BOOKS IN PRINT 1985-1986

This edition of BOOKS IN PRINT was
prepared by the R. R. Bowker Company's Data Services
Division in collaboration with the
Publication Systems Department.

Peter Simon, Vice President, Data Services
Ernest Lee, Managing Editor, Books in Print Database
Brian Phair, Project Manager
Rebecca Olmo, Project Coordinator
Basmattie Gravesande and John Thompson, Editorial Coordinators
Frank Accurso, Jane Bensel, Patricia Cahill, Domonique Fernandez,
Gene Gold, Yvonne Holness, Malcolm MacDermott, Karen Mayer,
Hyacinth Myers, Beverly Palacio, Joan Russell, Suzann Satmary,
Albert Simmonds, George Tibbetts, Joseph Tondi, Frances Walsh,
and Sonja Wright, Assistant Editors.

Publisher Directories:
Brenda Sutton-McElroy, Manager
Keith Schiffman, Project Manager
Sandra Bailey and Joseph Slater, Assistant Editors.

Bernard Kideckel, Manager, Computer Systems and Operations
Michael Gold, Manager, Systems Department
Betty Birdsell, Data Processing Manager
Jack Murphy, Operations Coordinator.

BOOKS IN PRINT 1985-1986

Volume 1
Authors
A-G

R.R.BOWKER COMPANY
New York & London

Published by R. R. Bowker Co.
205 East Forty-second Street, New York, N.Y. 10017

International Standard Book Numbers: Set 0-8352-2024-9
Vol. 1 0-8352-2025-7, Vol. 2 0-8352-2026-5
Vol. 3 0-8352-2027-3, Vol. 4 0-8352-2028-1
Vol. 5 0-8352-2030-3, Vol. 6 0-8352-2031-1
International Standard Serial Number 0068-0214
Library of Congress Catalog Card Number 4-12648

Printed and bound in the United States of America

DATABASES and PUBLICATIONS of the Department of Bibliography

BIPS DATABASE

Books in Print 1985-1986 was produced from the BIPS Database of the R. R. Bowker Company. This database is used to produce a complete, complementary line of bibliographic publications that give booksellers, librarians, publishers, and all other book, on-line, and microfiche users access to the latest bibliographic and ordering information. Following is a description of this database and its publications.

The bibliographic database was begun in 1948 primarily as a listing of titles included in Bowker's *Publishers' Trade List Annual (PTLA)*. The computerization of this database during the late nineteen-sixties using the Bibliographic Information Publication System (BIPS) made it possible for Bowker to expand the amount of information included in the bibliographic entries and to increase the number of essential tools of the trade we produced.

During the early nineteen-seventies the database was greatly expanded to include information from additional publishers whose titles were not included in *PTLA*. Since that time, the database has been composed of and compiled from information received on an on-going basis directly from publishers. Prior to each publication from the database, publishers review and correct their entries, providing current price, availability, and ordering information and update their list with recently published and forthcoming titles.

The database includes scholarly, popular, adult, juvenile, reprint, and all other types of books covering all subjects provided they are published or exclusively distributed in the United States and are available to the trade or to the general public for single or multiple copy purchase. All editions and bindings are included: hardcover, paperbound, library binding, perfect binding, boards, spiral binding, text editions, teachers' editions, and workbooks.

Bibles as such are excluded, although commentaries, histories, and versions other than the standard English are extensively covered. Free books, books priced at less than 25 cents, unbound materials, pamphlets, periodicals, serials, government publications, puzzles, calendars, maps, microforms, audio-visual materials, and most books available only to members of a particular organization, subscription-only titles or those sold only to schools are omitted. Spanish language books published outside of the United States are not included, but are covered in *Libros En Venta.*

Bibliographic entries contain the following information when available: author, co-author, editor, coeditor, translator, co-translator, title, original title, number of volumes, volume number, edition, whether or not reprinted, Library of Congress number, subject information, series information, language if other than English, whether or not illustrated, page numbers, grade range, date of publication, type of binding if other than cloth over boards, price, ISBN, imprint, publisher, and distributor, if other than the publisher.

In addition to the various publications described below, the full BIPS database is available for use through online services and microfiche. In these media, two years of out-of-print information are included as well.

Other databases of the Data Services Division include: Textbook Database, Publishers' Authority Database, Associations' Publications Database, Law Books Database, the American Book Publishing Record Database, Bowker's Serials Bibliography Database, and Bowker's Microcomputer Software Database.

Data Services Division's other publications include: *American Book Publishing Record, American Book Publishing Record Cumulative, 1876-1949, American Book Publishing Record Cumulative, 1950-1977, American Book Record Cumulative, 1980-1984, Art Books, 1950-1979, Art Books, 1980-1984, Associations' Publications in Print, Health Science Books, 1876-1982, Irregular Serials and Annuals, Law Books, 1876-1981, On Cassette, Performing Arts Books 1876-1981, Pure and Applied Science Books, 1876-1982, Ulrich's International Periodicals Directory, Weekly Record,* and *World Museum Publications.*

DESCRIPTION OF PUBLICATIONS

Books In Print

An annual publication listing all in-print and forthcoming titles from more than 18,200 publishers.

Indexes: *Author/Title/New Publishers & Distributors/Key to Publishers' & Distributors' Abbreviations/ Directory of U.S. Publishers & Distributors.*

Subject Guide to Books In Print

A companion volume to *Books In Print,* this annual lists all in-print and forthcoming titles except fiction, literature, poetry, and drama by one author, under approximately 63,500 Library of Congress (LC) subject headings.

Indexes: *Subject/Key to Publishers' & Distributors' Abbreviations*

Publishers, Distributors and Wholesalers of the United States

The main index of this publication contains the full name with editorial and ordering addresses for some 57,000 publishers currently listed in Bowker's Publisher Authority Database and active in the United

States. In addition, an ISBN index supplies the ISBN prefixes, a Key to Publishers' Abbreviations Index supplies the publishers' abbreviations from *Books In Print,* and a Wholesalers Index supplies the full name and addresses for United States Wholesalers. This directory is a useful companion tool to users of *Books In Print* as it increases the number of people who can use it simultaneously, and to librarians, booksellers, and others who need a comprehensive and up-to-date directory of U.S. publishing companies.
Indexes: *Publisher Name/ BIP Abbreviation/ ISBN Prefix/ Wholesalers*

Books In Print Supplement
An annual publication which updates *Books In Print* by listing all entries which have changes or additions to price, date of publication, ISBN, LC card number, or availability. Expands *Books In Print* by listing backlist titles new to the database and titles published since January or forthcoming through July. Expands *Subject Guide To Books In Print* by listing all new and forthcoming titles under LC subject headings.
Indexes: *Author/ Title/ Subject/ Key to Publishers' & Distributors' Abbreviations*

Books Out of Print
A companion publication to Books in Print listing titles declared out of print or out of stock indefinitely by publishers since 1981.
Indexes: *Title/ Author/ Key to Publishers' & Distributors' Abbreviations*

Books In Series In the United States
A publication listing in-print *and* out-of-print titles in popular, scholarly, and professional series.
Indexes: *Series Heading/ Series/ Author/ Title/ Subject Index to Series/ Directory of Publishers' & Distributors'*

Forthcoming Books
A bi-monthly cumulative publication listing forthcoming titles and titles published since July. Beginning with the November 1977 issue, an asterisk indicates titles new to the data base since the last issue. Beginning with the May 1981 issue, a separate index was added of publishers new to the database since the last issue.
Indexes: *Author/ Title/ New Publishers & Distributors/ Key to Publishers' & Distributors' Abbreviations*

Subject Guide To Forthcoming Books
A bi-monthly companion to *Forthcoming Books* covering the coming five-month season. Each issue overlaps and updates its predecessor. Adult and juvenile titles are listed under LC subject headings, as well as under additional headings created for literature, drama, and poetry by one author and for children's literature. In addition to their listing in the subject section, all titles for the juvenile market are listed by author in a separate section. Beginning with the July 1977 issue an asterisk indicates titles new to the data base since the last issue. Beginning with the May 1981 issue, a separate index was added of publishers new to the data base since the last issue.
Indexes: *Subject/ Juvenile Books/ New Publishers & Distributors/ Key to Publishers' & Distributors' Abbreviations*

Paperbound Books In Print
A semi-annual* publication listing all in-print and forthcoming paper trade and paper text editions. Entries are listed under approximately 470 subject headings.
Indexes: *Author/ Title/ Subject/ Key to Publishers' & Distributors' Abbreviations*
*semi-annual beginning 1978.

Children's Books In Print
An annual publication listing all books written for children. Grade or reading levels, where available, are indicated.
Indexes: *Author/ Title/ Illustrator/ Key to Publishers' & Distributors' Abbreviations*

Subject Guide To Children's Books In Print
A companion to *Children's Books In Print* this annual lists fiction and non-fiction titles under appropriate Sears or LC subject headings.
Indexes: *Subject/ Key to Publishers' & Distributors' Abbreviations*

Scientific And Technical Books And Serials In Print*
An annual subject selection of entries on science and technology *and* a selection of the same subject areas from the Bowker Serials Bibliography Data Base.
Indexes: *Book Section: Subject/ Author/ Title/ Key to Publishers' & Distributors' Abbreviations*
Serial Section: Subject/ Title
*beginning with the 1978 edition. Prior editions (1972, 1973, 1974) were titled *Scientific And Technical Books In Print* and did not include serial publications.

Computer Books and Serials in Print
A subject selection of entries on all aspects of computers. In addition to the Books in Print and Serials Bibliography Databases, Bowker's separate databases of legal titles, dictionaries, association publications and government information were thoroughly examined for inclusion of eligible entries. A Subject Area Directory provides access by broad areas to the LC subject headings used in the book.
Indexes: *Book Section: Subject/ Author/ Title/ Key to Publishers' & Distributors' Abbreviations*
Subject Area Directory
Serials Section: Subject/ Title

Medical And Health Care Books And Serials In Print*

An annual subject selection of entries on medicine, psychiatry, dentistry, nursing, and allied areas of the health field *and* a selection of the same subject areas from the Bowker Serials Bibliography Database.

Indexes: *Book Section: Subject/Author/ Title/Key to Publishers' & Distributors' Abbreviations*
Serial Section: Subject/Title

*beginning with the 1985 edition. Prior editions were titled *Medical Books And Serials In Print.*

Business and Economics Books And Serials In Print*

A subject selection of entries in the areas of economics, industry, finance, management, industrial psychology, vocational guidance, and other business-related topics *and* a selection of the same subject areas from the Bowker Serials Bibliography Database.

Indexes: *Book Section: Subject/Author/ Title/Key to Publishers' & Distributors' Abbreviations*
Serial Section: Subject/Title

*beginning with the 1981 edition. The 1973 and 1974 editions were titled *Business Books In Print* and did not include serial publications. The 1977 edition and its 1978 supplement were titled Business Books and Serials in Print.

Religious And Inspirational Books And Serials In Print

A subject selection of all entries on the world's religions and on allied religious and moral topics *and* a selection of the same subject areas from the Bowker Serials Bibliography Database. A Subject Area Directory provides access by broad areas to the subjects included. A Sacred Works Index provides a listing of the sacred books of the world's religions available in the U.S.

Indexes: *Book Section: Subject/Author/ Title/Key to Publishers' & Distributors' Abbreviations*
Subject Area Directory/
Sacred Works Index
Serial Section: Subject/Title

*beginning with the 1985 edition. Prior editions were titled *Religious Books and Serials In Print.*

Large Type Books In Print

An annual* publication listing all books which are produced in 14 point or larger type and intended for the visually handicapped. This volume is printed in 18 point type.

Indexes: *Subject/Textbook/Title/Author/ Key to Publishers' & Distributors' abbreviations*

*Annual beginning with 1982 edition. Previous editions were issued in 1970, 1976, 1978, and 1980.

OTHER DATABASES

Bowker's Microcomputer Software Database

This database contains information on thousands of microcomputer software packages, with detailed information on each one. Related databases contain information on hardware, peripheral hardware, manufacturers, software producers and distributors, user groups, and many other types of microcomputing-oriented organizations.

PUBLICATIONS:

Bowker's Complete Sourcebook of Personal Computing (annual), **Parent-Teacher's Microcomputing Sourcebook for Children 1985, Microcomputer Market Place, Retailers' Microcomputer Market Place** (semi-annual), and **Software Encyclopedia** (annual).

TEXTBOOK DATABASE

The Textbook Database was separated from the BIPS Database and expanded beyond the BIPS scope in 1973. Included are book and non-book materials for kindergarten through the first year of college as well as pedagogical material available and related to the educational world but not marketed to nor always available to the trade. The database includes all editions and bindings (hardcover, paperbound, boards, spiral binding, reprints) as well as kits, maps, audio-visual materials and other teaching aids. Bibliographic entries contain the same elements as on the BIPS Database.

PUBLICATIONS:

El-Hi Textbooks And Serials In Print

An annual publication listing in-print and forthcoming titles.

Indexes: *Subject/Title/Author/Series/ Key to Publishers' & Distributors' Abbreviations*

PUBLISHERS' AUTHORITY DATABASE

PUBLICATIONS:

Key to Publishers' and Distributors' Abbreviations

Provides the abbreviation, full name, ordering address, and ISBN prefix for all publishers and distributors whose bibliographic entries appear in the publication being indexed.

Directory of United States' Publishers, Distributors and Wholesalers

A listing of full name, editorial address, telephone number, and ISBN prefix for all active U.S. publishers, distributors and wholesalers currently on record in the files of the Department of Bibliography.

BOWKER SERIALS BIBLIOGRAPHY DATABASE

This Database contains up-to-date information on 128,000 serial titles published by 63,000 serial publishers and corporate authors around the world. Maintained by the Bowker Serials Bibliography Department.

PUBLICATIONS:

Ulrich's International Periodicals Directory (annual); **Irregular Serials and Annuals** (annual); **Ulrich's Quarterly,** a supplement to **Ulrich's** and **Irregular Serials; Sources of Serials,** an international directory of serial publishers and corporate authors and their titles by country.

ISBN
INTERNATIONAL STANDARD BOOK NUMBER

The 1985-1986 BOOKS IN PRINT is the seventh edition where each title or edition of a title is listed with an ISBN. All publishers were notified and requested to submit a valid ISBN for their titles.

During the past decade, the majority of the publishers complied with the requirements of the standard and implemented the ISBN. At present, approximately 97% of all new titles and all new editions are submitted for listing with a valid ISBN.

To fulfill the responsibility of accomplishing total book numbering, the ISBN Agency allocated the ISBN prefixes 0-317, 0-318, 0-685 and 0-686 to number the titles in the BOOKS IN PRINT database without an ISBN. Titles not having an ISBN at the closing date of this publication were assigned an ISBN with one of these prefixes by the International Standard Book Numbering Agency.

Titles numbered within the prefixes 0-317, 0-318, 0-685 and 0-686 are:

—Publishers who did not assign ISBN to their titles.

—Distributors with titles published and imported from countries not in the ISBN system, or not receiving the ISBN from the originating publisher.

—Errors from transposition and transcription which occurred in transmitting the ISBN to the BOOKS IN PRINT database.

All the ISBN listed in BOOKS IN PRINT are validated by using the check digit control, and only valid ISBN are listed in the BIP database.

All publishers participating in the ISBN system having titles numbered within the prefixes 0-317, 0-318, 0-685 and 0-686 will receive a computer printout, requesting them to submit the correct ISBN.

Publishers not participating in the ISBN system may request from the ISBN Agency the assignment of an ISBN Publisher Prefix, and start numbering their titles.

The Book Industry System Advisory Committee (BISAC) developed a standard format for data transmission, and many companies are already accepting orders transmitted on magnetic tape using the ISBN. Another standard format by BISAC for title updating is under development.

The ISBN Agency and the Data Services Division of the Bowker Company wish to express their appreciation to all publishers who collaborated in making the ISBN system the standard of the publishing industry.

For additional information related to the ISBN total numbering, please refer to Emery Koltay, Director of the ISBN/SAN Agency.

How to Use BOOKS IN PRINT 1985-1986

This 38th annual edition of *Books In Print* was produced from records stored on magnetic tape, edited by computer programs, and set in type by computer-controlled photocomposition. This edition, in six volumes, lists approximately 692,462 titles available from 18,200 United States publishers. Volumes 1, 2 and 3 are an alphabetically-arranged author index. Volumes 4, 5 and 6 are an alphabetically-arranged title index. Also included at the end of Volume 6 are three publisher indexes: a listing of all new publishers with titles listed for the first time in Books In Print 1985-1986; a listing of the active publishers in *Books In Print* arranged in the order of the abbreviation of publishers' or distributors' names used in each entry; and an alphabetical index of active United States publishers. All of these indexes include the International Standard Book Number prefix of the publishers participating in this system.

ALPHABETICAL ARRANGEMENT OF AUTHOR AND TITLE INDEXES

Within each index entries are filed alphabetically by word, with following exceptions:

Initial articles of titles in English, French, German, Italian and Spanish are deleted from the title index.

M', Mc and *Mac* are filed as if they were *Mac* and are interfiled with other names beginning with *Mac*; for example, Macan, MacAnally, Macardle, McAree, McArthur, Macarthur, M'Aulay, Macaulay, McAuley. Within a specific name grouping *Mc* and *Mac* are interfiled according to the given name of the author; for example, Macdonald, Agnes; McDonald, Alexander; MacDonald, Anne L.; McDonald, Austin F; MacDonald, Betty. Compound names are listed under the first part of the name, and cross-references appear under the last part of the name.

Entries beginning with initial letters (whether authors' given names, or titles) are filed first, e.g., Smith, H.C., names before Smith, Harold A.; B E A M A Directory comes before Baal, Babylon.

Numerals, including year dates, are written out in most cases and are filed alphabetically.

Seven Years in Tibet
Seventeen
Seventeen famous operas
Seventeen-Fifteen to the present
Seventeen party book
Seventeen reader
Seventeen century

U.S., UN, Dr., Mr., and St. are filed as though they were spelled out.

SPECIAL NOTE ON HOW TO FIND AN AUTHOR'S COMPLETE LISTING

In sorting author listings by computer it is not possible to group the entire listing for an author together unless a standard spelling and format for each name is used. The information in *Books In Print* comes directly from publishers or from their catalogs. Where publishers do not submit an author's name in consistent form, his listings in the author index may be divided into several groups.

Variant forms of an author's first and middle names may not be adjacent in the filing sequence, as in: Aiken, Conrad and Aiken, Conrad P. or Jung, C. G. or Jung, Carl G. For most surnames, variant forms of entry will fall close together, but for the most common surnames (Smith, Brown, etc.) it is suggested you check specifically for all variant forms of first and middle names.

Foreign names which may or may not be given with a prefix will not be adjacent in the filing sequence, such as Balzac and de Balzac and Goethe or von Goethe. German names with umlauts may appear in two alphabets because of the varying treatment of the umlauted vowel; Mu%ller, F. Max or Mueller, F. Max. Acronyms for names of corporate authors may appear in two or more groups of listings if one form is presented with no space between initials—UNESCO, and another with spaces, U N E S C O.

You will find cross-references to the variant forms of an author's name wherever we anticipated that his listings might not be filed together. To the extent practicable, we hope in future editions to reduce the number of variant forms of author's names in *Books In Print*.

INFORMATION INCLUDED IN AUTHOR AND TITLE ENTRIES

Entries include the following bibliographic information, when available: author, co-author, editor, co-editor, translator, co-translator, title, number of volumes, edition, Library of Congress number, series information, page numbers, language if other than English, whether or not illustrated, grade range, year of publication, type of binding if other than cloth over boards, price. International Standard Book Number, publisher's order number, imprint and publisher. When an entry includes the prices for both the hardcover and paperback editions, the publication date within the entry refers to the hardcover binding; however, when the paperback binding is the only one included in the entry, the publication date is the paperback publication date. (Information one the International Standard Book Numbering System developing in the

United States and other English-speaking countries is available from R.R. Bowker Co.)

GENERAL EDITORIAL POLICIES

In order to insure that the essential information in these listings is uniform, complete, and easy to find, the following editorial policies have been maintained:

When two authors or editors are responsible for a book, full bibliographic information is included in the author entry for the author or editor named first, and a cross-reference directs the user from the second author or editor to the primary entry; e.g., Wilson, Robert E., jt. auth. See Fensch, E. A. If more than two authors or editors are responsible for a certain publication, only the name of the first is given followed by *et al.*

Titles of single volumes as part of a set are given if the volumes are sold singly. Some series are also listed in the Title Index.

The Bible, the Book of Common Prayer, catechisms, hymnals and books of this type cannot always be recorded with full description. Since incomplete information is misleading, the user of this book is directed to the appropriate publisher's trade lists.

Every effort is made by most publishers to submit their material with consideration for its accuracy throughout the life of this edition of *Books In Print*. Most publishers anticipate price changes, list forthcoming books even if publication dates and prices are not set, and for the most part try not to list books that may shortly become unavailable. In spite of these efforts, a certain amount of unanticipated change in price will occur and a certain number of titles in this edition will become unavailable before the new edition of *Books In Print* is published. The *Books In Print Supplement 1985-1986* to be published in April 1986 will reflect any changes which have occurred in the interim. All prices are subject to change without notice.

Most prices are list prices. Lack of uniformity in publishers' data prohibits indicating trade discounts. A lower case "a" follows some of the trade edition prices and indicates that a specially priced library edition is available; "t" indicates a tentative price; "g" a guaranteed binding on a juvenile title; and "x" a short discount—20%, or less. Short discount (20% or less) information is generally supplied by publishers to Bowker for each publication. However, all publishers do not uniformly supply this information and Bowker can only make its best efforts to transmit this information when it is provided. PLB indicates a publishers' library binding. YA indicates that a title may be used for young adults.

An "i" following the price indicates an invoice price. Specific policies for such titles should be obtained from the individual publishers.

Publishers' and distributors' names, in most instances, are abbreviated. A key to these abbreviations will be found in the *Key to Publishers' & Distributors' Abbreviations* at the end of Volume 6. Entries in this "Key" are arranged alphabetically by the abbreviations used in the bibliographic entries. The full name, ISBN prefix, editorial address, telephone number, ordering address (if different from editorial address), and imprints follow the abbreviation. SAN (Standard Address Number) is a unique identification code for each address of each organization in or served by the book industry.

For example:

> **Bowker,** (Bowker, R. R., Co., 0-8352), 205 East Forty-second Street, New York, N.Y. 10017 Tel 212-916-1600 (SAN 214-1191); Order to P.O. Box 1807, Ann Arbor, MI 48106 (SAN 214-1205)

If an entry contains a "Pub by" note after the price, the title should be ordered from the company whose abbreviation appears at the end of the entry. For example, an entry for a book published by Melbourne U Pr., but distributed by International Scholarly Book Services, Inc., will convey this information in the form "Pub. by Melbourne U Pr." after the price with "Intl Schol Bk Serv." at the end of the entry.

Firms included in the *Key to Publishers' & Distributors' Abbreviations* listed with box number addresses only were solicited for complete street addresses to supplement the box numbers. This effort did increase the occurrence of street address and telephone numbers in this edition. In addition, a review of the editorial and ordering addresses included in the "Key" will provide a complete address profile of the firm.

Publishers and Distributors of the U.S.: This alphabetical index of publishers, following the "Key" at the end of Volume 6, is an index of all active United States publishers and distributors with titles represented in the Author and Title indexes.

The R. R. Bowker Company has used its best efforts in collecting and preparing material for inclusion in *Books In Print 1985-1986* but does not assume, and hereby disclaims any liability to any party for any loss or damage caused by errors or omissions in *Books In Print 1985-1986* whether such errors or omissions result from negligence, accident or any other cause.

TYPES OF PUBLICATIONS NOT FULLY REPRESENTED IN *Books In Print*

This edition of *Books In Print* indexes the listings of some 18,200 publishers—a total of 692,462 titles. Certain classes of publications are, however not represented in *Books In Print*. These include government publications, some professional law book publications, subscription reference sets and book club editions.

Books In Print 1985-1986 is not limited to information in the *Publishers' Trade List Annual.* Current information was obtained from all publishers in the BIPS Data Base. These publishers include regular contributors to Bowker's Advance Book Information system and less active publishers who responded to our request for *Books In Print 1985-1986* information. Publishers were asked to correct and update computer listings of the *Books In Print 1985-1986* master file. If this was not possible we obtained the latest edition of the publisher's trade order list. Every effort by correspondence, telephone and personal contact with publishers was made to get up-to-date, complete information on the in-print titles published and distributed in the United States for inclusion in *Books In Print 1985-1986*.

These criteria of inclusion were followed: Books must be available to the trade; this excludes books available only to numbers of a particular organization, subscription-only titles, or those sold only to schools. Books must be available for single copy purchase. No attempt was made to include things other than books, such as periodicals, puzzles, calendars, microforms, or audio-visual materials (unless accompanied by a text). Free material and material available only in quantities are also omitted.

Imported books must have a sole U.S. distributor. Distributors of Spanish language books published outside the U.S. have informed us that sole rights to these titles are not available. These books, therefore, are not listed in *Books In Print* but are fully covered in *Libros En Venta* and supplements to *Libros En Venta*. Some U.S. distributors of these books are listed in a special section of the *Key to Publishers' & Distributors' Abbreviations* in this year's edition. Distributors of books imported from Germany often do not have sole rights to these titles. These books listed in *Books In Print 1985-1986* as available from *one* distributor may also be available from other distributors of German books. For distributors of German titles, refer to the American Book Trade Directory, *31st edition*, also published by R. R. Bowker Company.

OTHER BIBLIOGRAPHIC PUBLICATIONS TO SUPPLEMENT *Books In Print*

Although *Books In Print* looks ahead, it cannot, of course, contain information that was unknown to the publishers when they submitted data in July. In April 1986 a *Books In Print Supplement* will be published, giving price changes, titles which have gone out-of-print and new books published or announced in the 6 months following the publication of *Books In Print*. This volume, arranged by author, title and subject, is priced tentatively at $119.95.

A tool for keeping up with new titles is *Forthcoming Books,* a separate bimonthly publication which provides author-title indexes to all books due to appear in the coming 5 month period. In addition, it cumulates all books that have appeared since July 1985, serving to keep your *Books In Print* up-to-date the year through. Yearly subscriptions are available at $90.00 U.S.A., single copies for $18.00 U.S.A.

Subject Guide to Forthcoming Books, companion to *Forthcoming Books,* is a separate bimonthly publication, giving by subject, all books due to appear in the coming 5 month period, providing new title information to supplement the annual *Subject Guide to Books in Print*. Yearly subscriptions are available at $60.00 U.S.A., single copies for $12.00 U.S.A. The combination rate for yearly subscriptions to both *Forthcoming Books* and its *Subject Guide* is $130.00 U.S.A.

Paperbound Books in Print includes all published and forthcoming paper trade and paper text editions published or exclusively distributed in the U.S. Beginning in 1978 a service of two complete editions published in the Spring and Fall replaces the old service of one base volume and two supplements. The complete service includes both the Spring and Fall volumes. Optional selection of either the Spring or Fall edition separately is also available. The Spring edition will be published in April 1986 and the Fall in October 1986. This service is priced at $145.00 a year or $82.50 per edition.

A complete description of other publications from the BIPS Data Base is included in preceding pages.

Publishers Weekly ($84.00 a year U.S.A.) and especially its forecasts, is another way of keeping up with later information about new books. The special announcement issues (Fall, Spring) are available separately at $4.95 ea. U.S.A.

All forecasts are, of course, necessarily incomplete, and to some extent inaccurate or unfulfilled. A record of the new books as actually published is therefore also available both in an author arrangement in the *Weekly Record* ($70.95 a year U.S.A.) and in a Dewey subject classification in the monthly *American Book Publishing Record* ($60.00 a year U.S.A.). The latter provides an author-title index. Both provide full cataloging information.

El-Hi Textbooks in Print, priced at $60.00, is somewhat more comprehensive than *Books In Print* when it comes to textbooks for elementary and secondary schools. *Bowker's Law Books and Serials in Print*, a new annual Bowker publication started in 1982, provides comprehensive coverage of law books, including many titles not found in *Books in Print. Bowker's Law Books and Serials in Print Update*, a monthly updating service to this annual, was published starting in 1983.

Out-of-print books may be sought through the columns of the *AB Bookman's Weekly,* Box AB, Clifton, New Jersey 07015.

Books Out-Of-Print listing over 225,000 titles declared out-of-print or out-of-stock indefinitely from 1981 through 1985 is available from R. R. Bowker.

Facsimiles of out-of-print books may also be obtained from University Microfilms Intl., 300 N. Zeeb Road, Ann Arbor, Michigan 48106.

KEY TO ABBREVIATIONS

a	after price, specially priced library edition available
abr.	abridged
adpt.	adapted
Amer.	American
annot.	annotation(s), annotated
ans.	answer(s)
app.	appendix
approx.	approximately
assn.	association
auth.	author
bd.	bound
bdg.	binding
bds.	boards
bibl(s).	bibliography(ies)
bk(s).	book, books
bklet(s)	booklets
Bro.	Brother
coll.	college
comm.	commission, committee
co.	company
cond.	condensed
comp(s).	compiler(s)
corp.	corporation
dept.	department
diag(s).	diagram(s)
dir.	director
disk	software disk or diskette
dist.	distributed
Div.	Division
doz.	dozen
ea.	each
ed.	editor, edited, edition
eds.	editions, editors
educ.	education
elem.	elementary
ency.	encyclopedia
Eng.	English
enl.	enlarged
exp.	expurgated
fac.	facsimile
fasc.	fascicule
fict.	fiction
fig(s).	figure(s)
for.	foreign
Fr.	French
frwd.	foreword
g	after price, guaranteed juvenile binding
gen.	general
Ger.	German
Gr.	Greek
gr.	grade, grades
hdbk.	handbook
i	invoice price—see publisher for specific pricing policies
ISBN	International Standard Book Number
i.t.a.	initial teaching alphabet
Illus.	illustrated, illustration(s), illustrator(s)
in prep.	in preparation
incl.	includes, including
inst.	institute
intro.	introduction
Ital.	Italian
Jr.	Junior
jt. auth.	joint author
jt. ed.	joint editor
k	kindergarten audience level
l.p.	long playing
ltd. ed.	limited edition
lab.	laboratory
lang(s).	language(s)
Lat.	Latin
lea.	leather
lib.	library
lit.	literature, literary
math.	mathematics
mod.	modern
mor.	morocco
MS, MSS	manuscript, manuscripts
natl.	national
no., nos.	number, numbers
o.p.	out of print
orig.	original text, not a reprint
o.s.i.	out of stock indefinitely
pap.	paper
photos	photographs, photographer
PLB	publisher's library binding
Pol.	Polish
pop. ed.	popular edition
Port.	Portuguese
prep.	preparation
probs.	problems
prog. bk.	programmed book
ps	preschool audience level
pseud.	pseudonym
pt(s).	part, parts
pub.	published, publisher, publishing
pubn.	publication
ref(s).	reference(s)
repr.	reprint
reprod(s).	reproduction(s)
rev.	revised
rpm.	revolution per minute (phono records)
Rus.	Russian
SAN	Standard Address Number
S&L	Signed and Limited
s.p.	school price
scp	single copy Direct to the Consumer Price
sec.	section
sel.	selected
ser.	series
Soc.	Society
sols.	solutions
Span.	Spanish
Sr. (after given name)	Senior
Sr. (before given name)	Sister
St.	Saint
subs.	subsidiary
subsc.	subscription
suppl.	supplement
t	after price, tentative price
tech.	technical
text ed.	text edition
tr.	translator, translated, translation
univ.	university
vol(s).	volume, volumes
wkbk.	workbook
x	after price, short discount (20% or less)
YA	young adult audience level
yrbk.	yearbook

BOOKS IN PRINT

1985-1986

VOLUME 1

AUTHORS

A-G

A

A. Mathematische Auswahl-Funktionen und Gesellschaftliche Entscheidungen. (Interdisciplinary Systems Research Ser.: No. 14). (Illus.). 343p. (Ger.). 1976. 37.95x (ISBN 0-8176-0814-1). Birkhauser.

A. A. U. P. Ohio Conference. History - 1949-1974. LC 74-620076. 1974. 1.00 (ISBN 0-88215-038-3). Ohio St U Lib.

A. & C. Black. Who's Who 1984-1985. 136th ed. 2500p. 1984. 110.00. Marquis.

A. C. Nielsen Co. The Business of Information, 1983, 2 vols. 1983. 300.00 (ISBN 0-942774-12-4). Info Indus.

A. D. Little, Inc., jt. ed. see Research Committee on Industrial & Municipal Wastes, ASME.

A E E World Energy Engineering Congress, 1st. Energy Engineering Technology: Proceedings. pap. 45.00 (ISBN 0-915586-15-0). Fairmont Pr.

A Editorial Staff. Construction Craft Jurisdiction Agreements. 216p. 1984. pap. text ed. 20.00 (ISBN 0-87179-459-4). BNA.

--Hazardous Materials Transport Guide. 378p. 1984. pap. text ed. 20.00 (ISBN 0-87179-462-4). BNA.

A. G. A. Operating Section. Operating Section Proceedings: Index: 1950-1969. 90p. 1970. pap. 3.00 (ISBN 0-318-12640-0, X50070). Am Gas Assn.

A. G. A. Pipeline Research Committee. AC Effects on Transmission Pipelines. 58p. 1978. pap. 20.00 (ISBN 0-318-12581-1, L51278). Am Gas Assn.

A. G. a Pipeline Research Committee. Manual for the Determination of Supercompressibility Factors of Natural Gas. 407p. 1963. pap. 12.00 (ISBN 0-318-12650-8, L00340). Am Gas Assn.

A. G. A.Pipeline Research Committee. Field Validation of Atmospheric Dispersion Models for Natural Gas Compressor Stations. 100p. pap. 20.00 (ISBN 0-318-12615-X, L51387). Am Gas Assn.

A. J. & Kirk, A. Life Cycle Cost Data. 140p. 1982. 40.00 (ISBN 0-318-17692-0); members 37.50 (ISBN 0-318-17693-9). Soc Am Value E.

A. J. Bicknell & Co. Bicknell's Victorian Buildings. LC 79-52830. (Illus.). 1980. pap. 5.50 (ISBN 0-486-23904-7). Dover.

A. J. Wilson Mining Journal Books Ltd. The Pick & the Pen. 318p. 1980. 26.00x (ISBN 0-900117-16-8, Pub. by Mining Journal England). State Mutual Bk.

A. J., jt. auth. see Schweitzer, Albert.

A L A see American Library Association.

A. M. Best Staff. Best's Directory of Recommended Insurance Attorneys. annual 1985. 40.00 (ISBN 0-317-07366-4). A M Best.

--Best's Directory of Recommended Insurance Adjusters. 1985. 35.00 (ISBN 0-317-07371-0). A M Best.

A P W A Research Foundation. Computer Assisted Mapping & Records Activity Manual. (CAMRAS: Pt. 1). 1979. 45.00 (ISBN 0-917084-31-4). Am Public Works.

A Panel of Leaders of the Christian Church & Teegarden, Kenneth L. Seeking God's Peace in a Nuclear Age. Osborn, Ronald, ed. 96p. (Orig.). 1985. pap. 2.50 (ISBN 0-8272-3422-8). CBP.

A, Peters J. Dictionary of Herpetology: Description of Words & Terms. (Illus.). 392p. 1981. lib. bdg. 15.00x (ISBN 0-02-850230-2). Lubrecht & Cramer.

A. R. E. New York Members. Economic Healing. rev. ed. 29p. 1974. pap. 1.50 (ISBN 0-87604-074-1). ARE Pr.

A. T. Kearney, Inc. Measuring & Improving Productivity in Physical Distribution. 1984. 50.00 (ISBN 0-318-03265-1); members 25.00 (ISBN 0-318-03266-X). Natl Coun Phys Dist.

AAAI Artificial Intelligence Conference, 1983. Proceedings. pap. 45.00 (ISBN 0-86576-065-9). W Kaufmann.

AAAI Artificial Intelligence Conference, 1980. Proceedings. pap. 40.00 (ISBN 0-86576-052-7). W Kaufmann.

AAAS-AAS Meeting, Dallas, Dec. 1968. Bioengineering & Cabin Ecology. (Science & Technology Ser.: Vol. 20). (Illus.). 1969. 20.00x (ISBN 0-87703-048-0, Pub. by Am Astronaut). Univelt Inc.

AABB Administrative Section Coordinating Committee, ed. Administrative Manual. 1984. write for info. three ring binder (ISBN 0-915355-08-6). Am Assn Blood.

A. Abd Al-Magid Haridi, jt. ed. see Butterworth, C. E.

Aaberg, J. C. Hymns & Hymnwriter of Denmark. 170p. Repr. of 1945 ed. 29.00 (ISBN 0-932051-28-6). Am Repr Serv.

Aaberg, Thomas M., jt. auth. see Machemer, Robert.

Aaboe, A. Episodes from the Early History of Mathematics. LC 63-21916. (New Mathematical Library: No. 13). 131p. 1975. pap. 8.75 (ISBN 0-88385-613-1). Math Assn.

AACD. Annotated Index 1981-1983. 165p. 1983. pap. text ed. 12.00 (ISBN 0-911547-02-9). Am Assn Coun Dev.

AACD Library, ed. Counseling Adults & Aging. (Shell Bibliography Ser.). 28p. 1983. pap. text ed. 7.50 (ISBN 0-317-04372-2, 72501W34). Am Assn Coun Dev.

Aaco Library. Guidance & Counseling Practices & Programs K-12. (Shell Bibliographies). 48p. 1983. pap. text ed. 7.50 (ISBN 0-911547-90-8, 7251ZW34). Am Assn Coun Dev.

--Shell Bibliography Package. 1983. pap. text ed. 84.50 (ISBN 0-911547-92-4, 72514W34). Am Assn Coun Dev.

Aaco Library, ed. Counseling Children & Adolescents. (Shell Bibliographies). 25p. 1983. pap. text ed. 7.50 (ISBN 0-911547-91-6, 72513W34). Am Assn Coun Dev.

--Counseling Minority Group Members. (Shell Bibliographies). 22p. 1983. pap. text ed. 7.50 (ISBN 0-911547-86-X, 72508W34). Am Assn Coun Dev.

--Counseling the Handicapped. (Shell Bibliographies Ser.). 35p. (Orig.). 1983. pap. text ed. 7.50 (ISBN 0-911547-83-5, 72505W34). Am Assn Coun Dev.

--Counselor Preparation & Supervision. (Shell Bibiographies). 23p. (Orig.). 1983. pap. text ed. 7.50 (ISBN 0-911547-81-9, 72503W34). Am Assn Coun Dev.

AACP. Shall I Study Pharmacy? 4th ed. 32p. 1980. pap. 0.45 (ISBN 0-937526-08-8). Am Assn Coll Pharm.

Aaen, Bernhard. No Appointment Needed. Van Dolson, Bobbie J., ed. 128p. 1981. pap. 5.95 (ISBN 0-8280-0025-5). Review & Herald.

AAG Consulting Services Panel. Suggestions for Self-Evaluation of Geography Programs with Self-Study Data Forms. 1974. pap. 2.00 (ISBN 0-89291-141-7). Assn Am Geographers.

Aagot, Raaen. Grass of the Earth. Scott, Franklyn D., ed. LC 78-15850. (Scandinavians in America Ser.). 1979. Repr. of 1950 ed. lib. bdg. 21.00x (ISBN 0-405-11658-6). Ayer Co Pubs.

Aagre, Scott & Martin, Lance. Calligraphy & Related Ornamentation. (Illus.). 96p. (Orig.). 1982. pap. 5.95. Lighthouse Hill Pub.

AAHPERD Research Consortium, ed. Encyclopedia of Physical Education, Fitness & Sports, 3 Vols. Incl. Sports, Dance, & Related Activities. 990p. 1977. 30.00 (ISBN 0-686-95403-3, 240-26756); Training, Environment, Nutrition, & Fitness. 630p. 1980. 38.00 (ISBN 0-686-95404-1, 240-26754); Philosophy, Programs & History. 721p. 1981. 38.00 (ISBN 0-686-95405-X, 240-27024). (Illus.). AAHPERD.

AAHPHERD. Dance Directory: Programs of Professional Preparation in American Colleges & Universities. 11th ed. 92p. 1983. 7.30 (ISBN 0-88314-257-0). Natl Dance Assn.

Aaken, Ernst Van see Van Aaken, Ernst.

Aaker, D. A. & Day, G. S. Marketing Research. 731p. 1983. 33.95 (ISBN 0-471-09740-3). Wiley.

Aaker, David A. Developing Business Strategies. LC 83-21906. (Ronald Series on Marketing Management: 1-372). 391p. 1984. 22.95 (ISBN 0-471-87179-6, Pub by Ronald Pr). Wiley.

--Multivariate Analysis in Marketing. 2nd ed. 1980. pap. text ed. 22.50 (ISBN 0-89426-029-4). Scientific Pr.

--Strategic Market Management. LC 83-21694. 336p. 1984. pap. 21.45 (ISBN 0-471-87110-9, Pub by Wiley). Wiley.

Aaker, David A. & Day, George S. Marketing Research: Private & Public Sector Decisions. 2nd ed. LC 79-18532. (Marketing Ser.). 731p. 1982. text ed. 29.95 (ISBN 0-471-00059-0). Wiley.

Aaker, David A. & Myers, John G. Advertising Management. 2nd ed. (Illus.). 560p. 1982. text ed. 31.95 (ISBN 0-13-016006-7). P-H.

Aaker, David A. & Day, George S., eds. Consumerism: Search for the Consumer Interest. 4th ed. LC 77-83163. (Illus.). 1982. pap. text ed. 12.95 (ISBN 0-02-900040-8). Free Pr.

Aal, Katharyn M. The Raccoon Book. LC 82-7831. (Illus.). 88p. 1982. pap. 5.95 (ISBN 0-935526-05-6). McBooks Pr.

Aal, Katharyn M. & Fulton, Alice. The Wings, the Vines. LC 82-24978. 96p. 1983. pap. 6.50 (ISBN 0-935526-07-2). McBooks Pr.

Aal, Katharyn M., ed. Rapunzel, Rapunzel: Poetry, Prose & Photographs by Women on the Subject of Hair. LC 79-28326. (Illus.). 128p. (Orig.). 1980. pap. 5.95 (ISBN 0-935526-00-5). McBooks Pr.

Aalami, B., jt. auth. see Williams, D. G.

Aaland, Mikkel. County Fair: Portraits. LC 81-10267. 96p. (Orig.). 1981. pap. 12.95 (ISBN 0-88496-172-9). Capra Pr.

--Sweat. Young, Noel, ed. LC 77-28114. (Illus.). 256p. 1978. pap. 7.95 (ISBN 0-88496-124-9). Capra Pr.

Aalders, jt. auth. see Herschberg.

Aalders, C. C. & Heynen, Will. Bible Studies Commentary - Genesis, 2 vols. Set. 29.95 (ISBN 0-310-43968-X). Zondervan.

Aalders, Carel A. V. & Bertouille, S., eds. Branches & Subsidiaries in the European Common Market: Legal & Tax Aspects. 2nd ed. 322p. 1976. 26.00 (ISBN 90-268-0830-5, Pub. by Kluwer Law Netherlands). Kluwer Academic.

Aalen, F. H. Man & the Landscape in Ireland. 343p. 1978. 40.00 (ISBN 0-12-041350-7). Acad Pr.

A.A.L.L. Proceedings of the Annual Meeting, 1981. Legal Information for the 1980's: Meeting the Needs of the Legal Profession. (AALL Publication Ser.). 45.00 (ISBN 0-317-31413-0). Rothman.

Aaltio. Finnish for Foreigners, Pt. I. 20.00 (ISBN 0-317-19051-2, F561); additional exercises 9.00 (ISBN 0-317-19052-0, F561E). Vanous.

--Finnish for Foreigners. Pt. II. 20.00 (ISBN 0-317-19054-7, F562); Pt. III. 18.50 (ISBN 0-317-19055-5, F566). Vanous.

Aaltio, M. Finnish for Foreigners, 3 vols. Set. pap. 40.00 (ISBN 0-686-66991-6). Vol. 1 (ISBN 9-5110-0397-6). Vol. 2 (ISBN 9-5110-1483-8). Vol. 3 (ISBN 9-5110-1919-8). Vol. 4 Oral Drills. pap. 10.00 (ISBN 9-5110-1231-2). Heinman.

Aaltio, M-H. Finnish for Foreigners: Pt 2, Lessons 26 to 40. 8th rev. ed. (Illus.). 192p. 1976. pap. text ed. 20.00x (ISBN 95-110-1483-8, F 562). Vanous.

Aaltio, M. J. Finnish for Foreigners, Pt. 1: Lessons 1-25. 10th ed. (Illus.). 254p. 1982. pap. text ed. 20.00x (ISBN 951-1-00397-6, F561); cassette A 45.00x; cassette B-E 100.00x. Vanous.

Aaltio, Maija H. Finnish Language Book for English Speaking People. 27.50 (ISBN 0-87559-107-8). Shalom.

Aaltio, Maija-Hellikki. Finnish for Foreigners, 2 vols. 1982. Vol. 1, 253p. includes 5 cassettes 85.00x (ISBN 0-88432-093-6, FN1); Vol. 2, 192p. includes 4 cassettes 60.00x (ISBN 0-88432-094-4, FN10). J Norton Pubs.

--Finnish for Foreigners (Korva Tarkkana) 102p. 1977. includes 1 cassette 25.00x (ISBN 0-88432-095-2, FN20). J Norton Pubs.

Aalto, Alvar. Alvar Aalto Furniture. Pallasmaa, Juhani, ed. (Illus.). 179p. 1985. 25.00 (ISBN 0-262-13206-0). MIT Pr.

--Synopsis: Painting, Architecture, Sculpture. 2nd ed. (Geschichte und Theorie der Architektur: No. 12). (Illus.). 240p. (English, German, French.). 1980. 81.95x (ISBN 0-8176-1109-6). Birkhauser.

Aamodt, Alice, jt. auth. see Johnson, Sylvia A.

Aamuna, pseud. Spitting Image. 1981. 9.95x (ISBN 0-917266-19-6). Vanilla.

Aandahl, Andrew R. Soil Teaching Aid. LC 79-12843. (Illus.). xxxii, 140p. 1979. pap. 100.00x with slide carousel (ISBN 0-8032-5902-6); tape cassette 5.00x (ISBN 0-8032-1012-4). U of Nebr Pr.

--Soils of the Great Plains: Land Use, Crops, & Grasses. LC 81-7435. (Illus.). xvi, 282p. 1982. 28.50x (ISBN 0-8032-1011-6). U of Nebr Pr.

Aanenson, Charles R. Indonesia. (World Education Ser.). (Illus.). 120p. 1979. pap. text ed. 4.00 (ISBN 0-910054-56-8). Am Assn Coll Registrars.

Aan-Ta-T'Loot & Pack, Raymond. Tlingit Designs & Carving Manual. LC 78-11887. (Illus.). 1978. 7.95 (ISBN 0-87564-862-2). Superior Pub.

AAOS. Instructional Course Lectures. LC 43-17054. (Vol. 32). (Illus.). 379p. 1983. text ed. 53.95 (ISBN 0-8016-0073-1). Mosby.

Aardema, Verna. Bimwili & the Zimwi. LC 85-4449. (Illus.). 32p. (ps-3). 1985. PLB 10.89 (ISBN 0-8037-0213-2); pap. 10.95 (ISBN 0-8037-0212-4). Dial Bks Young.

--Bringing the Rain to Kapiti Plain. LC 80-25886. (Illus.). 32p. (ps). 1981. pap. 12.95 (ISBN 0-8037-0809-2, 01258-370); PLB 12.89 (ISBN 0-8037-0807-6). Dial Bks Young.

--Bringing the Rain to Kapiti Plain. (Pied Piper Book). (Illus.). 32p. (ps-2). 1983. pap. 3.95 (ISBN 0-8037-0904-8, 0383-120). Dial Bks Young.

--Oh, Kojo! How Could You? LC 84-1710. (Illus.). 32p. (ps-3). 1984. 10.95 (ISBN 0-8037-0006-7, 01063-320); PLB 10.89 (ISBN 0-8037-0007-5). Dial Bks Young.

--What's So Funny, Ketu? LC 82-70195. (Illus.). 32p. (ps-2). 1982. 9.95 (ISBN 0-8037-9364-2); PLB 9.89 (ISBN 0-8037-9370-7). Dial Bks Young.

--Why Mosquitoes Buzz in People's Ears: A West African Tale. LC 77-71514. (Pied Piper Bk.). (Illus.). (ps-3). 1978. pap. 3.95 (ISBN 0-8037-6088-4, 0383-120). Dial Bks Young.

--Why Mosquitoes Buzz in People's Ears: A West African Tale. LC 74-2886. (Illus.). 32p. (ps-3). 1975. 11.95 (ISBN 0-8037-6089-2, 01160-350); PLB 11.89 (ISBN 0-8037-6087-6). Dial Bks Young.

Aardema, Verna, retold by. The Vinganance & the Tree Toad. LC 82-13473. (Illus.). 48p. (gr. 1-4). 1983. 12.95 (ISBN 0-7232-6217-9). Warne.

--Who's in Rabbit's House? LC 77-71514. (Illus.). 32p. (gr. k-3). 1977. 11.95 (ISBN 0-8037-9550-5); PLB 11.89 (ISBN 0-8037-9551-3). Dial Bks Young.

--Who's in Rabbit's House? LC 77-71514. (Pied Piper Bk.). (Illus.). 32p. (ps-3). 1979. pap. 3.95 (ISBN 0-8037-9549-1, 0383-120, Pied Piper Book). Dial Bks Young.

Aardweg, Gerard van den see Van den Aardweg, Gerard.

Aare, jt. auth. see Hansen.

Aarli, J. A. & Toender, O. Immunological Aspects of Neurological Diseases. (Monographs in Neural Sciences: Vol. 6). (Illus.). xiv, 190p. 1980. pap. 21.00 (ISBN 3-8055-0814-X). S Karger.

Aaron. Soups & Stews. (Easy Cooking Ser.). 1983. 4.95 (ISBN 0-8120-5533-0). Barron.

Aaron, Benjamin. Legal Status of Employee Benefit Rights Under Private Pension Plans. 1961. 10.00x (ISBN 0-256-00638-5). Irwin.

--The Strike: A Current Assessment. 1967. 1.00 (ISBN 0-89215-052-1). U Cal LA Indus Rel.

Aaron, Benjamin, jt. auth. see Blanpain, R.

Aaron, Benjamin, ed. Labor Courts & Grievance Settlement in Western Europe. LC 72-123628. 1971. 46.50x (ISBN 0-520-01757-9). U of Cal Pr.

Aaron, Benjamin, ed. see Conference of the Institute of Industrial Relations.

Aaron, Benjamin see Labor Law Group.

Aaron, Chester. Duchess. LC 81-47755. 192p. (YA) (gr. 7 up). 1982. 10.10i (ISBN 0-397-31947-9); PLB 11.89g (ISBN 0-397-31948-7). Lipp Jr Bks.

--Gideon. LC 81-48066. 192p. (YA) (gr. 7 up). 1982. 10.89 (ISBN 0-397-31992-4); PLB 9.89g (ISBN 0-397-31993-2). Lipp Jr Bks.

--Out of Sight, Out of Mind. LC 84-48356. 192p. (gr. 6-9). 1985. 11.06i (ISBN 0-397-32100-7); PLB 10.89g (ISBN 0-397-32101-5). Lipp Jr Bks.

Aaron, Daniel. Men of Good Hope: A Story of American Progressives. 1951. 25.00x (ISBN 0-19-501232-1). Oxford U Pr.

--Writers on the Left. LC 61-13349. 1977. pap. 9.95 (ISBN 0-19-519970-7, GB512, GB). Oxford U Pr.

--Writers on the Left: Episodes in American Literary Communism. LC 73-19759. 460p. 1974. Repr. of 1961 ed. lib. bdg. 31.50 (ISBN 0-374-90005-1). Octagon.

Aaron, Daniel, ed. American Men & Women of Letters, 24 vols. 1982. Set. pap. 148.95 (ISBN 0-87754-149-3). Chelsea Hse.

--The Inman Diary: A Public & Private Confession. (Illus.). 1600p. 1985. 50.00 (ISBN 0-674-45445-6); pre-Jan. 1986 39.95 (ISBN 0-317-20023-2). Harvard U Pr.

--Studies in Biography. (Harvard English Studies: No. 8). 200p. 1978. text ed. 16.00x (ISBN 0-674-84651-6); pap. text ed. 5.95x (ISBN 0-674-84652-4). Harvard U Pr.

Aaron, Daniel, ed. see Herrick, Robert.

Aaron, David. One Thousand One-Minute Lessons. 152p. 1985. 10.95 (ISBN 0-8059-2973-8). Dorrance.

Aaron, Elizabeth. Quilling: The Art of Paper Scroll Work. (Illus.). 120p. 1984. pap. 9.95 (ISBN 0-7134-4623-4, Pub. by Batsford England). David & Charles.

Aaron, Henry. On Social Welfare. LC 80-80680. (Illus.). 143p. 1980. 18.00 (ISBN 0-89011-549-4). Abt Bks.

--On Social Welfare. (Illus.). 144p. 1984. lib. bdg. 28.00 (ISBN 0-8191-4102-X). U Pr of Amer.

--Pillar to Post: Looking at Street Furniture. 192p. 1982. 60.00x (ISBN 0-7232-2762-4, Pub. by F Warne England). State Mutual Bk.

Aaron, Henry, ed. VAT Experiences of Some European Countries. 250p. 1981. 60.00 (ISBN 90-65-4402-40, Pub. by Kluwer Law Netherlands). Kluwer Academic.

Aaron, Henry J. Economic Effects of Social Security. LC 82-73654. (Studies of Government Finance). 100p. 1982. 12.95 (ISBN 0-8157-0030-X); pap. 6.95 (ISBN 0-8157-0029-6). Brookings.

--The Peculiar Problem of Taxing Life Insurance Companies. LC 83-70788. (Studies of Government Finance). 71p. 1983. pap. 6.95 (ISBN 0-8157-0031-8). Brookings.

--Politics & the Professors: The Great Society in Perspective. LC 77-91809. (Studies in Social Economics). 1978. 22.95 (ISBN 0-8157-0026-1); pap. 8.95 (ISBN 0-8157-0025-3). Brookings.

--Shelter & Subsidies: Who Benefits from Federal Housing Policies? LC 72-306. (Brookings Institution Studies in Social Economics Ser.). pap. 63.50 (ISBN 0-317-30177-2, 2025359). Bks Demand UMI.

--Who Pays the Property Tax? A New View. (Studies of Government Finance). 1975. 18.95 (ISBN 0-8157-0022-9); pap. 7.95 (ISBN 0-8157-0021-0). Brookings.

--Why Is Welfare So Hard to Reform? (Studies in Social Economics). 71p. 1973. pap. 6.95 (ISBN 0-8157-0019-9). Brookings.

Aaron, Henry J. & Galper, Harvey. Assessing Tax Reform. LC 84-45979. 175p. 1985. 22.95 (ISBN 0-8157-0038-5); pap. 8.95 (ISBN 0-8157-0037-7). Brookings.

Aaron, Henry J. & Schwartz, William B. The Painful Prescription: Rationing Hospital Care. LC 83-45962. 161p. 1984. 22.95 (ISBN 0-8157-0034-2); pap. 8.95 (ISBN 0-8157-0033-4). Brookings.

Aaron, Henry J., ed. Inflation & the Income Tax. LC 76-28669. (Studies of Government Finance). 1976. 29.95 (ISBN 0-8157-0024-5); pap. 10.95 (ISBN 0-8157-0023-7). Brookings.

--The Value-Added Tax: Lessons from Europe. LC 81-38475. (Studies of Government Finance). 120p. 1981. 18.95 (ISBN 0-8157-0028-8); pap. 7.95 (ISBN 0-8157-0027-X). Brookings.

Aaron, Henry J. & Boskin, Michael J., eds. The Economics of Taxation. (Studies of Government Finance). 1980. 28.95 (ISBN 0-8157-0014-8); pap. 11.95 (ISBN 0-8157-0013-X). Brookings.

Aaron, Henry J. & Burtless, Gary, eds. Retirement & Economic Behavior. LC 83-45962. (Studies in Social Economics). 352p. 1984. 31.95 (ISBN 0-8157-0036-9); pap. 11.95 (ISBN 0-8157-0035-0). Brookings.

Aaron, Henry J. & Pechman, Joseph A., eds. How Taxes Affect Economic Behavior. LC 81-1040. (Studies of Government Finance). 454p. 1981. 31.95 (ISBN 0-8157-0012-1); pap. 12.95 (ISBN 0-8157-0011-3). Brookings.

Aaron, James. The Gay Trivia Quiz Book. 224p. (Orig.). 1985. pap. 5.95 (ISBN 0-87795-638-3, Pub. by Priam). Arbor Hse.

Aaron, James, jt. auth. see Strasser, Maryland K.

Aaron, James E. & Shafter, Albert J. The Police Officer & Alcoholism. 84p. 1963. 9.75x (ISBN 0-398-00000-X). C C Thomas.

Aaron, James E. & Strasser, Marland K. Driving Task Instruction: Dual Control, Simulation, & Multiple-Car. 1974. pap. write for info. (ISBN 0-02-300040-6, 30004). Macmillan.

Aaron, James E., et al. First Aid Emergency Care: Prevention & Protection of Injuries. 2nd ed. 1979. pap. text ed. 14.95x (ISBN 0-02-300060-0). Macmillan.

Aaron, Jan. The Firm Upper Arms Book. 80p. 1985. 4.95 (ISBN 0-07-001482-5). McGraw.

--Gerald R. Ford: President of Destiny. LC 74-21356. (Illus.). 140p. 1975. 7.95 (ISBN 0-8303-0147-X). Fleet.

--India on Twenty Dollars a Day. 348p. 1985. pap. 9.95 (ISBN 0-671-49903-3). Frommer-Pasmantier.

--Plantworks: Indoor Gardening Made Easy. LC 74-21357. 208p. Date not set. 14.95 (ISBN 0-8303-0146-1). Fleet.

Aaron, Jan & Salom, Georgine S. The Art of Mexican Cooking. 1982. pap. 2.95 (ISBN 0-451-11433-7, AE1433, Sig). NAL.

Aaron, Jane E., ed. The Compact Reader. LC 83-61636. 384p. 1984. pap. text ed. 7.95 (ISBN 0-312-15306-6, Pub. by Bedford Bks); instr's manual avail. St Martin.

Aaron, Jonathan. Second Sight. Hecht, Anthony, ed. LC 81-48026. (National Poetry Ser.). 80p. 1982. 10.53i (ISBN 0-06-014969-8, HarpT); pap. 5.72i (ISBN 0-06-090944-7, CN-0944, HarpT). Har-Row.

Aaron, M. Audrey. Lovers Genteel or Gentile. LC 76-58666. 1977. 2.95 (ISBN 0-89301-042-1). U Pr of Idaho.

Aaron, Norma S., jt. auth. see Schwartz, Alice K.

Aaron, P. G., jt. ed. see Malatesha, R. N.

Aaron, Pietro. Libri Tres de Institutione Harmonica. (Monuments of Music & Music Literature in Facsimile, Ser. II: Vol. 67). 134p. (Lat.). 1975. Repr. of 1516 ed. 27.50x (ISBN 0-8450-2267-9). Broude.

--Lucidario in Musica di Alcune oppenioni Antiche et Moderne. (Monuments of Music & Music Literature in Facsimile: Ser. II, Vol. 68). (Illus.). 1978. Repr. of 1545 ed. 27.50 (ISBN 0-8450-2268-7). Broude.

--Trattato...di Canto Figurato. (Monuments of Music & Music Literature, Ser. II: Vol. 129). 1979. Repr. of 1525 ed. 30.00x (ISBN 0-8450-2329-2). Broude.

Aaron, R. I. Our Knowledge of Universals. (Studies in Philosophy: No. 40). 1975. lib. bdg. 22.95x (ISBN 0-8383-0108-8). Haskell.

Aaron, Richard I. Bankruptcy Law Fundamentals. LC 83-2735. 1984. 75.00 (ISBN 0-87632-432-4). Boardman.

--Bankruptcy Law Handbook. 1985. write for info. Boardman.

--John Locke. 3rd ed. 1971. 42.00x (ISBN 0-19-824355-3). Oxford U Pr.

Aaron, Roberto, jt. auth. see Rosner, Jonathan L.

Aaron, Robin, jt. auth. see Aaron, Ronald.

Aaron, Ronald & Aaron, Robin. Improve Your Physics Grade. 250p. (Orig.). 1984. pap. text ed. 13.50 (ISBN 0-471-89006-5). Wiley.

Aaron, Shirley L. A Study of Combined School-Public Libraries. LC 80-19785. (School Media Centers: Focus on Trends & Issues Ser.: No. 6). 120p. 1980. pap. 7.00x (ISBN 0-8389-3247-9). ALA.

Aaron, Shirley L. & Scales, Pat R., eds. School Library Media Annual, 1983, Vol. 1. 451p. 1983. lib. bdg. 35.00 (ISBN 0-87287-353-6). Libs Unl.

--School Library Media Annual 1984. 2nd., 2nd Annual Vol. ed. 450p. 1984. lib. bdg. 35.00 (ISBN 0-87287-434-6). Libs Unl.

--School Library Media Annual, 1985, Vol. 3. 450p. 1985. lib. bdg. 40.00 (ISBN 0-87287-475-3). Libs Unl.

Aaron, Thomas J. The Control of Police Discretion: The Danish Experience. 124p. 1966. 9.75x (ISBN 0-398-00001-8). C C Thomas.

Aaron, Thomas L. Sermon Notes & Outlines. pap. 1.00 (ISBN 0-911866-82-5). Advocate.

Aaron, Tossi, jt. auth. see Bisgaard, Erling.

Aaron, Tossi, ed. see Bisgaard, Erling & Stehouwer, Gulle.

Aaron, William M. Italic Writing. 1977. pap. 10.50 (ISBN 0-85458-311-4). Transatlantic.

Aaroni, Wallenod. Modern Hebrew Reader & Grammar. 208p. 1978. pap. 5.50 (ISBN 0-88328-002-7). Shilo Pub Hse.

Aaroni, Wallenrod. Fundamentals of Hebrew Grammar. 272p. 1978. pap. 5.50 (ISBN 0-88328-004-3). Shilo Pub Hse.

Aaronovitch, S. & Smith, R. The Political Economy of British Capitalism: A Marxist Analysis. 416p. 1982. 17.00 (ISBN 0-07-084121-7). McGraw.

Aaronovitch, Sam. The Road from Thatcherism. 138p. 1981. pap. text ed. 8.00x (ISBN 0-85315-534-8, Pub. by Lawrence & Wisart Ltd England). Humanities.

--The Ruling Class: A Study of British Finance Capital. LC 78-23485. 1979. Repr. of 1961 ed. lib. bdg. 24.75x (ISBN 0-313-20764-X, AARC). Greenwood.

Aaronovitch, Sam & Sawyer, Malcolm C. Big Business: Theoretical & Empirical Aspects of Concentration & Mergers in the United Kingdom. LC 74-34221. 350p. 1975. text ed. 44.50x (ISBN 0-8419-0196-1). Holmes & Meier.

Aarons, Alfred C. Issues in the Teaching of Standard English. 112p. 1974. 8.80 (ISBN 0-318-18143-6). Tchrs Eng Spkrs.

Aarons, Edward S. Assignment--Afghan Dragon. (Assignment Ser.). 1982. pap. 2.25 (ISBN 0-449-14085-7, GM). Fawcett.

--Assignment--Black Gold. (Assignment Ser.). 192p. (Orig.). 1980. pap. 1.95 (ISBN 0-449-13354-0, GM). Fawcett.

--Assignment--Ceylon. (Assignment Ser.). 208p. 1981. pap. 1.95 (ISBN 0-449-13583-7, GM). Fawcett.

--Assignment--Golden Girl. (Assignment Ser.). 1981. pap. 2.25 (ISBN 0-449-14140-3, GM). Fawcett.

--Assignment--Lili Lamaris. (Assignment Ser.). 1978. pap. 1.50 (ISBN 0-449-13934-4, GM). Fawcett.

--Assignment--Mermaid. (Assignment Ser.). 1981. pap. 1.75 (ISBN 0-449-14203-5, GM). Fawcett.

--Assignment--Sulu Sea. (Assignment Ser.). 160p. 1981. pap. 1.95 (ISBN 0-449-13875-5, GM). Fawcett.

--Assignment--the Girl in the Gondola. (Assignment Ser.). 1979. pap. 1.75 (ISBN 0-449-14165-9, GM). Fawcett.

--Assignment--Zoraya. (Assignment Ser.). 1981. pap. 1.95 (ISBN 0-449-14184-5, GM). Fawcett.

--Assignment Manchurian Doll. (Assignment Ser.). 1979. pap. 1.75 (ISBN 0-449-13449-0, GM). Fawcett.

--Dark Destiny. pap. 0.95 (ISBN 0-532-95239-1). Woodhill.

--Death Is My Shadow. 2nd ed. 160p. 1975. pap. 0.95 (ISBN 0-532-95371-1). Woodhill.

--Terror in the Town. 160p. 1974. pap. 0.95 (ISBN 0-532-15266-2). Woodhill.

Aarons, Howell, jt. auth. see Schweitzer, Burton L.

Aarons, Jules, ed. Solar System Radio Astronomy. LC 65-14086. 416p. 1965. 39.50x (ISBN 0-306-30192-X, Plenum Pr). Plenum Pub.

Aarons, Trudy & Koelsch, Francine. One Hundred & One Language Arts Activities. (Illus.). 1979. pap. text ed. 11.95 (ISBN 0-88450-795-5, 3053-B). Communication Skill.

--One Hundred & One Language Arts Activities. 134p. (Orig.). 1985. pap. text ed. 11.95 (ISBN 0-88450-922-2, 3053-B). Communication Skill.

--One Hundred & One Science Activities. 156p. (Orig.). 1981. pap. text ed. 11.95 (ISBN 0-88450-879-X, 7221-B). Communication Skill.

--One Hundred One Math Activities. 118p. 1981. pap. text ed. 11.95 (ISBN 0-88450-740-8, 2065-B). Communication Skill.

--One Hundred One Reading Activities. 125p. (ps-4). 1982. pap. text ed. 11.95 (ISBN 0-88450-833-1, 2079-B). Communication Skill.

Aarons, Victoria. Author As Character in the Works of Sholom Aleichem. LC 84-22703. (Studies in Art & Religious Interpretation: Vol. 3). 210p. 1985. 39.95x (ISBN 0-88946-553-3). E Mellen.

Aarons, Will B. Assignment: Death Ship. 192p. (Orig.). 1983. pap. 2.50 (ISBN 0-449-12440-1, GM). Fawcett.

Aaronson, D. & Rieber, R. W., eds. Psycholinguistic Research: Implications & Applications. 544p. 1979. 39.95x (ISBN 0-89859-149-X). L Erlbaum Assocs.

Aaronson, David E. Maryland Criminal Jury Instructions & Commentary. LC 75-2870. 453p. 1975. 25.00 (ISBN 0-87215-165-4). Michie Co.

Aaronson, David E., et al. Public Policy & Police Discretion. LC 83-11882. 1984. 25.00 (ISBN 0-87632-347-6). Boardman.

Aaronson, Doris & Rieber, Robert W., eds. Developmental Psycholinguistics & Communication Disorders, Vol. 263. (Annals of the New York Academy of Sciences). 287p. 1975. 22.00x (ISBN 0-89072-016-9). NY Acad Sci.

Aaronson, H. I., jt. ed. see Russell, K. C.

Aaronson, H. I., jt. ed. see Zackay, V. F.

Aaronson, Hubert I., ed. High-Temperature, High-Resolution Metallography. LC 67-26569. (Metallurgical Society Conferences Ser.: Vol. 38). pap. 97.80 (ISBN 0-317-10571-X, 2001527). Bks Demand UMI.

Aaronson, Hubert I. & Laughlin, David E., eds. International Conference on Solid-Solid Phase Transformations: Proceedings, Pittsburgh, 1981. (Illus.). 1610p. 1983. 70.00 (ISBN 0-89520-452-5); members 45.00 (ISBN 0-317-36279-8); student members 25.00 (ISBN 0-317-36280-1). ASM.

Aaronson, Ian A. & Cremin, B. J. Clinical Paediatric Uroradiology. (Illus.). 456p. 1984. text ed. 139.00 (ISBN 0-443-01852-9). Churchill.

Aaronson, Sheldon. Experimental Microbial Ecology. 1970. 46.00 (ISBN 0-12-041050-8). Acad Pr.

Aaronson, Sheldon, ed. Chemical Communication at the Microbial Level, Vols. I & II. 200p. 1982. Vol. I 200p. 67.00 (ISBN 0-8493-5319-X); Vol. II 200p. 67.00 (ISBN 0-8493-5320-3). CRC Pr.

Aaronson, Stuart A., et al, eds. Genetic & Phenotypic Markers of Tumors. 392p. 1984. 62.50x (ISBN 0-306-41817-7, Plenum Pr). Plenum Pub.

Aarre, Bent. Spinnaker Handling. LC 79-2728. (Illus.). 1980. 6.95i (ISBN 0-06-010019-2, HarpT). Har-Row.

Aarre, Bent, jt. auth. see Hansen, P. G.

Aarseth, Sigmund, jt. auth. see Miller, Margaret M.

Aarsleff, Hans. From Locke to Saussure: Essays on the Study of Language & Intellectual History. LC 81-10428. 474p. 1982. pap. 12.95x (ISBN 0-8166-0967-5). U of Minn Pr.

--Study of Language in England, Seventeen Eighty to Eighteen Sixty. LC 78-13573. 1979. Repr. of 1967 ed. lib. bdg. 24.75x (ISBN 0-313-21046-2, AASL). Greenwood.

--The Study of Language in England: Seventeen Eighty to Eighteen Sixty. 288p. 1984. pap. 14.95x (ISBN 0-8166-1253-6). U of Minn Pr.

Aarts, F. English Syntactic Structures: An Introduction to the Syntax of Present-Day Written English. (Institute of English Courses Ser.). 160p. 1982. 8.35 (ISBN 0-08-028634-8). Pergamon.

Aarts, F., jt. auth. see Janssens, G.

Aarts, F. G., et al, eds. The Best of DQR. (Costerus New Ser.: No. 43). 332p. 1984. pap. text ed. 32.75x (ISBN 90-6203-626-0, Pub. by Rodopi Holland). Humanities.

Aarts, J. & Maijs, W., eds. Corpus Linguistics. (Costerus New Ser.: No. 45). 229p. 1984. pap. text ed. 23.50x (ISBN 90-6203-696-1, Pub. by Rodopi Holland). Humanities.

Aarts, Jack W. Antitrust Policy Versus Economic Power. 1975. pap. 43.00 (ISBN 90-207-0473-7, Pub. by Martinus Nijhoff Netherlands). Kluwer Academic.

Aarts, N. J., ed. see European Congress on Thermography, 1st, Amsterdam, Jun 1974.

AAS - AAAS Symposium - Montreal - 1964. Towards Deeper Space Penetration. Van Driest, Edard R., ed. (Science & Technology Ser.: Vol. 2). 1964. 20.00x (ISBN 0-87703-030-8, Pub. by Am Astronaut). Univelt Inc.

Aas, E. J., jt. ed. see Anceau, F.

Aas, Kjell. The Allergic Child. Disch, Lizann, tr. (Illus.). 300p. 1971. 30.00x (ISBN 0-398-00002-6). C C Thomas.

--The Biochemical & Immunological Basis of Bronchial Asthma. (Illus.). 256p. 1972. 19.75x (ISBN 0-398-02213-5). C C Thomas.

--The Bronchial Provocation Test. (Illus.). 120p. 1975. 18.75x (ISBN 0-398-03208-4). C C Thomas.

AASA. New Forms for Community Education. 12.00 (ISBN 0-686-08744-5, 021-00414). Am Assn Sch Admin.

Aasen, A. O., et al, eds. Papers Dedicated to Egil Amundsen: On the Occasion of his 60th Birthday March 18, 1984. (Journal: European Surgical Research: Vol. 16, Supp. 2). (Illus.). iv, 172p. 1984. pap. 22.25 (ISBN 3-8055-3889-8). S Karger.

Aaseng, Nate. Baseball: It's Your Team. (You Are the Coach Ser.). (Illus.). 104p. (gr. 4 up). 1985. PLB 8.95 (ISBN 0-8225-1558-X). Lerner Pubns.

--Carl Lewis: Legend Chaser. LC 84-23348. (Achievers Ser.). (Illus.). 56p. (gr. 4 up). 1985. PLB 6.95 (ISBN 0-8225-0496-0). Lerner Pubns.

--Football: It's Your Team. (You Are the Coach Ser.). (Illus.). 104p. (gr. 4 up). 1985. PLB 8.95 (ISBN 0-8225-1557-1). Lerner Pubns.

--More with Less: The Future World of Buckminster Fuller. (Illus.). 80p. (gr. 4-10). 1986. PLB 9.95 (ISBN 0-8225-0498-7). Lerner Pubns.

--Pro Sports' Greatest Rivalries. (Sports Talk Ser.). (Illus.). 80p. (gr. 4 up). 1985. PLB 8.95 (ISBN 0-8225-1530-X). Lerner Pubns.

--You Are the Coach: College Basketball. (gr. k-12). 1986. pap. 2.25 (ISBN 0-440-99839-5, LFL). Dell.

Aaseng, Nathan. Baseball: You Are the Manager. LC 82-268. (You Are the Coach Ser.). (Illus.). 104p. (gr. 4up). 1983. PLB 8.95 (ISBN 0-8225-1552-0). Lerner Pubns.

--Baseball's Ace Relief Pitchers. LC 83-17585. (Sports Heroes Library). (Illus.). 80p. (gr. 4up). 1984. PLB 7.95 (ISBN 0-8225-1334-X). Lerner Pubns.

--Baseball's Brilliant Managers. LC 81-13643. (Sports Heroes Library). (Illus.). 80p. (gr. 4 up). 1982. PLB 7.95 (ISBN 0-8225-1071-5). Lerner Pubns.

--Baseball's Finest Pitchers. LC 80-12275. (Sports Heroes Library). (Illus.). 72p. (gr. 4 up). 1980. PLB 7.95 (ISBN 0-8225-1061-8). Lerner Pubns.

--Baseball's Greatest Teams. (Sports Talk Ser.). (Illus.). 80p. (gr. 4 up). 1985. PLB 8.95 (ISBN 0-8225-1526-1). Lerner Pubns.

--Baseball's Hottest Hitters. LC 83-711. (Sports Heroes Library). (Illus.). 80p. (gr. 4up). 1983. PLB 7.95 (ISBN 0-8225-1331-5). Lerner Pubns.

--Baseball's Power Hitters. LC 83-1025. (Sports Heroes Library). (Illus.). 80p. (gr. 4up). 1983. PLB 7.95 (ISBN 0-8225-1332-3). Lerner Pubns.

--Baseball's Worst Teams. (Sports Talk Ser.). (Illus.). 80p. (gr. 4 up). 1985. PLB 8.95 (ISBN 0-8225-1527-X). Lerner Pubns.

--Basketball: You Are the Coach. LC 82-17261. (You Are the Coach Ser.). (Illus.). 104p. (gr. 4up). 1983. PLB 8.95 (ISBN 0-8225-1553-9). Lerner Pubns.

--Basketball's High Flyers. LC 79-17137. (Sports Heroes Library). (Illus.). (gr. 4 up). 1980. PLB 7.95 (ISBN 0-8225-1058-8). Lerner Pubns.

--Basketball's Playmakers. LC 83-1041. (Sports Heroes Library). (Illus.). 80p. (gr. 4up). 1983. PLB 7.95 (ISBN 0-8225-1330-7). Lerner Pubns.

--Basketball's Power Players. (Sports Heroes Bks.). (Illus.). 80p. (gr. 4 up). 1985. PLB 7.95 (ISBN 0-8225-1342-0). Lerner Pubns.

--Basketball's Sharpshooters. LC 83-712. (Sports Heroes Library). (Illus.). 80p. (gr. 4up). 1983. PLB 7.95 (ISBN 0-8225-1329-3). Lerner Pubns.

--Batting Ninth for the Braves. (Pennypincher Bks.). 132p. (Orig.). (gr. 3-6). 1982. pap. 2.25 (ISBN 0-89191-708-X). Cook.

--Bruce Jenner: Decathlon Winner. LC 79-4497. (Achievers Ser.). (Illus.). (gr. 4-9). 1979. PLB 6.95 (ISBN 0-8225-0477-4). Lerner Pubns.

--College Basketball: You Are the Coach. LC 83-19996. (You Are the Coach Ser.). (Illus.). 104p. (gr. 4 up). 1984. lib. bdg. 8.95 (ISBN 0-8225-1555-5). Lerner Pubns.

--College Football: You Are the Coach. LC 83-22193. (You Are the Coach Ser.). (Illus.). (gr. 4 up). 1984. lib. bdg. 8.95 (ISBN 0-8225-1556-3). Lerner Pubns.

--Comeback Stars of Pro Sports. LC 83-737. (Sports Heroes Library). (Illus.). 80p. (gr. 4up). 1983. PLB 7.95 (ISBN 0-8225-1327-7). Lerner Pubns.

--Eric Heiden: Winner in Gold. LC 80-16982. (The Achievers Ser.). (Illus.). (gr. 4-9). 1980. PLB 6.95 (ISBN 0-8225-0481-2). Lerner Pubns.

--Football: You Are the Coach. LC 82-269. (You Are the Coach Ser.). (Illus.). 104p. (gr. 4up). 1983. PLB 8.95 (ISBN 0-8225-1551-2). Lerner Pubns.

--Football's Breakaway Backs. LC 80-16691. (Sports Heroes Library). (Illus.). 72p. (gr. 4 up). 1980. PLB 7.95 (ISBN 0-8225-1063-4). Lerner Pubns.

--Football's Crushing Blockers. LC 81-13681. (Sports Heroes Library). (Illus.). 80p. (gr. 6 up). 1982. PLB 7.95 (ISBN 0-8225-1074-X). Lerner Pubns.

--Football's Cunning Coaches. LC 80-29252. (The Sports Heroes Library). (Illus.). (gr. 4 up). 1981. PLB 7.95 (ISBN 0-8225-1065-0). Lerner Pubns.

--Football's Daring Defensive Backs. LC 83-17583. (Sports Heroes Library). (Illus.). 80p. (gr. 4up). 1984. PLB 7.95 (ISBN 0-8225-1335-8). Lerner Pubns.

--Football's Fierce Defenses. LC 79-16315. (The Sports Heroes Library). (Illus.). (gr. 4 up). 1980. PLB 7.95 (ISBN 0-8225-1057-X). Lerner Pubns.

--Football's Hard-Hitting Linebackers. LC 83-17566. (Sports Heroes Library). (Illus.). 80p. (gr. 4up). 1984. PLB 7.95 (ISBN 0-8225-1336-6). Lerner Pubns.

--Football's Most Controversial Calls. (Sports Talk Ser.). (Illus.). 96p. (gr. 4 up). 1985. 8.95 (ISBN 0-8225-1528-8). Lerner Pubns.

--Football's Most Shocking Upsets. (Sports Talk Ser.). (Illus.). 96p. (gr. 4 up). 1985. PLB 8.95 (ISBN 0-8225-1529-6). Lerner Pubns.

--Football's Punishing Pass Rushers. LC 83-17556. (Sports Heroes Library). (Illus.). 80p. (gr. 4up). 1984. PLB 7.95 (ISBN 0-8225-1338-2). Lerner Pubns.

--Football's Steadiest Kickers. LC 80-28863. (Sports Heroes Library). (Illus.). (gr. 4 up). 1981. PLB 7.95 (ISBN 0-8225-1069-3). Lerner Pubns.

--Football's Super Bowl Champions: I-VIII. LC 81-13659. (Sports Heroes Library). (Illus.). 80p. (gr. 4 up). 1982. PLB 7.95 (ISBN 0-8225-1072-3). Lerner Pubns.

--Football's Super Bowl Champions: IX-XVI. LC 82-10099. (Sports Heroes Library). (Illus.). 72p. (gr. 4 up). 1982. PLB 7.95 (ISBN 0-8225-1333-1). Lerner Pubns.

--Football's Sure-Handed Receivers. LC 80-17762. (Sports Heroes Library). (Illus.). 72p. (gr. 4 up). 1980. PLB 7.95 (ISBN 0-8225-1064-2). Lerner Pubns.

--Football's Toughest Tight Ends. LC 80-27803. (Sports Heroes Library). (Illus.). (gr. 4 up). 1981. PLB 7.95 (ISBN 0-8225-1070-7). Lerner Pubns.

--Football's Winning Quarterbacks. LC 80-12074. (Sports Heroes Library). (Illus.). (gr. 4 up). 1980. PLB 7.95 (ISBN 0-8225-1062-6). Lerner Pubns.

--Forty Two Red on Four. (Pennypincher Bks.). 132p. (gr. 6-9). 1983. 2.25 (ISBN 0-89191-754-3). Cook.

--Hockey: You Are the Coach. LC 82-17170. (You Are the Coach Ser.). (Illus.). 104p. (gr. 4up). 1983. PLB 8.95 (ISBN 0-8225-1554-7). Lerner Pubns.

--Hockey's Fearless Goalies. LC 83-17512. (Sports Heroes Library). (Illus.). 80p. (gr. 4 up). 1984. PLB 7.95 (ISBN 0-8225-1341-2). Lerner Pubns.

--Hockey's Super Scorers. LC 83-17511. (Sports Heroes Library). (Illus.). 80p. (gr. 4up). 1984. PLB 7.95 (ISBN 0-8225-1340-4). Lerner Pubns.

--I'm Learning, Lord, but I Still Need Help: Story Devotions for Boys. LC 81-65652. 112p. (Orig.). 1981. pap. 3.75 (ISBN 0-8066-1888-4, 10-3202). Augsburg.

--I'm Searching, Lord, but I Need Your Light. LC 82-72644. (Young Readers Ser.). 112p. (gr. 3-6). 1983. pap. 3.75 (ISBN 0-8066-1950-3, 10-3203). Augsburg.

--Little Giants of Pro Sports. LC 80-12031. (Sports Heroes Library). (Illus.). (gr. 4 up). 1980. PLB 7.95 (ISBN 0-8225-1059-6). Lerner Pubns.

--Memorable World Series Moments. LC 81-13725. (Sports Heroes Library). (Illus.). 80p. (gr. 4 up). 1982. PLB 7.95 (ISBN 0-8225-1073-1). Lerner Pubns.

--Pete Rose. LC 79-27377. (The Achievers Ser.). (Illus.). (gr. 4-9). 1981. PLB 6.95 (ISBN 0-8225-0480-4). Lerner Pubns.

--Steve Carlton: Baseball's Silent Strongman. LC 83-17516. (Achievers Ser.). (Illus.). 64p. (gr. 4 up). 1984. PLB 6.95 (ISBN 0-8225-0491-X). Lerner Pubns.

--Superstars Stopped Short. LC 81-12431. (Sports Heroes Library). (Illus.). 80p. (gr. 4 up). 1982. PLB 7.95 (ISBN 0-8225-1326-9). Lerner Pubns.

--Supersubs of Pro Sports. LC 83-738. (Sports Heroes Library). (Illus.). 80p. (gr. 4up). 1983. PLB 7.95 (ISBN 0-8225-1328-5). Lerner Pubns.

--Track's Magnificent Milers. LC 80-27404. (The Sports Heroes Library). (Illus.). (gr. 4 up). 1981. PLB 7.95 (ISBN 0-8225-1066-9). Lerner Pubns.

--Which Way Are You Leading Me, Lord? Bible Devotions for Boys. (Young Readers Ser.). 112p. (Orig.). 1984. pap. 3.75 (ISBN 0-8066-2113-3, 10-7099). Augsburg.

--Winners Never Quit: Athletes Who Beat the Odds. LC 80-12305. (Sports Heroes Library). (Illus.). (gr. 4 up). 1980. PLB 7.95 (ISBN 0-8225-1060-X). Lerner Pubns.

--Winning Men of Tennis. LC 80-28598. (Sports Heroes Library). (Illus.). (gr. 4 up). 1981. PLB 7.95 (ISBN 0-8225-1068-5). Lerner Pubns.

--Winning Women of Tennis. LC 81-6033. (The Sports Heroes Library). (Illus.). (gr. 4 up). 1981. PLB 7.95 (ISBN 0-8225-1067-7, AACR2). Lerner Pubns.

--World-Class Marathoners. LC 81-13660. (Sports Heroes Library). (Illus.). 80p. (gr. 4 up). 1982. PLB 7.95 (ISBN 0-8225-1325-0). Lerner Pubns.

--You Are the Coach: Basketball. 112p. (YA) (gr. 5 up). 1983. pap. 1.95 (ISBN 0-440-99128-5, LFL). Dell.

--You Are The Coach: College Football. (gr. k-6). 1985. pap. 2.25 (ISBN 0-440-99840-9, LFL). Dell.

--You Are the Coach: Football. 112p. (gr. 5 up). 1983. pap. 1.95 (ISBN 0-440-99136-6, LFL). Dell.

--You Are the Coach: Hockey. (gr. 5 up). 1984. pap. 1.95 (ISBN 0-440-99843-3, LFL). Dell.

--You Are the Manager: Baseball. 112p. (gr. 5 up). 1984. pap. 1.95 (ISBN 0-440-99829-8, LFL). Dell.

Aaseng, Rolf E. Basic Christian Teachings. LC 81-52276. 112p. (Orig.). 1982. pap. 4.95 (ISBN 0-8066-1908-2, 10-0547). Augsburg.

--Sense & Nonsense: A Word for Teens. 64p. 1976. pap. 2.50 (ISBN 0-8010-0090-4). Baker Bk.

Aaseth, Sigmund, jt. auth. see Miller, Margaret M.

Aasgaard, P. R., ed. see Sorrows, Gene.

Aasheim, Ashley. A Stillness at Sea. 368p. (Orig.). 1983. pap. 3.50 (ISBN 0-440-08250-1, Emerald). Dell.

--Vulcan Rising. 320p. (Orig.). 1982. pap. 3.50 (ISBN 0-440-19348-6). Dell.

AASHTO Administrative Subcommittee on Computer Technology. Computer Systems Index. 1985. 15.00 (ISBN 0-686-20962-1, CSI). AASHTO.

AATCC. Coated Fabrics. (Symposia Papers). 99p. 1976. 35.00 (ISBN 0-318-12150-6); members 19.00 (ISBN 0-318-12151-4). AATCC.

--Textile, Toxicological & Environmental Concerns. (Symposia Papers). 50p. 1980. 46.00 (ISBN 0-318-12187-5); members 25.00 (ISBN 0-318-12188-3). AATCC.

Aatec Publications, ed. Solar Census: Photovoltaics Edition. LC 84-71602. 200p. 1984. pap. 14.95 (ISBN 0-937948-05-5). Aatec Pubns.

Aatre, V. K. Network Theory & Filter Design. LC 80-84534. 432p. 1981. cloth 21.95x (ISBN 0-470-26934-0). Halsted Pr.

Aavani, Gholam R., tr. see Nasr, Seyyed H.

ABA Center of Professional Responsiblity. ABA-BNA Lawyers' Manual on Professional Conduct: Bibliography. 500p. 1985. pap. 35.00 (ISBN 0-87179-485-3). BNA.

ABA National Conference of Lawyers & Collection Agencies & American Law Institute-American Bar Association Committee on Continuing Professional Education. Debt Collection Law & Practice: ALI-ABA Course of Study Materials. LC 83-172718. 1983. pap. 40.00 (ISBN 0-318-00248-5). Am Law Inst.

ABA National Institute Staff. The Trial of an Antitrust Price-Fixing Case. 271p. 1981. looseleaf 75.00 (ISBN 0-317-30576-X). Amer Bar Assn.

ABA National Institutes. Arson for Profit: The Insurer's Defense. 170p. 1981. 50.00 (ISBN 0-686-47977-7). Amer Bar Assn.

ABA Special Committee on Centennial & Division of Communications. A Good Day at Saratoga. 59p. 1978. 4.95 (ISBN 0-686-47761-8). Amer Bar Assn.

ABA Special Committee on Youth Education for Citizenship. Mandate for Change: The Impact of Law on Educational Innovation. Henning, Joel F., et al, eds. LC 79-89342. 326p. 1979. pap. 9.95 (ISBN 0-89994-238-5). Soc Sci Ed.

ABA Standing Committee on Lawyers' Professional Liability. A Lawyers' Guide to Legal Malpractice Insurance. 124p. 1982. pap. 18.00 (414-0001). Amer Bar Assn.

Abad, Gemino H. A Formal Approach to Lyric Poetry. 1978. text ed. 20.00x (ISBN 0-8248-0632-8); pap. text ed. 16.00x (ISBN 0-8248-0643-3). UH Pr.

--In Another Light: Poems & Essays. 1976. text ed. 15.00x (ISBN 0-8248-0471-6). UH Pr.

Abad, Jerry & Abad, Valerie. Sound & Graphics: For the Apple II, IIe & Franklin Computers. (Illus., Orig.). (gr. 2-12). 1984. pap. text ed. 9.95 (ISBN 0-88190-351-5, BO351). Datamost.

Abad, Valerie, jt. auth. see Abad, Jerry.

Abad de Santillan, Diego. Ricardo Flores Magon: Apostle of the Mexican Social Revolution. (Mexico Ser.). 1979. lib. bdg. 59.95 (ISBN 0-8490-2998-8). Gordon Pr.

Abadi, Jacob. Britain's Withdrawal from the Middle East, 1947-1971: The Economic & Strategic Imperatives (1947-1971) (Leaders, Politics, & Social Change in the Islamic World: Vol. 2). 300p. 1983. 26.00 (ISBN 0-940670-19-4). Kingston Pr.

Abadie, Ann, jt. ed. see Fowler, Doreen.

Abadie, Ann J. & Dollarhide, Louis D., eds. Eudora Welty: A Form of Thanks. LC 78-13285. (Illus.). 1979. text ed. 9.95x (ISBN 0-87805-089-2). U Pr of Miss.

Abadie, Ann J., jt. ed. see Fowler, Doreen.

Abadie, Ann J., jt. ed. see Harrington, Evans.

Abadie, Daniel, jt. auth. see Hulten, Pontus.

Abadie, J., ed. Integer & Non-Linear Programming. 544p. 1970. 85.00 (ISBN 0-7204-2036-9). Elsevier.

Abadie, M. J., jt. auth. see Campbell, Joseph.

Abadie, M. J., jt. auth. see Raphael, Sally Jessy.

Abadinsky, Howard. The Criminal Elite: Professional & Organized Crime. LC 83-1445. (Contributions to Criminology & Penology: No. 1). (Illus.). xv, 190p. 1983. lib. bdg. 29.95 (ISBN 0-313-23833-2, ACE/). Greenwood.

--Discretionary Justice: An Introduction to Discretion in Criminal Justice. LC 84-2478. 192p. 1984. 24.75x (ISBN 0-398-05019-8). C C Thomas.

--The Mafia in America: An Oral History. LC 81-4338. 160p. 1981. 26.95 (ISBN 0-03-059587-8). Praeger.

--Organized Crime. LC 85-8963. 1985. lib. bdg. 23.95x (ISBN 0-8304-1165-8); text ed. 13.95x (ISBN 0-8304-1126-7). Nelson-Hall.

--Probation & Parole: Theory & Practice. 2nd ed. (Illus.). 480p. 1982. 28.95 (ISBN 0-13-715979-X). P-H.

Abadir, Akef, tr. see Mahfuz, Nagib.

Abagnale, Frank W., Jr. Catch Me If You Can. 1982. pap. 3.50 (ISBN 0-671-46287-3). PB.

Abailard, P. Sic et Non: A Critical Edition, 7 fascicles. Boyer, Blanche & McKeon, Richard, eds. Incl. Fascicle 1. (ISBN 0-226-00058-3);;; Fascicle 4. (ISBN 0-226-00061-3); Fascicle 5. (ISBN 0-226-00062-1); (ISBN 0-226-00064-8);. LC 74-7567. 1978. pap. text ed. 16.00x ea. O. P.; fascicles 1-7 complete in one clothbound vol. 130.00x (ISBN 0-226-00066-4). U of Chicago Pr.

Abailard, Pierre. Abailard's Christian Theology. McCullum, James R., tr. from Fr. LC 76-1128. 117p. 1976. Repr. of 1948 ed. lib. bdg. 14.50x (ISBN 0-915172-07-0). Richwood Pub.

--Abailard's Ethics. McCullum, James R., tr. from Fr. 93p. 1976. Repr. of 1935 ed. lib. bdg. 14.50x (ISBN 0-915172-08-9). Richwood Pub.

Abajian, Diane. Praying & Doing the Stations of the Cross with Children. (Illus.). 24p. (gr. 1-3). 1980. pap. 1.50 (ISBN 0-89622-118-0). Twenty-Third.

Abajian, James T. de see De Abajian, James T.

Abakanowicz, Magdalena, jt. auth. see Reichardt, Jasia.

Abalkin, L. I. The Economic System of Socialism. 139p. 1980. 5.95 (ISBN 0-8285-1705-3, Pub. by Progress Pubs USSR). Imported Pubns.

Abamson, Jeffrey A. Liberation & Its Limits: The Moral & Political Thought of Freud. LC 84-47681. 192p. 1984. 14.95 (ISBN 0-02-900210-9). Free Pr.

Abao, Tito. Who's Going to Win Tomorrow: How to Use Your Dreams for Fun & Profit. (Illus.). 80p. (Orig.). 1983. pap. 9.95 (ISBN 0-912651-00-8). TPA Publishing.

Abarbanel, Jerome. Redefining the Environment. (Key Issues Ser.: No. 9). 40p. 1972. pap. 2.00 (ISBN 0-87546-200-6). ILR Pr.

Abarbanel, Judah. The Philosophy of Love. Friedeberg-Seeley, F. & Barnes, J. H., trs. 1977. lib. bdg. 59.95 (ISBN 0-8490-2433-1). Gordon Pr.

Abarbanel, Karin, jt. auth. see Hillman, Howard.

Abarbenel, Don I. Abarbenel Al Hatorah, 3 Vols. (Heb.). Set. 45.00 (ISBN 0-87559-078-0). Shalom.

Abartis, Caesarea. The Tragicomic Construction of Cymberline & the Winter's Tale. (Salzburg Studies in English Literature: Jacobean Drama Studies: Vol. 73). (Orig.). 1977. pap. text ed. 25.50x (ISBN 0-391-01289-4). Humanities.

Abasiekong, Edet M. Integrated Rural Development in the Third World: Its Concepts, Problems & Prospects. (Illus.). 144p. 1982. 7.50 (ISBN 0-682-49750-9, University). Exposition Pr FL.

Abata, Russell M. Helps for the Scrupulous. LC 76-21430. (Orig.). 1976. pap. 2.50 (ISBN 0-89243-061-3, 41210). Liguori Pubns.

--How to Develop a Better Self-Image. LC 79-91440. (Orig.). 1980. pap. 2.95 (ISBN 0-89243-119-9, 41150). Liguori Pubns.

--Sexual Morality: Guidelines for Today's Catholic. 1975. pap. 1.50 (ISBN 0-89243-019-2, 29528). Liguori Pubns.

--Unlocking the Doors of Your Heart: A New Look at Love. LC 83-83442. 1984. pap. 4.25 (ISBN 0-89243-204-7). Liguori Pubns.

Abata, Russell M., jt. auth. see Weir, William.

Abate, Frank, jt. ed. see Urdang, Laurence.

Abate, Frank R., jt. ed. see Urdang, Laurence.

Abate, Susan & Lucia, Nancy. Consumer Power: Classroom Strategies for Consumer Education. 1983. pap. 14.95 (ISBN 0-673-16594-9). Scott F.

Abate, Yohannis, jt. auth. see Wubneh, Mulatu.

Abaya, Hernando J. The Making of a Subversive: A Memoir. (Illus.). iii, 236p. 1984. pap. 13.50x (ISBN 971-10-0154-3, Pub. by New Day Philippines). Cellar.

Abayakoon, Cyrus. Astro-Palmistry. LC 75-7187. (Illus.). 1975. 20.00 (ISBN 0-88231-012-7). ASI Pubs Inc.

Abba, Giuseppe C. The Diary of One of Garibaldi's Thousand. Vincent, E. R., tr. from Ital. LC 80-24181. (Oxford Library of Italian Classics). (Illus.). xxi, 166p. 1981. Repr. of 1962 ed. lib. bdg. 20.75x (ISBN 0-313-22446-3, ABDO). Greenwood.

Abba, R. Nature & Authority of the Bible. 349p. 1958. 8.95 (ISBN 0-227-67539-8). Attic Pr.

Abbad Y Lasierra, Inigo. Historia Geografica, Civil y Natural De la Isla De San Juan Bautista De Puerto Rico. 3rd ed. pap. 9.00 (ISBN 0-8477-0800-4). U of PR Pr.

Abbagnano, Nicola. Critical Existentialism. Langiulli, Nino, ed. 10.25 (ISBN 0-8446-0450-X). Peter Smith.

Abbas, B. M. The Ganges Water Dispute. 160p. 1982. text ed. 27.50x (ISBN 0-7069-2080-5, Pub. by Vikas India). Advent NY.

Abbas, H. & Khan, Emir A. Sufi Principles Action, Learning Methods, Imitators, Meeting-Places. (Sufi Research Ser.). 64p. 1982. pap. 4.95 (ISBN 0-86304-001-2, Pub. by Octagon Pr England). Ins Study Human.

Abbas, Ihsan, tr. see Issawi, Charles.

Abbas, Ihsan, tr. see Khuri, Ra'if.

Abbas, Ihsan, tr. see Khuri, Raif.

Abbas, K. A. I Am Not an Island: An Experiment in Autobiography. 1977. 12.50x (ISBN 0-88386-941-1). South Asia Bks.

--That Woman: Indira Gandhi's Seven Years in Power. 1973. 11.25 (ISBN 0-89684-553-2). Orient Bk Dist.

--The World Is My Village: A Novel of Modern India. 1984. 28.50x (ISBN 0-8364-1132-3, Pub. by Ajanta). South Asia Bks.

Abbas, Kathleen, jt. auth. see Johnston, Dorothy G.

Abbas, S. A., jt. auth. see Brecher, Irving.

Abbaschian, G. J. & David, S. A., eds. Grain Refinement in Castings & Welds: Proceedings, TMS Fall Meeting, St. Louis Missouri, 1982. LC 83-61027. (Illus.). 293p. 1983. 42.00 (ISBN 0-89520-457-6). Metal Soc.

Abbaschian, G. J., ed. see Engineering Foundation Conference on Modeling of Casting & Welding Processes II, New Hampshire, July 31 - August 5, 1983.

Abbasi, Abdul S. Echocardiographic Interpretation. (Illus.). 564p. 1981. 49.75x (ISBN 0-398-04153-9). C C Thomas.

Abbat, William. Colloquial Who's Who. LC 65-27204. 256p. Repr. of 1925 ed. 14.50 (ISBN 0-405-03660-4, Pub. by Blom). Ayer Co Pubs.

Abbate, Fred J., et al. Ethics & Energy. (Decisionmakers Bookshelf: Vol. 5). (Illus.). 1979. pap. 2.50 (ISBN 0-931032-05-9). Edison Electric.

Abbate, M. J., jt. auth. see Stammler, R.

Abbate, Marcia & LaChappelle, Nancy. Pictures, Please! A Language Supplement. (Illus.). 1979. looseleaf 39.00 (ISBN 0-88450-773-4, 3092-B). Communication Skill.

Abbate, Marcia S. & LaChappelle, Nancy B. Pictures, Please! An Articulation Supplement. 215p. 1984. 3-ring binder 39.00 (ISBN 0-88450-878-1, 2091-B). Communication Skill.

Abbazia, Patrick. John Paul Jones, America's First Naval Hero. Rahmas, D. Steve, ed. (Outstanding Personalities Ser: No. 86). 1976. lib. bdg. 3.50 incl. catalog cards (ISBN 0-87157-586-8); pap. 1.95 vinyl laminated covers (ISBN 0-87157-086-6). SamHar Pr.

--Nathanael Greene: Commander of the American Continental Army in the South. Rahmas, Steve, ed. (Outstanding Personalities Ser.: No. 87). (YA) (gr. 7-12). 1976. lib. bdg. 3.50 incl. catalog cards (ISBN 0-87157-587-6); pap. 1.95 vinyl laminated covers (ISBN 0-87157-087-4). SamHar Pr.

Abbe, Derek Van see Van Abbe, Derek.

Abbe, Donald R. Austin & the Reese River Mining District: Nevada's Forgotten Frontier. LC 84-20966. (History & Political Science Ser.: No. 19). (Illus.). 117p. (Orig.). 1985. pap. 6.95x (ISBN 0-87417-091-5). U of Nev Pr.

Abbe, Dorothy. The Dwiggins Marionettes: A Complete Experimental Theatre in Miniature. (Puppet Library Ser). 1970. 29.95 (ISBN 0-8238-0146-2). Plays.

--William Addison Dwiggins. 1974. 1.00 (ISBN 0-89073-018-0). Boston Public Lib.

Abbe, Dorothy, compiled by. Stencilled Ornament & Illustration. pap. 15.00 (ISBN 0-89073-064-4). Boston Public Lib.

Abbe, Elfriede. The Fern Herbal: Including the Ferns, the Horsetails, & the Club Mosses. LC 84-45439. (Illus.). 120p. 1985. 35.00x (ISBN 0-8014-1718-X). Cornell U Pr.

Abbe, George. Collected Poems. 1961. 5.95 (ISBN 0-87233-800-2). Bauhan.

--Dreams & Dissent, Poems 1961-1970. 5.95 (ISBN 0-87233-016-8). Bauhan.

--The Larks. (YA) 1974. pap. 3.95 (ISBN 0-87233-033-8). Bauhan.

--You & Contemporary Poetry. 1968. pap. 3.95 (ISBN 0-87233-010-9). Bauhan.

Abbe, Kathryn M., jt. auth. see Gill, Frances M.

Abbensetts, Michael. Samba. 1981. pap. 4.95 (ISBN 0-413-48140-9, NO. 2569). Methuen Inc.

Abbett, R. W. American Civil Engineering Practice, Vol. 3. LC 56-11255. Repr. of 1973 ed. 120.00 (ISBN 0-8357-9835-6, 2055091). Bks Demand UMI.

--Engineering Contracts & Specifications. 4th ed. LC 63-14072. 461p. 1963. 39.95x (ISBN 0-471-00035-3, Pub. by Wiley-Interscience). Wiley.

Abbey, Augustus. Technological Innovation: The R & D Work Environment. Dufey, Gunter, ed. LC 82-4883. (Research for Business Decisions Ser.: No. 49). 140p. 1982. 39.95 (ISBN 0-8357-1335-0). UMI Res Pr.

Abbey, Charles J. The English Church & Its Bishops, 1700-1800, 2 Vols. LC 77-130230. Repr. of 1887 ed. Set. 74.50 (ISBN 0-404-00290-0). AMS Pr.

Abbey, Dawn, ed. see Sutphen, Dick.

Abbey, Donald S. To Take the Money. LC 80-65745. 326p. 1980. 10.00 (ISBN 0-9604228-0-3). Allowance.

Abbey, Edward. Abbey's Road: Take the Other. 1979. pap. 6.75 (ISBN 0-525-03001-8, 0655-200). Dutton.

--Beyond the Wall. 1984. 14.95 (ISBN 0-03-069299-7); pap. 7.95 (ISBN 0-03-069301-2). HR&W.

--Black Sun. 160p. 1982. pap. 2.50 (ISBN 0-380-58503-0, 58503-0). Avon.

--Black Sun. LC 80-27953. 160p. 1981. pap. 5.95 (ISBN 0-88496-167-2). Capra Pr.

--The Brave Cowboy. LC 76-57530. (Zia Books). 277p. 1977. pap. 6.95 (ISBN 0-8263-0448-6). U of NM Pr.

--The Brave Cowboy. 320p. 1982. pap. 2.95 (ISBN 0-380-58966-4, 64386-3). Avon.

--Desert Solitaire. rev. ed. LC 80-28961. (Literature of the American Wilderness). (Illus.). 296p. 1981. Repr. of 1968 ed. 12.50 (ISBN 0-87905-070-5, Peregrine Smith). Gibbs M Smith.

--Desert Solitaire. 1970. pap. 8.95 (ISBN 0-671-20716-4, Touchstone Bks). S&S.

--Desert Solitaire: A Season in the Wilderness. 320p. 1985. pap. 3.00 (ISBN 0-345-32649-0). Ballantine.

--Down the River. LC 81-19429. (Illus.). 256p. 1982. 13.95 (ISBN 0-525-09524-1, 01355-400); pap. 7.95 (ISBN 0-525-47676-8, 0772-230). Dutton.

--Fire on the Mountain. LC 77-89434. (Zia Books). 1978. pap. 6.95 (ISBN 0-8263-0457-5). U of NM Pr.

--Fire on the Mountain. 192p. 1982. pap. 2.75 (ISBN 0-380-59519-2, 59519-2, Flare). Avon.

--Good News. 256p. 1980. pap. 6.95 (ISBN 0-525-03467-6, 0674-210). Dutton.

--The Journey Home: Some Words in Defense of the American West. 1977. pap. 7.95 (ISBN 0-525-03700-4, 0772-230). Dutton.

--The Monkey Wrench Gang. 400p. 1983. pap. 3.95 (ISBN 0-380-00741-X, 60073-0). Avon.

--The Monkey Wrench Gang. rev. ed. LC 75-831. (Illus.). 368p. 1985. ltd. ed. 75.00 (ISBN 0-942688-19-8); 17.95 (ISBN 0-942688-18-X). Dream Garden.

--Slumgullion Stew: An Edward Abbey Reader. 352p. 1984. 18.95 (ISBN 0-525-24284-8, 01840-550); pap. 8.95 (ISBN 0-525-48138-9, 0869-260). Dutton.

Abbey, Edward, jt. auth. see Blaustein, John.

Abbey, Edward, jt. auth. see Thollander, Earl.

Abbey, Edward, jt. auth. see Thoreau, Henry D.

Abbey, F., jt. auth. see Thomas, A. F.

Abbey, Harlan C., et al. Showing Your Horse. LC 72-96963. (Illus.). 1979. pap. 4.95 (ISBN 0-668-04792-5). Arco.

Abbey, Hermione, ed. Three Psalm Tunes by Thomas Tallis. 16p. (Orig.). 1982. pap. 2.50 (ISBN 0-939400-02-2). RWS Bks.

Abbey, James R., jt. auth. see Astroff, Milton T.

Abbey, Karin, jt. auth. see Evans, G. Edward.

Abbey, L., jt. ed. see Asprin, Robert L.

Abbey, Lester. A History of Music for Those Who Don't Want to Know Too Much About Music History. LC 80-124026. (Illus.). 278p. 1982. pap. 5.00 (ISBN 0-939400-03-0). RWS Bks.

Abbey, Lloyd. Destroyer & Preserver: Shelley's Poetic Skepticism. LC 79-9166. xiv, 171p. 1980. 15.50x (ISBN 0-8032-1001-9). U of Nebr Pr.

Abbey, Lynn. The Black Flame. 352p. pap. 2.75 (ISBN 0-441-06586-4). Ace Bks.

--The Black Flame. 1980. pap. 6.95 oversize (ISBN 0-441-06583-X). Ace Bks.

--The Black Flame. 384p. 1985. pap. 3.50 (ISBN 0-441-06587-2). Ace Bks.

--Daughter of the Bright Moon. 416p. 1985. pap. 3.50 (ISBN 0-441-13873-X, Pub. by Ace Science Fiction). Ace Bks.

--The Guardians. 1982. pap. 2.95 (ISBN 0-441-30589-X, Pub. by Ace Science Fiction). Ace Bks.

Abbey, Lynn, jt. auth. see Asprin, Robert L.

Abbey, Lynn, jt. ed. see Asprin, Robert L.

Abbey, Lynn, ed. see Asprin, Robert L.

Abbey, Merrill R. Communication in Pulpit & Parish. LC 72-14329. 238p. 1980. pap. 8.50 (ISBN 0-664-24312-6). Westminster.

--The Epic of United Methodist Preaching: A Profile in American Social History. 216p. (Orig.). 1983. lib. bdg. 24.00 (ISBN 0-8191-3691-3); pap. text ed. 12.00 (ISBN 0-8191-3692-1). U Pr of Amer.

Abbey, S. Goldsmith's & Silversmith's Handbook. 2nd rev. ed. (Illus.). 1968. 17.50 (ISBN 0-685-12021-X). Heinman.

Abbey, Staten. Book of Hillman Minx & Hunter. (Illus.). pap. 6.00x (ISBN 0-273-40039-8, SpS). Sportshelf.

--Book of the Rover. pap. 6.00x (ISBN 0-392-05798-0, SpS). Sportshelf.

--Book of the Triumph Two Thousand. pap. 6.00x (ISBN 0-392-05803-0, SpS). Sportshelf.

--Motorist Afloat. 14.50x (ISBN 0-392-01623-0, SpS). Sportshelf.

Abbey, Staton. Book of B.M.C. Eleven Hundred. pap. 6.00x (ISBN 0-392-02285-0, SpS). Sportshelf.

--Book of B.M.C. Minis. pap. 6.00x (ISBN 0-392-02299-0, SpS). Sportshelf.

--Book of Vauxhall Viva & Bedford Beagle. (Illus.). pap. 6.00x (ISBN 0-392-02366-0, SpS). Sportshelf.

Abbey, Stella K. Mother Goose Sweeps History. LC 13-275. (Illus.). 1967. 2.99 (ISBN 0-686-00888-X). S K Abbey.

Abbey, Wallace W. The Little Jewel. LC 84-14873. (Illus.). 244p. 1984. text ed. 39.00 (ISBN 0-930855-00-0). Pinon Productions.

Abbey-Harris, Nancy. Family Life Education: Homework for Parents & Teens. (Illus.). 82p. (Orig.). 1984. pap. 11.95 (ISBN 0-941816-11-7). Network Pubns.

Abbey-Harris, Nancy, jt. auth. see Todd, Kay R.

Abbiatico, Mario. Grandi Incisioni su Armi d'Oggi. (Illus.). Repr. of 1976 ed. 30.00 (ISBN 0-686-70832-6). Arma Pr.

Abbie, A. A. Studies in Physical Anthropology, Vols. 1 & 2. (AIAS Research & Regional Ser.: No. 5). (Illus., Orig.). 1975. Vol. 1. pap. text ed. 7.00x (ISBN 0-391-01880-9); Vol. 2. pap. text ed. 8.00x (ISBN 0-391-01881-7). Humanities.

Abbie, Leslie A. & Harrison, James Q. Economic Return to Investment in Irrigation in India, No. 536. 52p. 1982. pap. 3.00 (ISBN 0-8213-0083-0). World Bank.

Abbinanant, D., et al. Officiating Women's Sports. 1975. pap. text ed. 3.60x (ISBN 0-87563-079-0). Stipes.

Abbing, Roscam H. International Organizations in Europe & the Right to Health Care. 290p. 1979. pap. 42.00 (ISBN 90-26-8107-76, Pub. by Kluwer Law Netherlands). Kluwer Academic.

Abbo, Fred E. Steps to a Longer Life. LC 78-31661. 220p. 1979. pap. 4.95 (ISBN 0-89037-211-X). Anderson World.

Abbondante, Paul J., jt. auth. see Moliver, Donald M.

Abbot, jt. auth. see Sternberg.

Abbot, Abiel. Letters Written in the Interior of Cuba. facsimile ed. LC 75-37299. (Black Heritage Library Collection). Repr. of 1829 ed. 20.50 (ISBN 0-8369-8936-8). Ayer Co Pubs.

Abbot, Alexander S. The Philosophical, Psychological & Moral Degeneration of the American Pragmatists. (Illus.). 114p. 1980. 61.75 (ISBN 0-89266-257-3). Am Classical Coll Pr.

Abbot, Charles G. Adventures in the World of Science. 1958. 8.50 (ISBN 0-8183-0226-7). Pub Aff Pr.

Abbot, Claude C., ed. Early Mediaeval French Lyrics. 1979. Repr. of 1932 ed. lib. bdg. 25.00 (ISBN 0-8495-0218-7). Arden Lib.

Abbot, David. An Introduction to Reaction Kinetics. LC 67-7380. (Longman Concepts in Chemistry Ser.). pap. 40.00 (ISBN 0-317-09056-9, 2016336). Bks Demand UMI.

Abbot, David W. & Rogowsky, Edward T. Political Parties. 2nd ed. 1978. 19.95 (ISBN 0-395-30780-5). HM.

Abbot, Elisabeth, ed. see Pareto, Vilfredo.

Abbot, Evelyn. Pericles & the Golden Age of Athens. 1891. 25.00 (ISBN 0-8274-3926-1). R West.

Abbot, Francis E. Professor Royce's Libel. Bd. with A Public Remonstrance Addressed to the Board of Overseers of Harvard University. LC 75-3011. Repr. of 1892 ed. 11.50 (ISBN 0-404-59003-9). AMS Pr.

--Scientific Theism. LC 75-3012. (Philosophy in America Ser.). Repr. of 1885 ed. 21.50 (ISBN 0-404-59004-7). AMS Pr.

--The Syllogistic Philosophy or Prolegomena to Science, 2 vols. LC 75-3013. (Philosophy in Anerica Ser.). Repr. of 1906 ed. 51.00 set (ISBN 0-404-59005-5). AMS Pr.

--The Way Out of Agnosticism: Or the Philosophy of Free Religion. LC 75-3014. (Philosophy in America Ser.). Repr. of 1890 ed. 15.00 (ISBN 0-404-59008-X). AMS Pr.

Abbot, George. A Briefe Description of the Whole Worlde. LC 78-25701. (English Experience Ser.: No. 213). 68p. Repr. of 1599 ed. 9.50 (ISBN 90-221-0213-0). Walter J Johnson.

Abbot, Henry L. Beginning of Modern Submarine Warfare, under Captain-Lieutenant David Bushnell, Sappers & Miners, Army of the Revolution. (Illus.). xiv, 68p. (Facsimile of 1881 ed.). 1966. 12.50 (ISBN 0-208-00031-3, Archon). Shoe String.

Abbot, John & Bamberger, Eudes. The Abbey Psalter: The Book of Psalms Used by the Trappist Monks of Genesee Abbey. LC 81-80871. 368p. 1981. 24.95 (ISBN 0-8091-0316-8). Paulist Pr.

Abbot, P. Algebra. (Teach Yourself Ser.). 1980. pap. 4.95 (ISBN 0-679-10386-4). McKay.

Abbot, Philip & Levy, Michael B., eds. The Liberal Future in America: Essays in Renewal. LC 84-12834. (Contributions in Political Science Ser.: No. 123). (Illus.). vi, 210p. 1985. lib. bdg. 29.95 (ISBN 0-313-23761-1, ALF/). Greenwood.

Abbot, W. Panama & the Canal. 1976. lib. bdg. 59.95 (ISBN 0-8490-2404-8). Gordon Pr.

--Practical Geometry & Engineering Graphics. 8th ed. (Illus.). 1971. pap. text ed. 21.00x (ISBN 0-216-89450-6). Intl Ideas.

Abbot, W. W. The Royal Governors of Georgia, 1754-1775. LC 59-9568. (Institute of Early American History & Culture Ser.). x, 198p. 1959. 18.50 (ISBN 0-8078-0758-3). U of NC Pr.

Abbot, W. W., ed. The Papers of George Washington. LC 81-16307. (Colonial Ser.: Vol. 4). 495p. 1984. text ed. 30.00x (ISBN 0-8139-1006-4). U Pr of Va.

--The Papers of George Washington. LC 81-16307. (Colonial Ser.: Vol. 3). 512p. 1984. text ed. 30.00x (ISBN 0-8139-1003-X). U Pr of Va.

--The Papers of George Washington: June-September 1775. LC 81-16307. (Revolutionary Ser.: No. 1). 460p. 1985. text ed. 35.00x (ISBN 0-8139-1040-4). U Pr of Va.

Abbot, Wilbur C. Bibliography of Oliver Cromwell. 1929. Repr. 65.00 (ISBN 0-8482-7261-7). Norwood Edns.

Abbot, William W. The Colonial Origins of the United States 1607-1763. 139p. 1975. pap. text ed. 6.95 (ISBN 0-394-34161-9, RanC). Random.

Abbot, William W., ed. The Papers of George Washington, Vols. 1 & 2. LC 81-16307. (Colonial Ser. I). (Illus.). 1983. 35.00x ea. Vol. 1 (ISBN 0-8139-0912-0). Vol. 2 (ISBN 0-8139-0923-6). U Pr of Va.

Abbot, Willis J. Watching the World Go by. (American Newspapermen 1790-1933 Ser.). (Illus.). 358p. 1974. 17.50x (ISBN 0-8464-0033-2). Beekman Pubs.

Abbot-Smith, G., ed. A Manual Greek Lexicon of the New Testament. 528p. 45.00x (ISBN 0-567-01001-5, Pub. by T&T Clark Scotland). State Mutual Bk.

Abbott. Great Gatsby (Fitzgerald) (Book Notes Ser.). 1984. pap. 2.50 (ISBN 0-8120-3415-5). Barron.

--Large Software Development. 1985. 32.00 (ISBN 0-471-82646-4). Wiley.

Abbott & Anon. Railroads One Hundred Years Ago. (Sun Historical Ser.). (Illus.). 1980. 3.50 (ISBN 0-89540-048-0, SB-048). Sun Pub.

Abbott & Love, eds. Sappho Was a Right-On Woman. 1978. 8.95 (ISBN 0-8128-2406-7). Stein & Day.

Abbott, A. C., jt. ed. see Lamble, J. W.

Abbott, A. F. Ordinary Level Physics. 3rd ed. 1977. pap. text ed. 16.00x (ISBN 0-435-67005-0). Heinemann Ed.

Abbott, Abbe, jt. auth. see Green, Paul.

Abbott, Anthony, ed. Publisher's Trade List Annual Index, 1903-1963. 150p. 1980. lib. bdg. 49.50x (ISBN 0-930466-25-X). Meckler Pub.

--Publishers' Trade List Annual Index, 1964-1980. 175p. 1984. lib. bdg. 75.00 (ISBN 0-88736-015-7). Meckler Pub.

Abbott, Berenice. Berenice Abbott: Photographs. (Illus.). 1970. 22.50 (ISBN 0-8180-1412-1); pap. 13.95 (ISBN 0-8180-1413-X). Horizon.

--New York in the Thirties. LC 73-77375. Orig. Title: Changing New York. (Illus.). 112p. 1973. Repr. of 1939 ed. 6.50 (ISBN 0-486-22967-X). Dover.

--New York in the Thirties. Orig. Title: Changing New York. 15.00 (ISBN 0-8446-5000-5). Peter Smith.

--The World of Atget. (Illus.). 256p. 1980. 27.50 (ISBN 0-8180-1415-6). Horizon.

Abbott, C. B., jt. auth. see Lerner, Elaine.

Abbott, C. C. Boswell. 1985. 54.50 (ISBN 0-317-19960-9). Porter.

Abbott, Carl. Boosters & Businessmen: Popular Economic Thought & Urban Growth in the Antebellum Middle West. LC 80-1795. (Contributions in American Studies: No. 53). (Illus.). xii, 266p. 1981. lib. bdg. 29.95 (ISBN 0-313-22562-1, ABB/). Greenwood.

--The Great Extravaganza: Portland & the Lewis & Clark Exposition. LC 80-83179. (Illus.). 96p. 1981. pap. 6.95 (ISBN 0-87595-088-4). Oreg Hist Soc.

--The New Urban America: Growth & Politics in Sunbelt Cities. LC 80-22848. ix, 317p. 1981. 22.00 (ISBN 0-8078-1464-4); pap. 7.95x (ISBN 0-8078-4079-3). U of NC Pr.

--Portland: Gateway to the Northwest. 264p. 1985. 24.95 (ISBN 0-89781-155-0). Windsor Pubns Inc.

--Portland: Planning, Politics & Growth in a Twentieth-Century City. LC 82-21978. (Illus.). x, 350p. 1983. 25.00 (ISBN 0-8032-1008-6); pap. 12.95 (ISBN 0-8032-5906-9, BB 878, Bison). U of Nebr Pr.

Abbott, Carl, et al. Colorado: A History of the Centennial State. LC 81-68869. 1982. 17.50x (ISBN 0-87081-130-4); pap. 11.95 (ISBN 0-87081-128-2); pap. text ed. 8.95x (ISBN 0-87081-129-0). Colo Assoc.

Abbott, Charles C. The New York Bond Market, Nineteen Twenty to Nineteen Thirty. facsimile ed. LC 75-2618. (Wall Street & the Security Market Ser.). 1975. Repr. of 1937 ed. 24.50x (ISBN 0-405-06945-6). Ayer Co Pubs.

Abbott, Claude C. Boswell. 1978. lib. bdg. 10.00 (ISBN 0-8495-0123-7). Arden Lib.

--Boswell. 1980. Repr. of 1946 ed. lib. bdg. 8.50 (ISBN 0-89987-003-1). Darby Bks.

--Boswell. LC 73-10004. 1946. lib. bdg. 8.50 (ISBN 0-8414-2860-3). Folcroft.

--Boswell. 1979. 28.50 (ISBN 0-685-94327-5). Porter.

--Early Mediaeval French Lyrics. LC 75-12998. Repr. of 1932 ed. lib. bdg. 27.50 (ISBN 0-8414-3006-3). Folcroft.

--The Life & Times of George Darley: Poet & Critic. 1979. Repr. of 1928 ed. lib. bdg. 45.00 (ISBN 0-8495-0215-2). Arden Lib.

Abbott, Craig S. Marianne Moore: A Descriptive Bibliography. LC 76-5922. (Pittsburgh Series in Bibliography). 1977. 34.00x (ISBN 0-8229-3319-5). U of Pittsburgh Pr.

Abbott, Craig S., jt. auth. see Williams, William P.

Abbott, Daniel J., jt. auth. see Clinard, Marshall B.

Abbott, David. Basic Notes on Advanced Level Chemistry. pap. 6.50x (ISBN 0-392-08409-0, SpS). Sportshelf.

Abbott, David, ed. The Biographical Dictionary of Scientists: Astronomers. LC 84-9236. (The Biographical Dictionary of Scientists Ser.). 210p. 1984. 18.95x (ISBN 0-911745-80-7). P Bedrick Bks.

--The Biographical Dictionary of Scientists: Biologists. LC 84-10972. (The Biographical Dictionary of Scientists Ser.). 188p. 1984. 18.95x (ISBN 0-911745-82-3). P Bedrick Bks.
--The Biographical Dictionary of Scientists: Chemists. LC 84-9284. (The Biographical Dictionary of Scientists Ser.). 210p. 1984. 18.95x (ISBN 0-911745-81-5). P Bedrick Bks.
--The Biographical Dictionary of Scientists: Physicists. LC 84-9211. (The Biographical Dictionary of Scientists Ser.). 220p. 1984. 18.95x (ISBN 0-911745-79-3). P Bedrick Bks.
Abbott, David P. & Graham, Walter B. David P. Abbott's Book of Mysteries. (Illus.). 184p. 1985. text ed. 35.00x (ISBN 0-916638-33-2). Meyerbooks.
Abbott, David W., et al. Police, Politics & Race: The New York City Referendum on Civilian Review. 1969. pap. 3.00x (ISBN 0-674-68321-8). Harvard U Pr.
Abbott, Delila M. Days of Our Fathers. 247p. 1981. pap. 7.95 (ISBN 0-9607336-0-4). D M Abbott.
Abbott, Derek & Pollit, Kimball. Hill Housing: A Guide to Design & Construction. 304p. 1981. 34.50 (ISBN 0-8230-7259-2, Whitney Lib). Watson-Guptill.
Abbott, Diane L., et al. The Neighborhood's Catalogue: Lower East Side Planning & Design File. (Illus.). vi, 117p. 1981. 12.00 (ISBN 0-938744-18-6, R81-5). U of Wis Ctr Arch-Urban.
Abbott, Dorothy. Nothing's Changed: Diary of a Mastectomy. LC 81-65746. 224p. 1981. 11.95 (ISBN 0-8119-0423-7). Fell.
Abbott, Dorothy, ed. Mississippi Writers: Reflections of Childhood & Youth, Vol. 1: Fiction. LC 84-5131. (Center for the Study of Southern Culture Ser.). 1985. 35.00x (ISBN 0-87805-231-3); pap. 14.95 (ISBN 0-87805-232-1). U Pr of Miss.
Abbott, E. see Rahn, Carl.
Abbott, E. A. A Shakespearian Grammar. LC 72-3661. (Studies in Shakespeare, No. 24). 1972. Repr. of 1870 ed. lib. bdg. 59.95x (ISBN 0-8383-1571-2). Haskell.
Abbott, E. C. We Pointed Them North: Recollections of a Cowpuncher. 1976. pap. 7.95 (ISBN 0-8061-1366-9). U of Okla Pr.
Abbott, Earl L. & Solomon, Erwin S., eds. Instructions for Virginia & West Virginia, 3 vols. 2nd ed. 1962. with 1985 suppl. 90.00 (ISBN 0-87215-077-1); 1983 suppl. 25.00 (ISBN 0-87215-565-X); Suppl. 1985. 30.00 (ISBN 0-87215-871-3). Michie Co.
Abbott, Edith. Historical Aspects of the Immigration Problem: Select Documents. LC 69-18753. (American Immigration Collection Ser., No. 1). 1969. Repr. of 1926 ed. 36.50 (ISBN 0-405-00502-4). Ayer Co Pubs.
--Immigration: Select Documents & Case Records. LC 69-18754. (American Immigration Collection Ser., No. 1). 1969. Repr. of 1924 ed. 32.00 (ISBN 0-405-00501-6). Ayer Co Pubs.
--Some American Pioneers in American Social Welfare. (Midway Reprint Ser). 216p. 1937. pap. 8.75x (ISBN 0-226-00072-9). U of Chicago Pr.
--Tenements of Chicago, 1908-1935. LC 78-112535. (Rise of Urban America). (Illus.). 1970. Repr. of 1936 ed. lib. bdg. 37.50 (ISBN 0-405-02431-2). Ayer Co Pubs.
--Women in Industry: A Study in American Economic History. LC 70-89714. (American Labor, from Conspiracy to Collective Bargaining Ser.: No. 1). 408p. 1969. Repr. of 1910 ed. lib. bdg. 25.50 (ISBN 0-405-02101-1). Ayer Co Pubs.
Abbott, Edith & Breckinridge, S. P. The Family & Social Service in the 1920's. LC 74-169361. (Family in America Ser). 386p. 1972. 31.00 (ISBN 0-405-03885-2). Ayer Co Pubs.
Abbott, Edith & Breckinridge, Sophonisba P. Truancy & Non-Attendance in the Chicago Schools: A Study of the Social Aspects of the Compulsory Education & Child Labor Legislation of Illinois. LC 74-12526. (Rise of Urban America). 1970. Repr. of 1917 ed. 26.50 (ISBN 0-405-02432-0). Ayer Co Pubs.
Abbott, Edith, jt. auth. see Breckinridge, Sophonisba P.
Abbott, Edwin A. Flatland. (Illus.). 1978. Repr. of 1884 ed. 35.00 (ISBN 0-910330-21-2). Grant Dahlstrom.
--Flatland. (Illus.). 144p. 1983. pap. 4.33i (ISBN 0-06-463573-2, EH 573). B&N NY.
--Flatland: A Romance of Many Dimensions. 5th rev. ed. (Illus.). 108p. 1963. 12.50 (ISBN 0-451-51841-1, 06303). B&N Imports.
--Flatland: A Romance of Many Dimensions. 2nd ed. 1884. pap. 2.00 (ISBN 0-486-20001-9). Dover.
--Flatland: A Romance of Many Dimensions. (Illus.). 123p. 1982. 10.95 (ISBN 0-87523-199-3). Enslow Pubs.
--St. Thomas of Canterbury: His Death & Miracles, 2 vols. in 1. LC 80-18216. (The Crusades & Military Orders: Second Ser.). Repr. of 1898 ed. 55.00 (ISBN 0-404-16366-1). AMS Pr.
Abbott, Elisabeth, tr. see Artusi, Pellegrino.
Abbott, Elizabeth, tr. see Da Ponte, Lorenzo.
Abbott, Elizabeth, tr. see Soubiran, Andre.
Abbott, Evelyn. Index to Plato. 59.95 (ISBN 0-8490-0394-6). Gordon Pr.
--Pericles & the Golden Age of Athens. LC 79-77326. (Illus.). 1970. Repr. of 1897 ed. lib. bdg. 27.50 (ISBN 0-8154-0317-8). Cooper Sq.
--Pericles & the Golden Age of Athens. 59.95 (ISBN 0-8490-0813-1). Gordon Pr.
--Pericles & the Golden Age of Athens. 379p. 1982. Repr. of 1891 ed. lib. bdg. 50.00 (ISBN 0-89984-014-0). Century Bookbindery.
Abbott, Evelyn & Mansfield, E. D. Primer of Greek Grammar. 246p. 1977. 20.00x (ISBN 0-7156-1257-3, Pub. by Duckworth England); pap. 10.95x (ISBN 0-7156-1258-1, BPA 02519, Pub. by Duckworth England). Biblio Dist.
Abbott, Frank F. The Common People of Ancient Rome: Studies of Roman Life & Literature. LC 65-23487. (gr. 7 up). 1965. Repr. of 1911 ed. 12.00x (ISBN 0-8196-0157-8). Biblo.
--A History & Description of Roman Political Institutions. 3rd ed. LC 63-10766. 451p. (gr. 7 up). 1910. 12.00x (ISBN 0-8196-0117-9). Biblo.
--Roman Politics. LC 63-10295. (Our Debt to Greece & Rome Ser). Repr. of 1930 ed. 15.00 (ISBN 0-8154-0000-4). Cooper Sq.
--Society & Politics in Ancient Rome: Essays & Sketches. LC 63-10767. 267p. (gr. 7 up). 1909. 12.00x (ISBN 0-8196-0118-7). Biblo.
Abbott, G. The Beefeaters of the Tower of London. (Illus.). 96p. 1985. pap. 5.95 (ISBN 0-7153-8636-0). David & Charles.
--Ghosts of the Tower of London. (Illus.). 85p. pap. 6.50 (ISBN 0-434-00595-9, Pub. by W Heinemann Ltd). David & Charles.
--Great Escapes from the Tower of London. (Illus.). 128p. 1982. 6.50 (ISBN 0-434-00596-7, Pub. by W Heinemann Ltd). David & Charles.
Abbott, George C. International Indebtedness & the Developing Countries. LC 79-5070. 310p. 1979. 30.00 (ISBN 0-87332-149-9). M E Sharpe.
Abbott, George F. Macedonian Folklore. LC 76-51722. 1977. Repr. of 1903 ed. lib. bdg. 40.00 (ISBN 0-8414-2957-X). Folcroft.
Abbott, Grace. The Immigrant & the Community. LC 70-145468. (The American Immigration Library). xii, 303p. 1971. Repr. of 1917 ed. lib. bdg. 16.50x (ISBN 0-89198-000-8). Ozer.
Abbott, Grace, jt. auth. see Hockett, Betty.
Abbott, Grace, ed. The Child & State: Select Documents, 2 Vols. LC 68-57587. (Illus.). 1968. Repr. of 1938 ed. Set. lib. bdg. 53.75x (ISBN 0-8371-0279-0, ABCS). Greenwood.
--Ideas for Use with Two's & Three's. 176p. (Orig.). 1985. pap. 7.95 (ISBN 0-8341-1056-3). Beacon Hill.
Abbott, Graham & Little, Geoffrey, eds. The Respectable Sydney Merchant: A. B. Spark of Tempe. 1976. 27.00x (ISBN 0-424-00016-4, Pub. by Sydney U Pr). Intl Spec Bk.
Abbott, H. Porter. Diary Fiction: Writing As Action. LC 84-7111. 240p. 1984. 22.50x (ISBN 0-8014-1713-9). Cornell U Pr.
--The Fiction of Samuel Beckett: Form & Affect. LC 79-186102. (Perspectives in Criticism Ser.: No. 22). 1973. 40.00x (ISBN 0-520-02202-5). U of Cal Pr.
Abbott, Henry. Birch Bark Books of Henry Abbott: Sporting Adventures & Nature Observations in the Adirondacks in the Early 1900s. LC 80-11071. (Illus., Repr. of 1914 & 1932 eds.). 1980. 19.95 (ISBN 0-916346-40-4). Harbor Hill Bks.
Abbott, Ira H. & Von Doenhoff, Albert E. Theory of Wing Sections: Including a Summary of Airfoil Data. (Illus.). 1949. pap. 9.95 (ISBN 0-486-60586-8). Dover.
Abbott, Isabella A. & Dawson, E. Yale. How to Know the Seaweeds. 2nd ed. (Pictured Key Nature Ser.). 200p. 1978. Wire Coil. write for info. (ISBN 0-697-04892-6). Wm C Brown.
Abbott, Isabella A. & Hollenberg, George J. Marine Algae of California. LC 74-82774. (Illus.). 1976. 30.00x (ISBN 0-8047-0867-3). Stanford U Pr.
Abbott, J. Indian Ritual & Belief. Orig. Title: Keys of Power: A Study of Indian Religion & Ritual. 1985. Repr. of 1932 ed. 40.00x (ISBN 0-8364-1294-X, Pub. by Usha). South Asia Bks.
--Man-Machine Interface Design. 180p. 1982. pap. 27.35 (ISBN 0-471-89409-5). Wiley.
--On-Line Programming: A Management Guide. 64p. 1981. pap. 18.60 (ISBN 0-471-89415-X). Wiley.
Abbott, J. C. Marketing Problems & Improvement Programs. (Marketing Guides: No. 1). 220p. (Orig., 5th Printing 1975). 1958. pap. 13.25 (ISBN 92-5-101669-0, F273, FAO). Unipub.
Abbott, J. C. & Creupelandt, H. C. Agricultural Marketing Boards: Their Establishment & Operation. (Marketing Guides: No. 5). 236p. (3rd Printing 1974). 1966. pap. 15.50 (ISBN 92-5-101668-2, F14, FAO). Unipub.
Abbott, J. C., jt. auth. see Stewart, G. F.
Abbott, J. C., jt. auth. see Weirer, K.
Abbott, J. C., ed. Marketing Fruits & Vegetables: FAO Marketing Guide No. 2. 2nd, Rev. ed. (Plant Production & Protection Papers: No. 6). 181p. 1978. pap. 13.25 (ISBN 92-5-100594-X, F271, FAO). Unipub.
Abbott, J. C., et al. Rice Marketing. (Marketing Guides: No. 6). (Illus.). 189p. (Orig.). 1972. pap. 15.50 (ISBN 92-5-101540-6, F411, FAO). Unipub.
Abbott, Jack H. In the Belly of the Beast: Letters from Prison. 166p. 1981. 11.95 (ISBN 0-394-51858-6). Random.
--In the Belly of the Beast: Letters from Prison. LC 81-52257. 192p. 1982. pap. 2.95 (ISBN 0-394-70822-9, Vin). Random.
Abbott, Jacob. Charles I. (Makers of History). 285p. 1980. Repr. of 1903 ed. lib. bdg. 20.00 (ISBN 0-89984-002-7). Century Bookbindery.
--History of Alexander the Great. Repr. of 1854 ed. 20.00 (ISBN 0-686-20098-5). Quality Lib.
--History of Cyrus the Great. Repr. of 1852 ed. 20.00 (ISBN 0-686-20099-3). Quality Lib.
--History of Elizabeth, Queen of England. 252p. 1980. Repr. lib. bdg. 20.00 (ISBN 0-8492-3226-0). R West.
--History of Hannibal the Carthaginian. Repr. of 1854 ed. 20.00 (ISBN 0-686-20100-0). Quality Lib.
--History of Julius Caesar. Repr. of 1854 ed. 20.00 (ISBN 0-686-20101-9). Quality Lib.
--The History of Nero. Repr. of 1854 ed. 20.00 (ISBN 0-686-20102-7). Quality Lib.
--History of Pyrrhus. Repr. of 1854 ed. 20.00 (ISBN 0-686-20103-5). Quality Lib.
--Queen Elizabeth. 281p. 1982. Repr. of 1903 ed. lib. bdg. 25.00 (ISBN 0-89987-037-6). Darby Bks.
Abbott, James, ed. The Chauvenet Papers, 2 Vols. 312p. 1979. Vol. 1, 1979, 312p. 24.00 (ISBN 0-88385-425-2); Vol. 2, 1979, 282p. 24.00 (ISBN 0-88385-427-9). Math Assn.
--The Chauvenet Papers: A Collection of Prize-Winning Expository Papers in Mathematics. Set. 41.50 (ISBN 0-88385-439-2, CHV-012); members 31.00 (ISBN 0-317-30488-7); Vol. 1, 312p. 24.00 (ISBN 0-88385-425-2, CHV-01); members 18.50 (ISBN 0-88385-427-9); Vol. 2, 282p. 24.00 (ISBN 0-317-30489-5, CHV-02); members 18.50 (ISBN 0-317-30490-9). Math Assn.
Abbott, James H., tr. see Zea, Leopoldo.
Abbott, Jean, et al. Protocols for Prehospital Emergency Care. 2nd ed. 283p. 1984. 17.95 (ISBN 0-683-00044-6). Williams & Wilkins.
Abbott, Jeanne. The Substitute Bridegroom. 256p. 1985. pap. 2.50 (ISBN 0-449-20804-4, Crest). Fawcett.
Abbott, Jennie. A Wish for Tonight. (Turning Points Ser.: No. 8). 1984. pap. 2.25 (ISBN 0-451-13289-0, Sig Vista). NAL.
Abbott, Jere. Lautrec-Redon. LC 74-86435. (Museum of Modern Art Publications in Reprint Ser). (Illus.). 1970. Repr. of 1931 ed. 15.00 (ISBN 0-405-01527-5). Ayer Co Pubs.
Abbott, Jerry, jt. auth. see Barbe, Walter.
Abbott, Joe. On-Line Programming: A Management Guide. 110p. (Orig.). 1981. pap. 20.00x (ISBN 0-85012-295-3). Intl Pubns Serv.
Abbott, John. The Iranians: How They Live & Work. 168p. 1978. text ed. 9.95 (ISBN 0-03-042496-8, HoltC). HR&W.
Abbott, John, jt. auth. see Prillaman, Douglas.
Abbott, John L. John Hawkesworth, Eighteenth-Century Man of Letters. 316p. 1982. text ed. 22.50x (ISBN 0-299-08610-0). U of Wis Pr.
Abbott, John R. Footwear Evidence: The Examination, Identification & Comparison of Footwear Impressions. (Illus.). 100p. 1964. photocopy ed. 13.75x (ISBN 0-398-00003-4). C C Thomas.
Abbott, John S. History of Joseph Bonaparte: King of Naples & Italy. 391p. Repr. of 1869 ed. lib. bdg. 30.00 (ISBN 0-686-82064-9). Darby Bks.
--History of Madame Roland. 304p. 1981. Repr. of 1854 ed. lib. bdg. 25.00 (ISBN 0-8495-0068-0). Arden Lib.
--Joseph Bonaparte. (Makers of History). 391p. 1980. Repr. of 1903 ed. lib. bdg. 20.00 (ISBN 0-89984-049-3). Century Bookbindery.
--Life of John Paul Jones. xi, 359p. Date not set. Repr. of 1898 ed. 39.00 (ISBN 0-932051-77-4). Am Repr Serv.
--The Life of Kit Carson. (The Golden West Ser.). 1977. pap. 1.25 (ISBN 0-8439-0474-7, Leisure Bks). Dorchester Pub Co.
--The Mother at Home or, the Principles of Maternal Duty. LC 72-169366. (Family in America Ser). (Illus.). 198p. 1972. Repr. of 1834 ed. 14.00 (ISBN 0-405-03841-0). Ayer Co Pubs.
--South & North: Or, Impressions Received During a Trip to Cuba & the South. LC 78-90104. Repr. of 1860 ed. cancelled (ISBN 0-8371-2015-2). Greenwood.
Abbott, Judith A., et al. Identifying & Educating the Disadvantaged Gifted-Talented: Selected Proceedings of the Fifth Biennial National Conference on Disadvantaged Gifted-Talented. 116p. 11.95 (ISBN 0-318-02201-X). NSLTIGT.
Abbott, Justin E. The Life of Eknath. 198p. 1981. 15.00 (ISBN 0-89581-120-0). Asian Human Pr.
--Life of Eknath. cancelled (ISBN 0-8364-0746-6, Pub. by Motilal Banarsidass). South Asia Bks.
--The Life of Tukaram. 356p. 13.50 (ISBN 0-89581-121-9). Asian Human Pr.
Abbott, Justin E., ed. Life of Tukaram. Repr. of 1930 ed. cancelled (ISBN 0-8364-0791-1, Pub. by Motilal Banarsidass). South Asia Bks.
Abbott, Justin E., tr. from Sanskrit. Life of Tukaram. 346p. 1980. pap. text ed. 8.50 (ISBN 0-89684-251-7, Pub. by Motilal Banarsidass India). Orient Bk Dist.
Abbott, K. Company Law. 350p. 1982. 37.00x (ISBN 0-905435-28-1, Pub. by DP Pubns). State Mutual Bk.
Abbott, K. & Pendlebury, N. Business Law. 400p. 1982. 37.00x (ISBN 0-905435-22-2, Pub. by DP Pubns). State Mutual Bk.
Abbott, Katherine M. Old Paths & Legends of New England: Saunterings over Historic Roads with Glimpses of Picturesque Fields & Old Homesteads in Massachusetts, Rhode Island & New Hampshire. LC 76-75228. Repr. of 1903 ed. 40.00x (ISBN 0-8103-3564-6). Gale.
--Old Paths & Legends of the New England Border: Connecticut, Deerfield, Berkshire. LC 72-75227. 1970. Repr. of 1907 ed. 40.00x (ISBN 0-8103-3562-X). Gale.
Abbott, Keith. The Book of Rimbaud. 1977. sewn in wrappers 1.25 (ISBN 0-685-79999-9). New Rivers Pr.
--Erase Words. LC 76-58861. (Illus.). 1977. pap. 5.95 (ISBN 0-912652-35-7, Dynamite Books); pap. 10.95x signed ed. (ISBN 0-912652-36-5). Blue Wind.
--Gush. LC 75-9878. 140p. (Orig.). 1975. 14.95 (ISBN 0-912652-16-0, Dynamite Books); pap. 7.95 (ISBN 0-912652-17-9); signed ed. 24.95x (ISBN 0-912652-18-7). Blue Wind.
--Harum Scarum. LC 84-15003. (Illus.). 96p. (Orig.). 1984. pap. 8.95 (ISBN 0-918273-00-5). Coffee Hse.
--Mordecai of Monterey. LC 84-72513. (Illus.). 224p. 1985. 13.95 (ISBN 0-933944-10-1); pap. 8.95 (ISBN 0-933944-11-X). City Miner Bks.
--Putty. (Illus.). 1971. pap. 7.95 (ISBN 0-912652-31-4). Blue Wind.
--Rhino Ritz: An American Mystery. LC 78-23542. 1979. 19.95 (ISBN 0-912652-42-X, Dynamite Bks); pap. 9.95 (ISBN 0-912652-43-8); signed ed. 29.95x (ISBN 0-912652-44-6). Blue Wind.
Abbott, Kenneth A. Harmony & Individualism. (Asian Folklore & Social Life Monograph: No. 12). 1970. 19.00 (ISBN 0-89986-015-X). Oriental Bk Store.
Abbott, L. B. Special Effects: Wire, Tape & Rubber Band Styles. Turner, George E., tr. 275p. 1984. 29.95 (ISBN 0-935578-06-4). ASC Holding.
Abbott, L. W. Law Reporting in England Fourteen Eighty-Five to Fifteen Eighty-Five. (University of London Legal Ser.: No. 10). 372p. 1973. 110.00 (ISBN 0-485-13410-1, Pub. by Athlone Pr Ltd). Longwood Pub Group.
Abbott Langer & Associates, jt. auth. see Langer, Steven.
Abbott, Lawrence. The Listener's Book on Harmony. LC 74-27325. Repr. of 1943 ed. 19.50 (ISBN 0-404-12850-5). AMS Pr.
--Quality & Competition: An Essay in Economic Theory. LC 73-5261. (Illus.). 229p. 1973. Repr. of 1955 ed. lib. bdg. 15.00 (ISBN 0-8371-6883-X, ABQC). Greenwood.
Abbott, Lawrence F. The Letters of Archie Butt: Personal Aide to President Roosevelt. 1978. Repr. of 1924 ed. lib. bdg. 15.00 (ISBN 0-8492-3556-1). R West.
--Twelve Great Modernists. facs. ed. LC 76-84292. (Essay Index Reprint Ser). 1927. 20.25 (ISBN 0-8369-1118-0). Ayer Co Pubs.
Abbott, Lee K., Jr. The Heart Never Fits Its Wanting. 1980. 9.95 (ISBN 0-915996-05-7); pap. 5.95 (ISBN 0-915996-06-5). North Am Rev.
Abbott, Leonard. Pericles & the Metaphysics of Political Leadership, 2 vols. (Illus.). 387p. 1984. 247.50 (ISBN 0-89266-477-0). Am Classical Coll Pr.
Abbott, Lois A., et al. Taxonomic Analysis in Biology: Computers, Models & Databases. 320p. 1985. 35.00x (ISBN 0-231-04926-9); pap. 15.00x (ISBN 0-231-04927-7). Columbia U Pr.
Abbott, Lyman. Christianity & Social Problems. LC 4-3768. Repr. of 1896 ed. 30.00 (ISBN 0-384-00074-6). Johnson Repr.
--The Evolution of Christianity. (American Studies Ser.). Repr. of 1892 ed. 24.00 (ISBN 0-384-00075-4). Johnson Repr.
--The Evolution of Christianity. vi, 258p. Date not set. Repr. of 1919 ed. 34.00 (ISBN 0-318-04538-9). Am Repr Serv.
--Henry Ward Beecher. facs. ed. LC 78-89428. (Black Heritage Library Collection). 1903. 20.25 (ISBN 0-8369-8500-1). Ayer Co Pubs.
--Henry Ward Beecher. LC 80-19338. (American Men & Women of Letters Ser.). 475p. 1980. pap. 6.95 (ISBN 0-87754-163-9). Chelsea Hse.
Abbott, Lyman, et al. The New Puritanism: During the Semi-Centennial Celebration of Plymouth Church, N.Y., 1847-1897. LC 70-39672. (Essay Index Reprint Ser.). 19.00 (ISBN 0-8369-2732-X). Ayer Co Pubs.
Abbott, M., ed. see Benque, J. P., et al.
Abbott, M. B. Computational Hydraulics: Elements of the Theory of Free Surface Flows. LC 78-40148. (Water Resources Engineering Ser.). 324p. 1979. text ed. 64.95 (ISBN 0-273-01140-5). Pitman Pub MA.
Abbott, M. B. & Cunge, J. A. Engineering Applications of Computational Hydraulics. LC 81-2327. (Water Resources Engineering Ser.). 288p. 1982. 66.50 (ISBN 0-273-08512-3). Pitman Pub MA.
Abbott, M. B., jt. ed. see Larwood, G. P.
Abbott, M. M. & VanNess, H. C. Thermodynamics. (Schaum Outline Ser). 1972. pap. 9.95 (ISBN 0-07-000040-9). McGraw.
Abbott, M. M., jt. auth. see Van Ness, H. C.

Abbott, M. W. Browning & Meredith. 1979. 28.50 (ISBN 0-685-94328-3). Porter.

Abbott, Marguerite, jt. auth. see Franciscus, Marie L.

Abbott, Martha S., et al. Alternative Approaches to Educating Young Children. LC 76-47152. 91p. (gr. 3 up). 1976. pap. text ed. 7.95 (ISBN 0-89334-004-9). Humanics Ltd.

Abbott, Mary K. Invasive Radiologic Diagnostic Procedures. LC 78-2811. (Illus.). 1978. pap. text ed. 5.50x (ISBN 0-8036-0003-8). Davis Co.

Abbott, Mary W. Browning & Meredith. 1904. lib. bdg. 9.50 (ISBN 0-8414-2960-X). Folcroft.

--Browning & Meredith. Some Points of Similarity. 55p. 1980. Repr. of 1904 ed. lib. bdg. 10.00 (ISBN 0-8495-0150-4). Arden Lib.

Abbott, Nabia. Aishah: The Beloved of Mohammed. LC 73-6264. (The Middle East Ser.). Repr. of 1942 ed. 18.00 (ISBN 0-405-05318-5). Ayer Co Pubs.

--Quaranic Commentary & Tradition: Studies in Arabic Literary Papyri, Vol. 2. LC 56-5027. (Oriental Inst. Pubns. Ser: No. 76). 1967. 35.00x (ISBN 0-226-62177-4, OIP76). U of Chicago Pr.

--Studies in Arabic Literary Papyri: Language & Literature, Vol. 3. LC 56-5027. (Oriental Institute Pubns. Ser: No. 77). (Illus.). xvi, 216p. 1974. lib. bdg. 40.00x (ISBN 0-226-62178-2). U of Chicago Pr.

Abbott, Nabie. Two Queens of Baghdad, Mother & Wife of Harun Al-Rashid. LC 46-3799. pap. 73.80 (ISBN 0-317-11341-0, 2011225). Bks Demand UMI.

Abbott, Othman A. & Sheldon, Addison E. Recollections of a Pioneer Lawyer: A Special Publication of the Nebraska State Historical Society. (Illus.). 1929. write for info. Nebraska Hist.

Abbott, P. Calculus. (Teach Yourself Ser.). 1975. pap. 4.95 (ISBN 0-679-10391-0). McKay.

--Geometry. (Teach Yourself Ser.). 1973. pap. 6.95 (ISBN 0-679-10398-8). McKay.

--Trigonometry. (Teach Yourself Ser.). 1975. pap. 5.95 (ISBN 0-679-10409-7). McKay.

Abbott, P. E. Recipients of the Distinquished Conduct Medal 1855-1909. 112p. 1982. 40.00 (ISBN 0-903754-09-6, Pub. by Picton England). State Mutual Bk.

Abbott, P. E. & Tamplin, J. M. A. British Gallantry Awards. 334p. 1982. 69.00 (ISBN 0-902633-74-0, Pub. by Picton England). State Mutual Bk.

Abbott, Philip. The Family on Trial: Special Relationships in Modern Political Thought. LC 80-26964. 256p. 1981. 22.75x (ISBN 0-271-00282-4). Pa St U Pr.

--Furious Fancies: American Political Thought in the Post-Liberal Era. LC 79-7469. (Contributions in Political Science: No. 35). 1980. lib. bdg. 29.95 (ISBN 0-313-20945-6, AFF/). Greenwood.

Abbott, R. D., jt. auth. see Lunneborg, C. E.

Abbott, R. T., ed. see McDonald, Gary R. & Nybakken, James W.

Abbott, R. T., ed. see Say, Thomas.

Abbott, R. Tucker. The Best of the Nautilus: A Bicentennial Anthology of American Conchology. LC 75-41628. (Illus.). 280p. 1976. 13.95 (ISBN 0-915826-02-X). Am Malacologists.

--Collectible Shells of Southeastern U. S., Bahamas & the Caribbean. LC 84-192682. (Illus.). 68p. 1984. pap. 4.95 (ISBN 0-915826-13-5); pap. 8.95 waterproof ed. (ISBN 0-915826-14-3). Am Malacologists.

--Seashells of North America. Zim, Herbert S., ed. (Golden Field Guide Ser). (gr. 9 up). 1969. (Golden Pr); pap. 7.95 (ISBN 0-307-13657-4). Western Pub.

--Seashells of the World. Rev. ed. Zim, Herbert S., ed. (Golden Guide Ser). (gr. 9 up). 1985. pap. 2.95 (ISBN 0-307-24410-5, Golden Pr). Western Pub.

Abbott, R. Tucker, jt. auth. see Sandved, Kiell.

Abbott, R. Tucker, jt. auth. see Wagner, R. J.

Abbott, R. Tucker, ed. Indexes to the Nautilus: Geographical, Vols. 1-90, & Scientific Names, Vols. 61-90. 1979. Set. 24.00x (ISBN 0-915826-06-2). Am Malacologists.

Abbott, Raymond, jt. auth. see Marvin, John.

Abbott, Richard H. Cobbler in Congress: The Life of Henry Wilson, 1812-1875. LC 70-147856. (Illus.). 308p. 1972. 25.00x (ISBN 0-8131-1249-4). U Pr of Ky.

Abbott, Sally A. Esther: A Melodrama in Three Acts. (Orig.). Date not set. pap. write for info. (ISBN 0-937172-45-6). JLJ Pubs.

Abbott, Sandra. Castle of Evil. 1974. pap. 0.95 (ISBN 0-380-01087-9, 18044). Avon.

Abbott, Sheldon. Automotive Brakes: Text-Lab Manual. 1st ed. 1977. pap. 17.00 (ISBN 0-02-810150-2); tchrs manual 3.20 (ISBN 0-02-810160-X). Glencoe.

Abbott, Sheldon L. Automotive Brakes: A Text-Lab Manual. (Illus.). 1977. pap. 13.95x (ISBN 0-02-810150-2). Macmillan.

--Automotive Power Trains. LC 77-73274. 256p. 1978. pap. text ed. 17.00 (ISBN 0-02-810130-8); instrs'. manual 3.20 (ISBN 0-02-810140-5). Glencoe.

--Automotive Transmissions. 320p. 1980. pap. text ed. 17.00 (ISBN 0-02-810170-7); instr. manual 3.20 (ISBN 0-02-810180-4). Glencoe.

Abbott, Sheldon L. & Hinerman, Ivan D. Automotive Suspension & Steering. LC 74-25602. 377p. 1982. pap. text ed. 18.08 (ISBN 0-02-810350-5); instrs'. manual 3.20 (ISBN 0-02-810360-2). Glencoe.

Abbott, Shirley. The Art of Food. Glusker, Irwin, ed. LC 79-83704. (Illus.). 1979. 19.18i (ISBN 0-8487-0497-5). Oxmoor Hse.

--The National Museum of American History. (Illus.). 496p. 1981. 60.00 (ISBN 0-8109-1363-1). Abrams.

--Womenfolks: Growing Up Down South. LC 82-16880. 224p. 1983. 13.95 (ISBN 0-89919-156-8). Ticknor & Fields.

--Womenfolks: Growing Up Down South. LC 82-16880. 224p. 1984. pap. 6.95 (ISBN 0-89919-283-1). Ticknor & Fields.

Abbott, Stan. Holy Spirit: The Anointing of God. (Illus.). 86p. (Orig.). 1984. pap. 2.95 (ISBN 0-915545-00-4). S R Abbott Mini.

Abbott, Susan & Van Willigen, John, eds. Predicting Sociocultural Change. LC 79-10193. (Southern Anthropological Society Proceedings Ser.: No. 13). 158p. 1980. 14.00x (ISBN 0-8203-0477-8); pap. 7.00x (ISBN 0-8203-0484-0). U of Ga Pr.

Abbott, Susan W. Families of Early Milford, Connecticut. LC 78-66024. 875p. 1979. 38.50 (ISBN 0-8063-0838-9). Genealog Pub.

Abbott, T. K., ed. see Dublin University.

Abbott, Thomas K. Fundamental Principles of the Metaphysics of Morals Kant. 1949. pap. text ed. write for info. (ISBN 0-02-300140-2). Macmillan.

Abbott, Thomas K., tr. see Kant, Immanuel.

Abbott, Tucker & Dance, Peter. Compendium of Seashells: A Color Guide to More than 4000 of the World's Marine Shells. (Illus.). 400p. 1983. 50.00 (ISBN 0-525-93269-0, 04854-1460). Dutton.

Abbott, W. Technical Drawing. 4th ed. (Illus.). 1976. pap. 23.50x (ISBN 0-216-90210-X). Intl Ideas.

Abbott, W. C. New York in the American Revolution. LC 72-7428. (American History & Americana Ser., No. 47). 1973. Repr. of 1929 ed. lib. bdg. 49.95 (ISBN 0-8383-1668-9). Haskell.

Abbott, Walter F. Foundations of Modern Sociology: Study Guide & Workbook. 4th ed. 224p. 1985. pap. 10.95 (ISBN 0-13-330234-2). P-H.

Abbott, Walter M., ed. The Documents of Vatican II. pap. 3.50 (ISBN 0-686-19062-9, EC-101). US Catholic.

--The Documents of Vatican II: With Notes & Comments by Catholic, Protestant & Orthodox Authorities. LC 82-80350. 794p. 1974. pap. 6.95 (ISBN 0-8329-1115-1, Assn Pr). New Century.

Abbott, Ward. North. (Illus.). 1975. lib. bdg. 20.00 (ISBN 0-916908-38-0); pap. 1.50 (ISBN 0-916908-01-1). Place Herons.

Abbott, Wilbur C. Adventures in Reputation. LC 69-16486. (Essay & General Literature Index Reprint Ser). 1969. Repr. of 1935 ed. 21.50x (ISBN 0-8046-0517-3, Pub. by Kennikat). Assoc Faculty Pr.

--Conflicts with Oblivion. LC 68-8193. (Essay & General Literature Index Reprint Ser). 1969. Repr. of 1924 ed. 30.75x (ISBN 0-8046-0000-7, Pub. by Kennikat). Assoc Faculty Pr.

--Conflicts With Oblivion. 1924. 29.50x (ISBN 0-686-83509-3). Elliots Bks.

--The New Barbarians. facsimile ed. LC 75-179499. (Select Bibliographies Reprint Ser.). Repr. of 1925 ed. 17.00 (ISBN 0-8369-6628-7). Ayer Co Pubs.

Abbott, Willis J. The Early History of the United States Navy, 2 vols. (Illus.). 1985. Set. 191.75 (ISBN 0-89266-531-9). Am Classical Coll Pr.

--The Story of Our Army: From Colonial Days to the Present. 1977. lib. bdg. 59.95 (ISBN 0-8490-2684-9). Gordon Pr.

Abbott, Winston O. Letters from Chickadee Hill. (Illus.). 1978. 5.95 (ISBN 0-918114-04-7). Inspiration Conn.

Abbott-Smith, Nourma. Profile of an Artist: Ian Fairweather. (Illus.). 1979. 24.95x (ISBN 0-7022-1115-X). U of Queensland Pr.

Aboud, Francois M., jt. auth. see Shepherd, John T.

Abboud, Francois M., ed. Mechanics of Hypertension. (Hypertension Ser: Vol. 18). pap. 5.00 (ISBN 0-87493-001-4, 73-209A). Am Heart.

Abboud, P. F. & Abdel-Massih, E. T. Modern Standard Arabic: Intermediate Level, 3 vols. as a set. 1971. 13.00x set (ISBN 0-916798-09-7); write for info. tapes avail.; recorded exercises avail. to instructors 1.50. Dept NE Stud.

Abboud, P. F., et al. Elementary Modern Standard Arabic, 2 vols. rev. ed. 1983. Set. write for info. (ISBN 0-916798-06-2). Part One; xxi,634p; Pronunciation & writing; lessons 1-30. 18.95 (ISBN 0-521-27295-5); Part Two; viii,481p.; lessons 31-45. 15.95 (ISBN 0-521-27296-3); tapes avail. Cambridge U Pr.

Abboushi, Wasif. The Unmaking of Palestine. 230p. 1985. lib. bdg. 27.50x (ISBN 0-906559-20-0). Lynne Rienner.

Abbs, James H., jt. ed. see Bless, Diane M.

Abbs, Peter. English Within the Arts. 156p. (Orig.). 1982. pap. 8.50 (ISBN 0-89874-599-3). Krieger.

--Reclamations. LC 80-670038. 1980. text ed. 19.50x (ISBN 0-435-18024-X). Heinemann Ed.

--Root & Blossom: Essays on the Philosophy, Practice & Politics of English Teaching. 1976. text ed. 18.00x (ISBN 0-435-18028-2). Heinemann Ed.

Abbs, Peter & Carey, Graham. Proposal for a New College. 1977. pap. text ed. 6.50x (ISBN 0-435-80013-2). Heinemann Ed.

Abby Aldrich Rockefeller Folk Art Museum. Christmas Decorations from Williamsburg's Folk Art Collection. LC 76-41253. (Illus.). 80p. (Orig.). 1976. pap. 3.95 (ISBN 0-87935-040-7). Williamsburg.

Abcarian, Gilbert, jt. auth. see Chackerian, Richard.

Abcarian, Richard. Words in Flight: An Introduction to Poetry. LC 79-181898. 267p. 1972. pap. 11.50 (ISBN 0-534-00147-5). Krieger.

Abcarian, Richard & Klotz, Marvin, eds. The Experience of Fiction. LC 74-23048. (Illus.). 500p. 1975. pap. text ed. 13.95 (ISBN 0-312-27615-X); inst. manual avail. St Martin.

--Literature: The Human Experience. 3rd ed. LC 81-51834. 1260p. 1982. pap. text ed. 16.95 (ISBN 0-312-48795-9); Instr's. manual avail. St Martin.

--Literature: The Human Experience. 2nd rev. ed. LC 83-61605. 934p. 1984. pap. text ed. 14.95 (ISBN 0-312-48797-5); instr's manual avail. St Martin.

Abcarius, J. John. An English-Arabic Reader's Dictionary. 1974. 18.00x (ISBN 0-86685-063-5). Intl Bk Ctr.

Abcarius, Michel F. Palestine Through the Fog of Propaganda. LC 75-6418. (The Rise of Jewish Nationalism & the Middle East Ser). 240p. 1975. Repr. of 1946 ed. 18.00 (ISBN 0-88355-306-6). Hyperion Conn.

Abdalati, Hammudah. The Family Structure in Islam. LC 77-79635. 1976. 10.95 (ISBN 0-89259-004-1). Am Trust Pubns.

--Islam in Focus. 2nd ed. LC 75-4382. (Illus.). 211p. 1975. pap. 5.00 (ISBN 0-89259-000-9). Am Trust Pubns.

Abd-Al-Kahir Ibn-Tahir Ibn Muhammad, Abu M. Moslem Schisms & Sects: Being the History of the Various Philosophic Systems Developed in Islam. Seelye, Kate C., tr. LC 75-158216. (Columbia University Oriental Studies: No. 15). 1920. 20.00 (ISBN 0-404-50505-8). AMS Pr.

Abdalla, Ismail H., jt. ed. see Du Toit, Brian M.

Abdalla, Ismail-Sabri, et al. Images of the Arab Future. Talaat, Maissa, tr. LC 83-9762. 250p. 1983. 22.50 (ISBN 0-312-40935-4). St Martin.

Abdalla, Raqiya H. Sisters in Affliction: Circumcision & Infibulation of Women in Africa. 128p. 1983. cancelled (ISBN 0-86232-093-3, Pub. by Zed Pr England); pap. cancelled (ISBN 0-86232-094-1). Biblio Dist.

Abdallah, Hassan. Abdallah Dictionary of International Relations & Conference Terminology in English-Arabic. (Eng. & Arabic.). 1982. 40.00x (ISBN 0-86685-289-1). Intl Bk Ctr.

Abdallah, Maureen S. Middle East. LC 80-53900. (Countries Ser.). PLB 13.96 (ISBN 0-382-06417-8). Silver.

Abdallah, Wagdy M. Internal Accountability: An International Emphasis. Farmer, Richard, ed. LC 84-2662. (Research for Business Decisions Ser.: No. 68). 130p. 1984. 34.95 (ISBN 0-8357-1555-8). UMI Res Pr.

Abdallah, Yohanna Barnaba. Yao: The Chiikala Cha Wayao. new ed. Sanderson, M., tr. 132p. 1973. 26.00x (ISBN 0-7146-2462-4, BHA 02462, F Cass Co). Biblio Dist.

Abd Allah Ansarti, Khwajih. Munajat: The Intimate Prayers. Morris, Lawrence & Sarfeh, Rustam, trs. from Fari. LC 75-30173. (Eng. & Persian.). 1975. 7.50 (ISBN 0-917220-00-5). Khaneghah & Maktab.

Abd Al-Monem, Mufid Al-Guindi. Diccionario Espanol-Arabe de Verbos, Gramatica y Temas de Conversacion. 2nd ed. 368p. (Span. & Arabic.). 1974. pap. 13.95 (ISBN 84-7074-021-0, S-50423). French & Eur.

Abd al-Rahman al Jami. The Precious Pearl: Al-Durrah Al-Fakhirah. Heer, Nicholas L., tr. from Arabic. LC 78-126071. 1979. 39.50x (ISBN 0-87395-379-7). State U NY Pr.

Abd al-Rahman Isma'il. Folk Medicine in Modern Egypt: Being the Relevant Parts of the Tibb al-Rukka, or Old Wives' Medicine, of 'Abd al-Rahman Isma'il. LC 77-87651. (Anthropolgy Ser.). (Illus.). Repr. of 1934 ed. 19.00 (ISBN 0-404-16407-2). AMS Pr.

Abd Al-Wahhab Ibn'Ali, Taj Al-Din. Kitab Mu'id an-Ni'am Wa-Mubid an-Niqam. LC 78-53829. (Luzac's Semitic Text & Translation Ser.: Vol. 18). Repr. of 1908 ed. 32.50 (ISBN 0-404-11291-9). AMS Pr.

Abdeen, Adnan. English-Arabic Dictionary for Accounting & Finance. LC 79-41213. 280p. (Eng. & Arabic.). 1982. 26.95x (ISBN 0-471-27673-1, Pub. by Wiley-Interscience). Wiley.

--English-Arabic Dictionary of Accounting & Finance. 1981. 30.00x (ISBN 0-86685-275-1). Intl Bk Ctr.

Abdeen, Adnan M. & Shook, Dale N. The Saudi Financial System: In the Context of Western & Islamic Finance. LC 83-16978. 332p. 1984. 34.95x (ISBN 0-471-90346-9). Wiley.

Abdel-Aal & Smelzlee. Petroleum Economics & Engineering. (Chemical Processing & Engineering Ser.: Vol. 6). 1976. 49.75 (ISBN 0-8247-6293-2). Dekker.

Abdel-Barr, Hussein A. The Market Structure of International Oil with Special Reference to the Organization of Petroleum Exporting Countries. Bruchey, Stuart, ed. LC 78-22653. (Energy in the American Economy Ser.). (Illus.). 1979. lib. bdg. 30.50x (ISBN 0-405-11958-5). Ayer Co Pubs.

Abdel-Fadil, M. Development, Income Distribution & Social Change in Rural Egypt 1952-1970. LC 75-17114. (Department of Applied Economics, Occasional Papers Ser.: No. 45). 1976. pap. 17.95x (ISBN 0-521-29019-8). Cambridge U Pr.

--The Political Economy of Nasserism. LC 80-49995. (Cambridge Department of Applied Economics, Occasional Papers: No. 52). (Illus.). 140p. 1980. 32.50 (ISBN 0-521-22313-X); pap. 17.95 (ISBN 0-521-29446-0). Cambridge U Pr.

Abdel-Fettah, Y. M., ed. see IFAC-IFIP-IFORS Conference, 3rd, Rabat, Morocco, Nov. 1980.

Abd-El-Gawad, Tawfik. Technical Dictionary: Archtiecture & Building. 1319p. (Eng., Fr., Ger. & Arabic.). 1976. 35.00x (ISBN 0-686-44745-X, Pub. by Collets). State Mutual Bk.

Abdel Hai, Mohamed. Cultural Policy in the Sudan. (Studies & Documents on Cultural Policies). (Illus.). 43p. 1982. pap. 6.00 (ISBN 92-3-101938-4, U1214, UNESCO). Unipub.

Abdel-Hameed, M., et al, eds. Reliability Theory & Models: Stochastic Failure Models, Optimal Maintenance Policies, Life Testing, & Structure. (Notes & Reports in Computer & Applied Mathematics Ser.). 1984. 37.50 (ISBN 0-12-041420-1). Acad Pr.

Abdel-Khalek, Goudal, jt. ed. see Tignor, Robert L.

Abdel-Khalik, A. Rashad. The Economic Effects On Lessees of FASB Statement No. 13, Accounting for Leases. LC 81-68881. (The Financial Accounting Standards Board Research Report). 311p. (Orig.). 1981. pap. 20.00 (ISBN 0-910065-12-8). Finan Acct.

--Financial Reporting by Private Companies: Analysis & Diagnosis. LC 83-81884. (Research Reports Ser.). (Illus.). 155p. (Orig.). 1983. pap. 15.00 (ISBN 0-910065-17-9). Finan Acct.

Abdel-khalik, A. Rashad, ed. Government Regulation of Accounting & Information. LC 79-26555. (University of Florida Accounting Ser.: No. 11). (Illus.). vi, 320p. (Orig.). 1980. pap. 10.00 (ISBN 0-8130-0663-5). U Presses Fla.

--Internal Control & the Impact of the Foreign Corrupt Practices Act. LC 82-17480. (University of Florida Accounting Ser.: No. 12). (Illus.). 240p. 1982. pap. 8.00x (ISBN 0-8130-0730-5). U Presses Fla.

Abdel-khalik, Rashad & Keller, Thomas F. Earnings or Cash Flows: An Experiment on Functional Fixation & the Valuation of the Firm. (Studies in Accounting Research: Vol. 16). 101p. 6.00 (ISBN 0-86539-028-2); members. 4.00. Am Accounting.

Abdel-khalik, Rashad & Ajinkya, Bipin B., eds. Empirical Research in Accounting: A Methodological Viewpoint, Vol. 4. (Studies in Accounting Education). 125p. 1979. 6.00 (ISBN 0-86539-032-0); members 4.00. Am Accounting.

Abdella, Fay G. & Levine, Eugene. Better Patient Care Through Nursing Research. 2nd ed. 1978. write for info. (ISBN 0-02-300110-0). Macmillan.

Abdel-Malek, Anouar. Social Dialectics: Civilizations & Social Theory. Gonzalez, M., tr. from Fr. LC 80-25061. 207p. 1981. 34.50x (ISBN 0-87395-500-5); pap. 16.95x (ISBN 0-87395-502-1). State U NY Pr.

--Social Dialectics: Nation & Revolution. Gonzalez, M., tr. from Fr. LC 80-25061. 217p. 1981. 34.50x (ISBN 0-87395-501-3); pap. 17.95x (ISBN 0-87395-503-X). State U NY Pr.

Abdel-Malek, Anouar, jt. auth. see Anisuzzaman.

Abdel-Malek, Anouar, ed. Contemporary Arab Political Thought. 266p. 1983. 29.50x (ISBN 0-86232-077-1, Pub. by Zed Pr England); pap. 10.75x (ISBN 0-86232-074-7). Biblio Dist.

Abdel-Malek, Anouar & Blue, Gregory, eds. Science & Technology in the Transformation of the World. 497p. 1982. 36.25 (ISBN 92-808-0339-5, TUNU193, UNU). Unipub.

Abdel-Malek, Anouar & Pandeya, A. N., eds. Intellectual Creativity in Endogenous Culture. 632p. 1981. 36.25 (ISBN 92-808-0265-8, TUNU184, UNU). Unipub.

Abdel-Malek, Zaki N. The Closed-List Classes of Colloquial Egyptian Arabic. (Janua Linguarum, Ser. Practica: No. 128). 240p. (Orig.). 1972. pap. text ed. 26.40x (ISBN 90-2792-322-1). Mouton.

Abdel-Massih, E. T., jt. auth. see Abboud, P. F.

Abdel-Massih, Ernest. The Life & Miracles of Pope Kirillos VI. 139p. (Orig.). 1982. pap. text ed. 3.00 (ISBN 0-932098-20-7). St Mark Coptic Orthodox.

Abdel-Massih, Ernest T. Advanced Moroccan Arabic. LC 74-161877. 1974. pap. text ed. 13.00x (ISBN 0-932098-08-8). Ctr for NE & North African Stud.

--A Computerized Lexicon of Tamazight: Berber Dialect of Ayt Seghrouchen. LC 77-32220. (Berber.). 1971. pap. text ed. 12.00x (ISBN 0-932098-06-1). Ctr for NE & North African Stud.

--A Course in Spoken Tamazight: Berber Dialects of the Middle Atlas. LC 79-32218. 1970. pap. text ed. 12.00x (ISBN 0-932098-04-5). Ctr for NE & North African Stud.

--An Introduction to Egyptian Arabic. rev. ed. LC 75-24784. 1981. pap. text ed. 14.00x (ISBN 0-932098-09-6). Ctr for NE & North African Stud.

--An Introduction to Moroccan Arabic. rev. ed. LC 74-154239. 1982. pap. text ed. 15.00x (ISBN 0-932098-07-X). Ctr for NE & North African Stud.

--A Reference Grammar of Tamazight. LC 72-32219. 1970. pap. text ed. 12.00x (ISBN 0-932098-05-3). Ctr for NE & North African Stud.

--A Sample Lexicon of Pan-Arabic. LC 75-18985. (Arabic.). 1975. pap. text ed. 10.00x (ISBN 0-932098-10-X). Ctr for NE & North African Stud.

Abdel-Massih, Ernest T., et al. A Comprehensive Study of Egyptian Arabic: A Reference Grammar of Egyptian Arabic: Grammatical & Linguistic Terms in Dictionary Form, Vol. III. LC 76-24957. 1979. pap. text ed. 15.00x (ISBN 0-932098-13-4). Ctr for NE & North African Stud.

--A Comprehensive Study of Egyptian Arabic: Conversation, Texts, Folk Literature, Cultural, Ethnological & Socio-Linguistic Notes, Vol. 1. LC 76-24957. 1976. pap. text ed. 15.00x (ISBN 0-932098-11-8). Ctr for NE & North African Stud.

--A Comprehensive Study of Egyptian Arabic: Proverbs & Metaphoric Phrases, Vol. II. LC 76-24957. 1978. pap. text ed. 15.00x (ISBN 0-932098-12-6). Ctr for NE & North African Stud.

--A Comprehensive Study of Egyptian Arabic: Lexicon, Vol. IV. Incl. Pt. I. Egyptian Arabic - English: 34 Cultural Categories; Pt. II. English - Arabic: 34 Cultural Categories. LC 76-24957. 1979. pap. text ed. 15.00x (ISBN 0-932098-14-2). Ctr for NE & North African Stud.

Abdel-Massih, Ernest T., et al, trs. from Coptic. The Divine Liturgy of St. Basil the Great. 257p. 1982. pap. 7.00 (ISBN 0-932098-19-3). St Mark Coptic Orthodox.

Abdel-Nour, Jabbour. Arabe-Francais Dictionnaire. 1983. 40.00 (ISBN 0-86685-334-0). Intl Bk Ctr.

Abdel Wahab, Farouk, ed. & tr. Modern Egyptian Drama: An Anthology. LC 72-94939. (Studies in Middle Eastern Literatures: No. 3). 1974. 25.00x (ISBN 0-88297-005-4). Bibliotheca.

Abdel-Wahab, M. F., ed. Schistosomiasis in Egypt. 256p. 1982. 74.50 (ISBN 0-8493-6220-2). CRC Pr.

Abd-El-Wahed. Automotive Engineering Dictionary: English-French-German-Arabic. 436p. (Eng., Fr., Ger. & Arabic.). 1978. 45.00 (ISBN 0-686-92337-5). French & Eur.

--Radio & Television Dictionary. 320p. (Eng., Fr., Ger., Arabic.). 1980. 45.00 (ISBN 0-686-92395-2, M-9762). French & Eur.

--Refrigeration & Conditioning Dictionary. 395p. (Eng., Fr., Ger. & Arabic.). 1979. 45.00 (ISBN 0-686-97399-2, M-9756). French & Eur.

Abd-El-Wahed, A. M. Chemical Technology Dictionary: English, French-German-Arabic. 383p. (Eng., Fr., Ger. & Arabic.). 1974. 45.00 (ISBN 0-686-92502-5, M-9759). French & Eur.

--Iron & Steel Industry Dictionary. 441p. (Eng., Fr., Ger. & Arabic.). 1974. 45.00 (ISBN 0-686-92487-8, M-9760). French & Eur.

--Machine Tools Dictionary: English-French-German-Arabic. 334p. (Eng., Fr., Ger. & Arabic.). 1977. 45.00 (ISBN 0-686-92135-6, M-9757). French & Eur.

--Metal Forming Dictionary. 386p. (Eng., Fr., Ger. & Arabic.). 1978. 45.00 (ISBN 0-686-92426-6, M-9755). French & Eur.

Abd-el-Washed, ed. see Zimaity, M. A.

Abdill, George. Locomotive Engineer Album. (Encore Ed.). (Illus.). 9.95 (ISBN 0-87564-534-8). Superior Pub.

--Rails West. LC 60-14424. (Encore Ed.). (Illus.). 9.95 (ISBN 0-87564-516-X). Superior Pub.

--This Was Railroading. (Encore Ed.). (Illus.). 9.95 (ISBN 0-87564-535-6). Superior Pub.

Abdillah Ahmed Wied. Out of the Somali World. Date not set. price not set (ISBN 0-914110-13-6). Blyden Pr.

Abdo, David. Studies in Arabic Linguistics. (Arabic.). 1973. 15.00x (ISBN 0-86685-053-8). Intl Bk Ctr.

Abdrabboh, Bob. Saudi Arabia: Forces of Modernization. 125p. (Orig.). 1985. pap. 10.95 (ISBN 0-915597-19-5). Amana Bks.

Abdu, Hani R. Christian Psychology. 288p. 1981. 11.00 (ISBN 0-682-49643-X). Exposition Pr FL.

--The True Christian Science. 64p. 1981. 5.00 (ISBN 0-682-49632-4). Exposition Pr FL.

Abdul, Baha. The Promulgation of Universal Peace: Talks Delivered by Abdu'l-Baha during His Visit to the United States & Canada in 1912. 2nd ed. LC 81-21689. 470p. 1982. 19.95 (ISBN 0-87743-172-8, 103-039). Baha'i.

Abdul, M. A. The Quran, Sh. Tabarsi's Commentary. 15.95 (ISBN 0-317-01596-6). Kazi Pubns.

Abdul, Raoul, jt. ed. see Lomax, Alan.

Abdu'l-Baha. Christ's Promise Fulfilled. 1954. pap. 4.95 (ISBN 0-87743-049-7, 106-001). Baha'i.

--Huv Allah. (Illus.). 52p. (Persian.). 1984. Repr. 7.95 (ISBN 0-933770-26-X). Kalimat.

--Memorials of the Faithful. Gail, Marzieh, tr. LC 77-157797. 1971. 11.95 (ISBN 0-87743-041-1, 106-012). Baha'i.

--Secret of Divine Civilization. 2nd ed. Gail, Marzieh, tr. LC 56-12427. 1970. 13.95 (ISBN 0-87743-008-X, 106-006). Baha'i.

--Selections from the Writings of. Effendi, Shoghi & Gail, Marzieh, trs. 1978. 10.95 (ISBN 0-85398-081-0, 106-025); pap. 6.95 (ISBN 0-85398-084-5, 106-026); Lightweight. pap. 6.00 (ISBN 0-85398-136-1). Baha'i.

--Some Answered Questions. Barney, Laura C., tr. from Persian. LC 81-2467. xviii, 324p. 1981. 19.95 (ISBN 0-87743-162-0). Baha'i.

--Some Answered Questions. Barney, Laura C., tr. from Persian. LC 83-21353. xviii, 324p. 1984. Pocket sized. pap. 5.00 (ISBN 0-87743-190-6). Baha'i.

--Tablets of the Divine Plan. rev. ed. LC 76-10624. 1977. 13.95 (ISBN 0-87743-107-8, 106-010); pap. 6.95 (ISBN 0-87743-116-7, 106-011). Baha'i.

--A Traveler's Narrative: Written to Illustrate the Episode of the Bab. rev. ed. Browne, Edward G., tr. from Persian. LC 79-19025. 1980. 14.95 (ISBN 0-87743-134-5, 106-027); pap. 6.95 (ISBN 0-686-96668-6, 106-028). Baha'i.

--THe Wisdom of the Master. 1986. pap. 7.95 (ISBN 0-933770-35-9). Kalimat.

Abdu'l-Baha, jt. auth. see Baha'u'llah.

Abdu'l-Baha, jt. auth. see Baha'u'llah, Bab.

Abdu'l-Baha, jt. auth. see Baha'u'llah, the Bab.

Abdul-Baki, Houda S. A Select Annotated Bibliography on the Ethnic Minorities of Color & Women in Social Work Education. 1985. 10.00 (ISBN 0-533-05934-8). Vantage.

Abdulbhan, P., jt. ed. see Tabucanon, M. T.

Abdul Fattah Rashid Hamid. Self Knowledge & Spiritual Yearning. Quinlan, Hamid, ed. LC 82-70348. 116p. 1982. pap. 4.00 (ISBN 0-89259-027-0). Am Trust Pubns.

Abdulghani, Jasim. Iraq & Iran: The Years of Crisis. LC 84-47945. 288p. 1984. text ed. 28.50x (ISBN 0-8018-2519-9). Johns Hopkins.

Abdulhamid Jodah Al Sahhar. The Prophet's Biography Series for Children: Nos. 8, 9, 10. Shahnaz, Mary & Quinlan, Hamid, eds. Outaiba Elhuwaib, tr. from Arabic. LC 82-70350. Orig. Title: Kasas Alsyrah. 16p. 1982. pap. 1.10 (ISBN 0-89259-025-4). Am Trust Pubns.

Abdul-Haqq, Adiyah Akbar. Sharing Your Faith with a Muslim. 192p. (Orig.). 1980. pap. 5.95 (ISBN 0-87123-553-6, 210553). Bethany Hse.

Abdul Huq, A. M. & Aman, Mohammed M. Librarianship & the Third World. LC 76-30916. (Reference Library of Social Science Ser.: Vol. 40). 1977. lib. bdg. 55.00 (ISBN 0-8240-9897-8). Garland Pub.

Abdul-Jabbar, Kareem & Knobler, Jerry. Giant Steps: The Autobiography of Kareem Abdul-Jabbar. 336p. 1983. 14.95 (ISBN 0-553-05044-3). Bantam.

Abdul-Jabbar, Kareem & Knobler, Peter. Giant Steps. 352p. (Orig.). 1985. pap. 3.95 (ISBN 0-553-24511-2). Bantam.

Abdul-Karim, Aliyah. Power Skills in Reading, Bk. 1. 1979. pap. 4.95 (ISBN 0-07-000041-7). McGraw.

Abdul-Karim, R. Drugs During Pregnancy: Clinical Perspectives. (Illus.). 160p. 1981. text ed. 15.00x (ISBN 0-89313-050-8). G F Stickley.

Abdulla, Adnan K. Catharsis in Literature. LC 84-42839. 1985. 27.50x (ISBN 0-253-31323-6). Ind U Pr.

Abdulla, J. J. & McCarus, E. N. Kurdish Basic Course: Dialect of Sulaimania, Iraq. viii, 482p. 1967. pap. text ed. 9.00x (ISBN 0-916798-60-7). Dept NE Stud.

Abdulla, Ummi. Malabar Muslim Cookery. 112p. 1981. pap. text ed. 4.25x (ISBN 0-86131-241-4, Pub. by Orient Ltd India). Apt Bks.

Abdulla, V., tr. see Basheer, Vaikom M.

Abdullah, Achmed. Alien Souls. facs. ed. LC 75-121518. (Short Story Index Reprint Ser). 1922. 18.00 (ISBN 0-8369-3474-1). Ayer Co Pubs.

--Honourable Gentleman, & Others. facs. ed. LC 74-140324. (Short Story Index Reprint Ser). 1919. 17.00 (ISBN 0-8369-3716-3). Ayer Co Pubs.

--Swinging Caravan. LC 75-103485. (Short Story Index Reprint Ser.). 1925. 18.00 (ISBN 0-8369-3077-0). Ayer Co Pubs.

Abdullah, Achmed & Pakenham, Thomas C. Dreamers of Empire. facs. ed. LC 68-57300. (Essay Index Reprint Ser). 1929. 18.00 (ISBN 0-8369-0099-5). Ayer Co Pubs.

Abdullah, Achmed, tr. Lute & Scimitar: Poems & Ballads of Central Asia. 1977. lib. bdg. 59.95 (ISBN 0-8490-2188-X). Gordon Pr.

Abdullah, Achmed, et al. Ten-Foot Chain. facs. ed. LC 73-116924. (Short Story Index Reprint Ser). 1920. 13.00 (ISBN 0-8369-3426-1). Ayer Co Pubs.

Abdullah, Farooq. My Dismissal. 96p. 1985. text ed. 13.95x (ISBN 0-7069-2749-4, Pub. by Vikas India). Advent NY.

Abdullah, K. A., et al. Principles of Accounting. 600p. (Arabic.). 1983. pap. 16.00 (ISBN 0-471-87222-9). Wiley.

Abdullah, M., jt. auth. see Kuffel.

Abdullah, Mena & Mathew, Ray. The Time of the Peacock. LC 83-14618. 128p. 1983. 10.95 (ISBN 0-8149-0877-2). Vanguard.

Abdullah, Mohammed, jt. auth. see Morgan, J. Derald.

Abdullah, T. & Zeidenstein, S. Village Women of Bangladesh: Prospects for Change. (Women in Development Ser.: Vol. 4). (Illus.). 256p. 1981. 25.00 (ISBN 0-08-026795-5). Pergamon.

Abdullah, Taufik. Schools & Politics: The Kaum Muda Movement in West Sumatra 1927-1933. 257p. 1971. pap. 6.00 (ISBN 0-87763-010-0). Cornell Mod Indo.

Abdullah, Yahya Taher. The Mountain of Green Tea. Johnson-Davies, Denys, tr. from Arabic. LC 82-74250. 130p. 1983. pap. 7.00x (ISBN 0-89410-352-0). Three Continents.

Abdullah Al-Mani, Muhammad & Sbit As-Sbit, Abdul-Rahman. Cultural Policy in the Kingdom of Saudi Arabia. (Studies & Documents on Cultural Policies). (Illus.). 69p. 1981. pap. 9.25 (ISBN 92-3-101772-1, U1140, UNESCO). Unipub.

Abdulrahman, A. J., ed. Iraq. (World Bibliographical Ser.: No. 42). 162p. 1984. lib. bdg. 35.00 (ISBN 0-903450-73-9). ABC-Clio.

Abdul-Rauf, Muhammad. The Islamic View of Women & the Family. 1977. text ed. 11.95 (ISBN 0-8315-0156-1). Speller.

--A Muslim's Reflections on Democratic Capitalism. 1984. pap. 4.95 (ISBN 0-8447-3537-X). Am Enterprise.

Abdul-Rauf, Muhammed. Marriage in Islam: A Manual. LC 75-186483. 1972. 7.50 (ISBN 0-682-47431-2, Banner). Exposition Pr FL.

Abdushelishvili, M. G., et al. Contributions to the Physical Anthropology of Central Asia & the Caucasus. Field, Henry, ed. Heath, Barbara, tr. LC 79-158217. (Harvard University, Peabody Museum of Archaeology & Ethnology. Russian Translation Ser.: Vol. 3, No. 2). 1968. lib. bdg. 67.50 (ISBN 0-404-52645-4). AMS Pr.

Abdy, Edward S. Journal of a Residence & Tour in the United States of North America, from April, 1833, to October, 1834, 3 Vols. LC 69-16592. Repr. of 1835 ed. Set. 44.00x (ISBN 0-8371-2475-1, ABT&, Pub. by Negro U Pr). Greenwood.

Abdy, Georgiana B. A Victorian Potpourri, of Verses, Known, Unknown & Forgotten. 1979. Repr. of 1930 ed. lib. bdg. 25.00 (ISBN 0-8495-0214-4). Arden Lib.

--A Victorian Potpourri of Verses, Known, Unknown & Forgotten. 1977. Repr. of 1930 ed. 15.00 (ISBN 0-89984-241-0). Century Bookbindery.

Abdy, Jane. The French Poster. (Illus.). 1977. 11.95 (ISBN 0-89545-010-0); pap. 5.95 (ISBN 0-89545-011-9). Images Graphiques.

Abdy, Jane & Gere, Charlotte. The Souls. (Illus.). 176p. 1984. 19.95 (ISBN 0-283-98920-3, Pub. by Sidgwick & Jackson). Merrimack Pub Cir.

Abe & Malka. One Hundred Guitar Accompaniment Patterns. LC 73-92398. (Orig.). 1974. pap. 9.95 (ISBN 0-8256-2812-1, Amsco Music). Music Sales.

Abe, E. Hopf Algebras. LC 79-50912. (Cambridge Tracts in Mathematics Ser.: No. 74). 1980. 47.50 (ISBN 0-521-22240-0). Cambridge U Pr.

Abe, H. & Hoshi, M., eds. Diabetic Microangiopathy. (Frontiers in Diabetes Series: Vol. 3). (Illus.). xii, 500p. 1983. 117.50 (ISBN 3-8055-3787-5). S Karger.

Abe, K., jt. auth. see Tsuchida, E.

Abe, K., jt. ed. see Nagasawa, H.

Abe, Kobo. Inter Ice Age Four. Saunders, E. Dale, tr. from Jap. (Perigee Japanese Library). 240p. 1981. pap. 4.95 (ISBN 0-399-50519-9, Perigee). Putnam Pub Group.

--The Ruined Map. Sanders, E. Dale, tr. (The Perigee Japanese Library). (Illus.). 320p. 1981. pap. 5.95 (ISBN 0-399-50470-2, Perigee). Putnam Pub Group.

--The Secret Rendezvous. Carpenter, Juliet W., tr. (The Perigee Japanese Library). 192p. 1981. pap. 4.95 (ISBN 0-399-50501-6, Perigee). Putnam Pub Group.

--The Woman in the Dunes. 1972. pap. 4.95 (ISBN 0-394-71814-3, V814, Vin). Random.

Abe, Kobo, ed. The Man Who Turned Into a Stick: Three Related Plays. Keene, Donald, tr. 1975. 9.00x (ISBN 0-86008-147-8, Pub. by U of Tokyo Japan). Columbia U Pr.

Abe, Masao. Zen & Western Thought. LaFleur, William R., ed. LC 83-24153. 1985. text ed. 24.95x (ISBN 0-8248-0952-1). UH Pr.

Abe, Ryuzo, ed. Statistical Mechanics. Takahashi, Yasushi, tr. 178p. 1974. 20.00 (ISBN 0-86008-118-4, Pub. by U of Tokyo Japan). Columbia U Pr.

Abe, T. & Sherry, S. A New Approach to Reduction of Cardiac Death. 85p. 1979. 40.00 (ISBN 3-456-80804-6, Pub. by Holdan Bk Ltd UK). State Mutual Bk.

Abe, T. & Yamamaka, M., eds. Disseminated Intravascular Coagulation. (Bibliotheca Haematologica: No. 49). (Illus.). xiv, 356p. 1983. bound 84.00 (ISBN 3-8055-3726-3). S Karger.

Abear, Gerald J., ed. see Richardson, Robert M.

Abecassis De Laredo, E., ed. see Latin School of Physics, 14th Caracas, Venezuela July 10-28, 1972.

A Beckett, Arthur W. A Becketts of Punch. LC 69-17341. 1969. Repr. of 1903 ed. 40.00x (ISBN 0-8103-3518-2). Gale.

A'Beckett, Gilbert A. Comic History of England, 2 Vols. LC 72-158218. (Illus.). Repr. of 1898 ed. Set. 62.50 (ISBN 0-404-00300-1). AMS Pr.

Abed, Joanne. Education for All: Study in the U. S. for Foreign Students with Disabilities. 55p. (Orig.). 1985. 3.50 (ISBN 0-913957-04-6). Amideast.

Abedor, Allan J., jt. auth. see Bell, Norman T.

Abed-Rabbo, Samir. International Law & the Question of Palestine. (Illus.). 200p. (Orig.). 1985. 18.95 (ISBN 0-915597-21-7); pap. 9.95 (ISBN 0-317-19702-9). Amana Bks.

Abed-Rabbo, Samir, jt. auth. see Khawas, Mohamed.

Abee, Cleveland. A First Report on the Relations Between Climates & Crops: U.S. Department of Agriculture, Weather Bureau Bulletin,No. 36. Egerton, Frank N., 3rd, ed. LC 77-74200. (History of Ecology Ser.). 1978. Repr. of 1905 ed. lib. bdg. 30.00 (ISBN 0-405-10370-0). Ayer Co Pubs.

Abeel, Erica. Last Romance. 288p. 1985. pap. 6.95 (ISBN 0-380-89672-9). Avon.

Abeele, Alain van de see Van de Abeele, Alain.

Abeer Abu Saud. Qatari Women: Past & Present. (Illus.). 184p. 1984. text ed. 29.95 (ISBN 0-582-78372-0). Longman.

Abegg, Lynda R. & Grillot, Peggy J. Savvy Secs: Street Wise & Book Smart. Treloar, Millicent, ed. LC 84-91839. 140p. (Orig.). 1985. pap. 9.95 (ISBN 0-9614131-0-7). Abegg Grillot Ent.

Abegglen, James C. The Japanese Factory. rev. ed. LC 80-52878. 200p. 1985. pap. 6.25 (ISBN 0-8048-1372-8). C E Tuttle.

--The Japanese Factory: Aspects of Its Social Organization. Coser, Lewis A. & Powell, Walter W., eds. LC 79-6982. (Perennial Works in Sociology Ser.). (Illus.). 1979. Repr. of 1958 ed. lib. bdg. 15.00x (ISBN 0-405-12082-6). Ayer Co Pubs.

Abegglen, James C. & Stalk, George. Raisha, the Japanese Corporation: The New Competitors in World Business. LC 85-47552. 352p. 1985. 22.50 (ISBN 0-465-03711-9). Basic.

Abegglen, James C., jt. auth. see Warner, W. Lloyd.

Abegglen, James C., et al. U. S. - Japan Economic Relations: A Symposium on Critical Issues. LC 80-620017. (Research Papers & Policy Studies: No. 1). 68p. 1980. pap. 5.00x (ISBN 0-912966-25-4). IEAS.

Abegglen, Jean-Jacques. On Socialization in Hamadryas Baboons. LC 80-70316. (Illus.). 208p. 1984. 35.00 (ISBN 0-8387-5017-6). Bucknell U Pr.

Abegunrin, Olayiwola, jt. auth. see Newsum, H. E.

Abehsera, Michael. Healing Clay. 1978. pap. 7.95x (ISBN 0-317-07324-9, Regent House). B of A.

Abehsera, Michael, compiled by see Muramoto, Naboru.

Abehsera, Michel. Cooking for Life. 384p. 1976. pap. 4.95 (ISBN 0-380-00777-0, 35188). Avon.

--Zen Macrobiotic Cooking. 1970. pap. 3.50 (ISBN 0-380-01483-1, 60939-8). Avon.

--Zen Macrobiotic Cooking. 1971. pap. 7.95 (ISBN 0-8065-0893-0). Citadel Pr.

Abel, Alan. Don't Get Mad...Get Even! A Manual for Retaliation. (Illus.). 1983. 10.95 (ISBN 0-393-01614-5); pap. 4.95 (ISBN 0-393-30118-4). Norton.

--How to Thrive on Rejection: A Manual for Survival. LC 84-11320. (Illus., Orig.). 1984. 12.95 (ISBN 0-934878-44-7); pap. 5.95 (ISBN 0-934878-45-5). Dembner Bks.

Abel, Albert S. Towards a Constitutional Charter for Canada. 1980. pap. 8.50 (ISBN 0-8020-6399-3). U of Toronto Pr.

Abel, Alison M. Make Hay While the Sun Shines. (Illus.). 48p. 1977. 7.95 (ISBN 0-571-11006-1). Faber & Faber.

Abel, Andrew, ed. see Modigliani, Franco.

Abel, Andrew B. Investment & the Value of Capital. LC 78-75063. (Outstanding Dissertations in Economics Ser.). 1979. lib. bdg. 26.00 (ISBN 0-8240-4139-9). Garland Pub.

Abel, Annie H. The American Indian As Participant in the Civil War. LC 19-5303. (American Studies). Repr. of 1919 ed. 22.00 (ISBN 0-384-00080-0). Johnson Repr.

--The American Indian under Reconstruction. LC 25-10315. Repr. of 1925 ed. 24.00 (ISBN 0-384-00090-8). Johnson Repr.

--History of Events Resulting in Indian Consolidation West of the Mississippi. LC 76-158219. Repr. of 1908 ed. 14.50 (ISBN 0-404-07116-3). AMS Pr.

--Slaveholding Indians, 3 vols. Incl. Vol. 1. The American Indian As Slaveholder & Secessionist. 1919. Repr. 49.00 (ISBN 0-685-26252-9); Vol. 2. The American Indian As Participant in the Civil War. 1919. Repr. 49.00 (ISBN 0-685-26253-7); Vol. 3. The American Indian Under Reconstruction. 1919. Repr. 49.00 (ISBN 0-685-26254-5). LC 70-116268. 1925. Repr. Set. 125.00 (ISBN 0-403-00471-3). Scholarly.

Abel, Annie H., ed. Chardon's Journal at Fort Clark 1834-39. facs. ed. LC 77-140349. (Select Bibliographies Reprint Ser). 1932. 22.00 (ISBN 0-8369-5592-7). Ayer Co Pubs.

Abel, Annie H., ed. see Tappan, Lewis.

Abel, Armand, et al. Unity & Variety in Muslim Civilization. Von Grunebaum, Gustave E., ed. LC 55-11191. (Comparative Studies of Cultures & Civilizations: No. 7). pap. 99.30 (ISBN 0-317-11328-3, 2013614). Bks Demand UMI.

Abel, Bob & Valenti, Mike. Sports Quotes: The Insiders View of the Sports World. 288p. 1983. 16.95 (ISBN 0-87196-776-6). Facts on File.

Abel, Carl F. & Bach, Johan C. Carl Friedrich Abel & Johan Christian Bach. Brook, Barry S., et al, eds. LC 83-1435. (The Symphony Ser.). 400p. 1983. lib. bdg. 90.00 (ISBN 0-8240-3825-8). Garland Pub.

Abel, Charles F. & Marsh, Frank H. Punishment & Restitution: A Restitutionary Approach to Crime & the Criminal. LC 83-22837. (Contributions in Criminology & Penology Ser.: No. 5). (Illus.). 232p. 1984. lib. bdg. 29.95 (ISBN 0-313-23717-4, ABP/). Greenwood.

Abel, Christopher & Lewis, Colin M. Latin America, Economic Imperialism, & the State: The Political Economy of an External Connection from Independence to the Present. LC 84-9260. (Institute of Latin American Studies Monographs: Vol. 13). 540p. 1985. 52.00 (ISBN 0-485-17713-7, Pub. by Athlone Pr Ltd). Longwood Pub Group.

Abel, Christopher & Torrents, Nissa, eds. Spain: Conditional Democracy. LC 83-40172. 224p. 1984. 24.50 (ISBN 0-312-74959-7). St Martin.
Abel, Darrel. American Literature, 3 vols. Incl. Vol. 1. Colonial & Early American Writings. LC 61-18352. pap. text ed. 5.95 (ISBN 0-8120-0023-4); Vol. 2. Literature of the Atlantic Culture. pap. text ed. 6.95 (ISBN 0-8120-0024-2); Vol. 3. Masterworks of American Realism. pap. text ed. 5.95 (ISBN 0-8120-0025-0); Vol. 4. American Literature. (gr. 9-12). 1963. pap. Barron.
--Barron's Simplified Approach to Melville's Moby Dick. LC 65-25679. 1965. pap. 1.95 (ISBN 0-8120-0179-6). Barron.
Abel, Dominick. Guide to the Wines of the United States. 1979. 3.95 (ISBN 0-346-12427-1). Cornerstone.
Abel, Dorothy. The Tender Melody. 1984. 2.95 (ISBN 0-89081-428-7). Harvest Hse.
Abel, Dorothy L. The Candy Shoppe. LC 83-80876. (Rhapsody Romance Ser.). 192p. (Orig.). 1983. pap. 2.95 (ISBN 0-89081-388-4). Harvest Hse.
--Until Then. (Rhapsody Romance Ser.). 192p. 1984. 2.95 (ISBN 0-89081-417-1). Harvest Hse.
--The Whisper of Love. (Rhapsody Romances Ser.). 192p. (Orig.). 1983. pap. 2.95 (ISBN 0-89081-396-5). Harvest Hse.
Abel, E. L. Marihuana: The First Twelve Thousand Years. 1982. pap. 6.95 (ISBN 0-07-000047-6). McGraw.
Abel, E. W. & Stone, F. G. Organometallic Chemistry, Vols. 1-7. Incl. Vol. 1. 1971 Literature. 1972. 41.00 (ISBN 0-85186-501-1); Vol. 2. 1972 Literature. 1973. 49.00 (ISBN 0-85186-511-9); Vol. 3. 1973 Literature. 1974. 54.00 (ISBN 0-85186-521-6); Vol. 4. 1974 Literature. 1975. 68.00 (ISBN 0-85186-531-3); Vol. 5. 1975 Literature. 1976. 73.00 (ISBN 0-85186-541-0); Vol. 6. 1976 Literature. 1977. 86.00 (ISBN 0-85186-551-8); Vol. 7. 1978. 93.00 (ISBN 0-85186-561-5, Pub. by Royal Soc Chem London). LC 72-83459. Am Chemical.
Abel, Eli, ed. What's News: The Media in American Society. 300p. 1981. 18.95 (ISBN 0-87855-448-3); pap. 7.95 (ISBN 0-917616-41-3). Transaction Bks.
Abel, Elie, jt. auth. see Harriman, Averell.
Abel, Elie, jt. auth. see Kalb, Marvin.
Abel, Elie, ed. What's News: The Media in American Society. LC 81-81414. 296p. 1981. text ed. 18.95 (ISBN 0-87855-448-3); pap. text ed. 7.95 (ISBN 0-917616-41-3). ICS Pr.
Abel, Elizabeth. Writing & Sexual Difference. LC 82-11131. (Phoenix Ser.). 312p. 1983. pap. 8.95 (ISBN 0-226-00076-1). U of Chicago Pr.
Abel, Elizabeth & Abel, Emily K., eds. The Signs Reader: Women, Gender & the Scholarship. LC 83-5781. 304p. 1983. lib. bdg. 25.00x (ISBN 0-226-00074-5). U of Chicago Pr.
Abel, Elizabeth, et al, eds. The Voyage In: Fictions of Female Development. LC 82-40473. 374p. 1983. 25.00x (ISBN 0-87451-250-6); pap. 12.95x (ISBN 0-87451-251-4). U Pr of New Eng.
Abel, Emily K. Terminal Degrees: The Job Crisis in Higher Education. LC 83-26876. 240p. 1984. 26.95 (ISBN 0-03-068917-1). Praeger.
Abel, Emily K., jt. ed. see Abel, Elizabeth.
Abel, Ernest L. Ancient Views on the Origins of Life. LC 72-656. 93p. 1973. 15.00 (ISBN 0-8386-1198-2). Fairleigh Dickinson.
--A Dictionary of Drug Abuse Terms & Terminology. LC 83-22867. xi, 137p. 1984. 29.95 (ISBN 0-313-24095-7, ADD/). Greenwood.
--Drugs & Behavior: A Primer in Neuropsychopharmacology. LC 80-11313. 240p. 1982. Repr. of 1974 ed. lib. bdg. 16.50 (ISBN 0-89874-137-8). Krieger.
--Fetal Alcohol Syndrome & Fetal Alcohol Effects. 256p. 1984. 27.50x (ISBN 0-306-41427-9, Plenum Pr). Plenum Pub.
--Fetal Alcohol Syndrome, Vol. I: An Annotated & Comprehensive Bibliography. 144p. 1981. 52.00 (ISBN 0-8493-6192-3). CRC Pr.
--A Marihuana Dictionary: Words, Terms, Events & Persons Relating to Cannabis. LC 81-13427. xi, 136p. 1982. lib. bdg. 35.00 (ISBN 0-313-23252-0, ABM/). Greenwood.
--Marihuana: The First Twelve Thousand Years. LC 80-15606. 300p. 1980. 22.50x (ISBN 0-306-40496-6, Plenum Pr). Plenum Pub.
--Marihuana, Tobacco, Alcohol, & Reproduction. 256p. 1983. 88.00 (ISBN 0-8493-6480-9). CRC Pr.
--Psychoactive Drugs & Sex. 242p. 1985. 27.50x (ISBN 0-306-41869-X, Plenum Pr). Plenum Pub.
--The Roots of Anti-Semitism. LC 73-8286. 264p. 1975. 25.00 (ISBN 0-8386-1406-X). Fairleigh Dickinson.
--Smoking & Reproduction: A Comprehensive Bibliography. LC 82-15660. xviii, 163p. 1982. lib. bdg. 35.00 (ISBN 0-313-23663-1, ASR/). Greenwood.
--Smoking & Reproduction: An Annotated Bibliography. 160p. 1984. 50.00 (ISBN 0-8493-6481-7). CRC Pr.
Abel, Ernest L. & Buckley, Barbara E. The Handwriting on the Wall: Toward a Sociology & Psychology of Graffiti. LC 76-50408. (Contributions in Sociology: No. 27). 1977. lib. bdg. 37.50x (ISBN 0-8371-9475-X, AVJ/). Greenwood.
Abel, Ernest L., compiled by. Alcohol & Reproduction: A Bibliography. LC 82-6202. ix, 219p. 1982. lib. bdg. 29.95 (ISBN 0-313-23474-4, AAR/). Greenwood.
--A Comprehensive Guide to the Cannabis Literature. LC 78-20014. 1979. lib. bdg. 55.00 (ISBN 0-313-20721-6, ACG/). Greenwood.
--Dictionary of Alcohol Use & Abuse: Slang, Terms & Terminology. LC 85-22521. xvi, 189p. 1985. lib. bdg. 29.95 (ISBN 0-313-24631-9, ABA/). Greenwood.
--Drugs & Sex: A Bibliography. LC 83-5656. xvii, 129p. 1983. lib. bdg. 29.95 (ISBN 0-313-23941-X, ADS/). Greenwood.
--Fetal Alcohol Exposure & Effects: A Comprehensive Bibliography. LC 85-9864. 328p. 1985. lib. bdg. 45.00 (ISBN 0-313-24632-7, AFC/). Greenwood.
--Lead & Reproduction: A Comprehensive Bibliography. LC 84-12846. xxxvi, 118p. 1985. lib. bdg. 35.00 (ISBN 0-313-24604-1, ALR/). Greenwood.
--Narcotics & Reproduction: A Bibliography. LC 83-13252. xvii, 215p. 1983. lib. bdg. 29.95 (ISBN 0-313-24052-3, ABN/). Greenwood.
Abel, Ernest L., ed. The Scientific Study of Marihuana. LC 76-4508. 320p. 1976. 24.95x (ISBN 0-88229-144-0). Nelson-Hall.
Abel, Evelyn, tr. see Givet, Jacques.
Abel, Francis & McCutcheon, Ernest P. Cardiovascular Function: Principles & Applications. (Physiopathology Ser.). 1979. 45.00 (ISBN 0-316-00190-2). Little.
Abel, Francis L. & Newman, Walter H., eds. Functional Aspects of the Normal, Hypertrophied, & Failing Heart. (Developments in Cardiovascular Medicine Ser.). 1984. lib. bdg. 55.00 (ISBN 0-89838-665-9, Pub. by Martinus Nijhoff Netherlands). Kluwer Academic.
Abel, H., ed. Electrocardiology VI. (Advances in Cardiology: Vol. 28). (Illus.). xii, 248p. 1981. 67.00 (ISBN 3-8055-1185-X). S Karger.
Abel, H., ed. see Congress on Electrocardiology, 1st, Wiesbaden, Oct. 1974.
Abel, H., ed. see International Congress on Electrocardiology, 2nd, Varna, Oct. 1975.
Abel, I. W. Collective Bargaining: Labor Relations in Steel, Then & Now. LC 76-14369. (Benjamin Fairless Memorial Lectures). 84p. 1976. 10.00x (ISBN 0-915604-05-1). Columbia U Pr.
--Labor's Role in Building a Better Society. (Distinguished Lecturers Ser.: No. 2). 18p. 1972. pap. 1.00 (ISBN 0-87755-174-X). Bureau Busn UT.
Abel, John F., jt. auth. see Desai, C. S.
Abel, L., tr. see Pissarro, Camille.
Abel, Lionel. The Intellectual Follies: A Memoir of the Literary Venture in New York & Paris. 384p. 1984. 17.95 (ISBN 0-393-01841-5). Norton.
Abel, Martin E., ed. see Waugh, Frederick V.
Abel, Martin S. Occult Traumatic Lesions of the Cervical & Thoraco-Lumbar Vertebrae. 2nd ed. 386p. 1983. 42.50 (ISBN 0-87527-312-2). Green.
Abel, Mary, jt. auth. see Moe, Harold.
Abel, Michael. Backpacking Made Easy. 2nd ed. LC 75-8529. (Illus.). 128p. 1975. 10.95 (ISBN 0-87961-041-7); pap. 4.95 (ISBN 0-87961-040-9). Naturegraph.
Abel, Niels H. Oeuvres Completes, 2 vols in 1. Sylow, L. & Lie, S., eds. Set. 65.00 (ISBN 0-384-00103-3). Johnson Repr.
Abel, Othenio. Palaobiologie und Stammeschichte: Paleobiology & Phylogeny. Gould, Stephen J., ed. LC 79-8320. (The History of Paleontology Ser.). (Illus., Ger.). 1980. Repr. of 1929 ed. lib. bdg. 40.00x (ISBN 0-405-12701-4). Ayer Co Pubs.
Abel, Otto, tr. see Wattenbach, W.
Abel, Peter. Assembler for the IBM PC & PC XT. (Illus.). 1983. text ed. 21.95 (ISBN 0-8359-0110-6); pap. text ed. 18.95 (ISBN 0-8359-0153-X). Reston.
--COBOL Programming. 2nd ed. LC 84-9954. 1984. text ed. 23.95 (ISBN 0-8359-0835-6). Reston.
--Programming Assembler Language. 2nd ed. 1984. text ed. 26.95 (ISBN 0-8359-5661-X). Reston.
Abel, Reuben. Man Is the Measure: A Cordial Invitation to the Central Problems of Philosophy. LC 75-16646. (Illus.). 1976. 14.95 (ISBN 0-02-900140-4); pap. text ed. 12.95 (ISBN 0-02-900110-2). Free Pr.
--Pragmatic Humanism of F. C. S. Schiller. LC 70-158220. Repr. of 1955 ed. 18.50 (ISBN 0-404-00275-7). AMS Pr.
Abel, Reuben E., ed Humanistic Pragmatism: The Philosophy of F. C. S. Schiller. (Orig.). 1966. pap. text ed. 6.95 (ISBN 0-02-900120-X). Free Pr.
Abel, Richard. French Cinema: The First Wave, Nineteen Fifteen to Nineteen Twenty-Nine. LC 83-43057. (Illus.). 550p. 1984. 75.00 (ISBN 0-691-05408-8). Princeton U Pr.
--The Politics of Informal Justice: The American Experience, Vol. 1. LC 81-14920. (Studies on Law & Social Control Ser.). 352p. 1981. 29.50 (ISBN 0-12-041501-1). Acad Pr.
Abel, Richard, ed. The Politics of Informal Justice: Vol. 2, Comparative Studies. LC 81-14920. (Studies on Law & Social Control Ser.). 1981. 29.50 (ISBN 0-12-041502-X). Acad Pr.
Abel, Sally. How to Become a U. S. Citizen. LC 83-62116. 158p. 1983. pap. 9.95 (ISBN 0-917316-60-6). Nolo Pr.
Abel, Theodora M. Psychological Testing in Cultural Contexts. 1973. 9.95x (ISBN 0-8084-0363-X); pap. 6.95x (ISBN 0-8084-0364-8). New Coll U Pr.
Abel, Theodora M. & Metreaux, Rhoda. Culture & Psychotherapy. 1974. 11.95x (ISBN 0-8084-0368-0); pap. 8.95x (ISBN 0-8084-0369-9). New Coll U Pr.
Abel, Theodore F. Why Hitler Came into Power. LC 78-63647. (Studies in Fascism: Ideology & Practice). 344p. Repr. of 1938 ed. 35.00 (ISBN 0-404-16897-3). AMS Pr.
Abel, Wilhelm. Agricultural Fluctuations in Europe: From the Thirteenth to the Twentieth Centuries. Ordish, Olive, tr. LC 80-5072. 1980. 12.95 (ISBN 0-312-01465-1). St Martin.
Abelard, Heloise, jt. auth. see Abelard, Peter.
Abelard, Max. Magnificent Samarai. 1984. 22.00x (ISBN 0-901764-00-0, Pub. by P H Crompton Ltd UK). State Mutual Bk.
--Night of the Ninja. 1984. 25.00x (ISBN 0-901764-61-2, Pub. by P H Crompton Ltd UK). State Mutual Bk.
Abelard, May. Magnificent Samarai. 118p. (Orig.). 1969. pap. 3.95 (ISBN 0-317-27268-3). Unique Pubns.
Abelard, Peter. The Cruel Tragedy of My Life: The Autobiography of Peter Abelard. (Illus.). 131p. 1985. 97.45 (ISBN 0-89901-198-5). Found Class Reprints.
--Ethics. Luscombe, D. E., ed. (Oxford Medieval Texts Ser). 1971. 49.95X (ISBN 0-19-822217-3). Oxford U Pr.
--Historia Calamitatum: Story of My Misfortunes. 59.95 (ISBN 0-8490-0305-9). Gordon Pr.
Abelard, Peter & Abelard, Heloise. The Letters of Abelard & Heloise. Scott-Moncrieff, C. K., tr. LC 73-86442. xii, 264p. 1974. Repr. of 1942 ed. lib. bdg. 20.00 (ISBN 0-8154-0486-7). Cooper Sq.
Abele, Hyacinth & Niederheitman, Friedrich. The Violin: Its History & Construction. Broadhouse, John, tr. from Gr. LC 77-75188. 1977. Repr. of 1952 ed. lib. bdg. 25.00 (ISBN 0-89341-081-0). Longwood Pub Group.
Abele, Lawrence, jt. ed. see Bliss, Dorothy.
Abele, Rudolph Von see Von Abele, Rudolph.
Abele, Rudolph Von see Von Abele, Rudolph R.
Abele, Theodor A. Der Senat Unter Augustus. pap. 8.00 (ISBN 0-384-00130-0). Johnson Repr.
Abeles, B., jt. ed. see Chang, R. P.
Abeles, Frederick B. Ethylene in Plant Biology, 1973. 60.00 (ISBN 0-12-041450-3). Acad Pr.
Abeles, Harold & Hoffer, Charles K. Foundations of Music Education. (A Schrimer Book). 1983. 9.95 (ISBN 0-02-870050-3). Macmillan.
Abeles, M. Local Cortical Circuits: An Electrophysiological Study. (Studies of Brain Function: Vol. 6). (Illus.). 110p. 1982. 22.00 (ISBN 0-387-11034-8). Springer-Verlag.
Abeles, P W. & Bardham Roy, B K. Prestressed Concrete Designer's Handbook. 3rd ed. (Illus.). 550p. 1981. text ed. 45.00 (ISBN 0-7210-1227-2, Pub. by Viewpoint). Scholium Intl.
Abeles, Peter, jt. auth. see Schwartz, Harry.
Abeles, Ronald P., jt. ed. see Withey, Stephen B.
Abeles, Ronald P., jt. ed. see Riley, Matilda W.
Abeling, Theodor. Nibelungenlied und Seine Literatur: Eine Bibliographie und Vier Abhandlungen. LC 70-123508. (Bibliography & Reference Ser: No. 363). (Ger). 1970. Repr. of 1907 ed. lib. bdg. 23.50 (ISBN 0-8337-0003-0). B Franklin.
Abel-Khalik, A. Rashad & Keller, Thomas F., eds. The Impact of Accounting Research on Practice & Disclosure. LC 77-85520. 221p. 1978. 20.00 (ISBN 0-8223-0396-5). Duke.
Abelkis & Hudson, eds. Design of Fatigue & Fracture Resistant Structures - STP 761. 486p. 1982. 51.00 (ISBN 0-8031-0714-5, 04-761000-30). ASTM.
Abell, Aaron I. American Catholicism & Social Action: A Search for Social Justice, 1865-1950. LC 80-16876. 306p. 1980. Repr. of 1963 ed. lib. bdg. 27.50x (ISBN 0-313-22513-3, ABAC). Greenwood.
--Urban Impact on American Protestantism, 1865-1900. x, 275p. 1962. Repr. of 1943 ed. 18.50 (ISBN 0-208-00587-0, Archon). Shoe String.
Abell, Alphonse R. Recent Advances of Computers in Medicine: Guidebook for Research & Reference. LC 84-45003. 150p. 1984. 29.95 (ISBN 0-88164-166-9); pap. 21.95 (ISBN 0-88164-167-7). ABBE Pubs Assn.
Abell, D. Defining the Business: The Starting Point of Strategic Planning. 1980. 24.95 (ISBN 0-13-197814-4). P-H.
Abell, Derek F. & Hammond, John. Strategic Market Planning: Problems & Analytical Approaches. 1979. text ed. 32.95 (ISBN 0-13-851089-X). P-H.
Abell, George. Drama of the Universe. LC 77-22338. (Illus.). 1978. prof. ed. 29.95 (ISBN 0-03-043036-4, HoltC). HR&W.
--Drama of the Universe. 1978. pap. text ed. 32.95 (ISBN 0-03-022401-2, CBS C); instr's manual 8.95 (ISBN 0-03-039231-4). SCP.
--Exploration of the Universe. 4th ed. 1982. text ed. 36.95 (ISBN 0-03-058502-3, CBS C); instr's manual 20.00 (ISBN 0-03-058503-1). SCP.
--Realm of the Universe. 3rd ed. 1984. pap. text ed. 28.95 (ISBN 0-03-058504-X, CBS C); instr's manual 10.95 (ISBN 0-03-058506-6). SCP.
Abell, George & Peebles, P. J., eds. Objects of High Redshift: I. A. U. Symposium Los Angeles, Aug. 28 to 31, 1979. (International Astronomical Union Symposium Ser.: No. 92). 328p. 1980. lib. bdg. 42.00 (ISBN 90-277-1118-6, Pub. by Reidel Holland); pap. 21.00 (ISBN 90-277-1119-4). Kluwer Academic.
Abell, Howard, jt. auth. see Schuster, Bertram.
Abell, Parker. A Two-Faced Nation. 1985. 6.95 (ISBN 0-533-06463-5). Vantage.
Abell, Peter, jt. auth. see Proctor, Michael.
Abell, Peter, jt. ed. see Gilbert, G. Nigel.
Abell, Ron. Tap City. 256p. 1985. 14.95 (ISBN 0-316-00200-3). Little.
Abell, Tami, jt. auth. see Mulligan, Mary.
Abell, Troy D. Better Felt Than Said: The Holiness Pentecostal Experience in Southern Appalachia. LC 81-86285. 206p. 1982. 18.00 (ISBN 0-918954-35-5). Baylor Univ Pr.
Abell, Vivian & Farlie, Barbara L. Flower Craft. 192p. 1982. pap. 10.95 (ISBN 0-672-52150-4). Bobbs.
Abell, Vivian, jt. auth. see Farlie, Barbara.
Abell, Walter. Representation & Form. LC 79-138573. (Illus.). 1971. Repr. of 1936 ed. lib. bdg. 22.50x (ISBN 0-8371-5772-2, ABRF). Greenwood.
--Representation & Form: A Study of Aesthetic Values in Representational Art. LC 36-17784. 172p. 1936. Repr. 16.00x (ISBN 0-403-08900-X). Somerset Pub.
Abell, Wescott. The Shipwright's Trade. LC 81-71244. (Illus.). 227p. 1982. Repr. of 1949 ed. 16.00 (ISBN 0-87033-284-8). Cornell Maritime.
Abella, Irving & Troper, Harold. None is Too Many: Canada & the Jews of Europe, 1933-1948. LC 83-42864. 368p. 1983. 17.95 (ISBN 0-394-53328-3). Random.
Abella, Irving M. Nationalism, Communism & Canadian Labour: The CIO, the Communist Party, & the Canadian Congress of Labour, 1935-56. LC 72-80712. 304p. 1973. pap. 10.50 (ISBN 0-8020-6150-8). U of Toronto Pr.
--Nationalism, Communism, & Canadian Labour: The CIO, the Communist Party, & the Canadian Congress of Labour, 1935-1956. LC 72-80712. pap. 67.00 (ISBN 0-317-28714-1, 2020448). Bks Demand UMI.
Abella, Irving M., et al. The Influence of the United States on Canadian Development: Eleven Case Studies. Preston, Richard A., ed. LC 72-81337. (Duke University, Commonwealth-Studies Center Publication Ser.: No. 40). pap. 70.30 (ISBN 0-317-20428-9, 2023437). Bks Demand UMI.
Abella, Kay T. Building Successful Training Programs: A Step-by-Step Guide. 176p. 1986. text ed. 13.95x (ISBN 0-201-00100-4). Addison-Wesley.
Abells, Chana. The Children-We Remember. LC 82-23377. (Illus.). 48p. (gr. 4-8). 1983. 9.95 (ISBN 0-930494-20-2); pap. 5.95 (ISBN 0-930494-21-0). Kar Ben.
Abelman, Paul. Anatomy of Nakedness. (Illus.). 112p. 1985. 11.95 (ISBN 0-317-06236-0); pap. 8.95 (ISBN 0-910550-52-2). Elysium.
--Shoestring. LC 83-61259. 224p. 1984. 9.95 (ISBN 0-88186-376-9); pap. 3.50 (ISBN 0-88186-875-2). Parkwest Pubns.
--Shoestring's Finest Hour. LC 83-61267. 204p. 1983. 12.95 (ISBN 0-88186-375-0); pap. 3.95 (ISBN 0-88186-876-0). Parkwest Pubns.
--Tests: Maximum Characters in Any Play-5. 1981. pap. 6.95 (ISBN 0-413-31570-3, NO. 6474). Methuen Inc.
Abeloff, Diane. Medical Art: Graphics for Use. (Illus.). 252p. 1982. spiral 68.00 (ISBN 0-683-00033-0). Williams & Wilkins.
Abeloff, Martin D., ed. Complications of Cancer: Diagnosis & Management. LC 79-7563. 1980. text ed. 40.00x (ISBN 0-8018-2254-8). Johns Hopkins.
Abelow, Dan. Total Sex. 192p. 1981. pap. 3.50 (ISBN 0-441-81794-7). Ace Bks.
--Total Sex. LC 76-27127. (Illus.). 96p. 1977. pap. 6.95 (ISBN 0-448-12851-9, G&D). Putnam Pub Group.
--Total Sex. 1976. pap. 1.95 (ISBN 0-685-11829-0, Success). Merit Pubns.
Abelow, Dan, jt. auth. see Barr, Samuel J.
Abelow, Daniel & Hilpert, Edwin J. Communications in the Modern Corporate Environment. (Illus.). 224p. 1986. text ed. 27.00 (ISBN 0-13-153842-X). P-H.
Abels, Harriet. A Special Love. (Caprice Romance Ser.: No. 9). 192p. 1984. pap. 1.95 (ISBN 0-441-77788-0, Pub. by Tempo). Ace Bks.
Abels, Harriet & Schenk, Joyce. Seaside Heights. 1985. pap. 2.50 (ISBN 0-451-13671-3, Sig Vista). NAL.
Abels, Harriette S. Cupid Confusion. (Caprice Romance Ser.: No. 44). 160p. 1984. pap. 1.95 (ISBN 0-441-12574-3). Ace Bks.
--First Impression. (Caprice Romance Ser.: No. 50). 160p. 1984. pap. 2.25 (ISBN 0-441-23992-7, Pub. by Tempo). Ace Bks.
--A Forgotten World. Schroeder, Howard, ed. LC 79-4633. (Galaxy 1 Ser.). (Illus.). 48p. (gr. 3-5). 1979. PLB 7.95 (ISBN 0-89686-032-9). Crestwood Hse.
--A Good Sport. (Caprice Romance Ser.: No. 62). 160p. 1985. pap. 2.25 (ISBN 0-441-29848-6, Pub. by Tempo). Ace Bks.

--The Green Invasion. Schroeder, Howard, ed. LC 79-4639. (Galaxy I Ser.). (Illus.). 48p. (gr. 3-5). 1979. PLB 6.95 (ISBN 0-89686-030-2). Crestwood Hse.
--Medical Emergency. Schroeder, Howard, ed. LC 79-9823. (Galaxy I Ser.). (Illus.). 48p. (gr. 3-5). 1979. PLB 7.95 (ISBN 0-89686-029-9). Crestwood Hse.
--Meteor from the Moon. Schroeder, Howard, ed. LC 79-4650. (Galaxy I Ser.). (Illus.). 48p. (gr. 3-5). 1979. PLB 7.95 (ISBN 0-89686-025-6). Crestwood Hse.
--Mystery on Mars. Schroeder, Howard, ed. LC 79-9923. (Galaxy I Ser.). (Illus.). 48p. (gr. 3-5). 1979. PLB 7.95 (ISBN 0-89686-024-8). Crestwood Hse.
--A New Love For Lisa. 176p. pap. 1.95 (ISBN 0-441-57169-7). Ace Bks.
--Planet of Ice. Schroeder, Howard, ed. LC 79-9920. (Galaxy I Ser.). (Illus.). 48p. (gr. 3-5). 1979. PLB 7.95 (ISBN 0-89686-026-4). Crestwood Hse.
--The Silent Invaders. Schroeder, Howard, ed. LC 79-4644. (Galaxy I Ser.). (Illus.). 48p. (gr. 3-5). 1979. PLB 7.95 (ISBN 0-89686-031-0). Crestwood Hse.
--Strangers on NMA-6. Schroeder, Howard, ed. LC 79-4627. (Galaxy I Ser.). (Illus.). 48p. (gr. 3-5). 1979. PLB 7.95 (ISBN 0-89686-027-2). Crestwood Hse.
--Unwanted Visitors. Schroeder, Howard, ed. LC 79-9922. (Galaxy I Ser.). (Illus.). 48p. (gr. 3-5). 1979. PLB 7.95 (ISBN 0-89686-028-0). Crestwood Hse.
Abels, Harriette Sheffer. Follow Me, Love. (YA) 1978. 8.95 (ISBN 0-685-05586-8, Avalon). Bouregy.
Abels, Herriette S. Lucky in Love. (Caprice Ser.: No. 76). 144p. 1985. pap. 2.25 (ISBN 0-441-50440-X). Ace Bks.
Abels, Jules. Man on Fire: John Brown & the Cause of Liberty. LC 72-117961. pap. 116.00 (ISBN 0-317-28765-6, 2051680). Bks Demand UMI.
Abels, Linda F. Mosby's Manual of Critical Care: Practices & Procedures, 1979. LC 78-24358. (Illus.). 1979. pap. text ed. 23.95 (ISBN 0-8016-0055-3). Mosby.
Abels, Linda F., et al. Critical Care Nursing: Process & Practice. (Illus.). 825p. 1984. pap. text ed. 25.95 (ISBN 0-8016-0083-9). Mosby.
Abels, Paul & Murphy, Michael J. Administration in the Human Services: A Normative Systems Approach. (P-H Series in Social Work). (Illus.). 256p. 1981. text ed. 27.95 (ISBN 0-13-005850-5). P-H.
Abels, Richard. The Endangered Species Gourmet Cookbook. (Illus.). 112p. 1983. pap. 3.95 (ISBN 0-910937-07-9). Laranmark.
Abel-Smith, B. International Study of Health Expenditure & Its Relevance for Health Planning. (Public Health Paper: No. 32). (Also avail. in French, Russian & Spanish). 1967. pap. 2.80 (ISBN 92-4-130032-9). World Health.
Abel-Smith, Brian. Accounting for Health. 64p. 1973. 18.00x (ISBN 0-900889-37-3, Pub. by Kings Fund). State Mutual Bk.
--Cost Containment in Health Care: A Study of 12 European Countries 1977-1983. 123p. 1984. pap. text ed. 12.00x (ISBN 0-7199-1127-3, Pub. by Bedford England). Brookfield Pub Co.
--People Without Choices. (Eng. & Span.). 1973. 15.00x (ISBN 0-686-87127-8, Pub. by Intl Planned Parent). State Mutual Bk.
--The Poor & the Poorest. 78p. 1965. pap. text ed. 5.00x (ISBN 0-686-70854-7, Pub. by Bedford England). Brookfield Pub Co.
--Value for Money in Health Services. 1976. pap. text ed. 11.00x (ISBN 0-435-82006-0). Gower Pub Co.
Abel-Smith, Brian, jt. auth. see Titmuss, Richard M.
Abelson, Danny. The Muppets Take Manhattan: The Storybook Based on the Movie. LC 83-19153. (Illus.). 64p. (ps-4). 1984. 6.95 (ISBN 0-394-86386-0, BYR); PLB 7.99 (ISBN 0-394-96386-5, BYR). Random.
Abelson, H. & Sussman, G. Structure & Interpretation of Computer Programs. (MH-MIT Press Ser.). 1984. 32.50 (ISBN 0-07-000422-6). McGraw.
Abelson, Hal. Apple LOGO. (Illus.). 256p. 1982. pap. 18.95 (ISBN 0-07-000425-0, BYTE Bks). McGraw.
--LOGO for the Apple II. 1982. 18.95 (ISBN 0-07-000426-9, BYTE Bks). McGraw.
--TI LOGO. (Illus.). 1984. pap. 17.95 (ISBN 0-07-038459-2, BYTE Bks). McGraw.
Abelson, Harold & DiSessa, Andrea. Turtle Geometry: The Computer As a Medium for Exploring Mathematics. (Artificial Intelligence Ser.). (Illus.). 477p. 1981. text ed. 27.00x (ISBN 0-262-01063-1). MIT Pr.
Abelson, Harold & Sussman, Gerald J. Structure & Interpretation of Computer Programs. (Electrical Engineering & Computer Science Ser.). (Illus.). 400p. 1984. text ed. 34.95x (ISBN 0-262-01077-1). MIT Pr.
Abelson, Harold H. The Improvement of Intelligence Testing. LC 76-176502. (Columbia University Teachers College Contributions to Education: No. 273). Repr. of 1927 ed. 22.50 (ISBN 0-404-55273-0). AMS Pr.
Abelson, Herbert, jt. auth. see Karlins, Marvin.
Abelson, John see Schimmel, Paul.
Abelson, Joshua. Jewish Mysticism: An Introduction to Kabbalah. LC 80-54593. (The Judaic Studies Library: SHP 7). 192p. 1981. pap. 5.95 (ISBN 0-87203-096-2). Hermon.
Abelson, Neva M. Topics in Blood Banking. LC 74-8253. pap. 42.50 (ISBN 0-317-26672-1, 2055994). Bks Demand UMI.
Abelson, Paul. The Seven Liberal Arts: A Study in Medieval Culture. LC 76-176501. (Columbia University Teachers College, Contributions to Education Ser.: No. 11). Repr. of 1906 ed. 22.50 (ISBN 0-404-55011-8). AMS Pr.
Abelson, Philip H. Energy for Tomorrow. LC 75-1368. (Jessie & John Danz Lecture Ser). (Illus.). 64p. 1975. 10.00x (ISBN 0-295-95413-2); pap. 3.95x (ISBN 0-295-95414-0). U of Wash Pr.
--Enough of Pessimism: One Hundred Essays. 221p. 1985. text ed. write for info. (ISBN 0-87168-310-5); pap. text ed. write for info (ISBN 0-87168-274-5). AAAS.
Abelson, Philip H., ed. Biotechnology & Biological Frontiers. LC 84-21655. 516p. 1984. 29.95 (ISBN 0-87168-308-3); pap. 14.95 (ISBN 0-87168-266-4). AAAS.
--Energy: Use, Conservation & Supply. LC 74-29004. (Science Compendium Ser.: Vol. 1). 154p. 1974. casebound 10.00 (ISBN 0-87168-213-3); pap. 3.50 (ISBN 0-87168-223-0). AAAS.
--Food: Politics, Economics, Nutrition & Research. LC 75-18785. (Science Compendium Ser.: Vol. 2). (Illus.). 1975. casebound 10.00 (ISBN 0-87168-215-X). AAAS.
--Food: Politics, Economics, Nutrition & Research. 1976. 29.00 (ISBN 0-12-041652-2); pap. 17.00 (ISBN 0-12-041653-0). Acad Pr.
--Health Care: Regulation, Economics, Ethics, Practice. LC 78-67824. (AAAS Science Compendia Ser.: Vol. 7). 258p. 1978. 12.00 (ISBN 0-87168-302-4); pap. 5.00 (ISBN 0-87168-240-0). AAAS.
--Researches in Geochemistry, Vol. 2. LC 59-6755. 678p. 1967. 38.50 (ISBN 0-471-00167-8). Krieger.
Abelson, Philip H. & Dorfman, Mary, eds. Advanced Technology. LC 80-67368. (Science Compendia Ser.: Vol. 8). (Illus.). 144p. 1980. text ed. 14.00x (ISBN 0-87168-303-2); pap. text ed. 6.00x (ISBN 0-87168-249-4). AAAS.
Abelson, Philip H. & Hammond, Allen L., eds. Electronics: The Continuing Revolution. LC 77-77257. (Compendium Ser.: Vol. 5). 217p. casebound 10.00 (ISBN 0-87168-217-6); pap. 3.50 (ISBN 0-87168-230-3). AAAS.
--Energy Two: Use, Conservation & Supply. LC 78-59190. (Science Compendia Ser.: Vol. 6). 1978. 12.00 (ISBN 0-87168-300-8); pap. 5.00 (ISBN 0-87168-237-0). AAAS.
--Materials: Renewable & Nonrenewable Resources. LC 76-7295. (Science Compendium Ser.: Vol. 4). 196p. 1976. casebound 10.00 (ISBN 0-87168-216-8); pap. 3.50 (ISBN 0-87168-227-3). AAAS.
Abelson, Philip H. & Kulstad, Ruth, eds. The Science Centennial Review. LC 80-69480. (Science Compendia Ser.: Vol. 9). (Illus.). 188p. 1980. text ed. 14.00x (ISBN 0-87168-305-9); pap. text ed. 6.00x (ISBN 0-87168-250-8). AAAS.
Abelson, Philip H., et al, eds. Liquid Thermal Diffusion. AEC Technical Information Center. (National Nuclear Energy Ser.: Div. IX, Vol. 1). 258p. 1958. 22.00 (ISBN 0-87079-259-8, TID-5229); microfilm 10.00 (ISBN 0-87079-260-1, TID-5229). DOE.
--Neuroscience. LC 84-24524. (Illus.). 453p. 1985. text ed. 29.95 (ISBN 0-87168-309-1); pap. text ed. 14.95 (ISBN 0-87168-268-0). AAAS.
Abelson, Raziel. Persons: A Study in Philosophical Psychology. LC 76-19225. 1977. 22.50x (ISBN 0-312-60235-9). St Martin.
Abelson, Raziel & Friquegnon, Marie-Louise. The Philosophical Imagination: An Introduction to Philosophy. LC 76-28137. 1977. text ed. 24.95 (ISBN 0-312-60515-3). St Martin.
Abelson, Raziel & Friquegnon, Marie-Louise, eds. Ethics for Modern Life. 2nd ed. LC 81-48150. 428p. 1982. pap. text ed. 15.95 (ISBN 0-312-26601-4). St Martin.
Abelson, Robert, jt. auth. see Schank, Roger.
Abelson, Robert B., ed. Using Microcomputers in the Social Studies Classroom. LC 83-14925. (Orig.). 1983. pap. 9.95 (ISBN 0-89994-282-2). Soc Sci Ed.
Aben, Hillar. Integrated Photoelasticity. (Illus.). 1979. 48.00x (ISBN 0-07-000043-3). McGraw.
Abend, Allen C., et al. Facilities for Special Education Services: A Guide for Planning New & Renovated Schools. 160p. 1979. pap. 8.00 (ISBN 0-86586-033-5). Coun Exc Child.
Abend, Hallett. Pacific Charter: Our Destiny in Asia. LC 72-4478. (Essay Index Reprint Ser.). Repr. of 1943 ed. 18.00 (ISBN 0-8369-2932-2). Ayer Co Pubs.
Abend, Sander M. & Porder, Michael A. Borderline Patients: Psychoanalytic Perspectives. Fine, Bernard D., et al, eds. LC 83-12750. (Monographs of Kris Study Group Ser.: No. 7). viii, 255p. 1983. 27.50 (ISBN 0-8236-0576-0). Intl Univs Pr.
Abend, Sheldon, jt. auth. see Sauter, Joseph M.
Abendroth, Wolfgang. A Short History of the European Working Class. Jacobs, Nicholas, et al, trs. from Ger. LC 72-81766. 208p. 1972. pap. 5.95 (ISBN 0-85345-289-X). Monthly Rev.
--A Short History of the European Working Class. Rev. ed. Jacobs, Nicholas, et al, trs. 240p. (Orig.). 1985. 25.00 (ISBN 0-85345-694-1); pap. 9.00 (ISBN 0-85345-695-X). Monthly Rev.
Abenheim, Peter, jt. auth. see Masri, Allan.
Abensour, E. S., jt. auth. see Cepede, M.
Abensour, E. S., et al. Principles of Land Tenancy Legislation: A Comparative Study. Rev. ed. (Legislative Studies: No. 6). (Orig.). 1966. pap. 4.75 (ISBN 0-685-09401-4, F332, FAO). Unipub.
--Principles of Tenancy Legislation. (Legislative Studies: No. 2). 69p. (Orig.). 1957. pap. 5.25 (ISBN 92-5-101519-8, F333, FAO). Unipub.
Aber, Hal, jt. auth. see Aber, Linda W.
Aber, Ita. The Art of Judaic Needlework: Traditional & Contemporary Designs. (Illus.). 1979. pap. 3.95 encore (ISBN 0-684-17684-X). Scribner.
Aber, Linda W. & Aber, Hal. Bears Forever. (Stuck on Stickers Ser.: No. 5). (Illus.). 24p. (Orig.). (gr. 2-6). 1985. pap. 2.95. Scholastic Inc.
--Get the Message: Say It Quicker with A Sticker. (Stuck on Stickers Ser.: No. 7). (Illus.). 24p. (Orig.). (gr. 2-7). 1985. pap. 2.95 (ISBN 0-590-33607-X). Scholastic Inc.
--More Stuck on Stickers. (Stuck on Stickers Ser.). (Illus.). 48p. (Orig.). 1984. pap. 5.95 (ISBN 0-590-33360-7). Scholastic Inc.
--Rainbow Sticker Riot. (Stuck on Stickers Ser.). (Illus.). 24p. (Orig.). (gr. 2-6). 1985. pap. 2.95 (ISBN 0-590-33388-7). Scholastic Inc.
--Stickers Forever. (Stuck on Stickers Ser.: No. 4). (Illus.). 24p. pap. 2.95 (ISBN 0-590-33611-8). Scholastic Inc.
--Stuck on Stickers. (Illus.). 48p. (Orig.). (ps). 1984. pap. 5.95 (ISBN 0-590-33272-4). Scholastic Inc.
--Unicorn Fantascenes. (Stuck on Sticker Ser.: No. 6). (Illus.). 24p. (Orig.). 1985. pap. 2.95 (ISBN 0-590-33568-5). Scholastic Inc.
Aber, Ted. Adirondack Folks. LC 79-89617. (Illus.). 218p. 1982. Repr. of 1980 ed. 10.95 (ISBN 0-913710-08-3). North Country.
Aber, Ted & King, Stella. Tales from An Adirondack County. 1981. Repr. of 1961 ed. 9.95 (ISBN 0-913710-07-5). North Country.
Aber, William M. Behind the Begats: Conversations for Thanksgiving & Advent. 1977. pap. 3.75 (ISBN 0-89536-283-X). CSS of Ohio.
--A Lenten Zoo. 1973. pap. 3.50 (ISBN 0-89536-127-2). CSS of Ohio.
Aberbach, Alan D. The Ideas of Richard Wagner: An Examination & Analysis of His Major Aesthetic, Political, Economic, Social, & Religious Thoughts. 396p. (Orig.). 1984. lib. bdg. 26.75 (ISBN 0-8191-4145-3); pap. text ed. 15.50 (ISBN 0-8191-4146-1). U Pr of Amer.
Aberbach, David. At the Handles of the Lock. (Littman Library of Jewish Civilization). 29.95X (ISBN 0-19-710040-6). Oxford U Pr.
Aberbach, Joel & Walker, Jack. Detroit Longitudinal Study, 1967. 1974. codebook write for info (ISBN 0-89138-103-1). ICPSR.
Aberbach, Joel D. & Putnam, Robert D. Bureaucrats & Politicians in Western Democracies. 324p. 1982. pap. text ed. 9.95x (ISBN 0-674-08627-9). Harvard U Pr.
Aberbach, Joel D., et al. Bureaucrats & Politicians in Western Democracies. LC 81-2899. (Illus.). 336p. 1981. text ed. 29.50 (ISBN 0-674-08625-2). Harvard U Pr.
Aberbach, M. & Grossfeld, B. Targum Onkelos to Genesis. 45.00x (ISBN 0-87068-339-X). Ktav.
Abercrombie, A. Vaughn. His Everlasting Words. 80p. 7.95 (ISBN 0-89962-326-3). Todd & Honeywell.
Abercrombie, Barbara. Amanda & Heather & Company. LC 78-72117. (Illus.). (gr. k-3). 1979. 3.50 (ISBN 0-89799-086-2); pap. 1.50 (ISBN 0-89799-017-X). Dandelion Pr.
--Cat-Man's Daughter. LC 79-2676. 160p. (gr. 6-9). 1981. 10.53i (ISBN 0-06-020030-8); PLB 11.06 (ISBN 0-06-020031-6). HarpJ.
--Cat-Man's Daughter. 160p. (gr. 7 up). 1983. pap. 1.95 (ISBN 0-590-32727-5). Scholastic Inc.
--Good Riddance. LC 78-20197. 1979. 11.49 (ISBN 0-06-010021-4, HarpT). Har-Row.
--Run for Your Life. LC 83-13076. 276p. 1984. 12.95 (ISBN 0-688-01552-2). Morrow.
Abercrombie, D. The Elements of General Phonetics. 203p. 1967. 20.00x (ISBN 0-85224-028-7, Pub. by Edinburgh U Pr Scotland). Columbia U Pr.
Abercrombie, Jay. Walks & Rambles on the Delmarva Peninsula. (Walks & Rambles Ser.). (Illus.). 160p. (Orig.). 1985. pap. 7.95 (ISBN 0-942440-27-7). Backcountry Pubns.
Abercrombie, John R. Computer Methods for Literary Analysis. LC 84-7214. 176p. 1984. pap. 12.95 spiral bdg. (ISBN 0-8122-1177-4); IBM-PC (Dos 2.0) diskette 24.95 (ISBN 0-8122-3000-0); Apple diskette 24.95 (ISBN 0-8122-3001-9); Dec Rainbow diskette 24.95 (ISBN 0-8122-3002-7). U of Pa Pr.
Abercrombie, L. Poetry: Its Music & Meaning. 1979. 28.50 (ISBN 0-685-94339-9). Porter.
Abercrombie, Lascellas. A Plea for the Liberty of Interpreting. 1978. lib. bdg. 10.00 (ISBN 0-8495-0125-3). Arden Lib.
Abercrombie, Lascelles. Epic. LC 73-102222. (Select Bibliographies Reprint Ser.). 1914. 14.50 (ISBN 0-8369-5107-7). Ayer Co Pubs.
--Idea of Great Poetry. LC 73-99654. (Select Bibliographies Reprint Ser). 1925. 19.00 (ISBN 0-8369-5083-6). Ayer Co Pubs.
--The Idea of Great Poetry. LC 72-131601. 231p. 1925. Repr. 17.00x (ISBN 0-403-00488-8). Scholarly.
--Interludes & Poems. LC 79-50016. (One-Act Plays in Reprint Ser.). 1980. Repr. of 1928 ed. 22.50x (ISBN 0-8486-2040-2). Core Collection.
--Plea for the Liberty of Interpreting. LC 73-9721. 1930. lib. bdg. 8.50 (ISBN 0-8414-2862-X). Folcroft.
--The Poems of Lascelles Abercrombie. LC 83-45404. Repr. of 1930 ed. 49.50 (ISBN 0-404-20000-1). AMS Pr.
--Poetry: Its Music & Meaning. 1978. Repr. of 1932 ed. lib. bdg. 15.00 (ISBN 0-8495-0124-5). Arden Lib.
--Poetry: Its Music & Meaning. LC 72-194362. 1932. lib. bdg. 9.50 (ISBN 0-8414-3542-1). Folcroft.
--Principles of English Prosody, Pt. 1. LC 75-41000. (BCL Ser.: No. II). Repr. of 1923 ed. 15.00 (ISBN 0-404-14735-6). AMS Pr.
--Principles of Literary Criticism. LC 78-21288. 1979. Repr. of 1932 ed. lib. bdg. 22.50x (ISBN 0-313-20025-4, ABPL). Greenwood.
--Speculative Dialogues. 1971. Repr. of 1913 ed. 39.00 (ISBN 0-403-00799-2). Scholarly.
--The Theory of Poetry. LC 69-17712. 1969. Repr. of 1926 ed. 12.00x (ISBN 0-8196-0223-X). Biblo.
--The Theory of Poetry. LC 76-131602. 222p. 1924. Repr. 11.00x (ISBN 0-403-00489-6). Scholarly.
--Thomas Hardy, a Critical Study. LC 64-8920. 1964. Repr. of 1912 ed. 11.00x (ISBN 0-8462-0117-8). Russell.
Abercrombie, Lascelles, et al. Revaluations: Studies in Biography. LC 75-30773. (English Biography Ser., No. 31). 1975. lib. bdg. 49.95x (ISBN 0-8383-2106-2). Haskell.
Abercrombie, M. & Brachet, J., eds. Advances in Morphogenesis, 10 vols. Incl. Vol. 1. 1961 (ISBN 0-12-028601-7); Vol. 2. 1963 (ISBN 0-12-028602-5); Vol. 3. 1964. (ISBN 0-12-028603-3); Vol. 4. 1965 (ISBN 0-12-028604-1); Vol. 5. 1966 (ISBN 0-12-028605-X); Vol. 6. 1967 (ISBN 0-12-028606-8); Vol. 7. King, T. J., ed. 1968 (ISBN 0-12-028607-6); Vol. 8. King, T. J., ed. 1970 (ISBN 0-12-028608-4); Vol. 9. King, T. J., ed. 1971 (ISBN 0-12-028609-2); Vol. 10. 1973 (ISBN 0-12-028610-6). 75.00 ea. Acad Pr.
Abercrombie, M., et al. Diccionario de Biologia. 242p. (Span.). 1978. pap. 16.75 (ISBN 0-686-57336-6, S-50068). French & Eur.
--Dictionary of Biology. 6th ed. (Reference Ser.). (Orig.). 1951. pap. 5.95 (ISBN 0-14-051003-6). Penguin.
--The Penguin Dictionary of Biology. 1978. 12.95 (ISBN 0-670-27222-1). Viking.
Abercrombie, Nicholas. Class, Structure & Knowledge: Problems in the Sociology of Knowing. LC 79-9650. 1980. 27.00x (ISBN 0-8147-0571-5). NYU Pr.
Abercrombie, Nicholas & Urry, John. Capital, Labour & the Middle Classes. (Controversies in Sociology Ser.: No. 15). 176p. (Orig.). 1983. text ed. 21.95x (ISBN 0-04-301145-4); pap. text ed. 8.95x (ISBN 0-04-301146-2). Allen Unwin.
Abercrombie, Nicholas, et al. Dominant Ideology Thesis. 240p. 1980. text ed. 28.50x (ISBN 0-04-301117-9). Allen Unwin.
--The Dominant Ideology Thesis. 224p. 1984. pap. text ed. 9.95x (ISBN 0-04-301181-0). Allen Unwin.
--The Penguin Dictionary of Sociology. (Reference Ser.). 272p. 1984. pap. 5.95 (ISBN 0-14-051108-3). Penguin.
Abercrombie, Nigel. Artists & Their Public. 123p. 1975. pap. 6.00 (ISBN 92-3-101252-5, U39, UNESCO). Unipub.
--Cultural Policy in the United Kingdom. (Studies & Documents on Cultural Policies). 71p. 1982. pap. 7.50 (ISBN 92-3-102018-8, U1226, UNESCO). Unipub.
Abercrombie, Patrick, jt. ed. see Adshead, S. D.
Abercrombie, Stanley. Architecture As Art: An Esthetic Analysis. LC 83-23300. (Illus.). 192p. 1984. 24.95 (ISBN 0-442-20875-8). Van Nos Reinhold.
--Gwathmey Siegel. (Monograph Ser.). (Illus.). 120p. 1981. 19.95 (ISBN 0-8230-7257-6, Whitney Lib). Watson-Guptill.
Abercrombie, V. T. & Gaylord, Louise. Catering to Houston. LC 80-70604. 1981. 9.95. Brown Rabbit.
Abercrombie, V. T. & Williams, Helen, eds. Christmas in Texas. LC 79-66212. (Illus., Orig.). 1979. pap. 4.50 (ISBN 0-933988-00-1). Brown Rabbit.
Abercromby, John. The Pre- & Proto- Historic Finns, Both Eastern & Western, with the Magic Songs of the West Finns, 2 Vols. LC 70-144523. (Grimm Library: Nos. 9-10). Repr. of 1898 ed. Set. 65.00 (ISBN 0-404-53590-9). AMS Pr.
--A Study of the Bronze Age Pottery of Great Britain & Ireland: Its Associated Grave Goods, 2 vols. LC 77-86419. (Illus.). Repr. of 1912 ed. 70.00 set (ISBN 0-404-15850-1). AMS Pr.

Aberdeen, Scotland (Diocese) Registrum Episcopatus Aberdonensis: Ecclesie Cathedralis Aberdonensis Regesta Que Extant in Unum Collecta, 2 Vols. Innes, Cosmo, ed. LC 77-38504. (Maitland Club, Glasgow. Publications: No. 63). 1845. Set. 75.00 (ISBN 0-404-53065-6). AMS Pr.

Aberdo, E. J. & Thomas, L. J., eds. Directory of Agencies Serving the Deaf-Blind. 77p. 1980. 5.00 (ISBN 0-318-17870-2). H Keller Natl Ctr.

Aberg, F. A., ed. Medieval Moated Sites. (CBA Research Report Ser.: No. 17). 91p. 1978. pap. text ed. 18.45x (ISBN 0-900312-58-0, Pub. by Coun Brit Archaeology). Humanities.

Aberg, Gilbert S. Esther: A Play. LC 69-17410. (Illus.). 163p. 1969. 4.50 (ISBN 0-87601-001-X). Carnation.

Aberg, T., et al. Corpuscles & Radiation in Matter I. (Encyclopedia of Physics: Vol. 31). (Illus.). 670p. 1982. 131.20 (ISBN 0-387-11313-4). Springer-Verlag.

Aberg, Williams, ed. A Promise of Morning: Writings from Arizona Prisons. 1982. pap. 6.95 (ISBN 0-933188-21-8). Blue Moon Pr.

Aberlaitz & Buenaventura de Oreyegui, P. Diccionario Vasco-Castellano, Castellano-Vasco De Voces Comunes a Dos O Mas Dialectos Del Euskera. (Span.). 25.50 (ISBN 84-248-0014-1, S-21917). French & Eur.

Aberle, David F. The Peyote Religion among the Navaho. 2nd ed. LC 82-2562. (Illus.). 514p. 1982. lib. bdg. 35.00x (ISBN 0-226-00082-6); pap. text ed. 15.00x (ISBN 0-226-00083-4). U of Chicago Pr.

Aberle, S. B. De see De Aberle, S. B.

Aberman & Logan, A. Emergency Management of the Critically Ill. 1980. 61.50 (ISBN 0-8151-0003-5). Year Bk Med.

Abernathey, William J. & Clark, Kim B. Industrial Renaissance: Producing a Competitive Future in America. LC 82-72391. 1983. 19.00 (ISBN 0-465-03254-0). Basic.

Abernathy, Charles F. Civil Rights Cases & Materials. LC 79-24759. (American Casebook Ser.). 660p. 1980. text ed. 22.95 (ISBN 0-8299-2076-5). West Pub.

Abernathy, David & Perrin, Norman. Understanding the Teaching of Jesus. 288p. (Orig.). 1983. pap. 13.95 (ISBN 0-8164-2438-1, Pub. by Seabury). Winston Pr.

Abernathy, Estelle K. Pumpkin Corner. (Illus.). 160p. 1979. pap. 5.00 (ISBN 0-9608428-2-9). Straw Patchwork.

Abernathy, Francis E. Legends of Texas' Heroic Age. (Texas History Ser.). (Illus.). 108p. (Orig.). 1984. pap. text ed. 3.95x (ISBN 0-89641-143-5). American Pr.

Abernathy, Glenn. The Right of Assembly & Association. 2nd & rev. ed. LC 61-9384. 300p. 1981. pap. text ed. 9.95x (ISBN 0-87249-410-1). U of SC Pr.

Abernathy, M. Glenn. Civil Liberties under the Constitution. rev. ed. LC 85-1052. 700p. 1985. pap. text ed. 12.95x (ISBN 0-87249-455-1). U of SC Pr.

Abernathy, M. Glenn, et al. The Carter Years: The President & Policy Making. LC 83-40061. 219p. 1984. 22.50 (ISBN 0-312-12286-1). St Martin.

Abernathy, Mark, jt. auth. see Covello, Vincent.

Abernathy, Ruth. A Study of Expenditures & Service in Physical Education: An Analysis of Variations in Expenditure, Extent of Service, Personnel, Facilities, & Program of Physical Education in Selected Schools of New York State. LC 77-176685. (Columbia University. Teachers College, Contributions to Education: No. 904). Repr. of 1944 ed. 22.50 (ISBN 0-404-55904-2). AMS Pr.

Abernathy, Steve. Learning Safety First. (Science Ser.). 24p. (gr. 5-9). 1977. wkbk. 5.00 (ISBN 0-8209-0158-X, S-20). ESP.

Abernathy, William J. The Productivity Dilemma: Roadblock to Innovation in the Automobile Industry. LC 78-1034. (Illus.). 280p. 1978. text ed. 25.00x (ISBN 0-8018-2081-2). Johns Hopkins.

Abernathy, William J. & Clark, Kim B. Industrial Renaissance: Producing a Competitive Future for America. LC 82-72391. 194p. 1984. pap. 8.95 (ISBN 0-465-03255-9, CN-5125). Basic.

Abernethy, Byron R., ed. see Stockwell, Elisha, Jr.

Abernethy, Cecil see Anderson, Charles R.

Abernethy, David B. The Political Dilemma of Popular Education: An African Case. LC 69-13175. 1969. 27.50x (ISBN 0-8047-0703-0). Stanford U Pr.

Abernethy, E. M. Relationships Between Mental & Physical Growth. (Society for Research in Child Development Monographs: Vol. 1, No. 7). pap. 12.00 (ISBN 0-527-01492-3). Kraus Repr.

Abernethy, Francis, ed. Paisanos: A Folklore Miscellany. 1978. 10.50 (ISBN 0-88426-054-2). Encino Pr.

Abernethy, Francis, et al. Texas & Germany: Crosscurrents. Wilson, Joseph, ed. (Rice University Studies: Vol. 63, No. 3). (Illus.). 139p. 1977. pap. 10.00x (ISBN 0-89263-233-X). Rice Univ.

Abernethy, Francis E. How the Critters Created Texas. LC 82-80440. (Illus.). 40p. 1982. pap. 8.95 (ISBN 0-936650-01-X). E C Temple.

--Observations & Reflections on Texas Folklore. (Illus.). 151p. 1972. 10.00 (ISBN 0-88426-010-0). Encino Pr.

--Singin' Texas. LC 83-80205. (Illus.). 208p. (Orig.). 1983. 29.95 (ISBN 0-935014-07-1); pap. 19.95 (ISBN 0-935014-04-7). E-Heart Pr.

Abernethy, Francis E., ed. Built in Texas. (Publications of the Texas Folklore Society Ser.: No. 42). (Illus.). 288p. 1979. 24.50 (ISBN 0-935014-00-4). E-Heart Pr.

--Folk Art in Texas. (Texas Folklore Society Publications Ser.: Vol. XLV). (Illus.). 204p. 1985. 35.00 (ISBN 0-87074-210-8). SMU Press.

--Legendary Ladies of Texas. LC 80-68402. (Publications of the Texas Folklore Society No. 43 in Cooperation with the Texas Foundation for Women's Resources Women in Texas History Project). (Illus.). 236p. (Orig.). 1981. o.p 24.95 (ISBN 0-935014-01-2); pap. 12.95 (ISBN 0-935014-02-0). E-Heart Pr.

--Some Still Do: Essays on Texas Customs. new ed. (Publications of the Texas Folklore Society: Vol. 39). (Illus.). 125p. 1975. 10.00 (ISBN 0-88426-047-X). Encino Pr.

--Sonovagun Stew. (Texas Folklore Society Publications: No. 46). Date not set. price not set (ISBN 0-87074-211-6). SMU Press.

--T for Texas: A State Full of Folklore. LC 82-70089. (Texas Folklore Society Publications Ser.: No. 44). (Illus.). 250p. (Orig.). 1982. 15.95 (ISBN 0-935014-03-9). E-Heart Pr.

--Tales from the Big Thicket. (Illus.). 256p. 1966. 12.95 (ISBN 0-292-73636-3). U of Tex Pr.

--What's Going On? (Texas Folklore Society Publications: Vol. 40). (Illus.). 1976. 12.50 (ISBN 0-88426-049-6). Encino Pr.

Abernethy, George L. & Langford, Thomas A., eds. Philosophy of Religion: A Book of Readings. 2nd ed. 1968. write for info. (ISBN 0-02-300150-X, 30015). Macmillan.

Abernethy, Jane F. & Tune, Suelyn C. Made in Hawaii. LC 83-4895. (Kolowalu Bk.). (Illus.). 140p. (gr. 3-12). 1983. pap. 5.95 (ISBN 0-8248-0870-3). UH Pr.

Abernethy, Peter, et al. English Novel Explication: Supplement One to Jan. 1975. (Novel Explication Ser.). vii, 305p. 1976. 19.50 (ISBN 0-208-01464-0). Shoe String.

Abernethy, R. B. Measurement Uncertainty Handbook. rev. ed. 174p. 1980. pap. text ed. 16.95x (ISBN 0-87664-483-3). Instru Soc.

Abernethy, Rose & Lynn, Diana. Never Look Back. LC 84-90298. 43p. 1985. 6.95 (ISBN 0-533-06345-0). Vantage.

Abernethy, Thomas P. The Burr Conspiracy. 11.75 (ISBN 0-8446-1000-3). Peter Smith.

--From Frontier to Plantation in Tennessee: A Study in Frontier Democracy. LC 78-12038. (Illus.). 1979. Repr. lib. bdg. 27.50x (ISBN 0-313-21124-8, ABFF). Greenwood.

--South in the New Nation, 1789-1819. LC 61-15488. (History of the South Ser.: Vol. 4). (Illus.). xvi, 530p. 1961. 27.50x (ISBN 0-8071-0004-8); pap. 9.95x (ISBN 0-8071-0014-5). La State U Pr.

--Three Virginia Frontiers. 12.00 (ISBN 0-8446-1001-1). Peter Smith.

Abernethy, Virginia. Population Pressure & Cultural Adjustment. LC 78-11676. 189p. 1979. 24.95 (ISBN 0-87705-329-4). Human Sci Pr.

Abernethy, Virginia, ed. Frontiers in Medical Ethics: Applications in a Medical Setting. LC 79-26566. 216p. 1980. prof ref 29.95 (ISBN 0-88410-710-8). Ballinger Pub.

Abersold, John & Howard, Wayne. Cases in Labor Relations: An Arbitration Experience. (Orig.). 1967. pap. text ed. 15.95. P-H.

Abert, Geoffrey. After the Crash. rev. ed. 1982. pap. 3.95 (ISBN 0-451-11869-3, AE1869, Sig). NAL.

Abert, Hermann. Mozart's Don Giovanni. Gellhorn, Peter, tr. from Ger. (Eulenburg Music Bks.). (Illus.). 138p. 1982. Repr. of 1976 ed. 12.00 (ISBN 0-903873-11-7). Da Capo.

Abert, Hermann J. Grundprobleme der Operngeschichte. LC 80-2253. Repr. of 1926 ed. 14.00 (ISBN 0-404-18800-1). AMS Pr.

Abert, James G. Economic Policy & Planning in the Netherlands, 1950-1965. LC 69-15439. pap. 74.50 (ISBN 0-317-29594-2, 2021972). Bks Demand UMI.

Abert, James G., ed. Resource Recovery Guide, Vol. 1. 608p. 1983. 44.50 (ISBN 0-442-20235-0). Van Nos Reinhold.

Aberth, Oliver. Computable Analysis. new ed. (Illus.). 208p. 1980. text ed. 46.50 (ISBN 0-07-000079-4). McGraw.

Abeshouse, M. & Abeshouse, T. Music Video Trivia. 1985. pap. 2.95 (ISBN 0-380-89836-5). Avon.

Abeshouse, Mattew & Abeshouse, Tevin. The Amazing Pyramid Puzzle. (Orig.). Date not set. pap. 6.95 (ISBN 0-671-50455-X, Long Shadow Bks). PB.

Abeshouse, T., jt. auth. see Abeshouse, M.

Abeshouse, Tevin, jt. auth. see Abeshouse, Mattew.

Abey, Daniel E. & Harries, Keith D., eds. Crime: A Spatial Perspective. LC 80-14640. 320p. 1980. 31.50x (ISBN 0-231-04734-7). Columbia U Pr.

Abeyatunge, Lambert R. Cuisine Sri Lanka. 1985. 6.95 (ISBN 0-8062-2441-X). Carlton.

Abeyratne, Shyamala. Second-Generation Settlers & Their Impact on Land & Water Resources in the Gal Oya Irrigation Scheme, Sri Lanka. (Special Series on Resource Management: No. 3). 130p. (Orig.). 1982. pap. text ed. 8.90 (ISBN 0-86731-084-7). RDC Ctr Intl Stud.

Abeysekera, Dayalal. Regional Patterns of Intercensal & Lifetime Migration in Sri Lanka. LC 81-12540. (Papers of the East-West Population Institute: No. 75). v, 46p. (Orig.). 1981. pap. text ed. 1.25 (ISBN 0-86638-016-7). E W Center HI.

Abhayadatta. Buddha's Lions. Robinson, James, tr. from Tibean. (Tibetan Translation Ser.). (Illus.). 1979. 16.95 (ISBN 0-913546-60-7). Dharma Pub.

Abhayananda, Swami. Jnaneshvar: The Life & Works of the Celebrated 13th Century Indian Mystic-Poet. (Illus.). 200p. (Orig.). pap. cancelled (ISBN 0-914557-02-5). Atma Bks.

Abhedananda. Human Affection & Divine Love. 64p. 3.95 (ISBN 0-87481-610-6, Pub. by Ramakrishna Math Madras India). Vedanta Pr.

Abhedananda, Swami. The Complete Works of Swami Abhedananda, 11 vols. (Illus.). Set. 125.00x (ISBN 0-87481-621-1). Vedanta Pr.

--Doctrine of Karma. 5.95 (ISBN 0-87481-608-4). Vedanta Pr.

--How to Be a Yogi. 59.95 (ISBN 0-8490-0375-X). Gordon Pr.

--How to Be a Yogi. 6th ed. 64p. pap. 4.95 (ISBN 0-88697-040-7). Life Science.

--Reincarnation. 2.95 (ISBN 0-87481-604-1). Vedanta Pr.

--Yoga Psychology. 10.95 (ISBN 0-87481-614-9). Vedanta Pr.

Abhendananda. Songs Divine. Aiyer, P. S., tr. from Sanskrit. 69p. 1985. 6.50 (ISBN 0-87481-653-X, Pub. by Ramakrishna Math Madras India). Vedanta Pr.

Abhishiktananda. Prayer. LC 73-600. 88p. 1973. pap. 3.95 (ISBN 0-664-24973-6). Westminster.

Abhyankar, S. Ramification Theoretic Methods in Algebraic Geometry. (Annals of Mathematics Studies: No. 43). (Orig.). 1959. 17.50 (ISBN 0-691-08023-2, AM43). Princeton U Pr.

--Resolution of Singularities of Embedded Algebraic Surfaces. (Pure & Applied Mathematics Ser). 1966. 55.00 (ISBN 0-12-041956-4). Acad Pr.

Abhyankar, S. S. & Sathaye, A. M., eds. Geometric Theory of Algebraic Space Curves. LC 74-20717. (Lecture Notes in Mathematics: Vol. 423). xiv, 302p. 1974. pap. 19.00 (ISBN 0-387-06969-0). Springer-Verlag.

Abhyanker, S. S. Weighted Expansions for Canonical Desingularization. (Lecture Notes in Mathematics Ser.: Vol. 910). 236p. 1982. pap. 16.00 (ISBN 0-387-11195-6). Springer-Verlag.

Abian, Alexander. Linear Associative Algebras. 1972. text ed. 25.00 (ISBN 0-08-016564-8). Pergamon.

Abidi, A. H. China, Iran & the Persian Gulf. 325p. 1982. text ed. 32.75x (ISBN 0-391-02627-5). Humanities.

Abidin, Richard R. Parent Education & Intervention Handbook. 608p. 1980. 40.75x (ISBN 0-398-03937-2). C C Thomas.

--Parenting Skills: Workbook & Trainer's Manual. 2nd ed. LC 81-13314. 84p. 1982. 14.95 (ISBN 0-89885-118-1); lab manual 155 18.95 (ISBN 0-89885-117-3); Set. 24.95 (ISBN 0-89885-119-X). Human Sci Pr.

Abiko, Bonnie, tr. see Harada, Minoru.

Abiko, Bonnie F., tr. see Narazaki, Muneshige.

Abiko, Yasushi, jt. ed. see Winbury, Martin.

Abikoff, W. The Real Analytic Theory of Teichmueller Space. (Lecture Notes in Mathematics Ser.: Vol. 820). (Illus.). 144p. 1980. pap. 15.00 (ISBN 0-387-10237-X). Springer-Verlag.

Abikoff, William & Cornell, Gary. The BASIC Adam. LC 84-7532. (Series 1-999). 524p. 1984. pap. 14.95 (ISBN 0-471-80807-5, Pub. by Wiley Pr). Wiley.

Abikoff, William, jt. auth. see Cornell, Gary.

Abildness, Abby J. Biofeedback Strategies. (Illus.). 160p. (Orig.). 1982. pap. text ed. 24.00 (ISBN 0-910317-09-7). Am Occup Therapy.

Abilene Christian University Lectureship. Crowning Fifty Years. Thomas, J. D., ed. LC 68-21004. 1968. 9.95 (ISBN 0-89112-030-0). Bibl Res Pr.

Abimbola, Wande. Ifa Divination Poetry. LC 73-86025. 179p. 1977. text ed. 14.95x (ISBN 0-88357-023-8). Nok Pubs.

Abingdon Abbey. Accounts of the Obedientiars of Abingdon Abbey. 27.00 (ISBN 0-384-00140-8). Johnson Repr.

Abir, Mordechai. Ethiopia & the Red Sea: The Rise & Decline of the Solomonic Dynasty & Muslim-European Rivalry in the Region. 251p. 1980. 29.50x (ISBN 0-7146-3164-7, BHA 03164, F Cass Co). Biblio Dist.

--Oil, Power & Politics: Conflict in Arabia, the Red Sea & the Gulf. 210p. 1974. 29.50x (ISBN 0-7146-2990-1, BHA 02990, F Cass Co). Biblio Dist.

Abir, Mordechai & Yodfat, Aryeh. In the Direction of the Gulf: The Soviet Union & the Persian Gulf. 167p. 1977. 28.50x (ISBN 0-7146-3071-3, BHA 03071, F Cass Co). Biblio Dist.

Abirached, Robert, et al. Lectures D'Adamov Actes du Colloque International Wuerzberg 1981. (Etudes Litteraires Francaises Ser.: No. 27). 179p. (Orig., Fr.). 1983. pap. 23.00x (ISBN 3-87808-592-3, Pub by G N Verlag Germany). Benjamins North Am.

Abi-Saab, Georges. The United Nations Operation in the Congo, 1960-1964. (International Crises & the Role of Law Ser.). 1979. pap. 11.95x (ISBN 0-19-825323-0). Oxford U Pr.

Abi-Saab, Georges, ed. The Concept of International Organization. (Illus.). 245p. 1981. pap. 15.75 (ISBN 92-3-101742-X, U1094, UNESCO). Unipub.

Abisch, Roz, et al. Stories from Miss A. Perle, Ruth L., ed. (Alpha Vowel Books). (Illus.). (gr. k-1). 1977. pap. text ed. 2.75 (ISBN 0-89796-850-6). Arista Corp NY.

--Stories from Miss E. Perle, Ruth L., ed. (Alpha Vowel Books). (Illus.). (gr. k-1). 1977. pap. text ed. 2.75 (ISBN 0-89796-851-4). Arista Corp NY.

--Stories from Miss I. Perle, Ruth L., ed. (Alpha Vowel Books). (Illus.). (gr. k-1). 1977. pap. text ed. 2.75 (ISBN 0-89796-852-2). Arista Corp NY.

--Stories from Miss O. Perle, Ruth L., ed. (Alpha Vowel Books). (Illus.). (gr. k-1). 1977. pap. text ed. 2.75 (ISBN 0-89796-853-0). Arista Corp NY.

--Stories from Miss U. Perle, Ruth L., ed. (Alpha Vowel Books). (Illus.). (gr. k-1). 1977. pap. text ed. 2.75 (ISBN 0-89796-854-9). Arista Corp NY.

Abish, Walter. Alphabetical Africa. LC 73-89478. 160p. 1974. pap. 5.95 (ISBN 0-8112-0532-0). New Directions.

--How German Is It. LC 80-20838. 256p. 1980. 14.95 (ISBN 0-8112-0775-7); pap. 7.95 (ISBN 0-8112-0776-5, NDP508). New Directions.

--How German Is It. 195p. 1982. text ed. 15.25x (ISBN 0-85635-396-5, Pub. by Carcanet Pr England). Humanities.

--In the Future Perfect. LC 77-9443. 1977. 10.75 (ISBN 0-8112-0659-9); pap. 5.95 (ISBN 0-8112-0660-2, NDP440). New Directions.

--Minds Meet. LC 74-23315. 192p. 1975. 9.50 (ISBN 0-8112-0557-6); pap. 3.45 (ISBN 0-8112-0558-4, NDP387). New Directions.

Abish, Walter, et al see Messerli, Douglas.

Able, Augustus. George Meredith & Thomas Love Peacock: A Study in Literary Influence. 1933. lib. bdg. 15.00 (ISBN 0-8414-2864-6). Folcroft.

--George Meredith & Thomas Love Peacock. 1977. 16.50 (ISBN 0-685-86330-1). Porter.

Able, Augustus H. George Meredith & Thomas Love Peacock: A Study in Literary Influence. LC 78-90364. (New Index). 1970. Repr. of 1933 ed. 10.00 (ISBN 0-87753-000-9). Phaeton.

--George Meredith & Thomas Love Peacock. 1978. Repr. of 1933 ed. lib. bdg. 15.00 (ISBN 0-8495-0128-8). Arden Lib.

--George Meredith & Thomas Love Peacock. 59.95 (ISBN 0-8490-0224-9). Gordon Pr.

Able, Bill V., et al. Animal Science & Industry Laboratory Manual. 2nd ed. 1978. pap. text ed. 7.95 (ISBN 0-8403-2517-7). Kendall-Hunt.

Able, James E. Victims-Story of a Teen-Age Hooker. Ashton, Sylvia, ed. LC 78-53087. 1979. 15.95 (ISBN 0-87949-130-2). Ashley Bks.

Abler, David A. & Natti, Susanna. Cam Jansen & Mystery Carnival Prize. LC 84-3617. (Cam Jansen Adventure Ser.). (Illus.). 64p. (gr. 2-5). 1984. 8.95 (ISBN 0-670-20034-4, Viking Kestrel). Viking.

Abler, Ronald, et al. The Twin Cities of St. Paul & Minneapolis. LC 76-4801. (Contemporary Metropolitan Analysis Ser.). (Illus.). 1976. pap. 14.95x Prof ref (ISBN 0-88410-434-6). Ballinger Pub.

Abler, William. Shop Tactics: The Common-Sense Way of Using Tools & Working with Woods, Metals, Plastics & Glass. LC 76-28967. Orig. Title: The Sensuous Gadgeteer. (Illus.). 112p. 1977. lib. bdg. 12.90 (ISBN 0-914294-63-6); pap. 3.95 (ISBN 0-914294-64-4). Running Pr.

Ables. Mystery on the Delta. PLB 6.19 (ISBN 0-8313-0001-9). Lantern.

Ables, Billie S. & Brandsma, Jeffrey M. Therapy for Couples: A Clinician's Guide for Effective Treatment. LC 76-50698. (Social & Behavioral Science Ser.). 1977. text ed. 18.95x (ISBN 0-87589-312-0). Jossey-Bass.

Ables, Billie S., jt. auth. see Confer, William N.

Ables, Ernest D., ed. The Axis Deer in Texas. (Kleberg Studies in Natural Resources). (Illus.). 86p. 1977. pap. 5.95x (ISBN 0-89096-196-4). Tex A&M Univ Pr.

Abley, Mark, ed. see Palmer, Samuel.

Ablin. Prostatic Cancer. (Science Practice of Surgery Ser.: Vol. 1). 288p. 1981. 55.00 (ISBN 0-8247-1524-1). Dekker.

Ablin, R. J. Handbook of Cryosurgery. (Science & Practice of Surgery: Vol. 1). 1980. 75.00 (ISBN 0-8247-6981-3). Dekker.

Ablin, Richard J. Immunobiology of the Prostate. LC 79-50200. 320p. 1985. 22.50 (ISBN 0-87527-178-2). Green.

Ablon, jt. auth. see Olsen.

Ablon, Joan. Little People in America: The Social Dimensions of Dwarfism. LC 84-15910. 224p. 1984. 27.95 (ISBN 0-03-000118-8); pap. 14.95 (ISBN 0-03-000119-6). Praeger.

Ablon, L. J., et al. Series in Mathematics Modules, Pts. 7, 8, 9, 10, 11. Incl. Module 7. Trigonometry with Applications. LC 75-262499. 7.95 (ISBN 0-8465-0261-5); Module 8. Exponents & Logarithms. LC 75-35281 (ISBN 0-8465-0262-3); Module 9. Advanced Algebraic Techniques (ISBN 0-8465-0263-1); Module 10. Functions & Word Problems (ISBN 0-8465-0264-X); Module 11. Graphing Functions (ISBN 0-8465-0265-8). 1976. pap. 7.95 (ISBN 0-686-67410-3). Benjamin-Cummings.

Ablon, L. J., et al, eds. see Alton, E. V. & Gersting, J. L.

Ablon, Leon, et al. Series in Mathematics Modules, 5 Modules. 1981. pap. 8.95; Module 1. pap. 8.95 (ISBN 0-8053-0131-3); Module 2. pap. 8.95 (ISBN 0-8053-0132-1); Module 3. pap. 8.95 (ISBN 0-8053-0133-X); Module 4. pap. 8.95 (ISBN 0-8053-0134-8); Rationale. pap. 4.95 (ISBN 0-8053-0136-4). Benjamin-Cummings.

--The Steps in Mathematics Modules One Thru Five. 1981. pap. 30.95 (ISBN 0-8053-0140-2). Benjamin-Cummings.

Ablon, Leon J. see Fitts, Gary.

Ablon, Leon J., ed. see Fitts, Gary.

Ablon, Leon J., ed. see Siner, Helen B.

Ablon, Steven L., jt. ed. see Mack, John E.

Ablowitz, M. J. & Segur, H. Solitons & the Inverse Scattering Transform. LC 81-50600. (SIAM Studies in Applied Mathematics: No. 4). x, 425p. 1981. text ed. 57.00 (ISBN 0-89871-174-6). Soc Indus-Appl Math.

ABM Service Corp. National Directory of CB Radio Channels. LC 78-12796. 1979. 15.00 (ISBN 0-88280-064-7); pap. 7.95 (ISBN 0-88280-065-5). ETC Pubns.

Abma, John S. Introductory Psychology, 7 vols. 2nd ed. Incl. Vol. 1-Introductory to Psychology. 4.25x (ISBN 0-86589-007-2); Vol. 2-Learning. 4.25x (ISBN 0-86589-008-0); Vol. 3-the Physiological Bases of Behavior. 4.25x (ISBN 0-86589-009-9); Vol. 4-Individual Differences & Group Processes. 4.25x (ISBN 0-86589-010-2); Vol. 5-Motivation & Stress. 4.25x (ISBN 0-86589-011-0); Vol. 6-Mental Health. 4.25x (ISBN 0-86589-012-9); Vol. 7-Measurements, Statistics & Analysis. 4.25x (ISBN 0-86589-013-7). 1973. Set. 28.50x (ISBN 0-86589-006-4). Individual Learn.

Abney, Darrell H., et al. Computer Mathematics for Programmers. 1984. text ed. 18.00i (ISBN 0-12-042150-X). Acad Pr.

--Computer Mathematics for Programmers: Instructor's Manual. Date not set. text ed. price not set (ISBN 0-12-042151-8). Acad Pr.

Abney, Louise. Choral Speaking Arrangements for the Junior High. (gr. 7-9). 1973. text ed. 4.00 (ISBN 0-686-09419-0). Expression.

--Choral Speaking Arrangements for the Upper Grades. (gr. 4-8). 1973. text ed. 3.50 (ISBN 0-686-09417-4). Expression.

Abney, Louise & Rowe, Grace. Choral Speaking Arrangements for the Lower Grades. (gr. k-3). 1973. text ed. 3.50 (ISBN 0-686-09415-8). Expression.

Abney, W. D., jt. auth. see Robinson, Henry P.

Abo, Takaji, et al. Marshallese-English Dictionary. LC 76-26156. (Pali Language Texts Ser.: Micronezia). 624p. (Marshallese & Eng.). 1976. pap. text ed. 23.00x (ISBN 0-8248-0457-0). UH Pr.

Abodaber, David J. So You're Ready to Drive a Car. LC 81-28408. (Illus.). 128p. (gr. 7 up). 1981. 9.79 (ISBN 0-671-34058-1, 62928). Childrens.

Abodaher, David. Iacocca. 1985. pap. 3.95 (ISBN 0-317-31346-0). Zebra.

Abodaher, David J. Great Moments in Sports Car Racing. LC 80-26026. (Illus.). 96p. (gr. 4-6). 1981. PLB 9.29 (ISBN 0-671-33090-X). Messner.

Abodeely, John E., et al. The NLRB & the Appropriate Bargaining Unit. rev. ed. LC 80-85252. (Labor Relations & Public Policy Ser.: No. 3). 359p. 1981. pap. 20.00 (ISBN 0-89546-028-9). Indus Res Unit-Wharton.

Abolafia, Yossi. My Three Uncles. LC 84-4195. (Illus.). 32p. (gr. k-3). 1985. 11.75 (ISBN 0-688-04024-1); PLB 11.88 (ISBN 0-688-04025-X). Greenwillow.

Abonyi, George, jt. auth. see Higgins, Benjamin.

Abood, Doris M. Lebanon: Bridge Between East & West. LC 73-84565. (Illus.). 40p. (gr. 5-10). 1973. 3.50 (ISBN 0-913228-07-9). Dillon-Liederbach.

Abood, Edward F. Underground Man. LC 72-97331. 189p. 1973. pap. 5.95 (ISBN 0-88316-048-X). Chandler & Sharp.

Abood, Leo G., ed. see Conference Held at Silver Spring, Maryland, Mar. 1978.

Abott, R. Tucker. Collectible Florida. (Illus.). 68p. 1984. waterproof ed. 8.95 (ISBN 0-915826-12-7); pap. 4.95 (ISBN 0-915826-11-9). Am Malacologists.

Abouchar, Alan. Project Decision Making in the Public Sector. LC 83-49463. 192p. 1984. 20.00x (ISBN 0-669-08015-2). Lexington Bks.

--Soviet Planning & Spatial Efficiency: The Prewar Cement Industry. LC 70-126203. (Indiana University Russian & East European Ser.: Vol. 39). (Illus.). pap. 27.40 (ISBN 0-317-08589-1, 2015812). Bks Demand UMI.

--Transportation Economics & Public Policy: With Urban Extensions. LC 76-51828. 354p. 1982. 29.50 (ISBN 0-471-02101-6). Krieger.

Abouchar, Alan, ed. The Socialist Price Mechanism. LC 76-4219. 221p. 1977. 21.00 (ISBN 0-8223-0366-3). Duke.

Aboud, Antone, jt. auth. see Sterrett, Grace.

Aboud, Antone, ed. Plant Closing Legislation. (Key Issues Ser.: No. 27). 60p. 1984. pap. 6.00 (ISBN 0-87546-108-5). ILR Pr.

Aboud, Grace. Hiring & Training the Disadvantaged for Public Employment. (Key Issues Ser.: No. 11). 60p. 1973. pap. 2.00 (ISBN 0-87546-202-2). ILR Pr.

Aboud, Grace S. & Doherty, Robert E. Practices & Procedures under the Taylor Law: A Practical Guide in Narrative Form. 84p. 1974. pap. 2.00 (ISBN 0-87546-203-0). ILR Pr.

Aboukhaled, A. & Alfaro, A. Lysimeters. (Irrigation & Drainage Papers: No. 39). 74p. (2nd Printing 1983). 1982. pap. 7.50 (ISBN 92-5-101186-9, F2330, FAO). Unipub.

Aboulafia, Mitchell. The Self-Winding Circle: A Study of Hegel's System. LC 82-210652. 107p. 1982. 14.75 (ISBN 0-87527-307-6). Green.

Abouleish, Ezzat. Childbirth: A Joy Not a Suffering. (Illus.). 104p. 1975. pap. 4.95 (ISBN 0-8059-2176-1). Dorrance.

Aboul-Fetouh, Hilmi M. Morphological Study of Egyptian Colloquial Arabic. (Janua Linguarum, Ser. Practica: No. 33). 1969. pap. text ed. 24.80x (ISBN 90-2790-691-2). Mouton.

Abouna, George M., ed. Current Status of Clinical Organ Transplantation. LC 84-1553. (Developments in Surgery Ser.). 1984. lib. bdg. 61.00 (ISBN 0-89838-635-7, Pub. by Martinus Nijhoff Netherlands). Kluwer Academic.

Abou-Rass, Marwan, jt. ed. see Frank, Alfred L.

Abou-Sabe, Morad, ed. Microbial Genetics. LC 73-13002. (Benchmark Papers in Microbiology: Vol. 3). 451p. 1977. 57.95 (ISBN 0-87933-046-5). Van Nos Reinhold.

About, Edmond. The Man with the Broken Ear. Holt, Henry, tr. LC 74-15941. (Science Fiction Ser). 258p. 1975. Repr. of 1874 ed. 21.00x (ISBN 0-405-06271-0). Ayer Co Pubs.

Abowd, John M. An Econometric Model of the U. S. Market for Higher Education. LC 80-8615. (Outstanding Dissertations in Economics Ser.). 175p. 1984. lib. bdg. 24.00 (ISBN 0-8240-4166-6). Garland Pub.

Abragam, A. L'Effet Mossbauer. (Documents on Modern Physics Ser.). 76p. 1964. pap. 30.25 (ISBN 0-677-00015-4). Gordon.

--Principles of Nuclear Magnetism. (International Series of Monographs on Physics). 1961. pap. 29.50x (ISBN 0-19-852014-X). Oxford U Pr.

Abragam, A. & Goldman, M. Nuclear Magnetism: Order & Disorder. (International Series of Monographs in Physics). 1982. 89.00x (ISBN 0-19-851294-5). Oxford U Pr.

Abraham. Glycosylated Hemoglobins: Methods of Analysis & Clinical Applications. (Clinical & Biochemical Analysis Ser.). 280p. 1985. write for info. (ISBN 0-8247-7356-X). Dekker.

--Iconography of Sensory Nerve Endings. 1981. 79.00 (ISBN 0-9960071-8-0, Pub. by Akademiai Kaido Hungary). Heyden.

--Radioassay Systems in Clinical Endocrinology. (Basic & Clinical Endocrinology Ser.: Vol. 1). 904p. 1981. 85.00 (ISBN 0-8247-6953-8). Dekker.

Abraham & Pindar. Georgia Real Estate Sales Contracts. 2nd ed. incl. latest pocket part supplement 52.95 (ISBN 0-686-90369-2); separate pocket part supplement, 1984 20.95 (ISBN 0-686-90370-6). Harrison Co GA.

Abraham, A. Iconography of Sensory Nerve Endings. 1981. 79.00 (ISBN 0-9960071-9-9, Pub. by Akademiai Kaido Hungary). Heyden.

--Microscopic Innervation of the Heart & Blood Vessels in Vertebrates Including Man. 1969. 76.00 (ISBN 0-08-012342-2). Pergamon.

Abraham, A. J. Lebanon: A State of Seige. 85p. (Orig.). 1985. pap. 6.95 (ISBN 0-932269-21-4). Wyndham Hall.

--Lebanon at Mid-Century: Maronite-Druze Relations in Lebanon 1840-1860; a Prelude to Arab Nationalism. LC 80-6253. 156p. 1981. lib. bdg. 21.25 (ISBN 0-8191-1536-3); pap. text ed. 10.25 (ISBN 0-8191-1537-1). U Pr of Amer.

Abraham, Abraham K., et al, eds. Protein Synthesis. LC 83-26463. (Experimental Biology & Medicine Ser.). 480p. 1984. 59.50 (ISBN 0-89603-060-1). Humana.

Abraham, Antoine J. Khoumani, Islamic Fundamentalists & the Contributions of Islamic Sciences to Modern Civilization. 60p. (Orig.). 1985. pap. 5.95 (ISBN 0-932269-51-6). Wyndham Hall.

Abraham, Arthur. Cultural Policy in Sierra Leone. (Studies & Documents on Cultural Policies). (Illus.). 75p. 1979. pap. 6.25 (ISBN 92-3-101601-6, U885, UNESCO). Unipub.

Abraham, Arthur & Kopelman, David L. Federal Social Security. 358p. 1979. 35.00 (ISBN 0-686-26716-8). Am Law Inst.

Abraham, Arthur, et al. The Encyclopaedia Africana Dictionary of African Biography, Vol. 2: Sierra Leone-Zaire. Ofosu-Appiah, L. H., ed. LC 76-17954. (Illus.). 1979. 59.95 (ISBN 0-917256-06-9). Ref Pubns.

Abraham, Ashley P. Some Portraits of the Lake Poets & Their Homes. 1978. Repr. of 1914 ed. lib. bdg. 27.50 (ISBN 0-8495-0129-6). Arden Lib.

--Some Portraits of the Lake Poets, & Their Homes. LC 75-28026. 1975. Repr. of 1914 ed. lib. bdg. 27.50 (ISBN 0-8414-2874-3). Folcroft.

Abraham Ben Moses Ben Maimon. High Ways to Perfection of Abraham Maimonides. Rosenblatt, Samuel, tr. LC 74-158221. (Columbia University Oriental Studies: No. 27). 1927. 19.00 (ISBN 0-404-50517-1); Suppl., 1982. 35.00; Supp., 1983. 43.50. AMS Pr.

Abraham, Bovas & Ledolter, Johannes. Statistical Methods for Forecasting. LC 83-7006. (Probability & Mathematics Statistics Ser.). 480p. 1983. 36.95x (ISBN 0-471-86764-0, 1-346, Pub. by Wiley-Interscience). Wiley.

Abraham, C. & Thomas, A. Microeconomics: Optimal Decision Making by Private Firms & Public Authorities. Jones, D. V., tr. from Fr. LC 79-188001. Orig. Title: Microeconomic, Decisions Optimal dans L'enterprise et dans la Nation. (Illus.). 507p. 1973. lib. bdg. 60.50 (ISBN 90-277-0237-3, Pub. by Reidel Holland). Kluwer Academic.

Abraham, Claude. Tristan L'Hermite. (World Authors Ser.). 1980. lib. bdg. 16.95 (ISBN 0-8057-6411-9, Twayne). G K Hall.

Abraham, Claude K. Enfin Malherbe: The Influence of Malherbe on French Lyric Prosody, 1605-1674. LC 70-160042. 368p. 1971. 30.00x (ISBN 0-8131-1254-0). U Pr of Ky.

--Strangers: The Tragic World of Tristan l'Hermite. LC 66-64916. (University of Florida Humanities Monographs: No. 23). 1966. pap. 3.50 (ISBN 0-8130-0000-9). U Presses Fla.

Abraham, David. The Collapse of the Weimar Republic: Political Economy & Crisis. LC 80-8533. 550p. 1981. 36.00x (ISBN 0-691-05322-7). Princeton U Pr.

Abraham, Dorothye B. Je Suis Moi. 5.95 (ISBN 0-8062-2259-X). Carlton.

Abraham, E. P., jt. ed. see Baddiley, James.

Abraham, Eric & Steele, Jonathan. Andropov in Power: From Komsomol to Kremlin. LC 83-45157. (Illus.). 224p. 1984. 15.95 (ISBN 0-385-18911-7, Anchor Pr). Doubleday.

Abraham, F. & Tiller, W. A., eds. An Introduction to Computer Simulation in Applied Science. LC 72-83047. 220p. 1972. 29.50 (ISBN 0-306-30579-8, Plenum Pr). Plenum Pub.

Abraham, Farid F. & Tiller, William A., eds. An Introduction to Computer Simulation in Applied Science. LC 72-83047. pap. 58.30 (ISBN 0-317-30342-2, 2024714). Bks Demand UMI.

Abraham, Fern-Rae. Tin Craft. (Illus.). 42p. (Orig.). 1975. pap. 5.00 (ISBN 0-913270-05-9). Sunstone Pr.

Abraham, G. Nietzsche. 59.95 (ISBN 0-8490-0731-3). Gordon Pr.

--Nietzsche. LC 73-20387. (Nietzsche Ser., No. 89). 1974. lib. bdg. 49.95x (ISBN 0-8383-1764-2). Haskell.

--Sibelius: A Symposium. 59.95 (ISBN 0-8490-1051-9). Gordon Pr.

Abraham, George. Green Thumb Book of Fruit & Vegetable Gardening. LC 78-85000. (Illus.). 384p. 1981. pap. 6.95 (ISBN 0-13-365064-2). P-H.

--The Green Thumb Book of Indoor Gardening. 304p. 1982. pap. 6.95 (ISBN 0-13-365072-3). P-H.

Abraham, George R. & Abraham, Katherine. Your Last Diet Plan. (Illus.). 208p. (Orig.). 1983. pap. text ed. 9.95 casette incl. (ISBN 0-915469-00-6). Growth Assocs Inc.

Abraham, Gerald. The Concise Oxford History of Music. (Illus.). 1979. 45.00 (ISBN 0-19-311319-8); pap. 17.95 (ISBN 0-19-284010-X). Oxford U Pr.

--Dostoevski. LC 74-6398. (Studies in Dostoyevsky, No. 86). 1974. lib. bdg. 39.95x (ISBN 0-8383-1869-X). Haskell.

--Essays on Russian & East European Music. 1985. 24.95x (ISBN 0-19-311208-6). Oxford U Pr.

--Hundred Years of Music. 4th ed. 333p. 1974. 40.50x (ISBN 0-7156-1006-6, Pub. by Duckworth England); pap. 13.50x (ISBN 0-7156-0704-9, Pub. by Duckworth England). Biblio Dist.

--On Russian Music: Critical & Historical Studies of Glinka's Operas. facsimile ed. LC 73-134046. (Essay Index Reprint Ser.). 280p. 1982. Repr. of 1939 ed. lib. bdg. 11.00 (ISBN 0-8290-0786-5). Irvington.

--Tolstoy. LC 74-7018. (Studies in Tolstoy, No. 62). 1974. lib. bdg. 39.95x (ISBN 0-8383-1965-3). Haskell.

--Tradition of Western Music. LC 72-97738. (Ernest Bloch Lectures Ser). 1974. pap. 9.50x (ISBN 0-520-02615-2). U of Cal Pr.

Abraham, Gerald, jt. auth. see Calvocoressi, Michel D.

Abraham, Gerald, ed. The History of Music in Sound, Vols. 1-3. Incl. Vol. 3. Ars Nova & the Renaissance, 1350-1540. Westrup, J. A., ed. (Illus.). 1953 (ISBN 0-19-323102-6). 6.00. Oxford U Pr.

--The Music of Sibelius. LC 74-23413. (Music Reprint Ser.). 218p. 1975. Repr. of 1947 ed. lib. bdg. 27.50 (ISBN 0-306-70716-0). Da Capo.

--The Music of Tchaikovsky. (Illus.). 1974. pap. 5.95 (ISBN 0-393-00707-3, Norton Lib). Norton.

--The New Oxford History of Music, Vol. VIII: The Age of Beethoven, 1790-1830. (Illus.). 1982. 49.95x (ISBN 0-19-316308-X). Oxford U Pr.

Abraham, Gerald see Abraham, Gerald, et al.

Abraham, Gerald, ed. see Calvocoressi, M. D.

Abraham, Gerald, et al, eds. New Oxford History of Music. Incl. Vol. 1. Ancient & Oriental Music. Wellesz, Egon, ed. (15 plates). 1957. 49.95x (ISBN 0-19-316301-2); Vol. 2. Early Medieval Music up to 1300. Hughes, Dom Anselm, ed. 1954. 49.95x (ISBN 0-19-316302-0); Vol 3. Ars Nova & the Renaissance, 1300-1540. Hughes, Dom Anselm & Abraham, Gerald, eds. 1960. 49.95x (ISBN 0-19-316303-9); Vol. 4. The Age of Humanism, 1540-1630. Abraham, Gerald, ed. (Illus.). 1968. 49.95x (ISBN 0-19-316304-7); Vol. 7. The Age of Enlightenment, 1745-1790. Wellesz, Egon & Sternfeld, Frederick, eds. (Illus.). 1973. 49.95x (ISBN 0-19-316307-1); Vol. 10. Modern Age, 1890-1960. Cooper, Martin, ed. 1974. 49.95x (ISBN 0-19-316310-1). Oxford U Pr.

Abraham, Gerald E. Beethoven's Second-Period Quartets. LC 70-181101. 79p. 1942. Repr. 29.00 (ISBN 0-403-01500-6). Scholarly.

--Borodin: The Composer & His Music. LC 74-27324. (BCL Ser.: No. II). (Illus.). Repr. of 1927 ed. 18.60 (ISBN 0-404-12851-3). AMS Pr.

--Chopin's Musical Style. LC 79-25521. xii, 116p. 1980. Repr. of 1939 ed. lib. bdg. 24.75x (ISBN 0-313-22251-7, ABCM). Greenwood.

--Eight Soviet Composers. LC 71-106679. Repr. of 1943 ed. lib. bdg. 22.50 (ISBN 0-8371-3350-5, ABSC). Greenwood.

--On Russian Music. facs. ed. LC 73-134046. (Essay Index Reprint Ser.). 1939. 16.00 (ISBN 0-8369-1900-9). Ayer Co Pubs.

--On Russian Music. 1976. lib. bdg. 15.00x (ISBN 0-403-03757-3). Scholarly.

--On Russian Music: Critical & Historical Studies of Glinka's Operas. LC 39-32448. (Music Ser.: Practice & Theory). Repr. of 1939 ed. 23.00 (ISBN 0-384-00150-5). Johnson Repr.

--Rimsky-Korsakov. LC 75-41002. (BCL Ser.: No. II). Repr. of 1945 ed. 15.00 (ISBN 0-404-14500-0). AMS Pr.

--Studies in Russian Music. facs. ed. LC 68-20285. (Essay Index Reprint Ser). 1936. 18.00 (ISBN 0-8369-0133-9). Ayer Co Pubs.

--Studies in Russian Music. 1976. Repr. of 1935 ed. lib. bdg. 16.00x (ISBN 0-403-03700-X). Scholarly.

--Tchaikovsky. LC 78-58996. (Encore Music Editions). (Illus.). 1979. Repr. of 1945 ed. 14.50 (ISBN 0-88355-672-3). Hyperion Conn.

Abraham, Gerald E., ed. Grieg: A Symposium. LC 71-138196. 144p. 1972. Repr. of 1950 ed. lib. bdg. 15.00 (ISBN 0-8371-5549-5, ABGR). Greenwood.

--Handel: A Symposium. LC 80-11679. (Illus.). vi, 328p. 1980. Repr. of 1954 ed. lib. bdg. 32.50x (ISBN 0-313-22358-0, ABHA). Greenwood.

--Schumann: A Symposium. LC 77-8051. 1977. Repr. of 1952 ed. lib. bdg. 29.75x (ISBN 0-8371-9050-9, SCSY). Greenwood.

Abraham, Guy E., ed. Handbook of Radioimmunoassay, Pt. 1. (Clinical & Biochemical Analysis Ser.: Vol. 5). 1977. pap. 135.00 (ISBN 0-8247-7255-5). Dekker.

Abraham, Henry & Pfeffer, Irwin. Enjoying American History. (gr. 11-12). 1984. text ed. 20.00 (ISBN 0-87720-635-X, 273X); pap. 15.00 (ISBN 0-87720-634-1); Key 0.95 (ISBN 0-317-03301-8). Amsco Sch.

--Enjoying World History. (gr. 10-12). 1977. text ed. 12.92 (ISBN 0-87720-620-1); pap. text ed. 9.50 (ISBN 0-87720-618-X). AMSCO Sch.

Abraham, Henry see Cassel, Christine, et al.

Abraham, Henry J. Freedom & the Court: Civil Rights & Liberties in the United States. 4th ed. LC 81-745. 1982. 29.95x (ISBN 0-19-502960-7); pap. text ed. 10.95x (ISBN 0-19-502961-5). Oxford U Pr.

--The Judicial Process: An Introductory Analysis of the Courts of the United States, England, & France. 5th ed. Date not set. price not set (ISBN 0-19-503713-8). Oxford U Pr.

--The Judicial Process: An Introductory Analysis of the United States, England, & France. 4th ed. 1980. pap. 12.95x (ISBN 0-19-502613-6). Oxford U Pr.

--The Judiciary: The Supreme Court in the Governmental Process. 6th ed. 264p. 1983. pap. text ed. 15.00scp (ISBN 0-205-07981-4, 7679815). Allyn.

--Justices & Presidents: A Poltical History of Appointments to the Supreme Court. 2nd ed. LC 84-825. 407p. 1985. 24.95x (ISBN 0-19-503479-1); pap. 9.95x (ISBN 0-19-503480-5). Oxford U Pr.

Abraham, Herbert J. World Problems in the Classroom. LC 73-76702. 223p. (Orig.). 1973. pap. 6.25 (ISBN 0-685-31874-5, U729, UNESCO). Unipub.

Abraham, Horst. Skiing Right. LC 83-48651. (Illus.). 238p. (Orig.). 1984. pap. 12.45 (ISBN 0-06-250015-5, CN 4093, HarpR). Har-Row.

Abraham, Karl. Clinical Papers & Essays on Psycho-Analysis. Ellison, D. R. & Mass, Hilda, trs. LC 79-11099. (Classics in Psychoanalysis: No. 3). (Illus.). 1979. Repr. of 1955 ed. 27.50 (ISBN 0-87630-207-X). Brunner-Mazel.

--Dreams & Myths: A Study in Race Psychology. White, William A., tr. (Nervous & Mental Disease Monographs: No. 15). 19.00 (ISBN 0-384-00160-2). Johnson Repr.

Abraham, Katherine, jt. auth. see Abraham, George R.

Abraham, Kelly. Dreams & Myths: A Study in Race Psychology. 1976. lib. bdg. 59.95 (ISBN 0-8490-1734-3). Gordon Pr.

Abraham, Ken. Don't Bite the Apple 'Til You Check for Worms. 160p. (Orig.). 1985. pap. 5.95 (ISBN 0-8007-5190-6). Revell.

Abraham, Kurt. Threefold Method for Understanding the Seven Rays & Other Essays in Esoteric Psychology. LC 84-81567. 120p. (Orig.). 1984. pap. 6.95 (ISBN 0-9609002-1-7). Lampus Pr.

Abraham, Kurt B. Psychological Types & the Seven Rays, Vol. 1. LC 82-81863. 163p. (Orig.). 1983. pap. 6.95 (ISBN 0-9609002-0-9). Lampus Pr.

Abraham, M. Francis. Modern Sociological Theory. 1982. pap. 7.95x (ISBN 0-19-561384-8). Oxford U Pr.

Abraham, Michael R. & Pavelich, Michael J. Inquiries into Chemistry. (Illus.). 1979. 10.95x (ISBN 0-917974-32-8). Waveland Pr.

Abraham, Nicholas A. Doing Business in Egypt. Prinz, Karl E., ed. (Doing Business in the Middle East: Vol. 2). (Illus.). 280p. (Orig.). 1979. pap. text ed. 79.95x (ISBN 0-934592-00-4). Tradeship Pub Co.

--Doing Business in Kuwait. Prinz, Karl E., ed. (Doing Business in the Middle East: Vol. 3). (Illus.). 280p. (Orig.). 1981. pap. text ed. 79.95x (ISBN 0-934592-02-0). Tradeship Pub Co.

--Doing Business in Saudi Arabia. Hanna, Christine A., ed. (Doing Business in the Middle East: Vol. 1). (Illus.). 336p. (Orig.). 1980. pap. text ed. 79.95x (ISBN 0-934592-01-2). Tradeship Pub Co.

Abraham, Norma J. Erik of the Dragon Ships. LC 83-50987. 163p. (Orig.). 1983. pap. 3.50 (ISBN 0-912661-00-3). Woodsong Graph.

Abraham, Paul & Mackey, Daphne. Get Ready: Interactive Listening & Speaking. (Illus.). 176p. 1986. pap. text ed. 9.95 (ISBN 0-13-353913-X). P-H.

Abraham, Paul & Mackey, Joan. Contact U.S.A. An ESL Reading & Vocabulary Textbook. 200p. 1982. pap. text ed. 12.50 (ISBN 0-13-169599-1). P-H.

Abraham, R. & Marsden, J. E. Manifolds, Tensor Analysis, & Applications. LC 82-13737. 582p. 1983. text ed. 41.95 (ISBN 0-201-10168-8). Addison-Wesley.

Abraham, R. J. Nuclear Magnetic Resonance, Vols. 1-8. Incl. Vol. 1. 1970-71 Literature. 1972. 34.00 (ISBN 0-85186-252-7); Vol. 2. 1971-72 Literature. 1973. 38.00 (ISBN 0-85186-262-4); Vol. 3. 1972-73 Literature. 1974. 43.00 (ISBN 0-85186-272-1); Vol. 4. 1973-74 Literature. 1975. 45.00 (ISBN 0-85186-282-9); Vol. 5. 1974-75 Literature. 1976. 52.00 (ISBN 0-85186-292-6); Vol. 6. 1975-76 Literature. 1977. 54.00 (ISBN 0-85186-302-7); Vol. 7. 1976-77 Literature. 1978. 65.00 (ISBN 0-85186-312-4); Vol. 8. 1979. 73.00 (ISBN 0-85186-322-1, Pub. by Royal Soc Chem London). LC 72-78527. Am Chemical.

Abraham, R. J. & Loftus, P. Proton & Carbon-13 Nmr Spectroscopy: An Integrated Approach. 216p. 1978. 29.95 (ISBN 0-471-25576-9, Wiley Heyden). Wiley.

Abraham, Ralph. On Morphodynamics: Selected Papers. (Science Frontier Express Ser.). (Illus.). 255p. Date not set. pap. 25.00 (ISBN 0-942344-06-5). Aerial Pr.

Abraham, Ralph & Marsden, Jerrold E. Foundations of Mechanics: A Mathematical Exposition of Classical Mechanics with An Introduction to the Qualitative Theory of Dynamical Systems & Applications to the Three-Body Problem. 2nd rev. & enl. ed. 1978. 59.95 (ISBN 0-8053-0102-X). Benjamin-Cummings.

Abraham, Ralph & Shaw, Chris. Dynamics, the Geometry of Behavior. LC 81-71616. (Visual Mathematics Ser.). (Illus.). 240p. 1982. pap. text ed. 32.00 (ISBN 0-942344-01-4). Pt. 1, Periodic Behavior. Pts. 3 & 4 Future. Aerial Pr.

--Dynamics: The Geometry of Behavior: Pt. 2, Chaotic Behavior. (Visual Mathematics Ser.). (Illus.). 160p. 1983. pap. 26.00x (ISBN 0-942344-02-2). Aerial Pr.

--Dynamics: The Geometry of Behavior: Pt. 3, Global Behavior. (Visual Mathematical Ser.). (Illus.). 176p. 1985. pap. 26.00x (ISBN 0-942344-03-0). Aerial Pr.

Abraham, Ralph H. Complex Dynamical Systems: Selected Papers. (Science Frontier Express Ser.). (Illus.). 125p. Date not set. pap. 15.00 (ISBN 0-942344-07-3). Aerial Pr.

Abraham, Richard & Kochan, Lionel. The Making of Modern Russia. 2nd ed. LC 82-23079. 250p. 1984. 25.00x (ISBN 0-312-50703-8). St Martin.

Abraham, Richard, jt. auth. see Kochan, Lionel.

Abraham, Richard D., tr. see Navarro, Tomas.

Abraham, Robert M. Easy-to-Do Entertainments & Diversions with Cards, Strings, Coins, Paper & Matches. Orig. Title: Winter Nights Entertainments. (Illus.). 186p. 1933. pap. 3.50 (ISBN 0-486-20921-0). Dover.

--Tricks & Amusements. Orig. Title: Diversions & Pastimes with Cards, Strings, Coins, Paper & Matches. (Illus.). 1933. pap. 2.50 (ISBN 0-486-21127-4). Dover.

Abraham, Roger D. & Troike, Rudolph D., eds. Language & Cultural Diversity in American Education. 384p. 1972. pap. text ed. 16.95 (ISBN 0-13-522888-3). P-H.

Abraham, S. Tetraalkyl Halides. 1986. 100.00 (ISBN 0-08-026188-4). Pergamon.

Abraham, Samuel & Kiefer, Ferenc. Theory of Structural Semantics. (Janua Linguarum, Ser. Minor: No. 49). 1966. 11.20x (ISBN 90-2790-581-9). Mouton.

Abraham, Samuel V. Real Estate Dictionary & Reference Guide. McFadden, S. Michele & Wilson-Fulkerson, Roberta, eds. LC 79-9761. 1983. pap. text ed. 6.95x (ISBN 0-89262-059-5). Career Pub.

Abraham, Sidney, et al. Dietary Intake Source Data: United States, 1971-74. 1979. pap. text ed. 1.50 (ISBN 0-8406-0162-X). Natl Ctr Health Stats.

--Caloria & Selected Nutrient Values of Persons Age 1-74 Years, U. S., 1971-74. Stevenson, Taloria, ed. (Ser. 11: No. 209). 1978. pap. 1.50 (ISBN 0-8406-0147-6). Natl Ctr Health Stats.

--Serum Cholesterol Level of Adults 18-74 Years in the United States, 1971-1974. Stevenson, Taloria, ed. (Series Eleven: No. 205). 1977. pap. text ed. 1.50 (ISBN 0-8406-0111-5). Natl Ctr Health Stats.

--Total Serum Cholesterol Levels of Children 4-17 Years United States, 1971-1974. Shipp, Audrey, ed. (Series 11: No. 207). 1978. pap. text ed. 1.75 (ISBN 0-8406-0125-5). Natl Ctr Health Stats.

--Weight & Height of Adults 18-74 Years of Age: United States, 1971-1974. Akers, Karen, ed. (Series II: No. 211). 1978. pap. text ed. 1.75 (ISBN 0-8406-0142-5). Natl Ctr Health.

--Weight by Height & Age for Adults, 18-74 Years, United States, 1971-1974. Cox, Klaudia, ed. (Ser. 11: No. 208). 1978. pap. text ed. 1.75 (ISBN 0-8406-0141-7). Natl Ctr Health Stats.

--Preliminary Findings of the First Health & Nutrition Examination Survey, U.S., Nineteen Seventy-One to Nineteen Seventy-Two, Dietary Intake & Biochemical Findings. 70p. 1974. pap. 1.25 (ISBN 0-8406-0028-3). Natl Ctr Health Stats.

Abraham, Sidney, jt. auth. see Carroll, Margaret D.

Abraham, Suzanne A. & Jones, Derek L. Eating Disorders: The Facts. 1984. 12.95x (ISBN 0-19-261459-2). Oxford U Pr.

Abraham, W. E. Mind of Africa. LC 63-9733. (Nature of Human Society). 1963. pap. 3.95x (ISBN 0-226-00086-9, P233, Phoen). U of Chicago Pr.

Abraham, Werner. On the Formal Syntax of the West-Germania: Papers from the "Third Groninger Grammar Talks," Groningen, January 1981. (Linguistik Aktuel Ser.: No. 3). xi, 242p. 1983. 30.00x (ISBN 90-272-2723-3). Benjamins North Am.

Abraham, Werner, ed. Valence Semantic Case & Grammatical Relations. (Studies in Language Companion Ser.: No. 1). xiv, 729p. 1978. 50.00x (ISBN 90-272096-2-6). Benjamins North Am.

Abraham, William J. The Coming Great Revival: Recovering the Full Evangelical Tradition. LC 84-47710. 160p. 1984. 12.45 (ISBN 0-06-060035-7, HarpR). Har-Row.

--Divine Inspiration of Holy Scripture. 1981. 29.95x (ISBN 0-19-826659-6). Oxford U Pr.

--Divine Revelation & the Limits of Historical Criticism. 1982. 27.50x (ISBN 0-19-826665-0). Oxford U Pr.

--An Introduction to the Philosophy of Religion. 250p. 1985. pap. text ed. 19.95 (ISBN 0-13-491887-8). P-H.

Abraham, Williard. Living with Preschoolers. (Illus.). 160p. 1976. pap. 3.95 (ISBN 0-89019-055-0). O'Sullivan Woodside.

Abraham-Frois, Gilbert & Berrebi, E. Theory of Value, Prices & Accumulation: Two Mathematical Integrations of Marx, Von Neumann & Straffa. Kregel-Javaux, M. P., tr. LC 78-16277. (Illus., Fr.). 1979. 39.50 (ISBN 0-521-22385-7). Cambridge U Pr.

Abrahamian, Ervand. Iran Between Two Revolutions. LC 81-47905. (Princeton Studies on the Near East). 700p. 1982. 50.00 (ISBN 0-691-05342-1); pap. 17.50 (ISBN 0-691-10134-5). Princeton U Pr.

Abrahams, Cecil A. Alex La Guma. (World Authors Ser.). 1985. lib. bdg. 22.95 (ISBN 0-8057-6589-1, Twayne). G K Hall.

--William Blake's Fourfold Man. (Studien zur Germanistik, Anglistik und Komparatistik: Vol. 72). 387p. (Orig.). 1978. pap. 28.00x (ISBN 0-317-19122-5, Pub. by Bouvier Verlag W Germany). Benjamins North Am.

Abrahams, Cecila A. William Blake's Fourfold Man. 1982. 40.00x (ISBN 3-416-01418-9, Pub. by Bouvier Verlag Ger). State Mutual Bk.

Abrahams, Doug. Doug: Man & Missionary. 1983. pap. 3.95 (ISBN 0-85363-151-4). OMF Bks.

Abrahams, Douglas. An Introduction to BASIC Programming for Microcomputers. 2nd ed. 96p. 1984. 6.94x (ISBN 0-7715-0691-0); tchr's manual 6.94x (ISBN 0-7715-0791-7). Forkner.

Abrahams, Edith, jt. ed. see Tauben, Carol.

Abrahams, Edward. The Lyrical Left: Randolph Bourne, Alfred Stieglitz, & the Origins of Cultural Radicalism in America. (Illus.). 300p. 1986. price not set (ISBN 0-8139-1080-3). U Pr of Va.

Abrahams, Evelyn. Mum's the Word: The Wit & Wisdom of a Semi-Sweet Grandmother. 240p. 1985. 14.95 (ISBN 0-89586-401-0). H P Bks.

Abrahams, G. Chess. (Teach Yourself Ser.). 1975. pap. 4.95 (ISBN 0-679-10354-6). McKay.

Abrahams, Gerald. Brilliance in Chess. (Illus.). 1977. 14.95x (ISBN 0-8464-0208-4). Beekman Pubs.

--Morality & the Law. LC 71-580486. 256p. 1980. 15.00 (ISBN 0-7145-0662-1, Dist by Scribner); pap. 7.95 (ISBN 0-7145-0663-X). M Boyars.

--Technique in Chess. 2nd ed. 224p. 1973. pap. 4.00 (ISBN 0-486-22953-X). Dover.

Abrahams, Harold J. Heroic Efforts at Meteor Crater, Arizona: Selected Correspondence Between Daniel Moreau Barringer & Elihu Thomson. LC 78-75170. 480p. 1983. 35.00 (ISBN 0-8386-2399-9). Fairleigh Dickinson.

Abrahams, Harold J. & Savin, Marion B., eds. Selections from the Scientific Correspondence of Elihu Thomson. 1971. 35.00x (ISBN 0-262-01034-8). MIT Pr.

Abrahams, Howard. Making TV Pay Off. (Illus.). 1975. pap. 6.95 (ISBN 0-87005-140-7). Fairchild.

Abrahams, I. Campaigns in Palestine from Alexander the Great. (British Academy, London, Schweich Lectures on Biblical Archaeology Series, 1922). pap. 19.00 (ISBN 0-317-15777-9). Kraus Repr.

Abrahams, Israel. The Book of Delight & Other Papers. Katz, Steven, ed. LC 79-7124. (Jewish Philosophy, Mysticism & History of Ideas Ser.). 1980. Repr. of 1912 ed. lib. bdg. 26.50x (ISBN 0-405-12238-1). Ayer Co Pubs.

--By-Paths in Hebraic Bookland. LC 77-174368. Repr. of 1920 ed. 17.00 (ISBN 0-405-08177-4, Pub. by Blom Publications). Ayer Co Pubs.

--Jewish Life in the Middle Ages. LC 58-11933. (Temple Books). 1969. pap. text ed. 7.95x (ISBN 0-689-70001-6, T1). Atheneum.

--A Short History of Jewish Literature. 1906. Repr. 20.00 (ISBN 0-8274-3400-6). R West.

Abrahams, Israel, jt. auth. see Yellin, David.

Abrahams, Israel, ed. & tr. Hebrew Ethical Wills. new ed. LC 76-2898. (JPS Library of Jewish Classics). 742p. 1976. pap. 10.95 (ISBN 0-8276-0082-8, 389). Jewish Pubns.

Abrahams, Israel, tr. see Alon, Gedalyahu.

Abrahams, Israel, tr. see Cassuto, U.

Abrahams, Israel, tr. see Urbach, Ephraim E.

Abrahams, J. R. & Pridham, G. J. Semiconductor Circuits: Theory, Design & Experiment. 25.00 (ISBN 0-08-011652-3). Pergamon.

Abrahams, Joel P. & Crooks, Valerie C., eds. Geriatric Mental Health. 304p. 1984. 34.50 (ISBN 0-8089-1657-2, 790005). Grune.

Abrahams, K., et al, eds. Nuclear Structure. LC 81-7291. (NATO ASI Series B, Physics: Vol. 67). 442p. 1981. 69.50x (ISBN 0-306-40728-0, Plenum Pr). Plenum Pub.

Abrahams, P. H. & Webb, P. J. Clinical Anatomy of Practical Procedures: A Guide for Nurses, Students & Junior Doctors. (Illus.). 150p. (Orig.). 1975. pap. text ed. 17.95x (ISBN 0-8464-0250-5). Beekman Pubs.

Abrahams, Paul P. The Foreign Expansion of American Finance & Its Relationship to the Foreign Economic Policies of the United States, 1907-1921. Bruchey, Stuart & Bruchey, Eleanor, eds. LC 76-4762. (American Business Abroad Ser.). 1976. 21.00x (ISBN 0-405-09262-8). Ayer Co Pubs.

Abrahams, Peter. The Fury of Rachel Monette. 352p. 1982. pap. 3.50 (ISBN 0-671-41906-4). PB.

--Mine Boy. (African Writers Ser.). 1963. pap. text ed. 3.50x (ISBN 0-435-90006-4). Heinemann Ed.

--Path of Thunder. 279p. 1975. Repr. of 1948 ed. 8.95x (ISBN 0-911860-43-6). Chatham Bkseller.

--Tell Freedom. 311p. 1982. 4.95 (ISBN 0-571-11777-5). Faber & Faber.

--This Island Now. 256p. 1985. pap. 7.95 (ISBN 0-571-13439-4). Faber & Faber.

--Tongues of Fire. LC 82-1390. 312p. 1982. 12.95 (ISBN 0-87131-374-X). M Evans.

--Tongues of Fire. 1985. pap. 3.95 (ISBN 0-671-46419-1). PB.

--The View from Coyaba. LC 84-28746. 288p. 1985. 19.95 (ISBN 0-571-13288-X); pap. 8.95 (ISBN 0-571-13289-8). Faber & Faber.

--A Wreath for Udomo. LC 83-45608. Repr. of 1956 ed. 32.00 (ISBN 0-404-20001-X). AMS Pr.

Abrahams, Peter, jt. auth. see Weir, Jamie.

Abrahams, Peter, illus. Wreath for Udomo. (African-American Lib). 1971. pap. 1.95 (ISBN 0-02-048060-1, Collier). Macmillan.

Abrahams, R. G. The Nyamwezi Today: A Tanzanian People in the Seventies. LC 80-41012. (Changing Cultures Ser.). (Illus.). 176p. 1981. 37.50 (ISBN 0-521-22694-5); pap. 12.95 (ISBN 0-521-29619-6). Cambridge U Pr.

--Political Organization of Unyamwezi. (Cambridge Studies in Social Anthropology: No. 1). (Illus.). 1967. 34.50 (ISBN 0-521-04001-9). Cambridge U Pr.

Abrahams, Robert D. Sir David Salomons: Sound of Bow Bells. LC 62-12320. (Covenant Ser.). 158p. (gr. 6-10). 1962. 3.50 (ISBN 0-8276-0159-X, 286). Jewish Pubns.

Abrahams, Roger D. Afro-American Folktales: Stories from Black Traditions in the New World. LC 84-16601. (Fairytales & Folktale Library). 352p. 1985. 22.95 (ISBN 0-394-52755-0); pap. 11.95 (ISBN 0-394-72885-8). Pantheon.

--Deep Down in the Jungle: Negro Narrative Folklore from the Streets of Philadelphia. rev. ed. LC 78-124404. 1970. lib. bdg. 29.95x (ISBN 0-202-01091-0); pap. text ed. 14.95x (ISBN 0-202-01092-9). Aldine Pub.

--The Man-of-Words in the West Indies: Performance & the Emergence of Creole Culture. LC 82-16235. (Studies in Atlantic History & Culture). 240p. 1983. text ed. 24.50x (ISBN 0-8018-2838-4); pap. text ed. 12.95x (ISBN 0-8018-2839-2). Johns Hopkins.

Abrahams, Roger D., jt. auth. see Szwed, John F.

Abrahams, Roger D., ed. African Folktales: Traditional Stories of the Black World. LC 83-2474. (Fairy Tale & Folklore Library). 384p. 1983. 21.45 (ISBN 0-394-50236-1); pap. 10.95 (ISBN 0-394-72117-9). Pantheon.

--African Folktales: Traditional Stories of the Black World. (Pantheon Fairy Tale & Folklore Library Ser.). 1983. pap. 21.95. Random.

Abrahams, Roger D. & Rankin, Lois, eds. Counting out Rhymes: A Dictionary. (AFS Bibliographical & Special Ser.: Vol. 33). 263p. 1980. text ed. 19.95x (ISBN 0-292-71057-7). U of Tex Pr.

Abrahams, Roger D. & Szwed, John F., eds. After Africa: Extracts from British Travel Accounts & Journals of the Seventeenth, Eighteenth, & Nineteenth Centuries Concerning the Slaves, Their Manners, & Customs in the British West Indies. LC 82-20110. 480p. 1983. text ed. 47.50x (ISBN 0-300-02748-6); pap. text ed. 12.95x (ISBN 0-300-03030-4). Yale U Pr.

Abrahams, Roger D., jt. ed. see Bauman, Richard.

Abrahams, S. C., ed. Accuracy in X-Ray Intensity Measurements. (Transactions of the American Crystallographic Association Ser.: Vol. 1). 112p. 1965. pap. 15.00 (ISBN 0-686-60372-9). Polycrystal Bk Serv.

Abrahams, Thomas, ed. North American Directory & Reference Guide of Asian Indian Businesses & Independent Professional Practioners. 304p. pap. 22.95 (ISBN 0-933047-00-2). India Enterprises West.

Abrahams, William. Prize Stories 1985: The O. Henry Awards. LC 21-9372. 336p. 1985. 16.95 (ISBN 0-385-19477-3); pap. 8.95 (ISBN 0-385-19478-1). Doubleday.

Abrahams, William, jt. auth. see Stansky, Peter.

Abrahams, William, ed. Prize Stories of the Seventies: From the O. Henry Awards. 512p. 1981. pap. 4.95 (ISBN 0-671-41866-1). WSP.

--Prize Stories, 1982: The O. Henry Awards. LC 21-9372. 360p. 1982. 15.95 (ISBN 0-385-17563-9). Doubleday.

--Prize Stories 1983: The O. Henry Awards. LC 21-9372. 360p. 1983. 16.95 (ISBN 0-385-18115-9). Doubleday.

--Prize Stories 1984: The O. Henry Awards. LC 21-9372. 312p. 1984. 16.95 (ISBN 0-385-18844-7); pap. 8.95 (ISBN 0-385-18855-2). Doubleday.

Abrahams-Curiel, Diana, tr. see Linssen, Robert.

Abrahamse, Dorothy, ed. see Alexander, Paul F.

Abrahamsen, David. Confessions of Son of Sam. 256p. 1985. 19.95 (ISBN 0-231-05760-1). Columbia U Pr.

--Crime & the Human Mind. LC 69-14906. (Criminology, Law Enforcement, & Social Problems Ser.: No. 43). 1969. Repr. of 1944 ed. 15.00x (ISBN 0-87585-043-X). Patterson Smith.

--The Mind of the Accused: A Psychiatrist in the Courtroom. 252p. 1983. 15.95 (ISBN 0-671-47053-1). S&S.

--The Psychology of Crime. LC 59-13606. 1960. 27.50x (ISBN 0-231-02274-3). Columbia U Pr.

--The Psychology of Crime. LC 59-13606. pap. 93.00 (ISBN 0-317-26424-9, 2024976). Bks Demand UMI.

--Who Are the Guilty? A Study of Education & Crime. LC 70-143306. 340p. 1972. Repr. of 1952 ed. lib. bdg. 20.75x (ISBN 0-8371-5807-9, ABWG). Greenwood.

Abrahamsen, Samuel. Say It in Norwegian. (Orig.). 1957. pap. 2.25 (ISBN 0-486-20814-1). Dover.

Abrahamson, E. M. Body, Mind & Sugar. 1981. 13.95x (ISBN 0-686-76729-2). B Of A.

Abrahamson, E. M. & Pezet, A. W. Body, Mind & Sugar. (YA) 1977. pap. 4.95 (ISBN 0-380-00903-X, 64964-0). Avon.

--Body, Mind & Sugar. 3.95x (ISBN 0-380-47415-8). Cancer Control Soc.

Abrahamson, Edwin & Ostroy, Sanford E., eds. Molecular Processes in Vision. LC 80-29543. (Benchmark Papers in Biochemistry: Vol. 3). 448p. 1981. 57.95 (ISBN 0-87933-372-3). Van Nos Reinhold.

Abrahamson, I. A. Cataract Surgery. 384p. 1985. price not set (ISBN 0-07-000173-1). McGraw.

--Color Atlas of Anterior Segment Eye Diseases. (Illus.). 1974. 31.95 (ISBN 0-87489-055-1). Med Economics.

Abrahamson, Irving. Against Silence: The Voice & Vision of Elie Wiesel, 3 vols. 1984. Vol. 1. 60.00 set (ISBN 0-89604-075-5). Vol. 2 (ISBN 0-89604-076-3). Vol. 3 (ISBN 0-89604-077-1). Holocaust Pubns.

--Against Silence: The Voice & Vision of Elie Wiesel, 3 Vols. 356p. 1984. Vol. 1. 20.00 (ISBN 0-8052-5048-4); Vol. 2. 20.00 (ISBN 0-8052-5049-2); Vol. 3. 20.00 (ISBN 0-8052-5050-6). Schocken.

Abrams, Marshall D. & Stein, Philip G. Computer Hardware & Software: An Interdisciplinary Introduction. LC 72-3455. 1973. text ed. 31.95 (ISBN 0-201-00019-9). Addison-Wesley.

Abrams, Martha. Poems Uplifting & Thoughtful. Date not set. 6.00 (ISBN 0-8062-2418-5). Carlton.

Abrams, Maxine, jt. auth. see Flowers, Charles E., Jr.

Abrams, Meyer H. Mirror & the Lamp. 1953. 27.50x (ISBN 0-19-500465-5). Oxford U Pr.

--Mirror & the Lamp: Romantic Theory & the Critical Tradition. 1983. pap. 9.95 (ISBN 0-19-501471-5, 360, GB). Oxford U Pr.

Abrams, Meyer H., ed. Wordsworth: A Collection of Critical Essays. 1972. 12.95 (Spec). P-H.

Abrams, Natalie & Buckner, Michael D. Medical Ethics: A Clinical Textbook & Reference for the Health Care Professions. 848p. 1982. text ed. 50.00x (ISBN 0-262-01068-2, Pub. by Bradford); pap. text ed. 27.50x (ISBN 0-262-51024-3). MIT Pr.

Abrams, P. & McCulloch, A. Communes, Sociology & Society. LC 75-40985. (Themes in the Social Sciences Ser.: No. 3). 200p. 1976. 39.50 (ISBN 0-521-21188-3); pap. 11.95 (ISBN 0-521-29067-8). Cambridge U Pr.

Abrams, P. & Wrigley, E. A., eds. Towns in Societies. LC 77-82481. (Past & Present Publications). 1978. 39.50 (ISBN 0-521-21826-8); pap. 14.95 (ISBN 0-521-29594-7). Cambridge U Pr.

Abrams, P., et al, eds. Practice & Progress: British Sociology 1950-1980. 240p. 1981. text ed. 28.50x (ISBN 0-04-301131-4); pap. text ed. 12.50x (ISBN 0-04-301132-2). Allen Unwin.

Abrams, P. H. Urodynamics. (Clinical Practice in Urology Ser.). (Illus.). 236p. 1983. 46.00 (ISBN 0-387-11903-5). Springer-Verlag.

Abrams, Pepper, jt. auth. see Zolla, Susan.

Abrams, Philip. Historical Sociology. 400p. 1981. 60.00x (ISBN 0-7291-0111-8, Pub. by Open Bks England); pap. 30.00x (ISBN 0-7291-0106-1). State Mutual Bk.

--Historical Sociology. LC 82-61210. 372p. 1983. text ed. 34.95x (ISBN 0-8014-1578-0); pap. 14.95x (ISBN 0-8014-9243-2). Cornell U Pr.

--Origins of British Sociology: Eighteen Thirty-Four to Nineteen Fourteen: An Essay with Selected Papers. LC 68-54221. (Heritage of Sociology Ser). 472p. 1972. pap. 3.25x (ISBN 0-226-00171-7). U of Chicago Pr.

Abrams, Philip, ed. see Locke, John.

Abrams, R. & Essman, W. B., eds. Electroconvulsive Therapy: Biological Foundations & Clinical Applications. (Illus.). 320p. 1982. text ed. 47.50 (ISBN 0-89335-144-X). SP Med & Sci Bks.

Abrams, Ray H., ed. The American Family in World War Two. LC 79-169365. (Family in America Ser.). 196p. 1972. Repr. of 1943 ed. 19.00 (ISBN 0-405-03842-9). Ayer Co Pubs.

Abrams, Richard & Wexler, Paul. Medical Care of the Pregnant Patient. 404p. 1983. text ed. 42.50 (ISBN 0-316-00470-7). Little.

Abrams, Richard, ed. see Taylor, Michael A., et al.

Abrams, Richard I. & Hutchinson, Warner A. An Illustrated Life of Jesus: From The National Gallery of Art Collection. LC 81-17575. (Illus.). 1982. 40.00 (ISBN 0-687-01356-9); deluxe ed. 75.00 (ISBN 0-687-01358-5); ltd. ed. 300.00 (ISBN 0-687-01357-7). Abingdon.

Abrams, Richard I., jt. auth. see Bell, James B.

Abrams, Richard K., jt. auth. see Johnson, G. G.

Abrams, Richard M. The Burdens of Progress, 1900-1929. 1978. pap. text ed. 10.80 (ISBN 0-673-05778-X). Scott F.

Abrams, Richard M., ed. Issues of the Populist & Progressive Eras, 1892-1912. LC 76-625503. (Documentary History of the United States Ser.). 1970. 19.95x (ISBN 0-87249-164-1). U of SC Pr.

Abrams, Rita. At Your Age You're Having a What?! (Illus.). 108p. (Orig.). 1983. pap. 4.95 (ISBN 0-931432-17-0). Whatever Pub.

Abrams, Robert. Foundations of Political Analysis: An Introduction to the Theory of Collective Choice. LC 79-20850. 1980. 30.00x (ISBN 0-231-04480-1); pap. 14.00x. Columbia U Pr.

Abrams, Robert, et al. FLEX Review. LC 80-83395. 1980. pap. 29.50 (ISBN 0-87488-158-7). Med Exam.

Abrams, Robert E., selected by. Treasures of Disney Animation Art. (Illus.). 320p. 29.98 (ISBN 0-89659-315-0). Abbeville Pr.

Abrams, Ruth D. Not Alone with Cancer: A Guide for Those Who Care; What to Expect; What to Do. 128p. 1976. pap. 8.75x (ISBN 0-398-02973-3). C C Thomas.

Abrams, Stanley. Polygraph Handbook for Attorneys. LC 77-6074. (Illus.). 1977. 27.00x (ISBN 0-669-01598-9). Lexington Bks.

Abrams, Stanley, jt. auth. see Ansley, Norman.

Abrams, Stanley D. Guide to Maryland Zoning Decisions. 2nd ed. 391p. 1985. 45.00 (ISBN 0-87215-847-0). Michie Co.

--How to Win the Zoning Game. 389p. 1978. with 1982 suppl. 35.00 (ISBN 0-87215-203-0); 1982 Suppl. 15.00 (ISBN 0-87215-574-9). Michie Co.

Abrams, Stuart E., ed. see Fink, Robert S., et al.

Abrams, Walter H., jt. auth. see Holleb, Gordon P.

Abramskii, I. P. Smekh Sil'Nykh: O Khudo Zhnikakh Zhurnala 'Krokodil' 320p. 1977. 30.00x (ISBN 0-317-14299-2, Pub. by Collet's). State Mutual Bk.

Abramsky, Chimen & Williams, Beryl J., eds. Essays in Honour of E. H. Carr. (Illus.). viii, 387p. 1974. 25.00 (ISBN 0-208-01451-9, Archon). Shoe String.

Abramson, Alan J., jt. auth. see Salamon, Lester M.

Abramson, Albert. Electronic Motion Pictures: A History of the Television Camera. LC 74-4663. (Telecommunications Ser). (Illus.). 228p. 1974. Repr. of 1955 ed. 24.50 (ISBN 0-405-06031-9). Ayer Co Pubs.

Abramson, D. I. Circulatory Problems in Podiatry. (Karger Continuing Education Ser.: Vol. 7). (Illus.). xvi, 408p. 1985. 70.00 (ISBN 3-8055-3910-X). S Karger.

Abramson, D. I. & Miller, D. S. Vascular Problems in Musculoskeletal Disorders of the Limbs. (Illus.). 404p. 1981. 49.00 (ISBN 0-387-90524-3). Springer-Verlag.

Abramson, David H., jt. auth. see Sagerman, Robert H.

Abramson, David I. Circulatory Diseases of the Limbs: A Primer. 380p. 1978. 45.00 (ISBN 0-8089-1064-7, 790010). Grune.

Abramson, David I. & Casey, M. Beth. Self-Assessment of Current Knowledge in Peripheral Vascular Disorders. 1980. pap. 24.00 (ISBN 0-87488-291-5). Med Exam.

Abramson, David I. & Dorbin, Philip B. Blood Vessels & Lymphatics in Organ Systems. 1984. 89.00 (ISBN 0-12-042520-3). Acad Pr.

Abramson, David I., ed. Blood Vessels & Lymphatics. 1962. 90.00 (ISBN 0-12-042550-5). Acad Pr.

--Circulation in the Extremities. 1967. 85.00 (ISBN 0-12-042556-4). Acad Pr.

Abramson, Doris E. Negro Playwrights in the American Theatre, 1925-1959. LC 69-19457. pap. 87.80 (ISBN 0-317-29442-3, 2024289). Bks Demand UMI.

Abramson, Edward E., ed. Behavioral Approaches to Weight Control. LC 77-21042. (Behavior Therapy & Behavioral Medicine Ser.: Vol. 3). 1977. text ed. 12.95 (ISBN 0-8261-1900-X). Springer Pub.

Abramson, Glenda. Modern Hebrew Drama. LC 79-16608. (Illus.). 1979. 29.95x (ISBN 0-312-53988-6). St Martin.

Abramson, Glenda & Parfitt, Tudor, eds. The Great Transition: The Recovery of the Lost Centres of Modern Hebrew Literature. (Oxford Centre for Postgraduate Hebrew Studies). 250p. 1985. 38.50x (ISBN 0-8476-7437-1). Rowman.

Abramson, Glenda, tr. see Amichai, Yehuda.

Abramson, H. N., tr. see Rapoport, I. M.

Abramson, Harold A. Psychological Problems in the Father-Son Relationship. LC 71-81849. 1969. 7.50 (ISBN 0-8079-0154-7). October.

Abramson, Harvey. Theory & Application of a Bottom-up Syntax-Directed Translator. (ACM Monograph Ser.). 1973. 37.00 (ISBN 0-12-042650-1). Acad Pr.

Abramson, J. H. Survey Methods in Community Medicine: An Introduction to Epidemiological & Evaluative Studies. 3rd ed. 1984. pap. text ed. 13.00 (ISBN 0-443-03068-5). Churchill.

Abramson, J. H. & Peritz, E. Calculator Programs for the Health Sciences. (Illus.). 1983. text ed. 42.50x (ISBN 0-19-503187-3); pap. text ed. 24.95x (ISBN 0-19-503188-1). Oxford U Pr.

Abramson, Joan. The Invisible Woman: Discrimination in the Academic Profession. LC 74-32627. (Higher Education Ser.). 224p. 1975. 19.95x (ISBN 0-87589-256-6). Jossey-Bass.

--Old Boys-New Women: The Politics of Sex Discrimination. LC 79-65933. 270p. 1979. 34.95 (ISBN 0-03-049756-6); pap. 14.95 (ISBN 0-03-049751-5). Praeger.

--Practical Application of the Gas Laws to Pulmonary Physiology. 97p. (Orig.). 1981. pap. text ed. 8.95x (ISBN 0-89787-107-3). Gorsuch Scarisbrick.

Abramson, Joan, ed. Photographers of Old Hawaii. 3rd ed. LC 76-1504. (Illus.). 228p. 1981. 12.50 (ISBN 0-89610-082-0). Island Herit.

Abramson, Lillian & Robinson, Jessie. Alef Bet Fun. (Illus.). (gr. 2-4). 1957. pap. 3.95x (ISBN 0-8197-0028-2). Bloch.

Abramson, Lillian S. & Leiderman, Lillian T. Jewish Holiday Party Book: A Practical Guide to Parties Planned for Children Ages 5-12. 2nd ed. LC 54-11436. 1966. 4.95 (ISBN 0-8197-0051-7). Bloch.

Abramson, Marcia, jt. auth. see Reamer, Frederic.

Abramson, Mark. Sociological Theory: An Introduction to Concepts, Issues & Research. (Prentice Hall Series in Sociology). (Illus.). 288p. 1981. text ed. 27.95 (ISBN 0-13-820803-4). P-H.

Abramson, Mark A. see Wholey, Joseph S., et al.

Abramson, N. & Kuo, F., eds. Computer-Communications Networks. 1973. 41.95 (ISBN 0-13-165431-4). P-H.

Abramson, Nils. The Making & Evaluation of Holograms. LC 81-67905. 1981. 49.50 (ISBN 0-12-042820-2). Acad Pr.

Abramson, P. B., ed. Guidebook to Light Water Reactor Safety Analysis. LC 84-22447. (Proceedings of the International Centre for Heat & Mass Transfer Ser.). (Illus.). 393p. 1985. 89.95 (ISBN 0-89116-262-3). Hemisphere Pub.

Abramson, Paul. Personality. LC 80-474. 377p. 1980. text ed. 26.95 (ISBN 0-03-055726-7, HoltC); instr's. manual 25.00 (ISBN 0-03-055731-3). HR&W.

Abramson, Paul R. Political Attitudes in America. LC 82-13508. (Illus.). 353p. 1983. pap. text ed. 17.95 (ISBN 0-7167-1420-5). W H Freeman.

--Sarah: A Sexual Biography. (Sexual Behavior Ser.). 158p. 1984. 29.50x (ISBN 0-87395-862-4); pap. 9.95 (ISBN 0-87395-863-2). State U NY Pr.

Abramson, Paul R. & Aldrich, John H. Change & Continuity in the 1980 Election. rev. ed. LC 83-1961. 279p. 1983. pap. 9.25 (ISBN 0-87187-270-6). Congr Quarterly.

Abramson, Paul R., jt. auth. see Murray, Joan.

Abramson, Robert & Halset, Walter. Planning for Improved Enterprise Performance: A Guide for Managers & Consultants. International Labour Office, Geneva, ed. (Management Development Ser.: No. 15). (Illus., Orig.). 1982. pap. 11.40 (ISBN 92-2-102082-7). Intl Labour Office.

--Planning for Improved Enterprise Performance: Guide for Managers & Consultants. (Management Development Ser.: No. 15). 170p. (2nd Impression). 1981. pap. 11.40 (ISBN 92-2-102082-7, ILO210, ILO). Unipub.

Abramson, Samuel H., jt. auth. see Postal, Bernard.

Abramson, Sue. Extended Frames. 32p. 1981. spiral bdg. 10.00 (ISBN 0-930794-21-4). Station Hill Pr.

Abramson, Theodore, et al. Handbook of Vocational Education Evaluation. LC 78-24256. (Illus.). 624p. 1979. 40.00 (ISBN 0-8039-1078-9). Sage.

Abran, et al. Delta Data & Your Paper. LC 84-22102. 121p. 1984. pap. 16.95 (ISBN 0-471-90645-X). Wiley.

Abranson, Erik. Ships & Seafarers. LC 80-50953. (Adventures in History Ser.). PLB 12.68 (ISBN 0-382-06382-1). Silver.

Abranson, Lillian. Hanukkah ABC. (Illus.). (gr. 3-7). 1968. pap. 4.00 (ISBN 0-914080-60-1). Shulsinger Sales.

Abrash, Barbara, ed. Black African Literature in English since 1952. LC 67-29100. pap. 9.00 (ISBN 0-384-00201-3). Johnson Repr.

Abrash, Henry & Hardcastle, Kenneth. Chemistry. 1981. Repr. text ed. write for info. (ISBN 0-02-471100-4); lab. manual avail. (ISBN 0-02-471170-5); study guide avail. (ISBN 0-686-72522-0). Macmillan.

Abrash, Michael, jt. auth. see Illowsky, Dan.

Abrash, Michael, jt. auth. see Illowsky, Daniel.

Abrashkin, Raymond, jt. auth. see Williams, Jay.

Abravanal, Isaac. Principles of Faith (Rosh Amanah) (LLJC Ser.). 1982. 24.95x (ISBN 0-19-710045-7). Oxford U Pr.

Abravanel, Claude. Claude Debussy: A Bibliography. LC 72-90430. (Detroit Studies in Music Bibliography Ser.: No. 29). 1974. 5.00 (ISBN 0-911772-49-9); pap. 2.00 (ISBN 0-89990-007-0). Info Coord.

Abravanel, Eliott D. & King, Elizabeth A. Dr. Abravanel's Body Type Diet & Lifetime Nutrition Plan. (Illus.). 256p. 1983. 12.95 (ISBN 0-553-05036-2); pap. 3.95. Bantam.

Abravanel, Elliot D. & King, Elizabeth A. Dr. Abravanel's Body Type Program for Health, Fitness & Nutrition. 304p. 1985. 15.95 (ISBN 0-553-05074-5). Bantam.

Abravanel, Ernest, ed. see Stendhal.

Abravnel, Elliot D. & King, Elizabeth A. Dr. Abravnel's Body Type Diet & Lifetime Nutrition Plan. 256p. 1984. pap. 3.95 (ISBN 0-553-23973-2). Bantam.

Abray, Lorna J. The People's Reformation: Magistrates, Clergy & Commons in Strasbourg 1500-1598. LC 84-45805. 288p. 1985. text ed. 27.50x (ISBN 0-8014-1776-7). Cornell U Pr.

Abrera, Bernard. Moths of Australia. 96p. 1984. 37.00x (ISBN 0-317-07164-5, Pub. by FW Classey UK). State Mutual Bk.

Abrera, Dette L. Handyong. (Illus., Orig.). 1985. pap. 3.00 (ISBN 0-318-04253-3, Pub. By New Day Philippines). Cellar.

Abreu, Beatriz, ed. Physical Disabilities Manual. 380p. 1981. text ed. 47.50 (ISBN 0-89004-505-4). Raven.

Abreu, Jose L., tr. see Swokowski, Earl W.

Abreu, Manuel. Llegaron los Hippies. 112p. 1978. pap. 3.00 (ISBN 0-940238-24-1). Ediciones Huracan.

Abreu, Maria I. & Rameh, Clea. Portugues Contemporaneo, 2 vols. Incl. Vol. 1. 256p. pap. 7.95 (ISBN 0-87840-026-5); 11 cassettes 70.00 (ISBN 0-87840-048-6); 22 reel-to-reel tapes 120.00 (ISBN 0-87840-075-3); Vol. 2. 346p. pap. 7.95 (ISBN 0-87840-025-7); 10 cassettes 70.00 (ISBN 0-87840-049-4); 20 tapes 120.00 (ISBN 0-87840-076-1). LC 66-25520. 1971. Georgetown U Pr.

Abreu, Rosendo. The Cambridge Program for the GED Social Studies Test. (GED Preparation Ser.). (Illus.). 272p. (Orig.). 1981. pap. text ed. 6.66 (ISBN 0-8428-9388-1); Cambridge Exercise Book for the Social Studies Test. wkbk. 3.93 (ISBN 0-8428-9394-6). Cambridge Bk.

Abreu, Rosendo, jt. auth. see Lanzano, Susan.

Abreu-Gomez, Emilo. Canek: History & Legend of a Maya Hero. Davila, Mario L. & Wilson, Carter, trs. from Span. LC 75-32674. 1979. 19.50x (ISBN 0-520-03148-2); pap. 2.95 (ISBN 0-520-03982-3, CAL 441). U of Cal Pr.

Abri, Amir F., tr. see Mutahhari, Morteza.

Abrie, P. L. D. The Design of Impedance Matching Networks for Radio-Frequency & Microwave Amplifiers. 1985. text ed. 60.00 (ISBN 0-89006-172-6). Artech Hse.

Abriel, Vera. Too Near the Flame. LC 82-61844. 222p. (Orig.). 1983. pap. 1.75 (ISBN 0-943654-00-9). New Paradise Bks.

Abrikosov, A. A. Introduction to the Theory of Normal Metals. (Solid State Physics: Suppl. 12). 1972. 55.00 (ISBN 0-12-607772-X). Acad Pr.

Abrikosov, A. A. & Gorkov, L. P. Methods of Quantum Field Theory in Statistical Physics. Silverman, Richard, tr. from Rus. 368p. 1975. pap. 7.00 (ISBN 0-486-63228-8). Dover.

Abrikosov, N. K., ed. Semiconductor Materials. LC 62-21587. 139p. 1963. 27.50x (ISBN 0-306-10659-0, Consultants). Plenum Pub.

Abrikossow, Dmitrii I. Revelations of a Russian Diplomat: The Memoirs of Dmitrii I. Abrikossow. Lensen, George A., ed. LC 64-18426. (Washington Paperbacks on Russia & Asia Ser.: No. 5). (Illus.). 351p. 1968. 20.00x (ISBN 0-295-73911-8); pap. 6.95x (ISBN 0-295-97896-1, WPRA5). U of Wash Pr.

Abriksov, N. K., et al. Semiconducting Two-Six, Four-Six, & Five-Six Compounds. LC 69-12527. (Monographs in Semiconductor Physics Ser.: Vol. 3). 250p. 1969. 32.50x (ISBN 0-306-30389-2, Plenum Pr). Plenum Pub.

Abriola, Frank L. Broccoliville. (gr. 1 up). 1984. 4.95 (ISBN 0-533-05990-9). Vantage.

Abriola, L. M. Multiphase Migration of Organic Compounds in a Porous Medium: A Mathematical Model. (Lecture Notes in Engineering Ser.: Vol. 8). (Illus.). viii, 232p. 1984. pap. 15.00 (ISBN 0-387-13694-0). Springer-Verlag.

Abrishaman, M. & Putnam, A. Effect of Furnace Design on Combustion Noise. 49p. 1977. pap. 3.75 (ISBN 0-318-12604-4, M59077). Am Gas Assn.

Abro, A. The Evolution of Scientific Thought: From Newton to Einstein. 2nd ed. (Illus.). 481p. 1950. pap. 7.50 (ISBN 0-486-20002-7). Dover.

--The Rise of the New Physics. 2nd ed. (Illus.). 994p. 1951. pap. 6.95 ea.; Vol. 1. pap. (ISBN 0-486-20003-5); Vol. 2. pap. (ISBN 0-486-20004-3). Dover.

Abro, A. D' see Abro, A.

Abromeit, Heidrun. British Steel: An Industry Between the State & the Private Sector. 288p. 1985. 29.95 (ISBN 0-312-10541-X). St Martin.

Abromowitz, Milton & Stegun, Irene A., eds. Handbook of Mathematical Functions, with Formulas, Graphs, & Mathematical Tables. 10th ed. (National Bureau of Standards Applied Mathematics Ser.: No. 55). (Illus.). 1060p. 1972. 24.00 (ISBN 0-318-11730-4). Gov Printing Office.

Abroms, Gene M. & Greenfield, Norman S., eds. New Hospital Psychiatry: Proceedings of a Conference. LC 77-137633. 1971. 58.00 (ISBN 0-12-042850-4). Acad Pr.

Abroms, Israel F., jt. auth. see Scheiner, Albert P.

Abromson, Herman, ed. see Morley, Christopher.

Abromson, Morton. Painting in Rome During the Papacy of Clement VIII (1592-1605) LC 79-57512. (Outstanding Dissertations in the Fine Arts Ser.: No. 5). 425p. 1985. lib. bdg. 80.00 (ISBN 0-8240-3926-2). Garland Pub.

Abruscato, Joe & Hassard, Jack. The Earthpeople Activity Book: People, Places, Pleasures & Other Delights. LC 78-7602. (Illus.). 1978. 14.95 (ISBN 0-673-16359-8); pap. 12.95 (ISBN 0-673-16360-1). Scott F.

--Loving & Beyond: Science Teaching for the Humanistic Classroom. LC 75-19568. (Illus.). 1977. pap. 12.95 (ISBN 0-673-16383-0). Scott F.

--The Whole Cosmos Catalog of Science Activities for Kids of All Ages. LC 76-46463. (Illus.). 1977. pap. 12.95 (ISBN 0-673-16459-4). Scott F.

Abruscato, Joseph. Introduction to Teaching & the Study of Education. (Illus.). 416p. 1985. text ed. 25.95 (ISBN 0-13-498817-5). P-H.

--Teaching Children Science. (Illus.). 544p. 1982. 28.95 (ISBN 0-13-891754-X). P-H.

Abruzzo, James. Jobs in Arts & Media Management: What They Are & How to Get One. 1985. text ed. write for info. (ISBN 0-89676-090-1); pap. text ed. write for info. (ISBN 0-89676-073-1). Drama Bk.

Abs, Michael. Physiology & Behaviour of the Pigeon. 1983. 63.00 (ISBN 0-12-042950-0). Acad Pr.

Absalom, R. N. Comprehension of Spoken Italian. LC 76-21015. 1978. limp bdg. 5.95 (ISBN 0-521-29115-1). Cambridge U Pr.

--Passages for Translation from Italian. 1967. pap. 8.95x (ISBN 0-521-09431-3, 431). Cambridge U Pr.

Absalom, Stacy. Knave of Hearts. (Harlequin Romances Ser.). 192p. 1983. pap. 1.75 (ISBN 0-373-02581-5). Harlequin Bks.

Absar, Ilyas, jt. auth. see Van Wazer, John R.

Abse. Hysteria & Related Mental Disorders. 2nd ed. 1986. price not set. PSG Pub Co.

Abse, D. Wilfred. Speech & Reason: Language Disorder in Mental Disease & a Translation of Philipp Wegener's The Life of Speech. LC 72-163981. 1971. 25.00x (ISBN 0-8139-0344-0). U Pr of Va.

Abse, Dannie. Collected Poems. LC 76-21049. (Pitt Poetry Ser.). 1977. pap. 6.95 (ISBN 0-685-75151-1). U of Pittsburgh Pr.

--Dannie Abse. (Pocket Poet Ser.). 1963. pap. 2.00 (ISBN 0-8023-9036-6). Dufour.

--The Dogs of Pavlov. 128p. 1973. 13.50x (ISBN 0-85303-166-5, Pub. by Vallentine Mitchell England). Biblio Dist.

--Miscellany One. 108p. 1981. pap. 7.00 (ISBN 0-907476-00-7). Dufour.

--One-Legged on Ice. LC 82-20055. 64p. 1983. lib. bdg. 10.95x (ISBN 0-8203-0651-7); pap. 6.95 (ISBN 0-8203-0653-3). U of Ga Pr.

--A Poet in the Family. 198p. 1985. pap. 8.95 (ISBN 0-86051-280-0, Pub. by Salem Hse Ltd). Merrimack Pub Cir.

Abse, Dannie, ed. Best of the Poetry Year. (Poetry Dimension Annual: 6). 202p. 1979. 13.00x (ISBN 0-8476-2404-8). Rowman.

--Best of the Poetry Year: Poetry Dimension Annual 7. 160p. 1980. 15.00x (ISBN 0-8476-3255-5). Rowman.

--The Best of the Poetry Year: Poetry Dimension Annual, 5. 171p. 1978. 11.50x (ISBN 0-8476-3139-7). Rowman.

--Modern European Verse. (Pocket Poet Ser.). 1964. pap. 2.00 (ISBN 0-8023-9037-4). Dufour.

--Modern Poets in Focus, No. 1. 141p. 1973. 17.50x (ISBN 0-7130-0077-5, Pub by Woburn Pr England). Biblio Dist.

--My Medical School. (Illus.). 211p. 1978. 14.50x (ISBN 0-8476-3124-9). Rowman.

Abse, Joan. The Art Galleries of Britain & Ireland. (Illus.). 300p. 1985. pap. 8.95 (ISBN 0-86051-313-0, Pub. by Salem Hse Ltd). Merrimack Pub Cir.

--The Art Galleries of Britain & Ireland: A Guide to Their Collections. LC 75-24944. (Illus.). 248p. 1975. 24.50 (ISBN 0-8386-1850-2). Fairleigh Dickinson.

--John Ruskin: The Passionate Moralist. LC 81-47483. 1981. 18.50 (ISBN 0-394-51596-X). Knopf.

Abse, Joan, ed. My LSE. (Illus.). 223p. 1977. 14.50x (ISBN 0-8476-3125-7). Rowman.

Abshagen, Karl H. Kings, Lords & Gentlemen: Influence & Power of the English Upper Classes. 1977. 59.95 (ISBN 0-8490-2117-0). Gordon Pr.

Abshagen, U., ed. Clinical Pharmacology of Antianginal Drugs. (Handbook of Experimental Pharmacology Ser.: Vol. 76). (Illus.). 610p. 1985. 162.00 (ISBN 0-387-13110-8). Springer-Verlag.

Absher, Tom. Forms of Praise. LC 80-39926. 56p. 1981. 8.00 (ISBN 0-8142-0329-9). Ohio St U Pr.

Absher, W. O. Surry County, N. C., Court Minutes, 1768-1789, Vols. 1 & 2. 168p. pap. 18.50 (ISBN 0-89308-554-5). Southern Hist Pr.

--Surry County, N. C., Deed Books A, B, & C. 120p. 1981. Repr. 20.00 (ISBN 0-89308-172-8). Southern Hist Pr.

Abshire, David, ed. Egypt & Israel: Prospects for a New Era. 128p. (Orig.). 1979. pap. text ed. 5.95 (ISBN 0-87855-790-3). Transaction Bks.

Abshire, David M. & Allen, Richard V., eds. National Security. LC 63-17834. (Publications Ser.: No. 31). 1039p. 1963. 20.00x (ISBN 0-8179-1311-4). Hoover Inst Pr.

Abshire, Gary M. The Impact of Computers on Society & Ethics: A Bibliography. LC 80-65696. 120p. 1980. 17.95 (ISBN 0-916688-17-8, 12E). Creative Comp.

Abshire, Richard & Clair, William. Gants: Private Library Collection. 1985. mini-bound 6.95 (ISBN 0-938422-11-1). SOS Pubns CA.

Absolon, K. B., ed. The Intimate Billroth: The Intimate Story of the Founder of Modern Surgery. (Illus.). 240p. 1985. pap. 39.50 (ISBN 0-930329-05-8). Kabel Pubs.

Absolon, K. B., ed. & illus. see Absolon, Karel B.

Absolon, Karel B. Developmental Technology of Gastric Surgery. (Illus.). 152p. 1984. text ed. 65.00 (ISBN 0-930329-01-5); pap. text ed. 42.50 (ISBN 0-930329-00-7). KABEL Pubs.

--The Surgeon's Surgeon: Theodor Billroth (1829-1894, Vol. II. (Illus.). 232p. 1981. 28.50x (ISBN 0-87291-146-2). Coronado Pr.

--The Surgeon's Surgeon: Theodor Billroth, 1829-1894, Vol. 1. (Illus.). 1979. 15.00 (ISBN 0-87291-129-2). Coronado Pr.

--The Tale of the Bad Macocha & the Fable of the Underground Punkva River. Absolon, K. B., ed. & illus. (Moravian Tales, Legends, Myths Ser.). (Illus.). 40p. (Orig.). (gr. 4). 1984. pap. text ed. 16.00 (ISBN 0-930329-02-3). KABEL Pubs.

Abt, Clark C. The Social Audit: Problems & Possibilities. 1976. pap. 4.20x (ISBN 0-89011-489-7, REM-107). Abt Bks.

--A Strategy for Terminating Nuclear War. (Special Study Ser.). 200p. 1985. pap. 19.85x (ISBN 0-8133-7050-7). Westview.

Abt, Clark C., ed. The Evaluation of Social Programs. (Illus.). 503p. 1979. pap. 17.50 (ISBN 0-8039-4000-9). Sage.

--The Evaluation of Social Programs. LC 76-40712. (Illus.). 503p. 1977. 35.00 (ISBN 0-8039-0735-4). Sage.

--Perspectives on the Costs & Benefits of Applied Social Research. 300p. 1984. Repr. of 1978 ed. lib. bdg. 24.75 (ISBN 0-8191-4103-8). U Pr of Amer.

--Problems in American Social Policy Research. LC 79-55772. (Illus.). 1980. text ed. 24.00 (ISBN 0-89011-540-0). Abt Bks.

--Problems in American Social Policy Research. 300p. 1984. Repr. of 1980 ed. lib. bdg. 26.50 (ISBN 0-8191-4108-9). U Pr of Amer.

Abt, Clark C., et al, eds. Perspectives on the Costs & Benefits of Applied Social Research. LC 78-67240. 1979. text ed. 25.00 (ISBN 0-89011-520-6). Abt Bks.

Abt, E., tr. see Stark, W.

Abt, H. A., ed. Astrophysical Journal Supplement. 100.00 (ISBN 0-318-18120-7); members 40.00 (ISBN 0-318-18121-5). Am Astro Soc.

Abt, Henry E. The Care, Cure, & Education of the Crippled Child: A Study of American Social & Professional Facilities to Care for, Cure, & Educate Crippled Children. facsimile ed. LC 74-1659. (Children & Youth Ser.). (Illus.). 240p. 1974. Repr. of 1924 ed. 22.00x (ISBN 0-405-05941-8). Ayer Co Pubs.

Abt, L. E. & Riess, B. F., eds. Progress in Clinical Psychology. Incl. Vol. 4. 192p. 1960. 44.00 (ISBN 0-8089-0000-5, 790014); Vol. 5. 224p. 1962. 46.00 (ISBN 0-8089-0002-1, 790015); Vol. 7. 320p. 1966. 60.00 (ISBN 0-8089-0004-8); Vol. 8. Dreams & Dreaming. 200p. 1969. 48.00 (ISBN 0-8089-0005-6, 790018); Vol. 9. Clinical Psychology in Industrial Organization. 234p. 1971. 46.00 (ISBN 0-8089-0666-6, 790019). LC 52-12980. Grune.

Abt, Lawrence, jt. auth. see Stuart, Irving.

Abt, Lawrence E. & Stuart, Irving R. The Newer Therapies. 394p. 1982. 21.95 (ISBN 0-442-27942-6). Van Nos Reinhold.

--Social Psychology & Discretionary Law. 1979. 19.50 (ISBN 0-442-27907-8). Van Nos Reinhold.

Abt, Lawrence E., jt. auth. see Rosner, Stanley.

Abt, Samuel. Breakaway: The Nineteen Eighty-Four Tour de France. LC 85-2025. (Illus.). 224p. 1985. 15.95 (ISBN 0-394-54679-2). Random.

Abt, Vicki, et al. The Business of Risk: Commercial Gambling in Mainstream America. LC 85-7491. 375p. 1985. 29.95x (ISBN 0-7006-0280-1); pap. 14.95x (ISBN 0-7006-0281-X). U Pr of KS.

Abta, Nitza. The Complete Guide to Hair Replacement. 1975. 29.95x (ISBN 0-685-81806-3). New You Pub.

Abu-Ala, Maududi. Birth Control. pap. 4.50 (ISBN 0-686-18437-8). Kazi Pubns.

Abu al-Fida. Geographie d'Aboulfeda, 2 vols. in 3. Reinaud, M. & Guyard, S., trs. from Arabic. 1128p. (Fr.). Repr. of 1883 ed. lib. bdg. 180.00x set (ISBN 0-89241-181-3). Caratzas.

Abu Al-Hasan & Ahmed-Ibn Ibrahim. The Arithmetic of Al-Uqlidisi. Saidan, A. S., tr. 1978. lib. bdg. 103.00 (ISBN 90-277-0752-9, Pub. by Reidel Holland). Kluwer Academic.

Abu al-Tayyib Ahmad ibn al-Husan, jt. auth. see Al-Mutanabbi.

Abucewicz, John A. Fool's White. LC 82-72561. 236p. 1982. 10.00 (ISBN 0-933402-27-9). Charisma Pr.

Abuelo & Garfinkel, eds. Hereditary Aspects of Neurologic & Psychiatric Disorders. text ed. 22.95 (ISBN 0-938550-29-2). Acad Guild.

Abu-Ghazaleh, Adnan. American Missions in Syria. 120p. (Orig.). 1985. 16.95 (ISBN 0-915597-26-8); pap. 8.95 (ISBN 0-915597-25-X). Amana Bks.

Abu-Husayn, Abdul-Rahim. Provincial Leaderships in Syria Fifteen Seventy-Five to Sixteen Fifty. 230p. 1985. text ed. 29.95 (ISBN 0-8156-6072-3, Am U Beirut). Syracuse U Pr.

Abu-Izzedin, N. The Druzes: A New Study of Their History, Faith & Society. 246p. 1984. text ed. 23.50x (ISBN 90-04-06975-5, Pub. by E J Brill). Humanities.

Abu Jaber, Kamel S. Arab Ba'th Socialist Party History, Ideology, & Organization. LC 66-25181. 1966. 11.95x (ISBN 0-8156-0051-8). Syracuse U Pr.

Abu Khaldun Sati Al Husri. The Day of Maysalun: A Page from the Modern History of the Arabs. Glazer, Sidney, tr. from Arabic. LC 66-29228. 1966. pap. 2.75 (ISBN 0-916808-06-8). Mid East Inst.

Abu-Laban, Baha & Zeadey, Faith, eds. Arabs in America: Myths & Realities. (Monograph: No. 5). 256p. 1975. 12.95 (ISBN 0-914456-12-1). Assn Arab-Amer U Grads.

Abu-Laban, Baha, jt. ed. see Abu-Lughod, Ibrahim.

Abulafia, D. The Two Italies. LC 76-11069. (Cambridge Studies in Medieval Life & Thought Ser.: No. 9). (Illus.). 1977. 59.50 (ISBN 0-521-21211-1). Cambridge U Pr.

Abul-Fadl, Mirza. The Baha'i Proofs & A Short Sketch of the History & Lives of the Leaders of This Religion. Khan, Ali-Kuli, tr. from Arabic. LC 83-22486. (Illus.). xi, 305p. 1983. 16.95 (ISBN 0-87743-191-4). Baha'i.

Abu'l-Fadl, Mirza. Letters & Essays, 1886-1913. Cole, Juan R., tr. from Persian. (Illus.). 1985. 11.95 (ISBN 0-933770-36-7). Kalimat.

--Miracles & Metaphors. Cole, Juan R., tr. from Arabic. (Illus.). 220p. 1982. 11.95 (ISBN 0-933770-22-7). Kalimat.

Abu-L-Fazl. The Akbar Nama, 3 vols. Beveridge, Henry, tr. 2000p. 1971-73. Repr. Set. 85.00x (ISBN 0-89684-366-1). Orient Bk Dist.

Abuli, Sanchez. Torpedo Nineteen Thirty-Six, Vol. 2. Metz, Bernd, ed. Luciano, Dale, tr. from Span. (Torpedo 1936 Ser.). (Illus.). 96p. (Orig.). 1985. pap. 8.95 (ISBN 0-87416-014-6). Catalan Communs.

--Torpedo: 1936, Vol. 1. Metz, Bernd, ed. Rosenthal, David, tr. from Span. (Torpedo 1936 Ser.). (Illus.). 118p. (Orig.). 1984. pap. 8.95 (ISBN 0-87416-006-5). Catalan Communs.

Abu-Lughod, Ibrahim. Renewed Commitment & Positive Pragmatism: The Thirteenth Session of the Palestine National Council. (Occasional Papers: No. 4). 14p. (Orig.). 1977. pap. 1.50 (ISBN 0-937694-43-6). Assn Arab-Amer U Grads.

Abu-Lughod, Ibrahim & Said, Edward. Two Studies on the Palestinians Today & American Policy. (Information Paper: No. 17). 22p. (Orig.). 1976. pap. 2.75 (ISBN 0-937694-33-9). Assn Arab-Amer U Grads.

Abu-Lughod, Ibrahim, ed. The Arab-Israeli Confrontation of June 1967: An Arab Perspective. LC 74-107607. pap. 53.80 (ISBN 0-317-11281-3, 2014772). Bks Demand UMI.

--Palestinian Rights: Affirmation & Denial. 225p. 1982. 17.95 (ISBN 0-914456-22-9); pap. 7.95 (ISBN 0-914456-23-7). Medina Pr.

Abu-Lughod, Ibrahim & Abu-Laban, Baha, eds. Settler Regimes in Africa & the Arab World: The Illusion of Endurance. (Monograph: No. 4). 251p. 1974. 10.95 (ISBN 0-914456-06-7); pap. text ed. 6.95 (ISBN 0-914456-07-5). Assn Arab-Amer U Grads.

Abu-Lughod, Ibrahim A. Arab Rediscovery of Europe: A Study in Cultural Encounters. LC 62-21102. (Princeton Studies on the Near East). pap. 49.80 (ISBN 0-317-09885-3, 2000599). Bks Demand UMI.

Abu-Lughod, Janet. Cairo: One Thousand-One Years of the City Victorious. LC 73-112992. (Princeton Studies on the Near East). (Illus.). 1971. 55.00x (ISBN 0-691-03085-5). Princeton U Pr.

Abu-Lughod, Janet & Hay, Richard, Jr., eds. Third World Urbanization. 1980. pap. 9.95x (ISBN 0-416-60141-3, NO. 2866). Methuen Inc.

Abu-Lughod, Janet L. Rabat: Urban Apartheid in Morocco. LC 80-7508. (Princeton Studies on the Near East). (Illus.). 400p. 1981. 42.50 (ISBN 0-691-05315-4); pap. 16.00x (ISBN 0-691-10098-5). Princeton U Pr.

AbuNabaa, Abdel A. Marketing in Saudi Arabia. LC 83-17819. 240p. 1984. 29.95 (ISBN 0-03-069354-3). Praeger.

Abun-Nasr, J. M. A History of the Maghrib. 2nd ed. LC 74-25653. (Illus.). 432p. 1975. 54.50 (ISBN 0-521-20703-7); pap. 22.95 (ISBN 0-521-09927-7). Cambridge U Pr.

Abun-Nasr, Jamil M. A History of the Maghrib. 2nd ed. LC 74-25653. pap. 108.00 (ISBN 0-317-26070-7, 2024410). Bks Demand UMI.

Aburdene, Patricia, jt. auth. see Naisbitt, John.

Abu-Salih, M. & Awad, A. Introduction to Statistics. 344p. (Arabic.). 1983. pap. 15.00 (ISBN 0-471-87221-0). Wiley.

Abu-Saud, Mahmoud. Concept of Islam. Quinlan, Hamid, ed. LC 83-70184. 147p. 1983. pap. 5.00 (ISBN 0-89259-043-2). Am Trust Pubns.

Abu-Shumays, I. K., et al, eds. see Society for Industrial & Applied Mathematics-American Mathematical Society Symposia, New York, April, 1967.

Abu-Sumayah, Taysir. Arabic Language for Beginners. LC 87-8437. 1977. pap. 8.00 (ISBN 0-686-24781-7). Mid East Pub Co.

Abu'Umar, Muhammad Ibn Yusuf see Muhammad Ibn Yusuf, Abu'Umar.

Abu 'Uthman 'Amr Ibn Bahr Al-Jahiz. The Book of the Glory of the Black Race. Preston, William, ed. Cornell, Vincent J., tr. from Arabic. (Illus.). 92p. (Orig.). 1981. pap. 6.95x (ISBN 0-939222-00-0). Maga Dubh.

Aby, Carroll D. & Vaughn, Donald E., Jr. Financial Management Classics. LC 79-10710. (Illus.). 1979. pap. text ed. 19.50 (ISBN 0-673-16168-4). Scott F.

Aby, Carroll D. & Vaughn, Donald E., Jr., eds. Investment Classics. LC 78-27774. 1979. pap. text ed. 19.50 (ISBN 0-673-16174-9). Scott F.

Abzug, Bella & Kelber, Mim. Gender Gap Nineteen Eighty-Four: How Women Will Decide the Next Election. 256p. 1984. pap. 6.95 (ISBN 0-395-35484-6). HM.

Abzug, Robert H. Inside the Vicious Heart: Americans & the Liberation of Nazi Concentration Camps. LC 84-27252. (Illus.). 1985. 16.95 (ISBN 0-19-503597-6). Oxford U Pr.

--Passionate Liberator: Theodore Dwight Weld & the Dilemma of Reform. LC 80-11819. (Illus.). 1980. 27.50x (ISBN 0-19-502771-X). Oxford U Pr.

--Passionate Liberator: Theodore Dwight Weld & the Dilemma of Reform. 1980. pap. 8.95 (ISBN 0-19-503061-3, GB 683, GB). Oxford U Pr.

Academia Litterarum Borussicae, ed. Inscriptiones Graecae, 15 Vols. in 23 Pts. (Lat). 1873-1939. write for info. (ISBN 0-685-02032-0). De Gruyter.

Academic Committee on Soviet Jewry & the Anti-Defamation League. Perspectives on Soviet Jewry. 150p. pap. 2.50 (ISBN 0-686-95144-1). ADL.

Academic Computing Services, University of Kansas. Learning Z-BASIC on the Heath-Zenith Z-100. (Illus.). 304p. 1985. pap. 17.95 (ISBN 0-89303-621-8). Brady Comm.

Academie de Droit International. Receuil des Cours 1980. (No. IV). 380p. 1984. 50.00 (ISBN 90-247-2976-9, Pub. by Martinus Nijhoff Netherlands). Kluwer Academic.

Academy for Educational Development. Energy Conservation Idea Handbook. 1981. 17.00 (ISBN 0-02-900950-2). ACE.

Academy for Scientific Interrogation. Academy Lectures on Lie Detection, Vol. I. 112p. 1957. 13.75x (ISBN 0-398-00005-0). C C Thomas.

--Academy Lectures on Lie Detection, Vol. II. 168p. 1958. 19.75x (ISBN 0-398-04182-2). C C Thomas.

Academy Forum. Coal As an Energy Resource: Conflict & Consensus. 1977. pap. 12.50 (ISBN 0-309-02728-4). Natl Acad Pr.

--Research with Recombinant DNA. 1977. pap. text ed. 9.95 (ISBN 0-309-02641-5). Natl Acad Pr.

Academy Forum National Academy of Sciences. Energy: Future Alternatives & Risks. LC 74-13084. 202p. 1974. prof ref 18.50x (ISBN 0-88410-025-1). Ballinger Pub.

Academy Forum, National Academy of Science. Experiments & Research with Humans: Values in Conflicts. LC 75-13985. (Illus.). 224p. 1975. pap. 8.50 (ISBN 0-309-02347-5). Natl Acad Pr.

Academy Forum, National Academy of Sciences. Sweeteners: Issues & Uncertainties. LC 75-29990. vi, 259p. 1975. pap. 9.50 (ISBN 0-309-02407-2). Natl Acad Pr.

Academy of Criminal Justice Sciences Staff, jt. auth. see Hochstedler, Ellen.

Academy of Criminal Justice Sciences Staff & Decker, Scott H. Juvenile Justice Policy: Analyzing Trends & Outcomes. LC 83-21187. (Perspectives in Criminal Justice Ser.: No. 7). 1984. 20.00 (ISBN 0-8039-2197-7); pap. 9.95 (ISBN 0-8039-2198-5). Sage.

Academy of Engineering. Technology, Trade & the U. S. Economy. 1978. pap. 9.75 (ISBN 0-309-02761-6). Natl Acad Pr.

Academy of Leisure Sciences. Values & Leisure & Trends in Leisure Services. (New Directions in Leisure Ser.). 128p. (Orig.). 1983. pap. 9.95x (ISBN 0-910251-05-3). Venture PA.

Academy of Letters & Arts in America, ed. see Theriault, Harry.

Academy of Letters and Arts in America, ed. see Theriault, Harry.

Academy of Management, Annual Meeting, 39th, 1979. Proceedings. Huseman, Richard C., ed. LC 40-2886. (Illus.). 1979. pap. text ed. 11.00 (ISBN 0-915350-18-1). Acad of Mgmt.

Academy of Management, 40th Annual Meeting, 1980. Proceedings. Huseman, Richard C., ed. LC 40-2886. 436p. (Orig.). 1980. pap. text ed. 11.00 (ISBN 0-915350-19-X). Acad of Mgmt.

Academy of Motion Picture Arts & Sciences. Annual Index to Motion Picture Credits, 1979. Ramsay, Verna, ed. LC 79-644761. 430p. 1980. lib. bdg. 150.00 (ISBN 0-313-20951-0, AN79). Greenwood.

--Annual Index to Motion Picture Credits, 1978. Ramsey, Verna, ed. LC 79-644761. 1979. lib. bdg. 150.00 (ISBN 0-313-20950-2, AN78). Greenwood.

Academy of Motion Picture Arts & Science. Annual Index to Motion Picture Credits, 1981. LC 79-644761. 469p. 1982. lib. bdg. 150.00 (ISBN 0-686-82498-9, AN81). Greenwood.

Academy of Motion Picture Arts & Sciences. Annual Index to Motion Picture Credits, 1982. LC 79-644761. (Annual Index to Motion Picture Credits Ser.). 447p. 1983. lib. bdg. 150.00 (ISBN 0-313-24263-1, AN82). Greenwood.

Academy of Motion Pictures Arts & Sciences. Annual Index to Motion Picture Credits, 1980. LC 79-644761. 450p. 1981. lib. bdg. 150.00 (ISBN 0-313-20952-9, AN80). Greenwood.

Academy of Natural Sciences of Philadelphia. Catalog of the Library of the Academy of Natural Sciences of Philadelphia, 16 vols. 1972. Set. lib. bdg. 1595.00 (ISBN 0-8161-0946-X, Hall Library). G K Hall.

Academy of Political Science. Municipal Income Taxes: Proceedings, Vol. 28, No. 4. Connery, R. H., ed. 1968. 9.50 (ISBN 0-8446-1887-X). Peter Smith.

--The Soviet Union Since Khrushchev: New Trends & Old Problems. LC 65-23730. Repr. of 1965 ed. 16.00 (ISBN 0-527-00301-8). Kraus Repr.

Academy of Rajeeshism Staff, ed. see Rajneesh, Bhagwan S.

Academy of Rajneeshism, ed. Rajneeshism: An Introduction to Bhagwan Shree Rajneesh & His Religion. rev. 2nd ed. LC 83-62845. (Academy Ser.). (Illus.). 72p. 1983. pap. 3.00 (ISBN 0-88050-700-4). Rajneesh Found Intl.

Academy of Rajneeshism, ed. see Bhagwan Shree Rajneesh.

Academy of Rajneeshism Staff, ed. see Rajneesh, Bhagwan S.

Academy of Religion & Mental Health. Psychologial Testing for Ministerial Selection: Proceedings of the Seventh Academy Symposium. xiv, 271p. 1970. 25.00 (ISBN 0-8232-0850-8). Fordham.

--Psychological Testing for Ministerial Selection: Proceedings of the Seventh Academy Symposium. Bier, W. C., ed. LC 73-79568. 1970. 25.00 (ISBN 0-8232-0850-8). Fordham.

Academy of Sciences of the GDR, Berlin. Kants Gesammelte Schriften. 1983. Vols. 1-29, in 33 pts. pap. write for info. De Gruyter.

Academy of Television Arts & Sciences, compiled by. ATAS-UCLA Television Archives Catalog. 197p. (Orig.). 1982. pap. 18.70 (ISBN 0-913178-69-1). Redgrave Pub Co.

Academy of Traditional Chinese Medicine, Shanghai. Essentials of Chinese Acupuncture. (Illus.). 446p. 1981. 79.00 (ISBN 0-08-027995-3). Pergamon.

Academy of Traditional Chinese Medicine. An Outline of Chinese Acupuncture. 33.00 (ISBN 0-08-021545-9). Pergamon.

Academy of Traditional Chinese Medicine, Peking Staff. An Outline of Chinese Acupuncture. 305p. 17.50 (ISBN 0-317-31550-1). Chans Corp.

Academy of Rajneeshism, ed. see Rajneesh, Bhagwan Shree.

Acar, J., et al. Cardiopathies Valvulaires Acquises. (Illus.). 656p. (Fr.). 1985. 130.00 (ISBN 2-257-10441-2). S M P F Inc.

Acarnley, P. P. Stepping Motors: A Guide to Modern Theory & Practice. (IEE Control Engineering Ser.: No. 19). 160p. 1982. 48.00 (ISBN 0-906048-83-4, CEH19); pap. 29.00 (ISBN 0-906048-75-3, CEP19). Inst Elect Eng.

A. C. Bhaktivedanta Prabhupada. Sri Namamrta: The Holy Nectar of the Holy Name. (Illus.). 586p. 1982. pap. 12.95 (ISBN 0-89213-113-6). Bhaktivedanta.

Accademia Del Cimento. Essays of Natural Experiments Made in the Academie Del Cimento. Waller, R., tr. (Illus.). Repr. of 1684 ed. 18.00 (ISBN 0-384-00260-9). Johnson Repr.

Accame, Silvio. Il Dominio Romano in Grecia Dalla Guerra Acaica Ad Augusto. LC 75-7302. (Roman History Ser.). (Italian.). 1975. Repr. of 1946 ed. 19.00x (ISBN 0-405-07179-5). Ayer Co Pubs.

Accardi, L. & Frigerio, A., eds. Quantum Probability & Applications to the Quantum Theory of Irreversible Processes: Proceedings of the International Workshop Held at Villa Mondragone, Italy, Sept. 6-11, 1982. (Lecture Notes in Mathematics Ser.: Vol. 1055). vi, 411p. 1984. 21.50 (ISBN 0-387-12915-4). Springer-Verlag.

Accardo. Pediatrician & the Developmentally Delayed Child. (Illus.). 256p. 1978. text ed. 21.00 (ISBN 0-8391-1331-5). Univ Park.

Accardo, Pasquale J. Failure to Thrive in Infancy & Early Childhood: A Multidisciplinary Team Approach. (Illus.). 432p. 1981. text ed. 32.00 (ISBN 0-8391-1678-0). Univ Park.

Accenti, Umberto. Follia Plastica. (Illus.). 152p. 1985. text ed. 39.50 (ISBN 0-87663-882-5). Universe.

Acciardo, Marcia. Light Eating for Survival. (Illus.). 106p. (Orig.). 1978. pap. text ed. 5.95 (ISBN 0-933278-05-5). Twen Fir Cent.

Accola, R. D. Riemann Surfaces, Theta Functions, & Abelian Automorphisms Groups. LC 75-25928. (Lecture Notes in Mathematics: Vol. 483). iii, 105p. 1975. pap. text ed. 13.00 (ISBN 0-387-07398-1). Springer-Verlag.

Accolti, Pietro. Perspective for Artists. (Printed Sources of Western Arts Ser.). (Illus.). 168p. (Italian.). 1981. pap. 35.00 slipcase (ISBN 0-915346-60-5). A Wofsy Fine Arts.

Accone, Frank D., jt. ed. see Grout, Donald J.

Accounting Symposium, Ohio State Univ, 1968. Behavioral Aspects of Accounting Data for Performance Evaluation. Burns, Thomas J., ed. (Illus., Orig.). 1969. pap. 8.50x (ISBN 0-87776-304-6, AA4). Ohio St U Admin Sci.

Accounting Symposium, Ohio State Univ., 1972. Behavioral Experiments in Accounting: Papers, Critiques, Discussion, & Commentary. Burns, Thomas J., ed. (Illus.). 533p. 1972. pap. 8.50x (ISBN 0-87776-307-0, AA7). Ohio St U Admin Sci.

Ace, Juliet. Speak No Evil. 28p. pap. 1.95 (ISBN 0-86212-001-2). Falling Wall.

Ace, Stroker. Stand On It. 304p. 1983. pap. 2.95 (ISBN 0-380-63669-7, 63669-7). Avon.

Acebedo, Medara. How to Make Your Own Basic Patterns. (Illus.). 64p. 1982. 8.95 (ISBN 0-89962-245-3). Todd & Honeywell.

Acena, Albert. Washington Commonwealth Federation: Reform Politics & the Popular Front, 1935-1945. Burke, Robert F. & Freidel, F., eds. (Modern American History Ser.). 53.00 (ISBN 0-8240-5650-7). Garland Pub.

Acerrano, Anthony J. The Outdoorman's Emergency Manual. (Illus.). 352p. pap. 9.95 (ISBN 0-88317-036-1). Stoeger Pub Co.

--The Practical Hunter's Handbook. LC 83-60291. (Illus.). 1981. 11.95 (ISBN 0-8329-3427-5, Pub. by Winchester Pr). New Century.

Acers, Thomas E. Congenital Abnormalities of the Optic Nerve & Related Forebrain. LC 82-24962. (Illus.). 75p. 1983. 14.50. (ISBN 0-8121-0889-2). Lea & Febiger.

Acevedo, Eloy. The Answer to the Riddle of the Universe. 1982. 8.95 (ISBN 0-533-05343-9). Vantage.

Acevedo, Ramon L. Augusto D'halmar: Novelista (Estudio De Pasion y Muerte Del Cura Deusto) LC 76-8011. (Coleccion Mente y Palabra). 204p. (Orig., Span.). 1976. 6.25 (ISBN 0-8477-0530-7); pap. 5.00 (ISBN 0-8477-0531-5). U of PR Pr.

--La Novela Centroamericana: Desde el Popol-vuh Hasta los Umbrales de la Novela Actual. LC 81-10316. (Coleccion Mente y Palabra). 908p. 1981. 18.00 (ISBN 0-8477-0584-6); pap. 15.00 (ISBN 0-8477-0585-4). U of PR Pr.

Aceves, Joseph. Social Change in a Spanish Village. (Illus.). 144p. 1971. pap. 9.95 (ISBN 0-87073-755-4). Schenkman Bks Inc.

Aceves, Joseph & Douglass, William A. The Changing Faces of Rural Spain. 256p. 1976. 16.95 (ISBN 0-87073-011-8); pap. 11.95x (ISBN 0-87073-012-6). Schenkman Bks Inc.

Aceves, Joseph B. Cultural Anthropology. LC 77-14696. 1978. pap. text ed. 16.00 (ISBN 0-394-33353-5, RanC); wkbk. o.p. 5.95 (ISBN 0-394-33357-8). Random.

Aceves, Joseph B. & King, H. Gill. Introduction to Anthropology. LC 79-66304. 1979. text ed. 20.00 (ISBN 0-394-33288-1, RanC). Random.

Acha, Eduardo de see De Acha, Eduardo.

Acha, Eduardo De see De Acha, Eduardo.

Acha, Eduardo de see De Acha, Eduardo.

Achad, Frater. Ancient Mystical White Brotherhood. pap. 5.50 (ISBN 0-87707-068-7). De Vorss.

--Crystal Vision Through Crystal Gazing. (Illus.). 116p. 1976. Repr. of 1923 ed. 6.95 (ISBN 0-911662-60-X). Yoga.

--Melchizedek Truth Principles. pap. 5.50 (ISBN 0-87516-166-9). De Vorss.

--Parzival: The Chalice of Ecstasy. 82p. 1976. Repr. of 1923 ed. 6.95 (ISBN 0-911662-59-6). Yoga.

Achar, D. G. & Ruge, J. Joining of Aluminium to Steel with Particular Reference to Welding. (Monograph). 1981. 30.00 (ISBN 0-9960034-7-9, Pub. by Aluminium W Germany). Heyden.

Achar, S. T. Pediatrics in Developing Tropical Countries. 688p. 1979. 50.00x (ISBN 0-86125-186-5, Pub. by Orient Longman India). State Mutual Bk.

Acharius, E. Lichenographia Universalia. (Illus., Latin.). 1976. Repr. of 1810 ed. 104.95x (ISBN 0-916422-30-5, Pub. by Richmond Pub Co). Mad River.

--Synopsis Medica Lichenum. (Illus.). 424p. (Latin.). 1977. Repr. of 1814 ed. 89.95x (ISBN 0-916422-29-1, Pub. by Richmond Pub Co). Mad River.

Acharya, K. R., et al. Pre-University Chemistry, Vol. 1. 2nd & rev. ed. 267p. 1985. 15.95x (ISBN 0-7069-2665-X, Pub. by Vikas India). Advent NY.

Acharya, P. K. An Encyclopaedia of Hindu Architecture. 1979. Repr. 56.00x (ISBN 0-8364-0373-8). South Asia Bks.

Acharya, Pundit. Breath, Sleep, the Heart, & Life: The Revolutionary Health Yoga of Pundit Acharya. LC 74-24306. 300p. 1975. pap. 7.95 (ISBN 0-913922-09-9). Dawn Horse Pr.

Acharya, R. M. Sheep & Goat Breeds of India. (Animal Production & Health Papers: No. 30). 197p. 1982. pap. 14.50 (ISBN 92-5-101212-1, F2340, FAO). Unipub.

Acharya, Shankar N. Incentives for Resource Allocation: A Case Study of Sudan. (Working Paper: No. 367). iii, 113p. 1979. 5.00 (ISBN 0-686-36088-5, WP-367). World Bank.

Achebe, Chinua. Arrow of God. LC 75-79409. (Anchor Literary Library). 1969. pap. 4.95 (ISBN 0-385-01480-5, Anch). Doubleday.

--Beware Soul Brother. (African Writers Ser.). 1972. pap. text ed. 5.50x (ISBN 0-435-90120-6). Heinemann Ed.

--Chike & the River. 1966. text ed. 2.95x (ISBN 0-521-04003-5). Cambridge U Pr.

--A Man of the People. LC 66-22929. pap. 3.50 (ISBN 0-385-08616-4, Anch). Doubleday.

--No Longer at Ease. 1961. 11.95 (ISBN 0-8392-1077-9); pap. 6.95 (ISBN 0-8392-5008-8). Astor-Honor.

--No Longer at Ease. 1977. pap. 2.25 (ISBN 0-449-30847-2, Prem). Fawcett.

--No Longer at Ease. (African Writers Ser.). 1981. pap. text ed. 4.00x (ISBN 0-435-90003-X). Heinemann Ed.

--Things Fall Apart. LC 59-7114. 1959. 11.95 (ISBN 0-8392-1113-9); pap. 6.95 (ISBN 0-8392-5006-1). Astor-Honor.

--Things Fall Apart. 1978. pap. 2.50 (ISBN 0-449-24142-4, Crest). Fawcett.

--Things Fall Apart. (African Writers Ser.). pap. 3.00x (ISBN 0-435-90001-3). Heinemann Ed.

--The Trouble with Nigeria. x, 68p. 1984. pap. text ed. 4.00 (ISBN 0-435-90698-4). Heinemann Ed.

Achebe, Chinua & Iroaganachi, John. How the Leopard Got His Claws. LC 72-93382. (Illus.). 32p. (gr. 6 up). 1973. 5.95 (ISBN 0-89388-056-6). Okpaku Communications.

Achebe, Chinua & Innes, C. L., eds. African Short Stories. (African Writers Ser.: No. 270). 159p. (Orig.). 1985. pap. text ed. 5.00x (ISBN 0-435-90270-9). Heinemann Ed.

Acheley, Thomas. A Most Lamentable & Tragicall Historie, Conteyning the Tyrannie Which Violenta Executed Upon Her Lover Didaco. LC 77-6840. (English Experience Ser: No. 836). 1977. Repr. of 1576 ed. lib. bdg. 8.00 (ISBN 90-221-0836-8). Walter J Johnson.

Achelis, Elisabeth. World Calendar: Addresses & Occasional Papers Chronologically Arranged on the Progress of Calendar Reform Since 1930. LC 73-102214. Repr. of 1937 ed. 40.00x (ISBN 0-8103-3784-3). Gale.

Achen, Christopher H. Interpreting & Using Regression. LC 82-42675. (Quantitative Applications in the Social Sciences Ser.: No. 29). 88p. 1982. pap. 5.00 (ISBN 0-8039-1915-8). Sage.

Achen, Sven T. Symbols Around Us. 240p. 1981. pap. 9.95 (ISBN 0-442-28261-3). Van Nos Reinhold.

Achenbach, J. D. A Theory of Elasticity with Microstructure for Directionally Reinforced Composites. (International Centre for Mechanical Sciences Courses & Lectures: No. 167). (Illus.). 1976. pap. 24.00 (ISBN 0-387-81234-2). Springer-Verlag.

--Wave Propagation in Elastic Solids. (Applied Mathematics & Mechanics Ser.: Vol. 16). 400p. 1973-75. 85.00 (ISBN 0-444-10465-8, North-Holland); pap. 36.25 (ISBN 0-444-10840-8). Elsevier.

Achenbach, J. D. & Gausten, A. K. Ray Methods for Waves in Elastic Solids. (Monographs & Studies: No. 14). 300p. 1982. pap. text ed. 54.50 (ISBN 0-273-08453-4). Pitman Pub MA.

Achenbach, Thomas M. Developmental Psychopathology. 2nd ed. LC 82-2838. 770p. 1982. text ed. 35.50 (ISBN 0-471-05536-0, Pub by Wiley). Wiley.

--Research in Developmental Psychology: Concepts, Strategies, Methods. LC 77-81429. (Illus.). 1978. text ed. 24.95 (ISBN 0-02-900180-3). Free Pr.

Achenbach, Thomas M. & Edelbrock, Craig. Manual for the Child Behavior Checklist & Revised Child Behavior Profile. LC 83-50450. (Illus.). 230p. (Orig.). 1983. pap. 19.80 (ISBN 0-9611898-0-0). U of VT Psych.

Achenbaum, W. Andrew. Old Age in the New Land: The American Experience Since Seventeen Ninety. LC 77-28666. 1979. 25.00x (ISBN 0-8018-2107-X); pap. 8.95x (ISBN 0-8018-2355-2). Johns Hopkins.

--Shades of Gray: Old Age, American Values, & Federal Policies since 1920. 1982. text ed. 14.95 (ISBN 0-316-00652-1); pap. text ed. 8.95 (ISBN 0-316-00654-8). Little.

Achenbaum, W. Andrew, jt. ed. see Trattner, Walter I.

Acheson, Arthur. Mistress Davenant. (Works of Arthur Acheson Ser.). v, 332p. Date not set. Repr. of 1913 ed. 39.00 (ISBN 0-932051-54-5). Am Repr Serv.

--Shakespeare & the Rival Poet. LC 79-113535. 1903. 12.50 (ISBN 0-404-00277-3). AMS Pr.

--Shakespeare & the Rival Poet. 1973. Repr. of 1903 ed. 12.25 (ISBN 0-8274-1599-0). R West.

--Shakespeare, Chapman & Sir Thomas More. LC 72-113536. Repr. of 1931 ed. 23.00 (ISBN 0-404-00278-1). AMS Pr.

--Shakespeare's Lost Years in London. LC 79-152552. (Studies in Shakespeare, No. 24). 1971. Repr. lib. bdg. 51.95x (ISBN 0-8383-1235-7). Haskell.

--Shakespeare's Sonnet Story: 1592-1598. LC 72-164658. (Studies in Shakespeare, No. 24). 1971. Repr. of 1922 ed. lib. bdg. 69.95x (ISBN 0-8383-1322-1). Haskell.

Acheson, Cornell W. Assignment Trouble: Foreign Correspondent at Large. LC 83-59836. 351p. 1984. 12.95 (ISBN 0-533-05983-6). Vantage.

Acheson, Dean. A Citizen Looks at Congress. LC 74-11311. 124p. 1974. Repr. of 1957 ed. lib. bdg. 22.50 (ISBN 0-8371-7221-7, ACCL). Greenwood.

--A Democrat Looks at His Party. LC 76-48254. 1977. Repr. of 1955 ed. lib. bdg. 15.00x (ISBN 0-8371-9332-X, ACDL). Greenwood.

--Korean War. 1971. pap. text ed. 2.95x (ISBN 0-393-09978-4). Norton.

--Pattern of Responsibility. Bundy, McGeorge, ed. LC 75-128070. Repr. of 1952 ed. 27.50x (ISBN 0-678-03560-1). Kelley.

--Sketches from Life of Men I Have Known. LC 73-15165. (Illus.). 206p. 1974. Repr. of 1961 ed. lib. bdg. 15.00 (ISBN 0-8371-7172-5, ACSL). Greenwood.

Acheson, E. D., ed. see Gardner, M. J. & Winter, P. D.

Acheson, E. J., jt. auth. see Hutchinson, E. C.

Acheson, Edna L. The Construction of Junior Church School Curricula. LC 73-176503. Repr. of 1929 ed. 22.50 (ISBN 0-404-55331-1). AMS Pr.

Acheson, G. H. see International Congress on Pharmacology, 5th, San Francisco, 1972.

Acheson, Keith & Gall, Meredith. Techniques in the Clinical Supervision of Teachers. 1980. pap. text ed. 14.95x (ISBN 0-582-28121-0). Longman.

Acheson, Patricia C. Our Federal Government: How it Works: An Introduction to the United States Government. rev. ed. 307p. 1984. pap. 11.95 (ISBN 0-396-08312-9). Dodd.

Acheson, R. M. An Introduction to the Chemistry of Heterocyclic Compounds. 3rd ed. LC 76-21319. 501p. 1976. 57.50 (ISBN 0-471-00268-2, Pub. by Wiley-Interscience). Wiley.

Acheson, R. M., jt. ed. see Weissberger, Arnold.

Acheson, Sam. Dallas Yesterday. Milazzo, Lee, ed. LC 77-7326. (Bicentennial Series in American Studies: No. 6). 1977. 16.95 (ISBN 0-87074-160-8). SMU Press.

Acheson, Sam & O'Connell, Julie, eds. George Washington Diamond's Account of the Great Hanging at Gainesville, 1862. 1963. pap. 3.50 (ISBN 0-87611-001-4). Tex St Hist Assn.

Acheson, Sam H. Joe Bailey, the Last Democrat. facs. ed. LC 79-124222. (Select Bibliographies Reprint Ser). 1932. 22.00 (ISBN 0-8369-5199-9). Ayer Co Pubs.

--Thirty-Five Thousand Days in Texas: A History of the Dallas News & Its Forbears. LC 72-136510. (Illus.). xi, 337p. Repr. of 1938 ed. lib. bdg. 22.50x (ISBN 0-8371-5428-6, ACTD). Greenwood.

Achesone, James. The Military Garden: Instructions for All Young Souldiers. LC 74-80157. (English Experience Ser.: No. 637). 36p. 1974. Repr. of 1629 ed. 5.00 (ISBN 90-221-0637-3). Walter J Johnson.

Achilles, Paul S., ed. Psychology at Work. facsimile ed. LC 74-156602. (Essay Index Reprint Ser). Repr. of 1932 ed. 18.00 (ISBN 0-8369-2262-X). Ayer Co Pubs.

Achilles, Tatius. The Most Delectable & Pleasant History of Clitiphon & Leucippe. Burton, W., tr. LC 77-6841. (English Experience Ser.: No. 837). Repr. of 1597 ed. lib. bdg. 15.00 (ISBN 90-221-0837-6). Walter J Johnson.

Achilles Tatius. Clitophon & Leucippe. (Loeb Classical Library: No. 45). 12.50x (ISBN 0-674-99050-1). Harvard U Pr.

Achilli, Michele & Khaldi, Mohamed, eds. The Role of Arab Development Funds in the World Economy. LC 84-15907. 320p. 1984. 32.50 (ISBN 0-312-68921-7). St Martin.

Achinstein. Concept of Evidence. 1983. 7.95x (ISBN 0-317-06321-9). Oxford U Pr.

Achinstein, Asher. Buying Power of Labor & Post-War Cycles. LC 68-57563. (Columbia University Studies in the Social Sciences: No. 292). Repr. of 1927 ed. 16.50 (ISBN 0-404-51292-5). AMS Pr.

Achinstein, Peter. The Concept of Evidence. (ORP Ser.). 192p. (Orig.). 1983. pap. 7.95 (ISBN 0-19-875062-5). Oxford U Pr.

--Concepts of Science: A Philosophical Analysis. LC 68-15451. 279p. 1968. pap. 8.95x (ISBN 0-8018-1273-9). Johns Hopkins.

--The Nature of Explanation. (Illus.). 1983. 29.95x (ISBN 0-19-503215-2). Oxford U Pr.

Achinstein, Peter & Barker, Stephen F., eds. The Legacy of Logical Positivism in the Philosophy of Science. LC 69-15396. pap. 20.00 (ISBN 0-317-08931-5, 2006285). Bks Demand UMI.

Achinstein, Peter & Hannaway, Owen, eds. Observation, Experiment, & Hypothesis in Modern Physical Science. 1985. 37.50 (ISBN 0-262-01083-6). MIT Pr.

Achogar, Hugo. Mariposas Tropicales. 80p. (Span.). 1985. pap. 8.50 (ISBN 0-910061-30-0). Ediciones Norte.

Achon, M. A., jt. auth. see Wittfoht, A.

Achong, B. G., jt. ed. see Epstein, M. A.

Achor, Shirley. Mexican Americans in a Dallas Barrio. LC 77-22434. 202p. 1978. pap. 8.95x (ISBN 0-8165-0533-0). U of Ariz Pr.

Achte, K. A., et al. Alcoholic Psychoses in Finland. (The Finnish Foundation for Alcohol Studies: Vol. 19). 1969. 4.00x (ISBN 951-9192-08-5). Rutgers Ctr Alcohol.

Achtemeier, Elizabeth. The Committed Marriage. LC 76-7611. (Biblical Perspectives on Current Issues Ser.). 224p. 1976. pap. 8.95 (ISBN 0-664-24754-7). Westminster.

--The Community & Message of Isaiah Fifty Six-Sixty Six: A Theological Commentary. LC 81-52284. 160p. (Orig.). 1982. pap. 8.95 (ISBN 0-8066-1916-3, 10-1610). Augsburg.

--Creative Preaching: Finding the Words. LC 80-16890. (Abingdon Preacher's Library). 128p. (Orig.). 1980. pap. 5.95 (ISBN 0-687-09831-9). Abingdon.

--Deuteronomy, Jeremiah. McCurley, Foster R., ed. LC 77-15226. (Proclamation Commentaries: the Old Testament Witnesses for Preaching Ser.). 96p. (Orig.). 1978. pap. 3.95 (ISBN 0-8006-0590-X, 1-590). Fortress.

--The Old Testament & the Proclamation of the Gospel. LC 73-7863. 224p. 1980. pap. write for info. (ISBN 0-664-24287-1). Westminster.

--Preaching As Theology & Art. 144p. 1984. pap. 8.75 (ISBN 0-687-33828-X). Abingdon.

Achtemeier, Elizabeth, jt. auth. see Achtemeier, Paul J.

Achtemeier, Elizabeth, ed. see Carlston, Charles.

Achtemeier, Elizabeth, ed. see Clifford, Richard J. & Rockwell, Hays H.

Achtemeier, Elizabeth, ed. see Fiorenza, Elisabeth S. & Holmes, Urban T.

Achtemeier, Elizabeth, ed. see Fuller, Reginald H.

Achtemeier, Elizabeth, ed. see Perkins, Pheme.

Achtemeier, Elizabeth, et al, eds. see Achtemeier, Paul J. & Mebust, J. Leland.

Achtemeier, Elizabeth, et al, eds. see Borsch, Frederick H. & Napier, Davie.

Achtemeier, Elizabeth, et al, eds. see Burgess, Joseph A. & Winn, Albert C.

Achtemeier, Elizabeth, et al, eds. see Edwards, O. C., Jr. & Taylor, Gardner C.

Achtemeier, Elizabeth, et al, eds. see Fuller, Reginald H.

Achtemeier, Elizabeth, et al, eds. see Furnish, Victor P. & Thulin, Richard L.

Achtemeier, Elizabeth, et al, eds. see Harrisville, Roy A. & Hackett, Charles D.

Achtemeier, Elizabeth, et al, eds. see Jeske, Richard L. & Barr, Browne.

Achtemeier, Elizabeth, et al, eds. see Juel, Donald H. & Buttrick, David.

Achtemeier, Elizabeth, et al, eds. see Kee, Howard C. & Gomes, Peter J.

Achtemeier, Elizabeth, et al, eds. see Kingsbury, Jack D. & Pennington, Chester.

Achtemeier, Elizabeth, et al, eds. see Krentz, Edgar & Vogel, Arthur A.

Achtemeier, Elizabeth, et al, eds. see Micks, Marianne H. & Ridenhour, Thomas E.

Achtemeier, Elizabeth, et al, eds. see Minear, Paul S. & Adams, Harry B.

Achtemeier, Elizabeth, et al, eds. see Nieting, Lorenz.

Achtemeier, Elizabeth, et al, eds. see Pervo, Richard I. & Carl, William J., III.

Achtemeier, Elizabeth, et al, eds. see Reid, Richard & Crum, Milton, Jr.

Achtemeier, Elizabeth, et al, eds. see Saunders, Ernest W. & Craddock, Fred B.
Achtemeier, Elizabeth, et al, eds. see Thulin, Richard L.
Achtemeier, Elizabeth, et al, eds. see Tiede, David L. & Kavanagh, Aidan.
Achtemeier, Elizabeth, et al, eds. see Trotti, John B.
Achtemeier, Paul J. The Inspiration of Scripture: Problems & Proposals. LC 80-10286. (Biblical Perspectives on Current Issues). 188p. 1980. pap. 8.95 (ISBN 0-664-24313-4). Westminster.
--Invitation to Mark: A Commentary on the Gospel of Mark with Complete Text from the Jerusalem Bible. LC 77-91555. 1978. pap. 3.95 (ISBN 0-385-12213-6, Im). Doubleday.
--Mark. Krodel, Gerhard, ed. LC 74-26333. (Proclamation Commentaries: The New Testament Witnesses for Preaching Ser.). 128p. 1975. pap. 4.50 (ISBN 0-8006-0581-0, 1-581). Fortress.
--Romans: Interpretation: A Bible Commentary for Teaching & Preaching. Mays, James L., ed. LC 84-47796. 240p. 1985. 17.95 (ISBN 0-8042-3137-0). John Knox.
--Society of Biblical Literature: Seminar Papers Nineteen Eighty. (SBL Seminar Papers & Abstracts). pap. 9.00 (ISBN 0-89130-357-X, 06-09-19). Scholars Pr GA.
Achtemeier, Paul J. & Achtemeier, Elizabeth. The Old Testament Roots of Our Faith. LC 78-14659. 160p. 1979. pap. 5.95 (ISBN 0-8006-1348-1, 1-1348). Fortress.
Achtemeier, Paul J. & Mebust, J. Leland. Advent-Christmas. Achtemeier, Elizabeth, et al, eds. LC 79-7377. (Proclamation 2: Aids for Interpreting the Lessons of the Church Year, Ser. B). 64p. (Orig.). 1981. pap. 3.50 (ISBN 0-8006-4060-8, 1-4060). Fortress.
Achtemeier, Paul J. & Society of Biblical Literature, eds. Harper's Bible Dictionary. LC 85-42767. (Illus.). 1088p. 1985. 29.95 (ISBN 0-06-069862-4, HarpR). Har-Row.
Achtemeier, Paul J., ed. see Williamson, Lamar, Jr.
Achtemeier, Paul J., tr. see Marxsen, Willi.
Achtenberg, Anya. I Know What the Small Girl Knew. LC 82-81350. 80p. 1983. pap. 4.50 (ISBN 0-930100-11-5). Holy Cow.
Achtenberg, Joel, ed. Standard MUMPS: Pocket Guide. 1983. pap. 2.50 (ISBN 0-918118-26-3). MUMPS.
Achtenberg, Roberta, jt. auth. see National Lawyers Guild, San Francisco Bay Area Chapter, Anti-Sexism Committee.
Achterberg, E. & Lanz, K. Enzyklopadisches Lexikon Fur des Geld, Bank und Borsen Wesen, 2 vols. (Ger.). 1967. 240.00 set (ISBN 3-7819-0030-4, M-7364, Pub. by Fritz Knapp Verlag). French & Eur.
Achterberg, Jeanne. Imagery in Healing: Shamanism & Modern Medicine. LC 84-20748. (New Science Library Ser.). 256p. (Orig.). 1985. pap. 9.95 (ISBN 0-87773-307-4, 73031-3). Shambhala Pubns.
Achterberg, Jeanne & Lawlis, Frank. Bridges of the Bodymind. LC 80-16596. (Illus.). 1980. text ed. 19.50 (ISBN 0-918296-14-5). Inst Personality & Ability.
Achtermier, William O. Rhode Island Arms Makers & Gunsmiths: 1643-1883. LC 80-84583. (Illus.). 108p. 1980. 16.50 (ISBN 0-917218-15-9). Mowbray.
Achtert, Walter S. & Gibaldi, Joseph. The MLA Style Manual. 250p. 1985. 15.00 (ISBN 0-87352-136-6). Modern Lang.
Achtert, Walter S., jt. auth. see Gibaldi, Joseph.
Achtert, Walter S., compiled by. MLA Abstracts of Articles in Scholarly Journals, 1973. 409p. 1975. 35.00x (ISBN 0-87352-229-X). Modern Lang.
Achtmeier, Paul J., et al see Shelp, Earl E. & Sunderland, Ronald H.
ACI Committee Staff. Building Code Requirements for Reinforced Concrete: ACI 318-83. 1983. 31.00 (ISBN 0-317-17423-1). ACI.
--Building Code Requirements for Reinforced Concrete S-Metric Edition: ACI 318-83. 1983. 33.75 (ISBN 0-317-17428-2). ACI.
ACI Committee 116. Cement & Concrete Terminology. 1978. pap. 17.75 (ISBN 0-685-85102-8, 116R-78). ACI.
ACI Committee 209. Shrinkage & Creep in Concrete. (Bibliography: No. 10). 1972. pap. 36.25 (ISBN 0-685-85150-8, B-10) (ISBN 0-685-85151-6). ACI.
ACI Committee 224. Causes, Mechanism, & Control of Cracking in Concrete. (Bibliography: No. 9). 1971. pap. 36.25 (ISBN 0-685-85148-6, B-9). ACI.
ACI Committee 311. ACI Manual of Concrete Inspection. 7th ed. 1981. 33.95 (ISBN 0-685-85096-X, SP-2) (ISBN 0-685-85097-8). ACI.
ACI Committee 318. Building Code Requirements for Reinforced Concrete: ACI 318-77 ANSI A89.1-1972. 102p. 1977. 27.50 (ISBN 0-685-03451-8, 318-77). ACI.
--Building Code Requirements for Reinforced Concrete: ACI 318-71 ANSI A89.1-1972. 78p. 1971. 23.00 (ISBN 0-685-85075-7, 318-71). ACI.
--Building Code Requirements for Reinforced Concrete SI Metric Edition: ACI 318-71. 1975. 23.00 (ISBN 0-685-85081-1, 318-7 SI). ACI.
--Commentary on Building Code Requirements for Reinforced Concrete: ACI 318R-77. 132p. 1977. 27.50 (ISBN 0-685-03453-4, 318-77C) (ISBN 0-685-03454-2). ACI.
ACI Committee 340. Design Handbook in Accordance with the Strength Design Method of ACI 318-77: Columns, Vol. 2. 1978. binder 55.50 (ISBN 0-685-85093-5, SP-17A78). ACI.
ACI Committee 349. Code Requirements for Nuclear Safety Related Concrete Structures: ACI 349-80. 1980. 59.75 (ISBN 0-685-85087-0, 349-80) (ISBN 0-685-85088-9). ACI.
Acier, Marcel, ed. From Spanish Trenches. LC 78-63648. (Studies in Fascism: Ideology & Practice). 216p. Repr. of 1937 ed. 28.00 (ISBN 0-404-16898-1). AMS Pr.
Acierno, Louis J. Comprehensive Cardiac Rehabilitation & Prevention: A Model Program. LC 85-8381. (Illus.). xiv, 168p. 1985. 29.95 (ISBN 0-915163-00-4). Immergut & Siolek.
Acimovic, L. J. Problems of Security & Cooperation in Europe. 344p. 1981. 56.00 (ISBN 90-286-0190-2). Sijthoff & Noordhoff.
Ackart, Robert. Celebration of Soups. LC 81-43248. (Illus.). 272p. 1982. 19.95 (ISBN 0-385-15847-5). Doubleday.
--Celebration of Soups. LC 81-43248. (Illus.). 272p. 1982. pap. 10.95 (ISBN 0-385-18141-8, Dolp). Doubleday.
--A Celebration of Vegetables: Menus for Festive Meat-Free Dining. LC 77-76469. (Illus.). 1979. pap. 6.95 (ISBN 0-689-70581-6, 244). Atheneum.
--The Frugal Fish Cookbook. (Illus.). 320p. 1985. pap. 9.70i (ISBN 0-316-00645-9). Little.
--The Frugal Fish Cookbook: 300 Delicious Recipes for All Seasons. 320p. 1983. 17.45i (ISBN 0-316-00646-7). Little.
--Souffles, Mousses, Jellies & Creams. LC 79-55606. 224p. 1982. pap. 6.95 (ISBN 0-689-70631-6). Atheneum.
--Spirited Cooking: An Introduction to Wines in the Kitchen. LC 84-45059. 384p. 1984. 17.95 (ISBN 0-689-11471-0). Atheneum.
Ackenheil, Alfred. Day by Day with the Apostle Paul. 200p. 1983. 8.95 (ISBN 0-8423-0517-3). Tyndale.
--Day by Day with the Apostle Paul. 1983. pap. 5.95 (ISBN 0-8423-0518-1). Tyndale.
Acker, Arnold. How to Do Practical Construction Cost Estimates. Howell, J. N., ed. LC 84-72825. 165p. 1984. pap. 52.00 (ISBN 0-932223-00-1). Churchill Pr.
Acker, Duane. Animal Science & Industry. x ed. (Illus.). 720p. 1983. 33.95 (ISBN 0-13-037416-4). P-H.
Acker, H. & O'Regan, R. G., eds. Physiology of the Peripheral Arterial Chemoreceptors. xii, 494p. 1984. 149.00 (ISBN 0-444-80494-3, I-179-84, Biomedical Pr). Elsevier.
Acker, H., et al, eds. Chemoreception in the Carotid Body. LC 77-13691. (Illus.). 1977. pap. 36.00 (ISBN 0-387-08455-X). Springer-Verlag.
--Spheroids in Cancer Research. (Recent Results in Cancer Research Ser.: Vol. 95). (Illus.). 210p. 1984. 35.50 (ISBN 0-387-13691-6). Springer-Verlag.
Acker, Helen. Four Sons of Norway. facsimile ed. LC 72-117318. (Biography Index Reprint Ser.). 1948. 22.00 (ISBN 0-8369-8010-7). Ayer Co Pubs.
Acker, Kathy. The Adult Life of Toulouse Lautrec. LC 78-58943. (Viper's Tongue Bks.). (Illus., Orig.). 1978. pap. 4.50 (ISBN 0-931106-21-4, Dist. by Printed Matter). TVRT.
--The Adult Life of Toulouse Lautrec by Henri Toulouse Lautrec. LC 78-58942. 1978. pap. text ed. 6.00 (ISBN 0-931106-21-4). Printed Matter.
--Blood & Guts in High School. (Illus.). 176p. 1984. pap. 7.95 (ISBN 0-394-62334-7, E-959, Ever). Grove.
--Blood & Guts in High School. LC 84-48118. 176p. 1984. 19.50 (ISBN 0-394-54292-4). Grove.
--The Childlike Life of the Black Tarantula. rev. ed. LC 78-58942. (Viper's Tongue Bks.). (Orig.). 1978. pap. 4.00 (ISBN 0-931106-20-6, Dist. by Printed Matter). TVRT.
--The Childlike Life of the Black Tarantula by the Black Tarantula. LC 78-58943. 1978. pap. text ed. 6.00 (ISBN 0-931106-20-6). Printed Matter.
--Great Expectations. (Illus.). 128p. (Orig.). 1982. 5.95 (ISBN 0-940642-02-6); pap. write for info. (ISBN 0-940642-01-8). Re-Search Media.
--Great Expectations. 128p. 1982. 5.95 (ISBN 0-940170-04-3). Grove.
--Great Expectations. LC 83-48312. 128p. 1983. 12.50 (ISBN 0-394-53497-2, GP-873); pap. 6.95 (ISBN 0-394-62480-7, E863). Grove.
--Hello, I'm Erica Jong. (Contact Publications Ser.). (Illus.). 32p. (Orig.). 1982. pap. 3.00 (ISBN 0-936556-07-2). Contact Two.
--I Dreamt I Was a Nymphomaniac! Imagining. (Illus.). 116p. 1980. 4.00 (ISBN 0-936578-00-9). Travelers Digest Edns.
--N. Y. C. in Nineteen Seventy-Nine. (Illus.). 24p. (Orig.). 1981. pap. 3.00 (ISBN 0-917061-09-8). Top Stories.
Acker, Kathy & Cherches, Peter. Diana's Third Almanac. Ahern, Tom, ed. Waldrop, Keith, tr. 96p. (Orig.). 1982. pap. 4.95 (ISBN 0-933442-06-8). Dianas Bimonthly.
Acker, Louis S., jt. auth. see Sakoian, Frances.
Acker, Louis S, jt. auth. see Sakoian, Frances.
Acker, Robert F., et al, eds. Proceedings of the Third International Congress on Marine Corrosion & Fouling. 1974. 36.00x (ISBN 0-8101-0445-8). Northwestern U Pr.
Acker, Sandra. The World Yearbook of Education, 1984: Women & Education. 300p. 1984. 35.00 (ISBN 0-89397-176-6). Nichols Pub.
Acker, Sandra & Piper, David W., eds. Is Higher Education Fair to Women? 256p. 1984. pap. 24.00x (ISBN 1-85059-002-8, Pub. by NFER Nelson UK). Taylor & Francis.
Acker, William R., tr. from Chinese. Some Tang & Pre-Tang Texts on Chinese Painting. LC 78-20444. 1980. Repr. of 1954 ed. text ed. 32.50 (ISBN 0-88355-825-4). Hyperion Conn.
Ackerknecht, E. H. A Short History of Psychiatry. 2nd rev. ed. Wolff, Sula, tr. (Illus.). 1970. pap. 8.95x (ISBN 0-02-840070-4, 84007). Hafner.
Ackerknecht, E H. The World of Asciepios. 92p. 1966. 39.00 (ISBN 3-456-00004-9, Pub. by Holdan Bk Ltd UK). State Mutual Bk.
Ackerknecht, Erwin H. Malaria in the Upper Mississippi Valley: 1760-1900. Rosenkrantz, Barbara G., ed. LC 76-25650. (Public Health in America Ser.). (Illus.). 1977. Repr. of 1945 ed. lib. bdg. 15.00x (ISBN 0-405-09805-7). Ayer Co Pubs.
--Medicine & Ethnology: Selected Essays of Erwin H. Ackerknecht. Koelbing, H. & Walser, H., eds. LC 70-165334. Repr. of 1971 ed. 37.10 (ISBN 0-8357-9276-5, 2014022). Bks Demand UMI.
--Medicine at the Paris Hospital, 1794-1848. LC 66-23003. (Illus.). 242p. 1967. 19.50x (ISBN 0-8018-0002-1). Johns Hopkins.
--Rudolph Virchow: Doctor, Statesman, Anthropologist & Virchow-Bibliographie 1843-1901. Schwalbe, J. & Cohen, I. Bernard, eds. LC 80-2112. (Development of Science Ser.). (Illus.). 1981. Repr. of 1901 ed. lib. bdg. 45.00 two vols.in one (ISBN 0-405-13832-6). Ayer Co Pubs.
--A Short History of Medicine 1982. rev. ed. LC 81-48194. 304p. 1982. pap. 7.95x (ISBN 0-8018-2726-4). Johns Hopkins.
--Therapeutics: From the Primitives to the 20th Century. LC 72-88252. 1973. 18.95x (ISBN 0-02-840060-7). Hafner.
Ackerknecht, Lucy. Life Meanings for Future Teachers. LC 64-20969. 1964. 4.00 (ISBN 0-8022-0003-6). Philos Lib.
Ackerley, Chris & Clipper, Lawrence. A Companion to Under the Volcano. 492p. 1984. 36.50 (ISBN 0-7748-0199-9). U BC Pr.
Ackerley, J. My Dog, Tulip. LC 65-24027. 8.95 (ISBN 0-8303-0056-2). Fleet.
Ackerley, J. R. Hindoo Holiday: An Indian Journal. (Travel Library). 256p. 1984. pap. 5.95 (ISBN 0-14-009507-1). Penguin.
--We Think the World of You. LC 61-13183. 190p. 1981. pap. 5.95 (ISBN 0-916870-36-7). Creative Arts Bk.
Ackerley, Joe R. We Think the World of You. 1961. 10.00 (ISBN 0-685-06622-3). Astor-Honor.
Ackerly, Salley M., jt. auth. see Riekes, Linda.
Ackerly, Sally M., jt. auth. see Riekes, Linda.
Ackerman. Ancient Art & Greek Architecture. (History of Art Ser.). 1985. text ed. 61.00 (ISBN 0-8240-2411-7). Garland Pub.
--The Pathology of Malignant Melanoma. LC 81-8393. (Monographs in Dermatopathology, Vol. 1). 406p. 1981. 65.50x (ISBN 0-89352-132-9). Masson Pub.
Ackerman, A. Bernard. Histologic Diagnosis of Inflammatory Skin Diseases: A Method by Pattern Analysis. LC 76-49437. (Illus.). 1978. text ed. 84.50 (ISBN 0-8121-0581-8). Lea & Febiger.
--Your Skin Is Showing. 32p. (gr. 1 up). 1979. text ed. 7.00 (ISBN 0-89352-082-9). Masson Pub.
Ackerman, A. Bernard & Ragaz, Anna. The Lives of Lesions. (Illus.). 261p. 1984. 75.00 (ISBN 0-89352-095-0). Masson Pub.
Ackerman, A. Bernard, et al. Differential Diagnosis in Dermatopathology. LC 81-5982. (Illus.). 196p. 1982. text ed. 86.00 (ISBN 0-8121-0800-0). Lea & Febiger.
Ackerman, Adolph J. Billings & Water Power in Brazil. 141p. 1953. pap. 10.00x (ISBN 0-87262-319-X). Am Soc Civil Eng.
Ackerman, Al. Ack's Hacks. 16p. (Orig.). 1984. pap. 2.50 (ISBN 0-935350-11-X). Luna Bisonte.
Ackerman, Allan D., et al. In the Bank...or up the Chimney? A Dollars & Cents Guide to Energy-Saving Home Improvements. (Illus.). 1975. pap. 1.25x (ISBN 0-89011-477-3, ECR-107). Abt Bks.
Ackerman, Bruce. Reconstructing American Law. 128p. 1984. text ed. 16.00x (ISBN 0-674-75015-2); pap. text ed. 6.95x (ISBN 0-674-75016-0). Harvard U Pr.
Ackerman, Bruce A. Private Property & the Constitution. LC 76-47667. 1978. pap. 12.95x (ISBN 0-300-02237-9). Yale U Pr.
--Social Justice in the Liberal State. LC 80-12618. 408p. 1980. 35.00x (ISBN 0-300-02439-8, Y-401); pap. 10.95x (ISBN 0-300-02757-5). Yale U Pr.
Ackerman, Bruce A. & Hassler, William T. Clean Coal: Dirty Air. LC 80-1089. (Illus.). 175p. 1981. 25.00x (ISBN 0-300-02628-5); pap. 7.95x (ISBN 0-300-02643-9). Yale U Pr.
Ackerman, Bruce A., ed. Economic Foundations of Property Law. 329p. 1975. pap. 10.95 (ISBN 0-316-00644-0). Little.
Ackerman, Bruce A., et al. The Uncertain Search for Environmental Quality. LC 73-21305. (Illus.). 1974. 16.95 (ISBN 0-02-900200-1). Free Pr.
Ackerman, C. Mexico's Dilemma. 1976. lib. bdg. 59.95 (ISBN 0-8490-2253-3). Gordon Pr.
Ackerman, Carl. The Bible in Shakespeare. 1978. lib. bdg. 18.00 (ISBN 0-8495-0134-2). Arden Lib.
--Bible in Shakespeare. lib. bdg. 15.00 (ISBN 0-8414-2954-5). Folcroft.
Ackerman, Carolyn. Cooking with Kids. 76p. 1982. pap. 5.50 (ISBN 0-87659-104-7). Gryphon Hse.
Ackerman, D. G., et al. Destruction & Disposal of PCB'S by Thermal & Non-Thermal Methods. LC 82-22312. (Pollution Technology Review Ser.: No. 97). (Illus.). 417p. 1983. 48.00 (ISBN 0-8155-0934-0). Noyes.
Ackerman, Diane. Lady Faustus. LC 83-61564. 96p. 1983. 9.70 (ISBN 0-688-02396-7). Morrow.
--Lady Faustus. LC 85-3454. 96p. 1985. pap. 5.95 (ISBN 0-688-04829-3, Quill). Morrow.
--On Extended Wings. LC 84-45606. 288p. 1985. 14.95 (ISBN 0-689-11540-7). Atheneum.
--The Planets: A Cosmic Pastoral. LC 76-14840. (Illus.). 1976. 6.95 (ISBN 0-688-03088-2). Morrow.
--The Planets: A Cosmic Pastoral. (Illus.). 1977. pap. 4.95 (ISBN 0-688-08088-X). Morrow.
--Twilight of the Tenderfoot: A Western Memoir. LC 79-25181. 1980. 9.95 (ISBN 0-688-03605-8). Morrow.
--Wife of Light. LC 77-25297. 1978. 6.95 (ISBN 0-688-03286-9). Morrow.
--Wife of Light. LC 77-25297. 1979. pap. 4.95 (ISBN 0-688-08286-6). Morrow.
Ackerman, Diane, et al. Poems-Ackerman, Bolz & Steele. 1973. wrappers 1.00 (ISBN 0-685-37096-8). Stone-Marrow Pr.
Ackerman, Dorothy. A Quaker Looks at Yoga. LC 76-23909. (Orig.). 1976. pap. 5.00x (ISBN 0-87574-207-6, 207). Pendle Hill.
Ackerman, Edward A., jt. auth. see Whitaker, J. Russell.
Ackerman, Edward A., et al. Technology in American Water Development. LC 77-86377. (Resources for the Future, Inc. Publications). Repr. of 1959 ed. 47.50 (ISBN 0-404-60326-2). AMS Pr.
Ackerman, Eugene & Gatewood, Lael C. Mathematical Models in the Health Sciences: A Computer-Aided Approach. 1979. 25.00x (ISBN 0-8166-0864-4). U of Minn Pr.
Ackerman, Eugene, et al. Simulation of Infectious Disease Epidemics. (Illus.). 210p. 1984. 29.75x (ISBN 0-398-04900-9). C C Thomas.
Ackerman, Evelyn. Dressed for the Country: 1860-1900. Belloli, Andrea P., ed. (Illus.). 60p. (Orig.). 1984. pap. 10.95x (ISBN 0-87587-121-6). LA Co Art Mus.
Ackerman, Evelyn B. Village on the Seine: Tradition & Change in Bonneires, 1815-1914. LC 78-58071. (Illus.). 188p. 1978. 24.95x (ISBN 0-8014-1178-5). Cornell U Pr.
Ackerman, Forrest J. Lon of One Thousand Faces. (Illus.). 263p. (Orig.). 1983. 50.00 (ISBN 0-912189-00-2); pap. 10.00 (ISBN 0-912189-01-0). Morrison Rav.
--Mr. Monster's the Beauties & the Beasts. Stine, Hank, ed. LC 82-23441. (Illus.). 206p. (Orig.). pap. 12.95 cancelled (ISBN 0-89865-289-8). Donning Co.
Ackerman, Forrest J, jt. auth. see Strickland, A. W.
Ackerman, Forrest J., jt. auth. see Strickland, A. W.
Ackerman, Forrest J., ed. The Gernsback Awards, Vol. 1, 1926. LC 82-50927. (The Gernsback Awards Ser. 1926-1954). (Illus.). 320p. 1982. 14.95 (ISBN 0-943958-01-6). Triton Bks.
Ackerman, Frank. Hazardous to Our Wealth: Economic Policies in the Nineteen-Eighties. LC 83-51288. 200p. 1984. 20.00 (ISBN 0-89608-203-2); pap. 8.00 (ISBN 0-89608-202-4). South End Pr.
--Reaganomics: Rhetoric vs. Reality. 200p. 1982. 20.00 (ISBN 0-89608-142-7); pap. 7.50 (ISBN 0-89608-141-9). South End Pr.
Ackerman, G. Adolph. Hematology: Normal Morphology, a Visual Approach. LC 75-732666. 40p. 1973. text ed. 130.00x set with 100 slides (ISBN 0-8036-0015-1); text ed. 5.00x (ISBN 0-8036-0016-X). Davis Co.
Ackerman, Gerald M., jt. auth. see Zafran, Eric.
Ackerman, Gretchen P., jt. auth. see Ackerman, Robert W.
Ackerman, Hal. The War Against Women: Overcoming Female Abuse. (Orig.). 1985. pap. 1.50 (ISBN 0-89486-282-0). Hazelden.
Ackerman, J. M., jt. auth. see Shelton, J. L.
Ackerman, J. Mark. Operant Conditioning Techniques for the Classroom Teacher. 1972. pap. 9.75 (ISBN 0-673-07664-4). Scott F.
Ackerman, James S. Palladio. rev. ed. 1974. pap. 7.95 (ISBN 0-14-020845-3, Pelican). Penguin.
Ackerman, James S., et al. Teaching the Old Testament in English Classes. LC 72-93907. (English Curriculum Study Ser.). 512p. 1973. 20.00x (ISBN 0-253-35785-3); pap. 7.95x (ISBN 0-253-28850-9). Ind U Pr.
Ackerman, Jerrold & Lipsitz, Lawrence, eds. Instructional Television: Status & Directions. LC 76-54241. (Illus.). 240p. 1977. 26.95 (ISBN 0-87778-096-X). Educ Tech Pubns.
Ackerman, John. Welsh Dylan. (Illus.). 143p. 1982. pap. 6.95 (ISBN 0-586-08350-2, Pub. by Granada England). Academy Chi Pubs.
Ackerman, Joseph, et al, eds. see Farm Foundation & Resources for the Future, Inc.

Ackerman, Judy. Business Mathematics: Effective Problem Solving. 2nd ed. 1985. pap. text ed. 22.95 (ISBN 0-8359-0591-8). Reston.
Ackerman, Kenneth B. Practical Handbook of Warehousing. 2nd ed. 1985. price not set. Traffic Serv.
Ackerman, M. & Hermann, Robert. Sophus Lie's Eighteen Eighty Transformation Group Paper. LC 75-17416. (Lie Groups: History, Frontiers on Applications Ser.: No. 1). 1975. 55.00 (ISBN 0-915692-10-4). Math Sci Pr.
Ackerman, M., jt. auth. see Hermann, Robert.
Ackerman, Margaret E. & McKissick, Maureen L. Nevada Legislative Almanac Nineteen Eighty-Two. (Nevada Legislative Almanac: No. 1). (Illus.). 300p. (Orig.). (gr. 9 up). 1982. pap. 15.00 (ISBN 0-942112-01-6); pap. text ed. 10.00 (ISBN 0-686-32831-0). Ackerman-Rorex.
Ackerman, Nathan W. Psychodynamics of Family Life: Diagnosis & Treatment of Family Relationships. LC 58-13043. 1972. pap. 8.95x (ISBN 0-465-09503-8, TB5004). Basic.
--Treating the Troubled Family. LC 66-27943. 1966. pap. 8.95x (ISBN 0-465-09522-4, TB5023). Basic.
Ackerman, Norman. A Theory of Family Systems. 225p. 1984. 26.95 (ISBN 0-89876-032-1). Gardner Pr.
Ackerman, Paul & Kappelman, Murray. Signals: What Your Child Is Really Telling You. 1980. pap. 3.95 (ISBN 0-451-12186-4, AE2186, Sig). NAL.
Ackerman, Phyllis. Tapestry, the Mirror of Civilization. LC 74-108123. Repr. of 1933 ed. 31.50 (ISBN 0-404-00279-X). AMS Pr.
Ackerman, Phyllis, jt. ed. see Pope, Arthur U.
Ackerman, Robert. Monarch Notes on Hardy's Tess of the D'Urbervilles. (Orig.). pap. 2.95 (ISBN 0-671-00619-3). Monarch Pr.
Ackerman, Robert J. Children of Alcoholics: A Guidebook for Educators, Therapists, & Parents. 2nd ed. LC 78-55067. 215p. 1983. lib. bdg. 14.95x (ISBN 0-918452-50-3); pap. text ed. 9.95x (ISBN 0-918452-47-3). Learning Pubns.
Ackerman, Robert K. South Carolina Colonial Land Policies. LC 74-16184. (Tricentennial Studies: No. 9). 1977. 17.95x (ISBN 0-87249-254-0). U of SC Pr.
Ackerman, Robert W. Backgrounds to Medieval English Literature. (Orig.). 1967. 6.00 (ISBN 0-394-30627-9, RanC). Random.
--Index of the Arthurian Names in Middle English. LC 78-158222. (Stanford University, Stanford Studies in Language & Literature: No. 10). Repr. of 1952 ed. 24.00 (ISBN 0-404-51820-6). AMS Pr.
--The Social Challenge to Business. 384p. 1976. 25.00x (ISBN 0-674-81190-9). Harvard U Pr.
Ackerman, Robert W. & Ackerman, Gretchen P. Sir Frederic Madden: A Bibliography & Biographical Sketch. LC 78-68237. 150p. 1979. lib. bdg. 22.00 (ISBN 0-8240-9819-6). Garland Pub.
Ackerman, Robert W., jt. auth. see Toole, Virginia G.
Ackerman, Robert W. & Dahood, Roger, eds. Ancrene Riwle: Introduction & Part One. LC 83-21987. (Medieval & Renaissance Te xts & Studies: Vol. 31). 110p. 1984. 12.00 (ISBN 0-86698-055-5). Medieval & Renaissance NY.
Ackerman, Robert W., tr. see Chretien De Troyes.
Ackerman, Roy L. Bildung & Verbildung in the Prose Fiction Works of Otto Julius Bierbaum. (European University Studies, German Language & Literature: No. 1, Vol. 101). 95p. 1974. pap. 18.25 (ISBN 3-261-01424-5). P Lang Pubs.
Ackerman, Rudolf. Ackermann's Oxford. 1814. 15.00 (ISBN 0-89984-000-0). Century Bookbindery.
Ackerman, Walter. Out of Our People's Past: Sources for the Study of Jewish History. 1978. 7.50x (ISBN 0-8381-0221-2). United Syn Bk.
Ackerman, Wendayne, tr. see Kalff, Dora M.
Ackerman, Winona B. & Lohnes, Paul R. Research Methods for Nurses. (Illus.). 304p. 1981. text ed. 33.95x (ISBN 0-07-000182-0). McGraw.
Ackermann. Ackermann's Costume Plates: Women's Fashions in England, 1818-1828. Blum, Stella, ed. 14.25 (ISBN 0-8446-5727-1). Peter Smith.
Ackermann, A. S. Popular Fallacies, a Book of Common Errors: Explained & Corrected with Copious References to Authorities. 4th ed. LC 79-121184. 1970. Repr. of 1950 ed. 70.00x (ISBN 0-8103-3295-7). Gale.
Ackermann, Gertrude see Nute, Grace L.
Ackermann, J., ed. Uncertainty & Control. (Lecture Notes in Control & Information Sciences Ser.: Vol. 70). iv, 236p. 1985. pap. 16.00 (ISBN 0-387-15533-3). Springer-Verlag.
Ackermann, Jean. A Pride of Heroes: Candid Celebrations. v, 22p. (Orig.). (gr. 8-12). 1984. pap. 5.00 (ISBN 0-9614506-0-6). Box Four Twenty-Four.
Ackermann, L. V., jt. auth. see Hamperl, H.
Ackermann, Paul K., ed. Bertolt Brecht, Die Dreigroschenoper. (Suhrkamp-Insel Series in German Literature). 118p. (Ger. & Eng.). pap. 7.95 (ISBN 3-518-03049-3). Suhrkamp.
Ackermann, Paul K., ed. see Durrenmatt, Friedrich.
Ackermann, Paul K., ed. see Frisch, Max.
Ackermann, Philip G., jt. auth. see Bauer, John D.
Ackermann, Philip G., jt. auth. see Toro, Gelson.
Ackermann, Phillip G., jt. auth. see Remson, Susan T.
Ackermann, Robert J. Data, Instruments, & Theory: A Dialetical Approach to Understanding Science. LC 84-15938. 224p. 1985. 25.00x (ISBN 0-691-07296-5). Princeton U Pr.
--Religion As Critique. LC 84-16471. 184p. 1985. lib. bdg. 20.00x (ISBN 0-87023-462-5); pap. 8.95x (ISBN 0-87023-463-3). U of Mass Pr.
Ackermann, Roy L. The Role of the Trial in the School Prose of the Weimar Republic. (European University Studies: No. 1, Vol. 488). 138p. 1983. 16.20 (ISBN 3-261-04980-4). P Lang Pubs.
Ackermann, Rudolph. Ackermann's Costume Plates: Women's Fashions in England, 1818-1828. Blum, Stella, ed. (Illus.). 1979. pap. 5.00 (ISBN 0-486-23690-0). Dover.
Ackermann, W., jt. auth. see Hilbert, David.
Ackermann, William C., et al, eds. Man-Made Lakes: Their Problems & Environmental Effects. LC 73-86486. (Geophysical Monographs: Vol. 17). (Illus.). 847p. 1973. 35.00 (ISBN 0-87590-017-8). Am Geophysical.
Ackers, P., et al. Weirs & Fumes for Flow Measurement. LC 78-317. 327p. 1978. cloth 91.95x (ISBN 0-471-99637-8, Pub. by Wiley-Interscience). Wiley.
Ackerson, et al. Gateways to Science. 4th ed. 1982. write for info. laboratory bks. McGraw.
Ackerson, Robert C. The Encyclopedia of American Supercars. (Illus.). 144p. (YA) 1981. pap. 12.95 (ISBN 0-934780-10-2). Bookman Dan.
--Ferraris of the Seventies. (Source Bks.). (Illus.). 144p. 1984. pap. 12.95 (ISBN 0-934780-35-8). Bookman Dan.
--Lamborghini. (Source Bks.). (Illus.). 144p. 1984. pap. 12.95 (ISBN 0-934780-37-4). Bookman Dan.
--Mid-Size Fords, Mercs: A Source Book. (Source Book Ser.). (Illus.). 144p. (Orig.). 1984. pap. 12.95 (ISBN 0-934780-30-7). Bookman Dan.
--Mustangs. (Source Bks.). (Illus.). 144p. 1984. pap. 12.95 (ISBN 0-934780-41-2). Bookman Dan.
--Ranchero: A Source Book. (Source Book Ser.). (Illus.). 144p. (Orig.). pap. 12.95 (ISBN 0-934780-29-3). Bookman Dan.
--Shelby Cobras & Mustangs: A Source Book. (Source Book Ser.). (Illus.). 144p. (Orig.). 1984. pap. 12.95 (ISBN 0-934780-33-1). Bookman Dan.
Ackerson, Robert C., jt. auth. see Kimes, Beverly R.
Ackert, Patricia. Insights & Ideas: A Beginning Reader for Students of English as a Second Language. 219p. 1982. pap. text ed. 14.95 (ISBN 0-03-058322-5). HR&W.
--Please Write: A Beginning Composition Text for Students of ESL. (Illus.). 208p. 1986. pap. text ed. 11.95 (ISBN 0-13-683418-3). P-H.
Ackery, P. R. & Vane-Wright, R. I. Milkweed Butterflies. LC 83-7334. (Illus.). 450p. 1984. 75.00x (ISBN 0-8014-1688-4). Cornell U Pr.
Ackery, Phillip R., jt. auth. see Vane-Wright, Richard I.
Ackins, Ralph. Energy Machines. LC 79-27714. (Machine World). (Illus.). (gr. 2-4). 1980. PLB 14.65 (ISBN 0-8172-1336-8). Raintree Pubs.
Acklan, William H. Sterope: The Veiled Pleiad. facsimile ed. LC 78-38637. (Black Heritage Library Collection). Repr. of 1892 ed. 19.25 (ISBN 0-8369-8963-5). Ayer Co Pubs.
Ackland, Donald, et al. Broadman Comments: July-September, 1984. LC 45-437. 1984. pap. 2.50 (ISBN 0-8054-1486-X). Broadman.
Ackland, Donald F. Broadman Comments, April-June, 1984. LC 45-437. 1984. pap. 2.50 (ISBN 0-8054-1485-1). Broadman.
--Broadman Comments, April-June 1985. 1985. pap. 2.50 (ISBN 0-8054-1491-6). Broadman.
--Broadman Comments, October-December, 1985. 1985. pap. 2.50 (ISBN 0-8054-1493-2). Broadman.
--Day by Day with John. LC 81-67374. 1982. pap. 4.95 (ISBN 0-8054-5187-0). Broadman.
--Day by Day with the Prophets. LC 82-82950. 1983. pap. 4.50 (ISBN 0-8054-5193-5). Broadman.
Ackland, Donald F., et al. Broadman Comments, January-March, 1986. 1985. pap. 2.50 (ISBN 0-8054-1496-7). Broadman.
--Broadman Comments, July-September, 1985. 1985. pap. 2.50 (ISBN 0-8054-1492-4). Broadman.
--Broadman Comments 1985-86. 1985. pap. 5.95 (ISBN 0-8054-1489-4). Broadman.
Ackland, Donald P. Day by Day with the Master. LC 83-70209. 1985. pap. 5.95 (ISBN 0-8054-5196-X). Broadman.
Ackland, Valentine. The Nature of the Moment. LC 73-84871. 64p. 1974. 5.00 (ISBN 0-8112-0517-7). New Directions.
Acklen, Jeannette T., et al. Tennessee Records: Bible Records & Marriage Bonds. LC 67-28618. (Illus.). 521p. 1980. Repr. of 1933 ed. 22.50 (ISBN 0-8063-0000-0). Genealog Pub.
Ackley, Clifford S. Photografic Viewpoints. (MFA Bulletin Ser.: Vol. 80). (Illus.). 80p. 1984. pap. 6.95 (ISBN 0-87846-229-5). Mus Fine Arts Boston.
--Printmaking in the Age of Rembrandt. 368p. 1981. 70.00 (ISBN 0-87846-198-1, 719331). NYGS.
--Ten Painters & Sculptors Draw. Purvis, Cynthia M., ed. (Illus.). 17p. 1984. pap. 2.50 (ISBN 0-87846-246-5). Mus Fine Arts Boston.
Ackley, Clifford S., et al. The Modern Art of the Print: Selections from the Collection of Lois & Michael Torf. Spear, Judy, ed. LC 84-60501. (Illus., Orig.). 1984. pap. 19.95 (ISBN 0-87846-239-2). Mus Fine Arts Boston.
--Edgar Degas: The Painter As Printmaker, the Complete Prints of Edgar Degas. (Illus.). 348p. 1984. 49.00i (ISBN 0-87846-244-9, 210773). NYGS.
Ackley, Edith F. Marionettes: Easy to Make Fun to Use. (Illus.). (gr. 5-9). 1939. lib. bdg. 11.89 (ISBN 0-397-31409-4). Lipp Jr Bks.
Ackley, Gardner. Macroeconomic Theory & Policy. 738p. 1978. text ed. write for info. (ISBN 0-02-300290-5). Macmillan.
--Prospects for the U. S. Economy: Growth or Stagnation? LC 74-4906. (Richard J. Gonzalez Lectures Ser.: No. 5). 1974. pap. 1.00 (ISBN 0-87755-199-5). Bureau Busn UT.
Ackley, Gardner, et al. Economic Freedom, Stability & Growth. 1972. 8.40 (ISBN 0-932826-05-9); pap. 3.95 (ISBN 0-685-85517-1). New Issues MI.
Ackley, P. O. Home Gun Care & Repair. LC 69-16147. 192p. 1974. pap. 6.95 (ISBN 0-8117-2028-4). Stackpole.
Ackley, Phil. Get Wise: Studies in Proverbs. (Young Fisherman Bible Studyguides). (Illus.). 80p. (gr. 4-6). 1985. tchr's. ed. 4.95 (ISBN 0-87788-696-2); student ed. 2.95 (ISBN 0-87788-695-4). Shaw Pubs.
Ackley, Robert J. & Greer, Laura B. Spectrovision Inc. A Business Communication Simulation. (Business Communications Ser.: 1-321). 183p. 1984. pap. text ed. 12.95 (ISBN 0-471-86276-2, Pub by Wiley); tchr's. manual avail. (ISBN 0-471-87996-7). Wiley.
Ackman, R. G. & Metcalfe, L. D., eds. Analysis of Fatty Acids & Their Esters by Chromatographic Methods. 1976. 25.00 (ISBN 0-912474-07-6). Preston Pubns.
Ackoff, R. L. A Concept of Corporate Planning. LC 74-100318. 158p. 1969. cloth 28.95 (ISBN 0-471-00290-9, Pub. by Wiley-Interscience). Wiley.
--Progress in Operations Research, Vol. 1. LC 61-10415. (Operations Research Ser.: No. 5). Repr. of 1961 ed. 98.30 (ISBN 0-8357-9966-2, 2051575). Bks Demand UMI.
Ackoff, Russell & Emery, Fred. On Purposeful Systems. (Systems Inquiry Ser.). 296p. 1982. pap. text ed. 14.95x (ISBN 0-914105-00-0). Intersystems Pubns.
Ackoff, Russell L. The Art of Problem Solving: Accompanied by Ackoff's Fables. LC 78-5627. 214p. 1978. 23.95 (ISBN 0-471-04289-7, Pub. by Wiley-Interscience). Wiley.
--Creating the Corporate Future: Plan or Be Planned for. LC 80-28005. 297p. 1981. 23.95 (ISBN 0-471-09009-3). Wiley.
--Redesigning the Future: A Systems Approach to Societal Problems. LC 74-10627. 260p. 1974. 27.95 (ISBN 0-471-00296-8, Pub. by Wiley-Interscience). Wiley.
--Scientific Method: Optimizing Applied Research Decisions. LC 83-12060. 476p. 1984. Repr. of 1962 ed. text ed. 34.50 (ISBN 0-89874-661-2). Krieger.
Ackoff, Russell L., ed. Designing a National Scientific & Technological Communication System. LC 76-20150. 1976. 30.00x (ISBN 0-8122-7716-3). U of Pa Pr.
Ackoff, Russell L., et al. Revitalizing Western Economies: A New Agenda for Business & Government. LC 84-47977. (Management Ser.). 1984. 19.95x (ISBN 0-87589-609-X). Jossey-Bass.
--A Guide to Controlling Your Corporation's Future. LC 84-14772. 165p. 1983. cloth 19.95 (ISBN 0-471-88213-5, Pub. by Ronald Pr). Wiley.
Ackrill, J. L., ed. Aristotle the Philosopher. (Oxford Paperbacks University Ser.). (Orig.). 1981. pap. text ed. 7.95x (ISBN 0-19-289118-9). Oxford U Pr.
Ackrill, J. L., tr. see Aristotle.
Ackroyd, John, jt. auth. see Scheinmann, Feodor.
Ackroyd, Joyce, tr. from Japanese. Told Round a Brushwood Fire: The Autobiography of Arai Hakuseki (Oritaku Shiba no Ki) LC 79-3239. (Princeton Library of Asian Translations). 350p. 1980. 29.00x (ISBN 0-691-04671-9). Princeton U Pr.
Ackroyd, Joyce, tr. see Hakuseki, Arai.
Ackroyd, Peter. The Last Testament of Oscar Wilde. LC 83-47549. 192p. 1983. 12.45 (ISBN 0-06-015187-0, HarpT). Har-Row.
--The Last Testament of Oscar Wilde. LC 83-47549. 192p. (Orig.). 1985. pap. 3.80i (ISBN 0-06-080733-4, P733, PL). Har-Row.
--London Lickpenny. 1973. wrappers 3.00 (ISBN 0-686-08925-1); wrappers, signed with a holograph poem, limited to 26 copies 10.00 (ISBN 0-686-08926-X). Small Pr Dist.
--T. S. Eliot: A Life. (Illus.). 338p. 1984. 24.95 (ISBN 0-671-53043-7). S&S.
Ackroyd, Peter, ed. P. E. N. New Fiction One. 246p. 1985. 14.95 (ISBN 0-7043-2453-9, Pub. by Quartet Bks). Merrimack Pub Cir.
Ackroyd, Peter R. Exile & Restoration: A Study of Hebrew Thought of the Sixth Century B. C. LC 68-27689. (Old Testament Library). 302p. 1968. 14.95 (ISBN 0-664-20843-6). Westminster.
--First Book of Samuel: Cambridge Bible Commentary on the New English Bible. LC 77-128636. (Old Testament Ser.). (Illus.). 1971. 27.95 (ISBN 0-521-07965-9); pap. 9.95x (ISBN 0-521-09635-9). Cambridge U Pr.
--Israel under Babylon & Persia. (New Clarendon Bible Ser.). 1970. 14.95x (ISBN 0-19-836917-4). Oxford U Pr.
--The Second Book of Samuel: Cambridge Bible Commentary on the New English Bible. LC 76-58074. (Old Testament Ser.). (Illus.). 1977. 32.50 (ISBN 0-521-08633-7); pap. 11.95 (ISBN 0-521-09754-1). Cambridge U Pr.
Ackroyd, Ted J., ed. Health & Medical Economics: A Guide to Information Sources. LC 73-17567. (Economics Information Guide Ser.: Vol. 7). 1977. 60.00x (ISBN 0-8103-1390-1). Gale.
Acland, C. H. D. The Country Life Picture Book of the Lake District. (Illus.). 1983. 19.95 (ISBN 0-393-01733-8). Norton.
Acland, James H. Medieval Structure: The Gothic Vault. LC 72-76769. (Illus.). pap. 66.00 (ISBN 0-317-10651-1, 2016085). Bks Demand UMI.
Acland, Robert D. Microsurgery Practice Manual. LC 79-17533. (Illus.). 1979. pap. text ed. 19.95 (ISBN 0-8016-0076-6). Mosby.
ACLD. ACLD Pantry Cookbook. 300p. 1982. 5.00 (ISBN 0-686-36324-8, Dist. by ACLD). Rahija.
Acleto, Cesar O., et al, eds. Phycologia Latino-Americana, Vol. 1. (Illus.). 186p. (Span.). 1981. text ed. 21.00x (ISBN 3-7682-1297-1). Lubrecht & Cramer.
Acleto, O. & Bicudo, C., eds. Phycologia Latino-Americana, Vol. 2. 213p. 1984. text ed. 28.00x (ISBN 3-7682-1410-9). Lubrecht & Cramer.
Acloque, Genevieve see Croy, Genevieve, pseud.
ACMRR Working Party on FAO Regional Fisheries Councils & Commissions. Report of the Fifth Session of the Advisory Committee on Marine Resources Research: Rome, 1968. (Fisheries Reports: No. 56, Suppl. 2). 29p. 1968. pap. 7.50 (ISBN 0-686-92754-0, F1671, FAO). Unipub.
Acoca, Miguel, tr. see Timerman, Jacobo.
Acocella, Bart, et al. The All-Time All-Star Baseball Book. 368p. 1985. pap. 3.95 (ISBN 0-380-89530-7). Avon.
Acocella, J., jt. auth. see Calhoun, J.
Acocella, Joan, jt. auth. see Bootzin, Richard R.
Acock. Informal Logic Examples. 288p. 1985. write for info. (ISBN 0-534-04494-8). Wadsworth Pub.
Acomb, Evelyn M. French Laic Laws: 1879-1889. LC 67-18747. 1968. Repr. lib. bdg. 21.50 (ISBN 0-374-90038-8). Octagon.
Acomb, Frances. Anglophobia in France, 1763-1789. xiv, 167p. 1980. lib. bdg. 18.50 (ISBN 0-374-90036-1). Octagon.
--Mallet Du Pan (Seventeen Forty-Nine to Eighteen Hundred) A Career in Political Journalism. LC 72-96985. 330p. 1973. 21.75 (ISBN 0-8223-0295-0). Duke.
Aconcio, Giacomo. Darkness Discovered (Satans Stratagems) LC 78-9490. 1978. Repr. of 1651 ed. 45.00x (ISBN 0-8201-1313-1). Schol Facsimiles.
Acosta, Adalberto J. From Common Clay. 1978. 10.95 (ISBN 0-87141-059-1). Manyland.
Acosta, Antonio A. Imagenes. LC 85-50001. (Senda Poetica). 110p. (Orig., Span.). 1985. pap. 6.95 (ISBN 0-918454-47-6). Senda Nueva.
Acosta, Antonio A. & Calvo, Zoraida. Matematicas: Preparacion Para el Examen el Espanol De Equivalencia De la Escuela Superior. rev. ed. LC 80-25182. 272p. (Orig.). 1982. pap. 6.95 (ISBN 0-668-04821-2, 4821-2). Arco.
Acosta, Enrique V. & Fedoroff, Sergey, eds. Eleventh International Congress of Anatomy, Part A: Glial & Neuronal Cell Biology. LC 81-2778. (Progress in Clinical & Biological Research Ser.: Vol. 59A). 352p. 1981. 38.00 (ISBN 0-8451-0153-6). A R Liss.
Acosta, Enrique V. & Galina, Miguel A., eds. Eleventh International Congress of Anatomy, Part B: Advances in the Morphology of Cells & Tissues. LC 81-2778. (Progress in Clinical & Biological Research Ser.: Vol. 59B). 416p. 1981. 40.00 (ISBN 0-8451-0154-4). A R Liss.
Acosta, Enrique V., et al, eds. Eleventh International Congress of Anatomy, Part C: Biological Rhythms in Structure & Function. LC 81-2778. (Progress in Clinical & Biological Research Ser.: Vol. 59C). 260p. 1981. 28.00 (ISBN 0-8451-0155-2). A R Liss.
Acosta, Frank X., et al. Effective Psychotherapy for Low-Income & Minority Patients. LC 82-9053. 182p. 1982. pap. 14.95 (ISBN 0-306-40879-1, Plenum Pr). Plenum Pub.
Acosta, Ivan. El Super: (Tragi-Comdeia) Hernandez-Miyares, Julio E., ed. LC 80-68858. (Coleccion Teatro). 72p. (Orig., Span.). 1982. pap. 5.95 (ISBN 0-89729-271-5). Ediciones.
Acosta, Jorge R., tr. see Caso, Alfonso.
Acosta, Joseph De see De Acosta, Joseph.
Acosta, Mercedes De see De Acosta, Mercedes.
Acosta, Virgilio, et al. Fisica Moderna. (Span.). 1975. pap. text ed. 15.00 (ISBN 0-06-310010-X, IntlDept). Har-Row.
Acosta-Belen, Edna & Christensen, Eli H. The Puerto Rican Woman. LC 79-17638. 186p. 1979. 29.95 (ISBN 0-03-052466-0). Praeger.
Acosta-Belen, Edna, ed. Mujer en la sociedad puertorriquena. LC 80-69122. 240p. 1981. pap. 5.95 (ISBN 0-940238-28-4). Ediciones Huracan.
Acosta de Gonzalez, Fe. El Sistema Metrico (Modulo) (Coleccion Uprex; Serie Pedagogia: No. 57). (Span.). 1979. pap. text ed. 3.80 (ISBN 0-8477-2743-2). U of PR Pr.

A'Court, M. Estate Conveyancing. 208p. 1984. 31.20 (ISBN 0-08-039137-0). Pergamon.

Acquaah, Samuel O. A New Certificate Practical Chemistry. LC 83-82066. 112p. 1983. write for info (ISBN 0-8187-0054-8). Harlo Pr.

Acquaviva, Francis A. & Malone, Robert A. The Power of Positive Persuasion: A Professional's Guide to Communications. 96p. pap. 9.95 (RAMSCO 00200). Ramsco Pub.

Acquaviva, Samuel J. & Bortz, Seymour A., eds. Structural Ceramics & Design. 240p. 1969. 69.50 (ISBN 0-677-13550-5). Gordon.

--Structural Ceramics & Testing of Brittle Materials. 232p. 1968. 93.75 (ISBN 0-677-12770-7). Gordon.

Acredolo, Linda P., jt. ed. see Pick, Herbert L.

Acree, James E. Rhythmic Thoughts. 1981. cancelled (ISBN 0-533-04855-9). Vantage.

Acree, William E., Jr. Thermodynamic Properties of Nonelectro-Lyte Solutions. LC 83-9998. (Monograph). 1984. 65.00 (ISBN 0-12-043020-7). Acad Pr.

Acrelius, Israel. History of New Sweden; or the Settlements on the River Delaware. LC 70-141080. (Research Library of Colonial Americana). (Illus.). 1971. Repr. of 1874 ed. 40.00 (ISBN 0-405-03271-4). Ayer Co Pubs.

Acret, James. Architects & Engineers. 2nd ed. (Construction Law-Land Use Environmental Publications). 616p. 1984. 75.00 (ISBN 0-07-000222-3, Shepards-McGraw). McGraw.

--California Construction Law Manual. 3rd ed. LC 82-16747. (Construction Law-Land Use Environmental Publications). 398p. 1982. 70.00 (ISBN 0-07-000226-6, Shepards-McGraw). McGraw.

Acret, James & California Continuing Education of the Bar. Attorneys Guide to California Construction Contracts & Disputes. LC 75-39425. x, 473p. 1976. 55.00 (ISBN 0-88124-045-1). Cal Cont Ed Bar.

Acrivos, J. V., ed. Physics & Chemistry of Electrons & Ionsin Condensed Matter. 768p. 1984. 99.00 (ISBN 90-277-1799-0, Pub. by Reidel Holland). Kluwer Academic.

Acropolis Books Ltd. Xanadu. 1983. 25.00 (ISBN 0-87491-701-8). Natl Assn Home.

ACS Committee on Chemistry & Public Affairs. Chemistry & the Food System. LC 80-11194. 1980. 19.95 (ISBN 0-8412-0557-4); pap. 12.95 (ISBN 0-8412-0563-9). Am Chemical.

Acs, Zoltan J. The Changing Structure of the American Economy: Lessons from the Steel Industry. LC 84-15930. 268p. 1984. 35.95x (ISBN 0-03-001092-6). Praeger.

ACSM-ASP Fall Convention, Sept. 1982. Technical Papers. pap. 12.00 (ISBN 0-937294-39-X); pap. 7.00 members. ASP & RS.

Acson, Veneeta & Leeds, Richard L., eds. For Gordon H. Fairbanks. (Oceanic Linguistics Special Publications Ser.: No. 20). 320p. 1985. pap. text ed. 12.00x (ISBN 0-8248-0992-0). UH Pr.

Actemeier, Elizabeth, et al, eds. see Brown, Schuyler & Saliers, Don E.

Action for Older Persons, Inc. Staff. Your Retirement: How to Plan for a Secure Future. Page, Cynthia L., ed. LC 84-2820. (Illus.). 186p. (Orig.). 1984. pap. 7.95 (ISBN 0-668-05945-1). Arco.

Acton. Essays on Freedom & Power. 13.25 (ISBN 0-8446-0000-8). Peter Smith.

Acton, Bryan. Recipes for Prizewinning Wines. 125p. Date not set. pap. 5.95 (ISBN 0-900841-16-8, Pub. by Aztex Corp). Argus Bks.

Acton, Bryan, jt. auth. see Duncan, Peter.

Acton, Bryon & Duncan, Peter. Making Wines Like Those You Buy. (Illus.). 159p. Date not set. pap. 6.95 (ISBN 0-900841-03-6, Pub. by Aztex Corp). Argus Bks.

Acton, David, jt. auth. see Loring, John.

Acton, E. Alexander Herzen & the Role of the Intellectual Revolutionary. LC 78-56747. 1979. 29.95 (ISBN 0-521-22166-8). Cambridge U Pr.

Acton, Forman S. Numerical Methods That Work. (Illus.). 1970. text ed. 36.95 scp (ISBN 0-06-040161-3, HarpC). Har-Row.

Acton, Harold. Memoirs of an Aesthete. (Illus.). 426p. 1984. pap. 11.95 (ISBN 0-241-11373-3, Pub. by Hamish Hamilton England). David & Charles.

--Memoirs of an Aesthete. (Illus.). 426p. 1985. pap. 11.95 (ISBN 0-241-11373-3, Pub. by Hamish Hamilton England). David & Charles.

--Modern Chinese Poetry. lib. bdg. 79.95 (ISBN 0-87968-195-0). Krishna Pr.

--Nancy Mitford: A Memoir. (Illus.). 272p. 1984. pap. 9.95 (ISBN 0-241-11278-8, Pub. by Hamish Hamilton England). David & Charles.

--The Pazzi Conspiracy: The Plot Against the Medici. (Illus.). 1979. 14.95 (ISBN 0-500-25064-2). Thames Hudson.

--Three Extraordinary Ambassadors. LC 83-50109. (Walter Neurath Memorial Lectures). (Illus.). 64p. 1984. 12.95f (ISBN 0-500-55015-8). Thames-Hudson.

--Villas of Tuscany. (Illus.). 1984. 40.00 (ISBN 0-500-24085-X). Thames Hudson.

Acton, Henry. Religious Opinions & Example of Milton, Locke, & Newton. LC 71-158223. Repr. of 1833 ed. 11.50 (ISBN 0-404-00283-8). AMS Pr.

Acton, John. An Essay on Shooting. 316p. 1984. Repr. of 1789 ed. 39.00x (ISBN 0-85546-188-8, Pub. by Richmond Pub England). State Mutual Bk.

Acton, John E. The Correspondence of Lord Acton & Richard Simpson. Altholtz, Josef L., et al, eds. LC 75-112466. pap. 94.30 (ISBN 0-317-26130-4, 2024407). Bks Demand UMI.

--Essays in the Liberal Interpretation of History: Selected Papers. McNeill, willliam H., ed. LC 67-15313. (Classic European Historians Ser.). pap. 112.30 (ISBN 0-317-28214-X, 2020016). Bks Demand UMI.

--Historical Essays & Studies. facs. ed. Figgis, J. N. & Laurence, R. V., eds. LC 67-23171. (Essay Index Reprint Ser). 1907. 22.00 (ISBN 0-8369-0134-7). Ayer Co Pubs.

--History of Freedom, & Other Essays. facs. ed. Figgis, J. N. & Laurence, R. V., eds. LC 67-22048. (Essay Index Reprint Ser.). 1907. 26.50 (ISBN 0-8369-0135-5). Ayer Co Pubs.

--Lectures on the French Revolution. Figgis, John N. & Laurence, Reginald V., eds. LC 78-108814. (BCL Ser.: No. II). Repr. of 1910 ed. 24.50 (ISBN 0-404-00284-6). AMS Pr.

--Lord Acton & His Circle. Gasquet, Abbot, ed. LC 68-56781. (Research & Source Works Ser.: No. 269). (Illus.). 1969. Repr. of 1906 ed. 25.50 (ISBN 0-8337-1293-4). B Franklin.

--Lord Acton & His Circle. 1906. 17.00 (ISBN 0-8274-2983-5). R West.

Acton, Lord. Collected Works. 600.00 (ISBN 0-87968-883-1). Gordon Pr.

--Essays on Church & State. 12.00 (ISBN 0-8446-1505-6). Peter Smith.

--Lectures on Modern History. 59.95 (ISBN 0-8490-0496-9). Gordon Pr.

--Lectures on Modern History. Golin, E., ed. 11.50 (ISBN 0-8446-1504-8). Peter Smith.

--Lectures on the French Revolution. 59.95 (ISBN 0-8490-0499-3). Gordon Pr.

Acton, Lord see Acton, John E.

Acton, Ronald T. Immunobiological & Immunochemical Studies of the Oyster, Crassptrea Virginica. 144p. 1972. text ed. 29.50x (ISBN 0-8422-7034-5). Irvington.

Acton, Ronald T., ed. Cell Culture & Its Application. 1977. 60.00 (ISBN 0-12-043050-9). Acad Pr.

Acton, Ronald T. & Lynn, J. Daniel, eds. Eukaryotic Cell Cultures: Basics & Applications. (Advances in Experimental Medicine & Biology Ser.: Vol. 172). 566p. 1984. 75.00x (ISBN 0-306-41619-0, Plenum Pr). Plenum Pub.

Acton, Ronald T., et al. Invertebrate Immune Defense Mechanisms. 1973. 23.50x (ISBN 0-8422-7054-X). Irvington.

Acton, Susan, jt. auth. see Ross, Judith.

Acton, Susan, jt. auth. see Ross, Judity.

Acton, Thomas. Gypsies. LC 82-80194. (Surviving Peoples Ser.). (Illus.). 48p. (gr. 5 up). 1985. PLB 12.68 (ISBN 0-382-06645-6). Silver.

Acton, William. Prostitution, Considered in Its Moral, Social & Sanitary Aspects in London & Other Large Cities & Garrison Towns. 302p. 1972. Repr. of 1870 ed. 27.50x (ISBN 0-7146-2414-4, BHA 02414, F Cass Co). Biblio Dist.

Actor, Paul, jt. ed. see Eisenstein, Toby K.

Acuff, jt. auth. see Dean.

Acuff, Roy & Neely, William. Roy Acuff's Nashville: The Life & Good Times of Country Music. (Illus.). 224p. 1983. pap. 8.95 (ISBN 0-399-50874-0, Perigee). Putnam Pub Group.

Acuna, Rodolfo. East Los Angeles: A Community under Siege. (Monograph Ser.: No. 12). 550p. (Orig.). 1984. pap. 21.95 (ISBN 0-89551-065-0, S301). UCLA Chicano Stud.

--Occupied America: A History of Chicanos. 2nd ed. 1980. pap. text ed. 15.50 scp (ISBN 0-06-380352-6, HarpC). Har-Row.

--Sonoran Strongman: Ignacio Pesqueira & His Times. LC 72-92105. 179p. 1974. pap. 7.50x (ISBN 0-8165-0462-8). U of Ariz Pr.

Acuna, Victor E., jt. auth. see Riley, Eugene W.

Acupuncture News. How to Build-up a Successful Acupuncture Practice. new ed. 1976. 37.50x (ISBN 0-914322-04-4). Chans Corp.

Acupuncture Research Institute. Acupuncture Made Easy. 1976. 9.50 (ISBN 0-914322-03-6). Borden.

--Electro-Acupuncture. 1982. pap. 15.00 (ISBN 0-914322-05-2). Borden.

--A Guide for Application of Ryodoraku. 1976. pap. 5.00. Borden.

--An Outline of Chinese Acupuncture. 1976. pap. 17.50 (ISBN 0-87505-295-9). Borden.

Acus, Leah K. Quarreling Kids: Stop the Fighting & Develop Loving Relationship Within the Family. (Illus.). 192p. 1981. 12.95 (ISBN 0-13-748012-1, Spec); pap. 5.95 (ISBN 0-13-748004-0). P-H.

Acworth, A. W. Buildings of Architectural or Historic Interest in the British West Indies. pap. 10.00 (ISBN 0-384-00287-0). Johnson Repr.

Acworth, B. Swift. 1985. 54.50 (ISBN 0-317-19978-1). Porter.

Acworth, Bernard. Bird & Butterfly Mysteries. 1956. 10.00 (ISBN 0-8022-0004-4). Philos Lib.

--Swift. 1978. Repr. of 1947 ed. lib. bdg. 30.00 (ISBN 0-8414-2911-1). Folcroft.

--Swift. 250p. 1983. Repr. of 1947 ed. lib. bdg. 30.00 (ISBN 0-8492-3434-4). R West.

Acworth, Henry. Ballads of the Marathas in English. 59.95 (ISBN 0-87968-698-7). Gordon Pr.

Acworth, William M. The Elements of Railway Economics. LC 79-51854. 1980. Repr. of 1924 ed. 21.00 (ISBN 0-88355-948-X). Hyperion Conn.

Acyutananda, Swami, ed. Songs of the Vaisnava Acaryas. 1979. pap. 6.95 (ISBN 0-912776-56-0). Bhaktivedanta.

Aczel, J. Lectures on Functional Equations & Their Applications. (Mathematics in Science & Engineering). 1966. 82.00 (ISBN 0-12-043750-3). Acad Pr.

--On Applications & Theory of Functional Equations. 1969. 22.50 (ISBN 0-12-043756-2). Acad Pr.

--Vorlesungen Uber Funktionalgleichungen und Ihre Anwendungen. (Mathematische Reihe Ser.: No. 25). (Illus.). 331p. (Ger.). 1961. 44.95x (ISBN 0-8176-0002-7). Birkhauser.

Aczel, J. & Daroczy, Z. On Measures of Information & Their Characterizations. (Mathematics in Science & Engineering Ser.). 1975. 49.50 (ISBN 0-12-043760-0). Acad Pr.

Aczel, J., ed. Functional Equations: History, Applications & Theory. 1984. lib. bdg. 47.50 (ISBN 90-277-1706-0, Pub. by Reidel Holland). Kluwer Academic.

Aczel, Tamas & Meray, Tibor. The Revolt of the Mind. LC 74-20275. 449p. 1975. Repr. of 1960 ed. lib. bdg. 24.00x (ISBN 0-8371-7851-7, ACRM). Greenwood.

Ad Hoc Committee for Grading of Coronary Artery Disease. A Reporting System on Patients Evaluated for Coronary Artery Disease. 1975. pap. 2.00 (ISBN 0-87493-044-8, 73-315A). Am Heart.

Ad Hoc Group on Uniform Selection Guidelines, et al. A Professional & Legal Analysis of the Uniform Guidelines on Employee Selection Procedures. Erwin, Frank & Koral, Alan, eds. 226p. 1981. 39.95x (ISBN 0-939900-02-5). Am Soc Personnel.

Ad Hoc Library Committee of the National Association of Independent Schools, compiled by. Books for Secondary School Libraries. 844p. 1981. 34.95 (ISBN 0-8352-1111-8). Bowker.

Ad-Lib Consultants. Form Aides for Direct Response Marketing. LC 83-21497. (Illus.). 80p. 1983. pap. 9.95 (ISBN 0-912411-02-3). Ad-Lib.

--Form Aides for Successful Book Publishing. LC 83-60510. (Illus.). 52p. (Orig.). 1983. pap. 5.95 (ISBN 0-912411-00-7). Ad-Lib.

Ada, Alama F., tr. see Rohmer, Harriet.

Ada, Alma F., jt. auth. see Perl, Lila.

Ada, Alma F., tr. see Blume, Judy.

Ada, Alma F., tr. see Clifton, Lucille.

Ada, Alma F., tr. see Simon, Norma.

Ada, Alma F., tr. see Vigna, Judith.

Ada, Alma Flor, tr. see Williams, Barbara.

Ada, G. L., jt. auth. see Nossal, G. J.

Ada, G. L., ed. Contemporary Topics in Molecular Immunology, Vol. 3. LC 73-186260. (Illus.). 273p. 1974. 35.00x (ISBN 0-306-36103-5, Plenum Pr). Plenum Pub.

Ada, G. L., jt. ed. see Porter, R. R.

Adachi, Fumie, tr. from Jap. see Matsuya Piece-Goods Store.

Adachi, Fumie, tr. & illus. see Matsuya Piece-Goods Store.

Adachi, Geraldine, ed. see Chun, Richard.

Adachi, Geraldine, ed. see Demura, Fumio.

Adachi, Geraldine, ed. see Demura, Fumio & Ivan, Dan.

Adachi, Geraldine, ed. see Toguchi, Seikichi.

Adachi, Kelly. The Kids' Handbook. (Illus.). 112p. (gr. 1 up). 1985. 7.95 (ISBN 0-8184-0365-9); pap. 4.95 (ISBN 0-8184-0368-3). Lyle Stuart.

Adachi, M., et al. Sphingolipidoses & Allied Disorders, Vol. 1. Horrobin, D. F., ed. (Annual Research Reviews). 1979. 26.00 (ISBN 0-88831-055-2). Eden Pr.

Adademiderinninbund, Deutschen, ed. Die Frauenfrage in Deutschland Bibliographie 1931-1980, Vol.10. 957p. (Ger.). 1981. lib. bdg. 62.00 (ISBN 0-317-13559-7). K G Saur.

Adair & Rosenstock. Les Portes du Tonnere. (Fr.). 1984. pap. 3.50 (ISBN 0-380-86181-X, 86181). Avon.

Adair, jt. auth. see Amery.

Adair, Alvis V. Desegration: The Illusion of Black Progress. LC 83-25914. 208p. 1984. lib. bdg. 22.00 (ISBN 0-8191-3766-9); pap. text ed. 11.50 (ISBN 0-8191-3767-7). U Pr of Amer.

Adair, Audrey J. Ready-to-Use Music Activities Kit. LC 83-17480. 291p. 1984. pap. text ed. 24.95 (ISBN 0-13-762295-3, Parker). P-H.

Adair, Bryan. The Estimation of a State's Gross Product: A Procedure Applied to Texas. 69p. 1975. pap. 4.00 (ISBN 0-87755-220-7). Bureau Busn UT.

Adair, D., jt. auth. see Hamilton, W. H.

Adair, Denis. Thundergate, Book III: The Story of Canada. 1982. pap. 3.50 (ISBN 0-380-80952-4, 80952). Avon.

Adair, Dennis & Rosenstock, Janet. Bitter Shield: Book II - The Story of Canada. 288p. (Orig.). 1983. pap. 2.95 (ISBN 0-380-79053-X, 79053-X). Avon.

--Kanata, Book 1: The Story of Canada. 1981. pap. 3.95 (ISBN 0-380-77826-2, 83618-1). Avon.

--Kanata: The Story of Canada. 1983. pap. 3.50 (ISBN 0-380-81042-5, 81042-5). Avon.

--Tristes Murailles. (Fr.). 1983. pap. 3.50 (ISBN 0-380-83824-9, 83824-9). Avon.

--Victoria, Book V: The Story of Canada. 272p. 1983. pap. 3.50 (ISBN 0-380-85134-2, 85134). Avon.

--Wildfires, Bk. 4: The Story of Canada. 336p. pap. 3.50 (ISBN 0-380-82313-6, 82313-6). Avon.

Adair, Douglass. Fame & the Founding Fathers. Colbourn, H. Trevor, ed. & intro. by. LC 73-17356. 315p. 1974. 14.95x (ISBN 0-393-05499-3). Norton.

Adair, Douglass, ed. see Oliver, Peter.

Adair, Douglass, jt. ed. see Schutz, John A.

Adair, E. R. Sources for the History of the Council in the Sixteenth & Seventeenth Centuries. LC 70-118458. 1971. Repr. of 1924 ed. 16.50x (ISBN 0-8046-1206-4, Pub. by Kennikat). Assoc Faculty Pr.

Adair, Eleanor R., ed. Microwaves & Thermoregulation: Symposium. 1983. 55.00 (ISBN 0-12-044020-2). Acad Pr.

Adair, Frances E. A Little Leaven. Burgess, J. R., ed. 342p. 1984. Repr. 19.95 (ISBN 0-87797-065-3). Cherokee.

--A Little Leaven. LC 84-7831. 352p. 1984. 19.95 (ISBN 0-87797-065-3). Cherokee.

Adair, Gilbert. Alice Through the Needle's Eye: The Further Adventures of Lewis Carroll's "Alice". (Illus.). 192p. 1985. 11.95 (01160-350). Dutton.

--Hollywood's Vietnam. (Illus.). 192p. 1983. 11.95 (ISBN 0-86276-101-8). Proteus Pub NY.

Adair, Gilbert, tr. see Ciment, Michel.

Adair, Hunter. Shooting & the Countryside. (Illus.). 144p. 1984. 16.95 (ISBN 0-85362-214-0, Oriel); pap. 9.95 (ISBN 0-85362-215-9). Routledge & Kegan.

Adair, Ian, jt. auth. see Amery, Heather.

Adair, J. & Blitt. Training for Series (Trilogy, No. 1. 1978. text ed. 23.95x (ISBN 0-566-02110-2). Gower Pub Co.

--Training for Series (Trilogy, No. 2. 1978. text ed. 23.95x (ISBN 0-566-02111-0). Gower Pub Co.

Adair, James. History of the American Indians. (American Studies). Repr. of 1775 ed. 40.00 (ISBN 0-384-00305-2). Johnson Repr.

Adair, James B. Adair History & Genealogy. (Illus.). 1978. Repr. of 1924 ed. 27.50 (ISBN 0-89308-086-1). Southern Hist Pr.

Adair, James R. Saints Alive. facsimile ed. LC 76-117319. (Biography Index Reprint Ser). 1951. 18.00 (ISBN 0-8369-8011-5). Ayer Co Pubs.

Adair, James R. & Miller, Ted. Escape from Darkness. 156p. 1982. pap. 4.95 (ISBN 0-88207-318-4). Victor Bks.

Adair, James R., jt. auth. see Jorden, Paul J.

Adair, John. Action Centered Leadership. 208p. 1979. text ed. 36.50x (ISBN 0-566-02143-9). Gower Pub Co.

--Effective Leadership: A Self-Development Manual. 130p. 1983. text ed. 30.00x (ISBN 0-566-02411-X). Gower Pub Co.

--Founding Fathers. 322p. 1986. pap. price not set. Baker Bk.

--Founding Fathers: The Puritans in England & America. 314p. 1982. 24.95x (ISBN 0-460-04421-4, Pub. by J M Dent England). Biblio Dist.

--Management & Morality: The Problems & Opportunities of Social Capitalism. 196p. 1980. text ed. 28.25x (ISBN 0-566-02241-9). Gower Pub Co.

--Management Decision Making. 180p. 1985. text ed. 29.95 (ISBN 0-566-02530-2). Gower Pub Co.

--Navajo & Pueblo Silversmiths. (Civilization of the American Indian Ser.: No. 25). (Illus.). 1975. Repr. of 1944 ed. 14.95 (ISBN 0-8061-0133-4). U of Okla Pr.

--The Pilgrim's Way: Shrines & Saints in Britain & Ireland. (Illus.). 1978. 12.98 (ISBN 0-500-25061-8). Thames Hudson.

--The Skills of Leadership. 200p. 1984. 27.50 (ISBN 0-89397-195-2). Nichols Pub.

--Training for Communication. 205p. 1978. Repr. of 1973 ed. text ed. 23.95x (ISBN 0-566-02112-9). Gower Pub Co.

--Training for Decisions. 1981. 75.00x (ISBN 0-686-87409-9, Pub. by Brit Assn Comm England). State Mutual Bk.

--Training for Decisions. 166p. Repr. of 1971 ed. text ed. 23.95x (ISBN 0-566-02111-0). Gower Pub Co.

--Training for Leadership. 158p. 1982. Repr. of 1968 ed. text ed. 23.95x (ISBN 0-566-02110-2). Gower Pub Co.

Adair, John, jt. auth. see Leighton, Dorothea C.

Adair, John, jt. auth. see Worth, Sol.

Adair, John, jt. auth. see Young, Peter.

Adair, John & Despres, David, eds. A Handbook of Management Training Exercise, Vol. 11. 130p. 1978. 175.00 (ISBN 0-686-87408-0, Pub. by Brit Assn Comm England). State Mutual Bk.

Adair, John, et al. A Handbook of Management Training Exercises, Vol. 1. 160p. 1981. 150.00x (ISBN 0-686-87438-2). State Mutual Bk.

Adair, John G. The Human Subject: The Social Psychology of the Psychological Experiment. (Orig.). 1973. pap. text ed. 9.95 (ISBN 0-316-00700-5). Little.

Adair, Margo. Working Inside Out: Tools for Change. LC 84-22912. (Illus.). 427p. (Orig.). 1985. pap. 9.95 (ISBN 0-914728-50-4). Wingbow Pr.

Adajre, S. O. Try the Rabbit: A Handbook on Rabbit Raising for Beginners. (Illus.). 40p. (Orig.). 1984. pap. 5.75x (ISBN 0-946688-61-3, Pub. by Intermediate Tech England). Intermediate Tech.

Adal. The Evidence of Things Not Seen. LC 74-31350. (Photography Ser.). (Illus.). 1975. 21.50 (ISBN 0-306-70722-5); pap. 7.95 (ISBN 0-306-80013-6). Da Capo.

Adali-Mortty, Adali, jt. ed. see Awoonor, Kofi.

Adam, ed. see Baudelaire, Charles.

Adam, ed. see De Balzac, Honore.

Adam, ed. see Descartes, Rene.

Adam, A. Synthetic Adjuvants: Modern Concepts in Immunology. 288p. 1985. 25.00 (ISBN 0-471-86450-1). Wiley.

Adam, A. M., ed. see Plato.

Adam, Addie. Maggie Cameron, Cruise Nurse. (YA) 1978. 8.95 (ISBN 0-685-05591-4, Avalon). Bouregy.

Adam, Adolf. The Liturgical Year: Its History & Its Meaning after the Reform of the Liturgy. O'Connell, Matthew J., tr. from Ger. 1981. pap. 14.95 (ISBN 0-916134-47-4). Pueblo Pub Co.

Adam, Alfred. Antike Berichte ueber die Essener. 2nd ed. Burchard, Christoph, ed. (Kleine Texte fuer Vorlesungen und Uebungen, 182). 80p. 1972. pap. text ed. 7.90 (ISBN 3-11-004183-9). De Gruyter.

Adam, Antoine, jt. auth. see Diderot, Denis.

Adam, Antoine, jt. auth. see Pascal, Blaise.

Adam, Antoine, ed. see Voltaire.

Adam, Auste, jt. auth. see Adam, Helen.

Adam, B. A. The Survival of Domination: Inferiorization & Everyday Life. 1978. 27.50 (ISBN 0-444-99047-X, ASU/, Pub. by Elsevier). Greenwood.

Adam, Barry, ed. Homosexuality & the Social Sciences. Date not set. text ed. price not setx (ISBN 0-8290-1346-6). Irvington.

Adam, Ben. Astrologia-Una Antigua Conspiracion. 128p. 1978. 1.95 (ISBN 0-88113-007-9). Edit Betania.

Adam, Charles, jt. auth. see Descartes, Rene.

Adam, D. L. Mac see Agoston, G. A.

Adam, E., ed. Torrent of Portyngale. (EETS E.S.: No.51). Repr. of 1887 ed. 15.00 (ISBN 0-527-00257-7). Kraus Repr.

Adam, Elaine P., ed. American Foreign Relations, 1976: A Documentary Record. LC 78-53104. (A Council on Foreign Relations Book). 559p. 1978. 55.00x (ISBN 0-8147-7790-2). NYU Pr.

--American Foreign Relations, 1977: A Documentary Record. LC 78-57941. 1979. 55.00x (ISBN 0-8147-0567-7). NYU Pr.

--American Foreign Relations, 1978: A Documentary Record. LC 76-64024. (A Council on Foreign Relations Book). 1979. 55.00x (ISBN 0-8147-0570-7). NYU Pr.

Adam, Evelyn. To Be a Nurse. (Illus.). 118p. 1980. pap. 7.95 (ISBN 0-7216-1032-3). Saunders.

Adam, Everett E., Jr. & Ebert, Ronald J. Production & Operations Management: Concepts, Models & Behavior. 2nd ed. (Illus.). 736p. 1982. ref. ed. 31.95 (ISBN 0-13-724971-3). P-H.

Adam, Everett, Jr. & Ebert, Ronald J. Production & Operations Management: Concepts, Models & Behavior. 3rd ed. (Illus.). 800p. 1986. text ed. 31.95 (ISBN 0-13-724857-1). P-H.

Adam, Frank. What Is My Tartan? Or, the Clans of Scotland, with Their Septs & Dependents. 112p. 1983. pap. 5.00 (ISBN 0-912951-01-X). Scotpr.

Adam, G. Perception, Consciousness, Memory: Reflections of a Biologist. LC 73-20153. 229p. 1980. 29.50x (ISBN 0-306-30776-6, Plenum Pr). Plenum Pub.

Adam, G., ed. Biology of Memory. LC 73-154700. 250p. 1971. 29.50x (ISBN 0-306-30535-6, Plenum Pr). Plenum Pub.

Adam, G., ed. see Deutsche Gesellschaft Fur Biophysik, Annual Meeting, Konstanz, October 1979.

Adam, G., et al, eds. Brain & Behaviour: Proceedings of the 28th International Congress of Physiological Sciences, Budapest, 1980. LC 80-42186. (Advances in Physiological Sciences Ser.: Vol. 17). (Illus.). 500p. 1981. 66.00 (ISBN 0-08-027338-6). Pergamon.

Adam, Graeme M. Spain & Portugal, 2 vols. 1980. Set. lib. bdg. 199.00 (ISBN 0-8490-3183-4). Gordon Pr.

--Spain & Portugal. 1976. lib. bdg. 59.95 (ISBN 0-8490-2638-5). Gordon Pr.

Adam, Hamish & McLatchie, Greg. Competition Karate. (Illus.). 112p. (Orig.). 1985. pap. 8.95 (ISBN 0-7136-2465-5, Pub. by A & C Black UK). Sterling.

Adam, Hans C., jt. auth. see Fabian, Rainer.

Adam, Helen. The Bells of Dis. (Morning Coffee Chapbk.). (Illus.). 24p. 1985. pap. 10.00 (ISBN 0-915124-92-0). Coffee Hse.

--Ghosts & Grinning Shadows. 1979. pap. 4.00 (ISBN 0-914610-10-4). Hanging Loose.

--San Francisco's Burning. 1985. pap. 15.00 (ISBN 0-914610-33-3). Hanging Loose.

--Selected Poems & Ballads. LC 74-77378. (Publication Ser.: No. 5b). (Illus.). 60p. 1975. 7.00 (ISBN 0-914496-04-2). Helikon NY.

--Stone Cold Gothic. 7.00x (ISBN 0-318-04059-X); pap. 3.50x (ISBN 0-318-04060-3). Human Res Inst.

--Turn Again to Me. 1977. 7.00x (ISBN 0-686-22908-8); pap. 3.50x (ISBN 0-686-22909-6). Kulchur Foun.

Adam, Helen & Adam, Auste. Stone Cold Gothic. 1984. 7.00 (ISBN 0-317-16221-7); pap. 3.50 (ISBN 0-317-16222-5). Kulchur Foun.

Adam, Heribert. Modernizing Racial Domination: The Dynamics of South African Politics. LC 75-132422. (Perspectives on Southern Africa Ser.: No. 2). 1971. pap. 9.95x (ISBN 0-520-02251-3, CAMPUS229). U of Cal Pr.

Adam, Heribert & Giliomee, Hermann. Ethnic Power Mobilized: Can South Africa Change? LC 78-65492. 1979. 33.00x (ISBN 0-300-02377-4); pap. 8.95x (ISBN 0-300-02378-2, Y-349). Yale U Pr.

Adam, Ian, ed. This Particular Web: Essays on Middlemarch. LC 75-15844. 152p. 1975. 15.00x (ISBN 0-8020-5332-7). U of Toronto Pr.

Adam, J. G., jt. auth. see Balian, R.

Adam, J. H., ed. Longman Dictionary of Business English. 528p. 1982. 17.95 (ISBN 0-582-55552-3). Longman.

Adam, James. Religious Teachers of Greece. LC 72-2565. (Select Bibliographies Reprint Ser). 1972. Repr. of 1908 ed. 26.00 (ISBN 0-8369-6843-3). Ayer Co Pubs.

--The Religious Teachers of Greece. LC 65-22806. (Library of Religious & Philosophical Thought). Repr. of 1908 ed. lib. bdg. 35.00x (ISBN 0-678-09950-2, Reference Bk Pubs). Kelley.

Adam, James, jt. auth. see Adam, Robert.

Adam, James, ed. see Plato.

Adam, James M. Hypothermia - Ashore & Afloat: Proceedings of 3rd International " Action for Disaster " Conference, Aberdeen 1979. (Illus.). 216p. 1981. 32.50 (ISBN 0-08-025750-X). Pergamon.

Adam, Jan. Employment & Wage Policies in Poland, Czechoslovakia & Hungary Since 1950. LC 83-40125. 272p. 1985. 25.00 (ISBN 0-312-24457-6). St Martin.

Adam, Jan, ed. Employment Policies in the Soviet Union & Eastern Europe. LC 81-18289. 224p. 1982. 27.50 (ISBN 0-312-24462-2). St Martin.

--Wage Control & Inflation in the Soviet Bloc Countries. 266p. 1980. 38.95 (ISBN 0-03-057007-7). Praeger.

Adam, Jean-Michel. Linguistique et Discours Litteraire. new ed. (Collection L). (Orig., Fr.). 1976. pap. text ed. 19.95 (ISBN 0-685-66283-7). Larousse.

Adam, John & Adam, Nancy. Divorce: How & When to Let Go. pap. 4.95 (ISBN 0-13-216408-6). Divorce Res.

Adam, K. M., et al. Medical & Veterinary Protozoology. rev. ed. 1980. 50.00 (ISBN 0-443-00764-0). Churchill.

Adam, Karl. The Spirit of Catholicism. McCann, Dom J., tr. from German. 237p. 1981. Repr. of 1929 ed. lib. bdg. 30.00 (ISBN 0-89987-028-7). Darby Bks.

Adam, Karl & McCann, Dom J. The Spirit of Catholicism. 1979. pap. 4.50 (ISBN 0-385-14968-9, Im). Doubleday.

Adam, Kirstine, jt. auth. see Oswald, Ian.

Adam, Milan, ed. see Deyl, Zdenek.

Adam, Nabil R., jt. auth. see Dogramaci, Ali.

Adam, Nabil R. & Dogramaci, Ali, eds. Current Issues in Computer Simulation. LC 79-51696. 1979. 47.50 (ISBN 0-12-044120-9). Acad Pr.

--Productivity Analysis at the Organizational Level. (Productivity Analysis Studies). 192p. 1981. lib. bdg. 21.00 (ISBN 0-89838-038-3, Pub. by Martinus Nijhoff). Kluwer Academic.

Adam, Nancy, jt. auth. see Adam, John.

Adam, of Usk. Chronicon Adae de Usk, A.D. 1377 to 1421. Thompson, Edward M., ed. LC 78-63447. (Pilgrimages Ser.). 392p. 1980. Repr. of 1904 ed. 44.50 (ISBN 0-404-16367-X). AMS Pr.

Adam, Peter A., jt. ed. see Merkatz, Irwin R.

Adam, Robert. The Works in Architecture of Robert & James Adam, 3 vols. in 1. LC 78-67644. (Scottish Enlightenment Ser.). Repr. of 1788 ed. 135.00 (ISBN 0-404-17233-4). AMS Pr.

Adam, Robert & Adam, James. The Works in Architecture of Robert & James Adam. LC 78-62405. (Illus.). 144p. 1980. 50.00 (ISBN 0-486-23810-5). Dover.

Adam, Robert E. Oceans of the World: Syllabus. 1978. pap. text ed. 5.35 (ISBN 0-89420-041-0, 233021); cassette recordings 70.85 (ISBN 0-89420-166-2, 233000). Natl Book.

--U. S. Government: Executive Branch: Syllabus. (U. S. Government Ser.). (gr. 7-12). 1979. pap. text ed. 7.35 student syllabus (ISBN 0-89420-089-5, 194030); cassette recordings 150.05 (ISBN 0-89420-189-1, 194000). Natl Book.

Adam, Ruth. I'm Not Complaining. LC 83-23978. 352p. 1984. pap. 7.95 (ISBN 0-385-27961-2, Virago). Doubleday.

Adam, Ruth, jt. auth. see Muggeridge, Kitty.

Adam, T. R. Western Interests in the Pacific Realm. 10.00 (ISBN 0-8446-1507-2). Peter Smith.

Adam, Waldemar & Cilento, G., eds. Chemical & Biological Generation of Excited States. 1982. 59.50 (ISBN 0-12-044080-6). Acad Pr.

Adam, William S., et al. Microscopic Anatomy of the Dog: A Photographic Atlas. 304p. 1970. photocopy ed. 33.50x (ISBN 0-398-00006-9). C C Thomas.

Adamany, David. Financing Politics: Recent Wisconsin Elections. LC 79-84948. 318p. 1969. 27.50x (ISBN 0-299-05430-6). U of Wis Pr.

Adamany, David, jt. ed. see Keynes, Edward.

Adamany, David W. Financing Politics: Recent Wisconsin Elections. LC 79-84948. pap. 79.50 (ISBN 0-317-29010-X, 2023727). Bks Demand UMI.

Adamany, David W. & Agree, George E. Political Money: A Strategy for Campaign Financing in America. 2nd ed. LC 75-11351. 254p. 1980. pap. text ed. 7.95x (ISBN 0-8018-2377-3). Johns Hopkins.

Adamany, David W. & Agree, George E., eds. Political Money: A Strategy for Campaign Financing in America. LC 75-11351. 254p. 1975. 22.50x (ISBN 0-8018-1718-8); pap. text ed. 7.95x (ISBN 0-8018-2377-3). Johns Hopkins.

Adamaszek, Thaddeus, et al. Handbook of Job Proficiency Criteria: A GLAC Research Report. 80p. 1974. pap. 3.00 (ISBN 0-686-81170-4). Intl Personnel Mgmt.

Adamczyk. Black Dance: An Annotated Bibliography. 1985. lib. bdg. 33.50 (ISBN 0-8240-8808-5). Garland Pub.

Adamec, Cannie S., ed. Sex Roles: Origins, Influences & Implications for Women. 1980. 17.95 (ISBN 0-920792-00-6). Eden Pr.

Adamec, Ludwig. Afghanistan's Foreign Affairs to the Mid-Twentieth Century: Relations with the USSR, Germany, & Britain. LC 73-86450. 324p. 1974. pap. 12.50x (ISBN 0-8165-0459-8). U of Ariz Pr.

Adamek, Jiri. Theory of Mathematical Structures. 1983. lib. bdg. 59.50 (ISBN 90-277-1459-2, Pub. by Reidel Holland). Kluwer Academic.

Adamek, Josef. Centrally Planned Economies: Economic Overview 1984. (Report Ser.: No. 857). 72p. 1984. 100.00 (ISBN 0-8237-0298-7); members 20.00 (ISBN 0-317-36906-7). Conference Bd.

--Centrally Planned Economies: Economic Overview 1983. (Report Ser.: No. 841). (Illus.). 63p. (Orig.). 1983. pap. 50.00 (ISBN 0-8237-0281-2); pap. 10.00 member. Conference Bd.

Adames, Leonard, et al. Entrance. 1976. 2.00 (ISBN 0-912678-24-0). Greenfld Rev Pr.

Adamfio, Tawia. By Nkrumah's Side. 39.00x (ISBN 0-86036-176-4, Pub. by R Collings UK). State Mutual Bk.

Adami, Giuseppe, ed. Letters of Giacomo Puccini. Makin, Ena, tr. from It. LC 74-183316. (Illus.). 352p. 1973. pap. 7.50x (ISBN 0-8443-0036-5). Vienna Hse.

Adamiak, Richard. Justice & History in the Old Testament: The Evolution of Divine Retribution in the Historiographies of the Wilderness Generation. 1982. 12.95x (ISBN 0-939738-08-2). Zubal Inc.

--The Law Book Price Guide: A Market Value Reference for Antiquarian, Out-of-Print & Rare Law Books & Documents & Other Law-Related Material. Gastor, Joseph J., ed. xiv, 376p. 1983. lib. bdg. 75.00 (ISBN 0-9610650-0-1). Chicago Law Bk.

Adamic, K. J., jt. ed. see Herak, J. N.

Adamic, Louis. Dynamite, the Story of Class Violence in America. (Illus.). 1959. 12.00 (ISBN 0-8446-1002-X). Peter Smith.

--Eagle & the Roots. LC 75-108386. Repr. of 1952 ed. lib. bdg. 21.00x (ISBN 0-8371-3809-4, ADER). Greenwood.

--Grandsons: A Story of American Lives. LC 74-26092. 384p. 1983. Repr. of 1935 ed. 37.50 (ISBN 0-404-58401-2). AMS Pr.

--Laughing in the Jungle: An Autobiography of an Immigrant in America. LC 69-18755. (American Immigration Collection Ser., No. 1). 1969. Repr. of 1932 ed. 25.00 (ISBN 0-405-00503-2). Ayer Co Pubs.

--My America: 1928-1938. LC 76-2050. (FDR & the Era of the New Deal). 1976. Repr. of 1938 ed. lib. bdg. 59.50 (ISBN 0-306-70801-9). Da Capo.

--The Native's Return. LC 74-34412. 358p. 1975. Repr. of 1934 ed. lib. bdg. 23.50x (ISBN 0-8371-7965-3, ADNR). Greenwood.

--Robinson Jeffers: A Portrait. 1978. Repr. of 1929 ed. lib. bdg. 10.00 (ISBN 0-8495-0048-6). Arden Lib.

--Robinson Jeffers: A Portrait. LC 73-11375. 1929. lib. bdg. 16.50 (ISBN 0-8414-2881-6). Folcroft.

Adamic, Louis see Friedman, Leon.

Adamis, Eddie. BASIC Key Words: A User's Reference. LC 82-21759. 292p. 1983. pap. 14.95 (ISBN 0-471-86542-7, Pub. by Wiley Pr). Wiley.

--BASIC Key Words for the Apple III. LC 83-12327. 143p. 1984. pap. text ed. 14.95 (ISBN 0-471-88389-1, Pub. by Wiley Pr). Wiley.

--BASIC Keywords for the IBM PC. (IBM Personal Computer Ser.). 150p. 1984. pap. 14.95 (ISBN 0-471-88402-2, Pub. by Wiley Pr). Wiley.

--BASIC Subroutines for Commodore Computers. LC 82-21874. 312p. 1983. pap. text ed. 12.95 (ISBN 0-471-86541-9, Pub. by Wiley Pr). Wiley.

--Business BASIC for the Apple III: A Self Teaching Guide. LC 83-12328. 245p. 1984. pap. 16.95 (ISBN 0-471-88388-3, Pub. by Wiley Pr). Wiley.

--Business BASIC for the IBM PC. (IBM PC Ser.: No. 1-646). 200p. 1984. pap. 14.95 (ISBN 0-471-88401-4, Pub. by Wiley Pr). Wiley.

Adamjan, V. M., et al. Eleven Papers in Analysis. LC 51-5559. (Translations Ser.: No. 2, Vol. 95). 1970. 30.00 (ISBN 0-8218-1795-7, TRANS 2-95). Am Math.

--Nine Papers on Analysis. LC 78-5442. (Translation Ser.: No. 2, Vol. 111). 1978. 41.00 (ISBN 0-8218-3061-9, TRANS2-111). Am Math.

Adamnan, Saint. Vita Sancti Columbae. Reeves, William, ed. LC 79-174801. (Bannatyne Club, Edinburgh. Publications: No. 103). Repr. of 1857 ed. 45.00 (ISBN 0-404-52858-9). AMS Pr.

Adamo, Pat. A Guide to Pediatric Tracheostomy Care. (Illus.). 72p. 1981. spiral bdg. 12.75x (ISBN 0-398-04479-1). C C Thomas.

Adamo, Ralph. End of the World. LC 78-17913. (Lost Roads Poetry Ser.: No. 17). 1979. pap. 4.00 (ISBN 0-918786-18-5). Lost Roads.

--Sadness at the Private University. LC 77-79216. (Lost Roads Poetry Ser.: No. 3). 1978. 6.00 (ISBN 0-918786-04-5); pap. 3.00 (ISBN 0-918786-05-3). Lost Roads.

Adamou. Enpi Karate Kata Shotokan. 1984. 20.00 (ISBN 0-901764-59-0, Pub. by P H Crompton Ltd UK). State Mutual Bk.

Adamov, N. V., et al. Differential Equations. (Translations, Ser.: No. 1, Vol. 4). 1962. 24.00 (ISBN 0-8218-1604-7, TRANS 1-4). Am Math.

Adamovich, A., et al. Out of the Fire. 1980. 12.00 (ISBN 0-8285-1891-2, Pub. by Progress Pubs USSR). Imported Pubns.

Adamovich, Brenda L., et al, eds. Cognitive Rehabilitation of Closed Head Injured Patients: A Dynamic Approach. (Illus.). 220p. 1985. 25.00 (ISBN 0-933014-67-8). College-Hill.

Adamovich, David R. The Heart: Fundamentals of Electrocardiography, Exercise Physiology, & Exercise Stress Testing. LC 83-50971. (Illus.). 414p. (Orig.). 1984. pap. 29.95 (ISBN 0-914363-00-X). Sports Med Bks.

Adamovich, Shirley Gray. Reader in Library Technology. 236p. 1976. 28.50 (ISBN 0-313-24042-6, ZRJ/). Greenwood.

Adams. Congregational Dancing in Christian Worship. 161p. 1980. 4.95 (ISBN 0-318-16438-8). Sacred Dance Guild.

--Cosmic X-Ray Astronomy. 1980. 37.50 (ISBN 0-9960019-2-1, Pub. by A Hilger England). Heyden.

--Humor in the American Pulpit. 245p. 1981. 6.95 (ISBN 0-318-16444-2). Sacred Dance Guild.

--Italy at War. LC 82-3182. (World War II Ser.). lib. bdg. 22.60 (ISBN 0-8094-3449-0, Pub. by Time-Life). Silver.

--Othello (Shakespeare) (Book Notes). 1984. pap. 2.50 (ISBN 0-8120-3434-1). Barron.

--Personal Injury & Property Damage: Preparation for Trial. (The Law in North Carolina Ser.). incl. latest pocket part supplement 24.95 (ISBN 0-686-90945-3); separate pocket part supplement, 1982 for use in 1983 11.95 (ISBN 0-686-90946-1). Harrison Co GA.

--Single Variable Calculus. 624p. 1983. text ed. 24.95 (ISBN 0-201-10053-3). Addison-Wesley.

--Ysengrimus the Wolf. (Library of Medieval Literature). 1985. lib. bdg. 27.00 (ISBN 0-8240-8780-1). Garland Pub.

Adams & Bayless. Georgia Driving Laws & Safety Rules. 40p. 1984. 2.95 (ISBN 0-87797-088-2). Cherokee.

Adams & Corsellis, J. A. Greenfield's Neuropathology. 4th ed. 1126p. 1984. 147.50 (ISBN 0-471-82307-4). Wiley.

Adams & Hurless. Our United States Workbook. Rev. ed. 64p. 1982. 2.10 (ISBN 0-317-35480-9). New Readers.

Adams & Murray. Improving Your Health with Calcium & Phosphorus. 1978. 1.25x (ISBN 0-915962-25-X). Cancer Control soc.

--Improving Your Health with Vitamin C. 1978. 1.50x (ISBN 0-915962-23-3). Cancer Control Soc.

Adams, jt. auth. see Ferguson.

Adams, jt. auth. see Kakulas.

Adams, ed. Dancing Christmas Carols. (Illus.). 132p. 1978. 6.95 (ISBN 0-318-16440-X). Sacred Dance Guild.

Adams, ed. see De Dwyer.

Adams, A. Stalin & His Times. LC 70-183627. 1972. pap. text ed. 10.95 (ISBN 0-03-085094-0, HoltC). HR&W.

Adams, A. & Schots, C., eds. Biochemical & Biological Applications of Isotachophoresis: Proceedings of the 1st International Symposium, Baconfoy, May 1979. (Analytical Chemistry Symposia Ser.: Vol. 5). vii, 278p. 1980. 70.25 (ISBN 0-444-41891-1). Elsevier.

Adams, A., et al. Litterature francaise, 2 Vols. (Illus., Fr.). 79.95 ea. Larousse.

Adams, A. Dana, ed. Four Thousand Questions & Answers on the Bible. 1983. 4.25 (ISBN 0-8054-1148-8); pap. 2.25 (ISBN 0-8054-1149-6). Broadman.

Adams, A. E., et al. Atlas of Sedimentary Rocks under the Microscope. LC 83-12379. 104p. (Orig.). 1984. pap. 24.95x (ISBN 0-470-27476-X). Halsted Pr.

Adams, A. P. & Hahn, C. E. Principles & Practice of Blood-Gas Analysis. 2nd ed. LC 81-21709. (Illus.). 101p. 1982. pap. text ed. 19.50 (ISBN 0-443-02521-5). Churchill.

Adams, A. T. Explorations of Pierre Esprit Radisson. 10.00 (ISBN 0-87018-001-0). Ross.

Adams, Abigail. Letters, 2 vols. LC 72-78635. 1840. Repr. Set. 79.00x (ISBN 0-403-01935-4). Somerset Pub.

--New Letters of Abigail Adams, 1788-1801. Mitchell, Stewart, ed. LC 73-13398. (Illus.). 281p. 1973. Repr. of 1947 ed. lib. bdg. 20.25x (ISBN 0-8371-7055-9, ADNL). Greenwood.

Adams, Abigail & Adams, John. The Book of Abigail & John: Selected Letters of the Adams Family, 1762-1784. Butterfield, L. H., et al, eds. LC 74-27938. (Illus.). 450p. 1975. 25.00x (ISBN 0-674-07855-1); pap. 8.95 (ISBN 0-674-07854-3). Harvard U Pr.

Adams, Abigail, jt. auth. see Adams, John.

Adams, Adeline V. Amouretta Landscape & Other Stories. facsimile ed. LC 79-103486. (Short Story Index Reprint Ser.). 1922. 17.00 (ISBN 0-8369-3192-0). Ayer Co Pubs.

Adams, Adolph A., et al, eds. Methods for Studying Mononuclear Phagocytes. LC 81-20646. 1981. 75.00 (ISBN 0-12-044220-5). Acad Pr.

Adams, Adrian, tr. see Kourouma, Ahmado.

Adams, Adrian, tr. see Ousmane, Sembene.

Adams, Adrienne. The Christmas Party. LC 78-16230. (Aladdin Edition). (Illus.). (gr. k-2). 1978. reinforced bdg 12.95 (ISBN 0-684-15930-9, ScribJ); pap. 2.95 Aladdin edition (ISBN 0-689-70747-9). Scribner.

--Christmas Party. LC 78-16230. 1982p. 1982. pap. 2.95 (ISBN 0-689-70747-9, A-123, Aladdin). Atheneum.

--The Easter Egg Artists. LC 75-39301. (Illus.). 32p. (gr. k-3). 1976. reinforced bdg 12.95 (ISBN 0-684-14652-5, ScribJ); pap. 2.95 Aladdin Edition (ISBN 0-689-70479-8). Scribner.

--The Great Valentine's Day Balloon Race. LC 80-19527. (Illus.). 32p. (gr. k-3). 1980. 12.95 (ISBN 0-684-16640-2, ScribJ). Scribner.

--A Halloween Happening. (Illus.). 32p. (gr. k-3). 1981. 10.95 (ISBN 0-684-17166-X, ScribJ). Scribner.

--Poetry of Earth & Sky. LC 70-39577. (Illus.). 48p. (gr. 1-4). 1972. reinforced bdg. 6.95 (ISBN 0-684-13012-2, ScribJ). Scribner.

--The Shoemaker & the Elves. (Illus.). 32p. (gr. k-3). pap. 2.95 (ISBN 0-689-70480-1, A-107, Aladdin). Atheneum.

--Woggle of Witches. LC 70-161536. (Illus.). 32p. (ps-1). 1971. reinforced bdg. 12.95 (ISBN 0-684-12506-4, ScribJ); (ScribJ). Scribner.

--A Woggle of Witches. LC 70-161536. (Illus.). 32p. (Orig.). (gr. k-3). 1985. pap. 3.95 (ISBN 0-689-71050-X, A-164, Aladdin). Atheneum.

Adams, Adrienne & Andersen, Hans Christian. Thumbelina. LC 61-17282. (Illus.). (gr. k-4). 1961. reinforced bdg. 12.95 (ISBN 0-684-12705-9, ScribJ). Scribner.

Adams, Adrienne & Brothers Grimm. Hansel & Gretel. LC 74-14080. (Illus.). 32p. (gr. k-5). 1975. (ScribJ); pap. 2.95 (ISBN 0-684-16006-4, ScribJ). Scribner.

--Shoemaker & the Elves. LC 60-12607. (Illus.). (gr. k-4). 1960. reinforced bdg. 11.95 (ISBN 0-684-12982-5, ScribJ); pap. 2.95 (SBF3, ScribJ). Scribner.

Adams, Adrienne, illus. The Ugly Duckling. LC 65-21364. (Illus.). 1982. pap. 2.95 (ISBN 0-689-70748-7, A-124, Aladdin). Atheneum.

Adams, Agatha B. & Adams, Nicholson B. Contemporary Spanish Literature in English Translation. 1978. Repr. of 1929 ed. lib. bdg. 10.00 (ISBN 0-8482-0020-9). Norwood Edns.

Adams, Alexander B., ed. see Thoreau, Henry D.

Adams, Alice. Beautiful Girl. 240p. 1980. pap. 2.95 (ISBN 0-671-83218-2). WSP.

--Beautiful Girl. 1984. pap. 3.95 (ISBN 0-671-54688-0). WSP.

--Families & Survivors. 224p. 1984. pap. 5.95 (ISBN 0-14-007375-2). Penguin.

--Listening to Billie. 224p. 1984. pap. 5.95 (ISBN 0-14-007376-0). Penguin.

--Return Trips. Wilson, Victoria, ed. LC 85-40116. 208p. 1985. 14.95 (ISBN 0-394-53633-9). Knopf.

--Rich Rewards. LC 80-10214. 224p. 1980. 9.95 (ISBN 0-394-51101-8). Knopf.

--Rich Rewards. (Contemporary American Fiction Ser.). 205p. 1981. pap. 5.95 (ISBN 0-14-005918-0). Penguin.

--Superior Women. LC 84-47507. 374p. 1984. 16.45 (ISBN 0-394-53632-0). Knopf.

--Superior Women. 384p. 1985. pap. 3.95 (ISBN 0-449-20746-3, Crest). Fawcett.

--To See You Again. 1982. 13.50 (ISBN 0-394-52335-0). Knopf.

--To See You Again. (Contemporary American Fiction Ser.). 312p. 1983. pap. 5.95 (ISBN 0-14-006483-4). Penguin.

Adams, Alice D. The Neglected Period of Anti-Slavery in America 1808-1831. 307p. 1973. Repr. of 1908 ed. 16.95 (ISBN 0-87928-034-4). Corner Hse.

--Neglected Period of Anti-Slavery in America, 1808-1831. 1964. 11.50 (ISBN 0-8446-1003-8). Peter Smith.

Adams, Alicen. Changing Stations. (Illus.). 112p. 1983. 7.00 (ISBN 0-682-40141-2). Exposition Pr FL.

Adams, Alison, ed. The Romance of Yder. (Arthurian Studies: No. VIII). 259p. 1983. 29.50 (ISBN 0-85991-133-0, BAB-04929, Pub. by Boydell & Brewer). Longwood Pub Group.

Adams, Alto, Jr. A Cattleman's Backcountry Florida. LC 84-20890. (Illus.). 54p. 1985. pap. 12.00 (ISBN 0-8130-0809-3). U Presses Fla.

Adams, Andrew. Ninja. (Illus.). 1970. 7.95x (ISBN 0-685-00900-9). Wehman.

--Ninja, the Invisible Assassins. Alston, Pat, ed. LC 75-130760. (Ser. 302). (Illus.). 1970. 7.95 (ISBN 0-89750-030-X). Ohara Pubns.

Adams, Andy. Andy Adams' Campfire Tales. Hudson, Wilson M., ed. LC 75-29131. (Illus.). xxxii, 296p. 1976. 23.95x (ISBN 0-8032-0870-7); pap. 7.95 (ISBN 0-8032-5835-6, BB 615, Bison). U of Nebr Pr.

--Cattle Brands: A Collection of Western Campfire Stories. facsimile ed. LC 70-150534. (Short Story Index Reprint Ser.). Repr. of 1934 ed. 16.00 (ISBN 0-8369-3831-3). Ayer Co Pubs.

--Log of a Cowboy. (Classics Ser). (gr. 7 up). 1969. pap. 1.95 (ISBN 0-8049-0201-1, CL-201). Airmont.

--The Log of a Cowboy. Orig. Title: Public Domain. 1976. pap. 1.25 (ISBN 0-685-64012-4, LB344ZK, Leisure Bks). Dorchester Pub Co.

--The Log of a Cowboy. 387p. 1975. Repr. of 1903 ed. 16.95 (ISBN 0-87928-067-0). Corner Hse.

--The Log of a Cowboy. 20.95 (ISBN 0-88411-929-7, Pub. by Aeonian Pr). Amereon Ltd.

--The Log of a Cowboy: A Narrative of the Old Trail Days. LC 3-12817. (Illus.). x, 397p. 1964. 27.50x (ISBN 0-8032-1000-0); pap. 4.95 (ISBN 0-8032-5000-2, BB 192, Bison). U of Nebr Pr.

--Trail Drive. Rounds, Glen, ed. & illus. (Illus.). 256p. (YA) (gr. 7 up). 1965. 3.95 (ISBN 0-8234-0120-0). Holiday.

Adams, Ann. Travels with a Donkey. (Hindsight Saga Ser.). (Illus.). 92p. 1983. pap. 6.95 (ISBN 0-915433-09-5). Packrat WA.

Adams, Ann, ed. see Jones, Franklin, Sr.

Adams, Ann, et al. Reading for Survival in Today's Society, Vol. 1. LC 77-24017. 1978. 14.95 (ISBN 0-673-16421-7); pap. 12.95 (ISBN 0-673-16420-9). Scott F.

--Reading for Survival in Today's Society, Vol. 2. LC 77-24017. 1978. 14.95 (ISBN 0-673-16423-3); pap. 12.95 (ISBN 0-673-16422-5). Scott F.

Adams, Anna. The Ratio of One to a Stone. 25p. (Orig.). 1982. pap. 4.50 (ISBN 0-910829-02-0). First East.

Adams, Anne, ed. see Fowler, Alex D.

Adams, Anne, et al. Success in Reading & Writing: Grade 2. 1980. 14.95 (ISBN 0-673-16435-7). Scott F.

--Success in Kindergarten Reading & Writing. 1980. 13.95 (ISBN 0-673-16437-3). Scott F.

Adams, Anne H. Success in Beginning Reading & Writing: Grade 1. 1978. 14.95 (ISBN 0-673-16551-5). Scott F.

--Success in Reading & Writing: Grade 3. 1980. 14.95 (ISBN 0-673-16436-5). Scott F.

--Success in Reading & Writing: Phonics Sheets, Grade 1. 1978. pap. 6.95 (ISBN 0-673-16433-0). Scott F.

Adams, Anne H. & Bebensee, Elisabeth L. Success in Reading & Writing: Grade 6. 1983. 16.95 (ISBN 0-673-16586-8). Scott F.

Adams, Anne H., jt. auth. see London, Liz E.

Adams, Anne H., et al. Success in Reading & Writing. (gr. 5). 1982. 15.95 (ISBN 0-673-16546-9). Scott F.

--Success in Reading & Writing: Grade 4. 1982. 15.95 (ISBN 0-673-16545-0). Scott F.

Adams, Anne R. Tappan Zee Dress: Plain & Fancy, 1780-1930. (Illus.). 40p. Date not set. pap. 2.00 (ISBN 0-911183-20-5). Hist Soc Rocklan Cty.

Adams, Annie E., tr. see Brandenburg, Erich.

Adams, Ansel. Ansel Adams. LC 76-53306. (Illus.). 128p. 1972. 34.00 (ISBN 0-8212-0721-0, 043583). NYGS.

--Born Free & Equal. rev. ed. Medvec, Emily, ed. LC 84-21125. (Illus.). 44p. 1984. pap. 15.00 (ISBN 0-931547-00-8, BFE). Echolight Corp.

--The Camera. (The Ansel Adams Photography Ser.: Bk. 1). (Illus.). 1980. 16.50 (ISBN 0-8212-1092-0, 125121, Pub. by Museum Mod Art). NYGS.

--Examples: The Making of Forty Photographs. (Illus.). 192p. 1983. 39.00i (ISBN 0-8212-1551-5, 258636). NYGS.

--Images Nineteen Twenty Three to Nineteen Seventy-Four. (Illus.). 128p. 1981. 125.00 (ISBN 0-8212-1132-3, 382205). NYGS.

--Liliane de Cock. pap. 7.95 (ISBN 0-88360-038-2, Dist. by Univ. of Texas Pr.). Amon Carter.

--The Negative. (The New Ansel Adams Photography Ser.: Bk. 2). (Illus.). 288p. 1981. 18.95 (ISBN 0-8212-1131-5). NYGS.

--Photographs of the Southwest. LC 76-10034. (Illus.). 1976. 39.95 (ISBN 0-8212-0699-0, 706914); pap. 24.50i (ISBN 0-8212-1574-4, 702617). NYGS.

--Polaroid Land Photography. LC 78-7069. 1978. 19.45 (ISBN 0-8212-0729-6, 712744). NYGS.

--The Portfolios of Ansel Adams. 1981. pap. 22.00i (ISBN 0-8212-1122-6, 713953). NYGS.

--The Portfolios of Ansel Adams. LC 77-71628. (Illus.). 1977. 44.00i (ISBN 0-8212-0723-7, 713945). NYGS.

--The Print. LC 83-950. (Photography Ser.: Bk. 3). (Illus.). 224p. 1983. 19.45i (ISBN 0-8212-1526-4, 719307). NYGS.

--Singular Images. LC 73-93872. (Illus.). 1974. pap. 14.45i (ISBN 0-8212-0728-8, 792896). NYGS.

--Yosemite & the Range of Light. LC 78-72074. (Illus.). 1979. 100.00 (ISBN 0-8212-0750-4, 969605); pap. 24.50 (ISBN 0-8212-1523-X, 969591). NYGS.

Adams, Ansel & Austin, Mary. Taos Pueblo. LC 76-53307. (Illus.). 1977. ltd. ed. 500.00 (ISBN 0-8212-0722-9, 043591). NYGS.

Adams, Ansel & Newhall, Nancy. Death Valley. 4th. ed. (Illus.). 1970. (Dist. by Little, Brown); pap. 8.95 (ISBN 0-913832-02-2). Mus Graphics.

Adams, Ansel, et al. Death Valley. (Illus.). 1954. 8.95 (ISBN 0-8212-0724-5, 178012); pap. 8.95 (ISBN 0-8212-0725-3, 178004). NYGS.

Adams, Anthony & Jones, Esnor. Teaching Humanities in the Microelectronic Age. 128p. 1983. pap. 13.00x (ISBN 0-335-10196-8, Pub. by Open Univ Pr). Taylor & Francis.

Adams, Anthony, ed. New Directions in English Teaching. 245p. 1982. text ed. 30.00x (ISBN 0-905273-37-0, Pub. by Falmer Pr); pap. 16.00x (ISBN 0-905273-36-2, Pub. by Falmer Pr). Taylor & Francis.

Adams, Anthony, ed. see Mayrand, Lionel E., Jr. & Duchesne, Edmond J.

Adams, Arthur, jt. auth. see Weis, Frederick L.

Adams, Arthur B. Marketing Perishable Farm Products. LC 70-76718. (Columbia University Studies in the Social Sciences: No. 170). Repr. of 1916 ed. 17.50 (ISBN 0-404-51170-8). AMS Pr.

Adams, Arthur E., ed. Russian Revolution & Bolshevik Victory: Causes & Processes. 2nd ed. (Problems in European Civilization Ser.). (Orig.). 1972. pap. text ed. 5.50 (ISBN 0-669-81745-7). Heath.

Adams, Arthur G. Guide to the Catskills & the Region Around. 274p. 1977. pap. 12.00 (ISBN 0-89540-041-3, SB-041). Sun Pub.

--The Hudson: A Guidebook to the River. LC 79-14846. (Illus.). 424p. 1981. 21.95 (ISBN 0-87395-406-8). State U NY Pr.

--The Hudson Through the Years. LC 82-82934. (Illus.). 350p. 1983. 18.95 (ISBN 0-910389-00-4). Lind Grap Pubns.

Adams, Arthur G., et al. Guide to the Catskills with Trail Guide & Maps. (Illus.). 440p. 1975. pap. 7.95 (ISBN 0-915850-01-X); pap. 7.95 (ISBN 0-915850-02-8). Walking News Inc.

Adams, Arthur G., Jr., ed. The Hudson River in Literature: An Anthology. (Orig.). 1980. 24.50x (ISBN 0-87395-407-6). State U NY Pr.

Adams, Arthur M. Effective Leadership for Today's Church. LC 77-27547. 202p. 1978. pap. 6.95 (ISBN 0-664-24196-4). Westminster.

Adams, Arvil V. & Mangum, Garth L. The Lingering Crisis of Youth Unemployment. LC 78-16706. 152p. 1978. 11.95 (ISBN 0-911558-01-2). W E Upjohn.

Adams, B. B. & Hitt, Rodney, eds. Signals & Signal Symbols from the 1911 Railway Signal Dictionary. 2nd ed. (Train Shed Cyclopedia Ser, No. 27). (Illus.). pap. 2.50 (ISBN 0-912318-57-0). N K Gregg.

Adams, Barbara. Egyptian Mummies. (Shire Egyptology Ser.: No. 1). (Orig.). 1985. pap. 6.95 (ISBN 0-85263-699-7, Pub. by Shire Pubns England). Seven Hills Bks.

--Egyptian Objects in the Victoria & Albert Museum. (Egyptology Today Ser.: No. 3). 61p. 1977. pap. text ed. 29.50x (ISBN 0-85668-103-2, Pub. by Aris & Phillips England). Humanities.

--Like It Is: Facts & Feelings About Handicaps from Kids Who Know. (Illus.). (gr. 5 up). 1979. lib. bdg. 9.85 (ISBN 0-8027-6375-8). Walker & Co.

Adams, Barbara & Jaeschke, Richard. The Koptos Lions. 1983. 5.95 (ISBN 0-89326-100-9). Milwaukee Pub Mus.

Adams, Barry B., ed. see Bale, John.

Adams, Benson D. Ballistic Missile Defense. LC 74-165800. (Policy Sciences Book Ser.). pap. 72.00 (ISBN 0-317-09562-5, 2007765). Bks Demand UMI.

Adams, Berbert B. & Wood, Henry. Columbus & His Discovery of America. 88p. Repr. 29.00 (ISBN 0-932051-52-9). Am Repr Serv.

Adams, Bernard. London Illustrated 1604-1851: A Survey & Index of Topographical Books & Their Plates. (Illus.). 620p. 1983. lib. bdg. 110.00x (ISBN 0-85365-734-3, Co-Pub. by Lib Assn England). Oryx Pr.

Adams, Bert N. The Family: A Sociological Interpretation. 3rd ed. LC 81-80805. 530p. 1981. text ed. 26.95 (ISBN 0-395-30555-1); instr's manual 2.95 (ISBN 0-395-30556-X). HM.

Adams, Bert N. & Campbell, John L. Framing the Family: Contemporary Portraits. 531p. 1984. pap. 12.95x (ISBN 0-88133-079-5). Waveland Pr.

Adams, Beverly A. The New Fifteen Minute Gourmet: One Hundred Fifty Recipes You Can Prepare in Fifteen Minutes or Less, Plus 108 Quick Tips for Giving Any Meal an Elegant Flair. LC 81-22872. 112p. 1982. pap. 4.95 (ISBN 0-87491-490-6). Acropolis.

Adams, Bill. Trees for Southern Landscapes. LC 76-15457. (Illus.). 96p. (Orig.). 1976. pap. 6.95x (ISBN 0-88415-881-0, Pub. by Pacesetter Pr). Gulf Pub.

--Vegetable Growing for Southern Gardens. LC 75-18204. (Illus.). 96p. (Orig.). 1976. pap. 6.95x (ISBN 0-88415-889-6, Pub. by Pacesetter Pr). Gulf Pub.

Adams, Bob. The Official Hacker's Rules of Tennis. (Official Rules Ser.). (Illus.). 96p. (Orig.). 1982. pap. 3.95 (ISBN 0-937860-22-0). Adams Inc MA.

--The Official Hacker's Rules of Tennis. (Illus.). 96p. 1985. pap. 4.95 (ISBN 0-8092-5143-4). Contemp Bks.

Adams, Bob, ed. Career Paths: The Last Word in Career Guides. 246p. 1984. 7.95 (ISBN 0-937860-37-9). Adams Inc Ma.

Adams, Bob, tr. see Maston, T. B.

Adams, Brian. How to Succeed: Unique Techniques for Achieving Personal Goals. 1985. pap. 7.00 (ISBN 0-87980-413-0). Wilshire.

--Sales Cybernetics: New Scientific Techniques in Motivational Selling. 1985. pap. 7.00 (ISBN 0-87980-412-2). Wilshire.

Adams, Brian, jt. auth. see Shirley, Graham.

Adams, Brooks. America's Economic Supremacy. facsimile ed. LC 77-152155. (Essay Index Reprint Ser). Repr. of 1947 ed. 16.00 (ISBN 0-8369-2477-0). Ayer Co Pubs.

--Law of Civilization & Decay. 75.00 (ISBN 0-87968-235-3). Gordon Pr.

--Law of Civilization & Decay: An Essay on History. facsimile ed. LC 71-37125. (Essay Index Reprint Ser). Repr. of 1943 ed. 21.00 (ISBN 0-8369-2478-9). Ayer Co Pubs.

--The New Empire. 1967. 8.00 (ISBN 0-686-05050-9); pap. 3.75 (ISBN 0-686-05051-7). Frontier Press Calif.

Adams, Brooks, jt. auth. see McFadden, David R.

Adams, Bruce, ed. see Rapoport, Vitaly & Alexeev, Yuri.

Adams, C., ed. see Brizova, Joza, et al.

Adams, C. B., jt. auth. see Van Zwanenberg, Dinah.

Adams, C. D. Flowering Plants of Jamaica. 848p. 1972. 40.00x (ISBN 0-565-00841-2, Pub. by Brit Mus Nat Hist England). Sabbot-Natural Hist Bks.

--Flowering Plants of Jamaica. 848p. 1972. 78.50 (ISBN 0-686-78655-6, Pub. by Brit Mus Pubns England). State Mutual Bk.

Adams, C. F. & Adams, John Q. Life of John Adams, 2 Vols. LC 68-24969. (American Biography Ser., No. 32). 1969. Repr. lib. bdg. 79.95x (ISBN 0-8383-0151-7). Haskell.

Adams, C. G., jt. ed. see Hedley, R. H.

Adams, C. K. A Beginner's Guide to Computers & Microprocessors--with Projects. (Illus.). (gr. 10 up). 1978. pap. 9.25 (ISBN 0-8306-1015-4, 1015). TAB Bks.

Adams, C. R. The Eve Equation. 274p. 1981. 12.95 (ISBN 0-941654-00-1). Realm Bks.

Adams, C. R., tr. see Falbe, J.

Adams, C. W. Research on Multiple Sclerosis. (Illus.). 192p. 1972. photocopy ed. 24.75x (ISBN 0-398-02214-3). C C Thomas.

Adams, Candice. Diamond of Desire. (Orig.). 1983. pap. 2.95 (ISBN 0-440-01990-7). Dell.

--Fascination. (Love & Life Romance Ser.). 176p. (Orig.). 1982. pap. 1.75 (ISBN 0-345-30524-8). Ballantine.

--Finders Keepers. (Candlelight Ecstasy Supreme Ser.: No. 60). 288p. (Orig.). 1985. pap. 2.50 (ISBN 0-440-12509-X). Dell.

--Going Places. (Love & Life Romance Ser.). (Orig.). 1982. pap. write for info. (ISBN 0-345-30525-6). Ballantine.

--Legal & Tender, No. 6. 192p. 1983. pap. 1.95 (ISBN 0-515-06933-7). Jove Pubns.

--Not Too Perfect. (Candlelight Ecstasy Romance Ser.: No. 301). 192p. (Orig.). 1985. pap. 1.95 (ISBN 0-440-16451-6). Dell.

--Steal Away. (Candlelight Ecstasy Supreme Ser.: No. 40). 288p. (Orig.). 1984. pap. 2.50 (ISBN 0-440-17861-4). Dell.

--When Opposites Attract. (Candlelight Ecstasy Ser.: No. 232). (Orig.). 1984. pap. 1.95 (ISBN 0-440-19674-4). Dell.

Adams, Caren & Fay, Jennifer. No More Secrets: Protecting Your Child from Sexual Assault. LC 81-3931. 96p. (Orig.). 1981. pap. 4.95 (ISBN 0-915166-24-0). Impact Pubs Cal.

--Nobody Told Me It Was Rape. 25p. (Orig.). 1984. pap. 3.95 (ISBN 0-941816-13-3). Network Pubns.

Adams, Caren, et al. No Is Not Enough: Helping Teenagers Avoid Sexual Assault. LC 84-20506. 178p. (Orig.). 1984. pap. 6.95 (ISBN 0-915166-35-6). Impact Pubs Cal.

Adams, Carl & McElhaney, Dolly. Born with a Mission. Wallace, Mary H., ed. (Illus.). 240p. 1981. pap. 5.95 (ISBN 0-912315-15-6). Word Aflame.

Adams, Carl E., et al. Development of Design & Operational Criteria for Wastewater Treatment. LC 80-69077. (Illus.). 550p. 1980. text ed. 40.00 (ISBN 0-937976-00-8). Enviro Pr.

Adams, Carol. Ordinary Lives: A Hundred Years Ago. 230p. 1983. pap. 8.95 (ISBN 0-86068-239-0, Pub. by Virago Pr). Merrimack Pub Cir.

Adams, Carol & Laurikietis, Rae. The Gender Trap: A Closer Look at Sex Roles, Bk. 1: Education & Work. Sellers, Jill, ed. (Illus.). 119p. 1977. pap. 4.95 (ISBN 0-915864-09-6). Academy Chi Pubs.

--The Gender Trap: A Closer Look at Sex Roles, Bk. 2: Sex & Marriage. Sellers, Jill, ed. LC 77-22605. (Illus.). 124p. 1977. o. p. 9.95 (ISBN 0-915864-29-0); pap. 1.00 (ISBN 0-915864-11-8). Academy Chi Pubs.

--The Gender Trap: A Closer Look at Sex Roles, Bk. 3: Messages & Images. Sellers, Jill, ed. LC 77-22605. (Illus.). 124p. 1977. o. p. 9.95 (ISBN 0-915864-30-4); pap. 4.95 (ISBN 0-915864-13-4). Academy Chi Pubs.

Adams, Carol, et al. From Workshop to Warfare: The Lives of Medieval Women. LC 83-7323. (Women in History Ser.). 43p. 1984. pap. 3.95 (ISBN 0-521-27696-9). Cambridge U Pr.

--Under Control: Life in a Nineteenth Century Silk Factory. LC 83-7500. (Women in History Ser.). 1984. pap. 3.95 (ISBN 0-521-27481-8). Cambridge U pr.

Adams, Caroline, et al. Laboratory Manual for Principles of Biology. 3rd ed. 94p. 1984. pap. 8.95 (ISBN 0-88725-026-2). Hunter Textbks.

--Laboratory Manual for Principles of Biology. 2nd ed. (Illus.). 94p. 1979. pap. 7.95x lab manual (ISBN 0-89459-147-9). Hunter Textbks.

Adams, Carolyn. Stars over Texas. rev. ed. (Illus.). 128p. (gr. 1-6). 1983. 8.95 (ISBN 0-89015-411-2). Eakin Pubns.

Adams, Carolyn E. & Bogle, Irma. Study Guide & Review of Practical-Vocational Nursing. (Illus.). 464p. 1982. pap. text ed. 15.25 (ISBN 0-397-54347-6, 64-02895, Lippincott Nursing). Lippincott.

Adams, Catherine F. Nutritional Valve of Americans Foods in Common Units. 291p. 1981. pap. 8.50 (ISBN 0-318-11808-4). Gov Printing Office.

--Nutritive Value of American Foods in Common Units. (Agriculture Handbook Ser.). (Illus.). 291p. 1981. pap. 8.50 (ISBN 0-318-04553-2). Gov Printing Office.

Adams, Catherine G. & Macione, Alberta. Handbook of Psychatric & Mental Health Nursing. (Red Books Ser.). (Illus.). 495p. (Orig.). 1982. pap. 17.50 (ISBN 0-471-86983-X). Wiley.

Adams, Cecil. The Straight Dope. Zotti, Ed, ed. (Illus.). 320p. (Orig.). pap. 8.95 (ISBN 0-914091-54-9). Chicago Review.

Adams, Celeste, jt. auth. see Wong, Kwan S.

Adams, Charles. Memoir of Washington Irving. LC 70-148869. (Select Bibliographies Reprint Ser.). 1972. Repr. of 1870 ed. 17.00 (ISBN 0-8369-5641-9). Ayer Co Pubs.

Adams, Charles & Bamford, Katherine. Principles of Horticulture. (Illus.). 264p. 1984. pap. 23.00 (ISBN 0-434-90008-7, Pub. by W Heinemann Ltd). David & Charles.

Adams, Charles & Graves, Jim. Fight, Flight, Fraud: The Story of Taxation. LC 83-80155. (Illus.). 300p. 1983. 35.00 (ISBN 0-686-39619-7). Euro-Dutch Pub.

Adams, Charles C. Middletown Upper Houses. LC 83-2344. 900p. 1983. 60.00 (ISBN 0-914016-94-6). Phoenix Pub.

Adams, Charles C., 3rd. Guide to the Study of Animal Ecology. Edgerton, Frank N., ed. LC 77-74201. (History of Ecology Ser.). (Illus.). 1978. Repr. of 1913 ed. lib. bdg. 16.00x (ISBN 0-405-10371-9). Ayer Co Pubs.

Adams, Charles D. Demosthenes & His Influence. LC 63-10306. (Our Debt to Greece & Rome). 1930. 15.00 (ISBN 0-8154-0001-2). Cooper Sq.

--Demosthenes Influence. 1927. lib. bdg. 12.50 (ISBN 0-8414-9120-8). Folcroft.

Adams, Charles F. The Antinomian Controversy. LC 74-164507. 1976. Repr. of 1892 ed. lib. bdg. 25.00 (ISBN 0-306-70290-8). Da Capo.

--Charles Francis Adams, 1807-1886. Morse, John T., ed. 1900. 14.50 (ISBN 0-8274-2029-3). R West.

--Charles Francis Adams, 1807-1886, by His Son. Morse, John T., Jr., ed. LC 72-128955. (American Statesmen: No. 29). Repr. of 1900 ed. 22.00 (ISBN 0-404-50879-0). AMS Pr.

--Dialect Ballads. LC 78-166640. (Illus.). 1971. Repr. of 1888 ed. 19.00 (ISBN 0-403-01415-8). Scholarly.

--Diary of Charles Francis Adams, 6 vols. Incl. Vol. 1. January 1820 - June 1825. Donald, Aida D. & Donald, David, eds. (Illus.). lxvi, 469p; Vol. 2. July 1825 - September 1829. Donald, Aida D. & Donald, David, eds. (Illus.). xlv, 514p. Vols. 1 & 2. 60.00x (ISBN 0-674-20399-2); Vol. 3. September 1829 - February 1831. Friedlaender, Marc & Butterfield, L. H., eds. (Illus.). liv, 431p; Vol. 4. March 1831 - December 1832. Friedlaender, Marc & Butterfield, L. H., eds. (Illus.). xx, 502p. Vols. 3 & 4. 60.00x (ISBN 0-674-20401-8); January 1833 - October 1834. Friedlaender, Marc & Butterfield, L. H., eds.; November 1834 - June 1836. Friedlaender, Marc & Butterfield, L. H., eds. Vols. 5 & 6. 60.00x (ISBN 0-674-20402-6). LC 64-20588. (The Adams Papers, Ser. 1, Diaries). Harvard U Pr.

--Lee at Appomattox, & Other Papers. 2nd facs. ed. LC 77-134047. (Essay Index Reprint Ser). 1902. 25.50 (ISBN 0-8369-1901-7). Ayer Co Pubs.

--Life of John Adams, 2 Vols. LC 78-108455. 1971. Repr. of 1871 ed. 95.00 (ISBN 0-403-00470-5). Scholarly.

--Massachusetts, Its Historians & Its History: An Object Lesson. facsimile ed. LC 73-146849. (Select Bibliographies Reprint Ser). Repr. of 1893 ed. 11.00 (ISBN 0-8369-5616-8). Ayer Co Pubs.

--Massachusetts: Its Historians & Its History, an Object Lesson. (The Works of Charles Francis Adams Ser.). 110p. Repr. of 1893 ed. lib. bdg. 29.00 (ISBN 0-932051-10-3, Pub by Am Repr Serv). Am Biog Serv.

--Richard Henry Dana, 2 Vols. LC 67-23883. 1968. Repr. of 1890 ed. 43.00x (ISBN 0-8103-3038-5). Gale.

--Studies, Military & Diplomatic, 1775-1865. facs. ed. LC 73-150168. (Select Bibliographies Reprint Ser). 1911. 23.50 (ISBN 0-8369-5681-8). Ayer Co Pubs.

--Studies, Military & Diplomatic 1775-1865. LC 73-150168. 424p. 1982. Repr. of 1911 ed. 20.00 (ISBN 0-8290-0474-2). Irvington.

Adams, Charles F., ed. Antionomianism in the Colony of Massachusetts Bay, 1636-38, Including the Short Story & Documents. 1966. 26.00 (ISBN 0-8337-0010-3). B Franklin.

--Correspondence Between John Adams & Mercy Warren Relating to Her History of the American Revolution, July-August, 1807. LC 72-2586. (American Women Ser: Images & Realities). 202p. 1972. Repr. of 1878 ed. 19.00 (ISBN 0-405-04487-9). Ayer Co Pubs.

--Russian Memoirs of John Quincy Adams: His Diary from 1809 to 1814. LC 74-115501. (Russia Observed, Series 1). 1970. Repr. of 1874 ed. 26.50 (ISBN 0-405-03001-0). Ayer Co Pubs.

Adams, Charles F., ed. see Adams, John Q.

Adams, Charles F., ed. see Morton, Thomas.

Adams, Charles F., et al, eds. see Bradford, William.

Adams, Charles F., Jr. Charles Francis Adams. LC 80-24115. (American Statesmen Ser.). 425p. 1980. pap. 6.95 (ISBN 0-87754-181-7). Chelsea Hse.

--Railroads: Their Origin & Problems. Bruchey, Stuart, ed. LC 80-1294. (Railroads Ser.). 1981. Repr. of 1878 ed. lib. bdg. 20.00x (ISBN 0-405-13764-8). Ayer Co Pubs.

Adams, Charles F., Jr. & Adams, Henry. Chapters of Erie, & Other Essays. LC 66-22613. (Library of Early American Business & Industry: No. VIII). Repr. of 1871 ed. 35.00x (ISBN 0-678-00788-8). Kelley.

Adams, Charles F., Jr., jt. auth. see Nathan, Richard P.

Adams, Charles J. Ghost Stories of Berks County, Bk II. 150p. 1984. pap. 5.95 (ISBN 0-317-05485-6). C J Adams.

Adams, Charles J. & Seibold, David J. Legends of Long Beach Island. (Illus.). 110p. 1985. pap. 5.95 (ISBN 0-317-18688-4). C J Adams.

--Shipwrecks of Barnegat Inlet. (Illus.). 85p. 1984. pap. 4.95 (ISBN 0-317-05483-X). C J Adams.

Adams, Charles J., ed. Iranian Civilization & Culture: Essays in Honour of the 2500th Anniversary of the Founding of the Persian Empire. (Illus.). 1973. pap. 8.50 (ISBN 0-7735-9077-3). McGill-Queens U Pr.

--A Reader's Guide to the Great Religions. 2nd ed. LC 76-10496. 1977. 24.95 (ISBN 0-02-900240-0). Free Pr.

Adams, Charles J., III. Ghost Stories of Berks County (Pennsylvania) 215p. 1982. pap. 5.95 (ISBN 0-9610008-0-5). C J Adams.

Adams, Charles K. Basic Integrated Circuit Theory & Projects. (Illus.). 266p. (Orig.). 1984. 19.95 (ISBN 0-8306-0699-8); pap. 11.95 (ISBN 0-8306-1699-3, 1699). TAB Bks.

--Master Handbook of Microprocessor Chips. (Illus.). 378p. 1981. 18.95 (ISBN 0-8306-9633-4); pap. 11.50 (ISBN 0-8306-1299-8, 1299). TAB Bks.

Adams, Charles L., ed. see Evans-Wentz, W. Y.

Adams, Charles L., ed. see Waters, Frank.

Adams, Charles M. Randall Jarrell. 1978. Repr. of 1958 ed. lib. bdg. 10.00 (ISBN 0-8495-0028-1). Arden Lib.

--Randall Jarrell: A Bibliography. LC 74-8205. Repr. of 1958 ed. lib. bdg. 15.00 (ISBN 0-8414-2977-4). Folcroft.

Adams, Charles W. Oklahoma Discovery Practice Manual. 1986. price not set looseleaf (ISBN 0-409-25104-6). Butterworth TX.

Adams, Charles W., jt. auth. see Ryan, Robert H.

Adams, Chuck. Bowhunter's Digest. 2nd ed. LC 73-91589. (Illus.). 288p. 1981. pap. 11.95 (ISBN 0-910676-29-1, 7426). DBI.

--The Complete Book of Bowhunting. LC 82-62605. (Illus.). 1978. 16.95 (ISBN 0-8329-2714-7, Pub. by Winchester Pr). New Century.

--Complete Guide to Bowhunting Deer. LC 84-70734. 256p. 1984. pap. 11.95 (ISBN 0-910676-73-9). DBI.

--Digest Book of Duck & Goose Hunting. LC 79-51752. 96p. pap. 3.95 (ISBN 0-686-81356-1). DBI.

--The Lawless Ones. 1979. pap. 1.75 (ISBN 0-505-51399-4, Pub. by Tower Bks). Dorchester Pub Co.

--The Violent Breed. 1979. pap. 1.50 (ISBN 0-8439-0680-4, Leisure Bks). Dorchester Pub Co.

Adams, Clifton. The Grabhorn Bounty. 192p. 1983. pap. 2.25 (ISBN 0-441-30223-8). Ace Bks.

--Hard Times & Arnie Smith. 1976. pap. 1.75 (ISBN 0-441-31721-9). Ace Bks.

--The Last Days of Wolf Garnet. 192p. 1985. pap. 2.50 (ISBN 0-441-47085-8). Ace Bks.

--The Last Days of Wolf Garnett. 1982. pap. 2.25 (ISBN 0-441-47083-1). Ace Bks.

--A Partnership with Death. 192p. 1982. pap. 1.95 (ISBN 0-441-65202-6). Ace Bks.

--Shorty. (Illus.). 224p. 1982. pap. 2.25 (ISBN 0-441-76173-9, Pub. by Charter Bks). Ace Bks.

Adams, Clinton. American Lithographers, 1900-1960: The Artists & Their Printers. LC 83-51034. (Illus.). 344p. 1983. 65.00 (ISBN 0-8263-0660-8). U of NM Pr.

--Fritz Scholder: Lithographs. LC 75-9106. (Illus.). 1976. 24.95 (ISBN 0-8212-0689-3, 293768). NYGS.

Adams, Clinton, jt. auth. see Antreasian, Garo Z.

Adams, Constance J. Nurse Midwifery: Health Care for Women & Newborns. (Monograph Ser.). 330p. 1983. 26.00 (ISBN 0-8089-1570-3, 790027). Grune.

Adams, Corrine. English Speech Rhythm & the Foreign Learner. (Janua Linguarum, Series Practica: No. 69). 1979. text ed. 28.80x (ISBN 90-279-7716-X). Mouton.

Adams, Cynthia, jt. auth. see Haskew, Paul.

Adams, Cyril E., ed. Mammalian Egg Transfer. 256p. 1982. 72.50 (ISBN 0-8493-6140-0). CRC Pr.

Adams, D., et al, eds. Electronic Equipment Wiring & Assembling: Part One. (Engineering Craftsmen: No. G5). 1968. spiral bdg. 38.50x (ISBN 0-85083-014-1). Trans-Atlantic.

--Electronic Inspection & Test, 2 vols. (Engineering Craftsmen: No. G26). (Illus.). 1969. Set. s 69.95x (ISBN 0-85083-035-4). Trans-Atlantic.

Adams, D. K., et al. An Atlas of North American Affairs. 2nd ed. viii, 164p. 1979. 9.95 (ISBN 0-416-85650-0, NO.2858); pap. 9.95x (ISBN 0-416-85640-3, NO.2857). Methuen Inc.

Adams, D. M. Inorganic Solids: An Introduction to Concepts in Solid State Structural Chemistry. LC 73-16863. 336p. 1974. pap. 29.95x (ISBN 0-471-00471-5, Pub. by Wiley-Interscience). Wiley.

Adams, D. R., et al, eds. Static Electrical Equipment Testing. (Engineering Craftsmen: No. G21). (Illus.). 1969. spiral bdg. 45.00x (ISBN 0-89563-021-4). Intl Ideas.

Adams, Dale & Speicher, Dale. Twenty-Five Bicycle Tours in Eastern Pennsylvania: Day Trips & Overnights from Philadelphia to the Highlands. LC 84-6288. (Bicycle Tours Ser.). (Illus.). 168p. 1984. pap. 6.95 (ISBN 0-942440-19-6). Backcountry Pubns.

Adams, Dale W., et al. Undermining Rural Development with Cheap Credit. (Special Studies in Social, Political, & Economic Development Ser.). 350p. 1984. lib. bdg. 25.00x (ISBN 0-86531-768-2). Westview.

Adams, Dana & Thomson, Norman B. Intra-Aortic Balloon Counterpulsation: How To Do It. (Illus.). 188p. 1982. 12.50 (ISBN 0-9607588-0-1). St Francis Hosp.

Adams, Daniel. Brothers & Enemies. 384p. 1982. pap. 3.50 (ISBN 0-515-05854-8). Jove Pubns.

--Defiant Loves. 368p. (Orig.). 1984. pap. 3.95 (ISBN 0-515-07432-2). Jove Pubns.

Adams, Daniel J. Thomas Merton's Shared Contemplation: A Protestant Perspective. Doyle, Teresa A., ed. (Cistercian Studies: No. 62). 1979. 8.00 (ISBN 0-87907-862-6). Cistercian Pubns.

Adams, David. Another Place. (Stone Country Poetry Ser.: No. 9). (Illus., Orig.). 1980. pap. 5.95x (ISBN 0-930020-08-1). Stone Country.

--Essentials of Oral Biology. (Dental Ser.). (Illus.). 152p. 1981. text ed. 10.00 (ISBN 0-443-02095-7). Churchill.

Adams, David & Leigh, William E. Programming Business Systems with BASIC. 1984. text ed. 16.95 wkbk. (ISBN 0-538-10980-7, J98). SW Pub.

Adams, David, ed. see Mees, L. F.

Adams, David M. Inorganic Solids: An Introduction to Concepts in Solid-State Structural Chemistry. LC 73-16863. pap. 88.00 (ISBN 0-317-09025-9, 2051237). Bks Demand UMI.

--Inorganic Solids: An Introduction to Concepts in Solid-Stte Sructural Chemistry. LC 73-16863. pap. 88.00 (ISBN 0-317-30437-2, 2024928). Bks Demand UMI.

Adams, David R. Computer Information Systems Development: Management Principles & Case Studies. 1985. 19.50 (ISBN 0-538-10970-X, J97). SW Pub.

Adams, David R., et al. Computer Information Systems Development: Design & Implementation. 1985. text ed. 21.95 (ISBN 0-538-10860-6, J86). SW Pub.

Adams, David W. Childhood Malignancy: The Psychosocial Care of the Child & His Family. (Illus.). 200p. 1979. 20.75x (ISBN 0-398-03928-3). C C Thomas.

Adams, Dennis M., ed. Computers & Teacher Training: A Practical Guide. (Monographic Supplement to Computers in the Schools Ser.: Vol. 2). 152p. 1985. text ed. 22.95 (ISBN 0-86656-312-1, B312); 16.95 (ISBN 0-86656-378-4). Haworth Pr.

Adams, Dickinson W., jt. ed. see Jefferson, Thomas.

Adams, Dolph O. & Hanna, Michael G., Jr., eds. Contemporary Topics in Immunobiology, Vol. 13: Macrophage Action. 280p. 1984. 39.50 (ISBN 0-306-41536-4, Plenum Pr). Plenum Pub.

Adams, Donald K., ed. see Polidori.

Adams, Donald R. Canine Anatomy: A Systematic Study. (Illus.). 512p. 1985. text ed. 39.75x (ISBN 0-8138-0281-4). Iowa St U Pr.

Adams, Donald R., Jr. Finance & Enterprise in Early America: A Study of Stephen Girard's Bank, 1812-1831. LC 77-20301. 1978. 30.00x (ISBN 0-8122-7736-8). U of Pa Pr.

--Wage Rates in Philadelphia, Seventeen Ninety to Eighteen Thirty. facsimile ed. LC 75-2572. (Dissertations in American Economic History). (Illus.). 1975. Repr. of 1975 ed. 29.00x (ISBN 0-405-07253-8). Ayer Co Pubs.

Adams, Doris G. Iraq's People & Resources. LC 80-19079. (University of California Publications in Economics Ser.: Vol. XVIII). (Illus.), viii, 160p. 1980. Repr. of 1958 ed. lib. bdg. 24.75x (ISBN 0-313-22759-4, ADIP). Greenwood.

Adams, Doris Sutcliffe. Power of Darkness. 1978. pap. 1.95 (ISBN 0-8439-0567-0, Leisure Bks). Dorchester Pub Co.

Adams, Dorothy & Kurtz, Margaret. The Legal Secretary: Terminology & Transcription. (Illus.). 1980. text ed. 23.95 (ISBN 0-07-000330-0). McGraw.

--Technical Secretary: Terminology & Transcription. (Diamond Jubilee Ser.). 1967. 26.65 (ISBN 0-07-000320-3). McGraw.

Adams, Dorothy, jt. auth. see Kurtz, Margaret A.

Adams, Dottie, ed. see Memorial Hospital Auxiliary.

Adams, Doug. Changing Biblical Imagery & Artistic Identity in 20th Century Liturgical Dance. 1984. pap. 3.00 (ISBN 0-941500-31-4). Sharing Co.

--Congregational Dancing in Christian Worship. rev. ed. 1984. 4.95 (ISBN 0-941500-02-0). Sharing Co.

--Humor in the American Pulpit from George Whitefield Through Henry Ward Beecher. rev. ed. 1981. 6.95 (ISBN 0-941500-10-1). Sharing Co.

--Involving the People in Dancing Worship: Historic & Contemporary Patterns. 1975. 2.00 (ISBN 0-941500-11-X). Sharing Co.

--Meeting House to Camp Meeting: Toward a History of American Free Church Worship from 1620-1835. 160p. (Orig.). 1981. pap. text ed. 6.95 (ISBN 0-941500-26-8). Sharing Co.

--Sacred Dance with Senior Citizens in Churches, Convalescent Homes, & Retirement Homes. 1982. pap. 3.00 (ISBN 0-941500-27-6). Sharing Co.

Adams, Doug & Rock, Judith. Biblical Criteria in Modern Dance: Modern Dance As a Prophetic Form. 1979. 2.50 (ISBN 0-941500-01-2). Sharing Co.

Adams, Doug, jt. auth. see Fisher, Constance.

Adams, Doug, jt. auth. see Taylor, Margaret.

Adams, Doug, ed. Dancing Christmas Carols. LC 78-63292. 1978. pap. 7.95 (ISBN 0-89390-006-0). Resource Pubns.

Adams, Doug, ed. see Blessin, Ann M.

Adams, Doug, ed. see Fisher, Constance L.

Adams, Doug, ed. see Kirk, Martha A.

Adams, Doug, ed. see Lyon, Barbara.

Adams, Doug, ed. see MacLeod, Marian B.

Adams, Doug, ed. see Packard, Dane.

Adams, Doug, ed. see Reed, Carlynn.

Adams, Doug, ed. see Taylor, Margaret F.

Adams, Doug, ed. see Winton-Henry, Cynthia.

Adams, Douglas. Hitchhiker's Companion: The Original Galaxy Radio Scripts. 1985. pap. 9.95 (ISBN 0-318-04765-9). Harmony Pr.

--The Hitchhiker's Guide to the Galaxy. 224p. 1980. 9.95 (ISBN 0-517-54209-9); 10-copy pre-pack o.p. 99.50 (ISBN 0-517-54230-7). Crown.

--Hitchhiker's Guide to the Galaxy. 1984. pap. 3.95 (ISBN 0-671-52721-5). PB.

--The Hitchhiker's Trilogy: Omnibus Editon. 512p. 1984. 15.95 (ISBN 0-517-55200-0, Harmony). Crown.

--Life, the Universe & Everything. 240p. 1985. pap. 3.95 (ISBN 0-671-60107-5). PB.

--Life, the Universe & Everything: The Cosmic Conclusion to the Hitchhiker Trilogy. 1982. 9.95 (ISBN 0-517-54874-7, Harmony). Crown.

--The Restaurant at the End of the Universe. 256p. 1982. 9.95 (ISBN 0-517-54535-7, Harmony). Crown.

--Restaurant at the End of the Universe. 1982. pap. 3.95 (ISBN 0-671-49304-3). PB.

--So Long, & Thanks for All the Fish. 1984. 12.95 (ISBN 0-517-55439-9, Harmony). Crown.

--So Long & Thanks for All the Fish. 1985. pap. 3.95 (ISBN 0-671-52580-8). PB.

Adams, Douglas & Lloyd, John. The Meaning of Liff. 1984. 8.95 (ISBN 0-517-55347-3, Harmony). Crown.

Adams, Douglas P. Nomography: Theory & Application. viii, 198p. 1964. 22.50 (ISBN 0-208-00435-1, Archon). Shoe String.

Adams, E. The Logic of Conditionals: An Application of Probability to Deductive Logic. LC 75-20306. (Synthese Library: No. 86). 140p. 1975. lib. bdg. 29.00 (ISBN 90-277-0631-X, Pub. by Reidel Holland). Kluwer Academic.

Adams, E. C. Congaree Sketches. LC 27-13763. Repr. of 1927 ed. 15.00 (ISBN 0-527-00400-6). Kraus Repr.

Adams, E. D. & Ihas, G. G., eds. Quantum Fluids & Solids, 1983: AIP Conference Proceedings No. 103, Sanibel Island, Florida. LC 83-72240. 512p. 1983. lib. bdg. 39.75 (ISBN 0-88318-202-5). Am Inst Physics.

Adams, E. M. Philosophy & the Modern Mind: A Philosophical Critique of Modern Western Civilization. 244p. 1985. pap. text ed. 12.00 (ISBN 0-8191-4754-0). U Pr of Amer.

Adams, Earl. The Greyhound Handicapper. 100p. (Orig.). 1985. pap. 9.50 (ISBN 0-9612748-2-4). E Adams.

--Greyhound Handicapping Manual. 85p. (Orig.). 1981. pap. 9.50 (ISBN 0-9612748-0-8). E Adams.

--Handbook for Gamblers. 105p. 1983. pap. 9.50 (ISBN 0-9612748-1-6). E Adams.

Adams, Edgar. United States Store Cards. LC 80-70824. 1981. Repr. of 1920 ed. softcover 12.00 (ISBN 0-915262-60-6). S J Durst.

Adams, Edgar H. The Julius Guttag Collection of Latin American Coins. LC 74-80921. (Illus.). 532p. 1974. Repr. 35.00x (ISBN 0-88000-027-9). Quarterman.

Adams, Edith. The Charmkins Discover Big World. (Illus.). 24p. (gr. 3-5). 1983. 3.95 (ISBN 0-394-86116-7). Random.

--The Charmkins Discover Big World. (Illus.). 32p. 1984. Repr. of 1983 ed. 8.98 (ISBN 0-87660-011-9). I J E Bk Pub.

--My Little Pony & The New Friends. LC 84-60331. (My Little Pony Mini-Storybooks Ser.). (Illus.). 32p. (ps-3). 1984. pap. 1.25 (ISBN 0-394-86810-2, Pub. by BYR). Random.

--The Noisy Book Starring Yakety Yak. LC 82-50431. (Sweet Pickles Mini-Storybooks). (Illus.). (ps-k). 1983. pap. 1.25 (ISBN 0-394-85544-2). Random.

--Santa's Christmas Surprise. LC 85-60216. (Illus.). 14p. (gr. 2-6). 1985. bds. 3.95 (ISBN 0-394-87538-9, BYR). Random.

Adams, Edward B. Art Treasurers of Seoul. (Illus.). 182p. 1979. 26.00 (ISBN 0-8048-1467-8, Pub. by Seoul Intl Publishing House). C E Tuttle.

--Art Treasures of Seoul: With Walking Tours. (Illus.). 272p. 1980. 25.00 (ISBN 0-89860-018-9). Eastview.

--Herdboy & Weaver. (Korean Folk Story for Children Ser.). (Illus.). 32p. (gr. 3). 1981. 6.50 (ISBN 0-8048-1470-8, Pub by Seoul Intl Publishing House). C E Tuttle.

--Korea Guide. (Illus.). 1979. pap. 12.00 (ISBN 0-89860-026-X). Eastview.

--Korea Guide. rev. ed. LC 77-670017. (Illus.). 392p. 1983. pap. 19.50 (ISBN 0-8048-1466-X, Seoul Intl Publishing House). C E Tuttle.

--Korea's Kyongju. LC 79-670108. (Illus.). 379p. 1979. pap. 18.20 (ISBN 0-8048-1414-7, Pub. by Seoul Intl Publishing House). C E Tuttle.

--Palaces of Seoul. 1979. pap. 4.50 (ISBN 0-89860-027-8). Eastview.

--Palaces of Seoul. 2nd, rev. ed. LC 72-77238. (Illus.). 220p. 1982. pap. 13.00 (ISBN 0-8048-1416-3, Pub. by Seoul Intl Publishing House). C E Tuttle.

--Seoul: Nineteen Eighty-Eight Olympic Site. (Illus.). 57p. (Orig.). 1984. pap. 4.00 (ISBN 0-8048-1425-2, Pub. by Seoul Intl Publishing House). C E Tuttle.

--Through Gates of Seoul, 2 vols. LC 75-134506. (Illus.). 1974. Vol. 1. 13.00 (ISBN 0-8048-1419-8, Pub. by Seoul Intl Publishing House); Vol. 2. 15.60 (ISBN 0-8048-1420-1). C E Tuttle.

--Woodcutter & Nymph. (Korean Folk Story for Children Ser.). (Illus.). 32p. (gr. 3). 1982. 6.50 (ISBN 0-8048-1471-6, Pub by Seoul Intl Publishing House). C E Tuttle.

Adams, Edward B., ed. Blindman's Daughter. (Korean Folk Story for Children Ser.: Bk. 1). (Illus.). 32p. (gr. 3). 1981. 6.50 (ISBN 0-8048-1472-4, Pub. by Seoul Intl Publishing House). C E Tuttle.

--Korean Cinderella. (Korean Folk Story for Children Ser.: Bk. 4). (Illus.). 32p. (gr. 3). 1982. 6.50 (ISBN 0-8048-1473-2, Pub. by Seoul Intl Publishing House). C E Tuttle.

--Two Brothers & Their Magic Gourds. (Korean Folk Stories for Children Ser.). (Illus.). 32p. (gr. 3). 1981. 6.50 (ISBN 0-8048-1474-0, Pub. by Seoul Intl Tourist Korea). C E Tuttle.

Adams, Edward L. Word-Formation in Provencal. 37.00 (ISBN 0-384-38802-7). Johnson Repr.

Adams, Elaine P., jt. ed. see Lukenbill, W. Bernard.

Adams, Elbridge. Joseph Conrad: The Man. LC 72-2130. (Studies in Conrad, No. 8). 1972. Repr. of 1925 ed. lib. bdg. 28.95 (ISBN 0-8383-1487-2). Haskell.

Adams, Elbridge L. Joseph Conrad: The Man. 1978. Repr. of 1925 ed. lib. bdg. 15.00 (ISBN 0-8495-0136-9). Arden Lib.

Adams, Eldridge L. & Zelie, John S. Joseph Conrad: The Man & the Burial in Kent. LC 73-11289. 1925. lib. bdg. 12.00 (ISBN 0-8414-2883-2). Folcroft.

Adams, Eleanor B. Bio-Bibliography of Franciscan Authors in Colonial Central America. (Bibliographical Ser.). 1953. 10.00 (ISBN 0-88382-101-X). AAFH.

Adams, Eleanor B. & Chavez, Angelico, eds. The Missions of New Mexico, 1776: A Description by Fray Francisco Atanasio Dominguez with Other Contemporary Documents. LC 55-12223. 1975. Repr. of 1956 ed. 35.00x (ISBN 0-8263-0373-0). U of NM Pr.

Adams, Eleanor N. Old English Scholarship in England from 1556-1800. LC 70-91177. (Yale Studies in English Ser.: No. 55). 204p. 1970. Repr. of 1917 ed. 16.50 (ISBN 0-208-00913-2, Archon). Shoe String.

Adams, Elie M. Ethical Naturalism & the Modern World-View. LC 73-3019. 229p. 1973. Repr. of 1960 ed. lib. bdg. 15.00 (ISBN 0-8371-6820-1, ADEN). Greenwood.

Adams, Elizabeth & Redstone, David. Bow Porcelain. (Illus.). 240p. 1981. 60.00 (ISBN 0-571-11696-5). Faber & Faber.

Adams, Elizabeth, jt. auth. see Haggar, Reginald.

Adams, Ellen. The Scaredy Book. LC 82-50426. (Sweet Pickles Mini-Storybooks). (Illus.). 32p. (ps-k). 1983. pap. 1.25 (ISBN 0-394-85542-6). Random.

Adams, Elsie B. Bernard Shaw & the Aesthetes. LC 76-153421. 220p. 1972. 8.00 (ISBN 0-8142-0155-5). Ohio St U Pr.

Adams, Emma H. To & Fro in Southern California: With Sketches in Arizona & New Mexico. Cortes, Carlos E., ed. LC 76-1220. (Chicano Heritage Ser.). 1976. Repr. of 1887 ed. 22.00x (ISBN 0-405-09481-7). Ayer Co Pubs.

Adams, Ephraim D. British Interests & Activities in Texas, 1838-1846. 1963. 11.75 (ISBN 0-8446-1004-6). Peter Smith.

--Great Britain & the American Civil War, 2 vols. Set. 13.25 ea. (ISBN 0-8446-1005-4). Peter Smith.

--Power of Ideals in American History. LC 75-98025. (BCL Ser.: No. II). Repr. of 1913 ed. 14.50 (ISBN 0-404-00285-4). AMS Pr.

Adams, Eric. Francis Danby: Varieties of Poetic Landscape. LC 72-75185. (Illus.). pap. 80.00 (ISBN 0-317-10493-4, 2021973). Bks Demand UMI.

Adams, Eugene T., et al. American Idea. facs. ed. LC 73-117747. (Essay Index Reprint Ser.). 1942. 19.00 (ISBN 0-8369-1820-7). Ayer Co Pubs.

Adams, Evangeline. Astrology for Everyone. LC 81-3107. 1981. pap. 5.95 (ISBN 0-396-07985-7). Dodd.

Adams, Evelyn C. American Indian Education: Government Schools & Economic Progress. LC 70-165701. (American Education Ser, No. 2). 1972. Repr. of 1946 ed. 16.00 (ISBN 0-405-03690-6). Ayer Co Pubs.

Adams, F. C. Uncle Tom at Home: A Review of the Reviewers & Repudiators of Uncle Tom's Cabin by Mrs. Stowe. facsimile ed. LC 78-107789. (Select Bibliographies Reprint Ser). 1853. 18.00 (ISBN 0-8369-5210-3). Ayer Co Pubs.

Adams, F. Gerald & Klein, Lawrence R., eds. Industrial Policies for Growth & Competitiveness: An Economic Perspective, Vol. I. LC 82-48557. (Wharton Econometric Studies). 448p. 1983. 34.00x (ISBN 0-669-05412-7); pap. 16.95 (ISBN 0-669-10920-7). Lexington Bks.

Adams, F. Gerard & Behrman, Jere R. Commodity Exports & Economic Development: The Commodity Problem & Policies in Developing Countries. LC 81-47961. (The Wharton Econometric Studies). 352p. 1982. 29.50x (ISBN 0-669-05145-4). Lexington Bks.

--Econometric Modeling of World Commodity Policy. LC 77-18596. (The Wharton Econometric Studies Ser.). (Illus.). 240p. 1978. 26.00x (ISBN 0-669-02111-3). Lexington Bks.

Adams, F. Gerard & Glickman, Norman. Modeling the Multiregional Economic System: Perspectives for the Eighties. LC 79-48005. (Wharton Econometric Ser.). 320p. 1980. 30.00x (ISBN 0-669-03627-7). Lexington Bks.

Adams, F. Gerard & Hickman, Bert G., eds. Global Econometrics: Essays in Honor of Lawrence R. Klein. (Illus.). 448p. 1983. text ed. 45.00x (ISBN 0-262-01071-2). MIT Pr.

Adams, F. Gerard & Klein, Sonia, eds. Stabilizing World Commodity Markets. LC 77-7805. (The Wharton Econometric Studies Ser.: No. 1). 368p. 1978. 29.00x (ISBN 0-669-01622-5). Lexington Bks.

Adams, Faith. El Salvador: Beauty among the Ashes. (Discovering Our Heritage Ser.). (Illus.). 144p. (gr. 5 up). 1985. lib. bdg. 10.95 (ISBN 0-87518-309-3). Dillon.

Adams Family. Adams Family Correspondence, Vol. 4. Incl. Vol. 1. Dec. 1761-May 1776; Vol. 2. June 1776-Mar. 1778. 1963. Set. 60.00x (ISBN 0-674-00400-0); Vol. 3. Apr. 1778-Sep. 1780; Vol. 4. Oct. 1780-Sep. 1782. 1973. Set. 60.00x (ISBN 0-674-00405-1). LC 63-14964. (Adams Papers: No. 2). (Illus.). Harvard U Pr.

Adams, Fay G. The Initiation of an Activity Program into a Public School. LC 77-176504. (Columbia University. Teachers College. Contributions to Education: No. 598). Repr. of 1934 ed. 22.50 (ISBN 0-404-55598-5). AMS Pr.

Adams, Fay O. Some Famous American Schools. 341p. 1982. Repr. 50.00 (ISBN 0-8495-0221-7). Arden Lib.

Adams, Florence. Catch a Sunbeam: A Book of Solar Study & Experiments. LC 78-52820. (Illus.). (gr. 4-7). 1978. 10.95 (ISBN 0-15-215197-4, HJ). HarBraceJ.

--Make Your Own Baby Furniture. LC 80-10495. (Illus.). 224p. 1980. pap. 9.95 (ISBN 0-87131-320-0). M Evans.

Adams, Francis. Free School System of the United States. LC 73-89144. (American Education: Its Men, Institutions & Ideas, Ser. 1). 1969. Repr. of 1875 ed. 14.00 (ISBN 0-405-01380-9). Ayer Co Pubs.

--The Genuine Works of Hippocrates. 384p. 1972. Repr. of 1939 ed. 24.50 (ISBN 0-88275-002-X). Krieger.

Adams, Francis, ed. & tr. see Aretaeus.

Adams, Frand, compiled by. Packard Jukebox Sales Brochures, 1946-49: Including Remote Equipment. 70p. 1984. 10 Mil laminated covers, spiral bdg. 24.50 (ISBN 0-913599-00-X, R-242). AMR Pub Co.

Adams, Frank. Unearthing Seeds of Fire: The Idea of Highlander. LC 74-16653. 1975. 12.95 (ISBN 0-910244-79-0); pap. 7.95 (ISBN 0-89587-019-3). Blair.

--Wurlitzer Jukeboxes 1934-74. 242p. 1983. deluxe ed. 24.50 10 mil laminated, spiral bound (ISBN 0-913599-19-0). Amr Pub Co.

Adams, Frank & Horton, Myles. Unearthing Seeds of Fire: The Idea of Highlander. 239p. 1975. pap. 7.95 (ISBN 0-89587-019-3). Highlander.

Adams, Frank, ed. Duo-Art Technical Manual: A Compilation of Service Manuals, Technical Charts, Photos. (Illus.). 90p. 1984. Repr. Service Information Included. spiral bound 19.50 (ISBN 0-913599-45-X, R-36B). AMR Pub Co.

Adams, Frank, compiled by. Wurlitzer Jukebox Models of the 3700 Series: Service & Parts Manual "Americana" of 1973. 136p. 1984. Repr. of 1973 ed. 10 mil laminated covers, spiral bdg. 29.50 (ISBN 0-913599-09-3, R-251). AMR Pub Co.

--Wurlitzer Jukebox Service & Parts Manual: Model 5220 Wall Box & Steppers, (Includes Schematics & Brochure on the 5220 Series Wall Boxes. 36p. 1984. Repr. 10 mil laminated covers 14.50 (ISBN 0-913599-01-8, R-245). AMR Pub Co.

Adams, Frank, ed. Wurlitzer Jukeboxes, Vol. II. 168p. 1984. deluxe ed. 21.50 spiral bound (ISBN 0-913599-50-6, R-295). AMR Pub Co.

Adams, Frank, compiled by. Wurlitzer Jukeboxes, 1934-74. 242p. (Orig.). 1984. pap. 16.50 Spiral bdg. (ISBN 0-913599-43-3, R-232E). AMR Pub Co.

Adams, Frank, ed. see AMI Co.

Adams, Frank, ed. see AMI Company.

Adams, Frank, ed. see Ampion Piano Player Co.

Adams, Frank, ed. see Rock-Ola Mfg. Corp.

Adams, Frank, ed. see Rock-Ola Mfg. Corporation.

Adams, Frank, ed. see Seeburg Co.

Adams, Frank, ed. see Seeburg Company.

Adams, Frank, ed. see Seeburg Company Staff.

Adams, Frank, ed. see Seeburg Corp.

Adams, Frank, ed. see Wurlitzer Co.

Adams, Frank, ed. see Wurlitzer Company Staff.

Adams, Frank C. & Stephens, Clarence W. College & University Student Work Programs: Implications & Implementations. LC 77-112382. 281p. 1970. 10.00x (ISBN 0-8093-0467-8). S Ill U Pr.

Adams, Frank O. Sindon: A Layman's Guide to the Shroud of Turin. DeSalvo, John A., ed. LC 82-90138. (Illus.). 1982. 12.50 (ISBN 0-86700-008-2, Synergy Bks). P Walsh Pr.

Adams, Fred, ed. Soil Acidity & Liming. 2nd ed. 1984. 25.00 (ISBN 0-89118-080-X). Am Soc Agron.

Adams, Frederick B. Introduction to the Pierpont Morgan Library. Ryskamp, Charles, ed. LC 64-21147. 54p. 1974. pap. 4.00 (ISBN 0-87598-032-5). Pierpont Morgan.

Adams, Frederick C. Economic Diplomacy: The Export-Import Bank & American Foreign Policy, 1934-1939. LC 75-43758. 1976. 24.00x (ISBN 0-8262-0197-0). U of Mo Pr.

Adams, Frederick U. Conquest of the Tropics: The Story of the Creative Enterprises Conducted by the United Fruit Company. Bruchey, Stuart & Bruchey, Eleanor, eds. LC 76-4766. (American Business Abroad Ser.). (Illus.). 1976. Repr. of 1914 ed. 36.50x (ISBN 0-405-09263-6). Ayer Co Pubs.

--President John Smith: The Story of a Peaceful Revolution. LC 72-154428. (Utopian Literature Ser). (Illus.). 1971. Repr. of 1897 ed. 23.50 (ISBN 0-405-03511-X). Ayer Co Pubs.

Adams, G. B. Civilization During the Middle Ages. 75.00 (ISBN 0-87968-873-4). Gordon Pr.

--History of England from the Norman Conquest to the Death of John, 1066-1216. (Political History of England Monograph). Repr. of 1905 ed. 35.00 (ISBN 0-527-00847-8). Kraus Repr.

Adams, G. Donald. Museum Public Relations. (AASLH Management Ser.: Vol. 2). 1983. text ed. 21.00 (ISBN 0-910050-65-1). AASLH Pr.

Adams, G. E., ed. see L. H. Gray Conference (5th: 1973: University of Sussex).

Adams, Gary, jt. auth. see Sternberg, Les.

Adams, Gene M. & Dietrick, Ronald W. Exercise Physiology Primer. rev. ed. (Illus.). 225p. (Orig.). 1983. 14.95 (ISBN 0-942728-05-X). Custom Pub Co.

Adams, George. How to Photograph a Woman. 1979. pap. 5.95 (ISBN 0-380-43117-3, 43117-3). Avon.

--Nature Ever New: Essays on the Renewal of Agriculture. 1979. pap. 6.50 (ISBN 0-916786-40-4). St George Bk Serv.

--Physical & Ethereal Spaces. (Illus.). 71p. 1978. pap. 5.00 (ISBN 0-85440-328-0, Pub. by Steinerbooks). Anthroposophic.

--Universal Forces in Mechanics. Eberhart, Stephen, tr. from Ger. 87p. (Orig.). 1977. pap. 5.25 (ISBN 0-85440-325-6, Pub. by Steinerbooks). Anthroposophic.

Adams, George & Whicher, Olive. The Plant Between Sun & Earth. LC 82-50276. (Illus.). 224p. (Orig.). 1982. pap. 12.95 (ISBN 0-87773-232-9, 71231-5). Shambhala Pubns.

--The Plant Between Sun & Earth & the Science Physical & Ethereal Spaces. 2nd ed. (Illus.). 1980. pap. 33.95 (ISBN 0-85440-360-4, Pub. by Steinerbooks). Anthroposophic.

Adams, George, tr. see Steiner, Rudolf.

Adams, George, et al, trs. see Steiner, Rudolf.

Adams, George B. Civilization During the Middle Ages. 1906. Repr. 30.00 (ISBN 0-8274-2063-3). R West.

--Council & Courts in Anglo-Norman England. LC 64-66387. 1965. Repr. of 1926 ed. 10.00x (ISBN 0-8462-0552-1). Russell.

--History of England from the Norman Conquest to the Death of John. LC 77-5634. (The Political History of England Ser.: No. 2). Repr. of 1905 ed. 22.50 (ISBN 0-404-50772-7). AMS Pr.

--Medieval & Modern History. 1901. 15.00 (ISBN 0-8482-7276-5). Norwood Edns.

--Select Documents of English Constitutional History. 1930. 40.00 (ISBN 0-8482-3258-5). Norwood Edns.

Adams, George F. Essentials of Geriatric Medicine. 2nd ed. (Orig.). 1981. pap. text ed. 9.95x (ISBN 0-19-261352-9). Oxford U Pr.

Adams, George J. A Lecture on the Doctrine of Baptism for the Dead. new ed. (Orig.). 1983. pap. 1.00 (ISBN 0-942284-04-6). Restoration Re.

Adams, George L., jt. auth. see Moffic, H. Steven.

Adams, George P. Idealism & the Modern Age. LC 75-3015. (Philosophy in America Ser.). Repr. of 1919 ed. 18.00 (ISBN 0-404-59009-8). AMS Pr.

Adams, George R. Life on the Yukon, 1865-186. Pierce, Richard A., ed. (Alaska History Ser.: No. 22). (Illus.). 1982. 22.00x (ISBN 0-919642-96-9). Limestone Pr.

Adams, George R., jt. auth. see Nichols, Roger I.

Adams, George R., jt. ed. see Gardner, James B.

Adams, George W., ed. see Logan, Mary.

Adams, Gerald. Neighborhood Guide. Leonard, Jan, ed. LC 80-66584. (Savvy San Francisco Ser.). (Illus.). 64p. (Orig.). 1980. pap. 2.50 (ISBN 0-89395-049-1). Cal Living Bks.

Adams, Gerald & Crossman, Sharyn. Physical Attractiveness. LC 78-56850. 1979. 7.95 (ISBN 0-87212-122-4). Libra.

Adams, Gerald & Schvaneveldt, Jay D. Understanding Research Methods. LC 84-12543. 448p. 1984. pap. text ed. 24.95 (ISBN 0-317-14367-0). Longman.

Adams, Gerald D. Son of the Sioux. (Orig.). 1981. pap. 1.95 (ISBN 0-505-51703-5, Pub. by Tower Bks). Dorchester Pub Co.

Adams, Gerald R. & Gullotta, Thomas. Adolescent Life Experiences. LC 82-20748. (Psychology Ser.). 600p. 1983. text ed. 21.25 pub net (ISBN 0-534-01242-6). Brooks-Cole.

Adams, Gerard F., ed. Industrial Policies for Growth & Competitiveness: Empirical Studies, Vol. II. LC 84-48529. (Wharton Econometric Studies). 256p. 1985. 34.00x (ISBN 0-669-09593-1). Lexington Bks.

Adams, Gerry. Falls Memories. (Illus.). 144p. 1982. pap. 5.75 (ISBN 0-86322-013-4, Pub. by Brandon Bks). Longwood Pub Group.

Adams, Gilbert T., Jr. & Clarkson, Richard J. Texas Evidence Law Reporter, Vol. 1, No. 1. 16p. 1984. looseleaf with binder 60.00 (ISBN 0-409-25038-4). Butterworth TX.

Adams, Gleason R., jt. tr. see Latortue, Regine.

Adams, Gordon. The Politics of Defense Contracting: The Iron Triangle. 465p. 1981. 39.95 (ISBN 0-87855-457-2); pap. 15.00 (ISBN 0-87871-012-4). Transaction Bks.

Adams, Grace. Workers on Relief. LC 74-137154. (Poverty U.S.A. Historical Record Ser). 1971. Repr. of 1939 ed. 23.50 (ISBN 0-405-03091-6). Ayer Co Pubs.

Adams, Guy B. A Bibliography on a Human Theory of Organization, No. 1293. 1977. 5.50 (ISBN 0-686-19694-5). CPL Biblios.

Adams, H. Democracy & Esther: Two Novels. 12.75 (ISBN 0-8446-1008-9). Peter Smith.

--Gas & Its Uses. (Illus.). (gr. 4 up). 9.50x (ISBN 0-392-03081-0, LTB). Sportshelf.

--Mont-Saint-Michel & Chartres: A Study of 13th Century Unity. LC 81-47279. (Illus.). 448p. 1981. 38.00x (ISBN 0-691-03971-2); pap. 9.95x (ISBN 0-691-00335-1). Princeton U Pr.

--Trauma & Regeneration. (Acta Neurochirurgica: Supplement 32). (Illus.). 150p. 1983. pap. 27.60 (ISBN 0-387-81775-1). Springer-Verlag.

--Water & the Waterworks. (Illus.). (gr. 4 up). 9.50x (ISBN 0-392-05252-0, LTB). Sportshelf.

Adams, H., jt. auth. see Sand, George.

Adams, H. B. Jared Sparks & Alexis De Tocqueville. pap. 9.00 (ISBN 0-384-00325-7). Johnson Repr.

Adams, H. F. see Fernald, Mabel R.

Adams, H. Greg. Effective Supervisory Safety Salesmanship. LC 81-86317. (Illus.). 40p. 1982. Incl. transparency masters & slides. 3-ring binder 37.50 (ISBN 0-88061-028-X). Inst Pub GA.

Adams, H. M. Catalogue of Books Printed on the Continent of Europe, 2 Vols. 1967. Set. 415.00 (ISBN 0-521-06951-3). Cambridge U Pr.

Adams, H. P. Karl Marx in His Earlier Writings. LC 65-18180. 1972. pap. 2.95 (ISBN 0-689-70291-4, 185). Atheneum.

Adams, Harold. The Missing Moon. 256p. 1983. pap. 2.50 (ISBN 0-441-53401-5). Ace Bks.

--Murder. 256p. (Orig.). 1983. pap. 2.50 (ISBN 0-441-54706-0). Ace Bks.

--The Naked Liar. 1985. 15.95 (ISBN 0-89296-126-0). Mysterious Pr.

--Paint the Town Red. 224p. 1982. pap. 2.95 (ISBN 0-441-64600-X, Pub. by Charter Bks). Ace Bks.

Adams, Harold W. & Stringham, Ray. Lawyer's Management Principles: A Course for Assistants, Student Syllabus. (gr. 11-12). 1975. pap. text ed. 6.65 (ISBN 0-89420-079-8, 101028); cassette recordings 86.90 (ISBN 0-89420-200-6, 101000). Natl Book.

Adams, Harry & Simpson, R. W. Propjet '85. (Illus.). 148p. 1985. pap. 7.95 (ISBN 0-941024-10-5, Pub. by AvCom Intl). Aviation.

Adams, Harry B. Propjet 1984. (Illus.). 142p. 1984. pap. 5.95 (ISBN 0-941024-08-3). Avcom Intl.

Adams, Harry B., jt. auth. see Minear, Paul S.

Adams, Hazard. Blake & Yeats: The Contrary Vision. LC 68-27044. (With a new preface). 1968. Repr. of 1955 ed. 20.00x (ISBN 0-8462-1188-2). Russell.

--Critical Theory since Plato. 1267p. 1971. text ed. 29.95 (ISBN 0-15-516142-3, HC). HarBraceJ.

--Joyce Cary's Trilogies: Pursuit of the Particular Real. LC 83-3461. 1983. 20.00 (ISBN 0-8130-0759-3). U Presses Fla.

--Lady Gregory. (Irish Writers Ser.). 106p. 1973. 4.50 (ISBN 0-8387-1085-9); pap. 1.95 (ISBN 0-8387-1207-X). Bucknell U Pr.

--Philosophy of the Literary Symbolic. LC 82-24785. (Illus.). xiv, 466p. 1983. 37.50 (ISBN 0-8130-0743-7); pap. 17.50x (ISBN 0-8130-0771-2). U Presses Fla.

--William Blake: A Reading of Shorter Poems. 337p. 1983. Repr. of 1963 ed. lib. bdg. 39.50 (ISBN 0-8492-3449-2). R West.

--William Blake, a Reading of the Shorter Poems. 337p. 1980. Repr. of 1963 ed. lib. bdg. 30.00 (ISBN 0-8414-2913-8). Folcroft.

Adams, Helen B. And So I Stayed. 1978. 5.00 (ISBN 0-8233-0279-2). Golden Quill.

Adams, Helen J. Understanding Retrogrades. 80p. 1980. 5.50 (ISBN 0-86690-056-X, 1006-01). Am Fed Astrologers.

Adams, Henry. A Catalogue of the Books of John Quincy Adams Deposited in the Boston Athenaeum. (Illus.). 152p. 1938. 25.00 (ISBN 0-934552-17-7). Boston Athenaeum.

--The Degradation of the Democratic Dogma. 12.00 (ISBN 0-8446-1007-0). Peter Smith.

--Democracy, an American Novel. (Classics Ser). (YA) (gr. 9 up). pap. 1.50 (ISBN 0-8049-0164-3, CL-164). Airmont.

--Democracy: An American Novel. 1976. Repr. of 1883 ed. 49.00x (ISBN 0-403-05724-8, Regency). Scholarly.

--Democracy: An American Novel. 256p. 1982. pap. 1.98 (ISBN 0-517-54728-7, Harmony). Crown.

--Democracy: An American Novel. 1983. pap. 3.50 (ISBN 0-452-00651-1, Mer). NAL.

--Democracy: An American Novel. (Works of Henry Adams Ser.). 374p. Date not set. Repr. of 1908 ed. lib. bdg. 39.00 (ISBN 0-932051-17-0). Am Repr Serv.

--Deomocracy. 15.95 (ISBN 0-89190-525-1, Pub. by Am Repr). Amereon Ltd.

--The Education of Henry Adams. Samuels, Ernest, ed. (Riverside Edition Ser.). 600p. 1973. pap. 7.950 (ISBN 0-395-16620-9, RivEd). HM.

--Education of Henry Adams. 1961. pap. 9.95 (ISBN 0-395-08352-4, 3, SenEd). HM.

--The Education of Henry Adams. LC 19-7386. 529p. 1975. Repr. of 1918 ed. 17.95 (ISBN 0-910220-74-3). Berg.

--The Education of Henry Adams. 20.95 (ISBN 0-89190-844-7, Pub. by Am Repr). Amereon ltd.

--Esther. Spiller, Robert, ed. LC 38-18393. 1976. Repr. lib. bdg. 45.00x (ISBN 0-8201-1187-2). Schol Facsimiles.

--Historical Essays. Repr. of 1891 ed. 39.50x (ISBN 3-4870-4645-8). Adlers Foreign Bks.

--History of the United States of America During the Administrations of Jefferson & Madison. 9 vols. 1980. lib. bdg. 995.00 (ISBN 0-8490-3148-6). Gordon Pr.

--History of U. S. A. During the Administrations of Jefferson & Madison. abr. ed. Samuels, Ernest, ed. LC 78-66081. (Midway Reprints Ser.). 1979. pap. text ed. 17.00x (ISBN 0-226-00512-7, CAH). U of Chicago Pr.

--Italy at War. (World War II Ser.). 1982. 14.95 (ISBN 0-8094-3423-7). Time-Life.

--John Randolph. Morse, John T., Jr., ed. LC 70-128968. (American Statesmen: No. 16). 1898. 27.00 (ISBN 0-404-50865-0). AMS Pr.

--John Randolph. 11.25 (ISBN 0-8446-0451-8). Peter Smith.

--John Randolph. 13.95 (ISBN 0-89190-526-X, Pub. by Am Repr). Amereon Ltd.

--The Letters of Henry Adams, Volumes 1-3: 1858-1892. Levenson, J. C. & Samuels, Ernest, eds. (Illus.). 2016p. 1983. Set. text ed. 110.00x (ISBN 0-674-52685-6, Belknap Pr). Harvard U Pr.

--Letters to a Niece & Prayer to the Virgin of Chartres. La Farge, Mabel, ed. 1970. Repr. of 1920 ed. 29.00 (ISBN 0-403-00490-X). Scholarly.

--The Life of George Cabot Lodge. LC 78-16619. 1978. Repr. of 1911 ed. 40.00x (ISBN 0-8201-1316-6). Schol Facsimiles.

--Mont-Saint-Michel & Chartres. 75.00 (ISBN 0-87968-178-0). Gordon Pr.

--Mont Saint Michel & Chartres. LC 36-27246. 397p. 1978. 17.95 (ISBN 0-910220-94-8). Berg.

--Novels, Mont Saint Michel, The Education. Samuels, Ernest & Samuels, Jayne N., eds. LC 83-5448. 1264p. 1983. 27.50 (ISBN 0-940450-12-7, Pub. by Library of America). Literary Classics.

--Tahiti. Spiller, Robert E., ed. LC 47-3845. (Illus.). 216p. 1976. Repr. 45.00x (ISBN 0-8201-1213-5). Schol Facsimiles.

--Tahiti: Memoirs of Arii Taimai. 196p. 1968. Repr. of 1901 ed. 20.00 (ISBN 0-8398-0051-7). Parnassus Imprints.

--The United States in Eighteen Hundred. 142p. 1955. pap. 4.95x (ISBN 0-8014-9014-6). Cornell U Pr.

Adams, Henry, jt. auth. see Adams, Charles F., Jr.

Adams, Henry, ed. Documents Relating to New England Federalism, 1800-1815. 1964. Repr. of 1905 ed. 24.50 (ISBN 0-8337-0012-X). B Franklin.

Adams, Henry, et al. American Drawings & Watercolors in the Collection of the Museum of Art, Carnegie Institute. Maloy, Kate, ed. (Illus.). 320p. (Orig.). 1985. pap. 19.95 (ISBN 0-88039-009-3). Mus Art Carnegie.

Adams, Henry B. Mont-Saint-Michel & Chartres. LC 82-14018. 408p. 1982. 25.00 (ISBN 0-89783-019-9). Larlin Corp.

Adams, Henry C. Public Debts: An Essay in the Science of Finance. facsimile ed. LC 75-2619. (Wall Street & the Security Market Ser.). 1975. Repr. of 1898 ed. 32.00x (ISBN 0-405-06946-4). Ayer Co Pubs.

--Taxation in the United States 1789-1816. LC 78-63745. (Johns Hopkins University. Studies in the Social Sciences. Second Ser. 1884: 5-6). Repr. of 1884 ed. 11.50 (ISBN 0-404-61015-3). AMS Pr.

--Taxation in the United States: 1789-1816. LC 78-122836. (John Hopkins University. Studies, Series 2: Nos. 5-6). 1970. Repr. of 1884 ed. 13.50 (ISBN 0-8337-0014-6). B Franklin.

--Taxation in the United States: 1789-1816. pap. 9.00 (ISBN 0-384-00337-0). Johnson Repr.

--Two Essays: Relation of the State to Industrial Action & Economics & Jurisprudence. Dorfman, Joseph, ed. LC 75-76510. (Reprints of Economic Classics). Repr. of 1954 ed. 22.50x (ISBN 0-678-00494-3). Kelley.

--Wonder Book of Travellers' Tales. (Black & Gold Lib). (Illus.). 1942. 6.95 (ISBN 0-87140-998-4). Liveright.

Adams, Henry E. Abnormal Psychology. 696p. 1981. text ed. write for info. (ISBN 0-697-06636-3); pap. text ed. write for info. (ISBN 0-697-06641-X); instrs.' manual avail. (ISBN 0-697-06638-X). Wm C Brown.

Adams, Henry E. & Unikel, I. P. Issues & Trends in Behavior Therapy. (Illus.). 288p. 1973. spiral 32.50x (ISBN 0-398-02686-6). C C Thomas.

Adams, Henry E., jt. auth. see Tollison, C. David.

Adams, Henry E., ed. Handbook of Latin American Studies, Vol. 29: Social Sciences 1962-64. LC 36-32633. 1967. 30.00x (ISBN 0-8130-0001-7). U Presses Fla.

--Handbook of Latin American Studies, Vol. 30: Humanities 1965-1966. LC 36-32633. 1968. 30.00x (ISBN 0-8130-0266-4). U Presses Fla.

--Handbook of Latin American Studies, Vol. 32: Humanities 1966-1967. LC 36-32633. 1970. 35.00x (ISBN 0-8130-0316-4). U Presses Fla.

--Handbook of Latin American Studies, Vol. 31: Social Sciences 1963-1969. LC 36-32633. 1969. 35.00x (ISBN 0-8130-0294-X). U Presses Fla.

Adams, Henry E. & Sutker, Patricia B., eds. Comprehensive Handbook of Psychopathology. LC 83-19193. 1091p. 1984. 95.00x (ISBN 0-306-41222-5, Plenum Pr). Plenum Pub.

Adams, Henry E., jt. ed. see Pariseau, Earl J.

Adams, Henry F. Advertising & Its Mental Laws. LC 84-46033. (History of Advertising Ser.). 344p. 1985. lib. bdg. 40.00 (ISBN 0-8240-6727-4). Garland Pub.

Adams, Henry H. English Domestic or Homiletic Tragedy: 1575-1642. LC 65-16225. Repr. of 1943 ed. 17.00 (ISBN 0-405-08178-2, Pub. by Blom). Ayer Co Pubs.

--English Domestic: Or, Homiletic Tragedy 1575 to 1642. 228p. 1983. Repr. of 1943 ed. lib. bdg. 35.00 (ISBN 0-89760-074-6). Telegraph Bks.

--English Domestic Or, Homiletic Tragedy 1575-1642: Being an Account of the Development of the Tragedy of the Common Man Showing Its Great Dependence on Religious Morality, Illustrated with Striking Examples of the Interposition of Providence for the Amendment of Men's Manners. (Illus.). 228p. 1985. Repr. of 1943 ed. lib. bdg. 40.00 (ISBN 0-8482-7278-1). Norwood Edns.

--Witness to Power: The Life of Fleet Admiral William D. Leahy. (Illus.). 400p. 1985. 22.95 (ISBN 0-87021-338-5). Naval Inst Pr.

Adams, Henry H. & Hathaway, Baxter, eds. Dramatic Essays of the Neoclassic Age. LC 64-14692. 25.50 (ISBN 0-405-08179-0, Pub. by Blom). Ayer Co Pubs.

Adams, Henry M. Prussian-American Relations, Seventeen Seventy-Five to Eighteen Seventy-One. LC 79-25884. 135p. 1980. Repr. of 1960 ed. lib. bdg. 22.50x (ISBN 0-313-22270-3, ADPA). Greenwood.

Adams, Herbert B. The Church & Popular Education. LC 78-63876. (Johns Hopkins University. Studies in the Social Sciences. Eighteenth Ser. 1900: 8-9). Repr. of 1900 ed. 11.50 (ISBN 0-404-61132-X). AMS Pr.

--The Church & Popular Education. Repr. of 1900 ed. 10.00 (ISBN 0-384-00323-0). Johnson Repr.

--The Church & Popular Education. (The Works of Herbert B. Adams Ser.). 84p. 1985. Repr. of 1900 ed. lib. bdg. 29.00 (ISBN 0-318-03787-4). Am Repr Serv.

--The Germanic Origin of New England Towns. LC 78-63731. (Johns Hopkins University. Studies in the Social Sciences. First Ser. 1882-1883: 2). Repr. of 1882 ed. 11.50 (ISBN 0-404-61002-1). AMS Pr.

--The Germanic Origin of New England Towns. pap. 9.00 (ISBN 0-384-00331-1). Johnson Repr.

--Historical Scholarship in the U. S., 1876 to 1901. (The Works of Herbert B. Adams Ser.). 314p. Repr. of 1938 ed. lib. bdg. 49.00 (ISBN 0-318-03807-2). Am Repr Serv.

--Historical Scholarship in the United States, 1876-1901: As Revealed in the Correspondence of Herbert B. Adams. Holt, W. Stull, ed. LC 78-64173. (Johns Hopkins University. Studies in the Social Sciences. Fifty-Sixth Ser. 1938: 4). Repr. of 1938 ed. 14.00 (ISBN 0-404-61282-2). AMS Pr.

--Historical Scholarship in the United States, 1876-1901, As Revealed in the Correspondence of Herbert B. Adams. Holt, W. Stull, ed. LC 73-144852. 1971. Repr. of 1938 ed. 13.00 (ISBN 0-403-00819-0). Scholarly.

--Jared Sparks & Alexis De Tocqueville. LC 78-63867. (Johns Hopkins University. Studies in the Social Sciences. Sixteenth Ser. 1898: 12). Repr. of 1898 ed. 11.50 (ISBN 0-404-61123-0). AMS Pr.

--Jared Sparks & Alexis de Tocqueville. (The Works of Herbert B. Adams Ser.). 49p. 1985. Repr. of 1898 ed. lib. bdg. 29.00 (ISBN 0-318-03784-X). Am Repr Serv.

--Life & Writings of Jared Sparks, 2 Vols. facs. ed. LC 76-119924. (Select Bibliographies Reprint Ser). 1893. Set. 55.00 (ISBN 0-8369-5367-3). Ayer Co Pubs.

--Maryland's Influence in Founding a Nation. 123p. 1877. 6.50 (ISBN 0-686-36841-X). Md Hist.

--Maryland's Influence Upon Land Cessions to the U. S. LC 77-97563. Repr. of 1885 ed. 11.50 (ISBN 0-404-00286-2). AMS Pr.

--Maryland's Influence Upon Land Cessions to the United States: With Minor Papers on George Washington's Interest in Western Lands, the Potomac Company & a National University. Repr. of 1885 ed. 12.00 (ISBN 0-384-00329-X). Johnson Repr.

--Maryland's Influence Upon Land Cessions to the United States. LC 4-8520. 1885. 5.00x (ISBN 0-403-00136-6). Scholarly.

--Methods of Historical Study. LC 78-63742. (Johns Hopkins University. Studies in the Social Sciences. Second Ser. 1884: 1-2). Repr. of 1884 ed. 11.50 (ISBN 0-404-61012-9). AMS Pr.

--Methods of Historical Study. Repr. of 1884 ed. 14.00 (ISBN 0-384-00336-2). Johnson Repr.

--Norman Constables in America. LC 78-63738. (Johns Hopkins University. Studies in the Social Sciences. First Ser. 1882-1883: 8). Repr. of 1883 ed. 11.50 (ISBN 0-404-61008-0). AMS Pr.

--Norman Constables in America. pap. 9.00 (ISBN 0-384-00333-8). Johnson Repr.

--Notes on the Literature of Charities. LC 78-63774. (Johns Hopkins University. Studies in the Social Sciences. Fifth Ser. 1887: 8). Repr. of 1887 ed. 11.50 (ISBN 0-404-61040-4). AMS Pr.

--Notes on the Literature of Charities. pap. 9.00 (ISBN 0-384-00339-7). Johnson Repr.

--Notes on the Literature of Charities. (The Works of Herbert B. Adams Ser.). 48p. 1985. Repr. lib. bdg. 29.00 (ISBN 0-318-03786-6). Am Repr Serv.

--Public Educational Work in Baltimore. LC 78-63872. (Johns Hopkins University. Studies in the Social Sciences. Seventeenth Ser. 1899: 12). Repr. of 1899 ed. 11.50 (ISBN 0-404-61128-1). AMS Pr.

--Public Educational Work in Baltimore. pap. 9.00 (ISBN 0-384-00324-9). Johnson Repr.

--Saxon Tithing-Men in America. LC 78-63734. (Johns Hopkins University. Studies in the Social Sciences. First Ser. 1882-1883: 4). Repr. of 1883 ed. 11.50 (ISBN 0-404-61004-8). AMS Pr.

--Saxon Tithing-Men in America. pap. 9.00 (ISBN 0-384-00332-X). Johnson Repr.

--Seminary Libraries & University Extension. LC 78-63777. (Johns Hopkins University. Studies in the Social Sciences. Fifth Ser. 1887: 11). Repr. of 1887 ed. 11.50 (ISBN 0-404-61043-9). AMS Pr.

--Seminary Libraries & University Extension. pap. 9.00 (ISBN 0-384-00328-1). Johnson Repr.

--Seminary Libraries & University Extension. (The Works of Herbert B. Adams Ser.). 33p. 1985. Repr. of 1887 ed. lib. bdg. 29.00 (ISBN 0-318-03785-8). Am Repr Serv.

--Village Communities of Cape Anne & Salem. LC 78-63739. (Johns Hopkins University. Studies in the Social Sciences. First Ser. 1882-1883: 9-10). Repr. of 1883 ed. 11.50 (ISBN 0-404-61009-9). AMS Pr.

--Village Communities of Cape Anne & Salem, from the Historical Collections of the Essex Institute. pap. 9.00 (ISBN 0-384-00334-6). Johnson Repr.

Adams, Herbert B. & Wood, Henry. Columbus & His Discovery of America. LC 70-149681. (BCL Ser.: No. I). Repr. of 1892 ed. 11.50 (ISBN 0-404-00287-0). AMS Pr.

--Columbus & His Discovery of America. pap. 10.00 (ISBN 0-384-00326-5). Johnson Repr.

--Columbus & His Discovery of America. (The Works of Herbert B. Adams Ser.). 88p. Repr. of 1892 ed. lib. bdg. 39.00 (ISBN 0-318-03808-0). Am Repr Serv.

Adams, Herbert B. see Latane, John H.

Adams, Herbert B., et al. Seminary Notes & Historical Literature. LC 78-63798. (Johns Hopkins University. Studies in the Social Sciences. Eighth Ser. 1890: 11-12). Repr. of 1890 ed. 11.50 (ISBN 0-404-61063-3). AMS Pr.

--Seminary Notes on Recent Historical Literature. Repr. of 1890 ed. 12.00 (ISBN 0-384-00327-3). Johnson Repr.

Adams, Herbert F., jt. auth. see Cooke, Nelson M.

Adams, Herbert R., jt. auth. see Glatthorn, Allan A.

Adams, Howard, jt. auth. see Wagner, Bob.

Adams, Howard, jt. auth. see Wagner, Robert.

Adams, Howard, ed. Jefferson & the Arts: An Extended View. LC 76-21951. 1976. 16.95 (ISBN 0-8139-0931-7, National Gallery of Art). U Pr of Va.

Adams, Hugh. Modern Painting. (Mayflower Gallery). (Illus.). 1979. 12.50 (ISBN 0-8317-6062-1, Mayflower Bks); pap. 6.95 (ISBN 0-8317-6063-X). Smith Pubs.

Adams, I. H. Agrarian Landscape Terms: A Glossary for Historical Geography Ser. (Special Publication of the Institute of British Geographers: No. 9). 1980. 25.00 (ISBN 0-12-044180-2). Acad Pr.

Adams, Ian. S, Portrait of a Spy. LC 82-731. 192p. 1982. 11.95 (ISBN 0-89919-087-1). Ticknor & Fields.

Adams, J. Correspondence of John Adams & Thomas Jefferson. LC 25-20253. Repr. of 1925 ed. 23.00 (ISBN 0-527-00460-X). Kraus Repr.

--Journal of Pastoral Practice, Vol. I, No. 2. 1978. kivar 3.50 (ISBN 0-87552-024-3). Presby & Reformed.

--What About Nouthetic Counseling? 1976. kivar 2.50 (ISBN 0-87552-064-2). Presby & Reformed.

--What to Do about Worry. 1972. pap. 0.75 (ISBN 0-87552-065-0). Presby & Reformed.

Adams, J. & Rockmaker, G. Industrial Electricity: Principles & Practices. 3rd ed. 1985. 26.90 (ISBN 0-07-000327-0). McGraw.

Adams, J. & Wilson, N. S. Teach Yourself French. (Teach Yourself Ser.). pap. 3.95 (ISBN 0-679-10172-1). McKay.

Adams, J., et al. Teach Yourself German. (Teach Yourself Ser.). pap. 3.95 (ISBN 0-679-10174-8). McKay.

Adams, J. Alan, jt. auth. see Rogers, David F.

Adams, J. B. A Brief Guide to Rolls-Royce & Bentley Cars 1925-1965. (Illus.). 1976. pap. 9.95 (ISBN 0-87938-003-9, Pub. by Adams & Oliver Ltd. England). Motorbooks Intl.

Adams, J. D. Literary Frontiers. LC 51-9613. Repr. of 1951 ed. 16.00 (ISBN 0-527-00440-5). Kraus Repr.

Adams, J. D. & Whalley, J. The International Taxation of Multinational Enterprise in Developed Countries. LC 77-13. vii, 178p. 1977. lib. bdg. 25.00x (ISBN 0-8371-9530-6, ADI/). Greenwood.

Adams, J. D., jt. auth. see Margulies, N.

Adams, J. Donald. Copey of Harvard: A Biography of Charles Townsend Copeland. LC 72-6191. (Illus.). 306p. 1973. Repr. of 1960 ed. lib. bdg. 19.75x (ISBN 0-8371-6465-6, ADCO). Greenwood.

--The Magic & Mystery of Words. LC 74-10471. 117p. 1975. Repr. of 1963 ed. lib. bdg. 18.75 (ISBN 0-8371-7686-7, ADMW). Greenwood.

Adams, J. E. You Can Conquer Depression. 1.25 (ISBN 0-8010-0094-7). Baker Bk.

--You Can Defeat Anger. 0.95 (ISBN 0-8010-0092-0). Baker Bk.

--You Can Kick the Drug Habit. 1.25 (ISBN 0-8010-0095-5). Baker Bk.

--You Can Overcome Fear. 1.25 (ISBN 0-8010-0093-9). Baker Bk.

--You Can Stop Worrying. 1.25 (ISBN 0-8010-0097-1). Baker Bk.

--You Can Sweeten a Sour Marriage. 0.95 (ISBN 0-8010-0096-3). Baker Bk.

Adams, J. Frank. Infinite Loop Spaces. (Annals of Mathematics Studies Ser.: No. 90). 1978. 26.50 (ISBN 0-691-08207-3); pap. 12.50 (ISBN 0-691-08206-5). Princeton U Pr.

--Lectures on Lie Groups. LC 82-51014. (Midway Reprints Ser.). 168p. 1983. pap. text ed. 11.00x (ISBN 0-226-00530-5). U of Chicago Pr.

--Stable Homotopy. (Chicago Lectures in Mathematics Ser). 384p. 1974. pap. text ed. 10.00x (ISBN 0-226-00524-0). U of Chicago Pr.

--Stable Homotopy Theory. 3rd ed. LC 70-90867. (Lecture Notes in Mathematics: Vol. 3). 1969. pap. 10.70 (ISBN 0-387-04598-8). Springer-Verlag.

Adams, J. H. & Murray, Margaret F. Atlas of Post-Mortem Techniques in Neuropathology. LC 82-4313. (Illus.). 120p. 1982. 34.50 (ISBN 0-521-24121-9). Cambridge U Pr.

Adams, J. M., jt. auth. see Stadt, R.

Adams, J. Mack & Haden, Douglas H. Social Effects of Computer Use & Misuse. LC 76-10698. 326p. 1976. pap. 28.00 (ISBN 0-471-00463-4). Wiley.

Adams, J. McKee, jt. ed. see Callaway, Joseph A.

Adams, J. Michael. Career Change: A Planning Book. (Illus.). 208p. 1983. pap. text ed. 10.40 (ISBN 0-07-000401-3). McGraw.

Adams, J. Michael & Faux, David D. Printing Technology. 2nd ed. 1982. text ed. write for info. (ISBN 0-534-01016-4, Breton Pubs). Wadsworth Pub.

Adams, J. Michael, jt. auth. see Kagy, Frederick D.

Adams, J. N. The Text & Language of a Vulgar Latin Chronicle (Anonymus Valesianus11) 189p. 1981. 35.00x (ISBN 0-900587-33-4, Pub. by Inst Class Stud England). State Mutual Bk.

--The Vulgar Latin of the Letters of Claudius Terentianus (P. Mich. VIII, 467-75) 100p. 1977. 22.75x (ISBN 0-8476-1428-X). Rowman.

Adams, J. Q., Jr., ed. see Mason, John.

Adams, J. T. The Complete Concrete Masonry & Brick Handbook. 1979. pap. 19.95 (ISBN 0-442-20830-8). Van Nos Reinhold.

--The Complete Home Electrical Wiring Handbook. LC 78-21969. (Illus.). 1979. pap. 12.95 (ISBN 0-668-04525-6). Arco.

--New England in the Republic. (Illus.). 1958. 13.25 (ISBN 0-8446-1010-0). Peter Smith.

Adams, J. V. The Sociopath. LC 83-82208. 288p. 1983. pap. 3.50 (ISBN 0-9612454-0-9). Jackrabbit.

Adams, Jack. Wild Elephants in Captivity. LC 81-69851. (Illus.). 206p. 1981. pap. 20.00x (ISBN 0-942074-00-9). Ctr Study Elephants.

Adams, Jack A. Learning & Memory: An Introduction. rev. ed. 1980. 32.00x (ISBN 0-256-02314-X). Dorsey.

Adams, James. The Unnatural Alliance: Israel & South Africa. 224p. 1984. 18.95 (ISBN 0-7043-2373-7, Pub. by Quartet Bks). Merrimack Pub Cir.

Adams, James & Frischer, Patricia. Artist in the Market Place: Making your Living in the Fine Arts. LC 80-11273. 168p. 1980. 9.95 (ISBN 0-87131-315-4); pap. 5.95 (ISBN 0-87131-323-5). M Evans.

Adams, James D. Shape of Books to Come. facsimile ed. LC 72-167302. (Essay Index Reprint Ser). Repr. of 1944 ed. 18.00 (ISBN 0-8369-2479-7). Ayer Co Pubs.

Adams, James E. Electrical Principles & Practices. 2nd ed. 1973. text ed. 28.70 (ISBN 0-07-000281-9). McGraw.

--Liberacion: El Evangelo de Dios. 1980. pap. 2.95 (ISBN 0-686-70961-6). Banner of Truth.

--Three to Win. LC 77-72255. (Radiant Life Ser.). 125p. pap. 2.50 (ISBN 0-88243-906-5, 02-0906); tchr's ed 2.50 (ISBN 0-88243-176-5, 32-0176). Gospel Pub.

Adams, James F. Understanding Adolescence: Current Developments in Adolescent Psychology. 4th ed. 512p. 1980. text ed. 32.50 (ISBN 0-205-06931-2, 2469316). Allyn.

Adams, James F., ed. see Buchanan, Joseph.

Adams, James L. Conceptual Blockbusting: A Guide to Better Ideas. 2nd ed. (Illus.). 160p. 1980. 10.95 (ISBN 0-393-01223-9); pap. text ed. 5.95x (ISBN 0-393-95016-6). Norton.

--On Being Human Religiously. 1976. pap. 5.50 (ISBN 0-933840-04-7). Unitarian Univ.

--Paul Tillich's Philosophy of Culture, Science & Religion. LC 81-43775. 320p. 1982. lib. bdg. 26.25 (ISBN 0-8191-2221-1); pap. text ed. 13.00 (ISBN 0-8191-2222-X). U Pr of Amer.

Adams, James L., ed. see Holl, Karl.

Adams, James L., ed. see Tillich, Paul.

Adams, James L., tr. see Tillich, Paul.

Adams, James L., et al, eds. The Thought of Paul Tillich. 1985. 19.95 (ISBN 0-06-060072-1). Har-Row.

Adams, James M. Data Processing: An Introduction. LC 81-66793. (Data Processing Ser.). (Illus.). 253p. 1982. text ed. 14.60 (ISBN 0-8273-1616-X); tchr's. guide 5.25 (ISBN 0-8273-1617-8). Delmar.

Adams, James N. The Latin Sexual Vocabulary: Three Years of Confrontation. LC 82-82629. 284p. 1983. 27.50x (ISBN 0-8018-2968-2). Johns Hopkins.

Adams, James N., compiled by. Cumulative Index, Journal of the Illinois State Historical Society, Vols. 26-50. 710p. 1968. 20.00 (ISBN 0-912154-17-9). Ill St Hist Lib.

--General Index to Journal of the Illinois State Historical Society, Vols. 1-25. 714p. 1949. 20.00 (ISBN 0-912154-15-2). Ill St Hist Lib.

Adams, James R. Media Planning. 2nd ed. 232p. 1977. 36.75x (ISBN 0-220-66337-8, Pub. by Busn Bks England); pap. 14.50x. Brookfield Pub Co.

--Secrets of the Tax Revolt. LC 84-3765. 371p. 1984. 16.95 (ISBN 0-15-179998-9). HarBraceJ.

Adams, James R., jt. auth. see National Judicial College (U. S.).

Adams, James T. The Adams Family. 364p. 1979. Repr. of 1930 ed. lib. bdg. 25.00 (ISBN 0-89987-000-7). Darby Bks.

--The Adams Family. LC 73-21487. (Illus.). 364p. 1974. Repr. of 1930 ed. lib. bdg. 20.50x (ISBN 0-8371-6427-3, ADAF). Greenwood.

--Album of American History, 3 vols. rev. ed. LC 74-91746. (gr. 5 up). 1969. Set. 225.00 (ISBN 0-684-16848-0, ScribR). Scribner.

--The American: Making of a New Man. LC 72-6722. (BCL Ser.: No. I). Repr. of 1943 ed. 21.00 (ISBN 0-404-10639-0). AMS Pr.

--Death in the Dark. 1979. Repr. of 1941 ed. lib. bdg. 20.00 (ISBN 0-8495-0144-X). Arden Lib.

--Death in the Dark. LC 76-30618. 1977. Repr. of 1941 ed. lib. bdg. 20.00 (ISBN 0-8414-2884-0). Folcroft.

--The Epic of America. LC 80-19550. (Illus.). ix, 446p. 1980. Repr. of 1941 ed. lib. bdg. 32.50x (ISBN 0-313-22377-7, ADEA). Greenwood.

--Frontiers of American Culture: A Study of Adult Education in a Democracy. LC 72-6721. (BCL Ser.: No. I). Repr. of 1944 ed. 20.00 (ISBN 0-404-10638-2). AMS Pr.

--Henry Adams. 1933. 11.00 (ISBN 0-8274-2480-9). R West.

--Henry Adams. LC 73-131604. (Illus.). 1970. Repr. of 1933 ed. 10.50 (ISBN 0-403-00491-8). Scholarly.

--New England in the Republic, Seventeen Seventy-Six to Eighteen Fifty. (Works of James Truslow Adams). 438p. Date not set. Repr. lib. bdg. 49.00 (ISBN 0-932051-16-2). Am Repr Serv.

--New England in the Republic 1776-1850. LC 70-144854. Repr. of 1926 ed. 39.00 (ISBN 0-403-00821-2). Scholarly.

--Our Business Civilization: Some Aspects of Our American Culture. LC 75-92608. Repr. of 1929 ed. 17.50 (ISBN 0-404-00288-9). AMS Pr.

--Provincial Society, Sixteen Ninety to Seventeen Sixty-Three. LC 84-19128. (Illus.). xvii, 374p. 1984. Repr. of 1927 ed. lib. bdg. 45.00x (ISBN 0-313-24618-1, ADPS). Greenwood.

--Revolutionary New England, Sixteen Ninety One to Seventeen Seventy Six. LC 68-19139. 1968. Repr. of 1923 ed. 27.50 (ISBN 0-8154-0002-0). Cooper Sq.

--Revolutionary New England, 1691-1776. 469p. 1981. Repr. of 1923 ed. lib. bdg. 30.00 (ISBN 0-89760-013-4). Telegraph Bks.

--Tempo of Modern Life. facs. ed. LC 74-121444. (Essay Index Reprint Ser). 1931. 20.00 (ISBN 0-8369-1691-3). Ayer Co Pubs.

Adams, James T., et al, eds. see American Geographical Society of New York.

Adams, Jan S. & Waldman, Marilyn R., eds. Transnational Approaches of the Social Sciences: Readings in International Studies. LC 83-3560. (Illus.). 582p. (Orig.). 1983. lib. bdg. 36.75 (ISBN 0-8191-3161-X); pap. text ed. 22.00 (ISBN 0-8191-3162-8). U Pr of Amer.

Adams, Jane. Democracy & Social Ethics. (Works of Jane Addams Ser.). 281p. Date not set. Repr. of 1902 ed. lib. bdg. 29.00 (ISBN 0-932051-18-9). Am Repr Serv.

--Good Intentions. 320p. 1985. 14.95 (ISBN 0-453-00479-2). NAL.

--How to Sell What You Write. 1984. 10.95 (ISBN 0-399-12982-0, Putnam). Putnam Pub Group.

--How to Sell What You Write. 1985. pap. 6.95 (ISBN 0-399-51199-7, Perigee). Putnam Pub Group.

--Making Good: Conversations with Successful Men. LC 81-38434. 320p. 1981. 13.95 (ISBN 0-688-00674-4). Morrow.

--Tradeoffs. Golbitz, Pat, ed. LC 82-23917. 372p. 1983. 14.95 (ISBN 0-688-01366-X). Morrow.

--Tradeoffs. 372p. 1984. pap. 3.95 (ISBN 0-451-13100-2, Sig). NAL.

Adams, Jane I. Are You Ready for More on Your Dulcymore? 84p. 1982. pap. 8.95 (ISBN 0-941126-04-8). Meadowlark.

Adams, Jane L. An Education Curriculum for the Moderately, Severely & Profoundly Mentally Handicapped Pupil. 96p. 1980. pap. 13.75x spiral bdg. (ISBN 0-398-03264-5). C C Thomas.

Adams, Jay, ed. Journal of Pastoral Practice, Vol. III, No. 1. 1979. pap. 5.00 (ISBN 0-87552-027-8). Presby & Reformed.

--Journal of Pastoral Practice, Vol. III, No. 2. 1979. pap. 5.00 (ISBN 0-87552-028-6). Presby & Reformed.

Adams, Jay E. Back to the Blackboard. 163p. 1982. pap. 5.95 (ISBN 0-87552-075-8). Presby & Reformed.

--Big Umbrella. 273p. 1971. pap. 6.95 (ISBN 0-87552-010-3). Presby & Reformed.

--Capacitado para Orientar. Orig. Title: Competent to Counsel. 328p. (Span.). 1981. pap. 7.95 (ISBN 0-8254-1000-2). Kregel.

--Christ & Your Problems. 1976. pap. 1.25 (ISBN 0-8010-0035-1). Baker Bk.

--Christ & Your Problems. 33p. 1973. pap. 0.75 (ISBN 0-87552-011-1). Presby & Reformed.

--Christian Counselor's Casebook. (Companion Vol. to Christian Counselor's Manual). 1976. pap. 5.95 (ISBN 0-8010-0075-0). Baker Bk.

--Christian Counselor's Casebook. 223p. 1974. pap. 4.95 (ISBN 0-87552-012-X). Presby & Reformed.

--Christian Counselor's Manual. 1974. 10.95 (ISBN 0-8010-0071-8). Baker Bk.

--Christian Counselor's Manual. 490p. 1973. 10.95 (ISBN 0-87552-013-8). Presby & Reformed.

--The Christian Counselor's New Testament. 1977. 24.95 (ISBN 0-8010-0119-6). Baker Bk.

--Christian Counselor's New Testament. 770p. 1980. 24.95 (ISBN 0-87552-014-6). Presby & Reformed.

--Christian Counselor's Wordbook. 1981. pap. 1.95 (ISBN 0-8010-0172-2). Baker Bk.

--Christian Counselor's Wordbook: A Primer of Nouthetic Counseling. 90p. 1981. pap. 1.95 (ISBN 0-87552-069-3). Presby & Reformed.

--Christian Living in the Home. 1974. pap. 2.95 (ISBN 0-8010-0052-1). Baker Bk.

--Christian Living in the Home. 1972. pap. 2.95 (ISBN 0-87552-016-2). Presby & Reformed.

--Communicating with Twentieth Century Man. 41p. 1979. pap. 1.95 (ISBN 0-87552-008-1). Presby & Reformed.

--Competent to Counsel. 1977. pap. 4.95 (ISBN 0-8010-0047-5). Baker Bk.

--Competent to Counsel. 309p. 1970. pap. 4.95 (ISBN 0-87552-017-0). Presby & Reformed.

--Coping with Counseling Crises. 98p. 1976. pap. 2.95 (ISBN 0-87552-018-9). Presby & Reformed.

--Coping with Counseling Crises: First Aid for Christian Counselors. 1976. pap. 2.95 (ISBN 0-8010-0112-9). Baker Bk.

--Counseling & the Five Points of Calvinism. 1981. pap. 0.75 (ISBN 0-87552-072-3). Presby & Reformed.

--Four Weeks with God & Your Neighbor. pap. 2.50 (ISBN 0-8010-0140-4). Baker Bk.

--Four Weeks with God & Your Neighbor. 75p. 1978. pap. 2.50 (ISBN 0-87552-020-0). Presby & Reformed.

--Godliness Through Discipline. 1977. pap. 0.95 (ISBN 0-8010-0057-2). Baker Bk.

--Godliness Through Discipline. 1972. pap. 0.75 (ISBN 0-87552-021-9). Presby & Reformed.

--Grist from Adams' Mill. 96p. 1983. pap. 2.50 (ISBN 0-87552-079-0). Presby & Reformed.

--Helps for Counselors. (Orig.). 1980. pap. 2.50 (ISBN 0-8010-0156-0). Baker Bk.

--How to Handle Trouble. 66p. 1982. pap. 2.45 (ISBN 0-87552-076-6). Presby & Reformed.

--How to Help People Change. 1985. pap. 7.95 (ISBN 0-8010-0200-1). Baker Bk.

--How to Overcome Evil. (Direction Bks). 1978. pap. 1.95 (ISBN 0-8010-0126-9). Baker Bk.

--How to Overcome Evil. 116p. 1978. pap. 2.50 (ISBN 0-87552-022-7). Presby & Reformed.

--Insight & Creativity in Christian Counseling. 144p. 1982. pap. 3.95 (ISBN 0-87552-073-1). Presby & Reformed.

--Journal of Pastoral Practice, Vol. IV, No. II. pap. 5.00 (ISBN 0-8010-0169-2). Baker Bk.

--Journal of Pastoral Practice, Vol. 1, No. 1 - Winter, 1977. 1977. pap. 3.50 (ISBN 0-8010-0116-1). Baker Bk.

--Journal of Pastoral Practice, Vol. V, No. 1. 1981. pap. 5.00 (ISBN 0-87552-035-9). Presby & Reformed.

--Journal of Pastoral Practice, Vol. IV, No. 1. 1979. 5.00 (ISBN 0-87552-031-6). Presby & Reformed.

--Journal of Pastoral Practice, Vol. V, No.1. 1981. pap. 5.00 (ISBN 0-8010-0178-1). Baker Bk.

--Journal of Pastoral Practice, Vol. I, No. 2. 1977. pap. 3.50 (ISBN 0-8010-0125-0). Baker Bk.

--Journal of Pastoral Practice, Vol. V, No. 2. 1981. pap. 5.00 (ISBN 0-87552-036-7). Presby & Reformed.

--Journal of Pastoral Practice, Vol. V, No. 2. 1981. pap. 5.00 (ISBN 0-8010-0183-8). Baker Bk.

--Journal of Pastoral Practice, Vol. IV, No. 3. pap. 5.00 (ISBN 0-8010-0170-6). Baker Bk.

--Journal of Pastoral Practice, Vol. IV, No. 3. 1981. pap. 5.00 (ISBN 0-87552-033-2). Presby & Reformed.

--Journal of Pastoral Practice, Vol. V, No. 3. 3rd ed. 1982. pap. 5.00 (ISBN 0-87552-037-5). Presby & Reformed.

--Journal of Pastoral Practice, Vol. V, No 3. 1982. pap. 5.00 (ISBN 0-8010-0186-2). Baker Bk.

--Journal of Pastoral Practice, Vol. IV, No. 4. pap. 5.00 (ISBN 0-8010-0177-3). Baker Bk.

--Journal of Pastoral Practice, Vol. IV, No. 4. 1981. pap. 5.00 (ISBN 0-87552-034-0). Presby & Reformed.

--Journal of Pastoral Practice, Vol. V, No. 4. 4th ed. 1982. pap. 5.00 (ISBN 0-87552-038-3). Presby & Reformed.

--Language of Counseling. 90p. 1981. pap. 2.45 (ISBN 0-87552-009-X). Presby & Reformed.

--Language of Counseling. 1981. pap. 2.45 (ISBN 0-8010-0181-1). Baker Bk.

--Marriage, Divorce & Remarriage. 120p. 1981. pap. 3.50 (ISBN 0-8010-0168-4). Baker Bk.

--Marriage, Divorce & Remarriage. 115p. 1980. pap. 3.50 (ISBN 0-87552-068-5). Presby & Reformed.

--The Meaning & Mode of Baptism. 63p. 1975. pap. 2.45 (ISBN 0-87552-043-X). Presby & Reformed.

--More Than Redemption. 8.95 (ISBN 0-8010-0159-5). Baker Bk.

--More Than Redemption. 350p. 1979. pap. 8.95 (ISBN 0-87552-039-1). Presby & Reformed.

--Prayers for Troubled Times. (Direction Bks.). pap. 1.50 (ISBN 0-8010-0161-7). Baker Bk.

--Prayers for Troubled Times. 1979. pap. 1.50 (ISBN 0-87552-067-7). Presby & Reformed.

--Preaching to the Heart. 40p. 1983. pap. 1.75 (ISBN 0-87552-080-4). Presby & Reformed.

--Preaching with Purpose. 1983. pap. 5.95 (ISBN 0-87552-078-2). Presby & Reformed.

--Preaching with Purpose: A Comprehensive Textbook on Biblical Preaching. 1983. pap. 5.95 (ISBN 0-8010-0193-5). Baker Bk.

--Ready to Restore. (Orig.). 1981. pap. 3.50 (ISBN 0-8010-0171-4). Baker Bk.

--Ready to Restore. 1981. pap. 3.50 (ISBN 0-87552-070-7). Presby & Reformed.

--Shepherding God's Flock, 1 vol. ed. 1978. pap. 10.95 (ISBN 0-8010-0133-1). Baker Bk.

--Shepherding God's Flock. 1979. pap. 10.95 (ISBN 0-87552-058-8). Presby & Reformed.

--Solving Marriage Problems. 1983. pap. 4.50 (ISBN 0-8010-0197-8). Baker Bk.

--Solving Marriage Problems. 132p. 1983. pap. 4.95 (ISBN 0-87552-081-2). Presby & Reformed.

--Studies in Preach 1: Sermons of Charles Spurgeon. pap. 1.95 (ISBN 0-8010-0102-1). Baker Bk.

--Time Is at Hand. 1970. pap. 3.50 (ISBN 0-87552-060-X). Presby & Reformed.

--Truth Apparent: Essays on Biblical Preaching. 1982. pap. 4.95 (ISBN 0-87552-077-4). Presby & Reformed.

--Update on Christian Counseling, Vol. II. 1981. pap. 2.75 (ISBN 0-87552-071-5). Presby & Reformed.

--Update on Christian Counseling, Vol. 1. pap. 3.50 (ISBN 0-8010-0153-6). Baker Bk.

--Update on Christian Counseling, Vol. 1. 1979. pap. 3.50 (ISBN 0-87552-062-6). Presby & Reformed.

--Update on Christian Counseling, Vol. 2. 1981. pap. 2.75 (ISBN 0-8010-0180-3). Baker Bk.

--Use of Scripture in Counseling. (Direction Bks). 1976. pap. 2.95 (ISBN 0-8010-0099-8). Baker Bk.

--Use of Scripture in Counseling. 1975. pap. 2.95 (ISBN 0-87552-063-4). Presby & Reformed.

--What about Nouthetic Counseling? The Question & Answer Book. 1977. pap. 2.50 (ISBN 0-8010-0114-5). Baker Bk.

--What to Do about Worry. 1976. pap. 1.50 (ISBN 0-8010-0048-3). Baker Bk.

--What to Do on Thursday. 1982. pap. 3.95 (ISBN 0-87552-074-X). Presby & Reformed.

--What to do on Thursday: A Layman's Guide to the Practical Use of the Scriptures. 144p. 1982. pap. 3.95 (ISBN 0-8010-0188-9). Baker Bk.

Adams, Jay E., ed. Journal of Practical Practice, Vol. IV, No. 2. 1980. pap. 5.00 (ISBN 0-87552-032-4). Presby & Reformed.

Adams, Jay E., tr. New Testament in Everyday English. 1979. pap. 5.95 (ISBN 0-8010-0132-3). Baker Bk.

Adams, Jean, et al. Heroines of the Sky. facsimile ed. LC 78-99615. (Essay Index Reprint Ser.). 1942. 27.50 (ISBN 0-8369-1539-9). Ayer Co Pubs.

Adams, Jeff, ed. see Marquis, Don.

Adams, Jennifer A. The Solar Church. Hoffman, Douglas R., ed. LC 82-11281. 288p. (Orig.). 1982. pap. 9.95 (ISBN 0-8298-0482-X). Pilgrim NY.

Adams, Jennifer K. With All My Heart. Wallace, Mary, ed. (Illus.). 104p. 1984. pap. 4.95 (ISBN 0-912315-78-4). Word Aflame.

Adams, Jerome & Yoder, Janice D. Effective Leadership for Women & Men. 176p. 1985. text ed. 29.95 (ISBN 0-89391-168-2). Ablex Pub.

Adams, Jerry L., jt. auth. see Shipman, James T.

Adams, Joan. The People Connection to New Mexico. 3rd ed. 254p. 1985. pap. 7.95 (ISBN 0-9607818-1-1). Escortguide.

Adams, Joan & Whitridge, Jackie. ESCORTGUIDE: The People Connection to New Mexico. 2nd ed. 203p. 1982. pap. 6.95 (ISBN 0-9607818-0-3). Escortguide.

Adams, Joey. Joey Adams Ethnic Humor. 1979. pap. 1.25 (ISBN 0-532-12268-2). Woodhill.

--Joey Adams Joke Diary. 1979. pap. 1.95 (ISBN 0-532-19220-6). Woodhill.

--Live Longer Through Laughter. LC 83-40361. 228p. 1984. 14.95 (ISBN 0-8128-2955-7). Stein & Day.

Adams, John. Cases & Materials on Sale of Goods. 176p. 1982. pap. 15.50 (ISBN 0-7099-0509-2, Pub. by Croom Helm Ltd). Longwood Pub Group.

--Defense of the Constitution of Government of the United States of America, 3 Vols. Repr. of 1797 ed. Set. 185.00x (ISBN 3-511-05000-6). Adlers Foreign Bks.

--Diary & Autobiography of John Adams, 4 Vols. Butterfield, L. H., et al, eds. LC 60-5387. (The Adams Papers, Ser. 1, Diaries). (Illus.). Set. 90.00x (ISBN 0-674-20300-3). Harvard U Pr.

--Drowned Valley: The Piscataqua River Basin. LC 75-40868. (Illus.). 294p. 1976. 29.95 (ISBN 0-87451-123-2). U Pr of New Eng.

--Earliest Diary of John Adams: June 1753-April 1754, September 1758-January 1759. Butterfield, L. H., et al, eds. LC 66-14442. (The Adams Papers, Ser. 1, Diaries). (Illus.). 1966. 10.00x (ISBN 0-674-22000-5). Harvard U Pr.

--Educational Theories. (Educational Ser.). 1927. Repr. 12.50 (ISBN 0-8482-7267-6). Norwood Edns.

--Guerrilla Gardening: Fruits & Vegetables the Way They Used to Taste. LC 83-2033. (Illus.). 224p. 1984. 14.95 (ISBN 0-698-11225-3, Coward). Putnam Pub Group.

--Institutional Economics. 1980. lib. bdg. 18.95 (ISBN 0-89838-022-7). Kluwer Academic.

--International Economics: A Self Teaching Introduction to the Basic Concepts. 2nd ed. LC 78-65206. 1979. pap. text ed. 11.95 (ISBN 0-312-42106-0). St Martin.

--Letter of John Adams, Addressed to His Wife. (Works of John Adams Ser.). 286p. Date not set. Repr. lib. bdg. 59.00 (ISBN 0-932051-15-4). Am Repr Serv.

--Political Writings of John Adams. Peek, George A., Jr., ed. LC 54-4998. 1954. pap. 7.87 scp (ISBN 0-672-60010-2). Bobbs.

--The Political Writings of John Adams: Representative Selections. Peek, George A., ed. LC 54-4998. 1954. 37.50x (ISBN 0-672-50965-2). Irvington.

--Political Writings of John Adams: Representative Selections. Peek, George A., ed. LC 54-4998. 1954. pap. 6.95 (ISBN 0-8290-1767-4). Irvington.

--Remarks on the Country Extending from Cape Palmas to the River Congo. 265p. 1966. Repr. of 1823 ed. 25.00x (ISBN 0-7146-1783-0, BHA 01783, F Cass Co). Biblio Dist.

--Sketches Taken During Ten Voyages to Africa Between the Years 1786 & 1800. (Landmarks in Anthropology Ser). (Illus.). Repr. of 1822 ed. 13.00 (ISBN 0-384-00330-3). Johnson Repr.

--Transport Planning: Vision & Practice. 288p. (Orig.). 1981. pap. 17.50x (ISBN 0-7100-0844-9). Routledge & Kegan.

--The Works of John Adams, 10 vols. LC 78-128978. Repr. of 1856 ed. Set. 325.00 (ISBN 0-404-00310-9); 32.50 ea. AMS Pr.

--Works of John Adams, Second President of the United States, 10 Vols. facs. ed. LC 77-80620. (Select Bibliographies Reprint Ser.). Repr. of 1856 ed. Set. 410.00 (ISBN 0-8369-5020-8). Ayer Co Pubs.

Adams, John & Adams, Abigail. Familiar Letters of John Adams & His Wife Abigail Adams, During the Revolution. facs. ed. LC 79-117865. (Select Bibliographies Reprint Ser). 1875. 22.00 (ISBN 0-8369-5318-5). Ayer Co Pubs.

Adams, John & Igbal, Sabiha. Exports, Politics, & Economic Development: Pakistan, 1970-1982. LC 83-3515. (Replica Edition Ser.). 257p. 1983. softcover 24.00x (ISBN 0-86531-959-6). Westview.

Adams, John, jt. auth. see Adams, Abigail.

Adams, John, ed. A Comparative Atlas of America's Great Cities: Twenty Metropolitan Regions. LC 76-14268. (Illus.). 500p. 1976. 95.00x (ISBN 0-8166-0767-2). U of Minn Pr.

--The Contemporary International Economy: A Reader. 2nd ed. LC 84-51147. 550p. 1985. pap. text ed. 16.95 (ISBN 0-312-16672-9). St Martin.

Adams, John, et al. Warren-Adams Letters, Being Chiefly a Correspondence among John Adams, Samuel Adams, & James Warren, 2 Vols. LC 79-158225. 1917-25. Repr. of 1925 ed. Set. 85.00 (ISBN 0-404-06854-5). Vol. 1 (ISBN 0-404-06855-3). Vol. 2 (ISBN 0-404-06856-1). AMS Pr.

--Managing by Project Management. 168p. 1983. 18.00. Univ Tech.

Adams, John A. A Defense of the Constitutions of Government of the United States of America, 3 Vols. LC 69-11328. (American Constitutional & Legal History Ser). 1971. Repr. of 1788 ed. Set. lib. bdg. 165.00 (ISBN 0-306-71176-1). Da Capo.

Adams, John A. & Lowder, Wayne M., eds. Natural Radiation Environment. LC 64-12256. (Illus.). 1964. 35.00x (ISBN 0-226-00596-8). U of Chicago Pr.

Adams, John A., Jr. We Are the Aggies: The Texas A&M University Association of Former Students. LC 78-21782. (The Centennial Series of the Association of Former Students, Texas A&M University: No. 7). (Illus.). 244p. 1979. 18.50 (ISBN 0-89096-062-3). Tex A&M Univ Pr.

Adams, John C. Globe Playhouse: Its Design & Equipment. 2nd, rev. & enl. ed. (Illus.). 435p. 1966. Repr. of 1961 ed. 26.95x (ISBN 0-06-480014-8, 06304). B&N Imports.

--Outline of Fractures. 8th ed. LC 77-30525. (Illus.). 1984. pap. text ed. 12.00 (ISBN 0-443-02897-4). Churchill.

Adams, John C., ed. Outline of Orthopaedics. 9th ed. LC 80-40931. (Illus.). 486p. 1981. pap. text ed. 19.50 (ISBN 0-686-31316-X). Churchill.

Adams, John C., tr. see Pavlov, Dmitrii V.

Adams, John D. Introduction to TRS-80 Data Files. 102p. (Orig.). 1984. spiral binding 24.95 (ISBN 0-88006-066-2, CC7398). Green Pub Inc.

--Transforming Work. (Orig.). 1984. pap. text ed. 16.50 (ISBN 0-917917-00-6). Miles River.

--Understanding & Managing Stress: A Facilitator's Guide. LC 80-50474. 37p. 1980. pap. 49.50 pkg. with readings & workbook (ISBN 0-88390-157-9). Univ Assocs.

--Understanding & Managing Stress: A Workbook in Changing Life Styles. LC 80-50474. 101p. 1980. pap. 11.00 (ISBN 0-88390-157-9). Univ Assocs.

Adams, John D., ed. Understanding & Managing Stress: A Book of Readings. LC 80-50474. 217p. 1980. pap. 17.50 (ISBN 0-88390-158-7). Univ Assocs.

Adams, John F. Algebraic Topology: A Student's Guide. LC 75-163178. (London Mathematical Lecture Note Ser.: No. 4). (Illus.). 1972. 29.95 (ISBN 0-521-08076-2). Cambridge U Pr.

--Beekeeping. 1980. pap. 2.25 (ISBN 0-380-01043-7, 48124-3). Avon.

Adams, John G. Without Precedent. (Illus.). 1983. 17.50 (ISBN 0-393-01616-1). Norton.

--Without Precedent: The Story of the Death of McCarthyism. (Illus.). 1985. pap. 6.95 (ISBN 0-393-30230-X). Norton.

Adams, John H. The Black Pulpit Revolution in the United Methodist Church & Other Denominations. 100p. (Orig.). 1985. pap. 8.50x (ISBN 0-913491-05-5). Strug Comm Pr.

Adams, John L. Musicians' Autobiographies: An Annotated Bibliography of Writings Available in English 1800 to 1980. LC 82-17108. 126p. 1982. lib. bdg. 24.95x (ISBN 0-89950-049-8). McFarland & Co.

Adams, John M. Multiple Sclerosis--Scars of Childhood: New Horizons & Hope. 96p. 1977. 15.75x (ISBN 0-398-03595-4). C C Thomas.

Adams, John P. & Marschall, Richard. Milton Caniff, Rembrandt of the Comic Strip. rev. ed. LC 80-70395. (Illus.). 64p. 1981. pap. 6.95x (ISBN 0-918348-04-8). NBM.

Adams, John Q. Argument of John Quincy Adams Before the Supreme Court of the United States in the Case of the United States vs. Cinque & Others: Africans Captured in the Schonner Amistad. LC 71-82164. (Anti-Slavery Crusade in America Ser). 1969. Repr. of 1841 ed. 11.50 (ISBN 0-405-00601-2). Ayer Co Pubs.

--Argument of John Quincy Adams, Before the Supreme Court of the United States. LC 69-18972. Repr. of 1841 ed. 15.00x (ISBN 0-8371-4887-1, ADA&, Pub. by Negro U Pr). Greenwood.

--Diary of John Quincy Adams: 1794-1845. Nevins, Allan, ed. LC 68-8892. (American Classics Ser). 1969. Repr. of 1928 ed. 30.00 (ISBN 0-8044-1010-0). Ungar.

--John Adams, 2 vols. LC 80-24028. (American Statesmen Ser.). 920p. 1981. Set. pap. 13.95 (ISBN 0-87754-177-9). Chelsea Hse.

--Jubilee of the Constitution. LC 72-2657. (Select Bibliographies Reprint Ser). 1972. Repr. of 1839 ed. 12.00 (ISBN 0-8369-6844-1). Ayer Co Pubs.

--Memoirs of John Quincy Adams, 12 Vols. Adams, Charles F., ed. LC 71-134915. Repr. of 1887 ed. Set. lib. bdg. 420.00 (ISBN 0-404-00330-3); 35.00 ea. AMS Pr.

--Memoirs of John Quincy Adams, Comprising Portions of His Diary from 1795 to 1848, 12 Vols. facs. ed. Adams, Charles F., ed. LC 71-85454. (Select Bibliographies Reprint Ser). Set. 470.00 (ISBN 0-8369-5021-6). Ayer Co Pubs.

--Oberon: A Poetical Romance in Twelve Books. Faust, A. B., ed. 1983. Repr. of 1940 ed. lib. bdg. 75.00 (ISBN 0-89760-068-1). Telegraph Bks.

--Report of the Secretary of State Upon Weights & Measures: Prepared in Obedience to a Resolution of the House of Representatives of the Fourteenth of December, 1819. Cohen, I. Bernard, ed. LC 79-7945. (Three Centuries of Science in America Ser.). 1980. Repr. of 1821 ed. lib. bdg. 23.00x (ISBN 0-405-12526-7). Ayer Co Pubs.

--Speech of John Quincy Adams of Massachusetts, Upon the Right of the People, Men & Women, to Petition. LC 78-82163. (Anti-Slavery Crusade in America Ser). 1969. Repr. of 1838 ed. 11.50 (ISBN 0-405-00602-0). Ayer Co Pubs.

--Writings of John Quincy Adams, 7 Vols. Ford, Worthington C., ed. LC 68-30993. (Illus.). 1968. Repr. of 1917 ed. Set. lib. bdg. 180.00x (ISBN 0-8371-0280-4, ADWR). Greenwood.

Adams, John Q. & U. S. 26th Congress, 1st Session. Africans Taken in the Amistad. Bd. with Argument Before the Supreme Court of the United States, in the Case of the U. S. Apellants, Vs. Cinque, & Other Africans, Captured in the Schooner Amistad. Repr. of 1841 ed. 16.00 (ISBN 0-384-63130-4). Johnson Repr.

Adams, John Q., jt. auth. see Adams, C. F.

Adams, John Q., tr. see Gentz, Friedrich.

Adams, John Q., tr. see Gentz, Friedrich Von & Possony, Stefan T.

Adams, John Q., tr. see Wieland, Christopher M.

Adams, John Quincy. Report to Congress on Weights & Measures. LC 79-53271. Repr. of 1821 ed. 12.50x (ISBN 0-87081-084-7). Colo Assoc.

Adams, John R. Books & Authors of San Diego. 1966. pap. 7.50x (ISBN 0-916304-01-9). SDSU Press.

--Edward Everett Hale. (United States Authors Ser.). 1977. lib. bdg. 12.50 (ISBN 0-8057-7186-7, Twayne). G K Hall.

--Harriet Beecher Stowe. (Twayne's United States Authors Ser). 1963. pap. 5.95x (ISBN 0-8084-0150-5, T42, Twayne). New Coll U Pr.

Adams, John R., ed. see Stowe, Harriet Beecher.

Adams, John S., ed. see Marshall, John.

Adams, John W. Be Rich. 1985. pap. 1.50 (ISBN 0-9602166-1-8). Golden Key.

--Be What You Are: Love. 96p. 1983. pap. 4.95 (ISBN 0-9602166-0-X). Golden Key.

--How I Can Have Everything. (Illus.). 1978. pap. 2.00 (ISBN 0-685-93857-3). Golden Key.

--Positively Alive. 120p. 1985. pap. 4.95 (ISBN 0-9602166-3-4). Golden Key.

Adams, John W., ed. Monographs on the United States Large Cent of 1793 & 1794. LC 75-28712. (Illus.). 240p. 1977. 35.00x (ISBN 0-88000-071-6). Quarterman.

Adams, John W., tr. see Lungwitz, Anton.

Adams, Joseph. A Treatise on the Supposed Hereditary Properties of Diseases...(London, 1814) Rosenberg, Charles, ed. LC 83-48528. (The History of Hereditarian Thought Ser.). 125p. 1985. Repr. of 1814 ed. lib. bdg. 22.00 (ISBN 0-8240-5800-3). Garland Pub.

--Yeats & the Masks of Syntax: A Study in Connections. 190p. 1984. 20.00x (ISBN 0-231-04818-1). Columbia U Pr.

Adams, Joseph Q. Conventual Buildings of Blackfriars, London, & the Playhouses Constructed Therein. LC 76-113537. Repr. of 1917 ed. 11.50 (ISBN 0-404-00289-7). AMS Pr.

--Shakespearean Playhouses: A History of English Theatres from the Beginning to the Reformation. (Illus.). 1959. 18.00 (ISBN 0-8446-1009-7). Peter Smith.

Adams, Joseph Q., ed. Chief Pre-Shakespearen Dramas. LC 78-52734. (BCL Ser.: No. I & II). Repr. of 1924 ed. 62.50 (ISBN 0-404-18054-X). AMS Pr.

Adams, Joseph Q., jt. ed. see Bradley, Jesse F.

Adams, Joseph Q., ed. see Herbert, Henry.

Adams, Judith. Against the Gates of Hell. 152p. pap. 2.50 (ISBN 0-87509-232-2). Chr Pubns.

Adams, Judith A. Guide to Cheyenne, Magic City of the Plains. (Illus.). 46p. (Orig.). 1981. pap. 2.50 (ISBN 0-9606722-0-6). J A Ent.

--Working Mother's Survival Manual. (Illus.). 50p. (Orig.). 1982. pap. 3.00 (ISBN 0-9606722-1-4). J A Ent.

Adams, Judith-Anne & Dwyer, Margaret A. English for Academic Uses: A Writing Workbook. (Illus.). 208p. 1982. pap. text ed. 12.95 (ISBN 0-13-279653-8). P-H.

Adams, Julian. Freedom & Ethics in the Press. (Student Journalism Ser.). 182p. 1983. lib. bdg. 12.50 (ISBN 0-8239-0562-4). Rosen Group.

--The Student Journalist & Mass Communication. (Illus.). 190p. 1981. lib. bdg. 8.95 (ISBN 0-8239-0499-7); workbook 1.50 (ISBN 0-8239-0538-1). Rosen Group.

Adams, Julian & Stratton, Kenneth. Press Time. 3rd ed. 1975. text ed. 19.36 (ISBN 0-13-699041-X). P-H.

Adams, Kasey. Reach for the Sky: Brenden's Story. (Rapture Romance Ser.: No. 104). 1985. pap. 2.25 (ISBN 0-451-13019-7, Sig). NAL.

--Untamed Desire. (Rapture Romance Ser.: No. 35). 192p. 1983. pap. 1.95 (ISBN 0-451-12554-1, Sig). NAL.

--Winter's Promise. (Rapture Romance Ser.: No. 57). 1984. pap. 1.95 (ISBN 0-451-12809-5, Sig). NAL.

Adams, Katherine, intro. by see Baird, Wellesley.

Adams, Kathleen & MacNeilage, Linda. Assertiveness at Work: How to Increase Your Personal Power on the Job. (Illus.). 266p. 1982. 15.95 (ISBN 0-13-049502-6); pap. 7.95 (ISBN 0-13-049494-1). P-H.

Adams, Kathleen & Tiffany, Sharon. The Wild Woman: Amazon, Virgin & Matriarch in Anthropological Perspective. 152p. 1985. 15.95 (ISBN 0-87073-213-7); pap. 9.95 (ISBN 0-87073-243-9). Schenkman Bks Inc.

Adams, Kathleen J., jt. ed. see Hareven, Tamara K.

Adams, Kay A., jt. auth. see Crowe, Michael R.

Adams, Kay Angana & Walker, Jerry. Improving the Accountability of Career Education Programs: Evaluation Guidelines & Checklists. 103p. 1979. 6.75 (ISBN 0-318-15488-9, RD 168). Natl Ctr Res Voc Ed.

Adams, Kelly. Bittersweet Revenge. (Second Chance at Love Ser.: No. 47). (Orig.). 1982. pap. 1.75 (ISBN 0-515-06423-8). Jove Pubns.

--Restless Tides, No. 113. 192p. 1983. pap. 1.95 (ISBN 0-515-07201-X). Jove Pubns.

--Sunlight & Silver. (Second Chance at Love Ser.: No. 292). 192p. 1985. pap. 2.25 (ISBN 0-425-08514-7). Berkley Pub.

--Wildcatter's Kiss. (Second Chance at Love Ser.: No. 221). 192p. 1984. pap. 1.95 (ISBN 0-515-08116-7). Jove Pubns.

--Wildfire. (Second Chance At Love Ser.). 192p. 1985. pap. 1.95 (ISBN 0-425-08153-2). Berkley Pub.

Adams, Kenneth. Foolishness of God. 1981. pap. 5.95 (ISBN 0-87508-036-7). Chr Lit.

Adams, Kenneth, jt. ed. see Wesson, Donald R.

Adams, Kenneth M., jt. ed. see Grant, Igor.

Adams, Kramer. Covered Bridges of the West. LC 63-19906. (Illus.). 1963. 14.95 (ISBN 0-8310-7037-4). Howell-North.

Adams, L. Mink Raising. (Illus.). 188p. 1979. pap. 3.50 (ISBN 0-936622-15-6). A R Harding Pub.

Adams, L. & Llanas, A. Starting Reading: Materials for Elementary Reading Comprehension. (Materials for Language Practice Ser.). (Illus.). 96p. 1983. pap. 3.95 (ISBN 0-08-029435-9). Pergamon.

Adams, Lane. How Come Its Taking Me So Long? (Living Studies). 156p. 1985. pap. 5.95 (ISBN 0-8423-1491-1); leader's guide 2.95 (ISBN 0-8423-1492-X). Tyndale.

Adams, Lark E. & Lumpkin, Rosa S., eds. Journals of the South Carolina House of Representatives, 1785-1786. LC 79-18504. (State Records Ser.). 1979. lib. bdg. 34.95x (ISBN 0-87249-941-3). U of SC Pr.

Adams, Larry L. Walter Lippmann. (World Leaders Ser.). 1977. lib. bdg. 13.50 (ISBN 0-8057-7709-1, Twayne). G K Hall.

Adams, Laura. Existential Battles: The Growth of Norman Mailer. LC 74-27710. viii, 192p. 1976. 16.95x (ISBN 0-8214-0182-3, 82-81818); pap. 7.95x (ISBN 0-8214-0401-6, 82-81826). Ohio U Pr.

--Norman Mailer: A Comprehensive Bibliography. LC 74-14163. (Author Bibliographies Ser.: No. 20). 151p. 1974. 16.50 (ISBN 0-8108-0771-8). Scarecrow.

Adams, Laura, ed. Will the Real Norman Mailer Please Stand up. LC 73-83259. 288p. 1974. 21.50x (ISBN 0-8046-9066-9, Pub. by Kennikat). Assoc Faculty Pr.

Adams, Lauren. Medieval Pottery from Broadgate East Lincoln, 1973. (Lincoln Archaeological Trust Monography Ser.: Vol. XVII-I). 54p. 1977. pap. text ed. 12.00x (ISBN 0-686-74109-9, Pub. by Coun Brit Archaeological). Humanities.

Adams, Laurie & Coudert, Allison. Alice & the Boa Constrictor. LC 82-15769. (Illus.). 96p. (gr. 3-6). 1983. 9.95 (ISBN 0-395-33068-8). HM.

Adams, Lee M. The Table Rock Basin in Barry County, Missouri. Chapman, Carl H., ed. (Memoir Ser.: No. 1). (Illus.). 63p. (Orig.). 1950. pap. 1.00 (ISBN 0-943414-17-2). MO Arch Soc.

Adams, Leigh & Madara, Lynda. Great Expectations. 1980. pap. 7.95 (ISBN 0-395-29460-6). HM.

Adams, Lela C. Abstracts of Deed Books Five & Six: Henry County, Virginia, Oct. 1792-Dec. 1805. 232p. 1984. pap. 21.00 (ISBN 0-89308-360-7, VA 45). Southern Hist Pr.

--Abstracts of Deed Books One & Two: Henry County, Virginia, Feb. 1776-July 1784. 188p. 1983. pap. 18.50 (ISBN 0-89308-358-5, VA 43). Southern Hist Pr.

--Abstracts of Wills, Inventories & Accounts, Patrick County, Virginia, 1791-1823. 110p. 1972. pap. 15.00 (ISBN 0-89308-356-9, VA 42). Southern Hist Pr.

--Marriages of Patrick County, Virginia, 1791-1850. 165p. 1972. pap. 17.50 (ISBN 0-89308-357-7, VA 46). Southern Hist Pr.

Adams, Leon D. Leon D Adams' Commonsense Book of Wine. LC 75-6805. 240p. 1975. pap. 7.95 (ISBN 0-395-20540-9). HM.

--The Wines of America. 3rd, rev. ed. 640p. 1984. 22.95 (ISBN 0-07-000319-X). McGraw.

Adams, Leonard P. Public Attitudes Toward Unemployment Insurance: A Historical Account with Special Reference to Alleged Abuses. 98p. 1971. pap. 3.95 (ISBN 0-911558-31-4). W E Upjohn.

--Public Employment Service in Transition, 1933-1968: Evolution of a Placement Service into a Manpower Agency. LC 68-66941. (Cornell Studies in Industrial & Labor Relations: No. 16). 264p. 1969. pap. 3.50 (ISBN 0-87546-037-2); pap. 7.50 special hard bdg. (ISBN 0-87546-274-X). ILR Pr.

Adams, Leonard P. & Aronson, Robert L. Workers & Industrial Change. LC 73-22502. (Cornell Studies in Industrial & Labour Relations, Vol. 8). (Illus.). 209p. 1974. Repr. of 1957 ed. lib. bdg. 15.00 (ISBN 0-8371-6373-0, ADIC). Greenwood.

Adams, Lewis M. Live at the Church. 7.00 (ISBN 0-686-20820-X); pap. 3.50 (ISBN 0-686-20821-8). Kulchur Foun.

Adams, Louis J. Theory, Law, & Policy of Contemporary Japanese Treaties. LC 73-11245. 288p. 1974. lib. bdg. 21.00 (ISBN 0-379-00021-0). Oceana.

Adams, Louise M., jt. auth. see Adams, Rick.

Adams, Loyce. Managerial Psychology. 1965. 12.50 (ISBN 0-8158-0034-7). Chris Mass.

Adams, M. J. An Introduction to Optical Waveguides. LC 80-42059. 401p. 1981. cloth 63.95x (ISBN 0-471-27969-2, Pub. by Wiley Interscience). Wiley.

Adams, M. L., Jr., ed. Rotor Dynamical Instability. (AMD Ser.: Vol. 55). 100p. 1983. pap. text ed. 24.00 (ISBN 0-317-02645-3, G00227). ASME.

Adams, Margaret. Bailliere's Midwives Dictionary. 7th ed. (Illus.). 368p. 1983. pap. 6.75 (ISBN 0-7216-0815-9, Pub. by Bailliere-Tindall). Saunders.

--Warm & Tasty: A Wood Heat Stove Cookbook. LC 81-11338. 227p. (Orig.). 1981. pap. 6.95 (ISBN 0-914718-62-2). Pacific Search.

Adams, Margaret B. American Wood Heat Cookery. 2nd rev. ed. 252p. (Orig.). 1984. pap. 7.95 (ISBN 0-914718-91-6). Pacific Search.

Adams, Marilyn M., tr. see William Of Ockham.

Adams, Mark. How to Tell if It's Art. (Shortcuts to Ignorance Ser.). 98p. 1980. pap. 5.95 (ISBN 0-915433-07-9). Packrat WA.

--How to Write So People Will Know What You're Trying to Say. (Shortcuts to Ignorance Ser.). 16p. 1980. pap. 1.00 (ISBN 0-915433-05-2). Packrat WA.

Adams, Mark, jt. auth. see Rapoport, Bernard.

Adams, Mark, et al. How to Read the Wall Street Journal. (Shortcuts to Ignorance Ser.). 14p. 1980. pap. 1.00 (ISBN 0-915433-06-0). Packrat WA.

Adams, Marsha T., jt. auth. see Fry, Louis.

Adams, Martin. Identification & Early Detection of Stuttering. (Illus.). 200p. cancelled (ISBN 0-933014-70-8). College-Hill.

Adams, Martin R. Studies in the Literary Backgrounds of English Radicalism, with Special Reference to the French Revolution. LC 68-28591. (Illus.). 1968. Repr. of 1947 ed. lib. bdg. 24.75x (ISBN 0-8371-0000-3, ADSL). Greenwood.

Adams, Mary. Natural Flower Arranging. (Illus.). 120p. 1981. 18.95 (ISBN 0-7134-2677-2, Pub. by Batsford England). David & Charles.

Adams, Mary, ed. Modern State. LC 68-26225. 1969. Repr. of 1933 ed. 22.00x (ISBN 0-8046-0003-1, Pub. by Kennikat). Assoc Faculty Pr.

--Science in the Changing World. facs. ed. LC 68-29188. (Essay Index Reprint Ser). 1968. Repr. of 1933 ed. 18.00 (ISBN 0-8369-0136-3). Ayer Co Pubs.

--Science in the Changing World: (Julian Huxley, Bertrand Russell & J. B. S. Haldane) 1979. Repr. of 1933 ed. lib. bdg. 25.00 (ISBN 0-8495-0204-7). Arden Lib.

Adams, Mary, ed. see Ferrari, Guy.

Adams, Mary, tr. see Steiner, Rudolf.

Adams, Marylou. Brighten up at Breakfast: Helpful Tips for Heavenly Bodies. LC 81-51601. (Illus.). 120p. (gr. 2-7). 1981. plastic comb 7.95 (ISBN 0-9606248-0-5). Starbright.

Adams, Michael. Blind Man's Bluff. 1985. pap. 3.50 (ISBN 0-345-32205-3). Ballantine.

--Censorship: The Irish Experience. 266p. 1968. 15.00x (ISBN 0-7165-0018-3, BBA 03075, Pub. by Irish Academic Pr). Biblio Dist.

--The Untravelled World: A Memoir. 288p. (Orig.). 1984. 19.95 (ISBN 0-7043-2449-0, Pub. by Quartet Bks). Merrimack Pub Cir.

--The Writer's Mind: Making Writing Make Sense. 1984. pap. text ed. 13.00 (ISBN 0-673-15810-1). Scott F.

Adams, Michael & Mayhew, Christopher. Publish It Not: The Middle East Cover-Up. LC 76-363688. pap. 51.00 (ISBN 0-317-11305-4, 2016300). Bks Demand UMI.

Adams, Michael, tr. see Huber, Georges.

Adams, Michael, tr. see Illanes, Jose L.

Adams, Michael, tr. see Orlandis, Jose.

Adams, Michael C. Our Masters the Rebels: A Speculation on Union Military Failure in the East, 1861-1865. LC 78-17107. 1978. 16.50x (ISBN 0-674-64643-6). Harvard U Pr.

Adams, Mignon S. & Morris, Jacquelyn M. Teaching Library Skills for Academic Credit. LC 83-43238. 224p. 1985. lib. bdg. 29.50 (ISBN 0-89774-138-2). Oryx Pr.

Adams, Mildred. Garcia Lorca: Playwright & Poet. LC 77-77561. 1977. 8.95 (ISBN 0-8076-0873-4). Braziller.

Adams, Mildred, tr. see Arciniegas, German.

Adams, Mildred, tr. see Ortega Y Gasset, Jose.

Adams, Monni. Designs for Living: Symbolic Communication in African Art. (Illus.). 150p. 1982. pap. text ed. 12.00x (ISBN 0-674-19969-3). Carpenter Ctr.

Adams, Morely. In the Footsteps of Borrow & Fitzgerald. 1973. 30.00 (ISBN 0-8274-0821-8). R West.

Adams, Morley. Mudland. (Orig.). 1980. pap. 1.75 (ISBN 0-532-23146-5). Woodhill.

--Omar's Interpreter. 1978. Repr. of 1911 ed. lib. bdg. 25.00 (ISBN 0-8495-0023-0). Arden Lib.

--Omar's Interpreter: A New Life of Edward Fitzgerald. Repr. of 1911 ed. lib. bdg. 25.00 (ISBN 0-8414-2899-9). Folcroft.

Adams, N. Douglas. PC Wizardry on Wall Street: How to Use Your IBM & Compatibles to Invest in the Stock Market. 224p. 1985. 21.95 (ISBN 0-13-655010-X); pap. 14.95 (ISBN 0-13-655002-9). P-H.

Adams, Neal. Well Control Problems & Solutions. 683p. 1980. 69.95x (ISBN 0-87814-124-3). Pennwell Bks.

--Workover Well Control. 308p. 1981. 53.95x (ISBN 0-87814-142-1). Pennwell Bks.

Adams, Neal J. Drilling Engineering: A Complete Well Planning Approach. LC 84-1110. 1985. 84.95 (ISBN 0-87814-265-7). Pennwell Bks.

Adams, Nehemiah. Sable Cloud: A Southern Tale with Northern Comments. facs. ed. LC 78-138329. (Black Heritage Library Collection Ser). 1861. 16.25 (ISBN 0-8369-8721-7). Ayer Co Pubs.

--South-Side View of Slavery. facs. ed. LC 74-83939. (Black Heritage Library Collection Ser). 1854. 12.75 (ISBN 0-8369-8501-X). Ayer Co Pubs.

--South-Side View of Slavery. LC 71-80466. 1969. Repr. of 1855 ed. 21.00x (ISBN 0-8046-0529-7, Pub. by Kennikat). Assoc FAculty PR.

--South-Side View of Slavery: Or Three Months at the South, 1854. LC 69-16593. Repr. of 1854 ed. 17.50x (ISBN 0-8371-3563-X, ADS&). Greenwood.

Adams, Nelson B., ed. see Northup, George T.

Adams, Neville, tr. see Dreissig, Georg.

Adams, Nicholson B. The Romantic Dramas Garcia Gutierrez. 149p. 1.00 (ISBN 0-318-14303-8). Hispanic Inst.

--The Romantic Dramas of Garcia Gutierrez. 1976. lib. bdg. 59.95 (ISBN 0-8490-2542-7). Gordon Pr.

Adams, Nicholson B., jt. auth. see Adams, Agatha B.

Adams, Nicholson B. & Keller, John, eds. Espana en Su Literatura. rev. ed. (Illus.). 1972. text ed. 11.95x (ISBN 0-393-09452-9). Norton.

Adams, Nicholson B., et al. Spanish Literature: A Brief Survey. 3rd ed. (Quality Paperback Ser.: No. 38). 210p. (Orig.). 1974. pap. 3.95 (ISBN 0-8226-0038-2). Littlefield.

Adams, Nicholson B., et al, eds. Hispanoamerica En Su Literatura. 1965. 9.95x (ISBN 0-393-09660-2, NortonC). Norton.

Adams, Nigel. The Holden Mine. (From Discovery to Production, 1896-1938). 87p. 1981. pap. 5.00 (ISBN 0-917048-53-9). Wash St Hist Soc.

Adams, Noland. The Complete Corvette Restoration & Technical Guide 1953 Through 1962, Vol. I. LC 80-65894. (Illus.). 424p. 1980. 64.95 (ISBN 0-915038-14-5); leather edition 87.50 (ISBN 0-915038-22-6). Auto Quarterly.

Adams, Norman & Singer, Joe. Drawing Animals. (Illus.). 1979. 19.95 (ISBN 0-8230-1361-8). Watson-Guptill.

Adams, Norman R., tr. see Raming, Ida.

Adams, O. Eugene, Jr., jt. auth. see Black, Paul H.

Adams, O. R. Lameness in Horses. 3rd ed. LC 73-16030. (Illus.). 566p. 1974. text ed. 22.50 (ISBN 0-8121-0474-9). Lea & Febiger.

Adams, Oscar F. A Brief Handbook of American Authors. LC 77-21126. 1977. Repr. of 1884 ed. lib. bdg. 15.00 (ISBN 0-89341-450-6). Longwood Pub Group.

--A Brief Handbook of American Authors. 15.00 (ISBN 0-8274-1976-7). R West.

--Dictionary of American Authors. 5th ed. LC 68-2175. 1969. Repr. of 1904 ed. 42.00x (ISBN 0-8103-3148-9). Gale.

--A Dictionary of American Authors. 75.00 (ISBN 0-8490-0031-9). Gordon Pr.

--A Dictionary of American Authors. LC 77-15009. 1977. Repr. of 1897 ed. lib. bdg. 25.00 (ISBN 0-89341-456-5). Longwood Pub Group.

--Some Famous American Schools. (Educational Ser.). 1903. Repr. 20.00 (ISBN 0-8482-3260-7). Norwood Edns.

--The Story of Jane Austen's Life. 277p. 1980. Repr. of 1891 ed. lib. bdg. 35.00 (ISBN 0-8495-0060-5). Arden Lib.

--The Story of Jane Austen's Life. LC 74-14568. 1974. Repr. of 1891 ed. lib. bdg. 25.00 (ISBN 0-8414-2861-1). Folcroft.

Adams, Oscar S., jt. auth. see Deetz, Charles H.

Adams, P., illus. The Child's Play Museum. (Illus.). 1977. 5.50 (ISBN 0-85953-094-9, Pub. by Childs's Play England). Playspaces.

Adams, P. H. & Entwistle, P. F. An Annotated Bibliography of Gilpinia Hercyniae (Hartig) European Spruce. 1981. 30.00x (ISBN 0-85074-051-7, Pub. by For Lib Comm England). State Mutual Bk.

Adams, Pam. The Fairground. (Panorama Ser.). (Illus.). 32p. (ps). 1984. 8.00 (ISBN 0-85953-194-5, Child's Play England). Playspaces.

--Mrs. Honey's Hat. (Illus.). 24p. 1980. 5.50 (ISBN 0-85953-099-X, Pub. by Child's Play England). Playspaces.

--The Ocean. (Panoramas Ser.). 32p. (ps). 1984. 8.00 (ISBN 0-85953-193-7, Child's Play England). Playspaces.

Adams, Pam, illus. Angels. (Pre-Reading Ser.). (Illus.). 24p. (Orig.). 1974. 4.50 (ISBN 0-85953-034-5, Pub. by Child's Play England). Playspaces.

--The Best Things. (Pre-Reading Ser.). 24p. 1974. 4.50 (ISBN 0-85953-031-0, Pub. by Child's England). Playspaces.

--Day Dreams. (Imagination Ser.). (Illus.). 32p. (Orig.). 1978. 5.50 (ISBN 0-85953-105-8, Pub. by Child's Play England); pap. 4.00 (ISBN 0-85953-082-5). Playspaces.

--The Gingerbread Man. (Illus.). 24p. 1981. 5.50 (ISBN 0-85953-107-4, Pub. by Child's Play England). Playspaces.

--The House That Jack Built. (Books with Holes Ser.). (Illus.). 16p. 1978. 8.00 (ISBN 0-85953-076-0, Pub. by Child's Play England). Playspaces.

--How Many? (Motivation Ser.). (Illus.). 16p. (Orig.). 1975. pap. 2.00 (ISBN 0-85953-045-0, Pub. by Child's Play England). Playspaces.

--I-Spy ABC. (Books with Holes Ser.). (Illus.). 16p. 1978. 8.00 (ISBN 0-85953-066-3, Pub. by Child's Play England). Playspaces.

--If I Weren't Me. (Illus.). 24p. 1981. 5.50 (ISBN 0-85953-108-2, Pub. by Child's Play England). Playspaces.

--Letters & Words. (Motivation Ser.). (Illus.). 16p. (Orig.). 1975. pap. 2.00 (ISBN 0-85953-046-9, Pub. by Child's Play England). Playspaces.

--Magic. (Imagination Ser.). (Illus.). 32p. (Orig.). 1978. 5.50 (ISBN 0-85953-104-X, Pub. by Child's Play England); pap. 4.00 (ISBN 0-85953-081-7). Playspaces.

--Oh, Soldier! Soldier! (Books with Holes Ser.). (Illus.). 16p. 1978. 8.00 (ISBN 0-85953-093-0, Pub. by Child's Play England). Playspaces.

--Old MacDonald. (Books with Holes Ser.). (Illus.). 16p. 1978. 8.00 (ISBN 0-85953-054-X, Pub. by Child's Play England). Playspaces.

--Old Macdonald Had a Farm. (Books with Holes Ser.). (Illus., Orig.). 1975. pap. 5.00 (ISBN 0-85953-053-1, Pub. by Child's Play England). Playspaces.

--Same & Different. (Motivation Ser.). (Illus.). 16p. (Orig.). 1975. pap. 2.00 (ISBN 0-85953-043-4, Pub. by Child's Play England). Playspaces.

--Shopping Day. (Pre-Reading Ser.). (Illus.). 24p. 1974. 4.50 (ISBN 0-85953-033-7, Pub. by Child's Play England). Playspaces.

--There Was an Old Lady. (Books with Holes). (Illus.). 16p. 1975. 8.00 (ISBN 0-85953-021-3, Pub. by Child's Play England). Playspaces.

--There Was an Old Lady Who Swallowed a Fly. (Books with Holes Ser.). (Illus.). 16p. 1973. pap. 5.00 (ISBN 0-85953-018-3, Pub. by Child's Play England). Playspaces.

--There Were Ten in the Bed. (Illus.). 24p. 1979. 5.50 (ISBN 0-85953-095-7, Pub. by Childs's Play England). Playspaces.

--This Is the House That Jack Built. (Books with Holes Ser.). 16p. (Orig.). 1977. pap. 5.00 (ISBN 0-85953-075-2, Pub. by Child's Play England). Playspaces.

--This Old Man. (Books with Holes Ser.). (Illus.). 16p. (Orig.). pap. 5.00 (ISBN 0-85953-026-4, Pub. by Childs Play England). Playspaces.

--This Old Man. (Books with Holes). (Illus.). 16p. 8.00 (ISBN 0-85953-027-2, Pub. by Child's Play England). Playspaces.

--What Is It? (Motivation Ser.). (Illus., Orig.). 1975. pap. 2.00 (ISBN 0-85953-044-2, Pub. by Child's Play England). Playspaces.

--The Zoo. (Pre-Reading Ser.). (Illus.). 24p. 1974. 4.50 (ISBN 0-85953-032-9, Pub. by Child's Play England). Playspaces.

Adams, Pam & Jones, Ceri, illus. A Book of Ghosts. (Imagination Ser.). (Illus.). 32p. (Orig.). 1974. 5.50 (ISBN 0-85953-073-6, Pub. by Child's Play England); pap. 4.00 (ISBN 0-85953-028-0). Playspaces.

Adams, Patricia & Johnson, Vicki. Wild Animal Care & Rehabilitation Manual. 2nd ed. (Illus.). 136p. 1984. pap. 9.50 (ISBN 0-939294-14-1, SF-997-A4B). Beech Leaf.

Adams, Patsy. Ceramica Culina. (Comunidades y Culturas Peruanas: No. 7). 22p. 1976. pap. 1.65x (ISBN 0-88312-742-3); microfiche 1.93 (ISBN 0-88312-339-8). Summer Inst Ling.

--La Musica Culina y la Educacion Informal. (Comunidades y Culturas Peruanas: No. 10). 5p. 1976. pap. 1.00x (ISBN 0-88312-789-X); microfiche 1.93 (ISBN 0-88312-331-2). Summer Inst Ling.

Adams, Paul. The Complete Legal Guide for Your Small Business. LC 81-11445. (Wiley Series Small Business Management). 218p. 1982. 23.50 (ISBN 0-471-09436-6, Pub by Ronald Pr). Wiley.

--Health of the State. Gilbert, Neil & Specht, Harry, eds. LC 81-22647. (Studies in Social Welfare). 208p. 1982. 29.95 (ISBN 0-03-058628-3). Praeger.

--New Self-Hypnosis. pap. 5.00 (ISBN 0-87980-233-2). Wilshire.

Adams, Paul L. A Primer of Child Psychology. 2nd ed. 1982. 15.95 (ISBN 0-316-03726-5). Little.

Adams, Paul L., et al. Fatherless Children. LC 83-21894. (Child Mental Health Ser.: 1561). 407p. 1984. cloth 33.95x (ISBN 0-471-88765-X, Pub. by Wiley-Interscience). Wiley.

Adams, Pauline & Thornton, Emma S. A Populist Assualt: Sarah E. Van de Vort Emery on American Democracy 1862-1895. LC 82-60665. (Illus.). 146p. 1982. 13.95 (ISBN 0-87972-203-7); pap. 6.95 (ISBN 0-87972-204-5). Bowling Green Univ.

Adams, Percy G. Graces of Harmony: Alliteration, Assonance, & Consonance in Eighteenth-Century British Poetry. LC 76-1144. 268p. 1977. 21.00x (ISBN 0-8203-0399-2). U of Ga Pr.

--Travel Literature & the Evolution of the Novel. LC 83-19683. 384p. 1983. 30.00x (ISBN 0-8131-1492-6). U Pr of Ky.

--Travelers & Travel Liars, 1660-1800. LC 79-8906. (Illus.). 1980. pap. 5.95 (ISBN 0-486-23942-X). Dover.

Adams, Peter. The Art of Bonsai. 176p. 1981. 35.00x (ISBN 0-7063-5860-0, Pub. by Ward Lock Ed England). State Mutual BK.

--Fatal Necessity: British Intervention in New Zealand 1830-1847. 1978. 25.00x (ISBN 0-19-647950-9). Oxford U Pr.

Adams, Philip R. Walt Kuhn: A Classic Revival. (Illus.). 1978. pap. 1.00 (ISBN 0-88360-030-7). Amon Carter.

--Walt Kuhn, Painter: His Life & Work. LC 78-3502. (Illus.). 308p. 1978. 35.00 (ISBN 0-8142-0258-6). Ohio St U Pr.

Adams, Phyliss, et al. Etta Can Get It! (Double Scoop Ser.). (ps-2). 1982. pap. 2.50 (ISBN 0-87895-369-8); PLB 4.95 (ISBN 0-87895-169-5). Caroline Hse.

Adams, Phyllis, et al. Stop the Bed. (Double Scoop Ser.). (Illus.). 32p. (gr. k-3). 1982. PLB 4.95 (ISBN 0-695-41644-8, Dist. by Caroline Hse); pap. 2.25 (ISBN 0-695-31644-3). Modern Curr.

Adams, Phylliss, et al. Pippin at the Gym. (Double Scoop Ser.). (Illus.). 32p. (gr. k-3). 1983. PLB 4.95 (ISBN 0-695-41681-2, Dist. by Caroline Hse); pap. 2.25 (ISBN 0-695-31681-8). Modern Curr.

--Pippin Cleans Up. (Double Scoop Ser.). (Illus.). 32p. (gr. k-3). 1983. PLB 4.95 (ISBN 0-695-41680-4, Dist. by Caroline Hse); pap. 2.25 (ISBN 0-695-31680-X). Modern Curr.

--Pippin Eats Out. (Double Scoop Ser.). (Illus.). 32p. (gr. k-3). 1983. PLB 4.95 (ISBN 0-695-41679-0, Dist. by Caroline Hse); pap. 2.25 (ISBN 0-695-31679-6). Modern Curr.

--Pippin Goes to Work. (Double Scoop Ser.). (Illus.). 32p. (gr. k-3). 1983. PLB 4.95 (ISBN 0-695-41678-2, Dist. by Caroline Hse); pap. 2.25 (ISBN 0-695-31678-8). Modern Curr.

--Pippin Learns a Lot. (Double Scoop Ser.). (Illus.). 32p. (gr. k-3). 1983. PLB 4.95 (ISBN 0-695-41677-4, Dist. by Caroline Hse); pap. 2.25 (ISBN 0-695-31677-X). Modern Curr.

--Pippin's Lucky Penny. (Double Scoop Ser.). (Illus.). 32p. (gr. k-3). 1983. PLB 4.95 (ISBN 0-695-41682-0, Dist. by Caroline Hse); pap. 2.25 (ISBN 0-695-31682-6). Modern Curr.

--A Dog Is Not a Troll. (Double Scoop Ser.). (Illus.). 32p. (gr. k-3). 1982. lib. bdg. 4.95 (ISBN 0-695-41612-X, Dist. by Caroline Hse); pap. 2.25 (ISBN 0-695-31612-5). Modern Curr.

--Go, Wendall, Go! (Double Scoop Ser.). 32p. (gr. k-3). 1982. lib. bdg. 4.95 (ISBN 0-695-41614-6, Dist. by Caroline Hse); pap. 2.25 (ISBN 0-695-31614-1). Modern Curr.

--Hi Dog. (Double Scoop Ser.). 32p. (gr. k-3). 1982. lib. bdg. 4.95 (ISBN 0-695-41611-1, Dist. by Caroline Hse); pap. 2.25 (ISBN 0-695-31611-7). Modern Curr.

--A Troll, a Truck, & a Cookie. (Double Scoop Ser.). 32p. (gr. k-3). 1982. lib. bdg. 4.95 (ISBN 0-695-41617-0, Dist. by Caroline Hse); pap. 2.25 (ISBN 0-695-31617-6). Modern Curr.

--Go, Wendall, Go! (Double Scoop Ser.). (ps-2). 1982. pap. 2.50 (ISBN 0-87895-367-1); PLB 4.95 (ISBN 0-87895-167-9). Caroline Hse.

--Good Show. (Double Scoop Bks.). 32p. (gr. k-3). 1982. PLB 4.95 (ISBN 0-695-41648-0, Dist. by Caroline Hse); pap. 2.25 (ISBN 0-695-31648-6). Modern Curr.

--I Love Wheels. (Double Scoop Ser.). (Illus.). 32p. (gr. k-3). 1982. PLB 4.95 (ISBN 0-695-41615-4, Dist. by Caroline Hse); pap. 2.25 (ISBN 0-695-31615-X). Modern Curr.

--I Love Wheels. (Double Scoop Ser.). (ps-2). 1982. pap. 2.50 (ISBN 0-87895-368-X); PLB 4.95 (ISBN 0-87895-168-7). Caroline Hse.

--Jump In! Now! (Double Scoop Ser.). (Illus.). 32p. (gr. k-3). 1982. PLB 4.95 (ISBN 0-695-41645-6, Dist. by Caroline Hse); pap. 2.25 (ISBN 0-695-31645-1). Modern Curr.

--This Way Down. (Double Scoop Ser.). (Illus.). 32p. (gr. k-3). 1982. PLB 4.95 (ISBN 0-695-41647-2, Dist. by Caroline Hse); pap. 2.25 (ISBN 0-695-31647-8). Modern Curr.

--Time Out! (Double Scoop Ser.). (Illus.). 32p. (gr. k-3). 1982. PLB 4.95 (ISBN 0-695-41643-X, Dist. by Caroline Hse); pap. 2.25 (ISBN 0-695-31643-5). Modern Curr.

--A Troll, a Truck, & a Cookie. (Double Scoop Ser.). (ps-2). 1982. pap. 2.50 (ISBN 0-87895-371-X); PLB 4.95 (ISBN 0-87895-171-7). Caroline Hse.

--Where Is Here? (Double Scoop Ser.). (Illus.). 32p. (gr. k-3). 1982. PLB 4.95 (ISBN 0-695-41646-4, Dist. by Caroline Hse); pap. 2.25 (ISBN 0-695-31646-X). Modern Curr.

Adams, Priscilla, ed. Examining the Metric Issues. 85p. 1976. pap. 4.00 (ISBN 0-916148-08-4); subscribers 3.00. Am Natl.

Adams, Priscilla B. Thinking on Paper. 120p. 1985. pap. text ed. 3.75 (ISBN 0-88334-185-9). Ind Sch Pr.

Adams, Q. A. Neither Male nor Female. 4.95 (ISBN 0-89985-104-5). Christ Nations.

Adams, R. & Murray, F. All You Should Know about Arthritis. 3.25x (ISBN 0-915962-28-4). Cancer Control Soc.

Adams, R., jt. auth. see Christ, F.

Adams, R. A. Sobolev Spaces. (Pure & Applied Mathematics Ser.). 1975. 47.50 (ISBN 0-12-044150-0). Acad Pr.

Adams, R. Clark, jt. auth. see Poirot, James L.

Adams, R. D. & Lyon, G. Neurology of Hereditary Metabolic Diseases of Children. 1981. 60.00 (ISBN 0-07-000318-1). McGraw.

Adams, R. D. & Victor, M. Principles of Neurology. 3rd ed. 1216p. 1985. 65.00 (ISBN 0-07-000296-7). McGraw.

Adams, R. D. & Wake, W. C. Structural Adhesive Joints in Engineering. 320p. 1984. 52.50 (ISBN 0-85334-263-6, I-166-84, Pub. by Elsevier Applied Sci England). Elsevier.

Adams, R. F. English-Efik Dictionary. (Eng. & Efik.). 27.50 (ISBN 0-87559-056-X); thumb indexed 32.50 (ISBN 0-87559-057-8). Shalom.

Adams, R. J. Arms & the Wizard: Lloyd George & the Ministry of Munitions, 1915-1916. LC 77-16694. 272p. 1978. 17.50x (ISBN 0-89096-045-3). Tex A&M Univ Pr.

Adams, R. J., jt. auth. see Gadsden, S. R.

Adams, R. L. Cell Culture for Biochemists. Work, T. S. & Burdon, R. H., eds. (Laboratory Techniques in Biochemistry & Molecular Biology Ser.: Vol. 8, No. 1). 292p. 1980. 65.50 (ISBN 0-444-80248-7); pap. 27.00 (ISBN 0-444-80199-5). Elsevier.

--Farm Management Crop Manual. 1981. 25.00x (ISBN 0-686-76636-9, Pub. by Oxford & IBH India). State Mutual Bk.

Adams, R. L. & Burdon, R. H. Biochemistry of Nucleic Acids. 9th ed. 420p. 1981. 44.00x (ISBN 0-412-22680-4, NO. 6532, Pub. by Chapman & Hall England); pap. 21.00x (ISBN 0-412-22690-1, NO. 6531). Methuen Inc.

Adams, R. N. Electrochemistry at Solid Electrodes. (Monographs in Electroanalytical Chemistry & Electrochemistry: Vol. 1). 1969. soft cover 75.00 (ISBN 0-8247-7034-X). Dekker.

Adams, Ramon F. Come An' Get It: The Story of the Old Cowboy Cook. 171p. (Orig.). 1952. pap. 6.95 (ISBN 0-8061-1013-9). U of Okla Pr.

--A Fitting Death for Billy the Kid. LC 60-5112. (Illus.). 310p. 1982. 18.95 (ISBN 0-8061-0458-9); pap. 8.95 (ISBN 0-8061-1764-8). U of Okla Pr.

--The Language of the Railroader. LC 77-22346. 1977. 12.95 (ISBN 0-8061-1435-5). U of Okla Pr.

--The Language of the Railroader. LC 77-22346. pap. 50.50 (ISBN 0-317-27972-6, 2052152). Bks Demand UMI.

--More Burs Under the Saddle: Books & Histories of the West. LC 77-18606. 1979. 19.95 (ISBN 0-8061-1469-X). U of Okla Pr.

--Rampaging Herd: A Bibliography of Books & Pamphlets on Men & Events in the Cattle Industry. 464p. 38.00x (ISBN 0-939738-05-8). Zubal Inc.

--Six-Guns & Saddle Leather: A Bibliography of Books & Pamphlets on Western Outlaws & Gunmen. 808p. 48.00 (ISBN 0-939738-06-6). Zubal Inc.

--Six-Guns & Saddle Leather: A Bibliography of Books & Pamphlets on Western Outlaws & Gunmen. LC 54-5939. pap. cancelled (ISBN 0-317-10340-7, 2005815). Bks Demand UMI.

--Western Words: A Dictionary of the American West. LC 68-31369. 355p. 1975. pap. 11.95 (ISBN 0-8061-1173-9). U of Okla Pr.

Adams, Ramon F., ed. see Wolfenstine, Manfred R.

Adams, Ray. Serious Cycling for the Beginner. LC 77-73654. (Illus.). 88p. 1977. pap. 4.95 (ISBN 0-89037-115-6). Anderson World.

Adams, Raymond. Thoreau Library: A Catalogue. LC 73-16257. lib. bdg. 10.00 1936 (ISBN 0-8414-2941-3); lib. bdg. 10.00 1937 suppl. (ISBN 0-8414-2939-1). Folcroft.

--The Thoreau Library of Raymond Adams. LC 80-2502. Repr. of 1937 ed. 24.50 (ISBN 0-404-19050-2). AMS Pr.

--The Thoreau Library of Raymond Adams. 80p. 1980. Repr. of 1936 ed. lib. bdg. 15.00 (ISBN 0-8495-0063-X). Arden Lib.

Adams, Raymond & Chen, David. The Process of Educational Innovation: An International Perspective. (Illus.). 284p. (Co-published with Kogan Page, London). 1982. pap. 37.25 (ISBN 92-803-1096-8, U1191, UNESCO). Unipub.

Adams, Raymond D., jt. auth. see Haymaker, Webb.

Adams, Raymond D., jt. auth. see Isselbacher, Kurt J.

Adams, Raymond D., jt. auth. see Petersdorf, Robert G.

Adams, Raymond J., Jr. Avian Research at the Kalamazoo Nature Center 1970 to 1978. (Illus.). 86p. 1982. pap. 5.00 (ISBN 0-939294-11-7, QL 677-5-A2). Beech Leaf.

Adams, Reginald. The Parish Clerks of London: A History of the Worshipful Company of Parish Clerks of London. (Illus.). 152p. 1971. 45.00x (ISBN 0-8476-1380-1). Rowman.

Adams, Rex. Doctor's Amazing Speed Reducing Diet. LC 79-11343. 1979. 17.95 (ISBN 0-13-216275-X, Parker). P-H.

--Miracle Medicine Foods. LC 77-6245. 1977. pap. 4.95 (ISBN 0-13-585463-6, Reward). P-H.

--Miracle Medicine Foods. 1982. pap. 4.95 (ISBN 0-13-585471-7, Reward). P-H.

--Miracle Medicine Foods. 1984. pap. cancelled (ISBN 0-446-32343-8). Warner Bks.

Adams, Rhenna L., jt. auth. see Torrado de Marcano, Ester.

Adams, Richard. The Girl in a Swing. LC 79-3480. 1980. 11.95 (ISBN 0-394-51049-6). Knopf.

--The Girl in a Swing. 1980. pap. 3.95 (ISBN 0-451-13467-2, E9662, Sig). NAL.

--Maia. LC 84-48844. 960p. 1985. 19.45 (ISBN 0-394-52857-3). Knopf.

--Our Amazing Sun. LC 82-17419. (Question & Answer Bks.). (Illus.). 32p. (gr. 3-6). 1983. PLB 9.59 (ISBN 0-89375-890-6); pap. text ed. 1.95 (ISBN 0-89375-891-4). Troll Assocs.

--Our Wonderful Solar System. LC 82-17413. (Question & Answer Bks.). (Illus.). 32p. (gr. 3-6). 1983. PLB 9.59 (ISBN 0-89375-872-8); pap. text ed. 1.95 (ISBN 0-89375-873-6). Troll Assocs.

--The Plague Dogs. 1983. pap. 2.95 (ISBN 0-449-20503-7, Crest). Fawcett.

--Shardik. (YA) 1976. pap. 4.95 (ISBN 0-380-00516-6, 62554-7, Bard). Avon.

--The Ship's Cat. 1977. 7.95 (ISBN 0-394-42334-8). Knopf.

--The Unbroken Web. 1982. pap. 3.95 (ISBN 0-345-30368-7). Ballantine.

--The Unbroken Web. (Illus.). 144p. 1980. 1.98 (ISBN 0-517-54231-5). Crown.

--Watership Down. 1975. pap. 4.50 (ISBN 0-380-00293-0, 69837-4). Avon.

--Watership Down. LC 73-6044. 444p. (YA) (gr. 8 up). 1974. 16.95 (ISBN 0-02-700030-3, 70003). Macmillan.

Adams, Richard & Bayley, Nicola. The Tyger Voyage. 1976. 7.95 (ISBN 0-394-40796-2). Knopf.

Adams, Richard & Lockley, Ronald. Voyage Through the Antarctic. LC 82-48484. (Illus.). 160p. 1982. 13.95 (ISBN 0-394-52858-1). Knopf.

Adams, Richard, ed. Grimm's Fairy Tales. (Illus.). 160p. 1983. 13.95 (ISBN 0-7100-0912-7); pap. 9.95 (ISBN 0-7100-9997-5). Routledge & Kegan.

Adams, Richard E. Prehistoric Mesoamerica. 1977. 21.95 (ISBN 0-316-00890-7). Little.

Adams, Richard E. W. The Ceramics of Altar de Sacrificios. LC 72-126638. (Peabody Museum Papers: Vol. 63, No. 1). 1971. pap. 12.50x (ISBN 0-87365-180-4). Peabody Harvard.

Adams, Richard N. Community in the Andes: Problems & Progress in Muquiyauyo. LC 59-14164. (American Ethnological Society Monographs: No. 31). (Illus.). 1959. 15.00x (ISBN 0-295-73747-6). U of Wash Pr.

--Crucifixion by Power: Essays on Guatemalan National Social Structure, 1944-1966. 567p. 1970. 25.00x (ISBN 0-292-70035-0). U of Tex Pr.

--Energy & Structure: A Theory of Social Power. LC 74-19392. 371p. 1975. pap. 9.95x (ISBN 0-292-72013-0). U of Tex Pr.

--Paradoxical Harvest: Energy & Explanation in British History, 1870-1914. LC 81-21631. (ASA Rose Monograph). (Illus.). 160p. 1982. 34.50 (ISBN 0-521-24637-7); pap. 10.95 (ISBN 0-521-28866-5). Cambridge U Pr.

Adams, Richard N., jt. ed. see Fogelson, Raymond D.

Adams, Richard P. Faulkner: Myth & Motion. 1968. 29.00 (ISBN 0-691-06141-6). Princeton U Pr.

Adams, Rick & Adams, Louise M. The California Highway One Book. (Orig.). 1985. pap. 19.95 (ISBN 0-345-31855-2). Ballantine.

Adams, Rick, ed. see Klotter, John C.

Adams, Robert. Abysmal Gloom. (Illus.). 32p. 1984. laminated bds 11.95 (ISBN 0-584-62073-X, Pub. by Salem Hse Ltd). Merrimack Pub Cir.

--Beauty in Photography: Essays in Defense of Traditional Values. LC 81-66767. (Illus.). 128p. 1981. 12.50 (ISBN 0-89381-080-0). Aperture.

--Beauty in Photography: Essays in Defense of Traditional Values. LC 81-66767. 128p. 1985. pap. 7.95 (ISBN 0-89381-202-1). Aperture.

--Bili the Axe. (Horseclans Ser.: No. 10). 192p. 1983. pap. 2.95 (ISBN 0-451-12928-8, Sig). NAL.

--Castaways in Time. 1983. pap. 2.75 (ISBN 0-451-12664-5, Sig). NAL.

--A Cat of Silvery Hue. (Horseclans Ser.: No. 4). (Orig.). 1983. pap. 2.95 (ISBN 0-451-13305-6, AE3305, Sig). NAL.

--Champion of the Last Battle. (Horseclans Ser.: No. 11). 201p. 1983. pap. 2.95 (ISBN 0-451-13304-8, Sig). NAL.

--The Coming of the Horseclans. (Horseclans Ser.: No. 1). 1983. pap. 2.95 (ISBN 0-451-13748-5, AE3142, Sig). NAL.

--The Death of a Legend. (Horseclans Ser.: No. 8). 1983. pap. 2.95 (ISBN 0-451-12935-0, Sig). NAL.

--Denver: A Photographic Survey of the Metropolitan Area. LC 76-44035. (Illus.). 1977. 19.50 (ISBN 0-87081-101-0); pap. 10.00 (ISBN 0-87081-102-9). Colo Assoc.

--From the Missouri West. LC 79-57634. (Illus.). 64p. 1980. 20.00 (ISBN 0-89381-059-2); ltd. ed., 100 copies 400.00 (ISBN 0-89381-063-0); pap. 15.00 (ISBN 0-89381-098-3). Aperture.

--Horseclans Odyssey. (Horseclans Ser.: No. 7). (Orig.). 1983. pap. 2.95 (ISBN 0-451-12416-2, Sig). NAL.

--Horses of the North. (Horseclans Ser.: No. 13). 1985. pap. 2.50 (ISBN 0-451-13626-8, Sig). NAL.

--The Lost Museum: Glimpses of Vanished Originals. (Illus.). 255p. 1980. 25.00 (ISBN 0-670-44107-4, Studio). Viking.

--Our Lives & Our Children: Pictures Taken Near the Rocky Flats Nuclear Weapons Plant. LC 83-72991. (Illus.). 96p. 1984. pap. 12.50 (ISBN 0-89381-142-4). Aperture.

--The Patrimony. (Horseclans Ser.: No. 6). (Orig.). 1983. pap. 2.95 (ISBN 0-451-13300-5, AE3300, Sig). NAL.

--Revenge of the Horseclans. (Horseclans Ser.: No. 3). 1983. pap. 2.95 (ISBN 0-451-13306-4, AE3306, Sig). NAL.

--The Savage Mountains. (Horseclans Ser.: No. 5). (Orig.). 1983. pap. 2.95 (ISBN 0-451-12934-2, AE2934, Sig). NAL.

--Selections from the Strauss Photography Collection. LC 82-71437. 40p. (Orig.). 1982. pap. 7.95 (ISBN 0-914738-29-1). Denver Art Mus.

--The Seven Magical Jewels of Ireland. (Castaways in Time Ser.: No. 2). 1985. pap. 2.95 (ISBN 0-451-13340-4, Sig). NAL.

--Summer Nights: Photographs by Robert Adams. (Illus.). 48p. 1985. 25.00 (ISBN 0-89381-141-6). Aperture.

--Swords of the Horseclans. (Horseclans Ser.: No. 2). 1983. pap. 2.95 (ISBN 0-451-14025-7, E9988, Sig). NAL.

--The Witch Goddess. (Horseclans Ser.: No. 9). 1983. pap. 2.95 (ISBN 0-451-14027-3, AE1792, Sig). NAL.

--A Woman of the Horseclans. (Horseclans Ser.: No. 12). 208p. 1983. pap. 2.50 (ISBN 0-451-13367-6, Sig). NAL.

Adams, Robert, ed. The New Times Network: Groups & Centres for Personal Growth. 192p. 1983. pap. 8.95 (ISBN 0-7100-9355-1). Routledge & Kegan.

Adams, Robert & Norton, Andre, eds. Magic in Ithkar. 320p. 1985. pap. 6.95 (ISBN 0-8125-4740-3). Tor Bks.

Adams, Robert, jt. ed. see Norton, Andre.

Adams, Robert, et al. Dry Lands: Man & Plants. LC 78-65219. 1979. 35.00x (ISBN 0-312-22042-1). St Martin.

Adams, Robert E. A Companion to Shakespeare: The Non-Shakespearean Elizabethan Drama - An Introduction. LC 78-58821. 1978. pap. text ed. 12.00 (ISBN 0-8191-0540-6). U Pr of Amer.

--Encuentro con Jesus. (Illus.). 80p. 1977. pap. 1.50 (ISBN 0-311-04657-6). Casa Bautista.

Adams, Robert E., ed. How to Get Along in This World. 171p. pap. 8.95 (ISBN 0-911012-33-8). Nelson-Hall.

Adams, Robert J., et al. Introduction to Folklore. rev ed. LC 73-78365. (Illus.). 200p. 1974. pap. text ed. 6.96 (ISBN 0-88429-002-6). Collegiate Pub.

Adams, Robert L., ed. The Greater Chicago Job Bank: A Comprehensive Guide to Major Local Employers. (Job Bank Ser.). 272p. (Orig.). 1982. pap. 9.95 (ISBN 0-937860-05-0). Adams Inc MA.

Adams, Robert L. & Fiedler, J. Michael, eds. The Greater Chicago Job Bank. 2nd ed. (Job Bank Ser.). 1985. pap. 9.95 (ISBN 0-937860-35-2). Adams Inc MA.

--The Metropolitan New York Job Bank: Including Northern New Jersey, Long Island, Southwestern Connecticut & Westchester. 2nd ed ed. (Job Bank Ser.). 453p. 1983. pap. 9.95 (ISBN 0-937860-19-0). Adams Inc MA.

--The Metropolitan Washington Job Bank. (Job Bank Ser.). 1985. pap. 9.95 (ISBN 0-937860-39-5). Adams Inc MA.

--The Pennsylvania Job Bank. 2nd ed. (Job Bank Ser.). Date not set. pap. 9.95 (ISBN 0-937860-38-7). Adams Inc MA.

Adams, Robert L., et al, eds. The Boston Job Bank: A Comprehensive Guide to Major Employers Throughout Greater Boston. 2nd ed. (Job Bank Ser.). 280p. 1983. pap. 9.95 (ISBN 0-937860-18-2). Adams Inc MA.

--Greater Atlanta Job Bank: The/Job Hunters's Guide to Greater Atlanta. (Job Bank Ser.). 250p. (Orig.). 1983. pap. 9.95 (ISBN 0-937860-17-4). Adams Inc MA.

--Southern California Job Bank: A Comprehensive Guide to Major Local Employers. 2nd ed. (Job Bank Ser.). (Orig.). 1985. 9.95 (ISBN 0-937860-21-2). Adams Inc Ma.

Adams, Robert M. After Joyce: Studies in Fiction After Ulysses. 1977. 19.95x (ISBN 0-19-502168-1). Oxford U Pr.

--Bad Mouth: Fugitive Papers on the Dark Side. LC 76-50241. (Quantum Ser.). 1977. 19.95x (ISBN 0-520-03381-7); pap. 2.65 (ISBN 0-520-03530-5, CAL 375). U of Cal Pr.

--Decadent Societies. LC 82-73710. 208p. 1983. 16.00 (ISBN 0-86547-103-7). N Point Pr.

--Heartland of Cities: Surveys of Ancient Settlement & Land Use on the Central Floodplain of the Euphrates. LC 80-13995. (Illus.). 384p. 1981. lib. bdg. 45.00x (ISBN 0-226-00544-5). U of Chicago Pr.

--Ikon: John Milton & the Modern Critics. LC 72-152588. 231p. 1972. Repr. of 1955 ed. lib. bdg. 18.75 (ISBN 0-8371-6021-9, ADIK). Greenwood.

--The Land & Literature of England: A Historical Account. (Illus.). 1983. 29.95 (ISBN 0-393-01704-4). Norton.

--Land Behind Baghdad: A History of Settlement on the Diyala Plains. LC 65-17279. (Illus.). 1965. 22.00x (ISBN 0-226-00425-2). U of Chicago Pr.

--Milton & the Modern Critics. 256p. 1966. pap. 4.95x (ISBN 0-8014-9025-1, CP25). Cornell U Pr.

--Occupational Skin Disease. 496p. 1982. 83.50 (ISBN 0-8089-1494-4, 790026). Grune.

--The Roman Stamp: Frame & Facade in Some Forms of Neo-Classicism. LC 72-50241. (Illus.). 1974. 35.00x (ISBN 0-520-02345-5, CAL 395); pap. 6.95 (ISBN 0-520-03715-4). U of Cal Pr.

--Strains of Discord. facs. ed. LC 75-142601. (Essay Index Reprint Ser). 1958. 16.00 (ISBN 0-8369-1917-3). Ayer Co Pubs.

Adams, Robert M. & Nissen, Hans J. The Uruk Countryside: The Natural Setting of Urban Societies. LC 78-179489. 1972. 28.00x (ISBN 0-226-00500-3). U of Chicago Pr.

Adams, Robert M., ed. see Berkeley, George.

Adams, Robert M., ed. see De Voltaire, Francois M.

Adams, Robert M., ed. see Jonson, Ben.

Adams, Robert M., ed. & tr. see Machiavelli, Niccolo.

Adams, Robert M., ed. see Meredith, George.

Adams, Robert M., ed. & tr. see More, Thomas.

Adams, Robert M., ed. see Stendhal.

Adams, Robert M., tr. & intro. by see Villiers de l'Isle-Adam.

Adams, Robert M., et al. Essays on the Philosophy of Leibniz. Kulstad, Mark, ed. (Rice University Studies: Vol. 63, No. 4). 143p. 1978. pap. 10.00x (ISBN 0-89263-234-8). Rice Univ.

--The Fitness of Man's Environment. LC 68-20988. (Smithsonian Annual, No. 2). 205p. 1968. 17.50x (ISBN 0-87474-058-4). Smithsonian.

Adams, Robert P. Better Part of Valor: More, Erasmus, Colet & Vives on Humanism, War, & Peace, 1496-1535. LC 61-15064. (Illus.). 368p. 1962. 15.00x (ISBN 0-295-73722-0). U of Wash Pr.

Adams, Robert W. Adding Solar Heat to Your Home. (Illus.). 1979. 12.95 (ISBN 0-8306-9768-3); pap. 7.95 (ISBN 0-8306-1196-7, 1196). TAB Bks.

Adams, Robert W., jt. auth. see Kotecha, Ken C.

Adams, Roe R., III, jt. auth. see Consumer Guide Editors.

Adams, Roger, ed. Organic Reactions, Vol. 2. LC 42-20265. 470p. 1981. Repr. of 1944 ed. 31.50 (ISBN 0-89874-375-3). Krieger.

Adams, Roger J. The Eastern Portal of the North Transept at Chartres: Christological Rather Than Mariological. (Kultstatten der Gallisch-frankischen Kirche). 190p. 1982. pap. 27.90 (ISBN 3-8204-6902-8). P Lang Pubs.

Adams, Romanzo. Interracial Marriage in Hawaii: A Study of Mutually Conditioned Processes of Acculturation & Amalgamation. LC 69-14907. (Criminology, Law Enforcement, & Social Problems Ser.: No. 65). (Illus.). 1969. Repr. of 1937 ed. 12.00x (ISBN 0-87585-065-0). Patterson Smith.

--Interracial Marriage in Hawaii: A Study of the Mutually Conditioned Processes of Acculturation & Amalgamation. LC 75-96473. (BCL Ser.: No. I). Repr. of 1937 ed. 12.00 (ISBN 0-404-00293-5). AMS Pr.

Adams, Ronald C., et al. Games, Sports & Exercises for the Physically Handicapped. 3rd. ed. LC 81-7288. (Illus.). 430p. 1982. pap. 28.50 (ISBN 0-8121-0785-3). Lea & Febiger.

Adams, Ronald J., et al. Street Survival: Tactics for Armed Encounters. LC 79-57196. (Illus.). 416p. 1980. 25.95 (ISBN 0-935878-00-9). Calibre Pr.

Adams, Roy. The Sanctuary Doctrine: Three Approaches in the Seventh-day Adventist Church. (Andrews University Seminary Doctoral Dissertation Ser.: Vol. 1). viii, 327p. (Orig.). 1981. pap. 9.95 (ISBN 0-943872-33-2). Andrews Univ Pr.

Adams, Roy, jt. auth. see Kakacek, Keith.

Adams, Roy M. Estate Planning Manual for Trust Officers. LC 82-229355. (Illus.). Date not set. price not set. Am Bankers.

--When the Eyes Faded. 1983. 7.75 (ISBN 0-8062-2102-X). Carlton.

Adams, Roy N. & Denman, Eugene D. Wave Propagation & Turbulent Media. LC 66-30179. (Modern Analytic & Computational Methods in Science & Mathematics Ser.). pap. 33.50 (ISBN 0-317-08452-6, 2007766). Bks Demand UMI.

Adams, Royce W., Jr., jt. auth. see Carman, Robert A.

Adams, Russell E., jt. ed. see Lucas, Jay P.

Adams, Russell L. Great Negroes, Past & Present. 3rd rev. ed. Ross, David P., Jr., ed. LC 72-87924. (Orig.). 1976. 14.95 (ISBN 0-910030-07-3); pap. text ed. 9.95 (ISBN 0-910030-08-1); 9 portfolios of display prints 12.95 ea. Afro-Am.

Adams, Ruth. The Complete Home Guide to All the Vitamins. 432p. 1972. pap. 3.95 (ISBN 0-915962-05-5). Larchmont Bks.

--Eating in Eden. 206p. (Orig.). 1976. pap. 1.75 (ISBN 0-915962-16-0). Larchmont Bks.

--One Little Candle. 1981. Repr. of 1966 ed. text ed. 6.50 (ISBN 0-88053-314-5, S-251). Macoy Pub.

Adams, Ruth & Murray, Frank. All You Should Know about Arthritis. 256p. (Orig.). 1979. pap. 3.95 (ISBN 0-915962-28-4). Larchmont Bks.

--All You Should Know about Beverages for Your Health & Well Being. 288p. 1976. pap. 1.75 (ISBN 0-915962-17-9). Larchmont Bks.

--All You Should Know About Health Foods. 352p. pap. 3.95 (ISBN 0-915962-01-2). Larchmont Bks.

--Body, Mind, & the B Vitamins. rev. ed. 320p. 1972. pap. 3.25 (ISBN 0-915962-02-0). Larchmont Bks.

--The Good Seeds, the Rich Grains, the Hardy Nuts for a Healthier, Happier Life. rev. ed. 304p. 1973. pap. 1.75 (ISBN 0-915962-07-1). Larchmont Bks.

--Improving Your Health with Niacin. (Larchmont Preventive Health Library). 128p. (Orig.). 1978. pap. 1.75 (ISBN 0-915962-12-8). Larchmont Bks.

--Improving Your Health with Vitamin A. (Larchmont Preventive Health Library). 128p. (Orig.). 1978. pap. 1.25 (ISBN 0-915962-24-1). Larchmont Bks.

--Improving Your Health with Vitamin E. (Larchmont Preventive Health Library). 176p. (Orig.). 1978. pap. 1.50 (ISBN 0-915962-22-5). Larchmont Bks.

--Improving Your Health with Zinc. (Larchmont Preventive Health Library). 128p. (Orig.). 1978. pap. 1.50 (ISBN 0-915962-26-8). Larchmont Bks.

--Is Blood Sugar Making You a Nutritional Cripple? rev. ed. 176p. (Orig.). 1975. pap. 3.50 (ISBN 0-915962-11-X). Larchmont Bks.

--Mega-Vitamin Therapy: Addicts, Alcoholics & Mentally Ill. 1980. 3.25x (ISBN 0-915962-03-9). Cancer Control Soc.

--Megavitamin Therapy. 286p. (Orig.). 1973. pap. 3.95 (ISBN 0-915962-03-9). Larchmont Bks.

--Minerals: Kill or Cure. rev. ed. 368p. (Orig.). 1974. pap. 1.95 (ISBN 0-915962-16-0). Larchmont Bks.

--New High-Fiber Diet. 2.25x (ISBN 0-915962-21-7). Cancer Control Soc.

--The New High Fiber Diet. 320p. (Orig.). 1977. pap. 2.25 (ISBN 0-915962-21-7). Larchmont Bks.

--Seeds, Grains, Nuts. 1.75x (ISBN 0-915962-07-1). Cancer Control Soc.

--The Vitamin B-Six Book. 176p. (Orig.). 1980. pap. 2.95 (ISBN 0-915962-30-6). Larchmont Bks.

--Vitamin B-Twelve & Folic Acid. 176p. (Orig.). 1981. pap. 2.95 (ISBN 0-915962-31-4). Larchmont Bks.

--Vitamin C, the Powerhouse Vitamin. 192p. 1975. pap. 1.50 (ISBN 0-532-12187-2). Woodhill.

--Vitamin E, Wonder Worker of the 70's? 128p. 1972. pap. 1.50 (ISBN 0-532-12142-2). Woodhill.

Adamski, George. Inside the Spaceships: UFO Experiences of George Adamski 1952-1955. LC 80-80385. (Illus.). 296p. pap. 9.95 (ISBN 0-942176-01-4). GAF Intl.

Adamski, M. Patricia, jt. auth. see Brodsky, Edward.

Adamson, A. M. Marquesan Insects: Environment. (BMB Ser.: No. 139). Repr. of 1936 ed. 14.00 (ISBN 0-527-02245-4). Kraus Repr.

--Review of the Fauna of the Marquesas Islands & Discussion of Its Origin. (BMB Ser.: No. 159). Repr. of 1939 ed. 12.00 (ISBN 0-527-02267-5). Kraus Repr.

Adamson, Arthur. A Textbook of Physical Chemistry. 2nd ed. 953p. 1979. 27.25i (ISBN 0-12-044260-4); solutions manual 5.75i (ISBN 0-12-044265-5). Acad Pr.

Adamson, Arthur W. Physical Chemistry of Surfaces. 4th ed. 664p. 1982. 44.95 (ISBN 0-471-86729-2). Wiley.

--A Textbook of Physical Chemistry. 3rd ed. Date not set. text ed. price not set (ISBN 0-12-044255-8). Acad Pr.

--Understanding Physical Chemistry. 3rd ed. 1980. 21.95 (ISBN 0-8053-0128-3). Benjamin Cummings.

Adamson, Arthur W. & Fleischauer, Paul D., eds. Concepts of Inorganic Photochemistry. LC 84-5776. 456p. 1984. Repr. of 1975 ed. lib. bdg. 34.50 (ISBN 0-89874-762-7). Krieger.

Adamson, D. Bride's Carefree Cookbook: A Beginner's Book with General Directions. 18.50 (ISBN 0-87559-124-8). Shalom.

Adamson, Donald. Pascal: A Critical Biography. LC 81-8033. 200p. 1985. 28.50x (ISBN 0-389-20098-0, 06871). B&N Imports.

Adamson, Donald, tr. see Balzac, Honore de.

Adamson, Douglas. Charles Bear & the Mystery of the Forest, Bk. 1. 1975. pap. 3.50 (ISBN 0-686-15459-2). D Adamson.

Adamson, Edward. Art As Healing. Timlin, John, ed. (Illus.). 70p. (Orig.). 1984. pap. 10.95 (ISBN 0-89254-013-3). Nicolas-Hays.

Adamson, Elizabeth C. Mind Your Manners. (gr. 1-3). 1981. 4.95 (ISBN 0-86653-014-2, GA 243). Good Apple.

--Seek & Ye Shall Find: LDS Puzzle Fun for All Ages. 1975. pap. 3.95 (ISBN 0-88290-048-X). Horizon Utah.

Adamson, Gary W., jt. auth. see McDowell, Richard L.

Adamson, George, jt. auth. see Ingrams, Richard.

Adamson, George, tr. see Ingrams, Richard & Wells, John.

Adamson, Greg. We All Live on Three Mile Island: The Case Against Nuclear Power. (Illus.). 160p. 1982. lib. bdg. 15.00 (ISBN 0-909196-12-5); pap. 4.95 (ISBN 0-686-79301-3). Path Pr NY.

Adamson, Iain T. An Introduction to Field Theory. 2nd ed. LC 82-1164. 192p. 1982. 22.95 (ISBN 0-521-24388-2); pap. 11.95 (ISBN 0-521-28658-1). Cambridge U Pr.

Adamson, James. Commentary on the Epistle of James. (New International Commentary on the New Testament). 480p. 1976. 13.95 (ISBN 0-8028-2377-7). Eerdmans.

Adamson, Jane. Othello As Tragedy: Some Problems of Judgement & Feeling. LC 79-41437. 230p. 1980. 39.50 (ISBN 0-521-22368-7); pap. 13.95 (ISBN 0-521-29760-5). Cambridge U Pr.

Adamson, Jerome. With an Eye Toward Collecting California Paintings. 35p. Date not set. write for info. (ISBN 0-939370-05-0); pap. write for info. (ISBN 0-939370-04-2). DeRu's Fine Art.

Adamson, Joe. Groucho, Harpo, Chico & Sometimes Zeppo: A Celebration of the Marx Brothers. (Illus.). 1983. pap. 8.50 (ISBN 0-671-47072-8, Touchstone Bks). S&S.

--Tex Avery: King of Cartoons. (Quality Paperbacks Ser.). (Illus.). 238p. 1985. pap. 14.95 (ISBN 0-306-80248-1). Da Capo.

--The Walter Lantz Story. (Illus.). 240p. 1985. 19.95 (ISBN 0-399-13096-9). Putnam Pub Group.

Adamson, Joe, contrib. by see Directors Guild of America.

Adamson, John E. Externals & Essentials. facs. ed. LC 67-22049. (Essay Index Reprint Ser). 1933. 17.00 (ISBN 0-8369-0137-1). Ayer Co Pubs.

Adamson, John W. The Illiterate Anglo-Saxon & Other Essays in Education: Medieval & Modern. 1978. Repr. of 1946 ed. lib. bdg. 22.50 (ISBN 0-8495-0056-7). Arden Lib.

--Illiterate Anglo-Saxon & Other Essays on Education, Medieval & Modern. LC 74-1485. 1946. lib. bdg. 22.50 (ISBN 0-8414-2956-1). Folcroft.

--Pioneers of Modern Education in the Seventeenth Century. LC 79-165366. (Classics in Education Ser.). 1971. text ed. 9.75 (ISBN 0-8077-1006-7); pap. text ed. 7.00x (ISBN 0-8077-1008-3). Tchrs Coll.

Adamson, Joy. Born Free. LC 74-5073. (Illus.). (YA) 1974. pap. 3.95 (ISBN 0-394-71263-3, V-263, Vin). Random.

--Born Free: A Lioness of Two Worlds. (Illus.). (gr. 9 up). 1960. Pantheon.

--Queen of Shaba: The Story of an African Leopard. LC 80-7931. (A Helen & Kurt Wolff Bk.). (Illus.). 256p. 1980. 14.95 (ISBN 0-15-175651-1). HarBraceJ.

--Spotted Sphinx. LC 77-85008. (Helen & Kurt Wolff Bk.). 313p. 1969. 9.50 (ISBN 0-15-184795-9). HarBraceJ.

Adamson, Judith. Graham Greene & Cinema. 225p. 1984. 31.95 (ISBN 0-937664-65-0). Pilgrim Bks OK.

Adamson, Lauren, jt. auth. see Tronick, Edward.

Adamson, Leslie, jt. auth. see Harcus, Alfred.

Adamson, M. R., tr. see Maritain, Jacques.

Adamson, Madeleine & Borgos, Seth. This Mighty Dream: Social Protest Movements in the United States. (Illus.). 128p. Date not set. 19.95x (ISBN 0-7102-0040-4); pap. 9.95 (ISBN 0-7102-0042-0). Routledge & Kegan.

Adamson, Margot, tr. see Maritain, Jacques.

Adamson, Margot R. Treasury of Middle English Verse. LC 73-9719. 1930. lib. bdg. 30.00 (ISBN 0-8414-2858-1). Folcroft.

Adamson, Martha C., jt. ed. see Zamora, Gloria J.

Adamson, R., ed. see Jevons, W. Stanley.

Adamson, R. B., jt. auth. see Franklin, D.

Adamson, Robert. The Development of Modern Philosophy. facsimile ed. Sorley, W. R., ed. LC 76-165613. (Select Bibliographies Reprint Ser.). Repr. of 1903 ed. 23.50 (ISBN 0-8369-5920-5). Ayer Co Pubs.

--Fichte. (The Works of Robert Adamson Ser.). 222p. Repr. of 1881 ed. 29.00 (ISBN 0-932051-72-3). Am Repr Serv.

--Fichte: Philosophical Classics for English Readers. facsimile ed. LC 76-94262. (Select Bibliographies Reprint Ser). 1903. 19.00 (ISBN 0-8369-5036-4). Ayer Co Pubs.

--A Short History of Logic. Sorley, W. R., ed. (Reprints in Philosophy Ser.). Repr. of 1911 ed. lib. bdg. 39.50x (ISBN 0-697-00001-X). Irvington.

Adamson, T., ed. Folk-Tales of the Coast Salish. LC 36-2204. (American Folklore Society Memoirs Ser.). Repr. of 1934 ed. 37.00 (ISBN 0-527-01079-0). Kraus Repr.

Adamson, T. C., ed. see Project SQUID Workshop on Transonic Flow Problems in Turbomachinery, Feb. 1976.

Adamson, Thomas A. Inside Grant & Project Writing. Pavlina, Connie L., ed. LC 78-70335. 1979. ring binder 46.00x (ISBN 0-932724-00-0). PAM Pubs.

Adamson, Walter L. Hegemony & Revolution: A Study of Antonio Gramsci's Political & Cultural Theory. LC 79-64478. 1980. 35.00x (ISBN 0-520-03924-6, CAL 642); pap. 8.95 (ISBN 0-520-05057-6). U of Cal Pr.

--Marx & the Disillusionment of Marxism. LC 84-8622. 272p. 1985. 28.50x (ISBN 0-520-05285-4). U of Cal Pr.

Adamson, Wendy, jt. auth. see Gadler, Steve.

Adams-Smith, William N., jt. auth. see Dolan, John P.

Adams-Webber, J. R. Personal Construct Theory: Concepts & Applications. LC 78-8638. 239p. 1979. cloth 48.95x (ISBN 0-471-99669-6, Pub. by Wiley-Interscience). Wiley.

Adams-Webber, Jack R. see Mancuso, James C.

Adams-Webber, Jack & Mancuso, J. C. Applications of Personal Construct Theory. LC 83-98055. 1983. 39.50 (ISBN 0-12-044240-X). Acad Pr.

Adamthwaite, Anthony. The Lost Peace: International Relations in Europe 1918-1939. 250p. 1981. 25.00 (ISBN 0-312-49882-9). St Martin.

Adamthwaite, Anthony P. Anthony P. France & the Coming of the Second World War. (Illus.). 456p. 1977. 32.50x (ISBN 0-7146-3035-7, BHA 03035, F Cass Co). Biblio Dist.

--The Making of the Second World War. (Historical Problems - Studies & Documents). (Illus.). 1977. pap. text ed. 8.95x (ISBN 0-04-940051-7). Allen Unwin.

Adan, Avraham. On the Banks of the Suez: An Israeli General's Personal Account of the Yom Kippur War. LC 80-12322. (Illus.). 492p. 1980. 16.95 (ISBN 0-89141-043-0). Presidio Pr.

Adanov, Arthur. Two Plays: Professor Taranne & Ping-Pong. 1962. text ed. 13.50x (ISBN 0-391-01115-4). Humanities.

Adanson, M. Familles des Plantes, 2 vols. in 1. (Illus.). 1966. Repr. of 1763 ed. 70.00 (ISBN 3-7682-0345-X). Lubrecht & Cramer.

Adar, et al. The IBM Personal Computer: What You Should Know. rev. ed. LC 83-72637. 170p. 1984. pap. 14.95 (ISBN 0-89435-102-8). QED Info Sci.

Adar, L., jt. ed. see Smilansky, M.

Adar Publications, ed. see Doukhan, Jacques.

Adar Publications Staff, ed. see Doukhan, Jacques.

Adare, Viscount. Experiences in Spiritualism with Mr. D. D. Home. LC 75-36824. (Occult Ser.). 1976. Repr. of 1870 ed. 16.00x (ISBN 0-405-07937-0). Ayer Co Pubs.

Adas, A. & Touq, M. S. General Psychology: Arabic Translation. 2nd ed. 600p. 1985. write for info. (ISBN 0-471-80690-0). Wiley.

Adas, Michael. The Burma Delta: Economic Development & Social Change on an Asian Rice Frontier, 1852-1941. LC 73-15256. Repr. of 1974 ed. 68.00 (ISBN 0-8357-9772-4, 2015350). Bks Demand UMI.

--Prophets of Rebellion: Millenarian Protest Movements Against the European Colonial Order. LC 78-26775. xxix, 243p. 1979. 22.50 (ISBN 0-8078-1353-2). U of NC Pr.

Adasch, N., et al. Topological Vector Spaces: The Theory Without Convexity Conditions. (Lecture Notes in Mathematics: Vol. 639). 1978. pap. 14.00 (ISBN 0-387-08662-5). Springer-Verlag.

Adashko, J. George, tr. see Basov, N. G.

Adashko, J. George, tr. see Borisova, Z. U.

Adatto, I. J., jt. auth. see Snider, Arthur J.

Aday, Lu Ann, et al. Access to Medical Care in the U. S. Who Has It, Who Doesn't. LC 84-61463. 175p. 1984. pap. 24.95 (ISBN 0-931028-56-6). Pluribus Pr.

--Hospital-Physician Sponsored Primary Care: Marketing & Impact. LC 85-7569. 330p. 1985. pap. text ed. price not set (ISBN 0-910701-05-9, 00653). Health Admin Pr.

Aday, LuAnn, et al. Health Care in the U. S. Equitable for Whom? LC 79-21841. 415p. 1980. 29.95 (ISBN 0-8039-1373-7). Sage.

Adb al-Wahhab ibn Ali, Taj. Kitab Mu'id an-Ni'am Wa-Mubid an-Niqam: The Restorer of Favours & the Restrainer of Chastisements. LC 78-53829. (Luzac's Semitic Text & Translation Ser.: Vol. 18). 1978. Repr. of 1908 ed. 32.50 (ISBN 0-404-11291-9). AMS Pr.

Adby, P. & Fredman, A. My Big Picture Dictionary. (Illus.). 1985. 1.98 (ISBN 0-517-46813-1). Outlet Bk Co.

Adby, P. R. & Dempster, M. A. Introduction to Optimization Methods. (Mathematics Ser.). 1974. pap. 15.95x (ISBN 0-412-11040-7, NO.6001, Pub. by Chapman & Hall). Methuen Inc.

Adcock, A. The Booklover's London: Chaucer, Dickens, Gissing Goldsmith, Jonson, Lamb, Scott, Shakespeare. 1913. Repr. 20.00 (ISBN 0-8274-1959-7). R West.

--Famous Houses & Literary Shrines of London. with Seventy-Four Illustrations by Frederick Adcock (Shakespeare, Pope, Hogarth, Goldsmith, Reynolds, Boswell, Blake, Johnson, Lamb, Dickens) 1912. Repr. 35.00 (ISBN 0-8274-2335-7). R West.

Adcock, A. St. John. Admissions & Asides. LC 74-105759. 1970. Repr. of 1925 ed. 14.00x (ISBN 0-8046-0936-5, Pub. by Kennikat). Assoc Faculty Pr.

Adcock, Arthur S. Glory That Was Grub Street. facsimile ed. LC 72-99678. (Essay Index Reprint Ser.). 1928. 27.50 (ISBN 0-8369-1388-4). Ayer Co Pubs.

Adcock, Betty. Nettles: Poems by Betty Adcock. LC 83-726. 72p. 1983. pap. 5.95 (ISBN 0-8071-1103-1). La State U Pr.

Adcock, Carol P. Geometric Maze Designs. (International Design Library). (Illus.). 48p. (Orig.). 1984. pap. 3.50 (ISBN 0-88045-048-7). Stemmer Hse.

Adcock, Craig E. Marcel Duchamp's Notes from the "Large Glass". An N-Dimensional Analysis. Foster, Stephen, ed. LC 83-9192. (Studies in the Fine Arts: The Avant-Garde: No. 40). 420p. 1983. 49.95 (ISBN 0-8357-1454-3). UMI Res Pr.

Adcock, Don & Segal, Marilyn. From One to Two Years. LC 80-13835. (Play & Learn Ser.). (Illus.). 1980. pap. 4.95 (ISBN 0-916392-51-1). Oak Tree Pubns.

--From Two to Three Years. LC 80-13834. (Play & Learn Ser.). (Illus.). 1980. pap. 5.95 (ISBN 0-916392-52-X). Oak Tree Pubns.

--Making Friends: Ways of Encouraging Social Development in Young Children. (Illus.). 192p. 1983. 14.95 (ISBN 0-13-547174-5); pap. 6.95 (ISBN 0-13-547166-4). P-H.

--Play Together Grow Together: A Cooperative Curriculum for Teachers of Young Children. (Illus.). 142p. (Orig.). 1983. 8.95 (ISBN 0-914799-00-2). Mailman Family.

Adcock, Don, jt. auth. see Segal, Marilyn.

Adcock, Don, jt. auth. see Segal, Marilyn M.

Adcock, Doon, jt. auth. see Segal, Marilyn.

Adcock, Fleur, ed. The Oxford Book of Contemporary New Zealand Poetry. 1982. pap. 14.95x (ISBN 0-19-558092-3). Oxford U Pr.

Adcock, Frank E. The Greek & Macedonian Art of War. LC 57-10495. (Sather Classical Lectures Ser.: No. 30). 1974. pap. 3.50 (ISBN 0-520-00005-6, CAL54). U of Cal Pr.

--Roman Art of War under the Republic. rev ed. (Martin Classical Lectures: Vol. 8). 140p. 1970. Repr. of 1960 ed. 14.95 (ISBN 0-06-490017-7, 06306). B&N Imports.

--Roman Political Ideas & Practice. (Jerome Lecture Ser). 1959. pap. 4.95x (ISBN 0-472-06088-0, 88, AA). U of Mich Pr.

--Thucydides & His History. viii, 146p. 1973. Repr. of 1963 ed. 16.50 (ISBN 0-208-01314-8, Archon). Shoe String.

Adcock, Mabel & Blackwell, Elsie. Creative Activities. (Illus.). 1984. 4.95 (ISBN 0-87162-011-1, D3195). Warner Pr.

Adcock, St. John. Robert Louis Stevenson: His Life & His Personality. 1924. Repr. 25.00 (ISBN 0-8274-3294-1). R West.

Adcock, Steven. Steve Adcock's Partner Workout: A Two-Person Exercise System That Provides Aerobic Benefits, Strength Building, & Flexibility Techniques Without the Need for a Gym or a Single Piece of Equipment. (Illus.). 192p. 1984. 15.95 (ISBN 0-87131-447-9). M Evans.

Adcock, Thomas L. Precinct Nineteen. LC 84-6317. 288p. 1984. 15.95 (ISBN 0-385-18453-0). Doubleday.

Adda, J. Progress in Flavour Research, 1984: Proceedings of the 4th Weurman Flavour Research Symposium, Dourdan, France, 9-11 May, 1984. (Developments in Food Science: Vol. 10). 1985. 126.00 (ISBN 0-444-42432-6). Elsevier.

Addams, Charles. Creature Comforts. (Illus.). 96p. 1983. 9.95 (ISBN 0-671-43963-4, Fireside). S&S.

Addams, Charles & Aruego, Jose. A Treasury of Windmill Books. LC 81-48387. (Illus.). 64p. (gr. 3 up). 1982. PLB 8.79 (ISBN 0-671-44802-1). Messner.

Addams, Jane. Democracy & Social Ethics: And Other Essays. Repr. of 1902 ed. 24.00 (ISBN 0-403-00824-7). Scholarly.

--Excellent Becomes the Permanent. facsimile ed. LC 77-107680. (Essay Index Reprint Ser). 1932. 15.00 (ISBN 0-8369-1488-0). Ayer Co Pubs.

--My Friend, Julia Lathrop. facsimile ed. LC 74-1660. (Children & Youth Ser.). 246p. 1974. Repr. of 1935 ed. 22.00x (ISBN 0-405-05942-6). Ayer Co Pubs.

--A New Conscience & an Ancient Evil. LC 76-169367. (Family in America Ser). 236p. 1972. Repr. of 1912 ed. 22.00 (ISBN 0-405-03843-7). Ayer Co Pubs.

--Newer Ideals of Peace. LC 71-137523. (Peace Movement in America Ser). xviii, 243p. 1972. Repr. of 1907 ed. lib. bdg. 16.95x (ISBN 0-89198-050-4). Ozer.

--Peace & Bread in Time of War. LC 75-137524. (Peace Movement in America Ser). 269p. 1972. Repr. of 1922 ed. lib. bdg. 16.95x (ISBN 0-89198-051-2). Ozer.

--Peace & Bread in Time of War. (NASW Classics Ser.). 262p. 1983. 5.95 (ISBN 0-87101-110-7). Natl Assn Soc Wkrs.

--Social Thought of Jane Addams. Lasch, Christopher, ed. LC 82-7135. 300p. 1982. pap. text ed. 14.95x (ISBN 0-8290-0338-X). Irvington.

--The Spirit of Youth & the City Streets. LC 72-76862. 192p. 1972. 12.50x (ISBN 0-252-00276-8). U of Ill Pr.

--Twenty Years at Hull-House. pap. 3.95 (ISBN 0-451-51955-8, CE1843, Sig Classics). NAL.

Addams, Jane, et al. Child, the Clinic, & the Court. LC 72-137577. 1971. Repr. lib. bdg. 25.00 (ISBN 0-384-08782-5). Johnson Repr.

--Philanthropy & Social Progress: Seven Essays by Jane Addams, Robert A. Woods, Father J. O. S. Huntington, Prof. Franklin H. Giddings, & Bernard Bosanquet, Delivered Before the School of Applied Ethics at Plymouth, Mass. During the Session of 1892. facsimile ed. LC 79-95059. (Select Bibliographies Reprint Ser). 1893. 19.00 (ISBN 0-8369-5061-5). Ayer Co Pubs.

--Philanthropy & Social Progress: Seven Essays. LC 75-108221. (Criminology, Law Enforcement, & Social Problems Ser.: No. 104). (Index added). 1970. Repr. of 1893 ed. 10.00x (ISBN 0-87585-104-5). Patterson Smith.

Addams, Shay. From Apshai to Zork. Date not set. price not set. S&S.

Addanki, Sam & Kindrick, Shirley A. Renewed Health for Diabetics & Obese People. Brennan, R. O., ed. (Orig.). 1982. pap. 3.50 (ISBN 0-9609896-0-9). Nu-Diet.

Addanki, Sam, et al. Diabetes Breakthrough: Control Through Nutrition. 224p. (Orig.). 1982. pap. 2.95 (ISBN 0-523-42085-4). Pinnacle Bks.

Addelson, L. Building Failures. 128p. 1982. pap. text ed. 27.25x (ISBN 0-85139-768-9, Pub. by Architectural Pr England). Humanities.

Addenbrooke, Alice B. Mistress of the Mansion. (Illus., Orig.). 1959. pap. 2.95 (ISBN 0-87015-087-1). Pacific Bks.

Addeo, Edmond, jt. auth. see Wheeler, Virginia L.

Adderley, C. B. Transportation Not Necessary. LC 83-49228. (Crime & Punishment in England 1850-1922 Ser.). 134p. 1984. lib. bdg. 30.00 (ISBN 0-8240-6202-7). Garland Pub.

Adderly, James G. Stephen Remarx: The Story of a Venture into Ethics, 1893. Wolff, Robert L., ed. Bd. with The Christian. Caine, Thomas H. Repr. of 1897 ed. LC 75-485. (Victorian Fiction Ser). 1976. lib. bdg. 73.00 (ISBN 0-8240-1562-2). Garland Pub.

Addey, John M. Harmonic Anthology. 160p. 1976. 13.95 (ISBN 0-86690-061-6, 1009-01). Am Fed Astrologers.

--Selected Writings. 232p. 1976. 8.75 (ISBN 0-86690-057-8, 1011-01). Am Fed Astrologers.

Addicott, Frederick T. Abscission. LC 81-4065. (Illus.). 376p. 1982. 50.00x (ISBN 0-520-04288-3). U of Cal Pr.

Addicott, Fredrick T., ed. Abscisic Acid. LC 81-23406. 624p. 1983. 75.00 (ISBN 0-03-055831-X). Praeger.

Addicott, James, jt. ed. see English, John A.

Addinall, Eric & Ellington, Henry. Nuclear Power in Perspective. 200p. 1982. 26.50 (ISBN 0-89397-110-3). Nichols Pub.

Addinall, Eric, jt. auth. see Ellington, Henry.

Addington, A. C. The Royal House of Stuart: The Descendants of King James VI of Scotland, James I of England. (Illus.). 1976. Set. 175.00 (ISBN 0-317-27392-2, Pub. by C Skilton Ltd England). Vol. I, xiii, 430 pgs. Vol. II, xiii, 409 pgs. Vol. III, iii, 215 pgs. Heinman.

Addington, Cornelia & Addington, Jack. All about Prosperity & How You Can Prosper. LC 83-73342. (Orig.). 1984. pap. 4.95 (ISBN 0-87516-533-8). De Vorss.

Addington, Cornelia, jt. auth. see Addington, Jack.

Addington, Cornelia, jt. auth. see Addington, Jack E.

Addington, Jack & Addington, Cornelia. I Am the Way. LC 82-71191. 118p. (Orig.). 1982. pap. 3.95 (ISBN 0-87516-486-2). De Vorss.

--The Joy of Meditation. LC 78-75078. 1979. pap. 4.95 (ISBN 0-87516-292-4). De Vorss.

--The Perfect Power Within You. new ed. LC 73-87712. 167p. 1973. pap. 4.95 (ISBN 0-87516-179-0). De Vorss.

--Your Needs Met. 156p. 1982. pap. 3.95 (ISBN 0-87516-490-0). De Vorss.

Addington, Jack, jt. auth. see Addington, Cornelia.

Addington, Jack E. All about Goals & How to Achieve Them. LC 77-80016. 1977. pap. 4.95 (ISBN 0-87516-237-1). De Vorss.

--The Hidden Mystery of the Bible. LC 70-93549. 1969. 10.95 (ISBN 0-396-05975-9). Dodd.

--Psychogenesis: Everything Begins in the Mind. LC 79-145391. 1971. 10.95 (ISBN 0-396-06334-9). Dodd.

--Secret of Healing. 204p. 1979. pap. 7.95 (ISBN 0-911336-80-X). Sci of Mind.

Addington, Jack E. & Addington, Cornelia. Drawing the Larger Circle. 160p. (Orig.). 1985. pap. 5.95 (ISBN 0-87516-558-3). De Vorss.

Addington, Larry H. The Blitzkreig Era & the German General Staff, 1865-1941. LC 75-163955. (Illus.). Repr. of 1971 ed. 57.40 (ISBN 0-8357-9528-4, 2050453). Bks Demand UMI.

--The Patterns of War since the Eighteenth Century. LC 83-48902. (Illus.). 352p. (Orig.). 1984. 29.50x (ISBN 0-253-34305-4); pap. 10.95x (ISBN 0-253-20342-2, MB 342). Ind U Pr.

Addington, Lucile R. Lithic Illustration: Drawing Flaked Stone Artifacts for Publication. LC 85-8121. (Prehistoric Archeology & Ecology Ser.). (Illus.). 160p. 1985. lib. bdg. 29.99x (ISBN 0-226-00634-4); pap. 10.00x (ISBN 0-226-00635-2). U of Chicago Pr.

Addington, Robert M. History of Scott County, Virginia. LC 77-77267. (Illus.). 364p. 1977. Repr. of 1932 ed. 18.50 (ISBN 0-8063-0771-4). Regional.

Addington, W. W., jt. ed. see Banner, Arthur S.

Addington, Whitney W., ed. see Gracey, Douglas R.

Addink, A. D. & Spronk, N., eds. Exogenous & Endogenous Influences on Metabolic & Neural Control, Vol. 1, Invited Lectures: Proceedings of the Third Congress of the European Society for Comparative Physiology & Biochemistry, August 31-September 3, 1981, Noorwijkerhout Netherlands. (Illus.). 432p. 1982. 83.00 (ISBN 0-08-027986-4). Pergamon.

--Exogenous & Endogenous Influences on Metabolic & Neural Control, Vol. 2, Abstracts: Proceedings ot the Third Congress of the European Society for Compara07394366xxxlogy & Biochemistry, August 31-September 3, 1981, Noorwijkerhout,Netherlands. (Illus.). 260p. 1982. 55.00 (ISBN 0-08-028845-6). Pergamon.

Addis, Ann B., jt. auth. see Levin, Harry.

Addis, Denise, jt. auth. see Breman, Paul.

Addis, Don. The Great John K. 1983. pap. 3.95 (ISBN 0-911818-38-3, World Almanac). Newspaper Ent.

--The Great John L. LC 82-61791. 128p. (Orig.). 1983. pap. 3.95 (ISBN 0-911818-38-3). World Almanac.

Addis, J. M. Chinese Ceramics from Datable Tombs & Some Other Dated Material: A Handbook 1978. (Illus.). 184p. 1978. 105.00x (ISBN 0-85667-039-1, Pub. by Sotheby Pubns England). Biblio Dist.

--Chinese Porcelain from the Addis Collection: Twenty-Two Pieces of Chingtehchen Porcelain Presented to the British Museum. 92p. 1981. 80.00x (ISBN 0-7141-1410-3, Pub. by Brit Mus Pubns England). State Mutual Bk.

Addis, Laird. The Logic of Society: A Philosophical Study. LC 74-83131. 256p. 1975. 17.50x (ISBN 0-8166-0733-8). U of Minn Pr.

Addis, Patricia K. Through a Woman's I: An Annotated Bibliography of American Women's Autobiographical Writings, 1946-1976. LC 82-10813. 621p. 1983. 37.50 (ISBN 0-8108-1588-5). Scarecrow.

Addi-Shir, Al-Sayyid. Dictionary of Persian Loan Words in the Arabic Language. (Persian & Arabic.). 1980. 21.00x (ISBN 0-86685-128-3). Intl Bk Ctr.

Addison & Johnson. Boner's Ark. 128p. 1982. pap. 1.75 (ISBN 0-523-49002-X). Pinnacle Bks.

Addison, jt. auth. see Matheson.

Addison, A. W. & Cullen, W. R. Biological Aspects of Inorganic Chemistry. LC 76-44225. 410p. 1977. text ed. 35.00 (ISBN 0-471-02147-4). Krieger.

Addison, Agnes. Romanticism & the Gothic Revival. 1967. Repr. of 1938 ed. 10.00 (ISBN 0-87752-000-3). Gordian.

Addison, Alexander. Rise & Progress of Revolution. 1979. lib. bdg. 59.95 (ISBN 0-8490-3000-5). Gordon Pr.

Addison, C. C. The Chemistry of the Liquid Alkali Metals. 330p. 1984. 64.95 (ISBN 0-471-90508-9). Wiley.

Addison, C. C., ed. Inorganic Chemistry of the Main Group Elements, Vols. 1-5. LC 72-95028. Vol. 1 1973. 1971-72 literature 43.00 (ISBN 0-85186-752-9); Vol. 2 1974. 1972-73 literature 61.00 (ISBN 0-85186-762-6); Vol. 3 1976. 1973-74 literature 73.00 (ISBN 0-85186-772-3); Vol. 4 1977. 1974-75 literature 66.00 (ISBN 0-85186-782-0); Vol. 5 1978. 1975-76 literature 86.00 (ISBN 0-85186-792-8). Am Chemical.

Addison, Charles G. Damascus & Palmyra, 2 vols. in 1. LC 73-6265. (The Middle East Ser.). Repr. of 1838 ed. 35.50 (ISBN 0-405-05319-3). Ayer Co Pubs.

--The Knights Templar History. rev. ed. LC 76-29832. Repr. of 1912 ed. 47.50 (ISBN 0-404-15407-7). AMS Pr.

Addison, Charles M. The Theory & Practice of Mysticism. 1977. lib. bdg. 59.95 (ISBN 0-8490-2742-X). Gordon Pr.

Addison, Daniel D. Lucy Larcom: Life, Letters & Diary. facsimile ed. LC 74-154143. (Selected Bibliographies Reprint Ser). Repr. of 1894 ed. 20.00 (ISBN 0-8369-5759-8). Ayer Co Pubs.

--Lucy Larcom: Life, Letters & Diary. LC 75-99065. (Library of Lives & Letters). 1970. Repr. of 1894 ed. 40.00x (ISBN 0-8103-3611-1). Gale.

Addison, G. M., jt. auth. see Schwarz, V.

Addison, G. M., et al, eds. Organic Acidureas. 1984. lib. bdg. 37.50 (ISBN 0-85200-875-9, Pub. by MTP Pr England). Kluwer Academic.

--Trace Metals & Inherited Metabolic Disease. 144p. 1983. lib. bdg. 35.00 (ISBN 0-85200-750-7, Pub. by MTP Pr England). Kluwer Academic.

Addison, Harry W. RFD No. 3. LC 77-23069. 96p. 1977. 6.95 (ISBN 0-88289-161-8). Pelican.

--Write That Down for Me Daddy. LC 78-9028. (Illus.). 50p. (gr. 6-12). 1978. Repr. of 1974 ed. 4.95 (ISBN 0-88289-116-2). Pelican.

Addison, Hilda. Mary Webb. 1931. Repr. 15.00 (ISBN 0-8274-3867-2). R West.

Addison, J. The De Coverly Papers. Meek, Joseph, ed. (Works of J. Addison Ser.). 128p. Date not set. Repr. of 1920 ed. lib. bdg. 29.00 (ISBN 0-932051-22-7). Am Repr Serv.

Addison, J. W., et al, eds. The Theory of Models: Proceedings of the International Symposium at Berkeley, 1963. (Studies in Logic & the Foundations of Mathematics). xvi, 494p. 1965. 85.00 (ISBN 0-7204-2233-7, North-Holland). Elsevier.

Addison, James C. An Old-Spelling Edition of Thomas Lodge's a Margarite of America (1596) (Salzberg - Elizabethan Studies: No. 96). 247p. 1980. pap. text ed. 25.50x (ISBN 0-391-02323-3, Pub. by Inst Lit Austria). Humanities.

Addison, James T. The Christian Approach to the Moslem. LC 76-158227. (BCL Ser.: No. II). Repr. of 1942 ed. 24.50 (ISBN 0-404-00294-3). AMS Pr.

Addison, Jerome F. How Rules Eighteen & Eleven Can Succeed in Magnifying the Profit Potential of Commodity Futures Trading Operations. (Illus.). 129p. 1981. 69.85x (ISBN 0-918968-81-X). Inst Econ Fina.

Addison, John. Apartheid. (Today's World Ser.). (Illus.). 72p. (gr. 7-9). 1981. 14.95 (ISBN 0-7134-2485-0, Pub. by Batsford England). David & Charles.

Addison, John & Siebert, W. S. A Market for Labor: An Analytical Treatment. LC 78-10976. (Illus.). 1978. 29.90 (ISBN 0-673-16175-7). Scott F.

Addison, John, et al. Suleyman & the Ottoman Empire. Yapp, Malcolm & Killingray, Margaret, eds. (Illus.). (gr. 10). 1980. lib. bdg. 6.95 (ISBN 0-89908-038-3); pap. text ed. 2.45 (ISBN 0-89908-013-8). Greenhaven.

--Traditional Africa. Yapp, Malcolm, et al, eds. (World History Ser.). (Illus.). 32p. (gr. 10). 1980. lib. bdg. 6.95 (ISBN 0-89908-034-0); pap. text ed. 2.45 (ISBN 0-89908-009-X). Greenhaven.

Addison, John T., jt. auth. see Hirsch, Barry T.

Addison, Joseph. Addison: The Freeholder. Leheny, James, ed. 55.00x (ISBN 0-19-812494-5). Oxford U Pr.

--The Coverley Papers from the Spectator. 1980. Repr. lib. bdg. 29.00 (ISBN 0-686-71913-1). Scholarly.

--Critical Essays from the Spectator. Bond, Donald F., ed. (Orig.). 1970. pap. 5.95x (ISBN 0-19-501359-X). Oxford U Pr.

--Criticism of Milton's Paradise Lost, from the Spectator, 1711-12. large type ed. Arber, Edward, ed. 152p. 1983. pap. 15.00 (ISBN 0-87556-550-6). Saifer.

--Criticisms on Paradise Lost. (Works of Joseph Addison Ser.). 200p. Date not set. Repr. of 1892 ed. lib. bdg. 29.00 (ISBN 0-932051-91-X). Am Repr Serv.

--Dialogues on the Usefulness of Ancient Medals. LC 75-27883. (Renaissance & the Gods Ser.: Vol. 38). (Illus.). 1976. Repr. of 1726 ed. lib. bdg. 88.00 (ISBN 0-8240-2087-1). Garland Pub.

--Essays in Criticism & Literary Theory. Loftis, John, ed. LC 74-76968. (Crofts Classics Ser.). 1975. pap. text ed. 3.75x (ISBN 0-88295-106-8). Harlan Davidson.

--The Free-Holder, or Political Essays. 1976. Repr. of 1761 ed. 19.00 (ISBN 0-403-05788-4, Regency). Scholarly.

--The Freeholder: Or, Political Essays. (The Works of Joseph Addison Ser.). 311p. 1985. Repr. of 1716 ed. 39.00 (ISBN 0-932051-53-7). Am Repr Serv.

--Letters. Repr. of 1941 ed. 59.00x (ISBN 0-403-07201-8). Somerset Pub.

--Miscellaneous Works of Joseph Addison, 2 Vols. 1971. Repr. of 1914 ed. Set. 79.00 (ISBN 0-403-00825-5). Scholarly.

Addison, Joseph & Steele, Richard. Selected Essays from the Tatler, the Spectator, & the Guardian. McDonald, Daniel, ed. pap. text ed. 19.95x (ISBN 0-8290-0337-1). Irvington.

--Selections from The Tatler & The Spectator. 2nd ed. LC 79-97857. (Rinehart Editions). 1970. pap. text ed. 11.95 (ISBN 0-03-080790-5, HoltC). HR&W.

Addison, Joseph, et al. Spectator, 4 Vols. 1979. Repr. of 1945 ed. Vol. 1. 14.95x (ISBN 0-460-00164-7, Evman); Vol. 2. 14.95x (ISBN 0-460-00165-5); Vol. 3. 14.95x (ISBN 0-460-00166-3); Vol. 4. 14.95x (ISBN 0-460-00167-1). Biblio Dist.

Addison, Julia. Arts & Crafts in the Middle Ages. 59.95 (ISBN 0-87968-665-0). Gordon Pr.

Addison, Julian M. The Art of the Palazzo Pitti in Florence, 3 vols. (Illus.). 416p. 1985. Set. 247.50 (ISBN 0-86650-165-7). Gloucester Art.

Addison, Linda, et al. Balancing the Scale for the Disadvantaged Gifted: Presentations from the Fourth Biennial National Conference on Disadvantaged Gifted-Talented held January 11-12, 1980, New Orleans, Louisiana. 240p. 13.95 (ISBN 0-318-02145-5). NSLTIGT.

Addison, Linda, jt. auth. see National Conference on Disadvantaged Gifted-Talented, Fourth Biennial.

Addison, Medora C. Dreams & a Sword. LC 71-144719. (Yale Series of Younger Poets: No. 12). Repr. of 1922 ed. 18.00 (ISBN 0-404-53812-6). AMS Pr.

Addison, Robert, jt. auth. see Berland, Theodore.

Addison, W. E. Structural Principles in Inorganic Compounds. pap. 50.00 (ISBN 0-317-08948-X, 2006383). Bks Demand UMI.

Addison, Wendy, ed. see Bennett, J. G. & Montessori, Mario.

Addison, William. The English Country Parson: (Cowper, George Herbert, Kingsley, Sterne, Wordsworth) 1947. Repr. 20.00 (ISBN 0-8274-2254-7). R West.

--In the Steps of Charles Dickens. 1955. 20.00 (ISBN 0-8274-2567-8). R West.

--Local Styles of the English Parish Church. (Illus.). 192p. 1982. text ed. 35.00x (ISBN 0-8419-6401-7). Holmes & Meier.

--Worthy Dr. Fuller. 1951. Repr. 13.50 (ISBN 0-8274-3772-2). R West.

Addison, William G. The Renewed Church of the United Brethren, 1722-1930. (Church Historical Society London Ser.: No. 9). pap. 23.00 (ISBN 0-317-16445-7). Kraus Repr.

Addison, Sir William. The Old Roads of England. (Illus.). 144p. 1980. 27.00 (ISBN 0-7134-1714-5, Pub. by Batsford England). David & Charles.

Addiss, Stephen. A Japanese Eccentric: The Three Arts of Murase Taiitsu. LC 79-91682. (Illus.). 68p. 1979. pap. 5.95 (ISBN 0-89494-008-2). New Orleans Mus Art.

--Nanga Paintings. (Illus.). 91p. 1975. 17.00 (ISBN 0-903697-03-3, Pub. by R G Sawers UK); pap. 12.50 (ISBN 0-903697-20-3). C E Tuttle.

--Samurai Painters. LC 82-48781. (Great Japanese Art Ser.). (Illus.). 48p. 1982. 18.95 (ISBN 0-87011-563-4). Kodansha.

--The World of Kameda Bosai. LC 84-2004. (Illus.). 1984. pap. 16.95 (ISBN 0-89494-019-8). New Orleans Mus Art.

--The World of Kameda Bosai: The Calligraphy, Poetry, Painting & Artistic Circle of a Japanese Literatus. LC 84-2004. (Illus.). 128p. 1984. 35.00x (ISBN 0-7006-0251-8). U Pr of KS.

Addiss, Stephen, ed. Japanese Ghosts & Demons: Art of the Supernatural. (Illus.). 192p. 1985. 35.00 (ISBN 0-8076-1125-5); pap. 20.00 (ISBN 0-8076-1126-3). Braziller.

--Tokaido: Adventures on the Road in Old Japan. LC 80-53851. (Illus.). 120p. 1980. Set. pap. 16.00 (ISBN 0-913689-09-2); pap. 8.50 (ISBN 0-913689-06-8). Spencer Muse Art.

--Tokaido: On the Road -- Pilgrimage, Travel & Culture. LC 82-50299. (Illus.). 84p. (Orig.). 1982. pap. 6.00 (ISBN 0-913689-07-6). Spencer Muse Art.

Addiss, Stephen, et al. A Myriad of Autumn Leaves: Japanese Art from the Kurt & Millie Gitter Collection. LC 83-43150. (Illus.). 295p. 1983. pap. 29.95 (ISBN 0-89494-017-1). New Orleans Mus Art.

--A Myriad of Autumn Leaves: Japanese Art from the Kurt & Millie Gitter Collection. LC 83-43150. (Illus.). 298p. (Orig.). 1983. pap. 29.95 (ISBN 0-295-96242-9). U of Wash Pr.

Addition, Grace. Pantry Shelf Sampler Cookbook. Jack, Susan, ed. 240p. 1983. 15.95 (ISBN 0-930096-44-4). G Gannett.

Addkison, Andrew R. Cooking on a Woodburning Stove: 150 Down-Home Recipes. LC 80-831192. 108p. (Orig.). 1980. pap. 7.95 (ISBN 0-915190-28-1). Jalmar Pr.

Addkison, Roy & Sellick, Douglas. Running Dry: How to Conserve Water Indoors & Out. LC 81-40347. (Illus.). 120p. 1982. 12.95 (ISBN 0-8128-2836-4); pap. 8.95 (ISBN 0-8128-6136-1). Stein & Day.

Addleman, Frank G. The Winning Edge: Nutrition for Athletic Fitness & Performances. 228p. 1984. 16.95 (ISBN 0-13-961145-2); pap. 7.95 (ISBN 0-13-961137-1). P-H.

Addleshaw, Percy. Sir Philip Sidney. LC 77-113304. 1970. Repr. of 1909 ed. 28.75x (ISBN 0-8046-1005-3, Pub. by Kennikat). Assoc Faculty Pr.

Addley, Ann C. Lost Inheritance. 1982. 8.95 (ISBN 0-533-05165-7). Vantage.

Addo, Herb. Transforming the World Economy: Nine Critical Essays on the New International World Order. 320p. 1985. pap. text ed. 23.50x (ISBN 0-340-35633-2). Westview.

Addy, J. & Power, E. G. The Industrial Revolution Set. (Then & There Ser.). (Illus.). 158p. (Orig.). (gr. 9-12). 1980. pap. text ed. 18.35 (ISBN 0-582-20523-9). Longman.

Addy, John. The Textile Revolution. (Seminar Studies in History). (Illus.). 1976. pap. text ed. 6.25x (ISBN 0-582-35220-7). Longman.

Addy, John & Reeves, Marjorie. A Coal & Iron Community in the Industrial Revolution. (Then & There Ser.). (Illus.). 108p. (Orig.). (YA) (gr. 7-12). 1980. pap. text ed. 3.40 (ISBN 0-582-20456-9). Longman.

Addy, S. D. A Glossary of Words Used in the Neighbourhood of Sheffield: Including... & Customs. (English Dialect Society Publications Ser.: No. 57). pap. 38.00 (ISBN 0-317-15967-4). Kraus Repr.

Addy, S. O. A Supplement to the Sheffield Glossary. (English Dialect Society Publications Ser.: No. 62). pap. 15.00 (ISBN 0-317-15980-1). Kraus Repr.

Addy, Sharon. We Didn't Mean to. LC 80-24976. (Life & Living from a Child's Point of View Ser.). (Illus.). 32p. (gr. k-5). 1981. PLB 14.25 (ISBN 0-8172-1370-8). Raintree Pubs Ltd.

Addy, Sidney O. Church & Manor: A Study in English Economic History. LC 70-107902. (Illus.). Repr. of 1913 ed. 37.50x (ISBN 0-678-00632-6). Kelley.

--Folk Tales & Superstitions. 163p. 1973. Repr. of 1895 ed. 13.50x (ISBN 0-87471-142-8). Rowman.

Addyman, A. M., jt. auth. see Wilson, I. R.

Addyman, P. V. Excavations in York Nineteen Seventy-Three to Seventy-Four: Second Interim Report. (Excavations in York - Interim Reports Ser.: No. 2). 32p. 1976. pap. text ed. 6.50x (ISBN 0-900312-39-4, Pub. by Coun Brit Archaeology). Humanities.

Addyman, Peter & Morris, Richard, eds. The Archaeological Study of Churches. LC 77-365546. (Council for British Archaeology Research Report Ser.: No. 13). (Illus.). pap. 24.00 (ISBN 0-317-09531-5, 2014021). Bks Demand UMI.

Ade, Debi, jt. auth. see Burkes, Joyce M.

Ade, George. Artie, & Pink Marsh: Eighteen Ninety-Six to Eighteen Ninety-Seven. LC 63-22584. (Chicago in Fiction Ser). (Illus.). Repr. of 1963 ed. 59.00 (ISBN 0-8357-9641-8, 2015748). Bks Demand UMI.

--Bang! Bang! A Collection of Stories Intended to Recall Memories of the Nickel Library Days When Boys Were Superhuman & Murder a Fine Art. facsimile ed. LC 75-160929. (Short Story Index Reprint Ser.). Repr. of 1928 ed. 11.00 (ISBN 0-8369-3908-5). Ayer Co Pubs.

--Doc Horne: A Story of the Streets & Town. LC 77-104402. lib. bdg. 18.75x (ISBN 0-8398-0052-5); pap. text ed. 7.95x (ISBN 0-89197-734-1). Irvington.

--George Ade's "Stories of Benevolent Assimilation". Gianakos, Perry E., ed. v, 82p. (Orig.). 1985. pap. 7.50 (ISBN 971-10-0193-4, Pub. by New Day Philippines). Cellar.

--The Girl Proposition. LC 74-96872. (Illus.). lib. bdg. 24.50x (ISBN 0-8398-0053-3). Irvington.

--In Pastures New. LC 74-91072. Repr. of 1906 ed. lib. bdg. 24.50 (ISBN 0-8398-0054-1). Irvington.

--One Afternoon with Mark Twain. LC 74-3426. 1939. lib. bdg. 10.00 (ISBN 0-8414-2958-8). Folcroft.

--People You Know. (Works of George Ade Ser.). 224p. Date not set. Repr. of 1903 ed. 29.00 (ISBN 0-932051-62-6). Am Repr Serv.

--The Permanent Ade: The Living Writings of George Ade. Kelly, Fred C., ed. LC 78-58997. 1979. Repr. of 1947 ed. 27.75 (ISBN 0-88355-673-1). Hyperion Conn.

Ade, Robin. Fisher in the Hills. (Illus.). 128p. 1985. 18.95 (ISBN 0-233-97570-5, Pub. by A Deutsch England). David & Charles.

Ade, Walter, tr. from Fr. & see Merimee, Prosper.

Ade, Walter F., tr. see Lessing, Gotthold E.

Ade Ajayi, J. F., ed. see Davidson, Basil.

Ade Ajayi, J. F. see International Scientific Committee for the Drafting of a General History of Africa.

Adebonojo, Festus, et al. How Baby Grows. 1985. pap. 8.95 (ISBN 0-87795-695-2). Arbor Hse.

Adebonojo, Mary. Free to Choose. 1980. pap. 6.95 (ISBN 0-8170-0853-5). Judson.

Adede, Rose. Joel Litu: African Quaker. LC 82-81325. 32p. 1982. pap. 2.30x (ISBN 0-87574-243-2). Pendle Hill.

Adedeji, Adebayo. Nigerian Federal Finance: Its Development, Problems & Prospects. LC 77-80848. (Illus.). 308p. 1969. 35.00x (ISBN 0-8419-0010-8, Africana). Holmes & Meier.
Adedeji, Adebayo, ed. The Indigenization of African Economics. 410p. 1981. text ed. 29.50x (ISBN 0-8419-0708-0, Africana); pap. text ed. 12.50x (ISBN 0-8419-0709-9, Africana). Holmes & Meier.
Adedeji, Adebayo & Shaw, Timothy M., eds. Economic Crisis in Africa: African Perspectives on Development Problems & Potentials. LC 85-10763. 300p. 1985. lib. bdg. 27.50 (ISBN 0-931477-43-3). Lynne Rienner.
Adegbite, Edeward. Black Enterprise with the Third World. 1985. 5.75 (ISBN 0-8062-2372-3). Carlton.
Adei, Christopher Y. African Law South of the Sahara. 62p. (Orig.). 1981. write for info. Intl Inst Adv Stud.
Adekson, J. Bayo. Nigeria in Search of a Stable Civil-Military System. 145p. 1982. lib. bdg. 26.50x (ISBN 0-86531-289-3). Westview.
Adel, D. China & Her Neighbours. 337p. 1984. text ed. 25.50x (ISBN 0-391-03228-3, Pub by Deep & Deep India). Humanities.
Adelamn, Linda, et al. Gold Level Student Book. (Writing & Thinking Ser.). (Orig.). (gr. 6). 1984. wkbk. 3.00 (ISBN 0-88106-116-6, W610). Mastery Ed.
Adelberg, A., jt. auth. see Polimeni, R. S.
Adelberg, Edward A. & Slayman, Carolyn, eds. Current Topics in Membranes & Transport, Vol. 23: Genes & Proteins: Transport Proteins & Receptors. 1985. 52.00 (ISBN 0-12-153323-9). Acad Pr.
Adelberg, Tina Z., jt. ed. see Shelly, Maynard W.
Adelio. A Journey to Philadelphia: Or Memoirs of Charles Coleman Saunders. LC 78-64060. Repr. of 1804 ed. 37.50 (ISBN 0-404-17055-2). AMS Pr.
Adell, Judith, et al, eds. A Guide to Non-Sexist Children's Books. LC 75-34396. 149p. 1976. 11.95 (ISBN 0-915864-01-0); pap. 4.95 (ISBN 0-915864-02-9). Academy Chi Pubs.
Adelmam, M. A. The World Petroleum Market. 458p. 1973. 37.00 (ISBN 0-8018-1422-7). Resources Future.
Adelman, Allan G. & Goldman, Bernard S., eds. Unstable Angina: Recognition & Management. LC 80-13211. 358p. 1981. 36.00 (ISBN 0-88416-271-0). PSG Pub Co.
Adelman, Andrew & Bainum, Peter M., eds. International Space Technical Applications. (Science & Technology Ser.: Vol. 52). (Illus.). 186p. 1981. lib. bdg. 30.00x (ISBN 0-87703-152-5, Pub. by Am Astronaut); pap. text ed. 20.00x (ISBN 0-87703-153-3). Univelt Inc.
Adelman, Benjamin & Adelman, Saul J. Bound for the Stars: An Enthusiastic Look at the Opportunities & Challenges Space Exploration Offers. (Illus.). 368p. 1981. text ed. 17.95 (ISBN 0-13-080390-1, Spec); pap. text ed. 8.95 (ISBN 0-13-080382-0). P-H.
Adelman, Bob & Off the Wall Street Journal, Inc. Reagan Report. LC 84-4100. 64p. 1984. pap. 5.95 (ISBN 0-385-19516-8, Dolp). Doubleday.
Adelman, Clem, jt. auth. see Walker, Robert.
Adelman, Clem, ed. The Politics & Ethics of Evaluation. LC 83-40173. 160p. 1984. 22.50 (ISBN 0-312-62619-3). St Martin.
--Uttering, Muttering Collecting, Using & Reporting Talk for Social & Educational Research. 244p. 1981. 50.00x (ISBN 0-86216-042-1, Pub. by McIntyre England). State Mutual Bk.
Adelman, Conrad. How to Manage Your Sales Time. (Orig.). pap. 30.00x (ISBN 0-933738-00-5). IBMS Inc.
--Smarter Not Harder. (Orig.). 1979. pap. 50.00x (ISBN 0-933738-01-3). IBMS Inc.
--Smarter Not Harder. 2nd ed. 1981. 50.00x (ISBN 0-686-24979-8). IBMS Inc.
--Smarter Not Harder. 3rd ed. 1984. pap. 60.00 (ISBN 0-317-02253-9). IBMS Inc.
Adelman, Howard S. & Taylor, Linda. An Introduction to Learning Disabilities. 1986. text ed. 24.95 (ISBN 0-673-15902-7). Scott F.
--Learning Disabilities in Perspective. 1983. text ed. 23.80 (ISBN 0-673-15398-3). Scott F.
Adelman, Irma. Economic Growth & Resources: National & International Policies, Vol. IV. LC 79-4430. 1979. 40.00 (ISBN 0-312-23317-5). St Martin.
--Theories of Economic Growth & Development. 1961. 12.50x (ISBN 0-8047-0083-4); pap. 5.95x (ISBN 0-8047-0084-2). Stanford U Pr.
Adelman, Irma & Morris, Cynthia T. Economic Growth & Social Equity in Developing Countries. LC 73-80616. 260p. 1973. 22.50x (ISBN 0-8047-0837-1); pap. 7.95 (ISBN 0-8047-0888-6, SP136). Stanford U Pr.
Adelman, Irma & Morris, Cynthia Taft. Society, Politics, & Economic Development: A Quantitative Approach. 336p. 1967. 25.00x (ISBN 0-8018-0006-4); pap. 10.00x (ISBN 0-8018-1301-8). Johns Hopkins.
Adelman, Irma, jt. auth. see Sarris, Alexander H.
Adelman, Irma, ed. Practical Approaches to Development Planning: Korea's Second Five-Year Plan. LC 69-19467. 320p. 1969. 28.50x (ISBN 0-8018-1061-2). Johns Hopkins.
Adelman, J. King Lear: Twentieth Century Interpretations. 1978. 9.95 (ISBN 0-13-516195-9, Spec). P-H.
Adelman, Johnathan R. Revolution, Armies, & War. 230p. 1985. lib. bdg. 25.00x (ISBN 0-931477-53-0). Lynne Rienner.
Adelman, Jonathan R. The Revolutionary Armies: The Historical Development of the Soviet & the Chinese People's Liberation Armies. LC 79-7728. (Contributions in Political Science Ser.: No. 38). (Illus.). 1980. lib. bdg. 27.50 (ISBN 0-313-22026-3, ADR/). Greenwood.
Adelman, Jonathan R., ed. Communist Armies in Politics: Their Origins & Development. LC 82-70561. (Special Studies in Military Affairs). 225p. 1982. 27.50x (ISBN 0-89158-880-9). Westview.
--Terror & Communist Politics: The Role of the Secret Police in Communist States. (Special Study). 300p. 1984. pap. 25.00 (ISBN 0-86531-293-1). Westview.
Adelman, Kenneth L. African Realities. LC 80-15828. 170p. 1980. 19.50x (ISBN 0-8448-1376-1). Crane-Russak Co.
Adelman, Linda, et al. Gold Level Teacher Manual. (Writing & Thinking Ser.). (Orig.). (gr. 6). 1984. Tchr's Ed. 12.00 (ISBN 0-88106-110-7, W620). Mastery Ed.
--Green Level Student Book. (Writing & Thinking Ser.). (Orig.). (gr. 2). 1984. tchr's. ed. 3.00 (ISBN 0-88106-112-3, W210). Mastery Ed.
--Green Level Teacher Manual. (Writing & Thinking Ser.). (Orig.). (gr. 2). 1984. tchr's. ed. 12.00 (ISBN 0-88106-106-9, W220). Mastery Ed.
Adelman, M. A. The World Petroleum Market. LC 72-4029. (Resources for the Future Ser.). (Illus.). 456p. 1973. 37.00x (ISBN 0-8018-1422-7). Johns Hopkins.
Adelman, M. A., et al. Energy Resources in an Uncertain Future: Coal, Gas, Oil & Uranium Supply Forecasting. LC 81-10969. 472p. 1983. text ed. 45.00x prof ref (ISBN 0-88410-644-6). Ballinger Pub.
Adelman, Mara B., jt. auth. see Levine, Deena.
Adelman, Melvin. A Sporting Time: New York City & the Rise of Modern Athletics, 1820-70. (Sports in Society Ser.). (Illus.). 375p. Date not set. 30.00x (ISBN 0-317-20584-6). U of Ill Pr.
Adelman, Morris A. A & P: A Study in Price-Cost Behavior & Public Policy. LC 59-14733. (Economic Studies: No. 113). (Illus.). 1959. 30.00x (ISBN 0-674-00050-1). Harvard U Pr.
Adelman, Morris A., et al. Japan-U. S. Assembly: Proceedings of a Conference on the Threat to the World Economic Order, Vol. 2. 1976. 14.25 (ISBN 0-8447-2083-6); pap. 6.25 (ISBN 0-8447-2082-8). Am Enterprise.
Adelman, Nancy B., ed. see Johnson, Dauphen.
Adelman, Paul. Victorian Radicalism. LC 83-17545. 1984. 9.95 (ISBN 0-582-49197-5). Longman.
Adelman, Penina V. Miriam's Well: Rituals for Jewish Women Around the Year. LC 84-71828. (Illus.). 150p. (Orig.). 1985. pap. 9.95 (ISBN 0-930395-00-X). Biblio NY.
Adelman, Richard, et al, eds. Neural Regulatory Mechanisms During Aging. LC 80-26333. (Modern Aging Ser.: Vol. 1). 246p. 1980. 25.00 (ISBN 0-8451-2300-9). A R Liss.
Adelman, Richard C. & Roth, George S. Endocrine & Neuroendocrine Mechanisms of Aging. 232p. 1982. 68.00 (ISBN 0-8493-5811-6). CRC Pr.
Adelman, Richard C. & Roth, George S., eds. Altered Proteins & Aging. 192p. 1983. 49.50 (ISBN 0-8493-5812-4). CRC Pr.
--Testing the Theories of Aging. 304p. 1982. 78.00 (ISBN 0-8493-5829-9). CRC Pr.
Adelman, Richard C., et al. Enzyme Induction in Aging & Protein Synthesis. LC 74-6131. 172p. 1974. text ed. 21.50x (ISBN 0-8422-7222-4). Irvington.
Adelman, Saul J., jt. auth. see Adelman, Benjamin.
Adelman, Seymour, frwd. by. Rosenwald & Rosenbach, Two Philadelphia Bookmen: Catalogue of an Exhibition at the Rosenbach Museum & Library from the Lessing J. Rosenwald Collection at the Library of Congress, April 30 to July 31, 1983. (Illus.). 72p. 1983. pap. 10.00 (ISBN 0-939084-15-5). U Pr of Va.
Adelman, William. Haymarket Revisited. (Illus.). 136p. 1976. 15.00 (ISBN 0-916884-08-2); pap. 3.95 (ISBN 0-916884-03-1). Ill Labor Hist Soc.
--Pilsen & the West Side. (Illus.). 112p. 1982. 19.95 (Pub. by Illinois Labor History Society); pap. 6.95 (ISBN 0-916884-07-4). C H Kerr.
--Pilsen & the West Side. (Illus.). 100p. 1983. pap. 6.95 (ISBN 0-916884-07-4). Ill Labor Hist Soc.
--Touring Pullman. 46p. 1977. pap. 2.00 (ISBN 0-916884-05-8, Pub. by Illinois Labor History Society). C H Kerr.
--Touring Pullman. 2nd ed. LC 72-80226. 46p. 1977. pap. 2.50 (ISBN 0-916884-05-8). Ill Labor Hist Soc.
Adelman, William J., Jr. & Goldman, David E., eds. The Biophysical Approach to Excitable Systems: A Volume in Honor of Kenneth S. Cole on His 80th Birthday. LC 81-15759. 269p. 1981. 39.50x (ISBN 0-306-40784-1, Plenum Pr). Plenum Pub.
Adelmann. From This Valley. 1981. 5.95 (ISBN 0-934860-18-1). Adventure Pubns.
--Philosophical Investigations in the U. S. S. R. (Boston College Studies in Philosophy: No. 4). 1975. pap. 24.00 (ISBN 90-247-1724-8, Pub. by Martinus Nijhoff Netherlands). Kluwer Academic.
--Soviet Philosphy Revisited. (Boston College Studies in Philosophy: No. 5). 1977. 31.50 (ISBN 90-247-1977-1, Pub. by Martins Nijhoff Netherlands). Kluwer Academic.
Adelmann, F. J. Contemporary Chinese Philosophy. 1983. lib. bdg. 32.50 (ISBN 90-247-3057-0, Pub. by Martinus Nijhoff Netherlands). Kluwer Academic.
Adelmann, Howard B. Marcello Malpighi & the Evolution of Embryology, 5 Vols. (History of Science Ser.). 2548p. 1966. Set. boxed 200.00x (ISBN 0-8014-0004-X). Cornell U Pr.
Adelmann, Howard B., ed. & tr. from It. The Correspondence of Marcello Malpighi, 5 vols. Incl. Vol. 1. 1-214 Letters, 1658-1669; Vol. 2. 214-431 Letters, 1670-1683; Vol. 3. 432-724 Letters, 1684-1688; Vol. 4. 725-824 Letters, 1689-1692; Vol. 5. 825-1050 Letters, 1693-1694. LC 73-9867. (History of Science Ser). 2316p. 1975. boxed set 95.00x (ISBN 0-8014-0802-4). Cornell U Pr.
Adelmann, Howard B., ed. & tr. from Lat. The Embryological Treatises of Hieronymus Fabricius of Aquapendente, 2 vols. Incl. Vol. 1. The Formation of the Egg & of the Chick; Vol. 2. The Formed Fetus. (History of Science Ser.). (Illus.). xxiv, 907p. (A facsimile reprint of the latin text). 1967. 69.50x (ISBN 0-8014-0122-4). Cornell U Pr.
Adelmann, Marianne, ed. Musical Europe. (Illus.). 447p. pap. 7.95 (ISBN 0-8467-0031-X). Brown Bk.
Adelmann, Nora E. Directory of Life Care Communities: A Guide to Retirement Communities for Independent Living. LC 81-11626. 256p. 1981. 23.00 (ISBN 0-8242-0663-0). Wilson.
Adelphi. Effective Prayer. 36p. (Orig.). 1976. pap. 2.00 (ISBN 0-915235-02-1). United Res.
Adelphus, Johannes. Johannes Adelphus: Ausgewaehlte Schriften, 4 vols, Vol. 1, Barbarosssa. Gotzkowsky, Bodo, ed. (Ausgaben Deutscher Literatur des XV Bis XVIII Jahrhunderts). 1974. 84.00 (ISBN 3-11-003382-8); Vol. 2. 126.00; Vol. 3. 96.00. De Gruyter.
Adelson, et al. Continuing Education for the Health Professional: Educational & Administrative Methods. 249p. 1984. 29.95 (ISBN 0-89443-564-7). Aspen Systems.
Adelson, Daniel, ed. Man as the Measure: The Crossroads. LC 77-184153. (Community Psychology Ser: Vol. I). 146p. 1972. 19.95 (ISBN 0-87705-058-9); pap. text ed. 12.95 (ISBN 0-87705-023-6). Human Sci Pr.
Adelson, Daniel, jt. ed. see Klein, Donald.
Adelson, Daniel, ed. see Sarbin, Theodore R.
Adelson, David, jt. ed. see Mitchell, Howard.
Adelson, Dorothy. Operation Susannah. LC 82-541. 200p. 1982. 13.95 (ISBN 0-9607830-0-8, AACR2). Pemberley Pr.
Adelson, Howard L. American Numismatic Society Eighteen Fifty-Eight to Nineteen Fifty-Eight. (Illus.). 390p. 1958. 35.00 (ISBN 0-89722-045-5). Am Numismatic.
Adelson, Joseph. Inventing Adolescence: The Political Psychology of Everyday Schooling. 320p. 1985. 29.95 (ISBN 0-88738-026-3). Transaction Bks.
Adelson, Joseph, ed. Handbook of Adolescent Psychology. LC 79-21927. (Personality Processes Ser.). 624p. 1980. 52.50x (ISBN 0-471-03793-1, Pub. by Wiley-Interscience). Wiley.
Adelson, L. Crisis of Subjectivity: Botho Strauss's Challenge to West German Prose of the 1970's. (Amsterdamer Publikationen zur Sprache und Literatur: Band 56). 273p. 1984. pap. text ed. 28.25x (ISBN 90-6203-906-5, Pub. by Rodopi Holland). Humanities.
Adelson, Laurie & Tracht, Arthur. Aymara Weavings: Ceremonial Textiles of Colonial & 19th Century Bolivia. LC 83-14653. (Illus.). 160p. 1983. pap. 17.50 (ISBN 0-86528-022-3, ADAWP). SITES.
Adelson, Leone. Dandelions Don't Bite: The Story of Words. (Illus.). (gr. 5 up). 1972. PLB 6.99 (ISBN 0-394-92370-7). Pantheon.
Adelson, Leone, jt. auth. see Moore, Lillian.
Adelson, Lester. The Pathology of Homicide: A Vade Mecum for Pathologist, Prosecutor & Defense Counsel. (Illus.). 992p. 1974. 67.50x (ISBN 0-398-03000-6). C C Thomas.
Adelson, Sandra. Wrap Her in Light. LC 80-21014. 448p. 1981. 12.95 (ISBN 0-688-03753-4). Morrow.
--Wrap Her in Light. 432p. 1983. pap. 3.95 (ISBN 0-671-44162-0). PB.
Adel'son-Vel'skii, G. M., jt. auth. see Kuznetsov, O. P.
Adelsperger, Charlotte. When Your Child Hurts. 1985. pap. 5.50 (ISBN 0-8066-2161-3, 10-7088). Augsburg.
Adelstein, James, et al, eds. see Brill, A. Bertrand.
Adelstein, Michael. The Business of Better Writing. Samuels, Betty, ed. 200p. 1984. 36.00 (ISBN 0-910475-04-0). KET.
--Business of Better Writing. Incl. Exercises to Lesson 1. 19p (ISBN 0-910475-09-1); Exercises to Lesson 2. 14p (ISBN 0-910475-10-5); Exercises to Lesson 3. 12p (ISBN 0-910475-11-3); Exercises to Lesson 4. 16p (ISBN 0-910475-12-1). 1984. pap. 3.00 ea. KET.
--Introductory Test Better Writing: Lessons 5-12. Samuels, Betty, ed. (Business of Better Writing Ser.). 1984. write for info. wkbk. (ISBN 0-910475-08-3). KET.
--Introductory Test Grammar: Lessons 1-4. Samuels, Betty, ed. (Business of Better Writing Ser.). 1984. write for info. wkbk. (ISBN 0-910475-07-5). KET.
--Mastering Grammar: Lessons 1-4. Samuels, Betty, ed. (Business of Better Writing Ser.). 53p. 1984. wkbk. 12.00 (ISBN 0-910475-05-9). KET.
--Writing Business Letters, Lesson II. Samuels, Betty, ed. (Business of Better Writing Ser.). 16p. 1984. wkbk. 3.00 (ISBN 0-910475-19-9). KET.
--Writing Business Reports, Lesson 12. Samuels, Betty, ed. (Business of Better Writing Ser.). 15p. 1984. wkbk. 3.00 (ISBN 0-910475-20-2). KET.
--Writing Clearly, Lesson 7. Samuels, Betty, ed. (Business of Better Writing Ser.). 21p. 1984. Wkbk. 3.00 (ISBN 0-910475-15-6). KET.
--Writing Concisely, Lesson 8. Samuels, Betty, ed. (Business of Better Writing Ser.). 14p. 1984. wkbk. 3.00 (ISBN 0-910475-16-4). KET.
--Writing Correctly, Lesson 6. Samuels, Betty, ed. (Business of Better Writing Ser.). 14p. 1984. wkbk. 3.00 (ISBN 0-910475-14-8). KET.
--Writing Interestingly, Lesson 9. Samuels, Betty, ed. (Business of Better Writing Ser.). 19p. 1984. wkbk. 3.00 (ISBN 0-910475-17-2). KET.
--Writing Persuasively, Lesson 10. Samuels, Betty, ed. (Business of Better Writing Ser.). 15p. 1984. wkbk. 3.00 (ISBN 0-910475-18-0). KET.
--Writing Principles, Lesson 5. Samuels, Betty, ed. (Business of Better Writing Ser.). 14p. 1984. wkbk. 3.00 (ISBN 0-910475-13-X). KET.
--Writing Principles: Lessons 5-12. Samuels, Betty, ed. (Business of Better Writing Ser.). 110p. 1984. wkbk. 24.00 (ISBN 0-910475-06-7). KET.
Adelstein, Michael E. Fanny Burney. LC 68-24282. (English Authors Ser.). 1968. lib. bdg. 15.95 (ISBN 0-8057-1072-8). Irvington.
Adelstein, Michael E. & Pival, Jean G. The Reading Commitment. 2nd ed. 390p. 1982. pap. text ed. 13.95 (ISBN 0-15-575572-2, HC); instr's. manual avail. (ISBN 0-15-575573-0). HarBraceJ.
--The Writing Commitment. 3rd ed. 536p. 1984. text ed. 15.95 (ISBN 0-15-597833-0, HC); write for info. instr's manual (ISBN 0-15-597834-9). HarBraceJ.
Adelstein, Michael E. & Sparrow, W. Keats. Business Communications. 490p. 1983. text ed. 24.95 (ISBN 0-15-505612-3, HC); instr's. manual avail. (ISBN 0-15-505613-1); student wkbk. 7.95 (ISBN 0-15-505614-X). HarBraceJ.
Adelstein, Richard P. The Negotiated Guilty Plea: An Economic & Empirical Analysis. LC 79-53639. (Outstanding Dissertations in Economics Ser.). 350p. 1984. lib. bdg. 37.00 (ISBN 0-8240-4160-7). Garland Pub.
Adema. Guillaume Apollinaire. 12.95 (ISBN 0-685-37180-8). French & Eur.
Adema, ed. see Apollinaire, Guillaume.
Ademuni-Odeke. Protectionism & the Future of International Shipping: The Nature, Development & Role of Flag Discriminations & Preferences, Cargo Reservations & Sabotage Restrictions, State Intervention & Maritime Subsidies. LC 83-25055. 1984. text ed. 89.50 (ISBN 9-02-472918-1, Pub. by Martinus Nijhoff Netherlands). Kluwer Academic.
Ademuwagun, Z. A., et al, eds. African Therapeutic Systems. 1979. 35.00 (ISBN 0-918456-25-8). African Studies Assn.
Aden, et al. Electronic Countermeasures. Boyd, et al, eds. 1100p. 1978. Repr. of 1961 ed. 37.50 (ISBN 0-932146-00-7). Peninsula CA.
Aden, Carlin. Among the Drum Tuners. 1969. pap. 3.00 (ISBN 0-686-14900-9). Goliards Pr.
--The Seventh Gate. 1973. pap. 3.00 (ISBN 0-686-05617-5). Goliards Pr.
Aden, John M. Pope's Once & Future Kings: Satire & Politics in the Early Career. LC 78-16618. 1978. 18.00x (ISBN 0-87049-252-7). U of Tenn Pr.
--Something Like Horace: Studies in the Art & Allusion of Pope's Horatian Satires. LC 71-83208. 1969. 7.95x (ISBN 0-8265-1138-4). Vanderbilt U Pr.
Aden, John M., ed. Critical Opinions of John Dryden: A Dictionary. LC 63-9945. 1963. 14.95x (ISBN 0-8265-1062-0). Vanderbilt U Pr.
--The Critical Opinions of John Dryden: A Dictionary. (Vanderbilt University Press Bks.). 291p. 1967. 14.95 (ISBN 0-8265-1062-0). U of Ill Pr.
Adenaes, J., et al. Norway & the Second World War. (Tanum of Norway Tokens Ser). (Illus.). 1983. pap. 14.00x (ISBN 8-2518-1777-3, N406). Vanous.
Adeney, Carol, ed. This Morning with God. LC 68-28080. 1978. pap. 9.95 (ISBN 0-87784-870-X). Inter-Varsity.
Adeney, Miriam. God's Foreign Policy. LC 83-25343. 152p. (Orig.). 1984. pap. 6.95 (ISBN 0-8028-1968-0). Eerdmans.
Adeney, Walter D. The Books of Ezra & Nehemiah. 1980. 13.00 (ISBN 0-86524-050-7, 7004). Klock & Klock.
Adeney, Walter F. The Greek & Eastern Churches. LC 65-22087. (Library of Religious & Philosophical Thought). Repr. of 1908 ed. lib. bdg. 45.00x (ISBN 0-678-09951-0, Reference Bk Pubs). Kelley.
Adeniran, Iunde, jt. ed. see Connolly, Michael.

Adepoju, Aderanti. Selected Studies on the Dynamics, Patterns & Consequences of Migration: Medium-Sized Towns in Nigeria, Research & Policy Prospects, Vol. 4. (Reports & Papers in the Social Sciences: No. 53). 56p. 1983. pap. text ed. 6.00 (ISBN 92-3-102035-8, U1277, UNESCO). Unipub.

Ader, Emile B. Essentials of Socialism. LC 65-25683. (Orig.). (gr. 9 up). 1966. pap. text ed. 3.95 (ISBN 0-8120-0227-X). Barron.

Ader, Guillaume. Poesies De Guillaume Ader. Repr. of 1904 ed. 28.00 (ISBN 0-384-00338-9). Johnson Repr.

Ader, Robert, ed. Psychoneuroimmunology. LC 80-265. (Behavioral Medicine Ser.). 1981. 65.00 (ISBN 0-12-043780-5). Acad Pr.

Ader-Brin, Dianne, ed. see Ingebritsen, Karl J.

Adereth, Maxwell. The French Communist Party: From Comintern to 'the Colours of France': A Critical History, 1920-84. LC 84-9696. 352p. 1984. 38.50 (ISBN 0-7190-1083-7, Pub. by Manchester Univ Pr). Longwood Pub Group.

Ade-Ridder, Linda, jt. ed. see Brubaker, Timothy H.

Aderman, James. I'm Listening, Lord: Leader's Guide. Fischer, William E., ed. (Bible Class Course for Young Adults Ser.). 64p. 1984. pap. text ed. 2.95 (ISBN 0-938272-19-5). Wels Board.

--I'm Listening, Lord: Student's Guide. Fischer, William E., ed. (Bible Class Course for Young Adults Ser.). (Illus.). 48p. 1984. pap. text ed. 2.95 (ISBN 0-938272-18-7). Wels Board.

--Is He the One? Fischer, William E., ed. (Bible Class Course for Young Adults Ser.). (Illus.). 64p. (gr. 9-12). 1985. pap. 2.95 leaders guide (ISBN 0-938272-21-7); pap. 2.95 students guide (ISBN 0-938272-20-9). WELS Board.

Aderman, Ralph M., ed. The Quest for Social Justice: The Morris Franklin Memorial Lectures, 1970-1980. LC 81-50831. (Illus.). 384p. 1982. text ed. 21.50 (ISBN 0-299-08730-1). U of Wis Pr.

Aderman, Ralph M. & Kleinfield, Herbert L., eds. Letters of Washington Irving: Vol. IV, 1847-1859. (Critical Editions Program Ser.). 1982. lib. bdg. 46.95 (ISBN 0-8057-8525-6, Twayne). G K Hall.

Aderman, Ralph M., ed. see Rebreau, Liviu.

Aderman, Ralph M., et al, eds. Letters of Washington Irving: Vol. III, 1839-1846. (Critical Editions Program Ser.). 1982. lib. bdg. 52.00 (ISBN 0-8057-8524-8, Twayne). G K Hall.

Adermanm, Ralph M., et al, eds. Letters: Volume II, 1823-1838. (Critical Editions Program Ser.). 1979. 36.50 (ISBN 0-8057-8523-X, Twayne). G K Hall.

Aderton, Mimi & Liss, Douglas. The Book of Gross. (Illus.). 96p. (Orig.). 1983. pap. 3.95 (ISBN 0-8065-0838-8). Citadel Pr.

Ades, D. Dada & Surrealism. LC 77-76765. (Modern Movements in Art Ser.). 1978. pap. 2.95 (ISBN 0-8120-0877-4). Barron.

Ades, Dawn. Dali & Surrealism. LC 82-47545. (Icon Editions Ser.). (Illus.). 216p. 1982. 19.18i (ISBN 0-06-430295-4, HarpT). Har-Row.

Ades, Dawn & Forge, Andrew. Francis Bacon. (Illus.). 246p. 1985. 49.50 (ISBN 0-8109-0714-3). Abrams.

Ades, Dawn, et al. The Twentieth Century Posters. LC 83-73420. (Illus.). 224p. 1984. 45.00; pap. 24.95 (ISBN 0-89659-434-3). Abbeville Pr.

Ades, Hawley. Choral Arranging, Expanded Edition. 1983. 19.95x (ISBN 0-686-46895-3). Shawnee Pr.

Ades, Leslie J. Increasing Your Sales Potential. (Illus.). 272p. 1981. text ed. 13.41I (ISBN 0-06-040169-9, HarpC). Har-Row.

Adesanya, M. O. & Oloyede, E. O. Business Law in Nigeria. LC 77-188223. 320p. 1972. 38.50x (ISBN 0-8419-0115-5, Africana). Holmes & Meier.

Adewoye, O. The Judicial System in Southern Nigeria, 1854-1954: Law & Justice in a Dependency. (Ibadan History Ser.). 1977. text ed. 17.50x (ISBN 0-391-00735-1). Humanities.

Adewumi, Julius. The Unseen World. 1984. 6.95 (ISBN 0-533-05824-4). Vantage.

Adewunmi, Wole. Loan Management in Nigerian Banks: A Study of Efficiency. (Bangor Occasional Papers in Economics: Vol. 21). 100p. 1984. pap. text ed. 25.75x (ISBN 0-7083-0844-9, Pub. by Univ of Wales Pr England). Humanities.

Adey, Margaret, et al. Galeria Hispanica. 3rd ed. (Illus.). 1979. 26.64 (ISBN 0-07-000361-0). McGraw.

Adey, Philip, jt. auth. see Shayer, Michael.

Adey, R. A. & Brebbia, C. A. Basic Computational Techniques for Engineers. LC 83-5739. 208p. 29.50 (ISBN 0-471-88970-9, Pub. by Wiley-Interscience). Wiley.

Adey, R. A., ed. Engineering Software III: Proceedings of the Third International Conference. (Illus.). 1090p. 1983. 69.50 (ISBN 3-540-12207-9). Springer-Verlag.

--Engineering Software IV. 1200p. 1985. 118.00 (ISBN 0-318-11703-7). Springer Verlag.

Adey, Robert A., ed. Software for Engineering Problems. LC 83-81509. 130p. (Orig.). 1983. pap. 30.95x (ISBN 0-87201-832-6). Gulf Pub.

Adey, W. Ross & Lawrence, A. F., eds. Nonlinear Electrodynamics in Biological Systems. 616p. 1984. 89.50x (ISBN 0-306-41736-7, Plenum Pr). Plenum Pub.

Adey, Walter H., et al. Field Guidebook to the Reefs & Reef Communities of St. Croix, Virgin Islands. (Third International Symposium on Coral Reefs Ser.). (Illus.). 52p. 1977. pap. 5.00 (ISBN 0-932981-40-2). Univ Miami A R C.

Adgey, A. J. Acute Phase of Ischemic Heart Disease & Myocardial Infarction. 1982. text ed. 49.50 (ISBN 90-247-2675-1, Pub. by Martinus Nijhoff Netherlands). Kluwer Academic.

Adhemar, Jean. Influences Antiques dans L'Art du Moyen Age Francais: Recherches sur les Sources et les Themes d'Inspiration. (Warburg Institutes Studies: Vol. 7). Repr. of 1939 ed. 44.00 (ISBN 0-317-16471-6). Kraus Repr.

Adhemar, Jean see Porzio, Domenico, et al.

Adhemar, Jean & Cachin, Francoise, eds. Degas' Complete Graphic Work. (Illus.). 290p. (Fr.). 1983. 75.00x (ISBN 0-915346-89-3). A Wofsy Fine Arts.

Adhemar, Jean, notes by see Daumier, Honore.

Adhemar, Jean, ed. see Diderot.

Adhesive Age Magazine. The Adhesives Redbook: Adhesives Age Directory. 32.50 (ISBN 0-686-48218-2, 0501). T-C Pubns CA.

Adhikari, Gautam. Conflict & Civilization. 160p. 1980. text ed. 15.00x (ISBN 0-7069-1207-1, Pub. by Vikas India). Advent NY.

Adhikarya, Ronny & Middleton, John. Communication Planning at the Institutional Level: A Selected Annotated Bibliography. ix, 99p. (Orig.). 1979. pap. text ed. 6.00 (ISBN 0-86638-022-1). E W Center HI.

Adhvarindra, Dharmaraja. Vedanta-Paribhasa. Madhavananda, Swami, tr. (English & Sanskrit). pap. 3.25 (ISBN 0-87481-072-8). Vedanta Pr.

Adian, S. I. The Burnside Problem & Identities in Groups. Lennox, J. & Wiegold, J., trs. from Russian. (Ergebnisse der Mathematik und Ihrer Grenzgebiete: Vol. 95). 1979. 46.00 (ISBN 0-387-08728-1). Springer-Verlag.

Adian, S. T. & Higman, C. World Problems-Two. (Studies in Logic: Vol. 95). x, 578p. 1980. 93.75 (ISBN 0-444-85343-X). Elsevier.

Adiba, M., jt. auth. see Delobel, C.

Adibi, S. A., et al, eds. Branched Chain Amino & Keto Acids in Health & Disease. (Illus.). xiv, 572p. 1985. 63.50 (ISBN 3-8055-3996-7). S Karger.

Adickes, Erich. German Kantian Bibliography, 3 pts. in 1 vol. 1967. Repr. of 1896 ed. 40.50 (ISBN 0-8337-0017-0). B Franklin.

Adicks, Richard, ed. LeConte's Report on East Florida. LC 77-9286. 1978. 5.00 (ISBN 0-8130-0588-4). U Presses Fla.

Adidevananda, Swami, tr. see Srinivasadasa.

Adie, Donald W. Marinas: A Guide to Their Development & Design. 3rd ed. (Illus.). 336p. 1983. 82.50 (ISBN 0-89397-170-7). Nichols Pub.

Adie, Ian W. Oil, Politics, & Seapower: The Indian Ocean Vortex. LC 74-29073. (Strategy Paper Ser.: No. 24). 98p. 1975. 6.95x (ISBN 0-8448-0617-X). Crane-Russak Co.

Adie, R. & Poitras, G. Latin America: The Politics of Immobility. 1974. pap. 15.95 (ISBN 0-13-524272-X). P-H.

Adie, Raymond, ed. Antarctic Geology & Geophysics. (Illus.). 876p. 1973. 50.00x (ISBN 8-200-02253-6, Dist. by Columbia U Pr). Universitet.

Adiga, M. G. The Song of the Earth & Other Poems. Ramanujan, A. K., tr. from Kannada. (Writers Workshop Redbird Ser.). 1975. 8.00 (ISBN 0-88253-640-0); pap. text ed. 4.00 (ISBN 0-88253-639-7). Ind-US Inc.

Adigal, Ilango. Shilappadikaram: The Ankle Bracelet. Danielou, Alain, tr. LC 64-16823. (Orig.). 1964. 6.50 (ISBN 0-8112-0246-1); pap. 3.25 (ISBN 0-8112-0001-9, NDP162). New Directions.

Adinolfi, M., ed. Polymorphisms & Fertility. (Journal: Experimental & Clinical Immunogenetics: Vol. 2; No. 2). (Illus.). 88p. 1985. pap. 17.25 (ISBN 3-8055-4066-3). S Karger.

Adinolfi, Matteo & Giannelli, F. Paediatric Research: A Genetic Approach (Polani Festschrift) (Clinics in Developmental Ser.: No. 83). 245p. 1983. text ed. 29.75 (ISBN 0-433-00111-9). Lippincott.

Adirondack Mountain Club. Guide to the Northville-Placid Trail. LC 80-16626. (Illus.). 148p. 1980. pap. 5.00 (ISBN 0-935272-12-7). ADK Mtn Club.

Adirondack Mountain Club, Inc. Guide to Adirondack Trails: High Peaks Region. 11th ed. Burdick, Neal & Goodwin, Tony, eds. (Forest Preserve Ser.). (Illus.). 310p. 1985. pap. 10.95 (ISBN 0-935272-25-9). ADK Mtn Club.

Adi-Rubin, Margalit. Israeli Yemenite Embroidery. (Illus.). 84p. (Orig.). 1983. pap. 10.95 (ISBN 0-9611996-0-1). M A R.

Adiseshiah, Malcolm S. It Is Time to Begin: The Human Role in Development - Some Further Reflections for the Seventies. LC 72-83081. 182p. (Orig.). 1972. pap. 5.25 (ISBN 92-3-100954-0, U343, UNESCO). Unipub.

Adivar, Halide E. The Turkish Ordeal. LC 79-3081. (Illus.). 407p. 1981. Repr. of 1928 ed. 32.50 (ISBN 0-8305-0057-X). Hyperion Conn.

Adivar, Halide Edib. Turkey Faces West. LC 73-6266. (The Middle East Ser.). Repr. of 1930 ed. 21.00 (ISBN 0-405-05320-7). Ayer Co Pubs.

Adix, Vern. Theatre Scenecraft. 1957. 15.00 (ISBN 0-87602-013-9). Anchorage.

Adiyodi, K. G. & Adiyodi, R. G. Reproductive Biology of Invertebrates: Spermatogenesis & Sperm Function, Vol. 2. 692p. 1983. 94.00 (ISBN 0-471-90071-0). Wiley.

Adiyodi, K. G. & Adiyodi, Rita G. Reproductive Biology of Invertebrates, Oogenesis, Oviposition & Oosorption, Vol. 1. LC 81-16355. 770p. 1983. 117.95 (ISBN 0-471-10128-1, Pub. by Wiley-Interscience). Wiley.

Adiyodi, K. G., jt. auth. see Bell, W. J.

Adiyodi, R. G., jt. auth. see Adiyodi, K. G.

Adiyodi, Rita G., jt. auth. see Adiyodi, K. G.

Adizes, Ichak. How to Solve the Mismanagement Crisis: Diagnosis & Treatment of Management Problems. 300p. 1979. 19.95x (ISBN 0-8290-1326-1, Dist. by Irvington). Adizes Inst Inc.

Adjali, Mia. Of Life & Hope: Toward Effective Witness in Human Rights. (Orig.). 1979. pap. 2.95 (ISBN 0-377-00084-1). Friend Pr.

Adjan, S., et al. Eleven Papers on Number Theory, Algebra & Functions of a Complex Variable. LC 51-5559. (Translations, Ser.: No. 2, Vol. 46). 1965. 25.00 (ISBN 0-8218-1746-9, TRANS 2-46). Am Math.

Adjan, S. I., ed. Mathematical Logic, the Theory of Algorithms & the Theory of Sets: Dedicated to Academician Petr Sergeevic Novikov. LC 77-3359. (Proceedings of the Steklov Institute of Mathematics Ser.: No. 133). 1977. 66.00 (ISBN 0-8218-3033-3, STEKLO 133). Am Math.

Adjan, S I., ed. see Steklov Institute of Mathematics, Academy of Sciences, USSR, No. 85.

Adjare, Stephen. The Golden Insect: A Handbook on Beekeeping for Beginners. (Illus.). 104p. (Orig.). 1984. pap. 10.75x (ISBN 0-946688-60-5, Pub. by Intermediate Tech England). Intermediate Tech.

Adjaye, Joseph K. Diplomacy & Diplomats in Nineteenth Century Asante. 318p. (Orig.). 1985. pap. text ed. 14.00 (ISBN 0-8191-4303-0). U Pr of Amer.

--Diplomacy & Diplomats in Nineteenth Century Asante. 318p. 1985. lib. bdg. 23.50 (ISBN 0-8191-4302-2). U Pr of Amer.

Adjustment Administration, U.S. Department of Agriculture. Agricultural Adjustment. LC 75-27634. (World Food Supply Ser). (Illus.). 1976. Repr. of 1934 ed. 32.00x (ISBN 0-405-07776-9). Ayer Co Pubs.

Adke, S. R. & Manjunath, Shri S. An Introduction to Finite Markov Processes: Continuous Time Finite Markow Processes. 310p. 1984. 24.95x (ISBN 0-470-27457-3). Halsted Pr.

Adkins. Florida Criminal Law & Procedure. 5th ed. latest pocket part supplement 89.95_incl. (ISBN 0-686-90164-9); separate pocket part supplement, 1984 (for use in 1984) 37.95; separate pocket part supplement,1984 (for use in 1985) 37.95. Harrison Co GA.

--Florida Discovery, Civil & Criminal. 2nd ed. incl. latest pocket part supplement 60.95 (ISBN 0-686-90171-1); separate pocket part supplement, 1983 21.95 (ISBN 0-686-90172-X). Harrison Co GA.

Adkins, A. W. Poetic Craft in the Early Greek Elegists. LC 84-16203. 248p. 1985. lib. bdg. 38.00x (ISBN 0-226-00725-1). U of Chicago Pr.

Adkins, Arthur W. Merit & Responsibility: A Study in Greek Values. (Midway Reprint Ser). 396p. 1975. pap. text ed. 17.00x (ISBN 0-226-00728-6). U of Chicago Pr.

Adkins, Bruce, ed. Man & Technology: The Social & Cultural Challenge of Modern Technology. 320p. 1984. pap. text ed. 28.00x (ISBN 0-905332-30-X). Westview.

Adkins, C. J. Equilibrium Thermodynamics. 3rd ed. LC 82-23634. 1984. 39.50 (ISBN 0-521-25445-0); pap. 14.95 (ISBN 0-521-27456-7). Cambridge U Pr.

Adkins, Cecil. Orazio Vecchi's "L'Amfiparnaso". A New Edition of the Music with Historical & Analytical Essays. LC 76-15183. (Early Musical Masterworks--Critical Editions & Commentaries). (Illus.). vi, 111p. 1977. 23.00x (ISBN 0-8078-1287-0). U of NC Pr.

Adkins, Cheryl L., jt. auth. see Wells, Jane.

Adkins, Curtis P., jt. ed. see Yang, Winston L.

Adkins, Dorothy C. Test Construction: Development & Interpretation of Achievement Tests. 2nd ed. LC 73-89607. 1974. pap. 11.95 (ISBN 0-675-08845-3). Merrill.

Adkins, E. M., ed. Light Metals 1983: Proceedings, AIME Annual Meeting, Atlanta, 1983. LC 72-623660. (Illus.). 1254p. 1983. 55.00; members 32.00; student members 16.00. Metal Soc.

Adkins, Erle. Three Days to Tucson. 1981. pap. 1.95 (ISBN 0-89083-744-9). Zebra.

Adkins, H. E. Treatise on the Military Band. 1977. lib. bdg. 59.95 (ISBN 0-8490-2763-2). Gordon Pr.

Adkins, Hal. The Directory of Homebuilt Ultra Light Aircraft. (Illus.). 106p. (Orig.). 1982. pap. 10.00 (ISBN 0-910907-00-5). Haljan Pubns.

Adkins, Hazel, ed. Spinal Injury. (Clinics in Physical Therapy Ser.: Vol. 6). (Illus.). 288p. 1985. text ed. 32.00 (ISBN 0-317-27259-4). Churchill.

Adkins, J. S., jt. auth. see Bodwell, C. E.

Adkins, James C. & MacConnell, Marcia. Florida Motor Vehicle Law. LC 82-240257. (Florida Personal Injury Practice Service Ser.). Date not set. price not set. D & S Pub.

Adkins, Jan. Art & Industry of Sandcastles. (gr. k up). 1982. 7.95 (ISBN 0-8027-0336-4); pap. 4.95 (ISBN 0-8027-7205-6). Walker & Co.

--The Craft of Making Wine. LC 75-161106. (Illus.). 92p. 1984. pap. 4.95 (ISBN 0-8027-7233-1). Walker & Co.

--The Craft of Sail. LC 72-8734. (Illus.). 80p. 1973. 11.95 (ISBN 0-8027-0401-8). Walker & Co.

--The Craft of Sail: A Primer of Sailing. LC 72-87347. 64p. 1984. pap. 4.95 (ISBN 0-8027-7214-5). Walker & Co.

--Heavy Equipment. LC 80-15213. (Illus.). 32p. (gr. 1-4). 1980. 10.95 (ISBN 0-684-16641-0, ScribJ). Scribner.

--Inside: Seeing Beneath the Surface. 32p. 1984. pap. 4.95 (ISBN 0-8027-7215-3). Walker & Co.

--Letterbox: The Art & History of Letters. (Illus.). (gr. 3 up). 1981. 10.95 (ISBN 0-8027-6385-5); PLB 11.85 (ISBN 0-8027-6386-3). Walker & Co.

--Moving Heavy Things. (Illus.). (gr. 5 up). 1980. PLB 6.95 (ISBN 0-395-29206-9). HM.

--A Storm Without Rain. LC 82-20342. 192p. (gr. 7 up). 1983. 12.45i (ISBN 0-316-01084-7). Little.

--Symbols: A Silent Language. LC 78-2977. (Illus.). 64p. 1984. pap. 4.95 (ISBN 0-8027-7216-1). Walker & Co.

--Toolchest: A Primer of Woodcraft. Cuyler, Margery, ed. LC 72-81374. (Illus.). 48p. 1973. 6.95 (ISBN 0-8027-6153-4); pap. 4.95 (ISBN 0-8027-7218-8). Walker & Co.

--Wooden Ship. (Illus.). (gr. 5 up). 1978. 6.95 (ISBN 0-395-26449-9). HM.

--Workboats. (Illus.). 48p. (gr. 5 up). 1985. 12.95 (ISBN 0-684-18228-9). Scribner.

Adkins, Jan & Adkins, Jan. How a House Happens. (Illus.). 32p. (gr. 5 up). 1983. pap. 3.95 (ISBN 0-8027-7206-4). Walker & Co.

Adkins, Lesley & Adkins, Roy A. A Thesaurus of British Archaeology. LC 81-12898. (Illus.). 320p. 1982. 28.50 (ISBN 0-389-20245-2). B&N Imports.

Adkins, M. M., jt. auth. see Sanford, N. R.

Adkins, Nelson F., ed. see Paine, Thomas.

Adkins, Rose, jt. ed. see Polking, Kirk.

Adkins, Roy A., jt. auth. see Adkins, Lesley.

Adkins, W. S., jt. auth. see Winton, W. M.

Adkinson, A. Wyle & Fry, N., eds. The House of Horror: The Story of Hammer Films. LC 74-146693. 1974. 6.95 (ISBN 0-89388-163-5). Okpaku Communications.

Adkinson, Burton W. Heller Report Revisited. 1971. 15.00 (ISBN 0-942308-00-X). NFAIS.

Adkison, Ron. Hiker's Guide to California. LC 85-80604. (Illus.). 224p. (Orig.). 1986. pap. 8.95 (ISBN 0-934318-35-2). Falcon Pr MT.

Adlam, Brian H. The Book of Dorchester. 1981. 40.00x (ISBN 0-86023-141-0, Pub. by Barracuda England). State Mutual Bk.

Adlam, Diana, et al, eds. Ideology & Consciousness, No. 5. 1979. pap. text ed. 3.75x (ISBN 0-391-01189-8). Humanities.

--Ideology & Consciousness Autumn 1978, No. 4. pap. text ed. 3.75x (ISBN 0-391-01214-2). Humanities.

Adland, P. G. Growing Stock Levels & Productivity Coclusions from Thinning & Spacing Trails in Young Pinus Patula Stands in Southern Tanzania. 1978. 40.00x (ISBN 0-85074-048-7, Pub. by For Lib Comm England). State Mutual Bk.

Adlard, J. The Sports of Cruelty: Fairies, Folk-Songs, Charms & Other Country Matters in the Work of William Blake. 159p. 1972. text ed. 18.50x (ISBN 0-900821-08-6, Pub. by C Woolf UK). Humanities.

--Stenbock, Yeats & the Nineties. 113p. 1969. text ed. 21.50x (ISBN 0-317-13478-7, Pub. by C Woolf UK). Humanities.

Adlard, John, ed. Fruit of That Forbidden Tree: Restoration Poems, Songs & Jests on the Subject of Sensual Love. (Fyfield Ser.). 1980. 10.00x (ISBN 0-85635-146-6, Pub. by Carcanet New Pr England); pap. 8.00x (ISBN 0-85635-147-4). Humanities.

--John Wilmot, Earl of Rochester: The Debt to Pleasure. (The Fyfield Ser.). 136p. pap. 7.50 (ISBN 0-85635-092-3). Carcanet.

Adlard, P. G. & Richardson, K. F. Stand Density & Stem Taper in Pinus Patula: Schiede & Deppe. 1978. 30.00x (ISBN 0-85074-047-9, Pub. by For Lib Comm England). State Mutual Bk.

Adlard, P. G. & Smith, J. P. Growth & Growing Space. 1981. 30.00x (ISBN 0-85074-054-1, Pub. by For Lib Comm England). State Mutual Bk.

Adlard, P. G., et al. Wood Density Variation in Plantation-Grown Pinus Patula from the Viphya Plateau, Malawi. 1978. 40.00x (ISBN 0-85074-045-2, Pub. by For Lib Comm England). State Mutual Bk.

Adleman, Irma & Robinson, Sherman. Income Distribution Policy in Developing Countries: A Case Study of Korea. LC 76-14269. 1978. 27.50x (ISBN 0-8047-0925-4). Stanford U Pr.

Adleman, Nancy B., ed. see Wood, Elaine.

Adleman, Robert H. Sweetwater Fever. LC 83-12263. 500p. 1984. 16.95 (ISBN 0-07-000354-8). McGraw.

Adler. Corpus Rubenianum Ludwig Burchard: Landscapes I, Pt. XVIII. 1981. write for info. Wiley.

--The Itinerary of Benjamin of Tudela. Adler, Marcus N., tr. LC 68-9344. 1964. 8.95 (ISBN 0-87306-033-4). Feldheim.

Adler, Alan, ed. Science-Fiction & Horror Movies Posters in Full Color. 1977. pap. 8.95 (ISBN 0-486-23452-5). Dover.

--Theses, Resolutions & Manifestos of the First Four Congresses of the Third International. Holt, Alix & Holland, Barbara, trs. from Rus. Orig. Title: Kommunisticheskii Internatsional V Dokumentakh. 481p. 1980. 34.95 (ISBN 0-906133-12-2, Pub. by Pluto Pr); pap. 13.95 (ISBN 0-906133-13-0). Longwood Pub Group.

Adler, Alan, ed. see Weinstock, Nathan.

Adler, Alan, ed. & tr. see Weinstock, Nathan.

Adler, Alan, tr. see Guerin, Daniel.

Adler, Alan D., ed. Biological Role of Porphyrins & Related Structures. (Annals of the New York Academy of Sciences: Vol. 244). 694p. 1975. 60.00x (ISBN 0-89072-758-9). NY Acad Sci.

Adler, Alexandra. Guiding Human Misfits. new & rev. ed. LC 49-8697. Repr. of 1948 ed. 18.00 (ISBN 0-527-00590-8). Kraus Repr.

Adler, Alfred. Case of Mrs. A: The Diagnosis of a Life-Style. 2nd ed. Shulman, Bernard, ed. (Individual Psychology Pamphlets, Medical Pamphlet: No. 1). 1969. pap. 4.00x (ISBN 0-918560-00-4). A Adler Inst.

--Cooperation Between the Sexes: Writings on Women & Men, Love & Marriage, & Sexuality. abr. ed. Ansbacher, Heinz L. & Ansbacher, Rowena R., eds. 192p. 1982. pap. 3.95 (ISBN 0-393-30019-6). Norton.

--Cooperation Between the Sexes: Writings on Women, Love, Marriage & Its Disorders. LC 76-23804. 480p. 1980. Repr. of 1978 ed. 25.00 (ISBN 0-87668-443-6). Aronson.

--Education of the Individual. LC 73-90458. Repr. of 1958 ed. lib. bdg. 15.00 (ISBN 0-8371-2134-5, ADEI). Greenwood.

--Individual Psychology of Alfred Adler: A Systematic Presentation in Selections from His Writings. Ansbacher, Heinz L. & Ansbacher, Rowena R., eds. pap. 11.95xi (ISBN 0-06-131154-5, TB1154, Torch). Har-Row.

--The Neurotic Constitution. LC 74-39684. (Select Bibliographies Ser). 1972. Repr. of 1926 ed. 31.00 (ISBN 0-8369-9925-8). Ayer Co Pubs.

--The Pattern of Life. 2nd ed. LC 81-71160. pap. 10.00x (ISBN 0-918560-28-4). A Adler Inst.

--The Practice & Theory of Individual Psychology. 2nd ed. Radin, P., tr. (Quality Paperback: No. 209). 352p. 1973. pap. 4.95 (ISBN 0-8226-0209-1). Littlefield.

--Souvenirs Fresh & Rancid. LC 83-81147. 224p. 1982. 14.95 (ISBN 0-394-53218-X, GP868); pap. 5.95 (ISBN 0-394-62467-X). Grove.

--Study of Organ Inferiority & Its Psychical Compensation: Contribution to Clinical Medicine. Jeliffe, Smith E., tr. (Nervous & Mental Disease Monographs: No. 24). 19.00. Johnson Repr.

--Superiority & Social Interest: A Collection of Later Writings. 2nd. rev ed. Ansbacher, Heinz L. & Ansbacher, Rowena R., eds. 1970. 19.95 (ISBN 0-8101-0037-1). Northwestern U Pr.

--Superiority & Social Interest: A Collection of Later Writings. Ansbacher, Heinz L. & Ansbacher, Rowena R., eds. 1979. pap. 8.95 (ISBN 0-393-00910-6). Norton.

--Understanding Human Nature. 1978. pap. 2.25 (ISBN 0-449-30833-2, Prem). Fawcett.

Adler, Allan. FBI Charter Legislation Comparison: A Report Comparing the Proposed FBI Charter Act of 1979 With Attorney General Levi's Domestic Security Guidelines, the Recommendations of the Church Committee, & Other Proposals to Regulate FBI Investigative Activities. (Center for National Security Studies Reports: No. 103). 109p. 1979. 3.50 (ISBN 0-86566-011-5). Ctr Natl Security.

Adler, Allan & Halperin, Morton H., eds. Litigation under the Freedom of Information Act & Privacy Act: Nineteen Eighty-Three Edition. 8th ed. LC 82-72706. 350p. 1982. pap. 30.00 (ISBN 0-86566-025-5). Ctr Natl Security.

Adler, Allan, jt. ed. see Halperin, Morton H.

Adler, Andrew, ed. see Carey, MacDonald.

Adler, Andrew, ed. see Lanigan, Anne.

Adler, Andrew, ed. see Leibowitz, Alan.

Adler, Andrew, ed. see Sugar, Bert R.

Adler, Ann. A Family in West Germany. LC 85-6981. (Families the World over Ser.). (Illus.). 32p. (gr. 2-5). 1985. PLB 8.95 (ISBN 0-8225-1658-6). Lerner Pubns.

Adler, Anne G. & Baber, Elizabeth A. Retrospective Conversion: From Cards to Computer. LC 84-81656. (Library Hi-Tech: No. 2). 324p. 1984. 39.50 (ISBN 0-87650-177-3). Pierian.

Adler, Anne G., et al, eds. Automation in Libraries, 1978-1982: A LITA Bibliography. (Library Hi Tech Ser.: No. 1). 1983. 29.50 (ISBN 0-87650-157-9). Pierian.

Adler, Betty. H. L. M. The Mencken Bibliography, a Ten Year Supplement. 1971. 6.00 (ISBN 0-910556-02-4). Enoch Pratt.

--H.L.M. The Menchen Bibliography. LC 61-15699. pap. 97.30 (ISBN 0-317-10542-6, 2011471). Bks Demand UMI.

Adler, Betty & Hart, R.compiled by. Man of Letters: Census of H. L. Mencken's Correspondence. (Orig.). 1969. 7.00 (ISBN 0-910556-03-2). Enoch Pratt.

Adler, Bill. Bill Adler's Chance of a Lifetime. 224p. 1985. text ed. 15.50 (ISBN 0-446-51327-X). Warner Bks.

--Dear Lord. 120p. 1982. 4.95 (ISBN 0-8407-5266-0). Nelson.

--Dear Pastor. LC 80-24088. 120p. 1980. 4.95 (ISBN 0-8407-5218-0). Nelson.

--Letters from Camp. 1976. pap. 0.95 (ISBN 0-532-95431-9). Woodhill.

--The Reagan Wit. 120p. 1981. 6.95 (ISBN 0-89803-090-0). Green Hill.

--Ronnie & Nancy: A Very Special Love Story. (Illus.). 1985. 14.95 (ISBN 0-517-55845-9). Crown.

--Still More Letters from Camp. 144p. (Orig.). 1976. pap. 0.95 (ISBN 0-532-95416-5). Woodhill.

--The Wit and Wisdom of Jimmy Carter. 1977. 6.95 (ISBN 0-8065-0563-X). Citadel Pr.

Adler, Bill & Adler, Bill, Jr. The Wit & Wisdom of Wall Street. LC 83-70857. 87p. (Orig.). 1984. pap. 9.95 (ISBN 0-87094-575-0). Dow Jones-Irwin.

Adler, Bill & Chastain, Thomas. The Revenge of the Robins Family. LC 84-60791. 1928p. 1984. 10.95 (ISBN 0-688-03793-3). Morrow.

Adler, Bill & Chastin, Thomas. Who Killed the Robins Family? 192p. 1984. pap. 3.50 (ISBN 0-446-32314-4). Warner Bks.

Adler, Bill & Minear, Ralph E. The Joy of Living Salt-Free. (Illus.). 256p. 1984. 13.95 (ISBN 0-02-585060-1). Macmillan.

Adler, Bill, jt. auth. see Chaffee, Suzy.

Adler, Bill, jt. auth. see Chastain, Thomas.

Adler, Bill, jt. auth. see George, Phyllis.

Adler, Bill, jt. auth. see Minear, Ralph E.

Adler, Bill, jt. auth. see Myerson, Bess.

Adler, Bill, ed. Dear Grandma. 124p. 1985. 4.95 (ISBN 0-8407-5452-3). Nelson.

Adler, Bill, compiled by. Kids' Letters to President Reagan. LC 81-19472. (Illus.). 128p. 1982. 6.95 (ISBN 0-87131-370-7); pap. 4.95 (ISBN 0-87131-377-4). M Evans.

Adler, Bill, ed. Please Save My World: Children Speak Out Against Nuclear War. (Illus.). 80p. 1984. 8.95 (ISBN 0-87795-634-0). Arbor Hse.

--Wit & Wisdom of Bishop Fulton J. Sheen. LC 78-82959. 1969. pap. 3.50 (ISBN 0-385-02691-9, Im). Doubleday.

Adler, Bill, Jr. The Home Buyer's Guide. 1984. pap. 5.95 (ISBN 0-671-50533-5, Fireside). S&S.

Adler, C. S. Binding Ties. LC 84-15580. (Illus.). 192p. (YA) (gr. 7 up). 1985. 14.95 (ISBN 0-385-29293-7). Delacorte.

--The Cat That Was Left Behind. LC 80-28123. 160p. (gr. 3-6). 1981. 8.95 (ISBN 0-395-31020-2, Clarion). HM.

--Down by the River. (gr. 7-10). 1983. pap. text ed. 1.95 (ISBN 0-671-45288-6). Archway.

--The Evidence That Wasn't There. 192p. (gr. 5-9). 1982. 10.50 (ISBN 0-89919-117-7, Clarion). HM.

--Fly Free. LC 83-16599. 160p. (gr. 4-8). 1984. 10.95 (ISBN 0-698-20606-1, Coward). Putnam Pub Group.

--Footsteps on the Stairs. LC 81-15146. 160p. (gr. 4-6). 1982. 12.95 (ISBN 0-385-28303-2). Delacorte.

--Footsteps on the Stairs. 160p. (gr. 5-9). 1984. pap. 2.25 (ISBN 0-440-42654-5, YB). Dell.

--Get Lost, Little Brother. 144p. (gr. 4-7). 1983. 11.95 (ISBN 0-89919-154-1, Clarion). HM.

--In Our House Scott Is My Brother. LC 79-20693. 144p. (gr. 5-9). 1980. PLB 9.95 (ISBN 0-02-700140-7). Macmillan.

--The Magic of the Glits. LC 78-12149. (Illus.). 128p. (gr. 5-8). 1979. 9.95 (ISBN 0-02-700120-2). Macmillan.

--The Once in a While Hero. 112p. 1982. 8.95 (ISBN 0-698-20553-7, Coward). Putnam Pub Group.

--Roadside Valentine. LC 83-9394. 280p. (gr. 7 up). 1983. 9.95 (ISBN 0-02-700350-7). Macmillan.

--Roadside Valentine. 1984. pap. 2.25 (ISBN 0-399-21146-2). Putnam Pub Group.

--Shadows on Little Reef Bay. LC 83-15207. 180p. (gr. 6 up). 1984. PLB 10.95 (ISBN 0-89919-217-3, Clarion). HM.

--The Shell Lady's Daughter. LC 82-19801. 144p. (gr. 6 up). 1983. pap. 10.95 (ISBN 0-698-20580-4, Coward). Putnam Pub Group.

--The Shell Lady's Daughter. 144p. 1984. pap. 1.95 (ISBN 0-449-70095-X, Juniper). Fawcett.

--Shelter on Blue Barns Road. LC 80-24715. (Illus.). 144p. (gr. 5-9). 1981. 9.95 (ISBN 0-02-700280-2). Macmillan.

--Shelter on Blue Barns Road. 1982. pap. 1.75 (ISBN 0-451-11438-8, Sig Vista). NAL.

--Some Other Summer. LC 82-7161. 132p. (gr. 5-9). 1982. 9.95 (ISBN 0-02-700290-X). Macmillan.

Adler, C. S., ed. Goodbye, Pink Pig. 160p. (gr. 5-8). 1985. 12.95 (ISBN 0-399-21282-5, Putnam). Putnam Pub Group.

Adler, Chaim, jt. auth. see Inbar, Michael.

Adler, Charles S. We Are but a Moment's Sunlight: Understanding Death. 272p. 1976. pap. 1.95 (ISBN 0-671-48772-8). WSP.

Adler, Claire F. Modern Geometry. 2nd ed. 1967. text ed. 27.95 (ISBN 0-07-000421-8). McGraw.

Adler, Cy A. Ecological Fantasies: Death from Falling Watermelons. LC 73-80695. (Illus., Orig.). 1978. 24.00 (ISBN 0-914018-02-7). Green Eagle Pr.

Adler, Cyrus. I Have Considered the Days. (Illus.). 1969. 8.00x (ISBN 0-8381-3110-7). United Syn Bk.

--Jacob H. Schiff: His Life & Letters, 2 vols. LC 72-1474. (Select Bibliographies Reprint Ser.). 1929. Set. 42.00 (ISBN 0-8369-6818-2). Ayer Co Pubs.

--Jacob H. Schiff: His Life & Letters, 2 vols. Set. 250.00 (ISBN 0-8490-0431-4). Gordon Pr.

--Jacob H. Schiff: His Life & Letters, 2 Vols. 1968. Repr. of 1928 ed. Set. 39.00x (ISBN 0-403-00134-X). Scholarly.

Adler, Cyrus & Margalith, Aaron M. With Firmness in the Right: American Diplomatic Action Affecting Jews, 1840-1945. Davis, Moshe, ed. LC 77-70651. (America & the Holy Land Ser.). 1977. Repr. of 1946 ed. lib. bdg. 40.00x (ISBN 0-405-10222-4). Ayer Co Pubs.

Adler, David. All about the Moon. LC 82-17422. (Question & Answer Bks.). (Illus.). 32p. (gr. 3-6). 1983. PLB 9.59 (ISBN 0-89375-886-8); pap. text ed. 1.95 (ISBN 0-89375-887-6). Troll Assocs.

--Amazing Magnets. LC 82-17377. (Question & Answer Bks.). (Illus.). 32p. (gr. 3-6). 1983. PLB 9.59 (ISBN 0-89375-894-9); pap. text ed. 1.95 (ISBN 0-89375-895-7). Troll Assocs.

--Banks: Where the Money Is. (Money Power Bks.). (Illus.). 32p. (gr. 1-8). 1985. PLB 8.90 (ISBN 0-531-04878-0). Watts.

--Bunny Rabbit Rebus. LC 82-45574. (Illus.). 40p. (gr. 1-4). 1983. 7.64i (ISBN 0-690-04196-9); PLB 8.89g (ISBN 0-690-04197-7). Crowell Jr Bks.

--The Carsick Zebra & Other Animal Riddles. 64p. (Orig.). (gr. 1). 1985. pap. 1.95 (ISBN 0-553-15335-8). Bantam.

--The House on the Roof. LC 84-12555. (Illus.). 32p. (gr. 4). 9.95 (ISBN 0-930494-34-2); pap. 4.95 (ISBN 0-930494-28-8). Kar-Ben.

--Our Amazing Ocean. LC 82-17373. (Question & Answer Bks.). (Illus.). 32p. (gr. 3-6). 1983. PLB 9.59 (ISBN 0-89375-882-5); pap. text ed. 1.95 (ISBN 0-89375-883-3). Troll Assocs.

--Wonders of Energy. LC 82-20042. (Question & Answer Bks.). (Illus.). 32p. (gr. 3-6). 1983. PLB 9.59 (ISBN 0-89375-884-1); pap. text ed. 1.95 (ISBN 0-89375-885-X). Troll Assocs.

--World of Weather. LC 82-17398. (Question & Answer Bks.). (Illus.). 32p. (gr. 3-6). 1983. PLB 9.59 (ISBN 0-89375-870-1); pap. text ed. 1.95 (ISBN 0-89375-871-X). Troll Assocs.

Adler, David, et al, eds. Physical Properties of Amorphous Materials. 432p. 1985. 62.50x (ISBN 0-306-41907-6, Plenum Pr). Plenum Pub.

Adler, David A. All Kinds of Money. (Money Power Ser.). (Illus.). 32p. (gr. 1-4). 1984. lib. bdg. 8.60 (ISBN 0-531-04627-3). Watts.

--Bible Fun Book: Puzzles, Riddles, Magic, & More. (A Bonim Fun-to-Do Bk.). (Illus., Orig.). (gr. 1-5). 1979. pap. 3.95 (ISBN 0-88482-769-0). Hebrew Pub.

--Cam Jansen & the Mystery at the Monkey House. (Illus.). 64p. (gr. 2-5). 1985. 9.95 (ISBN 0-670-80782-6). Viking.

--Cam Jansen & the Mystery Monster Movie. LC 83-16693. (Cam Jansen Mystery Adventure Ser.). (Illus.). 64p. (gr. 2-5). 1984. 8.95 (ISBN 0-670-20035-2, Viking Kestrel). Viking.

--Cam Jansen & the Mystery of the Babe Ruth Baseball. LC 82-2621. (Cam Jansen Ser.: No. 6). (Illus.). 64p. (gr. 2-5). 1982. 8.95 (ISBN 0-670-20037-9). Viking.

--Cam Jansen & the Mystery of the Babe Ruth Baseball. (Illus.). 64p. (gr. 1-4). 1984. pap. 1.95 (ISBN 0-440-41020-7, YB). Dell.

--Cam Jansen & the Mystery of the Circus Clown. LC 82-50363. (Cam Jansen Mystery Adventure Ser.: No. 7). (Illus.). 64p. (gr. 2-4). 1983. 8.95 (ISBN 0-670-20036-0). Viking.

--Cam Jansen & the Mystery of the Circus Clown. 64p. (gr. 1-4). pap. 1.95 (ISBN 0-440-41021-5, YB). Dell.

--Cam Jansen & the Mystery of the Dinosaur Bones. LC 80-25132. (Cam Jansen Adventure Ser.). (Illus.). 64p. (gr. 2-5). 1981. 8.95 (ISBN 0-670-20040-9). Viking.

--Cam Jansen & the Mystery of the Dinosaur Bones. (No. 3). (Illus.). (gr. 1-4). 1983. pap. 1.95 (ISBN 0-440-41199-8, YB). Dell.

--Cam Jansen & the Mystery of the Gold Coins. LC 81-16158. (Cam Jansen Mystery Adventure Ser.: No. 5). (Illus.). 64p. (gr. 2-5). 1982. 8.95 (ISBN 0-670-20038-7). Viking.

--Cam Jansen & the Mystery of the Gold Coins. (Illus.). 64p. (gr. k-6). 1984. pap. 1.95 (ISBN 0-440-40996-9, YB). Dell.

--Cam Jansen & the Mystery of the Stolen Diamonds. LC 79-20695. (Cam Jansen Adventures Ser.). (Illus.). 64p. (gr. 2-5). 1980. 9.95 (ISBN 0-670-20039-5, Viking Kestrel). Viking.

--Cam Jansen & the Mystery of the Stolen Diamonds. (Illus.). (gr. 1-4). 1982. pap. 1.95 (ISBN 0-440-41111-4, YB). Dell.

--Cam Jansen & the Mystery of the Television Dog. LC 81-2207. (Illus.). 64p. (gr. 2-5). 1981. 7.95 (ISBN 0-670-20042-5). Viking.

--Cam Jansen & the Mystery of the Television Dog. (Illus.). 64p. (gr. 1-4). 1983. pap. 1.95 (ISBN 0-440-41196-3, YB). Dell.

--Cam Jansen & the Mystery of the U. F. O. (Illus.). (gr. 1-4). 1982. pap. 1.95 (ISBN 0-440-41142-4, YB). Dell.

--Cam Jansen & the Mystery of the U.F.O. LC 80-15580. (Cam Jansen Ser.). (Illus.). 64p. (gr. 7-10). 1980. 8.95 (ISBN 0-670-20041-7). Viking.

--The Carsick Zebra & Other Animal Riddles. LC 82-48750. (Illus.). 64p. (gr. 1-4). 1983. reinforced binding 8.95 (ISBN 0-8234-0479-X). Holiday.

--Eaton Stanley & the Mind Control Experiment. (Eaton Stanley Adventure Ser.). (Illus.). (gr. 2-6). 1985. 10.95 (ISBN 0-525-44117-4, 01063-320). Dutton.

--Eaton Stanley & the Mind Control Experiment. LC 84-21135. (Eaton Stanley Adventure Ser.). (Illus.). 96p. (gr. 2-6). 1985. 9.95 (ISBN 0-525-44117-4, 0966-290). Dutton.

--Finger Spelling Fun. LC 80-11411. (gr. 1-3). 1980. PLB 8.90 (ISBN 0-531-04140-9). Watts.

--The Fourth Floor Twins & the Fish Snitch Mystery. LC 84-25713. (The Fourth Floor Twins Ser.). 64p. 1985. 9.95 (ISBN 0-670-80087-2). Viking.

--Fourth Floor Twins & the Fortune Cookie Chase. LC 84-21924. 64p. 1985. 9.95 (ISBN 0-670-80641-2). Viking.

--Hanukkah Fun Book: Puzzles, Riddles, Magic & More. LC 76-47459. (Illus.). (gr. 3-7). 1976. pap. 3.95 (ISBN 0-88482-754-2, Bonim Bks). Hebrew Pub.

--Hanukkah Game Book: Games, Riddles, Puzzles & More. (Fun-to-Do Bk). (Illus.). (gr. 1-5). 1978. pap. 3.95 (ISBN 0-88482-764-X, Bonim Bks). Hebrew Pub.

--Hyperspace! Facts & Fun from All Over the Universe. LC 81-70404. (Illus.). 80p. (gr. 3-7). 1982. 10.95 (ISBN 0-670-38908-0); pap. 4.95 (ISBN 0-670-05117-9). Viking.

--Inflation: When Prices Go up, up, up. (Money Power Bks.). 32p. (gr. 1-6). 1985. PLB 8.90 (ISBN 0-531-04899-3). Watts.

--Jeffrey's Ghost & the Fifth Grade Dragon. LC 85-886. (Illus.). 64p. (gr. 2-5). 1985. 9.95 (ISBN 0-03-069281-4). HR&W.

--My Dog & the Key Mystery. LC 82-2790. (Easy-Read Storybook Ser.). (Illus.). (gr. k-3). 1982. 3.95 (ISBN 0-531-03555-7); PLB 8.60 (ISBN 0-531-04449-1). Watts.

--My Dog & the Knock Knock Mystery. LC 84-19213. (Illus.). 32p. (gr. 1-4). 1985. reinforced bdg. 11.95 (ISBN 0-8234-0551-6). Holiday.

--Our Golda: The Story of Golda Meir. LC 83-16798. (Illus.). 64p. (gr. 3-7). 1984. 10.95 (ISBN 0-670-53107-3, Viking Kestrel). Viking.

--Passover Fun Book: Puzzles, Riddles, Magic & More. (Bonim Fun-to-Do Bk.). (Illus.). (gr. k-5). 1978. saddlewire bdg. 3.95 (ISBN 0-88482-759-3, Bonim Bks). Hebrew Pub.

--A Picture Book of Hanukkah. LC 82-2942. (Illus.). 32p. (ps-3). 1982. reinforced bdg. 10.95 (ISBN 0-8234-0458-7). Holiday.

--A Picture Book of Hanukkah. LC 82-2942. (Illus.). (gr. k-3). 1985. pap. 5.95 (ISBN 0-8234-0574-5). Holiday.

--A Picture Book of Israel. LC 83-18613. (Illus.). 40p. (ps-3). 1984. reinforced bdg. 10.95 (ISBN 0-8234-0513-3). Holiday.

--A Picture Book of Jewish Holidays. LC 81-2765. (Illus.). 32p. (gr. k-3). 1981. reinforced bdg. 10.95 (ISBN 0-8234-0396-3). Holiday.

--A Picture Book of Passover. LC 81-6983. (Illus.). 32p. (ps-3). 1982. reinforced bdg. 10.95 (ISBN 0-8234-0439-0). Holiday.

--Prices Go Up... Prices Go Down. (Money Power Ser.). (Illus.). 32p. 1984. lib. bdg. 8.60 (ISBN 0-531-04628-1). Watts.

--Redwoods Are the Tallest Trees in the World. LC 77-4713. (A Let's-Read-and-Find-Out Science Bk). (Illus.). (gr. k-3). 1978. PLB 11.89 (ISBN 0-690-01368-X). Crowell Jr Bks.

--Roman Numerals. LC 77-2270. (Young Math Ser.). (Illus.). (gr. 1-4). 1977. PLB 11.89 (ISBN 0-690-01302-7). Crowell Jr Bks.

--Three-D, Two-D, One-D. LC 74-5156. (Young Math Ser.). (Illus.). 40p. (gr. k-3). 1974. 10.53i (ISBN 0-690-00456-7); 11.89plb. (ISBN 0-690-00543-1). Crowell Jr Bks.

--The Twisted Witch & Other Spooky Riddles. LC 85-909. (Illus.). 64p. (gr. 1-4). 1985. reinforced 8.95 (ISBN 0-8234-0571-0). Holiday.

Adler, Denise. Five Women. 1980. pap. 2.50 (ISBN 0-8423-0874-1). Tyndale.

--Jonah Bible Study. 1980. pap. 1.95 (ISBN 0-8423-1948-4). Tyndale.

Adler, Denise R. Jesus, the Man Who Changes Lives. 1982. pap. 2.50 (ISBN 0-8423-1872-0). Tyndale.

Adler, Dennis. Dennis Adler's High Country Prints Book. (Illus.). 1977. pap. 3.95 (ISBN 0-918688-01-9). Touchstone Pr Ore.

Adler, Diane & Shoemaker, Norma J., eds. AACN Organization & Management of Critical Care Facilities. LC 78-31498. (Illus.). 1979. text ed. 18.95 (ISBN 0-8016-0130-4). Mosby.

Adler, Doris R. Thomas Dekker: A Reference Guide. 330p. 1983. lib. bdg. 52.00 (ISBN 0-8161-8384-8, Hall Reference). G K Hall.

Adler, Dorothy R. British Investment in American Railways 1834-1898. Hidy, Muriel E., ed. LC 79-122437. 1970. 20.00 (ISBN 0-8139-0311-4). U Pr of Va.

Adler, Elizabeth & Adler, Richard. Needlepoint: A New Look. (Illus.). 176p. (Orig.). 1983. pap. 12.95 (ISBN 0-283-98936-X, Pub. by Sidgwick & Jackson). Merrimack Pub Cir.

Adler, Elizabeth, jt. auth. see Adler, Richard.

Adler, Emanuel, jt. ed. see Hanusch, Ferdinand.

Adler, Eve. Catullan Self-Revelation. Connor, W. R., ed. LC 80-2638. (Monographs in Classical Studies). (Illus.). 1981. lib. bdg. 24.00 (ISBN 0-405-14026-6). Ayer Co Pubs.

Adler, F. & Mueller, G. O., eds. Politics, Crime & the International Scene: An Inter-American Focus. x, 403p. 1972. pap. 6.00x (ISBN 0-8377-0203-8). Rothman.

Adler, F. W., jt. auth. see Hufbauer, G.

Adler, Felix. The Reconstruction of the Spiritual Ideal. LC 77-27148. (Hibbert Lectures: 1923). Repr. of 1924 ed. 20.00 (ISBN 0-404-60422-6). AMS Pr.

Adler, France-Michele. Sportsfashion. 192p. 1980. pap. 7.95 (ISBN 0-380-76075-4, 76075-4). Avon.

Adler, Franx, et al. The Home of the Learned Man: A Symposium on the Immigrant Scholar in America. Kosa, John, ed. LC 68-22380. 1968. 10.95x (ISBN 0-8084-0160-2). New Coll U Pr.

Adler, Freda. The Incidence of Female Criminality in the Contemporary World. 352p. 1981. 42.50x (ISBN 0-8147-0576-6); pap. 15.00 (ISBN 0-8147-0577-4). NYU Pr.

--Nations Not Obsessed with Crime. (Publications of the Comparative Criminal Law Project, Wayne State University Law School: Vol. 15). xxi, 204p. 1983. 27.50x (ISBN 0-8377-0216-X). Rothman.

--Nations Not Obsessed with Crime. (Wayne State University Law School Comparative Criminal Law Project Publicattion Ser.). 27.50 (ISBN 0-317-31426-2). Rothman.

--Sisters in Crime. 287p. 1985. pap. text ed. 8.95x (ISBN 0-88133-145-7). Waveland Pr.

Adler, Freda & Simon, Rita J. The Criminology of Deviant Women. LC 78-69555. (Illus.). 1979. pap. text ed. 16.50 (ISBN 0-395-26719-6). HM.

Adler, Freda, jt. auth. see Mueller, Gerhard.

Adler, G., ed. Molecular Crystals & Liquid Crystals Special Topics: Proceedings of the Fifth International Symposium on Organic Solid State Chemistry, Brandeis University, June 1978, 2 pts. 632p. 1979. 531.50 (ISBN 0-677-40265-1). Gordon.

Adler, G., ed. see Jung, Carl G.

Adler, Gehard, et al, eds. The Collected Works of C. G. Jung: The Psychogenesis of Mental Disease, No. 3. Hull, R. F., tr. (Bollingen Ser.: No. 20). 1960. pap. 35.00 (ISBN 0-691-09769-0). Princeton U Pr.

--The Collected Works of C. G. Jung: Two Essays on Analytical Psychology, No. 7. 2nd ed. Hull, R. F., tr. (Bollingen Ser.: No. 20). 1966. 28.00 (ISBN 0-691-09776-3); pap. 8.95 (ISBN 0-691-01782-4). Princeton U Pr.

Adler, George, ed. Organic Solid State Chemistry. 526p. 1969. 130.75 (ISBN 0-677-13200-X). Gordon.

Adler, George L., jt. ed. see Nanda, Ravinder.

Adler, Gerald. Borderline Psychopathology & Its Treatment. LC 84-24171. 272p. 1985. 25.00 (ISBN 0-87668-739-7). Aronson.

Adler, Gerald & Meyerson, Paul G. Confrontation in Psychotherapy. LC 84-45065. 392p. 1973. 30.00x (ISBN 0-87668-670-6). Aronson.

Adler, Gerard, et al, eds. The Collected Works of C. G. Jung: Aion - Researches into the Phenomenology of the Self, No. 9, Pt. II. 2nd ed. Hull, R. F., tr. (Bollingen Ser.: No. 20). 1968. 33.00 (ISBN 0-691-09759-3). Princeton U Pr.

--The Collected Works of C. G. Jung: Alchemical Studies, No. 13. Hull, R. F., tr. (Bollingen Ser.: No. 20). 1968. 37.50 (ISBN 0-691-09760-7). Princeton U Pr.

--The Collected Works of C. G. Jung: Bibliography of Jung's Writings, No.19. Hull, R. F., tr. (Bollingen Ser.: No. 20). 1978. 38.50 (ISBN 0-691-09893-X). Princeton U Pr.

--The Collected Works of C. G. Jung: Civilization in Transition, No. 10. 2nd ed. Hull, R. F., tr. (Bollingen Ser.: No. 20). 1970. 42.00 (ISBN 0-691-09762-3). Princeton U Pr.

--The Collected Works of C. G. Jung: Mysterium Coniunctionis, No. 14. 2nd ed. Hull, R. F., tr. (Bollingen Ser.: No. 20). 1970. 40.00 (ISBN 0-691-09766-6). Princeton U Pr.

--The Collected Works of C. G. Jung: Psychology & Alchemy, No. 12. 2nd ed. Hull, R. F., tr. (Bolingen Ser.: No. 20). 1968. 45.00 (ISBN 0-691-09771-2). Princeton U Pr.

--The Collected Works of C. G. Jung: Psychology & Religion - West & East, No. 11. 2nd ed. Hull, R. F., tr. (Bollingen Ser.: No. 20). 1969. 43.00 (ISBN 0-691-09772-0). Princeton U Pr.

--The Collected Works of C. G. Jung: Psychological Types, No. 6. Hull, R. F., tr. (Bollingen Ser.: No. 20). 1971. 50.00 (ISBN 0-691-09770-4); pap. 12.95 (ISBN 0-691-01813-8). Princeton U Pr.

--The Collected Works of C. G. Jung: Symbols of Transformation, No. 5. 2nd ed. Hull, R. F., tr. (Bollingen Ser.: No. 20). 1967. 45.00 (ISBN 0-691-09775-5). Princeton U Pr.

--The Collected Works of C. G. Jung: The Development of Personality, No. 17. Hull, R. F., tr. (Bollingen Ser.: No. 20). 1954. 26.50 (ISBN 0-691-09763-1). Princeton U Pr.

--The Collected Works of C. G. Jung: The Practice of Psychotherapy, No. 16. 2nd ed. Hull, R. F., tr. (Bollingen Ser.: No. 20). 1966. 37.50 (ISBN 0-691-09767-4). Princeton U Pr.

--The Collected Works of C. G. Jung: The Structure & Dynamics of the Psyche, No. 8. 2nd ed. Hull, R. F., tr. (Bollingen Ser.: No. 20). 1968. 42.00 (ISBN 0-691-09774-7). Princeton U Pr.

--The Collected Works of C. G. Jung: The Symbolic Life, No. 18. Hull, R. F., tr. (Bollingen Ser.: No. 20). 1976. 50.00 (ISBN 0-691-09892-1). Princeton U Pr.

Adler, Gerhard. Living Symbol. (Bollingen Series, No. 63). (Illus.). 1961. 37.50 (ISBN 0-691-09783-6). Princeton U Pr.

--Studies in Analytical Psychology. LC 67-10652. (Illus.). 1967. 9.00 (ISBN 0-913430-14-5). C G Jung Foun.

--Studies in Analytical Psychology. LC 68-28585. (Illus.). 1968. Repr. of 1948 ed. lib. bdg. 24.75x (ISBN 0-8371-0001-1, ADAP). Greenwood.

Adler, Gerhard & Jaffe, Aniela, eds. Selected Letters of C. G. Jung, Nineteen Nine to Nineteen Sixty-One. 256p. 1984. 22.50 (ISBN 0-691-09955-3); pap. 7.95 (ISBN 0-691-01860-X). Princeton U Pr.

Adler, Gerhard, ed. see International Congress for Analytical Psychology, 5th.

Adler, Gerhard, ed. see Jung, Carl G.

Adler, Gerhard, et al, eds. The Collected Works of C. G. Jung: Experimental Researches, No. 2. Hull, R. F., tr. (Bollingen Ser.: No. 20). 1973. 42.00 (ISBN 0-691-09764-X). Princeton U Pr.

--The Collected Works of C. G. Jung: General Index, No. 20. Hull, R. F. C., tr. (Bollingen Ser.: No. 20). 1978. 42.50x (ISBN 0-691-09867-0). Princeton U Pr.

--The Collected Works of C. G. Jung: Psychiatric Studies, No. 1. 2nd ed. Hull, R. F. C., tr. (Bollingen Ser.: No. 20). 1970. 35.00 (ISBN 0-691-09768-2); pap. 8.95 (ISBN 0-691-01855-3). Princeton U Pr.

--The Collected Works of C. G. Jung: The Archetypes & the Collective Unconscious, No. 9, Pt. I. 2nd ed. Hull, R. F., tr. (Bollingen Ser.: No. 20). 1968. 35.00 (ISBN 0-691-09761-5); pap. 14.95. Princeton U Pr.

--The Collected Works of C. G. Jung: The Spirit in Man, Art, & Literature, No. 15. Hull, R. F., tr. (Bollingen Ser.: No. 20). 1966. 21.00 (ISBN 0-691-09773-9); pap. 6.95x. Princeton U Pr.

Adler, Gerhard, et al, eds. see Jung, C. G.

Adler, H. I., jt. ed. see Lett, J. T.

Adler, Hans A. Sector & Project Planning in Transportation. LC 67-28574. (World Bank Staff Occasional Papers Ser.: No. 4). 96p. 1967. pap. 5.00x (ISBN 0-8018-0009-9). Johns Hopkins.

Adler, Helmut E., jt. ed. see Pastore, Nicholas.

Adler, Hermann. Anglo-Jewish Memories. 59.95 (ISBN 0-87968-636-7). Gordon Pr.

Adler, Howard. Commodore 64 & VIC-20 Computer Programs for Beginners. 96p. 1983. 8.95 (ISBN 0-86668-033-0). ARCsoft.

--One Hundred One Programming Tips & Tricks for the VIC-20 & Commodore 64. 128p. 1983. 8.95 (ISBN 0-86668-030-6). ARCsoft.

--Thirty-Four VIC-20 Computer Programs for Home, School & Office. 96p. 1983. 8.95 (ISBN 0-86668-029-2). Arcsoft.

--VIC-20 & Commodore 64 Computer Program Writing Workbook. 96p. 1983. 4.95 (ISBN 0-86668-811-0). ARCsoft.

Adler, Howard, jt. ed. see Lett, John T.

Adler, I. & Trombka, J. I. Geochemical Exploration of the Moon & the Planets. LC 78-127039. (Physics & Chemistry in Space Ser.: Vol. 3). (Illus.). 230p. 1970. 38.00 (ISBN 0-387-05228-3). Springer-Verlag.

Adler, Irene. Ballooning: High & Wild. LC 75-23406. (Illus.). 32p. (gr. 5-10). 1976. PLB 9.79 (ISBN 0-89375-001-8); pap. 2.50 (ISBN 0-89375-017-4). Troll Assocs.

Adler, Irving. Atomic Energy. LC 75-132946. (Illus.). (gr. 3-6). 1971. PLB 10.89 (ISBN 0-381-99613-1, AO6100, JD-J). Har-Row.

--The Environment. LC 75-35526. (Reason Why Ser.). (Illus.). 1976. PLB 10.89 (ISBN 0-381-99617-4, JD-J). Har-Row.

--Fire in Your Life. LC 55-9930. (Illus.). (YA) (gr. 5-9). 1955. PLB 10.89 (ISBN 0-381-99991-2, A27060, JD-J). Har-Row.

--Food. LC 76-54783. (The Reason Why Ser.). (Illus.). (gr. 2-5). 1977. PLB 10.98 (ISBN 0-381-90051-7, JD-J). Har-Row.

--Hot & Cold. rev. ed. LC 74-9357. (Illus.). 1975. PLB 10.89 (ISBN 0-381-99990-4, A34461, JD-J). Har-Row.

--How Life Began. rev. ed. LC 76-16161. (Illus.). (gr. 7 up). 1977. 11.06i (ISBN 0-381-99603-4, JD-J). Har-Row.

--The Impossible in Mathematics. LC 77-33757. (Illus.). 32p. 1957. pap. 2.50 (ISBN 0-87353-062-4). NCTM.

--Readings in Mathematics. 188p. 1972. pap. 5.60 (ISBN 0-663-24123-5). NCTM.

--The Stars: Decoding Their Messages. rev. ed. LC 77-27665. (Illus.). 128p. (gr. 5-12). 1980. 9.57i (ISBN 0-690-03993-X); PLB 11.89 (ISBN 0-690-03994-8). Crowell Jr Bks.

--Sun & Its Family. rev. ed. LC 68-57377. (Illus.). (gr. 5-9). 1969. PLB 10.89 (ISBN 0-381-99983-1, A76000, JD-J). Har-Row.

Adler, Irving & Adler, Ruth. Houses. LC 64-20708. (Reason Why Ser). (Illus.). (gr. 3-6). 1965. PLB 10.89 (ISBN 0-381-99967-X, A35060, JD-J). Har-Row.

--Insects & Plants. LC 62-19714. (Reason Why Ser). (Illus.). (gr. 3-6). 1962. PLB 10.89 (ISBN 0-381-99966-1, A38660, JD-J). Har-Row.

--Taste, Touch & Smell. LC 66-11448. (Reason Why Ser). (Illus.). (gr. 3-6). 1966. PLB 11.89 (ISBN 0-381-99953-X, A76400, JD-J). Har-Row.

Adler, Isidore. X-Ray Emission Spectrography in Geology. (Methods in Geochemistry & Geophysics: Vol. 4). xii, 258p. 1966. 68.00 (ISBN 0-444-40004-4). Elsevier.

Adler, Israel & Bayer, B. Yuval. (Studies of the Jewish Music Research Centre: Vol. IV). 266p. 1982. text ed. 42.50x (Pub. by Magnes Israel). Humanities.

Adler, J. A. Elsevier's Dictionary of Criminal Science. xv, 1460p. (Eng., Fr., Span., Ital., Port., Dutch, Swedish, & Ger., Polyglot). 1960. 149.00 (ISBN 0-444-40003-6). Elsevier.

Adler, Jack. A Consumer's Guide to Travel. LC 82-22195. 224p. (Orig.). 1983. pap. 8.95 (ISBN 0-88496-194-X). Capra Pr.

--Fundamentals of Group Child Care: A Textbook & Instructional Guide for Child Care Workers. LC 81-3597. 357p. 1981. text ed. 29.95x (ISBN 0-88410-198-3). Ballinger Pub.

Adler, Jacob. Laugh, Jew, Laugh. facs. ed. London, Abraham, tr. LC 77-116925. (Short Story Index Reprint Ser). 1936. 17.00 (ISBN 0-8369-3427-X). Ayer Co Pubs.

Adler, Jacob & Barrett, Gwynn W. The Diaries of Walter Murray Gibson, 1886-1887. LC 75-188977. (Illus.). 200p. 1973. 14.00x (ISBN 0-8248-0211-X). UH Pr.

Adler, Jacob, ed. see Liholiho, Alexander.

Adler, Jacob H. Reach of Art: A Study in the Prosody of Pope. LC 64-63900. (University of Florida Humanities Monographs: No. 16). 1964. pap. 4.00 (ISBN 0-8130-0002-5). U Presses Fla.

Adler, James R., jt. auth. see Delaney, Patrick R.

Adler, Jane W. Simple Justice: How Litigants Fare in the Pittsburgh Court Arbitration Program. LC 83-16016. 152p. 1983. 15.00 (ISBN 0-8330-0518-9). Rand Corp.

Adler, Jeremy. The Wedding & Other Marriages. LC 79-57082. 1980. pap. 8.00 (ISBN 0-940580-13-6). Green River.

Adler, Joseph & Doherty, Robert E., eds. Employment Security in the Public Sector: A Symposium. 68p. 1974. pap. 2.00 (ISBN 0-87546-204-9). ILR Pr.

Adler, Joshua. Philosophy of Judaism. 3.00 (ISBN 0-8022-0008-7). Philos Lib.

Adler, Joyce S. War in Melville's Imagination. (The Gotham Library). 208p. 1981. 27.00x (ISBN 0-8147-0574-X); pap. 13.50x (ISBN 0-8147-0575-8). NYU Pr.

Adler, Judith. Artists in Office. LC 78-55941. 350p. 1979. 16.95 (ISBN 0-87855-281-2). Transaction Bks.

Adler, K. The Art of Accompanying & Coaching. LC 79-147128. (Music Reprint Ser.). 260p. 1971. lib. bdg. 32.50 (ISBN 0-306-70360-2); pap. 7.95 (ISBN 0-306-80027-6). Da Capo.

Adler, Kief. Beyond the Staff of Life: A Wheatless, Dairyless Cookbook. LC 76-43076. 80p. (Orig.). 1976. 10.95 (ISBN 0-87961-076-X); pap. 4.95 (ISBN 0-87961-075-1). Naturegraph.

Adler, Kraig & Dennis, David M. New Tree Frogs of the Genus Hyla from the Cloud Forests of Western Guerrero, Mexico. (Occasional Papers: No. 7). 19p. 1972. pap. 2.25 (ISBN 0-686-79834-1). U of KS Mus Nat Hist.

Adler, Kurt. Phonetics & Diction in Singing: Italian, French, Spanish, German. LC 67-25073. (Illus., Orig.). 1967. pap. 7.95x (ISBN 0-8166-0446-0). U of Minn Pr.

Adler, L. Ludwig Wittgenstein: eine existenzielle Deutung. 1976. 17.25 (ISBN 3-8055-2390-4). S Karger.

Adler, L. W. & Castberg, C. Reading Hebrew. 1972. pap. 3.95x (ISBN 0-87441-042-8). Behrman.

Adler, Larry. Heroes of Soccer. LC 80-10209. (Illus.). 96p. (gr. 4-6). 1980. PLB 8.29 (ISBN 0-671-33095-0). Messner.

--Man with a Mission: Pele. LC 76-11007. (Sports Profiles Ser.). (Illus.). 48p. (gr. 4-11). 1976. PLB 13.31 (ISBN 0-8172-0142-4). Raintree Pubs.

Adler, Laszlo, jt. auth. see Fitting, Dale.

Adler, Laurie N., jt. auth. see Ensign, Marie.

Adler, Laurie N., jt. ed. see Ensign, Marie S.

Adler, Laurie N., jt. ed. see Evans, Donald D.

Adler, Lee & Mayer, Charles S. Managing the Marketing Research Function. LC 76-46447. (Monograph Ser.: No. 5). 1977. 11.00 (ISBN 0-87757-082-5). Am Mktg.

--Readings in Managing the Marketing Research Function. LC 80-11092. 1980. pap. 22.00 (ISBN 0-87757-136-8). Am Mktg.

Adler, Lenore L. This Is the Dachshund. 3rd ed. 1966. 12.95 (ISBN 0-87666-278-5, PS-637). TFH Pubns.

Adler, Leonore L. Cross-Cultural Research at Issue. 1982. 44.00 (ISBN 0-12-044280-9). Acad Pr.

Adler, Leonore L., ed. Issues in Cross-Cultural Research. (Annals of the New York Academy of Sciences: Vol. 285). 1977. 22.00x (ISBN 0-89072-031-2). NY Acad Sci.

Adler, Lucile. The Society of Anna. LC 73-92471. 1974. 12.95 (ISBN 0-89016-001-5); pap. 4.95 (ISBN 0-89016-023-6). Lightning Tree.

Adler, M. N., tr. see Signer, Michael A.

Adler, M. S. & Temple, V. A. Semiconductor Avalanche Breakdown Design Manual. 60p. 1979. 165.00x (ISBN 0-931690-10-2). Genium Pub.

Adler, M. W., et al, eds. Factors Affecting the Action of Narcotics. LC 78-2999. (Monographs of the Mario Negri Institute for Pharmacological Research). 796p. 1978. 70.50 (ISBN 0-89004-272-1). Raven.

Adler, Manfred. A Parent's Manual: Answers to Questions on Child Development & Child Rearing. 124p. 1971. 10.50x (ISBN 0-398-00010-7). C C Thomas.

Adler, Marcus N., tr. see Adler.

Adler, Margot. Drawing Down the Moon: Witches, Druids, Goddess-Worshippers & Other Pagans in America Today. LC 79-12023. (Illus.). 470p. 1981. pap. 10.95 (ISBN 0-8070-3237-9, BP 616). Beacon Pr.

Adler, Marvin S. & McCarroll, Jesse C. Elementary Teachers' Music Almanack: Timely Lesson Plans for Every Day of the School Year. (Illus.). 1978. 15.50x (ISBN 0-13-260836-7, Parker). P-H.

--Making Music Fun: A Complete Collection of Games, Puzzles & Activities for the Elementary Classroom. LC 81-9474. 248p. 1981. 16.50x (ISBN 0-13-547455-8, Parker). P-H.

Adler, Max K. Collective & Individual Bilingualism: A Sociolinguistic Study. 184p. (Orig.). 1977. pap. text ed. 14.00x (ISBN 3-87118-281-8, Pub. by Helmut Buske Verlag Hamburg). Benjamins North Am.

--Marxist Linguistic Theory & Community Practice: A Sociolinguistic Study. 232p. (Orig.). 1980. pap. text ed. 17.00x (ISBN 3-87118-419-5, Pub. by Helmut Buske Verlag Hamburg). Benjamins North Am.

--Naming & Addressing: A Sociolinguistic Study. 283p. 1978. lib. bdg. 20.00x (ISBN 3-87118-332-6, Pub. by Helmut Buske Verlag Hamburg). Benjamins North Am.

--Non-Vocal Language & Language Substitutes: A Sociolinguistic Study. 206p. (Orig.). 1979. pap. text ed. 14.00x (ISBN 3-87118-337-7, Pub. by Helmut Buske Verlag Hamburg). Benjamins North Am.

--Pidgins, Creoles & Lingua Franca: A Sociolinguistic Study. 146p. (Orig.). 1977. pap. text ed. 10.00x (ISBN 3-87118-282-6, Pub. by Helmut Buske Verlag Hamburg). Benjamins North Am.

--Sex Differences in Human Speech: A Sociolinguistic Study. 151p. 1978. lib. bdg. 14.00x (ISBN 3-87118-331-8, Pub. by Helmut Buske Verlag Hamburg). Benjamins North Am.

--Welsh & Other Dying Languages in Europe: A Sociolinguistic Study. 113p. (Orig.). 1977. pap. text ed. 10.00x (ISBN 3-87118-283-4, Pub. by Helmut Buske Verlag Hamburg). Benjamins North Am.

Adler, Melvin J. A Pragmatic Logic for Commands. (Pragmatics & Beyond Ser.: No.3). viii, 131p. 1980. pap. 16.00 (ISBN 90-272-2501-X). Benjamins North Am.

Adler, Michael & Asquith, Stewart, eds. Discretion & Welfare. (Studies in Social Policy & Welfare). 269p. 1981. text ed. 30.00x (ISBN 0-435-82009-5). Gower Pub Co.

Adler, Michael W. ABC of Sexually Transmitted Diseases. 1984. 10.50 (ISBN 0-7279-0121-4, Pub. by British Med Assoc Uk). Taylor & Francis.

Adler, Michele. Astrology & Your Future. 1977. pap. 1.95 (ISBN 0-89596-202-0, Argent Bks). Merit Pubns.

Adler, Morris. Voice Still Speaks. Chinitz, Jacob, ed. LC 68-57433. 1969. pap. text ed. 15.00x (ISBN 0-8197-0052-5). Bloch.

--The World of the Talmud. 2nd ed. LC 63-18390. 1963. pap. 4.95 (ISBN 0-8052-0058-4). Schocken.

Adler, Mortimer. Some Questions About Language. LC 75-1221. 203p. 1976. 19.95 (ISBN 0-87548-320-8). Open Court.

Adler, Mortimer, ed. Annals of America: Fourteen Ninety-Three to Nineteen Seventy-Three, 23 vols. (Illus.). (YA) (gr. 10 up). 1976. Set. 459.00 (ISBN 0-87827-199-6). Ency Brit Ed.

Adler, Mortimer, jt. ed. see Hutchins, Robert M.

Adler, Mortimer J. The Angels & Us. 205p. 1982. 11.95 (ISBN 0-02-500550-2). Macmillan.

--Aristotle for Everbody. 208p. 1980. pap. 3.95 (ISBN 0-553-24037-4). Bantam.

--Aristotle for Everyone: Difficult Thought Made Easy. 1978. 11.95 (ISBN 0-02-503100-7). Macmillan.

--Art & Prudence. Jowett, Garth S., ed. LC 77-11371. (Aspects of Film Ser.). 1978. Repr. of 1937 ed. lib. bdg. 59.50x (ISBN 0-405-11126-6). Ayer Co Pubs.

--Freedom: A Study of the Development of the Concept in the English & American Traditions of Philosophy. (Overview Studies). (Orig.). 1968. pap. 0.50x (ISBN 0-87343-007-7). Magi Bks.

--How to Speak How to Listen. Lippman, B., ed. 288p. 1985. pap. 7.95 (ISBN 0-02-079590-4, Collier). Macmillan.

--How to Speak-How to Listen: A Guide to Pleasurable & Profitable Conversation. (Illus.). 288p. 1983. 12.95 (ISBN 0-02-500570-7). Macmillan.

--How to Think About God: A Guide for the Twentieth-Century Pagan. 1980. 10.95 (ISBN 0-02-500540-5). Macmillan.

--Paideia Problems & Possibilities. 96p. 1983. 7.95 (ISBN 0-02-500220-1); pap. 3.95 (ISBN 0-02-013050-3). Macmillan.

--The Paideia Program: An Educational Syllabus. 160p. 1984. 8.95 (ISBN 0-02-500300-3); pap. 4.95 (ISBN 0-02-013040-6). Macmillan.

--The Paideia Proposal. 85p. 1982. 6.95 (ISBN 0-02-500240-6); pap. 2.95 (ISBN 0-02-064100-1). Macmillan.

--Saint Thomas & the Gentiles. (Aquinas Lecture). 1938. 7.95 (ISBN 0-87462-102-X). Marquette.

--Six Great Ideas. 243p. 1981. 12.95 (ISBN 0-02-500560-X). Macmillan.

--Six Great Ideas: Truth, Goodness, Beauty, Liberty, Equality, Justice. 256p. 1984. pap. 5.95 (ISBN 0-02-072020-3). Macmillan.

--Ten Philosophical Mistakes. 200p. 1985. 12.95 (ISBN 0-02-500330-5). Macmillan.

--A Vision of the Future: Twelve Ideas for a Better Life & a Better Society. 272p. 1984. 14.95 (ISBN 0-02-500280-5). Macmillan.

Adler, Mortimer J. & Mayer, Milton. Revolution in Education. LC 58-5534. 1958. 15.00x (ISBN 0-226-00765-0). U of Chicago Pr.

Adler, Mortimer J. & Van Doren, Charles. The Great Treasury of Western Thought: A Compendium of Important Statements & Comments on Man & His Institutions by the Great Thinkers in Western History. LC 77-154. 1700p. 1977. 37.50 (ISBN 0-8352-0833-8). Bowker.

--How to Read a Book. rev. ed. 1972. pap. 8.95 (ISBN 0-671-21209-5, Touchstone Bks). S&S.

Adler, Mortimer J., jt. auth. see Kelso, Louis O.

Adler, Mortimer J., jt. auth. see Michael, Jerome.

Adler, Mortimer J. & Van Doren, John, eds. The Great Ideas Today: An Annual. LC 72-7288. (Illus.). 480p. 1981. 11.00 (ISBN 0-85229-364-X). Ency Brit Inc.

Adler, Mortimer J., jt. ed. see Hutchins, Robert M.

Adler, Norman T., ed. Neuroendocrinology of Reproduction: Physiology & Behavior. LC 80-28245. 576p. 1981. 42.00x (ISBN 0-306-40600-4, Plenum Pr); pap. 18.95x (ISBN 0-306-40611-X). Plenum Pub.

Adler, Norman T., et al. Mating Reflexes. LC 74-9523. 148p. 1975. text ed. 26.50x (ISBN 0-8422-7236-4). Irvington.

Adler, P., et al. Fluorides & Human Health. (Monograph Ser: No. 59). 364p. 1970. 13.60 (ISBN 92-4-140059-5, 423). World Health.

Adler, Pat. Mineral King Guide. rev. ed. (Illus.). 48p. 1975. wrappers 1.50 (ISBN 0-910856-05-2). La Siesta.

Adler, Pat, ed. see Walker, Joseph R.

Adler, Patricia A. Wheeling & Dealing: An Ethnography of an Upper-Level Drug Dealing & Smuggling Community. LC 85-2644. 1985. 25.00 (ISBN 0-231-06060-2). Columbia U Pr.

Adler, Paul. Saucer Hill. (YA) 1979. pap. 1.95 (ISBN 0-380-47613-4, 47613). Avon.

Adler, Peggy. Second Adler Book of Puzzles & Riddles. LC 63-15912. (Illus.). (gr. 3-6). 1963. PLB 10.89 (ISBN 0-381-99946-7, A68801, JD-J). Har-Row.

Adler, Peter. Momentum: A Theory of Social Action. LC 81-2718. (Sociological Observations Ser.: Vol. 11). (Illus.). 191p. 1981. 25.00 (ISBN 0-8039-1307-9); pap. 12.50 (ISBN 0-8039-1581-0). Sage.

Adler, R. Introduction to General Relativity. 2nd ed. 1975. 51.95 (ISBN 0-07-000423-4). McGraw.

Adler, R. L. & Marcus, B. Topological Entropy & Equivalence of Dynamical Systems. LC 79-15040. (Memoirs Ser.: No. 219). 84p. 1981. pap. 13.00 (ISBN 0-8218-2219-5). Am Math.

Adler, R. L. & Weiss, B. Similarity of Automorphisms of the Torus. LC 52-42839. (Memoirs: No. 98). 43p. 1970. pap. 9.00 (ISBN 0-8218-1298-X, MEMO-98). Am Math.

Adler, Renata. Pitch Dark. LC 83-48133. 192p. 1983. 12.95 (ISBN 0-394-50374-0). Knopf.

--Speedboat. (Vintage Contemporaries Ser.). 192p. 1985. pap. 5.95 (ISBN 0-394-72753-3, Vin). Random.

Adler, Richard. All in the Family: A Critical Appraisal. LC 79-89505. 384p. 1979. 39.95x (ISBN 0-03-053996-X). Praeger.

Adler, Richard & Adler, Elizabeth. Needlepoint: A New Look. (Illus.). 176p. pap. 19.95 (ISBN 0-283-98797-9, Pub. by Sidgwick & Jackson). Merrimack Pub Cir.

Adler, Richard, jt. auth. see Adler, Elizabeth.

Adler, Richard, ed. Understanding Television: Essays on Television As a Social & Cultural Force. 456p. 1981. 39.50 (ISBN 0-03-055806-9); pap. text ed. 18.95 (ISBN 0-03-055801-8). Praeger.

Adler, Richard, jt. ed. see Arlen, Gary H.

Adler, Richard P. The Effects of Television Advertising on Children: Review & Recommendations. LC 78-24714. 352p. 1980. 33.50x (ISBN 0-669-02814-2). Lexington Bks.

Adler, Robert J. The Geometry of Random Fields. LC 80-40842. (Probability & Mathematical Statistics Ser.). 280p. 1981. 61.95x (ISBN 0-471-27844-0, Pub. by Wiley-Interscience). Wiley.

Adler, Rodney R. Vertical Transportation for Buildings. LC 73-104976. (Elsevier Architectural Science Ser.). pap. 59.50 (ISBN 0-317-11060-8, 2007760). Bks Demand UMI.

Adler, Roger, ed. see Carey, MacDonald.

Adler, Roger, ed. see Lanigan, Anne.

Adler, Roger, ed. see Leibowitz, Alan.

Adler, Roger, ed. see Sugar, Bert R.

Adler, Ron. Communicating at Work. 320p. 1983. text ed. 17.95 (ISBN 0-394-32788-8, RanC). Random.

Adler, Ronald. Communicating at Work. 2nd ed. 384p. 1986. text ed. write for info. (ISBN 0-394-34316-6, RanC). Random.

Adler, Ronald & Rosenfeld, Lawrence. Interplay: The Process of Interpersonal Communication. 2nd ed. 1983. pap. text ed. 17.95 (ISBN 0-03-062083-X). HR&W.

Adler, Ronald B. Confidence in Communication: A Guide to Assertive & Social Skills. LC 76-58530. 334p. 1977. pap. text ed. 19.95x (ISBN 0-03-016696-9, HoltC). HR&W.

Adler, Ronald B. & Towne, Neil. Looking Out-Looking in. 4th ed. LC 83-13044. 372p. 1984. text ed. 22.95 (ISBN 0-03-062997-7, HoltC). HR&W.

Adler, Roy D. Marketing & Society: Cases & Commentaries. (Illus.). 528p. 1981. 22.95 (ISBN 0-13-557074-3). P-H.

Adler, Rudolph J. Biblical Beginnings: Archaeology & the Roots of Scripture. (Illus.). 320p. 1985. 22.95 (ISBN 0-13-076233-4). P-H.

Adler, Ruth. A Day in the Life of the New York Times. 22.00 (ISBN 0-405-13782-6). Ayer Co Pubs.

--Women of the Shtetl: Through the Eye of Y. L. Peretz. LC 78-69895. (Illus.). 152p. 1979. 17.50 (ISBN 0-8386-2336-0). Fairleigh Dickinson.

--The Working Press. 22.00 (ISBN 0-405-13783-4). Ayer Co Pubs.

Adler, Ruth, jt. auth. see Adler, Irving.

Adler, Samuel. Sight Singing: Pitch, Interval, Rhythm. (Illus.). 1979. pap. text ed. 12.95x (ISBN 0-393-95052-2). Norton.

--The Study of Orchestration. 400p. 1982. text ed. 19.95x (ISBN 0-393-95188-X); wkbkx 7.95 (ISBN 0-393-95213-4); tapes 295.00 (ISBN 0-393-95217-7). Norton.

Adler, Sebastian J., frwd. by see Tigerman, Stanley & Lewin, Susan G.

Adler, Selig. Isolationist Impulse: Its Twentieth Century Reaction. LC 74-15551. 538p. 1974. Repr. of 1957 ed. lib. bdg. 75.00x (ISBN 0-8371-7822-3, ADII). Greenwood.

Adler, Shelley, jt. auth. see Goodman, Florence J.

Adler, Sol. A Clinician's Guide to Stuttering. (Illus.). 192p. 1966. 14.75x (ISBN 0-398-00008-5). C C Thomas.

--The Health & Education of the Economically Deprived Child. LC 67-26009. 194p. 1968. 10.50 (ISBN 0-87527-025-5). Green.

--The Non-Verbal Child: An Introduction to Pediatric Language Pathology. 3rd ed. (Illus.). 288p. 1983. 19.75x (ISBN 0-398-04791-X). C C Thomas.

--Poverty Children & Their Language: Implications for Teaching & Treating. 352p. 1979. pap. 15.00 (ISBN 0-8089-1194-5, 790030). Grune.

Adler, Sol, ed. Cultural Language Differences: Their Educational & Clinical-Professional Implications. 236p. 1985. 24.75x (ISBN 0-398-05030-9). C C Thomas.

--Early Identification & Intensive Remediation of Language Retarded Children. 280p. 1985. 29.50x (ISBN 0-398-05164-X). C C Thomas.

Adler, Sol, et al. A Curriculum Guide for Developing Communication Skills in the Preschool Child. 314p. 1983. spiral 27.50x (ISBN 0-398-04941-6). C C Thomas.

--An Interdisciplinary Intervention Program for the Moderately to Profoundly Language-Retarded Child. 120p. 1980. 26.00 (ISBN 0-8089-1301-8, 790029). Grune.

--A Communicative Skills Program for Day Care, Preschool & Early Elementary Teachers. 168p. 1982. spiral bdg. 15.75x (ISBN 0-398-04675-1). C C Thomas.

--Lesson Plans for the Infant & Toddler: A Sequential Oral Communications Program for Clinicians & Teachers. 238p. 1984. spiral 24.75x (ISBN 0-398-04983-1). C C Thomas.

Adler, Stephen. International Migration & Dependence. 256p. 1977. text ed. 44.95x (ISBN 0-566-00202-7). Gower Pub Co.

Adler, Stephen N., et al. Pocket Manual of Differential Diagnosis. 1982. pap. text ed. 10.95 (ISBN 0-316-01106-1). Little.

Adler, Stuart P., et al. Pediatric Case Studies. 1985. pap. text ed. write for info. (ISBN 0-87488-534-5). Med Exam.

Adler, Susan, jt. ed. see Kipnis, Lynne.

Adler, T. K., jt. ed. see Way, E. L.

Adler, Thomas P. & Woodman, Leonora. The Writer's Choices. 1985. text ed. 15.95x (ISBN 0-673-15584-6). Scott F.

Adler, Warren. American Sextet. LC 82-72050. 256p. 1982. 13.95 (ISBN 0-87795-414-3). Arbor Hse.

--Random Hearts. 272p. 1984. 13.95 (ISBN 0-02-500290-2). Macmillan.

--Random Hearts. 1985. pap. 3.95 (ISBN 0-451-13395-1, Sig). NAL.

--The War of the Roses. LC 80-23036. 272p. (Orig.). 1981. 10.95 (ISBN 0-446-51220-6). Warner Bks.

Adler, Winston, ed. see Fitch, Asa.

Adler, Wolfgang. Rubens: Landscapes. (A Harvey Miller Publication Ser.). (Illus.). 320p. 1982. 74.00 (ISBN 0-19-921027-6). Oxford U Pr.

Adlerblum, Nima H. Study of Gersonides in His Proper Perspective. LC 73-158229. Repr. of 1926 ed. 14.50 (ISBN 0-404-00296-X). AMS Pr.

Adlercreutz, R., et al, eds. Endocrinological Cancer: Ovarian Function & Disease. (International Congress Ser.: No. 515). 400p. 1981. 81.00 (ISBN 0-444-90149-3, Excerpta Medica). Elsevier.

Adler-Golden, Rachel & Gordon, Debbie. Beginning French for Preschoolers: A Montessori Handbook. LC 80-83136. (Illus.). 85p. 1980. pap. 12.95 (ISBN 0-915676-04-4). Ed Sys Pub.

Adleson, Joe & Williams, Bill. Hang Flight: Flight Instruction Manual for Beginner & Intermediate Pilots. (Illus.). 96p. 1975. pap. 3.95 (ISBN 0-911720-71-5, Pub. by Eco-Nautics). Aviation.

Adley, Robert. To China for Steam. (Illus.). 160p. 1984. 19.95 (ISBN 0-7137-1344-5, Pub. by Blandford Pr England). Sterling.

Adlington, William, tr. see Apuleius, Madaurensis.

Adlmann, Jan Von see Tomko, George P.

Adloff, Richard, jt. auth. see Thompson, Virginia.

Adloff, Richard, jt. auth. see Thompson, Virginia M.

Adloff, Richard, tr. see Gauze, Rene.

Adloff, Richard, tr. see Riviere, Claude.

Adloff, Richard, tr. see Tholomier, Robert.

Adloff, Virginia, tr. see Riviere, Claude.

Adman, Carl E. Physician Services in the Long Term Care Facility. 100p. 9.50 (ISBN 0-318-12750-4, 901-0024); members 6.50 (ISBN 0-318-12751-2, 901-00025). Am Health Care Assn.

Administracion De Fomento Economico. Puerto Rico y el Mar: Un Programa de Accion Sobre Asuntos Marinos. pap. 6.25 (ISBN 0-8477-2300-3). U of PR Pr.

Administrative Agencies. Ohio Monthly Record, Rules Issued During Nineteen Eighty-Four-Nineteen Eighty-Five. 1984. 180.00 (ISBN 0-8322-0116-2). Banks-Baldwin.

Admon, K., jt. auth. see Goldschmidt, Y.

Adnan, Etel. From A to Z Poetry. (Illus.). 30p. (Orig.). 1982. pap. 4.00 (ISBN 0-942996-00-3). Post Apollo Pr.

--The Indian Never Had a Horse & Other Poems. (Poetry Ser.). (Illus.). 114p. (Orig.). 1985. pap. 9.95 (ISBN 0-942996-03-8). Post Apollo Pr.

--Sitt Marie-Rose. Kleege, Georgina, tr. from Fr. 116p. (Orig.). 1982. pap. 7.50 (ISBN 0-942996-02-X, Dist. by Three Continents). Post Apollo Pr.

Adnan, Etel, et al. Russell Chatham. (Illus.). 72p. 1984. pap. 14.95 (ISBN 0-916947-01-7); write for info. signed, limited ed. (ISBN 0-916947-00-9). Winn Pub.

Adnani, Muhammad. Dictionary of Common Mistakes in Modern Written Arabic: Arabic-Arabic. (Arabic.). 30.00x (ISBN 0-86685-104-6). Intl Bk Ctr.

Adney, Edwin T. & Chapelle, Howard I. The Bark Canoes & Skin Boats of North America. 2nd ed. LC 64-62636. (Illus.). 242p. 1983. Repr. of 1964 ed. text ed. 19.95x (ISBN 0-87474-204-8). Smithsonian.

Ado, I. D., et al. Lie Groups. (Translations, Ser.: No. 1, Vol. 9). 534p. 1962. pap. 44.00 (ISBN 0-8218-1609-8, TRANS 1-9). Am Math.

Adoff, Arnold. All the Colors of the Race. LC 81-11777. (Illus.). 56p. (gr. 5 up). 1982. 11.75 (ISBN 0-688-00879-8); PLB 11.88 (ISBN 0-688-00880-1). Lothrop.

--Big Sister Tells Me That I'm Black. LC 75-32249. 32p. (gr. k-4). 1976. reinforced bdg. 5.95 (ISBN 0-03-014546-5). HR&W.

--Birds. LC 81-47753. (Illus.). 48p. (gr. k-5). 1982. 10.10i (ISBN 0-397-31949-5); PLB 9.89 (ISBN 0-397-31950-9). Lipp Jr Bks.

--Black Is Brown Is Tan. LC 73-9855. (Illus.). 32p. (ps-3). 1973. PLB 11.89 (ISBN 0-06-020084-7). HarpJ.

--The Cabbages are Chasing the Rabbits. LC 85-893. (Illus.). 32p. (gr. 5-8). 1985. 13.95 (ISBN 0-15-213875-7, HJ). HarBraceJ.

--Eats: Poems. LC 79-11300. (Illus.). (gr. 4 up). 1979. 11.75 (ISBN 0-688-41901-1); PLB 11.88 (ISBN 0-688-51901-6). Lothrop.

--Friend Dog. LC 80-7773. (Illus.). 48p. (gr. k-5). 1980. 8.95 (ISBN 0-397-31911-8); PLB 9.89 (ISBN 0-397-31912-6). Lipp Jr Bks.

--I am the Running Girl. LC 78-14083. (Illus.). 48p. (gr. 2-7). 1979. 9.57i (ISBN 0-06-020094-4); PLB 10.89 (ISBN 0-06-020095-2). HarpJ.

--Malcolm X. LC 70-94787. (Crocodile Paperbacks Ser.). (Illus.). 41p. (gr. 2-6). 1972. pap. 3.95 (ISBN 0-690-51415-8). Crowell Jr Bks.

--Malcolm X. LC 70-94787. (Biography Ser.). (Illus.). (gr. 2-5). 1970. PLB 10.89 (ISBN 0-690-51414-X). Crowell Jr Bks.

--Outside-Inside Poems. LC 79-22168. (Illus.). 32p. (gr. 4-6). 1981. 11.25 (ISBN 0-688-41942-9); PLB 11.88 (ISBN 0-688-51942-3). Lothrop.

--Today We Are Brother & Sister. LC 80-16075. (Illus.). 32p. (gr. 2-6). 1981. 11.25 (ISBN 0-688-41973-9); PLB 11.88 (ISBN 0-688-51973-3). Lothrop.

--Where Wild Willie. LC 76-21390. (Illus.). (ps-3). 1978. PLB 10.89 (ISBN 0-06-020093-6). HarpJ.

Adoff, Arnold, ed. I Am the Darker Brother: An Anthology of Modern Poems by Negro Americans. LC 68-12077. 128p. (gr. 7 up). 1968. 10.95 (ISBN 0-02-700080-X); pap. text ed. 4.95 (ISBN 0-02-041120-0). Macmillan.

--My Black Me: A Beginning Book of Black Poetry. LC 73-16445. 96p. (gr. 3 up). 1974. 8.50 (ISBN 0-525-35460-3). Dutton.

--The Poetry of Black America: Anthology of the Twentieth Century. LC 72-76518. 576p. (gr. 7 up). 1973. 23.50 (ISBN 0-06-020089-8); PLB 22.89 (ISBN 0-06-020090-1). HarpJ.

Adoko, Akena. From Obote to Obote. (Illus.). xx, 336p. 1983. text ed. 40.00x (ISBN 0-7069-2262-X, Pub. by Vikas India). Advent NY.

--Repressed Manhood. LC 81-51043. 185p. 1982. 7.95 (ISBN 0-533-05027-8). Vantage.

Adolf, Barbara & Rose, Karol. The Employer's Guide to Child Care: Developing Programs for Working Parents. LC 84-18003. 176p. 1985. 24.95x (ISBN 0-03-070541-X). Praeger.

Adolf, Erman. Die Religion der Aegypter. (Illus.). 1978. Repr. of 1934 ed. 19.20x (ISBN 3-11-005187-7). De Gruyter.

Adolf, Friedrich. From the Congo to the Niger & the Nile. (Illus.). Repr. of 1913 ed. 44.00x (ISBN 0-8371-2775-0, FCN&, Pub. by Negro U Pr). Greenwood.

Adolf, Mary M., ed. see GMA Research Corporation.

Adolfson, John A. & Berghage, Thomas E. Perception & Performance Underwater. LC 73-23009. 380p. 1974. 24.50 (ISBN 0-471-00900-8, Pub. by Wiley). Krieger.

Adolph, A. L. & Lorenz, Rita. Enzyme Diagnosis in Diseases of the Heart, Liver & Pancreas. (Illus.). 124p. 1982. pap. 22.00 (ISBN 3-8055-3079-X). S Karger.

Adolph, E. F. Origins of Physiological Regulations. 1968. 38.00 (ISBN 0-12-044360-0). Acad Pr.

Adolph, Edward F. Regulation of Size As Illustrated in Unicellular Organisms. (Illus.). 238p. 1931. 19.75x (ISBN 0-398-04184-9). C C Thomas.

Adolph, L. & Lorenz, Rita. Diagnostico enzimatico En las Enfermedades De corazon, higado y Pancreas. (Illus.). 126p. 1980. soft cover 7.75 (ISBN 3-8055-0506-X). S Karger.

--Enzymdiagnostik bei Herz-Leber-und Pankreaserkrankungen. (Ger.). 1978. 7.75 (ISBN 3-8055-2872-8). S Karger.

Adolphus, John L. Letters to Richard Heber, Esq., M. P. LC 72-7269. 1973. Repr. of 1822 ed. lib. bdg. 25.00 (ISBN 0-8414-0325-2). Folcroft.

Adolphus, Stephen H., ed. Equality Postponed: Continuing Barriers to Higher Education in the 1980s. 156p. (Orig.). 1984. pap. 12.95 (ISBN 0-87447-188-5). College Bd.

Adomatis, Hans-Joachim, et al, eds. see Murer, Jos.

Adomeit, Hannes. Soviet Risk Taking & Crisis Behavior: A Theoretical & Empirical Analysis. 450p. 1982. text ed. 37.50x (ISBN 0-04-335043-7). Allen Unwin.

--Soviet Risk Taking & Crisis Behavior: A Theoretical & Empirical Analysis. 450p. 1984. pap. text ed. 14.95x (ISBN 0-04-335051-8). Allen Unwin.

Adomeit, Hannes, tr. see Berner, Wolfgang, et al.

Adomeit, Ruth. Three Centuries of Thumb Bibles. LC 78-68238. (Garland Reference Library of Humanities). (Illus.). 435p. 1980. 73.00 (ISBN 0-8240-9818-8). Garland Pub.

Adomian, G., ed. Applied Stochastic Processes. LC 80-19890. 1980. 31.50 (ISBN 0-12-044380-5). Acad Pr.

Adomian, George, jt. auth. see Bellman, Richard.

Adomian, George, ed. Stochastic Systems: Monograph. (Mathematics in Science & Engineering Ser.). 345p. 1983. 49.50 (ISBN 0-12-044370-8). Acad Pr.

Adonis. Transformations of the Lover, Vol. 7. Hazo, Samuel, tr. from Arabic. LC 83-13283. (International Poetry Ser.). xiv, 95p. 1983. text ed. 18.95x (ISBN 0-8214-0754-6, 82-85223); pap. 10.95 (ISBN 0-8214-0755-4, 82-85231). Ohio U Pr.

Adorni, Sergio, jt. auth. see Primorac, Karen.

Adorno, D., jt. ed. see Casciani, C. U.

Adorno, Rolena, ed. From Oral to Written Expression: Native Andean Chronicles of the Early Colonial Period. Harrison, Regina & Urioste, George L. LC 82-3311. (Foreign & Comparative Studies Program, Latin American Ser.: No. 4). (Illus., Orig.). 1982. pap. text ed. 8.50x (ISBN 0-915984-95-4). Syracuse U Foreign Comp.

Adorno, T. W. Aesthetic Theory. Lenhardt, G., tr. from Ger. (The International Library of Phenomenology & Moral Sciences). 480p. 1984. 49.95X (ISBN 0-7100-9204-0). Routledge & Kegan.

Adorno, T. W. & Frenkel-Brunswik, Else. The Authoritarian Personality. Abridged ed. 1983. pap. 8.95 (ISBN 0-393-30042-0). Norton.

Adorno, Theodor. Against Epistemology, a Metacritique: Studies in Husserl & the Phenomenological Antinomies. Domingo, Willis, tr. from Ger. (Studies in Contemporary German Social Thought). 256p. 1983. 30.00x (ISBN 0-262-01073-9); pap. 8.95 (ISBN 0-262-51030-8). MIT Pr.

--In Search of Wagner. 160p. 1981. 14.50 (ISBN 0-8052-7087-6, Pub. by NLB England). Schocken.

--The Jargon of Authenticity. Tarnowski, Knut & Will, Frederic, trs. from Ger. LC 27-96701. 160p. 1973. text ed. 17.95 (ISBN 0-8101-0407-5); pap. text ed. 7.95 (ISBN 0-8101-0657-4). Northwestern U Pr.

--Minima Moralia. 15.50 (ISBN 0-8446-6135-X). Peter Smith.

--Minima Moralia: Reflections from Damaged Life. Jephcott, E. F., tr. from Ger. 1978. 11.95 (ISBN 0-902308-95-5, Pub by NLB). Schocken.

Adorno, Theodor W. Introduction to the Sociology of Music. Ashton, E. B., tr. from Ger. LC 75-33883. 1976. 16.95 (ISBN 0-8264-0119-8). Continuum.
--Negative Dialectics. 2nd ed. pap. 14.95x (ISBN 0-8264-0132-5). Continuum.
--Philosophy of Modern Music. LC 77-146298. 1973. 12.50 (ISBN 0-8164-9133-X). Continuum.
--Philosophy of Modern Music. rev. ed. 233p. 1980. pap. 10.95x (ISBN 0-8264-0138-4). Continuum.
--Prisms. Weber, Samuel & Weber, Shierry, trs. from Ger. 272p. 1982. pap. 6.95 (ISBN 0-262-51025-1). MIT Pr.
Adorno, Theodor W., jt. auth. see Horkheimer, Max.
Adorno, Theodore. Positivist Dispute in German Sociology. 1981. pap. text ed. 17.50x (ISBN 0-435-82656-5). Gower Pub Co.
Adouse, J., jt. auth. see Balian, R.
Adovasio, James M. Basketry Technology: A Guide to Identification & Analysis. LC 77-70388. (Manuals on Archeology Ser.: No. 1). (Illus.). x, 182p. 1977. 18.00x (ISBN 0-202-33035-4). Taraxacum.
Adrain, R. H., et al, eds. Reviews of Physiology, Biochemistry & Pharmacology, Vol. 90. (Illus.). 300p. 1981. 52.00 (ISBN 0-387-10657-X). Springer-Verlag.
Adriaansens, Hans P. Talcott Parsons & the Conceptual Dilemma. (International Library of Sociology). (Illus.). 224p. 1980. 29.95x (ISBN 0-7100-0519-9). Routledge & Kegan.
Adrian. CM: The Construction Management Process. (Illus.). 368p. 1981. text ed. 26.95 (ISBN 0-8359-0829-1). Reston.
Adrian & Alexander J. Worker's Rights, East, & West. 150p. 4.95 (ISBN 0-318-14690-8). League Indus Demo.
Adrian, A. A. Georgina Hogarth & the Dickens Circle. LC 57-14175. Repr. of 1957 ed. 23.00 (ISBN 0-527-01050-2). Kraus Repr.
Adrian, Arthur A. Dickens & the Parent-Child Relationship. LC 83-19505. (Illus.). xii, 169p. 1984. text ed. 22.95x (ISBN 0-8214-0735-X, 82-85041). Ohio U Pr.
Adrian, C. R. & Press, C. Governing Urban America. 5th ed. 1977. 33.95 (ISBN 0-07-000446-3). McGraw.
Adrian, Charles R., jt. auth. see Griffith, Ernest S.
Adrian, Charles R., jt. auth. see Williams, Oliver P.
Adrian, Cheri, jt. ed. see Barber, Joseph.
Adrian, Colin, ed. Urban Service Provision in Australia: Institutional Process & Geographic Outcome. 208p. 1985. 27.50 (ISBN 0-949614-04-1, Pub. by Croom Helm Ltd). Longwood Pub Group.
Adrian, Denis, jt. auth. see Kuh, Katharine.
Adrian, Dennis. Sight Out of Mind: Essays & Criticism on Art. Kuspit, Donald, ed. LC 85-8434. (Contemporary American Art Critics Ser.: No. 5). 225p. 1985. 32.95 (ISBN 0-8357-1676-7). UMI Res Pr.
Adrian, Dennis & Myers, Trent. Chicago: Some Other Traditions. LC 83-19563. 101p. 1983. 19.95 (ISBN 0-913883-00-X). Madison Art.
Adrian, E. D. The Basis of Sensation. Repr. of 1928 ed. 30.00 (ISBN 0-89987-038-4). Darby Bks.
Adrian, J. & Legrand, G. Dictionnaire de Biochimie Alimentaire et de Nutrition. 233p. (Fr.). 1981. 85.00 (ISBN 2-85206-094-9, M-9626). French & Eur.
Adrian, J., ed. Dictionary of Food, Nutrition & Biochemsitry. (Illus.). 240p. 1985. 29.00 (ISBN 0-89573-404-4, Pub. by Ellis Horwood Ltd UK). VCH Pubs.
Adrian, James. Building Construction Handbook. 1982. text ed. 39.95 (ISBN 0-8359-0580-2). Reston.
--Business Practices for Construction Management. LC 75-14999. 426p. 1975. 32.00 (ISBN 0-444-00169-7). Elsevier.
--Construction Accounting. LC 78-27746. (Illus.). 1979. text ed. 27.95 (ISBN 0-8359-0911-5). Reston.
--Construction Estimating. 1982. text ed. 28.95 (ISBN 0-8359-0925-5); instrs'. manual avail. (ISBN 0-8359-0926-3). Reston.
Adrian, James J. Microcomputers in the Construction Industry. 1984. text ed. 35.00 (ISBN 0-8359-4366-6). Reston.
Adrian, Mary. American Prairie Chicken. LC 68-21353. (Preserve Our Wildlife Ser.: No. 7). (Illus.). (gr. 2-6). 1968. 5.95g (ISBN 0-8038-0316-8); PLB 4.95 (ISBN 0-8038-0317-6). Hastings.
--A Day & a Night in a Tide Pool. LC 72-4743. (Balance in Nature Ser). (Illus.). 64p. (gr. 2-5). 1972. 6.95g (ISBN 0-8038-1549-2). Hastings.
--The Fireball Mystery. (Illus.). (gr. 2-6). 1977. 7.95 (ISBN 0-8038-2325-8). Hastings.
--Kite Mystery. LC 67-25609. (Illus.). (gr. 4-6). 1968. 7.95 (ISBN 0-8038-3937-5). Hastings.
--The Lightship Mystery. (gr. 4-6). 1969. 3.84 (ISBN 0-8038-4263-5). Hastings.
--The Mystery of the Dinosaur Graveyard. (Illus.). 128p. (gr. 4-7). 1982. PLB 9.95 (ISBN 0-8038-4738-6). Hastings.
--Skin Diving Mystery. 1978. 6.95 (ISBN 0-8038-6719-0). Hastings.
--Wildlife on the Watch. (Illus.). 64p. (gr. 2-6). 1974. PLB 6.95 (ISBN 0-8038-1550-0). Hastings.
Adrian, R. H. Reviews of Physiology, Biochemistry, & Pharmacology, Vol. 88. (Illus.). 264p. 1981. 54.00 (ISBN 0-387-10408-9). Springer-Verlag.
Adrian, R. H., ed. Reviews of Physiology, Biochemistry & Pharmacology, Vol. 73. LC 74-3674. (Illus.). 190p. 1975. 57.00 (ISBN 0-387-07357-4). Springer-Verlag.
--Reviews of Physiology, Biochemistry & Pharmacology, Vol. 79. LC 74-3674. 1977. 64.00 (ISBN 0-387-08326-X). Springer-Verlag.
--Reviews of Physiology, Biochemistry & Pharmacology, Vol. 89. (Illus.). 260p. 1981. 56.00 (ISBN 0-387-10495-X). Springer-Verlag.
--Reviews of Physiology, Biochemistry, & Pharmacology, Vol. 93. (Illus.). 220p. 1982. 45.00 (ISBN 0-387-11297-9). Springer-Verlag.
--Reviews of Physiology, Biochemistry, & Pharmacology, Vol. 95. (Illus.). 235p. 1983. 45.50 (ISBN 0-387-11736-9). Springer-Verlag.
Adrian, R. H., et al, eds. Reviews of Physiology, Biochemistry & Pharmacology, Vol. 70. (Illus.). 260p. 1974. 52.00 (ISBN 0-387-06716-7). Springer-Verlag.
--Reviews of Physiology, Biochemistry & Pharmacology, Vol. 71. (Illus.). vi, 175p. 1974. 57.00 (ISBN 0-387-06939-9). Springer-Verlag.
--Reviews of Physiology, Biochemistry & Pharmacology, Vol. 76. LC 74-3674. (Illus.). 1976. 71.00 (ISBN 0-387-07757-X). Springer-Verlag.
--Reviews of Physiology, Biochemistry & Pharmacology, Vol. 77. LC 74-3674. (Illus.). 1977. 74.00 (ISBN 0-387-07963-7). Springer-Verlag.
--Reviews of Physiology, Biochemistry & Pharmacology, Vol. 78. LC 74-3674. 1977. 61.00 (ISBN 0-387-07975-0). Springer-Verlag.
--Reviews of Physiology, Biochemistry & Pharmacology, Vol. 80. LC 74-3674. (Illus.). 1977. 56.00 (ISBN 0-387-08466-5). Springer-Verlag.
--Reviews of Physiology, Biochemistry & Pharmacology, Vol. 81. LC 74-3674. (Illus.). 1978. 56.00 (ISBN 0-387-08554-8). Springer-Verlag.
--Reviews of Physiology, Biochemistry & Pharmacology, Vol. 82. (Illus.). 1978. 52.00 (ISBN 0-387-08748-6). Springer-Verlag.
--Reviews of Physiology, Biochemistry & Pharmacology, Vol. 83. LC 74-3674. (Illus.). 1978. 51.00 (ISBN 0-387-08907-1). Springer-Verlag.
--Reviews of Physiology, Biochemistry & Pharmacology, Vol. 85. (Illus.). 1979. 51.00 (ISBN 0-387-09225-0). Springer-Verlag.
--Reviews of Physiology, Biochemistry & Pharmacology, Vol. 91. (Illus.). 240p. 1981. 42.00 (ISBN 0-387-10961-7). Springer-Verlag.
--Reviews of Physiology, Biochemistry, & Pharmacology, Vol. 92. (Illus.). 220p. 1982. 42.50 (ISBN 0-387-11105-0). Springer-Verlag.
--Reviews of Physiology, Biochemistry & Pharmacology, Vol. 94. (Illus.). 225p. 1982. 46.00 (ISBN 0-387-11701-6). Springer-Verlag.
--Reviews of Physiology, Biochemistry & Pharmacology, Vol. 96. (Illus.). 194p. 1983. 41.00 (ISBN 0-387-11849-7). Springer-Verlag.
--Reviews of Physiology, Biochemistry, & Pharmacology, Vol. 97. (Illus.). 176p. 1983. 37.50 (ISBN 0-387-12135-8). Springer-Verlag.
Adriance, Guy W. & Brison, Fred R. Propagation of Horticultural Plants. 2nd ed. LC 79-9753. 308p. 1979. Repr. of 1955 ed. lib. bdg. 19.50 (ISBN 0-88275-965-5). Krieger.
Adriani, Gotz. Cezanne Watercolors. Stockman, Russell M., tr. from Ger. (Illus.). 294p. 1983. 65.00 (ISBN 0-8109-0784-4). Abrams.
Adriani, John. The Chemistry & Physics of Anesthesia. 2nd ed. (Illus.). 862p. 1979. 39.75x (ISBN 0-398-00011-5). C C Thomas.
--Drugs: The Drug Industry & Prices. LC 70-176187. 192p. Date not set. 10.50 (ISBN 0-87527-196-0). Green.
--Labat's Regional Anesthesia: Techniques & Clinical Applications. 4th ed. (Modern Concepts of Medicine Ser.). (Illus.). 744p. 1985. 75.00 (ISBN 0-87527-187-1). Green.
--The Pharmacology of Anesthetic Drugs: A Syllabus for Students & Clinicians. 5th ed. (Illus.). 320p. 1977. 30.00x (ISBN 0-398-00013-1). C C Thomas.
--Techniques & Procedures of Anesthesia. 3rd ed. 668p. 1972. photocopy ed. 48.75x (ISBN 0-398-00015-8). C C Thomas.
Adriani, John & Eaton, Allen. The Law & Health Professionals: Fundamentals of the Law & Malpractice. 192p. Date not set. 10.50x (ISBN 0-87527-189-8). Green.
Adriano, Domy C. & Brisbin, I. Lehr, eds. Environmental Chemistry & Cycling Processes: Proceedings. LC 78-6603. (DOE Symposium Ser.). 943p. 1978. pap. 31.50 (ISBN 0-87079-302-0, CONF-760429); microfiche 4.50 (ISBN 0-87079-199-0, CONF-760429). DOE.
Adrianov, O. S. & Mering, T. A. Atlas of the Canine Brain. Ignatieff, E., tr. LC 64-63010. (Illus.). 349p. 1964. 35.00x (ISBN 0-916182-01-0). NPP Bks.
Adrichem, Christianus van. A Briefe Description of Hierusalem, Also a Mappe. Tymme, T., tr. LC 70-29008. (English Experience Ser.: No. 125). 1969. Repr. of 1595 ed. 21.00 (ISBN 90-221-0125-8). Walter J Johnson.
Adriel, Jean. Avatar. 285p. 1972. 8.95 (ISBN 0-940700-02-6); pap. 4.95 (ISBN 0-940700-01-8). Meher Baba Info.
Adrienne. Fast French. 181p. 1984. 12.95 (ISBN 0-393-01705-2); pap. 5.95 (ISBN 0-393-30105-2). Norton.
--French in Thirty-Two Lessons. (Gimmick Ser.). 1979. pap. 7.95 (ISBN 0-393-04531-5). Norton.
--German in Thirty-Two Lessons. (Gimmick Ser.). 1979. 10.95 (ISBN 0-393-04527-7); pap. 7.95 (ISBN 0-393-04533-1). Norton.
--El Gimmick, Espanol Hablado. 1977. pap. 5.95 (ISBN 0-393-04477-7). Norton.
--Le Gimmick, Francais Parle. 1977. 9.95 (ISBN 0-393-04438-6); pap. 5.95 (ISBN 0-393-04474-2). Norton.
--Der Gimmick, Gesprochenes Deutsch. 1977. pap. 6.95 (ISBN 0-393-04480-7). Norton.
--Gimmick I: Italiano Parlato. (The Gimmick Ser.). 185p. 1984. 12.95 (ISBN 0-393-01842-3); pap. 5.95 (ISBN 0-393-30149-4). Norton.
--Italian in Thirty-Two Lessons. 1983. 12.95 (ISBN 0-393-01617-X); pap. 6.95 (ISBN 0-393-30053-6). Norton.
--Spanish in Thirty Two Lessons. (Gimmick Ser.). 1980. pap. 5.95 (ISBN 0-393-00979-3). Norton.
Adrienne, Wade. The College & University Writing Venture. 2nd ed. 240p. 1985. pap. 15.95 (ISBN 0-8403-3652-7). Kendall Hunt.
Adrosko, Rita J. Natural Dyes & Home Dyeing. (Illus.). 1971. pap. 2.95 (ISBN 0-486-22688-3). Dover.
--Natural Dyes & Home Dyeing. Orig. Title: Natural Dyes in the United States. (Illus.). 11.25 (ISBN 0-8446-4500-1). Peter Smith.
Adrosko, Rita J., jt. auth. see Partridge, Virginia P.
Adshead, Gladys L. & Duff, Annis. Inheritance of Poetry. (Illus.). 424p. (gr. 7-9). 1948. 14.95 (ISBN 0-395-06537-2). HM.
Adshead, Janet. Study of Dance. 127p. 1981. 15.00 (ISBN 0-903102-66-8, Pub. by Dance Bks England). Princeton Bk Co.
Adshead, Janet & Layson, June, eds. Dance History: A Methodology for Study. 216p. 1983. pap. text ed. 15.95 (ISBN 0-903102-74-9, Pub. by Dance Bks England). Princeton Bk Co.
Adshead, S. A. Modernization of the Chinese Salt Administration, 1900-1920. LC 77-120315. (East Asian Ser.: No. 53). (Illus.). 1970. 17.50x (ISBN 0-674-58060-5). Harvard U Pr.
--Province & Politics in Late Imperial China. (Scandinavian Institute of Asian Studies, Monographs: No. 50). 200p. 1984. pap. text ed. 11.00x (ISBN 0-7007-0165-6, Pub. by Curzon Pr England). Humanities.
Adshead, S. D. & Abercrombie, Patrick, eds. Transactions of Conference Held March 9 to 13, 1914 at Liberty Buildings Liverpool. LC 84-48275. (Illus.). 168p. 1985. lib. bdg. 30.00 (ISBN 0-317-28841-5). Garland Pub.
Adshead, S. D., et al, eds. see Liverpool Town Planning & Housing Exhibition.
Adside, Joseph W. Attitudes in Sub-Communities. 1983. 6.95 (ISBN 0-8062-2133-X). Carlton.
Adsit, A., ed. Composites for Extreme Environments-STP 768. 188p. 1982. 24.00 (ISBN 0-8031-0698-X, 04-768000-33). ASTM.
Adson, John. Courtly Masquing Ayres, to 5 & 6 Parts, for Violins, Consorts, & Cornets. LC 77-6842. (English Experience Ser.: No. 838). 1977. Repr. of 1621 ed. lib. bdg. 16.00 (ISBN 90-221-0838-4). Walter J Johnson.
Aduddell, Robert M. & Cain, Louis P. Chicago's Future Service Economy Revisited: Locational Pressures & Manufacturing Decline. LC 82-245754. (Urban Insights Ser.: No. 9). 44p. 1981. pap. 2.00 (ISBN 0-911531-00-9). Loyola U Ctr Urban.
Adult Education Association. Administration of Continuing Education. 438p. 6.00 (ISBN 0-317-36198-8). A A A C E.
--The Guidance Function & Counseling Roles in an Adult Education Program. 70p. 4.00 (ISBN 0-317-36199-6). A A A C E.
--The Second Treasury of Techniques for Teaching Adults. 50p. 2.00 (ISBN 0-317-36201-1). A A A C E.
--You Can be a Successful Teacher of Adults. 186p. 6.00 (ISBN 0-317-36197-X). A A A C E.
Adult Education Association of the U. S. A., jt. auth. see ERIC.
Advaita Ashrama Staff. Ramakrishna: A Biography in Pictures. (Illus.). 1976. 30.00x (ISBN 0-87481-167-8). Vedanta Pr.
Advaita Ashrama Staff, ed. Altar Flowers: A Bouquet of Choicest Sanskrit Hymns. (Eng. & Sanskrit). 1974. pap. 5.95 (ISBN 0-87481-101-5). Vedanta Pr.
Advaita Ashrama Staff, compiled by. Life of Sri Ramakrishna. 12.00 (ISBN 0-87481-077-9). Vedanta Pr.
Advaita Ashrama Staff, ed. see Vivekananda, Swami.
Advanced Estate Planning & Administration Seminar. Fourth Annual Advanced Estate Planning & Administration Seminar: April 24-26, 1983, the Tides Inn, Irvington, Virginia. LC 83-160259. (Virginia Continuing Legal Education Ser.). 278p. 1984. write for info. Virginia Bar.
Advanced Investment Strategies Inc. Investment Tax Analyst: IBM PC Visicalc. (Wiley Professional Software Ser.). 60p. 1983. incl. disc 150.00x (ISBN 0-471-88953-9). Wiley.
Advanced Legal Education, Hamline University. Administrative Law. LC 83-139110. (Illus.). 422p. Date not set. price not set. Hamline Law.
Advanced Level Workshop on Education for Rural Development. Managing Education for Rural Development: Report. 1978. pap. 4.00 (ISBN 0-685-20398-0, UB61, UB). Unipub.
Advanced Medical Symposia, 11th, 1975 & Royal College of Physicians. Proceedings. Lant, A. F., ed. (Illus.). 1975. pap. text ed. 40.00x (ISBN 0-685-83067-5). State Mutual Bk.
Advanced Medicine Symposia, 10th, 1974 & Royal College of Physicians. Proceedings. Ledingham, J. G., ed. (Illus.). 1974. pap. text ed. 50.00x (ISBN 0-685-83066-7). State Mutual Bk.
Advanced Medicine Symposia, 7th, 1971. Proceedings. Boucher, I. A., ed. 1971. pap. text ed. 30.00x (ISBN 0-685-83065-9). State Mutual Bk.
Advanced Seminar, the University of Wisconsin, Madison, March-April, 1975. Theory & Application of Special Functions: Proceedings. Askey, Richard A., ed. (University of Wisconsin Mathematics Research Center Publications: No. 35). 1975. 29.50 (ISBN 0-12-064850-4). Acad Pr.
Advanced Study Institute, Bergen, Norway, 1965. Radiation Trapped in the Earth's Magnetic Field: Proceedings. McCormac, B. M., ed. (Astrophysics & Space Library: No. 5). 901p. 1966. lib. bdg. 79.00 (ISBN 90-277-0130-X, Pub. by Reidel Holland). Kluwer Academic.
Advanced Study Institute on Dynamics of Numbers in Populations. Dynamics of Populations: Proceedings. 1971. 52.00 (ISBN 9-0220-0355-8, PDC29, PUDOC). Unipub.
Advanced Summer Institute, Sheffield, England, 13-12 August, 1973. Magnetospheric Physics: Proceedings. McCormac, B. M., ed. LC 74-76472. (Astrophysics & Space Science Library: No. 44). 370p. 1974. lib. bdg. 66.00 (ISBN 90-277-0454-6, Pub. by Reidel Holland). Kluwer Academic.
Advances in Patient Care Conference, 4th, 1977. New Approaches to Counseling & Communication: How to Improve Your Skills in Patient Care: Proceedings. Zoog, Spring & Yarnall, Stephen R., eds. 1977. 20.00 (ISBN 0-917054-14-8). Med Communicat.
Advances in Patient, Care, Second Annual Conference, Feb. 15-22, 1975. Design & Use of Protocols: Proceedings. new ed. Kallstrom, Marta & Yarnall, Stephen, eds. (Illus.). 294p. 1975. 18.00 (ISBN 0-917054-02-4). Med Communications.
Advances in Photochemistry. Advances in Photochemistry, Vol. 7. LC 63-13592. pap. 106.00 (ISBN 0-317-09792-X, 2006493). Bks Demand UMI.
Advani, L. T. Horsepower Tables for Agitator Impellers. LC 76-2964. 175p. 1976. 29.95x (ISBN 0-87201-368-5). Gulf Pub.
Advani, Rukun. E. M. Forster As Critic. LC 84-45981. 256p. 1984. 29.00 (ISBN 0-7099-0545-9, Pub. by Croom Helm Ltd). Longwood Pub Group.
Advena, Jean C. Drug Abuse Bibliography for 1973. LC 79-116588. xli, 410p. 1975. 18.00x (ISBN 0-87875-057-6). Whitston Pub.
Advena, Jean C., ed. Drug Abuse Bibliography for 1970. LC 79-116588. 1971. 10.00x (ISBN 0-87875-016-9). Whitston Pub.
--Drug Abuse Bibliography for 1971. LC 79-116588. 400p. 1972. 15.00x (ISBN 0-87875-025-8). Whitston Pub.
--Drug Abuse Bibliography for 1972. LC 79-116588. xii, 472p. 1974. 18.00x (ISBN 0-87875-046-0). Whitston Pub.
Advena, Jean C., jt. ed. see Harding, Walter.
Adventurer Magazine. Adventurer. Nos. 1-140, 2 vols. 1753-1754. LC 68-58000. Repr. of 1754 ed. Set. 125.00 (ISBN 0-404-19300-5). AMS Pr.
Advertising & Marketing Management. Effective Marketing Management: Planning & Control Systems for Making Better & Faster Marketing Decisions. 188p. 25.00 (ISBN 0-318-13460-8, 1). Assn Natl Advertisers.
Advertising Photographers Association. Advertising Photography in Japan, Vol. 1. LC 83-117721. (Illus.). 288p. 1982. 59.50 (ISBN 0-87011-524-3). Kodansha.
Advertising Research Foundation. A Bibliography of Theory & Research Techniques in the Field of Human Motivation. LC 72-5274. 117p. 1972. Repr. of 1956 ed. lib. bdg. 18.75 (ISBN 0-8371-5723-4, BTRT). Greenwood.
Advertising Research Foundation Staff. Copy Testing: A Study Prepared for the Advertising Research Foundation. LC 84-46053. (History of Advertising Ser.). 137p. 1985. lib. bdg. 25.00 (ISBN 0-8240-6747-9). Garland Pub.
Advisory Board on Military Personnel Supplies, National Research Council. Hospital Patient Feeding Systems. 1982. pap. text ed. 15.50 (ISBN 0-309-03296-2). Natl Acad Pr.
Advisory Board on the Use of Volunteer Lawyers to Supplement Judicial Resources. Guidelines for the Use of Lawyers to Supplement Judicial Resources. LC 84-11574. 45p. (Orig.). 1984. pap. text ed. 5.00 (ISBN 0-89656-076-7). Natl Ctr St Courts.
Advisory Committee. The Community of Women & Men in the Church: A Study Program. (Orig.). 1978. pap. 1.95 (ISBN 0-377-00092-2). Friend Pr.
Advisory Committee For Assessment Of University Based Institutes For Research On Poverty. Policy & Program Research in a University Setting: A Case Study. LC 70-174752. 1971. pap. text ed. 4.50 (ISBN 0-309-01929-X). Natl Acad Pr.

Advisory Committee for the Co-ordination of Information Systems. Directory of United Nations Databases & Information Systems 1985. 323p. 1985. pap. 35.00 (ISBN 92-904-8295-8, UN84/0/5, UN). Unipub.

Advisory Committee on Marine Resources Research. Report on Marine Resources Research on Biological Accumulators: First Session, Rome, December 1974. (Fisheries Reports: No. 160). 18p. 1976. pap. 7.50 (ISBN 0-685-67377-4, F803, FAO). Unipub.

--Report on Marine Resources Research: 7th Session, Rome, 1973. (Fisheries Reports: No. 142). 49p. 1974. pap. 7.50 (ISBN 0-686-93972-7, F788, FAO). Unipub.

Advisory Committee on Marine Resources Research, 7th Session, Rome, 1973. The Scientific Advisory Function in International Fishery Management & Development Bodies: Report, Supplement 1. (Fisheries Reports: No. 142, Suppl. 1). 14p. 1974. pap. 7.50 (ISBN 0-686-93096-7, F787, FAO). Unipub.

Advisory Committee to the Dept of Housing & Urban Development. Revenue Sharing & the Planning Process: Shifting the Locus of Responsibility for Domestic Problem Solving. LC 74-6418. 108p. 1974. pap. 7.75 (ISBN 0-309-02214-2). Natl Acad Pr.

Advisory Group Meeting, Vienna, Jan. 27-31, 1975. Interpretation of Environmental Isotope & Hydrochemical Data in Groundwater Hydrology: Proceedings. (Panel Proceedings Ser.). (Illus.). 228p. (Orig.). 1976. pap. 25.25 (ISBN 92-0-141076-X, ISP429, IAEA). Unipub.

Advisory Service of Greater Porland Landmarks, Inc., Staff. Living with Old Houses. rev ed. LC 75-28985. (Illus.). 109p. 1985. Repr. of 1975 ed. vello bound 10.50 (ISBN 0-9600612-4-X). Greater Portland.

Ady, C. M., ed. see Armstrong, Edward.

Ady, Endre. Poems of Endre Ady. LC 74-75423. (Literature Ser.). (Illus.). 491p. 1969. 19.50 (ISBN 0-914648-00-4). Hungarian Cultural.

Ady, Julia M. Baldassare Castiglione: The Perfect Courtier, His Life & Letters, 1478-1529, 2 Vols. LC 75-154138. (BCL Ser.: No. I). Repr. of 1908 ed. Set. 74.50 (ISBN 0-404-09206-3). AMS Pr.

--Beatrice D'Este, Duchess of Milan, 1475-1497. LC 71-154137. Repr. of 1905 ed. 27.50 (ISBN 0-404-09204-7). AMS Pr.

--Christina of Denmark, Duchess of Milan & Lorraine, 1522-1590. LC 73-154140. Repr. of 1913 ed. 37.50 (ISBN 0-404-09205-5). AMS Pr.

--Isabella D'Este, Marchioness of Mantua, 1474-1539, 2 Vols. LC 79-154139. Repr. of 1907 ed. Set. 49.50 (ISBN 0-404-09214-4). AMS Pr.

--Jean Francois Millet, His Life & Letters. LC 73-155629. Repr. of 1896 ed. 28.50 (ISBN 0-404-00297-8). AMS Pr.

--Pilgrim's Way from Winchester to Canterbury. LC 71-158231. Repr. of 1893 ed. 17.50 (ISBN 0-404-01399-6). AMS Pr.

Ady, Mrs. Henry see Cartwright, Julia.

Ady, Ronald W. THe Investment Evaluator: How to Size up Your Investments at a Glance. 274p. 1984. 22.50 (ISBN 0-13-503673-9, Busn); pap. 9.95 (ISBN 0-317-07154-8). P-H.

--Making Money in Inflation, Deflation & Recession. 228p. 1976. pap. 3.95 (ISBN 0-13-547778-6). P-H.

Adye, A. M., ed. see Royal Society of London.

Adye, J. Payne. A Treatise on Court Marshall. 284p. Repr. of 1800 ed. 34.00 (ISBN 0-932051-70-7). Am Repr Serv.

Adye, John. Review of the Crimean War. 1973. 17.50x (ISBN 0-8464-0794-9). Beekman Pubs.

Adzei, Kwaku, ed. see Wood, Ernest.

Adzigian, Denise, ed. Encyclopedia of Governmental Advisory Organizations. 5th ed. 1000p. 1985. Set. 425.00x (ISBN 0-8103-0255-1). Gale.

Adzigian, Denise A., ed. Encyclopedia of Governmental Advisory Organizations. 4th ed. 800p. 1983. 390.00x (ISBN 0-8103-0254-3). Gale.

--New Governmental Advisory Organizations, 2 issues. 400p. 1984. pap. 290.00x (ISBN 0-8103-0252-7). Gale.

Adzigian, Joy, jt. auth. see Hobbs, A. Hoyt.

Adzigian, Joy, jt. auth. see Hobbs, Hoyt A.

AE. By Still Waters. 52p. 1971. Repr. of 1906 ed. 12.50x (ISBN 0-7165-1335-8, BBA 02042, Pub. by Cuala Press Ireland). Biblio Dist.

AE, pseud. Candle of Vision. LC 73-17195. 1974. pap. 2.25 (ISBN 0-8356-0445-4, Quest). Theos Pub Hse.

AE. Living Torch. Gibbon, M., ed. LC 72-111862. (Essay Index Reprint Ser). 1937. 21.50 (ISBN 0-8369-1625-5). Ayer Co Pubs.

--Passages from the Letters of AE to W. B. Yeats. 76p. 1971. Repr. of 1936 ed. 12.50x (ISBN 0-7165-1382-X, BBA 02044, Pub. by Cuala Press Ireland). Biblio Dist.

A. E., Von Vogt see Van Vogt, A. E.

AEA Resources for Business Staff & Jordan, Alan H. ACCU-Scan: Clerical Aptitude Test System. 1984. 950.00 (ISBN 0-318-04116-2). Add-Effect Assoc.

--ACCU-Scan: Marketing Aptitude Test System. 1984. 1250.00 (ISBN 0-940896-11-7). Add-Effect Assoc.

--Comprehensive Telemarketing Strategies & Techniques. 1984. 135.00 (ISBN 0-940896-14-1). Add-Effect Assoc.

--The Only Telemarketing Book You'll Ever Need, Vol. 3. 222p. 1984. 135.00 (ISBN 0-940896-13-3). Add-Effect Assoc.

Aeberhard, Peter & Casey, Patrick A. Reoperation for Postoperative Intraabdominal Sepsis. 178p. 1983. text ed. 49.50 (ISBN 3-456-81301-5, Pub. by Hans Huber Switzerland). J K Burgess.

Aebersold, JoAnn, et al. Critical Thinking, Critical Choices: An Integrated Curriculum in English for Academic Purposes, Vol. I-Reading & Writing. (Illus.). 200p. 1984. pap. text ed. 10.95 (ISBN 0-13-194100-3). P-H.

--Critical Thinking, Critical Choices: Listening & Speaking, Bk. 2. (Illus.). 256p. 1985. pap. text ed. 11.50 (ISBN 0-13-194127-5). P-H.

Aebi & Whitehead, eds. Maternal Nutrition During Pregnancy & Lactation. (Nestle Foundation Publication Ser.: No. 1). (Illus.). 354p. 1980. text ed. 31.00 (ISBN 3-456-80945-X, Pub. by Hans Huber Switzerland). J K Burgess.

Aebi, H. & Berger, E. Nutrition & Enzyme Regulation. (Current Problems in Clinical Biochemistry Ser.: Vol. 10). (Illus.). 144p. (Orig.). 1980. pap. text ed. 19.00 (ISBN 3-456-80931-X, Pub. by Hans Huber Switzerland). J K Burgess.

Aebi, H., et al. Problems in Nutrition Research Today. LC 81-66375. 1981. 33.00 (ISBN 0-12-044420-8). Acad Pr.

Aebi, H., et al, eds. Einfuehrung in die Praktische Biochemie. 3rd ed. xii, 462p. 1982. pap. 32.00 (ISBN 3-8055-3448-5). S Karger.

Aebi, Hans-J., jt. auth. see Spiegel, Rene.

Aebi, Harry & Aebi, Ormund. The Art & Adventure of Beekeeping. (Illus.). 186p. 1983. pap. 7.95 (ISBN 0-87857-483-2). Rodale Pr Inc.

Aebi, Ormund, jt. auth. see Aebi, Harry.

Aeby, Jacqueline. The Sea Gate. 1977. pap. 1.75 (ISBN 0-8439-0509-3, Leisure Bks). Dorchester Pub Co.

Aeby, Jacquelyn. The Pipes of Margaree. 1978. pap. 1.50 (ISBN 0-532-15348-0). Woodhill.

AEC Technical Information Center. Ecological Aspects of the Nuclear Age: Selected Readings in Radiation Ecology. LC 72-600120. 588p. 1972. pap. 22.75 (ISBN 0-87079-183-4, TID-25978); microfiche 4.50 (ISBN 0-87079-184-2, TID-25978). DOE.

--Magnetohydrodynamics: Power Generation & Theory. A Bibliography, 1957 to October 1975. 875p. 1975. pap. 57.50 (ISBN 0-87079-359-4, TID-3356); microfiche 4.50 (ISBN 0-87079-431-0, TID-3356). DOE.

--Symposium on Nuclear Energy & Latin American Development: Proceedings. 166p. 1968. pap. 15.00 (ISBN 0-87079-358-6, PRNC-112). DOE.

AEC Technical Information Center see Abelson, Philip H., et al.

AEC Technical Information Center, jt. auth. see Argonne National Laboratory.

AEC Technical Information Center see Cameron, A. E.

AEC Technical Information Center see Chastain, Joel W., Jr.

AEC Technical Information Center see Cooper, Raymond D. & Wood, Robert W.

AEC Technical Information Center see Fickeisen, D. H. & Schneider, M. J.

AEC Technical Information Center, jt. auth. see Glasstone, Samuel.

AEC Technical Information Center see Harrer, Joseph M. & Beckerley, James G.

AEC Technical Information Center, jt. auth. see Hutchison, Clyde A.

AEC Technical Information Center, jt. auth. see Jaech, John L.

AEC Technical Information Center see Katzin, Leonard I.

AEC Technical Information Center see Kline, A. Burt, Jr.

AEC Technical Information Center see Murphy, George M.

AEC Technical Information Center see Odum, Howard T. & Pigeon, Robert F.

AEC Technical Information Center see Quill, Lawrence L.

AEC Technical Information Center see Rockwell, Theodore, 3rd.

AEC Technical Information Center see Rodden, C. J.

AEC Technical Information Center see Rodden, Clement J.

AEC Technical Information Center, jt. auth. see Saenger, Eugene L.

AEC Technical Information Center, jt. auth. see Schaeffer, N. M.

AEC Technical Information Center see Seaborg, Glenn & Katzin, Leonard I.

AEC Technical Information Center, jt. auth. see Sesonske, Alexander.

AEC Technical Information Center see Slade, David H.

AEC Technical Information Center, jt. auth. see Van Cleave, Charles.

AEC Technical Information Center see Warner, J. C., et al.

AEC Technical Information Center see Wilimovsky, Norman J. & Wolfe, John N.

AEC Technical Information Center see Zirkle, Raymond E.

AECT Intellectual Freedom Commitee. Media, the Learner & Intellectual Freedom: A Handbook. (Orig.). 1979. pap. 8.95 (ISBN 0-89240-034-X); pap. 7.95 members. Assn Ed Comm Tech.

AECT, Program Standards Committee Task Force. College Learning Resources Programs. 1977. pap. 6.95 (ISBN 0-89240-005-6); pap. 5.95 members. Assn Ed Comm Tech.

Aegerter, Ernest E. Understanding Your Body: From Cells to Systems in Health & Disease. (Illus.). (YA) 1978. 12.95 (ISBN 0-89313-011-7); pap. 7.95 (ISBN 0-89313-012-5). G F Stickley Co.

Aegerter, Ernest E. & Kilpatrick, John A., Jr. Orthopedic Diseases: Physiology, Pathology, Radiology. 4th ed. LC 74-4551. (Illus.). 791p. 1975. text ed. 47.95 (ISBN 0-7216-1062-5). Saunders.

Aehegma, Aelbert C. Turtle Dance: Poems of Hawaii. Freed, Ray, ed. 72p. 1984. pap. 7.95 (ISBN 0-916467-00-7, 101A). Oceanic Pub Co.

AEI, ed. Telecommunication Switching: State of the Art Impact on Networks & Services, 2 pts. 1410p. 1984. Set. 195.00 (ISBN 0-444-86860-7, North-Holland). Elsevier.

Aelfric. Aelfric's Catholic Homilies: The Second Series Text. Godden, Malcolm, ed. (Early English Text Soc., Supplementary Ser.: No. 5). (Illus.). 1979. text ed. 54.00x (ISBN 0-19-722405-9). Oxford U Pr.

--Colloquy. Garmonsway, G. N., ed. (Old English Ser.). 1966. pap. text ed. 1.95x (ISBN 0-89197-563-2). Irvington.

--The Homilies of the Anglo-Saxon Church, 2 Vols. Thorpe, Benjamin, tr. Repr. of 1846 ed. 60.00 ea. (ISBN 0-384-00340-0). Johnson Repr.

--Lives of Three English Saints. Needham, G. I., ed. (Old English Ser.). 1966. pap. text ed. 9.95x (ISBN 0-89197-564-0). Irvington.

Aelfric, Abbot. A Testimonie of Antique. LC 73-36208. (English Experience Ser.: No. 214). Repr. of 1567 ed. 13.00 (ISBN 90-221-0214-9). Walter J Johnson.

Aelian, Claudius. On the Characteristics of Animals, 3 Vols. (Loeb Classical Library: No. 446, 448, 449). 1958. 12.50x ea. Vol. 1 (ISBN 0-674-99491-4). Vol. 2 (ISBN 0-674-99493-0). Vol. 3 (ISBN 0-674-99494-9). Harvard U Pr.

Aelianus, Tacitus. The Art of Embattailing an Army, or the Second Part of Aelian's Tacticks. Bingham, J., tr. LC 68-54605. (English Experience Ser.: No. 70). Repr. of 1629 ed. 21.00 (ISBN 90-221-0070-7). Walter J Johnson.

Aelinanus, Tacitus. The Tacticks of Aelign, Or Art of Embattailing An Army. Bingham, J., tr. LC 68-54606. (English Experience Ser.: No. 14). (Illus.). Repr. of 1616 ed. 42.00 (ISBN 90-221-0014-6). Walter J Johnson.

Aelred Of Rievaulx. Dialogue on the Soul. (Cistercian Fathers Ser.: No. 22). Orig. Title: De Anima. 1981. 10.95 (ISBN 0-87907-222-9). Cistercian Pubns.

--The Mirror of Charity. Connor, Elizabeth, tr. from Latin. (Cistercian Fathers Ser.: No. 17). Orig. Title: Speculum Caritatis. Date not set. write for info. (ISBN 0-87907-217-2); pap. write for info. (ISBN 0-87907-717-4). Cistercian Pubns.

Aemelius, Friedrich Ludwig. Das Fest der Winzer. (German Opera Ser.). 325p. 1985. lib. bdg. 65.00 (ISBN 0-8240-8860-3). Garland Pub.

Aemmer, Gail. Drawing Conclusions. (Stick-Out-Your-Neck Ser.). (Illus.). 20p. (gr. 2-3). 1985. pap. text ed. 4.95 (ISBN 0-88724-116-6, CD-0544). Carson-Dellos.

--Drawing Conclusions. (Stick-Out-Your-Neck Ser.). (Illus.). 20p. (gr. 5-6). 1985. pap. 4.95 (ISBN 0-88724-118-2, CD-0546). Carson-Dellos.

--Drawing Conclusions. (Stick-Out-Your-Neck Ser.). (Illus.). 20p. (gr. 3-4). 1985. pap. 4.95 (ISBN 0-88724-117-4, CD-0545). Carson-Dellos.

--Good Health Fun Book. (Stick-Out-Your-Neck Ser.). (Illus.). 32p. (ps-1). 1984. pap. 1.25 (ISBN 0-88724-062-3, CD-8053). Carson-Dellos.

--Read & Comprehend: Following Directions. (Stick-Out-Your-Neck Ser.). (Illus.). 20p. (gr. 3-4). pap. 4.95 (ISBN 0-88724-132-8, CD-0565). Carson-Dellos.

--Read & Comprehend: Following Directions. (Stick-Out-Your-Neck Ser.). (Illus.). 20p. (gr. 2-3). pap. 4.95 (ISBN 0-88724-131-X, CD-0564). Carson-Dellos.

--Read & Comprehend: Following Directions. (Stick-Out-Your-Neck Ser.). (Illus.). 20p. (gr. 1-2). 1985. pap. 4.95 (ISBN 0-88724-130-1, CD-0563). Carson-Dellos.

--Read & Comprehend: Main Ideas. (Stick-Out-Your-Neck Ser.). (Illus.). 20p. (gr. 2-3). 1985. pap. 4.95 (ISBN 0-88724-126-3, CD-0559). Carson-Dellos.

--Read & Comprehend: Sequencing. (Stick-Out-Your-Neck Ser.). (Illus.). 20p. (gr. 2-3). 1985. pap. 4.95 (ISBN 0-88724-145-X, CD-0554). Carson-Dellos.

--Read & Comprehend: Vocabulary Development. (Stick-Out-Your-Neck Ser.). (Illus.). 20p. (gr. 2-3). 1985. pap. 4.95 (ISBN 0-88724-121-2, CD-0549). Carson-Dellos.

--Sequencing. (Stick-Out-Your-Neck Ser.). (Illus.). 20p. (gr. 3-4). 1985. pap. 4.95 (ISBN 0-88724-146-8, CD-0555). Carson-Dellos.

--Sequencing. (Stick-Out-Your-Neck Ser.). (Illus.). 20p. (gr. 5-6). 1985. pap. 4.95 (ISBN 0-88724-147-6, CD-0556). Carson-Dellos.

--Thanksgiving Activity Book. (Stick-Out-Your-Neck Ser.). (Illus.). 32p. (gr. 3-6). 1982. pap. 1.79 (ISBN 0-88724-042-9, CD-8016). Carson-Dellos.

--Vocabulary Development. (Stick-Out-Your-Neck Ser.). (Illus.). 20p. (gr. 5-6). 1985. pap. 4.95 (ISBN 0-88724-123-9, CD-0551). Carson-Dellos.

--Vocabulary Development. (Stick-Out-Your-Neck Ser.). (Illus.). 20p. (gr. 3-4). pap. 4.95 (ISBN 0-88724-122-0, CD-0550). Carson-Dellos.

--Vocabulary Development. (Stick-Out-Your-Neck Ser.). (Illus.). 20p. (gr. 1-2). 1985. pap. 4.95 (ISBN 0-88724-120-4, CD-0548). Carson-Dellos.

Aemmer, Gail, jt. auth. see Clapsadle, Mark.

Aemmer, Gail, jt. auth. see Rittenour, Gary.

Aeneas Tacticus. Military Essays. Bd. with Military Essays. Asclepiodotus; Military Essays. Onasander. (Loeb Classical Library: No. 156). 12.50x (ISBN 0-674-99172-9). Harvard U Pr.

Aengus, Saint Martyrology of St. Aengus. pap. 12.50 (ISBN 0-686-25554-2). Eastern Orthodox.

Aeppli, Felix. Heart of Stone: The Definitive Rolling Stones Discography, 1962-1983. (Rock & Roll Reference Ser.: No. 17). 1985. indiv 29.50 (ISBN 0-87650-192-7); inst 39.50. Pierian.

Aereboe, Friedrich. Der Einfluss des Krieges Auf die Landwirtschaftliche Produktion in Deutschland. (Wirtschafts-Und Sozialgeschichte des Weltkrieges (Deutsche Serie)). (Ger.). 1927. 75.00x (ISBN 0-317-27455-4). Elliots Bks.

Aerial Photo. Aerial America: From Sea to Shining Sea. 1981. 4.75 (ISBN 0-936672-11-0). Aerial Photo.

Aero Education Associates. Introduction to Aviation. 1976. pap. 12.00 (ISBN 0-911721-35-5). Aviation.

Aero Medical Center Staff, tr. see Surgeon General, USAF.

Aero Publishers Aeronautical Staff. Junkers JU87. LC 66-22651. (Aero Ser: Vol. 8). 1966. pap. 3.95 (ISBN 0-8168-0528-8). Aero.

--Kamikaze. LC 66-19666. (Aero Ser: Vol. 7). 1966. pap. 3.95 (ISBN 0-8168-0524-5). Aero.

Aero Publishers, Inc. Aeronautical Staff. Airman's Information Manual-1985. 256p. 1985. pap. 6.75 (ISBN 0-8168-1364-7). Aero.

--Federal Aviation Regulations for Pilots, 1985. 128p. 1985. pap. 5.25 (ISBN 0-317-16938-6). Aero.

Aero, Rita & Weiner, Elliot. The Brain Game: Twenty-Seven Fun-to Take Aptitude Tests. 1983. pap. 9.95 FPT (ISBN 0-688-01923-4, Quill). Morrow.

--The Love Exam. LC 84-6857. (Illus.). 144p. (Orig.). 1984. pap. 9.95 (ISBN 0-688-03908-1, Quill). Morrow.

--The Mind Test. LC 81-2341. (Illus.). 192p. (Orig.). 1981. pap. 14.95 (ISBN 0-688-00401-6, Quill NY). Morrow.

--The Money Test: Nineteen Authoritative Personality & Intelligence Tests That Reveal Your Chances for Riches & Success. 1985. pap. 11.95 (ISBN 0-688-04357-7, Quill). Morrow.

Aero, Rita & Wing, R. L. The I Ching Coloring Book. (Illus.). 144p. 1984. pap. 7.95 (ISBN 0-385-18848-X, Dolp). Doubleday.

Aero, Rita, jt. auth. see Rheingold, Howard.

Aerodynamics & Ventilation of Vehicle Tunnels, 2nd International Symposium. Proceedings. 1977. text ed. 60.00x (ISBN 0-900983-51-5, Dist. by Air Science Co.). BHRA Fluid.

Aeronautical Staff. Messerschmitt ME109. LC 65-24307. (Aero Ser.: Vol. 1). (Illus.). 1965. pap. 3.95 (ISBN 0-8168-0500-8). Aero.

--Supermarine Spitfire. LC 66-22653. (Aero Ser: Vol. 10). 1966. pap. 3.95 (ISBN 0-8168-0536-9). Aero.

Aeronautical Staff of Aero Publishers, et al. Boeing P12, F4B. LC 66-17554. (Aero Ser.: Vol. 5). 1966. pap. 3.95 (ISBN 0-8168-0516-4). Aero.

--Curtiss P-40. LC 65-24307. (Aero Ser: Vol. 3). 1965. pap. 3.95 (ISBN 0-8168-0508-3). Aero.

--Heinkel HE162. LC 65-26827. (Aero Ser.: Vol. 4). 1965. pap. 3.95 (ISBN 0-8168-0512-1). Aero.

Aeronautical Staff of Aero Publishers. Nakajima KI-84. LC 65-24308. (Aero Ser: Vol. 2). (Illus.). 1965. pap. 3.95 (ISBN 0-8168-0504-0). Aero.

--Republic P-47. LC 66-19665. (Aero Ser: Vol. 6). 1966. pap. 3.95 (ISBN 0-8168-0520-2). Aero.

Aers, D., ed. see Milton, John.

Aers, David. Chaucer, Langland & the Creative Imagination. 1980. 26.95x (ISBN 0-7100-0351-X). Routledge & Kegan.

Aers, David, et al. Romanticism & Ideology. 240p. (Orig.). 1981. pap. 12.95X (ISBN 0-7100-0781-7). Routledge & Kegan.

--Literature, Language & Society in England 1580-1680. 230p. 1981. 28.50 (ISBN 0-389-20198-7, 06980). B&N Imports.

Aerstin, Frank & Street, Gary. Applied Chemical Process Design. LC 78-9104. (Illus.). 312p. 1978. 32.00x (ISBN 0-306-31088-0, Plenum Pr). Plenum Pub.

Aerts, Jan. Pigeon Racing: Advanced Techniques. (Illus.). 192p. 1981. pap. 7.95 (ISBN 0-571-11572-1). Faber & Faber.

Aesch, Alexander Gode Von see Gode, Alexander.

Aeschines. Aeschines Against Ctesiphon: On the Crown. Connor, W. R. & Richardson, Rufus B., eds. LC 78-18596. (Greek Texts & Commentaries Ser.). (Illus., Gr. & Eng.). 1979. Repr. of 1889 ed. lib. bdg. 21.00x (ISBN 0-405-11437-0). Ayer Co Pubs.

--Discours sur L'Ambasade. Connor, W. R., ed. LC 78-18585. (Greek Texts & Commentaries Ser.). (Gr. & Fr.). 1979. Repr. of 1902 ed. lib. bdg. 17.00x (ISBN 0-405-11427-3). Ayer Co Pubs.

--Speeches. (Loeb Classical Library: No. 106). 12.50x (ISBN 0-674-99118-4). Harvard U Pr.

Aeschinis. Aeschinis Orationes. E Codicibus Partim Nunc Primum Excussis, Edidit Scholia ex Parteinedita, Adiecit Ferdinandus Schultz. LC 72-7905. (Greek History Ser). (Gr. & Latin.). Repr. of 1865 ed. 19.00 (ISBN 0-405-04776-2). Ayer Co Pubs.

Aeschliman, Bonnie. Step by Step Microwave Cooking for Boys & Girls. (Illus.). 64p. (Orig.). (gr. k-7). 1985. pap. 3.50 (ISBN 0-8249-3049-5). Ideals.

Aeschliman, Gordon, jt. auth. see Wilson, Samuel.

Aeschliman, Michael D. The Restitution of Man: C. S. Lewis & the Case Against Scientism. 96p. (Orig.). 1983. pap. 4.95 (ISBN 0-8028-1950-8). Eerdmans.

Aeschylus. Aeschylus One: Oresteia, Agamemnon, the Libation Bearers, the Eumenides. Lattimore, Richmond, tr. & intro. by. LC 53-9655. 171p. 1969. pap. text ed. 6.00x (ISBN 0-226-30778-6, P306, Phoen). U of Chicago Pr.

--Aeschylus Two; Four Tragedies: Prometheus Bound, Seven Against Thebes, the Persians, the Suppliant Maidens. Grene, David & Lattimore, Richard, eds. Grene, David & Benardete, Seth G., trs. LC 56-11262. 1969. pap. text ed. 6.00x (ISBN 0-226-30779-4, P307, Phoen). U of Chicago Pr.

--Agamemnon. Lloyd-Jones, Hugh, tr. from Greek. Orig. Title: Oresteia. 1979. 20.00x (ISBN 0-7156-1365-0, BPA-02617, Pub. by Duckworth England); pap. text ed. 6.75x (ISBN 0-7156-1367-7, BPA-02522, Pub. by Duckworth England). Biblio Dist.

--Agamemnon. Denniston, J. D. & Page, Denys, eds. 1957. 15.95x (ISBN 0-19-814102-5). Oxford U Pr.

--Agamemnon, 3 Vols. Fraenkel, Eduard, ed. Set. 79.00x (ISBN 0-19-814101-7). Oxford U Pr.

--Agamemnon of Aeschylus, Bacchanals of Euripides. 59.95 (ISBN 0-87968-584-0). Gordon Pr.

--The Choephoroe. Murray, Gilbert, tr. 1923. pap. text ed. 3.95x (ISBN 0-04-882004-0). Allen Unwin.

--The Eumenides. Murray, Gilbert, tr. 1925. pap. text ed. 3.95x (ISBN 0-04-882007-5). Allen Unwin.

--The Libation Bearers: The Oresteia, Parts 2 & 3. Arnott, Peter D., ed. & tr. Bd. with The Eumenides. LC 64-25233. (Crofts Classics Ser.). 1964. pap. text ed. 1.25x (ISBN 0-88295-002-9). Harlan Davidson.

--The Oresteia. Raphael, F., et al, trs. LC 78-6013. (Greek & Roman Authors Ser.). 1979. 17.95 (ISBN 0-521-22060-2); pap. 6.95 (ISBN 0-521-29344-8). Cambridge U Pr.

--The Oresteia. Fagles, Robert, tr. from Gr. LC 74-489. 352p. 1975. 20.00 (ISBN 0-670-52832-3). Viking.

--The Oresteia: Agamemnon, the Liberation Bearers, the Eumenides. Fagles, Robert, tr. (Penguin Classics Ser.). 336p. 1984. pap. 3.50 (ISBN 0-14-044333-9). Penguin.

--Oresteian Trilogy. Vellacott, Philip, tr. Incl. Agamemnon; Choephori; Eumenides. (Classics Ser.). (Orig.). (YA) (gr. 9 up). 1956. pap. 3.50 (ISBN 0-14-044067-4). Penguin.

--Persians. Arrowsmith, William, ed. Lembke, Janey & Herington, C. J., trs. (The Greek Tragedy in New Translation Ser.). 1981. 19.95x (ISBN 0-19-502777-9). Oxford U Pr.

--Plays. Cookson, G. M., tr. from Greek. 1967. Repr. of 1960 ed. text ed. 9.95x (ISBN 0-460-00062-4, Evman). Biblio Dist.

--The Prometheus Bound. Connor, W. R., ed. LC 78-18612. (Greek Texts & Commentaries Ser.). (Illus.). 1979. Repr. of 1932 ed. lib. bdg. 17.00x (ISBN 0-405-11451-6). Ayer Co Pubs.

--Prometheus Bound. Anderson, Warren D., tr. (Orig.). 1963. pap. 4.24 scp (ISBN 0-672-60357-8, LLA143). Bobbs.

--Prometheus Bound. Arrowsmith, William, ed. Scully, James & Herington, C. John, trs. from Greek. (The Greek Tragedy in New Translations Ser.). 1975. 19.95x (ISBN 0-19-501934-2). Oxford U Pr.

--Prometheus Bound. Griffith, Mark, ed. LC 82-1301. (Cambridge Greek & Latin Classics Ser.). 270p. 1983. 42.50 (ISBN 0-521-24843-4); pap. 15.95 (ISBN 0-521-27011-1). Cambridge U Pr.

--Prometheus Bound & Other Plays. Vellacott, Philip, tr. Incl. Suppliants; Seven Against Thebes; Persians. (Classics Ser.). (Orig.). 1961. pap. 2.95 (ISBN 0-14-044112-3). Penguin.

--The Prometheus Bound & the Fragments of Prometheus Loosed. Wecklein, N., ed. Allen, F. D., tr. (College Classical Ser.). iv, 178p. (Orig., Greek & Ger.). 1981. lib. bdg. 25.00x (ISBN 0-89241-358-1); pap. text ed. 12.50x (ISBN 0-89241-126-0). Caratzas.

--Septem Quae Supersunt Tragoedias. Page, Denys L., ed. (Oxford Classical Texts). 1973. 14.95x (ISBN 0-19-814570-5). Oxford U Pr.

--The Seven Against Thebes. Murray, Gilbert, tr. 1935. pap. text ed. 3.95x (ISBN 0-04-882015-6). Allen Unwin.

--Seven Against Thebes. Hecht, Anthony & Bacon, Helen, trs. (Greek Tragedy Ser.). 1973. 19.95x (ISBN 0-19-501732-3). Oxford U Pr.

--The Suppliant Women. Murray, Gilbert, tr. 1930. pap. text ed. 3.95x (ISBN 0-04-882017-2). Allen Unwin.

--The Suppliants. Arrowsmith, William, ed. Lembke, Janet, tr. from Greek. (The Greek Tragedy in New Translations Ser.). 1975. 19.95x (ISBN 0-19-501933-4). Oxford U Pr.

--Tragedies, 2 vols. Incl. Vol. 1. Suppliant Maidens, Persians, Prometheus, Seven Against Thebes (ISBN 0-674-99160-5); Vol. 2. Agamemnon, Libation Bearers, Eumenides' Fragments (ISBN 0-674-99161-3). (Loeb Classical Library: No. 145-146). 12.50 ea. Harvard U Pr.

--Tragoediae. Wilamowitz-Moellendorf, Udalricus de, ed. 280p. 1985. 15.00 (ISBN 0-89005-412-6). Ares.

Aeschylus & Sophocles. An Anthology of Greek Tragedy. Cook, Albert & Dolin, Edwin, eds. Sylvester, William & Sugg, Alfred, trs. LC 83-452. (Dunquin Series: No. 15). (Illus.). 1983. pap. 15.00 (ISBN 0-88214-215-1). Spring Pubns.

Aeschylus see Fitts, Dudley.

Aeschylus see Hadas, Moses.

Aeschylus see Lind, Levi R.

Aeschylus see Oates, Whitney J. & O'Neill, Eugene, Jr.

Aeschylus see Robinson, Charles A., Jr.

Aesop. The Aesop for Children. Clauss, J., intro. by. (Illus., In Very Large Type). (gr. 1-12). 1976. lib. bdg. 18.95x (ISBN 0-88411-991-2, Pub. by Aeonian Pr). Amereon Ltd.

--The Aesop for Children. LC 84-60664. (Illus.). 96p. (gr. 2 up). 1984. pap. 9.95 (ISBN 0-528-82134-2). Rand.

--Aesop's & Other Fables. Green, Roger L., ed. 1971. Repr. of 1913 ed. 12.95x (ISBN 0-460-00657-6, Evman). Biblio Dist.

--Aesop's Fables. Winder, Blanche, ed. (Classics Ser). (Illus.). (gr. 4 up). pap. 1.50 (ISBN 0-8049-0081-7, CL-81). Airmont.

--Aesop's Fables. (Illus.). (gr. 4-6). 1947-63. Illustrated Junior Library. pap. 5.95 (IJL) (ISBN 0-448-11003-2, G&D); deluxe ed. 10.95 (ISBN 0-448-06003-5); Companion Library. companion lib. o.p. 2.95 (ISBN 0-448-05453-1); pap. ed (IJL) o.p. 4.95 (ISBN 0-686-76870-1). Putnam Pub Group.

--Aesop's Fables. (gr. 4-6). 1965. 4.95 (ISBN 0-88088-022-8). Peter Pauper.

--Aesop's Fables. White, Anne T., ed. (Illus.). (gr. 2-5). 1964. PLB 7.99 (ISBN 0-394-90895-3, BYR). Random.

--Aesop's Fables. McGovern, Ann, ed. (Illus., Orig.). (gr. 4-9). pap. 1.95 (ISBN 0-590-08002-4). Scholastic Inc.

--Aesop's Fables. LC 80-26265. (Illus.). 1981. 13.50 (ISBN 0-670-10643-7). Viking.

--Aesop's Fables. (Children's Illustrated Classics Ser.). (Illus.). 171p. 1975. Repr. of 1961 ed. 11.00x (ISBN 0-460-05049-4, BKA 01565, Pub. by J. M. Dent England). Biblio Dist.

--Aesop's Four Footed Fables. (Illus.). 42p. 1985. pap. 4.95 (ISBN 0-932458-29-7). Star Rover.

--The Book of the Subtyl Historyes & Fables of Esope. LC 76-177403. (English Experience Ser.: No. 439). 288p. Repr. of 1484 ed. 49.00 (ISBN 90-221-0439-7). Walter J Johnson.

--The Caldecott Aesop-Twenty Fables. LC 77-88424. (gr. 3-9). 1978. 12.95 (ISBN 0-385-12653-0). Doubleday.

--The City Mouse & the Country Mouse. (Pudgy Pal Board Bks.). (Illus.). 18p. (ps). 1985. 3.95 (ISBN 0-448-10226-9, G&D). Putnam Pub Group.

--Fables of Aesop. Handford, S. A., tr. (Classics Ser.). (Orig.). 1954. pap. 3.95 (ISBN 0-14-044043-7). Penguin.

--Favorite Animal Fables. (Illus.). 40p. (ps-3). 1984. 5.95 (ISBN 0-394-86773-4, Pub. by BYR). Random.

--The Grasshopper & the Ants. LC 85-51035. (Stories from Around the World Ser.). (Illus.). 28p. (ps-3). 1985. pap. 3.95 (ISBN 0-382-09152-3). Silver.

--The Hare & the Tortoise. LC 80-28162. (Illus.). 32p. (gr. k-2). 1981. PLB 7.89 (ISBN 0-89375-468-4); pap. text ed. 1.95 (ISBN 0-89375-469-2). Troll Assocs.

--The Lion & the Mouse. LC 80-28154. (Illus.). 32p. (gr. k-4). 1981. PLB 7.89 (ISBN 0-89375-466-8); pap. text ed. 1.95 (ISBN 0-89375-467-6). Troll Assocs.

--The Miller, His Son & Their Donkey. LC 85-7198. (Illus.). 32p. (gr. k-3). 1985. 10.95 (ISBN 0-03-005733-7). HR&W.

--The Morall Fabillis of Esope in Scottis Meter Be Maister Henrisone. LC 79-25964. (English Experience Ser.: No. 282). 104p. 1970. Repr. of 1570 ed. 14.00 (ISBN 90-221-0282-3). Walter J Johnson.

--Town Mouse & the Country Mouse. new ed. LC 78-18062. (Illus.). 32p. (gr. k-4). 1979. PLB 7.89 (ISBN 0-89375-131-6); pap. 1.95 (ISBN 0-89375-109-X). Troll Assocs.

Aesopus. The Book of Subtyl Histories & Fables of Esope. Bd. with The Siege of Rhodes. Caoursin, Guillaume. LC 76-14086. 1975. Repr. of 1484 ed. 60.00x (ISBN 0-8201-1154-6). Schol Facsimilies.

--Fables of Aesop, Vol. One: History of the Aesopic Fable. Jacobs, Joseph, ed. 1970. Repr. of 1889 ed. text ed. 24.50 (ISBN 0-8337-1818-5). B Franklin.

--Select Fables of Esop & Other Fabulists. new ed. Dodsley, Robert, ed. LC 70-161796. (Augustan Translators Ser.). Repr. of 1781 ed. 31.50 (ISBN 0-404-54101-1). AMS Pr.

--Ysopet-Avionnet: The Latin & French Texts. McKenzie, Kenneth & Oldfather, William A., eds. 22.00 (ISBN 0-384-36680-5). Johnson Repr.

Aeur. Old Man & the Sea: Hemingway. (Book Notes). 1984. pap. 2.50 (ISBN 0-8120-3432-5). Barron.

AEVAC, Inc., ed. see O'Keefe, Ruth A.

AFA. Mundane Data Nineteen Eighty Four. 5.00 (ISBN 0-318-01885-3). Am Fed Astrologers.

--Synopsis of Publications. 3.00 (ISBN 0-318-01887-X). Am Fed Astrologers.

Afanas'Ev, Aleksandr. Russian Fairy Tales. LC 44-37884. (Fairytales & Folklore Library). (gr. 6 up). 1976. pap. 8.95 (ISBN 0-394-73090-9). Pantheon.

Afanas'Ev, Aleksandr, ed. Russian Fairy Tales. Guterman, Norbert, tr. from Rus. LC 45-37884. (Fairytales & Folklore Library). (Illus.). 664p. 1975. Repr. of 1945 ed. 17.00 (ISBN 0-394-49914-X). Pantheon.

Afanasev, Aleksandr N. Erotic Tales of Old Russia. Perkov, Yury, tr. (Orig., Eng. & Rus.). 1980. pap. 6.95 (ISBN 0-933884-07-9). Berkeley Slavic.

Afanasiev, V. Fundamentos del Comunismos Cientifico. 294p. (Span.). 1977. 7.45 (ISBN 0-8285-1658-8, Pub. by Progress Pubs USSR). Imported Pubns.

Afanasyev, Alexander, compiled by. Russian Folk Tales. Chandler, Robert, tr. from Rus. LC 80-50746. (Illus.). 80p. 1982. pap. 9.95 (ISBN 0-87773-233-7, 71234-X). Shambhala Pubns.

--Russian Folk Tales: Illustrated by Ivan Bilibin. Chandler, Robert, tr. from Russian. LC 80-50746. (Illus.). 80p. 1980. 14.95 (ISBN 0-87773-195-0, 51353-3). Shambhala Pubns.

Afanasyev, V. Bourgeois Economic Thought 1930s-70s. 543p. 1983. pap. 5.95 (ISBN 0-8285-2591-9, Pub. by Progress Pubs USSR). Imported Pubns.

--Social Information & Regulation of Social Development. 363p. 1978. 5.95 (ISBN 0-8285-0437-7, Pub. by Progress Pubs USSR). Imported Pubns.

Afanasyev, V., tr. see Neporozhny, P.

Afanasyev, V. G. Marxist Philosophy. 1980. 8.95 (ISBN 0-8285-1848-3, Pub. by Progress Pubs USSR). Imported Pubns.

--Scientific & Technological Revolution: Its Impact on Management & Education. 320p. 1975. 4.25 (ISBN 0-8285-0435-0, Pub. by Progress Pubs USSR). Imported Pubns.

Afanasyev, V., tr. see Polukhin, P., et al.

Afansiev, V. & Zaikov, G. In the Realm of Catalysis. 116p. 1979. pap. 3.95 (ISBN 0-8285-0822-4, Pub. by Mir Pubs USSR). Imported Pubns.

Afansyev, V. Fundamentals of Scientific Communism. 214p. 1981. 3.95 (ISBN 0-8285-2234-0, Pub. by Progress Pubs USSR). Imported Pubns.

Af Enehjelm, Curt. Cages & Aviaries. Friese, U. Erich, tr. from Ger. Orig. Title: Kafige und Volieren. (Illus.). 160p. 1981. 9.95 (ISBN 0-87666-840-6, H-1039). TFH Pubns.

Affabee, Eric. Operation: Star Raider. 1985. pap. 1.95 (ISBN 0-345-32665-2). Ballantine.

--The Siege of the Dragonriders. (Wizards, Warriors & You Ser.: Bk. 2). (Illus.). 112p. 1984. pap. 2.50 (ISBN 0-380-88054-7, 88054-7). Avon.

Affifi, A. E. Mystical Philosophy of Muhyid Din Ibn-Ul-Arabi. 1964. 11.00x (ISBN 0-87902-035-0). Orientalia.

Affifi, Abul E. The Mystical Philosophy of Muhyid Din-Ibnul 'Arabi. LC 77-180312. (Mid-East Studies). Repr. of 1939 ed. 12.00 (ISBN 0-404-56205-1). AMS Pr.

Affinity Publishers Services Staff. Incorporating Form Sample Packet for the State of California. 7p. 1984. pap. 4.00 (ISBN 0-318-00822-X). Affinity Pub Serv.

Affleck & Gray. The Border Post (Albury) Almanac 1878. (Facsimile Ser.: No. 22). 126p. 1981. 13.95 (ISBN 0-908120-30-3, Pub. by Lib Australian Hist). Australia N U P.

Affleck, James, jt. ed. see Forrest, A. D.

Afflerbach, Lois & Franck, Marga, eds. The Emerging Field of Sociobibliography: The Collected Essays of Ilse Bry. LC 76-28644. (Contributions in Librarianship & Information Science: No. 19). 1977. lib. bdg. 35.00 (ISBN 0-8371-9289-7, BRB/). Greenwood.

Affley, G. M. Business Law: Workbook. 1st ed. (M & E Business Studies Ser.). 64p. 1984. text ed. 2.95 Brit. pds. (ISBN 0-7121-2404-7). Macdonald & Evans.

Affolter, F. & Stricker, E. Perceptual Processes As Prerequisites for Complex Human Behaviour. 179p. 1980. 60.00 (ISBN 3-456-80925-5, Pub. by Holdan Bk Ltd UK). State Mutual Bk.

Affolter, James M. A Monograph of the Genus Lilaeopsis (Umbelliferae) Anderson, Christiane, ed. LC 85-1291. (Systematic Botany Monographs: Vol. 6). (Illus.). 140p. (Orig.). 1985. pap. 18.00 (ISBN 0-912861-06-1). Am Soc Plant.

Affonso, Dyanne D. Impact of Cesarean Childbirth. LC 81-4429. (Illus.). 296p. 1981. 15.95x (ISBN 0-8036-0034-8). Davis Co.

Afford, Max. Mischief in the Air: Radio & Stage Plays. 1974. 14.95x (ISBN 0-7022-0957-0); pap. 8.50x (ISBN 0-7022-0918-X). U of Queensland Pr.

Affre, Jean, ed. see Moreau, Jean-Francois & Mazzara, Laure.

Affron, Charles. Cinema & Sentiment. LC 82-2687. (Illus.). 160p. 1982. lib. bdg. 22.00x (ISBN 0-226-00820-7). U of Chicago Pr.

--Stage for Poets: Studies in the Theatre of Hugo & Musset. LC 75-153847. (Princeton Essays in Literature Ser.). 1972. 28.00x (ISBN 0-691-06201-3). Princeton U Pr.

Affron, Mirella J. & Rubinstein, E., eds. The Last Metro, Francois Truffaut, Director. (Rutgers Films in Print Ser.). (Illus.). 160p. 1985. 25.00 (ISBN 0-8135-1065-1); pap. 10.00 (ISBN 0-8135-1066-X). Rutgers U Pr.

Afgan, N., jt. auth. see Bankoff, G.

Afgan, N., jt. ed. see Soloukhin, R. I.

Afgan, N., jt. ed. see Spalding, D. Brian.

Afgan, N., ed. see Summer Seminar, Heat & Mass Transfer in Buildings, Dubrovnik, Yugoslavia, Aug. 29-Sept. 3,1977.

Afgan, N., jt. ed. see Van Swaaij, W. P.

Afgan, N. H. & Schlunder, E. U. Heat Exchangers: Design & Theory. (Illus.). 928p. 1974. 89.50 (ISBN 0-07-000460-9). McGraw.

Afgan, Naim H., jt. ed. see Bankoff, S. George.

Afgan, Naim H., jt. ed. see Metzger, Darryl E.

Afgan, Naim H., jt. ed. see Spalding, D. Brian.

Afghan, B. K., jt. auth. see Chau, A. S.

Afghan, B. K. see Chau, S. Y.

Afghan, B. K. & Mackay, D., eds. Hydrocarbons & Halogenated Hydrocarbons in the Aquatic Environment. LC 79-26462. (Environmental Science Research Ser.: Vol. 16). 602p. 1980. 79.50x (ISBN 0-306-40329-3, Plenum Pr). Plenum Pub.

Afifi, A. A. & Azen, Stanley P. Statistical Analysis: A Computer Oriented Approach. 2nd ed. 1979. 22.50i (ISBN 0-12-044460-7). Acad Pr.

Afifi, Abdelmonem & Clark, Virginia. Computer-Aided Multivariate Analysis. (Illus.). 360p. 1984. 32.00 (ISBN 0-534-02786-5). Lifetime Learn.

Afifi, Abdelmonem & Clark, Virginia A. Computer-Aided Multivariate Analysis. 360p. 1984. 32.00 (ISBN 0-534-02786-5). Van Nos Reinhold.

Afifi, Adel K. & Bergman, Ronald A. Basic Neuroscience: A Structural & Functional Approach. 2nd ed. (Illus.). 605p. 1985. pap. 24.50 (ISBN 0-8067-0102-1). Urban & S.

Afifi, Adel K., jt. auth. see Bergman, Ronald A.

Afigbo, A. E. The Role of History as a Social Force. LC 79-88988. Date not set. price not set (ISBN 0-88357-013-0); pap. price not set (ISBN 0-88357-052-1). NOK Pubs.

--The Warrant Chiefs: Indirect Rule in Southeastern Nigeria, 1891-1929. (Ibadan History Ser.). 320p. 1972. text ed. 13.75x (ISBN 0-391-00215-5). Humanities.

AFIPS. National Computer Conference 1984: AFIPS Proceedings, Vol. 53. (Illus.). 1984. 80.00 (ISBN 0-88283-043-0). AFIPS Pr.

AFIPS Taxonomy Committee & Ashenhurst, Robert L. Taxonomy of Computer Science & Engineering. LC 79-57474. ix, 462p. 1980. 40.25 (ISBN 0-88283-008-2). AFIPS Pr.

Afkham Darbandi, tr. see Farid ud-Din Attar.

Afkhami, Gholam R. The Iranian Revolution: Thanatos on a National Scale. LC 85-61787. 276p. 1985. 25.00 (ISBN 0-916808-28-9). Mid East Inst.

Af Klintberg, Bengt. The Cursive Scandinavian Salve. (Orig.). 1967. pap. 3.50 (ISBN 0-89366-084-1). Ultramarine Pub.

AFL-CIO. AFL-CIO Manual for Shop Stewards. 68p. 1985. single copies free. AFL-CIO.

Aflaki. The Whirling Ecstasy. Huart, C., tr. (Illus.). 30p. (Orig.). 1973. pap. 1.95 (ISBN 0-915424-02-9, Prophecy Presswords). Sufi Islamia-Prophecy.

Aflalo, F. G., jt. ed. see Peek, Hedley.

Afnan, Ruhi. Great Prophets. 1960. 6.00 (ISBN 0-8022-0010-9). Philos Lib.

--The Revelation of Baha'u'llah & the Bab: Descartes Theory of Knowledge, Bk. 1. LC 75-109166. 1970. 7.50 (ISBN 0-8022-2307-9). Philos Lib.

--Zoroaster's Influence on Anaxagoras, the Greek Tragedians & Socrates. LC 68-18733. 1969. 5.00 (ISBN 0-8022-2250-1). Philos Lib.

--Zoroaster's Influence on Greek Thought. LC 64-20423. 1965. 7.50 (ISBN 0-8022-0011-7). Philos Lib.

Afnan, Ruhi M. Baha'u'llah & the Bab Confront Modern Thinkers: Spinoza: Concerning God, Bk. 2. LC 75-109166. 1977. 7.50 (ISBN 0-8022-2197-1). Philos Lib.

Afnan, Soheil M. Avicenna, His Life & Works. LC 79-8705. 298p. 1980. Repr. of 1958 ed. lib. bdg. 27.50x (ISBN 0-313-22198-7, AFAV). Greenwood.

Afraimovic, V. S., et al. Transactions of the Moscow Mathematical Society, Vol. 28 (1973) LC 65-7413. 1975. 76.00 (ISBN 0-8218-1628-4, MOSCOW-28). Am Math.

Afrasiabe, A. Ali, jt. auth. see Valenta, Lubomir.

Afrendras, Evangelos A. & Kuo, Eddie C., eds. Language & Society in Singapore. 1980. 22.95x (ISBN 9971-69-016-0, 82-93698, Pub. by Singapore U Pr); pap. 12.95x (ISBN 9971-69-017-9, 82-93706, Pub. by Singapore U Pr). Ohio U Pr.

Afriat, S. N. Demand Functions & the Slutsky Matrix. LC 79-83973. (Princeton Studies in Mathematical Economics: No. 7). 1980. 23.00 (ISBN 0-691-04222-5). Princeton U Pr.

--The Price Index. LC 77-2134. pap. 50.80 (ISBN 0-317-26069-3, 2024409). Bks Demand UMI.

Africa Information Service, ed. Return to the Source: Selected Speeches. Cabral, Amilcar. LC 74-7788. (Illus.). 128p. 1974. pap. 4.95 (ISBN 0-85345-347-0). Monthly Rev.

Africa Magazine & Economist, eds. Africa Nineteen Seventy-Four to Nineteen Seventy-Five. LC 68-6810. (Illus.). 200p. 1974. pap. text ed. 15.00x (ISBN 0-8419-0108-2, Africana). Holmes & Meier.

Africa, Thomas W. The Immense Majesty: A History of Rome & the Roman Empire. LC 73-14536. 1974. 24.95x (ISBN 0-88295-700-7). Harlan Davidson.

African Bibliographic Center. Proceedings, 6 vols, Vols. 1-6. Incl. (Vols. 1-3). lib. bdg. 27.50 (ISBN 0-8371-9911-5, SBA); (Vol. 4). lib. bdg. 27.50 (ISBN 0-8371-9912-3, SBB); (Vol. 5). lib. bdg. 27.50 (ISBN 0-8371-9913-1, SBC); (Vol. 3). lib. bdg. 33.00 (ISBN 0-8371-9914-X, SBD). LC 75-77167. (Special Bibliographic Ser). Repr. Set. lib. bdg. 150.00 (ISBN 0-8371-1066-1, SBF&). Greenwood.

--Proceedings, Vol. 7, Nos. 1-2. Incl. No. 1; No. 2. lib. bdg. 18.75 (ISBN 0-8371-3329-7, SBG&). (Special Bibliographic Ser.). Repr. Greenwood.

--Proceedings, Vol. 8, Nos. 1-2. Incl. No. 1. lib. bdg. 9.00; No. 2. lib. bdg. 12.00 (ISBN 0-8371-6262-9, SBI). (Special Bibliographic Ser.). Repr. Set. lib. bdg. 22.50 (ISBN 0-8371-9915-8, SBN&). Greenwood.

--A Short Guide to the Study of Ethiopia: A General Bibliography. Hidaru, Alula & Rahmato, Dessalegn, eds. LC 76-27128. (Special Bibliographic Ser.: No. 2). 192p. 1976. lib. bdg. 27.50x (ISBN 0-8371-9284-6, HE/A02). Greenwood.

African Education Commission. Education in East Africa. LC 78-100256. (Illus.). Repr. of 1925 ed. 24.75x (ISBN 0-8371-2914-1, EDE&, Pub. by Negro U Pr). Greenwood.

African Institution - London. Review of the Colonial Slave Registration Acts. facs. ed. LC 78-149860. (Black Heritage Library Collection). 1820. 14.50 (ISBN 0-8369-8742-X). Ayer Co Pubs.

African Studies Association of the United Kingdom, 1972. The Population Factor in African Studies: Proceedings. Moss, R. P. & Rathbone, R. J., eds. 209p. 1975. text ed. 17.00 (ISBN 0-8419-6200-6, Africana). Holmes & Meier.

Africano, Lillian. Passions. 288p. 1985. pap. 3.50 (ISBN 0-515-08103-5). Jove Pubns.

--Something Old, Something New. 384p. 1983. pap. 3.50 (ISBN 0-515-05865-3). Jove Pubns.

Africano, Lillian, jt. auth. see Stutman, Fred A.

Africanus, Sextus J. List of Olympian Victors. Rutgers, I., ed. 196p. 1980. 25.00 (ISBN 0-89005-351-0). Ares.

Afrow, Mitchell L., jt. auth. see Alpers, Byron J.

Afrukhtih, Yunis Khan. Khatirat-i Nuh Salih. (Illus., Persian.). 1983. 15.95 (ISBN 0-933770-20-0, P-31). Kalimat.

AFS-DIS, Conference, 1975. Quality Ductile Iron Production Today & Tomorrow: Proceedings. 347p. 40.00 (ISBN 0-317-32662-7, FC7510); members 20.00 (ISBN 0-317-32663-5). Am Foundrymen.

Afshar, F., et al. Stereotaxic Atlas of the Human Brainstem & Cerebellar Nuclei: A Variability Study. LC 76-5676. 256p. 1978. 223.50 (ISBN 0-89004-132-6). Raven.

Afshar, Freydoun. Taxonomic Revision of the Superspecific Groups of the Cretaceous & Cenozoic Tellinidae. LC 72-98019. (Geological Society of America Ser.: No. 119). pap. 57.80 (ISBN 0-317-28386-3, 2025467). Bks Demand UMI.

Afshar, Haleh, ed. Women, Work, & Ideology in the Third World. 280p. 1985. price not set (ISBN 0-422-79700-6, 9606, Pub. by Tavistock England); pap. price not set (ISBN 0-422-79710-3, 9607, Pub. by Tavistock England). Methuen Inc.

Aft, jt. auth. see Lawrence.

Aft, Lawrence. Wage & Salary Administration. 1985. text ed. 24.95 (ISBN 0-8359-8528-8); instr's. manual avail. (ISBN 0-8359-8529-6). Reston.

Aftalion, Albert. L' Oeuvre Economique de Simonde de Sismondi. 1968. Repr. of 1899 ed. 22.50 (ISBN 0-8337-0025-1). B Franklin.

Aftandilian, Gregory L. Armenia, Vision of a Republic: The Independence Lobby in America 1918-1927. (Illus.). 1980. 9.95 (ISBN 0-89182-027-2). Charles River Bks.

Aftel, Mandy. Death of a Rolling Stone: The Brian Jones Story. (Illus.). 192p. (Orig.). 1982. pap. 8.95 (ISBN 0-933328-37-0). Delilah Bks.

Aftel, Mandy & Lakoff, Robin T. When Talk Is Not Cheap: Or, How to Find the Right Therapist When You Don't Know Where to Begin. 224p. 1985. 17.50 (ISBN 0-446-51309-1). Warner Bks.

Aftenposten. Facts about Norway. Royal Ministry of Foreign Affairs Staff, ed. 96p. 1982. 9.00 (ISBN 0-317-19013-X, N451). Vanous.

Aftenposten, A., ed. Norway: Facts About. 18th ed. 1984. 10.00x (ISBN 82-516-0659-4, N451). Vanous.

Aftergood, Lilla, jt. auth. see Alfin-Slater, Roslyn B.

Afterman, Alan B. Accounting & Auditing Disclosure Manual, 1985. 1984. 72.00 (ISBN 0-88712-194-2). Warren.

Afterman, Allan. GAAP Practice Manual. 1985. 175.00 (ISBN 0-88712-198-5). Warren.

Afterman, Allan B. Compilation & Review Practice Manual. 460p. 1984. text ed. 65.00 (ISBN 0-88712-159-4). Warren.

Afzal-Ur-Rehman. Economic Doctrines of Islam, 4 Vols. 39.50 (ISBN 0-686-18354-1). Kazi Pubns.

Afzelius, A. Two Studies on Roman Expansion: An Original Anthology. LC 75-7301. (Roman History Ser.). (Ger.). 1975. Repr. of 1975 ed. 30.00x (ISBN 0-405-07178-7). Ayer Co Pubs.

Afzelius, B., jt. auth. see Bacetti, B.

Afzelius, Bjorn. Anatomy of the Cell. Satir, Birgit, tr. LC 66-13860. (Illus.). 1967. pap. 2.45x (ISBN 0-226-00851-7, P532, Phoen). U of Chicago Pr.

Agabekov, Grigorii S. OGPU: The Russian Secret Terror. Bunn, H. W., tr. from Fr. LC 74-10073. (Russian Studies: Perspectives on the Revolution Ser). 277p. 1974. Repr. of 1931 ed. 22.50 (ISBN 0-88355-181-0). Hyperion Conn.

Agabian, Nina & Eisen, Harvey. Molecular Biology of Host-Parasite Interactions. LC 84-7874. (UCLA Symposium on Molecular & Cellular Biology, New Ser.: Vol. 13). 380p. 1984. 78.00 (ISBN 0-8451-2612-1). A R Liss.

Agahd, Reinholdo, ed. see Varro, Marcus T.

Agajanian, A. H. Computer Technology: Logic, Memory, & Microprocessors; A Bibliography. 360p. 1978. 95.00x (ISBN 0-306-65174-2, IFI Plenum). Plenum Pub.

--Microelectronic Packaging: A Bibliography. LC 79-18930. (IFI Data Base Library). 254p. 1979. 85.00x (ISBN 0-306-65183-1, IFI Plenum). Plenum Pub.

--MOSFET Technologies: A Comprehensive Bibliography. LC 80-21773. 390p. 1980. 95.00x (ISBN 0-306-65193-9, IFI Plenum). Plenum Pub.

--Semiconducting Devices: A Bibliography of Fabrication Technology, Properties, & Applications. LC 76-42313. 968p. 1976. 135.00x (ISBN 0-306-65166-1, IFI Plenum). Plenum Pub.

Agajanian, A. H., ed. Ion Implantation in Microelectronics: A Comprehensive Bibliography. LC 81-10753. (Computer Science Information Guides Ser.: Vol. 1). 266p. 1981. lib. bdg. 85.00x (ISBN 0-306-65198-X, IFI Plenum). Plenum Pub.

Agajanian, Shaakeh S. Sonnets from the Portugese & the Love Sonnet Tradition. LC 84-20708. 117p. (Orig.). 1985. pap. 9.95 (ISBN 0-8022-2480-6). Philos Lib.

Agalloco, jt. auth. see Carleton.

Aganbegyan, A. G. Regional Studies for Planning & Projection. (Regional Planning Ser.: No. 7). 1979. text ed. write for info. Mouton.

Aganbegyan, A. G., ed. Preplanning Studies for Regional Development in Siberia. (Publications in Collaboration with the Institute of Social Studies). 1977. text ed. write for info (ISBN 0-686-22630-5). Mouton.

Aga-Oglu, Kamer. The Williams Collection of Far Eastern Ceramics, Chinese, Siamese, & Annamese Ceramic Wares: Selected from the Collection of Justice & Mrs. G. M. Williams in the U. of Mich. Museum of Anthropology. (Special Publications Ser.). (Illus.). 1972. pap. 4.00x (ISBN 0-932206-74-3). U Mich Mus Anthro.

Agapius, et al. The Rudder: Divine Canons of the Seven Decumenical & of Local Synods. Orthodox Christian Educational Society & Makrakis, Apostolos, eds. Cummings, Denver, tr. from Hellenic. Orig. Title: Pedalion. 1097p. 1957. 26.00x (ISBN 0-938366-00-9). Orthodox Chr.

Agar, A. W., et al. Principles & Practice of Electron Microscope Operation. (Practical Methods in Electron Microscopy: Vol. 2). 1974. 76.50 (ISBN 0-7204-4254-0, Biomedical Pr); pap. 27.75 (ISBN 0-7204-4255-9). Elsevier.

Agar, Augustus. Baltic Episode. LC 82-42935. (Illus.). 264p. 1983. 14.95 (ISBN 0-87021-910-3). Naval Inst Pr.

Agar, Frederick A. The Deacon at Work. 1923. 3.95 (ISBN 0-8170-0783-0). Judson.

Agar, H. Milton & Plato. 1985. 52.50 (ISBN 0-317-19968-4). Porter.

Agar, Herbert. People's Choice. LC 33-19369. (Illus.). 337p. 1969. Repr. of 1933 ed. 18.95 (ISBN 0-910220-01-8). Berg.

--The Perils of Democracy. LC 66-11684. (Background Ser.). 95p. 1965. 7.95 (ISBN 0-8023-1001-X). Dufour.

--Price of Power: America Since Nineteen Forty-Five. LC 57-8575. (Chicago History of American Civilization Ser). 1957. pap. 8.00x (ISBN 0-226-00937-8, CHAC1). U of Chicago Pr.

--The Price of Power: America since Nineteen Forty Five. LC 57-8575. (The Chicago History of American Civilization Ser.). pap. 53.00 (ISBN 0-317-09974-4, 2020018). Bks Demand UMI.

Agar, Herbert, jt. auth. see Chilton, Eleanor Carroll.

Agar, Herbert & Tate, Allen, eds. Who Owns America. facs. ed. LC 71-99616. (Essay Index Reprint Ser). 1936. 23.00 (ISBN 0-8369-1540-2). Ayer Co Pubs.

--Who Owns America? A New Declaration of Independence. LC 82-24752. 352p. 1983. pap. text ed. 14.25 (ISBN 0-8191-2767-1). U Pr of Amer.

Agar, Michael. Ripping & Running: A Formal Ethnograph of Urban Heroin Addicts. (Language, Thought & Culture: Advances in the Study of Cognition Ser.). 1973. 35.00 (ISBN 0-12-785020-1). Acad Pr.

Agar, Michael H. The Professional Stranger: An Informal Introduction to Ethnography. LC 79-8870. (Studies in Anthropology). 1980. 13.50 (ISBN 0-12-043850-X). Acad Pr.

Agar, N. S. & Board, P. G., eds. Red Blood Cells of Domestic Animals. xviii, 420p. 1983. 130.75 (ISBN 0-444-80455-2). Elsevier.

Agard, A. The Reportorie of Records at Westminster. LC 72-225. (English Experience Ser.: No. 291). 1971. Repr. of 1631 ed. 22.00 (ISBN 90-221-0291-2). Walter J Johnson.

Agard, F. B. Spoken Romanian. LC 74-1000. (Spoken Language Ser.). 140p. (gr. 9-12). 1976. pap. 12.00x Units 1-30 (ISBN 0-87950-315-7); 6 dual track cassettes 60.00x (ISBN 0-87950-317-3); bk. & cassettes 65.00x (ISBN 0-87950-314-9). Spoken Lang Serv.

Agard, F. B., et al. English for Speakers of Spanish (El Ingles Hablado) LC 75-26678. (English for Foreigners Ser.). xii, 403p. (Prog. Bk.). 1975. pap. 12.00x (ISBN 0-87950-307-6); 5 dual track cassettes 60.00x (ISBN 0-87950-311-4); book & cassettes 65.00x (ISBN 0-87950-312-2). Spoken Lang Serv.

Agard, Frederick B. Agards in America. 1975. 15.00 (ISBN 0-686-20851-X). Polyanthos.

--A Course in Romance Linguistics: A Diachronic View, Vol. 2. 256p. 1984. text ed. 19.95 (ISBN 0-87840-089-3). Georgetown U Pr.

--A Course in Romance Linguistics, Vol. 1: A Synchronic View. (Orig.). 1984. 19.95 (ISBN 0-87840-088-5). Georgetown U Pr.

Agard, Frederick B. & Di Pietro, Robert J. The Sounds of English & Italian. LC 65-25118. (Midway Reprint Ser). 76p. 1974. pap. text ed. 6.00x (ISBN 0-226-01020-1). U of Chicago Pr.

Agard, Frederick B., jt. auth. see Sola, Donald F.

Agard, John. Dig Away Two Hole Tim. 32p. 9.95 (ISBN 0-370-30421-7, Pub. by the Bodley Head). Merrimack Pub Cir.

Agard, Judith A., jt. auth. see Mopsik, Stanley I.

AGARD-NATO. Combustion & Propulsion: Colloquium on Energy Sources & Energy Conversion. (Agardographs Ser.: No. 81). 936p. 1967. 236.95 (ISBN 0-677-10560-6). Gordon.

--Fluid Dynamic Aspects of Space Flight, 2 vols. (Agardographs Ser.: No. 87). 1966. Vol. 1, 416p. 119.25 (ISBN 0-677-11560-1); Vol. 2, 362p. 94.95 (ISBN 0-677-11570-9); Set, 778p. 212.75 (ISBN 0-677-11440-0). Gordon.

--Instrumentation for High Speed Plasma Flow. (Agardographs Ser.: No. 96). 196p. 1966. 69.50 (ISBN 0-677-11020-0). Gordon.

--Low Temperature Oxidation. (Agardographs Ser.: No. 86). 426p. 1966. 119.25 (ISBN 0-677-10540-1). Gordon.

--Nuclear Thermal & Electric Rocket Propulsion. (Agardographs Ser.: No. 101). 650p. 1967. 172.25 (ISBN 0-677-11040-5). Gordon.

--Physics & Technology of Ion Motors. (Agardographs Ser.: No. 88). (Illus.). 438p. 1966. 119.25 (ISBN 0-677-10570-3). Gordon.

--Radar Techniques for Detection Tracking & Navigation. (Agardographs Ser.: No. 100). (Illus.). 616p. 1966. 164.25 (ISBN 0-677-11030-8). Gordon.

Agard, Walter R. The Greek Mind. LC 78-25755. (Anvil Ser.). 190p. 1979. pap. text ed. 6.95 (ISBN 0-88275-811-X). Krieger.

Agard, William R. Humanities for Our Time. facsimile ed. LC 68-29218. (Essay Index Reprint Ser: Univ. of Kansas Lectures in the Humanities). Repr. of 1949 ed. 17.00 (ISBN 0-8369-0554-7). Ayer Co Pubs.

Agardh, C. A. Species Algarum Rite Cognitae Cum Symonymus, Differentis Specificis et Descriptionibus Succinctis, 2 vols. 1970. Repr. of 1828 ed. 39.10 (ISBN 90-6123-001-2). Lubrecht & Cramer.

Agardy, Maria, jt. auth. see Lance, Kathryn.

Agarwal, A. N. Indian Economy. 1976. 12.00 (ISBN 0-7069-0391-9). Intl Bk Dist.

Agarwal, A. N. & Lal, Kundan. Economic Planning: Principles, Techniques & Practice. 1977. 10.50 (ISBN 0-686-21732-2). Intl Bk Dist.

Agarwal, B. D. & Broutman, L. J. Analysis & Performance of Fibre Composites. (SPE Monograph). (Illus.). 350p. 1980. 45.00 (ISBN 0-686-48244-1, 0801). T-C Pubns CA.

Agarwal, B. K. X-Ray Spectroscopy. (Springer Series in Optical Sciences: Vol. 15). (Illus.). 1979. 48.00 (ISBN 0-387-09268-4). Springer-Verlag.

Agarwal, Bhagwan D. & Broutman, Lawrence J. Analysis & Performance of Fiber Composites. LC 79-23740. (Society of Plastics Engineers Monograph Ser). 355p. 1980. 44.95x (ISBN 0-471-05928-5, Pub. by Wiley-Interscience). Wiley.

Agarwal, Bhoo, et al. A Humanistic Approach to Quality of Life: A Selected Bibliography, Nos. 1052-1054. 1976. 12.50 (ISBN 0-686-20398-4). CPL Biblios.

Agarwal, Bina. Cold Hearths & Barren Slopes: Woodfuel Crisis in the Third World. LC 85-61078. 160p. 1985. 16.00 (ISBN 0-913215-03-1). Riverdale Co.

--Mechanization in Indian Agriculture: An Analytical Study Based on the Punjab. 1984. 24.00x (ISBN 0-8364-1168-4, Pub. by Allied India). South Asia Bks.

--Monsoon-Poems. 1976. 8.00 (ISBN 0-89253-807-4); flexible cloth 4.00 (ISBN 0-89253-808-2). Ind-US Inc.

Agarwal, D. D., et al. Geometrical Drawing. 1984. text ed. 22.50x (ISBN 0-7069-0802-3, Pub. by Vikas India). Advent NY.

Agarwal, G. C., jt. ed. see Stark, L.

Agarwal, G. P., ed. see All India Symposium, Jabalpur, Feb. 24-27, 1978.

Agarwal, G. S. Quantum-Statistical Theories of Spontaneous Emission & Their Relation to Other Approaches. LC 25-9130. (Tracts in Modern Physics Ser: Vol. 70). 140p. 1974. 45.50 (ISBN 0-387-06630-6). Springer-Verlag.

Agarwal, G. S. & Dattagupta, S., eds. Stochastic Processes Formalism & Applications. (Lecture Notes in Physics: Vol. 184). 324p. 1983. pap. 19.00 (ISBN 0-387-12326-1). Springer-Verlag.

Agarwal, H. N. Administrative System of Nepal. 1976. 15.00 (ISBN 0-7069-0345-5). Intl Bk Dist.

Agarwal, J. C., jt. ed. see Yannopoulos, J. C.

Agarwal, K. K. Programming with Structured Flowcharts. 160p. 1984. pap. 12.00. Van Nos Reinhold.

Agarwal, Krishna K. Programming with Structured Flowcharts. 142p. 1984. pap. 12.00 (ISBN 0-89433-226-0). Petrocelli.

Agarwal, M. K., ed. Antihormones. 458p. 1979. 78.50 (ISBN 0-444-80119-7, Biomedical Pr). Elsevier.

--Bacterial Endotoxins & Host Response. x, 436p. 1981. 78.50 (ISBN 0-444-80301-7). Elsevier.

--Hormone Antagonists. (Illus.). 734p. 1982. 72.00x (ISBN 3-11-008613-1). De Gruyter.

--Principles of Recepterology. LC 83-15441. (Illus.). vii, 677p. 1983. 88.00x (ISBN 3-11-009558-0). De Gruyter.

--Streptozotocin: Fundamentals & Therapy. viii, 310p. 1981. 90.00 (ISBN 0-444-80302-5). Elsevier.

Agarwal, M. K. & Yoshida, M., eds. Immunopharmacology of Endotoxicosis: Proceedings of the 5th International Congress of Immunology Satellite Workshop. Kyoto, Japan, August 27, 1983. LC 84-7650. (Illus.). xiv, 376p. 1984. 68.00x (ISBN 3-11-009887-3). De Gruyter.

Agarwal, M. K., ed. see International Congress of Endocrinology.

Agarwal, Manmoohan. Paraguay: Economic Memorandum. v, 178p. 1979. pap. 15.00 (ISBN 0-686-36113-X, RC-7906). World Bank.

Agarwal, Manoj K., et al. Readings in Industrial Marketing. (Illus.). 256p. 1986. pap. text ed. 17.95 (ISBN 0-13-756545-3). P-H.

Agarwal, N. The Development of a Dual Economy. 192p. 1983. 49.00x (ISBN 0-317-20268-5, Pub. by K P Bagchi & Co India). State Mutual Bk.

Agarwal, R. J., jt. auth. see Birla Institute of Scientific Research, Economic Research Division.

Agarwal, R. S. Yoga of Perfect Sight. 3rd ed. 1979. pap. 14.00 (ISBN 0-89744-948-7). Auromere.

--Yoga of Perfect Sight: With Letters of Sri Aurobindo. (Illus.). 1974. pap. 5.45 (ISBN 0-89071-261-1). Matagiri.

Agarwal, S. C. John Keats: Selected Poems. viii, 346p. 1982. text ed. 35.00 (ISBN 0-7069-1761-8, Pub. by Vikas India). Advent NY.

Agarwal, S. C., ed. John Keats: Selected Poems. 255p. 1982. 40.00x (ISBN 0-7069-1761-8, Pub. by Garlandfold England); pap. 30.00x (ISBN 0-7069-1762-6). State Mutual Bk.

Agarwal, S. L. Labour Relations Law in India. 1978. 14.00x (ISBN 0-8364-0309-6). South Asia Bks.

Agarwal, S. N., ed. see Gandhi, M. K.

Agarwal, Surendra, jt. auth. see Kavalsky, Basil.

Agarwal, V. P. & Sharma, V. K., eds. Progress of Plant Ecology in India, Vol. 4. 167p. 1980. 10.00 (ISBN 0-686-82969-7, Pub. by Messers Today & Tomorrows Printers & Publishers India). Scholarly Pubns.

Agarwal, V. P., ed. see All India Symposium, Muzaffarnagar, Dec. 1976.

Agarwala, Amar N. Education for Business in a Developing Society. LC 75-625500. 1969. 6.50x (ISBN 0-87744-022-0). Mich St U Pr.

Agarwala, Amar N. & Singh, S. P., eds. Economics of Underdevelopment: A Series of Articles & Papers. 1963. pap. 8.95x (ISBN 0-19-560674-4). Oxford U Pr.

Agarwala, P. N. The History of Indian Business. 300p. 1985. text ed. 40.00x (ISBN 0-7069-2609-9, Pub. by Vikas India). Advent NY.

--India's Export Strategy. 384p. 1978. 18.00x (ISBN 0-7069-0653-5, Pub. by Vikas India). Advent NY.

--The New International Economic Order. (Studies on the New International Economic Order). 350p. 1983. 35.00 (ISBN 0-08-028823-5). Pergamon.

Agarwala, Ramgopal. Econometric Model of India, 1848-1961. 188p. 1970. 29.50x (ISBN 0-7146-1200-6, BHA 01200, F Cass Co). Biblio Dist.

Agarwala, S. N., ed. see Seminar on Population Growth & India's Economic Development.

Agarwala-Rogers, Rekha, jt. auth. see Rogers, Everett M.

Agassi. Towards a Rational Philosophical Anthropology. (The Van Leer Jerusalem Foundation Ser). 1977. lib. bdg. 30.00 (ISBN 90-247-2003-6, Pub. by Martinus Nijhoff Netherlands). Kluwer Academic.

Agassi, J., ed. Psychiatric Diagnosis. vii, 184p. 1981. pap. 20.00 (ISBN 0-86689-015-7). Balaban Intl Sci Serv.

Agassi, Joseph. Faraday As a Natural Philosopher. LC 73-151130. 1972. 23.00x (ISBN 0-226-01046-5). U of Chicago Pr.
--Science & Society: Selected Essays in the Sociology of Science. 539p. 1981. 79.00 (ISBN 90-277-1244-1, Pub. by Reidel Holland). Kluwer Academic.
--Technology: Philosophical & Social Aspects. 1986. lib. bdg. 39.50 (ISBN 90-277-2044-4, Pub. by Reidel Holland); pap. text ed. 19.95 (ISBN 90-277-2045-2). Kluwer Academic.
Agassi, Joseph, jt. auth. see Fried, Yehuda.
Agassi, Joseph & Cohen, Robert, eds. Scientific Philosophy Today. 1982. lib. bdg. 69.50 (ISBN 90-277-1262-X, Pub. by Reidel Netherlands); pap. text ed. 34.50 (ISBN 90-277-1263-8, Pub. by Reidel Holland). Kluwer Academic.
Agassi, Judith B. Comparing the Work Attitudes of Women & Men. LC 81-47552. 368p. 1983. 38.00 (ISBN 0-669-04657-4). Lexington Bks.
Agassiz, Alexander, jt. auth. see Agassiz, Elizabeth.
Agassiz, Elizabeth & Agassiz, Alexander. Seaside Studies in Natural History: Marine Animals of Massachusetts Bay. LC 75-125726. (American Environmental Studies). (Illus.). 1970. Repr. of 1865 ed. 23.50 (ISBN 0-405-02651-X). Ayer Co Pubs.
Agassiz, George R., ed. see Lyman, Theodore.
Agassiz, Jean L. Contributions to the Natural History of the United States of America, 4 Vols. in 2. Sterling, Keir B., ed. LC 77-81094. (Biologists & Their World Ser.). (Illus.). 1978. Repr. of 1862 ed. Set. lib. bdg. 120.00x (ISBN 0-405-10675-0); 60.00x ea. Vol. 1 (ISBN 0-405-10676-9). Vol. 2 (ISBN 0-405-10677-7). Ayer Co Pubs.
Agassiz, Louis. Essay on Classification. Lurie, Edward, ed. LC 62-19211. (The John Harvard Library). 1962. 18.00x (ISBN 0-674-26250-6). Harvard U Pr.
--Etudes Critiques les Mollusques Fossiles: Memoire les Trigonies et Monographic Des Myes (Critical Studies on Fossil Mollusks. Gould, Stephen J., ed. LC 79-8323. (History of Paleontology Ser.). (Illus., Fr.). 1980. Repr. of 1840 ed. lib. bdg. 68.50x (ISBN 0-405-12702-2). Ayer Co Pubs.
--Geological Sketches. 229p. 1985. Repr. of 1885 ed. 29.00 (ISBN 0-932051-24-3). Am Repr Serv.
--The Intelligence of Louis Agassiz: A Specimen Book of Scientific Writings; Selected, with an Introduction & Notes. Davenport, Guy, ed. LC 83-18504. x, 237p. 1983. Repr. of 1963 ed. lib. bdg. 42.50x (ISBN 0-313-24249-6, AGIN). Greenwood.
--Lake Superior: Its Physical Character: Vegetation, & Animals Compared with Those of Other & Similar Regions. LC 79-125727. (American Environmental Studies). 1970. Repr. of 1850 ed. 22.00 (ISBN 0-405-02652-8). Ayer Co Pubs.
--Methods of Study in Natural History. LC 72-125728. (American Environmental Studies). 1970. Repr. of 1863 ed. 20.00 (ISBN 0-405-02653-6). Ayer Co Pubs.
Agassiz, Louis & Gould, Augustus. Principles of Zoology, Touching the Structure, Development, Distribution, & Natural Arrangement of the Races of Animals Living & Extinct. LC 76-125729. (American Environmental Studies). (Illus.). 1970. Repr. of 1848 ed. 17.00 (ISBN 0-405-02654-4). Ayer Co Pubs.
Agate, James. Amazing Theatre. LC 76-91307. Repr. of 1939 ed. 22.00 (ISBN 0-405-08181-2, Pub by Blom Publications). Ayer Co Pubs.
--Around Cinemas. LC 72-169323. (Literature of the Cinema, Series 2). (Illus.). 286p. 1972. Repr. of 1946 ed. 20.00 (ISBN 0-405-03888-7). Ayer Co Pubs.
--Around Cinemas: Second Series. LC 76-169324. (Literature of Cinema, Series 2). (Illus.). 300p. 1972. Repr. of 1948 ed. 22.00 (ISBN 0-405-03889-5). Ayer Co Pubs.
--At Half-Past Eight: Essays on the Theatre 1921-1922. LC 70-91308. Repr. of 1923 ed. 22.00x (ISBN 0-405-08182-0, Pub. by Blom). Ayer Co Pubs.
--Brief Chronicles. LC 79-92223. 1971. Repr. of 1943 ed. lib. bdg. 22.00 (ISBN 0-405-08183-9, Pub. by Blom). Ayer Co Pubs.
--Buzz, Buzz. LC 73-91309. Repr. of 1918 ed. 18.00 (ISBN 0-405-08184-7, Pub. by Blom). Ayer Co Pubs.
--Contemporary Theatre, Nineteen Twenty-Five. LC 74-91407. Repr. of 1926 ed. 20.00 (ISBN 0-405-08187-1, Pub. by Blom). Ayer Co Pubs.
--Contemporary Theatre, Nineteen Twenty-Four. LC 74-91407. Repr. of 1925 ed. 22.00 (ISBN 0-405-08186-3, Pub. by Blom). Ayer Co Pubs.
--Contemporary Theatre, Nineteen Twenty-Six. LC 74-91407. Repr. of 1927 ed. 22.00 (ISBN 0-405-08188-X, Pub. by Blom). Ayer Co Pubs.
--Contemporary Theatre, Nineteen Twenty-Three. LC 74-91407. Repr. of 1924 ed. 22.00 (ISBN 0-405-08185-5, Pub. by Blom). Ayer Co Pubs.
--The Contemporary Theatre: 1923. 313p. 1983. Repr. of 1924 ed. text ed. 13.00x cancelled (ISBN 0-8290-1444-6). Irvington.
--Immoment Toys. LC 77-86884. Repr. of 1945 ed. 18.00 (ISBN 0-405-08189-8, Pub. by Blom). Ayer Co Pubs.
--More First Nights. LC 74-86886. Repr. of 1937 ed. 22.00 (ISBN 0-405-08190-1, Pub. by Blom). Ayer Co Pubs.
--Playgoing: An Essay. LC 72-83870. Repr. of 1937 ed. 16.00 (ISBN 0-405-08191-X, Pub. by Blom). Ayer Co Pubs.
--Rachel. LC 72-84504. 1928. 16.00 (ISBN 0-405-08192-8, Pub. by Blom). Ayer Co Pubs.
--Red Letter Nights. LC 71-91886. Repr. of 1944 ed. 22.00 (ISBN 0-405-08193-6, Pub. by Blom). Ayer Co Pubs.
--Short View of the English Stage 1900-1926. LC 75-91887. Repr. of 1926 ed. 19.00 (ISBN 0-405-08194-4, Pub. by Blom). Ayer Co Pubs.
--These Were Actors: Extracts from a Newspaper Cutting Book, 1811-1833. LC 72-91889. Repr. of 1943 ed. 14.00 (ISBN 0-405-08195-2, Pub. by Blom). Ayer Co Pubs.
--Those Were the Nights. LC 77-91890. Repr. of 1947 ed. 18.00 (ISBN 0-405-08196-0, Pub. by Blom). Ayer Co Pubs.
Agate, James E. Alarums & Excursions. facs. ed. LC 67-30169. (Essay Index Reprint Ser). 1922. 18.00 (ISBN 0-8369-0138-X). Ayer Co Pubs.
--Short View of the English Stage, 1900-1926. facsimile ed. LC 70-94263. (Select Bibliographies Reprint Ser). 1926. 17.00 (ISBN 0-8369-5037-2). Ayer Co Pubs.
Agate, James E., ed. The English Dramatic Critics: An Anthology, 1660-1932. LC 83-45688. Repr. of 1958 ed. 32.50 (ISBN 0-404-20003-6). AMS Pr.
Agate, May. Madame Sarah. LC 73-82817. 1945. Repr. of 1945 ed. 18.00 (ISBN 0-405-08197-9, Pub. by Blom). Ayer Co Pubs.
Agathangelos. History of the Armenians. Thomson, R. W., ed. & tr. LC 76-2613. (Illus.). 1977. 59.00x (ISBN 0-87395-323-1). State U NY Pr.
--Patmowtiwn Hayots: History of the Armenians. Thomson, Robert W., ed. LC 79-27282. (Classical Armenian Texts). 1980. Repr. of 1909 ed. 55.00x (ISBN 0-88206-027-9). Caravan Bks.
Agathias. Agathiae Myrinaei Historiarum Libri quinque. Keydell, Rudolfus, ed. (Corpus Fontium Historiae Byzantinae Ser. Berolinensis Vol. 2). 232p. (Lat). 1967. 40.40x (ISBN 3-11-001348-7). De Gruyter.
Agawa, Hiroyuki. The Reluctant Admiral: Yamamoto & the Imperial Navy. Bester, John, tr. LC 79-84652. 397p. 1982. 16.95 (ISBN 0-87011-355-0); pap. 6.50 (ISBN 0-87011-512-X). Kodansha.
Agay, Denes. Ballet Music. (Everybody's Favorite Ser.: Vol. 89). 1953. pap. 8.95 (ISBN 0-8256-2089-9). Music Sales.
--The Baroque Period: Masters of the Seventeenth & Eighteenth Century. (An Anthology of Piano Music Ser.: Vol. 1). 232p. 1981. pap. 12.95 (ISBN 0-8256-8041-7). Music Sales.
--Best Loved Songs of the American People. LC 74-4502. 416p. 1975. 17.95 (ISBN 0-385-00004-9); pap. 11.95 (ISBN 0-385-14006-1). Doubleday.
--The Classical Period: Haydn, Mozart, Beethoven & Their Contemporaries. (An Anthology of Piano Music Ser.: Vol. 2). 236p. 1981. pap. 12.95. Music Sales.
--Intermediate Grades: Classics to Moderns. (Music for Millions Ser.: Vol. 37). 1962. pap. 7.95 (ISBN 0-8256-4037-7). Music Sales.
--The Joy of Beethoven. 1983. pap. 5.95 (Pub. by Yorktown). Music Sales.
--The Joy of Chopin. 1984. pap. 5.95 (ISBN 0-8256-8027-1). Music Sales.
--The Joy of Claude Debussy. 1984. pap. 5.95 (ISBN 0-8256-8029-8, Yorktown). Music Sales.
--The Joy of Mozart. 1983. pap. 5.95 (ISBN 0-8256-8026-3, Pub. by Yorktown). Music Sales.
--The Joy of Piano. (Orig.). 1964. pap. 5.95 (ISBN 0-8256-8002-6, Yorktown). Music Sales.
--The Joy of Ragtime. 1974. pap. 5.95 (ISBN 0-8256-8016-6, Yorktown). Music Sales.
--The Joy of the Music of Denes Agay. 1980. pap. 5.95 (ISBN 0-8256-8024-7, Yorktown). Music Sales.
--More Easy Classics to Moderns. 160p. pap. 7.95 (ISBN 0-8256-4027-X). Music Sales.
--The Romantic Period: Masters of the 19th Century. (An Anthology of Piano Music Ser.: Vol. 3). 244p. 1971. pap. 12.95 (ISBN 0-8256-8043-3, Yorktown). Music Sales.
--Teaching Piano, 2 vols. in slipcase. (Illus.). 1981. 29.95 (ISBN 0-8256-8039-5). Music Sales.
--The Twentieth Century: Major Composers of Our Time. (An Anthology of Piano Music Ser.: Vol. 4). 238p. 1971. pap. 12.95 (ISBN 0-8256-8044-1, Yorktown). Music Sales.
Agay, Denes, ed. Easy Classics to Moderns. 160p. pap. 7.95 (ISBN 0-8256-4017-2). Music Sales.
Agazarian, Yvonne & Peters, Richard. The Visible & Invisible Group: Two Perspectives on Group Psychotherapy & Group Process. (Illus.). 304p. 1981. 29.95x (ISBN 0-7100-0692-6). Routledge & Kegan.
Agbodeka, Francis. African Politics & British Policy in the Gold Coast 1868-1900: A Study in the Forms & Force of Protest. LC 73-175916. (Legon History Ser.). Repr. of 1971 ed. 54.50 (ISBN 0-8357-9446-6, 2015285). Bks Demand UMI.
Agbor-Tabi, Peter. U. S. Bilateral Assistance in Africa: The Case of Cameroon. (Illus.). 192p. (Orig.). 1984. lib. bdg. 20.50 (ISBN 0-8191-3909-2); pap. text ed. 11.25 (ISBN 0-8191-3910-6). U Pr of Amer.
Agcaoili, T. D., ed. Philippine Writing: An Anthology. LC 76-98742. 1971. Repr. of 1953 ed. lib. bdg. 22.50x (ISBN 0-8371-3063-8, AGPW). Greenwood.
Agee, Anne & Kline, Gary. The Basic Writer's Book. 2nd ed. LC 84-22291. (Illus.). 448p. 1985. pap. text ed. 15.95 (ISBN 0-13-066176-7). P-H.
Agee, Bill. Collecting All Cures. (Illus.). 96p. (Orig.). 1975. pap. 5.95 (ISBN 0-89288-006-6). Maverick.
Agee, Doris. Edgar Cayce on E.S.P. 1969. pap. 3.50 (ISBN 0-446-32715-8). Warner Bks.
Agee, E. M. & Assai, T., eds. Cloud Dynamics. 1982. 49.50 (ISBN 90-277-1458-4, Pub. by Reidel Holland). Kluwer Academic.
Agee, Helene B. Facets of Goochland (Virginia) County's History. 1962. 5.95 (ISBN 0-685-47896-3). Dietz.
Agee, Hugh, ed. High Interest-Easy Reading: For Junior & Senior High School Students. 4th ed. 96p. 1984. 5.00 (ISBN 0-317-37058-8, 20954R); members 4.50 (ISBN 0-317-37059-6). Ncte.
Agee, Hugh, jt. ed. see Committee to Revise High Interest-Easy Reading.
Agee, James. Agee on Film, 2 vols. 488p. (Orig.). 1983. Vol. 1. pap. 7.95 (ISBN 0-399-50870-8, Wideview); Vol. II. pap. 7.95 (ISBN 0-399-50871-6). Putnam Pub Group.
--The Collected Short Prose of James Agee. LC 68-29549. 1978. Repr. of 1962 ed. 15.95 (ISBN 0-910220-92-1). Berg.
--Death in the Family. (Literature Ser). (gr. 10-12). 1970. pap. text ed. 5.67 (ISBN 0-87720-750-X). AMSCO Sch.
--Death in the Family. 320p. (YA) (gr. 10 up). 1971. pap. 3.95 (ISBN 0-553-23392-0). Bantam.
--James Agee: Selected Journalism. Ashdown, Paul, ed. LC 85-710. (Illus.). 228p. 1985. 17.95 (ISBN 0-87049-466-X). U of Tenn Pr.
--Permit Me Voyage. LC 70-144740. (The Yale Series of Younger Poets: No. 33). Repr. of 1934 ed. 18.00 (ISBN 0-404-53833-9). AMS Pr.
Agee, James & Evans, Walker. Let Us Now Praise Famous Men. 1978. pap. 2.50 (ISBN 0-345-27696-5). Ballantine.
--Let Us Now Praise Famous Men. (Illus.). 1960. 19.95 (ISBN 0-395-07330-8). HM.
--Let Us Now Praise Famous Men. 496p. 1980. pap. 11.95 (ISBN 0-395-29696-X). HM.
Agee, James & Phelps, Robert. Letters of James Agee to Father Flye. 2nd ed. LC 76-146717. 1978. Repr. 15.95 (ISBN 0-910220-91-3). Berg.
Agee, Joel. Twelve Years: An American Boyhood in East Germany. 324p. 1981. 14.95 (ISBN 0-374-27958-6); pap. 6.95 (ISBN 0-374-51715-0). FS&G.
Agee, Joel, tr. see Federspiel, J. F.
Agee, Joel, tr. see Rilke, Rainer M.
Agee, Joel, tr. see Sabarsky, Serge.
Agee, Joel, tr. see Stajner, Karlo.
Agee, Joel, tr. see Von Hentig, Hartmut.
Agee, Jon. Ellsworth. LC 83-2325. (Illus.). 32p. (ps-2). 1983. 10.95 (ISBN 0-394-85995-2, Pant Bks Young); PLB 10.99 (ISBN 0-394-95995-7). Pantheon.
--Ellsworth. (Illus.). (gr. 4-7). 10.95 (ISBN 0-394-85995-2). Random.
--If Snow Falls. LC 82-6549. (Illus.). 32p. (gr. 3-6). 1982. 5.95 (ISBN 0-394-85520-5); PLB 6.99 (ISBN 0-394-95520-X). Pantheon.
--Ludlow Laughs. (Illus.). 32p. (gr. 6 up). 12.95 (ISBN 0-374-34666-6). FS&G.
Agee, Jonis. Mercury. 1982. signed o. p. 30.00 (ISBN 0-915124-53-X, Pub. by Toothpaste); pap. 7.50 (ISBN 0-915124-50-5). Coffee Hse.
--Two Poems. (Orig.). 1981. pap. 6.00 (ISBN 0-915316-97-8). Pentagram.
Agee, Marvin H, jt. auth. see White, John A.
Agee, Philip. Inside the Company: CIA Diary. 672p. 1976. pap. 4.95 (ISBN 0-553-24311-X). Bantam.
--White Paper Whitewash: Philip Agee on the CIA & El Salvador. Poelchau, Warner, ed. 220p. 1981. casebound 12.95 (ISBN 0-940380-01-3); pap. 6.50 (ISBN 0-940380-00-5). Sheridan Square Pubns.
Agee, Richard J., ed. see Holzbauer, Ignaz.
Agee, Roy. Effective Study Habits. McFadden, S. Michele, ed. 1981. 0.50 ea. (ISBN 0-89262-026-9); pak of 30 14.50. Career Pub.
Agee, Rucker. Twenty Alabama Books. LC 75-44472. (Illus.). 1976. 8.95 (ISBN 0-912458-48-8). E A Seemann.
Agee, Vicki L. Treatment of the Violent Incorrigible Adolescent. LC 78-24653. (Illus.). 192p. 1979. 21.50x (ISBN 0-669-02811-8). Lexington Bks.
Agee, Warren K., ed. Mass Media in a Free Society. LC 69-16934. xiv, 98p. 1969. pap. 5.95x (ISBN 0-7006-0056-6). U Pr of KS.
--Press & the Public Interest. 1968. 9.00 (ISBN 0-8183-0200-3). Pub Aff Pr.
Agee, Warren K., et al. Introduction to Mass Communications. 8th ed. 599p. 1985. pap. text ed. 17.50 scp (ISBN 0-06-040177-X, HarpC). Har-Row.
--Introduction to Mass Communications. 7th ed. 498p. 1982. pap. text ed. 18.95 scp (ISBN 0-06-040175-3, HarpC); instr's. manual avail. (ISBN 0-06-360178-8). Har-Row.
--Perspectives on Mass Communications. 476p. 1982. pap. text ed. 14.50 scp (ISBN 0-06-040174-5, HarpC). Har-Row.
--Reporting & Writing the News. 384p. 1983. pap. text ed. 16.95 scp (ISBN 0-06-040173-7, HarpC); instr's. manual avail. (ISBN 0-06-365516-0). Har-Row.
Agee, Willaim C. Ralston Crawford: Painting & Visual Experience. (Illus.). 177p. 1983. 40.00 (ISBN 0-942642-08-2). Twelvetrees Pr.
Agee, William, jt. auth. see Rose, Barbara.
Agee, William C., intro. by. The Museum of Fine Arts, Houston: A Guide to the Collection. LC 80-81646. (Illus.). 248p. (Orig.). 1980. pap. 19.95 (ISBN 0-295-96071-X). U of Wash Pr.
Agehananda Bharati. The Tantric Tradition. LC 77-7204. 1977. Repr. of 1965 ed. lib. bdg. 21.00x (ISBN 0-8371-9660-4, AGTT). Greenwood.
Agel, Jerome. Sports at Random: Q & A. 1984. pap. 6.95 (ISBN 0-87795-541-7, Pub. by Priam). Arbor Hse.
Agel, Jerome & Boe, Eugene. Deliverance in Shanghai. LC 83-7349. 362p. 1983. 14.95 (ISBN 0-934878-32-3). Dembner Bks.
Agel, Jerome, ed. The Making of Kubrick's 2001. (Film Ser.). (YA) (RL 10). 1972. pap. 1.95 (ISBN 0-451-07139-5, J7139, Sig). NAL.
Agel, Jerome B. American at Random: Q. & A. LC 83-70474. (Illus.). 192p. 1983. 7.95 (ISBN 0-87795-455-0, Pub. by Priam). Arbor Hse.
--Beyond Trivia: Expanded Answers to America's Most Loved Trivia Game. 674p. 1985. pap. 8.95 (ISBN 0-671-54128-5). S&S.
--Test Your Word Power. 288p. (Orig.). 1985. pap. 2.95 (ISBN 0-345-30897-2). Ballantine.
Ageloff & Mojena. Applied Structured BASIC. LC 84-25835. 568p. 1985. write for info (ISBN 0-534-04740-8). Wadsworth Pub.
Ageloff, Roy & Mojena, Richard. Applied BASIC Programming. 464p. 1980. pap. text ed. write for info (ISBN 0-534-00808-9). Wadsworth Pub.
--Applied FORTRAN 77 Featuring Structured Programming. 624p. 1981. pap. text ed. write for info (ISBN 0-534-00961-1). Wadsworth Pub.
--Fundamentals of FORTRAN for Management. 1979. text ed. write for info. (ISBN 0-534-00710-4). Wadsworth Pub.
--Fundamentals of FORTRAN for Management. 443p. pap. write for info. Wadsworth Pub.
Agenbroad, Larry D. The Hudson-Meng Site: An Alberta Bison Kill in the Nebraska High Plains. LC 78-57606. (Illus.). 1978. pap. text ed. 12.75 (ISBN 0-8191-0530-9). U Pr of Amer.
Agence de Cooperation Culturelle et Technique, ed. Vocabulaire De L'oceanologie. 431p. (Fr.). 1976. pap. 49.95 (ISBN 0-686-57252-1, M-6560). French & Eur.
Agenjo, C. Enciclopedia de la Inspeccion Veterinaria y Analisis de los Alimentos. 1300p. (Span.). 1980. 170.00 (ISBN 0-686-97333-X, S-37346). French & Eur.
Agenjo Cecilia, Cesar. Enciclopedia de la Avicultura. 2nd ed. 990p. (Espn.). 1964. 59.95 (ISBN 84-239-6004-8, S-14560). French & Eur.
Ager, Anne. Cooking for Fun: Great Ideas for Casual Entertaining. (Illus.). 80p. 1985. pap. 4.95 (ISBN 0-317-26936-4). H P Bks.
Ager, D. V. The Liassic Rhynchonellidae, Pt. 1. 12.00 (ISBN 0-384-00470-9). Johnson Repr.
Ager, D. V., ed. see Meeting of European Geological Societies.
Ager, Derek V. The Geology of Europe. LC 80-40318. 535p. 1980. 53.95x (ISBN 0-470-26990-1). Halsted Pr.
--Nature of the Stratigraphical Record. 2nd ed. LC 80-22559. 136p. 1981. 19.95x (ISBN 0-470-27052-7). Halsted Pr.
Ager, Trygve M., tr. see Ager, Waldemar.
Ager, Trygve M., tr. see Rolvaag, O. E.
Ager, Trygve M., tr. see Rolvaag, Ole E.
Ager, Waldemar. Sons of the Old Country. Ager, Trygve M., tr. from Nor. LC 82-17484. Orig. Title: Gamlelandets Sonner. xvi, 255p. 1984. 19.95x (ISBN 0-8032-1016-7); pap. 6.95 (ISBN 0-8032-5905-0, BB 871, Bison). U of Nebr Pr.
Agerer, R. Zur Oekologie der Mykorrhiza Pilze. (Bibliotheca Mycologica Ser.: vol. 97). (Illus.). 160p. 1985. pap. text ed. 21.00x (ISBN 3-7682-1423-0). Lubrecht & Cramer.
Agerschou, Hans & Lundgren, Helge. Planning & Design of Ports & Marine Terminals. LC 83-7032. 320p. 1983. 74.95x (ISBN 0-471-90191-1, Pub. by Wiley-Interscience). Wiley.
Agerter, Sharlene R. & Glock, Waldo S. An Annotated Bibliography of Tree Growth & Growth Rings, 1950-1962. LC 64-17274. pap. 47.00 (ISBN 0-317-10270-2, 2055332). Bks Demand UMI.
Ageton, Suzanne S. Sexual Assault among Adolescents. LC 82-48573. 208p. 1983. 24.00x (ISBN 0-669-06322-3). Lexington Bks.
Agey, Denes. The Joy of Bach. 1968. pap. 5.95 (ISBN 0-8256-8011-5, Yorktown). Music Sales.
--The Joy of Baroque. 1974. pap. 5.95 (ISBN 0-8256-8015-8, Yorktown). Music Sales.
--The Joy of Boogie & Blues. 1968. pap. 5.95 (ISBN 0-8256-8010-7, Yorktown). Music Sales.
Ageyev, M. Novel with Cocaine. Heim, Michael H., tr. 240p. 1984. 15.95 (ISBN 0-525-24294-5, 01549-460). Dutton.
--Novel with Cocaine. Heim, Michael H., tr. from Rus. LC 85-42547. 224p. 1985. pap. 6.95 (ISBN 0-06-097000-6, PL 7000, PL). Har-Row.

Aggarwal, J. C. Landmarks in the History of Modern Indian Education. 424p. 1984. (Pub. by Vikas India); pap. text ed. 18.95x (ISBN 0-7069-2406-1). Advent NY.

--Teaching of History. 279p. 1983. text ed. 27.50x o. p. (ISBN 0-7069-2163-1, Pub. by Vikas India); pap. text ed. 8.95x (ISBN 0-7069-2164-X, Pub. by Vikas India). Advent NY.

Aggarwal, J. K. & Vidyasagar, M., eds. Nonlinear Systems: Stability Analysis. (Benchmark Papers in Electrical Engineering & Computer Science: Vol. 16). 1977. 70.50 (ISBN 0-12-786035-5). Acad Pr.

Aggarwal, J. K., jt. ed. see Arya, V. K.

Aggarwal, J. K., et al, eds. Computer Methods in Image Analysis. LC 76-50335. 1977. pap. 24.90 (ISBN 0-87942-090-1, PP00919). Inst Electrical.

Aggarwal, Manju. I Am a Hindu. (My Heritage Ser.). (Illus.). 32p. (gr. 2 up). 1985. PLB 9.40 (ISBN 0-531-10018-9). Watts.

--I Am a Muslim. (My Heritage Ser.). 32p. (gr. 2 up). 1985. PLB 9.40 (ISBN 0-531-10020-0). Watts.

--I Am a Sikh. (My Heritage Ser.). (Illus.). (gr. 2 up). 1985. PLB 9.40 (ISBN 0-531-10021-9). Watts.

Aggarwal, N. English in South Asia. 188p. 1982. text ed. 24.00x (ISBN 0-391-02966-5, Pub. by Indian Doc Serv India). Humanities.

Aggarwal, Narindar K. Bibliography of Studies in Hindi Language & Linguistics. 1978. 14.00x (ISBN 0-8364-0172-7). South Asia Bks.

Aggarwal, Narinder K. English in South Asia: A Bibliographic Survey of Resources. 1982. 28.00x (ISBN 0-8364-0853-5, Pub. by Indian DOC Service). South Asia Bks.

Aggarwal, Partap C. Caste, Religion & Power: An Indian Case Study. LC 72-900733. 270p. 1971. 10.00x (ISBN 0-89684-374-2). Orient Bk Dist.

--Halfway to Equality: Harijans of India. 1983. 22.00x (ISBN 0-8364-1043-2, Pub. by Manohar India). South Asia Bks.

Aggarwal, Raj. International Business Finance: A Bibliography of Selected Business & Academic Sources. 1984. 27.95 (ISBN 0-03-047191-5). Praeger.

Aggarwal, Raj & Khera, Inder. Management Science: Cases & Applications. LC 79-65492. 1979. pap. text ed. 16.95x (ISBN 0-8162-0096-3); avail sol. manual 6.00x. Holden-Day.

Aggarwal, Raj Kumar. The Management of Foreign Exchange: Optimal Policies for a Multinational Company. rev. ed. Bruchey, Stuart, ed. LC 80-563. (Multinational Corporations Ser.). 1980. lib. bdg. 22.00x (ISBN 0-405-13359-6). Ayer Co Pubs.

Aggarwal, S. L., ed. Block Polymers. LC 74-119054. 339p. 1970. 39.50x (ISBN 0-306-30481-3, Plenum Pr). Plenum Pub.

Aggarwal, Vinod K. Liberal Protectionism. LC 84-16460. 310p. 1985. 27.50x (ISBN 0-520-05396-6). U of Cal Pr.

Aggasiz, Jean L. Bibliographia Zoologiae Et Geologiae, 4 Vols. (Sources of Science Ser.: No. 20). Set. 275.00 (ISBN 0-384-00404-0). Johnson Repr.

Aggeler, Geoffrey. Anthony Burgess: The Artist As Novelist. LC 78-12200. (Illus.). 245p. 1979. 19.50 (ISBN 0-8173-7106-0). U of Ala Pr.

Agger, Ben, ed. Western Marxism: An Introduction. LC 78-21654. 1979. text ed. 19.50 (ISBN 0-673-16277-X). Scott F.

Agger, Eugene E. Budget in the American Commonwealths. LC 75-158232. (Columbia University Studies in the Social Sciences: No. 66). Repr. of 1907 ed. 18.50 (ISBN 0-404-51066-3). AMS Pr.

Agger, Jens P., ed. see Eisner, Will.

Agger, Lee. Women of Maine. (Illus.). 250p. 1982. pap. 10.95 (ISBN 0-930096-21-5). G Gannett.

--Women of New England, Vol. I. 1985. pap. 10.95 (ISBN 0-930096-55-X). G Gannett.

--Women of New England, Vol. II. 1986. pap. 10.95 (ISBN 0-317-19633-2). G Gannett.

Agger, Robert E. & Swanson, Bert. Rulers & the Ruled. rev. ed. (Illus.). 1984. text ed. cancelled (ISBN 0-8290-0104-2); pap. text ed. cancelled (ISBN 0-8290-0105-0). Irvington.

Agger, Simona G. Urban Self-Management: Planning for a New Society. LC 78-73223. Orig. Title: L' Autogesione Urbana. 256p. 1979. 25.00 (ISBN 0-87332-125-1). M E Sharpe.

Aggerholm, Paula N. Social Work & Health Sciences: Medical Analysis Index with Reference Bibliography. LC 85-47858. 150p. 1985. 29.95 (ISBN 0-88164-392-0); pap. 21.95 (ISBN 0-88164-393-9). ABBE Pubs Assn.

Aggrawal, J. C. Theory & Principles of Education. 400p. 1982. 41.00x (ISBN 0-7069-1418-X, Pub. by Garlandfold England). State Mutual Bk.

Aghadjian, Mollie. The Fourteenth Duchess. 1978. pap. 2.25 (ISBN 0-532-22138-9). Woodhill.

Aghazarian, Aram A., jt. auth. see Simons, Herbert W.

Agheana, Ion T. The Prose of Jorge Luis Borges: Existentialism & the Dynamics of Surprise. LC 84-47694. (American University Studies II (Romance Languages & Literature): Vol. 13). 336p. (Orig.). 1984. pap. text ed. 31.85 (ISBN 0-8204-0130-7). P Lang Pubs.

Aghnides, Nicolas P. Mohammedan Theories of Finance, with an Introduction to Mohammedan Law & a Bibliography. LC 72-82246. (Columbia University Studies in the Social Sciences: No. 166). Repr. of 1916 ed. 39.50 (ISBN 0-404-51166-X). AMS Pr.

Agich, George J. Responsibility in Health Care. 1982. 39.50 (ISBN 90-277-1417-7, Pub. by Reidell Holland). Kluwer Academic.

Agid, Susan R. Fair Employment Litigation: Proving & Defending a Title VII Case. 2nd ed. LC 79-83709. 1979. text ed. 40.00 (ISBN 0-685-94308-9, BI-1265). PLI.

Agin, Daniel, ed. Perspectives in Membrane Biophysics: A Tribute to Kenneth S. Cole. 324p. 1972. 69.50 (ISBN 0-677-15210-8). Gordon.

Aginsky, Bernard W. Kinship Systems & the Forms of Marriage. LC 36-6759. (AAA. M Ser.: No. 45). 1935. 11.00 (ISBN 0-527-00544-4). Kraus Repr.

Aginsky, Ethel G. A Grammar of the Mende Language. (Language Dissertations Ser.: No. 20). 1935. pap. 9.00 (ISBN 0-527-00766-8). Kraus Repr.

Agius, Pauline. China Teapots. Riley, Noel, ed. (Antique Pocket Guides). (Illus.). 64p. (Orig.). 1982. pap. 5.95 (ISBN 0-7188-2548-9, Pub. by Lutterworth Pr UK). Seven Hills Bks.

Agle, Nan H. Princess Mary of Maryland. LC 70-12561. (Illus.). viii, 109p. 1967. Repr. 35.00x (ISBN 0-8103-5029-7). Gale.

Agler-Beck, Gayle. Der Von Kuerenberg: Edition, Notes, & Commentary. (German Language & Literature Monographs Ser.: No. 4). xix, 230p. 1978. 28.00x (ISBN 90-272-0964-2). Benjamins North Am.

Agley, Lyn, jt. auth. see Chaudhury, Jackie.

Aglietta, Michel. A Theory of Capitalist Regulation: The U. S. Experience. 1979. 24.50 (ISBN 0-8052-7066-3, Pub. by NLB). Schocken.

Aglietti, Susan L., ed. Maternal Legacy: A Mother-Daughter Anthology. 104p. (Orig.). 1985. pap. text ed. 7.95 (ISBN 0-9614375-0-2). Vintage Forty-Five.

Aglionby, William. Painting Illustrated in Three Dialogues. (Printed Sources of Western Art Ser.). 418p. 1981. pap. 45.00 slipcase (ISBN 0-915346-50-8). A Wofsy Fine Arts.

Aglow Editors, compiled by. Come Celebrate Book. 266p. 1984. pap. 6.95 (ISBN 0-930756-78-9, 531018). Aglow Pubns.

Aglow Staff Editors. Aglow Prayer Diary. 421p. 1982. 9.95 (ISBN 0-930756-70-3); pap. text ed. 6.95 (ISBN 0-930756-93-2, 531014). Womens Aglow.

Aglow, Stanley H. Schematic Wiring Simplified. LC 83-2736. (Illus.). 180p. 14.95 (ISBN 0-912524-23-5). Busn news.

Agmon, Samuel. Lectures on Exponential Decay of Solutions of Second-Order Elliptic Equations. LC 82-14978. (Mathematical Notes Ser.: No. 29). 118p. 1983. 11.50 (ISBN 0-691-08318-5). Princeton U Pr.

Agmon, Tamir. Political Economy & Risk in World Financial Markets. LC 84-47550. (Illus.). 128p. 1985. 16.00 (ISBN 0-669-08339-9). Lexington Bks.

Agmon, Tamir & Kindleberger, Charles P., eds. Multinationals from Small Countries. 1977. 24.50x (ISBN 0-262-01050-X). MIT Pr.

Agmon, Tamir, et al, eds. The Future of the International Monetary System. LC 83-47657. 320p. 1984. 30.00 (ISBN 0-669-06721-0); pap. 15.00x (ISBN 0-669-09783-7). Lexington Bks.

Agnello, Virginia L. & Garcia, Cindy. Workbook for Voice Improvement. 2nd ed. 1983. pap. 6.25x (ISBN 0-8134-2284-1, 2284). Interstate.

Agner, Dwight. The Books of WAD, a Bibliography of the Books Designed by W. A. Dwiggins. rev. ed. LC 76-58639. (Illus.). 1977. ltd. 25.00 (ISBN 0-915346-26-5). A Wofsy Fine Arts.

--Father Catich's Visit with Bill Dwiggins. 16p. 1982. pap. 12.50 (ISBN 0-912960-14-0). Nightowl.

Agnes, Saint Old French Lives of Saint Agnes & Other Vernacular Versions of the Middle Ages. Denomy, Alexander J., ed. (HSRL Ser.). 1938. 25.00 (ISBN 0-527-01111-8). Kraus Repr.

Agnew, Allen F., jt. auth. see Speidel, David H.

Agnew, Allen F., ed. International Minerals: A National Perspective. (AAAS Selected Symposium 90 Ser.). 180p. 1983. 22.00x (ISBN 0-86531-622-8). Westview.

Agnew, Brad. Fort Gibson: Terminal on the Trail of Tears. LC 78-21391. (Illus.). 259p. 1980. 18.50 (ISBN 0-8061-1521-1). U of Okla Pr.

Agnew, Daniel. History of the Region of Pennsylvania North of the Ohio & West of the Allegheny River. LC 75-146371. (First American Frontier Ser). 1971. Repr. of 1887 ed. 16.00 (ISBN 0-405-02821-0). Ayer Co Pubs.

Agnew, George. Canadian Hospitals, Nineteen Twenty to Nineteen Seventy: A Dramatic Half Century. LC 73-78942. pap. 80.00 (ISBN 0-317-26857-0, 2023486). Bks Demand UMI.

Agnew, H. W., jt. auth. see Breithaupt, S.

Agnew, H. Wayne, jt. auth. see Breithaupt, Sandra.

Agnew, Hugh E. Outdoor Advertising. LC 84-46055. (The History of Advertising Ser.). 323p. 1985. lib. bdg. 35.00 (ISBN 0-8240-6749-5). Garland Pub.

Agnew, Irene, ed. Glossary of English & Russian Computer & Automated Control Systems Terminology. (Eng. & Rus.). 1978. soft covers 15.00 (ISBN 0-686-31723-8). Agnew Tech-Tran.

Agnew, Jeanne & Knapp, Robert C. Linear Algebra with Applications. 2nd ed. LC 82-20752. (Mathematics Ser.). 400p. text ed. 23.75 pub net (ISBN 0-534-01364-3). Brooks-Cole.

Agnew, Jeremy. Exploring the Colorado High Country. LC 77-77959. (Illus.). 1977. pap. 4.95 (ISBN 0-918944-00-7). Wildwood.

Agnew, John. Competition Law in the U. K. 224p. 1985. text ed. 24.50x (ISBN 0-04-343002-3); pap. text ed. 11.50x (ISBN 0-04-343003-1). Allen Unwin.

Agnew, John A., jt. auth. see Szymanski, Richard.

Agnew, John A., et al, eds. The City in Cultural Context. (Illus.). 352p. 1984. text ed. 30.00x (ISBN 0-04-301176-4); pap. text ed. 14.95x (ISBN 0-04-301177-2). Allen Unwin.

Agnew, Neil M. & Pike, S. W. The Science Game: An Introduction to Research in the Behavorial Sciences. 2nd ed. (P-H Ser. in Experimental Psychology). (Illus.). 1978. pap. 19.95 (ISBN 0-13-795260-0). P-H.

Agnew, Swanzie & Stubbs, Michael, eds. Malawi in Maps. LC 74-654433. (Graphic Perspectives of Developing Countries Ser). (Illus.). 141p. 1973. text ed. 35.00x (ISBN 0-8419-0127-9, Africana). Holmes & Meier.

Agnew, W. G., jt. ed. see Cornelius, W.

Agnihotri, O. P. & Gupta, B. K. Solar Selective Surfaces. LC 80-17392. (Wiley Alternate Energy Ser.). 215p. 1981. 44.95x (ISBN 0-471-06035-6, Pub. by Wiley-Interscience). Wiley.

Agnihotri, V. K. India & Other Poems. (Writers Workshop Redbird Book Ser.). 39p. 1975. 8.00 (ISBN 0-88253-562-5); pap. text ed. 4.00 (ISBN 0-88253-561-7). Ind-US Inc.

Agnoli, A., ed. Sixth Meeting of the Italian League Against Parkinson's Disease & Extrapyramidal Disorders, 1981. (Journal: Pharmacology: Vol. 22, No. 1). (Illus.). 96p. 1981. pap. 20.00 (ISBN 3-8055-2322-X). S Karger.

Agnoli, A., jt. ed. see Muller, E. E.

Agnoli, A., et al, eds. Aging Brain & Ergot Alkaloids. (Aging Ser.: Vol. 23). 464p. 1983. text ed. 59.00 (ISBN 0-89004-853-3). Raven.

Agnon, S. Y. The Bridal Canopy. Lask, I. M., tr. from Hebrew. LC 67-19455. 300p. 1967. pap. 8.95 (ISBN 0-8052-0182-3). Schocken.

--A Guest for the Night. Louvish, Misha, tr. from Hebrew. LC 68-13723. 492p. 1980. pap. 8.95 (ISBN 0-8052-0646-9). Schocken.

--In the Heart of the Seas: A Story of a Journey to the Land of Israel. Lask, I. M., tr. from Hebrew. LC 66-30349. (Illus.). 128p. 1980. pap. 4.95 (ISBN 0-8052-0647-7). Schocken.

--A Simple Story. Halkin, Hillel, tr. from Hebrew. 256p. 1985. 14.95 (ISBN 0-8052-3999-5). Schocken.

Agnon, Y. Days of Awe: A Treasury of Tradition, Legends & Learned Commentaries Concerning Rosh Hashanah, Yom Kippur & the Days Between. LC 48-8316. 1965. pap. 8.95 (ISBN 0-8052-0100-9). Schocken.

--Twenty-One Stories. Glatzer, Nahum N., ed. LC 71-108902. 1971. 10.00x (ISBN 0-8052-3350-4); pap. 8.95 (ISBN 0-8052-0313-3). Schocken.

--Two Tales. Incl. Betrothed; Edo & Enam. LC 65-25414. 1966. 4.95x (ISBN 0-8052-3271-0). Schocken.

Agnor. Future Interests. (The Law in Georgia Ser.). incl. latest pocket part supplement 24.95 (ISBN 0-686-90394-3); separate pocket part supplement, 1981 7.45 (ISBN 0-686-90395-1). Harrison Co GA.

--Georgia Evidence. incl. latest pocket part supplement 55.95 (ISBN 0-686-90329-3); separate pocket part supplement, 1984 28.95 (ISBN 0-686-90330-7). Harrison Co GA.

--Use of Discovery Under the Georgia Civil Practice Act. 3rd ed. 62.95 (ISBN 0-686-90310-2). Harrison Co GA.

Agnos, T. J. & Schatt, S. The Practical Law Enforcement Guide to Writing Field Reports, Grant Proposals, Memos, & Resumes. (Illus.). 136p. 1980. pap. 15.75x spiral (ISBN 0-398-04042-7). C C Thomas.

Agoncillo, Teodoro A. The Burden of Proof: The Vargas-Laurel Collaboration Case. 476p. 1985. text ed. 28.00x (ISBN 0-8248-0969-6, Pub. by U of Philippines Pr). UH Pr.

Agonito, Rosemary, ed. History of Ideas on Woman: A Source Book. LC 77-5061. 1978. pap. 8.95 (ISBN 0-399-50379-X, Perigee). Putnam Pub Group.

Agopian, Michael W. Parental Child-Stealing. LC 80-8591. (Illus.). 176p. 1981. 19.00x (ISBN 0-669-04152-1). Lexington Bks.

Agor, Barbara J. & Agor, Stewart C. Benjamin Franklin: American, Level 4. McConochie, Jean, ed. (Regents Readers Ser.). (Illus.). 80p. 1983. pap. text ed. 2.50 (ISBN 0-88345-527-7, 20999). Regents Pub.

Agor, Stewart C., jt. auth. see Agor, Barbara J.

Agor, Weston H. The Chilean Senate: Internal Distribution of Influence. (Latin American Monograph Ser.: No. 23). 228p. 1971. 15.00x (ISBN 0-292-70146-2). U of Tex Pr.

--Intuitive Management: Integrating Left & Right Brain Management Skills. (Illus.). 192p. 1984. 15.95 (ISBN 0-13-502733-0); pap. 7.95 (ISBN 0-13-502725-X). P-H.

Agosin, Marjorie. Conchali. LC 80-53518. (Senda Poetica). 55p. (Orig., Span.). 1980. pap. 4.95 (ISBN 0-918454-23-9). Senda Nueva.

--Las Desterradas del Paraiso Protagonistas en la Narrativa de Maria Luis Bombal. LC 83-60448. (Senda de Estudios y Ensayos). 127p. (Orig.). 1983. pap. 12.95 (ISBN 0-918454-32-8). Senda Nueva.

--Witches & Other Things. Miller, Yvette E., ed. Franzen, Cola, tr. from Span. LC 84-768. 91p. 1984. pap. 10.50 (ISBN 0-935480-16-1). Lat Am Lit Rev Pr.

Agostini, Beatrice, tr. see McConkey, James H.

Agostini, Franco. Math & Logic Games: A Book of Puzzles & Problems. Foulkes, Paul, tr. LC 83-1542. (Illus.). 184p. 1984. 18.95 (ISBN 0-87196-212-8). Facts on File.

Agostini de del Rio, Amelia. Gramatica y Teoria Literaria: Guion Para el Estudiante. 2nd ed. 9.00 (ISBN 0-8477-3104-9). U of PR Pr.

Agostino De Del Rio, Amelia. Unamuno Multiple: Antologia. LC 81-10347. (Colleccion Mente y Palabra). 416p. 1981. 8.00 (ISBN 0-8477-0582-X); pap. 7.00 (ISBN 0-8477-0583-8). U of PR Pr.

Agoston, G. A. Color Theory & Its Application in Art & Design. Mac Adam, D. L., et al, eds. (Springer Series in Optical Sciences: Vol. 19). (Illus.). 1979. 31.00 (ISBN 0-387-09654-X). Springer-Verlag.

Agoston, Max K. Algebraic Topology: A First Course. (Pure & Applied Mathematics Ser.: Vol.32). 376p. 1976. 34.75 (ISBN 0-8247-6351-3). Dekker.

Agoston, S., ed. Clinical Experiences with Norcuron R. (Current Clinical Practice Ser.: Vol. 6). 98p. 1983. 25.75 (ISBN 0-444-90331-3, I-330-83, Excerpta Medica). Elsevier.

Agoston, S., et al, eds. Clinical Experiences with Norcuron. (Current Clinical Practice Ser.: Vol. 11). 221p. 1984. 46.25 (ISBN 0-444-90379-8, I-010-84, Excerpta Medica). Elsevier.

Agoston, Tom. Blunder! How U. S. Gave Away Nazi Supersecrets. (Illus.). 224p. 1985. 15.95 (ISBN 0-396-08556-3). Dodd.

Agozino, Joseph R. How to Find a Job in Forestry Parks, & Wildlife Conservation. Keith, Claudia, ed. (Illus.). 75p. (Orig.). 1985. pap. 8.95 (ISBN 0-932753-00-0). Outdoor Comm.

Agrait, Gustavo. Beatus Ille En la Poesia Lirica Del Siglo De Oro. 4.65 (ISBN 0-8477-3100-6); pap. 3.75 (ISBN 0-8477-3101-4). U of PR Pr.

--De Hito en Hito: Siete Ensayos Sobre Literatura Espanola. LC 83-8864. 225p. (Span.). 1982. pap. write for info. (ISBN 0-8477-3508-7). U of PR Pr.

--Ocho Casos Extranos y Dos Casos Mas: Cuentos, 1930-1970. (UPREX, Ficcion: No. 4). pap. 1.85 (ISBN 0-8477-0004-6). U of PR Pr.

Agrali, Selman & Swift, Lloyd B. FSI Turkish Basic Course, Units 31-50. 1968. pap. text ed. 11.25X (ISBN 0-686-10794-2); cassettes o.p. 78.00x (ISBN 0-686-28546-8). Intl Learn Syst.

Agrali, Selman, jt. auth. see Swift, Lloyd B.

Agramonte, Roberto. Marti y Su Concepcion de la Sociedad Tomo II, Parte 2: Patria y Humanidad 1. LC 81-10377. (Illus.). 307p. Date not set. pap. price not set (ISBN 0-8477-3500-1). U of PR Pr.

--Marti y su Concepcion Del Mundo. 9.35 (ISBN 0-8477-3102-2); pap. 7.50 (ISBN 0-8477-3103-0). U of PR Pr.

--Sociologia: Curso Introductorio. LC 77-5905. (Illus.). 1978. pap. 10.00 (ISBN 0-8477-2443-3). U of PR Pr.

Agramonte, Roberto D. Teoria Sociologica: Exegesis de los Grandes Sistemas. LC 78-9810. 1024p. (Span.). 1979. pap. text ed. 15.00 (ISBN 0-8477-2487-5). U of PR Pr.

Agramonte, Roberto D. & Rosa, Portada de Rafael. Marti y su Concepcion de la Sociedad Tomo II, Parte 1: Teoria General de al Sociedad. (Illus.). 232p. 1979. pap. 4.95 (ISBN 0-8477-2467-0). U of PR Pr.

Agran, Larry. Cancer Connection: And What We Can Do About It. 1977. 10.95 (ISBN 0-395-25178-8). HM.

Agranoff, Ann, jt. auth. see Anderes, Fred.

Agranoff, B. W. & Aprison, M. H., eds. Advances in Neurochemistry, Vols. 1-3. Incl. Vol. 1. 322p. 1975. 39.50x (ISBN 0-306-39221-6); Vol. 2. 358p. 1977. 39.50x (ISBN 0-306-39222-4); Vol. 3. 318p. 1978. 39.50x (ISBN 0-306-39223-2). LC 75-8710. (Illus., Plenum Pr). Plenum Pub.

Agranoff, B. W., et al. Progress in Molecular & Subcellular Biology, Vol. 1. Hahn, F. E., et al, eds. (Illus.). 230p. 1969. 42.00 (ISBN 0-387-04674-7). Springer-Verlag.

Agranoff, Bernard W. & Aprison, M. H. Advances in Neurochemistry, Vol. 4. 242p. 1982. 32.50x (ISBN 0-306-40678-0, Plenum Pr). Plenum Pub.

Agranoff, Robert, ed. Human Services on a Limited Budget. LC 83-4388. (Practical Management Ser.). (Illus.). 240p. (Orig.). 1983. pap. 19.95 (ISBN 0-87326-038-4). Intl City Mgt.

Agranovic, Z. S., et al. Thirteen Papers on Functional Analysis. LC 51-5559. (Translations Ser.: No. 2, Vol. 90). 1970. 32.00 (ISBN 0-8218-1790-6, TRANS 2-90). Am Math.

Agranovich, V. M. & Ginzburg, V. Crystal Optics with Spatial Dispersion, & Excitons. 2nd ed. (Springer Series in Solid-State Sciences: Vol. 42). (Illus.). 455p. 1984. 49.00 (ISBN 0-387-11520-X). Springer-Verlag.

Agranovich, V. M. & Loudon, R., eds. Surface Excitations. Modern Problems in Condensed Matter Sciences, Vol. 9. Date not set. 129.75 (ISBN 0-444-86868-2, North-Holland). Elsevier.

Agranovich, V. M. & Mills, D. L., eds. Surface Polaritons: Electromagnetic Waves of Surfaces & Interfaces. (Modern Problems in Condensed Matter Sciences Ser.: Vol. 1). 704p. 1982. 147.00 (ISBN 0-444-86165-3). Elsevier.

Agranovich, Z. S. & Marchenko, V. A. Inverse Problem of Scattering Theory. Seckler, B. D., tr. (Russian Monographs and Texts on the Physical Sciences Ser.). 304p. 1963. 80.95 (ISBN 0-677-20010-2). Gordon.

Agranovitch, V. M. & Galanin, M. D. Electronic Excitation Energy Transfer in Condensed Matter. (Modern Problems in Condensed Matter Sciences Ser.: Vol. 3). xxiv, 372p. 1982. 95.75 (ISBN 0-444-86335-4). Elsevier.

Agranovitch, V. M. & Hochstrasser, R. M., eds. Spectroscopy & Excitation Dynamics of Condensed Molecular Systems. (Modern Problems in Condensed Matter Sciences Ser.: Vol. 4). xii, 702p. 1983. 166.00 (ISBN 0-444-86313-3). Elsevier.

Agranowitz, Aleen & McKeown, Milfred R. Aphasia Handbook: For Adults & Children. (Illus.). 336p. 1975. 18.50x (ISBN 0-398-00017-4). C C Thomas.

Agras, Stewart. Panic: Facing Fears, Phobias & Anxiety. LC 85-4378. 160p. 1985. text ed. 21.95 (ISBN 0-7167-1730-1); pap. text ed. 11.95 (ISBN 0-7167-1731-X). W H Freeman.

Agras, Stewart, ed. Behavior Modification: Principles & Clinical Applications. 2nd ed. 220p. 1978. 16.95 (ISBN 0-316-02031-1). Little.

Agras, W. Stewart, et al. Behavior Therapy: Toward an Applied Clinical Science. LC 78-32069. (Psychology Ser.). (Illus.). 173p. 1979. text ed. 19.95 (ISBN 0-7167-1086-2); pap. text ed. 10.95 (ISBN 0-7167-1087-0). W H Freeman.

Agrawal, A., ed. Bioprocess Parameter Control. (Advances in Biochemical Engineering-Biochemistry Ser.: Vol. 30). (Illus.). 210p. 1984. 39.50 (ISBN 0-387-13539-1). Springer-Verlag.

Agrawal, A. K. & Guppy, J. G. Decay Heat Removal & Natural Convection in Fast Breeder Reactors. 1981. 60.00 (ISBN 0-07-000540-0). McGraw.

Agrawal, A. N. Indian Agriculture. 556p. 1982. 42.00x (ISBN 0-7069-1378-7, Pub. by Garlandfold England). State Mutual Bk.

--Indian Economy. 7th rev. ed. 800p. 1982. 47.00x (ISBN 0-7069-1416-3, Pub. by Garlandfold England). State Mutual Bk.

--Indian Economy: Nature, Problems & Progress. 4th rev. & enl. ed. 848p. 1978. 15.00x (ISBN 0-7069-0391-9, Pub. by Vikas India). Advent NY.

--Indian Economy: Problems of Development & Planning. 10th & rev. ed. 680p. 1985. pap. text ed. 22.50x (ISBN 0-7069-2632-3, Pub. by Vikas India). Advent NY.

Agrawal, A. N. & Lal, Kundan. Economic Planning. 2nd rev. ed. xiii, 492p. 1981. (Pub. by Vikas India); pap. 13.95x (ISBN 0-7069-1542-9). Advent NY.

Agrawal, Ashok K. & Guppy, James G., eds. Decay Heat Removal & Natural Convection in Fast Breeder Reactors. LC 81-329. 423p. 1981. text ed. 75.95 (ISBN 0-89116-196-1). Hemisphere Pub.

Agrawal, D. & Chakravarti, D., eds. Essays in Indian Protohistory. 1980. text ed. 44.50x (ISBN 0-391-01866-3). Humanities.

Agrawal, D. P. The Archaeology of India. (Scandinavian Institute of Asian Studies Monograph: No.46). (Illus.). 294p. 1982. pap. text ed. 18.50x (ISBN 0-7007-0140-0). Humanities.

--The Archaeology of India: A Summary & Survey of Indian Pre-History. 320p. 1981. 40.00x (ISBN 0-7007-0140-0, Pub. by Curzon England). State Mutual Bk.

Agrawal, H. N. A Portrait of Nationalized Banks. 334p. 1980. text ed. 19.50x (ISBN 0-391-02130-3). Humanities.

Agrawal, J. K. Practicals in Engineering Chemistry. 1981. 25.00x (ISBN 0-686-72962-5, Pub. by Oxford & IBH India). State Mutual Bk.

Agrawal, M., jt. ed. see Radhakrishna.

Agrawal, O. P. Conservation of Paintings & MS of Southeast Asia. 1983. text ed. 99.95 (ISBN 0-408-10671-9). Butterworth.

Agrawal, Om, jt. auth. see Pohm, Arthur V.

Agrawal, R. P., jt. auth. see Misra, A.

Agrawal, R. R. Tradition & Experiment in the Poetry of James Thomson, 1700 to 1748. (Salzburg - Romantic Reassessment Ser.: No. 90). 273p. 1981. pap. text ed. 25.50x (ISBN 0-391-02343-8, Pub. by Salzburg Austria). Humanities.

Agrawal, R. S. Important Guidelines on Research Methodology. 48p. 1983. text ed. 8.95 (ISBN 0-86590-163-5). Apt Bks.

Agrawal, Subhash C. Metamodeling: A Study of Approximations in Queing Models. (Illus.). 220p. 1984. pap. 22.50x (ISBN 0-262-01080-1). MIT Pr.

Agrawal, Surendra P., jt. auth. see Hallbauer, Rosalie C.

Agrawala, A. K. & Tripathi, S. K., eds. Performance Eighty-Three: Proceedings of the International Symposium on Computer Performance Modelling, Measurement & Evaluation, 9th, College Park, Maryland, May 25-27, 1983. 488p. 1984. 49.00 (ISBN 0-444-86673-6, I-467-83, North Holland). Elsevier.

Agrawala, Ashok K. Foundations of Microprogramming: Architecture, Software & Applications. 1976. 59.50 (ISBN 0-12-045150-6). Acad Pr.

Agrawala, Ashok K., ed. Machine Recognition of Patterns. LC 76-53069. 1977. 49.85 (ISBN 0-87942-091-X, PC00844). Inst Electrical.

Agrawala, P. K. Goddesses in Ancient India. 180p. 1983. text ed. 43.00x (ISBN 0-391-02960-6). Humanities.

Agrawala, S. K., ed. Essays on the Law of Treaties: With Special Reference to India. 1972. 22.50x (ISBN 0-8046-8801-X, Pub. by Kennikat). Assoc Faculty Pr.

Agre, K, ed. Fire & Fuel Management in Mediterranean-Climate Ecosystems: Research Priorities & Programmes. (MAB Technical Notes: No. 11). (Illus.). 41p. 1979. pap. 6.25 (ISBN 92-3-101688-1, U920, UNESCO). Unipub.

Agreda, Mary. The Mystical City of God: A Popular Abridgement. abr. ed. Marison, Fiscar & Blatter, George J., trs. from Sp. LC 78-62255. 1978. pap. 15.00 (ISBN 0-89555-070-9). TAN Bks Pubs.

Agree, George E., jt. auth. see Adamany, David W.

Agree, George E., jt. ed. see Adamany, David W.

Agress, Frances, jt. auth. see Agress, Hyman.

Agress, Hyman & Agress, Frances. The Firing of Rabbi Levi. 1978. pap. 1.75 (ISBN 0-532-17190-X). Woodhill.

Agress, Hyman, jt. auth. see Gimpel, Max.

Agress, Lynne. The Feminine Irony: Women on Women in Early Nineteenth Century English Literature. (Illus.). 190p. 1984. pap. text ed. 11.50 (ISBN 0-8191-4156-9). U Pr of Amer.

Agrest, M. M. & Maksimov, M. S. Theory of Incomplete Cylindrical Functions & Their Applications. Fettis, H. E., et al, trs. from Rus. LC 78-139673. (Die Grundlehren der Mathematischen Wissenschaften: Vol. 160). (Illus.). 1971. 50.00 (ISBN 0-387-05111-2). Springer-Verlag.

Agresti, Alan. Analysis of Ordinal Categorical Data. LC 83-23535. (Probability & Mathematical Statistics-Applied Probablity & Statistics Section Ser.: 1-346). 287p. 1984. 35.95x (ISBN 0-471-89055-3, Pub. by Wiley-Interscience). Wiley.

Agresti, Alan & Agresti, Barbara F. Statistical Methods for the Social Sciences. (Illus.). 554p. 1979. text ed. 25.95x (ISBN 0-02-301100-9). Dellen Pub.

Agresti, Barbara F., jt. auth. see Agresti, Alan.

Agresti, Olivia R. David Lubin: A Study in Practical Idealism. 2nd ed. LC 41-53013. (Illus.). 1941. 5.00 (ISBN 0-911090-01-0). Pacific Bk Supply.

Agresto, John. The Supreme Court & Constitutional Democracy. LC 83-45928. 192p. 1984. pap. 7.95x (ISBN 0-8014-9277-7). Cornell U Pr.

Agresto, John & Riesenberg, Peter, eds. The Humanist As Citizen: The Uses of the Humanities. LC 81-4021. viii, 267p. 1981. 19.50x (ISBN 0-8078-1450-4). U of NC Pr.

Agria, John J. College Housing: A Critique of the Federal College Housing Loan Program. 1972. pap. 5.25 (ISBN 0-8447-3074-2). Am Enterprise.

Agricola, Erhard. Semantische Relationen im Text und im System. (Janua Linguarum, Ser. Minor: No. 113). 1972. pap. text ed. 14.00x (ISBN 90-279-1977-1). Mouton.

Agricola, Georgius. De Re Metallica. (Illus.). 1912. 19.95 (ISBN 0-486-60006-8). Dover.

Agricola, Johannes. Die Sprichwoertersammlungen, 2 vols. Gilman, Sander L., ed. (Ausgaben Deutscher Literatur des XV. Bis XVIII Jahrhunderts). 989p. 1971. 154.00x (ISBN 3-11-003710-6). De Gruyter.

Agricola, Martin. Musica instrumentalis deutsch 1528 und 1545, erste und vierte. Eitner, Robert, ed. (Publikation aelterer praktischer und theoretischer Musikwerke Ser.: Vol. XX). (Illus., Ger.). 1967. Repr. of 1896 ed. 30.00x (ISBN 0-8450-1720-9). Broude.

Agricola, S. & Von Schmettow, B. Planung & Verwirklichung Von Freizeitangeboten. Moeglichkeiten & Formen der Partizipation. Schmitz-Scherzer, R., ed. (Psychologische Praxis: Band 50). 1976. 10.75 (ISBN 3-8055-2361-0). S Karger.

Agricultural & Renewable Resources Board & Food & Nutrition Board, Natural Research Council. Fat Content & Composition of Animal Products. LC 76-6496. 254p. 1976. pap. 10.75 (ISBN 0-309-02440-4). Natl Acad Pr.

Agricultural Board. Accumulation of Nitrate. LC 72-84111. (Illus.). 144p. 1972. pap. 7.00 (ISBN 0-309-02038-7). Natl Acad Pr.

--Aquatic Animal Health. LC 73-15707. 46p. 1973. pap. 4.50 (ISBN 0-309-02142-1). Natl Acad Pr.

--Communication for Change with the Rural Disadvantaged. LC 72-186371. 1972. pap. 5.75 (ISBN 0-309-01942-7). Natl Acad Pr.

--Nutrient Requirements of Laboratory Animals. rev. 3rd ed. LC 54-60841. (Illus.). 128p. 1978. pap. 8.25 (ISBN 0-309-02767-5). Natl Acad Pr.

--Principles of Plant & Animal Pest Control, Vol. 1, Plant-Disease Development & Control. 1968. pap. 7.00 (ISBN 0-309-01596-0). Natl Acad Pr.

--Principles of Plant & Animal Pest Control, Vol. 2, Weed Control. 1968. pap. 11.50 (ISBN 0-309-01597-9). Natl Acad Pr.

--Quality of Rural Living. LC 78-184629. 160p. 1971. pap. 5.25 (ISBN 0-309-01940-0). Natl Acad Pr.

Agricultural Board, ed. see Animal Nutrition.

Agricultural Board - Division Of Biology And Agriculture. Guide to Environmental Research on Animals. LC 76-609948. (Illus., Orig.). 1971. pap. 12.75 (ISBN 0-309-01869-2). Natl Acad Pr.

Agricultural Board Division of Biology & Agriculture. Principles of Plant & Animal Pest Control, Vol. 3, Insect-Pest Management & Control. 1969. pap. 12.75 (ISBN 0-309-01695-9). Natl Acad Pr.

Agricultural Communicators in Education, ed. Clip Art, Bk. 4. (Illus.). 200p. 1978. pap. 14.95x (ISBN 0-8134-2039-3, 2039). Interstate.

Agricultural Communicators in Education. Communications Handbook. 4th ed. (Illus.). 224p. 1983. pap. text ed. 14.95x (ISBN 0-8134-2226-4, 2226). Interstate.

Agricultural Production Team. Report on India's Food Crisis & Steps to Meet It. LC 75-26294. (World Food Supply Ser). 1976. Repr. of 1959 ed. 21.00x (ISBN 0-405-07767-X). Ayer Co Pubs.

Agricultural Sector Symposium, 3rd. Increasing Agricultural Productivity: Proceedings. Davis, Ted J., ed. 307p. 1982. 15.00 (ISBN 0-8213-0099-7). World Bank.

Agricultural Tribunal of Investigation. Final Report: Presented to Parliament by Command of His Majesty. LC 75-26316. (World Food Supply Ser.). (Illus.). 1976. Repr. of 1924 ed. 32.00x (ISBN 0-405-07793-9). Ayer Co Pubs.

Agriculture & Renewable Resources Board, National Research Council. Urea & Other Nonprotein Nitrogen Compounds in Animal Nutrition. LC 76-8240. 1976. pap. 6.95 (ISBN 0-309-02444-7). Natl Acad Pr.

Agriculture Board. Principles of Plant & Animal Pest Control, Vol. 6, Effects Of Pesticides On Fruit & Vegetable Physiology. 1968. pap. 5.95 (ISBN 0-309-01698-3). Natl Acad Pr.

Agriculture Board, National Research Council. Genetic Engineering of Plants: Agricultural Research Opportunities & Policy Concerns. 1984. pap. text ed. 9.50 (ISBN 0-309-03434-5). Natl Acad Pr.

Agricutural Economics Dept., U. of Nanking, Chengtu. Economic Facts, 4 Vols. LC 78-74325. (The Modern Chinese Economy Ser.: Vol. 11). 1980. Set. lib. bdg. 200.00 (ISBN 0-8240-4260-3). Garland Pub.

Agrin, Alice R., jt. ed. see Briggs, Anne K.

Agrios, George N. Plant Pathology. 2nd ed. 1978. 25.00i (ISBN 0-12-044560-3). Acad Pr.

Agrippa, Cornelius. The Ladies' Oracle. 118p. 1983. pap. 5.95 (ISBN 0-374-18263-9). FS&G.

Agrippa von Nettesheim, Heinrich C. Three Books of Occult Philosophy or Magic. LC 79-8222. (Illus.). 304p. Repr. of 1898 ed. 39.50 (ISBN 0-404-18401-4). AMS Pr.

Agris, Paul F. The Modified Nucleosides of Transfer RNA: A Bibliography of Biochemical & Biophysical Studies From 1970-1979. LC 80-81197. 220p. 1980. 32.00 (ISBN 0-8451-0207-9). A R Liss.

Agris, Paul F. & Kopper, Randall A. The Modified Nucleosides of Transfer RNA, II: A Laboratory Manual of Genetic Analysis, Identification, & Sequence Determination. LC 80-81197. 320p. 1983. 38.00 (ISBN 0-8451-0225-7). A R Liss.

Agris, Paul F., ed. Biomolecular Structure & Function. 1978. 60.00 (ISBN 0-12-043950-6). Acad Pr.

Agronomov, A., et al. Problems & Exercises in Organic Chemistry. MIR Publishers, tr. 400p. 1975. 17.50x (ISBN 0-8464-0756-6). Beekman Pubs.

Agruso, Victor M., Jr. Learning in the Later Years: Principles of Educational Gerontology. (Educational Psychology Ser.). 1978. 21.00 (ISBN 0-12-045250-2). Acad Pr.

Agterberg, F. Mineral Energy Resource Evaluation: Probabilistic Methods. Date not set. price not set. Elsevier.

Aguayo, Carlos A. & Biaggi, Virgilio. Diccionario De Biologia Animal. LC 76-41882. (Span.). 1977. 15.00 (ISBN 0-8477-2318-6). U of PR Pr.

Aguayo, Jorge, tr. see Dewey, Melvil.

Aguda, T. A. see Simmonds, Kenneth R.

Aguda, T. Akinola. Commercial, Business, & Trade Laws: Zimbabwe. LC 82-73731. 1983. looseleaf 125.00 (ISBN 0-379-23003-8). Oceana.

Agudo, Philomena. Affirming the Human & the Holy. LC 79-1499. (Illus.). 101p. 1979. pap. 4.95 (ISBN 0-89571-006-4). Affirmation.

Agudo, Philomena, et al. Guilt: Issues of Emotional Living in an Age of Stress for Clergy & Religious. Kelley, Kathleen E., ed. LC 80-10747. 144p. 1980. pap. 5.00 (ISBN 0-89571-008-0). Affirmation.

Aguecheek. My Unknown Chum. 1912. 9.50 (ISBN 0-8159-6208-8). Devin.

Aguera, Helen & Diaz, Modesto. Lecturas Basicas: A Cultural Reader. 2nd ed. 1981. pap. text ed. 11.95 (ISBN 0-03-058109-5). HR&W.

Aguero, Kathleen & Goodman, Miriam. Thirsty Day & Permanent Wave. LC 76-55615. 88p. 1977. pap. 6.95 (ISBN 0-914086-17-0). Alicejamesbooks.

Aguiar, Myriam Y. Sueno (Rimas al Recuerdo) LC 84-80617. 64p. (Orig., Span.). 1984. pap. 6.00 (ISBN 0-89729-348-7). Ediciones.

Aguiar, Neuma, ed. The Structure of Brazilian Development. LC 78-55936. 258p. 1979. 19.95 (ISBN 0-87855-138-7). Transaction Bks.

Aguiar, Walter R. Maya Land in Color. (Profiles of America Ser.). (Illus.). 1978. 8.95 (ISBN 0-8038-4703-3). Hastings.

Aguila, F. del see Del Aguila, F., et al.

Aguila, Juan del. Cuba: Dilemmas of a Revolution. (Profiles: Nations of Contemporary Latin America Ser.). 175p. 1984. 30.00x (ISBN 0-86531-563-9); pap. text ed. 12.95x (ISBN 0-8133-0032-0). Westview.

Aguila, Pancho. Anti-Gravity. 48p. (Orig.). 1977. pap. 2.95 (ISBN 0-917744-24-1). Aldebaran Rev.

--Dark Smoke. LC 77-76904. 1977. pap. 2.50 (ISBN 0-915016-14-1). Second Coming.

--Hijacked. 1976. pap. 3.25 (ISBN 0-685-79277-3). Twowindows Pr.

Aguila, Richard. The Iroquois Restoration: Iroquois Diplomacy on the Colonial Frontier, 1701-1754. LC 82-135390. (Illus.). 286p. 1982. 18.95 (ISBN 0-8143-1717-0). Wayne St U Pr.

Aguilar, Alonso. Pan-Americanism from Monroe to the Present: A View from the Other Side. Zatz, Asa, tr. LC 68-13659. 192p. 1969. pap. 4.95 (ISBN 0-85345-098-6). Monthly Rev.

Aguilar, Enrique. El Crepusculo. 1971. 3.50 (ISBN 0-686-27937-9). Franciscan Inst.

--Pensiamentos Sobre la Cultura Intelectual y Moral. 1967. 7.00 (ISBN 0-686-27936-0). Franciscan Inst.

--Sinfonias Do Otono (Symphonies of Autumn) 1962. 3.50 (ISBN 0-686-17964-1). Franciscan Inst.

Aguilar, Juan F. & Gonzalez, Armando E., eds. Basic Latin American Legal Materials 1970-1975. (American Association of Law Libraries Publication Ser: No. 13). vi, 106p. 1977. pap. 12.50x (ISBN 0-8377-0111-2). Rothman.

Aguilar, Luis. Operation Zapata: The "Ultrasensitive" Report & Testimony of the Board of Inquiry on the Bay of Pigs. 384p. lib. bdg. 24.00 (ISBN 0-89093-377-4, Aletheia Bks); pap. 8.00 (ISBN 0-89093-376-6, Aletheia Bks). U Pubns Amer.

Aguilar, Luis E. De Como Se Me Murieron las Palabas y Otros Cuentos, Cantos y Cuestiones. (Illus.). 205p. (Span.). 1984. 9.95 (ISBN 0-317-19416-X). Ediciones.

Aguilar, Luis E., ed. & intro. by. Marxism in Latin America. rev. 2nd ed. LC 77-81331. 426p. 1978. 27.95 (ISBN 0-87722-106-5); pap. 9.95 (ISBN 0-87722-108-1). Temple U Pr.

Aguilar, Nona. No-Pill, No-Risk Birth Control. LC 79-55463. (Illus.). 1980. 12.95 (ISBN 0-89256-118-1); pap. 6.95 (ISBN 0-89256-129-7). Rawson Assocs.

Aguilar, Rodolfo J. Systems Analysis & Design in Engineering, Architecture, Construction, & Planning. (Civil Engineering & Engineering Mechanics Ser). (Illus.). 448p. 1973. ref. ed. 33.95 (ISBN 0-13-881458-9). P-H.

Aguilar-Henson, Marcela. Figura Cristalina. Cantu, Norma E., ed. (Illus.). 31p. (Orig.). 1983. pap. 5.00 (ISBN 0-913983-01-2). M & A Edns.

Aguilera, Donna & Messick, Janice. Crises Intervention: Theory & Methodology. 4th ed. LC 81-9470. (Illus.). 194p. 1981. pap. text ed. 13.95 (ISBN 0-8016-0087-1). Mosby.

Aguilera, Donna, jt. auth. see Topalis, Mary.

Aguilera, Donna C. & Messick, Janice M. Crisis Intervention: Therapy for Psychological Emergencies. (Mosby Medical Library). 1982. pap. 7.95 (ISBN 0-452-25369-1, Plume). NAL.

--Crisis Intervention: Therapy for Psychological Emergencies. LC 82-3535. (Mosby Medical Library). 146p. 1983. pap. 6.95 (ISBN 0-452-25369-1, 0086-3). Mosby.

Aguilera, Francisco, ed. Handbook of Latin American Studies, Vols. 15-20. 1968. lib. bdg. 35.00 ea. Octagon.

--Handbook of Latin American Studies, Vol. 14: 1948. LC 36-32633. 1948. 25.00x (ISBN 0-8130-0003-3). U Presses Fla.

Aguilera, Francisco & Shelby, Charmion, eds. Handbook of Latin American Studies, Vols. 12 & 13. LC 36-32633. Vol. 12, 1946. 25.00x (ISBN 0-8130-0004-1); Vol. 13, 1947. 25.00x (ISBN 0-8130-0005-X). U Presses Fla.

Aguilera, Robert. Naturally Fractured Reservoirs. 703p. 1980. 69.95x (ISBN 0-87814-122-7). Pennwell Bks.

Aguilera-Hellweg, Max, jt. ed. see Barasch, Marc.

Aguilera-Malta, Demetrio. Babelandia. Earle, Peter, tr. LC 84-9035. (Contemporary Literature Ser.). (Illus.). 375p. 1985. 17.50 (ISBN 0-89603-065-2). Humana.

--Don Goyo. Brushwood, John & Brushwood, Carolyn, trs. from Span. LC 80-81656. (Contemporary Literature Ser.). (Illus.). 208p. 1980. 14.95 (ISBN 0-89603-019-9). Humana.

--Seven Serpents & Seven Moons. Rabassa, Gregory, tr. 320p. 1981. pap. 3.50 (ISBN 0-380-54767-8, 54767-8, Bard). Avon.

--Seven Serpents & Seven Moons. Rabassa, Gregory, tr. from Sp. LC 79-10516. (Texas Pan American Ser.). 315p. 1979. 12.95 (ISBN 0-292-77552-0); pap. cancelled (ISBN 0-292-77555-5). U of Tex Pr.

Aguinaldo, Emilio & Pacis, Vicente A. Second Look at America. 9.95 (ISBN 0-8315-0051-4). Speller.

Aguirre. Genetische Phanomenologie und Reduktion. (Phaenomenologica Ser.: No. 38). 1970. lib. bdg. 24.00 (ISBN 90-247-5025-3, Pub. by Martinus Nijhoff Netherlands). Kluwer Academic.

Aguirre, Adalberto, Jr. An Experimental Sociolinguistic Study of Chicano Bilingualism. LC 78-62239. 1978. soft cover 11.00 (ISBN 0-88247-540-1). R & E Pubs.

Aguirre, Angela M. Vida y Critica Literaria De Enrique Pineyro. LC 81-51622. (Senda De Estudios y Ensayos). 274p. (Orig., Span.). 1981. pap. 11.95 (ISBN 0-918454-26-3). Senda Nueva.

Aguirre, Carlos A., et al. Taxation in Sub-Saharan Africa: Pt. I: Tax Policy & Administration in Sub-Saharan Africa & Pt. II: A Statistical Evaluation of Taxation in Sub-Saharan Africa, 2 pts. (Occasional Papers: No. 8). 73p. 1981. Set. pap. 5.00 (ISBN 0-317-04009-X). Intl Monetary.

Aguirre, Cliff. The Death Transition. LC 84-70901. 80p. (Orig.). 1985. pap. 7.95 (ISBN 0-916977-10-2). Cedar Data.

Aguirre, Fidel. El Magnetismo de Jose Marie. LC 84-82243. (Coleccion Cuba y sus Jueces). (Illus.). 207p. (Orig., Span.). 1985. pap. 9.95 (ISBN 0-89729-361-4). Ediciones.

Aguirre, L., jt. ed. see Pitcher, W. S.

Agulhon, Maurice. Marianne into Battle: Republican Imagery & Symbolism in France, 1789-1880. Lloyd, Janet, tr. (Illus.). 224p. 1981. 44.50 (ISBN 0-521-23577-4); pap. 15.95 (ISBN 0-521-28224-1). Cambridge U Pr.

--The Republic in the Village: The People of the War from the French Revolution to the Second Republic. Lloyd, Janet, tr. LC 81-17095. (Past & Present Publications). (Illus.). 438p. 1982. 49.50 (ISBN 0-521-23693-2). Cambridge U Pr.

--The Republican Experiment, Eighteen Forty-Eight to Eighteen Fifty-Two. LC 82-23461. (Cambridge History of Modern France: No. 2). (Illus.). 211p. 1983. 42.50 (ISBN 0-521-24829-9); pap. 10.95 (ISBN 0-521-28988-2). Cambridge U Pr.

--Une Ville Ouvriere au Temps du Socialisme Utopique: Toulon De 1815 a 1851. 2nd ed. (Civilisations et Societes: No. 18). 1977. pap. 16.80 (ISBN 90-2796-287-1). Mouton.

Agurell, Stig, et al. The Cannabinoids: Chemical, Pharmacologic & Therapeutic Aspects. 1984. 88.00 (ISBN 0-12-044620-0). Acad Pr.

Agursky, Mikhail. The Ideology of National Bolshevism. 350p. 1985. 37.50x (ISBN 0-8133-0139-4). Westview.

Agus, Irving A. Heroic Age of Franco-German Jewry. LC 75-94444. 1969. 20.00x (ISBN 0-8197-0053-3). Bloch.

--Rabbi Meir of Rothenburg: His Life & Work, 2 Vols. in 1. rev. ed. 1970. 45.00x (ISBN 0-87068-026-9). Ktav.

Agus, Jacob B. The Evolution of Jewish Thought. LC 73-2185. (The Jewish People; History, Religion, Literature Ser.). Repr. of 1959 ed. 30.00 (ISBN 0-405-05251-0). Ayer Co Pubs.

--High Priest of Rebirth: The Life, Times & Thought of Abraham Isaac Kuk. 2nd ed. 1972. 7.95x (ISBN 0-8197-0281-1). Bloch.

--Jewish Identity in an Age of Ideologies. LC 76-14230. 1978. 25.00 (ISBN 0-8044-5018-8). Ungar.

--The Jewish Quest: Essays on Basic Concepts of Jewish Theology. LC 83-258. 264p. 1983. 25.00x (ISBN 0-88125-012-0). Ktav.

--Vision & the Way: An Interpretation of Jewish Ethics. LC 65-25104. 1966. 12.50 (ISBN 0-8044-5029-3); pap. 5.50 (ISBN 0-8044-6002-7). Ungar.

Agus, Jacob B., et al, eds. The Jewish People: History, Religion, Literature, 41 bks. 1973. Set. 1106.50 (ISBN 0-405-05250-2). Ayer Co Pubs.

Agustini De El, Amelia see De Del Rio, Amelia Agostini.

Agutter, Jenny. Snap: Observations of Los Angeles & London. 1984. 29.95 (ISBN 0-7043-3433-X, Pub. by Quartet Bks). Merrimack Pub Cir.

Agyei, A. K., tr. see Ginzburg, V. L. & Kirzhnits, D. A.

Agyeman, Opoku. The Panafricanist World View. 284p. 1984. 13.95 (ISBN 0-89697-171-6). Intl Univ Pr.

Agyeman-Badu, Yaw & Osei-Hwedie, Kwaku. The Political Economy of Instability: Colonial Legacy, Inequality & Political Instability in Ghana. Raymond, Walter J., ed. LC 82-71488. (Illus.). 68p. (Orig.). 1982. pap. 2.50x (ISBN 0-931494-18-4). Brunswick Pub.

Agyeman-Badu, Yaw, jt. auth. see Osei-Hwedie, Kwaku.

AHA Clearinghouse for Hospital Management Engineering. Health Facility Design Using Quantitative Techniques: A Collection of Case Studies. 148p. 1982. pap. 18.75 (ISBN 0-87258-397-X, AHA-043170). Am Hospital.

AHA Clearinghouse for Hospital Management Engineering, compiled by. In-House Training Programs on Quantitative Techniques: A Collection of Case Studies. LC 82-11654. 148p. 1982. pap. text ed. 18.75 (ISBN 0-87258-369-4, AHA-133200). Am Hospital.

--Nurse Staffing Based on Patient Classification: An Examination of Cases Studies. LC 83-2561. 188p. 1983. pap. 20.00 (ISBN 0-87258-384-8, AHA-154150). Am Hospital.

Ahalt, J. Dawson, jt. auth. see Kosters, Marvin H.

Ahamd, S. I. & Fung, K. T. Introduction to Computer Design & Implementation. LC 80-21005. 271p. 1981. 27.95 (ISBN 0-914894-11-0). Computer Sci.

Ahana, Doris N. & Kunishi, Marilyn M. Cancer Care Protocols for Hospital & Home Care Use. LC 80-20348. 1981. pap. text ed. 25.50 (ISBN 0-8261-3291-X). Springer Pub.

Aharoni, Ada. The Second Exodus. LC 82-90872. 136p. 1983. 10.95 (ISBN 0-8059-2862-6). Dorrance.

Aharoni, Ada & Wolf, Thea. Thea: To Alexandria, Jerusalem, & Freedom. 112p. 1984. 8.95 (ISBN 0-8059-2922-3). Dorrance.

Aharoni, Dov. General Sharon's War Against Time Magazine. 1985. pap. 4.95 (ISBN 0-317-19512-3). Steimatzky Pub.

Aharoni, J. The Special Theory of Relativity. (Physics Ser.). 331p. 1985. pap. 8.00 (ISBN 0-486-64870-2). Dover.

Aharoni, Miriam, ed. see Aharoni, Yohanan.

Aharoni, Yair. Markets, Planning & Development: The Private & Public Sectors in Economic Development. LC 77-8200. 364p. 1977. prof ref 35.00x (ISBN 0-88410-659-4). Ballinger Pub.

--The No-Risk Society. LC 81-6144. (Chatham House Series on Change in American Politics). 240p. (Orig.). 1981. 25.00 (ISBN 0-934540-07-1); pap. text ed. 12.95x (ISBN 0-934540-06-3). Chatham Hse Pubs.

Aharoni, Yair, jt. ed. see Vernon, Raymond.

Aharoni, Yohanan. The Archaeology of the Land of Israel. Aharoni, Miriam, ed. Rainey, Anson F., tr. LC 81-14742. (Illus.). 364p. 1982. pap. 18.95 (ISBN 0-664-24430-0). Westminster.

--The Land of the Bible: A Historical Geography. rev. & enlarged ed. Rainey, A. F., tr. LC 80-14168. 496p. 1980. softcover 19.95 (ISBN 0-664-24266-9). Westminster.

Aharoni, Yohanon & Avi-Yonah, Michael. The Macmillan Bible Atlas. rev. ed. LC 77-4313. (Illus.). 183p. 1977. 25.95 (ISBN 0-02-500590-1). Macmillan.

Aharonian, Aharon G. Intermarriage & the Armenian-American Community. 118p. 1984. 21.00 (ISBN 0-9613300-0-7). A G Aharonian.

Aharonson, Ephraim F., et al, eds. Air Pollution & the Lung. LC 76-3488. 313p. 1976. 96.95x (ISBN 0-470-15049-1). Halsted Pr.

Ahart, Ottilie, ed. see Ticker, E M.

Ahearn, Arthur J., ed. Trace Analysis by Mass Spectrometry. 1972. 78.00 (ISBN 0-12-044650-2). Acad Pr.

Ahearn, Barry. Zukofsky's "A". An Introduction. LC 81-13000. 254p. 1983. 19.95 (ISBN 0-520-04378-2). U of Cal Pr.

--Zukofsky's "A". An Introduction. (Cal Ser.: No. 653). (Illus.). 272p. 1983. pap. 6.95 (ISBN 0-520-04965-9, CAL 653). U of Cal Pr.

Ahearn, Daniel J., Jr. Wages of Farm & Factory Laborers. LC 78-76649. (Columbia University Studies in the Social Sciences: No. 518). 1969. Repr. of 1945 ed. 20.00 (ISBN 0-404-51518-5). AMS Pr.

Ahearn, Daniel S. Federal Reserve Policy Reappraised, 1951-1959. LC 63-10522. 376p. 1963. 30.00x (ISBN 0-231-02575-0). Columbia U Pr.

Ahearn, Edward J. Rimbaud: Visions & Habitations. LC 82-2776. 383p. 1983. text ed. 34.50x (ISBN 0-520-04591-2). U of Cal Pr.

Ahearn, Frederick, jt. auth. see Cohen, Raquel.

Ahearn, Kevin, jt. auth. see Cirillo, Bob.

Aheizer, N. I., et al. Nine Papers on Analysis. LC 51-5559. (Translations Ser.: No. 2, Vol. 22). 1962. 30.00 (ISBN 0-8218-1722-1, TRANS 2-22). Am Math.

Ahemd, Akbar S. & Hart, David M., eds. Islam in Tribal Societies: From the Atlas to the Indus. 320p. (Orig.). 1984. pap. 21.95x (ISBN 0-7100-9320-9). Routledge & Kegan.

Ahern, Barnabas M. The Epistle to the Romans. 1979. 1.75 (ISBN 0-8199-0629-8). Franciscan Herald.

Ahern, C., jt. auth. see Hettich, M.

Ahern, Colleen, ed. see Budy, Andrea H.

Ahern, Colleen, ed. see Dragone, Carol.

Ahern, Colleen, ed. see Sandy, Stephen.

Ahern, Dee Dee. Money Signals. cancelled (ISBN 0-399-12253-2). Putnam Pub Group.

Ahern, Denise. Bread & the Wine, No. Sixteen. (Arch Bk.). (Illus.). 1979. 0.99 (ISBN 0-570-06127-X, 59-1245). Concordia.

Ahern, Emily M. Chinese Ritual & Politics. LC 80-41831. (Cambridge Studies in Social Anthropology: No. 34). (Illus.). 208p. 1982. 29.95 (ISBN 0-521-23690-8). Cambridge U Pr.

--Cult of the Dead in a Chinese Village. LC 72-97202. (Illus.). 296p. 1973. 22.50x (ISBN 0-8047-0835-5). Stanford U Pr.

Ahern, Emily M. & Gates, Hill, eds. The Anthropology of Taiwanese Society. LC 79-64212. xvi, 491p. 1981. 35.00x (ISBN 0-8047-1043-0). Stanford U Pr.

Ahern, Gerald J. West's Textbook of Cosmetology. 507p. 1980. pap. text ed. 21.95 (ISBN 0-8299-0343-7, IM); study guide 12.95 (ISBN 0-8299-0319-4); answers to study guide 1.95 (ISBN 0-8299-0354-2); state board review questions 5.75 (ISBN 0-8299-0375-5); answers to state board review questions 1.75 (ISBN 0-8299-0379-8). West Pub.

Ahern, James, jt. auth. see Peternel, Carolyn R.

Ahern, Jerry. Atrocity. (The Track Ser.: No. 2). 224p. 1984. pap. 2.50 (ISBN 0-373-62002-0). Harlequin Bks.

--The Confederate. 1983. pap. 3.25 (ISBN 0-8217-1285-3). Zebra.

--The Ninety-Nine. (The Track Ser.: No. 1). 224p. 1984. pap. 2.50 (ISBN 0-373-62001-2). Harlequin Bks.

--The Prophet. (The Survivalist Ser.: No. 7). 1984. pap. 2.50 (ISBN 0-8217-1339-6). Zebra.

--The Survivalist, No. 1: Total War. (Orig.). 1981. pap. 2.25 (ISBN 0-89083-768-6). Zebra.

--The Survivalist, No. 10: The Awakening. 1984. pap. 2.50 (ISBN 0-317-06370-7). Zebra.

--The Survivalist, No. 2: The Nightmare Begins. (Orig.). 1981. pap. 2.50 (ISBN 0-89083-810-0). Zebra.

--The Survivalist, No. 3: The Quest. (Illus.). 1981. pap. 2.50 (ISBN 0-89083-851-8). Zebra.

--The Survivalist, No. 4: The Doomsayer. (Orig.). 1981. pap. 2.50 (ISBN 0-89083-893-3). Zebra.

--The Survivalist, No. 5: The Web. 1983. pap. 2.50 (ISBN 0-8217-1145-8). Zebra.

--The Survivalist, No. 6: The Savage Horde. 1983. pap. 2.50 (ISBN 0-8217-1232-2). Zebra.

--The Survivalist, No. 7: The Prophet. 1984. pap. 2.50 (ISBN 0-8217-1339-6). Zebra.

--The Survivalist, No. 8: The End Is Coming. 1984. pap. 2.50 (ISBN 0-8217-1374-4). Zebra.

--The Survivalist, No. 9: Earth Fire. 240p. 1984. pap. 2.50 (ISBN 0-8217-1405-8). Zebra.

--The Survivalist: The Reprisal, No. 11. 1986. pap. 2.50 (ISBN 0-8217-1590-9). Zebra.

--The Takers. 1984. pap. 3.50 (ISBN 0-318-01910-8, Pub. by Worldwide). Harlequin Bks.

--Track: The Ninety-Nine. (Gold Eagle Ser.). Date not set. pap. price not set (Pub. by Worldwide). Harlequin Bks.

Ahern, John E. The Exergy Method of Energy Systems Analysis. LC 79-24500. 295p. 1980. 44.50x (ISBN 0-471-05494-1, Pub. by Wiley-Interscience). Wiley.

Ahern, Mary, jt. auth. see Malerstein, Abraham J.

Ahern, Maureen, tr. see Asturias, Miguel.

Ahern, Maureen, tr. see Cisneros, Antonio.

Ahern, Maureen, et al, trs. see Wieser, Nora J.

Ahern, Tom. The Capture of Trieste. 1978. 15.00 (ISBN 0-930900-45-6, Windfall Pr); pap. 4.00 (ISBN 0-930900-46-4). Burning Deck.

--Hecatombs of Lake. (Contemporary Literature Ser.: No. 21). 144p. 1984. 11.95 (ISBN 0-940650-29-0); signed ed. 20.00 (ISBN 0-940650-30-4). Sun & Moon MD.

--A Movie Starring the Late Cary Grant & an As-Yet Unsigned Actress. (The Treacle Story Ser.: No. 1). (Illus.). 32p. 1976. signed ed. 8.00 (ISBN 0-914232-07-X); pap. 2.50 (ISBN 0-914232-06-1). McPherson & Co.

--Self-Portraits. (Illus.). 7p. 1980. 4.99 (ISBN 0-933442-04-1). Dianas Bimonthly.

--Superbounce. (Burning Deck Poetry Ser.). 28p. 1983. pap. 3.00 (ISBN 0-930901-12-6). Burning Deck.

Ahern, Tom, ed. see Acker, Kathy & Cherches, Peter.

Ahern, Tom, et al. The Treacle Story Series, Vol. 1, Nos. 1-4. LC 76-43558. (Illus.). 172p. 1976. 10.00 (ISBN 0-914232-14-2). McPherson & Co.

Aherne, Brian. A Dreadful Man: The Story of George Sanders. 272p. 1981. pap. 2.75 (ISBN 0-425-04715-6). Berkley Pub.

Aherne, Dee Dee & Bliss, Betsy. The Economics of Being a Woman. 1977. pap. 3.95 (ISBN 0-07-000650-4). McGraw.

Aherne, William & Dunnill, Michael. Morphometry. 176p. 1982. text ed. 49.50 (ISBN 0-7131-4403-3). E Arnold.

Aherns, Donna, ed. see Lansky, Bruce.

AHI, pseud. Misty's Kaboodle. (AHI Ser.). (gr. 1 up). 1979. 4.25 (ISBN 0-931420-25-3). Pi Pr.

Ahier, John & Flude, Michael, eds. Contemporary Education Policy. (Illus.). 288p. 1983. pap. 19.50 (ISBN 0-7099-0512-2, Pub. by Croom Helm Ltd). Longwood Pub Group.

Ahiezer, N. I. & Krein, M. G. Some Questions in the Theory of Moments. LC 63-22077. (Translations of Mathematical Monographs: Vol. 2). 1974. Repr. of 1962 ed. 30.00 (ISBN 0-8218-1552-0, MMONO-2). Am Math.

Ahiezer, N. I., et al. Fifteen Papers on Algebra. LC 51-5559. (Translations Ser.: No. 2, Vol. 50). 1966. 39.00 (ISBN 0-8218-1750-7, TRANS 2-50). Am Math.

--Fifteen Papers on Real & Complex Functions, Series, Differential & Integral Equations. LC 51-5559. (Translations Ser.: No. 2, Vol. 86). 1970. 34.00 (ISBN 0-8218-1786-8, TRANS 2-86). Am Math.

Ahimaaz Ben Paltiel. Chronicle of Ahimaaz. Salzman, Marcus, tr. LC 79-158233. (Columbia University Oriental Studies: No. 18). Repr. of 1924 ed. 15.75 (ISBN 0-404-50508-2). AMS Pr.

Ahimeir, Ora, jt. auth. see Eisenstadt, S. N.

Ahituv, Niv & Neumann, Seev. Principles of Information Systems for Management. 544p. 1982. write for info. (ISBN 0-697-08154-0); solutions manual avail. (ISBN 0-697-08155-9). Wm C Brown.

--Principles of Information Systems for Management. 2nd ed. 560p. 1985. text ed. price not set (ISBN 0-697-08267-9); price not set solutions manual (ISBN 0-697-00884-3). Wm C Brown.

Ahkmatova, A. Soviet Russian Poetry of the Nineteen Fifties to Nineteen Seventies. 254p. 1981. 7.00 (ISBN 0-8285-2063-1, Pub. by Progress Pubs USSR). Imported Pubns.

Ahl, David H. The Commodore 64 Ideabook. (Ideabook Ser.: No. 6). (Illus.). 150p. (Orig.). 1984. pap. 8.95 (ISBN 0-916688-68-2, 68-2). Creative Comp.

--Computers in Mathematics: A Sourcebook of Ideas. LC 79-57487. (Illus.). 214p. 1979. pap. 15.95 (ISBN 0-916688-16-X, 12D). Creative Comp.

--The Epson HX-20 Ideabook. (The Ideabook Ser.). 142p. 1983. pap. 8.95 (ISBN 0-916688-52-6, 3S). Creative Comp.

--The Microsoft BASIC Ideabook. (Ideabook Ser.: No. 4). (Illus.). 144p. (Orig.). 1984. pap. 8.95 (ISBN 0-916688-67-4, 67-4). Creative Comp.

--The Texas Instruments Ideabook. (The Ideabook Ser.). 150p. 1983. pap. 8.95 (ISBN 0-916688-51-8, 3R). Creative Comp.

--The Timex-Sinclair 1000: Ideabook Ser. 149p. 1983. 8.95 (ISBN 0-916688-48-8, 3P). Creative Comp.

--The TRS-80 Model 100 Ideabook. (The Ideabook Ser.). (Illus.). 150p. 1984. pap. 8.95 (ISBN 0-916688-57-7, 4A). Creative Comp.

Ahl, David H. & North, Steve. More BASIC Computer Games. LC 78-74958. (Illus.). 186p. 1979. pap. 7.95 (ISBN 0-916688-09-7, 6C2). Creative Comp.

Ahl, David H., ed. BASIC Computer Games: Microcomputer Edition. LC 78-50028. (Illus.). 180p. 1978. pap. 7.95 (ISBN 0-916688-07-0, 6C). Creative Comp.

--BASIC Computer Games: Microcomputer Edition. LC 78-17624. (Illus.). 188p. 1978. pap. 7.95 (ISBN 0-89480-052-3, 215). Workman Pub.

--The Best of Creative Computing, Vol. 1. LC 76-438. (Illus.). 326p. 1976. pap. 12.95 (ISBN 0-916688-01-1, 6A). Creative Comp.

--The Best of Creative Computing, Vol. 2. LC 76-438. (Illus.). 323p. 1977. pap. 12.95 (ISBN 0-916688-03-8, 6B). Creative Comp.

--Big Computer Games. 160p. 1984. pap. 9.95 (ISBN 0-916688-40-2, 13C). Creative Comp.

--Computers in Science & Social Studies. 197p. 1983. pap. 14.95 (ISBN 0-916688-44-5, 9X). Creative Comp.

--More BASIC Computer Games. LC 80-57619. (Illus.). 188p. 1980. pap. 8.95 (ISBN 0-89480-137-6, 438). Workman Pub.

--More BASIC Computer Games: TRS-80. LC 78-50028. (Illus.). 196p. (Orig.). 1980. pap. 7.95 (ISBN 0-916688-19-4, 6C4). Creative Comp.

Ahl, David H. & Green, Burchenal, eds. Best of Creative Computing, Vol. 3. LC 76-438. (Illus.). 323p. 1980. pap. 12.95 (ISBN 0-916688-12-7, 12C). Creative Comp.

Ahl, Frederick. Lucan: An Introduction. LC 75-16926. (Studies in Classical Philology: Vol. 39). 400p. 1976. 32.50x (ISBN 0-8014-0837-7). Cornell U Pr.

--Metaformations: Soundplay & Wordplay in Ovid & Other Classical Poets. LC 84-23872. 336p. 1985. text ed. 29.95x (ISBN 0-8014-1762-7). Cornell U Pr.

Ahlberg, Allan. Funnybones. LC 79-24872. (Illus.). 32p. (gr. k-3). 1981. 11.75 (ISBN 0-688-80238-9); PLB 11.88 (ISBN 0-688-84238-0). Greenwillow.

--Red Nose Readers. Incl. Big Bad Pig. LC 84-27748 (ISBN 0-394-97194-9) (ISBN 0-394-87194-4); Fee Fi Fo Fum. LC 84-27745 (ISBN 0-394-97193-0) (ISBN 0-394-87193-6); Happy Worm. LC 84-27742 (ISBN 0-394-97196-5); Help (ISBN 0-394-97190-6) (ISBN 0-394-87190-1). (Illus.). 32p. (ps-2). 1985. PLB 5.99 ea. (BYR); pap. 3.95 ea. Random.

Ahlberg, Allan, jt. auth. see Ahlberg, Janet.

Ahlberg, Gudrun. Prothesis & Ekphora in Greek Geometric Art: Text & Figures, 2 vols. (Studies in Mediterranean Archaeology: No. XXXII). (Illus.). 1971. pap. text ed. 75.25x (ISBN 91-85058-50-5). Humanities.

Ahlberg, J. Harold, et al. Theory of Splines & Their Applications. (Mathematics in Science & Engineering Ser.: Vol. 38). 1967. 60.00 (ISBN 0-12-044750-9). Acad Pr.

Ahlberg, Janet & Ahlberg, Allan. The Baby's Catalogue. LC 82-9928. (Illus.). 32p. (gr. k up). 1983. PLB 11.45i (ISBN 0-316-02037-0, Pub. by Atlantic Monthly Pr.). Little.

--Each Peach Pear Plum. (Illus.). 32p. (ps-2). 1985. pap. 2.50 (ISBN 0-590-33581-2, Blue Ribbon Bks.). Scholastic Inc.

--Each Peach Pear Plum: An I-Spy Story. LC 79-16726. (Illus.). 32p. (gr. k-3). 1979. 10.95 (ISBN 0-670-28705-9). Viking.

--The Ha Ha Bonk Bonk Book. (Illus.). (gr. 3-7). 1982. pap. 2.95 (ISBN 0-14-031412-1, Puffin). Penguin.

--The Old Joke Book. (Illus.). (gr. 2-5). 1979. pap. 2.95 (ISBN 0-14-050333-1, Puffin). Penguin.

--The Old Joke Book. (Illus.). (gr. 3 up). 1977. 9.50 (ISBN 0-670-52273-2). Viking.
--Peek-a-Boo! LC 81-1925. (Illus.). (ps-1). 1981. 10.95 (ISBN 0-670-54598-8). Viking.
--Peek-a-Boo. (Picture Puffin Ser.). (Illus.). 32p. 1984. pap. 3.95 (ISBN 0-14-050107-X, Puffin). Penguin.
--Playmates. LC 84-40123. (Slot Books). 20p. (ps-3). 1985. pap. 7.95 (ISBN 0-670-55988-1, Viking Kestrel). Viking.
Ahlbom, Anders & Norell, Staffan. Introduction to Modern Epidemiology. Ahlbom, Gunilla, tr. from Swedish. LC 84-80586. 1984. pap. 7.50 (ISBN 0-917227-00-X). Epidemiology.
Ahlbom, Gunilla, tr. see Ahlbom, Anders & Norell, Staffan.
Ahlborn, Boye, et al, eds. Shock Tube & Shock Wave Research: Proceedings of the Eleventh International Symposium on Shock Tubes & Waves. LC 77-20168. (Illus.). 670p. 1978. 60.00x (ISBN 0-295-95582-1). U of Wash Pr.
Ahlborn, Richard. The Sculpted Saints of a Borderland Mission. LC 74-18171. (Illus.). 124p. 1974. pap. 7.50 (ISBN 0-915076-03-9). SW Mission.
Ahlborn, Richard E. The San Antonio Missions: Edward Everett & the American Occupation, 1847. LC 85-71971. (Illus.). 1985. price not set (ISBN 0-88360-076-5). Amon Carter.
Ahlborn, Richard E., jt. auth. see Marshall, Howard W.
Ahlbrandt, Roger, Jr. Flexible Code Enforcement: A Key Ingredient in Neighborhood Preservation Programming. 93p. 1976. 9.00 (ISBN 0-318-14942-7, N582); members 7.00 (ISBN 0-318-14943-5). NAHRO.
Ahlbrandt, Roger S. A New Public Policy for Neighborhood Preservation. 304p. 1979. 39.95 (ISBN 0-03-051321-9). HR&W.
Ahlbrandt, Roger S., et al. A New Public Policy for Neighborhood Preservation. LC 79-12363. 304p. 1979. 39.95 (ISBN 0-03-051321-9). Praeger.
Ahlbrandt, Roger S., Jr. Neighborhoods, People, & Community. (Environment, Development, & Public Policy: Cities & Development Ser.). 256p. 1984. 27.50x (ISBN 0-306-41542-9, Plenum Pr). Plenum Pub.
Ahlbrandt, T. A., jt. ed. see Brookfield, M. E.
Ahlburg, Allan, jt. auth. see Ahlburg, Janet.
Ahlburg, Janet & Ahlburg, Allan. Yum Yum. LC 84-40124. 20p. (ps-k). 1985. 7.95 (ISBN 0-670-79620-4). Viking.
Ahlem, Lloyd. Help for Families of the Mentally Ill. LC 12-2820. (Trauma Bks.: Ser. 2). 1983. pap. 2.75 (ISBN 0-570-08257-9). Concordia.
Ahlem, Lloyd H. Living with Stress. 2nd ed. LC 81-52939. 1982. pap. text ed. 2.50 (ISBN 0-8307-0801-4, 5017404). Regal.
Ahlers, Arvel & Amphoto Editorial Board. Where & How to Sell Your Photography. 9th ed. (Illus.). 1979. (Amphoto); pap. 10.95 (ISBN 0-8174-2166-1). Watson-Guptill.
Ahlers, Arvel W. Where & How to Sell Your Photographs. 8th ed. (Illus.). 1977. 14.95 (ISBN 0-8174-2424-5, Amphoto); pap. 10.95 (ISBN 0-8174-2166-1). Watson-Guptill.
Ahlers, David M. A New Look at Portfolio Management. Altman, Edward I. & Walter, Ingo, eds. LC 76-10448. (Contemporary Studies in Economic & Financial Analysis: Vol. 5). 1977. lib. bdg. 36.50 (ISBN 0-89232-012-5). Jai Pr.
Ahles, Harry E., ed. see MacKeever, Frank C.
Ahlfeld, Helmut, ed. Licht's International Sugar Economic Year Book & Directory, 1981. LC 51-36145. (Illus.). 486p. (Eng. & Ger.). 1981. 85.00x (ISBN 0-8002-2907-X). Intl Pubns Serv.
Ahlfors, L. V., et al. Some Problems of Mathematics & Physics. LC 76-4884. (Translations Ser.: No. 2, Vol. 104). 1976. 55.00 (ISBN 0-8218-3054-6, TRANS 2-104). Am Math.
Ahlfors, Lars. Complex Analysis. 3rd ed. (Illus.). 1979. text ed. 36.95 (ISBN 0-07-000657-1, C). McGraw.
Ahlfors, Lars, et al, eds. Advances in the Theory of Riemann Surfaces. LC 72-121729. (Annals of Mathematics Studies: No. 66). 1971. 35.00x (ISBN 0-691-08081-X). Princeton U Pr.
Ahlfors, Lars V. Lars Valerian Ahlfors: Collected Papers, 2 Vols. 544p. 1982. text ed. 65.00X ea. Vol. 1 (ISBN 0-8176-3075-9). Vol. 2 (ISBN 0-8176-3076-7). Set. text ed. 130.00x (ISBN 0-8176-3077-5). Birkhauser.
Ahlfors, Lars V., et al, eds. Contributions to Analysis: A Collection of Papers Dedicated to Lipman Bers. 1974. 82.50 (ISBN 0-12-044850-5). Acad Pr.
Ahlfors, U. G. Alcohol & Conflict. 1969. 4.00 (ISBN 951-9192-06-9). Rutgers Ctr Alcohol.
Ahlgren, C. E., jt. ed. see Kozlowski, T. T.
Ahlgren, Clifford & Ahlgren, Isabel. Lob Trees in the Wilderness. LC 83-16809. (Illus.). 232p. 1984. 29.50x (ISBN 0-8166-1264-1); pap. 12.95 (ISBN 0-8166-1262-5). U of Minn Pr.
Ahlgren, Isabel, jt. auth. see Ahlgren, Clifford.
Ahlheid, Frans. Quintilian: The Preface to Book VII & Comparable Passages in the Institutio Oratoria. 204p. (Orig.). 1983. pap. 26.00x (ISBN 90-6032-240-1, Pub. by B R Gruener Netherlands). Benjamins North Am.
Ahlijian, Gregory M. Reflections in My Quiet Hours. 1976. pap. 3.95 (ISBN 0-9601572-1-2). Court Scribe.
Ahlin, et al. Maxillofacial Orthopaedics: Clinical Approach for the Growing Child. (Illus.). 300p. 1984. text ed. 88.00 (ISBN 0-86715-150-1). Quint Pub Co.
Ahlqvist, Anders, ed. Papers from the Fifth International Conference on Historical Linguistics, Galway, April 6-10, 1981. (Current Issues in Linguistic Theory Ser.: 21). 527p. 1982. 54.00x (ISBN 90-272-3514-7). Benjamins North Am.
Ahlstrand, Alan. Datsun 200 SX 1980-1982. Jorgensen, Eric, ed. (Illus.). pap. text ed. 12.95 (ISBN 0-89287-339-6, A206). Clymer Pubns.
--Datsun 4-Wheel Drive Pickups: 1980-1983 Shop Manual. Wauson, Sydnie A., ed. (Illus., Orig.). 1981. pap. 12.95 (ISBN 0-89287-344-2, A207). Clymer Pubns.
--MGA-MGB All Models: 1956-1980 Service, Repair Handbook. Robinson, Jeff, ed. (Illus.). pap. 12.95 (ISBN 0-89287-279-9, A165). Clymer Pubns.
--Nissan Sentra Nineteen Eighty-Two to Nineteen Eighty-Three Gas & Diesel Shop Manual. Wauson, Sydnie & Hamlin, Steve, eds. (Illus.). 287p. (Orig.). 1984. pap. 13.95 (ISBN 0-89287-386-8, A208). Clymer Pubns.
--Toyota Celica 1982-1983 Shop Manual. Wauson, Sydnie A., ed. (Illus.). 270p. 1984. pap. 12.95 (ISBN 0-89287-391-4). Clymer Pubns.
--Toyota Tercel 1980-1982: Shop Manual. Wauson, Sidnie A., ed. (Illus., Orig.). pap. text ed. 12.95 (ISBN 0-89287-342-6, A295). Clymer Pubns.
Ahlstrand, Alan & Wauson, Sydnie A. Datsun 280ZX 1979-1983 Includes Turbo Shop Manual. (Illus.). pap. 12.95 (ISBN 0-89287-346-9). Clymer Pubns.
Ahlstrom, Elbert H. A Quantitative Study of Rotatoria in Terwilliger's Pond, Put-in Bay, Ohio. 1934. 1.00 (ISBN 0-86727-029-2). Ohio Bio Survey.
Ahlstrom, Goran. Engineers & Industrial Growth: Higher Technical Education & the Engineering Profession During the 19th & Early 20th Centuries: France, Germany, Sweden & England. (Illus.). 118p. 1982. 24.00 (ISBN 0-7099-0506-8, Pub. by Croom Helm Ltd). Longwood Pub Group.
Ahlstrom, Mark. Books. Schroeder, Howard, ed. LC 83-15206. (Technology (How Things are Made) Ser.). (Illus.). 48p. (gr. 4 up). 1983. PLB 8.95 (ISBN 0-89686-236-4). Crestwood Hse.
--Books. (gr. 4-6). PLB 11.95 (ISBN 0-516-30236-1). Childrens.
--The Canada Goose. Schroeder, Howard, ed. LC 83-24015. (Wildlife Ser.: Habits & Habitat). (Illus.). 48p. (gr. 4-5). 1984. PLB 9.95 (ISBN 0-89686-243-7). Crestwood Hse.
--The Foxes. Schroeder, Howard, ed. LC 83-5324. (Wildlife Habits & Habitat Ser.). (Illus.). 48p. (gr. 4-5). 1983. lib. bdg. 9.95 (ISBN 0-89686-220-8). Crestwood Hse.
--The Sheep. Schroeder, Howard, ed. LC 83-25215. (Wildlife Ser.: Habits & Habitat). (Illus.). 48p. (gr. 4-5). 1984. PLB 9.95 (ISBN 0-89686-248-8). Crestwood Hse.
--The Whitetail. Schroeder, Howard, ed. LC 83-6944. (Wildlife Habits & Habitat Ser.). (Illus.). 48p. (gr. 4-5). 1983. lib. bdg. 9.95 (ISBN 0-89686-224-0). Crestwood Hse.
Ahlstrom, S. E. Religious History of the American People, 2 vols. LC 75-22362. (Illus.). 720p. 1975. pap. 6.95 vol. 1 (ISBN 0-385-11164-9, Im); pap. 6.95 vol. 2 (ISBN 0-385-11165-7). Vol. 2. Doubleday.
--A Religious History of the American People. LC 72-151564. (Illus.). 1120p. 1972. 50.00x (ISBN 0-300-01475-9); pap. 15.95x (ISBN 0-300-01762-6). Yale U Pr.
Ahlstrom, Sydney E. & Carey, Jonathan S., eds. An American Reformation: A Documentary History of Unitarian Christianity. vi, 506p. 1984. 39.50x (ISBN 0-8195-5080-9). Wesleyan U Pr.
Ahlstrom, Trudy, ed. see Loeb, David V. & Brown, David W.
Ahlstrom, Trudy H. & Devine, J. T. California Wine Winners, 1983. 72p. (Orig.). 1984. pap. 4.95 (ISBN 0-9614025-0-4). VARIETAL FAIR.
--California Wine Winners, 1984. (Orig.). 1984. pap. 4.95 (ISBN 0-9614025-1-2). Varietal Fair.
--California Wine Winners 1985. (Orig.). 1985. pap. price not set (ISBN 0-9614025-2-0). Varietal Fair.
Ahlstrom, Winton M. & Havighurst, Robert J. Four Hundred Losers: Delinquent Boys in High School. LC 74-149914. (JOssey-Bass Behavioral Science Ser.). Repr. of 1971 ed. 65.50 (ISBN 0-8357-9321-4, 2013935). Bks Demand UMI.
Ahlstrom-Laakso, Salme. Drinking Habits Among Alcoholics. (The Finnish Foundation for Alcohol Studies: Vol. 21). 1975. 8.00. Rutgers Ctr Alcohol.
Ahlum, Carol & Fralley, Jacqueline M., eds. High School Feminist Studies. 157p. (Orig.). (gr. 9-12). 1976. pap. 6.95 (ISBN 0-912670-24-X). Feminist Pr.
Ahluwalia, B. K., ed. Muslims & India's Freedom Movement. 1985. 26.50x (ISBN 0-8364-1349-0, Pub. by Heritage India). South Asia Bks.
Ahluwalia, H. P. Climbing Everest. 1975. 5.00x (ISBN 0-7069-0414-1, Pub. by Vikas India). Advent NY.
--Faces of Everest. (Illus.). 1979. text ed. 50.00x (ISBN 0-7069-0563-6, Pub. by Vikas India). Advent NY.
--The Hermit Kingdom: Ladakh. (Illus.). 180p. 1981. text ed. 75.00x (ISBN 0-7069-1022-2, Pub. by Vikas India). Advent NY.
--Higher Than Everest: Memoirs of a Mountaineer. 1975. 9.00x (ISBN 0-7069-0268-8). Intl Bk Dist.
Ahluwalia, H. P., jt. auth. see Kumar, N.
Ahluwalia, Isher J. Behavior of Prices & Output in India. 1979. 16.00x (ISBN 0-8364-0508-0). South Asia Bks.
--Industrial Growth in India: Stagnation since the Mid-Sixties. (Illus.). 250p. 1985. 18.95 (ISBN 0-19-561787-8). Oxford U Pr.
Ahmad, Alia. Agricultural Stagnation under Population Pressure: The Case of Bangladesh. 246p. 1984. text ed. 27.95x (ISBN 0-7069-2577-7, Pub. by Vikas India). Advent NY.
Ahmad, Aliiaz, ed. see Ghalib, Miza A.
Ahmad, Aziz. A History of Islamic Sicily. 1975. 10.00x (ISBN 0-85224-274-3, Pub. by Edinburgh U Pr Scotland). Columbia U Pr.
--An Intellectual History of Islamic India. 1970. 13.00x (ISBN 0-85224-057-0, Pub. by Edinburgh U Pr Scotland). Columbia U Pr.
Ahmad, F., et al, eds. Differentiation & Development: Miami Winter Symposia, Vol. 15. 1978. 70.00 (ISBN 0-12-045450-5). Acad Pr.
Ahmad, Fazal, et al, eds. Miami Winter Symposium: Vol. 19: From Gene to Protein: Translation into Biotechnology (Symposium) (Serial Publication). 1982. 45.00 (ISBN 0-12-045560-9). Acad Pr.
Ahmad, G. Sayings of Muhammad. 7.50x (ISBN 0-87902-036-9). Orientalia.
Ahmad, Ghazi. Sayings of Muhammad. pap. 2.00 (ISBN 0-686-18342-8). Kazi Pubns.
Ahmad, I. Letters from the Great Turke. LC 72-164. (English Experience Ser.: No. 292). 16p. Repr. of 1606 ed. 7.00 (ISBN 90-221-0292-0). Walter J Johnson.
Ahmad, Imtiaz, ed. Caste & Social Stratification Among Muslims. 2nd ed. 1978. 15.00x (ISBN 0-8364-0050-X). South Asia Bks.
--Family, Kinship, & Marriage Among the Muslims. LC 77-74484. 1977. 17.50x (ISBN 0-88386-757-5). South Asia Bks.
--Modernization & Social Change among Muslims in India. 1983. 28.00x (ISBN 0-88386-892-X). South Asia Bks.
--Ritual & Religion among Muslims in India. 1982. 20.00x (ISBN 0-8364-0852-7, Pub. by Manohar India). South Asia Bks.
Ahmad, Iqbal, ed. see AIME Annual Meeting, New Orleans, 1979.
Ahmad, Jalal Al-e. Gharbzadegi: Weststruckness. Green, John & Alizadeh, Ahmad, trs. from Persian. LC 82-61280. (Illus.). 204p. (Orig.). 1982. text ed. 16.95 (ISBN 0-939214-08-3); pap. text ed. 9.95 (ISBN 0-939214-07-5). Mazda Pubs.
Ahmad, Jalal Al-e see Al-e Ahmad, Jalal.
Ahmad, Jaleel. Floating Exchange Rates & World Inflation. LC 83-16155. 259p. 1984. 40.00 (ISBN 0-312-29647-9). St Martin.
--Import Substitution, Trade & Development, Vol. 11. Altman, Edward I. & Walter, Ingo, eds. LC 76-52015. (Contemporary Studies in Economic & Financial Analysis). (Orig.). 1977. lib. bdg. 32.00 (ISBN 0-89232-055-9). Jai Pr.
Ahmad, Jusuf J. The Economics of Survival: The Role of Cost-Benefit Analysis in Environmental Decision Making. (Studies Ser.: Vol. 4). 79p. 1981. pap. 10.50 (ISBN 92-807-1042-7, UNEP063, UNEP). Unipub.
Ahmad, K. Islam & the West. pap. 2.00 (ISBN 0-686-18572-2). Kazi Pubns.
Ahmad, K., et al. Computers, Language Learning & Language Teaching. (New Directions in Language Teaching Ser.). (Illus.). 128p. Date not set. price not set (ISBN 0-521-26569-X); pap. price not set (ISBN 0-521-31957-9). Cambridge U Pr.
Ahmad, Khurshid. Family Life in Islam. 38p. (Orig.). 1974. pap. 2.25x (ISBN 0-86037-016-X, Pub by Islamic Found UK). New Era Pubns MI.
Ahmad, Khurshid & Ansari, Zafar I. Mawdudi: An Introduction to His Life & Thought. 44p. (Orig.). 1979. pap. 2.30x (ISBN 0-86037-038-0, Pub by Islamic Found UK). New Era Pubns MI.
Ahmad, Khurshid, ed. Islam: Its Meaning & Message. 279p. 1980. (Pub. by Islamic Council of Europe England); pap. 14.95x (ISBN 0-86037-000-3). Intl Spec Bk.
--Islam: Its Meaning & Message. 279p. (Orig.). 1976. pap. 8.50x (ISBN 0-86037-000-3, Pub. by Islamic Found UK). New Era Pubns MI.
--Studies in Islamic Economics. 390p. (Orig.). 1980. 31.50x (ISBN 0-86037-066-6, Pub. by Islamic Found UK); pap. 14.75x (ISBN 0-86037-067-4). New Era Pubns MI.
Ahmad, Khurshid & Kerr, David, eds. Christian Mission & Islamic Da'wah: Proceedings of the Chambesy Dialogue Consultation. 102p. (Orig.). 1982. pap. 4.25x (ISBN 0-86037-110-7, Pub. by Islamic Found UK). New Era Pubns MI.
Ahmad, Khurshid, tr. see Maududi, Abul A.
Ahmad, Khurshid, tr. see Mawdudi, Sayyid A.
Ahmad, M. Saiyid Ahmad Shahid. pap. 22.50 (ISBN 0-686-18311-8). Kazi Pubns.
--Teaching of Islam. 195p. 1984. Repr. of 1910 ed. text ed. 23.50x (ISBN 0-391-03331-X, Pub. by Cosmo India). Humanities.
Ahmad, M. F. & Katib, M. K. Principles of Electronics. 300p. (Arabic.). pap. 15.00 (ISBN 0-471-88556-8). Wiley.
Ahmad, Mufassir M. The Koran. LC 81-52147. (Illus.). 600p. 1981. pap. 30.00 (ISBN 0-940368-04-8). Tahrike Tarsile Quran.
Ahmad, Muzaffer. Public Enterprise in South Asia. (ICPE Monograph). 57p. 1982. pap. 10.00x (ISBN 92-9038-902-8, Pub. by Intl Ctr Pub Yugoslavia). Kumarian Pr.
Ahmad, N. Muslim Contribution to Geography. pap. 14.50 (ISBN 0-686-18450-5). Kazi Pubns.
Ahmad, Nafis. Muslim Contributions to Geography. (Illus.). 178p. (Orig.). 1981. pap. 9.75 (ISBN 0-88004-014-9). Sunwise Turn.
Ahmad, Najma P. Hindustani Music. 1984. 18.50x (ISBN 0-8364-1218-4, Pub. by Manohar India). South Asia Bks.
Ahmad, Nazir. University Library Practices in Developing Countries. (Illus.). 220p. 1985. 45.00x (ISBN 0-7103-0058-1). Routledge & Kegan.
Ahmad, Qazi. Indian Cities: Characteristics & Correlates. LC 65-28148. (Research Papers Ser.: No. 102). 184p. 1965. pap. 10.00 (ISBN 0-89065-012-8). U Chicago Dept Geog.
Ahmad, S. Introduction to Qur'anic Script. 168p. 1984. text ed. 30.00x (ISBN 0-391-03153-8, Pub. by Macmillan England). Humanities.
Ahmad, Saghir. Class & Power in a Punjabi Village. LC 76-1663. 1977. 8.95 (ISBN 0-85345-385-3). Monthly Rev.
Ahmad, Sami, ed. Herbivorous Insects: Host-Seeking Behavior & Mechanisms. LC 82-20717. 1983. 39.50 (ISBN 0-12-045580-3). Acad Pr.
Ahmad, Shahnon. Srengenge. Aveling, Harry, tr. (Writing in Asia Ser.). 1979. pap. text ed. 6.00x (ISBN 0-686-86037-3, 00240). Heinemann Ed.
Ahmad, Shair & Keener, Marvin, eds. Differential Equations. LC 80-16549. 1980. 33.00 (ISBN 0-12-045550-1). Acad Pr.
Ahmad, Sohrab, jt. auth. see Irons, Bruce.
Ahmad, Sultan. Approaches to Purchasing Power Parity & Real Product Comparisons Using Shortcuts & Reduced Information. (Working Paper: No. 418). ii, 60p. 1980. 3.00 (ISBN 0-686-36083-4, WP-0418). World Bank.
Ahmad, Syed. Introduction to Quranic Script. 1984. 28.50x (ISBN 0-317-13505-8, Pub. by Macmillan India). South Asia Bks.
Ahmad, Syed B. Introduction to Quranic Arabic Script. 10.00x (ISBN 0-317-20254-5). Intl Bk Ctr.
Ahmad, Yusuf J. Analyzing the Economic Options: Cost-Benefit Analysis in Differing Economic Systems. (Studies Ser.: Vol. 5). Date not set. pap. 16.00 (UNEP078, UNEP). Unipub.
--Evaluating the Environment: Application of Cost-Benefit Analysis in Environmental Protection Measures. (Studies Ser.: Vol. 6). pap. 12.50 (ISBN 92-807-1044-3, UNEP077, UNEP). Unipub.
Ahmad, Yusuf J. & Muller, Frank G., eds. Integrated Physical, Socio-Economic & Environmental Planning, Vol. 10. (Natural Resources & the Environment Ser.). (Illus.). 196p. 1982. 30.00 (ISBN 0-907567-18-5, TYP115, TYP); pap. 21.00 (ISBN 0-907567-19-3, TYP111). Unipub.
Ahmad, Ziauddin, et al. Money & Banking in Islam. 299p. (Orig.). 1983. pap. 12.25x (ISBN 0-939830-27-2, Pub. by Inst Pol Stud Pakistan). New Era Pubns MI.
Ahmad Ibn Yahya, Al-Baladuri. Origins of the Islamic State, 2 vols. Incl. Vol. 1. Hitti, Philip K., tr. Repr. of 1916 ed (ISBN 0-404-51694-7); Vol. 2. Murgotten, Francis C., tr. Repr. of 1924 ed (ISBN 0-404-51695-5). LC 76-82247. (Columbia University Studies in the Social Sciences: No. 163 & No. 163a). Set. 82.50 (ISBN 0-404-51163-5). AMS Pr.
Ahmadjian, Vernon. Flowering Plants of Massachusetts. LC 78-19690. (Illus.). 608p. 1979. 22.50 (ISBN 0-87023-265-7). U of Mass Pr.
Ahmadjian, Vernon & Hale, Mason E., eds. The Lichens. 1974. 77.50 (ISBN 0-12-044950-1). Acad Pr.
Ahmad Midhat Effendi. Osmanli Proverbs & Quaint Sayings. LC 77-87623. Repr. of 1898 ed. 37.00 (ISBN 0-404-16449-8). AMS Pr.
Ahmand, Nazeer, jt. auth. see Chang, Y. Austin.
Ahmann, J. Stanley. The Academic Achievement of Young Americans. LC 83-61783. (Fastback Ser.: No. 196). 50p. 1983. pap. 0.75 (ISBN 0-87367-196-1). Phi Delta Kappa.
Ahmann, Mathew, ed. see National Conference on Religion & Race.
Ahmann, Mathew H. The New Negro. LC 73-77031. 1969. Repr. of 1961 ed. 10.00x (ISBN 0-8196-0232-9). Biblo.
Ahmanson, Howard, Jr., et al. Giving to God's Work. Welty, William P., ed. LC 81-67214. 150p. 1981. 24.95x (ISBN 0-940240-00-9). Fieldstead Inst.
Ahmanson, John. Secret History: An Eyewitness Expose of the Rise of Mormonism. Archer, Gleason L., tr. from Danish. 1984. 9.95 (ISBN 0-8024-0277-1). Moody.
Ahmed, A. Karim, jt. auth. see Perera, Frederica.
Ahmed, A. Karim, jt. auth. see Perera, Frederica P.
Ahmed, A. Karim, jt. ed. see Norris, Ruth.

Ahmed, A. S. Millenium & Charisma among Pathans: A Critical Essay in Social Anthroplogy. (International Library of Anthropology Ser.). 1980. pap. 10.95x (ISBN 0-7100-0547-4). Routledge & Kegan.

Ahmed, Abkar S. Religion & Politics in Muslim Society: Order & Conflict in Pakistan. LC 82-14774. (Illus.). 225p. 1983. 42.50 (ISBN 0-521-24635-0). Cambridge U Pr.

Ahmed, Alice P., jt. ed. see Basheer, S.

Ahmed, Aziz. Gleanings from the Glorious Quran. 1981. pap. 14.95x (ISBN 0-19-577280-6). Oxford U Pr.

Ahmed, Bashiruddin, jt. auth. see Eldersveld, Samuel.

Ahmed, F. & Almond, D. C. Field Mapping for Geology Students. (Illus.). 88p. 1983. pap. 6.95x (ISBN 0-04-550031-2). Allen Unwin.

Ahmed, H. & Spreadbury, P. J. Analogue & Digital Electronics for Engineers. (Illus.). 300p. 1984. 39.50 (ISBN 0-521-26463-4); pap. 18.95 (ISBN 0-521-31910-2). Cambridge U Pr.

Ahmed, H. & Nixon, W. C., eds. Microcircuit Engineering. LC 79-8907. (Illus.). 1980. 57.50 (ISBN 0-521-23118-3). Cambridge U Pr.

Ahmed, Haroon, et al. Microcircuit Engineering. 1984. 33.00 (ISBN 0-12-044980-3). Acad Pr.

Ahmed, Iftikhar. Technological Change & Agrarian Structure: A Study of Bangladesh. International Labour Office, ed. xvi, 136p. (Orig.). 1981. pap. 8.55 (ISBN 92-2-102543-8). Intl Labour Office.

--Technology & Rural Women: Conceptual & Empirical Issues. (Illus.). 384p. 1985. text ed. 28.50x (ISBN 0-04-382043-3). Allen Unwin.

Ahmed, Iftikhar & Kinsey, Bill H., eds. Farm Equipment Innovations in Eastern & Central Southern Africa. LC 84-10181. 368p. 1984. text ed. 31.50x (ISBN 0-566-00697-9). Gower Pub Co.

Ahmed, J. U., jt. auth. see Krishnamoorthy, P. N.

Ahmed, K. Fanaticism, Intolerance & Islam. pap. 1.00 (ISBN 0-686-18491-2). Kazi Pubns.

--Principles of Islamic Education. 1.00 (ISBN 0-686-18355-X). Kazi Pubns.

Ahmed, M. Economics of Islam. 14.50 (ISBN 0-686-18350-9). Kazi Pubns.

--Polypropylene Fibers: Science & Technology. (Textile Science & Technology Ser.: Vol. 5). 766p. 1982. 127.75 (ISBN 0-444-42090-8). Elsevier.

Ahmed, Manzoor, jt. auth. see Coombs, Philip H.

Ahmed, Manzooruddin, ed. Contemporary Pakistan: Politics, Economy, Society. LC 79-51941. 245p. 1980. 19.95 (ISBN 0-89089-126-5). Carolina Acad Pr.

Ahmed, Mukhtar. Coloring of Plastics. LC 78-26186. 240p. 1979. 22.50 (ISBN 0-442-20267-9). Krieger.

--Coloring of Plastics: Theory & Practice. 1979. 24.50 (ISBN 0-442-20267-9). Van Nos Reinhold.

Ahmed, N. U. & Teo, K. L. Optimal Control of Distributed Parameter Systems. 1981. 89.00 (ISBN 0-444-00559-5). Elsevier.

Ahmed, Nasir & Natarajan, T. Discrete Time Systems & Signals. 1983. text ed. 33.95 (ISBN 0-8359-1375-9); solutions manual incl. (ISBN 0-8359-1376-7). Reston.

Ahmed, Osman S. The Potential Effects of Income Redistribution on Selected Growth Constraints: A Case Study of Kenya. LC 80-6093. (Illus.). 368p. (Orig.). 1982. lib. bdg. 29.00 (ISBN 0-8191-2112-6); pap. text ed. 15.50 (ISBN 0-8191-2113-4). U Pr of Amer.

Ahmed, P. Pregnancy, Childbirth & Parenthood. (Coping with Medical Issues Ser.: Vol. 2). 414p. 1981. 45.50 (ISBN 0-444-00558-7, Biomedical Pr). Elsevier.

Ahmed, P., jt. ed. see Kolkner, A.

Ahmed, P. I. & Coelho, G. V., eds. Toward a New Definition of Mental Health: Psychosocial Dimensions. LC 79-9066. (Current Topics in Mental Health Ser.). (Illus.). 504p. 1979. 39.50x (ISBN 0-306-40248-3, Plenum Pr). Plenum Pub.

Ahmed, Paul I. & Plog, Stanley C., eds. State Mental Hospitals: What Happens When They Close. (Illus.). 234p. 1976. 32.50x (ISBN 0-306-30897-5, Plenum Med Bk). Plenum Pub.

Ahmed, Paul I., jt. ed. see Plog, Stanley C.

Ahmed, Paul I., et al, eds. Coping with Juvenile Diabetes. (Illus.). 420p. 1985. 39.50x (ISBN 0-398-05073-2). C C Thomas.

Ahmed, Rafiuddin. The Bengal Muslims, Eighteen Seventy-One to Nineteen Six: A Quest for Identity. (Illus.). 1981. 32.50x (ISBN 0-19-561260-4). Oxford U Pr.

Ahmed, Sadiq. Public Finance in Egypt: Its Structure & Trends. (World Bank Staff Working Papers: No. 639). 112p. Date not set. 5.00 (ISBN 0-318-02947-2). World Bank.

Ahmed, Said B. The Swahili Chronicle of Ngazija. Harries, Lyndon, ed. (African Humanities Ser.). (Illus.). 136p. (Orig.). 1977. pap. text ed. 5.00 (ISBN 0-941934-20-9). Indiana Africa.

Ahmed, Shemsu-D-Din, ed. Legends of the Sufis. 1977. pap. 7.95 (ISBN 0-7229-5050-0). Theos Pub Hse.

Ahmed, Tariq. Religio-Political Ferment in North-West Frontier During the Mughal Period. 1983. 12.50x (ISBN 0-8364-1081-5, Pub. by Idarah). South Asia Bks.

Ahmed, Viqar & Amjad, Rashid. The Management of Pakistan's Economy, 1947-1982. (UGC Series in Economics). 327p. 1985. pap. 21.95 (ISBN 0-19-577316-0). Oxford U Pr.

Ahmed, Zia U., ed. Financial Profitability & Losses in Public Enterprises. 167p. 1982. pap. 20.00x (ISBN 92-9038-023-3, Pub. by Intl Ctr Pub Yugoslavia). Kumarian Pr.

--Pricing Policy & Investment Criteria in Public Enterprises. 297p. 1982. pap. 20.00x (ISBN 92-9038-024-1, Pub. by Intl Ctr Pub Yugoslavia). Kumarian Pr.

Ahmed ibn Fartua. History of the First Twelve Years of the Reign of Mai Idris Alooma of Burnu (1571-1583) Palmer, H. R., tr. 121p. 1970. Repr. of 1926 ed. 35.00x (ISBN 0-7146-1709-1, F Cass Co). Biblio Dist.

Ahmed-Ibn Ibrahim, jt. auth. see Abu Al-Hasan.

Ahmed Sabri. When I Was a Boy in Turkey. LC 77-87624. (Illus.). Repr. of 1924 ed. 18.50 (ISBN 0-404-16450-1). AMS Pr.

Ahmed-Ud-Din, Feroz. This Handful of Dust. (Redbird Bk.). 31p. 1975. 8.00 (ISBN 0-88253-835-7); pap. 4.80 (ISBN 0-88253-836-5). Ind-US Inc.

Ahmet, O. E., jt. ed. see Holod, Renata.

Ahmos Zu-Bolton. A Niggered Amen. 1975. 5.95 (ISBN 0-941490-11-4). Solo Pr.

Ahn, Chung-si. Social Development & Political Violence: A Cross-National Causal Attitude. (The Institute of Social Sciences International Studies Ser.: No. 3). 210p. 1981. text ed. 16.00x (ISBN 0-8248-0941-6). UH Pr.

Ahne, W., ed. Fish Diseases: Third COPRAQ-Session. (Proceedings in Life Sciences Ser.). (Illus.). 252p. 1980. 52.00 (ISBN 0-387-10406-2). Springer-Verlag.

Ahnebrink, L. The Beginnings of Naturalism in American Fiction, 1891-1903. (Essays & Studies on American Language & Literature: Vol. 9). pap. 15.00 (ISBN 0-317-16340-X). Kraus Repr.

--The Influence of Zola on Frank Norris. (Essays & Studies on American Language & Literature: Vol. 5). pap. 15.00 (ISBN 0-317-16337-X). Kraus Repr.

Ahnebrink, Lars. The Influence of Emile Zola on Frank Norris. 1978. Repr. of 1947 ed. lib. bdg. 16.00 (ISBN 0-8495-0041-9). Arden Lib.

--The Influence of Emile Zola on Frank Norris. LC 73-12457. Repr. of 1947 ed. lib. bdg. 15.00 (ISBN 0-8414-2873-5). Folcroft.

Ahnefeld, F. W., et al, eds. Parenteral Nutrition. Babad, A., tr. from Ger. LC 75-34213. (Illus.). 200p. 1975. pap. 21.00 (ISBN 0-387-07518-6). Springer-Verlag.

Ahner, Walter. Laboratory Manual in Chemistry. (gr. 11-12). 1964. pap. 7.75 (ISBN 0-87720-123-4). AMSCO Sch.

Ahner, Walter L. Workbook & Laboratory Manual in Chemistry. rev. ed. (Illus.). (gr. 11-12). 1964. pap. 8.92 (ISBN 0-87720-125-0). AMSCO Sch.

Ahner, Walter L. & Diamond, Sheldon R. Laboratory Manual in Physics. 2nd ed. (Orig.). (gr. 10-12). 1967. 7.33 (ISBN 0-87720-174-9); tchrs' ed. 4.55 (ISBN 0-87720-175-7). AMSCO Sch.

--Workbook & Laboratory Manual in Physics. 2nd ed. (Illus., Orig.). (gr. 11-12). 1967. wkbk. 9.25 (ISBN 0-87720-176-5). AMSCO Sch.

Ahner, Walter L. & Kastan, Harold G. Review Text in Physics. (Illus., Orig.). (gr. 10-12). 1966. pap. text ed. 7.42 (ISBN 0-87720-171-4). AMSCO Sch.

Ahnert, Frank. A General & Comprehensive Theoretical Model of Slope Profile Development. (Occasional Papers in Geography: No. 1). (Illus.). 95p. pap. 2.00 (ISBN 0-686-32710-1). U MD Geography.

Ahnert, Gerald T. Retracing the Butterfield Overland Trail Through Arizona. LC 73-83025. (Illus.). 112p. 12.00 (ISBN 0-87026-030-8). Westernlore.

Ahnlund, Nils G. Gustav Adolf, the Great. Roberts, Michael, tr. from Swedish. LC 83-10868. (Illus.). ix, 314p. 1983. Repr. of 1940 ed. lib. bdg. 39.75x (ISBN 0-313-24115-5, AHGU). Greenwood.

Aho, A. V., et al. Data Structures & Algorithms. 1982. 33.95 (ISBN 0-201-00023-7). Addison-Wesley.

Aho, Alfred & Hopcroft, John. The Design & Analysis of Computer Algorithms. 480p. 1974. text ed. 34.95 (ISBN 0-201-00029-6). Addison-Wesley.

Aho, Alfred V. & Ullman, Jeffrey D. Principles of Compiler Design. LC 77-73953. (Illus.). 1977. text ed. 34.95 (ISBN 0-201-00022-9). Addison-Wesley.

--Theory of Parsing, Translation, & Compiling, Vol. 2 Compiling. (Illus.). 471p. 1973. ref. ed. 40.95 (ISBN 0-13-914564-8). P-H.

--Theory of Parsing, Translation & Compiling: Vol. 1, Parsing. (Illus.). 592p. 1972. ref. ed. 40.95 (ISBN 0-13-914556-7). P-H.

Aho, Arnold J. Materials, Energies & Environmental Design. 1981. lib. bdg. 42.50 (ISBN 0-8240-7178-6). Garland Pub.

Aho, Gary L. William Morris: A Reference Guide. (Reference Guides to Literature Ser.). 420p. 1985. lib. bdg. 48.00 (ISBN 0-8161-8449-6). G K Hall.

Aho, Gerhard, et al. Glory in the Cross-Fruit of the Spirit from the Passion of Christ. 1984. pap. 7.95 (ISBN 0-570-03940-1, 12-2876). Concordia.

Aho, James. Credit Union Auditing. 381p. 54.95 (ISBN 0-318-17594-0). Credit Union Natl Assn.

Aho, James A. German Realpolitik & American Sociology: An Inquiry into the Sources & the Political Significance of the Sociology of Conflict. LC 73-21229. 346p. 1975. 24.50 (ISBN 0-8387-1453-6). Bucknell U Pr.

--Religious Mythology & the Art of War: Comparative Religious Symbolisms of Military Violence. LC 80-23465. (Contributions to the Study of Religion Ser.: No. 3). 264p. 1981. lib. bdg. 29.95 (ISBN 0-313-22564-8, ARM/). Greenwood.

Aho, Jennifer J. & Petras, John W. Learning about Sexual Abuse. LC 84-26028. (Illus.). 96p. (gr. 4-10). 1985. PLB 11.95 (ISBN 0-89490-114-1). Enslow Pubs.

Aho, John V. A Butterfly in the Greenhouse. (Orig.). 1984. pap. 4.95 (ISBN 0-9613629-0-1). J V Aho.

--A Clearing of Daisies. (Orig.). 1985. pap. 5.00 (ISBN 0-9613629-1-X). J V Aho.

Ahola, David J. Finnish-Americans & International Communism: A Study of Finnish-American Communism from Bolshevization to the Demise of the Third International. LC 81-40011. (Illus.). 356p. (Orig.). 1982. lib. bdg. 29.00 (ISBN 0-8191-1930-X); pap. text ed. 15.00 (ISBN 0-8191-1931-8). U Pr of Amer.

Ahonen, Lauri. Mission Growth: A Case Study on Finnish Free Foreign Missions. LC 84-12636. 96p. (Orig.). 1984. pap. 5.95 (ISBN 0-87808-335-9). William Carey Lib.

Ahrari, Mohammed E. The Dynamics of Oil Diplomacy: Conflict & Concensus. Bruchey, Stuart, ed. LC 80-608. (Multinational Corporations Ser.). 1980. lib. bdg. 45.00x (ISBN 0-405-13360-X). Ayer Co Pubs.

Ahrendt, Kenneth M. Community College Reading Programs. LC 74-31131. 69p. pap. text ed. 3.50 (ISBN 0-87207-930-9). Intl Reading.

Ahrendts, Juergen, ed. Bibliographie zur alteuropaeischen Religionsgeschichte II, 1965-1969: Eine interdisziplinaere Auswahl von Literatur zu den Rand-und Nachfolgekulturen der Antike in Europa unter besonderer Beruecksichtigung der nichtchristlichen Religionen. LC 68-86477. (Arbeiten Zur Fruehmittelalterforschung: Vol. 5). xxvi, 591p. 1974. 59.20x (ISBN 3-11-003398-4). De Gruyter.

Ahrens, Art & Gold, Eddie. Day by Day in Chicago Cub History. LC 81-86516. (Illus.). 352p. (Orig.). 1982. pap. 9.95 (ISBN 0-88011-048-1). Leisure Pr.

Ahrens, Art, jt. auth. see Gold, Eddie.

Ahrens, C. Donald. Meteorology Today. 2nd ed. (Illus.). 550p. 1985. pap. text ed. 29.95 (ISBN 0-314-85212-3). West Pub.

Ahrens, Carsten. Afoot in Penn's Woods. LC 84-70535. (Illus.). 128p. 1984. pap. 5.95 (ISBN 0-910042-46-2). Allegheny.

--Along Penn's Waterways. LC 84-73238. (Illus.). 128p. 1985. pap. 7.95 (ISBN 0-910042-49-7). Allegheny.

Ahrens, Christa, tr. see Kubler, Rolf.

Ahrens, Christa, tr. see Raethel, Heinz-Sigurd.

Ahrens, Christa, tr. see Thies, Dagmar.

Ahrens, Donald C. Meteorology Today: An Introduction to Weather, Climate & Environment. (Illus.). 528p. 1982. text ed. 27.95 (ISBN 0-314-63147-X). West Pub.

Ahrens, Donald L., et al. Concrete & Concrete Masonry. (Illus.). 1976. pap. text ed. 5.65x (ISBN 0-913163-09-0, 176). Hobar Pubns.

Ahrens, Herman C., Jr. Feeling Good about Yourself. (Orig.). 1983. pap. 1.25 (ISBN 0-8298-0644-X). Pilgrim NY.

--Keep in Touch. LC 78-14912. (Illus.). 96p. (Orig.). (gr. 7-12). 1978. pap. 4.95 (ISBN 0-8298-0351-3). Pilgrim NY.

--Life with Your Parents. (Looking Up Ser.). 24p. 1983. pap. 1.25 booklet (ISBN 0-8298-0667-9). Pilgrim NY.

Ahrens, Herman C., Jr., ed. Tune In. LC 68-54031. (Illus.). 1968. pap. 3.95 (ISBN 0-8298-0138-3). Pilgrim NY.

Ahrens, John. Preparing for the Future: An Essay on the Rights Future Generations. 44p. 1983. pap. 4.00 (ISBN 0-912051-00-0). Transaction Bks.

--Preparing for the Future: An Essay on the Rights of Future Generations. (Studies in Social Philosophy & Policy: No. 2). 44p. (Orig.). 1983. pap. 4.00 (ISBN 0-912051-00-0). Soc Phil Pol.

Ahrens, L., jt. auth. see Schlesselman, R.

Ahrens, L. H. Ionization Potentials: Some Variations, Implications & Applications. (Illus.). 100p. 1983. 32.00 (ISBN 0-08-025274-5). Pergamon.

--Physics & Chemistry of the Earth, Vol. 10. (Illus.). 270p. 1980. 105.00 (ISBN 0-08-020287-X). Pergamon.

Ahrens, Robert H., Jr. Monarch Notes on Aeschylus' Plays. (Orig.). pap. 3.95 (ISBN 0-671-00801-3). Monarch Pr.

Ahrensfeld, Janet, et al. Special Libraries: A Guide for Management. 2nd ed. LC 81-14487. 80p. 1981. pap. text ed. 15.50 (ISBN 0-87111-258-2). SLA.

Ahrentzen, Sherry. Children & the Built Environment: An Annotated Bibliography of Representative Research of Children & Housing, School Design & Environmental Stress. (Architecture Series: Bibliography: A-764). 62p. 1982. pap. 9.00 (ISBN 0-88066-156-9). Vance Biblios.

Ahrland, S; see Dunitz, J. D., et al.

Ahrweiler, Helene. Byzance: Les Pays et Les Territoires. 338p. 1976. 60.00x (ISBN 0-902089-85-4, Pub. by Variorum). State Mutual Bk.

Ahsan, Manazir. Islam: Faith & Practice. (Illus.). 48p. (Orig.). 1980. pap. 3.00 (ISBN 0-86037-001-1, Pub. by Islamic Found UK). New Era Pubns MI.

Ahsan, Syed M. Agricultural Insurance: A New Policy for Developing Countries. 1984. text ed. 36.95 (ISBN 0-566-00800-9). Gower Pub Co.

Ahsen, Akhter. Basic Concepts in Eidetic Psychotherapy. 434p. 1973. text ed. 35.00 (ISBN 0-913412-12-0). Brandon Hse.

--Eidetic Parents Test & Analysis. 256p. 1972. 35.00 (ISBN 0-913412-02-3). Brandon Hse.

--Manhunt in the Desert. 1979. pap. 9.95 (ISBN 0-913412-26-0). Brandon Hse.

--Oedipus at Thebes. LC 83-70541. 80p. (Orig.). 1984. pap. 9.95 (ISBN 0-913412-35-X). Brandon Hse.

--Psycheye. 288p. 1977. 30.00 (ISBN 0-913412-47-3). Brandon Hse.

--Rhea Complex: A Detour Around the Oedipus Complex. LC 84-72149. 279p. 1984. 35.00 (ISBN 0-913412-24-4). Brandon Hse.

--Trojan Horse: Imagery in Psychology, Literature, Art & Politics. LC 84-72150. 287p. 1984. 35.00 (ISBN 0-913412-20-1). Brandon Hse.

Ahsen, Akhter & Dolan, A. T., eds. Handbook of Imagery Research & Practice. LC 82-73889. 400p. (Orig.). 1985. pap. 45.00 (ISBN 0-913412-19-8). Brandon Hse.

AHSGR. Kuche Kochen. (Illus.). 238p. (gr. 9-12). 1973. pap. text ed. 5.50 (ISBN 0-914222-10-4). Am Hist Soc Ger.

Ahuja, C. Tragedy, Modern Temper & O'Neill. 207p. 1984. text ed. 20.50x (ISBN 0-391-02699-2). Humanities.

Ahuja, D., et al, eds. National Energy Data Systems. 511p. 1984. text ed. 30.50x (ISBN 0-391-03209-7, Pub. by Concept India). Humanities.

Ahuja, Elizabeth, jt. auth. see Roberts, Jean.

Ahuja, Elizabeth M., jt. auth. see Roberts, Jean.

Ahuja, H. N. Project Management: Techniques in Planning & Controlling Construction Projects. (Construction Management & Engineering Ser.). 470p. 1984. 54.95 (ISBN 0-471-87399-3). Wiley.

Ahuja, Hira N. Construction Performance Control by Networks. LC 76-4774. (Construction Management & Engineering Ser.). 636p. 1976. 67.50x (ISBN 0-471-00960-1, Pub. by Wiley-Interscience). Wiley.

--Successful Construction Cost Control. LC 80-10156. (Construction Management & Engineering Ser.). 388p. 1980. 56.95x (ISBN 0-471-05378-3, Pub. by Wiley-Interscience). Wiley.

Ahuja, Hira N. & Walsh, Michael A. Successful Methods in Cost Engineering. LC 82-17316. (Construction Management & Engineering Ser.). 379p. 1983. 51.95 (ISBN 0-471-86435-8, Pub. by Wiley Interscience). Wiley.

Ahuja, K. Idle Labour in Village India: A Study of Rajasthan. 1978. 12.50x (ISBN 0-8364-0280-4). South Asia Bks.

Ahuja, M. M., ed. Practice of Diabetes Mellitus. text ed. 32.50x (ISBN 0-7069-2183-6, Pub. by Vikas India). Advent NY.

Ahuja, Narendra & Schachter, Bruce J. Pattern Models. LC 82-11070. 309p. 1983. 45.95 (ISBN 0-471-86194-4, Pub. by Wiley-Interscience). Wiley.

Ahuja, S. P., jt. auth. see Manning, G. W.

Ahuja, Satinder, ed. Ultrahigh Resolution Chromatography. LC 84-2792. (ACS Symposium Ser.: No. 250). 231p. 1984. lib. bdg. 44.95x (ISBN 0-8412-0835-2). Am Chemical.

Ahuja, Sut, et al, eds. Chemical Analysis of the Environment & Other Techniques. LC 73-82575. 384p. 1973. 49.50x (ISBN 0-306-39305-0, Plenum Pr). Plenum Pub.

Ahuja, V. Design & Analysis of Computer Communication Networks. 1982. 41.95x (ISBN 0-07-000697-0). McGraw.

Ahuma, S. R. & Attoch. Gold Coast Nation & National Consciousness. 63p. 1971. Repr. of 1911 ed. 27.50x (ISBN 0-7146-1742-3, BHA 01742, F Cass Co). Biblio Dist.

Ahumada, Rodolfo. A History of Western Ontology from Thales to Heidegger. LC 78-60794. 1978. pap. text ed. 12.50 (ISBN 0-8191-0507-4). U Pr of Amer.

AIA Journal. New American Architecture. (Illus.). 1979. 9.95 (ISBN 0-07-000701-2). McGraw.

AIA Journal, ed. The Annual of American Architecture, 1981. (The Annual of American Architecture Ser.). (Illus.). 164p. 1981. 24.00x (ISBN 0-913962-36-8). Am Inst Arch.

AIA Research Corporation. Energy Conservation in Building Design. 1974. pap. 3.50 (ISBN 0-913962-17-1). Am Inst Arch.

--Passive Solar Design: A Short Bibliography for Practitioners. 1979. pap. 6.50x (ISBN 0-89934-040-7, A-007). Solar Energy Info.

--Passive Solar Design: A Survey of Monitored Buildings. 353p. 1979. pap. 39.50x (ISBN 0-930978-85-4, A008). Solar Energy Info.

--Passive Solar Research & Development Project Summaries. 1979. pap. 11.95x (ISBN 0-89934-041-5, A-011). Solar Energy Info.

--Solar Dwelling Design Concepts. 146p. 1981. pap. 9.95x (ISBN 0-930978-24-2, H-025). Solar Energy Info.

--A Survey of Passive Solar Buildings. 176p. 1979. pap. 16.50x (ISBN 0-930978-84-6, A-002-PP). Solar Energy Info.

AIA Research Corporation for U. S. Department of Housing & Urban Renewal. A Survey of Passive Solar Homes. 105p. 1981. pap. 14.50x (ISBN 0-89934-026-1, A017). Solar Energy Info.

AIAA-ASME Structures, Structural Dynamics & Material Conference (10th: 1969: New Orleans, Louisiana) Structures & Materials: Collection of Technical Papers, April 14-16, 1969. (Illus.). pap. 120.30 (ISBN 0-317-08388-0, 2016452). Bks Demand UMI.

AICHE Design Institute for Physical Property Data Staff, ed. Predicting Chemical Process Design Data Manual: Data Prediction Manual. 1983. 150.00 (ISBN 0-8169-0233-X); 125.00 (ISBN 0-317-03747-1). Am Inst Chem Eng.

Aichelburg. Einstein: His Influence on Physics, Philosophy, Politics. 26.50 (ISBN 0-9940012-2-3). Heyden.

Aichelburg, P. C. & Sexl, R. U., eds. Albert Einstein: His Influence on Physics, Philosophy & Politics. 1979. 26.50 (ISBN 0-9940012-2-3, Pub. by Vieweg & Sohn Germany). Heyden.

Aichele, Douglas B. & Olson, Melfried. Geometric Selections for Elementary & Middle School Teachers. 96p. 1981. 11.95 (ISBN 0-8106-1720-X). NEA.

Aichele, Douglas B., ed. Mathematics Teacher Education. 64p. 1978. pap. 7.50 (ISBN 0-8106-1618-1). NEA.

Aichele, George, Jr. The Limits of Story. (Semeia Studies). 1985. 15.75 (ISBN 0-89130-768-0, 06 06 13); pap. 10.50 (ISBN 0-89130-751-6). Scholars Pr GA.

--The Limits of Story. LC 84-48726. (Semeia Studies). 160p. 1985. pap. 8.95 (ISBN 0-8006-1513-1, 1-1513). Fortress.

Aichholz, V. Miller zu see Zu Aichholz, V. Miller, et al.

Aichhorn, August. Delinquency & Child Guidance: Selected Papers of August Aichhorn. Fleischmann, Otto, et al, eds. LC 64-8751. (Menninger Foundation Monograph Ser.: No. 1). 244p. 1967. text ed. 25.00 (ISBN 0-8236-1160-4). Intl Univs Pr.

--Wayward Youth. pap. 7.95 (ISBN 0-8101-0660-4). Northwestern U Pr.

Aichinger, Ilse. Bound Man, & Other Stories. facsimile ed. Mosbacher, Eric, tr. LC 72-144151. (Short Story Index Reprint Ser., Suppl. 1955-58). Repr. of 1956 ed. 10.00 (ISBN 0-8369-3766-X). Ayer Co Pubs.

--Selected Poetry & Prose. Chappel, Allen H., tr. from Ger. LC 83-14867. 141p. 1983. 16.00x (ISBN 0-937406-25-2); pap. 6.50 (ISBN 0-937406-24-4). Logbridge-Rhodes.

Aichinger, Ilse see Otten, Anna.

Aichinger, Peter. American Soldier in Fiction, Eighteen Eighty to Nineteen Sixty-Three: A History of Attitudes Toward Warfare & the Military Establishment. 144p. 1975. 8.50x (ISBN 0-8138-0100-1). Iowa St U Pr.

Aickin, M. Linear Statistical Analysis of Discrete Data. (Probability & Mathematical Statistics Ser.). 358p. 1983. 38.95 (ISBN 0-471-09774-8). Wiley.

Aickman, Robert. Intrusions. 216p. 1980. 17.50 (ISBN 0-575-02854-8, Pub. by Gollancz England). David & Charles.

Aid, Frances M., et al, eds. Colloquium on Hispanic Linguistics: 1975. LC 76-53729. 157p. 1976. pap. 6.95 (ISBN 0-87840-043-5). Georgetown U Pr.

Aidala, Joseph B. & Katz, Leon. Transients in Electric Circuits. (Illus.). 1980. text ed. 29.95 (ISBN 0-13-929943-2). P-H.

Aidala, Thomas, jt. auth. see Bruce, Curt.

Aidala, Thomas R. Hearst Castle: San Simeon. LC 81-6752. (Illus.). 240p. 1981. 45.00 (ISBN 0-933920-19-9). Hudson Hills.

Aidarova, L. Child Development & Education. 200p. 1982. 6.95 (ISBN 0-8285-2562-5, Pub. by Progress Pubs USSR). Imported Pubns.

Aidley, D. J. The Physiology of Excitable Cells. 2nd ed. LC 77-87375. (Illus.). 1979. 79.50 (ISBN 0-521-21913-2); pap. 24.95 (ISBN 0-521-29308-1). Cambridge U Pr.

Aidley, D J., jt. auth. see Keynes, R. D.

Aidley, D. J., ed. Animal Migration. LC 81-3905. (Society for Experimental Biology Seminar Ser.: No. 13). 1981. 44.50 (ISBN 0-521-23274-0); pap. 22.95 (ISBN 0-521-29888-1). Cambridge U Pr.

Aidoo, Ama A. Our Sister Kill Joy. LC 78-64625. 1979. 9.95 (ISBN 0-88357-064-5); pap. 4.95 (ISBN 0-88357-065-3). NOK Pubs.

Aiello, David. Man on a String. LC 80-20345. 1984. pap. 10.95 (ISBN 0-87949-193-0). Ashley Bks.

Aiello, Greg, jt. auth. see Perkins, Steve.

Aiello, J. R. & Baum, A., eds. Residential Crowding & Design. LC 79-357. (Illus.). 270p. 1979. 25.00x (ISBN 0-306-40205-X, Plenum Pr). Plenum Pub.

Aiello, Janet. Cats & Kittens Iron-on Transfer Patterns. (Illus., Orig.). 1983. pap. 2.25 (ISBN 0-486-24461-X). Dover.

Aiello, Joseph A. & Moore, Charles A. The College Writing Book. 1979. pap. text ed. 12.00 (ISBN 0-8403-1954-1, 40195402). Kendall-Hunt.

Aiello, Roger, jt. auth. see Sherrill, Chris.

Aifantis, E. C. & Davison, L., eds. Media with Microstructures & Wave Propagation: Proceedings of the Conference Held Houghton, Michigan, USA, January 1983. 260p. 1985. pap. 120.00 (ISBN 0-08-031661-1). Pergamon.

Aigler, Ralph W., et al. Cases on Property, 2 vols. 1339p. 1960. write for info. West Pub.

Aigner, D. J. & Goldberger, A. S., eds. Latent Variables in Socio-Economic Models. (Contributions to Economic Analysis: Vol. 103). 384p. 1977. 85.00 (ISBN 0-7204-0526-2, North-Holland). Elsevier.

Aigner, Hal. Adoption in America Coming of Age. 240p. Date not set. pap. 8.95 t (ISBN 0-937572-02-0). Paradigm Pr.

--Faint Trails: An Introduction to the Fundamentals of Adult Adoptee-Birth Parent Reunification Searches. 104p. (Orig.). 1980. pap. 4.95 (ISBN 0-937572-00-4). Paradigm Pr.

Aigner, Hal, ed. see Galloway, Russell.

Aigner, K., ed. Regionale Chemotherapie der Leber. (Beitraege zur Onkologie. Contributions to Oncology Ser.: Vol. 21). (Illus.). viii, 140p. 1985. 24.75 (ISBN 3-8055-4014-0). S Karger.

Aigner, K., jt. ed. see Schwemmle, K.

Aigner, Kurt W. Allistar Journey Through a Mind. LC 84-90092. 101p. 1985. 8.95 (ISBN 0-533-06159-8). Vantage.

Aigner, M. Combinatorial Theory. (Grundlehren der Mathemtischen Wissenschaften Ser.: Vol. 234). (Illus.). 1979. 53.50 (ISBN 0-387-90376-3). Springer-Verlag.

Aigner, M. & Jungnickel, D., eds. Geometries & Groups: Proceedings. (Lecture Notes in Mathematics Ser.: Vol. 893). 250p. 1981. pap. 19.00 (ISBN 0-387-11166-2). Springer-Verlag.

Aigner, Martin, ed. Higher Combinatorics. (Advanced Study Institutes Math & Physical Sciences Ser.: No. 31). 1977. lib. bdg. 31.50 (ISBN 90-277-0795-2, Pub. by Reidel Holland). Kluwer Academic.

Aigner, Stephen M., jt. auth. see Simons, Ronald L.

Aigner, T. Storm Depositional Systems. (Lecture Notes in Earth Sciences: Vol. 3). vii, 174p. 1985. pap. 14.50 (ISBN 0-387-15231-8). Springer-Verlag.

Aihara, Cornellia. The Calendar Cookbook. (Illus., Orig.). 1979. pap. 14.95 (ISBN 0-918860-32-6). G Ohsawa.

--The Do of Cooking. 230p. 1982. pap. 19.95 (ISBN 0-918860-39-3). G Ohsawa.

--The First Macrobiotic Cookbook. rev. ed. Rothman, Sandy & Ruggles, Laurel, eds. 160p. 1985. 8.95 (ISBN 0-918860-40-7). G Ohsawa.

--Macrobiotic Child Care. rev. ed. 65p. (Orig.). 1979. pap. 3.95 (ISBN 0-918860-34-2). G Ohsawa.

--Macrobiotic Kitchen. Orig. Title: Chico San Cookbook. (Illus.). 140p. 1976. pap. 9.95 (ISBN 0-87040-514-4). G Ohsawa.

--Macrobiotic Kitchen: Key to Good Health. (Illus.). 144p. 1982. pap. 9.95 (ISBN 0-87040-514-4). Japan Pubns USA.

Aihara, Herman. Acid & Alkaline. 2nd ed. (Orig.). 1980. pap. 2.50 (ISBN 0-918860-35-0). G Ohsawa.

--Basic Macrobiotics. LC 84-81359. (Illus.). 128p. pap. 9.95 (ISBN 0-87040-614-0). Japan Pubns USA.

--Learning from Salmon & Other Essays. Rothman, Sandy, ed. 157p. 1980. pap. 7.95 (ISBN 0-918860-37-7). G Ohsawa.

Aihara, Herman & De Langre, Jacques. Milk, A Myth of Civilization. (Illus.). 39p. 1984. pap. 4.50 (ISBN 0-916508-29-3). Happiness Pr.

--Seven Celtic Macrobiotic Principles. (Illus.). 23p. 1984. pap. 4.50 (ISBN 0-916508-30-7). Happiness Pr.

Aihara, Herman, ed. see Ohsawa, George.

Aihara, Herman, tr. see Hashimoto, Keizo.

Aijazuddin, F. S. Pahari Paintings & Sikh Portraits in the Lahore Museum. (Illus.). 101p. 1977. 100.00x (ISBN 0-85667-029-4, Pub. by Sotheby Parke Bernet England). Biblio Dist.

--Sikh Portraits by European Artists. (Illus.). 160p. 1979. 40.00x (ISBN 0-85667-059-6, Pub. by Sotheby Pubns England). Biblio Dist.

Aijmer, Goran. Economic Man in Sha Tin: Vegetable Gardeners in a Hong Kong Valley. (Scandanavian Institute of Asian Studies Monograph: No. 43). (Orig.). 1980. pap. text ed. 12.50x (ISBN 0-7007-0135-4). Humanities.

Aijmer, Goran, ed. Leadership on the China Coast. (Studies on Asian Topics, Scandinavian Institute of Asian Studies: No. 8). 192p. 1984. pap. text ed. 11.00x (ISBN 0-7007-0162-1, Pub. by Curzon Pr England). Humanities.

Aikat, Amulyachandra. On the Poetry of Matthew Arnold, Robert Browning & Rabindranath Tagore. 1978. lib. bdg. 30.00 (ISBN 0-8495-0053-2). Arden Lib.

--On the Poetry of Matthew Arnold, Robert Browning & Rabindranath Tagore. LC 72-13660. 1972. Repr. of 1921 ed. lib. bdg. 20.00 (ISBN 0-8414-1237-5). Folcroft.

Aikawa, Jerry K. Magnesium: It's Biologic Significance. 144p. 1981. 52.00 (ISBN 0-8493-5871-X). CRC Pr.

--Myxedema. 116p. 1961. 12.75x (ISBN 0-398-04185-7). C C Thomas.

--Relationship of Magnesium to Disease in Domestic Animals & in Humans. (Illus.). 160p. 1971. 16.75x (ISBN 0-398-02215-1). C C Thomas.

--Rocky Mountain Spotted Fever. (Illus.). 156p. 1966. photocopy ed. 18.75x (ISBN 0-398-00019-0). C C Thomas.

Aikawa, Masamichi & Sterling, Charles R. Intracellular Parasitic Protozoa. 1974. 22.00 (ISBN 0-12-045350-9). Acad Pr.

Aiken. Psychological Testing & Assessment. 5th ed. 1985. 26.27 (ISBN 0-205-08252-1, 798252). Allyn.

--Selected Letters of Conrad Aiken. Killorin, Joseph R., ed. LC 77-20620. (Illus.). 1978. 27.50x (ISBN 0-300-02180-1). Yale U Pr.

Aiken & Ward. Foreclosures & Confirmation of Sales. (The Law in Georgia Ser.). incl. latest pocket part supplement 24.95 (ISBN 0-686-90392-7); separate pocket part supplement, 1984 15.95 (ISBN 0-686-90393-5). Harrison Co GA.

Aiken, B. The Waiter-Waitress Manual. 1976. 10.16 (ISBN 0-07-000742-X). McGraw.

Aiken, C. Porter. Transition. 1978. pap. 5.00 (ISBN 0-933992-02-5). Coffee Break.

Aiken, Conrad. The Charnel Rose, Senlin: A Biography & Other Poems. LC 79-156910. (Studies in Poetry, No. 38). 1972. Repr. of 1918 ed. lib. bdg. 33.95x (ISBN 0-8383-1247-0). Haskell.

--Clerk's Journal. LC 70-152799. 1971. 12.00x (ISBN 0-87130-022-2); signed, ltd. ed. 50.00 (ISBN 0-87130-023-0). Eakins.

--The Collected Short Stories of Conrad Aiken. LC 81-84243. 566p. 1982. pap. 10.95 (ISBN 0-8052-0690-6). Schocken.

--Gehenna. LC 73-4672. Repr. of 1930 ed. lib. bdg. 17.50 (ISBN 0-8414-1734-2). Folcroft.

--Great Circle. 1985. 6.95 (ISBN 0-87795-706-1). Arbor Hse.

--A Heart for the Gods of Mexico. LC 73-11309. Repr. of 1939 ed. lib. bdg. 27.50 (ISBN 0-8414-2885-9). Folcroft.

--A Heart for the Gods of Mexico. 157p. 1983. Repr. of 1939 ed. lib. bdg. 30.00 (ISBN 0-8495-0082-6). Arden Lib.

--Jig of Forslin. 1964. pap. 2.50 (ISBN 0-8283-1443-8, 32, IPL). Branden Pub Co.

--Prelude: A Poem. 1978. lib. bdg. 25.00 (ISBN 0-8495-0037-0). Arden Lib.

--Prelude: A Poem. LC 73-4435. 1973. lib. bdg. 16.50 (ISBN 0-8414-1728-8). Folcroft.

--Selected Poems. LC 82-3234. 288p. 1982. pap. 9.95 (ISBN 0-8052-0718-X). Schocken.

--Silent Snow, Secret Snow. LC 83-71788. (Classic Short Stories Ser.). 32p. 1983. 8.95 (ISBN 0-87191-963-X). Creative Ed.

--Turns & Movies & Other Tales in Verse. 1978. Repr. of 1916 ed. lib. bdg. 30.00 (ISBN 0-8495-0054-0). Arden Lib.

--Turns & Movies & Other Tales in Verse. LC 73-18103. Repr. of 1916 ed. lib. bdg. 29.50 (ISBN 0-8414-2947-2). Folcroft.

Aiken, Conrad P. Collected Poems, Nineteen Sixteen to Nineteen Seventy. 2nd ed. LC 79-120179. 1970. 35.00 (ISBN 0-19-501258-5). Oxford U Pr.

--Scepticisms, Notes On Contemporary Poetry. Repr. of 1919 ed. 18.00 (ISBN 0-384-00525-X). Johnson Repr.

--Scepticisms: Notes on Contemporary Poetry. facs. ed. LC 67-30170. (Essay Index Reprint Ser). 1919. 16.00 (ISBN 0-8369-0140-1). Ayer Co Pubs.

--Short Stories. facsimile ed. LC 72-178434. (Short Story Index Reprint Ser.). Repr. of 1950 ed. 26.50 (ISBN 0-8369-4034-2). Ayer Co Pubs.

--Ushant: An Essay. 1971. 27.50x (ISBN 0-19-501452-9). Oxford U Pr.

Aiken, D. W. & Fuller, K. J. Living Volute of Africa. 1970. pap. 3.50 (ISBN 0-913792-01-2). Shell Cab.

Aiken, Dawn. Taming Butterflies. Draze, Dianne & Ryder, Dixie, eds. 96p. tchrs. ed. 10.00 (ISBN 0-931724-25-2). Dandy Lion.

Aiken, Diane. Writing Tips. (Part II). 1981. pap. 1.00 (ISBN 0-912452-34-X). Am Phys Therapy Assn.

--Writing Tips. 1980. pap. 1.00 (ISBN 0-912452-01-3). Am Phys Therapy Assn.

Aiken, G. R., et al. Humic Substances in Soil, Sediment & Water: Geochemistry, Isolation & Characterization. 688p. 1985. 59.95 (ISBN 0-471-88274-7). Wiley.

Aiken, George D., et al. Vermont for Every Season. LC 80-23320. (Illus.). 160p. 1980. 30.00 (ISBN 0-936896-00-0). VT Life Mag.

Aiken, Henry D. Reason & Conduct: New Bearings in Moral Philosophy. LC 77-26079. 1978. Repr. of 1962 ed. lib. bdg. 28.50 (ISBN 0-313-20083-1, AIRD). Greenwood.

Aiken, Henry D., ed. Age of Ideology. facs. ed. LC 77-117748. (Essay Index Reprint Ser). 1956. 19.00 (ISBN 0-8369-1821-5). Ayer Co Pubs.

--Age of Ideology: The Nineteenth Century Philosophers. (Orig.). pap. 2.95 (ISBN 0-451-62063-1, ME2063, Ment). NAL.

Aiken, Henry D., ed. see Hume, David.

Aiken, Howard, ed. see Symposium on the Application of Switching Theory in Space Technology (1962: Sunnyvale, CA).

Aiken, J. Carl. Paul Pepo Paddletail. 1984. 4.95 (ISBN 0-533-06112-1). Vantage.

Aiken, Janet R. English, Present & Past. 1979. Repr. of 1930 ed. lib. bdg. 22.50 (ISBN 0-8495-0205-5). Arden Lib.

Aiken, Jean. Black Hearts in Battersea. 224p. (gr. 5 up). pap. 1.95 (ISBN 0-440-90648-2, LFL). Dell.

Aiken, Jim. Walk the Moons Road. 352p. 1985. pap. 2.95 (ISBN 0-345-32169-3, Del Rey). Ballantine.

Aiken, Joan. Arabel & Mortimer. LC 79-6577. (Illus.). 144p. (gr. 4 up). 1981. 9.95a (ISBN 0-385-15642-1); PLB (ISBN 0-385-15643-X). Doubleday.

--Arabel & Mortimer. 160p. (gr. 3-7). 1983. pap. 2.25 (ISBN 0-440-40253-0, YB). Dell.

--Arabel's Raven. LC 73-81120. (Illus.). 128p. (gr. 4 up). 1974. 9.95 (ISBN 0-385-08675-X). Doubleday.

--Bridle the Wind. LC 83-5355. 224p. (gr. 7 up). 1983. 14.95 (ISBN 0-385-29301-1). Delacorte.

--Castle Barebane. LC 76-3467. 288p. (YA) 1976. 11.50 (ISBN 0-670-20628-8). Viking.

--Cluster of Separate Sparks. LC 79-17532. 1972. 6.95 (ISBN 0-385-02906-3). Doubleday.

--The Far Forests: Tales of Romance, Fantasy & Suspence. LC 77-356. 160p. (gr. 7 up). 1977. 9.95 (ISBN 0-670-30760-2). Viking.

--The Girl from Paris. (General Ser.). 1983. lib. bdg. 17.50 (ISBN 0-8161-3497-9, Large Print Bks). G K Hall.

--The Kingdom under the Sea: And Other Stories. (Illus.). 128p. (gr. 3-8). 1985. 12.95 (ISBN 0-224-61882-5, Pub. by Chatto & Windus). Merrimack.

--The Kingdom under the Sea & Other Stories. (Illus.). 128p. (gr. 3-8). 12.95 (ISBN 0-224-61882-2, Pub by Jonathan Cape). Merrimack Pub Cir.

--Mansfield Revisited. LC 84-13748. 192p. 1985. 13.95 (ISBN 0-385-19793-4). Doubleday.

--Midnight Is a Place. 288p. (gr. 7 up). 1974. 9.95 (ISBN 0-670-47483-5). Viking.

--Mortimer's Cross. LC 83-49475. (Charlotte Zolotow Bk.). (Illus.). 160p. (gr. 3-6). 1984. 11.06i (ISBN 0-06-020032-4); PLB 10.89g (ISBN 0-06-020033-2). HarpJ.

--Nightbirds on Nantucket. 243p. (gr. 5 up). pap. 1.95 (ISBN 0-440-96070-3, LFL). Dell.

--The Shadow Guests: A Novel. LC 80-65830. 144p. (gr. 7 up). 1980. 11.95 (ISBN 0-385-28889-1). Delacorte.

--The Skin Spinners: Poems. (Illus.). 96p. (gr. 7 up). 1976. 12.50 (ISBN 0-670-64950-3). Viking.

--A Touch of Chill. LC 79-3331. 124p. (YA) (gr. 7 up). 1980. 9.95 (ISBN 0-385-29310-0). Delacorte.

--Up the Chimney Down. LC 85-42642. (A Charlotte Zolotow Bk.). 256p. (gr. 5 up). 1985. 11.49i (ISBN 0-06-020036-7); PLB 11.89g (ISBN 0-06-020037-5). HarpJ.

--Voices in an Empty House. 1976. pap. 1.75 (ISBN 0-671-80795-1). WSP.

--The Way to Write for Children. 112p. 1982. 10.95 (ISBN 0-312-85839-6); pap. 4.95 (ISBN 0-312-85840-X). St Martin.

--The Wolves of Willoughby Chase. 176p. (gr. 5 up). 1981. pap. 2.50 (ISBN 0-440-99629-5, LE). Dell.

--The Wolves of Willoughby Chase. LC 63-18034. (Illus.). 168p. (gr. 4-6). 1962. 8.95 (ISBN 0-385-03594-2). Doubleday.

Aiken, Joan, tr. see De Segur, Comtesse.

Aiken, John. A Whisper in the Night: Tales of Terror & Suspense. LC 84-3247. 192p. (gr. 7 up). 1984. 14.95 (ISBN 0-385-29344-5). Delacorte.

Aiken, Joyce. The Portable Needlepoint Boutique. LC 76-53870. (Illus.). 1977. 10.95 (ISBN 0-8008-6416-6). Taplinger.

Aiken, Joyce & Laury, Jean Ray. The Total Tote Bag Book: Designer Totes to Craft & Carry. LC 76-11058. (Illus.). 128p. 1977. 12.50 (ISBN 0-8008-7793-4); pap. 5.95 (ISBN 0-8008-7794-2). Taplinger.

Aiken, Joyce, jt. auth. see Laury, Jean R.

Aiken, Lewis R. Later Life. 2nd ed. 1982. text ed. 26.95 (ISBN 0-03-059751-X). HR&W.

Aiken, Linda H. Nursing in the Nineteen Eighties: Crises, Opportunities, Challenges. 350p. 1982. (Lippincott Nursing); pap. text ed. 13.25 (ISBN 0-397-54406-5, 64-03547). Lippincott.

Aiken, Louis. Dying, Death & Bereavement. 340p. (Orig.). 1984. pap. text ed. 14.29 (ISBN 0-205-08251-3, 798251). Allyn.

--Psychology Testing & Assessment. 5th ed. 480p. 1984. text ed. 26.28 net (ISBN 0-205-08252-1, 798252). Allyn.

Aiken, M., jt. auth. see Zey-Ferrell, Mary.

Aiken, Michael, et al. Coordinating Human Services: New Strategies for Building Service Delivery Systems. LC 75-7544. (Social & Behavioral Science Ser.). (Illus.). 224p. 1975. 21.95x (ISBN 0-87589-260-4). Jossey-Bass.

Aiken, Pauline. Influence of the Latin Elegists on English Lyric Poetry 1600-1650. LC 78-91345. 1970. Repr. of 1932 ed. 9.00 (ISBN 0-87753-002-5). Phaeton.

Aiken, Ray J., et al. Legal Liabilities in Higher Education: Their Scope & Management. 329p. 1976. 5.10 (ISBN 0-317-06224-7). Assn Am Coll.

Aiken, Richard C. Stiff Computation. (Illus.). 400p. 1984. 75.00x (ISBN 0-19-503453-8). Oxford U Pr.

Aiken, Riley. Mexican Folktales from the Borderland. (Illus.). 1980. 12.95 (ISBN 0-87074-175-6). SMU Press.

Aiken, Robert. Memorials of Robert Burns: & of Some of His Comtemporaries & Their Descendants. 422p. 1980. Repr. lib. bdg. 50.00 (ISBN 0-8492-3420-4). R West.

Aiken, S. R. & Leigh, C. H. Development & Environment in Peninsular Malaysia. 1982. 34.50 (ISBN 0-07-099204-5). McGraw.

Aiken, W., jt. auth. see Faulkner, Theodore A.

Aiken, William & LaFollette, Hugh. World Hunger & Moral Obligation. 224p. 1977. pap. text ed. 15.95 (ISBN 0-13-967950-2). P-H.

Aiken, William & LaFollette, Hugh, eds. Whose Child? Children's Rights, Parental Authority, & State Power. LC 79-29741. (Quality Paperbacks: No. 358). 310p. 1980. pap. 8.95 (ISBN 0-8226-0358-6). Littlefield.

--Whose Child? Children's Rights, Parental Authority, & State Power. LC 79-27577. 310p. 1980. 27.50x (ISBN 0-8476-6282-9). Rowman.

Aiken, William A. & Henning, Basil D., eds. Conflict in Stuart England: Essays in Honour of Wallace Notestein. 271p. 1970. Repr. of 1960 ed. 19.50 (ISBN 0-208-01029-7, Archon). Shoe String.

Aiken, Wm. A. Conduct of the Earl of Nottingham: 1689-1694. (Yale Historical Pubs., Manuscripts & Edited Texts: No. XVII). 1941. 75.00x (ISBN 0-685-69786-X). Elliots Bks.

Aikens, C. Melvin. Excavations at Snake Rock Village & the Bear River No. 2 Site. LC 68-84289. (Utah Anthropological Papers: No. 87). Repr. of 1967 ed. 25.00 (ISBN 0-404-60687-3). AMS Pr.

--Excavations in Southwest Utah. LC 67-2918. (Glen Canyon Series: No. 27). Repr. of 1965 ed. 34.00 (ISBN 0-404-60676-8). AMS Pr.

--Fremont-Promontory-Plains Relationships. (Utah Anthropological Papers: No. 82). Repr. of 1966 ed. 21.00 (ISBN 0-404-60682-2). AMS Pr.

--Hogup Cave. (Utah Anthropological Papers: No. 93). Repr. of 1970 ed. 24.00 (ISBN 0-404-60693-8). AMS Pr.

--Hogup Cave. (University of Utah Anthropological Papers: No. 93). (Illus.). 1970. pap. 20.00x (ISBN 0-87480-081-1). U of Utah Pr.

--Virgin Kayenta Cultural Relationships. (Glen Canyon Series: No. 29). Repr. of 1966 ed. 22.50 (ISBN 0-404-60679-2). AMS Pr.

Aikens, C. Melvin & Higuchi, Takayasu. Prehistory of Japan. LC 80-70596. (Studies in Archaeology). 1981. 37.50 (ISBN 0-12-045280-4). Acad Pr.

Aikens, C. Melvin, jt. auth. see Fowler, Don D.

Aikens, C. Melvin, et al. Miscellaneous Collected Papers, Vols. 19-24. (University of Utah Anthropological Papers: No. 99). (Illus., Orig.). 1979. pap. text ed. 15.00x (ISBN 0-87480-152-4). U of Utah Pr.

Aikens, Charlotte. Hospital Management. Reverby, Susan, ed. LC 83-49146. (History of American Nursing Ser.). 488p. 1985. Repr. of 1911 ed. lib. bdg. 55.00 (ISBN 0-8240-6500-X). Garland Pub.

Aikens, David A., et al. Principles & Techniques for an Integrated Chemistry Laboratory. (Illus.). 420p. 1984. pap. text ed. 14.95x (ISBN 0-88133-102-3). Waveland Pr.

Aikin, J. Description of the Country from Thirty to Forty Miles Round Manchester. LC 67-19706. (Illus.). Repr. of 1795 ed. 50.00x (ISBN 0-678-00340-8). Kelley.

Aikin, Jim, et al. Pandora Eight: Role Expanding Science Fiction & Fantasy. Wickstrom, Lois & Lorrah, Jean, eds. (Illus.). 64p. 1981. 2.50 (ISBN 0-916176-16-9). Sproing.

Aikin, Judith P. German Baroque Drama. (World Authors Ser.). 1982. lib. bdg. 18.95 (ISBN 0-8057-6477-1, Twayne). G K Hall.

Aikin, Lucy. Memoirs of the Court of King Charles the First, 2 vols. 1833. Set. 50.00 (ISBN 0-8482-7277-3). Norwood Edns.

Aikin, W. A. The Voice: An Introduction to Practical Phonology. Rumsey, H. St. John, ed. LC 51-13505. pap. 43.80 (ISBN 0-317-09971-X, 2051248). Bks Demand UMI.

Aikins, Carrol, tr. see Grimm, George.

Aikins, John. Sex in Literature, Vol. 3. 1981. pap. 12.95 (ISBN 0-7145-3861-2); 25.00 (ISBN 0-7145-3668-7). Riverrun NY.

Aikman, Alexander B., ed. see Task Force on Principles for Assessing Judicial Resources.

Aikman, Ann, jt. auth. see McQuade, Walter.

Aikman, Duncan, ed. Taming of the Frontier. facs. ed. LC 67-26711. (Essay Index Reprint Ser). 1925. 20.00 (ISBN 0-8369-0141-X). Ayer Co Pubs.

Aikman, Lonnelle. Nature's Healing Arts: From Folk Medicine to Modern Drugs. LC 76-56997. (Special Publications Ser.: No. 12). (Illus.). 1977. avail. only from Natl. Geog. 6.95 (ISBN 0-87044-232-5); PLB 8.50 (ISBN 0-87044-237-6). Natl Geog.

--Nous le Peuple. 1982. pap. 3.00 (ISBN 0-916200-01-9). US Capital Hist.

--We, the People. LC 81-52034. text ed. 3.50 (ISBN 0-916200-00-0); pap. 2.00 (ISBN 0-916200-14-0). US Capital Hist.

--We the People: The Story of the United States Capitol. 13th ed. National Geographic Society, ed. (Illus.). 144p. 1985. pap. 4.50 (ISBN 0-916200-06-X). US Capital Hist.

--Wir, das Volk. 2nd ed. Vidal, Paul, tr. (Illus.). 144p. (Ger.). 1983. pap. 3.00 (ISBN 0-916200-02-7). US Capital Hist.

Aikman, Ralph & Schwartz, Rachel. Life Cycle Cost Analysis Handbook. 1977. pap. 18.00x (ISBN 0-89011-509-5, HMD-128). Abt Bks.

Aikman, William F., jt. auth. see Kotin, Lawrence.

Ailes, Catherine P. & Pardee, Arthur E., Jr. Cooperation in Science & Technology: An Evaluation of the U. S.-Soviet Agreement. (WVSS in Science, Technology & Society Ser.). 300p. 1985. pap. 26.00x (ISBN 0-8133-0204-8). Westview.

Ailes, Catherine P. & Rushing, Francis W. The Science Race: Training & Utilization of Scientists & Engineers, U. S. & U. S. S. R. LC 81-17516. 280p. 1982. 28.50x (ISBN 0-8448-1407-5). Crane-Russak Co.

Ailloni-Charas, Dan. Promotion: A Guide to Effective Promotional Planning, Strategies & Executions. LC 83-26017. (Marketing Management Ser.: 1-372). 281p. 1984. 29.95x (ISBN 0-471-08060-8, Pub. by Ronald Pr). Wiley.

Ailor, William H., ed. Atmospheric Corrosion. LC 82-2059. (Corrosion Monograph). 1056p. 1982. 172.50 (ISBN 0-471-86558-3, Pub. by Wiley-Interscience). Wiley.

Ailor, William H., Jr. Handbook on Corrosion Testing & Evaluation. LC 74-162423. (Corrosion Monograph). 873p. 1971. 99.50x (ISBN 0-471-00985-7, Pub. by Wiley-Interscience). Wiley.

Aiman, E. J., ed. Infertility: Diagnosis & Management. (Clinical Perspectives in Obstetrics & Gynocology Ser.). (Illus.). 260p. 1984. 48.00 (ISBN 0-387-90940-0). Springer-Verlag.

AIME Annual Meeting, Atlanta, 1977. Toughness Characterization & Specifications for HSLA and Structural Steels: Proceedings. Mangonon, P. L., Jr., ed. (Illus.). 391p. 40.00 (ISBN 0-89520-352-9); members 26.00 (ISBN 0-317-34900-7); student members 14.00 (ISBN 0-317-34901-5). ASM.

AIME Annual Meeting, New Orleans, 1979. Advanced Fibers & Composites for Elevated Temperatures: Proceedings. Ahmad, Iqbal & Norton, Bryan, eds. (Illus.). 253p. 36.00 (ISBN 0-89520-366-9); members 24.00 (ISBN 0-317-34855-8); student members 14.00 (ISBN 0-317-34856-6). ASM.

--Structure & Properties of Dual-Phase Steels: Proceedings. Kot, R. A. & Morris, J. W., eds. (Illus.). 362p. 40.00 (ISBN 0-89520-357-X); members 26.00 (ISBN 0-317-34894-9); student members 14.00 (ISBN 0-317-34895-7). ASM.

--Theory of Alloy Phase Formation: Proceedings. Bennett, L. H., ed. (Illus.). 525p. 45.00 (ISBN 0-89520-362-6); members 30.00 (ISBN 0-317-34896-5); student members 16.00 (ISBN 0-317-34897-3). ASM.

AIME 110th Annual Meeting, Chicago, Feb. 22-26, 1981. Process Minerology: Extractive Metallurgy, Mineral Exploration, Energy Resources. Hausen, Donald M., ed. 713p. 55.00 (ISBN 0-89520-379-0, 204); members 36.00 (ISBN 0-317-37179-7); student members 18.00 (ISBN 0-317-37180-0). Metal Soc.

AIME 111th Annual Meeting, Dallas, Feb. 15-17, 1982. Novel NDE Methods for Materials. Raith, B. B., ed. 200p. 36.00 (ISBN 0-89520-466-5, 235); members 24.00 (ISBN 0-317-37187-8); student members 12.00 (ISBN 0-317-37188-6). Metal Soc.

AIME 111th Annual Meeting, Dallas, Texas, Feb. 14-18, 1982. Metallurgy of Continuous-Annealed Sheet Steel. Mangonon, P. L. & Bramfitt, B. L., eds. (Proceedings). 488p. (..). 40.00 (ISBN 0-89520-450-9, 217); members 25.00 (ISBN 0-317-37157-6); student members 15.00 (ISBN 0-317-37158-4). Metal Soc.

AIME 113th Annual Meeting, Los Angeles, Feb. 27-29, 1984. Optimizing Materials for Nuclear Applications. Gelles, D. S. & Wiffen, F. W., eds. avail. Metal Soc.

AIME 114th Annual Meeting, New York, Feb. 1985. Microbiological Effects on Metallurgical Processes. Haas, L. A. & Clum, J. A., eds. avail. Metal Soc.

Aimeri de Narbonne. Aymeri De Narbonne, Chanson De Geste, 2 Vols. Set. 67.00 (ISBN 0-384-00535-7); Set. pap. 55.00 (ISBN 0-384-00536-5). Johnson Repr.

Aimeric De Belenoi. Poesies Du Troubadour Aimeric De Belenoi. Dumitrescu, Maria, ed. LC 80-2174. Repr. of 1935 ed. 33.50 (ISBN 0-404-19000-6). AMS Pr.

Aimeric De Peguilhan. Poems. LC 70-128941. Repr. of 1950 ed. 28.00 (ISBN 0-404-50724-7). AMS Pr.

Aimes, Angelica. Divided Heart. 352p. (Orig.). 1981. pap. 2.95 (ISBN 0-523-41264-9). Pinnacle Bks.

Aimes, Hubert S. History of Slavery in Cuba: 1511-1868. 1967. Repr. lib. bdg. 20.50x (ISBN 0-374-90076-0). Octagon.

Aina, Justin, ed. see Okhuereigbe, Andy, et al.

Ainbler, Eric. Judgement on Deltchev. 240p. 1985. pap. 2.95 (ISBN 0-425-07591-5). Berkley Pub.

Ainger, Alfred. Charles Lamb. Morley, John, ed. LC 68-58369. (English Men of Letters). Repr. of 1888 ed. lib. bdg 10.00 (ISBN 0-404-51701-3). AMS Pr.

--Charles Lamb. 186p. 1980. Repr. of 1888 ed. lib. bdg. 15.00 (ISBN 0-8495-0175-X). Arden Lib.

--Charles Lamb. 1888. Repr. 9.95 (ISBN 0-8274-2038-2). R West.

--Charles Lamb. LC 77-131605. 1970. Repr. of 1901 ed. 9.00 (ISBN 0-403-00492-6). Scholarly.

--Charles Lamb. 226p. 1982. Repr. of 1888 ed. lib. bdg. 25.00 (ISBN 0-89984-010-8). Century Bookbindery.

--Charles Lamb. 186p. 1983. Repr. of 1882 ed. lib. bdg. 20.00 (ISBN 0-8495-0234-9). Arden Lib.

--Crabbe. 210p. 1980. Repr. of 1903 ed. lib. bdg. 20.00 (ISBN 0-89987-001-5). Darby Bks.

--Crabbe. 1973. Repr. of 1903 ed. 10.00 (ISBN 0-8274-1587-7). R West.

--Lectures & Essays, 2vols. LC 76-158235. Repr. of 1905 ed. Set. 48.00 (ISBN 0-404-00360-5). AMS Pr.

--Lectures & Essays: (Shakespeare, Swift, Cowper, Burns, Scott, Lamb, Wordsworth, Chaucer, Stephen Phillips, Dickens, 2 vols. 1905. Repr. 50.00 (ISBN 0-8274-2814-6). R West.

--The Letters of Charles Lamb, 2 vols. 1888. Repr. Set. 30.00 (ISBN 0-8274-2835-9). R West.

--The Life & Letters of Alfred Ainger. Sichel, Edith, ed. 1906. Repr. 45.00 (ISBN 0-8274-3872-9). R West.

Ainger, Alfred, ed. see Lamb, Charles.

Ain-Globe, Leah, jt. ed. see Eisenberg, Azriel.

Ainis, Jeffery, jt. auth. see Russo, William.

Ainlay, Thomas, Jr. The Last Book. LC 84-22738. 254p. (Orig.). 1984. 18.00 (ISBN 0-943920-20-5); pap. 10.00 (ISBN 0-943920-18-3). Metamorphous Pr.

Ainley, David G. & LeResche, Robert E. Breeding Biology of the Adelie Penguin. LC 82-17573. (Illus.). 198p. 1983. text ed. 29.50x (ISBN 0-520-04838-5). U of Cal Pr.

Ainley, David G., et al. The Marine Ecology of Birds in the Ross Sea, Antarctica. 97p. 1984. 9.00 (ISBN 0-943610-39-7). Am Ornithologists.

Ainley, Stephen. Mathematical Puzzles. 147p. 1983. 12.95 (ISBN 0-13-561845-2); pap. 4.95 (ISBN 0-13-561837-1). P-H.

--Mathemtical Puzzles. 156p. 1982. 30.00x (ISBN 0-7135-1327-6, Pub. by Bell & Hyman England). State Mutual Bk.

Ainscow, Mel & Tweddle, David A. Preventing Classroom Failure: An Objectives Approach. LC 78-31618. 205p. 1979. 34.95x (ISBN 0-471-27564-6, Pub. by Wiley-Interscience). Wiley.

Ainsfeld, Evelyn R., jt. ed. see Ainsfeld, Michael H.

Ainsfeld, Michael H. & Ainsfeld, Evelyn R., eds. International Device GMP's. 225p. 1981. text ed. 165.00 (ISBN 0-935184-01-5). Interpharm.

Ainsley, Alix. The House of Whispering Aspens. 1985. pap. 2.95 (ISBN 0-8217-1611-5). Zebra.

Ainsley, Tom. Ainsley's New Complete Guide to Harness Racing. rev. ed. 1981. 17.95 (ISBN 0-671-25257-7). S&S.

Ainslie, Alan C. & Colwell, M. A. Practical Electronic Project Building. (Newnes Constructor's Guides Ser.). (Illus.). (gr. 10 up). 1976. pap. 6.95 (ISBN 0-408-00231-X, 5448-3). Hayden.

Ainslie, Douglas, tr. see Croce, Benedetto.

Ainslie, Hew. Scottish Songs, Ballads, & Poems. LC 75-144578. Repr. of 1855 ed. 18.00 (ISBN 0-404-08550-4). AMS Pr.

Ainslie, Ricardo C. The Psychology of Twinship. LC 84-19591. xvi, 204p. 1985. 18.95x (ISBN 0-8032-1017-5). U of Nebr Pr.

Ainslie, Ricardo C., ed. The Child & the Day Care Setting: Qualitative Variations & Development. LC 84-6836. 222p. 1984. 29.95x (ISBN 0-03-070291-7). Praeger.

Ainslie, Tom. Ainslie's Complete Guide to Thoroughbred Racing. rev. ed. 1979. 23.95 (ISBN 0-671-24632-1). S&S.

--Ainslie's Complete Hoyle. LC 74-32023. 544p. 1975. pap. 11.95 (ISBN 0-671-24779-4). S&S.

--Ainslie's Encyclopedia of Thoroughbred Handicapping. LC 78-9755. 1978. 19.95 (ISBN 0-688-03345-8); pap. 12.95 (ISBN 0-688-00466-0). Morrow.

--How to Gamble in a Casino: The Most Fun at the Least Risk. LC 78-31610. (Tome Ainslie-Winner's Circle Bk). (Illus.). 1979. 10.95 (ISBN 0-688-03460-8). Morrow.

Ainslie, Tom & Ledbetter, Bonnie. The Body Language of Horses: Revealing the Nature of Equine Needs, Wishes & Emotions & How Horses Communicate Them - for Owners, Breeders, Trainers, Riders & All Other Horse Lovers (Including Handicappers) LC 79-26995. (Illus.). 224p. 1980. 15.95 (ISBN 0-688-03620-1). Morrow.

Ainstein, Reuben. The Warsaw Ghetto Revolt. (Illus.). 238p. 1979. pap. 8.95 (ISBN 0-89604-007-0). Holocaust Pubns.

Ainsworth & Bisby. Dictionary of the Fungi. 663p. 1971. 75.00x (ISBN 0-85198-075-9, Pub. by CAB Bks England). State Mutual Bk.

Ainsworth & Bisby's. Dictionary of the Fungi. 663p. 1978. 75.00 (ISBN 0-85198-075-9, M-9711). French & Eur.

Ainsworth, Barbara A. Education Through Travel. LC 79-10235. 160p. 1979. 18.95x (ISBN 0-88229-365-6). Nelson-Hall.

Ainsworth, Barbara A. & Trautman, David H. English to Use. (Illus.). (YA) (gr. 7-12). 1983. 12.95 (ISBN 0-86601-070-X); 9.95 (ISBN 0-86601-072-6); 3.95 (ISBN 0-86601-110-2); 69.95 (ISBN 0-86601-145-5). Media Materials.

Ainsworth, Catherine H. American Calendar Customs, Vol. I. LC 79-52827. (Calendar Customs & Holidays Ser.). viii, 104p. (Orig.). 1979. pap. 10.00 (ISBN 0-933190-06-9). Clyde Pr.

--American Calendar Customs, Vol. II. LC 79-55784. (Calender Customs). v, 105p. (Orig.). 1980. pap. 10.00 (ISBN 0-933190-07-7). Clyde Pr.

--American Folk Foods. LC 84-72828. (Illus.). 224p. (Orig.). 1985. pap. 10.00x (ISBN 0-933190-12-3). Clyde Pr.

--Black & White & Said All over: Riddles. (Folklore Bks.). 36p. 1976. 3.00 (ISBN 0-933190-02-6). Clyde Pr.

--Family Life of Young Americans. LC 85-72144. 224p. (Orig.). 1985. pap. 10.00 (ISBN 0-933190-13-1); pap. text ed. 10.00 (ISBN 0-317-20731-8). Clyde Pr.

--Folktales of America, Vol. II. LC 80-66300. ix, 203p. (Orig.). 1981. pap. 10.00 (ISBN 0-933190-09-3). Clyde Pr.

--Folktales of America, Vol I. LC 80-66300. (Folktales & Legends Ser.). iv, 120p. 1980. pap. 10.00 (ISBN 0-933190-08-5). Clyde Pr.

--Games & Lore of Young Americans. LC 83-70191. vii, 244p. (Orig.). 1983. pap. 10.00x (ISBN 0-933190-10-7). Clyde Pr.

--Italian-American Folktales. LC 76-52643. (Folklore Bks.). xii, 180p. 1977. 10.00 (ISBN 0-933190-03-4). Clyde Pr.

--Jump Rope Verses Around the United States. (Folklore Bks.). 24p. 1976. 3.00 (ISBN 0-933190-01-8). Clyde Pr.

--Legends of New York State. 2nd ed. LC 78-54873. (Folklore Bks.). vi, 93p. 1983. 10.00 (ISBN 0-933190-11-5). Clyde Pr.

--Polish-American Folktales. LC 77-80771. (Folklore Bks.). x, 102p. 1977. 10.00 (ISBN 0-933190-04-2). Clyde Pr.

--Superstitions from Seven Towns of the United States. (Folklore Bks.). vi, 58p. 1973. 3.00 (ISBN 0-933190-00-X). Clyde Pr.

Ainsworth, Charles H., ed. Selected Readings for Introductory Anthropology. LC 74-11102. 150p. 1974. pap. text ed. 5.95x (ISBN 0-8422-0409-1). Irvington.

--Selected Readings for Introductory Sociology. 2nd ed. 176p. 1974. pap. text ed. 6.00x (ISBN 0-8422-0460-1). Irvington.

--Selected Readings for Marriage & the Family. LC 72-11042. 1973. 37.50x (ISBN 0-8422-5123-5). Irvington.

Ainsworth, Fay, ed. Better Boating: A Guide to Safety Afloat. LC 77-88516. (Illus.). 1982. Students Ed. 2.50 (ISBN 0-916682-31-5); Instr. Ed. 3.50 (ISBN 0-916682-30-7). Outdoor Empire.

--Snowmobile Safety & You. (Illus.). 1982. Student Ed. 1.95 (ISBN 0-916682-33-1); Instr. Ed. 2.95 (ISBN 0-916682-32-3). Outdoor Empire.

Ainsworth, Fay, ed. see Griffin, James S.

Ainsworth, Fay, ed. see Waltz, Julie.

Ainsworth, Frank & Fulcher, Leon C., eds. Group Care for Children. 308p. 1981. 23.00x (ISBN 0-422-77290-9, NO. 3540, Pub. by Tavistock England); pap. 11.95 (ISBN 0-422-77850-8, NO. 3541). Methuen Inc.

Ainsworth, Frank, jt. ed. see Fulcher, Leon C.

Ainsworth, Fred. Persephone. (Illus.). 40p. (Director's Production Script). 1977. pap. 6.50 (ISBN 0-88680-150-8). I E Clark.

Ainsworth, G. & Lavin, J. Hospital Administrators' Guide to Purchasing & Materials Management. 1981. 14.95 (ISBN 0-87489-193-0). Med Economics.

Ainsworth, G. C. Introduction to the History of Mycology. LC 75-21036. (Illus.). 350p. 1976. 54.50 (ISBN 0-521-21013-5). Cambridge U Pr.

--Introduction to the History of Plant Pathology. LC 80-40476. 220p. 1981. 75.00 (ISBN 0-521-23032-2). Cambridge U Pr.

Ainsworth, G. C. & Bisby. Dictionary of the Fungi (Including the Lichens) 7th Ed. ed. (Illus.). 412p. 1983. lib. bdg. 27.50 (ISBN 0-85198-515-7). Lubrecht & Cramer.

Ainsworth, Geoffrey C. & Sussman, A. S., eds. Fungi: An Advanced Treatise, 4 vols. LC 65-15769. Vol. 2, 1966. 90.00 (ISBN 0-12-045602-8); Vol. 3, 1968. 90.00 (ISBN 0-12-045603-6); Vol. 4A, 1973. 75.00 (ISBN 0-12-045604-4); Vol. 4B, 1973. 70.00 (ISBN 0-12-045644-3). Acad Pr.

Ainsworth, Henry. A True Confession of the Faith, Which Wee Falsley Called Brownists, Doo Hold. LC 78-26338. (English Experience Ser.: No. 158). 24p. 1969. Repr. of 1956 ed. 7.00 (ISBN 90-221-0158-4). Walter J Johnson.

Ainsworth, Henry & Johnson, Francis. An Apologie or Defence of Such True Christians As Are Commonly Called Brownists. LC 70-25742. (English Experience Ser.: No. 217). Repr. of 1604 ed. 16.00 (ISBN 90-221-0424-9). Walter J Johnson.

Ainsworth, J., ed. Index of Wills Proved in the Prerogative Court of Canterbury, Vol. 9: 1671-1675. Repr. of 1942 ed. 85.00 (ISBN 0-317-16425-2). Kraus Repr.

Ainsworth, Katherine A. The Man Who Captured Sunshine. LC 77-2183. (Illus.). 1978. 12.95 (ISBN 0-88280-054-X). ETC Pubns.

Ainsworth, Leonard H., jt. auth. see Ainsworth, Mary D.

Ainsworth, M. D. & Blehar, M. C. Patterns of Attachment: A Psychological Study of the Strange Situation. 416p. 1978. 39.95 (ISBN 0-89859-461-8). L Erlbaum Assocs.

Ainsworth, Martha. Family Planning Programs: The Client's Perspective. (Staff Working Paper: No. 676). 102p. 5.00 (ISBN 0-318-11943-9, WP 0676). World Bank.

Ainsworth, Mary D. & Ainsworth, Leonard H. Measuring Security in Personal Adjustment. LC 58-37947. 1958. pap. 28.00 (ISBN 0-317-08111-X, 2014110). Bks Demand UMI.

Ainsworth, Mary D. Salter. Infancy in Uganda: Infant Care & the Growth of Love. LC 67-16039. (Illus.). 496p. 1967. 40.00x (ISBN 0-8018-0010-2). Johns Hopkins.

Ainsworth, Oliver M., ed. see Milton, John.

Ainsworth, Ralph B. Rule Eighteen & Eleven As Instrument of Success in Commodity Futures Trading. (Illus.). 133p. 1983. 61.45x (ISBN 0-86654-078-4). Inst Econ Finan.

Ainsworth, Ralph M. Basic Principles of Successful Commodity Futures Speculation. (Illus.). 174p. 1983. 137.75x (ISBN 0-86654-069-5). Inst Econ Finan.

--Grain Trading As a Foundation for Total Futures Trading. (Illus.). 197p. 1980. 89.75x (ISBN 0-918968-74-7). Inst Econ Finan.

--Profitable Grain Trading. LC 80-53316. 256p. 1980. Repr. of 1933 ed. text ed. 25.00 (ISBN 0-934380-04-X). Traders Pr.

Ainsworth, Stanley. Galloping Sounds. (gr. 1-6). 1962. text ed. 3.00 (ISBN 0-686-00577-5). Expression.

--Positive Emotional Power: How to Manage Your Feelings. (Illus.). 256p. 1981. 12.95 (ISBN 0-13-687616-1); pap. 5.95 (ISBN 0-13-687608-0). P-H.

--Stuttering: What It Is & What to Do About It. LC 74-76252. (Speech & Hearing Ser.). 101p. (Orig.). 1975. pap. text ed. 4.95 (ISBN 0-8220-1805-5). Cliffs.

Ainsworth, Stanley & Fraser-Gruss, Jane. If Your Child Stutters: A Guide for Parents. rev. ed. 50p. (Orig.). 1981. pap. 1.00 (ISBN 0-933388-16-0). Speech Found Am.

Ainsworth, Thomas. Live or Die. 192p. 1983. 16.95 (ISBN 0-02-500640-1). Macmillan.

Ainsworth, Thomas, jt. auth. see O'Donnell, Michael P.

Ainsworth, Thomas H., Jr. Quality Assurance in Long Term Care. LC 77-70432. 200p. 1977. 38.00 (ISBN 0-912862-40-8). Aspen Systems.

Ainsworth, W. A. Mechanisms of Speech Recognitions. (International Ser. in Natural Philosophy). (Illus.). 140p. 1976. pap. text ed. 19.00 (ISBN 0-08-020394-9). Pergamon.

Ainsworth, W. Harrison. Old Saint Paul's. 1968. Repr. of 1911 ed. 9.95x (ISBN 0-460-00522-7, Evman). Biblio Dist.

Ainsworth, William H. Auriol: Or, the Elixir of Life. Reginald, R. & Menville, Douglas, eds. LC 75-46248. (Supernatural & Occult Fiction Ser.). (Illus.). 1976. Repr. of 1892 ed. lib. bdg. 21.00x (ISBN 0-405-08108-1). Ayer Co Pubs.

--Jack Sheppard: A Romance, 3 vols. in 2. LC 79-8224. (Illus.). Repr. of 1839 ed. Set. 84.50 (ISBN 0-404-61751-4). AMS Pr.

--Rookwood: A Romance, 3 vols. in 2. LC 79-8225. (Illus.). Repr. of 1850 ed. Set. 84.50 (ISBN 0-404-61758-1). AMS Pr.

Ainsworth-Davis, James R. Thomas H. Huxley. LC 70-158236. (English Men of Science: No. 2). Repr. of 1907 ed. 21.50 (ISBN 0-404-07892-3). AMS Pr.

Ainsworth-Land, George & Ainsworth-Land, Vaune. The Opportunity Discovery Process. 56p. 1982. 6.95 (ISBN 0-88047-001-1, 8204). DOK Pubs.

Ainsworth-Land, George & Ainswoth-Land, Vaune. Forwart to Basics. 112p. (Orig.). 1982. tchr's manual 8.95 (ISBN 0-88047-002-X, 8214). DOK Pubs.

Ainsworth-Land, Vaune & Fletcher, Norma. Casting a Spell. rev. ed. (Illus., Orig.). 1983. pap. text ed. 5.95 (ISBN 0-914634-65-8, 7909). DOK Pubs.

--Making Waves with Creative Problem-Solving. (Illus.). 52p. (Orig.). 1979. pap. text ed. 5.95 (ISBN 0-914634-66-6, 7913). DOK Pubs.

Ainsworth-Land, Vaune, jt. auth. see Ainsworth-Land, George.

Ainswoth-Land, Vaune, jt. auth. see Ainsworth-Land, George.

Ainsztein, R., tr. see Simonov, Konstantin M.

Ainsztein, Reuben. Warsaw Ghetto Revolt. LC 78-71295. (Illus.). 1979. pap. 4.95 (ISBN 0-8052-5007-7, Pub. by Holocaust Library). Schocken.

--The Warsaw Ghetto Revolt. (Illus.). 248p. pap. 4.95 (ISBN 0-686-95102-6). ADL.

Ainworth, Maryan W. & Brealy, John. Art & Autoradiography: Insights Into the Genesis pf Paintings of Rembrandt, Van Dyck, & Vermeer. Wasserman, Rosanne, ed. (Illus.). 112p. 1982. 35.00 (ISBN 0-87099-285-6); pap. 19.50 (ISBN 0-87099-286-4). Metro Mus Art.

AIP & American Academy of Arts & Sciences Joint Conference, Brookline, Mass., 1967 & 1969. Exploring the History of Nuclear Physics: Proceedings, No. 7. Weiner, Charles, ed. LC 72-81883. (Illus.). 271p. 1972. 13.00 (ISBN 0-88318-106-1). Am Inst Physics.

AIP Conference. Causality & Physical Theories: Proceedings, No. 16. Rolnick, William B., ed. LC 73-93420. 177p. 1974. 12.00x (ISBN 0-88318-115-0). Am Inst Physics.

--Experiments on High Energy Particle Collisions-1973: Proceedings, No. 12. Panvini, R. S., ed. LC 73-81705. 419p. 1973. 15.00 (ISBN 0-88318-111-8). Am Inst Physics.

--High Energy Collisions-1973: Proceedings, No. 15. Quigg, Chris, ed. LC 73-92324. 314p. 1973. 13.75x (ISBN 0-88318-114-2). Am Inst Physics.

--Magnetism & Magnetic Materials: Proceedings, 1973, 2 pts. Graham, C. D., Jr. & Rhyne, J. J., eds. LC 52-2468. (AIP Conference Proceedings: No. 18). 1974. 25.00x (ISBN 0-88318-117-7). Am Inst Physics.

--Pi-Pi Scattering-1973: AIP Conference Proceedings, No. 13. Williams, D. K. & Hagopian, V., eds. LC 73-81704. 361p. 1973. 14.00 (ISBN 0-88318-112-6). Am Inst Physics.

--Thermal Expansion: Proceedings, No. 17. Taylor, R. E. & Denman, G. L., eds. LC 73-94415. 1974. pap. 14.00 (ISBN 0-88318-116-9). Am Inst Physics.

--Topics in Statistical Mechanics & Biophysics-A Memorial to Julius L. Jackson: AIP Conference Proceedings, No. 27. Piccirelli, R. A., ed. LC 75-36309. 209p. 1976. 17.00 (ISBN 0-88318-126-6). Am Inst Physics.

--Transport Phenomena-1973: AIP Conference Proceedings No.27, No. 11. Kestin, J., ed. LC 73-80682. 346p. 1973. 14.00 (ISBN 0-88318-110-X). Am Inst Physics.

AIP Conference, Boston 1974. Experimental Meson Spectroscopy 1974: Proceedings, No. 21. Garelick, David A., ed. LC 74-82628. 452p. 1974. 19.00 (ISBN 0-88318-120-7). Am Inst Physics.

AIP Conference, Chicago, 1971. Magnetism & Magnetic Materials: Proceedings, 1971, 2 pts. Graham, C. D., Jr. & Rhyne, J. J., eds. LC 59-2468. (AIP Conference Proceedings: No. 5). 1573p. 1972. 22.00 (ISBN 0-88318-104-5). Am Inst Physics.

AIP Conference, Corning, N.Y., 1971. Thermal Expansion 1971: AIP Conference Proceedings, No. 3. Graham, M. G. & Hagy, H. E., eds. LC 72-76970. 311p. 1972. 13.00 (ISBN 0-88318-102-9). Am Inst Physics.

AIP Conference, Denver, 1972. Magnetism & Magnetic Materials: Proceedings, 1972, 2 pts. Graham, C. D., Jr. & Rhyne, J. J., eds. LC 72-623469. (AIP Conference Proceedings: No. 10). 1714p. 1973. 24.00x (ISBN 0-88318-109-6). Am Inst Physics.

AIP Conference, Philadelphia, April, 1972. Experimental Meson Spectroscopy 1972: Proceedings, No. 8. Kwan-Wu Lai & Rosenfeld, A. H., eds. LC 72-88226. (Illus.). 489p. 1972. 14.00 (ISBN 0-88318-107-X). Am Inst Physics.

AIP Conference, Philadelphia 1974. Neutrinos-1974: Proceedings, No. 22. Baltay, Charles, ed. LC 74-82413. 1974. 16.00 (ISBN 0-88318-121-5). Am Inst Physics.

AIP Conference, Princeton, 1970. Feedback & Dynamic Control of Plasmas: Proceedings, No. 1. Chu, T. K. & Hendel, H. W., eds. LC 70-141596. 364p. 1970. 14.00 (ISBN 0-88318-100-2). Am Inst Physics.

AIP Conference Proceeding No. 86, Adelaide, Australia, 1982. Momentum Wave Functions: Proceedings. Weigold, Erich, ed. LC 82-72375. 345p. 1982. lib. bdg. 34.00 (ISBN 0-88318-185-1). Am Inst Physics.

AIP Conference Proceedings, No. 20 Yorktown Heights. Tetrahedrally Bonded Amorphous Semiconductors: Proceedings, No. 20. Brodsky, M., et al, eds. LC 74-80145. 369p. 1974. 16.00 (ISBN 0-88318-119-3). Am Inst Physics.

AIP Conference Proceedings No. 84, APS-AISI, Leigh University, 1981. Physics in the Steel Industry: Proceedings. Schwerer, Fred C., ed. LC 82-72033. 409p. 1982. lib. bdg. 36.00 (ISBN 0-88318-183-5). Am Inst Physics.

AIP Conference Proceedings No. 85 Madsion, Wisconsin, 1982. Proton-Antiproton Collider Physics: Proceedings. Barger, V., et al, eds. LC 82-72141. 676p. 1982. lib. bdg. 42.00 (ISBN 0-88318-184-3). Am Inst Physics.

AIP Conference Proceedings No. 87, Fermilab School, Physics of High Energy Particle Accelerators: Proceedings. Carrigan, R. A., et al, eds. LC 82-72421. 960p. 1982. lib. bdg. 48.00 (ISBN 0-88318-186-X). Am Inst Physics.

AIP Conference Proceedings No. 88, La Jolla Institute, 1981. Mathematical Methods in Hydrodynamics & Integrability in Dynamical Systems: Proceedings. Tabor, Michael & Treve, Yvain M., eds. LC 82-72462. 352p. 1982. lib. bdg. 34.00 (ISBN 0-88318-187-8). Am Inst Physics.

AIP Conference Proceedings No. 89, Argonne National Laboratory, 1981. Neutron Scattering: Proceedings. Faber, John, Jr., ed. LC 82-73094. 397p. 1982. lib. bdg. 35.50 (ISBN 0-88318-188-6). Am Inst Physics.

AIP Conference Proceedings No. 90 Boulder, 1982. Laser Techniques for Extreme Ultraviolet Spectroscopy. McIlrath, T. J. & Freeman, R. R., eds. LC 82-73205. 497p. 1982. lib. bdg. 37.00 (ISBN 0-88318-189-4). Am Inst Physics.

AIP Conference Proceedings No. 90. Los Alamos, 1982. Laser Acceleration of Particles. Channell, Paul J., ed. LC 82-73361. 276p. 1982. lib. bdg. 32.00 (ISBN 0-88318-190-8). Am Inst Physics.

AIP Conference, Univ. of British Columbia, Vancouver, 1972. Cyclotrons 1972: Proceedings, No. 9. Burgerson, J. J. & Strathdee, A., eds. LC 72-92798. 836p. 1972. 19.00 (ISBN 0-88318-108-8). Am Inst Physics.

AIP Conference, Univ. of California at Irvine, Dec., 1971. Particle Physics 1971: Proceedings, No. 6. Bander, M., et al, eds. LC 72-81239. 185p. 1972. 11.00 (ISBN 0-88318-105-3). Am Inst Physics.

AIP Conference, Univ. of Rochester, 1971. Superconductivity in D- & F- Band Metals: AIP Conference Proceedings, No. 4. Douglass, D. H., ed. LC 74-188879. 375p. 1972. 14.00 (ISBN 0-88318-103-7). Am Inst Physics.

AIP International Conf., Williamsburg, 1976. Structure & Excitation of Amorphous Solids: Proceedings. Lucovsky, G. & Galeener, F. L., eds. LC 76-22279. (AIP Conference Proceedings: No. 31). 1976. 19.50 (ISBN 0-88318-130-4). Am Inst Physics.

Ai Qing. Selected Poems of Ai Qing. Eoyang, Eugene C., ed. LC 82-47956. 476p. (Orig., Chinese.). 1983. 27.50x (ISBN 0-253-34519-7); pap. 10.95x (ISBN 0-253-20302-3). Ind U Pr.

Aiqouni, K. H., ed. see Wohlfahrt, F.

Air Conditioning & Refrigeration Institute. Refrigeration & Air Conditioning. (Illus.). 1979. 32.95 (ISBN 0-13-770164-0). P-H.

Air, G., jt. ed. see Laver, G.

Air, Gillian M., jt. ed. see Laver, W. Graeme.

Air Movement & Control Assoc, Inc. AMCA Fan Applications Manual - Fans & Systems. 54p. 1973. 7.50 (ISBN 0-318-12230-8, 201); members 6.00 (ISBN 0-318-12231-6). Air Mvmt & Cont.

Air Movement & Control Association Inc. AMCA Fan Application Manual - Field Performance Measurements. 145p. 1976. 16.50 (ISBN 0-318-12228-6, 203); members 9.00 (ISBN 0-318-12229-4). Air Mvmt & Cont.

Air Movement & Control Association, Inc. Certified Ratings Program-Air Performance. 76p. 1983. 5.50 (ISBN 0-318-12232-4, 211); members 3.50 (ISBN 0-318-12233-2). Air Mvmt & Cont.

Air Pollution Control Association. Air Pollution Experiments for Junior & Senior High School Science Classes. 2nd ed. Hunter, Donald C. & Wohlers, Henry C., eds. 128p. (gr. 7-12). 1972. 1.50 (ISBN 0-318-12242-1, APX). Air Pollution Control Assoc.

--Air Pollution Meteorology. (APCA Reprint Ser.: Vol. 7). 112p. 1977. 9.00 (ISBN 0-318-12243-X, RS-7); members 6.00 (ISBN 0-318-12244-8). Air Pollution Control Assoc.

--Control of Air Emissions from Coke Plants: Proceedings of the Air Pollution Control Association, Technical Conference, Pittsburgh, PA, 1979. 192p. 1979. 12.50 (ISBN 0-318-12247-2, VIP-1); members 10.00 (ISBN 0-318-12248-0). Air Pollution Control Assoc.

--Electrostatic Precipitation of Fly Ash. (APCA Reprint Ser.: Vol. 8). 72p. 1977. 6.00 (ISBN 0-318-12253-7, RS-8); members 4.50 (ISBN 0-318-12254-5). Air Pollution Control Assoc.

--Recognition of Air Pollution Injury to Vegetation: A Pictorial Atlas. (Illus.). 112p. 1970. 15.00 (ISBN 0-318-12273-1, ATL); members 10.00 (ISBN 0-318-12274-X). Air Pollution Control Assoc.

Air Pollution Control Association Specialty Conference. Air Pollution Control in the Iron & Steel Industry: Proceedings, San Francisco, Ca., Jan 1981. 208p. 1981. 15.00 (ISBN 0-318-12240-5, SP-39); members 12.00 (ISBN 0-318-12241-3). Air Pollution Control Assoc.

--Dispersion Modeling from Complex Sources: Proceedings, St. Louis, Mo., April 1981. 344p. 1981. 17.00 (ISBN 0-318-12249-9, SP-41); members 13.00 (ISBN 0-318-12250-2). Air Pollution Control Assoc.

--Economic Incentives for Clean Air: Proceedings, San Francisco, Ca., Jan, 1981. 288p. 1981. 17.00 (ISBN 0-318-12251-0, SP-41); members 13.00 (ISBN 0-318-12252-9). Air Pollution Control Assoc.

Air Pollution Control Association Specialty Conference, Anaheim, CA, 1978. Emission Factors & Inventories. 213p. 1979. 12.50 (ISBN 0-318-12255-3, SP-28); members 10.00 (ISBN 0-318-12256-1). Air Pollution Control Assoc.

Air Pollution Control Association Specialty Conference, Minneapolis, 1978. Handbook of Methodology for the Assessment of Air Pollution Effects on Vegetation. 350p. 1979. 15.00 (ISBN 0-318-12259-6, SP-29); members 12.00 (ISBN 0-318-12260-X). Air Pollution Control Assoc.

Air Pollution Control Association Specialty Conference, New York, 1977. Hydrocarbon Control Feasibility: Its Impact on Air Quality. 160p. 1977. 10.00 (ISBN 0-318-12261-8, SP-23); members 8.00 (ISBN 0-318-12262-6). Air Pollution Control Assoc.

Air Pollution Control Association Specialty Conference, Pittsburgh, PA, 1980. Operation & Maintenance of Gas Cleaning Equipment. 190p. 1980. 15.00 (ISBN 0-318-12263-4, SP-35); members 12.00 (ISBN 0-318-12264-2). Air Pollution Control Assoc.

Air Pollution Control Association Specialty Conference, Houston, 1979. Ozone Oxidants: Interactions with the Total Environment II. 542p. 1980. 25.00 (ISBN 0-318-12265-0, SP-32); members 20.00 (ISBN 0-318-12266-9). Air Pollution Control Assoc.

Air Pollution Control Association Specialty Conference. The Proposed SOx & Particulate Standard: Proceedings, Atlanta, Ga. 300p. 1980. 18.00 (ISBN 0-318-12269-3, SP-38); members 15.00 (ISBN 0-318-12270-7). Air Pollution Control Assoc.

Air Pollution Control Association Specialty Conference, New Orleans, 1979. Quality Assurance in Air Pollution Measurement. 486p. 1979. 24.00 (ISBN 0-318-12271-5, SP-27); members 18.00 (ISBN 0-318-12272-3). Air Pollution Control Assoc.

Air Pollution Control Association Specialty Conference, Danvers, MA & Seattle, WA, 1980. Technical Basis for a Size Specific Particulate Standard, 2 pts. 336p. 1980. avail. Air Pollution Control Assoc.

Air Pollution Control Association Specialty Conference, Cambridge, MA. Toxic Substances in the Air Environment. 202p. 1977. 10.00 (ISBN 0-318-12280-4, SP-20); members 8.00 (ISBN 0-318-12281-2). Air Pollution Control Assoc.

Air Pollution Control Association Specialty Conference, Niagara Falls, NY, 1978. The User & Fabric Filtration Equipment III. 207p. 1978. 11.50 (ISBN 0-318-12284-7, SP-26); members 9.50 (ISBN 0-318-12285-5). Air Pollution Control Assoc.

Air Pollution Control Association Specialty Conference, Denver, 1979. View on Visibility: Regulatory & Scientific. 304p. 1980. 12.50 (ISBN 0-318-12286-3, SP-33); members 10.00 (ISBN 0-318-12287-1). Air Pollution Control Assoc.

Air Pollution Control Association Technical Conference, Niagara Falls, N.Y., Oct. 1980. Toxic Air Contaminants: Health Effects, Monitoring & Control. 256p. 1981. 17.00 (ISBN 0-318-12278-2, VIP-II); members 13.50 (ISBN 0-318-12279-0). Air Pollution Control Assoc.

Air Pollution Control Associaton Specialty Conference. Waste Treatment & Disposal Aspects: Combustion & Air Pollution Control Processes. 216p. 1981. 15.00 (ISBN 0-318-12288-X, SP-42); members 12.00 (ISBN 0-318-12289-8). Air Pollution Control Assoc.

Airasian, Peter W., et al. Minimal Competency Testing. LC 79-3994. (Illus.). 248p. 1979. 27.95 (ISBN 0-87778-138-9). Educ Tech Pubns.

Aird, Alisdair, ed. The Good Pub Guide, 1985. (Illus.). 600p. 1984. pap. 14.95 (ISBN 0-340-36087-9, Pub. by Hodder & Stoughton UK). David & Charles.

Aird, Catherine. Harms Way. 192p. (Orig.). 1985. pap. 2.95 (ISBN 0-553-25191-0). Bantam.

--His Burial Too. 208p. 1980. pap. 2.95 (ISBN 0-553-25441-3). Bantam.

--Last Respects. LC 82-45344. (Crime Club Ser.). 192p. 1982. 11.95 (ISBN 0-385-18256-2). Doubleday.

--Last Respects. 176p. 1984. pap. 2.50 (ISBN 0-553-23677-6). Bantam.

--A Late Phoenix. 176p. 1981. pap. 2.95 (ISBN 0-553-25442-1). Bantam.

--Parting Breath. 176p. pap. 2.75 (ISBN 0-553-24601-1). Bantam.

--The Religious Body. 176p. 1980. pap. 2.95 (ISBN 0-553-24602-X). Bantam.

--Some Die Eloquent. 208p. 1981. pap. 2.95 (ISBN 0-553-25110-4). Bantam.

Aird, Hazel B. & Ruddiman, Catherine. Henry Ford: Boy with Ideas. LC 83-15663. (Childhood of Famous Americans Ser). (Illus.). (gr. 3-7). 1959. 5.95 (ISBN 0-672-50078-7). Bobbs.

Aird, John S. The Size, Composition & Growth of the Population of Mainland China. LC 76-38047. Repr. of 1961 ed. 21.50 (ISBN 0-404-56901-3). AMS Pr.

Aird, Robert B., et al. The Epilepsies: A Critical Review. 320p. 1984. text ed. 57.50 (ISBN 0-89004-424-4). Raven.

Aires, C., jt. auth. see Michalson, D.

Airey, Colin, jt. ed. see Jowell, Roger.

Airey, Dennis D. Basic Mathematics. 1976. coil bdg. 10.95 (ISBN 0-88252-021-0). Paladin Hse.

Airey, Stephen, et al. Messer Rondo & Other Stories by Gay Men. 157p. (Orig.). 1983. pap. 6.50 (ISBN 0-907040-21-7, Pub. by GMP England). Alyson Pubns.

Airey, T., et al, eds. Aircraft Erecting. (Engineering Craftsmen: No. H34). (Illus.). 1977. spiral bdg. 39.95x (ISBN 0-85083-413-9). Trans-Atlantic.

Airey, W. T., et al. New Zealand: Chapters by W. T. G. Airey (and Others) LC 81-23727. (The United Nations Ser.). (Illus.). xvii, 329p. 1982. Repr. of 1947 ed. lib. bdg. 35.00x (ISBN 0-313-23410-8, BENZ). Greenwood.

Airguide Publications. Flight Guide Airport & Frequency Manual, Vol. 1: Western States. Navarre, Monte, ed. 1980. small binder 17.00 (ISBN 0-911721-14-2, Pub. by Airguide). Aviation.

--Flight Guide Airport & Frequency Manual, Vol. 2: Eastern & Central States. Navarre, Monte, ed. 1980. small binder 26.00 (ISBN 0-911721-15-0, Pub. by Airguide). Aviation.

Airhart, Arnold E. Beacon Bible Expositions: Vol. 5, Acts. Greathouse, William M. & Taylor, Willard H., eds. (Beacon Bible Exposition Ser.). 1977. 6.95 (ISBN 0-8341-0316-8). Beacon Hill.

Airlie, Catherine. One Summer's Day, Passing Strangers & Red Lotus. (Harlequin Romances (3-in-1) Ser.). 576p. 1984. pap. 3.95 (ISBN 0-373-20080-3). Harlequin Bks.

Airlie House, jt. auth. see Conference on the Environment.

Airlie, Mabel F. In Whig Society, Seventeen Seventy-Five to Eighteen Eighteen. 205p. 1980. Repr. of 1921 ed. lib. bdg. 30.00 (ISBN 0-8495-0219-5). Arden Lib.

--In Whig Society Seventeen Seventy-Five to Eighteen Eighteen. 205p. 1984. Repr. of 1921 ed. lib. bdg. 30.00 (ISBN 0-89987-048-1). Darby Bks.

Airlife Publishing Ltd., ed. Pooley's Flight Guide: United Kingdom & Ireland. 400p. 1982. 59.00x (ISBN 0-902037-07-2, Pub. by Airlife England). State Mutual Bk.

Airola, P. There Is a Cure for Arthritis. pap. 4.95 (ISBN 0-13-914671-7, Reward). P-H.

Airola, Paavo. The Airola Diet & Cookbook. Lines, Anni M., ed. (Illus.). 288p. 1981. 12.95 (ISBN 0-932090-11-7). Health Plus.

--The Airola Diet & Cookbook. (A Health Plus Bk.). 12.95 (ISBN 0-932090-11-7). Contemp Bks.

--Are You Confused? Salov, Leslie H., frwd. by. 224p. 1971. pap. 6.95 (ISBN 0-932090-04-4). Health Plus.

--Are You Confused? The Authoritative Answers to Controversial Questions. (A Health Plus Bk.). 224p. pap. 6.95 (ISBN 0-932090-04-4). Contemp Bks.

--Cancer: Causes, Prevention & Treatment. (A Health Plus Book). 48p. 2.00. Contemp Bks.

--Cancer: Causes, Prevention & Treatment-the Total Approach. 48p. 1972. pap. 2.00 (ISBN 0-932090-05-2). Health Plus.

--Everywoman's Book. (Illus.). 640p. 1979. cloth 17.95 (ISBN 0-932090-00-1). Health Plus.

--Everywoman's Book. (Illus.). 640p. 1982. pap. 12.95 (ISBN 0-932090-10-9). Health Plus.

--Everywoman's Book: Dr. Airola's Practical Guide to Holistic Health. (A Health Plus Bks.). 640p. 17.95; pap. 12.95. Contemp Bks.

--How to Get Well. 300p. 1974. cloth 12.95 (ISBN 0-932090-03-6). Health Plus.

--How to Get Well: Dr. Airola's Handbook of Natural Healing. (A Health Plus Bk.). 304p. 12.95 (ISBN 0-932090-03-6). Contemp Bks.

--How to Keep Slim, Healthy & Young with Juice Fasting. 1971. 4.95x (ISBN 0-686-32624-5). Cancer Control Soc.

--How to Keep Slim, Healthy & Young with Juice Fasting. 80p. 1971. pap. 4.95 (ISBN 0-932090-02-8). Health Plus.

--How to Keep Slim, Healthy & Young with Juice Fasting. (A Health Plus Bk.). 80p. 4.95 (ISBN 0-932090-02-8). Contemp Bks.

--Hypoglycemia: A Better Approach. 192p. 1977. pap. 6.95 (ISBN 0-932090-01-X). Health Plus.

--Hypoglycemia: A Better Approach. (A Health Plus Bk.). 192p. 6.95 (ISBN 0-317-30836-X). Contemp Bks.

--The Miracle of Garlic. 48p. 1978. pap. 2.00 (ISBN 0-932090-08-7). Health Plus.

--The Miracle of Garlic. (A Health Plus Bk.). 48p. 2.00 (ISBN 0-932090-08-7). Contemp Bks.

--Stop Hair Loss. 32p. 1965. pap. 2.00 (ISBN 0-932090-06-0). Health Plus.

--Swedish Beauty Secrets. 32p. 1972. pap. 2.00 (ISBN 0-932090-07-9). Health Plus.

--There Is a Cure for Arthritis. 4.95x (ISBN 0-13-914671-7). Cancer Control Soc.

--Worldwide Secrets for Staying Young. 206p. 1982. pap. 6.95 (ISBN 0-932090-12-5). Health Plus.

--Worldwide Secrets for Staying Young. (A Health Plus Bk.). 208p. 6.95 (ISBN 0-932090-12-5). Contemp Bks.

Airola, Paavo O. Health Secrets from Europe. LC 79-135618. 1971. pap. 2.50 (ISBN 0-668-02411-9). Arco.

Airola, Stephen, jt. auth. see Frankland, Phillip.

Airports Conference, Atlanta, 1971. Airports: Key to the Air Transportation System. LC 73-171782. pap. 74.30 (ISBN 0-317-10158-7, 2010118). Bks Demand UMI.

Airy, George B. Gravitation. rev. ed. 1969. pap. 2.50 (ISBN 0-911014-02-0). Neo Pr.

Airy, George B. & Cohen, I. Bernard, eds. Gravitation. LC 80-2113. (Development of Science Ser.). (Illus.). 1981. lib. bdg. 20.00x (ISBN 0-405-13833-4). Ayer Co Pubs.

Airy, O., ed. see Essex, Arthur C.

Airy, Osmund. Charles II. 59.95 (ISBN 0-87968-839-4). Gordon Pr.

--The English Restoration & Louis XIV. 1977. Repr. of 1900 ed. lib. bdg. 17.50 (ISBN 0-8492-0137-3). R West.

Airy, Osmund, ed. see Lauderdale, John M.

Aisenberg, Alan C. Glycolysis & Respiration of Tumors. 1960. 57.50 (ISBN 0-12-046250-8). Acad Pr.

Aisenberg, Irwin A. Terminology in Patent Claims, 2 vols. 1985. looseleaf 150.00 (546). Bender.

Aisenberg, Nadya. A Common Spring: Crime Novel & Classic. LC 79-84638. 1980. 15.95 (ISBN 0-87972-141-3); pap. 8.95 (ISBN 0-87972-142-1). Bowling Green Univ.

--The Justice-Worm. LC 80-53871. (Chapbook Ser.: No. 3). 64p. (Orig.). 1981. pap. 5.95 (ISBN 0-937672-02-5). Rowan Tree.

Aisenberg, Nadya, ed. see Dickens, Charles, et al.

Aisenberg, Ruth, jt. auth. see Kastenbaum, Robert.

Aiserman, Mark A., et al. Logic, Automata & Algorithms. (Mathematics in Science & Engineering Ser). (Rus). 1971. 80.50 (ISBN 0-12-046350-4). Acad Pr.

Aisiku, J U., jt. ed. see Fafunwa, A. Babs.

AISLIN, jt. auth. see Sarrazin, Johan.

Aisner, Joseph, ed. Cancer Treatment Research. Chang, Paul. (Developments in Oncology Ser.: Vol. 2). (Illus.). xvi, 272p. 1980. lib. bdg. 45.00 (ISBN 90-247-2358-2, Pub. by Martinus Nijhoff Netherlands). Kluwer Academic.

--Lung Cancer. (Contemporary Issues in Clinical Oncology: Vol. 3). (Illus.). 352p. 1984. text ed. 42.50 (ISBN 0-443-08251-0). Churchill.

Aissen, Judith. The Syntax of Causative Constructions. Hankamer, Jorge, ed. LC 78-66533. (Outstanding Dissertations in Linguistics Ser.). 1985. lib. bdg. 33.00 (ISBN 0-8240-9690-8). Garland Pub.

Aistrop, Jack. Enjoying Nature's Marvels. LC 61-9014. (Illus.). (gr. 5-9). 1960. 6.95 (ISBN 0-8149-0250-2). Vanguard.

--Enjoying Pets. LC 55-7891. (gr. 5-10). 6.95 (ISBN 0-8149-0251-0). Vanguard.

Aistrup, E. Denmark-Between Sound & Sea. 1979. 25.00x (ISBN 8-7142-7989-4, D-747). Vanous.

Aistrup, I. Danmark-Town & Country. 72p. 1984. pap. 25.00x (ISBN 87-14-28462-6, D-745). Vanous.

Aita, C. R., jt. ed. see SreeHarsha, K. S.

Aita, John. Congenital Facial Anomalies with Neurologic Defects: A Clinical Atlas. (Illus.). 352p. 1969. photocopy ed. 29.75x (ISBN 0-398-00021-2). C C Thomas.

Aita, John A. Neurocutaneous Diseases. 96p. 1966. 12.75x (ISBN 0-398-00020-4). C C Thomas.

--Neurologic Manifestations of General Diseases. 936p. 1975. 69.50x (ISBN 0-398-02675-0). C C Thomas.

Aitchison. Gauge Theories in Particle Physics. 1981. pap. 36.00 (ISBN 0-9960022-2-7, Pub. by Inst Physics England). Heyden.

Aitchison, Diane, et al. Aldine: Our District & Its Community Activity Manual. new ed. Hawke, Sharryl D. & Lyons, Beth, eds. 310p. 1984. 69.00 (ISBN 0-87746-007-8). Graphic Learning.

Aitchison, G. D. Moisture Equilibria & Moisture Changes in Soils Beneath Covered Areas. 1982. 59.00x (ISBN 0-686-97906-0, Pub. by CSIRO Australia). State Mutual Bk.

Aitchison, Ian J. An Informal Introduction to Gauge Field Theories. LC 81-21753. (Illus.). 150p. 1982. 24.95 (ISBN 0-521-24540-0). Cambridge U Pr.

Aitchison, Ian J. & Paton, J. E., eds. Progress in Nuclear Physics, Vol. 13: Rudolf Peierls & Theoretical Physics - Proceedings of the Peierls Symposium. 1977. 16.50 (ISBN 0-08-021621-8). Pergamon.

Aitchison, J. & Brown, J. A. Lognormal Distribution. (Cambridge Department of Applied Economic Monographs: No. 5). 1957. 37.50 (ISBN 0-521-04011-6). Cambridge U Pr.

Aitchison, J. & Dunsmore, I. R. Statistical Prediction Analysis. (Illus.). 284p. 1980. pap. 19.95 (ISBN 0-521-29858-X). Cambridge U Pr.

--Statistical Prediction Analysis. LC 74-25649. (Illus.). 276p. 1975. 52.50 (ISBN 0-521-20692-8). Cambridge U Pr.

Aitchison, Jean. The Articulate Mammal. 2nd rev. ed. LC 82-49138. (Illus.). 288p. 1983. text ed. 15.50x (ISBN 0-87663-422-6). Universe.

--The Articulate Mammal: An Introduction to Psycholinguistics. (Illus.). 1978. pap. 4.95 (ISBN 0-07-000736-5). McGraw.

--Language Change: Progress of Decay. LC 84-24092. 266p. 1985. 16.50x (ISBN 0-87663-456-0); pap. 7.95x (ISBN 0-87663-872-8). Universe.

Aitchison, Jean & Allen, C. G. Bibliography of Mono- & Multilingual Vocabularies, Thesauri, Subject Headings & Classification Schemes in the Social Sciences: Prepared by the Aslib Library. (Reports & Papers in the Social Sciences: No. 54). 101p. 1983. pap. 7.00 (ISBN 92-3-102072-2, U1272, UNESCO). Unipub.

Aitchison, Jean, compiled by. UNESCO Thesaurus: A Structured List of Descriptors for Indexing & Retrieving Literature in the fields of Education, Science, Social Science, Culture & Communication, 2 Vols. 1977. Set. 93.00 (ISBN 92-3-101469-2, U816, UNESCO). Vol. 1: Introduction, Classified Thesaurus, Permuted Index, Hierarchical Display, 485 p. Vol. 2: Alphabetical Thesaurus, 530 p. Unipub.

Aitchison, Jean, et al. Thesaurus on Youth. 1982. 195.00x (ISBN 0-86155-044-7, Pub. by Natl Youth Bur England). State Mutual Bk.

Aitchison, Robert, jt. auth. see Eimers, Robert.

Aitchison, Stewart. A Naturalist's Guide to Hiking the Grand Canyon. LC 84-15035. 172p. 1985. 16.95 (ISBN 0-13-610239-5); pap. 8.95 (ISBN 0-13-610221-2). P-H.

--A Naturalist's San Juan River Guide. LC 82-3718. (Illus.). 100p. (Orig.). 1983. pap. 10.95 waterproof ed (ISBN 0-87108-653-0). Pruett.

Aitelli, Peter & Dietrich, Deborah. Research Guide to Professional Corporate Law. LC 85-8695. (Legal Research Guides Ser.). vii, 86p. 1985. lib. bdg. 22.50 (ISBN 0-89941-453-2). W S Hein.

Aitelli, Peter & Dietrich, Debra M. Research Guide to Professional Corporation Law. LC 85-8695. Date not set. price not set (ISBN 0-89941-453-2). W S Hein.

Aithnard, K. M. Some Aspects of Cultural Policy in Togo. (Studies & Documents on Cultural Policies). (Illus.). 101p. 1976. pap. 5.00 (ISBN 92-3-101315-7, U622, UNESCO). Unipub.

Aitio, Antero, et al, eds. Biological Monitoring & Surveillance of Workers Exposed to Chemicals. LC 82-2946. (Illus.). 403p. 1983. text ed. 64.50 (ISBN 0-89116-253-4). Hemisphere Pub.

Aitken, A. J. & McDiarmid, M. P., eds. Bards & Makars. 250p. 1977. 75.00x (ISBN 0-85261-132-3, Pub. by U of Glasgow Pr Scotland). State Mutual Bk.

Aitken, A. J. & Stevenson, J. A., eds. A Dictionary of the Older Scottish Tongue, Pts. XXVII-XXXI. (Dictionary of the Older Scottish Tongue Ser.: Vol. 5). 620p. 1983. 180.00 (ISBN 0-08-028490-6). Pergamon.

--A Dictionary of the Older Scottish Tongue, Pt. 32: From the Twelfth Century to the End of the Seventeenth. 120p. 1985. pap. 41.50 (ISBN 0-08-030393-5). Pergamon.

Aitken, Alexander C. Determinants & Matrices. LC 82-24168. (University Mathematical Texts Ser.). 144p. 1983. Repr. of 1956 ed. lib. bdg. 32.50x (ISBN 0-313-23294-6, AIDE). Greenwood.

Aitken, Amy. Kate & Mona in the Jungle. LC 80-15110. (Illus.). 32p. (gr. k-2). 1981. PLB 9.95 (ISBN 0-02-700320-5). Bradbury Pr.

--Ruby! LC 78-21283. (Illus.). 32p. (gr. k-2). 1979. 9.95 (ISBN 0-02-700330-2). Bradbury Pr.

--Ruby, the Red Knight. LC 82-9590. (Illus.). 32p. (ps-2). 1983. PLB 12.95 (ISBN 0-02-700340-X). Bradbury Pr.

--Wanda's Circus. LC 84-20488. (Illus.). 32p. (ps-2). 1985. PLB 11.95 (ISBN 0-02-700370-1). Bradbury Pr.

Aitken, C., ed. Psychosomatics & Pleasure: Proceedings of the Twenty-Third Annual Conference of the Society for Psychosomatic Research Held at the Royal College of Physicians, London, 19-20 November 1979. 88p. 1981. pap. 22.00 (ISBN 0-08-026797-1). Pergamon.

Aitken, D. J., ed. World List of Universities, Other Institutions of Higher Education & University Organizations 1982-1984. 15th ed. 632p. 1983. text ed. 54.95x (ISBN 3-11-008914-9). De Gruyter.

Aitken, Dorothy. The Hunted. Phillips, Max, ed. (Daybreak). 128p. 1982. pap. 4.95 (ISBN 0-8163-0469-6). Pacific Pr Pub Assn.

Aitken, F. C. Sodium & Potassium in Nutrition of Mammals. 296p. 1976. cloth 50.00x (ISBN 0-85198-370-7, Pub. by CAB Bks England). State Mutual Bk.

Aitken, F. c. & Hankin, R. G. Vitamins in Feeds for Livestock. 230p. 1970. cloth 40.00x (ISBN 0-686-45671-8, Pub. by CAB Bks England). State Mutual Bk.

Aitken, G. A. Life of Richard Steele, 2 Vols. LC 68-24893. (English Biography Ser., No. 31). (Illus.). 1968. Repr. of 1889 ed. lib. bdg. 79.95x (ISBN 0-8383-0152-5). Haskell.

Aitken, G. A., ed. see Steele, Richard.

Aitken, G. W., ed. Optical Engineering for Cold Environments, Vol. 414. 231p. 42.00 (ISBN 0-89252-449-9). Photo-Optical.

Aitken, George, ed. see Defoe, Daniel.

Aitken, George A. Later Stuart Tracts. LC 64-16748. (Arber's an English Garner Ser.). 1964. Repr. of 1890 ed. 20.00 (ISBN 0-8154-0003-9). Cooper Sq.

Aitken, George A., ed. see Steele, Richard.

Aitken, Hannah, ed. A Forgotten Heritage: Original Folk Tales of Lowland Scotland. (Illus.). 168p. 1973. 11.00x (ISBN 0-87471-430-3). Rowman.

Aitken, Hugh G. The Continuous Wave: Technology & American Radio, 1900-1932. (Illus.). 588p. 1985. text ed. 67.50x (ISBN 0-691-08376-2); pap. text ed. 19.95x (ISBN 0-691-02390-5). Princeton U Pr.

--Scientific Management in Action: Taylorism at Watertown Arsenal, 1908-1915. (Illus.). 280p. 1985. 30.00 (ISBN 0-691-04241-1); pap. 12.95 (ISBN 0-691-00375-0). Princeton U Pr.

--Syntony & Spark-the Origins of Radio Technology. LC 75-34247. (Science, Culture & Society Ser.). cancelled (ISBN 0-8357-9989-1, 2051289). Bks Demand UMI.

Aitken, Hugh G., ed. Conference on the State & Economic Growth, New York, 1956. LC 59-9954. 10.00 (ISBN 0-527-03306-5). Kraus Repr.

Aitken, Hugh J. Syntony & Spark: The Origins of Radio. LC 84-26408. (Illus.). 368p. 1985. 38.50 (ISBN 0-691-08377-0); pap. 13.95 (ISBN 0-691-02392-1). Princeton U Pr.

Aitken, J. A., et al. Manual of Human Anatomy, Parts 1, 2, &3. 3rd ed. LC 74-33179. (Illus.). 1976. Pt. 1 Thorax, Abdomen, & Pelvis. pap. text ed. 13.75 (ISBN 0-443-01240-7); Pt. 2 Head & Neck. pap. text ed. 13.75 (ISBN 0-443-01241-5); Pt. 3 The Upper & Lower Limbs. pap. text ed. 12.50 (ISBN 0-443-01242-3). Churchill.

Aitken, John. Compilations of Litanies & Vesper Hymns. 25.00x (ISBN 0-87556-004-0). Saifer.

Aitken, John J., jt. auth. see Hansell, Michael H.

Aitken, M. J. Thermoluminescence Dating. (Studies in Archaeological Science). Date not set. price not set (ISBN 0-12-046380-6). Acad Pr.

Aitken, Michael, jt. ed. see Gaffikin, Michael.

Aitken, Robert. The Mind of Clover: Essays in Zen Buddhist Ethics. 224p. (Orig.). 1984. pap. 11.50 (ISBN 0-86547-158-4). N Point Pr.

--Taking the Path of Zen. LC 82-81475. (Illus.). 176p. (Orig.). 1982. pap. 9.50 (ISBN 0-86547-080-4). N Point Pr.

--A Zen Wave: Basho's Haiku & Zen. LC 78-13243. 1979. pap. 7.95 (ISBN 0-8348-0137-X). Weatherhill.

Aitken, Robert T. Ethnology of Tubuai. (BMB Ser.: No. 70). Repr. of 1930 ed. 24.00 (ISBN 0-527-02176-8). Kraus Repr.

Aitken, W. R., ed. Scottish Literature in English & Scots: A Guide to Information Sources. LC 73-16971. (American Literature, English Literature, & World Literature in English Ser.: Vol. 37). 400p. 1982. 60.00x (ISBN 0-8103-1249-2). Gale.

Aitken, W. R., ed. see MacDiarmid, Hugh.

Aitken, William, ed. see MacDiarmid, Hugh.

Aitken, Yvonne. Flowering Time, Climate & Growth. (Illus.). 193p. 1975. 36.00x (ISBN 0-522-84071-X, Pub. by Melbourne U Pr Australia). Intl Spec Bk.

Aitken-Swan, Jean. Fertility Control & the Medical Profession. 238p. 1977. 30.00x (ISBN 0-85664-463-3, Pub. by Croom Helm Ltd). Longwood Pub Group.

Aitkin, D. Stability & Change in Australian Politics. new ed. 400p. (Orig.). 1982. pap. text ed. 18.95 (ISBN 0-7081-0022-8, 1241, Pub. by ANUP Australia). Australia N U P.

Aitkin, Don. Stability & Change in Australian Politics. LC 76-56692. 1977. 26.00x (ISBN 0-312-75478-7). St Martin.

Aitkin, Don, ed. Surveys of Australian Political Science. 372p. 1985. text ed. 32.00x (ISBN 0-86861-548-X); pap. text ed. 16.00x (ISBN 0-86861-556-0). Allen Unwin.

Aitkin, Donald, et al. Australian National Political Attitudes, 1967. 1975. codebook write for info. (ISBN 0-89138-117-1). ICPSR.

Aitkin, Lindsay, jt. ed. see Syka, Josef.

Aitmatov, C. Cranes Fly Early. 91p. 1983. pap. 4.95 (ISBN 0-8285-2639-7, Pub. by Raduga Pubs USSR). Imported Pubns.

--Tales of the Mountains & the Steppes. 280p. 1973. 6.95 (ISBN 0-8285-0937-9, Pub. by Progress Pubs USSR). Imported Pubns.

Aitmatov, Chingiz. The Day Lasts More Than a Hundred Years. French, John, tr. from Rus. LC 83-115957. 368p. 1983. 10.95x (ISBN 0-253-11595-7). Ind U Pr.

Aitmatov, Chingiz & Mukhamedzhanov, Kaltai. The Ascent of Mount Fuji. 212p. 1975. pap. 4.95 (ISBN 0-374-51215-9). FS&G.

Aitmatov, Chinguiz. Tres Relatos. 280p. (Span.). 1978. 4.95 (ISBN 0-8285-1327-9, Pub. by Progress Pubs USSR). Imported Pubns.

Aiuti, F. & Wigzell, H., eds. Thymus, Thymic Hormones & T Lymphocytes. (Serono Symposia Ser.: No. 38). 1980. 60.00 (ISBN 0-12-046450-0). Acad Pr.

Aivanhov, Omraam M. Sexual Force or the Winged Dragon. MacNamara, Ann, tr. from Fr. (Izvor Collection: Vol. 205). (Illus.). 138p. pap. 4.95 (ISBN 2-85566-197-8). Prosveta Fran.

Aivanhov, Omraam M. Christmas & Easter in the Initiatic Tradition. MacNamara, Ann, tr. from Fr. (Izvor Collection: Vol. 209). (Illus.). 139p. (Orig.). pap. 4.95 (ISBN 2-85566-226-5). Prosveta Fran.

--Education Begins Before Birth. MacNamara, Ann, tr. from Fr. (Izvor Collection Ser.: Vol. 203). (Illus.). 168p. 1982. pap. 4.95 (ISBN 0-911857-02-8). Prosveta Fran.

--Freedom, the Spirit Triumphant. (Izvor Collection Ser.: Vol. 211). (Illus.). 138p. 1984. pap. 4.95 (ISBN 2-85566-244-3, Dist. by DeVorss & Co.). Prosveta Fran.

--Hope for the World: Spiritual Galvanoplasty. (Izvor Collection: Vol. 214). (Illus.). 187p. (Orig.). 1984. pap. 4.95 (ISBN 2-85566-264-8, Dist. by DeVorss & Co.). Prosveta Fran.

--Light Is a Living Spirit. (Izvor Collection Ser.: Vol. 212). (Illus.). 138p. (Orig.). 1983. pap. 4.95 (ISBN 2-85566-252-4, Dist. by DeVross & Co). Prosveta Fran.

--The Living Book of Nature. (Izvor Collection Ser.: Vol. 216). (Illus.). 216p. (Orig.). 1984. pap. 4.95 (ISBN 2-85566-304-0, Dist. by DeVorss & Co.). Prosveta Fran.

--Man Master of His Destiny. MacNamara, Ann, tr. from Fr. (Izvor Collection Ser.: Vol. 202). 194p. 1982. pap. 4.95 (ISBN 0-911857-01-X). Prosveta Fran.

--Man's Two Natures, Human & Divine. (Izvor Collection Ser.: Vol. 213). (Illus.). 152p. (Orig.). 1984. pap. 4.95 (ISBN 2-85566-253-2, Dist by DeVorss & Co.). Prosveta Fran.

--The Second Birth. (Complete Works of O. M. Aivanhov: Vol. 1). 210p. 1981. pap. 9.50 (ISBN 0-87516-418-8). De Vorss.

--Toward a Solar Civilization. MacNamara, Ann, tr. from Fr. (Izvor Collection: Vol. 201). (Illus.). 148p. 1982. pap. 4.95 (ISBN 0-911857-00-1). Prosveta Fran.

--The Tree of Knowledge of Good & Evil. MacNamara, Ann, tr. from Fr. (Izvor Collection: Vol. 210). (Illus.). 160p. (Orig.). pap. 4.95 (ISBN 2-85566-237-0). Prosveta Fran.

--The True Meaning of Christ's Teaching, Vol. 215. (Izvor Collection Ser.). (Illus.). 186p. (Orig.). 1984. pap. 4.95 (ISBN 0-911857-04-4, Dist. by DeVorss & Co.). Prosveta Fran.

--Under the Dove, the Reign of Peace. MacNamara, Ann, tr. from Fr. (Izvor Collection: Vol. 208). (Illus.). 143p. pap. 4.95 (ISBN 2-85566-229-X). Prosveta Fran.

--The Universal White Brotherhood Is Not a Sect. (Izvor Collection Ser.: Vol. 206). (Illus.). 197p. (Orig.). 1982. pap. 4.95 (ISBN 2-85566-194-3, Dist. by DeVross & Co). Prosveta Fran.

--What is a Spiritual Master? MacNamara, Ann, tr. from Fr. (Izvor Collection: Vol. 207). 185p. pap. 4.95 (ISBN 2-85566-230-3). Prosveta Fran.

--The Yoga of Nutrition. MacNamara, Ann, tr. from Fr. (Izvor Collection: Vol. 204). 130p. pap. 4.95 (ISBN 0-911857-03-6). Prosveta Fran.

Aivazjan, S. A., et al. Twenty-Two Papers on Statistics & Probability. LC 61-9803. (Selected Translations in Mathematical Statistics & Probability Ser.: Vol. 6). 1966. 35.00 (ISBN 0-8218-1456-7, STAPRO-6). Am Math.

Aiwass, jt. auth. see Crowley, Aleister.

Aixala, Jerome, ed. see Arrupe, Pedro.

Aixala, Jerome, tr. see Dalmases, Candido de.

Aiyar, K. N. Thirty Minor Upanishads: Including the Yoga Upanishads. 300p. 1980. Repr. of 1914 ed. 16.95 (ISBN 0-935548-00-9). Santarasa Pubns.

Aiyar, P. R. Monetary & Fiscal Economics. 690p. 1984. pap. text ed. 15.95x (ISBN 0-86590-525-8, Pub. by Sterling Pubs India). Apt Bks.

Aiyar, R. Ramachandra. Quest for News. 1979. 6.50x (ISBN 0-8364-0556-0, Pub. by Macmillan India). South Asia Bks.

Aiyar, R. Sadasiva. Introduction to Galsworthy's Plays. LC 73-9722. 1925. lib. bdg. 15.00 (ISBN 0-8414-2856-5). Folcroft.

Aiyepeku, Wilson O. International Socioeconomic Information Systems: An Evaluative Study of DEVSIS-Type Programs. 100p. 1983. pap. text ed. 8.00 (ISBN 0-88936-366-8, IDRCTS43, IDRC). Unipub.

Aiyer, Arjun, et al. Bibliographic Specifications for Display: University of California Union Catalog. rev. ed. (Working Paper: No. 1). 1979. 5.00 (ISBN 0-686-87236-3). UCDLA.

Aiyer, K. Narayanaswami, tr. Laghu-Yoga-Vasistha. 1971. 19.95 (ISBN 0-8356-7497-5). Theos Pub Hse.

Aiyer, P. S., tr. see Abhendananda.

Aizawa, Hirayasu. Metabolic Maps of Pesticides. (Ecotoxicology & Environmental Quality Ser.). 1982. 45.00 (ISBN 0-12-046480-2). Acad Pr.

Aizenberg, Edna. The Aleph Weaver: Biblical, Kabbalistic & Judaic Elements in Borges. 25.00 (ISBN 0-916379-12-4). Scripta.

Aizenberg, I. A. & Yuzhakov, A P. Integral Representations & Residues in Multidimensional Complex Analysis. LC 83-15549. (Translations of Mathematical Monographs: No. 58). 283p. 1983. 68.00 (ISBN 0-8218-4511-X). Am Math.

Aizenberg, L. A., jt. auth. see Dautov, Sh. A.

Aizenstat, A. J. Survival for All: The Alternative to Nuclear War with a Practical Plan for Total Denuclearization. LC 84-28231. 224p. 1985. 14.95 (ISBN 0-932755-14-3). Billner & Rouse.

Aizerman, M. A., et al. Seventeen Papers on Analysis. LC 51-5559. (Translations Ser.: No. 2, Vol. 26). 1963. 29.00 (ISBN 0-8218-1726-4, TRANS 2-26). Am Math.

--Sixteen Papers on Differential & Difference Equations, Functional Analysis, Games & Control. LC 51-5559. (Translations Ser.: No. 2, Vol. 87). 1970. 36.00 (ISBN 0-8218-1787-6, TRANS 2-87). Am Math.

--Thirty-One Invited Addresses at the International Congress of Mathematicians in Moscow 1966. LC 51-5559. (Translations Ser.: No. 2, Vol. 70). 1968. 35.00 (ISBN 0-8218-1770-1, TRANS 2-70). Am Math.

Ajaegbu, H. I. & Faniran, A. A New Approach to Practical Work in Geography. 2nd ed. 1973. text ed. 12.95x (ISBN 0-435-95041-X). Heinemann Ed.

Ajami, Fouad. The Arab Predicament: Arab Political Thought & Practice since 1967. LC 80-27457. 250p. 1982. 27.95 (ISBN 0-521-23914-1); pap. 10.95 (ISBN 0-521-27063-4). Cambridge U Pr.

--Human Rights & World Order Politics. 33p. (Orig.). 1978. pap. text ed. 2.00x (ISBN 0-87855-757-1). Transaction Bks.

Ajami, M. The Neckveins of Winter: The Controversy over Natural & Artificial Poetry in Medieval Arabic Literary Criticism. (Studies in Arabic Literature: No. 9). x, 84p. 1984. pap. text ed. 13.50x (ISBN 90-04-07016-8, Pub. by Brill Holland). Humanities.

Ajar, Emile see Gary, Romain, pseud.

Ajay, Stephen. Abracadabra. 1977. perfect bound in wrappers 2.50 (ISBN 0-685-88987-4). New Rivers Pr.

Ajaya, Swami. Psychotherapy East & West: A Unifying Paradigm. LC 83-22608. 320p. (Orig.). 1984. pap. 9.95 (ISBN 0-89389-087-1). Himalayan Pubs.

--Yoga Psychology: A Practical Guide to Meditation. rev. ed. LC 76-374539. 115p. 1976. pap. 4.95 (ISBN 0-89389-052-9). Himalayan Pubs.

Ajaya, Swami, jt. auth. see Rama, Swami.

Ajaya, Swami, ed. Foundations of Eastern & Western Psychology. LC 77-150885. 119p. (Orig.). 1977. pap. 3.95 (ISBN 0-89389-027-8). Himalayan Pubs.

--Living with the Himalayan Masters: Spiritual Experiences of Swami Rama. LC 80-82974. 490p. 1980. 14.95 (ISBN 0-89389-034-0); pap. 9.95 (ISBN 0-89389-070-7). Himalayan Intl.

--Meditational Therapy. LC 80-105520. 92p. (Orig.). 1977. pap. 3.95 (ISBN 0-89389-032-4). Himalayan Pubs.

--Psychology East & West. LC 77-150850. 103p. (Orig.). 1976. pap. 3.95 (ISBN 0-89389-019-7). Himalayan Pubs.

Ajayi, J. F. Christian Missions in Nigeria, Eighteen Forty-One to Eighteen Ninety-One: The Making of a New Elite. 1965. 17.95 (ISBN 0-8101-0038-X). Northwestern U Pr.

Ajayi, J. F. & Crowder, Michael, eds. Historical Atlas of Africa. LC 83-675975. 1985. 75.00 (ISBN 0-521-25353-5). Cambridge U Pr.

--The History of West Africa, Vol. 1. 2nd ed. 649p. 1976. 42.00x (ISBN 0-231-04102-0). Columbia U Pr.

Ajayi, Simeon & Ojo, Oladeji O. Money & Banking Analysis & Policy in the Nigerian Context. (Illus.). 272p. 1981. pap. text ed. 13.50x (ISBN 0-04-330318-8). Allen Unwin.

Ajdukiewicz, K. Problems & Theories of Philosophy. Quinton, A. & Skolimowski, H., trs. from Polish. LC 72-97878. 160p. 1973. pap. 7.95 (ISBN 0-521-09993-5). Cambridge U Pr.

Ajdukiewicz, Kazimierz. Scientific World Perspective & Other Essays: 1931-1963. Giedymin, Jerzy, ed. (Synthese Library: No. 108). 1977. lib. bdg. 66.00 (ISBN 90-277-0527-5, Pub. by Reidel Holland). Kluwer Academic.

Ajello, Libero E., et al. Histoplasmosis: Proceedings. (Illus.). 540p. 1971. photocopy ed. 65.50x (ISBN 0-398-02216-X). C C Thomas.

Ajemian, Ina & Mount, Balfour M., eds. The R. V. H. Manual on Palliative-Hospice Care: A Resource Book. pap. 34.00 (ISBN 0-405-13934-9). Ayer Co Pubs.

Ajemian, Peter. Gasping for Information at Reagan's EPA. 28p. 1984. pap. 5.00 (ISBN 0-937188-25-5). Pub Citizen Inc.

Ajemian, Shari & Newcomb, Sarah. Partially Sage: A Comic Look at Common Songs. LC 83-90154. 130p. (Orig.). 1983. pap. 8.95 (ISBN 0-9611994-0-7). Rob Lynn Pub.

Ajiboye, Goke. Abiku. 1983. 8.95 (ISBN 0-533-05110-X). Vantage.

Ajijola, A. D. Essence of Faith in Islam. pap. 12.50 (ISBN 0-686-63898-0). Kazi Pubns.

--Myth of the Cross. pap. 9.50 (ISBN 0-686-63907-3). Kazi Pubns.

Ajilvsgi, Geyata. Wild Flowers of the Big Thicket, East Texas, & Western Louisiana. LC 78-21781. (The W. L. Moody, Jr., Natural History Ser.: N0. 4). (Illus.). 448p. 1979. 17.50 (ISBN 0-89096-064-X); pap. 9.95 (ISBN 0-89096-065-8). Tex A&M Univ Pr.

--Wildflowers of Texas. (Illus.). 414p. 1984. 11.95 (ISBN 0-940672-15-4). Shearer Pub.

Ajinkya, Bipin B., jt. ed. see Abdel-khalik, Rashad.

Ajisafa, Ajawi K. The Laws & Customs of the Yoruba People. 1976. lib. bdg. 59.95 (ISBN 0-8490-2135-9). Gordon Pr.

Ajl, S. J., et al, eds. Microbial Toxins: A Comprehensive Treatise. Incl. Vol. 1. Bacterial Protein Toxins. 1970. 85.50 (ISBN 0-12-046501-9); Vol. 2A. Bacterial Protein Toxins. 1971. 71.50 (ISBN 0-12-046502-7); Vol. 3. Bacterial Protein Toxins. 1970. 85.50 (ISBN 0-12-046503-5); Vol. 4. Bacterial Endotoxins. 1971. 74.50 (ISBN 0-12-046504-3); Vol. 5. Bacterial Endotoxins. 1971. 82.50 (ISBN 0-12-046505-1); Vol. 6. Fundal Toxins. 1971. 85.50 (ISBN 0-12-046506-X); Vol. 7. Algal & Fungal Toxins. 1971. 71.50 (ISBN 0-12-046507-8); Vol. 8. Fungal Toxins. 1972. 71.50 (ISBN 0-12-046508-6). Acad Pr.

Ajmone-Marsan, C., jt. ed. see Pompeiano, O.

Ajmone-Marsan, Cosimo & Matthies, H., eds. Neuronal Plasticity & Memory Formation. (International Brain Research Organization Monograph Ser.: Vol. 9). 650p. 1982. text ed. 93.00 (ISBN 0-89004-681-6). Raven.

Ajmone-Marson, Cosimo, et al, eds. Neuropeptides & Neural Transmission. (International Brain Research Organization (IBRO) Monograph: Vol. 7). 412p. 1980. text ed. 65.00 (ISBN 0-89004-501-1). Raven.

Ajult, Hugh J. & Radler, Albert J., trs. The German Corporation Tax Law with 1980 Amendments. 2nd, rev. ed. (Series on International Taxation). 146p. 26.00 (ISBN 0-686-41018-1). Kluwer Academic.

A Juriaguerra, J. de see De Ajuriaguerra, J.

Ajuwon, Bade. Funeral Dirges of Yoruba Hunters. LC 78-64626. (Traditional African Literature Ser.). (Illus.). 134p. (Orig.). 1982. 18.95x (ISBN 0-88357-075-0). NOK Pubs.

Ajzen, Icek, jt. auth. see Fishbein, Martin.

Ajzenberg-Selove, Fay, ed. Nuclear Spectroscopy, 2 Pts. (Pure & Applied Physics Ser.: Vol. 9). 1960. 83.00 ea. Pt. A (ISBN 0-12-046850-6). Pt. B (ISBN 0-12-046851-4). Acad Pr.

Aka, Masago. The Moon Watching Party. Franklin, Paula, tr. from Japanese. LC 85-40406. 28p. (ps-3). 1985. pap. 3.95 (ISBN 0-382-09138-8). Silver.

Akabas, Sheila H. & Kurzman, Paul. Work, Workers, & Work Organizations: A View from Social Work. 272p. 1982. 24.95 (ISBN 0-13-965335-X). P-H.

Akademie Der Wissenschaften - Munich. Historische Kommission, Vols. 2, 3, 5-17, 19-24. Set. 1075.00 (ISBN 0-384-00550-0). Johnson Repr.

Akademiia Nauk SSSR. Sovetsko-Kitaiskie Otnosheniia, Nineteen Seventeen to Nineteen Fifty-Seven: Sbornik Dokumentov. Kurdiukov, I. F., et al, eds. LC 70-38048. (China, Classic & Contemporary Works in Reprint Ser). Repr. of 1959 ed. 32.50 (ISBN 0-404-56902-1). AMS Pr.

Akademiia Nauk SSSR & Institut khimicheskoi fiziki. Atlas of Electron Spin Resonance Spectra: Theoretically Calculated Multicomponent Symmetrical Spectra, Vol. 1. LC 63-21216. pap. 58.30 (ISBN 0-317-09765-2, 2003355). Bks Demand UMI.

Akademikerinnenbund, ed. Frauenfrage in Deutschland. 460p. lib. bdg. 23.50 (ISBN 0-317-20494-7). K G Saur.

Akagha, Fidelis S. Strategies for Economic Development in Africa. LC 84-90090. 149p. 1985. 13.95 (ISBN 0-533-06174-1). Vantage.

Akagi, R. H. Town Proprietors of the New England Colonies. 1963. 12.75 (ISBN 0-8446-1012-7). Peter Smith.

Akagi, Roy. Japan's Foreign Relations, Fifteen Forty-Two to Nineteen Thirty-Six: A Short History. (Studies in Japanese History & Civilization). (Illus.). 560p. 1979. Repr. of 1936 ed. 36.50 (ISBN 0-89093-260-3). U Pubns Amer.

Akaha, Tsuneo. Japan in Global Ocean Politics. 160p. 1985. text ed. 19.00x (ISBN 0-8248-0898-3). UH Pr.

Akahira, M. & Takeuchi, K. Asymptotic Efficiency of Statistical Estimators: Concepts & Higher Order Asymptotic Efficiency. (Lecture Notes in Statistics Ser.: Vol. 7). 256p. 1981. pap. 18.00 (ISBN 0-387-90576-6). Springer-Verlag.

Akai, H. & King, R. C., eds. The Ultrastructure & Functioning of Insect Cells. (Illus.). 195p. 1983. 28.00x (ISBN 4-930813-00-X, Pub. by Japan Sci Soc Japan). Intl Spec Bk.

Akai, Hiromu & King, Robert C., eds. Insect Ultrastructure, Vol. 1. LC 82-5268. 507p. 1982. text ed. 65.00 (ISBN 0-306-40923-2, Plenum Pr). Plenum Pub.

Akai, Hiromu, jt. ed. see King, Robert C.

Akana, Akaiko, tr. see Kaaiakamanu, D. M. & Akina, J. K.

Akanazarova, S. L. & Kafarov, V. V. Experiment Optimization in Chemistry & Chemical Engineering. MAtskovsky, V. M. & Repyev, A. P., trs. from Rus. 312p. 1982. 9.95 (ISBN 0-8285-2305-3, Pub. by Mir Pubs USSR). Imported Pubns.

Akao, Nobutoshi, ed. Japan's Economic Security. LC 82-10257. 1983. 27.50x (ISBN 0-312-44064-2). St Martin.

Akare, Thomas. The Slums. (African Writers Ser. No. 241). 188p. (Orig.). 1981. pap. 6.50x (ISBN 0-435-90241-5). Heinemann Ed.

Akasaka, T., jt. ed. see Kawata, K.

Akashi. Control Science & Technology for the Progress of Society: Proceedings, 7 Vols. LC 81-23491. (IFAC Proceedings). 3800p. 1982. Set. 825.00 (ISBN 0-08-027580-X); Vol. 1. 180.00 (ISBN 0-08-028713-1); Vol. 2. 180.00 (ISBN 0-08-028714-X); Vol. 3. 99.00 (ISBN 0-08-028715-8); Vol. 4. 125.00 (ISBN 0-08-028716-6); Vol. 5. 110.00 (ISBN 0-08-028717-4); Vol. 6. 99.00 (ISBN 0-08-028718-2); Vol. 7. 110.00 (ISBN 0-08-028719-0). Pergamon.

Akashi, H. Appropriate Technolgy & Education & Economic Management: Biological, Medical & Environmental Systems. (Control Science & Technology Ser.: Vol. 7). 110.00 (ISBN 0-08-028719-0). Pergamon.

Akashi, H., jt. auth. see International Federation of Automatic Control.

Akashi, H., ed. see IFAC Symposium, Kyoto, Japan, Aug. 1977.

Akasofu, S. I. Polar & Magnetospheric Substorms. (Astrophysics & Space Science Library: No.11). 280p. 1968. lib. bdg. 37.00 (ISBN 90-277-0108-3, Pub. by Reidel Holland). Kluwer Academic.

Akasofu, S. I., ed. Dynamics of the Magnetosphere. (Astrophysics & Space Science Library: No. 78). 1980. lib. bdg. 79.00 (ISBN 90-277-1052-X, Pub. by Reidel Holland). Kluwer Academic.

Akasofu, S. I. & Kan, J. R., eds. Physics of Auroral Arc Formation. (Geophysical Monograph Ser.: Vol. 25). 465p. 1981. 32.00 (ISBN 0-87590-050-X). Am Geophysical.

Akasofu, Syun-Ichi. Physics of Magnetospheric Substorms. new ed. (Astrophysics & Space Science Library: No. 47). 1976. lib. bdg. 95.00 (ISBN 90-277-0748-0, Pub. by Reidel Holland). Kluwer Academic.

Akazawa, Takeru, jt. ed. see Hanihara, Kazuro.

Akbar, M. J. India: The Siege Within. 320p. 1985. pap. 5.95 (ISBN 0-14-007576-3). Penguin.

Akbar, M. J., ed. The Wills Book of Excellence: The Olympics. (Illus.). 250p. 1984. text ed. 40.00x (ISBN 0-86131-521-9, Pub. by Orient Longman Ltd India). Apt Bks.

Ake, Claude. A Political Economy of Africa. LC 81-8415. (Illus.). 176p. (Orig.). 1982. pap. text ed. 9.95x (ISBN 0-582-64370-8). Longman.

--Revolutionary Pressures in Africa. 112p. 1978. 19.95x (ISBN 0-905762-14-2, Pub. by Zed Pr England); pap. 8.95x (ISBN 0-686-71681-7, Pub by Zed Pr England). Biblio Dist.

Akehurst, Michael. A Modern Introduction to International Law. 5th ed. 360p. 1984. text ed. 28.50x (ISBN 0-04-341025-1); pap. text ed. 12.95x (ISBN 0-04-341026-X). Allen Unwin.

Akehurst, Richard. Game Guns & Rifles: From Percussion to Hammerless Ejector in Britain. (Illus.). 192p. 1985. 19.95 (ISBN 0-85368-695-5, Pub. by Arms & Armour). Sterling.

Akel, Abdullatif A. Agony in Limbo. Ciulla, A. J., ed. (Illus.). 388p. Date not set. 17.95 (ISBN 0-913791-01-6). Rubicon Bks.

Akel, D'Ann, jt. auth. see Dinaburg, Kathy.

Akell, Robert B. & King, C. Judson. New Developments in Liquid-Liquid Extractors: Selected Papers from ISEC'83. LC 84-18578. (Alche Symposium Ser.: Vol. 80, No. 238). 177p. 1984. pap. 35.00 (ISBN 0-8169-0327-1); pap. 17.50 members (ISBN 0-317-17532-7). Am Inst Chem Eng.

Aken, J. E. Van see Van Aken, J. E.

Aken, Paul M. Van see Van Aken, Paul M., Jr.

Aken, William van see Hausser, Robert L. & Van Aken, William.

Akens, David S. John Glenn: First American in Space. 10.95 (ISBN 0-88411-900-9, Pub. by Aeonian Pr). Amereon Ltd.

--World's Greatest Leaders: The Akens Book of Supernatural Records. LC 80-52087. 1980. pap. 4.95 (ISBN 0-87397-181-7). Strode.

Akens, David S., jt. auth. see Shea, John J.

Akens, Helen M., jt. auth. see Brown, Virginia P.

Akenside, Mark. Poetical Works of Mark Akenside. Dyce, Alexander, ed. LC 71-94924. Repr. of 1845 ed. 15.00 (ISBN 0-404-00299-4). AMS Pr.

Akenson, Donald H. Between Two Revolutons: Islandmagee County Antrim, Seventeen Ninety-Eight to Nineteen Twenty. (Illus.). 221p. 1979. 19.50 (ISBN 0-208-01827-1, Archon). Shoe String.

--The Church of Ireland: Ecclesiastical Reform & Revolution, 1880-1885. LC 76-151565. pap. 81.40 (ISBN 0-317-08435-6, 2013197). Bks Demand UMI.

--Irish in Ontario: A Study in Rural History. 416p. 1985. 15.95 (ISBN 0-7735-0591-1). McGill Queens U Pr.

--A Mirror to Kathleen's Face: Education in Independent Ireland, 1922-1960. 240p. 1975. 17.50x (ISBN 0-7735-0203-3). McGill-Queens U Pr.

--A Protestant in Purgatory: Richard Whately, Archbishop of Dublin. (Conference on British Studies (CBS) Biography: Vol. II). xiii, 269p. 1981. 19.50 (ISBN 0-208-01917-0, Archon). Shoe String.

--The United States & Ireland. LC 73-82348. (American Foreign Policy Library). 210p. 1973. 16.00x (ISBN 0-674-92460-6). Harvard U Pr.

Aker, Brooke & Walsh, Arthur C. Mental Capacity: Medical & Legal Aspects of the Aging. LC 77-21256. 1977. 75.00 (ISBN 0-07-000756-X, Shepard). McGraw.

Aker, Frank. October 1973: The Arab-Israeli War. (Illus.). 180p. 1985. lib. bdg. 19.50 (ISBN 0-208-02066-7, Archon Bks). Shoe String.

Aker, George. Adult Education Procedures, Methods, & Techniques: A Classified & Annotated Bibliography 1953-1963. 1965. 5.00 (ISBN 0-87060-089-3, PRE 2). Syracuse U Cont Ed.

Aker, J. Brooke. Law of Wills in Pennsylvania: Drafting, Interpreting, Contesting, with Forms. LC 83-72488. (Illus.). 567p. 1983. 59.50 (ISBN 0-318-01450-5). Bisel Co.

Aker, J. Brooke & Shimer, Robert. How to Build a More Profitable Wills & Estates Practice. 2nd ed. 1977. 99.50 (ISBN 0-13-403055-9). Exec Reports.

Aker, J. Brooke & Walsh, Arthur C. Mental Capacity: Medical & Legal Aspects of the Aging. (Trial Publications). 372p. 1977. write for info. (Pub. By Shepard's-McGraw). McGraw.

Aker, Sharon, jt. auth. see Softsync Inc. Staff.

Aker, Sharon Z. Microsoft BASIC Programming for the Mac. 1985. pap. 17.95 (ISBN 0-673-18167-7). Scott F.

--T-S 2068 Basics & Beyond. LC 85-1777. 228p. 1985. pap. 9.95 (ISBN 0-673-18109-X). Scott F.

Akerberg, Hans, jt. auth. see Pettersson, Olof.

Akerlof, George A. An Economic Theorist's Book of Tales: Essays That Entertain the Consequences of New Assumptions in Economic Theory. (Illus.). 128p. 1984. 29.95 (ISBN 0-521-26323-9); pap. 8.95 (ISBN 0-521-26933-4). Cambridge U Pr.

Akerman, Forrest J., jt. auth. see Strickland, A. W.

Akerman, Joe. American Brahman: A History of the American Brahman Breed & the American Brahman Breeders Association. (Illus.). 384p. 1982. 17.50 (ISBN 0-318-12445-9); leather bound 52.50 (ISBN 0-318-12446-7). Am Brahman Breeders.

Akerman, Johan. Economic Progress & Economic Crises. LC 79-13175. (Illus.). 1980. Repr. of 1932 ed. lib. bdg. 19.50x (ISBN 0-87991-952-3). Porcupine Pr.
--Theory of Industrialism: Causal Analysis & Economic Plans. LC 80-21155. (Illus.). 1981. Repr. of 1960 ed. lib. bdg. 27.50x (ISBN 0-87991-859-4). Porcupine Pr.
Akerman, John Y. Tradesmen's Tokens, Current in London & Its Vicinity Between the Years 1648-1672. (Illus.). 1969. Repr. of 1849 ed. 22.50 (ISBN 0-8337-0029-4). B Franklin.
Akerman, John Y., ed. Letters from Roundhead Officers. LC 73-158237. (Bannatyne Club, Edinburgh. Publications: No. 101). Repr. of 1856 ed. 37.50 (ISBN 0-404-52849-X). AMS Pr.
Akerman, John Y., ed. see Guy, Henry.
Akeroyd, Richard H. He Is Nigh: An Exegesis of the Books of Daniel & Revelation. (Illus.). 1981. 8.95 (ISBN 0-916620-53-0). Portals Pr.
--He Made Us a Kingdom: The Principles to be Applied in Establishing Christ's Kingdon Now. 1985. 5.00 (ISBN 0-916620-79-4). Portals Pr.
--The Spiritual Quest of Albert Camus. LC 76-3324. 1976. 7.50 (ISBN 0-916620-03-4). Portals Pr.
--Through the Scent of Water: A Neo-Pauline Discourse on the Order of Christian Assembly. 1985. pap. 5.00 (ISBN 0-916620-71-9). Portals Pr.
Akeroyd, Richard H., tr. see Schlumberger, Jean.
Akers. Deviant Behavior. 3rd ed. 1984. write for info. (ISBN 0-534-03915-4). Wadsworth Pub.
Akers, Alan B. Krozair of Kregen. (The Krozair Cycle Ser.: No. 3). 1977. pap. 2.75 (ISBN 0-88677-037-8). DAW Bks.
--Renegade of Kregen. (The Krozair Cycle Ser.: No. 2). 1976. pap. 2.75 (ISBN 0-88677-035-1). DAW Bks.
--Tides of Kregen. (The Krozair Cycle Ser.: No. 1). 176p. 1976. pap. 2.75 (ISBN 0-88677-034-3). DAW Bks.
Akers, Carl. Carl Akers' Colorado. 1981. pap. 9.95 (ISBN 0-933472-53-6). Johnson Bks.
--Carl Akers' Comments. LC 79-83950. (Illus., Orig.). 1979. pap. 6.95 (ISBN 0-88342-242-5). Old Army.
Akers, Charles W. Abigail Adams: An American Woman. LC 79-2241. (Library of American Biography). 1980. 13.95 (ISBN 0-316-02041-9); pap. 6.95 (ISBN 0-316-02040-0). Little.
--The Divine Politician: Samuel Cooper & the American Revolution in Boston. LC 81-18917. (Illus.). 445p. 1982. 23.95x (ISBN 0-930350-19-7). NE U Pr.
Akers, Herbert A. Modern Mailroom Management. LC 78-18495. pap. 87.50 (ISBN 0-317-28206-9, 2055967). Bks Demand UMI.
Akers, Karen, ed. see Abraham, Sidney, et al.
Akers, Karen, ed. see Ford, Kathleen.
Akers, Lane, ed. see Charles, C. M.
Akers, Lynn R., jt. auth. see Ewen, Dale.
Akers, Michael J. Parenteral Quality Control: Sterility, Pyrogen, Particulate & Package Integrity Testing. (Advances in Parenteral Sciences Ser.). 256p. 1985. 55.00 (ISBN 0-8247-7357-8). Dekker.
Akers, Michael J., jt. auth. see Avis, Kenneth E.
Akers, R. J., ed. Foams. 1977. 55.00 (ISBN 0-12-047350-X). Acad Pr.
Akers, Ronald L. & Hawkins, Richard. Law & Control in Society. LC 74-22213. (Sociology Ser.). 384p. 1975. 25.95 (ISBN 0-13-526095-7). P-H.
Akers, Ronald L., jt. ed. see Krohn, Marvin D.
Akerson, Charles B. The Appraiser's Workbook. 262p. 1985. wkbk. 14.50 (ISBN 0-911780-75-0, 0075M). Am Inst Real Estate Appraisers.
--Capitalization Theory & Techniques Study Guide. 258p. 1984. pap. 14.50 spiral study guide (ISBN 0-911780-73-4). Am Inst Real Estate Appraisers.
Akerstrom, Malin. Crooks & Squares: Lifestyles of Thieves & Addicts in Comparison to Conventional People. 250p. 1985. 24.95 (ISBN 0-88738-058-1). Transaction Bks.
Akert, K., ed. Biological Order & Brain Organization: Selected Works of W. R. Hess. (Illus.). 347p. 1981. 61.00 (ISBN 0-387-10551-4). Springer-Verlag.
Akert, Konrad, jt. auth. see Emmers, Raimond.
Akeson, Nancy, jt. auth. see Harrel, Lois.
Akesson, N. B. & Yates, W. E. The Use of Aircraft for Mosquito Control, Oct. 1982. 96p. 10.00 (ISBN 0-686-84357-6). Am Mosquito.
--The Use of Aircraft in Agriculture. (Agricultural Development Papers: No. 94). (Illus.). 217p. 1974. pap. 12.25 (ISBN 92-5-100067-0, F488, FAO). Unipub.
Akesson, N. B., jt. ed. see Kaneko, T. M.
Akesson, Norman B. & Yates, Wesley E. Pesticide Application Equipment & Techniques. (Agricultural Services Bulletins: No. 38). 261p. 1979. pap. 18.75 (ISBN 92-5-100835-3, F1894, FAO). Unipub.
Akesson, Samuel K., ed. see True, Adiaha.
Akey, Denise, ed. Encyclopedia of Associations: National Organizations of the U. S, 2 pts, Vol. 1. 19th ed. LC 76-46129. 2000p. 1984. 195.00x (ISBN 0-8103-1690-0). Gale.
--New Associations & Projects. 19th ed. (Encyclopedia of Associations Ser.: Vol. 3). 1984. text ed. 190.00x (ISBN 0-8103-0130-X). Gale.
Akey, Denise S., ed. Encyclopedia of Associations: Geographic & Executive Index, Vol. 2. 19th ed. 1080p. 1984. 175.00x (ISBN 0-8103-1691-9). Gale.
Akgul. Topics in Relaxation & Ellipsoidal Methods. (Research Notes in Mathematics: No. 97). 336p. 1984. pap. text ed. 24.95 (ISBN 0-273-08634-0). Pitman Pub MA.
Akhadov, Ya Y. Dielectric Properties of Binary Solutions: A Data Handbook. 400p. 1981. 125.00 (ISBN 0-08-023600-6). Pergamon.
Akhand, Dorothea G. Student's Workbook of Grammar Exercises. (Pitt Series in English as a Second Language). 100p. (Orig.). 1976. pap. text ed. 4.95x (ISBN 0-8229-8206-4, Pub. by U Ctr Intl St). U of Pittsburgh Pr.
Akhandananda, Swami. Service of God in Man. 186p. 3.50 (ISBN 0-87481-503-7). Vedanta Pr.
Akhapkin, Yuri. First Decrees of Soviet Power. 1970 ed. 186p. 16.00 (ISBN 0-686-37391-X). Beekman Pubs.
Akhavi, Shahrough. Religion & Politics in Contemporary Iran. LC 79-22084. 1980. 39.50x (ISBN 0-87395-408-4); pap. 12.95x (ISBN 0-87395-456-4). State U NY Pr.
Akheizer, N. I. Theory of Linear Operators in Hilbert Space, Vol. 1. Everitt, N., ed. Dawson, E. R., tr. (Monographs & Studies: No. 9). 320p. 1980. text ed. 89.95 (ISBN 0-273-08495-X). Pitman Pub MA.
Akheizer, N. I. & Glazman, I. M. Theory of Linear Operators in Hilbert Space, Vol. 2. Everitt, N., ed. Dawson, E. R., tr. (Monographs & Studies: No. 10). 280p. 1980. text ed. 84.50 (ISBN 0-273-08496-8). Pitman Pub MA.
Akhemtov, N. Inorganic Chemistry. 640p. 1975. 19.95x (ISBN 0-8464-1262-4). Beekman Pubs.
Akhiezer, A. I., et al. Collective Oscillations in a Plasma. 1967. 26.00 (ISBN 0-08-011894-1). Pergamon.
Akhiezer, N. I. Theory of Approximation. Hyman, Charles J., tr. LC 56-11950. 1956. 16.50 (ISBN 0-8044-4019-0). Ungar.
Akhiezer, N. I. & Glazman, I. M. Theory of Linear Operators in Hilbert Space, 2 Vols. Nestell, Merlynd, tr. LC 60-53138. Vol. 1. 12.50 (ISBN 0-8044-4022-0); Vol. 2. 16.50 (ISBN 0-8044-4023-9). Ungar.
Akhiezev, A. I. & Peletminskii, S. V. Methods of Statistical Physics. Schukin, M., tr. (International Series in Natural Philosophy: Vol. 104). (Illus.). 462p. 1981. 59.00 (ISBN 0-08-025040-8). Pergamon.
Akhilananda, Swami. Hindu Psychology: Its Meaning for the West. pap. 12.00 (ISBN 0-8283-1353-9). Branden Pub Co.
--Hindu View of Christ. pap. 12.00 (ISBN 0-8283-1355-5). Branden Pub Co.
--Mental Health & Hindu Psychology. pap. 12.00 (ISBN 0-8283-1354-7). Branden Pub Co.
--Modern Problems & Religion. pap. 9.00 (ISBN 0-8283-1146-3). Branden Pub Co.
--Spiritual Practices. LC 78-175140. 1972. 12.00 (ISBN 0-8283-1350-4). Branden Pub Co.
Akhmadi, Heri. Breaking the Chains of Oppression of the Indonesian People: Defense Statement at His Trial on Charges of Insulting the Head of State, Bandung, June 7-10, 1979. (Translation Ser.: No. 59). 201p. 1981. 8.75 (ISBN 0-87763-001-1). Cornell Mod Indo.
Akhmanov, S. A. & Khoklov, R. V. Problems of Nonlinear Optics. Sen, R., ed. Jacobi, N., tr. from Russian. LC 78-131021. 310p. 1972. 61.50 (ISBN 0-677-30400-5). Gordon.
Akhmanova, O. English-Russian Dictionary. 613p. (Eng. & Rus.). 1975. 4.45 (ISBN 0-8285-0586-1, Pub. by Rus Lang Pubs USSR). Imported Pubns.
--Optimization of Natural Communication Systems. (Juana Linguarum, Ser. Minor: No. 92). 116p. 1977. 16.00 (ISBN 90-279-3146-1). Mouton.
Akhmanova, O. S. & Wilson, E. English-Russian Dictionary. 639p. (Rus. & Eng.). 1979. 9.95 (ISBN 0-686-97370-4, M-9115). French & Eur.
Akhmanova, O. S., et al. Exact Methods in Linguistic Research. Haynes, David G. & Mohr, Dolores V., trs. LC 63-19957. 1963. 44.00x (ISBN 0-520-00542-2). U of Cal Pr.
Akhmanova, Olga. Phonology, Morphonology, Morphology. LC 72-159459. (Janua Linguarum, Ser. Minor: No. 101). 135p. 1971. pap. text ed. 16.00x (ISBN 90-2791-748-5). Mouton.
Akhmanova, Olga & Mikael'An, Galina. Theory of Syntax in Modern Linguistics. LC 69-13300. (Janua Linguarum, Ser. Minor: No. 68). (Orig.). 1969. pap. text ed. 17.60x (ISBN 90-2790-683-1). Mouton.
Akhmatova, Anna. Anna Akhmatova: Selected Poems. Arndt, Walter, ed. Kemball, Robin & Proffer, Carl, trs. from Rus. 1976. pap. 5.95 (ISBN 0-88233-180-9). Ardis Pubs.
--Chetki. 1972. pap. 3.00 (ISBN 0-88233-029-2). Ardis Pubs.
--Poems. Coffin, Lyn, tr. from Rus. 1983. 15.50 (ISBN 0-393-01567-X); pap. 6.95 (ISBN 0-393-30014-5). Norton.
--Requiem & Poem Without a Hero. Thomas, D. M., tr. from Rus. LC 76-7252. 78p. 1976. 10.00x (ISBN 0-8214-0350-8, 82-82402); pap. 5.50 (ISBN 0-8214-0357-5, 82-82410). Ohio U Pr.
--Way of All the Earth. Thomas, D. M., tr. from Rus. LC 79-1953. 96p. 1980. 11.95x (ISBN 0-8214-0429-6, 82-83186); pap. 6.95 (ISBN 0-8214-0430-X, 82-83194). Ohio U Pr.
--You Will Hear Thunder: Poems. Thomas, D. M., tr. from Rus. LC 84-62245. 147p. 1985. text ed. 22.00x (ISBN 0-8214-0805-4); pap. text ed. 11.00x (ISBN 0-8214-0806-2). Ohio U Pr.
Akhmedov, Ismail. In & Out of Stalin's GRU. 1983. 20.00 (ISBN 0-89093-546-7). U Pubns Amer.
Akhmetov, N. General & Inorganic Chemistry. 670p. 1983. 13.95 (ISBN 0-8285-2567-6, Pub. by Mir Pubs USSR). Imported Pubns.
--Problems & Laboratory Experiments in Inorganic Chemistry. 256p. 1982. 8.95 (ISBN 0-8285-2443-2, Pub. by Mir Pubs USSR). Imported Pubns.
Akhmetov, Nail. Inorganic Chemistry. 565p. text ed. cancelled (ISBN 0-8290-1479-9). Irvington.
Akhrem, A. A. & Titov, Y. A. Total Steroid Synthesis. LC 69-12525. 362p. 1970. 45.00x (ISBN 0-306-30380-9, Plenum Pr). Plenum Pub.
Akhrem, A. A., et al. Birch Reduction of Aromatic Compounds. LC 70-183103. 132p. 1972. 45.00x (ISBN 0-306-65158-0, Plenum Pr). Plenum Pub.
Akhtar, S. Health Care in the People's Republic of China: A Bibliography with Abstracts. 182p. 1975. pap. 18.50 (ISBN 0-88936-044-8, IDRC38, IDRC). Unipub.
Akhtar, Salman, ed. New Psychiatric Syndromes: DSM-III & Beyond. LC 83-3785. 402p. 1983. 30.00 (ISBN 0-87668-614-5). Aronson.
Aki, Keiiti & Richards, Paul G. Quantitative Seismology: Theory & Methods, Vol. I. LC 79-17434. (Geology Bks.). (Illus.). 573p. 1980. text ed. 47.95 (ISBN 0-7167-1058-7). W H Freeman.
--Quantitative Seismology: Theory & Methods, Vol. II. LC 79-17434. (Geology Bks.). (Illus.). 389p. 1980. text ed. 47.95 (ISBN 0-7167-1059-5). W H Freeman.
Akian, Gail G., jt. auth. see Breton, Raymond.
Akiba, K. Bond Switch at Hypervalent Sulfur in Thiathiophtene Analogous Systems. (Sulfur Reports Ser.). Date not set. price not set flexicover (ISBN 3-7186-0037-4). Harwood Academic.
Akiba, T., jt. auth. see Horikoshi, K.
Akiba Ben Joseph. Book of Formation - Sepher Yetzirah. Stenring, Kurt, tr. 7.95x (ISBN 0-87068-008-0). Ktav.
Akihiro, Amano, et al. Japan-U. S. Assembly: Proceedings of a Conference of Japan-U.S. Economic Policy, Vol. 1. 1975. pap. 6.25 (ISBN 0-8447-2061-5). Am Enterprise.
Akillian, Michael. The Eating of Names. LC 83-7097. 64p. 1983. pap. 3.95 (ISBN 0-935102-13-2). Ashod Pr.
Akilon. Portrait of a Woman. Nandakumar, Prema, tr. from Indian. 1984. pap. 7.00x (ISBN 0-8364-1095-5, Pub. by Macmillan India). South Asia Bks.
Akilov, G. P., jt. auth. see Kantorovich, L. V.
Akim, Y. Desmanado. (Illus.). 15p. (Span.). 1978. pap. 0.99 (ISBN 0-8285-1291-4, Pub. by Progress Pubs USSR). Imported Pubns.
--Helpless Can't Do. 16p. 1977. pap. 0.99 (ISBN 0-686-86117-5, Pub. by Progress Pubs USSR). Imported Pubns.
Akimoto, Haruo, et al, eds. see Epilepsy International Symposium, 13th., et al.
Akimoto, S. & Manghnani, M. H. High Pressure Research in Geophysics. 1982. 113.00 (ISBN 90-277-1439-8, Pub. by Reidel Holland). Kluwer Academic.
Akimov, Vladimir. Vladimir Akimov on the Dilemmas of Russian Marxism 1895-1903: Two Texts in Translation. Frankel, Jonathan, ed. (Cambridge Studies in the History & Theory of Politics). (Illus.). 1969. 54.50 (ISBN 0-521-05029-4). Cambridge U Pr.
Akimov, Yu K. Scintillation Counters in High Energy Physics. 1965. 49.00 (ISBN 0-12-047450-6). Acad Pr.
Akimova, V. Vishnyakova see Vishnyakova-Akimova, Vera V.
Akimushkin, I. Adonde? y Como? 375p. (Span.). 1973. 5.95 (ISBN 0-8285-1462-3, Pub. by Mir Pubs USSR). Imported Pubns.
--Animal Travelers. 375p. 1973. pap. 3.45 (ISBN 0-8285-0814-3, Pub. by Mir Pubs USSR). Imported Pubns.
--Rare Animals. (Illus.). 16p. 1978. pap. 1.99 (ISBN 0-8285-8817-1, Pub. by Progress Pubs USSR). Imported Pubns.
Akimushkin, Igor. Builders in the Wild. Yankowskaya, Eleanor, tr. 24p. 1982. pap. 1.99 (ISBN 0-8285-2363-0, Pub. by Malysh Pubs USSR). Imported Pubns.
Akin, E. The Geometry of Population Genetics. (Lecture Notes in Biomathematics: Vol. 31). 205p. 1979. pap. 18.00 (ISBN 0-387-09711-2). Springer-Verlag.
Akin, Ethan. Hopf Bifuraction in the Two Locus Genetic Model. LC 83-6438. (Memoirs of the American Mathematical Society: No. 284). 192p. 1983. pap. 16.00 (ISBN 0-8218-2284-5). Am Math.
Akin, Herbert L. Clergy Compensation & Financial Planning Workbook. (Illus.). 100p. 1982. wkbk. 6.95 (ISBN 0-938736-05-1). Life Enrich.
--Nineteen Ninety-Nine. LC 81-80962. (Illus.). 260p. 1981. 4.95 (ISBN 0-938736-03-5). Life Enrich.
Akin, J. E. Application & Implementation of Finite Element Methods. LC 81-69597. (Computational Mathematics & Applications Ser.). 1982. 60.00 (ISBN 0-12-047650-9). Acad Pr.
--Applications & Implementation of Finite Element Methods. 1984. pap. 25.00 (ISBN 0-12-047652-5). Acad Pr.
Akin, J. E. & Gray, W. H., eds. Computer Technology in Fusion Energy Research: PVP-PB-31. 117p. 1978. 18.00 (ISBN 0-317-33466-2, H00136); members 9.00 (ISBN 0-317-33467-0). ASME.
Akin, James. Journal of James Akin. 32p. 1971. Repr. of 1919 ed. pap. 3.00 (ISBN 0-87770-029-X). Ye Galleon.
Akin, John S., et al. The Demand for Primary Health Services in the Third World. LC 84-18153. (Illus.). 208p. 1985. 39.95x (ISBN 0-8476-7355-3). Rowman & Allanheld.
Akin, Johnnye. Crayfish International Cookbook. Woolfolk, Doug, ed. (Illus.). 210p. (Orig.). 1981. spiral bd 9.95 (ISBN 0-86518-023-7). Moran Pub Corp.
Akin, Johnnye & Goltry, T. S. Terms Used in Whitewater Kayaking in Colorado. Bd. with Collegiate Slang: Aspects of Word Formation & Semantic Change. Seymour, Richard K; The Vocabulary of Race Relations in a Prison. Kantrowitz, Nathan. (Publications of the American Dialect Society: No. 51). 46p. 1969. pap. 4.15 (ISBN 0-8173-0651-X). U of Ala Pr.
Akin, Johnnye, et al, eds. Language Behavior: A Book of Readings in Communication. LC 77-110948. (Janua Linguarum, Ser. Major: No. 41). 1970. text ed. 38.40x (ISBN 90-2791-244-0). Mouton.
Akin, Katy. Impassioned Cows by Moonlight. 72p. 1975. pap. 3.00 (ISBN 0-914610-02-3). Hanging Loose.
Akin, Richard H. The Private Investigator's Basic Manual. 208p. 1979. 19.75x (ISBN 0-398-03520-2). C C Thomas.
Akin, William E. Technocracy & the American Dream: The Technocrat Movement, 1900-1941. LC 75-22651. 1977. 32.00x (ISBN 0-520-03110-5). U of Cal Pr.
Akina, J. K., jt. auth. see Kaaiakamanu, D. M.
Akiner, Shirin. Islamic Peoples of the Soviet Union. (Illus.). 451p. 1983. 50.00x (ISBN 0-7103-0025-5, Kegan Paul). Routledge & Kegan.
Akins, Dianna L., et al. The Hospitalized Child: Psychosocial Issues - an Abstracted Bibliography. LC 81-12007. (IFI Data Base Library). 302p. 1981. 75.00 (ISBN 0-306-65199-8, IFI Plenum). Plenum Pub.
Akins, F. R., et al. Behavioral Development of Nonhuman Primates: An Abstracted Bibliography. LC 79-26700. 314p. 1980. 85.00x (ISBN 0-306-65189-0, IFI Plenum). Plenum Pub.
--Parent-Child Separation: Psychosocial Effects on Development. 368p. 1981. 85.00x (ISBN 0-306-65196-3, IFI Plenum). Plenum Pub.
Akins, William R. ESP: Your Psychic Powers & How to Test Them. LC 79-23929. (gr. 4 up). 1980. PLB 8.90 (ISBN 0-531-02947-6). Watts.
Akinsanya, Adeoye. Multinationals in a Changing Environment: A Study of Business & Government Relations in the Third World. LC 83-24592. 208p. 1984. 34.95 (ISBN 0-03-059866-4). Praeger.
Akinsanya, Adeoye A. The Expropriation of Multinational Property in the Third World: Finance Trade & Investment. (Int'l Business Ser.). 400p. 1980. 39.95 (ISBN 0-03-055811-5). Praeger.
Akintoye, S. A. Emergent African States: Topics in Twentieth Century African History. 1977. pap. text ed. 10.95x (ISBN 0-582-60127-4). Longman.
--Revolution & Power Politics in Yoruvaland 1840-1893: Ibadan Expansion & the Rise of Ekitparapo. (Ibadan History Ser). 1971. text ed. 11.50x (ISBN 0-391-00168-X). Humanities.
Akira, Oki, jt. ed. see Reid, Anthony.
Akisada, Masayoshi & Fujimoto, Yoshihide. Soft Tissue Roentgenography in Diagnosis of Thyroid Cancer. LC 74-2582. 142p. 1974. 22.50x (ISBN 0-306-30783-9, Plenum Pr). Plenum Pub.
--Soft Tissue Roentgenography in Diagnosis of Thyroid Cancer: Detection of Psammoma Bodies by Spot-tangential Projection. LC 74-176722. pap. 35.80 (ISBN 0-317-27214-4, 2024710). Bks Demand UMI.
Akishev, K. Issyk Mound: The Art of the Ska in Kazakhstan. 132p. 1978. 40.00x (ISBN 0-317-14240-2, Pub. by Collet's). State Mutual Bk.
Akishina, A. Russian Speech Conventions for English-Speaking Students of Russian. 176p. 1983. pap. 3.95 (ISBN 0-8285-2762-8, Pub. by Rus Lang Pubs USSR). Imported Pubns.
Akita, George. Foundations of Constitutional Government in Modern Japan, 1868-1900. LC 65-13835. (East Asian Ser: No. 23). 1967. 18.50x (ISBN 0-674-31250-3). Harvard U Pr.
Akitt, J. W. NMR & Chemistry: An Introduction to the Fourier Transform-Multinuclear Era. 2nd ed. (Illus.). 224p. 1983. 39.95 (ISBN 0-412-24010-6, NO. 6807, Pub. by Chapman & Hall); pap. 17.95 (ISBN 0-412-24020-3, NO. 6808). Methuen Inc.
Akivis, M. A. & Goldberg, V. V. An Introduction to Linear Algebra & Tensors. rev. ed. Silverman, Richard A., ed. LC 77-78589. 1977. pap. 4.00 (ISBN 0-486-63545-7). Dover.
Akiwowo, Akinsola, jt. ed. see Dofny, Jacques.
Akiyama, Aisaburo. Buddhist Hand-Symbol. LC 78-72367. Repr. of 1939 ed. 22.50 (ISBN 0-404-17214-8). AMS Pr.

Akiyama, Carol. The Language of Air Travel in English-in-Flight Services. (English for Careers). (gr. 10 up). 1976. pap. 4.25 (ISBN 0-88345-255-3, 18501). Regents Pub.

Akiyama, Carol & Akiyama, Nobuo. Japanese at a Glance. (At a Glance Ser.). 256p. 1985. pap. 4.95 (ISBN 0-8120-2850-3). Barron.

Akiyama, Nobuo, jt. auth. see Akiyama, Carol.

Akiyama, Nubuo. SR Japanese. (SR Japanese Ser.). 1970. pap. text ed. 4.95 (ISBN 0-88499-125-3); tapebk. 3.95 (ISBN 0-88499-126-1); cassette set 135.00 (ISBN 0-88499-199-7); tape set 295.00 (ISBN 0-88499-198-9). Inst Mod Lang.

Akiyama, Takamasa & Duncan, Ronald C. Analysis of the World Coffee Market. (Working Paper: No. 7). v, 54p. 1982. pap. 3.00 (ISBN 0-686-39657-X, CP-0007). World Bank.

Akiyama, Terukazu & Matsubara, Saburo. Arts of China, Vol. 2: Buddhist Cave Temples. Soper, Alexander, tr. LC 68-17454. (Arts of China Ser: Vol. 2). (Illus.). 248p. 1973. 89.00 (ISBN 0-87011-089-6). Kodansha.

Akiyama, Terukazu, et al. Arts of China, Vol. 1: Neolithic Cultures to the T'ang Dynasty. LC 68-17454. (Arts of China Ser.: Vol. 1). (Illus.). 1973. 89.00 (ISBN 0-87011-064-0). Kodansha.

Akizuki, Tatsuichiro. Nagasaki, Nineteen-Forty-Five. Honeycombe, Gordon, ed. (Illus.). 168p. 1982. pap. 5.95 (ISBN 0-7043-3382-1, Pub. by Quartet England). Charles River Bks.

Akkas, N. Progress on Biomechanics. (NATO Advaned Study Institute Ser.). 395p. 1979. 37.50x (ISBN 90-286-0479-0). Sijthoff & Noordhoff.

Akkerman, Fokke. Studies in the Posthumous Works of Spinoza: On Style, Earliest Translation & Reception, Earliest & Modern Edition of Some Texts. vi, 285p. (Orig.). 1980. pap. 17.00x (ISBN 0-317-19838-6, Pub. by Boumas Boekhuis Netherlands). Benjamins North AM.

Akkermans, A. D., et al, eds. Frankia Symbioses: Proceedings of the Workshop on Frankia Symbioses, Wageningen, September 5-6, 1983. 258p. 1984. 50.00 (ISBN 90-247-2967-X, Pub. by Martinus Nijhoff Netherlands). Kluwer Academic.

Akkermans, L. M., et al, eds. Gastric & Gastroduodenal Motility. Read, R. W. LC 84-16090. (Surgical Science Ser.: Vol. 4). 244p. 1984. 40.00 (ISBN 0-03-000929-4). Praeger.

Akl, Selim G. Parallel Sorting Alogorithms. Date not set. 49.00 (ISBN 0-12-047680-0). Acad Pr.

Aklonis, John J. & MacKnight, William J. Introduction to Polymer Viscoelasticity. 2nd ed. LC 82-17528. 295p. 1983. 39.95x (ISBN 0-471-86729-2, Pub. by Wiley Interscience). Wiley.

Aklonis, John J., et al, eds. Introduction to Polymer Viscoelasticity. 249p. 1972. 34.95 (ISBN 0-471-01860-0). Wiley.

Akmajian, Adrian. Aspects of the Grammar of Focus in English. Hankamer, Jorge, ed. LC 78-66534. (Outstanding Dissertations in Linguistics Ser.). 1985. 45.00 (ISBN 0-8240-9691-6). Garland Pub.

Akmajian, Adrian, et al. Linguistics: An Introduction to Language & Communication. 2nd ed. 536p. 1984. text ed. 30.00x (ISBN 0-262-01078-X); pap. text ed. 16.95x (ISBN 0-262-51029-4). MIT Pr.

Akmanova, A. English-Russian Dictionary. 590p. (Eng. & Rus.). 1980. 25.00x (ISBN 0-569-00012-2, Pub. by Collet's). State Mutual Bk.

Akmanova, O. S. & Wilson, E. A. Russian-English Dictionary. 521p. (Rus. & Eng.). 1974. 4.45 (ISBN 0-8285-0607-8, Pub. by Rus Lang Pubs USSR). Imported Pubns.

Akoka, J., ed. Management of Distributed Data Processing: Proceedings of the International Conference, Paris, France, June 23-26, 1982. 294p. 1982. 40.50 (ISBN 0-444-86458-X, I-299-82, North Holland). Elsevier.

Akopjan, S. A., et al. Fifteen Papers on Analysis. LC 51-5559. (Translations Ser.: No. 2, Vol. 72). 1968. 35.00 (ISBN 0-8218-1772-8, TRANS 2-72). Am Math.

Akoun, et al. Encyclopedie de la Sociologie. new ed. 536p. (Fr.). 1975. 23.00x (ISBN 2-03-070101-7). Larousse.

Akoyunoglou, G. Cell Function & Differentiation, Pt. C. LC 82-21658. (Progress in Clinical & Biological Research Ser.: Vol. 102C). 382p. 1982. 42.00 (ISBN 0-8451-0167-6). A R Liss.

--Cell Function & Differentiation, Pt. B. LC 82-21658. (Progress in Clinical & Biological Research Ser.: Vol. 102B). 544p. 1982. 60.00 (ISBN 0-8451-0166-8). A R Liss.

--Cell Function & Differentiation: Pt. A, Erythroid Differentiation, Hormone-Gene Interaction, Glycoconjugates, Liposomes. LC 82-21658. (Progress in Clinical & Biological Research Ser.: Vol. 102A). 550p. 1982. 60.00 (ISBN 0-8451-0165-X). A R Liss.

Akoyunoglou, George, ed. Chloroplast Development, Vol. 5. 1104p. 1981. 102.00 (ISBN 0-86689-010-6, 992200075). Balaban Intl Sci Serv.

--PhotoPhysical Process Membrane Energization, Vol. 1. 792p. 75.00 (ISBN 0-86689-006-8, 992200032). Balaban Intl Sci Serv.

--Photosynthesis, 6 vols. (Illus.). 5570p. 1981. Set. text ed. 499.00; Vol. 1. text ed. 75.00 (ISBN 0-86689-012-2); Vol. 2. text ed. 108.00 (ISBN 0-86689-006-8); Vol. 3. text ed. 109.00 (ISBN 0-86689-008-4); Vol. 4. text ed. 79.00 (ISBN 0-86689-009-2); Vol. 5. text ed. 102.00 (ISBN 0-86689-010-6); Vol. 6. text ed. 75.00 (ISBN 0-86689-011-4). Balaban Intl Sci Serv.

--Photosynthetic Election Transport & Phophosphorylation, Vol. 2. 1114p. 108.00 (ISBN 0-86689-007-6, 992200040). Balaban Intl Sci Serv.

--Structure & Molecular Organization of the Photosynthetic Membrane, Vol. 3. 1112p. 109.00 (ISBN 0-86689-008-4, 992200040). Balaban Intl Sci Serv.

Akpabot, Samuel E. Ibibi Music in Nigerian Culture. (Illus.). 140p. 1975. 7.50x (ISBN 0-87013-193-1). Mich St U Pr.

Akpalu, Vinoko. When Sorrow-Song Descends on You. Barkan, Stanley H., ed. Awoonor, Kofi, tr. (Cross-Cultural Review Chapbook 14: African Ghanaian Poetry 1). 16p. (Ewe & Eng.). 1981. pap. 2.00 (ISBN 0-89304-813-5). Cross Cult.

Akpan, Moses E. African Goals & Diplomatic Strategies in the United Nations. LC 76-4263. (Illus.). 192p. 1976. 9.95 (ISBN 0-8158-0335-4). Chris Mass.

Akpan, Ntieyong U. Epitaph to Indirect Rule: Local Government in Africa. 204p. 1967. 28.50x (ISBN 0-7146-1043-7, BHA 01043, F Cass Co). Biblio Dist.

--Struggle for Succession, 1966-1970: Personal Account of the Nigerian Civil War. 220p. 1972. 24.00x (ISBN 0-7146-2930-8, BHA 02930, F Cass Co); pap. 9.95x (ISBN 0-7146-2949-9, BHA 02949, F Cass Co). Biblio Dist.

Akrasanee, Narangchai, jt. ed. see Rieger, H. C.

Akrasanee, Narongchai. Thailand & Asian Economic Cooperation. 162p. (Orig.). 1981. pap. text ed. 20.00x (ISBN 9971-902-10-9, Pub. by Inst Southeast Asian Stud). Gower Pub Co.

Akrasanee, Narongchai, ed. ASEAN-Japan Relations: Trade & Development. (Institute Southeast Asian Studies). 200p. (Orig.). 1984. pap. text ed. 26.00x (ISBN 9971-902-63-X). Gower Pub Co.

Akrasanee, Narongchai, et al, eds. Trade & Employment in Asia & the Pacific. 1977. pap. text ed. 15.00x (ISBN 0-8248-0573-9). UH Pr.

Akre, Nancy, ed. Miniatures. Cooper-Hewitt Museum. LC 82-72762. (Smithsonian Illustrated Library of Antiques Ser.). (Illus.). 128p. (Orig.). 1983. 9.95 (ISBN 0-910503-45-1). Cooper Hewitt Museum.

Akre, Nancy, ed. see Benjamin, Susan.

Akre, Nancy, ed. see Harting, Joan L.

Akre, Nancy, ed. see Johnson, Hugh, et al.

Akre, Nancy, ed. see Ketchum, William C., Jr.

Akre, Nancy, ed. see Moss, Gillian.

Akre, Nancy, et al, eds. see Dee, Elaine E.

Akre, Nancy, et al, eds. see Harris, John.

Akre, Nancy, et al, eds. see MacDonald, William L.

Akre, Nancy, et al, eds. see McFadden, David R.

Akre, Nancy, et al, eds. see Snowman, A. K.

Akridge, Garth H. Pupil Progress Policies & Practices. LC 70-176505. (Columbia University. Teachers College. Contributions to Education: No. 691). Repr. of 1937 ed. 22.50 (ISBN 0-404-55691-4). AMS Pr.

Akrigg, D. West Yorkshire P. T. E. 32p. 1984. 20.00x (ISBN 0-86093-092-0, Pub. by ORPC Ltd UK). State Mutual Bk.

Akrigg, G. P., ed. Letters of King James VI & I. LC 82-20135. 504p. 1984. lib. bdg. 38.50x (ISBN 0-520-04707-9). U of Cal Pr.

Akroyd, Robert. A Guide to Contracting for the Sale of Goods. 208p. (Orig.). 1984. pap. 17.95x (ISBN 0-7102-0005-6). Routledge & Kegan.

Aks, Pat. Lisa's Choice. 192p. 1981. pap. 1.95 (ISBN 0-448-16997-5, Pub. by Tempo). Ace Bks.

Aks, Patricia. Junior Prom. 176p. (Orig.). (gr. 7 up). 1982. pap. 1.95 (ISBN 0-590-32003-3, Wildfire). Scholastic Inc.

--Lisa's Choice. 160p. (Orig.). 1985. pap. 2.25 (ISBN 0-449-70097-6, Juniper). Fawcett.

--A New Kind of Love. 160p. 1982. pap. 1.95 (ISBN 0-449-70019-4, Juniper). Fawcett.

--No More Candy. 176p. (gr. 5 up). 1982. pap. 2.25 (ISBN 0-448-16958-4, Pub. by Tempo). Ace Bks.

--The Searching Heart. (YA) (gr. 7 up). 1983. pap. 1.95 (ISBN 0-449-70057-7, Juniper). Fawcett.

--Senior Prom. 176p. (Orig.). (gr. 7 up). 1985. pap. 2.25 (ISBN 0-590-33553-7, Wildfire). Scholastic Inc.

--Two by Two Romance, No. 3: Change of Heart. 192p. (Orig.). 1983. pap. 1.95 (ISBN 0-446-30803-X). Warner Bks.

--The Two Worlds of Jill. 192p. (Orig.). (gr. 7 up). 1981. pap. 1.95 (ISBN 0-590-31801-2, Wishing Star Bks). Scholastic Inc.

--You Don't Have to Be a Perfect Girl. 192p. (Orig.). (gr. 7-12). 1981. pap. 1.95 (ISBN 0-590-31397-5). Scholastic Inc.

Aksakov, S. Family Chronicle: Childhood Years of Bagrov Grandson. 540p. 1985. 14.95 (ISBN 0-8285-2906-X, Pub. by Raduga Pubs USSR). Imported Pubns.

--The Little Scarlet Flower. 30p. 1976. pap. 1.99 (ISBN 0-8285-1192-6, Pub. by Progress Pubs USSR). Imported Pubns.

Aksakov, S. T. The Family Chronicle. Beverley, M. C., tr. from Rus. LC 85-7977. 256p. 1985. Repr. of 1961 ed. lib. bdg. 35.00x (ISBN 0-313-24835-4, AKCH). Greenwood.

Aksakov, Sergei. A Russian Gentleman. Crankshaw, Edward, ed. Duff, J. D., tr. from Rus. (World's Classics Paperback Ser.). 1982. pap. 6.95 (ISBN 0-19-281573-3). Oxford U Pr.

--A Russian Schoolboy. Duff, J. D., tr. from Rus. (The World's Classics-Paperback Ser.). 1983. pap. 6.95 (ISBN 0-19-281575-X). Oxford U Pr.

--Years of Childhood. Duff, J. D., tr. from Rus. (The World's Classics-Paperback Ser.). 1983. pap. 7.95 (ISBN 0-19-281574-1). Oxford U Pr.

Aksakov, Sergei T. Memoirs of the Aksakov Family, 3 vols. Duff, J., tr. from Rus. Incl. Vol. 1. A Russian Gentleman. LC 76-23869. 15.50 (ISBN 0-88355-469-0); pap. 10.00 (ISBN 0-88355-470-4); Vol. II. Years of Childhood. LC 76-23870. 15.00 (ISBN 0-88355-471-2); pap. 10.00 (ISBN 0-88355-472-0); Vol III. A Russian Schoolboy. LC 76-23871. Repr. of 1917 ed. 15.05 (ISBN 0-88355-473-9); pap. 10.00 (ISBN 0-88355-474-7). (Classics of Russian Literature). 1977. Repr. of 1917 ed. Hyperion Conn.

Aksen, Gerald, et al. International Arbitration Between Private Parties & Governments: A Course Handbook. 471p. 1982. 35.00 (ISBN 0-317-11484-0, B4-6624). PLI.

Aksenov, Vasilii. Aristofaniana S Lyagushkami: Aristophaniana & the Frogs. LC 81-7000. (Illus.). 384p. (Rus.). 1981. pap. 11.50 (ISBN 0-938920-07-3). Hermitage.

--Bumazhnyi Peizazh. 140p. 1983. 21.50 (ISBN 0-88233-857-9); pap. 7.00 (ISBN 0-88233-858-7). Ardis Pubs.

--Skazhi Izium. 375p. 1985. 25.00 (ISBN 0-88233-518-9). Ardis Pubs.

Aksenov, Vasily. Ostrov Krym. 330p. (Rus.). 1981. pap. 12.50 (ISBN 0-88233-719-X). Ardis Pubs.

--Pravo na Ostrov. LC 83-8924. 180p. (Orig.). 1983. pap. 7.00 (ISBN 0-938920-34-0). Hermitage.

Aksenov, Vasily P. Ozhog. (Rus.). 1980. pap. 12.50 (ISBN 0-88233-601-0). Ardis Pubs.

--Zolotaia Nasha Zhelezka. (Rus.). 1979. pap. 6.50 (ISBN 0-88233-480-8). Ardis Pubs.

Aksenova, Ludmila, tr. see Volkov, M. & Dedova, V.

Aksomaitis, A., et al. Twenty-Nine Papers on Statistics & Probability. LC 61-9803. (Selected Translations in Mathematical Statistics & Probability Ser.: Vol. 9). 1971. 37.00 (ISBN 0-8218-1459-1, STAPRO-9). Am Math.

Aksyonov, Vasily. Our Golden Ironburg. Peterson, Ronald E., tr. from Rus. 200p. 1986. 23.50 (ISBN 0-88233-559-6). Ardis Pubs.

--Sobranie Sochinenii: Complete Works, Vol. 1. Meyer, Priscilla, ed. 250p. (Rus.). 1985. 25.00 (ISBN 0-87501-026-1). Ardis Pubs.

--Surplussed Barrelware. Wilkinson, Joel & Yastremski, Slava, eds. LC 84-6348. 228p. 1985. 23.50 (ISBN 0-88233-904-4). Ardis Pubs.

--Zatovarennaya Bochkotara - Randevu. 2nd ed. Poliak, Gregory, ed. (Illus.). 100p. (Orig., Russian.). pap. 7.50 (ISBN 0-940294-02-8). Silver Age Pub.

Aksyonov, Vasily, et al, eds. Metropol: A Literary Almanac. 1983. 24.95 (ISBN 0-393-01438-X). Norton.

Aksyonov, Vassily. The Burn. Glenny, Michael, tr. LC 84-42521. 528p. 1984. 18.95 (ISBN 0-394-52492-6). Random.

--The Burn: Late 60's-Early 70's, 3 bks. Glenny, Michael, tr. 528p. (Rus.). 1984. Set. 19.95 (ISBN 0-317-07248-X). HM.

--The Island of Crimea. Heim, Michael H., tr. pap. 16.95 (ISBN 0-394-52431-4). Random.

--The Island of Crimea. LC 84-7300. 384p. 1984. pap. 8.95 (ISBN 0-394-72765-7, Vin). Random.

Akutagawa, Ryunosuke. Exotic Japanese Stories. (Illus.). 480p. cloth 1964 6.95 (ISBN 0-87140-994-1); pap. 4.95 paper 1972 (ISBN 0-87140-264-5). Liveright.

--Hell Screen & Other Stories. Norman, W. H., tr. LC 78-98800. Repr. of 1948 ed. lib. bdg. 22.50x (ISBN 0-8371-3017-4, AKHS). Greenwood.

--Kappa. Shiojiri, Seiichi, tr. LC 71-98801. Repr. of 1951 ed. lib. bdg. 15.00 (ISBN 0-8371-3064-6, AKKA). Greenwood.

--Kappa: A Satire. Bownas, Geoffrey, tr. from Japanese. LC 79-157260. 1971. pap. 5.25 (ISBN 0-8048-0994-1). C E Tuttle.

--Rashomon & Other Stories. new ed. Takashi, Kojima, tr. LC 52-9665. (Illus.). 1970. pap. 3.95 (ISBN 0-87140-214-9). Liveright.

--Rashomon & Other Stories. Takashi, Kojima, tr. from Japanese. LC 83-72480. 102p. 1952. pap. 3.25 (ISBN 0-8048-1457-0). C E Tuttle.

Akuts, Timias, et al, eds. Historia Aguaruna, 3 vols. (Comunidades y Culturas Peruanas Ser.: No. 16). 1979. Set. pap. 15.20 (ISBN 0-88312-773-3); Tomo I, 235p. 3.60; Tomo II, 8.00; Tomo III. avail. 3.60microfiche. Summer Inst Ling.

Akyuz, O., jt. auth. see Odabasi, Halis.

Akzin, Benjamin & Drov, Yehezkel. Israel: High-Pressure Planning. LC 66-17521. (National Planning Ser.: No. 5). pap. 30.50 (ISBN 0-317-28995-0, 2020393). Bks Demand UMI.

Akzin, Benjamin, ed. Studies in Law, Vol. V. 259p. 1958. pap. 18.50x (Pub. by Magnes Israel). Humanities.

Al-Anon Family Group Haadquarters, Inc. Staff. Al-Anon Family Groups. LC 84-70191. 1984. 5.00 (ISBN 0-910034-54-0). Al-Anon.

Al-Anon Family Group Headquarters. Al-Anon's Twelve Steps & Twelve Traditions. LC 80-28087. 160p. 1983. 5.00 (ISBN 0-910034-24-9). Al-Anon.

Al-Anon Family Group Headquarters, Inc. Staff. Al-Anon Faces Alcholism. 2nd ed. LC 84-70190. 1984. 6.00 (ISBN 0-910034-55-9). Al-Anon.

Al-Anon Family Group Headquarters, Inc. Alateen: A Day At a Time. LC 83-70348. 1984. 4.50 (ISBN 0-910034-53-2). Al Anon.

--The Dilemma of the Alcoholic Marriage. LC 70-182133. 1983. 4.50 (ISBN 0-910034-18-4). Al-Anon.

--One Day at a Time in Al-Anon. LC 72-85153. 1984. 5.00 (ISBN 0-910034-21-4). Al-Anon.

Al Fateh-IFAC Workshop, 1st, Tripoli, Libya, May 1980 & El Hares, H. Automatic Control in Desalination & the Oil Industry: Appropriate Applications: Proceedings. Dali, T., ed. LC 81-23412. (Illus.). 209p. 1982. 50.00 (ISBN 0-08-028698-4, A115, A135). Pergamon.

Ala-Cla-La. AACR Two Revisions. LC 82-13719. 24p. 1982. pap. text ed. 2.50x. ALA.

ALA Government Documents Roundtable. Directory of Foreign Document Collections. LC 84-52793. 150p. 1985. pap. 20.00 (ISBN 0-89059-045-1, UPB134, UPB). Unipub.

ALA Resources & Technical Services Division. Microforms in Libraries: A Manual for Evaluation & Management. Spreitzer, Francis, ed. LC 85-6036. 96p. 1985. pap. text ed. 8.95x (ISBN 0-8389-3310-6). ALA.

ALA see American Library Association.

Alabado, Ceres S. Kangkong: 1896. (Illus.). 241p. (Orig., Tagalog.). 1984. pap. 5.00x (ISBN 971-10-0106-3, Pub. by New Day Philippines). Cellar.

Alabama ACEP, jt. auth. see Campbell, John E.

Alabama Law Institute & Thigpen, Richard A. The Alabama Project on Medicaid. LC 80-624165. Date not set. price not set. AL Law Inst.

Alabama Law Institute Staff. Alabama Probate Code: With Commentary. rev. ed. LC 83-131624. viii, 56p. 1982. write for info. Michie Co.

Alabama Pattern Jury Instructions Committee. Alabama Pattern Jury Instructions: Civil. LC 73-93831. 644p. 67.50; Suppl. 1984. 25.00; Suppl. 1982. 18.50. Lawyers Co-Op.

Alabaster, J. S. Habitat Modification & Freshwater Fisheries. (Illus.). 304p. 1985. text ed. 64.95 (ISBN 0-407-00418-1). Butterworth.

Alabaster, J. S., ed. Biological Monitoring of Inland Fisheries. 226p. 1977. 57.50 (ISBN 0-85334-719-0, Pub. by Elsevier Applied Sci England). Elsevier.

Alabaster, John S. Report of the EIFAC Workshop on Fish-Farm Effluents: Silkeborg, Denmark, May 26-28, 1981. (European Inland Fisheries Advisory Commission (EIFAC): Technical Papers: No. 41). 174p. 1982. pap. 12.75 (ISBN 92-5-101162-1, F2285, FAO). Unipub.

Alabaster, Oliver. What You Can Do to Prevent Cancer. 1985. 17.95 (ISBN 0-671-49537-2). S&S.

Alabaster, William. Sonnets. Story, G. M. & Gardner, Helen, eds. LC 83-45405. Repr. of 1959 ed. 20.00 (ISBN 0-404-20004-4). AMS Pr.

Al-Abdul-Razzak, Fatimah H. Marine Resources of Kuwait: Their Role in the Development of Non-Oil Resources. (Illus.). 300p. 1985. 55.00x (ISBN 0-7103-0069-7, Kegan Paul). Routledge & Kegan.

Al-Abidin, Zayn. Supplication: Makarim al-Akhlaq. Chittick, William C., tr. 30p. 1984. pap. 2.49 (ISBN 0-940368-45-5). Tahrike Tarsile Quran.

Alabiso, Frank P. & Hansen, James C. The Hyperactive Child in the Classroom. 336p. 1977. 25.75x (ISBN 0-398-03550-4). C C Thomas.

Alacevic, M., ed. Progress in Environmental Mutagenesis. (Developments in Toxicology & Environmental Science Ser.: Vol. 7). 1980. 58.50 (ISBN 0-444-80241-X). Elsevier.

Aladjem, Henrietta. The Sun Is My Enemy. LC 76-7733. 1977. pap. 6.95 (ISBN 0-8070-2171-7, BP537). Beacon Pr.

--Understanding Lupus: What It Is, How to Treat It, How to Cope with It. (Illus.). 272p. 1985. 15.95 (ISBN 0-684-18348-X, ScribT). Scribner.

Aladjem, Silvio & Vidyasagar, D. Atlas of Perinatology. (Illus.). 508p. 1982. 88.00 (ISBN 0-7216-1080-3). Saunders.

Alaeddinoglue, Gurdal N., et al, eds. Industrial Aspects of Biochemistry & Genetics, Volume 87. (NATO ASI Series A, Life Sciences). 227p. 1985. 45.00x (ISBN 0-306-41934-3, Plenum Pr). Plenum Pub.

Alagappan, M. V. Tears in Teardrop Island. 103p. 1985. text ed. 15.00x (ISBN 0-86590-593-2, Pub. by Sterling Pubs India). Apt Bks.

Alagic, S. & Arbib, M. A. The Design of Well-Structured & Correct Programs. LC 77-27087. (Texts & Monographs in Computer Science). 1978. 23.00 (ISBN 0-387-90299-6). Springer-Verlag.

Alagille, Daniel & Odievre, Michel. Liver & Biliary Tract Disease in Children. LC 79-12254. pap. 93.80 (ISBN 0-317-27961-0, 2055759). Bks Demand UMI.

Alagoa, E. J. King Boy of Brass. (African Historical Biographies Ser.). (Illus.). 48p. 1977. pap. text ed. 2.75x (ISBN 0-435-94471-1). Heinemann Ed.

Alagoa, Ebieberi J. The Small Brave City-State: A History of Nembe-Brass in the Niger Delta. LC 64-12722. pap. 47.30 (ISBN 0-317-27788-X, 2015351). Bks Demand UMI.

Al-Ahmad, Jalal. Plagued by the West: Gharbzadegi. Sprachman, Paul, tr. LC 81-18168. (Modern Persian Literature Ser.). 1983. 25.00x (ISBN 0-88206-047-3). Caravan Bks.

Alaia, Cheri, jt. auth. see Rafter, Rosalie.

Alain, pseud. Alain on Happiness. Cottrell, Robert D. & Cottrell, Jane E., trs. from Fr. LC 76-186356. Orig. Title: Propos Sur le Bonheur. 272p. 1973. 10.50 (ISBN 0-8044-5033-1); pap. 4.95 (ISBN 0-8044-6004-3). Ungar.

--The Gods. Pevear, Richard, tr. from Fr. LC 74-8291. 192p. 1974. 8.95 (ISBN 0-8112-0547-9); pap. 3.95 (ISBN 0-8112-0548-7, NDP382). New Directions.

Alain, ed. see Valery, Paul.

Alain, Hermano. Flora de Cuba, Vol. 5. 4.35 (ISBN 0-8477-2319-4); pap. 3.10 (ISBN 0-8477-2302-X). U of PR Pr.

Alain, Hermano, jt. auth. see Leon, H.

Alain-Fournier. Le Grand Meaulnes. Davison, Frank, tr. from Fr. (Penguin Classics Ser.). 1978. pap. 3.95 (ISBN 0-14-002466-2). Penguin.

Alain-Fournier, jt. auth. see Peguy, Charles.

Alain-Fournier, Henri. Grand Meaulnes. (Illus.). 1963. 36.65 (ISBN 0-685-11219-5); pap. 3.95 (ISBN 0-685-11220-9, 1000). French & Eur.

--Wanderer. 1981. pap. 3.95 (ISBN 0-452-00754-2, Mer). NAL.

Alais, Pierre & Metherell, Alexander F., eds. Acoustical Imaging, Vol. 10. LC 69-12533. 842p. 1981. 115.00x (ISBN 0-306-40725-6, Plenum Pr). Plenum Pub.

Alakoye, Adesanya. Tell Me How Willing Slaves Be. 1976. 1.25 (ISBN 0-686-15701-X). Energy Blacksouth.

Al-Alak, B. & Ford, J. D. The Housebuilding Market in the Middle East. 164p. 1979. 121.00x (ISBN 0-86010-153-3, Pub. by Graham & Trotman England). State Mutual Bk.

Alam. Handbook of Gasoline Automobiles, 2 vols. Vol. 3, 1925-1926. pap. 7.95 (ISBN 0-486-22690-5). Dover.

Alam, M. A. Elementary Calculations. 188p. 1981. 30.00x (ISBN 0-86125-715-4, Pub. by Orient Longman India). State Mutual Bk.

Alam, M. S., jt. ed. see Panvini, R. S.

Al-Amad, Hani. Cultural Policy in Jordan. (Studies & Documents on Cultural Policies). (Illus.). 87p. 1981. pap. 10.00 (ISBN 92-3-101749-7, U1139, UNESCO). Unipub.

Ala Maudoodi, Abul. Come Let Us Change This World. 4th ed. Siddique, Kaukab, intro. by. & tr. from Urdu. 151p. 1983. pap. 2.00 (ISBN 0-942978-05-6). Am Soc Ed & Rel.

Alameda Poets. Wings & Waves. Ford, Samuel E., ed. LC 76-2294. (Illus.). 99p. 1976. pap. 3.95 (ISBN 0-916734-01-3). Alameda.

Alameda Poets Editorial Committee. First Anthology of Poetry & Drawings. (Illus.). 1971. pap. 2.00 (ISBN 0-916734-00-5). Alameda.

Alamgir, Mohiuddin. Famine in South Asia: Political Economy of Mass Starvation. LC 80-13078. 448p. 1980. text ed. 45.00 (ISBN 0-89946-042-9). Oelgeschlager.

Alamuddin, Nura S. & Starr, Paul D. Crucial Bonds: Marriage Among the Lebanese Druze. LC 78-10465. 1980. 25.00x (ISBN 0-88206-024-4). Caravan Bks.

Alan. Mission with Mountbatten. 2nd ed. LC 77-4388. (Illus.). 1977. Repr. of 1972 ed. lib. bdg. 29.50x (ISBN 0-8371-9596-9, CJMM). Greenwood.

Alan, John, jt. auth. see Turner, Lou.

Alan, John, ed. Black Brown & Red: The Movement for Freedom among Black, Chicano, Latino, & Indian. (Illus.). 78p. (Orig.). 1975. pap. 0.75x (ISBN 0-686-32886-8). News & Letters MN.

Alan Of Tewkesbury. Alani Priors Cantuariensis Postea Abbatis Tewkesberiensis Scripta Quae Extant. Giles, J. A., ed. 1966. Repr. of 1848 ed. 24.00 (ISBN 0-8337-1340-X). B Franklin.

Alan, Ray. The Beirut Pipeline. 242p. 1980. 10.95 (ISBN 0-374-11018-2). FS&G.

Alan, Richard X. Enjoy The Sweetest Days of Love: A Man's Feeling on Love & Lovers. LC 83-91116. (Illus.). 72p. 1984. pap. 6.95 (ISBN 0-914317-00-8). Magic Ocean.

Alan Sloan, Inc., jt. auth. see Sea World Press.

Alanahally, Shrikrishna. The Woods. Taranath, Rajeeve, tr. from Kannada. Orig. Title: Kaadu. 112p. 1979. pap. 2.95 (ISBN 0-86578-091-9). Ind-US Inc.

Aland, Barbara, jt. auth. see Aland, Kurt.

Aland, K., ed. Synopsis of the Four Gospels. 1983. 5.95x (ISBN 0-8267-0500-6, 08564). Am Bible.

Aland, Karen L. Chinese Cooking: The Easy Wok Method. 1984. pap. 5.95 (ISBN 0-913880-06-X). Caroline Hse.

Aland, Kurt. A History of Christianity, Vol. 1: From the Beginnings to the Threshold of the Reformation. Schaaf, James L., tr. LC 84-47913. 464p. 24.95 (ISBN 0-8006-0725-2, 1-725). Fortress.

Aland, Kurt & Aland, Barbara. Der Text des Neuen Testaments. LC 82-56158. (Illus.). 342p. (Ger.). 1982. text ed. 15.00 (ISBN 3-438-06011-6). Am Bible.

Aland, Kurt, ed. Die Alten Uebersetzungen des Neuen Testaments, die Kirchenvaeterzitate und Lektionare: Der Gegenwaertige Stand Ihrer Erforschung und Ihre Bedeutung fuer die Griechische Textgeschichte. (Arbeiten zur neutestamentlichen Textforschung 5). xxiv, 590p. 1972. 62.40x (ISBN 3-11-004121-9). De Gruyter.

--Glanz und Niedergang der Deutschen Universitaet: 50 Jahre Deutscher Wissenschafts-Geschichte in Briefen an und Von Hans Lietzmann, 1892-1942. 1979. 63.20x (ISBN 3-11-004980-5). De Gruyter.

--Repertorium der Griechischen Christlichen Papyri, Pt.1: Biblische Papyri, Altes Testament, Neues Testament, Varia, Apokryphen. (Patristische Texte und Studien, Vol. 18). 473p. 1976. 63.20x (ISBN 3-11-004674-1). De Gruyter.

Aland, Kurt, jt. ed. see Institut fuer Neutestamentliche Textforschung, Muenster-Westf.

Aland, Kurt, et al, eds. The Greek New Testament. 3rd ed. 1983. 6.50x (ISBN 3-438-05110-9, 56491, Pub. by United Bible); With Dictionary. 8.50x (ISBN 3-438-05113-3, 56492). Am Bible.

Al-Ani & Shammas. Arabic: Phonology & Script. 1980. 9.00x (ISBN 0-917062-04-3). Intl Bk Ctr.

Al-Ani, Salman H. Arabic Phonology: An Acoustical & Physiological Investigation. (Janua Linguarum, Ser. Practica: No. 61). 1970. pap. text ed. 21.60 (ISBN 90-2790-727-7). Mouton.

Al-Ani, Salmon H., compiled by. Fred Walter Householder Bibliography. (Arcadia Bibliographica Virorum Eruditorum Ser.: Fasc. 6). 1984. 14.00 (ISBN 0-931922-16-X). Eurolingua.

Alanne, V. S. Finnish Dictionary: Suomalais-Englantilainen, Vol. 1. 3rd ed. (Finnish & Eng.). 1982. 85.00x (ISBN 95-100-1069-3, F563). Vanous.

--Finnish-English Dictionary. 85.00 (ISBN 0-317-19056-3, F563). Vanous.

--Finnish-English General Dictionary. 1111p. (Eng. & Finnish.). 1980. 75.00 (ISBN 951-0-01069-3, M-9658). French & Eur.

Alan Of Lille. The Art of Preaching. Evans, Gillian R., tr. (Cistercian Fathers Ser.: No. 23). (Orig., Lat.). 1981. pap. 13.95 (ISBN 0-87907-923-1). Cistercian Pubns.

Al-Ansary, Rahman. Qaryat Al-Fau: A Portrait of Pre-Islamic Civilization in Saudi Arabia. LC 81-21329. 1982. 37.50 (ISBN 0-312-65742-0). St Martin.

Alanzel, W., jt. auth. see Brown, T.

A Lapide, Cornelius. The Personality of St. Paul. 1959. 3.50 (ISBN 0-8198-5802-1); pap. 2.25 (ISBN 0-8198-5803-X). Dghtrs St Paul.

Alapuro, Risto, et al, eds. Small States in Comparative Perspective: Essays in Honour of Erik Allardt. (Norwegian University Press Pub. Ser.). 300p. 1985. 45.00 (ISBN 0-317-28025-2). Oxford U Pr.

Al-Arabi, Muhyiddin. The Seals of Wisdom. (Sacred Texts Ser.). (Illus., Orig.). 1983. pap. 6.50 (ISBN 0-88695-010-4). Concord Grove.

Alarcon, Francisco X., ed. see Herrera, Juan F.

Alarcon, Hernando R. de see Ruiz de Alarcon, Hernando.

Alarie, Julia & Conlon, Elizabeth. Book Report Boosters. Sussman, Ellen, ed. (Illus.). 44p. (Orig.). (gr. 3-6). 1983. pap. 5.95 (ISBN 0-933606-21-4, MS-619). Monkey Sisters.

--Green Thumb Grammar: Teaching Parts of Speech with Indoor Plants. (Illus.). 28p. (Orig.). (gr. 4-6). 1981. pap. text ed. 4.50 (ISBN 0-933606-13-3, MS-610). Monkey Sisters.

--Proofing Is in the Pudding. Sussman, Ellen, ed. (Illus.). 44p. (Orig.). (gr. 3-6). 1983. pap. text ed. 5.95 (ISBN 0-933606-22-2, MS620). Monkey Sisters.

--Purple Punctuation Pages: Exciting Detective Activities to Teach Punctuation. (Illus.). 28p. (Orig.). (gr. 4-6). 1981. pap. text ed. 4.50 (ISBN 0-933606-09-5, MS-607). Monkey Sisters.

--SOWHAT - Spelling Only Without A Test. Sussman, Ellen, ed. (Creative Assignments in Spelling Ser.). (Illus.). (gr. 3-6). 1980. pap. text ed. 5.95 (ISBN 0-933606-06-0, MS-605). Monkey Sisters.

--Tickle My Fancy: Creative Language Arts Activities, Written-Verbal-Artistic. Sussman, Ellen, ed. (Illus.). 48p. (Orig.). (gr. 4-6). 1980. pap. text ed. 5.95 (ISBN 0-933606-05-2, MS-606). Monkey Sisters.

Al-Arif, Ibn. Mahasin Al-Majalis. Elliott, William & Elliott, Abdulla, trs. 120p. 1980. text ed. 19.50x (ISBN 0-86127-102-5, Pub. by Avebury England). Humanities.

Al-Arif, Ismail. Iraq Reborn: A Firsthand Account of the 1958 Revolution & After. 1982. 9.50 (ISBN 0-533-05009-X). Vantage.

Alas, Leopoldo. His Only Son. Jones, Julie, tr. from Span. LC 80-20837. xxii, 218p. 1981. 22.50x (ISBN 0-8071-0759-X). La State U Pr.

--La Regenta. 736p. 1985. pap. 14.95 (ISBN 0-14-044346-0). Penguin.

--La Regenta. Rutherford, John, tr. from Span. LC 83-17886. 736p. 1984. 20.00 (ISBN 0-8203-0700-9). U of Ga Pr.

Al-Asfour, Taiba A. Changing Sea-Level along the North Coast of Kuwait Bay. 208p. 1982. 50.00x (ISBN 0-7103-0010-7). Routledge & Kegan.

Alaska Flyfishers. Fly Patterns of Alaska. (Illus.). 88p. (Orig.). 1983. pap. 11.95 (ISBN 0-936608-13-7). F Amato Pubns.

Alaska Geographic, ed. The Aleutian Islands. LC 80-17331. (Alaska Geographic Ser.: Vol. 7, No. 3). (Illus.). 224p. (Orig.). 1980. pap. 14.95 (ISBN 0-88240-145-9). Alaska Northwest.

--The Kotzebue Basin. LC 81-7910. (Alaska Geographic Ser.: Vol. 8, No. 3). (Illus., Orig.). 1981. pap. 12.95 album style (ISBN 0-88240-157-2). Alaska Northwest.

--A Photographic Geography of Alaska. rev. ed. (Alaska Geographic Ser.: Vol. 7, No. 2). (Illus.). 192p. (Orig.). 1983. pap. 15.95 (ISBN 0-88240-173-4). Alaska Northwest.

--Wrangell-Saint Elias: International Mountain Wilderness. LC 80-26210. (Alaska Geographic Ser.: Vol. 8, No. 1). (Illus., Orig.). 1981. pap. 9.95 album style (ISBN 0-88240-149-1). Alaska Northwest.

Alaska Geographic, jt. ed. see Alaska Magazine Staff.

Alaska Geographic Staff. Alaska National Interest Lands: D-2 Lands. LC 81-10979. (Alaska Geographic Ser.: Vol. 8, No. 4). (Illus.). 242p. (Orig.). 1981. pap. 14.95 album style (ISBN 0-88240-159-9). Alaska Northwest.

--Alaska's Farms & Gardens. (Alaska Geographic Ser.: Vol. 11; No. 2). (Illus.). 144p. (Orig.). 1984. pap. 12.95 album style (ISBN 0-88240-202-1). Alaska Northwest.

--Alaska's Glaciers. LC 81-20508. (Alaska Geographic Ser.: Vol. 9, No. 1). (Illus.). 144p. (Orig.). 1982. pap. 9.95 album style (ISBN 0-88240-167-X). Alaska Northwest.

--The Chilkat River Valley. (Alaska Geographic Ser.: Vol. II, No. 3). (Illus.). 112p. (Orig.). 1984. pap. 12.95 (ISBN 0-88240-203-X). Alaska Northwest.

--Nome, City of the Golden Beaches. (Alaska Geographic Ser.: Vol. 11, no. 1). (Illus.). 184p. 1984. pap. 14.95 (ISBN 0-88240-201-3, Alaska Geographic Society). Alaska Northwest.

--Southeast: Alaska's Panhandle. LC 72-92087. (Alaska Geographic: Vol. 5, No. 2). (Illus.). 1978. pap. 12.95 album style (ISBN 0-88240-107-6). Alaska Northwest.

--Up the Koyukuk. (Alaska Geographic Ser.: Vol. 10, no. 4). (Illus.). 152p. 1983. pap. 14.95 (ISBN 0-88240-200-5, Alaska Geographic Society). Alaska Northwest.

Alaska Geographic Staff, ed. Alaska Mammals. LC 81-976. (Alaska Geographic Ser.: Vol. 8, No. 2). (Illus.). 184p. (Orig.). 1981. pap. 12.95 (ISBN 0-88240-155-6). Alaska Northwest.

--Alaska Whales & Whaling. LC 72-92087. (Alaska Geographic Ser.: Vol. 5, No. 4). (Illus.). 144p. 1978. pap. 12.95 album style (ISBN 0-88240-114-9). Alaska Northwest.

--Alaska's Oil-Gas & Minerals Industry. (Alaska Geographic Ser.: Vol. 9, No. 4). pap. 12.95 Album Style (ISBN 0-88240-170-X). Alaska Northwest.

--Aurora Borealis. LC 72-92087. (Alaska Geographic Ser.: Vol. 6, No. 2). (Illus.). 1979. pap. 7.95 album style (ISBN 0-88240-124-6). Alaska Northwest.

--The Pribilofs: Island of the Seals. (Alaska Geographic Ser.: Vol. 9 No. 3). (Illus., Orig.). 1982. pap. 9.95 (ISBN 0-88240-169-6). Alaska Northwest.

--Sitka & Its Ocean-Island World. (Alaska Geographic Ser.: Vol. 9 No. 2). (Illus., Orig.). 1982. pap. 9.95 (ISBN 0-88240-168-8). Alaska Northwest.

--The Stikine River. LC 79-20674. (Alaska Geographic Ser.: Vol. 6, No. 4). (Illus.). 1979. pap. 9.95 (ISBN 0-88240-133-5). Alaska Northwest.

Alaska Magazine, ed. Alaska Wild Berry Guide & Cookbook. (Illus.). 216p. 1983. pap. 14.95 (ISBN 0-88240-229-3). Alaska Northwest.

--Bits & Pieces of Alaskan History: Vol. II: 1960-1974. (Illus.). pap. 14.95 (ISBN 0-88240-228-5). Alaska Northwest.

Alaska Magazine Editors. The Alaska Almanac: Facts about Alaska, 1985. 9th ed. (Illus.). 210p. (Orig.). 1985. pap. 5.95 (ISBN 0-88240-242-0). Alaska Northwest.

--Anchorage. LC 79-16616. (Alaska Town Ser.). (Illus., Orig.). 1979. pap. 2.95 (ISBN 0-88240-129-7). Alaska Northwest.

Alaska Magazine Editors, jt. auth. see Armstrong, Robert H.

Alaska Magazine Editors, ed. Bits & Pieces of Alaskan History, Vol. I: 1935-1959. LC 81-3618. (Illus.). 1981. pap. 14.95 (ISBN 0-88240-156-4). Alaska Northwest.

Alaska Magazine Staff, ed. Alaska: A Pictorial Geography. 1982. pap. 4.95 (ISBN 0-88240-231-5). Alaska Northwest.

Alaska Magazine Staff & Alaska Geographic, eds. Introduction to Alaska. (Illus.). 64p. 1983. pap. 4.95 (ISBN 0-88240-230-7). Alaska Northwest.

Alaska Sportsman's Council. The Alaskan Camp Cook. LC 62-22307. (Illus.). 1962. spiral bdg. 4.95 (ISBN 0-88240-000-2). Alaska Northwest.

Alaska Travel Publications Editors. Exploring Katmai National Monument & the Valley of Ten Thousand Smokes. LC 74-84798. (Illus.). 1975. 12.00 (ISBN 0-914164-02-3). Alaska Travel.

Al-Askari, Allama M. Hadith: A Probe into the History of. Haq, M. Fazal, tr. 120p. 1983. pap. 4.00 (ISBN 0-941724-16-6). Islamic Seminary.

Al-Askari, Salah, et al, eds. Essentials of Basic Sciences in Urology. (Illus.). 336p. 1980. 52.00 (ISBN 0-8089-1299-2, 790033). Grune.

Alastos, Doros. Cyprus in History: A Survey of 5,000 Years. rev., 2nd ed. (Illus.). 1977. 30.00 (ISBN 0-7228-0061-4). Heinman.

--Cyprus in History: A Survey of 5,000 Years. 428p. 1976. 49.00x (ISBN 0-7228-0006-1, Pub. by Yr Oriel Fach Pr). State Mutual Bk.

Alastos, Doros & Papacosma, S. Victor. Venizelos: Patriot, Statesman, Revolutionary. (CEES: 10). 1978. Repr. of 1940 ed. 22.00 (ISBN 0-87569-030-0). Academic Intl.

Alaszewski, Andy. Institutional Care & the Mentally Handicapped: The Mental Handicap Hospital. 224p. 1985. 21.50 (ISBN 0-7099-0564-5, Pub. by Croom Helm Ltd). Longwood Pub Group.

Alaszewski, Andy, jt. auth. see Ayer, Sam.

Alaszewski, Andy, jt. auth. see Haywood, Stuart.

Alatas, Syed Hussein. Intellectuals in Developing Societies. 130p. 1977. 25.00x (ISBN 0-7146-3004-7, BHA 03004, F Cass Co). Biblio Dist.

--Myth of the Lazy Native. 267p. 1977. 27.50x (ISBN 0-7146-3050-0, BHA 03050, F Cass Co). Biblio Dist.

Alatis, James E., ed. Studies in Honor of Albert H. Markwardt. 166p. 1972. 4.00 (ISBN 0-318-16647-X). Tchrs Eng Spkrs.

Alatis, James E. & Crymes, Ruth, eds. The Human Factors in ESL. 100p. 1977. 5.00 (ISBN 0-318-16643-7). Tchrs Eng Spkrs.

Alatis, James E. & Staczek, John J., eds. Perspectives on Bilingualism & Bilingual Education. 456p. (Orig.). 1985. pap. 12.95 (ISBN 0-87840-192-X). Georgetown U Pr.

Alatis, James E. & Tucker, G. Richard, eds. Georgetown University Round Table on Languages & Linguistics: Language in Public Life. LC 58-31607. (Georgetown Univ. Round Table Ser., 1979). 310p. (GURT 1979). 1980. pap. 8.95 (ISBN 0-87840-114-8). Georgetown U Pr.

Alatis, James E. & Twaddell, Kristie, eds. English as a Second Language in Bilingual Education. 360p. 1976. 8.25 (ISBN 0-318-16640-2). Tchrs Eng Spkrs.

Alatis, James E., et al, eds. The Second Language Classroom: Directions for the 1980's. Altman, Howard B. & Alatis, Penelope M. (Illus.). 1981. text ed. 14.95x (ISBN 0-19-502928-3); pap. text ed. 8.95x (ISBN 0-19-502929-1). Oxford U Pr.

--Gurt '83: Applied Linguistics & the Preparation of Second Language Teachers: Toward a Rationale. LC 58-31607. (Gurt Ser.). 416p. (Orig.). 1984. pap. 13.95 (ISBN 0-87840-118-0). Georgetown U Pr.

Alatis, Penelope M. see Alatis, James E., et al.

Alaux, Michel. Modern Fencing. 1981. pap. 9.95 (ISBN 0-684-16945-2, ScribT). Scribner.

Alavi, Abass, jt. auth. see Bohrer, Stanley P.

Alavi, Abass & Arger, Peter, eds. Abdomen, Vol. 3. (Multiple Imaging Procedures Ser.). 464p. 1980. 57.00 (ISBN 0-8089-1306-9, 790034). Grune.

Alavi, Bozorg. The Prison Papers of Bozorg Alavi: A Literary Odyssey. Raffat, Donne, ed. LC 85-8053. (Contemporary Issues in the Middle East Ser.). (Illus.). 256p. 1985. 28.00 (ISBN 0-8156-0195-6). Syracuse U Pr.

Alavi, Hamza, jt. ed. see Shanin, Teodor.

Alavi, Hamza, et al. Capitalism & Colonial Production: Essays on the Rise of Capitalism in Asia. (Illus.). 208p. 1982. 28.00 (ISBN 0-7099-0634-X, Pub. by Croom Helm Ltd). Longwood Pub Group.

Alavi, Y. & Lick, D. R., eds. Theory & Applications of Graphs: Proceedings, Michigan, May 11-15, 1976. (Lecture Notes in Mathematics: Vol. 642). 1978. pap. 31.00 (ISBN 0-387-08666-8). Springer-Verlag.

Alavi, Y., et al, eds. Graph Theory & Its Applications to Algorithms & Computer Science. 608p. 1985. 49.95 (ISBN 0-471-81635-3). Wiley.

Alavi, Y., et al, eds. see Conference on Graph Theory - Western Michigan University - Kalamazoo - 1972.

Alawar, Mohamed A., ed. A Concise Bibliography of Northern Chad & Fezzan in Southern Libya. 253p. 1983. lib. bdg. 32.00x (ISBN 0-906559-14-6, Menas Pr). Westview.

Alaxander, Frank, ed. see Levin, Beatrice.

Alaya, Flavia. William Sharp - "Fiona MacLeod", 1855-1905. LC 75-113183. (Illus.). 1970. 17.50x (ISBN 0-674-95345-2). Harvard U Pr.

Alazraki, Jaime. Jorge Luis Borges. LC 77-136494. (Essays on Modern Writers Ser.: No. 57). 48p. 1971. pap. 2.50 (ISBN 0-231-03283-8). Columbia U Pr.

Alazraki, Jaime & Ivask, Ivar, eds. The Final Island: The Fiction of Julio Cortazar. LC 77-21912. (Illus.). 1978. 17.95x (ISBN 0-8061-1436-3). U of Okla Pr.

Alazraki, Jaime, et al, eds. Homenaje a Andres Iduarte. (Illus., Eng. & Span.). 1976. 15.00 (ISBN 0-89217-000-X). American Hispanist.

Alazraki, N. P. & Mishkin, F. S., eds. Fundamentals of Nuclear Medicine. 208p. 1984. 12.00 (ISBN 0-317-17711-7). Soc Nuclear Med.

Alba. Alba's Medical Technology Board Examination Review, Vol. I. 10th ed. (Illus.). 1984. pap. text ed. 28.00 (ISBN 0-910224-10-2). Berkeley Sci.

--Alba's Medical Technology Board Examination Review, Vol. II. 5th ed. LC 72-172446. (Illus.). 489p. 1981. pap. text ed. 22.00 (ISBN 0-910224-06-4). Berkeley Sci.

Alba, Esther S. Teatro Cubano: Tres obras de Jose Antonio Ramos. (Caliban Rex, El Traidor y La recurva) LC 81-84199. 160p. (Orig., Span.). 1983. pap. 11.95 (ISBN 0-918454-30-1). Senda Nueva.

Alba, Francisco. The Population of Mexico: Trends, Issues, & Policies. LC 81-1432. 150p. 1981. 24.95 (ISBN 0-87855-359-2). Transaction Bks.

Alba, Joaquin De see De Alba, Joaquin.

Alba, Richard D. Italian Americans: Into the Twilight of Ethnicity. (Illus.). 240p. 1985. text ed. 16.95 (ISBN 0-13-506676-X); pap. text ed. 13.95 (ISBN 0-317-11601-0). P-H.

Alba, Richard D., ed. Ethnicity & Race in the U. S. A. Towards the Twenty First Century. 192p. 1985. 24.95x (ISBN 0-7102-0633-X). Routledge & Kegan.

Alba, Victor. The Communist Party in Spain. Smith, Vincent G., tr. from Span. LC 82-19339. 475p. 1983. 49.95 (ISBN 0-87855-464-5). Transaction Bks.

--Politics & the Labor Movement in Latin America. 1968. 30.00x (ISBN 0-8047-0193-8). Stanford U Pr.

--Transition in Spain: From Franco to Democracy. Lotito, Barbara, tr. LC 77-28117. 334p. 1978. 14.95 (ISBN 0-87855-225-1). Transaction Bks.

Alba, Victor, jt. auth. see Harris, Louis K.

Alba-Buffill, Elio. Los Estudios Cervantinos de Enrique Jose Varona. LC 78-73618. (Senda De Estudios y Ensayos Ser.). (Orig., Span.). 1979. pap. 9.95 (ISBN 0-918454-11-5). Senda Nueva.

Alba-Buffill, Elio & Feito, Francisco E. Indice de El Pensamiento: Cuba, 1879-1880. LC 77-75370. (Senda Bibliografica). (Orig., Span.). 1977. pap. 4.95 (ISBN 0-918454-00-X). Senda Nueva.

Alba-Buffill, Elio, jt. ed. see De La Solana Gutierrez, Alber to.

Albach, H. & Bergendahl, G., eds. Production Theory & Its Applications: Proceedings of a Workshop. (Lecture Notes in Economics & Mathematical Systems Ser.: Vol. 139). 1977. pap. 13.00 (ISBN 0-387-08062-7). Springer-Verlag.

Al Bahanna, H. M. The Arabian Gulf States: Their Legal & Political Status. 428p. 1979. 33.00x (ISBN 0-86010-174-6, Pub by Graham & Trotman England). State Mutual Bk.

Albaiges, J., jt. auth. see Second International Congress on Analytical Techniques in Environmental Chemistry.

Albaiges, J., ed. see International Congress on Analytical Techniques in Environmental Chemistry, Barcelona, 27-30 November 1978.

Albaiges, J., et al, eds. Chemistry & Analysis of Hydrocarbons in the Environment. LC 83-1603. (Current Topics in Environmental & Toxicological Chemistry Ser.: Vol. 5). 326p. 1983. 57.75 (ISBN 0-677-06140-4). Gordon.

Alban, Laureano. Autumn's Legacy. Fornoff, Frederick, tr. from Span. LC 82-6455. xiv, 77p. 1982. lib. bdg. 18.95x (ISBN 0-8214-0667-1, 82-84358); pap. 10.95 (ISBN 0-8214-0696-5, 82-84655). Ohio U Pr.

--THe Endless Voyage. Fornoff, Fredrick H., tr. from Span. LC 84-7526. (International Poetry Ser.: Vol. 8). Orig. Title: El viaje interminable. (Illus.). xxiv, 96p. 1984. text ed. 16.95x (ISBN 0-8214-0785-6, 82-85439); pap. 10.95 (ISBN 0-8214-0786-4). Ohio U Pr.

Albanese, Anthony A., ed. Bone Loss: Causes, Detection & Therapy. LC 77-24954. (Current Topics in Nutrition & Disease: Vol. 1). 220p. 1977. 25.00 (ISBN 0-8451-1600-2). A R Liss.

--Nutrition for the Elderly. LC 80-21565. (Current Topics in Nutrition & Disease: Vol. 3). 342p. 1980. 42.00 (ISBN 0-8451-1602-9). A R Liss.

Albanese, Catherine. Sons of the Fathers: The Civil Religion of the American Revolution. LC 76-17712. 288p. 1977. 29.95 (ISBN 0-87722-073-5). Temple U Pr.

Albanese, Catherine L. America: Religions & Religion. LC 80-21031. (The Wadsworth Series in Religion Studies). 389p. 1981. pap. write for info (ISBN 0-534-00928-X). Wadsworth Pub.

--Corresponding Motion: Transcendental Religion & the New America. LC 77-70329. 234p. 1977. 29.95 (ISBN 0-87722-098-0). Temple U Pr.

--King Crockett: Nature & Civility on the American Frontier. 1979. pap. 3.50x (ISBN 0-912296-40-2, Dist. by U Pr of Va). Am Antiquarian.

Albanese, Gayle, jt. auth. see Garrison, Eileen.

Albanese, Jay S. Dealing with Delinquency: An Investigation of Juvenile Justice. (Illus.). 138p. (Orig.). 1985. lib. bdg. 20.50 (ISBN 0-8191-4448-7); pap. text ed. 8.75 (ISBN 0-8191-4449-5). U Pr of Amer.

--Justice, Privacy, & Crime Control. 68p. (Orig.). 1984. pap. text ed. 7.25 (ISBN 0-8191-4173-9). U Pr of Amer.

--Myths & Realities of Crime & Justice: A Citizen's Guide. LC 83-72105. 140p. (Orig.). 1984. pap. 6.95 (ISBN 0-941614-01-8). Apocalypse Pub.

--Organizational Offenders: Why Solutions Fail to Political, Corporate, & Organized Crime. LC 81-69949. 170p. (Orig.). 1982. pap. 7.95 (ISBN 0-941614-00-X). Apocalypse Pub.

Albanese, Jay S., et al. Is Probation Working? A Guide for Managers & Methodologists. LC 80-6311. 190p. 1981. lib. bdg. 22.75 (ISBN 0-8191-1507-X); pap. text ed. 10.50 (ISBN 0-8191-1508-8). U Pr of Amer.

Albanese, Joseph. The Nurses' Drug Reference. 2nd ed. (Illus.). 1184p. 1981. 36.00x (ISBN 0-07-000767-5); pap. 28.00x (ISBN 0-07-000768-3). McGraw.

--The Nurses' Drug Reference: Nineteen Eighty-Two Drug Update. 128p. 1983. pap. 3.00 (ISBN 0-07-000769-1). McGraw.

Albanese, Joseph & Bond, Thomas. Drug Interactions: Basic Principles & Clinical Problems. (Illus.). 1978. pap. text ed. 19.95 (ISBN 0-07-000940-6). McGraw.

Albanese, Ralph, Jr. Le Dynamisme De la Peur Chez Moliere: Une Analyse Socio - Culturelle De Dom Juan, Tartuffe, et L'ecole Des Femmes. LC 76-9061. (Romance Monographs: No. 19). 1976. 20.00x (ISBN 84-399-5071-3). Romance.

Albanese, Robert. Managing: Toward Accountability for Performance. 3rd ed. 1981. 31.95x (ISBN 0-256-02505-3). Irwin.

Albanese, Rosetta T. One Thousand One Temple Avenue. 1985. 7.95 (ISBN 0-533-06541-0). Vantage.

Albani, Emma. Forty Years of Song. Farkas, Andrew, ed. LC 76-29924. (Opera Biographies). (Illus.). 1977. Repr. of 1911 ed. lib. bdg. 30.00x (ISBN 0-405-09667-4). Ayer Co Pubs.

Albano, A., et al, eds. Computer-Aided Database Design: The DATAID Project. 222p. 1985. 44.50 (ISBN 0-444-87735-5, North-Holland). Elsevier.

Albano, Charles. Transactional Analysis on the Job & Communicating with Subordinates. Rendero, Thomasine, ed. LC 75-20236. (Illus.). 184p. 1975. 9.95 (ISBN 0-8144-5401-1). AMACOM.

--Transactional Analysis on the Job & Communicating with Subordinates. rev. ed. Rendero, Thomasine, ed. LC 75-20236. pap. 45.80 (ISBN 0-317-27194-6, 2023928). Bks Demand UMI.

Albano, John. Ms. Pac-Man's Prize Pupil. (Golden Look-Look Books). (Illus.). 24p. (ps-3). 1983. pap. 1.50 (ISBN 0-307-11791-X, 11791, Golden Bks). Western Pub.

--Pac-Man & the Ghost Diggers. (Golden Look-Look Bks.). (Illus.). 24p. (ps-3). 1983. pap. 1.50 (ISBN 0-307-11790-1, 11790, Golden Bks). Western Pub.

Albano, Peter. The Seventh Carrier. 1983. pap. 3.25 (ISBN 0-8217-1271-3). Zebra.

Albans, Suzanne St. see St. Albans, Suzanne.

Albanse, Robert & Van Fleet, David D. Organizational Behavior: A Managerial Viewpoint. 640p. 1983. 33.95x (ISBN 0-03-050736-7); instr's. manual 19.95 (ISBN 0-03-050741-3). Dryden Pr.

Albany. The Fighting Saga of the SAS: Bk. 1, Warrior Caste. Date not set. pap. 2.95 (ISBN 0-523-42520-1). Pinnacle Bks.

Albany County Sessions. Minutes of the Commissioners for Detecting & Defeating Conspiracies in the State of New York, 3 vols. in 2. Paltsits, Victor H., ed. LC 72-1835. (Era of the American Revolution Ser.). (Illus.). 1972. Repr. of 1909 ed. Set. lib. bdg. 125.00 (ISBN 0-306-70504-4). Da Capo.

Albany, Eric A., ed. see Nuffield Foundation.

Albany, James. Mailed Fist. (The Fighting Saga of the SAS Ser.: Bk. 2). 192p. (Orig.). 1985. pap. 2.95 (ISBN 0-523-42522-8). Pinnacle Bks.

--Warrior Castle. (The Fighting Saga of the SAS Ser.: No. 1). 192p. (Orig.). 1985. pap. 2.95 (ISBN 0-523-42520-1). Pinnacle Bks.

Al-Barbar, Aghil M. Government & Politics in Libya, Nineteen Sixty-Nine to Nineteen Seventy-Eight: A Bibliography. (Public Administration Ser.: Bibliography P-388). 139p. 1979. pap. 14.50 (ISBN 0-88066-042-2). Vance Biblios.

Albarella, Jacqueline. The Basic Make-up Workbook. (Illus.). 1980. pap. 12.95 (ISBN 0-914620-03-7). Alpha Pr.

Albarella, Joan. Mirror Me. (Illus.). 50p. 1973. pap. 3.00 (ISBN 0-914620-01-0). Alpha Pr.

--Poems for the Asking. (Illus.). 24p. 1975. pap. 2.00 (ISBN 0-914620-02-9). Alpha Pr.

Albarracin-Sarmiento, Carlos. Estructura del 'Martin Fierro' (Purdue University Monographs in Romance Languages: No. 9). xx, 336p. (Span.). 1982. 40.00x (ISBN 90-272-1719-X). Benjamins North Am.

Al-Barrawi, Rashid. The Military Coup in Egypt. LC 79-2851. 269p. 1981. Repr. of 1952 ed. 23.00 (ISBN 0-8305-0027-8). Hyperion Conn.

Albas. Student Life & Exams: Stresses & Coping Strategies. 184p. 1984. pap. 10.95 (ISBN 0-8403-3362-5). Kendall-Hunt.

Al-Bashir, Faisal Safooq. A Structural Econometric Model of the Saudi Arabian Economy: Nineteen Sixty to Nineteen Seventy. LC 77-441. 144p. 1977. text ed. 36.50 (ISBN 0-471-02177-6). Krieger.

Albaugh, jt. auth. see Ehresman.

Albaugh, William A. III. A Photographic Supplement of Confederate Swords with Addendum. (Illus.). 278p. 1963. Repr. of 1979 ed. 24.95 (ISBN 0-943522-02-1). Moss Pubns VA.

Al-Bayati, Basil. Community & Unity. (Academy Architecture Ser.). (Illus.). 144p. 1983. 35.00 (ISBN 0-312-15298-1). St Martin.

Albeck, Chanoch. Einfuehrung in die Mischna. (Studia Judaica, 6). 493p. 1971. 33.60x (ISBN 3-11-006429-4). De Gruyter.

Albeda, W., et al, eds. Temporary Work in Modern Society, 2 pts. Incl. Pt. 1. 63.00 (ISBN 90-312-0070-0); Pt. 2. 44.00 (ISBN 90-312-0071-9). 1978. Set. 87.50 (ISBN 0-686-15415-0, Pub. by Kluwer Law Netherlands). Kluwer Academic.

Albee, Edward. American Dream & Zoo Story. pap. 2.95 (ISBN 0-451-13461-3, Sig). NAL.

--Counting the Ways & Listening: Two Plays. LC 76-53401. 1977. 7.95 (ISBN 0-689-10785-4). Atheneum.

--The Lady from Dubuque: A Play in Two Acts. pap. 3.35x (ISBN 0-686-69575-5). Dramatists Play.

--The Man Who Had Three Arms. LC 83-45493. 160p. Date not set. 12.95 (ISBN 0-689-11451-6). Atheneum.

--The Plays, Vol. 3. Incl. Seascape; Counting the Ways & Listening; All Over. 1982. pap. 9.95 (ISBN 0-689-70615-4). Atheneum.

--The Plays, Vol. 2: Tiny Alice, A Delicate Balance, Box, Quotations from Chairman Mao Tse-tung. LC 81-3616. 1981. pap. 9.95 (ISBN 0-689-70614-6). Atheneum.

--The Plays, Vol. 4: Everything in the Garden, Malcolm, the Ballad of the Sad Cafe. LC 81-3616. 512p. 1982. pap. 10.95 (ISBN 0-689-70616-2). Atheneum.

--Sandbox. Bd. with Death of Bessie Smith. 1964. pap. 2.95 (ISBN 0-451-12819-2, AE2819, Sig). NAL.

--Who's Afraid of Virginia Woolf? 256p. 1983. pap. 3.50 (ISBN 0-451-12125-2, Sig). NAL.

Albee, Edward see Strasberg, Lee.

Albee, Edward A. The Lady from Dubuque. LC 78-3192. 1980. 9.95 (ISBN 0-689-10925-3). Atheneum.

--Who's Afraid of Virginia Woolf? LC 62-17691. 1962. pap. text ed. 5.95x (ISBN 0-689-70565-4). Atheneum.

Albee, Ernest. History of English Utilitarianism. 59.95 (ISBN 0-8490-0327-X). Gordon Pr.

--History of English Utilitarianism. (Muirhead Library of Philosophy). 1957. Repr. of 1901 ed. text ed. 18.00x (ISBN 0-04-171001-0). Humanities.

Albee, George W. & Joffe, Justin M., eds. The Issues: An Overview of Primary Prevention. LC 76-53992. (Primary Prevention of Psychopathology Ser.: Vol. 1). (Illus.). 440p. 1977. 35.00x (ISBN 0-87451-135-6). U Pr of New Eng.

Albee, George W., jt. ed. see Joffe, Justin M.

Albee, George W., et al, eds. Promoting Sexual Responsibility & Preventing Sexual Problems. LC 82-40474. (Primary Prevention of Psychopathology Ser.: No. 7). (Illus.). 462p. 1983. 40.00x (ISBN 0-87451-248-4). U Pr of New Eng.

Albee, J. Remembrances of Emerson. 1985. 62.50 (ISBN 0-317-19973-0). Porter.

Albee, John. Remembrances of Emerson. LC 73-11303. 1974. Repr. of 1903 ed. lib. bdg. 12.50 (ISBN 0-8414-2877-8). Folcroft.

Albegov. Regional Development Modelling Theory & Practice. (Studies in Regional Science: Vol. 8). 1982. 53.25 (ISBN 0-444-86473-3). Elsevier.

Alber, A. Videotex-Teletext: Principle & Practices. 416p. 1985. 32.95 (ISBN 0-07-000957-0). McGraw.

Alber, Charles A., tr. see Semanov, V. I.

Alber, S. I., et al. Eleven Papers on Analysis. LC 51-5559. (Translations, Ser: No. 2, Vol. 14). 1964. Repr. of 1960 ed. 27.00 (ISBN 0-8218-1714-0, TRANS 2-14). Am Math.

Albera, A. E. Making Roses Behave. (Illus.). 1960. spiral bdg. 2.50 (ISBN 0-87505-244-4). Borden.

Alberda, Th. Production & Water Use of Several Food & Fodder Crops Under Irrigation in the Desert Area of Southwestern Peru. (Agricultural Research Reports: No. 928). (Illus.). 50p. 1985. pap. 7.50 (ISBN 90-220-0869-X, PDC291, Pudoc). Unipub.

Alberding, Faye V. Morrow & Miracles. (Illus.). 1983. 5.95 (ISBN 0-8062-2203-4). Carlton.

Alberes. Esthetique et Morale chez Giradoux. 1957. 24.95 (ISBN 0-685-33933-5). French & Eur.

Alberes, Rene M. & De Boisdeffre, Pierre. Kafka: The Torment of Man. Baskin, Wade, tr. 1968. pap. 1.95 (ISBN 0-8065-0109-X, 275). Citadel Pr.

Alberger, Particia L., ed. Winning Techniques for Athletic Fund Raising. 97p. 1981. 14.50 (ISBN 0-89964-188-1). Coun Adv & Supp Ed.

Alberger, Patricia, ed. How to Work Effectively with Alumni Boards. 81p. 1981. 14.50 (ISBN 0-89964-182-2). Coun Adv & Supp Ed.

Alberger, Patricia, jt. ed. see Carter, Virginia L.

Alberger, Patricia L., ed. Building Your Alumni Program. 100p. (Orig.). 1980. pap. 14.50 (ISBN 0-89964-165-2). Coun Adv & Supp Ed.

--How to Involve Alumni in Student Recruitment. 84p. 1983. 14.50 (ISBN 0-89964-208-X). Coun Adv & Supp Ed.

--How to Work Effectively with Alumni Boards. 81p. (Orig.). 1981. 14.50 (ISBN 0-89964-182-2). Coun Adv & Supp Ed.

--Student Alumni Associations & Foundations. 65p. (Orig.). 1980. pap. 14.50 (ISBN 0-89964-163-6). Coun Adv & Supp Ed.

--Student Alumni Associations & Foundations. 65p. 1980. 14.50 (ISBN 0-89964-163-6). Coun Adv & Supp Ed.

--Winning Techniques for Athletic Fund Raising. 97p. 1981. 14.50 (ISBN 0-89964-188-1). Coun Adv & Supp Ed.

Alberger, Patricia L. & Carter, Virginia L., eds. Communicating University Research. 200p. 1981. pap. 19.50 (ISBN 0-89964-171-7). Coun Adv & Supp Ed.

--Communicating University Research. 226p. 1981. 19.50 (ISBN 0-89964-171-7). Coun Adv & Supp Ed.

Alberger, Patricia L., jt. ed. see Smith, Virgina C.

Alberger, Patricia LaSalle see Carter, Virginia L. & LaSalle Alberger, Patricia.

Albergotti, J. Clifton. Mighty Is the Charm: Lectures on Science, Literature, & the Arts. LC 81-40158. (Illus.). 248p. (Orig.). 1982. lib. bdg. 26.00 (ISBN 0-8191-2207-6); pap. text ed. 12.25 (ISBN 0-8191-2208-4). U Pr of Amer.

Alberi, et al, eds. see Trieste.

Alberi, G. & Bajzer, Z., eds. Applications of Physics to Medicine & Biology: Proceedings of the International Conference, Trieste, Italy, March 30-April 3, 1982. 688p. 1983. 67.00x (ISBN 9971-950-42-1, Pub. by World Sci Singapore). Taylor & Francis.

Alberigo, Giuseppe, ed. Where Does the Church Stand, Vol. 146. (Concilium 1981). 128p. (Orig.). 1981. pap. 6.95 (ISBN 0-8164-2313-X, Pub. by Seabury). Winston Pr.

Alberione, James. Call to Total Consecration. 1974. 3.00 (ISBN 0-8198-0312-X); pap. 2.00 (ISBN 0-8198-0313-8). Dghtrs St Paul.

--Christ, Model & Reward of Religious. 1964. 5.00 (ISBN 0-8198-0023-6); pap. 4.00. Dghtrs St Paul.

--Designs for a Just Society. (Divine Master Ser.). 1976. 6.00 (ISBN 0-8198-0400-2); pap. 5.00 (ISBN 0-8198-0401-0); wkbk 0.60 (ISBN 0-8198-0402-9). Dghtrs St Paul.

--Eternal Wisdom. 7.00 (ISBN 0-8198-0502-5). Dghtrs St Paul.

--Insights into Religious Life. 1977. 3.00 (ISBN 0-8198-0424-X); pap. 2.00 (ISBN 0-8198-0425-8). Dghtrs St Paul.

--Last Things. (Orig.). 1965. 4.50 (ISBN 0-8198-0072-4). Dghtrs St Paul.

--Living Our Commitment. 1968. 4.00 (ISBN 0-8198-4411-X); pap. 3.00 (ISBN 0-8198-4412-8). Dghtrs St Paul.

--Lord, Teach Us to Pray. Daughters of St. Paul, tr. from Ital. 295p. 1982. 4.00 (ISBN 0-8198-4422-5, SP0408); pap. 3.00 (ISBN 0-8198-4423-3). Dghtrs St Paul.

--Mary, Queen of Apostles. rev. ed. 1976. 4.00 (ISBN 0-8198-0438-X); pap. 3.00 (ISBN 0-8198-0439-8). Dghtrs St Paul.

--Month with Saint Paul. 1952. pap. 2.25 (ISBN 0-8198-0104-6). Dghtrs St Paul.

--Paschal Mystery in Christian Living. Daughters Of St. Paul, tr. LC 68-28102. (St. Paul Editions). (Illus.). 1968. 3.95 (ISBN 0-8198-0114-3); pap. 2.95 (ISBN 0-8198-0115-1). Dghtrs St Paul.

--Pray Always. 1966. 4.00 (ISBN 0-8198-0126-7); pap. 3.00 (ISBN 0-8198-0127-5). Dghtrs St Paul.

--Queen of Apostles Prayerbook. 7.50 (ISBN 0-8198-0266-2); plastic bdg. 6.00 (ISBN 0-8198-0267-0). Dghtrs St Paul.

--Saint & Thought for Every Day. 1976. 4.50 (ISBN 0-8198-0471-1); pap. 3.50 (ISBN 0-8198-6800-0). Dghtrs St Paul.

--The Spirit in My Life. 1977. pap. 0.95 (ISBN 0-8198-0460-6). Dghtrs St Paul.

--Superior Follows the Master. (Orig.). 1965. pap. 2.00 (ISBN 0-8198-0153-4). Dghtrs St Paul.

--That Christ May Live in Me. 1980. 3.50 (ISBN 0-8198-7300-4); pap. 2.25 (ISBN 0-8198-7301-2). Dghtrs St Paul.

--Thoughts. 1973. 3.00 (ISBN 0-8198-0332-4). Dghtrs St Paul.

--A Time for Faith. 1978. 4.00 (ISBN 0-8198-0371-5); pap. 3.00 (ISBN 0-8198-0372-3). Dghtrs St Paul.

--Woman: Her Influence & Zeal. (Orig.). 1964. 3.50 (ISBN 0-8198-0176-3); pap. 1.25 (ISBN 0-8198-0177-1). Dghtrs St Paul.

Alberione, James J. Personality & Configuration with Christ. (Orig.). 3.50 (ISBN 0-8198-0120-8); pap. 2.50 (ISBN 0-8198-0121-6). Dghtrs St Paul.

Alberione, Rev. James. Glories & Virtues of Mary. 1970. 3.50 (ISBN 0-8198-3017-8); pap. 2.50 (ISBN 0-8198-3018-6). Dghtrs St Paul.

--Growing in Perfect Union. 1964. 3.00 (ISBN 0-8198-3019-4); pap. 2.00 (ISBN 0-8198-3020-8). Dghtrs St Paul.

Alberman, Eva, jt. auth. see Stanley, Fiona.

Alberoni, Francesco. Falling in Love. Venuti, Lawrence, tr. from Ital. LC 83-42757. 160p. 1984. 13.95 (ISBN 0-394-53007-1). Random.

--Movement & Institution. (European Perspectives Ser.). 448p. 1984. 45.00x (ISBN 0-231-04884-X). Columbia U Pr.

Alberry, Nicholas, ed. How to Save the World: A Fourth World Guide to the Politics of Scale. 192p. 1984. pap. 9.95 (ISBN 0-85500-209-3). Newcastle Pub.

Albers, Adriana. The Diary of a Mad Golf Wife or How to Begin. (Illus.). 96p. 1984. pap. 5.95 (ISBN 0-911433-02-3). HealthRight.

Albers, Anni. On Designing. LC 62-12321. (Illus.). 1962. pap. 7.95 (ISBN 0-8195-6019-7). Wesleyan U Pr.

--On Weaving. LC 65-19855. (Illus.). 1965. 23.00x (ISBN 0-8195-3059-X); pap. 9.95 (ISBN 0-8195-6031-6). Wesleyan U Pr.

Albers, D. J. & Steen, L. A., eds. Teaching Teachers, Teaching Students. 152p. 1981. 14.95x (ISBN 0-8176-3043-0). Birkhauser.

Albers, Donald J. & Alexanderson, G. L., eds. Mathematical People: Profiles & Interviews. 260p. 1985. 24.95 (ISBN 0-8176-3191-7). Birkhauser.

Albers, G., jt. ed. see Bernold, T.

Albers, Henry H. Management: The Basic Concepts. 2nd ed. LC 80-39780. 336p. 1982. lib. bdg. 19.50 (ISBN 0-89874-312-5). Krieger.

Albers, Henry H. & Schoer, Lowell A. Programmed Organization & Management Principles. LC 77-3561. 128p. 1977. pap. 7.50 (ISBN 0-88275-555-2). Krieger.

Albers, Henry H., jt. tr. see Natto, Ibrahim A.

Albers, Josef. Interaction of Color. rev ed. LC 74-15585. (Illus.). 74p. 1975. 18.50x (ISBN 0-300-01845-2); pap. 5.95 (ISBN 0-300-01846-0). Yale U Pr.

Albers, Michael D. The Terror. (Orig.). 1980. pap. 2.25 (ISBN 0-532-23311-5). Woodhill.

Albers, Patricia & Medicine, Beatrice. The Hidden Half: Studies of Plains Indian Women. LC 82-23906. 286p. (Orig.). 1983. lib. bdg. 25.50 (ISBN 0-8191-2956-9); pap. text ed. 13.25 (ISBN 0-8191-2957-7). U Pr of Amer.

Albers, R. Wayne, jt. auth. see Siegel, George J.

Albers, V. Underwater Sound. 1982. 52.95 (ISBN 0-87933-006-6). Van Nos Reinhold.

Albers, V. M., ed. Underwater Acoustics, Vol. 2. LC 62-8011. 429p. 1967. 69.50x (ISBN 0-306-37562-1, Plenum Pr). Plenum Pub.

Albers, Vernon M. Acoustical Society of America Suggested Experiments for Laboratory Courses in Acoustics & Vibrations. 2nd ed. LC 75-165357. 175p. 1973. text ed. 24.95x (ISBN 0-271-01104-1). Pa St U Pr.

--How to Use Woodworking Tools Effectively & Safely. (Illus.). 190p. 1974. 8.95 (ISBN 0-498-01851-2). A S Barnes.

--Underwater Acoustics Handbook. 2nd ed. LC 64-15069. (Illus.). 1965. 29.75x (ISBN 0-271-73106-0). Pa St U Pr.

--Underwater Acoustics Instrumentation. LC 76-84217. pap. 24.80 (ISBN 0-317-08626-X, 2051122). Bks Demand UMI.

Albers, Walter A., jt. ed. see Schwing, Richard C.

Albers, Walter A., Jr., ed. Physics of Opto-Electronic Materials. LC 73-173832. (General Motors Symposium Ser). 281p. 1971. 45.00 (ISBN 0-306-30558-5, Plenum Pr). Plenum Pub.

Albersheim, Walter J. The Conscience of Science & Other Essays. LC 82-50162. 237p. 1982. 12.50 (ISBN 0-912057-34-3, G-648). AMORC.

Albersmeier, Franz-Josef. Bild und Text: Beitraege zu Film und Literatur, 1976-1982. (European University Studies: No. 30, Vol. 12). 258p. (Ger.). 1983. 30.55 (ISBN 3-8204-7294-0). P Lang Pubs.

Alberson, Sarah D. Blue Sea Cookbook. Porter, Eleanor, ed. LC 67-29995. (Illus.). 1968. 9.95 (ISBN 0-8038-0689-2). Hastings.

Albert, et al. Great Traditions in Ethics. 394p. write for info. (ISBN 0-534-02815-2). Wadsworth Pub.

Albert, A. Human Pituitary Gonadotropins: A Workshop Conference. (Illus.). 448p. 1961. photocopy ed. 40.75x (ISBN 0-398-00023-9). C C Thomas.

Albert, A. & Serjeant, E. P. The Determination of Ionization Constants: A Laboratory Manual. 3rd ed. (Illus.). 150p. 1984. 33.00x (ISBN 0-412-24290-7, NO. 6848, Pub. by Chapman & Hall). Methuen Inc.

Albert, A. A., ed. Studies in Modern Algebra. LC 63-12777. (MAA Studies: No. 2). 190p. 1963. 16.50 (ISBN 0-88385-102-4). Math Assn.

Albert, A. A., ed. see Symposia in Pure Mathematics, New York, 1959.

Albert, A. Adrian. Fundamental Concepts of Higher Algebra. LC 81-2528. 1981. 4.95 (ISBN 0-936428-04-X). Polygonal Pub.

Albert, A. Adrian, ed. see Dickson, Leonard E.

Albert, Abraham A. Modern Higher Algebra. LC 38-2937. (University of Chicago Science Ser.). pap. 82.80 (ISBN 0-317-09455-6, 2016998). Bks Demand UMI.

--Solid Analytic Geometry. pap. 43.50 (ISBN 0-317-09471-8, 2016983). Bks Demand UMI.

--Structure of Algebras. LC 41-9. (Colloquium Pbns. Ser.: Vol. 24). 210p. 1980. pap. 33.00 (ISBN 0-8218-1024-3, COLL-24). Am Math.

Albert, Adelin, jt. ed. see Heusghem, Camille.

Albert, Adrian. Selective Toxicity: The Physico-Chemical Basis of Therapy. 7th Ed ed. 792p. 1985. text ed. 69.95 (ISBN 0-412-26010-7, NO. 9126, Pub. by Chapman & Hall England); pap. text ed. 34.95 (ISBN 0-412-26020-4, NO. 9127). Methuen Inc.

Albert, Adrien. Heterocyclic Chemistry: An Introduction. 547p. 1968. 62.00 (ISBN 0-485-11092-X, Pub. by Athlone Pr Ltd). Longwood Pub Group.

--Selective Toxicity: The Physico-Chemical Basis of Theory. 6th ed. LC 78-15491. 1979. pap. text ed. 19.95x (ISBN 0-412-23650-8). Halsted Pr.

Albert, Arthur. Regression & the Moore-Penrose Pseudo-Inverse. (Mathematics in Science & Engineering Ser.: Vol. 94). 1972. 35.00 (ISBN 0-12-048450-1). Acad Pr.

Albert, Bill. South America & the World Economy from Independence to 1930. (Studies in Economic & Social History). 88p. 1983. pap. text ed. 6.75x (ISBN 0-333-34223-2, 41241, Pub. by Macmillan England). Humanities.

Albert, Burton. Clubs for Kids. LC 82-90845. 112p. (Orig.). (gr. 4 up). 1983. pap. 4.95 (ISBN 0-345-30292-3). Ballantine.

--Code Busters! Levine, Abby, ed. (Illus.). 32p. (gr. 3-6). 1985. 10.25 (ISBN 0-8075-1235-4). A Whitman.

--Codes for Kids. LC 76-25456. (Activity Bks). (Illus.). (gr. 3 up). 1976. PLB 10.25 (ISBN 0-8075-1239-7). A Whitman.

--Mine, Yours, Ours. LC 77-9408. (Self-Starter Books). (Illus.). (ps). 1977. PLB 9.25 (ISBN 0-8075-5148-1). A Whitman.

--Sharks & Whales. LC 78-66936. (Deluxe Illustrated Ser.). (Illus.). (gr. 1-6). 1979. 5.95 (ISBN 0-448-48990-2, G&D); PLB 5.29 (ISBN 0-448-13620-1). Putnam Pub Group.

Albert, Burton, Jr. More Codes for Kids. Pacini, Kathy, ed. LC 79-245. (How-to Bks.). (Illus.). (gr. 3-6). 1979. PLB 10.25 (ISBN 0-8075-5270-4). A Whitman.

Albert, C. Figure Drawing Comes to Life. 1986. pap. cancelled (ISBN 0-442-20980-0). Van Nos Reinhold.

Albert, Daniel M. Granulomatous Inflammations of the Eye. LC 80-720243. (Lancaster Course in Opthalmic Histopathology Ser.). (Illus.). 21p. text ed. 43.00 (includes 31 slides) (ISBN 0-8036-3829-9). Davis Co.

--Jaeger's Atlas of Diseases of the Ocular Fundus. LC 75-180175. (Illus.). 165p. 1972. 52.50 (ISBN 0-7216-1085-4). Saunders.

Albert, Daniel M. & Puliafito, Carmen A. Melanomas of the Eye. LC 80-720254. (Lancaster Course in Opthalmic Histopathology Ser.). (Illus.). 19p. text ed. 43.00 (includes 31 slides) (ISBN 0-8036-3840-X). Davis Co.

Albert, Daniel M. & Sang, Delia N. Retinoblastoma & Pseudoglioma. LC 80-720253. (Lancaster Course in Ophthalmic Histopathology Ser.). (Illus.). 13p. text ed. 43.00 (incl. 30 slides) (ISBN 0-8036-3839-6). Davis Co.

Albert, Daniel M. & Scheie, Harold G. A History of Ophthalmology at the University of Pennsylvania. (Illus.). 420p. 1965. photocopy ed. 36.50x (ISBN 0-398-00024-7). C C Thomas.

Albert, Daniel M., et al. Herpesvirus: Recent Studies, 3 vols, Vol. 2. LC 73-13558. 1974. 22.50x (ISBN 0-8422-7169-4). Irvington.

Albert, Dave & Melvin, George F. New England Diesels. LC 75-27730. (Illus.). 1977. 28.95 (ISBN 0-916160-01-7). G R Cockle.

Albert, David. People Power: Applying Nonviolence Theory in the Nuclear Age. 64p. 1985. lib. bdg. 14.95 (ISBN 0-86571-064-3); pap. 2.45 (ISBN 0-86571-049-X). New Soc Pubs.

Albert, David H. Tell the American People: Perspectives on the Iranian Revolution. rev. ed. LC 80-83577. 1980. 14.95 (ISBN 0-86571-001-5); pap. 4.95 (ISBN 0-86571-003-1). New Soc Pubs.

Albert, David H., ed. Tell the American People: Perspectives on the Iranian Revolution. 1984. 14.95 (ISBN 0-86571-001-5); pap. 4.95 (ISBN 0-86571-003-1). Mizan Pr.

Albert, Don E. General Wesley Merritt. LC 80-13126. (Illus.). 1979. 15.00 (ISBN 0-935978-05-4); deluxe ed. 40.00 (ISBN 0-935978-06-2). Presidial.

Albert, Donna. Beautiful American Marine. LC 82-90348. (Illus.). 74p. (Orig.). 1982. pap. 5.95 (ISBN 0-9608924-0-0). DJA Writ Circle.

Albert, E. A History of English Literature. 1923. Repr. 20.00 (ISBN 0-8274-2506-6). R West.

Albert, E. D., et al, eds. Histocompatibility Testing, 1984. 820p. 1984. 98.00 (ISBN 0-387-13464-6). Springer-Verlag.

Albert, Edward. History of English Literature. 5th ed. Stone, J. A., rev. by. LC 79-54165. 1979. text ed. 28.50x cloth (ISBN 0-06-490145-9, BNB 06308); pap. text ed. 12.95x (ISBN 0-06-490146-7, BNB 06309). B&N Imports.

Albert, Ernest, jt. ed. see Gautherie, Michel.

Albert, Ethel M., jt. ed. see Vogt, Evon Z.

Albert, George & Hoffmann, Frank. The Cash Box Country Singles Charts, 1958-1982. LC 84-1266. 605p. 1984. 37.50 (ISBN 0-8108-1685-7). Scarecrow.

Albert, Gilbert. Les Champs et Les Forets. (Illus.). 28p. (Fr.). (gr. 6-8). 1984. pap. text ed. write for info. (ISBN 0-911409-46-7). Natl Mat Dev.

Albert, Gretchen D. Scribble Art: Kindergarten & Preschool. (Illus.). 85p. (ps-3). 1980. pap. text ed. 5.80 (ISBN 0-686-28105-5). GDA Pubns.

Albert, Hans. Treatise on Critical Reason. Rorty, Mary V., tr. LC 84-15095. 270p. 1985. text ed. 30.00x (ISBN 0-691-07295-7). Princeton U Pr.

Albert, Harold. Shape up. 1975. 5.75 (ISBN 0-89536-212-0). CSS of Ohio.

Albert, Harold & Morentz, James. The Compleat Sermon Program for Lent. 1982. 4.25 (ISBN 0-89536-533-2). CSS of Ohio.

Albert, Harry D., ed. see Stone, Michael H. & Forest, David.

Albert, Helen M. Serving Successful Salads: A Merchandising Cookbook. LC 75-33339. 192p. 1975. 17.95 (ISBN 0-8436-2068-4). Van Nos Reinhold.

Albert, Jamme. Sabaean Inscriptions from Mahram Bilgis (Marib) LC 62-10311. (American Foundation for the Study of Man Publications: Vol. 3). pap. 139.30 (ISBN 0-317-09904-3, 2005199). Bks Demand UMI.

Albert, Judith C. & Albert, Stewart E., eds. The Sixties Papers: Documents of a Rebellious Decade. 336p. 1984. 32.95 (ISBN 0-03-063617-5); pap. 16.95 (ISBN 0-03-063617-5). Praeger.

Albert, Kenneth J. How to Pick the Right Small Business Opportunity. 252p. 1980. pap. 6.95 (ISBN 0-07-000952-X). McGraw.

--How to Solve Business Problems: The Consultant's Approach to Business Problem Solving. LC 82-14956. 224p. 1983. 10.95 (ISBN 0-07-000753-5). McGraw.

--Straight Talk about Small Business. (Illus.). 256p. 1980. 21.50 (ISBN 0-07-000949-X). McGraw.

--Strategic Management Handbook. LC 82-17110. (Illus.). 544p. 1983. 57.50 (ISBN 0-07-000954-6). McGraw.

Albert, Kenneth S., ed. Drug Absorption & Disposition: Statistical Considerations. 152p. 1980. 18.00 (ISBN 0-917330-28-5). Am Pharm Assn.

Albert, Linda. Coping with Kids. 208p. 1984. pap. 2.95 (ISBN 0-345-31627-4). Ballantine.

--Coping with Kids & School. 196p. 1984. 13.95 (ISBN 0-525-24251-1, 01354-410). Dutton.

--Coping with Kids & School. 224p. 1985. pap. 2.95 (ISBN 0-345-32175-8). Ballantine.

--Linda Albert's Advice for Coping with Kids. 168p. 1982. 10.95 (ISBN 0-525-93262-3, 01063-320). Dutton.

Albert, Louise. But I'm Ready to Go. LC 76-9949. 204p. (gr. 6-8). 1976. 9.95 (ISBN 0-02-700310-8). Bradbury Pr.

Albert, M. L., et al. Clinical Aspects of Dysplasia. (Disorders of Human Communication Ser.: Vol. 2). (Illus.). 240p. 1981. 32.00 (ISBN 0-387-81617-8). Springer-Verlag.

Albert, Marillyn, ed. God, Grass & Grit: History of the Sherman County Trade Area. (Illus.). 440p. 1971. Vol. II 1975. 12.50 (ISBN 0-933512-23-6). Pioneer Bk Tx.

Albert, Martin L. & Obler, Loraine K. The Bilingual Brain: Neuropsychological & Neurolinguistic Aspects of Bilingualism. LC 78-51243. (Perspectives in Neurolinguistics & Psycholinguistics Ser.). 1978. 33.00 (ISBN 0-12-048750-0). Acad Pr.

Albert, Martin L., jt. auth. see Hecaen, Henri.

Albert, Martin L., jt. auth. see Obler, Loraine K.

Albert, Martin L., ed. Clinical Neurology of Aging. (Illus.). 544p. 1984. 55.00x (ISBN 0-19-503287-X). Oxford U Pr.

Albert, Marvin. Hidden Lives. 1982. pap. 3.95 (ISBN 0-440-13500-1). Dell.

--The Medusa Complex. LC 81-66972. 320p. 1981. 13.95 (ISBN 0-87795-341-4). Arbor Hse.

--The Medusa Complex. pap. 3.50 (ISBN 0-8217-1278-0). Zebra.

--A Nightmare in Dreamland. cancelled. Arbor Hse.

--Operation Lila. 1985. pap. 3.50 (ISBN 0-8217-1572-0). Zebra.

Albert, Marvin H. The Gargoyle Conspiracy. 288p. 1982. pap. 2.95 (ISBN 0-440-15239-9). Dell.

--Operation Lila. LC 82-72067. 304p. 1983. 14.95 (ISBN 0-87795-411-9). Arbor Hse.

Albert, Marvin H., jt. auth. see Seidman, Theodore R.

Albert, Maurice. Theatres de la foire, Sixteen Sixty to Seventeen Eighty-Nine. LC 78-135169. (Drama Ser.). 1971. Repr. of 1900 ed. 21.00 (ISBN 0-8337-0030-8). B Franklin.

Albert, Michael. Effective Management: Readings, Cases & Experiences. 220p. 1981. pap. text ed. 10.50 scp (ISBN 0-06-166407-3, HarpC); instr's. manual avail. (ISBN 0-06-360185-0). Har-Row.

--Effective Management: Readings, Cases, & Experiences. 2nd ed. LC 84-19800. 256p. 1985. pap. text ed. 13.50 scp (ISBN 0-06-040212-1, HarpC); instr's. manual avail. Har-Row.

--What Is to Be Undone: A Modern Revolutionary Discussion of Classical Left Ideologies. LC 74-18987. (Extending Horizons Ser.). 352p. 1975. 8.95 (ISBN 0-87558-075-0); pap. text ed. 3.95 (ISBN 0-87558-076-9). Porter Sargent.

Albert, Michael & Hahnel, Robin. Marxism & Socialist Theory. LC 80-85407. 300p. 1981. 20.00 (ISBN 0-686-71650-7); pap. 7.00 (ISBN 0-89608-075-7). South End Pr.

--Socialism Today & Tomorrow. LC 81-50138. 350p. 1981. 20.00 (ISBN 0-89608-078-1); pap. 9.50 (ISBN 0-89608-077-3). South End Pr.

--Unorthodox Marxism. LC 78-53575. 374p. 1978. 15.00 (ISBN 0-89608-005-6); pap. 7.00 (ISBN 0-89608-004-8). South End Pr.

Albert, Michael & Dellinger, David, eds. Beyond Survival: New Directions for the Disarmament Movement. 365p. 1983. 20.00 (ISBN 0-89608-176-1); pap. 8.00 (ISBN 0-89608-175-3). South End Pr.

Albert, Michel & Ball, James. Toward European Economic Recovery in the 1980s: Report for the European Parliament. LC 84-13362. (The Washington Papers: Vol. XII, No. 109). 176p. 1984. 7.95 (ISBN 0-03-001488-3). Praeger.

Albert, Mimi. The Second Story Man. LC 75-10743. 106p. 1975. 8.95 (ISBN 0-914590-12-X); pap. 3.95 (ISBN 0-914590-13-8). Fiction Coll.

Albert, Nancy E. Insider's Guide to Divorce in Illinois: The Practical Consumer Divorce Manual. 172p. (Orig.). 1984. pap. text ed. 12.95 (ISBN 0-9613998-0-5). N E Albert.

Albert, Octavia V. The House of Bondage. facsimile ed. LC 70-37580. (Black Heritage Library Collections). Repr. of 1890 ed. 14.50 (ISBN 0-8369-8956-2). Ayer Co Pubs.

Albert, Pedling. Animal School. LC 78-62002. (Orig.). 1978. 5.95 (ISBN 0-9602716-2-7); pap. 2.95 (ISBN 0-9602716-1-9). Paranoid Pubns.

Albert, Peter J. American Federation of Labor Records: The Samuel Gompers Era - Guide to a Joint Microfilm Publication. Miller, Harold L., ed. 67p. 1981. pap. 5.00 (ISBN 0-87020-190-5). State Hist Soc Wis.

Albert, Peter J., jt. auth. see Hoffman, Ronald.

Albert, Peter J. & Miller, Harold L., eds. The American Federation of Labor Records: The Samuel Gompers Era-Guide to a Joint Microfilm Edition. 67p. 1981. pap. text ed. 9.75 (ISBN 0-87020-190-5). Microfilming Corp.

Albert, Peter J., jt. ed. see Hoffman, Ronald.

Albert, Phyllis C. The Modernization of French Jewry: Consistory & Community in the Nineteenth Century. LC 76-50680. (Illus.). 472p. 1977. 35.00x (ISBN 0-87451-139-9). U Pr of New Eng.

Albert, Phyllis C., jt. ed. see Malino, Frances.

Albert, R. S., ed. Genius & Eminence: The Social Psychology of Creativity & Exceptional Achievement. (International Series in Experimental Social Psychology). 416p. 1983. 39.00 (ISBN 0-08-028105-2). Pergamon.

Albert, Renaud S., ed. A Tour de role. (Neuf Pieces en un Acte Ser.). 204p. (Fr.). (gr. 7-12). 1980. pap. 4.00 (ISBN 0-911409-11-4). Natl Mat Dev.

Albert, Richard C. Trolleys from the Mines: Street Railways of Centre, Clearfield, Indiana & Jefferson Counties, Pennsylvania. (Illus.). 100p. (Orig.). 1980. pap. 9.00 (ISBN 0-911940-32-4). Cox.

Albert, Ronald & Hahnewald, Harry, eds. Eight Language Dictionary of Medical Technology. LC 78-40828. 1979. 89.00 (ISBN 0-08-023763-0). Pergamon.

Albert, Roy E. Thorium: Its Industrial Hygiene Aspects. (U. S. Atomic Energy Commission Monographs). 1966. 17.50 (ISBN 0-12-048656-3). Acad Pr.

Albert, Salich, jt. auth. see Harrison, Sheldon P.

Albert, Sam. As Is. 140p. 1983. pap. 7.95 (ISBN 0-931694-20-5). Wampeter Pr.

Albert, Solomon N. Blood Volume & Extracellular Fluid Volume. 2nd ed. (Illus.). 336p. 1971. 33.50x (ISBN 0-398-02193-7). C C Thomas.

Albert, Solomon N., et al. The Hematocrit in Clinical Practice. (Illus.). 80p. 1965. 9.75x (ISBN 0-398-00025-5). C C Thomas.

Albert, Stewart E., jt. ed. see Albert, Judith C.

Albert, Stuart & Luck, Edward C., eds. On the Endings of Wars. (National University Publications, Political Science Ser.). 180p. 1980. 17.50x (ISBN 0-8046-9240-8, Pub. by Kennikat). Assoc Faculty Pr.

Albert, Walter, ed. Detective & Mystery Fiction: An International Bibliography of Secondary Sources. 800p. 1985. 60.00 (ISBN 0-941028-02-X). Brownstone Bks.

Albert, Walter, ed. see Cendrars, Blaise.

Albertelli, Pilo. Gli Eleati: Testimonianze & Frammenti. facsimile ed. LC 75-13249. (History of Ideas in Ancient Greece Ser.). (Italian.). 1976. Repr. of 1939 ed. 16.00x (ISBN 0-405-07286-4). Ayer Co Pubs.

Albertet de Sestero. Les Poesies Du Troubadour Albertet. Boutiere, Jean, ed. LC 80-2173. Repr. of 1937 ed. 24.50 (ISBN 0-404-19001-4). AMS Pr.

Alberti, Barbara. Delirium. Venuti, Lawrence, tr. from It. 256p. 1980. 12.95 (ISBN 0-374-13744-7). FS&G.

Alberti, Del & Laycock, Mary. The Correlation of Activity-Centered Science & Mathematics. 1975. 8.50 (ISBN 0-918932-07-6). Activity Resources.

Alberti, Delbert & Mason, George. Laboratory Laughter. (Math Is Everywhere Ser.). (Illus., Orig.). (gr. 2-9). 1974. pap. 6.50 (ISBN 0-918932-25-4). Activity Resources.

Alberti, F. H., jt. ed. see Sakamoto, N.

Alberti, Giorgio. Basic Needs in the Context of Social Change: The Case of Peru. 114p. (Orig.). 1981. pap. text ed. 8.00x (ISBN 92-64-12207-9). OECD.

Alberti, K. G., jt. auth. see Karran, S. J.

Alberti, K. G. & Krall, L. P., eds. The Diabetes Annual, Vol. 1. 1985. 70.50 (ISBN 0-444-90343-7, Excerpta Medica). Elsevier.

Alberti, K. G. & Price, C. P., eds. Recent Advances in Clinical Biochemistry, No. 2. LC 77-2344. (Recent Advances in Clinical Biochemistry Ser.). (Illus.). 1982. 47.50 (ISBN 0-443-02005-1). Churchill.

Alberti, Leon B. The Albertis of Florence: Leon Battista Albertis Della Famiglia. Guarino, Guido, tr. LC 75-124579. 351p. 1971. 30.00 (ISBN 0-8387-7736-8). Bucknell U Pr.

--De Re Aedificatoria. (Documents of Art & Architectural History Series 2: Vol. 1). 420p. (Latin.). Date not set. 45.00x (ISBN 0-89371-201-9). Broude Intl Edns.

--Family in Renaissance Florence: A Translation of I Libri Della Famiglia. Watkins, Renee Neu, tr. LC 75-79129. 1969. 19.95x (ISBN 0-87249-152-8). U of SC Pr.

--On Painting. rev. ed. Spencer, John R., tr. (Rare Masterpieces of Philosophy & Science). (Illus.). 1967. pap. 4.95x (ISBN 0-300-00001-4, Y175). Yale U Pr.

Alberti, Leone B. On Painting. (Printed Sources of Western Art Ser.). 128p. (Latin.). 1981. pap. 20.00 slipcase (ISBN 0-915346-55-9). A Wofsy Fine Arts.

--On Painting. Spencer, John R., tr. from Ital. LC 76-22485. (Illus.). 141p. 1976. Repr. of 1966 ed. lib. bdg. 20.00 (ISBN 0-8371-8974-8, ALOP). Greenwood.

Alberti, P. W., ed. Personal Hearing Protection in Industry. 622p. 1982. text ed. 82.50 (ISBN 0-89004-698-0). Raven.

Alberti, Peter M. & Uhlmann, Armin. Stochasticity & Partial Order. 1982. lib. bdg. 28.50 (ISBN 90-277-1350-2, Pub. by Reidel Holland). Kluwer Academic.

Alberti, R. E. & Emmons, M. L. Stand Up, Speak Out, Talk Back! 1984. pap. 3.50 (ISBN 0-671-54758-5). PB.

Alberti, Rafael. Concerning the Angels. (Poetry in Europe Ser.: No. 2). 1967. 6.50 (ISBN 0-8040-0055-7, 82-70373, Pub. by Swallow). Ohio U Pr.

--The Lost Grove: Autobiography of a Spanish Poet in Exile. Berns, Gabriel, ed. & tr. LC 74-79760. 1977. 21.00x (ISBN 0-520-02786-8); pap. 5.95 (ISBN 0-520-04265-4, CAL464). U of Cal Pr.

--The Other Shore: 100 Poems by Rafael Alberti. Chantikian, Kosrof, ed. Elgorriaga, Jose A. & Paul, Martin, trs. from Span. LC 80-84602. (Modern Poets in Translation Ser.: Vol. I). xiii, 234p. (Orig.). 1981. text ed. 20.00x (ISBN 0-916426-05-X); pap. 7.95 (ISBN 0-916426-06-8). KOSMOS.

--The Owl's Insomnia: Poems. Strand, Mark, tr. LC 73-81724. 1973. pap. 7.95 (ISBN 0-689-10585-1). Atheneum.

Alberti, Robert E. Your Perfect Write: The Manual for Self-Help Writers. 160p. (Orig.). 1985. pap. 9.95 (ISBN 0-915166-40-2). Impact Pubs Cal.

Alberti, Robert E. & Emmons, Michael L. Your Perfect Right: A Guide to Assertive Living. 4th ed. LC 81-20265. 224p. 1982. 8.95 (ISBN 0-915166-06-2); pap. 6.95 (ISBN 0-915166-05-4). Impact Pubs Cal.

Alberti, Santiago. Diccionari Castella-Catala, Catala-Castella, Mitja. 2nd ed. 584p. (Catalan & Castel.). 1978. 19.95 (ISBN 84-400-0761-2, S-31551). French & Eur.

--Diccionari de la Llengua Catalan. 3rd ed. 412p. (Catalan.). 1978. pap. 13.95 (ISBN 84-7246-058-4, S-50208). French & Eur.

--Diccionario Castella-Catala, Catala-Castella Petit. 2nd ed. 340p. (Castella & Catalan.). 1977. pap. 13.95 (ISBN 84-7246-057-6, S-50289). French & Eur.

--Diccionario Castella-Catala, Catala-Castella Gran. 9th ed. 1182p. (Castella & Catalan.). 1978. 44.95 (ISBN 84-7246-056-8, S-50294). French & Eur.

Albertina, Vienna, jt. auth. see Sammiung, Graphische.

Albertini, ed. Radioimmunoassay of Hormones, Proteins & Enzymes. (International Congress Ser.: Vol. 528). 1981. 61.00 (ISBN 0-444-90173-6). Elsevier.

Albertini, A. & Crosignani, P. G., eds. Progress in Perinatal Medicine: Biochemical & Biophysical Diagnostic Procedures. (International Congress Ser.: Vol. 614). 308p. 1984. 63.50 (ISBN 0-444-90370-4, I-456-83, Excerpta Medica). Elsevier.

Albertini, A. & Ekins, R. P., eds. Free Hormones in Blood: Proceedings of the Advanced Course on Free Hormone Assays & Neuropeptides, Venice, Italy, June 15-17, 1982. (Symposia of the Giovanni Lorenzini Foundation Ser.: Vol. 14). 392p. 1983. 70.25 (ISBN 0-444-80463-3, Biomedical Pr). Elsevier.

Albertini, A. & Elkins, R., eds. Monoclonal Antibodies & Developments in Immunoassay. (Symposia of the Giovanni Lorenzini Founadtion Ser.: Vol. 11). 1981. 68.00 (ISBN 0-444-80373-4). Elsevier.

Albertini, A. & Rigosa, C., eds. International Symposium on C-Peptide. (Illus.). 180p. 1979. text ed. 37.50x (ISBN 0-686-29670-2, Pub. by Piccin Italy). J K Burgess.

Albertini, A., et al, eds. Radioimmunoassay of Drugs & Hormones in Cardiovascular Medicine. (Symposia Giovanni Lorenzini Foundation: Vol. 3). 364p. 1979. 65.00 (ISBN 0-444-80176-6, North Holland). Elsevier.

--Ferritins & Isoferritins As Biochemical Markers: Proceedings of the Advanced Course on Ferritins & Isoferritins Held in Milan, May 17, 1984. (Symposia of the Giovanni Lorenzini Foundation Ser.: Vol. 19). 208p. 1984. 40.50 (ISBN 0-444-80607-5). Elsevier.

--Cost-Benefit & Predictive Value of Radioimmunoassay. (Symposia of the Giovanni Lorenzini Foundation Ser.: Vol. 18). 270p. 1984. 62.00 (ISBN 0-444-80618-0). Elsevier.

Albertini, A., jt. ed. see Godfraind, T.

Albertini, Jean. Dictionnaire Francais-Corse. 349p. (Fr. & Corse.). 1974. pap. 39.95 (ISBN 0-686-56891-5, M-6001). French & Eur.

Albertini, Jean, ed. see Rolland, Romain.

Albertini, Jose A. Tierra de Extranos. LC 82-8440. (Coleccion Caniqui Ser.). 160p. (Orig., Span.). 1983. pap. 9.95 (ISBN 0-89729-327-4). Ediciones.

Albertini, Luigi. The Origins of the War of Nineteen Hundred Fourteen, 3 vols. Massey, Isabella M., tr. from It. LC 80-12769. (Illus.). 1980. Repr. of 1952 ed. Set. lib. bdg. 130.00x (ISBN 0-313-22401-3, ALOW). Greenwood.

Albertini, Rudolf Von see Von Albertini, Rudolf & Wirz, Albert.

Albertini Von, Rudolf see Von Albertini, Rudolf.

Albertis, Gustave G. De see De Albertis, Gustave G.

Alberto, Paul & Troutman, Anne. Applied Behavior Analysis for Teachers. 448p. 1982. pap. text ed. 22.50 (ISBN 0-675-09840-8). Additional Supplements May Be Obtained From Publisher. Merrill.

Alberts, A. The Islands. Beekman, E. M., ed. Koning, Hans, tr. from Dutch. LC 82-21882. (Library of the Indies Ser.). Orig. Title: De Eilanden. 160p. 1983. lib. bdg. 13.00x (ISBN 0-87023-385-8). U of Mass Pr.

Alberts, Bruce & Fox, C. Fred, eds. Mechanistic Studies of DNA Replication & Genetic Recombination. (ICN-UCLA Symposia on Molecular & Cellular Biology Ser.: Vol. XIX). 1980. 66.00 (ISBN 0-12-048850-7). Acad Pr.

Alberts, Bruce, et al. Molecular Biology of the Cell. LC 82-15692. 1250p. 1983. lib. bdg. 37.95 (ISBN 0-8240-7282-0). Garland Pub.

Alberts, Cecil D. Game Power for Phonics. rev ed. (Illus., Orig.). 1972. text ed. 9.95 (ISBN 0-915048-00-0, 916220). Spin-A-Test Pub.

--Game Power for Phonics, Plus. 1981. 75.00 (ISBN 0-915048-04-3). Spin-A-Test Pub.

--Game Power for Phonics Professional Kit. (Illus.). 1978. 40.00 (ISBN 0-915048-02-7). Spin-a-Test Pub.

--Parent's Power for Phonics. new ed. (Illus.). 1978. pap. text ed. 25.00 (ISBN 0-915048-01-9). Spin-A-Test Pub.

Alberts, David S. & Surwit, Earl A., eds. Ovarian Cancer. (Cancer Treatment & Research Ser.). 1985. lib. bdg. 59.50 (ISBN 0-89838-676-4, Pub. by Martinus Nijhoff Netherlands). Kluwer Academic.

Alberts, Don E., ed. Rebels on the Rio Grande: The Civil War Journals of A. B. Peticolas. LC 84-17237. (Illus.). 192p. 1984. pap. 9.95 (ISBN 0-8263-0773-6). U of NM Pr.

Alberts, Jim. The Land of Two Moons. LC 83-90276. 243p. 1984. 12.95 (ISBN 0-533-05770-1). Vantage.

Alberts, Robert C. The Shaping of the Point: Pittsburgh's Renaissance Park. LC 79-26885. (Illus.). 264p. 1980. 14.95 (ISBN 0-8229-3422-1). U of Pittsburgh Pr.

Alberts, S. S. A Bibliography of the Works of Robinson Jeffers. LC 66-21849. 1966. 25.00 (ISBN 0-685-83031-4). Small Pr Dist.

Alberts, Tom. Agrarian Reform & Rural Poverty: A Case Study of Peru. (Replica Edition Ser.). 306p. 1983. softcover 27.50x (ISBN 0-86531-962-6). Westview.

Alberts, Ulvis. Poker Face. LC 80-70464. (Illus.). 144p. limited ed. 125.00 (ISBN 0-9605416-0-8); pap. 30.00 (ISBN 0-9605416-1-6). Angel City.

Alberts, William W. & Segall, Joel E., eds. Corporate Merger. LC 66-13888. (Studies in Business Society). 1966. 17.00x (ISBN 0-226-01233-6); pap. 4.95x (ISBN 0-226-01234-4, P563, Phoen). U of Chicago Pr.

Albertshauser, Marianne, compiled by see Frankfurt Book Fair Editors.

Albertson, Alice O. Nantucket Wild Flowers. LC 73-80640. (Illus.). 1973. Repr. of 1921 ed. 10.00 (ISBN 0-913728-02-0). Theophrastus.

Albertson, Chris. Bessie. LC 79-163353. 253p. 1982. pap. 7.95 (ISBN 0-8128-1700-1). Stein & Day.

Albertson, Dean. Roosevelt's Farmer: Claude R. Wickard in the New Deal. LC 74-23430. (Fdr & the Era of the New Deal Ser.). 1975. Repr. of 1961 ed. lib. bdg. 49.50 (ISBN 0-306-70702-0). Da Capo.

Albertson, Dorothy. RPM Unlimited: A Business Machines Practice Set. 2nd ed. (Illus.). (gr. 9-12). 1980. 10.76 (ISBN 0-07-000955-4). McGraw.

Albertson, Maurice L., et al. Fluid Mechanics for Engineers. 1960. text ed. 37.95 (ISBN 0-13-322578-X). P-H.

Albertson, Ralph. A Survey of Mutualistic Communities in America. LC 72-2934. (Communal Societies in America Ser.). Repr. of 1936 ed. 11.50 (ISBN 0-404-10700-1). AMS Pr.

Albertson, Rebecca. The Complete Book of Macra-Tack. 4th, rev. ed. (Illus.). 50p. (gr. 3-12). 1983. spiral 11.95 (ISBN 0-9611536-0-1). Macra-Tack Inc.

Albertson, Roger & Kocian, Patrick. The Original Woodstrippers Handbook. 106p. 1985. spiral binding 9.95 (ISBN 0-9611754-0-0). Wallace-Homestead.

Albertson, Sandra D., jt. auth. see Bean, Cheryl A.

Albertson, Sandra H. Endings & Beginnings: A Harvesting. 1980. 12.95 (ISBN 0-394-50627-8). Random.

Albertus, F. Tysk-Dansk: Dansk-Tysk Ordbog. 532p. (Danish & Ger.). 1982. 19.95 (ISBN 0-686-92489-4, M-1293). French & Eur.

Albertus, Frater. Alchemist's Handbook. LC 74-21127. 124p. 1974. cloth 12.50 (ISBN 0-87728-181-5). Weiser.

--The Seven Rays of the QBL. rev. ed. LC 84-51785. 1985. 39.95 (ISBN 0-87728-552-7). Weiser.

Albertus Magnus. The Boke of Secretes. LC 76-28227. (English Experience Ser.: No. 116). 168p. 1969. Repr. of 1525 ed. 15.00 (ISBN 90-221-0116-9). Walter J Johnson.

--The Book of Secrets of Albertus Magnus of the Virtues of Herbs, Stones & Certain Beasts; Also, a Book of the Marvels of the World. Best, Michael R. & Best, Michael R., eds. (Illus.). 1974. pap. 7.95 (ISBN 0-19-519786-0, GB421, GB). Oxford U Pr.

Alberty. Physical Chemistry. 7th ed. Date not set. price not set (ISBN 0-471-82577-8). Wiley.

Alberty, Beth & Weber, Lillian. Continuity & Connection in Curriculum. 1979. pap. 3.50 (ISBN 0-918374-03-0). Workshop Ctr.

Alberty, Beth & Dropkin, Ruth, eds. The Open Education Advisor: Training, Role & Function of Advisors to the Open Corridor Program. Descriptions of Specific Help to Teachers. 92p. 1975. pap. 3.50 (ISBN 0-918374-10-3). Workshop Ctr.

Alberty, Robert A. Physical Chemistry. 6th ed. LC 82-11058. 824p. 1983. text ed. 45.00 (ISBN 0-471-09284-3); solutions manual 14.95 (ISBN 0-471-87208-3). Wiley.

Alberty, Robert A. & Daniels, Farrington. Physical Chemistry SI Version. LC 78-14876. 692p. 1980. text ed. 38.00 (ISBN 0-471-05716-9); solutions manual 16.45 (ISBN 0-471-06376-2). Wiley.

Albery, E. H., et al. Cleft Lip & Palate: A Team Approach. (Illus.). 128p. 1985. write for info. (ISBN 0-7236-0700-1). PSG Pub Co.

Albery, Faxon F. Michael Ryan, Capitalist. LC 74-22766. (Labor Movement in Fiction & Non-Fiction). 1976. Repr. of 1913 ed. 16.00 (ISBN 0-404-58402-0). AMS Pr.

Albery, John. Electrode Kinetics. (Oxford Chemistry Ser). (Illus.). 1975. 32.50x (ISBN 0-19-855433-8). Oxford U Pr.

Albery, W. J. & Hitchman, M. L. Ring-Disc Electrodes. (Oxford Science Research Papers Ser). (Illus.). 1971. pap. 42.50x (ISBN 0-19-855349-8). Oxford U Pr.

Albeverio, S., ed. Infinite-Dimensional Analysis: Stochastic Processes. (Research Notes in Mathematics Ser.: No. 124). 250p. 1985. pap. text ed. 21.95 (ISBN 0-273-08684-7). Pitman Pub MA.

Albeverio, S., et al, eds. Stochastic Processes in Quantum Theory & Statistical Physics: Proceedings, Marseille, France, 1981. (Lecture Notes in Physics Ser.: Vol. 173). 337p. 1982. pap. 19.00 (ISBN 0-387-11956-6). Springer-Verlag.

--Stochastic Aspects of Classical & Quantum Systems. (Lecture Notes in Mathematics Ser.: Vol. 1109). ix, 227p. 1985. pap. 14.40 (ISBN 0-387-13914-1). Springer-Verlag.

--Resonances Models & Phenomena. (Lecture Notes in Physics Ser.: Vol. 211). vi, 359p. 1984. pap. 21.00 (ISBN 0-387-13880-3). Springer-Verlag.

Albi, Charles & Forrest, Kenton. The Moffat Tunnel, a Brief History. LC 78-603. (Illus.). 1978. pap. 2.95 (ISBN 0-918654-26-2). CO RR Mus.

Albi, Charles & Jones, William C. Otto Perry: Master Railroad Photographer. (Illus.). 336p. 1982. 30.00 (ISBN 0-918654-32-7). Co RR Mus.

Albi, Charles, jt. auth. see Forrest, Kenton.

Albi, Charles, jt. ed. see Jones, William C.

Albietz, Carol, jt. ed. see Rolih, Susan.

Albin, Edgar A., et al. Selections from the Permanent Collection of the Springfield Art Museum. Landwehr, William C., ed. LC 80-53333. 100p. (Orig.). 1980. pap. text ed. 9.95 (ISBN 0-934306-03-6). Springfield.

Albin, Francis M. Consumer Economics & Personal Money Management. (Illus.). 496p. 1982. 26.95 (ISBN 0-13-169490-1). P-H.

Albin, Leslie, ed. Information Processing in the U. S. Revised & Updated. 70p. 1985. 11.50 (ISBN 0-88283-047-3). AFIPS Pr.

Albin, Mel & Cavallo, Dominick. Family Life in America. (Illus.). 350p. 1980. 11.95 (ISBN 0-686-64847-1). Revisionary.

Albin, Mel, et al, eds. New Directions in Psychohistory: The Adelphi Papers in Honor of Erik H. Erikson. LC 78-4410. 240p. 1980. 29.50x (ISBN 0-669-02350-7). Lexington Bks.

Albin, Rochelle S. Emotions. Choices: Guides for Today's Woman. Vol. 1. LC 83-10187. 120p. 1983. pap. 6.95 (ISBN 0-664-24540-4). Westminster.

--Health & Beauty. LC 84-7459. (Choices: Guides for Today's Woman Ser.: Vol. 10). 116p. 1984. pap. 6.95 (ISBN 0-664-24543-9). Westminster.

Albini, B., ed. see International Convocation on Immunology, 6th.

Albini, Joseph L. American Mafia: Genesis of a Legend. LC 70-147120. (Orig.). 1971. 12.95x (ISBN 0-89197-014-2). Irvington.

Albinoni, Tomaso. Zenobia Regina di Palmireni. Brown, Howard M., ed. LC 76-21018. (Italian Opera 1640-1770 Ser.: Vol. 15). 1978. lib. bdg. 77.00 (ISBN 0-8240-2614-4). Garland Pub.

Albinski, Henry S. The Australian American Security Relationship in Regional & International Perspective. 1982. 32.50x (ISBN 0-312-06119-6). St Martin.

--Australian Policies & Attitudes Toward China. 1966. 50.00x (ISBN 0-691-03004-9). Princeton U Pr.

--Politics & Foreign Policy in Australia: The Impact of Vietnam & Conscription. LC 76-101128. Repr. of 1970 ed. 45.60 (ISBN 0-8357-9114-9, 2017878). Bks Demand UMI.

Albion, Mark S. Advertising's Hidden Effects: Manufacturers' Advertising & Retailing Pricing. LC 82-6776. 304p. 1983. 24.95 (ISBN 0-86569-111-8). Auburn Hse.

Albion, Mark S. & Farris, Paul. Advertising Controversy: Evidence on the Economic Effects of Advertising. LC 80-24645. 256p. 1981. 24.95 (ISBN 0-86569-057-X). Auburn Hse.

Albion, Robert G. Introduction to Military History. LC 75-158240. (Illus.). 1971. Repr. of 1929 ed. 29.00 (ISBN 0-404-00303-6). AMS Pr.

--The Makers of Naval Policy Seventeen Ninety-Eight to Nineteen Forty-Seven. Reed, Rowena, ed. LC 79-90772. 752p. 1980. 22.95x (ISBN 0-87021-360-1). Naval Inst Pr.

--The Makers of Naval Policy 1798-1947. (Illus.). 737p. 1980. 22.95 (ISBN 0-87021-360-1); bulk rates avail. Naval Inst Pr.

--Naval & Maritime History: An Annotated Bibliography. 4th rev. ed. LC 73-186863. 370p. 1972. 10.00 (ISBN 0-913372-05-6); pap. 5.00 (ISBN 0-913372-06-4). Mystic Seaport.

--The Rise of New York Port, Eighteen Fifteen to Eighteen Sixty. LC 83-27190. 485p. 1984. 24.95x (ISBN 0-930350-58-8); pap. 9.95x (ISBN 0-930350-59-6). NE U Pr.

Albion, Robert G., et al. New England & the Sea. LC 72-3694. (The American Maritime Library: Vol. 5). (Illus.). 303p. 1972. 15.95 (ISBN 0-8195-4052-8); pap. 9.00 (ISBN 0-913372-23-4); ltd. ed. 40.00 (ISBN 0-8195-4053-6). Mystic Seaport.

Albiruni. The Chronology of Ancient Nations. Sachau, Edward C., ed. xvi, 464p. Repr. of 1879 ed. lib. bdg. 90.00x (ISBN 0-89241-178-3). Caratzas.

Albis, Abelardo S. The Bell Ringer & Other Stories. 103p. (Orig.). 1982. pap. 4.75 (ISBN 0-686-37572-6, Pub. by New Day Philippines). Cellar.

Albisetti, James C. Secondary School Reform in Imperial Germany. LC 82-12223. 392p. 1983. 37.00x (ISBN 0-691-05373-1). Princeton U Pr.

Albohm, Marjorie. Health Care & The Female Athlete. (Orig.). 1981. pap. text ed. 6.95 (ISBN 0-87670-063-6). Athletic Inst.

Albone, D. J. & Payne, K. W. The Determination of Microgram Quantities of Sulphur & Other Elements in Rainwater by X-Ray Fluorescence Spectrometry, 1978. 1981. 40.00x (ISBN 0-686-97056-X, Pub. by W Spring England). State Mutual Bk.

Albone, Eric S. Mammalian Semiochemistry: The Investigation of Chemical Signals Between Mammals. LC 83-10231. 360p. 1984. 57.00x (ISBN 0-471-10253-9, Pub. by Wiley-Interscience). Wiley.

Alboni, Paolo. Intraventricular Conduction Disturbances: Developments in Cardiovascular Medicine, No. 12. 400p. 1981. 69.00 (ISBN 90-247-2483-X, Pub. by Martinus Nijhoff Netherlands). Kluwer Academic.

Alboni, Paolo, jt. auth. see Masoni, Antonio.

Alborn, et al. The Popular Smithsonian. 1976. pap. 0.95 (ISBN 0-87972-080-8). Bowling Green Univ.

Albornoz, Fernando, ed. The Auxiliaries. Quiroga, Roberto, tr. (Rotary Drilling Ser.: Unit I, Lesson 9). (Illus.). 60p. (Orig., Span.). 1983. pap. text ed. 5.00 (ISBN 0-88698-037-2, 2.10922). PETEX.

--The Drill Stem. 2nd ed. Quiroga, Roberto, tr. (Rotary Drilling Ser.: Unit I, Lesson 3). (Illus.). 51p. (Orig., Span.). 1983. pap. text ed. 5.00 (ISBN 0-88698-031-3, 2.10322). PETEX.

--The Rotary, Kelly, & Swivel. Quiroga, Roberto, tr. (Rotary Drilling Ser.: Unit I, Lesson 4). (Illus.). 69p. (Orig., Span.). 1982. pap. text ed. 5.00 (ISBN 0-88698-032-1, 2.10422). PETEX.

--The Rotary Rig & its Components. Carmona-Agosto, Vivian, tr. (Rotary Drilling Ser.: Unit I, Lesson 1). (Illus.). 47p. (Orig., Span.). 1980. pap. text ed. 5.00 (ISBN 0-88698-029-1, 2.10132). PETEX.

Albornoz, Fernando, tr. see Carmona-Agosto, Vivian.

Albornoz, Fernando, tr. see Leecraft, Jodie.

Alborough, Jez. Bare Bear. LC 83-25119. (Illus.). 32p. (gr. k up). 1984. PLB 6.99 (ISBN 0-394-96808-5); 4.95 (ISBN 0-394-86808-0). Knopf.

Albouy, Pierre, ed. see Hugo, Victor.

Albracht, James & Kurtz, Ray. Introduction to AG Metrics. text ed. 16.75x (ISBN 0-8134-1999-9). Interstate.

Albran, Kehlog. The Profit. 108p. (Orig.). 1973. pap. 2.95 (ISBN 0-8431-0260-8). Price Stern.

Albrand, Martha. Endure No Longer. 1973. pap. 1.25 (ISBN 0-380-01166-2, 17467). Avon.

--The Mask of Alexander. 1982. 15.00x (ISBN 0-7274-0321-4, Pub. by Severn Hse). State Mutual Bk.

--Remembered Anger. 1973. pap. 0.75 (ISBN 0-380-01523-4, 14464). Avon.

Albrecht, Adalbert, tr. see Aschaffenburg, Gustav.

Albrecht, Bob, et al. My TRS-80 Likes Me. 1980. pap. 2.50 (ISBN 0-318-01183-2). Radio Shack.

--Number Patterns. 1980. pap. 2.50 (ISBN 0-318-01184-0). Radio Shack.

--How to Play with Your Timex Sinclair 1000. 124p. PLB 12.95 (ISBN 0-395-34926-5); pap. 7.95 cancelled (ISBN 0-395-34919-2). HM.

--Atari BASIC. XL ed. (General Trade Books). 388p. 1985. pap. 14.95 (ISBN 0-471-80726-5). Wiley.

--TRS-80 BASIC: A Self Teaching Guide. LC 80-10268. (Self Teaching Guides Ser.: No. 1581). 351p. 1980. pap. 12.95 (ISBN 0-471-06466-1, Pub. by Wiley Pr). Wiley.

Albrecht, Bob L., et al. Atari BASIC. LC 79-12513. (Self-Teaching Guides). 333p. 1981. pap. text ed. 12.95 (ISBN 0-471-06496-3, Pub. by Wiley Pr). Wiley.

Albrecht, Carl W. & Watkins, Reed A. Cross-Reference to Names of Ohio Skippers & Butterflies: Insecta, Lepidoptera, Hesperoidea & Papilionoidea. 1983. 4.00 (ISBN 0-86727-095-0). Ohio Bio Survey.

Albrecht, D. G., ed. Recognition of Pattern & Form, Austin, Texas 1979: Proceedings. (Lecture Notes in Biomathematics: Vol. 44). 225p. 1982. pap. 17.00 (ISBN 0-387-11206-5). Springer-Verlag.

Albrecht, David Von, ed. Divorce in the "Liberal" Jurisdictions. 48p. 1955. pap. 2.50 (ISBN 0-87945-016-9). Fed Legal Pubn.

Albrecht, E. & Pepe, G., eds. Perinatal Endocrinology. (Research in Perinatal Medicine Ser.). 1985. 40.00 (ISBN 0-916859-11-8). Perinatology.

Albrecht, Earl. Altar Prayer Workbook B: (Common-Luth) 1984. 6.25 (ISBN 0-89536-688-6, 4865). CSS of Ohio.

Albrecht, F. Topics in Control Theory. (Lecture Notes in Mathematics: Vol. 63). 1968. pap. 10.70 (ISBN 0-387-04233-4). Springer-Verlag.

Albrecht, F. O. The Anatomy of the Red Locust (Nomadacris Septemfasciate Serville) 1956. 35.00x (ISBN 0-85135-067-4, Pub. by Centre Overseas Research). State Mutual Bk.

Albrecht, G., ed. Weyer's Warships of the World 1984-85: Flottentaschenbuch. LC 46-43961. (Weyer's Warships of the World Flottentaschenbuch Ser.). (Illus.). 736p. 1983. 64.95 (ISBN 0-933852-43-6). Nautical & Aviation.

Albrecht, Gary L., ed. The Sociology of Physical Disability & Rehabilitation. LC 75-33544. (Contemporary Community Health Ser.). (Illus.). 317p. 1982. pap. text ed. 8.95x (ISBN 0-8229-5341-2). U of Pittsburgh Pr.

--The Sociology of Physical Disability & Rehabilitation. LC 75-33544. (Contemporary Community Health Ser.). 1976. 16.95x (ISBN 0-8229-3312-8). U of Pittsburgh Pr.

Albrecht, Gene H. The Craniofacial Morphology of the Sulawesi Macaques: Multivariate Analysis As a Tool in Systematics. (Contributions to Primatology: Vol. 13). (Illus.). 1977. 31.50 (ISBN 3-8055-2694-6). S Karger.

Albrecht, Guenther. Lexikon Deutschsprachiger Schriftsteller, Vol. 1. (Ger.). 1974. 45.00 (ISBN 3-589-00091-0, M-7204). French & Eur.

--Lexikon Deutschsprachiger Schriftsteller, Vol. 2. (Ger.). 1974. 45.00 (ISBN 3-589-00092-9, M-7205). French & Eur.

Albrecht, H. J. Rheumatologie fuer die Praxis. (Unveraenderte Auflage: Vol. 2). (Illus.). 1979. pap. 17.50 (ISBN 3-8055-3047-1). S Karger.

Albrecht, J. & Collatz, L., eds. Finite Elemente und Differenzenverfahren: Proceedings, Technical Univ. of Clausthal, W. Germany, Sep. 25-27, 1974. (International Ser. of Numerical Mathematics: No. 28). 186p. (Ger.). 1975. 30.95x (ISBN 0-8176-0775-7). Birkhauser.

--Numerical Treatment of Free Boundary Value Problems. (International Series of Numerical Mathematics: Vol. 58). 350p. 1982. text ed. 36.95x (ISBN 0-8176-1277-7). Birkhauser.

--Numerische Behandlung von Eigenwertaufgaben. (International Ser. of Numerical Mathematics: Vol. 2, No. 43). (Illus.). 203p. (Ger.). pap. 32.95x (ISBN 3-7643-1067-7). Birkhauser.

--Numerische Methoden bei Differentialgleichungen und mit Funktionalanalytischen Hilfsmittein. (International Series on Numerical Mathematics: No. 19). (Illus.). 231p. (Ger.). 1974. 50.95 (ISBN 0-8176-0710-2). Birkhauser.

Albrecht, J., et al. Numerical Treatment of Eigenvalue Problems, Vol. 3. (International Series of Numerical Mathematics: Vol. 69). 216p. (Eng. & Ger.). 1984. 34.95 (ISBN 3-7643-1605-5). Birkhauser.

Albrecht, J., et al, eds. Numerische Behandlung von Differentialgleichungen Mit Besonderer Berucksichtigung Freier Randwertaufgaben. (International Series of Numerical Mathematics: No. 39). (Illus.). 280p. (Ger.). 1978. pap. 37.95 (ISBN 0-8176-0986-5). Birkhauser.

Albrecht, Jeanne, ed. see Renda, Richard D.

Albrecht, Julius & Collatz, Lothar, eds. Numerical Treatment of Integral Equations. (International Ser. of Numerical Mathematics Ser.: No. 53). 283p. 1981. pap. 38.95x (ISBN 0-8176-1105-3). Birkhauser.

Albrecht, Karl. Brain Building: Easy Games to Develop Your Problem Solving Skills. (Illus.). 96p. 1984. 13.95 (ISBN 0-13-081042-8); pap. 5.95 (ISBN 0-13-081034-7). P-H.

--Executive Tune-Up: Personal Effectiveness Skills for Business & Professional People. (Illus.). 224p. 1981. text ed. 13.95 (ISBN 0-13-294215-1, Spec); pap. text ed. 6.95 (ISBN 0-13-294207-0, Spec). P-H.

--Organization Development: A Total Systems Approach to Positive Change in Any Business Organization. 254p. 1983. 20.95 (ISBN 0-13-641696-9). P-H.

--Stress & the Manager: Making It Work for You. (Illus.). 1979. (Spec); pap. 6.95 (ISBN 0-13-852673-7). P-H.

--Successful Management by Objectives: An Action Manual. LC 77-14971. (Illus.). 1978. 14.95 (ISBN 0-13-863266-9, Spec); pap. 6.95 (ISBN 0-13-863258-8, Spec). P-H.

Albrecht, Karl & Churchill, Winton. Computers & Productivity. 300p. 1983. cancelled (ISBN 0-201-10148-3). Benjamin-Cummings.

Albrecht, Karl & Zemke, Ron. Service America! Doing Business in the New Economy. 235p. 1985. 19.95 (ISBN 0-87094-659-5). Dow Jones-Irwin.

Albrecht, Karl G., jt. auth. see Boshear, Walton C.

Albrecht, Maryann & Hall, Francine. The Management of Affirmative Action. new ed. LC 78-24516. (Illus.). 1979. text ed. 31.45 (ISBN 0-673-16108-0). Scott F.

Albrecht, Maryann H. Careers in Business: Exercises & Cases. LC 83-3580. 156p. 1983. pap. 18.45 (ISBN 0-471-87369-1). Wiley.

Albrecht, Maryann H., et al. Growing: A Woman's Guide to Career Satisfaction. 320p. 1979. pap. 14.95 (ISBN 0-942560-12-4). Brace Park.

Albrecht, Otto E. Four Latin Plays of St. Nicholas from the 12th Century Fleury Playbook. 1935. 17.50 (ISBN 0-8482-7271-4). Norwood Edns.

--Four Latin Plays of St. Nicholas from the 12th Century Fleury Play-Book. 1935. 20.00 (ISBN 0-686-21825-6). Quality Lib.

Albrecht, Otto E., jt. ed. see Westlake, Neda M.

Albrecht, Peggy. Eyes In the Bombax Tree, No. 2. (gr. 6-8). 1983. pap. 2.50 (ISBN 0-87508-652-7). Chr Lit.

--House of Congo Cross, No.3. (gr. 6-8). 1983. pap. 2.50 (ISBN 0-87508-651-9). Chr Lit.

--Secret of the Old House, No. 1. (gr. 6-8). 1983. pap. 2.50 (ISBN 0-317-01495-1). Chr Lit.

Albrecht, R. L., et al. BASIC for Home Computers. LC 78-9010. (Self-Teaching Guides). 336p. 1978. pap. 10.95x (ISBN 0-471-03204-2, Pub. by Wiley Pr). Wiley.

Albrecht, R. M, jt. ed. see Johari, Om.

Albrecht, R. M., jt. ed. see Johari, Om.

Albrecht, Robert C., ed. World of Short Fiction. LC 69-11841. 1970. pap. text ed. 10.95 (ISBN 0-02-900350-4). Free Pr.

Albrecht, Robert L. & Inman, Don. BASIC for Your TRS-80 Super. LC 81-16286. (Self-Teaching Guides Ser.: No. 1-581). 374p. 1982. pap. text ed. 10.95 (ISBN 0-471-09644-X, Pub. by Wiley Pr). Wiley.

Albrecht, Robert L., et al. BASIC. 2nd ed. LC 77-14998. (Self-Teaching Guide Ser.). 325p. 1978. pap. text ed. 12.95 (ISBN 0-471-03500-9, Pub. by Wiley Pr). Wiley.

Albrecht, Ruth, jt. auth. see Havighurst, Robert J.

Albrecht, Stan L., et al. Divorce & Remarriage: Problems, Adaptations & Adjustments. LC 82-24250. (Contributions in Women's Studies: No. 42). (Illus.). 256p. 1983. lib. bdg. 29.95 (ISBN 0-313-23616-X, ALD). Greenwood.

--Social Psychology. (P-H Series in Sociology). (Illus.). 1980. text ed. 27.95 (ISBN 0-13-817882-8). P-H.

Albrecht, Theodore. Ludwig Van Beethoven: A Guide to Reaearch. LC 84-48404. 500p. 1985. lib. bdg. 40.00 (ISBN 0-8240-8807-7). Garland Pub.

Albrecht, Ulrich. A Short Research Guide to Arms & Armed Forces. 1980. lib. bdg. 17.50x (ISBN 0-87196-423-6). Facts on File.

Albrecht, Val. Larger Than Life: Joe Namath. LC 75-42313. (Sports Profiles). (gr. 4-11). 1976. PLB 13.31 (ISBN 0-8172-0112-2). Raintree Pubs.

Albrecht, W. P. Hazlitt & the Creative Imagination. LC 65-26727. xii, 204p. 1965. 19.95x (ISBN 0-7006-0001-9). U Pr of KS.

--The Sublime Pleasures of Tragedy: A Study of Critical Theory from Dennis to Keats. LC 75-11896. x, 206p. 1975. 19.95x (ISBN 0-7006-0135-X). U Pr of KS.

Albrecht, W. S., et al. Deterring Fraud: The Internal Auditor's Perspective. 169p. 1984. text ed. 33.00 (ISBN 0-89413-117-6). Inst Inter Aud.

Albrecht, W. Steve. Money Wise. 198p. 1983. 7.95 (ISBN 0-87747-919-4). Deseret Bk.

Albrecht, W. Steve, et al. How to Detect & Prevent Business Fraud. 216p. 1982. 37.50 (ISBN 0-13-404707-9). P-H.

Albrecht, William A. The Albrecht Papers, Vol. I. Walters, Charles, Jr., ed. (Illus.). 515p. 1982. 18.75 (ISBN 0-911311-05-X). Halycon Hse.

Albrecht, William P. Economics. 4th ed. (Illus.). 784p. 1986. text ed. 31.95 (ISBN 0-13-224403-9). P-H.

--The Loathly Lady in "Thomas of Erceldoune". 1978. Repr. of 1954 ed. lib. bdg. 20.00 (ISBN 0-8495-0050-8). Arden Lib.

--The Loathly Lady in Thomas of Erceldoune. LC 74-18004. 1975. Repr. of 1954 ed. lib. bdg. 17.50 (ISBN 0-8414-3000-4). Norwood Edns.

--The Loathly Lady in "Thomas of Erceldoune". LC 55-62031. 127p. 1982. lib. bdg. 29.95x (ISBN 0-89370-722-8). Borgo Pr.

--William Hazlitt & the Malthusian Controversy. LC 70-85980. 1969. Repr. of 1950 ed. 21.00x (ISBN 0-8046-0597-1, Pub. by Kennikat). Assoc Faculty Pr.

Albrecht, William P., Jr. Economics. 3rd ed. (Illus.). 768p. 1983. text ed. 31.95 (ISBN 0-13-224345-8); study guide & wkbk. 12.95 (ISBN 0-13-224360-1). P-H.

--Macroeconomic Principles. 2nd ed. (Illus.). 448p. 1983. pap. text ed. 20.95 (ISBN 0-13-542787-8). P-H.

Albrecht, William P, Jr. Microeconomic Principles. (Illus.). 1979. study guide & wkbk. O.P. 11.95 (ISBN 0-13-227553-8). P-H.

Albrecht, William P., Jr. Microeconomic Principles. 2nd ed. (Illus.). 496p. 1983. pap. text ed. 20.95 (ISBN 0-13-581157-0). P-H.

Albrecht-Carrie, Rene. A Diplomatic History of Europe: Since the Congress of Vienna. rev. ed. 1973. pap. text ed. 23.50 scp (ISBN 0-06-040171-0, HarpC). Har-Row.

--Europe after Eighteen Fifteen. 5th ed. (Quality Paperback: No. 43). (Orig.). 1972. pap. 4.95 (ISBN 0-8226-0043-9). Littlefield.

--Europe Fifteen Hundred to Eighteen Forty-Eight. (Quality Paperback: No. 42). (Orig.). 1973. pap. 4.95 (ISBN 0-8226-0042-0). Littlefield.

--France, Europe & the Two World Wars. LC 74-6775. 346p. 1975. Repr. of 1961 ed. lib. bdg. 22.50x (ISBN 0-8371-7568-2, ALFR). Greenwood.

--Italy at the Paris Peace Conference. xiv, 575p. 1966. 30.00 (ISBN 0-208-00068-2, Archon); (Archon). Shoe String.

--Italy from Napoleon to Mussolini. LC 49-50178. 302p. 1950. pap. 10.50x (ISBN 0-231-08508-7). Columbia U Pr.

--Italy from Napoleon to Mussolini. 20.00 (ISBN 0-8446-1518-8). Peter Smith.

--Meaning of the First World War. (Illus., Orig.). 1965. 3.95 (ISBN 0-13-567370-4, Spec). P-H.

--Twentieth Century Europe. (Quality Paperback: No. 256). 283p. (Orig.). 1973. pap. 2.95 (ISBN 0-8226-0256-3). Littlefield.

Albrecht-Mathey, Elisabeth. The Printed Fabrics of Mulhouse & Alsace, 1750-1800. 1981. 40.00x (ISBN 0-85317-091-6, Pub. by Lewis Pubs). State Mutual Bk.

Albrektsson, T., jt. auth. see Lee, A. J.

Albright & Weiner. Wild about Brownies. (Wild about Ser.). 1985. pap. 5.95 (ISBN 0-8120-2911-9). Barron.

Albright, Arnita, jt. auth. see Albright, Hardie.

Albright, Barbara & Weiner, Leslie. Mostly Muffins. (Illus.). 96p. 1984. pap. 4.95 (ISBN 0-312-54916-4). St Martin.

Albright, C., jt. auth. see Donely, D.

Albright, Daniel. Lyricality in English Literature. LC 84-10455. xii, 276p. 1985. 24.50x (ISBN 0-8032-1019-1). U of Nebr Pr.

--Personality & Impersonality: Lawrence, Wolf & Mann. LC 77-23873. 1978. lib. bdg. 26.00x (ISBN 0-226-01249-2). U of Chicago Pr.

--Representation & the Imagination: Beckett, Kafka, Nabokov, & Schoenberg. LC 80-26976. (Chicago Originals Ser.). 256p. 1981. lib. bdg. 20.00x (ISBN 0-226-01252-2). U of Chicago Pr.

Albright, David E. The U. S. S. R. Sub-Saharan Africa in the 1980s. (Washington Papers: No. 101). 144p. 1983. 7.95 (ISBN 0-03-069344-6). Praeger.

Albright, David E., ed. Communism in Africa. LC 78-13813. 288p. 1980. 15.00x (ISBN 0-253-12814-5). Ind U Pr.

Albright, Evelyn M. Dramatic Publications in England: 1580-1640. LC 77-131246. 1971. Repr. of 1927 ed. text ed. 10.00x (ISBN 0-87752-127-1). Gordian.

--The Short Story: Its Principles & Structure. LC 73-15603. Repr. of 1907 ed. lib. bdg. 27.50 (ISBN 0-8414-2920-0). Folcroft.

Albright, Frank, jt. auth. see Bowen, Richard L.

Albright, Frank P. Johann Ludwig Eberhardt & His Salem Clocks. LC 77-18955. (Old Salem Ser.). x, 192p. 1978. 12.95 (ISBN 0-8078-1324-9). U of NC Pr.

Albright, George A. Anesthesia in Obstetrics. LC 76-62908. 1978. 37.50 (ISBN 0-201-00154-3, Med-Nurse). Addison-Wesley.

Albright, Gretchen E. Survival Sanctuary: A Scouts Guide to Preparedness. LC 80-54281. (Illus.). 146p. (Orig.). 1980. pap. 4.95 (ISBN 0-938064-00-2). Secure Futures.

Albright, H. D., ed. see Antoine, Andre.

Albright, Hardie & Albright, Arnita. Acting: The Creative Process. 3rd ed. 432p. 1980. pap. text ed. write for info (ISBN 0-534-00744-9). Wadsworth Pub.

Albright, Horace M. The Birth of the National Park Service: The Founding Years, 1913-1933. 350p. 1985. 19.95 (ISBN 0-935704-32-9); pap. 11.95 (ISBN 0-935704-33-7). Howe Brothers.

Albright, Horace M. & Taylor, Frank J. Oh, Ranger! rev. 14th ed. Jones, William R., ed. (Illus.). 176p. pap. 6.95 (ISBN 0-89646-068-1). Outbooks.

Albright-Knox Art Gallery. Thirty Seventh Western New York Exhibition. LC 78-53046. (Illus.). 1978. 3.50 (ISBN 0-914782-18-5). Buffalo Acad.

Albright-Knox Art Gallery & Nash, Steven A. Painting & Sculpture from Antiquity to Nineteen Forty-Two. LC 77-79651. (Illus.). 1979. 35.00 (ISBN 0-8478-0146-2); pap. 25.00 (ISBN 0-914782-17-7). Buffalo Acad.

Albright, Leonard. Administering Programs for Handicapped Students. (Professional Development Ser.: No. 3). 24p. (Orig.). 1979. pap. 3.00 (ISBN 0-89514-025-X, 10379). Am Voc Assn.

Albright, Lyle, et al. Pyrolysis: Theory & Industrial Practice. 446p. 1983. 65.00 (ISBN 0-12-048880-9). Acad Pr.

Albright, Lyle F. Processes for Major Addition-Type Plastics & Their Monomers. rev. ed. LC 80-12568. 300p. 1985. lib. bdg. 32.50 (ISBN 0-89874-074-6). Krieger.

Albright, Lyle F. & Baker, R. T., eds. Coke Formation on Metal Surfaces. LC 82-16335. (ACS Symposium Ser.: No. 202). 318p. 1982. lib. bdg. 38.95x (ISBN 0-8412-0745-3). Am Chemical.

Albright, Lyle F. & Crynes, Billy L., eds. Industrial & Laboratory Pyrolyses. LC 76-28733. (ACS Symposium Ser: No. 32). 1976. 39.95 (ISBN 0-8412-0337-7). Am Chemical.

Albright, Lyle F. & Goldsby, Arthur R., eds. Industrial & Laboratory Alkylations. LC 77-23973. (ACS Symposium Ser.: No. 55). 1977. 39.95 (ISBN 0-8412-0385-7). Am Chemical.

Albright, Lyle F. & Hanson, Carl, eds. Industrial & Laboratory Nitrations. LC 75-38712. (ACS Symposium Ser.: No. 22). 1976. 34.95 (ISBN 0-8412-0306-7). Am Chemical.

Albright, Madeleine K. Poland: The Role of the Press in Political Change. LC 83-16144. (The Washington Papers). 168p. 1983. 7.95 (ISBN 0-03-063696-5). Praeger.

Albright, Nanc T., illus. I Know an Old Lady Who Swallowed a Fly. (Flannel Board Ser.). (Illus., Orig.). (ps-6). pap. cancelled (ISBN 0-913545-10-4). Moonlight FL.

Albright, Nancy. A Little Meat Goes a Long Way. Geras, Charlie, ed. 240p. 1982. 14.95 (ISBN 0-87857-376-3, 07-005-0); pap. 10.95 (ISBN 0-87857-355-0, 07-005-1). Rodale Pr Inc.

--The Rodale Cookbook. 1982. pap. 7.95 (ISBN 0-345-30527-2). Ballantine.

Albright, Nancy T. Do Tell! Holiday Draw & Tell Stories. (Draw & Tell Stories). (ps-4). 1981. 4.50 (ISBN 0-913545-02-3). Moonlight FL.

Albright, Priscilla, jt. auth. see Albright, Rod.

Albright, Priscilla, jt. auth. see Albright, Rodney.

Albright, Rod & Albright, Priscilla. Walks in the Great Smokies. LC 79-4898. (Illus.). 192p. 1979. pap. 7.95 (ISBN 0-914788-14-0). East Woods.

Albright, Rodney & Albright, Priscilla. Short Walks on Long Island. 2nd, enl. ed. LC 74-75075. 132p. 1983. pap. 5.95 (ISBN 0-87106-920-2). Globe Pequot.

Albright, Roger. Old Houses, New Homes. LC 80-21288. (Illus.). 256p. 1981. pap. 9.95 (ISBN 0-8289-0396-4). Greene.

Albright, Ruth N. Vedic Declension of the Type Vrkis: A Contribution to the Study of the Feminine Noun Declension in Indo-European. (LD: No.1). 1927. pap. 16.00 (ISBN 0-527-00747-1). Kraus Repr.

Albright, Thomas. Art in the San Francisco Bay Area, 1945-1980: An Illustrated History. 360p. 1985. 60.00 (ISBN 0-520-05193-9); pap. 29.95 (ISBN 0-520-05518-7). U of Cal Pr.

Albright, Thomas & Butterfield, Jan. Oliver Jackson. LC 82-61511. (Illus.). 32p. (Orig.). 1982. pap. 10.95 (ISBN 0-932216-10-2). Seattle Art.

Albright, Thomas A. Orbital Interactions in Chemistry. LC 84-15310. 447p. 1985. 49.95 (ISBN 0-471-87393-4, Pub. by Wiley-Interscience). Wiley.

Albright, Verne. Horseback Across Three Americas. (Illus.). 204p. 1974. 10.00 (ISBN 0-912830-17-4). Printed Horse.

Albright, Victor E. Shakespearian Stage. LC 79-158241. Repr. of 1926 ed. 16.00 (ISBN 0-404-00304-4). AMS Pr.

Albright, W. Paul. Collective Bargaining: A Canadian Simulation. 2nd ed. 1981. pap. text ed. 6.95 (ISBN 0-8403-2428-6). Kendall-Hunt.

Albright, William F. Archaeology of Palestine. rev. ed. 11.25 (ISBN 0-8446-0003-2). Peter Smith.

--Biblical Period from Abraham to Ezra: A Historical Survey. pap. 4.95xi (ISBN 0-06-130102-7, TB102, Torch). Har-Row.

--The Proto-Sinaitic Inscriptions & Their Decipherment. LC 73-248003. (Harvard Theological Studies: No. 22). pap. 20.00 (ISBN 0-317-10139-0, 2017505). Bks Demand UMI.

--The Vocalization of the Egyptian Syllabic Orthography. (American Orient Ser.). 1934. pap. 16.00 (ISBN 0-685-13730-9). Kraus Repr.

--Yahweh & the Gods of Canaan: An Historical Analysis of Two Contrasting Faiths. 1978. Repr. of 1968 ed. 12.00x (ISBN 0-931464-01-3). Eisenbrauns.

Albright, William F. & Mann, C. S., eds. Matthew. LC 77-150875. (Anchor Bible Ser.: Vol. 26). 1971. 18.00 (ISBN 0-385-08658-X, Anchor Pr). Doubleday.

Albritton, Clarice. Beyond the Lighthouse. LC 77-83447. (Illus.). 1978. pap. 4.25 (ISBN 0-87516-243-6). De Vorss.

--The Untold Story: Jesus Son of God. LC 83-73188. 1983. pap. 5.95 (ISBN 0-318-00817-3). W P Brownell.

Albritton, Clarice & Newby, Grace. A Lamp Unto Our Faith. LC 76-24514. 1976. pap. 3.95 (ISBN 0-87516-218-5). De Vorss.

Albritton, Claude C. Philosophy of Geohistory. LC 74-10559. (Benchmark Papers in Geology Ser: Vol. 13). 400p. 1975. 66.00 (ISBN 0-12-786049-5). Acad Pr.

Albritton, Claude C., ed. Charles Lyell on North American Geology: An Original Anthology. LC 77-6524. (History of Geology Ser.). (Illus.). 1978. lib. bdg. 51.00 (ISBN 0-405-10446-4). Ayer Co Pubs.

--History of Geology Series, 37 vols. (Illus.). 1978. lib. bdg. 1286.50x (ISBN 0-405-10429-4). Ayer Co Pubs.

Albritton, Claude C., ed. see Association of American Geologists & Naturalists at Philadelphia, 1840 & 1841.

Albritton, Claude C., ed. see Clarke, John M.

Albritton, Claude C., ed. see Kirwan, Richard.

Albritton, Claude C., ed. see Literary & Philosophical Society of New York, May, 1814 & Clinton, Dewitt.

Albritton, Claude C., ed. see Marcou, Jules, Jr.

Albritton, Claude C., ed. see Mariotte, Edme.

Albritton, Claude C., jt. ed. see Merrill, George P.

Albritton, Claude C., Jr. Abyss of Time: Changing Conceptions of the Earth's Antiquity after the 16th Century. LC 79-57131. (Illus.). 252p. 1980. text ed. 14.95x (ISBN 0-87735-341-7); pap. text ed. 8.95x. Freeman Cooper.

Albritton, Claude C., Jr., ed. see Bakewell, Robert.

Albritton, Claude C., Jr., ed. see Buckland, William.

Albritton, Claude C., Jr., ed. see Cleaveland, Parker.

Albritton, Claude C., Jr., ed. see Conybeare, W. D. & Phillips, William.

Albritton, Claude C., Jr., ed. see Cuvier, Georges.

Albritton, Claude C., Jr., ed. see Davison, Charles.

Albritton, Claude C., Jr., ed. see Gilbert, Grove K.

Albritton, Claude C., Jr., ed. see Greenough, George B.

Albritton, Claude C., Jr., ed. see Hooke, Robert.

Albritton, Claude C., Jr., ed. see Lambrecht, K. & Quenstedt, W. A.

Albritton, Claude C., Jr., ed. see Lyell, Charles.

Albritton, Claude C., Jr., ed. see Miller, Hugh.

Albritton, Claude C., Jr., ed. see Moore, Nathaniel F.

Albritton, Claude C., Jr., ed. see Murray, John.

Albritton, Claude C., Jr., ed. see Parkinson, James.

Albritton, Claude C., Jr., ed. see Phillips, John.

Albritton, Claude C., Jr., ed. see Phillips, William.

Albritton, Claude C., Jr., ed. see Ray, John.

Albritton, Claude C., Jr., ed. see Scrope, George P.

Albritton, Claude C., Jr., ed. see Sherley, Thomas.

Albritton, Claude C., Jr., ed. see Whiston, William.

Albritton, Claude C., Jr., ed. see White, George W.

Albritton, Claude C., Jr., ed. see Whitehurst, John.

Albritton, Claude C., Jr., ed. see Woodward, Horace B.

Albritton, Claude C., Jr., ed. see Woodward, John.

Albritton, Harold D. Controversies in Real Property Valuation: A Commentary. 127p. 1982. 12.50 (ISBN 0-911780-60-2). Am Inst Real Estate Appraisers.

Albritton, Robert. A Japanese Reconstruction of Marxist Theory. 256p. 1985. 27.50 (ISBN 0-312-44061-8). St Martin.

Albro, John A., ed. see Shepard, Thomas.

Albronda, Mildred. Douglas Tilden: Portrait of a Deaf Sculptor. 1980. 11.95x (ISBN 0-932666-26-4); pap. 8.95x (ISBN 0-932666-03-5). T J Pubs.

Albrow, Martin, tr. see Luhmann, Niklas.

Albuquerque, Alfonso D' see D'Albuquerque, Alfonso.

Albuquerque, E. X. & Eldefrawi, A. T., eds. Myasthenia Gravis. (Illus.). 512p. 1983. 75.00 (ISBN 0-412-16310-1, NO. 6779, Pub. by Chapman & Hall). Methuen Inc.

Alburger, Mary A. Scottish Fiddlers & Their Music. (Illus.). 224p. 1983. 32.00 (ISBN 0-575-03174-3, Pub. by Gollancz England). David & Charles.

--The Violin Makers. 1978. 22.50 (ISBN 0-575-02442-9, Pub. by Gollancz England). David & Charles.

Alburo, Erlinda K., ed. Cebuano Folk Tales, 1 & 2, 2 vols. wrps. 3.50x (ISBN 0-686-09462-X). Cellar.

--Cebuano Folksongs One. (Illus.). 1978. pap. 2.25x (ISBN 0-686-24098-7, Pub. by San Carlos). Cellar.

Albury, Haziel L. Man-O-War, My Island Home: A History of an Outer Abaco Island. LC 77-87225. (Illus.). 167p. 1977. 9.00 (ISBN 0-935968-02-4). Holly Pr.

Albury, W. R. Condillac: Loqique. Bonnot de Condillac, Etienne, tr. LC 77-86228. 1980. 20.00 (ISBN 0-913870-38-2). Abaris Bks.

Albus, James S. Brains, Behavior, & Robotics. 400p. 1981. 21.95 (ISBN 0-07-000975-9). McGraw.

--Brains, Behavior & Robotics. 352p. 1981. write for info. New World Bks.

--Peoples' Capitalism: The Economics of the Robot Revolution. LC 75-44585. 157p. 1976. 10.50 (ISBN 0-917480-01-5); pap. 6.95 (ISBN 0-917480-00-7). New World Bks.

Al-Bustani, Abdullah. A Concise Arabic Dictionary (Al Wafi) (Arabic.). 1980. 40.00x (ISBN 0-86685-095-3). Intl Bk Ctr.

Al-Bustani, Butrus. Arabic-Arabic Dictionary Muhit Al Muhit. (Arabic.). 50.00x (ISBN 0-86685-096-1). Intl Bk Ctr.

Alcacer, Luis, ed. The Physics & Chemistry of Low Dimensional Solids. (NATO Advanced Study Institute Ser. C: Mathematical & Physical Sciences: No. 56). 436p. 1980. lib. bdg. 50.00 (ISBN 90-277-1144-5, Pub. by Reidel Holland). Kluwer Academic.

Alcala, A. Vocabulario Andaluz. 676p. (Span.). 1980. 47.95 (ISBN 84-249-1364-7, S-32726). French & Eur.

Alcala, Angel C. Philippine Land Vertebrates: Field Biology. 1976. wrps. 6.50x (ISBN 0-686-09425-5). Cellar.

Alcala, Gaspar. History of New Mexico, Sixteen-Ten. Espinos, Gilberto & Hodge, F. W., eds. LC 67-24716. (Quivira Society Publications, Vol. 4). 1967. Repr. of 1933 ed. 17.00 (ISBN 0-405-00074-X). Ayer Co Pubs.

Alcala, V. O., ed. A Bibliography of Education in the Caribbean. 1976. lib. bdg. 59.95 (ISBN 0-8490-1498-0). Gordon Pr.

Alcala, Yanez Y. & Rivera, Geronimo A. The Life & Adventures of Alonso, the Chattering Lay Brother & Servant of Many Masters. LC 80-2468. Repr. of 1845 ed. 57.50 (ISBN 0-404-19100-2). AMS Pr.

Alcalay. Basic Encyclopedia of Jewish Proverbs, Quotations, Folk Wisdom. 18.95 (ISBN 0-87677-153-3). Hartmore.

Alcalay, Ammiel, tr. see Kis, Danilo.

Alcalay, Klara, tr. see Kis, Danilo.

Alcalay, Reuben. Complete English-Hebrew, Hebrew-English Dictionary, 3 vols. 7180p. (Eng. & Hebrew.). 1980. Repr. of 1965 ed. 69.00 set (ISBN 0-89961-017-X). Vol. 1 (ISBN 0-89961-003-X). Vol. 2 (ISBN 0-89961-007-2). Vol. 3 (ISBN 0-89961-008-0). SBS Pub.

--The Massada English-Hebrew Student Dictionary. 734p. (Eng. & Hebrew.). 1980. Repr. 18.95 (ISBN 0-89961-006-4). SBS Pub.

Alcalay, Ruben. The Hebrew-English Dictionary, 2 vols. Incl. Vol. 1. Complete Hebrew-English Dictionary; Vol. 2. Complete English-Hebrew Dictionary (ISBN 0-87677-020-0). (Hebrew & Eng.). 1965. text ed. 50.00 ea. Prayer Bk.

Alcala-Zamora. Alcala-Zamora, Diccionario Frances-Espanol, Espanol-Frances. 960p. (Span. & Fr.). pap. 9.95 (ISBN 84-303-0094-5, S-50399). French & Eur.

--Alcala-Zamora, Diccionario Frances-Espanol, Espanol-Frances. 960p. (Span. & Fr.). 12.25 (ISBN 84-303-0093-7, S-50400). French & Eur.

Alcaly, Roger, jt. auth. see Mermelstein, David.

Alcamo, I. Edward. Microbiology. (Biology Ser.). (Illus.). 600p. 1983. text ed. 34.95 (ISBN 0-201-10068-1); Instrs' Manual 3.00 (ISBN 0-201-10069-X); study guide 10.95 (ISBN 0-201-11180-2); Laboratory Manual 13.95 (ISBN 0-201-11181-0) (ISBN 0-201-11182-9). Addison-Wesley.

Alcantara, Cynthia H. de see De Alcantara, Cynthia H.

Alcantara, Ruben R. Sakada: Filipino Adaptation in Hawaii. LC 80-5858. 202p. (Orig.). 1981. lib. bdg. 22.75 (ISBN 0-8191-1578-9); pap. text ed. 11.00 (ISBN 0-8191-1579-7). U Pr of Amer.

Alcantara, Ruben R. & Alconcel, Nancy S. The Filipinos in Hawaii: An Annotated Bibliography. LC 77-84531. (Hawaii Bibliographies Ser: No. 6). 1977. pap. text ed. 8.00x (ISBN 0-8248-0612-3). UH Pr.

Alcantara, S. Peter. A Golden Treatise of Mental Prayer. Hollings, G. S., ed. LC 77-18960. Repr. of 1978 ed. 35.20 (ISBN 0-8357-9135-1, 2019096). Bks Demand UMI.

Alcanter, Frank, jt. auth. see Odekirk, Glenn E.

Alcantud, Adela. Diccionario Bilingue De Psicologia. LC 78-50649. (Senda Lexicografica Ser.). (Span.). 1978. pap. 7.95 (ISBN 0-918454-05-0). Senda Nueva.

Alcaraz, Manuel, et al. Sexual Hormones: Influence on the Electrophysiology of the Brain. LC 74-4137. 223p. 1974. text ed. 28.00x (ISBN 0-8422-7214-3). Irvington.

Alcarez, Ramon, et al, eds. Other Side, or Notes for the History of the War Between Mexico & U. S. Ramsey, Albert C., tr. 1850. 40.50 (ISBN 0-8337-2902-0). B Franklin.

Alcedo, Antonio De see De Alcedo, Antonio.

Alcega, Juan de see De Alcega, Juan.

Al-Chalabi, Fadhil J. OPEC & the International Oil Industry: A Changing Structure. (Illus.). 1980. pap. 9.95 (ISBN 0-19-877155-X). Oxford U Pr.

ALCHE Educational Services Dept. Annual Staff. Applications Software Survey for Personal Computers 1984. 191p. 1984. pap. 40.00 (ISBN 0-8169-0316-6); pap. 20.00 members (ISBN 0-317-17534-3). Am Inst Chem Eng.

Alchemy, Jack. For Sex & Free Roadmaps. 1976. pap. 1.50 (ISBN 0-917402-01-4). Downtown Poets.

Alche's Equipment Testing Procedures Committee. Centrifugal Pumps. 2nd ed. 1984. pap. 16.00 (ISBN 0-8169-0320-4). Am Inst Chem Eng.

Alchian, Armen A. Economic Forces at Work. LC 77-1327. 1977. 10.00 (ISBN 0-913966-30-4, Liberty Pr); pap. 3.50 (ISBN 0-913966-35-5). Liberty Fund.

Alchian, Armen A. & Allen, William R. Exchange & Production: Competition, Coordination, & Control. 3rd ed. 496p. 1983. pap. text ed. write for info. (ISBN 0-534-01320-1). Wadsworth Pub.

Al-Chihabi, Emir. Dictionnaire des Termes Agricoles: Francais-Arabe. 2nd. ed. (Arabic & Fr.). 40.00 (ISBN 0-86685-305-7). Intl Bk Ctr.

Alchin, Carrie A. Ear Training for Teacher & Pupil. LC 74-27326. 152p. 1982. Repr. of 1904 ed. 19.00 (ISBN 0-404-12852-1). AMS Pr.

Alcholics Anonymous World Services, Inc. Dr. Bob & the Good Oldtimers & Pass it On. 1894. text ed. 12.50 combined gift package (ISBN 0-916856-13-5). AAWS.

Alchon, Guy. The Invisible Hand of Planning: Capitalism, Social Science, & the State in the 1920s. LC 84-42873. 250p. 1985. text ed. 25.00x (ISBN 0-691-04723-5). Princeton U Pr.

Alchourron, C. E. & Bulygin, E. Normative Systems. LC 75-170895. (Library of Exact Philosophy: Vol. 5). (Illus.). 1971. 31.00 (ISBN 0-387-81019-6). Springer-Verlag.

Alciphron, et al. Letters: Alciphron, Aelian, Philostratus. Warmington, E. H., ed. (Loeb Classical Library: No. 383). (Gr. & Eng.). 12.50x (ISBN 0-674-99421-3). Harvard U Pr.

Alcman. The Parthenon. Connor, W. R., ed. LC 78-81590. (Greek Texts Commentaries Ser.). 1979. Repr. of 1951 ed. lib. bdg. 17.00x (ISBN 0-405-11432-X). Ayer Co Pubs.

Alcock & Harris. Welfare Law & Order. 240p. 1982. text ed. 27.75x (ISBN 0-333-29490-4, Pub. by Macmillan England). Humanities.

Alcock, A. Materials for a Carcenological Fauna of India: 1895-1900, 6pts. in 1. 1968. 70.00 (ISBN 3-7682-0544-4). Lubrecht & Cramer.

Alcock, Anne. They're Off. (Illus.). 1979. 18.95 (ISBN 0-85131-299-3, BL187, Dist. by Miller). J A Allen.

Alcock, C. B. Principles of Pyrometallurgy. 1977. 60.00 (ISBN 0-12-048950-3). Acad Pr.

Alcock, C. B., ed. Electromotive Force Measurements in High-Temperature Systems. 227p. 1968. text ed. 28.75x (ISBN 0-686-32509-5). IMM North Am.

Alcock, Donald. Illustrating BASIC: A Simple Programming Language. (Illus.). 120p. 1977. 27.95 (ISBN 0-521-21703-2); pap. 10.95 (ISBN 0-521-21704-0). Cambridge U Pr.

--Illustrating FORTRAN. (Illus.). 132p. 1983. 19.95 (ISBN 0-521-24598-2); pap. 10.95 (ISBN 0-521-28810-X). Cambridge U Pr.

--Illustrating Superbasic on the Sinclair QL. (Illus.). 191p. 1985. pap. 11.95 (ISBN 0-521-31517-4). Cambridge U Pr.

Alcock, F. Trade & Travel in South America. 1976. lib. bdg. 59.95 (ISBN 0-8490-2754-3). Gordon Pr.

Alcock, Gudrun. Dooley's Lion: A Junior Novel. (Illus.). 112p. (gr. 3-7). 1985. text ed. 11.95 (ISBN 0-88045-066-5). Stemmer Hse.

Alcock, James E. Parapsychology-Science or Magic? A Psychological Perspective. (Foundations & Philosophy of Science & Technology Ser.). 300p. 1981. 39.00 (ISBN 0-08-025773-9); pap. 16.50 (ISBN 0-08-025772-0). Pergamon.

Alcock, John. Animal Behavior: An Evolutionary Approach. 3rd, rev. ed. LC 83-14420. (Illus.). 380p. 1983. text ed. 27.50 (ISBN 0-87893-021-3). Sinauer Assoc.

--Mons Perfectionis. LC 74-28823. (English Experience Ser.: No. 706). 1974. Repr. of 1497 ed. 6.00 (ISBN 90-221-0706-X). Walter J Johnson.

--Sonoran Desert Spring. LC 84-16468. (Illus.). 196p. 1985. 19.95 (ISBN 0-226-01258-1). U of Chicago Pr.

--Spousage of a Virgin to Christ. LC 74-80158. (English Experience Ser.: No. 638). (Illus.). 19p. 1974. Repr. of 1496 ed. 3.50 (ISBN 90-221-0638-1). Walter J Johnson.

Alcock, John, jt. auth. see Thornhill, Randy.

Alcock, Leslie. Arthur's Britain. 1970. pap. 5.95 (ISBN 0-14-021396-1, Pelican). Penguin.

Alcock, N. W. Cruck Construction: An Introduction & Catalogue. (CBA Research Reports Ser.: No. 42). 180p. 1981. pap. text ed. 24.50x (ISBN 0-906780-11-X, Pub. by Coun Brit Archaeology). Humanities.

Alcock, N. W., ed. Warwickshire Grazier & London Skinner, 1532 to 1555: The Account Book of Peter Temple & Thomas Heritage. (Records of Social & Economic History Ser.). (Illus.). 1981. 98.00x (ISBN 0-19-726008-X). Oxford U Pr.

Alcock, R. C. & Holland, F. C. British History: A Short History & Guide. 372p. 1982. 37.00x (ISBN 0-686-45765-X, Pub. by R C Alcock Ltd Scotland). State Mutual Bk.

--The Maltese Cross Cancellations of the United Kingdom. 2nd ed. 1982. 33.00x (ISBN 0-686-45770-6, Pub. by R C Alcock Ltd Scotland). State Mutual Bk.

Alcock, Randal H. Botanical Names for English Readers. LC 73-174935. xviii, 236p. 1971. Repr. of 1876 ed. 40.00x (ISBN 0-8103-3823-8). Gale.

Alcock, Roy. The Feedback Loop. 1984. 7.95 (ISBN 0-533-05880-5). Vantage.

Alcock, Rutherford. Capital of the Tycoon, 2 Vols. 1863. Set. 35.00x (ISBN 0-403-00241-9). Scholarly.

--Capital of the Tycoon: A Narrative of a Three Years' Residence in Japan, 2 Vols. LC 68-30995. (Illus.). 1968. Repr. of 1863 ed. Set. lib. bdg. 36.50x (ISBN 0-8371-1865-4, ALCT). Greenwood.

Alcock, T. The Life of Samuel of Kalahum. 144p. 1983. pap. text ed. 32.50x (ISBN 0-85668-219-5, Pub. by Aris & Phillips England). Humanities.

Alcock, Vivien. The Haunting of Cassie Palmer. LC 81-15230. 160p. (gr. 4-6). 1982. 9.95 (ISBN 0-385-28402-0). Delacorte.

--The Haunting of Cassie Palmer. (gr. k-12). 1985. pap. 2.50 (ISBN 0-440-43370-3, YB). Dell.

--The Stonewalkers. LC 82-13956. 192p. (gr. 4-6). 1983. 13.95 (ISBN 0-385-29233-3). Delacorte.

--The Stonewalkers. 192p. (gr. k-12). 1985. pap. 2.50 (ISBN 0-440-98198-0, LFL). Dell.

--The Sylvia Game. LC 84-3279. 192p. (gr. 4-6). 1984. 14.95 (ISBN 0-385-29341-0). Delacorte.

--Travelers by Night. LC 85-1663. (Illus.). 192p. (gr. 5-9). 1985. 14.95 (ISBN 0-385-29406-9). Delacorte.

Alcoholics Anonymous World Services, Inc. Los Doce Pasos y Las Doce Tradiciones. 196p. (Orig., Eng. & Span.). 1985. pap. 2.50 (ISBN 0-916856-16-X). AAWS.

Alcoholics Anonymous World Services Inc. Fifty Years of Gratitude. (Illus.). 78p. English. text ed. write for info. (ISBN 0-916856-14-3); French. text ed. write for info (ISBN 0-916856-15-1). AAWS.

Alcoholics Anonymous World Services, Inc. Staff. Pass It On: The Story of Bill Wilson & How the A. A. Message Reached the World. 432p. 1984. 6.50 (ISBN 0-916856-12-7). AAWS.

Alconcel, Nancy S., jt. auth. see Alcantara, Ruben R.

Alcorn, Alfred. The Pull of the Earth. 299p. 1985. 15.95 (ISBN 0-395-36804-9). HM.

Alcorn, Charles L., jt. auth. see Nicholson, Charles L.

Alcorn County Historical Association, ed. The History of Alcorn County, Mississippi, Vol. I. (Illus.). 645p. 1983. 57.00 (ISBN 0-88107-008-4). Natl ShareGraphics.

Alcorn, Edgar G. The Duties & Liabilities of Bank Directors. Bruchey, Stuart, ed. LC 80-1128. (The Rise of Commercial Banking Ser.). 1981. Repr. of 1908 ed. lib. bdg. 15.00x (ISBN 0-405-13628-5). Ayer Co Pubs.

Alcorn, George T., jt. ed. see Jordan, James M.

Alcorn, Gordon A. Silent Wings. (Illus.). 83p. 1982. pap. 4.95x (ISBN 0-87770-277-2). Ye Galleon.

Alcorn, Janis B. Huastec Mayan Ethnobotany. (Illus.). 992p. 1984. text ed. 40.00x (ISBN 0-292-71543-9). U of Tex Pr.

Alcorn, John. The Jolly Rogers: History of the 90th Bomb Group in WW II. LC 81-80465. (World War II Forces History Ser.). (Illus.). 212p. 1981. 18.95 (ISBN 0-911852-89-1). Aviation.

--The Nature Novel from Hardy to Lawrence. LC 76-17552. 139p. 1977. 21.00x (ISBN 0-231-04122-5). Columbia U Pr.

Alcorn, Pat. Success & Survival in the Family Owned Business. 256p. 1982. 23.50 (ISBN 0-07-000961-9). McGraw.

Alcorn, Paul A. Social Issues in Technology: A Format for Investigation. (Illus.). 240p. 1985. text ed. 22.95 (ISBN 0-13-815929-7). P-H.

Alcorn, Randy C. Christians in the Wake of the Sexual Revolution: Recovering Our Sexual Sanity. LC 85-4959. (Critical Concern Ser.). 1985. 13.95 (ISBN 0-88070-095-5). Multnomah.

Alcorn, Rowena. Timothy: Nez Perce Chief, Life & Times, 1800-1891. Date not set. price not set. Ye Galleon.

Alcorn, Samuel R. The World Is Yours-Enjoy Listening to International Radio. 64p. 1984. pap. 2.95 (ISBN 0-914542-14-1). Gilfer.

Alcorn, Wallace. Teacher's Guide to Elijah: Prophet of God. (Illus.). 1974. pap. 1.50 (ISBN 0-87227-022-X). Reg Baptist.

Alcott, A. Bronson. Concord Days. 10.00 (ISBN 0-87556-005-9). Saifer.

--Concord Lectures on Philosophy: Comprising Outlines of All the Lectures at the Concord Summer School of Philosophy in 1882. Bridgman, Raymond L., ed. 1969. 15.00x (ISBN 0-87556-006-7). Saifer.

--New Connecticut. 1970. Repr. of 1881 ed. 10.00 (ISBN 0-87556-007-5). Saifer.

--Sonnets & Canzonets. Repr. of 1882 ed. lib. bdg. 35.00 (ISBN 0-8482-0117-5). Norwood Edns.

--Sonnets & Canzonets. (Illus.). 1969. Repr. of 1882 ed. 10.00x (ISBN 0-87556-008-3). Saifer.

--Table Talk. 208p. 1969. 10.00x (ISBN 0-87556-010-5). Saifer.

--Tablets. 208p. 1969. Repr. of 1868 ed. 10.00x (ISBN 0-87556-011-3). Saifer.

--Tablets. 1868. 30.00 (ISBN 0-932062-02-4). Sharon Hill.

Alcott, A. Bronson, ed. Conversations with Children on the Gospels (Record of Conversations on the Gospels, Held in Mr. Alcott's School; Unfolding the Doctrine & Discipline of Human Culture, 2 vols. in 1. LC 72-4948. (The Romantic Tradition in American Literature Ser.). 616p. 1972. Repr. of 1836 ed. 40.00 (ISBN 0-405-04621-9). Ayer Co Pubs.

Alcott, Amos B. Ralph Waldo Emerson. 1978. lib. bdg. 59.95. Gordon Pr.

--Ralph Waldo Emerson. LC 68-24930. (American Biography Ser., No. 32). 1969. Repr. of 1881 ed. lib. bdg. 75.00x (ISBN 0-8383-0908-9). Haskell.

--Sonnets & Canzonets. LC 72-86166. Repr. of 1882 ed. 11.50 (ISBN 0-404-00305-2). AMS Pr.

Alcott, Bronson. Ralph Waldo Emerson. (Illus.). 81p. 1983. pap. 10.00 (ISBN 0-317-03735-8). Saifer.

Alcott, Edward B. Will Western Civilization Survive: Challenging Readings for Contemporary Times. 192p. 1981. pap. text ed. 10.95 (ISBN 0-8403-2370-0). Kendall-Hunt.

Alcott, John K. The Astrological Impact upon the Stock Market. (Illus.). 138p. 1981. 63.75x (ISBN 0-918968-80-1). Inst Econ Fina.

Alcott, Louisa M. Behind a Mask. 17.95 (ISBN 0-88411-096-6, Pub. by Aeonian Pr). Amereon Ltd.

--Works of Louisa May Alcott. 33.95 (ISBN 0-88411-173-3, Pub. by Aeonian Pr). Amereon Ltd.

Alcott, Louisa May. Behind a Mask: The Unknown Thrillers of Louisa May Alcott. Stern, Madeleine B., ed. LC 74-31046. (Illus.). 320p. 1975. 7.95 (ISBN 0-688-03370-9). Morrow.

--Diana & Persis. Elbert, Sarah, ed. LC 77-11663. (Individual Publications Ser.). (Illus.). 1978. lib. bdg. 9.50x (ISBN 0-405-10521-5). Ayer Co Pubs.

--Eight Cousins. (gr. 7 up). 1874. 14.45i (ISBN 0-316-03091-0). Little.

--Eight Cousins. (gr. k-6). 1986. pap. 4.95 (ISBN 0-440-42231-0, Pub. by Yearling Classics). Dell.

--Garland for Girls. (Louisa May Alcott Library). (gr. 5-9). 1971. Repr. 5.95 (ISBN 0-448-02360-1, G&D). Putnam Pub Group.

--Glimpses of Louisa: A Centennial Sampling of the Best Short Stories by Louisa May Alcott. (gr. 7 up). 1968. 8.95 (ISBN 0-316-03100-3). Little.

--Good Wives. (Puffin Classics Ser.). 320p. (gr. 3-7). 1983. pap. 2.25 (ISBN 0-14-035009-8, Puffin). Penguin.

--Good Wives. (Children's Illustrated Classics). (Illus.). 303p. 1974. Repr. of 1953 ed. 11.95x (ISBN 0-460-05019-2, Pub. by J. M. Dent England). Biblio Dist.

--Jack & Jill. (gr. 5 up). 1879. 15.45i (ISBN 0-316-03092-9). Little.

--Jo's Boys. (Children's Illustrated Classics Ser.). (Illus.). 335p. 1976. Repr. of 1960 ed. 10.95x (ISBN 0-460-05044-3, Pub. by J. M. Dent England). Biblio Dist.

--Jo's Boys. (Puffin Classics Ser.). 352p. 1984. pap. 2.25 (ISBN 0-14-035015-2, Puffin). Penguin.

--Jo's Boys & How They Turned Out. (gr. 7 up). 1886. 15.45i (ISBN 0-316-03093-7). Little.

--Little Men. (Classics Ser.). (Illus.). (gr. 5 up). 1969. pap. 1.95 (ISBN 0-8049-0194-5, CL-194). Airmont.

--Little Men. (Louisa May Alcott Library). (gr. 4-6). 1971. 5.95 (ISBN 0-448-02363-6, G&D). Putnam Pub Group.

--Little Men. (Illus.). (gr. 4-6). (G&D); deluxe ed. 10.95 (ISBN 0-448-06018-3). Putnam Pub Group.

--Little Men. (The Illustrated Junior Library). (Illus.). 384p. 1982. pap. 5.95 (ISBN 0-448-11018-0, G&D). Putnam Pub Group.

--Little Men. (gr. 7 up). 1871. 15.45 (ISBN 0-316-03094-5). Little.

--Little Men. LC 62-19969. 316p. 1962. pap. 3.95 (ISBN 0-02-041150-2, Collier). Macmillan.

--Little Men. 1983. Repr. lib. bdg. 18.95x (ISBN 0-89966-409-1). Buccaneer Bks.

--Little Men. (Children's Illustrated Classics). (Illus.). 350p. 1982. Repr. of 1957 ed. 11.45x (ISBN 0-460-05038-9, Pub. by J M Dent England). Biblio Dist.

--Little Men. (Puffin Classics Ser.). 240p. 1984. pap. 2.25 (ISBN 0-14-035018-7, Puffin). Penguin.

--Little Women. (gr. 4 up). 1978. pap. 2.25 (ISBN 0-448-17256-9, Pub. by Tempo). Ace Bks.

--Little Women. (Classics Ser). (Illus.). (gr. 6 up). pap. 2.50 (ISBN 0-8049-0106-6, CL-106). Airmont.

--Little Women. 1978. pap. text ed. 3.50x (ISBN 0-460-01248-7, Evman). Biblio Dist.

--Little Women. (Illus.). (gr. 4-6). 1981. Illustrated Junior Library. pap. 6.95 (ISBN 0-448-11019-9, G&D); deluxe ed. 11.95 (ISBN 0-448-06019-1); Companion Library 3.95 (ISBN 0-448-05466-3). Putnam Pub Group.

--Little Women. 59.95 (ISBN 0-8490-0547-7). Gordon Pr.

--Little Women. LC 68-21171. (Illus.). (gr. 7 up). 1868. 15.45 (ISBN 0-316-03095-3). Little.

--Little Women. Centennial ed. (Illus.). 1968. 16.95 (ISBN 0-316-03090-2). Little.

--Little Women. LC 62-20197. 544p. 1962. pap. 2.95 (ISBN 0-02-041230-4, Collier). Macmillan.

--Little Women. (Puffin Classics Ser.). 320p. (gr. 3-7). 1983. pap. 2.25 (ISBN 0-14-035008-X, Puffin). Penguin.

--Little Women. 1963. cloth 22.50 (ISBN 0-685-20188-0, 144-7). Saphrograph.

--Little Women. abr. ed. (Illus.). (gr. 5-8). pap. 2.25 (ISBN 0-590-08556-5). Scholastic Inc.

--Little Women. (Bambi Classics Ser.). (Illus.). 336p. (Orig.). 1981. pap. 3.95 (ISBN 0-89531-068-6, 0221-48). Sharon Pubns.

--Little Women. Barish, Wendy, ed. (Illus.). 576p. 1982. 14.95 (ISBN 0-671-44447-6). Wanderer Bks.

--Little Women. 1983. Repr. lib. bdg. 18.95x (ISBN 0-89966-408-3). Buccaneer Bks.

--Little Women. LC 81-15953. (Classics Ser.). (Illus.). 576p. (gr. 3 up). 1982. lib. bdg. 14.79 (ISBN 0-671-45651-2). Messner.

--Little Women. 1981. (Mod LibC). Modern Lib.

--Little Women. (Bantam Classics Ser.). 1984. pap. 2.95 (ISBN 0-553-21115-3). Bantam.

--Little Women. Bedell, Madelon, ed. (Modern Library College Edition). 730p. 1983. pap. text ed. 5.95 (ISBN 0-394-33187-7, RanC). Random.

--Little Women. (Children's Illustrated Classics). (Illus.). 314p. 1977. Repr. of 1948 ed. 11.95x (ISBN 0-460-05002-8, Pub. by J. M. Dent England). Biblio Dist.

--Little Women. 480p. 1983. pap. 2.95 (ISBN 0-451-51814-4, Sig Classic). NAL.

--Little Women. (Oxford Graded Readers Ser.). 48p. 1975. pap. text ed. 0.95x (ISBN 0-19-421804-X). Oxford U Pr.

--Little Women. LC 84-63128. (Illus.). 432p. 1985. 12.95 (ISBN 0-89577-209-4). RD Assn.

--Louisa May Alcott: Her Life Letters & Journals. 1928. 30.00 (ISBN 0-8274-2996-7). R West.

--Louisa's Wonder Book: An Unknown Alcott Juvenile. Stern, Madeline B., ed. (Juvenile Ser.: No. 1). Orig. Title: Will's Wonder Book. (Illus.). 1975. Repr. of 1870 ed. 7.50 (ISBN 0-916699-08-0). Clarke His.

--Old-Fashioned Girl. (Louisa May Alcott Library). (gr. 5-9). 1971. Repr. 5.95 (ISBN 0-448-02365-2, G&D). Putnam Pub Group.

--Old-Fashioned Girl. (Illus.). (gr. 7 up). 1869. 15.45i (ISBN 0-316-03096-1). Little.

--An Old-Fashioned Thanksgiving. LC 73-15698. (gr. 2-5). 1974. 11.49i (ISBN 0-397-31515-5). Lipp Jr Bks.

--On Picket Duty & Other Tales. 1972. Repr. of 1864 ed. lib. bdg. 18.00 (ISBN 0-8422-8000-6). Irvington.

--On Picket Duty & Other Tales. 1885. 17.00x (ISBN 0-403-04193-7). Somerset Pub.

--Rose in Bloom. (Louisa May Alcott Library). (gr. 5-9). 1971. Repr. 5.95 (ISBN 0-448-02366-0, G&D). Putnam Pub Group.

--Rose in Bloom. (Illus.). (gr. 7 up). 1876. 15.45i (ISBN 0-316-03098-8). Little.

--Rose In Bloom. 1986. pap. 4.95 (ISBN 0-317-20482-3, YB). Dell.

--Transcendental Wild Oats. LC 76-355426. (Illus.). 92p. (YA) 1981. 8.95 (ISBN 0-916782-21-2). Harvard Common Pr.

--Under the Lilacs. (Illus.). (gr. 7 up). 1877. 15.45i (ISBN 0-316-03099-6). Little.

--Work. LC 76-48849. (Studies in the Life of Women). (Illus.). (YA) 1977. lib. bdg. 10.50x (ISBN 0-8052-3656-2); pap. 5.95 (ISBN 0-8052-0563-2). Schocken.

--Work: A Story of Experience. Hardwick, Elizabeth, ed. LC 76-51662. (Rediscovered Fiction by American Women Ser.). (Illus.). 1977. Repr. of 1873 ed. lib. bdg. 27.00 (ISBN 0-405-10042-6). Ayer Co Pubs.

--Work: A Story of Experience. 1976. Repr. of 1875 ed. 25.00x (ISBN 0-403-05873-2, Regency). Scholarly.

Alcott, Louisa May & Parsons, Emily E. Hospital Sketches: Memoir of Emily Elizabeth Parsons Ser. Reverby, Susan, ed. LC 83-49142. (History of American Nursing). 261p. 1984. Repr. of 1880 ed. lib. bdg. 38.00 (ISBN 0-8240-6505-0). Garland Pub.

Alcott, Louisa May see Swan, D. K.

Alcott, William A. Confessions of a School Master. LC 77-89145. (American Education: Its Men, Institutions & Ideas Ser). 1969. Repr. of 1839 ed. 17.00 (ISBN 0-405-01381-7). Ayer Co Pubs.

--The Physiology of Marriage. LC 79-180551. (Medicine & Society in America Ser). 266p. 1972. Repr. of 1866 ed. 18.00 (ISBN 0-405-03931-X). Ayer Co Pubs.

--Vegetable Diet. 2nd rev. & enl. ed. LC 74-29280. Repr. of 1851 ed. 17.50 (ISBN 0-404-13400-9). AMS Pr.

--The Young Husband or, Duties of Man in the Marriage Relation. LC 70-169368. (Family in America Ser). (Illus.). 392p. 1972. Repr. of 1841 ed. 23.00 (ISBN 0-405-03844-5). Ayer Co Pubs.

--The Young Wife, or Duties of Woman in the Marriage Relation. LC 73-169369. (Family in America Ser). (Illus.). 382p. 1972. Repr. of 1837 ed. 23.00 (ISBN 0-405-03845-3). Ayer Co Pubs.

Alcover, Antoni M. & Moll, Francesc de B. Diccionari I Catala-Valencia-Balear, 10 vols. 2nd ed. 9850p. (Catalan.). 1975. Set. 200.00 (ISBN 84-273-0025-5, S-31549). French & Eur.

Alcover, Madeleine, et al. Studies in French. (Rice University Studies: Vol. 63, No. 1). 133p. 1977. pap. 10.00x (ISBN 0-89263-231-3). Rice Univ.

--Women in an Intellectual Context. Eifler, Margret E., ed. (Rice University Studies: Vol. 64, No. 1). 130p. 1978. pap. 10.00x (ISBN 0-89263-235-6). Rice Univ.

Alcyone, pseud. At the Feet of the Master. 1967. 4.50 (ISBN 0-8356-0098-X). Theos Pub Hse.

Alcyone. At the Feet of the Master. 1970. pap. 1.95 (ISBN 0-8356-0196-X, Quest). Theos Pub Hse.

--At the Feet of the Master. leatherette 2.50 (ISBN 0-911662-17-0). Yoga.

Ald, Roy. Jogging, Aerobics & Diet. Orig. Title: The Aerobic Joggers' Guide & Diet Plan. 192p. 1973. pap. 2.50 (ISBN 0-451-11977-0, AE1977, Sig). NAL.

Alda, Alan, jt. auth. see Alda, Arlene.

Alda, Arlene. Arlene Alda's ABC Book. LC 80-66261. (Illus.). 64p. (ps-2). 1981. pap. 8.95 (ISBN 0-89742-042-X). Celestial Arts.

--Matthew & His Dad. (Illus.). 48p. 1983. 7.95 (ISBN 0-671-45158-8, Little Simon). S&S.

--Sonya's Mommy Works. Klimo, Kate, ed. (Illus.). 48p. (ps-3). 1982. 7.95 (ISBN 0-671-45157-X, Little Simon). S&S.

--Sonya's Mommy Works. LC 82-6550. (Illus.). 48p. (ps-2). 1982. 9.29 (ISBN 0-671-46167-2). Messner.

Alda, Arlene & Alda, Alan. The Last Days of Mash. (Illus.). 128p. 1984. pap. 9.95 (ISBN 0-88101-008-1). Unicorn Pub.

Alda, Flora & Alda, Robert. Ninety-Nine Ways to Cook Pasta. 1980. 12.95 (ISBN 0-02-500740-8). Macmillan.

Alda, Frances. Men, Women & Tenors. LC 75-149653. Repr. of 1937 ed. 18.00 (ISBN 0-404-00306-0). AMS Pr.

--Men, Women & Tenors. facsimile ed. LC 72-107790. (Select Bibliographies Reprint Ser). 1937. 26.50 (ISBN 0-8369-5174-3). Ayer Co Pubs.

Alda, Robert, jt. auth. see Alda, Flora.

Al-Daffa, A. A. A Brief Exposition of Arabic & Islamic Scientific Heritage: Arabic Edition. LC 78-31087. 256p. 1979. 14.50 (ISBN 0-471-05348-1). Wiley.

--Modern Mathematics & Intellect: Arabic Edition. 96p. 1979. pap. text ed. 6.60 (ISBN 0-471-05139-X). Wiley.

Al-Daffa, A. A. & Shawki, G. Mathematical Sciences in Islamic Civilization, 2 vols. 400p. (Arabic.). 1985. Vol. 1. pap. 18.00 (ISBN 0-471-87557-0); Vol. 2. pap. 18.00 (ISBN 0-471-87282-2). Wiley.

Al-Daffa, Ali A. The Muslim Contribution to Mathematics. 1977. text ed. 23.50x (ISBN 0-391-00714-9). Humanities.

Al-Daffa, Ali A., jt. auth. see Stroyls, John J.

Aldag, Ramon & Brief, Arthur. Managing Organizational Behavior. (Illus.). 510p. 1980. text ed. 27.95 (ISBN 0-8299-0306-2). West Pub.

Aldag, Ramon J. & Brief, Arthur P. Task Design & Employee Motivation. 1979. pap. text ed. 13.70 (ISBN 0-673-15146-8). Scott F.

Aldan, D., et al, trs. see Steffen, Albert.

Aldan, Daisy. The Art & Craft of Poetry. LC 80-27694. 128p. 1981. 8.95 (ISBN 0-88427-047-5). North River.

--Between High Tides: Poems. 1978. pap. 5.95 (ISBN 0-913152-48-X, 0-9131520910). Folder Edns.

--Breakthrough. 1971. lib. bdg. 6.95 (ISBN 0-913152-02-1). Folder Edns.

--Contemporary Poetry & the Evolution of Consciousness. 1981. pap. 2.95 (ISBN 0-916786-54-4). St George Bk Serv.

--Destruction of Cathedrals & Other Poems. (Illus.). pap. 6.95 (ISBN 0-913152-18-8). Folder Edns.

--Foundation Stone Meditation by Rudolf Steiner. 1981. pap. 2.00 (ISBN 0-916786-53-6). St George Bk Serv.

--A Golden Story: Novella. 1979. pap. 5.95 (ISBN 0-913152-49-8). Folder Edns.

--Or Learn to Walk on Water: Poems by Daisy Aldan. 1971. 3.50 (ISBN 0-913152-20-X). Folder Edns.

--Stones: Poems by Daisy Aldan. 1973. 4.95 (ISBN 0-913152-15-3). Folder Edns.

--Verses for the Zodiac. 1975. sewn 7.95 (ISBN 0-913152-10-2); pap. 4.95 (ISBN 0-913152-16-1). Folder Edns.

Aldan, Daisy, tr. see Steffen, Albert.

Aldan, Daisy, tr. see Witzenman, Herbert.

Aldanov, Mark. Nightmare & Dawn. Carmichael, Joel, tr. LC 73-21489. 343p. 1974. Repr. of 1957 ed. lib. bdg. 35.00x (ISBN 0-8371-6406-0, ALND). Greenwood.

Aldanov, Mark A. Zagadka Tolstogo. LC 79-91652. (The Brown University Slavic Reprint Ser.: No. 7). pap. 34.50 (ISBN 0-317-28393-6, 2022394). Bks Demand UMI.

Aldaraca, Bridget, et al, eds. Nicaragua in Revolution: The Poets Speak. LC 80-16304. (Studies in Marxism: Vol. 5). 310p. (Bilingual: Spanish & English). 1980. 18.95x (ISBN 0-930656-10-5); pap. 8.95 (ISBN 0-930656-09-1). MEP Pubns.

Aldave, Barbara B., jt. auth. see Matthew Bender Firm.

Aldcroft, D. The British Economy Between the Wars. 153p. 1983. text ed. 17.50x (ISBN 0-86003-800-9, Pub. by Allan England); pap. text ed. 9.00x (ISBN 0-86003-900-5). Humanities.

Aldcroft, D., jt. ed. see Slaven, A.

Aldcroft, D. H. & Mort, D. Rail & Sea Transport. 280p. 1981. 39.00 (ISBN 0-08-026105-1). Pergamon.

Aldcroft, D. H. & Rodger, R., eds. Bibliography of European Economic & Social History. LC 83-12049. 290p. 1984. 37.50 (ISBN 0-7190-0944-8, Pub. by Manchester Univ Pr). Longwood Pub Group.

Aldcroft, D. H., jt. ed. see Cottrel, P. L.

Aldcroft, Derek & Fearon, Peter. Economic Growth in Twentieth-Century Britain. 1970. 11.50x (ISBN 0-333-10041-7). Humanities.

Aldcroft, Derek, jt. auth. see Buxton, Neil K.

Aldcroft, Derek, jt. auth. see Freeman, Michael.

Aldcroft, Derek H. From Versailles to Wall Street: The International Economy in the 1920's. LC 76-40824. (History of the World Economy in the 20th Century Ser.: Vol. 3). 1977. 38.50x (ISBN 0-520-03336-1); pap. 8.95 (ISBN 0-520-04506-8, CAL531). U of Cal Pr.

--From Versailles to Wall Street, 1919-1929. 1983. 16.00 (ISBN 0-8446-5968-1). Peter Smith.

--The Inter-War Economy: Britain 1919-1939. LC 70-20963. 441p. 1971. 27.50x (ISBN 0-231-03517-9). Columbia U Pr.

Aldcroft, Derek H. & Fearon, Peter, eds. British Economic Fluctuations: Seventeen Ninety to Nineteen Thirty-Nine. LC 77-178900. 1972. text ed. 25.00 (ISBN 0-312-10045-0). St Martin.

Aldcroft, Derek H. & Freeman, Michael J., eds. Transport in the Industrial Revolution. LC 82-62266. 228p. 1983. 23.50 (ISBN 0-7190-0839-5, Pub. by Manchester Univ Pr). Longwood Pub Group.

Aldebaran. Nixon & the Foxes of Watergate. pap. 4.95 (ISBN 0-918680-12-3). Griffon Hse.

Aldecoa, Ignacio. Cuentos. (Easy Readers Ser.). (Illus.). 1976. pap. text ed. 4.25 (ISBN 0-88436-283-3, 70274). EMC.

Alden, Betsey, jt. ed. see Castano, Francis A.

Alden, Carole. Word Processing with Your Coleco Adam. LC 84-51243. 175p. 1984. pap. 9.95 (ISBN 0-89588-182-9). SYBEX.

Alden, Carroll S. & Earle, Ralph. Makers of Naval Tradition. LC 76-167303. (Essay Index Reprint Ser.). Repr. of 1942 ed. 27.50 (ISBN 0-8369-2733-8). Ayer Co Pubs.

Alden, Dauril. Royal Government in Colonial Brazil: With Special Reference to the Administration of the Marquis of Lavradio, Viceroy, 1769-1779. LC 68-26064. (Illus.). 1968. 48.50x (ISBN 0-520-00008-0). U of Cal Pr.

Alden, Dauril, ed. Colonial Roots of Modern Brazil: Papers of the Newberry Library Conference. LC 78-174458. 1973. 42.50x (ISBN 0-520-02140-1). U of Cal Pr.

Alden, Dauril & Dean, Warren, eds. Essays Concerning the Socioeconomic History of Brazil & Portuguese India. LC 76-53761. (Illus.). 1977. 12.50 (ISBN 0-8130-0565-5). U Presses Fla.

Alden, Debby. If I Touch a Star Will I Sparkle Too? A Fans Guide to Meeting Stars. 220p. (Orig.). 1980. pap. text ed. 5.95 (ISBN 0-9604238-1-8). Dublin Pr.

Alden, Dion. Reckless Dreamer. 1985. pap. 3.50 (ISBN 0-317-29665-5). Bantam.

Alden, Douglas. Marcel Proust's Grasset Proofs. (Studies in the Romance Languages & Literatures: No. 193). 640p. 1978. pap. 23.50x (ISBN 0-8078-9193-2). U of NC Pr.

Alden, Douglas W., ed. French XX Bibliography: Critical & Biographical References for the Study of French Literature since 1885, Index to Nos. 31-35. (Orig.). 1984. pap. 40.00x (ISBN 0-933444-43-5). French Inst.

--French XX Bibliography: Critical & Biographical References for the Study of French Literature since 1885, No. 35. (Orig.). 1983. pap. 48.00x (ISBN 0-933444-42-7). French Inst.

--French XX Bibliography: Critical & Biographical References for the Study of French Literature since 1885, No. 36. (Orig.). 1984. pap. 48.00x (ISBN 0-933444-44-3). French Inst.

--Introduction to French Masterpieces. (Fr.). 1948. 29.95x (ISBN 0-89197-240-4); pap. text ed. 12.50x (ISBN 0-89197-241-2). Irvington.

Alden, Douglas W. & Brooks, Richard A., eds. A Critical Bibliography of French Literature: Vol. VI, Twentieth Century, 3 pts. 1980. 150.00x (ISBN 0-8156-2204-X). Syracuse U Pr.

Alden, Douglas W., et al, eds. French Twenty Bibliography: Critical & Biographical References for the Study of French Literature Since 1885, Nos. 1-35. Incl. Nos. 1-9. 1949-1957. pap. 4.00x ea.; No. 1. 1949. pap. (ISBN 0-933444-02-8); No. 2, 1950. pap. (ISBN 0-933444-03-6); No. 3. 1951. pap. (ISBN 0-933444-04-4); No. 4. 1952. pap. (ISBN 0-933444-05-2); No. 5. 1953. pap. (ISBN 0-933444-06-0); No. 6. 1954. pap. (ISBN 0-933444-07-9); No. 7. 1955. pap. (ISBN 0-933444-08-7); No. 8. 1956. pap. (ISBN 0-933444-09-5); No. 9. 1957. pap. (ISBN 0-933444-10-9); No. 10. 1958. Incl. Index To Nos. 1-10. pap. 7.00x (ISBN 0-933444-11-7); Nos. 11-16. pap. 6.00x ea.; No. 11. 1959. pap. (ISBN 0-933444-12-5); No. 12. 1960. pap. (ISBN 0-933444-13-3); No. 13. 1961. pap. (ISBN 0-933444-14-1); No. 14. 1962. pap. (ISBN 0-933444-15-X); No. 15. 1963. pap. (ISBN 0-933444-16-8); No. 16. 1964. pap. (ISBN 0-933444-17-6); Nos. 17-20. pap. 12.00x ea.; No. 17. 1965. pap. (ISBN 0-933444-18-4); No. 18. 1966. pap. (ISBN 0-933444-19-2); No. 19. 1967. pap. (ISBN 0-933444-20-6); No. 20. 1968. pap. (ISBN 0-933444-21-4); General Index to Nos. 11-20. Tussing, Ruth-Elaine, et al, eds. 1969. pap. 15.00x (ISBN 0-933444-22-2); No. 21. 1969. pap. 12.00x (ISBN 0-933444-23-0); Nos. 22-24. pap. 18.00x ea.; No. 22. 1970. pap. (ISBN 0-933444-24-9); No. 23. 1971. pap. (ISBN 0-933444-25-7); No. 24. 1972. pap. (ISBN 0-933444-26-5); No. 25. 1973. pap. 24.00x (ISBN 0-933444-27-3); Index to Nos. 21-25. Tussing, Ruth-Elaine, ed. 1974. pap. 26.00x (ISBN 0-933444-28-1); Nos. 26-27. pap. 30.00x ea.; No. 26. 1974. pap. (ISBN 0-933444-29-X); No. 27. 1975. pap. (ISBN 0-933444-30-3); No. 28, 1976. pap. 36.00x (ISBN 0-933444-31-1); No. 29, 1977. pap. 42.00x (ISBN 0-933444-33-8); No. 30, 1978. pap. 42.00x (ISBN 0-933444-34-6); General Index to Nos. 26-30. pap. 34.00x (ISBN 0-933444-38-9); No. 31, 1979. pap. 42.00x (ISBN 0-933444-36-2); No. 32, 1980. pap. 42.00 (ISBN 0-933444-37-0); No. 33, 1981. pap. 48.00 (ISBN 0-933444-40-0); No. 34,1982. pap. 48.00 (ISBN 0-933444-41-9). (Orig., Nos. 1-20, LC 49-3084; nos. 21-35, LC 77-648803. Nos. 1-20 originally published as French Seven Bibliography). 1949-83. Set. pap. 600.00x (ISBN 0-933444-01-X). French Inst.

Alden, Edmund K. The World's Representative Assemblies of Today: A Study in Comparative Legislation. LC 78-63817. (Johns Hopkins University. Studies in the Social Sciences. Eleventh Ser. 1893: No. 12). Repr. of 1893 ed. 11.50 (ISBN 0-404-61080-3). AMS Pr.

Alden, George H. New Governments West of the Alleghenies Before 1780: Introductory to a Study of the Organization & Admission of New States. LC 70-106117. (First American Frontier Ser). (Illus.). 1971. Repr. of 1897 ed. 10.00 (ISBN 0-405-02822-9). Ayer Co Pubs.

Alden, Henry M. Magazine Writing & the New Literature. facs. ed. LC 70-175686. (Select Bibliographies Reprint Ser.). Repr. of 1908 ed. 21.50 (ISBN 0-8369-5030-5). Ayer Co Pubs.

--A Study of Death: Works of Henry Mills Alden. (Works of Henry Mills Alden Ser.). vii, 335p. Date not set. Repr. of 1895 ed. 39.00 (ISBN 0-932051-54-5). Am Repr Serv.

Alden, Henry M., jt. ed. see Howells, William D.

Alden, J. E. Pre-Raphaelites & Oxford. LC 74-1477. 1948. lib. bdg. 10.00 (ISBN 0-8414-2964-2). Folcroft.

Alden, Jay. Backward Chaining: Teaching Task Performance. Langdon, Danny G., ed. LC 77-25132. (Instructional Design Library). (Illus.). 96p. 1978. 19.95 (ISBN 0-87778-110-9). Educ Tech Pubns.

Alden, John. European Americana: A Chronological Guide to Writings on the Americas Published in Europe 1493-1600, Vol. I. 467p. 1980. 80.00 (ISBN 0-918414-03-2). Readex Bks.

--The First South. 11.25 (ISBN 0-8446-1013-5). Peter Smith.

--The Fleet Submarine in the U. S. Navy. LC 78-61054. (Illus.). 280p. 1979. 32.95 (ISBN 0-87021-187-0). Naval Inst Pr.

--Stephen Sayre: American Revolutionary Adventurer. LC 82-771. 232p. 1983. text ed. 27.50x (ISBN 0-8071-1067-1). La State U Pr.

Alden, John & Landis, Dennis C. European Americana: A Chronological Guide to Works Printed in Europe Relating to the Americas, 1493-1776, 8 vols. 954p. 1982. Vol. 2, 1601-1650. 135.00 (ISBN 0-918414-09-1). Readex Bks.

Alden, John D. The Fleet Submarine in the United States Navy. (Illus.). 280p. 1979. 32.95 (ISBN 0-87021-187-0); bulk rates avail. Naval Inst Pr.

Alden, John L. & Kane, John M. Design of Industrial Ventilation Systems. 5th ed. (Illus.). 260p. 1982. 29.95 (ISBN 0-8311-1138-0). Indus Pr.

Alden, John R. American Revolution: Seventeen Seventy-Five to Seventeen Eighty-Three. (New American Nation Ser.). (Illus.). pap. 8.50xi (ISBN 0-06-133011-6, TB3011, Torch). Har-Row.

--First South. LC 61-10831. (Walter Lynwood Fleming Lectures). viii, 144p. 1971. pap. text ed. 4.95x (ISBN 0-8071-0204-0). La State U Pr.

--George Washington: A Biography. LC 83-25585. (Southern Biography Ser.). (Illus.). 344p. 1984. 19.95 (ISBN 0-8071-1153-8). La State U Pr.

--John Stuart & the Southern Colonial Frontier: A Study of Indian Relations, War, Trade, Land Problems in the Southern Wilderness, 1754-1775. LC 66-29459. (Illus.). 1966. Repr. of 1944 ed. 17.50x (ISBN 0-87752-001-1). Gordian.

--Robert Dinwiddie: Servant of the Crown. LC 72-86731. (Williamsburg in America Ser.). 1973. 6.95x (ISBN 0-8139-0440-4). U Pr of Va.

--South in the Revolution, 1763-1789. LC 57-12096. (History of the South Ser.: Vol. 3). (Illus.). xvi, 442p. 1957. 27.50x (ISBN 0-8071-0003-X); pap. 8.95x (ISBN 0-8071-0013-7). La State U Pr.

Alden, Laura. I Read about God's Care: Grade 2. rev. ed. (Basic Bible Readers Ser.). (Illus.). 128p. (gr. 2). 1983. text ed. 7.95 (ISBN 0-87239-662-2, 2952). Standard Pub.

--Learning About Fairies. LC 81-15502. (Learning About Ser.). (Illus.). 48p. (gr. 2-6). 1982. lib. bdg. 11.00 (ISBN 0-516-06532-7). Childrens.

--Saying I'm Sorry. LC 82-19945. (What's in a Word Ser.). (Illus.). 32p. (gr. 1-2). 1983. PLB 7.45 (ISBN 0-89565-247-1). Childs World.

--Saying I'm Sorry. (What's In a Word Ser.). (Illus.). 32p. (ps-2). 1983. 9.95 (ISBN 0-516-06324-3). Childrens.

--Sorry. LC 82-9660. (What Does it Mean? Ser.). (Illus.). 32p. (gr. 1-2). 1982. PLB 5.95 (ISBN 0-89565-236-6, 4897, Pub. by Childs World). Standard Pub.

--When. (Question Bks). (Illus.). 32p. (gr. k-2). 1983. 10.35 (ISBN 0-516-06592-0); pap. 2.95 (ISBN 0-516-46592-9). Childrens.

Alden, Laura F. & Mulligan, Lorraine G. Our Christmas Handbook, Vol. 2. Tester, Sylvia R., ed. LC 80-14587. (Illus.). 112p. 1982. PLB 6.95 (ISBN 0-89565-231-5, 3042, Pub. by Childs World). Standard Pub.

Alden, Maureen J. Bronze Age Population in the Argolid from the Evidence of Mycenaean Tombs. (Studies in Mediterranean Archaeology Ser.: NO. 15). 436p. 1981. pap. text ed. 48.50x (ISBN 91-86098-00-4, Pub. by Astroms Sweden). Humanities.

Alden, Peter. Finding the Birds in Western Mexico: A Guide to the State of Sonora, Sinaloa, & Nayarit. LC 68-9334. pap. 40.50 (ISBN 0-317-28654-4, 2055346). Bks Demand UMI.

Alden, Peter, jt. auth. see Peterson, Roger T.

Alden, Priscilla. Sex & the Triple Girl. LC 84-51912. (Illus.). 88p. (Orig.). 1984. pap. 4.95 (ISBN 0-931533-00-7). Shift Pub.

Alden, R. & Smith, R. Essays English & American. Repr. of 1918 ed. 10.00 (ISBN 0-8482-7268-4). Norwood Edns.

Alden, Raymond M. Alfred Tennyson, How to Know Him. LC 76-30812. 1977. lib. bdg. 35.00 (ISBN 0-8414-2969-3). Folcroft.

--The Art of Debate. 1904. 30.00 (ISBN 0-8274-3784-6). R West.

--An Introduction to Poetry. 1973. lib. bdg. 30.00 (ISBN 0-8414-3051-9). Folcroft.

--An Introduction to Poetry: For Students of English Literature. 371p. 1981. Repr. of 1909 ed. lib. bdg. 40.00 (ISBN 0-89987-030-9). Darby Bks.

--Rise of Formal Satire in England Under Classical Influence. LC 73-1450. Repr. of 1899 ed. lib. bdg. 17.50 (ISBN 0-8414-1706-7). Folcroft.

--Shakespeare. 1973. Repr. of 1922 ed. 27.00 (ISBN 0-8274-1666-0). R West.

--Shakespeare Handbook. facsimile ed. Campbell, Oscar J., ed. LC 75-109639. (Select Bibliographies Reprint Ser). 1932. 22.00 (ISBN 0-8369-5248-0). Ayer Co Pubs.

--A Shakespeare Handbook. 315p. Repr. of 1932 ed. lib. bdg. 21.00 (ISBN 0-8290-0787-3). Irvington.

--The Sonnets of Shakespeare: From the Quarto of 1609 with Varioum Readings & Commentary. 542p. 1981. Repr. of 1916 ed. lib. bdg. 200.00 (ISBN 0-89760-011-8). Telegraph Bks.

Alden, Raymond M., ed. English Verse. LC 77-121032. Repr. of 1929 ed. 21.50 (ISBN 0-404-00308-7). AMS Pr.

--English Verse. 450p. 1981. Repr. of 1903 ed. lib. bdg. 40.00 (ISBN 0-89760-006-1). Telegraph Bks.

--Poems of the English Race. facs. ed. LC 77-149099. (Granger Index Reprint Ser). 1921. 25.00 (ISBN 0-8369-6224-9). Ayer Co Pubs.

--Shakespeare. LC 73-113539. Repr. of 1922 ed. 27.50 (ISBN 0-404-00307-9). AMS Pr.

Alden, Robert L. Proverbs: A Commentary on an Ancient Book of Timeless Advice. 222p. 1984. 12.95 (ISBN 0-8010-0194-3). Baker Bk.

--Psalms: Songs of Discipleship, 3 vols. (Everyman's Bible Commentary Ser.). 1975. pap. 5.95 ea. Vol. 1 (ISBN 0-8024-2018-4). Vol. 2 (ISBN 0-8024-2019-2). Vol. 3 (ISBN 0-8024-2020-6). Moody.

Alden, S. F. Jane Austen. LC 77-6735. 1977. Repr. of 1899 ed. lib. bdg. 25.00 (ISBN 0-8414-6188-0). Folcroft.

Alden, Thomas. Scientific Management: The Essential Knowledge Which Everyone, but Absolutely Everyone Ought to Possess of the Main Guiding Principles Which Intelligent Men Follow in the Management of Their Business & Personal Affairs. (The Essential Knowledge Ser.). 1978. 58.45 (ISBN 0-89266-120-8). Am Classical Coll Pr.

Alden, Timothy. A Collection of American Epitaphs: Inscriptions with Occasional Notes, 5 vols. in 2. Kastenbaum, Robert, ed. LC 76-19556. (Death and Dying Ser.). 1977. Repr. of 1814 ed. lib. bdg. 90.00x (ISBN 0-405-09594-5). Ayer Co Pubs.

Alden, William L. Told by the Colonel. (Illus.). 1971. Repr. of 1893 ed. 19.00 (ISBN 0-403-01435-2). Scholarly.

Aldenham, Lord, ed. see Degeste, Beatrix Chanson.

Aldenhoff, J. B., jt. ed. see Emrich, H. M.

Aldenson, Simon C. How to Develop the Power of Abstract Thinking. (Illus.). 146p. 1981. 51.75 (ISBN 0-89266-315-4). Am Classical Coll Pr.

Alder, A. B. Methods in Computational Physics: Advances in Research & Applications, Vol. 18. Date not set. price not set (ISBN 0-12-460818-3). Acad Pr.

Alder, Alexandra. Guiding Human Misfits: A Practical Application of Individual Psychology. 88p. 1982. pap. 5.00x (ISBN 0-939654-00-8). Social Interest.

Alder, B., ed. see Kirkwood, John G.

Alder, B., et al, eds. Methods in Computational Physics: Advances in Research & Applications. Incl. Vol. 1. Statistical Physics. 1963. 68.00 (ISBN 0-12-460801-9); Vol. 2. Quantum Mechanics. 1963. 68.00 (ISBN 0-12-460802-7); Vol. 3. Fundamental Methods in Hydrodynamics. 1964. 68.00 (ISBN 0-12-460803-5); Vol. 4. Applications in Hydrodynamics. 1965. 68.00 (ISBN 0-12-460804-3); Vol. 5. Nuclear Particle Kinematics. 1966. 68.00 (ISBN 0-12-460805-1); Vol. 6. Nuclear Physics. 1967. 68.00 (ISBN 0-12-460806-X); Vol. 7. Astrophysics. 1967. 68.00 (ISBN 0-12-460807-8); Vol. 8. Energy Bands of Solids. 1968. 68.00 (ISBN 0-12-460808-6); Vol. 9. Plasma Physics. 1970. 71.50 (ISBN 0-12-460809-4); Vol. 10. Atomic & Molecular Scattering. 1971. 71.50 (ISBN 0-12-460810-8); Vol. 11. Seismology, Surface Waves & Earth Oscillations. Bolt, Bruce A., et al, eds. 1972. 63.50 (ISBN 0-12-460811-6); Vol. 12. Seismology, Body Waves & Sources. Bolt, Bruce A., ed. 1972. 63.50 (ISBN 0-12-460812-4); Vol. 13. Geophysics. Bolt, Bruce A., et al, eds. 1973. 90.00 (ISBN 0-12-460813-2); Vol. 14. Radio Astronomy. 1975. 68.50 (ISBN 0-12-460814-0); Vol. 15. Vibration Properties of Solids. Gilat, Gideon, et al, eds. 1976. 83.00 (ISBN 0-12-460815-9); Vol. 16. Computer Applications to Controlled Fusion Research. Killeen, John, ed. 1976. 89.50 (ISBN 0-12-460816-7); Vol. 17. General Circulation Models of the Atmosphere. Chang, Julius, ed. 1977. 71.50 (ISBN 0-12-460817-5); lib ed. 91.50 (ISBN 0-12-460878-7); microfiche 52.00 (ISBN 0-12-460879-5). Acad Pr.

Alder, David A. The Children of Chelm. (Story Book). (Illus.). (gr. 1-5). 1979. PLB 7.95 (ISBN 0-88482-772-0, Bonim Bks); pap. 3.95 (ISBN 0-88482-773-9, Bonim Bks). Hebrew Pub.

Alder, Douglas D. & Linden, Glenn M., eds. Teaching World History: Structured Inquiry Through a Historical-Anthropological Approach. 164p. 1976. 9.95 (ISBN 0-89994-195-8). Soc Sci Ed.

Alder, Felix. Creed & Deed: A Series of Discourses. LC 76-38430. (Religion in America Ser: 2). 254p. 1972. Repr. of 1877 ed. 17.00 (ISBN 0-405-04051-2). Ayer Co Pubs.

Alder, Henry L. & Roessler, Edward B. Introduction to Probability & Statistics. 6th ed. LC 76-13643. (Illus.). 426p. 1977. text ed. 26.95 (ISBN 0-7167-0467-6); answer book avail. W H Freeman.

Alder, Jane W. The Pace of Litigation: Conference Proceedings. LC 82-224463. (Illus.). 1982. write for info. Rand.

Alder, Jim. Guide to Services Selection in Low Rise Buildings. (Illus.). 160p. 1983. 26.50 (ISBN 0-89397-153-7). Nichols Pub.

Alder, Kurt & Winther, Aage, eds. Coulomb Excitation: A Collection of Reprints. (Perspectives in Physics Ser). 1966. 49.50 (ISBN 0-12-049250-4). Acad Pr.

Alder, Lory. Paris Is Fun: A Bilingual Guide. 1969. 7.95 (ISBN 0-7207-0225-9). Transatlantic.

Alder, Renata. Pitch Dark. 192p. 1985. pap. 5.95 (ISBN 0-553-34130-8). Bantam.

Alder, Vera S. Fifth Dimension. LC 78-16459. 240p. 1970. pap. 5.50 (ISBN 0-87728-055-X). Weiser.

--Finding of the Third Eye. 1973. pap. 5.95 (ISBN 0-87728-056-8). Weiser.

--Initiation of the World. 256p. 1979. pap. 6.95 (ISBN 0-87728-057-6). Weiser.

--Wisdom in Practice. 1970. pap. 4.95 (ISBN 0-87728-058-4). Weiser.

Alder, W. & Caillez, F. Forest Volume Estimation & Yield Prediction. (Forestry Papers: Vol. 22, Nos. 1 & 2). (Eng., Fr. & Span.). 1980. Set. pap. 21.50 (ISBN 92-5-100923-6, F2138, FAO). Vol. 1, Volume Estimation, 100 p. Vol. 2, Yield Prediction, 201 p. Unipub.

Alder, Warren. Twilight Child. 320p. 1985. 15.95 (ISBN 0-02-500360-7). Macmillan.

Alder, William H. & Nordin, Albert A. Immunological Techniques Applied to Aging Research. 256p. 1981. 77.00 (ISBN 0-8493-5809-4). CRC Pr.

Alderfer, Clayton, jt. ed. see Cooper, Cary L.

Alderfer, Clayton P. Existence, Relatedness & Growth: Human Needs in Organizational Settings. LC 78-156839. 1972. 17.95 (ISBN 0-02-900390-3). Free Pr.

Alderfer, Clayton P. & Cooper, Cary L., eds. Advances in Experimental Social Processes, Vol. 2. (Advances in Experimental Social Processes Ser.). 329p. 1980. 69.95x (ISBN 0-471-27623-5, Pub. by Wiley-Interscience). Wiley.

Alderfer, E. G. The Ephrata Commune: An Early American Counterculture. LC 85-1044. (Illus.). 288p. 1985. 22.95x (ISBN 0-8229-3813-8, Dist by Harper & Row Publishers); pap. 8.95 (ISBN 0-8229-4801-X). U of Pittsburgh Pr.

Alderfer, Gordon E., jt. ed. see Tolles, Frederick.

Alderfer, Harold F. Bibliography of African Government Nineteen Fifty to Nineteen Sixty-Six. 1967. pap. 5.00x (ISBN 0-87098-001-7). Livingston.

Alderfer, Helen, ed. Farthing in Her Hand: Stewardship for Women. LC 64-23376. 226p. 1964. pap. 3.95 (ISBN 0-8361-1515-5). Herald Pr.

Alderink, Larry J. Creation & Salvation in Ancient Orphism. LC 81-5772. (APA American Classical Studies Ser.). 1981. pap. 10.00 (ISBN 0-89130-502-5, 400408). Scholars Pr GA.

Alder-Karlsson, G. The Political Economy of East-West-South Cooperation. (Studien Uber Wirtschaftsund Systemvergleiche: Vol. 7). 1976. pap. 31.00 (ISBN 0-387-81385-3). Springer-Verlag.

Alderman. Pressure Groups & Government in Great Britain. 176p. 1984. pap. text ed. 6.95 (ISBN 0-582-29626-9). Longman.

Alderman & Hanley. Clinical Medicine for the Occupational Physician. (Occupational Safety & Health Ser.). 512p. 1982. 79.50 (ISBN 0-8247-1785-6). Dekker.

Alderman, Clifford L. Annie Oakley & the World of Her Time. LC 78-31838. (Illus.). 112p. (gr. 5-9). 1979. 10.95 (ISBN 0-02-700270-5, 70027). Macmillan.

--Story of the Thirteen Colonies. (Landmark Ser.). (Illus.). (gr. 5-9). 1966. PLB 5.99 (ISBN 0-394-90415-X, BYR). Random.

--You Can Be a Writer: A Career & Leisure Guide. LC 80-28306. 160p. (gr. 7 up). 1981. PLB 9.79 (ISBN 0-671-34047-6). Messner.

Alderman, E. A. & Harris, J. C., eds. Library of Southern Literature, 17 Vols. 1971. Repr. of 1909 ed. Set. lib. bdg. 740.00 (ISBN 0-384-32598-X); lib. bdg. 44.00 ea. Johnson Repr.

Alderman, Geoffrey. British Elections. 1978. 14.95 (ISBN 0-7134-0195-8, Pub. by Batsford England); pap. 14.95 (ISBN 0-7134-0196-6). David & Charles.

--The Jewish Community in British Politics. 1983. 34.95 (ISBN 0-19-827436-X). Oxford U Pr.

Alderman, Harold G. Nietzsche's Gift. LC 76-25612. xvi, 184p. 1977. 18.95x (ISBN 0-8214-0231-5, 82-82329); pap. 8.95x (ISBN 0-8214-0385-0, 82-82337). Ohio U Pr.

Alderman, Joy. Renewed in Strength. LC 74-18108. 1975. pap. 1.95 (ISBN 0-8170-0660-5). Judson.

Alderman, Karen Cleary, jt. auth. see Levitan, Sar A.

Alderman, Paul R., Jr. God's Spotlight on Tomorrow: Seven Sevens Concerning the Return of Christ. 1960. pap. 1.25 (ISBN 0-87213-010-X). Loizeaux.

Alderman, Richard & Dole, Richard F. A Transactional Guide to the Uniform Commercial Code. 2nd ed. 1349p. 1983. text ed. 150.00 (ISBN 0-8318-0400-9, B400). Am Law Inst.

Alderman, Richard M. Know Your Rights: The Peoples Lawyers Answers to Your Most Common Legal Questions. 192p. 1985. pap. 8.95 (ISBN 0-940672-31-6). Shearer Pub.

Alderman, Robert. How to Make More Money at Interior Design. 192p. 1982. 18.95 (ISBN 0-442-20876-6). Van Nos Reinhold.

--How to Make More Money at Interior Design. 192p. 1982. 18.95. Inter Design.

Alderman, Sharon & Wertenberger, Kathryn. Handwoven, Tailormade: A Tandem Guide to Fabric Designing, Weaving, Sewing & Tailoring. LC 82-81683. (Illus.). 147p. 1982. 17.50 (ISBN 0-934026-08-4). Interweave.

Alderman, Tom, jt. auth. see Singer, Sheri.

Alderson. Comic Postcard in English Life. (Illus.). 112p. lib. bdg. 10.95 (ISBN 0-317-36205-4). 50 plastic pages 3.50 ea. Deltiologists Am.

Alderson, jt. ed. see Maunder, W. F.

Alderson, A. D. & Iz, Fahir. The Oxford Turkish-English Dictionary. 3rd ed. 640p. 1985. 34.95 (ISBN 0-19-864124-9). Oxford U Pr.

Alderson, A. D. & Iz, Fahir, eds. Concise Oxford Turkish Dictionary. (Turkish.). 1959. 29.00x (ISBN 0-19-864109-5). Oxford U Pr.

Alderson, Anthony D. The Structure of the Ottoman Dynasty. LC 81-23751. xvi, 186p. 1982. Repr. of 1956 ed. lib. bdg. 49.75x (ISBN 0-313-22522-2, ALSO). Greenwood.

Alderson, Brian, compiled by. Cakes & Custards: Children's Rhymes. LC 75-24523. (Illus.). 176p. 1975. PLB 13.88 (ISBN 0-688-32050-3). Morrow.

Alderson, Brian, ed. see Darton, F. J.

Alderson, Brian, ed. see Lang, Andrew.

Alderson, Brian, tr. see Brothers Grimm.

Alderson, Brian, tr. see Hans Christian Andersen & Grandfather Drewsen.

Alderson, Frederick. Bicycles. (Junior Reference Ser.). (Illus.). 64p. (gr. 6 up). 1974. 8.95 (ISBN 0-7136-1464-1). Dufour.

--Outdoor Games. (Junior Reference Ser.). (Illus.). 64p. (gr. 6 up). 1980. 8.95 (ISBN 0-7136-2031-5). Dufour.

--View North: A Long Look at Northern England. LC 68-23825. (Illus.). 1968. 24.95x (ISBN 0-678-05577-7). Kelley.

Alderson, George & Sentman, Everett. How You Can Influence Congress: The Complete Handbook for the Citizen Lobbyist. 1979. pap. 9.95 (ISBN 0-87690-320-0). Dutton.

Alderson, J. C., ed. Evaluation: Lancaster Practical Papers in English Language Education, Vol. 6. (Lancaster Practical Papers Ser.). (Illus.). 176p. 1985. pap. 8.95 (ISBN 0-08-029462-6, Pub. by PPL). Pergamon.

Alderson, J. D. & Rushton, D. M. Morgan Sweeps the Board: The Three-Wheeler Story. (Illus.). 18.95 (ISBN 0-85614-050-3, F405). Haynes Pubns.

Alderson, John. Law & Disorder. 256p. 1984. 17.50 (ISBN 0-241-11259-1, Pub. by Hamish Hamilton England). David & Charles.

--Policing Freedom. 288p. 1979. 32.50x (ISBN 0-7121-1815-2, Pub. by Macdonald & Evans England). Trans-Atlantic.

Alderson, L. W. Gingko Leaves & Cello Grass. 1978. 5.00 (ISBN 0-686-24038-3); signed 7.50 (ISBN 0-686-85711-9). Bellevue Pr.

Alderson, Lawrence. Rare Breeds. (Shire Album Ser.: No. 118). (Illus.). 32p. (Orig.). 1984. pap. 2.95 (ISBN 0-85263-677-6, Pub. by Shire Pubns England). Seven Hills Bks.

Alderson, M. R., et al, eds. Hodgkin's Disease III: Occurence & Diagnosis. LC 73-23030. (Hodgkin's Disease Ser.: Vol. 3). 155p. 1974. text ed. 19.00x (ISBN 0-8422-7195-3). Irvington.

Alderson, Michael. International Mortality Statistics. 380p. 1981. 65.00x (ISBN 0-87196-514-3). Facts on File.

Alderson, Michael, ed. The Prevention of Cancer. (Management of Malignant Disease Ser.: No. 4). 304p. 1982. text ed. 49.50 (ISBN 0-7131-4401-7). E Arnold.

Alderson, Nannie T. & Smith, Helena H. A Bride Goes West. LC 42-12918. (Illus.). viii, 273p. 1969. pap. 5.95 (ISBN 0-8032-5001-0, BB 389, Bison). U of Nebr Pr.

Alderson, R. H., ed. Design of the Electron Microscope Laboratory. (Practical Methods in Electron Microscopy Ser.: Vol. 4). 1975. pap. 13.75 (ISBN 0-444-10816-5, North-Holland). Elsevier.

Alderson, William T. & Low, Shirley P. Interpretation of Historic Sites. LC 75-33292. (Illus.). 1976. pap. 9.50 (ISBN 0-910050-19-8). AASLH Pr.

Alderson, Wroe. Marketing Behavior & Executive Action. Assael, Henry, ed. LC 78-222. (Century of Marketing Ser.). 1978. Repr. of 1957 ed. lib. bdg. 40.00x (ISBN 0-405-11162-2). Ayer Co Pubs.

Alderton, David. Canaries. 80p. 1982. pap. 2.75 (ISBN 0-86230-044-4). Triplegate.

--Caring for Aquarium Fish. LC 83-62525. (Illus.). 112p. 1984. pap. 8.95 (ISBN 0-399-51017-6, G&D). Putnam Pub Group.

--Guide to Cage Birds. 120p. 1980. 15.75 (ISBN 0-904558-78-9). Saiga.

--Looking after Cage Birds. LC 82-11598. (Illus.). 128p. 1983. pap. 7.95 (ISBN 0-668-05710-6, 5710). Arco.

--Parrots, Lories & Cockatoos. 200p. 1982. 21.95 (ISBN 0-86230-041-X). Triplegate.

Alderton, Patricia, jt. auth. see Kerry, Iris.

Alderton, Patrick M. Sea Transport: Operation & Economics. 2nd ed. (Illus.). 1980. 22.50 (ISBN 0-900335-63-7). Heinman.

Alderton, Peggy. Peggy Alderton's Stay Young for Life! (Illus.). 338p. 1984. 15.95 (ISBN 0-915657-00-7); pap. 7.95 (ISBN 0-915657-01-5). Books World.

--The Vitamin, Mineral Connection. 30p. 1985. pap. 2.95 (ISBN 0-317-14757-9). Books World.

Alderwyck, A. How to Restore Wooden Body Framing. (Osprey Restoration Guide Ser.). (Illus.). 128p. 1984. text ed. 14.95 (ISBN 0-85045-590-1, Pub. by Osprey England). Motorbooks Intl.

Aldgate, Anthony. Cinema & History: British Newsreels & the Spanish Civil War. (Illus.). 1979. text ed. 31.75x (ISBN 0-85967-485-1). Humanities.

--Cinema & History: British Newsreels & the Spanish Civil War. (Illus., Orig.). 1980. pap. 12.95 (ISBN 0-85967-486-X). NY Zoetrope.

Aldgate, Anthony, jt. auth. see Richards, Jeffrey.

Aldhizer, Gerard & Krop, Thomas. The Doctors' Book on Hair Loss. (Illus.). 142p. 1983. 14.95 (ISBN 0-13-216598-8); pap. 7.95 (ISBN 0-13-216580-5). P-H.

Alding, Peter. Betrayed by Death. 192p. 1982. 10.95 (ISBN 0-8027-5465-1). Walker & Co.

--Betrayed by Death. LC 81-71203. (British Mystery Ser.). 175p. 1984. pap. 2.95 (ISBN 0-8027-3074-4). Walker & Co.

--A Man Condemned. LC 80-54822. 1981. 9.95 (ISBN 0-8027-5443-0). Walker & Co.

--A Man Condemned. 176p. 1983. pap. 2.95 (ISBN 0-8027-3018-3). Walker & Co.

--Murder Is Suspected. 184p. 1983. pap. 2.95 (ISBN 0-8027-3017-5). Walker & Co.

--Ransom Town. (British Mysteries Ser.). 1983. pap. 2.95 (ISBN 0-8027-3046-9). Walker & Co.

Aldington, ed. see Wilde, Oscar.

Aldington, Richard. A. E. Housman & W. B. Yeats. LC 73-3175. 1955. lib. bdg. 9.50 (ISBN 0-8414-1716-4). Folcroft.

--A. E. Housman & W. B. Yeats. 1978. 28.50 (ISBN 0-685-65704-3). Porter.

--Artifex: Sketches & Ideas. facsimile ed. (Essay Index Reprint Ser.). 1936. 20.00 (ISBN 0-8369-1438-4). Ayer Co Pubs.

--At All Costs. 1930. 20.00 (ISBN 0-932062-01-6). Sharon Hill.

--Balls, & Another Book for Suppression. LC 76-30429. 1977. Repr. of 1931 ed. lib. bdg. 10.00 (ISBN 0-8414-2964-2). Folcroft.

--A Book of "Characters". LC 78-16197. lib. bdg. 50.00 (ISBN 0-8414-1708-3). Folcroft.

--A Book of Characters from Theophrastus Joseph Hall, Sir Thomas Overbury, Nicolas Breton, John Earle, Thomas Fuller, & Other English Authors; Jean De la Bruyere, Vauvenargues, & Other French Authors. 559p. 1980. Repr. of 1924 ed. lib. bdg. 50.00 (ISBN 0-8482-0049-7). Norwood Edns.

--Collected Poems. LC 78-64002. (Des Imagistes: Literature of the Imagist Movement). 248p. Repr. of 1928 ed. 26.00 (ISBN 0-404-17075-7). AMS Pr.

--D. H. Lawrence. 1978. Repr. of 1935 ed. lib. bdg. 10.00 (ISBN 0-8495-0045-1). Arden Lib.

--D. H. Lawrence. 1982. lib. bdg. 34.50 (ISBN 0-685-86328-X). Porter.

--D. H. Lawrence: A Complete List of His Works, Together with a Critical Appreciation. LC 73-1263. lib. bdg. 10.00 (ISBN 0-8414-1700-8). Folcroft.

--D. H. Lawrence: An Appreciation. LC 76-462799. 1978. Repr. of 1930 ed. lib. bdg. 10.00 (ISBN 0-8492-0007-5). R West.

--D. H. Lawrence: An Indiscretion. LC 74-13379. Repr. of 1927 ed. lib. bdg. 10.00 (ISBN 0-8414-2995-2). Folcroft.

--D. H. Lawrence: Portrait of a Genius But-- 1961. pap. 1.50 (ISBN 0-02-001070-2, Collier). Macmillan.

--Death of a Hero. 480p. 1984. pap. 7.95 (ISBN 0-7012-0604-7, Pub. by Chatto & Windus-Hogarth Pr). Merrimack Pub Cir.

--Death of a Hero: A Novel. LC 73-144860. (Literature Ser.). 412p. 1972. Repr. of 1929 ed. 59.00 (ISBN 0-403-00828-X). Scholarly.

--Euripides Alcestis. 1930. 12.50 (ISBN 0-932062-00-8). Sharon Hill.

--Fifty Romance Lyric Poems. LC 73-13661. 1973. lib. bdg. 25.00 (ISBN 0-8414-2900-6). Folcroft.

--French Studies & Reviews. facs. ed. LC 67-23172. (Essay Index Reprint Ser.). 1926. 17.00 (ISBN 0-8369-0142-8). Ayer Co Pubs.

--French Studies & Reviews. LC 67-23172. (Essay Index Reprint Ser.). 247p. Repr. of 1926 ed. lib. bdg. 15.00 (ISBN 0-8290-0481-5). Irvington.

--Last Straws. LC 76-52454. 1977. lib. bdg. 15.00 (ISBN 0-8414-2973-1). Folcroft.

--Lawrence of Arabia: A Biographical Inquiry. LC 75-36506. (Illus.). 448p. 1976. Repr. of 1955 ed. lib. bdg. 31.50 (ISBN 0-8371-8634-X, ALLA). Greenwood.

--Life for Life's Sake: A Book of Reminiscences. LC 78-64003. (Des Imagistes). 416p. Repr. of 1941 ed. 42.50 (ISBN 0-404-17076-5). AMS Pr.

--Literary Studies & Reviews. facs. ed. LC 68-16901. (Essay Index Reprint Ser). 1924. 17.00 (ISBN 0-8369-0143-6). Ayer Co Pubs.

--A Passionate Prodigality: Letters to Alan Bird from Richard Aldington, 1949-1962. Benkovitz, Miriam J., ed. LC 75-23105. (Illus.). 376p. 1975. 20.00 (ISBN 0-87104-259-2). NY Pub Lib.

--Remy De Gourmont: A Modern Man of Letters. LC 74-28305. 1928. 10.00 (ISBN 0-8414-2855-7). Folcroft.

--Richard Aldington: Selected Critical Writing, 1928-1960. Kershaw, Alister, ed. LC 78-86189. (Crosscurrents-Modern Critique Ser.). 158p. 1970. 6.95 (ISBN 0-8093-0451-1). S Ill U Pr.

--Roads to Glory. facs. ed. (Short Story Index Reprint Ser). 1931. 18.00 (ISBN 0-8369-3666-3). Ayer Co Pubs.

--Voltaire. LC 77-21922. 1977. Repr. of 1925 ed. lib. bdg. 35.00 (ISBN 0-8414-1738-5). Folcroft.

--Voltaire. 278p. 1980. Repr. of 1925 ed. lib. bdg. 25.00 (ISBN 0-8492-3202-3). R West.

--W. Somerset Maugham: An Appreciation. LC 76-30814. 1977. lib. bdg. 10.00 (ISBN 0-8414-2953-7). Folcroft.

Aldington, Richard, ed. Oscar Wilde Selected Works with 12 Unpublished Letters. 553p. 1983. Repr. of 1946 ed. lib. bdg. 40.00 (ISBN 0-8495-0231-4). Arden Lib.

--The Poet's Translation Series, 2 vols. Incl. Series One. LC 78-64005 (ISBN 0-404-17101-X); Series Two. LC 78-64016 (ISBN 0-404-17102-8). (Des Imagistes: Literature of the Imagist Movement). Repr. of 1920 ed. Set. 49.00 (ISBN 0-404-17100-1); 25.00 ea. AMS Pr.

Aldington, Richard & Weintraub, eds. The Portable Oscar Wilde. rev. ed. LC 80-39827. 1981. 14.95 (ISBN 0-670-76743-3). Viking.

Aldington, Richard, ed. see Gourmont, Remy de.

Aldington, Richard, tr. see Benda, Julien.

Aldington, Richard, tr. see De Laclos, Choderlos.

Aldington, Richard, tr. see Gourmont, Remy de.

Aldington, Richard, tr. see Laclos, Pierre A.

Aldington, Richard, tr. see Nerval, Gerard de.

Aldington, William, tr. see Henley, W. E.

Aldis, A. S. Cardiff Royal Infirmary: 1883-1983. 60p. 1984. pap. text ed. 7.00x (ISBN 0-7083-0864-3, Pub. by Univ of Wales Pr England). Humanities.

Aldis, Harry G. List of Books Printed in Scotland Before 1700: Including Those Printed Furth of the Realm for Scottish Booksellers, with Brief Notes on the Printers & Stationers. LC 76-121214. (Edinburgh Bibliographical Society. Publications: Vol. 7). 1970. Repr. of 1904 ed. 20.50 (ISBN 0-8337-0032-4). B Franklin.

Aldis, Janet. The Queen of Letter Writers: Marquise De Sevigne Dame De Bourbilly, 1626-1696. 1977. Repr. of 1907 ed. lib. bdg. 27.50 (ISBN 0-8495-0015-X). Arden Lib.

--The Queen of Letter Writers: Marquise De Sevigne Dame De Bourbilly 1626-1696. 1973. Repr. of 1907 ed. 35.00 (ISBN 0-8274-1209-6). R West.

--The Queen of Letter Writers: Marquise De Sevigne Dame De Bourbilly 1626-1696. 1907. 35.00 (ISBN 0-932062-03-2). Sharon Hill.

Aldisert, Ruggero J. The Judicial Process, Readings, Materials & Cases. LC 17-1630. (American Casebook Ser.). 948p. 1976. text ed. 25.95 (ISBN 0-317-03451-0). West Pub.

--Readings, Materials & Cases in the Judicial Process. LC 76-1630. (American Casebook Ser.). 1976. 17.95 (ISBN 0-685-71458-6). West Pub.

Aldiss, Brian. Billion Year Spree: The True History of Science Fiction. LC 74-9868. 1974. pap. 3.95 (ISBN 0-8052-0450-4). Schocken.

--Earthworks. 1980. pap. 1.95 (ISBN 0-380-52159-8, 52159). Avon.

--Galaxies Like Grains of Sand. pap. 2.75 (ISBN 0-451-13416-8, Sig). NAL.

--Hothouse. 1984. pap. write for info. (ISBN 0-671-55930-3, Pub. by Baen Books). PB.

--Malacia Tapestry. 416p. 1981. pap. 2.75 (ISBN 0-441-51648-3). Ace Bks.

--New Arrivals, Old Encounters: Twelve Stories. LC 79-2642. 224p. 1979. 15.00 (ISBN 0-06-010055-9). Ultramarine Pub.

--A Report on Probability. 144p. 1980. pap. 1.95 (ISBN 0-380-52498-8, 52498-8). Avon.

--Seasons in Flight. LC 84-24329. 160p. 1986. 10.95 (ISBN 0-689-11538-5). Atheneum.

Aldiss, Brian, ed. Galactic Empires, Vol. I. (YA) 1979. pap. 2.25 (ISBN 0-380-42341-3, 42341). Avon.

Aldiss, Brian & Harrison, Harry, eds. Science Fiction Horizons, 2 vols. in 1. LC 74-15942. (Science Fiction Ser). (Illus.). 64p. 1975. Repr. 14.00x (ISBN 0-405-06320-2). Ayer Co Pubs.

Aldiss, Brian W. Frankenstein Unbound. 1974. 10.00 (ISBN 0-394-49079-7). Random.

--Helliconia Spring. LC 81-66036. 1982. 15.95 (ISBN 0-689-11196-7). Atheneum.

--Helliconia Spring. 384p. 1983. pap. 6.95 (ISBN 0-425-06186-8). Berkley Pub.

--Helliconia Spring. 480p. 1984. pap. 3.50 (ISBN 0-425-07328-9). Berkley Pub.

--Helliconia Summer. LC 83-45062. 384p. 1983. 16.95 (ISBN 0-689-11388-9). Atheneum.

--Helliconia Summer. 416p. 1984. pap. 6.95 (ISBN 0-425-07368-8). Berkley Pub.

--The Helliconia Trilogy, 3 vols. LC 84-45780. 1184p. 1985. Boxed Set. 50.00 (ISBN 0-689-11566-0). Atheneum.

--Helliconia Winter. LC 84-45607. 384p. 1985. 17.95 (ISBN 0-689-11541-5). Atheneum.

--The Malacia Tapestry. 416p. 1985. pap. 3.50 (ISBN 0-425-08079-X). Berkley Pub.

--The Saliva Tree. 1981. lib. bdg. 17.95 (ISBN 0-8398-2566-8, Gregg). G K Hall.

--This World & Nearer Ones: Essays Exploring the Familiar. LC 81-9179. (Illus.). 261p. 1981. pap. 6.95 (ISBN 0-87338-261-7). Kent St U Pr.

Aldiss, Margaret. The Work of Brian W. Aldiss: An Annotated Bibiography & Guide. (Bibliographies of Modern Authors: No. 9). 144p. 1985. lib. bdg. 19.95x (ISBN 0-89370-388-5); pap. text ed. 9.95x (ISBN 0-89370-488-1). Borgo Pr.

Aldman, B. & Chapon, A. The Biomechanics of Impact Trauma: Proceedings of the Symposium, Amalfi, May 31 - June 4, 1983. 1985. 74.00 (ISBN 0-444-86837-2, I-546-83, North-Holland). Elsevier.

Aldon, Edmund K. The World's Representative Assemblies of Today: A Study in Comparative Legislation. pap. 9.00 (ISBN 0-384-00640-X). Johnson Repr.

Al-Doory, Yousef. The Epidemiology of Human Mycotic Diseases. (Illus.). 364p. 1976. 36.50x (ISBN 0-398-03380-3). C C Thomas.

--Laboratory Medical Mycology. LC 79-22500. (Illus.). 410p. 1980. text ed. 24.50 (ISBN 0-8121-0695-4). Lea & Febiger.

Al-Doory, Yousef & Wagner, Gerald E. Aspergillosis. (Illus.). 286p. 1985. 29.75x (ISBN 0-398-05037-6). C C Thomas.

Al-Doory, Yousef & Domson, Joanne F., eds. Mould Allergy. LC 83-14951. (Illus.). 287p. 1984. text ed. 28.50 (ISBN 0-8121-0897-3). Lea & Febiger.

Aldous, Clarence M., jt. auth. see Mendall, Howard L.

Aldous, D. J., et al. Ecole d'Ete de Probabilites de Saint-Flour XIII, 1983. Hennequin, P. L., ed. (Lecture Notes in Mathematics Ser.: Vol, 1117). (Illus.). ix, 490p. 1985. pap. 25.80 (ISBN 0-387-15203-2). Springer-Verlag.

Aldous, Donald. Sound Systems. 1984. lib. bdg. 9.40 (ISBN 0-531-09224-0, Warwick). Watts.

Aldous, Joan. Family Careers: Developmental Change in Families. LC 77-15043. 358p. 1978. text ed. 28.50 (ISBN 0-471-02046-X). Wiley.

--Two Paychecks: Life in Dual Earner Families. (Sage Focus Editions: Vol. 56). (Illus.). 232p. 1982. 24.00 (ISBN 0-8039-1882-8); pap. 12.00 (ISBN 0-8039-1883-6). Sage.

Aldous, Joan & Dahl, Nancy, eds. International Bibliography of Research in Marriage & the Family, Vol. 2: 1965-1972. LC 67-63014. 1519p. 1974. 39.50x (ISBN 0-8166-0726-5). U of Minn Pr.

Aldous, Joan, jt. ed. see D'Antonio, William V.

Aldous, Tony. Illustrated London News Book of London's Villages. 1981. (Pub. by Secker & Warburg UK); pap. 12.50 (ISBN 0-436-01151-4, Pub. by Secker & Warburg UK). David & Charles.

Aldous, Tony, ed. Trees & Buildings. 95p. 1980. pap. 11.25 (ISBN 0-900630-73-6, Pub. by RIBA). Intl Spec Bk.

Aldred, Cyril. A Book of Tutankhmun. (Illus.). 1978. pap. 1.50 (ISBN 0-88388-059-8). Bellerophon Bks.

--Egypt to the End of the Old Kingdom. LC 82-80981. (Illus.). 1982. pap. 7.95f (ISBN 0-500-29001-6). Thames Hudson.

--Egyptian Art. LC 84-51309. (World of Art Ser.). (Illus.). 252p. 1985. pap. 9.95 (ISBN 0-500-20180-3). Thames Hudson.

--The Egyptians. 2nd, rev. & enl. ed. LC 83-50637. (Ancient Peoples & Places Ser.). (Illus.). 216p. 1984. 19.95 (ISBN 0-500-02104-X). Thames Hudson.

--Tut-Ankh-Amun-& His Friends. (gr. 8). pap. 2.50 (ISBN 0-88388-043-1). Bellerophon Bk.

Aldred, Guy. Bakunin. LC 79-179272. (Studies in Philosophy, No. 40). 1971. lib. bdg. 26.95x (ISBN 0-8383-1259-4). Haskell.

Aldred, Guy A. Bakunin's Writings. 59.95 (ISBN 0-87968-049-0). Gordon Pr.

Aldred, Jennifer, ed. Industrial Confrontation. 120p. 1984. 20.00 (ISBN 0-86861-480-7). Allen Unwin.

Aldred, Jennifer & Wilkes, John, eds. A Fractured Federation. 128p. 1983. text ed. 19.95x (ISBN 0-86861-109-3). Allen Unwin.

Aldred, William H., jt. auth. see Jones, Fred R.

Aldredge, John. Satisfaction: The Story of Mick Jagger. (Illus.). 160p. 1984. 17.95 (ISBN 0-86276-136-0); pap. 10.95 (ISBN 0-86276-135-2). Proteus Pub NY.

Aldrete, J. A. Intravenous Anesthesia. 1980. 67.95 (ISBN 0-8151-0106-6). Year Bk Med.

Aldrete, J. Antonio & Britt, Beverly A., eds. The International Symposium on Malignant Hyperthermia, Second, 1978: International Symposium. 592p. 1978. 54.00 (ISBN 0-8089-1073-6, 790035). Grune.

Aldrete, J. Antonio, jt. ed. see Guerra, Frank.

Aldrete, J. Antonio, et al, eds. Low Flow & Closed System Anesthesia. 352p. 1979. 52.00 (ISBN 0-8089-1176-7, 790036). Grune.

Aldrich, Alexander. How to Write a Book Which the Millions Will Want to Read. (Illus.). 127p. 1981. 47.55 (ISBN 0-89266-332-4). Am Classical Coll Pr.

Aldrich, B. S. Home-Coming. 16.95 (ISBN 0-8488-0067-2, Pub. by Amereon Hse). Amereon Ltd.

Aldrich, Bailey. Crowding Memories. 1920. 25.00 (ISBN 0-8274-2123-0). R West.

Aldrich, Bernard. The Ever-Rolling Stream. (Illus.). 176p. 1984. 16.50x (ISBN 0-04-799019-8). Allen Unwin.

Aldrich, Bess S. Across the Smiling Meadow. 15.95 (ISBN 0-8488-0068-0, Pub. by Amereon Hse). Amereon Ltd.

--The Cutters. 275p. 1975. Repr. of 1926 ed. lib. bdg. 16.95 (ISBN 0-88411-254-3, Pub. by Aeonian Pr). Amereon Ltd.

--The Drum Goes Dead. 339p. 1975. Repr. of 1941 ed. lib. bdg. 5.95x (ISBN 0-88411-256-X, Pub. by Aeonian Pr). Amereon Ltd.

--Journey into Christmas. 265p. Repr. of 1949 ed. lib. bdg. 15.95 (ISBN 0-88411-262-4, Pub. by Aeonian Pr). Amereon Ltd.

--Journey into Christmas & Other Stories. LC 85-8559. (Illus.). vi, 265p. 1985. pap. 7.50 (ISBN 0-8032-5908-5, BB 934, Bison). U of Nebr Pr.

--A Lantern in Her Hand. 278p. Repr. of 1928 ed. lib. bdg. 18.95 (ISBN 0-88411-260-8, Pub. by Aeonian Pr). Amereon Ltd.

--A Lantern in Her Hand. 1983. pap. 2.25 (ISBN 0-451-12287-9, Sig Vista). NAL.

--The Lieutenant's Lady. 275p. 1975. Repr. of 1942 ed. lib. bdg. 17.95 (ISBN 0-88411-252-7, Pub. by Aeonian Pr). Amereon Ltd.

--Man Who Caught the Weather & Other Stories. 293p. 1975. Repr. of 1936 ed. lib. bdg. 16.95 (ISBN 0-88411-258-6, Pub. by Aeonian Pr). Amereon Ltd.

--Miss Bishop. 336p. 1975. Repr. of 1933 ed. lib. bdg. 18.95 (ISBN 0-88411-255-1, Pub. by Aeonian Pr). Amereon Ltd.

--Miss Bishop. Large Print ed. LC 83-18098. 370p. 1984. Repr. of 1933 ed. 13.95 (ISBN 0-89621-505-9). Thorndike Pr.

--Mother Mason. 268p. 1975. Repr. of 1924 ed. lib. bdg. 15.95 (ISBN 0-88411-257-8, Pub. by Aeonian Pr). Amereon Ltd.

--New Bess Streeter Aldrich Reader. 320p. Repr. of 1979 ed. lib. bdg. 20.95x (ISBN 0-88411-263-2, Pub. by Aeonian Pr). Amereon Ltd.

--The Outsiders. 15.95 (ISBN 0-8488-0161-X, Pub by. Amereon Hse). Amereon Ltd.

--Rim of the Prairie. 296p. Repr. of 1925 ed. lib. bdg. 16.95x (ISBN 0-88411-259-4, Pub. by Aeonian Pr). Amereon Ltd.
--The Rim of the Prairie. LC 25-19624. xii, 352p. 1966. pap. 8.95 (ISBN 0-8032-5002-9, BB 347, Bison). U of Nebr Pr.
--Romance in G. Minor. 18.95 (ISBN 0-8488-0066-4, Pub. by Amereon Hse). Amereon Ltd.
--A Song of Years. 490p. 1975. Repr. of 1937 ed. lib. bdg. 23.95x (ISBN 0-88411-251-9, Pub. by Aeonian Pr). Amereon Ltd.
--Song of Years. 1985. pap. 2.95 (ISBN 0-451-13925-9, Sig Vista). NAL.
--Spring Came on Forever. 333p. Repr. of 1935 ed. lib. bdg. 18.95x (ISBN 0-88411-261-6, Pub. by Aeonian Pr). Amereon Ltd.
--Spring Came on Forever. LC 84-19671. viii, 334p. 1985. pap. 8.95 (ISBN 0-8032-5907-7, BB 904, Bison). U of Nebr Pr.
--The Victory of Connie Lee. 17.95 (ISBN 0-8488-0160-1, Pub. by Amereon Hse). Amereon Ltd.
--A White Bird Flying. 335p. 1975. Repr. of 1931 ed. lib. bdg. 18.95x (ISBN 0-88411-253-5, Pub. by Aeonian Pr). Amereon Ltd.
--A White Bird Flying. large print ed. LC 82-19254. 385p. 1983. Repr. of 1931 ed. 14.95 (ISBN 0-89621-410-9). Thorndike Pr.
--A White Bird Flying. (gr. 6 up). 1983. pap. 2.50 (ISBN 0-451-12462-6, AE2462, Sig Vista). NAL.

Aldrich, Charles R. Primitive Mind & Modern Civilization. LC 79-98401. Repr. of 1931 ed. 11.50 (ISBN 0-404-00309-5). AMS Pr.
--The Primitive Mind & Modern Civilization. LC 70-98206. xvii, 249p. Repr. of 1931 ed. lib. bdg. 15.00 (ISBN 0-8371-3240-1, ALPM). Greenwood.

Aldrich, Dawn. A Song for Mandy. (Magic Moments Ser.: No. 9). 1985. pap. 2.25 (ISBN 0-451-13422-2, Sig Vista). NAL.

Aldrich, Dorothy, jt. ed. see Schwartz, Dorothy.

Aldrich, Earl M., Jr. Modern Short Story in Peru. 224p. 1966. 25.00x (ISBN 0-299-03960-9). U of Wis Pr.

Aldrich, Elizabeth. Daily Use of the Ephemeris. 86p. avail. (ISBN 0-86690-286-4). Am Fed Astrologers.

Aldrich, Frank T., jt. auth. see Lounsbury, John F.

Aldrich, Henry. Cell Biology of Physarum & Didymium, Vol. 2. (Cell Biology Ser.). 1982. 65.00 (ISBN 0-12-049602-X). Acad Pr.

Aldrich, Henry & Daniel, John W., eds. Cell Biology of Physarum & Didymium: Vol. I, Organisms, Nucleus & Cell Cycle. LC 81-20483. (Cell Biology Ser.). 1982. 60.00 (ISBN 0-12-049601-1). Acad Pr.

Aldrich, Howard. Organizations & Environments. (P-H Ser. in Sociology). (Illus.). 1979. ref. 28.95 (ISBN 0-13-641431-1). P-H.

Aldrich, John F. Single Wing Offense with the Spinning Fullback. (Illus.). 176p. 1983. text ed. 16.95 (ISBN 0-8138-1643-2). Iowa St U Pr.

Aldrich, John H. Before the Convention: A Theory of Presidential Nomination Campaigns. LC 79-27752. (Illus.). 1980. lib. bdg. 25.00x (ISBN 0-226-01269-7); pap. 7.95x (ISBN 0-226-01270-0, P888, Phoen). U of Chicago Pr.

Aldrich, John H. & Nelson, Forrest D. Linear Probability, Logit, & Probit Models. LC 84-51766. 95p. 1984. pap. 5.00 (ISBN 0-8039-2133-0). Sage.

Aldrich, John H., jt. auth. see Abramson, Paul R.

Aldrich, Jonathan. Croquet Lover at the Dinner Table. LC 76-45630. 64p. 1977. 7.95 (ISBN 0-8262-0205-5). U of Mo Pr.
--Death of Michelangelo. Hunting, Constance, ed. 40p. (Orig.). 1985. pap. 6.95 (ISBN 0-913006-34-3). Puckerbrush.

Aldrich, Joseph C. Life-style Evangelism: Crossing Traditional Boundaries to Reach the Unbelieving World. LC 80-27615. (Critical Concern Bks.). 1981. 9.95 (ISBN 0-930014-46-4). Multnomah.
--Life-Style Evangelism: Crossing Traditional Boundaries to Reach the Unbelieving World. LC 80-27615. (Critical Concern Ser.). 246p. 1983. pap. 5.95 (ISBN 0-88070-023-8). Multnomah.
--Life-Style Evangelism: Study Guide. 1983. pap. 2.95 (ISBN 0-88070-020-3). Multnomah.
--Love for All Your Worth! LC 85-11420. 1985. pap. 5.95 (ISBN 0-88070-119-6). Multnomah.
--Secrets to Inner Beauty. LC 84-9970. 142p. 1984. pap. 5.95 (ISBN 0-88070-069-6). Multnomah.

Aldrich, Keith, tr. Apollodorus: The Library of Greek Mythology. 298p. 1975. 15.00x (ISBN 0-87291-072-5). Coronado Pr.

Aldrich, Mark & Buchele, Robert. The Economics of Comparable Worth. 200p. 1986. prof. ref. 29.95 (ISBN 0-88730-073-1). Ballinger Pub.

Aldrich, Michael. Videotex: Key to the Wired City. 144p. 1982. 29.00x (ISBN 0-907621-12-0, Pub. by Quiller Pr England). State Mutual Bk.

Aldrich, Mildred. Told in a French Garden, August, 1914. facsimile ed. (Short Story Index Reprint Ser.). 1916. 18.00 (ISBN 0-8369-3327-3). Ayer Co Pubs.

Aldrich, Nelson. In Herited Wealth. Date not set. price not set (ISBN 0-670-39824-1). Viking.

Aldrich, Nelson W. Tommy Hitchcock: An American Hero. 304p. 1985. 19.95 (ISBN 0-9611314-2-X). Fleet St Corp.

Aldrich, Pearl. The Impact of Mass Media. LC 75-1012. 192p. (gr. 10-12). 1975. pap. text ed. 6.50x (ISBN 0-8104-6000-9). Boynton Cook Pubs.

Aldrich, Pearl G. Everything You've Ever Heard about Grammar Ain't Necessarily So: A New Look at an Old Problem. (How to Improve Your Writing Ser.). (Illus.). 50p. (Orig.). 1987. pap. text ed. 6.95 (ISBN 0-915025-02-7). Res Ent Pubs.
--How to Decrease Wordiness: A Handbook with Models for Executives & Professionals. (How to Improve Your Writing Ser.). (Illus.). 75p. (Orig.). 1986. pap. text ed. 8.95 (ISBN 0-915025-01-9). Res Ent Pubs.
--How to Plan & Organize Your Writing: A Text-Workbook for Executives & Professionals. (How to Improve Your Writing Ser.). (Illus.). 125p. (Orig.). 1984. pap. text ed. 12.95 (ISBN 0-915025-00-0). Res Ent Pubs.
--Research Papers: A Beginner's Manual. (Orig.). 1976. pap. text ed. 6.95 (ISBN 0-316-03109-7). Little.

Aldrich, Peggy. The Aldrich Report. 1977. pap. text ed. 1.95 (ISBN 0-505-51158-4, BT51158, Pub. by Tower Bks). Dorchester Pub Co.
--My First. 1976. pap. 1.75 (ISBN 0-685-69148-9, LB355KK, Leisure Bks). Dorchester Pub Co.
--Nights in the Garden of Love. (Orig.). 1975. pap. 1.50 (ISBN 0-685-52939-8, LB256NK, Leisure Bks). Dorchester Pub Co.

Aldrich, Putnam. Ornamentation in J. S. Bach's Organ Works. LC 78-17258. (Music Reprint Ser.). (Illus.). 1978. Repr. of 1950 ed. lib. bdg. 19.50 (ISBN 0-306-77590-5). Da Capo.

Aldrich, R. J. Weed-Crop Ecology: Principles in Weed Management. text ed. write for info. (ISBN 0-534-02833-0). Wadsworth Pub.

Aldrich, Richard. Concert Life in New York, Nineteen Hundred to Nineteen Twenty-Three. facsimile ed. Johnson, Harold, ed. LC 78-156603. (Essay Index Reprint Ser). Repr. of 1941 ed. 36.00 (ISBN 0-8369-2263-8). Ayer Co Pubs.
--Musical Discourse, from the New York Times. facsimile ed. LC 67-28740. (Essay Index Reprint Ser). 1928. 18.00 (ISBN 0-8369-0144-4). Ayer Co Pubs.

Aldrich, Richard S. Gertrude Lawrence As Mrs. A: An Intimate Biography of the Great Star. LC 78-94600. Repr. of 1954 ed. lib. bdg. 24.75 (ISBN 0-8371-2469-7, ALGL). Greenwood.

Aldrich, Robert. Economy & Society in Burgundy since 1950. LC 83-40127. 256p. 1984. 27.50 (ISBN 0-312-23680-8). St Martin.

Aldrich, Robert, jt. ed. see Carroll, John M.

Aldrich, Ruth I., ed. see Holcroft, Thomas.

Aldrich, Samuel R., jt. auth. see Scott, Walter O.

Aldrich, Terry M. Rates of Return on Investment in Technical Education in the Ante-Bellum American Economy. LC 75-2573. (Dissertations in American Economic History). (Illus.). 1975. 34.50x (ISBN 0-405-07254-6). Ayer Co Pubs.

Aldrich, Thomas. The Story of a Bad Boy. Repr. of 1927 ed. lib. bdg. 27.00 (ISBN 0-8414-3052-7). Folcroft.

Aldrich, Thomas B. Marjorie Daw & Other People. facs. ed. (Short Story Index Reprint Ser.). 1873. 18.00 (ISBN 0-8369-3230-7). Ayer Co Pubs.
--Marjorie Daw & Other People. (The Works of Thomas Bailey Aldrich Ser.). 243p. Repr. of 1901 ed. 34.00 (ISBN 0-932051-71-5). Am Repr Serv.
--Marjorie Daw & Other Stories. facsimile ed. (Short Story Index Reprint Ser.). 1885. 16.00 (ISBN 0-8369-3231-5). Ayer Co Pubs.
--Marjorie Daw & Other Stories. 1972. Repr. of 1885 ed. lib. bdg. 15.00 (ISBN 0-8422-8001-4). Irvington.
--The Poems of Thomas Bailey Aldrich. 1977. Repr. of 1908 ed. lib. bdg. 27.50 (ISBN 0-8495-0016-8). Arden Lib.
--Ponkapog Papers. facs. ed. LC 70-84293. (Essay Index Reprint Ser). 1903. 12.25 (ISBN 0-8369-1073-7). Ayer Co Pubs.
--Sea Turn, & Other Matters. facs. ed. LC 76-81258. (Short Story Index Reprint Ser.). 1902. 18.00 (ISBN 0-8369-3010-X). Ayer Co Pubs.
--The Stillwater Tragedy. LC 68-20001. (Americans in Fiction Ser.). lib. bdg. 15.00 (ISBN 0-8398-0055-X); pap. text ed. 4.95x (ISBN 0-89197-949-2). Irvington.
--Two Bites at a Cherry, with Other Tales. 1972. Repr. of 1894 ed. lib. bdg. 24.00 (ISBN 0-8422-8002-2). Irvington.
--Writings of Thomas Bailey Aldrich, 9 Vols. Repr. of 1907 ed. Set. 202.50 (ISBN 0-404-00370-2); 22.50 ea. AMS Pr.

Aldrich, Virgil. Philosophy of Art. (Illus.). 1963. pap. 13.95 ref. ed. (ISBN 0-13-663765-5). P-H.

Aldrich, Winifred. Metric Pattern Cutting for Children's Wear: From 2-14 years. (Illus.). 160p. 1985. text ed. 19.95x (ISBN 0-00-383115-9, Pub. by Collins England). Sheridan.
--Metric Pattern Cutting: For Menswear Including Unisex Casual Clothes. (Illus.). 128p. 1980. text ed. 19.00 (ISBN 0-246-11219-0, Granada England). Brookfield Pub Co.
--Metric Pattern Cutting for Menswear: Including Unisex Casual Clothes. 128p. 1980. 16.00x (ISBN 0-246-11219-0, Pub. by Granada England). Sheridan.

Aldrich-Langen, Caroline. Australia. LC 83-19723. (World Education Ser.). (Illus.). 276p. (Orig.). 1983. pap. text ed. 5.00 (ISBN 0-910054-78-9). Am Assn Coll Registrars.

Aldridge, A. Owen. Thomas Paine's American Idealogy. LC 83-40239. 328p. 1984. 38.50 (ISBN 0-87413-260-6). U Delaware Pr.
--Voltaire & the Century of Light. LC 75-2978. 472p. 1975. 30.00x (ISBN 0-691-06287-0). Princeton U Pr.

Aldridge, Adele. Notpoems. 3rd ed. LC 72-23824. (Illus.). 56p. 1976. pap. 4.95 (ISBN 0-915600-01-3). Artists & Alchemists.
--Notpoems. LC 72-23824. 1976. pap. 5.95 (ISBN 0-8040-0753-5, 0753-5, Pub by Swallow, 82-74854). Ohio U Pr.

Aldridge, Adele & Davis, Frederic E. MacArt for the Macintosh: The Marriage of Art & Science. (Micropower Ser.). 224p. 1985. deluxe ed. 29.95 incl. diskette (ISBN 0-697-00735-9); pap. 16.95 (ISBN 0-697-00708-1). Wm C Brown.

Aldridge, Adele, jt. auth. see Ippolito, Donna.

Aldridge, Alan. Phantasia. (Orig.). 1982. pap. 14.95 (ISBN 0-345-30238-9). Ballantine.

Aldridge, Alan & Plomer, William. Butterfly Ball & the Grasshopper's Feast. (Illus.). 74p. (gr. 2-5). 1980. 10.95 (ISBN 0-224-00808-0, Pub. by Jonathan Cape). Merrimack Pub Cir.

Aldridge, Alan & Walker, Ted. The Lion's Cavalcade. (Illus.). 32p. (gr. 3 up). 1981. 10.95 (ISBN 0-224-01701-2, Pub. by Jonathan Cape). Merrimack Pub Cir.

Aldridge, Alan, ed. Beatles Illustrated Lyrics, Vol. 1. (Illus.). 160p. (Orig.). (gr. 7 up). 1980. pap. 10.95 (ISBN 0-440-50503-8, Dell Trade Pbks). Dell.
--Beatles Illustrated Lyrics, Vol. 2. 128p. (Orig.). (gr. 7 up). 1980. pap. 10.95 (ISBN 0-440-50504-6, Dell Trade Pbks). Dell.

Aldridge, Alexandra. The Scientific World View in Dystopia. Scholes, Robert, ed. LC 84-2724. (Studies in Speculative Fiction: No. 3). 108p. 1984. 24.95 (ISBN 0-8357-1572-8). UMI Res Pr.

Aldridge, Alfred O. Benjamin Franklin & Nature's God. LC 67-13409. pap. 71.80 (ISBN 0-317-20084-4, 2023365). Bks Demand UMI.

Aldridge, Betty. You Can Teach Preschoolers Successfully. (Training Successful Teachers Ser.). 48p. (Orig.). 1984. pap. 2.50 (ISBN 0-87239-805-6, 3205). Standard Pub.

Aldridge, Bill G., compiled by. Science & Engineering Technician Curriculum. 1976. Set. 75.00. Natl Sci Tchrs.

Aldridge, D. C., jt. auth. see Turner, W. B.

Aldridge, Daniel W., Jr., ed. The Aldridge Historically Black College Guide. 249p. 1983. pap. text ed. 12.95x (ISBN 0-317-03146-5). Aldridge Group.

Aldridge, Don. The Master Book of Environmental Education. 1981. pap. 25.00x (ISBN 0-686-81322-7, Pub. by GEO Abstracts England). State Mutual Bk.
--The Monster Book of Environmental Education. 29.50x (ISBN 0-686-78647-5, Pub. by GEO Abstracts England). State Mutual Bk.

Aldridge, E. E. Acoustical Holography. 46p. 1971. 39.00x (ISBN 0-900541-16-4, Pub. by Meadowfield Pr England). State Mutual Bk.

Aldridge, G. J., ed. see International Association Of Gerontology - 5th Congress.

Aldridge, James. The Broken Saddle. (Julia MacRae Ser.). 128p. (gr. 5 up). 1983. 8.95 (ISBN 0-531-04579-X, MacRae). Watts.

Aldridge, Jennifer & Tregorran, John. Ambridge: An English Village Through the Ages. 30.00x (ISBN 0-413-48350-9, Pub. by Borchester England). State Mutual Bk.

Aldridge, John W. After the Lost Generation. facs. ed. LC 79-142602. (Essay Index Reprint Ser). 1951. 20.00 (ISBN 0-8369-2141-0). Ayer Co Pubs.
--After the Lost Generation. 1985. 6.95 (ISBN 0-87795-757-6, Pub. by Library of Contemporary Americana). Arbor Hse.
--The American Novel & the Way We Live Now. 1983. 16.95 (ISBN 0-19-503198-9). Oxford U Pr.
--In Search of Heresy: American Literature in an Age of Conformity. LC 74-3618. 208p. 1974. Repr. of 1956 ed. lib. bdg. 82.50 (ISBN 0-8371-7452-X, ALSH). Greenwood.
--Time to Murder & Create: The Contemporary Novel in Crisis. LC 79-39113. (Essay Index Reprint Ser.). Repr. of 1966 ed. 26.50 (ISBN 0-8369-2682-X). Ayer Co Pubs.

Aldridge, John W., ed. Critiques & Essays on Modern Fiction, Nineteen Twenty to Nineteen Fifty-One: Representing the Achievement of Modern American & British Critics. 1952. text ed. 22.75 (ISBN 0-673-15650-8). Scott F.

Aldridge, M. V. English Quantifiers: A Study of Quantifying Expressions in Linguistic Science & Modern English Usage. 75.00 (ISBN 0-686-75546-4, Pub. by Avebury Pub England). State Mutual Bk.
--English Quantifiers: A Study of Quantifying Expressions in Linguistic Science & Modern English Usage. 288p. 1982. text ed. 46.25x (ISBN 0-86127-208-0, Pub. by Avebury England); pap. text ed. 31.00x (ISBN 0-86127-222-6). Humanities.

Aldridge, Marion D. The Pastor's Guidebook: A Manual for Worship. LC 83-70213. 1984. 9.95 (ISBN 0-8054-2312-5). Broadman.

Aldridge, Martha, et al. Beyond Management: Humanizing The Administrative Process. 180p. 1982. pap. 6.95 (ISBN 0-87414-025-0). U of Iowa Sch Soc Wk.

Aldridge, Mary, ed. see Ghose, Sri A.

Aldridge, Melanie. Paula's Feeling Angry. rev. ed. LC 79-10773. (A Values Ser.). (Illus.). (ps-3). 1979. PLB 4.95 (ISBN 0-89565-076-2). Childs World.

Aldridge, Meryl. British New Towns: A Programme Without a Policy. (International Library of Sociology). (Illus.). 1979. 32.50x (ISBN 0-7100-0356-0). Routledge & Kegan.

Aldridge, Richard. Red Pine, Black Ash. LC 80-18598. (Illus.). 144p. 1980. 10.00 (ISBN 0-89621-062-6). Thorndike Pr.

Aldridge, Robert C. Counterforce Syndrome: A Guide to U. S. Nuclear Weapons & Strategic Doctrine. rev. ed. (Illus.). 86p. 1979. pap. 4.95 (ISBN 0-89758-008-7). Inst Policy Stud.
--First Strike: The Pentagon's Strategy for Nuclear War. LC 82-61148. (Illus.). 300p. 1983. 20.00 (ISBN 0-89608-155-9); pap. 8.50 (ISBN 0-89608-154-0). South End Pr.

Aldridge, Sarah. All True Lovers. LC 78-59626. 340p. (Orig.). 1978. 6.95 (ISBN 0-930044-10-X). Naiad Pr.
--Cytherea's Breath. 1982. 6.95 (ISBN 0-930044-02-9). Naiad Pr.
--The Latecomer. 1982. 5.00 (ISBN 0-930044-00-2). Naiad Pr.
--Madame Aurora. 240p. (Orig.). 1983. pap. 7.95 (ISBN 0-930044-44-4). Naiad Pr.
--Misfortune's Friend. 288p. (Orig.). 1985. pap. 7.95 (ISBN 0-930044-67-3). Naiad Pr.
--The Nesting Place. 320p. (Orig.). 1982. pap. 6.95 (ISBN 0-930044-26-6). Naiad Pr.
--Tottie: The Tale of the Sixties. 181p. 1980. 5.95 (ISBN 0-930044-01-0). Naiad Pr.

Aldridge, W. N., jt. ed. see Matteis, F. De.

Aldrih, Winthrop. Artificial Poetry. 48p. 1981. 8.98 (ISBN 0-934276-02-1). Divisions.

Aldus, P. J. Mousetrap: Structure & Meaning in Hamlet. LC 76-42263. 1977. 27.50x (ISBN 0-8020-5329-7). U of Toronto Pr.

Aldwell, Edward & Schachter, Carl. Harmony & Voice Leading, Vol. I. 302p. 1978. text ed. 17.95 (ISBN 0-15-531515-3, HC); wkbk. 7.95 (ISBN 0-15-531516-1). HarBraceJ.
--Harmony & Voice Leading, Vol. 2. 276p. 1979. text ed. 17.95 (ISBN 0-15-531517-X, HC); wkbk. 7.95 (ISBN 0-15-531518-8). HarBraceJ.

Aldwinckle, Russell. Jesus: A Savior or the Savior? Religious Pluralism in Christian Perspective. LC 81-19033. 240p. 1982. 15.95x (ISBN 0-86554-023-3). Mercer Univ Pr.

Aldworth, Thomas. Shaping a Healthy Religion. 132p. 1985. 8.95 (ISBN 0-88347-176-0). Thomas More.

Aldyne, Nathan. Cobalt. 208p. 1986. pap. 2.95 (ISBN 0-345-32705-5). Ballantine.
--Slate. 192p. 1985. pap. 2.95 (ISBN 0-345-31366-6). Ballantine.
--Vermilion. 1980. pap. 2.75 (ISBN 0-380-76596-9, 81570-2). Avon.
--Vermilion. 1985. pap. 2.95 (ISBN 0-345-32706-3). Ballantine.

Aldyne, Nathen. Cobalt. 224p. 1982. pap. 2.75 (ISBN 0-380-81117-0, 81117-0). Avon.

Al-e Ahmad, Jalal. Lost in the Crowd. Green, John, et al, trs. from Farsi. LC 84-51088. 200p. 1985. 20.00; pap. 9.00 (ISBN 0-89410-443-8). Three Continents.
--The School Principal. Newton, John K., tr. (Studies in Middle Eastern Literatures: No. 4). 1983. pap. 11.95 (ISBN 0-88297-032-1). Bibliotheca.

Aleamoni, Lawrence M., jt. auth. see Kirkpatrick, J. Stephen.

Alechinsky, Pierre. Pierre Alechinsky; les Estampes, 1946-1972. 1973. 60.00 (ISBN 0-915346-17-6). A Wofsy Fine Arts.

Aledort, L. M., et al, eds. Outpatient Medicine. LC 78-51280. 335p. 1980. pap. text ed. 15.50 (ISBN 0-89004-354-X). Raven.

Aleem, A. A. Marine Resources of the United Arab Republic. (General Fisheries Council of the Mediterranean (GFCM): Studies & Reviews: No. 43). 22p. 1969. pap. 7.50 (ISBN 92-5-101962-2, F1803, FAO). Unipub.

Alefeld, F. Landwirtschaftliche Flora. 1966. Repr. of 1866 ed. lib. bdg. 42.70x (ISBN 3-87429-001-8). Lubrecht & Cramer.

Alefeld, G. & Grigorieff, R. D., eds. Fundamentals of Numerical Computation: International Conference. (Computing Supplementum: No. 2). (Illus.). 250p. 1980. pap. 57.90 (ISBN 0-387-81566-X). Springer-Verlag.

Alefeld, G. & Voelkl, J., eds. Hydrogen in Metals I: Basic Properties. (Topics in Applied Physics Ser.: Vol. 28). (Illus.). 1978. 64.00 (ISBN 0-387-08705-2). Springer-Verlag.
--Hydrogens in Metals II: Application - Oriented Properties. LC 78-4487. (Topics in Applied Physics Ser.: Vol. 29). (Illus.). 1978. 52.00 (ISBN 0-387-08883-0). Springer-Verlag.

Alefeld, Gotz & Herzberger, Jurgen. Introduction to Interval Computations. Rockne, Jon, tr. from Ger. (Computer Science & Applied Mathematics Ser.). 1983. 55.00 (ISBN 0-12-049820-0). Acad Pr.

Alegret Sanroma, Salvador. Doccionari De L'utillatage Quimic. 64p. (Cata.). 1977. pap. 8.75 (ISBN 84-7283-013-6, S-50061). French & Eur.

Alegria, Carmen, tr. see Camarda, Renato.

Alegria, Ciro. Broad & Alien Is the World. Onis, Harriet De, tr. from Span. 1973. Repr. 12.95 (ISBN 0-85036-282-2, Merlin Pr). Carrier Pigeon.

--Broad & Alien Is the World. De Onis, Harriet, tr. 434p. 1984. Repr. of 1941 ed. pap. text ed. 10.95 (ISBN 0-85036-282-2, Pub. by Merlin UK). Yorkville Bk.
--Broad & Alien Is the World. Onis, Harriet D., tr. from Span. LC 62-17709. 434p. 1973. 17.95 (ISBN 0-85036-171-0, Merlin Pr); pap. 12.95 (ISBN 0-85036-282-2, Merlin Pr). Dufour.
--Mundo es Ancho y Ajeno. Wade, G. E. & Stiefel, W. E., eds. (Span.). 1945. text ed. 28.50x (ISBN 0-89197-309-5); pap. text ed. 12.95x (ISBN 0-89197-310-9). Irvington.
Alegria, Claribel. Flowers from the Volcano. Forche, Carolyn, tr. from Span. LC 82-70893. (Pitt Poetry Ser.). 101p. 1982. 14.95 (ISBN 0-8229-3469-8); pap. 6.95 (ISBN 0-8229-5344-7). U of Pittsburgh Pr.
Alegria, Fernando. The Chilean Spring Discoveries. Miller, Yvette, ed. Fredman, Stephen, tr. from Span. LC 79-91641. 160p. (Orig.). 1980. cloth 15.95 (ISBN 0-935480-01-3); pap. 7.95 (ISBN 0-935480-00-5). Lat Am Lit Rev Pr.
--Instructions for Undressing the Human Race. (Illus., Orig., Span.). 1968. pap. 1.50 (ISBN 0-685-13650-7). Kayak.
--Nueva Historia de la Novela Hispanoamericana. 300p. (Span.). 1985. pap. 14.00 (ISBN 0-910061-29-7). Ediciones Norte.
--Retratos Contemporaneos. 247p. 1979. pap. text ed. 10.95 (ISBN 0-15-576680-5, HC). HarBraceJ.
Alegria, Fernando, et al, eds. Chilean Writers in Exile: Short Novels. Dagnino, Alfonso G. & Delano, Poli. LC 81-12567. (Crossing Press Translation Ser.). (Illus.). 176p. 1981. 18.95 (ISBN 0-89594-059-0); pap. 8.95 (ISBN 0-89594-060-4). Crossing Pr.
Alegria, Idsa, jt. auth. see Pico, Isabel.
Alegria, Idsa E., jt. ed. see Pico, Isabel.
Alegria, Ricardo E. Ball Courts & Ceremonial Plazas in the West Indies. (Publications in Anthropology Ser.: No. 79). 1983. pap. 12.50 (ISBN 0-913516-15-5). Yale U Anthro.
--Fort of San Jeronimo Del Boqueron. (Puerto Rico Ser.). 1979. lib. bdg. 59.95 (ISBN 0-8490-2921-X). Gordon Pr.
--Institute of Puerto Rican Culture. (Puerto Rico Ser.). 1979. lib. bdg. 59.95 (ISBN 0-8490-2948-1). Gordon Pr.
--Utuado Ceremonial Park. (Puerto Rico Ser.). 1979. lib. bdg. 59.95 (ISBN 0-8490-3013-7). Gordon Pr.
Alegria Ortega, Idsa E. La Comision Del Status De Puerto Rico: Su Historia y Significacion. LC 80-25739. 1981. pap. text ed. 6.00 (ISBN 0-8477-0869-1). U of PR Pr.
Aleichem, Sholem. Hanukah Money. LC 77-26693. (Illus.). 32p. (gr. k-3). 1978. 11.75 (ISBN 0-688-80120-X); PLB 11.88 (ISBN 0-688-84120-1). Greenwillow.
Aleichem, Sholom. The Adventures of Menahem-Mendl. LC 79-13506. 1979. pap. 4.95 (ISBN 0-399-50396-X, Perigee). Putnam Pub Group.
--From the Fair: The Autobiography of Sholom Aleichem. Leviant, Curt, tr. LC 84-17299. 336p. 1985. 20.00 (ISBN 0-670-80390-1). Viking.
--Holiday Tales of Sholom Aleichem. Shevrin, Aliza, tr. LC 79-753. (Illus.). (gr. 5 up). 1979. 10.95 (ISBN 0-684-16118-4, ScribJ). Scribner.
--Holiday Tales of Sholom Aleichem. Shevrin, Aliza, tr. LC 79-753. (Illus.). 145p. (Orig.). (gr. 5 up). 1985. pap. 4.95 (ISBN 0-689-71034-8, A-146, Aladdin). Atheneum.
--In the Storm. LC 83-19158. 224p. 1984. 15.95 (ISBN 0-399-12922-7, Putnam). Putnam Pub Group.
--In the Storm. Shevrin, Aliza, tr. 1985. pap. 6.95 (ISBN 0-452-25760-3, Plume). NAL.
--Inside Kasrilevke. LC 65-14829. (Illus.). 1968. pap. 4.95 (ISBN 0-8052-0173-4). Schocken.
--Marienbad. Shevrin, Aliza, tr. LC 83-27290. 228p. (Yiddish.). 1984. pap. 8.95 (ISBN 0-399-51013-3, Wideview). Putnam Pub Group.
--The Nightingale. Shevrin, Aliza, tr. 224p. 1985. 16.95 (ISBN 0-399-13098-5). Putnam Pub Group.
Aleinikoff, T. Alexander & Martin, David A. Immigration: Process & Policy. (American Casebook Ser.). 1000p. 1985. text ed. 30.95 (ISBN 0-314-90039-X). West Pub.
Aleixandre, Vicente. A Bird of Paper: Poems of Vicente Aleixandre. Barnstone, Willis & Garrison, David, trs. from Span. LC 82-80388. (International Poetry Ser.: Vol. 6). viii, 75p. 1982. lib. bdg. 16.95x (ISBN 0-8214-0661-2, 82-84317); pap. 10.95 (ISBN 0-8214-0662-0, 82-84325). Ohio U Pr.
--A Longing for the Light: Selected Poems of Vicente Aleixandre. Hyde, Lewis, ed. Kessler, Stephen, et al, trs. from Span. 284p. 1985. pap. 10.00 (ISBN 0-914742-89-2). Copper Canyon.
Alejandro, Carlos F. Diaz see Bacha, Edmar L. & Diaz Alejandro, Carlos F.
Alejandro, Carlos F. Diaz see Diaz Alejandro, Carlos F.
Alejandro, R. Everyday Tagalog. 1946. 4.00x (ISBN 0-686-00863-4). Colton Bk.
Alejandro, Reynaldo. The Flavor of Asia. LC 84-11117. 237p. 1984. 17.95 (ISBN 0-8253-0244-7). Beaufort Bks NY.
--The Philippine Cookbook. (Illus.). 288p. 1983. 17.95 (ISBN 0-698-11174-5, Coward). Putnam Pub Group.
--The Philippine Cookbook. (Illus.). 256p. 1985. pap. 8.95 (ISBN 0-399-51144-X, Perigee). Putnam Pub Group.
Alekhine, A. On the Road to the World Championship, Nineteen Twenty-Three to Twenty-Seven. Neat, K. P., ed. Feather, C. J., tr. LC 84-3051. (Pergamon Chess Ser.). (Illus.). 250p. 1984. 21.95 (ISBN 0-08-029731-5); pap. 15.95 (ISBN 0-08-029730-7). Pergamon.
Alekhine, Alexander. My Best Games of Chess, Nineteen Hundred & Eight to Nineteen Thirty-Seven. 581p. 1985. pap. 8.95 (ISBN 0-486-24941-7). Dover.
Alekhine, Alexander & Winter, E. G. One Hundred & Seven Great Chess Battles. (Illus.). 1980. pap. 17.50x (ISBN 0-19-217591-2). Oxford U Pr.
Alekhine, Alexander, ed. Book of the Nottingham International Chess Tournament, 10th to 28th August, 1936. 1937. pap. 5.00 (ISBN 0-486-20189-9). Dover.
Alekhine, Alexander, ed. see Watts, W. H.
Aleksander, I., ed. Artificial Vision for Robots. (Illus.). 234p. 1984. 37.50 (ISBN 0-412-00451-8, NO. 9001, Pub. by Chapman & Hall). Methuen Inc.
Aleksander, Igor. The Human Machine: A View of Intelligent Mechanisms. (Illus.). 1978. pap. text ed. 9.95x (ISBN 2-604-00023-7). Brookfield Pub Co.
Aleksander, Igor & Burnett, Piers. Reinventing Man: The Robot Becomes Reality. 1984. 17.95 (ISBN 0-03-063857-7). HR&W.
Aleksander, Igor & Hanna, F. Keith. Automata Theory: An Engineering Approach. LC 74-32509. (Computer Systems Engineering Ser.). 172p. 1975. 24.50x (ISBN 0-8448-0657-9). Crane-Russak Co.
Aleksander, Igor, ed. Computing Techniques for Robots. 276p. 1985. 39.50 (ISBN 0-412-01091-7, 9660). Methuen Inc.
--World Yearbook of Robotics Research & Development, 1985-1986. 2nd ed. 400p. 1985. 65.00x (ISBN 0-85038-933-X, Pub. by Kogan Page). Gale.
Aleksander, Igor, et al. Advanced Digital Information Systems. (Illus.). 576p. 1985. text ed. 39.95 (ISBN 0-13-011305-0). P-H.
Aleksandrjan, R. A., et al. Partial Differential Equations: Proceedings. LC 76-8428. (Translations Ser.: No. 2, Vol. 105). 1976. 62.00 (ISBN 0-8218-3055-4, TRANS 2-105). Am Math.
Aleksandrov, A. D. & Zalgaller, V. A. Intrinsic Geometry of Surfaces. LC 66-30492. (Translations of Mathematical Monographs: Vol. 15). 1967. 32.00 (ISBN 0-8218-1565-2, MMONO-15). Am Math.
Aleksandrov, A. D., ed. see Steklov Institute of Mathematics, Academy of Sciences, U S S R.
Aleksandrov, A. D., et al. Eleven Papers on Topology, Function Theory, & Differential Equations. LC 51-5559. (Translations Ser.: No. 2, Vol. 1). 1955. 26.00 (ISBN 0-8218-1701-9, TRANS 2-1). Am Math.
--Nine Papers on Topology, Lie Groups, & Differential Equations. LC 51-5559. (Translations Ser.: No. 2, Vol. 21). 1962. 33.00 (ISBN 0-8218-1721-3, TRANS 2-21). Am Math.
--Ten Papers on Differential Equations & Functional Analysis. LC 51-5559. (Translations Ser.: No. 2, Vol. 68). 1968. 35.00 (ISBN 0-8218-1768-X, TRANS 2-68). Am Math.
Aleksandrov, A. D., et al, eds. Mathematics: Its Content, Methods, & Meaning, 3 Vols. 2nd ed. Gould, S. H., tr. 1969. pap. 9.95 ea.; Vol. 1. pap. (ISBN 0-262-51005-7); Vol. 2. pap. (ISBN 0-262-51004-9); Vol. 3. pap. (ISBN 0-262-51003-0); pap. 27.50 set (ISBN 0-262-51014-6). MIT Pr.
Aleksandrov, I. V. Theory of Nuclear Magnetic Resonance. 1966. 45.00 (ISBN 0-12-049850-2). Acad Pr.
Aleksandrov, L. Growth of Crystalline Semi-Conductor Materials on Crystal Surfaces. (Thin-Films Science & Technology Ser.: Vol. 5). 1984. 98.25 (I-453-84). Elsevier.
Aleksandrov, P. S., et al. Ten Papers on Topology. LC 51-5559. (Translatons Ser.: No. 2, Vol. 30). 1963. 30.00 (ISBN 0-8218-1730-2, TRANS 2-30). Am Math.
--Transactions of the Moscow Mathematical Society, Vol. 31 (1974) LC 65-4713. 1976. 69.00 (ISBN 0-8218-1631-4, MOSCOW-31). Am Math.
Aleksandrov, Pavel S. Combinatorial Topology, 3 vols. Incl. Vol. 1. Introduction, Complexes, Coverings, Dimension. 1956 (ISBN 0-910670-01-3); Vol. 2. The Betti Groups. 1957 (ISBN 0-910670-02-1); Vol. 3. Homological Manifolds, Duality, Classification & Fixed Point Theorems. 1960 (ISBN 0-910670-03-X). LC 56-13930. (Illus.). 15.00x ea. Graylock.
Aleksandrov, Yu A. Bubble Chambers. Frisken, William R., tr. LC 66-14342. pap. 95.50 (ISBN 0-317-08533-6, 2055192). Bks Demand UMI.
Aleksandrova, V. D. The Arctic & Antarctic. Love, Doris, tr. from Russ. LC 79-41600. (Illus.). 200p. 1980. 42.50 (ISBN 0-521-23119-1). Cambridge U Pr.
Alekseev, F. A., ed. Soviet Advances in Nuclear Geophysics. LC 64-18194. 189p. 1965. 39.50x (ISBN 0-306-10708-2, Consultants). Plenum Pub.
Alekseev, P. M. English-Russian Glossary of Physics Terms. 288p. (Eng. & Rus.). 1980. 35.00x (ISBN 0-686-44696-8, Pub. by Collets). State Mutual Bk.
Alekseev, V. M., et al. Thirteen Papers on Differential Equations. LC 51-5559. (Translations Ser.: No. 2, Vol. 89). 1970. 35.00 (ISBN 0-8218-1789-2, TRANS 2-89). Am Math.
Alekseev, V. P., et al. Contributions to the Archaeology of Armenia. Field, Henry, ed. Krimgold, Arlene, tr. (Harvard University. Peabody Museum of Archeology & Ethnology. Russian Translation Ser. Three: No. 3). Repr. of 1968 ed. lib. bdg. 32.50 (ISBN 0-404-52646-2). AMS Pr.
Alekseeva, T. V. Artists of the Venetsianov School. 420p. 1982. 60.00x (ISBN 0-317-14223-2, Pub. by Collet's). State Mutual Bk.
Aleksich, Sue, jt. auth. see Schwartz, Linda.
Aleksinskii, Grigorii A. Modern Russia. Miall, Bernard, tr. LC 75-39045. (Russian Studies: Perspectives on the Revolution Ser). vi, 361p. 1977. Repr. of 1914 ed. 27.50 (ISBN 0-88355-422-4). Hyperion-Conn.
Aleksova, Blaga, jt. ed. see Wiseman, James.
Alem, Andre. Marquis d'Argenson et l'economie politique au debut du huitieme. LC 68-56757. (Research & Source Works Ser.: No. 242). (Fr). 1967. Repr. of 1900 ed. 19.50 (ISBN 0-8337-0033-2). B Franklin.
Aleman, Matheo. The Rogue or the Life or Guzman De Alfarache, 4 Vols. Mabbe, James, tr. (The Tudor Translations, Second Series: No. 2-5). Repr. of 1924 ed. Set. 180.00 (ISBN 0-404-51970-9); 45.00 ea. Vol. 1 (ISBN 0-404-51971-7). Vol. 2 (ISBN 0-404-51972-5). Vol. 3 (ISBN 0-404-51973-3). Vol. 4 (ISBN 0-404-51974-1). AMS Pr.
Aleman, Serafin. Juegos de Vida y Muerte: El Suicidio la Novela Galdosiana. LC 77-88535. 1978. pap. 7.95 (ISBN 0-89729-182-4). Ediciones.
Alemann, Johanna. The Pendulum of Choice. LC 80-81252. 175p. (Orig., Sidonie Flacco, M. ED., MFCC Subject Editor-Collaborator). 1980. pap. 10.00 (ISBN 0-936696-00-1). Maxim Pub.
Aleman Valdes, Miguel. Miguel Aleman contesta. LC 75-720022. (Mexico Ser.: No. 4). 66p. (Text in Spanish). 1976. pap. 2.95x (ISBN 0-292-75024-2). U of Tex Pr.
Alemany, Norah, tr. see Maury, Inez.
Alembert, Jean L. D' see D' Alembert, Jean L.
Alencar, Jose M. de. Iracema: The Honey Lips, a Legend of Brazil. Burton, Isabel, tr. 1976. lib. bdg. 59.95 (ISBN 0-8490-2076-X). Gordon Pr.
Alengry, Frank. Condorcet: Guide de la Revolution francaise, theoricien du droit constitutionnel et precurseur de la science sociale. LC 79-159691. xxiii, 891p. (Fr.). 1972. Repr. of 1904 ed. lib. bdg. 43.00 (ISBN 0-8337-3925-5). B Franklin.
Alenicyn, J. E., ed. see Steklov Institute of Mathematics, Academy of Sciences, U S S R, No. 94.
Alenicyn, Ju. E., et al. Fifteen Papers on Series & Functions of Complex Variables. LC 51-5559. (Translations Ser.: No. 2, Vol. 43). 1964. 27.00 (ISBN 0-8218-1743-4, TRANS 2-43). Am Math.
Alenier, Karren L. The Dancer's Muse. (Dialogues on Dance Ser.: No. 2). 25p. (Orig.). 1981. pap. 5.95 (ISBN 0-915380-12-9). Ommation Pr.
--Wandering on the Outside. 2nd ed. LC 74-30470. (Illus.). 1979. perfect bdg. 5.95 (ISBN 0-915380-00-5). Word Works.
Alenier, Karren L., ed. Whose Woods These Are. LC 83-50101. 176p. 1983. pap. 10.00 (ISBN 0-915380-18-8). Word Works.
Aler, Jan, ed. Proceedings of the Fifth International Congress of Aesthetics. 1968. pap. 140.00x (ISBN 90-2791-059-6). Mouton.
Aleramo, Sibilla. A Woman. Delmar, Rosalind, tr. from Italian. (Illus.). 200p. 1980. 12.95 (ISBN 0-520-04108-9); pap. 6.95 (ISBN 0-520-04949-7). U of Cal Pr.
Alerding, Kathy. Bending the Rules. (Candlelight Supreme Ser.: No. 91). (Orig.). 1895. pap. 2.25 (ISBN 0-440-10755-5). Dell.
--Calling the Shots. (Candlelight Ecstasy Ser.: No. 355). 1985. pap. 2.25 (ISBN 0-440-11054-8). Dell.
--With Open Arms. (Candlelight Supreme Ser.: No. 111). (Orig.). 1986. pap. 2.75 (ISBN 0-440-19620-5). Dell.
Alerich, W. N. Electrical Construction Wiring. (Illus.). 1971. 14.95 (ISBN 0-8269-1420-9). Am Technical.
Alerich, Walter. Electric Motor Control. 3rd, rev ed. 1983. 11.95 (ISBN 0-442-20862-6). Van Nos Reinhold.
Alerich, Walter N. Electric Motor Control. 3rd ed. LC 73-13484. (Electric Trades Ser.). (Illus.). 272p. 1983. pap. text ed. 13.80 (ISBN 0-8273-1365-9); instrs' guide 3.00 (ISBN 0-8273-1366-7); lab manual 6.80 (ISBN 0-8273-1369-1). Delmar.
--Electricity Four: AC Motors, Controls, Alternators. LC 79-93325. (Electrical Trades Ser.). 215p. 1981. pap. 9.60 (ISBN 0-8273-1363-2); instructor's guide 3.00 (ISBN 0-8273-1364-0). Delmar.
--Electricity Three: DC Motors & Generators, Controls, Transformers. LC 79-93324. (Electrical Trades Ser.). 224p. 1981. pap. 9.60 (ISBN 0-8273-1361-6); instructor's guide 3.00 (ISBN 0-8273-1362-4). Delmar.
Alerich, Walter N., jt. auth. see Herman, Stephen L.
Alers-Montalvo, Manual. The Puerto Rican Migrants of New York City. LC 83-45349. (Immigrant Communities & Ethnic Minorities in the United States & Canada Ser.). 1985. 30.00 (ISBN 0-404-19400-1). AMS Pr.
Alert, Daniel M., jt. auth. see Scheie, Harold G.
Ales, Anatole, ed. see Charles Louis De Bourbon.
Alesen, Lewis A. Mental Robots. LC 57-13125. 1957. pap. 1.50 (ISBN 0-87004-000-6). Caxton.
--Physician's Responsibility As a Leader. LC 53-10247. 1953. pap. 1.00 (ISBN 0-87004-001-4). Caxton.
Aleshin, V. G., jt. auth. see Nemoshkalenko, V. V.
Aleshire, Daniel O. A Christian Minister in the Making. Date not set. pap. 6.95 (ISBN 0-8054-2707-4). Broadman.
Aleshire, Joan. Cloud Train. LC 82-80305. 58p. 1982. 8.95 (ISBN 0-89672-099-3); pap. 4.95 (ISBN 0-89672-098-5). Tex Tech Pr.
Aleshkovsky, Yuz. Kangaroo. Glenny, Tamara, tr. from Russian. Date not set. 16.50 (ISBN 0-374-18068-7). FS&G.
--Nikolai Nikolaevich. 80p. (Rus.). 1980. pap. 4.50 (ISBN 0-88233-565-0). Ardis Pubs.
--Ruka: (Roman O Palache) LC 80-51176. 314p. (Rus.). 1980. pap. 16.50 (ISBN 0-89830-015-0). Russica Pubs.
Alesi, Gladys. How to Prepare for the U. S. Citizenship Test. LC 82-16417. 1982. pap. 7.95 (ISBN 0-8120-2525-3). Barron.
Alesi, Gladys & Pantell, Dora. Family Life in the U. S. A. (gr. 9-12). 1962. pap. text ed. 3.50 (ISBN 0-88345-370-3, 17391). Regents Pub.
Aleskjavicene, A., et al. Twenty-Four Papers on Statistics & Probability. LC 61-9803. (Selected Translations in Mathematical Statistics & Probability Ser.: Vol. 7). 1968. 37.00 (ISBN 0-8218-1457-5, STAPRO-7). Am Math.
--Twenty-Two Papers on Statistics & Probability. (Selected Translations in Mathematical Statistics & Probability: Vol. 11). 1973. 33.00 (ISBN 0-8218-1461-3, STAPRO-11). Am Math.
Al-Esman, Mashef, ed. Quran. (Arabic.). 25.00x (ISBN 0-86685-135-6). Intl Bk Ctr.
Alessandra, A. & Cathcart, J. The Business of Selling. 1984. text ed. 19.95 (ISBN 0-8359-0609-4); pap. text ed. 14.95 (ISBN 0-8359-0567-5). Reston.
Alessandra, Anthony. Selling by Objectives. 1982. text ed. 13.95 (ISBN 0-8359-6989-4); pap. 9.95 reward ed. (ISBN 0-8359-6988-6). Reston.
Alessandra, Anthony, jt. auth. see Hunsacker, Philip.
Alessandra, Anthony J. Non-Manipulative Selling. 1981. text ed. 19.95 (ISBN 0-8359-4936-2); pap. text ed. 14.95 (ISBN 0-8359-4935-4). Reston.
Alessandro, Nini. Ida Della Torre. Gossett, Philip, ed. (Italian Opera Ser., 1810-1840). 85.00 (ISBN 0-8240-6576-X). Garland Pub.
Alesse, Craig. Basic Thirty-Five mm Photo Guide. LC 79-54311. (Illus.). 110p. (Orig.). 1980. pap. 9.95 (ISBN 0-936262-00-1). Amherst Media.
Alessi, Dennis J., jt. auth. see American Nurses Association.
Alessi, Stephen M. & Trollip, Stanley. Computer-Based Instruction: Methods & Development. (Illus.). 480p. 1985. pap. text ed. 21.95 (ISBN 0-13-164161-1). P-H.
Alessi, Vincie. Evangelism in Your Church School. 1978. pap. 2.50 (ISBN 0-8170-0786-5). Judson.
--Programs for Lent & Easter, Vol. 2. 64p. 1983. pap. 5.95 (ISBN 0-8170-1016-5). Judson.
Alessi, Vincie, ed. Programs for Advent & Christmas. 1978. pap. 4.75 (ISBN 0-8170-0808-X). Judson.
--Programs for Advent & Christmas, Vol. 2. 64p. 1981. pap. 4.75 (ISBN 0-8170-0930-2). Judson.
--Programs for Lent & Easter. 1979. pap. 3.95 (ISBN 0-8170-0861-6). Judson.
Alessia, Joseph. The Poetry of Dino Frescobaldi: Romance Language & Literature. LC 83-5482. (American University Studies II: Vol. 2). 158p. (Orig.). 1983. pap. text ed. 15.80 (ISBN 0-8204-0008-4). P Lang Pubs.
Alessio. The Secretes of Alexis of Piemount. Warde, W., tr. from Fr. LC 74-28825. (English Experience Ser.: No. 707). 1975. Repr. of 1558 ed. 21.00 (ISBN 90-221-0707-8). Walter J Johnson.
Alessio, Luis & Munoz, Hector. Marriage & the Family: The Domestic Church. Owen, Aloysius, tr. from Span. LC 82-6853. 121p. 1982. pap. 3.95 (ISBN 0-8189-0433-X). Alba.
Alessio, Piemontese. A Booke Conteining...Experienced Medicines: The Fourth & Finall Booke of His Secretes. Androse, R., tr. LC 77-6846. (English Experience Ser.: No. 841). 1977. Repr. of 1569 ed. lib. bdg. 20.00 (ISBN 90-221-0841-4). Walter J Johnson.
--The Second Part of the Secretes of Maister Alexis of Piemont. Ward, W., tr. LC 77-6843. (English Experience Ser.: No. 839). 1977. Repr. of 1563 ed. lib. bdg. 17.50 (ISBN 90-221-0839-2). Walter J Johnson.
Aletrino, L. Six World Religions. Foran, Mary, tr. (Orig.). (gr. 12 up). 1969. pap. 4.95 (ISBN 0-8192-2000-0). Morehouse.
Aletti, Ann & Brinkley, Jeanne. Altering Ready-to-Wear Fashions. (gr. 10-12). 1976. text ed. 20.48 (ISBN 0-02-662180-0); avail. tchr's guide 1.28 (ISBN 0-02-662160-6). Bennett IL.
Aletto, P. Ross. Stretch Your Gas Dollars. LC 79-54982. (Illus.). 72p. (Orig.). 1979. pap. 2.95 (ISBN 0-935126-00-7). E & C Bks.
Aleveyev, M. Cherry Pool. 327p. 1978. pap. 6.45 (ISBN 0-8285-0938-7, Pub. by Progress Pubs USSR). Imported Pubns.
Alex, Ben, jt. auth. see Alex, Marlee.

Alexander, Floyce, ed. see Randall, Margaret.

Alexander, Frances. Mother Goose on the Rio Grande. (Illus.). 96p. 1983. pap. 4.95 (ISBN 0-8442-7641-3, 7641-3, Passport Bks). Natl Textbk.

Alexander, Frank. How to Make Your Own Trail Wines. (Illus.). 1978. pap. 1.95 (ISBN 0-916956-02-4). Kokono.

--I'm in Love with a Mannequin. LC 76-8767. (Illus.). 1976. pap. 1.95 (ISBN 0-916956-00-8). Kokono.

Alexander, Frank, ed. see Aycox, Frank.

Alexander, Frank, ed. see Capon, Jack.

Alexander, Frank, ed. see Evans, Jack.

Alexander, Frank, ed. see French, Ron & Horvat, Michael.

Alexander, Frank, ed. see Hall, Tom.

Alexander, Frank, ed. see Johnson, Ryerson.

Alexander, Frank, ed. see Kogan, Sheila.

Alexander, Frank, ed. see Stangl, Jean.

Alexander, Frank J. In the Hours of Meditation. pap. 1.75 (ISBN 0-87481-162-7). Vedanta Pr.

Alexander, Franz. Medical Value of Psychoanalysis. The, Chicago Institute for Psychoanalysis Staff, ed. LC 84-22475. (Classics in Psychoanalysis Monograph: No. 2). vi, 278p. 1985. text ed. 27.50 (ISBN 0-317-17978-0, 03285). Intl Univs Pr.

--Psychoanalysis & Psychotherapy. 1956. 5.50x (ISBN 0-393-01013-9, NortonC). Norton.

--Psychosomatische Medizin: Grundlagen und Anwendungsgebiete. 4th, rev. ed. (Illus.). xvi, 244p. (Ger.). 1985. pap. text ed. 19.20x (ISBN 3-11-010192-0). De Gruyter.

Alexander, Franz & Healy, William. Roots of Crime: Psychoanalytic Studies. LC 69-14908. (Criminology, Law Enforcement, & Social Problems Ser.: No. 68). 1969. Repr. of 1935 ed. 15.00x (ISBN 0-87585-068-5). Patterson Smith.

Alexander, Franz & Ross, Helen, eds. Impact of Freudian Psychiatry. 304p. 1961. pap. 3.95 (ISBN 0-226-01355-3, P62, Phoen). U of Chicago Pr.

--Twenty Years of Psychoanalysis. facsimile ed. LC 77-93312. (Essay Index Reprint Ser.). 1953. 25.50 (ISBN 0-8369-1541-0). Ayer Co Pubs.

Alexander, Franz, et al. Psychoanalytic Therapy: Principles & Application. LC 79-24893. xiv, 353p. 1980. 24.95x (ISBN 0-8032-1007-8); pap. 6.95x (ISBN 0-8032-5903-4, BB 732, Bison). U of Nebr Pr.

Alexander, Fred. Moving Frontiers. LC 69-16482. 1969. Repr. of 1947 ed. 13.50x (ISBN 0-8046-0522-X). Assoc Faculty Pr.

Alexander, G. & Williams, O. B., eds. The Pastoral Industries of Australia. LC 72-82759. (Illus.). 568p. 1973. 36.00x (ISBN 0-424-06540-1, Pub. by Sydney U Pr); pap. 31.00x (ISBN 0-424-06550-9, Pub by Sydney U Pr). Intl Spec Bk.

Alexander, G. M. The Prelude to the Truman Doctrine: British Policy in Greece, 1944-47. 1982. 46.00x (ISBN 0-19-822653-5). Oxford U Pr.

Alexander, George. George Alexander's Adventures in Dining. 224p. 15.00 (ISBN 0-930923-00-6). G Alexander.

Alexander, George J. Commercial Torts. 1973. text ed. 22.50x including 1979 suppl. (ISBN 0-87473-068-6). A Smith Co.

--Commercial Torts: 1979 Supplement. 1979. pap. text ed. 6.00x (ISBN 0-87473-179-8). A Smith Co.

Alexander, George L., jt. auth. see Craig, Gordon A.

Alexander, George M. The Handbook of Biblical Personalities. 320p. 1981. pap. 6.95 (ISBN 0-8164-2316-4, Pub. by Seabury). Winston Pr.

Alexander, George W. Letters on the Slave-Trade, Slavery & Emancipation. LC 73-83399. Repr. of 1842 ed. 17.50x (ISBN 0-8371-1730-5, ALS&, Pub. by Negro U Pr). Greenwood.

Alexander, Gerard L. Guide to Atlases - World, Regional, National, Thematic: An International Listing of Atlases Published Since 1950. LC 70-157728. 671p. 1971. 27.50 (ISBN 0-8108-0414-X). Scarecrow.

--Guide to Atlases Supplement, World, Regional, National, Thematic: An International Listing of Atlases Published 1971 Through 1975 with Comprehensive Indexes. LC 70-157728. 373p. 1977. 22.50 (ISBN 0-8108-1011-5). Scarecrow.

Alexander, Gerard L., jt. auth. see Kane, Joseph N.

Alexander, Gerda I. Fortis & Lenis in Germanic: Germanic Languages & Literature. (American University Studies I: Vol. 18). 183p. (Orig.). 1983. pap. text ed. 20.80 (ISBN 0-8204-0028-9). P Lang Pubs.

Alexander, Gilbert H. The Heart & Its Action: Roentgenkymographic Studies. LC 78-96979. (Illus.). 272p. 1971. 32.50 (ISBN 0-87527-001-8). Green.

Alexander, Gordon. General Zoology. 5th ed. (Illus., Orig.). 1964. pap. 5.95 (ISBN 0-06-460032-7, CO 32, COS). B&N NY.

Alexander, Gordon & Alexander, Douglas G. Biology. 9th ed. LC 77-118098. (Illus.). 1970. pap. 6.95 (ISBN 0-06-460004-1, CO 4, COS). B&N NY.

Alexander, Gordon J. & Francis, Jack C. Portfolio Analysis. 3rd ed. (Illus.). 400p. 1986. text ed. 28.95 (ISBN 0-13-686825-8). P-H.

Alexander, Grover, jt. ed. see Naumann, Albert.

Alexander, Guy. Silica & Me: The Career of an Industrial Chemist. LC 73-75723. (Chemistry in Action Ser.). 111p. 1973. pap. 7.95 (ISBN 0-8412-0162-5). Am Chemical.

Alexander, Guy B. Chromatography: An Adventure in Graduate School. LC 77-8637. (Chemistry in Action Ser.). 1977. pap. 5.95. Am Chemical.

Alexander, H. G., ed. The Leibniz Clarke Correspondence: Together with Extracts from Newton's "Principia" & "Opticks". (Philosophical Classics Ser.). 200p. 1976. pap. 15.00x (ISBN 0-06-490150-5, 06311). B&N Imports.

Alexander, H. T. African Tightrope: My Two Years As Nkrumah's Chief of Staff. 1966. 7.50 (ISBN 0-685-56706-0). Univ Place.

Alexander Hamilton Institute. Financial Sourcebook. 1984. Binder 110.00 (ISBN 0-88057-116-0). Exec Ent Inc.

Alexander, Harold L. V. Classifying Palmprints: A Complete System of Coding, Filing & Searching Palmprints. (Illus.). 136p. 1973. photocopy ed. 15.25x. C C Thomas.

Alexander, Harriet S. American & British Poetry: A Guide to the Criticism, 1925-1978. Hendrick, George & Gerstenberger, Donna, eds. LC 83-24114. xii, 486p. 1984. text ed. 46.00x (ISBN 0-8040-0848-5, Swallow). Ohio U Pr.

Alexander, Hartley. Manito Masks; Dramatizations, with Music, of American Indian Spirit Legends. LC 77-94335. (One-Act Plays in Reprint Ser.). (Illus.). 1978. Repr. of 1925 ed. 19.75x (ISBN 0-8486-2031-3). Core Collection.

Alexander, Hartley B. God & Man's Destiny: Inquiries into the Metaphysical Foundations of Faith. LC 75-3017. 1976. Repr. of 1936 ed. 16.50 (ISBN 0-404-59010-1). AMS Pr.

--Latin American Mythology. LC 63-19096. (Mythology of All Races Ser.: Vol. 11). (Illus.). 1964. Repr. of 1932 ed. 30.00 (ISBN 0-8154-0006-3). Cooper Sq.

--Letters to Teachers. 255p. 1919. 8.95 (ISBN 0-87548-263-5). Open Court.

--Nature & Human Nature: Essays Metaphysical & Historical. LC 75-3018. (Philosophy in America Ser.). Repr. of 1923 ed. 41.50 (ISBN 0-404-59011-X). AMS Pr.

--North American Mythology. LC 63-19095. (Mythology of All Races Ser.: Vol. 10). (Illus.). 1964. Repr. of 1932 ed. 30.00 (ISBN 0-8154-0007-1). Cooper Sq.

--The Problem of Metaphysics & the Meaning of Metaphysical Explanation. LC 72-38480. Repr. of 1902 ed. 14.00 (ISBN 0-404-00322-2). AMS Pr.

--The World's Rim: Great Mysteries of the North American Indians. LC 53-7703. (Illus.). xx, 259p. 1967. pap. 4.95 (ISBN 0-8032-5003-7, BB 160, Bison). U of Nebr Pr.

Alexander, Helene. Fans. (Costume Accessory Ser.). (Illus.). 96p. 1984. text ed. 13.95 (ISBN 0-7134-4276-X, Pub. by Batsford England). Drama Bk.

Alexander, Herbert, tr. see Mantegazza, Paolo.

Alexander, Herbert E. Campaign Money: Reform & Reality in the States. LC 76-21180. 1976. pap. text ed. 3.95 (ISBN 0-02-900420-9). Free Pr.

--Financing Politics, Money, Elections & Political Reform. 3rd ed. LC 83-21079. 230p. 1983. pap. 9.95 (ISBN 0-87187-280-3). Congr Quarterly.

--Money in Politics. 1972. 15.00 (ISBN 0-8183-0181-3). Pub Aff Pr.

Alexander, Herbert E. & Caiden, Gerald E. The Politics & Economics of Organized Crime. LC 84-48376. 192p. 1984. 20.00x (ISBN 0-669-09342-4). Lexington Bks.

Alexander, Herbert E. & Haggerty, Brian A. Financing the Nineteen-Eighty Election. LC 82-48863. 544p. 1983. 35.00 (ISBN 0-669-06375-4); pap. 17.00 (ISBN 0-669-09619-9). Lexington Bks.

Alexander, Herbert E., ed. Political Finance. LC 78-24439. (Sage Electoral Studies Yearbook: Vol. 5). (Illus.). pap. 68.00 (ISBN 0-317-08932-3, 2021867). Bks Demand UMI.

Alexander, Herbert E. & Lambert, Richard D., eds. Political Finance: Reform & Reality. LC 75-45503. (Annals Ser.: No. 425). 250p. 1976. 15.00 (ISBN 0-87761-200-5); pap. 7.95 (ISBN 0-87761-201-3). Am Acad Pol Soc Sci.

Alexander, Herman D. Laboratory Manual for Anatomy. 1978. wire coil bdg. 7.95 (ISBN 0-88252-080-6). Paladin Hse.

Alexander, Holmes. Aaron Burr, the Proud Pretender. LC 73-13412. (Illus.). 390p. 1973. Repr. of 1937 ed. lib. bdg. 21.75x (ISBN 0-8371-7128-8, ALAB). Greenwood.

--How to Read the Federalist. 1961. pap. 2.00 (ISBN 0-88279-124-9). Western Islands.

--Never Lose a War: Memoirs & Observations of a National Columnist. LC 83-18964. 158p. 1984. 14.95 (ISBN 0-8159-6223-1). Devin.

--Pen & Politics. LC 77-90747. 212p. 1970. 5.50 (ISBN 0-937058-07-6). West Va U Pr.

--Pen & Politics: The Autobiography of a Working Writer. 1970. 5.00 (ISBN 0-685-30815-4). McClain.

--Washington & Lee. LC 65-28197. 1966. 3.00 (ISBN 0-88279-210-5). Western Islands.

--With Friends Possessed. LC 75-92683. 1970. 5.95 (ISBN 0-87004-196-7). Caxton.

Alexander, Horace. Everyman's Struggle for Peace. 1983. pap. 5.00x (ISBN 0-87574-074-X, 074). Pendle Hill.

--Gandhi Remembered. LC 71-84674. (Orig.). 1969. pap. 5.00x (ISBN 0-87574-165-7). Pendle Hill.

--Gandhi Through Western Eyes. 200p. 1984. lib. bdg. 24.95 (ISBN 0-86571-045-7); pap. 8.95 (ISBN 0-86571-044-9). New Soc Pubs.

--Quakerism in India. 1983. pap. 5.00x (ISBN 0-87574-031-6, 031). Pendle Hill.

Alexander, Ian. The City Centre: Patterns & Problems. (Illus.). 248p. 1975. 27.50x (ISBN 0-85564-075-8, Pub. by U of W Austral Pr). Intl Spec Bk.

Alexander, Ian C. Office Location & Public Policy. LC 78-40206. (Topics in Applied Geography Ser.). pap. 31.30 (ISBN 0-317-20804-7, 2025273). Bks Demand UMI.

--Office Location & Public Policy. LC 78-40206. (Topics in Applied Geography Ser.). pap. 31.30 (ISBN 0-317-30105-5, 2025273). Bks Demand UMI.

Alexander, Ian C. see Diamond, Donald R. & McLoughlin, J. B.

Alexander, Ian W. French Literature & the Philosophy of Consciousness: Phenomenological Essays. LC 84-22918. 202p. 1985. 25.00 (ISBN 0-312-30495-1). St Martin.

Alexander, Irving E., jt. auth. see Shapiro, Kenneth.

Alexander J., jt. auth. see Adrian.

Alexander, J. A. Acts of the Apostles, 2 vols. in 1. (Banner of Truth Geneva Series Commentaries). 1980. 21.95 (ISBN 0-85151-309-3). Banner of Truth.

--Mark. (Geneva Series Commentaries). 1984. 12.95 (ISBN 0-85151-422-7). Banner of Truth.

Alexander, J. Estill & Filler, Ronald C. Attitudes & Reading. (Reading Aids Ser.). (Orig.). 1976. pap. text ed. 4.50 (ISBN 0-87207-222-3). Intl Reading.

Alexander, J. Estill, et al. Teaching Reading. 2nd ed. 1983. text ed. 24.95 (ISBN 0-316-03127-5); Teacher's Manual avail. (ISBN 0-316-03128-3). Little.

Alexander, J. H. The Lay of the Last Minstrel: Vol. 1-2, Three Essays. (Salzburg Studies in English Literature, Romantic Reassessment: No. 77). 1978. pap. text ed. 25.50x (ISBN 0-391-01290-8). Humanities.

--Marmion: Studies in Interpretation & Composition. (Salzburg-Romantic Reassessment Ser.: No. 30). 257p. 1981. pap. text ed. 25.50x (ISBN 0-391-02768-9, 40662, Pub. by Salzburg Austria). Humanities.

--The Reception of Scott's Poetry by His Correspondents, 2 vols. (SSEL Romantic Reassessment Ser.: No. 84). (Orig.). 1979. pap. text ed. 25.50x ea. Vol. I (ISBN 0-391-01291-6). Vol. II (ISBN 0-391-01292-4). Humanities.

--Two Studies in Romantic Reviewing: Edinburgh Reviewers & the English Tradition, Vol. 1. (Salzburg Studies in English Literature: No. 49). (Orig.). 1976. pap. text ed. 25.50x (ISBN 0-391-01293-2). Humanities.

--Two Studies in Romantic Reviewing: The Reviewing of Walter Scott's Poetry, 1805-1817, Vol. 2. (Salzburg Studies in English Literature Romantic Reassessment: No. 49). 1976. pap. text ed. 25.50x (ISBN 0-391-01294-0). Humanities.

Alexander, J. J. A History of Manuscripts Illuminated in the British Isles: Insular Manuscripts Sixth to Ninth Century, Vol. 1. (Illus.). 1978. 74.00x (ISBN 0-19-921008-X). Oxford U Pr.

Alexander, J. J., ed. The Decorated Letter. LC 78-6487. (Magnificent Paperback Ser.). 1978. 22.95 (ISBN 0-8076-0894-7); pap. 12.95 (ISBN 0-8076-0895-5). Braziller.

--Italian Renaissance Illuminations. LC 77-2841. (Magnificent Paperback Ser.). (Illus.). 1977. 19.95 (ISBN 0-8076-0863-7); pap. 11.95 (ISBN 0-8076-0864-5). Braziller.

--The Master of Mary of Burgundy: A Book of Hours for Engelbert of Nassau. LC 78-128576. 1970. slipcase 30.00 (ISBN 0-8076-0578-6). Braziller.

Alexander, J. L. Along the Starry Trail: Poems & Ceremonies. 1979. Repr. of 1954 ed. text ed. 3.00 (ISBN 0-88053-302-1, S-109). Macoy Pub.

Alexander, J. M. Strength of Materials: Fundamentals, Vol. 1. LC 80-42009. (Mechanical Engineering Ser.). 267p. 1981. 89.95x (ISBN 0-470-27119-1). Halsted Pr.

Alexander, J. O'Donel. Arthropods & Human Skin. (Illus.). 430p. 1984. 90.00 (ISBN 0-387-13235-X). Springer-Verlag.

Alexander, J. P., et al. Odd Order Group Actions & Witt Classification of Innerproducts. (Lecture Notes in Mathematics Ser: Vol. 625). 1977. pap. 18.00 (ISBN 0-387-08528-9). Springer-Verlag.

Alexander, J. W. Plan Para Memorizar las Escrituras. Orig. Title: Fire in My Bones. 48p. 1981. Repr. of 1979 ed. 1.75 (ISBN 0-311-03660-0). Casa Bautista.

--Thoughts on Preaching. 1975. 10.95 (ISBN 0-85151-210-0). Banner of Truth.

Alexander, J. Wesley & Good, Robert. Fundamentals of Clinical Immunology. LC 77-75530. (Illus.). 1977. pap. text ed. 16.00 (ISBN 0-7216-1101-X). Saunders.

Alexander, James & Parsons, Bruce V. Functional Family Therapy. LC 81-17058. (Counseling Ser.). 233p. 1982. text ed. 10.00 pub net (ISBN 0-8185-0485-4). Brooks-Cole.

Alexander, James A. A Brief Narrative of the Case & Trial of John Peter Zenger, Printer of the New York Weekly. 2nd ed. (Belknap Ser.). (Illus.). 953p. 1969. 17.50 (ISBN 0-674-08153-6). Harvard U Pr.

Alexander, James B. Early Babylonian Letters & Economic Texts. LC 78-63526. (Babylonian Inscriptions in the Collection of James B. Nies: 7). Repr. of 1943 ed. 30.00 (ISBN 0-404-60137-5). AMS Pr.

Alexander, James E. An Expedition of Discovery into the Interior of Africa, 2 Vols. (Illus.). Set. 50.00 (ISBN 0-384-00690-6). Johnson Repr.

Alexander, James I. Blue Coats-Black Skin: The Black Experience in New York City Police Department Since 1891. 1978. 6.95 (ISBN 0-682-49031-8, University). Exposition Pr FL.

--Blue Coats, Black Skin: The Black Experience in the New York City Police Department Since 1891. LC 77-92716. pap. 35.80 (ISBN 0-317-29165-3, 2055582). Bks Demand UMI.

Alexander, James P. Programmed Journalism Editing. new ed. (Illus.). (gr. 10-12). 1979. pap. text ed. 8.50x (ISBN 0-8138-1040-X). Iowa St U Pr.

--Programmed Journalism Writing. 1979. pap. text ed. 9.95x (ISBN 0-8138-1020-5). Iowa St U Pr.

Alexander, James W. Medieval World. LC 78-67276. 1979. pap. text ed. 3.75x (ISBN 0-88273-320-6). Forum Pr IL.

--Ranulf of Chester: A Relic of the Conquest. LC 83-3459. 208p. 1983. 16.50x (ISBN 0-8203-0673-8). U of Ga Pr.

Alexander, Jane, jt. auth. see Jacobs, Greta.

Alexander, Jason. In Praise of the Common Man. LC 80-54489. 86p. (Orig.). 1980. pap. 9.95 (ISBN 0-931826-02-0). Sitnalta Pr.

--Philosophy for Investors. LC 79-93363. 75p. (Orig.). 1979. pap. 9.95 (ISBN 0-931826-01-2). Sitnalta Pr.

--Why Johnny Can't Run, Swim, Pull, Dig, Slither, Etc. Porter, Deirdre J. G., ed. LC 78-58309. (Illus.). 206p. 1978. pap. text ed. 9.95 (ISBN 0-931826-00-4). Sitnalta Pr.

Alexander, Jean. Affidavits of Genius: Edgar Allan Poe & the French Critics, 1847-1924. LC 79-154033. 1971. 21.50x (ISBN 0-8046-9015-4, Pub by Kennikat). Assoc Faculty Pr.

--Let's Get Down to Cases. 32p. 0.25 (ISBN 0-686-74914-6). ADL.

--Venture of Form in the Novels of Virginia Woolf. LC 73-83260. 1974. 20.50x (ISBN 0-8046-9052-9, Pub by Kennikat). Assoc Faculty Pr.

Alexander, Jean, tr. see Timofeev, Lev.

Alexander, Jeffrey A. Nursing Unit Organization: Its Effects on Staff Professionalism. Kalisch, Philip & Kalisch, Beatrice, eds. LC 82-13485. (Nursing Management Studies: No. 4). 151p. 1982. 34.95 (ISBN 0-8357-1369-5). UMI Res Pr.

--Nursing Unit Organization: Its Effects on Staff Professionalism. LC 82-13485. (Studies in Nursing Management: No. 4). 151p. 1982. 34.95 (ISBN 0-317-12131-6). UMI Res Pr.

Alexander, Jeffrey C. The Modern Reconstruction of Classical Thought: Talcott Parsons. LC 75-17305. (Theoretical Logic in Sociology Ser.: Vol. 4). 1984. text ed. 39.50x (ISBN 0-520-04483-5, CAL 770); pap. 12.95 (ISBN 0-520-05615-9). U of Cal Pr.

--Theoretical Logic in Sociology: Positivism, Presuppositions, & Current Controversies, Vol. 1. LC 75-17305. 248p. 1982. 27.50x (ISBN 0-520-04480-0, CAL 767); pap. 9.95 (ISBN 0-520-05612-4). U of Cal Pr.

--Theoretical Logic in Sociology: The Antinomies of Classical Thought: Marx & Durkheim, Vol. 2. LC 82-40096. 560p. 1982. 37.50x (ISBN 0-520-04481-9, CAL 768); pap. 12.95 (ISBN 0-520-05613-2). U of Cal Pr.

--Theoretical Logic in Sociology, Vol. 3: The Classical Attempt at Theoretical Synthesis: Max Weber. LC 75-17305. 224p. 1983. text ed. 27.50x (ISBN 0-520-04482-7, CAL 769); pap. 12.95 (ISBN 0-520-05614-0). U of Cal Pr.

Alexander, Jerome & Elins, Roberta. Be Your Own Makeup Artist: Jerome Alexander's Complete Makeup Workshop. LC 82-48107. (Illus.). 128p. 1983. 16.30i (ISBN 0-06-015088-2, HarpT). Har-Row.

Alexander, Jessie L. Looking Back. (Illus.). 160p. 1982. 24.95 (ISBN 0-686-45748-X). At Speed Pr.

Alexander, Joan. Voices & Echoes: Tales from Colonial Women. (Illus.). 264p. 1984. 19.95 (ISBN 0-7043-2366-4, Pub. by Quartet Bks). Merrimack Pub Cir.

Alexander, Joe. Dare to Change: How to Program Yourself for Success. LC 83-25013. 240p. 1985. pap. 3.95 (ISBN 0-451-13523-7, Sig). NAL.

Alexander, Joel D., ed. The New Covenant Journal. (Historical Bks.: Vol. I). 48p. 1985. 1.95 (ISBN 0-933615-05-1). Inter-Travel Comms.

Alexander, John. The Collapse Therapy of Pulmonary Tuberculosis. (Illus.). 705p. 1937. photocopy ed. 56.75x (ISBN 0-398-04186-5). C C Thomas.

Alexander, John, jt. auth. see Graham, Gerald S.

Alexander, John D., Jr. Make a Chair from a Tree: An Introduction to Working Green Wood. LC 78-58222. (Illus.). 128p. 1978. pap. 8.95 (ISBN 0-918804-01-9, Dist. by W W Norton). Taunton.

Alexander, John F., ed. Fitness & Exercise. LC 72-96923. 1972. pap. 5.00 (ISBN 0-87670-855-6). Athletic Inst.

Alexander, John H. Mosby's Men. 180p. 1983. Repr. of 1907 ed. 22.50x (ISBN 0-913419-22-2). Butternut Pr.

Alexander, John J. & Steffel, Margaret J. Chemistry in the Laboratory. 374p. 1976. pap. text ed. 15.95 (ISBN 0-15-506466-5, HC); instructor's manual (ISBN 0-15-506469-X). HarBraceJ.

Alexander, John K. Render Them Submissive: Responses to Poverty in Philadelphia, 1760-1800. LC 79-22638. 248p. 1980. lib. bdg. 17.50x (ISBN 0-87023-289-4). U of Mass Pr.

Alexander, John L., et al. Handbook for Boys. (Illus.). (gr. 7-12). pap. 6.80x (ISBN 0-8395-3100-1, 3100). BSA.

Alexander, John R., jt. auth. see Henn, Harry G.

Alexander, John T. The Bubonic Plague in Early Modern Russia: Public Health & Urban Disaster. LC 79-3652. (Johns Hopkins University Studies in Political & Social Science: 98th Ser.). 1980. text ed. 35.00x (ISBN 0-8018-2322-6). Johns Hopkins.

--Emperor of the Cossacks: Pugachev & the Frontier Jacquerie of 1773-1775. (Illus.). 248p. 1973. pap. 6.00 (ISBN 0-87291-045-8). Coronado Pr.

Alexander, John T., ed. see Sugarbeet Congress, 1969, Salt Lake City.

Alexander, John T., tr. see Platonov, S. F.

Alexander, John W. Hope for a Troubled World. 32p. 1978. pap. 0.75 (ISBN 0-87784-165-9). Inter-Varsity.

--Scripture Memory One Hundred One. 1975. pap. 0.75 (ISBN 0-87784-153-5). Inter-Varsity.

--What Is Christianity. pap. 0.75 (ISBN 0-87784-133-0). Inter-Varsity.

Alexander, John W. & Gibson, L. Economic Geography. 2nd ed. 1979. 38.95 (ISBN 0-13-225151-5). P-H.

Alexander, Jon. American Personal Religious Accounts, 1600-1980: Toward an Inner History of America's Faiths. LC 83-21950. (Studies in American Religion: Vol. 8). 518p. 1984. 69.95x (ISBN 0-88946-654-8). E Mellen.

Alexander, Jon & Dimock, Giles, eds. Religion in Western Civilization Since the Reformation: Select Readings. 184p. 1983. pap. text ed. 6.50 (ISBN 0-8191-3391-4). U Pr of Amer.

Alexander, Joseph. Commentary on the Acts of the Apostles. 1979. 27.50 (ISBN 0-86524-025-6, 4401). Klock & Klock.

--Commentary on the Gospel of Mark. 1980. 16.75 (ISBN 0-86524-018-3, 4101). Klock & Klock.

Alexander, Joseph A. Isaiah, 2 Vols. 1981. Set. lib. bdg. 29.95 (ISBN 0-86524-072-8, 2302). Klock & Klock.

--Mark. (Thornapple Commentaries Ser.). 1980. pap. 8.95 (ISBN 0-8010-0150-1). Baker Bk.

--Matthew. (Thornapple Commentaries Ser.). 1980. pap. 8.95 (ISBN 0-8010-0146-3). Baker Bk.

Alexander, Joy, tr. see Nikkyo, Niwano.

Alexander, Joyce & Alexander, Dorsey. Messiah: Choruses from Handel's Messiah. 24p. (Calligraphy & Illus.). 1985. pap. 5.00 (ISBN 0-937686-10-7). Turtles Quill.

--Thaddeus. (Calligraphy & Illus.). 1972. pap. 3.00 (ISBN 0-686-05667-1). Turtles Quill.

Alexander, Joyce, jt. auth. see Alexander, Dorsey.

Alexander, Joyce & Alexander, Dorsey, illus. David: Psalm Twenty-Four. (Calligraphy & Illus.). 1970. pap. 4.00 (ISBN 0-912020-17-2). Turtles Quill.

--The Sea: Excerpts from Herman Melville. (Calligraphy & Illus.). 1970. pap. 4.00 (ISBN 0-912020-15-6). Turtles Quill.

--Shakespeare: Selected Sonnets. (Calligraphy & Illus.). 1974. pap. 4.00 (ISBN 0-686-05668-X). Turtles Quill.

Alexander, Joyce M., jt. auth. see Saaty, Thomas L.

Alexander, Judy. James Bond Story Book. (Illus.). 64p. (gr. 3 up). 1985. 6.95 (ISBN 0-448-18972-0, G&D). Putnam Pub Group.

Alexander, Karl. The Curse of the Vampire. 320p. (Orig.). 1982. pap. 2.95 (ISBN 0-523-43001-9). Pinnacle Bks.

--A Private Investigation. 1981. pap. 2.75 (ISBN 0-440-17141-5). Dell.

--A Private Investigation. 334p. 1982. 20.00x (ISBN 0-7278-0708-0, Pub. by Severn Hse). State Mutual Bk.

Alexander, Kate. Friends & Enemies. 304p. 1983. 12.95 (ISBN 0-312-30545-1). St Martin.

--Paths of Peace. LC 84-13246. 320p. 1984. 14.95 (ISBN 0-312-59801-7). St Martin.

Alexander, Kay, jt. auth. see Herberholz, Don.

Alexander, Ken. How to Start Your Own Mail Order Business. rev. ed. (Illus.). 1960. 7.95 (ISBN 0-87396-000-9). Stravon.

Alexander, Kenneth J., et al. Economist in Business. LC 67-30476. 1969. 22.50x (ISBN 0-678-06253-6). Kelley.

Alexander, Kern. School Law. LC 79-24471. 939p. 1980. text ed. 23.95 (ISBN 0-8299-2078-1). West Pub.

Alexander, Kern & Alexander, David. American Public School Law. 2nd ed. 900p. 1985. 27.95 (ISBN 0-314-85213-1). West Pub.

Alexander, Kern & Alexander, M. D. The Law of Schools, Students & Teachers in a Nutshell. LC 84-2409. (Nutshell Ser.). 409p. 1984. pap. text ed. 11.95 (ISBN 0-314-80555-9). West Pub.

Alexander, Kern & Solomon, Erwin. College & University Law. 802p. 1972. incl. 1976 suppl. 26.00 (ISBN 0-87215-146-8); 1976 suppl 7.00 (ISBN 0-87215-298-7). Michie Co.

Alexander, Kern & Jordan, K. Forbis, eds. Educational Need in the Public Economy. LC 75-33898. 1976. 12.00 (ISBN 0-8130-0530-2). U Presses Fla.

Alexander Kohut Memorial Foundation. Jewish Studies in Memory of Israel Abrahams. Katz, Steven, ed. LC 79-7164. (Jewish Philosophy, Mysticism & History of Ideas Ser.). (Illus.). 1980. Repr. of 1927 ed. lib. bdg. 45.00x (ISBN 0-405-12274-8). Ayer Co Pubs.

Alexander, L. G. For & Against. (English As a Second Language Bk.). 1975. pap. text ed. 4.25x (ISBN 0-582-52306-0). Longman.

Alexander, L. G. & Cornelius, E. T., Jr. COMP: Exercises in Comprehension & Composition. (English As a Second Language Bk.). (Illus.). 1978. pap. text ed. 3.80x (ISBN 0-582-79703-9). Longman.

Alexander, L. G see Allen, W. S.

Alexander, L. G. see Allen, W. S.

Alexander, L. G see Allen, W. S.

Alexander, L. G., ed. Longman Integrated Comprehension & Composition Series, 6 stages, Wave 1. Incl. Stage 1. Round the World. (Nonfiction). pap. 2.10x (ISBN 0-582-52295-1); Stage 3. Strange but True. (Nonfiction). pap. 2.10x (ISBN 0-582-52299-4); Stage 4. Spare Time. (Nonfiction). pap. 2.30x (ISBN 0-582-52289-7); Stage 4. The Search. (Fiction). pap. 2.30x (ISBN 0-582-52288-9); Stage 5. Flight. (Nonfiction). pap. 2.50x (ISBN 0-582-52291-9); Stage 6. People at Work. (Nonfiction). pap. 2.50x (ISBN 0-582-52293-5). (English As a Second Language Bk.). 1971-81. pap. Longman.

--Longman Integrated Comprehension & Composition Series, 6 stages, Wave 2. Incl. Stage 1. All in a Year. (Nonfiction). pap. 1.75 (ISBN 0-582-55330-X); Stage 1. It's in the Bag. (Fiction). pap. 1.90x (ISBN 0-582-55326-1); Stage 2. Mysteries. (Nonfiction). pap. 1.90x (ISBN 0-582-55331-8); Stage 2. Egyptian Cat. (Fiction). pap. 2.10x (ISBN 0-582-55327-X); Stage 3. Energy. (Nonfiction). pap. 2.30x (ISBN 0-582-55332-6); Stage 3. A Week by the Sea. (Fiction). pap. 2.30x (ISBN 0-582-55328-8); Stage 4. Food Matters. (Nonfiction). pap. 2.30x (ISBN 0-582-55333-4); Stage 4. Nobody Sings Like Ted. (Fiction). pap. 2.30x (ISBN 0-582-55329-6); Stage 5. Cities. (Nonfiction). pap. 2.50x (ISBN 0-582-55336-9); Stage 5. Untitled. (Fiction). pap. write for info. (ISBN 0-582-55334-2); Stage 6. Animal Behavior. (Nonfiction). pap. 2.50x (ISBN 0-582-55337-7); Stage 6. Untitled. (Fiction). pap. write for info. (ISBN 0-582-55335-0). (English As a Second Language Bk.). 1971-81. pap. tchr's. manual & key avail. Longman.

Alexander, L. G., et al. Take a Stand: Discussion Topics for Intermediate Adult Students. (English As a Second Language Bk.). (Illus.). 1978. pap. text ed. 3.95x (ISBN 0-582-79721-7); cassettes 10.50x (ISBN 0-582-79722-5). Longman.

Alexander, Lamar, jt. auth. see Parker, Barry.

Alexander, Laurence, ed. Downtown Planning & Development Annual, 1977. LC 77-641768. (Planning & Development Ser.). 1977. pap. 11.00 (ISBN 0-915910-08-X). Downtown Res.

Alexander, Laurence A., ed. Downtown District Action Guide. LC 79-116845. 1979. pap. 10.00 (ISBN 0-915910-15-2). Downtown Res.

--Downtown Mall Annual & Urban Design Report, Vol. 3. LC 75-646900. (Design Ser). (Illus.). 1977. pap. 11.00 (ISBN 0-915910-09-8). Downtown Res.

--Downtown Mall Annual & Urban Design Report, Vol. 4. LC 75-646900. (Design Ser.). (Illus.). 1978. pap. 11.00 (ISBN 0-915910-11-X). Downtown Res.

--Downtown Malls: An Annual Review, Vol. 2. LC 75-646900. (Design Ser.). (Illus.). 1976. pap. 11.00 (ISBN 0-915910-07-1). Downtown Res.

--Downtown Planning & Development Annual, 1978. LC 77-641768. (Planning & Development Ser.). 1978. pap. 11.00 (ISBN 0-915910-10-1). Downtown Res.

--Great Downtown Events! How to Build Crowds & Boost Business. LC 85-70520. (Illus., Orig.). 1985. pap. 39.50 (ISBN 0-915910-21-7). Downtown Res.

--How to Achieve Downtown Action in the 80's: Realistic Private & Public Implementation Techniques. LC 82-71571. 120p. 1982. pap. 45.00 (ISBN 0-915910-19-5). Downtown Res.

--Promoting Effectively for Downtown Business: Dynamic New Case Studies. LC 83-71250. (Illus.). 64p. (Orig.). 1983. pap. 27.50 (ISBN 0-915910-20-9). Downtown Res.

--Public Attitudes Toward Downtown Malls: A National Opinion Research Survey. LC 75-21099. (Illus.). 84p. 1975. pap. 17.50 (ISBN 0-915910-05-5). Downtown Res.

--Strategies for Stopping Shopping Centers: A Guidebook on Minimizing Excessive Shopping Center Growth. LC 80-65968. (Orig.). 1980. pap. 24.50 (ISBN 0-915910-17-9). Downtown Res.

--Winning Downtown Projects: A Photographic Case Study Report of Outstanding Downtown Developments. LC 81-66891. (Illus., Orig.). 1981. pap. 25.00 (ISBN 0-915910-18-7). Downtown Res.

Alexander, Laurence A., et al. Where Is Downtown Going? Twelve Expert Opinions. Spanbock, Marion H., ed. LC 79-119531. (Illus.). 1979. pap. 5.00 (ISBN 0-915910-14-4). Downtown Res.

Alexander, Leroy E., jt. auth. see Klug, Harold P.

Alexander, Lewis M. Marine Regionalism in the Southeast Asian Seas. LC 82-18216. (East-West Environment & Policy Institute Research Report: No. 11). v, 85p. (Orig.). 1982. pap. text ed. 3.00 (ISBN 0-86638-033-7). E W Center HI.

--Offshore Geography of Northwestern Europe. LC 63-9453. (Monograph: No. 3). 3.95 (ISBN 0-89291-082-8). Assn Am Geographers.

Alexander, Linda. Job Well Done. (Illus.). (gr. 1-4). PLB 6.19 (ISBN 0-8313-0002-7). Lantern.

Alexander, Lloyd. Beggar Queen. 224p. (gr. 6up). 1984. 11.95 (ISBN 0-525-44103-4, 01160-350). Dutton.

--The Beggar Queen. (gr. k-12). 1985. pap. 2.95 (ISBN 0-440-90548-6, LFL). Dell.

--Black Cauldron. 192p. (gr. 5-9). 1969. pap. 2.95 (ISBN 0-440-40649-8, YB). Dell.

--Black Cauldron. LC 65-13868. (Illus.). (gr. 5-9). 1965. reinforced bdg. 10.95 (ISBN 0-03-089687-8). HR&W.

--The Book of Three. 192p. (gr. 5-9). 1980. pap. 2.50 (ISBN 0-440-90702-0, LFL). Dell.

--Book of Three. LC 64-18250. (gr. 5-9). 1964. reinforced bdg. 10.95 (ISBN 0-03-089821-8, HR&W). HR&W.

--The Book of Three. (Prydain Chronicles Ser.). 192p. (gr. 5-9). pap. 2.75 (ISBN 0-440-40702-8, YB). Dell.

--The Castle of Llyr. 192p. (gr. 5-9). 1980. pap. 2.50 (ISBN 0-440-91125-7, LFL). Dell.

--Castle of Llyr. 192p. (gr. 5-9). 1969. pap. 2.75 (ISBN 0-440-41125-4, YB). Dell.

--Castle of Llyr. LC 66-13461. (gr. 5-9). 1966. reinforced bdg. 9.95 (ISBN 0-03-019066-5). HR&W.

--The Cat Who Wished to Be a Man. 120p. (gr. 4-7). 1973. 8.95 (ISBN 0-525-27545-2). Dutton.

--The First Two Lives of Lukas-Kasha. 224p. (gr. 7 up). 1982. pap. 2.25 (ISBN 0-440-42784-3, YB). Dell.

--The High King. 288p. (gr. 5-9). 1980. pap. 2.75 (ISBN 0-440-93574-1, LFL). Dell.

--The High King. LC 68-11833. (gr. 5-9). 1968. reinforced bdg. 10.95 (ISBN 0-03-089504-9). HR&W.

--The High King. 288p. (gr. 4-9). pap. 3.25 (ISBN 0-440-43574-9, YB). Dell.

--The Kestrel. 256p. (gr. 5 up). 1982. 10.95 (ISBN 0-525-45110-2, 01063-320). Dutton.

--The Kestrel. 256p. (YA) (gr. 7 up). 1983. pap. 2.75 (ISBN 0-440-94393-0, LFL). Dell.

--Marvelous Misadventures of Sebastian. LC 70-166879. (gr. 4 up). 1970. 14.95 (ISBN 0-525-34739-9, 01451-440). Dutton.

--Taran Wanderer. 272p. (YA) (gr. 5-9). 1980. pap. 2.50 (ISBN 0-440-98483-1, LFL). Dell.

--Taran Wanderer. 272p. (gr. 5-9). 1969. pap. 2.95 (ISBN 0-440-48483-9, YB). Dell.

--Taran Wanderer. LC 67-10230. (gr. 5-9). 1967. reinforced bdg. 9.95 (ISBN 0-03-089732-7). HR&W.

--Time Cat. (Illus.). 192p. (gr. 4-7). 1982. pap. 1.95 (ISBN 0-380-00195-0, 57422-5, Camelot). Avon.

--Time Cat. (gr. k-12). 1985. pap. 3.25 (ISBN 0-440-48677-7, YB). Dell.

--The Town Cats & Other Tales. 144p. (gr. 5 up). 1981. pap. 1.50 (ISBN 0-440-48989-X, YB). Dell.

--The Town Cats & Other Tales. (Illus.). (gr. 4-7). 1977. 11.95 (ISBN 0-525-41430-4, 01160-350). Dutton.

--Westmark. 192p. (gr. 5-9). 1982. pap. 2.50 (ISBN 0-440-99731-3, LFL). Dell.

--Westmark. LC 80-22242. (gr. 5 up). 1981. 11.95 (ISBN 0-525-42335-4, 01160-350). Dutton.

--The Wizard in the Tree. 144p. (gr. 5 up). 1981. pap. 1.75 (ISBN 0-440-49556-3, YB). Dell.

--The Wizard in the Tree. (Illus.). 144p. (gr. 4-7). 1974. 9.95 (ISBN 0-525-43128-4). Dutton.

Alexander, Lloyd, tr. see Eluard, Paul.

Alexander, Lloyd, tr. see Sartre, Jean-Paul.

Alexander, Louis. Beyond the Facts: A Guide to the Art of Feature Writing. 2nd ed. LC 82-1021. 300p. 1982. 18.95x (ISBN 0-87201-281-6). Gulf Pub.

Alexander, Louis, jt. auth. see Shafritz, Jay M.

Alexander, Louis C., ed. Autobiography of Shakespeare. LC 70-113361. 1970. Repr. of 1911 ed. 14.00x (ISBN 0-8046-1006-1, Pub. by Kennikat). Assoc Faculty Pr.

Alexander, Luther H. Participial Substantives of the "ata" Type in the Romance Languages. LC 76-38481. (Columbia University Studies in Romance Philology & Literature: No. 12). Repr. of 1912 ed. 16.50 (ISBN 0-404-50612-7). AMS Pr.

Alexander, Lynne. Safe Houses. LC 85-47594. 272p. 1985. 15.95 (ISBN 0-689-11606-3). Atheneum.

Alexander, M., ed. Advances in Microbial Ecology, Vol. 1. (Illus.). 280p. 1977. 39.50x (ISBN 0-306-38161-3, Plenum Pr). Plenum Pub.

--Advances in Microbial Ecology, Vol. 2. (Illus.). 311p. 1978. 39.50x (ISBN 0-306-38162-1, Plenum Pr). Plenum Pub.

--Advances in Microbial Ecology, Vol. 3. (Illus.). 237p. 1979. 47.50x (ISBN 0-306-40240-8, Plenum Pr). Plenum Pub.

--Advances in Microbial Ecology, Vol. 4. 262p. 1980. 39.50x (ISBN 0-306-40493-1, Plenum Pr). Plenum Pub.

--Advances in Microbial Ecology, Vol. 5. 262p. 1981. 39.50x (ISBN 0-306-40767-1, Plenum Pr). Plenum Pub.

Alexander, M. D., jt. auth. see Alexander, Kern.

Alexander, M. E., jt. auth. see Fielding, P. M.

Alexander, Margaret F. Learning to Nurse: Integrating Theory & Practice. LC 82-9568. (Studies in Nursing). (Illus.). 259p. 1983. pap. text ed. 14.00 (ISBN 0-443-02623-8). Churchill.

Alexander, Marguerite. A Reader's Guide to Shakespeare & His Contemporaries. LC 79-53435. (Reader's Guide Ser.). 386p. 1979. text ed. 24.50x (ISBN 0-06-490149-1, 06310). B&N Imports.

Alexander, Marsha. Demon Fire. 224p. (Orig.). 1982. pap. 2.50 (ISBN 0-523-41636-9). Pinnacle Bks.

Alexander, Martha. And My Mean Old Mother Will Be Sorry, Blackboard Bear. (Illus.). 32p. (ps-2). 1972. PLB 8.89 (ISBN 0-8037-0593-X). Dial Bks Young.

--And My Mean Old Mother Will Be Sorry, Blackboard Bear. LC 72-707. (Pied Piper Book). (Illus.). (gr. k-2). 1977. pap. 2.25 (ISBN 0-8037-0126-8). Dial Bks Young.

--Blackboard Bear. (Illus.). (gr. k-3). 1969. 7.95 (ISBN 0-8037-0651-0). Dial Bks Young.

--Blackboard Bear. (Pied Piper Book). (Illus.). (ps-2). 1977. pap. 2.50 (ISBN 0-8037-0629-4). Dial Bks Young.

--Bobo's Dream. LC 73-102825. (Pied Piper Book Ser.). (Illus.). (ps-2). 1978. pap. 1.75 (ISBN 0-8037-0971-4). Dial Bks Young.

--Bobo's Dream. LC 73-102825. (Illus.). (ps-2). 1970. 7.95 (ISBN 0-8037-0686-3). Dial Bks Young.

--Four Bears in a Box. 1981. boxed set 7.95 (ISBN 0-8037-2756-9). Dial Bks Young.

--How My Library Grew, By Dinah. (Illus.). 32p. 1983. 12.00 (ISBN 0-8242-0679-7). Wilson.

--I Sure Am Glad to See You, Blackboard Bear. LC 76-2280. (Illus.). (gr. k-2). 1976. 7.95 (ISBN 0-8037-4002-6); PLB 7.89 (ISBN 0-8037-4003-4). Dial Bks Young.

--I Sure Am Glad to See You, Blackboard Bear. LC 76-2280. (Pied Piper Book). (Illus.). 1979. pap. 1.75 (ISBN 0-8037-4008-5). Dial Bks Young.

--I'll Be the Horse If You'll Play with Me. LC 75-9207. (Illus.). 32p. (ps-2). 1975. 5.95 (ISBN 0-8037-5458-2, 0869-260); PLB 5.47 (ISBN 0-8037-5511-2). Dial Bks Young.

--I'll Be the Horse If You'll Play with Me. LC 75-9207. (Pied Piper Book). (Illus.). 32p. (ps-2). 1980. pap. 1.95 (ISBN 0-8037-5459-0). Dial Bks Young.

--I'll Protect You from the Jungle Beasts. LC 73-6015. (Illus.). 32p. (ps-2). 1973. 8.95 (ISBN 0-8037-4308-4, 0869-260); PLB 8.89 (ISBN 0-8037-4309-2). Dial Bks Young.

--I'll Protect You from the Jungle Beasts. LC 73-6015. (Pied Piper Book). (Illus.). 32p. (ps-2). 1980. pap. 1.95 (ISBN 0-8037-3900-1). Dial Bks Young.

--Maggie's Moon. LC 82-1575. (Illus.). 32p. (ps-2). 1982. 7.95 (ISBN 0-8037-5708-5); PLB 7.89 (ISBN 0-8037-5721-2). Dial Bks Young.

--Marty McGee's Space Lab, No Girls Allowed. LC 81-2497. 32p. (ps-3). 1981. 7.95 (ISBN 0-8037-5156-7, 0772-230); PLB 7.89 (ISBN 0-8037-5157-5). Dial Bks Young.

--Marty McGee's Space Lab, No Girls Allowed. (Illus.). 32p. (ps-2). 1983. 7.50 (ISBN 0-8037-5156-7); pap. 3.25 (ISBN 0-8037-0018-0, 0316-090). Dial Bks Young.

--Maybe a Monster. LC 68-28732. (Illus.). 32p. (ps-2). 1968. 8.95 (ISBN 0-8037-5508-2, 0869-260); PLB 8.89 (ISBN 0-8037-5513-9). Dial Bks Young.

--Maybe a Monster. LC 68-28732. (Pied Piper Book). (Illus.). 32p. (ps-3). 1979. pap. 1.75 (ISBN 0-8037-5389-6). Dial Bks Young.

--Move Over, Twerp. LC 80-21405. (Illus.). 32p. (ps-2). 1981. PLB 7.89 (ISBN 0-8037-6140-6). Dial Bks Young.

--No Ducks in Our Bathtub. LC 72-7598. (Pied Piper Bk.). (Illus.). (ps-2). 1977. pap. 2.95 (ISBN 0-8037-6380-8, 0286-090). Dial Bks Young.

--No Ducks in Our Bathtub. LC 72-7598. (Illus.). 32p. (ps-2). 1973. 8.95 (ISBN 0-8037-6239-9, 0869-260); PLB 8.89 (ISBN 0-8037-6217-8). Dial Bks Young.

--Nobody Asked Me If I Wanted a Baby Sister. LC 78-153731. (Illus.). (ps-2). 1971. 9.95 (ISBN 0-8037-6401-4, 0966-294); PLB 9.89 (ISBN 0-8037-6402-2, 0316-090); pap. 3.25 (ISBN 0-8037-6410-3). Dial Bks Young.

--Nobody Asked Me If I Wanted a Baby Sister. (Illus.). (gr. k-2). 1977. pap. 3.25 (ISBN 0-8037-6410-3, 0316-090, Pied Piper). Dial Bks Young.

--Out, Out, Out. LC 68-15251. (Illus.). (gr. k-3). 1968. 6.95 (ISBN 0-8037-6663-7). Dial Bks Young.

--Poems & Prayers for the Very Young. (Illus.). (ps-1). 1973. pap. 1.95 (ISBN 0-394-82705-8, BYR). Random.

--Three Magic Flip Books. Incl. The Magic Hat; The Magic Picture; The Magic Box. (Illus.). 1984. 3 bks. in a shrink-wrapped slipcase 5.95 (ISBN 0-8037-0051-2, 0578-170). Dial Bks Young.

--We Never Get to Do Anything. LC 78-121575. (Pied Piper Bk.). (Illus.). (ps-2). 1978. pap. 1.75 (ISBN 0-8037-9781-8). Dial Bks Young.

--We Never Get to Do Anything. (Illus.). (ps-3). 1970. 7.95 (ISBN 0-8037-9415-0); PLB 7.89 (ISBN 0-8037-9416-9). Dial Bks Young.
--We're in Big Trouble, Blackboard Bear. (Pied Piper Bk.). (Illus.). 32p. 1982. pap. 2.95 (ISBN 0-8037-9583-1). Dial Bks Young.
--We're in Big Trouble, Blackboard Bear. LC 79-20631. (Illus.). (ps-2). 1980. 6.95 (ISBN 0-8037-9741-9). Dial Bks Young.
--When the New Baby Comes, I'm Moving Out. LC 79-4275. (Pied Piper Bk.). (Illus.). 32p. (gr. k-3). 1981. pap. 2.95 (ISBN 0-8037-9563-7, 0286-090). Dial Bks Young.
--When the New Baby Comes, I'm Moving Out. LC 79-4275. (Illus.). (ps-2). 1979. 8.95 (ISBN 0-8037-9557-2); PLB 8.89 (ISBN 0-8037-9558-0, 0869-260). Dial Bks Young.
Alexander, Martin. Introduction to Soil Microbiology. 2nd ed. LC 77-1319. 467p. 1977. text ed. 38.50 (ISBN 0-471-02179-2); arabic translation avail. Wiley.
--Introduction to Soil Microbiology. 2nd ed. 573p. (Arabic.). 1982. pap. 18.00 (ISBN 0-471-06392-4). Wiley.
Alexander, Martin, ed. Biological Nitrogen Fixation: Ecology, Technology & Physiology. 248p. 1984. 42.50x (ISBN 0-306-41632-8, Plenum Pr). Plenum Pub.
Alexander, Mary J. Handbook of Decorative Design & Ornament. (Illus., Orig.). 5.95 (ISBN 0-8148-0395-4); pap. 2.95 (ISBN 0-8148-0396-2). L Amiel Pub.
Alexander, Mary Jean. Decorating Made Simple. LC 64-13823. (Made Simple Ser.). pap. 4.50 (ISBN 0-385-01695-6). Doubleday.
Alexander, Mary M. & Brown, Marie S. Pediatric History Taking & Physical Diagnosis for Nurses. 2nd ed. (Illus.). 1979. text ed. 32.00 (ISBN 0-07-001019-6); pap. text ed. 24.00 (ISBN 0-07-001018-8). McGraw.
Alexander, Matthias F. Constructive Conscious Control. 317p. 13.95 (ISBN 0-318-17655-6). Am Ctr Alexander Tech.
--The Use of the Self. 136p. 9.95 (ISBN 0-318-17654-8). Am Ctr Alexander Tech.
Alexander, Maxine, ed. Indians of the South. (Southern Exposure Ser.). (Illus.). 120p. (Orig.). 1985. pap. 4.00. Inst Southern Studies.
--Speaking for Ourselves: Women of the South. LC 84-7088. 304p. 1984. pap. 10.95 (ISBN 0-394-72275-2). Pantheon.
Alexander, Meena. The Bird's Bright Ring. 1976. 8.00 (ISBN 0-89253-811-2); flexible cloth 4.80 (ISBN 0-89253-812-0). Ind-US Inc.
--The Poetic Self: Towards a Phenomenology of Romanticism. 280p. 1980. text ed. 15.25x (ISBN 0-391-01754-3). Humanities.
Alexander, Megan. Blossoms in the Snow. (Superromances Ser.). 384p. 1984. pap. 2.95 (ISBN 0-373-70095-4, Pub. by Worldwide). Harlequin Bks.
--Contract for Marriage. (Superromances Ser.). 384p. 1982. pap. 2.50 (ISBN 0-373-70017-2, Pub. by Worldwide). Harlequin Bks.
Alexander, Melinda, jt. auth. see Hopkins, John A.
Alexander, Michael. The Poetic Achievement of Ezra Pound. LC 78-59449. 1979. 32.50x (ISBN 0-520-03739-1, CAL 525); pap. 6.95 (ISBN 0-520-04507-6). U of Cal Pr.
Alexander, Michael & Anand, Shushila. Queen Victoria's Maharajah: Duleep Singh, 1838-1893. LC 79-5426. (Illus.). 1980. 14.95 (ISBN 0-8008-6567-7). Taplinger.
Alexander, Michael, ed. Old English Literature. (History of Literature Ser.). (Illus.). 328p. 1983. 28.50 (ISBN 0-8052-3862-X). Schocken.
Alexander, Michael, tr. Beowulf. (Classics Ser). (Orig.). 1973. pap. 2.25 (ISBN 0-14-044268-5). Penguin.
--Earliest English Poems. (Classics Ser.). (Orig.). 1966. pap. 4.95 (ISBN 0-14-044172-7). Penguin.
Alexander, Michael V. Charles I's Lord Treasurer: Sir Richard Weston, Earl of Portland (1577-1635) LC 74-34370. xvii, 261p. 1975. text ed. 22.50 (ISBN 0-8078-1248-X). U of NC Pr.
Alexander, Michael Van Cleave see Van Cleave Alexander, Michael.
Alexander, Miles J. & Practicing Law Institute. Trademark Litigation: Pragmatic Tactics & Techniques of Winning. LC 83-62924. (Patents, Copyrights, Trademarks, & Literary Property Course Handbook Ser.: No. 173). 368p. 1983. 35.00. PLI.
Alexander, Milton J. Information Systems Analysis: Theory & Application. LC 73-89599. (Illus.). 432p. 1974. text ed. 28.95 (ISBN 0-574-19100-3, 13-2100); instr's guide avail. (ISBN 0-574-19101-1, 13-2101). SRA.
Alexander, Mithrapuram K. Yoga System. rev. ed. LC 77-140373. (Illus.). 1971. 8.95 (ISBN 0-8158-0257-9); pap. 6.95 (ISBN 0-686-66311-X). Chris Mass.
Alexander, Morris. Israel & Me. (Illus.). 278p. 1977. 14.50x (ISBN 0-87073-204-8). Schenkman Bks Inc.
Alexander, Myrna. After God's Heart. (Woman's Workshop Ser.). 160p. (Orig.). 1982. pap. 3.95 (ISBN 0-310-37141-4). Zondervan.
--Behold Your God: A Woman's Workshop on the Attributes of God. pap. 2.95 (ISBN 0-310-37131-7). Zondervan.
Alexander, Nancy. Father of Texas Geology: Robert T. Hill. LC 76-2621. (Bicentenial Series in American Studies: No. 4). (Illus.). 1976. 29.95 (ISBN 0-87074-152-7); pap. 15.95 (ISBN 0-87074-002-4). SMU Press.
Alexander, Nancy see Mallis, Jackie.
Alexander, Nancy J., jt. auth. see Parakkal, P. F.
Alexander, Noy. Let's Make Candy. Werner, Janet, ed. LC 65-19806. (Illus.). (YA) (gr. 9 up). 1965. pap. 4.25 (ISBN 0-8048-0361-7). C E Tuttle.
Alexander, P., jt. auth. see Bacq, Z. M.
Alexander, P., et al, eds. A Laboratory Manual of Analytical Methods of Protein Chemistry (Including Polypeptides, Vols. 2-5. Incl. Vol. 2. Composition, Structure & Reactivity of Protein. 1960. lib. bdg. 16.50 (ISBN 0-08-011398-2); Vol. 3. Determination of the Size & Shape of Protein in Molecules. 1961; Vol. 4. Protein Analysis. 1965; Vol. 5. 1968. 18.00 (ISBN 0-08-012677-4). Pergamon.
Alexander, P. C. Buddhism in Kerala. LC 78-72369. Repr. of 1949 ed. 37.50 (ISBN 0-404-17216-4). AMS Pr.
Alexander, P. E., ed. Electrolytes & Neuropsychiatric Disorders. (Illus.). 351p. 1981. text ed. 60.00 (ISBN 0-89335-122-9). SP Med & Sci Bks.
Alexander, Pamela. Navigable Waterways. LC 84-40666. (Series of Younger Poets: No. 80). 96p. 1985. text ed. 12.95x (ISBN 0-300-03331-1); pap. 5.95x (ISBN 0-300-03397-4). Yale U Pr.
Alexander, Pat. Nelson Children's Bible. 6.95 (ISBN 0-8407-5238-5). Nelson.
Alexander, Pat, ed. Eerdmans Book of Christian Poetry. 128p. 1981. 10.95 (ISBN 0-8028-3555-4). Eerdmans.
--Eerdmans' Concise Bible Encyclopedia. LC 80-19885. (Illus.). 256p. (Orig.). 1981. pap. 8.95 (ISBN 0-8028-1876-5). Eerdmans.
Alexander, Pat, jt. ed. see Alexander, David.
Alexander, Patricia & Muia, Joseph. Gifted Education: A Comprehensive Roadmap. LC 81-12707. 323p. 1982. text ed. 31.00 (ISBN 0-89443-383-0). Aspen Systems.
Alexander, Patricia, ed. Eerdmans' Family Encyclopedia of the Bible. (Illus.). 1978. 18.95 (ISBN 0-8028-3517-1). Eerdmans.
--The Life & Words of Jesus. LC 83-47715. (Illus.). 96p. 1983. 10.53 (ISBN 0-06-065255-1, HarpR). Har-Row.
Alexander, Patrick P. Mill & Carlyle. 1866. lib. bdg. 10.00 (ISBN 0-8414-2968-5). Folcroft.
Alexander, Paul. Sri Lankan Fishermen: Rural Capitalism & Peasant Society. (South Asia Monograph Ser.). 1982. pap. 20.00x (ISBN 0-908070-06-3, Pub. by Australian Nat Univ). South Asia Bks.
Alexander, Paul & Bridges, Laurie. Swamp Witch. 160p. pap. 2.25 (ISBN 0-553-25232-1). Bantam.
Alexander, Paul, jt. auth. see Bridges, Laurie.
Alexander, Paul, intro. by. Ariel Ascending: Writings about Sylvia Plath. LC 84-47616. 240p. (Orig.). 1984. pap. 9.57i (ISBN 0-06-091175-1, CN 1175, CN). Har-Row.
Alexander, Paul B. Land Utilization in the Karst Region of Zgornja Pivka, Slovenia. LC 75-9151. 132p. 1967. 6.00 (ISBN 0-686-28379-1). Studia Slovenica.
Alexander, Paul F. The Byzantine Apocalyptic Tradition. Abrahamse, Dorothy, ed. LC 82-23816. 248p. 1985. 28.50x (ISBN 0-520-04998-5). U of Cal pr.
Alexander, Paul J. Ancient World: To A.D. Three Hundred. 2nd ed. (Orig.). 1968. pap. text ed. write for info. (ISBN 0-02-301650-7, 30165). Macmillan.
--The Oracle of Baalbek: The Tiburtine Sibyl in Greek Dress. LC 75-27113. (Dumbarton Oaks Studies: Vol. 10). (Illus.). 151p. 1967. 12.00x (ISBN 0-88402-020-7). Dumbarton Oaks.
--The Patriarch Nicephorus of Constantinople: Ecclesiastical Policy & Image Worship in the Byzantine Empire. LC 78-63177. (Heresies Ser.: No. II). Repr. of 1958 ed. 31.00 (ISBN 0-404-16195-2). AMS Pr.
--Religious & Political History & Thought in the Byzantine Empire. 360p. 1980. 60.00x (ISBN 0-86078-016-3, Pub. by Variorum England). State Mutual Bk.
Alexander, Peter. Ideas, Qualities & Corpuscles: Locke & Boyle on the External World. 330p. 1985. 44.50 (ISBN 0-521-26707-2). Cambridge U Pr.
--Roy Campbell: A Biography. (Illus.). 29.95x (ISBN 0-19-211750-5). Oxford U Pr.
--Shakespeare's Henry Sixth & Richard Third. LC 73-732. 229p. 1973. Repr. lib. bdg. 19.00 (ISBN 0-374-90130-9). Octagon.
--Shakespeare's Henry VI & Richard III. 1978. Repr. of 1929 ed. lib. bdg. 25.00 (ISBN 0-8495-0052-4). Arden Lib.
--Shakespeare's Henry VI & Richard III. LC 73-7500. 1973. lib. bdg. 12.50 (ISBN 0-8414-1746-6). Folcroft.
--Shakespeare's Life & Art. LC 78-25749. 1979. Repr. of 1961 ed. lib. bdg. 27.50x (ISBN 0-313-20666-X, ALSA). Greenwood.
Alexander, Peter & Gill, Roger, eds. Utopias. LC 84-1897. 240p. 1985. 39.95 (ISBN 0-87548-364-X). Open Court.
Alexander, Peter, jt. ed. see Campbell, Roy.
Alexander, Philip S., ed. Judaism. LC 84-6199. (Textual Sources for the Study of Religion Ser.). 208p. 1984. 23.50x (ISBN 0-389-20477-3, BNB 08039). B&N Imports.
Alexander, Polly, jt. auth. see Choukas-Bradley, Melanie.
Alexander, R. C., ed. see Garrick, David.
Alexander, R. McNeill. Animal Mechanics. (Illus.). 312p. 1983. text ed. 30.00x (ISBN 0-632-00956-X). Blackwell Pubns.
--The Chordates. 2nd. ed. (Illus.). 500p. 1981. text ed. 75.00 (ISBN 0-521-23658-4); pap. text ed. 24.95 (ISBN 0-521-28141-5). Cambridge U Pr.
--The Invertebrates. LC 78-6275. (Illus.). 1979. 82.00 (ISBN 0-521-22120-X); pap. 24.95 (ISBN 0-521-29361-8). Cambridge U Pr.
--Locomotion of Animals. (Tertiary Level Biology Ser.). 192p. 1982. 35.00x (ISBN 0-412-00001-6, NO.5001, Pub. by Chapman & Hall); pap. 18.95x (ISBN 0-412-00011-3, NO. 5002). Methuen Inc.
--Optima for Animals. 120p. 1982. pap. text ed. 13.95 (ISBN 0-7131-2843-7). E Arnold.
Alexander, Ralph. Ezekiel. (Everyman's Bible Commentary Ser). 160p. (Orig.). 1976. pap. 4.95 (ISBN 0-8024-2026-5). Moody.
--Ezequiel (Comentario Biblico Portavoz) Orig. Title: Ezekiel (Everyman's Bible Commentary) 128p. (Span.). 1979. pap. 4.50 (ISBN 0-8254-1002-9). Kregel.
Alexander, Ralph W. & Sparlin, Don M. Physics Laboratory Manual. 176p. 1981. 12.95 (ISBN 0-8403-2289-5). Kendall-Hunt.
Alexander, Rena R. Charlie Tracks. 93p. 1984. 4.40 (ISBN 0-89697-226-7). Intl Univ Pr.
Alexander, Renee R. Basic Biochemical Methods. LC 84-13215. 1984. pap. 24.95 (ISBN 0-471-88027-2, Pub. by Wiley-Interscience). Wiley.
Alexander, Richard D. Darwinism & Human Affairs. LC 78-65829. (Jessie & John Danz Lecture Ser.). (Illus.). 342p. 1980. 25.00x (ISBN 0-295-95641-0); pap. 10.95x (ISBN 0-295-95901-0). U of Wash Pr.
Alexander, Richard D., jt. auth. see Otte, Daniel.
Alexander, Richard D., ed. Natural Selection & Social Behavior. Tinkle, Donald W. LC 80-65758. (Illus.). 544p. 1981. 49.95x (ISBN 0-913462-08-X). Chiron Pr.
Alexander, Robert, et al. The Communist Tide in Latin America: A Selected Treatment. Herman, Donald L., ed. LC 72-11900. (Quarterly Ser.). (Illus.). 1973. 10.00 (ISBN 0-87959-072-6). U of Tex H Ransom Ctr.
Alexander, Robert J. Bolivia: Past, Present, & Future of Its Politics. Wesson, Robert, ed. LC 81-22661. (Politics in Latin America Ser.). 184p. 1982. 28.95 (ISBN 0-03-061762-6). Praeger.
--Bolivian National Revolution. LC 73-20876. (Illus.). 302p. 1974. Repr. of 1958 ed. lib. bdg. 20.00x (ISBN 0-8371-5730-7, ALBN). Greenwood.
--Communist Party of Venezuela. LC 77-77320. (Studies Ser.: No. 24). 246p. 1969. 11.95x (ISBN 0-8179-3241-0); pap. 7.95 (ISBN 0-8179-3242-9). Hoover Inst Pr.
--Peron Era. LC 65-18783. 1965. Repr. of 1951 ed. 13.00x (ISBN 0-8462-0632-3). Russell.
--The Right Opposition: The Lovestoneites & the International Communist Opposition of the 1930's. LC 80-1711. (Contributions in Political Science Ser.: No. 54). 320p. 1981. lib. bdg. 35.00 (ISBN 0-313-22070-0, AOP/). Greenwood.
--Romulo Betancourt & the Transformation of Venezuela. LC 81-14684. 600p. 1982. 19.95 (ISBN 0-87855-450-5). Transaction Bks.
--The Tragedy of Chile. LC 77-91101. (Contributions in Political Science: No. 8). 1978. lib. bdg. 35.00x (ISBN 0-313-20034-3, ATC/). Greenwood.
--Trotskyism in Latin America. LC 71-187262. (Publications Ser.: No. 119). 303p. 1973. 13.95x (ISBN 0-8179-6191-7). Hoover Inst Pr.
Alexander, Robert J., ed. Aprismo: The Ideas & Doctrines of Victor Raul Haya de la Torre. LC 78-181083. 381p. 1973. 20.00x (ISBN 0-87338-125-4). Kent St U Pr.
--Political Parties of the Americas: Canada, Latin America, & the West Indies, 2 vols. LC 81-6952. (The Greenwood Historical Encyclopedia of the World's Political Parties Ser.). (Illus.). xxviii, 1274p. 1982. lib. bdg. 65.00x (ISBN 0-313-21474-3, APA/). Greenwood.
Alexander, Robert L. The Architecture of Maximilian Godefrey. LC 74-6810. (Johns Hopkins Studies in Nineteenth-Century Architecture). (Illus.). pap. 66.50 (ISBN 0-317-10603-1, 2020331). Bks Demand UMI.
Alexander, Robert S. Case Studies in Medical Physiology. 1977. pap. 11.95 (ISBN 0-316-03124-0). Little.
Alexander, Roberta S. North Carolina Faces the Freedmen: Race Relations During Presidential Reconstruction, 1865-67. (Illus.). 232p. 1985. 29.75 (ISBN 0-8223-0628-X). Duke.
Alexander, Robin, tr. see Falck-Ytter, Harald.
Alexander, Rodney & Sapery, Elizabeth, eds. The Shortchanged: Minorities & Women in Banking. LC 73-79033. 190p. 1973. 19.50x (ISBN 0-8046-7066-8, Pub. by Kennikat); pap. 9.95 (ISBN 0-8046-7067-6). Assoc Faculty Pr.
Alexander, Roland, jt. auth. see Weber, Dick.
Alexander, Roy. The Astrology of Choice. LC 83-6486. (Illus.). 173p. 1983. pap. 7.95 (ISBN 0-87728-563-2). Weiser.
--Chart Synthesis. 144p. 1984. pap. 9.95 (ISBN 0-85030-364-8). Newcastle Pub.
--Mehdi: Nothing Is Impossible. LC 77-95190. 1978. 10.95 (ISBN 0-87863-157-7). Farnswth Pub.
Alexander, Roy, jt. auth. see Newman, James A.
Alexander, Roy, jt. auth. see Roth, Charles B.
Alexander, S. Space, Time & Deity: The Gifford Lectures at Glasgow 1916-1918, 2 Vols. Set. 32.00 (ISBN 0-8446-1521-8). Peter Smith.
Alexander, Sally. Women's Work in Nineteenth Century London 1820-1850. 64p. (Orig.). 1984. pap. 5.25 (ISBN 0-904526-82-8, Pub by Journeyman Pr England). Flatiron Book Dist.
Alexander, Sally J., jt. ed. see Alexander, Chauncey A.
Alexander, Samuel. Art & Instinct. LC 73-16256. 1927. lib. bdg. 8.50 (ISBN 0-8414-2929-4). Folcroft.
--Locke. LC 73-102561. 1970. Repr. of 1908 ed. 14.00x (ISBN 0-8046-0717-6, Pub. by Kennikat). Assoc Faculty Pr.
--Philosophical & Literary Pieces. facsimile ed. LC 70-93313. (Essay Index Reprint Ser). 1940. 24.50 (ISBN 0-8369-1269-1). Ayer Co Pubs.
--Philosophical & Literary Pieces. LC 74-98207. Repr. of 1939 ed. lib. bdg. 18.50x (ISBN 0-8371-3241-X, ALPL). Greenwood.
Alexander, Sandy. Franchising & You. (Illus.). 1970. pap. 5.95 (ISBN 0-87505-306-8, Pub. by Lawrence). Borden.
Alexander, Scott. Advanced Rhinocerology. 9th ed. LC 81-51912. (Illus.). 128p. (Orig.). 1981. pap. 4.95 (ISBN 0-937382-01-9). Rhinos Pr.
--Rhinoceros Success. 16th ed. LC 80-51648. (Illus.). 123p. (Orig.). 1980. pap. 4.95 (ISBN 0-937382-00-0). Rhinos Pr.
Alexander, Scott R. Rhinocerotic Relativity. LC 83-60933. (Illus.). 120p. (Orig.). 1983. pap. 4.95 (ISBN 0-937382-02-7). Rhinos Pr.
Alexander, Shana. Nutcracker: Money, Madness, Murder-A Family Album. LC 85-7042. 456p. 1985. 17.95 (ISBN 0-385-19268-1). Doubleday.
--Very Much a Lady: The Untold Story of Jean Harris & Dr. Herman Tarnower. 1983. 17.00i (ISBN 0-316-03125-9). Little.
Alexander, Sharon K. From the Strawberry Patch. (Die-cut Cookbooks Ser.: No. 1). (Illus.). 1982. pap. 10.95 indexed (ISBN 0-9608126-0-1). ABC Enterprises.
Alexander, Sharon K. & Fairbairn, Kay. All American Apple Cookbook. LC 82-70679. (Die-Cut Cookbooks Ser.: No. 2). (Illus.). 120p. 1982. pap. text ed. 10.95 indexed (ISBN 0-9608126-1-X). ABC Enterprises.
Alexander, Sidney. The Hand of Michelangelo. LC 77-154999. 693p. 1977. pap. 12.95 (ISBN 0-8214-0235-8, 82-82378). Ohio U Pr.
--Lions & Foxes: Men & Ideas of the Italian Renaissance. LC 77-92250. (Illus.). xi, 375p. 1978. 20.00x (ISBN 0-8214-0404-0, 82-82956); pap. text ed. 11.95x (ISBN 0-8214-0394-X, 82-82964). Ohio U Pr.
--Marc Chagall: A Biography. (Illus.). 525p. 1979. 26.95x (ISBN 0-8464-1196-2). Beekman Pubs.
--Michelangelo the Florentine. LC 65-25109. 464p. 1965. pap. 14.95x (ISBN 0-8214-0236-6, 82-82386). Ohio U Pr.
--Nicodemus: The Roman Years of Michelangelo Buonarroti, 1534-1564. LC 84-5191. viii, 293p. 1984. 19.95 (ISBN 0-8214-0778-3). Ohio U Pr.
Alexander, Sidney, tr. see Guicciardini, Francesco.
Alexander, Sidney S., et al. Five Monographs on Business Income. LC 73-84377. 1973. Repr. of 1950 ed. text ed. 13.00 (ISBN 0-914348-00-0). Scholars Bk.
Alexander-Smith-Robin. Conflicts of Interest: Multiple Representations. LC 83-164423. (Problems in Professional Responsibility Ser.). 32p. 1983. pap. 4.00 (ISBN 0-317-01769-1). Amer Bar Assn.
Alexander, Stan & Broussard, Sharon. An Analysis of the Nineteen Seventy-Three Atlanta Elections. 1973. 3.00 (ISBN 0-686-36617-4). Voter Ed Proj.
--An Analysis of the 1973 Atlanta Elections. 1973. 3.00 (ISBN 0-686-38001-0). Voter Ed Proj.
Alexander, Stella. Church & State in Yugoslavia since Nineteen Forty-Five. LC 77-88668. (Soviet & East European Studies). 1979. 52.50 (ISBN 0-521-21942-6). Cambridge U Pr.
Alexander, Sue. Dear Phoebe. LC 83-23856. (Illus.). 32p. (ps-3). 1984. 10.45i (ISBN 0-316-03132-1). Little.
--Finding Your First Job. LC 79-26487. (Illus.). (YA) (gr. 9 up). 1980. 10.95 (ISBN 0-525-29725-1, 01063-320, Skinny Bk). Dutton.
--Marc the Magnificent. LC 78-3285. (Illus.). (gr. k-3). 1978. 4.95 (ISBN 0-394-83728-2); 5.99g (ISBN 0-394-93728-7). Pantheon.
--More Witch, Goblin & Ghost Stories. LC 78-3280. (An I AM READING Bk.). (Illus.). (gr. 1-4). 1978. PLB 7.99 (ISBN 0-394-93933-6). Pantheon.
--Nadia the Willful. LC 82-12602. (Illus.). 48p. (gr. k-3). 1983. 10.95 (ISBN 0-394-85265-6); PLB 10.99 (ISBN 0-394-95265-0). Pantheon.
--Small Plays for Special Days. LC 76-28424. (Illus.). 64p. (gr. 2-4). 1976. 8.95 (ISBN 0-395-28761-8, Clarion). HM.
--Small Plays for You & a Friend. LC 74-4019. (Illus.). 48p. (gr. 1-4). 1974. 6.95 (ISBN 0-395-28762-6, Clarion). HM.

--Whatever Happened to Uncle Albert? (Illus.). 128p. (gr. 3-6). 1980. 8.95 (ISBN 0-395-29104-6, Clarion); pap. 3.95 (ISBN 0-395-30061-4). HM.

--Witch, Goblin, & Ghost Are Back. LC 83-22157. (Illus.). 72p. (gr. 1-4). 1985. bds. 6.95 (ISBN 0-394-86296-1, Pant Bks Young); PLB 7.99 (ISBN 0-394-96296-6). Pantheon.

--Witch, Goblin & Ghost in the Haunted Woods. LC 80-20863. (I Am Reading Bk.). (Illus.). 72p. (gr. 1-4). 1981. 6.95 (ISBN 0-394-84443-2); PLB 7.99 (ISBN 0-394-94443-7). Pantheon.

--Witch, Goblin & Ghost's Book of Things to Do. LC 80-28930. (I Am Reading Bks.). (Illus.). 72p. (gr. 6-9). 1982. 6.95 (ISBN 0-394-84612-5); PLB 7.99 (ISBN 0-394-94612-X). Pantheon.

--Witch, Goblin, & Sometimes Ghost: Six Read-Alone Stories. LC 76-8657. (Illus.). (ps-3). 1976. PLB 7.99 (ISBN 0-394-93216-1). Pantheon.

--World Famous Muriel. LC 82-17186. (Illus.). (ps-3). 1984. 13.45i (ISBN 0-316-03131-3). Little.

--World Famous Muriel & the Scary Dragon. (Illus.). 48p. (gr. 1-3). 1985. 14.95 (ISBN 0-316-03134-8). Little.

Alexander, Susan. Un Reve Sans Vie. (Collection Harlequin Ser.). 192p. 1983. pap. 1.95 (ISBN 0-373-49343-6). Harlequin Bks.

Alexander, T. Adult-Child Interaction Test: A Projective Test for Use in Research. (SRCD. M Ser.). 1952. pap. 16.00 (ISBN 0-527-01555-5). Kraus Repr.

Alexander, T. G., jt. auth. see Woodruff, A. M.

Alexander, T. J. United States Postal Markings, Eighteen Fifty-One to Eighteen Sixty-One. (Illus.). 434p. 30.00 (ISBN 0-318-16828-6). US Phil Classics.

Alexander, T. John. Spanish Surname Recent Migrant Families: Life Cycle, Family, Socioeconomics & Housing Status. LC 78-68462. 1979. perfect bdg. 9.00 (ISBN 0-88247-555-X). R & E Pubs.

Alexander, Thea. Macro Study Series. Incl. How to Develop Your Macro Awareness; How to Live a Macro Lifestyle; How to Interpret Your Dreams from a Macro View; The Prophetess: Conversations with Rana; Simulataneous Time: Your Parallel Lives, Twin Souls, & Soul Mates; How to Do Personal Evolution Tutoring; The Macro Study Guide & Workbook. 30.00 set (ISBN 0-913080-12-8). Macro Bks.

--Twenty-One Fifty A.D. 281p. (Orig.). 1971. pap. 5.00 (ISBN 0-913080-03-9). Macro Bks.

--Two Thousand One Hundred & Fifty A. D. 288p. (Orig.). 1976. pap. 3.95 (ISBN 0-446-32214-8). Warner Bks.

Alexander, Thomas B. Thomas A. R. Nelson of East Tennessee. LC 56-63418. pap. 56.00 (ISBN 0-317-26107-X, 2024383). Bks Demand UMI.

Alexander, Thomas G. A Clash of Interests: Interior Department & Mountain West 1863-96. LC 77-80144. (Illus.). 1977. 4.95 (ISBN 0-8425-1480-5). Brigham.

--Mormonism in Transition: The Latterday Saints & Their Church, 1890-1930. LC 84-22164. 384p. 1986. 18.95 (ISBN 0-252-01185-6). U of Ill Pr.

Alexander, Thomas G. & Allen, James B. Mormons & Gentiles: A History of Salt Lake City. LC 84-15884. (The Western Urban History Ser.: Vol. V). (Illus.). 350p. 1984. 20.00 (ISBN 0-87108-664-6). Pruett.

Alexander, Thomas G., ed. see Cornwall, Rebecca & Arrington, Leonard J.

Alexander, Thomas G., ed. see Grant, Ulysses S.

Alexander, Thomas G., ed. see Nash, Gerald D., et al.

Alexander, Thomas G., ed. see Palmer, Richard F. & Butler, Karl D.

Alexander, Thomas G., ed. see Shipps, Jan, et al.

Alexander, Thomas G., jt. ed. see Poll, Richard D.

Alexander, Thomas L. Modular Study Guide-Lab Manual for Intermediate Algebra (Pre-Calculus) 408p. 1982. pap. text ed. 21.95 (ISBN 0-8403-3300-5, 40317001). Kendall-Hunt.

Alexander, Truman H. Loot. facsimile ed. LC 79-39077. (Black Heritage Library Collection). Repr. of 1932 ed. 15.50 (ISBN 0-8369-9015-3). Ayer Co Pubs.

Alexander, Uhlman S. Special Legislation Affecting Public Schools. LC 78-176507. (Columbia University. Teachers College. Contributions to Education: No. 353). Repr. of 1929 ed. 22.50 (ISBN 0-404-55353-2). AMS Pr.

Alexander, Van. First Chart. Haskell, Jimmie, ed. LC 70-182858. 112p. 1971. 9.95, incl. 2 records (ISBN 0-910468-01-X). Criterion Mus.

Alexander, Vicente. World Alone. Hyde, Lewis & Unger, David, trs. (Illus.). 76p. 1982. 17.50x (ISBN 0-915778-41-6); deluxe ed. 150.00x (ISBN 0-915778-42-4). Penmaen Pr.

Alexander, Virginia & Elliott, Colleen M. Pendleton District & Anderson County, S. C. Wills, Estates & Legal Records, 1793 to 1857. 350p. 1979. 35.00 (ISBN 0-89308-143-4). Southern Hist Pr.

Alexander, Virginia W. Maury County, Tennessee, Deed, Books A to F, 1807 to 1817. 248p. 1981. Repr. of 1965 ed. 22.50 (ISBN 0-89308-185-X). Southern Hist Pr.

Alexander, W. The EEC Rules of Competition. 204p. 1973. 22.00 (ISBN 90-268-0683-3, Pub. by Kluwer Law Nethrelands). Kluwer Academic.

--Film on the Left: American Documentary Film from 1931-1942. LC 80-8534. (Illus.). 364p. 1981. 35.00 (ISBN 0-691-04678-6, LPE); pap. 12.50x L.P.E. (ISBN 0-691-10111-6). Princeton U Pr.

Alexander, W., jt. auth. see Unruh, G.

Alexander, W. C. Short Synopsis of the Most Essential Points in Hawaiian Grammar. LC 68-13866. pap. 2.95 (ISBN 0-8048-0528-8). C E Tuttle.

Alexander, W. D., tr. see Remy, M. Jules.

Alexander, William. An Encouragement to Colonies. LC 68-54607. (English Experience Ser.: No. 63). (Illus.). 47p. 1968. Repr. of 1624 ed. 11.50 (ISBN 90-221-0063-4). Walter J Johnson.

--The History of Women from the Earliest Antiquity to the Present Time, 2 vols. LC 72-9610. Repr. of 1796 ed. 65.00 set (ISBN 0-404-57401-7). AMS Pr.

--Image of China. (Oresko-Jupiter Art Bks). (Illus.). 96p. 1981. 17.95 (ISBN 0-933516-82-7, Pub. by Oresko-Jupiter England). Hippocrene Bks.

--Notes & Sketches Illustrative of Northern Rural Life in the Eighteenth Century. LC 77-10060. 1977. Repr. of 1877 ed. lib. bdg. 25.00 (ISBN 0-8414-1701-6). Folcroft.

--The Tragedie of Darius. LC 72-6936. (English Experience Ser.: No. 293). 80p. Repr. of 1603 ed. 11.50 (ISBN 90-221-0293-9). Walter J Johnson.

Alexander, William J. An Introduction to the Poetry of Robert Browning. 1978. Repr. of 1889 ed. lib. bdg. 22.50 (ISBN 0-8495-0055-9). Arden Lib.

--An Introduction to the Poetry of Robert Browning. 210p. 1980. Repr. of 1889 ed. lib. bdg. 22.50 (ISBN 0-89987-006-6). Darby Bks.

--Introduction to the Poetry of Robert Browning. LC 74-8047. 1889. lib. bdg. 10.00 (ISBN 0-8414-2979-0). Folcroft.

Alexander, William M. Demonic Possession in the New Testament: Its Historical, Medical, & Theological Aspects. 1980. pap. 6.95 (ISBN 0-8010-0147-1). Baker Bk.

--State Leadership in Improving Instruction: A Study of the Leadership Service Function of State Education Departments, with Special Reference to Louisiana, Tennessee & Virginia. LC 71-176508. (Columbia University. Teachers College. Contributions to Education: No. 820). Repr. of 1940 ed. 22.50 (ISBN 0-404-55820-8). AMS Pr.

Alexander, William M. & George, Paul. Exemplary Middle School. 1981. pap. text ed. 27.95 (ISBN 0-03-052301-X, HoltC). HR&W.

Alexander, William P., jt. auth. see Krauss, Bob.

Alexander, William T. History of the Colored Race in America, Containing Also Their Ancient & Modern Life in Africa, the Origin & Development of Slavery, the Civil War. 2nd ed. LC 68-55867. (Illus.). Repr. of 1887 ed. 28.00x (ISBN 0-8371-0283-9, ALC&, Pub. by Negro U Pr). Greenwood.

Alexander, Yona & Chertoff, Mordecai, eds. Bibliography on Israel & Zionism. 1980. write for info. Herzl Pr.

Alexander, Yonah & Nanes, Allan. The United States & Iran: A Documentary History. 524p. lib. bdg. 24.00 (ISBN 0-89093-378-2, Aletheia Bks); pap. 8.00 (ISBN 0-686-96909-X, Aletheia Bks). U Pubns Amer.

Alexander, Yonah, jt. auth. see Cline, Ray S.

Alexander, Yonah, jt. auth. see Kilmarx, Robert A.

Alexander, Yonah, ed. Behavioral & Quantitative Perspectives on Terrorism. Gleason, John M. LC 80-39752. (Pergamon Press Series on International Politics). 300p. 1981. 39.00 (ISBN 0-08-025989-8). Pergamon.

--International Terrorism: National, Regional, & Global Perspectives. rev. ed. LC 75-8396. 414p. 1976. text ed. 39.95 (ISBN 0-275-09480-4). Praeger.

Alexander, Yonah & Ebinger, Charles, eds. Political Terrorism & Energy: The Threat & Response. 272p. 1982. 37.95 (ISBN 0-03-059344-1). Praeger.

Alexander, Yonah & Finger, Seymour M., eds. Terrorism: Interdisciplinary Perspectives. LC 77-7552. 1977. 17.50 (ISBN 0-89444-004-7). John Jay Pr.

Alexander, Yonah & Friedlander, Robert A., eds. Self-Determination: National, Regional, & Global Dimensions. LC 80-65075. (Special Studies in National & International Terrorism). 1980. 36.50 (ISBN 0-89158-090-5). Westview.

Alexander, Yonah & Kilmarx, Robert A., eds. Political Terrorism & Business: The Threat & the Response. LC 79-16374. 360p. 1979. 41.95 (ISBN 0-03-046686-5). Praeger.

Alexander, Yonah & Kittrie, Nicholas N. F., eds. Crescent & Star: Arab & Israeli Perspectives on the Middle East Conflict. LC 72-5797. (AMS Studies in Modern Society: Political & Social Issues). 37.50 (ISBN 0-404-10522-X); pap. 14.00 (ISBN 0-404-10523-8). AMS Pr.

Alexander, Yonah & Myers, Kenneth, eds. Terrorism in Europe. LC 81-21306. 230p. 1982. 25.00x (ISBN 0-312-79250-6). St Martin.

Alexander, Yonah & Nanes, Allan, eds. United States & Iran: A Documentary History. 450p. 1980. 24.00 (ISBN 0-89093-183-6); pap. 8.00 (ISBN 0-89093-184-4). U Pubns Amer.

Alexander, Yonah & O'Day, Alan, eds. Terrorism in Ireland. LC 83-3106. 277p. 1984. 25.00x (ISBN 0-312-79260-3). St Martin.

Alexander, Yonah, jt. ed. see Freedman, Lawrence Z.

Alexander, Yonah, jt. ed. see Rapoport, David.

Alexander, Yonah, jt. ed. see Rapoport, David C.

Alexander, Yonah, jt. ed. see Tavin, Eli.

Alexander, Yonah, et al. Terrorism: What Sould Be Our Response? 25p. 1982. 3.75 (ISBN 0-8447-2231-6). Am Enterprise.

Alexander, Yonah, et al, eds. Control of Terrorism: International Documents. LC 79-4384. 215p. 1979. 19.50x (ISBN 0-8448-1327-3). Crane-Russak Co.

--Terrorism: Theory & Practice. (Westview Special Studies in National & International Terrorism). 200p. 1979. pap. text ed. 13.50 (ISBN 0-86531-041-6). Westview.

Alexander, Ziggi, ed. see Seacole, Mary.

Alexanderson, E. Pauline & Wagner, Harvey A., eds. FERMI-I: New Age for Nuclear Power. LC 78-67176. (ANS Monograph). (Illus.). 1979. 27.80 (ISBN 0-89448-017-0, 690004). Am Nuclear Soc.

Alexanderson, G. L., jt. ed. see Albers, Donald J.

Alexanderson, Gerald L., jt. auth. see Hillman, Abraham P.

Alexandersson, G. The Baltic Straits. 1982. lib. bdg. 32.50 (ISBN 90-247-2595-X, Pub. by Martinus Nijhoff Netherlands). Kluwer Academic.

Alexandersson, Gunnar & Klevebring, Bjorn. World Resources: Energy Metals, Minerals. (Studies in Economic & Political Geography). 1978. 14.40x (ISBN 3-11-006577-0). De Gruyter.

Alexandersson, Jan & Hedman, Iwan. Leslie Charteris och Helgonet under 5 Decennier en Bio-Bibliografi. LC 85-11045. 124p. 1985. Repr. of 1973 ed. lib. bdg. 19.95x (ISBN 0-89370-874-7). Borgo Pr.

Alexandersson, Jan, jt. auth. see Hedman, Iwan.

Alexander The Great. Roman d'Alexandre, Vols. 1-7. (Elliott Monographs: Nos. 36-42). Repr. of 1955 ed. 169.00 (ISBN 0-527-02605-0). Kraus Repr.

Alexander-Williams, J. BIMR Gastroenterology Vol. 3: Large Intestine. new ed. 1983. text ed. 59.95 (ISBN 0-407-02289-9). Butterworth.

Alexander-Williams, J. & Irving, M., eds. Intestinal Fistulas. (Illus.). 240p. 1982. text ed. 37.00 (ISBN 0-7236-0555-6). PSG Pub Co.

Alexandra. Letters of the Tsaritsa to the Tsar, 1914-1916. LC 75-34991. (Russia: Perspectives on the Revolution Ser.). 478p. 1976. Repr. of 1924 ed. 35.75 (ISBN 0-88355-423-2). Hyperion-Conn.

Alexandratos, Nikos, et al. Agriculture from the Perspective of Population Growth: Some Results from "Agriculture Toward 2000". (Economic & Social Development Papers: No. 30). 100p. 1984. pap. 7.50 (ISBN 92-5-101365-9, F2484, FAO). Unipub.

Alexandre, A., et al. Road Traffic Noise. 1975. 33.50 (ISBN 0-85334-628-3, Pub. by Elsevier Applied Sci England). Elsevier.

Alexandrescu, S., ed. Transformational Grammar & the Rumanian Language. 97p. (Orig.). 1977. pap. 10.00x (ISBN 90-316-0144-6). Benjamins North Am.

Alexandrescu-Dersca, M. M. La Campagne De Timur En Anatolie (1402) 228p. 1977. 70.00x (ISBN 0-86078-015-5, Pub. by Variorum). State Mutual Bk.

Alexandria, Betty, pseud. Contigo (Poesias) LC 83-82881. (Coleccion Espejo de Paciencia). 63p. (Orig., Span.). 1984. pap. 6.95 (ISBN 0-89729-346-0). Ediciones.

Alexandrian, Sarane. Dictionnaire de la Peinture Surrealiste. 58p. (Fr.). 1973. 32.50 (ISBN 0-686-56823-0, M-6601). French & Eur.

--Seurat. (QLP Ser.). (Illus.). 96p. 1980. 9.95 (ISBN 0-517-54106-8). Crown.

--Surrealist Art. (The World of Art Ser.). (Illus.). 1985. pap. 9.95 (ISBN 0-500-20097-1). Thames Hudson.

Alexandrides, C. G. & Moschis, George P. Export Marketing Management. LC 76-12839. 202p. 1977. text ed. 35.95 (ISBN 0-275-23610-2). Praeger.

Alexandrides, C. G., ed. International Business Systems Perspectives. LC 72-619616. (Illus., Orig.). 1973. pap. 15.00 (ISBN 0-88406-000-4). Ga St U Busn Pub.

Alexandridis, E. The Pupil. Telger, T., tr. from Ger. (Illus.). 115p. 1985. 29.90 (ISBN 0-387-96109-7). Springer-Verlag.

Alexandridis, Nikitas A. Microprocessor Systems Design Concepts. LC 82-18189. 623p. 1984. text ed. 32.95 (ISBN 0-914894-66-8). Computer Sci.

Alexandroff, Alan S. The Logic of Diplomacy. LC 80-29544. (Sage Library of Social Research: Vol. 120). (Illus.). 199p. 1981. 24.00 (ISBN 0-8039-1572-1). Sage.

--The Logic of Diplomacy. LC 80-29544. (Sage Library of Social Research: Vol. 120). (Illus.). 199p. 1981. pap. 12.00 (ISBN 0-8039-1573-X). Sage.

Alexandroff, Paul. Elementary Concepts of Topology. Farley, Alan E., tr. 1961. pap. 2.50 (ISBN 0-486-60747-X). Dover.

Alexandroff, Paul S. & Hopf, H. Topologie. LC 65-21833. (Ger.). 17.50 (ISBN 0-8284-0197-7). Chelsea Pub.

Alexandrov, A. F., et al. Principles of Plasma Electrodynamics. (Springer Series in Electrophysics: Vol. 9). (Illus.). 510p. 1984. 49.50 (ISBN 0-387-12613-9). Springer-Verlag.

Alexandrov, Eugene A., compiled by. Mineral & Energy Resources of the USSR: A Selected Bibliography of Sources in English. 160p. 1980. pap. 10.00 (ISBN 0-913312-21-5). Am Geol.

Alexandrov, Paul S. Introduction to the Theory of Sets & Functions. write for info. (ISBN 0-685-07980-5). Chelsea Pub.

Alexandrov, S. V., et al. Las Fuezas Motrices del Proceso Revolucionario Mundial. 342p. 1984. 5.95 (ISBN 0-8285-2559-5, Pub. by Progress Pubs USSR). Imported Pubns.

Alexandrov, V., et al. Handful of Stars: Stories by Soviet Writers. Butler, Janet & Riordan, James, trs. 161p. (Russian.). 1983. 7.95 (ISBN 0-8285-2536-6, Pub by Raduga Pubs USSR). Imported Pubns.

Alexandrov, V. Y. Cells, Macromolecules, & Temperature. (Ecological Studies Ser: Vol. 21). 1977. 51.00 (ISBN 0-387-08026-0). Springer-Verlag.

Alexandrov, Vladimir E. Andrei Bely: The Major Symbolist Fiction. (Russian Research Center Studies: No. 83). 256p. 1985. text ed. 22.50x (ISBN 0-674-03646-8). Harvard U Pr.

Alexandrova, Vera. History of Soviet Literature. Ginsburg, Mirra, tr. from Rus. LC 70-156171. 1971. Repr. of 1963 ed. lib. bdg. 37.50 (ISBN 0-8371-6114-2, ALSL). Greenwood.

Alexandrowicz, Charles H. The Law of Global Communications. LC 79-163081. (International Legal Studies Ser). 195p. 1971. 22.00x (ISBN 0-231-03529-2). Columbia U Pr.

Alexandrowicz, Harry. Six Hundred Ninety-Nine Ways to Improve the Performance of Your Car. LC 79-93251. (Illus.). 192p. 1980. lib. bdg. 17.79 (ISBN 0-8069-5551-1). Sterling.

Alexanian, M., ed. see Summer Institute in Theoretical Physics, Mexico City, 1973.

Alexeev, Yuri, jt. auth. see Rapoport, Vitaly.

Alexeevsky, Petr. Ispoved Razvedchitsy Istoria Odnogo Pokhoda 1919-1937: Confessions of a Spy-History of an Operation 1919-1937. (Illus.). 70p. (Russian.). 1983. pap. 8.00x (ISBN 0-88669-063-3). Globus Pubs.

--Otets Savvatiy Dorogami Detstva: Father Savatiy Roads of Youth. (Illus.). 180p. (Orig., Russian.). 1983. pap. 12.00 (ISBN 0-88669-062-5). Globus Pubs.

Alexeiev, J. K., et al. Instrument & Observing Problems in Cold Climates. (Technical Note Ser.: No. 135). x, 30p. (Orig.). 1974. pap. 10.00 (ISBN 92-63-10384-4, W154, WMO). Unipub.

Alexenberg, Melvin. Alef Bet Zoo. (Illus.). (gr. 1-3). 1963. 4.00 (ISBN 0-914080-05-9). Shulsinger Sales.

Alexenberg, Melvin & Alexenberg, Miriam. Alef Bet Picture Dictionary. (Illus.). (gr. 1-3). 1963. 5.00 (ISBN 0-914080-06-7). Shulsinger Sales.

Alexenberg, Miriam, jt. auth. see Alexenberg, Melvin.

Alexeyev, M. Men at War. 413p. 1980. 9.60 (ISBN 0-8285-2035-6, Pub. by Progress Pubs USSR). Imported Pubns.

Alexeyev, R. USSR-FRG Relations: A New Stage. 240p. 1983. pap. 3.95 (ISBN 0-8285-2599-4, Pub. by Progress Pubs USSR). Imported Pubns.

Alexeyev, S. Stories about Magnitka. Belskaya, Natalia, tr. 102p. 1983. pap. 3.95 (ISBN 0-8285-2771-7, Pub. by Raduga Pubs USSR). Imported Pubns.

Alexeyev, Sergei. My First Book. Cook, Cathleen, tr. from Rus. (Illus.). 26p. (gr. k-3). 1983. pap. 1.99 (ISBN 0-8285-2490-4, Pub. by Progress Pubs. USSR). Imported Pubns.

Alexeyev, Vladimir. Quantitative Analysis. MIR Publishers, tr. from Rus. (Illus.). 563p. 1975. text ed. 17.95x (ISBN 0-8464-0774-4). Beekman Pubs.

--Quantitative Analysis. (Russian Monographs & Texts on the Physical Sciences). 501p. 1969. 67.25 (ISBN 0-677-20860-X). Gordon.

Alexeyeva, Ludmilla. Soviet Dissent: Contemporary Movements for National, Religious & Human Rights. Glad, John & Pearce, Carol, trs. from Rus. LC 84-11811. 1985. 35.00 (ISBN 0-8195-5124-4, Dist. by Harper). Wesleyan U Pr.

Alexeyeva, T. Venetsianov & His School. 239p. 1984. 45.00 (ISBN 0-8285-2951-5, Pub. by Aurura Pubs USSR). Imported Pubns.

Alexie, Angela. The Treacherous Heart. (Orig.). 1980. pap. 1.95 (ISBN 0-449-14312-0, GM). Fawcett.

--The Velvet Thorn. 320p. (Orig.). 1982. pap. 2.95 (ISBN 0-449-14502-6, GM). Fawcett.

Alexieva, M. & Paounova, E. English-Bulgarian Conversation Phrase Bk. 1982. pap. 8.50 (ISBN 0-686-46537-7). Heinman.

Alexieva, Marguerite, tr. see Dzhagarov, Georgi.

Alexieva, Marguerite, tr. see Kirilov, Nikolai & Kirk, Frank.

Alexieva, Marguerite, tr. see Panayotova, Dora.

Alexin, A. Crazy Evdokia. 192p. 1979. 4.45 (ISBN 0-8285-1126-8, Pub. by Progress Pubs USSR). Imported Pubns.

Alexis, Guillaume. Oeuvres Poetiques, 3 Vols. Set. 100.00 (ISBN 0-384-00710-4); Set. pap. 84.00 (ISBN 0-384-00711-2). Johnson Repr.

Alexis, Katina. Young Blood. 288p. (Orig.). 1982. pap. 2.95 (ISBN 0-523-48028-8). Pinnacle Bks.

Alexis, Marcus, et al. Black Consumer Profiles: Food Purchasing in the Inner City. (Illus.). 106p. 1980. pap. 4.00 (ISBN 0-87712-195-8). U Mich Busn Div Res.

Alexis Pub. Extraordinaire: Little Tidbits. (Illus.). 64p. 1984. pap. 5.00 (ISBN 0-682-40156-0). Exposition Pr FL.

Alexits. Approximation Theory. 1984. 34.00 (ISBN 0-9910001-0-2, Pub. by Akademiai Kaido Hungary). Heyden.

Alexopoulos, C. J., jt. auth. see Martin, G. W.

Alexopoulos, Constantine J. & Bold, Harold C. Algae & Fungi. 1967. pap. 12.95x (ISBN 0-02-301700-7, 30170). Macmillan.

Alexopoulos, Constantine J. & Mims, Charles W. Introductory Mycology. 3rd ed. LC 79-12514. 632p. 1979. text ed. 42.50 (ISBN 0-471-02214-4). Wiley.

Alexsandrov, Michail. On the Dynamics of Cables with Application to Marine Use. (University of Michigan Dept. of Naval Architecture & Marine Engineering Report Ser.: No. 76). pap. 20.00 (ISBN 0-317-28262-X, 2022630). Bks Demand UMI.

Alexy, George, jt. auth. see Rector, Russell.

Al-Eyd, Kadhim A. Oil Revenues & Accelerated Growth: Absorptive Capacity in Iraq. LC 79-18596. 206p. 1979. 39.95 (ISBN 0-03-053306-6). Praeger.

Aleyev, Yu G. Nekton. (Illus.). 1977. lib. bdg. 63.00 (ISBN 90-6193-560-1, Pub. by Junk Pubs Netherlands). Kluwer Academic.

Alfano, Genrose J. All-RN Nursing Staff. LC 81-80201. 133p. 1980. pap. text ed. 22.50 (ISBN 0-913654-68-X). Aspen Systems.

Alfano, Pete. Super Bowl Superstars: The Most Valuable Players in the NFL's Championship Game. LC 82-368. (Random House Sports Library). (Illus.). 144p. (gr. 5-9). 1982. pap. 2.95 (ISBN 0-394-85017-3). Random.

Alfano, R. R. Semiconductors Probed by Ultrafast Laser Spectroscopy, Vol. 1. 1985. 79.50 (ISBN 0-12-049901-0). Acad Pr.

--Semiconductors Probed by Ultrafast Laser Spectroscopy, Vol. 2. 1985. 85.00 (ISBN 0-12-049902-9). Acad Pr.

Alfano, R. R., ed. Biological Events Proved by Ultrafast Laser Spectroscopy. LC 82-1613. (Quantum Electronics Ser.). 1982. 59.00 (ISBN 0-12-049950-9). Acad Pr.

Al-Farabi. Short Commentary on Aristotle's Prior Analytics. Rescher, Nicholas, tr. LC 63-10581. pap. 33.00 (ISBN 0-317-09047-X, 2010487). Bks Demand UMI.

Al-Farabi, Abu N. & Zimmerman, F. W. Al-Farabi's Commentary & Short Treatise on Aristotle's 'De Interpretatione' 1981. text ed. 165.00x (ISBN 0-19-725959-6). Oxford U Pr.

Alfaro, A., jt. auth. see Aboukhaled, A.

Alfaro, Adolfo, jt. auth. see Martin, Genevieve A.

Alfaro, Angel G. Educacion y Cambio Social en Puerto Rico: Una Epoca Critica. 4.35 (ISBN 0-8477-2714-9); pap. 3.75 (ISBN 0-8477-2715-7). U of PR Pr.

Alfaro, Juan. Preguntas y Respuestas sobre la Biblia. 64p. (Spanish.). 1982. pap. 1.50 (ISBN 0-89243-162-8). Liguori Pubns.

Alfaro, Julian H., jt. auth. see Bomse, Marguerite D.

Alfaro, Ricardo J. Diccionario de Anglicismos. 2nd ed. 520p. (Span.). 29.95 (ISBN 84-249-1342-6, S-11836). French & Eur.

Alfaro Perez, Juan. Diccionario Maritimo y De Construccion Naval. 478p. (Span. & Eng.). 1976. leather 53.95 (ISBN 84-7079-081-1, S-50094). French & Eur.

Al-Farsey, Fouad. Saudi Arabia: A Case Study in Development. 20.00x (ISBN 0-905743-20-2). Intl Bk Ctr.

Al-Farsy, Fouad. Saudi Arabia: A Case Study in Development. 224p. (Orig.). 1982. pap. 17.50x (ISBN 0-7103-0005-0). Routledge & Kegan.

Alfaruqi, Ismael R., jt. auth. see Chan, Wing T.

Al Faruqi, Lois I., ed. An Annotated Glossary of Arabic Musical Terms. LC 81-4129. 536p. (Arabic & Eng.). 1981. lib. bdg. 49.95x (ISBN 0-313-20554-X, AFM/). Greenwood.

Alfassa, Maurice, jt. auth. see Mantoux, Paul.

Alfassa, Mira. Conversations. 133p. 1973. pap. 1.75 (ISBN 0-89071-246-8). Matagiri.

--Conversations: The Mother. 1973. pap. 1.75 (ISBN 0-89071-246-8). Matagiri.

--Flowers & Their Messages. (Illus.). 308p. 1980. pap. 14.95 (ISBN 0-89071-282-4). Matagiri.

--Glimpses of the Mother's Life, Vol. 1. Das, Nilima, ed. 259p. 1978. 9.50 (ISBN 0-89071-247-6). Matagiri.

--Glimpses of the Mother's Life, Vol. 2. Das, Nilima, ed. 335p. 1980. 11.00 (ISBN 0-89071-291-3). Matagiri.

--Health & Healing in Yoga. 305p. 1979. 6.00 (ISBN 0-89071-284-0, Pub. by Sri Aurobindo Ashram India); pap. 6.00 (ISBN 0-89071-283-2). Matagiri.

--The Mother on Herself. 84p. 1977. pap. 1.85 (ISBN 0-89071-248-4). Matagiri.

Alfassa, Mira, jt. auth. see Aurobindo.

Alfassy, Leo. Blues Hanon. 1980. pap. 6.95 (ISBN 0-8256-2224-7, Amsco Music). Music Sales.

--Boogie Woogie Hanon. 1980. pap. 6.95 (ISBN 0-8256-2222-0, Amsco Music). Music Sales.

--Children's Jazz Pieces. (Music for Millions Ser.: Vol. 56). 1969. pap. 4.95 (ISBN 0-8256-4056-3). Music Sales.

--Jazz Hanon. 1980. pap. 6.95 (ISBN 0-8256-2223-9, Amsco Music). Music Sales.

--The Piano Chord Finder. (Illus.). 40p. pap. 2.95 (ISBN 0-8256-2389-8). Music Sales.

Alfassy, Leo, ed. Baroque & Folk Tunes for Recorder. pap. 5.95 (ISBN 0-8256-2155-0, Amsco). Music Sales.

Al-Fatih, Zudhi. The Jews in Review: The World's Greatest Minds on Zionism. 1984. lib. bdg. 79.95 (ISBN 0-87700-581-8). Revisionist Pr.

Al-Fawaris, Abu. The Political Doctrine of the Isma'ilis. Makarim, Sami N., ed. LC 77-16600. 156p. 1977. 25.00x (ISBN 0-88206-016-3). Caravan Bks.

Alfeld, Louis & Graham, Alan K. Introduction to Urban Dynamics. LC 76-19725. 1976. 37.50x (ISBN 0-262-01054-2). MIT Pr.

Alfen, Nicholas Van see Van Alfen, Nicholas.

Alferi, Vincent. The Practical Guide to WordStar & MailMerge. 350p. pap. 18.95 (6305). Hayden.

Alferieff, E. E. Imperator Nikolaj Btoroj, kak tchelovjek sil'noj voli. LC 83-80987. 152p. 1983. pap. 8.00 (ISBN 0-317-29226-9). Holy Trinity.

Alferirff, E. E., ed. Pisoma Tsarskoj Semji iz Zatotchenija. LC 73-91829. (Illus.). 544p. 1974. 25.00 (ISBN 0-317-29225-0). Holy Trinity.

Alfers, et al. America's Second Century: Topical Readings, 1865-Present. 368p. 1983. pap. text ed. 9.95 (ISBN 0-8403-3157-6). Kendall-Hunt.

Alfian. Political Science in Indonesia. LC 82-95016. (Illus.). x, 58p. 1979. pap. 4.95x (ISBN 0-8214-0775-9). Ohio U Pr.

Alfidi, Ralph J., jt. ed. see Haaga, John R.

Alfieri, et al. Laboratory for General Botany. 1977. pap. text ed. 7.95 (ISBN 0-917962-00-1). Peek Pubns.

Alfieri, Dino. Dictators Face to Face. Moore, David, tr. LC 78-755. (Illus.). x, 307p. 1978. Repr. of 1954 ed. lib. bdg. 22.50x (ISBN 0-313-20285-0, ALDF). Greenwood.

Alfieri, Vittorio. The Prince & Letters. Corrigan, Beatrice & Molinaro, Julius A., trs. LC 75-185707. (Illus.). pap. 53.50 (ISBN 0-317-10076-9, 2019444). Bks Demand UMI.

--Tragedies of Vittorio Alfieri, 2 Vols. LC 75-98802. Repr. of 1876 ed. Set. lib. bdg. 37.50x (ISBN 0-8371-2885-4, ALTA). Greenwood.

Alfin-Slater, Roslyn & Kritchevsky, David, eds. Human Nutrition-A Comprehensive Treatise, Vol. 3A: Nutrition & the Adult-Macronutrients. LC 79-25119. (Illus.). 308p. 1980. 35.00x (ISBN 0-306-40287-4, Plenum Pr). Plenum Pub.

--Human Nutrition-A Comprehensive Treatise, Vol. 3B: Nutrition & the Adult- Micronutrients. LC 79-3888. (Illus.). 450p. 1980. 49.50x (ISBN 0-306-40288-2, Plenum Pr). Plenum Pub.

Alfin-Slater, Roslyn B. & Aftergood, Lilla. Nutrition for Today. (Contemporary Topics in Health Science Ser). 64p. 1973. pap. text ed. write for info. (ISBN 0-697-07340-8). Wm C Brown.

Alfoeldi, Andreas & Alfoeldi, Elisabeth. Die Kontorniat-Medaillons. (Antike Muenzen und Geschnittene Steine Ser., Vol. 6). 1976. 118.00x (ISBN 3-11-003484-0). De Gruyter.

Alfoeldi, Elisabeth, jt. auth. see Alfoeldi, Andreas.

Alfoeldy, Geza. Die Roemischen Inschriften von Tarraco, 2 vols. (Madrider Forschungen Ser.: Vol. 10). (Ger.). 1975. text & plate 128.00x (ISBN 3-11-004403-X). De Gruyter.

Alfoldi, Andras. A Conflict of Ideas in the Late Roman Empire: The Clash Between the Senate & Valentinian I. Mattingly, Harold, tr. LC 78-26781. 1979. Repr. of 1952 ed. lib. bdg. 18.75x (ISBN 0-313-20836-0, ALCI). Greenwood.

--A Conflict of Ideas in the Late Roman Empire: The Clash Between the Senate & Valentinian I. Mattingly, Harold, tr. LC 78-58998. 1979. Repr. of 1952 ed. 14.50 (ISBN 0-88355-674-X). Hyperion Conn.

Alfoldy, Geza. The Social History of Rome. Wood, John, tr. LC 85-11188. 224p. 1985. 27.50x (ISBN 0-389-20583-4, BNB 08141). B&N Imports.

Alfonsi, Ferdinando P. & Alfonsi, Sandra R. An Annotated Bibliography of Moravia Criticism in Italy & the English-Speaking World. LC 75-24084. (Reference Library of the Humanities: Vol. 30). 500p. 1975. lib. bdg. 34.00 (ISBN 0-8240-9982-6). Garland Pub.

Alfonsi, Petrus. The Disciplina Clericalis of Petrus Alfonsi. Hermes, Eberhard, ed. Quarrie, P. R., tr. LC 73-94434. (Islamic World Ser.). 250p. 1977. 34.50x (ISBN 0-520-02704-3). U of Cal Pr.

Alfonsi, Sandra R., jt. auth. see Alfonsi, Ferdinando P.

Alfonso, et al. Instructional Supervision: A Behavior System. 1985. 33.57 (ISBN 0-205-07142-2, 237142). Allyn.

Alfonso, Amelia B., et al. The Case of the Philippines. (Culture & Fertility Ser.). 67p. (Orig.). 1980. pap. text ed. 9.50x (ISBN 9971-902-14-1, Pub. by Inst Southeast Asian Stud). Gower Pub Co.

Alfonso, Antonio E. & Gardner, Bernard, eds. The Practice of Cancer Surgery. (Illus.). 496p. 1982. 48.50 (ISBN 0-8385-7861-6). ACC.

Alfonso, Felipe B., jt. ed. see Korten, David C.

Alfonso X. General Estoria: Part II, 2 vols. (Illus.). lxvii, 413p. 1957-1961. 50.00x (ISBN 0-942260-01-5); deluxe ed. 125.00x (ISBN 0-942260-02-3). Hispanic Seminary.

--Lapidario y Libro de las formas y ymagenes. Winget, Lynn W. & Diman, Roderic C., eds. (Spanish Ser.: No. 3). xix, 202p. 1980. 20.00x (ISBN 0-942260-12-0). Hispanic Seminary.

--Libro de las Cruzes. Kasten, L. A. & Kiddle, L. B., eds. (Illus.). xlvii, 173p. 1961. pap. 10.00x (ISBN 0-942260-03-1); deluxe ed. 20.00x. Hispanic Seminary.

Alfonso XI. Libro de la Monteria. Seniff, Dennis P., ed. (Spanish Ser.: No. 8). (Illus.). xlvi, 156p. 1983. 24.00x (ISBN 0-942260-27-9). Hispanic Seminary.

Alford, et al. One Hour Telecomputing. LC 84-9450. 1985. pap. text ed. 19.95 (ISBN 0-931543-01-0). IM Pr.

Alford, B. W. & Barker, T. C. History of the Carpenters Company. (Illus.). 271p. 1968. 23.00 (ISBN 0-208-00840-3, Archon). Shoe String.

Alford, Betty B. & Bogle, Margaret L. Nutrition During the Life Cycle. 384p. 1982. 29.95 (ISBN 0-13-627810-8). P-H.

Alford, C. Fred. Science & the Revenge of Nature: Marcuse & Habermas. LC 85-627. 208p. 1983. 24.50 (ISBN 0-8130-0817-4). U Presses Fla.

Alford, D., intro. by. Constitutional Crisis. 3.00 (ISBN 0-8315-0072-7). Speller.

Alford, D. V. & Upstone, M. E. Pest & Disease Control in Fruit & Hops. 97p. (Orig.). 1981. pap. 9.95x (ISBN 0-901436-60-7, Pub. by B C P C England). Intl Spec Bk.

--Pests & Disease Control in Fruit & Hops. 105p. 1980. 30.00x (ISBN 0-901436-60-7, Pub. by CAB Bks England). State Mutual Bk.

Alford, David V. A Colour Atlas of Fruit Pests: Their Recognition, Biology & Control. (Illus.). 310p. 1984. text ed. 58.00x (ISBN 0-7234-0816-5, Pub. by Wolfe Medical England). Sheridan.

Alford, Dean H. The Book of Genesis & Part of the Book of Exodus. 1979. 12.50 (ISBN 0-86524-001-9, 7002). Klock & Klock.

Alford, Delton L. Music in the Pentecostal Church. 113p. 1969. 5.25 (ISBN 0-87148-561-3); pap. 4.25 (ISBN 0-87148-562-1). Pathway Pr.

Alford, Harold D. Procedures for School District Reorganization. LC 75-176509. (Columbia University. Teachers College. Contributions to Education: No. 852). Repr. of 1942 ed. 22.50 (ISBN 0-404-55852-6). AMS Pr.

Alford, Harold J. Power & Conflict in Continuing Education. 272p. 1980. text ed. write for info. (ISBN 0-534-00849-6). Wadsworth Pub.

Alford, Henry. The New Testament for English Readers, 4 vols. 1983. Repr. of 1976 ed. 54.95 (ISBN 0-8010-0195-1). Baker Bk.

Alford, Henry S. Egyptian Soudan: Its Loss & Its Recovery. LC 77-97397. (Illus.). Repr. of 1898 ed. 24.75x (ISBN 0-8371-2647-9, ALE&, Pub. by Negro U Pr). Greenwood.

Alford, Jim. Track Athletics. (Competitive Sports Ser.). (Illus.). 64p. (gr. 7-12). 1984. 12.95 (ISBN 0-7134-4312-X, Pub. by Batsford England). David & Charles.

Alford, John A. & Seniff, Dennis P. Literature & Law in the Middle Ages: A Bibliography of Scholarship. LC 82-49117. 292p. 1985. lib. bdg. 48.00 (ISBN 0-8240-9211-2). Garland Pub.

Alford, Jonathan. The Soviet Union: Security Policies & Constraints. LC 85-2011. (Adelphi Library). 230p. 1985. 27.50 (ISBN 0-312-74901-5). St Martin.

Alford, Jonathan, ed. Arms Control & European Security. LC 83-40153. 160p. 1984. 22.50 (ISBN 0-312-04948-X). St Martin.

--Greece & Turkey: Adversity in Alliance. LC 83-40152. (Adelphi Library). 160p. 1984. 22.50 (ISBN 0-312-34715-4). St Martin.

--The Impact of New Military Technolgy. LC 80-67839. (Adelphi Library: Vol. 4). 140p. 1981. text ed. 33.50x (ISBN 0-916672-74-3). Allanheld.

--Sea Power & Influence: Old Issues & New Challenges. LC 80-67840. (Adelphi Library: Vol. 2). 224p. 1981. text ed. 33.50x (ISBN 0-916672-72-7). Allanheld.

Alford, Lady M. Needlework As Art. (Illus.). 1977. Repr. of 1886 ed. 33.00x (ISBN 0-7158-1072-3). Charles River Bks.

Alford, Leon P. The Laws of Management Applied to Manufacturing. (Management History Ser.: No. 23). 272p. 1974. Repr. of 1928 ed. 22.50 (ISBN 0-87960-035-7). Hive Pub.

Alford, M. H. & Alford, V. L. Russian-English Scientific & Technical Dictionary, 2 vols. LC 73-88348. (Rus. & Eng.). 1970. Set. 60.00 (ISBN 0-08-012227-2). Pergamon.

Alford, Mrs. Henry, ed. Life Journals & Letters of Henry Alford, 2 vols. vii, 542p. Repr. of 1874 ed. Set. 59.00 (ISBN 0-932051-71-5). Am Repr Serv.

Alford, Robert L. Tips on Testing: Strategies for Test-Taking. LC 79-88269. 1979. pap. text ed. 8.00 (ISBN 0-8191-0770-0). U Pr of Amer.

Alford, Robert R. Health Care Politics: Idealogical & Interest Groups Barriers to Reform. LC 74-75611. xiv, 294p. 1975. 27.50x (ISBN 0-226-01379-0); pap. 5.45x (ISBN 0-226-01380-4, Phoen). U of Chicago Pr.

--Party & Society: The Anglo-American Democracies. LC 72-9541. (Illus.). 396p. 1973. Repr. of 1964 ed. lib. bdg. 21.50x (ISBN 0-8371-6584-9, ALPS). Greenwood.

Alford, Robert R. & Friedland, Roger. Powers of Theory: Capitalism, the State & Democracy. 544p. Date not set. price not set (ISBN 0-521-30349-4); pap. price not set (ISBN 0-521-31635-9). Cambridge U Pr.

Alford, Roger C. The NSC800 Microprocessor Cookbook. (Illus.). 280p. 1983. 18.95 (ISBN 0-8306-0502-9, 1502); pap. 12.95 (ISBN 0-8306-1502-4). TAB Bks.

Alford, Steven E. Irony & Logic of the Romantic Imagination. LC 84-47533. (American University Studies III (Comparative Literature): Vol. 13). 180p. (Orig.). 1984. pap. text ed. 19.45 (ISBN 0-8204-0110-2). P Lang Pubs.

Alford, Terry W. Facility Planning, Design, & Construction of Rural Health Centers. LC 78-31993. (Rural Health Center Ser.). (Illus.). 256p. 1979. prof ref 25.00x (ISBN 0-88410-539-3); pap. 13.50x (ISBN 0-88410-545-8). Ballinger Pub.

Alford, Thomas W. Civilization: & the Story of the Shawnees-As Told to Florence Drake. (The Civilization of the American Indian Ser.: Vol. 13). (Illus.). 203p. 1980. 14.95 (ISBN 0-8061-1590-4); pap. 7.95 (ISBN 0-8061-1614-5). U of Okla Pr.

Alford, V. L., jt. auth. see Alford, M. H.

Alford, Violet. The Hobby Horse & Other Animal Masks. (Illus.). 211p. 1978. 15.00x (ISBN 0-8476-6194-6). Rowman.

--Introduction to English Folklore. 1978. Repr. of 1952 ed. lib. bdg. 22.50 (ISBN 0-8495-0105-9). Arden Lib.

--Introduction to English Folklore. LC 75-33843. 1975. Repr. of 1952 ed. lib. bdg. 32.50 (ISBN 0-8414-2893-X). Folcroft.

--Pyrenean Festivals: Calendar Customs, Music & Magic, Drama & Dance. LC 77-87730. 1977. Repr. of 1937 ed. 25.00 (ISBN 0-404-16577-X). AMS Pr.

Alfred Benzon Symposium - 1st. Role of Nucleotides for the Function & Conformation of Enzymes. Kalckar, H. M., et al, eds. 1970. 70.00 (ISBN 0-12-394550-X). Acad Pr.

Alfred Benzon Symposium - 3rd - Copenhagen & Lund, 1970, et al. Ion Homeostasis of the Brain: The Regulation of Hydrogen & Potassium Ion Concentrations in Central Intra- & Extracellular Fluids. Siesjo, B. K. & Sorensen, S. C., eds. 1971. 85.00 (ISBN 0-12-642850-6). Acad Pr.

Alfred Benzon Symposium 5th. Transport Mechanisms in Epithelia. Ussing, H. H., et al, eds. 1973. 65.00 (ISBN 0-12-709550-0). Acad Pr.

Alfred C. Kinsey Institute for Sex Research, Indiana University. Sex Studies Index: 1980. 1982. lib. bdg. 80.00 (ISBN 0-8161-0386-0, Hall Library). G K Hall.

Alfred, J. Tyrone & Cannon-Alfred, C. Medical Handbook for the Layman. 1969. 5.95 (ISBN 0-686-00411-6). Alfred.

Alfred Metzner Verlag GmbH, Frankfurt, jt. auth. see Hoffmann, Dietrich.

Alfred Metzner Verlag GmbH, Frankfurt, jt. auth. see Kolvenbach, Walter.

Alfred, Richard L. & Ivens, Stephen H. A Conceptual Framework for Institutional Research in Community Colleges. 1978. pap. 4.00 (ISBN 0-87447-022-6, 219299). College Bd.

Alfred, Richard L., ed. Institutional Impacts on Campus, Community, & Business Constituencies. LC 81-48566. (Community Colleges Ser.: No. 38). 1982. 8.95x (ISBN 0-87589-884-X). Jossey-Bass.

Alfred The Great. Whole Works of Alfred the Great, 3 Pts. in 2 Vols. Giles, J. A., ed. LC 73-86832. Repr. of 1858 ed. Set. 130.00 (ISBN 0-404-00380-X). Vol. 1 (ISBN 0-404-00381-8). Vol. 2 (ISBN 0-404-00382-6). AMS Pr.

Alfred, the Great. The Works of Alfred the Great, 2 vols. 1977. Set. lib. bdg. 250.00 (ISBN 0-8490-2843-4). Gordon Pr.

Alfreda. The Baby Occasion Uses for the Pledge, Task, Promise, Shower, That Occasion & Other Cards. 6p. (Orig.). 1985. pap. 2.00 (ISBN 0-913597-74-0, Pub. by Alpha Pyramis). Prosperity & Profits.

--Crust Variations, Potpourri Tea, Candy Apple, Rhyming Recipes & Eggplant Topping. 1985. pap. text ed. 1.50 (ISBN 0-318-04371-8). Prosperity & Profits.

--Fundraising Uses for the Promise, Commitment, Favor, Any Occasion & Others. 6p. (Orig.). 1985. pap. 2.00 (ISBN 0-913597-91-0, Pub. by Alpha Pyramis). Prosperity & Profits.

Alfreda, illus. Fruit Wraps: Suggestions for Use Plus Patterns. 10p. 1985. pap. 2.00 (ISBN 0-318-04417-X, Pub. by Alpha Pyramis). Prosperity & Profits.

--Vegetable & Fruit Wraps Pattern Book. 16p. 1985. pap. 3.95 (ISBN 0-318-04419-6, Pub. by Alpha Pyramis). Prosperity & Profits.

Alfredo, Gonzalez W. Dos y Dos Son Cinco y Otras 4 Comedias. LC 80-69553. (Coleccion Teatro). 255p. (Orig., Span.). 1984. pap. 9.95 (ISBN 0-89729-276-6). Ediciones.

Alfrey, T., Jr. Mechanical Behavior of High Polymers, Vol. 6. 1948. 29.50 (ISBN 0-470-39040-9). Krieger.

Alfs, Matthew. Concepts of Father, Son, & Holy Spirit: A Classification & Description of the Trinitarian & Non-Trinitarian Theologies Existent Within Christendom. LC 83-63213. 104p. 1984. lib. bdg. 12.95 (ISBN 0-9612964-0-2); pap. 7.95 (ISBN 0-9612964-1-0). Old Theology Bk Hse.

Alfsen, E. M. Compact Convex Sets & Boundary Integrals. LC 72-136352. (Ergebnisse der Mathematik und Ihrer Grenzgebiete: Vol. 57). (Illus.). 1971. 31.00 (ISBN 0-387-05090-6). Springer-Verlag.

Alfsen, Erik M. & Shultz, Frederick W. Non-Commutative Spectral Theory for Affine Function Spaces on Convex Sets. LC 76-18309. (Memoirs: No. 172). 120p. 1976. pap. 14.00 (ISBN 0-8218-1872-4, MEMO-172). Am Math.

Alft, E. C. Elgin: An American History. (Illus.). 368p. 1985. 14.95 (ISBN 0-916445-09-7). Crossroads Comm.

Alfven, H. Cosmic Plasma. 1981. 39.50 (ISBN 90-277-1151-8, Pub. by Reidel Holland). Kluwer Academic.

Alfven, H. & Arrhenius, G. Structure & Evolutionary History of the Solar System. LC 75-29444. (Geophysics & Astrophysics Monographs: No. 5). xvi, 280p. 1975. lib. bdg. 42.00 (ISBN 90-277-0611-5, Pub. by Reidel Holland); pap. 31.50 (ISBN 90-277-0660-3). Kluwer Academic.

Alfven, Hannes. Atom, Man, & the Universe: The Long Chain of Complications. Hoberman, John, tr. LC 69-15872. 110p. 1969. text ed. 13.95 (ISBN 0-7167-0327-0). W H Freeman.

--On the Origin of the Solar System. LC 72-9604. (International Series of Monographs on Physics). (Illus.). 194p. 1973. Repr. of 1954 ed. lib. bdg. 82.50 (ISBN 0-8371-6595-4, ALOS). Greenwood.

--Worlds-Antiworlds: Antimatter in Cosmology. Feichtner, Rudy, tr. LC 66-27947. (Illus.). 103p. 1966. 13.95 (ISBN 0-7167-0317-3). W H Freeman.

Algar, Ayla E. The Complete Book of Turkish Cooking. (Illus.). 250p. 1985. 29.95 (ISBN 0-7103-0101-4, Kegan Paul International). Routledge & Kegan.

Algar, Hamid. Mirza Malkum Khan: A Biographical Essay in 19th Century Iranian Modernism. LC 78-187750. 1973. 46.50x (ISBN 0-520-02217-3). U of Cal Pr.

--Religion & State in Iran, Seventeen Eighty-Five to Nineteen Six: The Role of the 'Ulama in the Qajar Period. LC 72-79959. (Near Eastern Center, UCLA; Ca. Library Reprint Ser.: No. 106). 1980. 34.50x (ISBN 0-520-04100-3). U of Cal Pr.

Algar, Hamid, jt. ed. see Khouri, Mounah A.

Algar, Hamid, ed. see Mutahhari, Ayatullah M.

Algar, Hamid, ed. see Shariati, Ali.

Algar, Hamid, tr. from Persian. Constitution of the Islamic Republic of Iran. 94p. 1980. 9.95 (ISBN 0-933782-07-1); pap. 2.95 (ISBN 0-933782-02-0). Mizan Pr.

Algar, Hamid, tr. see Khouri, Mounah A. & Algar, Hamid.

Algar, Hamid, tr. see Khumayni, Ruh A.

Algar, Hamid, tr. see Razi, Najm A.

Algar, Hamid, tr. see Shari'ati, Ali.

Algarin, Joanne P. Japanese Folk Literature: A Core Collection. 226p. 1982. 29.95 (ISBN 0-8352-1516-4). Bowker.

Algarin, Miguel. Body Bee Calling from the Twenty-First Century. LC 82-71654. 88p. (Orig.). 1982. pap. 5.00 (ISBN 0-934770-17-4). Arte Publico.

--On Call. 2nd ed. LC 79-9066. (Illus.). 80p. (Orig.). 1980. pap. 5.00x (ISBN 0-934770-03-4). Arte Publico.

--The Time Is Now. LC 83-72575. 80p. (Orig., Eng. & Span.). 1985. pap. 7.00 (ISBN 0-934770-33-6). Arte Publico.

Algarin, Miguel, tr. see Neruda, Pablo.

Algarotti, Francesco. Saggio Sopra la pittura. (Documents of Art & Architectural History, Series 2: Vol. 6). (Ital.). 1981. Repr. of 1763 ed. 27.50 (ISBN 0-686-90615-2). Broude Intl Edns.

Algazi, Linda, jt. auth. see Sklansky, Gloria J.

Algeo, John. Exercises in Contemporary English. 217p. (Orig.). 1974. pap. text ed. 10.95 (ISBN 0-15-512931-7, HC); instructor's key (ISBN 0-15-512932-5). HarBraceJ.

--On Defining the Proper Name. LC 73-9849. (University of Florida Humanities Monographs: No. 41). 94p. 1973. pap. 3.50 (ISBN 0-8130-0410-1). U Presses Fla.

--Problems in the Origins & Development of the English Language. 3rd ed. 288p. 1982. pap. 12.95 (ISBN 0-15-567609-1, HC); instr's key (ISBN 0-15-567610-5). HarBraceJ.

Algeo, John, jt. auth. see Pyles, Thomas.

Algeo, John, ed. Thomas Pyles: Selected Essays on English Usage. LC 78-18833. xiv, 223p. 1979. 18.00 (ISBN 0-8130-0542-6). U Presses Fla.

Algeo, Phillipa, ed. The Best of British Illustrators. 1979. 90.00x (ISBN 0-7148-2070-9, Pub. by Phaidon Pr). State Mutual Bk.

Alger, Abby L., tr. see De Solms, Marie T.

Alger, Chadwick F. & Hoovler, David G. You & Your Community in the World. (CISE Learning Packages in International Studies). 172p. 1978. pap. text ed. 4.00x (ISBN 0-317-34814-0). Learn Res Intl Stud.

Alger, Horatio. Adrift in the City: Or, Oliver Conrad's Plucky Fight. 1976. Repr. of 1895 ed. lib. bdg. 17.95x (ISBN 0-88411-810-X, Pub. by Aeonian Pr). Amereon Ltd.

--Brave & Bold: Or, the Fortunes of a Factory Boy. 1976. Repr. of 1874 ed. lib. bdg. 18.95 (ISBN 0-88411-811-8, Pub. by Aeonian Pr). Amereon Ltd.

--Dean Dunham; or, the Waterford Mystery. 275p. 1974. Repr. of 1891 ed. lib. bdg. 16.95 (ISBN 0-88411-801-0, Pub. by Aeonian Pr). Amereon Ltd.

--Digging the Gold: A Story of California. 1976. Repr. of 1892 ed. lib. bdg. 18.95 (ISBN 0-88411-816-9, Pub. by Aeonian Pr). Amereon Ltd.

--The Disagreeable Woman. 1976. lib. bdg. 11.95 (ISBN 0-88411-809-6, Pub. by Aeonian Pr). Amereon Ltd.

--Erie Train Boy. 249p. 1974. Repr. of 1890 ed. lib. bdg. 15.95x (ISBN 0-88411-802-9, Pub. by Aeonian Pr). Amereon Ltd.

--Frank & Fearless; or, the Fortunes of Jasper Kent. 322p. 1974. Repr. of 1897 ed. lib. bdg. 18.95 (ISBN 0-88411-803-7, Pub. by Aeonian Pr). Amereon Ltd.

--Getting Creamed on Wall Street. LC 85-70691. (Illus.). 60p. (Orig.). 1985. pap. 6.00 (ISBN 0-87034-075-1). Fraser Pub Co.

--Jack's Ward: Or, the Boy Guardian. 1976. Repr. of 1875 ed. lib. bdg. 17.15x (ISBN 0-88411-817-7, Pub. by Aeonian Pr). Amereon Ltd.

--Jed, the Poorhouse Boy. 1976. Repr. of 1889 ed. lib. bdg. 19.95 (ISBN 0-88411-814-2, Pub. by Aeonian Pr). Amereon Ltd.

--Luke Walton: Or, the Chicago Newsboy. 1976. Repr. of 1889 ed. lib. bdg. 18.95 (ISBN 0-88411-813-4, Pub. by Aeonian Pr). Amereon Ltd.

--Mark Manning's Mission; or, the Story of a Shoe Factory Boy. 268p. 1974. Repr. of 1905 ed. lib. bdg. 16.95 (ISBN 0-88411-804-5, Pub. by Aeonian Pr). Amereon Ltd.

--Phil the Fiddler: Or, the Story of a Young Street Musician. 1976. Repr. of 1872 ed. lib. bdg. 14.85x (ISBN 0-88411-815-0, Pub. by Aeonian Pr). Amereon Ltd.

--Ragged Dick & Mark the Matchboy. LC 62-21187. 382p. (Orig.). 1962. pap. 4.95 (ISBN 0-02-041390-4, Collier). Macmillan.

--Ralph Raymond's Heir. 125p. 1974. Repr. of 1892 ed. lib. bdg. 15.95x (ISBN 0-88411-805-3, Pub. by Aeonian Pr). Amereon Ltd.

--Rolling Stone; or, the Adventures of Wanderer. 294p. 1974. Repr. of 1902 ed. lib. bdg. 16.95x (ISBN 0-88411-806-1, Pub. by Aeonian Pr). Amereon Ltd.

--Tom, the Bootblack: Or, the Road to Success. 1976. Repr. of 1878 ed. lib. bdg. 15.95x (ISBN 0-88411-812-6). Amereon Ltd.

--The Train Boy. 1975. Repr. of 1883 ed. lib. bdg. 16.95x (ISBN 0-88411-807-X, Pub. by Aeonian Pr). Amereon Ltd.

--Young Captain Jack; or, Son of a Soldier. 267p. 1974. Repr. of 1901 ed. lib. bdg. 14.95x (ISBN 0-88411-808-8, Pub. by Aeonian Pr). Amereon Ltd.

Alger, Horatio, Jr. Alger Street: The Collected Poetry of Horatio Alger, Jr. Westgard, Gilbert K., 2nd, ed. 1964. 10.00x (ISBN 0-910324-08-5); leather, signed, limited ed. 25.00x (ISBN 0-910324-09-3). Canner.

--Bertha's Christmas Vision: An Autumn Sheaf. (Illus.). 248p. 1978. Repr. of 1856 ed. 22.50 (ISBN 0-686-35748-5). G K Westgard.

--The Disagreeable Woman: A Social Mystery. 190p. 1978. Repr. of 1895 ed. 24.00 (ISBN 0-686-35752-3). G K Westgard.

--Grand'ther Baldwin's Thanksgiving with Other Ballads & Poems. 125p. 1978. Repr. of 1875 ed. 16.50 (ISBN 0-686-35750-7). G K Westgard.

--Hugo, the Deformed. (Illus.). 84p. 1978. 19.50 (ISBN 0-686-37019-8). G K Westgard.

--Making His Mark. (Illus.). 307p. 1979. Repr. of 1901 ed. 30.00 (ISBN 0-686-35753-1). G K Westgard.

--Making His Way: Frank Courtney's Struggle Upward. LC 74-15724. (Popular Culture in America Ser.). 290p. 1975. Repr. 18.00x (ISBN 0-405-06361-X). Ayer Co Pubs.

--The New Schoolma'am: A Summer in North Sparta. 140p. 1976. Repr. of 1877 ed. 18.75 (ISBN 0-686-37020-1). G K Westgard.

--Nothing to Do: A Tilt at Our Best Society. (Illus.). 45p. 1978. Repr. of 1857 ed. 15.00 (ISBN 0-686-37021-X). G K Westgard.

--Number Ninety-One: The Adventures of a New York Telegraph Boy. (Illus.). 205p. 1977. Repr. of 1889 ed. 19.50 (ISBN 0-686-37022-8). G K Westgard.

--Ragged Dick & Struggling Upward. Bode, Carl, ed. (American Library). 304p. 1985. pap. 4.95 (ISBN 0-14-039033-2). Penguin.

--Struggling Upward or Luke Larkin's Luck. 160p. 1984. pap. 3.95 (ISBN 0-486-24737-6). Dover.

--Timothy Crump's Ward: The New Years Loan & What Became of It. 188p. 1977. Repr. of 1866 ed. 24.00 (ISBN 0-686-37023-6). G K Westgard.

--Tom Tracy: The Trials of a New York Newsboy. (Illus.). 208p. 1978. Repr. of 1888 ed. 21.00 (ISBN 0-686-35749-3). G K Westgard.

--Wait & Win: The Story of Jack Drumond's Fluck. (Illus.). 279p. 1979. Repr. of 1908 ed. 27.75 (ISBN 0-686-35756-6). G K Westgard.

Alger, Horatio, Sr. & Sheaf, J. P., Jr. Addresses Delivered at the Semi-Centennial Celebration of the Dedication of the First Unitarian Church, South Natick (Massachusetts) November 20, 1878. (Illus.). 41p. 1977. pap. 6.00 (ISBN 0-686-35760-4). G K Westgard.

Alger, John G. Napoleon's British Visitors & Captives, 1801-1815. LC 71-113541. Repr. of 1904 ed. 19.50 (ISBN 0-404-00324-9). AMS Pr.

--Paris in Seventeen Eighty-Nine to Seventeen Ninety-Four, Farewell Letters of Victims of the Guillotine. LC 78-113540. Repr. of 1902 ed. 34.50 (ISBN 0-404-00323-0). AMS Pr.

Alger, John I. The Quest for Victory: The History of the Principles of War. LC 81-13319. (Contributions in Military History Ser.: NO. 30). 344p. 1982. lib. bdg. 37.50 (ISBN 0-313-23322-5, AMM/). Greenwood.

Alger, Linda & Sanders, Priscilla. Good Health-Naturally! LC 83-80405. 144p. 1983. pap. 7.95 (ISBN 0-88290-217-2). Horizon-Utah.

Alger, P. L. Steinmetz: The Philosopher. 194p. 1965. 47.75 (ISBN 0-677-65170-8). Gordon.

Alger, Philip L. Induction Machines: Behavior & Uses. 2nd ed. 526p. 1970. 93.75 (ISBN 0-677-02390-1). Gordon.

Alger, Philip L., ed. The Human Side of Engineering. 170p. 1972. 46.25 (ISBN 0-677-65180-5). Gordon.

Alger, R. A. The Spanish-American War. 1976. lib. bdg. 59.95 (ISBN 0-8490-2644-X). Gordon Pr.

Alger, Ralph K. Basic Skills in Grammar, 2 Bks. (Illus.). pap. text ed. 4.87 ea.; Bk. 1. pap. text ed. (ISBN 0-8428-0004-2); Bk. 2. pap. text ed. (ISBN 0-8428-0005-0); Bk. 1. key 2.00 (ISBN 0-8428-0031-X); Bk. 2. key 2.00 (ISBN 0-8428-0032-8). Cambridge Bk.

Alger, Raymond S. Electron Paramagnetic Resonance: Techniques & Applications. LC 67-20255. pap. 150.50 (ISBN 0-317-08506-9, 2010180). Bks Demand UMI.

Alger, Russell A. Spanish-American War. facsimile ed. LC 78-146850. (Select Bibliographies Reprint Ser). Repr. of 1901 ed. 33.00 (ISBN 0-8369-5617-6). Ayer Co Pubs.

Alger, William R. Destiny of the Soul: Critical History of the Doctrine of a Future Life, 2 Vols. 10th ed. LC 68-19263. 1968. Repr. of 1880 ed. Set. lib. bdg. 43.25x (ISBN 0-8371-0003-8, ALDS). Greenwood.

--Life of Edwin Forest, 2 vols. LC 76-84505. 1877. Set. 44.00 (ISBN 0-405-08198-7, Pub. by Blom); 22.00 ea. Vol. 1 (ISBN 0-405-08199-5). Vol. 2 (ISBN 0-405-08200-2). Ayer Co Pubs.

Algerin, Miguel & Pinero, Miguel, eds. Nuyorican Poetry: An Anthology of Puerto Rican Words & Feelings. LC 75-22390. (Illus.). 192p. 1975. pap. 2.95 (ISBN 0-688-07966-0). Morrow.

Algernon, Cecil. Six Oxford Thinkers (Edward Gibbon, John Henry Newman, R. W. Church, James Anthony Froude, Walter Pater, Lord Morley of Blackburn) (Victorian Age Ser). 1909. Repr. 20.00 (ISBN 0-8482-3259-3). Norwood Edns.

Al-Ghazali. The Duties of Brotherhood in Islam. Holland, Muhtar, tr. from Arabic. 95p. (Orig.). 1980. pap. 4.50x (ISBN 0-86037-068-2, Pub. by Islamic Found UK). New Era Pubns MI.

--Inner Dimensions of Islamic Worship. Holland, Muhtar, tr. from Arabic. 142p. (Orig.). 1983. pap. 7.00x (ISBN 0-86037-125-5, Pub. by Islamic Found UK). New Era Pubns MI.

--On the Duties of Brotherhood. (ISBN 0-686-83895-5). Kazi Pubns.

Al-Ghazali, tr. see McCarthy, Richard J.

Al-Ghazzal, see Ghazzali, Al.

Al-Ghazzali. Alchemy of Happiness. 1964. 3.25x (ISBN 0-87902-055-5). Orientalia.

--The Book of Knowledge. 1970. 14.00x (ISBN 0-87902-106-3). Orientalia.

--Confessions of Al-Ghazzali. Watt, W. M., tr. 2.75x (ISBN 0-87902-059-8). Orientalia.

--Foundations of the Articles of Faith. 1969. 6.50x (ISBN 0-87902-058-X). Orientalia.

--Just Balance. 6.50 (ISBN 0-317-01603-2). Kazi Pubns.

--Mishkat Al-Anwar: A Niche for Lights. 1952. 3.95x (ISBN 0-87902-051-2). Orientalia.

--The Mysteries of Almsgiving. Faris, Nabik A., tr. 1966. 12.95x (ISBN 0-8156-6002-2, Am U Beirut). Syracuse U Pr.

--Mysteries of Fasting. 1970. 3.00x (ISBN 0-87902-052-0). Orientalia.

--Mysteries of Purity. 1966. 4.00x (ISBN 0-87902-053-9). Orientalia.

--On Divine Predicates & Their Attributes. 1970. 5.50x (ISBN 0-87902-057-1). Orientalia.

--Some Moral & Religious Teachings. 4.25x (ISBN 0-87902-056-3). Orientalia.

--Tahafut Al-Falasifah. 7.25x (ISBN 0-87902-054-7). Orientalia.

--Worship in Islam. Calverley, Edwin E., ed. LC 79-2860. 242p. 1981. Repr. of 1925 ed. 21.25 (ISBN 0-8305-0032-4). Hyperion Conn.

Al-Ghazzali, see Ghazzali, Al.

Al-Ghazzali, Muhammad. Our Beginning in Wisdom. 1975. Repr. lib. bdg. 18.00x (ISBN 0-374-90114-7). Octagon.

Algier, Ann S. & Algier, Keith W., eds. Improving Reading & Study Skills. LC 81-48565. (College Learning Assistance Ser.: No. 8). 1982. 9.95x (ISBN 0-87589-880-7). Jossey-Bass.

Algier, Keith W., jt. ed. see Algier, Ann S.

Algire, Tom, photos by. Wisconsin. LC 80-85370. (Illus.). 128p. (Text by Justin Isherwood). 1981. 28.50 (ISBN 0-912856-67-X). Graphic Arts Ctr.

Al-Gita, Kashif, ed. The Shia Origin & Faith. Haq, M. Fazal, tr. from Arabic. 284p. 1984. pap. 7.50 (ISBN 0-941724-23-9). Islamic Seminary.

Algosaibi, Ghazi, ed. & tr. from Arabic. Lyrics from Arabia. LC 82-74255. 125p. 1983. text ed. 15.00x (ISBN 0-89410-379-2); pap. 8.00x (ISBN 0-89410-380-6). Three Continents.

Algosaibi, Ghazi, ed. Lyrics from Arabia. Saleem, Qazi, tr. LC 84-51201. (Illus.). 100p. (Eng. & Arabic & Urdu.). 1985. 17.00 (ISBN 0-89410-446-2); pap. 8.00 (ISBN 0-89410-447-0). Three Continents.

Algosaibi, Ghazi A. Arabian Essays. 120p. 1982. 19.95x (ISBN 0-7103-0019-0, Kegan Paul). Routledge & Kegan.

--Arabian Essays. 120p. 1985. pap. 10.95x (ISBN 0-7103-0126-X, Kegan Paul International). Routledge & Kegan.

Algozin, Bruce. Blood Knot. (Orig.). 1982. pap. 2.95 (ISBN 0-8217-1073-7). Zebra.

--Lair of the Lich. LC 84-91356. (Endless Quest Books Ser.). (Illus.). 160p. (gr. 4-7). 1985. pap. 2.25 (ISBN 0-394-73964-7). Random.

Algozin, Keith, ed. see Rubel, Maximilien.

Algozzine, Bob, et al. Childhood Behavior Disorders: Applied Research & Educational Practice. LC 81-4360. 399p. 1981. text ed. 33.00 (ISBN 0-89443-345-8). Aspen Systems.

Algozzine, Robert. Problem Behavior Management: Educator's Resource Service. LC 82-1663. 350p. 1982. text ed. 85.00 looseleaf updated semi-annually (ISBN 0-89443-678-3). Aspen Systems.

Algozzine, Robert, jt. auth. see Ysselyke, James E.

Algren, Axel B., jt. auth. see Rowley, Frank B.

Algren, N. Chicago: City on the Make. 112p. 1983. pap. 5.95 (ISBN 0-07-001012-9). McGraw.

Algren, Nelson. The Devil's Stocking: A Last Interview by W. J. Weatherby. 1983. 16.95 (ISBN 0-87795-547-6); pap. 9.95 (ISBN 0-87795-548-4). Arbor Hse.

--The Man with the Golden Arm. 368p. 1977. pap. 5.95 (ISBN 0-14-004523-6). Penguin.

--The Neon Wilderness. 1960. 16.00 (ISBN 0-8446-1014-3). Peter Smith.

--A Walk on the Wild Side. LC 78-509. 346p. 1978. Repr. of 1956 ed. lib. bdg. 22.50x (ISBN 0-313-20294-X, ALWW). Greenwood.

--A Walk on the Wild Side. 352p. 1977. pap. 5.95 (ISBN 0-14-003565-6). Penguin.

Al-Hadad, Sabah. Agricultural Mathematics. 168p. 1981. pap. text ed. 10.95 (ISBN 0-8403-2450-2). Kendall-Hunt.

Al-Hadad, Sabah & Scott, C. H. College Algebra with Applications. 1978. text ed. 22.95 (ISBN 0-316-02044-3); tchr's. manur' avail. (ISBN 0-316-02045-1). Little.

Al-Haddad, Abdul-Rahman. Cultural Policy in the Yemen Arab Republic. (Studies & Documents on Cultural Policies). 74p. 1982. pap. text ed. 9.25 (ISBN 92-3-101976-7, U1267, UNESCO). Unipub.

Alhadeff, David A. Microeconomics & Human Behavior: Toward a New Synthesis of Economics & Psychology. LC 81-3356. (Illus.). 264p. 1982. 30.00x (ISBN 0-520-04353-7). U of Cal Pr.

--Monopoly & Competition in Banking. Bruchey, Stuart, ed. LC 80-1129. (The Rise of Commerical Banking Ser.). (Illus.). 1981. Repr. of 1954 ed. lib. bdg. 23.00x (ISBN 0-405-13629-3). Ayer Co Pubs.

Alhaji Sir Dawda Kairaba Jawara. The Shining Diadem. 75.00x (ISBN 0-86036-193-4, Pub. by R Collings UK). State Mutual Bk.

Al-Hajj, H., jt. auth. see Lufty, R.

Al-Hajj, H. A. Microscopic Techniques. 137p. (Arabic.). 1982. pap. 7.00 (ISBN 0-471-09671-7). Wiley.

Al-Hakim, Tawfig. The Return of Consciousness. Winder, Bayly, tr. from Arabic. (Studies in Near Eastern Civilization). 192p. 1985. 30.00x (ISBN 0-8147-1072-7). NYU Pr.

Al-Hakim, Tawfiq. Plays, Prefaces & Postscripts of Tawfiq Al-Hakim: Vol. 1-Theater of the Mind. Hutchins, William M., tr. LC 80-80887. 316p. (Orig.). 1981. 25.00 (ISBN 0-89410-148-X); pap. 12.00 (ISBN 0-89410-134-X). Three Continents.

--Plays, Prefaces & Postscripts of Tawfiq al-Hakim: Vol. 2-Theater of Society. Hutchins, William M., tr. LC 80-80887. (Orig.). 1984. 25.00 (ISBN 0-89410-280-X); pap. 12.00 (ISBN 0-89410-147-1). Three Continents.

--The Tree Climber: A Play. 2nd ed. Johnson-Davis, Denys, tr. from Arabic. LC 82-74256. (Illus.). 100p. 1985. 12.00 (ISBN 0-89410-204-4); pap. 7.00 (ISBN 0-89410-205-2). Three Continents.

Al-Hakim, Tewfik. Fate of a Cockroach & Other Plays. Johnson-Davies, Denys, tr. from Arabic. 184p. 1980. 15.00 (ISBN 0-89410-196-X); pap. 7.00 (ISBN 0-89410-197-8). Three Continents.

Alhambra. Diccionario Arabe-Espanol, Espanol-Arabe. 1252p. (Arabic & Span.). 17.95 (ISBN 84-303-0163-1, S-50424). French & Eur.

Al-Hamdani & Al-Hasan Ibn Ahmad. The Antiquities of South Arabia. Fairs, Nabih A., tr. from Arabic. LC 79-2864. (Illus.). 119p. 1981. Repr. of 1938 ed. 15.00 (ISBN 0-8305-0033-2). Hyperion Conn.

Alhamisi, Ahmed A. Holy Ghosts. new ed. LC 74-141234. 63p. 1972. 4.50 (ISBN 0-910296-38-3); pap. 2.50 (ISBN 0-685-26701-6). Broadside.

Alhamisi, Ahmed L. The Black Narrator. (Black Arts Publication Ser). 1966. pap. 1.00 (ISBN 0-685-42973-3). Broadside.

Al-Harizi, Judah. Tahkemoni of Judah Al-Harizi, Vol. 1. 1975. 14.95x (ISBN 0-8197-0055-X). Bloch.

--Tahkemoni of Judah Al-Harizi, Vol. 2. Reichert, Victor E., tr. from Heb. LC 65-1135. (Illus.). 504p. 1974. Vol. 2. 14.95x (ISBN 0-8197-0373-7). Bloch.

Al-Hasan Ibn Ahmad, jt. auth. see Al-Hamdani.

Alhashim, Dhia & Robertson, James W. Contemporary Issues in Accounting. LC 79-9840. (ITT Key Issue Lecture Ser.). 296p. 1979. text ed. 18.08 scp (ISBN 0-672-97331-6); pap. text ed. 10.28 scp (ISBN 0-672-97332-4). Bobbs.

Alhashim, Dhia D. & Robertson, James W. Accounting for Multinational Enterprises. LC 77-13732. (Key Issues Lecture Ser). 1978. scp o.p. 19.96 (ISBN 0-672-97209-3); pap. 11.49 scp (ISBN 0-672-97183-6). Bobbs.

AlHashim, Dhia D., jt. auth. see Arpan, Jeffrey S.

Al-Hassani, S. T., jt. ed. see Niku-Lari, A.

Alhazen. Opticae Thesaurus: Alhazeni Arabis Libri Septem, Nunc Primum Editi, Eiusdem Liber De Crepusculis et Nubium Ascensionibus. (Lat). Repr. of 1572 ed. 75.00 (ISBN 0-384-00730-9). Johnson Repr.

Alheritiere, Dominique. Environmental Impact Assessment & Agricultural Development: A Comparative Law Study. (Environment Papers: No. 2). 139p. (Eng. & Fr.). 1982. pap. 10.00 (ISBN 92-5-101110-9, F2292, FAO). Unipub.

Al-Hibri, A. Women & Islam. 106p. 1982. 19.50 (ISBN 0-08-027928-7). Pergamon.

Al-Hibri, A., ed. Hypatia, Issue No. 2. 100p. 1985. pap. 17.50 (ISBN 0-08-031851-7). Pergamon.

Al-Hibri, Azizah. Deontic Logic: A Comprehensive Appraisal & a View Proposal. LC 78-66422. 1978. pap. text ed. 11.00 (ISBN 0-8191-0303-9). U Pr of Amer.

Al-Hibri, Azizah, jt. auth. see Hickman, Larry.

Al-Hilali, Muhammad T., tr. from Arabic. Interpretation of the Meaning of "The Noble Qur'an", Vol. 1. (Illus.). 650p. 1986. 49.95x (ISBN 0-934905-00-2). Lawletters.

Al-Himyari, Ibn. Al-Rawd al-Mi'tar FiKhabar al-Aqtar. (Arabic.). 1975. 40.00x (ISBN 0-86685-358-8). Intl Bk Ctr.

Al-Husaini, Ishak M. The Moslem Brethren: The Greatest of the Modern Islamic Movements. LC 79-2866. 186p. 1981. Repr. of 1956 ed. 19.75 (ISBN 0-8305-0039-1). Hyperion Conn.

Al-Husayn al-Sulami, Ibn. The Book of Sufi Chivalry: Lessons to a Son of the Moment (Futuwwah) Bayrak, Tosun, tr. from Arabic. 1983. 8.95 (ISBN 0-89281-031-9). Inner Tradit.

Al-Husry, Khaldun S. Origins of Modern Arab Political Thought. LC 80-11794. Repr. of 1966 ed. 25.00x (ISBN 0-88206-037-6). Caravan Bks.

Ali, A. Ibn-As-Sikkit. pap. 1.25 (ISBN 0-686-18321-5). Kazi Pubns.

Ali, A., jt. ed. see Mamak, A.

Ali, A. A. Holy Qur'an, 2 Vols. 25.50x (ISBN 0-87902-038-5). Orientalia.

Ali, A. Yusuf, tr. Qur'an: The Holy. 1862p. (Eng. & Arabic.). 1983. text ed. 20.00 (ISBN 0-940368-32-3); pap. 10.00 (ISBN 0-940368-31-5). Tahrike Tarsile Quran.

Ali, Aamir. Assignment in Kashmir. (Orient Paperbacks Ser.). 200p. 1973. pap. 2.95 (ISBN 0-88253-246-4). Ind-US Inc.

ALI-ABA & American Association of Museums. Legal Problems of Museum Administration: Course of Study Transcripts. No. B224 - 1973. pap. 20.00 (ISBN 0-317-31042-9); No. B225 - 1974. pap. 20.00 (ISBN 0-317-31043-7); No. B226 - 1975. pap. 20.00 (ISBN 0-317-31044-5). Am Law Inst.

ALI-ABA Committee on Continuing Professional Education & Environmental Law Institute. Water & Air Pollution: ALI-ABA Course of Study Materials. LC 83-169811. (Illus.). ciii, 539p. Date not set. 40.00. Am Law Inst.

Ali, Abdullah. The Spirit & the Future of Islam, 2 vols. 155p. 1983. Set. 187.50x (ISBN 0-86722-051-1). Inst Econ Pol.

Ali, Abdullah Y. & Ali, Abdullah Y. The Meaning of the Glorious Qur'an, 2 Vols. Set. 24.00 (ISBN 0-686-37146-1). New World Press NY.

Ali, Abdullah Yusuf. A Cultural History of India During the British Period. LC 75-41006. Repr. of 1940 ed. 25.50 (ISBN 0-404-14723-2). AMS Pr.

Ali, Agha S. Bone-Sculpture. (Writers Workshop Redbird Ser.). 32p. 1975. Ind-US Inc.

Ali, Ahmed. Twilight in Delhi. 2nd ed. 290p. 1974. pap. 3.50 (ISBN 0-88253-281-2). Ind-US Inc.

--Twilight in Delhi. 320p. 1985. pap. 13.95x (ISBN 0-19-577328-4). Oxford U Pr.

Ali, Ahmed, ed. & tr. from Urdu. The Golden Tradition: An Anthology of Urdu Poetry. LC 72-10181. (Studies in Oriental Culture). 350p. 1973. 29.00x (ISBN 0-231-03687-6); pap. 10.00x (ISBN 0-231-03688-4). Columbia U Pr.

Ali, Asghar & Kumar, Krishan. Bibliography. 2nd rev. ed. 1980. text ed. 15.00x (ISBN 0-7069-0738-8, Pub. by Vikas India). Advent NY.

Ali, B. Hajjat-ul-Wada: Last Sermon. 1981. 1.25 (ISBN 0-686-97858-7). Kazi Pubns.

Ali, Chaudhri M. The Emergence of Pakistan. LC 79-163081. 418p. 1967. 35.00x (ISBN 0-231-02933-0). Columbia U Pr.

Ali, D. S., et al. Aspects of Medical Education in Developing Countries: Selected Papers Presented at the 2nd WHO Conference on Medical Education in the Eastern Mediterranean Region. (Public Health Papers Ser: No. 47). 113p. 1972. pap. 3.20 (ISBN 92-4-130047-7, 545). World Health.

Ali, Florence. Opposing Absolutes: Conviction & Convention in John Ford's Plays. (Salzburg Studies in English Literature, Jacobean Drama Studies: No.44). 1974. pap. text ed. 25.50x (ISBN 0-391-01295-9). Humanities.

Ali, Hazrat, jt. auth. see Muhammad.

Ali, I. Parents Guide. pap. 1.25 (ISBN 0-686-18435-1). Kazi Pubns.

Ali, Jamil. Determination of the Coordinates of Positions for the Correction of Distances Between Cities. 1967. 24.95x (ISBN 0-8156-6007-3, Am U Beirut). Syracuse U Pr.

Ali, Kamil, jt. auth. see Stanton, Timothy.

Ali, Khalid. Against All Odds. 1985. pap. 7.00 (ISBN 0-682-40183-8). Exposition Pr FL.

--A Second Chance. 1982. 7.95 (ISBN 0-533-05102-9). Vantage.

Ali, M., jt. auth. see Katyal, K. K.

Ali, M. A. & Anctil, M. Retinas of Fishes: An Atlas. LC 76-22204. (Illus.). 1976. 71.00 (ISBN 0-387-07840-1). Springer-Verlag.

Ali, M. A., ed. Environmental Physiology of Fishes. LC 80-22156. (NATO ASI Series A, Life Sciences: Vol. 35). 734p. 1981. 89.50x (ISBN 0-306-40574-1, Plenum Pr). Plenum Pub.

--Photoreception & Vision in Invertebrates. (NATO ASI Ser. A: Life Sciences: Vol. 74). 868p. 1984. 115.00 (ISBN 0-306-41626-3, Plenum Pr). Plenum Pub.

--Sensory Ecology: Review & Perspectives. LC 78-17597. (NATO ASI Series A, Life Sciences: Vol. 18). 607p. 1978. 69.50x (ISBN 0-306-40024-3, Plenum Pr). Plenum Pub.

--Vision in Fishes - New Approaches in Research. LC 75-8570. (Nato ASI Series A, Life Sciences: Vol. 1). 850p. 1975. 89.50x (ISBN 0-306-35601-5, Plenum Pr). Plenum Pub.

Ali, M. Athar. The Apparatus of Empire: Appointments & Titles in the Mughal Empire, 1574-1658. 400p. 1984. 74.00 (ISBN 0-19-561500-X). Oxford U Pr.

Ali, M. Khalil & Ewer, Michael S. Cancer & the Cardiopulmonary System. 254p. 1984. text ed. 54.50 (ISBN 0-89004-606-9). Raven.

Ali, M. M. Introduction to the Study of the Holy Qur'an. 4.95x (ISBN 0-87902-040-7). Orientalia.

Ali, Majid. FMG-VQE: Vol. 1, Basic Sciences. 2nd ed. 1983. pap. text ed. 16.95. Med Exam.

Ali, Majid & Fayemi, A. Olusegun. The Pathology of Maintenance Hemodialysis. (Illus.). 406p. 1982. 39.75x (ISBN 0-398-04588-7). C C Thomas.

Ali, Majid, et al. FMG Exam Review, Vol. 1: Basic Sciences. LC 78-61617. 1978. pap. 16.95 (ISBN 0-87488-124-2). Med Exam.

--Surgical Pathology Case Studies, Vol. 1. 1978. spiral bdg. 25.50 (ISBN 0-87488-068-8). Med Exam.

--Surgical Pathology Case Studies, Vol. 2. 1978. spiral bdg. 25.50 (ISBN 0-87488-089-0). Med Exam.

Ali, Masur & Pitre, B. G. Secondary Biology Workshop. 218p. 1981. 40.00 (ISBN 0-86131-054-3, Pub. by Orient Longman India). State Mutual Bk.

Ali, Maulana. A Manual of Hadith. (Arabic, Eng.). 1983. 15.00x (ISBN 0-7007-0110-9). Intl Bk Ctr.

Ali, Mir Amed, tr. from Arabic. The Message of the Qur'an. LC 82-80220. 660p. 1982. 15.00 (ISBN 0-940368-14-5); pap. 9.00 (ISBN 0-940368-13-7). Tahrike Tarsile Quran.

Ali, Mohamed. Ecological & Physiological Studies on the Alfalfa Ladybird. 1981. 50.00x (ISBN 0-569-08553-5, Pub. by Collet's). State Mutual Bk.

--Ecological & Physiological Studies on the Alfalfa Ladybird. 1979. 20.00 (ISBN 0-9960015-8-1, Pub. by Akademiai Kaido Hungary). Heyden.

Ali, Muhammad K., ed. Islamic Unity & Happiness. Pazargali, Alaedin, tr. from Persian. 1985. pap. 3.95 (ISBN 0-940368-47-1). Tahrike Tarsile Quran.

Ali, Muhammed K., ed. see Mutahhari, Murtaza.

Ali, Muhsin J. Scheherazade in England: A Study of Nineteenth-Century English Criticism of the Arabian Nights. LC 81-51662. (Illus.). 187p. (Orig.). 1981. 20.00x (ISBN 0-89410-246-X); pap. 10.00x (ISBN 0-89410-247-8). Three Continents.

Ali, N., et al. Transactions of the Moscow Mathematical Society, 1975. LC 65-4713. 1977. 62.00 (ISBN 0-8218-1632-2, MOSCOW-32). Am Math.

Ali, S. Teach Yourself Arabic. 9.50 (ISBN 0-686-83575-1). Kazi Pubns.

Ali, S. A. Resources for Future Economic Growth. 1979. text ed. 10.50x (ISBN 0-7069-0746-9, Pub. by Vikas India). Advent NY.

Ali, S. Husin. The Malays: Their Problems & Future. (Heinemann Asian Studies Ser.). viii, 143p. (Orig.). 1981. pap. 7.50x (ISBN 0-686-79033-2, 00153). Heinemann Ed.

Ali, S. V. Husain the Savior of Islam. LC 81-51900. 252p. 1981. 5.95 (ISBN 0-940368-05-6); pap. 3.95 (ISBN 0-940368-03-X). Tahrike Tarsile Quran.

Ali, S. V., tr. from Arabic. The Holy Qur'an. 550p. 1981. text ed. 9.00 (ISBN 0-940368-08-0); pap. 3.95 (ISBN 0-940368-07-2). Tahrike Tarsile Quran.

Ali, Salim. Fieldguide to the Birds of the Eastern Himalayas. (Illus.). 1978. 24.00x (ISBN 0-19-560595-0). Oxford U Pr.

Ali, Salim & Ripley, Dillon. Compact Edition of the Handbook of the Birds of India & Pakistan, Together with Those of Bangladesh, Nepal, Bhutan & Sri Lanka. (Illus.). 1983. 98.00x (ISBN 0-19-561245-0). Oxford U Pr.

Ali, Salim & Ripley, Dillon S. Handbook of the Birds of India & P akistan: Frogmouths to Pittas, Vol. 4. 2nd ed. (Illus.). 268p. 1983. 37.50x (ISBN 0-19-561551-4). Oxford U Pr.

Ali, Salim & Ripley, S. D. Handbook of the Birds of India & Pakistan, Vol. II: Megapodes to Crab Plover. 2nd ed. (Illus.). 1980. 37.50x (ISBN 0-19-561201-9). Oxford U Pr.

Ali, Salim & Ripley, S. Dillon. Handbook of the Birds of India & Pakistan: Together with Those of Nepal, Sikkim, Bhutan, & Ceylon, 10 vols. Incl. Vol. 2. Megapodes to Crab Plover. 362p. 1969; Vol. 3. Stone Curlews to Owls. 2nd ed. 1981. 37.50x (ISBN 0-19-561302-3); Vol. 4. Frogmouths to Pittas. 1970. 23.75x (ISBN 0-19-635275-4); Vol. 5. Larks to the Grey Hypocolius. 1972. 29.50x (ISBN 0-19-560166-1); Vol. 6. Cuckoo-Shrikes to Babaxes. 1971. 23.50x (ISBN 0-19-560101-7); Vol. 7. Laughing Thrushes to the Mangrove Whistler. 1972. 29.50x (ISBN 0-19-560263-3); Vol. 8. Warblers to Redstarts. 294p. 1973. 29.50x (ISBN 0-19-560291-9); Vol. 9. Robins to Wagtails. 322p. 1973. 29.50x (ISBN 0-19-560349-4); Vol. 10. Flowerpeckers to Buntings. 1974. 29.50x (ISBN 0-19-560385-0). (Illus.). Oxford U Pr.

--Handbook of the Birds of India & Pakistan: Vol. 1, Divers to Hawks. 2nd ed. (Illus.). 1978. 37.50x (ISBN 0-19-561115-2). Oxford U Pr.

Ali, Shahrazad. How Not to Eat Pork: Or Life Without the Pig. LC 85-70171. (Illus.). 120p. (Orig.). 1985. pap. 5.95 (ISBN 0-933405-00-6). Civilized Pubns.

Ali, Shanti S. & Ramchandani, R. R., eds. India & the Western Indian Ocean States: Towards Regional Cooperation in Development. 310p. 1981. 27.50x (ISBN 0-940500-85-X, Pub by Allied Pubs India). Asia Bk Corp.

Ali, Shaukat. Islamic Resurgence: A Short Essay & Bibliography. (Bibliography Ser.: No. 5). (Orig.). 1985. pap. 5.50 (ISBN 0-937694-68-1). Assn Arab-Amer U Grads.

Ali, Sheikh R. & Elliot, Jeffrey M. The Trilemma of World Oil Politics. LC 84-275. (Great Issues of the Day Ser.: No. 2). 192p. (Orig.). 1985. lib. bdg. 19.95x (ISBN 0-89370-168-8); pap. text ed. 9.95x (ISBN 0-89370-268-4). Borgo Pr.

Ali, Sheikh R., jt. auth. see Elliot, Jeffrey M.

Ali, Syed A. The Spirit of Islam: A History of the Evolution & Ideals of Islam with a Life of the Prophet. rev ed. 515p. 1974. Repr. of 1922 ed. text ed. 17.50x (ISBN 0-391-00341-0). Humanities.

Ali, Syed A. & Arif, Abu A. Labor Migration from Bangladesh to the Middle East. (Working Paper: No. 454). 396p. 1981. 5.00 (ISBN 0-686-36046-X, WP-0454). World Bank.

Ali, Syed A., tr. see Imam, Zainul A.

Ali, Tariq. Can Pakistan Survive? The Death of a State. 238p. 1984. 19.50 (ISBN 0-8052-7194-5, Pub. by NLB England); pap. 7.95 (ISBN 0-8052-7195-3). Schocken.

--An Indian Dynasty: The Story of the Nehru-Gandhi Family. 1985. 17.95 (ISBN 0-399-13074-8, Putnam). Putnam Pub Group.

--Trotsky for Beginners. (Illus.). 1980. 8.95 (ISBN 0-394-50921-8); pap. 4.95 (ISBN 0-394-73885-3). Pantheon.

Ali, Tariq, ed. The Stalinist Legacy: Its Impact on Twentieth Century World Politics. (History Ser.). 560p. 1985. pap. 7.95 (ISBN 0-14-022429-7). Penguin.

--The Stalinist Legacy: Its Impact on Twentieth Century World Politics. LC 85-14300. 551p. 1985. Repr. of 1984 ed. lib. bdg. 37.50x (ISBN 0-931477-56-5). Lynne Rienner.

Ali, Waleed, jt. auth. see Cepican, Bob.

Ali, Yousuf. Holy Quran. 450.00 (ISBN 0-317-14645-9). Kazi Pubns.

--The Holy Quran with Arabic Text Commentary & Translation. 25.75 (ISBN 0-686-18528-5). Kazi Pubns.

--An Interpretation of the Holy Quran with Arabic Text. 22.50 (ISBN 0-686-18338-X). Kazi Pubns.

Ali, Yusef. The Holy Quran. (Arabic & Eng.). 20.00x (ISBN 0-86685-167-4). Intl Bk Ctr.

Ali, Yusuf. The Holy Quran. LC 77-78098. 1915p. 14.00 (ISBN 0-89259-006-8). Am Trust Pubns.

Ali, Yusuf H. Spirit, Soul, Consciousness, Realization. 1975. pap. 3.50 (ISBN 0-913358-10-X). Shabazz Pr.

Ali, Zaki. Islam in the World. LC 74-180314. (Mid-East Studies). Repr. of 1947 ed. 31.00 (ISBN 0-404-56209-4). AMS Pr.

Aliaga, Barbara. Keyboarding for Kids. (Illus.). 96p. (Orig.). (gr. 1-6). 1985. pap. 8.50 (ISBN 0-88908-606-0, 9538, Pub. by Intl Self-Counsel Pr). TAB Bks.

--Learn to Type. 77p. Date not set. pap. 6.50 (ISBN 0-317-30531-X, 9508, Pub. by Intl Self-Counsel Pr). TAB Bks.

--Learn to Type Fast. 2nd ed. 77p. 1983. pap. 6.50 (ISBN 0-88908-914-0). Self Counsel Pr.

--Start & Run a Profitable Home Typing Business. 123p. (Orig.). 1984. pap. 9.95 (ISBN 0-88908-585-4, 9524). TAB Bks.

--Start & Run a Profitable Home Typing Business. 123p. 1984. pap. 9.95 (ISBN 0-88908-585-4). Self Counsel Pr.

Aliandro, H. Dicionario Ingles-Portugues. 402p. (Eng. & Port.). 1980. pap. 8.95 (ISBN 0-686-97638-X, M-9215). French & Eur.

--Dicionario Portugues-Ingles. 311p. (Port. & Eng.). 1980. pap. 8.95 (ISBN 0-686-97641-X, M-9216). French & Eur.

Aliano, Richard A. American Defense Policy from Eisenhower to Kennedy: The Politics of Changing Military Requirements, 1957-1961. LC 74-27709. xi, 309p. 1975. 18.50x (ISBN 0-8214-0181-5, 82-81792); pap. 8.95x (ISBN 0-8214-0406-7, 82-81800). Ohio U Pr.

Aliber, Robert Z. A Conceptual Approach to the Analysis of External Debt of the Developing Countries. (Working Paper: No. 421). 25p. 1980. pap. 3.00 (ISBN 0-686-39739-8, WP-0421). World Bank.

--Exchange Risk & Corporate International Finance. LC 78-4645. 1978. 32.95x (ISBN 0-470-26307-5). Halsted Pr.

--The International Money Game. 4th, rev. ed. LC 82-72393. 350p. 1983. 15.95 (ISBN 0-465-03377-6); pap. 8.95x (ISBN 0-465-03379-2). Basic.

--National Monetary Policies & the International Financial System. LC 74-75610. (Studies in Business & Society - Midway Reprint Ser.). 352p. 1982. pap. 18.00x (ISBN 0-226-01393-6). U of Chicago Pr.

--Your Money & Your Life: A Lifetime Approach to Money Management. LC 82-70843. 1982. 15.95 (ISBN 0-465-09340-X). Basic.

Aliber, Robert Z., jt. ed. see Shultz, George P.

Alibert-Kouraguine, Daniel. Prairie Dwellers. LC 83-50220. (Nature's Hidden World Ser.). 48p. (gr. 2 up). 1984. 12.68 (ISBN 0-382-06713-4). Silver.

--Prairie Dwellers. LC 83-50220. (Nature's Hidden World Ser.). (Illus.). 48p. (gr. 3 up). 1985. pap. 4.95 (ISBN 0-382-09150-7). Silver.

Aliboni, Roberto. The Red Sea Region: Local Actors & the Superpowers. LC 84-24024. (Contemporary Issues in the Middle East Ser.). 200p. 1985. text ed. 19.95x (ISBN 0-8156-2332-1). Syracuse U Pr.

Aliboni, Roberto, ed. Arab Industrialization & Economic Integration. LC 78-10632. 1979. 27.50 (ISBN 0-312-04702-9). St Martin.

Aliboni, Roberto, et al. Egypt's Economic Potential. 256p. 1984. 28.00 (ISBN 0-7099-1319-2, Pub. by Croom Helm Ltd). Longwood Pub Group.

Al-Ibrahim, Mohamed S., jt. auth. see Novick, Lloyd F.

Alibrandi, Tom. Burnout. 288p. (Orig.). 1981. pap. 2.75 (ISBN 0-523-41057-3). Pinnacle Bks.

--Custody. (Orig.). 1979. pap. 2.95 (ISBN 0-523-42262-8). Pinnacle Bks.

--Young Alcoholics. LC 77-87741. 1978. pap. 6.95 (ISBN 0-89638-014-9). CompCare.

Alibrandi, Tom & Armani, Frank H. Privileged Information. 256p. 1984. 15.95 (ISBN 0-396-08363-3). Dodd.

Alicata, Joseph E. & Jindrak, Karel. Angiostrongylosis in the Pacific & Southeast Asia. (Illus.). 120p. 1970. photocopy ed. 16.75x (ISBN 0-398-00028-X). C C Thomas.

Alicia. Psychic Poetry from the French Quarter. 39p. 1980. pap. 5.95 (ISBN 0-686-32519-2). Transitour.

Alico, Stella H. Benjamin Franklin-Martin Luther King Jr. (Pendulum Illustrated Biography Ser.). (Illus.). (gr. 4-12). 1979. text ed. 5.00 (ISBN 0-88301-365-7); pap. text ed. 1.95 (ISBN 0-88301-353-3); wkbk 1.25 (ISBN 0-88301-377-0). Pendulum Pr.

--Elvis Presley - The Beatles. (Pendulum Illustrated Biography Ser.). (Illus.). (gr. 4-12). 1979. text ed. 5.00 (ISBN 0-88301-364-9); pap. text ed. 1.95 (ISBN 0-88301-352-5); wkbk 1.25 (ISBN 0-88301-376-2). Pendulum Pr.

Alicoate, J. Film Daily Production Guide & Directors Annual of 1934. 1976. lib. bdg. 75.00 (ISBN 0-8490-1814-5). Gordon Pr.

--Film Daily Production Guide & Directors Annual of 1935. 1976. lib. bdg. 79.50 (ISBN 0-8490-1815-3). Gordon Pr.

--Film Daily Yearbook of Motion Pictures of 1930. 1976. lib. bdg. 79.95 (ISBN 0-8490-1818-8). Gordon Pr.

--Film Daily Yearbook of Motion Pictures of 1932. 1976. lib. bdg. 79.95 (ISBN 0-8490-1819-6). Gordon Pr.

--Film Daily Yearbook of Motion Pictures of 1935. 1976. lib. bdg. 79.95 (ISBN 0-8490-1820-X). Gordon Pr.

--Film Daily Yearbook of Motion Pictures of 1936. lib. bdg. 79.95 (ISBN 0-8490-1821-8). Gordon Pr.

--Film Daily Yearbook of Motion Pictures of 1922-1923. 1976. lib. bdg. 79.95 (ISBN 0-8490-1828-5). Gordon Pr.

Alicoate, J., ed. Film Daily Directors Annual & Production Guide of 1929. 1976. lib. bdg. 75.95 (ISBN 0-8490-1810-2). Gordon Pr.

--Film Daily Directors Annual & Production Guide of 1930. lib. bdg. 75.95 (ISBN 0-8490-1811-0). Gordon Pr.

--Film Daily Directors Annual & Production Guide of 1932. 1976. lib. bdg. 75.00 (ISBN 0-8490-1812-9). Gordon Pr.

--Film Daily Production Guide & Directors Annual of 1936. 1976. lib. bdg. 79.75 (ISBN 0-8490-1816-1). Gordon Pr.

--Film Daily Production Guide & Directors Annual of 1937. 1976. lib. bdg. 79.75 (ISBN 0-8490-1817-X). Gordon Pr.

--Film Daily Yearbook of Motion Pictures of 1940. 1976. lib. bdg. 75.00 (ISBN 0-8490-1822-6). Gordon Pr.

--Film Daily Yearbook of Motion Pictures of 1934. 1976. lib. bdg. 79.95 (ISBN 0-8490-1823-4). Gordon Pr.

--Film Daily Yearbook of Motion Pictures of 1933. 1976. lib. bdg. 79.95 (ISBN 0-8490-1824-2). Gordon Pr.

--Film Daily Yearbook of Motion Pictures of 1926. 1976. lib. bdg. 79.95 (ISBN 0-8490-1825-0). Gordon Pr.

--Film Daily Yearbook of Motion Pictures of 1939. 1976. lib. bdg. 79.95 (ISBN 0-8490-1826-9). Gordon Pr.

--Film Daily Yearbook of Motion Pictures of 1937. 1976. lib. bdg. 79.95 (ISBN 0-8490-1827-7). Gordon Pr.

--Film Daily Yearbook of Motion Pictures of 1921-1922. 1976. lib. bdg. 79.95 (ISBN 0-8490-1829-3). Gordon Pr.

Ali-El, Yusuf. Once upon a Ryme Tyme for Growing Minds. LC 83-90101. (Illus.). 90p. (gr. k-5). 1983. pap. 9.95 (ISBN 0-912475-09-9). Natl Res Unltd.

Alier, Verena Martinez see Martinez Alier, Verena.

Aliesan, Jody. As If It Will Matter. LC 78-63399. 60p. (Orig.). 1978. 15.00 (ISBN 0-931188-04-0); pap. 6.00 (ISBN 0-931188-03-2). Seal Pr Feminist.

--Soul Claiming. LC 75-23822. (Haystack Ser). (Illus.). 76p. 1975. 6.00 (ISBN 0-913142-16-6); pap. 3.50 (ISBN 0-913142-15-8). Mulch Pr.

Aliev, K., ed. Public Education in Soviet Azerbaijan: Appraisal of an Achievement. 239p. 1985. 22.50 (ISBN 92-803-1110-7, U1383, UNESCO). Unipub.

Aliev, M. R., jt. auth. see Papousek, D.

Alifano, Roberto. Recent Conversations with Borges. 1983. 14.95 (ISBN 0-911441-02-6); pap. 8.95 (ISBN 0-911441-03-4). Altamira Lascaux.

Alifano, Roberto, jt. auth. see Borges, Jorge L.

Alifano, Roberto, ed. Twenty-Four Conversations with Borges: Interviews by Roberto Alifano 1981-1983. Arauz, Nicomedes S., et al, trs. LC 83-49422. (Illus.). 157p. 1984. 17.95 (ISBN 0-394-53879-X, GP 921); pap. 8.95 (ISBN 0-394-62192-1, E 940). Grove.

Aliff, Gregory E., jt. auth. see Hahne, Robert L.

Alig, Marcia F. Daniel-Leina D. 1978. 8.05 (ISBN 0-685-30205-9). Nautilus Bks.

Alighiere, Dante. Paradiso. Ciardi, John, tr. 1970. pap. 3.50 (ISBN 0-451-62279-0, ME2279, Ment). NAL.

Alighieri, Dante. The Canzoniere of Dante Alighieri. xxxvi, 467p. Date not set. Repr. of 1835 ed. lib. bdg. 49.00 (ISBN 0-932051-93-6). Am Repr Serv.

--Dante's Inferno. Kilmer, Nicholas, tr. from Ital. (Illus., Orig.). 1985. pap. 9.95 (ISBN 0-8283-1884-0). Branden Pub Co.

--De Monarchia. 59.95 (ISBN 0-8490-0000-9). Gordon Pr.

--The Divine Comedy: Paradise, 2 vols. Norton, Charles E., tr. (Illus.). 251p. 1985. 157.85 (ISBN 0-89266-510-6). Am Classical Coll Pr.

--Divine Comedy: Paradiso, Vol. 3. Singleton, Charles S., tr. from Ital. (Bollinger Ser.: LXXX). (Illus.). 1982. pap. 14.95 (ISBN 0-691-01844-8). Princeton U Pr.

--The Inferno. Mandelbaum, Allen, tr. from Italian. (Bantam Classics Ser.). (Illus.). 350p. (gr. 9-12). 1982. pap. 2.50 (ISBN 0-553-21069-6). Bantam.

--The Inferno. Kilmer, Nicholas, tr. (Illus.). 1985. 19.50 (ISBN 0-937832-28-6). Dante U Am.

--Inferno. Cary, Henry F., tr. from Ital. (Illus.). 139p. 1985. 88.85 (ISBN 0-89266-525-4). Am Classical Coll Pr.

--The New Life. (Illus.). 115p. 1980. Repr. of 1867 ed. 79.85 (ISBN 0-89901-040-7). Found Class Reprints.

--The New Life. (Most Meaningful Classics in World Culture Ser.). (Illus.). 129p. 1983. 99.95. Found Class Reprints.

--The New Life. 77p. Repr. 29.00 (ISBN 0-932051-68-5). Am Repr Serv.

--Paradise. Cary, Henry F., tr. from Ital. (Illus.). 141p. 1985. 88.95 (ISBN 0-89266-527-0). Am Classical Coll Pr.

--Purgatory. Cary, Henry F., tr. from Ital. (Illus.). 137p. 1985. 93.25 (ISBN 0-89266-526-2). Am Classical Coll Pr.

Alighieri, Dante see Dante Alighieri.

Alihan, Milla. Corporate Etiquette. 1974. pap. 3.50 (ISBN 0-451-62143-3, ME2143, Ment). NAL.

Alihan, Milla A. Social Ecology, a Critical Analysis. LC 64-24804. 267p. Repr. of 1938 ed. 20.00 (ISBN 0-8154-0008-X). Cooper Sq.

Ali ibn Isma'il, A. H., et al. Al ibanah 'an usul addiyanah. Klein, W. C., tr. (American Oriental Ser.: Vol. 19). 1940. 18.00 (ISBN 0-527-02693-X). Kraus Repr.

Aliki. At Mary Bloom's. (Illus.). (gr. 1-3). 1978. pap. 2.95 (ISBN 0-14-050278-5, Puffin). Penguin.

--At Mary Bloom's. LC 75-45482. (Illus.). 32p. (gr. k-3). 1983. PLB 10.88 (ISBN 0-688-02481-5); 10.25 (ISBN 0-688-02480-7). Greenwillow.

--Corn Is Maize: The Gift of the Indians. LC 75-6928. (A Let's-Read-&-Find-Out Science Book Ser.). (Illus.). 40p. (gr. k-3). 1976. PLB 11.89 (ISBN 0-690-00975-5); pap. 3.95 (ISBN 0-690-04203-5, TYC-J). Crowell Jr Bks.

--Digging up Dinosaurs. LC 80-2250. (A Let's Read & Find Out Science Bk.). (Illus.). 40p. (gr. k-3). 1981. 10.53i (ISBN 0-690-04098-9); PLB 11.89 (ISBN 0-690-04099-7). Crowell Jr Bks.

--Dinosaurs Are Different. LC 84-45332. (A Let's-Read-&-Find-Out Science Bk.). (Illus.). 32p. (ps-3). 1985. 11.06i (ISBN 0-690-04456-9); PLB 11.89g (ISBN 0-690-04458-5). Crowell Jr Bks.

--Feelings. LC 84-4098. (Illus.). 32p. (gr. k-3). 1984. 10.25 (ISBN 0-688-03831-X); PLB 9.55 (ISBN 0-688-03832-8). Greenwillow.

--Fossils Tell of Long Ago. LC 78-170999. (A Let's-Read-&-Find-Out Science Bk). (Illus.). 40p. (gr. k-3). 1972. PLB 11.89 (ISBN 0-690-31379-9). Crowell Jr Bks.

--Fossils Tell of Long Ago. LC 78-170999. (A Trophy Let's-Read-&-Find-Out Bk.). (Illus.). 40p. (ps-3). 1983. pap. 3.80i (ISBN 0-06-445004-X, Trophy). HarpJ.

--Hush Little Baby. (Illus.). (ps-1). 1968. PLB 8.95x (ISBN 0-13-448167-4, Pub. by Treehouse); pap. 3.95 (ISBN 0-13-448175-5). P-H.

--Keep Your Mouth Closed, Dear. LC 66-19310. (Illus.). (gr. k-3). 1966. 9.95 (ISBN 0-8037-4416-1); PLB 9.89 (ISBN 0-8037-4418-8). Dial Bks Young.

--Keep Your Mouth Closed, Dear. LC 66-19310. (Pied Piper Book). (Illus.). 48p. (ps-2). 1980. pap. 2.50 (ISBN 0-8037-4420-X). Dial Bks Young.

--The Many Lives of Benjamin Franklin. (Illus.). (ps-2). 1977. PLB 6.95 (ISBN 0-13-556019-5). P-H.

--A Medieval Feast. LC 82-45923. (Illus.). 32p. (gr. 2-6). 1983. 10.53 (ISBN 0-690-04245-0); PLB 10.89 (ISBN 0-690-04246-9). Crowell Jr Bks.

--Mummies Made in Egypt. LC 77-26603. (Illus.). (gr. 2-6). 1979. 11.49i (ISBN 0-690-03858-5); PLB 11.89 (ISBN 0-690-03859-3). Crowell Jr Bks.

--Mummies Made in Egypt. LC 85-42746. (Trophy Nonfiction Bk.). (Illus.). 32p. (gr. 3-7). 1985. pap. 3.80i (ISBN 0-06-446011-8, Trophy). HarpJ.

--My Five Senses. LC 62-7150. (A Let's-Read-&-Find-Out Science Bk). (Illus.). (gr. k-3). 1962. PLB 11.89 (ISBN 0-690-56763-4). Crowell Jr Bks.

--My Hands. LC 62-12810. (A Let's-Read-&-Find-Out Science Bk). (Illus.). (gr. k-3). 1962. PLB 11.89 (ISBN 0-690-56834-7). Crowell Jr Bks.

--My Visit to the Dinosaurs. rev. ed. LC 85-47538. (A Let's-Read-&-Find-Out Science Bk.). (Illus.). 32p. (ps-3). 1985. 11.06i (ISBN 0-690-04422-4); PLB 11.89g (ISBN 0-690-04423-2). Crowell Jr Bks.

--My Visit to the Dinosaurs. rev. ed. LC 85-42748. (A Trophy Let's-Read-&-Find-Out Bk.). (Illus.). 32p. (ps-3). 1985. pap. 3.80i (ISBN 0-06-445020-1, Trophy). HarpJ.

--Story of Johnny Appleseed. (Illus.). (ps-2). 1963. lib. bdg. 9.95 (ISBN 0-13-850800-3); pap. 3.95 (ISBN 0-13-850818-6). P-H.

--The Twelve Months. LC 78-3554. (Illus.). 32p. (gr. k-3). 1978. 11.75 (ISBN 0-688-80164-1); PLB 11.88 (ISBN 0-688-84164-3). Greenwillow.

--The Two of Them. LC 79-10161. (Illus.). 32p. (gr. k-3). 1979. 11.75 (ISBN 0-688-80225-7); PLB 11.88 (ISBN 0-688-84225-9). Greenwillow.

--Use Your Head, Dear. LC 82-11911. (Illus.). 48p. (gr. k-3). 1983. 10.25 (ISBN 0-688-01811-4); PLB 10.88 (ISBN 0-688-01812-2). Greenwillow.

--We Are Best Friends. LC 81-6549. (Illus.). (gr. k-3). 1982. 10.75 (ISBN 0-688-00822-4); PLB 10.88 (ISBN 0-688-00823-2). Greenwillow.

--Wild & Woolly Mammoths. LC 76-18082. (A Let's-Read-&-Find-Out Science Bk.). (Illus.). (gr. k-3). 1977. PLB 11.89 (ISBN 0-690-01276-4). Crowell Jr Bks.

--Wild & Woolly Mammoths. LC 76-18082. (A Trophy Let's-Read-&-Find-Out Bk.). (Illus.). 40p. (ps-3). 1983. pap. 3.80i (ISBN 0-06-445005-8, Trophy). HarpJ.

Aliko, Hysni, jt. auth. see Kici, Gasper.

Alikonis, Justin J. Candy Technology. (Illus.). 1979. lib. bdg. 32.50 (ISBN 0-87055-280-5). AVI.

Ali Majid, et al. Pathology Review. 7th ed. (Medical Exam Review Ser.). 1980. pap. 12.75 (ISBN 0-87488-204-4). Med Exam.

Alimayo, Chikuyo, pseud. A Garden on Cement. (Essays on Black America Ser.). (Illus.). 224p. 1973. 7.95 (ISBN 0-9606692-0-5); pap. 3.95 (ISBN 0-9606692-1-3). Eko Pubns.

--Once Around the Track. (Illus.). (YA) 1974. 7.95 (ISBN 0-9606692-2-1); pap. 3.95 (ISBN 0-9606692-3-X). Eko Pubns.

Ali-Nadawi, Abul H. Prophet's Stories. Quinlan, Hamid, ed. El-Helbawy, Kamal, tr. from Arabic. LC 82-70453. (Illus.). 200p. (Orig.). Date not set. pap. 5.00 (ISBN 0-89259-038-6). Am Trust Pubns.

Alinder, James. The Contact Print, Nineteen Forty-Six to Nineteen Eighty-Two. LC 82-83985. (Untitled Ser.: No. 30). (Illus.). 52p. 1982. pap. 15.00 (ISBN 0-933286-32-5). Friends Photography.

Alinder, James, ed. Discovery & Recognition. LC 81-65401. (Untitled Ser.: No. 25). (Illus.). 56p. (Orig.). 1981. pap. 12.00 (ISBN 0-933286-24-4). Friends Photography.

--Nine Critics - Nine Photographs. LC 80-68803. (Untitled Ser.: No. 23). (Illus.). 56p. (Orig.). 1980. pap. 8.95 (ISBN 0-933286-21-X). Friends Photography.

Alinder, James, ed. see DeCarava, Roy.

Alinder, James, ed. see Featherstone, David.

Alinder, James, ed. see Giacomelli, Mario.

Alinder, James, ed. see Mark, Mary E.

Alinder, James, ed. see Morris, Wright.

Alinder, James, ed. see Nixon, Nicholas.

Alinder, James, ed. see Ollman, Arthur.

Alinder, James, ed. see Teske, Edmund.

Alinder, James, ed. see Wolcott, Marion P.

Alinder, James, ed. see Worth, Don.

Aling, Charles F. Egypt & Bible History: From Earliest Times to 1000 B.C. (Baker Studies in Biblical Archaeology). 144p. (Orig.). 1981. pap. 5.95 (ISBN 0-8010-0174-9). Baker Bk.

Alington, Adrian. The Amazing Test Match Crime. 256p. 1984. pap. 7.95 (ISBN 0-7012-0561-X, Pub. by Chatto & Windus-Hogarth Pr). Merrimack Pub Cir.

Alington, Adrian, et al. Beginnings. LC 76-105762. 1970. Repr. of 1935 ed. 14.00x (ISBN 0-8046-0937-3, Pub. by Kennikat). Assoc Faculty Pr.

--Beginnings. 200p. 1981. Repr. of 1935 ed. lib. bdg. 30.00 (ISBN 0-89760-076-2). Telegraph Bks.

--Beginnings: A. E. Coppard, A. J. Crowin, Wyndham Lewis, V. S. Pritchett, V. Sackville-West, Alec Waugh. 1935. Repr. 7.25 (ISBN 0-8274-3809-5). R West.

Alinsky, Saul. Reveille for Radicals. 1969. pap. 3.95 (ISBN 0-394-70568-8, V568, Vin). Random.

Alinsky, Saul D. Rules for Radicals. 224p. 1972. pap. 3.95 (ISBN 0-394-71736-8, V736, Vin). Random.

Alioto, Joseph L., et al, eds. Teilhard de Chardin: In Quest of the Perfection of Man. LC 72-9596. 290p. 1973. 24.50 (ISBN 0-8386-1258-X). Fairleigh Dickinson.

Aliotta, Antonio. The Idealistic Reaction Against Science. McCaskill, Agnes, tr. from It. LC 74-26246. (History, Philosophy & Sociology of Science Ser). 1975. Repr. of 1914 ed. 37.50x (ISBN 0-405-06576-0). Ayer Co Pubs.

Aliprantis, C. D. & Burkinshaw, O. Principles of Real Analysis. 288p. 1981. 33.50 (ISBN 0-444-00448-3). Elsevier.

Aliprantis, C. D., et al, eds. Advances in Equilibrium Theory. (Lecture Notes in Economics & Mathematical Systems Ser.: Vol. 244). 244p. 1985. pap. 17.30 (ISBN 0-387-15229-6). Springer-Verlag.

Aliprantis, Charalambos D. & Burkinshaw, Owen. Locally Solid Riesz Spaces. (Pure & Applied Mathematics Ser.). 1978. 47.50 (ISBN 0-12-050250-X). Acad Pr.

Aliprantis, Charalambous D. & Burkinshaw, Owen. Positive Operators. (Pure & Applied Mathematics Ser.). Date not set. price not set (ISBN 0-12-050260-7). Acad Pr.

Alireza, Marianne. At the Drop of a Veil. 1971. 15.95 (ISBN 0-395-12090-X). HM.

Alisin, V. V., jt. ed. see Kragelsky, I. V.

Alisjahbana, Takdir S. Language Planning for Modernization: The Case of Indonesian & Malaysian. (Contributions to the Sociology of Language Ser.: No. 14). 1976. pap. text ed. 13.60 (ISBN 90-279-7712-7). Mouton.

Alisky, Marvin. Historical Dictionary of Peru. LC 79-16488. (Latin American Historical Dictionaries Ser.: No. 20). 163p. 1979. 17.50 (ISBN 0-8108-1235-5). Scarecrow.

--Latin American Media: Guidance & Censorship. 266p. 1981. 24.95x (ISBN 0-8138-1525-8). Iowa St U Pr.

Alisky, Marvin, jt. auth. see Briggs, Donald C.

Alison, A. England in Eighteen Fifteen & Eighteen Forty-Five. 98p. 1971. Repr. of 1845 ed. 15.00x (ISBN 0-7165-1699-3, BBA 05044, Pub. by Irish Academic Pr Ireland). Biblio Dist.

Alison, Archibald. Essays on the Nature & Principle of Taste. 1968. Repr. of 1790 ed. 64.00x (ISBN 3-4870-2125-0). Adlers Foreign Bks.

--History of Europe from the Commencement of the French Revolution to the Restoration of the Bourbons, 14 Vols. 10th ed. LC 70-38482. Repr. of 1860 ed. Set. 665.00 (ISBN 0-404-00390-7); 47.50 ea. AMS Pr.

Alison, Linda, ed. see Neal, Richard G.

Alison, Malcolm, jt. auth. see Wright, Nicholas.

Alison, Richard. A Confutation of Brownisme. LC 68-54608. (English Experience Ser.: No. 9). 130p. 1968. Repr. of 1590 ed. 16.00 (ISBN 90-221-0009-X). Walter J Johnson.

Alison, Robert M. Breeding Biology & Behavior of the Oldsquaw (Clangula Hyemalis L.) 52p. 1975. 3.50 (ISBN 0-943610-18-4). Am Ornithologists.

Alisouskas, Vincent & Tomasi, Wayne. Digital & Data Communications. (Illus.). 320p. 1985. text ed. 32.95 (ISBN 0-13-212424-6). P-H.

Al-Issa, Ashan. Culture & Psychopathology. (Illus.). 464p. 1982. text ed. 35.95 (ISBN 0-8391-1679-9). Univ Park.

Al-Issa, Ihsan. The Psychopathology of Women. (Illus.). 1979. 15.95 (ISBN 0-13-736827-5, Spec); pap. 7.95 (ISBN 0-13-736819-4). P-H.

Al-Issa, Ihsan, ed. Gender & Psychopathology. (Personality & Psychopathology Ser.). 355p. 1982. 37.50 (ISBN 0-12-050350-6). Acad Pr.

Alissi, Albert & Casper, Max, eds. Time As a Factor in Groupwork: Time-Limited Group Experiences. LC 85-7636. (Social Work with Groups Ser.: Vol. 8, No. 2). 176p. 1985. text ed. 22.95 (ISBN 0-86656-409-8); pap. text ed. 16.95 (ISBN 0-86656-438-1). Haworth Pr.

Alissi, Albert S. Boys in Little Italy: A Comparison of Their Individual Value Orientations, Family Patterns, & Peer Group Associations. LC 77-90360. 1978. soft cover 11.95 (ISBN 0-88247-495-2). R & E Pubs.

Alissi, Albert S., ed. Perspectives on Social Group Work Practice: A Book of Readings. LC 79-7633. 1980. pap. text ed. 14.95 (ISBN 0-02-900480-2). Free Pr.

Alitto, Guy S. The Last Confucian: Liang Shu-Ming & the Chinese Dilemma of Modernity. (Center for Chinese Studies). (Illus.). 404p. 1984. pap. 9.95 (ISBN 0-520-05318-4, CAL 665). U of Cal Pr.

Alix, Ernest K. Ransom Kidnapping in America, 1874-1974: The Creation of a Capital Crime. LC 78-1985. (Perspectives in Sociology Ser.). 256p. 1978. 20.00x (ISBN 0-8093-0849-5). S Ill U Pr.

--Ransom Kidnapping in America, 1874-1974: The Creation of a Capital Crime. LC 78-1985. 256p. 1980. pap. 9.95x (ISBN 0-8093-0976-9). S Ill U Pr.

Alizadeh, Ahmad, tr. see Ahmad, Jalal Al-e.

Al-Jadir, Saad. Arab & Islamic Silver. (Illus.). 216p. 1983. 60.00 (ISBN 0-905743-23-7, Pub. by Salem Hse Ltd). Merrimack Pub Cir.

--Arab & Islamic Silver. (Illus.). 1983. 55.00x (ISBN 0-686-47157-1). Intl Bk Ctr.

Al-Jarallah, M. I. & Nawara, G. Project Management. (Illus.). 350p. 1984. 27.00 (ISBN 0-471-81189-0); pap. 18.00 (ISBN 0-471-88816-8). Wiley.

Al-Jarrahi, Abdussamad, ed. see Badawi, Gamal.

Al-Jarrahi, Abdussamad, tr. see Boisard, Marcel.

Aljian, George W. Purchasing Handbook. 3rd ed. 1152p. 1973. 59.95 (ISBN 0-07-001068-4). McGraw.

Al-Jundi, Sef. A Long May. LC 84-91284. 84p. 1985. 6.95 (ISBN 0-533-06354-X). Vantage.

Alk, Madelin & Redbook Editors, eds. Expectant Mother. 1983. pap. 3.50 (ISBN 0-671-49637-9). PB.

Al-Kasimi, Ali M. Linguistics & Bilingual Dictionaries. 1977. text ed. 21.00x (ISBN 90-04047-87-5). Humanities.

Alkazi, Roshen. Ancient Indian Costume. 1985. 44.00x (ISBN 0-8364-1334-2, Pub. by Art Heritage, India). South Asia Bks.

--Seventeen More Poems. (Writers Workshop Redbird Ser.). 1975. 8.00 (ISBN 0-88253-628-1); pap. text ed. 4.00 (ISBN 0-88253-627-3). Ind-US Inc.

--Seventeen Poems. 8.00 (ISBN 0-89253-549-0). Ind-US Inc.

Alkazin, D. M. Descriptive Geometry Workbook. (Illus.). 96p. 1985. pap. 6.95x (ISBN 0-911168-56-7); instructor's overlay 9.95x (ISBN 0-911168-57-5). Prakken.

Alkema, Chester J. Mask-Making. LC 80-54343. (Illus.). 96p. (gr. 3-7). 1983. pap. 6.95 (ISBN 0-8069-7744-2). Sterling.

Alkemade, C. J., et al. Metal Vapours In Flames. LC 82-421. (International Series in National Philosophy: Vol. 103). (Illus.). 1016p. 1982. 105.00 (ISBN 0-08-018061-2, A145). Pergamon.

Alkemade, Cornelis T. & Herrmann, Roland. Fundamentals of Analytical Flame Spectroscopy. LC 79-4376. 442p. 1979. 104.95 (ISBN 0-470-26710-0). Halsted Pr.

Alkemade, Dick Van see Van Alkemade, Dick, et al.

Alken & Sokeland. Urology. 1982. 20.95 (ISBN 0-8151-0108-2). Year Bk Med.

Alken, C. E., et al, eds. Encyclopedia of Urology, Vols. 28 5-7, 9, 11-13 & 15. Incl. Vol. 2. Physiology & Pathological Physiology. (Illus.). xx, 1009p. 1965. 247.80 (ISBN 0-387-03315-7); Vol. 5, Pt. 1. Diagnostic Radiology. (Illus.). xii, 533p. 1962. 188.80 (ISBN 0-387-02846-3); Vol. 6. Endoscopy. (Illus.). xxiv, 282p. 1959. 118.00 (ISBN 0-387-02419-0); Vol. 7, Pt. 1. Malformations. (Illus.). xiv, 479p. 1968. 129.80 (ISBN 0-387-04165-6); Vol. 9, Pt. 2. Inflammation Two: Specific Inflammations. (Illus.). xvi, 564p. 1959. 165.20 (ISBN 0-387-02420-4); Vol. 11, Pt. 1. Organic Diseases. (Illus.). xiv, 286p. 1967. 112.10 (ISBN 0-387-03859-0); Vol. 12. Functional Disturbances. (Illus.). xiv, 312p. 1960. 100.30 (ISBN 0-387-02551-0); Vol. 13, Pt. 2. Operative Urology Two. (Illus.). 280p. 1970. 97.40 (ISBN 0-387-05142-2); Vol. 15. Urology in Childhood. (Illus.). xvi, 353p. 1958. 106.20 (ISBN 0-387-02303-8); Vol. 15, Supplement. Urology in Childhood. Williams, D. I., et al. 1974. 87.40 (ISBN 0-387-06406-0). (Handbuch der Urologic). Springer-Verlag.

Alken, C. E., et al, eds. see Kuess, R. & Chatelain, C.

Alker, E. Franz Grillparzer: Ein Kampf Um Leben und Kunst. (Beitraege Zur Deutschen Literaturwissenschaft: No. 36). 19.00 (ISBN 0-384-00750-3). Johnson Repr.

Alker, Hayward R. Dialectical Logics for the Political Sciences. (Ponzan Studies: No. 7). 96p. 1982. pap. text ed. 13.45x (ISBN 90-6203-684-8, Pub. by Rodopi Holland). Humanities.

Alker, Hayward R. & Russett, Bruce M. World Politics in the General Asssembly. LC 65-22313. (Yale Studies in Political Science: No. 15). pap. 88.00 (ISBN 0-317-09370-3, 2021974). Bks Demand UMI.

Al-Khalesi, Yasin M. The Court of the Palms: A Functional Interpretation of the Mari Palace. LC 77-94987. (Bibliotheca Mesopotamica Ser.: Vol. 8). (Illus.). viii, 90p. 1978. 25.00x (ISBN 0-89003-029-4); pap. 14.50x o.s.i (ISBN 0-89003-030-8). Undena Pubns.

Al-Khui, Ayatullah A. Articles of Islamic Acts. Haq, M. Fazal, tr. from Arabic. 236p. 1983. pap. 6.00 (ISBN 0-941724-21-2). Islamic Seminary.

Al-Khuli, Muhammad A. Dictionary of Theoretical Linguistics: English-Arabic with Arabic-English Glossary. (Arabic & Eng.). 1983. 30.00x (ISBN 0-86685-306-5). Intl Bk Ctr.

Alkin, Glyn. Sound Recording & Reproduction. LC 80-41481. (Illus.). 226p. 1981. 16.95 (ISBN 0-240-51070-4). Focal Pr.

--TV Sound Operation. (Media Manuals Ser.). pap. 7.95 (ISBN 0-8038-7148-1). Hastings.

--TV Sound Operations. (Media Manual Ser.). (Illus.). 1975. pap. 14.95 (ISBN 0-240-50865-3). Focal Pr.

Alkin, Marvin C. & Solmon, Lewis C., eds. The Costs of Evaluation. (Sage Focus Editions: Vol. 60). 200p. 1983. 24.00 (ISBN 0-8039-1979-4); pap. 12.00 (ISBN 0-8039-1980-8). Sage.

Alkin, Marvin C., et al. Using Evaluations: Does Evaluation Make a Difference. LC 78-25780. (Sage Library of Social Research: Vol. 76). (Illus.). 269p. 1979. 28.00 (ISBN 0-8039-1177-7); pap. 14.00 (ISBN 0-8039-1178-5). Sage.

--Conducting Evaluations: Three Perspectives. LC 80-52791. 60p. (Orig.). 1980. pap. 2.95 (ISBN 0-87954-036-2). Foundation Ctr.

Al-Kindi. Medical Formulary or Aqrabadhin of al-Kindi. Levey, Martin, tr. (Medieval Science Pubns., No. 7). 424p. 1966. 35.00x (ISBN 0-299-03600-6). U of Wis Pr.

Al-Kindi, Ya'Qub I. Al-Kindi's Metaphysics: A Translation of Ya'qub Ibn Ishaq Al-Kindi's Treatise on First Philosophy (Fi-Al-Falsafah Al-Ula) Ivry, Alfred L., ed. LC 70-171182. 1974. 49.50x (ISBN 0-87395-092-5). State U NY Pr.

Alkins, Arthur C. Computers & Data Processing Today. (Plaid Ser.). 200p. 1983. pap. 9.95 (ISBN 0-87094-389-8). Dow Jones-Irwin.

Alkire, Leland, ed. New Periodical Title Abbreviations. 1984. pap. 125.00x (ISBN 0-8103-0339-6). Gale.

Alkire, Leland G., Jr. Periodical Title Abbreviations by Abbreviation, Vol. 1. 4th ed. 1100p. 1983. 140.00x (ISBN 0-8103-0538-0). Gale.

Alkire, Leland G., Jr., ed. Periodical Title Abbreviations by Title, Vol. 2. 4th ed. 1100p. 1983. 140.00x (ISBN 0-8103-0539-9). Gale.

Alkire, Leland G., Jr. & Westerman, Cheryl I., eds. Writer's Advisor. LC 84-24715. 375p. 1985. 60.00x (ISBN 0-8103-2093-2). Gale.

Alkire, Richard & Chin, Der-Tau, eds. Tutorial Lectures in Electrochemical Engineering & Technology II. (AIChE Symposium Ser.: Vol. 79, No. 229). 232p. 1983. pap. 45.00 (ISBN 0-317-05082-6). Am Inst Chem Eng.

Alkire, William. Coral Islanders. Goldschmidt, Walter, ed. LC 77-90673. (World of Man Ser.). (Illus.). 1978. text ed. 18.95x (ISBN 0-88295-618-3); pap. text ed. 9.95x (ISBN 0-88295-619-1). Harlan Davidson.

Alkon, Daniel L. & Farley, Joseph, eds. Primary Neural Substrates of Learning & Behavioral Change. LC 83-7681. 385p. 1984. 49.50 (ISBN 0-521-25472-8). Cambridge U Pr.

Alkon, Paul K. Defoe & Fictional Time. LC 78-6021. 288p. 1979. 23.00x (ISBN 0-8203-0458-1). U of Ga Pr.

Alkons, Nancy V. see Bottiglia, William F.

Alkow, Jacob. In Many Worlds. LC 84-52110. (Illus.). 260p. 1985. pap. 13.95 (ISBN 0-88400-111-3). Shengold.

Alksne, Z. K. & Ikaunieks, Ya Y. Carbon Stars. rev. ed. Baumert, J. H., ed. (Astronomy & Astrophysics Ser.: Vol. 11). Orig. Title: Uglerodnye Zvezdy. (Illus.). 192p. pap. 24.00 (ISBN 0-912918-16-0, 0016). Pachart Pub Hse.

All-European Conference for Directors of National Research Institutions in Education, 1st, Hamburg 1976. Educational Research in Europe: Proceedings. Carelli, M. Dino & Sachsenmeier, Peter, eds. 142p. 1977. pap. text ed. 14.00 (ISBN 90-265-0250-8, Pub. by Swets & Zeitlinger Netherlands). Hogrefe Intl.

All India Sociological Conference. Sociology, Social Research, & Social Problems in India. Saksena, R. N., ed. LC 77-27251. 1978. Repr. of 1961 ed. lib. bdg. 19.00x (ISBN 0-8371-7893-2, SSRP). Greenwood.

All India Symposium, Jabalpur, Feb. 24-27, 1978. Physiology of Parasitism: Proceedings. Agarwal, G. P. & Bilgrami, K. S., eds. (Current Trends in Life Sciences: Vol. 7). vi, 478p. 1979. 50.00 (ISBN 0-88065-004-4, Pub. by Messers Today & Tomorrows Printers & Publishers India). Scholarly Pubns.

All India Symposium, Muzaffarnagar, Dec. 1976. Advancement of Ecology: Proceedings. Agarwal, V. P. & Sharma, V. K., eds. (Current Trends in Life Sciences: Vol. 4). xxii, 218p. 1978. 22.50 (ISBN 0-88065-005-2, Pub. by Messers Today & Tomorrows Printers & Publishers India). Scholarly Pubns.

All-Union Conference on Radiation Chemistry, 1957. Radiation Electrochemical Processes: A Portion of Proceedings of the First All-Union Conference on Radiation Chemistry, 1957. pap. 20.00 (ISBN 0-317-27216-0, 2024709). Bks Demand UMI.

All-Union Conference on Radiation Chemistry, 1957. Radiation Chemistry of Aqueous Solutions: A Portion of Proceedings of the First All-Union Conference on Radiation Chemistry, 1957. pap. 20.00 (ISBN 0-317-27217-9, 2024708). Bks Demand UMI.

All-Union Scientific & Technical Conference on the Application of Isotopes. Application of Radioactive Isotopes in Microbiology, Vol. 2. 28p. 1959. 17.50x (ISBN 0-306-17023-X, Consultants). Plenum Pub.

--Application of Radioactive Isotopes in the Food & Fishing Industries & in Agriculture, Vol. 2. 94p. 1959. 35.00x (ISBN 0-306-17022-1, Consultants). Plenum Pub.

--Radiobiology, Vol. 4. 260p. 1959. 95.00x (ISBN 0-306-17024-8, Consultants). Plenum Pub.

Alla, M. Ata. Arab Sruggle for Economic Independence. 271p. 1974. 4.95 (ISBN 0-8285-2221-9, Pub. by Progress Pubs USSR). Imported Pubns.

Allaback, Steven. Alexander Solzhenitsyn. LC 77-92765. 1978. 9.95 (ISBN 0-8008-0167-9). Taplinger.

Allaben, Stanton D. Vermont Ski Trail Guide: Central Region. 129p. 1983. pap. 5.00 (ISBN 0-913109-01-0). Stanton Production.

Allaby, M. World Food Resources: Actual & Potential. 418p. 1977. 33.50 (ISBN 0-85334-731-X, Pub. by Elsevier Applied Sci England). Elsevier.

Allaby, Michael. Animal Artisans. LC 82-47962. 1982. 25.00 (ISBN 0-394-52451-9). Knopf.

--Dictionary of the Environment. 2nd, rev. ed. (Illus.). 608p. 1984. 55.00x (ISBN 0-8147-0582-0). NYU Pr.

--Making & Managing a Small Holding. LC 79-51103. (Making & Managing Ser.). (Illus.). 1980. 17.95 (ISBN 0-7153-7803-1). David & Charles.

Allaby, Michael & Bunyard, Peter. The Politics of Self-Sufficiency. 1980. 27.50x (ISBN 0-19-217695-1). Oxford U Pr.

Allaby, Michael & Crawford, Peter. The Curious Cat. (Illus.). 160p. 1983. 16.95 (ISBN 0-7181-2065-5, Pub. by Michael Joseph). Merrimack Pub Cir.

Allaby, Michael & Lovelock, James. The Greening of Mars. 176p. 1984. 11.95 (ISBN 0-312-35024-4, Pub. by Marek). St Martin.

Allaby, Michael, jt. auth. see Lovelock, James.

Alladi, K., ed. Number Theory. (Lecture Notes in Mathematics: Vol. 1122). vii, 217p. 1985. pap. 14.40 (ISBN 0-387-15222-9). Springer-Verlag.

--Number Theory, Mysore, India Nineteen Eighty-One: Proceedings. (Lecture Notes in Mathematics: Vol. 938). 177p. 1982. pap. 13.70 (ISBN 0-387-11568-4). Springer-Verlag.

Alladin, Bilzik. Story of Mohammad the Prophet. (Illus.). (gr. 3-10). 1979. 7.25 (ISBN 0-89744-139-7). Auromere.

Allain, Ernest. Oeuvre scolaire de la revolution, 1789-1802. LC 68-57257. (Research & Source Works Ser.: No. 278). (Fr). 1969. Repr. of 1891 ed. 29.50 (ISBN 0-8337-0039-1). B Franklin.

Allain, Louis J. Capital Investment Models of the Oil & Gas Industry: A Systems Approach. Bruchey, Stuart, ed. LC 78-22654. (Energy in the American Economy Ser.). (Illus.). 1979. lib. bdg. 42.00x (ISBN 0-405-11959-3). Ayer Co Pubs.

Allain, Marie-Francoise. The Other Man: Conversations with Graham Greene. Waldman, Guido, tr. 1983. 13.95 (ISBN 0-671-44767-X). S&S.

Allain, Mathe & Ancelet, Barry, eds. Litterature francais de la louisiana. (Anthologie Ser.). (Illus.). 360p. (Fr.). (gr. 10 up). 1981. pap. text ed. 7.00 (ISBN 0-911409-34-3). Natl Mat Dev.

Allain, Mathe, jt. ed. see Ancelet, Barry J.

Allain, Violet A. Futuristics & Education. LC 79-89541. (Fastback Ser.: No. 131). (Orig.). 1979. pap. 0.75 (ISBN 0-87367-131-7). Phi Delta Kappa.

Allaire, Anthony. Diary of Lieutenant Anthony Allaire of Fergusons Corps. LC 67-29025. (Eyewitness Accounts of the American Revolution Ser., No. 1). 1968. Repr. of 1881 ed. 13.00 (ISBN 0-405-01102-4). Ayer Co Pubs.

Allaire, Barbara & McNeil, Robert. Teaching Patient Relations in Hospitals: The Hows & Whys. LC 82-22765. (Illus.). 204p. 1983. 75.00 (ISBN 0-939450-43-7, 049150). AHPI.

Allaire, Pierre. Bird Species on Mined Lands. (Illus.). 72p. (Orig.). 1982. pap. text ed. 10.00 (ISBN 0-86607-010-9). Inst Mining & Minerals.

Allaire, Yvan & Miller, Roger E. L' Entreprise canadienne et la loi sur la francisation du milieu de travail. 80p. 1980. 5.00 (ISBN 0-88806-061-0, AQ-12). Inst C D Howe.

Allais, Maurice & Hagen, Ole, eds. Expected Utility Hypotheses & the Allais Paradox. (Theory & Decision Library: No. 21). 1979. lib. bdg. 87.00 (ISBN 90-277-0960-2, Pub. by Reidel Holland). Kluwer Academic.

Allal, M. & Chuta, E. Cottage Industries & Handicrafts: Some Guidelines for Employment Promotion. 2nd ed. 200p. 1984. 11.40 (ISBN 92-2-103029-6). Intl Labour Office.

Allama Sir Abdullah al-Mamun alsuhrawardy. The Sayings of Muhammad. LC 79-52559. (Islam Ser.). 1980. Repr. of 1941 ed. lib. bdg. 12.00x (ISBN 0-8369-9266-0). Ayer Co Pubs.

Allan, Ann G., jt. ed. see Allison, Anne M.

Allan, Bill & Hinchcliffe, Keith. Planning Policy Analysis & Public Spending: Theory & the Papua New Guinea Practice. 168p. 1982. text ed. 35.00x (ISBN 0-566-00496-8). Gower Pub Co.

Allan, Blaine. Nicholas Ray: A Guide to References & Resources. 1984. lib. bdg. 49.95 (ISBN 0-8161-8059-8, Hall Reference). G K Hall.

Allan, Boris. Introducing Pascal. (Illus.). 170p. 1984. pap. 13.95 (ISBN 0-246-12322-2, Pub. by Granada England). Sheridan.

--Pocket Guide: LOGO. (Pitman Programming Pocket Guides Ser.). 64p. (Orig.). 1984. pap. 6.95 (ISBN 0-273-02109-5). Pitman Pub MA.

Allan, Cecil J. Nineteen Forty-Eight British Railway Locomotives, Comb. Vol. 10.00x (ISBN 0-392-08815-0, SpS). Sportshelf.

Allan, D. F. Philosophy of Aristotle. 2nd ed. (Oxford Paperbacks University Ser.). 1970. pap. 7.95x (ISBN 0-19-888037-5). Oxford U Pr.

Allan, D. G. William Shipley: Founder of the Royal Society of Arts. 1979. 22.50 (ISBN 0-85967-483-5); pap. 9.95 (ISBN 0-85967-484-3). Scolar.

Allan, D. G. & Schofield, R. E. Stephen Hales: Scientist & Philanthropist. 1980. 50.00 (ISBN 0-85967-482-7). Scolar.

Allan, D. J., ed. & tr. see Stenzel, Julius.

Allan, David & Brown, Vinson. An Illustrated Guide to Common Rocks & Their Minerals. rev. 2nd ed. LC 76-7372. (Illus.). 60p. (Orig.). 1976. pap. 3.00 (ISBN 0-87961-054-9). Naturegraph.

Allan, David R., ed. Uncoated Groundwood Papers: Proceedings of the First Uncoated Groundwood Papers Conference, New York, New York, November 1983. LC 84-60473. (Illus.). 112p. (Orig.). pap. 97.00 (ISBN 0-87930-155-4). Miller Freeman.

Allan, Douglas, jt. auth. see Purchese, Gillean.

Allan, Duncan. Outlines of Animal Immunobiology. (Illus.). 168p. 1980. spiral bound 24.00 (ISBN 0-7216-0781-0, Pub. by Bailliere-Tindall). Saunders.

Allan, Edward J. Advanced American Idioms. LC 80-82155. (Advanced American English Ser.). 68p. (Orig.). 1983. pap. text ed. 3.75 (ISBN 0-936808-00-4). Eng Educ Serv.

Allan, Elizabeth, jt. auth. see Watson, Adam.

Allan, Elizabeth, ed. see International Association of Business Communications.

Allan, Elizabeth, ed. see International Association of Business Communicators.

Allan, Elizabeth P. The Life & Letters of Margaret Junkin Preston. 1978. Repr. of 1903 ed. lib. bdg. 20.00 (ISBN 0-8495-0026-5). Arden Lib.

Allan, Eric, jt. auth. see Blogg, Rowan.

Allan, F. D., ed. Allan's Lone Star Ballads. LC 72-135170. 1970. Repr. of 1874 ed. lib. bdg. 21.00 (ISBN 0-8337-0040-5). B Franklin.

Allan, Francis C. The Mauser Parabellum. Koss, Joseph P., Jr., ed. (Illus.). 75p. (Orig.). 1985. pap. 9.95 (ISBN 0-9614814-0-4). AK Enterprises.

Allan, George. Life of Sir Walter Scott, Baronet. LC 74-9795. 1834. 45.00 (ISBN 0-8414-2985-5). Folcroft.

--The Structure of Industry in Britain: A Study in Economic Change. 3rd ed. LC 66-70817. pap. 70.30 (ISBN 0-317-20851-9, 2025263). Bks Demand UMI.

Allan, Iris. White Sioux. 1969. 9.95 (ISBN 0-88826-021-0). Superior Pub.

Allan, J. The Sahara: Ecological Change & Early History. 146p. 1983. lib. bdg. 14.50x (ISBN 0-906559-04-9). Westview.

Allan, J. A. Libya: The Experience of Oil. 320p. 1981. lib. bdg. 36.50x (ISBN 0-86531-232-X). Westview.

Allan, J. A., ed. Libya Since Independence: Economic & Social Development. LC 82-42564. 1982. 22.50x (ISBN 0-312-48363-5). St Martin.

Allan, James. The Life of James Allan, the Celebrated Northumberland Piper: Containing His Travels, Adventures & Wonderful Escapes, Etc. LC 80-2469. Repr. of 1817 ed. 62.50 (ISBN 0-404-19101-0). AMS Pr.

--Under the Dragon Flag: My Experiences in the Chino-Japanese War. LC 72-82087. (Japan Library Ser.). 1973. Repr. of 1898 ed. lib. bdg. 15.00 (ISBN 0-8420-1383-0). Scholarly Res Inc.

Allan, James W. Islamic Metalwork: The Nuhad Es-Said Collection. (Illus.). 128p. 1982. text ed. 105.00x (ISBN 0-85667-164-9, Pub. by Sotheby Pubns England). Biblio Dist.

Allan, John. The Gospel According to Science Fiction: An Esoteric Religion of the Future? LC 76-6920. (Illus.). 1976. 3.75 (ISBN 0-916608-02-6). Quill Pubns.

--The Kingdom of God. pap. 2.50 (ISBN 0-87516-286-X). De Vorss.

--Mysteries. (Book of Beliefs). 1981. 9.95 (ISBN 0-89191-477-3, 54775). Cook.

Allan, John, et al. Conversations in Spirit. LC 81-66244. 112p. (Orig.). 1981. pap. 4.95 (ISBN 0-87516-452-8). De Vorss.

Allan, John J., 3rd. CAD Systems: Proceedings of the IFIP Working Conference on Computer Aided Design Systems, Austin, Texas, February 12-14, 1976. 458p. 1976. 64.00 (ISBN 0-7204-0472-X, North-Holland). Elsevier.

Allan, Joseph P. & Martin, Russell. Entering Space: An Astronaut's Odyssey. rev., enl. ed. (Illus.). 240p. (Orig.). 1985. 24.95 (ISBN 0-941434-76-1); pap. 16.95 (ISBN 0-941434-74-5). Stewart Tabori & Chang.

Allan, Leslie, et al. Promised Lands 1: Subdivisions in Deserts & Mountains, Vol. 1. LC 76-46735. (Promised Lands Ser.). (Illus.). 1976. pap. 20.00x (ISBN 0-918780-04-7). INFORM.

Allan, Lorraine, jt. ed. see Gibbon, John.

Allan, Mabel E. A Dream of Hunger Moss. (Illus.). (gr. 5 up). 1983. 10.95 (ISBN 0-396-08224-6). Dodd.

--The Horns of Danger. 192p. (gr. 7 up). 1981. 7.95 (ISBN 0-396-07987-3). Dodd.

--A Lovely Tomorrow. LC 79-6642. (gr. 7 up). 1980. 7.95 (ISBN 0-396-07813-3). Dodd.

--The Mills Down Below. LC 80-2782. 192p. (gr. 7 up). 1981. 7.95 (ISBN 0-396-07926-1). Dodd.

--Mystery in Arles. LC 64-23321. (gr. 7 up). 1964. 5.95 (ISBN 0-8149-0255-3). Vanguard.

--Mystery in Wales. LC 79-89664. (gr. 7 up). 1970. 5.95 (ISBN 0-8149-0664-8). Vanguard.

--A Strange Enchantment. (gr. 7 up). 1982. PLB 8.95 (ISBN 0-396-08044-8). Dodd.

Allan, Mea. Darwin & His Flowers: The Key to Natural Selection. LC 77-77261. (Illus.). 1977. 14.50 (ISBN 0-8008-2113-0). Taplinger.

--William Robinson: Eighteen Thirty-Eight to Nineteen Thirty-Five. (Illus.). 288p. 1983. 23.95 (ISBN 0-571-11865-8). Faber & Faber.

Allan, Morton. Morton Allan Directory of European Passenger Steamship Arrivals for the Years 1890 to 1930 at the Port of New York, & for the Years 1904 to 1926 at the Ports of New York, Philadelphia, Boston, & Baltimore. LC 78-65163. 268p. 1980. Repr. of 1931 ed. 15.00 (ISBN 0-8063-0830-3). Genealog Pub.

Allan, Mowbray. T. S. Eliot's Impersonal Theory of Poetry. LC 73-489. 189p. 1974. 18.00 (ISBN 0-8387-1311-4). Bucknell U Pr.

Allan Nairn & Associates. The Reign of ETS: The Corporation That Makes up Minds. LC 80-107761. (The Ralph Nader Report on the Educational Testing Service). 554p. (Orig.). 1980. pap. 30.00 (ISBN 0-936486-00-7). R Nader.

Allan, Nick & Allan, Rosie. One Hundred One Ways to Your Wife's-Husband's Heart. LC 83-13136. 1983. 4.95 (ISBN 0-8407-5298-9). Nelson.

Allan, P. B. The Book-Hunter at Home. 1979. Repr. of 1920 ed. lib. bdg. 50.00 (ISBN 0-8495-0146-6). Arden Lib.

--The Book Hunter at Home. 1977. lib. bdg. 59.95 (ISBN 0-8490-1526-X). Gordon Pr.

--Leaves from a Moth Hunter's Notebook. 45.00x (ISBN 0-317-07105-X, Pub. by EW Classey UK). State Mutual Bk.

--Talking of Moths. 340p. 1943. 30.00x (ISBN 0-317-07181-5, Pub. by FW Classey UK). State Mutual Bk.

Allan, Peta & Jolley, Moya. Nursing, Midwifery & Health Visiting since 1900. 316p. 1982. 18.95 (ISBN 0-686-83081-4); pap. 10.95 (ISBN 0-571-11840-2). Faber & Faber.

Allan, Pierre. Crisis Bargaining & the Arms Race: A Theoretical Model. LC 82-12846. (Peace Science Studies). 192p. 1983. prof ref 25.00x (ISBN 0-88410-911-9). Ballinger Pub.

Allan, R. N., jt. auth. see Billinton, R.

Allan, Richard G., et al. U. S. History - Two, 5 vols. Incl. Vol. 1: Modern America Takes Shape. 242p (ISBN 0-86624-005-5, UU4); Vol. 2: Imperialism to Progressivism. 192p (ISBN 0-86624-006-3, UU5); Vol. 3: War, Prosperity & Depression. 180p (ISBN 0-86624-007-1, UU6); Vol. 4: The Roosevelt Years of Depression & War. 184p (ISBN 0-86624-008-X, UU7); Vol. 5: The Cold War Years. 244p (ISBN 0-86624-009-8, UU8); Teacher's Guide. avail. (UV9); End of Unit Test. avail. (UV0). (Illus.). 1981. pap. text ed. 5.95 ea. Bilingual Ed Serv.

Allan, Robert F., et al. Collegefields: Youth from Delinquency to Freedom. 176p. (Orig.). 1981. text ed. 18.95x (ISBN 0-8290-0273-1); pap. text ed. 9.95x (ISBN 0-8290-0274-X). Irvington.

Allan, Rogers, et al, eds. The Countryside Handbook. 98p. 1985. pap. 10.00 (ISBN 0-7099-1948-4, Pub. by Croom Helm Ltd). Longwood Pub Group.

Allan, Ronald N., jt. ed. see Billinton, Roy.

Allan, Rosie, jt. auth. see Allan, Nick.

Allan, Sidney see Hartmann, Sadakichi, pseud.

Allan, Stella. A Mortal Affair. 192p. 1981. pap. 2.25 (ISBN 0-380-54775-9, 54775-9). Avon.

Allan, Ted. Love Is a Long Shot. 1985. pap. 3.50 (ISBN 0-380-69941-9). Avon.

--Willie the Squowse. (Illus.). (gr. 2 up). 1978. 8.95 (ISBN 0-8038-8086-3). Hastings.

Allan, Ted & Gordon, Sydney. The Scalpel, the Sword: The Story of Doctor Norman Bethune. rev. ed. LC 73-8059. 336p. 1974. pap. 5.95 (ISBN 0-85345-302-0). Monthly Rev.

Allan, Ted, ed. see Shaw, Arnold.

Allan, Thomas D. Satellite Microwave Remote Sensing. (Marine Science Ser.). 526p. 1983. 110.00x (ISBN 0-470-27397-6). Halsted Pr.

Allan, W. B. Fibre Optics: Theory & Practice. LC 72-95066. (Optical Physics & Engineering Ser.). 247p. 1973. 42.50x (ISBN 0-306-30735-9, Plenum Pr). Plenum Pub.

Allan, W. J. Power & Sail: A Complete Guide to Yachting & Boating in New Zealand. (Illus.). 228p. 1975. pap. 9.95 (ISBN 0-89955-370-2, Pub. by Heinemann Pubs New Zealand). Intl Spec Bk.

Allan, William. The African Husbandman. LC 75-17188. (Illus.). 1977. Repr. of 1965 ed. lib. bdg. 33.50x (ISBN 0-8371-8287-5, ALAH). Greenwood.

--The Army of Northern Virginia in 1862. 1984. 60.00 (ISBN 0-89029-077-6). Pr of Morningside.

--Land Holding & Land Usage Among the Plateau Tonga of Mazabuka District, a Reconnaissance Survey, 1945. LC 76-129937. (Illus.). Repr. of 1948 ed. cancelled (ISBN 0-8371-0305-3, ALH&, Pub. by Negro U Pr). Greenwood.

Allana, G. Eminent Muslim Freedom Fighters, 1562-1947. 347p. 1983. text ed. 35.00x (ISBN 0-86590-152-X). Apt Bks.

Allanbrook, Wye J. Rhythmic Gesture in Mozart: "Le Nozze Di Figaro" & "Don Giovanni". LC 83-9184. (Illus.). 396p. 1984. lib. bdg. 30.00x (ISBN 0-226-01403-7). U of Chicago Pr.

Alland, Alexander. Adaptation in Cultural Evolution: An Approach to Medical Anthropology. LC 78-100666. 203p. 1970. 28.00x (ISBN 0-231-03229-3); pap. 11.50x (ISBN 0-231-03997-2). Columbia U Pr.

--Human Diversity. LC 79-138293. 203p. 1971. 26.00x (ISBN 0-231-03227-7). Columbia U Pr.

Alland, Alexander, Jr. The Human Imperative. LC 77-183227. 185p. 1972. 21.00x (ISBN 0-231-03228-5); pap. 10.00x (ISBN 0-231-08301-7). Columbia U Pr.

--Human Nature: Darwin's View. 232p. 1985. 25.00x (ISBN 0-231-05898-5). Columbia U Pr.

--Playing with Form: Children Draw in Six Countries. LC 82-25269. (Illus.). 224p. 1983. 30.00x (ISBN 0-231-05608-7); pap. 15.00x (ISBN 0-231-05609-5). Columbia U Pr.

--To Be Human: An Introduction to Cultural Anthropology. 657p. 1980. text ed. 25.95 (ISBN 0-394-34402-2, RanC). Random.

--To Be Human: An Introduction to Cultural Anthropology. 388p. 1981. pap. text ed. 23.95 (ISBN 0-394-34406-5, RanC). Random.

Alland, Guy & Hemingway, Patricia D. The Auto Repair Primer. LC 77-18808. 1978. pap. 8.95 (ISBN 0-316-35528-3). Little.

Allansmith, Mathea R. The Eye & Immunology. LC 81-14163. (Illus.). 209p. 1982. text ed. 37.95 (ISBN 0-8016-0117-7). Mosby.

Allanson, B. R., ed. Lake Sibaya. (Monographiae Biologicae: No. 36). 1980. lib. bdg. 68.50 (ISBN 90-6193-088-X, Pub. by Junk Pubs Netherlands). Kluwer Academic.

Allanson, E. W., ed. Car Ownership Forecasting. (Transportation & Planning Ser.). 168p. 1982. 37.95 (ISBN 0-677-05690-7). Gordon.

Allara, David L., ed. Stabilization & Degradation of Polymers. Hawkins, Walter L. LC 78-10600. (Advances in Chemistry Ser.: No. 169). 1978. 49.95 (ISBN 0-8412-0381-4). Am Chemical.

Allard, Dean C., Jr. Spencer Fullerton Baird & the U.S. Fish Commission: A Study in the History of American Science. new ed. Sterling, Keir B., ed. LC 77-81138. (Biologists & Their World Ser.). 1978. lib. bdg. 33.00x (ISBN 0-405-10738-2). Ayer Co Pubs.

Allard, Francis X. A Structural & Semantic Analysis of the German Modal Moegen. (Standford German Studies: Vol. 6). 117p. 1975. pap. 19.60. P Lang Pubs.

Allard, G. F., et al, eds. High Speed Can Manufacture, 2 vols. (Engineering Craftsmen Ser.: No. H301). (Illus.). 1972. Set. spiral bdg. 69.95x (ISBN 0-85083-159-8). Intl Ideas.

Allard, Harry. Bumps in the Night. LC 78-22301. (Illus.). 32p. (gr. 3). 1979. 7.95a (ISBN 0-385-12942-4); PLB (ISBN 0-385-12943-2). Doubleday.

--Bumps in the Night. (Illus.). 48p. (gr. 1-4). 1984. pap. 2.25 (ISBN 0-553-15284-X, Skylark). Bantam.

--I Will Not Go to Market Today. LC 78-72474. (Pied Piper Book). (Illus.). 32p. (ps-2). 1981. pap. 2.75 (ISBN 0-8037-4178-2, Pied Piper Bk). Dial Bks Young.

--It's So Nice to Have a Wolf Around the House. (Illus.). 1979. pap. 2.95 (ISBN 0-385-15188-8, Zephyr); PLB write for info. (ISBN 0-385-11301-3). Doubleday.

--May I Stay? LC 77-3024. (Illus.). (ps-2). 1978. 6.95 (ISBN 0-13-566323-7). P-H.

--Miss Nelson Has a Field Day. LC 84-27791. (Illus.). 32p. (gr. k-3). 1985. 12.95 (ISBN 0-395-36690-9). HM.

--Miss Nelson Is Missing. (gr. k-3). 1978. pap. 1.95 (ISBN 0-590-11877-3). Scholastic Inc.

--Miss Nelson is Missing. 1985. pap. 3.95 (ISBN 0-317-31626-5). HM.

--The Stupids Die. (Illus.). (gr. k-3). 1981. 9.95 (ISBN 0-395-30347-8). HM.

--The Stupids Have a Ball. LC 77-27660. (Illus.). (gr. k-3). 1978. PLB 10.95 (ISBN 0-395-26497-9). HM.

--The Stupids Have a Ball. (Illus.). 32p. (gr. k-3). pap. 3.95 (ISBN 0-395-36169-9, 4-90940). HM.

--The Stupids Step Out. LC 73-21698. (Illus.). 32p. (gr. k-3). 1974. PLB 10.95 (ISBN 0-395-18513-0). HM.

--There's a Party at Mona's Tonight. LC 79-319. (Illus.). 32p. (gr. 3). 1981. 8.95a (ISBN 0-385-15186-1); PLB (ISBN 0-385-15187-X). Doubleday.

--There's a Party at Mona's Tonight. (Snuggle & Read Story Bks.). (Illus.). 32p. (ps-3). 1985. pap. 2.25 (ISBN 0-380-69920-6, Camelot). Avon.

Allard, Harry & Marshall, James. Miss Nelson is Back. (Illus.). (gr. k-3). 1982. PLB 8.95 (ISBN 0-395-32956-6). HM.

--Miss Nelson Is Missing! (Illus.). (gr. k-3). 1977. PLB 10.95 reinforced bdg. (ISBN 0-395-25296-2). HM.

--The Stupids Step Out. (Illus.). (gr. k-3). 1977. pap. 2.95 (ISBN 0-395-25377-2). HM.

Allard, Jean-Louis. Education for Freedom: The Philosophy of Education of Jacques Maritain. Nelson, Ralph C., tr. 130p. 1982. pap. text ed. 8.95 (ISBN 0-268-00909-0). U of Notre Dame Pr.

Allard, Jeannine. The Legende: The Story of Philippa & Aurelie. 128p. (Orig.). 1984. pap. text ed. 5.95 (ISBN 0-932870-50-3). Alyson Pubns.

Allard, Louis. La Comedie De Moeurs En France Au Dixneuvieme Siecle. LC 23-17333. (Harvard Studies in Romance Languages Monographs: Vol. 5). 1923. 41.00 (ISBN 0-527-01103-7). Kraus Repr.

Allard, Lucile E. A Study of the Leisure Activities of Certain Elementary School Teachers of Long Island. LC 70-176510. (Columbia University. Teachers College. Contributions to Education: No. 779). Repr. of 1939 ed. 17.50 (ISBN 0-404-55779-1). AMS Pr.

Allard, M., jt. auth. see Jacobs, J. J.

Allard, Matsuo. Bird Day Afternoon. 32p. 1978. 10.00 (ISBN 0-913719-07-2); pap. 3.50 (ISBN 0-913719-06-4). High-Coo Pr.

Allard, R. J. An Approach to Econometrics. LC 75-4614. 227p. 1974. 18.75 (ISBN 0-470-02311-2). Krieger.

Allard, Robert W. Principles of Plant Breeding. LC 60-14240. 485p. 1960. 37.50 (ISBN 0-471-02310-8). Wiley.

Allard, S. Metals: Thermal & Mechanical Data. 1969. 125.00 (ISBN 0-08-006588-0). Pergamon.

Allard, Sven. Russia & the Austrian State Treaty: A Case Study of Soviet Policy in Europe. LC 68-8176. 1970. 24.50x (ISBN 0-271-00083-X). Pa St U Pr.

Allard, William A. Vanishing Breed: Photographs of the Cowboy & the West. LC 82-60768. 1982. 34.95 (ISBN 0-8212-1505-1, 396934); deluxe ed. o. p. 125.00 (ISBN 0-8212-1524-8, 903396); pap. 14.45. NYGS.

Allard, William A., jt. auth. see Running, John.

Allardt, Erik & Andre, Nils, eds. Nordic Democracy: Ideas, Issues, & Institutions in Politics, Economy, Education, Social, & Cultural Affairs of Denmark, Finland, Iceland, Norway & Sweden. Friis, Erik J., et al. Valen, Henry & Wendt, Frantz, trs. from Danish, Swedish, Norwegian, Icelandic & Finish. LC 82-146587. (Illus.). 780p. 1981. 36.00X (ISBN 87-7429-040-1). Nordic Bks.

Allardt, Linda. The Names of the Survivors. LC 79-25878. 49p. 1979. 4.00 (ISBN 0-87886-108-4). Ithaca Hse.

Allardt, Linda see Emerson, Ralph Waldo.

Allardyce, Alexander, ed. see Ramsay, John.

Allasio, John. Practice RCT Math Exam, No. 12. (gr. 9-12). 1982. Set of 20. 7.50 (ISBN 0-937820-44-X). Westsea Pub.

Allasio, John, et al. Practice RCT Math Exam, No. 1. 1980. Set of 20. 7.50 (ISBN 0-937820-02-4). Westsea Pub.

--Practice RCT Math Exam, No. 2. 1980. Set of 20. 7.50 (ISBN 0-937820-03-2). Westsea Pub.

--Practice Rct Math Exam, No. 3. 1980. Set of 20. 7.50 (ISBN 0-937820-04-0). Westsea Pub.

--Practice RCT Math Exam, No. 5. 1980. Set of 20. 7.50 (ISBN 0-937820-06-7). Westsea Pub.

--Practice RCT Math Exam, No. 6. (gr. 9-12). 1981. Set Of 20. 7.50 (ISBN 0-937820-07-5). Westsea Pub.

--Practice RCT Math Exam, No. 7. (gr. 9-12). 1981. Set Of 20. 7.50 (ISBN 0-937820-08-3). Westsea Pub.

--Practice RCT Math Exam, No. 8. (gr. 9-12). 1981. Set Of 20. 7.50 (ISBN 0-937820-09-1). Westsea Pub.

--Practice RCT Math Exam, No. 9. (gr. 9-12). 1981. Set Of 20. 7.50 (ISBN 0-937820-21-0). Westsea Pub.

--Practice RCT Math Exam, No. 10. (gr. 9-12). Set of 20. 7.50 (ISBN 0-937820-40-7). Westsea Pub.

--Practice RCT Math Exam, No. 11. (gr. 9-12). 1982. Set of 20. 7.50 (ISBN 0-937820-42-3). Westsea Pub.

--Practice RCT Math Exams, No. 4. 1980. Set of 20. 7.50 (ISBN 0-937820-05-9). Westsea Pub.

--Practice RCT Math Exams: No. 1, Spanish Version. 1981. Set of 20. 8.50 (ISBN 0-937820-12-1); set includes 20 Westsea Original practice RCT Math exam booklets, 20 answer sheets, 1 answer key, 1 scoring conversion table. Westsea Pub.

--Practice RCT Math Exams: No. 2, Spanish Version. 1981. Set of 20. 8.50 (ISBN 0-937820-13-X); set includes 20 Westsea Original practice RCT Math exam booklets, 20 answer sheets, 1 answer key, 1 scoring conversion table. Westsea Pub.

--RCT Mathematics: A Workbook. 168p. (gr. 9-12). 1980. pap. 6.95 (ISBN 0-937820-00-8); ans. key 1.95 (ISBN 0-937820-01-6). Westsea Pub.

Allason, Julian, jt. auth. see Bradbeer, Robin.

Allason, Rupert. The Branch: British Metropolitan Police SpecialBranch. (Illus.). 288p. 1983. 18.95 (ISBN 0-436-01165-4, Pub. by Secker & Warburg UK). David & Charles.

Allaway, William & Shorrock, Hallem, eds. The International Aspects of Higher Education. (Westview Special Studies in Education). 150p. 1985. 14.50 (ISBN 0-8133-7083-3). Westview.

Allbaugh, Leland G. Crete: A Case Study of an Underdeveloped Area. LC 52-5849. pap. 154.50 (ISBN 0-317-08685-5, 2000029). Bks Demand UMI.

Allbeury, Ted. The Alpha List. 228p. 1979. 9.95 (ISBN 0-416-00771-6, NO.0197). Methuen Inc.

--The Alpha List. 208p. (Orig.). 1982. pap. 2.25 (ISBN 0-505-51771-X, Pub. by Tower Bks). Dorchester Pub Co.

--Children of Tender Years. 240p. Date not set. 14.95 (ISBN 0-8253-0306-0). Beaufort Bks NY.

--The Other Side of Silence. LC 83-47578. 320p. 1983. pap. 3.37i (ISBN 0-06-080669-9, P 669, PL). Har-Row.

--Palomino Blonde. LC 83-47576. 160p. 1983. pap. 2.84i (ISBN 0-06-080670-2, P 670, PL). Har-Row.

--Snowball. LC 83-4757. 224p. 1983. pap. 2.84i (ISBN 0-06-080671-0, P671, PL). Har-Row.

Allbirght, Viv. Ten Go Hopping. LC 85-13010. (Illus.). 29p. (gr. 2-5). 1985. 6.95 (ISBN 0-571-13473-4). Faber & Faber.

Allbritton, Bert. Victory over Depression. 128p. (Orig.). 1981. pap. 3.50 (ISBN 0-88368-104-8). Whitaker Hse.

Allbritton, Cliff. How to Get Married: And Stay That Way. LC 82-71219. (Orig.). 1983. pap. 5.50 (ISBN 0-8054-5653-8). Broadman.

Allbut, R. London Rambles with Charles Dickens. LC 74-1229. (Studies in Dickens, No. 52). 1974. lib. bdg. 47.95x (ISBN 0-8383-1779-0). Haskell.

--Rambles in Dickens' Land. LC 76-52947. (Studies in Dickens, No. 52). 1977. lib. bdg. 48.95x (ISBN 0-8383-2139-9). Haskell.

Allbut, Robert. Rambles in Dickens' Land. 1899. 17.50 (ISBN 0-8274-3240-2). R West.

Allbutt, Mary E., jt. ed. see Fraser, J. D.

Allbutt, T. C. Greek Medicine in Rome. LC 69-13230. Repr. of 1921 ed. 30.00 (ISBN 0-405-08201-0, Pub. by Blom). Ayer Co Pubs.

Allbutt, Thomas C. The Historical Relations of Medicine & Surgery to the End of the 16th Century. LC 75-23672. Repr. of 1905 ed. 14.00 (ISBN 0-404-13225-1). AMS Pr.

--Science & Medieval Thought. LC 75-23673. Repr. of 1901 ed. 19.50 (ISBN 0-404-13226-X). AMS Pr.

Allchin, A. L., rev. by see Thunberg, Lars.

Allchin, A. M. The Joy of All Creation: An Anglican Meditation on the Place of Mary. LC 84-72479. 162p. 1985. pap. 7.50 (ISBN 0-936384-24-7). Cowley Pubns.

--The Kingdom of Love & Knowledge: The Encounter Between Orthodoxy & the West. 224p. (Orig.). 1982. 14.95 (ISBN 0-8164-0532-8, Pub. by Seabury). Winston Pr.

--The Living Presence of the Past: The Dynamic of Christian Tradition. 192p. (Orig.). 1981. pap. 7.95 (ISBN 0-8164-2334-2, Pub. by Seabury). Winston Pr.

--The World Is a Wedding. 1978. 12.95x (ISBN 0-19-520079-9). Oxford U Pr.

--The World Is a Wedding: Explorations in Christian Spirituality. (Crossroad Paperback Ser.). 512p. 1982. pap. 6.95 (ISBN 0-8245-0411-9). Crossroad NY.

Allchin, Arthur M., jt. ed. see Coulson, John.

Allchin, Bridget & Allchin, Raymond. The Rise of Civilization in India & Pakistan. LC 82-1262. (World Archaeology Ser.). (Illus.). 352p. 1982. 57.50 (ISBN 0-521-24244-4); pap. 17.95 (ISBN 0-521-28550-X). Cambridge U Pr.

Allchin, Bridget, et al, eds. The Prehistory & Palaeogeography of the Great Indian Desert. 1978. 73.00 (ISBN 0-12-050450-2). Acad Pr.

Allchin, Bridget, et al, eds. see International Conference of the Association of South Asian Archaeologists in Western Europe, 6th.

Allchin, F. R. Neolithic Cattle-Keepers of Southern India. (University of Cambridge Oriental Pubs). 1963. 39.50 (ISBN 0-521-04018-3). Cambridge U Pr.

Allchin, F. R. & Hammond, N., eds. The Archaeology of Afghanistan: From Earliest Times to the Timurid Period 1978. 1979. 87.50 (ISBN 0-12-050440-5). Acad Pr.

Allchin, M. C. A History of Highland Locomotives. 128p. 30.00x (ISBN 0-86093-048-3, Pub. by ORPC Ltd UK). State Mutual Bk.

Allchin, Raymond, jt. auth. see Allchin, Bridget.

Allcock, H. R. Heteroatom Ring Systems & Polymers. 1967. 73.50 (ISBN 0-12-050550-9). Acad Pr.

--Phosphorus-Nitrogen Compounds: Cyclic, Linear, & High-Polymeric Systems. 1972. 85.50 (ISBN 0-12-050560-6). Acad Pr.

Allcock, John B., ed. see Durkheim, Emile.

Allcorn, Seth. Internal Auditing for Hospitals. LC 79-20072. 212p. 1980. text ed. 38.50 (ISBN 0-89443-163-3). Aspen Systems.

Allcroft, Arthur. A History of Sicily, 491-289 B.C. 1977. lib. bdg. 59.95 (ISBN 0-8490-1986-9). Gordon Pr.

Allday, D. Heken. Insurrection in Wales. 220p. 1982. 32.00 (ISBN 0-86138-001-0, Pub. by Terence Dalton England). State Mutual Bk.

Allderidge, Patricia. The Late Richard Dadd, Eighteen Seventeen to Eighteen Eighty-Six. (Illus.). 172p. 16.95 (ISBN 0-900874-79-1, Pub. by Salem Acad); pap. 9.95 (ISBN 0-900874-78-3). Merrimack Pub Cir.

Alldis, James. Animals As Friends: A Head Keeper Remembers London Zoo. LC 73-5275. (Illus.). 128p. 1973. 5.95 (ISBN 0-8008-0271-3). Taplinger.

Alldridge, J. C. Ilse Aichinger. LC 74-92613. (Modern German Authors: Texts & Contexts Vol. 2). 1969. 9.95 (ISBN 0-8023-1235-7). Dufour.

Alldridge, Thomas J. Sierra Leone As It Was & Is: Its Progress, People, Native Customs, & Undeveloped Wealth. 1976. lib. bdg. 59.95 (ISBN 0-8490-2602-4). Gordon Pr.

--Transformed Colony, Sierra Leone. LC 74-109313. (Illus.). Repr. of 1910 ed. 31.00x (ISBN 0-8371-3564-8, ASL&). Greenwood.

Alldritt, Keith. Eliot's Four Quartets: Poetry As Chamber Music. 141p. 1978. 18.50x (ISBN 0-7130-0161-5, Pub by Woburn Pr England). Biblio Dist.

Allee, et al. Basic Compounding & Processing of Rubber. Long, Harry, ed. (Illus.). xii, 237p. 1985. text ed. 10.00 (ISBN 0-912415-02-9). Rubber Division.

Allee, G. Franklin. God & the Timberwolf. 240p. 1985. pap. 8.95 (ISBN 0-8341-0956-5). Beacon Hill.

Allee, John G., jt. auth. see Demura, Fumio.

Allee, John G., ed. Webster's Dictionary for Everyday Use. pap. 3.80i (ISBN 0-06-463330-6, EH 330, EH). B&N NY.

Allee, John S. Product Liability. LC 84-7928. 1984. 35.00. NY Law Pub.

Allee, Warder C. Animal Aggregations, A Study in General Sociology. LC 75-41007. Repr. of 1931 ed. 28.00 (ISBN 0-404-14501-9). AMS Pr.

--The Social Life of Animals. LC 75-41008. Repr. of 1938 ed. 22.00 (ISBN 0-404-14639-2). AMS Pr.

Alleger, Daniel E., ed. Fertile Lands of Friendship: The Florida-Costa Rican Experiment in International Agricultural Cooperation. LC 62-20773. 1962. 6.50 (ISBN 0-8130-0007-6). U Presses Fla.

--Social Change & Aging in the Twentieth-Century. LC 53-12339. (Center for Gerontological Studies & Programs Ser.: No. 13). 1964. pap. 5.00 (ISBN 0-8130-0008-4). U Presses Fla.

Alleger, Daniel E., ed. see Bard, Samuel A.

Allegheny Trails Council, Boy Scouts of America & National Flag Foundation. Broad Stripes & Bright Stars. (Illus.). 61p. 1970. 4.95 (ISBN 0-318-15630-X). Natl Flag Foun.

Allego, Antonio M. This Time Yesterday. 109p. (Orig.). 1984. pap. 6.25x (ISBN 971-10-0152-7, Pub. by New Day Philippines). Cellar.

Allegra, Joseph E. Chemotherapy of Malignant Disease. 280p. 1985. 27.50 (ISBN 0-87527-349-1). Green.

Allegre, C. J. & Michard, G. Introduction to Geochemistry. Varney, R. N., tr. from Fr. LC 74-83871. (Geophysics & Astrophysics Monographs: No. 10). 1974. lib. bdg. 31.50 (ISBN 90-277-0497-X, Pub. by Reidel Holland); pap. text ed. 18.50 (ISBN 90-277-0498-8, Pub. by Reidel Holland). Kluwer Academic.

Allegre, C. J. & Hart, S. R., eds. Trace Elements in Igneous Petrology. (Developments in Petrology: Vol. 5). 1978. Repr. 72.50 (ISBN 0-444-41658-7). Elsevier.

Allegre, Carlos. A Lost Mine Called the Virgin of Guadalupe. 294p. (Orig.). 1984. pap. 3.50 (ISBN 0-930541-00-6). Santo Tomas Pr.

Allegri, T. H., Sr. Handling & Management of Hazardous Wastes. 350p. 1985. 34.50 (ISBN 0-412-00751-7, 9669, Pub. by Chapman & Hall England). Methuen Inc.

Allegri, Theodore H. Materials Handling: Principles & Applications. (Illus.). 480p. 1984. 42.50 (ISBN 0-442-20985-1). Van Nos Reinhold.

Allegro, J. M. Dead Sea Scrolls. 1956. pap. 4.95 (ISBN 0-14-020376-1, Pelican). Penguin.

Allegro, John. The Dead Sea Scrolls & the Christian Myth. LC 83-63566. (Illus.). 248p. 1984. 19.95 (ISBN 0-87975-241-6). Prometheus Bks.

--Physician, Heal Thyself. 85p. 1985. 13.95 (ISBN 0-87975-305-6). Prometheus Bks.

Allegro, John M. All Manner of Men. (Illus.). 186p. 1982. spiral 16.75x (ISBN 0-398-04575-5). C C Thomas.

Alleine, Joseph. Alarm. 1978. pap. 3.45 (ISBN 0-85151-081-7). Banner of Truth.

Alleine, Richard. Heaven Opened. (Summit Books). 1978. pap. 3.95 (ISBN 0-8010-0136-6). Baker Bk.
Allem, ed. see De Balzac, Honore.
Allem, ed. see De Beaumarchais, Pierre A.
Allem, ed. see De Musset, Alfred.
Allem, Maurice, ed. see Musset, Alfred de.
Allem, Maurice, ed. see Sainte-Beuve, Charles-Augustin.
Alleman, Herman C. Prayers for Boys. LC 81-142145. (gr. 4-9). pap. 4.95 (ISBN 0-8407-5241-5). Nelson.
Alleman, Richard. The Movie Lover's Guide to Hollywood: A Guide to Over 300 Attractions from the Glory Days of Motion Pictures. LC 84-48574. (Illus.). 288p. (Orig.). 1985. pap. 10.53i (ISBN 0-06-091262-6, CN 1262, CN). Har-Row.
Alleman-Brooks, Janet E., jt. auth. see Joyce, William W.
Allemand, Gordon L., jt. auth. see Townsend, Donald E.
Allemann, Beda, jt. ed. see Koppen, Erwin.
Allen. Antitrust & Trade Regulation. (The Law in North Carolina Ser.). 24.95 (ISBN 0-686-90932-1). Harrison Co GA.
--Computerized Inventory Procedures. 1986. pap. text ed. price not set wkbk. (ISBN 0-538-19040-X, S04). SW Pub.
--Faith, Hope & Love. 5.95 (ISBN 0-318-18178-9). WCTU.
--The Lady Name. 1985. pap. 3.95 (ISBN 0-02-765580-6). Warner Bks.
--The Latchkey Children. 8.95 (ISBN 0-19-277111-6, Pub. by Oxford U Pr Childrens). Merrimack Pub Cir.
--Pharaohs & Pyramids. (Time Traveler Books). (gr. 4-9). 1977. 7.95 (ISBN 0-86020-083-3, Usborne-Hayes); PLB 12.95 (ISBN 0-88110-103-6); pap. 4.95 (ISBN 0-86020-084-1). EDC.
--Secret of Abundant Living. 2.50 (ISBN 0-318-18181-9). WCTU.
--Sewing & Knitting. (Beginner's Guides Ser.). (gr. 4-9). 1979. PLB 11.95 (ISBN 0-88110-035-8); pap. 2.95 (ISBN 0-86020-311-5). EDC.
Allen & Foreman. Crowns & Bridges. 1986. price not set (ISBN 0-7236-0760-5). PSG Pub Co.
Allen & Simonsen. Corrections in America: An Introduction. 4th ed. 622p. 1986. text ed. price not set (ISBN 0-02-301770-8). Macmillan.
Allen, ed. Polymers with Unusual Properties. price not set (ISBN 0-471-88172-4). Wiley.
Allen, ed. see Choderlos De Laclos, P.
Allen, ed. see Hugo, Victor.
Allen, jt. auth. see Booz.
Allen, A. H. An Introduction to Prestressed Concrete. (Educational Ser.). (Illus.). 1978. pap. 17.50x (ISBN 0-7210-1090-3). Scholium Intl.
Allen, A. H., jt. auth. see McMurtrie, D. C.
Allen, A. H., ed. see McMurtrie, D. C.
Allen, A. L., et al. Practical Field Surveying & Computations. (Illus.). 688p. 1968. 37.00 (ISBN 0-434-90061-3, Pub. by W Heinemann Ltd). David & Charles.
Allen, A. M. A History of Verona. 1977. lib. bdg. 59.95 (ISBN 0-8490-2012-3). Gordon Pr.
Allen, Adrian, et al, eds. Mechanisms of Mucosal Protection in the Upper Gastrointestinal Tract. 416p. 1984. text ed. 58.50 (ISBN 0-89004-317-5). Raven.
Allen, Agnes. The Story of Sculpture. 2nd ed. (Illus.). 220p. 1967. 7.95 (ISBN 0-571-04601-0). Faber & Faber.
Allen, Alexander. Jonathan Edwards: 1703-1758. lib. bdg. 23.50 (ISBN 0-8337-3926-3). B Franklin.
--Travelling Ladies. 240p. 1981. 24.00x (ISBN 0-906379-16-4, Pub. by Jupiter England). State Mutual Bk.
Allen, Alexandra, jt. auth. see Arellano, Richard G.
Allen, Algernon R., jt. auth. see Annis, John R.
Allen, Alice, jt. auth. see Everett, Mark R.
Allen, Alice B. Simon Benson: Northwest Lumber King. LC 77-157143. 1970. 10.00 (ISBN 0-8323-0047-0). Binford.
Allen, Ann T. Satire & Society in Wilhelmine Germany: Kladderadatsch & Simplicissimus 1890-1914. LC 84-5114. (Illus.). 272p. 1984. 25.00x (ISBN 0-8131-1512-4). U Pr of KY.
Allen, Anne. Sports for the Handicapped. (gr. 6 up). 1981. 9.95 (ISBN 0-8027-6436-3); lib. bdg. 10.85 (ISBN 0-8027-6437-1). Walker & Co.
Allen, Archie E., jt. auth. see Lewis, John.
Allen, Ardelle. Ida. LC 79-17461. 96p. (Orig.). 1979. pap. 3.95 (ISBN 0-89621-040-5). Thorndike Pr.
Allen, Arnold O. Probability, Statistics & Queueing Theory: With Computer Science Application. (Computer Science & Applied Math Ser.). 1978. 35.00 (ISBN 0-12-051050-2). Acad Pr.
Allen, Arthur B. A Tale That Is Told: A Pageant of English Literature, 1900-1950. 223p. 1983. Repr. of 1960 ed. lib. bdg. 40.00 (ISBN 0-89987-044-9). Darby Bks.
Allen, Arthur J. A Whaler & Trader in the Arctic: Eighteen Ninety-Five to Nineteen Forty-Four. LC 78-2575. (Illus.). 1978. pap. 5.95 (ISBN 0-88240-105-X). Alaska Northwest.
Allen Associates. The New York Times American Studies Program, 3 Pt. Ser. 64p. 1981. pap. text ed. write for info. (ISBN 0-912853-07-7). Skills (ISBN 0-912853-09-3). Topics (ISBN 0-912853-08-5). NY Times.
Allen, B. L. Basic Anatomy: A Laboratory Manual: the Human Skeleton, the Cat. 2nd ed. (Illus.). 171p. 1980. 14.95 (ISBN 0-7167-1091-9). W H Freeman.
Allen, Barbara & Montell, William L. From Memory to History: Using Oral Sources in Local Historical Research. LC 81-3485. (Illus.). 176p. 1981. text ed. 12.50x cloth (ISBN 0-910050-51-1). AASLH Pr.
Allen, Barbara, et al. ECFMG - FMG: Pt. II. 2nd ed. 1983. pap. text ed. 16.95 (ISBN 0-87488-121-8). Med Exam.
--Barbara Allen's Bargain Book. Johnson, Sylvia, ed. (Illus.). 153p. (Orig.). 1981. pap. 4.95 (ISBN 0-942050-03-7). Southern-Lite.
Allen, Barbara A. National Boards Examination Review: For Part III. 1984. pap. write for info. (ISBN 0-87488-074-2). Med Exam.
Allen, Barbara A., jt. auth. see Allen, James R.
Allen, Barbara A., jt. ed. see Allen, James.
Allen, Barbara A., et al. FMG-VQE: Vol. 2, Clinical Sciences. 1983. pap. text ed. 16.95 (ISBN 0-87488-125-0). Med Exam.
Allen, Barry. Sports Illustrated Skin Diving & Snorkeling. LC 72-14150. 1973. pap. 2.95i (ISBN 0-397-00970-4, LP79). Har-Row.
Allen, Belton E. Microcomputer System Software & Languages. (Tutorial Texts Ser.). 231p. 1980. 20.00 (ISBN 0-8186-0340-2, Q340). IEEE Comp Soc.
Allen, Bem P. Social Behavior: Fact & Falsehood. LC 77-28709. 260p. 1978. 22.95x (ISBN 0-88229-393-1). Nelson-Hall.
Allen, Bem P. & Potkay, Charles R. Adjective Generation Technique (AGT) Research & Applications. 500p. 1984. text ed. 49.50x (ISBN 0-8290-0718-0). Irvington.
Allen Benj. & Co. & William Green Brothers Staff. Eighteen Ninety-Seven Watches. 1968. pap. 5.00 (ISBN 0-915706-11-3). Am Reprints.
Allen, Betsy. Connie Blair: The Brown Satchel Mystery. (gr. 6 up). 1978. pap. 1.25 (ISBN 0-448-14803-X, Pub. by Tempo). Ace Bks.
--Connie Blair: The Clue in Blue. (gr. 6 up). 1978. pap. 1.25 (ISBN 0-448-14802-1, Pub. by Tempo). Ace Bks.
--Connie Blair: The Mystery of the Ruby Queens. (gr. 6 up). 1978. pap. 1.25 (ISBN 0-448-14801-3, Pub. by Tempo). Ace Bks.
Allen, Beverly. Pier Paolo Pasolini: The Poetics of Heresy. (Illus.). 144p. (Orig.). 1982. pap. 25.00 (ISBN 0-915838-11-7). Anma Libri.
Allen, Beverly, jt. auth. see Allen, Ronald.
Allen, Beverly, et al, eds. The Defiant Muse: Italian Feminist Poems from the Middle Ages to the Present. 225p. (Orig., Ital.). 1985. text ed. 24.95 (ISBN 0-935312-48-X); pap. text ed. 9.95 (ISBN 0-935312-55-2). Feminist Pr.
Allen, Bill & Lyons, Lamont. Effective Teacher Evaluation. LC 76-21433. (Mandala Ser. in Education). 39p. 1981. pap. 3.95 (ISBN 0-916250-20-2). Irvington.
--Teacher Evaluation: A Color & Activity Book. LC 76-21433. (Mandala Ser. in Education). (Illus.). 1976. pap. 7.95 (ISBN 0-916250-18-0). Irvington.
Allen, Bill, jt. auth. see Hays, Dick.
Allen, Blaine. When God Says No. LC 81-9556. 168p. 1981. pap. 4.95 (ISBN 0-8407-5781-6). Nelson.
Allen, Blair H. Atlantis Trilogy. 1982. pap. 1.25 (ISBN 0-917458-09-5). Kent Pubns.
--Dreamwish of the Magician: Long Poem. 8p. (Orig.). 1983. pap. 1.00 (ISBN 0-917458-11-7). Kent Pubns.
Allen, Bob. George Jones: The Saga of an American Singer. LC 84-1541. (Illus.). 312p. 1984. 15.95 (ISBN 0-385-27906-X). Doubleday.
Allen, Brandt, jt. auth. see Rotch, William.
Allen, Brandt R. VisiCalc: Apple. 1984. pap. text ed. 10.95 (ISBN 0-8359-8410-9). Reston.
--VisiCalc: IBM. 1984. pap. text ed. 10.95 (ISBN 0-8359-8408-7). Reston.
--VisiCalc: TRS-80. 1984. pap. text ed. 10.95 (ISBN 0-8359-8409-5). Reston.
Allen, Bryan, jt. auth. see Scrivener, Len.
Allen, Bryan, ed. The World of Phyllis Haylor & Ballroom Dancing. (Ballroom Dance Ser.). 1985. lib. bdg. 79.95 (ISBN 0-87700-660-1). Revisionist Pr.
Allen, Bud & Bosta, Diana. Games Criminals Play: How You Can Profit by Knowing Them. LC 80-54225. 228p. 1981. 12.95 (ISBN 0-9605226-0-3). Rae John.
--How to Be a Successful Trainer: Without Being Tarred & Feathered. 62p. 1981. vinyl 8.95x (ISBN 0-9605226-8-9). Rae John.
--Library of Lesson Plans: Courtroom Demeanor. 95p. 1982. vinyl 39.95 (ISBN 0-939438-22-4). Rae John.
--Library of Lesson Plans: Creative Thinking & Problem Solving. 80p. 1982. vinyl 39.95 (ISBN 0-939438-19-4). Rae John.
--Library of Lesson Plans: Forty Hour Orientation Package. 82p. 1981. vinyl 39.95 (ISBN 0-9605226-4-6). Rae John.
--Library of Lesson Plans: How Administrators & Victims Can Handle a Hostage Situation. 100p. 1982. loose-leaf bdg. 49.95 (ISBN 0-939438-21-6). Rae John.
--Library of Lesson Plans: How to Handle Classroom Disturbances. 64p. 1982. vinyl 29.95 (ISBN 0-939438-20-8). Rae John.
--Library of Lesson Plans: Rape Prevention-How to Avoid It & What to Do If You Can't. 41p. 1981. vinyl 29.95 (ISBN 0-9605226-5-4). Rae John.
--Library of Lesson Plans: Stress Management. 64p. 1981. vinyl 49.95 (ISBN 0-939438-17-8). Rae John.
--Library of Lesson Plans: Team Building & Listening Workshop. 90p. 1981. vinyl 49.95 (ISBN 0-939438-16-X). Rae John.
--Library of Lesson Plans: The Anatomy of a Set up. 222p. 1981. looseleaf folder 59.95 (ISBN 0-939438-18-6). Rae John.
--Library of Lesson Plans: Vol. 1, Career Development. 285p. 1981. loose leaf bdg. 99.95 (ISBN 0-939438-02-X). Rae John.
--Library of Lesson Plans: Vol. 1, No. 1, Professionalism-What It Really Means. 50p. 1981. vinyl 29.95 (ISBN 0-939438-00-3). Rae John.
--Library of Lesson Plans: Vol. 1, No. 2, Report Writing. 105p. 1981. 39.95 (ISBN 0-9605226-1-1). Rae John.
--Library of Lesson Plans: Vol. 1, No. 3, How to Take Promotional Examinations & Oral Interviews. 74p. 1981. vinyl 29.95 (ISBN 0-9605226-3-8). Rae John.
--Library of Lesson Plans: Vol. 1, No. 4, How to Reduce Sick Leave. 57p. 1981. vinyl 29.95 (ISBN 0-939438-01-1). Rae John.
--Library of Lesson Plans: Vol. 2, No. 1 Basic Supervision. 73p. 1981. vinyl 29.95 (ISBN 0-939438-09-7). Rae John.
--Library of Lesson Plans: Vol. 2, No. 2, Discretionary Decision Making. 61p. 1981. vinyl 29.95 (ISBN 0-939438-10-0). Rae John.
--Library of Lesson Plans: Vol. 2, No. 3, Corrective Interviewing for Supervisors. 63p. 1981. vinyl 29.95 (ISBN 0-939438-11-9). Rae John.
--Library of Lesson Plans: Vol. 2, No. 4, Human Relations. 67p. 1981. vinyl 29.95 (ISBN 0-939438-12-7). Rae John.
--Library of Lesson Plans: Vol. 2, Supervision in Depth. 257p. 1981. loose leaf binder 99.95 (ISBN 0-939438-03-8). Rae John.
--Library of Lesson Plans: Vol. 3, Improving Staff-Inmate Relations. 256p. 1981. loose leaf binder 99.95 (ISBN 0-939438-04-6). Rae John.
--Library of Lesson Plans: Vol. 3, No. 1, How to Recognize & Handle Disturbed Inmates. 41p. 1981. vinyl 29.95 (ISBN 0-9605226-2-X). Rae John.
--Library of Lesson Plans: Vol. 3, No. 2, Counseling & Interviewing. 78p. 1981. vinyl 29.95 (ISBN 0-939438-06-2). Rae John.
--Library of Lesson Plans: Vol. 3, No. 3, Staff-Inmate Relations. 82p. 1981. vinyl 29.95 (ISBN 0-939438-07-0). Rae John.
--Library of Lesson Plans: Vol. 3, No. 4, Recognizing Signs of a Riot & What to Do About Them. 57p. 1981. vinyl 29.95 (ISBN 0-939438-08-9). Rae John.
--Library of Lesson Plans: Vol. 4, No. 1, Custodial Competence & Expectations. 79p. 1981. vinyl 29.95 (ISBN 0-939438-13-5). Rae John.
--Library of Lesson Plans: Vol. 4, No. 2, Transportation of Prisoners & How to Build a Transportation Kit. 41p. 1981. vinyl 29.95 (ISBN 0-9605226-6-2). Rae John.
--Library of Lesson Plans: Vol. 4, No. 3, What Most People Don't Know About Court Procedure. 42p. 1981. vinyl 29.95 (ISBN 0-939438-14-3). Rae John.
--Library of Lesson Plans: Vol. 4, No. 4, Search Techniques. 67p. 1981. vinyl 29.95 (ISBN 0-939438-15-1). Rae John.
--Library of Lesson Plans: Vol. 4, Techniques of Custodial Functions. 227p. 1981. looseleaf binder 99.95 (ISBN 0-939438-05-4). Rae John.
--Pure Gold. 87p. 1981. vinyl 8.95 (ISBN 0-9605226-7-0). Rae John.
Allen, C., jt. auth. see Harmon, T.
Allen, C. D. Ex-Libris, Essays of a Collector. 59.95 (ISBN 0-8490-0147-1). Gordon Pr.
Allen, C. F., et al. Heterocyclic Compounds, Vol. 12. LC 45-8533. 646p. 83.50 (ISBN 0-470-37851-4). Krieger.
Allen, C. G. A Short Economic History of Modern Japan. 4th ed. 272p. 1980. 27.50 (ISBN 0-312-71771-7). St Martin.
Allen, C. G., jt. auth. see Aitchison, Jean.
Allen, C. G., ed. Rulers & Government of the World: 1977-1978, 3 vols. Incl. Vol. I. Earliest Times to 1491. Ross, Martha, compiled by. LC 77-72342. 1978 (ISBN 0-85935-021-5); Vol. II. 1492 to 1929. Spuler, Bertold, compiled by. LC 77-70294. 1977 (ISBN 0-85935-009-6); Vol. III. 1930 to 1975. Spuler, Bertold, compiled by. LC 77-72339. 1978 (ISBN 0-85935-056-8). 49.50 ea.; Set. 135.00 (ISBN 0-85935-051-7). Bowker.
Allen, C. W. Astrophysical Quantities. 310p. 1976. text ed. 65.00 (ISBN 0-485-11150-0, Pub. by Athlone Pr Ltd). Longwood Pub Group.
--Walt Whitman Abroad. 1985. 48.50 (ISBN 0-317-19982-X). Porter.
--Walt Whitman Poet, Philosopher. 1985. 48.50 (ISBN 0-317-19984-6). Porter.
Allen, Cady H., jt. auth. see Rasooli, Jay M.
Allen, Carl P., jt. auth. see Moriarity, Shane.
Allen, Carleton K. Law in the Making. 7th ed. 1964. pap. 19.95x (ISBN 0-19-881029-6, OPB29). Oxford U Pr.
Allen, Carlos & Estudios, Guias de. Guia De Estudios Sobre Estudios En el Nuevo Testamento. (Illus.). 96p. 1981. pap. 3.50 (ISBN 0-311-43502-5). Casa Bautista.
Allen, Carol & Lustig, Herbert. Tea with Demons. LC 85-5066. 275p. 1985. 14.95 (ISBN 0-688-05093-X). Morrow.
Allen, Catherine. The New Lottie Moon Story. LC 79-52336. 1980. 8.95 (ISBN 0-8054-6319-4). Broadman.
Allen, Cecil J. Great Eastern Railway. 19.50x (ISBN 0-392-07857-0, SpS). Sportshelf.
--Modern Railways: Their Engineering, Equipment & Operation. LC 72-9045. (Illus.). 307p. 1973. Repr. of 1959 ed. lib. bdg. 24.75x (ISBN 0-8371-6565-2, ALMR). Greenwood.
Allen, Chaney. I'm Black & I'm Sober. LC 77-86454. 1978. pap. 6.95 (ISBN 0-89638-008-4). CompCare.
--I'm Black & I'm Sober. 280p. 1978. 6.95 (ISBN 0-318-15332-7). Natl Coun Alcoholism.
Allen, Charles. A Mountain in Tibet: The Search for Mount Kailas & the Sources of the Great Rivers of Asia. (Illus.). 256p. 1982. 27.50 (ISBN 0-233-97281-1). Andre Deutsch.
--A Mountain in Tibet: The Search for Mount Kailas & the Sources of the Great Rivers of Asia. (Illus.). 256p. 1982. 27.00 (ISBN 0-233-97281-1, Pub. by A Deutsch England). David & Charles.
--Notes of the Bacon-Shakespeare Question. 59.95 (ISBN 0-8490-0738-0). Gordon Pr.
--Notes on the Bacon-Shakespeare Question. LC 75-113542. Repr. of 1900 ed. 10.00 (ISBN 0-404-00326-5). AMS Pr.
--Plain Tales from the Raj. (Illus.). 240p. 1985. pap. 12.95 (ISBN 0-03-005862-7). HR&W.
--Pocket Dicionary of Ukulele Chords. pap. 1.50 (ISBN 0-934286-24-8). Kenyon.
--Pocket Dictionary of Baritone Ukulele Chords. pap. 1.50 (ISBN 0-934286-21-3). Kenyon.
--Pocket Dictionary of Mandolin Chords. pap. 1.50 (ISBN 0-934286-23-X). Kenyon.
--Pocket Dictionary of Tenor Banjo Chords. pap. 1.50 (ISBN 0-934286-20-5). Kenyon.
--The Touch of the Masters Hand. 128p. pap. 2.75 (ISBN 0-515-07378-4). Jove Pubns.
Allen, Charles & Dwivedi, Sharada. Lives of the Indian Princes. (Illus.). 352p. 1985. 24.95 (ISBN 0-517-55689-8). Crown.
Allen, Charles, jt. auth. see Ryder, George.
Allen, Charles, ed. Tales from the Dark Continent. 192p. 1979. 30.00x (ISBN 0-563-17754-3, Pub. by BBC Pubns). State Mutual Bk.
--Tales from the Dark Continent: Images of British Colonial Africa in the 20th Century. (Illus.). 166p. 1979. 19.95 (ISBN 0-233-97171-8, Pub. by A Deutsch England). David & Charles.
Allen, Charles D. American Book-Plates. LC 68-20212. (Illus.). 1968. 20.00 (ISBN 0-405-08203-7, Pub. by Blom). Ayer Co Pubs.
Allen, Charles F., jt. auth. see Allen, Ruth N.
Allen, Charles L. All Things Are Possible Through Prayer. 1984. pap. 3.95 (ISBN 0-515-08463-8, PV072). Jove Pubns.
--All Things Are Possible Through Prayer. 8.95 (ISBN 0-8007-0007-4); pap. 2.50 (ISBN 0-8007-8000-0, Spire Bks). Revell.
--Charles L. Allen Treasury. Wallis, Charles L., ed. 192p. 1970. 10.95 (ISBN 0-8007-0398-7). Revell.
--Faith, Hope, & Love. 192p. 1982. pap. 5.95 (ISBN 0-8007-5096-9, Power Bks). Revell.
--God's Psychiatry. 1984. pap. 2.95 (ISBN 0-515-08234-1). Jove Pubns.
--God's Psychiatry. 160p. 9.95 (ISBN 0-8007-0113-5); pap. 2.95 (ISBN 0-8007-8015-9, Spire Bks); pap. 5.95 (ISBN 0-8007-5010-1, Power Bks). Revell.
--Inspiring Thoughts for Your Marriage. 1985. 7.95 (ISBN 0-8007-1401-6). Revell.
--Joyful Living in the Fourth Dimension. 160p. 1983. 9.95 (ISBN 0-8007-1351-6). Revell.
--Life More Abundant. pap. 2.25 (ISBN 0-515-06412-2). Jove Pubns.
--The Miracle of Love. LC 72-5430. 128p. 1972. 7.95 (ISBN 0-8007-0543-2). Revell.
--Perfect Peace. 160p. 1979. 9.95 (ISBN 0-8007-1055-X). Revell.
--The Secret of Abundant Living. 160p. 1980. 8.95 (ISBN 0-8007-1123-8); Spire Bks. pap. 3.50 (ISBN 0-8007-8479-0). Revell.
--La Siquiatria de Dios. 176p. 1975. 2.75 (ISBN 0-88113-280-2). Edit Betania.
--Touch of the Master's Hand: Christ's Miracles for Today. 160p. 1956. pap. 2.75 (ISBN 0-8007-8093-0, Spire Bks). Revell.
--Twenty-Third Psalm. (Illus.). 62p. 1961. 7.95 (ISBN 0-8007-0330-8). Revell.
--Victory in the Valleys of Life. 128p. 1981. 8.95 (ISBN 0-8007-1271-4). Revell.
--Victory in the Valleys of Life. 128p. 1984. pap. 2.50 (ISBN 0-8007-8488-X, Spire Bks). Revell.
--When a Marriage Ends. 128p. 1985. 7.95 (ISBN 0-8007-1443-1). Revell.
--When You Lose a Loved One. 64p. 1959. 7.95 (ISBN 0-8007-0347-2). Revell.
--You Are Never Alone. 160p. 1978. 9.95 (ISBN 0-8007-0917-9). Revell.

--You Are Never Alone. 160p. 1984. pap. 5.95 (ISBN 0-8007-5145-0, Power Bks). Revell.

Allen, Charles L. & Biggs, Mouzon. When You Graduate. 64p. 1972. 7.95 (ISBN 0-8007-0527-0). Revell.

Allen, Charles L. & Parker, Mildred. How to Increase Your Sunday School Attendance. 128p. 1980. 8.95 (ISBN 0-8007-1088-6). Revell.

Allen, Charles L. & Rice, Helen S. The Prayerful Heart. 160p. (Orig.). 1981. pap. 5.95 (ISBN 0-8007-5073-X, Power Bks). Revell.

--When You Lose a Loved One-Life Is Forever. 128p. 1979. pap. 5.95 (ISBN 0-8007-5031-4, Power Bks). Revell.

Allen, Charlotte H. The Super Years. new ed. 160p. 1984. 8.95 (ISBN 0-8007-1349-4). Revell.

Allen, Charlotte V. Daddy's Girl. 1980. 10.95 (ISBN 0-671-61024-4, Wyndham). S&S.

--Destinies. 384p. 1984. pap. 3.95 (ISBN 0-425-07444-7). Berkley Pub.

--Hidden Meanings. 320p. 1985. pap. 3.95 (ISBN 0-425-07747-0). Berkley Pub.

--Intimate Friends. 336p. 1984. pap. 3.95 (ISBN 0-425-06591-X). Berkley Pub.

--Meet Me in Time. 400p. 1983. pap. 3.50 (ISBN 0-425-05964-2). Berkley Pub.

--Memories. 336p. 1984. pap. 3.50 (ISBN 0-425-07027-1). Berkley Pub.

--Pieces of Dreams. 1985. pap. 3.95 (ISBN 0-425-07582-6). Berkley Pub.

--Promises. 464p. 1981. pap. 2.95 (ISBN 0-7704-1676-4). Bantam.

--Promises. 464p. (Orig.). 1983. pap. 3.50 (ISBN 0-425-06167-1). Berkley Pub.

--Promises. 1984. pap. 3.95 (ISBN 0-425-07445-5). Berkley Pub.

Allen, Charlotte Vale. Daddy's Girl. 272p. 1984. pap. 3.50 (ISBN 0-425-06579-0). Berkley Pub.

Allen, Chris & Martin, Michel. Benin & the Congo: Politics, Economics & Society. Szajkowski, Bogdan, ed. LC 84-62671. (Marxist Regimes Ser.). (Illus.). 160p. 1986. lib. bdg. 22.50x (ISBN 0-931477-27-1); pap. text ed. 10.95x (ISBN 0-931477-28-X). Lynne Rienner.

Allen, Chris, jt. auth. see Kurtz, Edwin B.

Allen, Chris & Williams, Gavin, eds. Sub-Saharan Africa. LC 81-16902. (Sociology of "Developing Societies" Ser.). 240p. 1982. 18.00 (ISBN 0-85345-597-X); pap. 8.00 (ISBN 0-85345-598-8). Monthly Rev.

Allen, Christine. The Twelve Days of Turkey. (Illus.). 48p. 1983. pap. 2.95 (ISBN 0-89286-224-6). One Hund One Prods.

Allen, Christine M., jt. ed. see Stevens, Michael E.

Allen, Christopher & Johnson, R. W., eds. African Perspectives. LC 78-128497. (Illus.). 1971. 44.50 (ISBN 0-521-07948-9). Cambridge U Pr.

Allen, Clarence, jt. auth. see Allen, Roach V.

Allen, Clark L. Elementary Mathematics of Price Theory. 1966. pap. write for info. (ISBN 0-534-00655-8). Wadsworth Pub.

Allen, Clay. Range Trouble. 160p. 1982. 10.95 (ISBN 0-8027-4010-3). Walker & Co.

--Range Trouble. large print ed. LC 84-8766. 233p. 1984. Repr. of 1982 ed. 12.95 (ISBN 0-89621-563-6). Thorndike Pr.

Allen, Clifford. The Sexual Perversions & Abnormalities: A Study in the Psychology of Paraphilia. LC 78-27783. 1979. Repr. of 1949 ed. lib. bdg. 24.75x (ISBN 0-313-20627-9, ALSP). Greenwood.

Allen, Clifton J. Life Is Worth Your Best. LC 79-55004. (Orig.). 1980. pap. 4.50 (ISBN 0-8054-5276-1). Broadman.

Allen, Clifton J., et al, eds. Broadman Bible Commentary, 12 vols. Incl. Vol. 1, General Articles, Genesis-Exodus. rev. ed (ISBN 0-8054-1125-9); Vol. 2 (ISBN 0-8054-1102-X); Vol. 3 (ISBN 0-8054-1103-8); Vol. 4 (ISBN 0-8054-1104-6); Vol. 5 (ISBN 0-8054-1105-4); Vol. 6 (ISBN 0-8054-1106-2); Vol. 7 (ISBN 0-8054-1107-0); Vol. 8, General Articles, Matthew-Mark. rev. ed (ISBN 0-8054-1108-9); Vol. 9 (ISBN 0-8054-1109-7); Vol. 10 (ISBN 0-8054-1110-0); Vol. 11 (ISBN 0-8054-1111-9); Vol. 12 (ISBN 0-8054-1112-7). LC 78-93918. 1969. lib. bdg. 14.95 ea.; 175.00 set (ISBN 0-8054-1100-3). Broadman.

Allen, Clinton M. Some Effects Produced in an Individual by Knowledge of His Own Intellectual Level. LC 73-176511. (Columbia University. Teachers College. Contributions to Education: No. 401). Repr. of 1930 ed. 22.50 (ISBN 0-404-55401-6). AMS Pr.

Allen, Connie J., jt. auth. see Allen, Gerald R.

Allen, Curt, ed. see Kaufman, Jackie.

Allen, Cynthia L. Topics in Diachronic English Syntax. (Outstanding Dissertations in Linguistics Ser.). 425p. 1985. 53.00 (ISBN 0-8240-4550-5). Garland Pub.

Allen, D. Dancing Tales. (Shorey Historical Ser.). 95p. Repr. of 1951 ed. pap. 3.95 (ISBN 0-8466-0287-3, S287). Shorey.

Allen, D. E. & Dowling, J. P. Techniques for Nephropathology. 128p. 1981. 56.00 (ISBN 0-8493-5791-8). CRC Pr.

Allen, D. H. A Guide to the Economic Evaluation of Projects. 1981. 30.00x (ISBN 0-85295-131-0, Pub. by Inst Chem Eng England). State Mutual Bk.

Allen, D. I., jt. auth. see Bowman, M. A.

Allen, D. J. The Pathology of Tropical Food Legumes: Disease Resistance in Crop Imporovement. LC 82-20301. 413p. 1983. pap. text ed. 64.95x (ISBN 0-471-10232-6, Wiley-Interscience). Wiley.

Allen, D. J., ed. Plato: Republic, Bk. I. (Classical Texts Ser.). 142p. pap. 9.95x (ISBN 0-631-13884-6). Basil Blackwell.

Allen, D. J., et al, eds. Three-Dimensional Microanatomy of Cells & Tissue Surfaces. 1981. 90.00 (ISBN 0-444-00607-9). Elsevier.

Allen, D. K. Metallurgy Theory & Practice. (Illus.). 1969. 19.95 (ISBN 0-8269-3500-1). Am Technical.

Allen, Daniel. Bibliography of Discographies: Jazz, Vol. II. 200p. 1981. 35.00 (ISBN 0-8352-1342-0). Bowker.

Allen, Darrel J., jt. auth. see Mead, Daniel L.

Allen, David. Diesels in the North East. 112p. 30.00x (ISBN 0-86093-262-1, Pub. by ORPC Ltd UK). State Mutual Bk.

--Diesels Nationwide, Vol. 3. 128p. 30.00x (ISBN 0-86093-113-7, Pub. by ORPC Ltd UK). State Mutual Bk.

--English Teaching Since Nineteen Sixty-Five: How Much Growth? (Orig.). 1980. pap. text ed. 13.50x (ISBN 0-435-10051-3). Heinemann Ed.

--Finance: A Theoretical Introduction. LC 83-10934. 250p. 1983. 27.50 (ISBN 0-312-28944-8). St Martin.

--Funds Flow Management. 96p. 1980. pap. 4.95 (ISBN 0-434-90040-0, Pub. by W Heinemann Ltd). David & Charles.

--Hospital Planning. 197p. 1979. 60.00x (ISBN 0-272-79520-8, Pub. by Pitman Bks England). State Mutual Bk.

Allen, David & Kilkenny, Brian. Planned Beef Production. 2nd ed. (Illus.). 248p. (Orig.). 1984. pap. text ed. 17.95x (ISBN 0-246-12194-7, Pub by Granada England). Sheridan.

Allen, David & Pijpers, Alfred, eds. European Foreign Policy-Making & the Arab-Israeli Conflict. 1984. lib. bdg. 49.50 (ISBN 90-247-2965-3, Pub. by Martinus Nijhoff Netherlands). Kluwer Academic.

Allen, David B., jt. auth. see Getz, William L.

Allen, David E. Finance: A Theoretical Introduction. 336p. 1985. pap. 10.95x (ISBN 0-85520-540-7). Basil Blackwell.

Allen, David G. In English Ways: The Movement of Societies & the Transferal of English Local Law & Custom to Massachusetts Bay in the Seventeenth Century. LC 80-13198. (Institute of Early American History & Culture Ser.). xxi, 312p. 1981. 27.00x (ISBN 0-8078-1448-2). U of NC Pr.

--In English Ways: The Movement of Societies & the Transferal of English Local Law & Custom to Massachusetts Bay in the Seventeenth Century. 1982. pap. 7.95x (ISBN 0-393-95238-X). Norton.

Allen, David G., ed. see Webster, Daniel.

Allen, David G., et al, eds. Diary of John Quincy Adams: Nov. 1779-Dec. 1788, Vols. 1 & 2. LC 81-6197. (The Adams Papers Ser.). (Illus.). 1024p. 1982. Set. text ed. 60.00 (ISBN 0-674-20420-4). Harvard U Pr.

Allen, David H. Introduction to Aerospace Structural Analysis. LC 84-13194. 507p. 1985. 39.95 (ISBN 0-471-88839-7). Wiley.

Allen, David J. Sussex. (Shire County Guide Ser.: No. 4). (Illus.). 56p. (Orig.). 1984. pap. 4.95 (ISBN 0-85263-684-9, Pub. by Shire Pubns England). Seven Hills Bks.

Allen, David M. & Cady, Foster B. Analyzing Experimental Data by Regression. (Research Methods Ser.). (Illus.). 394p. 1982. 31.00 (ISBN 0-534-97963-7). Lifetime Learn.

--Analyzing Experimental Data by Regression. 394p. 1982. 31.00 (ISBN 0-534-97963-7). Van Nos Reinhold.

Allen, David R. Sir Aubrey: A Biography of C. Aubrey Smith. (Illus.). 172p. 1982. 31.50 (ISBN 0-241-10590-0, Pub. by Hamish Hamilton England). David & Charles.

--A Song for Cricket. (Illus.). 220p. 1983. 19.95 (ISBN 0-7207-1287-4, Pub. by Michael Joseph). Merrimack Pub cir.

Allen, David T. & Wells, John P. Passport to Good Health. LC 78-51737. 1978. 2.95 (ISBN 0-917634-02-0). Creative Infomatics.

Allen, David W. The Fear of Looking; or Scopophilic-Exhibitionistic Conflicts. LC 73-80875. 250p. 1974. 12.95x (ISBN 0-8139-0448-X). U Pr of Va.

Allen, Dell K. & Mortensen, Kay S. Metallurgy & Materials Science: Laboratory Manual. pap. 56.00 (ISBN 0-317-10273-7, 2011578). Bks Demand UMI.

Allen, Delmas J., jt. auth. see Pansky, Ben.

Allen, Derek & Nash, Dephne. Coins of the Ancient Celts. (Illus.). 265p. 1980. 26.50x (ISBN 0-85224-371-5, Pub. by Edinburgh U Pr Scotland). Columbia U Pr.

Allen, Devere. Fight for Peace, 2 vols. LC 74-147439. (Library of War & Peace; Histories of the Organized Peace Movement). Set. lib. bdg. 92.00 (ISBN 0-8240-0228-8); lib. bdg. 38.00 ea. Garland Pub.

--The Fight for Peace. LC 79-137525. (Peace Movement in America Ser). xi, 740p. 1972. Repr. of 1930 ed. lib. bdg. 37.95x (ISBN 0-89198-052-0). Ozer.

Allen, Devere, ed. Adventurous Americans. facsimile ed. LC 71-156604. (Essay Index Reprint Ser). Repr. of 1932 ed. 25.50 (ISBN 0-8369-2264-6). Ayer Co Pubs.

--Pacifism in the Modern World. Bd. with Pacifism in the Modern World. Randall, John H. LC 70-147446. (Library of War & Peace; Problems of the Organized Peace Movement: Selected Documents). lib. bdg. 46.00 (ISBN 0-8240-0236-9). Garland Pub.

--Pacifism in the Modern World. LC 72-137526. (Peace Movement in America Ser). xviii, 278p. 1972. Repr. of 1929 ed. lib. bdg. 18.95x (ISBN 0-89198-053-9). Ozer.

Allen, Diane van see Van Allen, Diane.

Allen, Dick. Overnight in the Guest House of the Mystic: Poems. LC 83-25620. 64p. 1984. text ed. 13.95 (ISBN 0-8071-1165-1); pap. 5.95 (ISBN 0-8071-1166-X). La State U Pr.

--Science Fiction: The Future. 2nd ed. 432p. 1983. pap. text ed. 14.95 (ISBN 0-15-578651-2, HC). HarBraceJ.

Allen, Dick & Chacko, David. Detective Fiction: Crime & Compromise. 481p. (Orig.). 1974. pap. text ed. 12.95 (ISBN 0-15-517408-8, HC). HarBraceJ.

Allen, Diogenes. Philosophy for Understanding Theology. LC 84-48510. 252p. pap. 14.95 (ISBN 0-8042-0688-0). John Knox.

--Three Outsiders: Pascal, Kierkegaard, Simone Weil. LC 82-83552. 150p. (Orig.). 1983. pap. 6.50 (ISBN 0-936384-08-5). Cowley Pubns.

--The Traces of God. LC 80-51570. 108p. (Orig.). 1981. pap. 6.00 (ISBN 0-936384-03-4). Cowley Pubns.

Allen, Don, ed. A Celebration of Poets. LC 67-18376. pap. 63.30 (ISBN 0-317-19829-7, 2023078). Bks Demand UMI.

Allen, Don A., jt. auth. see Davis, Lanny J.

Allen, Don C. The Harmonious Vision: Studies in Milton's Poetry. 1979. Repr. of 1970 ed. lib. bdg. 18.50x (ISBN 0-374-90139-2). Octagon.

--The Legend of Noah: Renaissance Rationalism in Art, Science, & Letters. LC 49-49065. (Reprint of Studies in Language & Literature Ser.: Vol. 33, No. 3-4, 1949). (Illus.). 1963. pap. 3.95x (ISBN 0-252-72516-6). U of Ill Pr.

--Mysteriously Meant: The Rediscovery of Pagan Symbolism & Allegorical Interpretation in the Renaissance. LC 77-105363. Repr. of 1970 ed. 69.60 (ISBN 0-8357-9279-X, 2015160). Bks Demand UMI.

--Star-Crossed Renaissance. 1966. Repr. lib. bdg. 23.00 (ISBN 0-374-90153-8). Octagon.

Allen, Don C., ed. Four Poets on Poetry. LC 80-20856. (Percy Graeme Turnbull Memorial Lectures on Poetry, 1958). 111p. 1980. Repr. of 1959 ed. lib. bdg. 24.75x (ISBN 0-313-22405-6, ALFP). Greenwood.

--The Moment of Poetry. LC 80-17079. (The Percy Graeme Turnbull Memorial Lectures on Poetry, 1961). 135p. 1980. Repr. of 1962 ed. lib. bdg. 24.75x (ISBN 0-313-22406-4, ALMP). Greenwood.

Allen, Don Cameron. The Harmonious Vision: Studies in Milton's Poetry. enl. ed. LC 79-117254. 166p. 1970. 14.95x (ISBN 0-8018-1191-0). Johns Hopkins.

Allen, Don L., et al. Periodontics for the Dental Hygienist. 3rd ed. LC 79-26079. (Illus.). 277p. 1980. text ed. 13.50 (ISBN 0-8121-0691-1). Lea & Febiger.

Allen, Donald & Butterick, George F. The Postmoderns: New American Poetry Revised. 1984. 17.50 (ISBN 0-8446-6082-5). Peter Smith.

Allen, Donald & Guy, Rebecca. Conversation Analysis: The Sociology of Talk. (Janua Linguarum, Ser. Minor: No. 200). 284p. 1978. pap. text ed. 26.00x (ISBN 90-279-3002-3). Mouton.

Allen, Donald & Butterick, George F., eds. The Postmoderns: The New American Poetry Revised. LC 79-52054. 480p. (Orig.). 1982. pap. 9.95 (ISBN 0-394-17458-5, E732, Ever). Grove.

Allen, Donald, ed. see Creeley, Robert.

Allen, Donald, ed. see Dorn, Edward.

Allen, Donald, ed. see Ginsberg, Allen.

Allen, Donald, ed. see Kerouac, Jack.

Allen, Donald, ed. see O'Hara, Frank.

Allen, Donald, ed. see Spicer, Jack.

Allen, Donald, ed. & intro. by see Welch, Lew.

Allen, Donald, ed. see Welch, Lew.

Allen, Donald, ed. see Whalen, Philip.

Allen, Donald M. & Taliman, Warren, eds. The Poetics of the New American Poetry. LC 73-6222. 1973. pap. 12.50 (ISBN 0-394-17801-7, E609, Ever). Grove.

Allen, Donald M., ed. see Lorca, Federico Garcia.

Allen, Donald M., tr. see Ionesco, Eugene.

Allen, Donald R. French Views of America in the 1930's. Freidel, Frank, ed. LC 78-62374. (Modern American History Ser.: Vol. 1). 1979. lib. bdg. 34.00 (ISBN 0-8240-3625-5). Garland Pub.

Allen, Donna. Fringe Benefits: Wages or Social Obligation? LC 75-627371. (Cornell Studies in Industrial & Labor Relations: No. 13). 288p. 1969. pap. 4.00 (ISBN 0-87546-006-2). ILR Pr.

Allen, Dorothea. Elementary Science Activities for Every Month of the School Year. LC 81-9503. 258p. 1981. 17.50 (ISBN 0-13-259952-X, Parker). P-H.

Allen, Dorothy. Baby Jesus. (Very First Bible Stories Ser.). 1983. 1.59 (ISBN 0-87162-275-0, D8504). Warner Pr.

Allen, Dorothy S. Plaster & Bisque Art: Gold Leafing, Hummel, Lacquer, Marble & Woodtone Finishes. Cole, Tom, ed. LC 80-70317. (Plaster Art, Step by Step Ser.). (Illus.). 56p. 1981. pap. 1.95 (ISBN 0-9605204-2-2). Dots Pubns.

--Plaster & Bisque Art: Special Finishes. Cole, Tom, ed. LC 80-70317. (Plaster Art Step by Step Ser.). (Illus.). 44p. (gr. 4 up). 1981. pap. 1.95 (ISBN 0-9605204-4-9). Dots Pubns.

--Plaster & Bisque Art: The Soft Touch Technique. Cole, Tom, ed. LC 80-70317. (Plaster Art Step by Step Ser.). (Illus.). 47p. (gr. 4 up). 1981. pap. 1.95 (ISBN 0-9605204-6-5). Dots Pubns.

--Plaster & Bisque Art with Acrylics. Cole, Tom, ed. LC 80-70317. (Plaster Art, Step by Step Ser.). (Illus.). 75p. 1981. pap. 1.95 (ISBN 0-9605204-1-4). Dots Pubns.

--Plaster & Bisque Art: With Transparent Watercolor. Cole, Tom, ed. LC 80-70317. (Plaster Art Step by Step Ser.). (Illus.). 57p. (gr. 4 up). 1981. pap. 1.95 (ISBN 0-9605204-5-7). Dots Pubns.

--Plaster Art: Step by Step. Cole, Tom, ed. LC 80-70317. (Illus.). 172p. (Orig.). 1981. pap. 7.95 (ISBN 0-9605204-0-6). Dots Pubns.

Allen, Dorothy S. & Cole, Tom. Plaster & Bisque Art: Mist, Museum Bronze, Pastel Chalk, Pearl & Suede Finishes. LC 80-70317. (Plaster Art Step by Step Ser.). (Illus.). 52p. (gr. 4 up). 1981. pap. 1.95 (ISBN 0-9605204-3-0). Dots Pubns.

Allen, Douglas. Structure & Creativity in Religion. (Religion & Reason Ser.: No. 14). 1978. 20.40x (ISBN 90-279-7594-9). Mouton.

Allen, Douglas & Doeing, Dennis. Mircea Eliade: An Annotated Bibliography. LC 78-68240. 284p. 1984. lib. bdg. 43.00 (ISBN 0-8240-9817-X). Garland Pub.

Allen, Douglas C. Principles of Forest Entomology. LC 84-8509. (Illus.). 224p. 1984. lab manual 13.95x (ISBN 0-8156-2318-6). Syracuse U Pr.

Allen, Douglas G. & Coufal, James E. Introduction to Forest Entomology: A Training Manual for Forest Technicians. LC 84-8510. (Illus.). 168p. 1984. pap. 12.95x (ISBN 0-8156-2319-4). Syracuse U Pr.

Allen, Dwight W., et al, eds. The Teacher's Handbook. 1971. 23.80 (ISBN 0-673-05880-8). Scott F.

Allen, E. Reason the Only Oracle of Man. LC 40-36196. Repr. of 1940 ed. 29.00 (ISBN 0-527-01240-8). Kraus Repr.

Allen, E. C. Coast Highway, No. 1. 192p. 1983. 12.95 (ISBN 0-8027-5569-0). Walker & Co.

Allen, E. F. Dictionary of Abbreviations & Symbols. 22.50 (ISBN 0-87559-167-1). Shalom.

--Guide to the National Parks of America. 59.95 (ISBN 0-8490-0272-9). Gordon Pr.

--Red Letter Days of Samuel Pepys. 59.95 (ISBN 0-8490-0937-5). Gordon Pr.

Allen, E. L. Freedom in God: A Guide to the Thought of Nicholas Berdyaev. 1978. lib. bdg. 8.50 (ISBN 0-8495-0049-4). Arden Lib.

--Freedom in God: A Guide to the Thought of Nicholas Berdyaev. LC 73-5751. lib. bdg. 12.50 (ISBN 0-8414-1740-7). Folcroft.

--From Plato to Nietzsche. Orig. Title: Guide Book to Western Thought. 192p. 1977. pap. 2.25 (ISBN 0-449-30768-9, Prem). Fawcett.

Allen, E. M. America's Story As Told in Postage Stamps. 69.95 (ISBN 0-87968-381-3). Gordon Pr.

Allen, E. Ross, jt. auth. see Neill, Wilfred T.

Allen, E. W. The Position of Foreign States Before National Courts, Chiefly in Continental Europe. LC 33-31666. Repr. of 1933 ed. 24.00 (ISBN 0-527-01200-9). Kraus Repr.

Allen, E. Waterhouse. How to Execute an Agency. LC 79-53977. (Illus., Orig.). 1980. pap. 3.95 (ISBN 0-9603338-1-9). Bark-Back.

Allen, Edgar L. Existentialism from Within. LC 72-7817. 185p. 1973. Repr. of 1953 ed. lib. bdg. 15.00 (ISBN 0-8371-6526-1, ALEX). Greenwood.

Allen, Edith B. Better Bible Games. (Paperback Program Ser). (Orig.). (YA) 1969. pap. 3.45 (ISBN 0-8010-0027-0). Baker Bk.

--One Hundred Bible Games. (Paperback Program Ser). (YA) 1968. pap. 3.50 (ISBN 0-8010-0033-5). Baker Bk.

Allen, Edward. How Buildings Work: The Natural Order of Architecture. (Illus.). 1980. 29.95 (ISBN 0-19-502605-5). Oxford U Pr.

--The Professional Handbook of Building Construction. 608p. 1985. price not set (ISBN 0-471-82524-7). Wiley.

--Stone Shelters. (Illus.). 1969. pap. 9.95 (ISBN 0-262-51010-3). MIT Pr.

Allen, Edward B. Early American Wall Paintings, 1710-1850. LC 77-77694. (Library of American Art Ser.). 1971. Repr. of 1926 ed. lib. bdg. 32.50 (ISBN 0-306-71332-2). Da Capo.

Allen, Edward B., ed. The Responsive House. LC 74-23518. 320p. 1974. 27.50x (ISBN 0-262-01040-2); pap. 15.00x (ISBN 0-262-51012-X). MIT Pr.

Allen, Edward D. Early American Wall Paintings. Wood, Serry, ed. (Visual Art Classics Ser). (Illus.). 1969. pap. text ed. 5.95 (ISBN 0-87282-002-5). CHB-ALF.

--Rollicking Pacific: Selection of Poems. (Shorey Historical Ser.). 118p. pap. 7.95 (ISBN 0-8466-0286-5, S286). Shorey.

Allen, Edward D. & Valette, Rebecca M. Classroom Techniques: Foreign Languages & English As a Second Language. 418p. (Orig.). 1977. pap. text ed. 15.95 (ISBN 0-15-507674-4, HC). HarBraceJ.

Allen, Edward D., et al. Habla Espanol: Essentials. 2nd ed. (Span.). 1982. text ed. 25.95 (ISBN 0-03-058304-7); instr's manual 19.95 (ISBN 0-03-058858-8); lab manual 11.95 (ISBN 0-03-058859-6); tapes avail. (ISBN 0-03-058861-8). HR&W.

--Habla Espanol? An Introductory Course. 2nd ed. LC 80-23174. 502p. 1981. text ed. 26.95 (ISBN 0-03-057196-0, HoltC); instr's manual 19.95 (ISBN 0-03-057197-9); wkbk. 11.95 (ISBN 0-03-057198-7); lab manual 11.95 (ISBN 0-03-057199-5); tapes 350.00 (ISBN 0-03-057201-0). HR&W.

Allen, Edward F. Complete Dream Book. 288p. 1967. pap. 2.95 (ISBN 0-446-30250-3). Warner Bks.

--How to Write & Speak Effective English. abr ed. 1977. pap. 1.95 (ISBN 0-449-30858-8, Prem). Fawcett.

--Red Letter Days of Samuel Pepys. 1910. Repr. 15.00 (ISBN 0-8274-3257-7). R West.

Allen, Edward J. Merchants of Menace-the Mafia: A Study of Organized Crime. (Illus.). 344p. 1962. photocopy ed. 25.50x (ISBN 0-398-04187-3). C C Thomas.

--The Second United Order among the Mormons. LC 73-38483. (Columbia University Studies in the Social Sciences: No. 419). Repr. of 1936 ed. 15.00 (ISBN 0-404-51419-7). AMS Pr.

Allen, Edward L. Energy & Economic Growth in the United States. 1979. text ed. 37.50x (ISBN 0-262-01062-3). MIT Pr.

Allen, Edward S. Freedom in Iowa: The Role of the Iowa Civil Liberties Union. 1977. 8.50x (ISBN 0-8138-0700-X). Iowa St U Pr.

Allen, Edward Van see Van Allen, Edward.

Allen, Eleanor. Home Sweet Home: A History of Housework. (Junior Reference Ser.). (Illus.). 64p. (gr. 6 up). 1979. 8.95 (ISBN 0-7136-1927-9). Dufour.

--Victorian Children. (Junior Reference Ser.). (Illus.). 64p. (gr. 6 up). 1979. 8.95 (ISBN 0-7136-1324-6). Dufour.

--Wartime Children, Nineteen Thirty-Nine to Nineteen Forty-Five. (Junior Reference Ser.). (Illus.). 64p. (gr. 6 up). 1978. 8.95 (ISBN 0-7136-1503-6). Dufour.

--Wash & Brush up. (Junior Reference Ser.). (Illus.). 64p. (gr. 7 up). 1977. 8.95 (ISBN 0-7136-1639-3). Dufour.

Allen, Eliot D. & Colbrunn, Ethel B. A Short Guide to Writing a Critical Review. new rev. ed. 1975. pap. 2.00 (ISBN 0-912112-20-4). Everett-Edwards.

--A Short Guide to Writing a Research Paper: Manuscript Form & Documentation. rev. ed. 1975. pap. 2.50 (ISBN 0-912112-19-0). Everett-Edwards.

--Student Writer's Guide. 5th ed. 1976. pap. text ed. 5.00 (ISBN 0-912112-18-2). Everett-Edwards.

Allen, Elizabeth. Lady Anne. 416p. 1985. pap. 3.95 (ISBN 0-446-32120-6). Warner Bks.

--A Woman's Place in the Novels of Henry James. LC 83-40159. 200p. 1984. 22.50 (ISBN 0-312-88653-5). St Martin.

Allen, Elizabeth, ed. see Noland, Ronald G., et al.

Allen, Elizabeth C. Mother, Can you Hear Me? LC 83-1455. 208p. 1983. 13.95 (ISBN 0-89696-194-X, An Everest House Book). Dodd.

Allen, Elizabeth E. Rebel. (Orig.). 1985. pap. 3.95 (ISBN 0-446-32551-1). Warner Bks.

Allen, Ellen G. Japanese Flower Arrangement: A Complete Primer. rev. ed. LC 62-21731. (Illus.). 1963. Repr. 8.25 (ISBN 0-8048-0293-9). C E Tuttle.

--Japanese Flower Arrangement in a Nutshell. (Illus., Orig.). pap. 4.50 (ISBN 0-8048-0295-5). C E Tuttle.

Allen, Elsa G. The History of American Ornithology Before Audubon. (Illus.). 1979. Repr. of 1951 ed. 45.00 (ISBN 0-934626-00-6). W G Arader.

Allen, Elsie. Pomo Basketmaking: A Supreme Art for the Weaver. Brown, Vinson, ed. (Illus.). 68p. 1972. 10.95 (ISBN 0-87961-017-4); pap. 4.95 (ISBN 0-87961-016-6). Naturegraph.

Allen, Eric. Black Powder Posse. 224p. 1985. pap. 2.50 (ISBN 0-8217-1567-4). Zebra.

--Ride to Revenge. (Orig.). 1979. pap. 1.95 (ISBN 0-89083-551-9). Zebra.

Allen, Ethan. Baseball Play & Strategy. 3rd ed. LC 81-17177. 456p. 1982. lib. bdg. 26.50 (ISBN 0-89874-450-4). Krieger.

--Narrative of Colonel Ethan Allen. 1961. pap. 1.50 (ISBN 0-87091-000-0, AE). Corinth Bks.

Allen, Ethel K., jt. auth. see Allen, O. N.

Allen, Eula. A Trilogy of Creation, 3 vols. rev. ed. Incl. Vol. 1. Before the Beginning. 1966 (ISBN 0-87604-054-7); Vol. 2. The River of Time. 1965 (ISBN 0-87604-055-5); Vol. 3. You Are Forever. 1966 (ISBN 0-87604-056-3). (Illus.). pap. 10.95 set (ISBN 0-87604-125-X); pap. 3.95 ea. ARE Pr.

Allen, Everett S. Children of the Light: The Rise & Fall of New Bedford Whaling & the Death of the Arctic Fleet. 320p. 1983. pap. 9.95 (ISBN 0-87645-123-4). Parnassus Imprints.

--Martha's Vineyard: An Elegy. 1982. 16.00 (ISBN 0-316-03257-3). Little.

--A Wind to Shake the World: The Story of the 1938 Hurricane. (Illus.). 1976. 17.45 (ISBN 0-316-03426-6). Little.

Allen, Everett T., et al. Pension Planning: Pensions, Profit Sharing & Other Deferred Compensation Plans. 5th ed. 1984. 25.95x (ISBN 0-256-03081-2). Irwin.

Allen, Evie A., tr. see Schyberg, Frederik.

Allen, Evlyn. Figuring It Out: Diet & Exercise for a Lovelier You. LC 77-74493. (Illus.). 1977. pap. 4.95 (ISBN 0-88290-078-1). Horizon Utah.

Allen, F. A., jt. auth. see Brace, Arthur William.

Allen, F. D., tr. see Aeschylus.

Allen, F. H. Letters of Robert Burns, 4 vols. Set. 450.00 (ISBN 0-8490-0512-4). Gordon Pr.

Allen, F. Sturges. Allen's Synonyms & Antonyms. pap. 4.33i (ISBN 0-06-463328-4, EH 328, EH). B&N NY.

Allen, Fay W. Waldo Emerson. (Illus.). 782p. 1982. pap. 10.95 (ISBN 0-14-006278-5). Penguin.

Allen, Frances C. Little Mouse's Wonderful Journey. (Arch Bks: Set 9). (Illus.). 32p. (ps-4). 1972. pap. 0.99 (ISBN 0-570-06069-9, 59-1187). Concordia.

Allen, Francis A. Borderland of Criminal Justice: Essays in Law & Criminology. LC 64-24972. 573p. 1964. 10.00x (ISBN 0-226-01416-9); pap. 2.45x (ISBN 0-226-01417-7, Phoen). U of Chicago Pr.

--Crimes of Politics: Political Dimensions of Criminal Justice. LC 73-93506. (Oliver Wendell Holmes Lectures: 1973). 128p. 1974. 10.00x (ISBN 0-674-17625-1). Harvard U Pr.

--The Decline of the Rehabilitative Ideal: Penal Policy & Social Purpose. LC 80-25098. (Storrs Lectures). 160p. 1981. 19.00x (ISBN 0-300-02565-3). Yale U Pr.

--Law, Intellect, & Education. (Michigan Faculty Ser.). 1979. lib. bdg. 12.00x (ISBN 0-472-09309-6, 09309); pap. 5.95 (ISBN 0-472-06309-X, 06309). U of Mich Pr.

Allen, Francis H. A Bibliography of Henry David Thoreau. LC 69-17930. 1969. Repr. of 1908 ed. 16.50 (ISBN 0-8337-0041-3). B Franklin.

Allen, Francis H., ed. A Bibliography of Henry David Thoreau. 17.00 (ISBN 0-384-00770-8). Johnson Repr.

Allen, Francis H., ed. see Thoreau, Henry D.

Allen, Frank C. A Critical Edition of Robert Browning's "Bishop Blougram's Apology". (Salzburg Studies in English Literature: Romantic Reassessment: No. 60). 243p. (Orig.). 1976. pap. 25.50x (ISBN 0-391-01296-7). Humanities.

Allen, Frank Kenyon, et al. Golfer's Bible. LC 68-11788. 1968. pap. 5.95 (ISBN 0-385-01402-3). Doubleday.

Allen, Fred. Much Ado About Me. 402p. Repr. of 1956 ed. lib. bdg. 20.95 (ISBN 0-88411-291-8, Pub. by Aeonian Pr). Amereon Ltd.

Allen, Frederick H. Psychotherapy with Children. LC 79-52647. vi, 311p. 1979. 23.50x (ISBN 0-8032-1002-7); pap. 5.95x (ISBN 0-8032-5900-X, BB 707, Bison). U of Nebr Pr.

Allen, Frederick L. The Big Change: America Transforms Itself, 1900-1950. LC 82-18395. xii, 308p. 1983. Repr. of 1952 ed. lib. bdg. 35.00x (ISBN 0-313-23791-3, ALBC). Greenwood.

--Big Change, America Transforms Itself, Nineteen Hundred to Nineteen Fifty. 1969. pap. 2.95i (ISBN 0-06-080150-6, P150, PL). Har-Row.

--Only Yesterday. pap. 3.80i (ISBN 0-06-080004-6, P4, PL). Har-Row.

--Only Yesterday: An Informal History of the Nineteen-Twenties. (Illus.). 370p. Date not set. Repr. of 1931 ed. lib. bdg. 30.00 (ISBN 0-89760-969-7). Telegraph Bks.

--Since Yesterday. 1972. pap. 3.37i (ISBN 0-06-080256-1, P256, PL). Har-Row.

Allen, G. & Oliver, R. Architectural Drawing. (Illus.). 200p. 1981. 35.00 (ISBN 0-8230-7043-3, Whitney Lib). Watson-Guptill.

Allen, G., et al, eds. Laboratory Techniques in Biochemistry & Molecular Biology: Vol. 9, Sequencing of Proteins & Peptides. 328p. 1981. 76.25 (ISBN 0-444-80275-4, Biomedical Pr); pap. 28.50 (ISBN 0-444-80254-1). Elsevier.

Allen, G. C. Appointment in Japan: Memories of Sixty Years. (Illus.). 196p. 1983. 25.00 (ISBN 0-485-11237-X, Pub. by Athlone Pr Ltd). Longwood Pub Group.

--The British Disease. 2nd ed. (Hobart Paper Ser.: No. 67). (Orig.). 1979. technical 5.95 (ISBN 0-255-36082-7). Transatlantic.

--British Industry & Economic Policy. 220p. 1979. text ed. 29.75x (ISBN 0-8419-5048-2). Holmes & Meier.

--How Japan Competes. (Institute of Economic Affairs Ser.: Hobart Paper 81). 1979. pap. 5.95 technical (ISBN 0-255-36113-0). Transatlantic.

--Japanese Economy. 238p. 1982. 11.95 (ISBN 0-312-44052-9). St Martin.

--Railways. (Illus.). (gr. 7 up). 9.50x (ISBN 0-392-04327-0, LTB). Sportshelf.

Allen, G. D. & Chui, Charles K. Elements of Calculus. LC 82-12874. (Mathematics Ser.). 512p. 1983. text ed. 23.50 pub net (ISBN 0-534-01188-8). Brooks-Cole.

Allen, G. E. Life & Science in the Twentieth Century. LC 77-83985. (History of Science Ser.). (Illus.). 1978. 34.50 (ISBN 0-521-21864-0); pap. 11.95 (ISBN 0-521-29296-4). Cambridge U Pr.

Allen, G. Freeman, jt. ed. see Whitehouse, P. B.

Allen, G. J. & Chinsky, J. M. Community Psychology & the Schools: A Behaviorally Oriented Multilevel Preventive Approach. 208p. 1976. 24.95x (ISBN 0-89859-439-1). L Erlbaum Assocs.

Allen, G. J., et al. Community Psychology & the Schools: A Behaviorally Oriented Multilevel Preventive Approach. LC 75-42469. 208p. 1976. 14.95x (ISBN 0-470-01368-0). Halsted Pr.

Allen, G. M., jt. auth. see Tozzer, Alfred M.

Allen, G. R. A Field Guide to Inland Fishes of Western Australia. (Illus.). 92p. 1982. pap. 15.00x (ISBN 0-7244-8409-4, Pub. by U of West Austral Pr). Intl Spec Bk.

Allen, G. R. & Cross, N. J. Rainbowfishes of Australia & Papua New Guinea. (Illus.). 160p. 1982. 19.95 (ISBN 0-87666-547-4, H-1047). TFH Pubns.

Allen, G. R. & Smethurst, R. G. Impact of Food Aid on Donor & Other Food Exporting Countries. (World Food Problems Ser.: No. 2). (Orig.). 1965. pap. 4.50 (ISBN 0-685-09389-1, F238, FAO). Unipub.

Allen, Gardner W., ed. see Dallas, Francis G.

Allen, Garland. Thomas Hunt Morgan: A Scientific Biography. LC 77-85526. (Illus.). 1978. text ed. 46.00x (ISBN 0-691-08200-6). Princeton U Pr.

Allen, Garland A., jt. auth. see Baker, Jeffrey J.

Allen, Garland E., jt. auth. see Baker, Jeffrey J.

Allen, Garland E., jt. auth. see Baker, Jeffrey J. W.

Allen, Garth. Taking the Kid Gloves Off Astrology. 52p. (Orig.). 1975. pap. 3.25 (ISBN 0-940058-02-2). Clancy Pubns.

Allen, Gary. Communist Revolution in the Streets. LC 66-28922. (Illus.). 1967. 5.00 (ISBN 0-88279-212-1). Western Islands.

--Jimmy Carter-Jimmy Carter. 96p. pap. 1.00 (ISBN 0-686-31145-0). Concord Pr.

--Jimmy Carter-Jimmy Carter. LC 76-27187. (Orig.). 1976. pap. 2.00 (ISBN 0-89245-006-1). Concord Bks.

--Kissinger. 1976. 6.50 (ISBN 0-89245-003-7). Devin.

--The Kissinger: The Secret Side of the Secretary of State. LC 76-14012. (Orig.). 1976. pap. 3.00 (ISBN 0-685-65508-3). Concord Bks.

--None Dare Call It Conspiracy. Date not set. 12.50 (ISBN 0-318-00910-2). Concord Pr.

--Richard Nixon: The Man Behind the Mask. 434p. pap. 4.95 (ISBN 0-686-31149-3). Concord Pr.

--Richard Nixon: The Man Behind the Mask. LC 73-31048. 433p. 1971. 8.00 (ISBN 0-88279-222-9). Western Islands.

--The Rockefeller File. 200p. pap. 2.00 (ISBN 0-686-31144-2). Concord Pr.

--The Rockefeller File. LC 75-39136. (Orig.). 1976. pap. 4.00 (ISBN 0-89245-001-0). Concord Bks.

--Tax Target: Washington. 1979. 8.95 (ISBN 0-89245-015-0); pap. 3.00 (ISBN 0-89245-014-2). Concord Bks.

--Ted Kennedy: In over His Head. 144p. pap. 4.95 (ISBN 0-686-31147-7). Concord Pr.

Allen, Gary, tr. from Ger. Kissinger: The Secret Side of the Secretary of State. 200p. softbound 5.00 (ISBN 0-686-31311-9); pap. 1.50 (ISBN 0-686-31312-7). Concord Pr.

Allen, Gay W. American Prosody. 1966. Repr. lib. bdg. 27.50 (ISBN 0-374-90133-3). Octagon.

--Aspects of Walt Whitman. 1978. Repr. of 1976 ed. lib. bdg. 40.00 (ISBN 0-8495-0101-6). Arden Lib.

--Aspects of Walt Whitman. LC 77-751. 1977. Repr. of 1961 ed. lib. bdg. 30.00 (ISBN 0-8414-2882-4). Folcroft.

--The Solitary Singer: A Critical Biography of Walt Whitman. LC 84-16462. (Illus.). xx, 620p. 1985. pap. 15.95 (ISBN 0-226-01435-5). U of Chicago Pr.

--Twenty-Five Years of Walt Whitman Bibliography, 1918-1942. LC 77-16478. 1978. Repr. lib. bdg. 10.00 (ISBN 0-8414-2942-1). Folcroft.

--Waldo Emerson: A Biography. LC 81-65275. (Illus.). 696p. 1981. 25.00 (ISBN 0-670-74866-8). Viking.

--Walt Whitman Abroad. 1978. Repr. of 1955 ed. lib. bdg. 30.00 (ISBN 0-8495-0108-3). Arden Lib.

--Walt Whitman Abroad. LC 75-20161. 1975. Repr. of 1955 ed. lib. bdg. 30.00 (ISBN 0-8414-2890-5). Folcroft.

--Walt Whitman As Man, Poet, & Legend. 260p. 1980. Repr. of 1961 ed. lib. bdg. 30.00 (ISBN 0-8414-2934-0). Folcroft.

--Walt Whitman As Man, Poet & Legend. LC 75-26974. 1975. Repr. of 1961 ed. lib. bdg. 20.00 (ISBN 0-8414-2851-4). Folcroft.

--Walt Whitman Handbook. 560p. 1962. 10.45 (ISBN 0-87532-050-3). Hendricks House.

--Walt Whitman: Man, Poet, Philosopher. 1978. Repr. of 1955 ed. lib. bdg. 12.50 (ISBN 0-8495-0107-5). Arden Lib.

--Walt Whitman: Man, Poet, Philosopher. LC 74-19353. 1974. Repr. of 1955 ed. lib. bdg. 15.00 (ISBN 0-8414-2863-8). Folcroft.

--William James. LC 79-629874. (Pamphlets on American Writers Ser.: No. 88). (Orig.). 1970. pap. 1.25x (ISBN 0-8166-0560-2, MPAW88). U of Minn Pr.

Allen, Gay W., jt. auth. see Pochmann, Henry A.

Allen, Gay W., ed. see Whitman, Walt.

Allen, Gay W., et al. American Poetry. (YA) 1965. text ed. 27.50 scp (ISBN 0-06-040220-2, HarpC). Har-Row.

Allen, Gay Wilson. Carl Sandburg. (Pamphlets on American Writers Ser: No. 101). (Orig.). 1972. pap. 1.25x (ISBN 0-8166-0644-7). U of Minn Pr.

--The New Walt Whitman Handbook. LC 74-21595. 423p. 1975. 30.00x (ISBN 0-8147-0556-1). NYU Pr.

--A Reader's Guide to Walt Whitman. 1971. Repr. lib. bdg. 19.00x (ISBN 0-374-90147-3). Octagon.

Allen, Gene P., jt. ed. see Wright, Nancy D.

Allen, Geoffrey F. Railways of the Twentieth Century. (Illus.). 1983. 27.50 (ISBN 0-393-01603-X). Norton.

Allen, Geoffrey F., ed. Jane's World Railways 1984-85. (Illus.). 800p. 1984. 125.00x (ISBN 0-7106-0802-0). Jane's Pub Inc.

--Jane's World Railways 1985-86. 27th ed. (Jane's Yearbooks). (Illus.). 800p. 1985. 125.00x (ISBN 0-7106-0818-7). Jane's Pub Inc.

Allen, George. The Agile Administrator. LC 79-65136. (Illus.). 136p. 1979. 12.95 (ISBN 0-933554-13-3); pap. 9.95 (ISBN 0-933554-12-5). Tempe Pubs.

--Blackjack Decision Tables. LC 84-50319. 36p. 1984. pap. 5.00 (ISBN 0-933554-19-2). Tempe Pubs.

--George Allen's New Handbook of Football Drills. 1974. 14.95 (ISBN 0-13-352716-6). P-H.

--Life of Philidor: Musician & Chess-Player. LC 70-139198. (Music Reprint Ser.). 1971. Repr. of 1863 ed. 25.00 (ISBN 0-306-70075-1). Da Capo.

--The Mental Game (The Inner Game of Bowling) LC 83-50980. (Illus.). 192p. 1983. pap. 12.95 (ISBN 0-933554-18-4). Tempe Pubs.

Allen, George & Olan, Ben. Pro & College Football's Fifty Greatest Games. LC 83-3800. 272p. 1983. 14.95 (ISBN 0-672-52778-2). Bobbs.

Allen, George & Ritger, Dick. The Complete Guide to Bowling Principles: The Encyclopedia of Principles. LC 81-85284. (The Encyclopedia of Bowling Instruction: Vol. 1). (Illus.). 280p. 1982. 17.95 (ISBN 0-933554-00-1); pap. 12.95 (ISBN 0-933554-01-X). Tempe Pubs.

--The Complete Guide to Bowling Strikes: The Encyclopedia of Strikes. LC 80-53200. (The Encyclopedia of Bowling Instruction Ser.: Vol. 2). (Illus.). 222p. 1981. 17.95 (ISBN 0-933554-02-8); pap. 12.95 (ISBN 0-933554-03-6). Tempe Pubs.

--Encyclopedia of Bowling Instruction, 3 vols. 1982. Set. 34.95 (ISBN 0-933554-14-1). Tempe Pubs.

Allen, George & Weiskopf, Don. Handbook of Winning Football. 1976. text ed. 29.56 (ISBN 0-205-04880-3, 624880). Allyn.

Allen, George, jt. auth. see Ritger, Dick.

Allen, George, tr. Book of the Dead; or, Going Forth by Day: Ideas of the Ancient Egyptians Concerning the Hereafter As Expressed in Their Own Terms. LC 74-10338. (Studies in Ancient Oriental Civilization Ser.: No. 37). 1974. pap. text ed. 20.00x (ISBN 0-226-62410-2). U of Chicago Pr.

Allen, George C. Japanese Industry: Its Recent Development & Present Condition. LC 75-30093. (Institute of Pacific Relations). Repr. of 1939 ed. 12.50 (ISBN 0-404-59501-4). AMS Pr.

--The Structure of Industry in Britain: A Study in Economic Change. 3rd ed. LC 66-70817. pap. 70.30 (ISBN 0-317-30112-8, 2025263). Bks Demand UMI.

Allen, George C. & Donnithorne, Audrey G. Western Enterprise in Far Eastern Economic Development, China & Japan. LC 54-1323. pap. 72.80 (ISBN 0-317-28695-1, 2055254). Bks Demand UMI.

Allen, George N. RI. LC 78-15913. 1978. 7.95. (ISBN 0-13-780932-8). P-H.

Allen, George R. The Graduate Students' Guide to Theses & Dissertations: A Practical Manual for Writing & Research. LC 73-3774. (Higher Education Ser.). 256p. 1973. 14.95x (ISBN 0-87589-182-9). Jossey-Bass.

Allen, George V. Rivals. 288p. 1985. pap. 3.95 (ISBN 0-445-20147-9, Pub. by Popular Lib). Warner Bks.

Allen, Gerald. Charles Moore. (Illus.). 128p. 1980. 19.95 (ISBN 0-8230-7375-0, Whitney Lib). Watson-Guptill.

Allen, Gerald D., et al, eds. Dental Analgesia. LC 78-55278. (Illus.). 258p. 1979. casebound 31.00 (ISBN 0-88416-153-6). PSG Pub Co.

Allen, Gerald L. Colorado Manufacturers with One Hundred or More Employees. 35p. 1985. 50.00 (ISBN 0-89478-088-3). U CO Busn Res Div.

--Directory of Colorado High Tech Manufacturers. 75p. 1985. 50.00 (ISBN 0-89478-086-7). U CO Busn Res Div.

--Directory of Colorado Manufacturers with International Sales. 75p. 1985. 50.00 (ISBN 0-89478-087-5). U CO Busn Res Div.

--Directory of Colorado Manufacturers, 1983-84. 380p. 1983. pap. text ed. 45.00 (ISBN 0-89478-103-0). U CO Busn Res Div.

--Directory of Colorado Manufacturers 1985-86. 390p. 1985. pap. text ed. 50.00 (ISBN 0-89478-085-9). U CO Busn Res Div.

Allen, Gerald L. & Montanari, J. Richard. Profile of Employment, Manpower Needs & Business Potential in the Boulder County Area. 155p. 1976. 25.00 (ISBN 0-686-64178-7). U CO Busn Res Div.

Allen, Gerald R. Cockatiel Handbook. 14.95 (ISBN 0-87666-956-9, PS-741). TFH Pubns.

--Damselfishes. (Illus.). 240p. 1975. 19.95 (ISBN 0-87666-034-0, H-950). TFH Pubns.

Allen, Gerald R. & Allen, Connie J. All about Cockatiels. (Illus.). 1977. 7.95 (ISBN 0-87666-757-4, PS-746). TFH Pubns.

Allen, Gilbert. In Everything: Poems Nineteen Seventy-Two to Nineteen Seventy-Nine. LC 81-82661. 75p. 1982. pap. 4.50x perfect bd. (ISBN 0-916418-37-5). Lotus.

Allen, Glover M. Extinct & Vanishing Mammals of the Western Hemisphere: With the Marine Species of All Oceans. LC 72-85661. xv, 620p. 1973. Repr. of 1942 ed. lib. bdg. 30.00 (ISBN 0-8154-0433-6). Cooper Sq.

Allen, Graham A. Sociology of Friendship & Kinship. (Studies in Sociology Ser.). (Orig.). 1979. text ed. 22.50x (ISBN 0-04-301104-7); pap. text ed. 9.95x (ISBN 0-04-301105-5). Allen Unwin.

Allen, Grant. An African Millionaire: Episodes in the Life of the Illustrious Colonel Clay. LC 75-32732. (Literature of Mystery & Detection). (Illus.). 1976. Repr. 24.50x (ISBN 0-405-07862-5). Ayer Co Pubs.

--An African Millionaire: Episodes in the Life of the Illustrious Colonel Clay. 1980. pap. 5.95 (ISBN 0-486-23992-6). Dover.

--The British Barbarians. LC 74-15943. (Science Fiction Ser.). (Illus.). 226p. 1975. Repr. 17.00x (ISBN 0-405-06272-9). Ayer Co Pubs.

--The British Barbarians. Fletcher, Ian & Stokes, John, eds. LC 76-20062. (Decadent Consciousness Ser.). 1977. lib. bdg. 46.00 (ISBN 0-8240-2751-5). Garland Pub.

--Charles Darwin. 1973. Repr. of 1888 ed. 15.00 (ISBN 0-8274-1805-1). R West.

--Early Britain: Anglo-Saxon Britain. (Illus.). 237p. 1980. Repr. of 1901 ed. lib. bdg. 25.00 (ISBN 0-89987-002-3). Darby Bks.

--The Evolution of the Idea of God. 1977. lib. bdg. 59.95 (ISBN 0-8490-1796-3). Gordon Pr.

--Falling in Love: With Other Essays on More Exact Branches of Science. LC 72-3357. (Essay Index Reprint Ser.). Repr. of 1889 ed. 21.00 (ISBN 0-8369-2884-9). Ayer Co Pubs.

--Miss Cayley's Adventures. LC 79-8227. (Illus.). Repr. of 1899 ed. 44.50 (ISBN 0-404-61756-5). AMS Pr.

--Physiological Aesthetics. 283p. 1980. Repr. of 1877 ed. lib. bdg. 35.00 (ISBN 0-8495-0064-8). Arden Lib.

--Post-Prandial Philosophy. Repr. of 1894 ed. lib. bdg. 20.00 (ISBN 0-8414-3055-1). Folcroft.

--The Story of the Plants. 1978. Repr. of 1904 ed. lib. bdg. 20.00 (ISBN 0-8495-0120-2). Arden Lib.

Allen, Grant, ed. see White, Gilbert.

Allen, Gwenfread E. Hawaii's War Years, 1941-1945. LC 70-136889. (Illus.). 1971. Repr. of 1950 ed. lib. bdg. 27.75 (ISBN 0-8371-5331-X, ALHW). Greenwood.

Allen, H. Direct Drilling & Reduced Cultivations. (Illus.). 219p. 22.95 (ISBN 0-85236-113-0, Pub. by Farming Pr Uk). Diamond Farm Bk.

Allen, H., jt. ed. see Heyward, D.

Allen, H. C. Anglo-American Predicament: British Commonwealth & United States & European Unity. 1969. 25.00 (ISBN 0-312-03675-2). St Martin.

--Keynotes & Characteristics with Comparisons. 319p. 1980. Repr. of 1959 ed. lib. bdg. 40.00 (ISBN 0-89987-005-8). Darby Bks.

Allen, H. C. & Hill, C. P., eds. British Essays in American History. LC 82-20916. x, 350p. 1983. Repr. of 1957 ed. lib. bdg. 39.75x (ISBN 0-313-23789-1, ALBE). Greenwood.

Allen, H. C. & Thompson, Roger, eds. Contrast & Connection: Bicentennial Essays in Anglo-American History. LC 76-7095. x, 373p. 1976. 20.00x (ISBN 0-8214-0355-9, 82-82485). Ohio U Pr.

Allen, H. G. & Bulson, P. S. Background to Buckling. (Illus.). 1980. text ed. 60.00x (ISBN 0-07-084100-4). McGraw.

Allen, H. Hugh & Nisker, Jeffrey A., eds. Cancer in Pregnancy. (Illus.). 288p. 1985. monograph 32.50 (ISBN 0-87993-235-X). Futura Pub.

Allen, H. J., jt. ed. see Wilbur, J. B.

Allen, H. W. The Romance of Wine. (Illus.). 9.25 (ISBN 0-8446-0004-0). Peter Smith.

Allen, H. Warner. Romance of Wine. LC 71-166424. (Illus.). 1971. pap. 3.50 (ISBN 0-486-21684-5). Dover.

Allen, Hannah. Homemaker's Guide to Foods for Pleasure & Health. LC 76-17403. (Illus., Orig.). 1976. pap. 2.95 (ISBN 0-914532-12-X). Natural Hygiene.

Allen, Harold & Frumkin, Deborah S. Harold Allen: Photographer & Teacher. DelliQuadri, Lyn & Rossen, Susan F., eds. LC 84-72695. (Illus.). 54p. (Orig.). 1984. pap. 7.95 (ISBN 0-86559-059-1). Art Inst Chi.

Allen, Harold B. Beach Haven & Other Stories. 200p. 1982. pap. 3.95 (ISBN 0-941418-00-6). Long Beach Isl Pr.

--The Linguistic Atlas of the Upper Midwest, 3 vols. Vol. 1, 425 p., 1973. 45.00x (ISBN 0-8166-0686-2); Vol. 2, 92 p., 1975. 45.00x (ISBN 0-8166-0756-7); Vol. 3, 362p., 1976. 45.00x (ISBN 0-8166-0789-3). Gale.

--Linguistics & English Linguistics. 2nd ed. LC 75-42974. (Goldentree Bibliographies in Language & Literature Ser.). 1977. pap. text ed. 16.95x (ISBN 0-88295-558-6). Harlan Davidson.

--Minor Dialect Areas of the Upper Midwest. Bd. with A Tentative Bibliography of Kentucky Speech. Woodbridge, Hensley C; The Language of Jazz Musicians. Hinton, Norman D. (Publications of the American Dialect Society: No. 30). 48p. 1958. pap. 1.65 (ISBN 0-8173-0630-7). U of Ala Pr.

--Semantic Confusion: A Report from Atlas Files. (Publications of the American Dialect Society: No. 33). 24p. 1960. pap. 2.20 (ISBN 0-8173-0633-1). U of Ala Pr.

--A Survey of the Teaching of English to Non-English Speakers in the United States. Cordasco, Francesco, ed. LC 77-90403. (Bilingual-Bicultural Education in the U.S. Ser.). 1978. Repr. of 1966 ed. lib. bdg. 20.00x (ISBN 0-405-11072-3). Ayer Co Pubs.

Allen, Harold B. & Linn, Michael D. Readings in Applied English Linguistics. LC 81-18663. 1981. pap. text ed. 15.00 (ISBN 0-394-32750-0, KnopfC). Knopf.

Allen, Harold J., jt. ed. see Wilbur, James B.

Allen, Harry C. Bush & Backwoods. LC 75-9110. 153p. 1975. Repr. of 1959 ed. lib. bdg. 22.50 (ISBN 0-8371-8135-6, ALBB). Greenwood.

Allen, Harry E. & Simonsen, Clifford E. Corrections in America. 3rd ed. 1981. text ed. write for info. (ISBN 0-02-471670-7). Macmillan.

Allen, Harry E., et al. Probation & Parole in America. LC 85-10093. 336p. 1985. 22.50x (ISBN 0-02-900440-3). Free Pr.

--Crime & Punishment: An Introduction to Criminology. LC 80-69715. (Illus.). 464p. 1981. text ed. 17.95 (ISBN 0-02-900460-8). Free Pr.

Allen, Harry S. & Volgyes, Ivan, eds. Israel, the Middle East, & U.S. Interests. LC 82-22357. 190p. 1983. 33.95 (ISBN 0-03-063431-8). Praeger.

Allen, Harvey. Du Bose Heyward: A Critical & Biographical Sketch. 1978. lib. bdg. 10.00 (ISBN 0-8495-0043-5). Arden Lib.

--Du Bose Heyward: Critical & Biographical Sketch. LC 73-5974. 1922. lib. bdg. 8.50 (ISBN 0-8414-1731-8). Folcroft.

Allen, Hattie L. & Curlin, Vashti. Barron's How to Prepare for the Practical Nurse Licensing Examination. LC 78-27122. 1979. pap. 7.95 (ISBN 0-8120-0603-8). Barron.

Allen, Hazel O. The Ward Sister: Role & Preparation. 192p. 1982. pap. 17.50 (ISBN 0-7216-0800-0, Pub. by Bailliere-Tindall). Saunders.

Allen, Helena G. The Betrayal of Liliuokalani: Last Queen of Hawaii, 1838-1917. LC 82-71912. (Illus.). 420p. 1983. 19.95 (ISBN 0-87062-144-0). A H Clark.

Allen, Henriette & Barbe, Walter. Reinforcement Drills in Basic Reading Skills, 32 Bks. 1981. Write for Info. Ctr Appl Res.

Allen, Henry. Fool's Mercy. 6.95 (ISBN 0-931848-62-8, Pub. by HM). Dryad Pr.

--Fool's Mercy. 285p. 1984. pap. 3.95 (ISBN 0-88184-091-2). Carroll & Graf.

Allen, Henry E. Turkish Transformation: A Study in Social & Religious Development. LC 68-57588. (Illus.). 1968. Repr. of 1935 ed. lib. bdg. 22.50x (ISBN 0-8371-0284-7, ALTT). Greenwood.

Allen, Henry J. & Gompers, Samuel. Party of the Third Part: The Story of the Kansas Industrial Relations Court. LC 74-156401. (American Labor Ser., No. 2). 1971. Repr. of 1920 ed. 20.00 (ISBN 0-405-02911-X). Ayer Co Pubs.

Allen, Henry T. Atnatanas: Natives of Copper River, Alaska. (Shorey Indian Ser.). 14p. 1970. pap. 2.95 (ISBN 0-8466-4015-5). Shorey.

--An Expedition to the Copper: Tanana & Koyukuk Rivers in 1885. (Illus.). 96p. 1975. 7.95 (ISBN 0-88240-300-1). Alaska Northwest.

Allen, Herb, ed. The Bread Game: The Realities of Foundation Fundraising. 4th rev. ed. 150p. 1981. pap. 9.95 (ISBN 0-9606198-1-X). Regional Young.

Allen, Hervey. Anthony Adverse. 1977. 12.95 (ISBN 0-03-028400-7). HR&W.

--Wampum & Old Gold. LC 70-144716. (The Yale Series of Younger Poets: No. 9). Repr. of 1921 ed. 18.00 (ISBN 0-404-53809-6). AMS Pr.

Allen, Hope E. Writings Ascribed to Richard Rolle Hermit of Hampole & Materials for His Biography. 568p. 1981. Repr. of 1927 ed. lib. bdg. 125.00 (ISBN 0-89987-023-6). Darby Bks.

--Writings Ascribed to Richard Rolle, Hermit of Hampole & Materials for His Biography. (MLA. MS Ser.). 1927. 44.00 (ISBN 0-527-01280-7). Kraus Repr.

Allen, Horace N. Korean Tales. LC 78-67682. (The Folktale). Repr. of 1889 ed. 19.50 (ISBN 0-404-16053-0). AMS Pr.

Allen, Horace T., Jr. A Handbook for the Lectionary. LC 80-19735. 254p. 1980. softcover 8.95 (ISBN 0-664-24347-9, A Geneva Press Pub.). Westminster.

Allen, Howard W. Poindexter of Washington: A Study in Progressive Politics. LC 80-20123. 352p. 1981. 28.95x (ISBN 0-8093-0952-1). S Ill U Pr.

Allen, Hugh. The House of Goodyear: A Story of Rubber & of Modern Business. LC 75-41745. (Companies & Men: Business Enterprises in America). (Illus.). 1976. Repr. of 1943 ed. 43.00x (ISBN 0-405-08063-8). Ayer Co Pubs.

Allen, Hugh D., et al. Workbook in Pediatric Echocardiography. (Illus.). 1978. pap. 26.50 (ISBN 0-8151-0109-0). Year Bk Med.

Allen, Ida B. Best Loved Recipes of the American People. LC 81-43453. 648p. 1982. pap. 8.95 (ISBN 0-385-18015-2, Dolp). Doubleday.

Allen, Ira. Natural & Political History of the State of Vermont. LC 69-19611. 1969. Repr. 13.95 (ISBN 0-8048-0419-2). C E Tuttle.

Allen, Ira M. The Teacher's Contractual Status As Revealed by an Analysis of American Court Decisions. LC 77-176512. (Columbia University. Teachers College. Contributions to Education: No. 304). Repr. of 1928 ed. 22.50 (ISBN 0-404-55304-4). AMS Pr.

Allen, Irene A., jt. auth. see Thompson, Richard A.

Allen, Irvin G. Historic Old Town Maryland. 1983. write for info. (ISBN 0-9612514-0-9). McClain.

Allen, Irving L. The Language of Ethnic Conflict. 168p. 1983. 22.00x (ISBN 0-231-05556-0); pap. 11.00x (ISBN 0-231-05557-9). Columbia U Pr.

Allen, Irving L., ed. New Towns & the Suburban Dream. (Interdisciplinary Urban Ser). 1976. 24.00x (ISBN 0-8046-9161-4, Pub. by Kennikat). Assoc Faculty Pr.

Allen, J. Anatomy of LISP. (Computer Science Ser.). (Illus.). 1978. 42.50 (ISBN 0-07-001115-X). McGraw.

Allen, J., et al, eds. Grinding, Vol. 1. (Engineering Craftsmen: No. H5). 1968. spiral bdg. 38.50x (ISBN 0-85083-013-3). Trans-Atlantic.

--Sunda & Sahul: Prehistoric Studies in Southeast Asia, Melenasia & Australia. 1977. 75.00 (ISBN 0-12-051250-5). Acad Pr.

Allen, J. C., jt. auth. see Hudson, N. G.

Allen, J. C. & Hamilton, R. J., eds. Rancidity in Foods. 198p. 1984. 44.50 (ISBN 0-85334-219-9, Pub. by Elsevier Applied Sci England). Elsevier.

Allen, J. Dev, jt. auth. see Wright, Leigh R.

Allen, J. F., et al. Illustrated Bible for Children. (Illus.). (ps up). 8.95 (ISBN 0-8407-5264-4). Nelson.

Allen, J. Garrott, ed. The Physiology & Treatment of Peptic Ulcer. LC 59-10421. pap. 61.50 (ISBN 0-317-26372-2, 2024109). Bks Demand UMI.

Allen, J. H. & Greenough, J. B. New Latin Grammar. Kittredge, G. L., et al, eds. (College Classical Ser.). 490p. 1975. lib. bdg. 25.00x (ISBN 0-89241-001-9); pap. 12.50x (ISBN 0-89241-331-X). Caratzas.

Allen, J. H. D. Portuguese Word-Formation with Suffixes. (LD Ser.). 1941. 12.00 (ISBN 0-527-00779-X). Kraus Repr.

Allen, J. L. & Medley, M. W., Jr. Microwave Circuit Design Using Programmable Calculators. (Illus.). 279p. 1980. 54.00 (ISBN 0-89006-089-4). Artech Hse.

Allen, J. P. & Widdowson, H. G. English in Physical Science. (English in Focus Ser). (Illus.). 1974. Student's Edition. pap. 9.95x (ISBN 0-19-437510-2); Tchr's Edition. 12.00x (ISBN 0-19-437504-8). Oxford U Pr.

Allen, J. R. Experiments in Physical Sedimentology. 64p. (Orig.). 1985. pap. text ed. 7.95x (ISBN 0-04-551066-0). Allen Unwin.

--Sedimentary Structures, 2 Vols. (Developments in Sedimentology Ser.: Vol. 30B). 594p. 1982. Vol. 1. 110.75 (ISBN 0-444-41935-7); Vol. 2. 110.75 (ISBN 0-444-41945-4). Elsevier.

--Sedimentary Structures: Their Character & Physical Basis, Pts. A & B. (Developments in Sedimentology Ser.: Vol. 30). 1984. pap. 57.50 (ISBN 0-444-42232-3). Elsevier.

Allen, J. Romilly. Celtic Art in Pagan & Christian Times. 1977. lib. bdg. 69.95 (ISBN 0-8490-1589-8). Gordon Pr.

Allen, J. S. Neutrino. (Investigations in Physics Ser.: No. 5). 1958. 22.50 (ISBN 0-691-08009-7). Princeton U Pr.

Allen, J. W. A History of Political Thought in the Sixteenth Century. 576p. 1977. Repr. of 1928 ed. 29.50x (ISBN 0-87471-885-6). Rowman.

Allen, J. W., jt. auth. see Seccombe, Thomas.

Allen, J. W., ed. & intro. by. Tendi: A Swahili Classical Verse Form. LC 78-147117. 502p. 1971. text ed. 59.50x (ISBN 0-8419-0075-2, Africana). Holmes & Meier.

Allen, Jack. Education in the Eighties: Social Studies. 140p. 1981. pap. 9.95 (ISBN 0-8106-3163-6). NEA.

Allen, Jack & Moristo, Dennis. An Introduction to the BIA Affairs. 27p. 1971. pap. 2.00 (ISBN 0-935626-22-0). U Cal AISC.

Allen, James. All These Things Added. 192p. 1983. pap. 9.50 (ISBN 0-89540-129-0, SB-129). Sun Pub.

--As a Man Thinketh. pap. 1.00 (ISBN 0-87516-000-X). De Vorss.

--As a Man Thinketh. 1959. 3.95 (ISBN 0-399-12829-8, G&D). Putnam Pub Group.

--As a Man Thinketh. LC 77-77691. 1976. text ed. 6.00 (ISBN 0-912472-21-9). Miller Bks.

--As a Man Thinketh. 4.95 (ISBN 0-88088-037-6). Peter Pauper.

--As a Man Thinketh. (Inspirational Classics Ser.). 64p. 6.95 (ISBN 0-8007-1142-4). Revell.

--As a Man Thinketh. 88p. 1983. pap. 4.50 (ISBN 0-89540-136-3, SB-136). Sun Pub.

--As a Man Thinketh. 4.95 (ISBN 0-529-05908-8, F12); pap. 2.95 (ISBN 0-529-05906-1, D6). World Bible.

--As You Thinketh: Update & Revision of James Allen's Classic "As a Man Thinketh". rev. ed. 88p. 1984. pap. 5.95 (ISBN 0-914295-03-9). Univ Life Sci.

--From Passion to Peace. 64p. 1981. pap. 3.50 (ISBN 0-89540-077-4, SB-077). Sun Pub.

--From Poverty to Power. 184p. 1980. pap. 7.50 (ISBN 0-89540-061-8, SB-061). Sun Pub.

--The Life Triumphant. 112p. 1983. pap. 6.50 (ISBN 0-89540-125-8, SB-125). Sun Pub.

--Morning & Evening Thoughts. 80p. 1983. pap. 4.00 (ISBN 0-89540-137-1, SB-137). Sun Pub.

Allen, James & Allen, Barbara A., eds. Psychiatry. 7th ed. (Medical Examination Review Book: Vol 7). 1982. 12.75 (ISBN 0-87488-107-2). Med Exam.

Allen, James, et al. Inspiration Three, Vol. 1: Three Famous Classics in One Book. LC 73-80032. (Pivot Family Reader Ser.). 128p. 1973. pap. 2.50 (ISBN 0-87983-041-7). Keats.

Allen, James A. Studies in Innovation in the Steel & Chemical Industries. LC 68-583. 246p. 1967. lib. bdg. 27.50x (ISBN 0-678-06790-2). Kelley.

Allen, James A. Van see Van Allen, James A.

Allen, James B. Great Lakes & Plain Songs. Holley, Barbara, ed. (T. S. Eliot Chapbook Ser.: No. 3). (Orig.). Date not set. pap. 3.75 (ISBN 0-933494-31-9). Earthwise Pubs.

Allen, James B., jt. auth. see Alexander, Thomas G.

Allen, James B., ed. see Clayton, William.

Allen, James C. & Beam, Thomas R. Infectious Disease for the House Officer. (HO). (Illus.). 196p. 1982. pap. 10.95 (ISBN 0-683-00069-1). Williams & Wilkins.

Allen, James E. The Negro in New York. 1964. 5.00 (ISBN 0-682-42082-4). Exposition Pr FL.

Allen, James E. & Bender, Deborah. Managing Teenage Pregnancy: Access to Abortion, Contraception & Sex Education. LC 79-89009. 332p. 1980. 39.95 (ISBN 0-03-053991-9). Praeger.

Allen, James H. May's Manual of Diseases of the Eye. LC 74-10746. 442p. 1974. Repr. of 1968 ed. 24.50 (ISBN 0-88275-190-5). Krieger.

Allen, James J. European Common Market & the G.A.T.T. facsimile of 1960 ed. 1970. 6.00 (ISBN 0-87419-008-8). U Pr of Wash.

Allen, James L. Blue-Grass Region of Kentucky: And Other Kentucky Articles. LC 74-39712. (Essay Index Reprint Ser.). Repr. of 1892 ed. 25.50 (ISBN 0-8369-2734-6). Ayer Co Pubs.

--The Choir Invisible. LC 73-86169. Repr. of 1897 ed. 7.50 (ISBN 0-404-00327-3). AMS Pr.

--The Choir Invisible. 1974. pap. 0.95 (ISBN 0-380-00035-0, 19570). Avon.

--Choir Invisible. 1897. 7.00x (ISBN 0-403-00000-9). Scholarly.

--The Choir Invisible. 361p. 1982. lib. bdg. 25.00 (ISBN 0-89987-038-4). Darby Bks.

--The Choir Invisible. 361p. 1983. Repr. of 1905 ed. lib. bdg. 20.00 (ISBN 0-89984-019-1). Century Bookbindery.

--Flute & Violin & Other Kentucky Tales & Romances. facsimile ed. LC 78-98555. (Short Story Index Reprint Ser.). 1891. 16.00 (ISBN 0-8369-3129-7). Ayer Co Pubs.

--A Kentucky Cardinal. LC 68-20002. (Americans in Fiction Ser.). lib. bdg. 16.50 (ISBN 0-8398-0056-8); pap. text ed. 2.95x (ISBN 0-89197-818-6). Irvington.

--A Kentucky Cardinal, Aftermath, & Other Selected Works. Bottorff, William K., ed. (Masterworks of Literature Ser). 1967. 7.95x (ISBN 0-8084-0200-5); pap. 4.95x (ISBN 0-8084-0201-3). New Coll U Pr.

--Landmark. facsimile ed. LC 70-110177. (Short Story Index Reprint Ser.). 1925. 14.50 (ISBN 0-8369-3328-1). Ayer Co Pubs.

--Mettle of the Pasture. LC 74-94468. Repr. of 1903 ed. 14.00 (ISBN 0-404-00328-1). AMS Pr.

--Mettle of the Pasture. LC 3-15441. 1969. Repr. of 1903 ed. 13.00x (ISBN 0-403-00137-4). Scholarly.

--The Reign of Law: A Tale of the Kentucky Hemp Fields. facsimile ed. LC 77-164556. (American Fiction Reprint Ser). Repr. of 1900 ed. 31.00 (ISBN 0-8369-7032-2). Ayer Co Pubs.

Allen, James Lovic. Yeats's Epitaph: A Key to Symbolic Unity in His Life & Work. LC 80-5848. 282p. (Orig.). 1982. lib. bdg. 27.25 (ISBN 0-8191-2592-X); pap. text ed. 13.00 (ISBN 0-8191-2593-8). U Pr of Amer.

Allen, James P. The Inflection of the Verb in the Pyramid Texts. (Bibliotheca Aegyptia: Vol. 2). 785p. 1984. 76.00x (ISBN 0-89003-086-3); pap. 56.00x (ISBN 0-89003-087-1). Undena Pubns.

Allen, James R. & Allen, Barbara A. Psychiatry: Guide to Treatment. 2nd ed. 1983. pap. text ed. 27.50 (ISBN 0-87488-716-X). Med Exam.

--Textbook Study Guide of Psychiatry. 2nd. ed. (Medical Examination Review Book: Vol. 7A). 1978. 13.95 (ISBN 0-87488-156-0). Med Exam.

Allen, James S. Popular French Romanticism: Authors, Readers, & Books in the 19th Century. LC 80-27129. (Illus.). 320p. 1981. 20.00x (ISBN 0-8156-2232-5). Syracuse U Pr.

--Reconstruction: The Battle for Democracy. LC 37-34604. 256p. 1955. pap. 2.25 (ISBN 0-7178-0169-1). Intl Pubs Co.

--The Romance of Commerce & Culture: Capitalism, Modernism & the Chicago-Aspen Crusade for Cultural Reform. LC 83-4816. 352p. 1983. lib. bdg. 27.50x (ISBN 0-226-01458-4). U of Chicago Pr.

Allen, James S., ed. see Lenin, Vladimir I.

Allen, James T. First Year of Greek. rev. ed. 1931. text ed. write for info. (ISBN 0-02-301750-3). Macmillan.

--Greek Theatre of the Fifth Century Before Christ. LC 68-2221. (Studies in Drama, No. 39). 1969. Repr. of 1919 ed. lib. bdg. 39.95x (ISBN 0-8383-0647-0). Haskell.

--Stage Antiquities of the Greeks & Romans & Their Influence. LC 63-10266. (Our Debt to Greece & Rome Ser). (Illus.). Repr. of 1930 ed. 15.00 (ISBN 0-8154-0009-8). Cooper Sq.

Allen, Jan. Diesels in East Anglia. 80p. 30.00x (ISBN 0-86093-105-6, Pub. by ORPC Ltd UK). State Mutual Bk.

Allen, Jan C. Fifty-Five Years of East Anglian Steam. 108p. 30.00x (ISBN 0-86093-182-X, Pub. by ORPC Ltd UK). State Mutual Bk.

--Gleneagles to Glastonbury. 96p. 42.00x (ISBN 0-86093-351-2, Pub. by ORPC Ltd UK). State Mutual Bk.

Allen, Jane A., ed. see Day, Holliday D.

Allen, Jane E., jt. auth. see Groff, John M.

Allen, Janet. Collage: The Art of Making Pictures from Odds & Ends. 80p. 1981. pap. 7.95 (ISBN 0-8120-2289-0). Barron.

Allen, Janice, jt. auth. see Allen, Jerry.

Allen, Jay, tr. see Mengin, Robert.

Allen, Jeanne T., ed. Now, Voyager. LC 84-40144. (Wisconsin-Warner Brothers Screenplay Ser.). 1984. 17.50x (ISBN 0-299-09790-0); pap. 6.95 (ISBN 0-299-09794-3). U of Wis Pr.

Allen, Jeffery. Nosy Mrs. Rat. LC 84-19618. (Illus.). 32p. (ps-3). 1985. 11.95 (ISBN 0-670-80880-6). Viking.

Allen, Jeffrey. Mary Alice, Operator Number Nine. (Illus.). 32p. (gr. 1-3). 1976. 9.70 (ISBN 0-316-03425-8). Little.

--Mary Alice, Operator Number Nine. (Illus.). (gr. 2-8). 1978. pap. 2.95 (ISBN 0-14-050265-3, Puffin). Penguin.

Allen, Jeffrey, et al. Finding the Right Job at Mid-Life. 168p. 1985. 12.95 (ISBN 0-671-53058-5); pap. 6.95 (ISBN 0-671-55548-0). S&S.

Allen, Jelisaveta & Sevcenko, Ihor, eds. Dumbarton Oakes Bibliographies Based on Byzantinische Zeitschrift: Series II, Literature in Various Byzantine Disciplines, 1892-1977. 408p. 1982. Vol. 1: Epigraphy. 96.00 (ISBN 0-7201-1586-8). Mansell.

Allen, Jelisaveta S., ed. Dumbarton Oaks Bibliographies Based on "Byzantinische Zeitschrift". LC 72-81538. (Ser. 1, Literature on Byzantine Art: Vol. 1, Parts 1 & 2, by Location). 1095p. 1973. Set. 72.00 (ISBN 0-7201-0217-0). Mansell.

--Dumbarton Oaks Bibliographies Based on "Byzantinische Zeitschrift" Literature on Byzantine Art 1892-1967, Vol. 2, by Categories. 614p. 1976. 64.00 (ISBN 0-7201-0218-9). Mansell.

Allen, Jerry. The Adventures of Mark Twain. 12.00 (ISBN 0-8446-0453-4). Peter Smith.

Allen, Jerry & Allen, Janice. Halia Language Course. 68p. 1965. pap. 1.93x (ISBN 0-88312-771-7); microfiche 1.50 (ISBN 0-88312-393-2). Summer Inst Ling.

Allen, Jerry, ed. see Conrad, Joseph.

Allen, Jim & Curnow, Wystan. New Art: Some Recent New Zealand Sculpture & Past Object Art. (Illus.). 1976. 9.95 (ISBN 0-424-00093-8, Pub. by Heinemann Pub New Zealand). Intl Spec Bk.

Allen, Jo, jt. auth. see Fearing, Bertie B.

Allen, Jo Harvey. Cheek To Cheek: Poems & Excerpts From Interviews. Robertson, Kirk, ed. (Windriver Ser.). 64p. (Orig.). 1983. pap. 6.00 (ISBN 0-916918-22-X); pap. text ed. 25.00 (ISBN 0-916918-23-8). Duck Down.

Allen, Joan M. Candles & Carnival Lights: The Catholic Sensibility of F. Scott Fitzgerald. LC 77-82752. 1978. 25.00x (ISBN 0-8147-0563-4); pap. 13.50x (ISBN 0-8147-0564-2). NYU Pr.

Allen, Joel A. The American Bisons Living & Extinct. LC 73-17790. (Natural Sciences in America Ser.). (Illus.). 295p. 1974. Repr. 21.00x (ISBN 0-405-05701-6). Ayer Co Pubs.

--History of the North American Pinnipeds: A Monograph of the Walruses, Sea-Lions, Sea-Bears & Seals of North America. LC 73-17792. (Natural Sciences in America Ser.). (Illus.). 806p. 1974. Repr. 53.00x (ISBN 0-405-05702-4). Ayer Co Pubs.

Allen, John. Assault with a Deadly Weapon: The Autobiography of a Street Criminal. Kelly, Dianne H. & Heyma, K., eds. 1978. pap. 5.95 (ISBN 0-07-001073-0). McGraw.

--Drama in Schools. 1981. pap. text ed. 10.00x (ISBN 0-435-18033-9). Heinemann Ed.

--A History of the Theatre in Europe. LC 83-6050. (Illus.). 320p. 1983. 24.50x (ISBN 0-389-20398-X, BNB 07283). B&N Imports.

--Masters of European Drama. 192p. 1981. 25.00x (ISBN 0-234-77574-2, Pub. by Dobson Bks England). State Mutual Bk.

--Notes of Noteworthy Men. 1978. Repr. lib. bdg. 30.00 (ISBN 0-8492-0093-8). R West.

--Super Profile: Ford GT40. 56p. 1983. 9.95 (ISBN 0-85429-332-9, F332). Haynes Pubns.

Allen, John & Hammond, Paul. The Magnificent Gateway: A Geology of the Columbia River Gorge. LC 79-2714. (Illus.). 150p. 1979. pap. 8.50 (ISBN 0-917304-10-1). Timber.

Allen, John see Massey, Doreen, et al.

Allen, John, ed. Three Medieval Plays: The Coventry Nativity Play, Everyman, Master Pierre Pathelin. 1968. pap. 3.50x (ISBN 0-87830-529-7). Theatre Arts.

Allen, John C. Inquiry into the Rise & Growth of the Royal Prerogative in England. new ed. 1962. Repr. of 1849 ed. 22.50 (ISBN 0-8337-0042-1). B Franklin.

Allen, John E. Aerodynamics: The Science of Fluid in Motion. 2nd ed. (Illus.). 205p. 1982. 27.50 (ISBN 0-07-001074-9). McGraw.

--Newspaper Designing. 1977. Repr. of 1947 ed. lib. bdg. 15.00 (ISBN 0-686-19822-0). Havertown Bks.

Allen, John H. Judah's Sceptre & Joseph's Birthright. 1946. 8.00 (ISBN 0-685-08809-X). Destiny.

Allen, John Houghton. The Southwest. LC 76-57532. (Zia Books). 1977. pap. 5.95 (ISBN 0-8263-0446-X). U of NM Pr.

Allen, John J. Don Quixote: Hero or Fool, Pt. II. LC 71-625420. (University of Florida Humanities Monographs: No. 46). vii, 118p. 1979. pap. 6.50 (ISBN 0-8130-0630-9). U Presses Fla.

--Don Quixote: Hero or Fool? A Study in Narrative Technique, Pt. 1. LC 71-625420. (University of Florida Humanities Monographs: No. 29). 1969. pap. 3.75 (ISBN 0-8130-0268-0). U Presses Fla.

--The Reconstruction of a Spanish Golden-Age Playhouse: El Corral del Principe (1583-1744) LC 83-1241. (Illus.). xii, 129p. 1984. 25.00 (ISBN 0-8130-0755-0). U Presses Fla.

Allen, John L. Passage Through the Garden: Lewis & Clark & the Image of the American Northwest. LC 74-14512. pap. 110.00 (ISBN 0-317-28195-X, 2022773). Bks Demand UMI.

Allen, John R. Physical Geology. (Introducing Geology Ser.). 1975. pap. text ed. 11.95x (ISBN 0-04-550022-3). Allen Unwin.

--Physical Processes of Sedimentation: An Introduction. (Earth Science Ser.). (Illus.). 1970. pap. text ed. 11.95x (ISBN 0-04-551014-8). Allen Unwin.

--Principles of Physical Sedimentology. (Illus.). 400p. 1985. text ed. 40.00x (ISBN 0-04-551095-4); pap. text ed. 24.95x (ISBN 0-04-551096-2). Allen Unwin.

Allen, John R., et al. Thinking about TLC LOGO. 236p. 1984. pap. 17.45 (ISBN 0-03-064116-0). HR&W.

--Thinking about TLC LOGO: For Mattel Aquarius. LC 83-10771. 220p. 1983. pap. 14.95 (ISBN 0-03-064114-4). HR&W.

Allen, John S., tr. see Cremer, Lothar.

Allen, John T. What Every Manager Needs to Know about Quality Circles & Participative Management. 32p. 1985. pap. 4.95 (ISBN 0-937670-34-0). Quality Circle.

Allen, John W. It Happened in Southern Illinois. 1973. 6.00 (ISBN 0-686-11834-0). Univ Graphics.

--Legends & Lore of Southern Illinois. 1973. 6.00 (ISBN 0-686-11835-9). Univ Graphics.

Allen, John W., jt. auth. see Seccombe, Thomas.

Allen, John W., et al. The Foundations of Free Enterprise. 24p. 1979. 1.00 (ISBN 0-86599-004-2). Ctr Educ Res.

Allen, Jonathan. A Bad Case of Animal Nonsense. LC 81-47137. (Illus.). 64p. (gr. 2-5). 1981. 10.00 (ISBN 0-87923-398-2). Godine.

--From Text to Speech: The System. (Cambridge Studies in Speech Science & Communication). (Illus.). 300p. Date not set. price not set (ISBN 0-521-30641-8). Cambridge U Pr.

Allen, Jonathan, ed. March Fourth: Scientists, Students & Society. 1970. pap. 4.95x (ISBN 0-262-51008-1). MIT Pr.

Allen, Jordan. Cavern of Silver. 1983. 11.95 (ISBN 0-8027-4014-6). Walker & Co.

--Texas Fever. 224p. (Orig.). 1980. pap. 1.95 (ISBN 0-89083-664-7). Zebra.

Allen, Joseph. Battles of the British Navy, 2 vols. 1977. Set. lib. bdg. 250.00 (ISBN 0-8490-1480-8). Gordon Pr.

Allen, Joseph C. Weatherwise & Otherwise: The Best of Yankee's Oracle, Bk. 1. Silitch, Clarissa M., ed. LC 73-93979. (Illus.). 64p. (Orig.). 1974. pap. 1.95 (ISBN 0-911658-60-2, 3024). Yankee Bks.

Allen, Joseph H. Our Liberal Movement in Theology: Chiefly As Shown in Recollections of the History of Unitarianism in New England. 3rd ed. LC 73-38432. (Religion in America, Ser. 2). 230p. 1972. Repr. of 1892 ed. 20.00 (ISBN 0-405-04053-9). Ayer Co Pubs.

Allen, Joseph J., jt. auth. see Metropolitan Philip Saliba.

Allen, Joseph J., ed. Orthodox Synthesis: The Unity of Theological Thought. 231p. (Orig.). 1981. pap. 8.95 (ISBN 0-913836-84-2). St Vladimirs.

Allen, Joseph L. Love & Conflict: A Covenantal Model of Christian Ethics. 336p. 1984. pap. 12.95 (ISBN 0-687-22806-9). Abingdon.

Allen, Joyce E. Sense & Sensitivity in Gymnastics. 1969. pap. text ed. 6.00x (ISBN 0-435-80020-5). Heinemann Ed.

Allen, Judson B. The Ethical Poetic of the Later Middle Ages: A Decorum of Convenient Discussion. 360p. 1981. 45.00x (ISBN 0-8020-2370-3). U of Toronto Pr.

--Friar As Critic: Literary Attitudes in the Later Middle Ages. LC 77-123037. 1971. 11.50x (ISBN 0-8265-1158-9). Vanderbilt U Pr.

Allen, Judson B. & Moritz, Theresa A. A Distinction of Stories: The Medieval Unity of Chaucer's Fair Chain of Narratives for Canterbury. LC 80-26629. 270p. 1981. 20.00 (ISBN 0-8142-0310-8). Ohio St U Pr.

Allen, Judy. Guide to Stamps & Stamp Collecting. (Hobby Guides Ser.). (gr. 2-5). 1981. 7.95 (ISBN 0-86020-549-5, Usborne-Hayes); PLB 12.95 (ISBN 0-88110-027-7); pap. 4.95 (ISBN 0-86020-548-7). EDC.

--In London. (Nicholson Guides). (Illus.). 128p. (Orig.). 1983. pap. 4.95 (ISBN 0-905522-69-9, Pub. by Auto Assn-British Tourist Authority England). Merrimack Pub Cir.

Allen, Julia, tr. see Saudray, Nicholas.

Allen, Juliet V. What Do I Do When...? A Handbook for Parents & Other Beleaguered Adults. LC 83-12903. 224p. (Orig.). 1983. pap. 6.95 (ISBN 0-915166-23-2). Impact Pubs Cal.

Allen, June. The Other Side of the Elephant. (Illus.). 1977. 5.95 (ISBN 0-914634-45-3, 7719). DOK Pubs.

Allen, June, tr. see Garin, Eugenio.

Allen, K. Aileen, et al, eds. Early Intervention: A Team Approach. LC 78-17065. (Illus.). 512p. 1978. 14.00 (ISBN 0-8391-0896-6). Pro Ed.

Allen, K. Eileen. Mainstreaming in Early Childhood Education. LC 78-74838. (Early Childhood Education Ser.). (Illus.). 260p. (Orig.). 1980. pap. text ed. 13.20 (ISBN 0-8273-1692-5); instructor's guide O. S. 3.60 (ISBN 0-8273-1693-3). Delmar.

Allen, K. Eileen & Goetz, Elizabeth M. Early Childhood Education: Special Problems, Special Solutions. LC 82-4029. 349p. 1982. 32.00 (ISBN 0-89443-657-0). Aspen Systems.

Allen, K. Eileen & Hart, Betty. The Early Years: Arrangements for Learning. (Illus.). 384p. 1984. 25.95 (ISBN 0-13-223149-2). P-H.

Allen, K. Eileen, jt. ed. see Goetz, Elizabeth M.

Allen, K. Radway. Conservation & Management of Whales. LC 79-90505. (Washington Sea Grant). (Illus.). 120p. 1980. 15.00x (ISBN 0-295-95706-9). U of Wash Pr.

Allen, K. W., ed. Adhesion, Vols. 1-5. 1977-81. Vol. 1. 48.00 (ISBN 0-85334-735-2, Pub. by Elsevier Applied Sci England); Vol. 2. 44.50 (ISBN 0-85334-743-3); Vol. 3. 48.00 (ISBN 0-85334-808-1); Vol. 4. 48.00 (ISBN 0-85334-861-8); Vol. 5. 48.00 (ISBN 0-85334-929-0). Elsevier.

--Adhesion, Vol. 6. (Illus.). x, 210p. 1983. 64.75 (ISBN 0-85334-106-0, Pub. by Elsevier Applied Sci England). Elsevier.

--Adhesion, Vol. 7. (Illus.). 271p. 1983. 64.75 (ISBN 0-85334-195-8, Pub. by Elsevier Applied Sci England). Elsevier.

--Adhesion, Vol. 8. (Illus.). 220p. 1984. 64.75 (ISBN 0-85334-252-0, I-518-83, Pub. by Elsevier Applied Sci England). Elsevier.

--Adhesion: Papers from the Annual Conference on Adhesion & Adhesives, 22nd, City University, London, UK, Vol. 9. 198p. 1985. 52.50 (ISBN 0-85334-328-4, Pub. by Elsevier Applied Sci England). Elsevier.

Allen, Karen M. The Human-Animal Bond: An Annotated Bibliography. LC 85-1916. 246p. 1985. 17.50 (ISBN 0-8108-1792-6). Scarecrow.

Allen, Keith, jt. ed. see Stavrakas, Nick.

Allen, Ken. Cooking Wild. (Illus.). 160p. 1985. pap. 10.95 (ISBN 0-930096-53-3). G Gannett.

Allen, Kenneth. Fountain of Youth: Life Extension Guide. 12.95 (ISBN 0-911505-16-4). Lifecraft.

--Great Warriors. LC 80-50952. (Adventures in History Ser.). PLB 12.68 (ISBN 0-382-06384-8). Silver.

Allen, Kerry K. The Wichita Experience: Mobilizing Corporate Resources to Meet Community Needs. 51p. 1978. pap. 3.65 (ISBN 0-318-17141-4, C12). Natl Ctr Cit Involv.

Allen, Kerry K. & Chapin, Isolde. Volunteers from the Workplace. 312p. 1979. pap. 8.95 (ISBN 0-318-17140-6, C19). Natl Ctr Cit Involv.

Allen, Kevin & Yuill, Douglas. Small Area Employment Forecasting. 264p. 1978. text ed. 44.50x (ISBN 0-566-00201-9). Gower Pub Co.

Allen, L., jt. auth. see Knight, P. L.

Allen, L. A. Making Managerial Planning More Effective. 320p. 1982. 31.50 (ISBN 0-07-001078-1). McGraw.

Allen, L. David. Asimov's Foundation Trilogy & Other Works: Notes. 1977. pap. 2.50 (ISBN 0-8220-0212-4). Cliffs.

--Herbert's Dune & Other Works Notes. 101p. 1975. pap. text ed. 3.50 (ISBN 0-8220-0419-4). Cliffs.

--The Prince & the Pauper Notes. 77p. (Orig.). 1980. pap. text ed. 3.25 (ISBN 0-8220-1096-8). Cliffs.

--Science Fiction: An Introduction. 187p. (Orig.). 1973. pap. text ed. 4.95 (ISBN 0-8220-1169-7). Cliffs.

Allen, L. David & Roberts, James L. Connecticut Yankee in King Arthur's Court Notes. 64p. (Orig.). (gr. 9-12). 1982. pap. 2.95 (ISBN 0-8220-0324-4). Cliffs.

Allen, L. David, Jr. Animal Farm Notes. (Orig.). 1981. pap. 2.75 (ISBN 0-8220-0174-8). Cliffs.

Allen, Laine. Undercover Kisses. (Second Chance at Love Ser.: No. 276). 192p. 1985. pap. 2.25 (ISBN 0-425-08286-5). Berkley Pub.

Allen, Laura G. Contemporary Hopi Pottery. (Illus., Orig.). 1984. pap. 8.95 (ISBN 0-89734-055-8). Mus Northern Ariz.

Allen, Laura J. Ottie & the Star. LC 78-22485. (Early I Can Read Bk.). (Illus.). 32p. (ps-3). 1979. PLB 8.89 (ISBN 0-06-020108-8). HarpJ.

--Rollo & Tweedy & the Case of the Missing Cheese. LC 82-47731. (Illus.). 48p. (gr. k-3). 1983. 11.49 (ISBN 0-06-020096-0); PLB 11.89 (ISBN 0-06-020097-9). HarpJ.

Allen, Layman. Equations: Game of Creative Mathematics. 12.00 (ISBN 0-911624-38-4); tchrs' manual 1.75 (ISBN 0-911624-11-2). Wffn Proof.

--WFF: Beginner's Game of Modern Logic. 2.50 (ISBN 0-911624-01-5). Wffn Proof.

--Wffn Proof: Game of Modern Logic. 15.00 (ISBN 0-911624-36-8). Wffn Proof.

Allen, Layman, et al. Queries & Theories: Game of Science & Language. 15.00 (ISBN 0-911624-42-2). Wffn Proof.

Allen, Layman E. The Meditation Game: Strategy. pap. 2.00 (ISBN 0-911624-41-4). Wffn Proof.

--Real Numbers: Arithmetic. 2.50 (ISBN 0-911624-04-X). Wffn Proof.

Allen, Layman E. & Ross, Joan. IMP (Instructional Math Play) Kits: Individual Solitare Kits. 15.00 (ISBN 0-911624-18-X). Wffn Proof.

Allen, Layman E., et al. On-Sets: Game of Set Theory. 12.00 (ISBN 0-911624-37-6). Wffn Proof.

--On-Words: The Game of Word Structures. 12.00 (ISBN 0-911624-40-6). Wffn Proof.

Allen, Lee, ed. see Rommel, Erwin.

Allen, Leslie. Joel, Obadiah, Jonah, Micah. (New International Commentary on Old Testament Ser.). 16.95 (ISBN 0-8028-2373-4). Eerdmans.

Allen, Linda. Stepping Stones. 72p. (YA) (gr. 7-12). 1984. 16.95 (ISBN 0-7134-1265-8, Pub. by Batsford England). David & Charles.

Allen, Linda, jt. auth. see Meyer, Carolyn.

Allen, Linda, jt. auth. see Tudor, Tasha.

Allen, Lochie J. & Kinney, Edward C., eds. Bio-Engineering Symposium for Fish Culture: Proceedings. 307p. 1981. text ed. 24.00 (ISBN 0-913235-25-3). AM Fisheries Soc.

Allen, Loring. OPEC Oil. LC 79-19284. 288p. 1979. text ed. 35.00 (ISBN 0-89946-002-X). Oelgeschlager.

--Venezuelan Economic Development: A Politico-Economic Analysis. Altman, Edward I. & Walter, Ingo, eds. LC 76-10395. (Contemporary Studies in Economic & Financial Analysis: Vol. 7). 1977. lib. bdg. 36.50 (ISBN 0-89232-011-7). Jai Pr.

Allen, Louis. Burma: The Longest War Nineteen Forty-One to Nineteen Forty-Five. (Illus.). 686p. 1985. 29.95 (ISBN 0-312-10858-3). St Martin.

--The End of the War in Asia. (Illus.). 1976. 24.95x (ISBN 0-8464-0043-X). Beekman Pubs.

--Singapore, Nineteen Forty-One to Nineteen Forty-Two. Frankland, Noble & Dowling, Christopher, eds. LC 79-52236. (The Politics & Strategy of the Second World War). 343p. 1979. 27.50 (ISBN 0-87413-160-X). U Delaware Pr.

Allen, Louis A. Management Profession. (Management Ser.). 1964. 32.95 (ISBN 0-07-001375-6). McGraw.

--Professional Management. 256p. 1973. 32.95 (ISBN 0-07-001110-9). McGraw.

Allen, Lynn A., jt. auth. see Kisner, Carolyn.

Allen, M. & Finlay, D. Radiological Guide to Fracture Diagnosis. (Illus.). 255p. Date not set. price not set (Pub. by Bailliere-Tindall). Saunders.

Allen, M. B., III. Collocation Techniques for Modeling Compositional Flows in Oil Reservoirs. (Lecture Notes in Engineering: Vol. 6). 216p. 1984. pap. 14.00 (ISBN 0-387-13096-9). Springer Verlag.

Allen, M. Cecil. The Mirror of the Passing World. 1978. Repr. of 1928 ed. lib. bdg. 15.00 (ISBN 0-8482-0115-9). Norwood Edns.

--Painters of the Modern Mind. Repr. of 1929 ed. 15.00 (ISBN 0-8482-3254-2). Norwood Edns.

Allen, M. J., jt. auth. see Calder, D. G.

Allen, M. W. & Noffsinger, Ella M. A Revision of the Marine Nematodes of the Superfamily Draconematoidea Filipjev 1918. (Publications in Zoology Ser.: Vol. 109). 1978. 16.00x (ISBN 0-520-09583-9). U of Cal Pr.

Allen, Marc. Friends & Lovers: How to Create the Relationships You Want. 128p. 1985. 6.95 (ISBN 0-931432-22-7). Whatever Pub.

Allen, Marcus. Astrology for the New Age: An Intuitive Approach. LC 79-10433. 129p. 1979. pap. 5.95 (ISBN 0-931432-03-0). Whatever Pub.

--Astrology for the New Age: An Intuitive Approach. LC 79-10433. 128p. (Orig.). 1984. pap. 5.95 (ISBN 0-916360-22-9). CRCS Pubns NV.

--Tantra for the West: A Guide to Personal Freedom. LC 80-316. 235p. 1981. pap. 7.95 (ISBN 0-931432-06-5). Whatever Pub.

Allen, Margaret, jt. auth. see Ghertman, Michel.

Allen, Margaret, ed. The Times One Thousand. 144p. 1984. 34.50 (ISBN 0-89730-148-X, Pub. by Times Bks). News Bks Intl.

--The Times One Thousand, 1982-1983: Leading Companies in Britain & Overseas. 16th ed. LC 72-617301. (Illus.). 132p. 1982. 52.50x (ISBN 0-7230-0242-8). Intl Pubns Serv.

--The Times One Thousand, 1984-85. 112p. 1985. 34.50 (ISBN 0-89730-161-7, Pub by Times Bks). News Bks Intl.

Allen, Margaret V. The Achievement of Margaret Fuller. LC 79-1732. 1979. 24.95x (ISBN 0-271-00215-8). Pa St U Pr.

Allen, Marjorie N. One, Two, Three---Ah-Choo! (Illus.). 64p. (gr. 3-5). 1980. PLB 6.99 (ISBN 0-698-30718-6, Coward). Putnam Pub Group.

Allen, Mark. Falconry in Arabia. LC 82-6163. 1982. 40.00 (ISBN 0-8289-0481-2). Greene.

--Seeds to the Wind: Poems, Songs, Meditations. LC 79-10662. (Illus.). 119p. 1979. 10.00 (ISBN 0-931432-05-7); pap. 5.95 (ISBN 0-931432-04-9). Whatever Pub.

Allen, Marshall B. Manual of Neurosurgery. LC 77-25278. (Illus.). 296p. 1977. pap. 27.00 (ISBN 0-8391-1174-6). Univ Park.

Allen, Marshall B., Jr., jt. auth. see El Gammal, Taher.

Allen, Marshall B., Jr., ed. see Symposium on the Pituitary, Medical College of Georgia, Augusta, Georgia, May 20-22, 1976.

Allen, Martha. Meet the Monkeys. LC 78-26211. (Illus.). 93p. (gr. 2-5). 1979. 6.95 (ISBN 0-13-574202-1). P-H.

Allen, Martha D. Real Live Monsters. (Illus.). 58p. 1978. 5.95 (ISBN 0-13-766568-7). P-H.

Allen, Martin. Red Saturday. LC 84-28747. 150p. (Orig.). 1985. pap. 8.95 (ISBN 0-571-13477-7). Faber & Faber.

Allen, Mary. Animals in American Literature. LC 82-17369. (Illus.). 224p. 1983. 14.95x (ISBN 0-252-00975-4). U of Ill Pr.

--The Necessary Blankness: Women in Major American Fiction of the Sixties. LC 75-38780. 250p. 1976. 15.95x (ISBN 0-252-00519-8). U of Ill Pr.

--Portrait Photography in Practice. (Photography in Practice Ser.). (Illus.). 144p. 1985. 22.50 (ISBN 0-7153-8410-4). David & Charles.

Allen, Mary, jt. ed. see Reiser, Virginia.

Allen, Mary B., ed. Comparative Biochemistry of Photoreactive Systems. 1960. 71.50 (ISBN 0-12-051750-7). Acad Pr.

Allen, Mary C; see Youtz, Phillip N.

Allen, Mary J. & Yen, Wendy M. Introduction to Measurement Theory. LC 78-25821. 1979. text ed. 22.00 pub net (ISBN 0-8185-0283-5). Brooks-Cole.

Allen, Mary M., ed. see International Science & Technology, Inc.

Allen, Mary S. Pioneer Policewomen. Heyneman, Julie H., ed. LC 71-156001. Repr. of 1925 ed. 23.50 (ISBN 0-404-09100-8). AMS Pr.

Allen, Mearle L. Welcome to the Stork Club. LC 79-5424. 300p. 1980. 14.95 (ISBN 0-498-02395-8). A S Barnes.

Allen, Melanie, jt. auth. see Fry, William, Jr.

Allen, Michael. Poe & the British Magazine Tradition. 1978. Repr. of 1969 ed. lib. bdg. 35.00 (ISBN 0-8495-0100-8). Arden Lib.

--Spence & the Holiday Murders. LC 78-51976. 1978. 7.95 (ISBN 0-8027-5390-6). Walker & Co.

--Spence at Marlby Manor. LC 81-71191. 192p. 1982. 11.95 (ISBN 0-8027-5469-4). Walker & Co.

--Spence at Marlby Manor. 1984. pap. 3.25 (ISBN 0-440-17821-5). Dell.

--Spence at the Blue Bazaar. 1981. pap. 2.25 (ISBN 0-440-18308-1). Dell.

--Spence at the Blue Bazaar. 1979. 7.95 (ISBN 0-8027-5408-2). Walker & Co.

Allen, Michael & Mokherjee, Sal. Women in India & Nepal. 1982. pap. 24.00 (ISBN 0-908070-07-1, Pub. by Australia Nat Univ). South Asia Bks.

Allen, Michael, ed. Vanuatu: Politics, Economics & Ritual in Island Melanesia. LC 81-65767. (Studies in Population). 425p. 1981. 47.50 (ISBN 0-12-051450-8). Acad Pr.

Allen, Michael G. British Family Cars of the Fifties. (Illus.). 200p. 1986. 20.95 (ISBN 0-85429-471-6, Pub. by G T Foulis Ltd). Interbook.

Allen, Michael G. & McEwin, Kenneth. Middle Level Social Studies: From Theory to Practice. 58p. 1983. 4.95 (ISBN 0-318-16920-7, NMSA 012). Natl Middle Schl.

Allen, Michael J. The Platonism of Marsilio Ficino: A Study of His Phaedrus Commentary, Its Sources & Genesis. LC 83-18187. (Center for Medieval & Renaissance Studies: No. 21). 290p. 1984. text ed. 30.00x (ISBN 0-520-05152-1). U of Cal Pr.

Allen, Michael J., ed. Marsilio Ficino & the Phaedran Charioteer. LC 80-20439. (Center for Medieval & Renaissance Studies, UCLA: No. 14). 1981. 33.50x (ISBN 0-520-04222-0). U of Cal Pr.

--Marsilio Ficino: The Philebus Commentary. LC 73-80826. (California Library Reprint Ser.: No. 101). 1975. 50.00x (ISBN 0-520-03977-7). U of Cal Pr.

Allen, Michael J., ed. see Shakespeare, William.

Allen, Michael S. We Are Called Human: The Poetry of Richard Hugo. LC 81-69840. 160p. 1982. text ed. 15.00x (ISBN 0-938626-07-8). U of Ark Pr.

Allen, Milton F. Acupinch Cramp Relief...in Seconds. (Illus.). 64p. 1981. pap. 1.95 (ISBN 0-9607456-0-2). Acupinch.

Allen, Milton H. Why Do Good People Suffer? LC 82-82949. 1983. pap. 4.95 (ISBN 0-8054-5208-7). Broadman.

Allen, Morse S. Satire of John Marston. LC 65-26460. (Studies in Drama, No. 39). 1969. Repr. of 1920 ed. lib. bdg. 45.95x (ISBN 0-8383-0500-8). Haskell.

Allen, Morse S., jt. auth. see Hughes, Arthur H.

Allen, Myron S. Psycho-Dynamic Synthesis. LC 66-17160. 248p. 1979. Repr. of 1966 ed. soft cover 11.95 (ISBN 0-918936-07-1). Astara.

Allen, Myrtle. The Ballymaloe Cookbook. (Illus.). 203p. (Orig.). 1984. pap. 9.95 (ISBN 0-7171-1339-6, Pub. by Gill & Macmillan Ireland). Irish Bks Media.

Allen, N. S., jt. auth. see Bark, L. S.

Allen, N. S., jt. auth. see McKellar, J. F.

Allen, N. S., ed. Degradation & Stablisation of Polymers. (Illus.). 384p. 1983. 70.50 (ISBN 0-85334-194-X, Pub. by Elsevier Applied Sci England). Elsevier.

--Developments in Polymer Photochemistry, Vols. 1-3. Vol. 1, 1980. 42.75 (ISBN 0-85334-911-8, Pub. by Elsevier Applied Sci England); Vol. 2, 1981. 68.50 (ISBN 0-85334-936-3); Vol. 3, 1982. 81.50 (ISBN 0-85334-978-9). Elsevier.

Allen, N. S. & McKellar, J. F., eds. Photochemistry of Dyed & Pigmented Polymers. 296p. 1980. 52.00 (ISBN 0-85334-898-7, Pub. by Elsevier Applied Sci England). Elsevier.

Allen, N. S. & Schnabel, W., eds. Photochemistry & Photophysics of Polymers. 440p. 1984. 126.00 (ISBN 0-85334-269-5, I-256-84, Pub. by Elsevier Applied Sci England). Elsevier.

Allen, Nancy. Film Study Collections: A Guide to Their Development & Use. LC 78-20935. 1979. 18.50 (ISBN 0-8044-2001-7). Ungar.

--Homicide: Perspectives on Prevention. LC 79-11841. 192p. 1980. text ed. 24.95 (ISBN 0-87705-382-0); pap. text ed. 12.95 (ISBN 0-87705-412-6). Human Sci Pr.

Allen, Nancy & Carringer, Robert. An Annotated Catalog of Unpublished Film & Television Scripts in the University of Illinois Library at Urban-Champaign, No. 7. LC 83-5110. (Robert B. Downs Publication Fund Ser.: No. V). 125p. 1983. pap. 15.00 for info. (ISBN 0-87845-069-6). U of Ill Lib Info Sci.

Allen, Nancy, et al. Cuckoo Two. 348p. 1982. pap. 9.95 (ISBN 0-89716-110-6). Peanut Butter.

Allen, Nancy M. When Your Mind Goes Blank: A Resource Book of Word Lists & Activities. (Orig.). 1984. pap. text ed. 15.95 (ISBN 0-913956-15-5). EBSCO Ind.

Allen, Naomi, intro. by see Trotsky, Leon.

Allen, Naomi, ed. see Trotsky, Leon.

Allen, Nathan. The Opium Trade as Carried on in India & China. LC 77-91524. 1977. Repr. of 1853 ed. lib. bdg. 12.50 (ISBN 0-89341-504-9). Longwood Pub Group.

Allen, Ned B. Sources of John Dryden's Comedies. LC 67-21718. 1967. Repr. of 1935 ed. 12.50x (ISBN 0-87752-002-X). Gordian.

--The Sources of John Dryden's Comedies. LC 77-9975. 1978. Repr. of 1935 ed. lib. bdg. 25.00 (ISBN 0-8492-0016-4). R West.

Allen, Norma C. & Gulczynski, Diane. Operating Room Technician Examination Review. 3rd ed. 1984. pap. text ed. write for info. (ISBN 0-87488-651-1). Med Exam.

Allen, Norman. New Century Vest-Pocket: Webster Dictionary. rev. ed. LC 81-84631. 304p. 1975. pap. 2.95 (ISBN 0-8329-1536-X). New Century.

Allen, O. N. & Allen, Ethel K. The Leguminosae: A Source Book of Characteristics, Uses & Nodulation. LC 80-5104. (Illus.). 878p. 1981. 65.00x (ISBN 0-299-08400-0). U of Wis Pr.

Allen, Oliver. Atmosphere. LC 82-16768. (Planet Earth Ser.). 1983. lib. bdg. 19.94 (ISBN 0-8094-4337-6, Pub. by Time-Life). Silver.

--The Pacific Navigators. Time-Life Books Editors, ed. (The Seafarers Ser.). (Illus.). 176p. 1980. 13.95 (ISBN 0-8094-2685-4). Time-Life.

--The Windjammers. Time-Life Books, ed. (The Seafarers Ser.). 1979. 13.95 (ISBN 0-8094-2703-6). Time-Life.

Allen, Oliver E. The Airline Builders. LC 80-15249. (Epic of Flight Ser.). lib. bdg. 21.27 (ISBN 0-8094-3284-6, Pub. by Time-Life). Silver.

--The Airline Builders. Time-Life Books, ed. (The Epic of Flight Ser.). (Illus.). 175p. 1981. 14.95 (ISBN 0-8094-3283-8). Time Life.

--The Pacific Navigators. LC 80-13963. (Seafarers Ser.). lib. bdg. 21.27 (ISBN 0-8094-2686-2). Silver.

--The Vegetable Gardener's Journal. (Illus.). 120p. 1985. 14.95 (ISBN 0-941434-63-X). Stewart Tabori & Chang.

--The Windjammers. LC 78-10819. (The Seafarers Ser.). (Illus.). (gr. 7 up). 1979. lib. bdg. 21.27 (ISBN 0-8094-2704-4, Pub. by Time-Life). Silver.

Allen, Opal S. Narcissa Whitman. (Illus.). 1959. 9.95 (ISBN 0-8323-0049-7). Binford.

Allen, P. The Cambridge Apostles. LC 77-82482. (Illus.). 1979. 44.50 (ISBN 0-521-21803-9). Cambridge U Pr.

--Sales & Sales Management. 2nd ed. (Illus.). 288p. 1979. pap. 11.95x (ISBN 0-7121-1962-0, Pub. by Macdonald & Evans England). Trans-Atlantic.

Allen, P. David & Watson, Dorothy J., eds. Findings of Research in Miscue Analysis: Classroom Implications. LC 76-45092. 1976. 11.00 (ISBN 0-8141-1733-3). NCTE.

Allen, P. E., ed. Catalogue of the Newspaper Library, Colindale, 8 vols. Incl. Vol. 1. London. 564p; Vol. 2. England & Wales, Scotland, Ireland. 672p; Vol. 3. Aden-New Guinea. 496p; Vol. 4. New Zealand-Zanzibar. 320p; Vol. 5. Titles A-E. 600p; Vol. 6. Titles F-L. 480p; Vol. 7. Titles M-R. 496p; Vol. 8. Titles S-Z. 512p. 1975. 300.00 (ISBN 0-7141-0352-7, Pub. by British Lib). Longwood Pub Group.

Allen, P. G., et al. Bioeconomics of Aquaculture. (Developments in Aquaculture & Fisheries Science Ser.: Vol. 13). 1984. 75.00 (ISBN 0-444-42301-X, I-102-84). Elsevier.

Allen, P. S. Erasmus' Services to Learning. 1974. lib. bdg. 59.95 (ISBN 0-8490-0123-4). Gordon Pr.

Allen, P. S., ed. see Erasmus.

Allen, Pamela. Bertie & the Bear. (Illus.). 32p. (gr. k-3). 1984. 10.95 (ISBN 0-698-20600-2, Coward); pap. 4.95 (ISBN 0-698-20607-X, Coward). Putnam Pub Group.

--Free Space: A Perspective on the Small Group in Women's Liberation. (Illus., Orig.). 1971. pap. 2.00 (ISBN 0-87810-006-7). Times Change.

--Who Sank the Boat? (Illus.). 32p. (ps-3). 1983. 10.95 (ISBN 0-698-20576-6, Coward). Putnam Pub Group.

--Who Sank the Boat? (Illus.). 32p. (ps-k). 1985. pap. 4.95 (ISBN 0-698-20622-3, Coward). Putnam Pub Group.

Allen, Pat & DeRuiter, Gerald L. Backpacking in Michigan. LC 81-11598. (Illus.). 1982. pap. 8.95 (ISBN 0-472-06331-6). U of Mich Pr.

Allen, Pat, ed. see Gale, Jack L.

Allen, Pat, ed. see Levine, Mark L.

Allen, Patricia. Barriers & Bridges. 1984. 5.95 (ISBN 0-533-06160-1). Vantage.

--Cycles: Every Woman's Guide to Menstruation. 192p. (Orig.). 1983. pap. 3.50 (ISBN 0-523-42145-1). Pinnacle Bks.

Allen, Patricia, ed. see Scavo, Janet.

Allen, Patricia S., jt. auth. see Klausmeier, Herbert J.

Allen, Paul. A History of the American Revolution, 2 vols. LC 72-10761. (American Revolutionary Ser.). Repr. of 1822 ed. Vol. 1. lib. bdg. 46.00x (ISBN 0-8290-0369-X); Vol. 2. lib. bdg. 44.00x (ISBN 0-686-96756-9). Irvington.

--The Life of Charles Brockden Brown. LC 75-25800. 424p. 1975. lib. bdg. 60.00x (ISBN 0-8201-1160-0). Schol Facsimiles.

Allen, Paul A. How to Keep Your Company Out of Court: The Practical Legal Guide for Growing Businesses. LC 83-11176. 1983. 22.50 (ISBN 0-13-411132-X, Busn); pap. 9.95 (ISBN 0-13-411140-0). P-H.

Allen, Paul H. The Rain Forests of Golfo Dulce. LC 77-76150. (Illus.). 1956. 30.00x (ISBN 0-8047-0955-6). Stanford U Pr.

Allen, Paul M. Rudolf Steiner: The Man & His Work. 1976. pap. 1.00 (ISBN 0-916786-01-3). St George Bk Serv.

--Vladimir Soloviev: Russian Mystic, Vol. 9. LC 72-81592. (Spiritual Science Library). (Illus.). 544p. 1978. lib. bdg. 20.00 (ISBN 0-89345-032-4, Spiritual Sci Lib); pap. 10.00 (ISBN 0-89345-213-0, Steinerbks). Garber Comm.

Allen, Paul M., ed. A Christian Rosenkreutz Anthology, Vol. 10. 2nd, rev. ed. LC 68-13130. (Illus.). 640p. 1981. Repr. of 1968 ed. lib. bdg. 65.00 (ISBN 0-89345-009-X, Steinbooks Spiritual Sci Lib). Garber Comm.

Allen, Paul M., ed. see Steiner, Rudolf, et al.

Allen, Paul M., ed. see Steiner, Rudolf.

Allen, Paula G. The Blind Lion. LC 74-10806. (Orig.). 1974. pap. 2.00x (ISBN 0-914476-31-9). Thorp Springs.

--Shadow Country. 149p. 1982. pap. 7.50 (ISBN 0-935626-26-3). U Cal AISC.

--The Woman Who Owned the Shadows. LC 83-50233. 217p. (Orig.). 1983. pap. 8.95 (ISBN 0-933216-07-6). Spinsters Ink.

Allen, Paula G., ed. Studies in American Indian Literature: Critical Essays & Course Designs. LC 82-12516. (MLA Commission on the Literatures & Languages of America Ser.). 384p. 1983. 30.00x (ISBN 0-87352-354-7); pap. 14.50x (ISBN 0-87352-355-5). Modern Lang.

Allen, Penelope J. Leaves from the Family Tree. 372p. 1982. 40.00 (ISBN 0-89308-227-9). Southern Hist Pr.

--Tennessee Soldiers in the Revolution: A Roster of Soldiers Living During the Revolutionary War in the Counties of Washington & Sullivan. LC 75-970. 71p. 1982. pap. 5.00 (ISBN 0-8063-0666-1). Genealog Pub.

Allen, Peter. The Ninety-One Before Linbergh. (Illus.). 19.95 (ISBN 0-911139-03-6). Flying Bks.

--Skyblazer. 1985. pap. 2.95 (ISBN 0-931773-20-2). Critics Choice Paper.

--The Windsor Secret: New Revelations of the Nazi Connection. LC 84-4246. (Illus.). 272p. 1984. 17.95 (ISBN 0-8128-2975-1). Stein & Day.

Allen, Peter, ed. The Affluent Market. 227p. 1984. pap. 985.00 (ISBN 0-931634-36-9). FIND-SVP.

--Artificial Intelligence: A Market Assessment. 200p. 1984. pap. 1250.00 (ISBN 0-931634-44-X). FIND-SVP.

--Conductive Plastics. 240p. 1984. pap. 1250.00 (ISBN 0-931634-43-1). FIND-SVP.

--Diagnosis Related Groups. 200p. 1984. pap. 995.00 (ISBN 0-931634-38-5). FIND-SVP.

--Free-Standing & Office-Based Ambulatory Care: Surgicenters, Emergency Clinics, Occupational Clinics, & Office-Based Surgery. 2nd ed. 208p. 1984. pap. 985.00 (ISBN 0-931634-33-4). FIND-SVP.

--Hazardous Waste Management. 300p. 1984. pap. 985.00 (ISBN 0-931634-41-5). FIND-SVP.

--Home-Care Products & Services. 295p. 1985. pap. 1475.00 (ISBN 0-931634-27-X). FIND-SVP.

--The Ice Cream Market. 222p. 1984. pap. 985.00 (ISBN 0-931634-42-3). FIND-SVP.

--The Market for Children's Toys & Games. 200p. 1985. pap. 1250.00 (ISBN 0-931634-49-0). FIND-SVP.

--The Market for Physical Fitness & Exercise Equipment. 336p. 1984. pap. 995.00 (ISBN 0-931634-45-8). FIND-SVP.

--The Maturity Market: Americans 55 & Over. 200p. 1985. pap. 995.00 (ISBN 0-931634-47-4). FIND-SVP.

--Medical Prosthetic Devices & Artificial Organs. 279p. 1983. pap. 1250.00 (ISBN 0-931634-35-0). FIND-SVP.

--Microcomputer Software Distribution. 180p. 1984. pap. 985.00 (ISBN 0-931634-34-2). FIND-SVP.

--Microwave Cooking: Ovens, Ovenwares, Food & Packaging. 300p. 1983. pap. 985.00 (ISBN 0-931634-28-8). FIND-SVP.

--The Noninstitutional Senior Market for Healthcare Products & Services. 2nd ed. 250p. 1984. pap. 1250.00 (ISBN 0-931634-46-6). FIND-SVP.

--The Pasta Market. 2nd ed. 218p. 1983. pap. 985.00 (ISBN 0-931634-32-6). FIND-SVP.

--Processed Foods Packaging. 250p. 1982. pap. 985.00 (ISBN 0-931634-25-3). FIND-SVP.

--The Self-Care Market: The Market for Do-It-Yourself Diagnostic Devices. 200p. 1985. pap. 1475.00 (ISBN 0-931634-26-1). FIND-SVP.

--The Semiconductor Industry. 310p. 1984. pap. 985.00 (ISBN 0-931634-40-7). FIND-SVP.

--The Small Appliance Industry. 400p. (Orig.). 1983. pap. 985.00 (ISBN 0-931634-30-X). FIND-SVP.

--Superalloys. 295p. 1984. pap. 985.00 (ISBN 0-931634-37-7). FIND-SVP.

--The U. S. Bottled Water Market. 3rd ed. 200p. 1985. pap. 1475.00 (ISBN 0-931634-31-8). FIND-SVP.

--The U. S. Hispanic Market. 260p. 1984. pap. 995.00 (ISBN 0-931634-48-2). FIND-SVP.

--The World Market for High Technology Industrial Ceramics. 200p. 1985. pap. 1475.00 (ISBN 0-931634-29-6). FIND-SVP.

Allen, Peter M. Plays for Assembly. (Illus.). 143p. 1978. 22.00x (ISBN 0-7217-3019-1, Pub. by Schofield & Sims UK). State Mutual Bk.

--Vladimir Soloviev: Russian Mystic. (Illus.). 448p. (Orig.). 1978. pap. 10.95 (ISBN 0-8334-1750-9, Pub. by Garber Communications). Anthroposophic.

Allen, Peter M., jt. ed. see Schieve, William C.

Allen, Peter S. & Lazio, Carlos, eds. Archaeology on Film. 240p. 1983. 10.00 (ISBN 0-318-17843-5); members 7.50 (ISBN 0-318-17844-3). Archaeological Inst.

Allen, Phil, et al. Energy, Matter, & Form. 2nd ed. Hills, Christopher, ed. LC 77-84873. (Illus.). 311p. 1977. pap. 11.95 (ISBN 0-916438-07-4). Univ of Trees.

Allen, Philip. North Atlantic Pilot. Date not set. pns (ISBN 0-393-03244-2). Norton.

Allen, Philip, jt. auth. see Huelsman, Lawrence P.

Allen, Philip W. Tumors & Proliferations of Adipose Tissue: A Clinicopathologic Approach. LC 80-28916. (Masson Monographs in Diagnostic Pathology: Vol. 1). 200p. 1981. text ed. 45.50x (ISBN 0-89352-057-8). Masson Pub.

Allen, Phillip E. & Sinencio, Edgar S. Switched Capacitor Circuits. 608p. 1984. 56.50 (ISBN 0-442-20873-1). Van Nos Reinhold.

Allen, Phyllis, jt. auth. see Mullins, William.

Allen, Phyllis A. Mammalian Physiology Level II. (Illus.). 144p. 1981. pap. text ed. 17.95x (ISBN 0-7121-1283-9). Trans-Atlantic.

Allen, Phyllis S. Beginning of Interior Environment. 5th rev. ed. (Illus.). 384p. 1985. text ed. write for info. (ISBN 0-8087-0098-7); write for info. (ISBN 0-8087-0001-4). Burgess.

Allen, Polly R. & Kenen, Peter B. Asset Markets & Exchange Rates: Modeling an Open Economy. Abridged ed. LC 79-16874. 352p. 1983. pap. 18.95 (ISBN 0-521-27406-0). Cambridge U Pr.

--Asset Markets, Exchange Rates, & Economic Integration. LC 79-16874. (Illus.). 1980. 69.50 (ISBN 0-521-22982-0). Cambridge U Pr.

Allen, Prudence. The Concept of Women: The Aristotelian Revolution 750 B. C. to 1250 A. D. 512p. 1985. text ed. 42.00 (ISBN 0-920792-43-X). Eden Pr.

Allen, R. Colour Chemistry. 1982. 29.95 (ISBN 0-442-30669-5). Van Nos Reinhold.

Allen, R. C. How to Build a Fortune in Commodities. 1972. 25.00 (ISBN 0-910228-03-5). Best Bks.

--How to Build a Fortune in Commodities. 1983. 25.00 (ISBN 0-686-40440-8). Windsor.

--Immortal Words of Jesus Christ. 1981. pap. 4.95 (ISBN 0-910228-11-6). Best Bks.

--Professional Trading System. 1983. 45.00 (ISBN 0-910228-10-8). Best Bks.

--The Professional Trading System. 1983. 45.00 (ISBN 0-686-40439-4). Windsor.

--The Secret of Success. 192p. 1965. 8.95 (ISBN 0-910228-01-9); pap. 4.95 (ISBN 0-910228-02-7). Best Bks.

Allen, R. D. Optical Microscopy. 320p. 1985. write for info. (ISBN 0-444-00848-9, Biomedical Pr). Elsevier.

Allen, R. E. The Attalid Kingdom: A Constitutional Kingdom. (Illus.). 1983. text ed. 42.00x (ISBN 0-19-814845-3). Oxford U Pr.
--Plato's Parmenides: Translation & Analysis. LC 82-7051. xv, 331p. 1983. 25.00x (ISBN 0-8166-1070-3). U of Minn Pr.
--The Pocket Oxford Dictionary of Current English. 7th ed. 900p. 1984. 11.95 (ISBN 0-19-861133-1). Oxford U Pr.
--Socrates & Legal Obligation. 176p. 1981. 17.50x (ISBN 0-8166-0962-4); pap. 8.95x (ISBN 0-8166-0965-9). U of Minn Pr.
Allen, R. E., jt. ed. see Furley, David J.
Allen, R. E., tr. The Dialogues of Plato: Euthyphro; Apology; Crito; Meno; Gorgias; Menexenus, Vol. I. LC 84-17349. 384p. 1985. text ed. 30.00 (ISBN 0-300-03226-9). Yale U Pr.
Allen, R. Earl. Funeral Source Book. (Preaching Helps Ser.). (Orig.). 1984. pap. 3.50 (ISBN 0-8010-0076-9). Baker Bk.
--Good Morning, Lord: Devotionals for Times of Sorrow. (Good Morning, Lord Ser.). 96p. 1983. 4.95 (ISBN 0-8010-0191-9). Baker Bk.
--Good Morning, Lord: Devotions for Hospital Patients. 96p. 1975. 4.95 (ISBN 0-8010-0079-3). Baker Bk.
--Just When You Need Him. (Contempo Ser). pap. 0.95 (ISBN 0-8010-0074-2). Baker Bk.
--Let It Begin in Me. LC 84-19934. 1985. pap. 3.25 (ISBN 0-8054-5005-X). Broadman.
--A Man Like No Other. 132p. 1984. pap. 2.95 (ISBN 0-89693-374-1). Victor Bks.
Allen, R. F., ed. Computers & the Humanities: Proceedings of the Symposium, Raleigh, NC. June 6-8, 1983. 300p. 1984. write for info. (North-Holland). Elsevier.
Allen, R. F., jt. ed. see Burnham, P. C.
Allen, R H., jt. ed. see Webb, L R.
Allen, R. H., et al. Part-Time Farming in the Southeast. LC 74-165677. (Research Monograph: Vol. 9). 1971. Repr. of 1937 ed. lib. bdg. 39.50 (ISBN 0-306-70341-6). Da Capo.
Allen, R. I. & Stewart, Ian, eds. Estimating & Projecting Input-Output Coefficients. 1975p. 1975. PLB 27.50x (ISBN 0-678-08071-2). Kelley.
Allen, R. J. & Lientz, Bennett P. Systems in Action. LC 77-16546. 1978. text ed. 20.60 (ISBN 0-673-16149-8); pap. text ed. 16.85 (ISBN 0-673-16150-1). Scott F.
Allen, R. L. Colour Chemistry. (Studies in Modern Chemistry Ser.). 336p. 1971. 34.50x (ISBN 0-306-50002-7, Plenum Pr). Plenum Pub.
Allen, R. L., jt. auth. see Saunders, K. H.
Allen, R. R., et al. Learning Language Through Communication: A Functional Perspective. 384p. 1985. text ed. write for info. (ISBN 0-534-05316-5). Wadsworth Pub.
Allen, Rae, ed. see Sulkin, S. E.
Allen, Randy L. Bottom Line Issues in Retailing. 310p. 1984. 16.95 (ISBN 0-8019-7409-7); pap. 10.95 (ISBN 0-8019-7410-0). Chilton.
Allen, Reginald E. Greek Philosophy: Thales to Aristotle. LC 66-10363. (Orig.). 1966. pap. text ed. 11.95 (ISBN 0-02-900500-0). Free Pr.
--Greek Philosophy: Thales to Aristotle. 2nd ed. LC 84-26067. 432p. 1985. pap. 9.95x (ISBN 0-02-900660-0). Free Pr.
Allen, Rex W. & Von Karolyi, Ilona. Hospital Planning Handbook. LC 75-30599. 242p. 1976. text ed. 34.95x (ISBN 0-471-02319-1, Pub. by Wiley-Interscience). Wiley.
Allen, Richard. Imperialism & Nationalism in the Fertile Crescent: Sources & Prospects of the Arab-Israeli Conflict. (Illus.). 1974. 29.95x (ISBN 0-19-501782-X). Oxford U Pr.
--Imperialism & Nationalism in the Fertile Crescent: Sources & Prospects of the Arab-Israeli Conflict. (An Encore Reprint Ser.). 700p. 1985. Repr. softcover 40.00x (ISBN 0-8133-0134-3). Westview.
--The Life Experience & Gospel Labors of the Rt. Rev. Richard Allen. 96p. (Orig.). 1983. pap. 3.95 (ISBN 0-687-21844-6). Abingdon.
Allen, Richard B., jt. auth. see Schafer, William J.
Allen, Richard B., ed. Atlantic Fishermans Handbook. (Illus.). 482p. (Orig.). 1982. pap. 9.00 (ISBN 0-9608932-0-2). Fisheries Comm.
Allen, Richard C., jt. auth. see Shampine, Lawrence F.
Allen, Richard C., ed. Mental Health in America: The Years of Crisis. LC 78-71070. (Illus.). 1979. 29.50 (ISBN 0-8379-4901-7, 031084). Marquis.
Allen, Richard C., et al, eds. Readings in Law & Psychiatry. LC 74-24384. pap. 160.00 (ISBN 0-317-09569-2, 2004407). Bks Demand UMI.
Allen, Richard C., Jr., jt. auth. see Sanchez, David A.
Allen, Richard E., tr. see Konrad, George
Allen, Richard E., tr. see Konrad, George & Szelenyi, Ivan.
Allen, Richard F., jt. auth. see Menon, Y. Keshava.
Allen, Richard G., et al. American Government, 3 vols. Incl. Vol. 1. Origins of American Government & Citizenship: Political Parties & Elections. 156p (ISBN 0-86624-035-7, US0); Vol. 2. The Birth of Our Nation-Congress & the Laws-The President & His Cabinet. 256p (ISBN 0-86624-036-5, US1); Vol. 3. The Courts & Liberty: The World at Our Doorstep. 174p (ISBN 0-86624-037-3, US2). (Illus.). 1981. pap. text ed. write for info.; write for info. tchr's guide (US3); write for info. end-of-unit test (US4). Bilingual Ed Serv.
--U. S. History - One, 4 vols. Incl. Vol. 1: America - Its Discovery, Independence & Early Problems. 290p (ISBN 0-86624-001-2, UT1); Vol. 2: Strengthening the New Nation. 270p (ISBN 0-86624-002-0, UT2); Vol. 3: The Republic Expands. 192p (ISBN 0-86624-003-9, UT3); Vol. 4: Expansion, Destruction & Reconstruction. 156p (ISBN 0-86624-004-7, UT4); Teacher's Guide. avail. (UT5); End of Unit Test. avail. (UT6). (Illus.). 1981. pap. text ed. 5.95 ea. Bilingual Ed Serv.
Allen, Richard H. An Annotated Arthur Schnitzler Bibliography. (Studies in the Germanic Languages & Literatures Ser.: No.56). xiii, 151p. 1966. 12.50x (ISBN 0-8078-8056-6). U of NC Pr.
--Star Names: Their Lore & Meaning. rev. ed. 1963. pap. 7.95 (ISBN 0-486-21079-0). Dover.
--Star Names: Their Lore & Meaning. Orig. Title: Star-Names & Their Meanings. 16.00 (ISBN 0-8446-1527-7). Peter Smith.
Allen, Richard J. How to Write A Nothing Down Offer So That Everyone Wins: A Casebook of Alternate Real Estate Investing. 315p. 1982. 49.95 (ISBN 0-943402-00-X). Allen Group.
Allen, Richard J., jt. ed. see Jacobs, Frederic.
Allen, Richard K. Common Intertidal Invertebrates of Southern California. 1976. 11.95 (ISBN 0-917962-10-9). Peek Pubns.
Allen, Richard P., jt. auth. see Joseph, William J.
Allen, Richard P., jt. auth. see Safer, Daniel J.
Allen, Richard S. Old North Country Bridges: Upstate New York. (Illus.). 112p. 1983. 16.95 (ISBN 0-932052-28-2). North Country.
Allen, Richard V., jt. auth. see Lee, Dorris M.
Allen, Richard V., ed. Yearbook on International Communist Affairs, 1969. LC 67-31024. (Publications Ser.: No. 92). 1970. 25.00 (ISBN 0-8179-1921-X). Hoover Inst Pr.
Allen, Richard V., jt. ed. see Abshire, David M.
Allen, Roach V. Language Experiences in Communication. LC 75-31011. (Illus.). 512p. 1976. text ed. 26.95 (ISBN 0-395-18624-2); instr's. manual 1.50 (ISBN 0-395-18798-2). HM.
Allen, Roach V. & Allen, Clarence. Language Experience Activities. 2nd ed. (Illus.). 384p. 1982. pap. 15.95 (ISBN 0-395-31802-5). HM.
Allen, Robert. Blues & Ballads. LC 75-302484. 103p. 1974. 3.95 (ISBN 0-87886-047-9). Ithaca Hse.
--A Child's Book of Animals. (Illus.). 64p. (ps-1). 1981. 3.95 (ISBN 0-448-41056-7, G&D). Putnam Pub Group.
--Easy Money in Hard Times. 15.95 (ISBN 0-911505-12-1). Lifecraft.
--Hot & Cold & in Between. 1985. 3.50 (ISBN 0-89536-717-3, 5801). CSS of Ohio.
--How to Save the World. (Illus.). 150p. 1980. cloth 14.95 (ISBN 0-389-20011-5, IUCN79, IUCN); 7.50 (IUCN120). Unipub.
--How to Save the World: Strategy for World Conservation. (Illus.). 150p. 1980. 18.95x (ISBN 0-389-20011-5, 06786). B&N Imports.
--How to Save the World: Strategy for World Conservation. (Illus.). 144p. 1981. pap. 1.95 (ISBN 0-8226-0366-7). Littlefield.
--The Loyal Americans. (Illus.). 208p. 1983. pap. 14.95 (ISBN 0-660-10753-8, 56420-7, Pub. by Natl Mus Canada). U of Chicago Pr.
--No Risk Real Estate. 1985. 15.95 (ISBN 0-911505-19-9). Lifecraft.
--No Risk Real Estate: Property Analysis Guide. 9.95 (ISBN 0-911505-25-3). Lifecraft.
--No Risk Real Estate: Property Buyer's Guide. 9.95 (ISBN 0-911505-26-1). Lifecraft.
--No Risk Real Estate: Property Manager's Guide. 9.95 (ISBN 0-911505-28-8). Lifecraft.
--No Risk Real Estate: Property Rental Guide. 9.95 (ISBN 0-911505-27-X). Lifecraft.
--No Risk Real Estate: Property Seller's Guide. 9.95 (ISBN 0-911505-29-6). Lifecraft.
--One-Two-Three: First Counting Book. (Illus.). 72p. (ps-1). 1981. 3.95 (ISBN 0-448-41055-9, G&D). Putnam Pub Group.
--Reluctant Reformers: The Impact of Racism on American Social Reform Movements. LC 73-85495. 1974. 10.95 (ISBN 0-88258-002-7); pap. 6.95 (ISBN 0-88258-026-4). Howard U Pr.
Allen, Robert, jt. auth. see Greene, Lorne.
Allen, Robert & Maurer, H. Rainer, eds. Electrophoresis & Isoelectric Focusing in Polyacrylamide Gel: Advances of Methods & Theories, Biochemical & Clinical Applications. LC 73-94225. (Illus.). 1974. 44.00x (ISBN 3-11-004344-0). De Gruyter.
Allen, Robert, ed. see Martin, James & Keavent, Timothy.
Allen, Robert A. Billy Sunday: Homerun to Heaven. Rock, Louise, ed. (The Sowers Ser.). (gr. 3-7). 1985. 8.95 (ISBN 0-88062-124-9); pap. 4.95 (ISBN 0-88062-125-7). Mott Media.
Allen, Robert C. Speaking of Soap Operas. LC 84-21894. x, 246p. 1985. 27.50x (ISBN 0-8078-1643-4); pap. 9.95x (ISBN 0-8078-4129-3). U of NC Pr.
--Vaudeville & Film. Jowett, Garth S., ed. LC 79-6667. (Dissertations on Film, 1980 Ser.). 1980. lib. bdg. 35.50x (ISBN 0-405-12901-7). Ayer Co Pubs.
Allen, Robert C. & Gomery, Douglas. Film History: Theory & Practice. 248p. 1985. text ed. 14.95 (ISBN 0-394-35040-5, RanC). Random.
Allen, Robert C., et al. Gel Electrophoresis & Isoelectric Focusing of Proteins: Selected Techniques. LC 84-12694. (Illus.). xiii, 255p. 1984. 39.95 (ISBN 3-11-007853-8). De Gruyter.
Allen, Robert C., et al, eds. Marker Proteins in Inflammation: Proceedings of the Symposium; Lyon, France, April 22-25, 1981. Suskind, Robert M. (Illus.). 608p. 1982. 74.00 (ISBN 3-11-008625-5). De Gruyter.
Allen, Robert D. & Wolfe, Thomas E. The Allen & Wolfe Illustrated Dictionary of Real Estate. LC 82-13445. (Real Estate for Professional Practitioners Ser.). 266p. 1983. 28.95 (ISBN 0-471-09415-3, Pub. by Wiley-Interscience). Wiley.
Allen, Robert D. & Kamiya, Noburo, eds. Primitive Motile Systems in Cell Biology. 1964. 83.00 (ISBN 0-12-052950-5). Acad Pr.
Allen, Robert D. & Wolfe, Thomas E., eds. The Real Estate Almanac. LC 80-12417. (Real Estate for Professional Practitioners Ser.). pap. 117.00 (ISBN 0-317-10964-2, 2055413). Bks Demand UMI.
Allen, Robert E. & Keaveny, Timothy J. Contemporary Labor Relations. 672p. 1983. text ed. 34.95 (ISBN 0-201-00047-4); instr's manual 20.00 (ISBN 0-201-00048-2). Addison-Wesley.
Allen, Robert F. Nutrition. (Lifegain Program for Changing Our Health Cultures Ser.). 45p. 1981. pap. 5.95 (ISBN 0-318-03839-0). Human Res Inst.
--Physical Fitness. (Lifegain Program for Changing Our Health Cultures Ser.). 41p. pap. 5.95 (ISBN 0-318-03840-4). Human Res Inst.
--Smoking. (Lifegain Program for Changing Our Health Cultures Ser.). 35p. 1981. pap. 5.95 (ISBN 0-318-03838-2). Human Res Inst.
--Stress Reduction. (Lifegain Program for Changing Our Health Cultures Ser.). 37p. (Orig.). 1981. pap. 5.95 (ISBN 0-318-03841-2). Human Res Inst.
--Weight Control. (Lifegain Program for Changing Our Health Cultures Ser.). 31p. 1981. pap. 5.95 (ISBN 0-318-03837-4). Human Res Inst.
Allen, Robert F. & Kraft, Charlotte. Beat the System: A Way to Create More Human Environments. Nealton, William R., ed. 294p. 1980. Repr. 15.95 (ISBN 0-07-001080-3). Human Res Inst.
--The Organizational Unconscious: How to Create the Organizational Environment. (Illus.). 229p. 1982. 14.95 (ISBN 0-13-641381-1); pap. 6.95 (ISBN 0-13-641373-0). P-H.
Allen, Robert F. & Linde, Shirley. Lifegain: The Exciting New Program That Will Change Your Health & Your Life. 248p. 1981. 12.95 (ISBN 0-318-03729-7). Human Res Inst.
Allen, Robert G. Creating Wealth. 1983. 17.95 (ISBN 0-671-44281-3). S&S.
--Nothing Down. 1980. 16.95 (ISBN 0-671-24748-4). S&S.
--Nothing Down: How to Buy Real Estate with Little or No Money Down. rev. ed. 320p. 1984. 16.95 (ISBN 0-671-50469-X). S&S.
Allen, Robert L. Black Awakening in Capitalist America: An Analytic History. LC 69-20059. pap. 5.50 (ISBN 0-385-07718-1, Anch). Doubleday.
--Soviet Economic Warfare. 1960. 12.00 (ISBN 0-8183-0209-7). Pub Aff Pr.
--Verb System of Present-Day American English. 2nd ed. (Janua Linguarum, Ser. Practica: No. 24). (Orig.). 1983. pap. text ed. 18.00x (ISBN 90-2790-643-2). Mouton.
Allen, Robert L., et al. Working Sentences. 1975. pap. text ed. 12.00 scp (ISBN 0-690-00770-1, HarpC); instr's manual avail. (ISBN 0-06-360210-5). Harper Row.
Allen, Robert M. Elements of Rorschach Interpretation, with an Extended Bibliography. LC 54-6098. (Illus.). pap. 60.50 (ISBN 0-317-10583-3, 2010424). Bks Demand UMI.
--Student's Rorschach Manual: An Introduction to Administering, Scoring & Interpreting Researcher's Psychodiagnostic Inkblot Test. rev. ed. LC 77-14710. 361p. 1978. text ed. 30.00 (ISBN 0-8236-6201-2). Intl Univs Pr.
--Variables in Personality Theory & Personality Testing: An Interpretation. 108p. 1965. 9.75x (ISBN 0-398-00030-1). C C Thomas.
Allen, Robert M. & Cortazzo, Arnold D. Psychosocial & Educational Aspects & Problems of Mental Retardation. 136p. 1970. 14.75x (ISBN 0-398-00031-X). C C Thomas.
Allen, Robert M. & Jefferson, Thomas W. Psychological Evaluation of the Cerebral Palsied Person: Intellectual, Personality, & Vocational Applications. (Illus.). 100p. 1962. 10.50x (ISBN 0-398-04188-1). C C Thomas.
Allen, Robert M. & Cortazzo, Arnold D., eds. Psycholinguistic Development in Children: Implications for Children with Developmental Disabilities. LC 72-92899. (Illus.). 93p. 1974. 6.95x (ISBN 0-87024-260-1). U of Miami Pr.
Allen, Robert M., et al. Theories of Cognitive Development: Implications for the Mentally Retarded. LC 72-92899. (Illus.). 1973. 9.95x (ISBN 0-87024-249-0). U of Miami Pr.
Allen, Robert M., et al, eds. The Role of Genetics in Mental Retardation. LC 73-143453. (Illus.). 1971. 7.95x (ISBN 0-87024-197-4). U of Miami Pr.
Allen, Robert P. Roseate Spoonbill. (Illus.). 7.00 (ISBN 0-8446-1528-5). Peter Smith.
Allen, Robert R., ed. The Dialogue Called Funus, Trans. of Erasmus' Colloquy, 1534: A Very Pleasant Dialogue Called the Epicure. Gerrand, tr. (Renaissance English Text Society Ser.: Vol. 3). 10.00 (ISBN 0-911028-10-2). Newberry.
Allen, Robert R., jt. ed. see Korshin, Paul J.
Allen, Robert S. Lucky Foward. 1977. pap. 1.75 (ISBN 0-532-17150-0). Woodhill.
--Patton's Third U.S. Army Lucky Forward. 320p. 1974. pap. 1.95 (ISBN 0-532-19104-8). Woodhill.
Allen, Robert S., jt. auth. see Pearson, Drew.
Allen, Robert S., ed. Our Fair City. LC 73-19124. (Politics & People Ser.). 396p. 1974. Repr. 26.50x (ISBN 0-405-05851-9). Ayer Co Pubs.
Allen, Robert W., jt. auth. see Porter, Lyman W.
Allen, Robert Y. & Spohn, Robert F. Selling Dynamics. (Marketing Ser.). 512p. 1984. text ed. 33.95 (ISBN 0-07-001161-3). McGraw.
Allen, Rodney, jt. ed. see Cowart, Marie.
Allen, Rodney F. Energy Education: Goals & Practices. LC 79-93115. (Fastback Ser.: No. 139). (Orig.). 1980. pap. 0.75 (ISBN 0-87367-139-2). Phi Delta Kappa.
Allen, Rodney F., et al. Deciding How to Live on Spaceship Earth. LC 73-81184. (Decision-Making Skills Ser.). (Illus.). 134p. (Orig.). (gr. 10-12). 1973. pap. text ed. 4.89 (ISBN 0-88343-669-8). McDougal-Littell.
Allen, Roger. The Arabic Novel: An Historical & Critical Introduction. LC 82-3235. 200p. 1982. pap. 15.00x (ISBN 0-8156-2276-7). Syracuse U Pr.
Allen, Roger, jt. ed. see Ringold, Fran.
Allen, Roger, tr. see Jabra, Jabra I.
Allen, Roger, tr. see Mahfuz, Nagib.
Allen, Roger B. Common Sense Discipline: What to Say & Do When Children Misbehave. (Illus.). 86p. (Orig.). 1984. pap. 4.95 (ISBN 0-916979-00-8). Common Sen Pubns.
Allen, Roger H. Real Estate Investment & Taxation. 1984. text ed. 14.95 (ISBN 0-538-19610-6, S61). SW Pub.
Allen, Roland. The Compulsion of the Spirit: A Roland Allen Reader. Long, Charles H. & Paton, David, eds. 160p. 1983. pap. 4.50 (ISBN 0-88028-025-5). Forward Movement.
--The Compulsion of the Spirit: A Roland Allen Reader. Paton, David & Long, Charles H., eds. LC 83-14006. pap. 39.50 (ISBN 0-317-30156-X, 2025338). Bks Demand UMI.
--Missionary Methods: St. Paul's or Our's? 1962. pap. 4.95x (ISBN 0-8028-1001-2). Eerdmans.
--The Spontaneous Expansion of the Church. 1962. pap. 4.95 (ISBN 0-8028-1002-0). Eerdmans.
Allen, Ron & McKerrow, Ray E. Pragmatics of Public Communication. 208p. 1981. pap. text ed. 9.95 (ISBN 0-8403-2494-4). Kendall-Hunt.
Allen, Ronald & Allen, Beverly. Liberated Traditionalism: Men & Women in Balance. LC 85-8969. (Critical Concern Bks.). 1985. 9.95 (ISBN 0-88070-112-9). Multnomah.
Allen, Ronald & Kuhns, Richard. Constitutional Criminal Procedure. LC 84-80836. 1985. text ed. 32.00 (ISBN 0-316-03415-0). Little.
Allen, Ronald B. The Majesty of Man: The Dignity of Being Human. LC 84-984. (Critical Concern Ser.). 1984. 11.95 (ISBN 0-88070-065-3). Multnomah.
--Praise! a Matter of Life & Breath. LC 80-23894. 248p. 1980. pap. 5.95 (ISBN 0-8407-5733-6). Nelson.
--When Song Is New. LC 83-8286. 240p. 1983. pap. 5.95 (ISBN 0-8407-5825-1). Nelson.
Allen, Ronald B., et al. Worship: Rediscovering the Missing Jewel. LC 82-2198. (Critical Concern Ser.). 180p. 1982. 9.95 (ISBN 0-930014-86-3). Multnomah.
Allen, Ronald J. Contemporary Biblical Interpretation for Preaching. 160p. 1984. pap. 9.50 (ISBN 0-8170-1002-5). Judson.
--Our Eyes Can Be Opened: Preaching the Miracle Stories of the Synoptic Gospels Today. LC 81-43679. 146p. 1983. pap. text ed. 9.25 (ISBN 0-8191-2671-3). U Pr of Amer.
Allen, Rosamund. King Horn: An Edition Based on Cambridge University Manuscript Library. Edwards, A. S., ed. LC 83-49067. (Medieval Texts Ser.). 427p. 1984. lib. bdg. 66.00 (ISBN 0-8240-9425-5). Garland Pub.
Allen, Rosemary & Purkis, Andrew. Health in the Round: Voluntary Action & Antenatal Services. 104p. (Orig.). 1983. pap. text ed. 12.25 (ISBN 0-7199-1077-3, Pub. by Bedford England). Brookfield Pub Co.
Allen, Ross. How to Keep Snakes in Captivity. rev. ed. LC 76-184098. pap. 2.95 (ISBN 0-8200-0304-2). Great Outdoors.
Allen, Rowena, tr. & illus. see Fisher, Robert.
Allen, Roy F. German Expressionist Poetry. (World Authors Ser.). 1979. lib. bdg. 15.50 (ISBN 0-8057-6386-4, Twayne). G K Hall.
--Literary Life in German Expressionism & the Berlin Circles. Foster, Stephen, ed. LC 82-4762. (Studies in the Fine Arts: The Avant-Garde: No. 25). 414p. 1983. 59.95 (ISBN 0-8357-1315-6). UMI Res Pr.
Allen, Roy G. Macro-Economic Theory. LC 67-12508. 1968. pap. 10.95 (ISBN 0-312-50330-X). St Martin.
--Mathematical Analysis for Economists. rev. ed. 1969. pap. 13.95 (ISBN 0-312-52185-5). St Martin.

Allen, Rupert C. Psyche & Symbol in the Theater of Federico Garcia Lorca: Perlimplin, Yerma, Blood Wedding. LC 74-7285. 234p. 1974. 14.50x (ISBN 0-292-76418-9). U of Tex Pr.

--Symbolic Experience: A Study of Poems by Pedro Salinas. LC 81-10307. 180p. 1982. text ed. 20.00 (ISBN 0-8173-0081-3). U of Ala Pr.

--The Symbolic World of Federico Garcia Lorca. LC 72-80890. 1972. 17.50 (ISBN 0-8263-0245-9). Lib Soc Sci.

Allen, Ruth. What's the Matter with Christy? LC 82-8036. 110p. (Orig.). 1982. pap. 3.95 (ISBN 0-87123-629-X, 210629). Bethany Hse.

Allen, Ruth N. & Allen, Charles F. Twenty-Two Common Herbs. (Illus.). 1968. pap. 2.00 (ISBN 0-8283-1161-7). Branden Pub Co.

Allen, S., jt. ed. see Miles, E.

Allen, Sally, jt. auth. see Foreman, Dale I.

Allen, Sam. Locks & Alarms. (Illus.). 352p. (Orig.). 1984. 21.95 (ISBN 0-8306-0359-X); pap. 15.95 (ISBN 0-8306-0259-3, 1559). TAB Bks.

--The Wood Finisher's Handbook. LC 84-8557. (Illus.). 192p. (Orig.). 1985. pap. 9.95 (ISBN 0-8069-7914-3). Sterling.

Allen, Samuel. Paul Vesey's Ledger. (Heritage Ser.). 1975. pap. 2.50 (ISBN 0-685-50388-7). Broadside.

--Poems from Africa. LC 75-184976. (Poems of the World Ser.). (Illus.). (gr. 9-12). 1973. 10.53i (ISBN 0-690-62975-3). Crowell Jr Bks.

Allen, Sandra G., ed. The Terrier Lovers Cookbook. 1977. 10.00 (ISBN 0-9600722-2-5). Skye Terrier.

Allen, Sarah. A Cleaner World. (Cambridge Dinosaur Information Ser.). (Illus.). 26p. (gr. 7-10). 1983. pap. 1.95 (ISBN 0-521-27200-9). Cambridge U Pr.

Allen, Shirley S. Samuel Phelps & Sadler's Wells Theatre. LC 72-120259. (Illus.). 1971. 42.00x (ISBN 0-8195-4029-3). Wesleyan U Pr.

Allen Smith Co. Editorial Staff. Ohio Police Officers' Manual. 5th ed. 1979. pap. text ed. 9.00x (ISBN 0-87473-123-2). A Smith Co.

Allen Smith Co. Staff. Drugs in Litigation: Damage Awards Involving Prescription & Nonprescription Drugs. 520p. 1982. pap. text ed. 35.00x (ISBN 0-87473-153-4). A Smith Co.

Allen, Stephen A., 3rd, jt. auth. see Lorsch, Jay W.

Allen, Stephen D., jt. auth. see Koneman, Elmer W.

Allen, Steve. Explaining China. (Illus.). 320p. 1980. Outlet 2.98 (ISBN 0-517-54062-2, Michelman Bks). Crown.

--Funny People. LC 80-5895. 288p. 1982. 12.95 (ISBN 0-8128-2764-3). Stein & Day.

--Funny People. 336p. 1984. pap. 3.50 (ISBN 0-8128-8011-0). Stein & Day.

--How to Make a Speech. 224p. 1985. 15.95 (ISBN 0-07-001164-8). McGraw.

--More Funny People. LC 82-42553. 336p. 1982. 14.95 (ISBN 0-8128-2884-4). Stein & Day.

--Ripoff: A Report on Moral Collapse & Corruption in America. 1979. 9.95 (ISBN 0-8184-0249-0). Lyle Stuart.

--The Talk Show Murders. 1983. pap. 2.95 (ISBN 0-440-18480-0). Dell.

Allen, Steven. Girls on the Tenth Floor, & Other Stories. facs. ed. LC 78-128718. (Short Story Index Reprint Ser). 1958. 14.00 (ISBN 0-8369-3608-6). Ayer Co Pubs.

Allen, Stuart D., jt. auth. see Link, Albert N.

Allen, Sture & Petofi, Janos S., eds. Aspects of Automatized Text Processing, Vol. 17. (Paper in Textlinguistics Ser.). 194p. (Orig.). 1979. pap. text ed. 14.00x (ISBN 3-87118-363-6, Pub. by Helmut Buske Verlag Hamburg). Benjamins North Am.

Allen, Sue. Victorian Bookbindings: A Pictorial Survey. rev. ed. LC 76-7420. (No. 4). 1976. 3 color fiches incl. 28.00 (ISBN 0-226-68787-2, Chicago Visual Lib). U of Chicago Pr.

Allen, Susan E. The Frontier Nursing Service Oral History Project: An Annotated Guide. Birdwhistell, Terry L., ed. (University of Kentucky Libraries Occasional Papers: No. 9). 50p. (Orig.). 1985. pap. 15.00 (ISBN 0-917519-05-1). U of KY Libs.

Allen, Susan W. & Talbot, Karen H. Preparing Preschoolers. 150p. (Orig.). 1981. pap. 9.95 (ISBN 0-88290-160-5, 2047). Horizon Utah.

--Projects for Preschoolers. 72p. (Orig.). 1981. pap. 12.95 (ISBN 0-88290-161-3, 2048). Horizon Utah.

Allen, T. Particle Size Measurement. 3rd ed. (Powder Technology Ser.). 1981. 64.00x (ISBN 0-412-15410-2, NO. 6386, Pub. by Chapman & Hall). Methuen Inc.

Allen, T., ed. see Particle Size Analysis Conference.

Allen, T., ed. see Particle Size Analysis, Loughborough University of Technology, 4th, 1981.

Allen, T. D. Navahos Have Five Fingers. LC 63-17167. (The Civilization of the American Indian Ser.: Vol. 68). (Illus.). 249p. 1982. 17.95 (ISBN 0-8061-0575-5); pap. 8.95 (ISBN 0-8061-1765-6). U of Okla Pr.

--Writing to Create Ourselves: New Approaches for Teachers, Students, & Writers. LC 82-1878. 255p. 1982. 16.95x (ISBN 0-8061-1768-0). U of Okla Pr.

Allen, T. D., jt. auth. see Mitchell, Emerson B.

Allen, T. Diener, jt. auth. see Autry, Gloria D.

Allen, T. E., ed. Oil Spill Chemical Dispersants: Research, Experience, & Recommendations - STP 840. 448p. 1984. 54.00 (ISBN 0-8031-0400-6, 04-840000-24). ASTM.

Allen, T. Earl, jt. auth. see Miller, David K.

Allen, T. F. Encyclopaedia of Pure Materia Medica, 12 vols. 1979. Set. 900.00x (ISBN 0-686-78731-5, Pub. by Bks India England). State Mutual Bk.

--Encyclopedia of Pure Materia Medica, 12 vols. 1979. Set. 900.00x (ISBN 0-686-78827-3, Pub. by Bks India England). State Mutual Bk.

Allen, T. F. & Starr, Thomas B. Hierarchy: Perspectives for Ecological Complexity. LC 81-22010. (Illus.). 1982. lib. bdg. 27.50x (ISBN 0-226-01431-2). U of Chicago Pr.

Allen, T. G., jt. auth. see Chapman, G. w.

Allen, T. Harrell. The Bottom Line: Communicating in the Organization. LC 78-24521. (Illus.). 180p. 1979. text ed. 19.95x (ISBN 0-88229-405-9). Nelson-Hall.

--New Methods in Social Science Research: Policy Sciences & Futures Research. LC 76-12840. (Praeger Special Studies). 176p. 1978. 34.95 (ISBN 0-275-23630-7). Praeger.

Allen, T. O. & Roberts, Alan P. Production Operations, 2 vols. 2nd ed. 1982. Set. 90.00 (ISBN 0-317-13016-1); Vol. 1, 290p. 47.50 (ISBN 0-930972-05-8); Vol. 2, 250p. 47.50 (ISBN 0-930972-04-X). Oil & Gas.

Allen, T. W., ed. see Homer.

Allen, Thomas & Keefer, Raymond. General Chemistry Experiments. 1982. wire coil bdg. 5.95 (ISBN 0-88252-085-7). Paladin Hse.

Allen, Thomas B. Vanishing Wildlife of North America. LC 73-833. (Special Publications Ser.). 1974. avail. only from Natl. Geog. 6.95 (ISBN 0-87044-129-9). Natl Geog.

--Where the Children Live. (Illus.). 27p. 1981. 10.95 (ISBN 0-13-957126-4). P-H.

Allen, Thomas B., jt. auth. see Polmar, Norman.

Allen, Thomas B., ed. Images of the World: Photography at the National Geographic. 2nd 1984 ed. (Illus.). 396p. 1981. deluxe 28.95 (ISBN 0-87044-394-1). Natl Geog.

Allen, Thomas B., ed. see Nowak, Ronald, et al.

Allen, Thomas B., et al. Earth's Amazing Animals. Parker, Ceilia I., ed. LC 83-17324. (Illus.). 208p. 1983. 18.95 (ISBN 0-912186-48-8). Natl Wildlife.

Allen, Thomas J. Managing the Flow of Technology. 336p. 1977. pap. text ed. 12.50x (ISBN 0-262-51027-8). MIT Pr.

Allen, Thomas L. & Keefer, Raymond M. Chemistry: Experiment & Theory. 2nd ed. 742p. 1982. text ed. 31.95 scp (ISBN 0-06-040209-1, HarpC); solution manual scp 3.95 (ISBN 0-06-040211-3); instr's. manual avail. (ISBN 0-06-360203-2). Har-Row.

Allen, Thomas O. & Roberts, Alan P. Production Operations: Well Completions, Workover, & Stimulation, 2 Vols. (Illus.). 530p. 1982. 89.95 set (ISBN 0-930972-00-7); each 47.50 (ISBN 0-317-00456-5). Pennwell Bks.

Allen, Thomas P., jt. auth. see Polmar, Norman.

Allen, Thomas T., tr. see Guyon, Madame.

Allen, Thomas W. The ASEAN Report, 2 vols. Wain, Barry, ed. Incl. Vol. 1. A Comparative Assessment of the ASEAN Countries; Vol. 2. The Evolution & Programs of ASEAN: The Asian Wall Street Journal. LC 80-110683. (Illus.). 414p. 1980. Set. pap. 125.00x (ISBN 0-295-95740-9, 80-110683). U of Wash Pr.

Allen, Tom. Those Buried Texans, No Stone Unturned. LC 80-82288. (Illus.). 192p. (Orig.). 1980. pap. 6.95 (ISBN 0-937460-25-7). Hendrick-Long.

Allen, Tom, ed. see Marler, Peter R., et al.

Allen, Trevor B. Grammar of Resigaro, 3 vols. 533p. 1976. microfiche (6) 6.66x (ISBN 0-88312-349-5). Summer Inst Ling.

Allen, Trevor R. Vocabulario Resegaro. (Documentos De Trabajo: No. 16). 151p. (Orig., Span.). 1979. microfiche 1.60 (ISBN 0-88312-371-1). Summer Inst Ling.

Allen, V. L., jt. ed. see Levin, J. R.

Allen, Vera, ed. see Larsen, Phyllis.

Allen, Vernon L., ed. Children As Teachers: Theory & Research on Tutoring. (Educational Psychology Ser.). 1976. 39.00 (ISBN 0-12-052640-9). Acad Pr.

Allen, Vernon L. & Scheibe, Karl E., eds. The Social Context of Conduct: Psychological Writings of Theodore R. Sarbin. LC 81-5864. 288p. 1982. 34.95 (ISBN 0-03-059716-1). Praeger.

Allen, Vernon L. & Van de Vliert, Evert, eds. Role Transitions. (NATO Conference Series III, Human Factors: Vol. 23). 384p. 1984. 49.50x (ISBN 0-306-41506-2, Plenum Pr). Plenum Pub.

Allen, Vernon L., jt. ed. see Magnusson, David.

Allen, Victor L. Social Analysis: A Marxist Critique & Alternative. LC 75-327627. pap. 84.50 (ISBN 0-317-09619-2, 2010049). Bks Demand UMI.

Allen, Victoria. The New Uncle Tom's Cabin. 118p. 1980. 20.00x (ISBN 0-86116-134-3, Pub. by New Horizon England). State Mutual Bk.

Allen, Virginia F. Inside English. 1983. pap. text ed. 8.25 (ISBN 0-88345-491-2, 21181). Regents Pub.

--Techniques in Teaching Vocabulary. (Teaching Techniques in English as a Second or Foreign Language Ser.). (Illus., Orig.). 1983. pap. 4.95x (ISBN 0-19-434130-5). Oxford U Pr.

Allen, Virginia F. & Forman, Sidney. English As a Second Language: A Comprehensive Bibliography. Cordasco, Francesco, ed. LC 77-90404. (Bilingual-Bicultural Education in the U. S. Ser.). 1978. Repr. of 1967 ed. lib. bdg. 25.50x (ISBN 0-405-11073-1). Ayer Co Pubs.

Allen, Virginia F, et al, eds. The Student Dictionary. 1984. pap. 9.50 (ISBN 0-582-79890-6). Caroline Hse.

Allen, Virginia G., jt. auth. see Fox, Sharon E.

Allen, Virginia M. The Femme Fatale: Erotic & Fatal Muse. 300p. 1983. 25.00X (ISBN 0-87875-267-6). Whitston Pub.

Allen, Virginia P. Before the Pattern: An Idea Book for Drawing Garment Designs. 1975. softcover 2.95 (ISBN 0-686-11167-2). Spinning Spool.

--Beyond the Pattern: A Guide to Creative Sewing & Design with Knit Fabrics. LC 73-91225. 1973. softcover 9.95 (ISBN 0-686-09884-6); lib. bdg. 15.95 (ISBN 0-686-09885-4). Spinning Spool.

Allen, W., et al. Newcastle Disease Vaccines: Their Production & Use. (Animal Production & Health Papers: No. 10). 163p. 1978. pap. 14.25 (ISBN 92-5-100484-6, F1602, FAO). Unipub.

Allen, W. A. Know Your Car. 3rd ed. (Illus.). 1974. 11.50 (ISBN 0-8269-0163-8). Am Technical.

Allen, W. B. & Lloyd, Gorden, eds. The Essential Antifederalist. LC 85-5303. 292p. (Orig.). 1985. lib. bdg. 24.50 (ISBN 0-8191-4631-5, Ctr Study Constitution); pap. 9.75 (ISBN 0-8191-4632-3). U Pr of Amer.

Allen, W. D. Philosophies of Music History: A Study of General Histories of Music, 1600-1960. 15.00 (ISBN 0-8446-1529-3). Peter Smith.

Allen, W. E. A History of the Georgian People. 1978. lib. bdg. 75.00 (ISBN 0-8490-1998-2). Gordon Pr.

--Sucesos de las Islas Filipinos, by Antonio Marga, 1609, 2 vols. Mango, Anthony, tr. 1971. 45.00x (ISBN 0-686-79459-1, Pub. by Hakluyt Soc England). Vol. 1, 368 P. Vol. 2, 271 P. State Mutual Bk.

Allen, W. E., ed. see Finney, Charles G.

Allen, W. Gore. Renaissance in the North. facsimile ed. LC 79-111810. (Essay Index Reprint Ser.). 1946. 18.00 (ISBN 0-8369-1590-9). Ayer Co Pubs.

Allen, W. S. Vox Latina. 2nd ed. LC 78-1153. (Illus.). 1978. 22.95 (ISBN 0-521-22049-1). Cambridge U Pr.

Allen, W. S., ed. Longman Structural Readers, 4 bks. Incl; Modern Short Stories (ISBN 0-582-53777-0). (English As a Second Language Bk.). (Basic vocabulary about 1800 words). 1965-81. pap. 2.35x ea. Longman.

--Longman Structural Readers, 14 bks. Incl. Car Thieves. Alexander, L. G (ISBN 0-582-53705-3); Detectives from Scotland Yard. Cox, Alwyn (ISBN 0-582-53704-5); The Flying Spy. Cox, Alwyn (ISBN 0-582-53709-6); Green Island. Eyre, A. G (ISBN 0-582-53703-7); The House Near the Sea. Musman, R (ISBN 0-582-53707-X); Kate & the Clock. Dunkling, L (ISBN 0-582-53708-8); King Henry. Shakespeare, William (ISBN 0-582-53702-9); Mr. Punch. Alexander, L. G (ISBN 0-582-53706-1); Operation Janus. Alexander, L. G (ISBN 0-582-53713-4); Pele: Nick & the Motorbike. Byrne, Donn. 1.65 ea (ISBN 0-582-52969-7); The Prisoners. Byrne, Donn (ISBN 0-582-53701-0); Scoops: Especially for Young Readers. see sep. entry; Sherlock Holmes & the Dancing Men. Doyle, Arthur Conan (ISBN 0-582-53677-4); The Storm. Musman, Richard; Nick & the Motorbike. Byrne, Donn. 1.65 (ISBN 0-582-52969-7). (English As a Second Language Bk.). (Basic vocabulary about 300 words). 1965-81. pap. 1.65x ea.; pap. 17.85 Handy Pack (ISBN 0-582-53064-4). Longman.

--Longman Structural Readers, 13 bks, Stage 2. Incl. April Fool's Day. Alexander, L. G (ISBN 0-582-53719-3); The Boy & the Donkey. Turvey, Celia (ISBN 0-582-53723-1); Don Quixote & Sancho Panza. Cervantes (ISBN 0-582-53718-5); Hamad the Diver: A Tale As Told by His Grandson (ISBN 0-582-53720-7); Island of the Volcanoes. Byrne, Donn (ISBN 0-582-53715-0); The Lost Love & Other Stories (ISBN 0-582-53690-1); On the Road. Byrne, Donn (ISBN 0-582-53716-9); Pop Festival. Serraillier, Ian (ISBN 0-582-53714-2); Professor Boffin's Unbrella. Alexander, L. G (ISBN 0-582-53724-X); The Stone Mother & Child. Heaton, J. B (ISBN 0-582-53722-3); Worth a Fortune. Alexander, L. G (ISBN 0-582-53721-5); Adventure Story. Alexander, L. G. pap. 1.75 (ISBN 0-582-53045-8); Inspector Thackeray Arrives. James, Kenneth. pap. 1.75 (ISBN 0-582-53340-6). (English As a Second Language Bk.). (Basic vocabulary about 500 words). 1965-81. pap. 1.75x ea.; pap. 18.90 Handy Pack. Longman.

--Longman Structural Readers, 17 bks, Stage 3. Incl. Clint Magee. Alexander, L. G (ISBN 0-582-53682-0); Stage 4. Computers (ISBN 0-582-53334-1); Dangerous Game. Harris, William (ISBN 0-582-53681-2); David Copperfield. Dickens, Charles (ISBN 0-582-53734-7); Everest the Hard Way. Bonington, Chris & Grant, Neville. (ISBN 0-582-52337-0); How Life Began. Jones, Lewis (ISBN 0-582-53812-2); Inspector Thackeray Calls. James, Kenneth & Mullen, Lloyd. (ISBN 0-582-53745-2); Operation Mastermind. Alexander, L. G (ISBN 0-582-53741-X); Round the World in Eighty Days. Verne, Jules (ISBN 0-582-53731-2); SOS in Space. Jones, Lewis; Stunt! Jones, Lewis (ISBN 0-582-53680-4); Survive the Savage Sea. Robertson, Douglas & Kingsbury, Ray. (ISBN 0-582-52548-9); Tales from Arab History (ISBN 0-582-53733-9); The World Under the Sea. Wright, Andrew & Buckby, M.. (English As a Second Language Bk.). (Basic vocabulary about 750 words). 1965-81. pap. 1.85x ea. Longman.

--Longman Structural Readers, 18 bks, Stage 4. Incl; Eight Ghost Stories. Burton, S. H (ISBN 0-582-54078-X); The Energy Crisis. Walsh, Gordon; Fair Play! Sport, Money & Success in the World Today. McLean, Alan (ISBN 0-582-52516-0); I Can Jump Puddles. Marshall, Alan (ISBN 0-582-53672-3); Me, Myself & I: Seven Science Fiction Stories (ISBN 0-582-53844-0); Nothing to Fear & Other Stories. Hartley, L. P., et al. (ISBN 0-582-53109-8); Oil. Wymer, N; The Prisoner of Zenda. Hope, Anthony (ISBN 0-582-53746-0); Race to the South Pole. Jones, Lewis & Brett, Bernard. (ISBN 0-582-53848-3); Silas Marner. Eliot, George (ISBN 0-582-53751-7); Water. Jones, Lewis (ISBN 0-582-53684-7). (English As a Second Language Bk.). (Basic vocabulary about 1100 words). 1965-81. pap. 1.95x ea.; LSR Handy Pack Stage 4 21.00 (ISBN 0-582-53067-9). Longman.

--Longman Structural Readers, 9 bks, Stage 5. Incl. The Adventures of Tom Sawyer. Twain, Mark (ISBN 0-582-53761-4); Hard Times. Dickens, Charles (ISBN 0-582-53831-9); Inspector Thackeray Investigates. James, Kenneth & Mullen, Lloyd. (ISBN 0-582-53774-6); Kidnapped. Stevenson, Robert Louis (ISBN 0-582-53762-2); The Valentine Generation & Other Stories. Updike, John, et al. (ISBN 0-582-53108-X); Your Choice? A Self-Defense Guide to Advertising. Williams, Alma (ISBN 0-582-53849-1). (English As a Second Language Bk.). (Basic vocabulary about 1500 words). 1965-81. pap. 2.25x ea. Longman.

Allen, W. Sidney. Accent & Rhythm: Prosodic Features of Latin & Greek. LC 72-91361. (Studies in Linguistics). 432p. 1973. 72.50 (ISBN 0-521-20098-9). Cambridge U Pr.

--Sandhi: The Theoretical, Phonetic, & Historical Bases of Word-Junction in Sanskrit. (Janua Linguarum Ser. Minor: No. 17). 1972. pap. text ed. 12.80x (ISBN 90-2792-360-4). Mouton.

--Vox Graeca. 2nd ed. (Illus.). 1968. 22.95 (ISBN 0-521-20626-X). Cambridge U Pr.

Allen, Wallace W. A Design for News. LC 81-2022. (Illus.). 1981. spiral bdg. 10.95 (ISBN 0-932272-04-5). Minneapolis Tribune.

Allen, Walter. As I Walked Down New Grub Street. LC 81-69852. 1982. lib. bdg. 15.00x (ISBN 0-226-01433-9). U of Chicago Pr.

--Governor Chamberlain's Administration in South Carolina: A Chapter of Reconstruction in the Southern States. facsimile ed. LC 73-95060. (Select Bibliographies Reprint Ser). 1888. 38.50 (ISBN 0-8369-5062-3). Ayer Co Pubs.

--Governor Chamberlain's Administration in South Carolina: A Chapter of Reconstruction in the Southern States. LC 78-79817. Repr. of 1888 ed. 24.75x (ISBN 0-8371-0283-9, ALG&, Pub. by Negro U Pr). Greenwood.

--The Novel to-Day. 1978. Repr. of 1955 ed. lib. bdg. 10.00 (ISBN 0-8495-0030-3). Arden Lib.

--Novel To-Day. LC 73-15717. 1955. lib. bdg. 12.50 (ISBN 0-8414-2924-3). Folcroft.

--The Short Story in English. 1981. 25.00x (ISBN 0-19-812666-2). Oxford U Pr.

--Six Great Novelists. LC 73-5556. 1955. lib. bdg. 27.50 (ISBN 0-8414-1737-7). Folcroft.

--Six Great Novelists. 1985. 52.50 (ISBN 0-317-19976-5). Porter.

Allen, Walter C., ed. Serial Publications in Large Libraries. LC 74-629637. (Allerton Park Institute Ser.: No. 16). 194p. 1970. 6.00x (ISBN 0-87845-011-4). U of Ill Lib Info Sci.

--Studies in Jazz Discography: No. 1. LC 78-5037. 1978. Repr. of 1971 ed. lib. bdg. 22.50x (ISBN 0-313-20407-1, ALJD). Greenwood.

Allen, Walter E. Arnold Bennett. LC 76-148344. Repr. of 1949 ed. 7.50 (ISBN 0-404-08716-7). AMS Pr.

--Reading a Novel. 1978. Repr. of 1956 ed. lib. bdg. 12.50 (ISBN 0-8495-0109-1). Arden Lib.

--Reading a Novel. LC 72-194361. 1949. 9.50 (ISBN 0-8414-2924-3). Folcroft.

--Six Great Novelists. 1978. Repr. of 1955 ed. lib. bdg. 30.00 (ISBN 0-8495-0106-7). Arden Lib.

Allen, Walter P. Easy Crossword Puzzles for People Learning English. 1956. pap. 2.50 (ISBN 0-87789-026-9). Eng Language.

--More Easy Crossword Puzzles for People Learning English. 1970. pap. 2.50 (ISBN 0-87789-031-5). Eng Language.

Allen, Ward, ed. & tr. Translating for King James: Notes Made by a Translator of King James's Bible. LC 69-17535. xi, 155p. (Eng.). 1969. 10.00x (ISBN 0-8265-1136-8). Vanderbilt U Pr.

Allen, Warren, jt. auth. see Klooster, Dale H.

Allen, Warren D. Our Marching Civilization. LC 77-25408. (Music Reprint Ser.). 1978. Repr. of 1943 ed. lib. bdg. 21.50 (ISBN 0-306-77568-9). Da Capo.

Allen, Warren W. Accounting Tutorial. 3rd ed. (Orig.). (gr. 9-12). 1985. pap. text ed. 2.75 wkbk. (ISBN 0-538-02190-X, B19). SW Pub.

--Computerized Payroll Procedures. (Orig.). (gr. 9-12). 1985. pap. text ed. 2.95 wkbk. (ISBN 0-538-02180-2, B18). SW Pub.

Allen, Warren W., jt. auth. see Klooster, Dale H.

Allen, Will W., ed. Banneker: The Afro-American Astronomer. facsimile ed. LC 77-168504. (Black Heritage Library Collection). Repr. of 1921 ed. 10.00 (ISBN 0-8369-8858-2). Ayer Co Pubs.

Allen, William. The Fire in the Birdbath: And Other Disturbances. 1986. 13.95 (ISBN 0-393-02249-8). Norton.

Allen, William & Thomson, T. R. Narrative of the Expedition Sent by Her Majesty's Government to the River Niger in 1841, 2 Vols. (Illus.). Repr. of 1848 ed. Set. 85.00 (ISBN 0-384-00803-8). Johnson Repr.

Allen, William & Thomson, T. R. H. A Narrative of the Expedition Sent by Her Majesty's Government to the River Niger in 1841 under the Command of Captain H.D. Trotter, 2 vols. 1968. Repr. of 1848 ed. Set. 85.00x (ISBN 0-7146-1784-9, BHA 01784, F Cass Co). Biblio Dist.

Allen, William see Cecil, William.

Allen, William A., jt. auth. see Hopper, C. Edmund.

Allen, William A., et al. How Drugs Can Affect Your Life: The Effects of Drugs on Safety & Well-Being, with Special Emphasis on Prevention of Drug Use. (Illus.). 218p. 1983. pap. 14.75x (ISBN 0-398-04810-X). C C Thomas.

Allen, William C. The Annals of Haywood County, North Carolina: Historical, Sociological, & Genealogical. LC 77-24593. (Illus.). 1977. Repr. of 1935 ed. 36.50 (ISBN 0-87152-251-9). Reprint.

Allen, William F., et al, eds. Slave Songs of the United States. facs. ed. LC 72-138330. (Black Heritage Library Collection Ser). 1867. Repr. of 1867 ed. 15.00 (ISBN 0-8369-8722-5). Ayer Co Pubs.

--Slave Songs of the United States. 1960. 11.25 (ISBN 0-8446-1411-4). Peter Smith.

Allen, William G. American Prejudice Against Color. LC 75-82165. (Anti-Slavery Crusade in America Ser). 1969. Repr. of 1853 ed. 11.00 (ISBN 0-405-00603-9). Ayer Co Pubs.

--Wheatley, Banneker & Horton. facs. ed. LC 77-133145. (Black Heritage Library Collection Ser). 1849. Repr. of 1849 ed. 7.00 (ISBN 0-8369-8657-1). Ayer Co Pubs.

Allen, William H., Jr. How to Raise & Train Pigeons. LC 58-7602. (Illus.). 160p. 1982. 13.95 (ISBN 0-8069-3706-8); lib. bdg. 16.79 (ISBN 0-8069-3707-6). Sterling.

--Pigeons: How to Raise & Train Them. pap. 2.00 (ISBN 0-87980-118-2). Wilshire.

Allen, William O. Two Hundred Years: The History of the Society for Promoting Christian Knowledge, 1698-1898. LC 76-135171. (Research & Source Works Ser.: No. 622). 1971. Repr. of 1898 ed. 32.00 (ISBN 0-8337-0044-8). B Franklin.

Allen, William R. Modern Autobody Repair. 1985. text ed. 24.95 (ISBN 0-8359-4525-1); wkbk avail. (ISBN 0-8359-4526-X). Reston.

Allen, William R. & Bragaw, Louis K. Social Forces & the Manager: Readings & Cases. LC 81-10402. (Wiley Series in Management). 502p. 1982. pap. text ed. 27.45 (ISBN 0-471-08611-8); tchrs'. ed. (ISBN 0-471-08933-8). Wiley.

Allen, William R., jt. auth. see Alchian, Armen A.

Allen, William S. The Nazi Seizure of Power: The Experience of a Single German Town, 1930-1935. 2nd, rev. ed. 416p. 1984. 18.95 (ISBN 0-531-09935-0, EE22); pap. 9.95 (ISBN 0-531-06439-5, EE27). Watts.

--A Study in Latin Prognosis. LC 70-176513. (Columbia University. Teachers College. Contributions to Education: No. 135). Repr. of 1923 ed. 22.50 (ISBN 0-404-55135-1). AMS Pr.

Allen, Woody. The Floating Light Bulb. 1982. 10.50 (ISBN 0-394-52415-2). Random.

--Getting Even. 1971. 10.95 (ISBN 0-394-47348-5). Random.

--Getting Even. 128p. pap. 2.95 (ISBN 0-394-72640-5, V-640, Vin). Random.

--Play It Again, Sam. LC 75-85621. 1969. 10.00 (ISBN 0-394-40663-X). Random.

--Side Effects. 160p. 1981. pap. 2.75 (ISBN 0-345-29653-2). Ballantine.

--Side Effects. 1980. 8.95 (ISBN 0-394-51104-2). Random.

--Sleeper. 1978. 7.95 (ISBN 0-394-50051-2). Random.

--Without Feathers. 224p. 1983. pap. 2.95 (ISBN 0-345-30128-5). Ballantine.

Allen, Zachariah. The Practical Tourist; or, Sketches of the State of the Useful Arts, & of Society, Scenery in Great Britain, France & Holland, 2 vols. in 1. LC 73-38258. (The Evolution of Capitalism Ser.). 896p. 1972. Repr. of 1832 ed. 52.00x (ISBN 0-405-04111-X). Ayer Co Pubs.

AllenBaugh, Carl. Coins Questions & Answers. 4th, rev. ed. Krause Publications Staff, ed. LC 76-1543. (Illus.). 200p. 1985. pap. write for info. (ISBN 0-87341-075-0). Krause Pubns.

Allen-Brown, Patricia, ed. see Long, Leslie, et al.

Allen-Browne, Patricia, ed. see Fritz, Jack.

Allen-Browne, Patricia, ed. see Rowbotham, George E.

Allenby, R. B. Rings, Fields & Groups. 304p. 1983. pap. text ed. 23.50 (ISBN 0-7131-3476-3). E Arnold.

Allendale, John & Homes, R. C. Sailorman Between the Wars. 205p. 1981. 35.00x (ISBN 0-905540-09-3, Pub. by Hollewell Pubns). State Mutual Bk.

Allende, Isabel. The House of the Spirits. Goerner, Lee, ed. Bogin, Magda, tr. LC 84-48516. 400p. 1985. 17.95 (ISBN 0-394-53907-9). Knopf.

Allende, S. La Voi Chiliene Vers le Socialisme. (Publications Gramma Ser.). 174p. 1974. pap. 31.25 (ISBN 0-677-50845-X). Gordon.

Allender, Dan B., jt. auth. see Crabb, Lawrence J., Jr.

Allender, Michael, jt. auth. see Tennant, Alan.

Allendoerfer, C. B., ed. see Symposium in Pure Mathematics, - Tempe, Ariz., - 1960.

Allendoerfer, Carl B. & Oakley, Cletus O. Fundamentals of Freshman Mathematics. 3rd ed. (Illus.). 1972. text ed. 32.95 (ISBN 0-07-001366-7). McGraw.

Allendoerfer, Carl B., et al. Elementary Functions. 1976. text ed. 27.95 (ISBN 0-07-001371-3). McGraw.

Allendoerfer, Robert D. Explorations in Chemistry. 64p. 1985. pap. text ed. 35.00 (ISBN 0-13-295866-X). P-H.

Allendorf, Katherine. Applique. LC 72-13333. (Early Craft Bks.). (Illus.). 36p. (gr. 1-4). 1973. PLB 4.95 (ISBN 0-8225-0851-6). Lerner Pubns.

Allen-Meares, Paula, et al. Social Work Services in Schools. (Illus.). 304p. 1986. text ed. 32.95 (ISBN 0-13-819665-6). P H.

Alleno, Gene P., jt. ed. see Wright, Nancy D.

Allenov, M. M. Alexander Andreyevich Ivanov. 204p. 1980. 35.00x (ISBN 0-317-14213-5, Pub. by Collet's). State Mutual Bk.

Allen-Shore, Lena. The Little Shoes & the Cry from Warsaw. 25p. 1983. pap. 2.95 (ISBN 0-88400-095-8). Shengold.

--Ten Steps in the Land of Life. LC 82-61165. 1983. 13.95 (ISBN 0-88400-088-5); pap. 6.95 (ISBN 0-88400-089-3). Shengold.

Allen-Shore, Lena, jt. auth. see Herzig, Jakub.

Allenson, Robert D., compiled by. John Henry Newman, 1801-1890: A Preliminary Register of Editions from 1818 to 1890. 1976. pap. text ed. 2.00x (ISBN 0-8401-0050-7, Aleph Pr). A R Allenson.

Allenspach, Heinz. Flexible Working Hours. 2nd ed. 1978. 8.75 (ISBN 92-2-101198-4). Intl Labour Office.

--Flexible Working Hours. v, 64p. (2nd Impression). 1978. pap. 10.00 (ISBN 92-2-101198-4, ILO59, ILO). Unipub.

Allensworth, Carl, et al. The Complete Play Production Handbook Revised & Updated. LC 81-48151. (Illus.). 384p. 1982. 14.38i (ISBN 0-06-015000-9, HarpT); pap. 8.61i (ISBN 0-06-463558-9, EH-558). Har-Row.

Allensworth, Don T. Land Planning Law. 272p. 1981. 38.95 (ISBN 0-03-057039-5). Praeger.

Allentuch, Harriet R. Madame de Sevigne: A Portrait in Letters. LC 78-16378. 1978. Repr. of 1963 ed. lib. bdg. 22.50x (ISBN 0-313-20537-X, ALMS). Greenwood.

Allentuck, Andrew J. & Bivens, Gordon E. Consumer Choice: The Economics of Personal Living. 510p. 1977. text ed. 19.95 (ISBN 0-15-513456-6, HC); instr's manual avail. (ISBN 0-15-513457-4); study guide 7.95 (ISBN 0-15-513458-2). HarBraceJ.

Allentuck, Marcia, ed. Achievement of Isaac Bashevis Singer. LC 69-19747. (Crosscurrents-Modern Critique Ser.). 197p. 1969. 9.95x (ISBN 0-8093-0383-3). S Ill U Pr.

Allentuck, Marcia Epstein, intro. by. John Graham's System & Dialectics of Art. LC 74-160670. (Illus.). 224p. 1971. ann. from unpubl. writings 20.00x (ISBN 0-8018-1100-7). Johns Hopkins.

Allenworth, Don T. City Planning Politics. 286p. 1980. 39.95 (ISBN 0-03-052716-3). HR&W.

Aller, Doris, jt. auth. see Aller, Paul.

Aller, Lawrence H. Atoms, Stars, & Nebulae. Rev. ed. LC 76-134951. (The Harvard Books on Astronomy). (Illus.). pap. 90.80 (ISBN 0-317-09183-2, 2019508). Bks Demand UMI.

--Physics of Therman Gaseous Nebulae: Physical Processes in Gaseous Nebulae. 1984. lib. bdg. 49.50 (ISBN 90-277-1814-8, Pub. by Reidel Holland). Kluwer Academic.

Aller, Lawrence H. & McLaughlin, Dean B., eds. Stellar Structures. Midway rep. ed. LC 63-16723. (Stars & Stellar Systems Ser.: Vol. 8). (Illus.). 1981. pap. 35.00x (ISBN 0-226-45969-1). U of Chicago Pr.

Aller, Lawrence H., jt. ed. see Middlehurst, Barbara M.

Aller, Paul & Aller, Doris. Build Your Own Adobe. (Illus.). 1946. 10.95x (ISBN 0-8047-0993-9). Stanford U Pr.

Allergy Information Association. The Food Allergy Cookbook: Diets Unlimited for Limited Diets. 148p. 1984. pap. 6.95 (ISBN 0-312-29765-3). St Martin.

Allerhand, Annette, jt. auth. see Flatto, Edwin.

Allers, Robert D. Divorce, Children, & the School. LC 81-84079. 158p. 1982. text ed. 14.95x (ISBN 0-916622-22-3). Princeton Bk Co.

Allers, Rudolf. Character Education in Adolescence. (Educational Ser.). 1940. Repr. 10.00 (ISBN 0-8482-7264-1). Norwood Edns.

--Existentialism & Psychiatry: Four Lectures. 120p. 1961. 12.75x (ISBN 0-398-05131-3). C C Thomas.

Allert, Kathy. Kate Greenaway Paper Dolls. (Illus.). 32p. (Orig.). 1981. pap. 3.50 (ISBN 0-486-24153-X). Dover.

Allert, Kathy, illus. The Get Along Gang on the Go. (Get Along Gang Ser.). (Illus.). 12p. (Orig.). (gr. 2-4). 1984. pap. 2.95 (ISBN 0-590-33198-1). Scholastic Inc.

--Meet the Get Along Gang. (The Get Along Gang Ser.). (Illus.). 12p. (Orig.). (gr. 2-4). 1984. 2.95 (ISBN 0-590-33197-3). Scholastic Inc.

--Traditional Folk Costumes of Europe Paper Dolls in Full Color. (Toy Books, Paper Dolls Ser.). (Illus.). 32p. (Orig.). (gr. 3up). 1984. pap. 3.50 (ISBN 0-486-24571-3). Dover.

Allerton, D. J. Essentials of Grammatical Theory: A Consensus View of Syntax & Morphology. 1979. pap. 12.95x (ISBN 0-7100-0278-5). Routledge & Kegan.

--Valency & the English Verb. 1983. 27.50 (ISBN 0-12-052980-7). Acad Pr.

Allerton, D. J., et al, eds. Function & Context in Linguistics Analysis. LC 78-11603. 1979. 32.50 (ISBN 0-521-22429-2). Cambridge U Pr.

Allery, Ginny. Corn Songs. 60p. (Orig.). 1983. pap. 4.25 (ISBN 0-940248-16-6). Guild Pr.

Alles, jt. auth. see Florio, A. E.

Alles, Wesley F., jt. auth. see Eddy, James M.

Alleton, V. Les Adverbes en Chinois Moderne. (Materiaux Pour L'etude De L'extreme-Orient Moderne et Contemporain, Etudes Linguistiques: No. 4). 1972. pap. 16.40x (ISBN 90-2796-989-2). Mouton.

Allett, John. New Liberalism: The Political Economy of J.A. Hobson. 268p. 1981. 30.00x (ISBN 0-8020-5558-3). U of Toronto Pr.

Alley, Brian & Cargill, Jennifer S. Keeping Track of What You Spend: The Librarian's Guide to Simple Bookkeeping. LC 81-11289. 108p. 1982. pap. 25.00 (ISBN 0-912700-79-3). Oryx Pr.

Alley, Brian, jt. auth. see Cargill, Jennifer S.

Alley, Cora, jt. auth. see Alley, Steve.

Alley, Gloria. This Very Madness. LC 77-86737. 95p. 1977. 6.00 (ISBN 0-8233-0270-9). Golden Quill.

Alley, Gordon & Deshler, Donald. Teaching the Learning Disabled Adolescent: Strategies & Methods. 360p. 1979. text ed. 24.95 (ISBN 0-89108-094-5). Love Pub Co.

Alley, Hartley, jt. auth. see Alley, Jean.

Alley, Henry. Through Glass. LC-79-21296. (American Land Ser.: Vol. 1). 191p. (Orig.). 1979. 12.95 (ISBN 0-916078-06-X); pap. 7.95 (ISBN 0-916078-07-8). Iris Pr.

Alley, Jean & Alley, Hartley. Southern Indiana. LC 65-11797. (Illus.). 128p. 1965. pap. 6.95x (ISBN 0-253-18291-3). Ind U Pr.

Alley, Reuben E. History of the University of Richmond: 1830-1971. LC 76-54906. 1977. 14.95x (ISBN 0-8139-0700-4). U Pr of Va.

Alley, Rewi. Peking Opera. (Illus.). 103p. (Orig.). 1984. pap. 14.95 (ISBN 0-8351-1617-4). China Bks.

--Six Americans in China. (Illus.). 234p. (Orig.). 1985. pap. 5.95 (ISBN 0-8351-1547-X). China Bks.

Alley, Rewi, jt. auth. see Burchett, Wilford.

Alley, Rewi, tr. Folk Poems From China's Minority. (Illus.). 147p. 1982. pap. 7.95 (ISBN 0-8351-1104-0). China Bks.

Alley, Rewi, tr. from Chinese. Light & Shadow along a Great Road. 403p. 1984. text ed. 10.95 (ISBN 0-8351-1516-X). China Bks.

Alley, Robert. The Ghost in Dobbs Diner. LC 81-4864. (Illus.). 48p. (ps-3). 1981. 5.95 (ISBN 0-8193-1055-7). Parents.

--Stab. 224p. 1982. pap. 2.50 (ISBN 0-345-30689-9). Ballantine.

--Still of the Night. 224p. (Orig.). 1982. pap. 2.50 (ISBN 0-345-30689-9). Ballantine.

Alley, Robert, ed. James Madison on Religious Liberty. LC 85-42957. 350p. 1985. 20.95 (ISBN 0-87975-298-X). Prometheus Bks.

Alley, Robert S., jt. auth. see Newcomb, Horace.

Alley, Robert S., jt. ed. see Rose, Brian.

Alley, Roderic. New Zealand & the Pacific. (Replica Edition). (Illus.). 300p. 1983. soft cover 32.00x (ISBN 0-86531-929-4). Westview.

Alley, Ronald. Graham Sutherland. (Illus.). 184p. pap. 14.95 (ISBN 0-905005-48-1, Pub. by Salem Hse Ltd). Merrimack Pub Cir.

--Paule Vezelay. (Illus.). 47p. pap. 5.95 (ISBN 0-905005-19-8, Pub. by Salem Hse Ltd). Merrimack Pub Cir.

Alley, Ronald, compiled by. Catalogue of the Tate Gallery's Collection of Modern Art Other Than Works by British Artists. (Illus.). 822p. 1981. 120.00x (ISBN 0-85667-102-9, Pub. by Sotheby Pubns England). Biblio Dist.

Alley, Sam, et al. Case Studies of Mental Health Paraprofessionals: Twelve Effective Programs. LC 79-11081. 272p. 1979. 29.95 (ISBN 0-87705-416-9). Human Sci Pr.

Alley, Sam, et al, eds. Paraprofessionals in Mental Health: Theory & Practice. LC 79-11115. 336p. 1979. 34.95 (ISBN 0-87705-420-7). Human Sci Pr.

Alley, Steve & Alley, Cora. Creative Dramatics for Children's Church. LC 78-65586. (Life After Christ Ser.). (Illus.). 1979. pap. 6.95 (ISBN 0-87239-246-5, 3362). Standard Pub.

Alley, Walter, jt. auth. see Billiet, Walter E.

Alleyn, Edward. Alleyn Papers: A Collection of Original Documents Illustrative of the Life & Times of Edward Alleyn & of the Early English Stage. LC 79-113543. Repr. of 1843 ed. 14.00 (ISBN 0-404-00329-X). AMS Pr.

Alleyne, M., jt. auth. see Nash, Rose.

Allfrey, Phyliss S. The Orchid House. 2nd ed. LC 84-51090. 235p. 1985. 20.00 (ISBN 0-89410-433-0); pap. 10.00 (ISBN 0-89410-434-9). Three Continents.

Allfrey, V. G., et al, eds. Organization & Expression of Chromosomes, LSRR 4. (Dahlem Workshop Reports Ser.: L.S.R.R. No. 4). 349p. 1976. pap. 36.50x (ISBN 0-89573-088-X). VCH Pubs.

Allgaier, Karl. Der Einfluss Bernhards von Clairvaux auf Gottfried von Strassburg. (European University Studies Ser.: No. 1, Vol. 641). 185p. (Ger.). 1983. 24.20 (ISBN 3-8204-7541-9). P Lang Pubs.

Allgair, John, jt. auth. see Williamson, Darcy.

Allgeier, Albert, jt. auth. see Allgeier, Elizabeth.

Allgeier, Arthur. Die Chester Beatty-Papyri Zum Pentateuch. 12.00 (ISBN 0-384-00860-7). Johnson Repr.

--Die Psalmen der Vulgata: Ihre Eigenart. 22.00 (ISBN 0-384-00870-4). Johnson Repr.

Allgeier, Elizabeth & Allgeier, Albert. Sexual Interactions. 660p. 1983. text ed. 22.95 (ISBN 0-669-03536-X). Heath.

Allgeier, Elizabeth & McCormick, Naomi, eds. Changing Boundaries: Gender Roles & Sexual Behavior. LC 82-60885. 347p. 1982. pap. 13.95 (ISBN 0-87484-536-X). Mayfield Pub.

Allgoewer, M. The Dynamic Compression Plate (DCP) LC 73-13494. (Illus.). 1978. pap. 19.00 (ISBN 0-387-06466-4). Springer-Verlag.

Allgoewer, M., et al, eds. Progress in Surgery, 2 vols. (Illus.). 1973. Vol. 11. 28.25 (ISBN 3-8055-1379-8); Vol. 12. 58.75 (ISBN 3-8055-1617-7). S Karger.

--Progress in Surgery, Vol. 8. 1970. 28.25 (ISBN 3-8055-0430-6). S Karger.

--Progress in Surgery, Vol. 9. 1971. 28.75 (ISBN 3-8055-0431-4). S Karger.

--Progress in Surgery, Vol. 10. (Illus.). x, 132p. 1972. 23.50 (ISBN 3-8055-1285-6). S Karger.

--Progress in Surgery, Vol. 13. 300p. 1974. 59.25 (ISBN 3-8055-1741-6). S Karger.

--Progress in Surgery, Vol. 14. x, 192p. 1975. 39.25 (ISBN 3-8055-2181-2). S Karger.

Allgood, Dave & Allgood, Stephanie. Merry Bear Book of Dreams: A Book to Read & Color. 2nd ed. (Illus.). 36p. (ps-3). 1985. pap. 2.25 (ISBN 0-933103-00-X). Merry Bears.

Allgood, J. H., et al. Mexico: The Fertilizer Industry. (Technical Bulletin Ser.: T-16). (Illus.). 60p. (Orig.). 1979. pap. 4.00 (ISBN 0-88090-015-6). Intl Fertilizer.

Allgood, Stephanie, jt. auth. see Allgood, Dave.

Allgower, M. & Arder, F., eds. State of the Art of Surgery, Nineteen Seventy-Nine to Nineteen Eighty. 116p. 1980. pap. 7.10 (ISBN 0-387-10136-5). Springer-Verlag.

Allgower, M., et al, eds. ASIF - Technique for Internal Fixation of Fractures. 1975. ring binder 187.00 (ISBN 0-387-92105-2). Springer-Verlag.

Allhands, James L. Looking Back Over Ninety-Eight Years: Autobiography of James L. Allhands. 1978. 25.00x (ISBN 0-932612-07-5). Pepperdine U Pr.

Alliance Against Sexual Coersion. Fighting Sexual Harassment: An Advocacy Handbook. rev. ed. 96p. (Orig.). 1981. pap. 3.95 (ISBN 0-932870-14-7). Alyson Pubns.

Alliance of Guardian Angels, Inc., jt. auth. see Sliwa, Curtis.

Allianz Versicherungs-AG & Muenchner Rueckversicherungs-Gesellschaft, eds. Handbook of Loss Prevention. Cahn-Speyer, P., tr. from Ger. 1978. 46.70 (ISBN 0-387-07822-3). Springer-Verlag.

Alliband, Terry. Catalysts of Development: Voluntary Agencies in India. LC 82-83115. (Library of Management for Development Ser.). xii, 114p. (Orig.). 1983. pap. text ed. 12.50x (ISBN 0-931816-27-0). Kumarian Pr.

Allibert, M. Life of St. Benedict. facsimile ed. LC 70-168505. (Black Heritage Library Collection). Repr. of 1835 ed. 17.25 (ISBN 0-8369-8859-0). Ayer Co Pubs.

Allibone, S. Austin. Critical Dictionary of English Literature & British & American Authors, 3 Vols. LC 67-295. 1965. Repr. of 1872 ed. Set. 195.00x (ISBN 0-8103-3017-2). Gale.

Allibone, Samuel. Critical Dictionary of English Literature & British & American Authors, 3 vols. 300.00 (ISBN 0-87968-965-X). Gordon Pr.
--Poetical Quotations from Chaucer to Tennyson. 59.95 (ISBN 0-8490-0855-7). Gordon Pr.
--Prose Quotations from Socrates to Macaulay. 59.95 (ISBN 0-8490-0902-2). Gordon Pr.
Allibone, Samuel A. Prose Quotations from Socrates to Macauley. LC 68-30642. 764p. 1973. Repr. of 1876 ed. 37.00x (ISBN 0-8103-3181-0). Gale.
Allibone, T. E. The Royal Society & Its Dining Clubs. LC 75-35793. 1976. text ed. 62.00 (ISBN 0-08-020493-7). Pergamon.
Allibone, T. E., jt. auth. see Hartcup, G.
Allibrant, Ronald. The Psychological Foundation of Economics. (Illus.). 127p. 1983. 79.85x (ISBN 0-86654-087-3). Inst Econ Finan.
Allied Chemical Corporation, jt. auth. see Mastroianni, M. J.
Allies, Jabez. On the Ancient British, Roman & Saxon Antiquities & Folk-Lore of Worcestershire. 2nd ed. Dorson, Richard M., ed. LC 77-70577. (International Folklore Ser.). (Illus.). 1977. Repr. of 1852 ed. lib. bdg. 38.50x (ISBN 0-405-10078-7). Ayer Co Pubs.
Allies, Mary H. Three Catholic Reformers of the Fifteenth Century. facsimile ed. LC 73-38755. (Essay Index Reprint Ser). Repr. of 1878 ed. 13.00 (ISBN 0-8369-2633-1). Ayer Co Pubs.
Allies, Mary H., tr. see Joannes, Damascenus.
Alliger, G. & Sjothun, I. J., eds. Vulcanization of Elastomers: Principles & Practice of Vulcanization of Commercial Rubbers. LC 78-8167. 1978. Repr. of 1964 ed. lib. bdg. 24.50 (ISBN 0-88275-686-9). Krieger.
Allihn, Wolf-Eberhard. Schueler-Erwartungen an den Paedagogik-Unterricht am Gymnasium, Vol. 9. (Studien zur Pedagogik der Schule). 227p. (Ger.). 1983. 25.25 (ISBN 3-8204-7769-1). P Lang Pubs.
Allilueva, Svetlana. The Faraway Music. 1985. 20.00x (ISBN 0-8364-1359-8, Pub. by Lancer India). South Asia Bks.
Alliluyeva, Svetlana. Twenty Letters to a Friend. McMillan, Priscilla J., tr. 1967. 11.49i (ISBN 0-06-010099-0, HarpT). Har-Row.
Allin, Alfred, tr. see Keysser, Christian.
Allin, Craig W. The Politics of Wilderness Preservation. LC 81-6234. (Contributions in Political Science Ser.: No. 64). 344p. 1982. lib. bdg. 29.95 (ISBN 0-313-21458-1, ALP/). Greenwood.
Allin, John. Circus Life. (Illus.). 48p. (ps-5). 1983. 9.95 (ISBN 0-7207-1344-7, Pub. by Michael Joseph). Merrimack Pub Cir.
Allin, John, jt. auth. see Wesker, Arnold.
Allin, Lawrence C. The United States Naval Institute, Intellectual Forum of the New Navy: 1873-1889. new ed. 381p. (Orig.). 1978. pap. 38.00x (ISBN 0-89126-066-8). MA-AH Pub.
Allin, Richard. The Southern Legislative Dictionary. 36p. 1983. pap. 3.95 (ISBN 0-914546-50-3). Rose Pub.
Allin, Richard & Fisher, Goerge. The Second Southern Legislative Dictionary. (Illus.). 36p. 1984. pap. 3.95 (ISBN 0-914546-56-2). Rose Pub.
Alling, N. L. Real Elliptic Curves. (North-Holland Mathematics Studies: Vol. 54). 350p. 1981. 47.00 (ISBN 0-444-86233-1, North-Holland). Elsevier.
Alling, N. L. & Greenleaf, N. Foundation of the Theory of Klein Surfaces. LC 73-172693. (Lecture Notes in Mathematics: Vol. 219). ix, 117p. 1971. pap. 11.00 (ISBN 0-387-05577-0). Springer-Verlag.
Allinger, N. L., jt. ed. see Eliel, E. L.
Allinger, N. L., et al. Topics in Stereochemistry, Vol. 14. 315p. 1983. 108.00 (ISBN 0-471-89858-9, Pub. by Wiley-Interscience). Wiley.
Allinger, Norman, et al. Topics in Stereochemistry, Vol. 13. LC 61-13943. 489p. 1982. 100.00 (ISBN 0-471-05680-4, Pub. by Wiley-Interscience). Wiley.
Allinger, Norman L., jt. ed. see Burkert, Ulrich.
Allinger, Norman L., jt. ed. see Eliel, Ernest L.
Allinger, Norman L., et al. Organic Chemistry. 2nd ed. LC 75-18431. 1976. 38.95x (ISBN 0-87901-050-9). Worth.
Allingham, Helen & Williams, E. Baumer, eds. Letters to William Allingham. LC 70-148739. Repr. of 1911 ed. 24.50 (ISBN 0-404-00343-5). AMS Pr.
Allingham, Margery. The Allingham Case Book. 13.95 (ISBN 0-89190-915-X, Pub. by Am Repr). Amereon Ltd.
--The Black Dudley Murder. 176p. Repr. of 1929 ed. lib. bdg. 12.95x (ISBN 0-89190-188-4, Pub. by River City Pr). Amereon Ltd.
--The Black Dudley Murder. 1976. pap. 1.25 (ISBN 0-532-12386-7). Woodhill.
--Black Plumes. 1976. Repr. of 1940 ed. lib. bdg. 15.95 (ISBN 0-89190-191-4, Pub. by River City Pr). Amereon Ltd.
--Cargo of Eagles. 14.95 (ISBN 0-317-27919-X, Pub. by Aeonian Pr). Amereon Ltd.
--Case of the Late Pig. 1980. cancelled (ISBN 0-434-01886-4, Pub. by W Heinemann Ltd). David & Charles.
--The China Governess. 1976. Repr. of 1964 ed. lib. bdg. 14.95 (ISBN 0-89190-192-2, Pub. by River City Pr). Amereon Ltd.
--The China Governess. 1978. pap. 1.50 (ISBN 0-532-15314-6). Woodhill.
--Coronor's Pidgin. 14.95 (ISBN 0-89190-177-9, Pub. by Am Repr). Amereon ltd.
--Crime at Black Dudley. 1980. cancelled (ISBN 0-434-01872-4, Pub. by W Heinemann Ltd). David & Charles.
--Dancers in Mourning. 284p. Repr. of 1937 ed. lib. bdg. 16.95x (ISBN 0-89190-189-2, Pub. by River City Pr). Amereon Ltd.
--Dancers in Mourning. 256p. 1984. pap. text ed. 2.95 (ISBN 0-553-24852-9). Bantam.
--Deadly Duo. 1976. Repr. of 1949 ed. lib. bdg. 12.95 (ISBN 0-89190-193-0, Pub. by River City Pr). Amereon Ltd.
--Death of a Ghost. 1976. Repr. of 1934 ed. lib. bdg. 12.95 (ISBN 0-89190-195-7, Pub. by River City Pr). Amereon Ltd.
--The Fashion in Shrouds. 1976. Repr. of 1938 ed. lib. bdg. 17.95x (ISBN 0-89190-194-9, Pub. by River City Pr). Amereon Ltd.
--Fashion in Shrouds. 1976. pap. 1.50 (ISBN 0-532-15196-8). Woodhill.
--Fashion in Shrouds. 1979. 16.95 (ISBN 0-434-01875-9, Pub. by W Heinemann Ltd). David & Charles.
--The Fear Sign. 192p. Repr. of 1933 ed. lib. bdg. 13.95x (ISBN 0-89190-190-6, Pub. by River City Pr). Amereon Ltd.
--The Fear Sign. 1976. pap. 1.50 (ISBN 0-532-12419-7). Woodhill.
--Flowers for the Judge. 1980. cancelled (ISBN 0-434-01876-7, Pub by W Heinemann). David & Charles.
--Flowers for the Judge. 256p. pap. text ed. 2.95 (ISBN 0-553-24190-7). Bantam.
--Look to the Lady. 1980. 16.95 (ISBN 0-434-01878-3, Pub. by W Heinemann Ltd). David & Charles.
--The Margery Allingham Omnibus. Incl. Mystery Mile; The Crime at Black Dudley; Look to the Lady. 592p. 1983. pap. 7.95 (ISBN 0-14-006058-8). Penguin.
--The Mind Reader. 16.95 (ISBN 0-89190-179-5, Pub. by Am Repr). Amereon Ltd.
--Mr. Campion & Others. 1980. cancelled (ISBN 0-434-01879-1, Pub by W Heinemann Ltd). David & Charles.
--More Work for the Undertaker. (Orig.). 1952. pap. 3.50 (ISBN 0-14-000864-0). Penguin.
--More Work for the Undertaker. 1980. cancelled (ISBN 0-434-01878-3, Pub by W Heinemann Ltd). David & Charles.
--More Work for the Undertaker. 15.95 (ISBN 0-89190-180-9, Pub. by Am Repr). Amereon Ltd.
--Mystery Mile. 18.95 (ISBN 0-89190-178-7, Pub. by Am Repr). Amereon Ltd.
--No Love Lost. 1980. cancelled (ISBN 0-434-01881-3, Pub. by W Heinemann Ltd). David & Charles.
--The Patient at Peacock's Hall. 10.95 (ISBN 0-89190-165-5, Pub. by Am Repr). Amereon Ltd.
--Pearls Before Swine. 192p. Repr. of 1945 ed. lib. bdg. 13.95x (ISBN 0-89190-196-5, Pub. by River City Pr). Amereon Ltd.
--Police at the Funeral. 1976. pap. 1.50 (ISBN 0-532-15219-0). Woodhill.
--Safer Than Love. 10.95 (ISBN 0-89190-166-3, Pub. by Am Repr). Amereon Ltd.
--Sweet Danger. 1950. pap. 3.50 (ISBN 0-14-000769-5). Penguin.
--Sweet Danger. 1980. cancelled (ISBN 0-434-01883-X, Pub. by W Heinemann Ltd). David & Charles.
--Tether's End. 176p. Repr. of 1958 ed. lib. bdg. 12.95x (ISBN 0-89190-197-3, Pub. by River City Pr). Amereon Ltd.
--The Tiger in the Smoke. 223p. Repr. of 1952 ed. lib. bdg. 14.95x (ISBN 0-89190-198-1, Pub. by River City Pr). Amereon Ltd.
--The Tiger in the Smoke. 240p. 1985. pap. 2.95 (ISBN 0-553-24814-6). Bantam.
--Traitor's Purse. 176p. Repr. of 1941 ed. lib. bdg. 12.95 (ISBN 0-89190-199-X, Pub. by River City Pr). Amereon Ltd.
Allingham, Michael. Value. LC 82-6018. 105p. 1983. 22.50x (ISBN 0-312-83611-2). St Martin.
Allingham, W. Ballad Book. facs. ed. LC 76-76931. (Granger Index Reprint Ser.). 1864. 19.00 (ISBN 0-8369-6000-9). Ayer Co Pubs.
--Ballad Book. 1864. Repr. 10.75 (ISBN 0-8274-3811-7). R West.
Allingham, William. A Diary: Lives & Letters. Norwich, John J., intro. by. 416p. 1985. pap. 5.95 (ISBN 0-317-19386-4). Penguin.
--Fifty Modern Poems. LC 74-148740. Repr. of 1865 ed. 16.50 (ISBN 0-404-00344-3). AMS Pr.
--Laurence Bloomfield in Ireland: A Modern Poem. LC 71-148742. Repr. of 1864 ed. 22.00 (ISBN 0-404-00346-X). AMS Pr.
--Poems. LC 78-148741. Repr. of 1850 ed. 11.00 (ISBN 0-404-00345-1). AMS Pr.
--Robin Redbreast, & Other Verses. LC 78-74507. (Children's Literature Reprint Ser.). (Illus.). (gr. 2-4). 1979. Repr. of 1930 ed. 17.50x (ISBN 0-8486-0007-X). Core Collection.
--Sixteen Poems. Yeats, W. B., ed. 48p. 1971. Repr. of 1905 ed. 12.50x (ISBN 0-7165-1333-1, BBA 02045, Pub. by Cuala Press Ireland). Biblio Dist.
--Songs, Ballads, & Stories. LC 75-148743. Repr. of 1877 ed. 24.00 (ISBN 0-404-00347-8). AMS Pr.
Allington, Richard. Smelling. LC 79-27147. (Beginning to Learn about Ser.). (Illus.). 32p. (ps-2). 1985. pap. 9.27 (ISBN 0-8172-2488-2). Raintree Pubs.
--Spring. Krull, Kathleen. LC 80-25093. (Beginning to Learn about Ser.). (Illus.). 32p. (ps-2). 1985. pap. 9.75g (ISBN 0-8172-2489-0). Raintree Pubs.
Allington, Richard L. Autumn. Krull, Kathleen. LC 80-25190. (Beginning to Learn about Ser.). (Illus.). 32p. (ps-2). 1985. pap. 9.27 (ISBN 0-8172-2476-9). Raintree Pubs.
--Colors. LC 79-19116. (Beginning to Learn About Ser.). (Illus.). (gr. k-2). 1979. PLB 14.25 (ISBN 0-8172-1280-9). Raintree Pubs.
--Colors. LC 79-19116. (Beginning to Learn about Ser.). (Illus.). 32p. (gr. k-2). 1985. pap. 9.27 (ISBN 0-8172-2477-7). Raintree Pubs.
--Feelings. LC 79-27549. (Beginning to Learn about Ser.). (Illus.). 32p. (ps-2). 1985. pap. 9.27 (ISBN 0-8172-2478-5). Raintree Pubs.
--Hearing. LC 79-28387. (Beginning to Learn about Ser.). (Illus.). 32p. (ps-2). 1985. pap. 9.27 (ISBN 0-8172-2479-3). Raintree Pubs.
--Letters. LC 82-9785. (Beginning to Learn About). (Illus.). 32p. (gr. 1-2). 1983. PLB 14.25 (ISBN 0-8172-1384-8). Raintree Pubs.
--Looking. LC 79-27083. (Beginning to Learn about Ser.). (Illus.). 32p. (ps-2). 1985. pap. 9.27 (ISBN 0-8172-2481-5). Raintree Pubs.
--Numbers. LC 79-19200. (Beginning to Learn about Ser.). (Illus.). 32p. (gr. k-2). 1985. pap. 9.27 (ISBN 0-8172-1278-7). Raintree Pubs.
--Opposites. LC 79-20525. (Beginning to Learn About Ser.). (Illus.). (gr. k-2). 1979. PLB 14.25 (ISBN 0-8172-1279-5). Raintree Pubs.
--Opposites. LC 79-20525. (Beginning to Learn about Ser.). (Illus.). 32p. (gr. k-2). 1985. pap. 9.27 (ISBN 0-8172-2484-X). Raintree Pubs.
--Shapes. LC 79-19852. (Beginning to Learn About Ser.). (Illus.). (gr. k-2). 1979. PLB 14.25 (ISBN 0-8172-1277-9). Raintree Pubs.
--Shapes. LC 79-19852. (Beginning to Learn about Ser.). (Illus.). 32p. (gr. k-2). 1985. pap. 9.27 (ISBN 0-8172-2487-4). Raintree Pubs.
--Stories. Krull, Kathleen. LC 82-10208. (Beginning to Learn about Ser.). (Illus.). 32p. (gr. 1-2). 1985. pap. 9.27 (ISBN 0-8172-2490-4). Raintree Pubs.
--Summer. Krull, Kathleen. LC 80-25097. (Beginning to Learn about Ser.). (Illus.). 32p. (ps-2). 1985. pap. 9.27 (ISBN 0-8172-2491-2). Raintree Pubs.
--Talking. Krull, Kathleen. LC 80-17021. (Beginning to Learn about Ser.). (Illus.). 32p. (ps-2). 1985. pap. 9.27 (ISBN 0-8172-2492-0). Raintree Pubs.
--Tasting. LC 79-29662. (Beginninng to Learn about Ser.). (Illus.). 32p. (ps-2). 1985. pap. 9.27 (ISBN 0-8172-2493-9). Raintree Pubs.
--Thinking. Krull, Kathleen. LC 80-15390. (Beginning to Learn about Ser.). (Illus.). 32p. (ps-2). 1985. pap. 9.97g (ISBN 0-8172-2494-7). Raintree Pubs.
--Time. Krull, Kathleen. LC 82-10170. (Beginning to Learn about Ser.). (Illus.). 32p. (gr. 1-2). 1985. pap. 9.27 (ISBN 0-8172-2495-5). Raintree Pubs.
--Touching. LC 79-28398. (Beginning to Learn about Ser.). (Illus.). 32p. (ps-2). 1985. pap. 9.27 (ISBN 0-8172-2496-3). Raintree pubs.
--Winter. Krull, Kathleen. LC 80-25115. (Beginning to Learn about Ser.). (Illus.). 32p. (ps-2). 1985. pap. 9.27 (ISBN 0-8172-2497-1). Raintree Pubs.
--Words. Krull, Kathleen. LC 82-9787. (Beginning to Learn about Ser.). (Illus.). 32p. (gr. 1-2). 1985. pap. 9.27 (ISBN 0-8172-2498-X). Raintree Pubs.
--Writing. Krull, Kathleen. LC 80-15334. (Beginning to Learn about Ser.). (Illus.). 32p. (ps-2). 1985. pap. 9.27 (ISBN 0-8172-2499-8). Raintree Pubs.
Allington, Richard L. & Krull, Kathleen. Autumn. LC 80-25190. (Beginning to Learn About Ser.). (Illus.). 32p. (ps-2). 1981. PLB 14.25 (ISBN 0-8172-1343-0). Raintree Pubs.
--Feelings. LC 79-27549. (Beginning to Learn About). (Illus.). 32p. (ps-2). 1980. PLB 14.25 (ISBN 0-8172-1295-7). Raintree Pubs.
--Hearing. LC 79-28387. (Beginning to Learn About). (Illus.). 32p. (ps-2). 1980. PLB 14.25 (ISBN 0-8172-1291-4). Raintree Pubs.
--Letters. LC 82-9785. (Beginning to Learn about Ser.). (Illus.). 32p. (gr. 1-2). 1985. pap. 9.27 (ISBN 0-8172-2480-7). Raintree Pubs.
--Looking. LC 79-27083. (Beginning to Learn about). (Illus.). 32p. (ps-2). 1980. PLB 14.25 (ISBN 0-8172-1290-6). Raintree Pubs.
--Measuring. LC 82-9840. (Beginning to Learn About Ser.). (Illus.). 32p. (gr. 1-2). 1983. PLB 14.25 (ISBN 0-8172-1389-9). Raintree Pubs.
--Measuring. LC 82-9840. (Beginning to Learn about Ser.). (Illus.). 32p. (gr. 1-2). 1985. pap. 9.27 (ISBN 0-8172-1389-9). Raintree Pubs.
--Reading. LC 80-16547. (Beginning to Learn About). (Illus.). 32p. (ps-2). 1980. PLB 14.25 (ISBN 0-8172-1322-8). Raintree Pubs.
--Reading. LC 80-16547. (Beginning to Learn about Ser.). (Illus.). 32p. (gr. k-2). 1985. pap. 9.27 (ISBN 0-8172-2485-8). Raintree Pubs.
--Science. LC 82-101711. (Beginning to Learn about). (Illus.). 32p. (gr. 1-2). 1983. PLB 14.25 (ISBN 0-8172-1387-2). Raintree Pubs.
--Science. LC 82-10171. (Beginning to Learn about Ser.). (Illus.). 32p. (gr. 1-2). 1985. pap. 9.27 (ISBN 0-8172-2486-6). Raintree Pubs.
--Smelling. LC 79-27147. (Beginning to Learn About). (Illus.). 32p. (ps-2). 1980. PLB 14.25 (ISBN 0-8172-1293-0). Raintree Pubs.
--Spring. LC 80-25093. (Beginning to Learn About Ser.). (Illus.). 32p. (ps-2). 1981. PLB 14.25 (ISBN 0-8172-1342-2). Raintree Pubs.
--Stories. LC 82-10208. (Beginning to Learn About). (Illus.). 32p. (gr. 1-2). 1983. PLB 14.25 (ISBN 0-8172-1386-4). Raintree Pubs.
--Summer. LC 80-25097. (Beginning to Learn About). (Illus.). 32p. (gr. k-2). 1981. PLB 14.25 (ISBN 0-8172-1341-4). Raintree Pubs.
--Talking. LC 80-17021. (Beginning to Learn About). (Illus.). 32p. (ps-2). 1980. PLB 14.25 (ISBN 0-8172-1320-1). Raintree Pubs.
--Tasting. LC 79-29662. (Beginning to Learn About). (Illus.). 32p. (ps-2). 1980. PLB 14.25 (ISBN 0-8172-1292-2). Raintree Pubs.
--Thinking. LC 80-15390. (Beginning to Learn About). (Illus.). 32p. (ps-2). 1980. PLB 14.25 (ISBN 0-8172-1319-8). Raintree Pubs.
--Time. (Beginning to Learn about). (Illus.). 32p. (gr. 1-2). 1983. PLB 14.25 (ISBN 0-8172-1388-0). Raintree Pubs.
--Touching. LC 79-28393. (Beginning to Learn About). (Illus.). 32p. (ps-2). 1980. PLB 14.25 (ISBN 0-8172-1294-9). Raintree Pubs.
--Winter. LC 80-25115. (Beginning to Learn About Ser.). (Illus.). 32p. (ps-2). 1981. PLB 14.25 (ISBN 0-8172-1340-6). Raintree Pubs.
--Words. LC 82-9787. (Beginning to Learn About Ser.). (Illus.). 32p. (gr. 1-2). 1983. PLB 14.25 (ISBN 0-8172-1385-6). Raintree Pubs.
--Writing. LC 80-15334. (Beginning to Learn About). (Illus.). 32p. (ps-2). 1980. PLB 14.25 (ISBN 0-8172-1321-X). Raintree Pubs.
Allington, Richard L. & Strange, Michael. Learning Through Reading in the Content Areas. 1980. pap. text ed. 9.95 (ISBN 0-669-01375-7). Heath.
Allinson, A., jt. auth. see De Beaumont, E.
Allinson, A. R., ed. War Diary of the Emperor Frederick the Third, 1870-1871. LC 77-114529. (Illus.). 1971. Repr. of 1926 ed. lib. bdg. 22.75x (ISBN 0-8371-4824-3, FRWD). Greenwood.
Allinson, Alfred, tr. see France, Anatole.
Allinson, Alfred, tr. see Maeterlinck, M.
Allinson, Anne C. Children of the Way. facsimile ed. LC 74-103490. (Short Story Index Reprint Ser.). 1923. 17.00 (ISBN 0-8369-3232-3). Ayer Co Pubs.
--Selected Essays. facs. ed. LC 68-55836. (Essay Index Reprint Ser). 1933. 18.00 (ISBN 0-8369-0146-0). Ayer Co Pubs.
Allinson, Anne C., jt. auth. see Allinson, Francis G.
Allinson, Beverley. Mitzi's Magic Garden. LC 77-155567. (Venture Ser.). (Illus.). (gr. 1). 1971. PLB 7.47 (ISBN 0-8116-6702-2). Garrard.
Allinson, Christopher. Bureaucratic Personality & Organization Structure. LC 84-18680. 168p. 1984. text ed. 34.50 (ISBN 0-566-00712-6). Gower Pub Co.
Allinson, E. P. & Penrose, Boies. The City Government of Philadelphia. pap. 9.00 (ISBN 0-384-00873-9). Johnson Repr.
Allinson, Edward P. Philadelphia, Sixteen Eighty-One to Eighteen Eighty-Seven: A History of Municipal Development. LC 78-64246. (Johns Hopkins University. Studies in the Social Sciences. Extra Volumes: 2). Repr. of 1887 ed. 30.50 (ISBN 0-404-61351-9). AMS Pr.
Allinson, Edward P. & Penrose, Boies. The City Government of Philadelphia. LC 78-63768. (Johns Hopkins University. Studies in the Social Sciences. Fifth Ser. 1887: 1-2). Repr. of 1887 ed. 11.50 (ISBN 0-404-61035-8). AMS Pr.
Allinson, Elaine S. Daniel's Question: A Cesarean Birth Story. (Illus.). 13p. (ps-5). 1981. staple bdg. 2.95 (ISBN 0-9606960-0-8). Willow Tree NY.
Allinson, Francis G. Lucian, Satirist & Artist. LC 63-10286. (Our Debt to Greece & Rome Ser). Repr. of 1930 ed. 15.00 (ISBN 0-8154-0010-1). Cooper Sq.
Allinson, Francis G. & Allinson, Anne C. Greek Lands & Letters. 1909. 30.00 (ISBN 0-8274-3928-8). R West.
Allinson, Frank G., tr. see Menander of Athens.
Allinson, Gary D. Japanese Urbanism: Industry & Politics in Kariya, 1872-1972. LC 74-84141. (Center for Japanese & Korean Studies, U. C. Berkeley). 296p. 1975. 42.50x (ISBN 0-520-02842-2). U of Cal Pr.
--Suburban Tokyo: A Comparative Study in Politics & Social Change. LC 78-62852. (Center for Japanese & Korean Studies, U. C. Berkeley). 1979. 38.50x (ISBN 0-520-03768-5). U of Cal Pr.
Allinson, Richard, ed. Status Offenders & the Juvenile Justice System: An Anthology. 216p. 1978. 6.00 (ISBN 0-318-15375-0); bulk rates avail. Natl Coun Crime.
Allinson, Russel R. Drug Abuse: Why It Happens & How to Prevent It. LC 84-7369. 130p. (Orig.). 1984. pap. 9.95 (ISBN 0-9612990-1-0). Valley Publishing.
Allinson, T. R. Hygienic Medicine: A Rational Way to Treat Disease. 1974. lib. bdg. 69.95 (ISBN 0-87700-279-7). Revisionist Pr.
Allio, Robert J. & Pennington, Malcom W., eds. Corporate Planning: Techniques & Applications. LC 78-25803. pap. 111.50 (ISBN 0-317-27068-0, 2023537). Bks Demand UMI.
Allione, Tsultrim. Women of Wisdom. (Illus.). 224p. (Orig.). 1985. pap. 12.95 (ISBN 0-7102-0240-7). Routledge & Kegan.
Alliot, Maurice. Le Culte d'Horus a Edfou: Au Temps des Ptolemees, 2 Vols, Pt. 2. 1979. 80.00x (ISBN 0-86685-335-9). Intl Bk Ctr.
Allioux, Alain, jt. auth. see Giono, Jean.

Allis, Frederick S., Jr., ed. see Colonial Society of Massachusetts.

Allis, Jeannette B. West Indian Literature: An Index to Criticism, 1930-1975. (Reference Bks.). 1981. lib. bdg. 35.50 (ISBN 0-8161-8266-3, Hall Reference). G K Hall.

Allis, Oswald T. Bible Numerics. 1949. pap. 0.50 (ISBN 0-87552-100-2). Presby & Reformed.

--The Five Books of Moses. 1977. pap. 5.95 (ISBN 0-8010-0108-0). Baker Bk.

--Five Books of Moses. 1949. pap. 5.95 (ISBN 0-87552-102-9). Presby & Reformed.

--God Spake by Moses. 1951. pap. 3.95 (ISBN 0-87552-103-7). Presby & Reformed.

--God Spake by Moses: An Exposition of the Pentateuch. 1951. pap. 3.95 (ISBN 0-8010-0109-9). Baker Bk.

--Prophecy & the Church. 1977. pap. 5.95 (ISBN 0-8010-0110-2). Baker Bk.

--Prophecy & the Church. 1945. pap. 5.95 (ISBN 0-87552-104-5). Presby & Reformed.

--Unity of Isaiah. 1952. pap. 4.50 (ISBN 0-87552-105-3). Presby & Reformed.

--The Unity of Isaiah: A Study in Prophecy. 1974. pap. 4.50 (ISBN 0-8010-0111-0). Baker Bk.

Allis, Samuel, jt. auth. see Dunbar, John.

Allision, Dean & Henderson, Bruce. Empire of Deceit. LC 84-18731. 384p. 1985. 17.95 (ISBN 0-385-18933-8). Doubleday.

Allison, A. C. Lysosomes. rev. ed. Head, J. J., ed. LC 76-29372. (Carolina Biology Readers Ser.). (Illus.). 16p. (gr. 11 up). 1977. pap. 1.60 (ISBN 0-89278-258-7, 45-9658). Carolina Biological.

Allison, A. C., jt. auth. see Gregoriadis, G.

Allison, A. C., ed. Structure & Function of Plasma Proteins, Vol. 1. LC 72-77046. 325p. 1974. 35.00x (ISBN 0-306-35081-5, Plenum Pr). Plenum Pub.

--Structure & Function of Plasma Proteins, Vol. 2. LC 74-95071. 436p. 1976. 49.50x (ISBN 0-306-35082-3, Plenum Pr). Plenum Pub.

Allison, A. F. & Goldsmith, V. F. Titles of English Books (& of Foreign Books Printed in England) An Alphabetical Finding List by Title of Books Published Under the Author's Name, Pseudonym, or Initials Volume One: 1475-1640. 176p. 1976. 26.00 (ISBN 0-208-01619-8, Archon). Shoe String.

--Titles of English Books (& of Foreign Books Printed in England) An Alphabetical Finding-List by Title of Books Published Under the Author's Name, Pseudonym, or, Initials, Volume Two, 1641-1700. 318p. 1977. 37.50 (ISBN 0-208-01625-2, Archon). Shoe String.

Allison, Alexander W. The Norton Anthology of Poetry. 3rd ed. Barrows, Herbert, et al, eds. 1983. Regular Ed. pap. 17.95 (ISBN 0-393-95242-8); Shorter Ed. 13.95x (ISBN 0-393-95224-X); reference guide avail. (ISBN 0-393-95247-9). Norton.

Allison, Alexander W., et al. Masterpieces of the Drama. 4th ed. 1978. pap. text ed. write for info. (ISBN 0-02-301910-7). Macmillan.

--Masterpieces of the Drama. 5th ed. 1185p. 1986. pap. text ed. price not set (ISBN 0-02-301970-0). Macmillan.

Allison, Alida. The Children's Manners Book. (Illus.). 32p. (Orig.). 1981. pap. 3.95 (ISBN 0-8431-0437-6). Price Stern.

--The Sweet Dreams Book. 32p. 1984. pap. 3.95 (ISBN 0-8431-1037-6). Price Stern.

--The Toddler's Potty Book. 32p. (ps). 1985. softcover 3.95 (ISBN 0-8431-0673-5). Price Stern.

Allison, Andrew. Managing the Microminicomputer Explosion: A Guide for Manufacturers, Users & Third Party Participants. (Illus.). 250p. (Orig.). 1983. pap. 985.00 (ISBN 0-914405-00-4). Electronic Trend.

Allison, Andrew M., et al. The Real Thomas Jefferson. 2nd ed. (American Classic Ser.). (Illus.). 709p. 15.95 (ISBN 0-88080-005-4); pap. 11.95 (ISBN 0-88080-006-2). Natl Ctr Constitutional.

--The Real Benjamin Franklin. (American Classic Ser.). (Illus.). xx, 504p. (Orig.). 1982. 14.95 (ISBN 0-88080-000-3); pap. 9.95 (ISBN 0-88080-001-1). Natl Ctr Constitutional.

Allison, Anne M. & Allan, Ann G., eds. OCLC: A National Library Network. LC 78-11948. (Illus.). 248p. 1979. pap. text ed. 18.95x (ISBN 0-89490-019-6). Enslow Pubs.

Allison, C. FitzSimons. Fear, Love, & Worship. pap. 4.95 (ISBN 0-8164-2020-3, SP17, Pub. by Seabury). Winston Pr.

--Guilt, Anger, & God. 1972. pap. 5.95 (ISBN 0-8164-2091-2, Pub. by Seabury). Winston Pr.

--The Rise of Moralism. LC 84-61194. 262p. (Orig.). pap. 8.95 (ISBN 0-8192-1353-5). Morehouse.

Allison, Charles E. History of Yonkers. LC 84-12826. (Illus.). 464p. 1984. 45.00 (ISBN 0-916346-51-X). Harbor Hill Bks.

Allison, Dale C., Jr. The End of the Ages Has Come: An Early Interpretation of the Passion & Resurrection of Jesus. LC 85-47732. 208p. 1985. 19.95 (ISBN 0-8006-0753-8, 1-753). Fortress.

Allison, David B., ed. The New Nietzsche: Contemporary Styles of Interpretation. 302p. 1985. pap. text ed. 7.95x (ISBN 0-262-51034-0). MIT Pr.

Allison, David B., tr. see Derrida, Jacques.

Allison, Donald H., jt. auth. see Perrott, Ronald M.

Allison, Dorothy. The Women Who Hate Me. LC 84-121194. 1983. pap. 4.50 (ISBN 0-9602284-2-X). Long Haul.

Allison, Dorothy & Jacobson, Scott. Dorothy Allison: A Psychic Story. (Orig.). 1980. pap. 2.50 (ISBN 0-515-05304-X). Jove Pubns.

Allison, Elizabeth. Dance of Desire. (Rapture Romance Ser.: No. 24). 192p. (Orig.). 1983. pap. 1.95 (ISBN 0-451-12477-4, Sig). NAL.

Allison, Elliot, et al. Monadnock Sightings: Birds of Dublin, N. H. (Including Gerald H. Thayer's List of 1909) LC 79-13478. (Illus., Orig.). 1979. pap. 5.00x (ISBN 0-87233-051-6). Bauhan.

Allison, Ellyn, ed. see Fahy, Everett.

Allison, Eric, jt. auth. see Allison, Mary A.

Allison, F. C., jt. auth. see Klaften, B.

Allison, G. Mini English-Thai-English Dictionary. 460p. (Eng. & Thai.). 1979. pap. 9.95 (ISBN 0-686-92176-3, M-9900). French & Eur.

Allison, Gordon H. Easy Thai: An Introduction to the Thai Language. LC 69-12085. 120p. (Orig.). 1969. pap. 6.25 (ISBN 0-8048-0159-2). C E Tuttle.

Allison, Graham, ed. see Kennedy, Robert F.

Allison, Graham T. Essence of Decision: Explaining the Cuban Missile Crisis. 338p. 1971. pap. 10.95 (ISBN 0-316-03436-3). Little.

--Land Policy in Developing Countries. (Monograph: No. 84-4). (Illus.). 72p. 1984. pap. text ed. 6.00 (ISBN 0-318-04689-X). Lincoln Inst Land.

Allison, Graham T., et al, eds. Hawks, Doves, & Owls: An Agenda for Avoiding Nuclear War. LC 84-29485. 1985. 14.95 (ISBN 0-393-01995-0). Norton.

Allison, Henry E. Kant's Transcendental Idealism: An Interpretation & Defense. LC 83-5756. 400p. 1984. text ed. 33.50x (ISBN 0-300-03002-9). Yale U Pr.

--Lessing & the Enlightenment: His Philosophy of Religion & Its Relation to Eighteenth-Century Thought. LC 66-11080. pap. 57.50 (ISBN 0-317-08206-X, 2010041). Bks Demand UMI.

Allison, Henry E., ed. see Immanuel.

Allison, Ira S. Geology of Pluvial Lake Chewaucan, Lake County, Oregon. LC 81-22415. (Studies in Geology: No. 11). (Illus.). 80p. 1982. pap. 7.95x (ISBN 0-87071-069-9). Oreg St U Pr.

Allison, Ira S. & Palmer, Donald F. Geology: The Science of a Changing Earth. 7th ed. (Illus.). 1980. text ed. 28.95 o. p. (ISBN 0-07-001123-0); pap. text ed. 26.95x (ISBN 0-07-001121-4). McGraw.

Allison, J. B., jt. ed. see Munro, Hamish N.

Allison, J. M., ed. Concerning the Education of a Prince: Correspondence of the Princess of Nassau-Saarbruck 13 June - 15 November 1758. 1941. 39.50x (ISBN 0-686-51358-4). Elliots Bks.

Allison, J. P., ed. Criteria for Quality of Petroleum Products. Institute of Petroleum. 286p. 1973. 39.00 (ISBN 0-85334-469-8, Pub. by Elsevier Applied Sci England). Elsevier.

Allison, James. Behavioral Economics. 240p. 1983. 28.95x (ISBN 0-03-063400-8). Praeger.

Allison, James P., jt. ed. see Tom, Baldwin H.

Allison, Joel, et al. The Interpretation of Psychological Tests. 1968. text ed. 25.31 scp (ISBN 0-06-040229-6, HarpC). Har-Row.

Allison, John G., ed. Pathology & Management of Lymphoma. 264p. 1984. 32.50 (ISBN 0-87993-207-4). Futura Pub.

Allison, John M. Lamoignon de Malesherbes: Defender & Reformer of the French Monarchy, 1721-1794. 1938. 49.50x (ISBN 0-686-83605-7). Elliots Bks.

--Thiers & the French Monarchy. (Illus.). xi, 379p. 1968. Repr. of 1926 ed. 27.00 (ISBN 0-208-00017-8, Archon). Shoe String.

Allison, Joseph D. The Bible Study Resource Guide. rev. ed. 228p. 1984. pap. 6.95 (ISBN 0-8407-5927-4). Nelson.

--Setting Goals That Count. 128p. 1985. pap. 4.95 (ISBN 0-310-60941-0, Pub. by Chosen Bks). Zondervan.

Allison, K. J., ed. A History of the County of York: East Riding, Vol. V. (The Victorian History of the Counties of England Ser.). (Illus.). 208p. 1984. 149.00x (ISBN 0-19-722760-0). Oxford U Pr.

--Victoria History of the Counties of England: York East Riding, Vol. 4. (Illus.). 1979. 110.00x (ISBN 0-19-722752-X). Oxford U Pr.

Allison, Karen. Teaching Children As the Spirit Leads. LC 77-81946. 1978. pap. 4.95 (ISBN 0-88270-192-4, Pub. by Logos). Bridge Pub.

Allison, Karen J. A View from the Islands: The Samal of Tawi-tawi. LC 81-85309. (Museum Ser.). 50p. (Orig.). 1984. pap. 6.90 (ISBN 0-88312-168-9). Summer Inst Ling.

Allison, Lincoln. Environmental Planning: A Political & Philosophical Analysis. 134p. 1975. 9.50x (ISBN 0-87471-692-6). Rowman.

--Right Principles: A Conservative Philosophy of Politics. LC 84-11084. 224p. 1984. 24.95x (ISBN 0-631-13475-1). Basil Blackwell.

Allison, Linda. Blood & Guts. (The Brown Paper School). (Illus.). (gr. 5-12). 1976. 13.45i (ISBN 0-316-03442-8); pap. 7.70i (ISBN 0-316-03443-6). Little.

--The Reasons for Seasons: The Great Cosmic Megagalactic Trip Without Moving from Your Chair. (A Brown Paper School Book). (Illus.). 128p. (gr. 4 up). 1975. 13.45 (ISBN 0-316-03439-8); pap. 7.70i (ISBN 0-316-03440-1). Little.

--Trash Artists Workshop. LC 80-84184. (Craft Workshop Ser.). (gr. 3-8). pap. 7.95 (ISBN 0-8224-9780-8). Pitman Learning.

Allison, Linda & Katz, David. Gee Wiz! How to Mix Art & Science or the Art of Thinking Scientifically. LC 83-9834. (Brown Paper School Bks.). (Illus.). 128p. (gr. 4 up). 1983. PLB 13.45i (ISBN 0-316-03444-4); pap. 7.70i (ISBN 0-316-03445-2). Little.

Allison, Mary A. & Allison, Eric. Managing Up, Managing Down: How to Be a Better Manager & Get What You Want from Your Boss & Staff. 1984. pap. 7.95 (ISBN 0-346-12639-8). Cornerstone.

Allison, Paul D. Processes of Stratification in Science. Zuckerman, Harriet & Merton, Robert K., eds. LC 80-13567. (Dissertations on Sociology Ser.). 1980. lib. bdg. 23.00x (ISBN 0-405-12946-7). Ayer Co Pubs.

Allison, Peter B., ed. Labor, Worklife & Industrial Relations: Sources of Information. LC 84-4539. (Behavioral & Social Sciences Librarian Ser.: Vol. 3, No. 3). 128p. 1984. text ed. 19.95 (ISBN 0-86656-317-2, B317). Haworth Pr.

Allison, Philip. The New Forest. 1981. 45.00x (ISBN 0-686-75453-0, Pub. by Cave Pubns England). State Mutual Bk.

Allison, R. Bruce. Democrats in Exile 1968-1972: Political Confessions of a New England Liberal. LC 74-78096. 160p. 1974. pap. 6.00 (ISBN 0-913370-02-9, Sol Press). Wisconsin Bks.

--Travel Journal-Europe & North Africa. 1979. pap. 5.95 (ISBN 0-913370-03-7, Sol Press). Wisconsin Bks.

Allison, R. Bruce & Durbin, Elizabeth. Wisconsin's Famous & Historic Trees. (Illus.). 120p. pap. 14.95 (ISBN 0-913370-14-2). Wisconsin Bks.

Allison, Ross. I Saw Time. 80p. Date not set. 12.95 (ISBN 0-89016-085-6); pap. 6.95 (ISBN 0-89016-084-8). Lightning Tree.

Allison, Roy. Finland's Relation with the Soviet Union, 1944-1984. LC 84-17694. 272p. 1985. 29.95 (ISBN 0-312-29066-7). St Martin.

Allison, Samuel D. & Johnson, June. VD Manual for Teachers. 7.95 (ISBN 0-87523-077-6). Emerson.

Allison, Sidney. Bantams. (Illus.). 300p. 1983. 19.95 (ISBN 0-88962-191-8, Pub by Mosaic Pr Cananda); pap. 12.95 (ISBN 0-88962-190-X). Flatiron Book Dist.

Allison, Sonia. Bisto Book of Meat Cookery. LC 80-66429. (Illus.). 128p. 1980. 14.95 (ISBN 0-7153-7893-7). David & Charles.

--Book of Microwave Cookery. LC 77-91467. (Illus.). 1978. 12.95 (ISBN 0-7153-7525-3). David & Charles.

--Cooking in Style: Gourmet Recipes Without Meat or Fish. (Illus.). 176p. 1980. 19.95 (ISBN 0-241-10352-5, Pub. by Hamish Hamilton England). David & Charles.

--The English Biscuit & Cookie Book. (Illus.). 80p. 1983. 7.95 (ISBN 0-312-25347-8). St Martin.

--I Can't Cook. (Illus.). 192p. 1984. 16.95 (ISBN 0-241-11124-2, Pub. by Hamish Hamilton England). David & Charles.

--Making Gifts with Food. (Illus.). 64p. 1982. 7.50 (ISBN 0-7153-8264-0). David & Charles.

--A Pleasure to Cook. (Illus.). 256p. 1984. 16.95 (ISBN 0-241-10843-8, Pub. by Hamish Hamilton England). David & Charles.

--Sonia Allison's Home Baking Book. (Illus.). 240p. 1983. 18.95 (ISBN 0-7153-8159-8). David & Charles.

--Sonia Allison's New Complete Microwave Cookery. (Illus.). 256p. 1985. 17.50 (ISBN 0-7182-1560-5, Pub. by Kaye & Ward). David & Charles.

--Spirited Cooking: With Liqueurs, Spirit & Wines. LC 81-68254. (Illus.). 128p. 1982. 18.95 (ISBN 0-7153-8015-X). David & Charles.

Allison, Thomas. English Religious Life in the Eighth Century. LC 75-106708. Repr. of 1929 ed. lib. bdg. 15.00 (ISBN 0-8371-3438-2, ALRL). Greenwood.

--English Religious Life in the Eighth Century As Illustrated by Contemporary Letters. LC 70-136409. Repr. of 1929 ed. 9.00 (ISBN 0-404-00348-6). AMS Pr.

--Pioneers of English Learning. 1978. lib. bdg. 20.00 (ISBN 0-8495-0104-0). Arden Lib.

--Pioneers of English Learning. LC 74-22133. 1974. Repr. of 1932 ed. lib. bdg. 15.00 (ISBN 0-8414-3004-7). Folcroft.

Allison, W. H. Inventory of Unpublished Material for American Religion History in Protestant Church Archives & Other Repositories. (CI.G Ser.). 1910. 21.00 (ISBN 0-527-00683-1). Kraus Repr.

Allison, William H. & Barnes, W. W. Baptist Ecclesiology: An Original Anthology. Gaustad, Edwin S., ed. LC 79-52582. (The Baptist Tradition Ser.). 1980. lib. bdg. 21.00x (ISBN 0-405-12449-X). Ayer Co Pubs.

Allison-Booth, William. Devil's Island: Revelations of the French Penal Settlements in Guiana. LC 71-162504. (Illus.). 1971. Repr. of 1931 ed. 40.00x (ISBN 0-8103-3761-4). Gale.

Alliss, Peter. The Duke. LC 99-943935. 192p. 1984. 14.95 (ISBN 0-450-04924-8, New Eng Lib). David & Charles.

--The Shell Book of Golf. LC 81-65956. (Illus.). 224p. 1981. 24.00 (ISBN 0-7153-7988-7). David & Charles.

Allister, Barbara. Mischievous Matchmaker. 1985. pap. 2.50 (ISBN 0-451-13478-8, Sig). NAL.

--Prudent Partnership. 1984. pap. 2.25 (ISBN 0-451-13054-5, Sig). NAL.

Allister, Ray. Friese-Greene: Close-Up of an Inventor. LC 71-169339. (Arno Press Cinema Program). (Illus.). 212p. 1972. Repr. of 1948 ed. 17.00 (ISBN 0-405-03908-5). Ayer Co Pubs.

Allitt, Patrick. Founders of America. LC 82-61636. (In Profile Ser.). 1983. 12.68 (ISBN 0-382-06641-3). Silver.

Allix, Charles. Carriage Clocks: Their History & Development. (Illus.). 484p. 1974. 59.50 (ISBN 0-902028-25-1). Antique Collect.

--Carriage Clocks, Their History & Development. (Illus.). 1974. 59.50 (ISBN 0-902028-25-1). Apollo.

Allkin, Robert & Bisby, Frank. Databases in Systematics. (Systematics Association Special Ser.: Vol. 26). 1984. 49.50 (ISBN 0-12-053040-6). Acad Pr.

Allman, Audean S, et al. Curriculum Development: A Reflection of Programmatic Trends. (Illus.). 231p. (Orig.). 1980. pap. text ed. 9.95x (ISBN 0-89641-049-8). American Pr.

Allman, C. B. Lewis Wetzel, Indian Fighter. (Illus.). 1961. 9.95 (ISBN 0-8159-6107-3). Devin.

Allman, Eileen J. Player King & Adversary: Two Faces of Play in Shakespeare. LC 79-15365. xii, 324p. 1980. 27.50x (ISBN 0-8071-0592-9). La State U Pr.

Allman, Ethel. Moments. 64p. 1983. 5.95 (ISBN 0-89962-328-X). Todd & Honeywell.

Allman, Fred L., jt. auth. see Ryan, Allan J.

Allman, Fred L., Jr. Care & Conditioning of the Pitching Arm: For Little League Baseball. Darden, Ellington, ed. LC 77-76068. (Physical Fitness & Sports Medicine Ser.). (Illus.). 1977. pap. 3.95 (ISBN 0-89305-008-3). Anna Pub.

Allman, George J. Greek Geometry from Thales to Euclid. facsimile ed. LC 75-13250. (History of Ideas in Ancient Greece Ser.). 1976. Repr. of 1889 ed. 18.00x (ISBN 0-405-07287-2). Ayer Co Pubs.

Allman, Janet, jt. auth. see Tabberer, Ralph.

Allman, John. Clio's Children. LC 84-22659. 96p. 1985. 16.95 (ISBN 0-8112-0935-0); pap. 7.95 (ISBN 0-8112-0936-9, NDP590). New Directions.

--Walking Four Ways in the Wind. LC 79-83974. (Princeton Series of Contemporary Poets). 1979. 12.95x (ISBN 0-691-06402-4); pap. 5.95x (ISBN 0-691-01359-4). Princeton U Pr.

Allman, Lawrence R. & Jaffe, Dennis T., eds. Readings in Adult Psychology: Contemporary Perspectives. 2nd ed. 407p. 1982. pap. text ed. 10.95 scp (ISBN 0-06-040234-2, HarpC). Har-Row.

Allman, Margaret see Chuan, Helen.

Allman, Marie Von see Nemiro, Beverly & Von Allman, Marie.

Allman, Paul. Exploring Careers in Video. (Exploring Careers Ser.). 144p. 1985. lib. bdg. 8.97 (ISBN 0-8239-0623-X). Rosen Group.

Allman, Ruth. Alaska Sourdough: The Real Stuff by a Real Alaskan. LC 76-13604. 1976. pap. 6.95 (ISBN 0-88240-085-1). Alaska Northwest.

--Canaan Valley & the Black Bear. 3rd ed. 1976. 6.00 (ISBN 0-87012-220-7). McClain.

--Fifty Years of Seniors. 1981. 8.00 (ISBN 0-87012-419-6). McClain.

Allman, Ruth C. Roots in Tucker County. 1979. 7.00 (ISBN 0-87012-328-9). McClain.

Allman, S. Audean, et al. Environmental Education: A Promise for the Future. 196p. 1982. pap. text ed. 8.95x (ISBN 0-89641-085-4). American Pr.

Allman, T. D. Unmanifest Destiny. LC 84-4224. 480p. 1984. 19.95 (ISBN 0-385-27464-5, Dial). Doubleday.

Allmand. War, Literature, & Politics in the Late Middle Ages. 216p. 1982. 50.00x (ISBN 0-85323-273-3, Pub. by Liverpool Univ England). State Mutual Bk.

Allmand, C. T. Lancastrian Normandy, 1415-1450: The History of a Medieval Occupation. (Illus.). 1983. 47.50x (ISBN 0-19-822642-X). Oxford U Pr.

Allmand, C. T. & Armstrong, C. A., eds. English Suits Before the Parlement of Paris, 1420-1436, Vol. 26. (Camden Fourth Ser.). 328p. 1982. text ed. 15.00 (ISBN 0-86193-095-9, BAB-04695, Pub. by Boydell & Brewer). Longwood Pub Group.

Allmen, Jean-Jacques Von, ed. Vocabulaire Biblique. 320p. (Fr.). 1964. pap. 24.95 (ISBN 0-686-57248-3, M-6759). French & Eur.

Allmers, Nancy M. & Verderame, Joan A. Surgical Technology Examination Review. LC 81-10925. 176p. 1982. pap. 15.95 (ISBN 0-668-05114-0). ACC.

Allnat, John W. Transmitted-Picture Assessment. LC 82-21895. 303p. 1983. 42.95x (ISBN 0-471-90113-X, Pub. by Wiley-Interscience). Wiley.

Allnutt, Frank. Unlocking the Mystery of the Force. Rev. ed. LC 83-72138. 208p. 1983. pap. 2.95 (ISBN 0-934374-02-3). Allnutt Pub.

Allnutt, Frank, jt. ed. see Galvin, John.

Allocca, John & Stuart, Allen. Electronic Instrumentation. 1983. text ed. 29.95 (ISBN 0-8359-1633-2). Reston.

Allocca, John A., jt. auth. see Levenson, Harold.

Allock, H. R. & Lampe, F. W. Contemporary Polymer Chemistry. 1981. 45.95 (ISBN 0-13-170258-0). P-H.

Allon, Natalie. Urban Life Styles. 250p. 1979. pap. text ed. write for info. (ISBN 0-697-07558-3). Wm C Brown.

Allor, David J. The Planning Commissioners Guide. LC 83-62938. (Illus.). 186p. 1983. 13.95 (ISBN 0-918286-30-1); 10 copies or more 11.95 ea. Planners Pr.

Allot, Robert. England's Parnassus: Or, the Choysest Flowers of Our Moderne Poets. LC 72-167. (English Experience Ser.: No. 216). 510p. Repr. of 1600 ed. 62.00 (ISBN 90-221-0216-5). Walter J Johnson.

--Wits Theatre of the World. LC 70-17131. (English Experience Ser.: No. 359). 560p. Repr. of 1599 ed. 51.00 (ISBN 90-221-0359-5). Walter J Johnson.

Allott, Antony N. Essays in African Law, with Special Reference to the Law of Ghana. LC 74-30925. 323p. 1975. Repr. of 1960 ed. lib. bdg. 19.00x (ISBN 0-8371-7885-1, ALAL). Greenwood.

Allott, Kenneth. The Poems of William Habington. 208p. 1969. 35.00x (ISBN 0-85323-272-5, Pub. by Liverpool Univ England). State Mutual Bk.

Allott, Kenneth & Farris, Miriam. Art of Graham Greene. LC 63-15146. (Illus.). 1963. Repr. of 1951 ed. 15.00x (ISBN 0-8462-0371-5). Russell.

Allott, Kenneth, ed. The Poems of Matthew Arnold. 2nd ed. (Longman Annotated English Poets Ser.). 1979. pap. text ed. 19.95x (ISBN 0-582-48679-3). Longman.

--Writers & Their Background: Matthew Arnold. LC 75-15339. (Writers & Their Background Ser.). xxvi, 353p. 1976. 20.00x (ISBN 0-8214-0197-1, 82-82022); pap. 10.00x (ISBN 0-8214-0198-X, 82-82030). Ohio U Pr.

Allott, Miram, ed. Essays on Shelly: Liverpool Texts & Studies, Vol. 19. 312p. 1982. 60.00x (ISBN 0-85323-294-6, Pub. by Liverpool Univ England). State Mutual Bk.

Allott, Miriam, ed. Essays on Shelley. LC 81-12885. (English Texts & Studies). 304p. 1982. 28.50x (ISBN 0-389-20127-8, 06903). B&N Imports.

--The Poems of John Keats. (Longman Annotated English Poets Ser.). (Illus.). 1971. pap. text ed. 18.95x (ISBN 0-582-48457-X). Longman.

Allott, R. V., jt. auth. see Moore, C. J.

Alloway, B. S. & Mills, G. M., eds. Aspects of Educational Technology: New Directions in Education & Training Technology, Vol. 18. (Aspects of Education Ser.). 250p. 1985. 35.00 (ISBN 0-89397-211-8). Nichols Pub.

Alloway, David N., jt. auth. see Cordasco, Francesco.

Alloway, David N., jt. ed. see Cordasco, Francesco.

Alloway, Lawrence. Network: Art & the Complex Present. Kuspit, Donald, ed. LC 83-24201. (Contemporary American Art Critics Ser.: No. 1). 324p. 1984. 29.95 (ISBN 0-8357-1519-1). UMI Res Pr.

--Realism & Latin American Painting in the 70s. (Illus., Span. & Eng.). 1980. pap. 3.50 (ISBN 0-89192-312-8, Pub. by Ctr Inter-Am Relations). Interbk Inc.

--Roy Lichtenstein. LC 83-2788. (Modern Masters Ser.). (Illus.). 128p. 1983. 29.95 (ISBN 0-89659-330-4); pap. 16.95 (ISBN 0-89659-331-2). Abbeville Pr.

--Topics in American Art Since 1945. (Illus.). 320p. 1975. text ed. 12.95x (ISBN 0-393-04401-7); pap. text ed. 9.95x (ISBN 0-393-09237-2). Norton.

Alloway, Lawrence & Kuspit, Donald B. The Idea of the Post-Modern: Who is Teaching It? 64p. (Orig.). 1981. pap. 3.95 (ISBN 0-686-91785-5). Henry Art.

Alloway, Lawrence, et al. Urban Encounters: Art Architecture Audience. (Illus.). 1980. 15.00 (ISBN 0-88454-055-3). U of Pa Contemp Art.

Alloway, Thomas, ed. Communication & Affect-a Comparative Approach. 1972. 33.00 (ISBN 0-12-053050-3). Acad Pr.

Alloway, Thomas, et al, eds. Attachment Behavior. LC 76-45647. (Illus.). 237p. 1977. 29.50x (ISBN 0-306-35903-0, Plenum Pr). Plenum Pub.

Alloyd Corporation. Coating of Copper Wire for Severe Environment Electrical Insulation. 56p. 1962. 8.40 (ISBN 0-317-34499-4, 19). Intl Copper.

Allphin, Clela. Women in the Plays of Henrik Ibsen. 1974. lib. bdg. 79.95 (ISBN 0-87700-211-8). Revisionist Pr.

Allphin, McKay. Eternal Grit: Up-to-Heaven Insights & Down-to-Earth Wisdom. LC 78-70363. 1978. 7.95 (ISBN 0-88290-102-8). Horizon Utah.

Allport, D. C. Block Copolymers. James, W. H., ed. (Illus.). 620p. 1973. 64.75 (ISBN 0-85334-557-0, Pub. by Elsevier Applied Sci England). Elsevier.

Allport, Floyd H. Institutional Behaviour: Essays. LC 71-90460. Repr. of 1933 ed. lib. bdg. 20.75x (ISBN 0-8371-2145-0, ALIB). Greenwood.

--Social Psychology. (Illus.). 30.00 (ISBN 0-384-00890-9). Johnson Repr.

Allport, G. W., et al, eds. see Conference On Educational Problems Of Special Cultural Groups - Teachers College - Columbia University - 1949.

Allport, Gordon, ed. Letters from Jenny. LC 65-18327. (Illus., Orig.). 1965. pap. 3.95 (ISBN 0-15-650700-5, Harv). HarBraceJ.

Allport, Gordon, ed. see James, William.

Allport, Gordon W. ABC's of Scapegoating. 40p. 2.50 (ISBN 0-88464-028-0). ADL.

--Becoming: Basic Considerations for a Psychology of Personality. (Terry Lectures Ser.). 1955. pap. 4.95x (ISBN 0-300-00002-2, Y20). Yale U Pr.

--Individual & His Religion. 1967. pap. 4.95 (ISBN 0-02-083130-7). Macmillan.

--The Nature of Personality: Selected Papers. LC 74-2795. 220p. 1975. Repr. of 1950 ed. lib. bdg. 24.75x (ISBN 0-8371-7432-5, ALNP). Greenwood.

--The Nature of Prejudice. special ed. 1979. special ed. 7.64 (ISBN 0-201-00178-0); pap. 5.95 (ISBN 0-201-00179-9). Addison-Wesley.

--The Nature of Prejudice. 496p. pap. 5.95 (ISBN 0-686-95007-0). ADL.

--Personality & Social Encounter: Selected Essays. LC 80-39538. x, 388p. 1981. pap. text ed. 17.00x (ISBN 0-226-01494-0). U of Chicago Pr.

--Trait-Names: Psycho-Lexical Study. Bd. with Psychological Studies of Heiman Variability. Miles, Walter R., ed. pap. 29.00 (ISBN 0-317-17949-7). Kraus Repr.

Allport, Gordon W. & Postman, Leo. Psychology of Rumor. LC 65-18784. (Illus.). 1965. Repr. of 1947 ed. 20.00x (ISBN 0-8462-0564-5). Russell.

Allport, Gordon W., jt. auth. see Cantril, Hadley.

Allport, Gordon W., et al. Study of Values. 3rd ed. test booklets 14.64 (ISBN 0-395-08460-1); instrs' manual 2.40 (ISBN 0-395-08466-0). HM.

Allport, J. A. & Stewart, C. M. Economics. 2nd ed. LC 77-28479. 1978. 19.95 (ISBN 0-521-22013-0). Cambridge U Pr.

Allred, G. Hugh. How to Strengthen Your Marriage & Family. LC 76-19047. Orig. Title: On the Level. (Illus.). 424p. 1976. pap. 8.95 (ISBN 0-8425-0960-7). Brigham.

Allred, G. T., jt. auth. see Kuwahara, Y.

Allred, Gordon. Dori the Mallard. (Illus.). (gr. 5 up). 1968. 6.95 (ISBN 0-8392-3052-4). Astor-Honor.

--Hungry Journey. 160p. 1973. pap. 2.50 (ISBN 0-89036-000-6). Hawkes Pub Inc.

--Lonesome Coyote. (gr. 6-11). 1969. 4.25 (ISBN 0-8313-0003-5); PLB 6.19 (ISBN 0-685-13775-9). Lantern.

--Old Crackfoot. (Illus.). (gr. 5 up). 1965. 6.95 (ISBN 0-8392-3051-6). Astor-Honor.

Allred, Gordon T. God the Father. 1979. 7.95 (ISBN 0-87747-746-9). Deseret Bk.

--Starfire. LC 81-67182. 190p. 1981. 6.95 (ISBN 0-87747-871-6). Deseret Bk.

Allred, Hugh & Allred, Steven. How to Make a Good Mission Great. 66p. 1978. pap. 1.25 (ISBN 0-87747-761-2). Deseret Bk.

--How to Make a Good Mission Great. LC 78-7974. 1978. 4.95 (ISBN 0-87747-703-5). Deseret Bk.

Allred, John. The Measurement of Library Services. 1979. 90.00x (ISBN 0-86176-024-7, Pub. by MCB Pubns). State Mutual Bk.

Allred, Mary. Grandmother Poppy & the Children's Tea Party. LC 84-4933. (Illus.). (gr. k-3). 1984. 5.95 (ISBN 0-8054-4292-8, 4242-92). Broadman.

--Grandmother Poppy & the Funny-Looking Bird. LC 81-65832. (gr. k-3). 1981. bds. 5.95 (ISBN 0-8054-4269-3, 4242-69). Broadman.

--The Move to a New House. (Illus.). (gr. k-3). 1979. 4.95 (ISBN 0-8054-4252-9, 4242-52). Broadman.

Allred, Morrell. Beaver Behavior: Architect of Fame & Bane! (Illus.). 80p. 10.95 (ISBN 0-87961-154-5); pap. 4.95 (ISBN 0-87961-155-3). Naturegraph.

Allred, Steven, jt. auth. see Allred, Hugh.

Allred, V. Dean. Oil Shale Processing Technology. LC 81-65818. (Illus.). 240p. 1982. 60.00 (ISBN 0-86563-001-1). Ctr Prof Adv.

Allsburg, Chris Van see Van Allsburg, Chris.

Allsen, Philip E. Conditioning & Physical Fitness: Current Answers to Relevant Questions. 304p. 1978. pap. text ed. write for info. (ISBN 0-697-07148-0). Wm C Brown.

Allsen, Philip E. & Harrison, Joyce M. Philip Allsen's Total Fitness for Life. 1985. pap. 9.95 (ISBN 0-697-00545-3); computerized ed. (Apple II Series & IBM (both on one diskette) 19.95 (ISBN 0-697-00536-4). Wm C Brown.

Allsen, Philip E. & Witbeck, Alan R. Racquetball. 3rd ed. (Physical Education Activities Ser.). 112p. 1980. pap. text ed. write for info. (ISBN 0-697-07172-3). Wm C Brown.

--Racquetball: Trade Edition. 4th ed. (Exploring Sports Ser.). 92p. 1983. pap. 4.95 (ISBN 0-697-09963-6). Wm C Brown.

Allsen, Philip E., jt. auth. see Fisher, A. Garth.

Allsen, Philip E., jt. auth. see Fisher, Garth A.

Allsen, Philip E., et al. Fitness for Life: An Individualized Approach. 3rd ed. 208p. 1984. pap. text ed. write for info (ISBN 0-697-07475-7); write for info instr's manual (ISBN 0-697-07460-9). Wm C Brown.

Allsop, Bruce. A History of Renaissance Architecture. LC 59-2405. 228p. 1959. Repr. 59.00x (ISBN 0-403-04103-1). Somerset Pub.

Allsop, D. F. & Kennedy, D. Pressure Diecasting: The Technology of the Casting & the Die, Pt. 2. (Materials Engineering Practice Ser.). (Illus.). 186p. 1983. 30.00 (ISBN 0-08-027615-6); pap. 14.00 (ISBN 0-08-027614-8). Pergamon.

Allsop, Fred W. History of the Arkansas Press for a Hundred Years. (Illus.). 1978. Repr. of 1922 ed. 25.00 (ISBN 0-89308-073-X). Southern Hist Pr.

Allsop, Judy. Health Policy & the National Health Service. LC 83-995. (Social Policy in Modern Britain). 1983. 13.95 (ISBN 0-582-29599-8). Longman.

Allsop, Michael, jt. auth. see Heal, Carolyn.

Allsopp, Bruce. A Modern Theory of Architechture. 1978. 16.50 (ISBN 0-7100-8611-3). Routledge & Kegan.

--A Modern Theory of Architecture. (Illus.). 112p. (Orig.). 1981. pap. 8.95 (ISBN 0-7100-0950-X). Routledge & Kegan.

--Social Responsibility & the Responsible Society. 208p. (Orig.). 1985. pap. 19.95x (ISBN 0-85362-220-5, Oriel). Routledge & Kegan.

Allsopp, Michael. Management in the Professions: Guidelines to Improved Professional Performance. 201p. 1979. text ed. 31.50x (ISBN 0-220-67011-0, Pub. by Busn Bks England). Brookfield Pub Co.

--Survival in Business. 139p. 1977. text ed. 24.50x (ISBN 0-220-66320-3, Pub. by Busn Bks England). Brookfield Pub Co.

Allston, Aaron. Lands of Mystery. Mallonee, Dennis, ed. (Hero System Ser.). (Illus.). 96p. (Orig.). 1985. pap. 9.95 (ISBN 0-917481-60-7). Hero Games.

--Trail of the Gold Spike. Mallonee, Dennis, ed. (Hero System Ser.). (Illus.). 32p. (Orig.). 1984. pap. 5.95 (ISBN 0-917481-51-8). Hero Games.

Allston, Aaron, jt. auth. see Robinson, Andrew.

Allston, Aaron, ed. see Peterson, Steve & MacDonald, George.

Allston, Aaron, et al. Justice, Inc: The Role-Playing Game of the 20's & 30's. Peterson, Steve, ed. (Hero System Ser.). (Illus.). 176p. (Orig.). 1984. boxed ed. 14.95 (ISBN 0-917481-50-X). Hero Games.

Allston, Washington. Lectures on Art, & Poems, 1850, & Monaldi, 1841. LC 67-10124. 1967. 60.00x (ISBN 0-8201-1001-9). Schol Facsimiles.

--Lectures on Art-Poems. LC 75-171379. (Library of American Art Ser.). 1972. Repr. of 1892 ed. lib. bdg. 42.50 (ISBN 0-306-70414-5). Da Capo.

Allstroem, Carl M. Dictionary of Royal Lineage of Europe & Other Countries, 2 vols. 1976. lib. bdg. 250.00 (ISBN 0-8490-1722-X). Gordon Pr.

Allstrom, Elizabeth. Let's Play a Story. (Orig.). 1957. pap. 2.95 (ISBN 0-377-47072-4). Friend Pr.

Allsup, James O. The Magic Circle: A Study of Shelley's Concept of Love. (Literary Criticism Ser.). 1976. 11.95x (ISBN 0-8046-9117-7, Pub. by Kennikat). Assoc Faculty Pr.

Allswang, John. Physician's Guide to Computers & Computing. (Orig.). 1985. pap. write for info. (ISBN 0-8385-7851-9). ACC.

Allswang, John M. A House for All Peoples: Ethnic Politics in Chicago, 1890-1936. LC 76-119810. (Illus.). 264p. 1971. 24.00x (ISBN 0-8131-1226-5). U Pr of Ky.

--Macintosh: The Definitive User's Guide. LC 84-24226. (Illus.). 256p. 1985. pap. 15.95 (ISBN 0-89303-649-8). Brady Comm.

--The New Deal & American Politics 1930-1940. 155p. 1978. pap. text ed. 6.95 (ISBN 0-394-34162-7, RanC). Random.

--The Political Behavior of Chicago's Ethnic Groups, 1918-1932. LC 80-837. (American Ethnic Groups Ser.). 1981. lib. bdg. 32.00x (ISBN 0-405-13401-0). Ayer Co Pubs.

Allswang, John M., et al. Computer Power for Physicians. 225p. pap. cancelled (ISBN 0-89588-197-7). SYBEX.

Allswede, Jerry L., jt. ed. see Heiser, Edward J.

Allt, P., ed. see Yeats, William B.

Allt, Peter. Some Aspects of the Life & Works of James Augustine Joyce. 1978. Repr. lib. bdg. 10.00 (ISBN 0-8495-0111-3). Arden Lib.

--Some Aspects of the Life & Works of James Augustine Joyce. 50p. 1980. Repr. of 1942 ed. lib. bdg. 8.50 (ISBN 0-89987-026-0). Darby Bks.

--Some Aspects of the Life & Works of James Augustine Joyce. LC 74-2083. 1952. lib. bdg. 10.00 (ISBN 0-8414-2962-6). Folcroft.

Allton, David. Valuing Outdoor Recreation Benefits: An Annotated Bibliography. (Public Administration Ser.: P 258). 1979. pap. 5.00 (ISBN 0-88066-024-4). Vance Biblios.

Alluisi, Earl A. & Fleishman, Edwin A., eds. Stress & Performance Effectiveness. (Human Performance & Productivity Ser.: Vol. 3). 256p. 1982. text ed. 29.95x (ISBN 0-89859-091-4). L Erlbaum Assocs.

Allum, Faith T. Respite. (Illus.). 48p. (Orig.). 1985. pap. 4.95 (ISBN 0-9613349-2-4). F T Allum.

--Seasons & Love. (Illus.). 44p. (Orig.). 1984. pap. 4.95 (ISBN 0-9613349-1-6). F T Allum.

--White Water, Pebbles & Love. (Illus.). 48p. (Orig.). (gr. 6 up). 1984. pap. 4.95 (ISBN 0-9613349-0-8). F T Allum.

Allum, J. A. Photogeology & Regional Mapping. 1966. 25.00 (ISBN 0-08-012033-4); pap. 9.95 (ISBN 0-08-012032-6). Pergamon.

Allum, P. A. Italy: Republic Without Government? LC 73-20230. (Comparative Modern Governments Ser.). (Illus.). 267p. 1974. pap. 5.95x (ISBN 0-393-09302-6). Norton.

--Politics & Society in Post-war Naples. LC 75-174259. pap. 106.50 (ISBN 0-317-26136-3, 2024408). Bks Demand UMI.

Allums, Betty, ed. see Allums, Charles.

Allums, Charles. Sing a New Song. Allums, Betty, ed. (Illus.). 135p. (Orig.). 1984. pap. 8.75 (ISBN 0-932211-00-3). Bay Area Cross.

Allums, J. Larry, ed. Allen Tate & the Poetic Way. LC 83-49360. (American University Studies III (Comparative Literature Ser.): Vol. 10). 214p. (Orig.). 1984. pap. text ed. cancelled (ISBN 0-8204-0089-0). P Lang Pubs.

Allums, John, jt. auth. see Saye, Albert.

Allums, John F., jt. auth. see Saye, Albert B.

Alluntis, Felix, illus. John Duns Scotus: God & Creatures; the Quodlibetal Questions. Wolter, Allan B., tr. from Lat. LC 80-28098. Orig. Title: Quaestiones Quodlibetales. 548p. pap. 16.95x (ISBN 0-8132-0557-3). Cath U Pr.

Alluri, F. M., jt. auth. see Lawani, S. M.

Allvin. Basic Musicianship: An Introduction to Music Fundamentals with Computer Assistance. 1985. write for info (ISBN 0-534-04059-4). Wadsworth Pub.

Allvine. The Greatest Fox of Them All. 5.95 (ISBN 0-8184-0035-8). Lyle Stuart.

Allvine, Fred C. & Patterson, James M. Competition Ltd, the Marketing of Gasoline. LC 70-180491. pap. 65.40 (ISBN 0-317-28578-5, 2055197). Bks Demand UMI.

--Highway Robbery: An Analysis of the Gasoline Crisis. LC 74-1598. (Illus.). Repr. of 1974 ed. 51.90 (ISBN 0-8357-9216-1, 2017606). Bks Demand UMI.

Allward & McLeavy. London's Airports. pap. 5.00x (ISBN 0-392-07308-0, SpS). Sportshelf.

Allward, Maurice. An Illustrated History of Seaplanes & Flying Boats. (Illus.). 1980. cancelled (ISBN 0-904978-54-0). Transatlantic.

Allwood, J., et al, eds. Logic in Linguistics. LC 76-46855. (Cambridge Textbooks in Linguistics Ser.). (Illus.). 1977. 34.50 (ISBN 0-521-21496-3); pap. 12.95 (ISBN 0-521-29174-7). Cambridge U Pr.

Allwood, Martin, ed. Modern Scandinavian Poetry. LC 81-38320. 400p. 1982. 22.50 (ISBN 0-8112-0818-4). New Directions.

Allwood, Martin S., tr. see Aurell, Tage.

Allworth, Edward. Nationalities of the Soviet East: Publications & Writing Systems, a Bibliographical Directory & Transliteration Tables for Iranian & Turkic-Language Publications, 1818-1945 U.S. Libraries. LC 73-110143. (Middle East Institute Ser). (Illus.). 451p. 1971. 35.00x (ISBN 0-231-03274-9). Columbia U Pr.

Allworth, Edward, ed. Ethnic Russia in the U. S. S. R. The Dilemma of Dominance. LC 79-22959. (Pergamon Policy Studies Ser.). 270p. 1980. 44.00 (ISBN 0-08-023700-2). Pergamon.

--The Nationality Question in Soviet Central Asia. LC 72-85986. (Special Studies in International Politics & Government). 1973. 79.50x (ISBN 0-275-28659-2). Irvington.

--Soviet Nationality Problems. LC 77-166211. (Illus.). 296p. 1971. 30.00x (ISBN 0-231-03493-8). Columbia U Pr.

Allworth, Edward, tr. see Sinasi, Ibrahim.

Allworth, Louise M. Battle Ground, in & Around: A Pictorial Drama of Early Northwest Pioneer Life. 2nd ed. LC 75-43292. (Illus.). 400p. 1984. Repr. of 1976 ed. 30.00x (ISBN 0-9613899-0-7). Write Stuff.

Allworth, S. T. Introduction to Real-Time Software Design. 140p. 1981. pap. 14.95 (ISBN 0-387-91175-8). Springer-Verlag.

Allworthy, A. W. The Petition Against God: The Full Story Behind RM-2493. LC 75-43375. (Illus.). 150p. 1976. pap. 3.95 (ISBN 0-686-16824-0, Pub. by Christ the Light). Mho & Mho.

Allyn, Charles, ed. see Allyn, Rube.

Allyn, Jane, jt. auth. see Cooper, Montgomery.

Allyn, Jennifer. Forgiveness. (Love & Life Romance Ser.). 176p. (Orig.). 1983. pap. 1.75 (ISBN 0-345-31082-9). Ballantine.

Allyn, John. Forty-Seven Ronin Story. LC 70-121274. (Illus.). 1970. 4.75 (ISBN 0-8048-0196-7). C E Tuttle.

--Kon Ichikawa: A Guide to References & Resources. (Performing Arts: Film-Directors Ser.). 1985. lib. bdg. 45.00 (ISBN 0-8161-8520-4). G K Hall.

Allyn, Mildred V. About Aging: A Catalog of Films Supplement. 10.95 (ISBN 0-686-94880-7). Hollander Co.

Allyn, Mildred V., compiled by. About Aging: A Catalog of Films. 4th ed. LC 79-64804. 1979. pap. 12.00x (ISBN 0-88474-091-9, 05726-6). Lexington Bks.

Allyn, Mildred V., ed. About Aging: A Catalog of Films, (1981 Supplement to Fourth Edition) LC 81-6693. 105p. 1981. pap. 11.00x (ISBN 0-88474-126-5, 05725-8). Lexington Bks.

Allyn, Rube. Dictionary of Fishes. LC 52-334. (Orig.). pap. 4.95 (ISBN 0-8200-0101-5). Great Outdoors.

--Fishermen's Handbook. (Orig.). pap. 2.95 (ISBN 0-8200-0103-1). Great Outdoors.

--Florida Fishes. Allyn, Charles, ed. LC 74-14516. (Illus., Orig.). 1969. pap. 2.95 (ISBN 0-8200-0108-2). Great Outdoors.

--How to Cook Your Catch. (Orig.). pap. 1.95 (ISBN 0-8200-0801-X). Great Outdoors.

Allyn, Stan. Heave To! You'll Drown Yourselves! 2nd ed. LC 82-72425. (Illus.). 160p. 1984. pap. 6.50 (ISBN 0-8323-0409-3). Binford.

Allyne, Kerry. Coral Cay. (Harlequin Presents Ser.). 192p. 1982. pap. 1.75 (ISBN 0-373-10513-4). Harlequin Bks.

--Mixed Feelings. (Harlequin Romances Ser.). 192p. 1982. pap. 1.50 (ISBN 0-373-02479-7). Harlequin Bks.

--Somewhere to Call Home. (Harlequin Romances Ser.). 192p. 1983. pap. 1.75 (ISBN 0-373-02593-9). Harlequin Bks.

--Spring Fever. (Harlequin Romances Ser.). 192p. 1983. pap. 1.50 (ISBN 0-373-02527-0). Harlequin Bks.

--Ton Rire Comme un Soleil. (Collection Harlequin Ser.). 192p. 1983. pap. 1.95 (ISBN 0-373-49346-0). Harlequin Bks.

Allyson, June & Leighton, Frances S. June Allyson. 288p. 1983. pap. 3.50 (ISBN 0-425-06251-1). Berkley Pub.

Alm, Alvin & Weiner, Robert, eds. Oil Shock: Policy Response & Implementation. LC 83-22459. 256p. 1984. prof. ref 29.95x (ISBN 0-88410-900-3). Ballinger Pub.

Alm, Alvin L. Coal Myths & Environmental Realities: Industrial Fuel-Use Decisions in a Time of Change. (Special Studies in Natural Resources & Energy Management). 135p. 1984. 19.00x (ISBN 0-86531-712-7). Westview.

Almaas, A. H. The Elixir of Enlightenment. LC 84-50159. 64p. (Orig.). 1984. pap. 3.95 (ISBN 0-87728-613-2). Weiser.

Almack, Edward. Eikon Basilike, or the King's Book. 1979. Repr. of 1907 ed. lib. bdg. 30.00 (ISBN 0-8495-0140-7). Arden Lib.

Almack, John C., ed. Modern School Administration. facs. ed. LC 78-121445. (Essay Index Reprint Ser). 1933. 21.50 (ISBN 0-8369-1902-5). Ayer Co Pubs.

Almack, M. R. see Sloan, Louise L.

Almagno, Romano S. & Harkins, Conrad L., eds. Studies Honoring Ignatius Charles Brady O. F. M. (Theology Ser). 1976. 25.00 (ISBN 0-686-17960-9). Franciscan Inst.

Almagno, Stephen, pref. by see Wright, John.

Almagor, Uri. Pastoral Partners: Affinity & Bond Partnership Among the Dassanetch of South-West Ethiopia. LC 78-4128. 258p. 1978. text ed. 45.00x (ISBN 0-8419-0384-0, Africana). Holmes & Meier.

Almagor, Uri, jt. ed. see Baxter, P. T.

Almagro, Bertha R. Early American Medical Imprints 1668-1820: Subject, Name & Format Index to the Microfilm Collection. LC 81-12077. 240p. 1981. 50.00 (ISBN 0-89235-027-X). Res Pubns Conn.

Al-Mahasin Yusuf, Abu, jt. auth. see Taghribirdi, Ibn.

Almaini, A. E. Electronic Logic Systems. (Illus.). 448p. 1986. text ed. 36.95 (ISBN 0-13-251752-3). P-H.

Alman, Brian M. Self-Hypnosis: A Complete Manual for Health & Self-Change. LC 83-17173. (Illus.). 280p. 1983. pap. 19.95 (ISBN 0-913801-05-4). Intl Health Pub.

Alman, David. World Full of Strangers. LC 74-29040. (The Labor Movement in Fiction & Non-Fiction Ser.). Repr. of 1949 ed. 24.00 (ISBN 0-404-58521-3). AMS Pr.

Alman, Isadora. Aural Sex & Verbal Intercourse. 176p. (Orig.). 1984. pap. 8.50 (ISBN 0-940208-09-1). Down There Pr.

Alman, John, ed. see Wilkes, John.

Almana, Mohammed A. Arabia Unified: A Portrait of Ibn Saud. LC 84-62429. (Illus.). 352p. (Orig.). 1985. text ed. 29.95 (ISBN 0-930244-05-2); pap. text ed. 9.95 (ISBN 0-930244-06-0). North American Inc.

Almand, Joan & Wooderson, Joy. Establishing Values. LC 76-17147. 1976. pap. 1.99 (ISBN 0-87148-283-5). Pathway Pr.

Almand, Joan, jt. auth. see Flinn, Avril.

Almaney, A. J. & Alwan, A. J. Communicating with the Arabs: A Handbook for the Business Executive. LC 81-70668. (Illus.). 296p. 1982. pap. 17.95x (ISBN 0-917974-81-6). Waveland Pr.

Al Manfaloute, Mustapha. Al Sha'er: The Poet. (Arabic.). pap. 12.00x (ISBN 0-86685-369-3). Intl Bk Ctr.

Almansa, Andres De & Mendoza, Andres De. Two Royall Entertainments, Lately Given to Charles, Prince of Great Britaine, by Philip the Fourth of Spaine. LC 77-6847. (English Experience Ser.: No. 842). 1977. Repr. of 1623 ed. lib. bdg. 8.00 (ISBN 90-221-0842-2). Walter J Johnson.

Almansi, Guido & Henderson, Simon. Harold Pinter. LC 82-22902. (Contemporary Writers Ser.). 96p. 1983. pap. 4.75 (ISBN 0-416-31710-3, NO. 3560). Methuen Inc.

Almansi, Guido & Merry, Bruce. Montale: The Private Language of Poetry. 167p. 1977. 14.00x (ISBN 0-85224-298-0, Pub. by Edinburgh U Pr Scotland). Columbia U Pr.

Almanza, Francisco, tr. see Dobson, James.

Almanza, Francisco G., tr. see Baker, R. A.

Al-Maqqari, Ahmed, ed. History of the Mohammedan Dynasties in Spain, 2 Vols. De Gayangos, P., tr. 1969. Repr. of 1840 ed. Set. 175.00 (ISBN 0-384-35253-7). Johnson Repr.

Al-Marayati, Abid A. Diplomatic History of Modern Iraq. 1961. 9.95 (ISBN 0-8315-0108-1). Speller.

Al-Marayati, Abid A., ed. International Relations of the Middle East & North Africa. 500p. 1984. text ed. 22.50x (ISBN 0-87073-824-0); pap. 15.95 (ISBN 0-87073-830-5). Schenkman Bks Inc.

Almaraz, Carlos. Carlos Almaraz: Paintings. LC 83-82616. (Illus.). 3p. (Orig.). 1983. pap. 1.00 (ISBN 0-934418-19-5). La Jolla Mus Contemp Art.

Almaraz, Felix D., Jr. Tragic Cavalier: Governor Manuel Salcedo of Texas, 1808-1813. 218p. 1981. pap. text ed. 6.95 (ISBN 0-292-78039-7). U of Tex Pr.

Almarik, Andrei. Involuntary Journey to Siberia. Harari, Manya & Hayward, Max, trs. LC 75-117568. (A Helen & Kurt Wolff Bk.). 297p. 1971. pap. 6.95 (ISBN 0-15-645393-2, Harv). HarBraceJ.

Al-Mashat, Abdul-Monem M. National Security in the Third World. (Replica Edition Ser.). 140p. 1985. softcover 16.00x (ISBN 0-86531-834-4). Westview.

Almayrac, G., tr. see Bouisson, Maurice.

Al-Mazini, Ibrahim A. Al-Mazini's Egypt: Midu & His Accomplices; Return to a Beginning; The Fugitive. Hutchins, William, ed. & tr. from Arabic. LC 82-50878. 185p. 1983. 18.00 (ISBN 0-89410-332-6); pap. 8.00 (ISBN 0-89410-333-4). Three Continents.

Almazov, A. B. Electronic Properties of Semiconducting Solid Solutions. LC 68-18820. (Illus.). 82p. 1968. 25.00x (ISBN 0-306-10808-9, Consultants). Plenum Pub.

Almeda, Frank, Jr. Systematics of the Genus Monochaetum (Melastomataceae) in Mexico & Central America. (U. C. Publications in Botany Ser.: Vol. 75). 1978. 18.50x (ISBN 0-520-09587-1). U of Cal Pr.

Almeder, Robert. The Philosophy of Charles S. Peirce: A Critical Introduction. Rescher, Nicholas, ed. (American Philosophical Quarterly Library of Philosophy). 224p. 1980. 27.50x (ISBN 0-8476-6854-1). Rowman.

Almeder, Robert, ed. Praxis & Reason: Studies in the Philosophy of Nicholas Rescher. LC 81-43602. (Nicholas Rescher Ser.). 276p. (Orig.). 1982. lib. bdg. 28.75 (ISBN 0-8191-2648-9); pap. text ed. 13.75 (ISBN 0-8191-2649-7). U Pr of Amer.

Almeder, Robert E., jt. auth. see Humber, James M.

Almeder, Robert F., jt. ed. see Humber, James M.

Almedingen, E. M. The Crimson Oak. LC 82-12556. 112p. (gr. 6-9). 1983. pap. 9.95 (ISBN 0-698-20569-3, Coward). Putnam Pub Group.

--Tomorrow Will Come. 256p. pap. 7.95 (ISBN 0-85115-220-1). Academy Chi Pubs.

Almeida. Enciclopedia del Whisky. (Span.). 1978. 23.50 (ISBN 0-686-92195-X, S-37337). French & Eur.

--Sinn und Inhalt in der Genetischen Phanomenologica E. Husserls. (Phaenomenologica Ser: No. 47). 1972. lib. bdg. 31.50 (ISBN 90-247-1318-8, Pub. by Martinus Nijhoff Netherlands). Kluwer Academic.

Almeida, Bira. Capoeira: A Brazilian Art Form. 2nd ed. (Illus.). 152p. 1982. pap. 7.95 (ISBN 0-938190-09-1). North Atlantic.

--Capoeira: History, Philosophy, & Practice. (Illus.). 224p. 1985. 25.00 (ISBN 0-938190-30-X); pap. 12.95 (ISBN 0-938190-29-6). North Atlantic.

Almeida, Hermione De see De Almeida, Hermione.

Almeida, Irene M., ed. see Silka, Henry P.

Almeida, Jose, et al. Descubrir y Crear. 2nd ed. (Illus.). 430p. (Span.). 1981. text ed. 23.95 scp (ISBN 0-06-040224-5, HarpC); scp tape manual 10.95 (ISBN 0-06-044563-7); instr's. manual avail. (ISBN 0-06-360251-2); tapes scp 331.00 (ISBN 0-06-047497-1). Har-Row.

Almeida, Laurindo. Guitar Tutor. 9.95 (ISBN 0-910468-03-6). Criterion Mus.

Almeida, Onesimo, ed. The Sea Within. Monteiro, George, tr. from Port. LC 83-80877. (Illus.). 115p. (Orig.). 1983. pap. 3.50 (ISBN 0-943722-09-8). Gavea-Brown.

Almeida, Onesimo T., ed. Jose Rodrigues Migueis: Lisbon in Manhattan. LC 83-83071. 250p. (Orig.). 1985. pap. 7.50 (ISBN 0-943722-10-1). Gavea-Brown.

Almeida, Onesimo T., ed. see Joao Teixeira de Medeiros.

Almeida, Philip. How to Decorate a Dump. (Illus.). 144p. 1983. 17.95 (ISBN 0-8184-0346-2). Lyle Stuart.

Almeida, Renato. Historia da Musica Braisliera. (Ballroom Dance Ser.). 1985. lib. bdg. 79.50 (ISBN 0-87700-831-0). Revisionist Pr.

Almen, William J. Five Hundred Drugs the Alcoholic Should Avoid. 40p. 1983. 1.50 (ISBN 0-89486-166-2). Hazelden.

Almendros, Nestor. A Man with a Camera. Belash, Rachel P., tr. from Fr. LC 84-1689. (Illus.). 288p. 1984. 15.95 (ISBN 0-374-20172-2). FS&G.

Almers, Ambrose J. How to Build by Yourself Scientifically the Log Cabin of Your Dreams. (Illus.). 187p. 1982. 175.55 (ISBN 0-86650-029-4). Gloucester Art.

Almgren, F. J., Jr. Existence & Regularity Almost Everywhere of Solutions to Ellipic Variational Problems with Constraints. LC 75-41603. (Memoirs: No. 165). 199p. 1976. pap. 15.00 (ISBN 0-8218-1865-1, MEMO-165). Am Math.

Alminaque, Conrado. El Indio Pampero en la Literatura Gauchesca. LC 81-69534. (Coleccion Polymita Ser.). 57p. (Span.). 1981. pap. 5.95 (ISBN 0-89729-305-3). Ediciones.

Almirol, Edwin B. Ethnic Identity & Social Negotiation: A Study of a Filipino Community in California. LC 83-45347. (Immigrants Communities & Ethnic Minorities in the United States & Canada Ser.). 1985. 47.50 (ISBN 0-404-19401-X). AMS Pr.

Almirudas, Hiram, ed. El Fruto del Espiritu. 112p. (Span.). 1979. pap. 3.50 (ISBN 0-87148-303-3). Pathway Pr.

Almirudus, Hiram, ed. Antologia de Homilias Biblicas, Vol. IV. 162p. (Span.). 1981. 6.95 (ISBN 0-87148-025-5). Pathway Pr.

--Antologia de Homilias Biblicas, Vol. V. 158p. (Span.). 1982. 6.95 (ISBN 0-87148-026-3). Pathway Pr.

--Antologia de Homilias Biblicas, Vol. VI. 158p. (Span.). 1982. 6.95 (ISBN 0-87148-027-1). Pathway Pr.

--Antologia de Homilias Biblicas, Vol. III. 148p. (Span.). 1980. 6.95 (ISBN 0-87148-024-7). Pathway Pr.

--Antologia de Homilias Biblicas, Vol. I. 159p. (Span.). 1977. 6.95 (ISBN 0-87148-022-0). Pathway Pr.

--Antologia de Homilias Biblicas, Vol. II. 159p. (Span.). 1979. 6.95 (ISBN 0-87148-023-9). Pathway Pr.

--Los Dones del Espiritu. 88p. (Span.). 1978. pap. 2.75 (ISBN 0-87148-520-6). Pathway Pr.

Almli, C. Robert & Finger, Stanley, eds. Early Brain Damage, Vol. 1: Research Orientation & Clinical Observations. (Behavioral Biology Ser.). 1984. 49.50 (ISBN 0-12-052901-7). Acad Pr.

--Early Brain Damage, Vol. 2: Neurobiology & Behavior. (Behavioral Biology Ser.). 1984. 49.50 (ISBN 0-12-052902-5). Acad Pr.

Al-Moajil, Abdullah H. & Benharbit, Abdelali. Basic Mathematics: A Pre-Calculus Course for Science & Engineering. LC 80-41685. 308p. 1981. 44.95x (ISBN 0-471-27941-2, Pub. by Wiley Interscience). Wiley.

Almogi, Yosef. Total Commitment. LC 81-70146. (Illus.). 320p. 1982. 20.00 (ISBN 0-8453-4749-7). Cornwall Bks.

Almon, Bert. Gary Snyder. LC 79-53650. (Western Writers Ser.: No. 37). (Illus.). 47p. (Orig.). 1979. pap. 2.00x (ISBN 0-88430-061-7). Boise St Univ.

--Nuclear Family. 31p. (Orig.). 1979. pap. 3.00 (ISBN 0-88235-040-4). San Marcos.

--The Return, & Other Poems. 52p. 1968. pap. 3.00 (ISBN 0-88235-002-1). San Marcos.

--Taking Possession. 1976. 5.25 (ISBN 0-941490-17-3). Solo Pr.

Almon, John, ed. A Collection of Papers Relative to the Dispute Between Great Britain & America, 1764-1775. LC 70-146272. (Era of the American Revolution Ser). 1971. Repr. of 1777 ed. lib. bdg. 39.50 (ISBN 0-306-70127-8). Da Capo.

Almon, John, compiled by. Collection of Political Tracts, 3 vols. LC 75-31109. Repr. of 1766 ed. 80.00 set (ISBN 0-404-13620-6). AMS Pr.

Almon, Muriel, tr. see Ludwig, Otto.

Almond, D. C., jt. auth. see Ahmed, F.

Almond, E. A., et al, eds. Science of Hard Materials 1984. Warren, R. R. (Institute of Conference Ser.: 75). 1000p. 1985. 120.00 (ISBN 0-85498-166-7, Pub. by A Hilger England). Heyden.

Almond, Gabriel. The American People & Foreign Policy. 2nd ed. LC 77-7019. 1977. Repr. of 1960 ed. lib. bdg. 22.75 (ISBN 0-8371-9617-5, ALAM). Greenwood.

Almond, Gabriel & Verba, Sidney. Civic Culture Study, 1959-1960. 1974. codebook write for info. (ISBN 0-89138-065-5). ICPSR.

Almond, Gabriel, jt. ed. see Smelser, Neil J.

Almond, Gabriel A. & Powell, G. Bingham, Jr. Comparative Politics: Systems, Process, & Policy. 2nd ed. (The Little, Brown Series in Comparative Politics). 1978. pap. text ed. 14.95 (ISBN 0-316-03498-3). Little.

Almond, Gabriel A. & Verba, Sidney. The Civic Culture: Political Attitudes & Democracy in Five Nations. (The Little, Brown Series in Comparative Politics). 379p. 1965. pap. text ed. 13.95 (ISBN 0-316-03493-2). Little.

--Civic Culture: Political Attitudes & Democracy in Five Nations. (Center of International Studies Ser.). 1963. 32.50 (ISBN 0-691-07503-4). Princeton U Pr.

Almond, Gabriel A. & Coleman, James S., eds. Politics of the Developing Areas. (Center of International Studies Ser.). 1960. pap. 13.50 (ISBN 0-691-02165-1). Princeton U Pr.

Almond, Gabriel A. & Verba, Sidney, eds. The Civic Culture Revisited. 421p. 1980. pap. text ed. 13.95 (ISBN 0-316-03490-8). Little.

Almond, Gabriel A., et al. Comparative Politics Today: A World View. 3rd ed. 1984. text ed. 24.95 (ISBN 0-316-03488-6); tchr's. manual avail. (ISBN 0-316-03489-4). Little.

--The Civic Culture: Political Attitudes & Democracy in Five Nations. LC 63-12666. pap. cancelled (ISBN 0-317-07753-8, 2051837). Bks Demand UMI.

Almond, Gabriel A., et al, eds. Progress & Its Discontents. LC 81-11643. 550p. 1982. 30.00 (ISBN 0-520-04478-9). U of Cal Pr.

Almond Growers Exchange Staff & Schmidt, Michelle. The New Almond Cookery. 208p. 1984. 19.95 (ISBN 0-671-52490-9). S&S.

Almond, J. D. Magdalene. 1985. 25.00 (ISBN 0-318-04119-7); pap. 13.50 (ISBN 0-318-04120-0). CLCB Pr.

Almond, Joseph P. Plumbers' Handbook. 7th ed. LC 82-1342. (Illus.). 1985. pap. 9.95 (ISBN 0-672-23419-X). Audel.

Almond, Joseph P., Sr. Plumbers' Handbook. 6th ed. LC 82-1342. 1982. 9.95 (ISBN 0-672-23370-3). Bobbs.

--The Plumbers Handbook. rev. ed. (Audel Ser.). 1985. pap. text ed. 9.95 (ISBN 0-672-23419-X). G K Hall.

Almond, Philip C. Mystical Experience & Religious Doctrine: An Investigation of the Study of Mysticism in World Religions. (Religion & Reason: No. 26). 197p. 1982. text ed. 27.20 (ISBN 90-279-3160-7). Mouton.

--Rudolf Otto: An Introduction to His Philosophical Theology. LC 83-19865. (Studies in Religion). 182p. 1984. 23.00x (ISBN 0-8078-1589-6). U of NC Pr.

Almond, Richard. The Healing Community: Dynamics of the Therapeutic Milieu. LC 73-17733. 468p. 1974. 30.00x (ISBN 0-87668-111-9). Aronson.

Almond, T., tr. see Bartknecht, W.

Al-Moosa, Abdulrasool & McLachlan, Keith. Immigrant Labour in Kuwait. LC 84-29316. 176p. 1985. 29.00 (ISBN 0-7099-3554-4, Pub. by Croom Helm Ltd). Longwood Pub Group.

Almoster Ferreira, M. A., ed. Ionic Processes in the Gas Phase. lib. bdg. 46.50 (ISBN 0-318-00435-6, Pub. by Reidel Holland). Kluwer Academic.

Almozning, Albert. Hand Shadow Magic for Classroom & Home Activities. (Illus.). 92p. 1984. 12.95 (ISBN 0-87396-096-3). Stravon.

Almoznino, A. Hand Shadows. LC 70-105956. (Illus.). 1969. 7.95 (ISBN 0-87396-026-2); pap. 3.95 (ISBN 0-87396-027-0). Stravon.

Almquist, Alan J., jt. auth. see Heizer, Robert F.

Almquist, Bo & Dorson, Richard M., eds. Hereditas: Essays & Studies Presented to Professor Seamus O Duilearga. LC 80-737. (Folklore of the World Ser.). (Illus.). 1980. Repr. of 1975 ed. lib. bdg. 45.00x (ISBN 0-405-13301-4). Ayer Co Pubs.

Almquist, C. J. Sara Videbeck-the Chapel. Benson, Adolph B., tr. from Swedish. LC 77-185449. (Library of Scandinavian Literature). 1972. lib. bdg. 6.75x (ISBN 0-8057-3354-X). Irvington.

Almquist, Elizabeth, et al. Sociology: Women, Men & Society. (Illus.). 1978. pap. text ed. 19.95 (ISBN 0-8299-0174-4); instrs.' manual avail. (ISBN 0-8299-0450-6). West Pub.

Almquist, Elizabeth M., jt. auth. see Angrist, Shirley S.

Almquist, Jane. Mountmellick Work: Irish White Embroidery. (Illus.). 64p. 1985. pap. 11.95 (ISBN 0-85219-616-4, Pub. by Batsford England). David & Charles.

Almqvist, C. J. Sara Videbeck - the Chapel. Benson, Adolph B., tr. from Swedish. LC 77-185499. (Library of Scandinavian Literature: Vol. 13). 1972. 6.95x (ISBN 0-89067-009-9). Am Scandinavian.

Almroth, S. & Greiner, T. The Economic Value of Breast-Feeding. (Food & Nutrition Papers: No. 11). 97p. 1979. pap. 8.25 (ISBN 92-5-100797-7, F1865, FAO). Unipub.

Al-Mufid, Shaykh. Kitab Al-Irshad. Howard, I. K., tr. from Arabic. 606p. 1982. 18.00 (ISBN 0-940368-12-9); pap. 9.00 (ISBN 0-940368-11-0). Tahrike Tarsile Quran.

Al'muhamedov, M. I., et al. Stability & Dynamic Systems. (Translations Series: No. 1, Vol. 5). 1962. 27.00 (ISBN 0-8218-1605-5, TRANS 1-5). Am Math.

Al Muhiyaddin, Mohammed A. A Comparative Study of the Religions of Today. 1984. 15.95 (ISBN 0-533-05963-1). Vantage.

Al-Mukaffah. Kalilat wa Dumma: Short Stories in Arabic. 1983. pap. 15.00x (ISBN 0-317-20295-2). Intl Bk Ctr.

Al-Mutanabbi & Abu al-Tayyib Ahmad ibn al-Husan. Poems of al-Mutanabbi: A Selection with Introduction, Translations & Notes. Arberry, A. J., tr. LC 66-17060. pap. 40.30 (ISBN 0-317-09928-0, 2051447). Bks Demand UMI.

Al-Muzaffar, Muhammad. The Faith of Shi'a Islam. LC 83-50153. 80p. pap. 4.00 (ISBN 0-940368-26-9). Tahrike Tarsile Quran.

Almy, Amy B. At Christmas Time the World Grows Young. facs. ed. LC 70-116926. (Short Story Index Reprint Ser). 1939. 13.00 (ISBN 0-8369-3428-8). Ayer Co Pubs.

Almy, Millie & Genishi, Celia. Ways of Studying Children: An Observational Manual for Early Childhood Teachers. 2nd ed. LC 79-13881. 1979. pap. text ed. 9.95x (ISBN 0-8077-2551-X). Tchrs Coll.

Almy, Millie, et al. Logical Thinking in Second Grade. LC 73-117980. (Illus.). 1970. pap. text ed. 6.95x (ISBN 0-8077-1016-4). Tchrs Coll.

--Studying School Children in Uganda: Four Reports of Exploratory Research. LC 74-122748. Repr. of 1970 ed. 21.30 (ISBN 0-8357-9607-8, 2017763). Bks Demand UMI.

Almy, Millie C. Children's Experiences Prior to First Grade & Success in Beginning Reading. LC 71-176516. (Columbia University. Teachers College. Contributions to Education: No. 954). Repr. of 1949 ed. 22.50 (ISBN 0-404-55954-9). AMS Pr.

Almy, Millie C., et al. Young Children's Thinking: Studies of Some Aspects of Piaget's Theory. LC 66-16091. (Illus.). pap. 42.00 (ISBN 0-317-10467-5, 2013176). Bks Demand UMI.

Almy, Richard R. Improving Real Property Assessment: A Reference Manual. LC 78-70575. 444p. 1978. 25.00 (ISBN 0-88329-010-3). Intl Assess.

--Land Record Systems in the United States. (Research & Information Ser.). 53p. 1979. 11.50 (ISBN 0-88329-044-8). Intl Assess.

Almy, Richard R., et al. Improving Real Property Assessment: A Reference Manual. LC 78-70575. 1978. 25.00 (ISBN 0-88329-010-3). Intl Assess.

Al-Nahari, Abdulaziz M. The Role of National Libraries in Developing Countries. Anwar, Mumtaz A. & Tashkandy, Abbas S., eds. 174p. 1984. 27.00 (ISBN 0-7201-1696-1). Mansell.

--The Role of National Libraries in Developing Countries. 174p. 1984. 37.00 (ISBN 0-7201-1696-1). Wilson.

Alnasrawi, Abbas. Arab Oil & United States Energy Requirements. (Monograph No. 16). 42p. (Orig.). 1982. pap. 5.95 (ISBN 0-937694-52-5). Assn Arab-Amer U Grads.

--Oil, Saudi Arabia & the Decade of Arab Failure, 1973-1983. LC 83-71815. 130p. (Orig.). 1983. 95.00 (ISBN 0-913177-00-8); pap. 10.00 (ISBN 0-913177-01-6). Arab Petro Res.

--OPEC in a Changing World Economy. LC 84-7196. 208p. 1985. text ed. 22.50x (ISBN 0-8018-3216-0). Johns Hopkins.

Alo, R. A. & Shapiro, H. L. Normal Topological Spaces. LC 73-79304. (Tracts in Mathematics Ser.: No. 65). (Illus.). 250p. 1974. 49.50 (ISBN 0-521-20271-X). Cambridge U Pr.

Alo, R. A., et al, eds. TOPO 72: General Topology & Its Applications. LC 74-390. (Lecture Notes in Mathematics: Vol. 378). xiv, 651p. 1974. pap. 31.00 (ISBN 0-387-06741-8). Springer-Verlag.

Alock, Norman Z. & CPRI Researchers. Global Models & Projections of Arms, War, & Development 1982. 1978. 4.00 (ISBN 0-318-01703-2). Peace Res Lab.

Aloff, Mindy. Night Lights. Gale, Vi, ed. LC 79-84510. (Prescott First Book). (Illus.). 1979. ltd. ed. 20.00 (ISBN 0-915986-13-2); pap. 5.00 (ISBN 0-915986-14-0). Prescott St Pr.

Aloff, Mindy & Cohen, Marty. On the Nile. 4p. 1978. pap. 1.00 (ISBN 0-932264-23-9). Trask Hse Bks.

Alofs, John W. Modern Sales Technique for Ophthalmic Dispensing. LC 84-61608. 1984. 25.00 (ISBN 0-87873-056-7). Prof Press.

Alofsin, Dorothy. America's Triumph: Stories of American Jewish Heroes. facs. ed. LC 72-148205. (Biography Index Reprint Ser.). 1949. 22.00 (ISBN 0-8369-8052-2). Ayer Co Pubs.

Alogna, Maria & Hull, Nancy. Balance Your Act: A Book for Adults with Diabetes. (Illus.). 96p. (Orig.). 1984. pap. text ed. 5.00 (ISBN 0-939838-14-1). Pritchett & Hull.

Alogozzine, Bob, jt. auth. see Ysseldyke, James E.

Aloha Magazine Staff, ed. Aloha. (Illus.). casebound 19.95 (ISBN 0-317-11881-1); pap. Cancelled (ISBN 0-317-11882-X). Mutual Pub HI.

Aloi, G. Restaurants (Architecture) (Illus.). 1972. 50.00 (ISBN 0-685-25486-0). Heinman.

Aloi, R. Fifty Villas of Our Time. (Illus.). 1970. 40.00 (ISBN 0-685-47307-4). Heinman.

--Museums: Architecture, Technics. (Illus.). 1962. 50.00 (ISBN 0-685-12032-5). Heinman.

Aloi, R. & Bassi, C. Hospitals (Architecture) (Illus.). 1972. 50.00 (ISBN 0-685-30577-5). Heinman.

Aloia, Roland. Membrane Fluidity in Biology, Vol. 2: General Principles. LC 82-11535. 336p. 1983. 43.00 (ISBN 0-12-053002-3). Acad Pr.

Aloia, Roland C., ed. Membrane Fluidity in Biology: Concepts of Membrane Structure, Vol. 1. 1982. 45.00 (ISBN 0-12-053001-5). Acad Pr.

Aloia, Roland C. & Boggs, Joan M., eds. Membrane Fluidity in Biology: Cellular Aspects & Disease Processes, Vol. 3. Date not set. 64.50 (ISBN 0-12-053003-1). Acad Pr.

--Membrane Fluidity in Biology: Cellular Activities, Vol. 4. Date not set. price not set (ISBN 0-12-053004-X). Acad Pr.

Aloisi, Ralph M. & Hyun, Jayson. Immunodiagnostics. LC 83-16264. (Laboratory & Research Methods in Biology & Medicine Ser.: Vol. 8). 304p. 1983. 36.00 (ISBN 0-8451-1657-6). A R Liss.

Alokeranjan, Dasgupta. Roots in the Void: Baul Songs of Bengal. 1983. 5.00x (ISBN 0-8364-0972-8, Pub. by KP Bagchi India). South Asia Bks.

Alon, D., tr. see Sagi, Nana.

Alon, Gedaliah. The Jews in Their Land in the Talmudic Age, Vol. 1. Gershon, Levi, tr. from Hebrew. 324p. 1980. text ed. 25.50x (ISBN 965-223-352-8, Pub. by Magnes Israel). Humanities.

Alon, Gedalyahu. Jews, Judaism & the Classical World. Abrahams, Israel, tr. from Hebrew. 499p. 1977. text ed. 36.50x (Pub. by Magnes Israel). Humanities.

Alon, Hanan. Countering Palestinian Terrorism in Israel: Toward a Policy Analysis of Countermeasures. LC 81-124569. (Series in International Security & Arms Control: N-1567-FF). (Illus.). xxiii, 271p. 1980. 20.00. Rand Corp.

Alon, Mati. The Unavoidable Surgery. 1982. 12.95 (ISBN 0-533-05388-9). Vantage.

Alonso, Eutimio. Cana Roja. LC 80-65446. (Coleccion Polymita). 348p. (Orig., Span.). 1982. pap. 14.95 (ISBN 0-89729-251-0). Ediciones.

Alonso, Irma T., jt. auth. see Dutta, Manoranjan.

Alonso, J. L. & Tarrach, R., eds. Quantum Chromodynamics: Proceedings. (Lecture Notes in Physics: Vol. 113). 306p. 1980. pap. 26.00 (ISBN 0-387-09731-7). Springer-Verlag.

Alonso, J. M. Althea. LC 76-2875. 1976. 11.95 (ISBN 0-914590-24-3); pap. 4.95 (ISBN 0-914590-25-1). Fiction Coll.

Alonso, J. R. Simple: BASIC Programs for Business Applications. 1981. 21.95 (ISBN 0-13-809897-2); pap. 14.95 (ISBN 0-13-809889-1). P-H.

Alonso, Joaquin M. The Secret of Fatima Fact & Legend. Dominican Nuns of the Perpetual Rosary, tr. from Span. LC 79-13182. (Illus.). 1979. 8.95 (ISBN 0-911218-14-9); pap. 3.95 (ISBN 0-911218-15-7). Ravengate Pr.

Alonso, Lou, ed. see Raynor, Sherry & Drouillard, Richard.

Alonso, Manuel. El Gibaro: An English Translation, 2 vols. in 1. (Studies in Puerto Rican Culture, Literature & History). 1980. lib. bdg. 75.00 (ISBN 0-8490-2926-0). Gordon Pr.

Alonso, Marcelo. Crisis in Central America. LC 83-61052. 1984. pap. 7.95 (ISBN 0-89226-022-X, Pub. by Wash Inst DC). Paragon Hse.

Alonso, Marcelo & Finn, Edward J. Fundamental University Physics, 2 vols. 2nd ed. Incl. Vol. 1. Mechanics. 1979. text ed. 17.95 (ISBN 0-201-00076-8); Vol. 2. Fields & Waves. 1983. text ed. 19.95 (ISBN 0-201-00077-6). 1980. Addison-Wesley.

Alonso, Marcelo & Valk, Henry. Quantum Mechanics: Principles & Applications. 1986. Repr. of 1973 ed. lib. bdg. price not set (ISBN 0-89874-894-1). Krieger.

Alonso, Marcelo, et al. Central America in Crisis. 1984. pap. 9.95 (ISBN 0-89226-022-X, Pub. by Wash Inst DC). Paragon Hse.

Alonso, Martin. Diccionario del Espanol Moderno. 5th ed. 1100p. (Span.). 1978. 66.00 (ISBN 84-03-27061-5, S-12229). French & Eur.

Alonso, Nina. This Body. LC 70-168711. (Orig.). 1971. pap. 5.95 (ISBN 0-87923-043-6). Godine.

Alonso, Ose Rizal Y see Rizal Y Alonso, Jose.

Alonso, Ricardo. Cimarron. LC 78-25876. (The Wesleyan Poetry Program: Vol. 94). 1978. 15.00x (ISBN 0-8195-2094-2); pap. 6.95 (ISBN 0-8195-1094-7). Wesleyan U Pr.

Alonso, William. Location & Land Use: Toward a General Theory of Land Rent. LC 63-17193. (Joint Center for Urban Studies Publications Ser). (Illus.). 1964. 16.50x (ISBN 0-674-53700-9). Harvard U Pr.

Alonso, William, jt. ed. see Friedmann, John.

Alonso-Conchiero, jt. auth. see IFAC Symposium, Laxenburg, Austria, Mar. 1983.

Alonso-Conchiero, A., ed. see IFAC Conference, Guadalajara City, Mexico, Jan. 1983.

Alonso de Quesada, Alba. Towards a Cultural Policy for Honduras. (Studies & Documents on Cultural Policies). (Illus.). 73p. 1978. pap. 5.25 (ISBN 92-3-101520-6, U875, UNESCO). Unipub.

Alonso-de Ruiz, Patricia, tr. see Saccomanno, Geno.

Alonzo, Gisela P. Distant Fever. 231p. 1984. 6.95 (ISBN 0-89697-172-4). Intl Univ Pr.

Al-Otaiba, M. S. OPEC & the Petroleum Industry. 208p. 1976. 25.00 (ISBN 0-85664-262-2, Pub. by Croom helm Ltd). Longwood Pub Group.

Al-Otaiba, Mana S. Essays on Petroleum. 176p. 1982. 21.50 (ISBN 0-7099-1921-2, Pub. by Croom Helm Ltd). Longwood Pub Group.

--The Petroleum Concession Agreements of the United Arab Emirates: Adu Dhabi 1939-1981, 2 vols. 1982. Set. 165.00 (ISBN 0-7099-1915-8, Pub. by Croom Helm Ltd). Longwood Pub Group.

Al-Otaiba, Mana Saeed. Petroleum & the Economy of the United Arab Emirates. 304p. 1977. 90.00 (ISBN 0-85664-519-2, Pub. by Croom Helm Ltd). Longwood Pub Group.

Alotta, Robert I. Number Two: A Look at the Vice Presidency. LC 81-2109. (Illus.). 256p. (gr. 8 up). 1981. PLB 10.79 (ISBN 0-671-41628-6). Messner.

--Old Names & New Places. LC 78-20915. (Illus.). 112p. 1979. 8.95 (ISBN 0-664-32647-1). Westminster.

--Street Names of Philadelphia. LC 75-14689. 158p. 1975. 10.95 (ISBN 0-87722-046-8). Temple U Pr.

Alouf, J. E., et al, eds. Bacterial Protein Toxins. (Fems Symposia Ser.). 1984. 26.00 (ISBN 0-12-053080-5). Acad Pr.

Alovert, Nina. Baryshnikov in Russia. Huntoon, Irene, tr. from Rus. LC 83-13012. 224p. 1984. 30.00 (ISBN 0-03-062589-0). HR&W.

Alpander, Guvenc G. Human Resources Management Planning. 320p. 1982. 24.95 (ISBN 0-8144-5750-9); pap. 9.95 (ISBN 0-8144-7578-7). AMACOM.

Alpar, John J., jt. auth. see Fechner, Paul.

Alpar, Murat. Memet, the Foreign Worker: Poems. Taylor, Alexander, tr. LC 80-16550. 1980. pap. 3.50 (ISBN 0-915306-19-0). Curbstone.

Alpatov. Artistic Problems of the Italian Renaissance. 286p. 1976. 60.00x (ISBN 0-317-14222-4, Pub. by Collet's). State Mutual Bk.

Alpatov, Mikhail V. Geschichte der Altrussischen Kunst. (Illus., Ger.). Repr. 60.00 (ISBN 0-384-00910-7). Johnson Repr.

--Russian Impact on Art. Wolf, Martin L., ed. Litvinov, Ivy, tr. LC 75-90461. Repr. of 1950 ed. lib. bdg. 37.50x (ISBN 0-8371-2160-4, ALRA). Greenwood.

Alpaugh, Craig. Bad for Business. (Orig.). 1985. pap. text ed. 4.00 (ISBN 0-88734-307-4). Players Pr.

--Filthy Habit. (Orig.). 1985. pap. text ed. 4.00 (ISBN 0-88734-311-2). Players Pr.

Alpaugh, Patricia & Haney, Margaret. Counseling the Older Adult. 9.95 (ISBN 0-686-94882-3). Hollander Co.

--Counseling the Older Adult: A Training Manual. LC 77-99241. 1978. 10.00x (ISBN 0-88474-043-9, 05727-4). Lexington Bks.

Alpenvereins Buchereio, Munich. Kataloge der Alpenvereins Bucherei: Catalogs of the Alpine Association Library, 2 pts. Incl. Pt. 1. Autorenkatalog,Author Catalog, 3 vols. 300.00 (ISBN 0-8161-0849-8); Pt. 2. Sachkatalog,Subject Catalog, 3 vols. 297.00 (ISBN 0-8161-0101-9). 1970 (Hall Library). G K Hall.

Alper, A. M., ed. High Temperature Oxides. Incl. Part 1. Magnesia, Lime & Chrome Refractories. 1970 (ISBN 0-12-053301-4); Part 2. Oxides of Rare Earths, Titanium, Zirconium, Hafnium, Niobium & Tantalum. 1970 (ISBN 0-12-053302-2); Part 3. MgO Al203, BcO Ceramics. 1970 (ISBN 0-12-053303-0); Part 4. Refractory Glasses, Glass-Ceramics & Ceramics. 1971 (ISBN 0-12-053304-9). 72.00 ea. Acad Pr.

Alper, Allan M., ed. Phase Diagrams: Materials Science & Technology Vol. 5: Crystal Chemistry, Stoichiometry, Spinodal Decomposition, Properties of Inorganic Phases. (Refractory Materials Ser.: Vol. 6-V). 1978. 70.00 (ISBN 0-12-053205-0). Acad Pr.

Alper, Allen, ed. Phase Diagrams: Materials Science & Technology. Incl. Part 1. Theory, Principles & Techniques of Phase Diagrams. 1970. 77.00 (ISBN 0-12-053201-8); Part 2. The Use of Phase Diagrams in Metals, Refractories, Ceramics, Glass & Electronic Materials. 1970. 77.00 (ISBN 0-12-053202-6); Part 3. The Use of Phase Diagrams in Electronic Materials & Glass Technology. 1970. 77.00 (ISBN 0-12-053203-4); Pt. 4. The Use of Phase Diagrams in Technical Materials. 1976. 72.00 (ISBN 0-12-053204-2). (Refractory Materials Ser: Vol. 6). Acad Pr.

Alper, B. S. Prisons Inside Out: Alternatives in Correctional Reform. LC 74-2268. 1975. pap. 12.95 prof ref (ISBN 0-88410-211-4). Ballinger Pub.

Alper, Benedict S. & Nichols, Lawrence T. Beyond the Courtroom: Community Justice & Programs in Conflict Resolution. LC 78-20376. 320p. 1981. 21.00x (ISBN 0-669-02724-3). Lexington Bks.

Alper, Howard. Transition Metal Organometallics in Organic Synthesis, 2 vols. (Organic Chemistry Ser.). Vol. 1, 1976. 66.00 (ISBN 0-12-053101-1); Vol. 2, 1978. 43.50 (ISBN 0-12-053102-X). Acad Pr.

Alper, Lynne & Holmberg, Meg. Parents, Kids, & Computers. LC 84-50360. (Illus.). 145p. (Orig.). 1984. pap. 4.95 (ISBN 0-89588-151-9). SYBEX.

--Parents, Kids & the Commodore 64. 110p. 1984. pap. 9.95 (ISBN 0-89588-234-5). SYBEX.

Alper, T. Cellular Radiobiology. LC 78-68331. (Illus.). 1979. 54.50 (ISBN 0-521-22411-X); pap. 18.95 (ISBN 0-521-29479-7). Cambridge U Pr.

Alperin, David S., ed. see Interstate Bureau of Regulations.

Alperin, Melvin & Alperin, Stanley, eds. Directory of Major Medical Libraries Worldwide. 1978. 86.00x (ISBN 0-916524-07-8, 506). US Direct Serv.

Alperin, Richard J. Rimmonim Bells: Ten Generations of the Behrman, Drucker, Hahn, Stockler & Sztynberg Families Plus Ten Related Lines. LC 80-65119. (Illus.). 249p. 1980. 39.95x (ISBN 0-9603932-0-X). Junius Inc.

Alperin, Sondra P., ed. Guide Book to Florida Nursing Homes. 1979. 19.95 (ISBN 0-916524-12-4). US Direct Serv.

Alperin, Stanley, ed. Directory of Medical Schools Worldwide. 3rd ed. LC 77-93356. 1982. text ed. 24.95 (ISBN 0-916524-17-5). US Direct Serv.

--Directory of Medical Schools Worldwide. 4th ed. Date not set. price not set (ISBN 0-916524-25-6). US Direct Serv.

--The Federal Hospital Phone Book: 1983-84. pap. 24.99 (ISBN 0-916524-19-1). US Direct Serv.

--Hospital Phone Book-Canada 1985-86. pap. 75.00 (ISBN 0-916524-23-X). US Direct Serv.

--The Hospital Phone Book: 1983-84. pap. 29.95 (ISBN 0-916524-18-3). US Direct Serv.

--Hospital Phone Book 1985-86. pap. 34.99 (ISBN 0-916524-22-1). US Direct Serv.

--Insurance Phone Book & Directory: 1984-85. 1984. 59.95 (ISBN 0-916524-21-3). US Direct Serv.

--U. S. Medical Directory 1983-84. 6th ed. LC 72-92344. 1983. 89.95 (ISBN 0-916524-20-5). US Direct Serv.

Alperin, Stanley, jt. ed. see Alperin, Melvin.

Alpern, Andrew. Handbook of Specialty Elements in Architecture. (Illus.). 448p. 1982. 49.50 (ISBN 0-07-001360-8). McGraw.

Alpern, Gerald D. Divorce: Rights of Passage. 247p. 1983. pap. text ed. 9.95 (ISBN 0-912397-00-4). Psych Dev Pubns.

Alpern, Henry. March of Philosophy. LC 68-15817. 1968. Repr. of 1933 ed. 22.50x (ISBN 0-8046-0008-2, Pub. by Kennikat). Assoc Faculty Pr.

Alpern, Hymen, jt. auth. see Martel, Jose.

Alperovitch, A., et al, eds. Evaluation of Efficacy of Medical Action. 536p. 1980. 78.75 (ISBN 0-444-85379-0). Elsevier.

Alperovitch, I. M., et al. Magnetotellurics in Oil Exploration in the U.S.S.R. Keller, G. V., tr. Vozoff, K. & Asten, M., eds. 65p. 1982. pap. 12.00 (ISBN 0-931830-19-2). Soc Exploration.

Alperovitz, Gar. Atomic Diplomacy: Hiroshima & Potsdam. rev. ed. 416p. 1985. pap. 7.95 (ISBN 0-14-008337-5). Penguin.

Alperovitz, Gar & Faux, Jeff. Rebuilding America: A Blueprint for the New Economy. 1984. 19.50 (ISBN 0-394-53200-7); pap. 10.95 (ISBN 0-394-71619-1). Pantheon.

Alperovitz, Gar, ed. American Economic Policy: Problems & Prospects. Skurski, Roger. LC 83-40592. 256p. 1984. text ed. 20.95 (ISBN 0-268-00612-1, 85-06131); pap. text ed. 9.95 (ISBN 0-268-00613-X, 85-06123). U of Notre Dame Pr.

Alpers, Anthony. Life of Katherine Mansfield. 1982. pap. 7.95 (ISBN 0-14-006219-X). Penguin.

Alpers, Antony. The Life of Katherine Mansfield. (Illus.). 1980. 16.95 (ISBN 0-670-42805-1). Viking.

Alpers, Byron J. & Afrow, Mitchell L. Carpentry. (Shoptalk-Vocational Reading Skills). (gr. 9-12). 1978. pap. text ed. 7.88 (ISBN 0-205-05820-5, 4958209). Allyn.

--Metal & Machines. (Shoptalk - Vocational Reading Skills Ser.). (gr. 9-12). 1978. pap. text ed. 7.88 (ISBN 0-205-05823-X, 4958233); tchr's guide 8.40 (ISBN 0-205-05824-8, 4958241). Allyn.

--You & Your Work. (Shoptalk - Vocational Reading Skills). (gr. 9-12). 1978. pap. text ed. 7.88 (ISBN 0-205-05825-6, 495825X). Allyn.

Alpers, David H., et al. Manual of Nutritional Therapeutics. (Little, Brown Spiral Manual Ser.). 457p. 1983. Spiral bdg. 16.95 (ISBN 0-316-03509-2). Little.

Alpers, Edward A. Ivory & Slaves in East Central Africa: Changing Patterns of International Trade to the Later Nineteenth Century. LC 73-93046. (Illus.). 1974. 38.50x (ISBN 0-520-02689-6). U of Cal Pr.

Alpers, Edward A. & Fontaine, Pierre-Michel, eds. Walter Rodney, Revolutionary & Scholar: A Tribute. LC 82-4509. (CAAS Special Publications Ser.). (Illus.). 200p. (Orig.). 1983. 17.95 (ISBN 0-934934-09-6); pap. 10.95x (ISBN 0-934934-08-8). Ctr Afro-Am Stud.

Alpers, Leonard, jt. auth. see Kuhn, Dolores.

Alpers, Lynne, jt. auth. see Blumenfeld, Esther.

Alpers, Paul. The Singer of the Eclogues: A Study of Virgilian Pastoral. LC 77-93465. 1979. 27.50x (ISBN 0-520-03651-4). U of Cal Pr.

Alpers, Paul J. Poetry of "The Faerie Queene". LC 80-50217. 432p. 1982. 25.00; pap. 10.00 (ISBN 0-8262-0383-3). U of MO Pr.

Alpers, Svetlana. The Art of Describing: Dutch Art in the Seventeenth Century. LC 82-6969. (Illus.). 1983. 42.50x (ISBN 0-226-01512-2). U of Chicago Pr.

--The Art of Describing: Dutch Art in the Seventeenth Century. LC 82-6969. (Illus.). xxviii, 274p. 1984. pap. 19.95 (ISBN 0-226-01513-0). U of Chicago Pr.

Alpert. Florida Law of Damages. 2nd ed. incl. latest pocket part supplement 80.95 (ISBN 0-686-90167-3); separate pocket part supplement, 1984 (for use in 1985) 16.95 (ISBN 0-686-90168-1). Harrison Co GA.

--Motor Vehicle No-Fault Law: Alpert's Florida. rev. ed. 225p. 1985. 39.95 (ISBN 0-317-20127-1). Harrison Co GA.

--Products Liability. (The Law in Florida Ser.). incl. latest pocket part supplement 24.95 (ISBN 0-686-90256-4); separate pocket part supplement, 1983 22.45 (ISBN 0-686-90257-2); separate 1984 Supplementary Insert to 1983 Supplement 14.95. Harrison Co GA.

Alpert & Murphy. Florida Workmen's Compensation Law. 3 Ed. ed. incl. latest separately bound cumulative supplement 96.95 (ISBN 0-686-90214-9); separately bound cumulative supplement, 1983 54.95 (ISBN 0-686-90215-7); 1984 insert 18.95. Harrison Co GA.

Alpert, Augusta. The Solving of Problem-Situations by Preschool Children. LC 74-176514. (Columbia University. Teachers College. Contributions to Education: No. 323). Repr. of 1928 ed. 22.50 (ISBN 0-404-55323-0). AMS Pr.

Alpert, Carl. Technion: The Story of Israel's Institute of Technology. LC 82-11556. (Illus.). 439p. 1983. 25.00x (ISBN 0-87203-102-0). Hermon.

Alpert, Elliot & Hirai, Hidematsu, eds. Oncodevelopmental Biology & Medicine, Vol. 417. 92.00x (ISBN 0-89766-228-8); pap. 92.00x (ISBN 0-89766-229-6). NY Acad Sci.

Alpert, Elliot, jt. ed. see Hirai, Hidematsu.

Alpert, Geoffrey P. Legal Rights of Prisoners: An Analysis of Legal Aid. LC 78-4343. (Illus.). 192p. 1978. 24.50x (ISBN 0-669-02347-7). Lexington Bks.

Alpert, Geoffrey P., ed. Legal Rights of Prisoners. LC 80-17241. (Sage Criminal Justice System Annuals: Vol. 14). (Illus.). 280p. 1980. 28.00 (ISBN 0-8039-1188-2). Sage.

--Legal Rights of Prisoners. LC 80-17241. (Sage Criminal Justice System Annuals: Vol. 14). (Illus.). 280p. 1980. pap. 14.00 (ISBN 0-8039-1189-0). Sage.

Alpert, George. The Queens. LC 74-30498. (Photography Ser). (Illus., Orig.). 1975. pap. 5.95 (ISBN 0-306-80012-8). Da Capo.

Alpert, George & Leogrande, Ernest. A Second Chance to Live: The Suicide Syndrome. LC 75-20452. (Photography Ser.). (Illus.). 90p. 1976. lib. bdg. 19.50 (ISBN 0-306-70751-9); pap. 6.95 (ISBN 0-306-80023-3). Da Capo.

Alpert, Hollis. Burton. 272p. 1986. 16.95 (ISBN 0-399-13093-4). Putnam Pub Group.

Al'pert, I. L. Radio Wave Propagation & the Ionosphere. LC 61-17727. pap. 101.00 (ISBN 0-317-09200-6, 2020656). Bks Demand UMI.

Alpert, Jane. Growing up Underground. LC 82-62184. 372p. 1983. pap. 6.70 (ISBN 0-688-01396-1, Quill). Morrow.

Alpert, Jonathan L. Florida Settlement & Release. LC 82-246638. (Illus.). xi, 151p. 1982. 35.95; separate pocket part supplement, 1984 13.95. Harrison Co GA.

Alpert, Joseph E., jt. auth. see Dalen, James E.

Alpert, Joseph S. The Heart Attack Handbook: A Commonsense Guide to Prevention, Treatment, Recovery & Staying Well. 256p. 1984. 14.45; pap. 6.70i. Little.

--The Heart Attack Handbook: A Commonsense Guide to Treatment, Recovery & Staying Well. 2nd ed. 180p. 1984. 12.45i (ISBN 0-316-03507-6); pap. 4.70i (ISBN 0-316-03506-8). Little.

--Physiopathology of the Cardiovascular System. (Physiopathology Ser.). 348p. 1984. pap. text ed. 19.95 (ISBN 0-316-03504-1). Little.

Alpert, Joseph S. & Francis, Gary S. Manual of Coronary Care. 3rd ed. (The Spiral Manual Ser.). 190p. 1984. 16.95 (ISBN 0-316-03508-4). Little.

Alpert, Joseph S. & Rippe, James M. Manual of Cardiovascular Diagnosis & Therapy. (Little, Brown SPIRAL TM Manual Ser.). 1980. 16.95 (ISBN 0-316-03502-5). Little.

--Manual of Cardiovascular Diagnosis & Therapy. (Spiral Manual Ser.). 400p. 1984. spiral bdg. 17.95 (ISBN 0-316-03510-6). Little.

Alpert, Joseph S., jt. auth. see Gore, Joel M.

Alpert, Judith, et al. Psychological Consultation in Educational Settings: A Casebook for Working with Administrators, Teachers, Students, & Community. LC 82-8995. (Social & Behavioral Science Ser.). 1982. text ed. 22.95x (ISBN 0-87589-528-X). Jossey Bass.

Alpert, Judith L. & Meyers, Joel. Training in Consultation: Perspectives from Mental Health, Behavioral & Organizational Consultation. 268p. 1983. 21.50x (ISBN 0-398-04801-0). C C Thomas.

Alpert, M. E., et al. Chemical & Radionuclide Food Contamination. (Illus.). 220p. 1973. text ed. 29.50x (ISBN 0-8422-7091-4). Irvington.

Alpert, Martin A. Cardiac Arrhythmias. (Illus.). 256p. 1980. pap. 28.50 (ISBN 0-8151-0118-X). Year Bk Med.

Alpert, Michael, tr. Two Spanish Picaresque Novels. Incl. Lazarillo De Tormes; Swindler. Quevedo, Francisco. (Classics Ser). (Orig.). 1969. pap. 4.95 (ISBN 0-14-044211-1). Penguin.

Alpert, Murray. Controversies in Schizophrenia: Changes & Constancies. (Proceedings of the American Psychopathological Association). text ed. 42.50 (ISBN 0-89862-375-8). Guilford Pr.

Alpert, Nancy L. Religion & Psychology: A Medical Subject Analysis & Research Index with Bibliography. LC 83-71657. 150p. 1985. 29.95 (ISBN 0-88164-034-4); pap. 21.95 (ISBN 0-88164-035-2). ABBE Pubs Assn.

Alpert, Nelson L., et al. IR-Theory & Practice of Infrared Spectroscopy. rev. 2nd ed. LC 70-107535. 394p. 1970. 45.00 (ISBN 0-306-30399-X, Plenum Pr); pap. 8.95 (ISBN 0-306-20001-5, Plenum Pr). Plenum Pub.

--IR-Theory & Practice of Infrared Spectroscopy. LC 73-12968. 394p. 1973. pap. text ed. 8.95x (ISBN 0-306-20001-5, Rosetta). Plenum Pub.

Alpert, Norman. Cardiac Hypertrophy. 642p. 1971. 82.00 (ISBN 0-12-053550-5). Acad Pr.

Alpert, Norman R., ed. Myocardial Hypertrophy & Failure. (Perspectives in Cardiovascular Research Ser.: Vol. 7). (Illus.). 720p. 1983. text ed. 99.00 (ISBN 0-89004-743-X). Raven.

Alpert, Ronald L. & Ward, Edward J. Evaluating Unsprinklered Fire Hazards. 5.35 (ISBN 0-318-00407-0, TR83-2). Society Fire Protect.

Alpert, Stephen P. & Smith, Kenneth E. Amusement Tokens of the United States & Canada. LC 79-88433. (Illus.). 136p. (Orig.). 1979. pap. 24.95 (ISBN 0-934422-20-6). Mead Pub Corp.

Alpert, Stuart W., jt. auth. see Taylor, Delores A.

Alpert, Y. L. The Near-Earth & Interplanetary Plasma: General Properties & Fundamental Theory, Vol. 1. 175p. 1983. 72.50 (ISBN 0-521-24364-5). Cambridge U Pr.

--The Near-Earth & Interplanetary Plasma: Plasma Flow, Plasma Waves & Oscillations, Vol. 2. LC 82-12879. 150p. 1983. 62.50 (ISBN 0-521-24601-6). Cambridge U Pr.

Al'pert, Y. L. Radio Wave Propagation & the Ionosphere, Vol. 1: The Ionosphere. 2nd ed. LC 75-167674. (Illus.). 430p. 1973. 45.00x (ISBN 0-306-17141-4, Consultants). Plenum Pub.

--Waves & Satellites in the Near-Earth Plasma. LC 74-19475. (Studies in Soviet Science: Physical Sciences). (Illus.). 196p. 1974. 45.00 (ISBN 0-306-10910-7, Consultants). Plenum Pub.

Al'pert, Y. L. & Fligel', D. S. Propagation of ELF & VLF Waves Near the Earth. LC 69-12526. 171p. 1970. 32.50x (ISBN 0-306-10836-4, Consultants). Plenum Pub.

--Propagation of ELF & VLF Waves Near the Earth. LC 75-167674. (Illus.). 280p. 1974. 42.50x (ISBN 0-306-17142-2, Consultants). Plenum Pub.

Al'pert, Y. L., et al. Space Physics with Artificial Satellites. LC 64-23253. 240p. 1965. 42.50x (ISBN 0-306-10727-9, Consultants). Plenum Pub.

Alpert, Yakov L., ed. Radio Wave Propagation & the Ionosphere: Propagation of Electromagnetic Waves Near the Earth, Vol. 2. 2nd ed. LC 75-167674. 268p. 1974. 42.50x (ISBN 0-306-17142-2, Plenum Pr). Plenum Pub.

Alpha Pyramis. Candle Molds from Food Containers: Poem with Bibliography. 1985. pap. text ed. 1.00 (ISBN 0-913597-83-X, Pub. by Alpha Pyramis). Prosperity & Profits.

--Candles in Rituals, Folklore, Etc. A Bibliography. 21p. (Orig.). 1985. pap. text ed. 2.75 (ISBN 0-318-04374-2, Alpha Pyramis). Prosperity & Profits.

--Coffee Substitution Poem. 6p. 1984. pap. text ed. 1.00 (ISBN 0-913597-48-1, Pub. by Alpha Pyramis). Prosperity & Profits.

--Family Business & Small Business Suggestions Rhyming Poetry Recital. 16p. 1985. pap. text ed. 2.95 (ISBN 0-913597-92-9, Pub. by Alpha Pyramis). Prosperity & Profits.

--Fashion Poetry Recital Book One. 14p. 1984. pap. text ed. 3.00 (ISBN 0-913597-60-0, Pub. by Alpha Pyramis). Prosperity & Profits.

--Fashion Poetry Recital Book Two. 14p. 1984. pap. text ed. 3.00 (ISBN 0-913597-61-9, Pub. by Alpha Pyramis). Prosperity & Profits.

--Gourmet Food Poems, Appetizing Ideas: Book One. 13p. 1984. pap. text ed. 2.50 (ISBN 0-913597-62-7, Pub. by Alpha Pyramis). Prosperity & Profits.

--New Age Consciousness & Awareness Poetry, Bk. 1. 15p. 1985. pap. 3.95 (ISBN 0-913597-59-7, Pub. by Alpha Pyramis). Prosperity & Profits.

--Old Fashioned Baby Foods, Powders, Oils, etc. 10p. 1985. pap. text ed. 1.50 (ISBN 0-318-04418-8, Pub. by Alpha Pyramis). Prosperity & Profits.

--Recycling Simulation Activity Sessions, Vol. 1. 60p. 1984. 15.95 (ISBN 0-913597-57-0, Pub. by Alpha Pyramis). Prosperity & Profits.

--Rhyming Pattern, Bk. 1. 8p. 1984. pap. text ed. 7.95 (ISBN 0-913597-46-5, Pub. by Alpha Pyramis). Prosperity & Profits.

--Rhyming Recipe & Cookbook, Vol. 1. 21p. 1984. pap. text ed. 5.95 (ISBN 0-913597-50-3, Pub. by Alpha Pyramis). Prosperity & Profits.

--Roses As Food, Medicine, Cosmetics, Etc. A Rosy Rhyme Book. 10p. 1984. pap. text ed. 2.35 (ISBN 0-913597-69-4, Pub. by Alpha Pyramis). Prosperity & Profits.

--Small Business Services Suggestions; Poetry, Bk. 1. 38p. 1948. pap. text ed. 4.75 (ISBN 0-913597-45-7, Pub. by Alpha Pyramis). Prosperity & Profits.

--Tea Poetry Book of Medicinal Uses, Bk. 1. 11p. 1984. pap. text ed. 1.00 (ISBN 0-913597-54-6, Pub. by Alpha Pyramis). Prosperity & Profits.

--Telemarketing Rhymes, Verses & Poetry. 28p. 1985. pap. text ed. 4.95 (ISBN 0-913597-90-2, Alpha Pyramis). Prosperity & Profits.

--Vinegar Use Poetry Pages. 30p. 1984. pap. text ed. 1.50 (ISBN 0-913597-66-X, Pub. by Alpha Pyramis). Prosperity & Profits.

Alpha Pyramis Business Division Staff, tr. Answering Services, Mail Services & Executive Office Services Located in 10 U. S. Cities: Atlanta, Houston, Detroit, Miami, Chicago, New York, Phoenix, Denver, Minneapolis & New Orleans; A Reference. 40p. 1984. pap. 6.95 (Pub. by Alpha Pyramis). Prosperity & Profits.

Alpha Pyramis Cookbook Division. Cook's Helper Recipe Ingredient Substitution Cookbook. 50p. 1985. pap. text ed. 6.95 (ISBN 0-913597-87-2, Pub. by Alpha Pyramis). Prosperity & Profits.

Alpha Pyramis Educational Division. Coupons, Cashoffs, etc. Seminar or Workshop Workbook. 21p. 1984. pap. text ed. 10.95 (ISBN 0-913597-23-6, Pub. by Alpha Pyramis). Prosperity & Profits.

--Fundraising Projects Seminar: Workshop Workbook. 50p. 1984. pap. text ed. 9.95 (ISBN 0-913597-24-4, Pub. by Alpha Pyramis). Prosperity & Profits.

Alpha Pyramis Publishing Co. Staff. Gift Basket Idea Index. 86p. 1985. pap. 6.95 (ISBN 0-913597-72-4, Pub. by Alpha Pyramis). Prosperity & Profits.

Alpha Pyramis Research Center. Answering Services, Mail Services, & Executive Office Services Located in Canada. 15p. 1984. pap. text ed. 3.00 (ISBN 0-913597-34-1, Pub. by Alpha Pyramis). Prosperity & Profits.

Alpha Pyramis Research Division. Alchemy: A Bibliography. 50p. 1984. pap. 3.75 (ISBN 0-913597-40-6, Pub. by Alpha Pyramis). Prosperity & Profits.

--Almost Butter: Alternative Butter Recipe Book. 1984. pap. 2.50 (ISBN 0-913597-72-4, Pub. by Alpha Pyramis). Prosperity & Profits.

--Almost Milk: Milk Alternative. 15p. 1984. pap. 1.75 (ISBN 0-913597-72-4, Pub. by Alpha Pyramis). Prosperity & Profits.

--Ancient Egypt: A Bibliography. 50p. 1984. pap. 3.75 (ISBN 0-913597-39-2, Pub. by Alpha Pyramis). Prosperity & Profits.

--Answering Services, Mail Services & Executive Office Services Located in Singapore. 10p. 1984. pap. text ed. 4.95 (ISBN 0-913597-35-X, Pub. by Alpha Pyramis). Prosperity & Profits.

--Answering Services, Mail Services, & Executive Office Services Located in London. 10p. 1984. pap. text ed. 2.00 (ISBN 0-913597-37-6, Pub. by Alpha Pyramis). Prosperity & Profits.

--Black American History: Rhyme One. 30p. 1984. pap. text ed. 3.95 (ISBN 0-913597-53-8, Pub. by Alpha Pyramis). Prosperity & Profits.

--Business Start Up Fees: An International Directory. 100p. 1983. text ed. 17.95 (ISBN 0-913597-01-5, Pub. by Alpha Pyramis). Prosperity & Profits.

--Dude Ranches, Lodges, Country Inns etc. An International Index of Books & References. 126p. 1983. text ed. 17.95 (ISBN 0-913597-14-7, Pub. by Alpha Pyramis). Prosperity & Profits.

--Farmers Markets: An International Directory. 160p. 1983. text ed. 9.95 (ISBN 0-913597-03-1, Pub. by Alpha Pyramis). Prosperity & Profits.

--Home Exchanges, Time Sharing, Bed & Breakfast Organizations: An International Directory. 200p. 1983. text ed. 9.95 (ISBN 0-913597-04-X, Pub. by Alpha Pyramis). Prosperity & Profits.

--Honey Plant Source: Alphabet Poem. (Alphabet Poem Ser.). 6p. 1984. pap. text ed. 1.00 (ISBN 0-913597-44-9, Pub. by Alpha Pyramis). Prosperity & Profits.

--Incorporating Fees: An International Directory. 60p. 1983. text ed. 6.75 (ISBN 0-913597-05-8, Pub. by Alpha Pyramis). Prosperity & Profits.

--Natural & Hot Springs: An International Directory. 75p. 1983. text ed. 4.75 (ISBN 0-913597-07-4, Pub. by Alpha Pyramis). Prosperity & Profits.

--Non-Bank Safe Deposit Boxes: An International Directory. 215p. 1983. text ed. 19.95 (ISBN 0-913597-08-2, Pub. by Alpha Pyramis). Prosperity & Profits.

--Recyclable Scrap: Places to Locate; An International Directory. 150p. 1983. text ed. 16.95 (ISBN 0-913597-09-0, Pub. by Alpha Pyramis). Prosperity & Profits.

--Self Storage Units or Warehouses: An International Directory. 300p. 1983. text ed. 17.95 (ISBN 0-913597-12-0, Pub. by Alpha Pyramis). Prosperity & Profits.

Alpha Pyramis Research Division Staff. Almost Sugar: Sweet Alternatives. 12p. 1984. pap. 1.75 (ISBN 0-913597-10-4, Pub. by Alpha Pyramis). Prosperity & Profits.

--Baby & Infant Thrift Book: Thrifty Suggestions. 6p. 1985. pap. text ed. 1.50 (ISBN 0-318-04416-1, Pub. by Alpha Pyramis). Prosperity & Profits.

--Carob: A Bibliography. 1984. pap. 3.50 (Pub. by Alpha Pyramis). Prosperity & Profits.

--Castor Oil Beauty, Medicinal & Other Uses. 1984. pap. 1.75 (Pub. by Alpha Pyramis). Prosperity & Profits.

--Freemasonry: A Bibliography. 60p. Date not set. pap. 3.00 (ISBN 0-913597-38-4, Pub. by Alpha Pyramis). Prosperity & Profits.

--Geo the Geography Airplane: A Geography Reference. 43p. 1984. pap. text ed. 3.95 (ISBN 0-913597-52-X, Pub. by Alpha Pyramis). Prosperity & Profits.

--Not Quite Hamburger Meat: Imitation Hamburger Meat Recipe Book. 20p. 1984. pap. 3.75 (ISBN 0-913597-68-6, Pub. by Alpha Pyramis). Prosperity & Profits.

Alpha Pyramis Staff. The Any Occasion Card, the All Occasion Card, & the Promise Card: Rhyming Suggestions for Use Plus Greeting Cards. 14p. 1984. pap. text ed. 2.00 (ISBN 0-913597-18-X, Pub. by Alpha Pyramis). Prosperity & Profits.

--The Appreciation Card, the Recycler Notice, & the Reminder Card. (Rhyming Suggestions for Use Plus Greeting Cards Ser.). 13p. 1984. pap. 2.00 (ISBN 0-913597-19-8, Pub. by Alpha Pyramis). Prosperity & Profits.

--Catering Services: Creative Suggestion Pages. 16p. (Orig.). 1985. pap. text ed. 4.00 (ISBN 0-913597-89-9, Pub. by Alpha Pyramis). Prosperity & Profits.

--Coupon Search: How to Locate Coupons, Forms, Etc. 1986. pap. text ed. 5.25 (ISBN 0-318-12005-4, Pub. by Alpha Pyramis). Prosperity & Profits.

--Dear Departed: Poetry for the Occasion. 20p. 1984. pap. text ed. 2.95 (ISBN 0-913597-67-8, Pub. by Alpha Pyramis). Prosperity & Profits.

--One Six & One-Half Ounce Can of Tuna Ingredient Substitution Cookbook. 18p. 1985. pap. text ed. 4.95 (ISBN 0-913597-88-0, Pub. by Alpha Pyramis). Prosperity & Profits.

--The Travel Inquiry Card, Daily Housekeeping Itinerary, & Daily Babysitter Instruction Card: Suggestions for Use Plus Cards. 10p. 1984. pap. 2.00 (ISBN 0-913597-20-1, Pub. by Alpha Pyramis). Prosperity & Profits.

Alpha Pyramis World Business Division, tr. Singapore Survival Address Guide. 15p. 1984. pap. 4.00 (ISBN 0-913597-43-0, Pub. by Alpha Pyramis). Prosperity & Profits.

Alpha Research & Development, Inc. Investigation of Adhesives for Use with Copper Hydrolytic & Thermal Stability. 53p. 1966. 7.95 (ISBN 0-317-34531-1, 79). Intl Copper.

Alphand, Adolphe. Les Promenades de Paris. (Illus.). 464p. 1984. Repr. of 1873 ed. text ed. 75.00 (ISBN 0-910413-06-1). Princeton Arch.

Alphandery, Paul. Les Idees Morales Chez les Heterodoxes Latins Au Debut Du Xiiie Siecle. LC 78-63184. (Heresies of the Early Christian & Medieval Era: Second Ser.). Repr. of 1903 ed. 27.50 (ISBN 0-404-16198-7). AMS Pr.

Alpharetta, Georgia, jt. auth. see Twing, J. W.

Alphen, Corry Van see Van Alphen, Corry.

Alphen, J. Van see Van Alphen, J.

Alphonso-Karkala, John B. Comparative World Literature: Seven Essays. 98p. 1976. lib. bdg. 9.95 (ISBN 0-89253-048-0). Ind-US Inc.

Alphonso-Karkala, John B., ed. Vedic Vision. 80p. 1980. pap. 4.50 (ISBN 0-86578-004-8). Ind-US Inc.

Alphonsus, Mary. St. Rose of Lima. LC 81-86444. 304p. 1982. pap. 8.00 (ISBN 0-89555-172-1). TAN Bks Pubs.

Alpiar, Ronald. Computer Data & Mass Storage. (Illus.). pap. cancelled (ISBN 0-85012-175-2). Intl Pubns Serv.

Alpin & Dowd. Anderson's Ohio Criminal Practice & Procedure, 2 vols. 2300p. 1979. 155.00; 1984 suppl. incl. Anderson Pub Co.

Alpiner, Jerome G. Handbook of Adult Rehabilitative Audiology. 2nd ed. (Illus.). 402p. 1982. lib. bdg. 35.00 (ISBN 0-683-00076-4). Williams & Wilkins.

Alps, Glen. Glen Alps Retrospective: The Collagraph Idea, Nineteen Fifty-Six to Nineteen Eighty. Bellevue Art Museum, ed. LC 79-54958. (Illus.). pap. 4.95 (ISBN 0-295-95703-4). U of Wash Pr.

Al-Qadi, Wadad, ed. Studia Arabica et Islamia: Festschrift for Ihsan Abbas. 1981. 175.00x (ISBN 0-8156-6058-8, Am U Beirut). Syracuse U Pr.

Al-Qaradawi, Yusuf. The Lawful & the Prohibited in Islam. Siddiqui, Mohammed M., tr. from Arabic. LC 80-81562. Orig. Title: Al-Halal Wal-Haram Fil Islam. 355p. (Orig., Eng.). 1981. write for info. (ISBN 0-89259-016-5); pap. write for info. (ISBN 0-686-85630-9). Am Trust Pubns.

Al-Qazzaz, Ayad. Arab World: Handbook for Teachers. pap. 12.00x (ISBN 0-86685-328-6). Intl Bk Ctr.

--Women in the Arab World: An Annotated Bibliography. (Bibliography Ser.: No. 2). 39p. (Orig.). 1975. pap. text ed. 2.50 (ISBN 0-937694-15-0). Assn Arab-Amer U Grads.

--Women in the Middle East & North Africa: An Annotated Bibliography. (Center for Middle Eastern Studies Monograph: No. 2). 190p. 1977. pap. 7.50x (ISBN 0-292-79009-0). U of Tex Pr.

Al-Qazzaz, Ayad & Oweiss, Ibrahim. Two Studies on Israel. (Information Papers: No. 13). 29p. (Orig.). 1974. pap. text ed. 2.75 (ISBN 0-937694-29-0). Assn Arab-Amer U Grads.

Al-Qibrisi, Shaykh N. Mercy Oceans: Teachings of Maulana Abdullah al-Faiza ad-Daghestani. 190p. (Orig.). 1980. pap. 4.75x (ISBN 0-939830-11-6, Pub. by Leon). New Era Pubns MI.

Al-Qirqisani, Ya'Qub. Kitab Al-Anwar Wal-Maraoib: Code of Karaite Law, 3 vols. Incl. Vol. 1. First Discourse - Historical Introduction; Second Discourse - Philosophical & Theological Principles of JurisPrudence; Vol. 2. Third Discourse - Criticism of Sectarian Doctrines; Fourth Discourse - Methods of Construction & Interpretation of Law; Vol. 3. Fifth Discourse - Circumcion - Sabbath; Sixth Discourse - Civil & Criminal Law Liturgy. pap. 49.50 ea. in arabic; Set. pap. 125.00x (ISBN 0-686-52167-6). Elliots Bks.

Alquie, Ferdinand, ed. Entretiens Sur le Surrealisme. (Decades Du Centre Culturel International De Cerisy-la-Salle, Nouvelle Ser.: No. 8). (Illus.). 1968. pap. 30.80x (ISBN 90-279-6018-6). Mouton.

Alquie, Ferdinand, ed. see Descartes, Rene.

Alquist, Tom. Getting Your Way with Parents. LC 80-68888. 128p. (Orig.). (YA) 1981. pap. 3.95 (ISBN 0-89636-065-2). Accent Bks.

Al-Radi, S. Phlamaudhi Vounari: A Sanctuary Site in Cyprus. (Studies in Mediterranean Archaeology Ser.: Vol. LXV). 136p. 1983. pap. text ed. 40.75x (ISBN 91-86098-10-1, Pub. by Paul Astroms Sweden). Humanities.

Al-Raheb, Hani. The Zionist Character in the English Novel. 220p. 1985. pap. 8.95 (ISBN 0-86232-364-9, Pub. by Zed Pr England). Biblio Dist.

Al Rashid, Ibrahim. Saudi Arabia Enters the Modern World: Secret U. S. Documents on the Emergence of the Kingdom of Saudi Arabia As a World Power, 1936-1949, 2 vols. (Documents on the History of Arabia Ser.: Vols. 4 & 5). 1980. Set. lib. bdg. 44.95x set (ISBN 0-89712-056-6). Documentary Pubns.

Al-Rashid, Ibrahim. The Struggle Between the Two Princes: The Kingdom of Saudi Arabia in the Final Days of IBN Saud. (Documents on the History of Arabia Ser.: Vol. VIII). 276p. 1985. text ed. 39.95x (ISBN 0-89712-112-0). Documentary Pubns.

--Yemen Under the Rule of Iman Ahmad. (Documents on the History of Arabia Ser.: Vol. VII). 244p. 1985. text ed. 39.95x (ISBN 0-89712-059-0). Documentary Pubns.

Al-Rashid, Ibrahim, ed. Yemen Enters the Modern World: Secret U. S. Documents on the Rise of the Second Power on the Arabian Peninsula. (Documents on the History of Arabia Ser.: Vol. 6). 1984. ltd. ed. 500 copies 34.95x (ISBN 0-89712-058-2). Documentary Pubns.

Al-Rashid, Rashid A. Pediatric Cancer Chemotherapy. (Medical Outline Ser.). 1979. 33.00 (ISBN 0-87488-685-6); pap. 25.00 (ISBN 0-87488-663-5). Med Exam.

--Pediatric Hematology Case Studies. 1984. pap. text ed. write for info. (ISBN 0-87488-279-6). Med Exam.

Al-Rawi, Ali, rev. by see Daoud, Hazim S.

Alreck, Pamela L. & Settle, Robert B. The Survey Research Handbook. LC 84-71129. 350p. 1985. 37.50 (ISBN 0-87094-529-7). Dow Jones-Irwin.

--The Survey Research Handbook. 1985. pap. 18.95x (ISBN 0-256-03174-6). Irwin.

Alred, Gerald J., et al. Business & Technical Writing: An Annotated Bibliography of Books, 1880-1980. LC 80-29211. 249p. 1981. 15.00 (ISBN 0-8108-1397-1). Scarecrow.

Alred, Gerald J., jt. auth. see Brusaw, Charles T.

Alric, Abbe H. Sketches of a Journey on Two Oceans& to the Interior of America & of a Civil War in Northern Lower California. Jones, Norah E., tr. Nunis, Doyce B., ed. (Baja California Travels Ser.: No. 24). 215p. (Fr.). 1971. 20.00 (ISBN 0-87093-224-1). Dawsons.

Alridge, A. Owen. Early American Literature: A Comparatist Perspective. LC 82-47580. 288p. 1982. 25.00x (ISBN 0-691-06517-9). Princeton U Pr.

Al-Rumi, Yakut. Moujam al Buldan, 5 vols. 50.00x (ISBN 0-86685-359-6). Intl Bk Ctr.

Al-Sabah, Y. S. F. The Oil Economy of Kuwait. 176p. 1981. 29.95x (ISBN 0-7103-0003-4). Routledge & Kegan.

Al-Sabi, Hilal. Rusum Dar Al-Khila Fah (Rules & Regulations of Abbasid Court) Salem, Elie A., ed. 1977. 19.95x (ISBN 0-8156-6046-4, Am U Beirut). Syracuse U Pr.

Al-Sadi, H. N. Seismic Exploration. (Astronomisch-Geophysikalische Reihe Ser.: No. 7). 150p. 1980. 30.95x (ISBN 0-8176-1007-3). Birkhauser.

Al-Sadr, Ayatullah B. He His Messenger & His Message. x ed. Ansari, M. A., tr. from Arabic. 116p. pap. 6.00 (ISBN 0-941724-12-3). Islamic Seminary.

Al Sadr, Muhammad B. Awaited Saviour. 110p. 1983. pap. text ed. 4.00 (ISBN 0-686-90398-6). Islamic Seminary.

--Islam & Schools of Economics. Ansari, M. A., tr. 160p. 1983. pap. text ed. 6.00 (ISBN 0-686-90405-2). Islamic Seminary.

Alsaker, Rasmus. Conquering Colds & Sinus Infections. 2nd ed. 1979. pap. 1.75 (ISBN 0-532-17200-0). Woodhill.

Al-Saleh, Khairat. Fabled Cities, Princes & Jinn from Arabic Myths & Legends. (Illus.). 132p. 1985. 15.95 (ISBN 0-8052-3926-X). Schocken.

Al-Salem, Faisal S. Ecological Dimensions of Development Administration. 1977. 15.00x (ISBN 0-686-12054-X). Intl Bk Dist.

Al-Salman, S. A. Foundation of Algebra. 250p. (Arabic.). 1985. pap. 15.00 (ISBN 0-471-88218-6). Wiley.

Al-Sarraf, Hassan S. Programming with BASIC. 200p. (Arabic.). 1985. pap. 13.00 (ISBN 0-471-80970-5). Wiley.

Al-Sayari, S. S. & Zoetl, J. G., eds. Quaternary Period in Saudi Arabia One. (Illus.). 1978. 61.00 (ISBN 0-387-81448-5). Springer-Verlag.

Al-Sayed, Abdul M. Social Ethics of Islam: Classical Islamic Political Theory & Practice. 1982. 14.95 (ISBN 0-533-04671-8). Vantage.

Al-Sayyid-Marsot, A. L., ed. Society & the Sexes in Medieval Islam. LC 79-63268. (Giorgio Levi Della Vida Biennial Conference Ser.: Vol. 6). 149p. 1979. pap. 18.50x (ISBN 0-89003-033-2). Undena Pubns.

Al-Sayyid Marsot, Afaf L. Egypt in the Reign of Mohammad Ali. LC 83-5241. (Cambridge Middle East Library). (Illus.). 320p. 1984. 49.50 (ISBN 0-521-24795-0); pap. 17.95 (ISBN 0-521-28968-8). Cambridge U Pr.

Al-Sayyid-Marsot, Afaf L. Egypt's Liberal Experiment, 1922-1936. LC 75-22659. 1977. 39.50x (ISBN 0-520-03109-1). U of Cal Pr.

Alsberg, Carl L. Combination in the American Bread-Baking Industry: With Some Observations on the Mergers of 1924-25. LC 73-1987. (Big Business; Economic Power in a Free Society Ser.). Repr. of 1926 ed. 10.00 (ISBN 0-405-05071-2). Ayer Co Pubs.

Alsberg, John. Modern Art & Its Enigma: Art Theories from 1800 to 1950 Based upon the Writings of This Period's Artists & Philosophers. 192p. 1983. 19.95x (ISBN 0-297-78347-5, GWN 04898, Pub. by Weidenfeld & Nicolson England). Biblio Dist.

Alsburg, Chris Van see Van Alsburg, Chris.

ALSC Library Service to the Disadvantaged Child Committee. I Read...I See...I Hear...I Learn. 112p. 1971. write for info. (ISBN 0-8389-3124-3). Assn Library Serv.

Alschuler, Alfred S. Developing Achievement Motivation in Adolescents: Education for Human Growth. LC 72-84336. 330p. 1973. 27.95 (ISBN 0-87778-037-4). Educ Tech Pubns.

--School Discipline: A Socially Literate Solution. 1980. text ed. 19.95 (ISBN 0-07-001127-3). McGraw.

--Teacher Burnout. 96p. 1980. 6.95 (ISBN 0-8106-1680-7). NEA.

Alschuler, Rose H. & Hattwick, LaBerta W. Painting & Personality: A Study of Young Children. rev. & abr. ed. LC 75-75966. (Illus.). 1969. 24.00x (ISBN 0-226-01566-1). U of Chicago Pr.

Alsen, Eberhard. Salinger's Glass Stories As A Composite Novel. LC 82-50411. 300p. 1984. 22.50X (ISBN 0-87875-243-9). Whitston Pub.

Alsever, Robert N. & Gotlin, Ronald W. Handbook of Endocrine Tests in Adults & Children. 2nd ed. (Illus.). 260p. 1978. pap. 22.25 (ISBN 0-8151-0126-0). Year Bk Med.

Alsfeld, Drysdale. The Perplexing Art by Matthias Grunewald & His Most Impressive Paintings. (The Art Library of the Great Masters of the World). (Illus.). 117p. 1983. 81.75x (ISBN 0-86650-087-1). Gloucester Art.

Al-Shahi, Ahmed, jt. ed. see MacEoin, Denis.

Al-Shaikly, Salah, jt. auth. see Mani, Salah A.

Al-Shaikly, Salah, ed. see MacKillop, Andrew.

Alsheler, Joseph. Rifleman of Ohio. 432p. 1981. Repr. lib. bdg. 19.95 (ISBN 0-89968-226-X). Lightyear.

Alsina, Claudi. Vocabulari Catala De Matematica Basica. 48p. (Catalan.). 1977. pap. 8.75 (ISBN 84-85008-06-5, S-50127). French & Eur.

Alsmeyer, D. & Atkins, A. G., eds. Guide to Science & Technology in the Asia Pacific Area. 540p. 150.00x (ISBN 0-582-90100-6, Pub. by Longman). Gale.

Alsmeyer, Marie B. The Way of the WAVES: Women in the Navy. LC 81-81450. 186p. 1981. pap. 12.50x (ISBN 0-9606152-0-2). Hamba Bks.

Alsmeyer, Marie B., ed. Old Waves Tales: Navy Women: Memories of World War II. LC 82-82517. (Illus.). 56p. (Orig.). 1982. pap. 4.95x (ISBN 0-9606152-1-0). Hamba Bks.

Alsobrook, Rosalyn. The Thorn Bush Blooms. 304p. (Orig.). 1981. pap. 2.95 (ISBN 0-505-51753-1, Pub. by Tower Bks). Dorchester Pub Co.

Alson, Jeff, jt. auth. see Gray, Charles, Jr.

Alson, R. E. see Runeckles, V. C., et al.

Alsop, Em B., ed. Greatness of Woodrow Wilson 1856-1956. LC 70-95331. (Essay & General Literature Index Reprint Ser). 1971. Repr. of 1956 ed. 21.00x (ISBN 0-8046-1395-8, Pub. by Kennikat). Assoc Faculty Pr.

Alsop, George. Character of the Province of Maryland. LC 74-39491. (Select Bibliographies Reprint Series). 1972. Repr. of 1902 ed. 10.00 (ISBN 0-8369-9900-2). Ayer Co Pubs.

Alsop, John R. An Index to the Revised Bauer Arndt, Gingrich Greek Lexicon. 2nd ed. (Gr.). 1981. 14.95 (ISBN 0-310-44031-9, 6773P). Zondervan.

Alsop, Joseph. FDR. large print ed. LC 82-5870. (Illus.). 303p. 1982. Repr. of 1982 ed. 13.95 (ISBN 0-89621-369-2). Thorndike Pr.

--FDR: A Centenary Remembrance. LC 81-68381. (Illus.). 256p. 1982. 25.00 (ISBN 0-670-30454-9). Viking.

--FDR: A Centenary Remembrance 1882-1945. (Illus.). 1982. pap. 3.50 (ISBN 0-671-45891-4). WSP.

--The Rare Art Traditions: A History of Art Collecting & Its Linked Phenomena. LC 81-47218. (Illus.). 464p. 1982. 57.64i (ISBN 0-06-010091-5, HarpT). Har-Row.

--The Rare Art Traditions: A History of Art Collecting & Its Linked Phenomena Wherever They Have Appeared. LC 81-47218. (The A. W. Mellon Lectures in the Fine Arts, Bollingen Ser.: No. 35). (Illus.). 500p. 1981. 27.50x (ISBN 0-691-03974-7). Princeton U Pr.

Alsop, Joseph & Catledge, Turner. The One Hundred Sixty-Eight Days. LC 72-2362. (American Constitutional & Legal History Ser). 324p. 1973. Repr. of 1938 ed. lib. bdg. 39.50 (ISBN 0-306-70481-1). Da Capo.

Alsop, Joseph W. From the Silent Earth: A Report of the Greek Bronze Age. LC 81-4122. (Illus.). xviii, 296p. 1981. Repr. of 1964 ed. lib. bdg. 39.00x (ISBN 0-313-23014-5, ALFS). Greenwood.

Alsop, Reese F. Back Talk. LC 80-10084. 1981. 6.95 (ISBN 0-87233-053-2). Bauhan.

Alsop, Richard. The Echo with Other Poems. LC 70-104403. Repr. of 1807 ed. lib. bdg. 18.00 (ISBN 0-8398-0057-6). Irvington.

Alsop, Stewart. Stay of Execution: A Sort of Memoir. LC 73-13691. 1973. 12.45i (ISBN 0-397-00897-X). Har-Row.

Alsop, Stewart & Branden, Thomas. Sub Rosa: The O.S.S. & American Espionage. LC 64-57431. 272p. 1964. pap. 1.65 (ISBN 0-15-686300-6, Harv). HarBraceJ.

Alsop, Susan M. The Congress Dances. 1985. pap. 3.95 (ISBN 0-671-55680-0). WSP.

--The Congress Dances: Vienna 1814-1815. LC 83-48781. 240p. 1984. 15.86 (ISBN 0-06-015280-X, HarpT). Har-Row.

--Lady Sackville: A Biography. 288p. 1983. pap. 3.95 (ISBN 0-380-63701-4, 63701-4, Discus). Avon.

--Yankees at the Court. 1985. pap. 4.95 (ISBN 0-671-55799-8). WSP.

Al-Sowayegh, Abdulaziz. Arab Petropolitics. LC 83-40196. 224p. 1984. 25.00 (ISBN 0-312-04718-5). St Martin.

Alspach, JoAnn G. The Educational Process in Critical Care Nursing. LC 82-2090. (Illus.). 432p. 1982. pap. text ed. 24.95 (ISBN 0-8016-0141-X). Mosby.

Alspach, Russell K. Irish Poetry, from the English Invasion to 1798. 2nd rev. ed. LC 75-28807. Repr. of 1960 ed. 16.50 (ISBN 0-404-13800-4). AMS Pr.

Alssid, Michael W. Dryden's Rhymed Heroic Tragedies: A Critical Study of the Plays & of Their Place in Dryden's Poetry, 2 vols. (Salzburg Studies in English Literature, Poetic Drama & Poetic Theory: No. 7). 429p. 1974. Set. pap. text ed. 50.75x (ISBN 0-391-01298-3). Humanities.

Alston, Anna & Sharp, Angela. Working in the Travel Business. 1982. 26.00x (ISBN 0-7134-1496-0, Pub. by Careers Con England). State Mutual Bk.

Alston, Anna, jt. auth. see Parker, Julia.

Alston, Denise, jt. auth. see Pettigrew, Thomas.

Alston, Edith & Cutler, David. Emergency Room: Confessions of an E. R. Doctor. 368p. 1984. 19.95 (ISBN 0-15-128755-4). HarBraceJ.

Alston, Elizabeth. Muffins: Sixty Sweet & Savory Recipes from Old Favorites to New. 96p. 1985. 8.95 (ISBN 0-517-55587-5, C N Potter Bks). Crown.

Alston, Frank M., et al. Contracting with the Federal Government. LC 83-17008. 525p. 1984. 55.00x (ISBN 0-471-87078-1, Pub. by Ronald Pr). Wiley.

Alston, Jacquelyn G. Comparative Nationalism: Definitions & Interpretations & the Black American & British West African Experience to 1947. 2nd ed. LC 85-80588. 283p. (Orig.). 1985. pap. 10.95 (ISBN 0-9614733-6-3). Hist Dimensions.

Alston, Lee J. & Bruchey, Stuart, eds. Costs of Contracting & the Decline of Tenancy in the South, 1930-1960. LC 84-48302. (American Economic History Ser.). 109p. 1985. lib. bdg. 20.00 (ISBN 0-8240-6650-2). Garland Pub.

Alston, Liviu L. Railways & Energy. 94p. 3.00 (ISBN 0-318-02821-2, WP0634). World Bank.

Alston, Liviu L., ed. High-Voltage Technology. (United Kingdom Atomic Energy Authority, Harwell Post-Graduate Ser.). (Illus.). pap. 106.50 (ISBN 0-317-09403-3, 2051952). Bks Demand UMI.

Alston, Pat, ed. see Adams, Andrew.

Alston, Pat, ed. see Fong, Leo T.

Alston, Patrick L. Education & the State in Tsarist Russia. LC 68-26775. 1969. 27.50x (ISBN 0-8047-0681-6). Stanford U Pr.

Alston, Philip & Tomasevski, Katarina. The Right to Food. 1984. text ed. 36.50 (ISBN 90-247-3087-2, Pub. by Martinus Nijhoff Netherlands). Kluwer Academic.

Alston, Philip, ed. see Vasek, Karel.

Alston, R. C. & Jannetta, M. J. Bibliography, Machine-Readable Cataloguing & the ESTC. 248p. (Orig.). 1978. pap. 18.00 (ISBN 0-904654-17-6, Pub. by British Lib). Longwood Pub Group.

Alston, Raymond, tr. see Szonyi, Erzsebet.

Alston, Richard. Partnership Administration: A Practical Guide for Professional Firms. Phillips, Jim, ed. 218p. 1982. 60.00x (ISBN 0-686-45858-3, Pub. by Pubns Sec Templegate Pr England). State Mutual Bk.

Alston, Richard M. Commercial Irrigation Enterprise: The Fear of Water Monopoly & the Genesis of Market Distortion in the Nineteenth Century American West. LC 77-14752. (Dissertations in American Economic History Ser.). 1978. 27.50 (ISBN 0-405-11025-1). Ayer Co Pubs.

--The Individual vs. the Public Interest: Political Idiology & National Forest Policy. (Replica Edition Ser.). 200p. 1982. softcover 24.00x (ISBN 0-86531-950-2). Westview.

Alston, Steven. Of Peace, Love & Light. 64p. 1983. 5.95 (ISBN 0-89962-338-7). Todd & Honeywell.

Alston, Walter, et al. Complete Baseball Handbook: Strategies & Techniques for Winning. 2nd ed. 543p. 1984. 27.95x (ISBN 0-205-08109-6, 628109, Pub. by Longwood Div). Allyn.

Alston, William P. Philosophy of Language. (Orig.). 1964. pap. 13.95 ref. ed. (ISBN 0-13-663799-X). P-H.

Alston, William P. & Brandt, Richard B. The Problems of Philosophy: Introductory Readings. 3rd ed. 1978. text ed. 31.79 (ISBN 0-205-06110-9, 6061109). Allyn.

Alstrom, T., jt. ed. see Graesbeck, R.

Alstyn, Dorothy Van see Van Alstyn, E. Dorothy & Osborne, E.

Alstyne, Arvo Van see Sato, Sho.

Alstyne, Arvo Van see Van Alstyne, Arvo.

Alstyne, Arvo Van see Van Alstyne, Arvo, et al.

Alstyne, Dorothy Van see Van Alstyne, Dorothy.

Alstyne, Judith S. van see Van Alstyne, Judith S.

Alstyne, Richard van see Van Alstyne, Richard.

Alstyne, Richard W. Van see Van Alstyne, Richard W.

Alstyne, William van see Van Alstyne, William.

Alsup, John E., tr. see Goppelt, Leonard.

Alsup, Rea T. The Vocational Development of Welfare-Supported Youth. LC 74-28606. 1975. soft bdg. 11.95. R & E Pubs.

Alswang, Hope, jt. auth. see Peirce, Donald C.

Alswang, Hope, jt. auth. see Peirce, Donald.

Alsworth, Marydean. Gleanings from Alta California. LC 80-68882. 139p. (Orig.). 1980. pap. 15.00 (ISBN 0-939052-00-8). Dean Pubns.

--More Gleanings from Alta California. LC 82-72383. 146p. (Orig.). 1982. pap. 18.00 (ISBN 0-939052-01-6). Dean Pubns.

Alszeghy, Zoltan & Flick, Maurizio. Introductory Theology. 1983. 8.95 (ISBN 0-87193-198-2). Dimension Bks.

Alt, A. Tilo, jt. ed. see Phelps, Leland R.

Alt, David. Physical Geology: A Process Approach. 400p. 1982. text ed. write for info. (ISBN 0-534-01034-2). Wadsworth Pub.

Alt, David & Hyndman, Donald. Roadside Geology of Northern California. LC 74-81834. (Roadside Geology Ser.). (Illus.). 244p. 1975. pap. 9.95 (ISBN 0-87842-055-X). Mountain Pr.

--Roadside Geology of Oregon. LC 77-2581. (Roadside Geology Ser.). (Illus.). 268p. 1978. pap. 9.95 (ISBN 0-87842-063-0). Mountain Pr.

--Roadside Geology of the Northern Rockies. LC 72-78039. (Roadside Geology Ser.). (Illus.). 280p. 1976. pap. 9.95 (ISBN 0-87842-029-0). Mountain Pr.

--Roadside Geology of Washington. (Roadside Geology Ser.). (Illus.). 320p. (Orig.). 1984. pap. 9.95 (ISBN 0-87842-160-2). Mountain Pr.

--Rocks, Ice, & Water. LC 73-78910. (Roadside Geology Ser.). (Illus.). 104p. 1973. pap. 4.95 (ISBN 0-87842-041-X). Mountain Pr.

Alt, E. Winifred. Index to Handicrafts, Modelmaking & Workshop Projects, Suppl. 4. LC 36-27324. (The Useful Reference Ser. of Library Bks: Vol. 96). 1969. lib. bdg. 16.00x (ISBN 0-87305-096-7). Faxon.

Alt, Edith, jt. auth. see Alt, Herschel.

Alt, Franz. Peace Is Possible: The Politics of the Sermon on the Mount. Neugroschel, Joachim, tr. from Ger. 136p. 1985. 12.95 (ISBN 0-8052-3969-3). Schocken.

Alt, Franz L. Advances in Computers, Vol. 23. LC 59-15761. 1984. 52.00 (ISBN 0-12-012123-9). Acad Pr.

--Electronic Digital Computers: Their Uses in Science & Engineering. (Applied Mathematics & Mechanics Ser: Vol. 4). 1958. 65.00 (ISBN 0-12-053650-1). Acad Pr.

Alt, Franz L., et al, eds. Advances in Computers. Incl. Vol. 1. 1960. 80.00 (ISBN 0-12-012101-8); Vol. 2. 1961. 80.00 (ISBN 0-12-012102-6); Vol. 3. Alt, Franz L. & Rubinoff, M., eds. 1962. 80.00 (ISBN 0-12-012103-4); Vol. 4. 1964. 80.00 (ISBN 0-12-012104-2); Vol. 5. 1964. 80.00 (ISBN 0-12-012105-0); Vol. 6. 1966. 80.00 (ISBN 0-12-012106-9); Vol. 7. 1966. 80.00 (ISBN 0-12-012107-7); Vol. 8. 1967. 80.00 (ISBN 0-12-012108-5); Vol. 9. 1969. 80.00 (ISBN 0-12-012109-3); Vol. 10. Freiberger, Walter, ed. 1970. 80.00 (ISBN 0-12-012110-7); Vol. 11. Yovits, Marshall C., ed. 1971. 80.00 (ISBN 0-12-012111-5); Vol. 12. Rubinoff, M. & Finerman, A., eds. 1972. 80.00 (ISBN 0-12-012112-3); Vol. 13. Yovits, Marshall C. & Rubinoff, Morris, eds. 1975. 80.00 (ISBN 0-12-012113-1); Vol. 14. 1976. 75.00 (ISBN 0-12-012114-X); Vol. 15. 1976. 75.00 (ISBN 0-12-012115-8); Vol. 16. 1978. 75.00 (ISBN 0-12-012116-6); Vol. 17. 1978. 70.00 (ISBN 0-12-012117-4). LC 59-15761. Acad Pr.

Alt, Herschel & Alt, Edith. Russia's Children. 1963. 12.95x (ISBN 0-8084-0383-4). New Coll U Pr.

--Russia's Children: A First Report on Child Welfare in the Soviet Union. LC 75-18353. 240p. 1975. Repr. of 1959 ed. lib. bdg. 25.00x (ISBN 0-8371-8330-8, ALRC). Greenwood.

Alt, James E. The Politics of Economic Decline. LC 78-67295. 1979. 37.50 (ISBN 0-521-22327-X). Cambridge U Pr.

Alt, James E. & Chrystal, K. Alec. Political Economics. LC 82-23721. (California Series on Social Choice & Political Economy). 1983. text ed. 26.50x (ISBN 0-520-04934-9); pap. 8.95 (ISBN 0-520-04983-7, CAL 672). U of Cal Pr.

Alt, Jeannette, jt. auth. see Stolte, H.

Alt, M. B., jt. auth. see Miles, R. S.

Alt, M. S., et al, eds. Encyclopedia of Ohio Associations. 1977. 5.00x (ISBN 0-88215-044-8). Ohio St U Lib.

Alt, Ruth R. & Kirkland, Mary L. Steps to Composition: A Pre-Composition Workbook for Students of English As a Second Language. 321p. 1973. pap. 7.00 (ISBN 0-87840-175-X). Georgetown U Pr.

Alta. I Am Not a Practicing Angel. LC 74-32443. 80p. 1975. 13.95 (ISBN 0-912278-54-4); pap. 4.95 (ISBN 0-912278-55-2). Crossing Pr.

--Momma: A Start on All the Untold Stories. LC 74-79105. (Illus.). 80p. (Orig.). (YA) 1974. pap. 2.50 (ISBN 0-87810-028-8). Times Change.

Al-Tabari, Aby J. The History of Al-Tabari, Vol. XXVII: The Abbasid Revolution. Yar-Shater, Ehsan, ed. Williams, John A., tr. from Arabic. (Near Eastern Studies). 192p. 1985. 29.50x (ISBN 0-87395-884-5). State U NY Pr.

Al-Tabataba'I, Muhammed H. Shi'ite Islam. Nasr, Seyyed H., tr. LC 74-8289. 1979. 39.50x (ISBN 0-87395-272-3); pap. 13.95x (ISBN 0-87395-390-8). State U NY Pr.

Altabe, David F. Temas y Dialogos. 4th ed. LC 83-22669. 232p. (Span.). 1984. pap. 14.95 (ISBN 0-03-063564-0). HR&W.

Altaf, Zafar. Pakistani Entrepreneurs: Their Development, Characteristics & Attitudes. (Illus.). 244p. 1983. 27.25 (ISBN 0-7099-0520-3, Pub. by Croom Helm Ltd). Longwood Pub Group.

Al-Tajir, Mahdi A. Language & Linguistic Origins in Bahrain: The Baharnah Dialect of Arabic. (Library of Arab Linguistics). 188p. 1983. 50.00x (ISBN 0-7103-0024-7). Routledge & Kegan.

Altamira Y Crevea, Rafael. History of Spanish Civilization. Volkov, P., tr. LC 77-22622. Repr. of 1930 ed. 28.50 (ISBN 0-404-16030-1). AMS Pr.

Altan, Taylan & Oh, Soo-Ik. Metal Forming: Fundamentals & Applications. 1983. 84.00 (ISBN 0-87170-167-7). ASM.

Altankov, Nikolay G. The Bulgarian-Americans. LC 78-1012. 1979. perfect 10.00 (ISBN 0-918660-09-2). Ragusan Pr.

Altaras, Jakob. Radiologic Atlas of the Colon & Rectum. Dimitrijevic, George D., ed. Orig. Title: Radiologischer Atlas Kolon und Rectum. (Illus.). 318p. 1983. text ed. 65.00 (ISBN 0-8067-0141-2). Urban & S.

ALTAS Corporation, ed. Proceedings of the Workshop on Economic & Operational Requirements & Status of Large Scale Wind Systems. 447p. 1979. pap. 39.95x (ISBN 0-89934-022-9, W-029). Solar Energy Info.

Altasen, J., et al. Immortality. 733p. 1978. 7.45 (ISBN 0-8285-0939-5, Pub. by Progress Pubs USSR). Imported Pubns.

Altbach, Edith H. Woman in America. 1972. pap. text ed. 3.95x (ISBN 0-669-63453-0). Heath.

Altbach, Edith H., ed. From Feminism to Liberation. LC 70-137492. 328p. 1980. text ed. 15.95x (ISBN 0-686-63316-4); pap. text ed. 8.95x (ISBN 0-686-63316-4). Schenkman Bks inc.

Altbach, Edith H., et al, eds. German Feminism: Readings in Politics & Literature. 352p. 1984. 39.50x (ISBN 0-87395-840-3); pap. 12.95x (ISBN 0-87395-841-1). State U NY Pr.

Altbach, Philip, jt. auth. see Chitnis, Suma.

Altbach, Philip, jt. auth. see Singh, Amrik.

Altbach, Philip & Berdahl, Robert O., eds. Higher Education in American Society. LC 81-82204. 326p. 1981. 24.95 (ISBN 0-87975-165-7); pap. 13.95 (ISBN 0-87975-166-5). Prometheus Bks.

Altbach, Philip, et al. Academic Supermarkets: A Critical Case Study of a Multiversity. LC 71-173853. (Jossey-Bass Higher Education Ser.). Repr. of 1971 ed. 97.50 (ISBN 0-8357-9294-3, 2013791). Bks Demand UMI.

Altbach, Philip G. Comparative Higher Education Abroad: Bibliography & Analysis. 288p. 1976. pap. 5.50 (ISBN 0-89192-222-9, Pub. by ICED). Interbk Inc.

--Comparative Higher Education: Research Trends & Bibliography. 218p. 1979. 31.00x (ISBN 0-7201-0825-X). Mansell.

Altbach, Philip G. & Kelly, David H. Higher Education in Developing Nations: A Selected Bibliography. 1974. pap. 6.00 (ISBN 0-89192-221-0, Pub. by ICED). Interbk Inc.

Altbach, Philip G. & Rathgeber, Eva-Maria. Publishing in the Third World: Trend Report & Bibliography. LC 80-20146. 200p. 1980. 36.95 (ISBN 0-03-055931-6). Praeger.

Altbach, Philip G. & Uphoff, Norman T. The Student Internationals. LC 72-12980. 214p. 1973. 13.00 (ISBN 0-8108-0578-2). Scarecrow.

Altbach, Philip G., ed. Student Politics: Perspectives for the Eighties. LC 81-2725. 276p. 1981. 17.50 (ISBN 0-8108-1430-7). Scarecrow.

Altbach, Philip G. & Kelly, Gail P., eds. Education & the Colonial Experience. 2nd, rev. ed. 320p. 1984. pap. 12.95x (ISBN 0-87855-958-2). Transaction Bks.

Altbach, Philip G. & Lambert, Richard D., eds. The Academic Profession. LC 80-65242. (Annals of the American Academy of Political & Social Science: No. 448). 1980. 15.00 (ISBN 0-87761-248-X); pap. 7.95 (ISBN 0-87761-249-8). Am Acad Pol Soc Sci.

Altbach, Philip G. & Laufer, Robert, eds. Students Protest. LC 72-160738. (Annals Ser: No. 395). 1971. pap. 7.95 (ISBN 0-87761-138-6). Am Acad Pol Soc Sci.

Altbach, Philip G., ed. see Eisemon, Thomas O.

Altbach, Philip G., et al. Research on Foreign Students & International Study: An Overview & Bibliography. LC 85-3372. 416p. 1985. 35.95 (ISBN 0-03-071922-4). Praeger.

--International Bibliography of Comparative Education. LC 81-962. 316p. 1981. 47.95 (ISBN 0-03-056881-1). Praeger.

Altbach, Philip G., et al, eds. Publishing in the Third World: Knowledge & Development. LC 84-27920. 240p. 1985. text ed. 35.00x (ISBN 0-435-08006-7). Heinemann Ed.

--Excellence in Education. 300p. 1985. 24.95 (ISBN 0-87975-296-3); pap. 12.95 (ISBN 0-87975-301-3). Prometheus Bks.

Altbach, Phillip G., et al. Comparative Education. 1982. text ed. write for info. (ISBN 0-02-301920-4). Macmillan.

Altbauer, Mosha & Lunt, Horace G., eds. An Early Slavonic Psalter from Rus' Vol. 1: Phoreproduction. LC 78-59967. (Harvard Ukrainian Research Institute, Sources & Documents Ser.). 1979. text ed. 15.00x (ISBN 0-674-22310-1). Harvard U Pr.

Altekar, A. S. The Position of Women in Hindu Civilization. 1978. 21.00 (ISBN 0-89684-273-8); pap. 9.95 (ISBN 0-89684-485-4). Orient Bk Dist.

--State & Government in Ancient India. 1977. 8.50 (ISBN 0-89684-321-1). Orient Bk Dist.

Altemeier, William A., ed. Manual on Control of Infection in Surgical Patients. 2nd ed. (Illus.). 324p. 1984. text ed. 37.50 (ISBN 0-397-50575-2, 65-07362, Lippincott Medical). Lippincott.

Altemeyer, A., jt. auth. see Bucksch, H.

Altemus, Eleanor W. Chestnut Hill's Main Street Shopping, 1930-1935: Philadelphia's Provincial Section with International Flavor. 112p. 1984. 8.95 (ISBN 0-8059-2948-7). Dorrance.

Alten. Audio in Media. 2nd ed. 1986. text ed. write for info (ISBN 0-534-06156-7). Wadsworth Pub.

Altena, Hans, compiled by. Playbook for Christian Theatre. (Good Things for Youth Leaders Ser.). pap. 3.95 (ISBN 0-8010-0166-8). Baker Bk.

Altena, I. van Regteren see Van Regteren Altena, I.

Altenbach, J. Scott. Locomotor Morphology of the Vampire Bat, Desmodus Rotundus. (ASM Special Publication Ser.: No. 6). (Illus.). vi, 137p. 1979. 12.00 (ISBN 0-943612-05-5). Am Soc Mammalogists.

Altenberg, G. A. & Ubaldi, V. Dizionario Italiano-Tedesco, Tedesco-Italian. 395p. (Ger. & Ital.). 1979. leatherette 6.95 (ISBN 0-686-97349-6, M-9176). French & Eur.

Altenbernd, Lynn. Anthology: An Introduction to Literature. 1977. write for info. (ISBN 0-02-301960-3, 30196). Macmillan.

Altenbernd, Lynn & Lewis, Leslie L. Handbook for the Study of Drama. rev. ed. (Orig.). 1966. pap. text ed. write for info. (ISBN 0-02-301940-9, 30194). Macmillan.

--Handbook for the Study of Poetry. rev. ed. (Orig.). 1966. pap. text ed. write for info. (ISBN 0-02-301930-1, 30193). Macmillan.

--Introduction to Literature: Poems. 3rd ed. 800p. 1975. pap. text ed. write for info. (ISBN 0-02-302060-1, 30206). Macmillan.

--Introduction to Literature: Stories. 3rd ed. 1980. pap. write for info. (ISBN 0-02-302070-9). Macmillan.

Altenburg, J. Ernst. Trumpeters' & Kettledrummers' Art (1795) Tarr, Edward H., tr. from Ger. LC 74-4026. (Illus.). 168p. 1974. 12.00 (ISBN 0-914282-01-8). Brass Pr.

Altengarten, James S. & Molyneaux, Gary A. The History, Philosophy & Methodology of Geography: A Bibliography Selected for Education & Research, No. 957. 1976. 5.50 (ISBN 0-686-20385-2). CPL Biblios.

Altenpohl, D. Aluminium Viewed from Within. 1982. 42.00 (ISBN 0-9960034-3-6, Pub. by Aluminium W Germany). Heyden.

Altenpohl, D. G., et al. Materials in World Perspective. (Materials Research & Engineering Ser.: Vol. 1). (Illus.). 208p. 1980. pap. 39.00 (ISBN 0-387-10037-7). Springer-Verlag.

Altenstetter, Christa & Bjorkman, James W. Federal-State Health Policies & Impacts: The Politics of Implementation. LC 78-62173. (Illus.). 1978. pap. text ed. 9.25 (ISBN 0-8191-0503-1). U Pr of Amer.

Altenstetter, Christa, ed. Innovation in Health Policy & Service Delivery: A Cross-National Perspective. LC 80-39617. (Research on Service Delivery, Vol. 3). 320p. 1981. text ed. 35.00 (ISBN 0-89946-078-X). Oelgeschlager.

Alter & Dunn. Solid Waste Conversion to Energy. (Pollution Engineering & Technology Ser.: Vol. 11). 184p. 1980. 39.75 (ISBN 0-8247-6917-1). Dekker.

Alter, Aaron A., et al. Medical Technology Examination Review Book, Vol. 1. 4th ed. 1977. spiral bdg. 12.75 (ISBN 0-87488-451-9). Med Exam.

--Medical Technology Examination Review Book, Vol. 2. 4th ed. 1978. spiral bdg. 12.75 (ISBN 0-87488-452-7). Med Exam.

Alter, Arnold. Champion! The Story of Amazing Race Horses. LC 83-60114. (Strange but True Ser.). 1983. 10.00 (ISBN 0-382-06684-7). Silver.

Alter, Dinsmore, et al. Pictorial Astronomy. 5th ed. LC 81-47878. (Illus.). 384p. 1983. 19.18i (ISBN 0-06-181019-3, HarpT). Har-Row.

Alter, Eric. Deseret. 352p. (Orig.). 1983. pap. 3.50 (ISBN 0-523-41483-8). Pinnacle Bks.

--The Dukes of Hazzard: Gone Racin' 224p. (Orig.). 1983. pap. 2.50 (ISBN 0-446-30324-0). Warner Bks.

Alter, G. & Ruprecht, J. Catalogue of Star Clusters & Associations. 1970. 65.00 (ISBN 0-9960008-7-9, Pub. by Akademiai Kaido Hungary). Heyden.

--The System of Open Star Clusters & the Galaxy Atlas of Open Star Clusters. 1963. 66.00 (ISBN 0-12-054250-1). Acad Pr.

Alter, G., tr. see Ulehla, Ivan, et al.

Alter, G., et al, eds. Catalogue of Star Clusters & Associations. 2nd ed. 80.00x (ISBN 0-685-27543-4). Adlers Foreign Bks.

Alter, Henry C. Of Messages & Media: Teaching & Learning by Public Television. (Notes & Essays Ser.: No. 58). 1968. pap. text ed. 2.00 (ISBN 0-87060-022-2, NES 58). Syracuse U Cont Ed.

Alter, Iska. The Good Man's Dilemma: Social Criticism in the Fiction of Bernard Malamud. LC 79-8836. (AMS Studies in Modern Literature Ser.: No. 5). 1981. 29.50 (ISBN 0-404-18038-8). AMS Pr.

Alter, J. Cecil. Early Utah Journalism. LC 79-98803. Repr. of 1938 ed. lib. bdg. 22.50x (ISBN 0-8371-3065-4, ALUJ). Greenwood.

--Jim Bridger. (Illus.). 1979. 18.95 (ISBN 0-8061-0546-1); pap. 9.95 (ISBN 0-8061-1509-2). U of Okla Pr.

Alter, Jonathan, jt. auth. see Peters, Charles.

Alter, Joseph D. Life after Fifty: Your Guide to Health & Happiness. (Illus.). 144p. 1983. 10.95 (ISBN 0-89313-060-5). G F Stickley.

Alter, Judith M. Luke & the Van Zandt County War. LC 84-101. (A Sundance Book Ser.). (Illus.). 144p. (gr. 4 up). 1984. 10.95 (ISBN 0-912646-88-8). Tex Christian.

Alter, Judy. After Pa Was Shot. (gr. 7-9). 1978. PLB 11.88 (ISBN 0-688-32136-4). Morrow.

--Dorothy Johnson. LC 80-70458. (Western Writers Ser.: No. 44). (Illus.). 47p. (Orig.). 1980. pap. 2.00x (ISBN 0-88430-068-4). Boise St Univ.

--Stewart Edward White. LC 75-7011. (Western Writers Ser.: No. 18). (Illus., Orig.). 1975. pap. 2.00x (ISBN 0-88430-017-X). Boise St Univ.

--Surviving Exercise: Judy Alter's Safe & Sane Exercise Program. 1983. 11.95 (ISBN 0-395-33112-9); pap. 5.95 (ISBN 0-395-33113-7). HM.

Alter, Judy & Roach, Joyce G., eds. Texas & Christmas: A Collection of Traditions, Memories & Folklore. LC 83-4717. (Illus.). 96p. 1983. pap. 6.50 (ISBN 0-912646-81-0). Tex Christian.

Alter, M., jt. auth. see Schaumann, B.

Alter, Maria P. The Concept of Physician in the Writings of Hans Carossa & Arthur Schnitzler. (European University Studies, German Language & Literature: Ser. 1, Vol. 43). 104p. 1971. pap. 14.05 (ISBN 3-261-00042-2). P Lang Pubs.

Alter, Reinhard. Gottfried Benn: The Artist & Politics (1910-1934) (Australian & New Zealand Studies in German Language & Literature: Vol. 8). 149p. 1976. pap. 18.25 (ISBN 3-261-01871-2). P Lang Pubs.

Alter, Richard C. The Tired Tourist's Concise Guide to Florence. rev. ed. (Illus.). 1978. pap. 3.00 (ISBN 0-89726-000-7). Foldabook Pub.

--The Tired Tourist's Concise Guide to London. LC 78-55944. (Illus.). 1978. pap. 3.00 (ISBN 0-89726-002-3). Foldabook Pub.

--The Tired Tourist's Concise Guide to Paris. LC 78-75278. (Illus.). 1979. pap. 3.00 (ISBN 0-89726-005-8). Foldabook Pub.

--The Tired Tourist's Concise Guide to Rome. LC 79-57049. (Illus.). 1980. pap. 3.00 (ISBN 0-89726-031-7). Foldabook Pub.

Alter, Robert. The Art of Biblical Narrative. LC 80-68958. 208p. 1981. 14.95 (ISBN 0-465-00424-5). Basic.

--The Art of Biblical Narrative. LC 80-68958. 195p. 1983. pap. 7.95 (ISBN 0-465-00427-X, CN-5099). Basic.

--The Art of Biblical Poetry. LC 85-47550. 272p. 1985. 17.95 (ISBN 0-465-00430-X). Basic.

--Defenses of the Imagination: Jewish Writers & Modern Historical Crisis. LC 77-87244. 292p. 1978. 8.50 (ISBN 0-8276-0097-6, 410). Jewish Pubns.

--Motives for Fiction. LC 83-10829. 248p. 1984. text ed. 20.00x (ISBN 0-674-58762-6). Harvard U Pr.

--Partial Magic: The Novel As Self-Conscious Genre. LC 74-77725. 1975. 28.50x (ISBN 0-520-02755-8); pap. 3.95 (ISBN 0-520-03732-4). U of Cal Pr.

Alter, Robert, ed. Modern Hebrew Literature. LC 75-9928. (Library of Jewish Studies). 384p. 1975. pap. text ed. 9.95x (ISBN 0-87441-235-8); cloth 15.95x. Behrman.

Alter, Stephen. Neglected Lives. LC 78-5838. 192p. 1978. 8.95 (ISBN 0-374-22024-7). FS&G.

--Silk & Steel. 327p. 1980. 11.95 (ISBN 0-374-26411-2). FS&G.

Alter, Steven L. Decision Support Systems: Current Practice & Continuing Challenges. LC 78-67960. 1979. text ed. 27.95 (ISBN 0-201-00193-4). Addison-Wesley.

Alterman, Ira. Do Diapers Give You Leprosy? What Every Parent Should Know about Bringing Up Babies. 96p. 1984. pap. 3.95 (ISBN 0-8092-5365-8). Contemp Bks.

--Games for the John. (Illus.). 96p. 1984. pap. 3.95 (ISBN 0-8092-5368-2). Contemp Bks.

--Games You Can Play with Your Pussy Cat: And Lots of Other Stuff Cat Owners Should Know. (Illus.). 96p. 1984. pap. 3.95 (ISBN 0-8092-5369-0). Contemp Bks.

--Picking up Girls. (Illus.). 96p. 1984. pap. 3.95 (ISBN 0-8092-5360-7). Contemp Bks.

--Sex Manual for People over Thirty. 96p. 1984. pap. 3.95 (ISBN 0-8092-5354-2). Contemp Bks.

Alterman, Ira, jt. auth. see Schmidt, Allen H.

Alterman, Jack, jt. auth. see Darmstadter, Joel.

Alterman, Jack, jt. auth. see Dunkerley, Joy.

Alternative Defence Commission. Defence Without the Bomb. LC 83-6239. 320p. (Orig.). 1983. pap. 9.00x (ISBN 0-8002-3080-9). Taylor & Francis.

Alternative Museum. The Art of Appropriation & the Appropriation Art. (Illus.). pap. price not set (ISBN 0-932075-03-7). Alternative Mus.

--Machiko Itatani. (Illus.). 1985. pap. price not set (ISBN 0-932075-04-5). Alternative Mus.

Alternative Museum Staff. Emilio Cruz: Recent Painting & Drawing. LC 84-73546. (Illus., Orig.). 1985. pap. text ed. 4.00 (ISBN 0-932075-00-2). Alternative Mus.

--Endangerd Species: The Art of Staying Alive. (Illus.). 1986. pap. price not set (ISBN 0-932075-05-3). Alternative Mus.

--Southern Exposure: Not a Regional Exhibition. LC 85-71155. (Illus.). 56p. (Orig.). 1985. pap. text ed. 6.00 (ISBN 0-932075-02-9). Alternative Mus.

Alternative Museum Staff. Disinformation: The Manufacture of Consent. LC 85-70365. (Illus.). 64p. (Orig.). 1985. pap. text ed. 8.00 (ISBN 0-932075-01-0). Alternative Mus.

Alternative Press Center. Alternative Press Index. 100p. 1969. ann. subscr. 25.00 (ISBN 0-318-12304-5); back issues avail. Alternative Pr Ctr.

Alternatives Staff. The Kit 'n' Kaboodle Book: The Idea Book for Children. 96p. 2.50 (ISBN 0-317-32269-9). Alternatives.

--The Mother Earth News Handbook of Homemade Power. 374p. 2.50 (ISBN 0-317-32271-0). Alternatives.

--Nutrition Scoreboard: Your Guide to Better Eating. 102p. 2.25 (ISBN 0-317-32275-3); scoreboard poster 2.00 (ISBN 0-317-32276-1). Alternatives.

Altevogt, tr. see Rensch, Bernard.

Altfeld, E. Milton. The Jews' Struggle for Religious & Civil Liberty in Maryland. LC 78-99859. (Civil Liberties in American History Ser). 1970. Repr. of 1924 ed. lib. bdg. 29.50 (ISBN 0-306-71859-6). Da Capo.

Altfelder, Klaus. Lexikon der Unternehmensfuehrung. (Ger.). 1973. 65.00 (ISBN 3-470-56191-5, M-7219). French & Eur.

Altfest, Lewis J. & Lechner, Alan B. Introduction to Business. pap. 5.95x (ISBN 0-06-460171-4, CO 7001, COS). B&N NY.

Altgeld, John P. The Cost of Something for Nothing. 59.95 (ISBN 0-87968-948-X). Gordon Pr.

--Live Questions. 59.95 (ISBN 0-8490-0548-5). Gordon Pr.

--Live Questions: Including Our Penal Machinery & Its Victims. LC 79-156003. (Foundations of Criminal Justice Ser.). Repr. of 1890 ed. 18.00 (ISBN 0-404-09103-2). AMS Pr.

--Mind & Spirit of John Peter Altgeld. facs. ed. Christman, Henry M., ed. LC 70-128200. (Essay Index Reprint Ser.). 1960. 15.00 (ISBN 0-8369-1860-6). Ayer Co Pubs.

--The Mind & Spirit of John Peter Altgeld: Selected Writings & Addresses. Christman, Henry M., ed. LC 70-128200. (Essay Index Reprint Ser.). 185p. Repr. of 1960 ed. lib. bdg. 14.00 (ISBN 0-8290-0801-2). Irvington.

--Reasons for Pardoning the Haymarket Anarchists. 80p. lib. bdg. 14.95 (ISBN 0-88286-149-2); pap. 4.95 (ISBN 0-88286-124-7). C H Kerr.

Altgelt & Gouw. Chromatography in Petroleum Analysis. (Chromatographic Science Ser.: Vol. 11). 1979. 85.00 (ISBN 0-8247-6790-X). Dekker.

Alth, Charlotte & Alth, Max. Be Your Own Contractor: The Affordable Way to Home Ownership. (Illus.). 232p. 1984. pap. 12.95 (ISBN 0-8306-0154-6, 1554). TAB Bks.

--Constructing & Maintaining Your Well & Septic System. (Illus.). 240p. 1984. 19.95 (ISBN 0-8306-0654-8, 1654); pap. 12.95 (ISBN 0-8306-1654-3). TAB Bks.

Alth, Charlotte, jt. auth. see Alth, Max.

Alth, Max. All about Bikes & Bicycling. 181p. 1981. 25.00x (ISBN 0-561-00204-5, Pub. by Bailey & Swinfen South Africa). State Mutual Bk.

--All about Locks & Locksmithing. (Illus.). 1972. pap. 4.50 (ISBN 0-8015-0151-2, Hawthorn). Dutton.

--Do-It-Yourself Plumbing. LC 74-27320. (A Popular Science Bk.). (Illus.). 316p. 1975. 14.37i (ISBN 0-06-010122-9, HarpT). Har-Row.

--Motorcycles & Motorcycling. (First Bks.). (Illus.). (gr. 4 up). 1979. PLB 8.90 s&l (ISBN 0-531-02945-X). Watts.

Alth, Max & Alth, Charlotte. Disastrous Hurricanes & Tornadoes. LC 81-7544. (First Bks.). (Illus.). 72p. (gr. 4 up). 1981. lib. bdg. 8.90 (ISBN 0-531-04327-4). Watts.

--The Furniture Buyer's Handbook: How to Buy, Arrange, Maintain & Repair Furniture. (Illus.). 1980. 14.95 (ISBN 0-8027-0636-3); pap. 9.95 (ISBN 0-8027-7155-6). Walker & Co.

Alth, Max, jt. auth. see Alth, Charlotte.

Althaus, Catherine & French-Hodges, Peter F. Cook Now, Dine Later. rev. ed. LC 84-26083. 243p. 1985. pap. 8.95 (ISBN 0-571-13559-5). Faber & Faber.

Althaus, D. & Wortmann, F. X. Stuttgart's Profile Catalog: Experimental Results from the Laminar Wind Tunnel of the Institute for Aero- and Gas-Dynamics. 1981. 125.00 (ISBN 0-9940013-0-4, Pub. by Vieweg & Sohn Germany). Heyden.

Althaus, F., et al, eds. ADP-Ribosylation of Proteins. (Proceedings in Life Sciences Ser.). (Illus.). 585p. 1985. 89.50 (ISBN 0-387-15598-8). Springer Verlag.

Althaus, Hans. Lexikon der Grammatischen Linguistik. (Ger.). 1973. 95.00 (ISBN 3-484-10186-5, M-7256). French & Eur.

Althaus, Hans P. Die Cambridger Loewenfabel von 1382: Untersuchung und Edition eines defektiven Textes. (Quellen und Forschungen Zur Sprach-und Kulturgeschichte der Germanischen Voelker Ser.). (Illus.). 238p. 1971. 40.40x (ISBN 3-11-003939-7). De Gruyter.

Althaus, Joan N., et al. Nursing Decentralization: The El Camino Experience. LC 81-83018. 215p. 1981. text ed. 31.50 (ISBN 0-913654-76-0). Aspen Systems.

Althaus, Paul. The Ethics of Martin Luther. Schultz, Robert C., tr. from Ger. LC 72-164552. 192p. 1972. pap. 8.95 (ISBN 0-8006-1709-6, 1-1709). Fortress.
--Fact & Faith in the Kerygma of Today. Cairas, David, tr. 89p. 1978. Repr. of 1959 ed. lib. bdg. 15.00x (ISBN 0-313-20446-2, ALFA). Greenwood.
--Theology of Martin Luther. Schultz, Robert C., tr. from Ger. LC 66-17345. 480p. 1966. 16.95 (ISBN 0-8006-0060-6, 1-60). Fortress.
Althea. Bridges. (Cambridge Books for Children). (Illus.). 32p. (gr. 10-12). 1983. pap. 2.50 (ISBN 0-521-27170-3). Cambridge U Pr.
--Building a House. (Cambridge Books for Children). (Illus.). 26p. (gr. 7-10). 1983. pap. 1.95 (ISBN 0-521-27152-5). Cambridge U Pr.
--Going on a Train. (Cambridge Books for Children). (Illus.). 26p. 1983. pap. 1.95 (ISBN 0-521-27150-9). Cambridge U Pr.
--How Life Began. (Cambridge Books for Children). (Illus.). 26p. (gr. 7-10). 1983. pap. 1.95 (ISBN 0-521-27167-3). Cambridge U Pr.
--Life in a Castle. (Cambridge Books for Children). (Illus.). 32p. (gr. 10-12). 1983. pap. 2.50 (ISBN 0-521-27169-X). Cambridge U Pr.
--Machines on a Farm. (Cambridge Books for Children). (Illus.). 26p. (gr. 7-10). 1983. pap. 1.95 (ISBN 0-521-27156-8). Cambridge U Pr.
--Making a Book. (Cambridge Books for Children). (Illus.). 26p. (gr. 7-10). 1983. pap. 1.95 (ISBN 0-521-27159-2). Cambridge U Pr.
--Man Flies On. (Cambridge Books for Children). (Illus.). 32p. (gr. 10-12). 1983. pap. 2.50 (ISBN 0-521-27173-8). Cambridge U Pr.
--Man in the Sky. (Cambridge Books for Children). (Illus.). 32p. (gr. 10-12). 1983. pap. 2.50 (ISBN 0-521-27172-X). Cambridge U Pr.
--Mountain Homes. (Natural History Ser.). 24p. 1985. write for info (ISBN 0-521-30296-X); pap. write for info (ISBN 0-521-31620-0). Cambridge U Pr.
--Rainforest Homes. (Natural History Ser.). 24p. 1985. write for info (ISBN 0-521-30295-1); pap. write for info (ISBN 0-521-31619-7). Cambridge U Pr.
--The School Fair. (Cambridge Books for Children). (Illus.). 26p. (gr. 7-10). 1983. pap. 1.95 (ISBN 0-521-27166-5). Cambridge U Pr.
--Signposts of the Sea. (Cambridge Books for Children). (Illus.). 32p. (gr. 10-12). 1983. pap. 2.50 (ISBN 0-521-27171-1). Cambridge U Pr.
--Undersea Homes. (Natural History Ser.). 24p. 1985. write for info. (ISBN 0-521-30297-8); pap. write for info. (ISBN 0-521-31621-9). Cambridge U Pr.
--Visiting a Museum. (Cambridge Books for Children). 26p. (gr. 7-10). 1983. pap. 1.95 (ISBN 0-521-27160-6). Cambridge U Pr.
Altheide & Johnson. Bureaucratic Propaganda. 1980. text ed. 27.14 (ISBN 0-205-06716-6, 8161716). Allyn.
Altheide, David L. Creating Reality: How TV News Distorts Events. LC 76-22602. (Sage Library of Social Research: Vol. 33). 1976. 24.00 (ISBN 0-8039-0671-4); pap. 12.00 (ISBN 0-8039-0672-2). Sage.
--Media Power. LC 84-22876. 288p. 1985. 29.00 (ISBN 0-8039-2411-9); pap. 14.95 (ISBN 0-8039-2410-0). Sage.
Altheide, David L. & Snow, Robert P. Media Logic. LC 78-19646. (SAGE Library of Social Research: No. 89). (Illus.). 256p. 1979. 24.00 (ISBN 0-8039-1296-X); pap. 12.00 (ISBN 0-8039-1297-8). Sage.
Altheim, Franz & Stiehl, Ruth. Christentum am Roten Meer, Vol. 2. 1973. 136.00x (ISBN 3-11-003791-2). De Gruyter.
--Geschichte Mittelasiens im Altertum. (Illus., Ger.). 1970. 132.00x (ISBN 3-11-002677-5). De Gruyter.
Althen, Gary. The Handbook of Foreign Student Advising. LC 83-82532. 208p. 1984. 19.95 (ISBN 0-933662-53-X); softcover 15.95 (ISBN 0-933662-55-6). Intercult Pr.
Althen, Gary, ed. Learning Across Cultures. 153p. (Orig.). 1981. pap. text ed. 1.00 (ISBN 0-912207-05-1). Natl Assn Foreign Students.
Alther, Lisa. Kinflicks. 1977. pap. 3.95 (ISBN 0-451-11985-1, AE1985, Sig). NAL.
--Original Sins. LC 80-22823. 608p. 1981. 13.95 (ISBN 0-394-51685-0). Knopf.
--Original Sins. 1985. pap. 4.50 (ISBN 0-451-13966-6, AE1448, Sig). NAL.
--Other Women. LC 84-47873. 1984. 15.95 (ISBN 0-394-53936-2). Knopf.
--Other Women. 1985. pap. 4.50 (ISBN 0-451-13894-5, Sig). NAL.
Altherr, Thomas L., ed. Procreation or Pleasure? Sexual Attitudes in American Histroy. LC 83-12. 178p. 1983. pap. text ed. 8.50 (ISBN 0-89874-609-4). Krieger.
Althoen, Steven C. & Bumcrot, Robert J. Finite Mathematics. (Illus.). 1978. text ed. 16.95x (ISBN 0-393-09046-9). Norton.
--Matrix Methods in Finite Mathematics: An Introduction with Applications to Business & Industry. new ed. 350p. 1976. text ed. 26.95x (ISBN 0-393-09192-9). Norton.
Althoen, Steven C. & Gavlick, Paul K. College Algebra via the Theory of Equations. (Illus.). 450p. 1985. pap. text ed. write for info. (ISBN 0-912675-14-4). Ardsley.
Althoff, Karl F. The Magna Charta of the Christian Church. Grimm, Werner, tr. from Ger. 19p. 1982. pap. 3.00 (ISBN 0-919924-15-8, Pub. by Steiner Book Centre Canada). Anthroposophic.
Althoff, Philip, jt. ed. see Leachman, Robert B.
Altholtz, Josef L., et al, eds. see Acton, John E.
Altholz, et al. Type Right! A Complete Program for Business Typewriting. LC 78-73160. 1980. text ed. 17.20 (ISBN 0-8224-2128-3); tchrs' manual o.p. 7.96 (ISBN 0-8224-2129-1); stationary supplies 7.80 (ISBN 0-8224-2131-3); classroom mgmt manual (3 ring binder) 1981 30.00 (ISBN 0-8224-2132-1). Glencoe.
Altholz, Josef L., ed. The Mind & Art of Victorian England. 1976. 19.50x (ISBN 0-8166-0772-9). U of Minn Pr.
Althouse, Andrew & Turnquist, C. H. Modern Refrigeration & Air Conditioning. LC 81-20002. (Illus.). 1012p. 1982. text ed. 26.00x (ISBN 0-87006-340-5); lab manual 5.28x (ISBN 0-87006-422-3). Goodheart.
Althouse, Andrew D. & Turnquist, Carl H. Modern Welding. rev. ed. (Illus.). 1984. text ed. 21.00 (ISBN 0-87006-433-9). Goodheart.
Althouse, Larry & Althouse, Valere. You Can Save Your Breast: One Woman's Experience With Radiation Therapy. LC 81-18721. 192p. 1982. 12.95 (ISBN 0-393-01507-6). Norton.
--You Can Save Your Breast: One Woman's Experience with Radiation Therapy. 192p. 1984. pap. 5.95 (ISBN 0-393-30161-3). Norton.
Althouse, LaVonne. When Jew & Christian Meet. (Illus.). 1966. pap. 1.50 (ISBN 0-377-36221-2). Friend Pr.
Althouse, Lawrence. Rediscovering the Gift of Healing. 2nd ed. 144p. 1983. Repr. of 1977 ed. pap. 5.95 (ISBN 0-87728-604-3). Weiser.
Althouse, Rosemary. The Young Child: Learning with Understanding. LC 81-4600. 1981. text ed. 18.95x (ISBN 0-8077-2658-3). Tchrs Coll.
Althouse, Valere, jt. auth. see Althouse, Larry.
Althusius, Johannes. Politica Methodice Digesta of Johannes Althusius. Mayer, J. P., ed. LC 78-67326. (European Political Thought Ser.). 1979. Repr. of 1932 ed. lib. bdg. 39.00x (ISBN 0-405-11673-X). Ayer Co Pubs.
Althusser, Louis. For Marx. Brewster, Ben, tr. from Ger. 1979. pap. 12.00 (ISBN 0-8052-7018-3, Pub. by Verso). Schocken.
--Lenin & Philosophy & Other Essays. Brewster, Ben, tr. from Fr. LC 78-178710. 256p. 1972. pap. 5.95 (ISBN 0-85345-213-X). Monthly Rev.
--Politics & History: Montesquieu, Rousseau, Hegel, Marx. 1978. pap. 7.95 (ISBN 0-8052-7136-8, Pub by NLB). Schocken.
Althusser, Louis & Balibar, Etienne. Reading Capital. 1979. pap. 10.25 (ISBN 0-8052-7016-7, Pub by NLB). Schocken.
Altick, Richard & Lunceford, Andrea. Preface to Critical Reading. 6th ed. 1984. pap. text ed. 15.95 (ISBN 0-03-061373-6). HR&W.
Altick, Richard D. The Art of Literary Research. 3rd ed. 1982. 16.95x (ISBN 0-393-95176-6). Norton.
--Art of Literary Research. 2nd, rev. ed. 1975. 11.95x (ISBN 0-393-09227-5, NortonC). Norton.
--The Cowden Clarkes. LC 73-136895. (Illus.). 268p. 1973. Repr. of 1948 ed. lib. bdg. 24.75x (ISBN 0-8371-5338-7, ALCC). Greenwood.
--English Common Reader: A Social History of the Mass Reading Public, 1800-1900. LC 57-6975. (Midway Reprints Ser.). 1983. 16.00x (ISBN 0-226-01539-4). U of Chicago Pr.
--Lives & Letters: A History of Literary Biographies in England & America. LC 78-13952. 1979. Repr. of 1965 ed. lib. bdg. 32.50x (ISBN 0-313-21116-7, ALLL). Greenwood.
--Scholar Adventurers. 1966. pap. text ed. 9.95 (ISBN 0-02-900580-9). Free Pr.
--The Shows of London. LC 77-2755. 1978. 35.00 (ISBN 0-674-80731-6, Belknap Pr). Harvard U Pr.
--Victorian People & Ideas. (Illus.). 338p. 1974. pap. 8.95x (ISBN 0-393-09376-X). Norton.
--Victorian Studies in Scarlet. LC 70-103962. 1970. 7.95 (ISBN 0-393-08605-4). Norton.
Altick, Richard D. & Wright, Andrew. Selective Bibliography for the Study of English & American Literature. 6th ed. 1978. pap. text ed. write for info (ISBN 0-02-302110-1). Macmillan.
Altick, Richard D. & Matthews, William R., eds. Guide to Doctoral Dissertations in Victorian Literature, 1886-1958. LC 73-715. 119p. 1973. Repr. of 1960 ed. lib. bdg. 18.75 (ISBN 0-8371-6787-6, ALGD). Greenwood.
Altick, Richard D., ed. see Browning, Robert.
Altick, Richard D., ed. see Carlyle, Thomas.
Altieri, Charles. Act & Quality: A Theory of Literary Meaning & Humanistic Understanding. LC 81-2147. 352p. 1981. lib. bdg. 27.50x (ISBN 0-87023-327-0); pap. 12.90x (ISBN 0-87023-428-5). U of Mass Pr.
--Enlarging the Temple: New Directions in American Poetry During the 1960's. LC 77-89773. 256p. 1979. 22.50 (ISBN 0-8387-2127-3); pap. 9.95 (ISBN 0-8387-5012-5). Bucknell U Pr.
--Self & Sensibility in Contemporary American Poetry. LC 83-7855. (Cambridge Studies in American Literature & Culture). 240p. 1984. 24.95 (ISBN 0-521-25396-9). Cambridge U Pr.
Altieri, Charles F. Modern Poetry. LC 76-4656. (Goldentree Bibliographies in Language & Literature Ser.). 1980. pap. text ed. 14.95 (ISBN 0-88295-550-0). Harlan Davidson.
Altieri, James. Spearheaders: A Personal History of Darby's Rangers. LC 79-18951. Repr. of 1960 ed. 15.95 (ISBN 0-89201-061-4). Zenger Pub.
Altieri, V. J. & American Gas Association Committee on Revision of the Gas Chemists Handbook. Gas Analysis & Testing of Gaseous Materials. 567p. 1945. 5.00 (ISBN 0-318-12626-5, X51145). Am Gas Assn.
Altieri de Barreto, Carmen G. El Lexico De la Delincuencia En Puerto Rico. (UPREX, C. Sociales: No. 18). (Span.). pap. 1.85 (ISBN 0-8477-0018-6). U of PR Pr.
Altimir, Oscar. The Extent of Poverty in Latin American. rev. ed. LC 82-8533. (World Bank Staff Working Papers: No. 522). (Orig.). 1982. pap. text ed. 3.00 (ISBN 0-8213-0012-1). World Bank.
Altimiras, J. Sailing Knots. Willis, Tom, tr. 128p. 1984. 12.95 (ISBN 0-668-06266-5). Arco.
Altimonte, Paul, jt. auth. see Labuz, Ronald A.
Alting. Manufacturing Engineering Processes. (Manufacturing Engineering & Materials Processing Ser.: Vol. 7). 384p. 1982. 49.50 (ISBN 0-8247-1528-4). Dekker.
Alting, J. H., jt. auth. see Buning, W. De Cock.
Alting von Gesau, Frans A. & Pelkmans, Jacques, eds. National Economic Security: Perceptions, Threats, & Policies. 253p. 1983. pap. 9.95 (ISBN 0-87855-946-9, Pub. by J F K Inst Netherlands). Transaction Bks.
Alting von Geusau, F. A. Uncertain Detente. 310p. 1979. 47.50x (ISBN 90-286-0818-4). Sijthoff & Noordhoff.
Alting von Geuseau, Frans A., ed. Allies in a Turbulent World: Challenges to U. S. & Eastern European Cooperation. LC 82-47776. (Illus.). 192p. 1982. 27.50x (ISBN 0-669-05581-6). Lexington Bks.
Altizer, Thomas, et al. Deconstruction & Theology. 176p. 1982. 14.95 (ISBN 0-8245-0475-5); pap. 8.95 (ISBN 0-8245-0412-7). Crossroad NY.
Altizer, Thomas J. The Descent into Hell: A Study of the Radical Reversal of the Christain Consciousness. 222p. 1979. pap. 6.95 (ISBN 0-8164-1194-8, Pub. by Seabury). Winston Pr.
--History as Apocalypse. LC 84-16289. (SUNY Series in Religion). 250p. 1985. lib. bdg. 34.50x (ISBN 0-88706-013-7); pap. text ed. 10.95x (ISBN 0-88706-014-5). State U NY Pr.
--Mircea Eliade & the Dialectic of the Sacred. LC 73-15398. 219p. 1975. Repr. of 1963 ed. lib. bdg. 22.50 (ISBN 0-8371-7196-2, ALME). Greenwood.
--New Apocalypse: The Radical Christian Vision of William Blake. 1967. 8.50 (ISBN 0-87013-108-7). Mich St U Pr.
--Total Presence: The Language of Jesus & the Language of Today. 128p. 1980. 9.95 (ISBN 0-8164-0461-5, Pub. by Seabury). Winston Pr.
Altizer, Thomas J., jt. ed. see Griffin, David R.
Altland, Millard, jt. auth. see Cornell, William A.
Altmaier, Elizabeth M. & Meyer, Merle. Applied Specialties in Psychology. 600p. 1985. text ed. 27.00 (ISBN 0-394-35060-X, RanC). Random.
Altman. Contractors & Contractor Direction Theory & Applications: A New Approach to Solving Equations. (Lecture Notes in Pure & Applied Math Ser.: Vol. 32). 1977. 55.00 (ISBN 0-8247-6672-5). Dekker.
Altman & Weil. How to Manage Your Law Office. 1973. Updates avail. 80.00 (ISBN 0-685-40615-6, 356); looseleaf 1983 37.50; looseleaf 1984 39.50. Bender.
Altman & Ziporyn. Speck: The Untold Story of a Mass Murderer. LC 83-82679. 1984. pap. 8.95 (ISBN 0-87319-025-4). C Hallberg.
Altman, Arnold & Schwartz, Allen D. Malignant Diseases of Infancy, Childhood & Adolescence. 2nd ed. (Major Problems in Clinical Pediatrics Ser.: Vol. 18). 1983. text ed. 69.50 (ISBN 0-7216-1211-3). Saunders.
Altman, Barry J. Biomedical Equipment Database. 203p. 1984. 196.00x (ISBN 0-930844-12-2). Quest Pub.
Altman, Dennis. Coming Out in the Seventies. 192p. 1980. pap. 5.95 (ISBN 0-932870-05-8). Alyson Pubns.
--The Homosexualization of America. LC 82-73959. 256p. 1983. pap. 10.95 (ISBN 0-8070-4143-2, BP-654). Beacon Pr.
--The Homosexualization of America: The Americanization of the Homosexual. 252p. 1982. 13.95 (ISBN 0-312-38888-8). St Martin.
--Politics of An Epidemic: AIDS in the Mind of America. 240p. 1986. 15.95 (ISBN 0-385-19523-0). Doubleday.
--Rehearsals for Change. 215p. 1982. pap. 6.95 (ISBN 0-00-635716-4, Pub by W Collins). Intl Spec Bk.
Altman, Devra L. A Manual for Small & Medium-sized Law Libraries. LC 76-372536. (Research Contributions of the American Bar Foundation: 1976, No. 2). pap. 20.00 (ISBN 0-317-26202-5, 2052129). Bks Demand UMI.
Altman, Donald E. Contingency Table Analysis in Geographic Research: A Bibliographic Essay, No. 898. 1975. 6.00 (ISBN 0-686-20371-2). CPL Biblios.
Altman, Douglas G., jt. auth. see Gore, Sheila M.
Altman, Edward & Subrahmanyam, Marti G. Recent Advances in Corporate Finance. 1985. 30.00 (ISBN 0-87094-560-2). Dow Jones-Irwin.
Altman, Edward I. Corporate Financial Distress: A Complete Guide to Predicting, Avoiding & Dealing with Bankruptcy. LC 82-16103. (Professional Banking & Finance Ser.). 368p. 1983. 34.95 (ISBN 0-471-08707-6, Pub. by Wiley-Interscience). Wiley.
Altman, Edward I. & Subrahmanyam, Marti G. Recent Advances in Corporate Finance. 1985. pap. 18.95x (ISBN 0-256-03279-3). Irwin.
Altman, Edward I., ed. Financial Handbook. 5th ed. LC 81-10473. 1344p. 1981. 69.95x (ISBN 0-471-07727-5, Pub. by Ronald Pr). Wiley.
Altman, Edward I. & Sametz, Arnold W., eds. Financial Crises: Institutions & Markets in a Fragile Environment. LC 77-2308. (Illus.). pap. 76.00 (ISBN 0-317-09318-5, 2022497). Bks Demand UMI.
Altman, Edward I. & Walter, Ingo, eds. Contemporary Studies in Economic & Financial Analysis: Import Dependence & Economic Vulnerability. 1983. 40.00 (ISBN 0-89232-392-2). Jai Pr.
--Contemporary Studies in Economic & Financial Anaylsis: Innovations in Bond Portfolio Management, Vol. 41. 1983. 45.00 (ISBN 0-89232-320-5). Jai Pr.
--Contemporary Studies in Economic & Financial Analysis: Problems in Financing Small Business, Pt. 1. 1983. 40.00 (ISBN 0-89232-390-6). Jai Pr.
--Contemporary Studies in Economic & Financial Analysis: Sources of Financing for Small Business, Pt. 2. 1983. 40.00 (ISBN 0-89232-391-4). Jai Pr.
Altman, Edward I., ed. see Ahlers, David M.
Altman, Edward I., ed. see Ahmad, Jaleel.
Altman, Edward I., ed. see Allen, Loring.
Altman, Edward I., ed. see Altman, Edward I., et al.
Altman, Edward I., ed. see Balbkins, Nicholas.
Altman, Edward I., ed. see Bierwag, G. O.
Altman, Edward I., ed. see Bloch, Ernest & Schwartz, Robert A.
Altman, Edward I., ed. see Dreyer, Jacob S.
Altman, Edward I., ed. see Fewings, David R.
Altman, Edward I., ed. see Ghatak, Subrata.
Altman, Edward I., ed. see Gladwin, Thomas N.
Altman, Edward I., ed. see Hallwood, Paul.
Altman, Edward I., ed. see Hunt, Lacy H.
Altman, Edward I., ed. see Kaufman, George G.
Altman, Edward I., ed. see Kobrin, Stephen J.
Altman, Edward I., ed. see Levich, Richard M.
Altman, Edward I., ed. see Newfarmer, Richard.
Altman, Edward I., ed. see Oh, John.
Altman, Edward I., ed. see Oldfield, George S., Jr.
Altman, Edward I., ed. see Parry, Thomas G.
Altman, Edward I., ed. see Pastre, Oliver.
Altman, Edward I., ed. see Ramsey, James B.
Altman, Edward I., ed. see Roxburgh, Nigel.
Altman, Edward I., ed. see Sciberras, Edmond.
Altman, Edward I., ed. see Siebert, Horst, et al.
Altman, Edward I., ed. see Sinkey, Joseph F., Jr.
Altman, Edward I., ed. see Stapleton, Richard.
Altman, Edward I., ed. see Thompson, John K.
Altman, Edward I., ed. see Uri, Noel D.
Altman, Edward I., et al. Application of Classification Techniques in Business, Banking & Finance, Vol. 3. Walter, Ingo & Altman, Edward I., eds. LC 76-5759. (Contemporary Studies in Economic & Financial Analysis). 325p. 1981. lib. bdg. 47.50 (ISBN 0-89232-004-4). Jai Pr.
Altman, Edward V., ed. see Walker, William B.
Altman, Ellen. Local Public Library Administration. 2nd ed. 260p. 1980. lib. bdg. 20.00x (ISBN 0-8389-0307-X). ALA.
Altman, Ellen & Plate, Kenneth. Problems in Library Supervision. (The Libraries & Information Sciences Ser.). Date not set. price not set (ISBN 0-89391-111-9). Ablex Pub.
Altman, H. B., jt. auth. see Hibbs, Michele.
Altman, Howard B. see Alatis, James E., et al.
Altman, Ida & Lockhart, James, eds. Provinces of Early Mexico: Variants of Spanish American Regional Evolution. LC 76-620055. (Latin American Studies: Vol. 36). (Illus.). 1976. text ed. 12.00 (ISBN 0-87903-036-4); pap. 11.95 (ISBN 0-87903-110-7). UCLA Lat Am Ctr.
Altman, Irving & Baiardi, Peter. Investment Recovery. LC 76-26926. (AMA Management Briefing Ser.). pap. 20.00 (ISBN 0-317-28461-4, 2051304). Bks Demand UMI.
Altman, Irwin. The Environment & Social Behavior. 256p. 1981. pap. text ed. 14.95x (ISBN 0-8290-0639-7). Irvington.
Altman, Irwin & Chemers, Martin M. Culture & Environmental. Altman, Irwin & Stokols, Daniel, eds. (Environment & Behavior Ser.: No. 2). (Illus.). 337p. 1984. pap. 13.95 (ISBN 0-521-31970-6). Cambridge U Pr.
Altman, Irwin & Taylor, Dalmas A. Social Penetration: The Development of Interpersonal Relationships. 212p. 1983. pap. text ed. 12.95x (ISBN 0-8290-1046-7). Irvington.
Altman, Irwin & Wohlwill, J. F., eds. Human Behavior & Environment, Vol. 1. (Illus.). 316p. 1976. 32.50x (ISBN 0-306-33301-5, Plenum Pr). Plenum Pub.
--Human Behavior & Environment, Vol. 2: Advances in Theory & Research. (Illus.). 358p. 1977. 32.50x (ISBN 0-306-33302-3, Plenum Pr). Plenum Pub.

--Human Behavior & Environment, Vol. 3: Children & the Environment. (Illus.). 316p. 1978. 32.50x (ISBN 0-306-40090-1, Plenum Pr). Plenum Pub.

Altman, Irwin & Wohlwill, Joachim F., eds. Behavior & the Natural Environment. LC 83-7285. (Human Behavior & Environment Ser.: No. 6). (Illus.). 346p. 1983. 35.00 (ISBN 0-306-41099-0). Plenum Pub.

Altman, Irwin, ed. see Altman, Irwin & Chemers, Martin M.

Altman, Irwin, ed. see Cone, John D. & Hayes, Steven C.

Altman, Irwin, ed. see Wicker, Allan W.

Altman, Irwin, ed. see Zeisel, John.

Altman, Irwin, ed. see Zube, Ervin H.

Altman, Irwin, et al, eds. Human Behavior & Environment, Vol. 4: Environment & Culture. (Illus.). 368p. 1980. 32.50x (ISBN 0-306-40367-6, Plenum Pr). Plenum Pub.

--Elderly People & the Environment. (Human Behavior & Environment Ser.: Vol. 7). 362p. 1984. 39.50x (ISBN 0-306-41429-5, Plenum Pr). Plenum Pub.

--Human Behavior & Environment, Vol. 5: Transportation & Behavior. LC 76-382942. 301p. 1982. 32.50 (ISBN 0-306-40773-6, Plenum Pr). Plenum Pub.

Altman, J. & Bayer, S. Development of the Cranial Nerve Ganglia & Related Nuclei in the Rat. (Advances in Anatomy, Embroyology & Cell Biology Ser.: Vol. 74). (Illus.). 100p. 1982. pap. 27.00 (ISBN 0-387-11337-1). Springer-Verlag.

Altman, J. & Bayer, S. A. The Development of the Rat Spinal Chord. (Advances in Anatomy, Embryology & Cell Biology Ser.: Vol. 58). (Illus.). 160p. 1984. pap. 25.00 (ISBN 0-387-13119-1). Springer-Verlag.

Altman, J. C. & Nieuwenhuysen, J. P. The Economic Status of Australian Aborigines. LC 78-14917. 1979. 44.50 (ISBN 0-521-22421-7). Cambridge U Pr.

Altman, Janet G. Epistolarity: Approaches to a Form. LC 81-16866. 242p. 1982. 20.00x (ISBN 0-8142-0313-2). Ohio St U Pr.

Altman, Joel B. The Tudor Play of Mind: Rhetorical Inquiry & the Development of Elizabethan Drama. LC 76-52022. 1978. 38.50x (ISBN 0-520-03427-9). U of Cal Pr.

Altman, Joseph. Organic Foundations of Animal Behavior. LC 65-18350. (Illus.). 1966. text ed. 37.50x (ISBN 0-03-052230-7); pap. text ed. 14.95x (ISBN 0-89197-871-2). Irvington.

Altman, Kurt I. Radiation Biochemistry, 2 vols. Incl. Vol. 1. Cells. Okada, Shigefumi (ISBN 0-12-054501-2); Vol. 2. Tissues & Body Fluids. Altman, Kurt I. & Gerber, Georg B. (ISBN 0-12-054502-0). 1970. 75.00 ea.. Acad Pr.

Altman, Lawrence K. Who Goes First! The Story of Self-Experimentation in Medicine. LC 84-18807. 416p. 1985. 19.45 (ISBN 0-394-50382-1). Random.

Altman, Leon L. The Dream in Psychoanalysis. rev. ed. LC 75-13572. 280p. (Orig.). 1975. text ed. 27.50 (ISBN 0-8236-1431-X). Intl Univs Pr.

Altman, Liza & Gonella, Ronald R., eds. Great Events Two As Reported in the New York Times: Program Guide. 107p. (gr. 7-12). 1980. pap. text ed. 7.95 (ISBN 0-667-00600-1). Microfilming Corp.

Altman, Louis. The Law of Unfair Competition Trademarks & Monopolies: 1933-1984, 9 Vols. LC 81-7639. 650.00 (ISBN 0-317-20372-X). Callaghan.

Altman, M. Dicionario Tecnico Contabil: Portugues-Ingles, Ingles-Portugues. 126p. (Port. & Eng.). 1980. pap. 14.95 (ISBN 0-686-97637-1, M-9355). French & Eur.

Altman, Marjorie & Crocker, Ruth, eds. Social Groupwork & Alcoholism. LC 82-2998. (Social Work with Groups Ser.: Vol. 5, No. 1). 92p. 1982. text ed. 19.95 (ISBN 0-917724-94-1, B94); pap. text ed. 10.95 (ISBN 0-86656-439-X). Haworth Pr.

Altman, Michael L. Standards Relating to Juvenile Records & Information Systems. LC 77-3228. (IJA-ABA Juvenile Justice Standards Project Ser.). 208p. 1980. prof ref 22.50 (ISBN 0-88410-247-5); pap. 12.50 (ISBN 0-88410-819-8). Ballinger Pub.

Altman, Millys N. Racing in Her Blood. LC 79-3018. (gr. 7 up). 1980. PLB 8.89 (ISBN 0-397-31895-2). Lipp Jr Bks.

Altman, Nat. Ahimsa: Dynamic Compassion. LC 80-51548. 150p. (Orig.). 1981. pap. 4.95 (ISBN 0-8356-0537-X, Quest). Theos Pub Hse.

Altman, Nathaniel. The Chiropractic Alternative. LC 79-93020. 208p. 1981. pap. 5.95 (ISBN 0-87477-237-0). J P Tarcher.

--The Palmistry Workbook. (Illus.). 160p. (Orig.). pap. 12.95 (ISBN 0-85030-352-4, Pub. by Aquarian Pr England). Sterling.

--Total Vegetarian Cooking. LC 80-85343. 1981. pap. 2.95 (ISBN 0-87983-246-0). Keats.

--Where the Vegetarians Eat: Nat Altman's Pocket Guide to 250 Vegetarian Restaurants in the U. S. & Canada. LC 82-80698. 1982. pap. 4.95 (ISBN 0-87983-280-0). Keats.

Altman, Norman H., jt. ed. see Melby, Edward C., Jr.

Altman, P. L., ed. Pathology of Laboratory Mice & Rats. (Biology Databook Ser.). 700p. 1985. 140.00 (ISBN 0-08-030077-4, Pub. by Aberdeen Scotland). Pergamon.

Altman, Philip L. & Dittmer, Dorothy S., eds. Biology Data Book, 3 vols. 2nd ed. Incl. Vol. 1. 1972 (ISBN 0-913822-06-X); Vol. 2. 1973 (ISBN 0-913822-08-6); Vol. 3. 1974 (ISBN 0-913822-07-8). LC 72-87738. (Biological Handbooks). (Illus.). 60.00 ea.; Set. 150.00. Pergamon.

--Environmental Biology. LC 66-27592. (Biological Handbks). (Illus.). 694p. 1966. 20.00 (ISBN 0-913822-03-5). Pergamon.

--Respiration & Circulation. rev. ed. LC 70-137563. (Biological Handbks). (Illus.). xxv, 930p. 1971. 60.00 (ISBN 0-08-030067-7). Pergamon.

Altman, Philip L. & Katz, Dorothy D., eds. Cell Biology. LC 75-42787. (Biological Handbks: Vol. 1). (Illus.). 1976. 55.00 (ISBN 0-913822-10-8). Pergamon.

--Inbred & Genetically Defined Strains of Laboratory Animals. Incl. Pt. 1. Mouse & Rat. 65.00 (ISBN 0-913822-12-4); Pt. 2. Hamster, Guinea Pig, Rabbit & Chicken. 50.00 (ISBN 0-913822-13-2). LC 78-73555. (Biological Handbooks: Vol. 3). (Illus.). 1979. Set. 100.00 (ISBN 0-913822-14-0). Pergamon.

Altman, Phyllis. Bram Fischer, Q. C. rev. ed. 6p. 1975. 0.60 (ISBN 0-317-20229-4). IDAFSA.

Altman, Ralph. Availability for Work: A Study in Unemployment Compensation. LC 68-8935. (Illus.). 1968. Repr. of 1950 ed. lib. bdg. 19.00x (ISBN 0-8371-0004-6, ALAW). Greenwood.

Altman, Rick, ed. Genre: The Musical. (BFI Readers in Film Ser.). 180p. 1983. pap. 10.95x (ISBN 0-7100-0817-1). Routledge & Kegan.

Altman, S. P. Orbital Hodograph Analysis. (Science & Technology Ser.: Vol. 3). 1965. 20.00x (ISBN 0-87703-031-6, Pub. by Am Astronaut). Univelt Inc.

Altman, Sheldon. Acupuncture for Animals. 300p. 25.00 (ISBN 0-317-31551-X). Chans Corp.

Altman, Sidney, ed. Transfer RNA. (MIT Press Cell Monograph Ser.: No. 2). 1978. text ed. 47.50x (ISBN 0-262-01056-9). MIT Pr.

Altman, Sig. Comic Image of the Jew: Explorations of a Pop Culture Phenomenon. LC 71-146161. 234p. 1971. 22.50 (ISBN 0-8386-7869-6). Fairleigh Dickinson.

Altman, Steven & Hodgetts, Richard M. Readings in Organizational Behavior. 1979. pap. text ed. 15.95 (ISBN 0-7216-1140-0). HR&W.

Altman, Steven, et al. Organizational Behavior: Theory & Practice. 1985. text ed. 24.00i (ISBN 0-12-054750-3); instr's. manual avail. (ISBN 0-12-054751-1). Acad Pr.

Altman, Stuart & Sapolsky, Harvey M., eds. Federal Health Programs: Improving the Health-Care System? LC 79-48059. (The University Health Policy Consortium Ser.). 272p. 1981. pap. text ed. 14.00x (ISBN 0-669-06371-1). Lexington Bks.

Altman, Stuart A. Social Communication Among the Primates. LC 65-25120. (Midway Reprints Ser.). (Illus.). xiv, 392p. 1982. pap. text ed. 18.00x (ISBN 0-226-01597-1). U of Chicago Pr.

Altman, Stuart H., et al. Ambulatory Care: Problems of Cost & Access. LC 82-49054. (University Health Policy Consortium Ser.). 256p. 1983. 26.50x (ISBN 0-669-06401-7). Lexington Bks.

Altman, Wilfred, et al. T. V. From Monopoly to Competition, & Back. (Institute of Economic Affairs Hobart Papers Ser.: No. 15). pap. 2.50 technical (ISBN 0-685-20638-6). Transatlantic.

Altmann, et al, eds. Current Topics in Pathology, Vol. 58. LC 56-49162. (Illus.). 190p. 1973. 70.80 (ISBN 0-387-06405-2). Springer-Verlag.

Altmann, A., ed. see Israeli, Isaac.

Altmann, Alexander. Essays in Jewish Intellectual History. LC 80-54471. 336p. 1981. 30.00x (ISBN 0-87451-192-5). U Pr of New Eng.

--Studies in Religious Philosophy & Mysticism. (New Reprints in Essay & General Literature Index Ser.). 1975. Repr. of 1969 ed. 24.25 (ISBN 0-518-10194-0). Ayer Co Pubs.

Altmann, Alexander, intro. by see Mendelssohn, Moses.

Altmann, Horst. Poisonous Plants & Animals. (Illus.). 150p. 1981. pap. 5.95 (ISBN 0-7011-2526-8, Pub. by Chatto & Windus). Merrimack Pub Cir.

Altmann, Jeanne. Baboon Mothers & Infants. LC 79-21568. (Illus.). 1980. text ed. 18.50x (ISBN 0-674-05856-9); pap. text ed. 8.95x (ISBN 0-674-05857-7). Harvard U Pr.

Altmann, Simon L. Induced Representations in Crystals & Molecules: Point, Space & Nonrigid Molecule Groups. 1978. 59.50 (ISBN 0-12-054650-7). Acad Pr.

Altmann, Walter. Die Romischen Grabaltare der Kaiserzeit. facsimile ed. LC 75-10626. (Ancient Religion & Mythology Ser.). (Illus., Ger.). 1975. Repr. of 1905 ed. 26.50x (ISBN 0-405-07002-0). Ayer Co Pubs.

Altmann, Wilhelm, ed. see Haydn, Joseph.

Altmeyer, A. P., jt. auth. see Bucksch, H.

Altmeyer, Arthur J. Formative Years of Social Security. (Illus.). 328p. 1966. 27.50x (ISBN 0-299-03820-3); pap. 8.95x (ISBN 0-299-03824-6). U of Wis Pr.

Altmeyer, Jean J. Histoire des relations commerciales et diplomatiques des Pays-Bas avec le nord de l'Europe pendant le sixieme siecle. LC 66-20684. 1970. Repr. of 1840 ed. lib. bdg. 32.00 (ISBN 0-8337-0052-9). B Franklin.

Altoma, Salih J. Problems of Diglossia in Arabic: A Comparative Study of Classical & Iraqi Arabic. LC 69-11663. (Middle Eastern Monographs Ser: No. 21). 1969. pap. text ed. 4.50x (ISBN 0-674-70775-3). Harvard U Pr.

Altomara, Rita E. Hollywood on the Palisades: A Filmography of Silent Feaures Made in Fort Lee, New Jersey 1903-1927. 120p. 1983. lib. bdg. 42.00 (ISBN 0-8240-9225-2). Garland Pub.

Alton, Albert. In God's Hands. Garfield Publications, ed. 272p. (Orig.). 1984. pap. 5.95 (ISBN 0-9609856-1-1). Garfield Pubns.

Alton, E. V. & Gersting, J. L. Module SI: Metric System. Ablon, L. J., et al, eds. LC 76-58669. (Ser. in Mathematical Modules). 1977. pap. text ed. 11.95 (ISBN 0-8465-0266-6). Benjamin-Cummings.

Alton, G. G. & Jones, Lois M. Laboratory Techniques in Brucellosis. 2nd ed. (Monograph Ser: No. 55). (Illus.). 92p. (Eng, Fr, Rus, & Span.). 1975. 14.00 (ISBN 92-4-140055-2). World Health.

Alton, Robert. Violin & Cello Building & Repairing. 1976. Repr. of 1946 ed. lib. bdg. 39.00x (ISBN 0-403-03758-1). Scholarly.

Alton, Walter G., Jr. Malpractice: A Trial Lawyer's Advice for Physicians. 1977. 19.95 (ISBN 0-316-03500-9). Little.

Alton, Wright. The Third Eye, Book I. (The Third Eye Bks.). 160p. (Orig.). Date not set. pap. 10.95. Creat Gospel Prod A Wright.

Altounyan, R. E., ed. see Symposium on Asthma & Chronic Bronchitis in Children & Their Prognosis into Adult Life, 3rd, Davos, 1969.

Altounyan, Taqui. In Aleppo Once. (Illus.). 1971. 9.50 (ISBN 0-7195-1922-5). Transatlantic.

Altounyon, Taqui. Through the Year in the Middle East. (Through the Year Ser.). (Illus.). 72p. (YA) (gr. 7-10). 1983. 14.95 (ISBN 0-7134-4075-9, Pub. by Batsford England). David & Charles.

Altov, Genrikh & Zhuravlyova, Valentina. Ballad of the Stars. 300p. 1982. 15.75 (ISBN 0-02-501740-3). Macmillan.

Al'tov, V. A., et al, eds. Stabilization of Superconducting Magnetic Systems. LC 77-8618. (International Cryogenics Monographs Ser.). 338p. 1977. 52.50x (ISBN 0-306-30943-2, Plenum Pr). Plenum Pub.

Al'tovskii, M. E., et al. Origin of Oil & Oil Deposits. LC 60-13948. 107p. 1961. 30.00x (ISBN 0-306-10564-0, Consultants). Plenum Pub.

Altrocchi, John. Abnormal Behavior. 755p. 1980. text ed. 30.95 (ISBN 0-15-500370-4, HC); instructor's manual with tests avail. (ISBN 0-15-500371-2). HarBraceJ.

Altrocchi, Julia C. Wolves Against the Moon. LC 79-103313. 1980. 17.50 (ISBN 0-912382-02-3). Black Letter.

Altrocchi, Rudolph. Sleuthing in the Stacks. LC 68-26239. 1968. Repr. of 1944 ed. 21.50x (ISBN 0-8046-0009-0, Pub. by Kennikat). Assoc Faculty Pr.

Altrocchi, Rudolph, tr. see Sommi-Picenardi, Girolamo.

Altschiller, Donald. Transportation in America. (The Reference Shelf Ser.: Vol. 54, No. 3). 204p. 1982. text ed. 8.00 (ISBN 0-8242-0667-3). Wilson.

Altschul, Aaron & Wilcke, Harold L., eds. New Protein Foods, Vol. 5: Seed Storage Proteins. (Food Science & Technology Ser.). 1985. 94.50 (ISBN 0-12-054805-4). Acad Pr.

Altschul, Aaron A., ed. New Protein Foods. (Food Science & Technology Ser.). 1974. Vol. 1A, 1974. 85.00 (ISBN 0-12-054801-1); Vol. 2B 1976. 70.00 (ISBN 0-12-054802-X). Acad Pr.

--New Protein Foods Vol. 4. LC 72-12188. (Food Science & Technology Ser.). 1981. Pt. B. 65.00 (ISBN 0-12-054804-6). Acad Pr.

Altschul, Aaron M., jt. auth. see Symposium on Evaluation of World Resources, Atlantic City, 1965.

Altschul, Aaron M. & Wilcke, Harold L., eds. New Protein Foods Vol. 3, Animal Protein Supplies, Part A. (Food Science & Technology Ser.). 1978. 75.00 (ISBN 0-12-054803-8). Acad Pr.

Altschul, Aaron M., jt. ed. see Scrimshaw, Nevin S.

Altschul, B. J., jt. auth. see LaFray-Young, Joyce.

Altschul, Carlos, tr. see Cardenal, Ernesto.

Altschul, Michael. Anglo-Norman England: Ten Sixty-Six to Eleven Fifty-Four. LC 78-80816. (Conference on British Studies, Bibliographical Handbooks Ser.). pap. 23.00 (ISBN 0-317-10590-6, 2022432). Bks Demand UMI.

--A Baronial Family in Medieval England: The Clares, 1217-1314. LC 78-64244. (Johns Hopkins University. Studies in the Social Sciences. Eighty-Third Ser. 1965: 2). Repr. of 1965 ed. 27.00 (ISBN 0-404-61349-7). AMS Pr.

--A Baronial Family in Medieval England: The Clares, 1217-1314. LC 65-22947. (Johns Hopkins University Studies in Historical & Political Science: Series 83, No. 2). pap. 88.00 (ISBN 0-317-09205-7, 2004926). Bks Demand UMI.

Altschul, Monique, tr. see Cardenal, Ernesto.

Altschul, Siri V. Drugs & Foods from Little Known Plants: Notes in Harvard University Herbaria. LC 72-85145. 1973. 35.00x (ISBN 0-674-21676-8). Harvard U Pr.

Altschuld, James W., et al. From Idea to Action: Career Guidance Plans of Rural & Small Schools. 291p. 1978. 14.60 (ISBN 0-318-15477-3, RD148). Natl Ctr Res Voc Ed.

Altschule, Mark D. Nutritional Factors in General Medicine: Effects of Stress & Distorted Diets. 200p. 1978. 20.75x (ISBN 0-398-03736-1). C C Thomas.

--Roots of Modern Psychiatry. 2nd ed. LC 65-12656. (Illus.). 216p. 1965. 45.00 (ISBN 0-8089-0011-0). Grune.

--What Medicine Is about: Using Its Past to Improve Its Future. (Library Associates Historical Publications). 100p. 1975. 7.95 (ISBN 0-686-15547-5). F A Countway.

Altschule, Mark D., jt. auth. see Valeri, C. Robert.

Altschule, Mark D., ed. Frontiers of Pineal Physiology. 1974. 37.50x (ISBN 0-262-01041-0). MIT Pr.

Altschuler, Allen, tr. see Sergeev-Tsienskii, Sergei N.

Altschuler, Bruce E. Keeping a Finger on the Public Pulse: Private Polling & Presidential Elections. LC 81-6965. (Contributions in Political Science Ser.: No. 72). (Illus.). 197p. 1982. lib. bdg. 27.50 (ISBN 0-313-23046-3, AKF/). Greenwood.

Altschuler, David, ed. The Precious Legacy: Judaic Treasures from the Czechoslavak State Collection. (Illus.). 256p. (Orig.). 1983. 40.00 (ISBN 0-671-49448-1); pap. 17.50 (ISBN 0-671-49498-8). Summit Bks.

Altschuler, Glenn C. Andrew M. White, Educator, Historian, Diplomat. LC 78-58065. (Illus.). 296p. 1978. 27.50x (ISBN 0-8014-1156-4). Cornell U Pr.

--Race, Ethnicity, & Class in American Social Thought, 1865-1919. (American History Ser.). 168p. (Orig.). 1982. pap. text ed. 7.95x (ISBN 0-88295-808-9). Harlan Davidson.

Altschuler, Glenn C. & Saltzgaber, Jan M. Revivalism, Social Conscience, & Community in the Burned-Over District: The Trial of Rhoda Bement. (Illus.). 184p. 1983. 24.95x (ISBN 0-8014-1541-1); pap. 8.95x (ISBN 0-8014-9246-7). Cornell U Pr.

Altschuler, Mark. Your Passport to Making It Abroad. 2.95 (ISBN 0-8315-0133-2). Speller.

Altschuler, Richard A., et al, eds. Neurobiology of Hearing: The Cochlea. 1985. text ed. price not set (ISBN 0-89004-925-4). Raven.

Altschull, J. Herbert. Agents of Power. LC 83-14906. (Annenberg Longman Communication Ser.). 320p. (Orig.). 1983. text ed. 29.95 (ISBN 0-582-28417-1); pap. text ed. 15.95 (ISBN 0-582-28418-X). Longman.

Altschuller, G. S. Creativity as An Exact Science. (Studies in Cybernetics: Vol. 5). 332p. 1984. 54.00 (ISBN 0-677-21230-5). Gordon.

Altsheler, Joseph. Before the Dawn. 1976. lib. bdg. 16.70x (ISBN 0-89968-000-3). Lightyear.

--Border Watch. 1976. lib. bdg. 21.95 (ISBN 0-89968-001-1). Lightyear.

--The Border Watch. (The Young Trailer Ser.). 319p. 1984. lib. bdg. 21.95x (ISBN 0-89966-485-7). Buccaneer Bks.

--Eyes of the Woods. 1976. lib. bdg. 19.95 (ISBN 0-89968-145-X). Lightyear.

--The Eyes of the Woods. (The Young Trailer Ser.). 319p. 1984. Repr. lib. bdg. 19.95x (ISBN 0-89966-481-4). Buccaneer Bks.

--The Forest Runners. 1976. lib. bdg. 19.95 (ISBN 0-89968-002-X). Lightyear.

--The Forest Runners. (The Young Trailer Ser.). 319p. Repr. lib. bdg. 19.95x (ISBN 0-89966-480-6). Buccaneer Bks.

--Free Rangers. 350p. 1981. Repr. lib. bdg. 19.95 (ISBN 0-89968-225-1). Lightyear.

--The Free Rangers. (The Young Trailer Ser.). 319p. 1984. Repr. lib. bdg. 19.95x (ISBN 0-89966-482-2). Buccaneer Bks.

--The Great Sioux Trail. 18.95 (ISBN 0-89190-825-0, Pub. by Am Repr). Amereon Ltd.

--In Hostile Red. 1976. lib. bdg. 15.80x (ISBN 0-89968-003-8). Lightyear.

--The Rifleman of the Ohio. (The Young Trailer Ser.). 319p. 1984. Repr. lib. bdg. 20.95 (ISBN 0-89966-483-0). Buccaneer Bks.

--The Rock of Chicamauga. 18.95 (ISBN 0-8488-0071-0, Pub. by Amereon Hse). Amereon Ltd.

--The Scouts of Stonewall. 1976. lib. bdg. 19.95 (ISBN 0-89968-004-6). Lightyear.

--The Scouts of Stonewall. 19.95 (ISBN 0-8488-0070-2, Pub. by Amereon Hse). Amereon Ltd.

--Scouts of the Valley. 345p. 1981. Repr. lib. bdg. 19.95 (ISBN 0-89968-227-8). Lightyear.

--The Scouts of the Valley. (The Young Trailer Ser.). 319p. 1984. Repr. lib. bdg. 21.95 (ISBN 0-89966-484-9). Buccaneer Bks.

--The Tree of Appomattox. 19.95 (ISBN 0-317-27924-6, Pub. by Amereon Hse). Amereon Ltd.

--The Young Trailers. 1976. lib. bdg. 18.95 (ISBN 0-89968-005-4). Lightyear.

--The Young Trailers. (The Young Trailer Ser.). Repr. lib. bdg. 19.95x (ISBN 0-89966-479-2). Buccaneer Bks.

--The Young Trailers. 19.95 (ISBN 0-89190-824-2, Pub. by Am Repr). Amereon ltd.

Altsheler, Joseph A. Apache Gold. 1976. Repr. of 1913 ed. lib. bdg. 19.95x (ISBN 0-88411-941-6, Pub. by Aeonian Pr). Amereon Ltd.

--The Great Sioux Trail. (The Texan Ser.). 1985. write for info. (Pub. by J M C & Co). Amereon Ltd.

--The Guns of Bull Run. 1976. Repr. of 1914 ed. lib. bdg. 18.95 (ISBN 0-88411-942-4, Pub. by Aeonian Pr). Amereon Ltd.

--The Guns of Shiloh. 1976. Repr. of 1914 ed. lib. bdg. 18.95 (ISBN 0-88411-943-2, Pub. by Aeonian Pr). Amereon Ltd.

--Horseman of the Plains. 1976. Repr. of 1910 ed. lib. bdg. 20.95 (ISBN 0-88411-946-7, Pub. by Aeonian Pr). Amereon Ltd.

--The Hosts of the Air: The Story of a Quest in the Great War. 327p. Repr. of 1932 ed. lib. bdg. 17.95 (ISBN 0-88411-947-5, Pub. by Aeonian Pr). Amereon Ltd.

--The Keepers of the Trail: A Story of the Great Woods. 323p. Repr. of 1916 ed. lib. bdg. 17.95 (ISBN 0-88411-948-3, Pub. by Aeonian Pr). Amereon Ltd.

--The Lost Hunters: A Story of Wild Man & Great Beasts. 311p. Repr. of 1918 ed. lib. bdg. 17.95 (ISBN 0-88411-949-1, Pub. by Aeonian Pr). Amereon Ltd.

--The Masters of the Peaks: A Story of the Great North Woods. 311p. Repr. of 1918 ed. lib. bdg. 17.95 (ISBN 0-88411-938-6, Pub. by Aeonian Pr). Amereon Ltd.

--The Quest of the Four: A Story of the Comanches & Buena Vista. 386p. Repr. of 1911 ed. lib. bdg. 16.95x (ISBN 0-88411-939-4, Pub. by Aeonian Pr). Amereon Ltd.

--The Rock of Chicamauga: A Story of the Western Crisis. (The Joseph A. Altsheler Civil War Ser.). 1985. 17.95 (Pub. by J M C & Co). Amereon Ltd.

--The Scouts of Stonewall: The Story of the Great Valley Campaign. (The Joseph A. Altshelter Civil War Ser.). 1985. 18.95. Amereon Ltd.

--Shades of the Wilderness: A Story of Lee's Great Stand. 312p. Repr. of 1916 ed. lib. bdg. 18.95x (ISBN 0-88411-940-8, Pub. by Aeonian Pr). Amereon Ltd.

--The Shadow of the North. 357p. 1976. Repr. of 1917 ed. lib. bdg. 17.95x (ISBN 0-88411-944-0, Pub. by Aeonian Pr). Amereon Ltd.

--The Star of Gettysburg. 1976. Repr. of 1915 ed. lib. bdg. 19.95x (ISBN 0-88411-945-9, Pub. by Aeonian Pr). Amereon Ltd.

--The Sword of Antietam: The Story of the Nation's Crisis. (The Joseph A. Altsheler Civil War Ser.). 1985. 19.95 (ISBN 0-317-28286-7, Pub. by J M C & Co). Amereon Ltd.

--The Texan Scouts. (The Texan Ser.). 1985. write for info. (Pub. by J M C & Co). Amereon Ltd.

--The Texan Star. (The Texan Ser.). 1985. write for info. (Pub. by J M C & Co). Amereon Ltd.

--The Texan Triumph. (The Texan Ser.). 1985. write for info. (Pub. by J M C & Co). Amereon Ltd.

--The Tree of Appomattox: A Story of the Civil War's Close. (The Joseph A. Altsheler Civil War Ser.). 1985. 18.95 (ISBN 0-317-28292-1, Pub. by J M C & Co). Amereon Ltd.

Altshuler, Alan, ed. Transportation & Communication Policy. new ed. 1977. pap. 8.00 (ISBN 0-918592-22-4). Policy Studies.

Altshuler, Alan, et al. The Future of the Automobile: The Report of MIT's International Automobile Program. 1984. 16.95 (ISBN 0-262-01081-X). MIT Pr.

Altshuler, Alan A. The City Planning Process: A Political Analysis. LC 65-25498. 466p. 1969. pap. 12.95x (ISBN 0-8014-9081-2, CP81). Cornell U Pr.

--The City Planning Process: A Political Analysis. 466p. 1965. 22.50 (ISBN 0-318-12942-6); members 20.50 (ISBN 0-318-12943-4); pap. 5.95 (ISBN 0-318-12944-2). Am Plan Assn.

Altshuler, Alan A. & Thomas, Norman C., eds. Politics of the Federal Bureaucracy. 2nd ed. 1977. pap. text ed. 19.50 scp (ISBN 0-06-040246-6, HarpC). Har-Row.

Altshuler, Alan A., et al. The Urban Transportation System: Politics & Policy Innovation. 1979. pap. 16.50x (ISBN 0-262-51023-5). MIT Pr.

Altshuler, Constance W. Starting with Defiance: Nineteenth Century Arizona Military Posts. (Historical Monograph: No. 7). (Illus.). 88p. 1983. pap. 8.00 (ISBN 0-910037-20-5). AZ Hist Soc.

Altshuler, David, ed. see Neusner, Jacob.

Altshuler, David, ed. see Zamir, Yaron.

Altshuler, David A. Hitler's War Against the Jews - the Holocaust: A Young Reader's Version of the War Against the Jews: 1933-1945 by Lucy Dawidowicz. LC 78-5418. (Illus.). 1978. 8.95x (ISBN 0-87441-293-5); pap. 6.50x (ISBN 0-87441-222-6). Behrman.

Altshuler, G. see Huth, F., et al.

Altshuler, H. L., jt. ed. see Burch, N.

Altshuler, Kenneth, jt. ed. see Rush, A. John.

Altshuler, Mark. Predtechi Slavianofilstva v Russkoi Literature. 370p. 1984. 35.00 (ISBN 0-88233-181-7). Ardis Pubs.

Altshuler, Thelma, jt. auth. see Janaro, Richard.

Altshuller, Marc, intro. by. Izbrannye Rasskazy Shestidesyatykh. LC 84-28696. 348p. 1985. pap. 13.50 (ISBN 0-938920-52-9). Hermitage.

Altstein, Howard, jt. auth. see Simon, Rita J.

Altszuler, N., et al. Insulin Two. Hasselblatt, A. & Brushhausen, F. V., eds. (Handbook of Experimental Pharmacology, Vol. 32, Pt. 2). (Illus.). 880p. 1975. 172.00 (ISBN 0-387-07006-0). Springer-Verlag.

Al Tulab, Munjid see Tulab, Munjid al & Mashreq, Dar el.

Altum, Bernard. Der Vogel und Sein Leben. Sterling, Keir B., ed. LC 77-81082. (Biologists & Their World Ser.). (Ger.). 1978. Repr. of 1868 ed. lib. bdg. 17.00x (ISBN 0-405-10652-1). Ayer Co Pubs.

Al Tunisi, Khayr. Surest Path: The Political Treatise of a Nineteenth-Century Muslim Statesman. Brown, Leon C., tr. LC 67-25399. (Middle Eastern Monographs Ser: No. 16). pap. 5.00x (ISBN 0-674-85695-3). Harvard U Pr.

Altura, B. M., jt. auth. see Kaley, G.

Altura, B. M., ed. Ionic Regulation of the Microcirculation. (Advances in Microcirculation: Vol. 11). (Illus.). x, 174p. 1982. 63.50 (ISBN 3-8055-3429-9). S Karger.

--Vascular Endothelium & Basement Membranes. (Advances in Microcirculation: Vol. 9). (Illus.). 1979. 26.00 (ISBN 3-8055-3054-4). S Karger.

Altura, B. M. & Altura, Bella T., eds. Dietary Minerals & Cardiovascular Disease. (Journal: Magnesium: Vol. 1, No. 3-6). (Illus.). vi, 188p. 1983. pap. 55.50 (ISBN 3-8055-3682-8). S Karger.

Altura, B. M. & Kruck, F., eds. Interactions of Magnesium & Potassium on Cardiac & Vascular Smooth Muscle. (Journal: Magnesium: Vol. 3, No. 4-6, 1984). (Illus.). iv, 192p. 1985. pap. 37.25 (ISBN 3-8055-4149-X). S Karger.

Altura, B. M., jt. ed. see Durlach, J.

Altura, Bella T., jt. ed. see Altura, B. M.

Altura, Burton M. & Saba, Thomas M., eds. Pathophysiology of the Reticuloendothelial System. 248p. 1981. text ed. 35.00 (ISBN 0-89004-441-4). Raven.

Altura, Burton M., et al, eds. Handbook of Shock & Trauma: Vol. 1: Basic Science. 484p. 1983. text ed. 70.50. Raven.

Altvater, Helen. From Eight to Eighty (Young Adult Poetry) 100p. (Orig.). 1981. pap. 4.95 (ISBN 0-933906-17-X). Gusto Pr.

Altwein, J. E., jt. ed. see Jacobi, G. H.

Alty, J. L., jt. auth. see Coombs, M. J.

Al-Udhari, Abdullah. Voice Without Passport. 1974. sewn in wrappers 1.25 (ISBN 0-685-78970-5, Pub. by Menard Pr). Small Pr Dist.

Al-Udhari, Abdullah, tr. Fireflies in the Dark. 1974. saddlestitched in wrappers 1.25 (ISBN 0-685-78971-3, Pub. by Menard Pr). Small Pr Dist.

--A Mirror for Autumn. 1974. saddlestitched in wrappers 1.25 (ISBN 0-685-78972-1, Pub. by Menard Pr). Small Pr Dist.

Aluf, I. A., et al. Lenin & the Leagues of Struggle. 227p. 1983. 7.95 (ISBN 0-8285-2625-7, Pub. by Progress pubs USSR). Imported Pubns.

Aluise, John J. The Physician as Manager. 357p. 1980. 29.95 (ISBN 0-318-17265-8). Soc Tchrs Fam Med.

Aluko, Olajide. Essays on Nigerian Foreign Policy. 1981. text ed. 28.50x (ISBN 0-04-327062-X). Allen Unwin.

Aluko, Olajide, ed. Ghana & Nigeria 1957-1970: A Study in Inter-African Discord. LC 75-1614. (Illus.). 275p. 1976. text ed. 22.50x (ISBN 0-06-490163-7, 06313). B&N Imports.

Aluko, Olajide & Shaw, Timothy M., eds. Southern Africa in the 1980s. 320p. 1985. text ed. 35.00x (ISBN 0-04-320169-5). Allen Unwin.

Aluko, Olajide, jt. ed. see Shaw, Timothy M.

Aluko, T. M. Chief the Honourable Minister. (African Writers Ser.). 1970. pap. text ed. 5.00x (ISBN 0-435-90070-6). Heinemann Ed.

--His Worshipful Majesty. (African Writers Ser.). 1973. pap. text ed. 5.00x (ISBN 0-435-90130-3). Heinemann Ed.

--Kinsman & Foreman. (African Writers Ser.). 1968. pap. text ed. 4.00x (ISBN 0-435-90032-3). Heinemann Ed.

--One Man, One Matchet. (African Writers Ser.). 1965. pap. text ed. 6.00x (ISBN 0-435-90011-0). Heinemann Ed.

--One Man, One Wife. (African Writers Ser.). 1967. pap. text ed. 4.00x (ISBN 0-435-90030-7). Heinemann Ed.

--Wrong Ones in the Dock. (African Writers Ser.: No. 242). 195p. 1982. pap. text ed. 6.00x (ISBN 0-435-90242-3). Heinemann Ed.

Aluminium Association. Aluminium Industry Energy Conservation Workshop, 7: Proceedings. 357p. 1983. 102.00 (ISBN 0-9911000-8-5, Pub. by Aluminium W Germany). Heyden.

Aluminium-Zentrade, ed. European Aluminium Statistics, 1982. 1983. 24.00 (ISBN 0-9911000-4-2, Pub. by Aluminium W Germany). Heyden.

Aluminium-Zentrale, ed. Aluminium & the Automobile. 1981. 81.00 (ISBN 0-9960034-4-4, Pub. by Aluminium W Germany). Heyden.

Aluminium-Zentrale Editors. European Aluminium Statistics. 1980. 18.00 (ISBN 0-9960034-5-2, Pub. by Aluminium W Germany). Heyden.

Aluminium Zentrale Staff. European Aluminum Statistics. 20p. 1984. pap. 24.00 (ISBN 0-9911002-0-4). Heyden.

Aluri, Rao & Robinson, Judith. A Guide to U. S. Government Scientific & Technical Resources. 259p. 1983. lib. bdg. 23.50 (ISBN 0-87287-377-3). Libs Unl.

Aluri, Rao, jt. auth. see Yannarella, Philip A.

Alurista. Floricanto En Aztlan. (Creative Ser.). (Illus.). 1971. text ed. 19.95 (ISBN 0-89551-004-9); pap. 14.95 (ISBN 0-89551-023-5). UCLA Chicano Stud.

--Return: Poems Collected & New. LC 81-68424. 176p. (Eng. & Span.). 1982. pap. 10.00x (ISBN 0-916950-24-7). Biling Rev-Pr.

--Spik in Glyph? LC 81-65312. 64p. (Orig.). 1981. pap. 5.00 (ISBN 0-934770-09-3). Arte Publico.

Alurista & Xelina, eds. Southwest Tales: A Contemporary Collection. 176p. 1985. pap. 8.00 (ISBN 0-939558-09-2). Maize Pr.

Alurista, ed. see Candelaria, Cordelia.

Alurista, ed. see Cobian, Ricardo.

Alurista, ed. see Griep-Ruiz, L. J.

Alurista, ed. see Keller, Gary D.

Alurista, ed. see Morales, Alejandro.

Alurralde, Carlos. A Statement of the Laws of Argentina in Matters Affecting Business. 1976. lib. bdg. 134.95 (ISBN 0-8490-2666-0). Gordon Pr.

Alvan, Bond. Memoir of the Rev. Pliny Fisk: Late Missionary to Palestine. Davis, Moshe, ed. LC 77-70683. (America & the Holy Land Ser.). 1977. Repr. of 1828 ed. lib. bdg. 33.00x (ISBN 0-405-10230-5). Ayer Co Pubs.

Alvar, Manuel. Estudios Lexicos: Primera Serie. (Dialect Ser.: No. 6). (Illus.). 216p. 1984. 17.50x (ISBN 0-942260-31-7). Hispanic Seminary.

Alvarado, Alfredo, jt. auth. see Bornemisza, Elmer.

Alvarado, Manuel & Stewart, John. Made for Television: Euston Films Limited. (Orig.). 1985. pap. 11.95 (ISBN 0-85170-172-8, 9374). Methuen Inc.

Alvarado, Manuel, jt. auth. see Tulloch, John.

Alvarado, P. De see De Alvarado, Pedro.

Alvarado, Pedro De see De Alvarado, Pedro.

Alvarado-Morales, Manuel. La Ciudad de Mexico ante la Fundacion de la Armada de Barlovento: Historia de una Encrucijada 1635-1643. 284p. (Span.). 1984. pap. 8.50 (ISBN 0-317-17292-1). U of PR Pr.

Alvardo, Arturo R. Cronica De Aztlan. LC 77-85180. (Illus.). 1977. pap. 6.00 (ISBN 0-88412-107-0). Tonatiuh-Quinto Sol Intl.

Alvarenga, Beatriz. Fisica General, Vol. I. (Span.). 1980. pap. text ed. 8.60 (ISBN 0-06-310011-8, Pub. by HarLA Mexico). Har-Row.

--Fisica General, Vol. II. (Span.). 1980. pap. text ed. 9.30 (ISBN 0-06-310014-2, Pub. by HarLA Mexico). Har-Row.

--Fisica General. 2nd ed. 1024p. (Span.). 1983. pap. text ed. write for info (ISBN 0-06-310016-9, Pub. by HarLA Mexico). Har-Row.

Alvarenga, Beatriz & Alvarenga, Maximo. Fisica General. 1976. text ed. 12.40 (ISBN 0-06-310012-6, IntlDept). Har-Row.

Alvarenga, Maximo, jt. auth. see Alvarenga, Beatriz.

Alvarenga, Oneyda. Musica Popular Brasileira. 1976. lib. bdg. 59.95 (ISBN 0-8490-2308-4). Gordon Pr.

Alvares, Claude A. Homo Faber: Technology & Culture in India, China & the West from 1500 to the Present Day. xvi, 275p. 1980. lib. bdg. 47.50 (ISBN 90-247-2283-7). Kluwer Academic.

Alvares, Francisco. Narrative of the Portuguese Embassy to Abyssinia During the Years 1520-1527. LC 70-126273. (Hakluyt Society First Ser.: No. 64). 1970. lib. bdg. 32.00 (ISBN 0-8337-0053-7). B Franklin.

--The Prester John of the Indies: A True Relation of the Lands of the Prester John, Being the Narrative. Beckingham, C. F. & Huntingford, G. W., eds. Lord Stanley of Alderley, tr. (Hakluyt Society Works Ser. II: Vols. 114-115). 74.00 (ISBN 0-317-16034-6). Kraus Repr.

Alvarez, A. The Biggest Game in Town. 200p. 1983. 13.95 (ISBN 0-395-33964-2). HM.

--The Biggest Game in Town. 1985. pap. 7.95 (ISBN 0-395-38351-X). HM.

--Stewards of Excellence: Studies in Modern English & American Poets. LC 70-159035. 1971. Repr. of 1958 ed. text ed. 12.00x (ISBN 0-87752-152-2). Gordian.

Alvarez, A., ed. see Hardy, Thomas.

Alvarez, A., et al. Progress of Continental Law in the Nineteenth Century. Register, L. B., tr. (Continental Legal History Ser.: Vol. 11). (Illus.). xlix, 558p. 1969. Repr. of 1918 ed. 37.50x (ISBN 0-8377-1900-3). Rothman.

Alvarez, Abdon P. Financial & Operational Audit. 1981. 6.75 (ISBN 0-8062-1836-3). Carlton.

Alvarez, Francisco C. New Horizons for the Third World. 1976. pap. 8.00 (ISBN 0-8183-0246-1). Pub Aff Pr.

Alvarez, Francisco E., jt. auth. see Feliciano, Alberto R.

Alvarez, Gabrqel C., jt. ed. see Arce, Wilfredo F.

Alvarez, Ines, tr. see McNaught, Harry.

Alvarez, Ines, tr. see Provensen, Martin & Provensen, Alice.

Alvarez, J., et al. Microcomputers As Management Tools in the Sugar Cane Industry. 206p. 1985. 55.75 (ISBN 0-444-42425-3). Elsevier.

Alvarez, J. Mateos. Vocabulario Teologico del Evangelio de Saint Juan. 310p. (Span.). 1980. pap. 13.95 (ISBN 84-7057-270-9, S-33107). French & Eur.

Alvarez, Josefina R. De see De Alvarez, Josefina R.

Alvarez, Joseph. Politics in America. Liberty, Gene, ed. LC 76-128850. (Understanding Bks.). (Illus.). (gr. 4-9). 1971. PLB 8.95 (ISBN 0-87191-068-3). Creative Ed.

Alvarez, Joseph A. Elements of Composition. 360p. 1985. pap. text ed. 12.95 (ISBN 0-15-522077-2, HC); instr's manual avail. (ISBN 0-15-522078-0). HarBraceJ.

--The Elements of Technical Writing. 208p. 1980. pap. text ed. 11.95 (ISBN 0-15-522160-4, HC); instructor's manual avail. (ISBN 0-15-522161-2). HarBraceJ.

Alvarez, Juan & Kwapil, Marie J. Five Stories: Cinco Cuentos. (Eng. & Span.). (gr. k-4). 1972. 2.95x (ISBN 0-685-32664-0). Leslie Pr.

Alvarez, Julia. Homecoming. Pack, Robert, ed. LC 83-49391. (Poetry Ser.). 96p. 1984. 12.50 (ISBN 0-394-53855-2, GP889); pap. 5.95 (ISBN 0-394-62052-6, E903). Grove.

Alvarez, L. W., ed. Strong Interactions. (Italian Physical Society Ser.: Course 33). 1966. 75.00 (ISBN 0-12-368833-7). Acad Pr.

Alvarez, Louis. The New Orleans Bicycle Book. (Illus.). 168p. (Orig.). 1984. pap. 5.95 (ISBN 0-9614451-0-6). Little Nemo Pr.

Alvarez, Lynne. The Dreaming Man. 95p. (Orig.). 1984. pap. 6.50 (ISBN 0-943862-15-9). Waterfront NJ.

Alvarez, Manuel. Seven Years at Sea. 220p. 1983. lib. bdg. 15.95 (ISBN 0-919573-20-7); pap. 7.95 (ISBN 0-919573-21-5). Left Bank.

--Tall Soldier: My Forty Year Search for the Man Who Saved My Life. 236p. 1980. lib. bdg. 15.95 (ISBN 0-919573-04-5); pap. 7.95 (ISBN 0-919573-19-3). Left Bank.

Alvarez, Maria V., jt. auth. see Norman, Jill.

Alvarez, Max J. Index to Motion Pictures Reviewed by Variety, 1907-1980. LC 81-23236. 520p. 1982. 35.00 (ISBN 0-8108-1515-X). Scarecrow.

Alvarez, Nicolas E. Analisis Arquetipico, Mitico y Simbolico de Pedro Paramo. LC 83-80471. (Coleccion Polymita Ser.). 139p. (Orig., Span.). 1983. pap. 12.00 (ISBN 0-89729-330-4). Ediciones.

Alvarez, Octavio. The Celestial Brides: A Study in Mythology & Archaeology. LC 77-91208. (Illus.). 1978. 30.00 (ISBN 0-9601520-0-8). H Reichner.

Alvarez, Octavio, et al. Report on Library & Information Science Education in the United States. LC 75-620121. (Student Contribution Ser.: No. 7). 1975. pap. 5.00 (ISBN 0-911808-11-6). U of Md Lib Serv.

Alvarez, Paul, jt. ed. see Voros, Gerald J.

Alvarez, Paul H., jt. ed. see Voros, Gerald J.

Alvarez, Roberto, jt. auth. see Bagley, Bruce.

Alvarez, Roberto, tr. see Rhee, Jhoon.

Alvarez, Rodolfo, et al. Discrimination in Organizations: Using Social Indicators to Manage Social Change. LC 78-62567. (Social & Behavioral Science Ser.). 1979. text ed. 29.95x (ISBN 0-87589-429-1). Jossey-Bass.

Alvarez, Russell R De see De Alvarez, Russell R.

Alvarez, Russell R. de see De Alvarez, Russell R.

Alvarez, Ticul. A New Subspecies of Ground Squirrel (Spermophilus Spilosoma) from Tamaulipas, Mexico. (Museum Ser.: Vol. 14, No. 8). 4p. 1962. pap. 1.25 (ISBN 0-317-04910-0). U of KS Mus Nat Hist.

--A New Subspecies of Wood Rat (Neotoma) from Northeastern Mexico. (Museum Ser.: Vol. 14, No. 11). 5p. 1962. pap. 1.25 (ISBN 0-317-04911-9). U of KS Mus Nat Hist.

--The Recent Mammals of Tamaulipas, Mexico. (Museum Ser.: Vol. 14, No. 15). 111p. 1963. 5.75 (ISBN 0-317-04912-7). U of KS Mus Nat Hist.

--Taxonomic Status of Some Mice of the Peromyscus Boylii Group in Eastern Mexico, with Description of a New Subspecies. (Museum Ser.: Vol. 14, No. 7). 10p. 1961. pap. 1.25 (ISBN 0-317-04908-9). U of KS Mus Nat Hist.

Alvarez, Ticul, jt. auth. see Hall, E. Raymond.

Alvarez, Ticul, jt. auth. see Jones, J. Knox, Jr.

Alvarez, Walter C. Alvarez on Alvarez. LC 76-47216. (Illus., Orig.). 1977. pap. 5.95 (ISBN 0-89407-005-3). Strawberry Hill.

Alvarez-Altman, Grace, et al, eds. Names in Literature. (The International Library of Names). 400p. 1985. 29.50x (ISBN 0-8290-1221-4). Irvington.

Alvarez-Borland, Isabel. Discontinuidad y Ruptura en Guillermo Cabrera Infante. LC 82-84325. 144p. 1983. pap. text ed. 9.95 (ISBN 0-935318-09-7). Edins Hispamerica.

Alvarez-Detrell, Tamara & Paulson, Michael G. Suivez La Piste. 62p. (Orig.). 1983. pap. 8.75 wkbk. (ISBN 0-8191-3068-0). U Pr of Amer.

Alvarez-Detrell, Tamara, jt. auth. see Paulson, Michael G.

Alvarez-Detrell, Tamara & Paulson, Michael G., eds. The Gambling Mania On & Off the Stage in Pre-Revolutionary France. LC 81-43819. 192p. (Orig.). 1982. lib. bdg. 24.00 (ISBN 0-8191-2586-5); pap. text ed. 11.25 (ISBN 0-8191-2587-3). U Pr of Amer.

Alvarez De Williams, Anita. Travelers Among the Cucapa. (Baja California Travels Ser.: No. 34). 1975. 24.00 (ISBN 0-87093-234-9). Dawsons.

Alvarez-Mena, Sergio C., jt. auth. see Frank, Martin J.

Alvarez Nazario, Manuel. El Influjo Indigena En el Espanol De Puerto Rico. LC 76-1826. (Coleccion Mente y Palabra). vi, 216p. (Orig., Span.). 1977. 6.25 (ISBN 0-8477-0526-9); pap. 5.00 (ISBN 0-8477-0527-7). U of PR Pr.

Alvarez-Pereyre, Jacques. The Poetry of Commitment in South Africa. Wake, Clive, tr. from Fr. (Studies in African Literature). x, 278p. (Orig.). 1985. pap. text ed. 17.50x (ISBN 0-435-91056-6). Heinemann Ed.

Alvaro, Albert M., ed. see Santos, Elsie S.

Alverdes, F. Social Life in the Animal World. LC 27-17110. Repr. of 1927 ed. 17.00 (ISBN 0-527-01700-0). Kraus Repr.

Alvernaz, Bill. Expanding Your IBM PC: A Guide for Beginners. (Illus.). 256p. 1984. pap. 16.95 (ISBN 0-89303-445-2). Brady Comm.

Alverson, Dayton L., jt. ed. see Pruter, A. T.

Alverson, Hoyt. Mind in the Heart of Darkness: Value & Self-Identity Among the Tswana of Southern Africa. LC 78-4909. (Illus.). 1978. 27.00x (ISBN 0-300-02244-1). Yale U Pr.

Alves, Dora. The Anzus Partners. LC 94-9598. (Significant Issue Ser.: Vol. 6, No. 8). 80p. 1984. 6.95 (ISBN 0-89206-056-5). CSI Studies.

Alves, J. Controlling Financial Performance: A Multiplan Business User's Guide. pap. 19.50 (ISBN 0-930764-87-0). Van Nos Reinhold.

--Planning & Budgeting for Higher Profits: An IBM-PC Business User's Guide. incl. disk 39.95 (ISBN 0-930764-77-3); disk 29.95 (ISBN 0-930764-70-6). Van Nos Reinhold.

--Planning & Budgeting for Higher Profits: A 1-2-3-Business User's Guide. incl. disk 39.95 (ISBN 0-930764-93-5). Van Nos Reinhold.

Alves, Jeff & Curtin, Dennis. Planning & Budgeting for Higher Profits: An Apple Business User's Guide. 144p. 1983. pap. 14.95 (ISBN 0-930764-62-5). Van Nos Reinhold.

--Planning & Budgeting for Higher Profits: An IBM-PC Business User's Guide. 156p. 1983. pap. 14.95 (ISBN 0-930764-61-7). Van Nos Reinhold.

Alves, Jeff, jt. auth. see Curtin, Dennis.

Alves, Jeff, et al. Planning & Budgeting: A 1-2-3 Business User's Guide. 1983. pap. 16.95 (ISBN 0-930764-74-9); disk set 39.95 (ISBN 0-930764-93-5); disk 29.95 (ISBN 0-930764-94-3). Van Nos Reinhold.

Alves, Jefffey, jt. auth. see Curtin, Dennis.

Alves, Jeffrey & Curtin, Dennis. Planning & Budgeting-IBM Version. (Illus.). 224p. (Orig.). 1983. pap. 15.50 (ISBN 0-930764-61-7). Curtin & London.

Alves, Jeffrey, jt. auth. see Curtin, Dennis.

Alves, Jeffrey R. & Curtin, Dennis P. Planning & Budgeting. (A One-Two-Three Business User's Guide Ser.). (Illus.). 176p. (Orig.). 1983. pap. 17.50 (ISBN 0-930764-74-9). Curtin & London.

--Planning & Budgeting with Lotus Symphony. (Illus.). 144p. 1984. pap. 19.50 (ISBN 0-88703-010-6). Van Nos Reinhold.

Alves, Jeffrey R. & Maupin, J. David. Controlling Financial Performance: Lotus 1-2-3 on the DEC Rainbow. (Rainbow Business Ser.). 200p. 1985. 25.00 (ISBN 0-932376-68-1, EY-00038-DP). Digital Pr.

Alves, Jeffrey R., et al. Planning & Budgeting for Higher Profits: A Multiplan Business User's Guide. (Illus.). 160p. 1984. pap. 16.95 (ISBN 0-930764-88-9). Van Nos Reinhold.

Alves, Joseph T. Confidentiality in Social Work. LC 84-721. xvi, 268p. 1984. Repr. of 1959 ed. lib. bdg. 35.00x (ISBN 0-313-24459-6, ALC0). Greenwood.

Alves, Maria H. The State & Opposition in Military Brazil. (Institute of Latin America Studies Monography Ser.: No. 63). (Illus.). 256p. 1985. text ed. 22.50x (ISBN 0-292-77598-9). U of Tex Pr.

--State & Opposition in Military Brazil. (Latin American Monographs: No. 63). 368p. 1985. 22.50 (ISBN 0-292-77598-9). U of Tex Pr.

Alves, Mario. Dream a Little, Live a Lot. 1982. 8.95 (ISBN 0-533-05456-7). Vantage.

Alves, Michael J., jt. ed. see Cassidy, Daniel J.

Alves, Robert. Sketches of a History of Literature. LC 67-18714. 1967. Repr. of 1794 ed. 35.00x (ISBN 0-8201-1002-7). Schol Facsimiles.

Alves, Rubem. Protestantism & Repression: A Brazilian Case Study. Drury, John, tr. from Portuguese. LC 82-3594. 256p. (Orig.). 1985. pap. 11.95 (ISBN 0-88344-098-9). Orbis Bks.

--What Is Religion? Vinzant, Don, tr. from Portugese. LC 83-19398. Orig. Title: O Que E Religiao. 96p. (Orig.). 1984. pap. 4.95 (ISBN 0-88344-705-3). Orbis Bks.

Alvey, Edward, Jr. History of Mary Washington College, 1908-1972. LC 73-92624. (Illus.). 500p. 1974. 10.00x (ISBN 0-8139-0528-1). U Pr of Va.

Alvey, N. G. & Galwey, P. Lane. An Introduction to Genstat. 1982. 18.00 (ISBN 0-12-055550-6). Acad Pr.

Alvey, R. Gerald. Dulcimer Maker: The Craft of Homer Ledford. LC 82-40463. (Illus.). 200p. 1984. 18.00x (ISBN 0-8131-1447-0). U Pr of Ky.

Alvi, Effraim. The Amador Study on Aging, Nutrition, & Stress. LC 84-51500. (Illus.). 116p. 1984. pap. 14.95 (ISBN 0-918493-02-1). Sierra Pub Co.

--Sir Kenyon's History of the Book of Books. (Illus.). 135p. 1985. 35.00; pap. 17.95 (ISBN 0-918493-07-2). Sierra Pub Co.

Alvim, Paulo De T. see De T. Alvim, Paulo.

Alvin, Juliette. Music for the Handicapped Child. 1976. pap. 9.95x (ISBN 0-19-314920-6). Oxford U Pr.

--Music Therapy. 1984. 29.00x (ISBN 0-906549-38-8, Pub. by J Clare Bks UK). State Mutual Bk.

--Music Therapy for the Autistic Child. 1979. pap. 9.95x (ISBN 0-19-317414-6). Oxford U Pr.

Alvin, Julius. Gross Gifts. pap. 2.50 (ISBN 0-8217-1111-3). Zebra.

--Gross Jokes. 1983. pap. 2.50 (ISBN 0-317-02501-5). Zebra.

--Totally Gross Jokes. pap. 2.50 (ISBN 0-8217-1333-7). Zebra.

--Utterly Gross Jokes. 1984. pap. 2.50 (ISBN 0-8217-1350-7). Zebra.

Alvin, K. L., jt. auth. see Cutler, E. F.

Alvino, James, jt. auth. see Gifted Children Newsletter Staff.

Alvis, John & West, Thomas, eds. Shakespeare As Political Thinker. LC 79-51946. 306p. 1980. lib. bdg. 22.95 (ISBN 0-89089-097-8); pap. 10.75 (ISBN 0-89089-096-X). Carolina Acad Pr.

Alvisi, C. Investigative Ultrasonology: Technical Advances, No. 1. 250p. 1979. 50.00x (ISBN 0-686-91723-5, Pub. by Pitman Bks England). State Mutual Bk.

--Investigative Ultrasonology Two: Clinical Advances. 344p. 1981. 70.00x (ISBN 0-272-79576-3, Pub. by Pitman Bks England). State Mutual Bk.

Alvisi, C. & Hill, C. R. Investigative Ultrasonlogy Two: Clinical Advances. 256p. text ed. cancelled (ISBN 0-272-79576-3). Pitman Pub MA.

Alvisi, C. & Hill, C. R., eds. Investigative Ultrasonology. 200p. 1981. text ed. 48.00x (ISBN 0-8464-1221-7). Beekman Pubs.

Alvisi, C., jt. ed. see Hill, C. R.

Alvord, C. W. & Carter, C. E., eds. Trade & Politics: 1767-1769. LC 24-27219. (Illinois Historical Collections Ser.: Vol. 16). 1921. 7.50 (ISBN 0-912154-04-7). Ill St Hist Lib.

Alvord, Clarence W. The Illinois Country Sixteen Seventy-Three to Eighteen Eighteen. (The American West Ser.). 1965. 7.00 (ISBN 0-8294-0000-1). Loyola.

Alvord, Clarence W. & Carter, Clarence E., eds. Invitation Serieuse Aux Habitants Des Illinois Byun Habitant Des Kaskaskias. Repr. of 1908 ed. 16.50 (ISBN 0-8337-0038-3). B Franklin.

Alvord, David W., jt. auth. see Wass, Stan.

Alvord, E. C., Jr., jt. auth. see Kies, Marian W.

Alvord, Jack R. Home Token Economy: An Incentive Program for Children & Their Parents. (Orig.). 1973. pap. 6.95 guide & ten behavior charts (ISBN 0-87822-106-9, 1069); 10 behavior charts 5.95 (ISBN 0-87822-107-7, 1071). Res Press.

Alvord, Katharine T., ed. Document Retrieval: Sources & Services. 3rd ed. 247p. 1985. 60.00 (ISBN 0-940004-04-6). Info Store.

Alvstad, Linda, jt. auth. see Schomas, Rhonda.

Al-Wahab, Ibrahim. Law Dictionary (English-Arabic) 320p. (Eng. & Arabic.). 1972. 20.00x (ISBN 0-86685-082-1). Intl Bk Ctr.

Al-Wahhab, Muhammad I. Kitab Al Tawhid. 120p. (Orig., Arabic.). 1978. pap. 2.35x (ISBN 0-939830-20-5, Pub. by IIFSO Kuwait). New Era Pubns MI.

Alwall, N., et al, eds. see International Congress of Nephrology, 4th, Stockholm, 1969.

Alwan, A. J., jt. auth. see Almaney, A. J.

Alwan, Mohamed. Algeria Before the United Nations. 1959. 8.95 (ISBN 0-8315-0064-6). Speller.

Alward, Ron & Shapiro, Andy. Low-Cost Passive Solar Greenhouses: A Design & Construction Guide. (Illus.). 176p. 1982. pap. 10.95 (ISBN 0-684-17503-7, ScribT). Scribner.

Alwi Bin Alhady. Malay Customs & Traditions. LC 77-87477. (Illus.). 152p. Repr. of 1967 ed. 21.50 (ISBN 0-404-16789-6). AMS Pr.

Alwin, Duane F., ed. Survey Design & Analysis: Current Issues. LC 77-95433. (Sage Contemporary Social Science Issues: No. 46). 1978. pap. 7.50 (ISBN 0-8039-1021-5). Sage.

Alwin, John A. Between the Mountains: A Portrait of Eastern Washington. LC 84-61945. (Northwest Geographer Ser.: No. 1). (Illus.). 128p. 1984. pap. 13.95 (ISBN 0-9613787-0-0). NW Panorama.

--Eastern Montana: A Portrait of the Land & Its People. (Montana Geographic Ser.: No. 2). (Illus.). 128p. 1982. pap. 12.95 (ISBN 0-938314-02-5). MT Mag.

--Western Montana: A Portrait of the Land & Its People. (The Montana Geographic Ser.: No. 5). (Illus.). 152p. (Orig.). 1983. pap. 12.95 (ISBN 0-938314-07-6). MT Mag.

Alwin, John A., ed. see Scott, M. Douglas & Scott, Suvi A.

Alwin, Robert, et al. Algebra Programmed, Pt. 3. 2nd ed. 1980. pap. text ed. 23.95 (ISBN 0-13-021931-2). P-H.

Alwin, Robert H. & Hackworth, Robert D. Algebra Programmed, Pt. 2. 2nd ed. (Illus.). 1978. pap. text ed. 18.95 (ISBN 0-13-022020-5). P-H.

--Algebra Programmed, Pt. 1. 2nd ed. (Illus.). 1978. pap. text ed. 18.95 (ISBN 0-13-022038-8). P-H.

Alwin, Robert H., et al. Algebra Text: Intermediate. (Illus.). 1974. pap. 26.95 ref. ed. (ISBN 0-13-022400-6). P-H.

--Algebra Text: Elementary. (Illus.). 424p. 1974. pap. 26.95 ref. ed. (ISBN 0-13-022293-3). P-H.

Alwine, Nevin S., ed. Readings for Foundation of Education. 121p. 1969. pap. text ed. 9.95x (ISBN 0-8290-1310-5). Irvington.

Alwitt, Linda F. & Mitchell, Andrew A., eds. Psychological Processes & Advertising Effects: Theory, Research, & Applications. 320p. 1985. text ed. 29.95 (ISBN 0-89859-515-0). L Erlbaum Assocs.

Alwitt, Robert S. Oxide-Electrolyte Interfaces: Proceedings of Symposium Papers Held at the 142nd Meeting of the Society. LC 73-75171. pap. 77.50 (ISBN 0-317-08905-6, 2051820). Bks Demand UMI.

Alworth, E. Paul, jt. ed. see Hayden, Donald E.

Aly, H. H. Lectures on Particles & Fields. 385p. 1970. 85.75 (ISBN 0-677-13740-0). Gordon.

Aly, Lucile. John G. Neihardt. LC 76-45135. (Western Writers Ser.: No. 25). 1976. pap. 2.00x (ISBN 0-88430-024-2). Boise St Univ.

Aly, Lucile F. John G. Neihardt: A Critical Biography. (Melville Studies in American Culture). (Illus.). 307p. 1977. pap. text ed. 26.25x (ISBN 90-6203-109-9). Humanities.

Aly, Osman M., jt. auth. see Faust, Samuel D.

Aly, R. see Maibach, H.

Aly, Raza & Shinefield, Henry R. Bacterial Interference. 192p. 1982. 62.00 (ISBN 0-8493-6285-7). CRC Pr.

Al-Yassin, Ibrahim M. Growth Potential of Dental Epithelium in Tissue Culture. 180p. 1985. 55.00x (ISBN 0-7103-0073-5, Kegan Paul). Routledge & Kegan.

Al-Yassini, Ayman. Religion & State in the Kingdom of Saudi Arabia. (WVSS on the Middle East Ser.). 190p. 1985. 30.00x (ISBN 0-8133-0058-4). Westview.

Alyea, Blanche R., jt. auth. see Alyea, Paul E.

Alyea, Elmer C. & Meek, Devon W., eds. Catalytic Aspects of Metal Phosphine Complexes. LC 81-12903. (Advances in Chemistry Ser.: No. 196). 1981. 69.95 (ISBN 0-8412-0601-5). Am Chemical.

Alyea, Hubert N. & Dutton, F. B. Tested Demonstrations in Chemistry. 6th ed. 1962. 10.90 (ISBN 0-910362-07-6). Chem Educ.

Alyea, Paul E. & Alyea, Blanche R. Fairhope, 1894-1954: The Story of a Single Tax Colony. LC 76-42716. (Communal Societies in America Ser.). Repr. of 1956 ed. 32.50 (ISBN 0-404-60051-4). AMS Pr.

Alyeshmreni, Mansoor, tr. see Bahar, Mehrdad.

Alyn, Irene B., jt. auth. see Gillies, Dee A.

Alyn, Marjory. The Sound of Anthems: A Novel of Ireland. LC 83-10901. 211p. 1983. 13.95 (ISBN 0-312-74600-8). St Martin.

Alyson Publications Staff. The Gay Almanac. 150p. (Orig.). Date not set. pap. text ed. price not set (ISBN 0-932870-19-8). Alyson Pubns.

Alyson, Sasha, ed. Young, Gay & Proud. rev. ed. (Illus., Orig.). (YA) (gr. 9-12). 1980. pap. 2.95 (ISBN 0-932870-01-5). Alyson Pubns.

Alzado, Lyle & Moe, Doug. Still Hungry: THe Autobiography of Lyle Alzado. LC 85-47762. 320p. 1985. 15.95 (ISBN 0-553-05113-X). Bantam.

Alzaga, Florinda. Las Ansias De Infinito En la Avellaneda. LC 79-51297. (Colleccion Polymita). (Illus.). 1979. pap. 9.00 (ISBN 0-89729-169-7). Ediciones.

Al-Zay, Saleh Y. Infectious Skin Diseases: Medical Subject Analysis & Research Bibliography. LC 84-45667. 150p. 1984. 29.95 (ISBN 0-88164-206-1); pap. 21.95 (ISBN 0-88164-207-X). ABBE Pubs Assn.

Alzheimer's Disease & Related Disorders Association. Understanding Alzheimer's Disease. 256p. 1985. 15.95 (ISBN 0-684-18475-3, ScribT). Scribner.

Alzofon, David. Mastering Guitar. LC 80-24682. 1981. 11.95 (ISBN 0-671-25421-9, Fireside). S&S.

Alzona, Encarnacion. Some French Contemporary Opinions of the Russian Revolution of 1905. LC 70-158244. (Columbia University Studies in the Social Sciences: No. 228). Repr. of 1921 ed. 12.50 (ISBN 0-404-51228-3). AMS Pr.

Al-Zubayr, Basha. Black Ivory: Or, the Story of El Ziebeir Pasha, Slaver & Sultan, As Told by Himself. LC 71-100265. Repr. of 1913 ed. 15.00 (ISBN 0-8371-2868-4, JBI&, Pub. by Negro U Pr). Greenwood.

Alzugaray, J. J. Voces Extranjeras en el Lengua Technologico. (Span. & Eng.). 1980. pap. 9.95 (ISBN 0-686-92477-0, S-33100). French & Eur.

Am Anthro Assn. Guide to Departments of Anthropology: 1983-1984. 22nd ed. 1983. pap. 20.00 (ISBN 0-686-40414-9). Am Anthro Assn.

Am. Assn. of Medical Colleges. International Health Perspectives: An Introduction in Five Volumes, 5 vols. Waddell, Wendy & Pierleoni, Robert, eds. 1977. pap. text ed. 27.50 set (ISBN 0-8261-2490-9). Springer Pub.

Am-Fem Company. International Directory of Amateur Female Fighting. 1985. pap. 25.00 (ISBN 0-686-32796-9). AM FEM Co.

Am. Jnl. Nursing Co. The AJN Question & Answer Book: 2001 Practice Questions to Access. 388p. 1985. 14.95 (ISBN 0-683-09539-0). Williams & Wilkins.

Am. School Band Directory Association Staff, ed. ASBDA Curriculum Guide. 1974. pap. 15.00 (ISBN 0-913650-19-6). Columbia Pictures.

AMA Committee on Exercise & Physical Fitness. Guide to Prescribing Exercise Programs. 1976. 1.00 (ISBN 0-89970-050-0, OP-447). AMA.

Amabile, T. M. The Social Psychology of Creativity. (Springer Series in Social Psychology). (Illus.). 245p. 1983. 29.00 (ISBN 0-387-90830-7). Springer-Verlag.

Amabile, Teresa M & Stubbs, Margaret L., eds. Psychological Research in the Classroom: Issues for Educators & Researchers. LC 81-21114. (General Psychology Ser.: No. 108). (Illus.). 280p. 1982. 29.00 (ISBN 0-08-028042-0, J120); pap. 12.95 (ISBN 0-08-028041-2). Pergamon.

Amacher, A. Loren. Pediatric Head Injuries Handbook. (Illus.). 200p. 1985. 37.50 (ISBN 0-87527-337-8). Green.

Amacher, Ethel S. & Eaddy, Virginia B. Using Play Techniques in Interviewing Children. 111p. 1983. cancelled (ISBN 0-318-01079-8). U of Tenn Sch.

Amacher, P., jt. ed. see Gardner, L. I.

Amacher, Peter. Freud's Neurological Education & Its Influence on Psychoanalytic Theory. LC 65-19461. (Psychological Issues Monograph: No. 16, Vol. 4, No. 4). 93p. (Orig.). 1966. text ed. 17.50 (ISBN 0-8236-2040-9). Intl Univs Pr.

Amacher, Peter, ed. see Conference on Propranolol & Schizophrenia, Santa Ynez, Calif., Dec. 5-8, 1976, et al.

Amacher, Richard & Lange, Victor, eds. New Perspectives in German Literary Criticism. LC 78-12472. 1979. 46.00 (ISBN 0-691-06380-X). Princeton U Pr.

Amacher, Richard E. Benjamin Franklin. (Twayne's United States Authors Ser.). 1962. pap. 5.95x (ISBN 0-8084-0059-2, T12, Twayne). New Coll U Pr.

--Edward Albee. rev. ed. (United States Authors Ser.). 1982. lib. bdg. 13.50 (ISBN 0-8057-7349-5, Twayne). G K Hall.

Amacher, Richard E. & Rule, Margaret, eds. Edward Albee at Home & Abroad: A Bibliography, 1958 June, 1968. LC 73-158245. (AMS Studies in Modern Literature: No. 1). Repr. of 1973 ed. 29.50 (ISBN 0-404-07945-8). AMS Pr.

Amacher, Ryan C. Principles of Macroeconomics. 1983. text ed. 15.70 (ISBN 0-538-08170-8, H17). SW Pub.

--Principles of Microeconomics. 1983. text ed. 15.70 (ISBN 0-538-08160-0, H16). SW Pub.

Amacher, Ryan C. & Sweeney, Richard J., eds. The Law of the Sea: U.S. Interests & Alternatives. LC 76-1303. (Conference Proceedings Ser.). 196p. 1976. 14.25 (ISBN 0-8447-2073-9); pap. 6.25 (ISBN 0-8447-2072-0). Am Enterprise.

Amacher, Ryan C., et al, eds. Challenges to a Liberal International Economic Order. 1979. 17.25 (ISBN 0-8447-2151-4); pap. 9.25 (ISBN 0-8447-2152-2). Am Enterprise.

--The Economic Approach to Public Policy: Selected Readings. LC 75-38425. 528p. 1976. pap. 12.95x (ISBN 0-8014-9860-0). Cornell U Pr.

Amacker, Robert, ed. see Lo, Benjamin P., et al.

Amada, Gerald. A Guide to Psychotherapy. LC 82-21918. (Illus.). 128p. (Orig.). 1983. lib. bdg. 22.00 (ISBN 0-8191-2928-3); pap. text ed. 9.25 (ISBN 0-8191-2929-1). U Pr of Amer.

--Mental Health & Authoritarianism on the College Campus. LC 79-66480. 1979. pap. text ed. 15.00 (ISBN 0-8191-0831-6). U Pr of Amer.

Amaded, Douglas, et al. EDRA, 1983. Potter, James J., ed. (EDRA Proceedings Ser.). 1983. 33.00 (ISBN 0-939922-06-1). EDRA.

Amadei, B. Rock Anisotropy & the Theory of Stress Measurements. (Lecture Notes in Engineering Ser.: Vol. 2). 478p. 1983. pap. 29.00 (ISBN 0-387-12388-1). Springer-Verlag.

Amadeus Of Lausanne, jt. auth. see Bernard Of Clairvaux.

Amadi, Adolphe O. African Libraries: Western Tradition & Colonial Brainwashing. LC 80-29593. 277p. 1981. 16.00 (ISBN 0-8108-1409-9). Scarecrow.

Amadi, Elechi. The Concubine. (African Writers Ser.). 1966. pap. text ed. 4.00x (ISBN 0-435-90025-0). Heinemann Ed.

--Ethics in Nigerian Culture. 128p. (Orig.). 1982. pap. text ed. 7.50x (ISBN 0-435-89030-1). Heinemann Ed.

--The Great Ponds. (African Writers Ser.). 1970. pap. text ed. 4.00x (ISBN 0-435-90044-7). Heinemann Ed.

--Isiburu. (Secondary Readers Ser.). 1973. pap. text ed. 3.00x (ISBN 0-435-92508-3). Heinemann Ed.

--The Slave. (African Writers Ser.). 1979. pap. text ed. 5.00x (ISBN 0-435-90210-5). Heinemann Ed.

--Sunset in Biafra. (African Writers Ser.). 1973. pap. text ed. 5.00x (ISBN 0-435-90140-0). Heinemann Ed.

Amadie, Jimmy. Harmonic Foundation for Jazz & Popular Music. LC 81-670040. 168p. (Orig.). 1981. pap. text ed. 24.95 (ISBN 0-9613035-0-6). Thornton Pubns.

Amado, Jorge. Dona Flor & Her Two Husbands. 1977. pap. 4.95 (ISBN 0-380-01796-2, 60044-7, Bard). Avon.

--Gabriela, Clove & Cinnamon. 1974. pap. 4.95 (ISBN 0-380-01205-7, 60208-3, Bard). Avon.

--Home Is the Sailor. 1979. pap. 2.75 (ISBN 0-380-45187-5, Bard). Avon.

--Jubiaba. Neves, Margaret A., tr. from Port. 304p. 1984. pap. 4.50 (ISBN 0-380-88567-0, Bard). Avon.

--Pen, Sword, Camisole: A Fable to Kindle a Hope. Lane, Helen R., tr. LC 84-48301. 288p. 1985. 15.95 (ISBN 0-87923-552-7). Godine.
--Sea of Death. Rabassa, Gregory, tr. from Port. 288p. 1984. pap. 4.50 (ISBN 0-380-88559-X, Bard). Avon.
--Shepherds of the Night. 1978. pap. 3.95 (ISBN 0-380-39990-3, 58768-8, Bard). Avon.
--The Swallow & the Tom Cat: A Love Story. Merello, Barbara S., tr. from Port. (Illus.). 96p. 1982. 10.95 (ISBN 0-385-28984-7, E Friede). Delacorte.
--Tent of Miracles. 1978. pap. 3.95 (ISBN 0-380-41020-6, 54916-6, Bard). Avon.
--Tereza Batista: Home from the Wars. 1977. pap. 2.95 (ISBN 0-380-01752-0, 34645-1, Bard). Avon.
--Tieta. 688p. 1980. pap. 4.95 (ISBN 0-380-50815-X, 50815-X, Bard). Avon.
--Tieta. Merello, Barbara S., tr. LC 78-11470. 1979. 12.95 (ISBN 0-394-50139-X). Knopf.
--The Two Deaths of Quincas Wateryell. 1980. pap. 2.50 (ISBN 0-380-50047-7, 50047-7, Bard). Avon.
--The Violent Land. 1979. pap. 2.75 (ISBN 0-380-47696-7, 47696-7, Bard). Avon.

Amador, Antonio A., jt. auth. see Leo, F. Damian.

Amador, E. F. Martinez. Diccionario Aleman-Espanol, Espanol-Aleman. 1616p. (Ger. & Span.). 50.95 (ISBN 84-303-0117-8, S-12381). French & Eur.

Amador, E. M. Martinez. Diccionario Frances-Espanol, Espanol-Frances. 1568p. (Span. & Fr.). 1974. 47.95 (ISBN 84-303-0091-0, S-13282). French & Eur.
--Diccionario Ingles-Espanol, Espanol-Ingles. 1504p. (Span. & Eng.). 47.95 (ISBN 84-303-0105-4, S-2789). French & Eur.
--Diccionario Italiano-Espanol, Espanol-Italiano. 1440p. (Span. & Ital.). 50.95 (ISBN 84-303-0133-X, S-12383). French & Eur.
--Diccionario Manual Aleman-Espanol, Spanisch-Deutsch. 17th ed. 936p. (Ger. & Span.). 1977. 5.95 (ISBN 84-7183-002-7, S-50382). French & Eur.
--Diccionario Manual Amador Aleman-Espanol, Espanol-Aleman. 1400p. (Ger. & Span.). 17.95 (ISBN 84-303-0118-6, S-50385). French & Eur.
--Diccionario Manual Amador Frances-Espanol y Espanol-Frances. 944p. (Span. & Fr.). 1975. 17.95 (ISBN 84-303-0100-3, S-50401). French & Eur.

Amador, Luis V. Brain Tumors in the Young. (Illus.). 918p. 1983. 125.00x (ISBN 0-398-04697-2). C C Thomas.

Amaducci, S. Asbestos: Directory of Unpublished Studies. 1982. 45.00 (ISBN 90-277-1414-2, Pub. by Reidel Holland). Kluwer Academic.

Amaducci, S., ed. Asbestos: Directory of Research & Documentation Centres. 1982. 52.00 (ISBN 90-277-1415-0, Pub. by Reidel Holland). Kluwer Academic.

Amai, Robert L., jt. auth. see Clark, Ronald D.

Amaldas, Swami. Christian Yogic Meditation. (Ways of Prayer Ser.: Vol. 8). pap. 5.95 (ISBN 0-89453-368-1). M Glazier.

Amaldev, Jerry. India: Raga for the Piano. (Frances Clark Library for Piano Students). 32p. (Orig.). (gr. k-12). 1981. pap. text ed. 5.95 (ISBN 0-87487-104-2). Birch Tree Gr.

Amaldi, E., et al. Electroproduction at Low Energy & Hadron Form Factors. (Springer Tracts in Modern Physics: Vol. 83). (Illus.). 1979. 37.00 (ISBN 0-387-08998-5). Springer-Verlag.

Amaldi, Ginestra. The Nature of Matter: Physical Theory from Thales to Fermi. Astbury, Peter, tr. LC 66-12133. 1982. pap. 11.00x (ISBN 0-226-01661-7). U of Chicago Pr.

Amalric, P., ed. see International Symposium on Fluorescein Angiography, Albi, 1969.

Amalrich, Andrei. Will the Soviet Union Survive Until 1984. 13.25 (ISBN 0-8446-5844-8). Peter Smith.

Amalrik, Andrei. Nose! Nose? No-Se & Other Plays. Weissbort, Daniel, tr. from Rus. & intro. by. LC 72-90507. (Orig.). 1973. pap. 2.95 (ISBN 0-15-667350-9, Harv). HarBraceJ.
--Notes of a Revolutionary. Daniels, Guy, tr. LC 81-48120. 1982. 16.95 (ISBN 0-394-41756-9). Knopf.
--Will the Soviet Union Survive Until 1984? rev. & expanded ed. LC 79-2026. 1981. pap. 5.95i (ISBN 0-06-090732-0, CN 732, CN). Har-Row.

Amal'ryk, Andrei. Zapiski Dissidenta. 368p. (Rus.). 1982. 24.50 (ISBN 0-88233-750-5); pap. 14.00 (ISBN 0-686-85664-3). Ardis Pubs.

Aman, Mohammed M. Arab Periodicals & Serials: A Classified Directory. LC 78-68242. (Reference Library of Social Sciences Ser.). 1979. 44.00 (ISBN 0-8240-9816-1). Garland Pub.

Aman, Mohammed M., jt. auth. see Abdul Huq, A. M.

Aman, Mohammed M., ed. Cataloging & Classification of Non-Western Material: Concerns, Issues, & Practices. (Neal Shuman Professional Bk). 376p. 1980. lib. bdg. 37.50x (ISBN 0-912700-06-8). Oryx Pr.

Aman, Reinhold, ed. Ernest Borneman Festschrift. LC 77-649633. (Maledicta: the International Journal of Verbal Aggression: Vol. III, No. 1). (Illus.). 1979. pap. 10.00 (ISBN 0-916500-53-5). Maledicta.
--G. Legman Festschrift. LC 78-69966. (Maledicta: International Journal of Verbal Aggression: Vol. 1 No. 2). 1978. pap. 10.00 (ISBN 0-916500-51-9). Maledicta.
--How Do They Do It? A Collection of Wordplays Revealing the Sexual Proclivities of Man & Beast. 64p. 1983. pap. 5.00 (ISBN 0-916500-09-8). Maledicta.
--Maledicta 1977. LC 76-649633. (Maledicta: the International Journal of Verbal Aggression Ser.: Vol. 1 No. 1 & 2). 1978. pap. 20.00 (ISBN 0-916500-50-0). Maledicta.
--Maledicta 1978. LC 77-649633. (Maledicta: International Journal of Verbal Aggression Ser.: Vol. 2, No. 1-2). (Illus.). 1979. pap. 20.00 (ISBN 0-916500-52-7). Maledicta.
--Maledicta 1979. LC 77-649633. (Maledicta: International Journal of Verbal Aggression Ser.: Vol. 3, Nos. 1-2). (Illus.). 320p. 1980. pap. 20.00 (ISBN 0-916500-54-3). Maledicta.
--Maledicta 1980. LC 77-649633. (Maledicta: International Journal of Verbal Aggression Ser.: Vol. 4, No. 1 & 2). (Illus.). 320p. 1980. pap. 20.00 (ISBN 0-916500-55-1). Maledicta.
--Maledicta 1981. LC 77-649633. (Maledicta: the International Journal of Verbal Aggression: Vol. 5, Nos. 1 & 2). (Illus.). 352p. 1982. pap. 23.50 (ISBN 0-916500-25-X). Maledicta.
--Maledicta 1982. LC 77-649633. (Maledicta: International Journal of Verbal Aggression Ser.: Vol. 6, Nos. 1 & 2). (Illus.). 320p. 1983. pap. 23.50 (ISBN 0-916500-26-8). Maledicta.
--Maledicta 1983: Peter Tamony Festschrift. LC 77-649633. (Maledicta: International Journal of Verbal Aggression Ser.: Vol. 7). (Illus.). 320p. 1984. pap. 23.50 (ISBN 0-916500-27-6). Maledicta.
--Maledicta (1984-85) LC 77-649633. (Maledicta: International Journal of Verbal Aggression Ser.: Vol. 8). (Illus.). 320p. 1985. pap. 23.50 (ISBN 0-916500-28-4). Maledicta.

Aman, Reinhold, ed. see Raeithel, Gert.

Aman, Reinhold A., ed. see Morse, A. Reynolds.

Amanat, Abbas. Cities & Trade: Consul Abbott on the Economy of Iran, 1847-1866. 256p. 1984. 29.00 (ISBN 0-86372-006-4, Pub. by Ithaca England). Evergreen Dist.

Amandry, Pierre. La Mantique Apollinienne a Delphes: Essai Sur le Fonctionnement De L'Oracle. facsimile ed. LC 75-10627. (Ancient Religion & Mythology Ser.). (Illus., Fr.). 1976. Repr. of 1950 ed. 23.50x (ISBN 0-405-07003-9). Ayer Co Pubs.

Amann, Anton, ed. Open Care for the Elderly in Seven European Countries: A Pilot Study in the Possibilities & Limits of Care. LC 80-40816. 238p. 1980. 43.00 (ISBN 0-08-025215-X). Pergamon.

Amann, Charles A., jt. ed. see Mattavi, James N.

Amann, Dick. How to Make the Purchased Part Cycle Work to Your Company's Advantage. LC 76-52041. (Illus.). 250p. 1977. 19.95 (ISBN 0-917194-03-9); looseleaf 49.95 (ISBN 0-917194-05-5). Prog Studies.

Amann, Dick & Smith, Dick. Forgotten Women of Computer History. Whitson, Dick, ed. (Illus.). 1978. pap. 9.95 (ISBN 0-917194-09-8). Prog Studies.

Amann, Eric. Cicada Voices: Selected Haiku of Eric Amann, 1966-1979. Swede, George, intro. by. 64p. (Orig.). 1983. 20.00 (ISBN 0-913719-26-9); pap. 7.00 (ISBN 0-913719-25-0). High-Coo Pr.

Amann, H., et al, eds. Applications of Nonlinear Analysis in the Physical Sciences. LC 80-21067. (Surveys & References Ser.: No. 6). 352p. 1981. text ed. 81.95 (ISBN 0-273-08501-8). Pitman Pub MA.

Amann, Herbert. Gewoehnliche Differentialgleichungen. 497p. 1983. 23.60 (ISBN 3-11-009573-4). De Gruyter.

Amann, R., et al, eds. The Technological Level of Soviet Industry. LC 77-76298. (Illus.). 1977. 62.00x (ISBN 0-300-02076-7). Yale U Pr.

Amann, Ronald & Cooper, Julian, eds. Industrial Innovation in the Soviet Union. LC 81-70484. 512p. 1982. text ed. 68.00x (ISBN 0-300-02772-9). Yale U Pr.

Amann, Rupert, ed. Prospects for Sexing Mammalian Sperm. LC 82-70138. 1982. pap. text ed. 24.50x (ISBN 0-87081-134-7). Colo Assoc.

Amanne, E. Dictionnaire de Theologie Catholigue. (Fr.). Set. pap. 1995.00 (ISBN 0-686-56893-1, M-6003). French & Eur.

Amant, Kristi, ed. see Arrants, Cheryl & Asbjornsen, Jan.

Amante, Peggy, jt. auth. see Pollitt, Ernesto.

Amantea, Carlos. A Pervert's Diary. 375p. 1986. pap. 14.95 (ISBN 0-917320-08-5). Mho & Mho.

Amanuddin, Syed. Adventures of Atman: An Epic of the Soul. 1977. pap. 3.00 (ISBN 0-912206-61-6). Poetry Eastwest.
--The Age of Female Eunuchs. 1974. pap. 3.00 (ISBN 0-912206-58-6). Poetry Eastwest.
--Gems & Germs: With English French Urdu Versions. Ford, Peter & Chaudhry, Mokhtar, trs. (Illus.). 1978. pap. 5.00 (ISBN 0-912206-60-8). Poetry Eastwest.
--Lightning & Love. 64p. (Orig.). 1973. pap. 3.00 (ISBN 0-912206-57-8). Poetry Eastwest.
--Poems of Protest. 32p. 1972. pap. 2.00 (ISBN 0-912206-54-3). Poetry Eastwest.
--System Shaker: Plays. 48p. 1972. pap. 2.00 (ISBN 0-912206-56-X). Poetry Eastwest.
--World Poetry in English: Essays & Interviews. 179p. 1981. text ed. 15.50x (ISBN 0-391-02790-5, 41054, Pub. by Sterling India). Humanities.

Amanuddin, Syed, jt. ed. see Diesendorf, Margaret.

Amanullah, Syed. Expenditures, Staff, & Salaries of Planning Agencies, 1978. (PAS Reports: No. 334). 64p. 1978. 10.00 (ISBN 0-318-12989-2). Am Plan Assn.

Amar, E., et al, eds. Analyse Complexe. (Lecture Notes in Mathematics Ser.: Vol. 1094). ix, 185p. 1984. pap. 12.00 (ISBN 0-387-13886-2). Springer-Verlag.

Amar, Jules. The Human Motor. (Physical Education Reprint Ser.). (Illus.). 1972. Repr. of 1920 ed. lib. bdg. 28.50x (ISBN 0-697-00060-5). Irvington.
--The Physiology of Industrial Organization & the Re-Employment of the Disabled. Kent, A. F., ed. Miall, Bernard, tr. LC 73-10379. (Management History Ser.: No. 34). (Illus.). 400p. 1973. Repr. of 1918 ed. 25.00 (ISBN 0-87960-036-5). Hive Pub.

Amara, Roy. Toward Understanding the Social Impact of Computers. 136p. 1974. 10.50 (ISBN 0-318-14427-1, R29). Inst Future.

Amara, Roy & Institute for the Future. The Ten Year Forecast. 160p. incl., with membership, annually. Inst Future.

Amara, Roy & Lipinski, Hubert. Climate Change to the Year Two Thousand: A Survey of Expert Opinion. 129p. 1978. free. Inst Future.

Amara, Roy C. & Lipinski, Andrew J. Business Planning for an Uncertain Future: Scenarios & Strategies. (PPS on Business & Economics Ser.). 200p. 1983. 28.00 (ISBN 0-08-027545-1). Pergamon.

Amaral, Anne, jt. auth. see Ansari, Mary B.

Amaral, Anthony. Movie Horses: The Fascinating Techniques of Training. pap. 2.00 (ISBN 0-87980-274-X). Wilshire.
--Mustang: Life & Legends of Nevada's Wild Horses. LC 76-53821. (Lancehead Ser.). (Illus.). xiv, 156p. 1977. 9.00 (ISBN 0-87417-046-X). U of Nev Pr.

Amaral, David. Lusophone African Liberators: The University Years. (Graduate Student Paper Competition Ser.). 20p. (Orig.). 1979. pap. text ed. 2.00 (ISBN 0-941934-27-6). Indiana Africa.

Amarant, Julius J. Tall Baseball Stories. 1979. 6.95 (ISBN 0-89962-013-2). Todd & Honeywell.

Amarasinghe, Upali. Dryden & the Pope in the Early Nineteenth Century: A Study of Changing Literary Taste, 1800-1830. LC 62-52188. pap. 64.00 (ISBN 0-317-28394-4, 2022433). Bks Demand UMI.

Amari, S. Differential-Geometrical Methods in Statistics. (Lecture Notes in Statistics Ser.: Vol. 28). (Illus.). v, 290p. 1985. pap. 19.60 (ISBN 0-387-96056-2). Springer-Verlag.

Amari, S. & Arbib, M. A., eds. Competition & Cooperation in Neural Nets, Kyoto, Japan, 1982: Proceedings. (Lecture Notes in Biomathematics: Vol. 45). 441p. 1982. pap. 28.00 (ISBN 0-387-11574-9). Springer-Verlag.

Amari, Suad. Cooking the Lebanese Way. (Easy Menu Ethnic Cookbooks). (Illus.). 48p. (gr. 5 up). 1985. PLB 8.95 (ISBN 0-8225-0913-X). Lerner Pubns.

Amaria, P. J, et al. Arctic Systems. LC 77-3871. (NATO Conference Series II, Systems Science: Vol. 2). 956p. 1977. 115.00x (ISBN 0-306-32842-9, Plenum Pr). Plenum Pub.

Amari-Amir, Lisa, ed. see Diamond, Carlin J.

Amarillo Genealogical Society, ed. Texas Panhandle Forefathers, Vol. I. (Illus.). 388p. 1983. 50.00 (ISBN 0-88107-011-4). Natl ShareGraphics.

Amaro-Reyes, Jose A., jt. auth. see Gould, David J.

Amarshu, Azeem, et al. Development & Dependency: The Political Economy of Papua New Guinea. (Illus.). 1979. text ed. 35.00x (ISBN 0-19-550582-4). Oxford U Pr.

Amary, Issam B. Creative Recreation for the Mentally Retarded. (Illus.). 128p. 1975. 14.75x (ISBN 0-398-03292-0). C C Thomas.
--Effective Meal Planning & Food Preparation for the Mentally Retarded-Developmentally Disabled: Comprehensive & Innovative Teaching Methods. (Illus.). 232p. 1979. 21.50x (ISBN 0-398-03882-1). C C Thomas.
--The Rights of the Mentally Retarded-Developmentally Disabled to Treatment & Education. (Illus.). 216p. 1980. 17.50x (ISBN 0-398-03946-1). C C Thomas.
--Social Awareness, Hygiene, & Sex Education for the Mentally Retarded-Developmentally Disabled. (Illus.). 208p. 1980. 15.50x (ISBN 0-398-04096-6). C C Thomas.

Amastae, Jon & Elias-Olivares, Lucia, eds. Spanish in the United States: Sociolinguistic Aspects. LC 81-15437. (Illus.). 448p. 1982. 59.50 (ISBN 0-521-24448-X); pap. 19.95 (ISBN 0-521-28689-1). Cambridge U Pr.

Amateau, Maurice F., jt. ed. see Hack, John E.

Amateur Hockey Association of the U. S. Hockey Coaching. (Illus.). 248p. 1982. 29.95 (ISBN 0-684-17457-X, ScribT). Scribner.

Amati, Alfonso. The Teachings of the False Prophets of Mankind. (Human Development Library Bk.). (Illus.). 93p. 1984. pap. 39.75x (ISBN 0-89266-444-4). Am Classical Coll Pr.
--The Three Major Contemporary Cultural Tragedies of Mankind. (Illus.). 1977. 42.40 (ISBN 0-89266-080-5). Am Classical Coll Pr.

Amato. L' Ystoire de li Normant: Et la Chronique De Robert Viscart Par Aime, Moine Du Mont-Cassin. 43.00 (ISBN 0-384-01030-X); pap. 37.00 (ISBN 0-384-01031-8). Johnson Repr.

Amato, Benedetto A. Labor in Pregnancy: Medical Subject Analysis & Research Bibliography. LC 84-45643. 150p. 1984. 29.95 (ISBN 0-88164-192-8); pap. 21.95 (ISBN 0-88164-193-6). ABBE Pubs Assn.

Amato, Florence C. Fundamentals of Medical Science for Medical Record Personnel. 334p. 37.95 (ISBN 0-89443-567-1). Aspen Systems.

Amato, Francis. Guide to Computer Magazines, 1985 Edition. LC 84-91752. 144p. 1985. pap. 9.95 (ISBN 0-911061-11-8). S Davis Pub.

Amato, Janet D' see D'Amato, Janet & D'Amato, Alex.

Amato, Joseph. Countryside, Mirror of Ourselves. 2nd ed. (Illus.). 60p. 1983. pap. 3.50. V Amati.
--Death Book. 120p. 1985. 13.95 (ISBN 0-933180-66-7). Ellis Pr.
--Ethics, Living or Dead? xii, 132p. 1982. write for info. (ISBN 0-9614119-0-2, Co-Pub Portals Press). V Amati.

Amato, Joseph A. Death Book: Terrors, Consolations, Contradictions & Paradoxes. 1985. write for info. (ISBN 0-9614119-1-0, Co-Pub Ellis Press). V Amati.
--Ethics: Living or Dead? Themes in Contemporary Values. 1982. 10.50 (ISBN 0-916620-62-X). Portals Pr.

Amato, Joseph A., II. Guilt & Gratitude: A Study of the Origins of Contemporary Conscience. LC 81-6991. (Contributions in Philosophy Ser.: No. 20). xxv, 218p. 1982. lib. bdg. 29.95 (ISBN 0-313-22946-5, AGG/). Greenwood.

Amato, Nelida M. Problemas Administrativos Del Poder Judicial En Puerto Rico. pap. 3.75 (ISBN 0-8477-2210-4). U of PR Pr.

Amato, P. R., jt. auth. see Smithson, M.

Amato, Pete. Our Grandmothers' Cures & Remedies. LC 84-91323. 38p. 1985. 6.95 (ISBN 0-533-06410-4). Vantage.

Amatora, Sr. Mary. The Queen's Heart of Gold: The Complete Story of Our Lady of Beauraing. LC 78-188443. 1972. 7.50 (ISBN 0-682-47467-3, Banner); pap. 5.00 (ISBN 0-682-47480-0, Banner). Exposition Pr FL.
--The Queen's Portrait: The Story of Guadalupe. LC 74-188442. 1972. 7.50 (ISBN 0-682-47468-1, Lochinvar); (Lochinvar). Exposition Pr FL.
--El Retrato de la Reina: La Historia de Nuestra Senora de Guadalupe. 1972. 7.50 (ISBN 0-682-47542-4, Lochinvar); pap. 5.00 (ISBN 0-682-47548-3, Lochinvar). Exposition Pr FL.

Amatulla, Shakurra. Get Your Money, Honey! A Student's Guide to Staying Alive. 2nd ed. LC 84-1647. 1984. pap. 4.95 (ISBN 0-915383-01-2). For Us Pubns.
--Get Your Money Honey! A Student's Guide to Staying Alive. 2nd rev. ed. LC 84-1647. (Illus.). 70p. 1984. pap. 4.95 (ISBN 0-915383-01-2). For Us Pubns.

Amatuzzi, Joseph R. Television & the School. LC 82-60522. 125p. 1983. pap. 14.95 (ISBN 0-88247-676-9). R & E Pubs.

Amatya, Shaphalya. Some Aspects of Cultural Policy in Nepal. (Studies & Documents on Cultural Policies). 220p. 1983. pap. text ed. 7.50 (ISBN 92-3-102069-2, U1297, UNESCO). Unipub.

Amauri, Maurice & DeCraon, Pierre. Les Chansons Attribuees Aux Seigneurs De Craon. Langfors, Arthur, ed. LC 80-2160. (Societe Neo-Philologique De Helsingfors, Memoires Ser.: Vol. 6). 1981. Repr. of 1917 ed. 17.50 (ISBN 0-404-19020-0). AMS Pr.

Amavis, R. & Smeets, J., eds. Principles & Methods for Determining Ecological Criteria on Hydrobiocenoses. LC 76-14624. 1976. pap. text ed. 89.00 (ISBN 0-08-021233-6). Pergamon.

Amavis, R., et al, eds. Hardness of Drinking Water & Public Health: Proceedings. 1976. 89.00 (ISBN 0-08-020898-3). Pergamon.

Amaya, Mario. Art Nouveau. (Illus.). 168p. 1985. pap. 9.95 (ISBN 0-8052-0784-8). Schocken.

Amayo, R. K. & Stewart, I. Infinite-Dimensional Lie Algebras. 436p. 1974. 62.50x (ISBN 90-286-0144-9). Sijthoff & Noordhoff.

Amayo, R. K., ed. Algebra Carbondale Nineteen Eighty: Proceedings. (Lecture Notes in Mathematics Ser.: Vol. 848). 298p. 1981. pap. 22.00 (ISBN 0-387-10573-5). Springer-Verlag.

Amazigo, John C. & Rubenfeld, Lester A. Advanced Calculus: And Its Applications to the Engineering & Physical Sciences. LC 80-283. 407p. 1980. text ed. 36.45 (ISBN 0-471-04934-4). Wiley.

Ambarcumjan, G. A., et al. Thirty-Five Papers on Statistics & Probability. LC 61-9803. (Selected Translations in Mathematical Statistics & Probability Ser.: Vol. 4). 1963. 32.00 (ISBN 0-8218-1454-0, STAPRO-4). Am Math.

Ambard, L. & Trautmann, S. Ultrafiltration. Monnier, A., tr. (Illus.). 80p. 1960. 9.75x (ISBN 0-398-04189-X). C C Thomas.

Ambartzumian, R. V. Combinatorial Integral Geometry: With Applications to Mathemaitcal Stereology. LC 81-14773. (Probability & Mathematical Statistics). 220p. 1982. 52.95 (ISBN 0-471-27977-3, Pub. by Wiley-Interscience). Wiley.

Ambasz, Emilio. The Architecture of Luis Barragan. LC 74-21724. (Illus.). 1976. 27.50 (ISBN 0-87070-234-3); pap. 15.95 (ISBN 0-87070-233-5). Museum Mod Art.

Ambedkar, Bhimrao R. Pakistan or Partition of India. LC 77-179171. (South & Southeast Asia Studies). Repr. of 1945 ed. 32.50 (ISBN 0-404-54801-6). AMS Pr.

Amber, John T., ed. see Clayton, Joseph D.

Amber, John T., ed. see Dougan, John C.

Amber, Lee. Chosen. rev ed. LC 81-51985. 176p. 1981. pap. 3.95 (ISBN 0-88449-079-3, A424025). Vision Hse.

Amber, Reuben. Color Therapy. pap. 9.95x (ISBN 0-943358-04-3). Aurora Press.

Amberg, G., intro. by. Film Society Programmes, Nineteen Twenty-Five to Nineteen Thirty-Nine. LC 77-103815. (Contemporary Art Ser). 1971. Repr. of 1925 ed. 32.00 (ISBN 0-405-00741-8). Ayer Co Pubs.

Amberg, George. Ballet in America. (Series in Dance). (Illus.). xv, 244p. 1983. Repr. of 1949 ed. lib. bdg. 35.00 (ISBN 0-306-76154-8). Da Capo.

Amberg, George, et al. Art of Cinema: Selected Essays. LC 75-124020. (Arno Press Cinema Program). (Illus.). 106p. 1972. Repr. of 1971 ed. 12.00 (ISBN 0-405-03924-7). Ayer Co Pubs.

Amberger, Ronald, et al. Canal Boats, Interurbans & Trolleys: A History of the Rochester Subway. LC 80-82783. (Orig.). 1985. 12.95 (ISBN 0-9605296-1-6). Natl Rail Rochester.

Amberley, John R. An Analysis of Religious Belief. LC 76-161318. (Atheist Viewpoint Ser.). 745p. 1972. Repr. of 1877 ed. 41.00 (ISBN 0-405-03621-3). Ayer Co Pubs.

--An Analysis of Religious Belief. 59.95 (ISBN 0-87968-619-7). Gordon Pr.

Ambers, Henry J. The Dirigible & the Future. rev. ed. LC 81-69805. 70p. 1981. pap. 5.00 (ISBN 0-686-85921-9). Edelweiss Pr.

--The Unfinished Building. LC 74-19535. 400p. 1974. 8.95 (ISBN 0-9600874-2-7). Edelweiss Pr.

--The Waltzer. LC 76-114002. 320p. 1970. 6.95 (ISBN 0-685-26764-4). Edelweiss Pr.

Amberson, Max, ed. see Peterson, Paul, et al.

Amberson, Max L., ed. see Bishop, Douglas D.

Amberson, Max L., ed. see Shinn, Glen C. & Weston, Curtis.

Amberson, Max L., ed. see Stewart, Robert.

Amberson, Talmadge R. Reaching Out to People. LC 79-55435. 1979. pap. 5.95 (ISBN 0-8054-6321-6). Broadman.

Ambio Magazine. The Aftermath: The Human & Ecological Consequences of Nuclear War. 1983. 14.95 (ISBN 0-394-53446-8); pap. 7.95 (ISBN 0-394-72042-3). Random.

Ambirajan, S. Classical Political Economy & British Policy in India. LC 76-21020. (South Asian Studies: No. 21). (Illus.). 1978. 52.50 (ISBN 0-521-21415-7). Cambridge U Pr.

Amble, Bruce R. & Bradley, Richard W. Pupils As Persons: Case Studies in Pupil Personnel Work. LC 73-6532. 1973. 11.00 (ISBN 0-7002-2439-4, 0-910328-19-6). Carroll Pr.

Ambler, B. G. Alfred Lord Tennyson: His Homes & His Haunts. lib. bdg. 15.00 (ISBN 0-8414-2902-2). Folcroft.

Ambler, Charles H. Thomas Ritchie: A Study in Virginia Politics. (Law, Politics & History Ser). 1970. Repr. of 1913 ed. lib. bdg. 35.00 (ISBN 0-306-70092-1). Da Capo.

Ambler, Charles H., ed. Correspondence of Robert M. T. Hunter, 1826-1876. LC 76-75307. (American Scene Ser). 1971. Repr. of 1918 ed. lib. bdg. 49.50 (ISBN 0-306-71257-1). Da Capo.

Ambler, Effie. Russian Journalism & Politics, Eighteen Sixty-One to Eighteen Eighty-One: The Career of Aleksei Suvorin. LC 72-173671. 265p. 1972. 14.50x (ISBN 0-8143-1461-9). Wayne St U Pr.

Ambler, Eric. Background to Danger. 256p. 1985. pap. 2.95 (ISBN 0-425-06420-4). Berkley Pub.

--The Care of Time. 277p. 1981. 11.95 (ISBN 0-374-11897-3). FS&G.

--The Care of Time. 288p. 1985. pap. 2.95 (ISBN 0-425-07280-0). Berkley Pub.

--The Care of Time. 288p. 1986. pap. 2.95 (ISBN 0-425-08894-4). Berkley Pub.

--Cause for Alarm. 246p. Repr. of 1939 ed. lib. bdg. 15.95x (ISBN 0-89190-466-2, Pub. by River City Pr). Amereon Ltd.

--Cause for Alarm. 256p. 1985. pap. 2.95 (ISBN 0-425-07029-8). Berkley Pub.

--A Coffin for Dimitrios. 214p. Repr. of 1937 ed. lib. bdg. 15.95x (ISBN 0-89190-461-1, Pub. by River City Pr). Amereon Ltd.

--A Coffin for Dimitrios. 224p. 1983. pap. 2.95 (ISBN 0-425-06408-5). Berkley Pub.

--Doctor Frigo. LC 81-70068. 1982. pap. 7.95 (ISBN 0-689-70617-0, 276). Atheneum.

--Epitaph for a Spy. 201p. Repr. of 1952 ed. lib. bdg. 13.95x (ISBN 0-89190-462-X, Pub. by River City Pr). Amereon Ltd.

--Epitaph for a Spy. 224p. 1985. pap. 2.95 (ISBN 0-425-06564-2). Berkley Pub.

--Journey into Fear. 256p. 1983. pap. 2.95 (ISBN 0-425-06391-7). Berkley Pub.

--Judgement on Deltchev. 229p. Repr. of 1951 ed. lib. bdg. 14.95x (ISBN 0-89190-463-8, Pub. by River City Pr). Amereon Ltd.

--The Levanter. LC 81-70069. 1982. pap. 7.95 (ISBN 0-689-70618-9, 277). Atheneum.

--The Levanter. 17.95 (ISBN 0-88411-296-9, Pub. by Aeonian Pr). Amereon Ltd.

--The Light of Day. 215p. Repr. of 1962 ed. lib. bdg. 13.95x (ISBN 0-89190-464-6, Pub. by River City Pr). Amereon Ltd.

--The Light of Day. 224p. 1985. pap. 2.95 (ISBN 0-425-07455-2). Berkley Pub.

--Passage of Arms. 224p. 1985. pap. 2.95 (ISBN 0-425-07137-5). Berkley Pub.

--The Schirmer Inheritance. 224p. 1984. pap. 2.95 (ISBN 0-425-07302-5). Berkley Pub.

--Siege of the Villa Lipp. 17.95 (ISBN 0-89190-465-4, Pub. by Am Repr). Amereon Ltd.

--State of Siege. 160p. 1985. pap. 2.95 (ISBN 0-425-06768-8). Berkley Pub.

Ambler, J. R., jt. auth. see Lambert, Marjorie F.

Ambler, J. Richard. The Anasazi: Prehistoric Peoples of the Four Corners Region. 3rd ed. LC 77-76509. (Illus.). 1983. pap. 5.95 (ISBN 0-89734-005-1). Mus Northern Ariz.

--Caldwell Village. LC 68-28353. (Utah Anthropological Papers: No. 84). 1966. 30.00 (ISBN 0-404-60684-9). AMS Pr.

Ambler, John, et al, eds. Soviet & East European Transport Problems. 288p. 1985. 32.50 (ISBN 0-312-74757-8). St Martin.

Ambler, John S. The French Army in Politics, 1945-1962. LC 65-26274. 439p. 1966. 6.50 (ISBN 0-8142-0018-4). Ohio St U Pr.

Ambler, John S., ed. The French Socialist Experiment. LC 84-707. 250p. 1985. text ed. 27.50 (ISBN 0-89727-057-6); pap. text ed. 12.95 (ISBN 0-89727-065-7). ISHI PA.

Ambler, John S., et al. Papers in Political Science. (Rice University Studies: Vol. 54, No. 3). 88p. 1968. pap. 10.00x (ISBN 0-89263-197-X). Rice Univ.

Ambler, Nancy M., ed. see Valerio, Joseph M. & Friedman, Daniel.

Ambler, Vic. Basketball. (Illus.). 96p. 1979. pap. 6.50 (ISBN 0-571-11284-6). Faber & Faber.

--Basketball. (Competitive Sports Ser.). (Illus.). 64p. (gr. 7-12). 1984. 12.95 (ISBN 0-7134-4423-1, Pub. by Batsford England). David & Charles.

Ambraseys, N. N. & Melville, C. P. A History of Persian Earthquakes. LC 81-15540. (Cambridge Earth Science Ser.). (Illus.). 400p. 1982. 64.50 (ISBN 0-521-24112-X). Cambridge U Pr.

Ambre, John J., jt. auth. see Atkinson, Arthur J., Jr.

Ambrester, Marcus L. & Julian, Faye D. Speech Communication Reader. 217p. (Orig.). 1983. pap. text ed. 9.95x (ISBN 0-88133-013-2). Waveland Pr.

Ambrester, Marcus L. & Strause, Glynis Holm. A Rhetoric of Interpersonal Communication. 336p. (Orig.). 1984. pap. text ed. 13.95x (ISBN 0-88133-036-1). Waveland Pr.

Ambrogi, Fabio, jt. ed. see Fudenberg, H. Hugh.

Ambron, Sueann R. & Brodzinsky, David M. Lifespan Human Development. 2nd ed. 658p. 1982. text ed. 29.95 (ISBN 0-03-059144-5, HoltC); wkbk. 11.95 (ISBN 0-03-059811-7); instructor's manual 25.00 (ISBN 0-03-059863-X). HR&W.

Ambron, Sueann R. & Salkind. Child Development. 4th ed. 1984. text ed. 30.95 (ISBN 0-03-063302-8). HR&W.

Ambrose, A., jt. auth. see Lazerowitz, M.

Ambrose, A. J., ed. Jane's Merchant Shipping Review. 2nd ed. (Jane's Review Ser.). (Illus.). 160p. 1984. 17.95 (ISBN 0-7106-0302-9). Jane's Pub Inc.

--Jane's Merchant Shipping Review. 3rd ed. (Illus.). 176p. 1985. 17.95 (ISBN 0-7106-0332-0). Jane's Pub Inc.

Ambrose, Alice. Essays in Analysis. (Muirhead Library of Philosophy). 1966. text ed. 18.00x (ISBN 0-04-110001-8). Humanities.

Ambrose, Alice, jt. auth. see Lazerowitz, Morris.

Ambrose, Alice, ed. Wittgenstein's Lectures, Cambridge 1932-1935: From the Notes of Alice Ambrose & Margaret Macdonald. 225p. 1979. 25.00x (ISBN 0-8476-6151-2). Rowman.

Ambrose, Alice & Lazerowitz, Morris, eds. G. E. Moore: Essays in Retrospect. (Muirhead Library of Philosophy). 1970. text ed. 19.00x (ISBN 0-04-192023-6). Humanities.

--Ludwig Wittgenstein: Philosophy & Language. (Muirhead Library of Philosophy). 1972. text ed. 39.00x (ISBN 0-391-00190-6). Humanities.

Ambrose, Alice, ed. see Wittgenstein, Ludwig.

Ambrose, Amie S. Chinese Flora & Fauna Designs. (International Design Library). (Illus.). 48p. 1985. pap. 3.50 (ISBN 0-88045-062-2). Stemmer Hse.

--Japanese Nature Designs. (International Design Library). (Illus.). 48p. (Orig.). 1982. pap. 3.50 (ISBN 0-88045-013-4). Stemmer Hse.

--Japanese Woodblock Print Designs to Color. (The International Design Library). (Illus.). 48p. 1982. pap. 3.50 (ISBN 0-916144-95-X). Stemmer Hse.

Ambrose, Andrew, ed. Jane's Merchant Shipping Review. (Jane's Reviews Ser.). 150p. 1983. 17.95 (ISBN 0-86720-663-2). Jane's Pub Inc.

Ambrose, D. Gas Chromatography. 2nd ed. LC 72-169709. 227p. 1971. 16.50 (ISBN 0-442-20362-4, Pub. by Van Nos Reinhold). Krieger.

Ambrose, David, et al. D.A.R.Y.L. Movie Storybook. (Collector Books with Stickers). (Illus.). 22p. (gr. 5-8). 1985. pap. 1.95 (ISBN 0-89954-386-3). Antioch Pub Co.

Ambrose, David P., jt. auth. see Willet, Shelagh M.

Ambrose, E. J. Cell Biology. 2nd ed. (Illus.). 576p. 1978. pap. text ed. 19.95 (ISBN 0-8391-1236-X). Univ Park.

--The Nature & Origin of the Biological World. 190p. 1982. 58.95X (ISBN 0-470-27513-8); pap. 26.95X (ISBN 0-470-27514-6). Halsted Pr.

Ambrose, E. J. & Roe, F. J. C. The Biology of Cancer. 2nd ed. LC 74-26860. 315p. 1975. 74.95x (ISBN 0-470-02527-1). Halsted Pr.

Ambrose, G. & Newbold, G. A Handbook of Medical Hypnosis. 4th ed. 1980. text ed. 25.95 (ISBN 0-7216-0700-4, Pub. by Bailliere-Tindall). Saunders.

Ambrose, Harrison W. & Ambrose, Katherine P. A Handbook of Biological Investigation. 3rd ed. 170p. (Orig.). 1981. pap. text ed. 8.95 (ISBN 0-89459-148-7). Hunter Textbks.

Ambrose, James. Building Structures Primer. 2nd ed. LC 81-4336. 136p. 1981. 30.95 (ISBN 0-471-08678-9, Pub. by Wiley-Interscience). Wiley.

--Simplified Design of Building Foundations. LC 80-39880. 338p. 1981. 34.95x (ISBN 0-471-06267-7, Pub. by Wiley-Interscience). Wiley.

--Simplified Design of Building Structures. LC 79-413. 268p. 1979. 34.95 (ISBN 0-471-04721-X, Pub. by Wiley-Interscience). Wiley.

Ambrose, James & Vergun, Dimitry. Seismic Design of Buildings. 288p. 38.95 (ISBN 0-471-88979-2). Wiley.

--Simplified Building Design for Wind & Earthquake Forces. LC 79-26660. 142p. 1980. 37.50x (ISBN 0-471-05013-X, Pub. by Wiley-Interscience). Wiley.

Ambrose, James, jt. auth. see Parker, Harry.

Ambrose, James, ed. see Parker, Harry.

Ambrose, John T. & Shimanuki, H. The Beekeeper's Manual. (Illus.). 400p. 86. 39.95x (ISBN 0-03-058689-5). Praeger.

Ambrose, John W., jt. auth. see Buehner, William J.

Ambrose, Joseph G. The Dan Breen Story. 120p. 1981. pap. 4.95 (ISBN 0-85342-663-5, Pub. by Mercier Pr Ireland). Irish Bks Media.

Ambrose, Katherine P., jt. auth. see Ambrose, Harrison W.

Ambrose, Kay. Ballet-Lover's Companion. (Illus.). (YA) 1949. 6.95 (ISBN 0-394-40800-4). Knopf.

--Ballet-Lover's Pocket-Book. (Illus.). 1945. 8.95 (ISBN 0-394-40802-0). Knopf.

--Ballet-Student's Primer. (Illus.). (YA) 1954. 7.95 (ISBN 0-394-40804-7). Knopf.

--Classical Dances & Costumes of India. LC 83-40197. (Illus.). 115p. 1984. 22.50 (ISBN 0-312-14263-3). St Martin.

Ambrose, M. Happy Way to Numbers. rev. ed. (readiness). 1974. pap. text ed. 6.72 (ISBN 0-03-088439-X, HoltE); tchr's ed. o.p. 6.04 (ISBN 0-03-064765-7). HR&W.

Ambrose, Mark, jt. ed. see Walker, Jane.

Ambrose, Peter & Harper, John. Surviving Divorce: Men Beyond Marriage. LC 82-22717. 226p. 1983. text ed. 25.95x (ISBN 0-86598-122-1). Rowman & Allanheld.

Ambrose, St. Complete Letters. LC 67-28583. (Fathers of the Church Ser.: Vol. 26). 515p. 1954. 26.95x (ISBN 0-8132-0026-1). Cath U Pr.

--Hexameron Paradise, Cain & Abel. LC 77-81354. (Fathers of the Church Ser.: Vol. 42). 449p. 1961. 29.95x (ISBN 0-8132-0042-3). Cath U Pr.

--Seven Exegetical Works: Isaac, or the Soul, Death as a Good, Jacob & the Happy Life, Joseph, the Patriarchs, Flight from the World, The Prayer of Job & David. (Fathers of the Church Ser.: Vol. 65). 447p. 1972. 29.95x (ISBN 0-8132-0065-2). Cath U Pr.

--Theological & Dogmatic Works. (Fathers of the Church Ser.: Vol. 44). 343p. 1963. 21.95x (ISBN 0-8132-0044-X). Cath U Pr.

Ambrose, St., jt. auth. see Gregory Nazianzen, St.

Ambrose, Stephen. Eisenhower, 2 vols. Incl. Soldier, General of the Army: President-Elect, 1890-1952. Vol. I (ISBN 0-671-60564-X); The President. Vol. II (ISBN 0-671-60565-8). 1985. pap. 12.95 ea. (Touchstone). S&S.

--Rise to Globalism. 4th ed. 368p. (Orig.). 1985. pap. 7.95 (ISBN 0-14-022622-2). Penguin.

Ambrose, Stephen E. Duty, Honor, Country: A History of West Point. LC 66-14372. pap. 93.80 (ISBN 0-317-29740-6, 2015684). Bks Demand UMI.

--Eisenhower & Berlin, Nineteen Forty-Five: The Decision to Halt at the Elbe. (Essays in American History Ser). (Illus.). 1967. pap. 5.95x (ISBN 0-393-09730-7). Norton.

--Eisenhower, Vol. I: Soldier, General of the Army, President-Elect 1890-1952. 640p. 1983. 23.00 (ISBN 0-671-44069-1). S&S.

--Eisenhower, Vol. 2: The President. LC 83-9892. (Illus.). 752p. 1984. 24.95 (ISBN 0-671-49901-7). S&S.

--Ike: Abilene to Berlin. LC 73-5474. (Illus.). 192p. (gr. 7 up). 1973. PLB 12.89 (ISBN 0-06-020076-6). HarpJ.

--Pegasus Bridge: June 6, 1944. 208p. 1985. 15.95 (ISBN 0-671-52374-0). S&S.

--Rise to Globalism: American Foreign Policy since 1938. 3rd rev. ed. 428p. 1976. pap. 6.95 (ISBN 0-14-021247-7, Pelican). Penguin.

Ambrose, Stephen E. & Immerman, Richard H. Milton S. Eisenhower: Educational Statesman. LC 83-4. (Illus.). 352p. 1983. 22.50x (ISBN 0-8018-2988-7). Johns Hopkins.

Ambrose, Stephen E. & Barber, James A., Jr., eds. The Military & American Society. LC 77-163236. 1973. pap. text ed. 11.95 (ISBN 0-02-900550-7). Free Pr.

Ambrose, W. & Duerden, P. Archaeometry: An Australian Perspective. 391p. 1984. pap. text ed. 24.95 (ISBN 0-86784-239-3, 1612, Pub. by ANUP Australia). Australia N U P.

Ambrose, W. Haydn, jt. auth. see Packer, Wilfred T.

Ambrose, William G. College Algebra. (Illus.). 320p. 1976. text ed. write for info. (ISBN 0-02-302520-4, 30252). Macmillan.

Ambrosi, Antonio. Mas Alla de Los Paralelos. 184p. 1983. pap. 3.95 (ISBN 0-89922-209-9). Edit Caribe.

Ambrosi, Hans. Where the Great German Wines Grow. Pringle, Thom & Hamilton, Gavin, trs. (Illus.). 248p. 1976. 12.95 (ISBN 0-8038-8070-7). Hastings.

Ambrosio, Joe. Rock Rhythms for the Young. 24p. 1984. pap. 5.95 (ISBN 0-938170-06-6). Wimbledon Music.

Ambrosios, Hieromonk, jt. auth. see Chrysostomos, Archimandrite.

Ambrosius, Edgar E. Mechanical Measurement & Instrumentation. LC 66-21850. (Illus.). pap. 148.50 (ISBN 0-317-11128-0, 2013037). Bks Demand UMI.

Ambrosius, Saint Concerning the Mysteries. 1977. pap. 1.25 (ISBN 0-686-19348-2). Eastern Orthodox.

--Opera, 3 Vols. Set. 210.00 (ISBN 0-384-01038-5). Johnson Repr.

Ambroz, Oton. Realignment of World Power. LC 73-149631. 744p. 1972. Vol. 1. 13.95 ea. (ISBN 0-8315-0114-6); Vol. 2. (ISBN 0-8315-0115-4). Speller.

Ambroziak, A. Semiconductor Photoelectric Devices. 344p. 1970. 93.75 (ISBN 0-677-61800-X). Gordon.

Ambrozic, Aloysius M. The Hidden Kingdom: A Reductional-Critical Study of the References to the Kingdom of God in Mark's Gospel. LC 72-89100. (Catholic Biblical Quarterly Monographs: No. 2). xi, 280p. 1972. pap. 9.00 (ISBN 0-915170-01-9). Catholic Biblical.

Ambrozy, Andras. Electronic Noise. (Series in Electrical Engineering). (Illus.). 284p. 1982. text ed. 44.50x (ISBN 0-07-001124-9). McGraw.

Ambrus, J. L., ed. Pentoxifylline, Pharmacological & Clinical Research. 20.00 (ISBN 0-915340-05-4). PJD Pubns.

Ambrus, J. L., et al, eds. Advances in Some Aspects of Osteoporosis. 1985. 24.95 (ISBN 0-915340-13-5). PJD Pubns.

Ambrus, Victor. Grandma, Felix, & Mustapha Biscuit. LC 82-2133. (Illus.). 32p. (gr. k-3). 1982. 11.75 (ISBN 0-688-01285-X); lib. bdg. 11.88 (ISBN 0-688-01287-6). Morrow.

Ambrus, Victor G. Blackbeard the Pirate. (Illus.). 32p. (gr. 2-9). 1983. bds. 10.95 (ISBN 0-19-279771-9, Pub by Oxford U Pr Childrens). Merrimack Pub Cir.

--Blackbeard the Pirate. (Illus.). (gr. 1-3). 1983. pap. 9.95 (ISBN 0-19-279771-9). Oxford U Pr.

--Dracula: Everything You Always Wanted to Know But Were Too Afraid to Ask. (Illus.). 32p. (gr. 2-9). 1983. 10.95 (ISBN 0-19-279746-8, Pub by Oxford U Pr Childrens); pap. 5.95 (ISBN 0-19-272121-6). Merrimack Pub Cir.

--Dracula's Bedtime Storybook: Tales to Keep You Awake at Night. (Illus.). 32p. 1982. bds. 10.95 laminated (ISBN 0-19-279762-X, Pub. by Oxford U Pr Childrens); pap. 5.95 (ISBN 0-19-272077-5, Pub. by Oxford U Pr Childrens). Merrimack Pub Cir.

--Dracula's Everything You Always Wanted to Know But Were too Afraid to Ask. bds. 10.95 laminated (ISBN 0-318-12041-0, Pub. by Oxford U Pr Childrens). Merrimack Pub Cir.

--Under the Double Eagle. (Illus.). 48p. 1982. 11.95 (ISBN 0-19-279722-0, Pub. by Oxford U Pr Childrens). Merrimack Pub Cir.

Ambulando, Solvitur. In the Hudson Highlands. (Illus.). 320p. 1977. Repr. of 1945 ed. 8.95 (ISBN 0-915850-08-7). Walking News Inc.

Ambulatory ECG Monitoring, First National Conference. Proceedings. Jacobsen, Nancy & Yarnall, Stephen, eds. (Illus.). 150p. 1976. 16.50 (ISBN 0-917054-08-3). Med Communications.

Ambursley, Fitzroy. The New Jewel Revolution in Grenada, 1979-1983. 208p. 1985. 26.00 (ISBN 0-8052-7245-3, Pub. by NLB England); pap. 7.50 (ISBN 0-8052-7246-1). Schocken.

Ambursley, Fitzroy & Cohen, Robin, eds. Crisis in the Caribbean. LC 83-42524. 288p. 1984. 26.00 (ISBN 0-85345-630-5); pap. 10.00 (ISBN 0-85345-631-3). Monthly Rev.

Ambuter, Carolyn. Complete Book of Needlepoint. LC 70-178814. (Illus.). 1972. 12.95i (ISBN 0-690-00337-4). T y Crowell.

--Open Canvas. LC 82-60066. (Illus.). 304p. 1982. cloth 22.50 (ISBN 0-89480-170-8, 352); pap. 14.95 (ISBN 0-89480-171-6, 493). Workman Pub.

AMC Maine Mountain Guide Book Committee. AMC Guide to Mount Desert Island & Acadia National Park. 3rd ed. (Illus.). 40p. 1984. pap. 3.50 (ISBN 0-910146-52-7). Appalach Mtn.

AMC Maine Mountain Guide Book Committee, ed. AMC Maine Mountain Guide. 5th ed. (Illus.). 308p. 1985. pap. 9.95 (ISBN 0-910146-54-3). Appalach Mtn.

AMC River Guide Committee. AMC River Guide: MA-CT-RI. Schweiker, Roioli, ed. (Illus.). 204p. (Orig.). 1985. pap. 8.95 (ISBN 0-910146-56-X). Appalach Mtn.

AMC River Guide Committee see Schweiker, Roioli.

Amchin, Jess & Leflar, Robert B. The Hazards of Intra-Ocular Lenses. 81p. 1982. 5.00. Pub Citizen Inc.

Amdrup, E., jt. ed. see Rehfeld, J. F.

Amdur, Neil, jt. auth. see Evert-Lloyd, Chris.

Amdur, Nikki. One of Us. LC 81-65847. (Illus.). (gr. 3-6). 1981. 8.95 (ISBN 0-8037-6742-0); PLB 8.89 (ISBN 0-8037-6743-9). Dial Bks Young.

Amdursky, Robert S. Third Annual Institute on Municipal Finance Law. (Real Estate Law & Practice Course Handbook: Vol. 249). 726p. 1984. 35.00 (ISBN 0-317-11473-5, N4-4429). PLI.

Ameco Publishing. Radio Amateur Log Book. 1965. spiral bdg. 1.50 (ISBN 0-912146-09-5). AMECO.

Amedeo, Douglas & Golledge, Reginald G. An Introduction to Scientific Reasoning in Geography. LC 84-9656. 448p. 1985. Repr. of 1975 ed. lib. bdg. write for info. (ISBN 0-89874-764-3). Krieger.

Amedroz, H. F., tr. see Miskawayh, et al.

Ameen, Mark. A Circle of Sirens. LC 85-2129. 140p. (Orig.). 1985. pap. 6.95 (ISBN 0-933322-21-6). Sea Horse.

Ameer, B., et al. Pharmacy Practice for the Geriatric Patient. Brown, C. H., ed. Date not set. pap. text ed. price not set. Health Con NC.

Ameiss, Albert P. & Kargas, Nicholas A. Accountant's Desk Handbook. 2nd rev. ed. 437p. 1982. 41.50 (ISBN 0-13-001461-3). P-H.

Amelar, Richard D., et al. Male Infertility. LC 76-50145. (Illus.). 258p. 1977. text ed. 28.95 (ISBN 0-7216-1214-8). Saunders.

Amelin, B., jt. auth. see Pinkevich, A.

Amelinckx, S. The Direct Observation of Dislocations. (Solid State Physics Ser.: Suppl. 6). 1964. 75.00 (ISBN 0-12-607766-5). Acad Pr.

Amelinckx, S., et al. Diffraction & Imaging Techniques in Materials Science, 2 vols, Vols. 1& 2. 2nd rev. ed. 1978. Set. 134.00 (ISBN 0-444-85130-5, North-Holland); Vol. 1: Electron Microscopy. 76.75 (ISBN 0-444-85128-3); Vol. 2: Imaging & Diffraction Techniques. 76.50 (ISBN 0-444-85129-1). Elsevier.

Amelinckx, S., et al, eds. Solid State Dosimetry. 744p. 1970. 149.25 (ISBN 0-677-13470-3). Gordon.

Amelineau, D. Contes romans de l'Egypte chretienne, 2 vols. LC 78-20122. (Collection de contes et de chansons populaires: Vols. 13-14). Repr. of 1888 ed. Set. 43.00 (ISBN 0-404-60396-3). AMS Pr.

Ameling, W., ed. First European Simulation Congress: ESC 83. (Informatik-Fachberichte Ser.: Vol. 71). 653p. 1983. pap. 27.60 (ISBN 0-387-12723-2). Springer Verlag.

Amembal, Sudhir P., jt. auth. see Isom, Terry A.

Amemiya, Takeshi. Advanced Econometrics. (Illus.). 576p. 1985. text ed. 39.50x (ISBN 0-674-00560-0). Harvard U Pr.

Amen, Carol. Changing Problems into Challenges. (Uplook Ser.). 1972. pap. 0.79 (ISBN 0-8163-0068-2, 03109-6). Pacific Pr Pub Assn.

--Don't Forget Thank You. (Uplook Ser.). 32p. 1981. pap. 0.79 (ISBN 0-8163-0370-3). Pacific Pr Pub Assn.

--Hyacinths to Feed the Soul. LC 74-33850. (Better Living Ser.). 64p. 1975. pap. text ed. 0.99 (ISBN 0-8127-0094-5). Review & Herald.

--Love Is the Motive. LC 77-12655. (Better Living Ser.). 1977. pap. 0.99 (ISBN 0-8127-0153-4). Review & Herald.

--Pass It on Talents. (Uplook Ser.). 29p. 1978. pap. 0.79 (ISBN 0-317-00061-6). Pacific Pr Pub Assn.

--Teetering on the Tightrope. LC 79-18718. (Orion Ser.). 1979. pap. 2.95 (ISBN 0-8127-0250-6). Review & Herald.

Amen, Carol V. Love Goes 'Round the Circle. (Better Living Ser.). pap. 0.99 (ISBN 0-8280-1268-7). Review & Herald.

Amen, E. W. see Ortmann, Otto.

Amen, Michael M. American Foreign Policy in Greece 1944-1949: Economic, Military & Institutional Aspects. (European University Studies: Series 31, Political Science: Vol. 13). 310p. 1978. 37.25 (ISBN 3-261-02436-4). P Lang Pubs.

Amen, Ronald J., jt. ed. see Spiller, Gene A.

Amend, Karen, jt. auth. see Ruiz, Mary S.

Amend, Karen S., jt. auth. see Ruiz, Mary.

Amendola, B. E. & Amendola, M. A., eds. Radiation Oncology. 350p. 1984. 56.50 (ISBN 0-444-00846-2, Biomedical Pr). Elsevier.

--Recent Trends in Radiation Oncology & Related Fields: Proceedings of the Spring Symposium in Radiation Oncology, Second Annual Conference April 15-17, 1983. 315p. 1983. 56.50 (ISBN 0-444-00846-2). Elsevier.

Amendola, J. Ice Carving Made Easy. (Illus.). pap. 20.00x (ISBN 0-685-47434-8). Corner.

Amendola, Joseph. Baker's Manual for Quantity Baking & Pastry Making. rev., 3rd ed. (Illus.). 220p. 1972. 14.50 (ISBN 0-8104-9458-2). Hayden.

--Ice Carving Made Easy. rev. ed. (Illus.). 88p. 1970. pap. 18.95 (ISBN 0-911202-10-2). Radio City.

--Understanding Baking. 216p. 1970. pap. 14.95 (ISBN 0-8436-0521-9). Van Nos Reinhold.

Amendola, Joseph & Berrini, James. Practical Cooking & Baking for Schools & Institutions. (Illus.). 1971. 12.95 (ISBN 0-8104-9457-4). Hayden.

Amendola, Joseph, jt. auth. see Wilkinson, Jule.

Amendola, M. A., jt. ed. see Amendola, B. E.

Amendola, Sal. Perspective for the Artist. (Illus.). 64p. (Orig.). 1983. pap. 4.95 (Pentalic). Taplinger.

Ament, jt. auth. see Reiff.

Ament, Istvan. A Systematic Approach to Classical Ballet: A Four-Year Program. LC 85-6215. (Illus.). 352p. (Orig.). 1985. lib. bdg. 26.50 (ISBN 0-8191-4689-7); pap. text ed. 12.75 (ISBN 0-8191-4690-0). U Pr of Amer.

Ament, Susan, jt. auth. see Sherwin, Byron.

Amenta, Peter S. Histology & Embryology Review. 2nd ed. LC 82-11322. (Illus.). 208p. 1983. pap. 13.95 (ISBN 0-668-05486-7). ACC.

Amenta, Peter S., ed. Histology. 3rd ed. (Medical Outline Ser.). 1983. spiral bdg. 16.50 (ISBN 0-87488-662-7). Med Exam.

Amenzade, Y. W. The Theory of Elasticity. 284p. 1979. 8.45 (ISBN 0-8285-1522-0, Pub. by Mir Pubs USSR). Imported Pubns.

Amer, R. A. & Schwarz, H. R. Contributions to the Approximation Problem of Electrical Filters. (Mitteilungen Institut Fur Angewandte Math, ETH, Zurich Ser.: No. 9). 99p. 1964. pap. 20.95x (ISBN 0-8176-0004-3). Birkhauser.

Amerdongen, C. Van see Koncz, T.

Ameri, Houshang. Politics & Process in the Specialized Agencies of the United Nations. 304p. 1982. text ed. 46.00x (ISBN 0-566-00538-7). Gower Pub Co.

America Pulpwood Association. Chain Saw Manual. Modified ed. 118p. 1980. pap. text ed. 6.25x (ISBN 0-8134-2133-0). Interstate.

America, R. & Anderson, B. Moving Ahead: Black Managers in American Business. LC 78-3642. 1978. 24.95 (ISBN 0-07-001355-1). McGraw.

American Academy & Institute of Arts & Letters. American Academy & Institute of Arts & Letters Proceedings, No. 32. 100p. 1982. 12.00 (ISBN 0-915974-26-6). Am Acad Inst Arts.

American Academy for Jewish Research. Louis Ginzberg Jubilee Volume on the Occasion of His 70th Birthday, 2 Vols. (Eng-Heb). 1945. Set. 28.00 (ISBN 0-527-02359-0). Kraus Repr.

American Academy in Rome. American Academy in Rome. Incl. American Academy in Rome. (Memoirs: No. 24). (Illus.). 264p. 1956. 30.50 (ISBN 0-318-12312-6); American Academy in Rome. (Memoirs: No. 25). (Illus.). 193p. 1957. 24.50 (ISBN 0-318-12313-4); American Academy in Rome. (Memoirs: No. 27). (Illus.). 224p. 19.00 (ISBN 0-318-12314-2); American Academy in Rome. (Memoirs: No. 34). (Illus.). 280p. 1980. 30.50 (ISBN 0-318-12315-0). (Memoirs: No. 1). (Illus.). 172p. 1917. 30.50 (ISBN 0-318-12311-8). Am Acad Rome.

--The Imperialism of Mid-Republican Rome. (Papers & Monographs: No. 29). 194p. 1984. 16.50 (ISBN 0-318-18020-0). Am Acad Rome.

American Academy of Arts & Letters. Academy Papers. facs. ed. LC 70-117749. (Essay Index Reprint Ser). 1925. 19.00 (ISBN 0-8369-1641-7). Ayer Co Pubs.

American Academy Of Arts And Letters. Commemorative Tributes of the Academy, 1905-1941. facs. ed. LC 68-20286. (Essay Index Reprint Ser). 1942. 21.50 (ISBN 0-8369-0147-9). Ayer Co Pubs.

American Academy of Arts & Letters Staff. Four Addresses in Commemoration of the Twentieth Anniversary of the Founding of the Academy: Academy Publ., No. 54. facs. ed. LC 67-22068. (Essay Index Reprint Ser). 1926. 12.00 (ISBN 0-8369-0148-7). Ayer Co Pubs.

American Academy of Arts & Sciences, jt. auth. see Miller, Steven E.

American Academy of Arts and Sciences, Boston. Science & the Modern Mind: A Symposium. facsimile ed. Gerald, Holton, ed. LC 70-167304. (Essay Index Reprint Ser). Repr. of 1958 ed. 12.00 (ISBN 0-8369-2446-0). Ayer Co Pubs.

American Academy of Gnathologic Orthopedics. American Academy of Gnathologic Orthopedics Roster. (Illus.). 120p. pap. avail. Am Acad Gnatho.

American Academy of Orthopaedic Surgeons. American Academy of Orthopaedic Surgeons: Instructional Course Lectures, Vols. 21-29. Incl. Vol. 21. 1972; Vol. 22. 1973; Vol. 23. 1974; Vol. 24. 328p. 1975; Vol. 25. 1976; Vol. 26. 1977; Vol. 27. 1978; Vol. 28. 1979; Vol. 29. 156p. 1980. 46.50 (ISBN 0-8016-0047-2). LC 43-17054. Mosby.

--Atlas of Limb Prosthetics: Surgical & Prosthetic Principles. LC 80-16572. (Illus.). 668p. 1981. 85.95 (ISBN 0-8016-0058-8). Mosby.

--Atlas of Orthotics: Biomechanical Principals & Applications. LC 75-22185. (Illus.). 508p. 1975. 65.95 (ISBN 0-8016-0021-9). Mosby.

--Instructional Course Lectures, Vol. XXX. LC 43-17054. (Illus.). 496p. 1981. text ed. 61.95 (ISBN 0-8016-0048-0). Mosby.

American Academy of Orthopaedic Surgeons, Symposium on Total Joint Replacement of the Upper Extremity. Proceedings. LC 81-18677. (Illus.). 321p. 1982. text ed. 47.95 (ISBN 0-8016-0017-0). Mosby.

American Academy of Orthopaedic Surgeons. Symposium on Heritable Disorders of Connective Tissue. LC 82-6333. (Illus.). 380p. 1982. text ed. 55.95 (ISBN 0-8016-0129-0). Mosby.

--Symposium on the Athlete's Knee: Surgical Repair & Reconstruction. LC 80-19414. (Illus.). 218p. 1981. text ed. 52.95 (ISBN 0-8016-0077-4). Mosby.

--Symposium on the Foot & Ankle. Kiene, Richard H. & Johnson, Kenneth A., eds. LC 82-21716. (Illus.). 259p. 1983. text ed. 47.50 (ISBN 0-8016-0133-9). Mosby.

--Symposium on the Foot & Leg in Running Sports. LC 82-8188. (Illus.). 184p. 1982. text ed. 41.95 (ISBN 0-8016-0054-5). Mosby.

--Symposium on the Lumbar Spine. LC 81-11043. (Illus.). 259p. 1981. text ed. 51.95 (ISBN 0-8016-0080-4). Mosby.

--Symposium on Trauma to the Leg & Its Sequelae. LC 81-11104. (Illus.). 388p. 1981. text ed. 59.50 (ISBN 0-8016-0081-2). Mosby.

American Academy of Orthopedic Surgeons. Instructional Course Lectures, Vol. 31. LC 43-10754. (Illus.). 282p. 1982. text ed. 49.95 (ISBN 0-8016-0062-6). Mosby.

--Joint Motion: Method of Measuring & Recording. (Illus.). 1972. pap. 3.75 (ISBN 0-443-00270-3). Churchill.

--Symposium on Idiopathic Low Back Pain. White, Agustus A. & Gordon, Stephen L., eds. (Illus.). 492p. 1982. text ed. 56.95 (ISBN 0-8016-0059-6). Mosby.

American Academy of Pediatrics. Child Health Services & Pediatric Education: Report of the Committee for the Study of Child Health Services. facsimile ed. LC 74-1661. (Children & Youth Ser.). 304p. 1974. Repr. of 1949 ed. 24.50x (ISBN 0-405-05943-4). Ayer Co Pubs.

American Academy Of Pediatrics, jt. auth. see American Medical Association.

American Academy of Podiatric Sports Medecine. Sports Medicine Eighty: A Review by the Members of the American Academy of Podiatric Sports Medicine, Pt. 1. Rinaldi, Robert R. & Sabia, Michael L., eds. LC 80-66360. (Archives of Podiatric Medicine & Foot Surgery: Supplement III). (Illus.). 200p. 1980. pap. 15.00 (ISBN 0-87993-141-8). Futura Pub.

American Academy of Political & Social Science, 79th. Adjusting to Scarcity: Proceedings. Lambert, Richard D. & Wolfgang, Marvin E., eds. LC 74-29624. (Annals Ser.: No. 420). 250p. 1975. pap. 7.95 (ISBN 0-87761-191-2). Am Acad Pol Soc Sci.

American Academy of Political & Social Science. American Negro. Young, Donald R., ed. LC 28-29716. Repr. of 1928 ed. 23.00 (ISBN 0-527-02100-8). Kraus Repr.

American Academy Of Political And Social Science. America's Race Problems. LC 75-78759. Repr. of 1901 ed. 15.00 (ISBN 0-8371-1385-7, ARP&, Pub. by Negro U Pr). Greenwood.

American Academy of Political & Social Science. America's Race Problems. LC 72-95419. (Studies in Black History & Culture, No. 54). 1970. Repr. of 1901 ed. lib. bdg. 48.95x (ISBN 0-8383-0959-3). Haskell.

--Annals of the American Academy of Political & Social Science. LC 76-112556. (Literature of Cinema Ser). Repr. of 1970 ed. 19.00 (ISBN 0-405-01601-8). Ayer Co Pubs.

American Academy of Political & Social Science & Greene, Lee S., eds. City Bosses & Political Machines. LC 72-14147. (Essay Index Reprint Ser.). Repr. of 1964 ed. 18.75 (ISBN 0-518-10000-6). Ayer Co Pubs.

American Academy of Political & Social Science, Annual Meeting, 83rd. The Environment & the Quality of Life: A World View: Proceedings. Wolfgang, Marvin E. & Ginsberg, Ralph B., eds. LC 79-50266. (Annals: No. 444). 1979. 15.00 (ISBN 0-87761-240-4); pap. 7.95 (ISBN 0-87761-241-2). Am Acad Pol Soc Sci.

American Academy Of Political And Social Science. Negro's Progress in Fifty Years. LC 71-92737. Repr. of 1913 ed. 19.75x (ISBN 0-8371-2187-6, NEP&, Pub. by Negro U Pr). Greenwood.

American Academy of Political & Social Science, Philadelphia. The Police & the Crime Problem. Sellin, Thorsten, ed. Repr. of 1929 ed. 24.50 (ISBN 0-404-09145-8). AMS Pr.

--Prisons in Transformation: Proceedings. Sellin, Thorsten, ed. LC 79-90462. 227p. 1974. Repr. of 1954 ed. lib. bdg. 22.50 (ISBN 0-8371-6170-3, PRIT). Greenwood.

American Academy of Political & Social Science. Reform in Administration of Justice. LC 79-156961. (Foundations of Criminal Justice Ser.). Repr. of 1914 ed. 16.00 (ISBN 0-404-09101-6). AMS Pr.

--The Revolution, the Constitution & America's Third Century, 2 vols. 1980. 50.00x (ISBN 0-8122-7763-5); manual 4.95x (ISBN 0-686-77594-5). U of Pa Pr.

American Accounting Association. Accounting & Reporting Standards for Corporate Financial Statements & Preceding Statements & Supplements. 64p. 1.00 (ISBN 0-318-12336-3); members 0.50 (ISBN 0-318-12337-1). Am Accounting.

American Air Mail Society. American Air Mail Catalogue, 5 vols. 2138p. (Vol. 1, 478p.; Vol. 2, 521p.; Vol. 3, 520p.; Vol. 4, 619p.). Vol. 1,2 & 3. 12.50, ea. (ISBN 0-318-12354-1); Vol. 4. 18.00 (ISBN 0-318-12355-X); Vol. 5. fall 1984 avail. Am Air Mail.

--Ellington-Zwisler Pocket Mail Catalog, 2 Vols. 180p. 1973. 10.00 ea.; Set. 17.50 (ISBN 0-318-12360-6); for members 8.00 (ISBN 0-318-12361-4). Am Air Mail.

American Alliance. Shaping the Body Politic. 9.95x (ISBN 0-317-06643-9). AAHPERD.

American Alliance for Health, Physical Education, Recreation & Dance. Basketball Skills Test Manual: Boys & Girls. 1984. soft bdg. 5.25x (ISBN 0-88314-265-1). AAHPERD.

American Alliance for Health, Physical Education & Recreation. Best of Challenge, 3 vols. Incl. Vol. 1. Articles from the Dec. 1965 Through May-June 1970 Issues (ISBN 0-88314-032-2, 245-25124); Vol. 2. Articles from the Sep.-Oct. 1970 Through May-June 1973 Issues (ISBN 0-88314-033-0, 245-25562); Vol. 3. Articles from Sept. 73-May 76 (ISBN 0-88314-034-9). pap. 4.95x ea. AAHPERD.

--Children's Dance. rev. ed. 1981. pap. 9.40x (ISBN 0-88314-041-1). AAHPERD.

American Alliance for Health Physical Recreation & Dance. Dance Heritage. (Focus on Dance: VIII). 96p. 1977. 8.65 (ISBN 0-88314-073-X, 243-25952). AAHPERD.

American Alliance for Health, Physical Education, Recreation & Dance. Directories of Professional Preparation Programs in Physical Education: Directory of Graduate Physical Education Programs. 80p. 1982. 6.50 (ISBN 0-88314-058-6). AAHPERD.

--Directories of Professional Preparation Programs in Physical Education: Directory of Undergraduate Physical Education Programs. 96p. 1982. 6.50 (ISBN 0-88314-059-4). AAHPERD.

--The Drug Alternative. 96p. 1974. 3.10 (ISBN 0-88314-061-6, 244-25604). AAHPERD.

--Echoes of Influence for Elementary School Physical Education. 151p. 1977. 9.70 (ISBN 0-88314-063-2, 245-25980). AAHPERD.

--Encyclopedia of Physical Education, Fitness & Sports: Sports, Dance & Related Activities. 973p. 1977. 39.90 (ISBN 0-317-31994-9). AAHPERD.

--Encyclopedia of Physical Education, Fitness, & Sports: Training, Environment, Nutrition & Fitness. 614p. 1980. 39.90 (ISBN 0-317-31995-7, 240-26754). AAHPERD.

American Alliance for Health, Physical Education & Recreation. Field Hockey Guide 1984-86. (NAGWS Sports Guides Ser.). pap. 3.95x (ISBN 0-88314-286-4). AAHPERD.

--Focus on Dance: Dance Therapy, Vol. 7. 80p. 1974. pap. 8.65x (ISBN 0-88314-072-1, 243-25570). AAHPERD.

American Alliance for Health, Physical Education Recreation & Dance. Gymnastics Guide: 1982-1984. (NAGWS Sports Guides Ser.). plastic bdg. 6.95 (ISBN 0-88314-085-3). AAHPERD.

American Alliance for Health, Physical Education & Recreation. Health Education. 252p. 1975. pap. 6.25 (ISBN 0-88314-097-7). AAHPERD.

American Alliance for Health, Physical Education, Recreation & Dance. Health Education Teaching Ideas: Secondary. 1984. soft bdg. 6.85 (ISBN 0-88314-238-4). AAHPERD.

American Alliance for Health Physical Education Recreation & Dance. Health, Physical Education, Recreation & Dance for the Older Adult: A Modular Approach. 264p. 1980. 9.40 (ISBN 0-88314-101-9, 245-26766). AAHPERD.

American Alliance for Health, Physical Education, Recreation & Dance. Ideas II: A Sharing of Teaching Practices by Secondary School Physical Education Practitioners. 1984. soft bdg. 9.95x (ISBN 0-88314-264-3). AAHPERD.

--Leisure Today - Selected Readings, Vol. III. 1984. pap. 12.95x (ISBN 0-88314-287-2). AAHPERD.

American Alliance for Health, Physical Education & Recreation. Movement Activities for Places & Spaces. 48p. 1978. pap. 3.95 (ISBN 0-88314-133-7). AAHPERD.

--Special Olympics Instructional Manual: From Beginners to Champions. 128p. 1972. pap. 6.55x (ISBN 0-88314-173-6). AAHPERD.

American Alliance for Health, Physical Education, & Recreation. Sports Skill Test Manuals for Ages 10-18, 8 bks. Incl. Bk. 1. Archery (Boys & Girls (ISBN 0-88314-178-7, 242-07328); Bk. 2. Basketball (Boys; Bk. 3 o.p. Basketball (Girls (ISBN 0-88314-179-5). (242-07736); Bk. 4. Football (Boys (ISBN 0-88314-180-9). (242-07644); Bk. 5. Softball (Boys (ISBN 0-88314-181-7); Bk. 6. Softball (Girls; Bk. 7. Volleyball (Boys & Girls (ISBN 0-88314-182-5). (242-07946). pap. 3.95 ea. AAHPERD.

American Alliance for Health, Physical Education & Recreation. Swimnastics Is Fun, Vol. 1. 1975. 7.30 (ISBN 0-88314-185-X). AAHPERD.

American Alliance for Health, Physical Education, Recreation & Dance. Tennis Group Instruction, II. (NASPE Sports Guides Ser.). 64p. 1984. soft bdg. 7.95 (ISBN 0-88314-263-5, 245-26704). AAHPERD.
--Tennis Guide: 1984-1986. 1984. 3.95 (ISBN 0-88314-282-1). AAHPERD.
--Track & Field Guide, 1983-1985. (NACWS Sports Guides Ser.). soft bdg. 3.95 (ISBN 0-88314-267-8). AAHPERD.
--Training, Environment, Nutrition, & Fitness. (Encyclopedia of Physical Education, Fitness & Sports). (Illus.). 614p. 1980. 39.90 (ISBN 0-317-32060-2, 240-26754). AAHPERD.
--Volley Ball Guide: June 1984-June 1985. (NAGWS Sports Guides Ser.). 1984. 4.95 (ISBN 0-88314-284-8). AAHPERD.
American Alliance for Health, Physical Education & Recreation. Volleyball Scorebook. pap. 3.00 (ISBN 0-88314-169-8). AAHPERD.
American & British Committee for the International Greek New Testament Project. The New Testament in Greek: The Gospel According to St. Luke, Vol. 3, Pt. 1. (The New Testament in Greek Ser.). 1983. 98.00x (ISBN 0-19-826167-5). Oxford U Pr.
American Animal Hospital Association Annual Meeting, 1981. Scientific Proceedings. 408p. 7.50 (ISBN 0-318-17665-3); members 5.00 (ISBN 0-318-17666-1). Am Animal Hosp Assoc.
American Animal Hospital Association Annual Meeting. Scientific Proceedings. 534p. 1982. 7.50 (ISBN 0-318-17694-7); members 5.00 (ISBN 0-318-17695-5). Am Animal Hosp Assoc.
--Scientific Proceedings. 485p. 1983. 7.50 (ISBN 0-318-17696-3); members 5.00 (ISBN 0-318-17697-1). Am Animal Hosp Assoc.
--Scientific Proceedings. 467p. 1984. 30.00 (ISBN 0-318-17698-X); members 10.00 (ISBN 0-318-17699-8). Am Animal Hosp Assoc.
American Anti-Slave Society. Slavery & the Internal Slave Trade in the U. S. LC 70-92411. 1841. Repr. 16.00 (ISBN 0-403-00146-3). Scholarly.
American Anti-Slavery Society. American Anti-Slavery Reporter, Nos. 1-8. Repr. of 1834 ed. 25.00 (ISBN 0-8371-3053-0, AAR&, Pub. by Negro U Pr). Greenwood.
--Anti-Slavery Examiner, Nos. 1-14. 1836-1845. Repr. 61.00x (ISBN 0-8371-3219-3, ASE&, Pub. by Negro U Pr). Greenwood.
--Anti-Slavery History of the John Brown Year. LC 76-76852. Repr. of 1861 ed. 22.50x (ISBN 0-8371-1165-X, ASH&, Pub. by Negro U Pr). Greenwood.
--Anti-Slavery History of the John Brown Year: Being the Twenty-Seventh Report of the American Anti-Slavery Society. LC 70-82169. (Anti-Slavery Crusade in America Ser.). 1969. Repr. of 1861 ed. 15.00 (ISBN 0-405-00604-7). Ayer Co Pubs.
--Anti-Slavery Record, Vols. 1-3. 1835-1837. Repr. cancelled (ISBN 0-8371-3054-9, ANR&, Pub. by Negro U Pr). Greenwood.
--Anti-Slavery Tracts: Second Series, Nos. 1-25. 2nd ed. 1855-1861. Repr. 99.00x (ISBN 0-8371-9106-8, AST&, Pub. by Negro U Pr). Greenwood.
--Legion of Liberty & Force of Truth, Containing the Thoughts, Words, & Deeds of Some Prominent Apostles, Champions, & Martyrs. LC 71-82199. (Anti-Slavery Crusade in America Ser.). (Illus.). 1969. Repr. of 1844 ed. 16.00 (ISBN 0-405-00605-5). Ayer Co Pubs.
--Proceedings of the American Anti-Slavery Society at Its Third Decade. LC 79-82166. (Anti-Slavery Crusade in America Ser). 1969. Repr. of 1864 ed. 9.00 (ISBN 0-405-00606-3). Ayer Co Pubs.
--Proceedings of the American Anti-Slavery Society at Its Third Decade. LC 77-97417. 15.00x (ISBN 0-8371-2725-4, AAS&). Greenwood.
American Anti-Slavery Society - Philadelphia -1853. Proceedings of the American Anti-Slavery Society at Its Second Decade. LC 78-111562. Repr. of 1854 ed. 17.50x (ISBN 0-8371-4583-X, AAQ&). Greenwood.
American Antiquarian Society. Catalogue of the Manuscript Collections of the American Antiquarian Society, 40 Vols. 1979. lib. bdg. 390.00 (ISBN 0-8161-0258-9, Hall Library). G K Hall.
--Transactions & Collections, 12 Vols. Set. 460.00 (ISBN 0-384-01057-1); Set. pap. 400.00 (ISBN 0-685-02203-X). Johnson Repr.
American Antiquarian Society & Tate, Thad W. The Discovery & Development of the Southern Colonial Landscape, Six Commentators: Proceedings, American Antiquarian Society, October 1983. 22p. 1984. pap. 3.25 (ISBN 0-912296-63-1). Am Antiquarian.
American Arbitration Association. Commerical Arbitration Rules of the American Arbitration Association Annoted (As Amended & in Effect February 1, 1984) write for info. Amer Bar Assn.
--Dictionary of Arbitration & Its Terms. LC 70-94692. 334p. 1970. lib. bdg. 21.00 (ISBN 0-379-00386-4). Oceana.
--Lawyers' Arbitration Letters, 1970 to 1979. LC 80-39817. 1981. 19.95 (ISBN 0-02-900570-1). Free Pr.
--New Strategies for Peaceful Resolution of International Business Disputes. LC 78-158817. 252p. 1972. 11.50 (ISBN 0-379-00066-0). Oceana.
--Yearbook: Commercial Arbitration, Vol. I. 268p. 1976. 15.80 (ISBN 0-318-12393-2). Am Arbitration.
American Arbitration Association Conference. Dispute Resolution Training: The State of the Art. 116p. 5.00 (ISBN 0-318-12375-4); members 3.75 (ISBN 0-318-12376-2). Am Arbitration.
--The Future of Labor Arbitration in America. 320p. 10.00 (ISBN 0-318-12381-9); members 7.50 (ISBN 0-318-12382-7). Am Arbitration.
American Arbitration Association Staff & McCarthy, Jane E. Negotiating Settlements: A Guide to Environmental Mediation. LC 84-70963. 107p. 1984. 10.00 (ISBN 0-318-04282-7). Am Arbitration.
American Artist Magazine. American Artist Diary Nineteen Eighty-Four. (Annual Ser.). (Illus.). 232p. 1983. 12.95 (ISBN 0-8230-0196-2). Watson-Guptill.
American Artists' Congress. Graphic Works of the American '30s. (Quality Paperbacks Ser.). (Illus.). 1977. pap. 7.95 (ISBN 0-306-80078-0). Da Capo.
American Artists Magazine Staff, ed. Learning from the Pros. (Illus.). 80p. 1984. pap. 6.95 (ISBN 0-8230-2680-9). Watson-Guptill.
American Assembly. Arms Control. facs. ed. LC 75-117750. (Essay Index Reprint Ser). 1961. 18.00 (ISBN 0-8369-1780-4). Ayer Co Pubs.
--Economic Security for Americans. facs. ed. LC 72-111811. (Essay Index Reprint Ser). 1954. 25.50 (ISBN 0-8369-1640-9). Ayer Co Pubs.
--Ethnic Relations in America. LC 82-552. pap. 48.50 (ISBN 0-317-29321-4, 2022328). Bks Demand UMI.
--The Nuclear Power Controversy. Murphy, Arthur W., ed. LC 76-40017. pap. 36.50 (ISBN 0-317-10099-8, 2015398). Bks Demand UMI.
--Outer Space: Prospects for Man & Society. rev. ed. Bloomfield, Lincoln P., ed. LC 72-3391. (Essay Index Reprint Ser.). Repr. of 1968 ed. 17.00 (ISBN 0-8369-2886-5). Ayer Co Pubs.
--Secretary of State. facs. ed. LC 73-133511. (Select Bibliographies Reprint Ser). 1960. 17.00 (ISBN 0-8369-5543-9). Ayer Co Pubs.
--United States & Africa. facs. ed. LC 75-117751. (Essay Index Reprint Ser). 1963. 20.00 (ISBN 0-8369-1781-2). Ayer Co Pubs.
--The United States & the Far East. 2nd ed. Thorp, Willard L., ed. LC 62-12831. pap. 48.00 (ISBN 0-317-08145-4, 2050840). Bks Demand UMI.
--U. S. Monetary Policy. facsimile & rev. ed. Jacoby, Neil H., ed. LC 79-164586. (Select Bibliographies Reprint Ser). Repr. of 1964 ed. 18.00 (ISBN 0-8369-5702-4). Ayer Co Pubs.
American Assembly & Stevens, G. G. The United States & the Middle East. (New Reprints in Essay & General Literature Index Ser.). 1975. Repr. of 1964 ed. 20.25 (ISBN 0-518-10195-9, 10195). Ayer Co Pubs.
American Assembly of Collegiate Schools of Business & European Foundation for Management Development, eds. Management for the Twenty-First Century: Education & Development. 1982. lib. bdg. 17.00 (ISBN 0-89838-097-9). Kluwer-Nijhoff.
American Assembly Staff. Global Companies: The Political Economy of World Business. Ball, George W., ed. LC 75-5557. pap. 48.00 (ISBN 0-317-27773-1, 2015397). Bks Demand UMI.
American Assn. of Homes for the Aging Staff. Continuing Care Issues for Nonprofit Providers. Cloud, Deborah A., ed. LC 84-73167. 65p. 1985. pap. text ed. 12.00x (ISBN 0-943774-23-3, 23-3). Am Assn Homes.
--The Volunteer Leader: Essays on the Role of Trustees of Nonprofit Facilities & Services for the Aging. Cloud, Deborah A., ed. LC 84-73168. 146p. (Orig.). 1985. pap. text ed. 10.00x (ISBN 0-943774-24-1, 24-1). Am Assn Homes.
American Association for Artifical Intelligence. Artificial Intelligence: Proceedings of the National Conference, 4th, 1984. 500p. 1984. pap. 45.00 (ISBN 0-86576-080-2). W Kaufmann.
American Association for Artifical Intelligence, National Conference on Artificial Intelligence, AAAI 82, Pittsburgh, Pa., Aug. 1982. Proceedings. 437p. (Orig.). 1982. pap. text ed. 45.00x (ISBN 0-86576-043-8). W Kaufmann.
American Association for Artificial Intelligence. Annual Naitonal Conference on Artificial Intelligence, 1st: Proceedings. (Illus.). 349p. 1980. 40.00 (ISBN 0-86576-052-7). Amer Artificial.
American Association for Artificial Intelligence National Conference, 1982. Artificial Intelligence: Proceedings. 1982. 45.00 (ISBN 0-86576-043-8). W Kaufmann.
American Association for Artificial Intelligence. Artificial Intelligence: Proceedings of the First Annual National Conference, 1980. (Illus.). 350p. 1980. 40.00 (ISBN 0-86576-052-7). W Kaufmann.
--Artificial Intelligence: Proceedings of the National Conference, 1983. (Illus.). 368p. (Orig.). 1983. 45.00 (ISBN 0-86576-065-9). W Kaufmann.
American Association for Artificial Intelligence Staff. Artificial Intelligence: Proceedings of the National Conference, 1984. (Illus.). 500p. 1984. ref. ed. 45.00 (ISBN 0-86576-080-2). Amer Artificial.
American Association for Artificial Intelligence. National Conference on Artificial Intelligence: Proceedings, 18-20 August 1982. (Illus.). 455p. 1982. 45.00 (ISBN 0-86576-043-8). Amer Artificial.
American Association for Ethiopian Jews. Jewish Survival: The Tale of Three Communities. 115p. 8.50 (ISBN 0-318-12399-1). Am Assn Ethiopian Jews.
American Association for Gifted Children. The Gifted Child. Witty, Paul, ed. LC 79-148630. 338p. 1972. Repr. of 1951 ed. lib. bdg. 21.50x (ISBN 0-8371-6002-2, AAGC). Greenwood.
--Gifted Child, the Family & the Community. Miller, Bernard S. & Price, Merle, eds. 246p. 1981. 17.50 (ISBN 0-8027-0673-8). Walker & Co.
--On Being Gifted. LC 78-58622. 1979. pap. 8.95 (ISBN 0-8027-7138-6). Walker & Co.
--Reaching Out: Advocacy for the Gifted & Talented. Tannenbaum, Abraham J., ed. LC 80-14342. (Perspectives on Gifted & Talented Education Ser.). (Orig.). 1980. pap. text ed. 5.75x (ISBN 0-8077-2591-9). Tchrs Coll.
American Association for the Advancement of Science - Symposia Presented at the Chicago Meeting. Aging, Some Social & Biological Aspects: Proceedings. Shock, Nathan W., ed. LC 73-167305. (Essay Index Reprint Ser.). Repr. of 1960 ed. 33.00 (ISBN 0-8369-2735-4). Ayer Co Pubs.
American Association for the Advancement of Science Staff. Astronomical Photoelectric Photometry. Wood, Frank B., ed. LC 53-12745. pap. 37.30 (ISBN 0-317-07843-7, 2000204). Bks Demand UMI.
American Association for the Advancement of Science, Section, L, 1949. Boston Studies in the Philosophy of Science, Vol. 11: Philosophical Foundations of Science, Proceedings. Seeger, R. J. & Cohen, R. S., eds. LC 73-83555. (Synthese Library: No. 58). 545p. 1974. 66.00 (ISBN 90-277-0390-6, Pub. by Reidel Holland); pap. 34.00 (ISBN 90-277-0376-0). Kluwer Academic.
American Association for the Advancement of Science. The Breaking of Minds & Bodies. Stover, Eric & Nightingale, Elena O., eds. LC 85-4512. 352p. 1985. 21.95 (ISBN 0-7167-1732-8); pap. 11.95 (ISBN 0-7167-1733-6). W H Freeman.
American Association for the Advancement of Science, Dallas, December, 1968. Global Effects of Environmental Pollution: A Symposium. Singer, S. F., ed. LC 78-118129. 218p. 1970. lib. bdg. 26.00 (ISBN 90-277-0151-2, Pub. by Reidel Holland). Kluwer Academic.
American Association for the Advancement of Science. Ground Level Climatology: A Symposium Presented at the Berkeley Meeting of the American Association for the Advancement of Science. Shaw, Robert H., ed. LC 67-29427. (American Association for the Advancement of Science Publication: No. 86). pap. 101.80 (ISBN 0-317-09580-3, 2015168). Bks Demand UMI.
--Industrial Science, Present & Future. facs. ed. Christman, Rutch C. & Bonnell, Allen T., eds. LC 70-90598. (Essay Index Reprint Ser). 1952. 17.00 (ISBN 0-8369-1201-2). Ayer Co Pubs.
American Association for the Advancement of Science, et al. National Energy Policy Conference: Proceedings. (AAAS Report: No. 77-R-5). 1977. pap. 6.00 (ISBN 0-87168-247-8). AAAS.
American Association For The Advancement Of Science - New York - 1949. Present State of Physics. facsimile ed. Brackett, Frederick S., ed. LC 75-99617. (Essay Index Reprint Ser.). 1954. 27.50 (ISBN 0-8369-1542-9). Ayer Co Pubs.
American Association for the Advancement of Science, Section on Engineering Staff. Systems of Units, National & International Aspects: A Symposium Organized by Section M on Engineering. Kayan, Carl F., ed. LC 59-15335. (American Association for the Advancement of Science Ser.: No. 57). pap. 76.80 (ISBN 0-317-27548-8, 2015170). Bks Demand UMI.
American Association for the Cure of Inebriates. Proceedings: 1870 to 1875. Grob, Gerald N., ed. LC 80-1271. (Addiction in America Ser.). 1981. lib. bdg. 45.00x (ISBN 0-405-13565-3). Ayer Co Pubs.
American Association for the International Commission of Jurists. Human Rights & U.S. Foreign Policy: The First Decade, 1973-1983. LC 84-305. 1984. 5.00 (ISBN 0-916265-00-5). Am Assn Intl Comm Jurists.
American Association for the Study & Cure of Inebiety. The Disease of Inebriety from Alcohol, Opium & Other Narcotic Drugs: Its Etiology, Pathology Treatment & Medico-Legal Relations. Grob, Gerald N., ed. LC 80-1210. (Addiction in America Ser.). 1981. Repr. of 1893 ed. lib. bdg. 35.00x (ISBN 0-405-13566-1). Ayer Co Pubs.
American Association for the Study & Prevention of Infant Mortality Meeting, 1st, New Haven, 1909. Transactions. facsimile ed. LC 74-1663. (Children & Youth Ser.). 356p. 1974. Repr. of 1910 ed. 26.50x (ISBN 0-405-05944-2). Ayer Co Pubs.
American Association of Collegiate Registrars & Admissions Officers Staff. The AACRAO Survey of Grading Policies in Member Institutions: A Report. pap. 20.00 (ISBN 0-317-26624-1, 2024078). Bks Demand UMI.
--Academic Record & Transcript Guide. pap. 20.00 (ISBN 0-317-26620-9, 2024076). Bks Demand UMI.
American Association of Collegiate Registrars & Admissions Officers. Certification of Students under Veterans Laws: Information for Certifying Officials & Other Advisers of Veterans, Their Dependents or Survivors & Service Persons. pap. 25.50 (ISBN 0-317-20523-4, 2022849). Bks Demand UMI.
American Association of Collegiate Registrars & Admissions Officers Staff. The Registrar's Guide to Facilities Planning & Management. pap. 20.00 (ISBN 0-317-26608-X, 2024074). Bks Demand UMI.
American Association of Collegiate Registrars & Admisssions Officers Staff. Retention of Records: A Guide for Retention & Disposal of Student Records. pap. 20.00 (ISBN 0-317-26604-7, 2024073). Bks Demand uMI.
American Association of Collegiate Registrars & Admission Officers Staff. Survey of the Management & Utilization of Electronics Data Processing Systems in Admission, Records, & Registration, 1969-70. pap. 34.80 (ISBN 0-317-26616-0, 2024076). Bks Demand UMI.
American Association of Critical Care Nurses. Core Curriculum for Critical Care Nurses. 2nd ed. Borg, Nan, ed. 400p. 1981. soft cover 21.95 (ISBN 0-7216-1215-6). Saunders.
American Association of Critical-Care Nurses. Critical Care Nursing of Children & Adolescents. Oakes, Annalee, ed. (Illus.). 750p. 1981. pap. 16.50 (ISBN 0-7216-1003-X). Saunders.
American Association of Critical Care Nurses. Critical Care Nursing of the Multi-Injured Patient. Mann, James K. & Oakes, Annalee R, eds. LC 79-67787. (Illus.). 168p. 1980. pap. 13.00 (ISBN 0-7216-1002-1). Saunders.
American Association of Critical-Care Nurses. High-Risk Perinatal Nursing. Vestal, Katherine W. & McKenzie, Carol, eds. (Illus.). 672p. 1983. pap. 24.50 (ISBN 0-7216-1005-6). Saunders.
American Association of Critical Care Nurses. Methods in Critical Care. Millar, Sally, et al, eds. LC 79-67786. (Illus.). 484p. 1980. pap. 22.50 (ISBN 0-7216-1006-4). Saunders.
--Standards of Nursing Care of the Critically Ill. (Illus.). 368p. 1980. pap. text ed. 14.95 (ISBN 0-8359-7061-2). Reston.
American Association of Diabetes Educators. AADE Reference Manual for Evaluation of Diabetes Education Programs. 26p. 1982. pap. text ed. 4.00 (ISBN 0-686-39261-2). Am Assn Diabetes Ed.
--Healthy Eating for Healthy Growing: A Children's Coloring Book. 26p. (gr. 1-6). 1983. 0.75 (ISBN 0-686-39262-0). Am Assn Diabetes Ed.
American Association of Homes for the Aging. Directory of Members, 1985. LC 78-741009. 200p. 1985. pap. 12.00 (ISBN 0-943774-21-7, 21-7); members 6.00 (ISBN 0-317-14353-0); pap. 100.00 business firms (ISBN 0-317-14354-9); pap. 6.00 members, retirees (ISBN 0-317-14355-7). Am Assn Homes.
American Association of Homes for the Aging Staff. Guide to Caring for the Mentally Impaired Elderly. LC 84-73166. Orig. Title: Does It Really Matter If It's Tuesday? 134p. (Orig.). 1985. pap. text ed. 20.00x (ISBN 0-943774-22-5, 22-5). Am Assn Homes.
American Association of Laboratory Animal Science, New Jersey, 1970. Environmental Variables in Animal Experimentation: Symposium. Magalhaes, Hulda, ed. LC 72-3526. (Illus.). 146p. 1974. 15.00 (ISBN 0-8387-1231-2). Bucknell U Pr.
American Association of Law Libraries, jt. auth. see Wisneski, Martin E.
American Association of Law Librarians & Dyer, Susan K. Manual of Procedures for Private Law Libraries: 1984 Supplement. LC 84-11589. (AALL Publication Ser.: No. 21). ix, 130p. 1984. 18.50x. Am Assn Law Libs.
American Association of Law Libraries. Providing Legal Services for Prisoners: A Tool for Correctional Administrators. Rev. ed. 104p. 1982. pap. 10.00 (ISBN 0-942974-02-6). Am Correctional.
American Association of Museums. A Statistical Survey of Museums in the United States & Canada. LC 75-21957. (America in Two Centuries Ser). 1976. Repr. of 1965 ed. 13.00x (ISBN 0-405-07735-1). Ayer Co Pubs.
American Association of Museums, jt. auth. see ALI-ABA.
American Association of Petroleum Geologists (26th: 1941: Houston) Staff. Possible Future Oil Provinces of the United States & Canada. Levorsen, A. I., ed. LC 41-23448. pap. 40.00 (ISBN 0-317-29056-8, 2023744). Bks Demand UMI.
American Association of Retired Persons, jt. auth. see National Retired Teachers Association.
American Association of School Administrators. AASA Convention Reporter 1982. 6.00 (ISBN 0-318-01760-1, 021-00103). Am Assn Sch Admin.
--AASA Convention Reporter 1983. 6.00 (ISBN 0-318-01757-1, 021-0010). Am Assn Sch Admin.

American Association of School Admin. AASA Convention Reporter, 1984. 36p. (Orig.). 1984. pap. 6.00 (ISBN 0-87652-063-8). Am Assn Sch Admin.

--AASA Convention Reporter, 1985. Lewis, Anne, ed. 40p. (Orig.). 1985. pap. 6.00 (ISBN 0-87652-064-6). Am Assn Sch Admin.

American Association of School Administrators. The Administrative Leadership Team. (Superintendent Career Development Ser.). 3.50 (ISBN 0-686-36524-0, 021-00820). Am Assn Sch Admin.

American Association Of School Administrators & National School Boards Association. Administrative Team Contracts. (Administrative Team Career Development Ser.: Bk. 5). 3.50 (ISBN 0-318-01737-7, 021-00855X). Am Assn Sch Admin.

American Association of School Administrators. American Elementary & Secondary Schools Abroad. rev. ed. 1976. pap. 2.50 (ISBN 0-686-16896-8, 021-00618). Am Assn Sch Admin.

American Association of School Administrators & National School Boards Association. The Board's Role in Selecting the Administrative Team. (Administrative Team Career Development Ser.: Bk. 3). 6.95 (ISBN 0-318-01725-3, 021-00848). Am Assn Sch Admin.

American Association of School Administrators. Building Morale... Motivating Staff: Problems & Solutions. 11.95 (ISBN 0-318-01771-7, 021-00834). Am Assn Sch Admin.

American Association of School Admin. Building Public Confidence in Our Schools. 13p. (Orig.). 1983. pap. 0.60 (ISBN 0-87652-075-1). Am Assn Sch Admin.

--Business & Industry: Patterns in Education. 9p. (Orig.). 1984. pap. 0.45 (ISBN 0-87652-067-0). Am Assn Sch Admin.

American Association of School Administrators. Collective Bargaining: Problems & Solutions. 10.95 (ISBN 0-318-01775-X, 021-00330). Am Assn Sch Admin.

--Community Education: Managing for Success. 9.95 (ISBN 0-686-36532-1, 021-00202). Am Assn Sch Admin.

American Association of School Administrators & National School Boards Association. Compensating the Administrative Team. (Administrative Team Career Development Ser.: Bk. 2). 3.50 (ISBN 0-318-01723-7, 021-00844). Am Assn Sch Admin.

--Compensating the Administrative Team (Full Report) (Administrative Team Career Developement Ser.: Bk. 4). 15.00 (ISBN 0-318-01732-6, 021-00850). Am Assn Sch Admin.

American Association of School Administrators. Compensating the Superintendent: Full Report. 15.00 (ISBN 0-686-36526-7, 021-00825). Am Assn Sch Admin.

--Compensating the Superintendent: Summary Report. (Superintendent Career Development Ser.). 3.50 (ISBN 0-686-36523-2, 021-00819). Am Assn Sch Admin.

--The Competency Movement: Problems & Solutions. 8.95 (ISBN 0-318-01777-6, 021-00510). Am Assn Sch Admin.

--Creative Ideas for Small Schools. 10.95 (ISBN 0-318-01713-X, 021-00842). Am Assn Sch Admin.

American Association of School Admin. Declining Enrollment, Closing Schools. 80p. (Orig.). 1981. pap. 10.95 (ISBN 0-87652-084-0). Am Assn Sch Admin.

American Association of School Administrators. Educational Management Tools for the Practicing School Administrator. 5.00 (ISBN 0-686-36529-1, 021-00337). Am Assn Sch Admin.

--Effective Instructional Management. 12.95 (ISBN 0-318-01706-7, 021-00838). Am Assn Sch Admin.

American Association of School Administration. Evaluating Educational Personnel. 10.95 (ISBN 0-318-01712-1). Am Assn Sch Admin.

American Association of School Administrators. Evaluating Educational Programs. 10.95 (ISBN 0-318-01711-3, 021-00852). Am Assn Sch Admin.

--Evaluating the Superintendent. (Superintendent Career Development Ser.). 3.50 (ISBN 0-686-36525-9, 021-00821). Am Assn Sch Admin.

American Association of School Administrators, ed. The Excellence Report: Using It to Improve Your School. 16p. (Orig.). 1983. pap. 1.00 (ISBN 0-87652-061-1). Am Assn Sch Admin.

American Association of School Administrators & National School Boards Association. Goal Setting & Evaluation of School Boards. 3.50 (ISBN 0-318-01717-2, 021-00203). Am Assn Sch Admin.

American Association of School Admin. High Tech for Schools: Problems & Solutions. Neill, Shirley B., ed. 96p. (Orig.). 1984. pap. 12.95 (ISBN 0-87652-076-X). Am Assn Sch Admin.

--Holding Effective Board Meetings. 100p[illegible](Orig.). 1984. pap. 10.95 (ISBN 0-87652-077-8[illegible]Am Assn Sch Admin.

--Improving Math & Science Education: [illegible]oblems & Solutions. Neill, Shirley B., ed. 92p. ([illegible].). 1985. pap. 13.95 (ISBN 0-87652-072-7). A[illegible]ssn Sch Admin.

American Association of School Admin[illegible]tion. A Look at Sex Equality in School Ad[illegible]stration in the U. S. Territories. 5.00 (ISBN 0-[illegible]-01745-8, 021-0082). Am Assn Sch Admin.

American Association of School Admin. Perspectives on Racial Minority & Women School Administrators. 341p. (Orig.). 1983. pap. 6.50 (ISBN 0-87652-081-6). Am Assn Sch Admin.

American Association of School Administration. Recent Trends in Representation of Women & Minorities in School Administration & Problems in Documentation. 5.00 (ISBN 0-318-01741-5, 021-00910). Am Assn Sch Admin.

American Association of School Administrators. The Role of the Principal in Effective Schools: Problems & Solutions. 12.95 (ISBN 0-318-01769-5, 021-00822). Am Assn Sch Admin.

American Association of School Administrators & National School Boards Association. Roles & Relationships: School Boards & Superintendents. 3.50 (ISBN 0-318-01720-2, 021-00204). Am Assn Sch Admin.

American Association of School Administration. School Energy Management. Shirley Hanson Associates, Inc., ed. 10.00 (ISBN 0-318-01749-0, 021-00520). Am Assn Sch Admin.

American Association of School Administrators & National School Boards Association. Selecting the Administrative Team. (Administrative Team Career Development Ser.: Bk. 1). 9.95 (ISBN 0-318-01721-0, 021-00846). Am Assn Sch Admin.

American Association of School Administrators. Staff Development in Small & Rural Schools. (Small Schools Ser.: No. 1). 4.50 (ISBN 0-318-01716-4, 021-00835). Am Assn Sch Admin.

--Teaching Writing: Problems & Solutions. 11.95 (ISBN 0-318-01772-5, 021-00901). Am Assn Sch Admin.

--Time on Task. 6.95 (ISBN 0-318-01709-1, 021-00870). Am Assn Sch Admin.

American Association of School Librarians. Certification Model for Professional School Media Personnel. 40p. 1976. pap. 4.00x (ISBN 0-8389-3179-0). ALA.

--Media Programs: District & School. 136p. 1975. pap. text ed. 4.00 (ISBN 0-8389-3159-6). ALA.

American Association of School Librarians, Knapp School Libraries Project. Realization: The Final Report of the Knapp School Libraries Project. Sullivan, Peggy, ed. LC 68-29658. pap. 102.50 (ISBN 0-317-27855-X, 2024216). Bks Demand UMI.

American Association Of Teacher Educators In Agriculture. Summaries of Studies in Agricultural Education 1963-1965. 1968. pap. 3.00x (ISBN 0-8134-1070-3, 1070). Interstate.

--Summaries of Studies in Agricultural Education 1965-1967. 1970. pap. text ed. 4.00x (ISBN 0-8134-1134-3, 1134). Interstate.

American Association of Teachers of French. Bilingual Education & FLES: Keeping the Child in Focus. Kunkle, John F., ed. (Reports of the FLES & Bilingual Education Section). 71p. (Orig.). 1975. pap. 8.00x (ISBN 0-87352-168-4). Modern Lang.

--FLES & Bilingual Education: Getting the Word Out. Kunkle, John F., ed. (Reports of the FLES & Bilingual Education Section). 71p. (Orig.). 1974. pap. 8.00x (ISBN 0-87352-167-6, FF74). Modern Lang.

--FLES: Foreign Language Teaching Techniques in FLES & Bilingual Settings. Kunkle, John F. & Cipriani, Anita A., eds. (Reports of the FLES Committee). 184p. (Orig.). 1973. pap. 8.00x (ISBN 0-87352-166-8). Modern Lang.

--FLES: Goals & Guides. Lipton, Gladys C. & Spaar-Rauch, Virginia, eds. (Reports of the FLES Committee). ix, 75p. (Orig.). 1971. pap. 8.00x (ISBN 0-87352-164-1, FF71). Modern Lang.

--FLES: USA Success Stories. Lipton, Gladys C. & Bourque, Edward H., eds. (Reports of the FLES Committee). 85p. (Orig.). 1972. pap. 8.00x (ISBN 0-87352-165-X, FF72). Modern Lang.

American Association of Textile Chemists & Colorists. Buyer's Guide. 280p. 40.00 (ISBN 0-318-12148-4); members 20.00 (ISBN 0-318-12149-2); in TCC subscr. incl. AATCC.

--Dyers World: 1980's Theory to Practice. (Symposia Papers). 116p. 46.00 (ISBN 0-318-12154-9); members 25.00 (ISBN 0-318-12155-7). AATCC.

--Face to Face with the Environmental Problems. (Symposia Papers). 118p. 1975. 35.00 (ISBN 0-318-12156-5); members 19.00 (ISBN 0-318-12157-3). AATCC.

--Flock Technology. (Symposia Papers). 104p. 1971. 27.00 (ISBN 0-318-12159-X); members 16.00 (ISBN 0-318-12160-3). AATCC.

--Practical Dyeing Problems: Analysis & Solutions. (Symposia Papers). 184p. 1977. 46.00 (ISBN 0-318-12165-4); members 25.00 (ISBN 0-318-12166-2). AATCC.

--Technical Manual. 400p. 63.00 (ISBN 0-318-12171-9); members 34.00 (ISBN 0-318-12172-7). AATCC.

--Textile Flammability. 214p. 1975. 55.00 (ISBN 0-318-12173-5); members 29.00 (ISBN 0-318-12174-3). AATCC.

--The Textile Industry & the Environment. (Symposia Papers). 56p. 1981. 46.00 (ISBN 0-318-12175-1); members 25.00 (ISBN 0-318-12176-X). AATCC.

--The Textile Industry & the Environment. (Symposia Papers). 152p. 1973. 27.00 (ISBN 0-318-12177-8); 16.00 (ISBN 0-318-12178-6). AATCC.

--The Textile Industry & the Environment. (Symposia Papers). 144p. 1971. 27.00 (ISBN 0-318-12179-4); members 16.00 (ISBN 0-318-12180-8). AATCC.

--Textile Printing. (Symposia Papers). 166p. 1975. 35.00 (ISBN 0-318-12181-6); members 19.00 (ISBN 0-318-12182-4). AATCC.

--Textile Printing: Meeting the Challenge of the 80's. (Symposia Papers). 89p. 1978. 46.00 (ISBN 0-318-12183-2); members 25.00 (ISBN 0-318-12184-0). AATCC.

--Textile Technology-Ecology Interface. (Symposia Papers). 94p. 1977. 46.00 (ISBN 0-318-12185-9); members 25.00 (ISBN 0-318-12186-7). AATCC.

American Association of University Instructors in Accounting. Proceedings, 3 vols. Brief, Richard P., ed. LC 80-1468. (Dimensions of Accounting Theory & Practice Ser.). 1981. lib. bdg. 114.50 (ISBN 0-405-13498-3). Ayer Co Pubs.

American Association on Mental Deficiency. Data Banks & Automated Information Systems on Mental Retardation & Developmental Disabilities in the United States. 100p. 1978. 5.50 (ISBN 0-317-32302-4). Am Assn Mental.

American Astronautical Society. Advances in the Astronautical Sciences. Incl. Vol. 6. Sixth Annual Meeting, New York, 1960. Jacobs, H. & Burgess, E., eds. 45.00x (ISBN 0-87703-007-3); Vol. 9. Fourth Western Regional Meeting, San Francisco, 1961. Jacobs, H. & Burgess, E., eds. 45.00x (ISBN 0-87703-010-3); Vol. 11. Eighth Annual Meeting, Washington, 1962. 45.00x (ISBN 0-87703-012-X); Vol. 13. Ninth Annual Meeting, Interplanetary Missions, Los Angeles, 1963. Burgess, E., ed. 45.00x (ISBN 0-87703-014-6). Am Astronaut). Univelt Inc.

--Lunar Flight Problems. Fleisig, R., ed. (Advances in the Astronautical Sciences Ser.: Vol. 18). 1964. 45.00x (ISBN 0-87703-020-0, Pub. by Am Astronaut). Univelt inc.

--Post Apollo Space Exploration, 2 Vols. (Advances in Astronautical Ser.: Vol. 20). 1966. Set. 85.00x (ISBN 0-87703-022-7, Pub. by Am Astronaut). Univelt Inc.

American Astronautical Society Annual Meeting, San Francisco, Oct. 1977. The Industrialization of Space: Proceedings. Van Patten, R. A., et al, eds. LC 57-43769. (Advances in the Astronautical Sciences: Vol. 36). (Illus.). 1978. Pt. I. lib. bdg. 55.00x (ISBN 0-87703-094-4, Pub. by Am Astronaut); Pt. II. lib. bdg. 45.00x (ISBN 0-87703-095-2); microfiche suppl. 15.00x (ISBN 0-87703-121-5). Univelt Inc.

American Automobile Association. Handicapped Driver's Mobility Guide. 1981. pap. 0.55 (ISBN 0-916748-00-6, 3772). AAA.

--Sportsmanlike Driving. rev. ed. Cranford, Carolyn E., ed. (Illus.). (gr. 10-12). 1979. text ed. 16.40 (ISBN 0-07-001330-6); pap. text ed. 10.72 (ISBN 0-07-001331-4). McGraw.

American Automobile Association Staff. AAA Road Atlas, 1986. (Illus.). 144p. 1985. pap. 5.95 (ISBN 0-916748-03-0). AAA.

American Banker Association, et al. Bankruptcy Manual. LC 85-135509. (Illus.). 371p. 1985. 97.00. Am Bankers.

American Bankers Association. Bank Dividend Policy. 81p. 1970. 4.50 (ISBN 0-317-32365-2, 270400); members 3.50 (ISBN 0-317-32366-0). Am Bankers.

--Bank Investments. 313p. 1978. 16.00 (ISBN 0-317-32367-9, 051100); members 13.00 (ISBN 0-317-32368-7); instructor's manual 10.00 (ISBN 0-317-32369-5, 251100); members 8.00 (ISBN 0-317-32370-9). Am Bankers.

--The Bank Tellers Job: A Day to Day Reference Guide. 128p. 1980. 31.00 (ISBN 0-317-32371-7, 049700); members 25.00 (ISBN 0-317-32372-5). Am Bankers.

--Commercial Banks & Investment Banking. 112p. 1979. 6.25 (ISBN 0-317-32375-X, 185500); members 5.00 (ISBN 0-317-32376-8). Am Bankers.

--Concepts of Secured Transactions. (Loan & Discount Ser.: Book 4). 71p. 1979. 12.50 (ISBN 0-317-32377-6, 167700); members 10.00 (ISBN 0-317-32378-4). Am Bankers.

--Federal Laws Impacting Insurance Activities of Banks. LC 84-236759. 40p. Date not set. price not set. Am Bankers.

--Federal Reserve Float: Trends & Options. 53p. 1980. 12.00 (ISBN 0-317-32387-3, 186300); members 10.00 (ISBN 0-317-32388-1). Am Bankers.

--The Future of Trust Institutions: Golembe Report. 175p. 1977. 1-4 copies 42.00 ea. (365400); members 28.00 ea.; 5 & over 28.50 ea.; members 19.00 ea. Am Bankers.

--Getting Started in Telecommunications Management. 260p. 1980. 30.00 (ISBN 0-317-32391-1, 063900); members 25.00 (ISBN 0-317-32392-X). Am Bankers.

--Guidelines for Forming & Managing a Bank-Owned Agricultural Credit Corporation. LC 82-228669. (Illus.). Date not set. price not set. Am Bankers.

--A New Frontier for Business Opportunities: A Handbook for Private Initiative in Community Revitalization. 101p. 1980. 7.50 (ISBN 0-317-32399-7, 029900); members 5.00 (ISBN 0-317-32400-4). Am Bankers.

--The Promissory Note. (Loan & Discount Ser.: Book 1). 98p. 1979. 12.50 (ISBN 0-317-32405-5, 167000); members 10.00 (ISBN 0-317-32406-3). Am Bankers.

--Retail Bank Credit Referral Directory. 124p. 1980. 17.25 (ISBN 0-317-32409-8, 208400); members 15.00 (ISBN 0-317-32410-1). Am Bankers.

--The Retention & Destruction of Bank Records. 196p. 1979. 22.00 (ISBN 0-317-32411-X, 062700); members 17.50 (ISBN 0-317-32412-8). Am Bankers.

--The Retention of Bank Records. rev. ed. LC 85-119139. 171p. Date not set. price not set. Am Bankers.

American Bankers Association, jt. auth. see O'Connor, William J.

American Bankers Association Office of the General Counsel. Summary of State Banking Legislation, Winter 1981. LC 84-189202. write for info. Amer Bar Assn.

American Bankers Association. Office of the General Counsel. Summary of State Legislation-Savings Banks, Credit unions, Savings & Loan Associations. LC 84-189061. Date not set. price not set. Am Bankers.

American Bankers Assoication. Branch Management: A Selection of Contemporary Readings. 320p. 1980. 16.25 (ISBN 0-317-32373-3, 051600); members 13.00 (ISBN 0-317-32374-1). Am Bankers.

American Bantam Car Company. Bantam Model BRC Jeep, 1941 Prototype: TM-10-1205. Post, Dan R., ed. LC 75-185932. (Illus.). 128p. 1971. pap. 12.95 (ISBN 0-911160-44-2). Post-Era.

American Bar Assn. Shakespeare Cross-Examination: A Complication of Articles First Appearing on the American Bar Association Journal. 125p. 1961. 5.00 (ISBN 0-686-47950-5). Amer Bar Assn.

American Bar Association. ABA Standards for Criminal Justice, 4 vols. LC 79-91936. 1980. Set. 215.00 (ISBN 0-316-03709-5); 57.00 ea.; 1982 supplement 32.00 (ISBN 0-316-00093-0). Little.

--Administrative Law Review, 1949-1984, 1-36 vols. Incl. Administrative Law Review, 1-9 vols. 30.00 ea; Administrative Law Review, 10-18 vols. 32.50 ea.; Administrative Law Review, 19-36 vols. 37.50 ea.. Set. 1165.00x (ISBN 0-686-89382-4). Rothman.

--Child Snatching: The Legal Response to the Abduction of Children. LC 81-65945. 206p. (Orig.). 1981. pap. text ed. 19.00x (ISBN 0-89707-036-4, 5130018). Amer Bar Assn.

--Cost Accounting for Law Firms. 59p. 1984. pap. 25.00 (ISBN 0-89707-127-1). Amer Bar Assn.

--Cumulative Index of the American Bar Association Journal: Volumes One Through Fifty, Covering the Years 1915 Through 1964. 333p. 1971. vol. 18.00 ea. Amer Bar Assn.

--Federal Regulation of Consumer Credit. 1981. 48.50. Warren.

--Interlocking Directorates Under Section Eight of the Clayton Act. 67p. 1984. pap. 35.00 (ISBN 0-89707-151-4). Amer Bar Assn.

--Legal Status of Prisoners. 106p. 1983. 30.00 (ISBN 0-316-03720-6); pap. 10.00 (ISBN 0-316-03722-2). Little.

--Manual of Class Action Notice Forms. LC 79-50160. 320p. 1979. pap. 10.00 (ISBN 0-686-47785-5, 5030023). Amer Bar Assn.

--Model Code of Professional Responsibility & Code of Judicial Conduct: As Amended August, 1980. LC 83-202790. v, 71p. 1982. 2.50 (561-0010). Amer Bar Assn.

--The Remedies Phase of an EEO Case: A Study Guide for the ABA Videolaw Seminar. 537p. Date not set. price not set. Amer Bar Assn.

--Serving Two Masters: The Law of Lawyer Disqualification. 54p. 1984. 7.95 (ISBN 0-89707-149-2). Amer Bar Assn.

--Supplement to Standards for Criminal Justice, 1985. 1985. pap. write for info. Little.

American Bar Association & American Law Institute - American Bar Association Committee on Continuing Professional Education. The Distribution of Products at Wholesale & Retail: ALI-ABA Course of Study Materials. LC 84-104370. write for info. Am law Inst.

American Bar Association & Anderrson, Charlotte C. Through the Legal Looking Glass, Reflections of Peoples & Cultures: A Handbook for Educators. LC 82-157433. (Intercom Ser.: No. 100). (Illus.). 40p. 1981. 4.00. Global Perspectives.

American Bar Association & JAD Lawyers Conference. Explaining the Courts: Materials & Sources. LC 82-74359. x, 102p. 1983. write for info. (ISBN 0-89707-108-5, 410-0001). Amer Bar Assn.

American Bar Association, jt. auth. see Cox, Henry B.

American Bar Association, jt. auth. see Committee on Jury Standards.

American Bar Association Action Commission to Reduce Court Costs & Delay. Attacking Litigation Costs & Delay: Project Reports & Research Findings Supporting the Final Report of the Action Commission to Reduce Court Costs & Delay. LC 85-123500. (Illus.). vi, 318p. write for info. Amer Bar Assn.

American Bar Association. Action Commission to Reduce Court Cost & Delay. Evaluation of Telephone-Conferencing in Civil & Criminal Court Cases: Joint Project of the Institute for Court Management & the American Bar Association Action Commission to Reduce Court Costs & Delay. LC 84-164743. Date not set. price not set. ICM Denver.

American Bar Association. Commission in the Mentally Disabled, et al. Mental Disability Law: A Primer. LC 84-244127. write for info. Amer Bar Assn.

American Bar Association. Committee on Comparative Procedure & Practice, jt. auth. see Cone, Sydney M.

American Bar Association Committee on Continuing Professional Education, jt. auth. see American Law Institute.

American Bar Association, Committee on Selection, Training, & Utilization of Lawyers, jt. auth. see Munneke, Gary A.

American Bar Association Committee on Privacy, jt. auth. see National Symposium on Personal Privacy & Informational Technology October 4-7, 1981.

American Bar Association. Committee on Corporate Laws. Model Business Corporation Act Annotated: Revised Model Business Corporation Act (1984), Professioanl Corporation Supplement, Close Corporation Supplement, with Officaiial Comments & Reporter's Annotations. 3rd ed. LC 85-13133. Date not set. price not set (ISBN 0-15-004389-9). Amer Bar Assn.

American Bar Association Committee on Corporate Laws. Revised Model Business Corporation Act: Adopted by Committee on Corporate Laws of the Section of Corporation, Banking & Business Law of the American Bar Association Spring 1984: Offical Text with Offical Comments & Statutory Cross References. LC 85-5238. write for info. Amer Bar Assn.

American Bar Association, Discovery Committee, jt. auth. see American Law Institute-American Bar Association Committee on Continuing Professional Education.

American Bar Association, Division of Communications. Law & Marriage: Your Legal Guide. LC 83-150958. 64p. 1983. pap. 1.00 (235-0004). Amer Bar Assn.

American Bar Association Forum Committee on the Contruction Industry. Emerging Trends in Construction Law. LC 84-247811. (Illus.). write for info. Amer Bar Assn.

American Bar Association Forum Committee on Entertainment & Sports Industries & American Bar Association Section of Patent Trademark & Copyright Law. Seven Years of the New Copyright Act: Report, Analysis, & Predictions for the Future, October 26-27, 1984. write for info. Amer Bar Assn.

American Bar Association, Professional Education Publications. Guidelines for a Corporate Law Dept. Manual. LC 79-88508. 65p. (Orig.). 1980. pap. 35.00 (ISBN 0-89707-023-2, 577-0017). Amer Bar Assn.

American Bar Association Public Utility Section. Public Utility Law: Proceedings of the Section of Public Utility Law of the American Bar Association, Atlanta, Georgia, August 1-3, 1983. LC 84-189239. 60p. Date not set. price not set. Amer Bar Assn.

American Bar Association. Section of Antitrust Law, jt. auth. see Pasahow, Lynn H.

American Bar Association Section of Law Staff, jt. auth. see American Law Institute-American Bar Association Committe on Continuing Professional Education Staff.

American Bar Association Section of Patent Trademark & Copyright Law, jt. auth. see American Bar Association Forum Committee on Entertainment & Sports Industries.

American Bar Association Section of Antitrust Law Staff & Loftis, James R. Antitrust Law Developments. 2nd ed. LC 84-153173. 900p. 1984. 75.00 (ISBN 0-89707-137-9). Amer Bar Assn.

American Bar Association Section of Litigation. The Litigation Manual: A Primer for Trial Lawyers. LC 83-71715. (Illus.). v, 285p. 1983. 40.00 (ISBN 0-89707-106-9, 531-0037). Amer Bar Assn.

American Bar Association; Section of Economics of Law Practice Staff, et al. Locate. LC 84-117646. (Monographs). (Illus.). x, 200p. 1984. 28.00 (ISBN 0-89707-148-4). Amer Bar Assn.

American Bar Association, Section of Taxation. Subchapter S Revision Act of 1982: ALI-ABA Video Law Review Study Materials. LC 83-188726. xii, 124p. Date not set. price not set. Am Law Inst.

American Bar Association Section of Taxation & American Law Institute-American Bar Association Committee on Continuing Professional Education. Tax Reform Act of 1984: ALI-ABA Course of Study Materials. LC 85-138566. Date not set. price not set. Am Law Inst.

American Bar Association. Special Committee on Lawyers' Public Service Responsibility, jt. auth. see Lardent, Esther F.

American Bar Association Special Committee on Housing & Urban Development Law, ed. see Floodplains & Wetlands-Legal Constraints & Options Institute & Loyola University of Chicago.

American Bar Association Special Committee on Election Law & Voter Participation & Conference on the Federal Election Commission. The Federal Election Commission: Conference Highlights, Washington, D.C., March 1982. LC 82-72032. 8p. 1982. 2.00 (357-0007). Amer Bar Assn.

American Bar Association Special Committee on Dispute Resolution, et al. Problem Solving Through Mediation: Conference Proceedings, December 1-2, 1983, John Jay College of Criminal Justice. LC 85-123815. 144p. write for info. Amer Bar Assn.

American Bar Association. Special Committee on the Tort Liability System & Shapo, Marshall S. Towards a Jurisprudence of Injury: The Continuing Creation of a System of Substantive Justice in American Tort Law: Report to the American Bar Association. LC 85-112535. Date not set. price not set. Amer Bar Assn.

American Bar Association Staff. Flying Solo: A Survival Guide for the Solo Lawyer. 362p. 1984. pap. 39.95 (ISBN 0-89707-104-2). Amer Bar Assn.

--The Use of Economists in Antitrust Litigation. 81p. 1984. pap. 35.00 (ISBN 0-89707-145-X). Amer Bar Assn.

American Bar Association Standing Committee on Professional Discipline & Center for Professional Responsibility. The Judicial Response to Lawyer Misconduct. LC 84-177336. 225p. 1984. 25.00. Amer Bar Assn.

American Bar Association Standing Committee on Unauthorized Practice of the Law. Model Rules for Advisory Opinions on Unauthorized Practice of the Law. LC 84-251160. 10p. write for info. Amer Bar Assn.

American Bar Association's Section of Labor & Employment Law. Employment Discrimination Law: 1983 Supplement. 2nd. ed. 240p. 1984. pap. 17.50 (ISBN 0-87179-452-7). BNA.

American Bar Foundation. Judical Performance Polls. i, 108p. 1977. 5.00 (ISBN 0-910058-81-4). Am Bar Foun.

--Sample Incorporating Indenture 1967: All Registered Issues. 22p. 1967. pap. 1.00 (ISBN 0-910058-29-6). Amer Bar Assn.

--Sources of our Liberties: With a Postscript 1978; Bibliographical Note by Stanley N. Katz. Deluxe Rev. ed. 488p. 1978. 50.00 (ISBN 0-910058-91-1); pap. 7.50 (ISBN 0-910058-90-3). Amer Bar Assn.

American Bar Foundation Publisher. Commentaries on Model Debenture Indenture Provisions, 1965; Model Debenture Indenture Provisions, All Registered Issues, 1967; & Certain Negotiable Provisions Which May Be Included in a Particular Incorporating Indenture. Bd. with Model Debenture Indenture Provisions, All Registered Issues, 1967; Certain Negotiable Provisions Which May Be Included in a Particular Incorporating Indenture. LC 79-127110. 609p. 1971. 100.00 (ISBN 0-910058-00-8). Am Bar Foun.

--Sample Incorporating Indenture. Bd. with Model Debenture Indenture Provisions, 1965. 18p. 1965. pap. 1.00 (ISBN 0-910058-27-X). Am Bar Foun.

American Bar Foundation Staff. Model Debenture Indenture Provisions: All Registered Issues, 1967. 78p. 1967. pap. 2.00 (ISBN 0-910058-29-6). Am Bar Foun.

--Sample Incorporating Indenture & Model Debenture Indenture Provisions 1965. 120p. 1965. 5.00 (ISBN 0-910058-25-3). Amer Bar Assn.

American Bas Association. Section of Public Contract Law & State & Local Government Law. Identifying & Prosecuting Fraud & Abuse in State & Local Contracting. LC 84-192395. Date not set. price not set. Amer Bar Assn.

American Bed & Breakfast Association Staff. A Treasury of Bed & Breakfast. 2nd ed. Sonke, Sarah W. & Wilson, Patricia P., eds. (Illus.). 168p. 1985. pap. 12.95 (ISBN 0-934473-01-3). Am Bed & Breakfast.

American Book Collector, ed. Directory of Specialized American Bookdealers, 1981-1982. 1981. 19.95 (ISBN 0-89679-005-3). Moretus Pr.

American Book Collector Magazine Staff, compiled by. Directory of Specialized American Bookdealers, 1984-1985. 2nd ed. xiv, 344p. 1984. lib. bdg. 35.00 (ISBN 0-89679-012-6). Moretus Pr.

American Booksellers Association. A Manual on Bookselling: How to Open & Run Your Own Bookstore. rev. ed. Cobb, Sanford, ed. 352p. (Harmony); pap. 4.95 (ISBN 0-517-51647-0). Crown.

American Bookseller's Association, ed. A Manual on Bookselling: How to Open & Run Your Own Bookstore. 3rd ed. (Illus.). 416p. 1980. 15.95 (ISBN 0-517-53705-2, Harmony); pap. 8.95 (ISBN 0-517-53706-0, Harmony). Crown.

American Bureau of Metal Statistics Inc. ABMS Non-Ferrous Metal Data Publication. annual ed. 1978. 25.00 (ISBN 0-685-91837-8). Am Bur Metal.

American Bureau of Metal Statistics Staff, compiled by. ABMS Non-Ferrous Metal Data Publication: 1974 Yearbook. rev. ed. Incl. 1974 Yearbook. American Bureau of Metal Statistics Staff, ed. 1975 (ISBN 0-910064-09-1); 1975 Yearbook. American Bureau of Metal Statistics Staff, ed. 1976 (ISBN 0-910064-09-1). LC 21-15719. 1975. 70.00 (ISBN 0-910064-08-3). Am Bur Metal.

American Bureau of Metal Statistics Staff, ed. ABMS Non-Ferrous Metal Data Publication: 1975 Yearbook. rev. ed. LC 21-15719. 1976. 70.00 (ISBN 0-910064-09-1). Am Bur Metal.

--ABMS Non-Ferrous Metal Data Publication: 1976 Year Book. rev. ed. LC 21-15719. 1977. 70.00 (ISBN 0-910064-10-5). Am Bur Metal.

American Bureau of Metal Statistics Editorial Staff, ed. Fifty-Second Annual Yearbook. 1973. 70.00 (ISBN 0-685-39802-1). Am Bur Metal.

American Bureau of Metal Statistics Inc. Non-Ferrous Metal Data Yearbook, 1978. (Illus.). 1979. 70.00 (ISBN 0-686-51336-3). Am Bur Metal.

--Non-Ferrous Metal Data Yearbook, 1979. (Illus.). 1980. yrbk. 70.00 (ISBN 0-686-61434-8). Am Bur Metal.

American Bureau of Metal Statistics Staff, compiled by. Year Book of the American Bureau of Metal Statistics. annual 1972. 70.00 (ISBN 0-910064-05-9). Am Bur Metal.

--Year Book of the American Bureau of Metal Statistics. LC 21-15719. 1973. 70.00 (ISBN 0-910064-06-7). Am Bur Metal.

American Camping Association. Guide to a Counselor-in-Training Program. 32p. 1974. pap. 2.00 (ISBN 0-87603-020-7). Am Camping.

American Camping Association Publicaions Committee, ed. Sing. 95p. 1978. pap. 1.50 (ISBN 0-87603-037-1, SO 01). Am Camping.

American Canal Society. The Best from American Canals. (Illus.). 88p. 1983. pap. 6.00 (ISBN 0-933788-32-0). Am Canal Soc.

--The Best from American Canals, No. 1. (Illus.). 88p. 1980. 6.00 (ISBN 0-933788-32-0). Am Canal & Transport.

American Canal Society Staff. The Best from American Canals, No. 2. (Illus.). 88p. 1984. 8.00 (ISBN 0-933788-45-2). Am Canal & Transport.

American Cancer Society. American Cancer Society - What It Is. 24p. avail. (5618). Am Cancer NY.

--Cook It in Massachusetts. 192p. 1981. pap. 6.00 (ISBN 0-686-31481-6). Am Cancer Mass.

--High Country Cooking in Colorado. 192p. 1981. pap. 7.00 (ISBN 0-686-31478-6). Am Cancer Colo.

--I Love New York Cooking from Other Lands. 192p. 1981. pap. 5.00 (ISBN 0-686-31485-9). Am Cancer Syracuse.

--Iowa: The Place to Cook. 192p. 1981. pap. 6.00 (ISBN 0-686-31479-4). Am Cancer Iowa.

--Maryland's Flavors. 192p. 1981. pap. 6.00 (ISBN 0-686-31480-8). Am Cancer MD.

--Seasonal Samplings. 192p. 1981. pap. 6.00 (ISBN 0-686-31482-4). Am Cancer Mich.

--Show Me Missouri Cooking for Company Cookbook, 1982. 192p. 1982. pap. 6.00 (ISBN 0-686-31483-2). Am Cancer MO.

--Show Me Missouri Four Seasons Cookbook, 1983. 1983. pap. 6.00 (ISBN 0-686-43081-6). Am Cancer MO.

--A Slice of the Big Apple. 192p. 1982. pap. 6.00 (ISBN 0-686-31486-7). Am Cancer Forest Hills.

--Stop Smoking Program Guide. 184p. avail. (5003). Am Cancer NY.

--Target Five - Report to the Board of Directions. 82p. avail. Am Cancer NY.

--A Taste of New Hampshire. 192p. 1981. pap. 5.00 (ISBN 0-686-31484-0). Am Cancer NH.

--Wyoming Frontier Cooking. 136p. 1981. pap. 6.00 (ISBN 0-686-31488-3). Am Cancer WY.

--Youth Looks at Cancer. 68p. avail. (2044). Am Cancer NY.

American Cancer Society, Minnesota Division Inc. Look What's Cooking Now: Minnesota Heritage Cookbook II. Zelickson, Sue, ed. 1985. pap. 10.00 (ISBN 0-9602796-1-X). Am Cancer Minn.

American Cancer Society Staff. Mississippi Memories, Vol. II. 190p. 1983. pap. 7.50 (ISBN 0-318-04093-X). Am Cancer MS.

American Catholic Historic Association. Catholic Philosophy of History, Vol. 3. facs. ed. LC 67-23190. (Essay Index Reprint Ser). 1936. 16.00 (ISBN 0-8369-0285-8). Ayer Co Pubs.

American Catholic Philosophical Association. Ethics & Other Knowledge: Proceedings, Vol. 31. 1957. 18.00 (ISBN 0-384-14760-7). Johnson Repr.

--Natural Law & International Relations, Vol. 24. 1950. 18.00 (ISBN 0-384-40940-7). Johnson Repr.

--Philosophy & the Experimental Sciences: Proceedings, Vol. 26. 1952. 18.00 (ISBN 0-384-46400-9). Johnson Repr.

--Role of the Christian Philosopher, Proceedings. 1958. 18.00 (ISBN 0-384-51830-3). Johnson Repr.

American Ceramic Society, Inc. American Ceramic Society Bulletin. 1550p. (B). avail., monthly; members free. Am Ceramic.

American Chain Association, compiled by. Chains for Power Transmission & Materials Handling: Design & Applications Handbook. (Mechanical Engineering Ser.: Vol. 18). (Illus.). 368p. 1982. 35.00 (ISBN 0-8247-1701-5). Dekker.

American Chamber of Commerce in Hong Kong. Doing Business in Today's Hong Kong. 1980. 15.00 (ISBN 0-686-32786-1). A M Newman.

--Living in Hong Kong. 248p. 1981. 15.00 (ISBN 0-686-22824-3). A M Newman.

American Chamber of Commerce in Japan. ACCJ Directory of Members. (Illus.). 1984. 45.00 (ISBN 0-686-12229-1). A M Newman.

--Exporting to Japan. 1982. 10.00 (ISBN 0-686-37954-3). A M Newman.

--Living in Japan. 9th, rev. ed. 1983. 15.00 (ISBN 0-686-16964-6). A M Newman.

American Chamber of Commerce in Korea. Living in Korea: 1984 Ed. 1984. 14.00 (ISBN 0-686-23876-1). A M Newman.

American Chamber of Commerce in the Philipines. Living in the Philipines. 1980. 12.00 (ISBN 0-686-32785-3). A M Newman.

American Chemical Society. Emulsion Polymerization: An International Symposium Sponsored by the Division of Polymer Chemistry, Inc. at the 169th Meeting of the American Chemical Society, Philadelphia, Penn., April 8-10, 1975. Piirma, Irja & Gardon, John L., eds. LC 75-44458. (American Chemical Society. ACS: No. 24). (Illus.). pap. 103.80 (ISBN 0-317-09441-6, 2019528). Bks Demand UMI.

--Handbook for Authors. LC 78-6401. 1978. 19.95 (ISBN 0-8412-0425-X); pap. 9.95 (ISBN 0-8412-0430-6). Am Chemical.

--New Approaches to Pest Control & Eradication: A Symposium Sponsored by the Pesticides Subdivision of the Division of Agricultural & Food Chemistry at the 142nd Meeting. Hall, Stanley A., ed. LC 63-19396. (American Chemical Society, Advances in Chemistry Ser.: No. 41). pap. 21.50 (ISBN 0-317-09566-8, 2019530). Bks Demand UMI.

American Chemical Society, Division of Fuel Chemistry. Chemistry & Geochemistry of Oil Shales: Preprints of Papers Presented at Seattle, Washington, March 20-25, 1983. (American Chemical Society, Division of Fuel Chemistry, Preprints of Papers Ser.: Vol. 28, No. 3). pap. 62.80 (ISBN 0-317-28800-8, 2020320). Bks Demand UMI.

--Chemistry of Low Rank Coals: Supercritical Phenomena. (American Chemical Society, Division of Fuel Chemistry, Preprints of Papers: Vol. 28, No. 4). pap. 106.00 (ISBN 0-317-29913-1, 2021767). Bks Demand UMI.

--Coal Gasification Chemistry: Flash Hydrogenation of Coal; Pyrolysis Reactions of Coal; Government Role in Fuel R & D; Henry H. Storch Award Symposium (&) General Papers Presented at Washington, D. C., September 10-14, 1979. (Preprints of Papers Ser.: Vol. 24, No. 3). pap. 77.00 (ISBN 0-317-29986-7, 2051824). Bks Demand UMI.

--Environmental Control in Synfuels Processes: Catalytic Reactions Involving Synthesis Gas. (Preprints of Papers: Vol. 25, No. 2). pap. 54.00 (ISBN 0-317-28249-2, 2012122). Bks Demand UMI.

--Fundamentals of Gas-Carbon Reactions; Chemistry & Characterization of Coal Macerals; General Papers: Coal to Liquid Products; General Papers: Chemistry & Characterization of Fossil Fuels: Preprints of Papers Presented at Seattle, Washington, March 20-25, 1983. (American Chemical Society, Division of Fuel Chemistry, Preprints of Papers: Vol. 28, No. 1). pap. 55.00 (ISBN 0-317-30066-0, 2020265). Bks Demand UMI.

--Oil Shale, Tar Sands, & Related Materials: General Papers: Storch Award Symposium: Preprints of Papers Presented at San Francisco, California, August 24-29, 1980. (Preprints of Papers: Vol. 25, No. 3). pap. 74.50 (ISBN 0-317-28241-7, 2013279). Bks Demand UMI.

American Chemical Society Division of Fuel Chemistry. Physical Methods for Fossil Fuels Characterization, Coal Gasification, Pyrolysis & Biomass: Presented at Miami Beach, FL, April 28 May 3, 1985, Vol. 7. (American Chemical Society Division of Fuel Chemistry Preprints of Papers Ser.: Vol. 30). pap. 108.80 (ISBN 0-317-28033-3, 2025564). Bks Demand UMI.

American Chemical Society, Division of Organic Chemistry. & Industrial & Engineering Chemistry. System of Nomenclature for Terpene Hydrocarbons: Acyclics, Monocyclics, Bicyclics. LC 55-4170. (American Chemical Society Advances in Chemistry Series: No. 14). pap. 37.50 (ISBN 0-317-08703-7, 2050183). Bks Demand UMI.

American Chemical Society,164th National Meeting. Biogenesis of Plant Cell Wall Polysaccharides: Proceedings. Loewus, Frank, ed. 1973. 94.00 (ISB[illegible]0-12-455350-8). Acad Pr.

Americ[illegible] Chemistry Society. Chemistry of Mineral Matt[illegible] & Ash in Coal, Vol. 29. (American Chem[illegible]y Society Division of Fuel Chemistry Prep[illegible] of Papers: No. 4). pap. 92.50 (ISBN 0-317-[illegible]0-6, 2024163). Bks Demand UMI.

American Civil Liberties Union, jt. auth. see Robertson, John A.

American Classical League. Greek Numismatic Art. (Illus.). 60p. 0.80 (ISBN 0-318-12453-X, B33). Amer Classical.

--Roman Family Life. (Illus.). 62p. 3.30 (ISBN 0-318-12456-4, B39). Amer Classical.
--The Roman House. 62p. 3.30 (ISBN 0-318-12457-2, B30). Amer Classical.
--Roman Sport & Entertainment. (Illus.). 62p. 3.30 (ISBN 0-318-12459-9, B31). Amer Classical.
--Roman Towns. (Illus.). 60p. 3.30 (ISBN 0-318-12460-2, 53). Amer Classical.

American Classical Studies Editors. A Collection of the Historically Most Famous Orations Delivered by the Men Who Built the United States Politically & Spiritually, 2 vols. (Illus.). 317p. 1985. Set. 197.50 (ISBN 0-89901-229-9). Found Class Reprints.

American College of Emergency Physicians Staff. Emergency Medicine: A Comprehensive Study Guide. 1056p. 1984. 85.00 (ISBN 0-07-001439-6). McGraw.

American College of Foot Surgeons. Complications in Foot Surgery: Prevention & Management. LC 75-28130. pap. 63.30 (ISBN 0-317-30007-5, 2051867). Bks Demand UMI.

American College of Radiology. Radiologists Guide to Detection of Early Breast Cancer by Mammography, Thermography, & Xeroradiography. 169p. 10.00 (ISBN 0-318-12467-X); members 7.50 (ISBN 0-318-12468-8). Am Coll Radiology.
--Technologist's Guide to Detection of Early Breast Cancer by Mammography, Thermography, & Xeroradiography. 118p. 10.00 (ISBN 0-318-12470-X); members 7.50 (ISBN 0-318-12471-8). Am Coll Radiology.

American College of Sports Medicine. Exercise & Aging: The Scientific Basis. Smith, Everett L. & Serfass, Robert C., eds. LC 80-24700. (Illus.). 191p. 1981. text ed. 17.95x (ISBN 0-89490-042-0). Enslow Pubs.

American College of Sports Medicine, ed. Guidelines for Graded Exercise Testing & Exercise Prescription. 2nd ed. LC 80-19484. 151p. 1980. pap. 6.50 (ISBN 0-8121-0769-1). Lea & Febiger.

American College of Surgeons. Early Care of the Injured Patient. 3rd ed. (Illus.). 1982. text ed. 29.95 (ISBN 0-7216-1165-6). Saunders.
--Manual of Surgical Intensive Care. Kinney, John M., ed. LC 76-51009. (Illus.). 1977. text ed. 18.95 (ISBN 0-7216-1180-X). Saunders.
--Manual of Surgical Nutrition. Ballinger, Walter F., ed. LC 75-19840. (Illus.). 527p. 1975. text ed. 27.95 (ISBN 0-7216-1525-2). Saunders.

American College of Surgeons Staff. A List of the Fellows: 1913. ix, 187p. Repr. of 1913 ed. 29.00 (ISBN 0-932051-29-4). Am Repr Serv.

American College of Trial Lawyers, et al. Civil Trial Manual, Vol. 2. 2nd ed. LC 81-65817. 1980. write for info. Am Law Inst.

American College Testing Program. College Planning-Search Book. 10th ed. (Illus.). 309p. (Orig.). 1984. pap. text ed. 6.00 (ISBN 0-937734-07-1). Am Coll Testing.

American Colortype Company. Cut & Assemble Paper Dollhouse Furniture. 1981. pap. 3.50 (ISBN 0-486-24150-5). Dover.

American Concrete Institute. Abeles Symposium: Fatigue of Concrete. LC 73-92588. (American Concrete Institute Ser.: SP-41). (Illus.). pap. 89.50 (ISBN 0-317-10268-0, 2013340). Bks Demand UMI.
--Behavior of Concrete under Temperature Extremes. LC 73-85854. (American Concrete Institute. Publication: No. SP-39). (Illus.). pap. 53.50 (ISBN 0-317-10013-0, 2004296). Bks Demand UMI.
--Bibliography on Prestressed Concrete. 2nd ed. (American Concrete Institute. Bibliography: No. 1). pap. 26.50 (ISBN 0-317-10001-7, 2004254). Bks Demand UMI.
--Concrete Bridge Design: Papers Presented to the First International Symposium on Concrete Bridge Design, Toronto, 1967. LC 68-54701. (American Concrete Institute Publications: SP-23). (Illus.). pap. 160.00 (ISBN 0-317-10038-6, 2003079). Bks Demand UMI.
--Concrete Design: United States & European Practices. LC 78-72044. (American Concrete Institute. Publication: No. SP-59). (Illus.). pap. 88.00 (ISBN 0-317-10026-2, 2022762). Bks Demand UMI.
--Concrete for Nuclear Reactors, 3 vols. LC 72-81007. (American Concrete Institute Publication Ser.: No. SP-34). (Illus.). Vol. 1. pap. 160.00 (ISBN 0-317-10390-3, 2012301); Vol. 2. pap. 135.30 (ISBN 0-317-10391-1); Vol. 3. pap. 142.30 (ISBN 0-317-10392-X). Bks Demand UMI.
--Designing for Effects of Creep, Shrinkage, Temperature in Concrete Structures. LC 78-156591. (American Concrete Institute. Publication: No. SP-27). (Illus.). pap. 107.00 (ISBN 0-317-10018-1, 2004492). Bks Demand UMI.
--Impact of Computers on the Practice of Structural Engineering in Concrete. LC 72-78494. (American Concrete Institute Publication Ser.: SP-33). (Illus.). pap. 80.00 (ISBN 0-317-10253-2, 2012300). Bks Demand UMI.
--Models for Concrete Structures. LC 79-103139. (American Concrete Institute Publications: SP-24). (Illus.). pap. 125.80 (ISBN 0-317-10043-2, 2022760). Bks Demand UMI.
--Polymers in Concrete. LC 73-86176. (American Concrete Institute Publication Ser.: No. SP-40). (Illus.). pap. 92.00 (ISBN 0-317-10006-8, 2004294). Bks Demand UMI.
--Polymers in Concrete: International Symposium. LC 78-73077. (American Concrete Institute, Publication: SP-58). pap. 106.50 (ISBN 0-317-27232-2, 2025082). Bks Demand UMI.
--Reinforced Concrete Columns. LC 75-8454. (American Concrete Institute Publications: SP-50). (Illus.). pap. 80.00 (ISBN 0-317-10048-3, 2022761). Bks Demand UMI.
--Response of Multistory Concrete Structures to Lateral Forces. LC 72-93775. (American Concrete Institute Publications Ser.: SP-36). (Illus.). pap. 80.00 (ISBN 0-317-10936-7, 2002352). Bks Demand UMI.
--Roadways & Airport Pavements. LC 75-10374. (American Concrete Institute Publications: SP-51). (Illus.). pap. 72.80 (ISBN 0-317-10031-9, 2017593). Bks Demand UMI.

American Concrete Institute & Jenny, Daniel P. Lightweight Concrete. LC 71-162468. (American Concrete Institute Publications Ser.: SP-29). (Illus.). pap. 83.30 (ISBN 0-317-10986-3, 2003080). Bks Demand UMI.

American Concrete Institute, Committee 318. Commentary on Building Code Requirements for Reinforced Concrete (ACI 318-63) Report of ACI Committee 318, Standard Building Code. LC 65-6942. (American Concrete Institute. Publication.: No. SP-10). pap. 25.00 (ISBN 0-317-09982-5, 2002351). Bks Demand UMI.

American Concrete Institute Staff. Shear in Reinforced Concrete. LC 73-94112. (American Concrete Institute, Publication Ser.: SP-42). (Illus.). Vol. 1. pap. 108.30 (ISBN 0-317-10241-9); Vol. 2. pap. 131.00 (ISBN 0-317-10242-7). Bks Demand UMI.

American Congress on Surveying & Mapping Fall Convention, Portland, 1969. Technical Papers. 378p. 5.00 (ISBN 0-317-32474-8, T633); members 3.00 (ISBN 0-317-32475-6). Am Congrs Survey.

American Consulting Engineers Council. ACEC Membership Directory, 1984-85. 413p. 1983. 50.00 (ISBN 0-686-60620-5). Am Consul Eng.
--Consulting Engineering Practice Manual. Cohen, Stanley, ed. (Illus.). 192p. 1981. 34.50 (ISBN 0-07-001352-7). McGraw.
--Guidelines for Ad Hoc Collaboration Agreements Between Consulting Firms. 54p. 1977. member 10.00 (ISBN 0-686-48325-1); non-member 15.00 (ISBN 0-686-48326-X). Am Consul Eng.

American Contract Bridge League Editorial Staff, ed. The Official Encyclopedia of Bridge. 4th., rev., expanded ed. 1984. 27.95 (ISBN 0-517-55272-8). Crown.

American Correctional Association. Annual Congress of Correction, 111th: Proceedings. 192p. (Orig.). 1982. pap. 10.00 (ISBN 0-942974-09-3). Am Correctional.
--Annual Congress of Correction, 118th: Proceedings. 168p. (Orig.). 1984. pap. 10.00x (ISBN 0-942974-65-4). Am Correctional.
--Correctional Career Logbook. 52p. (Orig.). 1982. pap. 4.50 (ISBN 0-942974-01-8). Am Correctional.
--Correctional Law: An Updated Bibliography of Selected Books & Articles. Rev. ed. 44p. 1982. pap. 4.00 (ISBN 0-942974-15-8). Am Correctional.
--Handbook on Correctional Classification: Programming for Treatment & Reintegration. (Criminal Justice Ser). 320p. 1978. pap. text ed. 10.50 (ISBN 0-87084-004-5). Anderson Pub Co.

American Correctional Association & Hippchen, Leonard J. Handbook on Correctional Classification: Programming for Treatment & Reintegration. LC 78-65636. (Criminal Justice Ser.). 172p. 1978. pap. text ed. 10.50 (ISBN 0-87084-005-3). Anderson Pub Co.

American Correctional Association. Legal Responsibility & Authority of Correctional Officers. Rev. ed. 64p. 1982. pap. 3.50 (ISBN 0-942974-11-5). Am Correctional.

American Correctional Association Staff. Classification. (Series 1: No. 4). 87p. (Orig.). 1981. pap. 5.00 (ISBN 0-942974-21-2). Am Correctional.
--Classification as a Management Tool: Theories & Models for Decision-Makers. 160p. (Orig.). 1982. pap. 9.00 (ISBN 0-942974-40-9). Am Correctional.
--Community Corrections. (Series 1: No. 5). 79p. (Orig.). 1981. pap. 5.00 (ISBN 0-942974-20-4). Am Correctional.
--Correctional Management. (Series 1: No. 2). 40p. (Orig.). 1981. pap. 5.00 (ISBN 0-686-37661-7). Am Correctional.
--Corrections & Public Awareness. (Series 2: No. 1). 25p. (Orig.). 1981. pap. 3.50 (ISBN 0-942974-22-0). Am Correctional.
--Guidelines for Adult Parole Authorities: Adult Probation & Parole Field Services. 281p. (Orig.). 1981. pap. 15.00 (ISBN 0-942974-33-6). Am Correctional.
--Guidelines for the Development of Policies & Procedures: Adult Community Residential Services. 220p. (Orig.). 1981. pap. 15.00 (ISBN 0-942974-32-8). Am Correctional.
--Guidelines for the Development of Policies & Procedures: Adult Correctional Institutions. 500p. (Orig.). 1981. pap. 20.00 (ISBN 0-942974-30-1). Am Correctional.
--Model Correctional Rules & Regulations. rev. ed. 50p. 1979. pap. 4.50 (ISBN 0-942974-13-1). Am Correctional.
--Probation & Parole Directory. 480p. (Orig.). 1981. pap. 25.00 (ISBN 0-942974-05-0). Am Correctional.
--Probation & Parole Directory: United States & Canada 1985. rev. ed. Travisono, Diana N. & Reilly, Jonna M., eds. 519p. (Orig.). 1985. pap. 35.00 (ISBN 0-942974-53-0). Am Correctional.

American Correctional Staff. Correctional Officers: Power, Pressure & Responsibility. 42p. (Orig.). 1983. pap. 4.00 (ISBN 0-942974-57-3). Am Correctional.

American Council of Learned. Concise Dictionary of American Biography. 3rd ed. LC 80-13892. 1980. lib. bdg. 75.00 (ISBN 0-684-16631-3, ScribR). Scribner.

American Council of Learned Societies, ed. Concise Dictionary of Scientific Biography. 1981. 70.00 (ISBN 0-684-16650-X, ScribR). Scribner.
--Dictionary of American Biography, 17 vols. LC 44-41895. Set. text ed. 1100.00 set includes supplements 1-7 (ISBN 0-684-17323-9, ScribR). Scribner.
--Dictionary of American Biography, Supplement 7. 1981. lib. bdg. 65.00 (ISBN 0-684-16794-8, ScribR). Scribner.
--Dictionary of American Biography: Biographical Index Guide. (Orig.). 1981. pap. 12.95 (ISBN 0-684-17152-X, ScribR). Scribner.

American Council Of Learned Societies Devoted To Humanistic Studies - Conference Of Secretaries. Studies in the History of Culture. facs. ed. LC 70-86728. (Essay Index Reprint Ser). 1942. 25.50 (ISBN 0-8369-1170-9). Ayer Co Pubs.

American Council of Otolaryngology. Pocket Guide to Antimicrobial Therapy in Otolaryngology. 60p. 4.00 (ISBN 0-318-12309-6); members 2.00 (ISBN 0-318-12310-X). Am Acad Otolary.

American Council on Education. General Education: Explorations in Evaluation; the Final Report. LC 72-138574. (Illus.). xxiii, 302p. Repr. of 1954 ed. lib. bdg. 15.00x (ISBN 0-8371-5773-0, ACGE). Greenwood.
--Youth & the Future: A General Report of the American Youth Commission. LC 73-7694. 296p. 1973. Repr. of 1942 ed. lib. bdg. 17.75x (ISBN 0-8371-6937-2, YOFU). Greenwood.

American Council on Education & Bauer, David G. The Complete Grants Sourcebook for Higher Sourcebook for Higher Education. 2nd ed. 608p. 1985. 85.00 (ISBN 0-02-901950-8). Macmillan.

American Council on Education, ed. American Universities & Colleges. 12th ed. 2176p. 1983. text ed. 99.50x (ISBN 3-11-008433-3). De Gruyter.

American Craft Council. Enamel: A Bibliography. rev. ed. 1978. 2.70 (ISBN 0-88321-029-0). Am Craft.
--Jewelry U. S. A. (Illus.). 64p. 1984. write for info. (ISBN 0-88321-053-3). AM Craft.
--Metal: A Bibliography. rev. ed. 1979. 4.70 (ISBN 0-88321-037-1). Am Craft.

American Crystallographic Association. Motion in Molecules: Calculation of Crystal Packing & Non-Bonded Forces. (Program & Abstracts Ser.: Vol.12, No. 1). 58p. 1984. pap. 5.00 (ISBN 0-317-05920-3). Polycrystal Bk Serv.

American Crystallographic Association Programs & Abstracts. Small Angle Scattering: Perspectives in Crystallography at Atomic Resolution. 1983. pap. 5.00 (ISBN 0-686-45047-7). Polycrystal Bk Serv.

American Crystallographic Association. Thirty-Second Annual Denver X-ray Conference: Summer Meeting, Snowmass, CO. Program & Abstracts. (Series 2: Vol. 11, No. 2). 72p. 1983. pap. 5.00 (ISBN 0-317-03259-3). Polycrystal Bk Serv.

American Crystallographic Association, ed. Workshop on Calculation of Crystal Packing & Non-Bonded Forces. 1984. 15.00 (ISBN 0-317-12233-9). Polycrystal Bk Serv.

American Demographics Magazine Editors, ed. State Demographics: Population Profiles of the 50 States. LC 83-70909. 300p. 1984. 59.50 (ISBN 0-87094-451-7). Dow Jones-Irwin.

American Dental Association - Bureau of Library & Indexing Service. Index to Dental Literature. 1981. annual cumulative 100.00 (ISBN 0-934510-11-3); quarterly cumulative 125.00 (ISBN 0-686-77270-9). Am Dental.

American Dental Association-Council on Dental Therapeutics. Accepted Dental Therapeutics. 39th ed. 1982. 15.00 (ISBN 0-934510-10-5). Am Dental.

American Diabetes Association & American Dietetic Association. The American Diabetes Association & the American Dietetic Association Family Cookbook, Vol. II. (Illus.). 400p. 1984. 15.95 (ISBN 0-13-024910-6). P-H.
--American Dietetic Association Family Cookbook. LC 80-16722. 320p. 1980. 14.95 (ISBN 0-13-024901-7). P-H.
--Family Cookbook, Vol. II. 448p. 1984. 15.95. Am Diabetes.

American Diabetes Association & Sims, Dorothea. Diabetes: Reach for Health & Freedom. 171p. 1984. 9.95. Am Diabetes.

American Dietetic Association. Handbook of Clinical Dietetics. LC 80-11317. 480p. 1981. text ed. 27.50x (ISBN 0-300-02256-5). Yale U Pr.

American Dietetic Association, jt. auth. see American Diabetes Association.

American Economic Association & Royal Economic Society. Surveys of Economic Theory. Robinson, E. A., ed. Incl. Vol. 1. Money, Interest & Welfare. (Illus.). 222p. 1965; Vol. 2. Growth & Development. (Illus.). 272p. 1965; Vol. 3. Resource Allocation. 224p. 1966. 19.95 (ISBN 0-312-77875-9). St Martin.

American Economic Association, ed. Readings in the Social Control of Industry. LC 72-14175. (Essay Index Reprint Ser.). Repr. of 1942 ed. 27.50 (ISBN 0-518-10001-4). Ayer Co Pubs.

American Economic Association Committee, compiled by. Readings in Business Cycle Theory. LC 76-29403. (BCL Ser.). 736p. Repr. of 1951 ed. 33.50 (ISBN 0-686-77531-7). AMS Pr.
--Readings in the Theory of Income Distribution. LC 76-29414. (BCL II Ser.). Repr. of 1946 ed. 45.00 (ISBN 0-404-15332-1). AMS Pr.

American Electrican Magazine Staff. Electrical Designs. 1984. pap. 10.95 (ISBN 0-917914-22-8). Lindsay Pubns.

American Enterprise Institute, ed. Candidates, Nineteen Eighty: Where They Stand. 1980. pap. 4.25 (ISBN 0-8447-1336-8). Am Enterprise.

American Enterprise Institute for Public Policy Research. How Can Our Physical Environment Best be Controlled & Developed? (American Enterprise Institute for Public Policy Research. High School Debate Ser.). pap. 31.30 (ISBN 0-317-09965-5, 2017087). Bks Demand UMI.
--Proposed Procedures for a Limited Constitutional Convention: 1984, 98th Congress, 2d Session. LC 84-244484. 40p. 1984. 3.95 (ISBN 0-8447-0262-5). Am Enterprise.
--Toxic Torts: Proposals for Compensating Victims of Hazardous Substances: 1984, 98th Congress, 2nd Session. LC 84-243006. 32p. 1984. 3.95 (ISBN 0-8447-0260-9). Am Enterprise.

American Enterprise Institute for Public Policy Research, et al. War Powers & the Constitution. (AEI Forum Ser.: No. 61). write for info. Amer Bar Assn.

American Ethnological Society. American Indian Intellectuals: 1976 Proceedings. Liberty, Margot, ed. (Illus.). 1978. pap. text ed. 18.95 (ISBN 0-8299-0223-6). West Pub.
--Forms of Play of Native North Americans: Proceedings. Norbeck, Edward & Ferrer, Claire R., eds. (Illus.). 1979. pap. text ed. 17.50 (ISBN 0-8299-0262-7). West Pub.
--Publications of the American Ethnological Society, Vols. 1-17, 19, & 21. Repr. of 1951 ed. 820.00 (ISBN 0-404-58150-1). AMS Pr.

American Ethnological Society & Bennett, John W. The New Ethnicity, Perspectives from Ethnology: Proceedings. (AES Ser). 1975. pap. text ed. 18.95 (ISBN 0-8299-0032-2). West Pub.

American Ethnological Society, 1974. American Anthropology, the Early Years: Proceedings. Murra, John V., ed. (AES Ser). (Illus.). 235p. 1976. pap. text ed. 18.95 (ISBN 0-8299-0097-7). West Pub.

American-European Symposium, Vienna, Nov. 3-5, 1975, Sponsored by Physicians Associated for Continuing Education, Johns Hopkins University, & the University of Vienna & the Univ. of Innesbruck. Prostatic Disease: Proceedings. Marberger, H., et al, eds. LC 75-42905. (Progress in Clinical & Biological Research Ser.: Vol. 6). 432p. 1976. 42.00x (ISBN 0-8451-0006-8). A R Liss.

American Express. American Express International Traveler's Pocket Dictionaries & Phrase Books. 240p. 1984. pap. 5.95 ea. Fr (ISBN 0-671-47029-9). Ger (ISBN 0-671-47030-2). Ital (ISBN 0-671-47031-0). Span (ISBN 0-671-47028-0). S&S.

American Fabrics Magazine, ed. Encyclopedia of Textiles. 3rd ed. (Illus.). 656p. 1980. 49.95 (ISBN 0-13-276576-4, Busn). P-H.

American Family Records Association. AFRA Member Directory & Ancestral Surname Registry, Vol. 2. Baldwin, Betty C. & Karns, Kermit B., eds. 40p. 1985. pap. 3.95 (ISBN 0-913233-03-X). AFRA.

American Family Records Association Staff. AFRA Member Directory & Ancestral Surname Registry, 1984, Vol. 1. Baker, Shirley R. & Karns, Kermit B., eds. 1984. Vol. 1, 57p. pap. 3.95 (ISBN 0-913233-02-1). AFRA.

American Family Records Association. List of Pupils, Mount Gilead Rural School, District 22, Clay County, Missouri, 1915-16-1945-46. 32p. 1983. pap. 5.00 (ISBN 0-913233-01-3). AFRA.

American Family Records Association Staff. Trails West: The Genealogy of the Ohio Territory. Neblock, Nita, ed. (Illus.). 46p. 1985. pap. 3.95 (ISBN 0-913233-04-8). AFRA.

American Federation of Arts. Cultural Resources of Boston. (Orig.). 1965. 5.00 (ISBN 0-8079-0030-3); pap. 2.00 (ISBN 0-8079-0031-1). October.
--New Chinese Landscape. (Illus., Orig.). 1966. pap. 2.00 (ISBN 0-8079-0093-1). October.
--Thirty-Third Biennial Exhibition of Art, Venice, 1966. (Illus.). 1966. 5.00 (ISBN 0-8079-0123-7); pap. 2.00 (ISBN 0-8079-0124-5). October.

American Federation of Arts, jt. auth. see Center for Inter-American Relations.

American Federation of Labor. American Federation of Labor: History, Encyclopedia, Reference Book, 3 vols. Roberts, William C. & Erb, Mary, eds. LC 77-3562. 1977. lib. bdg. 197.75x set (ISBN 0-8371-9568-3, AFLH); Vol. 1. lib. bdg. 30.00 (ISBN 0-8371-9569-1, AFLI); Vol. 2. lib. bdg. 25.00 (ISBN 0-8371-9570-5, AFLJ); Vol. 3, Pt. 1. lib. bdg. 45.00 (ISBN 0-8371-9571-3, AFLK); Vol. 3, Pt. 2. lib. bdg. 55.00 (ISBN 0-8371-9572-1, AFLL); Vol. 3, Pt. 3. lib. bdg. 40.00 (ISBN 0-8371-9598-5, AFLM). Greenwood.

--Reports of the Proceedings of the Annual Conventions of the American Federation of Labor, 74 vols. in 58. Repr. of 1955 ed. Set. 2480.00 (ISBN 0-685-56820-2). AMS Pr.

American Federation of Teachers & the Doctorate Association, ed. Early Childhood Education. (Doctorate Association Ser.). (Illus.). 1977. pap. 10.95 (ISBN 0-89529-007-3). Avery Pub.

American Feed Manufacturers Association. Feed Manufacturing Technology. Pfost, Harry, ed. 1976. 50.00 (ISBN 0-686-00374-8). AG Pr.

American Film Institute. Filmmakers on Filmmaking, 2 vols. McBride, Joseph, ed. LC 83-4722. 1983. 15.95 ea. Vol. 1, 224p (ISBN 0-87477-266-4). Vol. 2, 240p (ISBN 0-87477-267-2). pap. 7.95 ea. Vol. 1, 224p (ISBN 0-87477-249-4). Vol. 2, 240p (ISBN 0-87477-250-8). J P Tarcher.

--Guide to College Courses in Film & Television. LC 75-15345. 1975. pap. 6.95 (ISBN 0-87491-030-7). Acropolis.

American Film Institute, ed. American Film Heritage. LC 72-3813. (Illus.). 200p. 1972. pap. 7.95 (ISBN 0-87491-336-5). Acropolis.

American Film Institute, compiled by. American Film Institute Catalog of Motion Pictures. Incl. Feature Films 1921-1930, 2 vols. 1653p. 1971. Set. 139.00 (ISBN 0-8352-0440-5). LC 79-128587. Bowker.

American Film Institute Staff, ed. The American Film Institute Factfile. 1984. pap. 140.00 library slipcase (ISBN 0-89093-571-8, Co-pub. by Am Film Inst). U Pubns Amer.

American Fire Journal. Skull Sessions, Vol. 1. 103p. 27.50 (ISBN 0-317-34561-3). Intl Fire Serv.

American Fisheries Society Fish Health Section see McDaniel, D. W.

American Fisheries Society Northeastern Division see Johnson, R. E.

American Fisheries Society Southern Division see Bonn, E. W, et al.

American Folklife Center. Ethnic Recordings in America: A Neglected Heritage. LC 80-607133. (Studies in American Folklife: No. 1). (Illus.). xiii, 269p. 1982. 13.00 (ISBN 0-8444-0339-3). Lib Congress.

American Football Coaches Assoc., compiled by. Football Coaching. 224p. 1981. 19.95 (ISBN 0-684-17149-X, ScribT). Scribner.

American for Health Physical Education Recreation & Dance. Dance Therapy. (Focus on Dance: VII). 80p. 1974. 8.65 (ISBN 0-88314-072-1, 243-25570). AAHPERD.

American Foresters Society & Wildlife Society. Choices in Silviculture for American Forests. LC 81-51229. (Illus.). 88p. (Orig.). 1981. pap. 4.00 (ISBN 0-939970-09-0). Soc Am Foresters.

American Forestry Association. Trees Every Boy & Girl Should Know. 4.50 (ISBN 0-686-26729-X, 31). Am Forestry.

American Foundation. Medical Research: A Midcentury Survey, 2 vols. LC 77-13559. 1977. Repr. of 1955 ed. lib. bdg. 93.50x (ISBN 0-8371-9863-1, AMFO). Greenwood.

American Foundation for the Blind (New York) Dictionary Catalog of the M. C. Migel Memorial Library, 2 Vols. 1966. Set. lib. bdg. 156.00 (ISBN 0-8161-0705-X, Hall Library). G K Hall.

American Foundrymen Society. Electric Ironmelting Conference Proceedings, 2nd, 1974. 167p. 30.00 (ISBN 0-317-32659-7, FC7509); members 15.00 (ISBN 0-317-32660-0). Am Foundrymen.

American Friends of the Chinese People. China Today. 1934-42. Repr. lib. bdg. 205.00x (ISBN 0-8371-9142-4, CT00). Greenwood.

American Friends Service Committee. A Compassionate Peace: A Future for the Middle East. (Illus.). 226p. 1982. pap. 5.95 (ISBN 0-8090-1399-1). Hill & Wang.

--A Compassionate Peace: A Future for the Middle East. 1981. 6.95 (ISBN 0-686-95355-X). Am Fr Serv Comm.

--Struggle for Justice: A Report on Crime & Punishment in America. 186p. 1971. 4.50 (ISBN 0-8090-8927-0); pap. 4.95 (ISBN 0-8090-1363-0). Hill & Wang.

American Friends Service Committee of San Francisco. Taking Charge of Our Lives: Living Responsibly in the World. Bodner, Joan, ed. LC 83-48981. (Illus.). 256p. 1984. pap. 9.57 (ISBN 0-06-250019-8, CN 4085, HarpR). Har-Row.

American Gas Association. Gas Engineers Handbook. Segeler, C. George, ed. LC 65-17328. (Illus.). 1550p. 1965. 75.00 (ISBN 0-8311-3011-3). Indus Pr.

--Glossary for the Gas Industry. rev. ed. 83p. 1975. pap. 3.50 (ISBN 0-318-12635-4, F50000). Am Gas Assn.

--Methane. (Special Report Ser.). 200p. 1983. 375.00 (ISBN 0-8247-7072-2). Dekker.

American Gas Association & Payne, F. William. Guide to New Natural Gas Utilization Technologies. LC 83-49499. 300p. 1984. text ed. 39.00 (ISBN 0-915586-94-0). Fairmont Pr.

American Gas Association Committee on Revision of the Gas Chemists Handbook, jt. auth. see Altieri, V. J.

American Gas Association Pipeline Research Committee, jt. auth. see Gideon, D. N.

American Gas Association Pipeline Research Committee, jt. auth. see Hardy, H. Reginald, Jr.

American Gas Association. Policy Evaluation & Analysis Group. New Technologies for Gas Energy Supply & Efficient Use: 1983 Update. LC 83-174168. (Illus.). 43p. Date not set. price not set. Am Gas Assn.

American Genealogical Research Institute Staff. How to Trace Your Family Tree. LC 73-88881. 200p. 1975. pap. 3.95 (ISBN 0-385-09885-5, Dolp). Doubleday.

American Geographical Society Library New York. Author, Title, Subject & Geographic Catalogs of the Glaciology Collection, Department of Exploration & Field Research, 3 vols. 1971. Set. 298.00 (ISBN 0-8161-0922-2, Hall Library). G K Hall.

--Research Catalogue of the American Geographical Society, 15 Vols. (Illus.). 1962. Set. 1450.00 (ISBN 0-8161-0628-2, Hall Library). G K Hall.

American Geographical Society Library-New York. Research Catalogue of the American Geographical Society: First Supplement, 2 pts. Incl. Pt. 1. Regional Catalogue, 2 vols. 1972. lib. bdg. 260.00 (ISBN 0-8161-0999-0); Pt. 2. Topical Catalogue, 2 vols. 1974. lib. bdg. 265.00 (ISBN 0-8161-1083-2). Hall Library). G K Hall.

American Geographical Society, Map Department, New York. Index to Maps in Books & Periodicals, First Supplement. 1971. lib. bdg. 110.00 (ISBN 0-8161-0806-4, Hall Library). G K Hall.

--Index to Maps in Books & Periodicals, 10 vols. 1968. Set. lib. bdg. 990.00 (ISBN 0-8161-0753-X, Hall Library). G K Hall.

--Index to Maps in Books & Periodicals, Second Suppl. 1976. lib. bdg. 110.00 (ISBN 0-8161-0995-8, Hall Library). G K Hall.

American Geographical Society of New York. New England's Prospect: 1933. Adams, James T., et al, eds. LC 78-111763. Repr. of 1933 ed. 34.00 (ISBN 0-404-00354-0). AMS Pr.

--Oriental Explorations & Studies, 6 vols. & map vol. Repr. of 1928 ed. 350.00 set (ISBN 0-404-60230-4). AMS Pr.

--Pioneer Settlement. facsimile ed. LC 74-90599. (Essay Index Reprint Ser). 1932. 31.00 (ISBN 0-8369-1241-1). Ayer Co Pubs.

American Geological Institute. Deep Sea Drilling Project, Legs 1-25. (AGI Reprint Ser.: No. 1). 1975. 10.00 (ISBN 0-913312-16-9). Am Geol.

--Deep Sea Drilling Project, Legs 26-44. (AGI Reprint Ser.: No. 2). 1976. 10.00 (ISBN 0-913312-17-7). Am Geol.

--Deep Sea Drilling Project, Legs 45-62. LC 78-74943. (AGI Reprint Ser.: No. 4). 1979. pap. 10.00 (ISBN 0-913312-12-6). Am Geol.

--Dictionary of Geological Terms. 3rd rev. ed. LC 82-45315. (Illus.). 576p. 1984. 19.95 (ISBN 0-385-18100-0, Anchor Pr); pap. 7.95 (ISBN 0-385-18101-9, Anchor Pr). Doubleday.

--Directory of the Geologic Division, U.S. Geological Survey. (Illus.). 144p. 1980. pap. 10.00 (ISBN 0-913312-45-2). Am Geol.

--Geology: Science & Profession. 1976. pap. 1.00 (ISBN 0-913312-19-3). Am Geol.

American Greetings Corp. Strawberry Shortcake & the Catnabbing. LC 81-85697. (Strawberry Shortcake Little Pops Ser.). (Illus.). 12p. (ps-3). 1982. pap. 2.50 (ISBN 0-394-85292-3). Random.

--Strawberry Shortcake & the Fake Cake Surprise. LC 81-85539. (Strawberry Shortcake Little Pops Ser.). (Illus.). 12p. (ps-3). 1982. pap. 2.50 (ISBN 0-394-85330-X). Random.

--Strawberry Shortcake & the Picnic Plot. LC 81-52980. (Strawberry Shortcake Little Pops Ser.). (Illus.). 12p. (ps-3). 1982. pap. 2.50 (ISBN 0-394-85232-X). Random.

American Greetings Corp., jt. auth. see Razzi, Jim.

American Health Foundation. The American Health Foundation Guide to Lifespan Health. (Illus.). 288p. 1984. 19.95 (ISBN 0-396-08373-0). Dodd.

--The Book of Health: A Complete Guide to Making Health Last a Lifetime. Wynder, Ernst L., ed. (Illus.). 736p. 1981. 19.95 (ISBN 0-531-09929-6). Watts.

American Health Research Institute. Depression: Medical Subject Analysis & Research Directory with Bibliography. Bartone, J. C., et al, eds. LC 81-71808. 133p. 1982. 29.95 (ISBN 0-941864-30-8); pap. 21.95 (ISBN 0-941864-31-6). ABBE Pubs Assn.

--Medical Subject Analysis of a Selected Bibliography Concerning General Counseling. Bartone, J. C., ed. LC 81-71268. 266p. 1982. 39.95 (ISBN 0-941864-18-9); pap. 29.95 (ISBN 0-941864-19-7). ABBE Pubs Assn.

--Neurotic Disorders: Medical Subject Analysis & Research Guide with Bibliography. Bartone, John C., ed. LC 83-45531. 149p. 1984. 29.95 (ISBN 0-88164-118-9); pap. 21.95 (ISBN 0-88164-119-7). ABBE Pubs Assn.

--Rape Victims, Offenders, Treatment & Jurisprudence: Medical Subject Analysis & Research Guide. Bartone, John C., ed. LC 83-45537. 140p. 1984. 29.95 (ISBN 0-88164-122-7); pap. 21.95 (ISBN 0-88164-123-5). ABBE Pubs Assn.

--Science, Medicine & Psychology of Personality: Subject Analyses with Bibliography. Bartone, John C., ed. LC 83-45529. 145p. 1985. 29.95 (ISBN 0-88164-124-3); pap. 21.95 (ISBN 0-88164-125-1). ABBE Pubs Assn.

--Sex Behavior: Medical Subject Analysis & Research Bibliography. LC 84-45662. 150p. 1985. 29.95 (ISBN 0-88164-204-5); pap. 21.95 (ISBN 0-88164-205-3). ABBE Pubs Assn.

American Health Research Institute Ltd. Anxiety: Medical Subject Analysis & Research Directory with Bibliography. Bartone, J. C., et al, eds. LC 81-71807. 120p. 1982. 29.95 (ISBN 0-941864-28-6); pap. 21.95 (ISBN 0-941864-29-4). ABBE Pubs Assn.

American Health Research Institute, Ltd. Cannabis (Marijuana) & Cannabinoids: Medical Subject Research Directory with Bibliography. Bartone, John C., ed. LC 82-72018. 105p. 1982. 29.95 (ISBN 0-941864-52-9); pap. 21.95 (ISBN 0-941864-53-7). ABBE Pubs Assn.

American Health Research Institute LTD. Genetic Engineering & Cell Intervention: Guidebook for Medicine, & Science. Bartone, John C., ed. LC 83-46106. 150p. 1984. 29.95 (ISBN 0-88164-146-4); pap. 21.95 (ISBN 0-88164-147-2). ABBE Pubs Assn.

American Health Research Institute, Ltd. Gunshot Wounds in Crime & Medicine: A Medical Subject Analysis & Research Index With Bibliography. Bartone, John C., ed. LC 83-70085. 218p. 1983. 39.95 (ISBN 0-941864-82-0); pap. 34.95 (ISBN 0-941864-83-9). ABBE Pubs Assn.

--Intelligence: International Survey with Research Subject Index & Bibliography. Bartone, John C., ed. LC 82-72014. 115p. 1982. 29.95 (ISBN 0-941864-44-8); pap. 21.95 (ISBN 0-941864-45-6). ABBE Pubs Assn.

American Health Research Institute Ltd. International Bibliography & Medical Subject Index of Crime Publications. Bartone, J. C., ed. LC 81-71266. 155p. 1982. 29.95 (ISBN 0-941864-14-6); pap. 19.95 (ISBN 0-941864-15-4). ABBE Pubs Assn.

--Medical & Psychological Subject Classification of Persuasive Communication Literature. Bartone, J. C., ed. LC 81-71264. 121p. 1982. 29.95 (ISBN 0-941864-10-3); pap. 21.95 (ISBN 0-941864-11-1). ABBE Pubs Assn.

--Medical Subject Research Directory & Bibliography of Iatrology, Iatrogenesis & Iatrogenic Diseases. Bartone, J. C., ed. LC 81-71263. 272p. 1982. 39.95 (ISBN 0-941864-08-1); pap. 29.95 (ISBN 0-941864-09-X). ABBE Pubs Assn.

--Medical Subject Research Directory of Medical Malpractice Exclusive of Iatrology. Bartone, J. C., ed. LC 81-71270. 132p. 1982. 29.95 (ISBN 0-941864-22-7); pap. 21.95 (ISBN 0-941864-23-5). ABBE Pubs Assn.

--Medical Subject Research Index of International Bibliography Concerning Cocaine. Bartone, J. C., ed. LC 81-71267. 198p. 1982. 34.95 (ISBN 0-941864-16-2); pap. 29.95 (ISBN 0-941864-17-0). ABBE Pubs Assn.

--Medical Subjects Directory & Bibliography for Psychosomatic Medicine. Bartone, J. C., ed. LC 81-71262. 120p. 1982. 29.95 (ISBN 0-941864-06-5); pap. 21.95 (ISBN 0-941864-07-3). ABBE Pubs Assn.

American Health Research Institute, Ltd. Mental Disorders: Medical Research Subject Directory on the Occurrence, Diagnosis, Etiology & Therapy with Bibliography. Bartone, John C., ed. LC 82-72019. 142p. 1982. 29.95 (ISBN 0-941864-54-5); pap. 21.95 (ISBN 0-941864-55-3). ABBE Pubs Assn.

--Patients: A Medical Subject Analysis & Research Index with Bibliography. Bartone, John C., ed. LC 82-72029. 150p. 1985. 29.95 (ISBN 0-941864-74-X); pap. 21.95 (ISBN 0-941864-75-8). ABBE Pubs Assn.

--Psycho-Physiological Disorders: General & Medical Research Subject Directory with Bibliography. Bartone, John C., ed. LC 82-72012. 236p. 1982. 39.95 (ISBN 0-941864-40-5); pap. 29.95 (ISBN 0-941864-41-3). ABBE Pubs Assn.

--Stress: Medical Subject Analysis & Research Directory with Bibliography. Bartone, John C., ed. LC 81-71806. 106p. 1982. 29.95 (ISBN 0-941864-27-8); pap. 21.95 (ISBN 0-941864-26-X). ABBE Pubs Assn.

American Health Research Institute Ltd. Women & Women's Rights: A Medical, Psychological & International Subject Survey with Research Index & Bibliography. Bartone, John C., ed. LC 83-70089. 146p. 1984. 29.95 (ISBN 0-88164-98-7); pap. 21.95 (ISBN 0-941864-99-5). ABBE Pubs Assn.

American Health Research Institute Staff. Abstracting & Indexing: Research Subject Analysis Index with Reference Bibliography. LC 85-478733. 150p. 1985. 29.95 (ISBN 0-88164-419-6); pap. 21.95 (ISBN 0-317-15190-8). ABBE Pubs Assn.

--Accidents of All Types Forms: Medical Analysis Index with Research Bibliography. LC 85-47574. 150p. 1985. 29.95 (ISBN 0-88164-322-X); pap. 21.95 (ISBN 0-88164-323-8). ABBE Pubs Assn.

--Decision Making in Health Sciences: Medical Analysis Index with Reference Bibliography. LC 85-48752. 150p. 1985. 29.95 (ISBN 0-88164-378-5); pap. 21.95 (ISBN 0-88164-379-3). ABBE Pubs Assn.

--Disasters & Disaster Planning: Medical Analysis Index with Research Bibliography. LC 85-47857. 150p. 1985. 29.95 (ISBN 0-88164-390-4); pap. 21.95 (ISBN 0-88164-391-2). ABBE Pubs Assn.

--Drug Therapy in Health, Medicine & Disease: Subject Analysis Index with Reference Bibliography. LC 85-47872. 150p. 1985. 29.95 (ISBN 0-88164-416-1); pap. 21.95 (ISBN 0-88164-417-X). ABBE Pubs Assn.

--Efficiency & Performance in Health Sciences: Medical Analysis Index with Reference Bibliography. LC 85-47847. 150p. 1985. 29.95 (ISBN 0-88164-366-1); pap. 21.95 (ISBN 0-88164-367-X). ABBE Pubs Assn.

--International Cooperation in Medicine & Science: Subject Analysis Index with Research Bibliography. LC 85-47585. 150p. 1985. 29.95 (ISBN 0-88164-344-0); pap. 21.95 (ISBN 0-88164-345-9). ABBE Pubs Assn.

--Medical Research on Students: A Subject Analysis with Bibliography. LC 84-45736. 150p. 1985. 29.95 (ISBN 0-88164-250-9); pap. 21.95 (ISBN 0-88164-251-7). ABBE Pubs Assn.

--Mental & Intelligence Tests: Medical Subject Analysis with Research Bibliography. LC 84-45652. 150p. 1985. 29.95 (ISBN 0-88164-226-6); pap. 21.95 (ISBN 0-88164-227-4). ABBE Pubs Assn.

--Personality Tests & Inventory: Medical Subject Analysis with Bibliography. LC 84-45659. 150p. 1985. 29.95 (ISBN 0-88164-212-6); pap. 21.95 (ISBN 0-88164-213-4). ABBE Pubs Assn.

--Sex Disorders: Medical Subject Analysis & Research Guidebook with Bibliography. Bartone, John C., ed. LC 84-45866. 150p. 1985. 29.95 (ISBN 0-88164-288-6); pap. 21.95 (ISBN 0-88164-289-4). ABBE Pubs Assn.

--Weather, Health & Biomedicine: Subject Analysis Index with Research Bibliography. LC 85-47846. 150p. 1985. 29.95 (ISBN 0-88164-354-8); pap. 21.95 (ISBN 0-88164-355-6). ABBE Pubs Assn.

American Heart Association. The American Heart Association Cookbook. 1985. pap. 10.95 (ISBN 0-345-32819-1). Ballantine.

American Heart Association, Scientific Sessions, 52nd. Abstracts. (AHA Monograph: No. 65). 1979. pap. 8.00 (ISBN 0-686-58031-1). Am Heart.

American Heart Association Scientific Sessions, 51st. Abstracts. (AHA Momograph: No. 61). 1978. pap. 8.00 (ISBN 0-686-59598-X, 73-047-A). Am Heart.

American Heart Association Scientific Sessions, 50th. Abstracts. pap. 8.00 (ISBN 0-87493-059-6, 73-043-A). Am Heart.

American Heritage. Diccionario Ingles. 1981. 9.95 (ISBN 0-395-31254-X); pap. 7.95 (ISBN 0-395-31255-8). HM.

--Exercises to Accompany American Heritage Dictionary. 1977. 1.20 (ISBN 0-395-26171-6). HM.

--Historical Houses of America. pap. 6.95 (ISBN 0-686-60941-7, 24711-5, Fireside). S&S.

--The Word Book. LC 76-698. 1976. 3.95 (ISBN 0-395-24521-4). HM.

American Heritage Editors, jt. auth. see Catton, Bruce.

American Heritage Editors, ed. American Heritage School Dictionary. LC 72-75557. 1977. 10.95 (ISBN 0-395-24792-6). HM.

American Heritage Magazine, jt. auth. see UPI.

American Heritage Magazine, compiled by. A Sense of History: The Best Writing from American Heritage. 700p. 1985. 24.95 (ISBN 0-8281-1175-8). Am Heritage.

American Heritage Staff. Concise American Heritage Dictionary. LC 76-4047. 1980. 7.95 (ISBN 0-395-24522-2). HM.

American Historical Assn. War As a Social Institution: The Historian's Perspective. Clarkson, Jessie D. & Cochran, Thomas C., eds. LC 73-38408. Repr. of 1941 ed. 18.00 (ISBN 0-404-01575-1). AMS Pr.

American Historical Association, ed. see American Jewish Historical Society, et al.

American Historical Association - Committee for the Study of War Documents. A Catalogue of Files & Microfilms of the German Foreign Ministry Archives, 1867-1920. LC 59-2654. Repr. of 1959 ed. 71.00 (ISBN 0-527-02150-4). Kraus Repr.

American Home Editors. American Home Garden Book & Plant Encyclopedia. LC 63-19657. (Illus.). 512p. 1964. pap. 8.95 (ISBN 0-87131-035-X). M Evans.

American Home Food Staff, ed. The American Home All-Purpose Cookbook. LC 66-23272. (Illus.). 572p. 1978. pap. 7.95 (ISBN 0-87131-268-9). M Evans.

American Honey Institute. Good & Wholesome Honey Recipes. 112p. 1985. pap. 3.95 (ISBN 0-486-24945-X). Dover.

American Honey Institute, ed. Old Favorite Honey Recipes. (Illus.). 1977. pap. 3.50 (ISBN 0-916638-03-0). Meyerbooks.

American Horticultural Society. North American Horticulture. 448p. 1982. 50.00 (ISBN 0-684-17604-1, ScribT). Scribner.

American Hospital Association. Auxiliary Gift & Coffee Shop Management. LC 76-26604. 152p. (Orig.). 1976. pap. 18.75 (ISBN 0-87258-155-1, 019111). AHPI.

--Auxiliary: New Concepts, New Directions. LC 74-22174. 236p. (Orig.). 1974. pap. 24.50 (ISBN 0-87258-160-8, 019110); pap. 19.60 members. AHPI.

--Auxiliary Self-Evaluation Program. 32p. 1978. pap. 8.75 (AHA-019112). AHPI.

--Catalog of the Library of the American Hospital Association, Asa S. Bacon Memorial Chicago Library, 5 vols. 1976. Set. lib. bdg. 480.00 (ISBN 0-8161-1210-X, Hall Library). G K Hall.

--Cumulative Index of Hospital Literature: 1965-1969. 864p. 1970. 125.00 (ISBN 0-87258-055-5, AHA-121003). Am Hospital.

--Cumulative Index of Hospital Literature: 1955-1959. Incl. 1955-1959. 460p. 1960. casebound 125.00 (ISBN 0-87258-329-5, AHA-121002); 1950-1954. 540p. 1955. 125.00 (ISBN 0-87258-328-7, AHA-121001). Am Hospital.

--Cumulative Index of Hospital Literature: 1970-1974. 1004p. 1976. casebound 125.00 (ISBN 0-87258-192-6, AHA-121004). Am Hospital.

--Cumulative Index of Hospital Literature: 1975-1977. 564p. 1979. casebound 125.00 (ISBN 0-87258-260-4, AHA-121005). Am Hospital.

--Directory of Architects for Health Facilities, 1983. 5th ed. LC 80-641180. 56p. 1983. pap. 30.00 (ISBN 0-87258-415-1, AHA-043111). AHPI.

--Directory of Multihospital Systems. 5th ed. 100p. 1985. pap. 49.95 (ISBN 0-939450-42-9, 103155). AHPI.

--Fire Safety Training in Health Care Institutions. LC 75-20295. (Illus.). 60p. 1975. pap. 10.00 (ISBN 0-87258-163-2, 181147). AHPI.

--Guide for Preparation of Constitution & Bylaws for General Hospitals. Rev. ed. LC 81-2788. 32p. 1981. 12.50 (ISBN 0-87258-123-3, 118130). AHPI.

--The Hospital Admitting Department. LC 85-7401. (Illus.). 100p. (Orig.). 1977. pap. 18.75 (ISBN 0-939450-64-X, AHA-004155). AHPI.

--The Hospital Admitting Department. 90p. 1977. 18.75 (ISBN 0-87258-200-0, 1105P); members 15.00 (ISBN 0-318-12846-2). Am Med Record Assn.

--Hospital Computer Systems Planning: Preparation of Request for Proposal. LC 84-2880. 124p. 1980. 28.00 (ISBN 0-939450-19-4, 040145). AHPI.

--Hospital Housekeeping Handbook. (Illus.). 144p. 1980. 22.50 (ISBN 0-87258-273-6, 085125). AHPI.

--Hospital Literature Index: 1978, Vol. 34. 350p. 125.00 (ISBN 0-87258-347-3, AHA-121340). Am Hospital.

--Hospital Literature Index: 1979, Vol. 35. Dunlap, Alice, et al, eds. 736p. 1980. 125.00 (ISBN 0-87258-346-5, AHA-121350). Am Hospital.

--Hospital Statistics: Data from the American Hospital Association Annual Survey, 1981. 240p. 1982. pap. text ed. 40.00 (ISBN 0-87258-364-3, AHA-082082). Am Hospital.

--Hospital Statistics: Data from the American Hospital Association 1977 Annual Survey. (Illus.). 1978. pap. 12.50 (ISBN 0-87258-224-8, 082078). Am Hospital.

--Hospital Statistics: Data from the American Hospital Association 1972 Annual Survey. (Illus.). 224p. 1973. pap. 9.50 (ISBN 0-87258-127-6, 082073). Am Hospital.

--Hospital Statistics: Data from the American Hospital Association 1973 Annual Survey. (Illus.). 225p. 1974. pap. 9.50 (ISBN 0-87258-158-6, 082074). Am Hospital.

--Hospital Statistics: Data from the American Hospital Association 1974 Annual Survey. (Illus.). 230p. 1975. pap. 9.50 (ISBN 0-87258-167-5, 082075). Am Hospital.

--Hospital Statistics: Data from the American Hospital Association 1978 Annual Survey. (Illus.). 244p. 1979. pap. 15.00 (ISBN 0-87258-257-4, 082079). Am Hospital.

--Hospital Statistics: Data from the American Hospital Association 1975 Annual Survey. (Illus.). 232p. 1976. pap. 9.50 (ISBN 0-87258-185-3, 082076). Am Hospital.

--Hospital Statistics: Data from the American Hospital Association 1976 Annual Survey. (Illus.). 246p. 1977. pap. 12.50 (ISBN 0-87258-204-3, 082077). Am Hospital.

--Hospital Statistics: Data from the American Hospital Association 1979 Annual Survey. 256p. 1980. pap. 18.75 (ISBN 0-87258-282-5, 082080). Am Hospital.

--Hospital Statistics: Data from the American Hospital Association 1980 Annual Survey. 256p. 1981. pap. 26.25 (ISBN 0-87258-312-0, AHA-082081). Am Hospital.

--ICD-9-CM Coding Handbook for Entry-Level Coders, with Answers. LC 84-6242. 348p. 1979. pap. text ed. 23.75 (ISBN 0-939450-23-2, 148165); supplements (148162). AHPI.

--Implementing Patient Education in the Hospital. LC 79-4292. (Illus.). 316p. 1979. pap. 34.25 (ISBN 0-939450-50-X, AHA-070188). AHPI.

--Internal Control, Internal Auditing, & Operations Auditing for Hospitals. LC 79-15042. (Financial Management Ser). 104p. 1979. pap. 22.50 (ISBN 0-87258-272-8, 061108). AHPI.

--Staff Manual for Teaching Patients about Chronic Obstructive Pulmonary Diseases. LC 82-6856. (Illus.). 456p. 1982. 3-ring binder 47.50 (ISBN 0-87258-372-4, 070120). AHPI.

American Hospital Association & National Safety Council. Safety Guide for Health Care Institutions. 3rd ed. 160p. 1983. 35.00 (ISBN 0-87258-302-3, 181136). AHPI.

American Hospital Association, et al. Sharing Responsibility for Patient Safety. 24p. 1979. 8.75 (ISBN 0-87258-248-5, 178152). AHPI.

American Hospital Association Clearinghouse for Hospital Management Engineering, ed. Computer-Assisted Medical Record Systems: An Examination of Case Studies. 148p. 1982. pap. 18.75 (ISBN 0-87258-375-9, AHA-148200). Am Hospital.

American Hotel & Motel Association. Uniform System of Accounts & Expense Dictionary for Small Hotels & Motels. (Illus.). 157p. 1981. Repr. 15.00 (ISBN 0-86612-001-7). Educ Inst Am Hotel.

American Institute. AAI Policy Kit. 1984. 5.75 (ISBN 0-686-95947-7). IIA.

American Institute, ed. Reading in Economics. 2nd ed. LC 81-66115. 189p. 1981. pap. 12.00 (ISBN 0-89463-028-8). Am Inst Property.

American Institute Architects. Architectural Graphic Standards. 7th ed. Ramsey, Charles G. & Sleeper, Harold R., eds. LC 80-18151. 785p. 1981. 115.00 (ISBN 0-471-04683-3). Wiley.

American Institute for Character Education Staff. Character Education Curriculum: Living with Me & Others Including Our Rights & Responsibilities, Level G. (Illus.). 140p. (gr. 7-9). 1981. tchr's. ed. 80.00 (ISBN 0-913413-06-2). Am Inst Char Ed.

--Character Education Curriculum: The Happy Life Series. (Illus.). (ps). 1981. tchr's. ed. 89.95 (ISBN 0-913413-00-3). Am Inst Char Ed.

--Character Education Curriculum: The Happy Life Series plus Living with Me & Others Including Our Rights & Responsibilities, Levels A-E. (Illus.). (gr. 1-6). 1974. Set. 509.70 (ISBN 0-913413-08-9); tchr's. ed. 69.95 ea. Level A, 124p (ISBN 0-913413-01-1). Level B, 127p (ISBN 0-913413-02-X). Level C, 148p (ISBN 0-913413-03-8). Level D, 152p (ISBN 0-913413-04-6). Level E, 160p (ISBN 0-913413-05-4). Am Inst Char Ed.

American Institute for Paralegal Studies & Nemeth, Charles P. Paralegal Handbook: Theory, Practice & Materials. (Illus.). 608p. 1986. text ed. 39.95 (ISBN 0-13-648593-6). P-H.

American Institute for Property & Liability Underwriters. Code of Professional Ethics. LC 79-50832. 1979. 3.00 (ISBN 0-89463-021-0, CPCU 10). Am Inst Property.

American Institute of Accountants. Fiftieth Anniversary Celebration. LC 82-48350. (Accountancy in Transition Ser.). 568p. 1982. lib. bdg. 66.00 (ISBN 0-8240-5302-8). Garland Pub.

--Library Catalogue. LC 82-48337. (Accountancy in Transition Ser.). 242p. 1982. lib. bdg. 28.00 (ISBN 0-8240-5303-6). Garland Pub.

American Institute of Architects. The Architect's Guide to Facility Programming. 304p. 1981. 39.95 (ISBN 0-07-001490-6). McGraw.

--Architect's Handbook of Energy Practice: Active Solar Systems. (Illus.). 58p. 1982. pap. 7.50 (ISBN 0-913962-54-6). Am Inst Arch.

--Architect's Handbook of Energy Practice: Building Envelope. (Illus.). 42p. 1982. pap. 7.50 (ISBN 0-913962-51-1). Am Inst Arch.

--Architect's Handbook of Energy Practice: Climate & Site. (Illus.). 55p. 1982. pap. 7.50 (ISBN 0-913962-50-3). Am Inst Arch.

--Architect's Handbook of Energy Practice. (Monograph Ser.). 600p. 1982. 85.00 (ISBN 0-913962-43-0). Am Inst Arch.

--Architect's Handbook of Energy Practice: Daylighting. (Illus.). 48p. 1982. pap. 7.50 (ISBN 0-913962-52-X). Am Inst Arch.

--Architect's Handbook of Energy Practice: HVAC Systems. (Illus.). 54p. 1982. pap. 7.50 (ISBN 0-913962-53-8). Am Inst Arch.

--Architect's Handbook of Energy Practice: Photovoltaics. (Illus.). 56p. 1982. pap. 18.00x (ISBN 0-913962-56-2). Am Inst Arch.

--Architect's Handbook of Energy Practice: Shading & Sun Control. (Illus.). 48p. 1982. pap. 7.50 (ISBN 0-913962-49-X). Am Inst Arch.

--Architect's Handbook of Energy Practice: Thermal Transfer Through the Envelope. (Illus.). 51p. 1982. pap. 7.50 (ISBN 0-913962-55-4). Am Inst Arch.

--Architect's Handbook of Professional Practice. looseleaf 68.00 (ISBN 0-913962-13-9); annual handbook supplement service 17.50 (ISBN 0-685-27662-7). Am Inst Arch.

--The Building Systems Integration Handbook. 1985. 84.95 (ISBN 0-471-86238-X). Wiley.

--Compensation Guidelines for Architectural & Engineering Services. 2nd ed. LC 77-90943. 1977. pap. 19.95x (ISBN 0-913962-03-1); pap. 16.00 member. Am Inst Arch.

--Glossary of Construction Industry Terms. pap. 2.20 (ISBN 0-913962-18-X); pap. 1.55 member. Am Inst Arch.

--Materials Components & Design: An Integrated Approach Handbook. Rush, Richard D., ed. 500p. 1985. 84.95x. Wiley.

American Institute of Architects, ed. The Sourcebook. 100p. 1981. 3 ring binder 10.50 (ISBN 0-913962-45-7); members 10.00. Am Inst Arch.

American Institute of Certified Public Accountants. Continuing Professional Education Division, jt. auth. see Gorenberg, Hyman.

American Institute of Certified Public Accountants. Continuing Professional Education Division, jt. auth. see McKeen, Gregory B.

American Institute of Certified Public Accountants Staff. Accountant's Index: Twentieth Supplement, January 1971 to December 1971 (Inclusive) LC 21-10690. pap. 160.00 (ISBN 0-317-29037-1, 2023751). Bks Demand UMI.

--Accountant's Index: Twenty-Fifth Supplement, January-December, 1976. Kubat, Jane, ed. LC 21-10690. pap. 160.00 (ISBN 0-317-29035-5, 2023755). Bks Demand UMI.

American Institute of Certified Public Accountants. Accountant's Index: Twenty-Second Supplement, January-December 1973. Hegge, Karen L., ed. LC 21-10690. pap. 160.00 (ISBN 0-317-30027-X, 2023752). Bks Demand UMI.

American Institute of Certified Public Accountants Staff. Accountants' Index: Twenty-Sixth Supplement, January-December, 1977, 2 Vols. Kubat, Jane, ed. LC 21-10690. Vol. 1. pap. 160.00 (ISBN 0-317-29042-8, 2023756); Vol. 2. pap. 160.00 (ISBN 0-317-29043-6). Bks Demand UMI.

American Institute of Certified Public Accountants. Accountants' Index: Twenty-Third Supplement, January-December 1974. Simmons, Karen H., ed. LC 21-10690. pap. 160.00 (ISBN 0-317-30031-8, 2023753). Bks Demand UMI.

--Accountants' Index: 1981-30th Supplement. 1982. 57.00 (ISBN 0-685-58296-5). Am Inst CPA.

--Accountants' Index: 1982, 31st Supplement. 1983. 60.00 (ISBN 0-317-02601-1). Am Inst CPA.

--Accounting by Agricultural Producers & Agricultural Coorperatives. pap. 20.30 (ISBN 0-317-26578-4, 2023960). Bks Demand UMI.

--Accounting Practice: Selected Questions & Unofficial Answers Indexed to Content Specification Outline. Blum, James D. & Dexter, David S., eds. LC 84-160638. pap. 66.80 (ISBN 0-317-27243-8, 2025093). Bks Demand UMI.

--Accounting Theory: Selected Questions & Unofficial Answers Indexed to Content Specification Outline. Blum, James D. & Rhuda, Charles A., eds. LC 84-160551. pap. 27.80 (ISBN 0-317-27244-6, 2025094). Bks Demand UMI.

--Accounting Trends & Techniques, 1983: Survey of Accounting Practices Followed in Stockholders' Reports. 36th ed. 450p. 1983. pap. 42.00 (ISBN 0-685-47687-1). Am Inst CPA.

--Auditing: Selected Questions & Unofficial Answers Indexed to Content Specification Outline. Blum, James D., ed. pap. 27.50 (ISBN 0-317-27246-2, 2025096). Bks Demand UMI.

--Auditors' Reports on Comparative Financial Statements. (Financial Report Survey Ser.: No. 18). 1979. pap. 11.00 (ISBN 0-686-70236-0). Am Inst CPA.

--Audits of Banks: Prepared by the Banking Committee. LC 83-134099. pap. 51.50 (ISBN 0-317-29322-2, 2023969). Bks Demand UMI.

--Audits of Brokers & Dealers in Securities. 2nd ed. pap. 61.30 (ISBN 0-317-27241-1, 2025091). Bks Demand UMI.

--Audits of Entities with Oil & Gas Producing Activities: Proposed Audit & Accounting Guide, April 25, 1984. (Exposure Draft Ser.). pap. 25.30 (ISBN 0-317-30386-4, 2024762). Bks Demand UMI.

--Audits of Federal Financial Assistance to State & Local Governmental Units: Proposed Audit Guide, 1984. pap. 30.50 (ISBN 0-317-27237-3, 2025087). Bks Demand UMI.

--Audits of Investment Companies: Proposed Audit & Accounting Guide, 1985. (Exposure Draft Ser.). pap. 46.50 (ISBN 0-317-27238-1, 2025088). Bks Demand UMI.

--Audits of State & Local Governmental Units: Proposed Audit & Accounting Guide, October 19, 1984. (Exposure Draft Ser.). pap. 47.80 (ISBN 0-317-30388-0, 2024759). Bks Demand UMI.

--Business Law: Selected Questions & Unofficial Answers Indexed to Content Specification Outline. Blum, James D. & Goldstein, Mark S., eds. LC 84-189048. pap. 37.80 (ISBN 0-317-27245-4, 2025095). Bks Demand UMI.

--Codification of Statements of Auditing Standards, Numbers 1 to 47. pap. 160.00 (ISBN 0-317-27236-5, 2025086). Bks Demand UMI.

--Codification of Statements on Standards for Accounting & Review Services: Nos. 1-5. pap. 23.50 (ISBN 0-317-27242-X, 2025092). Bks Demand UMI.

American Institute of Certified Public Accountants. Federal Election Campaign Guide Task Force. Compliance with Federal Election Campaign Requirements: A Guide for Candidates. 4th ed. LC 83-208707. 216p. 1983. 22.00. Am Inst CPA.

American Institute of Certified Public Accountants. Departures from the Auditor's Standard Report. (Financial Report Survey Ser.: No. 7). 1975. pap. 10.00 (ISBN 0-685-65410-9). Am Inst CPA.

American Institute of Certified Public Accountants Staff. EDP Engagement: Assisting Clients in Software Contract Negotiations. LC 84-188421. (Management Advisory Services Practice Aids Ser.). Date not set. price not set. Am Inst CPA.

American Institute of Certified Public Accountants. Guidance for an Experiment on Reporting Current Value Information for Real Estate. pap. 20.00 (ISBN 0-317-27248-9). Bks Demand UMI.

American Institute of Certified Public Accountants. Committee on State Legislation. Manual for State Legislative Programs. 2nd ed. LC 82-199346. 53p. Date not set. write for info. Am Inst CPA.

American Institute of Certified Public Accountants. Reporting Results of Operations. (Financial Report Survey Ser.: No. 3). 1974. 9.50 (ISBN 0-685-47688-X). Am Inst CPA.

--Review of the Structure & Operations of the SEC Practice Section: Report of the SECPS Review Committee. pap. 21.50 (ISBN 0-317-27247-0, 2025097). Bks Demand UMI.

--Summary of Operations & Related Management Discussion & Analysis. (Financial Report Survey Ser.: No. 6). 1975. pap. 12.00 (ISBN 0-685-65411-7). Am Inst CPA.

American Institute of Chemical Engineers National Meeting, Philadelphia June 8-12, 1980. Loss Prevention, Vol. 14. Chemical Engineering Progress, ed. 186p. 1981. Vol. 14. pap. 32.00 (ISBN 0-8169-0195-3, T-72); pap. 17.00 members (ISBN 0-317-03759-5). Am Inst Chem Eng.

American Institute Of Chemical Engineers. Twenty-Five Years of Chemical Engineering Progress. facs. ed. Kirkpatrick, S. D., ed. LC 68-55837. (Essay Index Reprint Ser). 1933. 20.00 (ISBN 0-8369-0149-5). Ayer Co Pubs.

American Institute of Discussion. Make up Your Own Mind, Bks. 1 & 2. Pollis, Adamantia, ed. Incl. Bk. 1. Contemporary Editorials. 1964. pap. 1.00 (ISBN 0-910092-01-X); Bk. 2. Contemporary Political Issues. 1966. pap. 2.25 (ISBN 0-910092-02-8). pap. Am Inst Disc.

American Institute of Graphic Arts. Symbol Signs. (Visual Communication Bks). (Illus.). 192p. (Orig.). 1981. pap. 12.95 (ISBN 0-8038-6777-8). Hastings.

American Institute of Industrial Engineers. Industrial Engineering Terminology. 398p. 1985. 79.50 (ISBN 0-471-80270-0). Wiley.

American Institute Of Law & Criminology. Journal of the American Institute of Law & Criminology. LC 71-154571. (Police in America Ser). 1971. Repr. of 1910 ed. 15.00 (ISBN 0-405-03361-3). Ayer Co Pubs.

American Institute of Maintenance. The Contract Cleaner Companion. LC 79-55158. 162p. 1982. pap. 34.95x (ISBN 0-9609052-0-0). Am Inst Maint.

--Floor Care Guide. 149p. 1982. pap. 5.95x (ISBN 0-9609052-1-9). Am Inst Maint.

--Handy Maintenance Tips. 80p. 1982. pap. 3.00 (ISBN 0-9609052-4-3). Am Inst Maint.

--Selection & Care of Cleaning Equipment. 86p. 1982. pap. 3.00 (ISBN 0-9609052-3-5). Am Inst Maint.

American Institute of Physics. American Institute of Physics Handbook. 3rd ed. LC 71-109244. (Illus.). 2368p. 1972. 99.50 (ISBN 0-07-001485-X). McGraw.

American Institute Of Real Estate Appraisers. Appraisal Journal Bibliography, 1932-1969. 171p. 1970. pap. 5.00 (ISBN 0-911780-22-X). Am Inst Real Estate Appraisers.

--The Appraisal of Real Estate. 8th ed. (Illus.). 742p. 1983. text ed. 27.50 (ISBN 0-911780-69-6). Am Inst Real Estate Appraisers.

American Institute of Real Estate Appraisers, ed. The Appraisal of Rural Property. (Illus.). 434p. 1983. 28.50 (ISBN 0-911780-56-4). Am Inst Real Estate Appraisers.

--Condemnation Appraisal Practice, Vol. 2. 738p. 1973. 15.00 (ISBN 0-911780-32-7). Am Inst Real Estate Appraisers.

American Institute of Real Estate Appraisers. Readings in Market Value. 231p. 1981. pap. 10.50 (ISBN 0-911780-57-2). Am Inst Real Estate Appraisers.

--Real Estate Appraisal Bibliography. 346p. 1940-1972. 7.00 (ISBN 0-318-15191-X, NO. 21-1017). Natl Assoc Realtors.

American Institute of Real Estate Appraisers & Rushmore, Stephen. The Valuation of Hotels & Motels. 120p. 18.00 (ISBN 0-318-15198-7, NO. 21-1022). Natl Assoc Realtors.

American Institute of Timber Construction (AITC) Timber Construction Manual. 704p. 1985. 34.95 (ISBN 0-471-82758-4). Wiley.

American Institutes for Research. Resource Directory: Organization & Publications that Promote Sex Equity in Postsecondary Education. 1982. 10.00 (ISBN 0-317-06233-6). Assn Am Coll.

American Institutes for Research, jt. auth. see National Board of Medical Examiners.

American Iris Society. Basic Iris Culture. (Illus.). 1982. 1.25 (ISBN 0-9601242-3-3). Am Iris.

American Jewish Archives, Cincinnati. Manuscript Catalog of the American Jewish Archives, 4 vols. 1971. Set. lib. bdg. 400.00 (ISBN 0-8161-0899-4, Hall Library). G K Hall.

--Manuscript Catalog of the American Jewish Archives, Cincinnati: First Supplement. 1978. lib. bdg. 105.00 (ISBN 0-8161-0934-6, Hall Library). G K Hall.

American Jewish Historical Society, et al. The Palestine Question in American History. American Historical Association, ed. 14.00 (ISBN 0-405-11521-0). Ayer Co Pubs.

American Joint Committee on Cancer. Manual for Staging of Cancer. 2nd ed. Beahrs, Oliver H. & Myers, Max H., eds. (Illus.). 220p. 1983. pap. text ed. 17.50 (ISBN 0-397-50594-9, 65-07594, Lippincott Medical). Lippincott.

American Journal of Nursing Co. AJN 1985: Nursing Board Reviews for the NCLEX-RN Examination. (Illus.). 810p. 1985. 17.95 (ISBN 0-683-09501-3). Williams & Wilkins.

American Journal of Nursing Company. AJN Nursing Boards Review 1985. (Illus.). 808p. 1984. pap. 17.95 (ISBN 0-935236-42-2). Nurseco.

--The AJN Question & Answer Book for RN-NCLEX Evaluation. 220p. (Orig.). pap. 14.95 (ISBN 0-935236-39-2). Nurseco.

American Journal of Nursing, New York. Catalog of the Sophia F. Palmer Memorial Library, 2 vols. 1973. Set. lib. bdg. 190.00 (ISBN 0-8161-1066-2, Hall Library). G K Hall.

American Kennel Club. The Complete Dog Book. 17th ed. LC 85-4296. (Illus.). 768p. 1985. 16.95 (ISBN 0-87605-463-7). Howell Bk.

American Kennel Club Staff, jt. auth. see Barnes, Duncan.

American Labor Conference on International Affairs. Modern Review, Vols. 1-3, No. 2. 1947-50. Repr. lib. bdg. 64.00x (ISBN 0-8371-9203-X, MR00). Greenwood.

American Law Inst., American Bar Assoc. Committee on Continuing Professional Education, jt. auth. see Emory Univ. School of Law.

American Law Inst., American Bar Assoc. Committee on Continuing Professional Education. Complex Litigation: ALI-ABA Course of Study Materials. LC 83-108091. 1982. write for info. Am Law Inst.

--Tax Shelters Under Attack: ALI-ABA Course of Study Materials. LC 83-105446. 1982. write for info. Am Law Inst.

American Law Institute. Federal Estate & Gift Tax Project: Study on Generation-Skipping Transfers Under the Federal Estate Tax: Discussion Draft No. 1 (March 28, 1984) LC 84-220055. 1984. write for info. Am Law Inst.

--Federal Income Tax Project. LC 84-155263. Date not set. price not set. AM Law Inst.

--Restatement of Judgements, Second, Volumes 1-3. 2nd ed. Meehan, Violet, ed. 1982. Vol. 1-3, 1415 Pgs. text ed. write for info. (ISBN 0-314-66807-1). Am Law Inst.

--Restatement of the Law, Second, Restitution. LC 84-127641. 228p. Date not set. price not set. Am Law Inst.

American Law Institute & American Bar Association Committee on Continuing Professional Education. New Pension Legislation: ALI-ABA Video Law Review Study Materials. LC 83-108222. Date not set. price not set. Am LAw Inst.

American Law Institute & Casner, A. James. Restatement of the Law, Second, Property: Second, Donative Transfers. LC 83-2563. 1983. 50.00 (ISBN 0-314-73634-4); 50.00 (ISBN 0-314-73635-2). Am Law Inst.

American Law Institute & Massachusetts Continuing Legal Education-Inc. Hospital Operation & Management: A Review of Significant Developments. LC 83-169702. ix, 142p. Date not set. price not set. Am Law Inst.

American Law Institute & National Conference of Commissioners on Uniform State Laws. Uniform Commercial Code: 1972 Amendments to Article 9. 304p. 1978. 3.95 (ISBN 0-686-90969-0). Am Law Inst.

American Law Institute & National Conference of Commissioners on Uniforms State Laws. Uniform Commercial Code: 1977 Amendments to Article 8. 249p. 1978. 3.95 (ISBN 0-686-90957-7). Am Law Inst.

American Law Institute & National Conference of Commissioners on Uniform State Laws. Uniforms Commercial Code. 994p. 1978. 9.50 (ISBN 0-686-90955-0). Am Law Inst.

American Law Institute, jt. auth. see Gustafson, Charles H.

American Law Institute, jt. auth. see Shepard's Citations, Inc.

American Law Institute-American Bar Association Committee on Continuing Professional Education, jt. auth. see ABA National Conference of Lawyers & Collection Agencies.

American Law Institute-American Bar Association Committee on Continuing Professional Education, jt. auth. see University of Colorado-Boulder School of Law.

American Law Institute-American Bar Association Committee on Continuing Professional Education, jt. auth. see Conference on Life Insurance Company Products.

American Law Institute - American Bar Association Committee on Continuing Professional Education, jt. auth. see American Bar Association.

American Law Institute-American Bar Association Committee on Continuing Professional Education Staff, jt. auth. see American Society of International Law Staff.

American Law Institute-American Bar Association Committee on Continuing Professional Education, jt. auth. see Federal Bar Association. Securities Law Committee.

American Law Institute-American Bar Association Committee on Continuing Professional Education, jt. auth. see Stanford University, School of Law.

American Law Institute-American Bar Association Committee on Continuing Professional Education, jt. auth. see Environmental Law Institute.

American Law Institute-American Bar Association Committee on Continuing Professional Education, jt. auth. see Haynsworth, Harry J.

American Law Institute-American Bar Association Committee on Continuing Professional Education, jt. auth. see Massachusetts Continuing Legal Education Inc. (1982-).

American Law Institute-American Bar Association Committee on Continuing Professional Education, jt. auth. see American Bar Association Section of Taxation.

American Law Institute-American Bar Association Committee on Continuing Professional Education. Advanced Labor & Employment Law, 1984: ALI-ABI Course of Study Materials. LC 84-224025. 1984. write for info. Am Law Inst.

--Advocacy & Evidence: Courtroom Warriors & Their Weapons. LC 83-229679. (ALI-ABA Course of Study Materials Ser.). x, 359p. write for info. Am Law Inst.

American Law Institute-American Bar Association Committee on Continuing Professional Education Staff. Airline Labor & Employment Law: A Comprehensive Analysis. LC 84-219051. (Illus.). 697p. 1984. write for info. Am Law Inst.

American Law Institute-American Bar Association Committee on Continuing Professional Education. Basic Law of Pensions & Deferred Compensation: ALI-ABA Course of Study Materials. LC 84-117415. (Illus.). write for info. Am Law Inst.

American Law Institute-American Bar Association Committee on Continuing Professional Education Staff. Business Reorganization under the Bankruptcy Code: ALI-ABA Course of Study Materials. LC 84-228560. 491p. 1984. write for info. Am Law Inst.

American Law Institute-American Bar Association Committee on Continuing Professional Education. Business Reorganizations Under the Bankruptcy Code: ALI-ABA Course of Study Materials. LC 84-103165. xi, 608p. 1983. write for info. Am Law Inst.

--Civil Practice & Litigation in Federal & State Courts, 2 vols. LC 83-233293. (Resource Materials Ser.). 1794p. 1981. 60.00 (R133). Am Law Inst.

American Law Institute-American Bar Association Committee on Continuing Professional Education Staff. Computer Law: ALI-ABA Course of Study Materials. LC 84-223486. 578p. 1984. write for info. Am Law Inst.

American Law Institute-American Bar Association Committee on Continuing Professional Education, ed. Continuing Legal Education for Professional Competence & Responsibility: Since Arden House II. LC 84-70380. 322p. 1984. pap. text ed. 25.00 (ISBN 0-8318-0427-0, B427). Am Law Inst.

American Law Institute-American Bar Association Committee on Continuing Professional Education. Corporate Government Relations & Lobbying: ALI-ABA Course of Study Materials. LC 85-110266. 285p. Date not set. price not set. Am Law Inst.

--Designing Qualified Plans to Meet the 1982-1984 Statutory Requirements: Model Plans & Provisions: ALI-ABA Video Law Review Study Materials. LC 85-109910. (Illus.). Date not set. price not set. Am Law Inst.

American Law Institute-American Bar Association Committee on Continuing Professional Education, et al. The Economic Recovery Tax Act of 1981: Study Outline. LC 81-70588. xlvi, 394p. 1981. write for info. Am Law Inst.

American Law Institute-American Bar Association Committe on Continuing Professional Education. Eminent Domain & Land Valuation Litigation: ALI-ABA Course of Study Materials. write for info. Amer Bar Assn.

American Law Institute-American Bar Association Committee on Continuing Professional Education. Equitable Distribution: Litigation & Discovery Techniques: ALI-ABA Video Law Review Study Materials. LC 84-195222. xiv, 109p. write for info. Amer Bar Assn.

--Fundamentals of Bankruptcy Law: ALI-ABA Course of Study Materials. LC 83-179083. 1983. 30.00 (ISBN 0-318-00250-7). Am Law Inst.

--Growing Companies: Tax & Business Planning for the 80s: ALI-ABA Course of Study Materials. Date not set. price not set. Am Law Inst.

American Law Institute-American Bar Association Course of Study. Insuring Corporate Personnel & Professional Advisions Under Expanding Concepts of Responsibility: Course of Study Transcript. 303p. 1970. pap. 8.25 (ISBN 0-317-32229-X, B240). Am Law Inst.

American Law Institute. American Bar Association, ed. International Trade for the Nonspecialist, 2 vols. 3rd ed. (Resource Materials Ser.). 1063p. (Orig.). 1984. pap. 60.00 (ISBN 0-8318-0146-8, R146). Am Law Inst.

American Law Institute-American Bar Association Committee on Continuing Professional Education. Investment Company Regulation & Compliance: ALI-ABA Course of Study Materials. Date not set. price not set. Am Law Inst.

American Law Institute-American Bar Association Joint Committee. Law & Computers in the Mid-Sixties: Course of Study Transcript. 399p. 1966. pap. 2.18 (ISBN 0-317-32232-X, B239). Am Law Inst.

American Law Institute-American Bar Association Committee on Continuing Professional Education & Deer, Richard E. The Lawyer's Basic Corporate Practice Manual. 3rd ed. LC 84-72759. 320p. Date not set. price not set (ISBN 0-8318-0468-8). Am Law Inst.

American Law Institute-American Bar Association Committee on Continuing Professional Education. Major Changes in Insurance Company Investments, Governance, Subsidiaries, & Separate Accounts: ALI-ABA Course of Study Materials. LC 84-105487. x, 148p. 1983. write for info. Am Law Inst.

--Medical Products Liability & Preventive Law: ALI-ABA Course of Study Materials. (Illus.). x, 514p. Date not set. price not set. Am Law Inst.

--A Model Peer Review System. 275p. 1980. 25.00 (ISBN 0-686-77589-9, B218). Am Law Inst.

American Law Institute-American Bar Association Advisory Committee. A Model Peer Review System. 275p. 1980. pap. 25.00 (ISBN 0-317-32244-3, B218). Am Law Inst.

American Law Institute-American Bar Association Committee on Continuing Professional Education. Modern Real Estate Transactions, 2 vols. 5th ed. LC 84-228519. (Resource Materials Ser.). (Illus.). 1469p. 1984. 60.00 (ISBN 0-8318-0148-4, R148). Am Law Inst.

--Paper & Electronic Payments Litigation. LC 83-143788. (Illus.). xii, 347p. Date not set. price not set. Am Law Inst.

--Planning Techniques for Large Estates, 2 vols. LC 84-103580. (ALI-ABA Course of Study Materials Ser.). Date not set. price not set. Am Law Inst.

--Planning Techniques in Divorce Transactions under the Tax Reform Act of 1984: Video Law Review Study Materials. 159p. Date not set. price not set. Am Law Inst.

American Law Institute-American Bar Association Committee on Continuing Professional Education, et al. Postmortem Estate Planning. LC 76-4993. xiii, 154p. 1976. Incl. suppl. 22.00 (B195); Suppl. only. pap. 2.00 (B196). Am Law Inst.

American Law Institute-American Bar Association. The Practical Lawyer's Law Office Management Manual, No. 5. 218p. 1984. pap. 15.00 (ISBN 0-317-12707-1, F125). Am Law Inst.

American Law Institute-American Bar Association Committee on Continuing Professional Education Staff. The Practical Lawyer's Manual of Business Forms & Checklists. LC 84-71224. (Illus.). 230p. 1984. pap. 15.00 (F129). Am Law Inst.

American Law Institute-American Bar Association. The Practical Lawyer's Manual on Lawyer-Client Relations. 197p. 1983. pap. 15.00 (ISBN 0-317-12708-X, F127). Am Law Inst.

--The Practical Lawyer's Manual on Real Property Law, No. 2. 209p. 1983. pap. 15.00 (ISBN 0-317-12709-8, F126). Am Law Inst.

American Law Institute-American Bar Association Committee on Continuing Professional Education Staff. Products Liability: ALI-ABA Course of Study Materials. LC 84-222936. ix, 167p. Date not set. price not set. Am Law Inst.

American Law Institute-American Bar Association Committee on Continuing Professional Education. Real Estate Folio. LC 84-73129. (Illus.). 121p. Date not set. price not set. Am Law Inst.

--Retirement Planning for Small Business & Professionals Entering the Top-Heavy & Parity Age: ALI-ABA Video Law Review Study Materials. LC 84-166979. (Illus.). xiv, 290p. Date not set. price not set. Am Law Inst.

--Structured Settlements: ALI-ABA Video Law Review Study Materials. LC 84-210146. 95p. 1985. price not set. Am Law Inst.

American Law Institute-American Bar Association Committee on Continuing Professional Education & American Bar Association, Discovery Committee. Taking & Defending Depositions: ALI-ABA Video Law Review -Satellite Videolaw Seminar: Materials. LC 84-192327. (Illus.). vii, 525p. Date not set. price not set. Am Law Inst.

American Law Institute-American Bar Association Committee on Continuing Professional Education. Tax & Business Planning for the Growth Oriented Business, 2 vols. LC 82-111897. (Resource Materials Ser.). 1591p. 1981. 60.00 (R129). Am Law Inst.

--Tax Reform Act of 1984: An Overview: ALI-ABA Video Law Review Study Materials. LC 85-107799. Date not set. price not set. Am Law INst.

American Law Institute-American Bar Association Committe on Continuing Professional Education Staff & American Bar Association Section of Law Staff. Tax Shelter Legislation: ALI-ABA & ABA Section of Taxation Course of Study Materials. write for info. Amer Bar Assn.

American Law Institute-American Bar Association Committee on Continuing Professional Education. Unfair Competition, Trademarks & Copyrights: ALI-ABA Course of Study Materials. LC 83-215704. ix, 128p. Date not set. price not set. Am Law Inst.

American Law Institute Staff. Federal Income Tax Project: Subchapter K. 592p. 1984. 65.00 (ISBN 0-8318-5695-5, 5695). Am Law Inst.

American Law Institute Staff, ed. Partnerships: UPA, ULPA, Securities, Taxation & Bankruptcy. 683p. (Orig.). 1985. pap. 40.00 (ISBN 0-8318-0150-6). Am Law Inst.

American League of Professional Baseball Clubs. American League Red Book Nineteen Eighty-Two. (Illus.). 100p. 1982. pap. 6.95 (ISBN 0-933484-55-0). M G Book Graphics.

American Legion. National Americanism Commission. Isms: A Review of Alien Isms, Revolutionary Communism, & Their Active Sympathizers in the United States. 2nd ed. Grob, Gerald, ed. LC 76-46092. (Anti-Movements in America). (Illus.). 1977. Repr. 22.00x (ISBN 0-405-09965-7). Ayer Co Pubs.

American Legislative Exchange Council, jt. auth. see Butcher, James.

American Library Assn., jt. auth. see Ladenson, Alex.

American Library Association. American Library Association Index to General Literature, 3 vols. Incl. Vol. 1. Basic Volume. 90.00 (ISBN 0-87650-017-3); Vol. 2. Supplement. 39.50 (ISBN 0-87650-018-1); Vol. 3. Author Index. LC 76-143240. (Cumulative Author Index Ser.: No. 4). 1971. 39.50 (ISBN 0-87650-019-X). LC 79-143240. 155.00 set (ISBN 0-685-24375-3). Pierian.

--An Index to General Literature: The ALA Index. facs ed. LC 72-165612. (Essay Index Reprint Ser.). 44.00 (ISBN 0-8369-2382-0). Ayer Co Pubs.

--Librarian's Copyright Kit. 1982. 15 documents 15.00x (ISBN 0-8389-3276-2). ALA.

--Notable Children's Books, 1940-1959: Prepared by the Book Reevaluation Committee. LC 66-24177. pap. 20.00 (ISBN 0-317-26833-3, 2024213). Bks Demand UMI.

--Personnel Organization & Procedure: A Manual Suggested for Use in Public Libraries. 2nd ed. LC 68-21023. pap. 20.00 (ISBN 0-317-26831-7, 2024214). Bks Demand UMI.

--Subject Index to Poetry for Children & Young People. Sell, Violet, compiled by. LC 82-73702. 1982. 99.99 (ISBN 0-8486-0013-4). Core Collection.

American Library Association, jt. auth. see Association of College & Research Libraries.

American Library Association, et al. New Copyright Law: Questions Teachers & Librarians Ask. 72p. 1977. pap. text ed. 3.00 (ISBN 0-8389-3214-2). ALA.

American Library Association. Book Catalogs Committee, RTSD. Guidelines for Book Catalogs. LC 77-1248. 1977. pap. text ed. 5.00x (ISBN 0-8389-3190-1). ALA.

American Library Association Centennial Celebration. Libraries & the Life of the Mind in America: Addresses. LC 77-3288. 144p. 1977. lib. bdg. 10.00x (ISBN 0-8389-0238-3). ALA.

American Library Association - Children's Services Division. Notable Children's Books, 1940-1970. LC 77-641. 94p. 1977. pap. 4.00x (ISBN 0-8389-3182-0). ALA.

American Library Association Committee on Bibliography, ed. see Richardson, Ernest C.

American Library Association Committee On Intellectual Freedom-1st Conference-New York-1952. Freedom of Communication: Proceedings. facsimile ed. Dix, William & Bixler, Paul, eds. LC 71-104989. (Essay Index Reprint Ser). 1954. 18.00 (ISBN 0-8369-1439-2). Ayer Co Pubs.

American Library Association Committee on Cataloging Staff. Guidelines for Using AACR2 Chapter Nine for Cataloging Microcomputer Software. LC 84-11168. 34p. 1984. pap. text ed. 4.50x (ISBN 0-8389-5651-3). ALA.

American Library Association, Library Research Round Table. Library Research Round Table: 1977 Research Forums Proceedings: Meetings Held at the 96th Annual Conference of the American Library Association, 1977. Curran, Charles C., ed. LC 79-15300. (Monograph Publishing: Sponsor Ser.). pap. 74.80 (ISBN 0-317-28289-1, 2019859). Bks Demand UMI.

American Library Association, Library Administration Division, Buildings & Equipment Section, Buildings for College & University Libraries Committee. Running Out of Space: What Are the Alternatives. LC 78-1796. 172p. 1978. pap. 15.00x (ISBN 0-8389-3215-0). ALA.

American Library Association Office for Intellectual Freedom. Censorship Litigation & the Schools. LC 82-24458. xii, 161p. 1983. pap. text ed. 17.50x (ISBN 0-8389-3279-7). ALA.

--Intellectual Freedom Manual. 2nd. ed. LC 83-9958. xxx, 210p. 1983. pap. text ed. 15.00x (ISBN 0-8389-3283-5). ALA.

American Library Association, Public Library Association. The Library Connection: Essays Written in Praise of Public Libraries. LC 77-24687. 96p. 1977. pap. 5.00x (ISBN 0-8389-3202-9). ALA.

American Library Association Reference & Subscription Books Review Committee. Reference & Subscription Books Reviews, 1979-80. LC 73-159565. 148p. 1981. pap. 20.00x (ISBN 0-8389-3256-8). ALA.

American Library Association Resources & Technical Services Division Filing Committee. ALA Filing Rules. LC 80-22186. 59p. 1980. pap. 5.00x (ISBN 0-8389-3255-X). ALA.

American Library Association, Resources & Technical Services Division. Guidelines for Handling Library Orders for Inprint Monographic Publications. LC 83-22307. 22p. 1984. pap. text ed. 3.00x (ISBN 0-8389-3299-1). ALA.

American Library Association Staff. ALA Handbook of Organization & Membership Directory, 1984-1985. LC 80-649998. 708p. 1984. pap. text ed. 20.00x (ISBN 0-8389-5667-X). ALA.

--Curriculum Alternatives: Experiments in School Library Media. LC 74-12070. pap. 63.30 (ISBN 0-317-26285-8, 2024261). Bks Demand UMI.

--Directory of Outreach Services in Public Libraries. pap. 160.00 (ISBN 0-317-26558-X, 2023944). Bks Demand UMI.

--Library Effectiveness: A State of the Art: Papers from a 1980 ALA Preconference, 1980. pap. 105.80 (ISBN 0-317-26562-8, 2023949). Bks Demand UMI.

American Library Association, Young Adult Services Division. African Encounter: A Selected Bibliography of Books, Films, & Other Materials for Promoting an Understanding of Africa among Young Adults. LC 63-22444. pap. 20.00 (ISBN 0-317-10473-X, 2001782). Bks Demand UMI.

American Machines & Foundry Co. Silencers, Patterns, & Principles, Vol. II. (Illus.). 78p. 1969. pap. 12.95 (ISBN 0-87364-018-7). Paladin Pr.

American Machinist. Metalforming: Modern Machines, Methods & Tooling for Engineers & Operating Personnel. 288p. 1982. text ed. 36.50 (ISBN 0-07-001546-5). McGraw.

American Machinist Magazine. Tools of Our Trade. LC 82-7773. 1982. 35.50 (ISBN 0-07-001547-3). McGraw.

American Machinist Magazine Staff. Best of American Machinist Magazine, Jan-Jun 1909. 1985. pap. 9.95 (ISBN 0-917914-26-0). Lindsay Pubns.

--Metalcutting: Today's Techniques for Engineers & Shop Personnel. 1979. 31.50 (ISBN 0-07-001545-7). McGraw.

American Mamagement Associations, Research & Development Division. Achieving Full Value from R & D Dollars. LC 62-3195. (American Management Associations Management Reports: No. 69). pap. 27.30 (ISBN 0-317-09908-6, 2000324). Bks Demand UMI.

American Management Association. Managing Industrial Energy Conservation. LC 77-22251. (An American Management Associations' Management Briefing Ser.). (Illus.). pap. 20.00 (ISBN 0-317-11154-X, 2050200). Bks Demand UMI.

American Management Association Staff. New Products, New Profits: Company Experiences in New Product Planning. Marting, Elizabeth, ed. LC 64-12772. pap. 75.80 (ISBN 0-317-27181-4, 2023919). Bks Demand UMI.

American Map Corp. Commercial Atlas. rev. ed. 1978. 65.00 (ISBN 0-8416-9558-X). Am Map.

--Executive Sales Control Atlas. rev. ed. 1978. 94.75 (ISBN 0-8416-9557-1). Am Map.

--Student Atlas of the Bible. (Series 9500: No. 9559). (Illus.). 1978. 2.95 (ISBN 0-8416-9559-8); span. lang. ed. avail. Am Map.

American Map Corporation. Atlas Mundial, No. 9555. rev. ed. (Illus.). (gr. 7-12). 1979. pap. 1.75 (ISBN 0-8416-9555-5). Am Map.

--Business Control Atlas of the United States & Canada: 1979 Edition. (Series 6500). 1981. plastic spiral bdg. 16.95 (ISBN 0-8416-9701-9). Am Map.

--General World Atlas, No. 9550. rev. ed. 1981. 1.50 (ISBN 0-8416-9550-4). Am Map.

--Master Sales Control Atlas. rev. ed. 1981. 484.95 (ISBN 0-8416-9560-1). Am Map.

--Scholastic World Atlas: No. 9552. (gr. 7-9). 1981. pap. 2.75 (ISBN 0-8416-9552-0). Am Map.

--Students Indexed World Atlas, No. 9551. (Illus.). (gr. 7-12). 1983. pap. 1.50 (ISBN 0-8416-9551-2); pap. spanish ed. avail. Am Map.

American Map Corporation, jt. auth. see U. S. Naval Institute.

American Map Corporation, ed. Atlas Mundial. (Illus.). (gr. 7-12). 1982. pap. 1.75 (ISBN 0-8416-9555-5); pap. spanish ed. avail. Am Map.

American Marketing Association. Research Frontiers in Marketing: Dialogues & Directions: 1978 Educators' Proceedings. Jain, Subhash C., ed. LC 78-8596. (American Marketing Association, Proceedings Ser.: 43). pap. 113.80 (ISBN 0-317-20083-6, 2023364). Bks Demand UMI.

American Marketing Association & Weidenbaum, Murray L. The Military Market in the United States. LC 63-4878. pap. 20.00 (ISBN 0-317-08150-0, 2002173). Bks Demand UMI.

American Mathematical Society. Mathematical Reviews Cumulative Author Indexes. Incl. Twenty Volume Author Index of Mathematical Reviews, 1940-59, 2 pts. 1977. 350.00 set (ISBN 0-685-22496-1, MREVIN 40-59); Author Index of Mathematical Reviews, 1960-64, 2 pts. 1966. 275.00 set (ISBN 0-8218-0026-4, MREVIN 60-64); Author Index of Mathematical Reviews, 1965-72. 1974. 550.00 (ISBN 0-8218-0027-2, MREVIN 65-72). Repr. Am Math.

--Norbert Wiener, 1894-1964. 1982. Repr. of 1966 ed. 20.00 (ISBN 0-8218-0030-2, NW). Am Math.

--Space Mathematics, 3 vols. Rosser, J. B., ed. Incl. Pt.1. LC 66-20435. (Vol. 5). 1979. paper 41.00 (ISBN 0-8218-1105-3, LAM-5); Pt. 2. LC 66-20437. (Vol. 6). 1974. Repr. of 1966 ed. 33.00 (ISBN 0-8218-1106-1, LAM-6); Pt. 3. LC 66-20435. (Vol. 5-7). 1966. 35.00 (ISBN 0-8218-1107-X, LAM-7). LC 66-20435. (Lectures in Applied Mathematics Ser). Am Math.

American Mathematical Society, tr. see Detlovs, V. K., et al.

American Mathematical Society Special Session, San Francisco, Jan, 1974. A Crash Course on Kleinian Groups: Proceedings. Bers, L. & Kra, I., eds. (Lecture Notes in Mathematics Ser.: Vol. 400). vii, 130p. 1974. pap. 13.00 (ISBN 0-387-06840-6). Springer-Verlag.

American Medical Association. Allied Health Education Directory. 11th ed. 284p. 1984. pap. 14.00 (ISBN 0-317-12511-7, OP 159). AMA.

--Allied Health Education Directory. 12th ed. 1984. pap. 14.00 (ISBN 0-317-12527-3, OP 182). AMA.

--The AMA Handbook of First Aid & Emergency Care. (Illus.). 256p. 1980. 6.95 (ISBN 0-394-73668-0). Random.

--American Health Care Issues & Facts. 72p. 1984. pap. 6.00 (ISBN 0-317-12502-8, OP 038). AMA.

--Current Procedural Terminology 1984. 466p. 1984. pap. 25.00 (ISBN 0-317-12539-7, OP 341). AMA.

--Distribution of Physicians, Hospitals, & Hospital Beds in the U. S., 1970. 329p. 1970. pap. 5.00 (ISBN 0-89970-035-7, OP-347). AMA.

--Drug Evaluations. 312p. 1983. 64.00 (ISBN 0-7216-1107-9). Saunders.

--Family Medical Guide. (Illus.). 832p. 1982. 29.95 (ISBN 0-394-51015-1). Random.

--Freestanding Ambulatory Surgical Center. 60p. 1984. pap. 9.00 (ISBN 0-317-12530-3, OP 222). AMA.

--The Impaired Physician. 173p. 1984. pap. 4.50 (ISBN 0-317-12505-2, OP 129). AMA.

--Medical Education in the U. S. 1983. 160p. 1984. pap. 5.00 (ISBN 0-317-12538-9, OP 318). AMA.

--Medical Evaluation for Healthy People. 131p. 1984. pap. 3.00 (ISBN 0-317-12525-7, OP 171). AMA.

--Medicolegal Forms with Legal Analysis. 1973. pap. 2.50 (ISBN 0-89970-062-4, OP109). AMA.

--Medicolegal Forms with Legal Analysis. LC 83-105672. 1982. write for info. AMA.

--Mental Retardation: A Handbook for the Primary Physician. 3rd ed. 134p. 1976. pap. 2.00 (ISBN 0-686-15736-2, OP-314). AMA.

--Optimum Timetable for Starting Your Practice. 216p. 1984. pap. 5.00 (ISBN 0-317-12529-X, OP 216). AMA.

--Reports on the Council on Scientific Affairs of the AMA-1982. 185p. 1984. pap. 7.50 (ISBN 0-317-12540-0, OP 360). AMA.

--Socio-Economic Characteristics of Medical Practice, 1983. 156p. 1984. pap. 12.00 (ISBN 0-317-12518-4, OP 165). AMA.

American Medical Association & American Academy Of Pediatrics. Growing Pains. Michaelson, Mike, ed. 1969. pap. 2.25 (ISBN 0-89970-049-7, OP244). AMA.

American Medical Association & Institute for Strategic Management. Campaign Groundwork: Strategy, Planning, & Management. LC 84-235180. (Illus.). 1984. write for info. AMA.

American Medical Association & Melek, Jacques. Cancer-Birth Control Pills: Cause & Effect, Relationship, Benefits vs. Risks. (Illus.). 500p. (Orig.). 1984. pap. 19.85. Sunbright Bks.

American Medical Association, et al. Computer Assisted Medical Practice: AMA's Role. 1971. pap. 1.75 (ISBN 0-89970-028-4, OP377). AMA.

American Medical Association, Division of Library & Archival Services. Index to Medical Socioeconomic Literature, 1962-1970, 4 vols. 1980. lib. bdg. 310.00 (ISBN 0-8161-0338-0, Hall Library). G K Hall.

American Medical Association Judicial Council. Opinion & Report of the Judicial Council: 1977. 1977. pap. 2.00 (ISBN 0-89970-065-9). AMA.

American Medical Association Staff. Guides to the Evaluation of Permanent Impairment. 2nd ed. LC 74-151606. (Illus.). 245p. 1984. 25.00 (ISBN 0-89970-161-2). AMA.

American Medical Society & Melek, Jacques. Cancer & All You Need to Know to Avoid It. (Illus.). 500p. (Orig.). 1984. pap. text ed. 24.95 (ISBN 0-942330-39-0). Sunbright Bks.

American Mercury. The American Mercury: A Selection of Distinguished Articles. Spivak, Lawrence E. & Angoff, Charles, eds. LC 75-41009. (BCL Ser.: No. II). Repr. of 1944 ed. 24.50 (ISBN 0-404-14765-8). AMS Pr.

--Readings from the American Mercury. facs. ed. Knight, G. C., ed. LC 68-16902. (Essay Index Reprint Ser.). 1926. 18.00 (ISBN 0-8369-0150-9). Ayer Co Pubs.

American Meteorological Society, jt. auth. see Harris, Miles F.

American Meteorological Society - Boston. Cumulated Bibliography & Index to Meteorological & Geoastrophysical Abstracts: 1950-1969. 1972. Author Sequence, 9 Vols. 1395.00 (ISBN 0-8161-0942-7, Hall Library); Dec. Class, 4 Vols. 835.00 (ISBN 0-8161-0183-3). G K Hall.

American Metric Journal Editors. Metric in a Nutshell. 2nd ed. Hopkins, Robert A., ed. LC 76-19477. 1977. 8.95 (ISBN 0-917240-06-5). Am Metric.

American Micro Systems. Mos Integrated Circuits: Theory, Fabrication, Design & Systems Applications of MOS LSI. Penny, William M. & Lau, Lillian, eds. LC 79-1039. 494p. 1979. Repr. of 1972 ed. 27.50 (ISBN 0-88275-897-7). Krieger.

American Mosquito Control Association. Ground Equipment & Insecticides for Mosquito Control: Bulletin Number Two. Rev. ed. 101p. (B). 1968. 2.00 (ISBN 0-318-12860-8). Am Mosquito.

--Manual for Mosquito Rearing & Experimental Techniques: Bulletin No. 5. 105p. (B). 1970. 3.50 (ISBN 0-318-12862-4). Am Mosquito.

--The Use of Aircraft in the Control of Mosquitoes: Bulletin Number One. rev. ed. 108p. (B). 1982. 10.00 (ISBN 0-318-12864-0). Am Mosquito.

American Mothers Committee, Bicentennial Project 1974-1976, compiled by. Mothers of Achievement in American History: 1776-1976. LC 76-461. (Illus.). 1976. 14.50 (ISBN 0-8048-1201-2). C E Tuttle.

American Museum of Natural History, jt. auth. see Perkins, John.

American Museum of Natural History, ed. Research Catalog of the Library of the American Museum of Natural History: Authors, 13 vols. 1977. lib. bdg. 1200.00 (ISBN 0-8161-0064-0, Hall Library). G K Hall.

American National Red Cross Annual Scientific Symposium, 10th, Washington, D.C., May 1978. The Blood Platelet in Transfusion Therapy: Proceedings. Greenwalt, Tibor J. & Jamieson, G. A., eds. LC 78-19683. (Progress in Clinical & Biological Research: Vol. 28). 348p. 1979. 47.00 (ISBN 0-8451-0028-9). A R Liss.

American National Red Cross Annual Scientific Symposium, 9th, Washington, D. C., May 1977. Blood Substitutes & Plasma Expanders: Proceedings. Jamieson, G. A. & Greenwalt, Tibor J., eds. LC 77-29169. (Progress in Clinical & Biological Research Ser.: Vol. 19). 354p. 1978. 55.00 (ISBN 0-8451-0019-X). A R Liss.

American National Red Cross Symposium, Washington, Oct., 1971. Development of Plasma Derivatives for Clinical Use: Proceedings. Jamieson, G. A., ed. (Vox Sanguinis: Vol. 23, Nos. 1-2). (Illus.). 1972. pap. 23.00 (ISBN 3-8055-1483-2). S Karger.

American National Standard Committee Z39 on Library Work & Information Sciences. American National Standard for Synoptics, Z39.34-1977. 6.00 (ISBN 0-686-02642-X). ANSI.

American National Standards Committee, X3, Information Processing System. American National Dictionary for Information Systems. LC 83-73087. 350p. 1984. 32.50 (ISBN 0-87094-503-3). Dow Jones-Irwin.

American National Standards Committee Z39 on Library Work & Information Sceinces. American National Standard for the Development of Identification Codes for Use by the Bibliographic Community: Z39.33-1977. 5.00 (ISBN 0-686-10588-5). ANSI.

American National Standards Institute, Standards Committee Z39 on Library & Information Sciences. American National Standard for Basic Criteria for Indexes, Z39.4. 1984. 7.00. ANSI.

American National Standards Institute, Z39 on Library Work & Information Sciences. American National Standard for Identification Code for the Book Industry, Z39.43. 1980. 5.00 (ISBN 0-686-38030-4, Z39.43). ANSI.

American National Standards Institute Z39 on Library Work & Information Sciences. American National Standard for Order Form for Single Titles of Library Materials in 3-Inch by 5-Inch Format, Z39.30. 1982. 6.00 (ISBN 0-686-38032-0). ANSI.

American National Standards Institute Staff, ed. ANSI A58: Minimum Design Loads for Buildings & Other Structures. 100p. 1982. pap. 12.00x (ISBN 0-87262-367-X). Am Soc Civil Eng.

American Negro Academy. American Negro Academy Occasional Papers Nos. 1-22. LC 77-94134. (The American Negro: His History & Literatrue, Ser. No. 3). 1970. 32.00 (ISBN 0-405-01913-0). Ayer Co Pubs.

American Nuclear Society Executive Conference. Pan American Nuclear Technology Exchange. 448p. pap. 38.00 (ISBN 0-317-33003-9, 650008). Am Nuclear Soc.

American Nuclear Society Standards Committee Staff, jt. auth. see Amorosi, A.

American Nuclear Society, Topical Symposium Las Vegas, Sept. 1978. Uranium Resources - an International Assessment: Proceedings. 445p. softcover 25.00 (ISBN 0-317-33084-5, 700034). Am Nuclear Soc.

American Numismatic Society. Dictionary & Auction Catalogues of the Library of the American Numismatic Society, New York, 7 Vols. 1962. Set. lib. bdg. 595.00 (ISBN 0-685-11673-5, Hall Library); lib. bdg. 695.00 dictionary catalog, 7 vols. (ISBN 0-8161-0630-4); lib. bdg. 100.00 auction catalog, 1 vol. (ISBN 0-8161-0102-7). G K Hall.

--A Survey of Numismatic Research, 1966-71, 3 vols. 1973. 40.00 set (ISBN 0-89722-069-2). Am Numismatic.

American Numismatic Society, New York. Dictionary & Auction Catalogues of the Library of the American Numismatic Society: First Supplement 1962-67. 1967. lib. bdg. 110.00 (ISBN 0-8161-0788-2, Hall Library). G K Hall.

--Dictionary & Auction Catalogues of the Library of the American Numismatic Society, Second Supplement. 1973. lib. bdg. 110.00 (ISBN 0-8161-1058-1, Hall Library). G K Hall.

American Nurses Association & Alessi, Dennis J. Proving Sex-Based Wage Discrimination under Federal Law. LC 84-208867. Date not set. price not set. ANA.

American Office of War Information, et al. KZ: Herausgegeben vom Amerikanischen Kriegsinformationsamt in Auftrag des Oberbefehlshabers der Alliierten Streitkrafte. Baer, Kathy & Anderson, Terry, trs. from Ger. LC 83-60802. (Illus.). 54p. 1983. pap. 3.00 (ISBN 0-912313-00-5). Witness Holocaust.

American Oil Chemists Society, jt. auth. see Kabara, Jon J.

American Oil Chemists Society, jt. auth. see Perkins, E. G.

American Oil Chemists Society, jt. auth. see Pryde, Everett H.

American Oil Chemists Society, jt. auth. see Sosis, Paul.

American Oil Chemists Society, jt. auth. see Wood, Randall.

American Ornithologists' Union, ed. see Mengel, Robert M.

American Ornithologists' Union, jt. ed. see Sibley, Charles G.

American Ornithologists' Union, ed. see Van Tets, Gerard F.

American Outdoor Safety League Staff. Emergency Survival Handbook. 48p. 2.95 (ISBN 0-89886-052-0). Mountaineers.

American Petroleum Institiute. Manual of Petroleum Measurement Standards. LC 80-67080. (Chapter 11.1 -- Volume Correction Factors: Vol. VI). (Illus.). 563p. 1980. write for info. (ISBN 0-89364-027-1). Am Petroleum.

American Petroleum Institute. Energy in America: Progress & Potential. LC 81-12706. (Illus.). 40p. 1981. pap. text ed. write for info. (ISBN 0-89364-042-5). Am Petroleum.

--Manual of Petroleum Measurement Standards. LC 80-67080. (Chapter 11.1 -- Volume Correction Factors: Vol. II). (Illus.). 592p. 1980. write for info. (ISBN 0-89364-023-9). Am Petroleum.

--Manual of Petroleum Measurement Standards. LC 80-67080. (Chapter 11.1 -- Volume Correction Factors: Vol. III). (Illus.). 563p. 1980. write for info. (ISBN 0-89364-024-7). Am Petroleum.

--Manual of Petroleum Measurement Standards. LC 80-67080. (Chapter 11.1 -- Volume Correction Factors: Vol. IV). (Illus.). 878p. 1980. write for info. (ISBN 0-89364-025-5). Am Petroleum.

--Manual of Petroleum Measurement Standard. LC 80-67080. (Chapter 11.1 --Volume Corrections Factors: Vol. V). (Illus.). 812p. 1980. write for info. (ISBN 0-89364-026-3). Am Petroleum.

--Manual of Petroleum Measurement Standards. (Chapter 11.1 -- Volume Corrections Factors: Vol. VIII). (Illus.). 881p. 1980. write for info. (ISBN 0-89364-030-1). Am Petroleum.

--Manual of Petroleum Measurement Standards. LC 80-67080. (Chapter 11.1 -- Volume Correction Factors: Vol. IX). (Illus.). 587p. 1980. write for info. (ISBN 0-89364-032-8). Am Petroleum.

--Manual of Petroleum Measurement Standard. LC 80-67080. (Chapter 11.1 -- Volume Correction Factors: Vol. X). (Illus.). 420p. 1980. write for info. (ISBN 0-89364-033-6). Am Petroleum.

--Manual of Petroleum Measurement Standards. (Chapter 11.1 -- Vol. Correction Factors). (Illus.). 1980. write for info. (ISBN 0-89364-021-2). Am Petroleum.

--Manual of Petroleum Measurement Standards. LC 80-67080. (Chapter 11.1 -- Volume Correction Factors). 1980. write for info. (ISBN 0-89364-035-2). Am Petroleum.

--Manual of Petroleum Measurements Standards. LC 80-67080. (Chapter 11.1 -- Volume Correction Factors: Vol. VII). (Illus.). 958p. 1980. write for info. (ISBN 0-89364-029-8). Am Petroleum.

--Manual Relating to Federal Excise Taxes on Petroleum Products. 8th ed. LC 84-210587. 150p. Date not set. price not set. Am Petroleum.

--Two Energy Futures: A National Choice for the 80's. 2nd ed. LC 80-24004. (Illus.). 166p. 1982. pap. text ed. write for info. (ISBN 0-89364-037-9). Am Petroleum.

--Two Energy Futures: A National Choice for the 80's. LC 82-73749. (Illus.). 196p. 1982. pap. write for info. (ISBN 0-89364-048-4). Am Petroleum.

American Petroleum Institute, Research Project 42. Properties of Hydrocarbons of High Molecular Weight Synthesized by Research Project 42 of the American Petroleum Institute, the Pennsylvania State University College of Science, University Park, Penn., 1940-1961. LC 72-8620. pap. 20.00 (ISBN 0-317-10723-2, 2004349). Bks Demand UMI.

American Petroleum Institute Staff. Two Energy Futures: A National Choice for the Eighty's. rev. ed. LC 81-7926. (Illus.). 187p. 1981. pap. text ed. write for info. (ISBN 0-89364-041-7). Am Petroleum.

American Pharmaceutical Association. Computer Sources: A Practical Guide for Pharmacists. Casler, Robin E., ed. 1982. pap. text ed. 18.00 (ISBN 0-917330-38-2). Am Pharm Assn.

--Evaluations of Drug Interactions: 1976. 2nd ed. LC 76-14501. 24.00 (ISBN 0-917330-10-2); 1978 supplement 9.00 (ISBN 0-917330-20-X); Set. 30.00. Am Pharm Assn.

American Pharmaceutical Association Task Force on Pharmacy Education. Final Report of the Task Force on Pharmacy Education. LC 84-24502. 128p. 1984. pap. 25.00 (ISBN 0-917330-52-8). Am Pharm Assn.

American Pharmaceutical Association. Handbook of Nonprescription Drugs. 7th ed. 1982. text ed. 45.00 (ISBN 0-917330-40-4). Am Pharm Assn.

--The Right Drug to the Right Patient. 161p. 1977. three-ring binder 27.00 (ISBN 0-917330-44-7). Am Pharm Assn.

American Pharmaceutical Association Committee on Tableting Specifications. Tableting Specification Manual. rev. ed. (Illus.). 39p. 1981. pap. text ed. 42.00 (ISBN 0-917330-36-6). Am Pharm Assn.

American Pharmaceutical Association. Your Guide to Non-Prescription Drugs. (Illus.). 500p. Date not set. price not set (ISBN 0-8290-1580-9). Irvington.

American Philatelic Society. APS Stamp Identifier. 66p. 1982. pap. 2.00 (ISBN 0-933580-10-X). Am Philatelic Society.

American Philosophical Society. Aspects of American Liberty. LC 76-50180. (Memoirs Ser.: Vol.118). (Illus.). 1977. 15.00 (ISBN 0-87169-118-3). Am Philos.

--Catalogue of Instruments & Models. Multhauf, Robert P., ed. LC 61-14630. (Memoirs Ser.: Vol. 53). (Illus.). 1961. 8.00 (ISBN 0-87169-053-5). Am Philos.

--Catalogue of Portraits & Other Works of Art. LC 61-14631. (Memoirs Ser.: Vol. 54). (Illus.). 1961. 8.00 (ISBN 0-87169-054-3). Am Philos.

--Early Transactions. facsimile ed. LC 77-76993. (Memoirs Ser.: Vol. 77). 1969. pap. 7.00 (ISBN 0-87169-077-2). Am Philos.

--Year Book. LC 39-2034. pap. 1.50 ea. 1937-1967 (ISBN 0-87169-991-5); pap. 3.00 ea. 1968-1970; pap. 5.00 ea. 1979-1981; pap. 10.50 ea. Am Philos.

American Philosophical Society Staff, jt. auth. see King, Cornelia S.

American Philosophical Society Staff, ed. see Library Staff & Smith, Murphy D.

American Physical Fitness Research Inst., ed. Here's to Wellness: A Common-Sense Guide to Health of Mind & Body. 256p. 1984. 10.95 (ISBN 0-8149-0887-X). Vanguard.

American Physical Society Conference, New York City, Feb. 2-5, 1976. Materials Technology: Proceedings. Chynoweth, A. G. & Walsh, W. M., eds. LC 76-27967. (AIP Conference Proceedings: No. 32). 1976. 18.00 (ISBN 0-88318-131-2). Am Inst Physics.

American Physical Therapy Association & Courseware, Inc. Staff. Competencies in Physical Therapy: An Analysis of Practice. 1979. looseleaf binder 34.50 (ISBN 0-89805-002-2). Am Phys Therapy Assn.

American Physiologial Society. Handbook of Physiology: Circulation, Section 2, the Cardiovascular System, 3 vols. Berne, Robert & Sperelakis, Nick, eds. Incl. Vol. 1. Heart; Vol. 2. Vascular Smooth Muscle; Vol. 3. Microcirculation. 1979. 130.00 (ISBN 0-683-00605-3). Williams & Wilkins.

American Physiological Society. High Altitude & Man. (Clinical Physiology Ser.). 207p. 1984. 39.00 (ISBN 0-683-08945-5). Waverly Pr.

--Reactions to Environmental Agents. Falk, Hans L. & Murphy, S. D., eds. (Handbook of Physiology: Section 9). (Illus.). 667p. 1977. 80.00 (ISBN 0-683-03000-0). Williams & Wilkins.

American Physiological Society & Kandel, Eric R. The Nervous System, Section 1: Cellular Biology of Neurona, 2 bks, Vol. 1. 1238p. 1977. Set. 135.00 (ISBN 0-683-04505-9). Williams & Wilkins.

American Physiological Society & Kitchell, Ralph L. Animal Pain: Perception & Alleviation. 231p. 1983. 39.95 (ISBN 0-683-04625-X). Waverly Pr.

American Physiological Society & Peachey, Lee D. Skeletal Muscle. (Handbook of Physiology Ser.: Section 10). 700p. 1983. 145.00 (ISBN 0-683-06805-9). Waverly Pr.

American Physiological Society, et al. The Cardiovascular System: Section 2, Vol. 2: Vascular Smooth Muscle. (APS Handbk. of Physiology). (Illus.). 700p. 1980. lib. bdg. 95.00 (ISBN 0-683-00606-1). Williams & Wilkins.

American Phytopathological Society - Sourcebook Committee. Sourcebook of Laboratory Exercises in Plant Pathology. Kelman, Arthur, ed. (Illus.). 388p. 1967. 19.95 (ISBN 0-7167-0813-2). W H Freeman.

American Political Science Association, & Committee on American Legislatures. American State Legislatures. Zeller, Belle, ed. LC 73-92294. Repr. of 1954 ed. lib. bdg. 15.00 (ISBN 0-8371-2434-4, AMSL). Greenwood.

American Political Science Association. Toward a More Responsible Two-Party System: A Report. pap. 10.00 (ISBN 0-384-01065-2). Johnson Repr.

American Prepaid Legal Services Institute Staff & Clark, J. Anthony. State Regulation of Prepaid Legal Services in Brief. LC 84-151210. 1984. 12.50. Am Prepaid.

American Presbyterian Mission. The Isle of Palms: Sketches of Hainan. LC 78-74354. (The Modern Chinese Economy Ser.: Vol. 21). 141p. 1980. lib. bdg. 20.00 (ISBN 0-8240-4269-7). Garland Pub.

American Production & Inventory Control Society. APICS Training Aid Style Manual. LC 82-74467. 80p. 1983. pap. 15.00 (ISBN 0-935406-23-9). Am Prod & Inventory.

American Production & Inventory Control Society, ed. APICS 26th Annual Conference Proceedings. LC 79-640341. 711p. 1983. pap. 30.00 (ISBN 0-935406-33-6, 40633). Am Prod & Inventory.

--Bar Coding Reprints. LC 83-70845. 132p. 1983. pap. 10.50 (ISBN 0-935406-25-5). Am Prod & Inventory.

--Bar Coding Seminar Proceedings: September 1983. LC 83-72510. 66p. 1983. pap. 6.00 (ISBN 0-935406-30-1, 40630). Am Prod & Inventory.

American Production & Inventory Control Society. Microprocessor Seminar Proceedings: January-February 1984. LC 83-73538. 287p. 1984. pap. 17.00 (ISBN 0-935406-40-9, 40640). Am Prod & Inventory.

American Production & Inventory Control Society, ed. MRO Stores Seminar Proceedings: 1984. LC 84-71082. 161p. 1984. pap. 10.00 (ISBN 0-935406-49-2). Am Prod & Inventory.

American Production & Inventory Control Society Staff, ed. Process Industries Seminar Proceedings. LC 83-71959. 66p. 1983. pap. 6.00 (ISBN 0-935406-29-8). Am Prod & Inventory.

American Production & Inventory Control Society, ed. Readings in Computers & Software. LC 84-72234. 64p. 1984. pap. 9.00 (ISBN 0-935406-56-5, 40656). Am Prod & Inventory.

--Readings in Management & Personal Development. LC 84-72232. 84p. 1984. pap. 14.00 (ISBN 0-935406-54-9, 40654). Am Prod & Inventory.

--Readings in Material & Capacity Requirements Planning. LC 84-72231. 84p. 1984. pap. 9.00 (ISBN 0-935406-53-0, 40653). Am Prod & Inventory.

--Readings in Production & Inventory Control & Planning. LC 84-72230. 213p. 1984. pap. 9.00 (ISBN 0-935406-52-2, 40652). Am Prod & Inventory.

--Readings in Production & Inventory Control Interfaces. LC 84-72233. 69p. 1984. pap. 9.00 (ISBN 0-935406-55-7, 40655). Am Prod & Inventory.

--Readings in Productivity Improvements. LC 84-72235. 134p. 1984. pap. 11.00 (ISBN 0-935406-57-3, 40657). Am Prod & Inventory.

--Readings in Zero Inventory. LC 84-72229. 175p. 1984. pap. 13.00 (ISBN 0-935406-51-4, 40651). Am Prod & Inventory.

--Service Parts Seminar Proceedings: September 1983. LC 83-72512. 90p. 1983. pap. 6.00 (ISBN 0-935406-31-X, 40631). Am Prod & Inventory.

--Synergy '84 Conference Proceedings. LC 84-72542. 231p. 1984. 30.00 (ISBN 0-935406-58-1). Am Prod & Inventory.

American Production & Inventory Control Society. Zero Inventories Seminar Proceedings, 1984. LC 84-71081. 87p. 1984. pap. 8.00 (ISBN 0-935406-48-4). Am Prod & Inventory.

American Production & Inventory Control Society, ed. Zero Inventories Seminar Proceedings: September 1983. LC 83-72511. 82p. 1983. pap. 6.00 (ISBN 0-935406-32-8, 40632). Am Prod & Inventory.

--Zero Inventory Philosophy & Practices Seminar Proceedings. LC 84-72852. 473p. 1984. pap. 30.00 (ISBN 0-935406-61-1, 40661). Am Prod & Inventory.

American Productivity Center, jt. auth. see Kendrick, John W.

American Products & Inventory Control Society, jt. auth. see Hall, Robert W.

American Psychiatric Assn., ed. A Psychiatric Glossary. 5th ed. 1980. text ed. 12.95 (ISBN 0-316-03656-0). Little.

American Psychiatric Association. Biofeedback: Task Force Report Nineteen. LC 80-66989. (Monographs). 128p. 1981. 11.00x (ISBN 0-89042-219-2, 42-219-2). Am Psychiatric.

--Continuing Medical Education Syllabus. 330p. 1984. pap. 15.00x (ISBN 0-89042-084-X, 42-084-X). Am Psychiatric.

--Diagnostic & Statistical Manual of Mental Disorders (DSM-III) 3rd ed ed. LC 79-55868. (Illus.). 512p. 1980. Casebound. 32.00x (ISBN 0-89042-041-6, 42-041-6); pap. 25.00x (ISBN 0-89042-042-4, 42-042-4). Am Psychiatric.

--Electroconvulsive Therapy. LC 78-69521. (Task Force Report: No. 14). 212p. 1978. pap. 12.00x (ISBN 0-89042-214-1, 42-214-1). Am Psychiatric.

--Issues in Forensic Psychiatry. 264p. 1984. pap. text ed. 15.00x (ISBN 0-88048-045-9, 48-045-9). Am Psychiatric.

--Psychosocial Aspects of Nuclear Developments, Task Force Report, Twenty, No. 20. LC 82-71902. (Monographs). 103p. 1982. 12.00x (ISBN 0-89042-220-6, 42-220-6). Am Psychiatric.

--Quick Reference to the Biographical Directory. 452p. 1984. pap. text ed. 18.00 (ISBN 0-89042-183-8, 42-183-8). Am Psychiatric.

--Quick Reference to the Diagnostic Criteria from DSM-III. (Illus.). 272p. 1980. 12.95x (ISBN 0-89042-043-2, 42-043-2). Am Psychiatric.

--Tardive Dyskinesia, Task Force Report Eighteen. LC 80-65372. (Monographs). (Illus.). 212p. 1980. 12.00x (ISBN 0-89042-218-4, 42-218-4). Am Psychiatric.

American Psychoanalytic Association, Committee on Indexing. Cumulative Index of the Journal of the American Psychoanalytic Association: 1953-1974, Vols. 1-22. LC 75-37247. 1975. unbound 40.00 (ISBN 0-685-64601-7); bound 55.00 (ISBN 0-8236-1091-8). Intl Univs Pr.

American Psychological Association. Changing Attitudes: Student Booklet. (Human Behavior Curriculum Project Ser.). 64p. (Orig.). (gr. 9-12). 1981. pap. text ed. 3.95x (ISBN 0-8077-2621-4). Tchrs Coll.

--Changing Attitudes: Teachers Handbook & Duplication Masters. (Human Behavior Curriculum Project Ser.). 50p. (Orig.). (gr. 9-12). 1981. 9.95x (ISBN 0-8077-2622-2). Tchrs Coll.

--Conditioning & Learning: Student Booklet. (Human Behavior Curriculum Project Ser.). 64p. (gr. 9-12). 1981. pap. text ed. 3.95x (ISBN 0-8077-2623-0). Tchrs Coll.

--Conditioning & Learning: Teachers Handbook & Duplication Masters. (Human Behavior Curriculum Project Ser.). (gr. 9-12). 1981. 9.95x (ISBN 0-8077-2624-9). Tchrs Coll.

--Ethical Principles in the Conduct of Research with Human Participants. 80p. 1983. pap. 8.50 (ISBN 0-912704-83-7). Am Psychol.

--Language & Communication: Student Booklet. (Human Behavior Curriculum Peoject Ser.). 60p. (Orig.). (gr. 9-12). 1981. pap. text ed. 3.95x (ISBN 0-8077-2625-7). Tchrs Coll.

--Language & Communication: Teachers Handbook & Duplication Masters. (Human Behavior Curriculum Project Ser.). (Orig.). (gr. 9-12). 1981. pap. 9.95x (ISBN 0-8077-2626-5). Tchrs Coll.

--Natural Behavior in Humans & Animals. (Human Behavior Curriculum Project Ser.). 55p. (Orig.). 1981. pap. text ed. 3.95x (ISBN 0-8077-2613-3); tchrs. manual & duplication masters 9.95x (ISBN 0-8077-2614-1). Tchrs Coll.

--School Life & Organizational Psychology. (Human Behavior Curriculum Project Ser.). 64p. (Orig.). 1981. pap. text ed. 3.95x (ISBN 0-8077-2617-6); tchrs. manual & duplication masters 9.95x (ISBN 0-8077-2618-4). Tchrs Coll.

--Social Influences on Behavior: Student Booklet. (Human Behavior Curriculum Project Ser.). 80p. (Orig.). (gr. 9-12). 1981. pap. text ed. 3.95x (ISBN 0-8077-2619-2). Tchrs Coll.

--Social Influences on Behavior: Teachers Handbook. (Human Behavior Curriculum Project Ser.). 48p. (Orig.). (gr. 9-12). 1981. pap. 9.95 (ISBN 0-8077-2620-6). Tchrs Coll.

American Psychological Association, et al. States of Consciousness. (Human Behavior Curriculum Project Ser.). 55p. 1981. pap. text ed. 3.95x (ISBN 0-8077-2615-X); tchrs. manual & duplication masters 9.95x (ISBN 0-8077-2616-8). Tchrs Coll.

American Psychological Association. Studying Personality: Student Booklet. (Human Behavior Curriculum Project Ser.). 75p. (Orig.). (gr. 9-12). 1981. pap. text ed. 3.95x (ISBN 0-8077-2627-3). Tchrs Coll.

--Studying Personality: Teachers Manual & Duplication Masters. (Human Behavior Curriculum Project Ser.). (Orig.). (gr. 9-12). 1981. pap. 9.95x (ISBN 0-8077-2628-1). Tchrs Coll.

American Psychological Association Committee on the Standardizing of Procedure in Experimental Tests. Report. Woodworth, R. S., ed. Bd. with Tests of Practical Mental Classification. Healy, W. H. Repr. of 1911 ed; Some Types of Attention. McComas, H. C. Repr. of 1911 ed; On the Functions of the Cerebrum. Franz, S. I. Repr. of 1911 ed. (Psychology Monographs General & Applied: Vol. 13). pap. 29.00 (ISBN 0-317-17941-1). Kraus Repr.

American Psychological Association, Division 27. Issues in Community Psychology & Preventive Mental Health. LC 75-140047. 161p. (Orig.). 1971. 19.95 (ISBN 0-87705-022-8); pap. 9.95 (ISBN 0-87705-027-9). Human Sci Pr.

American Psychological Association Staff. Graduate Study in Psychology & Associated Fields: 1984 with 1985 Addendum. Rev. ed. 546p. 1985. pap. 15.50 (1220035). Am Psychol.

American Psychology Association Committee on Teaching of Psychology see Richardson, Florence.

American Psychopathological Association Publications. Neurobiological Aspects of Psychopathology: Proceedings, Vol. 25. Zubin, Joseph & Shagass, C., eds. (Illus.). 442p. 1969. 79.00 (ISBN 0-8089-0562-7, 794985). Grune.

American Psychopathological Association. Psychopathology & Psychopharmacology: Proceedings of the Sixty-Second Annual Meeting. Cole, Jonathon O., et al, eds. LC 72-12347. pap. 78.00 (ISBN 0-317-19879-3, 2023091). Bks Demand UMI.

American Psychopathological Association Publications. Psychopathology of Adolescence: Proceedings, Vol. 26. Zubin, Joseph & Freedman, Alfred, eds. 354p. 1970. 68.50 (ISBN 0-8089-0558-9, 794986). Grune.

American Psychopathological Association. Trends of Mental Disease. Grob, Gerald N., ed. LC 78-22547. (Historical Issues in Mental Health Ser.). (Illus.). 1979. Repr. of 1945 ed. lib. bdg. 14.00x (ISBN 0-405-11901-1). Ayer Co Pubs.

American Public Health Assn., jt. ed. see Kramer, Morton.

American Public Health Association. Guide to Medical Care Administration, 2 vols. Incl. Vol. 1. Concepts & Principles. LC 72-82743. 114p. 1965. 6.50 (ISBN 0-87553-011-7, 056); Vol. 2. Medical Care Appraisal. 221p. 1969. 7.50 (ISBN 0-87553-012-5, 057). Am Pub Health.

American Public Health Association Staff. Standard Methods for the Examination of Dairy Products. 14th ed. Marth, Elmer H., ed. LC 78-72892. 439p. 1978. cancelled 30.00x (ISBN 0-87553-084-2, 025). Am Pub Health.

American Public Welfare Association. Public Welfare Directory, 1982-83. Weinstein, Amy, ed. LC 41-4981. 448p. (Orig.). 1982. pap. 40.00x (ISBN 0-910106-13-4). Am Pub Welfare.

--Public Welfare Directory, 1983-84. Weinstein, Amy, ed. LC 41-4981. 456p. 1983. pap. 40.00 (ISBN 0-910106-14-2). Am Pub Welfare.

--Public Welfare Directory 1984-85. Weinstein, Amy, ed. LC 41-4981. 464p. 1984. pap. 50.00 (ISBN 0-910106-15-0). Am Pub Welfare.

American Public Works Association. History of Public Works in the United States, 1776-1976. LC 76-11513. 1976. 20.00 (ISBN 0-917084-03-9). Am Public Works.

American Public Works Association Street Sanitation Committee. Street Cleaning Practice. 2nd ed. (American Public Works Association Research Foundation Projects Ser.: No. 105). pap. 110.00 (ISBN 0-317-09892-6, 2015936). Bks Demand UMI.

American Quaternary Association. Biennial Meeting, 7th, 1982. Character & Timing of Rapid Environmental & Climatic Changes: Abstracts. 188p. 5.00 (ISBN 0-318-16892-8). Am Quaternary Assn.

American Quaternary Association. Biennial Meeting, 1st, 1970. Climatic Changes from Fourteen Thousand to Nine Thousand Years Ago: Abstracts. 167p. 5.00 (ISBN 0-318-13126-9). Am Quaternary Assn.

American Radio Relay League. The ARRL Antenna Anthology. LC 78-71955. 1979. 4.00 (ISBN 0-87259-775-X). Am Radio.

--FM & Repeaters for the Radio Amateur. LC 72-96087. pap. 5.00 (ISBN 0-87259-454-8). Am Radio.

--Hints & Kinks. LC 33-14685. 4.00 (ISBN 0-87259-710-5). Am Radio.

--Radio Frequency Interference. 1984. 3.00 (ISBN 0-87259-425-4). Am Radio.

--Understanding Amateur Radio. LC 63-10833. 5.00 (ISBN 0-87259-603-6). Am Radio.

American Radio Relay League Inc. The Beginner's Guide to Amateur Radio. (Illus.). 208p. 1982. 24.95 (ISBN 0-13-072157-3); pap. 14.95 (ISBN 0-13-072140-9). P-H.

American Red Cross Seventh Annual Scientific Symposium, Washington, D.C., May 1975. Trace Components of Plasma: Isolation & Clinical Significance, Proceedings. Jamieson, G. A. & Greenwalt, Tibor J., eds. LC 75-38563. (Progress in Clinical & Biological Research: Vol. 5). 440p. 1976. 57.00 (ISBN 0-8451-0005-X). A R Liss.

American Scandinavian Foundation. Index Nordicus: A Cumulative Index to English-Language Periodicals on Scandinavian Studies. 1980. lib. bdg. 85.00 (ISBN 0-8161-0080-2, Hall Library). G K Hall.

American School Band Directors Association, ed. The ASBDA Curriculum Guide: Reference Book for School Band Directors. LC 73-75694. 1973. 20.00 (ISBN 0-913650-00-5). Columbia Pictures.

American School Health Association. Health Instruction: Guidelines for Planning Health Education Programs K-12. 136p. 1983. pap. text ed. 8.95 (ISBN 0-8403-2955-5). Kendall-Hunt.

American School Health Association & the Pharmaceutical Manufacturers Association Curriculum Guide Rewrite Committee. Teaching about Drugs. 3rd ed. 213p. 1985. pap. text ed. 13.95 (ISBN 0-89917-447-7). Tichenor Pub.

American School of Classical Studies at Athens. Catalogue of the Gennadius Library. American School of Classical Studies at Athens, 7 Vols. 1968. 695.00 (ISBN 0-8161-0707-6, Hall Library). G K Hall.
--Catalogue of the Gennadius Library. American School of Classical Studies at Athens, First Supplement. 1973. lib. bdg. 125.00 (ISBN 0-8161-0835-8, Hall Library). G K Hall.
--Catalogue of the Gennadius Library. American School of Classical Studies at Athenss, Second Supplement. 1981. lib. bdg. 170.00 (ISBN 0-8161-0011-X, Hall Library). G K Hall.
American School of Classical Studies at Athens Staff. Studies in Athenian Architecture, Sculpture & Topography. LC 81-14994. (Hesperia Ser.: Suppl. 20). 1982. 15.00x (ISBN 0-686-85626-0). Am Sch Athens.
--Studies in Attic Epigraphy, History & Topography. LC 81-26460. (Hesperia Ser.: Suppl. 19). 1982. 15.00x (ISBN 0-87661-519-1). Am Sch Athens.
American School of Needlework. The Great Afghan Book. Thomas, Mary, ed. LC 80-68389. (Illus.). 160p. 1981. 17.95 (ISBN 0-8069-5444-2, Columbia Hse). Sterling.
--The Great Christmas Craft Book. (Illus.). 144p. 1983. 17.95 (ISBN 0-8069-5498-1). Sterling.
--The Great Christmas Crochet Book. (Illus.). 144p. 1982. 17.95 (ISBN 0-8069-5452-3). Sterling.
--Great Craft Quilts Book. (Illus.). 144p. 1984. 18.95 (ISBN 0-8069-5538-4). Sterling.
--Great Crochet Bazaar Book. LC 81-85030. (Illus.). 160p. 1982. 17.95 (ISBN 0-8069-5456-6). Sterling.
--The Great Granny Crochet Book. LC 78-73380. (Illus.). 1979. 12.95 (ISBN 0-13-363838-3). P-H.
American Society for Electroplated Plastics Staff. Standards & Guidelines for Electroplated Plastics. 3rd ed. (Illus.). 160p. 1984. 36.00 (ISBN 0-13-842310-5). P-H.
American Society for Engineering Education. Papers on Scientific Management. LC 75-6637. (Management History Ser.: No. 72). Orig. Title: American Society for the Promotion of Engineering Education Proceedings. (Illus.). 228p. 1975. Repr. of 1912 ed. 22.50 (ISBN 0-87960-110-8). Hive Pub.
American Society for Hospital Central Service Personnel. Ethylene Oxide Use in Hospitals: A Manual for Health Care Personnel. LC 82-13871. (Illus.). 176p. 1982. pap. 52.50 (ISBN 0-939450-35-6, 031180); pap. 42.00 members. AHPI.
American Society for Hospital Engineering of the American Hospital Association. Controlling Waste Anesthetic Gases. (Illus.). 52p. 1980. 10.75 (ISBN 0-87258-307-4, AHA-181152, Pub. by AHPI). Am Hospital.
American Society for Hospital Engineering. Hospital Engineering Handbook. (Illus.). 348p. 1980. 35.00 (ISBN 0-87258-311-2, 055120). AHPI.
American Society for Hospital Engineering of the American Hospital Association. Medical Equipment Management in Hospitals. 1982 ed. 704p. 1982. pap. 60.00 (ISBN 0-939450-32-1, 190105). AHPI.
American Society for Hospital Engineering & American Society for Hospital Purchasing & Materials Management. Silver Recovery for Hospitals. LC 80-19943. 36p. 1980. pap. 10.00 (ISBN 0-87258-331-7, 172100). AHPI.
American Society for Hospital Food Service Administrators. Hospital Food Service Management Review. LC 80-11834. 80p. (Orig.). 1980. pap. 12.50 (ISBN 0-87258-292-2, 046160). AHPI.
American Society for Hospital Marketing & Public Relations of the American Hospital Hospital Association. A Basic Guide to Hospital Marketing & Public Relations. 2nd ed. LC 83-21354. 102p. 1984. 33.75 (ISBN 0-939450-41-0, 166121). AHPI.
American Society for Hospital Purchasing & Materials Management, jt. auth. see American Society for Hospital Engineering.
American Society for Information Science, jt. ed. see Knowledge Industry Publications.
American Society for Legal History. Essays in Jurisprudence in Honor of Roscoe Pound. Newman, Ralph A., ed. LC 73-10750. (Illus.). 670p. 1973. Repr. of 1962 ed. lib. bdg. 34.00x (ISBN 0-8371-7023-0, EJRP). Greenwood.
American Society for Materials & Testing. Computer Automation of Materials Testing, STP 710. (710). 235p. 1980. 21.75x (ISBN 0-8031-0267-4, 04-710000-32). ASTM.
--Corrosion & Degradation of Implant Materials, STP 684. 369p. 1979. 37.75x (ISBN 0-8031-0313-1, 04-684000-27). ASTM.
--Crack Arrest Methodology & Applications, STP 711. 452p. 1980. 44.75x (ISBN 0-8031-0317-4, 04-711000-30). ASTM.
--Low-Temperature Pumpability Characteristics of Engine Oils in Full-Scale Engines, DS 57. 104p. 1975. pap. 16.00 (ISBN 0-8031-0392-1, 05-057000-12). ASTM.
--Manual of Coating Work for Light-Water Nuclear Power Primary Containment & Other Safety-Related Facilities, 1st ed. (Illus.). 201p. 1979. 57.50x (ISBN 0-8031-0394-8, 03-401079-14). ASTM.
American Society for Metal. Wear & Fracture Prevention: Proceedings of a Conference Held May 21-22, 1980, Peoria, Illinois. LC 81-67226. (Materials-Metalworking Technology Ser.). pap. 79.80 (ISBN 0-317-26752-3, 2024351). Bks Demand UMI.
American Society for Metals. Carburizing & Carbonitriding. LC 76-55702. pap. 58.30 (ISBN 0-317-20679-6, 2025145). Bks Demand UMI.
--Casting Design Handbook: Prepared from the Contributions of 18 Committees (Sponsored by the United States Air Force & the American Society for Metals) LC 62-53240. (Illus.). pap. 86.00 (ISBN 0-317-10976-6, 2013216). Bks Demand UMI.
--Control of Distortion & Residual Stress in Weldments: Proceedings of an International Conference. Saperstein, Z. Phillip, ed. LC 77-13326. (Materials-Metalworking Technology Ser.). pap. 23.30 (ISBN 0-317-19836-X, 2023059). Bks Demand UMI.
--Hydrogen Damage: A Discriminative Selection of Outstanding Articles & Papers from the Scientific Literature. Beachem, Cedric D., ed. LC 77-14966. pap. 105.50 (ISBN 0-317-26763-9, 2024346). Bks Demand UMI.
--Influence of Metallurgy on Hole Making Operations: Drilling, Reaming, Tapping & Others. Tipnis, Vijay A., compiled by. LC 77-13357. (Materials-Metalworking Technology Ser.). (Illus.). pap. 54.00 (ISBN 0-317-09756-3, 2019491). Bks Demand UMI.
--Influence of Metallurgy on Machinability: An International Symposium, Proceedings. Tipnis, Vijay A., compiled by. LC 75-29683. (Materials-Metalworking Technology Ser.: No. 7). (Illus.). pap. 120.00 (ISBN 0-317-09746-6, 2019477). Bks Demand UMI.
--The Inhomogeneity of Plastic Deformation: Papers Presented at a Seminar of the American Society for Metals. LC 72-95850. pap. 82.00 (ISBN 0-317-10482-9, 2019484). Bks Demand UMI.
--Materials Engineering in the Arctic: Proceedings of an International Conference, St. Jovite, Quebec, Canada, Sept. 27 - Oct. 1, 1976. LC 77-4214. (Illus.). pap. 85.80 (ISBN 0-317-08329-5, 2019495). Bks Demand UMI.
--The Metallurgical Evolution of Stainless Steels: A Discriminative Selection of Outstanding Articles & Papers from the Scientific Literature. Pickering, F. B., ed. LC 79-12994. pap. 121.80 (ISBN 0-317-27687-5, 2019495). Bks Demand UMI.
--New Trends in Materials Processing: Papers Presented at a Seminar of the American Society for Metals, October 19-20, 1974. LC 75-42155. (Illus.). pap. 92.80 (ISBN 0-317-11145-0, 2019476). Bks Demand UMI.
--Nondestructive Evaluation in the Nuclear Industry: Proceedings of an International Conference, 13-155 February, 1978, Salt Lake City, Utah. Natesh, R., ed. LC 78-25552. (Materials Metalworking Technology Ser.). pap. 134.00 (ISBN 0-317-27705-7, 2019488). Bks Demand UMI.
--Polymeric Materials: Relationships Between Structure & Mechanical Behavior: Papers Presented at a Seminar of the American Society for Metals. LC 74-20127. pap. 156.50 (ISBN 0-317-09007-0, 2015494). Bks Demand UMI.
--Source Book on Cold Forming: A Discriminative Selection of Outstanding Articles from the Periodical Literature. LC 75-6855. (American Society for Metals. Engineering Bookshelf Ser.). (Illus.). pap. 93.80 (ISBN 0-317-11151-5, 2019501). Bks Demand UMI.
--Source Book on Industrial Alloy & Engineering Data: A Comprehensive Collection of Alloy & Engineering Data in Tabular & Graphical Form. LC 77-28985. pap. 120.80 (ISBN 0-317-26761-2, 2024347). Bks Demand UMI.
--Source Book on Powder Metallurgy: A Comprehensive Collection of Oustanding Articles from the Periodical & Reference Literature. Bradbury, Samuel, ed. LC 78-24466. pap. 109.80 (ISBN 0-317-26758-2, 2024348). Bks Demand UMI.
--Source Book on Wear Control Technology: A Comprehensive Collection of Outstanding Articles from the Periodical & Reference Literature. Rigney, David A. & Glaeser, W. A., eds. LC 78-12162. (ASM Engineering Bookshelf Ser.). pap. 116.00 (ISBN 0-317-26756-6, 2024349). Bks Demand UMI.
--Specialized Cleaning, Finishing & Coating Processes: Proceedings of a Conference Held February 5-6, 1980, Los Angeles, California. LC 81-2755. (Materials-Metalworking Technology Ser.). pap. 106.00 (ISBN 0-317-26754-X, 2024350). Bks Demand UMI.
--Welding & Brazing of Carbon Steels. Davis, Charles A., ed. LC 76-44372. Book 3: Resistance Welding. pap. 37.80 (ISBN 0-317-26234-3, 2052147); Book 4: Gas Welding & Brazing. pap. 43.00 (ISBN 0-317-26235-1). Bks Demand UMI.
American Society for Metals Staff. Diffusion: Papers Presented at a Seminar of the American Society for Metals, October 14 & 15, 1972. LC 73-88315. pap. 95.80 (2019479). Bks Demand UMI.
--Nondestructive Evaluation in the Nuclear Industry: An International Conference, 13-15 February, 1978, Salt Lake City, Utah, Proceedings. Natesh, R., ed. LC 78-25552. (Materials-Metalworking Technology Ser.). (Illus.). pap. 134.00 (ISBN 0-317-09715-6, 2019488). Bks Demand UMI.
--Phase Transformations & Related Phenomena in Steels: Papers Presented at the E. C. Bain Seminar of the American Society for Metals. LC 72-95849. pap. 24.50 (ISBN 0-317-27682-4, 2019496). Bks Demand UMI.
--Prevention of Structural Failures: The Role of NDT, Fracture Mechanics & Failure Analysis: Proceedings of Two Annual Forums, 19-22 June, 1977 & 14-16 June 1976, Tarpon Springs, Florida. LC 78-15388. (Materials-Metalworking Technology Ser.). (Illus.). pap. 90.00 (ISBN 0-317-09726-1, 2019489). Bks Demand UMI.
American Society for Metals Staff & Kostesoja, Victor A. Properties & Selection of Tool Materials. LC 75-26829. pap. 80.00 (ISBN 0-317-27717-0, 2019483). Bks Demand UMI.
American Society for Metals Staff. Source Book in Failure Analysis: A Discriminative Selection of Outstanding Articles & Case Histories from the Periodical Literature. American Society for Metals Staff, the Periodical Publication Department, ed. LC 74-22347. (ASM Engineering Bookshelf Ser.). (Illus.). pap. 103.50 (ISBN 0-317-09642-7, 2019492). Bks Demand UMI.
--Source Book on Ductile Iron: A Discriminative Selection of Outstanding Articles from the Periodical & Reference Literature. Rauch, A. H., ed. LC 77-9278. (ASM Engineering Bookshelf Ser.). pap. 100.00 (ISBN 0-317-27679-4, 2019500). Bks Demand UMI.
--Source Book on Heat Treating: A Discriminative Selection of Outstanding Articles from the Literature Periodicals. LC 75-25598. (ASM Engineering Bookshelf Ser.: Vol. 1: Materials & Processes). (Illus.). pap. 99.50 (ISBN 0-317-09661-3, 2051904). Bks Demand UMI.
--Source Book on Maraging Steels: A Comprehensive Collection of Outstanding Articles from the Periodical & Reference Literature. Decker, Raymond F., compiled by. LC 79-13743. (AMS Engineering Bookself Ser.). (Illus.). pap. 100.00 (ISBN 0-317-09610-9, 2019493). Bks Demand UMI.
--Source Book on Stainless Steels: A Discriminative Selection of Outstanding Articles from the Periodical & Reference Literature. American Society for Metals Staff, The Periodical Publication Department, compiled by. LC 76-867. (ASM Engineering Bookshelf Ser.). (Illus.). pap. 104.00 (ISBN 0-317-09622-2, 2019497). Bks Demand UMI.
--Welding of HSLA Structural Steels: Proceedings of an International Conference. Rothwell, A. B. & Gray, Malcolm J., eds. LC 78-18220. (Materials Metalworking Technology Ser.). pap. 160.00 (ISBN 0-317-27699-9, 2019490). Bks Demand UMI.
American Society for Metals Staff, The Periodical Publication Department, compiled by see American Society for Metals Staff.
American Society for Metals Staff, the Periodical Publication Department, ed. see American Society for Metals Staff.
American Society for Personnel Administration. Work in the Twenty-First Century. (Orig.). 1984. pap. text ed. 5.95 (ISBN 0-939900-06-8). Am Soc Personnel.
American Society for Political & Legal Philosophy. Authority. Freidrich, Carl J., ed. LC 81-7114. (Nomos One Ser.). viii, 234p. 1981. Repr. of 1958 ed. lib. bdg. 25.00x (ISBN 0-313-23185-0, AMAU). Greenwood.
American Society for Reformation Research, ed. see Christensen, Carl C.
American Society for Surgery of the Hand. The Hand: Examination & Diagnosis. 2nd ed. LC 82-4140. (Illus.). 115p. 1983. pap. text ed. 6.95 (ISBN 0-443-02310-7). Churchill.
American Society for Testing & Institute of Petroleum. Petroleum Measurement Tables. 1973. (Pub. by Elsevier Applied Sci England); British Ed. 39.00 (ISBN 0-444-39994-1); Metric Ed. 48.00 (ISBN 0-444-39993-3). Elsevier.
American Society for Testing & Material. Annual Book of ASTM Standards, 1983, 66 vols. LC 40-10712. pap. write for info. (2025472). Bks Demand UMI.
American Society for Testing & Materials. Application of Advanced & Nuclear Physics to Testing Materials. LC 65-19687. (American Society for Testing & Materials Ser.: Special Technical Publication, No. 373). pap. 35.30 (ISBN 0-317-10989-8, 2000739). Bks Demand UMI.
American Society for Testing & Materials, Committee E-4 on Metallography. Applications of Modern Metallographic Techniques. LC 78-114749. (American Society for Testing & Materials Special Technical Publications: No. 480). pap. 70.00 (ISBN 0-317-10388-1, 2016594). Bks Demand UMI.
American Society for Testing & Materials. ASTM Specifications for Structural Steel. pap. 58.50 (ISBN 0-317-26541-5, 2023991). Bks Demand UMI.
American Society for Testing & Materials, Committee F-16 on Fasteners. ASTM Standards on Fasteners. 1st ed. LC 78-108362. pap. 84.00 (ISBN 0-317-11195-7, 2015509). Bks Demand UMI.
American Society for Testing & Materials. ASTM Viscosity Index Calculated from Kinematic Viscosity. LC 65-24834. (American Society for Testing & Materials, ASTM Data Ser.: No. DS 39a). pap. 160.00 (ISBN 0-317-29824-0, 2019952). Bks Demand UMI.
--ASTM Viscosity Tables for Kinematic Viscosity Conversions & Viscosity Index Calculations, STP 43C. 35p. 1972. pap. 10.00 (ISBN 0-8031-0766-8, 04-043030-12). ASTM.
--Cleaning Stainless Steel: A Symposium. LC 73-80188. (American Society for Testing & Materials Special Technical Publications Ser.: 538). (Illus.). pap. 59.50 (ISBN 0-317-10763-1, 2009068). Bks Demand UMI.
--Compaction of Soils. LC 65-18214. (American Society for Testing & Materials: Special Technical Publication, No. 377). pap. 35.30 (ISBN 0-317-10980-4, 2000734). Bks Demand UMI.
--Compilation & Index of Trade Names, Specifications, & Producers of Stainless Alloys & Superalloys. LC 72-91409. (ASTM Data Ser.: DS45A). pap. 20.00 (ISBN 0-317-08287-6, 2019652). Bks Demand UMI.
--Determination of Nonmetallic Compounds in Steel: A Symposium. LC 66-12290. (American Society for Testing & Materials Special Technical Publication Ser.: No. 393). pap. 25.80 (ISBN 0-317-09781-4, 2000967). Bks Demand UMI.
--Effects of High-Energy Radiation on Inorganic Substances: A Symposium. LC 66-21923. (American Society for Testing & Materials Special Technical Publication Ser.: No. 400). pap. 44.00 (ISBN 0-317-09791-1, 2000937). Bks Demand UMI.
--Electron Fractography: A Symposium Presented At the 70th Annual Meeting, American Society for Testing & Materials, Boston, Mass., 25-30 June 1967. LC 68-15547. (ASTM Special Technical Publication Ser.: No. 436). pap. 59.00 (ISBN 0-317-29816-X, 2016593). Bks Demand UMI.
--Erosion by Cavitation or Impingement: A Symposium. LC 67-12411. (American Society for Testing & Materials Series, Special Technical Publication: No. 408). pap. 73.00 (ISBN 0-317-11247-3, 2000975). Bks Demand UMI.
--Evaluation of Relative Density & Its Role in Geotechnical Projects Involving Cohesionless Soils. Selig, E. T. & Ladd, R. S., eds. LC 72-90704. pap. 129.00 (ISBN 0-317-26539-3, 2023989). Bks Demand UMI.
American Society for Testing & Materials, et al. Fatigue at Elevated Temperatures. Carden, A. E., ed. LC 73-76958. (American Society for Testing & Materials Special Technical Publications Ser.: 520). (Illus.). pap. 160.00 (ISBN 0-317-11056-X). Bks Demand UMI.
American Society for Testing & Materials. Fatigue Crack Propagation. LC 67-14532. (Special Technical Publication Ser.: No. 415). pap. 138.00 (ISBN 0-317-11250-3, 2001125). Bks Demand UMI.
--Fifty Years of Progress in Metallographic Techniques. LC 67-26105. (American Society for Testing & Materials, Special Technical Publications: 430). pap. 103.80 (ISBN 0-317-10307-5, 2000876). Bks Demand UMI.
--Fire Risk Assessment: A Symposium. Castino, G. T. & Harmathy, T. Z., eds. LC 81-68807. (ASTM Special Technical Publication: No. 762). pap. 27.80 (ISBN 0-317-26540-7, 2023990). Bks Demand UMI.
--Flow & Fracture of Metals & Alloys in Nuclear Environments. LC 65-16810. (American Society for Testing & Materials. Special Technical Publication: No. 380). pap. 119.30 (ISBN 0-317-08035-0, 2000740). Bks Demand UMI.
--Fracture Toughness Testing & Its Applications: A Symposium Presented at the Sixty-Seventh Annual Meeting, American Society for Testing & Materials, Chicago, Ill., 1964. LC 65-16811. (American Society for Testing & Materials. Special Technical Publication: No. 381). pap. 105.80 (ISBN 0-317-08197-7, 2015506). Bks Demand UMI.
--Handbook of Vapor Degreasing. LC 76-1382. (ASTM Special Technical Publication: No. 310A). pap. 20.00 (ISBN 0-317-26535-0, 2023986). Bks Demand UMI.
--Hot Corrosion: Problems Associated with Gas Turbines. LC 67-17473. (American Society for Testing & Materials Special Technical Publication Ser.: No. 421). pap. 75.80 (ISBN 0-317-10925-1, 2001123). Bks Demand UMI.
--Laser Induced Damage in Optical Materials, 1976: Proceedings of a Symposium. Glass, Alexander J. & Guenther, Arthur H., eds. LC 76-600074. pap. 103.00 (ISBN 0-317-27764-2, 2015510). Bks Demand UMI.
--Manual on Industrial Water & Industrial Waste Water. 2nd. ed. LC 67-4371. (American Society for Testing & Materials Special Technical Publications Ser.: 148-I). pap. 160.00 (ISBN 0-317-10882-4, 2000636). Bks Demand UMI.

--Manual on Low Cycle Fatigue Testing. LC 70-97730. (ASTM Special Technical Publication: No. 465). pap. 52.50 (ISBN 0-317-26536-9, 2023987). Bks Demand UMI.

--Measurement of Dielectric Properties under Space Conditions. LC 67-17472. (American Society for Testing & Materials. Special Technical Publication: No. 420). pap. 26.50 (ISBN 0-317-08047-4, 2001119). Bks Demand UMI.

American Society for Testing & Materials Ser. The Microstructure of Bronze Sinterings. LC 62-20903. (American Society for Testing & Materials Ser.: Special Technical Publication, No. 323). pap. 20.00 (ISBN 0-317-10788-7, 2000130). Bks Demand UMI.

American Society for Testing & Materials Staff & Wilson, M. A. Nondestructive Rapid Identification of Metals & Alloys by Spot Test. LC 73-90275. (American Society for Testing & Materials; Special Technical Publication Ser.: 550). pap. 20.00 (ISBN 0-317-08730-4, 2006068). Bks Demand UMI.

American Society for Testing & Materials. Orientation Effects in the Mechanical Behavior of Anisotropic Structural Materials. LC 66-29104. (American Society for Testing & Materials Ser.: Special Technical Publication, No. 405). pap. 24.30 (ISBN 0-317-10967-7, 2000703). Bks Demand UMI.

--Paint Testing Manual: Physical & Chemical Examination of Paints, Varnishes, Lacquers & Colors. 13th ed. Sward, G. G., ed. LC 75-186850. (ASTM Special Technical Publication Ser.: No. 500). pap. 153.00 (ISBN 0-317-20535-8, 2022835). Bks Demand UMI.

American Society for Testing & Materials Staff. Papers on Industrial Water & Industrial Waste. LC 63-12705. (American Society for Testing & Materials Special Technical Publication Ser.: No. 337). pap. 20.00 (ISBN 0-317-09816-0, 2000143). Bks Demand UMI.

American Society for Testing & Materials. Plane Strain Crack Toughness: Testing of High Strength Metallic Materials. LC 66-29517. (American Society for Testing & Materials, Special Technical Publication Ser.: No. 410). pap. 34.00 (ISBN 0-317-08331-7, 2051707). Bks Demand UMI.

--Progress in Flaw Growth & Fracture Toughness Testing: Proceedings of the 1972 National Symposium on Fracture Mechanics, Philadelphia, PA, 28-30, 1972. LC 73-76198. (American Society for Testing & Materials Special Technical Publication: No. 536). pap. 125.30 (ISBN 0-317-10700-3, 2022546). Bks Demand UMI.

--Radiation Effects in Electronics. LC 65-18216. (American Society for Testing & Materials. Special Technical Publication: No. 384). pap. 60.80 (ISBN 0-317-08042-3, 2000743). Bks Demand UMI.

--Sealant Technology in Glazing Systems: A Symposium. LC 77-83433. (ASTM Special Technical Publication: 638). pap. 29.00 (ISBN 0-317-20575-7, 2022516). Bks Demand UMI.

American Society for Testing & Materials Staff. Skid Resistance of Highway Pavements. LC 72-97870. (American Society for Testing & Materials. Special Technical Publication Ser.: No. 530). pap. 41.30 (ISBN 0-317-11157-4, 2016438). Bks Demand UMI.

American Society for Testing & Materials. Space Radiation Effects. LC 64-14650. (American Society for Testing & Materials Ser.: Special Technical Publication, No. 363). pap. 41.30 (ISBN 0-317-11242-2, 2000753). Bks Demand UMI.

American Society for Testing & Materials Staff. Specifications for Carbon & Alloy-Steel Plates for Pressure Vessels. pap. 46.50 (ISBN 0-317-28482-7, 2019125). Bks Demand UMI.

American Society for Testing & Materials. Stress Corrosion Cracking: The Slow Strain-Rate Technique - STP 665. 441p. 1979. 39.75x (ISBN 0-8031-0579-7, 04-665000-27). ASTM.

American Society for Testing & Materials Staff. Stress Corrosion Testing. LC 67-20038. (American Society for Testing & Materials Ser.: Special Technical Publication, No. 425). pap. 97.00 (ISBN 0-317-11257-0, 2001144). Bks Demand UMI.

American Society for Testing & Materials. Structural Fatigue in Aircraft. LC 66-28344. (American Society for Testing & Materials. Special Technical Publication Ser.: No. 404). pap. 51.80 (ISBN 0-317-09263-4, 2001130). Bks Demand UMI.

--Structure & Properties of Ultrahigh-Strength Steels. LC 65-19686. (American Society for Testing & Materials Ser.: Special Technical Publication, No. 370). pap. 56.80 (ISBN 0-317-11239-2, 2000741). Bks Demand UMI.

--Symposium on Cleaning & Materials Processing for Electronics & Space Apparatus. LC 63-15794. (American Society for Testing & Materials: Special Technical Publication: No. 342). pap. 68.30 (ISBN 0-317-08016-4, 2000138). Bks Demand UMI.

--Symposium on Dynamic Behavior of Materials. LC 63-20729. (American Society for Testing & Materials. Special Technical Publication Ser.: No. 336). pap. 80.80 (ISBN 0-317-10854-9, 2000144). Bks Demand UMI.

--Symposium on Fatigue Tests of Aircraft Structures: Low-Cycle, Full-Scale, & Helicopters. LC 63-15793. (American Society for Testing & Materials. Special Technical Publication Ser.: No. 338). pap. 69.80 (ISBN 0-317-09223-5, 2000142). Bks Demand UMI.

--Symposium on Lubricants for Automotive Equipment. LC 63-15729. (American Society for Testing & Materials. Special Technical Publication Ser.: No. 334). pap. 64.80 (ISBN 0-317-09152-2, 2000122). Bks Demand UMI.

--Symposium on Materials for Aircraft, Missiles, & Space Vehicles. LC 63-20730. (American Society for Testing & Materials. Special Technical Publication Ser.: 345). pap. 37.30 (ISBN 0-317-09214-6, 2000136). Bks Demand UMI.

--Symposium on Radiation Effects on Metals & Neutron Dosimetry. LC 63-12698. (American Society for Testing & Materials Ser.: Special Technical Publication, No. 341). pap. 103.80 (ISBN 0-317-10870-0, 2000139). Bks Demand UMI.

--Symposium on Recent Developments in Nondestructive Testing of Missiles & Rockets. (American Society for Testing & Materials. Special Technical Publication Ser.: No. 350). pap. 30.30 (ISBN 0-317-09141-7, 2000116). Bks Demand UMI.

--Symposium on Spectrochemical Analysis for Trace Elements. LC 58-3176. (American Society for Testing & Materials Special Technical Publications Ser: No. 221). pap. 21.30 (ISBN 0-317-09810-1, 2000112). Bks Demand UMI.

--Symposium on Spectroscopy. LC 60-9523. (American Society for Testing & Materials, Special Technical Publication: No. 269). pap. 62.80 (ISBN 0-317-09560-9, 2000106). Bks Demand UMI.

--Symposium on Standards for Filament-Wound Reinforced Plastics. LC 62-22246. (American Society for Testing & Materials Ser.: Special Technical Publication, No. 327). pap. 84.00 (ISBN 0-317-10780-1, 2000120). Bks Demand UMI.

--Symposium on Stress-Strain-Time-Temperature Relationships in Materials. LC 62-22248. (American Society for Testing & Materials: Special Publication, No. 325). pap. 33.80 (ISBN 0-317-10835-2, 2000133). Bks Demand UMI.

--Symposium on the Chemical & Physical Effects of High-Energy Radiation on Inorganic Substances. LC 64-14646. (American Society for Testing & Materials Special Technical Publication Ser.: No. 359). pap. 29.80 (ISBN 0-317-09795-4, 2000748). Bks Demand UMI.

--Techniques of Electron Microscopy, Diffraction, & Microprobe Analysis. (American Society for Testing & Materials Special Technical Publication: No. 372). pap. 23.80 (ISBN 0-317-09550-1, 2000730). Bks Demand UMI.

American Society for Testing & Materials, Committee A-1 on Steel. Temper Embrittlement of Alloy Steels: A Symposium Presented at the Seventy-Fourth Annual Meeting, American Society for Testing & Materials. LC 73-185535. (American Society for Testing & Materials Ser.: No. 499). pap. 35.30 (ISBN 0-317-10341-5, 2015504). Bks Demand UMI.

American Society for Testing & Materials. Testing for Prediction of Material Performance in Structures & Components: A Symposium. Presented at the Annual Meeting, American Society & Materials. LC 72-79572. (American Society for Testing & Materials. Special Technical Publication: No.515). pap. 79.80 (ISBN 0-317-08194-2, 2015505). Bks Demand UMI.

--Testing Techniques for Rock Mechanics. LC 66-24783. (American Society for Testing & Materials Ser.: Special Technical Publication, No. 402). pap. 76.00 (ISBN 0-317-11253-8, 2001129). Bks Demand UMI.

--Thermal Transmission Measurements of Insulation - STP 660. 458p. 1979. 39.50x (ISBN 0-8031-0589-4, 04-660000-10). ASTM.

--Unified Numbering System for Metals & Alloys: And Cross Index of Chemically-Similar Specification - A Joint Activity of the Society of Automotive Engineers, American Society for Testing & Materials. LC 77-89064. (American Society for Testing & Materials Ser.: No. DS-56A). pap. 72.00 (ISBN 0-317-29433-4, 2024296). Bks Demand UMI.

--Unified Numbering System for Metals & Alloys: Metals & Alloys Currently Covered by UNS Numbers, July, 1974. LC 75-309848. pap. 46.50 (ISBN 0-317-11264-3, 2021525). Bks Demand UMI.

--Water Quality Criteria. LC 67-14533. (American Society for Testing & Materials. Special Technical Publication Ser.: 416). pap. 31.80 (ISBN 0-317-10923-5, 2000707). Bks Demand UMI.

--X-Ray & Optical Emission Analysis of High-Temperature Alloys: A Symposium. LC 65-18213. (American Society for Testing & Materials Special Technical Publication Ser.: No. 376). pap. 20.00 (ISBN 0-317-09803-9, 2000851). Bks Demand UMI.

American Society for Testing Materials, Committee E-3 on Chemical Analysis of Metals Special Publication. Some Fundamentals of Analytical Chemistry: A Symposium Presented at the Seventy-Sixth Annual Meeting, American Societyfor Testing & Materials. LC 74-81159. (American Society for Testing & Materials Ser.: No. 564). (Illus.). pap. 21.80 (ISBN 0-317-09329-0, 2015507). Bks Demand UMI.

American Society for Training & Development (ASTD) Contemporary Organization Development: Current Thinking & Applications. Warrick, D. D., ed. 1984. 24.95 (ISBN 0-673-18032-8). Scott F.

American Society for Training & Development Inc. Quality of Work Life: Perspectives for Business & the Public Sector. Skrovan, Daniel J., ed. 208p. 1983. text ed. 18.95 (ISBN 0-201-07755-8). Addison-Wesley.

American Society of African Culture. Pan-Africanism Reconsidered. LC 76-3618. 376p. 1976. Repr. of 1962 ed. lib. bdg. 22.75x (ISBN 0-8371-8792-3, ASPA). Greenwood.

American Society of Agricultural Engineers, ed. Irrigation Scheduling for Water & Energy Conservation in the 1980's. LC 81-70534. 231p. 1981. pap. 19.50 (ISBN 0-916150-42-9). Am Soc Ag Eng.

American Society of Appraisers. Appraisal of Farmland: Use-Value Assessment Laws & Property Taxation, No. 8. new ed. LC 78-74140. (Monograph). 1979. pap. 5.00 (ISBN 0-937828-17-3). Am Soc Appraisers.

American Society of Association Executives Communication Section. Publishing with a Purpose: A Guide to Association Publishing. Jorpeland, Marshall, ed. 72p. (Orig.). 1982. pap. text ed. 20.00 (ISBN 0-88034-002-9). Am Soc Assn Execs.

American Society of Civil Engineers, jt. auth. see Coastal Engineering International Conference, 15th, Honolulu, Hawaii, July 1976.

American Society of Civil Engineers, compiled By see ASCE Professional Activities Committee Conference, March 1977.

American Society of Civil Engineers, compiled By see ASCE Urban Transportation Division, May 1973.

American Society of Civil Engineers, compiled By see ASCE Waterway, Port Coastal & Ocean Division Conference, Charleston, Nov. 1977.

American Society of Civil Engineers, compiled By see Coastal Engineering International Conference, 16th, Hamburg, Germany, Aug. 1978.

American Society of Civil Engineers, compiled By see Engineering Foundation Conference, Jan. 1978.

American Society of Civil Engineers, compiled By see Engineering Foundation Conference, Nov. 1976.

American Society of Civil Engineers, ed. see Environmental Impact Analysis Research Council at the Chicago National Convention, Oct. 1978.

American Society of Civil Engineers, compiled by see International Conference, 14th, Copenhagen, Denmark, June 1974.

American Society of Civil Engineering, compiled by. Readings in Cost Engineering. 730p. 1979. pap. 49.00x (ISBN 0-87262-147-2). Am Soc Civil Eng.

American Society of Civil Engineers, Conference, North Carolina State Univ., May 1977. Advances in Civil Engineering Through Engineering Mechanics: Proceedings. 634p. 1977. pap. 36.00x (ISBN 0-87262-087-5). Am Soc Civil Eng.

American Society of Civil Engineers, Irrigation & Drainage Division. Age of Changing Priorities for Land & Water: Irrigation & Drainage Division Specialty Conference, Spokane, Washington, September 26-28, 1972. LC 73-155132. pap. 123.00 (ISBN 0-317-10781-X, 2007866). Bks Demand UMI.

American Society of Civil Engineers. Agricultural & Urban Considerations in Irrigation & Drainage: Selected Papers from Specialty Conference, Fort Collins, Colorado, April 22-24. pap. 160.00 (ISBN 0-317-10872-7, 2022520). Bks Demand UMI.

--Airport Terminal Facilities: ASCE-AOCI Specialty Conference, Houston, Texas. pap. 83.80 (ISBN 0-317-10973-1, 2004909). Bks Demand UMI.

--Airports: Challenges of the Future. LC 76-371620. pap. 54.80 (ISBN 0-317-10152-8, 2010119). Bks Demand UMI.

American Society of Civil Engineers, compiled By. Applied Techniques for Cold Environments, 2 vols. 1183p. 1978. pap. 64.00x (ISBN 0-87262-182-0). Am Soc Civil Eng.

--ASCE-ICE-CSCE: Predicting & Designing for Natural & Man Made Hazards, 1978. 300p. 1979. pap. 30.00x (ISBN 0-87262-187-1). Am Soc Civil Eng.

--Assessment of Resources & Needs in Highway Technology Education. 227p. 1975. pap. 10.00x (ISBN 0-87262-117-0). Am Soc Civil Eng.

--Award Winning ASCE Papers in Geotechnical Engineering, 1950-59. 819p. 1977. pap. 32.00x (ISBN 0-87262-092-1). Am Soc Civil Eng.

--Bicycle-Pedestrian Planning & Design. 708p. 1974. pap. 22.50x (ISBN 0-87262-065-4). Am Soc Civil Eng.

--Bicycle Transportation: A Civil Engineers's Notebook for Bicycle Facilities. LC 80-70171. 193p. 1980. pap. 15.50x (ISBN 0-87262-260-6). Am Soc Civil Eng.

--Broadening Horizons: Transportation & Development Around the Pacific. LC 80-66122. 432p. 1980. pap. 32.00x (ISBN 0-87262-244-4). Am Soc Civil Eng.

--Case Studies of Applied Advanced Data Collection & Management. LC 80-65303. 416p. 1980. pap. 29.00x (ISBN 0-87262-037-9). Am Soc Civil Eng.

American Society of Civil Engineers. Coastal Engineering: Proceedings of 10th Conference, Tokyo, Japan, September, 1966, 2 vols, Vols. 1 & 2. pap. 160.00 ea. (2019545). Bks Demand UMI.

--Coastal Structures Seventy-Nine: A Specialty Conference on the Design, Construction, Maintenance, & Performance of Port & Coastal Structures, March 14-16, 1979, Alexandria, Va, 2 vols. Vol. 1. pap. 160.00 (ISBN 0-317-19859-9, 2023159); Vol. 2. pap. 144.30 (ISBN 0-317-19860-2). Bks Demand UMI.

American Society of Civil Engineers, compiled By. Composite or Mixed Steel: Concrete Construction for Buildings. 160p. 1977. pap. 11.50x (ISBN 0-87262-079-4). Am Soc Civil Eng.

--Computer Pricing Practices. LC 80-65829. (Manual & Report on Engineering Practice Ser.: No. 59). 20p. 1980. pap. 7.50x (ISBN 0-87262-029-8). Am Soc Civil Eng.

American Society of Civil Engineers. Computing in Civil Engineering: Conference. (Illus.). pap. 160.00 (ISBN 0-317-08312-0, 2019544). Bks Demand UMI.

American Society of Civil Engineers, ed. Computing in Civil Engineering, 1980. 34.00 (ISBN 0-686-46785-X). Am Soc Civil Eng.

American Society of Civil Engineers & Norris, G. M., eds. Cone Penetration Testing & Experience. LC 81-69229. 485p. 1981. pap. 34.75x (ISBN 0-87262-284-3). Am Soc Civil Eng.

American Society of Civil Engineers, compiled By. Conservation & Utilization of Water & Energy Resources. 541p. 1979. pap. 34.75x (ISBN 0-87262-189-8). Am Soc Civil Eng.

--Consulting Engineering: A Guide for the Engagement of Engineering Services. (Manual & Report on Engineering Practice Ser.: No. 45). 96p. 1975. pap. 8.00x (ISBN 0-87262-276-2). Am Soc Civil Eng.

--Consumptive Use of Water & Irrigation Water Requirements. 227p. 1974. pap. 10.75x (ISBN 0-87262-068-9). Am Soc Civil Eng.

--Contribution of Irrigation & Drainage to the World Food Supply. 430p. 1975. pap. 22.00x (ISBN 0-87262-114-6). Am Soc Civil Eng.

--Converting Existing Hydro-Electric Dams & Reservoirs into Pumped Storage Facilities. 607p. 1975. pap. 19.00x (ISBN 0-87262-120-0). Am Soc Civil Eng.

American Society of Civil Engineers. Cumulative Index to ASCE Publications: 1975-1979. 1192p. 1979. 40.00x (ISBN 0-87262-175-8). Am Soc Civil Eng.

--Cumulative Index to ASCE Publications 1960-1969. 928p. 1970. 20.00x (ISBN 0-87262-232-0). Am Soc Civil Eng.

--Cumulative Index to ASCE Publications 1970-1974. 1066p. 1974. 24.00x (ISBN 0-87262-233-9). Am Soc Civil Eng.

--Current Geotechnical Practice in Mine Waste Disposal: Papers Collected by the Committee on Embankment Dams & Slopes of the Geotechnical Engineering Division. LC 79-106963. pap. 66.50 (ISBN 0-317-11260-0, 2019542). Bks Demand UMI.

American Society of Civil Engineers, compiled By. Current Research on Tall Buildings. 140p. 1972. pap. 5.50 (ISBN 0-87262-039-5). Am Soc Civil Eng.

--The Current State of Knowledge of Lifeline Earthquake Engineering. 486p. 1977. pap. 23.00x (ISBN 0-87262-086-7). Am Soc Civil Eng.

--Definitions of Surveying & Associated Terms. (Manual & Report on Engineering Practice Ser.: No. 34). 218p. 1978. pap. 8.00x (ISBN 0-87262-211-8). Am Soc Civil Eng.

American Society of Civil Engineers. Design & Construction of Steel Chimney Liners. LC 80-475728. pap. 56.50 (ISBN 0-317-29141-6, 2025017). Bks Demand UMI.

American Society of Civil Engineers, compiled By. Design of Cylindrical Concrete Shell Roofs. (Manual & Report on Engineering Practice Ser.: No. 31). 185p. 1952. pap. 6.75x (ISBN 0-87262-209-6). Am Soc Civil Eng.

--Design of Foundations for Control of Settlement. 600p. 1966. pap. 29.50x (ISBN 0-87262-007-7). Am Soc Civil Eng.

--Design of Steel Transmission Pole Structures. 82p. 1978. pap. 6.00x (ISBN 0-87262-139-1). Am Soc Civil Eng.

--Design of Structures to Resist Nuclear Weapons Effects. (Manual & Report on Engineering Practice Ser.: No. 42). 172p. 1961. pap. 8.00x (ISBN 0-87262-218-5). Am Soc Civil Eng.

--Design of Water Intake Stuctures for Fish Protection. LC 81-70988. 175p. 1982. pap. 18.50x (ISBN 0-87262-291-6). Am Soc Civil Eng.

American Society of Civil Engineers & O'Neill, Michale W., eds. Drilled Piers & Caissons. LC 81-69227. 159p. 1981. 17.25x (ISBN 0-87262-285-1). Am Soc Civil Eng.

American Society of Civil Engineers, compiled By. Dynamic Planning for Environmental Quality in the 1980's. 281p. 1978. pap. 19.75x (ISBN 0-87262-098-0). Am Soc Civil Eng.
--Earth Reinforcement. 910p. 1979. pap. 40.00x (ISBN 0-87262-144-8). Am Soc Civil Eng.
--Economical Construction of Concrete Dams. 566p. 1972. pap. 19.75x (ISBN 0-87262-043-3). Am Soc Civil Eng.

American Society of Civil Engineers & Steyert, Richard D., eds. The Economics of High-Rise Apartment Buildings of Alternate Design Configuration. 187p. 1972. pap. 6.00x (ISBN 0-87262-038-7). Am Soc Civil Eng.

American Society of Civil Engineers, compiled By. Effective Project Management Techniques. 83p. 1973. pap. 5.00x (ISBN 0-87262-058-1). Am Soc Civil Eng.

American Society of Civil Engineers, Power Division. Electric Power Today & Tomorrow: Conference Papers, Power Division Specialty Conference, Denver, Colorado, August 18-20, 1965. LC 65-6824. pap. 160.00 (ISBN 0-317-10126-9, 2004905). Bks Demand UMI.

American Society of Civil Engineers. Engineering & Contracting Procedure for Foundations: Responsibilities of the Contracting Parties. LC 42-229. (American Society of Civil Engineers Manuals of Engineering Practice Ser.: No. 8). pap. 20.00 (ISBN 0-317-08381-3, 2016450). Bks Demand UMI.

American Society of Civil Engineers, compiled By. Engineering Ethics. 118p. 1975. pap. 7.00x (ISBN 0-87262-173-1). Am Soc Civil Eng.

American Society of Civil Engineers, Irrigation & Drainage Division. Environmental Aspects of Irrigation & Drainage: Proceedings of Specialty Conference, July 21-23, 1976. pap. 160.00 (ISBN 0-317-10817-4, 2016457). Bks Demand UMI.

American Society of Civil Engineers, compiled By. Environmental Effects of Large Dams. 229p. 1978. pap. 9.00x (ISBN 0-87262-125-1). Am Soc Civil Eng.

American Society of Civil Engineers Staff, compiled By. Environmental Impacts of International Civil Engineering Projects & Practices. 263p. 1978. pap. 18.00x (ISBN 0-87262-129-4). Am Soc Civil Eng.

American Society of Civil Engineers, compiled by. Evaluation, Maintenance & Upgrading of Wood Structures: A Guide & Commentary. LC 82-72779. 434p. 1982. pap. 13.00x (ISBN 0-87262-317-3). Am Soc Civil Eng.

American Society of Civil Engineers Staff & Water Pollution Control Federation Staff, eds. Existing Sewer Evaluation & Rehabilitation. (Manual & Report on Engineering Practice Ser.: No. 62). 116p. 1983. pap. 18.00x (ISBN 0-87262-389-0). Am Soc Civil Eng.

American Society of Civil Engineers, compiled By. Fatigue Life of Prestressed Concrete Beams. 96p. 1977. pap. 7.00x (ISBN 0-87262-094-8). Am Soc Civil Eng.
--Financing & Charges for Wastewater Systems. 2nd ed. 120p. 1984. pap. 35.00x (ISBN 0-87262-432-3). Am Soc Civil Eng.
--Finite Element Analysis of Reinforced Concrete. LC 82-71691. 553p. 1982. pap. 39.00x (ISBN 0-87262-307-6). Am Soc Civil Eng.

American Society of Civil Engineers. Flexural Mechanics of Reinforced Concrete: Proceedings of the International Symposium, Miami, Fla., Nov. 10-12, 1964. LC 66-402. (Illus.). pap. 150.00 (ISBN 0-317-10957-X, 2002788). Bks Demand UMI.

American Society of Civil Engineers & American Water Works Association, eds. Glossary: Water & Wastewater Control Engineering. LC 80-70933. 398p. 1969. 25.00x (ISBN 0-87262-262-2). Am Soc Civil Eng.

American Society of Civil Engineers & Water Pollution Control Federation. Gravity Sanitary Sewer Design & Construction. LC 81-69182. (Manual & Report on Engineering Practice Ser.: No. 60). 291p. 1982. 20.00x (ISBN 0-87262-313-0). Am Soc Civil Eng.

American Society of Civil Engineers, compiled By. Ground Water Management. (Manual & Report on Engineering Practice Ser.: No. 40). 230p. 1972. pap. 16.00x (ISBN 0-87262-216-9). Am Soc Civil Eng.
--Guide for The Field Testing of Bridges. LC 80-69154. 76p. 1980. pap. 12.00x (ISBN 0-87262-255-X). Am Soc Civil Eng.
--Guide to Investigation of Structural Failures. 84p. 1979. pap. 6.50x (ISBN 0-87262-184-7). Am Soc Civil Eng.
--Guide to Right of Way Survey Practices. 13p. 1981. pap. 6.00x (ISBN 0-87262-279-7). Am Soc Civil Eng.
--A Guide to Urban Arterial Systems. LC 81-69231. 368p. 1981. pap. 24.00x (ISBN 0-87262-280-0). Am Soc Civil Eng.

American Society of Civil Engineers & Kemp, Emory C., eds. Historic Preservation of Engineering Works. LC 81-69030. 329p. 1981. pap. 29.00x (ISBN 0-87262-278-9). Am Soc Civil Eng.

American Society of Civil Engineers, compiled by. Hydraulic Engineering & the Environment. 474p. 1973. pap. 12.50x (ISBN 0-87262-054-9). Am Soc Civil Eng.
--Implementing Highway Safety Improvements. LC 79-93190. 313p. 1980. pap. 22.50x (ISBN 0-87262-009-3). Am Soc Civil Eng.
--Inspection, Maintenance & Rehabilitation of Old Dams. 956p. 1974. pap. 34.00x (ISBN 0-87262-061-1). Am Soc Civil Eng.
--International Air Transportation Conference. 424p. 1977. pap. 28.00x (ISBN 0-87262-093-X). Am Soc Civil Eng.
--International Air Transportation Conference, 2 vols. 834p. 1979. Set. pap. 59.00x (ISBN 0-87262-201-0). Am Soc Civil Eng.
--International Seminar on Probabilistic & Extreme Load Design of Nuclear Plant Facilities. 454p. 1979. pap. 27.00x (ISBN 0-87262-146-4). Am Soc Civil Eng.

American Society of Civil Engineers, ed. Introductory Manual on Computer Services. (Manual & Report on Engineering Practice Ser.: No. 61). 92p. 1983. pap. 16.00x (ISBN 0-87262-366-1). Am Soc Civil Eng.

American Society of Civil Engineers, compiled by. Is Water Quality Enhancement Feasible? 137p. 1970. pap. 11.75x (ISBN 0-87262-025-5). Am Soc Civil Eng.

American Society of Civil Engineers & Klohn, Charles H., eds. Joint Usage of Utility & Transportation Corridors. LC 81-68750. 127p. 1981. pap. 15.50x (ISBN 0-87262-277-0). Am Soc Civil Eng.

American Society of Civil Engineers, Special Committee on Irrigation. Letter Symbols & Glossary for Hydraulics: With Special Reference to Irrigation. LC 42-233. (American Society of Civil Engineers, Manuals of Engineering Practice: No. 11). pap. 20.00 (ISBN 0-317-29810-0, 2052000). Bks Demand UMI.

American Society of Civil Engineers & Smith, D. J., Jr., eds. Lifeline Earthquake Engineering: The Current State of Knowledge. LC 81-67748. 360p. 1981. pap. 28.00x (ISBN 0-87262-274-6). Am Soc Civil Eng.

American Society of Civil Engineers & Yong, R. N., eds. Limit Equilibrium, Plasticity & Generalized Stress-Strain in Geotechnical Engineering. LC 81-69233. 875p. 1981. pap. 55.75x (ISBN 0-87262-282-7). Am Soc Civil Eng.

American Society of Civil Engineers, compiled by. Management of Engineering of Control Systems for Water Pipelines. 141p. 1978. pap. 16.25x (ISBN 0-87262-132-4). Am Soc Civil Eng.
--Mathematical Model of Aggregate Plant Production. 115p. 1974. pap. 6.50x (ISBN 0-87262-071-9). Am Soc Civil Eng.
--Metal Bridges. 444p. 1974. pap. 49.00x (ISBN 0-87262-101-4). Am Soc Civil Eng.
--Modes of Transportation. 156p. 1968. pap. 8.75x (ISBN 0-87262-021-2). Am Soc Civil Eng.
--Need for National Policy for the Use of Underground Space. 238p. 1973. pap. 14.50x (ISBN 0-87262-102-2). Am Soc Civil Eng.
--New Horizons in Rock Mechanics. 795p. 1973. 25.00x (ISBN 0-87262-050-6). Am Soc Civil Eng.
--Nuclear Facilities Siting. LC 82-73507. 64p. 1982. pap. 11.75x (ISBN 0-87262-344-0). Am Soc Civil Eng.
--Nuclear Waste Management. LC 82-73506. 52p. 1982. pap. 11.75x (ISBN 0-87262-343-2). Am Soc Civil Eng.

American Society of Civil Engineers. Placement & Improvement of Soil to Support Structures: Specialty Conference held at Cambridge, MA, August 26-28, 1968. LC 72-185397. (Illus.). pap. 111.50 (ISBN 0-317-08328-7, 2019535). Bks Demand UMI.

American Society of Civil Engineers Staff, compiled by. Ports '77, 2 Vols. 997p. 1977. pap. 36.00x (ISBN 0-87262-084-0). Am Soc Civil Eng.

American Society of Civil Engineers & Shinozuka, M., eds. Probabilistic Methods in Structural Engineering. LC 81-69228. 415p. 1981. pap. 30.00x (ISBN 0-87262-286-X). Am Soc Civil Eng.

American Society of Civil Engineers, compiled by. Public Works & Society. 255p. 1974. pap. 17.00x (ISBN 0-87262-064-6). Am Soc Civil Eng.
--Quality System in Construction. 210p. 1974. pap. 11.00x (ISBN 0-87262-073-5). Am Soc Civil Eng.
--Reaeration Research. 376p. 1979. pap. 26.00x (ISBN 0-87262-142-1). Am Soc Civil Eng.
--Reducing Risk & Liability Through Better Specifications & Inspections. LC 82-70874. 165p. 1982. pap. 18.75x (ISBN 0-87262-301-7). Am Soc Civil Eng.

American Society of Civil Engineers Staff. Reinforced Concrete Floor Slabs: Research & Design. (Reinforced Concrete Research Council Ser.: No. 20). pap. 53.80 (ISBN 0-317-27661-1, 2010543). Bks Demand UMI.

American Society of Civil Engineers, Engineering Mechanics Division. The Relation of Engineering Mechanics Research to the Practice of Civil Engineering: Engineering Mechanics Division Specialty Conference, Washington, D.C., October 12-14, 1966. LC 67-1660. (Illus.). pap. 160.00 (ISBN 0-317-11018-7, 2004904). Bks Demand UMI.

American Society of Civil Engineers, compiled by. Report on Small Craft Harbors. (Manual & Report on Engineering Practice Ser.: No. 50). 145p. 1969. pap. 10.00x (ISBN 0-87262-224-X). Am Soc Civil Eng.

American Society of Civil Engineers, et al. Residential Streets: Objective Principles & Design Considerations. LC 74-19958. 48p. 1974. pap. 6.00 (ISBN 0-87420-559-X, R06); pap. 4.50 members. Natl Assn Home.

American Society of Civil Engineers, compiled by. Seismic Performance of Low Rise Buildings: State-of-the-Art & Research Needs. LC 81-6930. 221p. 1981. pap. 20.50x (ISBN 0-87262-283-5). Am Soc Civil Eng.
--Shear Strength of Cohesive Soils. 1170p. 1960. pap. 37.50x (ISBN 0-87262-004-2). Am Soc Civil Eng.
--Site Characterization & Exploration. 401p. 1979. pap. 15.00x (ISBN 0-87262-186-3). Am Soc Civil Eng.

American Society of Civil Engineers Staff. Social & Ecological Aspects of Irrigation & Drainage: Selected Papers. LC 75-30807. pap. 95.30 (ISBN 0-317-10978-2, 2007865). Bks Demand UMI.

American Society of Civil Engineers. Soil Improvement: History, Capabilities, & Outlook: Report by the Committee on Placement & Improvement of Soils of the Geotechnical Engineering Division of the American Society of Civil Engineers. LC 78-104862. (Illus.). pap. 46.50 (ISBN 0-317-08310-4, 2019549). Bks Demand UMI.

American Society of Civil Engineers, compiled by. Solid Waste Research & Development Needs for Emerging Coal Technologies. 268p. 1979. pap. 21.50x (ISBN 0-87262-199-5). Am Soc Civil Eng.

American Society of Civil Engineers, Aero-Space Transport Division Staff. Space Age Facilities: Papers, Specialty Conference, Cocoa Beach, Fl., November 17-19, 1965. LC 68-23. pap. 99.50 (ISBN 0-317-10983-9, 2004908). BKs Demand UMI.

American Society of Civil Engineers, compiled by. Stability of Structures Under Static & Dynamic Loads. 820p. 1977. pap. 30.00x (ISBN 0-87262-095-6). Am Soc Civil Eng.

American Society of Civil Engineers. State-of-the-Art Report on Air-Supported Structures. LC 79-125997. (Illus.). pap. 25.80 (ISBN 0-317-10911-1, 2019556). Bks Demand UMI.
--Structural Failures: Modes, Causes, Responsibilities. (Illus.). pap. 27.80 (ISBN 0-317-08323-6, 2019539). Bks Demand UMI.

American Society of Civil Engineers, compiled by. Subsurface Exploration for Underground Excavation & Heavy Construction. 404p. 1974. pap. 13.50x (ISBN 0-87262-105-7). Am Soc Civil Eng.

American Society of Civil Engineers. Transactions of the American Society of Civil Engineers, Vol. 144. 1979. 22.50x (ISBN 0-87262-236-3). Am Soc Civil Eng.

American Society of Civil Engineers, compiled by. Transactions of the American Society of Civil Engineers, Vol. 146, 1981. 1056p. 1982. 52.50x (ISBN 0-87262-309-2). Am Soc Civil Eng.
--Transportation & Energy. 456p. 1978. pap. 15.00x (ISBN 0-87262-135-9). Am Soc Civil Eng.
--Wastewater Treatment Plant Design. (Manual & Report on Engineering Practice Ser.: No. 36). 574p. 1977. 20.00x (ISBN 0-87262-213-4). Am Soc Civil Eng.

American Society of Civil Engineers. Water Systems Seventy-Nine: Proceedings of the ASCE Water Resources Planning & Management Division Specialty Conference, University of Houston, Hilton Hotel Center, February 25-28, 1979. LC 79-105513. pap. 59.30 (ISBN 0-317-10837-9, 2019548). Bks Demand UMI.

American Society of Composers. Authors & Publishers (ASCAP) Copyright Law Symposium: Proceedings. LC 40-8341. No. 25. 24.00x (ISBN 0-231-04866-1). Columbia U Pr.

American Society of Composers, Authors, & Publishers Staff. American Society of Composers, Authors, & Publishers Copyright Law Symposium, No. 31. 1984. 24.00 (ISBN 0-231-05766-0). Columbia U Pr.

American Society of Composers, Authors & Publishers, ed. ASCAP Symphonic Catalog 1977. 3rd ed. LC 77-133. 1977. pap. 27.50 (ISBN 0-8352-0910-5). Bowker.

American Society of Composers, Authors & Publishers. Copyright Law Symposium, No. 24. 1980. 24.00x (ISBN 0-231-04864-5). Columbia U Pr.

American Society of Composers, Authors, & Publishers. Copyright Law Symposium, No. 21: Proceedings. LC 40-8341. 1974. 24.00x (ISBN 0-231-03834-8). Columbia U Pr.

American Society of Composers, Authors & Publishers (ASCAP) Copyright Law Symposium: Proceedings. Incl. No. 4. 1952. 24.00x (ISBN 0-231-02081-3); No. 5. 1954. 24.00x (ISBN 0-231-02025-2); No. 6. 1955. 24.00x (ISBN 0-231-02091-0); No. 8. 1957. 24.00x (ISBN 0-231-02192-5); 1958. 24.00x (ISBN 0-231-02318-9); No. 10. 1959. 24.00x (ISBN 0-231-02351-0); No. 11. 1962. 24.00x (ISBN 0-231-02528-9); No; No. 14; 1967. 24.00x (ISBN 0-231-03004-5); No. 16. 1968. 24.00x (ISBN 0-231-03167-X); No. 17. 1969. 24.00x (ISBN 0-231-03235-8); No. 18. 1970. 24.00x (ISBN 0-231-03411-3); No. 19. 1971. 24.00x (ISBN 0-231-03521-7); No. 20. 24.00x (ISBN 0-231-03636-1). LC 40-8341. Columbia U Pr.

American Society of Consultant Pharmacists, et al. Detecting & Counting Medication Errors in Long Term Care Facilities. (Illus., Orig.). 1984. pap. text ed. 30.00 (ISBN 0-934322-04-X); members 20.00. Am Soc Consult Phar.

American Society of Criminology, jt. auth. see Waldo, Gordon P.

American Society of Hospital Pharmacists. Consumer Drug Digest. 496p. 1982. 19.95 (ISBN 0-87196-554-2); pap. 9.95 (ISBN 0-87196-686-7). Facts on File.
--Handbook of Injectable Drugs. 159p. 1981. pap. text ed. 17.95 (ISBN 0-471-09131-6, Pub. by Wiley Med). Wiley.
--Sourcebook on Clinical Pharmacy. 2nd ed. LC 79-24069. (Illus.). 404p. 1980. text ed. 20.00 (ISBN 0-88416-303-2). PSG Pub Co.

American Society of Hospital Pharmacists, ed. Sourcebook on Unit Dose Drug Distribution Systems. (Illus.). 1978. pap. 25.00 (ISBN 0-930530-06-3). Am Soc Hosp Pharm.

American Society of Industrial Security Staff, ed. Security Management: Readings from Security Management Magazine. 288p. 1984. text ed. 22.95 (ISBN 0-409-95099-8). Butterworth.

American Society of International Law Staff & American Law Institute-American Bar Association Committee on Continuing Professional Education Staff. International Criminal Law: ALI-ABA Course of Study Materials. LC 83-108201. viii, 223p. 1982. write for info. Am Law Inst.

American Society of Journalists & Authors Staff. The ASJA Handbook: A Writers' Guide to Ethical & Economic Issues. 1985. pap. 5.95 (ISBN 0-317-31355-X). Am Soc Jrnl & Auth.

American Society of Journalists & Authors. The Complete Guide to Writing Nonfiction. Evans, Glen, ed. LC 83-16935. 870p. 1983. 24.95 (ISBN 0-89879-117-0). Writers Digest.
--A Treasury of Tips for Writers. Weisbord, Marvin, ed. LC 79-11859. 174p. 1981. pap. 6.95 (ISBN 0-89879-050-6). Writers Digest.

American Society of Magazine Photographers. ASMP Bk. 3. (Illus.). 475p. 1984. 39.95 (ISBN 0-912417-03-X). Annuals Pub Co.
--ASMP Bk. 4: The Annual of Professional Photography. (Illus.). 450p. 1985. 39.95 (ISBN 0-912417-04-8). Contemp Bks.
--ASMP Book 2. 500p. 1983. 39.95 (ISBN 0-912417-00-5). Annuals Pub Co.

American Society of Magazine Photographers Staff. Professional Photography Annual, Bk. 4. 450p. 1985. 39.95 (ISBN 0-912417-04-8). Annuals Pub Co.

American Society of Mechanical Engineering, ed. see Kulwiecv, Raymond A., et al.

American Society of Mechanical Engineers. Advances in Bioengineering, 1976: Presented at the Winter Meeting of the American Society of Mechanical Engineers, New York, N. Y., Dec. 5-10, 1976. Smith, Charles R., ed. (Illus.). pap. 20.00 (ISBN 0-317-08130-6, 2016867). Bks Demand UMI.
--ASME Handbook: Engineering Tables. 1956. 84.50 (ISBN 0-07-001516-3). McGraw.
--ASME Handbook: Metals Engineering-Design. 2nd ed. 1964. 72.50 (ISBN 0-07-001518-X). McGraw.

American Society of Mechanical Engineers, Research Committee on High Temperature Steam Generation. Behavior of Superheater Alloys in High Temperature, High Pressure Steam. Lien, George E., ed. LC 66-19905. (Illus.). pap. 29.80 (ISBN 0-317-08449-6, 2016886). Bks Demand UMI.

American Society of Mechanical Engineers. Cavitation State of Knowledge: Discussions Presented At the ASME Fluids Engineering & Applied Mechanics Conference, Northwestern University, Evanston, Illinois, June 16-18, 1969. Robertson, J. M. & Wislicenus, G. F., eds. LC 73-173121. pap. 20.00 (ISBN 0-317-29797-X, 2016853). Bks Demand UMI.
--Combustion Fundamentals for Waste Incineration. LC 74-19743. pap. 56.00 (ISBN 0-317-27801-0, 2024182). Bks Demand UMI.
--Computers in Flow Predictions & Fluid Dynamics Experiments. Ghia, K. N., et al, eds. LC 81-69010. pap. 60.50 (ISBN 0-317-19851-3, 2023147). Bks Demand UMI.

--Computing in Applied Mechanics: Presented at the Winter Annual Meeting of the ASME, New York City, December 5-10, 1976. LC 76-28858. (American Society of Mechanical Engineers, Applied Mechanics Division: Vol. 18). pap. 46.50 (ISBN 0-317-26614-4, 2024186). Bks Demand UMI.

--Control of Manufacturing Processes & Robotic Systems. 292p. 1983. 50.00 (ISBN 0-317-06828-8, H00279). ASME.

American Society of Mechanical Engineers, Lubrication Division. Diagnosing Machinery Health: Presented at the Winter Annual Meeting of the American Society of Mechanical Engineers, San Francisco, California, December 10-15, 1978. Dill, J. F. & Petrovic, W. K., eds. LC 78-59891. pap. 20.00 (ISBN 0-317-11179-5, 2015394). Bks Demand UMI.

American Society of Mechanical Engineers. Differential Games: Theory & Applications. LC 74-128583. pap. 36.80 (ISBN 0-317-08724-X, 2013312). Bks Demand UMI.

American Society of Mechanical Engineers, Research Committee on Industrial Wastes. Disposal of Industrial Wastes by Combustion, Vol. 2. LC 73-63622. pap. 20.00 (ISBN 0-317-10960-X, 2006134). Bks Demand UMI.

American Society of Mechanical Engineers. Dynamics of Structured Solids. Hermann, George, ed. LC 68-58743. pap. 28.50 (ISBN 0-317-08722-3, 2016807). Bks Demand UMI.

--Energy Conservation in Building Heating & Air Conditioning Systems. Gopal, R., et al, eds. LC 78-60047. pap. 27.30 (ISBN 0-317-19849-1, 2023146). Bks Demand UMI.

American Society of Mechanical Engineers, Heat Transfer Division Staff. Environmental Effects of Thermal Discharges: The Elements in Formulating a Rational Public Policy. LC 77-139496. pap. 20.00 (ISBN 0-317-11241-4, 2016910). Bks Demand UMI.

American Society of Mechanical Engineers. Fatigue Life Technology: Presented at the 22nd Annual International Gas Turbine Conference, Philadelphia, Pa., March 27-31, 1977. Cruse, T. A. & Gallagher, J. P., eds. LC 77-70040. pap. 30.50 (ISBN 0-317-29901-8, 2019350). Bks Demand UMI.

American Society of Mechanical Engineers, Applied Mechanics Division. Finite Elasticity: Presented at the Winter Annual Meeting of American Society of Mechanical Engineerings, Atlanta, Georgia, 1977. Rivlin, R. S., ed. LC 77-89014. (American Society of Mechanical Engineers: AMD; Vol. 27). pap. 39.50 (ISBN 0-317-13000-5, 2020934). Bks Demand UMI.

American Society of Mechanical Engineers, et al. Flow Studies in Air & Water Pollution: Presented at the Joint Meeting of the Fluids Engineering Division & the Applied Mechanics Division, Georgia Institute of Technology, Atlanta, GA, June, 1973. Arndt, Roger E., ed. LC 73-80154. pap. 58.00 (ISBN 0-317-11237-6, 2016839). Bks Demand UMI.

American Society of Mechanical Engineering. Fluids Engineering Division. Fluid Mechanics of Combustion: Papers Presented at Joint Fluids Engineering & CSME Conference, Montreal, Quebec, May 13-15, 1974. Dussourd, J. L., et al, eds. LC 74-78505. pap. 68.30 (ISBN 0-317-08509-3, 2051718). Bks Demand UMI.

American Society of Mechanical Engineers. The Generation of Isochronous Stress-Strain Curves: Papers Presented at the Winter Annual Meeting of ASME, New York, NY, November 26-30, 1972. LC 72-93459. (Illus.). pap. 22.80 (ISBN 0-317-08421-6, 2016821). Bks Demand UMI.

--Heat Transfer in Low Reynolds Number Flow. Brown, George A & Moszynski, Jerzy R, eds. LC 70-180676. pap. 20.00 (ISBN 0-317-08519-0, 2010126). Bks Demand UMI.

American Society of Mechanical Engineers. Heat Transfer Division. Heat Transfer in Solar Energy Systems: Presented at the Winter Annual Meeting of the American Society of Mechanical Engineers, Atlanta, Georgia, Nov. 27-Dec. 2, 1977. Howell, J. R. & Min, T., eds. LC 77-89012. pap. 35.30 (ISBN 0-317-08530-1, 2051730). Bks Demand UMI.

American Society of Mechanical Engineers. Indexes to Nineteen-Eighty Publications. (Transactions of American Society of Mechanical Engineers: Vol. 103). pap. 55.30 (ISBN 0-317-09799-7, 2016916). Bks Demand UMI.

--Interactive Computer Graphics in Engineering: Presented at the Winter Annual Meeting of the American Society of Mechanical Engineers, New York, N.Y. December 5-10-, 1976. Hulbert, L. E., ed. LC 77-77033. pap. 21.00 (ISBN 0-317-07994-8, 2051328). Bks Demand UMI.

--Isolation of Mechanical Vibration, Impact, & Noise: A Colloquium Presented at the ASME Design Engineering Technical Conference, Cincinnati, Ohio, Sept. 1973. Snowdon, John C. & Ungar, Eric E., eds. LC 73-84652. (ASME Applied Mechanics Division Ser.: Vol. 1). pap. 69.00 (ISBN 0-317-08486-0, 2051536). Bks Demand UMI.

--Loss Prevention of Rotating Machinery: Papers Presented at ASME Petroleum Division Conference, Houston, Texas, September 1971. LC 71-187881. pap. 20.00 (ISBN 0-317-11090-X, 2011328). Bks Demand UMI.

American Society of Mechanical Engineers, Research Committee on Metal Cutting Data & Bibliography. Manual on Cutting of Metals, with Single-Point Tools. 2nd ed. LC 53-1487. pap. 140.00 (ISBN 0-317-11012-8, 2004723). Bks Demand UMI.

American Society of Mechanical Engineers. Marine Propulsion: Presented at the Winter Annual Meting of the ASME, New York, NY, December 5-10, 1976. Sladky, J., ed. LC 76-28850. (American Society of Mechanical Engineers. Ocean Engineering Division Ser.: Vol. 2). (Illus.). pap. 58.80 (ISBN 0-317-09793-8, 2016815). Bks Demand UMI.

American Society of Mechanical Enginners. Measurement in Polyphase Flows: Papers Presented at the Winter Annual Meeting of the American Society of Mechanical Engineers, San Francisco, California, Dec. 10-15, 1978. Stock, David E., ed. LC 78-68328. pap. 32.80 (ISBN 0-317-08555-7, 2051712). Bks Demand UMI.

American Society of Mechanical Engineers. Modeling, Simulation, Testing & Measurements for Solar Energy Systems: Presented at the Winter Annual Meeting of ASME, San Francisco, CA., December 10-15, 1978. Nash, J. M. & Smok, J. T., eds. LC 78-67977. pap. 26.80 (ISBN 0-317-26621-7, 2024183). Bks Demand UMI.

--Pressure Vessels: A Workbook for Engineers. Hicks, E. J., ed. LC 81-111549. pap. 20.00 (ISBN 0-317-29757-0, 2017372). Bks Demand UMI.

--PTFE Seals in Reciprocating Compressors: Manual of Material Selection, Design & Operating Practices. LC 74-32657. pap. 22.50 (ISBN 0-317-11225-2, 2016824). Bks Demand UMI.

--Report on Diesel & Gas Engines Power Costs, 1974: Data for 1972 & Previous Years. pap. 20.00 (ISBN 0-317-08172-1, 2013318). Bks Demand UMI.

--Risers, Arctic Design Criteria, Equipment Reliability in Hydrocarbon Processing: A Workbook for Engineers, Presented at 37th Petroleum Mechanical Engineering Workshop & Conference, September 13-15, 1981, Dallas, Texas. Kozik, Thomas J., ed. LC 81-186405. pap. 62.50 (ISBN 0-317-29899-2, 2019351). Bks Demand UMI.

--Robotics Research & Advanced Application: Presented at the Winter Annual Meeting of ASME, Phoenix, Arizona, November 14-19,1982. Book, Wayne J., ed. LC 82-73173. pap. 73.30 (ISBN 0-317-26618-7, 2024184). Bks Demand UMI.

--The Role of Nucleation in Boiling & Cavitation: Symposium Presented at Joint Fluids Engineering, Heat Transfer & Lubrication Conference, Detroit, Michigan, May 26-27, 1970. pap. 20.00 (ISBN 0-317-09023-2, 2016877). Bks Demand UMI.

--Stochastic Problems in Control. LC 68-8579. pap. 31.00 (ISBN 0-317-08716-9, 2016484). Bks Demand UMI.

American Society of Mechanical Engineers, Committee on Nucleonics Heat Transfer. Survey of Nucleonic Heat Transfer Research & Development. LC 72-185848. (American Society of Mechanical Engineers, Heat Transfer Division Ser.: Vol. 1). pap. 20.00 (ISBN 0-317-09936-1, 2016900). Bks Demand UMI.

American Society of Mechanical Engineers. Rubber & Plastic Division. Symposium on Graphite Fiber Composites: An Integrated Approach to Their Development & Use Presented at ASME Winter Meeting, Pittsburgh, PA., Nov. 1967. LC 67-31228. pap. 20.00 (ISBN 0-317-08656-1, 2012303). Bks Demand UMI.

American Society of Mechanical Engineers. Theory of Machines & Mechanisms, 2 Vols. 1979. Set. 75.00 (ISBN 0-317-06827-X). Vol. 1, 1607p (G00148). Vol. 2, 1654p (G00149). ASME.

--Thermophysical Properties: Proceedings of the Fourth Symposium, University of Maryland, College Park, Maryland, 1968. Moszynski, J. R., ed. LC 59-1391. pap. 121.50 (ISBN 0-317-29841-0, 2051923). Bks Demand UMI.

--Turbomachinery Developments in Steam & Gas Turbines: Presented at the Winter Annual Meeting of the American Society of Mechanical Engineers, Atlanta, Georgia, November 27-December 2, 1977. Steltz, W. G., ed. LC 77-88002. (Illus.). pap. 26.00 (ISBN 0-317-11146-9, 2013321). Bks Demand UMI.

American Society of Mechnical Engineers. Singular Perturbations: Order Reduction in Control System Design. LC 72-87029. pap. 20.00 (ISBN 0-317-08441-0, 2012304). Bks Demand UMI.

--Stochastic Processes in Dynamical Problems. LC 71-105935. pap. 30.30 (ISBN 0-317-27786-3, 2024180). Bks Demand UMI.

American Society of Pediatric Neurosurgery, ed. Concepts in Pediatric Neurosurgery, No. 2. (Illus.). x, 222p. 1982. 81.00 (ISBN 3-8055-3454-X). S Karger.

--Concepts in Pediatric Neurosurgery, No. 1. (Illus.). x, 238p. 1981. 81.00 (ISBN 3-8055-2904-X). S Karger.

American Society of Photogrammetry, ed. Eighth Biennial Workshop on Color Aerial Photography in the Plant Sciences & Related Fields. 167p. pap. 16.00 (17.00 member) (ISBN 0-937294-34-9). ASP & RS.

American Society of Photogrammetry. Proceedings: Second Technology Exchange Week in Panama. 724p. (Eng & Sp.). 1982. eng. ed. (10.00 member) 14.00 (ISBN 0-937294-53-5); sp. ed. (10.00 member) 14.00 (ISBN 0-937294-54-3). ASP & RS.

--Workshop for Automated Photogrammetry & Cartography of Highways & Transport Systems. 138p. 1981. 14.00 (ISBN 0-937294-33-0); pap. 9.00 members. ASP & RS.

American Society of Planning Officials. Planned Unit Development Ordinances. 1973. 6.00 (ISBN 0-685-71649-X). Urban Land.

American Society of Real Estate Counselors. Real Estate Counseling. (Illus.). 352p. 1984. text ed. 27.95 (ISBN 0-686-90138-X). P-H.

--Real Estate Counseling: A Professional Approach to Problem Solving. 144p. pap. 5.00 (ISBN 0-318-13260-5). Am Soc REC.

American Society Of Tool & Manufacturing Engineers. ASTME Die Design Handbook. 2nd ed. Wilson, Frank W., ed. 1965. 74.50 (ISBN 0-07-001523-6). McGraw.

American Society of Tool & Manufacturing Engineers Staff. Fundamentals of Tool Design. (Illus.). 1962. text ed. 32.95 (ISBN 0-13-344861-4). P-H.

American Society of Tool & Manufacturing Engineers, Non-Traditional Machining Processes Subdivision. Non-Traditional Machining Processes. Springborn, R. K., ed. LC 67-17078. (American Society of Tool & Manufacturing Engineers Data Ser.). pap. 47.50 (ISBN 0-317-11170-1, 2051198). Bks Demand UMI.

American Society of Tool & Manufacturing Engineers. Pneumatic Controls for Industrial Application: A Practical & Comprehensive Presentation of Pneumatic Control System Fundamentals, Control Devices, Associated Facilities, & Application Circuitry for Manual, Semiautomatic, & Automatic Industrial Operations. Wilson, Frank W., ed. LC 65-13379. (Manufacturing Data Ser.). pap. 43.50 (ISBN 0-317-27763-4, 2024178). Bks Demand UMI.

American Society of Zoologists. Molecular Aspects of Early Development. Malacinski, George M. & Klein, William H., eds. 316p. 1984. 47.50x (ISBN 0-306-41496-1, Plenum Pr). Plenum Pub.

American Sociological Society. The Family. LC 78-169370. (Family in America Ser). 226p. 1972. Repr. of 1909 ed. 20.00 (ISBN 0-405-03846-1). Ayer Co Pubs.

--Social Problems - Social Processes: Selected Papers from the Proceedings of the American Sociological Society, 1932. facs. ed. Bogardus, E. S., ed. LC 67-23173. (Essay Index Reprint Ser). 1933. 17.00 (ISBN 0-8369-0151-7). Ayer Co Pubs.

American Solar Energy Society Staff. American Solar Energy Society Membership Directory 1982-83 & Guide to Programs. 120p. 1982. pap. text ed. 45.00x (ISBN 0-89553-049-X). Am Solar Energy.

American Standard, Inc. Expendable Cores for Copper Alloy Die Casting. 49p. 1970. 7.35 (ISBN 0-317-34524-9, 132). Intl Copper.

American States Organization. Inter-American Commission on Human Rights: Annual Report 1981-1982. iv, 136p. 1982. 7.00 (ISBN 0-8270-1644-1). OAS.

--The OAS & the Evolution of the Inter-American System. 46p. 1981. 5.00. OAS.

--Proceedings of the Twelfth Regular Session of the General Assembly of the OAS: Washington D.C.-November 15-21,1982, 2 vols. 1982. write for info. OAS.

American Statistical Association, jt. auth. see National Council of Teachers of Mathematics.

American Steel & Wire Co. Secrets of Piano Construction. LC 85-9122. Orig. Title: Piano Tone Building. (Illus.). 292p. 1985. pap. 12.95 (ISBN 0-911572-16-3, A-132). Vestal.

American Studies Symposium, 3rd, University of Florence, May 27-29, 1969. Gli Italiani Negli Stati Uniti-Italians in the United States: Proceedings. LC 74-17932. (Italian American Experience Ser.). (Illus.). 1975. Repr. 37.50x (ISBN 0-405-06404-7). Ayer Co Pubs.

American Sunbeam Staff. Weather Made to Whose Order? (Illus.). 56p. Date not set. 2.00 (ISBN 0-918700-04-3). Duverus Pub.

American Telephone & Telegraph Co. Engineering Economy: A Manager's Guide to Economic Decision Making. 3rd ed. 1977. 59.50 (ISBN 0-07-001530-9). McGraw.

American Temperance Society. Permanent Temperance Documents of the American Temperance Society. LC 77-38433. (Religion in America, Ser. 2). 566p. 1972. Repr. of 1835 ed. 38.50 (ISBN 0-405-04054-7). Ayer Co Pubs.

American Theatre Planning Board. Theatre Check List: A Guide to the Planning & Construction of Proscenium & Open Stage Theatres. rev ed. LC 69-19619. (Illus.). 1983. pap. 12.00x (ISBN 0-8195-6005-7). Wesleyan U Pr.

American Tract Society. The American Tract Society Documents, Eighteen Twenty-Four to Nineteen Twenty-Five. LC 74-38434. (Religion in America, Ser. 2). 484p. 1972. Repr. of 1874 ed. 29.00 (ISBN 0-405-04055-5). Ayer Co Pubs.

--American Tract Society: Homes & Hospitals. 1973. Repr. of 1873 ed. lib. bdg. 25.00 (ISBN 0-87821-274-4). Milford Hse.

--Enormity of the Slave-Trade. facs. ed. LC 77-133153. (Black Heritage Library Collection Ser.). 12.00 (ISBN 0-8369-8708-X). Ayer Co Pubs.

American Trade Union Delegation to the Soviet Union. Soviet Russia in the Second Decade. Chase, Stuart, et al, eds. LC 72-8432. (Select Bibliographies Reprint Ser.). 1973. Repr. of 1928 ed. 18.25 (ISBN 0-8369-6961-8). Ayer Co Pubs.

American Trucking Assn. ATA Hazardous Materials Tariff. 1983. pap. text ed. 18.25 (ISBN 0-88711-061-4). Am Trucking Assns.

--Best of the Front-Line Supervisor, Vol. 1. 32p. 1977. pap. text ed. 3.00 (ISBN 0-88711-058-4). Am Trucking Assns.

--Bulletin Advisory Service, 3 vols. 1983. Set. 195.00 (ISBN 0-88711-066-5); Vol. 1. 63.00 (ISBN 0-88711-063-0); Vol. 2. 63.00 (ISBN 0-88711-064-9); Vol. 3. 90.00. Am Trucking Assns.

--Effective Truck Terminal Planning & Operations. 131p. 1980. pap. text ed. 45.00 (ISBN 0-88711-055-X). Am Trucking Assns.

--Fundamentals of Transporting Hazardous Materials. 174p. 1982. pap. text ed. 4.50 (ISBN 0-88711-051-7). Am Trucking Assns.

--Fundamentals of Transporting Hazardous Wastes. 173p. 1980. pap. text ed. 4.50 (ISBN 0-88711-049-5). Am Trucking Assns.

--Hazardous Materials Handbook. 239p. 1982. pap. text ed. 4.50 (ISBN 0-88711-050-9). Am Trucking Assns.

--Shipper-Motor Carrier Dock Planning Manual. 69p. 1969. pap. text ed. 10.00 (ISBN 0-88711-054-1). Am Trucking Assns.

--TOC Guide for Training Terminal Personnel. 277p. 1974. text ed. 20.00 (ISBN 0-88711-056-8). Am Trucking Assns.

American Trucking Assn., jt. auth. see Davis, Bob J.

American Trucking Assoc. Guide to Weighing, Inspection & Accessorial Services. 1980. pap. text ed. 25.00 (ISBN 0-88711-048-7). Am Trucking Assns.

American Type Founders Co. Specimens of Type, Brass Rulers & Dashes, Ornaments & Borders, Society Emblems, Check Lines, Cuts, Initials & Other Productions of the American Type Founders Co. Bidwell, John, ed. (Nineteenth Century Book Arts & Printing History Ser.). 80.00 (ISBN 0-8240-3889-4). Garland Pub.

American Unitarian Association. From Servitude to Service. Cremin, Lawrence A. & Barnard, Frederick A., eds. LC 74-101402. (American Education: Its Men, Institutions & Ideas, Ser. 1). 1969. Repr. of 1905 ed. 16.00 (ISBN 0-405-01382-5). Ayer Co Pubs.

American Universities Field Staff. City & Nation in the Developing World: AUFS Readings, Vol. 2. LC 66-29570. (Illus.). 256p. 1968. 6.50 (ISBN 0-910116-62-8). U Field Staff Intl.

--Developing World: AUFS Readings, Vol. 1. LC 66-29570. (Illus.). 256p. 1966. pap. 3.00 (ISBN 0-910116-61-X). U Field Staff Intl.

--A Select Bibliography: Asia, Africa, Eastern Europe, Latin America. LC 60-10482. 358p. (Orig.). 1960. 8.50 (ISBN 0-910116-50-4); Cumulative Suppl. 1961-71. 12.50 (ISBN 0-910116-85-7). U Fleld Staff Intl.

American Urological Association. History of Urology, 2 vols. Ballanger, Edgard G., et al, eds. LC 75-23674. Repr. of 1933 ed. 63.50 set (ISBN 0-404-13300-2). AMS Pr.

American Vacuum Society Education Comm., ed. Experimental Vacuum Science & Technology. 288p. 1973. 65.00 (ISBN 0-8247-6068-9). Dekker.

American Water Resources Association. Proceedings of the Fourth American Water Resources Conference Held November 18-22, 1968, Commodore Hotel, New York, New York. Cohen, Philip & Francisco, Martha N., eds. (American Water Resources Association Proceedings Ser.: No. 6). pap. 160.00 (ISBN 0-317-28825-3, 2017811). Bks Demand UMI.

American Water Works Association. American National Standard for Thickness Design or Cast-Iron Pipe: C101-A21.1-67(R77) 88p. 1977. 9.00 (ISBN 0-89867-107-8, 43101); 6.75, with membership (ISBN 0-317-33291-0). Am Water Wks Assn.

Ames, Daniel T. Ames on Forgery, Its Detection & Illustration with Numerous Causes Celebres. (Illus.). 293p. 1981. Repr. of 1901 ed. lib. bdg. 27.00x (ISBN 0-8377-0208-9). Rothman.
Ames, David A. & Gracey, Colin B. Good Genes? Emerging Values for Science, Religion & Society. (Illus.). 136p. 1984. pap. 3.60 (ISBN 0-88028-034-4). Forward Movement.
Ames, David W. & King, Anthony V. Glossary of Hausa Music & Its Social Contexts. LC 76-164884. 1971. 14.95x (ISBN 0-8101-0361-3). Northwestern U Pr.
Ames, Delano. Corpse Diplomatique. LC 82-48239. 256p. 1983. pap. 2.84i (ISBN 0-06-080637-0, P 637, PL). Har-Row.
--For Old Crime's Sake. LC 82-47790. 256p. 1983. pap. 2.84i (ISBN 0-06-080629-X, P 629, PL). Har-Row.
--Murder, Maestro, Please. LC 82-47791. 224p. 1983. pap. 3.37i (ISBN 0-06-080630-3, P 630, PL). Har-Row.
--She Shall Have Murder. LC 82-48240. 272p. 1983. pap. 2.84i (ISBN 0-06-080638-9, P 638, PL). Har-Row.
Ames, Evelyn. Dust on a Precipice. LC 80-26142. 1981. 7.95 (ISBN 0-87233-055-9); pap. 4.95 (ISBN 0-87233-067-2). Bauhan.
--Glimpse of Eden. LC 67-11908. 1977. 13.95 (ISBN 0-910220-80-8). Berg.
Ames, F. Kashmir Shawl. (Illus.). 1985. 69.50 (ISBN 0-907462-62-6). Antique Collect.
Ames, Felicia. The Bird You Care for. Date not set. pap. 1.75 (ISBN 0-451-07527-7, E7527, Sig). NAL.
--The Cat You Care For. 1968. pap. 3.50 (ISBN 0-451-13041-3, Sig). NAL.
Ames, Fisher. Works of Fisher Ames, 2 vols. Ames, Seth, ed. LC 73-146132. (Research & Source Works Ser.: No. 711). 1971. Repr. of 1854 ed. Set. lib. bdg. 48.50 (ISBN 0-8337-0063-4). B Franklin.
Ames, Frederick C., et al, eds. Current Controversies in Breast Cancer. (Illus.). 671p. 1984. text ed. 65.00x (ISBN 0-292-71093-3). U of Tex Pr.
Ames, Gerald & Wyler, Rose. Magic Secrets. LC 67-4229. (I Can Read Ser. Bk.). (Illus.). 64p. (gr. k-3). 1967. PLB 9.89 (ISBN 0-06-020069-3). HarpJ.
--Magic Secrets. LC 67-4229. (I Can Read Ser.). (Illus.). 1978. pap. 1.95 (ISBN 0-06-444007-9, Trophy). HarpJ.
--Prove It! LC 62-21288. (Science I Can Read Bk). (Illus.). 64p. (gr. k-3). 1963. PLB 9.89 (ISBN 0-06-020051-0). HarpJ.
--Spooky Tricks. LC 68-16822. (I Can Read Bk.). (Illus.). 64p. (gr. k-3). 1968. PLB 9.89 (ISBN 0-06-026634-1). HarpJ.
--Story of the Ice Age. LC 56-6816. (Illus.). 82p. (gr. 3-7). 1956. PLB 9.89 (ISBN 0-06-020066-9). HarpJ.
Ames, Gerald, jt. auth. see Wyler, Rose.
Ames, Gesell A., et al. The Child from Five to Ten. rev. ed. LC 76-5123. (Illus.). 1977. 19.18i (ISBN 0-06-011501-7, HarpT). Har-Row.
Ames, Herman, et al, eds. X, Y, Z Letters. (BCL History Ser). 1899. 19.00x (ISBN 0-403-00035-1). Scholarly.
Ames, Herman V. John C. Calhoun & the Secession Movement of 1850. facsimile ed. LC 71-169749. (Select Bibliographies Reprint Ser). Repr. of 1918 ed. 12.00 (ISBN 0-8369-5892-6). Ayer Co Pubs.
--Proposed Amendments to the Constitution of the U. S., During the First Century of Its History. LC 73-135173. 1970. Repr. of 1896 ed. lib. bdg. 26.00 (ISBN 0-8337-0060-X). B Franklin.
Ames, Herman V., ed. State Documents on Federal Relations. LC 78-77697. (American Constitutional & Legal History Ser). 1970. Repr. of 1900 ed. lib. bdg. 42.50 (ISBN 0-306-71335-7). Da Capo.
Ames, J. Systems Study of Odorous Industrial Processes, 1979. 1981. 75.00x (ISBN 0-686-97144-2, Pub. by W Spring England). State Mutual Bk.
Ames, James B. Lectures on Legal History & Miscellaneous Legal Essays. 1976. lib. bdg. 59.95 (ISBN 0-8490-2137-5). Gordon Pr.
Ames, Jerry & Siegelman, Jim. The Book of Tap. (Illus.). 224p. 1977. McKay.
Ames, Jessie D. Changing Character of Lynching: Review of Lynching 1931-1941, with a Discussion of Recent Developments in This Field. LC 78-158249. Repr. of 1942 ed. 11.50 (ISBN 0-404-00134-3). AMS Pr.
Ames, John, jt. auth. see Richards, Renee.
Ames, John, jt. auth. see Uelsmann, Jerry N.
Ames, John G. & U.S. Dept. of the Interior, Division of New Documents. Comprehensive Index to the Publications of the United States Government, 2 vols. LC 5-32405. (Illus.). Repr. of 1905 ed. Set. 140.00 (ISBN 0-384-01103-9). Johnson Repr.
Ames, Joseph B. The Bladed Barrier. Reginald, R. & Melville, Douglas, eds. LC 77-84193. (Lost Race & Adult Fantasy Ser.). 1978. Repr. of 1929 ed. lib. bdg. 32.00x (ISBN 0-405-10951-2). Ayer Co Pubs.
Ames, Julius R., jt. auth. see Branagan, Thomas.
Ames, Kenneth J. The Religious Language of Thomas Traherne's Centuries. (Religion & Literature Ser.). 1979. lib. bdg. 59.95 (ISBN 0-87700-260-6). Revisionist Pr.
Ames, Kenneth L., jt. ed. see Schless, Nancy H.
Ames, L. B. & Rodell, J. L. Rorshach Responses in Old Age. LC 53-12914. Orig. Title: Old Age Rorshach Responses. 1973. 27.50 (ISBN 0-87630-064-6). Brunner-Mazel.
Ames, L. B., et al. Child Rorschach Responses. LC 72-93599. 320p. 1974. 27.50 (ISBN 0-87630-042-5). Brunner-Mazel.
--Adolescent Rorschach Responses. LC 77-132889. 330p. 1971. 27.50 (ISBN 0-87630-041-7). Brunner-Mazel.
Ames, Lee. Draw Fifty Horses. LC 81-43496. (Illus.). 64p. (gr. 4 up). 1984. 9.95 (ISBN 0-385-17640-6); PLB 9.95 (ISBN 0-385-17641-4). Doubleday.
--My Animal Friends, No. 7236. Lawrence, Leslie & Weingartner, Ronald, eds. (Bright Beginnings II Ser.). (Illus.). 40p. (gr. k-4). 1982. pap. 1.39 (ISBN 0-88049-006-3, 7235). Milton Bradley Co.
--Sprouting About, No. 7236. Lawrence, Leslie & Weingartner, Ronald, eds. (Bright Beginnings II Ser.). (Illus.). 40p. (gr. k-4). 1982. pap. 1.39 (ISBN 0-88049-005-5, 7234). Milton Bradley Co.
--Under the Big Top, No. 7236. Lawrence, Leslie & Weingartner, Ronald, eds. (Bright Beginnings II Ser.). (Illus.). 40p. (gr. k-4). 1982. pap. 1.39 (ISBN 0-88049-004-7, 7733). Milton Bradley Co.
Ames, Lee J. The Dot, Line & Shape Connection: How to Be Driven to Abstraction. LC 80-695. (Illus.). 64p. 1982. 12.95 (ISBN 0-385-14402-4). Doubleday.
--Draw Draw Draw. LC 62-7025. 47p. (gr. 3-9). 1962. 8.95a (ISBN 0-385-12767-7); PLB (ISBN 0-385-03388-5). Doubleday.
--Draw Fifty Airplanes, Aircraft & Spacecraft. LC 76-51554. 64p. (gr. 1 up). 1977. 9.95a (ISBN 0-385-12235-7); PLB (ISBN 0-385-12236-5). Doubleday.
--Draw Fifty Animals. LC 73-13083. (Illus.). 64p. (gr. 3-7). 1974. 9.95a (ISBN 0-385-07712-2); PLB (ISBN 0-385-07726-2). Doubleday.
--Draw Fifty Animals. LC 73-13083. (Illus.). 64p. 1985. pap. 4.95 (ISBN 0-385-19519-2, Zephyr). Doubleday.
--Draw Fifty Athletes. LC 83-45569. (Illus.). 64p. (gr. 4-6). 1985. 10.95 (ISBN 0-385-19055-7); lib. bdg. 10.95 (ISBN 0-385-19056-5). Doubleday.
--Draw Fifty Boats, Ships, Trucks & Trains. LC 75-19011. 64p. (gr. 1 up). 1976. 9.95a (ISBN 0-385-08903-1); PLB (ISBN 0-385-08904-X). Doubleday.
--Draw Fifty Buildings & Other Structures. LC 79-7483. (Illus.). 64p. (gr. 2 up). 1980. 9.95a (ISBN 0-385-14400-8); PLB (ISBN 0-385-14401-6). Doubleday.
--Draw Fifty Dinosaurs & Other Prehistoric Animals. LC 76-7285. 64p. (gr. 1 up). 1977. pap. 8.95 (ISBN 0-385-11134-7). Doubleday.
--Draw Fifty Dinosaurs & Other Prehistoric Animals. LC 76-7285. (Illus.). 64p. 1985. pap. 4.95 (ISBN 0-385-19520-6, Pub. by BFYR). Doubleday.
--Draw Fifty Dogs. LC 79-6853. (Illus.). 64p. (gr. 4-6). 1981. 9.95a (ISBN 0-385-15686-3); PLB (ISBN 0-385-15687-1). Doubleday.
--Draw Fifty Famous Cartoons. LC 78-1176. 64p. 1979. 9.95a (ISBN 0-385-13661-7); PLB (ISBN 0-385-13662-5). Doubleday.
--Draw Fifty Famous Cartoons. LC 78-1176. (Illus.). 64p. 1985. pap. 4.95 (ISBN 0-385-19521-4, Pub. by BFYR). Doubleday.
--Draw Fifty Famous Faces. LC 77-15878. (gr. 1 up). 1978. 9.95a (ISBN 0-385-13217-4); PLB (ISBN 0-385-13218-2). Doubleday.
--Draw Fifty Famous Stars: As Selected by Rona Barrett's Hollywood Magazine. LC 81-43238. (Illus.). 64p. (gr. 4-6). 1982. 8.95 (ISBN 0-385-15688-X); lib. bdg. 8.95 (ISBN 0-385-15689-8). Doubleday.
--Draw Fifty Monsters, Creepy Creatures, Superheroes, Demons, Dragons, Nerds, Dirts, Ghouls, Giants, Vampires, Zombies, & Other Curiosa... LC 80-3006. (Illus.). 64p. (gr. 1 up). 1983. 9.95a (ISBN 0-385-17637-6); PLB (ISBN 0-385-17638-4). Doubleday.
--Draw Fifty Vehicles. LC 77-94862. (gr. 1 up). 1978. pap. 3.50 (ISBN 0-385-14154-8, Zephyr). Doubleday.
--How to Draw Star Wars Heroes, Creatures, Spaceships & Other Fantastic Things. LC 83-22921. (Illus.). 80p. (gr. 3-7). 1984. pap. 4.95 (ISBN 0-394-86489-1, BYR). Random.
--Make Twenty-Five Crayon Drawings of the Circus. LC 76-6034. (Illus.). 64p. 1980. 8.95a (ISBN 0-385-15210-8); PLB (ISBN 0-385-15211-6). Doubleday.
--Make Twenty-Five Felt Tip Drawings Out West. LC 79-8554. (Illus.). 64p. 1980. 8.95a (ISBN 0-385-15208-6); PLB (ISBN 0-385-15209-4). Doubleday.
Ames, Lois, jt. ed. see Sexton, Linda G.
Ames, Louise B. Your Three Year Old. 1980. 6.95 (ISBN 0-385-29142-6, Delta). Dell.
--Your Two Year Old. 1980. 6.95 (ISBN 0-385-29141-8, Delta). Dell.
Ames, Louise B. & Chase, Joan A. Don't Push Your Preschooler. rev. ed. LC 80-8192. 240p. 1981. 13.41i (ISBN 0-06-010083-4, HarpT). Har-Row.
Ames, Louise B. & Haber, Carol C. Your Seven Year Old: Life in a Minor Key. (Illus.). 154p. 1985. 12.95 (ISBN 0-385-29382-8). Delacorte.
Ames, Louise B. & Ilg. Your Three-Year Old: Friend or Enemy. 1980. pap. 6.95 (ISBN 0-385-29142-6, Delta). Dell.
--Your Two Year Old: Terrible or Tender. 1980. pap. 6.95 (ISBN 0-385-29141-8, Delta). Dell.
Ames, Louise B. & Ilg, Frances L. Your Five Year Old. 1981. 6.95 (ISBN 0-385-29145-0, Delta). Dell.
--Your Five Year Old: Sunny & Serene. 1981. pap. 6.95 (ISBN 0-385-29145-0, Delta). Dell.
--Your Four Year Old. 1981. 6.95 (ISBN 0-385-29143-4, Delta). Dell.
--Your Four Year Old: Wild & Wonderful. 1980. pap. 6.95 (ISBN 0-385-29143-4, Delta). Dell.
Ames, Louise B., jt. auth. see Ilg, Frances L.
Ames, Louise B., et al. The Gesell Institute's Child from One to Six: Evaluating the Behavior of the Pre-School Child. LC 79-1795. (Illus.). 1979. 14.37i (ISBN 0-06-010087-7, HarpT). Har-Row.
--Your Six-Year-Old, 1981. pap. 6.95 (ISBN 0-385-29146-9, Delta). Dell.
--He Hit Me First: When Brothers & Sisters Fight. LC 82-1565. 1982. 14.95 (ISBN 0-934878-18-8). Dembner Bks.
--He Hit Me First: When Brothers & Sisters Fight. LC 82-1565. 190p. 1983. pap. 7.95 (ISBN 0-934878-34-X). Dembner Bks.
--Your One-Year-Old: The Fun-Loving, Fussy 12- to 24-Month-Old. (Illus.). 1982. 11.95 (ISBN 0-385-29186-8). Delacorte.
--Your One-Year-Old: The Fun-Loving, Fussy 12-to-24-Month Old. (Illus.). 1983. pap. 6.95 (ISBN 0-385-29206-6, Delta). Dell.
Ames, Louise B., jt. auth. see Ilg, Frances L.
Ames, M. A., et al, eds. Pharmacokinetics of Anticancer Agents in Humans. 300p. 1984. 113.50 (ISBN 0-444-80518-4, I-021-84, Biomedical Pr). Elsevier.
Ames, Margery E., jt. ed. see Nelson, Ted.
Ames, Marjorie. Miniature Macrame for Dollhouses. 1981. pap. 2.25 (ISBN 0-486-23960-8). Dover.
Ames, Mary. From a New England Woman's Diary in Dixie in 1865. LC 70-78760. Repr. of 1906 ed. 15.00x (ISBN 0-8371-1386-5, AMD&, Pub. by Negro U Pr). Greenwood.
Ames, Mary E. Outcome Uncertain: Science & the Political Process. LC 77-81692. (Orig.). 1978. casebound 13.95x (ISBN 0-89461-028-7). Comm Pr Inc.
--Outcome Uncertain: Science & the Political Process. 1982. pap. 3.50 (ISBN 0-380-59535-4, 59535-4, Discus). Avon.
Ames, Michael D. & Wellsfry, Norval L. Small Business Management. (Illus.). 450p. 1983. text ed. 26.95 (ISBN 0-314-69631-8). West Pub.
Ames, Michael M. Museums, the Public & Anthropology: A Study in the Anthropology of Anthropology. 140p. 1985. 12.50 (ISBN 0-7748-0213-8). U BC Pr.
Ames, Mildred. Anna to the Infinite Power. 204p. (gr. 7 up). 1981. 11.95 (ISBN 0-684-16855-3, ScribJ). Scribner.
--Anna to the Infinite Power. 208p. (gr. 7 up). 1985. pap. 2.25 (ISBN 0-590-33732-7, Point). Scholastic Inc.
--Cassandra-Jamie. LC 85-40297. 152p. (gr. 6-8). 1985. 12.95 (ISBN 0-684-18472-9). Scribner.
--The Dancing Madness: A Novel. LC 80-65831. 144p. (gr. 7 up). 1980. 8.95 (ISBN 0-385-28113-7). Delacorte.
--Philo Potts, or the Helping Hand Strikes Again. LC 82-6008. 192p. (gr. 4-6). 1982. 11.95 (ISBN 0-684-17625-4, ScribJ). Scribner.
--The Silver Link, the Silken Tie. LC 83-20337. 224p. (gr. 7 up). 1984. 12.95 (ISBN 0-684-18065-0, ScribJ). Scribner.
Ames, Nathaniel. Essays, Humor & Poems of Nathaniel Ames: Father & Son, of Dedham, Mass., from Their Almanacks, 1726-1775. Briggs, Samuel, ed. (Rediscovering America Ser). 1970. Repr. of 1891 ed. 36.00 (ISBN 0-384-05810-8). Johnson Repr.
Ames, Oakes. Orchidaceae: Illustrations & Studies of the Family Orchidaceae Volume IV: the Genus Habenaria in North America. (Orchid Ser.). (Illus.). 1980. Repr. of 1910 ed. text ed. 25.00 (ISBN 0-930576-23-3). E M Coleman Ent.
--Orchids in Retrospect: A Collection of Essays on the Orchidaceae. (Orchid Ser.). (Illus.). 1980. Repr. of 1948 ed. text ed. 15.00 (ISBN 0-930576-21-7). E M Coleman Ent.
Ames, Oakes & Correl, Donovan S. Orchids of Guatemala & Belize. (Nature Ser.). 800p. 1985. pap. 14.95 (ISBN 0-486-24834-8). Dover.
Ames, Oaks. Studies In the Family Corchidaceae, 7 Vols. (Illus.). 1610p. 1982. Repr. Set. 145.00 (ISBN 0-9608918-0-3); 27.00 ea. Vol. I (ISBN 0-9608918-1-1). Vol. II (ISBN 0-9608918-2-X). Vol. III (ISBN 0-9608918-3-8). Vol. IV. (ISBN 0-9608918-4-6); Vol. V. (ISBN 0-9608918-5-4); Vol. VI. (ISBN 0-9608918-6-2). Vol. VII (ISBN 0-9608918-7-0). Twin Oaks Bks.
Ames, Percy. Milton Memorial Lectures 1909. LC 65-15895. (Studies in Milton, No. 22). 1969. Repr. of 1909 ed. lib. bdg. 39.95x (ISBN 0-8383-0501-6). Haskell.
Ames, Percy W. Chaucer Memorial Lectures: 1900. 1978. Repr. of 1900 ed. lib. bdg. 25.00 (ISBN 0-8495-0103-2). Arden Lib.
--Chaucer Memorial Lectures 1900. LC 73-7771. 1900. lib. bdg. 30.00 (ISBN 0-8414-2850-6). Folcroft.
--Milton Memorial Lectures. 1974. Repr. 25.00 (ISBN 0-8274-2738-7). R West.
Ames, Robert. Off Road Desert Survival Handbook. (Illus.). 64p. (Orig.). 1981. pap. 3.95 (ISBN 0-89632-008-1). Del Oeste.
--Off Road Drivers Handbook. LC 77-92562. (Illus.). 176p. 1981. pap. 6.95 (ISBN 0-89632-002-2). Del Oeste.
Ames, Roger T. The Art of Rulership: A Study in Ancient Chinese Political Thought. LC 82-25917. 293p. 1983. 25.00x (ISBN 0-8248-0825-8). UH Pr.
Ames, Russell A. A Gentleman from Indiana: The Life & Times of Ned Ames - In Memory of Edward Elbridge Ames (1881-1952) (Illus., Orig.). 1978. pap. 10.50 (ISBN 0-686-24637-3). S A Shopen.
Ames, Russell E. & Ames, Carole. Research on Motivation in Education: Student Motivation, Vol. 1. LC 83-12315. 1984. 36.50 (ISBN 0-12-056701-6). Acad Pr.
Ames, Russell E., jt. auth. see Ames, Carole.
Ames, Ruth M. God's Plenty. 288p. 1984. 12.95 (ISBN 0-8294-0426-0). Loyola.
Ames, Samuel, jt. auth. see Angell, Joseph.
Ames, Scribner. Marsden Hartley in Maine. 1972. 5.95 (ISBN 0-89101-025-4). U Maine Orono.
Ames, Seth, ed. Works of Fisher Ames, 2 Vols. LC 69-14409. (American Public Figures Ser.). 1969. Repr. of 1854 ed. Set. lib. bdg. 89.50 (ISBN 0-306-71122-2). Da Capo.
--Works of Fisher Ames, 2 vol. set. LC 81-13568. 1984. 30.00 set (ISBN 0-86597-013-0); pap. 15.00 set (ISBN 0-86597-016-5). Liberty Fund.
Ames, Seth, ed. see Ames, Fisher.
Ames, Sue Ann, jt. auth. see Kneisl, Carol R.
Ames, Susie M. Reading, Writing & Arithmetic in Virginia, 1607-1699: Other Cultural Topics. (Illus., Orig.). 1957. pap. 2.95 (ISBN 0-8139-0139-1). U Pr of Va.
--Studies of the Virginia Eastern Shore in the Seventeenth Century. LC 73-76918. (Illus.). x, 274p. 1973. Repr. of 1940 ed. 17.00x (ISBN 0-8462-1730-9). Russell.
Ames, Susie M., ed. County Court Records of Accomack-Northampton, Virginia, 1640-1645. LC 72-90670. (Virginia Historical Society Documents Ser.: No. 10). 1973. 20.00x (ISBN 0-8139-0394-7). U Pr of Va.
Ames, Terrance, ed. Amphicroia. (Illus.). 40p. 1978. pap. 7.50x (ISBN 0-914974-27-0). Holmgangers.
Ames, V. M. Andre Gide. LC 47-11811. Repr. of 1947 ed. 22.00 (ISBN 0-527-02350-7). Kraus Repr.
Ames, Van M. Introduction to Beauty. facs. ed. LC 68-14895. (Essay Index Reprint Ser). 1931. 19.00 (ISBN 0-8369-0152-5). Ayer Co Pubs.
Ames, Van Meter. Zen & American Thought. 1978. Repr. of 1962 ed. lib. bdg. 26.50 (ISBN 0-313-20066-1, AMZA). Greenwood.
Ames, W. F. Numerical Solution of Partial Differential Equations. 2nd ed. 1977. 47.00 (ISBN 0-12-056760-1). Acad Pr.
Ames, W. F., ed. Nonlinear Partial Differential Equations: A Symposium on Methods of Solution. 1967. 72.00 (ISBN 0-12-056754-7). Acad Pr.
--Nonlinear Partial Differential Equations in Engineering, 2 vols. (Mathematics in Science & Engineering Ser). Vol. 1, 1965. 75.00 (ISBN 0-12-056756-3); Vol. 2, 1972. 75.00 (ISBN 0-12-056755-5). Acad Pr.
Ames, W. F. & Vichnevetsky, R., eds. Modelling & Simulation in Engineering: Proceedings of the IMACS World Conference on Systems Simulation & Scientific Computation, Tenth, Montreal, Canada, 8-13 Aug., 1982. (IMACS Transactions on Scientific Computation Ser.: Vol. III). 340p. 1983. 49.00 (ISBN 0-444-86609-4, I-296-83, North Holland). Elsevier.
Ames, W. F., et al, eds. Scientific Computing: Proceedings of the IMACS World Congress on Systems, Simulation, & Scientific Computation, Tenth, Montreal, Canada, 8-13 Aug., 1982. (IMACS Transactions on Scientific Computation Ser.: Vol. 1). 364p. 1983. 51.00 (ISBN 0-444-86607-8, North Holland). Elsevier.
Ames, Walter L. Police & Community in Japan. LC 80-12642. (Illus.). 300p. 1981. 27.50x (ISBN 0-520-04070-8). U of Cal Pr.
Ames, William. Conscience with the Power & Cases Thereof. LC 74-28826. (English Experience Ser.: No. 708). 1975. Repr. of 1639 ed. 35.00 (ISBN 9-0221-0708-6). Walter J Johnson.
--The Marrow of Theology. Eusden, John D., ed. & tr. from Latin. Orig. Title: Medulla Theologiae. xiv, 354p. 1983. pap. 14.95 (ISBN 0-939464-14-4). Labyrinth Pr.
--Technometry. Gibbs, Lee W., tr. from Lat. LC 78-65117. (Haney Foundation Ser.). (Illus.). 1979. 30.00x (ISBN 0-8122-7756-2). U of Pa Pr.
Ames, William, tr. see Ovsiannikov, L. V.
Ames, William F., ed. Nonlinear Ordinary Differential Equations in Transport Processes. (Mathematics in Science & Engineering: Vol. 42). 1968. 55.00 (ISBN 0-12-056753-9). Acad Pr.
Ames, Winter. Bird of Paradise. (Second Chance at Love Ser.: No. 18). 192p. (Orig.). 1981. pap. 1.75 (ISBN 0-515-05977-3). Jove Pubns.
Ames, Winthrop. What Shall We Name the Baby? 1984. pap. 4.80. PB.
Ames, Winthrop, ed. What Shall We Name the Baby. (Illus.). 1959. pap. 4.95 (ISBN 0-671-81210-6, Fireside). S&S.

--What Shall We Name the Baby? pap. 2.95 (ISBN 0-671-54152-8). PB.
Ames-Lewis, Francis. Drawing in Early Renaissance Italy. LC 81-40434. (Illus.). 196p. 1983. 47.00x (ISBN 0-300-02551-3, Y-447); pap. 14.95 (ISBN 0-300-02978-0). Yale U Pr.
--The Library & Manuscripts of Piero Di Cosimo De'Medici. LC 83-48687. (Theses from the Courtauld Institute of Art Ser.). (Illus.). 655p. 1984. lib. bdg. 80.00 (ISBN 0-8240-5975-1). Garland Pub.
Ames-Lewis, Francis & Wright, Joanne. Drawing in the Italian Renaissance Workshop. (Illus.). 328p. (Orig.). pap. 15.95 (ISBN 0-905209-31-1, Pub. by Victoria & Albert Mus UK). Faber & Faber.
AMETEK. Solar Energy Handbook: Theory & Application. LC 78-14646. 1979. 18.50x (ISBN 0-8019-6776-7). Chilton.
AMETEK Inc. Power Systems Group. Solar Energy Handbook: Theory & Applications of Solar-Generated Electricity. 2nd ed. LC 81-71091. 1984. 37.50 (ISBN 0-8019-7154-3). Chilton.
Amev, Lloyd R. & Egginton, Don A. Management Accounting: A Conceptual Approach. LC 73-86099. (Longman Business Studies Ser.). pap. 160.00 (ISBN 0-317-27726-X, 2025224). Bks Demand UMI.
Amey, J., jt. auth. see Coveney, James.
Amey, Leonard, jt. ed. see Engledow, Frank.
Amey, Lloyd R. Budget Planning & Control Systems. LC 79-12494. 290p. 1979. text ed. 32.95 (ISBN 0-273-01343-2). Pitman Pub MA.
Amey, Peter. Imperialism. Yapp, Malcolm, et al, eds. (World History Ser.). (Illus.). (gr. 10). 1980. lib. bdg. 6.95 (ISBN 0-89908-226-2); pap. text ed. 2.45 (ISBN 0-89908-201-7). Greenhaven.
--Pax Romana. Yapp, Malcolm, et al, eds. (World History Ser.). (Illus.). 32p. (gr. 10). 1980. lib. bdg. 6.95 (ISBN 0-89908-027-8); pap. text ed. 2.45 (ISBN 0-89908-002-2). Greenhaven.
--The Scientific Revolution. Yapp, Malcolm, et al, eds. (World History Ser.). (Illus.). (gr. 10). 1980. lib. bdg. 6.95 (ISBN 0-89908-132-0); pap. text ed. 2.45 (ISBN 0-89908-107-X). Greenhaven.
Amey, Peter, et al. Leonardo Da Vinci. Yapp, Malcolm, et al, eds. (World History Ser.). (Illus.). (gr. 10). 1980. lib. bdg. 6.95 (ISBN 0-89908-041-3); pap. text ed. 2.45 (ISBN 0-89908-016-2). Greenhaven.
--Luther, Erasmus & Loyola. Yapp, Malcolm, et al, eds. (World History Ser.). (Illus.). (gr. 10). 1980. lib. bdg. 6.95 (ISBN 0-89908-043-X); pap. text ed. 2.45 (ISBN 0-89908-018-9). Greenhaven.
Amey, Vera E., jt. auth. see Eaton, Margaret H.
Amherst, William A. & Thomson, Basil, eds. The Discovery of the Solomon Islands by Alvaro de Mendana in 1568, 2 vols. in 1. (Hakluyt Society Works Ser.: No. 2, Vols. 7 & 8). (Illus.). Repr. of 1901 ed. 72.00 (ISBN 0-317-16022-2). Kraus Repr.
AMI Co. AMI Model D-80 Service Manual of 1952: Including Parts List. Adams, Frank, ed. 116p. 1984. Repr. of 1952 ed. spiral bdg. 24.50 (ISBN 0-913599-18-2, R264). AMR Pub Co.
AMI Company. AMI Jukebox Model D-40 Service Manual & Parts List of 1951. Adams, Frank, ed. 102p. 1984. Repr. of 1951 ed. spiral bound, laminated covers 24.50 (ISBN 0-913599-18-2, R-270). AMR Pub Co.
Ami Press. The Message of Marienfried. 20p. 1983. 1.00 (ISBN 0-911988-50-5). AMI Pr.
AMI Press Staff. Five Homilies for First Saturdays. 46p. 1984. 1.50 (ISBN 0-911988-61-0). AMI Pr.
Amichai, Yehuda. Amen. LC 76-50164. 1977. 7.95i (ISBN 0-06-010090-7, HarpT); pap. 4.95i (ISBN 0-06-010089-3, TD-278, HarpT). Har-Row.
--Great Tranquility: Questions & Answers. Abramson, Glenda & Parfitt, Tudor, trs. from Hebrew. 96p. 1983. 12.45i (ISBN 0-06-015188-9, HarpT). Har-Row.
--Great Tranquility: Questions & Answers. Abramson, Glenda & Parfitt, Tudor, trs. from Hebrew. LC 83-47550. 96p. 1983. pap. 7.64i (ISBN 0-06-091085-2, CN 1085, CN). Har-Row.
--Love Poems. Abramson, Glenda & Parfitt, Tudor, trs. LC 80-8680. 128p. 1981. 12.02i (ISBN 0-06-014848-9, HarpT). Har-Row.
--Love Poems. Abramson, Glenda & Parfitt, Tudor, trs. LC 80-8680. 128p. 1981. pap. 7.64i (ISBN 0-06-090873-4, CN 873, CN). Har-Row.
--Not of This Time, Not of This Place. Katz, Shlomo, tr. from Hebrew. 345p. 1973. 15.00x (ISBN 0-85303-180-0, Pub. by Vallentine Mitchell England). Biblio Dist.
--Time. LC 78-66388. 1979. 10.53i (ISBN 0-06-010088-5, HarpT). Har-Row.
--Travels. Nevo, Ruth, tr. 145p. (Orig., Eng. & Hebrew.). 1986. 13.95 (ISBN 0-317-27458-9); pap. 8.95. Sheep Meadow.
--The World Is a Room, & Other Stories. 197p. 1984. 13.95 (ISBN 0-8276-0234-0). Jewish Pubns.
Amichai, Yehuda, ed. see Pagis, Dan.
Amichai, Yehuda, ed. see Yeshurun, Avoth.
Amici, R., et al. Cerebellar Tumors: Clinical Analysis & Physiopathologic Correlations. (Monographs in Neural Sciences: Vol. 4). 1976. pap. 27.25 (ISBN 3-8055-2358-0). S Karger.
Amicis, E. De see De Amicis, E.
Amicis, Edmondo de see De Amicis, Edmondo.
Amick, Louis S., ed. see Small, Rosemary K.
Amico, et al. All about Simulation, Nineteen Eighty-Four, Vol. 14. (Norfolk Ser.: No. 1). 30.00 (ISBN 0-317-17124-0). Soc Computer Sim.
Amideast Staff. Education in the Middle East. Keenum, Deborah G. & Schmida, Leslie C., eds. LC 83-72989. (Illus.). 150p. 1983. professional ref. 17.00 (ISBN 0-913957-00-3). Amideast.
--Orientation Handbook: An Introduction to Living & Studying in the United States. (Illus.). 77p. 1984. 3.50 (ISBN 0-913957-01-1). AMIDEAST.
Amidei, Nancy. Hunger in the Eighties: A Primer. Perry, Cecilia, ed. 166p. (Orig.). 1984. pap. write for info. (ISBN 0-934220-06-9). Food Res Action.
Amidei, Rosemary E., compiled by. Environment: The Human Impact, Selections from the Science Teacher. 1973. pap. 7.50 (ISBN 0-87355-001-3). Natl Sci Tchrs.
Amidon, Beulah E., ed. Democracy's Challenge to Education. facsimile ed. LC 74-128201. (Essay Index Reprint Ser). Repr. of 1940 ed. 21.00 (ISBN 0-8369-2265-4). Ayer Co Pubs.
Amiel, A., et al. Coronary Artery Diseases. (Diagnostic & Therapeutic Imaging Approaches Ser.). (Illus.). 250p. 1984. 49.50 (ISBN 0-387-13209-0). Springer-Verlag.
Amiel, Henri F. Amiel's Journal. 1976. lib. bdg. 59.95 (ISBN 0-8490-1421-2). Gordon Pr.
--Jacques Rousseau. 94p. 1980. Repr. of 1922 ed. lib. bdg. 17.50 (ISBN 0-8482-3250-X). Norwood Edns.
Amiel, Henri-F. Jean Jacques Rousseau. 1973. Repr. of 1922 ed. 10.00 (ISBN 0-8274-1400-5). R West.
Amiel, Henri-Frederic. Jean Jacques Rousseau. Brooks, Van Wyck, tr. 1979. Repr. of 1922 ed. lib. bdg. 10.00 (ISBN 0-8414-3026-8). Folcroft.
Amiel, Joseph. Birthright. LC 84-18507. 496p. 1985. 16.95 (ISBN 0-689-11508-3). Atheneum.
Amiel, Leon. Homage to Chagall. (Twentieth Century Art Ser.). (Illus.). 1982. 19.95 (ISBN 0-8148-0725-9). L Amiel Pub.
Amiel, M. & Moreau, J. F., eds. Contrast Media in Radiology, Appraisal & Prospects, Lyon 1981: Proceedings. (Illus.). 370p. 1982. 32.50 (ISBN 0-387-11534-X). Springer-Verlag.
Amiel, S., ed. Nondestructive Activation Analysis: With Nuclear Reactors & Radioactive Neutron Sources. (Studies in Analytical Chemistry: Vol. 3). 1981. 76.75 (ISBN 0-444-41942-X). Elsevier.
Amiel-Tison, Claudine & Grenier, Albert. Neurologic Examination of the Infant & Newborn. Steichen, Jean J., tr. (Illus.). 148p. 1983. 39.50 (ISBN 0-89352-164-7). Masson Pub.
Amiet, Pierre. Art of the Ancient Near East. (Illus.). 620p. 1980. 125.00 (ISBN 0-8109-0638-4, 0638-4). Abrams.
Amiet, William A. Literature by Languages: A Roll Call. 1979. Repr. of 1932 ed. lib. bdg. 35.00 (ISBN 0-8495-0207-1). Arden Lib.
Amigo, Eleanor & Neuffer, Mark. Beyond the Adirondacks: The Story of St. Regis Paper Company. LC 80-1798. (Contributions in Economics & Economic History Ser.: No. 35). (Illus.). xi, 219p. 1980. lib. bdg. 27.50x (ISBN 0-313-22735-7, AFN/). Greenwood.
Amihud, Yakov, ed. Bidding & Auctioning for Procurement & Allocation: Proceedings of a Conference at the Center for Applied Economics, New York University. LC 75-27104. 220p. 1976. 32.50x (ISBN 0-8147-0558-8). NYU Pr.
Amihud, Yakov, et al, eds. Market Making & the Changing Structure of the Securities Industry. LC 83-48658. (A Salomon Brothers Center Bk.). 336p. 1985. 33.50x (ISBN 0-669-07335-0). Lexington Bks.
Amin, Bakhita & Hall, Marjorie. Sisters under the Sun: The Story of Sudanese Women. LC 81-17153. (Illus.). 1982. text ed. 30.00x (ISBN 0-582-78017-9). Longman.
Amin, Galal. Food Supply & Economic Development with Special Reference to Egypt. 132p. 1966. 28.50x (ISBN 0-7146-1201-4, BHA 01201, F Cass Co). Biblio Dist.
Amin, Galal A. Food Supply & Economic Development with Special Reference to Egypt. LC 67-1159. (Illus.). 1966. 27.50x (ISBN 0-678-05022-8). Kelley.
Amin, Karima, jt. auth. see Stanford, Barbara D.
Amin, Mohamed, jt. auth. see Khalfan, Zulf M.
Amin, Mohamed, et al. Journey Through Pakistan. (Illus.). 256p. 1982. 39.95 (ISBN 0-370-30489-6, Pub. by the Bodley Head). Merrimack Pub Cir.
Amin, R. & Faruqee, F. Fertility & Its Regulation in Bangladesh. (Working Paper: No. 383). iv, 50p. 1980. 5.00 (ISBN 0-686-36196-2, WP-0383). World Bank.
Amin, Samir. Accumulation on a World Scale, 2 vols. in 1. LC 72-92028. 666p. 1978. Set. pap. 9.50 (ISBN 0-85345-430-2). Monthly Rev.
--The Arab Economy Today. Pallis, M., tr. from French. 128p. 1982. 25.00x (ISBN 0-86232-081-X, Pub. by Zed Pr England). Biblio Dist.
--The Arab Economy Today. 128p. 1982. pap. 7.50x (ISBN 0-86232-043-7, Pub. by Zed Pr England). Biblio Dist.
--The Arab Nation. 1982. lib. bdg. 34.50 (ISBN 0-686-47940-8). Porter.
--The Arab Nation: Nationalism & Class Struggle. 116p. 1978. 19.95x (ISBN 0-905762-22-3, Pub. by Zed Pr England); pap. 6.50x (ISBN 0-905762-23-1, Pub. by Zed Pr England). Biblio Dist.
--Class & Nation, Historically & in the Current Crisis. LC 79-3022. 292p. 1980. 15.50 (ISBN 0-85345-522-8). Monthly Rev.
--The Future of Maoism. Finkelstein, Norman, tr. from Fr. LC 82-48035. 128p. 1983. 12.00 (ISBN 0-85345-622-4); pap. 6.50 (ISBN 0-85345-623-2). Monthly Rev.
--Imperialism & Unequal Development. LC 77-7619. 267p. 1977. 12.95 (ISBN 0-85345-418-3). Monthly Rev.
--The Law of Value & Historical Materialism. Pearce, Brian, tr. from Fr. LC 78-15210. 144p. 1979. pap. 5.95 (ISBN 0-85345-517-1). Monthly Rev.
--Neo-Colonialism in West Africa. McDonagh, Francis, tr. from Fr. LC 74-7784. 320p. 1976. pap. 5.95 (ISBN 0-85345-373-X). Monthly Rev.
--Unequal Development: An Essay on the Social Formations of Peripheral Capitalism. Pearce, Brian, tr. from Fr. LC 75-15364. 1977. pap. 8.50 (ISBN 0-85345-433-7). Monthly Rev.
Amin, Samir, ed. Human Resources, Employment & Development, Vol. V: Developing Countries. LC 82-23163. 336p. 1984. 35.00 (ISBN 0-312-39959-6). St Martin.
Amin, Samir, ed. see International African Seminar.
Amin, Samir, et al. Dynamics of Global Crisis. LC 81-84739. 256p. 1982. pap. 8.00 (ISBN 0-85345-606-2). Monthly Rev.
Amin, Shahid. Sugarcane & Sugar in Gorakpur: An Inquiry into Peasant Production for Capitalist Enterprises in Colonial India. (Illus.). 1984. 29.95x (ISBN 0-19-561545-X). Oxford U Pr.
Amin, Tahir. Afghanistan Crisis: Implications & Options for Muslim World, Iran & Pakistan. 144p. (Orig.). 1982. pap. 8.00 (ISBN 0-939830-28-0, Pub. by Inst Pol Stud Pakistan). New Era Pubns MI.
Amini, Johari. Let's Go Some Where. 1970. pap. 1.00 (ISBN 0-88378-011-9). Third World.
Aminoff, David, ed. Blood & Tissue Antigens: A Symposium Volume. 1970. 84.00 (ISBN 0-12-057050-5). Acad Pr.
Aminoff, Michael J. Electrodiagnosis in Clinical Neurology. 1980. text ed. 49.00 (ISBN 0-443-08021-6). Churchill.
Aminoldesel, Gus T. Death Comes to the Dentist. (Murders in Miniature Ser.: No. 2). (Illus.). 16p. (Orig.). 1984. pap. 1.00x (ISBN 0-938338-79-X). Winds World Pr.
Aminzade, Ronald. Class, Politics, & Early Industrial Capitalism: A Study of Mid-Nineteenth-Century Toulouse, France. LC 80-28284. (European Social History Ser.). (Illus.). 230p. 1981. 39.50x (ISBN 0-87395-528-5); pap. 15.95x (ISBN 0-87395-529-3). State U NY Pr.
Amir, Jehoshua, tr. see Schalit, Abraham.
Amir, Menachem. Patterns in Forcible Rape. LC 79-14022. 1971. 29.00x (ISBN 0-226-01734-6). U of Chicago Pr.
Amir, Yehuda & Sharan, Shlomo. School Desegregation. 288p. 1984. text ed. 24.95 (ISBN 0-89859-335-2). L Erlbaum Assocs.
Amira, Karl Von see Von Amira, Karl.
Amiran, David H. K. & Wilson, Andrew H., eds. Coastal Deserts: Their Natural & Human Environments. LC 73-76305. 207p. 1973. 22.50x (ISBN 0-8165-0312-5). U of Ariz Pr.
Amiri, Imamu see Harrison, Paul C.
Amiri, Imanu see Harrison, Paul C.
Amirie, Abbas, ed. The Persian Gulf & Indian Ocean in International Politics. 1975. 15.00x (ISBN 0-8139-0846-9). U Pr of Va.
Amir-Moez, Ali R. & Menzel, Donald H. Fun with Numbers, Lines & Angles. 32p. (gr. 3-6). 1981. pap. 2.50 (ISBN 0-87534-179-9). Highlights.
Amirsadeghi, Hossein, ed. Security Dimensions of the Persian Gulf. 320p. 1981. 35.00x (ISBN 0-312-70915-3). St Martin.
--Twentieth Century Iran. LC 77-9569. (Illus.). 328p. 1977. text ed. 45.00x (ISBN 0-8419-0325-5). Holmes & Meier.
Amirthanayagam, G. & Harrex, S. C., eds. Only Connect: Literary Perspectives East & West. 335p. 1981. pap. text ed. 20.45x (ISBN 0-7258-0197-2, Pub. by Flinders U Australia). Humanities.
Amirthanayagam, Guy. Asian & Western Writers in Dialogue. 224p. 1982. text ed. 24.50x (ISBN 0-333-27341-9, Pub. by Macmillan England). Humanities.
Amirthanayagam, Guy, ed. Writers in East-West Encounter: New Cultural Bearings. 240p. 1981. text ed. 25.50x (ISBN 0-333-27342-7, Pub. by Macmillan England). Humanities.
Amis, Edward S. Solvent Effects on Reaction Rates & Mechanisms. 1966. 73.50 (ISBN 0-12-057350-4). Acad Pr.
Amis, Edward S. & Hinton, James F. Solvent Effects on Chemical Phenomena. 1973. Vol. 1. 83.00 (ISBN 0-12-057301-6). Acad Pr.
Amis, John. Amiscellany: My Life, My Music. LC 85-1552. (Illus.). 280p. 1985. 24.95 (ISBN 0-571-13490-4). Faber & Faber.
Amis, Kingsley. The Alteration. LC 76-18961. 1977. 9.95 (ISBN 0-670-11522-3). Viking.
--Collected Poems, 1944-1979. 162p. 1980. 10.00 (ISBN 0-670-22910-5). Viking.
--The Faber Popular Reciter. Amis, Kingsley, ed. 256p. 1979. 17.95 (ISBN 0-571-11287-0); pap. 7.95 (ISBN 0-571-11339-7). Faber & Faber.
--Harold's Years: Impressions of the Harold Wilson Era. 12.95 (ISBN 0-7043-2143-2, Pub. by Quartet England). Charles River Bks.
--Jake's Thing. 1980. pap. 4.95 (ISBN 0-14-005096-5). Penguin.
--Jake's Thing. 1979. 11.95 (ISBN 0-670-40471-3). Viking.
--Lucky Jim. 1976. pap. 3.95 (ISBN 0-14-001648-1). Penguin.
--Lucky Jim. 15.95 (ISBN 0-317-28086-4, Pub. by Aeonian Pr). Amereon Ltd.
--New Maps of Hell. LC 74-15944. (Science Fiction Ser). 161p. 1975. Repr. 13.00x (ISBN 0-405-06321-0). Ayer Co Pubs.
--Stanley & the Women. 256p. 1985. 16.95 (ISBN 0-671-60317-5). Summit.
Amis, Kingsley, ed. The New Oxford Book of English Light Verse. 1978. 18.95 (ISBN 0-19-211862-5). Oxford U Pr.
Amis, Kingsley & Conquest, Robert, eds. Spectrum: A Science Fiction Anthology. 13.95 (ISBN 0-8488-0105-9, Pub. by Amereon Hse). Amereon Ltd.
Amis, Lola J. Native Son Notes. (Orig.). 1971. pap. 3.25 (ISBN 0-8220-0874-2). Cliffs.
Amis, Martin. Money: A Suicide Note. (Fiction Ser.). 368p. 1985. 16.95 (ISBN 0-670-80440-1). Viking.
--Other People. 1982. pap. 3.95 (ISBN 0-14-006006-5). Penguin.
Amishai-Maisels, Ziva. Gauguin's Religious Themes. Freedberg, S. J., ed. (Outstanding Dissertations in Fine Arts Ser.). (Illus.). 670p. 1985. Repr. of 1970 ed. 75.00 (ISBN 0-8240-6863-7). Garland Pub.
Amiss, John M. & Jones, Franklin D. The Use of Handbook Tables & Formulas. 22nd ed. Ryffel, Henry H., ed. LC 75-10949. (Illus.). 224p. 1984. 9.95 (ISBN 0-8311-1156-9). Indus Pr.
Amissah, A. N. The Contribution of the Courts to Government: A West African View. 1981. text ed. 62.00x (ISBN 0-19-825356-7). Oxford U Pr.
Amit, D. J. Field Theory: The Renormalization Group & Critical Phenomena. 2nd ed. 400p. 1984. 56.00x (ISBN 9971-966-10-7, Pub. by World Sci Singapore); pap. 26.00x (ISBN 9971-966-11-5). Taylor & Francis.
Amit, D. J., jt. ed. see Wiser, N.
Amit, Raphael, jt. ed. see Avriel, Mordecai.
Amitsur, S. A & Saltman, D. J., eds. Algebraists' Homage: Papers in Ring Theory & Related Topics. LC 82-18934. (Contemporary Mathematics Ser.: vol. 13). 412p. 1982. pap. 32.00 (ISBN 0-8218-5013-X, CONM/13). Am Math.
Amjad, Rashid. Private Industrial Investment in Pakistan, 1960-1970. LC 81-17996. (Cambridge South Asian Studies: No. 26). 256p. 1983. 47.50 (ISBN 0-521-23261-9). Cambridge U Pr.
Amjad, Rashid, jt. auth. see Ahmed, Viqar.
Amjad, Rashid, ed. The Development of Labou-Intensive Industry in ASEAN Countries. 337p. 1981. 15.00 (ISBN 92-2-102750-3); pap. 10.00 (ISBN 92-2-102751-1). Intl Labour Office.
Amjad-Ali, Charles & Pitcher, W. Alvin, eds. Liberation & Ethics: Essays in Religious Social Ethics in Honor of Gibson Winter. LC 83-73425. (Studies in Religion & Society). 233p. 1985. text ed. 24.95x (ISBN 0-913348-22-8). Ctr Sci Study.
Amkreutz, Johann, jt. ed. see Wilhelm, Carl.
Amlaw, Mary. From Praying Never to Praying Always. 100p. (Orig.). 1985. pap. 5.95 (ISBN 0-916134-69-5). Pueblo Pub Co.
Amling, Frederick. Investments. 5th ed. (Illus.). 704p. 1984. 30.95 (ISBN 0-13-504324-7). P-H.
--Principles of Investment. 3rd ed. (Plaid Ser.). 198p. 1983. pap. 12.95 (ISBN 0-87094-336-7). Dow Jones-Irwin.
Amling, Frederick & Droms, William C. Personal Financial Management. 1982. 28.95x (ISBN 0-256-02319-0). Irwin.
Amling, Frederick & Droms, William G. The Dow Jones-Irwin Guide to Personal Financial Planning. LC 81-67117. 514p. 1982. 24.95 (ISBN 0-87094-265-4). Dow Jones-Irwin.
Amlung, Susan, ed. see League of Women Voters of New York State.
Amman, F. & Wilson, R., eds. Energy Demand & Efficient Use. LC 81-2803. (Ettore Majorana International Science Series; Physical Sciences: Vol. 9). 470p. 1981. 75.00x (ISBN 0-306-40732-9, Plenum Pr). Plenum Pub.
Amman, J. C. A Dissertation on Speech. Baker, C., tr. (Eng.). 1966. 5.00 (ISBN 0-934454-29-9). Lubrecht & Cramer.
Amman, Jost. Kunstbuchlin: Two Hundred & Ninety-Three Renaissance Woodcuts for Artists & Illustrators. (Illus.). 10.25 (ISBN 0-8446-1532-3). Peter Smith.
--Two Hundred Ninety-Three Rennaissance Woodcuts for Artists & Illustrators: Jost Amman's Kunstbuchlein. LC 68-14561. 1968. pap. 5.95 (ISBN 0-486-21987-9). Dover.
Amman, Jost & Sachs, Hans. Book of Trades (Standebuch) Appelbaum, Stanley, tr. from Ger. LC 72-75581. (Pictorial Archive Ser.). Orig. Title: Eygentliche Beschreibung Aller Stande Auff Erden. (Illus.). 1973. Repr. of 1568 ed. 4.95 (ISBN 0-486-22886-X). Dover.
--The Book of Trades (Standebuch) (Illus.). 13.25 (ISBN 0-8446-4618-0). Peter Smith.
Amman, L. A. Self Liberation. 1981. pap. 8.95 (ISBN 0-87728-511-X). Weiser.

Ammann, Herman. Canterbury Tale from the Wife of Bath. (Illus.). 33p. (Director's Production Script). 1970. pap. 6.00 (ISBN 0-88680-019-6). I E Clark.

Ammann, Hermann. Ghost for Rosanda. (Illus.). 47p. (Director's Production Script). 1974. pap. 5.00 (ISBN 0-88680-072-2). I E Clark.

--Little Match Girl. (Illus.). 36p. (Director's Production Script). 1970. pap. 6.00 (ISBN 0-88680-112-5). I E Clark.

--Magic Well. (Illus.). 37p. (Director's Production Script). 1972. pap. 5.00 (ISBN 0-88680-123-0). I E Clark.

--Steadfast Tin Soldier. (Illus.). 29p. (Director's production Script). 1969. pap. 5.00 (ISBN 0-88680-187-7). I E Clark.

Ammann, Karl, jt. auth. see Ammann, Kathrine.

Ammann, Kathrine & Ammann, Karl. Cheetah. (Illus.). 136p. 1985. 29.95 (ISBN 0-668-06259-2). Arco.

Ammar, Hamed. Growing up in an Egyptian Village. 1967. lib. bdg. 23.00x (ISBN 0-374-90171-6). Octagon.

Amme, Carl H., Jr. NATO Without France: A Strategic Appraisal. LC 67-31025. (Publications Ser.: No. 67). (Illus.). 195p. 1967. 9.95x (ISBN 0-8179-1671-7). Hoover Inst Pr.

Ammen, C. W. Casting Aluminum. (Illus.). 252p. (Orig.). 1985. 18.95 (ISBN 0-8306-0910-5, 1910); pap. 11.95 (ISBN 0-8306-1910-0). TAB Bks.

--Casting Brass. (Illus.). 252p. (Orig.). 1985. 18.95 (ISBN 0-8306-0810-9, 1810); pap. 11.95 (ISBN 0-8306-1810-4). TAB Bks.

--Casting Iron. (Illus.). 196p. 1984. o.p 15.95 (ISBN 0-8306-0210-0, 1610); pap. 10.25 (ISBN 0-8306-0610-6). TAB Bks.

--The Complete Handbook of Sand Casting. (Illus.). 1979. pap. 9.95 (ISBN 0-8306-1043-X, 1043). TAB Bks.

--Constructing & Using Wood Patterns. (Illus.). 266p. 1983. 17.95 (ISBN 0-8306-0110-4, 1510); pap. 12.50 (ISBN 0-8306-1510-5). TAB Bks.

--Lost Wax Investment Casting. LC 76-8598. 1977. pap. 9.25 (ISBN 0-8306-6725-3, 725). TAB Bks.

--Recovery & Refining of Precious Metals. LC 83-12355. (Illus.). 400p. 1984. pap. 24.95 (ISBN 0-442-20934-7). Van Nos Reinhold.

Ammende, Ewald. Human Life in Russia. (Illus.). xii, 320p. Repr. of 1936 ed. 13.95x (ISBN 0-939738-54-6). Zubal Inc.

Ammer, Christine. The A to Z of Women's Health: A Concise Encyclopedia. 448p. 1983. 19.95 (ISBN 0-87196-785-5). Facts on File.

--Harper's Dictionary of Music. LC 77-134280. (Illus.). 1972. 20.14i (ISBN 0-06-010113-X, HarpT). Har-Row.

--Harper's Dictionary of Music. (Illus.). 414p. 1973. pap. 5.50 (ISBN 0-06-463347-0, EH 347). B&N NY.

--Musician's Handbook of Foreign Terms. 1971. pap. 7.95 (ISBN 0-02-870100-3). Schirmer Bks.

--Unsung: A History of Women in American Music. LC 79-52324. (Contributions in Women's Studies: No. 14). 1980. lib. bdg. 29.95x (ISBN 0-313-22007-7, AMU/, AMU). Greenwood.

Ammer, Christine & Ammer, Dean S. Dictionary of Business & Economics. rev. & expanded ed. 508p. 1984. 29.95 (ISBN 0-02-900790-9). Free Pr.

Ammer, Christine & Sidley, Nathan T. The Common Sense Guide to Mental Health Care. LC 82-14850. 1982. pap. 11.95 (ISBN 0-86616-019-1). Greene.

Ammer, Dean S. Materials Management & Purchasing. 4th ed. 1980. 33.95x (ISBN 0-256-02146-5). Irwin.

--Profit-Conscious Purchasing: A Treasury of Newly-Developed Cost-Reduction Methods. 75.50 (ISBN 0-85013-086-7). Dartnell Corp.

--Purchasing & Materials Management for Health-Care Institutions. 2nd ed. LC 83-47985. 288p. 1983. 21.50x (ISBN 0-669-04908-5). Lexington Bks.

Ammer, Dean S., jt. auth. see Ammer, Christine.

Ammerman, Albert J. & Cavalli-Sforza, L. L. The Neolithic Transition & the Genetics of Populations in Europe. LC 84-42587. (Illus.). 196p. 1984. text ed. 25.00x (ISBN 0-691-08357-6). Princeton U Pr.

Ammerman, David. In the Common Cause: American Response to the Coercive Acts of 1774. LC 74-2417. pap. 46.00 (ISBN 0-317-30462-3, 2024835). Bks Demand UMI.

Ammerman, David L., jt. ed. see Tate, Thad W.

Ammerman, Gale. Your Future in Food Technology Careers. rev. ed. LC 74-17126. (Careers in Depth Ser.). (Illus.). 160p. (YA) (gr. 7-12). 1980. PLB 8.97 (ISBN 0-8239-0528-4). Rosen Group.

Ammerman, Leila T. Inspiring Devotional Programs for Women's Groups. (Paperback Program Ser). 1971. pap. 3.50 (ISBN 0-8010-0015-7). Baker Bk.

--Installation Services That Inspire. LC 81-67371. 1982. pap. 5.50 (ISBN 0-8054-3616-2). Broadman.

Ammianus, Marcellinus. Auszuge Aus Ammianus Marcellinus. pap. 10.00 (ISBN 0-384-01130-6). Johnson Repr.

Ammianus Marcellinus. Roman History, 3 Vols. (Loeb Classical Library: No. 300, 315, 331). 12.50x ea. Vol. 1, Bks. 14-19 (ISBN 0-674-99331-4). Vol. 2, Bks. 20-26 (ISBN 0-674-99348-9). Vol. 3, Bks. 27-31 (ISBN 0-674-99365-9). Harvard U Pr.

Ammirati, J. F., et al. Poisonous Mushrooms of the Northern United States & Canada. (Illus.). Date not set. 75.00 (ISBN 0-8166-1407-5). U of Minn Pr.

Ammirati, Joseph F., jt. auth. see Laursen, Gary A.

Ammirato, Philip, et al, eds. Handbook of Plant Cell Culture: Crop Species, Vol. 3. (Handbook of Plant Cell Culture Ser.). 650p. 1984. 53.00 (ISBN 0-02-949010-3). Macmillan.

Ammon, Friedrich von see Von Ammon, Friedrich.

Ammon, G. A. Soviet Navy in War & Peace. 160p. 1981. 5.80 (ISBN 0-8285-2223-5, Pub. by Progress Pubs USSR). Imported Pubns.

Ammon, Harry. The Genet Mission. (Essays in American History Ser.). 208p. 1973. 6.95x (ISBN 0-393-05475-6); pap. text ed. 3.95x (ISBN 0-393-09420-0). Norton.

Ammon, Jeanne E. & Etzel, Mary E. Sensorimotor Organization in Reach & Prehension: A Developmental Model. 1977. pap. 2.50 (ISBN 0-912452-19-6). Am Phys Therapy Assn.

Ammon, Solomon R. History & Present Development of Indian Schools in the United States. LC 75-5367. 1975. Repr. of 1935 ed. soft bdg. 10.95 (ISBN 0-88247-345-X). R & E Pubs.

Ammon, Ulrich, ed. Dialect & Standard in Highly Industrialized Societies. (International Journal of the Sociology of Language: No. 21). 1979. text ed. 14.40x (ISBN 90-279-7858-1). Mouton.

Ammons, A. R. Briefings. LC 70-119696. 1971. 6.00 (ISBN 0-393-04326-6). Norton.

--A Coast of Trees. 1981. 12.95 (ISBN 0-393-01447-9); pap. 4.95 (ISBN 0-393-00051-6). Norton.

--Collected Poems: 1951-1971. 396p. 1972. 17.50 (ISBN 0-393-04241-3). Norton.

--Corsons Inlet. 1965. 5.95 (ISBN 0-393-04463-7). Norton.

--Diversifications: Poems. 98p. 1975. 6.95 (ISBN 0-393-04414-9). Norton.

--Lake Effect Country: Poems. 1983. 15.50 (ISBN 0-393-01702-8); pap. 5.95 (ISBN 0-393-30104-4). Norton.

--Northfield Poems. 1966. 5.95 (ISBN 0-393-04462-9). Norton.

--Selected Longer Poems. 1980. 14.95 (ISBN 0-393-01297-2); pap. 4.95 (ISBN 0-393-00962-9). Norton.

--The Selected Poems: Nineteen Fifty One-Nineteen Seventy Seven. 1977. pap. 5.95 (ISBN 0-393-04470-X). Norton.

--The Snow Poems. 1977. 12.50 (ISBN 0-393-04467-X). Norton.

--Worldly Hopes: Poems. 51p. 1982. 12.95 (ISBN 0-393-01518-1); pap. 5.95 (ISBN 0-393-00081-8). Norton.

Ammons, David. Municipal Productivity: A Comparison of Fourteen High-Quality Service Cities. LC 83-17821. 320p. 1984. 32.95 (ISBN 0-03-069387-X). Praeger.

Ammons, Elizabeth. Edith Wharton's Argument with America. LC 79-48000. 222p. 1980. 17.00x (ISBN 0-8203-0513-8). U of Ga Pr.

Ammons, Nelle P., jt. auth. see Core, Earl L.

Ammons, Pamela, et al. Skiing for Women. (Illus.). 1979. 9.95 (ISBN 0-88280-052-3); pap. 5.95 (ISBN 0-88280-053-1). ETC Pubns.

Amnesty International. Democratic Republic of Afghanistan: Background Briefing on Amnesty International's Concerns. LC 84-224230. write for info. Amnesty Intl USA.

--Prisoners of Conscience in the USSR: Their Treatment & Conditions. 220p. 1981. 25.00x (ISBN 0-905898-09-5, Pub. by Quartermaine England). State Mutual Bk.

--Torture in the Eighties. (Illus.). 224p. 1984. pap. 5.95 (ISBN 0-939994-06-2). Amnesty Intl USA.

Amnesty International & Terry, Fernando B. Peru, Torture & Extrajudicial Executions: Letter of Amnesty International to President Fernando Belaunde Terry, August 1983. LC 84-223588. Date not set. price not set. Amnesty Intl USA.

Amnesty International Publications. Amnesty International Report 1984. 392p. 1984. pap. 6.95. Dodd.

Amnesty International Staff. Memeorandum to the Head of State Concerning Amnesty International's Mission to Zaire in July 1981. LC 84-193671. (Illus.). write for info. Amer Bar Assn.

Amnesty International U. S. A. Human Rights Violations in the Phillipines: An Account of Torture Disappearance, Extrajudicial Executions & Illegal Detention. LC 82-241911. Date not set. price not set. Amnesty Intl USA.

Amneus, Daniel. The Mystery of Macbeth. 1983. 10.00 (ISBN 0-9610864-0-8); pap. 7.00 (ISBN 0-9610864-1-6). Primrose Pr.

Amneus, Nils. Does Chance or Justice Rule Our Lives? 97p. 1972. pap. 2.00 (ISBN 0-913004-08-1). Point Loma Pub.

--Life's Riddle. 1975. pap. 5.25 (ISBN 0-913004-26-X). Point Loma Pub.

Amoako, Kingsley Y. Balance of Payments Problems & Exchange Rate Policy: The Ghanaian Experience. 25.00 (ISBN 0-8240-4149-6). Garland Pub.

Amodeo, Sandy. Julian, Julian. 1984. 22.00 (ISBN 0-318-03661-4); pap. 11.00 (ISBN 0-318-03663-0) (ISBN 0-318-03664-9). CLCB Pr.

Amodia, Jose. Franco's Political Legacy: From Dictatorship to Facade Democracy. 348p. 1977. 17.50x (ISBN 0-87471-937-2). Rowman.

Amoia, Alba. The Italian Theatre Today: Twelve Interviews. LC 76-51033. 1977. 12.50x (ISBN 0-87875-107-6). Whitston Pub.

Amoia, Alba, et al, trs. from Fr. An Anthology of Modern Belgian Theatre. LC 81-50286. 288p. 1981. 22.50x (ISBN 0-87875-215-3). Whitston Pub.

Amon, Aline. The Earth Is Sore: Native Americans on Nature. LC 80-36854. (Illus.). 96p. (gr. 5 up). 1981. PLB 9.95 (ISBN 0-689-30798-5). Atheneum.

--Orangutan: Endangered Ape. LC 76-41354. (Illus.). 160p. (gr. 4-6). 1977. 7.95 (ISBN 0-689-30563-X). Atheneum.

Amon Carter Museum. Amon Carter Museum: Nineteen Sixty-One to Nineteen Seventy-Seven. LC 77-81806. (Illus.). 47p. 1977. pap. 3.50 (ISBN 0-88360-028-5). Amon Carter.

--Future Directions for Museums of American Art. LC 80-80501. 68p. 1980. pap. 7.95 (ISBN 0-88360-033-1). Amon Carter.

Amon Carter Museum, jt. auth. see Palmquist, Peter E.

Amon, Rene, et al. Steel Design for Engineers & Architects. 432p. 1982. 39.50 (ISBN 0-442-20297-0). Van Nos Reinhold.

Amon, Von. Broken Dolls. LC 81-14943. 1985. 16.95 (ISBN 0-87949-183-3). Ashley Bks.

Amonoo, Ben. Ghana, 1957-1966: Politics of Institutional Dualism. 288p. 1981. text ed. 35.00x (ISBN 0-04-320147-4). Allen Unwin.

Amoore, John E. Molecular Basis of Odor. (Illus.). 216p. 1970. 21.00x (ISBN 0-398-00039-5). C C Thomas.

Amoore, Susannah, et al. Poetry Introduction, No. 6. LC 70-424610. 112p. (Orig.). 1985. pap. 7.95 (ISBN 0-571-13543-9). Faber & Faber.

Amor, J. B. Everybody is an Idiot. 1982. 6.95 (ISBN 0-533-05224-6). Vantage.

AMORC, ed. see Poole, Cecil A.

AMORC, tr. see Bernard, Raymond.

AMORC Staff, tr. see Bernard, Raymond.

AMORC Staff, tr. see Cerve, Wishar S.

AMORC Staff, tr. see Cihlar, Many.

AMORC Staff, tr. see Lewis, H. Spencer.

AMORC Staff, tr. see Lewis, Ralph M.

AMORC Staff, tr. see Poole, Cecil A.

AMORC Staff, tr. see Ramatherio, Sri.

AMORC Staff, tr. see Validivar.

Amore, Adelaide, ed. A Woman's Inner World: Selected Poetry & Prose of Anne Bradstreet. LC 82-40198. 152p. (Orig.). 1982. lib. bdg. 22.25 (ISBN 0-8191-2639-X); pap. text ed. 9.25 (ISBN 0-8191-2640-3). U Pr of Amer.

Amore, Roy C. & Shinn, Larry D. Lustful Maidens & Ascetic Kings: Buddhist & Hindu Stories of Life. (Illus.). 176p. 1981. text ed. 18.95x (ISBN 0-19-502838-4); pap. 6.95 (ISBN 0-19-502839-2). Oxford U Pr.

Amore, Roy C., ed. Developments in Buddhist Thought: Canadian Contributions to Buddhist Studies. 196p. 1979. pap. text ed. 9.75x (ISBN 0-919812-11-2, Pub. by Wilfrid Laurier U Pr Canada). Humanities.

Amoretti, Giovanni see Marchione, Margherita & Scalia, S. Eugene.

Amoriell, Amelia & Lindbeck, Susan. Chesapeake Colors. LC 82-60329. (Illus.). 48p. 1982. pap. 2.95 (ISBN 0-87033-298-8). Tidewater.

Amoros, Andres. Bibliografia de Francisco Ayala. 95p. (Sp., Reprinted from Bibliothecay Hispana Novissima). 1973. Repr. 2.00 (ISBN 0-317-34205-3). Hispanic Soc.

Amoros, Jose L., et al. The Laue Method. 1975. 78.00 (ISBN 0-12-057450-0). Acad Pr.

Amorosi, A. & American Nuclear Society Standards Committee Staff. Survey on Usefulness & Future Emphasis of the ANS Standards Effort. LC 83-181285. (Illus.). ii, 44p. 1983. 25.00 (ISBN 0-317-12891-4). Am Nuclear Soc.

Amorosi, Ray. Flim Flam. 64p. 1980. 8.50 (ISBN 0-89924-030-5); pap. 5.00 (ISBN 0-89924-029-1). Lynx Hse.

--A Generous Wall. LC 76-27961. 1976. pap. 4.50 (ISBN 0-89924-008-9). Lynx Hse.

Amoroso, G. G. & Passina, V. Stone Decay & Conservation: Atmospheric Pollution, Cleaning, Consolidation & Protection. (Materials Science Monographs: Vol. 11). 453p. 1983. 98.00 (ISBN 0-444-42146-7, I-269-83). Elsevier.

Amoroso, S. & Ingargiola, G. Ada: An Introduction to Program Design & Coding. 368p. 1985. text ed. 32.50 (ISBN 0-273-01818-3). Pitman Pub MA.

Amort, Eusebio. Vetus Disciplina Canocorum Regularium & Saecularium ex Documentis Magna Parte Hucusque Ineditis a Temporibus Apostolicis ad Saeculum XVII. 1112p. 1747. text ed. 248.40x (ISBN 0-576-99833-8, Pub. by Gregg Intl Pubs England). Gregg Intl.

Amory, Anne R., jt. auth. see Hammond, Mason.

Amory, Cleveland. Man Kind? 9.95x. Cancer Control Soc.

--The Proper Bostonians. 384p. 1984. pap. 9.95 (ISBN 0-940160-25-0). Parnassus Imprints.

--The Trouble with Nowadays: A Curmudgeon Strikes Back. LC 79-52255. 1979. 10.00 (ISBN 0-87795-238-8). Arbor Hse.

Amory, Hugh. Bute Broadsides in the Houghton Library Harvard University, Guide & Index to the Microfilm Collection. LC 81-11939. 98p. 1981. 50.00 (ISBN 0-89235-025-3). Res Pubns Conn.

Amory, Mark, ed. The Letters of Evelyn Waugh. 684p. 1982. pap. 8.95 (ISBN 0-14-004595-3). Penguin.

Amory, Martha B. The Domestic & Artistic Life of John Singleton Copley. LC 71-77698. (Library of American Art Ser.). 1969. Repr. of 1882 ed. lib. bdg. 49.50 (ISBN 0-306-71336-5). Da Capo.

--Domestic & Artistic Life of John Singleton Copley, R.A. facs. ed. LC 70-119925. (Select Bibliographies Reprint Ser.). 1882. 27.50 (ISBN 0-8369-5368-1). Ayer Co Pubs.

Amory, Thomas C. Military Services & Public Life of Major-General John Sullivan. LC 68-26264. 1968. Repr. of 1868 ed. 24.50x (ISBN 0-8046-0011-2, Pub. by Kennikat). Assoc Faculty Pr.

Amos, Arthur K., Jr. Time, Space, & Value: The Narrative Structure of the "New Arcadia". LC 74-30862. 203p. 1976. 20.00 (ISBN 0-8387-1614-8). Bucknell U Pr.

Amos, Ashley C. Linguistic Means of Determining the Dates of Old English Literary Texts. LC 79-89570. 1980. 22.00x (ISBN 0-910956-70-7). Medieval Acad.

Amos, Bernard, ed. Progress in Immunology. 1971. 153.00 (ISBN 0-12-057550-7). Acad Pr.

Amos, D. A Fisherman's Guide to Echo Soundings & Sonar Equipment: Acoustic Fish Detection Instruments. (Marine Bulletin Ser.: No. 41). 68p. 1980. 2.00 (ISBN 0-938412-30-2, P870). URI MAS.

--Single Vessel Midwater Trawling. (Marine Bulletin Ser.: No. 43). 30p. 1980. 2.00 (ISBN 0-938412-26-4, P872). URI MAS.

Amos, D. Bernard, et al, eds. Immune Mechanisms & Disease. LC 79-19241. 1979. 44.00 (ISBN 0-12-055850-5). Acad Pr.

Amos, Dan. Soils & Its Uses. 1979. text ed. 15.95 (ISBN 0-8359-7038-8); instrs' manual avail. (ISBN 0-8359-7039-6). Reston.

Amos, H. D. & Lang, A. G. These Were the Greeks. LC 81-71846. (Illus.). 224p. (Orig.). 1982. pap. 12.95 (ISBN 0-8023-1275-6). Dufour.

Amos, Harriet E. Cotton City: Urban Development in Antebellum Mobile. LC 84-189. (Illus.). 320p. 1985. 34.50 (ISBN 0-8173-0218-2). U of Ala Pr.

Amos, John M. & Sarchet, Bernard R. Management for Engineers. (Series in Industrial Systems Engineering). (Illus.). 384p. 1981. text ed. 25.95 (ISBN 0-13-549402-8). P-H.

Amos, John W. Arab-Israeli Military Political Relations: Arab Perceptions & the Politics of Escalation. 1979. text ed. 46.00 (ISBN 0-08-023865-3). Pergamon.

Amos, Linda K., et al. Patterns in Education: The Unfolding of Nursing. 178p. 1985. 18.95 (ISBN 0-88737-140-X, 15-1974). Natl League Nurse.

Amos, Martha T. Fanny & the Indy 500 Trophy. (Illus.). 48p. (gr. 1-6). 1985. 5.95 (ISBN 0-8059-2990-8). Dorrance.

--Fanny Runs in Honolulu. (Illus.). 48p. 1981. 5.00 (ISBN 0-682-49718-5). Exposition Pr FL.

--Fanny Runs the Bass Lake Runaround. (Illus.). 48p. (gr. 1-6). 1983. 5.95 (ISBN 0-8059-2861-8). Dorrance.

--Fanny the Soccer Star. (Illus.). 1979. 5.50 (ISBN 0-682-49455-0). Exposition Pr FL.

Amos, Peter. Side Effects. 176p. 1983. 10.95 (ISBN 0-312-72332-6). St Martin.

Amos, S. W. Dictionary of Electronics. 336p. 1981. 39.95 (ISBN 0-408-00331-6). Butterworth.

Amos, Sheldon. Lectures on International Law: Delivered in the Middle Temple Hall to the Students of the Inns of Court. xii, 136p. 1983. Repr. of 1874 ed. lib. bdg. 24.00x (ISBN 0-8377-0215-1). Rothman.

--Political & Legal Remedies for War. 254p. 1982. Repr. of 1880 ed. lib. bdg. 24.00x (ISBN 0-8377-0213-5). Rothman.

--Science of Law. (The International Scientific Ser.: Vol. X). xx, 417p. 1982. Repr. of 1875 ed. lib. bdg. 32.50x (ISBN 0-8377-0209-7). Rothman.

--Systematic View of the Science of Jurisprudence. xxii, 545p. 1982. Repr. of 1872 ed. lib. bdg. 39.50x (ISBN 0-8377-0210-0). Rothman.

Amos, Stephen, jt. auth. see Amos, William.

Amos, W. B. & Duckett, J. G., eds. Prokaryotic & Euraryotic Flagella. LC 81-38467. (Society for Experimental Biology Symposia: No. 35). 450p. 1982. 87.50 (ISBN 0-521-24228-2). Cambridge U Pr.

Amos, W. M. Basic Immunology. 210p. 1981. text ed. 14.95 (ISBN 0-407-00178-6). Butterworth.

Amos, William & Amos, Stephen. Atlantic & Gulf Coasts. Date not set. price not set. Knopf.

--Atlantic Coast. Elliott, Charles, ed. LC 84-48676. (Audubon Society Nature Guides Ser.). (Illus.). 256p. 1985. pap. 14.95 (ISBN 0-394-73109-3). Knopf.

Amos, William E. & Manella, Raymond L. Readings in the Administration of Institutions for Delinquent Youth. 228p. 1965. 18.75x (ISBN 0-398-00041-7). C C Thomas.

Amos, William E. & Orem, Reginald C. Managing Student Behavior. LC 67-26008. pap. 41.80 (ISBN 0-317-29232-3, 2055538). Bks Demand UMI.

Amos, William E. & Williams, David E. Community Counseling. LC 71-154110. 244p. 1972. 10.00 (ISBN 0-87527-092-1). Green.

Amos, William E., jt. ed. see Newman, Charles L.

Amos, William E., ed. see Stevens, George L.

Amos, William H. Life in Ponds & Streams. Crump, Donald J., ed. LC 81-47745. (Books for Young Explorers Ser.: Set 8). 32p. (ps-3). 1981. 12.20 (ISBN 0-87044-404-2). Natl Geog.
--Wildlife of the Islands. (Wildlife Habitat Ser.). (Illus.). 1980. 19.95 (ISBN 0-8109-1763-7). Abrams.
--Wildlife of the Rivers. LC 80-21928. (Wildlife Habitat Ser.). (Illus.). 232p. 1981. 19.95 (ISBN 0-8109-1767-X). Abrams.
Amos, William H. see National Geographic Society.
Amos, Winsom. Like a Dream. 15p. 1971. pap. 1.00x (ISBN 0-9600520-1-1). W Amos.
--Oriole to Black Mood. (Black Literature Ser.). (Illus.). 24p. (Orig.). 1973. pap. 1.00x. W Amos.
--Surprise! 63p. (Orig.). 1982. pap. 2.00 (ISBN 0-932510-01-9). Soma Pr.
--Youth Poems. (Illus.). 24p. (Orig.). (gr. 6-12). 1983. pap. 1.75 (ISBN 0-932510-00-0). Soma Pr.
Amos Bad Heart Bull, see Bad Heart Bull, Amos & Blish, Helen H.
Amoss, Berthe. The Chalk Cross. LC 75-4778. 160p. (gr. 6 up). 1976. 6.95 (ISBN 0-395-28887-8, Clarion). HM.
--The Loup Garou. LC 79-20536. (Illus.). 48p. (ps-4). 1979. 7.95 (ISBN 0-88289-189-8). Pelican.
--Secret Lives. 192p. (gr. 1-9). 1981. pap. 1.95 (ISBN 0-440-47904-5, YB). Dell.
--Secret Lives. LC 79-16717. (gr. 5 up). 1979. 8.95 (ISBN 0-316-03740-0, Pub. by Atlantic-Little Brown). Little.
Amoss, Harold L., ed. see Western Resources Conference, 3rd, Colorado State University, 1961.
Amoss, Pamela T. & Harrell, Stevan, eds. Other Ways of Growing Old: Anthropological Perspectives. LC 79-66056. 1981. 22.50x (ISBN 0-8047-1072-4); pap. 7.95 (ISBN 0-8047-1153-4, SP 13). Stanford U Pr.
Amour, Louis L' see L'Amour, Louis.
Amours, Francois J., ed. Scottish Alliterative Poems in Riming Stanzas. 43.50 (ISBN 0-384-01135-7). Johnson Repr.
Amowitz, Georgette W. And After the Journey. (Educational Dance Score Registry Ser.: No. 9). (Illus.). 14p. 1984. dance score 20.00 (ISBN 0-932582-38-9). Dance Notation.
Ampalavanar, Rajeswary. The Indian Minority & Political Change in Malaya: 1945-1957. (East Asian Historical Monographs). (Illus.). 1981. 37.50x (ISBN 0-19-580473-2). Oxford U Pr.
Ampco Metal Division. Properties of Incramute I Castings. 85p. 1974. 12.75 (ISBN 0-317-34541-9, 209). Intl Copper.
Ampco Metal, Inc. The Establishment of Foundry Procedures & Evaluation of Mechanical & Chemical Criteria (of INCRAMET 800) as Pertinent to Industries Other than Glass Making. 86p. 1965. 12.90 (ISBN 0-317-34522-2, 52). Intl Copper.
Amper, Julie, ed. see Byrd, Robert.
Amper, Julie, ed. see Christian, Mary B.
Amper, Julie, ed. see Cormley, Beatrice.
Amper, Julie, ed. see Hines, Anna G.
Amper, Julie, ed. see Hopper, Nancy J.
Ampere, Jean J. Melanges d'Histoire Litteraire et de Litterature, 2 Vols. (Classics in Art & Literary Criticism Ser). (Fr). Repr. of 1867 ed. Set. lib. bdg. 85.00 (ISBN 0-384-01203-5). Johnson Repr.
Amphlett, C. B., ed. Uses of Cyclotrons in Chemistry, Metallurgy & Biology. (Illus.). 1970. 32.75 (ISBN 0-8088-0029-9). Davey.
Amphlett, Hilda. Who Was Shakespeare? LC 72-126768. Repr. of 1955 ed. 21.50 (ISBN 0-404-00325-7). AMS Pr.
Amphlett, John & Rea, Carleton. Botany of Worcestershire. 688p. 50.00x (ISBN 0-7158-1338-2, Pub. by EP Pub England). State Mutual Bk.
Amphoto Corporation. Thirty-Five Millimeter Photography Simplified. rev. ed. (Modern Photo Guides Ser). (Illus.). 96p. 1974. Repr. 7.95t (ISBN 0-13-918888-6, Spec). P-H.
Amphoto Editorial Board, jt. auth. see Ahlers, Arvel.
Amphoto Staff, ed. Landscape Photography. (Illus.). 144p. 1984. 27.50 (ISBN 0-8174-4154-9, Amphoto). Watson-Guptill.
Amphoux, Nancy, tr. see Deshimaru, Taisen.
Amphoux, Nancy, tr. see Troyat, Henri.
Ampion Piano Player Co. How to Test & Regulate the Artecho, Apollo & Celco Reproducing Medium. Adams, Frank, ed. (Illus.). 24p. 1984. Repr. deluxe ed. 12.95 (ISBN 0-913599-44-1, R-286). AMR Pub Co.
Ampola, Mary G. Metabolic Diseases in Pediatric Practice. 1982. text ed. 35.00 (ISBN 0-316-03796-6). Little.
Amprimoz, Alexandre L. La Poesie Erotique de Germain Nouveau: Une Lecture des Valentines. (Stanford French & Italian Studies: Vol. 28). 128p. 1983. pap. 25.00 (ISBN 0-915838-09-5). Anma Libri.
Amr, et al. Energy Systems in the United States. (Energy, Power & Environment Ser.: Vol. 12). 1981. 69.75 (ISBN 0-8247-1275-7). Dekker.
AMR Publishing Company Staff, ed. see Seeburg Corporation.
Amram, David. Makers of Hebrew Books in Italy. 350p. 1983. 55.00 (ISBN 0-87556-013-X). Saifer.
--Vibrations: The Adventures & Musical Times of David Amram. LC 79-24422. (Illus.). 469p. 1980. Repr. of 1968 ed. lib. bdg. 32.50x (ISBN 0-313-22230-4, AMVI). Greenwood.
Amranand, P. & Gaas, W. Macroeconomic & Distributional Implications of Sectoral Policy Interventions: The Case of Energy & Rice in Thailand. 200p. 5.00 (ISBN 0-318-02815-8, WP0627). World Bank.
Amrein, W. O. Non-Relativistic Quantum Dynamics. viii, 237p. 1981. pap. 34.50 (ISBN 90-277-1324-3, Pub. by Reidell Holland). Kluwer Academic.
Amrine, Bill, ed. see Amrine, Lowell.
Amrine, Frederick, tr. see Steiner, Rudolf.
Amrine, Harold & Ritchey, John A. Manufacturing Organization & Management. 4th ed. (Illus.). 576p. 1982. 32.95 (ISBN 0-13-555748-8). P-H.
Amrine, Lowell. Sierra Railroad: A Portfolio. Amrine, Bill, ed. (Illus.). 32p. 1980. pap. 6.95 (ISBN 0-936616-01-6). Galliard Pr.
Amrine, Lowell & Jamieson, Tom. Six Axle Quartet: An Essay of Diesel Portraiture. LC 80-65901. (Illus.). 96p. 1980. pap. 12.95 (ISBN 0-936616-00-8). Galliard Pr.
Amritachandra. Purushartha-Siddhyupaya (Jaina-Pravachana-Rahasya-Kosha) Prasada, Ajit, ed. & tr. LC 73-3838. (The Sacred Books of the Jainas: No. 4). Repr. of 1933 ed. 22.50 (ISBN 0-404-57704-0). AMS Pr.
Amritananda Das. Foundations of Gandhian Economics. LC 79-17126. 1980. 19.95 (ISBN 0-312-30005-0). St Martin.
Amsalem, Michel A. Technology Choice in Developing Countries: The Textile & Pulp & Paper Industries. (Illus.). 224p. 1983. 30.00x (ISBN 0-262-01072-0). MIT Pr.
Amsbury. Bridge: Bidding Naturally. 1979. pap. 9.95 (ISBN 0-7134-1620-3, Pub. by Batsford England). David & Charles.
--Data Structures: From Arrays to Priority Queues. 544p. 1985. write for info. (ISBN 0-534-04590-1). Wadsworth Pub.
Amsbury, Joe & Payne, Dick. Bridge: Step-by-Step Card Play-No Trumps. (Illus.). 176p. 1981. (Pub. by Batsford England); pap. 9.95 (ISBN 0-7134-4154-2). David & Charles.
Amsbury, Wayne. Structured BASIC & Beyond. LC 80-18382. 310p. 1980. pap. 19.95 (ISBN 0-914894-16-1). Computer Sci.
Amsden, Alice H. International Firms & Labour in Kenya, 1945-1970. 186p. 1971. 30.00x (ISBN 0-7146-2581-7, F Cass Co). Biblio Dist.
Amsden, Alice H., ed. The Economics of Women & Work. LC 80-15970. 1980. pap. 12.95 (ISBN 0-312-23671-9). St Martin.
Amsden, Charles A. Navaho Weaving, Its Technic & History. (Beautiful Rio Grande Classic Ser.). (Illus.). 460p. Repr. of 1934 ed. 20.00 (ISBN 0-87380-017-6). Rio Grande.
--Prehistoric Southwesterners from Basketmaker to Pueblo. LC 76-43642. Repr. of 1949 ed. 25.00 (ISBN 0-404-15477-8). AMS Pr.
--Prehistoric Southwesterners from Basketmaker to Pueblo. 1976. Repr. of 1949 ed. 5.00 (ISBN 0-916561-57-7). Southwest Mus.
Amsden, Constance, ed. see Myers, John A.
Amsden, Davida M. & Amsden, Robert T., eds. QC Circles: Applications, Tools & Theory. 174p. 10.00 (ISBN 0-318-13230-3, 104); members 8.50 (ISBN 0-318-13231-1). Am Soc QC.
Amsden, Monroe. Archeological Reconnaisance in Sonora. (Illus.). 51p. 1970. Repr. of 1928 ed. 5.00 (ISBN 0-916561-08-9). Southwest Mus.
Amsden, Robert T., jt. auth. see Cleary, Michael J.
Amsden, Robert T., jt. ed. see Amsden, Davida M.
Amsden, Thomas W. Stratigraphy & Paleontology of the Brownsport Formation (Silurian) of Western Tennessee. 1949. 85.00x (ISBN 0-686-50033-4). Elliots Bks.
AMSE. Spent Nuclear Fuel Heat Transfer; Fuel Casks & Transfer Operations: Proceedings of AMSE, Annual Winter Meeting, December 1971. Groetch, D. J. & Todreas, N., eds. LC 79-180673. (American Society of Mechanical Engineers, Heat Transfer Division Ser.: Vol. 2). pap. 20.00 (ISBN 0-317-09924-8, 2016901). Bks Demand UMI.
Amse-De Jong, Tine H. The Meaning of the Finite Verb Forms in the Old Church Slavonic Codex Suprasliensis: A Synchronic Study. (Slavistic Printings & Reprintings Ser.: No. 319). 228p. (Orig.). 1974. pap. text ed. 36.00x (ISBN 90-2793-012-0). Mouton.
Amsel. Judaism & Psychology. pap. 4.95 (ISBN 0-87306-064-4). Feldheim.
Amsel, Abram & Rashotte, Michael E. Mechanisms of Adaptive Behavior: Clark L. Hull's Theoretical Papers with Commentary. 560p. 1984. 35.00 (ISBN 0-231-05792-X). Columbia U Pr.
Amsel, Avrohom. Rational Irrational Man: Torah Psychology. 1976. 9.95 (ISBN 0-87306-129-2). Feldheim.
Amsenga, B. J., et al, eds. Miscellanea Slavica: To Honour the Memor of Jan M. Meijer. 542p. 1983. pap. text ed. 69.50x (ISBN 90-6203-606-6, Pub. by Rodopi Holland). Humanities.
--Voz'Mi Na Radost', Festschrift in Honour of Jeanne Van der Eng-Liedmeier: A Collection of Articles by Slavists All over the World, Presented to Jeanne Van der Eng on the Occasion of her 65th Birthday. 446p. (Eng., Ger., Russ.). 1980. pap. 39.00x (ISBN 90-9000-171-9). Benjamins North Am.
AMSS. Some Aspects of the Economics of Zakah. Date not set. price not set (ISBN 0-89259-019-X). Am Trust Pubns.
Amstead, B. H., et al. Manufacturing Processes. 7th ed. LC 78-16185. 739p. 1979. SI Version. text ed. 44.00x (ISBN 0-471-03575-0); 48.95 (ISBN 0-471-06245-6); solutions manual avail. Wiley.
Amstell, I. Joel. What You Should Know about Advertising. LC 69-19797. (Business Almanac Ser.: No. 17). (Illus.). 83p. 1969. 5.95 (ISBN 0-379-11217-5). Oceana.
Amster, Gerald & Asbell, Bernard. Transit Point Moscow. LC 84-10788. 256p. 1985. 15.95 (ISBN 0-03-064156-X). HR&W.
Amster, Warren. Neighbors of the Earth. (Illus.). 87p. (Orig.). 1984. pap. 5.95 (ISBN 0-86700-012-0). P Walsh Pr.
Amsterdam, Anthony G. Trial Manual Four for the Defense of Criminal Cases, 2 vols. 4th ed. 950p. 1984. looseleaf 175.00 (ISBN 0-317-30882-3, B440). Am Law Inst.
--Trial Manual Three for the Defense of Criminal Cases. 794p. 1977. looseleaf 35.00 (ISBN 0-317-30884-X, B181). Am Law Inst.
--Trial Manual Three for the Defense of Criminal Cases Supplement, No. 2. 304p. 1978. pap. 20.00 (ISBN 0-317-30887-4, B180). Am Law Inst.
Amsterdam, E. A. & James, W. E. Cardiac Ischemia & Arrhythmias. 1980. 55.50 (ISBN 0-8151-4848-8). Year Bk Med.
Amsterdam, E. A., ed. Drugs in Cardiovascular Disease. (Journal: Cardiology: Vol. 72, No. 5-6). (Illus.). viii, 148p. 1985. pap. 30.25 (ISBN 3-8055-4081-7). S Karger.
Amsterdam, Ezra A. & Holmes, Ann M. Take Care of Your Heart. (Illus.). 356p. 1984. 14.95 (ISBN 0-87196-731-6). Facts on File.
Amsterdam, Ezra A., et al, eds. Exercise in Cardiovascular Health & Disease. LC 77-82741. (Illus.). 1977. 42.50 (ISBN 0-914316-11-7). Yorke Med.
Amsterdam, Morton. The Distal Extension Case-Tooth-Tissue Borne Removable Appliance. Cohen, D. Walter, ed. (Continuing Dental Education Series). 128p. 1981. pap. 18.00 (ISBN 0-931386-30-6). Quint Pub Co.
Amsterdamska, Olga, tr. see Karpinski, Jakub.
Amsterdamski, Stefan. Between Experience & Metaphysics: Philosophical Problems of the Evolution of Science. Michalowski, P., tr. from Pol. LC 75-2184. (Boston Studies in the Philosophy of Science: No. 35). xviii, 193p. 1975. lib. bdg. 29.00 (ISBN 90-277-0568-2, Pub. by Reidel Holland); pap. 16.00 (ISBN 90-277-0580-1). Kluwer Academic.
Amstey, Marvin S., ed. Virus Infection in Pregnancy. (Monograph in Neonatology Ser.). 256p. 1984. 37.50 (ISBN 0-8089-1609-2, 790080). Grune.
Amstrup, C. R., et al. Suggested Fertilizer-Related Policies for Government & International Agencies. (Technical Bulletin T-10). 67p. (Orig.). 1978. pap. 4.00 (ISBN 0-88090-009-1). Intl Fertilizer.
Amstutz, Arnold E. Computer Simulation of Competitive Market Response. (Illus.). 1967. pap. 12.50x (ISBN 0-262-51009-X). MIT Pr.
Amstutz, Beverly. Benjamin & the Bible Donkeys. (Illus.). 36p. (gr. k-7). 1981. pap. 2.50x (ISBN 0-937836-03-6). Precious Res.
--The Fly Has Lots of Eyes. (Illus.). 34p. (gr. k-9). 1981. pap. 2.50x (ISBN 0-937836-04-4). Precious Res.
--I Love My Foster Grandparents. (Illus.). 24p. (gr. k-7). 1981. pap. 2.50x (ISBN 0-937836-06-0). Precious Res.
--Moccasins & Sneakers. (Illus.). 24p. (gr. k-7). 1980. pap. 2.50x (ISBN 0-937836-02-8). Precious Res.
--Sharing Is Fun. (Illus.). 24p. (gr. k-7). 1979. pap. 2.50x (ISBN 0-937836-00-1). Precious Res.
--Sprouts: A Diary for the Foster Child. (Illus.). 38p. (Orig.). (gr. k-7). 1982. pap. 2.50x (ISBN 0-937836-07-9). Precious Res.
--That Boy, That Girl. LC 80-80372. (Illus.). 24p. (gr. k-7). 1979. pap. 2.50x (ISBN 0-937836-01-X). Precious Res.
--Too Big for the Bag. (Illus.). (gr. k-7). 1981. pap. 2.50x (ISBN 0-937836-05-2). Precious Res.
--Touch Me Not! (Illus.). 20p. (ps-7). 1983. pap. 2.50x (ISBN 0-937836-09-5). Precious Res.
--You Are Number One! (Illus.). 30p. (gr. k-9). 1982. pap. 2.50x (ISBN 0-937836-08-7). Precious Res.
Amstutz, Eveline. Caterina. 1978. pap. 2.25 (ISBN 0-8439-0575-1, Leisure Bks). Dorchester Pub Co.
Amstutz, G. Glossary of Mining Geology. 196p. (Eng., Span., Fr. & Ger.). 1971. 36.50 (ISBN 3-432-01667-0, M-7428, Pub. by F. Enke). French & Eur.
Amstutz, G. C., ed. Ore Genesis: The State of the Art. (Illus.). 780p. 1982. 69.00 (ISBN 0-387-11139-5). Springer-Verlag.
--Spilites & Spilitic Rocks. (International Union of Geological Sciences: Ser. A, No. 4). (Illus.). 450p. 1974. 46.00 (ISBN 0-387-06448-6). Springer-Verlag.
Amstutz, G. C. & Bernard, A. J., eds. Ores in Sediments. (International Union of Geological Sciences: Ser. a, No. 3). (Illus.). 1973. pap. 36.00 (ISBN 0-387-05712-9). Springer-Verlag.
Amstutz, H. Clair. Growing up to Love: A Guide to Sex Education for Parents. rev. ed. LC 56-11527. (Illus.). 112p. (YA) (gr. 9 up). 1966. pap. 0.95 (ISBN 0-8361-1535-X). Herald Pr.
--Marriage in Today's World. LC 78-955. 160p. 1978. pap. 5.95 (ISBN 0-8361-1849-9). Herald Pr.
Amstutz, H. E., ed. Bovine Medicine & Surgery, Vols. I & II. LC 80-68110. (Illus.). 1272p. 1980. 96.50 (ISBN 0-939674-06-8). Am Vet Pubns.
Amstutz, H. E., et al, eds. Equine Medicine & Surgery, Vols. I & II. LC 81-70196. (Illus.). 1456p. 1982. 98.50 (ISBN 0-939674-04-1). Am Vet Pubns.
Amstutz, Mark R. Economics & Foreign Policy: A Guide to Information Sources. LC 74-11566. (Vol. 7). 1977. 60.00x (ISBN 0-8103-1321-9). Gale.
--An Introduction to Political Science: The Management of Conflict. 1982. pap. text ed. 15.80 (ISBN 0-673-16053-X). Scott F.
Amter, Joseph A. Vietnam Verdict: A Citizen's History. LC 82-8274. (Illus.). 448p. 1982. 17.50 (ISBN 0-8264-0193-7). Continuum.
--Vietnam Verdict: A Citizen's History. LC 82-8274. (Illus.). 448p. 1984. pap. 9.95 (ISBN 0-8264-0235-6). Continuum.
Amthor, Terry K. The CloudLords of Tanara. (Illus.). 64p. (YA) (gr. 10-12). 1984. pap. 10.00 (ISBN 0-915795-17-5). Iron Crown Ent Inc.
--The Court of Ardor in Southern Middle-Earth. (Illus.). 52p. 1983. 10.00 (ISBN 0-915795-06-X). Iron Crown Ent Inc.
Amthor, Terry K. & Johnston, Olivia H. The Iron Wind. II ed. (Illus.). 52p. (YA) (gr. 10-12). 1984. pap. 8.00 (ISBN 0-915795-23-X). Iron Crown Ent Inc.
Amthor, Terry K., jt. auth. see Barrett, Kevin.
Amukotuwa, Sarath, et al. Radio Database International. Magne, Lawrence & Jensen, Don, eds. (Illus.). 200p. (Orig.). 1983. pap. 9.95 (ISBN 0-914941-00-3). Intl Broadcasting Serv.
Amundsen, Dirsten. A New Look at the Silenced Majority: Women & American Democracy. LC 76-58411. 160p. 1977. 8.95 (ISBN 0-13-615336-4, Spec). P-H.
Amundsen, Kirsten. Norway, NATO & the Forgotten Soviet Challenge. LC 81-80337. (Policy Papers in International Affairs Ser.: No. 14). (Illus.). iv, 50p. 1981. pap. 3.95x (ISBN 0-87725-514-8). U of Cal Intl St.
Amundsen, Lou. Cardiac Rehabilitation. (Clinics in Physical Therapy Ser.: Vol. 1). (Illus.). 224p. 1981. text ed. 20.00 (ISBN 0-443-08147-6). Churchill.
Amundsen, Louis R., et al. Energy Cost of Rehabilitation Calisthenics: 1979. 1980. pap. 2.50 (ISBN 0-912452-24-2). Am Phys Therapy Assn.
Amundsen, Roald. To the North Magnetic Pole & Through the Northwest Passage. facs. ed. 36p. pap. 3.95 (ISBN 0-8466-0149-4, S149). Shorey.
Amundsen, Roald E. The North West Passage: Being the Record of a Voyage of Exploration of the Ship Gjoa 1903-1907, 2 vols. LC 74-5824. Repr. of 1908 ed. Set. 50.00 (ISBN 0-404-11625-6). AMS Pr.
Amundson, Neal R. Mathematical Methods in Chemical Engineering: Matrices & Their Application. 1966. ref. ed. 42.95 (ISBN 0-13-561084-2). P-H.
Amundson, Neal R., jt. auth. see Ramkrishna, Doraiswami.
Amur, G. S. The Concept of Comedy. LC 77-1166. 1977. lib. bdg. 30.00 (ISBN 0-8414-2878-6). Folcroft.
--The Concept of Comedy. 219p. 1981. Repr. of 1963 ed. lib. bdg. 37.00 (ISBN 0-89760-009-6). Telegraph Bks.
--Images & Impressions. 1980. text ed. 12.00x (ISBN 0-391-01917-1). Humanities.
--Manohar Malgonkar. (Indian Writers Ser.). 1976. 8.50 (ISBN 0-89253-506-7). Ind-US Inc.
Amur, G. S., et al, eds. Indian Readings in Commonwealth Literature. 175p. 1985. text ed. 27.50x (ISBN 0-86590-734-X, Pub. by Sterling Pubs India). APT Bks.
--Essays on Comparative Literature & Linguistics. viii, 174p. 1984. text ed. 18.95x (ISBN 0-86590-228-3, Pub. by Sterling Pubs India). Apt Bks.
Amusement & Music Operators Association. Computers & Coin-Op. 1985. 7.00 (ISBN 0-318-04202-9). AMOA.
--Cost of Doing Business 1983. 1984. 25.00 (ISBN 0-318-04201-0). AMOA.
--Location. 1985. 15.00 (ISBN 0-318-04203-7). AMOA.
--Yearly Who's Who Membership Directory. 1984. 150.00 (ISBN 0-318-03293-7). AMOA.
Amuzegar, Jahangir. Comparative Economics: National Priorities, Policies, & Performance. 1981. text ed. 20.95 (ISBN 0-316-03801-6). Little.
--Iran: An Economic Profile. LC 77-5286. 1977. 12.95 (ISBN 0-916808-14-9). Mid East Inst.
Amuzegar, Jahangir & Fekrat, M. Ali. Iran: Economic Development Under Dualistic Conditions. LC 79-153044. (Publications of the Center for Middle Eastern Studies Ser.: No. 7). 1971. 13.00x (ISBN 0-226-01754-0). U of Chicago Pr.

Amuzegar, Jahngir. Oil Exporters' Economic Development in an Interdependent World. (Occasional Papers: No. 18). 99p. 1983. pap. 5.00 (ISBN 0-317-04016-2). Intl Monetary.

Amy, Ernest F. Text of Chaucer's Legend of Good Women. LC 65-21088. (Studies in Chaucer, No. 6). 1969. Repr. of 1918 ed. lib. bdg. 39.95 (ISBN 0-8383-0502-4). Haskell.

Amy, Francisco J., ed. Musa Bilingue: Bilingual Edition. 1977. lib. bdg. 59.95 (ISBN 0-8490-2306-8). Gordon Pr.

Amy, Gary L. & Knocke, William R., eds. Register of Environmental Engineering Graduate Programs. 5th ed. LC 84-70854. 626p. 1984. pap. 30.00 (ISBN 0-917567-00-5). Assn Environ Eng.

Amy, William O. & Recob, James B. Human Nature in the Christian Tradition. LC 82-45049. 118p. (Orig.). 1982. lib. bdg. 22.25 (ISBN 0-8191-2512-1); pap. text ed. 8.75 (ISBN 0-8191-2513-X). U Pr of Amer.

Amy Ong Tsui & Bogue, Donald J. Declining World Fertility: Trends, Causes, Implications. (Population Bulletin Ser.: Vol. 33 No. 4). 55p. (B). 4.00 (ISBN 0-317-35637-2); bulk rates avail. Population Ref.

Amyot, C. Grant. The Italian Communist Party. 1981. 26.00 (ISBN 0-312-43920-2). St Martin.

Amyot, Jacques, tr. see Plutarch.

Amyot, T., et al, eds. A Supplement to Dodsley's Old Plays, Vol. 1: The Chester Plays, a Collection of Mysteries. (Shakespeare Society of London Publications: Vol. 1). pap. 52.00 (ISBN 0-317-17942-X). Kraus Repr.

--A Supplement to Dodsley's Old Plays, Vol. 2: Ludus Coventriae, a Collection of Mysteries; The Marriage of Wit & Wisdom; The Moral Play of Wit & Science. (Shakespeare Society of London Publications: Vol. 2). pap. 52.00 (ISBN 0-317-17943-8). Kraus Repr.

Amyot, T, et al, eds. A Supplement to Dodsley's Old Plays, Vol. 3: Patient Grissil, a Play; Sir Thomas More, a Play; Ralph Roister Doister, a Comedy; The Tragedie of Gorboduc. (Shakespeare Society of London Publications: Vol. 3). pap. 52.00 (ISBN 0-317-17944-6). Kraus Repr.

Amyot, T., et al, eds. A Supplement to Dodsley's Old Plays, Vol. 4: The First Sketch of Shakespeare's Merry Wives of Windsor; the First Sketches of the Second & Third Parts of Henry VI; the True Tragedy of Richard III; the Old Taming of the Shrew. (Shakespeare Societyof London Publications: Vol. 4). pap. 52.00 (ISBN 0-317-17945-4). Kraus Repr.

Amyx, D. A. & Lawrence, Patricia. Archaic Corinthian Pottery & the Anaploga Well. LC 75-4551. (Corinth Ser.: Vol. 7, Pt. 2). (Illus.). 1976. 35.00x (ISBN 0-87661-072-6, NK4647). Am Sch Athens.

Amyx, James W., et al. Petroleum Reservoir Engineering Physical Properties. 1960. 52.95 (ISBN 0-07-001600-3). McGraw.

Amzallag, et al, eds. Low-Cycle Fatigue & Life Prediction- STP 770. 646p. 1982. 60.00 (ISBN 0-8031-0713-7, 04-770000-30). ASTM.

An, Tai Sung. North Korea: A Political Handbook. LC 83-16307. (Illus.). 294p. 1983. lib. bdg. 35.00 (ISBN 0-8420-2205-8). Scholarly Res Inc.

Ana, Julio De Santa see De Santa Ana, Julio.

Anabarlian, H. An Introduction to Multiplan-86 Spreadsheeting on the DEC Rainbow 100: McGraw-Hill Version. (Personnal Programming Ser.). 416p. 1984. 1.00 (ISBN 0-07-001709-3). McGraw.

Anachem Inc Staff & Sandia National Laboratories. Solar Heating Materials Handbook: Environmental & Safety Considerations for Selection. (Illus.). 286p. 1984. pap. 28.95x (H051). Solar Energy Info.

Anacker, H., et al. Endoscopic Retrograde Pancreaticocholangiography. LC 76-50000. 1977. 43.00 (ISBN 0-387-08008-2). Springer-Verlag.

Anacker, Robert, jt. auth. see Burgdorfer, Willy.

Anad, Mubarak, jt. auth. see Kennedy, Scott.

Anaejionu, Paul. X-Ray Diffraction Study to Assess the Potential Economic-Pharmaceutical Uses for Nigerian Clays. (Science & Development in Africa Ser.). 1979. pap. 10.00x (ISBN 0-914970-22-4). Conch Mag.

Anaejionu, Paul, et al, eds. Space & Society: Challenges & Choices. (Science & Technology Ser.: Vol. 59). (Illus.). 442p. (Orig.). 1984. lib. bdg. 55.00x (ISBN 0-87703-204-1, Pub. by Am Astro Soc); pap. text ed. 35.00x (ISBN 0-87703-205-X). Univelt Inc.

Anafulu, Joseph C. The Ibo-Speaking Peoples of Southern Nigeria: A Selected Annotated List of Writings, 1627 to 1970. 321p. 1981. lib. bdg. 55.00 (ISBN 3-601-00006-7). Kraus Intl.

Anagnostakos, Nicholas, jt. auth. see Tortora, Gerald J.

Anagnostakos, Nicholas P., jt. auth. see Tortora, Gerard.

Anagnostakos, Nicholas P., jt. auth. see Tortora, Gerard J.

Anagnostakos, Nicholos, jt. auth. see Tortora, Gerald.

Anagnostopoulos, Athan, tr. see Kakavelakis, Demetris.

Anak, Gde Agung. Twenty Years Indonesian Foreign Policy 1945-1965. LC 72-93180. 1973. text ed. 46.00x (ISBN 0-686-22635-6). Mouton.

Analysis Instrumentation Division, et al. Productivity Through Control Technology: Proceedings of the Joint Symposium, Houston, Texas, 1983. LC 83-205565. 238p. 1983. pap. text ed. 36.00x (ISBN 0-87664-783-2). Instru Soc.

Analysis Instrumentation Symposium, 26th, Baton Rouge, 1980. Analysis Instrumentation, Vol. 18: Proceedings. Bd. with Vol. 14. Instrument Maintenance Management. 156p. 1980. pap. text ed. 24.00x (ISBN 0-87664-471-X). Instru Soc.

Analysis Instrumentation Symposium, 27th, St. Louis, 1981. Analysis Instrumentation, Vol. 19: Proceedings. 144p. pap. text ed. 24.00x (ISBN 0-87664-521-X). Instru Soc.

Analysis Instrumentation Symposium, 28th, 1982. Analysis Instrumentation, Vol. 20: Proceedings. 114p. 1982. pap. text ed. 20.00x (ISBN 0-87664-687-9). Instru Soc.

Analytical Sciences Corp-Technical Staff. Applied Optimal Estimation. Gelb, Arthur, ed. LC 74-1604. (Illus.). 382p. 1974. pap. text ed. 14.95x (ISBN 0-262-57048-3). MIT Pr.

Ananaba, Wogu. The Trade Union Movement in Africa: Promise & Performance. 1979. 27.50x (ISBN 0-312-81221-3). St Martin.

--The Trade Union Movement in Nigeria. LC 72-106044. 1970. text ed. 29.50x (ISBN 0-8419-0039-6, Africana). Holmes & Meier.

Ananchenko, S. N., ed. International Symposium on Frontiers of Bioorganic Chemistry & Molecular Biology, Moscow & Tashkent, U.S.S.R., 1978: Proceedings. (IUPAC Symposium Ser.). (Illus.). 435p. 1980. 110.00 (ISBN 0-08-023967-6). Pergamon.

Anand, Balwant S. Guru Tegh Bahadur. 1979. text ed. 11.95 (ISBN 0-89684-076-X, Pub. by Sterling New Delhi). Orient Bk Dist.

Anand, D. K. Introduction to Control Systems. 2nd ed. LC 83-6320. (International Series on Systems & Control: Vol. 8). (Illus.). 448p. 1983. 55.00 (ISBN 0-08-030002-2); pap. 25.00 (ISBN 0-08-030001-4). Pergamon.

Anand, Davinder K. & Cunniff, Patrick. Engineering Mechanics: Dynamics. 450p. 1984. scp 29.10 (ISBN 0-205-07785-4, 327785). Allyn.

--Engineering Mechanics: Statics. 450p. 1984. scp 42.11 (ISBN 0-205-07784-6, 327810). Allyn.

Anand, Davinder K. & Cunniff, Patrick F. Engineering Mechanics: Statics & Dynamics. 900p. 1984. scp 29.10 (ISBN 0-205-07810-9, 327784). Allyn.

Anand, J. P., jt. auth. see Namboodiri, P. K.

Anand, Kewal K. Indian Philosophy: The Concept of Karma. 396p. 1982. 34.95 (ISBN 0-940500-91-4, Pub by Bharatiya Vidya Prakashan India). Asia Bk Corp.

Anand, M. & Singh, G., eds. Maharaja Ranjit Singh as Patron of the Arts. 138p. 1982. text ed. 38.25x (ISBN 0-391-02668-3). Humanities.

Anand, Mulk R. Across the Black Waters. (Orient Paperbacks Ser.). 322p. 1980. pap. 5.95 (ISBN 0-86578-081-1). Ind-US Inc.

--Album of Indian Paintings. (Illus.). 1979. 14.00 (ISBN 0-89744-191-5); pap. 10.00 (ISBN 0-89744-192-3). Auromere.

--Apology for Heroism. (Mayfair Paperbacks Ser.). 203p. 1975. pap. 3.60 (ISBN 0-86578-074-9). Ind-US Inc.

--The Barber's Trade Union & Other Stories. 175p. 1983. pap. 3.00 (ISBN 0-86578-145-1). Ind-US Inc.

--Between Tears & Laughter. 171p. 1974. Ind-US Inc.

--The Big Heart. rev. ed. 231p. 1980. 19.95 (ISBN 0-86578-086-2); pap. 3.95 (ISBN 0-86578-144-3). Ind-US Inc.

--Confession of a Lover. 404p. 1976. pap. 5.75 (ISBN 0-86578-073-0). Ind-US Inc.

--Gauri. (Mayfair Paperbacks Ser.). 256p. 1981. pap. 4.00 (ISBN 0-86578-067-6). Ind-US Inc.

--Maya of Mohenjo-Daro. 3rd ed. (Illus.). 24p. (Orig.). (gr. k-3). 1980. pap. 2.00 (ISBN 0-89744-214-8, Pub. by Children's Bk Trust India). Auromere.

--Morning Face. 571p. 1980. pap. 5.75 (ISBN 0-86578-062-5). Ind-US Inc.

--Seven Little-Known Birds of the Inner Eye. LC 77-72601. (Illus.). 1978. 17.50 (ISBN 0-8048-0936-4). C E Tuttle.

--Untouchable. (Mayfair Paperbacks Ser.). 226p. 1983. pap. 5.00 (ISBN 0-86578-068-4). Ind-US Inc.

--Untouchable. 181p. 1974. pap. 2.75 (ISBN 0-88253-280-4). Ind-US Inc.

Anand, Mulk R., ed. Kama Sutra of Vatsyayana. 276p. 1981. text ed. 125.50x (ISBN 0-391-02224-5). Humanities.

--The Kama Sutra of Vatsyayana. 1982. 175.00x (ISBN 0-85692-093-2, Pub. by J M Dent). State Mutual Bk.

Anand, Mulk Raj & Hutheasing, Krishina N. The Book of Indian Beauty. LC 80-52066. (Illus.). 1981. 12.95 (ISBN 0-8048-1180-6). C E Tuttle.

Anand, N. K. & Srivastava, G. Pediatric Emergencies. 310p. 1985. text ed. 35.00x (ISBN 0-7069-2693-5, Pub. by Vikas India). Advent NY.

Anand, Narender K., jt. auth. see Srivastava, Girish.

Anand, Nirmal, jt. auth. see Anand, Raj K.

Anand, R. P. Cultural Factors in International Relations. 1981. 20.00x (ISBN 0-8364-0727-X, Pub. by Abhinav India). South Asia Bks.

--New States & International Law. 1972. 6.50x (ISBN 0-686-20280-5). Intl Bk Dist.

--Origin & Development of the Law of the Sea. 1983. lib. bdg. 49.50 (ISBN 90-247-2617-4, Pub. by Martinus Nijhoff Netherlands). Kluwer Academic.

Anand, Raj K. & Anand, Nirmal. Diet for Healthy Living. 65p. (Orig.). 1985. pap. 3.95 (ISBN 0-318-04445-5). Raj Anand.

Anand, Satyapal. University Without Walls: Correspondence Education in India. 69p. 1979. text ed. 15.00x (ISBN 0-7069-0826-0, Pub. by Vikas India). Advent NY.

Anand, Shahla. Choice Ruminations on English Literature. 240p. 1983. pap. text ed. 12.25 (ISBN 0-8191-3284-5). U Pr of Amer.

--Of Costliest Emblem: Paradise Lost & the Emblem Tradition. LC 78-59853. (Illus.). 1978. pap. text ed. 13.25 (ISBN 0-8191-0556-2). U Pr of Amer.

Anand, Shushila, jt. auth. see Alexander, Michael.

Anand, Sudhir. Inequality & Poverty in Malaysia: Measurement & Decomposition. (WBRP Ser.). (Illus.). 1981. text ed. 27.50x (ISBN 0-19-520153-1). Oxford U Pr.

Anand, Uma. The Tale of Lumbdoom, The Long-Tailed Langoor. (Illus.). 1968. 1.00 (ISBN 0-88253-325-8). Ind-US Inc.

Anand, V. K. Conflict in Nagaland. 1981. 18.50x (ISBN 0-8364-0683-4, Pub. by Chanakya India). South Asia Bks.

--Nagaland in Transition. 1968. 10.50 (ISBN 0-686-20277-5). Intl Bk Dist.

Anand, V. S. Savarkar: A Study in the Evolution of Indian Nationalism. 95p. 1967. pap. text ed. 8.00x (Pub. by C Woolf UK). Humanities.

Anand, Valerie. The Disputed Crown. 320p. 1982. 14.95 (ISBN 0-684-17629-7, ScribT). Scribner.

--To a Native Shore. 304p. 1984. 15.95 (ISBN 0-684-18007-3, ScribT). Scribner.

Ananda. Spiritual Practice. pap. 3.00 (ISBN 0-87481-155-4). Vedanta Pr.

Ananda Marga Editors. Ananda Marga: Serving the People of North America. (Illus.). 24p. (Orig.). 1982. pap. 1.00 (ISBN 0-88476-022-7). Ananda Marga.

Ananda, Peter, jt. ed. see Kozicki, Richard J.

Ananda Publications. The Ananda Cookbook: Easy to Prepare Recipes for the Vegetarian Gourmet. 252p. 1985. pap. 9.95 (ISBN 0-916124-26-6). Ananda.

Ananda, Sita. Love the Sunshine with Sprouts. pap. 9.95x (ISBN 0-317-07321-4, Regent House). B of A.

Anandam, Kamala, jt. auth. see Kelly, J. Terence.

Ananda-Maitreya. The Religion of Burma & Other Papers. LC 77-87482. Repr. of 1929 ed. 31.50 (ISBN 0-404-16790-X). AMS Pr.

Anandamurti, Shrii S. A Guide to Human Conduct. LC 80-70792. 55p. 1981. pap. 3.00 (ISBN 0-88476-010-3). Ananda Marga.

Anandamurti, Shrii Shrii. Namami Krsnasundaram - Salutations to Lord Krsna. 252p. 1981. pap. 4.00 (ISBN 0-686-95432-7). Ananda Marga.

Anandanagar. Caryacarya, Vol. I & II. Vol. I - 37 p. pap. 2.00 (ISBN 0-686-95445-9); Vol. II - 49 p. pap. 1.00 (ISBN 0-686-99507-4). Ananda Marga.

Anand Kumar, T. C., ed. see International Primatological Society, 7th Congress, Bangalore, January 1979.

Anand Kumar, T. C., ed. see International Symposium on Neuroendocrine Regulation of Fertiltity.

Anan'eva, A. A., et al. Ceramic Acoustic Detectors. LC 65-11334. 122p. 1965. 35.00x (ISBN 0-306-10702-3, Consultants). Plenum Pub.

Anania, Michael. Color of Dust. LC 71-11681. (New Poetry Ser.: No. 40). 70p. 1970. 6.50 (ISBN 0-8040-0048-4, 82-70324, Pub. by Swallow); pap. 4.50 (ISBN 0-8040-0049-2, 82-70332, Pub. by Swallow). Ohio U Pr.

--Constructions - Variations. 36p. 1985. 3.00 (ISBN 0-317-27399-X). Spoon Riv Poetry.

--The Red Menace. 150p. (Orig.). 1984. 13.95 (ISBN 0-938410-19-9). Thunder's Mouth.

--Riversongs: Poems. LC 78-12900. 1979. 10.00x (ISBN 0-252-00717-4). U of Ill Pr.

Anania, Michael, ed. New Poetry Anthology I. LC 69-20470. 111p. (Orig.). 1969. 7.95x (ISBN 0-8040-0224-X, 82-71538, Pub. by Swallow); pap. 4.95x (ISBN 0-8040-0225-8, 82-71546, Pub. by Swallow). Ohio U Pr.

Ananichev, K. Environment: International Aspects. 207p. 1976. pap. 2.45 (ISBN 0-8285-0430-X, Pub. by Progress Pubs USSR). Imported Pubns.

Ananicz, Frank. The Red Overcoat & other Stories. 24p. 1983. pap. 3.00 (ISBN 0-933292-12-0). Arts End.

Ananikian, Mardiros H. Armenian Mythology & African Mythology. (Mythology of All Races Ser.: Vol. VII). Repr. of 1932 ed. 30.00 (ISBN 0-8154-0011-X). Cooper Sq.

Ananikyan, R. Yerevan: A Guide. 95p. 1982. 8.00 (ISBN 0-8285-2297-9, Pub. by Progress Pubs USSR). Imported Pubns.

Anan Isho, compiled by. The Wit & Wisdom of the Christian Fathers of Egypt: The Syrian Version of the Apophthegmata Patrum. Wallis Budge, Ernest A., tr. LC 80-2354. Repr. of 1934 ed. 53.50 (ISBN 0-404-18900-8). AMS Pr.

Anantanarayanan, M. The Silver Pilgrimage. (Indian Novels Ser.). 160p. 1976. pap. 2.75 (ISBN 0-89253-022-7). Ind-US Inc.

Anantaraman, V., et al, eds. Human Resource Management: Concepts & Perspectives. 342p. 1984. text ed. 23.95x (ISBN 9971-69-090-X, Pub. by Singapore U Pr); pap. text ed. 16.95x (ISBN 9971-69-091-8, Pub. by Singapore U Pr). Ohio U Pr.

Anantendra-Yati. Vedanta-Sara-Sangraha. Mahadevan, T. M., tr. 1974. pap. 3.50 (ISBN 0-89744-124-9, Pub. by Ganesh & Co. India). Auromere.

Ananthakrishnan, R., et al. Human Biochemical Genetics. LC 73-645. 147p. 1973. text ed. 22.50x (ISBN 0-8422-7095-7). Irvington.

Ananthakrishnan, T. N. The Biology of Gall Insects. 400p. 1985. text ed. 49.50 (ISBN 0-7131-2906-9). E Arnold.

Ananthakrishnan, T. N., jt. auth. see Murthy, V. A.

Ananthanarayan, R. Introduction to Medical Microbiology. 288p. 1984. pap. text ed. 15.95 (ISBN 0-86131-454-9, Pub. by Orient Longman India). Apt Bks.

Ananthanarayan, R. & Paniker, C. K. Textbook of Microbiology. 608p. 1979. 25.00x (ISBN 0-86131-032-2, Pub. by Orient Longman India). State Mutual Bk.

Ananthanarayan, R. & Paniker, Jayaram. Textbook of Microbiology. 2nd ed. (Illus.). 618p. 1982. pap. text ed. 25.00x (ISBN 0-86131-293-7, Pub. by Orient Longman Ltd India). Apt Bks.

Anantharaman, T. R., ed. Metallic Glasses: Production, Properties & Applications. 300p. 1984. 58.00 (ISBN 0-87849-525-8). Trans Tech.

Ananyeva, G. E., et al. An Outline Theory of Population. 1980. 8.45 (ISBN 0-8285-1764-9, Pub. by Progress Pubs USSR). Imported Pubns.

Ananyi, Christ. Phoenix Ascent. LC 83-91408. 70p. 1985. 7.95 (ISBN 0-533-06031-1). Vantage.

Anarchism, Bob. Anarchism: There's Nothing More Revolutionary Than Marxism-Lenisim, Mao Tsetung Thoughts. 32p. 1982. 2.25 (ISBN 0-89851-060-0). RCP Pubns.

Anas, Alex, ed. Residential Location Markets & Urban Transportation: Economic Theory, Econometrics & Policy Analysis with Discrete Choice Models. 257p. 1982. 39.50 (ISBN 0-12-057920-0). Acad Pr.

Anast, C. S., jt. ed. see DeLuca, H. F.

Anastaplo, George. The Artist As Thinker: From Shakespeare to Joyce. LC 82-6502. xvi, 499p. 1983. lib. bdg. 35.00x (ISBN 0-8040-0416-1, 82-75612, Swallow); pap. 16.00x (ISBN 0-8040-0417-X, 82-75620, Swallow). Ohio U Pr.

--The Constitutionalist: Notes on the First Amendment. LC 72-165793. 1971. 25.00 (ISBN 0-87074-004-0). SMU Press.

--Human Being & Citizen: Essays on Virtue, Freedom & the Common Good. LC 75-21909. xiv, 332p. 1975. 22.00x (ISBN 0-8040-0677-6, 82-73757, Pub. by Swallow). Ohio U Pr.

--Human Being & Citizen: Essays on Virtue, Freedom & the Common Good. LC 75-21909. 1978. pap. 8.95 (ISBN 0-8040-0678-4, 82-73765, Pub. by Swallow). Ohio U Pr.

Anastas, Lila. Your Career in Nursing. (Illus.). 210p. 1984. pap. text ed. 9.95 (ISBN 0-88737-074-8, 41-1952). Natl League Nurse.

Anastasas, Florence H. And They Called Him Amos: The Story of John Amos Comenius-a Woodcut in Words. LC 73-86540. 1973. 10.00 (ISBN 0-682-47814-8, University). Exposition Pr FL.

--Belshazzar: Prince of Babylon. (Illus.). 304p. 1982. 15.00 (ISBN 0-682-49818-1, University). Exposition Pr FL.

--The Legend of Good Women: Written in Praise of Women Faithful in Love. 1976. 10.00 (ISBN 0-682-48385-0, University). Exposition Pr FL.

Anastasescu, D., jt. ed. see Avram, C.

Anastasi, A. see Ruckwick, Christian A.

Anastasi, Agatha D. Caporetto. (Orig.). 1979. pap. 2.75 (ISBN 0-89083-543-8). Zebra.

--A Time for Roses. (Orig.). 1982. pap. 3.50 (ISBN 0-89083-946-8). Zebra.

Anastasi, Anne. Differential Psychology. 3rd ed. (Illus.). 1958. text ed. write for info. (ISBN 0-02-302800-9, 30280). Macmillan.

--Fields of Applied Psychology. 2nd ed. (Illus.). 1979. text ed. 33.95 (ISBN 0-07-001602-X). McGraw.

--Individual Difference. LC 65-25851. (Perspectives in Psychology Ser.). 1965. pap. 78.80 (ISBN 0-317-08082-2, 2051293). Bks Demand UMI.

--Psychological Testing. 5th ed. 768p. 1982. text ed. write for info. (ISBN 0-02-302960-9). Macmillan.

Anastasi, Anne, et al. Validation of a Biographical Inventory As a Predictor of College Success. (Research Monograph: No. 1). 1960. pap. 5.00 (ISBN 0-87447-099-4, 200080). College Bd.

Anastasi, T. Speaking of Selling. 1983. cassette & wkbk. 59.95 (ISBN 0-8436-0877-3). Van Nos Reinhold.

Anastasi, Thomas E., Jr. Desk Guide to Communication. 2nd ed. 286p. 1981. 17.95 (ISBN 0-8436-0855-2). Van Nos Reinhold.

--How to Manage.., 4 vols. Incl. How to Manage Your Writing. 123p (ISBN 0-932078-46-X); How to Manage Your Speaking. 128p (ISBN 0-932078-45-1); How to Manage Your Reading. 129p (ISBN 0-932078-44-3); Face to Face Communication. 198p (ISBN 0-932078-47-8). 1974. pap. 6.50 ea.; pap. 24.50 set of four (ISBN 0-932078-43-5). GE Tech Prom & Train.

--Listen! Techniques for Improving Communication Skills. 122p. 1982. pap. 11.95 (ISBN 0-8436-0864-1). Van Nos Reinhold.

Anastasia, Salvatore & Willig, Paul M. Structure of Factors. new ed. LC 72-78469. 1974. 30.00x (ISBN 0-917448-04-9). Algorithmics.

Anastasio, Dina. Big Bird Can Share. (Sesame Street Growing-Up Bks.). (Illus.). 32p. (ps-k). 1985. 2.50 (ISBN 0-307-12016-3, 12016, Pub. by Golden Bks). Western Pub.

--Conversation Kickers. 1979. pap. 1.50 (ISBN 0-8431-0656-5). Price Stern.

--Everybody's Invited to Dudley's Party Except... !! (Write-It-Yourself Bks.). (Illus.). 48p. 1980. pap. 1.75 (ISBN 0-8431-0277-2). Price Stern.

--The Little Scouts. (Illus.). 32p. (Orig.). (gr. 1-3). 1985. pap. 1.95 (ISBN 0-590-33465-4). Scholastic Inc.

--My Family Book. (My Bks.). 48p. 1982. pap. 1.75 (ISBN 0-8431-0615-8). Price Stern.

--My Own Book. (My Bks.). 1975. pap. 1.75 (ISBN 0-8431-0367-1). Price Stern.

--My Personal Book. (My Bks.). 48p. 1980. 1.75 (ISBN 0-8431-0677-8). Price Stern.

--My Private Book. (My Bks.). 48p. 1979. pap. 1.75 (ISBN 0-8431-0662-X). Price Stern.

--My School Book. (My Bks.). 48p. 1981. pap. 1.75 (ISBN 0-8431-0499-6). Price Stern.

--My Special Book. (My Bks.). 48p. 1980. 1.75 (ISBN 0-8431-0270-5). Price Stern.

--My Wish Book. (My Bks.). 48p. 1981. pap. 1.75 (ISBN 0-8431-0698-0). Price Stern.

--A Question of Time. (Illus.). 96p. (gr. 4-6). 1983. pap. 1.95 (ISBN 0-590-62028-2, Apple Paperbacks). Scholastic Inc.

--Romper Room Book of ABC's. LC 84-24651. (Illus.). 32p. (ps-3). 1985. 4.95 (ISBN 0-385-18313-5). Doubleday.

--Romper Room Book of Colors. LC 84-24650. (Illus.). 32p. (ps-3). 1985. 4.95 (ISBN 0-385-18314-3). Doubleday.

--Romper Room Book of One, Two, Threes. LC 84-24649. (Illus.). 32p. (ps-3). 1985. 4.95 (ISBN 0-385-18312-7). Doubleday.

--Romper Room Book of Shapes. LC 84-24648. (Illus.). 32p. (ps-3). 1985. 4.95 (ISBN 0-385-18315-1). Doubleday.

--Somebody Kidnapped the Mayor & Hid Her in... !! (Write-It-Yourself Bks.). (Illus.). 48p. 1980. pap. 1.75 (ISBN 0-8431-0279-9). Price Stern.

Anastasio, Dino. My Secret Book. (My Bks.). 48p. 1978. pap. 1.75 (ISBN 0-8431-0441-4). Price Stern.

Anastasio, William T., ed. see Hall, Viviana C.

Anastasiou, C. J. Ascomycetes & Fungi Imperfecti from the Salton Sea. 1963. 6.40 (ISBN 3-7682-0210-0). Lubrecht & Cramer.

Anastasiou, Clifford J. Teachers, Children, & Things. 2nd ed. 1979. pap. text ed. 9.95 (ISBN 0-03-923360-X, Pub. by HR&W Canada). HR&W.

Anastasiow, Nicholas. Identifying the Developmentally Delayed Child. LC 81-21838. (Illus.). 200p. 1982. 21.00 (ISBN 0-8391-1729-9). Pro Ed.

--Oral Language: Expression of Thought. 1971. 2.00 (ISBN 0-87207-840-X). Intl Reading.

Anastasiow, Nicholas J. Child Development & Special Education: A Psycho-biological Perspective. (Illus.). 320p. (Orig.). 1985. pap. text ed. 21.95 (ISBN 0-933716-53-2, 532). P-H Brookes.

Anastasiow, Nicholas J. & Hanes, Michael L. Language Patterns of Poverty Children. (Illus.). 176p. 1976. 15.25x (ISBN 0-398-03499-0). C C Thomas.

Anastasiow, Nicholas J., jt. ed. see Harel, Shaul.

Anastasiow, Nicholas J., et al. Language & Reading Strategies for Poverty Children. LC 81-22030. (Illus.). 232p. 1982. pap. 16.00 (ISBN 0-936104-80-5, 13471). Pro Ed.

Anastasoff, Christ. The Bulgarians: From Their Arrival in the Balkans to Modern Times--Thirteen Centuries of History. (Illus.). 1977. 20.00 (ISBN 0-682-48899-2, University). Exposition Pr FL.

Anastassiades, M. A., ed. Solar Eclipses & the Ionosphere. LC 71-119056. 307p. 1970. 34.50x (ISBN 0-306-30480-5, Plenum Pr). Plenum Pub.

Anastly, Indira. Rural Women of India. 482p. 1982. 39.95 (ISBN 0-317-12339-4, Pub. by B R Pub Delhi). Asia Bk Corp.

Anastos, Ernie & Levin, Jack. Twixt: Teens Yesterday & Today. (Illus.). 244p. 1983. 22.95 (ISBN 0-531-09890-7); pap. 9.95 (ISBN 0-531-09953-9). Watts.

Anastos, G., tr. see Pomerantzev, B. I.

Anastos, Milton V. Studies in Byzantine Intellectual History. 432p. 1980. 78.00x (ISBN 0-86078-031-7, Pub. by Variorum England). State Mutual Bk.

Anatol, Karl W., jt. auth. see Applbaum, Ronald L.

Anatoli, A. Babi Yar: A Document in the Form of a Novel. Floyd, David, tr. from Rus. LC 78-74649. 1979. Repr. of 1970 ed. lib. bdg. 15.00x (ISBN 0-8376-0432-X). Bentley.

Anatolius, Bishop of Mohilew & Mstislaw. Greek Orthodox Faith: Scriptural Presentation. Bjerring, Nicholas, tr. from Rus. 1974. pap. 1.00 (ISBN 0-686-10205-3). Eastern Orthodox.

Anawalt, Patricia R. Indian Clothing Before Cortes: Mesoamerican Costumes from the Codices. LC 80-5942. (The Civilization of the American Indian Ser.: Vol. 156). (Illus.). 252p. 1981. 45.00 (ISBN 0-8061-1650-1). U of Okla Pr.

Anaya, Rudolfo. The Adventures of Juan Chicaspatas. LC 84-72301. (Orig.). 1984. pap. 5.00 (ISBN 0-934770-45-X). Arte Publico.

Anaya, Rudolfo, tr. see Griego, Jose & Maestas.

Anaya, Rudolfo A. Bless Me, Ultima. LC 75-29996. 249p. 1976. pap. 10.95 (ISBN 0-89229-002-1). Tonatiuh-Quinto Sol Intl.

--Heart of Aztlan. LC 76-55065. 1976. pap. 7.00 (ISBN 0-685-78786-9). Editorial Justa.

--The Silence of the LLano. LC 82-50703. 1982. pap. 8.00 (ISBN 0-89229-009-9). Tonatiuh-Quinto Sol Intl.

--Tortuga. LC 79-89689. 1979. pap. 7.00 (ISBN 0-915808-34-X). Editorial Justa.

Anaya, Rudolfo A. & Marquez, Antonio, eds. Cuentos Chicanos: A Short Story Anthology. 224p. 1984. 19.95 (ISBN 0-8263-0771-X); pap. 9.95 (ISBN 0-8263-0772-8). U of NM Pr.

Anbar, Ada. How to Choose a Nursery School: A Parents' Guide to Preschool Education. LC 81-16872. (Illus.). 174p. 1982. 12.95 (ISBN 0-87015-233-5). Pacific Bks.

Anbar, Michael. The Genesis of Life. 400p. 1986. text ed. 34.00 (ISBN 0-02-949030-8). Macmillan.

Anbar, Michael, jt. ed. see Reiser, Stanley J.

Anbarlian, H. An Introduction to Multiplan-86 Spreadsheeting on the DEC Rainbow 100: DEC Version. (Personnal Programming Ser.). 416p. 1984. 1.00 (ISBN 0-07-001735-2). McGraw.

--An Introduction to SuperCalc Spreadsheeting on the Osborne. incl. diskette 49.95 (ISBN 0-07-001701-8, BYTE Bks). McGraw.

--An Introduction to Vu-Calc Spreadsheeting for the Timex-Sinclair 2000 & the Sinclair ZX Spectrum. 448p. 1983. pap. 27.95 (ISBN 0-07-001698-4, BYTE Bks). McGraw.

Anbarlian, Harry. An Introduction to Multiplan: Spreadsheeting on the Hewlett Packard 75C. 1984. pap. 22.95 (ISBN 0-07-079407-3). McGraw.

--An Introduction to VisiCalc Matrixing for Apple & IBM. (Personal Computing Ser.). 260p. 1982. pap. 26.95 (ISBN 0-07-001605-4, BYTE Bks). McGraw.

--An Introduction to VisiCalc Spreadsheeting on the ZX-81 & Timex-Sinclair 1000. 272p. 1983. pap. text ed. 26.95 (ISBN 0-07-001699-2). McGraw.

--Spreadsheeting on the TRS-80 Color Computer. (Personal Computing Ser.). 320p. 1983. 22.95 (ISBN 0-07-001595-3, BYTE Bks); incl. cassettes 39.95 (ISBN 0-07-079110-4). McGraw.

Anbian, Robert. Bohemian Airs & Other Kefs. LC 81-90581. (Literature Ser.: No. 1). (Illus.). 74p. (Orig.). 1982. pap. 6.00 (ISBN 0-941842-00-2). Night Horn Books.

Anbury, Thomas. Travels Through the Interior Parts of America in a Series of Letters by an Officer, 2 Vols. LC 75-76553. (Eyewitness Accounts of the American Revolution Ser., No. 2). (Illus.). 1969. Repr. of 1789 ed. Set. 41.00 (ISBN 0-405-01140-7). Vol. 1 #20.50 (ISBN 0-405-01141-5). Vol. 2_#20.50 (ISBN 0-405-01142-3). Ayer Co Pubs.

Ance, Louis & Hazenfield, Robert. Phones on Your Own. 1984. pap. 10.05. Reston.

Anceau, F. & Aas, E. J., eds. VLSI Design of Digital Systems: Conference on Very Large Scale Integration, Trondheim, Norway, Aug. 16-19, 1983. xii, 468p. 1984. 56.00 (ISBN 0-444-86751-1, I-023-84, North-Holland). Elsevier.

Ancel, Jerry, jt. auth. see Peebles, David.

Ancel, Marc. Suspended Sentence. (Cambridge Studies in Criminology). 1971. text ed. 6.95x (ISBN 0-435-82020-6). Gower Pub Co.

Ancel, Martin. The Authoritarians. Martin, Edythe, ed. LC 74-83390. (Illus.). 1977. lib. bdg. 15.95x (ISBN 0-685-81148-4). Pleasure Trove.

--Mira Conquistador. 1974. 15.95x (ISBN 0-685-52987-8). Pleasure Trove.

Ancelet, Barry, jt. ed. see Allain, Mathe.

Ancelet, Barry, tr. see Gould, Philip.

Ancelet, Barry, et al, eds. see Spitzer, Nicholas.

Ancelet, Barry J. & Morgan, Elemore, Jr. The Makers of Cajun Music: Musiciens cadiens et creoles. LC 83-21863. (Illus.). 160p. 1984. 24.95 (ISBN 0-292-75078-1); pap. 14.95 (ISBN 0-292-75079-X). U of Tex Pr.

Ancelet, Barry J. & Allain, Mathe, eds. Acadie Tropicale: Poesie de Louisiane. LC 83-71352. (Editions de la Nouvelle Acadie). (Illus.). 72p. 1983. pap. text ed. 5.00 (ISBN 0-940984-11-3). U of SW LA Ctr LA Studies.

Anchell, Melvin. Sex & Insanity. LC 83-81798. 169p. 1983. pap. 7.95 (ISBN 0-89420-238-3, 110020, Halcyon). Natl Book.

Ancheta, Celadonio A., ed. The Wainwright Papers: Historial Documents of World War II in the Philippines, Vols. 3 & 4. (Illus.). 217p. (Orig.). 1982. each o.p. 18.50x (ISBN 0-686-37568-8, Pub. by New Day Philippines); pap. 9.50 each (ISBN 0-686-37569-6). Cellar.

--The Wainwright Papers: Historical Documents of World War II in the Philippines, 1 of 4, Vol. 1. (Illus.). 220p. 1980. (Pub. by New Day Publishers Philippines); pap. 8.75x (ISBN 0-686-30675-9). Cellar.

Ancheta, Jocelyn, ed. see Metro Deaf Senior Citizens Inc.

Anchin, Jack C. & Kiesler, Donald J., eds. Handbook of Interpersonal Psychotherapy. (Pergamon General Psychology Ser.). 368p. 1981. 35.00 (ISBN 0-08-025959-6). Pergamon.

Anchor, R. D. Design of Liquid-Retaining Concrete Structures. LC 80-29093. 153p. 1981. 59.95x (ISBN 0-470-27163-X). Halsted Pr.

Anchor, Robert. The Enlightenment Tradition. LC 78-62855. 1979. 21.50x (ISBN 0-520-03805-3, CAL 411); pap. 5.95 (ISBN 0-520-03784-7). U of Cal Pr.

Anchor, Robert, tr. see Lukacs, Georg.

Anchors, Scott & Schroeder, Charles. Making Yourself at Home: A Practical Guide to Restructuring & Personalizing Your Residence Hall Environment, No. 24. 50p. 1978. 4.00 (ISBN 0-911547-53-3, 72168W34); 3.25 ea. Am Assn Coun Dev.

An Chunyang. Suzhou: A Garden City. (Illus.). 142p. 1984. pap. 17.95 (ISBN 0-8351-1051-6). China Bks.

Ancikov, A. M., et al. Seventeen Papers on Topology & Differential Geometry. LC 51-5559. (Translations Ser.: No. 2, Vol. 92). 1970. 35.00 (ISBN 0-8218-1792-2, TRANS 2-92). Am Math.

Ancinec, G. Dennis, et al. Natural History of Southern California. rev. ed. (Illus.). 375p. 1985. pap. text ed. 15.95x (ISBN 0-917962-84-2). Peek Pubns.

Anckarsvard, Karin. Doctor's Boy. MacMillan, Annabelle, tr. LC 65-12330. (Illus.). (gr. 4-7). 1965. 5.50 (ISBN 0-15-223925-1, HJ). HarBraceJ.

--Mysterious Schoolmaster. MacMillan, Annabelle, tr. LC 59-10170. (Illus.). (gr. 3-7). 1965. pap. 2.95 (ISBN 0-15-663971-8, VoyB). HarBraceJ.

--Robber Ghost. MacMillan, Annabelle, tr. LC 61-6307. (Illus.). (gr. 4-6). 1968. pap. 3.95 (ISBN 0-15-678350-9, VoyB). HarBraceJ.

Ancona, George. Bananas: From Manolo to Margie. (Illus.). 48p. (gr. 3-6). 1982. 11.50 (ISBN 0-89919-100-2, Clarion). HM.

--Dancing Is. (Illus.). 48p. (gr. 1-3). 1981. 10.75 (ISBN 0-525-28490-7, 01044-310). Dutton.

--Freighters: Cargo Ships & the People Who Work Them. LC 83-45059. (Illus.). 64p. (gr. 2-6). 1985. 12.45i (ISBN 0-690-04358-9); PLB 12.89g (ISBN 0-690-04359-7). Crowell Jr Bks.

--Helping Out. LC 84-14995. (ps-4). 1985. 12.95 (ISBN 0-89919-278-5, Clarion). HM.

--I Feel: A Picture Book of Emotions. (Illus.). (ps-1). 1977. 11.95 (ISBN 0-525-32525-5, 01160-350). Dutton.

--It's a Baby! LC 79-10453. (Illus.). (gr. k-3). 1979. 10.95 (ISBN 0-525-32598-0, 01064-310). Dutton.

--Monster Movers. LC 83-5504. (Illus.). 48p. (gr. 2-5). 1983. 11.95 (ISBN 0-525-44063-1, 01160-350). Dutton.

--Monster on Wheels. (Illus.). 48p. (gr. 3 up). 1974. 9.95 (ISBN 0-525-35155-8). Dutton.

--Sheep Dog. LC 84-20100. (Illus.). 64p. (gr. 5 up). 1985. 11.75 (ISBN 0-688-04118-3); PLB 11.88 (ISBN 0-688-04119-1). Lothrop.

--Team Work. LC 82-45579. (Illus.). 48p. (gr. 3-6). 1983. 11.49i (ISBN 0-690-04247-7); PLB 11.89g (ISBN 0-690-04248-5). Crowell Jr Bks.

Ancona, L. Enciclopedia Tematica De Psicologia. 1892p. (Span.). 1980. 155.00 (ISBN 0-686-35908-9, S-35828). French & Eur.

Ancona, Toni. St. Jude & "His People". 1985. 10.95 (ISBN 0-533-06604-2). Vantage.

Ancowitz, Arthur M. Strokes & Their Prevention. (Orig.). pap. 2.75 (ISBN 0-515-05723-1). Jove Pubns.

Ancrom, Nancy. A Fair Straight Ahead. (Orig.). 1981. limited edn. 15.00 (ISBN 0-939290-03-0); pap. 2.00 (ISBN 0-939290-02-2). Window Edns.

Anctil, M., jt. auth. see Ali, M. A.

Anctil, Pierre. A Franco-American Bibliography: New England. 137p. 1979. pap. 5.25 (ISBN 0-911409-36-X). Natl Mat Dev.

Andacht, Sandra. Joe Franklin's Show Biz Memorabilia. LC 84-51258. 160p. 1985. pap. text ed. 15.95 (ISBN 0-87069-435-9). Wallace-Homestead.

--The Orientalia Journal Annual of Articles, Vol. 1. (Illus.). 144p. (Orig.). 1981. pap. 9.95 (ISBN 0-9607616-0-8). S Andacht.

--The Orientalia Journal of Articles, Vol. 1. (Illus.). 144p. 1985. pap. 9.95 (ISBN 0-9607616-0-8). Wallace-Homestead.

--Treasury of Satsuma. 160p. 1981. 24.95 (ISBN 0-87069-318-2); price guide 1.50 (ISBN 0-87069-319-0). Wallace-Homestead.

Andacht, Sandra & Garthe, Nancy. Wallace-Homestead Price Guide to Oriental Antiques. 2nd ed. (Illus.). 303p. 1985. pap. 19.95 (ISBN 0-87069-382-4). Wallace-Homestead.

Andacht, Sandra, et al. Price Guide to Oriental Antiques. 2nd ed. 303p. 1981. pap. 19.95 (ISBN 0-87069-382-4). Wallace-Homestead.

Andagoya, Pascual De see De Andagoya, Pascval.

Andamo, Evelyn M., ed. Guide to Program Evaluation for Physical Therapy & Occupational Therapy Services. LC 84-8962. 151p. 1984. text ed. 24.95 (ISBN 0-86656-261-3, B261). Haworth Pr.

Anday, Melih C. Rain One Step Away. Halman, Talat & Swann, Brian, trs. LC 80-68880. 1980. 7.50 (ISBN 0-910350-00-0). Charioteer.

Andaya, Barbara W. & Andaya, Leonard Y. A History of Malaysia. LC 82-42612. 350p. 1984. pap. 14.95 (ISBN 0-312-38121-2). St Martin.

Andaya, Barbara W. & Matheson, Virginia, trs. The Precious Gift. Orig. Title: Tuhft al-Nafis. (Illus.). 1982. 55.00x (ISBN 0-19-582507-1). Oxford U Pr.

Andaya, Leonard Y., jt. auth. see Andaya, Barbara W.

Andel, G. Van see Van Andel, G. J.

Andel, Tjeerd H., et al. Cenozoic History & Paleoceanography of the Central Equatorial Pacific Ocean: A Regional Synthesis Deep Sea Drilling Project Data. LC 75-20815. (Geological Society of America Memoir Ser.: No. 143). pap. 57.80 (ISBN 0-317-29104-1, 2023732). Bks Demand UMI.

Andel, Tjeerd H. van. New Views on an Old Planet: Continental Drift & the History of the Earth. (Illus.). 272p. 1985. 19.95 (ISBN 0-521-30084-3). Cambridge U Pr.

Andelin, Aubrey. Man of Steel & Velvet. 288p. pap. 3.95 (ISBN 0-553-23363-7). Bantam.

Andelin, Aubrey P. Man of Steel & Velvet. 12.95 (ISBN 0-911094-03-2). Pacific Santa Barbara.

Andelin, Helen. Fascinating Womanhood. 320p. 1980. pap. 3.95 (ISBN 0-553-22706-8). Bantam.

Andelin, Helen B. All about Raising Children. 1981. 12.95 (ISBN 0-911094-07-5). Pacific Santa Barbara.

--The Fascinating Girl. LC 71-106916. 12.95 (ISBN 0-911094-01-6). Pacific Santa Barbara.

--Fascinating Womanhood. 12.95 (ISBN 0-911094-00-8). Pacific Santa Barbara.

--La Mujer Encantadora. (Span.). 7.95 (ISBN 0-911094-08-3). Pacific Santa Barbara.

Andelson, Robert V. Critics of Henry George. LC 78-66791. 416p. 1979. 28.50 (ISBN 0-8386-2350-6). Fairleigh Dickinson.

Andelson, Robert V., ed. Critics of Henry George. 424p. 1979. 15.00 (ISBN 0-8386-2350-6). Schalkenbach.

Andemicael, Berhanykun. The OAU & the UN: Relations Between the Organization of African Unity & the United Nations. LC 74-84658. 350p. 1976. text ed. 37.50x (ISBN 0-8419-0186-4, Africana). Holmes & Meier.

Andemicael, Berhanykun, ed. Regionalism & the U. N. System. LC 79-14018. 603p. 1979. lib. bdg. 54.00 (ISBN 0-379-00591-3). Oceana.

Andemichael, B. Regionalism & the United Nations. 623p. 1979. 45.00x (ISBN 90-286-0109-0). Sijthoff & Noordhoff.

Andenaes, Johannes. General Part of the Criminal Law of Norway. Ogle, T. P., tr. (New York University Criminal Law & Research Center Pubns: No. 3). xxiii, 346p. 1965. 22.50x (ISBN 0-8377-0202-X). Rothman.

--Punishment & Deterrence. LC 73-90883. 1974. text ed. 12.50x (ISBN 0-472-08013-X). U of Mich Pr.

Ander, O. F. & Nordstrom, Oscar L. The American Origin of the Augustana Synod & Contemporary Lutheran Periodicals, 1851-1860. LC 43-9754. (Augustana Historical Society Ser.: Vol. 9). 192p. 1942. pap. 3.00 (ISBN 0-910184-09-7). Augustana.

Ander, O. F., ed. Lincoln Images: Augustana College Centennial Essays. LC 60-12543. (Augustana College Library Ser.: No. 29). (Illus.). 161p. 1960. 6.95x (ISBN 0-910182-29-9). Augustana Coll.

Ander, O. Fritiof. The Cultural Heritage of the Swedish Immigrant. Scott, Franklyn D., ed. LC 78-15203. (Scandinavians in America Ser.). 1979. Repr. of 1956 ed. lib. bdg. 16.00x (ISBN 0-405-11629-2). Ayer Co Pubs.

Ander, O. Fritiof, ed. The John Hauberg Historical Essays. LC 54-14973. (Augustana College Library Ser.: No. 26). 70p. 1954. 4.50x (ISBN 0-910182-21-3). Augustana Coll.

Ander, Oscar F. T. N. Hasselquist. Scott, Franklyn D., ed. LC 78-15208. (Scandinavians in America Ser.). 1979. Repr. of 1931 ed. lib. bdg. 21.00x (ISBN 0-405-11630-6). Ayer Co Pubs.

Ander, Tjeerd van see Van Andel, Tjeerd.

Anderberg, Michael R. Cluster Analysis for Applications. (Probability & Mathematical Statistics: Vol. 19). 1973. 45.00 (ISBN 0-12-057650-3). Acad Pr.

Andereck, Paul & Pence, Richard. Computer Genealogy: A Guide to Research Through High Technology. LC 84-72693. (Illus.). 280p. (Orig.). 1985. pap. 12.95 (ISBN 0-916489-02-7). Ancestry.

Ander Egg, Ezequiel. Diccionario del Trabajo Social. 424p. (Span.). 1977. pap. 12.25 (ISBN 84-280-0606-7, S-50011). French & Eur.

Anderegg, G., ed. see International Union of Pure & Applied Chemistry.

Anderegg, Michael A. David Lean. (Fimmakers Ser.). 1984. lib. bdg. 21.95 (ISBN 0-8057-9298-8, Twayne). G K Hall.

--William Wyler. (Filmmakers Ser.). 1979. lib. bdg. 13.50 (ISBN 0-8057-9268-6, Twayne). G K Hall.

Andereggen, Anton. Blueprint for Crisis Preparedness. LC 81-80199. (Illus.). 200p. (Orig.). 1981. pap. 10.00 (ISBN 0-938942-00-X). Pacific Gallery.

--Verbes Francais: Formes et Emplois a l'Usage des Etudiants de Langue Etrangere. LC 84-60827. 228p. (Orig., Fr.). 1984. text ed. 22.00 (ISBN 0-938942-03-4); pap. text ed. 7.50. Pacific Gallery.

Anderer, Paul. Other Worlds: Arishima Takeo & the Bounds of Modern Japanese Fiction. 224p. 1984. 25.00x (ISBN 0-231-05884-5). Columbia U Pr.

Anderes, Fred & Agranoff, Ann. Ice Palaces. LC 83-6061. (Illus.). 132p. 1983. 29.95 (ISBN 0-89659-391-6); pap. 16.95 (ISBN 0-89659-393-2). Abbeville Pr.

Anderhalden, A., ed. Das Behinderte Kind. Roelli, H. J. (Paediatrische Fortbildungskurse fuer die Praxis: Vol. 56). (Illus.). vi, 110p. 1982. pap. 22.75 (ISBN 3-8055-3493-0). S Karger.

Anderheggen, George C. Willie the Weenie Whiner. (Illus.). 20p. (Orig.). 1983. 3.95 (ISBN 0-910717-01-X). Bookling Pub.

--A Wish for Your Christmas. (Illus.). 13p. (Orig.). 1982. write for info. Bookling Pub.

Anderhub, Beth. Manual of Abdominal Sonography. (Illus.). 256p. 1983. text ed. 37.50 (ISBN 0-8391-1804-X, 18589). Univ Park.

Anderhub, Rita, jt. auth. see Polek, David.

Anderman, Janusz. Poland under Black Light. Short, Andrew & Taylor, Nina, trs. from Pol. (Readers International Ser.). (Illus.). 150p. 1985. 12.50 (ISBN 0-930523-13-X, Dist. by Persea Books). Readers Intl.

Anderrson, Charlotte C., jt. auth. see American Bar Association.

Anders, Evan. Boss Rule in South Texas: The Progressive Era. 335p. 1982. 19.95 (ISBN 0-292-70736-3). U of Tex Pr.

Anders, Evelyn, jt. auth. see Becker, Esther.

Anders, Evelyn, jt. auth. see Becker, Esther R.

Anders, Frank L. The Custer Trail: A Narrative of the Line of March of Troops Serving in the Department of Dakota in the Campaign Against Hostile Sioux, 1876, Fort Abraham Lincoln to the Montana Line. Carroll, John M., ed. (Illus.). 148p. 1983. 55.00x (ISBN 0-87062-147-5). A H Clark.

Anders, Gerhard, et al, eds. The Economics of Mineral Extraction. Gramm, W. Phillip. LC 79-22949. 334p. 1980. 49.95x (ISBN 0-03-053171-3). Praeger.

Anders, Henry R. Shakespeare's Books. LC 76-158251. Repr. of 1904 ed. 12.50 (ISBN 0-404-00355-9). AMS Pr.

--Shakespeare's Books. 1973. Repr. of 1904 ed. 12.00 (ISBN 0-8274-1668-7). R West.

Anders, Isabel, jt. auth. see Williamsen, Glen.

Anders, Isabel, ed. see Kuntzleman, Charles T. & Runyon, Daniel V.

Anders, James E., Sr. Industrial Hydraulics Troubleshooting. (Illus.). 192p. 1983. 29.75 (ISBN 0-07-001592-9). McGraw.

Anders, Jaroslaw, tr. see Herbert, Zbigniew.

Anders, Julia. Counterfeit Honeymoon. (Orig.). 1980. pap. 1.50 (ISBN 0-440-11138-2). Dell.

Anders, K. T. Legacy of Fear. 224p. 1985. pap. 2.95 (ISBN 0-380-89515-3). Avon.

Anders, Karl. Murder to Order. (Illus.). 1967. 6.95 (ISBN 0-8159-6207-X). Devin.

Anders, Leslie. Gentle Knight: The Life & Times of Major General Edwin Forrest Harding. LC 84-27839. (Illus.). 300p. 1985. 27.50x (ISBN 0-87338-314-1). Kent St U pr.

--The Twenty-First Missouri: From Home Guard to Union Regiment. LC 75-64. (Contributions in Military History: No. 11). (Illus.). 1975. lib. bdg. 29.95x (ISBN 0-8371-7962-9, AVI/). Greenwood.

Anders, M. W. Bioactivation of Foreign Compounds. (Biochemical Pharmacology & Toxicology Ser.). 1985. 85.00 (ISBN 0-12-059480-3). Acad Pr.

Anders, N. L., et al. An Evaluation of Potential Export Markers for Selected U. S. Fish Products. 3.00 (ISBN 0-943676-21-5). MD Sea Grant Col.

Anders, Nedda C. Applique Old & New, Including Patchwork & Embroidery. LC 75-19756. (Illus.). 128p. 1976. pap. 3.00 (ISBN 0-486-23246-8). Dover.

Anders, Phil. How to Lose Friends & Influence Enemies. 2nd, rev. ed. LC 81-82862. (Illus.). 120p. (Orig.). 1982. pap. 4.95 (ISBN 0-943304-00-8). PZA Enterp.

Anders, Rebecca. Ali the Desert Fox. Hammarberg, Dyan, tr. from Fr. LC 76-29469. (Animal Friends Books): (Illus.). (gr. k-4). 1977. PLB 5.95g (ISBN 0-87614-076-2). Carolrhoda Bks.

--Careers in a Library. LC 77-90159. (Early Career Bks.). (Illus.). (gr. 2-5). 1978. PLB 5.95 (ISBN 0-8225-0334-4). Lerner Pubns.

--Clover the Calf. Hammarberg, Dyan, tr. from Fr. LC 76-29448. (Animal Friends Bks.). (Illus.). (gr. k-4). 1977. PLB 5.95g (ISBN 0-87614-073-8). Carolrhoda Bks.

--Dolly the Donkey. Hammarberg, Dyan, tr. LC 76-1283. (The Animal Friends Bks). (Illus.). 24p. (Eng.). (gr. k-4). 1976. PLB 5.95g (ISBN 0-87614-062-2). Carolrhoda Bks.

--A Look at Aging. LC 75-38467. (Awarness Bks.). (Illus.). 36p. (gr. 3-6). 1976. PLB 4.95 (ISBN 0-8225-1304-8). Lerner Pubns.

--A Look at Alcoholism. LC 77-12981. (Awareness Bks.). (Illus.). (gr. 3-6). 1977. PLB 4.95 (ISBN 0-8225-1311-0). Lerner Pubns.

--A Look at Death. LC 77-14182. (Awareness Bks.). (gr. 3-6). 1977. PLB 4.95 (ISBN 0-8225-1308-0). Lerner Pubns.

--A Look at Drug Abuse. LC 77-12982. (Awareness Bks.). (Illus.). (gr. 3-6). 1977. PLB 4.95 (ISBN 0-8225-1309-9). Lerner Pubns.

--A Look at Mental Retardation. LC 75-38466. (Lerner Awareness Bks.). (Illus.). 36p. (gr. 3-6). 1976. PLB 4.95 (ISBN 0-8225-1303-X). Lerner Pubns.

--A Look at Prejudice & Understanding. LC 75-38469. (Awareness Bks.). (Illus.). 36p. (gr. 3-6). 1976. PLB 4.95 (ISBN 0-8225-1306-4). Lerner Pubns.

--Lorito the Parrot. Hammarberg, Dyan, tr. from Fr. LC 76-1208. (The Animal Friends Bks). (Illus.). 24p. (gr. k-4). 1976. PLB 5.95g (ISBN 0-87614-068-1). Carolrhoda Bks.

--Whiskers the Rabbit. Hammarberg, Dyan, tr. from Fr. LC 76-1236. (The Animal Friends Bks). (Illus.). 24p. (Eng.). (gr. k-4). 1976. PLB 5.95g (ISBN 0-87614-070-3). Carolrhoda Bks.

--Winslow the Hamster. Hammarberg, Dyan, tr. from Fr. LC 76-40966. (Animal Friends Books). (Illus.). (gr. k-4). 1977. PLB 5.95g (ISBN 0-87614-078-9). Carolrhoda Bks.

Anders, W. An Army in Exile: The Story of the Second Polish Corps. (Allied Forces Ser.: No. 1). (Illus.). 319p. 1981. Repr. of 1949 ed. 18.95 (ISBN 0-89839-043-5). Battery Pr.

Andersch, Alfred. Efraim's Book. Manheim, Ralph, tr. 304p. 1984. pap. 6.95 (ISBN 0-14-004621-6). Penguin.

--Die Kirschen Der Freiheit & Selected Stories. Russ, C. A. H., ed. 177p. (Orig., Ger.). pap. text ed. 7.00x (ISBN 0-435-38000-1). Heinemann Ed.

Andersdatter, Karha. The Girl Who Struggled with Death. Date not set. price not set (ISBN 0-911051-14-7). Plain View.

Andersdatter, Karla. The Rising of the Flesh. 96p. (Orig.). 1983. pap. 5.95 (ISBN 0-911051-00-7). Plain View.

--To a Chinese Girl Singing. 36p. 1984. chapbook 6.00 (ISBN 0-911051-07-4). Plain View.

Andersdatter, Karla M. Follow the Blue Butterfly. (Illus.). (gr. 4-8). 1980. 6.00 (ISBN 0-935430-00-8). In Between.

--I Don't Know Whether to Laugh or Cry Cause I Lost the Map to Where I Was Going. LC 78-1144. 1978. pap. 2.50 (ISBN 0-915016-20-6). Second Coming.

Andersdutter, Karla. Anazazi Woman. (Fastbook 1985 Ser.). 20p. 1985. 6.00 (ISBN 0-911051-19-8). Plain View.

Andersen. Greatest Power in the Universe. pap. 5.00 (ISBN 0-87980-339-8). Wilshire.

--Vikings of the West. 103p. 1981. 13.00 (ISBN 0-317-19027-X, N508). Vanous.

Andersen, A. C., ed. Beagle As an Experimental Dog. LC 79-83321. (Illus.). 616p. 1970. 20.50x (ISBN 0-8138-0169-9). Iowa St U Pr.

Andersen, A. C., et al. Dogs & Other Large Mammals in Aging Research, Vol. 1. LC 74-8039. 168p. 1974. text ed. 21.50x (ISBN 0-8422-7226-7). Irvington.

Andersen, Alfred F. Liberating the Early American Dream: As a Way to Transcend the Capitalists-Communist Dilemma Nonviolently. LC 85-51336. (Illus.). xiii, 272p. (Orig.). 1985. 24.50 (ISBN 0-931803-02-0, Dist. by Transaction Books); pap. 12.50 (ISBN 0-931803-01-2). Paine Inst.

Andersen, Allen C. & Simpson, Miriam E. The Ovary & Reproductive Cycle of the Dog (Beagle) LC 72-83492. (Illus.). 1973. text ed. 30.00x (ISBN 0-87672-007-6). Geron-X.

Andersen, Anker. Budgeting for Data Processing. 49p. pap. 6.95 (ISBN 0-86641-089-9, 82141). Natl Assn Accts.

Andersen, Ann H., jt. ed. see Huck, Virginia.

Andersen, Arlow W. The Immigrant Takes His Stand: The Norwegian-American Press & Public Affairs, 1847-1872. LC 70-138098. vii, 176p. Repr. of 1953 ed. lib. bdg. 18.75 (ISBN 0-8371-5674-2, ANIS). Greenwood.

Andersen, Arnold E. Practical Comprehensive Treatment of Anorexia Nervosa & Bulimia. LC 84-47958. (Series in Contemporary Medicine & Public Health). 224p. 1985. text ed. 28.50X (ISBN 0-8018-2442-7). Johns Hopkins.

Andersen, Arthur, et al. Federal Taxes Affecting Real Estate. 5th ed. 477p. 1981. looseleaf 70.00 (ISBN 0-686-46428-1, 815). Inst Real Estate.

--Tax Shelters: The Basics. rev. ed. LC 84-48134. 144p. 1985. 15.34i (ISBN 0-06-015382-2, HarpT). Har-Row.

Andersen, Arthur W. Bee Prepared with Honey: 140 Delicious Honey Recipes. LC 75-17102. (Illus.). 144p. (Orig.). 1975. pap. 6.95 (ISBN 0-88290-053-6). Horizon Utah.

Andersen, Benny. Benny Andersen: Selected Poems. Taylor, Alexander, tr. from Dan. LC 75-3477. (The Lockert Library of Poetry in Translation). 150p. 1975. 17.00x (ISBN 0-691-06285-4); pap. 5.95 (ISBN 0-691-01319-5). Princeton U Pr.

--The Pillows. LC 83-7166. 182p. 1983. 7.50 (ISBN 0-915306-37-9). Curbstone.

--Selected Stories. LC 82-23459. 120p. 1983. pap. 6.00 (ISBN 0-915306-25-5). Curbstone.

Andersen, Blaine W. The Analysis & Design of Pneumatic Systems. LC 76-16767. 314p. 1976. Repr. of 1967 ed. text ed. 21.50 (ISBN 0-88275-435-1). Krieger.

Andersen, Brian & Andersen, Kevon. Prisons of the Deep. LC 84-47711. (Illus.). 160p. (Orig.). 1985. pap. 10.53 (ISBN 0-06-250020-1, HarpT). Har-Row.

Andersen, C. A., ed. Microprobe Analysis. LC 72-8837. 586p. 1973. 43.00 (ISBN 0-471-02835-5). Krieger.

Andersen, Carl E. Andersen on Financial Planning: How to Increase & Preserve Your Money No Matter How Much You Make. 250p. 1985. 19.95 (ISBN 0-87094-663-3). Dow Jones-Irwin.

--Andersen on Mutual Funds. 1984. 15.95 (ISBN 0-673-15931-0). Scott F.

Andersen, Carl M. Classroom Activities for Modifying Misbehavior in Children. 1974. pap. 6.40x (ISBN 0-87628-203-6). Ctr Appl Res.

Andersen, Christopher, jt. auth. see Myers, Albert.

Andersen, Clifton R. & Cateora, Philip R., eds. Marketing Insights: Selected Readings. 3rd ed. LC 74-82804. (Illus.). 561p. 1974. pap. 7.95x (ISBN 0-914872-01-X). Austin Pr.

Andersen, D. P., et al, eds. see International Symposium on Fish Biologics.

Andersen, Dan W., ed. see Herrick, Virgil E.

Andersen, David, jt. auth. see Roberts, Nancy.

Andersen, David W. & Brooker, Wendell. Expanding Your Church School Program: Planning Elective Classes for Adults. 88p. 1983. pap. 4.95 (ISBN 0-8170-1009-2). Judson.

Andersen, Dick. Symphony Encore: Program Notes. (Illus.). 325p. 21.95 (ISBN 0-89588-247-7). Sybex.

Andersen, Dick & Cobb, Douglas. One-Two-Three Tips, Tricks, & Traps. 360p. 1984. pap. 16.95 (ISBN 0-88022-110-0, 127). Que Corp.

Andersen, Dines. A Pali Reader with Notes & Glossary. 1976. Repr. of 1901 ed. 39.00x (ISBN 0-403-05978-X, Regency). Scholarly.

Andersen, Dines & Smith, Helmer, eds. The Sutta-Nipata. LC 78-70124. Repr. of 1913 ed. 27.00 (ISBN 0-404-17383-7). AMS Pr.

Andersen, E. B. Discrete Statistical Models with Social Science Applications. 383p. 1980. 64.00 (ISBN 0-444-85334-0, North Holland). Elsevier.

Andersen, Edwin D., jt. auth. see Lund, Charles.

Andersen, Francis I. The Hebrew Verbless Clause in the Pentateuch. (SBL Monograph). 8.95 (ISBN 0-89130-321-9, 06-00-14). Scholars Pr GA.

--Job. Wiseman, D. J., ed. LC 76-12298. (Tyndale Old Testament Commentary Ser.). 1976. 10.95 (ISBN 0-87784-869-6); pap. 6.95 (ISBN 0-87784-263-9). Inter-Varsity.

--The Sentence in Biblical Hebrew. (Janua Linguarum, Ser. Practica: No. 231). 209p. 1974. pap. text ed. 23.20x (ISBN 90-2792-673-5). Mouton.

Andersen, Francis I. & Forbes, A. Dean. Eight Minor Prophets: A Linguistic Concordance. (Computer Bible Ser.: Vol. X). 1976. pap. 25.00 (ISBN 0-935106-11-1). Biblical Res Assocs.

--A Linguistic Concordance of Ruth & Jonah: Hebrew Vocabulary & Idiom. (Computer Bible Ser.: Vol. IX). 1976. pap. 15.00 (ISBN 0-935106-12-X). Biblical Res Assocs.

Andersen, Georg & Dean, Edith. Interior Decorating: A Reflection of the Creator's Design. 192p. 1983. 15.95 (ISBN 0-87123-288-X). Bethany Hse.

Andersen, Gerda M. Say It in Danish. (Orig.). pap. 2.50 (ISBN 0-486-20818-4). Dover.

Andersen, Gosta-Esping. Politics Against Markets: The Social Democratic Road to Power. LC 84-42882. 376p. 1985. text ed. 32.50x (ISBN 0-691-09408-X). Princeton U Pr.

Andersen, Gretchen. Creative Exploration in Crafts. (Illus.). 368p. 1976. 21.95 (ISBN 0-87909-169-X). Reston.

Andersen, H. A. & Hohl, E. Studies in Cassius Dio & Herodian. LC 75-7342. (Roman History Ser.). (Illus., Ger.). 1975. Repr. of 1975 ed. 17.00x (ISBN 0-405-07063-2). Ayer Co Pubs.

Andersen, Hans C. The Nightingale. LC 85-2765. (Illus.). 32p. (gr. 4-8). 1985. pap. 12.95 (ISBN 0-15-257427-1). HarBraceJ.

Andersen, Hans Christian. Andersen's Fairy Tales. (Illustrated Junior Library). (Illus.). 352p. pap. 10.95 (ISBN 0-448-11005-9, G&D); deluxe ed. 5.95 (ISBN 0-448-06005-1). Putnam Pub Group.

--Andersen's Fairy Tales. (Bambi Classics Ser.). (Illus.). 204p. (Orig.). 1981. pap. 3.95 (ISBN 0-89531-052-X, 0221-48). Sharon Pubns.

--Andersen's Fairy Tales. LC 83-1357. (Illus.). 300p. 1983. 15.95 (ISBN 0-671-47559-2). Wanderer Bks.

--Andersen's Fairy Tales. (Classics Ser.). (Illus.). (gr. 3 up). pap. 1.25 (ISBN 0-8049-0169-4). Airmont.

--Complete Fairy Tales & Stories. LC 73-83583. (ps up). 24.95 (ISBN 0-385-01901-7). Doubleday.

--Dulac's the Snow Queen. LC 76-7308. (Illus.). 144p. (ps up). 7.95 (ISBN 0-385-11678-0). Doubleday.

--Eighty Fairy Tales. Keigwin, R. P., tr. LC 82-47882. 483p. 1982. 14.45 (ISBN 0-394-52523-X). Pantheon.

--Eighty Tales. Keigwin, R. P., tr. 394p. 1982. 7.95 (ISBN 0-394-71055-X). Random.

--Emperor & the Nightingale. (Silver Series of Puppet Plays). pap. 1.50 (ISBN 0-8283-1248-6). Branden Pub Co.

--Emperor & the Nightingale. LC 78-18065. (Illus.). 32p. (gr. k-4). 1979. PLB 7.89 (ISBN 0-89375-134-0); pap. 1.95 (ISBN 0-89375-112-X). Troll Assocs.

--The Emperor's New Clothes. Rockwell, Anne, retold by. & illus. LC 81-43313. (Illus.). 32p. (ps-3). 1982. 9.57i (ISBN 0-690-04150-0); PLB 9.89 (ISBN 0-690-04149-7). Crowell Jr Bks.

--Emperor's New Clothes. (Illus.). 48p. (gr. k-3). 1949. PLB 7.95 (ISBN 0-395-18415-0). HM.

--The Emperor's New Clothes. (Illus.). 48p. (gr. k-3). 1979. pap. 2.50 (ISBN 0-395-28594-1). HM.

--Emperor's New Clothes. Delano, Jack & Delano, Irene, eds. (Illus.). 1971. (BYR). Random.

--Emperor's New Clothes. (gr. k-3). 1971. pap. 1.75 (ISBN 0-590-02941-X). Scholastic Inc.

--Emperor's New Clothes. LC 78-18063. (Illus.). 32p. (gr. k-4). 1979. PLB 7.89 (ISBN 0-89375-132-4); pap. 1.95 (ISBN 0-89375-110-3). Troll Assocs.

--The Emperor's New Clothes. (Hans Christian Andersen Story Bks.). 28p. (gr. 3-6). 1985. PLB 5.95 (ISBN 0-87239-862-5, 4982). Standard Pub.

--The Emperor's Nightingale. Haugaard, Erik, tr. LC 81-40417. (Moonlight Editions Ser.). (Illus.). 34p. 1981. 5.95 (ISBN 0-8052-3780-1, Moonlight Edns). Schocken.

--Fairy Tales. (gr. k up). 1985. pap. 12.95 (ISBN 0-245-54269-8). Beaufort Bks NY.

--Fir Tree. LC 73-121800. (Illus.). 48p. (gr. 3-6). 1970. 10.53 (ISBN 0-06-020077-4); PLB 11.89 (ISBN 0-06-020078-2). HarpJ.

--The Fir Tree. (Collection of Fairy Tales Ser.). (Illus.). 40p. 1983. 7.95 (ISBN 0-87191-949-4). Creative Ed.

--First Three Tales. 3rd ed. pap. 5.00x (ISBN 87-14-27297-0, D715). Vanous.

--Hans Andersen: His Classic Fairy Tales. LC 77-74792. (Illus.). 196p. (gr. 1 up). 1978. 15.95 (ISBN 0-385-13364-2). Doubleday.

--Hans Andersen's Fairy Tales. Lewis, Naomi, ed. (Puffin Story Bk.). (Illus.). 176p. 1981. pap. 2.95 (ISBN 0-14-030333-2, Puffin). Penguin.

--Hans Andersen's Fairy Tales. Roberton, E. Jean, ed. LC 79-64120. (Illus.). (gr. 3-9). 1979. lib. bdg. 9.95x (ISBN 0-8052-3719-4); pap. 4.50 (ISBN 0-8052-0632-9). Schocken.

--Hans Andersen's Fairy Tales. LC 79-20407. (Illus.). 96p. 1980. 9.95 (ISBN 0-8052-3732-1). Schocken.

--Hans Andersen's Fairy Tales: A Selection. Kingsland, L. W., tr. from Danish. (WC-P Ser.). (Illus.). 493p. 1985. pap. 4.95 (ISBN 0-19-281699-3). Oxford U Pr.

--Hans Christian Andersen Fairy Tales. 1982. Repr. lib. bdg. 18.95x (ISBN 0-89966-388-5). Buccaneer Bks.

--Hans Christian Andersen's Fairy Tales. (Classics Ser.). (gr. 3 up). pap. 1.50 (ISBN 0-8049-0169-4, CL-169). Airmont.

--It's Absolutely True. (Hans Christian Andersen Story Bks.). 28p. (gr. 3-6). 1985. PLB 5.95 (ISBN 0-87239-861-7, 4981). Standard Pub.

--Kate Greenaway's Original Drawings for the Snow Queen. Boner, Charles, tr. LC 81-40406. (Illus.). 64p. 1981. 12.95 (ISBN 0-8052-3776-3). Schocken.

--Little Match Girl. LC 68-28050. (Illus.). (gr. k-3). 1968. PLB 12.95 (ISBN 0-395-21625-7); pap. 1.95 (ISBN 0-395-13712-8). HM.

--The Little Match Girl. (Hans Christian Andersen Story Bks.). 28p. (gr. 3-6). 1985. PLB 5.95 (ISBN 0-87239-863-3, 4983). Standard Pub.

--Little Mermaid. 3rd ed. 1981. pap. 6.00x (ISBN 87-14-27781-6, D714). Vanous.

--The Little Mermaid. Bell, Anthea, tr. from Ger. LC 84-9490. (Illus.). 32p. (gr. 2 up). 1984. 12.95 (ISBN 0-907234-59-3, Pub. by Picture Bk Studio USA). Neugebauer Pr.

--Michael Hague's Favorite Hans Christian Andersen Fairy Tales. LC 81-47455. (Illus.). 176p. (gr. 4 up). 1981. 16.95 (ISBN 0-03-059528-2). HR&W.

--New Tales, Eighteen Forty-Three. Incl. The Angel; The Nightingale; Sweethearts; The Ugly Duckling. 1973. pap. 6.00x (ISBN 8-7142-7349-7, D743). Vanous.

--The Nightingale. LC 73-17648. (Illus.). 32p. (gr. k-3). 1974. PLB 10.89 (ISBN 0-200-00133-7, AbS-J). Har-Row.

--Nightingale. Le Gallienne, Eva, tr. LC 64-18574. (Illus.). 48p. (gr. 3 up). 1965. 12.45i (ISBN 0-06-023780-5); PLB 12.89 (ISBN 0-06-023781-3). HarpJ.

--The Nightingale. Bell, Anthea, tr. from Ger. LC 84-9492. Orig. Title: Die Nachtigall. (Illus.). 28p. (Orig.). (gr. 1 up). Date not set. pap. 7.50 (ISBN 0-907234-68-2, Pub. by Picture Bk Studio USA). Neugebauer Pr.

--The Nightingale. LC 84-9492. (gr. 1up). 1984. 11.95 (ISBN 0-907234-57-7, Pub. by Picture Bk Studio USA). Neugebauer Pr.

--The Nightingale. Le Gallienne, Eve, tr. (Illus.). (ps-3). 13.50 (ISBN 0-317-13383-7). Har-Row.

--The Nightingale. Le Gallienne, Eva, tr. from Danish. LC 64-18574. (A Trophy Picture Bk.). (Illus.). 40p. (ps up). 1985. pap. 6.68i (ISBN 0-06-443070-7, Trophy). HarpJ.

--The Nightingale. (Illus.). 32p. (ps up). 1985. 12.95 (ISBN 0-517-55211-6). Crown.

--The Princess & the Pea. LC 77-12707. (Illus.). (ps-2). 1978. 10.95 (ISBN 0-395-28807-X, Clarion). HM.

--The Princess & the Pea. Stevens, Janet, adapted by. & illus. LC 81-13395. (Illus.). 32p. (gr. k-2). 1982. reinforced bdg. 11.95 (ISBN 0-8234-0442-0). Holiday.

--The Princess & the Pea. Boada, Francesc, adapted by. Northam, Leland, tr. from Span. LC 85-40496. (Illus.). 24p. (ps-3). 1985. 3.95 (ISBN 0-382-09144-2). Silver.

--The Red Shoes. (Children's Theatre Playscript Ser.). 1969. pap. 2.50x (ISBN 0-88020-048-0). Coach Hse.

--The Red Shoes. Bell, Anthea, tr. from Danish. LC 82-61836. 36p. 1983. 11.95 (ISBN 0-907234-26-7, Pub. by Picture Bk Studio USA). Neugebauer Pr.

--The Snow Queen. Naomi, adapted by. LC 68-17218. (Illus.). 32p. (ps-5). 8.95 (ISBN 0-87592-048-9). Scroll Pr.

--Snow Queen. Magito, Suria & Weil, Rudolf, eds. LC 59-15639. 1960. pap. 3.50x (ISBN 0-87830-538-6). Theatre Arts.

--The Snow Queen. Lewis, Naomi, adapted by. (Illus.). (ps-3). 1982. pap. 3.50 (ISBN 0-14-050294-7, Puffin). Penguin.
--The Snow Queen. LC 82-70199. (Illus.). 40p. (gr. k up). 1982. 12.95 (ISBN 0-8037-8011-7, 01258-370); PLB 12.89 (ISBN 0-8037-8029-X). Dial Bks Young.
--The Snow Queen. LC 83-71172. (Collection of Fairy Tales Ser.). 48p. 1984. 7.95 (ISBN 0-87191-950-8). Creative Ed.
--The Snow Queen. Le Gallienne, Eva, tr. from Danish. LC 83-47711. (Illus.). 128p. (ps up). 1985. 13.41i (ISBN 0-06-023694-9); PLB 13.89g (ISBN 0-06-023695-7). HarpJ.
--The Snow Queen. LC 85-42797. (Illus.). 64p. 1985. 17.95 (ISBN 0-02-743610-1). Macmillan.
--The Snow Queen: A New Adapted Version by Naomi Lewis. LC 78-10462. (Illus.). (gr. k-3). 1979. 10.95 (ISBN 0-670-65378-0). Viking.
--Snow White. Saunders, Robert, ed. Bell, Anthea, tr. from Ger. (Illus.). 40p. (gr. 1 up). 1985. 12.95 (ISBN 0-88708-012-X, Pub. by Picture Bk Studio USA). Neugebauer Pr.
--The Steadfast Tin Soldier. LC 79-4325. (Illus.). (ps-4). 1979. 8.95 (ISBN 0-395-28964-5, Clarion). HM.
--The Steadfast Tin Soldier. (Illus.). 32p. (gr. 1-4). 1981. 8.95 (ISBN 0-13-846295-X). P-H.
--The Steadfast Tin Soldier. LC 83-9360. (Illus.). 32p. 1983. 14.95 (ISBN 0-316-03949-7). Little.
--The Steadfast Tin Soldier. (Collection of Fairy Tales Ser.). (Illus.). 32p. 1983. 7.95 (ISBN 0-87191-948-6). Creative Ed.
--Stories from Hans Andersen. LC 79-50552. (Illus.). 1979. 35.00 (ISBN 0-913870-79-X). Abaris Bks.
--The Stories of Hans Andersen. Mathias, Robert, retold by. LC 85-61399. (Illus.). 80p. (ps-4). 1985. 11.45 (ISBN 0-382-09153-1). Silver.
--The Swineherd. Bell, Anthea, tr. from Danish. LC 81-14173. (Illus.). (gr. k-3). 1982. 11.75 (ISBN 0-688-00929-8); lib. bdg. 11.88 (ISBN 0-688-00930-1). Morrow.
--The Swineherd. Bell, Anthea, tr. from Ger. Orig. Title: Der Schweinehirt. (Illus.). 28p. (gr. 1 up). Date not set. pap. 7.50 (ISBN 0-88708-102-9, Pub. by Picture Bk Studio USA). Neugebauer Pr.
--Tales & Stories by Hans Christian Andersen. Conroy, Patricia & Rossel, Sven H., trs. LC 80-50867. (Illus.). 316p. 1980. 22.50x (ISBN 0-295-95769-7); pap. 9.95 (ISBN 0-295-95936-3). U of Wash Pr.
--Thumbelina. LC 79-50146. (Illus.). (ps-3). 1979. 12.95 (ISBN 0-8037-8815-0, 01258-370); PLB 12.89 (ISBN 0-8037-8814-2). Dial Bks Young.
--Thumbelina. new ed. LC 78-18080. (Illus.). 32p. (gr. k-4). 1979. PLB 7.89 (ISBN 0-89375-141-3); pap. 1.95 (ISBN 0-89375-119-7). Troll Assocs.
--Thumbelina. (Hans Christian Andersen Story Bks.). 28p. (gr. 3-6). 1985. PLB 5.95 (ISBN 0-87239-864-1, 4984). Standard Pub.
--Thumbelina. Saunders, Robert, ed. Bell, Anthea, tr. from Ger. (Illus.). 28p. (gr. 1 up). 1985. 11.95 (ISBN 0-88708-006-5, Pub. by Picture Bk Studio USA). Neugebauer Pr.
--Thumbelina. LC 79-50146. (Illus.). 32p. (ps-3). 1985. pap. 4.95 (ISBN 0-8037-0232-9, Pied Piper). Dial Bks Young.
--Thumbeline. Winston, Richard & Winston, Clara, trs. from Danish. LC 80-13012. Orig. Title: Tommelise. (Illus.). 40p. (gr. k-3). 1980. 12.50 (ISBN 0-688-22235-8); PLB 12.88 (ISBN 0-688-32235-2). Morrow.
--Thumbeline. Bell, Anthea, tr. from Ger. LC 84-9461. Orig. Title: Tommelise. (Illus.). 28p. (gr. 1 up). Date not set. pap. 7.50 (ISBN 0-907234-66-6, Pub. by Picture Bk Studio USA). Neugebauer Pr.
--Thumbeline, The Nightingale, The Swineherd, 3 vols. Bell, Anthea, tr. from Ger. Orig. Title: Tommelise, Die Nachtigall, Der Schweinehirt. (Illus.). 84p. (gr. 1 up). pap. cancelled (Pub. by Picture Bk Studio USA). Neugebauer Pr.
--The Ugly Duckling. LC 75-145207. (Illus.). 32p. (ps-3). 8.95 (ISBN 0-87592-055-1). Scroll Pr.
--Ugly Duckling. new ed. LC 78-18059. (Illus.). 32p. (gr. k-4). 1979. PLB 7.89 (ISBN 0-89375-128-6); pap. 1.95 (ISBN 0-89375-106-5). Troll Assocs.
--The Ugly Duckling. LC 84-52782. (Tell Me a Story Ser.). 18p. (ps-1). 1985. 3.75 (ISBN 0-382-09071-3). Silver.
--The Ugly Duckling. Stewart, Anne, tr. LC 84-25927. Orig. Title: Den grimme a elling. (Illus.). 24p. (gr. k-3). 1985. 11.75 (ISBN 0-688-04951-6). Greenwillow.
--The Wild Swans. LC 81-65843. 40p. (gr. k up). 1981. 10.95 (ISBN 0-8037-9381-2); PLB 10.89 (ISBN 0-8037-9391-X). Dial Bks Young.
--The Wild Swans. LC 80-27685. (Illus.). 32p. (gr. k-2). 1981. PLB 7.89 (ISBN 0-89375-480-3); pap. text ed. 1.95 (ISBN 0-89375-481-1). Troll Assocs.
--The Wild Swans. Lewis, Naomi, tr. LC 83-15805. (Illus.). 32p. 11.95 (ISBN 0-911745-36-X). P Bedrick Bks.
Andersen, Hans Christian, jt. auth. see Adams, Adrienne.
Andersen, Hans Christian, jt. auth. see Brown, Marcia.
Andersen, Hans Christian see Swan, D. K.
Andersen, Hans H., ed. Bibliography & Index of Experimental Range & Stopping Power Data. LC 77-22415. 1978. text ed. 57.00 (ISBN 0-08-021604-8). Pergamon.
Andersen, Hans H. & Ziegler, James F., eds. Hydrogen Stopping Powers & Ranges in All Elements, Vol. 3. LC 77-3068. 1977. text ed. 47.00 (ISBN 0-08-021605-6). Pergamon.
Andersen, Hans O. & Koutnik, Paul G. Toward More Effective Science Instruction in Secondary Education. 1972. write for info. (ISBN 0-02-303200-6, 30320). Macmillan.
Andersen, Howard A., jt. auth. see Moersch, Herman J.
Andersen, Ian. Making Money. LC 77-93232. 1978. 10.00 (ISBN 0-8149-0797-0). Vanguard.
--Turning the Tables on Las Vegas. 1978. pap. 2.95 (ISBN 0-394-72509-3, Vin). Random.
--Turning the Tables on Las Vegas. LC 76-12005. (Illus.). 224p. 1976. 10.00 (ISBN 0-8149-0776-8). Vanguard.
Andersen, Isabelle. Gentle Asylum: Life at a Mental Hospital. 1976. 8.95 (ISBN 0-8264-0108-2). Continuum.
Andersen, J. E., ed. Light Metals 1982: Proceedings, AIME Annual Meeting, Dallas, 1982. LC 72-623660. (Illus.). 1170p. 1981. 55.00. Metal Soc.
Andersen, Johannes C. Maori Life in Ao-tea. LC 75-35221. Repr. of 1907 ed. 56.00 (ISBN 0-404-14400-4). AMS Pr.
--Maori Music, with Its Polynesian Background. LC 75-35222. Repr. of 1934 ed. 42.00 (ISBN 0-404-14401-2). AMS Pr.
--Maori String Figures. LC 75-35223. Repr. of 1927 ed. 27.50 (ISBN 0-404-14402-0). AMS Pr.
--The Maori Tohunga & His Spirit World. LC 75-35224. Repr. of 1948 ed. 15.00 (ISBN 0-404-14403-9). AMS Pr.
--Myths & Legends of the Polynesians. LC 75-35170. (Illus.). Repr. of 1931 ed. 43.50 (ISBN 0-404-14200-1). AMS Pr.
Andersen, Juel. Curry Primer: A Grammar of Spice Cookery. (Illus.). 64p. pap. 4.50 (ISBN 0-916870-79-0). Creative Arts Bk.
--Juel Andersen's Curry Primer: A Grammar of Spice Cookery. LC 84-45102. 64p. (Orig.). 1984. pap. 4.50 (ISBN 0-916870-79-0). Creative Arts Bk.
--Juel Andersen's Sesame Primer. (Illus.). 64p. (Orig.). 1983. pap. 3.95 (ISBN 0-916870-66-9). Creative Arts Bk.
--Juel Andersen's Tofu Fantasies. (Illus.). 83p. (Orig.). 1982. pap. 4.95 (ISBN 0-916870-44-8). Creative Arts Bks.
--Juel Andersen's Tofu Primer: A Beginner's Book of Bean Cake Cookery. LC 84-71565. (Illus.). 64p. (Orig.). 1981. pap. 4.50 (ISBN 0-916870-33-2). Creative Arts Bk.
--Sesame Primer. (Illus.). 64p. pap. 3.95 (ISBN 0-916870-66-9). Creative Arts Bk.
--Tofu Fantasies: A Collectiion of Incomparable Dessert Recipes. (Illus.). 80p. pap. 4.95 (ISBN 0-916870-44-8). Creative Arts Bk.
Andersen, Juel & Andersen, Sigrid. Tofu Primer: A Beginner's Book of Bean Cake Cookery. (Illus.). 64p. pap. 4.50 (ISBN 0-916870-33-2). Creative Arts Bk.
Andersen, Juel, jt. auth. see Bauer, Cathy.
Andersen, Juel, jt. auth. see Clute, Robin.
Andersen, Juel, jt. auth. see Ford, Richard.
Andersen, K. E. & Maibach, H. I., eds. Contact Allergy Predictive Test in Guinea Pigs. (Current Problems in Dermatology: Vol. 14). (Illus.). viii, 250p. 1985. 77.25 (ISBN 3-8055-4053-1). S Karger.
Andersen, K. Lange, et al. Fundamentals of Exercise Testing. 116p. 1970. pap. 9.60 (ISBN 92-4-156001-0, 241). World Health.
Andersen, Karen B. What's the Matter, Sylvie, Can't You Ride? LC 80-12514. (Illus.). 32p. (ps-3). 1981. 9.95 (ISBN 0-8037-9607-2, 0966-290); PLB 9.89 (ISBN 0-8037-9621-8). Dial Bks Young.
Andersen, Kenneth E. Persuasion: Theory & Practice. 2nd ed. (Illus.). 431p. 1983. pap. text ed. 16.95x (ISBN 0-89641-117-6). American Pr.
Andersen, Kenneth W. & Jones, J. Knox, Jr. Mammals of Northwestern South Dakota. (Museum Ser.: Vol. 19, No. 5). 33p. 1971. pap. 1.75 (ISBN 0-317-04914-3). U of KS Mus Nat Hist.
Andersen, Kevon, jt. auth. see Andersen, Brian.
Andersen, Knud C. Catalogue of the Chiroptera in the Collection of the British Museum, Vol. 1. Megachiroptera. 2nd ed. (Illus.). 72.00 (ISBN 0-384-01395-3). Johnson Repr.
Andersen, Kristi. Creation of a Democratic Majority, Nineteen Twenty-Eight to Nineteen Thirty-Six. LC 78-11660. (Illus.). 1979. lib. bdg. 14.00x (ISBN 0-226-01884-9). U of Chicago Pr.
Andersen, Kurt. The Real Thing. LC 81-7043. 192p. (Orig.). 1982. pap. 5.25 (ISBN 0-03-060037-5, Owl Bks). HR&W.
Andersen, Linda. Classroom Activities for Helping Perceptually Handicapped Children. 1974. pap. 6.40x (ISBN 0-87628-201-X). Ctr Appl Res.
--Love Adds the Chocolate. 1984. 4.95 (ISBN 0-8010-0198-6). Baker Bk.
Andersen, Loren. Theo-History: The Parallel Covenants Theory. 120p. 1983. pap. 4.25 (ISBN 0-9611310-0-4). Day Bk Co.
Andersen, Mary A., ed. The Civil War Diary of Allen Morgan Geer. LC 77-3830. 1977. 15.00 (ISBN 0-686-22707-7). R C Appleman.
Andersen, N. R. & Malahoff, A., eds. The Fate of Fossil Fuel CO2 in the Oceans. LC 77-11099. (Marine Science Ser.: Vol. 6). 749p. 1977. 95.00x (ISBN 0-306-35506-X, Plenum Pr). Plenum Pub.
Andersen, Neil R. & Zahuranec, Bernard J., eds. Oceanic Sound Scattering Prediction. LC 77-3445. (Marine Science Ser.: Vol. 5). 859p. 1977. 110.00x (ISBN 0-306-35505-1, Plenum Pr). Plenum Pub.
Andersen, Niels T. Sunrise Over Jordan: A Twenty-First Century College. LC 82-84240. 283p. 1982. 11.95 (ISBN 0-910213-01-1); pap. 6.95 (ISBN 0-910213-00-3). Jordan Pub.
Andersen, P. Vikings of the West-Expansion of Norway in Middle Ages. (Tanum of Norway Tokens Ser). (Illus.). pap. 13.00x (ISBN 82-518-0026-9, N508). Vanous.
Andersen, Paul. Index to Coinage Magazine, Vols. 1-16: 1965-1980. LC 81-68956. 21p. (Orig.). (gr. 8 up). 1981. pap. 2.95 (ISBN 0-9604720-2-9). P Andersen.
--Let's Collect Type Coins. LC 81-90057. (Illus.). 57p. 1981. pap. 2.95 (ISBN 0-9604720-1-0). P Andersen.
--Obsolete Fractional Coinage of the United States. LC 79-55915. (Illus.). 67p. (Orig.). (gr. 9 up). 1980. pap. 2.95 (ISBN 0-9604720-0-2). P Andersen.
--Statically Indeterminate Structures: Their Analysis & Design. LC 52-11520. (Illus.). pap. 81.50 (ISBN 0-317-10804-2, 2012568). Bks Demand UMI.
--Substructure Analysis & Design. 2nd ed. LC 56-6804. pap. 87.00 (ISBN 0-317-08677-4, 2012446). Bks Demand UMI.
--United States Five-Cent Pieces, 1792-1982. LC 82-90453. (Illus.). 54p. (Orig.). 1982. pap. 2.95 (ISBN 0-9604720-3-7). P Andersen.
Andersen, Paul & Nordby, Gene M. Introduction to Structural Mechanics. LC 60-13150. pap. 88.00 (ISBN 0-317-10800-X, 2012445). Bks Demand UMI.
Andersen, R. & Barlag, R. They Were There. 1977. pap. 4.50 (ISBN 0-570-03769-7, 12-2704). Concordia.
Andersen, Raoul, ed. North Atlantic Maritime Cultures. (World Anthropology Ser.). 1979. text ed. 32.80x (ISBN 90-279-7830-1). Mouton.
Andersen, Richard. Devotional Guide Book for Board & Committee Chairpersons. 1982. pap. 2.95 (ISBN 0-570-03845-6, 12-2948). Concordia.
--Devotions for Church School Teachers. LC 76-2158. 64p. 1976. pap. 2.25 (ISBN 0-570-03722-0, 12-2624). Concordia.
--Inspirational Meditations for Sunday Church School Teachers. 1980. pap. 2.25 (ISBN 0-570-03810-3, 12-2919). Concordia.
--A Little Library of Inspiration for Sunday School Teachers. 1982. pap. 2.25 (ISBN 0-570-03846-4, 12-2949). Concordia.
--Positive Power of Christian Partnership. 1982. pap. 1.95 (ISBN 0-570-03844-8, 12-2947). Concordia.
--Straight Cut Ditch. Hammond, Debbie, ed. LC 79-7034. 1979. 14.95 (ISBN 0-87949-139-6). Ashley Bks.
Andersen, Richard & Deffner, Donald. For Example... 1978. pap. 7.95 (ISBN 0-570-03766-2, 12-2701). Concordia.
Andersen, Rikki. Tall & Terrific. LC 84-24659. 192p. 1985. 17.95 (ISBN 0-385-19452-8). Doubleday.
Andersen, Roger W., ed. The Acquisition & Use of Spanish & English as First & Second Languages. 181p. 1979. 6.50 (ISBN 0-318-16632-1). Tchrs Eng Spkrs.
--New Dimensions in Second Language Acquisition Research. (Illus.). 232p. (Orig.). 1981. pap. text ed. 17.95 (ISBN 0-88377-180-2). Newbury Hse.
--Pidginization & Creolization as Language Acquisition. 337p. 1983. 20.95 (ISBN 0-88377-266-3). Newbury Hse.
--Second Languages: A Cross-Linguistic Perspective. 1984. pap. text ed. 24.95. Newbury Hse.
Andersen, Ron, jt. auth. see Wei, C. C.
Andersen, Ron, jt. auth. see Wei, Kathie.
Andersen, Ronald, et al. Total Survey Error: Applications to Improve Health Surveys. LC 79-88104. (Social & Behavioral Science Ser.). 1979. text ed. 25.95x (ISBN 0-87589-409-7). Jossey-Bass.
Andersen, Ruth O see Roth, David M.
Andersen, S., et al, eds. Atomic Collisions in Solids: Conference, No. IV. 476p. 1972. 132.95 (ISBN 0-677-04660-X). Gordon.
Andersen, Sigrid, jt. auth. see Andersen, Juel.
Andersen, Sigrid, jt. auth. see Clute, Robin.
Andersen, Svend. Ideal und Singularitat: Uber die Funktion des Gottesbegriffes in Kants theoretischer Philosophie. 278p. 1983. 28.80 (ISBN 3-11-009649-8). De Gruyter.
Andersen, Svend E. & Holstein, Bjorn E. Ausbildung Im Gefangnis: Lebenshilfe fur Gefangene der Skadhauge-Plan im Daenischen Strafvolizug. (Strafvollzug, Ranggruppen, Soziale Hillen, Vol. 3). xi, 162p. (Ger.). 1982. 20.00. P Lang Pubs.
Andersen, Theodore A. A Century of Banking in Wisconsin. Bruchey, Stuart, ed. LC 80-1130. (The Rise of Commerical Banking Ser.). 1981. Repr. of 1954 ed. lib. bdg. 20.00x (ISBN 0-405-13630-7). Ayer Co Pubs.
Andersen, U. S. Secret Power of the Pyramids. 1977. pap. 5.00 (ISBN 0-87980-343-6). Wilshire.
Andersen, Uell S. Magic in Your Mind. pap. 6.00 (ISBN 0-87980-089-5). Wilshire.
--Secret of Secrets. pap. 6.00 (ISBN 0-87980-134-4). Wilshire.
--Success Cybernetics. pap. 6.00 (ISBN 0-87980-155-7). Wilshire.
--Three Magic Words. pap. 5.00 (ISBN 0-87980-165-4). Wilshire.
Andersen, Verlan. Many Are Called but Few Are Chosen. 96p. 1967. pap. 2.95 (ISBN 0-89036-002-2). Hawkes Pub Inc.
Andersen, William D. Genealogists in the United States & Canada, 1984. 65p. (Orig.). 1984. pap. 10.00 (ISBN 0-930373-01-4). W D Andersen.
Andersen, William R., jt. ed. see Roady, Thomas G., Jr.
Andersen, Yvonne. Make Your Own Animated Movies. (Illus.). (gr. 4 up). 1970. 15.45 (ISBN 0-316-03940-3). Little.
Andersland, Orlando B. & Anderson, Duwayne, eds. Geotechnical Engineering for Cold Regions. (Illus.). 1978. text ed. 52.00x (ISBN 0-07-001615-1). McGraw.
Andersohn, Gunter. Cacti & Succulents. (Illus.). 316p. 1983. 19.95 (ISBN 0-7158-0839-7, Pub by EP Publishing England). Sterling.
Anderson. Absorption of Ionizing Radiation. (Illus.). 448p. 1984. text ed. 49.50 (ISBN 0-8391-1821-X, 19860). Univ Park.
--Adventures in the Biology Laboratory. 1978. 9.00 (ISBN 0-942788-03-6). Marginal Med.
--Astro Delineator Kit. 14.25 (ISBN 0-318-01828-4). Am Fed Astrologers.
--Bank Security. 1981. text ed. 29.95 (ISBN 0-409-95038-6). Butterworth.
--Cold Victory. 2.75 (ISBN 0-317-31833-0). Tor Bks.
--Conflict. pap. 2.95 (ISBN 0-317-31838-1). Tor Bks.
--Explorations. 2.50 (ISBN 0-317-31845-4). Tor Bks.
--Fantasy. 2.50 (ISBN 0-317-31846-2). Tor Bks.
--Guardians of Time. pap. 2.95 (ISBN 0-317-31854-3). Tor Bks.
--Long Night. 2.95 (ISBN 0-317-31862-4). Tor Bks.
--Marmaduke: Ever Lovin' Marmaduke, No. 2. 1.95 (ISBN 0-317-31787-3). Tor Bks.
--Midsummer Tempest. 2.95 (ISBN 0-317-31868-3). Tor Bks.
--Mini Tours & Mystery Tours. (Illus.). 107p. 1981. pap. 6.95 (ISBN 0-937050-17-2). Stonehenge.
--Modern Compressible Flow: With Historical Perspective. (Mechanical Engineering Ser.). 1982. 45.00 (ISBN 0-07-001654-2). McGraw.
--Morphology of Congenital Heart Disease. (Illus.). 160p. 1983. text ed. 40.00 (ISBN 0-8391-1830-9, 19933). Univ Park.
--New America. 2.95 (ISBN 0-317-31869-1). Tor Bks.
--Software Construction Set for the IBM PC & PCjr. 1985. 18.95 (ISBN 0-8104-6353-9). Hayden.
--Teach What You Preach. 1982. pap. 8.95 (ISBN 0-8298-0481-1). Pilgrim NY.
Anderson & Bereitner. Thinking Games, 2 bks. Incl. Bk. 1. LC 79-57429 (ISBN 0-8224-6941-3); Bk. 2. LC 80-65124 (ISBN 0-8224-6942-1). 1980. pap. 6.50 ea. Pitman Learning.
Anderson & Grant. Heard at the Nineteenth. (Illus.). 15.00x (ISBN 0-392-03209-0, SpS). Sportshelf.
Anderson & Kober. Reading & Study Skills for the Urban College Student. 248p. 1984. pap. text ed. 16.95 (ISBN 0-8403-3356-0). Kendall-Hunt.
Anderson & Kosslyn. Tutorials in Learning & Memory. (Illus.). 336p. 1983. case 24.95 (ISBN 0-7167-1570-8); pap. text ed. 13.95 (ISBN 0-7167-1571-6). W H Freeman.
Anderson & Lawrence. Integrating Music in the Classroom. 368p. 1984. write for info. (ISBN 0-534-03933-2). Wadsworth Pub.
Anderson & McLean. Design of Experiments. (Illus.). 450p. 22.50 (ISBN 0-318-13206-0, P6). Am Soc QC.
Anderson & Savary, Louis M. Passages. (Illus.). 224p. 1972. pap. 12.45i (ISBN 0-06-067065-7, RD 51, HarpR). Har-Row.
Anderson & Sobieski. Introduction to Microbiology. 2nd ed. LC 79-20560. 1980. pap. 26.95 (ISBN 0-8016-0206-8). Mosby.
Anderson, jt. auth. see Farmer.
Anderson, jt. auth. see McLean.
Anderson, jt. auth. see Pantaleo.
Anderson, jt. auth. see Webster.
Anderson, jt. auth. see Willer.
Anderson, jt. ed. see Lowe.
Anderson, et al. Canyon De Chelly: The Story Behind the Scenery. LC 79-157461. (Illus.). 1971. 8.95 (ISBN 0-916122-34-4); pap. 3.75 (ISBN 0-916122-09-3). KC Pubns.
Anderson, A. A. Experiences & Impressions: The Autobiography of Colonel A. A. Anderson. facs. ed. LC 72-124223. (Select Bibliographies Reprint Ser). 1933. 19.00 (ISBN 0-8369-5411-4). Ayer Co Pubs.
Anderson, A. E., Jr. & Foraker, Alvan G. Pathology of Disruptive Pulmonary Emphysema. (Illus.). 256p. 1976. 23.75x (ISBN 0-398-03528-8). C C Thomas.
Anderson, A. Grant. New Zealand in Maps. (Graphic Perspectives of Developing Countries Ser.). 144p. 1978. 42.50x (ISBN 0-8419-0324-7). Holmes & Meier.

Anderson, A. J. The Artistic Side of Photography in Theory & Practice. LC 72-9179. (The Literature of Photography Ser.). Repr. of 1910 ed. 26.50 (ISBN 0-405-04890-4). Ayer Co Pubs.

--E. B. White: A Bibliography. LC 78-2783. (Author Bibliographies Ser.: No. 37). 205p. 1978. 17.50 (ISBN 0-8108-1121-9). Scarecrow.

--Problems in Library Management. LC 81-8153. (Library Science Text). 282p. 1981. text ed. 27.00 (ISBN 0-87287-261-0); pap. text ed. 20.00 (ISBN 0-87287-264-5). Libs Unl.

Anderson, A. L. The Way. 1978. pap. 2.50 (ISBN 0-8100-0006-7, 12N1715). Northwest Pub.

Anderson, A. S. Allen M. Anderson, Abraham B. Grimes & John Hamrick Families & Descendents. 1983. 30.50 (ISBN 0-9609958-0-3). McClain.

Anderson, A. W. Speed up Your Reading. LC 74-99614. 1968. pap. 8.75x (ISBN 0-85564-027-8, Pub. by U of W Austral Pr). Intl Spec Bk.

Anderson, Adam. Historical & Chronolgical Deduction of the Origin of Commerce 1801, 4 vols. 1981. write for info. (ISBN 0-08-027639-3, HE 046); microfiche 225.00 (ISBN 0-686-79343-9). Pergamon.

--Historical & Chronological Account of the Origin of Commerce, 4 vols. LC 67-20805. Repr. of 1801 ed. 250.00x (ISBN 0-678-00259-2). Kelley.

Anderson, Alan, Jr., ed. see Smith, Dwight.

Anderson, Alan R. & Belnap, Nuel D., Jr. Entailment: The Logic of Relevance & Necessity, Vol. 1. LC 72-14016. 567p. 1975. 50.00 (ISBN 0-691-07192-6). Princeton U Pr.

Anderson, Alan R., ed. Minds & Machines. (Orig.). 1964. pap. 12.95 ref. ed. (ISBN 0-13-583393-0). P-H.

Anderson, Alan R., et al, eds. The Logical Enterprise. LC 74-20084. 288p. 1975. 27.00x (ISBN 0-300-01790-1). Yale U Pr.

Anderson, Alastair S. Roman Military Tombstones. (Shire Archaeology Ser.: No. 19). (Illus., Orig.). 1983. pap. 5.95 (ISBN 0-85263-571-0, Pub. by Shire Pubns England). Seven Hills Bks.

Anderson, Albert A., tr. see Dufrenne, Mikel.

Anderson, Alexander W. How We Got Our Flowers. (Illus.). 10.75 (ISBN 0-8446-1533-1). Peter Smith.

Anderson, Alexandra, jt. auth. see Cohen, Randy.

Anderson, Alexandra, tr. see Leger, Fernand.

Anderson, Anders H. Bibliography of Arizona Ornithology. LC 76-163008. 241p. (Orig.). 1972. pap. 7.95x (ISBN 0-8165-0313-3). U of Ariz Pr.

Anderson, Anders H. & Anderson, Anne. The Cactus Wren. LC 72-77133. 226p. 1973. pap. 8.95 (ISBN 0-8165-0314-1). U of Ariz Pr.

Anderson, Andrew R. Alexander's Gate, Gog & Magog & the Inclosed Nations. 1932. 7.50x (ISBN 0-910956-07-3). Medieval Acad.

Anderson, Andy. Effective Methods of Church Growth. 1985. pap. 5.95 (ISBN 0-8054-3237-X). Broadman.

--Fasting Changed My Life. LC 77-82404. 1977. pap. 3.50 (ISBN 0-8054-5259-1). Broadman.

--Hungary Nineteen Fifty-Six. 1976. pap. 1.90x (ISBN 0-934868-01-8). Black & Red.

Anderson, Anita & Martin, Tracy. Mastering FORTH. 216p. 1984. pap. 17.95 (ISBN 0-89303-660-9). Brady Comm.

Anderson, Anker. Graphing Financial Information. 50p. pap. 6.95 (ISBN 0-86641-086-4, 82138). Natl Assn Accts.

Anderson, Ann K. I Gave God Time. 1982. 7.95 (ISBN 0-8423-1560-8); pap. 5.95 1984 (ISBN 0-8423-1559-4). Tyndale.

--Taste of Tears, Touch of God. (Illus.). 176p. 1985. 9.95 (ISBN 0-8407-9025-2). Nelson.

Anderson, Anna E. Pain: The Essence of a Mental Illness. 64p. 1979. 5.00 (ISBN 0-682-49527-1). Exposition Pr FL.

--Woman in the Wraparound Skirt. 152p. 1979. 7.50 (ISBN 0-682-49450-X). Exposition Pr FL.

Anderson, Anne. Interpreting Pottery. LC 84-61545. (Illus.). 208p. 1985. 27.50x (ISBN 0-87663-743-8). Universe.

Anderson, Anne, jt. auth. see Anderson, Anders H.

Anderson, Anne, jt. ed. see McPherson, Ann.

Anderson, Anne S. & Pitre, Marianne R. Land Claims of Hancock County, Mississippi Filed April 2nd 1894. 50p. 1985. lib. bdg. 15.00 (ISBN 0-318-04436-6). L W Anderson Genealogical.

Anderson, Annelise G. The Business of Organized Crime: A Cosa Nostra Family. (Publications 201 Ser.). (Illus.). 200p. 1979. 13.95x (ISBN 0-8179-7011-8). Hoover Inst Pr.

Anderson, Anthony. The Man Who Was H. M. Bateman. (Illus.). 224p. 1982. 19.95 (ISBN 0-03-061459-7). HR&W.

Anderson, Anthony, ed. The Raman Effect, Vol. 1. LC 77-134788. pap. 104.00 (ISBN 0-317-08513-1, 2055067). Bks Demand UMI.

Anderson, Arthur J. Grammatical Examples, Exercises, & Review: For Use with "Rules of the Aztec Language". LC 73-80997. 1973. pap. text ed. 10.00x (ISBN 0-87480-065-X). U of Utah Pr.

--Problems in Intellectual Freedom & Censorship. LC 74-4107. (Bowker Series in Problem-Centered Approaches to Librarianship). pap. 54.80 (ISBN 0-317-19839-4, 2023054). Bks Demand UMI.

--Rules of the Aztec Language: Classical Nahuatl Grammar. LC 72-88553. 1973. pap. text ed. 10.00x (ISBN 0-87480-023-4). U of Utah Pr.

Anderson, Arthur J. & Dibble, Charles E. The Florentine Codex: General History of the Things of New Spain, Introductory Volume. (The Florentine Codex Ser.). 1982. 35.00x (ISBN 0-87480-205-9). U of Utah Pr.

Anderson, Arthur J., tr. see Leon-Portilla, Miguel.

Anderson, Arthur J., tr. see Sahagun, Bernardino de.

Anderson, Arthur J., et al. Beyond the Codices: The Nahua View of Colonial Mexico. LC 74-29801. (Latin American Studies Center UCLA Ser.: Vol. 27). 225p. 1976. 44.00s (ISBN 0-520-02974-7). U of Cal Pr.

Anderson, Arthur L. Divided We Stand: Institutional Religion As a Reflection of Pluralism & Integration in America. LC 78-61582. 1978. pap. text ed. 9.95 (ISBN 0-8403-1935-5). Kendall-Hunt.

Anderson, Arthur W. Pension Mathematics for Actuaries. 1985. text ed. 49.00 (ISBN 0-9614420-1-8). A W Anderson.

--Wild Beasts & Angels. 1979. pap. 4.50 (ISBN 0-910452-43-1). Covenant.

Anderson, Arvid & Jascourt, Hugh D., eds. Trends in Public Sector Labor Relations. 278p. 1975. pap. 11.00 non-members; members 10.00. Intl Personnel Mgmt.

Anderson, Arvid C. Masters of Music. facsimile ed. LC 70-117320. (Biography Index Reprint Ser.). 1948. 17.00 (ISBN 0-8369-8012-3). Ayer Co Pubs.

Anderson, Austin G., jt. ed. see Withgott, Coleen K.

Anderson, Ava V. The Manhunt Was a Biggie (With Some Waiting) (Illus.). 144p. 1983. 10.95 (ISBN 0-89962-327-1). Todd & Honeywell.

Anderson, B. & Shapiro, P. Emergency Childbirth Handbook. 1982. pap. 7.95 (ISBN 0-442-20979-7). Van Nos Reinhold.

Anderson, B., jt. auth. see America, R.

Anderson, B. D. & Arbib, M. A. Foundations of System Theory Finitary & Infinitary Conditions. (Lecture Notes in Economics & Math Systems: Vol. 115). 93p. 1976. pap. 13.00 (ISBN 0-387-07611-5). Springer-Verlag.

Anderson, B. D., jt. auth. see Clements, D. J.

Anderson, B. D. & Ljung, L., eds. Adaptive Control. 232p. 1984. pap. 40.00 (ISBN 0-08-031660-3). Pergamon.

Anderson, B. L., ed. Capital Accumulation in the Industrial Revolution. (Rowman & Littlefield University Library). 212p. 1974. 13.50x (ISBN 0-87471-401-X). Rowman.

Anderson, B. Ray. How to Save Fifty Percent or More on Your Income Tax - Legally. 256p. 1983. 14.95 (ISBN 0-02-501980-5). Macmillan.

--How You Can Use Inflation to Beat IRS: All the Legal Ways to Keep Your Money for Yourself & Your Family... Without Getting in Trouble with the IRS. LC 80-8429. (Illus.). 448p. 1981. 16.30i (ISBN 0-06-014825-X, HarpT). Har-Row.

Anderson, B. Robert. Professional Sales Management. (Illus.). 432p. 1981. text ed. 27.95 (ISBN 0-13-725879-8). P-H.

--Professional Selling. (Illus.). 400p. 1981. text ed. 25.95 (ISBN 0-13-725960-3). P-H.

Anderson, B. W. Gem Testing. 9th rev. ed. 1980. 39.95 (ISBN 0-408-00440-1). Butterworth.

Anderson, Barbara. Kierkegaard: A Fiction. 1974. 14.95x (ISBN 0-8156-0100-X). Syracuse U Pr.

--Ordinary Days. (Porch Chapbook Ser.: No. 6). 1981. pap. 3.50 (ISBN 0-932968-17-1). Porch Pubns.

Anderson, Barbara & Anderson, Douglas. Chaco Canyon: Center of a Culture. rev. ed. Jackson, Earl, ed. LC 75-18206. 60p. (Orig.). 1981. pap. 5.00 (ISBN 0-911408-57-6). SW Pks Mnmts.

Anderson, Barbara & Shapiro, Pamela. Obstetrics for the Nurse. 272p. 1981. 17.95 (ISBN 0-442-21840-0). Van Nos Reinhold.

Anderson, Barbara & Shapiro, Pamela J. Obstetrics for the Nurse. 4th ed. LC 83-71048. 1984. pap. text ed. 14.40 (ISBN 0-8273-2194-5); instrs' guide 4.20 (ISBN 0-8273-2195-3). Delmar.

Anderson, Barbara, jt. auth. see Anderson, Douglas.

Anderson, Barbara, jt. auth. see Coale, Ansley J.

Anderson, Barbara A. Internal Migration During Modernization in Late Nineteenth-Century Russia. LC 80-7509. (Illus.). 248p. 1980. 26.50 (ISBN 0-691-09386-5). Princeton U Pr.

Anderson, Barbara B. & Anderson, Cletus. Costume Design. 1984. text ed. 28.95 (ISBN 0-03-060383-8). HR&W.

Anderson, Barbara G. The Aging Game: Success, Sanity & Sex After Sixty. LC 79-18293. (McGraw-Hill Paperbacks Ser.). 252p. 1981. pap. 4.95 (ISBN 0-07-001761-1). McGraw.

--The Aging Game: Success, Sanity & Sex After Sixty. LC 79-18293. 1979. 12.95 (ISBN 0-07-001760-3). McGraw.

Anderson, Barbara G., jt. auth. see Anderson, Robert T.

Anderson, Barbara G., jt. auth. see Clark, Margaret.

Anderson, Barbara S., jt. auth. see Hopkins, Bruce R.

Anderson, Barry, jt. auth. see Tobin, Gary A.

Anderson, Barry F. The Complete Thinker: A Handbook of Techniques for Creative & Critical Problem Solving. (Illus.). 224p. 1980. (Spec); pap. 4.95 (ISBN 0-13-164582-X). P-H.

--Psychology Experiment: An Introduction to the Scientific Method. 2nd ed. LC 77-133827. (Orig.). 1970. pap. text ed. 11.00 pub net (ISBN 0-8185-0100-6). Brooks-Cole.

Anderson, Barry F., et al. Concepts in Judgement & Decision Research: Definitions, Sources, Interrelations, Comments. LC 81-7345. 320p. 1981. 39.95x (ISBN 0-03-059337-9). Praeger.

Anderson, Basil W. Gem Testing. (Illus.). 1959. 13.95 (ISBN 0-87523-082-2). Emerson.

Anderson, Benedict. Imagined Communities: Reflections on the Origin & Spread of Nationalism. 288p. 1983. 24.00 (ISBN 0-8052-7177-5, Pub. by NLB England); pap. 6.50 (ISBN 0-8052-7178-3). Schocken.

Anderson, Benedict & Kahin, Audrey, eds. Interpreting Indonesian Politics: Thirteen Contributions to the Debate, 1964-1981. (Interim Reports Ser.). 164p. (Orig.). 1982. 9.00 (ISBN 0-87763-028-3). Cornell Mod Indo.

Anderson, Benedict, tr. see Simatupang, T. B.

Anderson, Benedict R. Mythology & the Tolerance of the Javanese. 3rd ed. 77p. Repr. of 1965 ed. 5.00 (ISBN 0-87763-023-2). Cornell Mod Indo.

--Some Aspects of Indonesian Politics under the Japanese Occupation: 1944-1945. LC 61-66733. (Cornell University Modern Indosnesia Project Interim Reports Ser.). pap. 34.00 (ISBN 0-317-11172-8, 2010810). Bks Demand UMI.

Anderson, Benedict R. & McVey, Ruth T. A Preliminary Analysis of the October 1, 1965 Coup in Indonesia: Interim Report. 162p. 1971. pap. 6.00 (ISBN 0-87763-008-9). Cornell Mod Indo.

Anderson, Benedict R., tr. see Sjahrir, Sutan.

Anderson, Benedict R., et al. A Preliminary Analysis of the October 1, 1965 Coup in Indonesia. LC 71-30341. (Cornell University, Modern Indonesia Project, Interim Reports Ser.). pap. 45.00 (ISBN 0-317-11107-8, 2021675). Bks Demand UMI.

Anderson, Benjamin. Narrative of a Journey to Musardu: The Capitol of the Mandingoes. 172p. 1971. 28.50x (ISBN 0-7146-1785-7, BHA 01785, F Cass Co). Biblio Dist.

Anderson, Benjamin M. Economics & the Public Welfare: Financial & Economic History of the United States, 1914-1946. LC 79-20911. 1980. 11.00 (ISBN 0-913966-68-1, Liberty Pr); pap. 5.00 (ISBN 0-913966-69-X). Liberty Fund.

Anderson, Benjamin M., Jr. Social Value: A Study in Economic Theory Critical & Constructive. LC 65-26357. Repr. of 1911 ed. 22.50x (ISBN 0-678-00177-4). Kelley.

Anderson, Berhard W., jt. auth. see Noth, Martin.

Anderson, Bern. By Sea & by River: The Naval History of the Civil War. LC 77-6473. (Illus.). 1977. Repr. of 1962 ed. lib. bdg. 39.75 (ISBN 0-8371-9651-5, ANBS). Greenwood.

Anderson, Bernhard W. The Eighth Century Prophets: Amos, Hosea, Isaiah, Micah. McCurley, Foster R., ed. LC 78-54545. (Proclamation Commentaries: the Old Testament Witnesses for Preaching). 132p. 1978. pap. 5.95 (ISBN 0-8006-0595-0, 1-595). Fortress.

--The Living Word of the Bible. LC 78-27108. 118p. 1979. pap. 4.95 (ISBN 0-664-24247-2). Westminster.

--Out of the Depths: The Psalms Speak for Us Today. Revised & Expanded ed. LC 83-19801. 254p. 1983. pap. 11.95 (ISBN 0-664-24504-8). Westminster.

--Understanding the Old Testament. 3rd ed. 608p. 1975. 28.95 (ISBN 0-13-936153-7). P-H.

--The Unfolding Drama of the Bible. rev. ed. LC 78-14057. 1971. pap. 2.95 (ISBN 0-8329-1068-6, Assn Pr). New Century.

Anderson, Bernhard W., ed. Creation in the Old Testament. LC 83-48910. (Issues in Religion & Theology Ser.). 192p. 1984. pap. 6.95 (ISBN 0-8006-1768-1, 1-768). Fortress.

Anderson, Bernice, jt. auth. see Mortlock, Allan J.

Anderson, Bernice E., jt. auth. see Lesnik, Milton.

Anderson, Bert M. Write True to Yourself So You Sell: 19 Lessons in Folios. write for info. (ISBN 0-917628-02-0). Coraco.

Anderson, Betty & Joels, Rosie W. Teaching Reading to Students with Limited English Proficiencies. 74p. 1985. 14.75x (ISBN 0-398-05179-8). C C Thomas.

Anderson, Betty A., et al. The Childbearing Family, Vol. 1: Pregnancy & Family Health. 2nd ed. (Illus.). 1979. pap. text ed. 22.95 (ISBN 0-07-001683-6). McGraw.

--The Childbearing Family, Vol. 2: Interruptions in Family Health During Pregnancy. 2nd ed. (Illus.). 1979. pap. text ed. 22.95 (ISBN 0-07-001684-4). McGraw.

Anderson, Beverly, jt. auth. see McConnell, Adeline.

Anderson, Beverly, jt. auth. see McConnell, Adeline P.

Anderson, Beverly M. & Hamilton, Donna M. The New High Altitude Cookbook. LC 80-5287. (Illus.). 320p. 1980. 16.95 (ISBN 0-394-51308-8). Random.

Anderson, Bijorn & Hedberg, Neils B. The Impact of Systems Change in Organizations, No. 2. (Information System Ser.). 356p. 1979. 47.50x (ISBN 90-286-0549-5). Sijthoff & Noordhoff.

Anderson, Bill. Navigation Exercises for Yachtsmen. 2nd ed. 1981. 15.00x (ISBN 0-540-07275-3, Pub. by Stanford Maritime England). State Mutual Bk.

Anderson, Bo, jt. auth. see Davis, Nanette J.

Anderson, Bob. Beartooth Country: Montana's Absaroka-Beartooth Mountains. (The Montana Geographic Ser.: No. 7). (Illus.). 112p. (Orig.). 1984. pap. 13.95 (ISBN 0-938314-13-0). MT Mag.

--Stretching. Kahn, Lloyd, ed. LC 79-5567. (Illus.). 192p. (Orig.). 1980. pap. 8.95 (ISBN 0-394-73874-8). Shelter Pubns.

--Stretching: For Everyday Fitness & for Running, Tennis, Cycling, Swimming, Golf, Walking, Skiing & Other Sports. (Illus.). 1980. pap. 8.95 (ISBN 0-394-73874-8). Random.

Anderson, Bob, ed. Complete Runner, Vol. II. (Illus.). 464p. 1982. 14.95 (ISBN 0-89037-078-8). Anderson World.

--Sport-Source. LC 75-16003. (Illus.). 430p. (Orig.). 1975. 18.95 (ISBN 0-89037-061-3). Anderson World.

Anderson, Bobby. Bull Shot. LC 84-60040. (Illus., Orig.). Date not set. pap. 10.00 (ISBN 0-88100-039-6). MuhlBut Pr.

Anderson, Bobby D. The Law & the Teacher in Mississippi: A Guide for Teachers, Administrators, & Potential Teachers. LC 74-25673. 176p. 1975. pap. text ed. 1.67x (ISBN 0-87805-067-1). U Pr of Miss.

Anderson, Brad. Encore, Marmaduke! Encore. 1985. pap. 1.95 (ISBN 0-451-14021-4, Sig). NAL.

--Everlovin' Marmaduke (II) 256p. (Orig.). 1985. pap. 2.50 (ISBN 0-8125-7342-0). Tor Bks.

--Marmaduke Hams It Up. 256p. (Orig.). 1986. pap. 2.95 (ISBN 0-317-30236-1, Dist. by Warner Pub Services & St. Martin). Tor Bks.

--Marmaduke Sounds Off. 1985. pap. 1.95 (ISBN 0-451-13675-6, Sig). NAL.

--Marmaduke, Super Dog. (Illus.). 104p. (Orig.). 1983. pap. 3.95 (ISBN 0-8362-1212-6). Andrews McMeel Parker.

--Marmaduke Take Two. 1984. pap. 1.95 (ISBN 0-451-13287-4, Sig). NAL.

--Marmaduke...Again? (gr. 5 up). 1977. pap. 1.50 (ISBN 0-590-09085-2). Scholastic Inc.

--More Marmaduke. (gr. 7-12). 1974. pap. 1.50 (ISBN 0-590-06113-5). Scholastic Inc.

Anderson, Brad & Leeming, Dorothy. Marmaduke Rides Again. (Illus.). (gr. 5-8). 1972. pap. 1.50 (ISBN 0-590-08072-5). Scholastic Inc.

Anderson, Brent E., jt. auth. see Claremont, Christopher.

Anderson, Brian & Moore, John B. Optimal Filtering. 1979. 42.95 (ISBN 0-13-638122-7). P-H.

Anderson, Brian, ed. see Lang, Andrew.

Anderson, Bruce. The New Solar Home Book. (Illus.). 256p. (Orig.). 1985. pap. 16.95 (ISBN 0-931790-70-0). Brick Hse Pub.

--The Price of a Perfect Baby. LC 83-22382. 192p. 1984. pap. 4.95 (ISBN 0-87123-426-2). Bethany Hse.

Anderson, Bruce & Riordan, Michael. The Solar Home Book: Heating, Cooling, & Designing with the Sun. LC 76-29494. (Illus.). 298p. 1976. pap. 10.95 (ISBN 0-917352-01-7); pap. 8.50 members. Natl Assn Home.

Anderson, Bruce & Wells, Malcolm. Passive Solar Energy. 1981. pap. 10.95 (ISBN 0-931790-09-3). Brick Hse Pub.

--Passive Solar Energy: The Homeowners Guide to Natural Heating & Cooling. (Illus.). 208p. (Orig.). 1982. 29.95 (ISBN 0-471-88651-3, Pub. by Brick Hse Pub). Wiley.

Anderson, Bruce, compiled by. Passive Solar Design Handbook. (Illus.). 752p. 1984. 55.00 (ISBN 0-442-20810-3). Van Nos Reinhold.

Anderson, Bruce, et al see Sharer, Robert J.

Anderson, Bruce L. Let Us Make Man. LC 80-80561. (Orig.). 1980. pap. 4.95 (ISBN 0-88270-430-3, Haven Bks). Bridge Pub.

Anderson, Bruce N. Solar Energy: Fundamentals in Building Design. LC 76-45467. (Illus.). 1977. 42.25 (ISBN 0-07-001751-4). McGraw.

Anderson, Buegel C. Homeopathic Remedies for Physicians. 1982. pap. 8.95x (ISBN 0-317-07320-6, Regent House). B of A.

Anderson, Burton. Burton Anderson's Guide to Italian Wines. 160p. 1984. pap. 8.95 (ISBN 0-671-53022-4). S&S.

--The Simon & Schuster Pocket Guide to Italian Wines. 1982. 5.95 (ISBN 0-671-45234-7). S&S.

--Vino: The Wine & Winemakers of Italy. (Illus.). 416p. 1980. 19.95 (ISBN 0-316-03948-9, Pub. by Atlantic Monthly Pr). Little.

Anderson, Byron. A Bibliography of Master's Theses & Doctoral Dissertations on Milwaukee Topics, 1911-1977. LC 80-27261. 136p. (Orig.). 1981. pap. 5.00 (ISBN 0-87020-202-2). State Hist Soc Wis.

Anderson, C. Manual for the Examination of Bone. 128p. 1982. 47.00 (ISBN 0-8493-0725-2). CRC Pr.

--A Monograph of the Mexican & Central American Species of Trixis (Compositae, No. 22(3) (Memoirs of the New York Botanical Garden Series). 68p. 1972. 8.00 (ISBN 0-317-35519-8). NY Botanical.

Anderson, C. Alan. God in a Nutshell. (Illus.). 28p. (Orig.). 1981. pap. 3.00 (ISBN 0-9607532-0-6). Squantum Pr.

--The Problem Is God: The Selection & Care of Your Personal God. (Illus.). 304p. (Orig.). 1985. pap. 9.95 (ISBN 0-913299-02-2). Stillpoint.

Anderson, C. Dixon. Spanish in Context: A Basic Course. (Illus.). 1978. text ed. 26.95 (ISBN 0-13-824235-6); pap. 11.95 student wkbk (ISBN 0-13-824243-7); tapes 240.00 (ISBN 0-13-824292-5). P-H.

Anderson, C. K. & Jones, W. G., eds. Germ Cell Tumours. 450p. cancelled (ISBN 0-85066-223-0). Taylor & Francis.

Anderson, C. K., et al, eds. Germ Cell Tumours: Proceedings, University of Leeds, March 24-24, 1981. LC 81-83947. 448p. 1981. 44.00 (ISBN 0-8451-3001-3). A R Liss.

Anderson, C. L., jt. auth. see Green, Lawrence W.

Anderson, C. N., ed. see Kohner, Frederick.

Anderson, C. W. Billy & Blaze. 1971. pap. 3.95 (ISBN 0-02-041420-X, Collier). Macmillan.

--Blaze & the Forest Fire. 1972. pap. 3.95 (ISBN 0-02-041410-2, Collier). Macmillan.

--Blaze & the Lost Quarry. LC 66-10356. (Illus.). 48p. (ps-3). 1973. pap. 2.95 (ISBN 0-02-041440-4, Collier). Macmillan.

--Complete Book of Horses & Horsemanship. LC 63-16746. 182p. 1973. pap. 2.95 (ISBN 0-02-041460-9, Collier). Macmillan.

--Lonesome Little Colt. LC 61-12352. (Illus.). 48p. (gr. k-3). 1974. pap. 3.95 (ISBN 0-02-041490-0, Collier). Macmillan.

Anderson, Carl & Fox, John. Hold-Em for Winners: Gamesmam Hold-Em. 1982. 14.95 (ISBN 0-940416-03-4). Bacchus Pr.

Anderson, Carl A. & Gribbin, William J., eds. Emblem of Freedom: The American Family in the 1980's. LC 80-69955. 139p. 1981. lib. bdg. 12.95 (ISBN 0-89089-193-1). Carolina Acad Pr.

Anderson, Carl E., jt. ed. see Schneider, Howard A.

Anderson, Carl L. Poe in Northlight: The Scandinavian Response to His Life & Work. LC 72-88734. 1973. 15.75 (ISBN 0-8223-0275-6). Duke.

Anderson, Carl L. & Creswell, William H., Jr. School Health Practice. 7th ed. LC 79-27664. (Illus.). 1980. text ed. 22.95 (ISBN 0-8016-0216-5). Mosby.

Anderson, Carl L., ed. see Roos, Rosalie.

Anderson, Carl L., tr. see Roos, Rosalie.

Anderson, Carl R. Management: Skills, Functions & Organization Performance. 800p. 1984. text ed. write for info (ISBN 0-697-08228-8); instr's manual avail. (ISBN 0-697-00228-4); instr's manual for wkbk avail. (ISBN 0-697-00271-3); transparencies avail. (ISBN 0-697-00288-8); wkbk. avail. (ISBN 0-697-00248-9); test item file avail. (ISBN 0-697-00360-4). Wm C Brown.

Anderson, Carl R., jt. auth. see Paine, Frank T.

Anderson, Carle. Choices, Chances, Changes: A Guide to Making Informed Choice About Your Untimely Pregnancy. 62p. 5.00 (ISBN 0-318-13873-5). CUB.

Anderson, Carol & Stewart, Susan. Mastering Resistance: A Practical Guide to Family Therapy. LC 82-21033. (Family Therapy Ser.). 251p. 1983. text ed. 20.00 (ISBN 0-89862-044-9, 2044). Guilford Pr.

Anderson, Carol, jt. ed. see Luber, Raymond F.

Anderson, Carol L., jt. auth. see Fraley, Ruth A.

Anderson, Carolyn & Haller, Jackie. Brain Stretchers-Book I. 1975. pap. 6.95 (ISBN 0-910974-87-X). Midwest Pubns.

Anderson, Catherine. In the Mother Tongue. LC 83-82377. 61p. 1983. 12.95 (ISBN 0-914086-47-2); pap. 6.95 (ISBN 0-914086-46-4). Alicejamesbooks.

Anderson, Cay M. Here Comes Jonathan. LC 82-81067. (Illus.). 36p. (Orig.). (ps-1). 1982. pap. 12.50 spiral bound (ISBN 0-941478-04-1). Paraclete Pr.

Anderson, Charles. A City & Its Cinemas. 96p. 1983. 20.00x (ISBN 0-905459-63-6, Pub. by Redcliffe Pr Ltd). State Mutual Bk.

--Political Economy of Social Class. 384p. 1974. text ed. 26.95 (ISBN 0-13-685149-5). P-H.

Anderson, Charles & Travis, L. D. Psychology & the Liberal Consensus. 200p. 1983. text ed. 17.75x (ISBN 0-88920-127-7, 40911, Pub. by Wilfrid Laurier U Pr). Humanities.

Anderson, Charles, ed. see James, Henry.

Anderson, Charles A. & Schnaper, Miriam. School & Society in England: Social Backgrounds of Oxford & Cambridge Students. LC 70-138142. 34p. 1972. Repr. of 1952 ed. lib. bdg. 15.00 (ISBN 0-8371-5599-1, ANSS). Greenwood.

Anderson, Charles B., jt. auth. see Klippel, Allen P.

Anderson, Charles D., ed. Outlaws of the Old West. (Great Adventures of History Ser.). 1973. pap. 1.50 (ISBN 0-87687-012-4, BM012). Mankind Pub.

Anderson, Charles R. Emily Dickinson's Poetry: Stairway of Surprise. LC 82-15844. (Illus.). xvii, 334p. 1982. Repr. of 1963 ed. lib. bdg. 42.50x (ISBN 0-313-23733-6, ANED). Greenwood.

--The Grunts. LC 76-4153. (Illus.). 204p. 1976. 14.95 (ISBN 0-89141-003-1). Presidio Pr.

--The Grunts. 256p. 1984. pap. 3.50 (ISBN 0-425-07119-7). Berkley Pub.

--Person, Place & Thing in Henry James's Novels. LC 77-75619. xx, 192p. 1977. 21.00 (ISBN 0-8223-0395-7). Duke.

--Vietnam: The Other War. LC 81-15677. (Illus.). 244p. 1982. 13.95 (ISBN 0-89141-137-2). Presidio Pr.

Anderson, Charles R., ed. Centennial Edition of the Works of Sidney Lanier, 10 vols. Incl. Vol. 1. Poems & Poem Outlines. 396p (ISBN 0-8018-0029-3); Vol. 2. The Science of English Verse & Essays on Music. Baum, Paull F., ed. 389p (ISBN 0-8018-0030-7); Vol. 3. Shakespeare & His Forerunners. Malone, Kemp, ed. 443p (ISBN 0-8018-0031-5); Vol. 4. The English Novel & Essays on Literature. Gohdes, Clarence & Malone, Kemp, eds. 411p (ISBN 0-8018-0032-3); Vol. 5. Tiger Lilies & Southern Prose. Greever, Garland & Abernethy, Cecil, eds. 407p (ISBN 0-8018-0033-1); Vol. 6. Florida & Miscellaneous Prose. Graham, Philip, ed. 437p (ISBN 0-8018-0034-X); Vols. 7-10. Letters. Anderson, Charles R. & Starke, Aubrey H., eds. (Vol. 7). Vol. 7, 401p (ISBN 0-8018-0035-8). Vol. 8, 450p. Vol. 9, 575p. Vol. 10, 542p. 4241p. 1945. 32.50x ea.; Set. 285.00x (ISBN 0-8018-0028-5). Johns Hopkins.

--Journal of a Cruise to the Pacific Ocean, 1842-1844, in the Frigate United States with Notes on Herman Melville. LC 70-158282. Repr. of 1937 ed. 16.50 (ISBN 0-404-00356-7). AMS Pr.

Anderson, Charles S. Augsburg Historical Atlas of Christianity in the Middle Ages & Reformation. LC 67-11723. 1973. pap. 8.95 (ISBN 0-8066-1317-3, 10-0521). Augsburg.

--Faith & Freedom: The Christian Faith According to the Lutheran Confessions. LC 76-27087. 1977. pap. 6.50 (ISBN 0-8066-1558-3, 10-2170). Augsburg.

Anderson, Charles S., ed. see Prenter, Regin.

Anderson, Charles W. Political Economy of Modern Spain: Policy-Making in an Authoritarian System. LC 72-106036. (Illus.). 298p. 1970. 27.50x (ISBN 0-299-05611-2); pap. 10.95x (ISBN 0-299-05614-7). U of Wis Pr.

Anderson, Charles W., jt. auth. see Glade, William P., Jr.

Anderson, Charles W. see Solo, Robert A.

Anderson, Charlotte C., jt. auth. see Winston, Barbara J.

Anderson, Cheryl A. Better Bulletin Boards. rev. ed. (Bridges for Ideas Handbook Ser.). 1981. pap. text ed. 6.00x (ISBN 0-913648-10-8). U Tex Austin Film Lib.

--Lettering Techniques. 3rd. ed. (Bridges for Ideas Handbook Ser.). 1982. pap. text ed. 6.00x (ISBN 0-913648-06-X). U Tex Austin Film Lib.

Anderson, Chester. Fox & Hare. LC 80-66869. (Illus.). 192p. 1980. 13.95 (ISBN 0-9601428-0-0); pap. 6.95 (ISBN 0-9601428-9-4). Entwhistle Bks.

Anderson, Chester G. Word Index to James Joyce's Stephen Hero. 185p. 1980. Repr. of 1958 ed. lib. bdg. 35.00 (ISBN 0-8495-0220-9). Arden Lib.

--Words Index to James Joyce's Stephen Hero. LC 76-49592. 1977. lib. bdg. 20.00 (ISBN 0-8414-2961-8). Folcroft.

Anderson, Chester G., ed. Growing Up in Minnesota: Ten Writers Remember Their Childhoods. LC 75-40546. 1976. 10.95 (ISBN 0-8166-0765-6); pap. 6.95 (ISBN 0-8166-0921-7). U of Minn Pr.

Anderson, Chester G., ed. see Joyce, James.

Anderson, Christian & Hawes, J. L. Basic Experimental Chemistry: A Laboratory Manual for Beginning Students. rev. ed. 1971. pap. 21.95 (ISBN 0-8053-0222-0). Benjamin-Cummings.

Anderson, Christiane, ed. see Affolter, James M.

Anderson, Christiane, ed. see Elisens, Wayne J.

Anderson, Christiane, ed. see Elvander, Patrick E. & Wells, Elizabeth F.

Anderson, Christiane, ed. see Schlessman, Mark A.

Anderson, Christiane, ed. see Standley, Lisa A.

Anderson, Christopher, jt. auth. see Myers, Albert.

Anderson, Christopher A. The Man & Woman Relationship: A New Center for the Universe. LC 85-71216. 1985. 25.00 (ISBN 0-931353-00-9). Andersons Pubns.

--To Cassandra: Early Years. LC 85-71217. 1985. pap. 10.00 (ISBN 0-931353-01-7). Andersons Pubns.

Anderson, Claire, ed. see League of Woman Voters of New York State.

Anderson, Clarence A. Minnesota Unemployment Insurance Guide. 1984. spiral bdg 37.50 (ISBN 0-86678-065-3). Butterworth MN.

Anderson, Clarence W. Billy & Blaze. LC 62-14797. (Illus.). (gr. k-3). 1969. 10.95x (ISBN 0-02-701880-6); pap. 3.95x (ISBN 0-02-041420-X). Macmillan.

--Blaze & the Forest Fire. LC 62-14797. (Illus.). (gr. k-3). 1969. 10.95x (ISBN 0-02-702080-0); pap. 3.95 (ISBN 0-02-041410-2). Macmillan.

--Blaze & the Gray Spotted Pony. LC 68-10997. (Illus.). (ps-2). 1968. 10.95 (ISBN 0-02-701150-X); pap. 2.95x (ISBN 0-02-041480-3). Macmillan.

--Blaze & the Indian Cave. LC 64-14529. (Illus.). (gr. 1-3). 1971. 9.95 (ISBN 0-02-702470-9). Macmillan.

--Blaze & the Mountain Lion. LC 59-22393. (gr. 1-3). 1969. 10.95 (ISBN 0-02-702630-2). Macmillan.

--Blaze & Thunderbolt. LC 55-14874. (Illus.). (gr. 1-3). 1969. 10.95 (ISBN 0-02-702870-4). Macmillan.

--Blaze Finds Forgotten Roads. LC 76-117970. (Illus.). (gr. k-3). 1970. 10.95 (ISBN 0-02-701340-5). Macmillan.

--Phantom, Son of the Gray Ghost. LC 69-18233. (Illus.). 96p. (gr. 4-6). 1969. 8.95 (ISBN 0-02-701350-2). Macmillan.

Anderson, Cletus, jt. auth. see Anderson, Barbara B.

Anderson, Craig. Science Fiction Films of the Seventies. LC 83-42898. (Illus.). 275p. 1985. pap. 15.95x (ISBN 0-89950-086-2). McFarland & Co.

Anderson, Curtis B., et al. Chemistry: Principles & Applications. 1973. text ed. 24.95x (ISBN 0-669-73833-6); instructors' manual free (ISBN 0-669-81919-0). Heath.

Anderson, Cynthia K., jt. ed. see Russell, Earl B.

Anderson, D. Pound's Cavalcanti: An Edition of the Translations, Notes & Essays. 1982. 27.00 (ISBN 0-691-06519-5). Princeton U Pr.

Anderson, D., et al. Schools to Grow in: An Evaluation of Secondary Colleges. LC 80-69743. 162p. 1981. pap. text ed. 6.95 (ISBN 0-7081-1014-2, 550, Pub. by ANUP Australia). Australia N U P.

Anderson, D., et al, eds. Pipe & Tube Fabrication. 2nd ed. (Engineering Craftsmen: No. D3). (Illus.). 1978. spiral bdg. 39.95x (ISBN 0-85083-415-5). Intl Ideas.

Anderson, D. A., et al. Computational Fluid Mechanics & Heat Transfer. LC 83-18614. (Series in Computational Methods in Mechanics & Thermal Sciences). 624p. 1984. 45.00 (ISBN 0-07-050328-1). McGraw.

Anderson, D. C. Evaluating Curriculum Proposals: A Critical Guide. LC 80-23324. 178p. 1981. 32.95x (ISBN 0-470-27075-6). Halsted Pr.

Anderson, D. C. & Large, D. M. Self Assessment in Clinical Medicine. 128p. 1981. pap. text ed. 9.25 (ISBN 0-632-00676-5, B-0201-7). Mosby.

Anderson, D. C., ed. Strategies for Professional Development Evaluation by Classroom Experience. 1979. 20.00x (ISBN 0-905484-20-7, Pub. by Nafferton England). State Mutual Bk.

--Strategies for Professional Development: Self Assessment in the N. H. S. Techniques for Monitoring & Research. 1980. 20.00x (ISBN 0-905484-35-5, Pub. by Nafferton England). State Mutual Bk.

Anderson, D. Carl. Trial by Death & Fire. LC 80-14446. (Orion Ser.). 160p. 1980. pap. 3.95 (ISBN 0-8127-0292-1). Review & Herald.

Anderson, D. Chris & Borkowski, John G. Experimental Psychology: Research Tactics & Their Applications. 1978. text ed. 22.75 (ISBN 0-673-07866-3). Scott F.

Anderson, D. Chris, jt. auth. see Borkowski, John G.

Anderson, D. D. Analyzing Time Series: Proceedings of the International Time Series Meeting, Guernsey, Oct. 1979. 1980. 76.75 (ISBN 0-444-85464-9). Elsevier.

Anderson, D. G. New Practice Readers, 7 Bks. 1978. Bks. A-E. pap. text ed. 6.92 ea.; Bks. F-G. pap. text ed. 7.44 ea. McGraw.

Anderson, D. H. Compartmental Modeling & Tracer Kinetics. (Lecture Notes in Biomathematics: Vol. 50). 302p. 1983. pap. 20.00 (ISBN 0-387-12303-2). Springer-Verlag.

Anderson, D. J. & Kikkawa, J. Community Ecology: Pattern & Process. (Illus.). 400p. 1985. text ed. 50.00x (ISBN 0-632-01062-2); pap. text ed. 28.00x (ISBN 0-632-01063-0). Blackwell Sci.

Anderson, D. J., jt. auth. see Gillison, A. N.

Anderson, D. J., ed. Physiology: Past, Present, & Future: A Symposium in Honour of Yngve Zotterman, University of Bristol, July 11 & 12, 1979. LC 80-40957. (Illus.). 168p. 1980. 32.00 (ISBN 0-08-025480-2). Pergamon.

Anderson, D. J., jt. ed. see Gillison, A. N.

Anderson, D. R., et al. Instructional Programming for the Handicapped Student. (Illus.). 1024p. 1976. pap. 37.50x (ISBN 0-398-03340-4). C C Thomas.

Anderson, D. S. & Blakers, C. Transition from School: An Annotated Bibliography on Recent Australian Studies. 286p. (Orig.). 1980. pap. text ed. 8.95 (ISBN 0-7081-1015-0, 0149, Pub. by ANUP Australia). Australia N U P.

Anderson, D. V. Illusions of Power: A History of the Washington Public Power Supply System. LC 84-18329. 176p. 1985. 29.95 (ISBN 0-03-000369-5). Praeger.

Anderson, Dan. American Freestyle Karate. LC 81-50512. (Illus.). 200p. 1981. pap. 7.95 (ISBN 0-86568-021-3). Unique Pubns.

Anderson, Daniel, jt. ed. see Bryant, Jennings.

Anderson, Daniel A. Psychopathology of Denial. 52p. 1981. 3.95 (ISBN 0-89486-143-3). Hazelden.

Anderson, Daniel J. Anxiety-Conflicts & Chemical Dependency. 40p. (Orig.). 1976. pap. 1.30 (ISBN 0-89486-047-X). Hazelden.

--The Joy & Sorrows of Sobriety. 28p. (Orig.). 1977. pap. 1.95 (ISBN 0-89486-035-6). Hazelden.

--Perspectives on Treatment: The Minnesota Experience. 60p. 1981. 3.95 (ISBN 0-89486-133-6). Hazelden.

Anderson, Daniel J., et al. Applied Research: Impact on Decision Making. 22p. 1978. pap. 5.95 (ISBN 0-89486-043-7). Hazelden.

Anderson, Darryl, ed. Atmospheric Science & Power Production. 860p. 1984. pap. 29.50 (ISBN 0-87079-126-5, DOE/TIC-27601); microfiche 4.50 (ISBN 0-87079-231-8, DOE/TIC-27601). DOE.

Anderson, Dave. More Funny Things on the Way to Church. Wilcox, Tim, ed. (Continued Applied Christianity Ser.). 1983. pap. 4.50 (ISBN 0-570-03893-6, 12-2975). Concordia.

--The Story of Football. (Illus.). 192p. (gr. 5 up). 1985. 13.00 (ISBN 0-688-05634-2, Morrow Junior Books); pap. 8.95 (ISBN 0-688-05635-0). Morrow.

Anderson, Dave & Wilcox, Tim. A Funny Thing Happened on the Way to Church. 1981. pap. 4.50 (ISBN 0-570-03834-0, 12YY2799). Concordia.

Anderson, Dave, jt. auth. see Iooss, Walter, Jr.

Anderson, Dave, jt. auth. see Madden, John.

Anderson, Dave, ed. The Red Smith Reader. LC 83-5879. 320p. 1983. pap. 5.95 (ISBN 0-394-71750-3, Vin). Random.

Anderson, David. The Life & Times of Walter Watton, M. D. LC 85-71216. 196p. 1985. 14.95 (ISBN 0-89227-111-6). Commonwealth Pr.

--The Net in the Bay: Or, Journal of a Visit to Moose & Albany. 22.00 (ISBN 0-384-01401-1). Johnson Repr.

--The Piano Makers. (Illus.). 56p. (gr. 8-12). 1982. 10.95 (ISBN 0-394-85353-9); PLB 10.99 (ISBN 0-394-95353-3). Pantheon.

Anderson, David & Benjaminson, Peter. Investigative Reporting. LC 75-23896. (Midland Bks.: No. 196). 320p. 1976. pap. 8.95x (ISBN 0-253-20196-9). Ind U Pr.

Anderson, David & Holland, I. I., eds. Forests & Forestry. 3rd ed. (gr. 10-12). 1982. 19.65 (ISBN 0-8134-2169-1); text ed. 14.75x. Interstate.

Anderson, David & Winter, Jeremy S., eds. Adrenal Cortex. (BIMR Clinical Endocrinology Ser.: Vol. 4). 352p. 1985. text ed. 99.95 (ISBN 0-407-02275-9). Butterworth.

Anderson, David, tr. from Greek. On the Divine Images: St. John of Damascus. LC 80-13409. 106p. 1980. pap. 3.95 (ISBN 0-913836-62-1). St Vladimirs.

Anderson, David, tr. see St. Basil The Great.

Anderson, David, et al. Homeopathic Remedies for Physicians, Laymen & Therapists. LC 78-102966. 140p. 1978. pap. 4.95 (ISBN 0-89389-037-5). Himalayan Pubs.

--Linear Programming for Decision Making: An Applications Approach. LC 74-1138. 280p. 1974. text ed. 28.95 (ISBN 0-8299-0008-X); tchrs. manual avail. (ISBN 0-8299-0014-4). West Pub.

Anderson, David D. Barron's Simplified Approach to Anderson's Winesburg, Ohio. LC 67-24537. (Orig.). (gr. 11 up). 1967. pap. text ed. 1.95 (ISBN 0-8120-0261-X). Barron.

--Brand Whitlock. (Twayne's United States Authors Ser.). 1968. pap. 5.95x (ISBN 0-8084-0342-7, T-129, Twayne). New Coll U Pr.

--Critical Essays on Sherwood Anderson. (Critical Essays on American Literature Ser.). 1981. 26.00 (ISBN 0-8161-8421-6, Twayne). G K Hall.

--Louis Bromfield. (Twayne's United States Authors Ser). 1964. pap. 5.95x (ISBN 0-8084-0204-8, T55, Twayne). New Coll U Pr.

--William Jennings Bryan. (United States Authors Ser.). 1981. lib. bdg. 13.00 (ISBN 0-8057-7294-4, Twayne). G K Hall.

Anderson, David D., ed. Michigan: A State Anthology: Writings About the Great Lake State, 1641-1981, Selected from Diaries, Journals, Histories, Fiction, & Verse. (Literature of the States Ser.: Vol. 1). 1982. 48.00x (ISBN 0-8103-1620-X, Pub. by Bruccoli). Gale.

Anderson, David L. Imperialism & Idealism: American Diplomats in China, 1861-1898. LC 84-48544. (Illus.). 256p. 1985. 24.95 (ISBN 0-253-32918-3). Ind U Pr.

Anderson, David L., jt. auth. see Graetzerk, Hans G.

Anderson, David L., compiled by. Symbolism: A Bibliography of Symbolism as an International & Multi-Disciplinary Movement. LC 74-17460. 160p. 1975. 35.00x (ISBN 0-8147-0555-3). NYU Pr.

Anderson, David L. & Cohen, I. Bernard, eds. The Discovery of the Electron. LC 80-2114. (Development of Science Ser.). (Illus.). 1981. lib. bdg. 15.00x (ISBN 0-405-13834-2). Ayer Co Pubs.

Anderson, David L., et al. The Dynamics of Government Programs for Urban Indians in the Prairie Provinces. 628p. 1984. pap. text ed. 19.95 (ISBN 0-920380-99-9, Pub. by Inst Res Pub Canada). Brookfield Pub Co.

Anderson, David N. & Hall, Beverly A., eds. Geothermal Exploration in the First Quarter Century. (Special Report Ser.: No. 3). (Illus.). 200p. 1973. 12.00 (ISBN 0-934412-00-6); pap. 10.00 (ISBN 0-934412-03-0). Geothermal.

Anderson, David N. & Lund, John W., eds. Direct Utilization of Geothermal Energy: A Technical Handbook. (Special Report Ser.: No. 7). (Illus.). 251p. 1979. pap. 10.00 (ISBN 0-934412-07-3). Geothermal.

Anderson, David R. Quotations from Chairman Calvin. (Illus.). 38p. 1984. pap. 2.95 (ISBN 0-933467-00-1). Brick Alley Books Press.

--Rex Stout. (Recognitions Ser.). 145p. 1984. 12.95 (ISBN 0-8044-2005-X); pap. 7.95 (ISBN 0-8044-6009-4). Ungar.

Anderson, David R. & Sweeney, Dennis J. Quantitative Methods for Business. 2nd ed. (Illus.). 656p. 1983. text ed. 30.95 (ISBN 0-314-69633-4); study guide 10.95 (ISBN 0-314-71075-2); write for info. test bank (ISBN 0-314-71077-9); instr's. manual avail. (ISBN 0-314-71076-0). West Pub.

--Statistics for Business & Economics. 2nd ed. (Illus.). 600p. 1984. text ed. 23.95 (ISBN 0-314-77811-X); tchrs.' manual avail. (ISBN 0-314-77814-4); student ed. avail. (ISBN 0-314-77818-7); sample package & test bank avail. West Pub.

Anderson, David R. & Sweeney, Dennis J. Quantitative Methods for Business: International Edition. 2nd ed. 668p. 1983. pap. text ed. write for info (ISBN 0-314-68850-1). West Pub.

Anderson, David R., et al. An Introduction to Management Science. 3rd ed. (Illus.). 700p. 1982. text ed. 31.95 (ISBN 0-314-63149-6). West Pub.

--Statistics for Business & Economics-International Edition. (Illus.). 600p. 1984. 17.00 (ISBN 0-314-77822-5). West Pub.

--An Introduction to Management Science: Quantitative Approaches to Decision Making. 4th ed. (Illus.). 752p. 1985. text ed. 30.95 (ISBN 0-314-85214-X). West Pub.

Anderson, Deb. Being a Friend Means... (Sparkler Bks.). (Illus.). (gr. k-2). 1985. plastic comb bndg. 2.95 (ISBN 0-89191-932-5, 59329). Cook.

--GOd Gives Me a Smile. 24p. (ps-5). 1985. lib. bdg. 3.95 (ISBN 0-89191-669-5). Cook.

--God Is the Greatest. 24p. (ps-5). 1985. lib. bdg. 3.95 (ISBN 0-89191-673-3). Cook.

--Thank You, God. (Sparkler Bks.). (Illus.). (gr. k-2). 1985. plastic comb bdg. 2.95 (ISBN 0-89191-931-7, 59311). Cook.

Anderson, Debby. God Is with Me. (Happy Day Bks.). (Illus.). 24p. (ps-2). 1984. 1.39 (ISBN 0-87239-734-3, 3704). Standard Pub.

--God Loves Even Me. (Happy Day Bks.). (Illus.). 24p. (ps-2). 1985. 1.39 (ISBN 0-87239-873-0, 3673). Standard Pub.

Anderson, Deborah, jt. auth. see Evans, Mary J.

Anderson, Debra, jt. auth. see Aves, Diane.

Anderson, Decima M. Computer Programming: FORTRAN IV. (Illus., Orig.). 1966. pap. 24.95 (ISBN 0-13-164822-5). P-H.

Anderson, Denna J., jt. auth. see Cox, Beverly J.

Anderson, Dennis. Small Industry in Developing Countries: A Discussion of Issues. LC 82-11130. (World Bank Staff Working Papers: No. 518). (Orig.). 1982. pap. 3.00 (ISBN 0-8213-0006-7). World Bank.

Anderson, Dennis & Khambata, Farida. Financing Small Scale Industry & Agriculture in Developing Countries: The Merits & Limitations of Commercial Policies. LC 82-8664. (World Bank Staff Working Papers: No. 519). (Orig.). 1982. pap. 3.00 (ISBN 0-8213-0007-5). World Bank.

--Small Enterprises & Development Policy in the Philippines: A Case Study. (Working Paper: No. 468). 239p. 1981. 5.00 (ISBN 0-686-36178-4, WP-0468). World Bank.

Anderson, Dennis & Leiserson, Mark. Rural Enterprise & Nonfarm Employment. (Working Paper). 87p. 1978. 5.00 (ISBN 0-686-36150-4, PP-7802). World Bank.

Anderson, Dennis, jt. auth. see Turvey, Ralph.

Anderson, Dennis A. Baptism and... (Orig.). 1977. pap. 3.50 (ISBN 0-89536-021-7). CSS of Ohio.

--Searching for Faith Within a Confused Society. 104p. 1976. pap. 4.50 (ISBN 0-89536-206-6). CSS of Ohio.

Anderson, Diann L., jt. auth. see Cosgriff, James H., Jr.

Anderson, Dice R. William Branch Giles: A Study in the Politics of Virginia & the Nation from 1790 to 1830. 1966. 13.25 (ISBN 0-8446-1028-3). Peter Smith.

Anderson, Dines. A Pali Reader. 130p. Date not set. Repr. 29.00 (ISBN 0-932051-66-9). Am Repr Serv.

Anderson, Donald D. The Status of Deer in Kansas. (Miscellaneous Publications Ser.: No. 39). 36p. 1964. pap. 2.00 (ISBN 0-317-04916-X). U of KS Mus Nat Hist.

Anderson, Donald K., Jr. John Ford. (English Authors Ser.). lib. bdg. 13.50 (ISBN 0-8057-1204-6, Twayne). G K Hall.

Anderson, Donald K., Jr., ed. see Ford, John.

Anderson, Donald L. Better Than Blessed. 1981. pap. 2.50 (ISBN 0-8423-0144-5). Tyndale.

Anderson, Donald L. & Raun, Donald L. Information Analysis in Management Accounting. LC 77-14938. (Wiley Series in Accounting & Information Systems). 706p. 1978. 46.50x (ISBN 0-471-02815-0). Wiley.

Anderson, Donna K. Charles T. Griffes: An Annotated Bibliography-Discography. LC 75-23552. (Bibliographies in American Music Ser.: No. 3). 1977. 12.00 (ISBN 0-911772-87-1). Info Coord.

--The Works of Charles T. Griffes: A Descriptive Catalogue. Buelow, George, ed. LC 83-4983. (Studies in Musicology: No. 68). 588p. 1983. 64.95 (ISBN 0-8357-1419-5). UMI Res Pr.

Anderson, Dorothy B. & McClean, Lenora J., eds. Identifying Suicide Potential. LC 78-140045. 112p. 1971. text ed. 16.95 (ISBN 0-87705-024-4). Human Sci Pr.

Anderson, Dorothy I., ed. see Channing, Edward T.

Anderson, Dorothy M. The Era of the Summer Estates: Swampscott, Massachusetts 1870-1940. LC 84-26324. (Illus.). 160p. 1985. 15.00 (ISBN 0-914659-10-3). Phoenix Pub.

--Women, Design, & the Cambridge School. LC 80-81341. (Illus.). 246p. 1980. 15.95 (ISBN 0-914886-10-X). PDA Pubs.

Anderson, Dorothy P. Leader's Guide for Jay E. Adams's Christian Living in the Home: A Teaching Manual for Use in Adult Study Groups. (Orig.). 1977. pap. 2.95 (ISBN 0-934688-05-2). Great Comm Pubns.

Anderson, Doug. Picture Puzzles for Armchair Detectives. LC 82-19344. (Illus.). 128p. (gr. 4-8). 1983. O.P. 7.95 (ISBN 0-8069-4670-9); PLB 9.99 O.P. (ISBN 0-8069-4671-7); pap. 3.95 (ISBN 0-8069-7718-3). Sterling.

Anderson, Douglas. The One Real Poem Is Life. LC 72-93478. 1973. 5.95 (ISBN 0-8076-0669-3). Braziller.

--The Planet of Waters. 135p. (Orig.). 1983. pap. 6.95 (ISBN 0-912549-00-9). Bread and Butter.

Anderson, Douglas & Anderson, Barbara. Chaco Canyon. 2nd., rev. ed. Jackson, Earl, ed. LC 75-18206. (Popular Ser: No. 17). (Illus., Orig.). 1976. pap. 5.00 (ISBN 0-911408-38-X). SW Pks Mnmts.

Anderson, Douglas & Itule, Bruce. Contemporary News Reporting. 352p. 1984. pap. 16.95 (ISBN 0-394-32891-4). Random.

Anderson, Douglas, jt. auth. see Anderson, Barbara.

Anderson, Douglas, ed. see Baldwin, Skip.

Anderson, Douglas, jt. ed. see Drance, Stephen M.

Anderson, Douglas A. New Approaches to Family Pastoral Care. LC 79-8898. (Creative Pastoral Care & Counseling Ser.). 96p. (Orig.). 1980. pap. 4.50 (ISBN 0-8006-0564-0, 1-564). Fortress.

--Washington Merry-Go-Round of Libel Actions. LC 79-18126. 352p. 1980. 24.95x (ISBN 0-88229-547-0); pap. 12.95 (ISBN 0-88229-746-5). Nelson-Hall.

Anderson, Douglas D. Regulatory Politics & Electric Utilities. 191p. 1981. 24.95 (ISBN 0-86569-058-8). Auburn Hse.

Anderson, Douglas P. Diseases of Fishes, Book 4: Fish Immunology. Snieszko, S. F. & Axelrod, Herbert R., eds. (Illus.). 240p. 1974. pap. 19.95 (ISBN 0-87666-036-7, PS-209). Tfh Pubns.

Anderson, Douglas R. Testing the Field of Vision. LC 81-14045. (Illus.). 301p. 1982. text ed. 45.95 (ISBN 0-8016-0207-6). Mosby.

Anderson, Douglas R., jt. ed. see Lichter, Paul R.

Anderson, Duane. Eastern Iowa Prehistory. 90p. 1981. 10.95 (ISBN 0-8138-1865-6). Iowa St U Pr.

--Western Iowa Prehistory. Facsimile ed. (Illus.). 86p. 1975. 6.95x (ISBN 0-8138-2223-8). Iowa St U Pr.

Anderson, Duane C. & Semken, Holmes, eds. The Cherokee Excavations: Holocene Ecology & Human Adaptations in Northwestern Iowa. (Studies in Archaeology). 1980. 36.50 (ISBN 0-12-058260-0). Acad Pr.

Anderson, Duwayne, jt. ed. see Andersland, Orlando B.

Anderson, Dwight G. Abraham Lincoln: The Quest for Immortality. LC 81-13738. 1982. 16.95 (ISBN 0-394-49173-4). Knopf.

Anderson, E. Frederick. The Development of Leadership & Organization Building in the Black Community of Los Angeles from 1900 Through World War II. LC 79-93305. 155p. 1980. 13.95 (ISBN 0-86548-000-1). R & E Pubs.

Anderson, E. N. The Floating World of Castle Peak Bay. (American Anthropological Association-Anthropological Studies: No. 4). pap. 69.80 (ISBN 0-317-10012-2, 2000776). Bks Demand UMI.

Anderson, E. N., jt. auth. see Cate, James L.

Anderson, E. P. & Ley, C. J. Projecting a Picture of Home Economics: Public Relations in Secondary Programs. 1982. 4.00 (ISBN 0-686-38743-0, A261-08454). Home Econ Educ.

Anderson, E. Ruth. Contemporary American Composers: A Biographical Dictionary. 2nd ed. 1982. lib. bdg. 65.00 (ISBN 0-8161-8223-X, Hall Reference). G K Hall.

Anderson, E. V., tr. see Kubizek, August.

Anderson, E. W. The Principles of Navigation. LC 66-70107. (Illus.). 654p. 1979. 25.00 (ISBN 0-370-00311-X, Pub. by the Bodley Head). Merrimack Pub Cir.

Anderson, Earl R. Cynewulf: Structure, Style, & Theme in His Poetry. LC 81-65464. 248p. 1983. 32.00 (ISBN 0-8386-3091-X). Fairleigh Dickinson.

Anderson, Earl W. The Teacher's Contract & Other Legal Phases of Teacher Status. LC 78-176515. (Columbia University. Teachers College. Contributions to Education: No. 246). Repr. of 1927 ed. 22.50 (ISBN 0-404-55246-3). AMS Pr.

Anderson, Eben M. Key of the Keelson. LC 84-90213. 55p. 1985. 6.95 (ISBN 0-533-06266-7). Vantage.

--There's the Sea. LC 84-90214. (Illus.). 61p. 1985. 6.95 (ISBN 0-533-06265-9). Vantage.

Anderson, Edgar. The Considered Landscape: Essays. 1985. 7.00 (ISBN 0-317-29431-8). White Pine.

--Plants, Man & Life. rev. ed. LC 52-5870. (YA) (gr. 9 up). 1967. pap. 3.95 (ISBN 0-520-00021-8, CAL142). U of Cal Pr.

Anderson, Edith H. & Reed, Suellen B. Innovative Approaches to Baccalaureate Programs in Nursing. 50p. 1979. 5.95 (ISBN 0-88737-206-6, 15-1804). Natl League Nurse.

Anderson, Edward. Hungry Men. (Penguin Fiction Ser.). 288p. 1985. pap. 5.95 (ISBN 0-14-007374-4). Penguin.

Anderson, Edward C. Florida Territory in 1844: The Diary of Master Edward Clifford Anderson USN. Hoole, W. Stanley, ed. LC 76-16071. 113p. 1977. 10.25 (ISBN 0-8173-5111-6). U of Ala Pr.

Anderson, Edward E. Fundamentals of Solar Thermal Energy Conversion. LC 81-22852. 576p. 1983. text ed. 38.95 (ISBN 0-201-00008-3). Addison-Wesley.

Anderson, Edward F. Peyote: The Divine Cactus. LC 79-20173. 248p. 1980. pap. 9.95 (ISBN 0-8165-0613-2). U of Ariz Pr.

Anderson, Edwin. Electric Machines & Transformers. 2nd ed. 1985. text ed. 28.95 (ISBN 0-8359-1618-9). Reston.

Anderson, Edwin P. Air Conditioning: Home & Commercial. 2nd ed. LC 83-223476. 1984. 14.95 (ISBN 0-672-23397-5). Audel.

--Gas Engine Manual. 3rd ed. LC 76-45883. 1985. 12.95 (ISBN 0-8161-1707-1). Audel.

--Home Appliance Servicing. 4th ed. LC 83-5984. (Audel Ser.). 608p. 15.95 (ISBN 0-672-23379-7). G K Hall.

--Refrigeration: Home & Commercial. 2nd ed. LC 83-22379. 1984. 16.95 (ISBN 0-672-23396-7). Audel.

Anderson, Edwin P. & Miller, Rex. Electric Motors. 4th ed. LC 82-17788. (Audel Ser.). 1983. 12.95 (ISBN 0-672-23376-2). G K Hall.

--Home Appliance Servicing. 4th ed. LC 83-5984. 1983. 15.95 (ISBN 0-672-23379-7). Audel.

--Refrigeration: Home & Commercial. LC 83-22379. 736p. 1984. 16.95 (ISBN 0-672-23396-7). G K Hall.

Anderson, Edwin P., jt. auth. see Miller, Rex.

Anderson, Einar. History & Beliefs of Mormonism. LC 81-13671. Orig. Title: Inside Story of Mormonism. 176p. 1981. pap. 5.95 (ISBN 0-8254-2122-5). Kregel.

Anderson, Elaine. The Central Railroad of New Jersey's First Hundred Years: 1849-1949. Lee, James & Metz, Lance, eds. LC 84-21449. (Illus.). 238p. (Orig.). 1984. pap. 14.00 (ISBN 0-930973-00-3, TF25, C43A 53). Ctr Canal Hist.

--With God's Help Flowers Bloom. 1978. pap. 4.95 (ISBN 0-89137-411-6); study guide 2.85 (ISBN 0-89137-412-4). Quality Pubns.

Anderson, Elaine, jt. auth. see Kurten, Bjorn.

Anderson, Elaine S. Speaking with Style: The Sociolinguistic Skills of Children. 250p. 1985. 29.00 (ISBN 0-7099-0559-9, Pub. by Croom Helm Ltd). Longwood Pub Group.

Anderson, Elaine V., jt. auth. see Tompkins, Phillip K.

Anderson, Elbridge. Through the Awakening Eye, Poems. (Illus.). 1976. pap. 4.00 (ISBN 0-915242-08-7). Pygmalion Pr.

Anderson, Eleanor C., illus. Gifts for Alcestis. 93p. 1985. 9.95 (ISBN 0-533-05798-1). Vantage.

Anderson, Elijah. A Place on the Corner: Identity & Rank Among Black Streetcorner Men. LC 78-1879. (Studies of Urban Society). 1978. 20.00x (ISBN 0-226-01953-5); pap. 9.00x (ISBN 0-226-01954-3). U of Chicago Pr.

Anderson, Elisabeth, et al. Cabin Comments: A Journal of Life in Jackson Hole. LC 80-53090. (Illus.). 286p. (gr. 7-12). 1980. 14.75 (ISBN 0-933160-08-9); pap. 7.75 (ISBN 0-933160-09-7). Teton Bkshop.

Anderson, Elizabeth. Fisherman's Catch. 1981. pap. 6.95 (ISBN 0-910286-85-X). Boxwood.

Anderson, Elizabeth, et al, eds. see Robbins, Roland.

Anderson, Elizabeth B. Annapolis: A Walk Through History. LC 83-40548. (Illus.). 152p. 1984. pap. 5.95 (ISBN 0-87033-311-9). Tidewater.

Anderson, Elizabeth L., ed. Newspaper Libraries in the U. S. & Canada: An SLA Directory. 2nd ed. LC 80-25188. 328p. 1980. pap. 18.50 (ISBN 0-87111-265-5). SLA.

Anderson, Elizabeth M. Disabled Schoolchild: A Study of Integration in Primary Schools. 377p. 1973. pap. 14.95x (ISBN 0-416-78190-X, NO.2062). Methuen Inc.

Anderson, Elizabeth M. & Clarke, Lynda. Disability in Adolescence. 400p. 1982. 32.00 (ISBN 0-416-72730-1, 3766); pap. 14.95 (ISBN 0-416-72740-9, 3767). Methuen Inc.

Anderson, Elizabeth Y. Faith in the Furnace. LC 84-72818. (Illus.). 1985. 10.00 (ISBN 0-9614002-0-X). E Y Anderson.

Anderson, Ella. Crooked Signpost. 1975. pap. 1.95 (ISBN 0-87508-656-X). Chr Lit.

--Jo-Jo. 1975. pap. 1.95 (ISBN 0-87508-693-4). Chr Lit.

Anderson, Ella J. The Teacher's Friend. 1970. pap. 3.85x (ISBN 0-87813-905-2). Christian Light.

Anderson, Ellen K. Pregnancy Workbook. (Illus.). 96p. (Orig.). 1983. pap. 8.95 (ISBN 0-939374-01-3). Homefront Graphics.

Anderson, Ellen McCarty see McCarty Anderson, Ellen.

Anderson, Elliot & Kinzie, Mary, eds. The Little Magazine in America: A Modern Documentary History. pap. 14.95 (ISBN 0-317-06427-4). Pushcart Pr.

Anderson, Elliott & Kinzie, Mary, eds. The Little Magazine in America: A Modern, Documentary History. 1979. 35.00 (ISBN 0-916366-04-9). Pushcart Pr.

Anderson, Elliott, jt. ed. see Hayman, David.

Anderson, Elmer. Introduction to Modern Physics. 1982. text ed. 35.95 (ISBN 0-03-058512-0, CBS C); Instr's manual 20.00 (ISBN 0-03-058513-9). SCP.

--Modern Physics & Quantum Mechanics. 1971. text ed. 35.95 (ISBN 0-7216-1220-2, CBS C). SCP.

Anderson, Elwood G. Therapy for Young Stutterers: The Kopp Method. LC 74-96726. 113p. 1970. text ed. 8.95x (ISBN 0-8143-1413-9). Wayne St U Pr.

Anderson, Emily. The Letters of Mozart & His Family. 2nd, rev. ed. (Illus.). 1985. slipcased 50.00 (ISBN 0-393-02248-X). Norton.

Anderson, Emily, ed. The Letters of Beethoven. (Illus.). 1985. slipcased 75.00 (ISBN 0-393-02247-1). Norton.

Anderson, Emily A., ed. English Poetry, Nineteen Hundred to Nineteen Fifty: A Guide to Information Sources. (American Literature, English Literature & World Literatures in English Information Guide Ser.). 350p. 1982. 60.00x (ISBN 0-8103-1360-X). Gale.

Anderson, Emily F. Between Two Seasons. 32p. (Orig.). 1984. pap. 1.75 (ISBN 0-916727-01-7). Namaste Pr.

Anderson, Emma D. & Campbell, Mary J. In the Shadow of the Himalayas. 1942. 10.00 (ISBN 0-8495-0226-8). Arden Lib.

--In the Shadow of the Himalayas: A Historical Narrative of the Missions of the United Presbyterian Church of North America as Conducted in the Punjab, India 1855-1940. 373p. 1983. Repr. of 1942 ed. lib. bdg. 45.00 (ISBN 0-89987-042-2). Darby Bks.

Anderson, Enid. Crafts & the Disabled. (Illus.). 168p. 1981. 19.95 (ISBN 0-7134-2181-9, Pub. by Batsford England). David & Charles.

--The Technique of Soft Toy Making. (Illus.). 144p. 1982. 16.95 (ISBN 0-7134-2391-9, Pub. by Batsford England). David & Charles.

Anderson, Enoch & Bellas, Henry H. Personal Recollections of Captain Enoch Anderson, an Officer of the Delaware Regiments in the Revolutionary War. LC 76-140851. (Eyewitness Accounts of the American Revolution Ser., No. 3). 1970. Repr. of 1896 ed. 11.50 (ISBN 0-405-01221-7). Ayer Co Pubs.

Anderson, Eric. Plane Safety & Survival. LC 78-8247. 1978. 7.95 (ISBN 0-8168-7508-1); pap. 5.95 (ISBN 0-8168-7510-3). Aero.

--Race & Politics in North Carolina, 1872 to 1901: The Black Second. LC 80-13622. xiii, 379p. 1980. 32.50x (ISBN 0-8071-0685-2); pap. 12.95x (ISBN 0-8071-0784-0). La State U Pr.

Anderson, Eric, jt. auth. see Ingraham, F.

Anderson, Eric A. & Earle, George, eds. Design & Aesthetics in Wood. LC 75-171186. 1972. 34.50x (ISBN 0-87395-216-2). State U NY Pr.

Anderson, Eric G. The Pilot's Health. (Illus.). 288p. (Orig.). 1984. pap. 15.50 (ISBN 0-8306-2346-9, 2346). TAB Bks.

Anderson, Erica, ed. see Schweitzer, Albert.

Anderson, Erland. Harmonious Madness: A Study of Musical Metaphors in the Poetry of Coleridge, Shelley & Keats. (Salzburg Studies in English Literature, Romantic Reassessment Ser.: No. 12). 321p. 1975. pap. text ed. 25.50x (ISBN 0-391-01299-1). Humanities.

Anderson, Ernest C. & Sullivan, Elizabeth M., eds. Impact of Energy Production on Human Health: An Evaluation of Means for Assessment: Proceedings. LC 76-22540. (ERDA Symposium Ser.). 152p. 1976. pap. 11.75 (ISBN 0-87079-032-3, CONF-751022); microfiche 4.50 (ISBN 0-87079-245-8, CONF-751022). DOE.

Anderson, Eskil. Asbestos & Jade in the Kobuk River Region of Alaska. facs. ed. (Shorey Prospecting Ser.). 26p. pap. 3.95 (ISBN 0-8466-0037-4, S37). Shorey.

Anderson, Ethel. Song of Hager to the Patriarch Abraham. 10.00 (ISBN 0-392-04747-0, ABC). Sportshelf.

Anderson, Eugene & Anderson, Marja L. Mountain & Water: Essays on the Cultural Ecology of South Coastal China. (Asian Folklore & Social Life Monograph: No. 54). 194p. 1973. photo copy 25.00 (ISBN 0-89986-051-6). Oriental Bk Store.

Anderson, Eugene, et al. Self-Esteem for Tots to Teens: Five Principles for Raising Confident Children. 207p. (Orig.). 1984. pap. 4.95 (ISBN 0-88166-043-4). Meadowbrook.

Anderson, Eugene N. First Moroccan Crisis, 1904-1906. 420p. 1966. Repr. of 1930 ed. 27.50 (ISBN 0-208-00294-4, Archon). Shoe String.

--Nationalism & Cultural Crisis in Prussia, 1806-1815. 1967. lib. bdg. 24.50x (ISBN 0-374-90228-3). Octagon.

--Social & Political Conflict in Prussia, 1858-1864. 1968. lib. bdg. 31.50x (ISBN 0-374-90266-6). Octagon.

Anderson, Eugene N., ed. see Kehr, Eckart.

Anderson, Evelyn M. Good Morning, Lord: Devotions for Women. (Good Morning Lord Ser.). 1971. 4.95 (ISBN 0-8010-0023-8). Baker Bk.

Anderson, Evelyn M., jt. ed. see Carney, Andrew L.

Anderson, Everett, et al. The Meiotic Process, I: Pairing, Recombination & Chromosome Movements. LC 72-6123. (Illus.). 189p. 1972. 29.50x (ISBN 0-8422-7019-1). Irvington.

Anderson, Farris. Alfonso Sastre. LC 78-125251. (World Authors Ser.). 1971. lib. bdg. 15.95 (ISBN 0-8057-2802-3). Irvington.

Anderson, Ferguson & Williams, Brian. Practical Management of the Elderly. 4th ed. 368p. 1983. casebound 29.95 (ISBN 0-632-01061-4, B0237-8). Mosby.

Anderson, Fletcher & Hopkinson, Ann. Rivers of the Southwest: A Boater's Guide to the Rivers of Colorado, New Mexico, Utah, & Arizona. LC 81-20990. (Illus.). 200p. (Orig.). 1982. pap. 13.95 (ISBN 0-87108-607-7). Pruett.

Anderson, Florence M. Religious Cults Associated with the Amazons. LC 73-158253. Repr. of 1912 ed. 16.00 (ISBN 0-404-00749-X). AMS Pr.

Anderson, Frances E. Art for All the Children: A Creative Sourcebook for the Impaired Child. (Illus.). 288p. 1978. 20.75x (ISBN 0-398-03737-X). C C Thomas.

Anderson, Frances J. Classroom Newspaper Activities: A Resource for Teachers, Grades k-8. (Illus.). 226p. (Orig.). 1985. spiral bound 19.75x (ISBN 0-398-05145-3). C C Thomas.

Anderson, Francis I. The Hebrew Verbless Clause in the Pentateuch. 128p. 1970. pap. 8.95 (ISBN 0-89130-321-9, 06-00-14); pap. 5.95 members (ISBN 0-317-35697-6). Scholars Pr GA.

Anderson, Frank, jt. ed. see Wegner, Bob.

Anderson, Frank, et al. Nineteen Eighty Census Socio-Economic Fact Book: North Central Texas Region. 275p. (Orig.). 1984. pap. 30.00 (ISBN 0-936440-50-3). Inst Urban Studies.

Anderson, Frank G. Southwestern Archaeology: A Bibliography. 1982. lib. bdg. 91.00 (ISBN 0-8240-9554-5). Garland Pub.

Anderson, Frank J. German Book Illustrations Through Fifteen Hundred: Herbals, 2 vols. (Illustrated Bartsch Ser.: Vol. 90). 1983. 120.00 (ISBN 0-89835-059-X). Abaris Bks.

--An Illustrated History of the Herbals. LC 77-8821. (Illus.). 270p. 1977. 30.00x (ISBN 0-231-04002-4). Columbia U Pr.

--An Illustrated History of the Herbals. (Illus.). 270p. 1985. pap. 11.95x (ISBN 0-231-08380-7). Columbia U Pr.

--Riches of the Earth. (Illus.). 224p. 1981. 24.95 (ISBN 0-8317-7739-7, Rutledge Pr). Smith Pubs.

--Submarines, Diving, & the Underwater World: A Bibliography. ix, 238p. 1975. 25.00 (ISBN 0-208-01508-6, Archon). Shoe String.

Anderson, Frank M. The Constitution & Other Select Documents. 1978. Repr. of 1904 ed. lib. bdg. 75.00 (ISBN 0-8495-0132-6). Arden Lib.

Anderson, Frank M. & Hershey, Amos S. Handbook for the Diplomatic History of Europe, Asia & Africa, 1870-1914. LC 70-75528. Repr. of 1918 ed. cancelled (ISBN 0-8371-1011-4, AND&, Pub. by Negro U Pr). Greenwood.

Anderson, Frank R. Quality Controlled Investing: Or How to Avoid the Pick & Pray Method. LC 78-7607. 160p. 1978. 39.95 (ISBN 0-471-04382-6, Pub. by Wiley-Interscience). Wiley.

Anderson, Fred. A People's Army: Massachusetts Soldiers & Society in the Seven Years' War. LC 84-2344. (Institute of Early American History & Culture at Williamsburg, Virginia, Ser.). (Illus.). 292p. 1984. 28.00x (ISBN 0-8078-1611-6). U of NC Pr.

Anderson, Fred, jt. auth. see Sahn, David J.

Anderson, Fred A. The Complete PFE Study Reference. 96p. (Orig.). 1983. pap. 18.95 (ISBN 0-939570-01-7). Skills Improvement.

--How to Cut Your Mortgage in Half. 112p. (Orig.). 1984. pap. 9.95 (ISBN 0-939570-06-8). Skills Improvement.

--How to Get Your College Degree Without Going to College. 104p. (Orig.). 1983. pap. 11.95 (ISBN 0-939570-03-3). Skills Improvement.

--How to Master Test Taking. Anderson, Hannelore, ed. LC 81-90062. 72p. (Orig.). 1981. pap. 7.95 (ISBN 0-939570-00-9). Skills Improvement.

--Practice Employment Tests, Vol. 1. 42p. (Orig.). 1983. pap. 9.95 (ISBN 0-939570-04-1). Skills Improvement.

--Scoring High on Medical & Health Sciences Exams. 48p. (Orig.). 1983. pap. 5.95 (ISBN 0-939570-02-5). Skills Improvement.

Anderson, Frederick & Daniels, Robert H. NEPA in the Courts: A Legal Analysis of the National Environmental Policy Act. LC 73-12345. (Resources for the Future Ser). 339p. 1973. pap. 9.95x (ISBN 0-8018-1559-2). Johns Hopkins.

Anderson, Frederick, ed. see Hempl, George.

Anderson, Frederick, ed. & intro. by see Twain, Mark.

Anderson, Frederick, et al, eds. see Twain, Mark.

Anderson, Frederick, et al, eds. see Twain, Mark & Howells, William D.

Anderson, Frederick I. Quad-Cities: Joined by a River. rev. ed. (Illus.). 262p. 1984. 27.95 (ISBN 0-317-19762-2). Lee Enterprises.

Anderson, Frederick R. & Daniels, Robert H. NEPA in the Courts: A Legal Analysis of the National Environmental Policy Act. 340p. 1973. pap. 9.95 (ISBN 0-8018-1559-2). Resources Future.

Anderson, Frederick R. & Kneese, Allen V. Environmental Improvement Through Economic Incentives. 208p. 1978. 18.50 (ISBN 0-8018-2000-6); pap. 6.00 (ISBN 0-8018-2100-2). Resources Future.

Anderson, Frederick R. & Mandelker, Daniel R. Environmental Protection: Law & Policy. LC 83-82691. 1127p. 1984. text ed. 31.00 (ISBN 0-316-03950-0). Little.

Anderson, Frederick R., et al. Environmental Improvement Through Economic Incentives. LC 76-47400. (Resources for the Future Ser.). 208p. 1978. text ed. 18.50x (ISBN 0-8018-2000-6); pap. text ed. 6.00x (ISBN 0-8018-2100-2). Johns Hopkins.

Anderson, Fulton H. Francis Bacon: His Career & His Thought. LC 77-18070. (The Aresnberg Lectures: 2nd Ser. 1957). 1978. Repr. of 1962 ed. lib. bdg. 28.50 (ISBN 0-313-20108-0, ANFB). Greenwood.

Anderson, Fulton H., ed. The New Organon: Bacon. 1960. pap. text ed. write for info. (ISBN 0-02-303380-0). Macmillan.

Anderson, Fulton H., ed. see Bacon, Francis.

Anderson, G. A. Surgery with Coefficients. (Lecture Notes in Mathematics: Vol. 591). 1977. 13.00 (ISBN 3-540-08250-6). Springer-Verlag.

Anderson, G. L., ed. Asian Literature in English: A Guide to Information Sources. (American Literature, English Literature & World Literatures in English Information Guide Ser.: Vol. 31). 300p. 1981. 60.00x (ISBN 0-8103-1362-6). Gale.

Anderson, G. L, ed. Masterpieces of the Orient. 1961. pap. 11.95x (ISBN 0-393-09542-8, NortonC); expanded pap. 1976 18.95x (ISBN 0-393-09196-1). Norton.

Anderson, G. Lester, ed. Educating for the Professions. LC 66-19134. (National Society for the Study of Education Yearbooks Ser: No. 61, Pt. 2). 1962. 6.50x (ISBN 0-226-60064-5). U of Chicago Pr.

Anderson, G. W. The History & Religion of Israel. (New Clarendon Bible Ser.). (Illus.). 1966. pap. 10.95x (ISBN 0-19-836915-8). Oxford U Pr.

--Tradition & Interpretation. 1979. 32.50x (ISBN 0-19-826315-5). Oxford U Pr.

Anderson, Gail S., jt. auth. see Anderson, Hal W.

Anderson, Garrett. Brennan's Book. 1976. text ed. 16.95x (ISBN 0-8464-0207-6). Beekman Pubs.

Anderson, Gary. Film to Video Post-Production. 175p. 1986. 34.95 (ISBN 0-86729-155-9). Knowledge Indus.

--Searching for the Ideal in Congregational Growth. 67p. (Orig.). 1974. pap. 3.75 (ISBN 0-89536-207-4). CSS of Ohio.

Anderson, Gary & Watson, Nancy. Programmed Power Phonics: A Simplified Method of Word Identification. 1978. 8.95 (ISBN 0-8403-1882-0). Kendall-Hunt.

Anderson, Gary, jt. ed. see Goldstone, Richard H.

Anderson, Gary C. Kinsmen of Another Kind: Dakota-White Relations in the Upper Mississippi Valley, 1650-1862. LC 83-23411. xvi, 384p. 1984. 25.00x (ISBN 0-8032-1018-3). U of Nebr Pr.

Anderson, Gary H. Video Editing & Post-Production: A Professional Guide. LC 83-25124. (Video Bookshelf Ser.). 165p. 1984. professional 34.95 (ISBN 0-86729-070-6); pap. 24.95 students ed. (ISBN 0-86729-114-1, 521-BW). Knowledge Indus.

Anderson, Gaylene, ed. Primary Primer: Simplified Piano Duets for Young Latter-day Saints. (Illus.). 32p. (Orig.). 1982. pap. 3.95 (ISBN 0-941214-10-9). Signature Bks.

Anderson, Gene. Coring & Core Analysis Handbook. LC 74-33713. 200p. 1975. 39.95 (ISBN 0-87814-058-1). Pennwell Bks.

--Coyote Space. (Kestrel Ser.: No. 6). 28p. 1983. pap. 3.00 (ISBN 0-914974-38-6). Holmgangers.

Anderson, Gene C. & Raff, Beverly, eds. Newborn Behavioral Organization: Nursing Research &Implications. LC 79-2597. (Alan R. Liss Ser.: Vol. 15, No. 7). 1979. 29.00 (ISBN 0-8451-1032-2). March of Dimes.

Anderson, Gene C., ed. see First National Foundation-March of Dimes Perinatal Nursing Research Roundtable Conference Chicago, Ill.

Anderson, George & Johnson, Pamela. Digest Book of Physical Fitness. LC 79-50061. 96p. pap. 3.95 (ISBN 0-695-81284-X). DBI.

Anderson, George B. How to Make Your Sales Meetings Come Alive. 1973. 75.50 (ISBN 0-85013-058-1). Dartnell Corp.

--One Hundred Booming Years. Row, H. J. & Stupek, D., eds. (Illus.). 305p. 1980. 32.50 (ISBN 0-9604136-0-X). Bucyrus-Erie Co.

Anderson, George B. & Johnson, Pamela J. Physical Fitness Digest. LC 79-50058. (Illus.). 288p. 1979. pap. 7.95 (ISBN 0-695-81275-0). DBI.

Anderson, George E., et al. Treaty Making & Treaty Rejection by the Federal Government in California 1850-1852. (No. 9). 1978. pap. 7.95 (ISBN 0-87919-071-X). Ballena Pr.

Anderson, George K. Breadloaf School of English: The First Fifty Years. 1969. pap. 3.50x (ISBN 0-910408-15-7). Coll Store.

--The Legend of the Wandering Jew. LC 65-14290. 503p. 45.00x (ISBN 0-87057-094-3). U Pr of New Eng.

--Literature of the Anglo-Saxons. LC 61-13776. (Illus.). 1962. Repr. of 1949 ed. 20.00x (ISBN 0-8462-0109-7). Russell.

Anderson, George K. & Buckler, William E. The Literature of England: Single Volume Edition. 2nd ed. 1967. 26.65 (ISBN 0-673-05656-2). Scott F.

Anderson, George K. & Warnock, Robert. The World in Literature, 2 vols. rev. ed. 1967. 21.70. Vol. 1 (ISBN 0-673-05636-8). Vol. 2 (ISBN 0-673-05637-6). Scott F.

--The World in Literature: Bk. 3. 1967. pap. 11.90.; Bk. 3. (ISBN 0-673-05653-8). Scott F.

Anderson, George K., tr. The Saga of the Volsungs. LC 80-65685. 272p. 1982. 29.50 (ISBN 0-87413-172-3). U Delaware Pr.

Anderson, George K., et al. The Literature of England. 3rd ed. Incl. Vol. 1. From the Middle Ages Through the Eighteenth Century. 1979. pap. text ed. 15.45x (ISBN 0-673-15156-5); Vol. 2. From the Romantic Period to the Present. 1979. pap. text ed. 15.45x (ISBN 0-673-15157-3). 1979. text ed. 27.90 (ISBN 0-673-15155-7). Scott F.

Anderson, George L. Essays in Kansas History: In Memorium. Williams, Burton J., ed. 1977. 7.50x (ISBN 0-87291-086-5). Coronado Pr.

--Essays on the History of Banking. 217p. 1972. 6.50x (ISBN 0-87291-037-7). Coronado Pr.

Anderson, George M. The Work of Adalbert Johann Volck, 1828-1912: Who Chose for His Name the Anagram, V. Blada, 1861-1865. (Illus.). 222p. 1970. 20.00 (ISBN 0-938420-19-4). Md Hist.

Anderson, George W. A Critical Introduction to the Old Testament. (Studies in Theology). 262p. 1959. pap. 13.50x (ISBN 0-7156-0077-X, Pub. by Duckworth England). Biblio Dist.

Anderson, Gerald & Stransky, Thomas, eds. Mission Trends: Faith Meets Faith, No. 5. LC 81-80983. 320p. (Orig.). 1981. pap. 3.95 (ISBN 0-8091-2356-8). Paulist Pr.

--Mission Trends: Liberation Theologies in North America & Europe, No. 4. LC 78-70827. 1978. pap. 3.95 (ISBN 0-8028-1709-2). Eerdmans.

Anderson, Gerald D. Fascists, Communists, & the National Government: Civil Liberties in Great Britain, 1931-1937. LC 82-10985. 256p. 1983. text ed. 20.00 (ISBN 0-8262-0388-4). U of Mo Pr.

Anderson, Gerald F., jt. auth. see Settgast, Edward E.

Anderson, Gerald H. Asian Voices in Christian Theology. LC 75-13795. pap. 83.30 (ISBN 0-317-20690-7, 2025115). Bks Demand UMI.

Anderson, Gerald H. & Stansky, Thomas. Missions Trends, No. 2. LC 75-29836. 1975. pap. 3.95 (ISBN 0-8028-1624-X). Eerdmans.

Anderson, Gerald H. & Stranskey, Thomas F. Mission Trends: "Evangelization", No. 2. LC 75-29836. (Mission Trend Ser.). 288p. 1976. pap. 3.45 (ISBN 0-8091-1900-5). Paulist Pr.

Anderson, Gerald H., ed. Witnessing to the Kingdom: Melbourne & Beyond. LC 82-3530. 176p. (Orig.). 1982. pap. 7.95 (ISBN 0-88344-708-8). Orbis Bks.

Anderson, Gerald H. & Stansky, Thomas F., eds. Mission Trends: Third World Theologies, No. 3. LC 76-24451. (Mission Trend Ser.). 264p. 1976. pap. 3.45 (ISBN 0-8091-1984-6). Paulist Pr.

Anderson, Gerald H. & Stransky, Thomas F., eds. Christ's Lordship & Religious Pluralism. LC 80-25406. 256p. (Orig.). 1981. pap. 8.95 (ISBN 0-88344-088-1). Orbis Bks.

--Mission Trends: Crucial Issues in Mission Today, No. 1. LC 74-81222. (Mission Trend Ser.). (Orig.). 1974. pap. 3.45 (ISBN 0-8091-1843-2). Paulist Pr.

--Mission Trends: Current Issues in Mission Today, No. 1. LC 74-81222. 1974. pap. 3.95 (ISBN 0-8028-1483-2). Eerdmans.

--Mission Trends: Faith Meets Faith, No. 5. (Mission Trends Ser.). 320p. (Orig.). 1981. pap. 3.95 (ISBN 0-8028-1821-8). Eerdmans.

Anderson, Gerald H. & Stransky, Thomas R., eds. Missions Trends, No. 3. (Mission Trends Ser.). (Orig.). 1976. pap. 3.95 (ISBN 0-8028-1654-1). Eerdmans.

Anderson, Gerald H., jt. ed. see Stransky, Thomas.

Anderson, Gillian B., ed. Freedom's Voice in Poetry & Song. LC 77-78353. 1977. 65.00 (ISBN 0-8420-2124-8). Scholarly Res Inc.

Anderson, Glenn P., ed. Covenant Roots: Sources & Affirmations. Jansson, Fred O., et al, trs. from Swedish. 238p. (Orig.). 1980. pap. 6.95 (ISBN 0-910452-46-6). Covenant.

Anderson, Godfrey T. Spicer: Leader with the Common Touch. Wheeler, Gerald, ed. LC 83-3279. (Illus.). 128p. (Orig.). 1983. pap. 5.95 (ISBN 0-8280-0150-2). Review & Herald.

Anderson, Gordon A. Latin Compositions in the Sixth Fasciale of the Notre-Dame Manuscript Wolfenbuttel 1099. (Wissenschaftliche Abhandlungen-Musicological Studies Ser.: Vol. 24). Pt. 1. lib. bdg. 50.00 (ISBN 0-931902-02-9); Pt. 2. lib. bdg. 50.00 (ISBN 0-931902-03-7). Inst Mediaeval Mus.

Anderson, Gordon A., ed. Notre-Dame & Related Conductus. (Gesamtausbaben-Collected Works Ser.: Vol. X). 140p. Pt. 3. lib. bdg. 70.00 (ISBN 0-912024-17-8); Pt. 5. lib. bdg. 45.00 (ISBN 0-931902-11-8); Pt. 6. lib. bdg. 70.00 (ISBN 0-912024-18-6); Pt. 8. lib. bdg. 47.50 (ISBN 0-931902-12-6). Inst Mediaeval Mus.

Anderson, Gordon A. & Dittmer, Luther, eds. Canberra, Nan Kivell Collecton. (Veroffentlichungen Mittelalterlicher Musikhandschriften - Publications of Mediaeval Musical Manuscripts Ser.: Vol. 13). (Eng & Ger.). 1981. lib. bdg. 37.50 (ISBN 0-912024-13-5). Inst Mediaeval Mus.

Anderson, Gordon S. A Whole Language Approach to Reading. LC 84-13229. (Illus.). 642p. (Orig.). 1984. lib. bdg. 37.50 (ISBN 0-8191-4196-8); pap. text ed. 25.00 (ISBN 0-8191-4197-6). U Pr of Amer.

Anderson, Gordon T., ed. see Mitchell, Alice & Szerny, Carl.

Anderson, Gordon T., ed. see Salvaggio, Jerry L.

Anderson, Grace F. The Incompetent Cat & Other Animal Tails. 144p. 1985. pap. 2.95 (ISBN 0-88207-495-4). Victor Bks.

--Skunk for Rent & Other Animal Tails. 120p. (gr. 1 up). 1982. pap. 2.95 (ISBN 0-88207-493-8). Victor Bks.

Anderson, Graham. Ancient Fiction: The Novel in the Graeco-Roman World. LC 84-12319. 256p. 1984. 28.50x (ISBN 0-389-20516-8). B&N Imports.

--Eros Sophistes: Ancient Novelists at Play. LC 81-16573. (American Philological Association American Classical Studies). 1981. pap. 12.75 (ISBN 0-89130-547-5, 40-04-09). Scholars Pr GA.

--Philostratus: Biography & Belles-Lettres in the Second Century A. D. 352p. 1985. 37.50 (ISBN 0-7099-0575-0, Pub. by Croom Helm Ltd). Longwood Pub Group.

Anderson, Greg, jt. auth. see O'Harra, Doug.

Anderson, Gregory L. Victorian Clerks. (Illus.). 1976. lib. bdg. 22.50x (ISBN 0-678-06794-5). Kelley.

Anderson, Gretchen, ed. The Louisa May Alcott Cookbook. (Illus.). 96p. (gr. 3 up). 1985. 10.95 (ISBN 0-316-03951-9). Little.

Anderson, Gunnar, jt. ed. see Radnitzky, Gerard.

Anderson, H. Frank Wilmot (Furnley Maurice) 1955. 8.50x (ISBN 0-522-83505-8, Pub. by Melbourne U Pr Australia). Intl Spec Bk.

Anderson, H., ed. Gospel of Mark. (New Century Bible Ser.). 384p. 1976. 12.50 (ISBN 0-551-00579-3). Attic Pr.

Anderson, H. George, tr. see Thielicke, Helmut.

Anderson, H. H. Centrifugal Pumps. 2nd ed. 470p. 1972. 84.00 (ISBN 0-85461-076-6, Pub by Trade & Tech England). Brookfield Pub Co.

Anderson, H. William, jt. auth. see Fisk, Marion J.

Anderson, Hal W. & Anderson, Gail S. Mom & Dad Are Divorced, but I'm Not: Parenting After Divorce. LC 80-27602. 284p. 1981. 21.95x (ISBN 0-88229-522-5). Nelson-Hall.

Anderson, Hamilton H., et al. Amebiasis: Pathology, Diagnosis, Chemotherapy. (Illus.). 448p. 1953. photocopy ed. 32.50x (ISBN 0-398-04190-3). C C Thomas.

Anderson, Hannelore, ed. see Anderson, Fred A.

Anderson, Hans C. Pictures of Trave. 1871. 30.00 (ISBN 0-89984-001-9). Century Bookbindery.

Anderson, Harry H. & Olson, Frederick I. Milwaukee: At the Gathering of the Waters. (Illus.). 224p. 1985. 24.95 (ISBN 0-938076-06-X). Milwaukee County.

Anderson, Heddy. A Labyrinth of Thoughts. (Illus.). 1982. 5.95 (ISBN 0-533-05157-6). Vantage.

Anderson, Heidi M., jt. auth. see Anderson, John M.

Anderson, Helen T. The Descendants of Jonathan Hiller. (Illus.). 284p. 1983. 30.00 (ISBN 0-932334-62-8). Heart of the Lakes.

Anderson, Henry, jt. auth. see London, Joan.

Anderson, Henry M., jt. auth. see Radlauer, Ruth.

Anderson, Henry P. The Bracero Program in California: With Particular Reference to Health Status, Attitudes, & Practices. Cortes, Carlos E., ed. LC 76-1225. (Chicano Heritage Ser.). (Illus.). 1976. 25.50x (ISBN 0-405-09482-5). Ayer Co Pubs.

Anderson, Henry R. & Raiborn, Mitchell H. Basic Cost Accounting Concepts. LC 76-12017. (Illus.). 720p. 1977. text ed. 31.95 (ISBN 0-395-20646-4). HM.

Anderson, Henry W. The Modern Food Service Industry: An Introductory Guide. 350p. 1977. text ed. write for info. (ISBN 0-697-08407-8). Wm C Brown.

Anderson, Herbert. The Family & Pastor Care: Theology & Pastoral Care. pap. 5.95 (ISBN 0-317-02963-0). Fortress.

--The Family & Pastoral Care. Browining, Don S., ed. LC 83-48914. (Theology & Pastoral Care Ser.). 128p. pap. 6.95 (ISBN 0-8006-1728-2, 1-1728). Fortress.

Anderson, Herbert, jt. auth. see Mitchell, Kenneth R.

Anderson, Herbert L., ed. Physics Vade Mecum. LC 81-69849. 340p. 1981. 25.00 (ISBN 0-88318-289-0). Am Inst Physics.

Anderson, Herman. Package of Love for Young & Old. 1980. 3.50 (ISBN 0-934860-12-2). Adventure Pubns.

Anderson, Hershel M. & Bailey, Andrew D. Economics & Business Finance. (Certificate in Management Accounting Review). (Illus.). 227p. 1984. 98.50 (ISBN 0-918937-06-X); cassette tapes 500.00 (ISBN 0-918937-12-4). Malibu Pub.

Anderson, Hershel M. & Giese, J. W. Taxes, Current Pronouncements, & Updated CMA Questions: 1984-1985. (Illus.). 238p. 1984. 19.95 (ISBN 0-918937-05-1). Malibu Pub.

Anderson, Hershel M., jt. auth. see Sommerfeld, Ray M.

Anderson Hospital. Neoplasms of the Skin & Malignant Melanoma. (Illus.). 1976. 58.50 (ISBN 0-8151-0213-5). Year Bk Med.

Anderson Hospital Staff. Cancer Patient Care at M. D. Anderson Hospital & Tumor Institute. (Illus.). 1976. 96.95 (ISBN 0-8151-0217-8). Year Bk Med.

Anderson, Howard, ed. see Lewis, Matthew.

Anderson, Howard, ed. see Sterne, Laurence.

Anderson, Howard, et al, eds. Familiar Letter in the Eighteenth Century. LC 66-17466. 1968. pap. 7.95x (ISBN 0-7006-0003-5). U Pr of KS.

Anderson, Howard C., jt. auth. see Forrest, Herbert E.

Anderson, Howard J. Major Employment Law Principles Established by the EEOC, the OFCCP & the Courts. LC 80-607842. pap. 29.30 (ISBN 0-317-26774-4, 2024340). Bks Demand UMI.

--New Techniques in Labor Dispute Resolution: A Report of the 23rd Conference of the Association of Labor Mediation Agencies. LC 76-13538. pap. 64.80 (ISBN 0-317-26770-1, 2024342). Bks Demand UMI.

--Primer of Labor Relations. 22nd ed. 172p. 1983. pap. 15.00 (ISBN 0-87179-438-1). BNA.

Anderson, Howard L. Amado Maurilio Pena, Jr. Young, Robert S., ed. (Illus.). 230p. 1981. 75.00 (ISBN 0-9607068-0-1). R S Young.

Anderson, Howard P. Forgotten Railways: The East Midlands. (Forgotten Railways of Great Britain Ser.). (Illus.). 208p. 1985. 19.95 (ISBN 0-946537-20-8). David & Charles.

Anderson, Howard R., ed. see Kublin, Hyman.

Anderson, Howard R., ed. see Logan, Rayford W. & Cohen, Irving S.

Anderson, Howard R., jt. ed. see Wade, Richard C.

Anderson, Hoyt. The Disabled Homemaker. (Illus.). 356p. 1981. photocopy ed. 33.75x (ISBN 0-398-04077-X). C C Thomas.

Anderson, Hugh. Gold-Digger's Songbook: When I First Landed Here, Vol. 1. (Studies in Australian Folklore: No. 2). (Illus.). 80p. (Orig.). 1985. pap. 11.95 (ISBN 0-9596490-9-3). Legacy Bks.

--The Gospel of Mark. rev. ed. (New Century Bible Commentary Ser.). 384p. 1981. pap. 8.95 (ISBN 0-8028-1887-0). Eerdmans.

Anderson, I., ed. Surveys in Combinatorics, 1985. (London Mathematical Society Lecture Note Ser.: No. 103). 180p. Date not set. pap. price not set. (ISBN 0-521-31524-7). Cambridge U Pr.

Anderson, I., jt. ed. see Proctor, D. S.

Anderson, I. G., ed. Councils, Committees & Boards: A Handbook of Advisory, Cunsultative, Executive & Similar Bodies in British Public Life. 4th ed. 409p. 1980. 100.00x (ISBN 0-900246-32-4). Intl Pubns Serv.

--Current Asian & Australasian Directories: A Guide to Directories Published in or Relating to All Countries in Asia, Australasia & Oceania. LC 79-318525. 1978. 92.00x (ISBN 0-900246-25-1). Gale.

--Current British Directories. 9th ed. LC 53-26894. 1979. 110.00x. Intl Pubns Serv.

--Current British Directories. 10th ed. 275p. 1984. 120.00x (ISBN 0-900246-40-5, Pub. by CBD Res Ltd). Gale.

--Current British Directories: A Guide to the Directories Published in Great Britain, Ireland, British Commonwealth & South Africa. 9th ed. 369p. 1979. 110.00x (ISBN 0-900246-31-6). Gale.

--Directory of European Associations, 2 vols. 2nd ed. Incl. Pt. 1. National Industrial, Trade & Professional Associations. 557p. 1976. 175.00 (ISBN 0-900246-19-7); Pt. 2. National Learned, Scientific & Technical Societies. 349p. 1979. 130.00 (ISBN 0-900246-29-4). LC 76-11697. 906p. (Eng, Fr. & Ger.). Intl Pubns Serv.

--Directory of European Associations: National Industrial, Trade & Professional Associations, Pt. 1, Vol. 1. 3rd ed. 500p. 1981. 195.00x (ISBN 0-900246-35-9, Pub. by CBD Research Ltd.). Gale.

Anderson, Ian. A First Course in Combinatorial Mathematics. (Illus.). 1979. pap. text ed. 12.95x (ISBN 0-19-859617-0). Oxford U Pr.

Anderson, Ian S. A Tangle of Otters. (Illus.). 78p. 1985. 15.95 (ISBN 0-7188-2616-7, Pub. by Salem Hse Ltd). Merrimack Pub Cir.

Anderson, Iona L. The Effectiveness of an Open Classroom Approach on Second Language Acquisition. LC 78-62238. 1978. soft cover 10.00 (ISBN 0-88247-541-X). R & E Pubs.

Anderson, Irvine H. Aramco, the United States, & Saudi Arabia: A Study of the Dynamics of Foreign Oil Policy, 1933-1950. LC 80-8535. 288p. 1981. 23.50x (ISBN 0-691-04679-4). Princeton U Pr.

Anderson, Irvine H., Jr. The Standard-Vacuum Oil Company & United States East Asian Policy, 1933-1941. 280p. 1975. 27.50x (ISBN 0-691-04629-8). Princeton U Pr.

Anderson, Isaac, tr. see Christiansen, Sigurd.

Anderson, J. The Multiple Choice Questions in Medicine. 2nd ed. 234p. pap. text ed. cancelled (ISBN 0-272-79642-5, Pub. by Pitman Bks Ltd UK). Pitman Pub MA.

Anderson, J. & Mikhail, E. Introduction to Surveying. 720p. 1984. 32.95 (ISBN 0-07-001653-4). McGraw.

Anderson, J., ed. Chemisorption & Reactions on Metallic Films, 2 vols. (Physical Chemistry Ser: Vol. 24). 1971. Vol. 1. 88.00 (ISBN 0-12-058001-2); Vol. 2. 60.00 (ISBN 0-12-058002-0). Acad Pr.

--Medical Informatics Europe 1978: First Congress of the European Federation for Medical Informatics, Proceedings, Cambridge, England, Sept. 4-8, 1978. (Lecture Notes in Medical Informatics: Vol. 1). (Illus.). 1978. pap. 37.00 (ISBN 0-387-08916-0). Springer-Verlag.

Anderson, J. & Forsythe, J. M., eds. Medinfo 1974: Proceedings of the World Conference on Medical Informatics, August 5-10, 1974, 2 vols. LC 74-83267. 1192p. 1975. Set. 127.75 (ISBN 0-444-10771-1, North-Holland). Elsevier.

Anderson, J., jt. ed. see Pinciroli, F.

Anderson, J., jt. ed. see Laudet, M.

Anderson, J. A. Real Analysis. 356p. 1969. 92.50 (ISBN 0-677-61460-8). Gordon.

Anderson, J. A., jt. auth. see Grahame, R.

Anderson, J. A., ed. Self-Medication. 132p. 1979. text ed. 19.00 (ISBN 0-85200-282-3). Univ Park.

Anderson, J. A., jt. ed. see Hinton, G. E.

Anderson, J. C. & Hum, D. M. Data & Formulae for Engineering Students. 3rd ed. 70p. 1983. 11.00 (ISBN 0-08-029982-2); pap. 5.00 (ISBN 0-08-029981-4). Pergamon.

Anderson, J. C., jt. auth. see Lewis, B.

Anderson, J. D. Introduction to Flight. 2nd ed. 576p. 1985. 35.95 (ISBN 0-07-001639-9). McGraw.

--The Peoples of India. (Illus.). xii, 118p. 1983. text ed. 15.00x (ISBN 0-86590-151-1). Apt Bks.

Anderson, J. D., et al, eds. Nuclear Isospin. 1969. 82.50 (ISBN 0-12-058150-7). Acad Pr.

Anderson, J. E. Organization & Financing of Self-Help Education in Kenya. LC 72-94388. (Financing Educational Systems: Country Case Studies). 70p. (Orig.). 1973. pap. 5.00 (ISBN 92-803-1054-2, U439, UNESCO). Unipub.

Anderson, J. E., tr. see Bloch, Marc.

Anderson, J. E., tr. see Lefebvre, Georges.

Anderson, J. G. The Structure of Western Europe. 1978. pap. text ed. 14.00 (ISBN 0-08-022046-0). Pergamon.

Anderson, J. G. & Owen, T. R. The Structure of the British Isles. 2nd ed. LC 80-41075. (Illus.). 242p. 1980. 35.00 (ISBN 0-08-023998-6); pap. 14.50 (ISBN 0-08-023997-8). Pergamon.

Anderson, J. G. C. & Owen, T. R. Field Geology in Britain's Isles. 1983. 35.00 (ISBN 0-08-022054-1); pap. 16.00 (ISBN 0-08-022055-X). Pergamon.

Anderson, J. I. I Can Read About Dogs & Puppies. LC 72-96953. (Illus.). (gr. 2-4). 1973. pap. 1.50 (ISBN 0-89375-053-0). Troll Assocs.

--I Can Read About Johnny Appleseed. new ed. LC 76-54445. (Illus.). (gr. 2-5). 1977. pap. 1.50 (ISBN 0-89375-037-9). Troll Assocs.

--I Can Read About Paul Bunyan. new ed. LC 76-54494. (Illus.). (gr. 2-5). 1977. pap. 1.50 (ISBN 0-89375-041-7). Troll Assocs.

--I Can Read About Pecos Bill. new ed. LC 76-54575. (Illus.). (gr. 2-5). 1977. pap. 1.50 (ISBN 0-89375-042-5). Troll Assocs.

--I Can Read About the First Thanksgiving. new ed. LC 76-54400. (Illus.). (gr. 2-5). 1977. pap. 1.50 (ISBN 0-89375-034-4). Troll Assocs.

--I Can Read About Whales & Dolphins. LC 72-96955. (Illus.). (gr. 2-4). 1973. pap. 1.50 (ISBN 0-89375-052-2). Troll Assocs.

Anderson, J. J. Newcastle upon Tyne. (Records of Early English Drama Ser.). (Illus.). 264p. 1982. 45.00x (ISBN 0-8020-5610-5). U of Toronto Pr.

Anderson, J. J., ed. Parturient Hypocalcemia. 1970. 60.00 (ISBN 0-12-058350-X). Acad Pr.

Anderson, J. J., jt. ed. see Cawley, A. C.

Anderson, J. K. Ancient Greek Horsemanship. LC 61-6780. (Illus.). 1961. 42.00x (ISBN 0-520-00023-4). U of Cal Pr.

--Genetic Engineering: The Ethical Issues. 128p. (Orig.). 1982. pap. 4.95 (ISBN 0-310-45051-9). Zondervan.

--Hunting in the Ancient World. 200p. 1985. 32.50x (ISBN 0-520-05197-1). U of Cal Pr.

--Xenophon. (Classical Life & Letters Ser.). 216p. 1979. 40.50x (ISBN 0-7156-0702-2, 616, Pub. by Duckworth England); pap. 12.50x (Pub. by Duckworth England). Biblio Dist.

Anderson, J. K., ed. see Smith, Henry R.

Anderson, J. Kerby. Life, Death & Beyond. 1980. pap. 4.95 (ISBN 0-310-41571-3). Zondervan.

Anderson, J. M. Ecology for Environmental Sciences: Biosphere Ecosystems & Man. LC 81-3349. (Resources & Environmental Science Ser.). 208p. 1981. 19.95x (ISBN 0-470-27216-3); pap. 24.95. Halsted Pr.

Anderson, J. M., jt. auth. see Lass, R.

Anderson, J. M. & Macfadyen, A., eds. The Role of Terrestrial & Aquatic Organisms in Decomposition Processes. LC 76-9830. (British Ecological Society Symposia Ser.). 474p. 1976. 63.95x (ISBN 0-470-15105-6). Halsted Pr.

Anderson, J. M., tr. see Heidegger, Martin.

Anderson, J. M., et al, eds. Invertebrate-Microbial Interactions: Joint Symposium of the British Mycological Society & the British Ecological Society Held at the University of Exeter, September 1982. LC 83-14416. (British Mycological Society Symposium Ser.: No. 6). (Illus.). 349p. 1984. 79.50 (ISBN 0-521-25395-0). Cambridge U Pr.

Anderson, J. N. Evidence for the Resurrection. pap. 0.75 (ISBN 0-87784-124-1). Inter-Varsity.

--The World's Religions. rev. ed. LC 75-26654. 1976. pap. 5.95 (ISBN 0-8028-1636-3). Eerdmans.

Anderson, J. N. & Queneau, P. E., eds. Pyrometallurgical Processes in Nonferrous Metallurgy. LC 67-26570. (Metallurgical Society Conferences: Vol. 39). pap. 132.30 (ISBN 0-317-10578-7, 2001528). Bks Demand UMI.

Anderson, J. R. Death in the North Sea. LC 75-34487. 192p. 1976. pap. 2.50 (ISBN 0-8128-7063-8). Stein & Day.

--High Mountains & Cold Seas: A Biography of H. W. Tilman. LC 80-81520. (Illus.). 364p. 1980. 20.00 (ISBN 0-89886-008-3). Mountaineers.

--Muir's Textbook of Pathology. 10th ed. (Illus.). 1976. pap. text ed. 47.75 (ISBN 0-8151-0166-X). Year Bk Med.

--Muir's Textbook of Pathology. 1120p. 1980. pap. text ed. 42.50 (ISBN 0-7131-4357-6). E Arnold.

--Sprig of Sea Lavender. 1980. pap. 2.25 (ISBN 0-440-18321-9). Dell.

--Structure of Metallic Catalysts. 1975. 74.00 (ISBN 0-12-057150-1). Acad Pr.

Anderson, J. R. & Bower, G. H. Human Associative Memory. 538p. 1973. text ed. 39.95x (ISBN 0-89859-108-2). L Erlbaum Assocs.

Anderson, J. R., ed. Catalysis-Science & Technology, Vol. 1. Boudart, M. (Illus.). 320p. 1981. 76.50 (ISBN 0-387-10353-8). Springer-Verlag.

Anderson, J. R. & Boudart, M., eds. Catalysis, Vol. 5. (Science & Technology Ser.). (Illus.). 280p. 1984. 54.00 (ISBN 0-387-12665-1). Springer-Verlag.

--Catalysis-Science & Technology, Vol. 2. (Illus.). 280p. 1981. 72.00 (ISBN 0-387-10593-X). Springer-Verlag.

--Catalysis: Science & Technology, Vol. 3. (Illus.). 290p. 1982. 58.00 (ISBN 0-387-11634-6). Springer-Verlag.

--Catalysis: Science & Technology, Vol. 6. (Illus.). 320p. 1984. 49.00 (ISBN 0-387-12815-8). Springer-Verlag.

Anderson, J. R., et al. Autoimmunity: Clinical & Experimental. (Illus.). 504p. 1967. photocopy ed. 49.50x (ISBN 0-398-00043-3). C C Thomas.

Anderson, J. V. Company Law. 500p. 1979. 79.00x (ISBN 0-906501-03-2, Pub. by Keenan England); paper 32.50x (ISBN 0-906501-02-4). State Mutual Bk.

Anderson, Jack. City Joys. LC 75-11117. 1975. 2.00 (ISBN 0-913722-06-5, Pub. by Release). Small Pr Dist.

--The Clouds of That Country. 1982. pap. 4.50 (ISBN 0-914610-29-5). Hanging Loose.

--The Nutcracker Ballet. LC 79-1307. (Illus.). 1979. 14.95 (ISBN 0-8317-6486-4, Mayflower Bks). Smith Pubs.

--The One & Only: The Ballet Russe de Monte Carlo. LC 81-67267. (Illus.). 400p. 1981. 25.00 (ISBN 0-87127-127-3). Dance Horiz.

--Washington Expose. 1967. 15.00 (ISBN 0-8183-0219-4). Pub Aff Pr.

Anderson, Jack & Boyd, James. Fiasco. LC 80-45037. 386p. 1983. 17.50 (ISBN 0-8129-0943-7). Times Bks.

Anderson, Jack & Kidner, John. Alice in Blunderland. LC 83-6352. (Illus.). 183p. 1983. 12.95 (ISBN 0-87491-448-5); pap. 7.95 (ISBN 0-87491-446-9). Acropolis.

Anderson, Jack, jt. auth. see Van Gogh, Anna.

Anderson, Jack, ed. see Van Gogh, Anna.

Anderson, Jack A. & Little, J. Wesley. Change & Innovation in Education. LC 74-11415. 116p. 1974. pap. text ed. 7.95x (ISBN 0-8422-0453-9). Irvington.

Anderson, Jack W., jt. auth. see Neff, Jerry M.

Anderson, Jacqulyn. Dewey Decimal & Sears Update: Supplement to How to Classify, Catalog, & Maintain Media. 1981. Repr. saddle wire 2.75 (ISBN 0-8054-3705-3). Broadman.

Anderson, Jacqulyn, compiled by. How to Administer & Promote a Church Media Library. 1985. pap. 5.95 (ISBN 0-8054-3711-8). Broadman.

--How to Classify & Catalog Media. 1985. pap. 5.95 (ISBN 0-8054-3709-6). Broadman.

--How to Process Media. 1985. pap. 5.95 (ISBN 0-8054-3710-X). Broadman.

Anderson, James. Abolition of Death. (Walker British Paperback Mysteries Ser.). 192p. 1985. pap. 2.95 (ISBN 0-8027-3132-5). Walker & Co.

--The Affair of the Blood-Stained Egg Cosy. 256p. 1978. pap. 2.95 (ISBN 0-380-01919-1, 63826-6). Avon.

--The Affair of the Mutilated Mink Coat. 304p. (Orig.). (YA) 1981. pap. 2.95 (ISBN 0-380-78964-7, 60187-7). Avon.

--Alpha List. (Walker British Paperback Mysteries Ser.). 192p. 1985. pap. 2.95 (ISBN 0-8027-3129-5). Walker & Co.

--British Novels of the Twentieth Century. 1978. Repr. of 1959 ed. lib. bdg. 6.50 (ISBN 0-8495-0040-0). Arden Lib.

--British Novels of the Twentieth Century. LC 73-15660. 1959. lib. bdg. 8.50 (ISBN 0-8414-2918-9). Folcroft.

--Diabetes. 288p. 1983. pap. 3.50 (ISBN 0-446-30593-6). Warner Bks.

--The Murder of Sherlock Holmes. 208p. 1985. pap. 2.95 (ISBN 0-380-89702-4). Avon.

--Observations on the Means of Exciting a Spirit of National Industry. LC 68-25541. Repr. of 1777 ed. 45.00x (ISBN 0-678-00391-2). Kelley.

Anderson, James & Tatro, Earl E. Shop Theory. 6th ed. (Illus.). 576p. (gr. 9-11). 1974. text ed. 25.40 (ISBN 0-07-001612-7). McGraw.

Anderson, James, jt. auth. see Larson, Jeffry H.

Anderson, James see Massey, Doreen, et al.

Anderson, James, ed. Economic Regulatory Policy. 1975. pap. 8.00 (ISBN 0-918592-12-7). Policy Studies.

Anderson, James & Duncan, Simon, eds. Redundant Spaces in Cities & Regions? (Special Publication Institute of British Geographers Ser.: No. 15). 1983. 49.00 (ISBN 0-12-058480-8). Acad Pr.

Anderson, James A. A Comparative Analysis of Selected Income Measurement Theories in Financial Accounting, Vol. 12. (Studies in Accounting Research). 120p. 1976. 6.00 (ISBN 0-86539-024-X); nonmembers 4.00. Am Accounting.

--Encina & Virgil. LC 74-75722. (Romance Monographs: No. 8). 1974. 10.00x (ISBN 84-399-2158-6); pap. 8.00x (ISBN 8-4399-2158-6). Romance.

Anderson, James A., jt. auth. see Ploghoft, Milton E.

Anderson, James D. & Jones, Ezra E. The Management of Ministry. LC 76-62942. 1978. 13.41i (ISBN 0-06-060235-X, HarpR). Har-Row.

--Ministry of the Laity. LC 84-48211. 224p. 1985. 15.34 (ISBN 0-06-060194-9, HarpR). Har-Row.

Anderson, James D., jt. ed. see Catala, Rafael.

Anderson, James D., jt. ed. see Franklin, Vincent P.

Anderson, James E. Cases in Public Policy-Making. 2nd ed. 1982. pap. text ed. 16.95 (ISBN 0-03-058208-3). HR&W.

--Grant's Atlas of Anatomy. 8th ed. (Illus.). 640p. 1983. 38.50 (ISBN 0-683-00211-2). Williams & Wilkins.

--Public Policy-Making. 2nd ed. LC 73-8174. 188p. 1978. lib. bdg. 13.50 (ISBN 0-88275-737-7). Krieger.

--Public Policy-Making. 3rd ed. 1984. pap. text ed. 16.95 (ISBN 0-03-062394-4). HR&W.

Anderson, James E. & Hazelton, Jared E. Managing Macroeconomic Policy: The Johnson Presidency. (Administrative History of the Johnson Presidency Ser.). (Illus.). 256p. 1986. text ed. 27.50x (ISBN 0-292-75084-6). U of Tex Pr.

Anderson, James E. & Hazleton, Jared E. Managing Macroeconomic Policy: The Johnson Presidency. (Illus.). 256p. 1985. 27.50 (ISBN 0-292-75084-6). U of Tex Pr.

Anderson, James E., ed. Economic Regulatory Policies. LC 76-44023. 232p. 1977. pap. 8.95x (ISBN 0-8093-0818-5). S Ill U Pr.

Anderson, James E., et al. Public Policy & Politics in America. 2nd ed. LC 83-21066. (Political Science Ser.). 450p. 1984. text ed. 15.50 pub net (ISBN 0-534-03094-7). Brooks-Cole.

--Texas Politics: An Introduction. 4th ed. 355p. 1984. pap. text ed. 11.95 scp (ISBN 0-06-040264-4, HarpC); instr's manual scp 1.88 (ISBN 0-06-360272-5). Har-Row.

Anderson, James F. Bond of Being: An Essay on Analogy & Existence. LC 77-91752. Repr. of 1949 ed. lib. bdg. 15.75x (ISBN 0-8371-2435-2, ANBB). Greenwood.

--Introduction to the Metaphysics of St. Thomas Aquinas. LC 53-6515. 1969. pap. 5.95 (ISBN 0-89526-970-8). Regnery-Gateway.

Anderson, James F., ed. Contemporary Economic Issues & Answers. 181p. 1978. text ed. 19.00x (ISBN 0-8422-5275-4). Irvington.

Anderson, James F. see Thomas Aquinas, St.

Anderson, James G. Bureaucracy in Education. LC 68-31016. pap. 60.00 (ISBN 0-317-20663-X, 2024143). Bks Demand UMI.

Anderson, James L. Principles of Relativity Physics. 1967. text ed. 35.00 (ISBN 0-12-058450-6). Acad Pr.

Anderson, James L. & Cohen, Martin. The West Point Fitness & Diet Book. 1978. pap. 3.95 (ISBN 0-380-01894-2, 37242-8). Avon.

--The West Point Fitness & Diet Book. 256p. 1981. pap. 2.95 (ISBN 0-380-54205-6, 54205-6). Avon.

Anderson, James L., jt. auth. see Kennett, Lee.

Anderson, James L., et al, eds. see Krakauer, Lewis J.

Anderson, James M. Structural Aspects of Language Change. (Linguistics Library Ser.). (Illus.). 1973. pap. text ed. 14.95x (ISBN 0-582-55033-5). Longman.

Anderson, James M. & Creore, JoAnn. Readings in Romance Linguistics. (Illus.). 472p. (Orig.). 1972. pap. text ed. 26.00x (ISBN 90-2792-303-5). Mouton.

Anderson, James M. & Kim, Sung W., eds. Recent Advance in Drug Delivery Systems. 406p. 1984. 65.00x (ISBN 0-306-41627-1, Plenum Pr). Plenum Pub.

Anderson, James N. Islamic Law in the Modern World. LC 75-31816. 106p. 1976. Repr. of 1959 ed. lib. bdg. 22.50 (ISBN 0-8371-8451-7, ANIL). Greenwood.

Anderson, James V., jt. auth. see Schenk, Fredrick J.

Anderson, James W. Diabetes: A Practical New Guide to Healthy Living. LC 81-66801. (Illus.). 112p. 1982. 12.95 (ISBN 0-668-05328-3, 5328); pap. 7.95 (ISBN 0-668-05330-5, 5330). Arco.

Anderson, James W., et al. Family Medicine Review. 200p. 1985. Boxed Set. 520.00 (ISBN 0-918473-07-1). Sci-Thru-Media.

Anderson, Jamie G., jt. auth. see Giammattei, Victor M.

Anderson, Jane. Inn Perspective: A Guide to New England Country Inns. LC 74-1785. (Illus.). 288p. 1976. pap. 4.95i (ISBN 0-06-010137-7, HarpT, TD-223, HarpT). Har-Row.

Anderson, Jane & Longnion, Bonnie. A Good Man & Other Stories. (Follet Adult Basic Reading Comprehension Program Ser.). 64p. pap. 4.33 (ISBN 0-8428-2256-9). Cambridge Bk.

--Hello, World & Other Stories. (Follet Adult Basic Reading Comprehension Program Ser.). 64p. pap. 3.47 (ISBN 0-8428-2250-X). Cambridge Bk.

Anderson, Jane, et al. Easy Money the Hard Way & Other Stories. (Follett Adult Basic Reading Comprehension Program Ser.). 64p. pap. 3.47 (ISBN 0-8428-2254-2). Cambridge Bk.
--A Hard Night's Run. (Follet Adult Basic Reading Comprehension Program Ser.). 64p. pap. 3.47 (ISBN 0-8428-2251-8). Cambridge Bk.
--Instructional Guide to the Follet Adult Basic Reading Comprehension Program: Instructional Guide for All Books. (Follet Adult Basic Reading Comprehension Program Ser.). 112p. pap. 3.47 (ISBN 0-8428-2258-5). Cambridge Bk.
--The Lucky Break & Other Stories. (Follet Adult Basic Reading Comprehension Program Ser.). 64p. pap. 3.47 (ISBN 0-8428-2255-0). Cambridge Bk.
--One Letter Too Many & Other Stories. (Follet Adult Basic Reading Comprehension Program Ser.). 64p. pap. 3.47 (ISBN 0-8428-2252-6). Cambridge Bk.
--Run for Your Life & Other Stories. (Follett Adult Basic Reading Comprehension Program Ser.). 64p. pap. 3.47 (ISBN 0-8428-2257-7). Cambridge Bk.
--Stay Alive & Other Stories. (Follet Adult Basic Reading Comprehension Program Ser.). 64p. pap. 3.47 (ISBN 0-8428-2253-4). Cambridge Bk.
Anderson, Janet. A Hug for a New Friend. (Hugga Bunch Ser.). (Illus.). 40p. (ps). Date not set. 4.00 (ISBN 0-910313-88-1). Parker Bro.
Anderson, Janet S. The Happy Birthday Hug. (Hugga Bunch Ser.). (Illus.). 32p. (ps-3). 1985. pap. 0.99 (ISBN 0-87372-006-7); 3.50 (ISBN 0-910313-90-3). Parker Bro.
Anderson, Jani. Bringing down the Moon: Fifteen Tales of Fantasy & Terror. LC 85-10904. (Illus.). 224p. (Orig.). 1985. cloth 15.95 (ISBN 0-917053-03-6); pap. 7.95 (ISBN 0-917053-02-8). Space And.
Anderson, Janice. British Library Guide to Visitors. 1982. 20.00x (ISBN 0-7123-0009-0, Pub. by Brit Lib England). State Mutual Bk.
--The British Library: The Reference Division Collections. (Illus.). 80p. (Orig.). 1983. pap. 2.95 (ISBN 0-7123-0009-0, Pub. by British Lib). Longwood Pub Group.
Anderson, Janice & Swinglehurst, Edmund. Scottish Walks & Legends: The Lowlands & East Scotland. (Walks & Legends Ser.). (Illus.). 184p. 1982. pap. 4.95 (ISBN 0-583-13443-2, Pub. by Granada England). Academy Chi Pubs.
Anderson, Janice R. Atlas of Skeletal Muscle Pathology. 1985. lib. bdg. 95.00 (ISBN 0-85200-325-0, Pub. by MTP Pr England). Kluwer Academic.
Anderson, Jay. The Living History Sourcebook. Date not set. price not set. AASLH Pr.
--Time Machines: The World of Living History. (Illus.). 224p. 1984. 19.95 (ISBN 0-910050-71-6). AASLH Pr.
Anderson, Jaynie, ed. see Wind, Edgar.
Anderson, Jean. The Grass Roots Cookbook. LC 77-4472. 1977. pap. 8.95 1983 (ISBN 0-8129-6330-X). Times Bks.
--Jean Anderson Cooks: Her Kitchen Reference & Recipe Collection. LC 82-7884. (Illus.). 672p. 1982. 19.95 (ISBN 0-688-01325-2). Morrow.
--Jean Anderson's Green Thumb Preserving Guide: The Best & Safest Ways to Can & Freeze, Dry & Store, Pickle, Preserve & Relish Home-Grown Vegetables & Fruits. LC 84-15883. (Illus.). 240p. 1985. pap. 6.95 (ISBN 0-688-04190-6, Quill). Morrow.
--Jean Anderson's New Processor Cooking. LC 83-61742. 1983. 17.50 (ISBN 0-688-02254-5). Morrow.
--Jean Anderson's Processor Cooking. LC 78-27880. (Illus.). 1979. 14.95 (ISBN 0-688-03389-X). Morrow.
--Unforbidden Sweets. LC 82-72070. (Illus.). 1982. 15.00 (ISBN 0-87795-433-X). Arbor Hse.
--Unforbidden Sweets. 1983. pap. 6.95 (ISBN 0-87795-543-3, Pub. by Priam). Arbor Hse.
Anderson, Jean & Buchan, Ruth. Half a Can of Tomatoe Paste & Other Culinary Dilemmas. LC 79-3385. 1980. 14.37i (ISBN 0-06-010147-4, HarpT). Har-Row.
Anderson, Jean & Hanna, Elaine. The Doubleday Cookbook: Complete Contemporary Cooking. LC 75-1000. 1344p. 1975. White. 16.95; Red. 16.95 (ISBN 0-385-18037-3); Green. 16.95 (ISBN 0-385-18038-1). Doubleday.
--New Doubleday Cookbook. (Illus.). 984p. 1985. 16.95 (ISBN 0-385-19577-X). Doubleday.
Anderson, Jean, jt. auth. see Kasten, Lloyd.
Anderson, Jeff & Moussa, Sameh. Useful dBASE Applications. 250p. (Orig.). pap. 15.95 (ISBN 0-915381-80-X). Wordware Pub.
Anderson, Jennifer. The Thinking Woman's Beauty Book. 1979. pap. 4.95 (ISBN 0-380-46375-X). Avon.
Anderson, Jennifer, ed. see Woodman, Bill.
Anderson, Jerry D. Success Strategies for Investment Real Estate: The Professionals Guide to Better Service & Increased Commissions. Berlin, Helene, ed. LC 82-61402. (Illus.). 322p. (Orig.). 1982. pap. text ed. 17.95 (ISBN 0-913652-33-4, BK 153); pap. text ed. 14.36 members. Realtors Natl.
Anderson, Jervis. Guns in American Life. LC 83-43195. 128p. 1984. 12.45 (ISBN 0-394-53598-7). Random.
--This Was Harlem: A Cultural Portrait, 1900-1950. (Illus.). 400p. 1982. 17.95 (ISBN 0-374-27623-4); pap. 10.95 (ISBN 0-374-51757-6). FS&G.
Anderson, Jessica. The Only Daughter. (Fiction Ser.). 256p. 1985. 15.95 (ISBN 0-670-80431-2). Viking.
--Tirra Lirra by the River. 160p. 1984. pap. 4.95 (ISBN 0-14-006945-3). Penguin.
Anderson, Jim. How to Live Rent Free, Job-Free, Tax-Free in the 1980's into the 1990's, Vol. 2. LC 78-113752. 376p. (One $10 real estate study tape free with either book purchased see notice inside book). 1980. lib. bdg. 25.00 (ISBN 0-932574-02-5); text ed. 15.00 (ISBN 0-932574-03-3). Brun Pr.
--Jim Anderson's Lively Talking Book: 90 Secrets on Living Rent-Free, Job-Free, & Tax-Free. LC 81-740007. for five, one-hour tape cassettes 50.00 (ISBN 0-932574-04-1); 10.00 ea. Brun Pr.
--Selling: High-Level into Mega-Level Selling in 3 Years. 300p. (A proven formula to earn six-figures quickly). Date not set. 25.00 (ISBN 0-932574-08-4). Brun Pr.
Anderson, Joan. Christmas on the Prairie. LC 85-4095. (Illus.). 48p. (gr. 2-6). 1985. 13.95 (ISBN 0-89919-307-2, Clarion). HM.
--The First Thanksgiving Feast. LC 84-5803. (Illus.). 48p. (gr. 2-6). 1984. PLB 12.95 (ISBN 0-89919-287-4, Clarion). HM.
--The Glorious Fourth in Prairie Town. (Illus.). 48p. (gr. 2-6). 1986. 12.50 (ISBN 0-688-06246-6); PLB 12.88 (ISBN 0-688-06247-4). Morrow.
Anderson, Joan W. The Best of Both Worlds: A Guide to Home-Based Careers. LC 82-4283. 188p. (Orig.). 1982. 10.95 (ISBN 0-932620-14-0). Betterway Pubns.
--Dear World: Don't Spin So Fast, I'm Having Trouble Hanging On. LC 82-73131. 160p. 1982. pap. 4.95 (ISBN 0-87029-188-2, 20280-4). Abbey.
--Teen is a Four-Letter Word: A Survival Kit for Parents. LC 82-25114. 140p. 1983. pap. 5.95 (ISBN 0-932620-19-1). Betterway Pubns.
Anderson, Joanna, jt. auth. see Benson, Jean.
Anderson, Joanne, jt. auth. see Benson, Jean.
Anderson, Jock. A Dynamic Simulation Model of the World Jute Economy. (Working Paper: No. 391). 39p. 1980. pap. 3.00 (ISBN 0-686-39658-8, WP-0391). World Bank.
Anderson, Jock, et al. Agricultural Decision Analysis. (Illus.). 344p. 1977. text ed. 24.95x (ISBN 0-8138-0401-9). Iowa St U Pr.
Anderson, Johan G., jt. auth. see Hencerson, Mayda.
Anderson, Johannes E. Myths & Legends of the Polynesians. LC 69-13509. (Illus.). (gr. 9 up). 1969. Repr. of 1928 ed. 37.50 (ISBN 0-8048-0414-1). C E Tuttle.
Anderson, John. Basic Forms of Shotokan Karate. 1984. 25.00 (ISBN 0-901764-33-7, Pub. by P H Crompton Ltd UK). State Mutual Bk.
--Bassai Dai Karate Kata (Shotokan) 1984. 20.00 (ISBN 0-901764-18-3, Pub. by P H Crompton Ltd UK). State Mutual Bk.
--Bassai-Dai: Shotokan Advanced Karate Katas No. 2. (Illus.). 32p. (Orig.). 1974. pap. 3.95 (ISBN 0-317-27148-2). Unique Pubns.
--The Deaf & Dumb Child's Picture Defining & Reading Book. 59.95 (ISBN 0-8490-0006-8). Gordon Pr.
--Education & Inquiry. Phillips, D. Z., ed. (Values & Philosophical Inquiry Ser.). 228p. 1980. 28.50x (ISBN 0-389-20075-1, 06847). B&N Imports.
--English Intercourse with Siam in the Seventeenth Century. 1976. Repr. of 1890 ed. 69.00 (ISBN 0-403-05983-6, Regency). Scholarly.
--An Essay Concerning Aspect: Some Considerations of a General Character Arising from the Abbe Darrigol's Analysis of the Basque Verb. (Janua Linguarum Ser. Minor: No. 167). 1973. pap. text ed. 13.60x (ISBN 90-2792-408-2). Mouton.
--Mackinaws Down the Missouri. Barrett, Glenn, ed. LC 73-79903. (Western Text Society Ser.). 105p. 1973. 7.50 (ISBN 0-87421-059-3); pap. 5.50 (ISBN 0-87421-090-9). Utah St U Pr.
--On Case Grammar: Prolegomena to a Theory of Grammatical Relations. (Croom Helm Linguistic Ser.). 1977. text ed. 26.50x (ISBN 0-391-00758-0). Humanities.
--Reptilia & Batrachia. (Zoology of Egypt Ser.: No. 1). (Illus.). 1965. Repr. of 1898 ed. 105.00 (ISBN 3-7682-0240-2). Lubrecht & Cramer.
--The Story of the Life of John Anderson, the Fugitive Slave. facsimile ed. Twelvetrees, Harper, ed. LC 72-164378. (Black Heritage Library Collection). Repr. of 1863 ed. 16.50 (ISBN 0-8369-8837-X). Ayer Co Pubs.
Anderson, John & Fulop-Miller, Rene. The American Theatre, & the Motion Picture in America. (English Literary Reference, House Ser). Repr. of 1938 ed. lib. bdg. 42.00 (ISBN 0-384-01435-6). Johnson Repr.
Anderson, John, jt. auth. see De Blassie, Richard R.
Anderson, John, jt. auth. see Foster, Josephine.
Anderson, John, ed. Language Form & Linguistic Variation: Papers Dedicated to Angus McIntosh. (Current Issues in Linguistic Theory Ser.: No. 15). 496p. 1982. 55.00x (ISBN 90-272-3506-6). Benjamins North Am.
Anderson, John, jt. auth. see Snapp, Allen.
Anderson, John B. The American Economy We Need: But Won't Get from the Republicans or the Democrats. LC 83-48832. 370p. 1984. 17.95 (ISBN 0-689-11464-8). Atheneum.
Anderson, John C. Cosmic Omelet. LC 79-89328. 1980. 5.95 (ISBN 0-87212-102-X). Libra.
Anderson, John C., et al, eds. Material Requirements Planning: A Study of Implementation & Practice. LC 81-68514. 58p. 1981. pap. 13.50 (ISBN 0-935406-03-4). Am Prod & Inventory.
Anderson, John D. Gasdynamic Lasers: An Introduction. (Quantum Electronic Ser.). 1976. 44.00 (ISBN 0-12-056950-7). Acad Pr.
Anderson, John D. & Ikime, Obaro. West Africa in the Nineteenth & Twentieth-Centuries. 1972. pap. text ed. 5.95x (ISBN 0-435-94008-2). Heinemann Ed.
Anderson, John D., ed. see William of St. Thierry.
Anderson, John D. & Kennan, Elizabeth T., trs. Bernard of Clairvaux: Consideration: Advice to a Pope. LC 75-27953. (Cistercian Fathers Ser.: No. 37). 1976. 5.00 (ISBN 0-87907-137-0). Cistercian Pubns.
Anderson, John E., jt. auth. see Committee on the Infant & Preschool Child.
Anderson, John E., jt. auth. see Goodenough, Florence L.
Anderson, John F., jt. auth. see Berdie, Douglas R.
Anderson, John G. Technical Shop Mathematics. 2nd ed. (Illus.). 500p. 1983. 20.95 (ISBN 0-8311-1145-3); Answer Manual avail. Indus Pr.
Anderson, John J. Commodore 64 Sight & Sound. (Illus.). 224p. (Orig.). 1984. pap. 12.95 (ISBN 0-916688-58-5, 58-5). Creative Comp.
--Dietary Excesses & Health Disease Implications. (Illus.). 1984. pap. 18.95 (ISBN 0-938938-13-4). Health Sci Consort.
--The Insider's Guide to the Macintosh: Tips, Shortcuts & Helpful Hints from the Professionals. (Illus.). 240p. (Orig.). pap. cancelled (ISBN 0-916688-93-3, 933). Creative Comp.
Anderson, John J., ed. The Creative Commodore 64. (Illus.). 256p. (Orig.). pap. cancelled (ISBN 0-916688-77-1, 77-1). Creative Comp.
Anderson, John J., et al. Cenozoic Geology of Southwestern High Plateaus of Utah. LC 75-10395. (Geological Society of America Ser.: No. 160). pap. 33.50 (ISBN 0-317-28376-6, 2025457). Bks Demand UMI.
Anderson, John K. Alexander the Great. 1981. pap. 3.50 (ISBN 0-88388-085-7). Bellerophon Bks.
--Horses & Riding. 48p. (gr. 7-9). 1979. pap. 2.50 (ISBN 0-88388-066-0). Bellerophon Bks.
--Tales of Great Dragons. (Illus.). 64p. 1980. pap. 3.50 (ISBN 0-88388-075-X). Bellerophon Bks.
Anderson, John M. Grammar of Case: Towards a Localistic Theory. LC 71-145602. (Studies in Linguistics Ser: No. 4). (Illus.). 1971. 47.50 (ISBN 0-521-08035-5); pap. 15.95 (ISBN 0-521-29057-0). Cambridge U Pr.
--The Individual & the New World. LC 55-649. 1955. pap. 4.95 (ISBN 0-932540-02-3). Dialogue Pr Man World.
--The Realm of Art. LC 67-16195. 1967. 18.75x (ISBN 0-271-73124-9); pap. 8.75x (ISBN 0-271-01180-7). Pa St U Pr.
--The Truth of Freedom. LC 78-26932. 1978. pap. 2.95 (ISBN 0-932540-01-5). Dialogue Pr Man World.
Anderson, John M. & Anderson, Heidi M. Paleoflora of Southern Africa: Vol. 1 Molteno Formation Triassic. 200p. 1984. lib. bdg. 45.00 (ISBN 90-6191-283-0, Pub. by Balkema RSA). IPS.
Anderson, John M., ed. see Calhoun, John C.
Anderson, John M., et al, eds. Historical Linguistics, 2 vols. (Linguistic Ser.: Vol. 12). 1976. Vol. 1: Syntax, Morphology, Internal & Comparative Reconstruction. pap. 29.75 (ISBN 0-7204-6195-2, North-Holland); Vol. 2: Theory & Description in Phonology. pap. 29.75 (ISBN 0-7204-6196-0); Set. pap. 59.75 (ISBN 0-444-10675-8). Elsevier.
Anderson, John N. & Storer, Roy. Immediate & Replacement Dentures. 3rd. ed. (Illus.). 364p. 1981. text ed. 26.75 (ISBN 0-632-00507-6, B 0211-4). Mosby.
Anderson, John O. & Brendel, Doug. Cry of the Innocents. LC 85-70539. 1985. pap. 3.50 (ISBN 0-88270-586-5). Bridge Pub.
Anderson, John O., jt. auth. see Garbutt, Cameron W.
Anderson, John P. Book of British Topography: Classified Catalogue of Topographical Works in the Library of the British Museum Relating to Great Britain & Ireland. LC 77-113836. 472p. 1970. Repr. of 1881 ed. 25.00 (ISBN 0-8063-0401-4). Genealog Pub.
--A Study of the Relationships Between Certain Aspects of Parental Behavior & Attitudes & the Behavior of Junior High School Pupils. LC 72-176519. (Columbia University. Teachers College. Contributions to Education: No. 809). Repr. of 1940 ed. 22.50 (ISBN 0-404-55809-7). AMS Pr.
Anderson, John Q. The Liberating Gods: Emerson on Poets & Poetry. LC 72-121682. 1971. 7.95x (ISBN 0-87024-157-5). U of Miami Pr.
Anderson, John Q., ed. Tales of Frontier Texas: 1830-1860. 315p. 1984. Repr. 15.95 (ISBN 0-87074-202-7). SMU Press.
--Texas Folk Medicine, Vol. 5. (Texas Folklore Society Paisano Books Ser.). 1970. 10.00 (ISBN 0-88426-013-5). Encino Pr.
Anderson, John Q., et al, eds. Southwestern American Literature: A Bibliography. LC 76-3121. 445p. 1980. 25.00 (ISBN 0-8040-0683-0, 82-75745, SB). Ohio U Pr.
Anderson, John R. The Architecture of Cognition. (Cognitive Science Ser.: No. 5). (Illus.). 352p. 1983. text ed. 25.00x (ISBN 0-674-04425-8). Harvard U Pr.
--Cognitive Psychology & Its Implications. LC 80-14354. (Psychology Ser.). (Illus.). 503p. 1980. text ed. 20.95 (ISBN 0-7167-1197-4). W H Freeman.
--Cognitive Psychology & Its Implications. 2nd ed. LC 84-18687. (Psychology Ser.). (Illus.). 472p. 1985. text ed. 25.95 (ISBN 0-7167-1686-0). W H Freeman.
--Death in the Caribbean. 159p. 1984. pap. 2.95 (ISBN 0-8128-8026-9). Stein & Day.
--Death in the Channel. Date not set. pap. cancelled (ISBN 0-8128-8112-5). Stein & Day.
--Death in the Greenhouse: A Colonel Peter Blair Mystery. 192p. 1983. 11.95 (ISBN 0-684-17872-9, ScribT). Scribner.
--Language, Memory, & Thought. LC 76-21791. 546p. 1976. text ed. 39.95x (ISBN 0-89859-107-4). L Erlbaum Assocs.
Anderson, John R. & Bower, Gordon H. Human Associative Memory: A Brief Edition. LC 79-28349. 288p. 1980. 19.95x (ISBN 0-89859-020-5). L Erlbaum Assocs.
Anderson, John R., ed. Cognitive Skills & Their Acquisition. (Carnegie-Mellon Symposia on Cognition Ser.). 384p. 1981. text ed. 36.00x (ISBN 0-89859-093-0). L Erlbaum Assocs.
Anderson, John W. Bioenergetics of Autotrophs & Heterotrophs. (Studies in Biology: No. 126). 64p. 1980. pap. text ed. 8.95 (ISBN 0-7131-2807-0). E Arnold.
Anderson, Jon. Cypresses. 37p. 1981. 45.00x (ISBN 0-915308-25-8). Graywolf.
--Death & Friends. LC 70-117469. (Pitt Poetry Ser). 1970. 12.95 (ISBN 0-8229-3202-4). U of Pittsburgh Pr.
--In Sepia. LC 73-13310. (Pitt Poetry Ser). 1974. 12.95 (ISBN 0-8229-3278-4); pap. 5.95 (ISBN 0-8229-5245-9). U of Pittsburgh Pr.
--Looking for Jonathan. LC 68-12734. (Pitt Poetry Ser). 1968. 12.95 (ISBN 0-8229-3141-9). U of Pittsburgh Pr.
--The Milky Way. LC 82-11491. (The American Poetry Ser.: Vol. 25). 125p. 1983. 14.95 (ISBN 0-88001-006-1). Ecco Pr.
Anderson, Joseph. Counseling Through Group Process. 288p. 1984. text ed. 25.50x (ISBN 0-8261-4620-1). Springer Pub.
--Prayerbook: Hebrew Teacher's Guide. Simon, Ethelyn & Kelman, Victoria, eds. (Orig.). 1985. pap. text ed. 4.95 (ISBN 0-939144-10-7). EKS Pub Co.
Anderson, Joseph & Lipshitz, Devora. Tall Tales Told & Retold in Biblical Hebrew. (Illus.). 96p. (Orig., Hebrew.). 1983. pap. text ed. 8.95 (ISBN 0-939144-07-7). EKS Pub Co.
Anderson, Joseph & Seelig, Alisse. Tall Tales Teacher's Guide. Simon, Ethelyn & Nelson, Beth, eds. (Illus.). 80p. (Orig.). 1983. pap. text ed. 4.95 (ISBN 0-939144-08-5). EKS Pub Co.
Anderson, Joseph, jt. auth. see Simon, Ethelyn.
Anderson, Joseph, et al. Prayerbook Hebrew the Easy Way. Simon, Ethelyn, ed. 264p. (Orig.). 1984. pap. text ed. 14.95 (ISBN 0-939144-09-3). Eks Pub Co.
Anderson, Joseph C., jt. auth. see Fischer, Asma Z.
Anderson, Joseph L. & Richie, Donald. The Japanese Film: Art & Industry (Expanded Edition) LC 81-47985. (Illus.). 500p. 1982. 43.00 (ISBN 0-691-05351-0); pap. 11.95 (ISBN 0-691-00792-6). Princeton U Pr.
Anderson, Joseph M. Modeling Analysis for Retirement Income Policy: Background & Overview. 88p. (Orig.). 1980. pap. 10.00 (ISBN 0-86643-008-3). Employee Benefit.
Anderson, Judith. Outspoken Women: Speeches by American Women Reformers 1635-1935. 288p. 1984. pap. text ed. 14.95 (ISBN 0-8403-3298-X). Kendall Hunt.
Anderson, Judith H. Biographical Truth: The Representation of Historical Persons in Tudor-Stuart Writing. LC 83-14520. 243p. 1984. 23.00x (ISBN 0-300-03085-1). Yale U Pr.
Anderson, Judith I. William Howard Taft: An Intimate History. (Illus.). 1981. 17.95 (ISBN 0-393-01462-2). Norton.
Anderson, Julian G. The Good News & How It Spread. (The New Testament in Everyday American English Ser: Vol. I). (Illus.). 1975. pap. 2.95 (ISBN 0-9602128-0-9). Anderson Publ.
--The New Testament in Everyday American English (EAE) (Illus.). 896p. 1984. pap. 4.95 (ISBN 0-9602128-4-1). Anderson Publ.
--The Story of Jesus the Messiah, Four Gospels. LC 76-52054. (A Life of Christ Wkbk). (Illus.). (gr. 6-12). 1977. pap. 3.95 (ISBN 0-9602128-1-7). Anderson Publ.
--The Story of Jesus the Messiah, Old Testament. (An Old Testament Wkbk). (Illus.). (gr. 6-12). 1977. pap. 3.95 (ISBN 0-9602128-2-5). Anderson Publ.
Anderson, Justo C. Historia De los Bautistas Tomo I: Sus Bases y Principios. 1978. pap. 5.75 (ISBN 0-311-15036-5). Casa Bautista.
Anderson, K. & Mafera, G. Italiensk-Dansk Ordbog. 485p. (Ital. & Danish.). 1980. 29.95 (ISBN 87-01-83431-2, M-1286). French & Eur.
Anderson, K., ed. see Ingram, H. E.

Anderson, Karen. Wartime Women: Sex Roles, Family Relations, & the Status of Women During World War II. LC 80-1703. (Contributions in Women's Studies: No. 20). 198p. 1981. lib. bdg. 27.50x (ISBN 0-313-20884-0, AWW/). Greenwood.

Anderson, Karen & Milliren, Alan. Structured Experiences for Integration of Handicapped Children. LC 83-9949. 390p. 1983. 30.50 (ISBN 0-89443-877-8). Aspen Systems.

Anderson, Karen, jt. auth. see Anderson, Poul.

Anderson, Karen E., jt. auth. see Cass, Lee H.

Anderson, Kari J., compiled by. Pacific Telecommunications Conference '83: Directions. 124p. 1983. pap. text ed. 20.00x (ISBN 0-8248-0925-4, Pac Telecom). UH Pr.

Anderson, Kathleen. Your Baby, Your Birth: A Guide to Alternatives. 300p. 1984. write for info. (ISBN 0-917982-14-2). Cougar Bks.

Anderson, Kathleen C. Fresh from the Farm: Where to Buy Food from Farmers. pap. cancelled (ISBN 0-917982-21-5). Cougar Bks.

Anderson, Kay. Municipal Disclosure Standards Sourcebook, Vol. 7. (Municipal Securities Regulation Ser.). 1978. pap. text ed. 60.00x (ISBN 0-916450-18-X). Coun on Municipal.

Anderson, Kay W. Don't Forget Me, Mommy! LC 81-85048. (Illus.). 118p. (Orig.). 1982. pap. 6.95. Marin Pub.

Anderson, Ken & Carlson, Morry. Games for All Occasions. pap. 2.95 (ISBN 0-310-20152-7). Zondervan.

Anderson, Ken & Clay, Jack. The Art of Quarterbacking. 1984. 19.95 (ISBN 0-671-47651-3, Linden Pr); pap. 10.95 (ISBN 0-671-50724-9). S&S.

Anderson, Ken, jt. auth. see Berger, Bill.

Anderson, Ken E., jt. auth. see Berger, Bill D.

Anderson, Kenneth. The Gourmet's Guide to Fish & Shellfish. LC 84-42596. (Gourmet's Guide Ser.). (Illus.). 128p. (Orig.). 1984. pap. 6.95 (ISBN 0-688-02503-X, Quill). Morrow.

--Orphan Drugs. 1983. 17.95 (ISBN 0-671-47172-4, Linden Pr); pap. 7.95 (ISBN 0-671-49521-6). S&S.

--Orphan Drugs: Your Complete Guide to Effective, Proven Medications Available Outside the U. S. & How to Get Them. 288p. 1983. 17.95 (ISBN 0-671-47172-4, Linden Pr); pap. 7.95 (ISBN 0-671-49521-6). S&S.

--The Pocket Guide to Coffees & Teas. (Illus.). 144p. 1982. pap. 5.95 (ISBN 0-399-50600-4, Perigee); pap. 59.50 10-copy counter prepack (ISBN 0-399-50630-6). Putnam Pub Group.

Anderson, Kenneth & Harmo, Lois. The Prentice-Hall Dictionary of Nutrition & Health. LC 84-11590. 257p. 1985. 18.95 (ISBN 0-13-695610-6); pap. 9.95 (ISBN 0-13-695602-5). P-H.

Anderson, Kenneth, ed. The Accredited Resident Manager Profile, 1984. 24p. (Orig.). 1984. pap. 13.50 (ISBN 0-912104-76-7). Inst Real Estate.

--Computer Applications in Property Management Accounting. 4th ed. 64p. 1983. pap. text ed. 16.50 (ISBN 0-912104-71-6, 990). Inst Real Estate.

--Expense Analysis: Condominiums, Cooperatives, & Planned Unit Developments. 1978. pap. 10.00 (ISBN 0-912104-33-3). Inst Real Estate.

--Expense Analysis: Condominiums, Cooperatives, & Planned Unit Developments. 1979. lib. bdg. 10.00 (ISBN 0-912104-41-4). Inst Real Estate.

--Income-Expense Analysis: Apartments. 1978. pap. 22.50 (ISBN 0-912104-32-5). Inst Real Estate.

--Income-Expense Analysis: Apartments. 1979. pap. 22.50 (ISBN 0-912104-39-2). Inst Real Estate.

--Income-Expense Analysis: Apartments Condominums & Cooperatives, 1977. 1977. pap. 17.50 (ISBN 0-912104-27-9). Inst Real Estate.

--Income-Expense Analysis: Suburban Office Buildings, 1977. 1977. pap. 7.50 (ISBN 0-912104-28-7). Inst Real Estate.

--Income-Expense Analysis: Suburban Office Buildings. 1978. pap. 10.00 (ISBN 0-912104-34-1). Inst Real Estate.

--Income-Expense Analysis: Suburban Office Buildings. 1979. lib. bdg. 15.00 (ISBN 0-912104-40-6). Inst Real Estate.

Anderson, Kenneth & Ruiz, Stacey, eds. Expense Analysis: Condominiums, Cooperatives & Planned Unit Developments, 1984. 152p. (Orig.). 1984. pap. 44.95 (ISBN 0-912104-79-1). Inst Real Estate.

--Income-Expense Analysis: Apartments, 1984. 224p. (Orig.). 1984. pap. 75.50 (ISBN 0-912104-77-5). Inst Real Estate.

--Income-Expense Analysis: Office Buildings (Downtown & Suburban), 1984. 224p. (Orig.). 1984. pap. 75.50 (ISBN 0-912104-78-3). Inst Real Estate.

Anderson, Kenneth E., jt. auth. see Berger, Bill D.

Anderson, Kenneth N. Eagle Claw Fish Cookbook. LC 77-89549. (Illus.). 1978. 9.95 (ISBN 0-916752-17-8). Dorison Hse.

Anderson, Kenneth R. Lease Escalators & Other Pass-Through Clauses: 1984. 2nd rev. ed. 35p. 1984. pap. 13.50 (ISBN 0-912104-70-8, 989). Inst Real Estate.

Anderson, Kenneth R. & Ruiz, Stacey L., eds. Expense Analysis: Condominiums, Cooperatives, & Planned Unit Developments. 136p. 1982. pap. 19.50 (ISBN 0-912104-63-5). Inst Real Estate.

--Expense Analysis: Condominiums, Cooperatives, & Planned Unit Developments, 1983 Edition. 152p. (Orig.). 1983. pap. 55.00 (ISBN 0-912104-74-0, 85803). Inst Real Estate.

--Income-Expense Analysis: Apartments, 1983. 224p. (Orig.). 1983. pap. 61.95 (ISBN 0-912104-72-4, 85503). Inst Real Estate.

--Income-Expense Analysis: Office Buildings. 200p. (Orig.). 1982. pap. 29.50 (ISBN 0-912104-65-1). Inst Real Estate.

--Income-Expense Analysis: Office Buildings, 1983 Edition. 224p. 1983. pap. 61.95 (ISBN 0-912104-73-2, 84203). Inst Real Estate.

Anderson, Kenneth R., ed. see Institute of Real Estate Management.

Anderson, Kent, ed. Career Education & the Art Teaching Profession. 48p. 1980. 6.95 (ISBN 0-937652-12-1). Natl Art Ed.

--Television Fraud: The History & Implications of the Quiz Show Scandals. LC 77-94755. (Contributions in American Studies: No. 39). lib. bdg. 27.50x (ISBN 0-313-20321-0, ATF/). Greenwood.

Anderson, Kim E. & Scott, Ronald M. Fundamentals of Industrial Toxicology. LC 80-69428. (Illus.). 120p. 1981. text ed. 24.95 (ISBN 0-250-40378-1). Butterworth.

Anderson, Knud. Danmark: The Training Ship under the Dannebrog & The Stars & Stripes. Ko, Suzanne M., tr. from Danish. LC 85-60389. (Illus.). 238p. 1985. 15.95 (ISBN 0-933748-08-6, Pub. by Samlerens Forlag Denmark). Nordic Bks.

Anderson, Kristen & DuBreuil, Linda. The Wholesome Hooker. 1978. pap. 1.75 (ISBN 0-505-51280-7, Pub. by Tower Bks). Dorchester Pub Co.

Anderson, Kym & Baldwin, Robert E. The Political Market for Protection in Industrial Countries: Empirical Evidence. (Working Paper: No. 492). 28p. 1981. pap. 3.00 (ISBN 0-686-39772-X, WP-0492). World Bank.

Anderson, Kym & George, Aurelia, eds. Australian Agriculture & Newly Industrialising Asia: Isssues for Research. LC 80-69631. (Australia-Japan Economic Relations Research Project-Monograph: No. 4). 462p. 1981. pap. text ed. 7.00 (ISBN 0-9596197-3-9, 0104, Pub. by ANUP Australia). Australia N U P.

Anderson, L. H. & Encausse, Gerard. Occult Science. 1955. 7.95 (ISBN 0-932785-35-2). Philos Pub.

Anderson, L. L. & Tillman, D. A., eds. Fuels from Waste. 1977. 55.00 (ISBN 0-12-056450-5). Acad Pr.

Anderson, L. O. Construction Guides for Exposed Wood Decks. 82p. 1982. pap. 5.00 (ISBN 0-318-11769-X). Gov Printing Office.

--How to Build a Wood-Frame House. Orig. Title: Wood-Frame House Construction. (Illus.). 233p. 1970. pap. 5.50 (ISBN 0-486-22954-8). Dover.

--How to Build a Wood-Frame House. LC 73-77635. 1973. lib. bdg. 15.00x (ISBN 0-88307-541-5). Gannon.

Anderson, L. O. & Zornig, Harold F. Build Your Own Low Cost Home. 200p. 1972. pap. 9.95 (ISBN 0-486-21525-3). Dover.

--Build Your Own Low-Cost Home: Complete Working Drawings & Specifications for Eleven Homes. 18.25 (ISBN 0-8446-4703-9). Peter Smith.

Anderson, L. O. & Winslow, Taylor F., illus. Wood-Frame House Construction. rev. ed. (Illus.). 1976. pap. 9.75 (ISBN 0-910460-20-5). Craftsman.

Anderson, L. O., et al. Wood Decks: Construction & Maintenance. LC 79-91405. (Illus.). 128p. 1980. pap. 6.95 (ISBN 0-8069-8794-4). Sterling.

Anderson, L. V., jt. auth. see Hayden.

Anderson, L. W. Light & Color. LC 77-27460. (Read About Science). (Illus.). (gr. k-3). 1978. PLB 14.25 (ISBN 0-8393-0077-8). Raintree Pubs.

Anderson, La Vere. Allan Pinkerton: First Private Eye. LC 77-182270. (Americans All Ser.). (Illus.). 96p. (gr. 3-6). 1972. PLB 7.98 (ISBN 0-8116-4575-4). Garrard.

Anderson, Larry E., ed. see Zimmerman, John J.

Anderson, Larry L. & Tillman, David A. Synthetic Fuels from Coal: Overview & Assessment. LC 79-17786. 158p. 1979. 40.00 (ISBN 0-471-01784-1, Pub. by Wiley-Interscience). Wiley.

--Synthetic Fuels from Coal: Overview & Assessment. LC 79-17786. (A Wiley-Interscience Publication). pap. 43.00 (ISBN 0-317-26175-4, 2025184). Bks Demand UMI.

Anderson, Lascelles & Windham, Douglas M., eds. Education & Development: Issues in the Analysis & Planning of Post-Colonial Societies. LC 81-47562. 240p. 1982. 28.50x (ISBN 0-669-04654-X). Lexington Bks.

Anderson, Laurens & Unger, Frank M., eds. Bacterial Lipopolysacharides: Structure, Synthesis, & Biological Activities. LC 83-158282. (ACS Symposium Ser.: No. 231). 325p. 1983. lib. bdg. 44.95x (ISBN 0-8412-0800-X). Am Chemical.

Anderson, Laurie. United States. LC 82-48315. (Illus.). 224p. 1984. 28.80i (ISBN 0-06-015243-5, HarpT). Har-Row.

--United States. LC 83-48315. (Illus.). 224p. 1984. pap. 19.18i (ISBN 0-06-091110-7, CN 1110, CN). Har-Row.

--Words in Reverse. 16p. (Orig.). 1979. pap. 3.00 (ISBN 0-917061-02-0). Top Stories.

Anderson, LaVere. Abe Lincoln & the River Robbers. LC 79-148089. (Regional American Stories Ser.). (Illus.). 64p. (gr. 3-6). 1971. PLB 7.47 (ISBN 0-8116-4251-8). Garrard.

--Allan Pinkerton. 96p. (gr. k-6). pap. 1.25 (ISBN 0-440-40210-7, YB). Dell.

--Balto: Sled Dog of Alaska. LC 75-45464. (Famous Animal Stories Ser.). (Illus.). 48p. (gr. 2-5). 1976. PLB 7.68 (ISBN 0-8116-4859-1). Garrard.

--Mary McLeod Bethune: Teacher with a Dream. LC 75-25765. (Discovery Bks.). (Illus.). 80p. (gr. 2-5). 1976. PLB 7.47 (ISBN 0-8116-6321-3). Garrard.

--Mary Todd Lincoln: President's Wife. LC 74-18303. (Discovery Ser.). (Illus.). 80p. (gr. 2-5). 1975. PLB 7.47 (ISBN 0-8116-6316-7). Garrard.

--Saddles & Sabers: Black Men of the Old West. LC 74-18122. (Toward Freedom Ser.). (Illus.). (gr. 5-9). 1975. PLB 4.47 (ISBN 0-8116-4805-2). Garrard.

--Sitting Bull: Great Sioux Chief. LC 70-120462. (Indians Ser). (Illus.). (gr. 2-5). 1970. PLB 6.69 (ISBN 0-8116-6608-5). Garrard.

--Story of Johnny Appleseed. LC 73-17255. (American Folktales Ser.). (Illus.). (gr. 2-5). 1974. PLB 7.47 (ISBN 0-8116-4040-X). Garrard.

--Svea: The Dancing Moose. LC 77-13922. (Famous Animal Ser.). (Illus.). (gr. 3). 1978. PLB 7.68 (ISBN 0-8116-4862-1). Garrard.

--Tad Lincoln: Abe's Son. LC 70-151987. (Discovery Ser.). (Illus.). (gr. 2-5). 1971. PLB 7.47 (ISBN 0-8116-6307-8). Garrard.

Anderson, Lavina F., jt. auth. see Zirker, Sherri M.

Anderson, Lee. Progressive Perspective. 1985. pap. text ed. 19.95 (ISBN 0-8359-5778-0). Reston.

--Smile in the Sun. (YA) 1983. 8.95 (ISBN 0-8034-8312-0, Avalon). Bouregy.

Anderson, Lee F., et al. Legislative Roll-Call Analysis. (Handbooks for Research in Political Behavior). 1966. 12.95 (ISBN 0-8101-0052-5). Northwestern U Pr.

Anderson, Lee P., jt. auth. see Greaves, Edward R.

Anderson, Leland I., jt. auth. see Ratzlaff, John T.

Anderson, Leonard. Electric Machines & Transformers. (Illus.). 336p. 1980. text ed. 28.95 (ISBN 0-8359-1615-4); instr's. manual free (ISBN 0-8359-1616-2). Reston.

--Electric Transmission Line Fundamentals. 1984. text ed. 35.95 (ISBN 0-8359-1597-2). Reston.

Anderson, Leone C. Learning about Towers & Dungeons. LC 82-9639. (Learning about Ser.). 48p. (gr. 2-6). 1982. PLB 11.00 (ISBN 0-516-06538-6). Childrens.

--My Friend Next Door. LC 83-7440. (Illus.). 32p. (gr. 1-3). 1983. PLB 4.95 (ISBN 0-89693-212-5). Dandelion Hse.

--Surprise at Muddy Creek. LC 84-7072. (Illus.). 32p. (gr. 1-2). 1984. lib. bdg. 4.95 (ISBN 0-89693-222-2). Dandelion Hse.

--The Wonderful Shrinking Shirt. Fay, Ann, ed. LC 83-1297. (Just for Fun Bks.). (Illus.). (gr. k-2). 1983. PLB 10.75 (ISBN 0-8075-9171-8). A Whitman.

Anderson, Leroy. Leroy Anderson: Twenty-Five Melodies for Piano Solo. Orig. Title: Leroy Anderson (Almost Complete) (Illus.). 1980. pap. 9.95 (ISBN 0-486-24067-3). Dover.

Anderson, Leslie. Industrial Information Systems. 1980. 69.00x (ISBN 0-86176-034-4, Pub. by MCB Pubns). State Mutual Bk.

Anderson, Lester G. Land-Grant Universities & Their Continuing Challenge. 366p. 1976. 15.00x (ISBN 0-87013-198-2). Mich St U Pr.

Anderson, Lewis E., jt. auth. see Crum, Howard A.

Anderson, Lewis F. The Anglo-Saxon Scop. LC 73-1780. 1974. Repr. of 1902 ed. lib. bdg. 10.00 (ISBN 0-8414-1703-2). Folcroft.

Anderson, Lewis F., compiled by. Pestalozzi. LC 75-130984. Repr. of 1931 ed. 14.00 (ISBN 0-404-00357-5). AMS Pr.

Anderson, Lewis F., ed. see Pestalozzi, Johann H.

Anderson, Linda. Person You Are. 1978. text ed. 14.10 (ISBN 0-913310-42-5). PAR Inc.

--We Can't All Be Heroes, You Know. LC 84-16359. 208p. 1985. 14.95 (ISBN 0-89919-333-1). Ticknor & Fields.

Anderson, Linda, jt. auth. see Collins, Marcia R.

Anderson, Linda A., ed. see Whitlock, Ruth.

Anderson, Lindsay. About John Ford. (Illus.). 1983. 17.95 (ISBN 0-07-001626-7); pap. 9.95 (ISBN 0-07-001624-0). McGraw.

--Making a Film. LC 76-52087. (Classics of Film Literature Ser.: Vol. 1). (Illus.). 1977. Repr. of 1952 ed. lib. bdg. 22.00 (ISBN 0-8240-2863-5). Garland Pub.

Anderson, Linnea, et al. Nutrition in Health & Disease. 17th ed. (Illus.). 794p. 1982. text ed. 26.50 (ISBN 0-397-54282-8, 64-02085, Lippincott Nursing). Lippincott.

Anderson, Lonzo. The Halloween Party. LC 74-8193. (Illus.). (ps-2). 1974. (ScribJ); pap. 2.95 (ISBN 0-684-16004-8, ScribJ). Scribner.

Anderson, Lorin. Charles Bonnet & the Order of the Known. 1982. lib. bdg. 37.00 (ISBN 90-277-1389-8, Pub. by Reidel Holland). Kluwer Academic.

Anderson, Lorin W., jt. auth. see Block, James H.

Anderson, Lorin W., jt. auth. see University of South Carolina.

Anderson, Lorin W., ed. Time & School Learning: Theory, Research & Practice. LC 83-11009. 240p. 1983. 25.00 (ISBN 0-312-80505-5). St Martin.

Anderson, Lorin W. & Carroll, John B., eds. Perspectives on School Learning: Selected Writings of John B. Carroll. 440p. 1985. text ed. 39.95 (ISBN 0-89859-343-3). L Erlbaum Assocs.

Anderson, Lorraine. Leathercraft. LC 74-33529. (Early Craft Bks). (Illus.). 32p. (gr. 1-4). 1975. PLB 4.95 (ISBN 0-8225-0872-9). Lerner Pubns.

Anderson, Lou A., ed. see Harrell, Billie J.

Anderson, Louis W. Light & Color. LC 77-27460. (Read about Science Ser.). (Illus.). 48p. (gr. 2-5). 1983. pap. 9.27g (ISBN 0-8393-0297-5). Raintree Pubs.

Anderson, Lowell, jt. auth. see McKenzie, Dennis J.

Anderson, Lucia. Mammals & Their Milk. (Illus.). 48p. (gr. 3-6). 1985. 11.95 (ISBN 0-396-08315-3). Dodd.

--The Smallest Life Around Us. LC 77-15858. (Illus.). (gr. 2-4). 1978. reinforced lib. bdg. 7.95 (ISBN 0-517-53227-1). Crown.

Anderson, Luleen S. Sunday Came Early This Week. 140p. 1982. pap. 8.95 (ISBN 0-87073-575-6). Schenkman Bks Inc.

Anderson, Lydia. Folk Dancing. LC 81-3071. (First Bks.). (gr. 4 up). 1981. PLB 8.90 (ISBN 0-531-04193-X). Watts.

--Immigration. (Impact Ser.). 96p. (gr. 7 up). 1981. lib. bdg. 9.90 (ISBN 0-531-04335-5). Watts.

--Nigeria Cameroon Central Africa. LC 80-23042. (First Bks.). (gr. 4 up). 1981. PLB 8.90 (ISBN 0-531-04276-6). Watts.

Anderson, Lynn. Exploring Careers in Library Science. (Careers in Depth Ser.). 144p. 1985. lib. bdg. 8.97 (ISBN 0-8239-0642-6). Rosen Group.

--Steps to Life. (Twentieth Century Sermons Ser.). 1977. 11.95 (ISBN 0-89112-310-5). Bibl Res Pr.

Anderson, Lynn, ed. A Study of the Feasibility of No-Fault Automobile Insurance for Texas. (Policy Research Project Reports Ser.: No. 10). 85p. 1975. pap. 3.00 (ISBN 0-89940-607-6). LBJ Sch Pub Aff.

Anderson, Lynne, jt. auth. see Terry, Ellen.

Anderson, M. Help for Families of a Depressed Person. LC 12-2821. (Trauma Bks.: Ser. 2). 1983. pap. 2.75 ea. (ISBN 0-570-08258-7); Set. pap. 11.95. Concordia.

Anderson, M. & Lee, R. Efficiency in Lighting. Gyftopoulos, Elias P. & Cohen, Karen C., eds. (Industrial Energy-Conservation Manuals: No. 10). (Illus.). 104p. 1982. loose-leaf 20.00x (ISBN 0-262-01066-6). MIT Pr.

Anderson, M., ed. see Metos, Thomas H.

Anderson, M. B., tr. see Hugo, Victor.

Anderson, M. G. & Burt, T. P. Hydrological Forecasting. (Geomorphology Ser.). 1985. 54.95 (ISBN 0-471-90614-X). Wiley.

Anderson, M. S. Europe in the Eighteenth Century 1713-1783. 2nd ed. (A General History of Europe Ser.). 1976. pap. text ed. 14.95 (ISBN 0-582-48672-6). Longman.

Anderson, M. S., jt. ed. see Hatton, R.

Anderson, Mabel, et al. That All Children May Learn We Must Learn: Looking Forward to Teaching. 2nd,1971 ed. LC 78-165217. (Illus.). 1972. pap. 3.60x (ISBN 0-87173-032-4). ACEI.

Anderson, Madelyn K. Counting on You: The U. S. Census. LC 79-67813. (Illus.). 96p. 1980. 9.95 (ISBN 0-686-63972-3). Vanguard.

--Greenland: Island at the Top of the World. LC 82-46003. (Illus.). 127p. (gr. 5-8). 1983. 10.95 (ISBN 0-396-08139-8). Dodd.

--Oil in Troubled Waters: Cleaning up Oil Spills. LC 80-21139. (Illus.). 128p. 1983. 9.95 (ISBN 0-8149-0842-X). Vanguard.

Anderson, Madelyn K., ed. see Burns, Sheila L.

Anderson, Maggie. Years That Answer. LC 79-2610. 1980. (HarpT); pap. 5.95 (ISBN 0-06-090760-6, CN 760). Har-Row.

Anderson, Malcolm, ed. Frontier Regions in Western Europe. 144p. 1983. text ed. 30.00x (ISBN 0-7146-3217-1, BHA 03217, F Cass Co). Biblio Dist.

Anderson, Marcia, jt. auth. see Jones, Benjamin.

Anderson, Marcia J. & Schmidt, Barbara A. Directory of Degree Programs in Nursing. 320p. 1984. lib. bdg. 29.95 (ISBN 0-668-05757-2, 5757-2). Arco.

Anderson, Margaret. Arabic Materials in English Translation: A Bibliography of Works from the Pre-Islamic Period to 1977 Arabic. 1980. lib. bdg. 25.00 (ISBN 0-8161-7954-9, Hall Reference). G K Hall.

--Fiery Fountains: Continuation & Crisis to 1950. LC 70-92707. (Illus.). 1969. pap. 8.95 (ISBN 0-8180-0211-5). Horizon.

--In the Keep of Time. LC 76-29671. (gr. 4 up). 1977. PLB 6.99 (ISBN 0-394-93434-2). Knopf.

--Light in the Mountain. LC 81-14266. (Illus.). 192p. (gr. 5-9). 1982. PLB 9.99 (ISBN 0-394-94791-6). Knopf.

--Louise: Her Flight to Freedom from Russia. LC 77-71626. 134p. 1977. pap. 2.95 (ISBN 0-87788-517-6). Shaw Pubs.

--The Mists of Time. LC 83-19555. 192p. (gr. 4 up). 1984. PLB 10.99 (ISBN 0-394-96573-6); 10.95 (ISBN 0-394-86573-1). Knopf.

--Momentos Felices Con Dios. 192p. 1977. 3.25 (ISBN 0-88113-312-4). Edit Betania.

--My Thirty Years' War, an Autobiography. LC 76-136511. (Illus.). 1971. Repr. of 1930 ed. lib. bdg. 19.75x (ISBN 0-8371-5429-4, ANTY). Greenwood.

--My Thirty Years' War: Beginnings & Battles to 1930. LC 76-92706. (Illus.). 1969. pap. 9.95 (ISBN 0-8180-0210-7). Horizon.
--Strange Necessity: Resolutions & Reminiscence to 1969. LC 73-92708. (Illus.). 1969. pap. 8.95 (ISBN 0-8180-0212-3). Horizon.
--The Unknowable Gurdjieff. 1st 1973 ed. (Illus.). 212p. (Orig.). 1969. pap. 7.50 (ISBN 0-87728-219-6). Weiser.
Anderson, Margaret, ed. Little Review Anthology. 1970. 10.00 (ISBN 0-8180-1123-8); pap. 4.95 (ISBN 0-8180-1154-8). Horizon.
Anderson, Margaret, ed. see Jansky, Robert C.
Anderson, Margaret, ed. see Pelletier, Robert.
Anderson, Margaret J. The Brain on Quartz Mountain. LC 81-23658. (Capers Ser.). (Illus.). 128p. (gr. 3-6). 1982. 1.95 (ISBN 0-394-85385-7); PLB 4.99 (ISBN 0-394-95385-1). Knopf.
--The Christian Writer's Handbook. rev. ed. LC 82-48917. 288p. 1983. 8.61i (ISBN 0-06-060195-7, RD/246, HarpR). Har-Row.
--Help for Families of Stroke Victims. 1981. pap. 8.75 (ISBN 0-570-08252-8, 12YY2924). Concordia.
--I Want the Truth. 96p. 1969. pap. 1.25 (ISBN 0-88243-531-0, 02-0531). Gospel Pub.
--In the Circle of Time. LC 78-10156. (gr. 5-9). 1979. PLB 6.99 (ISBN 0-394-94029-6). Knopf.
--The Journey of the Shadow Bairns. 196p. (gr. 5-9). 1980. PLB 8.99 (ISBN 0-394-94511-5). Knopf.
--The Journey of the Shadow Bairns. 184p. (gr. 4-6). 1983. pap. 1.95 (ISBN 0-590-32023-8, Apple Paperbacks). Scholastic Inc.
Anderson, Margaret L. Windthorst: A Political Biography. 1981. 72.00x (ISBN 0-19-822578-4). Oxford U Pr.
Anderson, Margaret M. Insect Friends & Enemies. (Illus.). 64p. 1981. 7.50 (ISBN 0-682-49689-8). Exposition Pr FL.
Anderson, Marian S., ed. Weekend Projects for the Radio Amateur, Vol. 1. LC 79-89723. 61p. 1979. pap. 3.00 (ISBN 0-87259-816-0). Am Radio.
Anderson, Maribeth Meyers see Gordon, David & Meyers-Anderson, Maribeth.
Anderson, Marilyn. Guatemalan Textiles Today. (Illus.). 1978. 24.50 (ISBN 0-8230-2158-0). Watson-Guptill.
Anderson, Marina. The Crayon Design Workbook. (Illus.). 40p. (Orig.). 1985. pap. 5.00 (ISBN 0-932946-23-2). Yours Truly.
Anderson, Marja L., jt. auth. see Anderson, Eugene.
Anderson, Marjorie C. Kings & Kingship in Early Scotland. rev. ed. 304p. 1981. 20.00x (ISBN 0-7073-0179-3, Pub. by Scottish Academic Pr Scotland). Columbia U Pr.
Anderson, Mark. The Broken Boat. LC 78-14534. 75p. 1978. 3.50 (ISBN 0-87886-104-1). Ithaca Hse.
Anderson, Mark A. The Homzas' Son. 1984. cancelled (ISBN 0-533-05187-8). Vantage.
Anderson, Marlene & Brearley, Joan McD. This Is the Saint Bernard. (Illus.). 1973. 17.95 (ISBN 0-87666-376-5, PS-698). TFH Pubns.
Anderson, Martha, jt. auth. see Biedermann, Gertrude.
Anderson, Martha G. & Arnoldi, Mary Jo. Art in Achebe's: Things Fall Apart & Arrow of God. (Graduate Student Paper Competition Ser.: No. 1). (Illus., Orig.). 1978. pap. text ed. 2.00 (ISBN 0-941934-25-X). Indiana Africa.
Anderson, Martin. Registration & the Draft. 424p. 1982. 19.95 (ISBN 0-8179-7421-0, P242). Hoover Inst Pr.
--Welfare: The Political Economy of Welfare Reform in the United States. 1978. 16.95x (ISBN 0-8179-6811-3). Hoover Inst Pr.
Anderson, Martin, ed. Conscription: A Select & Annotated Bibliography. LC 75-41906. (Bibliographical Ser.: No. 57). 472p. 1976. 19.95x (ISBN 0-8179-2571-6). Hoover Inst Pr.
--The Military Draft: Selected Readings on Conscription, No. 258. LC 81-84641. (Publication Ser.). 630p. 1982. 19.95x (ISBN 0-8179-7581-0). Hoover Inst Pr.
Anderson, Marty, ed. see Carter, Les.
Anderson, Marty, ed. see Case, Richard, et al.
Anderson, Marty, ed. see Flournoy, Richard L., et al.
Anderson, Marty, ed. see Houmes, Dan & Meier, Paul.
Anderson, Marty, ed. see Meier, Richard, et al.
Anderson, Marvin W. Battle for the Gospel: Bible & Reformation. LC 77-91119. 1978. pap. 4.95 (ISBN 0-8010-0121-8). Baker Bk.
Anderson, Mary. Catch Me, I'M Falling in Love. LC 85-3744. (Illus.). 144p. (gr. 7 up). 1985. 14.95 (ISBN 0-385-29409-3). Delacorte.
--The Catnapping Caper. LC 83-15655. (Escapade Ser.). 128p. (gr. 4-6). Date not set. cancelled (ISBN 0-689-31378-0). Atheneum.
--Colour Healing. 1975. pap. 2.50 (ISBN 0-85030-170-X). Weiser.
--A Comparative Study of the English-Speaking & Spanish-Speaking Beginners in the Public Schools. LC 74-83361. 1975. Repr. of 1951 ed. soft bdg. 10.95 (ISBN 0-88247-346-8). R & E Pubs.
--Divination: How to Use Unusual Methods. (Paths to Inner Power Ser.). 1974. pap. 1.25 (ISBN 0-87728-229-3). Weiser.
--Emma's Search for Something. LC 73-76313. (Illus.). 164p. (gr. 4-6). 1973. 5.95 (ISBN 0-689-30104-9). Atheneum.
--Forever Ahbra. LC 81-1926. 204p. (gr. 5-10). 1981. 9.95 (ISBN 0-689-30839-6). Atheneum.
--Matilda's Masterpiece. LC 76-40981. (Illus.). 192p. (gr. 3-7). 1977. 6.95 (ISBN 0-689-30565-6). Atheneum.
--The Menopause. LC 82-25303. 128p. 1983. pap. 4.95 (ISBN 0-571-13071-2). Faber & Faber.
--The Mystery of the Missing Painting. (Cat's Eye Mysteries Ser.). 208p. (gr. 3-6). 1983. pap. 1.95 (ISBN 0-590-32783-6). Scholastic Inc.
--Numerology: The Secret Power of Numbers. (Paths to Inner Power Ser.). 1972. pap. 2.50 (ISBN 0-85030-183-1). Weiser.
--Palmistry. (Paths to Inner Power Ser.). 1973. pap. 2.50 (ISBN 0-85030-164-5). Weiser.
--PATHS-How to Read Palmistry. 1981. pap. 4.95x (ISBN 0-317-07308-7, Regent House). B of A.
--PATHS Numerology-Secret Power. pap. 4.95x (ISBN 0-317-07306-0, Regent House). B of A.
--Pregnancy after Thirty. 128p. (Orig.). 1984. pap. 7.95 (ISBN 0-571-13355-X). Faber & Faber.
--R. I. S. K. LC 83-6428. (Escapade Ser.). 128p. (gr. 3-7). 1983. 3.95 (ISBN 0-689-31371-3). Atheneum.
--The Rise & Fall of a Teen-Age Wacko. LC 80-12396. 180p. (gr. 5-9). 1980. 9.95 (ISBN 0-689-30767-5). Atheneum.
--The Rise & Fall of a Teen Age Wacko. 1982. pap. 2.25 (ISBN 0-553-24027-7). Bantam.
--Step on a Crack. LC 77-22767. 192p. (gr. 4-8). 1978. 10.95 (ISBN 0-689-30610-5). Atheneum.
--Step on a Crack. 192p. 1985. pap. 2.25 (ISBN 0-553-24889-8). Bantam.
--That's Not My Style. LC 82-13772. 168p. (gr. 7 up). 1983. 11.95 (ISBN 0-689-30968-6). Atheneum.
--Tune in Tomorrow. LC 83-15656. 192p. (gr. 5 up). 1984. 11.95 (ISBN 0-689-31009-9). Atheneum.
--Tune in Tomorrow. 192p. (gr. 7 up). 1985. pap. 2.50 (ISBN 0-380-69870-6, Flare). Avon.
--Woman at Work. LC 73-13451. (Illus.). 266p. 1973. Repr. of 1951 ed. lib. bdg. 20.75 (ISBN 0-8371-7133-4, ANWW). Greenwood.
--You Can't Get There from Here. LC 81-10813. 216p. (gr. 7 up). 1982. PLB 10.95 (ISBN 0-689-30903-1). Atheneum.
--You Can't Get There from Here. 208p. 1983. pap. 2.25 (ISBN 0-441-94981-9). Ace Bks.
Anderson, Mary, jt. auth. see Ashby, Eric.
Anderson, Mary, ed. see Burnett, C. W.
Anderson, Mary Jo & Hayes, Arlene S. Building Blocks to Concept Mastery: Workbook. 130p. (gr. k-7). 1982. wkbk 29.95 (ISBN 0-88450-834-X, 2087-B). Communication Skill.
Anderson, Mary P., jt. auth. see Wang, Herbert F.
Anderson, Mary R. Art in a Desacralized World: Nineteenth Century France & England. 186p. (Orig.). 1984. lib. bdg. 21.75 (ISBN 0-8191-4147-X); pap. text ed. 11.25 (ISBN 0-8191-4148-8). U Pr of Amer.
Anderson, Mathew S. Historians & Eighteenth-Century Europe 1715-1789. 1979. 42.00x (ISBN 0-19-822548-2). Oxford U Pr.
Anderson, Matthew S. Eighteenth Century Europe, 1713-1789. (Orig.). 1968. pap. 6.95x (ISBN 0-19-500285-7). Oxford U Pr.
Anderson, Maxwell. Dramatist in America: Letters of Maxwell Anderson 1912-1958. Avery, Laurence G., ed. LC 77-4491. (Illus.). lxxxiii, 366p. 1977. 32.50 (ISBN 0-8078-1309-5). U of NC Pr.
--Four Verse Plays. Incl. High Tor; Winterset; Elizabeth the Queen; Mary of Scotland. LC 59-1731. 560p. (Orig.). 1959. pap. 9.95 (ISBN 0-15-633329-5, Harv). HarBraceJ.
--Notes on a Dream. Avery, Laurence G., ed. LC 70-633716. (Illus.). 1971. 5.95 (ISBN 0-87959-056-4). U of Tex H Ransom Ctr.
--Off Broadway: Essays About the Theatre. LC 75-77699. (Theater, Film, & the Performing Arts Ser.). 92p. 1971. Repr. of 1947 ed. lib. bdg. 19.50 (ISBN 0-306-71337-3). Da Capo.
--You Who Have Dreams. 1978. Repr. lib. bdg. 27.50 (ISBN 0-8495-0102-4). Arden Lib.
--You Who Have Dreams. LC 76-39796. 1976. Repr. of 1925 ed. lib. bdg. 18.50 (ISBN 0-8414-2996-0). Folcroft.
Anderson, Maxwell see Halline, Allan G.
Anderson, Maxwell see MacGowan, Kenneth.
Anderson, Maxwell, et al. Bases of Artistic Creation. 1969. lib. bdg. 10.00 (ISBN 0-374-90190-2). Octagon.
Anderson, Melville B., tr. see Hugo, Victor.
Anderson, Michael. Approaches to the History of the Western Family: 1500-1914. (Studies in Economic & Social History). 96p. 1980. pap. text ed. 6.00x (ISBN 0-333-24065-0, Pub. by Macmillan England). Humanities.
--Family Structure in Nineteenth Century Lancashire. LC 79-164448. (Cambridge Studies in Sociology: No. 5). pap. 60.00 (ISBN 0-317-26074-X, 2024412). Bks Demand UMI.
Anderson, Michael, jt. ed. see Medine, Allen.
Anderson, Michael, et al. Crowell's Handbook of Contemporary Drama. LC 79-158714. 1971. 10.00i (ISBN 0-690-22643-8). T Y Crowell.
Anderson, Michael H. Madison Avenue in Asia: Politics & Transnational Advertising. LC 81-69078. (Illus.). 380p. 1984. 39.50 (ISBN 0-8386-3101-0). Fairleigh Dickinson.
Anderson, Michael H., jt. ed. see Richstad, Jim.
Anderson, Michael J. & Wake Forest University School of Law. North Carolina Workers' Compensation Manual. LC 84-114925. (Illus.). 413p. 1983. 55.00. Wake Forest Law.
Anderson, Michael J., jt. auth. see Wake Forest University School of Law.
Anderson, Mignon H. Mostly Womenfolk & a Man or Two: A Collection. 1976. 4.25 (ISBN 0-88378-075-5). Third World.
Anderson, Mildred C., jt. auth. see Plaut, Thomas R.
Anderson, Miles H. Functional Bracing of the Upper Extremities: The Rationale, Principles, & Techniques of Upper Extremity Bracing to Prevent Deformities & Restore Function. (Illus.). 480p. 1958. photocopy ed. 37.50x (ISBN 0-398-04192-X). C C Thomas.
--Upper Extremities Orthotics. (Illus.). 476p. 1979. photocopy ed. 43.50x (ISBN 0-398-00044-1). C C Thomas.
Anderson, Miles H., ed. A Manual of Lower Extremities Orthotics. (Illus.). 552p. 1978. 49.50x (ISBN 0-398-02217-8). C C Thomas.
Anderson, Miles H., et al. Clinical Prosthetics for Physicians & Therapists: A Handbook of Clinical Practices Related to Artificial Limbs. (Illus.). 396p. 1959. photocopy ed. 36.50x (ISBN 0-398-04191-1). C C Thomas.
--Manual of Above Knee Wood Socket Prosthetics. rev. ed. (Illus.). 296p. 1980. ed. 34.50xspiral (ISBN 0-398-04071-0). C C Thomas.
Anderson, Moira & Martin, Netta. Moira Anderson's Scotland. (Illus.). 160p. 1983. 19.95 (ISBN 0-7188-2518-7, Pub. by Salem Hse Ltd). Merrimack Pub Cir.
Anderson, Montgomery D. & Blodgett, Ralph H. Fluctuations in General Business. (Illus.). 192p. 1977. 9.75 (ISBN 0-8158-0338-9). Chris Mass.
Anderson, Muriel, ed. Easter in the Country. 96p. 1977. pap. 5.95 (ISBN 0-89821-017-8). Reiman Assocs.
Anderson, N. The Electromagnetic Field. LC 68-16585. 124p. 1968. 24.50x (ISBN 0-306-30373-6, Plenum Pr). Plenum Pub.
Anderson, N. & Waller, P. J., eds. The Epidemiology & Control of Gastrointestinal Parasites of Cattle in Australia. (Illus.). xii, 90p. (Orig.). 1983. pap. text ed. 9.50x (ISBN 0-643-03517-6, Pub. by CSIRO). Intl Spec Bk.
Anderson, N., tr. see Bjorck, Ake & Dahlquist, Germund.
Anderson, N. G. From Concept to Production: A Management Approach. 300p. 1975. cancelled (ISBN 0-85066-082-3). Taylor & Francis.
Anderson, Nancy. Work with Passion: How to Do What You Love for a Living. 308p. 1984. 15.95 (ISBN 0-88184-099-8, Co-published with Carroll & Graf). Whatever Pub.
--Work with Passion: How to Do What You Love for a Living. 224p. 1984. 15.95 (ISBN 0-88184-099-8). Carroll & Graf.
Anderson, Nancy D., ed. French Mathematical Seminars. LC 78-10797. 1978. 20.00 (ISBN 0-8218-0063-9, FRENCHSEM); members 6.90. Am Math.
Anderson, Neil. The Ha Ha Book. LC 83-83324. (Illus.). 64p. (Orig.). 1984. pap. 4.95 (ISBN 0-915811-01-4). H J Kramer Inc.
--Singing Man. Rinzler, Allen, ed. 216p. (Orig.). 1984. pap. 8.95 (ISBN 0-915811-02-2). H J Kramer Inc.
Anderson, Neil V., ed. Veterinary Gastroenterology. LC 79-20234. (Illus.). 720p. 1980. text ed. 65.00 (ISBN 0-8121-0632-6). Lea & Febiger.
Anderson, Nels. Men on the Move. LC 74-7427. (FDR & the Era of the New Deal Ser.). xii, 357p. 1974. Repr. of 1940 ed. lib. bdg. 45.00 (ISBN 0-306-70588-5). Da Capo.
--The Right to Work. LC 70-136835. (Illus.). 152p. 1973. Repr. of 1938 ed. lib. bdg. 15.00 (ISBN 0-8371-5264-X, ANRW). Greenwood.
Anderson, Netta C. & Udden, Johan A. Fossil Mastodon & Mammoth Remains in Illinois & Iowa, & Proboscidian Fossils of the Pleistocene Deposits in Illinois & Iowa. LC 6-20234. (Augustana College Library Publication Ser.: No. 5). 57p. 1905. pap. 1.00 (ISBN 0-910182-03-5). Augustana Coll.
Anderson, Niels B., et al. Managing Computer Impacts. Ginzberg, Michael, ed. (Computer-Based Information Systems in Organizations Ser.). 288p. 1986. text ed. 35.00 (ISBN 0-89391-358-8). Ablex Pub.
Anderson, Norma R. An Elfindale Story. LC 81-5977. (Illus.). 36p. (Orig.). (gr. 1-6). 1981. pap. 5.95 (ISBN 0-913504-64-5). Lowell Pr.
Anderson, Norman. Christianity & World Religions. rev. ed. LC 84-115291. 192p. 1984. pap. 6.95 (ISBN 0-87784-981-1). Inter-Varsity.
--Islamic Law in Africa. new ed. 396p. 1970. 35.00x (ISBN 0-7146-1905-1, BHA 01905, F Cass Co). Biblio Dist.
--Jesus Christ: The Witness of History. LC 84-15703. 210p. 1985. pap. 6.95 (ISBN 0-87784-336-8). Inter-Varsity.
--The Kingdom of Saudi Arabia. 256p. 1984. 100.00 (ISBN 0-905743-28-8, Pub. by Stacey Intl Pubs UK). State Mutual Bk.
--Law Reform in the Muslim World. (University of London Legal Ser.: No. 11). 239p. 1976. 42.50 (ISBN 0-485-13411-X, Pub. by Athlone Pr Ltd). Longwood Pub Group.
--Methods of Information Integration Theory, Vol. 2. 1982. 47.50 (ISBN 0-12-058102-7). Acad Pr.
--The Mystery of the Incarnation. LC 79-13879. 1979. pap. 3.95 (ISBN 0-87784-530-1). Inter-Varsity.
--The Teachings of Jesus. LC 83-4312. (The Jesus Library). 216p. 1983. pap. 6.95 (ISBN 0-87784-926-9). Inter-Varsity.
Anderson, Norman & Brown, Walter. Rescue: The Young American Medal for Bravery. (Illus.). 128p. (gr. 5 up). 1983. 10.95 (ISBN 0-8027-6487-8). Walker & Co.
Anderson, Norman & Weiss, Margene, eds. Interspace & the Inward Sphere: Essays on Romantic & Victorian Self. LC 78-58247. 1978. pap. 5.00 (ISBN 0-934312-01-X). Essays in Lit W Ill U.
Anderson, Norman A. Instrumentation for Process Measurement & Control. LC 78-14643. 384p. 1980. 19.95 (ISBN 0-8019-6766-X). Chilton.
Anderson, Norman D. & Brown, Walter R. Ferris Wheels. LC 83-3959. (Illus.). 64p. (gr. 3-7). 1983. 10.95 (ISBN 0-394-85460-8, Pant Bks Young); PLB 10.99 (ISBN 0-394-95460-2). Pantheon.
--Fireworks! Pyrotechnics on Display. LC 82-45995. (Illus.). 96p. (gr. 4 up). 1983. 9.95 (ISBN 0-396-08142-8). Dodd.
--Halley's Comet. (Illus.). 80p. (gr. 4 up). 1981. 8.95 (ISBN 0-396-07974-1). Dodd.
--Lemurs. LC 84-8097. (A Skylight Bk.). (Illus.). 64p. (gr. 2-5). 1984. PLB 9.95 (ISBN 0-396-08454-0). Dodd.
Anderson, Norman D., jt. auth. see Brown, Walter R.
Anderson, Norman D., jt. auth. see Simpson, Ronald D.
Anderson, Norman E. & Macdermot, C. G. PA-Four Locomotive. LC 78-51249. (Illus.). 128p. 1978. 25.00 (ISBN 0-89685-035-8). Chatham Pub CA.
Anderson, Norman H. Foundations of Information Integration Theory: Foundations, Vol. 1. LC 80-1769. (Information Integration Ser.). 1981. 44.00 (ISBN 0-12-058101-9). Acad Pr.
Anderson, O. Outline of Business Law. 1964p. pap. 4.95 (ISBN 0-318-02921-9). Biblio Dist.
Anderson, O. D. Time Series Analysis: Theory & Practice, No. 2. 1983. 47.00 (ISBN 0-444-86536-5). Elsevier.
Anderson, O. D. & Perryman, M. R. Applied Time Series Analysis. 1982. 68.00 (ISBN 0-444-86424-5, I-182-82A). Elsevier.
Anderson, O. D., ed. Forecasting Public Utilities. 1980. 63.75 (ISBN 0-444-86046-0). Elsevier.
--Time Series Analysis, Theory & Practice: Proceedings of the Conference, Nottingham, March 1983, Vol. 5. 1984. 59.25 (ISBN 0-444-87568-9, I-438-84, North-Holland). Elsevier.
--Time Series Analysis, Theory & Practice: Proceedings of the Conference, Toronto, Aug. 18-21, 1983, Vol. 7. 312p. 1985. 59.25 (ISBN 0-444-87684-7, North-Holland). Elsevier.
--Time Series Analysis Theory & Practice, No. 3. 302p. 1983. 64.00 (ISBN 0-444-86625-6, I-117-83, North Holland). Elsevier.
--Time Series Analysis: Theory & Practice, No. 4. 352p. 1983. 72.50 (ISBN 0-444-86731-7, I-253-83). Elsevier.
--Time Series: Proceedings of the International Conference, Held at Nottingham University, March, 1979. 1980. 85.00 (ISBN 0-444-85418-5). Elsevier.
Anderson, O. D. & Ord, J. K., eds. Time Series Analysis, Theory & Practice-Hydrological, Geophysical & Spatial Applications: Proceedings of the Conference, Toronto, Aug. 10-14, 1983, Vol. 6. 308p. 1985. 59.25 (ISBN 0-444-87683-9, North-Holland). Elsevier.
Anderson, O. D. & Perryman, M. R., eds. Time Series Analysis: Proceedings of the International Conference, Held in Houston, Texas, August, 1980. 1981. 83.00 (ISBN 0-444-86177-7). Elsevier.
Anderson, O. D., et al, eds. Time Series Analysis: Theory & Practice: Proceedings of the International Conference, Valencia, Spain, June 22-26, 1981, No. 1. 756p. 1982. 85.00 (ISBN 0-444-86337-0). Elsevier.
Anderson, O. J. Outline of Business Law. (Quality Paperback: No. 79). (Orig.). 1975. pap. 4.95 (ISBN 0-8226-0079-X). Littlefield.
Anderson, O. R. Radiolaria. (Illus.). 350p. 1983. 65.00 (ISBN 0-387-90832-3). Springer-Verlag.
Anderson, O. Roger. The Experience of Science: A New Perspective for Laboratory Teaching. LC 75-37967. 1976. pap. text ed. 8.95x (ISBN 0-8077-2489-0). Tchrs Coll.
Anderson, O. S. The Seafarer. 1978. Repr. lib. bdg. 10.00 (ISBN 0-8495-0110-5). Arden Lib.
--Seafarer: A Interpretation. LC 73-9785. 1937. lib. bdg. 12.50 (ISBN 0-8414-2866-2). Folcroft.
Anderson, Odin & Weeks, Lewis. Sociology of Health Care: An Inquiry Anthology. (Illus.). 340p. Date not set. pap. text ed. price not set (ISBN 0-914904-78-7). Health Admin Pr.
Anderson, Odin, et al. HMOS Development: Patterns & Prospects. LC 84-61462. 400p. 1985. 34.95 (ISBN 0-931028-57-4). Pluribus Pr.

Anderson, Odin W. The American Health Services: A Growth Enterprise since 1875. LC 85-796. 300p. 1985. text ed. 29.00 (ISBN 0-910701-02-4, 00652). Health Admin Pr.

--Health Care: Can There Be Equity? the United States, Sweden, & England. LC 72-7449. Repr. of 1972 ed. 56.10 (ISBN 0-8357-9902-6, 2019524). Bks Demand UMI.

--The Uneasy Equilibrium: Private & Public Financing of Health Services in the United States, 1875-1965. 1968. pap. 7.95x (ISBN 0-8084-0305-2). New Coll U Pr.

Anderson, Odin W., jt. auth. see Anderson, Ronald.

Anderson, Odin W., jt. auth. see Sinai, Nathan.

Anderson, Olive M. Utopia in Upper Michigan. LC 81-84595. 1982. pap. 4.50 (ISBN 0-918616-10-7). Northern Mich.

Anderson, Olof W. The Treasure Vault of Atlantis. Reginald, R. & Melville, Douglas, eds. LC 77-84194. (Lost Race & Adult Fantasy Ser.). 1978. Repr. of 1925 ed. lib. bdg. 26.50x (ISBN 0-405-10952-0). Ayer Co Pubs.

Anderson, Olov B. Bushu: A Key to the "Radicals" of Japanese Language. (SIAS Monograph). 87p. 1981. pap. text ed. 9.25x (ISBN 0-7007-0127-3, Pub. by Curzon England). Humanities.

--A Concordance to Five Systems of Transcription for Standard Chinese. 230p. (Chinese.). 1982. pap. text ed. 22.50 (ISBN 0-7007-0080-3, Pub. by Curzon Pr England). Apt Bks.

--An Investiation into the Present State of Standard Chinese Pronunciation: A Comparison of Kuo-Yu & Putong Hua, Pt. 2. 220p. 1981. pap. text ed. 10.50x (ISBN 0-7007-0082-X, Pub. by Curzon Pr England). Humanities.

--An Investigation into the Present State of Chinese Pronunciation, Part 2a: A Comparison of KUO2 YU3 & Putong-Hua. 220p. 1975. pap. text ed. 13.25x (ISBN 91-44112-71-8). Humanities.

--An Investigation into the Present State of Standard Chinese Pronounciation, Part 1a: A Companion Volume to R. H. Mathews Chinese Dictionary. 2nd, rev. ed. 210p. 1978. text ed. 21.25x (ISBN 91-44152-21-3). Humanities.

--An Investigation into the Present State of Standard Chinese Pronunciation: Character Register, Pt. 1B. 160p. 1981. pap. text ed. 13.25x (ISBN 0-7007-0157-5, Pub. by Curzon Pr England). Humanities.

--An Investigation into the Present State of Standard Chinese Pronunciation: Character Register, Pt. 16. 160p. 1981. 35.00x (ISBN 0-686-79443-5, Pub. by Curzon England). State Mutual Bk.

Anderson, Osborne P. A Voice from Harper's Ferry. LC 72-8569. (Black Heritage Library Collection). 1972. Repr. of 1861 ed. 15.50 (ISBN 0-8369-9182-6). Ayer Co Pubs.

--A Voice from Harper's Ferry. Copeland, Vince, ed. 102p. 1974. pap. 2.00 (ISBN 0-89567-048-8). WV Pubs.

--A Voice from Harper's Ferry. 102p. 2.00 (ISBN 0-89567-048-8). World View Pubns.

Anderson, P. D. In Its Own Image: The Cinematic Vision of Hollywood. LC 77-22903. (Dissertations on Film Ser.). 1978. lib. bdg. 24.50x (ISBN 0-405-10749-8). Ayer Co Pubs.

Anderson, P. M. & Fouad, A. A. Power System Control & Stability. 1977. 48.95x (ISBN 0-8138-1245-3). Iowa St U Pr.

Anderson, P. W. Basic Notions of Condensed Matter Physics: Frontiers in Physics. (No. 55). 1984. 42.95 (ISBN 0-8053-0220-4); pap. 24.95 (ISBN 0-8053-0219-0). Benjamin-Cummings.

--Concepts in Solids: Lectures on the Theory of Solids. (Frontiers in Physics Ser.: No. 10). 1963. pap. 27.95 (ISBN 0-8053-0229-8). Benjamin-Cummings.

Anderson, Patricia. The Course of Empire: The Erie Canal & the New York Landscape, 1825-1875. LC 84-60498. (Illus.). 90p. (Orig.). 1984. pap. 14.95 (ISBN 0-295-96214-3). U of Wash Pr.

Anderson, Patricia A. Promoted to Glory: The Apotheosis of George Washington. (Illus.). 68p. (Orig.). 1980. pap. 8.75 (ISBN 0-87391-017-6). Smith Coll.

Anderson, Patricia M. & Rubin, Leonard G. Marketing Communications for Retailers. (Illus.). 560p. 1986. text ed. 28.95 (ISBN 0-13-557091-3). P-H.

Anderson, Patrick. Lords of the Earth. LC 82-45235. 600p. 1984. 17.95 (ISBN 0-385-15979-X). Doubleday.

Anderson, Paul. Building Christian Character. (Trinity Teen Curriculum Ser.). 48p. 1984. Repr. student wkbk. 3.95 (ISBN 0-87123-436-X, 210436); tchr's. guide 3.95 (ISBN 0-87123-430-0). Bethany Hse.

--Ensign Flandry. 288p. 1985. pap. 2.95 (ISBN 0-441-20729-4). Ace Bks.

--The High Crusade. 176p. 1983. pap. 2.50 (ISBN 0-425-06257-6). Berkley Pub.

--Orbit Unlimited. 160p. 1984. pap. 2.50 (ISBN 0-441-63754-X, Pub. by Ace Science Fiction). Ace Bks.

--Reptiles of Missouri. LC 64-14411. (Illus.). 1965. 21.00x (ISBN 0-8262-0027-3). U of Mo Pr.

--A Stone in Heaven. 256p. 1985. pap. 2.95 (ISBN 0-441-78658-8, Pub. by Ace Science Fiction). Ace Bks.

--Terrorists from Tomorrow. 192p. (Orig.). 1985. pap. 2.95 (ISBN 0-931773-39-3). Critics Choice Paper.

--Three Hearts & Three Lions. 176p. 1984. pap. 2.50 (ISBN 0-441-80821-2). Ace Bks.

Anderson, Paul & Brockmann, John, eds. New Essays in Technical & Scientific Communications: Theory, Research, & Practice. (Baywood Technical Communication Ser.: Vol. 2). 272p. (Orig.). 1983. pap. text ed. 18.00x (ISBN 0-89503-036-5). Baywood Pub.

Anderson, Paul & Ryan, Michael, eds. AMA Winter Educators' Conference, 1984: Scientific Method in Marketing. LC 84-10989. (Illus.). 299p. (Orig.). 1984. pap. text ed. 24.00 (ISBN 0-87757-170-8). Am Mktg.

Anderson, Paul, et al. The Three of Us. 1974. saddlestitched in wrappers 1.00 (ISBN 0-685-79028-2). Small Pr Dist.

Anderson, Paul B. People, Church & State in Modern Russia. LC 79-5204. 240p. 1980. Repr. of 1944 ed. 21.00 (ISBN 0-8305-0058-8). Hyperion Conn.

Anderson, Paul D. Basic Human Anatomy & Physiology: Clinical Implications for the Health Professionals. LC 83-23511. 450p. 1984. pap. text ed. 16.00x pub net (ISBN 0-534-03089-0). Wadsworth Health.

--Laboratory Manual & Study Guide for Clinical Anatomy & Physiology for Allied Health Sciences. LC 75-21143. (Illus.). Repr. of 1976 ed. 43.40 (ISBN 0-8357-9549-7, 2016689). Bks Demand UMI.

Anderson, Paul E. Tax Planning of Real Estate. 7th ed. 242p. 1977. Incl. 1980 & 1982 suppl. pap. 17.50 (ISBN 0-317-30808-4, B438); Suppl. 1982 only. pap. 5.00 (ISBN 0-317-30809-2, B430). Am Law Inst.

Anderson, Paul G. Brass Solo & Study Guide. 15.00 (ISBN 0-686-15889-X). Instrumental Co.

Anderson, Paul K. Word Order Typology & Comparative Constructions. (Current Issues in Linguistic Theory (CILT) Ser.: Vol. 25). 240p. 1983. 29.00x (ISBN 90-272-3517-1). Benjamins North Am.

Anderson, Paul L. The Fine Art of Photography. LC 72-9180. (The Literature of Photography Ser.). Repr. of 1919 ed. 31.00 (ISBN 0-405-04891-2). Ayer Co Pubs.

--For Freedom & for Gaul. 1931. 15.00 (ISBN 0-686-20090-X). Quality Lib.

--Slave of Catiline. LC 57-9446. 255p. (gr. 7-11). 1930. 10.00x (ISBN 0-8196-0101-2). Biblo.

--A Slave of Catiline. 225p. 9.90 (ISBN 0-318-12462-9, B202). Amer Classical.

--Swords in the North. LC 57-9448. 270p. (gr. 7-11). 1935. 10.00x (ISBN 0-8196-0103-9). Biblo.

--With the Eagles. LC 57-9447. (Illus.). (gr. 7-11). 1929. 12.00x (ISBN 0-8196-0100-4). Biblo.

Anderson, Paul M. Analysis of Faulted Power Systems. (Illus.). 846p. 1973. 33.50x (ISBN 0-8138-1270-4). Iowa St U Pr.

Anderson, Paul R. & Fisch, Max H. Philosophy in America from Puritans to James. 1969. lib. bdg. 31.50x (ISBN 0-374-90248-8). Octagon.

Anderson, Paul S. Storytelling with the Flannel Board, 3 Bks. LC 21-650. 270p. (ps). 1963. Bk.1. 12.95 (ISBN 0-513-00105-0). Denison.

--Storytelling with the Flannel Board, 3 Bks. LC 21-650. 260p. (ps). 1970. Bk. 2. 12.95 (ISBN 0-513-00137-9). Denison.

Anderson, Paul S. & Lapp, Diane. Language Skills in Elementary Education. 3rd ed. 1979. text ed. write for info. (ISBN 0-02-303140-9). Macmillan.

Anderson, Pauline & Burkard, Martha. The Dental Assistant. 4th rev. ed. (Dental Assisting Ser.). (Illus.). 400p. 1982. pap. text ed. 15.80 (ISBN 0-8273-1436-1); instr's. guide 3.60 (ISBN 0-8273-1915-0). Delmar.

Anderson, Pauline & Clifford, Susan B. Dental Radiology. rev. ed. LC 79-56352. (Dental Assisting Ser.). (Illus.). 152p. 1981. pap. text ed. 9.80 (ISBN 0-8273-1871-5); instructor's guide 2.20 (ISBN 0-8273-1872-3). Delmar.

Anderson, Pauline C. The Dental Assistant. 3rd ed. 372p. 1981. 17.95 (ISBN 0-442-21873-7). Van Nos Reinhold.

Anderson, Pauline H. The Library in the Independent School. 42p. 1980. pap. 7.75 (ISBN 0-934338-43-4). NAIS.

--Library Media Leadership in Academic Secondary Schools. 240p. 1985. 26.00 (ISBN 0-208-02048-9, Lib Prof Pubs); pap. 16.50x (ISBN 0-208-02049-7). Shoe String.

Anderson, Pauline R., ed. see Kehr, Eckart.

Anderson, Peggy. Children's Hospital. LC 81-47650. 512p. 1985. 17.26 (ISBN 0-06-015089-0, HarpT). Har-Row.

--Nurse. 1984. pap. 3.95 (ISBN 0-425-07487-0). Berkley Pub.

Anderson, Peggy L. Denver Handwriting Analysis. 80p. 1983. pap. 12.50 manual & wall chart (ISBN 0-87879-334-8). Acad Therapy.

Anderson, Penny. The Big Storm. (gr. 1-3). 1982. text ed. 4.95 (ISBN 0-89693-206-0, Sonflower Bks). SP Pubns.

--The Big Storm. LC 82-7433. (Illus.). 32p. (gr. 3-4). 1982. lib. bdg. 4.95 (ISBN 0-89693-206-0). Dandelion Hse.

--Feeling Frustrated. (What's In a Word Ser.). (Illus.). 32p. (ps-2). 1983. 9.95 (ISBN 0-516-06323-5). Childrens.

Anderson, Penny, tr. see Landry, Monica & Olivier, Julien.

Anderson, Penny S. Feeling Frustrated. LC 82-19910. (What's in a Word Ser.). (Illus.). 32p. (gr. 1-2). 1983. PLB 7.45 (ISBN 0-89565-245-5). Childs World.

--Frustrated. LC 82-4492. (What Does it Mean? Ser.). (Illus.). 32p. (gr. 1-2). 1982. PLB 5.95 (ISBN 0-89565-237-4, 4896, Pub. by Childs World). Standard Pub.

--A Pretty Good Team. LC 79-15928. (Handling Difficult Times Ser.). (Illus.). (gr. 1-4). 1979. PLB 5.95 (ISBN 0-89565-097-5). Childs World.

--The Sound of the Bell. LC 83-7453. (Illus.). 32p. (gr. 3-4). 1983. PLB 4.95 (ISBN 0-89693-217-6). Dandelion Hse.

Anderson, Perry. Argument Within English Marxism. 224p. 1980. text ed. 19.50x (ISBN 0-8052-7083-3, Pub by NLB England); pap. 8.00 (ISBN 0-8052-7082-5). Schocken.

--Considerations on Western Marxism. 1976. 13.50x (ISBN 0-8052-7014-0, Pub. by Verso); pap. 6.95 (ISBN 0-8052-7070-1, Pub. by NLB). Schocken.

--In the Tracks of Historical Materialism. LC 84-110. (The Wellek Library Lectures). 120p. 1984. 15.00x (ISBN 0-226-01788-5). U of Chicago Pr.

--In the Tracks of Historical Materialism. (The Wellek Library Lectures). 112p. 1985. pap. 5.95 (ISBN 0-8052-7238-0, Pub. by NLB England). Schocken.

--Lineages of the Absolutist State. 1979. 17.50x (ISBN 0-8052-7025-6); pap. 9.95 (ISBN 0-8052-7059-0, Pub. by Verso). Schocken.

--Passages from Antiquity to Feudalism. 1978. pap. 7.75 (ISBN 0-8052-7051-5, Pub. by NLB). Schocken.

Anderson, Peter. In Search of the New England Coyote. LC 81-86602. (Illus.). 228p. (Orig.). 1983. pap. 9.95 (ISBN 0-87106-966-0). Globe Pequot.

--Robert Stewart, Earl of Orkney, Lord of Shetland, 1533-1593. 222p. 1982. text ed. 32.00x (ISBN 0-85976-082-0, Pub. by John Donald Scotland). Humanities.

Anderson, Philip A. Church Meetings That Matter. LC 65-13499. (Orig.). 1965. pap. 3.95 (ISBN 0-8298-0019-0). Pilgrim NY.

Anderson, Philip J. One Body... Many Members. 35p. 1983. pap. 1.95 (ISBN 0-910452-53-9). Covenant.

Anderson, Philip M., ed. Integrating Reading, Writing, & Thinking. 51p. 1983. 3.75 (ISBN 0-317-36728-5, 23503); members 3.25 (ISBN 0-317-36729-3). NCTE.

Anderson, Philip N. Computers & the Radio Amateur. (Illus.). 224p. 1982. 25.95 (ISBN 0-13-166306-2). P-H.

Anderson, Poul. Agent of the Terran Empire. (Dominic Flandry Ser.: No. 3). 1980. pap. 2.75 (ISBN 0-441-01070-9, Pub. by Ace Science Fiction). Ace Bks.

--Agent of Vega. 1983. pap. 2.50 (ISBN 0-441-01076-8). Ace Bks.

--The Avatar. 1980. pap. 2.50 (ISBN 0-425-04861-6). Berkley Pub.

--The Best of Poul Anderson. 1976. pap. 2.25 (ISBN 0-671-83140-2). PB.

--Book of Poul Anderson. (Science Fiction Ser.). 1978. pap. 2.95 (ISBN 0-87997-868-6, UE1868). DAW Bks.

--Brain Wave. 176p. 1985. pap. 2.50 (ISBN 0-345-32521-4). Ballantine.

--The Broken Sword. (A Del Rey Bk.). 1983. pap. 2.75 (ISBN 0-345-31171-X). Ballantine.

--The Broken Sword. 1981. pap. 2.50 (ISBN 0-345-29860-8, Del Rey). Ballantine.

--Cold Victory. (The Psychotechnic League Ser.). 284p. (Orig.). 1982. pap. 2.75 (ISBN 0-523-48527-1). Pinnacle Bks.

--Conflict. 288p. (Orig.). 1983. pap. 2.95 (ISBN 0-523-48572-7, Pinnacle Bks). Tor Bks.

--The Corridors of Time. 192p. (Orig.). 1981. pap. 2.25 (ISBN 0-425-05048-3). Berkley Pub.

--Dialogue with Darkness. 320p. 1985. pap. 2.95 (ISBN 0-8125-3083-7). Tor Bks.

--The Earth Book of Stormgate. 448p. 1983. pap. 2.95 (ISBN 0-425-05933-2). Berkley Pub.

--The Enemy Stars. 160p. pap. 1.95 (ISBN 0-425-04339-8). Berkley Pub.

--Ensign Flandry. 1979. lib. bdg. 11.95 (ISBN 0-8398-2526-9, Gregg). G K Hall.

--Explorations. 320p. 1980. pap. 2.50 (ISBN 0-523-48517-4). Pinnacle Bks.

--Fantasy. 336p. 1981. pap. 2.50 (ISBN 0-523-48515-8). Pinnacle Bks.

--Fire Time. 256p. 1980. pap. 2.25 (ISBN 0-345-28692-8). Ballantine.

--Fire Time. 288p. 1984. pap. 2.95 (ISBN 0-671-55900-1). PB.

--Flandry of Terra. 304p. 1985. pap. 2.95 (ISBN 0-317-13514-7). Ace Bks.

--The Game of Empire. 288p. 1985. pap. 3.50 (ISBN 0-671-55959-1, Pub. by Baen Books). PB.

--The Gods Laughed. 320p. 1982. pap. 2.95 (ISBN 0-523-48550-6, Pinnacle Bks). Tor Bks.

--The Golden Slave. 256p. (Orig.). 1980. pap. 2.25 (ISBN 0-89083-651-5). Zebra.

--The Guardians of Time. rev. ed. 256p. 1981. pap. 2.95 (ISBN 0-523-48579-4). Pinnacle Bks.

--The Last Viking. 1980. pap. cancelled (ISBN 0-89083-573-X). Zebra.

--The Last Viking: Book One, The Golden Horn. 272p. (Orig.). 1980. pap. text ed. 2.50 (ISBN 0-89083-597-7). Zebra.

--The Long Night. (Tor Bks.). 320p. (Orig.). 1983. pap. 2.95 (ISBN 0-523-48582-4). Pinnacle Bks.

--A Midsummer Tempest. 320p. (Orig.). 1984. pap. 2.95 (ISBN 0-8125-3079-9). Tor Bks.

--A Midsummer Tempest. 320p. 1985. pap. 2.95 (ISBN 0-317-30239-6, Dist. by Warner Pub Services & St. Martin). Tor Bks.

--Mirkheim. (Polesotechnic League Ser.: No. 4). 224p. 1983. pap. 2.50 (ISBN 0-425-05863-8). Berkley Pub.

--New America. 288p. 1983. pap. 2.95 (ISBN 0-523-48553-0, Pinnacle Bks). Tor Bks.

--The Night Face & Other Stories. (Science Fiction, Worlds of Poul Anderson Ser.). 1978. lib. bdg. 10.50 (ISBN 0-8398-2412-2, Gregg). G K Hall.

--The Nightface. 160p. 1981. pap. 1.95 (ISBN 0-441-57451-3). Ace Bks.

--Orion Shall Rise. 480p. 1983. 16.50 (ISBN 0-671-46492-2, Timescape); pap. 8.50 (ISBN 0-671-46495-7, Timescape). PB.

--Orion Shall Rise. 1984. pap. 3.95 (ISBN 0-671-82842-8). PB.

--Past Times. (Orig.). 1984. pap. 2.95 (ISBN 0-8125-3081-0). Tor Bks.

--The Psychotechnic League. 1985. pap. 2.95 (ISBN 0-8125-3059-4). Tor Bks.

--Psychotechnic League: Starship. 2.75 (ISBN 0-317-31886-1). Tor Bks.

--The Road of the Sea Horse. (The Last Viking Ser.: No. 2). 400p. (Orig.). 1980. pap. 2.50 (ISBN 0-89083-610-8). Zebra.

--Rogue Sword. 256p. (Orig.). 1980. pap. 2.25 (ISBN 0-89083-638-8). Zebra.

--Satan's World. (Polesotechnic League Ser.: No. 3). 224p. 1983. pap. 2.25 (ISBN 0-425-05851-4). Berkley Pub.

--Seven Conquests. 1984. pap. 2.95 (ISBN 0-671-55914-1, Pub. by Baen Bks). PB.

--Shield. (Orig.). 1982. pap. 2.50 (ISBN 0-425-04704-0). Berkley Pub.

--Sign of the Raven. (The Last Viking Ser.: No. 3). (Orig.). 1981. pap. 2.50 (ISBN 0-686-96926-X). Zebra.

--The Sign of the Raven. (The Last Viking Ser.: No. 2). 352p. (Orig.). 1980. pap. 2.50 (ISBN 0-89083-625-6). Zebra.

--Starship. (The Psychotechnic League Ser.: Vol. III). 288p. (Orig.). 1982. pap. 2.75 (ISBN 0-523-48533-6, Pinnacle Bks). Tor Bks.

--Tales Of The Flying Mountains. 288p. (Orig.). 1984. pap. 2.95 (ISBN 0-8125-3073-X). Tor Bks.

--Time Patrolman. 288p. (Orig.). 1983. pap. 2.95 (ISBN 0-8125-3076-4, Pinnacle Bks). Tor Bks.

--The Trouble Twisters. 1983. pap. 2.25 (ISBN 0-425-05822-0). Berkley Pub.

--Twilight World. 256p. (Orig.). 1983. pap. 2.75 (ISBN 0-523-48561-1). Tor Bks.

--Vault of the Ages. 1980. pap. 1.95 (ISBN 0-425-04336-3). Berkley Pub.

--Vault of the Ages. 1979. lib. bdg. 11.95 (ISBN 0-8398-2521-8, Gregg). G K Hall.

--Winners. 288p. 1981. pap. 2.75 (ISBN 0-523-48507-7, Pinnacle Bks). Tor Bks.

Anderson, Poul & Anderson, Karen. The Unicorn Trade. 288p. (Orig.). 1984. pap. 2.95 (ISBN 0-8125-3085-3). Tor Bks.

Anderson, Poul & Broxon, Mildred D. The Demon of Scattery. Baen, Jim, ed. 1980. pap. 2.25 (ISBN 0-441-14251-6). Ace Bks.

Anderson, Poul & Dickson, Gordon R. Earthman's Burden. 192p. 1979. pap. 2.95 (ISBN 0-380-47993-1, 47993-1, Camelot). Avon.

--Hoka! 224p. (Orig.). 1983. pap. 8.95 (ISBN 0-671-43021-1, Wallaby). S&S.

--Hoka! 256p. (Orig.). 1984. pap. 2.75 (ISBN 0-8125-3567-7). Tor Bks.

Anderson, Poul, tr. The Method of Holding the Three Ones. (Studies on Asian Topics: No. 1). (Orig.). 1980. pap. text ed. 7.50x (ISBN 0-7007-0113-3). Humanities.

Anderson, Poul, et al. Berserker Base. 320p. (Orig.). 1985. pap. 6.95 (ISBN 0-8125-5322-5). Tor Bks.

Anderson Publishing. Anderson's Will Forms & Clauses, Vol. 7. 234p. 1984. text ed. 42.50 (ISBN 0-87084-042-8). Supplement 1979-80. Supplement 1984. Anderson Pub Co.

Anderson, R. Anglo-Scandinavian Law Dictionary. 1977. pap. 15.00x (ISBN 82-00-02365-6, Dist. by Columbia U Pr). Universitet.

--The Great Historical Power Centers Which Dominate the World & the Destinies of Mankind. (Illus.). 1977. 67.25 (ISBN 0-89266-067-8). Am Classical Coll Pr.

--Individualizing Educational Materials for Special Children in the Mainstream. LC 78-4147. (Illus.). 416p. 1978. 18.00 (ISBN 0-8391-1253-X). Pro Ed.

Anderson, R., jt. auth. see Sharrock, W.

Anderson, R., et al. The Administrative Secretary. 2nd ed. 1976. 26.30 (ISBN 0-07-001747-6). McGraw.

Anderson, R. A. Abandon Earth: Last Call. Douglas, Herb & Torkelson, T. R., eds. (RWD Ser.). 64p. 1982. pap. 3.95 (ISBN 0-8163-0476-9). Pacific Pr Pub Assn.

--Occult Explosion. 94p. 1984. pap. 4.95 (ISBN 0-8163-0548-X). Pacific Pr Pub Assn.

--Signs & Wonders: The International Theological Commentary on Daniel. Holmgren, Frederick & Knight, George A., eds. (The International Theological Commentary Ser.). 192p. (Orig.). 1984. pap. 7.95 (ISBN 0-8028-1038-1). Eerdmans.

--Unfolding Daniel. LC 75-16526. (Dimension Ser.). 192p. 1975. pap. 5.95 (ISBN 0-8163-0180-8, 21390-0). Pacific Pr Pub Assn.
--With Plunkett in Ireland: The Co-Op Organiser's Story. (Co-Operative Studies). 308p. 1983. pap. 10.00x (ISBN 0-7165-0513-4, Pub. by Irish Academic Pr Ireland). Biblio Dist.
Anderson, R. B. Norse Mythology or the Religion of Our Forefathers. LC 77-6879. 1977. Repr. of 1891 ed. lib. bdg. 25.00 (ISBN 0-89341-147-7). Longwood Pub Group.
Anderson, R. B., tr. see Brandes, Georg M.
Anderson, R. B., tr. see Winkel Horn, F.
Anderson, R. C. History of Crosville Motor Services. LC 81-65955. (Illus.). 160p. 1981. 19.95 (ISBN 0-7153-8088-5). David & Charles.
--The History of the Midland Red. (Illus.). 192p. 1984. 24.95 (ISBN 0-7153-8465-1). David & Charles.
--Naval Wars in the Levant, 1559 to 1853: A Study in Geopolitics & Naval Strategy. 620p. 1952. 75.00x (ISBN 0-85323-112-5, Pub. by Liverpool Univ England). State Mutual Bk.
--The Rigging of Ships: In the Days of the Spiritsail Topmast, 1600-1720. LC 82-71502. (Illus.). 320p. 1982. Repr. 25.00 (ISBN 0-87033-294-5). Cornell Maritime.
Anderson, R. C. & Frankis, G. A History of the Western National. LC 79-51082. (Illus.). 1979. 19.95 (ISBN 0-7153-7771-X). David & Charles.
Anderson, R. C. & Frankis, G. G. A History of Royal Blue Express Services. (Illus.). 218p. 1985. 18.95 (ISBN 0-7153-8654-9). David & Charles.
Anderson, R. C., jt. auth. see Anderson, Romola.
Anderson, R. C. & May, R. M., eds. Population Biology of Infectious Diseases: Berlin, 1982. (Dahlem Workshop Reports: Vol. 25). (Illus.). 320p. 1982. 23.00 (ISBN 0-387-11650-8). Springer-Verlag.
Anderson, R. C., et al, eds. Learning to Read in American Schools. LC 83-20701. 320p. 1984. text ed. 29.95x (ISBN 0-89859-219-4). L Erlbaum Assocs.
Anderson, R. D. Education & Opportunity in Victorian Scotland: Schools & Universities. 384p. 1983. 59.00 (ISBN 0-19-822696-9). Oxford U Pr.
--France Eighteen-Seventy to Nineteen-Fourteen: Politics & Society. 224p. 1984. pap. 9.95x (ISBN 0-7102-0175-3). Routledge & Kegan.
Anderson, R. D., ed. Symposium on Infinite Dimensional Topology. LC 69-17445. (Annals of Mathematic Studies, 69). 230p. 1972. text ed. 29.00x (ISBN 0-691-08087-9). Princeton U Pr.
Anderson, R. Earle. Liberia, America's African Friend. LC 76-24842. (Illus.). 305p. 1976. Repr. of 1952 ed. lib. bdg. 21.50x (ISBN 0-8371-8999-3, ANLI). Greenwood.
Anderson, R. G. Business Systems. (Illus.). 240p. (Orig.). 1977. pap. 14.95x (ISBN 0-7121-0254-X, Pub. by Macdonald & Evans England). Trans-Atlantic.
--Concise Dictionary of Data Processing & Computer Terms. 2nd ed. 149p. 1984. 23.50x (ISBN 0-7121-0435-6). Trans-Atlantic.
--Data Processing & Management Information Systems. 4th ed. (Illus.). 480p. 1983. pap. text ed. 15.95x (ISBN 0-7121-0431-3). Trans-Atlantic.
--Data Processing: Foundation Skills. 96p. (Orig.). 1985. pap. 11.95x (ISBN 0-7121-0193-4). Trans-Atlantic.
--Dictionary of Data Processing & Computer Terms. 112p. 1982. 23.50x (ISBN 0-7121-0429-1). Trans-Atlantic.
--A Dictionary of Management Terms. 122p. 1983. pap. 17.95 (ISBN 0-7121-0434-8). Trans-Atlantic.
--Microcomputing. 2nd ed. (Illus.). 210p. 1984. pap. text ed. 01.95x. Trans-Atlantic.
--Organisation & Methods. 2nd ed. 384p. (Orig.). 1980. pap. text ed. 13.95x (ISBN 0-7121-1536-6). Trans-Atlantic.
Anderson, R. J. & Sharrock, W. W., eds. Applied Sociological Perspectives. (Illus.). 192p. 1984. text ed. 22.50 (ISBN 0-04-301167-5); pap. text ed. 7.95 (ISBN 0-04-301168-3). Allen Unwin.
Anderson, R. L. & Ibragimov, N. H. Lie-Backlund Transformations in Applications. LC 78-78207. (SIAM Studies in Applied Mathematics: No. 1). x, 124p. 1979. text ed. 17.50 (ISBN 0-89871-151-7). Soc Indus-Appl Math.
Anderson, R. L., Jr. The Abominable Spaceman. LC 79-90732. (Aries Adventures Ser.: No. 1). 182p. (Orig.). (gr. 5-8). 1979. pap. 3.95 (ISBN 0-935138-00-5). Hobby Horse.
Anderson, R. M., et al, eds. Population Dynamics: (the Twentieth Symposium of the British Ecological Society) (British Ecological Society Symposia Ser.). 434p. 1977. 99.95x (ISBN 0-470-26816-6). Halsted Pr.
Anderson, R. S., ed. Nutrition & Behavior in Dogs & Cats: Proceedings of the First Nordic Symposium on Small Animal Veterinary Medicine, Oslo, Norway, September 15-18, 1982. LC 83-17281. 246p. 1983. 30.00 (ISBN 0-08-029778-1). Pergamon.
--Nutrition of the Dog & Cat: Proceedings of an International Symposium 26 June 1978, Hanover. LC 80-40449. (Illus.). 212p. 1980. 37.00 (ISBN 0-08-025526-4). Pergamon.
Anderson, R. S. & De Hoog, F. R., eds. Application & Numberical Solution of Intergral Equations. (Mechanics Analysis Ser.: No. 6). 265p. 1980. 27.50x (ISBN 90-286-0450-2). Sijthoff & Noordhoff.
Anderson, R. T., jt. auth. see Lakner, A. A.
Anderson, R. T., et al. Large Rotating Machine Winding. (Illus.). 201p. 1981. Repr. of 1969 ed. spiral 52.50x (ISBN 0-89563-049-4). Intl Ideas.
Anderson, R. T., et al, eds. Electrical Fitting, Vol. 1. (Engineering Craftsmen: No. G3). (Illus.). 1968. spiral bdg. 39.95x (ISBN 0-85083-015-X). Trans-Atlantic.
--Rotating Electrical Equipment Winding & Building, 2 vols. (Engineering Craftsmen: No. G2). (Illus.). 1969. Set. spiral bdg. 79.95x (ISBN 0-85083-030-3). Intl Ideas.
Anderson, Rachel. Little Angel Comes to Stay. (An Eagle Bk.). (Illus.). 64p. (gr. 3-7). 1984. bds. 9.95 laminated (ISBN 0-19-271472-4, Pub. by Oxford U Pr Childrens). Merrimack Pub Cir.
--Moffat's Road. (Illus.). 256p. (gr. 3-6). 1980. 8.95 (ISBN 0-224-01381-5, Pub. by Jonathan Cape). Merrimack Pub Cir.
--The Poacher's Son. (Illus.). 137p. 1983. text ed. 11.95 (ISBN 0-19-271468-6, Pub. by Oxford U Pr Childrens). Merrimack Pub Cir.
Anderson, Ralph E. & Carter, Irl. Human Behavior in the Social Environment: A Social Systems Approach. 3rd ed. LC 83-25783. 272p. 1984. text ed. 24.95x (ISBN 0-202-36035-0); pap. text ed. 12.95x (ISBN 0-202-36036-9). Aldine Pub.
Anderson, Ralph R., ed. Relaxin. LC 81-19962. (Advances in Experimental Medicine & Biology Ser.: Vol. 143). 372p. 1982. 52.50 (ISBN 0-306-40901-1, Plenum Pr). Plenum Pub.
Anderson, Ralph R., jt. ed. see Johnson, J. Alan.
Anderson, Rasmos B., tr. see Bjornson, Bjornstjerne.
Anderson, Ray S. On Being Human: Essays in Theological Anthropology. 234p. (Orig.). 1982. pap. 9.95 (ISBN 0-8028-1926-5). Eerdmans.
--Theological Foundations for Ministry. LC 78-13613. 1978. pap. 8.95 (ISBN 0-8028-1776-9). Eerdmans.
Anderson, Ray S. & Guernsey, Dennis B. On Being Family: Essays on a Social Theology of the Family. 192p. (Orig.). 1985. pap. 11.95 (ISBN 0-8028-1990-7). Eerdmans.
Anderson, Raymond L., jt. auth. see Maass, Arthur.
Anderson, Reed. Federico Garcia Lorca. (Modern Dramatists Ser.). 192p. 1984. 19.50 (ISBN 0-394-54137-5); pap. 7.95 (ISBN 0-394-62264-2, GP952, Ever). Grove.
Anderson, Richard. Abortion Pro & Con: (Debater's Manual) 1977. pap. 3.00x (ISBN 0-686-31357-7). Right to Life.
--Robert Coover. (United States Authors Ser.). 1981. lib. bdg. 13.50 (ISBN 0-8057-7330-4, Twayne). G K Hall.
Anderson, Richard, jt. auth. see Greenberg, Michael R.
Anderson, Richard, ed. see Shea, Maggie.
Anderson, Richard C. Business Systems: The Fabric of Management. LC 73-17244. (Illus.). 124p. 7.95 (ISBN 0-913842-06-0). Correlan Pubns.
--Communication: The Vital Artery. LC 73-2682. (Illus.). 83p. 7.95 (ISBN 0-913842-02-8). Correlan Pubns.
--The Manager: A Profile. LC 72-7667. (Illus.). 71p. 7.95 (ISBN 0-913842-00-1). Correlan Pubns.
--Motivation: The Master Key. LC 72-7668. (Illus.). 92p. 7.95 (ISBN 0-913842-01-X). Correlan Pubns.
--Thought Starters. (Illus.). 105p. 12.95 (ISBN 0-913842-04-4). Correlan Pubns.
Anderson, Richard C. & Dobyns, L. R. Time: The Irretrievable Asset. LC 73-12755. (Illus.). 75p. 7.95 (ISBN 0-913842-05-2). Correlan Pubns.
Anderson, Richard C. & Faust, Gerald W. Educational Psychology: The Science of Instruction & Learning. LC 79-184191. (Illus.). 620p. 1973. pap. text ed. 20.95 scp (ISBN 0-06-040277-6, HarpC); instr's manual avail. (ISBN 0-06-360270-9). Har-Row.
Anderson, Richard C., et al. Schooling & the Acquisition of Knowledge. 464p. 1977. text ed. 29.95x (ISBN 0-89859-109-0). L Erlbaum Assocs.
Anderson, Richard D., ed. see Packel, Edward W.
Anderson, Richard E. Strategic Policy Changes at Private Colleges. LC 77-13257. Repr. of 1977 ed. 21.30 (2013172). Bks Demand UMI.
Anderson, Richard E. & Kasl, Elizabeth. The Costs of Financing of Adult Education & Training. LC 81-47276. (Illus.). 352p. 1982. 33.00x (ISBN 0-669-04570-5). Lexington Bks.
Anderson, Richard F., jt. auth. see Greenberg, Michael R.
Anderson, Richard J. & Hofman, Peter L. Alternative Energy Sources for the United States. 19p. 1975. pap. 2.50x (ISBN 0-87855-743-1). Transaction Bks.
Anderson, Richard L. Art in Primitive Societies. (Illus.). 1979. pap. 19.95 ref. ed. (ISBN 0-13-048108-4). P-H.
--Investigating the Book of Mormon Witnesses. LC 80-26626. (Illus.). 206p. 1981. 6.95 (ISBN 0-87747-846-5). Deseret Bk.
--Understanding Paul. LC 83-72103. 448p. 1983. 10.95 (ISBN 0-87747-984-4). Deseret Bk.
Anderson, Rob. Students As Real People: Interpersonal Communication & Education. (gr. 10 up). 1978. pap. 7.00x (ISBN 0-8104-5764-4). Boynton Cook Pubs.
Anderson, Rob, jt. auth. see Whipple, Andy.
Anderson, Robert. Artillery Officer in the Mexican War, 1846-1847: Letters of Robert Anderson. facsimile ed. LC 74-148870. (Select Bibliographies Reprint Ser). Repr. of 1911 ed. 24.50 (ISBN 0-8369-5642-7). Ayer Co Pubs.
--The Coming Prince. LC 63-11464. (Sir Robert Anderson Library). 1975. pap. 6.95 (ISBN 0-8254-2115-2). Kregel.
--Criminals & Crime: Some Facts & Suggestions, London 1907. LC 83-49250. (Crime & Punishment in England, 1850-1922 Ser.). 182p. 1984. lib. bdg. 35.00 (ISBN 0-8240-6221-3). Garland Pub.
--Forgotten Truths. LC 80-17526. (Sir Robert Anderson Library). 1980. pap. 3.95 (ISBN 0-8254-2130-6). Kregel.
--The Gospel & Its Ministry. LC 78-9539. (Sir Robert Anderson Library). 1978. pap. 4.50 (ISBN 0-8254-2126-8). Kregel.
--The Life of Tobias Smollett. 1806. Repr. 15.00 (ISBN 0-8274-2872-3). R West.
--The Lord from Heaven. LC 78-9533. (Sir Robert Anderson Library). 1978. pap. 3.50 (ISBN 0-8254-2127-6). Kregel.
--El Principe que ha de Venir. Orig. Title: The Coming Prince. 288p. (Span.). 1980. pap. 5.95 (ISBN 0-8254-1021-5). Kregel.
--Redemption Truths. LC 80-16161. (Sir Robert Anderson Library). Orig. Title: For Us Men. 192p. 1980. pap. 3.95 (ISBN 0-8254-2131-4). Kregel.
--The Silence of God. LC 78-9528. (Sir Robert Anderson Library). 1978. pap. 4.95 (ISBN 0-8254-2128-4). Kregel.
--El Silencio de Dios. Orig. Title: The Silence of God. 192p. (Span.). 1981. pap. 3.25 (ISBN 0-8254-1022-3). Kregel.
--Spanish American Modernism: A Selected Bibliography. LC 73-82616. pap. 47.80 (ISBN 0-317-26809-0, 2024315). Bks Demand UMI.
--Spirit Manifestations & "the Gift of Tongues". pap. 0.75 (ISBN 0-87213-015-0). Loizeaux.
--Story of Extinct Civilizations of the West. 59.95 (ISBN 0-8490-1133-7). Gordon Pr.
--Stress Power! How to Turn Tension into Energy. LC 78-8308. 248p. 1978. 29.95 (ISBN 0-87705-328-6). Human Sci Pr.
--Types in Hebrews. LC 78-9545. (Sir Robert Anderson Library). 1978. pap. 4.50 (ISBN 0-8254-2129-2). Kregel.
--Wagner: A Biography, with a Survey of Books, Editions, & Recordings. (Concertgoers Companion Ser.). 154p. 1980. 16.50 (ISBN 0-208-01677-5, Linnet). Shoe String.
Anderson, Robert, jt. auth. see Cartwright, Ann.
Anderson, Robert, jt. auth. see Haast, William E.
Anderson, Robert, jt. auth. see Kroc, Ray.
Anderson, Robert see Strasberg, Lee.
Anderson, Robert, jt. auth. see Wolf, James M.
Anderson, Robert, ed. Semasia: Beitrage zur Germanisch-Romanischen Sprachforschung, Band 5. (Orig.). 1980. pap. text ed. 20.00x (ISBN 0-391-02047-1). Humanities.
Anderson, Robert A. Cooks & Bakers. 192p. 1982. pap. 2.95 (ISBN 0-380-79590-6, 87429-6). Avon.
--Stress Power! How to Turn Tension into Energy. LC 78-8308. 248p. 1981. pap. 14.95 (ISBN 0-89885-093-2). Human Sci Pr.
Anderson, Robert B. The Fischer-Tropsch Synthesis (Monograph) LC 83-15762. 1984. 55.00 (ISBN 0-12-058460-3). Acad Pr.
Anderson, Robert B., ed. Experimental Methods in Catalytic Research. LC 68-18652. Vol. 1 1968. 91.50 (ISBN 0-12-058650-9); Vol. 2 1976. 70.00 (ISBN 0-12-058660-6); Vol. 3 1976. 75.00 (ISBN 0-12-058662-2). Acad Pr.
Anderson, Robert C. The Effective Pastor: A Practical Guide to the Ministry. 1985. 14.95 (ISBN 0-8024-6359-2). Moody.
Anderson, Robert C., ed. Inspection of Metals: Visual Examination, Vol. 1. 1983. 45.00 (ISBN 0-87170-159-6). ASM.
Anderson, Robert D. Avoiding Malpractice for the California Nurse. 2nd ed. 112p. 1982. pap. text ed. 31.50 Home Study Course (ISBN 0-942028-03-1); Reference Book 10.00 (ISBN 0-942028-07-4). Anderson R.
--Legal Boundaries of California Nursing Practice. 3rd ed. 221p. 1984. text ed. 35.00 home study course (ISBN 0-942028-12-0); pap. 15.00 reference book (ISBN 0-942028-14-7). Anderson R.
--Legal Boundaries of Iowa Nursing Practice. LC 84-223730. 122p. 1984. pap. text ed. 28.00 home study course (ISBN 0-942028-12-0); reference bk. 12.00 (ISBN 0-942028-13-9). Anderson R.
--Legal Boundaries of Minnesota Nursing Practice. 100p. (Orig.). 1982. pap. text ed. 42.00 Home Study Course (ISBN 0-942028-06-6); Reference Book 12.00 (ISBN 0-942028-10-4). Anderson R.
Anderson, Robert D., ed. Legal Boundaries of Florida Nursing Practice. 2nd ed. 208p. (Orig.). 1985. pap. 42.00 home study course (ISBN 0-942028-15-5); reference book 15.00 (ISBN 0-942028-16-3). Anderson R.
Anderson, Robert E. The Merchant Marine & World Frontiers. LC 78-5585. (Illus.). xvii, 205p. 1978. Repr. of 1945 ed. lib. bdg. 20.50x (ISBN 0-313-20437-3, ANMM). Greenwood.
--The Story of Extinct Civilizations of the East. 1977. Repr. of 1904 ed. lib. bdg. 25.00 (ISBN 0-8492-0138-1). R West.
Anderson, Robert F. Hume's First Principles. LC 65-18415. xvi, 189p. 1966. 16.50x (ISBN 0-8032-0000-5). U of Nebr Pr.
Anderson, Robert H. & Becker, Anton E. Cardiac Anatomy. (Illus.). 252p. 1983. text ed. 110.00 (ISBN 0-443-02232-1). Churchill.
Anderson, Robert H., jt. auth. see Becker, Anton E.
Anderson, Robert H., jt. auth. see Losekoot, Tom G.
Anderson, Robert H., jt. auth. see Shinebourne, Elliot A.
Anderson, Robert H., jt. auth. see Wilcox, Benson R.
Anderson, Robert H. & MacArtney, Fergus J., eds. Paediatric Cardiology, No. 5. LC 82-22063. (Pediatric Cardiology Ser.). (Illus.). 476p. 1983. text ed. 79.00 (ISBN 0-443-02589-4). Churchill.
Anderson, Robert H. & Shinebourne, Elliot A., eds. Paediatric Cardiology Vol. 1, 1977. (Illus.). 1978. text ed. 63.50 (ISBN 0-443-01623-2). Churchill.
Anderson, Robert J. & Schrier, Robert W. Clinical Uses of Drugs in Patients with Kidney & Liver Disease. (Illus.). 368p. 1981. text ed. 39.00 (ISBN 0-7216-1239-3). Saunders.
Anderson, Robert J., jt. ed. see Campos-Lopez, Enrique.
Anderson, Robert J., et al. Clinical Use of Drugs in Renal Failure. (Illus.). 264p. 1978. 25.75x (ISBN 0-398-03400-1). C C Thomas.
Anderson, Robert M. American Law of Zoning, 5 vols. 2nd ed. LC 68-28408. 1976. 287.50 (ISBN 0-686-14539-9, 024A); Suppl. 1984. 39.50; Suppl. 1983. 36.00. Lawyers Co-Op.
--Law of Zoning in Pennsylvania. LC 82-82349. (Pennsylvania Practice Library). 1982. 149.00; Suppl. 1984. 26.00; Suppl. 1983. 20.00. Lawyers Co-op.
--New York Zoning Law & Practice. 3rd ed. LC 84-81189. 1984. 125.00 (ISBN 0-318-03855-2). Lawyers Co-Op.
--Vision of the Disinherited: The Making of American Pentecostalism. 1979. 24.95x (ISBN 0-19-502502-4). Oxford U Pr.
Anderson, Robert M. & Romfh, Richard F. Technique in the Use of Surgical Tools. (Illus.). 187p. 1980. pap. 13.95x (ISBN 0-8385-8841-7). ACC.
Anderson, Robert M., et al. Instructional Resources for Teachers of the Culturally Disadvantaged & Exceptional. 320p. 1971. 24.50x (ISBN 0-398-00045-X). C C Thomas.
--Divided Loyalties: Whistle-Blowing at Bart. LC 79-89588. (Science & Society: A Purdue University Series in Science, Technology, & Human Values: Vol. 4). (Illus.). 400p. 1980. pap. 4.95 (ISBN 0-931682-09-6). Purdue Univ.
Anderson, Robert M., jt. auth. see Greer, John G.
Anderson, Robert M., Jr., jt. ed. see Maxwell, Grover.
Anderson, Robert N., et al. Filipinos in Rural Hawaii. LC 83-9274. 198p. 1984. pap. text ed. 12.95x (ISBN 0-8248-0821-5). UH Pr.
Anderson, Robert O. Fundamentals of the Petroleum Industry. LC 84-40271. (Illus.). 400p. 1984. 29.95 (ISBN 0-8061-1909-8). U of Okla Pr.
Anderson, Robert P. & Halcomb, Charles G. Learning Disabilities-Minimal Brain Dysfunction: Research Perspectives & Applications. (Illus.). 296p. 1976. 24.50x (ISBN 0-398-03395-1). C C Thomas.
Anderson, Robert S. Metallic Cartridge Reloading. LC 81-70996. (Illus.). 320p. 1982. pap. 13.95 (ISBN 0-910676-39-9). DBI.
Anderson, Robert S., ed. Gun Digest Hunting Annual 1986. 3rd ed. (Illus.). 256p. 1985. pap. 12.95 (ISBN 0-910676-90-9). DBI.
--Reloading for Shotgunners. 2nd ed. (Illus.). 256p. 1985. pap. 11.95 (ISBN 0-910676-92-5). DBI.
Anderson, Robert S., et al, eds. Science, Politics, & the Agricultural Revolution in Asia. (Selected Symposium Ser.: No. 70). 450p. 1982. lib. bdg. 36.50x (ISBN 0-86531-320-2). Westview.
Anderson, Robert T. Denmark: Success of a Developing Nation. (Illus.). 186p. 1975. 15.95x (ISBN 0-87073-738-4); pap. text ed. 9.95x (ISBN 0-87073-739-2). Schenkman Bks Inc.
--Studies in Samaritan Manuscripts & Artifacts: The Chamberlain-Warren Collection. LC 78-52697. (American Schools of Oriental Research Monograph: Vol. 1). 99p. 1978. text ed. 8.00x (ISBN 0-89757-402-8, Am Sch Orient Res). Eisenbrauns.
Anderson, Robert T. & Anderson, Barbara G. The Vanishing Village: Danish Maritime Community. LC 77-87704. Repr. of 1964 ed. 28.00 (ISBN 0-404-16498-6). AMS Pr.
Anderson, Robert V. Simplifying the Complicated in Real Estate & Appraising. LC 84-70613. (Illus.). 1984. write for info. (ISBN 0-910436-27-4). Conway Data.
Anderson, Robert W. Party Politics in Puerto Rico. 1965. 20.00x (ISBN 0-8047-0253-5). Stanford U Pr.
Anderson, Robin. Between Two Wars: The Story of Pope Pius XI. 1978. 7.95 (ISBN 0-8199-0687-5). Franciscan Herald.
--St. Pius V - A Brief Account of His Life, Times, Virtues & Miracles. LC 78-55637. 1978. pap. 2.50 (ISBN 0-89555-068-7). TAN Bks Pubs.
Anderson, Rodney D. Outcasts in Their Own Land: Mexican Industrial Workers, 1906-1911. LC 74-28896. (The Origins of Modern Mexico Ser.). (Illus.). 407p. 1976. 17.50 (ISBN 0-87580-054-8). N Ill U Pr.

Anderson, Rodney J. The External Audit, Vol. 2E. (Pitman Series in Finance & Accounting). 537p. 1985. text ed. 49.95 (ISBN 0-7730-4308-X). Pitman Pub MA.

Anderson, Rolph & Hair, Joseph. Sales Management. Donnelly, Paul, ed. LC 82-23014. (Random House Business Division Ser.). 576p. 1983. text ed. 26.00 (ISBN 0-394-32293-2, RanC). Random.

Anderson, Romola & Anderson, R. C. The Sailing Ship: Six Thousand Years of History. LC 79-177507. 22.00 (ISBN 0-405-08205-3). Ayer Co Pubs.

Anderson, Ron. Boiler Efficiency Manual. (Illus.). 128p. 1986. text ed. 24.95 (ISBN 0-13-079724-3). P-H.

Anderson, Ron, jt. auth. see Wei, C. C.

Anderson, Ronald & Anderson, Odin W. A Decade of Health Services: Social Survey Trends in Use & Expenditure. LC 67-30125. (University of Chicago, Graduate School of Business, Studies in Business & Society). pap. 66.00 (ISBN 0-317-26636-5, 2024081). Bks Demand UMI.

Anderson, Ronald A. Couch on Insurance, 24 vols. 2nd ed. LC 59-1915. 1971. 1350.00 set (ISBN 0-686-14510-0). Lawyers Co-Op.

--Government & Business. 1981. text ed. 21.95 (ISBN 0-538-08570-3, H57). SW Pub.

--Hotelman's Basic Law. 15.75 (ISBN 0-914770-00-4). Littoral Develop.

--Insurer's Tort Law. 14.30 (ISBN 0-914770-01-2). Littoral Develop.

--Running a Professional Corporation. 7.50 (ISBN 0-914770-02-0). Littoral Develop.

--Social Forces & the Law. 1981. pap. text ed. 9.75 (ISBN 0-538-12300-1, L30). SW Pub.

--Uniform Commercial Code, 7 vols. 3rd ed. LC 81-837763. 1981. 385.00 (ISBN 0-686-14491-0); legal forms vol. 99.00 (ISBN 0-686-14492-9); pleading & practice forms 2 vols. 99.00 (ISBN 0-686-14493-7). Lawyers Co-Op.

Anderson, Ronald A., et al. Business Law: Comprehensive Volume. 1984. text ed. 22.40 (ISBN 0-538-12660-4, L66). SW Pub.

Anderson, Ronald H. Selecting & Developing Media for Instruction. 2nd ed. 192p. 1983. text ed. 24.95 (ISBN 0-442-20976-2). Van-Nos-Reinhold.

Anderson, Ronald T. Agent's Legal Responsibility. LC 80-83690. 168p. 1980. text ed. 12.75 (ISBN 0-87218-307-6). Natl Underwriter.

--Automating Your Agency Book. LC 82-60877. 288p. 1982. text ed. 16.35 (ISBN 0-87218-321-1). Natl Underwriter.

Anderson, Ronald T., jt. auth. see Hammes, Carol A.

Anderson, Ronald W. From BASIC to Pascal. (Illus.). 324p. 18.95 (ISBN 0-8306-2466-X, 1466); pap. 11.50 (ISBN 0-8306-1466-4, 1466). TAB Bks.

Anderson, Ronald W., ed. The Industrial Organization of Futures Markets. LC 83-48029. 320p. 1984. 28.50 (ISBN 0-669-06836-5). Lexington Bks.

Anderson, Ross & Perry, Barbara. The Diversions of Keramos: American Clay Sculpture, 1925-1950. Grover-Rogoff, Annis & Kuchta, Ronald A., eds. LC 83-82416. (Illus.). 118p. (Orig.). 1983. pap. text ed. 12.00 (ISBN 0-914407-00-7). Everson Mus.

Anderson, Roy, jt. auth. see Fox, Greg.

Anderson, Roy A. Unfolding the Revelation. LC 61-10884. (Dimension Ser.). 223p. 1961. pap. 5.95 (ISBN 0-8163-0027-5, 21400-7). Pacific Pr Pub Assn.

Anderson, Roy C. The Markets & Fairs of England & Wales. (Illus.). 192p. 1985. pap. 9.95 (ISBN 0-7135-2527-4, Pub. by Salem Hse Ltd). Merrimack Pub Cir.

Anderson, Roy C. & Frankis, G. History of the Royal Blue Express Services. LC 72-91235. 1970. 17.95x (ISBN 0-678-05649-8). Kelley.

Anderson, Roy C., jt. ed. see Davis, John W.

Anderson, Roy M. Population Dynamics & Infectious Disease. (Illus.). 376p. 1982. 39.95x (ISBN 0-412-21610-8, NO. 6655, Pub. by Chapman & Hall). Methuen Inc.

Anderson, Roy N. The Disabled Man & His Vocational Adjustment: A Study of the Types of Jobs Held by 4,404 Orthopedic Cases in Relation to the Specific Disability. Phillips, William R. & Rosenberg, Janet, eds. LC 79-6893. (Physically Handicapped in Society Ser.). 1980. Repr. of 1932 ed. lib. bdg. 14.00x (ISBN 0-405-13104-6). Ayer Co Pubs.

Anderson, Roy R., jt. auth. see Seibert, Robert F.

Anderson, Russell E. Biological Paths to Energy Self-Reliance. 400p. 1979. pap. 14.95 (ISBN 0-442-20872-3). Van Nos Reinhold.

Anderson, Ruth. Gallegan Provinces of Spain: Pontevedra & la Coruna. (Illus.). 1939. 7.00 (ISBN 0-87535-047-X). Hispanic Soc.

Anderson, Ruth, jt. auth. see Woolsey, Raymond H.

Anderson, Ruth I., et al. Word Finder. 4th ed. (gr. 9-12). 1974. pap. 3.95 (ISBN 0-8224-3355-9). Pitman Learning.

Anderson, Ruth L. Lost Hill. (Illus.). (gr. 4-6). 1976. pap. 2.25 (ISBN 0-933892-06-3). Child Focus Co.

--Mark of the Land. 320p. (Orig.). 1983. pap. 5.95x (ISBN 0-933892-15-2). Child Focus Co.

Anderson, Ruth M. Costumes Painted by Sorolla in His Provinces of Spain. (Illus.). 1957. 6.00 (ISBN 0-87535-091-7). Hispanic Soc.

--Gallegan Provinces of Spain: Pontevedra & La Caruna. (Illus.). 496p. 1953. 7.00 (ISBN 0-317-00544-8, Pub. by Hispanic Soc). Interbk Inc.

--Hispanic Costume Fourteen Eighty to Fifteen Thirty. LC 78-66860. (Hispanic Notes & Monographs: Peninsular). (Illus.). 1979. 29.00 (ISBN 0-87535-126-3). Hispanic Soc.

--Hispanic Costume, 1480-1530. (Illus.). 303p. 1979. 29.00 (ISBN 0-87535-126-3, Pub. by Hispanic Soc). Interbk Inc.

--Spanish Costume: Extremadura. (Illus.). 1951. 11.00 (ISBN 0-87535-067-4). Hispanic Soc.

--Spanish Costume: Extremadura. (Illus.). 342p. 1951. 11.00 (ISBN 0-317-00618-5, Pub. by Hispanic Soc). Interbk Inc.

Anderson, S. D. & Woodhead, R. W. Project Manpower Management: Management Process in Construction Practice. LC 80-22090. 264p. 1981. 48.50x (ISBN 0-471-95979-0, Pub. by Wiley-Interscience). Wiley.

Anderson, S. I., et al, eds. Differential Geometric Methods in Mathematical Physics. (Lecture Notes in Mathematics Ser.: Vol. 905). 309p. 1982. pap. 20.00 (ISBN 0-387-11197-2). Springer-Verlag.

Anderson, S. W., jt. auth. see Anderson, W. L.

Anderson, Samuel W., jt. ed. see Parkins, Charles W.

Anderson, Sandra, jt. auth. see Golden, Charles J.

Anderson, Sandra V. & Bauwens, Eleanor E. Chronic Health Problems: Concepts & Application. LC 80-29482. (Illus.). 336p. 1981. pap. 18.95 (ISBN 0-8016-0199-1). Mosby.

Anderson, Sandra Van Dam see Van Dam Anderson, Sandra & Simkin, Penny.

Anderson, Sarah T. Lewises, Meriwethers & Their Kin. LC 84-80082. (Illus.). 652p. 1984. Repr. of 1938 ed. 35.00 (ISBN 0-8063-1072-3). Genealog Pub.

Anderson, Scarvia B. & Ball, Samuel. The Profession & Practice of Program Evaluation. LC 78-1154. (Social & Behavioral Science & Higher Education Ser). (Illus.). 1978. text ed. 19.95x (ISBN 0-87589-375-9). Jossey-Bass.

Anderson, Scarvia B. & Coburn, Louisa V., eds. Academic Testing & the Consumer. LC 81-48587. (Testing & Measurement Ser.: No. 16). 1982. 9.95x (ISBN 0-87589-930-7). Jossey-Bass.

Anderson, Scarvia B. & Helmick, John S., eds. On Educational Testing: Intelligence, Performance Standards, Test Anxiety, & Latent Traits. LC 83-48155. (Social & Behavioral Science Ser.). 1983. text ed. 23.95x (ISBN 0-87589-576-X). Jossey-Bass.

Anderson, Scarvia B., et al. Encyclopedia of Educational Evaluation: Concepts & Techniques for Evaluating Education & Training Programs. LC 74-6736. (Higher Education Ser.). 544p. 1975. 27.95x (ISBN 0-87589-238-8). Jossey-Bass.

Anderson, Scott. First the Answer, Then the Question. (Laughter Library). (Illus.). 48p. (Orig.). 1983. pap. 1.75 (ISBN 0-8431-0548-8). Price Stern.

--Funniest Baseball Stories of the Century. rev. ed. (Laughter Library). (Orig.). 1979. pap. 1.75 (ISBN 0-8431-0539-9). Price Stern.

--Funniest Football Stories of the Century. (Laughter Library). (Orig.). 1979. pap. 1.75 (ISBN 0-8431-0538-0). Price Stern.

Anderson, Scott & Bryne, James. Mega-Tips: How to Get & Keep Any Restaurant Job. 150p. 1984. pap. 5.95 (ISBN 0-396-08359-5). Dodd.

Anderson, Scott, jt. auth. see Burgum, Thomas.

Anderson, Sharon, et al. Statistical Methods for Comparative Studies: Techniques for Bias Reduction. LC 79-27220. (Wiley Series in Probability & Mathematical Statistics: Applied Probability & Statistics). 289p. 1980. 38.95x (ISBN 0-471-04838-0, Pub. by Wiley-Interscience). Wiley.

Anderson, Sheridan. Baron Von Mabel's Backpacking. (Illus.). 96p. (Orig.). 1980. pap. 4.95 (ISBN 0-89620-082-5). Rip Off.

--Curtis Creek Manifesto. (Illus.). 48p. (Orig.). 1978. pap. 5.00 (ISBN 0-936608-06-4). F Amato Pubns.

Anderson, Sherwood. Alice & the Lost Novel. 1978. Repr. of 1929 ed. lib. bdg. 8.50 (ISBN 0-8495-0019-2). Arden Lib.

--Beyond Desire. (Black & Gold Lib). (Illus.). cloth 1961 6.95 (ISBN 0-87140-991-7); pap. 2.45 paper 1970 (ISBN 0-87140-206-8). Liveright.

--Buck Fever Papers. Taylor, Welford D., ed. LC 73-151252. (Illus.). 250p. 1971. 20.00x (ISBN 0-8139-0322-X). U Pr of Va.

--Dark Laughter. 17.95 (ISBN 0-88411-277-2, Pub. by Aeonian Pr). Amereon Ltd.

--Hometown. 1975. Repr. of 1940 ed. 15.00x (ISBN 0-911858-11-3). Appel.

--Kit Brandon. 1985. 6.95 (ISBN 0-87795-707-X). Arbor Hse.

--Letters to Bab: Sherwood Anderson to Marietta D. Finley, 1916-33. Sutton, William A., ed. LC 83-18258. 376p. 1985. 24.95 (ISBN 0-252-00979-7). U of Ill Pr.

--Mid-American Chants. LC 78-14240. 1978. Repr. of 1918 ed. lib. bdg. 18.50 (ISBN 0-8414-3007-1). Folcroft.

--Mid-American Chants. 68p. (Orig.). 1972. pap. 3.50 (ISBN 0-686-05065-7). Frontier Press Calif.

--Mid-American Chants. 82p. 1980. Repr. of 1923 ed. lib. bdg. 22.50 (ISBN 0-8482-0047-0). Norwood Edns.

--The Modern Writer. 1978. Repr. of 1925 ed. lib. bdg. 10.00 (ISBN 0-8495-0112-1). Arden Lib.

--The Modern Writer. LC 76-40963. 1976. Repr. of 1925 ed. lib. bdg. 20.00 (ISBN 0-8414-2992-8). Folcroft.

--Nearer the Grass Roots. 1978. Repr. of 1929 ed. lib. bdg. 10.00 (ISBN 0-8495-0117-2). Arden Lib.

--Nearer the Grass Roots. LC 76-49847. 1977. lib. bdg. 18.50 (ISBN 0-8414-2986-3). Folcroft.

--No Swank. LC 70-105302. 1970. Repr. of 1934 ed. 8.95x (ISBN 0-911858-06-7). Appel.

--Perhaps Women. LC 76-105301. 1970. Repr. of 1931 ed. 8.95x (ISBN 0-911858-05-9). Appel.

--Portable Sherwood Anderson. (Viking Portable Library). 1977. pap. 6.95 (ISBN 0-14-015076-5). Penguin.

--Puzzled America. 1970. Repr. of 1935 ed. 12.00x (ISBN 0-911858-07-5). Appel.

--Sherwood Anderson: Selected Letters. Modlin, Charles E., ed. LC 83-6530. (Illus.). 280p. 1983. text ed. 24.95x (ISBN 0-87049-404-X). U of Tenn Pr.

--Sherwood Anderson's Notebook 1926. LC 72-105299. 1970. 10.00x (ISBN 0-911858-03-2). Appel.

--A Story Teller's Tale. 22.95 (ISBN 0-88411-278-0, Pub. by Aeonian Pr). Amereon Ltd.

--The Teller's Tales: Short Stories. Gado, Frank, intro. by. LC 83-80751. (Signature Ser.). 229p. (Orig.). 1983. pap. 14.75 (ISBN 0-912756-09-8); pap. text ed. 3.95 (ISBN 0-912756-08-X). Union Coll.

--Winesburg, Ohio. 1976. pap. 2.95 (ISBN 0-14-000609-5). Penguin.

--Winesburg, Ohio: Text & Criticism. Ferres, John, ed. (Viking Critical Library: No. 1). 1977. pap. 7.95 (ISBN 0-14-015501-5). Penguin.

--The Writer at His Craft. Salzman, Jack, et al, eds. 1978. 22.50x (ISBN 0-911858-37-7). Appel.

Anderson, Shirley. A Matter of Choice. (Orig.). 1979. pap. 1.95 (ISBN 0-532-23320-4). Woodhill.

Anderson, Sparky & Ewald, Dan. Bless You Boys: Diary of the Detroit Tigers' 1984 Season, Through the World Series. rev. ed. (Illus.). 263p. 1985. 13.95 (ISBN 0-8092-5267-8); pap. 7.95 (ISBN 0-8092-5245-7). Contemp Bks.

Anderson, Stanley F. & Hull, Raymond. Art of Making Beer. rev. ed. 1971. pap. 5.95 (ISBN 0-8015-0380-9, 0578-170, Hawthorn). Dutton.

--Art of Making Wine. 1971. pap. 4.50 (ISBN 0-8015-0390-6, 0437-130, Hawthorn). Dutton.

Anderson, Stanley H. Wildlife Resource Management. 528p. 1985. text ed. 29.95 (ISBN 0-675-20337-6). Merrill.

Anderson, Stanley H., jt. auth. see Purdom, P. Walton.

Anderson, Stanley V. The Nordic Council: A Study of Scandinavian Regionalism. LC 67-21202. 1967. 9.50x (ISBN 0-89067-046-3). Am Scandinavian.

--Nordic Council: A Study of Scandinavian Regionalism. LC 67-21202. (American-Scandinavian Foundation Studies). (Illus.). 212p. 1967. 25.00x (ISBN 0-295-97865-1). U of Wash Pr.

Anderson, Stanley V. & Moore, John E., eds. Transcript of Ombudsman Workshop: Recent Experience in the United States. LC 72-5772. 294p. (Orig., Ombudsman workshop, Honolulu, May 5-7, 1971). 1972. pap. 3.00x (ISBN 0-87772-154-8). Inst Gov Stud Berk.

Anderson, Stephen O., jt. auth. see Bishop, Richard C.

Anderson, Stephen R. The Organization of Phonology. 1974. 39.50 (ISBN 0-12-785031-7). Acad Pr.

--Phonology in the Twentieth Century: Theories of Rules & Theories of Representations. LC 85-2773. 384p. 1985. lib. bdg. 40.00x (ISBN 0-226-01915-2); pap. text ed. 17.50x (ISBN 0-226-01916-0). U of Chicago Pr.

Anderson, Stuart. Race & Rapprochement. LC 79-24185. 240p. 1981. 23.50 (ISBN 0-8386-3001-4). Fairleigh Dickinson.

Anderson, Sue L. Shadows Across the Bayou. 1977. pap. 1.50 (ISBN 0-532-15298-0). Woodhill.

Anderson, Suzan K. Mirror of Sumari. (Illus.). 32p. (ps-6). 1985. 13.95x (ISBN 0-942494-93-8, #129). Coleman Pub.

Anderson, Sven A. Viking Enterprise. LC 77-158254. (Columbia University Studies in the Social Sciences: No. 424). Repr. of 1936 ed. 16.50 (ISBN 0-404-51424-3). AMS Pr.

Anderson, Sydney. The Baculum in Microtine Rodents. (Museum Ser.: Vol. 12, No. 3). 36p. 1960. pap. 2.00 (ISBN 0-317-04935-6). U of KS Mus Nat Hist.

--Distribution, Variation, & Relationships of the Montane Vole, Microtus Montanus. (Museum Ser.: Vol. 9, No. 17). 97p. 1959. 5.00 (ISBN 0-317-04924-0). U of KS Mus Nat Hist.

--Extensions of Known Ranges of Mexican Bats. (Museum Ser.: Vol. 9, No. 9). 5p. 1956. pap. 1.25 (ISBN 0-317-04921-6). U of KS Mus Nat Hist.

--Mammals of Mesa Verde National Park, Colorado. (Museum Ser.: Vol. 14, No. 3). 39p. 1961. pap. 2.25 (ISBN 0-317-04937-2). U of KS Mus Nat Hist.

--Mammals of the Grand Mesa, Colorado. (Museum Ser.: Vol. 9, No. 16). 10p. 1959. pap. 1.25 (ISBN 0-317-04923-2). U of KS Mus Nat Hist.

--Neotropical Bats from Western Mexico. (Museum Ser.: Vol. 14, No. 1). 8p. 1960. pap. 1.25 (ISBN 0-317-04936-4). U of KS Mus Nat Hist.

--Subspeciation in the Meadow Mouse, Microtus Montanus, in Wyoming & Colorado. (Museum Ser.: Vol. 7, No. 7). 18p. 1954. pap. 1.25 (ISBN 0-317-04917-8). U of KS Mus Nat Hist.

--Subspeciation in the Meadow Mouse, Microtus Pennsylvanicus, in Wyoming, Colorado & Adjacent Areas. (Museum Ser.: Vol. 9, No. 4). 20p. 1956. pap. 1.25 (ISBN 0-317-04919-4). U of KS Mus Nat Hist.

Anderson, Sydney & Jones, J. Knox, Jr. Orders & Families of Recent Mammals of the World. LC 83-21806. 686p. 1984. 54.95 (ISBN 0-471-08493-X, Pub. by Wiley-Interscience). Wiley.

--Records of Harvest Mice, Reithrodontomys, from Central America, with Description of a New Subspecies from Nicaragua. (Museum Ser.: Vol. 9, No. 19). 11p. 1960. pap. 1.25 (ISBN 0-317-04926-7). U of KS Mus Nat Hist.

Anderson, Sydney, ed. Simon & Schuster's Guide to Mammals. (Illus.). 512p. 1984. 30.95 (ISBN 0-671-43727-5); pap. 10.95 (ISBN 0-671-42805-5). S&S.

Anderson, T. & Randell, B., eds. Computing Systems Reliability. LC 78-75253. (Illus.). 1979. 52.50 (ISBN 0-521-22767-4). Cambridge U Pr.

Anderson, T. B., jt. auth. see Williams, S. H.

Anderson, T. W. An Introduction to Multivariate Statistical Analysis. 2nd ed. LC 84-7334. (In Probability & Mathematical Statistics (1-345)). 675p. 1984. text ed. 44.95 (ISBN 0-471-88987-3, Pub. by Wiley-Interscience). Wiley.

Anderson, T. W. & Sclove, Stanley L. An Introduction to the Statistical Analysis of Data. LC 77-78890. (Illus.). 1978. text ed. 29.50 (ISBN 0-395-15045-0); solutions manual 7.95 (ISBN 0-395-15046-9). HM.

Anderson, T. W., et al. A Bibliography of Multivariate Statistical Analysis. LC 76-54249. 1977. Repr. of 1972 ed. lib. bdg. 36.50 (ISBN 0-88275-477-7). Krieger.

Anderson, Ted R. Population Studies of European Sparrows in North America. (Occasional Papers: No. 70). 58p. 1978. pap. 3.25 (ISBN 0-317-04581-4). U of KS Mus Nat Hist.

Anderson, Teresa, tr. see Neruda, Pablo.

Anderson, Terry, ed. Water Rights: Scarce Resource Allocation, Bureaucracy & the Environment. LC 83-3855. (Pacific Institute on Public Policy Research Ser.). 376p. 1983. prof ref 35.00 (ISBN 0-88410-389-7). Ballinger Pub.

Anderson, Terry, tr. see American Office of War Information, et al.

Anderson, Terry H. The United States, Great Britain, & the Cold War: 1944-1947. LC 80-25838. 256p. 1981. text ed. 20.00x (ISBN 0-8262-0328-0). U of Mo Pr.

Anderson, Terry H., jt. auth. see Bond, Charles A., Jr.

Anderson, Terry L. The Economic Growth of Seventeenth-Century New England: A Measurement of Regional Income. LC 75-2574. (Dissertations in American Economic History). (Illus.). 1975. 22.00x (ISBN 0-405-07255-4). Ayer Co Pubs.

--Water Crisis: Ending the Policy Drought. LC 83-48046. 136p. 1983. text ed. 15.00x (ISBN 0-8018-3087-7); pap. text ed. 7.95x (ISBN 0-8018-3088-5). Johns Hopkins.

Anderson, Terry L., ed. Water Rights: Scarce Resource Allocation, Bureaucracy, & the Environment. LC 83-3855. (Illus.). 374p. 1983. pap. 12.95 (ISBN 0-88410-390-0). PIPPR.

Anderson, Terry L., jt. auth. see North, Douglas C.

Anderson, Theodore W. Statistical Analysis of Time Series. LC 70-126222. (Probability & Mathematical Statistics Ser.). 704p. 1971. 53.50x (ISBN 0-471-02900-9). Wiley.

Anderson, Theresa. Speaking in Sign. 1979. pap. 1.50 (ISBN 0-931122-16-3). West End.

Anderson, Thomas C. The Foundation & Structure of Sartrean Ethics. LC 79-11762. 1979. 22.50x (ISBN 0-7006-0191-0). U Pr of KS.

Anderson, Thomas D. Geopolitics of the Caribbean: Ministates in a Wider World. LC 83-21200. (Politics in Latin America, A Hoover Institution Ser.). 192p. 1984. 26.95 (ISBN 0-03-070553-3). Praeger.

Anderson, Thomas D., jt. auth. see Norwine, Jim.

Anderson, Thomas J. & Trotter, W. Word Processing. LC 73-94097. (Illus.). 192p. 1974. 23.95 (ISBN 0-8144-5356-2); user's manual 9.95. AMACOM.

Anderson, Thomas J. & Trotter, William R. Word Processing Users' Manual. LC 73-94097. 1976. pap. 12.95 (ISBN 0-8144-5424-0). AMACOM.

Anderson, Thomas P. Matanza: El Salvador's Communist Revolt of 1932. LC 78-146885. (Illus.). xii, 175p. 1971. 19.50x (ISBN 0-8032-0794-8). U of Nebr Pr.

--Politics in Central America: Guatemala, El Salvador, Honduras, & Nicaragua. Wesson, Robert, ed. LC 81-15787. (Politics in Latin America, A Hoover Institution Ser.). 240p. 1982. 29.95 (ISBN 0-03-060618-7). Praeger.

--Politics in Central America: Guatemala, El Salvador, Honduras, & Nicaragua. LC 81-15787. (Illus.). 240p. 1984. pap. 14.95 (ISBN 0-03-070762-5). Praeger.

--The War of the Dispossessed: Honduras & El Salvador, 1969. LC 80-24080. (Illus.). xiv, 203p. 1981. 16.95x (ISBN 0-8032-1009-4). U of Nebr Pr.

Anderson, Thomas P. & Springer, Robert W., eds. Advances in Plasma Dynamics: Proceedings of the 6th Biennial Gas Dynamics Symposium: August 25-27, 1965. LC 58-5928. pap. 85.30 (ISBN 0-317-08973-0, 2015310). Bks Demand UMI.

Anderson, Thomas P., ed. see Northwestern University, Evanston, Ill.

Anderson, Totten J., jt. auth. see Rodee, Carlton C.

Anderson, Troels & Atkins, Guy. Asger Jorn. LC 82-60792. (Illus.). 98p. 1982. pap. 9.00 (ISBN 0-89207-034-X). S R Guggenheim.

Anderson, Troels, jt. auth. see Atkins, Guy.

Anderson, Troyer S. The Command of the Howe Brothers During the American Revolution. LC 72-4221. vii, 368p. 1972. Repr. of 1936 ed. lib. bdg. 27.50x (ISBN 0-374-90198-8). Octagon.

--Command of the Howe Brothers During the Amercan Revolution. LC 77-144861. 1971. Repr. of 1936 ed. 25.00x (ISBN 0-403-00816-6). Scholarly.

Anderson, Tucker W. Counseling the Handicapped Client: A Series of Training Modules. 113p. 1983. pap. text ed. 7.00 (ISBN 0-911547-28-2, 72143W34). Am Assn Coun Dev.

Anderson, U. S. Three Magic Words. 3.00x (ISBN 0-685-70722-9). Wehman.

Anderson, Urton & Holman, Richard. Quality Assurance for Internal Auditing. (Illus.). 176p. 1983. text ed. 60.00 (ISBN 0-89413-098-6, 510). Inst Inter Aud.

Anderson, V. Elving, et al, eds. Genetic Basis of the Epilepsies. 400p. 1982. text ed. 70.00 (ISBN 0-89004-676-X). Raven.

Anderson, V. Elving, jt. ed. see Sheppard, John R.

Anderson, V. R. & Fox, G. K. A Pictorial Record of L. M. S. Architecture. 300p. 70.00x (ISBN 0-86093-083-1, Pub. by ORPC Ltd UK). State Mutual Bk.

Anderson, V. S. King of the Roses. LC 83-3005. 384p. 1983. 14.95 (ISBN 0-312-45512-7). St Martin.

Anderson, V. V. Psychiatry in Industry. Stein, Leon, ed. LC 77-70477. (Work Ser.). 1977. Repr. of 1929 ed. lib. bdg. 32.00x (ISBN 0-405-10151-1). Ayer Co Pubs.

Anderson, Valborg, ed. & tr. see Strindberg, August.

Anderson, Velma I. Wisps by the Way. 48p. (Orig.). 1983. pap. write for info. (ISBN 0-89279-052-0). V I Anderson.

Anderson, Vernon E. & Gruhn, William T. Principles & Practices of Secondary Education. 2nd ed. LC 62-11648. Repr. of 1962 ed. 130.80 (ISBN 0-8357-9958-1, 2012463). Bks Demand UMI.

Anderson, Victor D. Bibliografia Municipal Geografica Puertorriquena. LC 78-18780. 1979. pap. 6.25 (ISBN 0-8477-2007-1). U of PR Pr.

Anderson, Vincent P. Reaction to Religious Elements in the Poetry of Robert Browning: Introduction & Annotated Bibliography. LC 82-50407. 350p. 1984. 25.00X (ISBN 0-87875-221-8). Whitston Pub.

Anderson, Virgil A. Training the Speaking Voice. 3rd ed. (Illus.). 1977. text ed. 19.95x (ISBN 0-19-502150-9). Oxford U Pr.

Anderson, Virgil A. & Newby, Hayes. Improving the Child's Speech. 2nd ed. (Illus.). 1973. text ed. 16.95x (ISBN 0-19-501708-0). Oxford U Pr.

Anderson, Virgil L. & McLean, Robert A. Design of Experiments: A Realistic Approach. (Statistics, Textbks & Monographs: Vol. 5). 440p. 1974. 29.75 (ISBN 0-8247-6131-6). Dekker.

Anderson, Virginia P. Mountain View. LC 84-3149. 1984. pap. 4.95 (ISBN 0-8054-7322-X). Broadman.

Anderson, Vivian, tr. see Piaget, Jean, et al.

Anderson, W. A. & Scotti, W. A. Synopsis of Pathology. 10th ed. LC 80-13985. (Illus.). 786p. 1980. pap. text ed. 29.95 (ISBN 0-8016-0231-9). Mosby.

Anderson, W. A. & Sadler, W., eds. Perspectives in Differentiation & Hypertrophy. 1982. 88.50 (ISBN 0-444-00696-6). Elsevier.

Anderson, W. A. D. & Kissane, John M. Pathology. 7th ed. LC 77-1052. (Illus.). 1977. 74.95 (ISBN 0-8016-0186-X). Mosby.

Anderson, W. Ferguson & Judge, T. G., eds. Geriatric Medicine. 1974. 59.50 (ISBN 0-12-057250-8). Acad Pr.

Anderson, W. French, et al, eds. Cooley's Anemia Symposium, 4th. LC 80-17575. (Annals of the New York Academy of Sciences: Vol. 344). 448p. 1980. 81.00x (ISBN 0-89766-076-5). NY Acad Sci.

Anderson, W. H. National Income Theory & Its Price Theoretic Foundations. (Economic Handbook Ser.). (Illus.). 1979. text ed. 55.00x (ISBN 0-07-001670-4). McGraw.

Anderson, W. H. & Putallaz, Ann. Macroeconomics. (Illus.). 480p. 1983. pap. text ed. 20.95 (ISBN 0-13-542811-4). P-H.

Anderson, W. J. MSC-Nastran: Interactive Training Program. 482p. 1983. pap. 31.50 (ISBN 0-471-89109-6). Wiley.

Anderson, W. J., ed. Bearing Design - Historical Aspects, Present Technology, & Future Problems. 212p. 1980. 30.00 (ISBN 0-317-33438-7, H00160); members 15.00 (ISBN 0-317-33439-5). ASME.

Anderson, W. J., jt. ed. see Marwaha, J.

Anderson, W. L. Railroad Track Briefs for the Plant Engineer. (Illus.). 1979. 10.00 (ISBN 0-682-49448-8). Exposition Pr FL.

Anderson, W. L. & Anderson, S. W. The Debonair Bachelor: A Guide to Love & Laughter. LC 81-82186. (Illus.). 128p. 1983. 19.95 (ISBN 0-940452-00-6). Marduk Manumit.

Anderson, W. L. & Stageberg, N. C., eds. Introductory Readings on Language. 4th ed. LC 74-16229. 1975. pap. text ed. 17.95 (ISBN 0-03-089578-2, HoltC). HR&W.

Anderson, W. P., ed. Ion Transport in Plants. 1973. 97.00 (ISBN 0-12-058250-3). Acad Pr.

Anderson, W. R. Viking Explorers & the Columbus Fraud: Pros & the Con Man. LC 81-90279. (Illus.). 150p. 1982. 11.45 (ISBN 0-9607070-1-8); pap. 9.45 (ISBN 0-9607070-0-X). Valhalla Pr.

Anderson, W. Steve & Cox, Don R. The Technical Reader: Readings in Technical Business & Scientific Communication. 2nd ed. LC 83-26410. 357p. 1984. pap. text ed. 14.95 (ISBN 0-03-062396-0, HoltC). HR&W.

Anderson, W. Thomas, Jr., et al. Multidimensional Marketing: Managerial, Societal & Philosophical. LC 75-13358. (Illus.). 323p. (Orig.). 1976. pap. text ed. 7.95x (ISBN 0-914872-06-0). Austin Pr.

Anderson, Wallace E., jt. ed. see Edwards, Jonathan.

Anderson, Walt. The Sutter Buttes: A Naturalist's View. LC 82-90753. 346p. 1983. 18.95 (ISBN 0-9610722-0-2). Nat Select.

Anderson, Walter. Kleinere Arbeiten zur Volkskunde. (Asian Folklore & Social Life Monograph: No. 52). 170p. (Eng. & Ger.). 1973. 15.00 (ISBN 0-89986-049-4). Oriental Bk Store.

--A Place of Power: The American Episode in Human Evolution. LC 76-12809. 1976. pap. text ed. 15.80 (ISBN 0-673-16268-0). Scott F.

Anderson, Walter, illus. An Alphabet. LC 84-7291. (Illus.). 64p. 1984. pap. 9.95 (ISBN 0-87805-224-0). U Pr of Miss.

Anderson, Walter I. The Horn Island Logs of Walter Inglis Anderson. Sugg, Redding S., Jr., ed. LC 82-11067. 1985. 35.00 (ISBN 0-87805-168-6). U Pr of Miss.

--Robinson: The Pleasant History of an Unusual Cat. LC 82-10897. (Illus.). 72p. 1982. 12.95 (ISBN 0-87805-170-8). U Pr of Miss.

Anderson, Walter T. Rethinking Liberalism. 1983. pap. 4.95 (ISBN 0-380-84848-1, 84848, Discus). Avon.

--The Upstart Spring: Esalen & the Awakening of a Generation. (Illus.). 320p. 1983. pap. 11.95 (ISBN 0-201-11035-0). Addison-Wesley.

Anderson, Warren D. Prometheus Bound (Aeschylus) 1963. pap. text ed. write for info. (ISBN 0-02-303130-1). Macmillan.

Anderson, Warren D., tr. see Aeschylus.

Anderson, Warren H. Vanishing Roadside America. LC 81-11529. 144p. 1981. ltd. ed. 50.00 (ISBN 0-8165-0746-5); pap. 14.95 (ISBN 0-8165-0754-6). U of Ariz Pr.

Anderson, Wayne. A Mouse's Tale. LC 83-48170. (Illus.). 32p. (gr. 1-4). 1984. 12.02i (ISBN 0-06-020109-6); PLB 11.89g (ISBN 0-06-020110-X). HarpJ.

Anderson, Wayne, jt. auth. see Dickinson, Peter.

Anderson, Wayne, jt. auth. see Getchell, Bud.

Anderson, Wayne F, et al. The Effective Local Government Manager. LC 82-180. (Municipal Management Ser.). (Illus.). 1983. text ed. 33.00 (ISBN 0-87326-027-9); pap. text ed. 25.00 (ISBN 0-87326-028-7). Intl City Mgt.

Anderson, Wayne F., et al, eds. Managing Human Services. LC 77-2464. (Municipal Management Ser.). (Illus.). 591p. 1977. text ed. 30.00 (ISBN 0-87326-017-1). Intl City Mgt.

Anderson, Wayne I. Geology of Iowa: Over Two Billion Years of Change. (Illus.). 268p. 1983. 32.50x (ISBN 0-8138-0803-0); pap. 17.95 (ISBN 0-8138-1505-3). Iowa St U Pr.

Anderson, Wendell B. At Rock-Standing-in-Time. (Illus.). 56p. (Orig.). 1984. pap. 2.50 (ISBN 0-916727-02-5). Namaste Pr.

Anderson, Wendell G., ed. What Are the Subject Matter Boundaries. LC 67-21864. (Illus.). 1967. pap. text ed. 2.00x (ISBN 0-8134-0941-1, 941). Interstate.

Anderson, Wilbert L. The Country Town: A Study of Rural Evolution. LC 73-11914. (Metropolitan America Ser.). 318p. 1974. Repr. 23.50x (ISBN 0-405-05382-7). Ayer Co Pubs.

Anderson, Wilda C. Between the Library & the Laboratory: The Language of Chemistry in Eighteenth-Century France. LC 84-47942. 1985. text ed. 22.50x (ISBN 0-8018-3229-2). Johns Hopkins.

Anderson, Willard. Wheel of Fortune. 1985. 11.95 (ISBN 0-317-28984-5). Vantage.

Anderson, Willard V., ed. Easy-to-Build Model Railroad Structures. (Illus.). 96p. (Orig.). 1958. pap. 4.50 (ISBN 0-89024-514-2). Kalmbach.

Anderson, William. Boyd's Pathology for the Surgeon. LC 65-10285. (Illus.). Repr. of 1967 ed. 120.00 (ISBN 0-8357-9534-9, 2013060). Bks Demand UMI.

--Dante the Maker. (Crossroad Paperback Ser.). 512p. 1982. pap. 12.95 (ISBN 0-8245-0414-3). Crossroad NY.

--Dante the Maker. (Illus.). 1981. 35.00 (ISBN 0-7100-0322-6). Routledge & Kegan.

--In His Light: A Path into Catholic Belief. 216p. 1979. pap. 5.50 (ISBN 0-697-01716-8). Wm C Brown.

--Intergovernmental Relations in Review. LC 73-16639. (Intergovernmental Realtions in the U.S. Research Monograph: No. 10). 178p. 1974. Repr. of 1960 ed. lib. bdg. 22.50x (ISBN 0-8371-7208-X, ANIG). Greenwood.

--Japanese Wood-Engravings: Their History, Technique & Characteristics. LC 77-94541. 1979. Repr. of 1908 ed. lib. bdg. 30.00 (ISBN 0-89341-223-6). Longwood Pub Group.

--Journeying in His Light. 160p. 1982. wire coil 4.95 (ISBN 0-697-01858-X). Wm C Brown.

--Journeying Through the R.C.I.A. 160p. 1984. wire coil 5.75 (ISBN 0-697-01941-1). Wm C Brown.

--Journeying Toward Baptism. 1984. wire coil 5.75 (ISBN 0-697-02002-9). Wm C Brown.

--Journeying Toward Marriage. (Journeying with Christ Ser.). 176p. 1985. pap. 6.75 (ISBN 0-697-02059-2). Wm C Brown.

--The Nation & the States, Rivals or Partners? LC 73-16640. 263p. 1974. Repr. of 1955 ed. lib. bdg. 45.00 (ISBN 0-8371-7210-1, ANNS). Greenwood.

--The Pictorial Arts of Japan. LC 77-94540. 1979. Repr. of 1886 ed. lib. bdg. 35.00 (ISBN 0-89341-222-8). Longwood Pub Group.

--The Rise of the Gothic. (Illus.). 1985. 29.95 (ISBN 0-88162-109-9, Pub. by Salem Hse Ltd). Merrimack Pub Cir.

--Teaching the Physically Handicapped to Swim. (Illus.). 1969. 12.00 (ISBN 0-571-08236-X). Transatlantic.

--The Wild Man from Sugar Creek: The Political Career of Eugene Talmadge. LC 74-82002. (Illus.). xviii, 268p. 1975. 25.00x (ISBN 0-8071-0088-9); pap. 7.95x (ISBN 0-8071-0170-2). La State U Pr.

Anderson, William A. & Dynes, Russell R. Social Movements, Violence, & Change: The May Movement in Curacao. LC 75-6769. (Illus.). 185p. 1975. 12.50 (ISBN 0-8142-0240-3). Ohio St U Pr.

Anderson, William E. & Scott, W. Stephen. Bankruptcy: A Georgia Law Practice System. (Law Practice Systems Ser.). 420p. 1984. 75.00 (ISBN 0-87215-719-9, 69820). Michie Co.

Anderson, William E., jt. auth. see Glover, J. Littleton, Jr.

Anderson, William G. Analysis of Teaching Physical Education. LC 79-20074. 1980. pap. 11.95 (ISBN 0-8016-0179-7). Mosby.

--The Price of Liberty: The Public Debt of the American Revolution. LC 82-17420. 1983. 20.00x (ISBN 0-8139-0975-9). U Pr of Va.

Anderson, William H., jt. auth. see Stowers, Walter H.

Anderson, William J. The Architecture of Ancient Greece. LC 75-41010. Repr. of 1927 ed. 30.00 (ISBN 0-404-14725-9). AMS Pr.

Anderson, William J. & Spiers, Richard P. The Architecture of Ancient Rome: An Account of Its Historic Development. LC 27-24681. 202p. 1927. Repr. 49.00x (ISBN 0-403-08618-3). Somerset Pub.

Anderson, William J., et al. The Architecture of Ancient Rome. facsimile ed. LC 71-37326. (Select Bibliographies Reprint Ser). Repr. of 1927 ed. 51.00 (ISBN 0-8369-6675-9). Ayer Co Pubs.

Anderson, William K., ed. Protestantism. facs. ed. LC 69-18918. (Essay Index Reprint Ser). 1944. 17.50 (ISBN 0-8369-1018-4). Ayer Co Pubs.

Anderson, William L. & Lewis, James A. A Guide to Cherokee Documents in Foreign Archives. LC 83-4636. (Native American Bibliography Ser.: No. 4). 770p. 1983. 37.50 (ISBN 0-8108-1630-X). Scarecrow.

Anderson, William M. The Rocky Mountain Journals of William Marshall Anderson: The West in 1834. Morgan, Dale L. & Harris, Eleanor T., eds. LC 66-25064. (Huntington Library Publications). pap. 107.50 (ISBN 0-317-29233-1, 2055539). Bks Demand UMI.

Anderson, William P. Aspects of the Theology of Karl Barth. LC 81-40163. 198p. (Orig.). 1981. lib. bdg. 22.00 (ISBN 0-8191-1748-X); pap. text ed. 12.50 (ISBN 0-8191-1749-8). U Pr of Amer.

Anderson, William R., ed. see McVaugh, Rogers.

Anderson, William S. Essays on Roman Satire. LC 81-47906. 480p. 1982. cloth 30.00 (ISBN 0-691-05347-2); pap. 13.50 (ISBN 0-691-00791-8). Princeton U Pr.

Anderson, William S., ed. Ovid's Metamorphoses, Bks. 6-10. LC 78-160488. (APA Ser.: Vol. 2). 550p. 1978. pap. 12.95x (ISBN 0-8061-1456-8). U of Okla Pr.

Anderson, William T. Laura Wilder of Mansfield: Laura Ingalls Wilder Biography. (Laura Ingalls Wilder Family Ser.). (Illus.). 36p. 1982. pap. 3.50 (ISBN 0-9610088-1-4). Anderson MI.

--Laura's Rose: The Story of Rose Wilder Lane. (Laura Ingalls Wilder Family Ser.). (Illus.). 48p. (Orig.). 1984. pap. text ed. 3.50 (ISBN 0-9610088-3-0). Anderson MI.

--The Story of the Ingalls. (Laura Ingalls Wilder Family Ser.). (Illus.). 40p. (Orig.). 1971. pap. text ed. 3.50 (ISBN 0-9610088-0-6). Anderson MI.

--The Story of the Wilders. (Laura Ingalls Wilder Family Ser.). (Illus.). 32p. 1983. pap. 3.50 (ISBN 0-9610088-2-2). Anderson MI.

--A Wilder in the West: Eliza Jane's Story of a Lady Homesteader. (Laura Ingalls Wilder Family Ser.). (Illus.). 40p. 1985. pap. 3.50 (ISBN 0-9610088-4-9). Anderson MI.

Anderson, Winifred, et al. Negotiating the Special Education Maze: A Guide for Parents & Teachers. (Illus.). 156p. 1982. 16.95 (ISBN 0-13-611129-7); pap. 7.95 (ISBN 0-13-611111-4). P-H.

Anderson, Wood P. Weed Science: Principles. 2nd ed. (Illus.). 650p. 1983. text ed. 37.95 (ISBN 0-314-69632-6). West Pub.

Anderson-Evangelista, Anita. Hypnosis: A Journey into the Mind. LC 79-5134. (Illus.). 256p. 1981. pap. 6.95 (ISBN 0-668-05134-5). Arco.

--Hypnosis: A Journey into the Mind. LC 79-27817. (Illus.). 256p. 1980. 10.95 (ISBN 0-668-04908-1, 4908-1). Arco.

Anderson-Imbert, E. & Florit, E. Literatura Hispanoamericana, Antologia E Introduccion Historica, 2 Vols. rev ed. LC 70-86101. (Span). 1970. pap. text ed. 19.00 (HoltC); Vol. 1. 27.95 (ISBN 0-03-083454-6); Vol. 2. 27.95 (ISBN 0-03-083455-4). HR&W.

Anderson Imbert, Enrique. Other Side of the Mirrow (el Grimorio) Reade, Isabel, tr. LC 66-11155. (Contemporary Latin American Classic). 239p. 1966. 7.95x (ISBN 0-8093-0227-6). S Ill U Pr.

Anderson-Imbert, Enrique. Spanish American Literature: A History, 2 Vols. 2nd rev. & enl. ed. LC 70-75087. (Waynebooks Ser: Vols. 28-29). pap. 5.95x ea; Vol. 1, 1492-1910, 451 p. pap. (ISBN 0-8143-1386-8); Vol. 2, 1910-1963, 345 p. pap. (ISBN 0-8143-1388-4). Wayne St U Pr.

Anderson-Imbert, Enrique & Kiddle, Lawrence B., eds. Veinte Cuentos Espanoles del Siglo Veinte. (Orig., Span.). (gr. 10-12). 1961. pap. text ed. 16.95 (ISBN 0-13-941567-X). P-H.

--Veinte Cuentos Hispanoamericanos del Siglo Veinte. (Orig., Span.). 1956. pap. 16.95 (ISBN 0-13-941575-0). P-H.

Anderson-Khlief, Susan. Divorced But Not Disasterous: How to Improve the Ties Between Single-Parent Mothers, Divorced Fathers & the Children. 178p. 1982. 11.95 (ISBN 0-13-215632-6); pap. 5.95 (ISBN 0-13-215624-5). P-H.

Anderson-Sannes, Barbara. Alma on the Mississippi, 1848-1932. Doyle, Michael, et al, eds. LC 80-68241. (Illus.). 198p. (Orig.). 1980. pap. 11.95 (ISBN 0-9604684-0-4). Alma Hist Soc.

Anderson Sweeney, David R. & Williams, Thomas A. Introduction to Statistics: An Applications Approach. (Illus.). 750p. text ed. 27.50 (ISBN 0-8299-0361-5). West Pub.

Andersson, et al. Regional & Industrial Development Theories, Models & Empirical Evidence. (Studies in Regional Science & Urban Economics: Vol. 11). 1984. 55.75 (ISBN 0-444-87595-6). Elsevier.

Andersson, Ake E. & Holmberg, Ingvar, eds. Demographic, Economic & Social Interactions. LC 76-2042. 368p. 1977. prof ref 30.00 (ISBN 0-88410-045-6). Ballinger Pub.

Andersson, Aron. Mediaeval Drinking Bowls of Silver Found in Sweden. (Illus.). 118p. 1983. text ed. 15.50x (ISBN 91-7402-121-4, Pub. by Almqvist & Wiksell Sweden). Humanities.

Andersson, Bjorn. Science Teaching & the Development of Thinking. (Goteborg Studies in Educational Sciences: No. 20). (Illus.). 1976. pap. text ed. 18.75x (ISBN 91-7346-026-5). Humanities.

Andersson, Christiane & Talbot, Charles. From a Mighty Fortress: Prints, Drawings, & Books in the Age of Luther, 1483-1546. (Illus.). 410p. (Orig.). 1983. pap. 15.00 (ISBN 0-89558-091-8). Detroit Inst Arts.

Andersson, Efraim. Churches at the Grass Roots: A Study in Congo-Brazzaville. Barton, Dorothea M., tr. from Fr. (World Studies of Churches in Mission). 1968. pap. 3.95 (ISBN 0-377-82811-4, Pub. by Lutterworth England). Friend Pr.

Andersson, Gunnar, ed. Rationality in Science & Politics. 1983. lib. bdg. write for info (Pub. by D. Reidel Holland). Kluwer Academic.

Andersson, Gunnar B., jt. auth. see Chaffin, Don B.

Andersson, Hans. Strindberg's Master Olof & Shakespeare. LC 72-195260. 1952. lib. bdg. 10.00 (ISBN 0-8414-2966-9). Folcroft.

--Strindberg's Master Olof & Shakespeare. (Essays & Studies on English Language & Literature: Vol. 11). Repr. of 1952 ed. 15.00 (ISBN 0-317-16347-7). Kraus Repr.

Andersson, Ingvar. A History of Sweden. Hannay, Carolyn, tr. from Swed. LC 75-8717. (Illus.). 461p. 1975. Repr. of 1968 ed. lib. bdg. 27.25x (ISBN 0-8371-8044-9, ANHS). Greenwood.

Andersson, Johan G. Children of the Yellow Earth. 1973. pap. 4.95x (ISBN 0-262-51011-1). MIT Pr.

--Children of the Yellow Earth: Studies in Prehistoric China. 1976. lib. bdg. 59.95 (ISBN 0-8490-1602-9). Gordon Pr.

Andersson, L., ed. Diagnostic Radiology, Supplement: Radionuclides in Urology- Urological Ultrasonography- Percutaneous Puncture Nephrostomy. LC 58-4788. (Handbuch der Urology-Encyclopedia of Urology: Vol. 5, Pt. 1). (Illus.). 1977. 64.00 (ISBN 0-387-07896-7). Springer-Verlag.

Andersson, Ola. Studies in the Prehistory of Psychoneuroses: The Etiology of Psychoneuroses & Some Related Themes in Sigmund Freud's Scientific Writings & Letters, 1886-1896. 245p. 1962. pap. text ed. 20.00x (ISBN 0-686-27249-8). Gach Bks.

Andersson, Otto. The Bowed Harp. Schlesinger, Kathleen, tr. from Ger. LC 77-8733. 1977. Repr. of 1930 ed. lib. bdg. 30.00 (ISBN 0-89341-080-2). Longwood Pub Group.
Andersson, Otto E. The Bowed Harp, a Study in the History of Early Musical Instruments. rev. ed. Schlesinger, Kathleen, ed. Stenback, Mary, tr. Repr. of 1930 ed. 29.00 (ISBN 0-404-56503-4). AMS Pr.
Andersson, S., jt. ed. see Holle, F.
Andersson, S. I. & Doebner, H. D., eds. Non-linear Partial Differential Operators & Quantization Procedures. (Lecture Notes in Mathematics: Vol. 1037). 334p. 1983. pap. 17.00 (ISBN 0-387-12710-0). Springer Verlag.
Andersson, Theodore. Carlos Maria Ocantos, Argentine Novelist: A Study of Indigenous French & Spanish Elements in His Work. LC 70-38485. (Yale Romanic Studies: No. 8). Repr. of 1934 ed. 22.00 (ISBN 0-404-53208-X). AMS Pr.
--A Guide to Family Reading in Two Languages: The Preschool Years. 81p. (Orig.). 1981. pap. 1.25 (ISBN 0-89755-055-2). Natl Clearinghse Bilingual Ed.
Andersson, Theodore & Boyer, Mildred. Bilingual Schooling in the United States, 2 vols. LC 76-5907. 1976. Repr. of 1970 ed. 42.50 set (ISBN 0-87917-050-6). Ethridge.
--Bilingual Schooling in the United States. 2nd ed. LC 77-89939. 1978. pap. text ed. 18.50x (ISBN 0-931052-08-4, EB-001). AAR-Tantalus.
--Bilingual Schooling in the United States. 2nd ed. LC 77-89939. xx, 474p. 1984. Repr. of 1978 ed. text ed. 18.50x (ISBN 0-931052-08-4). AAR Tantalus.
Andersson, Theodore see Kellenberger, Hunter.
Andersson, Theodore M. The Legend of Brynhild. (Islandica Ser.: Vol. XLII). 288p. 1980. 29.95x (ISBN 0-8014-1302-8). Cornell U Pr.
Anderton, Basil. Fragrance Among Old Volumes: Essays & Idylls of a Book Lover. facs. ed. LC 67-30171. (Essay Index Reprint Ser). 1910. 17.00 (ISBN 0-8369-0153-3). Ayer Co Pubs.
--Sketches from a Library Window. facs. ed. LC 68-16903. (Essay Index Reprint Ser). 1923. 15.00 (ISBN 0-8369-0154-1). Ayer Co Pubs.
Anderton, Craig. Electronic Projects for Musicians. rev. ed. (Illus.). 140p. pap. 14.95 (ISBN 0-8256-9502-3). Music Sales.
--Guitar Gadgets. 1983. pap. 14.95 (ISBN 0-8256-2214-X, Amsco Music). Music Sales.
--Home Recording for Musicians. (Illus.). 300p. pap. 14.95 (ISBN 0-89122-019-4). Music Sales.
Anderton, David. B-29 Super Fortress at War. (Illus.). 1978. 19.95 (ISBN 0-684-15884-1, ScribT). Scribner.
--Republic F-105 Thunderchief. (Illus.). 200p. 1983. 19.95 (ISBN 0-85045-530-8, Pub. by Osprey England). Motorbooks Intl.
Anderton, H. Orsmond, ed. see Melvill, David.
Anderton, Johana G. Collector's Encyclopedia of Cloth Dolls. LC 82-51232. 376p. 1985. 39.95 (ISBN 0-87069-402-2). Wallace-Homestead.
--More Twentieth Century Dolls, Vol. 2, I-Z. (Illus.). 365p. 19.95 (ISBN 0-87069-292-5). Wallace-Homestead.
--More Twentieth Century Dolls: Vol. 1, A-H. (Illus.). 1979. 19.95 (ISBN 0-87069-273-9). Wallace-Homestead.
--Sewing for Twentieth Century Dolls. (Illus.). 264p. 19.95 (ISBN 0-87069-276-3). Wallace-Homestead.
--Twentieth Century Dolls: From Bisque to Vinyl. rev. ed. (Illus.). 29.95 (ISBN 0-87069-272-0). Wallace-Homestead.
Anderton, Nancy. Forms. (gr. 7-12). 1983. pap. 5.00 (ISBN 0-8224-3056-8). Pitman Learning.
Anderton, Nancy, ed. see McGuire, Marion L. & Bumpus, Marguerite J.
Anderton, R., et al. A Dynamic Stratigraphy of the British Isles. (Illus.). 1979. text ed. 35.00x (ISBN 0-04-551027-X); pap. text ed. 22.95x (ISBN 0-04-551028-8). Allen Unwin.
Andia, Ernest. The Complex World of My Thoughts. 112p. 1984. 8.95 (ISBN 0-89962-342-5). Todd & Honeywell.
--The Iron on Call. 1983. 11.95 (ISBN 0-533-05847-3). Vantage.
Andino, Alberto. Frutos De Mi Trasplante. LC 79-52356. (Coleccion Caniqui). 102p. (Span.). 1980. pap. 5.95 (ISBN 0-89729-230-8). Ediciones.
Andison, Mabelle L., tr. see Bergson, Henri L.
Andjelic, Alex & Hearns, Doug. European Hockey Drill Book. pap. 8.95 (ISBN 0-7706-0037-9). Van Nos Reinhold.
Andler, Kenneth. Mission to Fort No. Four. (N. H.-Vermont Historiettes). (Illus.). 64p. (gr. 6-7). 1975. 4.95 (ISBN 0-915892-04-9); pap. 1.95 (ISBN 0-915892-15-4). Regional Ctr Educ.
Ando. Comprehensive Atlas of Maxillofacial Radiology. 1985. price not set (ISBN 0-912791-17-9). Ishiyaku Euro.
Ando, Albert, et al. The Structure & Reform of the U. S. Tax System. 184p. 1985. 16.95 (ISBN 0-262-01086-0). MIT Pr.
Ando, Albert, et al, eds. Monetary Policy in Our Times. (Illus.). 356p. 1985. text ed. 25.00x (ISBN 0-262-01082-8). MIT Pr.
Ando, Cheryl, tr. see Suwa, Shigeo & Suwa, Shizuko.
Ando, Hirofumi, jt. auth. see Ness, Gayl D.
Ando, Isal & Webb, Graham A. Theory of NMR Parameters. 1984. 57.50 (ISBN 0-12-056820-9). Acad Pr.
Ando, Sadao, ed. A Descriptive Syntax of Christopher Marlowe's Language. 721p. 1976. 70.00 (ISBN 0-86008-162-1, Pub. by U of Tokyo Japan). Columbia U Pr.
Ando, Shoei. Zen & American Transcendentalism. 1970. 14.95 (ISBN 0-89346-022-2, Pub. by Hokuseido Pr). Heian Intl.
Ando, T., et al. Protamines: Isolation, Characterization, Structure & Function. LC 73-77821. (Molecular Biology, Biochemistry & Biophysics Ser: Vol. 12). (Illus.). 114p. 1973. 34.00 (ISBN 0-387-06221-1). Springer-Verlag.
Ando, W. Photo Oxidation of Organo-Sulfur Compounds. (Sulfur Reports Ser.). 80p. 1981. flexicover 22.00 (ISBN 3-7186-0073-0). Harwood Academic.
Ando, Y. Concert Hall Acoustics. (Springer Series in Electrophysics: Vol. 17). (Illus.). 170p. 1985. 41.50 (ISBN 0-387-13505-7). Springer-Verlag.
Andoh, Elizabeth. At Home with Japanese Cooking. LC 79-3501. (Illus.). 228p. 1980. 15.00 (ISBN 0-394-41219-2). Knopf.
Andolenko, S. Badges of Imperial Russia Including Military, Civil & Religious. Werlich, R., tr. (Illus.). 1983. lib. bdg. 36.00 (ISBN 0-685-00798-7). Quaker.
Andolfi, Maurizio. Family Therapy: An Interactional Approach. LC 78-27741. 186p. 1979. 24.95x (ISBN 0-306-40200-9, Plenum Pr). Plenum Pub.
Andolfi, Maurizio & Angelo, Claudio. Behind the Family Mask: Therapeutic Changes in Rigid Family Systems. LC 82-22817. 184p. 1983. 22.50 (ISBN 0-87630-330-0). Brunner-Mazel.
Andolfi, Maurizio, ed. Dimensions of Family Therapy. Zwerling, Israel. LC 79-25485. (Guilford Family Therapy Ser.). 280p. 1980. text ed. 20.00 (ISBN 0-89862-601-3). Guilford Pr.
Andolsen, Barbara H., et al, eds. Women's Consciousness, Women's Conscience: A Reader in Feminist Ethics. 340p. 1985. 24.95 (ISBN 0-86683-958-5, AY8540, Pub. by Seabury). Winston Pr.
Andonov, B. T., compiled by. Nuclear Power Economics, Vol. 1. (Bibliographical Ser.: No. 13). 145p. 1966. pap. (ISBN 92-0-154064-7, STI/PUB/21/13, IAEA). Unipub.
Andor, Jozsef. Frame Semantics & the Typology of Actions. (Pragmatics & Beyond Ser.). 120p. 1986. pap. 18.00 (ISBN 90-272-2521-4). Benjamins North Am.
Andors, Phyllis. The Unfinished Liberation of Chinese Women, 1949-1980. LC 81-48323. 224p. 1983. 22.50x (ISBN 0-253-36022-6). Ind U Pr.
Andors, Stephen, ed. Workers & Workplaces in Revolutionary China. Mathews, Jay, et al, trs. LC 76-53710. (The China Book Project Ser.). 440p. 1977. 30.00 (ISBN 0-87332-094-8). M E Sharpe.
Andothers, A, jt. auth. see Murray, H.
Andover, James J., ed. see Barzman, Sol.
Andover, James J., ed. see Berman, Ben.
Andover, James J., ed. see Bryan, William H.
Andover, James J., ed. see Mott, Sheryl S.
Andover, James J., jt. ed. see Nelson, Lester.
Andover, James J., ed. see Rutherford, R. D.
Andover, James J., ed. see Schermerhorn, Derick D.
Andover, James J., ed. see Taylor, Mary S.
Andover, James J., ed. see Viscione, Jerry A.
Andover, James J., ed. see Weintraub, Benjamin.
Andracki, Stanislaw. Immigration of Orientals into Canada with Special Reference to Chinese. Daniels, Roger, ed. LC 78-54806. (Asian Experience in North America Ser.). (Illus.). 1979. lib. bdg. 21.00x (ISBN 0-405-11262-9). Ayer Co Pubs.
Andrade. Introduccion a la Ciencia Politica. 400p. (Span.). 1982. pap. text ed. write for info. (ISBN 0-06-310030-4, Pub. by HarLA Mexico). Har-Row.
Andrade, Carlos D. The Minus Sign. De Araujo, Virginia, ed. (Illus.). 160p. 1981. 17.50 (ISBN 0-933806-03-5). Black Swan CT.
Andrade, E. N. An Approach to Modern Physics. 11.25 (ISBN 0-8446-0456-9). Peter Smith.
--Isaac Newton. 1979. Repr. of 1950 ed. lib. bdg. 16.00 (ISBN 0-8414-3014-4). Folcroft.
--Isaac Newton. 1950. 17.50 (ISBN 0-932062-04-0). Sharon Hill.
--Rutherford & the Nature of the Atom. (Illus.). 11.25 (ISBN 0-8446-2053-X). Peter Smith.
Andrade, E. N., intro. by. Classics in Science. LC 71-122975. (Essay & General Literature Index Reprint Ser). 1971. Repr. of 1960 ed. 23.50x (ISBN 0-8046-1356-7, Pub. by Kennikat). Assoc Faculty Pr.
Andrade, Edward N. Sir Isaac Newton. LC 79-15162. 140p. 1979. Repr. of 1958 ed. lib. bdg. 22.50x (ISBN 0-313-22022-0, ANNE). Greenwood.
Andrade, Eugenio de see De Andrade, Eugenio.
Andrade, John M. World Police & Paramilitary Forces. 300p. 1985. 90.00x (ISBN 0-943818-14-1). Stockton Pr.
Andrade, Jose M., ed. see National Gallery of Art.
Andrade, Joseph D., ed. Hydrogels for Medical & Related Applications. LC 76-28170. (ACS Symposium Ser: No. 31). 1976. 29.95 (ISBN 0-8412-0338-5). Am Chemical.
--Surface & Interfacial Aspects of Biomedical Polymers, Vol. 1: Surface Chemistry & Physics. 486p. 1985. 69.50x (ISBN 0-306-41741-3, Plenum Pr). Plenum Pub.
Andrade, Luis. Instrumentos De Placer. (Pimienta Collection Ser). 1976. pap. 1.25 (ISBN 0-88473-252-5). Fiesta Pub.
Andrade, Luis F., et al: The Political, Economic & Labor Climate in Brazil. rev. ed. (Multinational Industrial Relations Ser.: No. 4). (Illus.). 300p. 1986. pap. 20.00 (ISBN 0-89546-057-2). Indus Res Unit-Wharton.
Andrade, M. J., ed. Folk-Lore from the Dominican Republic. LC 33-10559. (American Folklore Social Theories Ser.). Repr. of 1930 ed. 37.00 (ISBN 0-527-01075-8). Kraus Repr.
Andrade, Magdalema, jt. auth. see Terrell, Tracy David.
Andrade, Manuel C. The Land & People of Northeast Brazil. Johnson, Dennis V., tr. from Port. LC 79-2309. 1980. 19.95x (ISBN 0-8263-0520-2). U of NM Pr.
Andrade, Manuel C. de see Andrade, Manuel C.
Andrade, Manuel J. Folklore de la Republica Dominicana, 2 vols. 1976. Set. lib. bdg. 250.00 (ISBN 0-8490-1850-1). Gordon Pr.
--Quileute. pap. 5.00 (ISBN 0-685-71707-0). J J Augustin.
--Quileute Texts. LC 75-82358. (Columbia Univ. Contributions to Anthropology Ser.: Vol. 12). Repr. of 1931 ed. 27.50 (ISBN 0-404-50562-7). AMS Pr.
Andrade, Mario D. Fraulein. Hollingworth, Margaret R., tr. 1977. lib. bdg. 59.95 (ISBN 0-8490-1864-1). Gordon Pr.
Andrade, Mario De. Hallucinated City. Tomlins, Jack E., tr. LC 68-20547. (Eng. & Port.). 1968. 7.95 (ISBN 0-8265-1113-9). Vanderbilt U Pr.
Andrade, Mario De see Andrade, Mario De.
Andrade, Oswald De see De Andrade, Oswald.
Andrade, Rafael, et al, eds. Cancer of the Skin: Biology-Diagnosis-Management. LC 73-91274. (Illus.). 1661p. 1976. text ed. 100.00x set (ISBN 0-7216-1247-4); Vol. 1. text ed. 50.00 (ISBN 0-7216-1245-8); Vol. 2. text ed. 50.00 (ISBN 0-7216-1246-6). Saunders.
Andrade, Sally, jt. auth. see Chapa, Evey.
Andrade, Sally J., ed. Latino Families in the United States: A Resourcebook for Family Life Education. LC 82-22321. (Illus.). 176p. (Orig., Eng. & Span.). 1983. pap. text ed. 14.00 (ISBN 0-934586-10-1). Plan Parent.
Andrade, Victor. My Missions for Revolutionary Bolivia 1944-1962. LC 76-6656. (Pitt Latin American Ser). Repr. of 1976 ed. 54.30 (ISBN 0-8357-9758-9, 2017863). Bks Demand UMI.
Andrae, Gunilla. Industry in West Ghana. 181p. 1982. pap. 24.50x (ISBN 0-8419-9739-X). Holmes & Meier.
Andrae, Tor. Mohammed: The Man & His Faith. facsimile ed. Menzel, Theophil, tr. LC 79-160954. (Select Bibliographies Reprint Ser). Repr. of 1936 ed. 19.00 (ISBN 0-8369-5821-7). Ayer Co Pubs.
Andrain, Charles F. Social Policies in Western Industrial Societies. LC 85-10840. (Research Ser.: No. 61). (Illus.). xi, 256p. 1985. pap. 11.95x (ISBN 0-87725-161-4). U of Cal Intl St.
Andras, L. How to Say It in Hungarian. 6th ed. 1984. 5.00 (ISBN 0-317-18966-2, H275). Vanous.
Andras, L. T. & Murval, M. How to Say It in Hungarian: An English-Hungarian Phrase-Book with Lists of Words. 6th ed. (Illus., Eng. & Hungarian.). 1979. 7.50 (ISBN 9-6317-4194-X). Heinman.
Andras, L. T. & Murval, M., eds. How to Say It in Hungarian. 238p. 1985. pap. 4.95 (ISBN 0-87052-158-6). Hippocrene Bks.
Andras, M. Hungarian: How to Say It in. 6th ed. 1979. 5.00x (ISBN 9-6317-4194-X, H275). Vanous.
Andrasik, Frank, jt. auth. see Blanchard, Edward B.
Andrasik, Frank, jt. ed. see Matson, Johnny L.
Andrasko, Kenneth, jt. auth. see Halevi, Marcus.
Andrasko, Kenneth, ed. see Setnicka, Timothy J.
Andrassy, Gyula. Bismarck, Andrassy, & Their Successors. 18.25 (ISBN 0-8369-7101-9, 7935). Ayer Co Pubs.
Andrassy, Juraj. International Law & the Resources of the Sea. LC 76-130960. (International Legal Studies). (Illus.). 191p. 1970. 26.00x (ISBN 0-231-03409-1). Columbia U Pr.
Andrassy, Stella. The Solar Cookbook. LC 79-88818. 128p. 1981. pap. 5.95 (ISBN 0-87100-142-X, 2142). Morgan.
Andre. Corporations: Formation with Forms. (The Law in Louisiana Ser.). incl. latest pocket part supplement 24.95 (ISBN 0-686-90596-2); separate pocket part supplement, 1983 9.45. Harrison Co GA.
--Course Alphabetique et Methodique de Droit Canon, 2 vols. Migne, J. P., ed. (Encyclopedie Theologique Ser.: Vols. 9-10). 1318p. (Fr.). Repr. of 1845 ed. lib. bdg. 168.00x (ISBN 0-89241-234-8). Caratzas.
--Dictionnaire Alphabetique, Theorique et Pratique de Droit Civil Ecclesiastique, 2 vols. Migne, J. P., ed. (Troisieme et Derniere Encyclopedie Theologique Ser.: Vols. 64-65). 1332p. (Fr.). Repr. of 1873 ed. lib. bdg. 170.00x (ISBN 0-89241-328-X). Caratzas.
Andre, Evelyn, compiled by. Rejoice & Sing Praise: A Collection of Songs & Materials to Be Used with Elementary Boys & Girls. LC 77-1604. 1977. pap. 9.95 (ISBN 0-687-35930-9). Abingdon.
--Sing & Be Joyful: Enjoying Music with Young Children. LC 79-14787. 1979. pap. 7.95 (ISBN 0-687-38547-4). Abingdon.
Andre, Evelyn M. Places I Like to Be. LC 79-23964. (Illus.). (gr. k-11). 1980. 7.75g (ISBN 0-687-31540-9). Abingdon.
Andre, F. & Herman, D. Synchronization of Parallel Programs. (Scientific Computation Ser.). 144p. 1985. text ed. 20.00x (ISBN 0-262-01085-2). MIT Pr.
Andre, G. David, the Man after God's Own Heart. (Let's Discuss It Ser.). pap. 2.50 (ISBN 0-88172-134-4). Believers Bkshelf.
--Gideon, Samson & Other Judges of Israel. (Let's Discuss It Ser.). pap. 1.95 (ISBN 0-88172-132-8). Believers Bkshelf.
--Jeremiah, the Prophet. (Let's Discuss It Ser.). pap. 1.95 (ISBN 0-88172-135-2). Believers Bkshelf.
--Moses, the Man of God. 47p. pap. 1.95 (ISBN 0-88172-131-X). Believers Bkshelf.
Andre, J., et al, eds. Quantum Theory of Polymers. (NATO Advanced Study Inst. Ser.). 1978. lib. bdg. 45.00 (ISBN 90-277-0870-3, Pub. by Reidel Holland). Kluwer Academic.
Andre, J. J., jt. auth. see Simon, J.
Andre, J. M., et al, eds. Recent Advances in the Quantum Theory of Polymers: Proceedings. (Lecture Notes in Physics: Vol. 113). 306p. 1980. pap. 26.00 (ISBN 3-540-09731-7). Springer-Verlag.
Andre, Jean, ed. The Sperm Cell. 1983. 71.75 (ISBN 90-247-2784-7, Pub. by Martinus Nijhoff Netherlands). Kluwer Academic.
Andre, Jean-Marie & Ladik, Janos, eds. Electronic Structure of Polymers & Molecular Crystals. LC 75-12643. (NATO ASI Series B, Physics: Vol. 9). 704p. 1975. 95.00x (ISBN 0-306-35709-7, Plenum Pr). Plenum Pub.
Andre, Jean-Marie, jt. ed. see Ladik, Janos.
Andre, Johann. Belmont und Constnze. (German Opera Ser.). 300p. 1985. lib. bdg. 65.00 (ISBN 0-8240-8855-7). Garland Pub.
--Der Topfer (Hanau, 1773) Lampedo (Darmstadt, 1779) Fernando und Yariko (Munich, 1784) Bauman, Thomas, ed. (German Opera Ser., 1770-1800). 75.00 (ISBN 0-8240-8858-1). Garland Pub.
Andre, John. Major Andre's Journal. LC 67-29031. (Eyewitness Accounts of the American Revolution Ser.: No. 1). 1968. Repr. of 1930 ed. 16.00 (ISBN 0-405-01103-2). Ayer Co Pubs.
Andre, Lucien St. see St. Andre, Lucien.
Andre, Lyn. Good Morning World. LC 74-31663. (Illus.). 1975. 10.95 (ISBN 0-930422-06-6). Dennis-Landman.
Andre, Michael. Letters Home. 24p. 1979. pap. 1.50 (ISBN 0-916696-14-6). Cross Country.
--Studying the Ground for Holes. LC 78-5184. (Illus.). 1978. pap. 3.00 (ISBN 0-913722-14-6, Pub by Release). Small Pr Dist.
Andre, Michael, ed. Unmuzzled Ox Anthology, No. 15. Barnes, Djuna, et al. (Illus.). pap. 4.95 (ISBN 0-686-28478-X). Unmuzzled Ox.
Andre, Michael, ed. see Cage, John, et al.
Andre, Michael, ed. see Corso, Gregory.
Andre, Michael, ed. see Wright, James, et al.
Andre, Michael, et al, eds. see Stafford, William.
Andre, Nevin, jt. auth. see Palmore, Phyllis.
Andre, Nils, jt. ed. see Allardt, Erik.
Andre, Rae. Homemakers: The Forgotten Workers. LC 80-21258. 320p. 1981. 20.00x (ISBN 0-226-01993-4); pap. 8.95 (ISBN 0-226-01994-2). U of Chicago Pr.
Andre, Rae & Ward, Peter. The Fifty-Nine Second Employee: How to Stay One Second Ahead of Your One-Minute Manager. 112p. 1984. pap. 5.95 (ISBN 0-395-35630-X). HM.
Andrea, Alfred J. & Schmokel, W. The Living Past: Western Historiographical Traditions. LC 81-20878. 314p. 1982. Repr. of 1975 ed. 18.50 (ISBN 0-89874-152-1). Krieger.
Andrea, Raymond. Technique of the Disciple. 4th ed. 187p. 1981. pap. 9.00 (ISBN 0-912057-12-2, G-643). AMORC.
--The Technique of the Master. 12th ed. 1981. 9.00 (ISBN 0-912057-10-6, G-513). AMORC.
Andrea, Raymund. La Tecnica del Maestro. 173p. (Orig., Span.). 1984. pap. 7.00 (ISBN 0-912057-85-8, GS-513). AMORC.
Andreach, Robert J. Studies in Structure: The Stages of the Spiritual Life in Four Modern Authors. LC 64-24755. xii, 177p. 1965. 20.00 (ISBN 0-8232-0630-0). Fordham.
--Studies in Structure: The Stages of the Spiritual Life in Four Modern Authors. xii, 177p. 1965. 20.00 (ISBN 0-317-26951-8). Fordham.
Andreades, A. History of the Bank of England. 59.95 (ISBN 0-87968-254-X). Gordon Pr.
Andreades, A. M. History of the Bank of England. Meredith, C., tr. 455p. 1966. 35.00x (ISBN 0-7146-1203-0, BHA 01203, F Cass Co). Biblio Dist.
Andreades, A. M. & Finley, Moses, eds. A History of Greek Public Finance, Vol. I. rev. & enl. ed. Brown, Carroll N., tr. LC 79-4959. (Ancient Economic History Ser.). 1980. Repr. of 1933 ed. lib. bdg. 37.00x (ISBN 0-405-12347-7). Ayer Co Pubs.

Andreades, Andreas M. History of the Bank of England, 1640 to 1903. 4th ed. Meredith, C., tr. LC 66-31537. Repr. of 1909 ed. 35.00x (ISBN 0-678-05023-6). Kelley.

Andreadis, Harriette, ed. see Lyly, John.

Andreae, B. The Economics of Tropical Agriculture. 170p. 1980. 50.00x (ISBN 0-85198-453-3, Pub. by CAB Bks England). State Mutual Bk.

Andreae, Bernard. The Art of Rome. LC 75-8855. (Illus.). 1978. 125.00 (ISBN 0-8109-0626-0). Abrams.

Andreae, Bernd. Allgemeine Agrargeographie. (Sammlung Goeschen Ser.: No. 2624). (Illus.). 219p. (Ger.). 1984. pap. text ed. 11.90x (ISBN 3-11-010076-2). De Gruyter.

--Farming, Development, & Space: A World Agricultural Geography. (Illus.). 345p. 1981. 31.20 (ISBN 3-11-007632-2). De Gruyter.

Andreae, Christine. Seances & Spiritualists. LC 74-8044. (Weird & Horrible Library). (Illus.). 160p. (gr. 6 up). 1974. pap. 1.95 (ISBN 0-397-31583-X). Lipp Jr Bks.

Andreae, J. P. Fockema. An Important Chapter from the History of Legal Interpretation. 1983. Repr. of 1948 ed. lib. bdg. 30.00 (ISBN 0-89941-274-2). W S Hein.

Andreae, John H. Thinking with the Teachable Machine. 1978. 37.00 (ISBN 0-12-060050-1). Acad Pr.

Andreani, Dominico, et al, eds. Current Views on Hypoglycemia & Glucagon: Proceedings. LC 79-41558. (Serono Symposia: No. 30). 1980. 69.50 (ISBN 0-12-058680-0). Acad Pr.

Andreano, Ralph & Siegfried, John J., eds. The Economics of Crime. LC 78-8601. 426p. 1980. pap. text ed. 10.50x (ISBN 0-470-26837-9). Halsted Pr.

Andreas. Energy-Efficient Electric Motors. (Electrical Engineering & Electronic Ser.: Vol. 15). 200p. 1982. 35.00 (ISBN 0-8247-1786-4). Dekker.

Andreas, Alfred T. History of Chicago: From the Earliest Period to the Present Time, 3 vols. facsimile ed. LC 75-80. (Mid-American Frontier Ser.). (Illus.). 1975. Repr. of 1884 ed. Set. 260.00x (ISBN 0-405-06846-8); Vol. 1. 77.00x (ISBN 0-405-06847-6); Vol. 2. 86.00x (ISBN 0-405-06848-4); Vol. 3. 101.50x (ISBN 0-405-06849-2). Ayer Co Pubs.

Andreas, Barbara, et al. Ohio Endangered & Threatened Vascular Plants: Abstract of State-Listed Taxa. McCance, Robert M., Jr. & Burns, James F., eds. LC 84-620010. xii, 635p. (Orig.). 1984. pap. 15.00 (ISBN 0-931079-00-4). Ohio Nat Res.

Andreas, Burton G. Experimental Psychology. 2nd ed. LC 78-171910. (Series in Psychology). (Illus.). 1972. pap. 155.50 (ISBN 0-317-08136-5, 2055488). Bks Demand UMI.

Andreas, Carol. Nothing Is As It Should Be: A North American Woman in Chile. LC 76-7836. (Illus.). 140p. 1976. pap. text ed. 8.95x (ISBN 0-87073-779-1). Schenkman Bks Inc.

--Sex & Caste in America. 1971. 12.95 (ISBN 0-13-807420-8, Spec); pap. 2.95 (ISBN 0-13-807438-0). P-H.

--When Women Rebel: The Rise of Popular Feminism in Peru. 1985. 19.95 (ISBN 0-88208-197-7); pap. 12.95 (ISBN 0-88208-196-9). Lawrence Hill.

Andreas, Connirae, ed. see Bandler, Richard.

Andreas, Connirae, ed. see Bandler, Richard & Grinder, John.

Andreas, Connirae, ed. see Grinder, John & Bandler, Richard.

Andreas, Osborn. Henry James & the Expanding Horizon. LC 72-90463. Repr. of 1948 ed. lib. bdg. 24.75 (ISBN 0-8371-2133-7, ANJH). Greenwood.

--Joseph Conrad: A Study in Non-Conformity. 212p. 1969. Repr. of 1959 ed. 17.50 (ISBN 0-208-00790-3, Archon). Shoe String.

Andreas, Steve, ed. see Bandler, Richard & Grinder, John.

Andreas, Steve, tr. see Bandler, Richard.

Andreas Capellanus. Art of Courtly Love. Parry, John J., tr. 1969. pap. text ed. 6.95x (ISBN 0-393-09848-6, NortonC). Norton.

Andreasen, A. & Gardner, D., eds. Diffusing Marketing Theory & Research: The Contributions of Bauer, Green, Kotler & Levitt. LC 78-1544. (Proceedings Ser.). 1979. 13.00 (ISBN 0-87757-116-3). Am Mktg.

Andreasen, Alan R. The Disadvantaged Consumer. LC 75-2805. (Illus.). 1975. 21.95 (ISBN 0-02-900690-2). Free Pr.

Andreasen, Alan R. & Sturdivant, Frederick D., eds. Minorities & Marketing: Research Challenges. LC 77-6819. pap. 37.50 (ISBN 0-317-27630-1, 2014626). Bks Demand UMI.

Andreasen, J. O. Traumatic Injuries of the Teeth. 2nd ed. (Illus.). 462p. 1981. 75.00 (ISBN 0-7216-1249-0). Saunders.

Andreasen, M. Myrup, et al. Design for Assembly. 189p. (Eng.). 1983. 41.50 (ISBN 0-387-12544-2). Springer-Verlag.

--Design for Assembly. 189p. 1983. 46.00 (ISBN 0-317-18026-6). Robot Inst Am.

Andreasen, Nancy. The Broken Brain: The Biological Revolution in Psychiatry. LC 83-48782. (Illus.). 288p. 1985. pap. 8.95 (ISBN 0-06-091272-3, PL 1272, PL). Har-Row.

Andreasen, Nancy C. The Broken Brain: The Biological Revolution in Psychiatry. LC 83-48782. (Illus.). 304p. 1984. 17.26i (ISBN 0-06-015281-8, HarpT). Har-Row.

--Can Schizophrenia Be Localized in the Brain? (Progress in Psychiatry Ser.). 100p. 1985. casebound 15.95x (ISBN 0-88048-084-X, 48-084-X). Am Psychiatric.

Andreasen, Niels-Erik. The Christian Use of Time. LC 78-847. 1978. pap. 5.50 (ISBN 0-687-07630-7). Abingdon.

Andreasen, Niels-Erik A. The Old Testament Sabbath: A Tradition-Historical Investigation. LC 72-88671. (Society of Biblical Literature. Dissertation Ser.). 1974. pap. 9.00 (ISBN 0-89130-683-8, 060107). Scholars Pr GA.

Andreason, Neils-Erik. Rest & Redemption: A Study of the Biblical Sabbath. (Andrews University Monographs, Studies in Religion: Vol. XI). vii, 137p. 1978. pap. 3.95 (ISBN 0-943872-11-1). Andrews Univ Pr.

Andreas-Salome, L. Frederic Nietzsche. 310p. 1971. 30.25 (ISBN 0-677-50405-5). Gordon.

Andreassen, A. T., jt. auth. see Ansteinsson, J.

Andreassi, John L. Psychophysiology: Human Behavior & Physiological Response. 1980. pap. 15.95x (ISBN 0-19-502581-4). Oxford U Pr.

Andreassi, Michael W. & MacRae, C. Duncan. Homeowner Income Tax Provisions & Metropolitan Housing Markets: A Simulation Study. LC 81-51624. 78p. 1981. pap. 9.00x (ISBN 0-87766-297-5, URI 29900). Urban Inst.

Andrecht, Venus C. The Herb Lady's Notebook, an Outrageous Herbal. LC 83-63072. (Illus.). 170p. (Orig.). 1984. pap. 9.95 (ISBN 0-9604342-4-0). Ransom Hill.

--The Outrageous Herb Lady: How to Make a Mint in Selling & Multi-Level Marketing. McWhorter, Margaret L., ed. LC 82-60388. 144p. (Orig.). 1982. pap. 6.95 (ISBN 0-9604342-2-4). Ransom Hill.

Andree, E. M., et al, trs. see Palmberg, Mai.

Andree, Herb, jt. auth. see Young, Noel.

Andree, Josephine & Andree, Richard. Cryptarithms. 1978. pap. 2.95 (ISBN 0-686-23790-0); instructor's manual 2.00 (ISBN 0-686-28564-6). Mu Alpha Theta.

--Logic Unlocks. 1979. pap. 2.00 (ISBN 0-686-28235-3); tchr's ed. 2.00. Mu Alpha Theta.

Andree, Josephine P., jt. auth. see Andree, Richard V.

Andree, Josephine P., ed. Chips from the Mathematical Log. (YA) 1966. pap. 2.00 (ISBN 0-686-00750-6). Mu Alpha Theta.

--Lines from the O. U. Mathematics Letter. Incl. Vol. 1. Number Extensions. pap. 1.60 (ISBN 0-685-39271-6); Vol. 2. Theory of Games. pap. 0.95 (ISBN 0-685-39272-4); Vol. 3. Geometric Extensions. pap. 1.60 (ISBN 0-685-39273-2). (gr. 9-12). 1971. Vol. 1, Number Expressions, 102p, 1.60. pap. Vol. 2, Theory of Games, 42p, .95. Vol. 3, Geometric Extensions, 102p, 1.60. NCTM.

--Lines from the O. U. Mathematics Letter. Incl. Vol. 1, Number Extensions. 1.00; Vol. 2, Theory of GAmes. 0.75; Vol. 3, Geometric Extensions. 1.25. Mu Alpha Theta.

Andree, Josephine P, ed. More Chips from the Mathematical Log. pap. 1.25 (ISBN 0-686-00324-1). Mu Alpha Theta.

Andree, Mary. Movie Trivia! Everything You Always Knew About Movies...but Thought You Forgot. Pohl, Jude C., ed. 70p. (Orig.). 1977. pap. 3.95 (ISBN 0-939332-01-9). Pohl Assoc.

Andree, Richard, jt. auth. see Andree, Josephine.

Andree, Richard V. & Andree, Josephine P. Explore Computing with the TRS-80 & with Programming in BASIC. (Illus.). 256p. 1982. pap. text ed. 12.95 (ISBN 0-13-296137-7). P-H.

Andree, Robert G. Collective Negotiations: A Guide to School Board-Teacher Relations. LC 74-121401. 1970. 39.50x (ISBN 0-89197-704-X). Irvington.

Andreen, Gustav. The Idyl in German Literature. LC 6-19423. (Augustana College Library Publication Ser.: No. 3). 96p. 1902. pap. 1.00 (ISBN 0-910182-01-9). Augustana Coll.

Andreev, A. E., et al. Twelve Papers on Function Theory, Probability, & Differential Equations. LC 51-5559. (Translations Ser.: No. 2, Vol. 8). 1957. 43.00 (ISBN 0-8218-1708-6, TRANS 2-8). Am Math.

Andreev, Boris V. Sleep Therapy in Neuroses. Haigh, Basil, tr. LC 60-13947. (International Behavioral Science Ser.). pap. 30.30 (ISBN 0-317-09869-1, 2020659). Bks Demand UMI.

Andreev, K. Konstantinopol'skie Patriarkhi Ot Vremeni Khalkidonskago Sobora Do Fotiya. LC 80-2353. Repr. of 1895 ed. 38.50 (ISBN 0-404-18901-6). AMS Pr.

Andreev, Leonid N. He Who Gets Slapped: A Play in Four Acts. Zilboorg, Gregory, tr. LC 74-14348. (Illus.). 193p. 1975. Repr. of 1922 ed. lib. bdg. 24.75 (ISBN 0-8371-7796-0, ANHW). Greenwood.

--Little Angel, & Other Stories. facsimile ed. LC 78-167439. (Short Story Index Reprint Ser.). Repr. of 1915 ed. 18.00 (ISBN 0-8369-3965-4). Ayer Co Pubs.

--Plays by Leonid Andreyeff: The Life of Man, the Black Maskers, the Sabine Women. Meader, Clarence L. & Scott, Fred N., trs. from Russian. LC 80-2885. (BCL Ser.: I & II). Repr. of 1915 ed. 29.00 (ISBN 0-404-18057-4). AMS Pr.

--When the King Loses His Head, & Other Stories. facs. ed. Wolfe, Archibald J., tr. LC 74-116927. (Short Story Index Reprint Ser.). 1919. 19.00 (ISBN 0-8369-3429-6). Ayer Co Pubs.

Andreev, N. N., jt. auth. see Kapustina, O. A.

Andreev, V. C. Skin Manifestations in Visceral Cancer. (Current Problems in Dermatology: Vol. 8). (Illus.). 1978. pap. 42.25 (ISBN 3-8055-2878-7). S Karger.

Andreeva, N. K. Atlas of Helminths (Strongylata) of Domestic Wild Ruminants of Kazakhstan. 206p. 1981. 75.00x (ISBN 0-686-72943-9, Pub. by Oxford & IBH India). State Mutual Bk.

Andreeva, Svetlana I., jt. auth. see Collias, Eugene E.

Andreichin, L., et al. How to Write Bulgarian. 454p. 1981. 25.00 (ISBN 0-686-97390-9, M-9832). French & Eur.

Andreichina, K., et al. Russian-Bulgarian Phraseological Dictionary. Vlasova, ed. 582p. (Rus. & Bulgarian.). 1980. 65.00 (ISBN 0-686-97416-6, M-9830). French & Eur.

Andreis, Flavio. Colloquial Italian. (Colloquial Ser.). 244p. (Orig.). 1983. pap. 8.95 (ISBN 0-7100-0876-7). Routledge & Kegan.

Andrejcak, Dawna M. Because the Death of a Rose. Holley, Barbara, ed. (T.S. Eliot Memorial Chapbook Ser.: Vol. 1). write for info. (ISBN 0-933494-21-1). Earthwise Pubs.

Andrejko, Dennis A., jt. auth. see Wright, David.

Andren, Arvid. Arkeologins Marodorer. (Studies in Mediterranean Archaeology, Pocketbook: No. 19). 122p. (Swedish.). 1983. pap. text ed. 23.50x (ISBN 9-186-09803-9, Pub. by Paul Astroms Sweden). Humanities.

Andren, John, Jr., et al. IBM PC to Apple II BASIC Program Translation. 100p. 1984. 15.00. Med Software.

Andren, Nils & Birnbaum, Karl E. Belgrade & Beyond: The CSCE Process in Perspective. (East West Perspectives Ser.: No. 5). 27.50x (ISBN 90-286-0250-X). Sijthoff & Noordhoff.

Andreoli, Kathleen G., et al. Comprehensive Cardiac Care: A Text for Nurses, Physicians & Other Health Practitioners. 5th ed. LC 82-12570. (Illus.). 556p. 1983. pap. text ed. 19.95 (ISBN 0-8016-0265-3). Mosby.

Andreoli, M., jt. ed. see Cassano, C.

Andreoli, Thomas E., et al, eds. Physiology of Membrane Disorders. LC 78-4071. (Illus.). 1148p. 1978. 85.00x (ISBN 0-306-31054-6, Plenum Med. Bk.). Plenum Pub.

--Membrane Physiology. 482p. 1980. pap. text ed. 19.95x (ISBN 0-306-40432-X, Plenum Pr). Plenum Pub.

Andreoli, V. M., et al, eds. Transmethylations & the Central Nervous System. (Psychiatry Ser.: Vol. 18). (Illus.). 1978. 38.00 (ISBN 0-387-08693-5). Springer-Verlag.

Andreoni, A., jt. ed. see Cubeddu, R.

Andreoni, Jill, jt. auth. see Duren, Donald.

Andreoni, Patricia A. The Complete Legal Secretarial Course. 460p. 1983. scp 25.00 (ISBN 0-205-07791-9, 177791). Allyn.

Andreopoulos, Spyros, ed. National Health Insurance: Can We Learn from Canada? LC 81-5786. 296p. 1983. Repr. of 1975 ed. lib. bdg. 19.50 (ISBN 0-89874-347-8). Krieger.

Andreotti, A. & Stoll, W. Analytic & Algebraic Dependence of Meromorphic Functions. (Lecture Notes in Mathematics: Vol. 234). iii, 390p. 1971. pap. 13.00 (ISBN 0-387-05670-X). Springer-Verlag.

Andreotti, Aldo. Complexes of Partial Differential Operators. LC 75-8440. (Yale Mathematical Monographs: No. 6). pap. 15.00 (ISBN 0-8357-9106-8, 2016793). Bks Demand UMI.

Andres, jt. auth. see McClusky.

Andres, A., et al. Analytical Chemistry Progress. (Topics in Current Chemistry. Fortschritte der Chemischen Forschung Ser.: Vol. 126). (Illus.). 120p. 1984. 27.00 (ISBN 0-387-13596-0). Springer-Verlag.

Andres, C. K., jt. auth. see Smith, R. C.

Andres, Glenn & Hunisak, John. The Art of Florence. LC 83-6394. Orig. Title: Arte en Firenze. (Illus.). 560p. 1986. 150.00 (ISBN 0-89659-402-5). Abbeville Pr.

Andres, M. F. Diccionario Espanol de Sinonimos y Equivalencias. 8th ed. 444p. (Span.). 1979. 17.50 (ISBN 84-7003-072-8, S-12233). French & Eur.

Andres, P. & Murai, T. How to Say It in Hungarian. 238p. 1980. 20.00x (ISBN 0-569-00222-2, Pub. by Collet's). State Mutual Bk.

Andres, P. G., et al. Basic Mathematics for Engineers. LC 55-8369. 776p. 1944. 41.50 (ISBN 0-471-02937-8). Wiley.

Andres, R. & Hazzard, W. R. Principles of Geriatric Medicine. 1024p. 1984. 60.00 (ISBN 0-07-001781-6). McGraw.

Andres, Tomas D. Management by Filipino Values: A Sequel to Understanding Filipino Values. vi, 276p. (Orig.). 1985. pap. 12.25 (ISBN 971-10-0209-4, Pub. by New Day Philippines). Cellar.

--Understanding Filipino Values: A Management Approach. 180p. 1981. pap. 7.00x (ISBN 0-686-32452-8, Pub. by New Day Philippines). Cellar.

Andresen, A. F. & Maeland, A., eds. Hydrides for Energy Storage: Proceedings of an International Symposium Held in Norway, Aug. 1977. 1978. text ed. 105.00 (ISBN 0-08-022715-5). Pergamon.

Andresen, Karl. Lexikon der Alten Welt. (Ger.). 1965. 395.00 (ISBN 3-7608-0137-4, M-7281). French & Eur.

Andresen, Robert L., jt. ed. see Boydston, Jo Ann.

Andresen, William, et al. Laboratory Inquiries into Concepts of Biology. 4th ed. 1984. pap. text ed. 11.95 (ISBN 0-8403-3354-4, 40335401). Kendall-Hunt.

Andreski, Stanislav. Max Weber's Insights & Errors. (International Library of Sociology). 147p. 1985. 27.50x (ISBN 0-7102-0051-X). Routledge & Kegan.

--Military Organization & Society. LC 68-27161. 1968. pap. 10.95x (ISBN 0-520-00026-9, CAMPUS 7). U of Cal Pr.

Andreski, Stanislav, ed. & tr. Max Weber on Capitalism, Bureaucracy & Religion. (A Selection of Texts Ser.). 192p. 1983. text ed. 22.95x (ISBN 0-04-301147-0); pap. text ed. 7.95x (ISBN 0-04-301148-9). Allen Unwin.

Andreski, Stanislav, ed. see Spencer, Herbert.

Andreson, Steve. The Orienteering Book. LC 77-73875. (Illus.). 100p. 1977. pap. 3.95 (ISBN 0-89037-118-0). Anderson World.

Andress, Barbara. Music Experiences in Early Childhood. LC 79-26605. 198p. (Orig.). 1980. pap. text ed. 18.95 (ISBN 0-03-021771-7, HoltC). HR&W.

Andress, J. Glacial Isostasy. 1982. 56.95 (ISBN 0-87933-051-1). Van Nos Reinhold.

Andress, Lesley. Caper. 1980. lib. bdg. 14.95 (ISBN 0-8161-3117-1, Large Print Bks). G K Hall.

Andressohn, John C. Ancestry & Life of Godfrey of Bouillon. LC 70-38379. (Biography Index Reprints - Social Science Ser.: No. 5). Repr. of 1947 ed. 15.50 (ISBN 0-8369-8114-6). Ayer Co Pubs.

Andretta, R. A. Shakespeare's Romances. 128p. 1982. 39.00x (ISBN 0-7069-1420-1, Pub. by Garlandfold England). State Mutual Bk.

Andretta, Richard A. Shakespeare's Romances. 152p. 1981. text ed. 15.00x (ISBN 0-7069-1420-1, Pub. by Vikas India). Advent NY.

Andreu, Helene C. Jazz Dance: An Adult Beginner's Guide. 184p. 1983. 15.95 (ISBN 0-13-509968-4); pap. 7.95 (ISBN 0-13-509950-1). P-H.

Andreucci, Vittorio E., ed. Acute Renal Failure. 1984. lib. bdg. 99.50 (ISBN 0-89838-627-6, Pub. by Martinus Nijhoff Netherlands). Kluwer Academic.

Andrew. Computational Methods in Operations Research. (Cybernetics & Systems Ser.). 1984. 25.00 (ISBN 0-9901002-9-4, Pub. by Abacus England). Heyden.

Andrew, A. M. Artificial Intelligence. 1983. 26.00 (ISBN 0-85626-165-3, Pub. by Abacus England). Heyden.

Andrew, A. Piatt. Statistics for the United States, 1867-1909. LC 82-48223. (Gold, Money, Inflation & Deflation Ser.). 282p. 1983. lib. bdg. 39.00 (ISBN 0-8240-5249-8). Garland Pub.

Andrew, A. Piatt & Kent, Frederick I. Banking Problems. Bruchey, Stuart, ed. LC 80-1178. (The Rise of Commercial Banking Ser.). 1981. Repr. of 1910 ed. lib. bdg. 18.00x (ISBN 0-405-13631-5). Ayer Co Pubs.

Andrew, Arthur & Shaff, Victor, eds. Corrugated Containers Waste Control Handbook for Supervisors & Operators. (TAPPI Press Report). 51p. 1976. 4.95 (ISBN 0-317-35998-3, 01-01-RO61). TAPPI.

Andrew, Brother. Is Life So Dear? 164p. 1985. pap. 4.95 (ISBN 0-8407-5976-2). Nelson.

Andrew, Bryan H., ed. Interstellar Molecules. (International Astronomical Union Symposia: No. 87). 500p. 1980. PLB 76.50 (ISBN 90-277-1160-7, Pub. by Reidel Holland); pap. 34.00 (ISBN 90-277-1161-5, Pub. by Reidel Holland). Kluwer Academic.

Andrew, C. S. & Kamprath, E. J. Mineral Nutrition of Legumes in Tropical & Subtropical Soils. 415p. 1978. 36.00 (ISBN 0-643-00311-8, C014, CSIRO). Unipub.

Andrew, C. S. & Kamprath, E. J., eds. Mineral Nutrition of Legumes in Tropical & Subtropical Soils. 1979. 28.00x (ISBN 0-643-00311-8, Pub. by CSIRO). Intl Spec Bk.

Andrew, Chris O. & Hildebrand, Peter E. Planning & Conducting Applied Agricultural Research. 96p. 1982. 13.00 (ISBN 0-86531-461-6); pap. text ed. 8.50x (ISBN 0-86531-460-8). Westview.

Andrew, Christopher & Dilks, David, eds. Missing Dimension: Governments & Intelligence Communities in the Twentieth Century. LC 84-2513. 308p. 1984. 27.95x (ISBN 0-252-01157-0). U of Ill Pr.

Andrew, Christopher M. & Kanya-Forstner, A. S. The Climax of French Imperial Expansion, 1914-1924. LC 80-53435. 302p. 1981. 32.50x (ISBN 0-8047-1101-1). Stanford U Pr.

Andrew, David S. Louis Sullivan & the Polemics of Modern Architecture: The Present Against the Past. LC 83-18164. (Illus.). 195p. 1985. 19.95 (ISBN 0-252-01044-2). U of Ill Pr.

Andrew, Dick. Even YOU Can Share Your Faith. 45p. (gr. 5-8). 1981. tchrs'. ed. 3.25 (ISBN 0-914936-47-6); student ed. 4.25 (ISBN 0-914936-48-4). Bible Temple.

Andrew, Dudley. Film & the Aura of Art. LC 84-1788. (Illus.). 240p. 1984. text ed. 25.00x (ISBN 0-691-06585-3). Princeton U Pr.

Andrew, Dudley & Andrew, Paul. Kenji Mizoguchi: A Guide to References & Resources. 336p. 1981. lib. bdg. 36.50 (ISBN 0-8161-8469-0, Hall Reference). G K Hall.

Andrew, Dudley J. Concepts in Film Theory. LC 83-17365. (Galaxy Bks.). 350p. 1984. 16.95 (ISBN 0-19-503394-9, GB); pap. 7.95 (ISBN 0-19-503428-7). Oxford U Pr.

Andrew, Edwin R. Nuclear Magnetic Resonance. (Cambridge Monographs on Physics Ser.). 1956. 52.50 (ISBN 0-521-04030-2). Cambridge U Pr.

Andrew, G. & Harlow, H. F. Performance of Macaque Monkeys on a Test of the Concept of Generalized Triangularity. LC 48-10876. (Comp Psych Monographs). pap. 8.00 (ISBN 0-527-24935-1). Kraus Repr.

Andrew, J. Dudley. The Major Film Theories: An Introduction. (Illus., Orig.). 1976. pap. 7.95 (ISBN 0-19-501991-1, 450, GB). Oxford U Pr.

Andrew, Jean. Tempo Easy Crosswords, No. 2. 1982. pap. 1.25 (ISBN 0-448-17153-8, Pub. by Tempo). Ace Bks.

Andrew, Joe. Russian Writers & Society in the Second Half of the 19th Century. 238p. 1982. text ed. 40.50x (ISBN 0-391-02216-4). Humanities.

--Writers & Society During the Rise of Russian Realism. 208p. 1980. text ed. 28.00x (ISBN 0-333-25912-2). Humanities.

Andrew, Joe, tr. see Pike, Christopher.

Andrew, Joe, jt. tr. see Pike, Christopher.

Andrew, John A., III. Rebuilding the Christian Commonwealth: New England Congregationalists & Foreign Missions, 1800-1830. LC 75-38214. 240p. 1976. 22.00x (ISBN 0-8131-1333-4). U Pr of Ky.

Andrew, Kenneth. Hong Kong Detective. (Illus.). 15.00 (ISBN 0-392-03260-0, LTB). Sportshelf.

Andrew, Larry D. & Andrew, Patricia. Math Exercises (in Addition) 1980. pap. 1.45 (ISBN 0-931992-36-2). Penns Valley.

--Math Exercises (in Division) 1980. pap. 1.45 (ISBN 0-931992-39-7). Penns Valley.

--Math Exercises (in Multiplication) 1980. pap. 1.45 (ISBN 0-931992-38-9). Penns Valley.

--Math Exercises (in Subtraction) 1980. pap. 1.45 (ISBN 0-931992-37-0). Penns Valley.

Andrew, Laurel B. The Early Temples of the Mormons: The Architecture of the Millennial Kingdom in the American West. LC 77-23971. (Illus.). 1978. 22.50x (ISBN 0-87395-358-4). State U NY Pr.

Andrew, Malcolm. The Gawain-Poet: An Annotated Bibliography, 1839-1977. LC 78-68243. (Garland Reference Library of the Humanities: No. 129). 1980. lib. bdg. 43.00 (ISBN 0-8240-9815-3). Garland Pub.

Andrew, Malcolm, ed. Two Early Renaissance Bird Poems: The Harmony of Birds & the Parliament Birds. LC 83-48646. 120p. 1984. 18.00 (ISBN 0-918016-73-8). Folger Bks.

Andrew, Malcolm & Waldron, Ronald, eds. The Poems of the Pearl Manuscript. LC 78-64464. (York Medieval Texts, Second Ser.). 1979. 55.00x (ISBN 0-520-03794-4, CAMPUS 292); pap. 11.95x (ISBN 0-520-04631-5). U of Cal Pr.

Andrew, Malcolm H. & Russell, A. Denver. The Revival of Injured Microbes. (Society for Applied Bacteria Symposium Ser.). 1984. 44.00 (ISBN 0-12-058520-0). Acad Pr.

Andrew, Murray, jt. auth. see Evans, Arthur J.

Andrew, Nancy, tr. see Murakami, Ryu.

Andrew, Nicholas J., ed. see Dryden, John.

Andrew, Patricia, jt. auth. see Andrew, Larry D.

Andrew, Paul, jt. auth. see Andrew, Dudley.

Andrew, R. J. & Huber, Ernst. Evolution of Facial Expression: Two Accounts. Incl. The Origin & Evolution of the Calls & Facial Expressions of the Primates. 1963; Evolution of Facial Musculature & Facial Expression. 1931. LC 72-344. (Body Movement Ser.: Perspectives in Research). 312p. 1972. Repr. of 1972 ed. 23.00 (ISBN 0-405-03143-2). Ayer Co Pubs.

Andrew, Ralph, jt. auth. see Sacks, Seymour.

Andrew, Robert. The Lucky Dream & Number Book. 144p. 1966. pap. 2.50 (ISBN 0-446-30842-0). Warner Bks.

Andrew, Samuel O. Postscript on Beowulf. 1978. Repr. of 1948 ed. lib. bdg. 20.00 (ISBN 0-8482-0118-3). Norwood Edns.

--Postscript on Beowulf. 158p. 1980. Repr. of 1948 ed. lib. bdg. 20.00 (ISBN 0-8492-3225-2). R West.

--Syntax & Style in Old English. LC 66-13220. 1966. Repr. of 1940 ed. 14.00x (ISBN 0-8462-0762-1). Russell.

Andrew, Warren. Anatomy of Aging in Man & Animals. LC 73-92018. (Illus.). 259p. 1971. 71.50 (ISBN 0-8089-0640-2, 790101). Grune.

--Six Anatomists Worth Knowing. LC 73-707. 280p. Date not set. 13.50 (ISBN 0-87527-174-X). Green.

Andrew, William G. & Williams, H. B. Applied Instrumentation in the Process Industries, Vol. 1: A Survey. 2nd ed. LC 79-9418. 407p. 1979. 45.95x (ISBN 0-87201-382-0). Gulf Pub.

--Applied Instrumentation in the Process Industries, Vol. 2: Practical Guidelines. 2nd ed. LC 79-9418. 312p. 1980. 45.95x (ISBN 0-87201-383-9). Gulf Pub.

--Applied Instrumentation in the Process Industries, Vol. 3: Engineering Data & Resource Material. 2nd ed. LC 79-9418. 520p. 1982. 45.95x (ISBN 0-87201-384-7). Gulf Pub.

Andrew, William W. Otto H. Bacher. 283p. 1981. pap. text ed. 30.00 (ISBN 0-86652-016-3). Know Unltd.

Andrewartha, H. G. The Ecological Web: More on the Distribution & Abundance of Animals. LC 84-70. (Illus.). 560p. 1985. lib. bdg. 35.00x (ISBN 0-226-02033-9). U of Chicago Pr.

Andrewartha, H. G. & Birch, L. C. Distribution & Abundance of Animals. LC 54-13016. (Illus.). 1954. 35.00x (ISBN 0-226-02026-6). U of Chicago Pr.

--Selections from the Distribution & Abundance of Animals. LC 82-6948. (Illus.). 288p. 1982. lib. bdg. 25.00x (ISBN 0-226-02031-2); pap. 9.00x (ISBN 0-226-02032-0). U of Chicago Pr.

Andrewartha, Herbert G. Introduction to the Study of Animal Populations. 2nd. ed. LC 73-135741. (Illus.). xvii, 281p. 1971. 12.00x (ISBN 0-226-02029-0, P519, Phoen). U of Chicago Pr.

Andrewe, L., tr. see Hieronymus, Von Braunschweig.

Andrewes, A. The Greek Tyrants. 1956. pap. 12.00x (ISBN 0-09-029564-1, Hutchinson U Lib). Humanities.

Andrewes, Antony. The Greeks. 1978. pap. 7.95 (ISBN 0-393-00877-0, N877, Norton Lib). Norton.

Andrewes, Christopher & Walton, John R. Viral & Bacterial Zoonoses. (Illus.). 120p. 1977. pap. 5.00 (ISBN 0-7216-0782-9, Pub. by Bailliere-Tindall). Saunders.

Andrewes, Christopher, et al. Viruses of Verebrates. 4th ed. 431p. 1978. 37.50 (ISBN 0-7216-0701-2, Pub. by Bailliere-Tindall). Saunders.

Andrewes, Sir Christopher. Natural History of Viruses. (World Naturalist Series). (Illus.). 1967. 10.00x (ISBN 0-393-06277-5). Norton.

Andrewes, Lancelot. Complete Works, 11 vols. Wilson, J. P. & Bliss, J., eds. LC 78-158257. (BCL Ser.: No. 1). Repr. of 1854 ed. Set. 445.00 (ISBN 0-404-52020-0). AMS Pr.

--Lancelot Andrewes & His Private Devotions. Whyte, Alexander, ed. (Summit Bks.). 240p. (Orig.). 1981. pap. 3.95 (ISBN 0-8010-0176-5). Baker Bk.

--Private Devotions of Lancelot Andrewes. Brightman, F. E., tr. & intro. by. 15.25 (ISBN 0-8446-1534-X). Peter Smith.

Andrewes, S., ed. see Eltringham, R., et al.

Andrewes, William & Atwood, Seth. The Time Museum: An Introduction. Chandler, Bruce, ed. (Illus.). 32p. (Orig.). 1983. pap. 4.95 (ISBN 0-912947-00-4). Time Museum.

Andrews. BASIC Theory of Structures. (Illus.). 160p. 1985. pap. text ed. 15.95 (ISBN 0-408-01357-5). Butterworth.

--Pig Plantagenet. 2.95 (ISBN 0-317-31879-9). Tor Bks.

Andrews & Houston. Adult Learners: A Research Study. 1981. 5.00 (ISBN 0-686-38071-1). Assn Tchr Ed.

Andrews & Sansone. Who Runs the Rivers: Dams & Decisions in the New West. 452p. 1983. 12.00 (ISBN 0-318-04411-0). Stanford Enviro.

Andrews, jt. auth. see Waterman.

Andrews, A. Australasian Tokens & Coins. (Illus.). 1982. Repr. of 1921 ed. lib. bdg. 35.00 (ISBN 0-942666-10-0). S J Durst.

Andrews, Albert H., Jr. & Polanyi, Thomas. Microscopic & Endoscopic Surgery with the Carbon Dioxide Laser. LC 81-15989. (Illus.). 386p. 1982. 47.00 (ISBN 0-7236-7009-9). PSG Pub Co.

Andrews, Alexander. History of British Journalism: From the Foundation of the Newspaper Press in England to the Repeal of the Stamp Act, 2 Vols. LC 68-24958. (British History Ser., No. 30). 1969. Repr. of 1859 ed. lib. bdg. 79.95x (ISBN 0-8383-0154-1). Haskell.

--History of British Journalism from the Foundation of the Newspaper Press in England to the Repeal of the Stamp Act in 1855, 2 Vols. 1968. Set. 59.00x (ISBN 0-403-00139-0). Scholarly.

Andrews, Allen. Castle Crespin. 240p. 1984. pap. 2.95 (ISBN 0-8125-3097-7). Tor Bks.

--The Pig Plantagenet. 288p. 1984. pap. 2.95 (ISBN 0-8125-3094-2, Pinnacle Bks). Tor Bks.

Andrews, Anthony P. Maya Salt Production & Trade. LC 83-9306. 173p. 1983. 16.95x (ISBN 0-8165-0813-5). U of Ariz Pr.

Andrews, Anthony T. Electrophoresis: Theory, Techniques, & Biochemical & Clinical Applications. (Monographs on Physical Biochemistry Ser.). (Illus.). 1981. 59.00x (ISBN 0-19-854626-2). Oxford U Pr.

Andrews, Arthur. A Dog-Eared Book. Young, Billie, ed. LC 73-83475. 1974. 8.95 (ISBN 0-87949-015-2). Ashley Bks.

--The First Settlement of the Murray 1835-1845: And a Short Account of Over Two Hundred Runs 1835-1880. (Facsimile Ser. No.23). 196p. 1981. 15.00 (ISBN 0-908120-28-1, Pub. by Lib Australian Hist). Australia N U P.

Andrews, Barbara. Add a Dash of Love. (Candlelight Ectasy Ser.: No. 385). (Orig.). 1985. pap. 2.25 (ISBN 0-440-10017-8). Dell.

--Emerald Fire. (Candlelight Ecstasy Supreme Ser.: No. 2). 288p. 1983. pap. 2.50 (ISBN 0-440-12301-1). Dell.

--Happily Ever After. (Candlelight Ecstasy Ser.: No. 278). 192p. (Orig.). 1984. pap. 1.95 (ISBN 0-440-13439-0). Dell.

--Love Trap. (Candlelight Ecstasy Ser.: No. 86). (Orig.). 1982. pap. 1.95 (ISBN 0-440-14601-1). Dell.

--Loving Lessons. (Candlelight Ecstasy Ser.: No. 338). 1985. pap. 2.25 (ISBN 0-440-15108-2). Dell.

--Midnight Magic. (Candlelight Ecstasy Ser.: No. 215). 192p. (Orig.). 1984. pap. 1.95 (ISBN 0-440-15618-1). Dell.

--My Kind of Love. (Candlelight Ecstasy Romance Ser.: No. 298). 192p. (Orig.). 1985. pap. 1.95 (ISBN 0-440-16202-5). Dell.

--A Novel Affair. (Candlelight Ecstasy Ser.: No. 317). (Orig.). 1985. pap. 1.95 (ISBN 0-440-16079-0). Dell.

--Passionate Deceiver. (Candlelight Ecstasy Ser.: No. 176). 192p. (Orig.). 1983. pap. 1.95 (ISBN 0-440-16919-4). Dell.

--Reach for the Sky. (Candlelight Supreme Ser.: No. 73). (Orig.). 1985. pap. 2.75 (ISBN 0-440-17242-X). Dell.

--Seduced by a Stranger. (Candlelight Ecstasy Ser.: No. 405). 1986. pap. 2.25 (ISBN 0-440-17635-2). Dell.

--Shady Business. (Candlelight Ecstasy Supreme Ser.: No. 23). (Orig.). 1984. pap. 2.50 (ISBN 0-440-17797-9). Dell.

--Stand-In Lover. (Candlelight Ectasy: No. 363). (Orig.). 1985. pap. 2.25 (ISBN 0-440-18276-X). Dell.

--Stolen Promises. (Candlelight Ecstacy Ser.: No. 111). (Orig.). 1983. pap. 1.95 (ISBN 0-440-17522-4). Dell.

--This Bittersweet Love. (Candlelight Ecstasy Ser.: No. 127). (Orig.). 1983. pap. 1.95 (ISBN 0-440-18797-4). Dell.

Andrews, Barry G. & Wilde, William H., eds. Australian Literature to Nineteen Hundred: A Guide to Information Sources. LC 74-11521. (American Literature, English Literature & World Literatures in English Information Guide Ser.: Vol. 22). 472p. 1980. 60.00x (ISBN 0-8103-1215-8). Gale.

Andrews, Bart. I Love Lucy Book. LC 84-6033. (Illus.). 448p. 1985. pap. 10.95 (ISBN 0-385-19033-6, Dolp). Doubleday.

--The Super Official TV Trivia Quiz Book. 1985. pap. 3.95 (ISBN 0-451-13507-5, Sig). NAL.

--The TV Fun Book. (Illus.). 92p. (Orig.). 1981. pap. 1.95 (ISBN 0-590-31699-0). Scholastic Inc.

Andrews, Bart & Juilliard, Ahrgus. Holy Mackerel! The Amos 'n' Andy Story. (Illus.). 256p. 1986. 14.95 (ISBN 0-525-24354-2). Dutton.

Andrews, Bart & Watson, Thomas. Loving Lucy. (Illus.). 383p. 1982. pap. 9.95 (ISBN 0-312-49975-2). St Martin.

Andrews, Betty. Close to the Bone. (Illus.). 18p. 1984. deluxe ed. 100.00 (ISBN 0-9614597-1-9); pap. 15.00 (ISBN 0-9614597-0-0). Ninja Pr.

--Plowing the Wind. 50p. 1985. pap. 15.00 (ISBN 0-9614597-2-7); deluxe ed. 45.00 (ISBN 0-9614597-3-5). Ninja Pr.

Andrews, Beverly. What Time Is It, Nana? 136p. 1982. 7.50 (ISBN 0-682-49795-9). Exposition Pr FL.

Andrews, Billy. Outstanding Weather Phenomena in the Ark-La-Tex. Hughes, Jeff, ed. LC 84-2938. (Illus.). 216p. (Orig.). 1984. pap. text ed. 10.50 (ISBN 0-910653-11-9, 8101-E). Archival Servs.

Andrews, Bruce. Film Noir. (Burning Deck Poetry Ser). 1978. pap. 15.00 signed ed. (ISBN 0-930900-47-2). Burning Deck.

Andrews, Bruce & Bennett, John M. Joint Words. 1979. 1.50 (ISBN 0-686-73441-6). Luna Bisonte.

Andrews, Bruce & Bernstein, Charles. The L-A-N-G-U-A-G-E Book. LC 83-376. (Poetics of the New Ser.). 310p. (Orig.). 1984. pap. 12.95 (ISBN 0-8093-1106-2). S Ill U Pr.

Andrews, Bruce, et al. Translations, "C". Wellman, Don, et al, eds. Rothenberg, Jerome, et al, trs. (Translations: Experiments in Reading Ser.). 104p. (Orig.). 1983. pap. 4.50 (ISBN 0-686-88655-0). O ARS.

Andrews, Bruce J., jt. auth. see Andrews, Keith L.

Andrews, Burton. The Law-Analysis & Synthesis. rev., 2nd ed. (Introduction to Law). 354p. 1980. 19.00x (ISBN 0-686-31006-3). Liberty Bk.

Andrews, C. C. Brazil, Its Condition & Prospects. 1976. lib. bdg. 59.95 (ISBN 0-87968-783-5). Gordon Pr.

Andrews, C. E. The Writing & Reading of Verse. 1973. Repr. of 1934 ed. 35.00 (ISBN 0-8274-1667-9). R West.

Andrews, C. E. & Precival, M. O. Poetry of the Nineties. 297p. 1980. Repr. lib. bdg. 25.00 (ISBN 0-8492-0099-7). R West.

Andrews, C. E. & Percival, M. O., eds. Poetry of the Nineties. facsimile ed. LC 78-116392. (Granger Index Reprint Ser). 1926. 18.00 (ISBN 0-8369-6133-1). Ayer Co Pubs.

--Poetry of the Nineties. 297p. 1981. Repr. of 1926 ed. lib. bdg. 40.00 (ISBN 0-89987-029-5). Darby Bks.

Andrews, C. F. & Morgan, E. B. Supermarine Aircraft since Nineteen Fourteen. (Illus.). 352p. 1981. 29.95 (ISBN 0-370-10018-2, Pub. by the Bodley Head). Merrimack Pub Cir.

Andrews, C. F., ed. see Gandhi, Mahatma.

Andrews, C. L. Story of Sitka. 142p. pap. 9.95 (ISBN 0-8466-0094-3, S94). Shorey.

Andrews, C. M. Guide to the Materials for American History, to 1783 in the Public Record Office of Great Britain, 2 Vols. (C1.G Ser.). 1912-1914. Set. 51.00 (ISBN 0-527-00686-6). Kraus Repr.

--The Old English Manor. 59.95 (ISBN 0-8490-0758-5). Gordon Pr.

--The River Towns of Connecticut: A Study of Wethersfield, Hartford & Windsor. Repr. of 1889 ed. 14.00 (ISBN 0-384-01454-2). Johnson Repr.

Andrews, C. M. & Davenport, F. G. Guide to the Manuscript Materials for the History of the United States to 1783. (C1.G Ser.). 1908. 41.00 (ISBN 0-527-00685-8). Kraus Repr.

Andrews, C. S. Dublin Made Me. 312p. 1979. 18.00 (ISBN 0-85342-606-6, Pub. by Mercier Pr Ireland). Irish Bk Ctr.

--Man of No Property. (Andrew's Biography Ser.: Vol. 2). 327p. 1982. 26.50 (ISBN 0-85342-680-5, Pub. by Mercier Pr Ireland). Irish Bk Ctr.

Andrews, C. S. & Kamprath, E. J. Mineral Nutrition of Legumes in Tropical & Subtropical Soils. 415p. 1982. 60.00x (Pub. by CSIRO Australia). State Mutual Bk.

Andrews, Carol. The British Museum Book of the Rosetta Stone. LC 85-9010. (Illus.). 64p. 1985. 10.95 (ISBN 0-87226-033-X); pap. 4.95 (ISBN 0-87226-034-8). P Bedrick Bks.

--Egyptian Mummies. (Illus.). 72p. 1984. pap. 6.95 (ISBN 0-674-24152-5). Harvard U Pr.

--The Rosetta Stone. 32p. 1982. pap. 25.00x (ISBN 0-7141-0931-2, Pub. by Brit Mus Pubns England). State Mutual Bk.

Andrews, Carol, jt. auth. see Hamilton-Paterson, James.

Andrews, Charles C. History of the New York African Free-Schools, from Their Establishment in 1787, to the Present Time. LC 68-55868. (Illus.). Repr. of 1830 ed. cancelled (ISBN 0-8371-1064-5). Greenwood.

Andrews, Charles F. John White of Mashonaland. LC 79-91660. Repr. of 1935 ed. cancelled (ISBN 0-8371-2070-5, ANW&, Pub. by Negro U Pr). Greenwood.

Andrews, Charles J. Fell's International Coin Book. 8th rev. ed. LC 81-65741. (Illus.). 324p. 1983. 14.95 (ISBN 0-8119-0594-2); pap. 9.95 (ISBN 0-8119-0587-X). Fell.

--Fell's United States Coin Book. 10th rev. ed. LC 58-2168. (Illus.). 176p. 1983. 11.95 (ISBN 0-8119-0595-0); pap. 7.95 (ISBN 0-8119-0588-8). Fell.

Andrews, Charles M. British Committees, Commissions, & Councils of Trade & Plantations: 1622-1675. LC 78-63925. (Johns Hopkins University. Studies in the Social Sciences. Twenty-Sixth, 1908: 1-3). Repr. of 1908 ed. 11.50 (ISBN 0-404-61175-3). AMS Pr.

--British Committees, Commissions & Councils of Trade & Plantations, 1622-1675. LC 8-22803. (John Hopkins University Studies in Historical & Political Science: No. 26). Repr. of 1908 ed. 12.00 (ISBN 0-527-02550-X). Kraus Repr.

--Colonial Background of the American Revolution: Four Essays in American Colonial History. rev. ed. LC 31-2404. 1961. pap. 8.95x (ISBN 0-300-00004-9, Y44). Yale U Pr.

--Colonial Folkways. 1919. 8.50x (ISBN 0-686-83505-0). Elliots Bks.

--Colonial Period of American History: The Settlements, 3 vols. Vol. 1 1934. 52.00x (ISBN 0-300-00269-6); Vol. 2 1936. 42.00x (ISBN 0-300-00271-8); Vol. 3 1937. 42.00x (ISBN 0-300-00272-6). Yale U Pr.

--Colonial Self-Government, 1652-1689. LC 73-98630. Repr. of 1904 ed. 12.50 (ISBN 0-404-00359-1). AMS Pr.

--Colonial Self-Government, 1652-1689. LC 4-32334. 1904. 11.00 (ISBN 0-403-00138-2). Scholarly.

--Fathers of New England. 1919. 8.50x (ISBN 0-686-83545-X). Elliots Bks.

--The Old English Manor: A Study in English Economic History. LC 78-64257. (Johns Hopkins University. Studies in the Social Sciences. Extra Volumes: 12). Repr. of 1892 ed. 25.50 (ISBN 0-404-61360-8). AMS Pr.

--Our Earliest Colonial Settlements: Their Diversities of Origin & Later Characteristics. 185p. 1959. pap. 6.95x (ISBN 0-8014-9016-2, CP16). Cornell U Pr.

--The River Towns of Connecticut: A Study of Wethersfield, Hartford & Windsor. LC 78-63790. (Johns Hopkins University. Studies in the Social Sciences. Seventh Ser. 1889: 7-9). Repr. of 1889 ed. 11.50 (ISBN 0-404-61055-2). AMS Pr.

Andrews, Charles M see Johnson, Allen & Nevins, Allan.

Andrews, Charles M., ed. Narratives of the Insurrections, Sixteen Seventy-Five to Sixteen Ninety. (Original Narratives). 414p. 1967. Repr. of 1915 ed. 21.50x (ISBN 0-06-480028-8, 06316). B&N Imports.

Andrews, Charles M., jt. ed. see Andrews, Evangeline W.

Andrews, Charlton. The Drama to-Day. 1975. Repr. of 1913 ed. 25.00 (ISBN 0-8274-4099-5). R West.

--Technique of Play Writing. 1975. Repr. of 1915 ed. 20.00 (ISBN 0-8274-4100-2). R West.

Andrews, Christopher, et al. Viruses of Vertebrates. 4th ed. 1978. text ed. 37.50 (ISBN 0-02-857150-9). Macmillan.

Andrews, Christopher C. Minnesota & Dacotah: In Letters Descriptive of a Tour Through the Northwest... facsimile ed. LC 75-81. (Mid-American Frontier Ser.). 1975. Repr. of 1857 ed. 17.00x (ISBN 0-405-06850-6). Ayer Co Pubs.

Andrews, Clarence. Growing up in the Midwest. 216p. 1981. 12.95 (ISBN 0-8138-0250-4). Iowa St U Pr.

Andrews, Clarence A. Chicago in Story: A Literary History. (Illus.). 414p. 1983. lib. bdg. 19.95 (ISBN 0-934582-03-3). Midwest Heritage.

--A Literary History of Iowa. LC 72-76305. 301p. 1972. 22.00x (ISBN 0-87745-032-3); pap. 9.00x (ISBN 0-87745-053-6). U of Iowa Pr.

Andrews, Clarence A., ed. Clarence Andrews' Christmas in Iowa. LC 79-89445. (Illus.). 128p. 1979. 7.95 (ISBN 0-934582-00-9). Midwest Heritage.

--Growing Up in Iowa. (Illus.). 1978. 9.95 (ISBN 0-8138-0801-4). Iowa St U Pr.

Andrews, Clarence A., ed. see Childs, Marquis & Engel, Paul.

Andrews, Clarence A., tr. see Gravel, Fern.

Andrews, Clarence E. Richard Brome: A Study of His Life & Works. (Yales Studies in English Ser.: No. 46). vi, 140p. 1972. Repr. of 1913 ed. 16.50 (ISBN 0-208-01122-6, Archon). Shoe String.

Andrews, Clarence L. Wrangell & the Gold of the Cassiar. 61p. pap. 4.95 (ISBN 0-8466-0267-9, S267). Shorey.

Andrews, Colman. Best Restaurants, Los Angeles. rev. ed. LC 84-7491. (Best Restaurants Ser.). (Illus.). 272p. 1984. pap. 4.95 (ISBN 0-89286-236-X). One Hund One Prods.

Andrews, Craig, jt. auth. see Benson, Carl.

Andrews, D. E., jt. ed. see Kennedy, C. W.

Andrews, D. F. & Herzberg, A. M. Data. (Statistics Ser.). (Illus.). 460p. 1985. 39.00 (ISBN 0-387-96125-9). Springer Verlag.

Andrews, D. F., et al. Robust Estimates of Location: Survey & Advances. LC 72-39019. 376p. 1972. pap. 9.95 (ISBN 0-691-08116-6). Princeton U Pr.

Andrews, David. Your Rights to Social Security Benefits. LC 81-9787. 192p. 1981. 12.95 (ISBN 0-87196-600-X); pap. 4.95 (ISBN 0-87196-601-8). Facts on File.

Andrews, Deborah. C. & Andrews, William D. Write for Results: How to Write Successful Memos, Letters, Summaries, Abstracts, Proposals, Reports, & Articles. (Orig.). 1982. pap. text ed. 8.95 (ISBN 0-316-04209-9). Little.

Andrews, Deborah C. & Blickle, Margaret D. Technical Writing: Principles & Forms. 2nd ed. 1982. text ed. write for info. (ISBN 0-02-303470-X). Macmillan.

Andrews, Denison. Hammock: How to Make Your Own & Lie in It. 2nd ed. LC 77-18433. (Illus.). 120p. 1978. pap. 2.95 (ISBN 0-89480-028-0, 178). Workman Pub.

Andrews, Dorothy W. God's World & Johhny. (YA) 1983. pap. 3.95 (ISBN 0-318-01335-5). Rod & Staff.

Andrews, E. H., ed. Developments in Polymer Fracture, Vol. 1. (Illus.). 348p. 1982. 64.75 (ISBN 0-85334-819-7, Pub. by Elsevier Applied Sci England). Elsevier.

Andrews, Earl & Dickens, Albert, eds. Voices from the Big House. LC 72-86910. 192p. 1972. 7.00 (ISBN 0-8187-0009-2). Harlo Pr.

Andrews, Edmund & Andrews, Irene D. A Comparative Dictionary of the Tahitian Language: Tahitian-English with an English-Tahitian Finding List. LC 75-35171. (Eng. & Tahitian.). Repr. of 1944 ed. 23.00 (ISBN 0-404-14201-X). AMS Pr.

Andrews, Edward D. The Community Industries of the Shakers. LC 77-187478. (The American Utopian Adventure Ser.). (Illus.). 322p. 1973. Repr. of 1932 ed. lib. bdg. 25.00x (ISBN 0-87991-010-0). Porcupine Pr.

--Gift to Be Simple. (Illus.). 1940. pap. 3.50 (ISBN 0-486-20022-1). Dover.

--Gift to Be Simple: Songs, Dances & Rituals of the American Shakers. (Illus.). 12.75 (ISBN 0-8446-1536-6). Peter Smith.

--People Called Shakers. new & enl. ed. 15.00 (ISBN 0-8446-1535-8). Peter Smith.

--People Called Shakers: A Search for the Perfect Society. (Illus.). 1953. pap. 5.50 (ISBN 0-486-21081-2). Dover.

Andrews, Edward D. & Andrews, F. Shaker Furniture: The Craftsmanship of an American Communal Sect. (Illus.). 14.75 (ISBN 0-8446-1537-4). Peter Smith.

Andrews, Edward D. & Andrews, Faith. Religion In Wood: A Book of Shaker Furniture. LC 66-12722. (Illus.). 128p. 1966. 20.00 (ISBN 0-253-17360-4); pap. 7.95x (ISBN 0-253-20286-8). Ind U Pr.

--Shaker Furniture: The Craftsmanship of an American Communal Sect. (Illus.). pap. 5.95 (ISBN 0-486-20679-3). Dover.

--Visions of the Heavenly Sphere: A Study in Shaker Religious Art. LC 79-83652. (Illus.). pap. 29.50 (ISBN 0-317-10386-5, 2017650). Bks Demand UMI.

--Work & Workshop among the Shakers. (Illus.). 224p. 1982. pap. 6.00 (ISBN 0-486-24382-6). Dover.

--Work & Worship among the Shakers. 1983. 13.25 (ISBN 0-8446-5942-8). Peter Smith.

Andrews, Edwin J., et al, eds. Spontaneous Animal Models of Human Disease, Vol. 1. (American College of Laboratory Animal Medicine Ser.). 1979. 70.00 (ISBN 0-12-058501-4). Acad Pr.

--Spontaneous Animal Models of Human Disease, Vol. 2. LC 78-20039. (American College of Laboratory Animal Medicine Ser.). 1980. 66.00 (ISBN 0-12-058502-2); Set. 110.00. Acad Pr.

Andrews, Elaine K. Civil Defense in the Nuclear Age. (Impact Ser.). (Illus.). 96p. (gr. 7 up). 1985. lib. bdg. 10.90 (ISBN 0-531-04853-5). Watts.

Andrews, Eliza F. The War-Time Journal of a Georgia Girl. King, Spencer B., ed. & intro. by. LC 75-39489. 416p. 1981. Repr. of 1960 ed. bds. 14.95 (ISBN 0-87797-033-5). Cherokee.

Andrews, Elizabeth. Ulster Folklore. 1978. Repr. of 1913 ed. lib. bdg. 30.00 (ISBN 0-8495-0113-X). Arden Lib.

--Ulster Folklore. LC 74-13592. 1974. Repr. of 1913 ed. lib. bdg. 17.50 (ISBN 0-88305-006-4). Norwood Edns.

Andrews, Elsie M. Facing & Fulfilling the Later Years. LC 68-16318. (Orig.). 1968. pap. 2.30x (ISBN 0-87574-157-6). Pendle Hill.

Andrews, Emily S. & Employee Benefit Research Institute Staff. The Changing Profile of Pensions in America. 1985. pap. 18.00 (ISBN 0-86643-038-5). Employee Benefit.

Andrews, Emma. The Films of Michael Caine. Castell, David, ed. (The Films of...Ser.). (Illus.). (gr. 7-12). 1978. Repr. of 1974 ed. PLB 6.95 (ISBN 0-912616-90-3). Greenhaven.

--The Films of Sean Connery. Castell, David, ed. (The Films of...Ser.). (Illus.). (gr. 7-12). 1978. Repr. of 1974 ed. PLB 6.95 (ISBN 0-912616-85-7). Greenhaven.

Andrews, Ernest E. The Emotionally Disturbed Family. LC 73-17734. 256p. 1974. 22.50x (ISBN 0-87668-112-7). Aronson.

Andrews, Ethan. Slavery & the Domestic Slave Trade in the U. S. LC 74-92412. 1836. 12.00 (ISBN 0-403-00148-X). Scholarly.

Andrews, Ethan A. Slavery & the Domestic Slave-Trade in the United States. facs. ed. LC 76-138331. (Black Heritage Library Collection Ser). 1836. 14.25 (ISBN 0-8369-8723-3). Ayer Co Pubs.

Andrews, Eva L., jt. ed. see Frizzell, Dorothy B.

Andrews, Evangeline W. & Andrews, Charles M., eds. Jonathan Dickinson's Journal. LC 61-11399. (Florida Classics). Orig. Title: God's Protecting Providence. (Illus.). 109p. pap. 5.95 (ISBN 0-912451-00-9). Florida Classics.

Andrews, F., jt. auth. see Andrews, Edward D.

Andrews, F., ed. Scientific Productivity. LC 78-21978. (Illus.). 1979. 44.50 (ISBN 0-521-22586-8). Cambridge U Pr.

Andrews, F. David, ed. Lost Peoples of the Middle East: Documents on the Struggle for Survival & Independence of the Kurds, Assyrians, & other Minority Races in the Middle East. 1983. ltd. 350 copies 34.95x (ISBN 0-89712-101-5). Documentary Pubns.

Andrews, F. Emerson. Foundation Watcher. LC 73-7398. 1973. 7.50 (ISBN 0-685-40252-5). Franklin & Marsh.

--New Numbers. 168p. 10.00 (ISBN 0-317-36274-7). Dozenal.

--Numbers, Please. 2nd enlarged ed. LC 77-20492. 1977. pap. 5.95x (ISBN 0-8077-2545-5). Tchrs Coll.

--Philanthropic Giving. 318p. 1950. 9.95x (ISBN 0-87154-022-3). Russell Sage.

Andrews, F. Emerson, ed. Legal Instruments of Foundations. LC 58-9443. 318p. 1958. 10.95x (ISBN 0-87154-020-7). Russell Sage.

Andrews, F. T. Building Mechanical Systems. 2nd ed. LC 75-11895. 412p. 1976. 24.50 (ISBN 0-88275-322-3). Krieger.

Andrews, Faith, jt. auth. see Andrews, Edward D.

Andrews, Fannie F. The Holy Land Under Mandate, 2 vols. LC 75-6417. (The Rise of Jewish Nationalism & the Middle East Ser). 797p. 1976. Repr. of 1931 ed. Set. 55.00 (ISBN 0-88355-304-X) (ISBN 0-88355-303-1). Hyperion Conn.

Andrews, Felicia. Riverwitch. (Orig.). 1980. pap. 2.75 (ISBN 0-515-05861-0). Jove Pubns.

--Seacliff. 368p. 1984. pap. 3.50 (ISBN 0-441-75640-9). Ace Bks.

--Silver Huntress. 1983. pap. 3.50 (ISBN 0-441-76609-9). Ace Bks.

--The Velvet Heart. 384p. 1985. pap. 3.95 (ISBN 0-441-86072-9, Pub. by Charter Bks). Ace Bks.

Andrews, Frank C. Equilibrium Statistical Mechanics. 2nd ed. LC 74-17197. 255p. 1975. 29.95x (ISBN 0-471-03123-2, Pub. by Wiley-Interscience). Wiley.

--Thermodynamics: Principles & Applications. LC 77-150607. Repr. of 1971 ed. 75.00 (ISBN 0-8357-9993-X, 2055278). Bks Demand UMI.

Andrews, Frank M. & Messenger, Robert C. Multivariate Nominal Scale Analysis: A Report on a New Analysis Technique & a Computer Program. LC 72-629721. 114p. 1973. 12.00x (ISBN 0-87944-135-6). Inst Soc Res.

Andrews, Frank M. & Withey, Stephen B. Social Indicators of Well-Being: Americans' Perception of Life Quality. LC 76-26179. (Illus.). 476p. 1976. 29.50x (ISBN 0-306-30935-1, Plenum Pr). Plenum Pub.

Andrews, Frank M., jt. auth. see Pelz, Donald C.

Andrews, Frank M., ed. Scientific Productivity: The Effectiveness of Research Groups in Six Countries. 469p. (Co-published with Cambridge University Press). 1979. pap. 29.95 (ISBN 92-3-101599-0, UM42, UNESCO). Unipub.

Andrews, Frank M., jt. ed. see Szalai, Alexander.

Andrews, Frank M., et al. A Guide for Selecting Statistical Techniques for Analyzing Social Science Data. 2nd ed. LC 74-620117. 80p. 1981. pap. 8.00x (ISBN 0-87944-274-3). Inst Soc Res.

--Multiple Classification Analysis: A Report on a Computer Program for Multiple Regression Using Categorical Predictors. rev. ed. LC 73-620206. 105p. 1973. cloth 12.00x (ISBN 0-87944-148-8); pap. 8.00x (ISBN 0-87944-055-4). Inst Soc Res.

Andrews, Fred. My Dog. (Illus.). 72p. (Orig.). 1976. pap. 4.95 (ISBN 0-915112-09-4). Seattle Bk.

Andrews, Fred, jt. auth. see Stein, Aurel.

Andrews, G. Reid. The Afro-Argentines of Buenos Aires, Eighteen Hundred to Nineteen Hundred. LC 80-5105. 304p. 1980. 25.00x (ISBN 0-299-08290-3). U of Wis Pr.

Andrews, G. S. Exfoliative Cytology. (Illus.). 120p. 1971. 15.50x (ISBN 0-398-01288-0). C C Thomas.

Andrews, Garnett, Jr. Reminiscences of an Old Georgia Lawyer. LC 84-12652. 112p. 1984. Repr. of 1870 ed. 9.95 (ISBN 0-87797-078-5). Cherokee.

Andrews, George. Extra-Terrestrials among Us. (Psi-Tech Ser.). (Illus.). 240p. (Orig.). 1985. pap. 9.95 (ISBN 0-87542-010-9, L-010). Llewellyn Pubns.

Andrews, George E. Encyclopedia of Mathematics & Its Applications: The Theory of Partitions, Vol. 2. 1984. 34.50 (ISBN 0-521-30222-6). Cambridge U Pr.

--Number Theory: The Theory of Partitions. LC 76-41770. (Encyclopedia of Mathematics & Its Applications: Vol. 2). (Illus.). 1976. text ed. 32.00 (ISBN 0-201-13501-9). Addison-Wesley.

--On the General Rogers-Ramanujan Theorem. LC 74-18067. (Memoirs: No. 152). 86p. 1974. pap. 10.00 (ISBN 0-8218-1852-X, MEMO-152). Am Math.

--Partitions: Yesterday & Today. 56p. (Orig.). 1980. pap. text ed. 5.00 (ISBN 0-9597579-0-2). Australia N U P.

--Stet. LC 84-3059. (Memoirs: No. 301). 48p. 1984. pap. 8.00 (ISBN 0-8218-2302-7). Am Math.

Andrews, George E. see Scedrov, Andrej.

Andrews, George E., ed. Percy Alexander MacMahon: Collected Papers: Combinatorics, Vol. 1. LC 77-28962. (Mathematicians of Our Time Ser.). 1978. 100.00x (ISBN 0-262-13121-8). MIT Pr.

Andrews, George F. Maya Cities: Placemaking & Urbanization. LC 73-19390. (Civilization of the American Indian Ser.: Vol. 131). (Illus.). 488p. 1975. 35.00 (ISBN 0-8061-1187-9). U of Okla Pr.

Andrews, Gini. Esther: The Star & the Sceptre. 288p. 1981. pap. 6.95 (ISBN 0-310-20181-0). Zondervan.

--Your Half of the Apple. pap. 4.95 (ISBN 0-310-20171-3). Zondervan.

Andrews, Glenn, jt. auth. see Sobol, Donald J.

Andrews, Gould A., jt. ed. see Kniseley, Ralph M.

Andrews, Gould A., et al, eds. Radioactive Pharmaceuticals: Proceedings. LC 66-60068. (AEC Symposium Ser.). 702p. 1966. pap. 25.50 (ISBN 0-87079-325-X, CONF-651111); microfiche 4.50 (ISBN 0-87079-326-8, CONF-651111). DOE.

Andrews, Gregory E., ed. Tax Incentives for Historic Preservation. rev. ed. LC 79-93052. (Illus.). 240p. 1981. pap. 12.95 (ISBN 0-89133-096-8). Preservation Pr.

Andrews, H. E. Coleoptera: Carabidae-Carabinae. (Fauna of British India Ser.: Vol. 1). (Illus.). xxvii, 433p. 30.00 (ISBN 0-88065-006-0, Pub. by Messers Today & Tomorrows Printers & Publishers India). Scholarly Pubns.

Andrews, H. E., ed. Coleoptera: Carabidae-Harpalinae 1. (Fauna of British India Ser.: Vol. 2). (Illus.). xvi, 340p. 1977. Repr. of 1935 ed. 25.00 (ISBN 0-88065-009-5, Pub. by Messers Today & Tomorrows Printers & Publishers India). Scholarly Pubns.

Andrews, H. K., jt. auth. see Morris, Reginald O.

Andrews, Hans A. Evaluating for Excellence. 160p. 1985. text ed. 12.95 (ISBN 0-913507-04-0); pap. text ed. 6.95 (ISBN 0-317-14535-5). New Forums.

Andrews, Harry C. Computer Techniques in Image Processing. 1970. 44.00 (ISBN 0-12-058550-2). Acad Pr.

--Introduction to Mathematical Techniques in Pattern Recognition. LC 82-6543. 262p. 1983. Repr. of 1972 ed. 27.50 (ISBN 0-89874-506-3). Krieger.

--Tutorial & Selected Papers in Digital Image Processing. 748p. 1978. 25.00 (ISBN 0-317-34769-1); 19.00, members (ISBN 0-317-34770-5). SPIE.

Andrews, Harry C. & Hunt, B. R. Digital Image Restoration. (Signal Processing Ser.). (Illus.). 1977. 41.95 (ISBN 0-13-214213-9). P-H.

Andrews, Heber J. How to Avoid Bicycle Theft: Complete Handbook for Parents & Owners. 2nd ed. LC 84-90406. (Illus.). 64p. (Orig.). 1985. pap. text ed. 5.95x (ISBN 0-9609596-1-0). Hands Off.

Andrews, Henry N. The Fossil Hunters: In Search of Ancient Plants. LC 79-24101. (Illus.). 420p. 1980. 37.50x (ISBN 0-8014-1248-X). Cornell U Pr.

Andrews, Henry N., jt. auth. see Gensel, Patricia G.

Andrews, Herbert K. The Technique of Byrd's Vocal Polyphony. LC 79-25357. 306p. 1980. Repr. of 1966 ed. lib. bdg. 42.50x (ISBN 0-313-22252-5, ANTB). Greenwood.

Andrews, Hilda, ed. & intro. by see Byrd, William.

Andrews, Hilda, ed. see Byrd, William.

Andrews, Hilda, tr. see Cortot, Alfred.

Andrews, Hilda, tr. see Marliave, Joseph De.

Andrews, Hilda, tr. see Walicki, Andrzei.

Andrews, Howard, jt. auth. see Lapp, Ralph.

Andrews, I. Pompeii. (Introduction to the History of Mankind Ser.). 1978. 4.95 (ISBN 0-521-20973-0). Cambridge U Pr.

Andrews, Ian. Boudicca's Revolt. (Introduction to the History of Mankind Ser.). 1972. 4.50 (ISBN 0-521-08031-2). Cambridge U Pr.

--Pompeii. LC 80-7447. (Cambridge Topic Bks.). (Illus.). (gr. 5-10). 1980. PLB 7.95 (ISBN 0-8225-1220-3). Lerner Pubns.

Andrews, Irene D., jt. auth. see Andrews, Edmund.

Andrews, Israel D. Communication from the Secretary of the Treasury. LC 75-22797. (America in Two Centuries Ser). 1976. Repr. of 1853 ed. 68.50x (ISBN 0-405-07668-1). Ayer Co Pubs.

Andrews, J. Price Guide to Antique Furniture. (Illus.). 1978. 39.50 (ISBN 0-902028-70-7). Apollo.

--Price Guide to British Antique Furniture. (Illus.). 1985. 39.50 (ISBN 0-907462-79-0). Antique Collect.

--Price Guide to Victorian, Edwardian & Nineteen Twenty Furniture. (Illus.). 1980. 39.50 (ISBN 0-902028-89-8). Apollo.

Andrews, J. & Von Hahn, H. P., eds. Geriatrics for Everyday Practice. (Illus.). viii, 220p. 1981. pap. 16.75 (ISBN 3-8055-1803-X). S Karger.

Andrews, J. & Williams, E. Woodford, eds. Iron, Anemia, & Old Age. (Gerontologia Clinica: Vol. 13, No. 1-2). 1971. pap. 9.50 (ISBN 3-8055-0889-1). S Karger.

Andrews, J., ed. see International Congress of the International Association of Gerontology, 10th.

Andrews, J. A. Human Rights in Criminal Procedure. 1982. lib. bdg. 85.00 (ISBN 90-247-2552-6, Pub. by Martinus Nijhoff Netherlands). Kluwer Academic.

--What Is Communism & Other Anarchist Essays. James, Bob, ed. (Illus.). 190p. (Orig.). 1984. pap. 12.95 (ISBN 0-949300-00-4). Left Bank.

Andrews, J. A. & Hirst, M. Evidence. (Criminal Law Library). 512p. 1987. 39.00 (ISBN 0-08-039237-7, Pub. by Waterlow). Pergamon.

Andrews, J. Austin & Wardian, Jeanne. Introduction to Music Fundamentals. 4th ed. 1978. pap. text ed. 22.95 (ISBN 0-13-489575-4). P-H.

Andrews, J. Austin & Wardian, Jeanne F. Introduction to Music Fundamentals. 5th ed. 256p. 1986. pap. text ed. 21.95 (ISBN 0-13-489584-3). P-H.

Andrews, J. B. Contes Ligures, traditions de Riviere. LC 78-20125. (Collection de contes et de chansons populaires: Vol. 17). Repr. of 1892 ed. 21.50 (ISBN 0-404-60367-X). AMS Pr.

Andrews, J. Cutler. The North Reports the Civil War. LC 84-22087. (Illus.). 829p. 1985. pap. 19.95 (ISBN 0-8229-5370-6). U of Pittsburgh Pr.

--Pittsburgh's Post-Gazette. LC 76-98805. Repr. of 1936 ed. lib. bdg. 18.75 (ISBN 0-8371-2956-7, ANPP). Greenwood.

--Pittsburgh's Post-Gazette: The First Newspaper West of the Alleghenies. (American Studies Ser.). 1969. Repr. of 1936 ed. 24.00 (ISBN 0-384-01455-0). Johnson Repr.

--The South Reports the Civil War. LC 84-25610. (Illus.). 627p. 1985. pap. 19.95 (ISBN 0-8229-5902-X). U of Pittsburgh Pr.

Andrews, J. D., ed. One Child Indivisible. LC 75-3790. 283p. 1975. pap. text ed. 2.75 (ISBN 0-912674-46-6, NAEYC 109). Natl Assn Child Ed.

Andrews, J. David. Choosing the Best Form for Your Poem: An Illustrated Guide to Fifteen Noteworthy Verse Forms. 92p. (gr. 6-12). 1979. pap. 6.50 (ISBN 0-686-29306-1); pap. text ed. 5.50 (ISBN 0-686-29307-X). Planetary Pr.

--Full Moon Is Rising: "Lost Haiku" of Matsuo Basho (1644-1694) & Travel Haiku of Matsuo Basho, a New Rendering. LC 75-32845. (Illus.). 1976. 12.00 (ISBN 0-8283-1651-1). Branden Pub Co.

--New Sonnets from Shakespeare: Thirty Famous Passages & Thirty New Sonnets from Shakespeare's Best-Loved Plays. 71p. (gr. 8-12). 1979. pap. 5.00 (ISBN 0-686-29305-3). Planetary Pr.

--Oh, My Comet, Shine! Found Haiku and Senryu, Based on "Thought Forms" by Mirtala Bentov. 60p. (Orig.). 1979. pap. 5.00 (ISBN 0-686-29308-8). Planetary Pr.

Andrews, J. David, ed. see Andrews, Melvin B.

Andrews, J. H. Irish Maps. (Irish Heritage Ser.). (Illus.). 26p. 1983. pap. 3.95 (ISBN 0-900346-23-X, Pub. by Salem Hse Ltd). Merrimack Pub Cir.

--A Short History of the Development of Street Railway Transportation in Philadelphia. (Illus.). 43p. 1979. pap. 2.50 (ISBN 0-911940-30-8). Cox.

Andrews, J. J. The Well-Built Elephant: A Tribute to American Eccentricity. (Illus.). 160p. 1983. pap. 16.95 (ISBN 0-312-92936-6). Congdon & Weed.

--The Well-Built Elephant & Other Roadside Attractions: A Tribute to American Eccentricity. LC 83-11107. (Illus.). 146p. 1983. pap. 16.95 (ISBN 0-312-92936-6). St Martin.

Andrews, J. Richard. Introduction to Classical Nahuatl. LC 74-30370. 752p. 1975. Set. 60.00x (ISBN 0-292-73802-1); text ed. 42.50x (ISBN 0-292-73804-8); wkbk. 17.50x (ISBN 0-292-73805-6). U of Tex Pr.

Andrews, J. Richard, ed. see Ruiz de Alarcon, Hernando.

Andrews, J. S. A Study of German Hymns in Current English Hymnals. (German Language & Literature-European University Studies: No. 1, Vol. 614). 398p. 1982. pap. 36.30 (ISBN 3-261-05068-3). P Lang Pubs.

Andrews, J. T. Quaternary Environments: The Eastern Canadian Arctic, Baffin Bay & West Greenland. (Illus.). 750p. 1985. text ed. 75.00x (ISBN 0-04-551094-6). Allen Unwin.

Andrews, J. T., et al. Nuclear Medicine: Clinical & Technological Bases. LC 77-5040. pap. 145.00 (ISBN 0-317-07739-2, 2015188). Bks Demand UMI.

Andrews, James D. Five-Seven-Five: Contemporary Verse in the Classic Haiku Form. 63p. 1974. 5.00 (ISBN 0-8233-0210-5). Golden Quill.

--Six Hundred Ships: Sonnets. 1975. 5.00 (ISBN 0-8233-0227-X). Golden Quill.

Andrews, James E. & Burgess, Joseph A. An Invitation to Action: The Luthern-Reformed Dialogue, Ser. III, 1981-1983; A Study of Ministry, Sacraments & Recognition. LC 84-47885. 144p. 1984. pap. 2.00 (ISBN 0-8006-1818-1, 1-1818). Fortress.

Andrews, James R. The Practice of Rhetorical Criticism. 288p. 1983. text ed. 20.95 (ISBN 0-02-303490-4). Macmillan.

Andrews, James R., ed. A Choice of Worlds: The Practice & Criticism of Public Discourse. (Auer Ser.). 1973. pap. text ed. 10.95 scp (ISBN 0-06-040291-1, HarpC). Har-Row.

Andrews, Jan. Ella: An Elephant-Unelephant. (Mini Books for Mini Hands Ser.). (Illus., Fr & Eng.). (gr. k-3). 1977. 0.95 (ISBN 0-912766-24-7); pap. 0.69 (ISBN 0-88776-063-5). Tundra Bks.

Andrews, Janice H. The Janan Curriculum: A Pre-School-Kindergarten Teachers Handbook. Linsel, Barbara & Dresser, Ginny, eds. (Illus.). 200p. pap. 16.95 (ISBN 0-9607458-4-X). Arts Pubns.

Andrews, Jean. Peppers: The Domesticated Capsicums. (Illus.). 186p. 1984. 35.00 (ISBN 0-292-76486-3). U of Tex Pr.

--Texas Shells: A Field Guide. (Elma Dill Russell Spencer Foundation Ser.: No. 11). (Illus.). 201p. 1981. pap. 8.95 (ISBN 0-292-72431-4). U of Tex Pr.

Andrews, Jenne. Reunion. 59p. (Orig.). 1983. pap. 6.00 (ISBN 0-89924-038-0). Lynx Hse.

Andrews, Jenne, et al, eds. Women Poets of the Twin Cities Anthology. 1977. pap. 3.60 (ISBN 0-917266-12-9). Vanilla.

Andrews, Jim, jt. auth. see Andrews, Judy.

Andrews, Joel, jt. auth. see Holmes, David.

Andrews, John. Adaptable Birds. (Dent Wildlife Bks.). (Illus.). 47p. 1985. 8.50x (ISBN 0-460-06061-9, BKA 05284, Pub. by J M Dent England). Biblio Dist.

--The Price Guide to Antique Furniture. 2nd ed. (Price Guide Ser.). (Illus.). 290p. 1978. 39.50 (ISBN 0-902028-70-7). Antique Collect.

--The Price Guide to Victorian, Edwardian & 1920's Furniture. (Price Guide Ser.). (Illus.). 218p. 1980. 39.50 (ISBN 0-902028-89-8). Antique Collect.

--The Price Guide to Victorian Furniture. (Price Guide Ser.). (Illus.). 346p. 1973. 21.50 (ISBN 0-902028-18-9). Antique Collect.

Andrews, John & Taylor, Jennifer. John Andrews Architecture: A Performing Art. (Illus.). 1982. 45.00x (ISBN 0-19-550557-3); pap. 19.95 (ISBN 0-19-554355-6). Oxford U Pr.

Andrews, John, jt. auth. see Taylor, Jennifer.

Andrews, John, ed. Discovering Walks in Suffolk. (Discovering Ser.: No. 263). (Illus.). 1983. pap. 3.95 (ISBN 0-85263-559-1, Pub. by Shire Pubns England). Seven Hills Bks.

Andrews, John B., jt. auth. see Commons, John R.

Andrews, John B. & Bliss, W. D., eds. History of Women in Trade Unions (Report on Conditions of Women & Child Wage-Earners in the United States, Vol. X; 61st Congress, 2nd Session, Senate Document No. 645) LC 74-3925. (Women in America Ser). 236p. 1974. Repr. of 1911 ed. 17.00x (ISBN 0-405-06071-8). Ayer Co Pubs.

Andrews, John C. The Airborne Album, Vol. 1. Philips, James M., ed. LC 81-82475. (Illus.). 52p. 1981. 5.95 (ISBN 0-932572-07-3). Phillips Pubns.

--Such Are the Valiant. (Inflation Fighter Ser.). 160p. 1982. pap. write for info. (ISBN 0-8439-1122-0, Leisure Bks). Dorchester Pub Co.

--Such Are the Valiant. 1978. pap. 1.50 (ISBN 0-505-51314-5, Pub. by Tower Bks). Dorchester Pub Co.

Andrews, John D., ed. Strengthening the Teaching Assistant Faculty. LC 84-82381. (Teaching & Learning Ser.: No. 22). (Orig.). 1985. pap. text ed. 9.95x (ISBN 0-87589-772-X). Jossey-Bass.

Andrews, John F., ed. William Shakespeare: His World, His Work, His Influence, 3 vols. 1985. lib. bdg. 180.00 (ISBN 0-684-17851-6, ScribR). Scribner.

Andrews, John M., et al, eds. Amyotrophic Lateral Sclerosis: Recent Research Trends. 1977. 27.50 (ISBN 0-12-059750-0). Acad Pr.

Andrews, John N. & Marsden, Carl A., eds. Tomorrow in the Making. LC 72-546. (Essay Index Reprint Ser.). Repr. of 1939 ed. 27.50 (ISBN 0-8369-2782-6). Ayer Co Pubs.

Andrews, John R. The Ghost Towns of Amador. (Illus.). 1978. pap. 3.95 (ISBN 0-913548-54-5, Valley Calif). Western Tanager.

Andrews, John S., tr. see Ernestus, Horst & Plassman, Engelbert.

Andrews, John T. A Geomorphological Study of Post-Glacial Uplift: With Particular Reference to Arctic Canada. (Special Publication of the Institute of British Geographers Ser.: No. 2). 1980. 25.00 (ISBN 0-12-058580-4). Acad Pr.

Andrews, John T. & Andrews, Martha, eds. Quarternary Studies on Baffin Island, West Greenland & Baffin Bay. 400p. cancelled (ISBN 0-08-027559-1). Pergamon.

Andrews, John W. A. D. Twenty-One Hundred. LC 71-82113. (Illus.). 1969. 12.00 (ISBN 0-8283-1033-5). Branden Pub Co.

--First Flight. 12.00 (ISBN 0-8283-1228-1). Branden Pub Co.

--Hill Country North. 12.00 (ISBN 0-8283-1226-5). Branden Pub Co.

--Prelude to Icaros. 1966. pap. 6.00 (ISBN 0-8283-1227-3). Branden Pub Co.

--Triptych for the Atomic Age. 12.00 (ISBN 0-8283-1281-8). Branden Pub Co.

Andrews, Joseph. Journey from Buenos Aires Undertaken on Behalf of the Chilian & Peruvian Mining Assn., 1825-26, 2 Vols. LC 74-128437. Repr. of 1827 ed. Set. 49.50 (ISBN 0-404-00410-5). AMS Pr.

Andrews, Joseph & Coffin, George. Win at Hearts. (Bridge & Other Card Games Ser.). (Illus.). 96p. (Orig.). pap. 2.95 (ISBN 0-486-24406-7). Dover.

Andrews, Judy & Andrews, Jim. Family Boating. (Illus.). 160p. 1983. 14.95 (ISBN 0-370-30407-1, Pub by The Bodley Head); pap. 7.95 (ISBN 0-370-30473-X). Merrimack Pub Cir.

Andrews, Julian, ed. & tr. see Tassi, Roberto.

Andrews, K. R. & Hair, P. E., eds. The Westward Enterprise: English Activities in Ireland, the Atlantic & America, 1480 to 1650. 332p. 1979. 53.00x (ISBN 0-85323-453-1, Pub. by Liverpool Univ England). State Mutual Bk.

Andrews, K. R., et al, eds. Westward Enterprise: English Activites in Ireland, the Atlantic & America 1480-1650. LC 79-13801. 326p. 1979. 19.95x (ISBN 0-8143-1647-6). Wayne St U Pr.

Andrews, K. W., et al, eds. Interpretation of Electron Diffraction Patterns. 2nd ed. 239p. 1971. 42.50x (ISBN 0-306-30534-8, Plenum Pr). Plenum Pub.

Andrews, Keith L. & Andrews, Bruce J. Commuter Calisthenics: An Exercise Program for Busy People's Travel Time. (Illus.). 122p. (Orig.). 1982. pap. 6.95 (ISBN 0-943364-11-6). Fitness Alt Pr.

Andrews, Kenneth R. The Concept of Corporate Strategy. rev. ed. LC 79-56086. 1980. 16.95 (ISBN 0-87094-208-5). Dow Jones-Irwin.

--Trade, Plunder & Settlement: Maritime Enterprise & the Genesis of the British Empire, 1480-1630. 404p. 1985. 49.50 (ISBN 0-521-25760-3); pap. 16.95 (ISBN 0-521-27698-5). Cambridge U Pr.

Andrews, Kenneth R., ed. English Privateering Voyages to the West Indies 1588-1595. (Hakluyt Society Works Ser.: No. 2, Vol. 111). Repr. of 1959 ed. 48.00 (ISBN 0-317-16032-X). Kraus Repr.

--The Last Voyage of Drake & Hawkins. 284p. 1972. 50.00x (ISBN 0-686-79462-1, Pub. by Hakluyt Soc England). State Mutual Bk.

Andrews, Kevin. The Flight of Ikaros: Travels in Greece During a Civil War. (Adventure & Exploration Ser.). 240p. 1985. pap. 5.95 (ISBN 0-14-009531-4). Penguin.

Andrews, L., jt. auth. see Karlins, M.

Andrews, Larry C. Ordinary Differential Equations. 1982. text ed. 27.75 (ISBN 0-673-15800-4). Scott F.

Andrews, Lewis M. & Karlins, Marvin. Requiem for Democracy? LC 71-149092. 1971. pap. text ed. 8.95 (ISBN 0-03-078120-5, HoltC). HR&W.

Andrews, Lewis M., jt. auth. see Karlins, Marvin.

Andrews, Mrs. Lewis R., et al, eds. Maryland's Way Cook Book. LC 64-25429. (Illus.). 372p. 1963. casebound 10.95 (ISBN 0-910688-01-X). Hammond-Harwood.

Andrews, Linda, jt. auth. see Leggett, Linda.

Andrews, Linton & Taylor, H. A. Lords & Laborers of the Press: Men Who Fashioned the Modern British Newspaper. LC 77-93879. (New Horizons in Journalism Ser). (Illus.). 352p. 1970. 12.50x (ISBN 0-8093-0432-5). S Ill U Pr.

Andrews, Lori. New Conceptions. 304p. 1983. 14.95 (ISBN 0-312-56610-7). St Martin.

Andrews, Lori B. New Conceptions. 1985. pap. 3.95 (ISBN 0-345-32307-6). Ballantine.

Andrews, Lorrin. A Dictionary of the Hawaiian Language. LC 72-89745. (Hawaiian.). 1973. 17.50 (ISBN 0-8048-1087-7). C E Tuttle.

--Grammar of the Hawaiian Language. LC 75-35173. Repr. of 1854 ed. 13.50 (ISBN 0-404-14202-8). AMS Pr.

Andrews, Lucilla. The Lights of London. 224p. 1985. 14.95 (ISBN 0-434-02130-X, Pub. by W Heinemann Ltd.). David & Charles.

Andrews, Lyman. Kaleidoscope. LC 74-160170. 96p. 1979. (Dist by Scribner); pap. 5.95 (ISBN 0-7145-1025-4). M Boyars.

Andrews, Lynn V. Flight of the Seventh Moon: The Teaching of the Shields. LC 83-48414. (Illus.). 208p. 1984. 13.41i (ISBN 0-06-250027-9, HarpR). Har-Row.

--Flight of the Seventh Moon: The Teaching of the Shields. LC 83-48414. 208p. 1985. pap. 6.68 (ISBN 0-06-250028-7, HarpR). Har-Row.

--Jaguar Woman: And the Wisdom of the Butterfly Tree. LC 84-48762. 192p. 1985. 15.34 (ISBN 0-06-250029-5, HarpR). Har-Row.

--Medicine Woman. LC 81-47546. 224p. 1983. pap. 6.68i (ISBN 0-06-250026-0, CN 4062, HarpR). Har-Row.

Andrews, M. Doris, ed. see Ash, Martha C.

Andrews, M. E. Gregg Office Job Training Program, Classroom Installation. Incl. Mail Clerk (ISBN 0-07-001811-1); File Clerk; Payroll Clerk (ISBN 0-07-001815-4); Typist (ISBN 0-07-001817-0); Clerk Typist (ISBN 0-07-001819-7); Accounts Payable Clerk (ISBN 0-07-001821-9); Accounts Receivable Clerk (ISBN 0-07-001823-5); Order Clerk (ISBN 0-07-001825-1); Credit Clerk (ISBN 0-07-001827-8); Stock Control Clerk (ISBN 0-07-001829-4); Office Cashier (ISBN 0-07-001831-6); Purchasing Clerk (ISBN 0-07-001833-2); Traffic Clerk. (ISBN 0-07-001835-9); Personnel Clerk (ISBN 0-07-001837-5); Billing Clerk (ISBN 0-07-001839-1). 1973. training manual 5.12 ea. McGraw.

Andrews, M. E., jt. auth. see Mulkerne, D. D.

Andrews, Malcolm. Dickens on England & the English. LC 78-27539. (Illus.). 201p. 1979. text ed. 26.50x (ISBN 0-06-490186-6, 06317). B&N Imports.

Andrews, Marietta M. My Studio Window: Sketches of the Pageant of Washington Life. 1928. 30.00 (ISBN 0-932062-05-9). Sharon Hill.

Andrews, Mark. Atari Roots: Atari Assembly Language. (Orig.). 1984. pap. 14.95 (ISBN 0-88190-171-7, BO171). Datamost.

--Blackout. 1978. pap. 1.50 (ISBN 0-8439-0525-5, Leisure Bks). Dorchester Pub Co.

--The Return of Jack the Ripper. 1977. pap. 1.75 (ISBN 0-8439-0476-3, Leisure Bks). Dorchester Pub Co.

--Satan's Manor. 288p. 1982. pap. 3.25 (ISBN 0-8439-1175-1, Leisure Bks). Dorchester Pub Co.

--Satan's Manor. 288p. 1983. pap. 2.95 (ISBN 0-8439-2014-9, Leisure Bks). Dorchester Pub Co.

Andrews, Marta, et al. Platicas: Conversational Spanish. LC 80-84024. 304p. 1981. pap. text ed. 14.50 (ISBN 0-8403-2328-X). Kendall-Hunt.

Andrews, Martha, jt. ed. see Andrews, John T.

Andrews, Mary. Bob & the Guides. facsimile ed. LC 77-163019. (Short Story Index Reprint Ser.). Repr. of 1906 ed. 21.50 (ISBN 0-8369-3933-6). Ayer Co Pubs.

Andrews, Mary R. His Soul Goes Marching on (Lincoln) Repr. of 1922 ed. 12.50 (ISBN 0-89987-160-7). Darby Bks.

--A Lost Commander: Florence Nightingale. 299p. Repr. of 1933 ed. lib. bdg. 45.00 (ISBN 0-918377-63-3). Russell Pr.

Andrews, Mason. Aldo Rossi: 1959-1983. Arnell, Peter & Bickford, Ted, eds. LC 83-42923. (Illus.). 320p. 45.00 (ISBN 0-8478-0498-4); pap. 29.95 (ISBN 0-8478-0499-2). Rizzoli Intl.

Andrews, Melvin B. Carolina Adventures: Brief Sketches of Growing Up in Eastern North Carolina at the Turn of the Century (1889-1915) Andrews, J. David, ed. (Illus.). 92p. (Orig.). 1979. pap. 5.00 (ISBN 0-686-29310-X). Planetary Pr.

Andrews, Michael. The Life That Lives on Man. LC 76-53299. (Illus.). 1978. pap. 4.95 (ISBN 0-8008-4820-9). Taplinger.

--Principles of Firmware Engineering in Microprogram Control. LC 80-19386. (Illus.). 347p. 1980. 36.95 (ISBN 0-914894-63-3). Computer Sci.

--Programming Microprocessor Interface for Control & Instrumentation. (Illus.). 368p. 1982. 39.95 (ISBN 0-13-729996-6). P-H.

Andrews, Michael & Carrell, John. Valuing Private Companies. 100p. 1982. 45.00x (ISBN 0-686-45859-1, Pub. by Pubns Sec Templegate Pr England). State Mutual Bk.

Andrews, Michael A. The Flight of the Condor: A Wildlife Exploration of the Andes. LC 81-48533. (Illus.). 158p. 1982. 22.50 (ISBN 0-316-03958-6). Little.

Andrews, Michael F., ed. Aesthetic Form of Education. LC 58-11799. (Illus.). pap. 28.80 (ISBN 0-317-10521-3, 2019471). Bks Demand UMI.

Andrews, Michale & Rook, Alan. Merging for Profit: How to Win in the Take-over Game. 240p. 1982. 60.00x (ISBN 0-686-45857-5, Pub. by Pubns Sec Templegate Pr England). State Mutual Bk.

Andrews, Mildred & Riddle, Pauline. Church Organ Method. 123p. 1973. pap. 15.00 (ISBN 0-8258-0050-1, 04904). Fischer Inc NY.

Andrews, Miriam. Fifty Poems. LC 70-135873. (Orig.). 1971. pap. 5.00 (ISBN 0-8283-1304-0). Branden Pub Co.

Andrews, Nancy, ed. see Shipley, Margaret.

Andrews, Nicola. Forbidden Melody. (Second Chance at Love Ser.: No. 139). 192p. 1983. pap. 1.95 (ISBN 0-515-07227-3). Jove Pubns.

--Head over Heels. (Second Chance at Love Ser.: No. 200). 192p. 1984. pap. 1.95 (ISBN 0-515-07816-6). Jove Pubns.

--Reckless Desire. (Second Chance at Love Ser.: No. 180). 192p. 1984. pap. 1.95 (ISBN 0-515-07595-7). Jove Pubns.

--Rules of the Game. (Second Chance at Love Ser.: No. 218). 192p. 1984. pap. 1.95 (ISBN 0-515-08074-8). Jove Pubns.

Andrews, Oliver. Living Materials: A Sculptor's Handbook. LC 77-71057. (Illus.). 348p. 1983. 45.00 (ISBN 0-520-03447-3). U of Cal Pr.

Andrews, Oliver, Jr; see Bird, Thomas E.

Andrews, Ondre H., ed. see Huston, Harvey.

Andrews, P. Transfinite Type Theory with Type Variables. (Studies in Logic: Vol. 3). 1965. 17.00 (ISBN 0-7204-2234-5, North Holland). Elsevier.

Andrews, P. B. Facies & Genesis of a Hurricane-Washover Fan, St. Joseph Island, Central Texas Coast. (Report of Investigations Ser.: RI 67). (Illus.). 147p. 1970. 3.00 (ISBN 0-318-03167-1). Bur Econ Geology.

Andrews, Patrick. The Bent Star. 192p. (Orig.). 1982. pap. 2.25 (ISBN 0-505-51843-0, Pub. by Tower Bks). Dorchester Pub Co.

--The Kiowa Flats Raiders. (Orig.). 1980. pap. 1.75 (ISBN 0-532-23145-7). Woodhill.

Andrews, Peter. Country Inns of America: Southwest. Gardner, Roberta H., ed. (Illus.). 96p. (Orig.). 1982. pap. 10.25 (ISBN 0-03-059179-1, Owl Bks). HR&W.

Andrews, Peter & Layhe, Robert. Excavations on Black Mesa, 1980: A Descriptive Report. LC 82-72189. (Research Paper: No. 24). (Illus.). xv, 360p. 1982. pap. 10.00 (ISBN 0-88104-003-7). Center Archaeo.

Andrews, Peter, jt. auth. see Busk, Fred.

Andrews, Peter, ed. Country Inns of America, 3 vols. Incl. Vol. I. New England & the Maritimes (ISBN 0-03-042836-X); Vol. II. The Mid Atlantic & the South (ISBN 0-03-042841-6); Vol. III. The Pacific Coast & the Southwest. LC 77-71352. (Illus.). 1978. 16.00 ea. HR&W.

--Country Inns of America: Southeast. Gardner, Roberta H., tr. (Illus.). 96p. (Orig.). 1982. pap. 10.25 (ISBN 0-03-059178-3, Owl Bks). HR&W.

Andrews, Peter, et al. California. (Country Inns of America Ser.). (Illus.). 96p. (Orig.). 1983. 25.00 (ISBN 0-03-062756-7); pap. 9.95 (ISBN 0-03-043726-1). HR&W.

--Lower New England. LC 79-22906. (Country Inns of America Ser.). (Illus.). 96p. (Orig.). 1980. pap. 9.95 (ISBN 0-03-043716-4). HR&W.

--New York & Mid-Atlantic. LC 79-22906. (Country Inns of America Ser.). (Illus.). 96p. (Orig.). 1980. pap. 9.95 (ISBN 0-03-043721-0). HR&W.

--Upper New England. LC 79-22906. (Country Inns of America Ser.). (Illus.). 96p. (Orig.). 1980. pap. 9.95 (ISBN 0-03-043711-3). HR&W.

Andrews, Philip W. On Competition in Economic Theory. LC 81-6246. ix, 141p. 1981. Repr. of 1964 ed. lib. bdg. 19.75x (ISBN 0-313-23053-6, ANOC). Greenwood.

Andrews, Ralph. Glory Days of Logging. encore ed. LC 56-58157. 1956. 9.95 (ISBN 0-87564-905-X). Superior Pub.

Andrews, Ralph W. Heroes of the Western Woods. (Illus.). 1979. pap. 6.95 (ISBN 0-87564-908-4). Superior Pub.

--Redwood Classic. (Illus.). 174p. 1985. pap. 12.95 (ISBN 0-88740-049-3). Schiffer.

--This Was Logging. 1954. 19.95 (ISBN 0-87564-901-7). Superior Pub.

--This Was Logging: Drama in the Northwest Timber Country. (Illus.). 157p. 1985. pap. 9.95 (ISBN 0-88740-035-3). Schiffer.

--Timber: Loggers Challenge the Great Northwest Forests. (Illus.). 182p. 1985. pap. 11.95 (ISBN 0-88740-036-1). Schiffer.

Andrews, Richard B. State Economic Development: Wisconsin's Planning Methods & Potentials. LC 68-9014. (Land Economics Monographs, No. 2). (Illus.). 116p. 1968. pap. 7.00x (ISBN 0-299-95023-9). U of Wis Pr.

--Urban Land Economics & Public Policy. LC 77-122281. 1971. 16.95 (ISBN 0-02-900710-0). Free Pr.

Andrews, Richard B., ed. Urban Land Use Policy. LC 70-169230. 1972. 22.95 (ISBN 0-02-900700-3). Free Pr.

Andrews, Richard M. The Geo-Political Significance of the European Empires. (Illus.). 167p. 1984. 89.50x (ISBN 0-86722-081-3). Inst Econ Pol.

Andrews, Robert & Ericson, E. E. Teaching Industrial Education: Principles & Practices. 1976. pap. text ed. 13.92 (ISBN 0-02-665790-2). Bennett IL.

Andrews, Robert C., jt. auth. see Bush, Clifford L.

Andrews, Ronald, jt. auth. see Frith, James.

Andrews, Roy C. Ends of the Earth. LC 78-164078. (Towers Bks). (Illus.). x, 355p. 1972. Repr. of 1929 ed. 40.00x (ISBN 0-8103-3923-4). Gale.

--On the Trail of Ancient Man. 1926. 30.00 (ISBN 0-8495-0227-6). Arden Lib.

--On the Trail of Ancient Man. 1926. 25.00 (ISBN 0-8482-3253-4). Norwood Edns.

Andrews, Ruth, ed. How to Know American Folk Art: Eleven Experts Discuss Many Aspects of the Field. 1977. pap. 6.95 (ISBN 0-525-47460-9). Dutton.

Andrews, S. Mahala, et al, eds. Problems in Vertebrate Evolution. (Linnean Society Symposium Ser.). 1977. 70.00 (ISBN 0-12-059950-3). Acad Pr.

Andrews, S. W. Be a Wine & Beer Judge. (Illus.). 110p. Date not set. pap. 3.95 (ISBN 0-900841-47-8, Pub. by Aztex Corp). Argus Bks.

Andrews, Samuel J. Christianity & Anti-Christianity in Their Final Conflict. 1982. lib. bdg. 15.00 (ISBN 0-86524-084-1, 9804). Klock & Klock.

Andrews, Samuel J. & Gifford, E. H. Man & the Incarnation: The Study of Philippians 2 & Psalm 110. 1981. lib. bdg. 15.00 (ISBN 0-86524-078-7, 9510). Klock & Klock.

Andrews, Sandy. Crested China. (Illus.). 304p. 1985. 26.95 (ISBN 0-903852-11-X, Pub. by Milestone Pubns UK). Seven Hills Bks.

Andrews, Sandy & Pine, Nicholas. The Price Guide to Crested China, 1985. (Illus.). 288p. 1985. 17.95 (ISBN 0-903852-44-6, Pub. by Milestone Pubns UK). Seven Hills Bks.

Andrews, Sephen P. Love, Marriage & Divorce. 121p. Date not set. Repr. of 1899 ed. 29.00 (ISBN 0-932051-63-4). Am Repr Serv.

Andrews, Sheila. The No-Cooking Fruitarian Recipe Book. (Illus.). 1976. pap. 5.00 (ISBN 0-7225-0290-7). Newbury Bks.

Andrews, Sherry, jt. auth. see Roberts, Patti.

Andrews, Sherry, jt. auth. see Roberts, Patty.

Andrews, Sidney. South Since the War. LC 69-18546. (American Negro: His History & Literature Ser., No. 2). 1969. Repr. of 1866 ed. 16.00 (ISBN 0-405-01847-9). Ayer Co Pubs.

Andrews, Siri, ed. Hewins Lectures, Nineteen Forty-Seven to Nineteen Sixty-Two. LC 63-21644. 1963. pap. 6.00 (ISBN 0-87675-056-0). Horn Bk.

Andrews, Stephen P. Primary Synopsis of Universology & Alwato: The New Scientific Universal Language. Stern, Madeleine B., ed. 1971. 12.50x (ISBN 0-87730-007-0). M&S Pr.

--The Science of Society. 69.95 (ISBN 0-8490-1003-9). Gordon Pr.

--Sovereignty of the Individual. 59.95 (ISBN 0-8490-1094-2). Gordon Pr.

Andrews, Stephen P., ed. Love, Marriage, & Divorce, & the Sovereignty of the Individual. LC 78-67573. (Free Love in America). Repr. of 1853 ed. 14.50 (ISBN 0-404-60962-7). AMS Pr.

Andrews, Stephen P., et al. Love, Marriage, & Divorce. Shively, Charles, ed. 1975. 15.00x (ISBN 0-87730-010-0). M&S Pr.

Andrews, Stephen Pearl. The Science of Society. Shively, Charles, ed. 184p. 1970. 15.00 (ISBN 0-87730-004-6). M&S Pr.

Andrews, Stephenson B., ed. Bacon's Castle Surry County, Virginia. LC 84-70846. (Illus.). 92p. 1984. pap. 24.95 (ISBN 0-917565-00-2). Assn Preserv Va.

Andrews, Susyn. Ilex in Paris. 150p. 20.00 (ISBN 0-318-17310-7). Holly Soc.

Andrews, Terry. The Story of Harold. (Illus.). 1980. pap. 2.95 (ISBN 0-380-49965-7, 49965-7, Bard). Avon.

Andrews, Theodora. A Bibliography of Drug Abuse: Supplement 1977 - 1980. LC 81-8194. 312p. 1981. lib. bdg. 27.50 (ISBN 0-87287-252-1). Libs Unl.

--Substance Abuse Materials for School Libraries: An Annotated Bibliography. 225p. 1984. lib. bdg. 22.50 (ISBN 0-87287-476-1). Libs Unl.

Andrews, Theodora, et al. Bibliography on Herbs, Herbal Remedies, Natural Foods, & Unconventional Treatment. LC 82-128. 344p. 1982. lib. bdg. 30.00 (ISBN 0-87287-288-2). Libs Unl.

Andrews, Thomas F., ed. see Cooke, Edward & Rogers, Woodes.

Andrews, V. C. Flowers in the Attic. 1982. pap. 3.95 (ISBN 0-671-46297-0). PB.

--Flowers in the Attic. (Reader's Request Ser.). 1983. lib. bdg. 18.95 (ISBN 0-8161-3428-6, Large Print Bks). G K Hall.

--Flowers in the Attic. Incl. If there be Thorns; Petals on the Wind; Seeds of Yesterday. 1984. pap. 15.80 boxed set (ISBN 0-671-90083-8). PB.

--Heaven. (Orig.). 1985. pap. 4.50 (ISBN 0-671-52542-5). PB.

--If There Be Thorns. 1982. pap. 3.95 (ISBN 0-671-46300-4). PB.

--If There Be Thorns. (Reader's Request Ser.). 1983. lib. bdg. 18.95 (ISBN 0-8161-3429-4, Large Print Bks). G K Hall.

--My Sweet Audrina. 368p. 1982. 14.50 (ISBN 0-671-44327-5, Poseidon). PB.

--My Sweet Audrina. 1982. 14.50 (ISBN 0-686-81877-6, Pub. by Poseidon). S&S.

--My Sweet Audrina. 1983. pap. 3.95 (ISBN 0-671-46820-0). PB.

--Petals on the Wind. 1982. pap. 3.95 (ISBN 0-671-46299-7). PB.

--Petals on the Wind. (Reader's Request Ser.). 1983. lib. bdg. 19.95 (ISBN 0-8161-3427-8, Large Print Bks). G K Hall.

--Seeds of Yesterday. 1983. write for info. (Pub. by Poseidon). S&S.

--Seeds of Yesterday. (Orig.). 1984. pap. 3.95 (ISBN 0-671-44328-3). PB.

Andrews, Victor L., et al. Financial Management: Cases & Readings. 3rd ed. 1982. 32.95x (ISBN 0-256-02621-1). Irwin.

Andrews, W. Guide to the Study of Environmental Pollution. 1972. text ed. 12.40 (ISBN 0-13-370858-6); pap. text ed. 9.84 (ISBN 0-13-370833-0). P-H.

--Guide to the Study of Freshwater Ecology. 1971. 11.36 (ISBN 0-13-370866-7); pap. text ed. 10.84 (ISBN 0-13-370759-8). P-H.

Andrews, W., et al. Guide to the Study of Terrestrial Ecology. 1974. lib. bdg. 12.40 (ISBN 0-13-370940-X); pap. text ed. 10.84 (ISBN 0-13-370932-9). P-H.

--Urban Studies. 1976. pap. text ed. 17.44 (ISBN 0-13-939280-7); tchr's guide o.p. 4.00 (ISBN 0-13-939454-0). P-H.

Andrews, W. L. Among My Books. 59.95 (ISBN 0-87968-616-2). Gordon Pr.

--Gossip About Book Collecting, 2 vols. 250.00 (ISBN 0-8490-0253-2). Gordon Pr.

--Jean Grolier. 59.95 (ISBN 0-8490-0437-3). Gordon Pr.

--New York As Washington Knew It After the Revolution. 59.95 (ISBN 0-8490-0726-7). Gordon Pr.

--The Old Booksellers of New York. 59.95 (ISBN 0-8490-0753-4). Gordon Pr.

Andrews, W. P., ed. see Brooks, Charles T.

Andrews, W. S., et al. Magic Squares & Cubes. 1917. pap. 6.95 (ISBN 0-486-20658-0). Dover.

Andrews, W. T. A Waif -A Prince. facsimile ed. LC 73-37581. (Black Heritage Library Collection). Repr. of 1895 ed. 18.50 (ISBN 0-8369-8957-0). Ayer Co Pubs.

Andrews, W. T., ed. Critics on D. H. Lawrence. LC 77-159294. (Readings in Literary Criticism Ser: No. 9). 1979. pap. 5.95x (ISBN 0-87024-207-5). U of Miami Pr.

--Critics on Shakespeare. (Readings in Literary Criticism). 1973. pap. text ed. 7.95x (ISBN 0-04-821034-X). Allen Unwin.

Andrews, Walter G. An Introduction to Ottoman Poetry. LC 74-27615. (Studies in Middle Eastern Literatures: No. 7). 1976. 17.50x (ISBN 0-88297-012-7); pap. 14.95x (ISBN 0-88297-034-8). Bibliotheca.

--Poetry's Voice, Society's Song: Ottoman Lyric Poetry. LC 84-7351. (Publications on the Near East Ser.: No. 1). 1985. pap. 25.00 (ISBN 0-295-96153-8). U of Wash Pr.

Andrews, Wayne. Architecture, Ambition, & Americans: A Social History of American Architecture. rev. ed. LC 78-50786. (Illus.). 1978. 24.95 (ISBN 0-02-900770-4). Free Pr.

--Architecture, Ambition, & Americans: A Social History of American Architecture. rev. ed. LC 78-50786. (Illus.). 1979. pap. text ed. 12.95 (ISBN 0-02-900750-X). Free Pr.

--Architecture in America. rev. ed. LC 77-4273. (Illus.). 1977. pap. 8.95 (ISBN 0-689-70549-2). Atheneum.

--Architecture in Michigan. Rev. & enlarged ed. LC 67-26428. (Illus.). 182p. 1982. o. p. 22.00x (ISBN 0-8143-1718-9); pap. 13.95 (ISBN 0-8143-1719-7). Wayne St U Pr.

--Architecture in New England: A Photographic History. LC 80-7766. (Illus.). 202p. (Orig.). 1980. pap. 9.95i (ISBN 0-06-430106-0, IN 106, Icon Edns). Har-Row.

--Architecture in New York: A Photographic History. (Icon Editions). (Illus.). 212p. 1973. pap. 8.95i (ISBN 0-06-430042-0, IN-42, HarpT). Har-Row.

--Pride of the South: A Social History of Southern Architecture. LC 78-3214. (Illus.). 1979. 20.00 (ISBN 0-689-10931-8); pap. 10.95 (ISBN 0-689-70579-4). Atheneum.

--Voltaire. LC 80-29565. (Illus.). 1981. 13.95 (ISBN 0-8112-0800-1); pap. 6.95 (ISBN 0-8112-0802-8, NDP519). New Directions.

Andrews, Wendy. Are We There Yet? 160p. (gr. 7 up). 1985. 11.95 (ISBN 0-448-47758-0). Putnam Pub Group.

--The Supergirl Storybook. LC 84-3320. (Illus.). 64p. 1984. 6.95 (ISBN 0-399-21075-X, Putnam); 83.40 sets of 12 (ISBN 0-399-21077-6). Putnam Pub Group.

Andrews, William. At the Sign of the Barber's Pole. LC 74-77164. 1969. Repr. of 1904 ed. 35.00x (ISBN 0-8103-3846-7). Gale.

--Doctor in History, Literature, Folklore. LC 74-99779. 1970. Repr. of 1896 ed. 40.00x (ISBN 0-8103-3595-6). Gale.

--The Doctor in History, Literature, Folklore. 59.95 (ISBN 0-8490-0052-1). Gordon Pr.

--Modern Merry Men: Authors in the Lighter Vein in the Victorian Era. Repr. of 1904 ed. 35.00 (ISBN 0-8274-4143-6). R West.

--Old Time Punishments. 251p. 1975. Repr. of 1890 ed. 16.00 (ISBN 0-87928-056-5). Corner Hse.

--Old Time Punishments. LC 78-124585. 1970. Repr. of 1890 ed. 30.00x (ISBN 0-8103-3841-6). Gale.

Andrews, William, ed. Antiquities & Curiosities of the Church: Folklore & Historical Traditions About English Churches. LC 77-87673. Repr. of 1897 ed. 20.00 (ISBN 0-404-16465-X). AMS Pr.

--The Lawyer in History, Literature & Humour. 276p. 1982. Repr. of 1896 ed. lib. bdg. 27.50x (ISBN 0-8377-0211-9). Rothman.

--Legal Lore: Curiosities of Law & Lawyers. xii, 117p. 1982. Repr. of 1897 ed. lib. bdg. 22.50x (ISBN 0-8377-0845-1). Rothman.

Andrews, William D. Basic Federal Income Taxation. 2nd ed. 1979. text ed. 30.35 (ISBN 0-316-04213-7). Little.

--Basic Federal Income Taxation. 3rd ed. LC 84-82457. 1985. text ed. write for info. (ISBN 0-316-04228-5). Little.

--Basic Federal Income Taxation: 1983 Supplement. 1984. pap. text ed. 11.00 (ISBN 0-316-04230-7). Little.

--Federal Income Taxation of Corporate Transactions. 2nd ed. 1979. text ed. 31.00 (ISBN 0-316-04212-9). Little.

--Federal Income Taxation of Corporate Transactions, 1982 Supplement. 1982. pap. 7.95 (ISBN 0-316-04224-2). Little.

Andrews, William D., jt. auth. see Andrews, Deborah. C.

Andrews, William D. & Surrey, Stanley S., eds. Federal Income Tax Project Subchapter C: Proposals on Corporate Acquisitions & Dispositions & Reporter's Study on Corporate Distributions (1982) LC 82-71580. xxvi, 551p. 1983. 65.00 (ISBN 0-686-82168-8, 5650). Am Law Inst.

Andrews, William G. French Politics & Algeria: The Process of Policy Formation 1954-1962. LC 62-15310. (Orig.). 1962. pap. text ed. 11.95x (ISBN 0-89197-179-3). Irvington.

--Presidential Government in Gaullist France: A Study of Executive Legislative Relations, 1958-1974. LC 82-222528. 320p. 1982. 39.50x (ISBN 0-87395-604-4); pap. 13.95x (ISBN 0-87395-605-2). State U NY Pr.

Andrews, William G., ed. International Handbook of Political Science. LC 81-6245. (Illus.). xii, 464p. 1982. lib. bdg. 55.00 (ISBN 0-313-22889-2, AIH/). Greenwood.

--The Politics of International Crises. 160p. 1970. pap. 9.50 (ISBN 0-317-14748-X). Krieger.

Andrews, William G. & Hoffman, Stanley, eds. The Impact of the Fifth Republic on France. LC 80-14651. 270p. pap. 11.95x (ISBN 0-87395-440-8). State U NY Pr.

Andrews, William G. & Hoffmann, Stanley, eds. The Fifth Republic at Twenty. 500p. 1980. 42.50x (ISBN 0-87395-413-0). State U NY Pr.

Andrews, William L. Critical Essays on W. E. B. DuBois. (Critical Essays in American Literature Ser.). 1985. lib. bdg. 35.00 (ISBN 0-8161-8688-X). G K Hall.

--The Literary Career of Charles W. Chesnutt. LC 79-25875. (Southern Literary Studies). 300p. 1980. 27.50x (ISBN 0-8071-0673-9). La State U Pr.

Andrews, William L., ed. Literary Romanticism in America. LC 80-24365. xviii, 136p. 1981. 14.95x (ISBN 0-8071-0760-3). La State U Pr.

Andrews, William P. Goethe's Key to Faust. 59.95 (ISBN 0-8490-0245-1). Gordon Pr.

Andrews, William R. The Village War: Vietnamese Communist Revolutionary Activities in Dihn Tuong Province, 1960-1964. LC 73-80584. 192p. 1973. 15.00x (ISBN 0-8262-0150-4). U of Mo Pr.

Andrews, Zelle, ed. War in Slow Motion. 128p. (Orig.). 1985. pap. 6.95 (ISBN 0-8298-0553-2). Pilgrim Ny.

Andrews, Zelle W. War in Slow Motion: The Economic & Social Impact of Militarism. 1985. 6.95 (ISBN 0-377-00155-4). Friend Pr.

Andrews-Rusiecka, Hilda, tr. see Walicki, Andrzej.

Andreyev, A., et al. The Komsomol: Question & Answers. 1980. pap. 2.95 (ISBN 0-8285-1827-0, Pub. by Progress Pubs USSR). Imported Pubns.

Andreyev, I. The Noncapitalist Way. 195p. 1977. 3.95 (ISBN 0-8285-0247-1, Pub. by Progress Pubs USSR). Imported Pubns.

Andreyev, I. L. Engel's "The Part Played by Labour in the Transition from Ape to Man". 80p. 1985. pap. 1.45 (ISBN 0-8285-2982-5, Pub. by Progress Pubs USSR). Imported Pubns.

Andreyev, I. M. Ockerki po Istoriji Russkoi Literaturi XIX Vjeka. 316p. 1968. pap. text ed. 10.00 (ISBN 0-317-30303-1). Holy Trinity.

--Pravoslavno-Khristijanskaja Apologetika. 92p. 1965. pap. text ed. 5.00 (ISBN 0-317-30249-3). Holy Trinity.

--Pravoslavno-Khristijanskoe Nravstvennoje Bogoslovije. 148p. 1966. pap. text ed. 5.00 (ISBN 0-317-30264-7). Holy Trinity.

Andreyev, L. N. Selected Stories. Shotton, M. H., ed. (Library of Russian Classics). 112p. pap. text ed. 9.95x (ISBN 0-900186-10-0). Basil Blackwell.

--Silence. Goldberg, Isaac, ed. Lowe, W. H., tr. (International Pocket Library). pap. 3.00 (ISBN 0-8283-1450-0). Branden Pub Co.

Andreyev, Leonid see Goldberg, Isaac.

Andreyev, Olga C. Cold Spring in Russia. Carlisle, Michael, tr. from Russian. 1978. 15.00 (ISBN 0-88233-303-8). Ardis Pubs.

Andreyev, Vladimir. Gamailis & Other Tales from Stalin's Russia. Berry, Fred, tr. LC 75-17671. 240p. 1975. Repr. of 1963 ed. lib. bdg. 18.75 (ISBN 0-8371-8231-X, ANGA). Greenwood.

Andreyev, Y. Soviet Russian Literature: Selected Reading. 879p. 1980. 17.00 (ISBN 0-8285-2095-X, Pub. by Progress Pubs USSR). Imported Pubns.

Andrian, Charles F. Foundations of Comparative Politics: A Policy Perspective. 1983. pub net 15.00 (ISBN 0-534-01377-5, 82-17791). Brooks-Cole.

Andrian, G. W. Fondo y Forma: Literature, Language, Grammar Review. 1970. text ed. write for info. (ISBN 0-02-303420-3). Macmillan.

Andrian, Gustave W. Modern Spanish Prose: An Introductory Reader with a Selection of Poetry. 3rd ed. 1977. pap. text ed. 13.95 (ISBN 0-02-303430-0). Macmillan.

Andrian, Gustave W. & Davies, Jane. Pret a Lire. 1980. pap. write for info. (ISBN 0-02-303440-8). Macmillan.

Andrianov, A. N., et al. Thirteen Papers on Group Theory, Algebraic Geometry & Algebraic Topology. LC 51-5559. (Translations Ser.: No. 2, Vol. 66). 1968. 35.00 (ISBN 0-8218-1766-3, TRANS 2-66). Am Math.

Andrianov, A N, et al, eds. Algebra, Theory of Numbers & Their Applications. LC 80-28539. (STEKLO Ser.: No. 148). 1980. 102.00 (ISBN 0-8218-3046-5). Am Math.

Andrianova, Z. S., et al. Seismic Love Waves. LC 66-19935. 91p. 1967. 25.00x (ISBN 0-306-10786-4, Consultants). Plenum Pub.

Andric, I., et al, eds. Particle Physics 1980. 1981. 91.50 (ISBN 0-444-86174-2). Elsevier.

Andric, Ivo. The Bridge of the Drina. Edwards, Lovett F., tr. from Serbo-Croat. 1977. pap. 8.95 (ISBN 0-226-02045-2, P746, Phoen). U of Chicago Pr.

--Devil's Yard. Johnstone, Kenneth, tr. LC 75-15692. 137p. 1975. Repr. of 1962 ed. lib. bdg. 24.75 (ISBN 0-8371-8218-2, ANDY). Greenwood.

Andriekus, Leonardas. Eternal Dream. 1980. 6.00 (ISBN 0-87141-061-3). Manyland.

Andrien, Kenneth J. Crisis & Decline: The Viceroyalty of Peru in the Seventeenth Century. LC 84-23436. (Illus.). 288p. 1985. text ed. 27.50 (ISBN 0-8263-0791-4). U of NM Pr.

Andrieu, Lucette, ed. Dommage Qu'elle Soit une P...(Tis Pity She's a Whore) De John Ford: Vitalite et Devenie Scenique De la Tragedie, 2 vols. (Salzburg Studies in English Literature, Jacobean Studies Drama Ser.: Nos. 52-53). (Illus.). 1975. Set. pap. text ed. 50.75x (ISBN 0-391-01300-9). Humanities.

Andrijanov, V. G. Meteorological & Hydrological Data Required in Planning the Development of Water Resources. (Operational Hydrology Reports: No. 5). 42p. 1975. pap. 10.00 (ISBN 92-63-10419-0, W261, WMO). Unipub.

Andriola, Mary R., jt. auth. see Epstein, Charles M.

Andriole, Stephen, ed. Microcomputer Decision Support Systems: Design, Implementation & Evaluation. 1985. pap. write for info. (ISBN 0-89435-173-7). Qed Info Sci.

Andriole, Stephen J. Computer-Based National Information Systems: A Sourcebook. (Illus.). 250p. 1984. 24.95 (ISBN 0-89433-255-4). Petrocelli.

--Corporate Crisis Management. LC 84-19068. (Illus.). 250p. 1984. text ed. 29.95 (ISBN 0-89433-216-3). Petrocelli.

--Handbook of Problem Solving. (Illus.). 327p. 1983. text ed. 25.00 (ISBN 0-89433-186-8). Petrocelli.

--Interactive Computer Based Systems. (Illus.). 198p. 1983. 16.95 (ISBN 0-89433-191-4). Petrocelli.

--Interactive Computer Based Systems Design & Development. 1983. 16.95 (ISBN 0-89433-191-4). Van Nos Reinhold.

--Software Development Tools: A Source Book. (Illus.). 300p. 1985. 29.95 (ISBN 0-89433-272-4). Van Nos Reinhold.

Andriole, Stephen J. & Hopple, Gerald W. Revolution & Political Instability: Applied Research Methods. LC 83-40704. 27.95 (ISBN 0-312-05774-1). St Martin.

--Revolution & Political Instability: Applied Research Methods. LC 83-40704. 198p. 1984. 27.95 (ISBN 0-312-67991-2). St Martin.

Andriole, Stephen J., ed. Applications in Artificial Intelligence. 1985. 49.95 (ISBN 0-89433-219-8). Petrocelli.

--The Future of Information Processing Technology: A Source Book. 1985. 29.95 (ISBN 0-89433-263-5). Petrocelli.

--Software Development Tools: A Source Book. (Illus.). 240p. 1986. text ed. 29.95 (ISBN 0-89433-272-4). Petrocelli.

--Software Validation, Verification, Testing & Documentation: A Source Book. 1985. 49.50 (ISBN 0-89433-269-4). Petrocelli.

Andriole, Stephen J. & Nagler, Gordon R., eds. Navy Command & Control. LC 85-72109. (AFCEA C31 Ser.: Vol. III). 320p. 1985. 29.95 (ISBN 0-916159-04-3). Set. AFCEA Intl Pr.

Andriole, Stephen J. & Paschall, Lee M., eds. Air & Satellite Communications. LC 84-72110. (AFCEA C31 Ser.: Vol. II). (Illus.). 373p. 1985. 29.95 (ISBN 0-916159-03-5). AFCEA Intl Pr.

Andriole, Stephen J., jt. ed. see Boyes, Jon L.

Andriole, Stephen J., jt. ed. see Hopple, Gerald W.

Andris, William. Liberty Street. LC 80-51206. 460p. 1980. 14.95 (ISBN 0-9604278-0-5). St Basil Pr.

Andrist, Friedrich. Mares, Foals & Foaling. Dent, A., tr. pap. 2.75 (ISBN 0-85131-053-2, BL714, Dist. by Miller). J A Allen.

Andrist, Ralph K. The Erie Canal. LC 64-13898. (American Heritage Junior Library). 154p. (YA) (gr. 7 up). 1964. PLB 15.89 (ISBN 0-06-020101-0). HarpJ.

--Long Death. (Illus.). 1969. pap. 7.95 (ISBN 0-02-030290-8, Collier). Macmillan.

Andrist, Ralph K., ed. see Johnson, Herbert A.

Androgeus, John C., ed. The Lost Gospel of the Ages: Key to Immortality & Companion to the Holy Bible. (Illus.). 979p. 1978. pap. text ed. 95.00 (ISBN 0-9609802-3-7). Life Science.

Andronescu, Serban. Bye Cadmos: A Journal of Aesthetic Analogies. 5.00 (ISBN 0-917944-00-3). Am Inst Writing Res.

--English-Rumanian Dictionary. (Eng. & Romanian.). 24.50 (ISBN 0-87557-064-X, 064-X). Saphrograph.

--Rumanian-English Dictionary. 24.50 (ISBN 0-87557-063-1). Saphrograph.

--Who's Who in Romanian America. LC 76-46879. 1976. 35.00 (ISBN 0-917944-01-1). Am Inst Writing Res.

Andronicos, Manolis. The Acropolis: The Monuments & the Museum. (Athenon Illustrated Guides Ser.). (Illus.). 80p. 1983. pap. 14.95 (ISBN 0-88332-310-9, 8245, Pub. by Ekdotike Athenon Greecee). Larousse.

--Delphi. (Athenon Illustrated Guides Ser.). (Illus.). 80p. 1983. pap. 8.95 (ISBN 0-88332-298-6, 8232, Pub. by Ekdotike Athenon Greece). Larousse.

--Herakleion Museum. (Athenon Illustrated Guides Ser.). (Illus.). 80p. 1983. pap. 8.95 (ISBN 0-88332-301-X, 8235, Pub. by Ekdotike Athenon Greece). Larousse.

--National Museum. (Athenon Illustrated Guides Ser.). (Illus.). 96p. 1983. pap. 8.95 (ISBN 0-88332-296-X, 8240, Pub. by Ekdotike Athenon Greece). Larousse.

--Olympia. (Athenon Illustrated Guides Ser.). (Illus.). 80p. 1983. pap. 8.95 (ISBN 0-88332-300-1, 8242, Pub. by Ekdotike Athenon Greece). Larousse.

--Thessalonike Museum. (Athenon Illustrated Guides Ser.). (Illus.). 79p. 1984. pap. 10.95 (ISBN 0-88332-342-7, 8256, Pub. by Ekdotike Athenon Greece). Larousse.

--Vergina, the Prehistoric Necropolis & the Hellenistic Palace. (Studies in Mediterranean Archaeology Ser.: No. 13). (Illus.). 1964. pap. text ed. 5.25x (ISBN 91-85058-12-2). Humanities.

Andronicos, Manolis, et al. Philip of Macedon. Hatzopoulos, Miltiades B. & Loukopoulos, Louisa D., eds. (Illus.). 254p. 1980. 50.00 (ISBN 0-89241-330-1). Caratzas.

Andronicus, M., et al. The Greek Museums. 1981. 90.00x (ISBN 0-686-75404-2). State Mutual Bk.

Andronikashvili, E. L., jt. auth. see Lifshits, Evgenii M.

Andronikos, M., et al. Greek Museums. (Illus.). 420p. 1975. 75.00 (ISBN 0-89241-005-1). Caratzas.

--The Greek Museums. Incl. Acropolis. soft bd. 7.50 (ISBN 0-89241-006-X); Benaki. soft bd. 7.50 (ISBN 0-89241-015-9); Byzantine. soft bd. 7.50 (ISBN 0-89241-014-0); Cyprus. soft bd. 7.50 (ISBN 0-89241-011-6); Delphi. oft bd. 7.50 (ISBN 0-89241-008-6); Herakleion. soft bd. 7.50 (ISBN 89241-012-4-2); National. soft bd. 9.00 (ISBN 0-89241-007-8); Olympia. soft bd. 7.50 (ISBN 0-89241-009-4); Pella. soft bd. 7.50 (ISBN 0-89241-010-8); Thessalonike. soft bd. 7.50 (ISBN 0-89241-013-2). (Illus.). 1977. Caratzas.

Andronikos, Manolis. The Acropolis. Hionides, Harry, tr. from Gr. (Greek Museums Ser.). (Illus.). 48p. 1975. pap. 9.50 (ISBN 0-89241-006-X). Caratzas.

--Delphi. Cicellis, Kay, tr. from Gr. (Greek Museums Ser.). (Illus.). 52p. 1975. pap. 9.50 (ISBN 0-89241-008-6). Caratzas.

--The Finds from the Royal Tombs at Vergina. 1981. 15.50x (ISBN 0-85672-204-9, Pub. by Brit Acad England). State Mutual Bk.

--Herakleion Museum & Archaeological Sites of Crete. new ed. Lidell, Robert, tr. from Gr. (The Greek Museum Ser.). (Illus.). 56p. (Orig.). 1975. pap. 7.50 (ISBN 0-89241-012-4). Caratzas.

--National Museum. Jongh, Brian De, tr. from Gr. (Greek Museums Ser.). (Illus.). 114p. 1975. pap. 12.95 (ISBN 0-89241-007-8). Caratzas.

--Olympia. new ed. Cicellis, Kay, tr. from Gr. (The Greek Museums Ser). (Illus.). 52p. 1975. pap. 9.50 (ISBN 0-89241-009-4). Caratzas.

--Pella Museum. Cicellis, Kay, tr. from Gr. (The Greek Museums Ser). (Illus.). 28p. (Orig.). 1975. pap. 9.50 (ISBN 0-89241-010-8). Caratzas.

--Thessalonike Archaeological Museum. Cicellis, Kay, tr. (The Greek Museums Ser). (Illus.). 32p. (Orig.). 1975. pap. 9.50 (ISBN 0-89241-013-2). Caratzas.

Andronikov, Iraklii. Lermontov: Pictures, Watercolours & Drawings. 246p. 1982. 60.00x (ISBN 0-317-14250-X, Pub. by Collet's). State Mutual Bk.

Andronis, Constantine. Apostolos Makrakis--An Evaluation of Half a Century. 369p. (Orig.). 1966. pap. 4.00x (ISBN 0-938366-33-5). Orthodox Chr.

Andronov, A. A., et al. Eleven Papers on Differential Equations & Two in Information Theory. LC 51-5559. (Translations, Ser.: No. 2, Vol. 33). 1963. 35.00 (ISBN 0-8218-1733-7, TRANS 2-33). Am Math.

--Seven Papers on Equations Related to Mechanics & Heat. LC 51-5559. (Translations Ser.: No. 2, Vol. 75). 1968. 34.00 (ISBN 0-8218-1775-2, TRANS 2-75). Am Math.

Andropov, Y. V. Speeches & Writings. (Leaders of the World Ser.). 192p. 1983. 20.00 (ISBN 0-08-028177-X); pap. 11.50 (ISBN 0-08-028182-6). Pergamon.

--Speeches & Writings. 2nd, enl. ed. LC 83-19340. (Leaders of the World Ser.). 386p. 1983. 25.00 (ISBN 0-08-031287-X). Pergamon.

Andropova, Y. V. Speeches, Articles & Interviews: Andropova. 1984. write for info. (ISBN 0-8364-1165-X, Pub. by Allied India). South Asia Bks.

Andros, Phil. Below the Belt & Other Stories by Phil Andros. LC 82-3141. (Perineum Press Bk.). 140p. (Orig.). 1982. pap. 6.95 (ISBN 0-912516-75-5). Grey Fox.

--The Boys in Blue. LC 83-20108. (Perineum Press Bk.). 156p. 1984. pap. 6.95 (ISBN 0-912516-85-2). Grey Fox.

--Different Strokes. LC 83-18430. (Perineum Press Bk.). 160p. 1984. pap. 6.95 (ISBN 0-912516-86-0). Grey Fox.

--Greek Ways. LC 83-18438. (Perineum Press Bk.). 170p. 1984. pap. 7.95 (ISBN 0-912516-84-4). Grey Fox.

--My Brother, My Self. LC 83-5487. (Perineum Press Bk.). 150p. 1983. pap. 6.95 (ISBN 0-912516-77-1). Grey Fox.

--Roman Conquests. LC 83-5486. (Perineum Press Bk.). 162p. 1983. pap. 6.95 (ISBN 0-912516-76-3). Grey Fox.

--Shuttlecock. LC 83-18434. (Perineum Press Bk.). 184p. 1984. pap. 7.95 (ISBN 0-912516-78-X). Grey Fox.

Andros, Phil, pseud. Stud. rev, abr. ed. 216p. 1982. pap. 6.95 (ISBN 0-932870-02-3). Alyson Pubns.

Androse, R., tr. see Alessio, Piemontese.

Andross, Matilda E. Alone with God. (Stories That Win Ser.). 1961. pap. 0.99 (ISBN 0-8163-0133-6, 01500-8). Pacific Pr Pub Assn.

Androulakis, G. & Pissiotis, C., eds. European Society for Surgical Research, 18th Congress, Athens 1983: Abstracts. (Journal--European Surgical Research: Vol. 15, Suppl. 1). (Illus.). iv, 120p. 1983. pap. 29.25 (ISBN 3-8055-3781-6). S Karger.

Andrulis, Richard S. Adult Assessment: A Source Book of Tests & Measures of Human Behavior. 340p. 1977. pap. 35.50x spiral (ISBN 0-398-03603-9). C C Thomas.

Andrunakievic, V. A., et al. Transactions of the Moscow Mathematical Society, Vol. 29 (1973) 1976. 66.00 (ISBN 0-8218-1629-2, MOSCOW-29). Am Math.

--Twelve Papers on Topology, Algebra & Number Theory. LC 51-5559. (Translations Ser.: No. 2, Vol. 52). 1966. 36.00 (ISBN 0-8218-1752-3, TRANS 2-52). Am Math.

Andrus, Ann T., jt. auth. see Miller, Ruth M.

Andrus, Hyrum L. Joseph Smith & World Government. 144p. 1972. pap. 3.95 (ISBN 0-89036-032-4). Hawkes Pub Inc.

--Joseph Smith, the Man & the Seer. 6.95 (ISBN 0-87747-131-2). Deseret Bk.

Andrus, J. Russell & Mohammed, Azizali F. Trade, Finance, & Development in Pakistan. 1966. 22.50x (ISBN 0-8047-0126-1). Stanford U Pr.

Andrus, Lisa F. Measure & Design in American Painting, 1760-1860. LC 76-23601. (Outstanding Dissertations in the Fine Arts-American). (Illus.). 1977. Repr. lib. bdg. 68.00 (ISBN 0-8240-2675-6). Garland Pub.

Andrus, Ruth. A Tentative Inventory of the Habits of Children from Two to Four Years of Age. LC 77-176520. (Columbia University. Teachers College. Contributions to Eduation: No. 160). Repr. of 1924 ed. 22.50 (ISBN 0-404-55160-2). AMS Pr.

Andrushkiw, Vira. Lessons for Nurseries for English-Speaking Children. 2nd rev. ed. 68p. 1978. pap. 3.00 (ISBN 0-317-36111-2). UNWLA.

Andruskiw, Olga, jt. ed. see Conway, Mary E.

Andrusyshen, C. H. & Kirkconnell, Watson, trs. The Poetical Works of Taras Shevchenko. LC 66-2188. (Illus.). 1964. 25.00x (ISBN 0-8020-3114-5). U of Toronto Pr.

Andrusz, Gregory D. Housing & Urban Development in the U. S. S. R. (SUNY Series in Urban Public Policy). 350p. 1985. lib. bdg. 39.50x (ISBN 0-317-17642-0); pap. text ed. 14.95x (ISBN 0-317-17643-9). State U NY Pr.

Andry, Andrew C. & Schepp, Steven. How Babies Are Made. LC 99-944003. (Illus.). 88p. (ps up). 1984. pap. 6.70i (ISBN 0-316-04227-7). Little.

Andry, Carl F. Paul & the Early Christians. LC 81-40766. (Illus.). 148p. (Orig.). 1982. lib. bdg. 22.50 (ISBN 0-8191-1935-0); pap. text ed. 10.00 (ISBN 0-8191-1936-9). U Pr of Amer.

Andrysiak, Therese, jt. auth. see Cohen, Sidney.

Andrzej, Tymowski. The Strike in Gdansk. 50p. pap. 3.00 (ISBN 0-317-36701-3). Kosciuszko.

Andrzejewski, tr. see Cawl, Farrax M.

Andrzejewski, A., et al. Housing Programmes: The Role of Public Health Agencies. (Public Health Papers Ser: No. 25). 197p. (Eng, Fr, Rus, & Span.). 1964. pap. 3.60 (ISBN 92-4-130025-6). World Health.

Andrzejewski, B. W. Islamic Literature of Somalia. (Hans Wolff Memorial Lecture Ser.). 48p. 1983. pap. text ed. 5.00 (ISBN 0-941934-47-0). Indiana Africa.

Andrzejewski, B. W., et al. Literature in African Languages. 600p. 1985. write for info. (ISBN 0-521-25646-1). Cambridge U Pr.

Andrzejewski, Jerzy. Ashes & Diamonds. Welsh, D. J., tr. from Pol. (Penguin Writers from the Other Europe Ser.). 1980. pap. 4.95 (ISBN 0-14-005277-1). Penguin.

--The Inquisitors. Syrop, Konrad, tr. from Polish. LC 76-6896. 1976. Repr. of 1960 ed. lib. bdg. 18.75 (ISBN 0-8371-8868-7, ANIN). Greenwood.

Andujar, Julio I. Mastering Spanish Verbs. (Orig.). 1968. pap. text ed. 4.50 (ISBN 0-88345-100-X, 17452). Regents Pub.

Andujar, Julio I. & Dixson, Robert J. Graded Exercises in Spanish. (Orig.). (gr. 11 up). 1970. pap. text ed. 4.75 (ISBN 0-88345-059-3, 17450); answer key 1.50 (ISBN 0-685-19798-0, 18117). Regents Pub.

--Workbook in Everyday Spanish, 2 bks. rev. ed. (gr. 9 up). 1973. Bk. 1. pap. text ed. 5.25 (ISBN 0-88345-188-3, 18085); Bk. 2. pap. text ed. 5.25 (ISBN 0-88345-189-1, 18086); answer key 2.50 (ISBN 0-685-19804-9, 18087). Regents Pub.

Andujar, Julio I., jt. auth. see Dixson, Robert J.

Andujar, Julio I., ed. see Clarey, M. Elizabeth & Dixson, Robert J.

Andujar, Maria D. & Iglesias, Jose L. Mecanografia Al Dia. rev. ed. (YA) (gr. 10 up). 1977. pap. text ed. 3.50 (ISBN 0-88345-306-1, 18482). Regents Pub.

Andy, Orlando J. & Stephan, Hienz. The Septum of the Cat. (Illus.). 96p. 1964. photocopy ed. 12.75x (ISBN 0-398-00048-4). C C Thomas.

Anechiarico, Frank, jt. auth. see Lewis, Eugene.

Anees, Munawar A., ed. see Hamarneh, Sami K.

ANEF. The Status of Education in Nepal, 8 papers. 76p. 1982. 14.00 (ISBN 0-318-17089-2, 71). Am-Nepal Ed.

--Summer Seminar in Kathmandu, 1975, 9 papers. 119p. (Selected Papers). 1975. 15.00 (ISBN 0-318-17090-6, 74). Am-Nepal Ed.

Anell, Lars. Recession, the Western Economies & the Changing World Order. 1981. 25.00 (ISBN 0-312-66576-8). St Martin.

--Recession, the Western Economies & the Changing World Order. 181p. 1981. pap. 9.50 (ISBN 0-86187-243-6). F Pinter Pubs.

Anell, Lars & Nygren, Birgitta. The Developing Countries & the World Economic Order. 208p. 1980. pap. 9.95x (ISBN 0-416-74630-6, NO.2002). Methuen Inc.

--The Developing Countries & the World Economic Order. LC 80-5094. 230p. 1980. 27.50 (ISBN 0-312-19658-X). St Martin.

Anello, Rose & Shuster, Tillie. A Guide for Non-Profit Shelter Operators in New York City: Negotiating the Public Assistance System on Behalf of Homeless Adults. 98p. (Orig.). 1984. pap. 6.50 (ISBN 0-88156-031-6). Comm Serv Soc Ny.

Anema, Durlynn. Don't Get Fired: Thirteen Ways to Hold Your Job. (Illus.). 64p. (gr. 7-12). 1978. pap. text ed. 3.95 (ISBN 0-915510-24-3). Janus Bks.

--Get Hired: Thirteen Ways to Get a Job. (Illus.). 64p. (gr. 7-12). 1979. pap. text ed. 3.95 (ISBN 0-915510-35-9). Janus Bks.

--Sharing an Apartment. Padial, Antonia, ed. (On Your Own Ser.). (Illus.). 64p. (gr. 9 up). 1982. pap. text ed. 3.95 (ISBN 0-915510-60-X). Janus Bks.

Anene, J. C. Southern Nigeria in Transition, Eighteen Eighty-Five - Nineteen Six. 1966. 34.50 (ISBN 0-521-04033-7). Cambridge U Pr.

Anene, Joseph C. & Brown, Godfrey, eds. Africa in the Nineteenth & Twentieth Centuries. (Illus.). 1979. pap. text ed. 14.25x (ISBN 0-391-00216-3). Humanities.

ANEP. European Petroleum Year Book, 1981-82. 15th ed. LC 72-16515. (Illus.). 644p. (Eng., Fr. & Ger.). 1981. 80.00x (ISBN 0-8002-2958-4). Intl Pubns Serv.

Anesaki, M. Buddhist Art in Its Relation to Buddhist Ideals. LC 76-39816. (Illus.). 1978. Repr. of 1923 ed. lib. bdg. 50.00 (ISBN 0-87817-197-5). Hacker.

Anesaki, Masaharu. Art, Life & Nature in Japan. LC 77-109705. (Illus.). 1971. Repr. of 1933 ed. lib. bdg. 22.50 (ISBN 0-8371-4196-6, ANNJ). Greenwood.

--Art, Life & Nature in Japan. LC 72-77520. (Illus.). 191p. 1973. pap. 6.50 (ISBN 0-8048-1486-4). C E Tuttle.

--History of Japanese Religion. LC 63-19395. 1963. Repr. of 1930 ed. 23.50 (ISBN 0-8048-0248-3). C E Tuttle.

--Katam Karaniyam: Lectures, Essays & Studies. LC 78-72369. Repr. of 1934 ed. 32.50 (ISBN 0-404-17216-4). AMS Pr.

Anesaki, Masaharu see Ferguson, John C.

Anesaki, Masharu. Nichiren: The Buddhist Prophet. 1916. 11.25 (ISBN 0-8446-1029-1). Peter Smith.

Anfinsen, C. B., ed. Aspects of Protein Biosynthesis, Pt. A. 1970. 72.00 (ISBN 0-12-058701-7). Acad Pr.

Anfinsen, C. B. & Schechter, Alan N., eds. Current Topics in Biochemistry. 1974. 40.00 (ISBN 0-12-058751-3). Acad Pr.

Anfinsen, C. B., et al. Current Topics in Biochemistry: National Institute of Health Lectures in Biomedical Sciences. 1972. pap. 45.00 (ISBN 0-12-058750-5). Acad Pr.

Anfinsen, C. B., et al, eds. Advances in Protein Chemistry, Vol. 34. (Serial Publication Ser.). 1981. 60.00 (ISBN 0-12-034234-0). Acad Pr.

--Current Research in Oncology. 1973. pap. 40.00 (ISBN 0-12-058752-1). Acad Pr.

Anfuso, Dominick, ed. see Ketwig, John.

Anfuso, Dominick, ed. see North, James.

Anfuso, Joseph & Sczepanski, David. Efrain Rios Montt - Servant or Dictator? The Real Story of Guatemala's Controversial "Born Again" President. LC 84-7553. pap. 5.95 (ISBN 0-88449-110-2, A424705). Vision Hse.

Anfuso, Nella & Gianuario, Annibale. Le Tre Arianne di Claudio Monteverdi. LC 77-452198. (Nuova Metodologia, Studi Musicologici: No. 5). (Illus.). 37p. (Orig., Ital.). 1975. pap. 8.00 (ISBN 0-934082-14-6, Pub. by SP Quaranta Quattro Florence Italy). Theodore Front.

Ang, A. H. & Tang, W. H. Probability Concepts in Engineering Planning & Design, Vol. 1. LC 75-5892. 409p. 1975. text ed. 44.50x (ISBN 0-471-03200-X). Wiley.

Ang, Alfredo H-S & Tang, Wilson H. Probability Concepts in Engineering Planning & Design, Vol. II. LC 75-5892. 562p. 1984. text ed. 42.50 (ISBN 0-471-03201-8). Wiley.

Angadi, Patricia. The Governess. 192p. 1985. 15.95 (ISBN 0-575-03485-8, Pub. by Gollancz England). David & Charles.

Angas, George F. Savage Life & Scenes in Australia & New Zealand: Being an Artist's Impressions of Countries & People at the Antipodes, 2 Vols. in 1. 2nd ed. (Illus.). 1967. 28.00 (ISBN 0-384-01465-8). Johnson Repr.

Angehrn, Emil. Freiheit und System Bei Hegel. 1977. 58.40x (ISBN 3-11-006969-5). De Gruyter.

Angel, Allen. Elementary Algebra: A Practical Approach. (Illus.). 544p. 1985. pap. text ed. 25.95 (ISBN 0-13-252784-7). P-H.

Angel, Allen R. Intermediate Algebra: A Practical Approach. (Illus.). 448p. 1986. pap. text ed. 26.95 (ISBN 0-13-469859-2). P-H.

Angel, Aubie, et al, eds. The Adipocyte & Obesity: Cellular & Molecular Mechanisms. 328p. 1983. text ed. 46.00 (ISBN 0-89004-946-7). Raven.

Angel, Edward & Bellman, Richard. Dynamic Programming & Partial Differential Equations. (Mathematics in Science & Engineering Ser: Vol. 88). 1972. 60.00 (ISBN 0-12-057950-2). Acad Pr.

Angel, Gerry & Petronko, Diane. Developing the New Assertive Nurse: Essential for Advancement. 256p. 1983. pap. text ed. 15.95 (ISBN 0-8261-3511-0). Springer Pub.

Angel, Heather. The Book of Close-Up Photography. LC 82-48716. (Illus.). 168p. 1983. 17.95 (ISBN 0-394-53232-5). Knopf.

--The Book of Nature Photography. LC 81-48106. 1982. 16.50 (ISBN 0-394-52467-5). Knopf.

--The Book of Nature Photography. 160p. 1982. 45.00x (ISBN 0-85223-227-6, Pub. by Ebury Pr England). State Mutual Bk.

--A Camera in the Garden. (Illus.). 160p. 1985. 19.95 (ISBN 0-907621-34-1, Pub by Salem Hse Ltd). Merrimack Pub Cir.

--Heather Angel's Countryside. (Illus.). 160p. 1983. 19.95 (ISBN 0-7181-2219-4, Pub. by Michael Joseph); pap. 12.95 (ISBN 0-7181-2284-4). Merrimack Pub Cir.

--Nature Photography: Its Arts & Techniques. (Illus.). 200p. 1980. Repr. of 1972 ed. text ed. 14.95 (ISBN 0-85242-670-4, 3105). Morgan.

Angel, Heather & Wolseley, Pat. The Water Naturalist. 192p. 1982. 19.95 (ISBN 0-87196-642-5). Facts on File.

Angel, Heather, et al. The Natural History of Britain & Ireland. (Illus.). 256p. 1985. pap. 14.95 (ISBN 0-7181-2557-6, Pub. by Michael Joseph). Merrimack Pub Cir.

Angel, J. L. The People. LC 73-139121. (Lerna Ser: Vol. 2). (Illus.). 1971. 17.50x (ISBN 0-87661-302-4). Am Sch Athens.

Angel, J. Lawrence. The People of Lerna: Analysis of a Prehistoric Aegean Population. LC 73-139121. (Illus.). 160p. 1971. 19.95x (ISBN 0-87474-098-3). Smithsonian.

Angel, J. R. & Boyce, P. J., eds. Independence & Alliance: Australia in World Affairs - Nineteen Seventy-Six to Nineteen Eighty. 368p. 1983. text ed. 37.50x (ISBN 0-86861-173-5). Allen Unwin.

Angel, Juvenal L. The Complete Resume & Job Getter's Guide. 1985. pap. 8.95 (Wallaby). PB.

Angel, M. V. Progress in Oceanography, Vol. 8. (Illus.). 296p. 1980. 115.00 (ISBN 0-08-022963-8). Pergamon.

Angel, M. V. & O'Brien, J. Progress in Oceanography, Vol. 9, Nos. 1-4. (Illus.). 246p. 1982. 115.00 (ISBN 0-08-027116-2). Pergamon.

Angel, M. V. & O'Brien, J., eds. Progress in Oceanography, Vol. 10. (Illus.). 226p. 1982. 106.00 (ISBN 0-08-029121-X). Pergamon.

Angel, M. V. & O'Brien, J. J., eds. Progress in Oceanography, Vol. 12. (Illus.). 470p. 1984. 150.00 (ISBN 0-08-031504-6). Pergamon.

--Progress in Oceanography, Vol. 13. (Illus.). 520p. 1985. 160.00 (ISBN 0-08-032724-9, Pub. by Aberdeen Scotland). Pergamon.

Angel, Marc D. La America. 240p. 1982. 15.95 (ISBN 0-8276-0205-7). Jewish Pubns.

--The Jews of Rhodes: The History of a Sephardic Community. 2nd ed. LC 77-93661. 1980. 12.50 (ISBN 0-87203-091-1). Hermon.

Angel, Marc D., ed. Studies in Sephardic Culture: The David N. Barocas Memorial Volume. LC 79-92737. (Illus.). 190p. 1980. 15.00 (ISBN 0-87203-090-3). Hermon.

Angelo, Valenti. Golden Gate. LC 74-17918. (Italian American Experience Ser.). (Illus.). 278p. 1975. Repr. 17.00x (ISBN 0-405-06391-1). Ayer Co Pubs.

Angeloglou, Christopher & Schofield, Jack, eds. Successful Nature Photography: How to Take Beautiful Pictures of the Living World. 240p. 1983. 24.95 (ISBN 0-8174-5925-1, Amphoto). Watson-Guptill.

Angeloglou, George, tr. see Tsakonas, Demetrios.

Angelopoulos, Angelos. A Global Plan for Employment: A New Marshall Plan. 234p. 1983. 29.95x (ISBN 0-03-063798-8); pap. text ed. 5.50x (ISBN 0-03-063847-X). Praeger.

--The Third World & the Rich Countries: Prospects for the Year 2000. LC 72-75694. (Special Studies in International Economics & Development). 1972. text ed. 37.50x (ISBN 0-275-28608-8). Irvington.

Angelou, Maya. And Still I Rise. 1978. 8.95 (ISBN 0-394-50252-3). Random.

--Gather Together in My Name. 192p. (gr. 9 up). 1975. pap. 3.50 (ISBN 0-553-25159-7). Bantam.

--Gather Together in My Name. 1974. 15.95 (ISBN 0-394-48692-7). Random.

--The Heart of a Woman. LC 81-40232. 288p. 1981. 12.50 (ISBN 0-394-51273-1). Random.

--Heart of a Woman. 1983. pap. 3.95 (ISBN 0-553-24689-5). Bantam.

--I Know Why the Caged Bird Sings. (gr. 9-12). 1971. pap. 3.50 (ISBN 0-553-23779-9). Bantam.

--I Know Why the Caged Bird Sings. 1970. 14.95 (ISBN 0-394-42986-9). Random.

--Just Give Me a Cool Drink of Water 'for I Die. 1971. 9.95 (ISBN 0-394-47142-3). Random.

--Oh Pray My Wings Are Gonna Fit Me Well. 1975. 10.95 (ISBN 0-394-49951-4). Random.

--Singin' & Swingin' & Gettin' Merry Like Christmas. (gr. 8-12). 1977. pap. 3.95 (ISBN 0-553-25199-6). Bantam.

--Singin' & Swingin' & Gettin' Merry Like Christmas. 1976. 13.95 (ISBN 0-394-40545-5). Random.

Angelov, Dimitar. Les Balkans au Moyen Age: A Bulgarie des Bogomils aux Turcs. 322p. 1978. 60.00x (ISBN 0-86078-019-8, Pub. by Variorum). State Mutual Bk.

Angels of Easter Seal, Youngstown, Ohio. Angels & Friends Favorite Recipes. (Illus.). 436p. 1981. 9.50 (ISBN 0-9613501-0-5). Angels Easter.

Angelsen, Bjorn, jt. auth. see Hatle, Liv.

Angelucci, Enzo. Encyclopedie Des Avions. 28p. (Fr.). 1976. 65.00 (ISBN 0-686-56894-X, M-6004). French & Eur.

--World Encyclopedia of Civil Aircraft, from Leonardo da Vinci to the Present. LC 82-4642. (Illus.). 414p. 1982. 24.95 (ISBN 0-517-54724-4). Crown.

Angelucci, Enzo & Cucari, Attilio. Encyclopedie Des Navires. 366p. (Fr., It.). 69.95 (ISBN 0-686-56895-8, M-6005). French & Eur.

Angelucci, Enzo & Matricardi, Paolo. World Aircraft: Commercial, 1935-1960. LC 79-51520. (Illus.). 1979. pap. 7.95 (ISBN 0-528-88206-6). Rand.

--World Aircraft: Military, 1945-1960. (Illus.). 1980. pap. 7.95 (ISBN 0-528-88205-8). Rand.

Anger, Kathryn. Breakout. LC 79-55871. (Feminist Novels Ser.). 128p. (Orig.). 1977. pap. 4.95 (ISBN 0-935772-01-4). Diotima Bks.

--Lockout. LC 79-57121. (Feminist Novels Ser.). 100p. 1975. pap. 4.95 (ISBN 0-935772-02-2). Diotima Bks.

--Override. LC 79-57122. (Feminist Novels Ser.). 100p. 1976. pap. 4.95 (ISBN 0-935772-03-0). Diotima Bks.

--Pilgrimage. LC 84-73307. (Feminist Novels Ser.). 98p. (Orig.). 1982. 4.95. Diotima Bks.

Anger, Kenneth. Hollywood Babylon. 1981. pap. 5.95 (ISBN 0-440-15325-5). Dell.

--Hollywood Babylon II. (Illus.). 288p. 1984. 24.95 (ISBN 0-525-24271-6, 02422-730). Dutton.

--Hollywood Babylon II. 1985. pap. 12.95 (ISBN 0-452-25721-2, Plume). NAL.

Anger, Per. With R. Wallenberg in Budapest. LC 80-84245. (Illus.). 191p. 1981. pap. 8.95 (ISBN 0-89604-047-X). Holocaust Pubns.

--With Raoul Wallenberg in Budapest: Memories of the War Years in Hungary. (Illus.). 1981. 8.95 (ISBN 0-8052-5027-1, Pub. by Holocaust Library); pap. 6.95 (ISBN 0-8052-5026-3, Pub. by Holocaust Library). Schocken.

--With Raoul Wallenberg in Budapest: Memories of the War Years in Hungary. Paul, David M. & Paul, Margareta, trs. from Swedish. (Illus.). 192p. 8.95 (ISBN 0-686-95103-4); pap. 4.95 (ISBN 0-686-99464-7). ADL.

Anger, Y., jt. auth. see Feigl, F.

Anger, Y., jt. auth. see Feigl, Fritz.

Angerbauer, George J. Principles of DC & AC Circuits. 2nd ed. 750p. 1985. 24.00 (ISBN 0-318-04389-0); write for info. (ISBN 0-534-04206-6); study guide 11.00 (ISBN 0-534-04204-X, 77F6059); write for info. (ISBN 0-534-04205-8). Breton Pubs.

Angerer, Hugo, et al, eds. see Riepel, Joseph, et al.

Angerer, J. & Schaller, K. H., eds. Analyses of Hazardous Substances in Biological Materials, Vol. 1. (Commission for the Investigation of Health Hazards of Chemical Compounds in the Work Area Ser.). 222p. 1985. lib. bdg. 36.00 (ISBN 0-89573-075-8). VCH Pubs.

Angerhausen, M. & Becker, A. The Anatomy of the Commodore 64. Kesten, D., tr. from German. 300p. 1983. pap. 19.95 (ISBN 0-916439-00-3). Abacus Soft.

Angermeier, W. F. Evolution des Operanten Lernens. (Illus.). x, 230p. 1983. 50.75 (ISBN 3-8055-3522-8). S Karger.

--The Evolution of Operant Learning & Memory. (Illus.). xii, 204p. 1984. text ed. 84.00 (ISBN 3-8055-3736-0). S Karger.

Angermeier, Wilhelm F. Evolution of Operant Learning & Memory. 216p. 1984. 114.00. Transaction Bks.

Angermeyer, John, jt. auth. see Waite, Mitchell.

Angers, Joann. Meeting the Forgiving Jesus: A Child's First Penance Book. 32p. 1984. pap. 1.75 (ISBN 0-89243-201-2). Liguori Pubns.

Angers, JoAnn M. My Beginning Mass Book. (Illus.). 32p. (Orig.). (gr. 1-4). 1978. pap. 1.95 (ISBN 0-89622-082-6). Twenty-Third.

Angers, Marilynn M. & Angers, William P. Creating Your Own Career for Job Satisfaction. LC 82-61718. 170p. (Orig.). 1983. pap. 9.95 (ISBN 0-910793-00-X). Marlborough Pr.

Angers, Trent & McDonough, Sue, eds. Acadiana Profile's Cajun Cooking. (Illus.). 240p. spiral bdg. 8.50 (ISBN 0-939524-00-7). Angers Pub.

Angers, William P., jt. auth. see Angers, Marilynn M.

Angeville, A. d' Essai sur la Statistique De la Population Francaise: Consideree Sous Quelque-Uns De Ses Rapports Physiques et Moraux. (Reeditions: No. 6). 1970. 44.40 (ISBN 0-686-20911-7). Mouton.

Angevine, C. D., et al, eds. The Immunochemistry & Biochemistry of Connective Tissue & Its Disease States. (Rheumatology: Vol. 3). 1970. 34.50 (ISBN 3-8055-0622-8). S Karger.

Angevine, Erma. People -- Their Power: The Rural Electric Fact Book. rev. ed. (Illus.). 196p. 1981. pap. 3.75 (ISBN 0-686-31129-9). Natl Rural.

Angevine, Jay B., Jr. & Cotman, Carl W. Principles of Neuroanatomy. (Illus.). 1981. 36.95x (ISBN 0-19-502885-6); pap. 18.95x (ISBN 0-19-502886-4). Oxford U Pr.

Angevine, Jay B., Jr., ed. see Womack, Lester.

Angha, Shah M. The Hidden Angles of Love. 128p. 1985. Repr. lib. bdg. 19.95x (ISBN 0-89370-894-1). Borgo Pr.

Anghelov, S. Socialist Internationalism: Theory & Practice of International Relations of a New Type. 507p. 1982. pap. 2.95 (ISBN 0-8285-2299-5, Pub. by Progress Pubs USSR). Imported Pubns.

Anghiera, Pietro D' see D'Anghiera, Pietro.

Anghileri, Leopold J., ed. General Processes of Radiotracer Localization, Vol. I. 272p. 1982. 78.00 (ISBN 0-8493-6027-7). CRC Pr.

--General Processes of Radiotracer Localization, Vol. II. 272p. 1982. 78.00 (ISBN 0-8493-6028-5). CRC Pr.

--The Role of Calcium in Biological Systems, Vol. III. 1982. 75.00 (ISBN 0-8493-6282-2). CRC Pr.

Anghileri, Leopold J. & Tuffet-Anghileri, Anne M., eds. The Role of Calcium in Biological Systems, Vol. I. 288p. 1982. 81.00 (ISBN 0-8493-6280-6). CRC Pr.

Angier, Bradford. At Home in the Woods: Living the Life of Thoreau Today. (Illus.). 1971. pap. 3.95 (ISBN 0-02-062120-5, Collier). Macmillan.

--Backcountry Basics. 368p. 19.95 (ISBN 0-8117-0112-3). Stackpole.

--The Competence Factor: Skills That Make the Difference in Outdoor Sports. (Illus.). 160p. 1983. pap. 7.95 (ISBN 0-8117-2189-2). Stackpole.

--Feasting Free on Wild Edibles. LC 72-6088. (Illus.). 320p. 1972. pap. 8.95 (ISBN 0-8117-2006-3). Stackpole.

--Field Guide to Edible Wild Plants. LC 73-23042. (Illus.). 256p. 1974. pap. 9.95 (ISBN 0-8117-2018-7). Stackpole.

--Field Guide to Medicinal Wild Plants. LC 78-19112. (Illus.). 320p. 1978. pap. 14.95 (ISBN 0-8117-2076-4). Stackpole.

--Home Cookbook of Wild Meat & Game. LC 81-23233. (Illus.). 192p. 1982. pap. 9.95 (ISBN 0-8117-2134-5). Stackpole.

--Home in Your Pack: A Modern Handbook of Back Packing. (Illus.). 288p. 1972. pap. 3.95 (ISBN 0-02-062130-2, Collier). Macmillan.

--How to Live in the Woods on Pennies a Day. LC 70-140741. (Illus.). 192p. 1971. pap. 7.95 (ISBN 0-8117-2009-8). Stackpole.

--How to Stay Alive in the Woods. Orig. Title: Living off the Country. 1962. pap. 3.95 (ISBN 0-02-028050-5, Collier). Macmillan.

--How to Stay Alive in the Woods. 1983. 13.50 (ISBN 0-8446-5964-9). Peter Smith.

--Looking for Gold. LC 74-23258. (Illus.). 224p. 1981. pap. 8.95 (ISBN 0-8117-2034-9). Stackpole.

--The Master Backwoodsman. 1979. pap. 4.95 (ISBN 0-449-90012-6, Columbine). Fawcett.

--The Master Backwoodsman. 224p. 1984. pap. 5.95 (ISBN 0-449-90126-2, Columbine). Fawcett.

--The Master Backwoodsman. 224p. 1984. pap. 5.95 (ISBN 0-317-07486-5). Ballantine.

--One Acre & Security: How to Live off the Earth Without Ruining It. 1973. pap. 4.95 (ISBN 0-394-71963-8, Vin). Random.

--Survival with Style. 1974. pap. 4.95 (ISBN 0-394-71982-4, V-982, Vin). Random.

--We Like It Wild. (Illus.). 176p. 1973. pap. 3.95 (ISBN 0-02-097200-8, Collier). Macmillan.

--Wilderness Neighbors. LC 76-26303. 228p. 1982. pap. 7.95 (ISBN 0-8128-6100-0). Stein & Day.

Angier, Bradford & Angier, Vena. How to Build Your Home in the Woods. (Illus.). Sheridan.

Angier, Bradford & Corcoran, Barbara. Ask for Love & They Give You Rice Pudding. 160p. (gr. 7 up). 1977. 6.95 (ISBN 0-395-25300-4). HM.

Angier, Bradford & Taylor, Zack. Camping-on-the-Go Cookery. (Illus.). 160p. 1983. pap. 9.95 (ISBN 0-8117-2156-6). Stackpole.

--Introduction to Canoeing. LC 73-519. (Illus.). 192p. (Orig.). 1981. pap. 8.95 (ISBN 0-8117-2010-1). Stackpole.

Angier, Bradford & Whitney, Peter J. At Home in the Desert. Schnell, Judith, ed. LC 84-39. (Illus.). 160p. 1984. pap. 10.95 (ISBN 0-8117-2153-1). Stackpole.

Angier, Bradford, jt. auth. see Kodet, E. Russel.

Angier, R. H. Firearm Blueing & Browning. 160p. 1936. 12.95 (ISBN 0-686-76905-8). Stackpole.

Angier, R. P. see Bridges, James W.

Angier, R. P. see Kitson, Harry D.

Angier, Roswell. A Kind of Life: Conversations in the Combat Zone. LC 76-536. (Illus.). 1976. 17.95 (ISBN 0-89169-002-6). Addison Hse.

Angier, Vena, jt. auth. see Angier, Bradford.

Angieski, S. Biochemical Aspects of Renal Function. Dubach, C., ed. 242p. 1975. 75.00 (ISBN 3-456-80208-0, Pub. by Holdan Bk Ltd UK). State Mutual Bk.

Angiletta, Anthony M., et al, eds. The State of Western European Studies: Implications for Collection Development. LC 84-12803. (Collection Management: Vol. 6, No. 1/2). 273p. 1984. text ed. 29.95 (ISBN 0-86656-354-7, B354). Haworth Pr.

Angilly, Richard. Chants: A Zen Wind. 136p. (Orig.). 1980. pap. 5.95x (ISBN 0-931290-28-7). Blue Dragon.

--Organic Music. (Illus.). 80p. (Orig.). 1980. pap. 4.95x (ISBN 0-931290-26-0). Blue Dragon.

--Poems of Illumination. (Illus., Orig.). 1980. pap. 4.95x (ISBN 0-931290-27-9). Blue Dragon.

Angilly, Richard, ed. see Gilbert, Donald.

Angino, E. D. & Long, D. T., eds. Geochemistry of Bismuth. LC 78-24291. (Benchmark Papers in Geology: Vol. 49). 432p. 1979. 58.95 (ISBN 0-87933-234-4). Van Nos Reinhold.

Angiolillo, Paul F. Armed Forces' Foreign Language Teaching. 440p. 1947. 7.75x (ISBN 0-913298-58-1). S F Vanni.

--A Criminal As Hero: Angelo Duca. LC 78-15431. 1979. 19.95x (ISBN 0-7006-0184-8). U Pr of KS.

Angione, Genevieve. All Bisque & Half Bisque Dolls. LC 76-77265. (Illus.). 357p. 1981. Repr. 25.00 (ISBN 0-916838-39-0). Schiffer.

Angira, Jared. Silent Voices. (African Writers Ser.). 1972. pap. text ed. 5.50x (ISBN 0-435-90111-7). Heinemann Ed.

Anglade, Christian & Fortin, Carlos, eds. The State & Capital Accumulation in Latin America: Brazil, Chile, Mexico. LC 84-12015. (Pitt Latin American Ser.). (Illus.). 240p. 1985. 21.95x (ISBN 0-8229-1144-2). U of Pittsburgh Pr.

Anglade, Joseph. Histoire Sommaire De la Litterature Meridionale Au Moyen Age. LC 74-38486. Repr. of 1921 ed. 21.50 (ISBN 0-404-08343-9). AMS Pr.

--Troubadours, Leur Vies, Leurs Oeuvres Leur Influence. LC 78-38487. Repr. of 1908 ed. 22.00 (ISBN 0-404-08344-7). AMS Pr.

Anglade, Joseph, ed. Leys D'amors, Manuscrit Inedit De L'academie Des Jeux Floraux, 4 Vols. Repr. of 1919 ed. 80.00 (ISBN 0-384-32499-1). Johnson Repr.

Anglars, Judith. Si loin Pour T'Aimer. (Collection Colombine Ser.). 192p. 1983. pap. 1.95 (ISBN 0-373-48087-3). Harlequin Bks.

Angle, Burr, ed. Hints & Tips for Plastic Modeling. (Illus.). 1980. pap. 4.75 (ISBN 0-89024-546-0). Kalmbach.

Angle, Burr, ed. see Banks, Michael.

Angle, Burr, ed. see Beckman, Bob.

Angle, Burr, ed. see Berliner, Don.

Angle, Burr, ed. see Marks, Fred M.

Angle, Burr, ed. see Marks, Fred & Winter, William.

Angle, Burr, ed. see Paine, Sheperd.

Angle, Burr, ed. see Poling, Mitch.

Angle, Burr, ed. see Pratt, Douglas R.

Angle, Burr, ed. see Sarpolus, Dick.

Angle, Burr, ed. see Schroder, Jack E.

Angle, Burr, ed. see Siposs, George G.

Angle, Burr, ed. see Staszak, E. R.

Angle, Burr, ed. see Thorne, Peter.

Angle, Burr, ed. see Wilkins, Lester.

Angle, Burr, ed. see Willard, Ken.

Angle, Harold L., jt. auth. see Perry, James L.

Angle, John. Language Maintenançe, Language Shift, & Occupational Achievement in the United States. LC 77-91426. 1978. soft cover 10.00 (ISBN 0-88247-542-8). R & E Pubs.

Angle, Paul. On a Variety of Subjects. 1974. 6.25 (ISBN 0-940550-05-9). Caxton Club.

Angle, Paul & Davis, William C. Pictorial History of the Civil War Years. LC 84-24678. 256p. 1985. pap. 12.95 (ISBN 0-385-18551-0). Doubleday.

Angle, Paul M. Bloody Williamson. 1952. 12.95 (ISBN 0-394-41720-8). Knopf.

--The Great Chicago Fire: October 8-10, 1871. LC 78-156094. (Illus.). 122p. 1971. 7.50 (ISBN 0-913820-01-6). Chicago Hist.

--On a Variety of Subjects. LC 74-82578. 192p. 1974. 6.95 (ISBN 0-913820-04-0). Chicago Hist.

--A Shelf of Lincoln Books. LC 72-6403. 142p. 1972. Repr. of 1946 ed. lib. bdg. 18.75 (ISBN 0-8371-6491-5, ANLB). Greenwood.

--A Shelf of Lincoln Books: A Critical, Selective Bibliography of Lincolniana. LC 46-25256. pap. 40.50 (ISBN 0-317-10291-5, 2050456). Bks Demand UMI.

Angle, Paul M., ed. Abraham Lincoln, by Some Men Who Knew Him. facsimile ed. LC 78-90601. (Essay Index Reprint Ser). 1950. 13.00 (ISBN 0-8369-1242-X). Ayer Co Pubs.

--Created Equal: The Complete Lincoln-Douglas Debates of 1858. LC 58-6885. 1958. 12.95 (ISBN 0-226-02087-8). U of Chicago Pr.

--Created Equal? The Complete Lincoln-Douglas Debates of 1858. LC 58-6885. xxxiv, 422p. (Orig.). 1985. pap. 14.00x (ISBN 0-226-02085-1). U of Chicago Pr.

--The Lincoln Reader. LC 80-25663. (Illus.). xii, 564p. 1981. Repr. of 1947 ed. lib. bdg. 49.50x (ISBN 0-313-22757-8, ANLR). Greenwood.

--The Lincoln Reader. 26.95 (ISBN 0-89190-866-8, Pub. by Am Repr). Amereon Ltd.

Angle, Robert O. Handbook of Probate Law, 2 vols. 4th, rev. ed. 659p. 1983. pap. text ed. 51.50 (ISBN 0-89074-089-5). Lega Bks.

Anglemeyer, Mary, ed. see International Institute for Environment & Development (I.I.E.D.).

Anglemyer, Mary & Seagraves, Eleanor R., eds. The Natural Environment: An Annotated Bibliography on Attitudes & Values. LC 83-600232. 268p. 1984. 25.00x (ISBN 0-87474-220-X, ANNE). Smithsonian.

Anglemyer, Mary, ed. see International Institute for Environment & Development (I.I.E.D.).

Anglemyer, Mary, et al, eds. A Search for Environmental Ethics: An Initial Bibliography. LC 80-15026. 119p. 1982. Repr. text ed. 12.50x (ISBN 0-87474-212-9). Smithsonian.

Anglesea, Martyn, notes by. Birds of Ireland. (Illus.). 120p. with slip case 460.00 (ISBN 0-85640-297-4, Pub. by Blackstaff Pr); limited ed. 750.00 (ISBN 0-317-02588-0). Longwood Pub Group.

Anglesey, Marquess of. A History of British Cavalry Eighteen Sixteen Nineteen Nineteen, Vol. 2: 1851-1871. (Illus.). 519p. 1975. 35.00 (ISBN 0-208-01468-3, Archon). Shoe String.

--A History of the British Cavalry, Eighteen Fifty-One to Eighteen Seventy-One, Vol. 2. (Illus.). 519p. 1983. Repr. 50.00 (ISBN 0-85052-174-2, Pub. by Secker & Warburg England). David & Charles.

--A History of the British Cavalry, Eighteen Sixteen to Eighteen Fifty, Vol. 1. (Illus.). 336p. 1983. Repr. 60.00 (ISBN 0-85052-112-2, Pub. by Secker & Warburg UK). David & Charles.

--A History of the British Cavalry 1816-1919, Vol. 1: 1816-1850. (Illus.). 336p. 1973. 27.50 (ISBN 0-208-01404-7, Archon). Shoe String.

Anglesey, Marquess Of see Anglesey, Marquess of.

Anglesey, Zoe. Something More Than Force: Poems for Guatemala, 1971-1981. 48p. 1982. signed & numbered ed. 15.00x (ISBN 0-938566-13-X). Adastra Pr.

--Something More than Force: Poems for Guatemala, 1971-1982. 2nd ed. 48p. 1984. pap. 3.50 (ISBN 0-938566-21-0). Adastra Pr.

Anglesio, Enrico. Treatment of Hodgkin's Disease. Rentchnick, P., ed. LC 68-56205. (Recent Results in Cancer Research: Vol. 18). 1969. 20.00 (ISBN 0-387-04681-X). Springer-Verlag.

Anglin, Betty. They Never Asked For Help: A Study on the Needs of Elderly Retarded People in Metro Toronto. 62p. 1981. 2.50 (ISBN 0-318-15727-6, 1014). NIMR.

Anglin, C. S., jt. auth. see Silverthorne, Nelles.

Anglin, D. L., jt. auth. see Crouse, W. H.

Anglin, D. L., jt. auth. see Crouse, William H.

Anglin, Don L., jt. auth. see Crouse, William H.

Anglin, Donald L., jt. auth. see Crouse, William H.

Anglin, Douglas, et al. Canada, Scandinavia & Southern Africa. Shaw, Timothy & Widstrand, Carl, eds. (Scandinavia Institute of African Studies, Uppsala). 1979. text ed. 25.50 (ISBN 0-8419-9735-7). Holmes & Meier.

Anglin, Douglas G., jt. auth. see Shaw, Timothy M.

Anglin, Douglas G., et al, eds. Conflict & Change in Southern Africa: Papers from a Scandinavian-Canadian Conference. LC 78-70693. 1978. pap. text ed. 13.00 (ISBN 0-8191-0647-X). U Pr of Amer.

Anglin, E. Warren. Seven Thunderers Utter Their Voices: History & Verse by Verse Study in the Book of Revelation of the Bible. 2nd ed. 176p. (Orig.). pap. 7.95 (ISBN 0-318-04199-5). Total Comm Ministries.

Anglin, Jeremey M., ed. see Bruner, Jerome S.

Anglin, Leo W., Jr., et al. Teaching: What It's All About. 372p. 1982. text ed. 20.35 scp (ISBN 0-397-47399-0, HarpC); instr's manual avail. (ISBN 0-06-379335-0). Har-Row.

Anglin, R. L., Jr., ed. Energy in the Man-Built Environment. LC 81-67745. 728p. 1982. pap. 47.00x (ISBN 0-87262-297-5). Am Soc Civil Eng.

Anglo-American Committee of Inquiry on Palestine. The Jewish Case Before the Anglo-American Committee of Inquiry on Palestine: Statements & Memoranda. LC 75-12168. (The Rise of Jewish Nationalism & the Middle East Ser.). x, 686p. 1976. Repr. of 1947 ed. 43.50 (ISBN 0-88355-361-9). Hyperion Conn.

Anglo, Mick. Man Eats Man: The Story of Cannibalism. 160p. 1981. 18.00x (ISBN 0-904041-76-X, Pub. by Jupiter England). State Mutual Bk.

Anglo-Swedenish Literary Foundation, London. Modern Swedish Short Stories. 30.00 (ISBN 0-8369-4261-2, 6063). Ayer Co Pubs.

Anglo, Sydney, ed. The Damned Art. 258p. 1985. pap. 9.95 (ISBN 0-7102-0684-4). Routledge & Kegan.

--Great Tournament Roll of Westminster. 1968. boxed 105.00x (ISBN 0-19-821340-9). Oxford U Pr.

Anglund, Joan W. Almost a Rainbow: A Book of Poems. (Illus.). 64p. 1980. 6.95 (ISBN 0-394-50072-5). Random.

--Amor Est Sensus Quidam Peculiaris. Lyne, G. M., tr. LC 68-25184. (Illus., Latin.). (gr. 8 up). 1968. 2.50 (ISBN 0-15-203231-2, HJ). HarBraceJ.

--Baby Brother. LC 84-15121. (Illus.). 40p. (ps-k). 1985. lib. bdg. 6.99 (ISBN 0-394-96837-9, BYR); pap. 5.95 (ISBN 0-394-86837-4). Random.

--Brave Cowboy. LC 59-5627. (Illus.). (ps-2). 1959. 5.95 (ISBN 0-15-211956-6, HJ). HarBraceJ.

--Childhood Is a Time of Innocence: Twentieth Anniversary Edition. LC 65-20974. (Illus.). 32p. (gr. k up). 1984. Repr. of 1964 ed. 6.95 (ISBN 0-15-216952-0, HJ). HarBraceJ.

--Christmas Candy Book. (Illus.). 1983. 5.95 (ISBN 0-915696-63-0). Determined Prods.

--A Christmas Cookie Book. LC 77-78293. (Illus.). 1982. Repr. of 1977 ed. 3.95 (ISBN 0-915696-07-X). Determined Prods.

--Christmas Is a Time of Giving. LC 61-10106. (Illus.). (gr. k-3). 1961. 7.95 (ISBN 0-15-217863-5, HJ). HarBraceJ.

--Cup of Sun: A Book of Poems. LC 67-24870. (Illus.). 1967. 6.95 (ISBN 0-15-123390-X). HarBraceJ.

--Do You Love Someone? LC 76-152692. (Illus.). 32p. (gr. 7 up). 1971. 4.95 (ISBN 0-15-224190-6, HJ). HarBraceJ.

--Emily & Adam, 3 bks. Incl. The Emily Book. LC 78-20719; The Adam Book. LC 78-20720; The Emily & Adam Book of Opposites. LC 78-20722. (Illus.). (ps-1). 1979. Boxed Set. 5.95 (ISBN 0-394-84254-5, BYR). Random.

--A Friend Is Someone Who Likes You: Silver Anniversary Edition. LC 58-8624. (Illus.). 32p. 1983. PLB 6.95 (ISBN 0-15-229678-6, HJ). HarBraceJ.

--A Gift of Love, 5 vols. (Illus.). 32p. 1980. Set. pap. 8.95 (ISBN 0-15-634741-5, VoyB). HarBraceJ.

--God Is Love. (Illus.). (gr. 1 up). 5.95 (ISBN 0-317-13661-5). Determined Prods.

--In a Pumpkin Shell. LC 60-10243. (Illus.). (ps-2). 1977. pap. 4.95 (ISBN 0-15-644425-9, VoyB). HarBraceJ.

--In a Pumpkin Shell: A Mother Goose ABC. LC 60-10243. (gr. k-3). 1960. 9.95 (ISBN 0-15-238269-0, HJ). HarBraceJ.

--The Joan Walsh Anglund Storybook. LC 78-55913. (Illus.). (ps-2). 1978. 8.95 (ISBN 0-394-83803-3, BYR); PLB 8.99 (ISBN 0-394-93803-8). Random.

--Love Is a Special Way of Feeling. LC 60-6224. (Illus.). (gr. 1 up). 1960. 4.95 (ISBN 0-15-249725-0, HJ). HarBraceJ.

--Love Is a Special Way of Feeling: Silver Anniversary Edition. LC 84-19296. (Illus.). 32p. 1985. Repr. of 1960 ed. 6.95 (ISBN 0-15-249724-2, HJ). HarBraceJ.

--Love One Another. LC 81-67305. (Illus.). 5.95 (ISBN 0-915696-45-2). Determined Prods.

--Memories of the Heart. 1984. 6.95 (ISBN 0-394-53576-6). Random.

--Morning Is a Little Child. LC 69-11592. (Illus.). (gr. 4-6). 1969. 7.95 (ISBN 0-15-255652-4, HJ). HarBraceJ.

--Nibble Nibble Mousekin: A Tale of Hansel & Gretel. LC 62-14422. (Illus.). (ps-3). 1962. 9.95 (ISBN 0-15-257400-X, HJ). HarBraceJ.

--Nibble Nibble Mousekin: A Tale of Hansel & Gretel. LC 62-14422. (Illus.). (gr. k-3). 1977. pap. 4.95 (ISBN 0-15-665588-8, VoyB). HarBraceJ.

--Rainbow Love. LC 82-70028. (Illus.). 1982. 5.95 (ISBN 0-915696-51-7). Determined Prods.

--Spring Is a New Beginning. LC 63-7892. (Illus.). (gr. k-3). 1963. 7.95 (ISBN 0-15-278161-7, HJ). HarBraceJ.

--Teddy Bear Tales. LC 85-2238. (Illus.). 48p. 1985. bds. 6.95 (ISBN 0-394-87171-5, BYR); PLB 7.99 (ISBN 0-394-97171-X, BYR). Random.

Anglund, Joan Walsh. Baby's First Book. (Cuddle Cloth Books). (Illus.). 12p. (ps). 1985. 2.95 (ISBN 0-394-87470-6, BYR). Random.

--The Joan Walsh Anglund Coloring Book. (Illus.). 64p. (ps-3). 1984. pap. 2.95 saddle-stitched (ISBN 0-394-86875-7, Pub. by BYR). Random.

--See the Year. LC 84-60248. (Chunky Bks.). (Illus.). 28p. (ps). 1984. bds. 2.95 (ISBN 0-394-86641-X, Pub. by BYR). Random.

Anglund, JoanWalsh. A Christmas Book. (Illus.). 48p. (gr. k-3). 1983. 6.95 (ISBN 0-394-85551-5); PLB 7.99 (ISBN 0-394-95551-X). Random.

Anglure, Ogier D' see D' Anglure, Ogier.

Angnostopoulos, Athan, tr. see Seferis, George.

Angoff, Allan & Dingwall, Eric J. Abnormal Hypnotic Phenomena, a Survey of Nineteenth-Century Cases, Vol. 4: The United States of America, Great Britain. LC 68-85483. pap. 47.50 (ISBN 0-317-11298-8, 2003094). Bks Demand UMI.

Angoff, Allan, ed. Public Relations for Libraries: Essays in Communications Techniques. LC 72-776. (Contributions in Librarianship & Information Science: No. 5). 1973. lib. bdg. 29.95x (ISBN 0-8371-6060-X, ANP/). Greenwood.

Angoff, Allan, ed. see International Conference, Amsterdam, Aug. 23-25, 1972.

Angoff, Allan, ed. see International Conference, France, 1971.

Angoff, Allan, ed. see International Conference London, Aug. 29-30, 1973.

Angoff, Allan, ed. see London Times Staff.

Angoff, Allan, ed. see Proceedings of an International Conference, France, June 16-18, 1969.

Angoff, Charles. Adventures in Heaven. facs. ed. LC 76-132110. (Short Story Index Reprint Ser). 1945. 12.00 (ISBN 0-8369-3667-1). Ayer Co Pubs.

--Bell of Time. 1966. 4.00 (ISBN 0-87141-018-4). Manyland.

--Emma Lazarus: Poet, Jewish Activist, Pioneer Zionist. LC 79-11570. (Illus.). 1979. pap. 2.00 (ISBN 0-916790-01-0). Jewish Hist.

--Fathers of Classical Music. facs. ed. LC 73-84294. (Essay Index Reprint Ser). 1947. 18.00 (ISBN 0-8369-1119-9). Ayer Co Pubs.

--Prayers at Midnight. 1971. 2.00 (ISBN 0-87141-036-2). Manyland.

--When I Was a Boy in Boston. facs. ed. LC 70-132111. (Short Story Index Reprint Ser.). 1947. 14.50 (ISBN 0-8369-3668-X). Ayer Co Pubs.

Angoff, Charles, ed. Biology & the Future of Man: Papers by Nathan Hershey & Merril Eisenbud. LC 77-92564. (The Leverton Lecture Ser: No. 6). 52p. 1978. 9.50 (ISBN 0-8386-2222-4). Fairleigh Dickinson.

--Stories from the Literary Review. LC 68-21271. 312p. 1969. 20.00 (ISBN 0-8386-6899-2). Fairleigh Dickinson.

Angoff, Charles & Decker, Clarence R., eds. Modern Stories from Many Lands. 2nd enl. ed. 434p. 1972. 7.95 (ISBN 0-87141-040-0). Manyland.

Angoff, Charles & Povey, John, eds. African Writing Today. (Illus.). 1969. 10.00 (ISBN 0-87141-029-X). Manyland.

Angoff, Charles, ed. see American Mercury.

Angoff, Charles, ed. see Cherry, Conrad, et al.

Angoff, Charles, intro. by see Nathan, George J.

Angoff, Charles, jt. ed. see Spivak, Lawrence E.

Angoff, Charles, ed. see Wallace, Emily M. & Burke, Kenneth.

Angold, M. J. A Byzantine Government in Exile: Government & Society Under the Laskairds of Nicaea 1204-1261. 1975. 42.50x (ISBN 0-19-821854-0). Oxford U Pr.

Angold, Michael. The Byzantine Empire Ten Twenty-Five to Twelve Hundred Four: A Political History. (Illus.). 336p. 1985. text ed. 35.00 (ISBN 0-582-49060-X); pap. text ed. 16.95 (ISBN 0-582-49061-8). Longman.

Angolia, J. R. For Fuhrer & Fatherland: Military Awards of the Third Reich. rev. ed. (Illus.). 448p. 1985. 24.95 (ISBN 0-912138-32-7). Bender Pub CA.

Angolia, John R. Belt Buckles & Brocades of the Third Reich. (Illus.). 192p. 1982. 15.95 (ISBN 0-912138-23-8). Bender Pub CA.

--Cloth Insignia of the SS. (Illus.). 400p. 1983. 24.95 (ISBN 0-912138-28-9). Bender Pub CA.

--On the Field of Honor: A History of the Knight's Cross Bearers, Vol. 1. (Illus.). 288p. 1979. 17.95 (ISBN 0-912138-19-X). Bender Pub CA.

--On the Field of Honor: A History of the Knight's Cross Bearers, Vol. 2. (Illus.). 368p. 1981. 17.95 (ISBN 0-912138-21-1). Bender Pub CA.

Angolia, John R. & Schlicht, Adolf. Traditions & Uniforms of the German Army 1933-1945. (Vol. 1). (Illus.). 448p. 1985. 24.95 (ISBN 0-912138-30-0). Bender Pub CA.

Angos. Endgame Artillery. i, 109p. 1982. pap. 10.95 (ISBN 0-938650-18-1). Thinkers Pr.

Angreova, R., jt. auth. see Stamov, Stefan.

Angress, R. K. The Early German Epigram: A Study in Baroque Poetry. LC 70-111501. (Studies in Germanic Languages & Literatures: No. 2). 136p. 1971. 12.00x (ISBN 0-8131-1231-1). U Pr of Ky.

Angress, Werner T. Stillborn Revolution. pap. 132.30 (ISBN 0-317-09317-7, 2000030). Bks Demand UMI.

Angrilli, Albert & Helfat, Lucile. Child Psychology. LC 80-7764. 180p. (Orig.). 1981. pap. 3.95 (ISBN 0-06-460189-7, COS 189, COS). B&N NY.

Angrist, B., et al, eds. Recent Advances in Neuropsychopharmacology: Selected Papers from the 12th Congress of the Collegium Internationale Neuro-Psychopharmacologicum Goteborg, Sweden, 22-26 June, 1980. (Illus.). 422p. 1981. 88.00 (ISBN 0-08-026382-8). Pergamon.

Angrist, Shirley S. & Almquist, Elizabeth M. Careers & Contingencies: How College Women Juggle with Gender. LC 73-88666. 1975. 22.00x (ISBN 0-8046-7100-1, Pub. by Kennikat). Assoc Faculty Pr.

Angrist, Shirley S., et al. Women After Treatment: A Study of Former Mental Patients & Their Normal Neighbors. LC 68-20043. 1968. 24.00x (ISBN 0-89197-471-7); pap. text ed. 6.95x (ISBN 0-89197-472-5). Irvington.

Angrist, Stanley W. Direct Energy Conversion. 4th ed. 520p. 1982. text ed. 45.03 (ISBN 0-205-07758-7, 327758); solutions manual free (ISBN 0-205-07759-5, 3277593L). Allyn.

Angrosino, Michael, jt. auth. see Crane, Julia.

Angrosino, Michael V., ed. Do Applied Anthropologists Apply Anthropology? LC 75-32126. (Southern Anthropological Society Proceedings Ser: No. 10). 144p. 1976. pap. 6.00x (ISBN 0-8203-0393-3). U of Ga Pr.

Angst, J. The Origins of Depression: Current Concepts & Approaches. (Dahlem Workshop Reports, Life Sciences Research Report: Vol. 26). (Illus.). 456p. 1983. 22.00 (ISBN 0-387-12451-9). Springer-Verlag.

Angst, J., jt. auth. see Ernst, C.

Angst, Jules, jt. auth. see Kline, Nathan.

Angstrom, M., jt. auth. see Ruben.

Anguiano, Marina. Country Children's Art. Humphries, B., tr. (Illus.). 160p. cancelled (ISBN 0-87905-405-0, Pub. by Mexican Min Ed Mexico). Gibbs M Smith.

Anguizola, Gustave. Philippe Bunau-Varilla: The Man Behind the Panama Canal. LC 79-13673. (Illus.). 480p. 1980. text ed. 28.95x (ISBN 0-88229-397-4). Nelson-Hall.

Angulo, D. & Sanchez, A. E. Corpus of Spanish Drawings, 1400-1600, Vols. 1 & 2. (Illus.). 1975. Vol. 2. 74.00x (ISBN 0-19-921022-5). Oxford U Pr.

Angulo, Diego & Perez-Sanchez, A. E. A Corpus of Spanish Drawings: Valencia: 1600-1700, Vol. IV. Bumpus, Judith, tr. (A Corpus of Spanish Drawings Ser.). (Illus.). 1984. 95.00x (ISBN 0-19-921039-X). Oxford U Pr.

--A Corpus of Spanish Drawings, Vol. III: Seville Sixteen Hundred to Sixteen Fifty. Bumpus, Judith, tr. 1984. 74.00x (ISBN 0-19-921031-4). Oxford U Pr.

Angulo, Gui de see Angulo, Jaime de.

Angulo, Jaime de. Jaime in Taos: Jaime de Angulo Letters & The Witch. De Angulo, Gui, ed. (Illus.). 228p. 13.95 (ISBN 0-87286-167-8); pap. 6.95 (ISBN 0-87286-165-1). City Lights.

Angulo, Jaime De see De Angulo, Jaime.

Angus, jt. ed. see Orwell.

Angus, Anne D. Computer People. (Illus.). 1970. 9.50 (ISBN 0-571-08288-2). Transatlantic.

Angus, Donald, ed. see Tennent, Arthur.

Angus, Douglas, ed. Best Short Stories of the Modern Age. 1978. pap. 2.50 (ISBN 0-449-30816-2, Prem). Fawcett.

Angus, Douglas & Angus, Sylvia, eds. Contemporary American Short Stories. 1978. pap. 2.95 (ISBN 0-449-30832-4, Prem). Fawcett.

--Great Modern European Short Stories. 1977. pap. 2.50 (ISBN 0-449-30781-6, Prem). Fawcett.

Angus, Fay. How to Do Everything Right & Live to Regret It: Confessions of a Harried Housewife. LC 82-48425. 192p. 1983. 10.53i (ISBN 0-686-82600-0, HarpR). Har-Row.

--Running Around in Spiritual Circles. LC 85-42768. 192p. 1985. 13.95 (ISBN 0-06-060238-4, HarpR). Har-Row.

Angus, Frances R. French Poetry: An Anthology 1100-1925. 1977. Repr. of 1928 ed. 15.00 (ISBN 0-89984-040-X). Century Bookbindery.

Angus, H. T. Cast Iron: Physical & Engineering Properties. 2nd ed. 542p. 1976. 139.95 (ISBN 0-408-70933-2). Butterworth.

Angus, Ian, ed. see Orwell, George.

Angus, Ian H. Technique & Enlightment: Limits of Instrumental Reason. LC 83-27363. (Current Continental Research Ser.). 172p. (Orig.). 1984. lib. bdg. 21.50 (ISBN 0-8191-3815-0, Ctr Adv Ctr Phenom); pap. text ed. 11.25 (ISBN 0-8191-3816-9, Ctr Adv Ctr Phenom). U Pr of Amer.

Angus, James A., jt. ed. see Korner, Paul I.

Angus, Joseph. Hand-book for the English Tongue. 1868. 20.00 (ISBN 0-8274-2458-2). R West.

Angus, Margaret. The Old Stones of Kingston: Its Buildings Before 1867. LC 66-6913. (Illus.). 1966. pap. 13.50 (ISBN 0-8020-6419-1). U of Toronto Pr.

--The Old Stones of Kingston: Its Buildings Before Eighteen Sixty-Seven. LC 66-6913. (Illus.). 1980. pap. 13.50 (ISBN 0-8020-6419-1). U of Toronto Pr.

Angus, Robert B., Jr., jt. auth. see Dearness, John L.

Angus, S. The Environment of Early Christianity. 1977. lib. bdg. 59.95 (ISBN 0-8490-1778-5). Gordon Pr.

--International Thermodynamic Tables of the Fluid State. Incl. Vol. 1: Argon. 39.00 (ISBN 0-08-020822-3); Vol. 3: Carbon Dioxide. 88.00 (ISBN 0-08-020924-6); Vol. 4: Helium. 56.00 (ISBN 0-08-020957-2). Pergamon.

--The Religious Quests of the Graeco-Roman World. 1929. 30.00 (ISBN 0-686-20108-6). Quality Lib.

Angus, S., ed. International Thermodynamic Tables of the Fluid State-5. 1978. text ed. 72.00 (ISBN 0-08-021981-0). Pergamon.

--International Thermodynamic Tables of the Fluid State-6. 1979. text ed. 97.00 (ISBN 0-08-022372-9). Pergamon.

--International Thermodynamic Tables of the Fluid State-7. 1980. text ed. 110.00 (ISBN 0-08-022373-7). Pergamon.

Angus, S., et al, eds. International Thermodynamic Tables of the Fluid State 8. Chlorine (Tentative Tables) (Chemical Data Ser.: No. 31). (Illus.). 168p. 1984. 47.50 (ISBN 0-08-030713-2). Pergamon.

Angus, Samuel. The Environment of Early Christianity. facsimile ed. LC 75-157322. (Select Bibliographies Reprint Ser). Repr. of 1915 ed. 17.00 (ISBN 0-8369-5781-4). Ayer Co Pubs.

--The Mystery Religions. LC 74-12637. 360p. 1975. pap. 5.95 (ISBN 0-486-23124-0). Dover.

--The Mystery Religions & Christianity. 1977. lib. bdg. 59.95 (ISBN 0-8490-2314-9). Gordon Pr.

--The Religious Quests of the Graeco-Roman World: A Study in the Historical Background of Early Christianity. LC 66-30791. 1929. 15.00x (ISBN 0-8196-0196-9). Biblo.

Angus, Sylvia, jt. ed. see Angus, Douglas.

Angus, W. Seats of the Nobility & Gentry in Great Britain & Wales. Hunt, John D., ed. LC 79-56977. (The English Landscape Garden Ser.). 190p. 1982. lib. bdg. 33.00 (ISBN 0-8240-0172-9). Garland Pub.

Angus-Butterworth, Lionel M. Ten Master Historians. facs. ed. LC 69-18919. (Essay Index Reprint Ser). 1961. 16.00 (ISBN 0-8369-0000-6). Ayer Co Pubs.

Angyal, Andras. Neurosis & Treatment: A Holistic Theory. (Psychoanalysis Examined & Re-Examined Ser.). 328p. 1982. lib. bdg. 27.50 (ISBN 0-306-79709-7). Da Capo.

Angyal, Andrew J. Loren Eiseley. LC 82-25483. (United States Authors Ser.). 1983. lib. bdg. 16.95 (ISBN 0-8057-7381-9, Twayne). G K Hall.

Anhalt, Istvan. Alternate Voices: Essays on Contemporary Vocal & Choral Composition. (Illus.). 336p. 1984. 35.00x (ISBN 0-8020-5531-1). U of Toronto Pr.

Anhalt, John P., jt. auth. see Gerson, Benjamin.

Anheuser-Busch Brewing Co. Budweiser Cookbook. (Illus.). 80p. (Orig.). 1983. pap. 4.95 (ISBN 0-8249-3025-8). Ideals.

Anholt, Uni V. In Search of Heffalumps. (Illus.). 88p. (Orig.). pap. 2.95 (ISBN 0-9601996-0-8). Beeberry Bks.

Anh-Viet, Tu Dien. English-Vietnamese Dictionary. 1560p. (Eng. & Vietnamese.). 1975. 99.00x (ISBN 0-686-44716-6, Pub. by Collets). State Mutual Bk.

Ani, Moukhtar, jt. ed. see Stowasser, Karl.

Aniakor, Chike C., jt. auth. see Cole, Herbert M.

Anicar, Thom. Secret Sex: Male Erotic Fantasies. (Orig.). 1976. pap. 3.95 (ISBN 0-451-12306-9, Sig). NAL.

Anido, A., ed. see International Symposium, 6th, Geneva, Apr 23-25, 1975, et al.

Aniebo, I. N. The Anonymity of Sacrifice. (African Writers Ser.). 1974. pap. text ed. 4.50x (ISBN 0-435-90148-6). Heinemann Ed.

--The Journey Within. LC 79-304442. (African Writers Ser.). 1978. pap. text ed. 5.50x (ISBN 0-435-90206-7). Heinemann Ed.

Aniebo, I. N. C. Of Wives, Talismans & the Dead. (African Writers Ser.: No. 253). 154p. 1984. pap. text ed. 7.50x (ISBN 0-435-90253-9). Heinemann Ed.

Anifowose, F. O. The Violence & Politics in Nigeria: A Case-Study of the Tiv & Yoruba. LC 79-88590. 1982. 22.95x (ISBN 0-88357-083-1); pap. 9.95 (ISBN 0-88357-084-X). NOK Pubs.

Anikin, A. A Science in Its Youth. 389p. 1975. 6.95 (ISBN 0-8285-3118-8, Pub. by Progress Pubs USSR). Imported Pubns.

Anikin, Andrei V. A Science In Its Youth. Cook, K. M., tr. from Rus. LC 78-31568. 389p. 1979. pap. 3.50 (ISBN 0-7178-0503-4). Intl Pubs Co.

Anikin, Andreiv. Gold: The Yellow Devil. LC 83-274. Orig. Title: Zheltyi d iavol. 272p. (Rus.). 1984. 5.95 (ISBN 0-7178-0599-9). Intl Pubs Co.

Anikouchine, William & Sternberg, Richard. The World Ocean. 2nd ed. (Illus.). 512p. 1981. 31.95 (ISBN 0-13-967778-X). P-H.

Anikst, M. & Turchin, V. Country Estates Around Moscow from the History of Russian Estate Culture of the 17th, 18th, & 19th Centuries. 398p. 1979. 150.00x (ISBN 0-317-14227-5, Pub. by Collet's). State Mutual Bk.

Animal Behavior Society Symposium, 1977. Behavioral Significance of Color: Proceedings. new ed. Burtt, Edward H., Jr., ed. LC 77-14618. 1979. lib. bdg. 52.50 (ISBN 0-8240-7016-X, Garland STPM Pr). Garland Pub.

Animal Medical Center Staff & Kay, William J. The Complete Book of Cat Health. (Illus.). 288p. 1985. 19.95 (ISBN 0-02-502350-0). Macmillan.

Animal Nutrition. Nutrient Requirements of Poultry. 7th rev ed. Agricultural Board, ed. LC 54-60841. (Nutrient Requirements of Domestic Animals Ser). 62p. 1978. pap. 8.95 (ISBN 0-309-02725-X). Natl Acad Pr.

Animuccia, Giovanni. Missarum Liber Primus. 218p. 1982. Repr. of 1567 ed. 120.00x (ISBN 0-576-28220-0, Pub. by Gregg Intl Dist Ctr England). State Mutual Bk.

Anirvan. Buddhiyoga of the Gita & Other Essays. 1984. 16.00x (ISBN 0-8364-1120-X, Pub. by Biblia Impex). South Asia Bks.

Anisfeld, Evelyn R., jt. ed. see Anisfeld, Michael H.

Anisfeld, Michael H. & Anisfeld, Evelyn R., eds. International Drug GMP's. 2nd ed. 250p. 1983. text ed. 180.00 (ISBN 0-935184-02-3). Interpharm.
Anisfeld, Moshe. Language Development from Birth to Three. LC 83-82493. 306p. 1984. text ed. 29.95x (ISBN 0-89859-284-4). L Erlbaum Assocs.
Anisman, H. & Bignami, G., eds. Psychopharmacology of Aversively Motivated Behavior. LC 77-17998. (Illus.). 576p. 1978. 55.00x (ISBN 0-306-31055-4, Plenum Pr). Plenum Pub.
Anisovich, V. V., et al. Quark Model & High Energy Collisions. 280p. 1984. 35.00x (ISBN 9971-966-68-9, Pub. by World Sci Singapore). Taylor & Francis.
Anisson du Perron, J., jt. auth. see Mai-Aru.
Anisuzzaman & Abdel-Malek, Anouar. Culture & Thought in the Transformation of the World. LC 84-40079. 105p. 1984. 19.95 (ISBN 0-312-17865-4). St Martin.
Anjaria, D. C. From Existence to Life. 1984. 5.95 (ISBN 0-533-05657-8). Vantage.
Anjaria, S. J., et al. Developments in International Trade Policy. (Occasional Papers: No. 16). 124p. 1982. pap. 5.00 (ISBN 0-317-04015-4). Intl Monetary.
--Trade Policy Developments in Industrial Countries. (Occasional Papers: No. 5). 56p. 1981. pap. 5.00 (ISBN 0-317-04006-5). Intl Monetary.
Anjaria, Shailendra J. Trade Policy Issues & Developments. (Occasional Papers). 1985. pap. 7.50 (ISBN 0-317-19914-5). Intl Monetary.
Anjaria, Shailendra J., et al. Payments Arrangements & the Expansion of Trade in Eastern & Southern Africa. (Occasional Papers: No. 11). 52p. 1982. pap. 5.00 (ISBN 0-317-04011-1). Intl Monetary.
Anjomani, Ardeshir & Kruse, David. Impact of Current Office Space Development on the Future Distribution of Employment & Population in the Dallas-Fort Worth Area. 66p. (Orig.). 1983. pap. 20.00 (ISBN 0-936440-51-1). Inst Urban Studies.
Anjomani, Ardeshir & Rowe, Nick. Effects of Employment Growth in Selected Employment Centers in the Dallas-Fort Worth Metropolitan Region. (Illus.). 86p. 1983. pap. 20.00 (ISBN 0-936440-55-4). Inst Urban Studies.
Anjomani, Ardeshir, et al. Residential Mobility Patterns in Dallas-Fort Worth & San Antonio: Determinants of Move, Racial Succession & Female-Headed Households. 111p. (Orig.). 1985. pap. 15.00 (ISBN 0-936440-59-7). Inst Urban Studies.
Anjou, Lars A. The History of the Reformation in Sweden. Mason, Henry M., tr. from Swedish. LC 83-45598. Date not set. Repr. of 1859 ed. 62.50 (ISBN 0-404-19866-X). AMS Pr.
Anjou, Robert. Dinah, Now... A Novel. LC 85-80351. 210p. (Orig.). 1985. pap. 10.95 (ISBN 0-9613373-1-1). Jasper Assocs.
--A Shadow of My Days: A Short-Story Collection. 1984. pap. 8.95 (ISBN 0-9613373-0-3). Jasper Assocs.
Ank, John A., jt. auth. see Breyer, Donald E.
Ankel-Simons, Friderun. A Survey of Living Primates & Their Anatomy. 288p. 1983. pap. text ed. write for info. (ISBN 0-02-303500-5). Macmillan.
Ankenbruck, John. Five Forts. LC 72-91181. 1976. pap. 1.95 (ISBN 0-686-16304-4). Lions Head.
--Voice of the Turtle. LC 75-75071. 1976. pap. 1.95 (ISBN 0-686-15471-1). Lions Head.
Anker, Hans, jt. auth. see Klinger, Julius.
Anker, J. Bird Books & Bird Art. lib. bdg. 80.00 (ISBN 90-6193-993-3, Pub. by Junk Pubs Netherlands). Kluwer Academic.
Anker, Jean. Bird Books & Bird Art: An Outline of the Literary History & Iconography of Descriptive Ornithology, Based Principally on the Collection in the University Library at Copenhagen. LC 73-17795. (Natural Sciences in America Ser.). (Illus.). 326p. 1974. Repr. 23.50x (ISBN 0-405-05705-9). Ayer Co Pubs.
Anker, Richard. Reproductive Behavior in Households of Rural Gujaret: Social, Economic & Community Factors. 152p. 1982. text ed. 13.50x (ISBN 0-391-02719-0, Pub. by Concept). Humanities.
Anker, Richard & Knowles, James C. Population Growth, Employment, & Economic-Demographic Interactions in Kenya: Bachue, Kenya. 754p. 1984. 50.00x (ISBN 0-312-63146-4). St Martin.
Anker, Richard, jt. ed. see Bodrova, Valentina.
Anker, Richard, ed. see International Labour Office Staff.
Anker, Richard, et al, eds. Women's Roles & Population Trends in the Third World. 288p. 1981. 33.50 (ISBN 0-7099-0508-4, Pub. by Croom Helm Ltd). Longwood Pub Group.
Ankerl, Guy. Overurbanization in Tropical Africa 1970-2000: Rapid Urbanization, Social Problems, & Solutions. LC 84-52309. 134p. 1984. pap. 7.25 (ISBN 0-932269-06-0). Wyndham Hall.
Ankerl, Guy C. Beyond Monopoly Capitalism & Monopoly Socialism: Distributive Justice in a Competitive Society. text ed. 108p. 1978. 13.25 (ISBN 0-87073-938-7). Schenkman Bks Inc.
--Experimental Sociology of Architecture: A Guide to Theory, Research & Literature. (New Babylon Studies in the Social Sciences Ser.: No. 36). 550p. 1981. 50.00 (ISBN 90-279-3219-0); pap. 19.95 (ISBN 90-279-3440-1). Mouton.
Ankersmit, F. R. Narrative Logic: A Semantic Analysis of the Historian's Language. 1983. lib. bdg. 39.50 (ISBN 90-247-2731-6, Pub. by Martinus Nijhoff Netherlands). Kluwer-Academic.
Ankerson, Dudley. Agrarian Warlord: Saturnino Cedillo & the Mexican Revolution in San Luis Potosi. LC 84-20683. 303p. 1985. 32.00 (ISBN 0-87580-101-3). N Ill U Pr.
Ankerst, Jaro, et al. Cell Surface Alteration As a Result of a Malignant Transformation. LC 72-13690. (Illus.). 237p. 1973. No. 2. text ed. 24.00x (ISBN 0-8422-7053-1); No. 1. text ed. 25.00x (ISBN 0-8422-7055-8). Irvington.
Anklam, Patricia, et al. Engineering a Compiler: VAX-11 Code Generation & Optimization. (Illus.). 269p. 1982. 28.00 (ISBN 0-932376-19-3, EY-0001-DP). Digital Pr.
Ankli, Robert E. Gross Farm Revenue in Pre-Civil War Illinois. Bruchley, Stuart, ed. LC 76-39820. (Nineteen Seventy-Seven Dissertations Ser.). (Illus.). 1977. lib. bdg. 35.50x (ISBN 0-405-09901-0). Ayer Co Pubs.
Ankner, William & Bivens, William E. Getting To Work: Northeast Perspectives on Rural Public Transportation & Economic Development. LC 83-72711. 98p. 1983. pap. 7.50 (ISBN 0-914193-03-1). Coalition NE Govn.
Ankori, Zvi. Karaites in Byzantium: The Formative Years, 970-1100. LC 71-158258. (Columbia University Studies in the Social Sciences: No. 597). Repr. of 1959 ed. 28.50 (ISBN 0-404-51597-5). AMS Pr.
Ankowitz, Arthur. Strokes & Their Prevention. 1980. pap. 4.95x (ISBN 0-317-07303-6, Regent House). B of A.
Ankrum, Freeman. Sidelights on Brethren History. (Illus.). 174p. 1962. 1.25 (ISBN 0-87178-788-1). Brethren.
Anku, Vincent. What to Know about the Treatment of Cancer: Clear, Sensible Answers to the Questions Asked by Cancer Patients, Their Families & Friends from a Concerned Physicians & Specialist in the Day-to-Day Treatement of Cancer. LC 84-20148. (Illus.). 152p. (Orig.). 1984. pap. 7.95 (ISBN 0-88089-002-9). Madrona Pubs.
Anliot, Sture F. The Vascular Flora of Glen Helen, Clifton Gorge, & John Bryan State Parks. 1973. 3.50 (ISBN 0-86727-064-0). Ohio Bio Survey.
Anlyan, William G., et al. The Future of Medical Education. Graves, Judy, ed. LC 72-97153. pap. 52.50 (ISBN 0-317-20085-2, 2023366). Bks Demand UMI.
ANMC Tariff Task Group Staff. Standard Reference Tables for Metric Conversion of Transporation Tariffs. rev. ed. 90p. 1982. 19.00 (ISBN 0-686-47622-0). Am Natl.
Ann Arbor Publishers Editorial Staff. Cursive Tracking. large type, reusable ed. 32p. (gr. 2-8). 1973. 5.00 (ISBN 0-89039-015-0). Ann Arbor FL.
--Cursive Writing One: Reusable Edition. (Cursive Writing Ser.). 64p. (gr. 2-3). 1977. wkbk. 6.50 (ISBN 0-89039-204-8). Ann Arbor FL.
--Manuscript Writing, 2 levels. Reusable ed. (Manuscript Writing Ser.). (gr. 1-3). 1978. Level one. 6.00 (ISBN 0-89039-235-8); Level two. 6.00 (ISBN 0-89039-212-9). Ann Arbor FL.
--Manuscript Writing: Words Book 1 & 2. Reusable ed. (Manuscript Writing Words Ser.). (gr. 3-6). Book 1. 6.50 (ISBN 0-89039-214-5); Book 2. 6.50 (ISBN 0-89039-216-1). Ann Arbor FL.
--Symbol Discrimination Series: Books 1, 2, 3, 4, 5, & 6. Reusable ed. (Symbol Discrimination Series). (Illus.). 16p. (gr. k-1). 1974. 3.00 ea.; Book 1. 3.00 (ISBN 0-89039-078-9); Book 2. 3.00 (ISBN 0-89039-079-7); Book 3. 3.00 (ISBN 0-89039-080-0); Book 4. 3.00 (ISBN 0-89039-081-9); Book 5. 3.00 (ISBN 0-89039-082-7); Book 6. 3.00 (ISBN 0-89039-083-5). Ann Arbor FL.
Ann, Fay, ed. see Corey, Dorothy.
Ann, Fay, ed. see Nixon, Joan L.
Ann, Lee S. Regional Security Developments & Stability in Southeast Asia. 60p. (Orig.). 1980. pap. text ed. 10.00x (ISBN 0-566-04010-7, Pub. by Inst Southeast Asian). Gower Pub Co.
Ann, Lee Soo, ed. Economic Relations Between West Asia & Southeast Asia. 256p. 1978. pap. text ed. 25.00x (ISBN 0-566-04003-4, Pub. by Inst Southeast Asian Stud). Gower Pub Co.
Anna, Contesse De Bremont see De Bremont Anna, Contesse.
Anna, James W. How to Write Your Life Story. LC 76-1761. (Illus.). 1976. pap. 3.95 (ISBN 0-89305-000-8). Anna Pub.
Anna, Timothy E. The Fall of the Royal Government in Mexico City. LC 77-17790. xxviii, 289p. 1978. 23.50x (ISBN 0-8032-0957-6). U of Nebr Pr.
--The Fall of the Royal Government in Peru. LC 79-9142. xiv, 291p. 1980. 22.50x (ISBN 0-8032-1004-3). U of Nebr Pr.
--Spain & the Loss of America. LC 82-11118. xxiv, 343p. 1983. 26.50x (ISBN 0-8032-1014-0). U of Nebr Pr.
Annabella. Passion's Pawn. 1978. pap. 2.25 (ISBN 0-440-06937-8). Dell.
--The Polreath Women. 1978. pap. 2.50 (ISBN 0-440-07031-7). Dell.
Annable, James E. The Price of Industrial Labor: The Role of Wages in Business Cycles & Economic Growth. LC 83-48131. 272p. 1984. 35.00x (ISBN 0-669-06952-3); pap. text ed. 15.00 (ISBN 0-669-09781-0). Lexington Bks.
Annaloro, John. The Software Publishing Handbook: A Complete Guide to Writing & Marketing Computer Programs. 320p. (Orig.). 1985. pap. 19.95 (ISBN 0-915391-13-9, Pub. by Microtrend). Slawson Comm.
Annan, Noel. Leslie Stephen: The Godless Victorian. LC 84-42512. (Illus.). 384p. 1984. 24.50 (ISBN 0-394-53061-6). Random.
Annan, Noel, ed. see Stephen, Leslie.
Annan, Noel G. Leslie Stephen, His Thought & Character in Relation to His Time. LC 75-30015. Repr. of 1951 ed. 23.00 (ISBN 0-404-14021-1). AMS Pr.
--Leslie Stephen: His Thought & Character in Relation to His Time. Metzger, Walter P., ed. LC 76-55199. (The Academic Profession Ser.). (Illus.). 1977. Repr. of 1952 ed. lib. bdg. 26.50x (ISBN 0-405-10028-0). Ayer Co Pubs.
Annan, Thomas. Photographs of the Old Closes & Streets of Glasgow, 1868-1877. (Eighteen Sixty-Eight to Eighteen Seventy-Seven). (Illus.). 96p. 1977. pap. 5.00 (ISBN 0-486-23442-8). Dover.
--Photographs of the Old Closes & Streets of Glasgow, 1868-1877. 11.75 (ISBN 0-8446-5550-3). Peter Smith.
Annandale, N. Coelenterata, Polyzoa: Freshwater Sponges, Hydroids, & Polyzoa. (Illus.). vii, 262p. 1972. Repr. of 1911 ed. 10.00 (ISBN 0-88065-015-X, Pub. by Messers Today & Tomorrows Printers & Publishers India). Scholarly Pubns.
Annandale, Nelson. The Faroes & Iceland: Studies in Island Life. LC 77-87701. 280p. Repr. of 1905 ed. 27.50 (ISBN 0-404-16495-1). AMS Pr.
Annandale, Nelson & Robinson, H. C. Fasciculi Malayeneses: Anthropological & Zoological Results of an Expedition to Perak & the Siamese Malay States, 1901-1902. LC 77-87478. 1977. Repr. of 1904 ed. 22.50 (ISBN 0-404-16791-8). AMS Pr.
Annarino, Anthony A. & Kahms, Frederick W. First Aid, Safety, & Family Health Emergencies: Study Guide. 2nd ed. 1979. pap. text ed. 6.95x (ISBN 0-8087-0063-4). Burgess.
Annarino, Anthony A., et al. Curriculum Theory & Design in Physical Education. 2nd ed. LC 80-282. (Illus.). 1980. text ed. 21.95 (ISBN 0-8016-0297-1). Mosby.
Annas, George J., jt. ed. see Milunsky, Aubrey.
Annas, George J., et al. Informed Consent to Human Experimentation: The Subject's Dilemma. LC 77-2266. 360p. 1977. prof ref 30.00 (ISBN 0-88410-147-9). Ballinger Pub.
--The Rights of Doctors, Nurses, & Allied Health Professionals: 1981. 400p. 1983. pap. 12.95 professional reference (ISBN 0-88410-992-5). Ballinger Pub.
Annas, Julia. An Introduction to Plato's Republic. 1981. pap. text ed. 18.95x (ISBN 0-19-827429-7). Oxford U Pr.
Annas, Julia & Barnes, Jonathan. The Modes of Scepticism: Ancient Texts & Modern Interpretations. 216p. 1985. 29.50 (ISBN 0-521-25682-8); pap. 9.95 (ISBN 0-521-27644-6). Cambridge U Pr.
Annas, Julia, ed. Oxford Studies in Ancient Philosophy, Vol. I: 1983. (Oxford Studies in Ancient Philosophy). 1983. 39.95x (ISBN 0-19-824687-0); pap. 19.95x (ISBN 0-19-824705-2). Oxford U Pr.
--Oxford Studies in Ancient Philosophy, Vol. 2. 312p. 1984. text ed. 29.95x (ISBN 0-19-824769-9); pap. text ed. 14.95x (ISBN 0-19-824768-0). Oxford U Pr.
Annas, Julia, ed. see Aristotle.
Anne. To the Whole World: An Open Letter. 1978. pap. 2.50 (ISBN 0-914350-33-1). Vulcan Bks.
Anne, Fay, ed. see Heide, Florence P. & Heide, Roxanne.
Anne, W. Now what Do I Do for Fun. (Orig.). 1985. pap. 0.85 (ISBN 0-89486-297-9). Hazelden.
Annechild, Annette. Annette Annechild's Seafood Wok. 1985. pap. 9.95 (ISBN 0-671-55398-4, Wallaby). PB.
--Annette Annechild's Wok Your Way Skinny 30-Day Menu Plan. 1984. 8.95 (ISBN 0-671-50034-1, Wallaby). S&S.
--Food Processor Cookbook. 160p. 1983. pap. 8.95 (ISBN 0-671-45391-2, Wallaby). S&S.
Annechild, Annette & Bennett, Russell. Recipe for a Great Affair: How to Cater Your Own Party...or Anybody Else's. LC 81-11806. 207p. 1981. pap. 9.95 (ISBN 0-671-42411-4, Wallaby). S&S.
Annegan, Charles, ed. see Baird, Samuel E.
Annemann, Ted. Annemann's Card Magic. LC 77-75234. (Illus.). 1977. pap. 3.50 (ISBN 0-486-23522-X). Dover.
--Annemann's Card Magic, 2 vols. in 1. Orig. Title: Full Deck of Impromptu Card Tricks, & Miracles of Card Magic. (Illus.). 11.50 (ISBN 0-8446-5551-1). Peter Smith.
Annemann, Theodore. Practical Mental Logic. (Illus.). 310p. (Orig.). 1983. pap. 5.95 (ISBN 0-486-24426-1). Dover.
Annen, Sharon, tr. see Desnos, Robert.
Annenberg, Maurice, intro. by. A Typographical Journey Through the Inland Printer 1883-1900. LC 77-89269. casebound 45.00 (ISBN 0-916526-04-6). Maran Pub.
Annenkov, Georges P., intro. by. Russian Stage & Costume Designs for the Ballet, Opera & Theatre. (Illus.). 64p. 1967. pap. 6.00 (ISBN 0-88397-063-5). Intl Exhibit Foun.
Annese, Lucius. Pope John Paul II in America. LC 79-56497. 1980. 50.00 (ISBN 0-933402-10-4). Charisma Pr.
--The Purpose of Authority? LC 78-72295. (Orig.). 1978. 50.00 (ISBN 0-933402-12-0). Charisma Pr.
--Write & Publish. LC 79-57036. 89p. 1980. 50.00 (ISBN 0-933402-13-9). Charisma Pr.
Annesley, Mabel. As the Sight Is Bent. 14.50 (ISBN 0-392-02142-0, SpS). Sportshelf.
Annesley, Samuel. Puritan Sermons, Sixteen Fifty-Nine To Sixteen Eighty-Nine Being the Morning Exercises at Cripplegate, St. Giles in the Fields & in Southwark: By 75 Ministers of the Gospel in or Near London, with Notes & Translations by James Nichols, 6 vols. Nichols, James, ed. 4200p. 1981. Set. lib. bdg. 120.00 (ISBN 0-686-32108-1). R O Roberts.
Annesley, Samuel, et al. Puritan Sermons, 1659-1689, 6 vols. Nichols, James, ed. 4220p. 1981. Repr. of 1845 ed. lib. bdg. 120.00 set (ISBN 0-939464-07-1). Labyrinth Pr.
Annest, Joseph L. & Mahaffey, Kathryn. Blood Lead Levels for Persons Ages 6 Months to 74 Years: United States, 1976-1980. Cox, Kaludia, ed. (Series 11-233). 50p. 1984. pap. text ed. 1.95 (ISBN 0-8406-0291-X). Natl Ctr Health Stats.
Annett, Marian. Left, Right, Hand & Brain: The Right Shift Theory. 488p. 1985. text ed. 39.95 (ISBN 0-86377-018-5). L Erlbaum Assocs.
Annett, Philippa. Naturally Healthy. (Illus.). 160p. 1984. 12.95 (ISBN 0-7182-1570-2, Pub. by Kaye & Ward). David & Charles.
Annett, Ross H., Jr. & Samuelson, G. Allen. Dictionary of Coleoptera Collections of North America: Canada Through Panama. 1969. 6.95 (ISBN 0-916846-05-9). World Natural Hist.
Annexton, May & Schillinger, Brent. Coping with Skin Care. (Coping with Ser.). 1981. lib. bdg. 8.97 (ISBN 0-8239-0525-X). Rosen Group.
Annie & Elizakeany. Heroes of Asgard. (Facsimile Classics Ser.). (Illus.). 1979. 6.95 (ISBN 0-8317-4475-8, Mayflower Bks). Smith Pubs.
Annino, R. & Driver, R. Personal Computers in Scientific & Engineering Applications. 1985. 39.95 (ISBN 0-471-79978-5). Wiley.
Annis, John R. & Allen, Algernon R. An Atlas of Canine Surgery: Basic Surgical Procedures with Emphasis on the Gastrointestinal & Urogenital Systems. LC 67-29212. pap. 58.80 (ISBN 0-317-28610-2, 2055414). Bks Demand UMI.
Annis, L., et al, eds. Turning, Vol. 1. 2nd ed. (Engineering Craftsmen: No. H2). (Illus.). 1977. spiral bdg. 37.50x (ISBN 0-85083-403-1). Intl Ideas.
Annis, Linda F. The Child Before Birth. LC 77-3112. (Illus.). 194p. 1978. 29.95x (ISBN 0-8014-1039-8); pap. 8.95x (ISBN 0-8014-9168-1). Cornell U Pr.
--Study Techniques. 136p. 1983. pap. text ed. write for info. (ISBN 0-697-06069-1). Wm C Brown.
Annis, Verle L. The Architecture of Antigua Guatemala, 1543-1773. (Illus.). 1968. 40.00 (ISBN 0-686-11833-2). R Reed.
Annixter, Jane & Annixter, Paul. Buffalo Chief. 220p. (gr. 7 up). 1958. 6.95 (ISBN 0-8234-0015-8). Holiday.
--The Last Monster. LC 80-7978. (gr. 4-6). 1980. 6.95 (ISBN 0-15-243614-6, HJ). HarBraceJ.
Annixter, Paul. The Best Nature Stories of Paul Annixter. LC 74-9347. 192p. (gr. 7 up). 1974. 6.95 (ISBN 0-88208-043-1). Lawrence Hill.
--Devil of the Woods. facs. ed. LC 70-81259. (Short Story Index Reprint Ser., Vol. 1). 1958. 17.00 (ISBN 0-8369-3011-8). Ayer Co Pubs.
--Wilderness Ways. 1979. Repr. of 1931 ed. lib. bdg. 30.00 (ISBN 0-8492-0094-6). R West.
Annixter, Paul, jt. auth. see Annixter, Jane.
Anno, J. N., jt. auth. see Walowit, J. A.
Anno, Mitsumasa. Anno's Alphabet: An Adventure in Imagination. LC 73-21652. (Illus.). 64p. (gr. k up). 1975. 10.53i (ISBN 0-690-00540-7); PLB 11.89 (ISBN 0-690-00541-5). Crowell Jr Bks.
--Anno's Animals. LC 79-11721. (Illus.). 1979. 7.95 (ISBN 0-529-05545-7, Philomel); PLB 7.99 (ISBN 0-529-05546-5). Putnam Pub Group.
--Anno's Britain. (Illus.). 48p. 1982. 10.95 (ISBN 0-399-20861-5, Philomel); pap. 5.95 (ISBN 0-399-21249-3). Putnam Pub Group.
--Anno's Counting Book. LC 76-28977. (Illus.). (ps-3). 1977. 11.49i (ISBN 0-690-01287-X); PLB 11.89 (ISBN 0-690-01288-8). Crowell Jr Bks.
--Anno's Counting House. (Illus.). 48p. 1982. 12.95 (ISBN 0-399-20896-8, Philomel). Putnam Pub Group.
--Anno's Journey. 48p. 1981. 10.95 (ISBN 0-399-20762-7, Philomel); pap. 5.95 (ISBN 0-399-20952-2, Philomel). Putnam Pub Group.
--Anno's Medieval World. LC 79-28367. 32p. (gr. 3 up). 1980. 12.95 (ISBN 0-399-20742-2, Philomel); PLB 12.99 (ISBN 0-399-61153-3). Putnam Pub Group.

--Anno's Mysterious Multiplying Jar. LC 82-22413. (Illus.). 48p. (gr. 3 up). 1983. pap. 12.95 (ISBN 0-399-20951-4, Philomel). Putnam Pub Group.

--Dr. Anno's Magical Midnight Circus. Weatherby, Meredith, tr. from Japanese. LC 72-78598. (Illus.). 28p. 1972. 6.50 (ISBN 0-8348-2011-0). Weatherhill.

--Topsy-Turvies: Pictures to Stretch the Imagination. LC 71-96054. (Illus.). 28p. (gr. k-5). 1970. 6.50 (ISBN 0-8348-2004-8). Weatherhill.

--The Unique World of Mitsumasa Anno: Selected Works 1968-1977. Morse, Samuel, tr. LC 80-12827. (Illus.). 64p. (gr. 7 up). 1980. 19.95 (ISBN 0-399-20743-0, Philomel). Putnam Pub Group.

--Upside-Downers: More Pictures to Stretch the Imagination. Weatherby, Meredith & Trumbull, Suzanne, trs. from Japanese. LC 71-157269. (Illus.). 28p. (gr. k-6). 1971. 6.50 (ISBN 0-8348-2005-6). Weatherhill.

Anno, Mitsumasa, jt. auth. see Nozaki, Akihiro.

Anno, Mitsumasa, illus. Anno's Flea Market. LC 83-21954. (Illus.). 44p. 1984. 11.95 (ISBN 0-399-21031-8, Philomel). Putnam Pub Group.

--Anno's Italy. (Illus.). 48p. 1984. 10.95 (ISBN 0-399-20770-8, Philomel); pap. 5.95 (ISBN 0-399-21032-6, Philomel). Putnam Pub Group.

--Anno's U. S. A. LC 83-13107. (Illus.). (gr. 3 up). 1983. 10.95 (ISBN 0-399-20974-3, Philomel); signed limited ed. 35.00 (ISBN 0-399-21053-9). Putnam Pub Group.

Annon, Jack S. Behavioral Treatment of Sexual Problems: Vol. 2, Intensive Therapy. (Illus.). 370p. (Orig.). 1975. pap. 14.50 (ISBN 0-917688-01-5). Enabling Syst.

Annual Birth Defects Conference, San Francisco, Ca., 1978. Diagnostic Approaches to the Malformed Fetus, Abortus, Stillborn, & Deceased Newborn: Annual Review of Birth Defects, 1978 Part a. Golbus, Mitchell S. & Hall, Bryan D., eds. LC 79-2369. (Birth Defects: Original Article Ser.: Vol. 15, No. 5a). 206p. 1979. 29.00x (ISBN 0-8451-1028-4). A R Liss.

Annual Birth Defects Conference, 1978. San Francisco, Ca. Penetrance & Variability in Malformation Syndromes: Proceedings, Annual Review of Birth Defects, 1978, Pt. B. O'Donnell, James J. & Hall, Bryan D., eds. LC 79-5115. (Birth Defects: Original Article Ser.: Vol. XV, No. 5B). 396p. 1979. 55.00x (ISBN 0-8451-1029-2). A R Liss.

Annual Chicago Symposium on Neoplasm Immunity, 2nd, Chicago, 1974. Neoplasm Immunity: Theory & Application: Proceedings. Crispen, Ray G., ed. LC 75-18796. 1975. 15.00 (ISBN 0-915314-02-9). Inst Tuberculosis.

Annual Chicago Symposium, 4th Chicago, 1975. Neoplasm Immunity: Mechanisms: Proceedings. Crispen, Ray G., ed. LC 76-8600. (Neoplasm Immunity Ser.). 1977. 18.00 (ISBN 0-915314-03-7). Inst Tuberculosis.

Annual Clinical Conference on Cancer, 22nd. Immunotherapy of Human Cancer: Proceedings. M. D. Anderson Hospital & Tumor Institute, ed. LC 77-17701. (Illus.). 437p. 1978. 59.00 (ISBN 0-89004-263-2). Raven.

Annual Conference for Psychosomatic Research, 20th, London, Nov. 15-16, 1976. The Psychosomatic Approach to Prevention of Disease: Proceedings. Carruthers, M. & Priest, R., eds. 1978. pap. text ed. 24.00 (ISBN 0-08-022253-6). Pergamon.

Annual Conference of the Royal Institute of British Architects, U. of Hull, 14-17 July, 1976. Architecture: Opportunities, Achievements: Report. Goldstein, Barbara, ed. (Illus.). 1977. pap. 8.75x (ISBN 0-900630-59-0, Pub. by RIBA). Intl Spec Bk.

Annual Conference on Magnetic Materials, 22nd, Pittsburgh, June 15-18, 1976. Magnetism & Magnetic Materials: Proceedings, 1976. LC 76-47106. (AIP Conference Proceedings: No. 34). 1976. 19.50 (ISBN 0-88318-133-9). Am Inst Physics.

Annual Conference on Shock, 3rd, Lake of the Ozarks, Missouri, June 1980. Advances in Shock Research: Proceedings, Vol. 5, Pt. 1. Lefer, Allan M., ed. LC 79-63007. 188p. 1981. 29.00x (ISBN 0-8451-0604-X). A R Liss.

--Advances in Shock Research: Proceedings, Vol. 6, Pt. 2. Schumer, William, et al, eds. LC 79-63007. 196p. 1981. 29.00x (ISBN 0-8451-0605-8). A R Liss.

Annual Educators Conference Chicago, Illinois, August, 1980. Marketing in the Eighties, Changes & Challenges: Proceedings. Bagozzi, Richard P., et al, eds. LC 80-15934. (No. 46). (Illus., Orig.). 1980. pap. text ed. 30.00 (ISBN 0-87757-141-4). Am Mktg.

Annual Hormone Research Symposium, 1st, 1974. Hormone Research I: Proceedings. Norvell, M. & Shellenberger, T., eds. (Illus.). 142p. 1976. text ed. 39.95 (ISBN 0-89116-009-4). Hemisphere Pub.

Annual Hormone Research Symposium, 2nd, 1975. Hormone Research II: Proceedings. Norvell, M. J. & Shellenberger, T. E., eds. (Illus.). 266p. 1976. text ed. 39.95 (ISBN 0-89116-039-6). Hemisphere Pub.

Annual Hormone Research Symposium, 3rd, 1976. Hormone Research III: Proceedings. new ed. Norvell, M. J. & Shellenberger, T. E., eds. (Illus.). 372p. 1977. text ed. 39.95 (ISBN 0-89116-070-1). Hemisphere Pub.

Annual Legal Conference on the Representation of Aliens 1978-1983. In Defense of the Alien: Proceedings, 6 vols. Fragomen, Austin L. & Tomasi, Lydio F., eds. (In Defense of the Alien Ser.). 144p. 1979. lib. bdg. 14.95 ea. Vol. I (ISBN 0-913256-41-2). Vol. II (ISBN 0-913256-53-6). Vol. III. Vol. IV (ISBN 0-913256-55-2). Vol. V (ISBN 0-913256-61-7). Vol. VI (ISBN 0-913256-65-X). Ctr Migration.

Annual Meeting Education Sessions. Tutorial Lecture Series: Proceedings. 1969. pap. text ed. 10.00 (ISBN 0-915414-48-1). Inst Environ Sci.

Annual Meeting of I.E.S. Environmental Science-Challenge to E-E Education in the Seventies! 1972 Tutorial Proceedings. (Illus.). 1972. pap. text ed. 8.00 (ISBN 0-915414-46-5); pap. text ed. 6.40 members. Inst Environ Sci.

Annual Meeting of the American Society of Psychopathology, 4th, Belmont, Mass., October 1969. Conscious & Unconscious Expressive Art: Theories, Methodology & Pathographies - Proceedings. Jakab, Irene, ed. (Psychiatry & Art: Vol. 3). (Illus.). 1971. 24.75 (ISBN 3-8055-1190-6). S Karger.

Annual Meeting of the Deutsche Gesellschaft Fuer Neurochirurgie, Heidelberg, May 1-3, 1975, et al. Brain Hypoxia Pain: Proceedings. Penzholz, H. & Brock, M., eds. (Advances in Neurosurgery: Vol. 3). (Illus.). 480p. 1975. pap. 48.00 (ISBN 0-387-07466-X). Springer-Verlag.

Annual Meeting of the Institute of Environmental Sciences, Boston, 1970. The Environmental Challenge of the 70's: Proceedings. LC 62-38584. (Illus.). 1970. pap. text ed. 20.00 (ISBN 0-915414-10-4). Inst Environ Sci.

Annual Meeting of the Institute of Environmental Sciences, 12th, 1966. The Environments & Man: Proceedings. LC 62-38584. (Illus.). 1966. pap. text ed. 8.00 (ISBN 0-915414-06-6). Inst Environ Sci.

Annual Meeting of the Institute of Environmental Sciences, 6th, 1960. Hyper-Environments...Space Frontier: Proceedings. (Illus.). 1960. pap. text ed. 8.00 (ISBN 0-915414-00-7). Inst Environ Sci.

Annual Meeting of the Institute of Environmental Sciences, 16th, 1970. Living Environments. (Nineteen-Seventy Tutorial Lecture Ser.). 1970. pap. text ed. 12.00 (ISBN 0-915414-47-3). Inst Environ Sci.

Annual Meeting of the Institute of Environmental Sciences, 8th, 1962. Product Improvement Through Environmental Science: Proceedings. LC 62-38584. (Illus.). 1962. pap. text ed. 8.00 (ISBN 0-915414-02-3). Inst Environ Sci.

Annual Meeting of the Institute of Environmental Sciences, 19th, Realism (Assessment) of Career Education in the Environmental Sciences. (Illus.). 1973. pap. text ed. 8.00 (ISBN 0-915414-45-7). Inst Environ Sci.

Annual Meeting of the Institute of Environmental Sciences, 10, 1964. Reliability vs. Reality: Proceedings. LC 62-38584. (Illus.). 1964. pap. text ed. 7.00 (ISBN 0-915414-04-X). Inst Environ Sci.

Annual Meeting of the International Continence Society, 6th, Antwerp, Sept. 1976. Proceedings. Coolsaet, B., ed. (Urologia Internationalis: Vol. 33, No. 1-3). 1978. pap. 31.50 (ISBN 3-8055-2898-1). S Karger.

Annual Meeting of the Japanese Society for Stereotactic & Functional Neurosurgery, 15th, Maebashi, October 1976. Recent Studies on the Human Thalamus: Proceedings. Gildenberg, Ph. L. & Ohye, C., eds. (Applied Neurophysiology: Vol. 39, No. 3-4). (Illus.). 1977. 24.75 (ISBN 3-8055-2847-7). S Karger.

Annual Meeting of the Materials Research Society, Cambridge, 1979. Ion Implantation Metallurgy: Proceedings. Preece, Carolyn M. & Hirvoen, J. K., eds. (Illus.). 197p. 26.00 (ISBN 0-89520-364-2); members 16.00 (ISBN 0-317-34880-9); student members 9.00 (ISBN 0-317-34881-7). ASM.

Annual Meeting on Brain Edema, 24th, 1973. Brain Edema, Pathophysiology & Therapy, Cerebello Pontine Angle Tumors, Diagnosis & Surgery: Proceedings. Schuermann, et al, eds. LC 73-14237. (Advances in Neurosurgery Ser.: Vol. 1). (Illus.). 400p. 1974. pap. 41.00 (ISBN 0-387-06486-9). Springer-Verlag.

Annual Meeting, 1st, North Carolina, July 1923. Papers Read at the Meeting of Grand Dragons Knights of the Ku Klux Klan. Grob, Gerald, ed. LC 76-46086. (Anti-Movements in America Ser). 1977. Repr. of 1923 ed. lib. bdg. 17.00x (ISBN 0-405-09959-2). Ayer Co Pubs.

Annual of Trade Mark Design. Book of American Trademarks, Vol. 7. Carter, David E., ed. LC 72-76493. (Illus.). 1980. 16.50 (ISBN 0-910158-61-4). Art Dir.

Annual Office of Children's Service. Children's Books, 1982. 1981. pap. 1.50 (ISBN 0-87104-660-1, Branch Lib). NY Pub Lib.

Annual Office of Children's Services. Children's Books, 1984. 1984. pap. 2.00 (ISBN 0-87104-671-7). NY Pub Lib.

Annual Oholo Biological Conference, 21st, Israel, March 1976. Host-Parasite Relationships in Systemic Mycoses: Proceedings. Beemer, A. M., et al, eds. Incl. Methodology, Pathology & Immunology, Pt. I. (Contributions to Microbiology & Immunology: Vol. 3) (ISBN 3-8055-2443-9); Specific Diseases & Therapy, Pt. II. (Contributions to Microbiology & Immunology: Vol. 4) (ISBN 3-8055-2444-7). (Illus.). 1978. pap. 33.25 ea. S Karger.

Annual Research Conference, 11th & 12th, UCLA, 1968-1969. Problems in Contract Negotiation & Problems & Goals in Manpower Policy: Proceedings. 1970. 2.00 (ISBN 0-89215-030-0). U Cal LA Indus Rel.

Annual Research Conference, 13th, UCLA, 1970. The Generation Gap: Implications for Labor-Management Relations: Proceedings. 2.00 (ISBN 0-89215-031-9). U Cal LA Indus Rel.

Annual Research Conference, 14th, UCLA, 1972. National Incomes Policy & Manpower Problems: Proceedings. 2.00 (ISBN 0-89215-032-7). U Cal LA Indus Rel.

Annual Research Conference, 8th, UCLA, 1965. Research Conference on Labor Relations: Proceedings. 2.00 (ISBN 0-89215-028-9). U Cal LA Indus Rel.

Annual Research Conference, 9th, UCLA, 1966. The City & the World of Work-A Critical Examination of Life in Los Angeles & Urban America in the Mid-Sixties: Proceedings. 2.00 (ISBN 0-89215-029-7). U Cal LA Indus Rel.

Annual San Francisco Cancer Symposium, 12th, San Francisco, Calif., March 4-5, 1977. Renaissance of Interstitial Brachytherapy: Proceedings. Vaeth, J. M., ed. (Frontiers of Radiation Therapy and Oncology: Vol. 12). (Illus.). 1977. 50.25 (ISBN 3-8055-2706-3). S Karger.

Annual Symposium on Fundamental Cancer Research, No. 31. Carcinogens: Identification & Mechanisms of Action. Griffin, A. Clark & Shaw, Charles R., eds. LC 78-23366. 505p. 1979. text ed. 65.00 (ISBN 0-89004-286-1). Raven.

Annual Technical Meeting of Institute of Environmental Sciences April, 1977. Environmental Technology '77: Proceedings of the 23rd Annual Technical Meeting of the Institute of Environmental Sciences, Los Angeles. LC 62-38584. (Illus.). 1977. pap. text ed. 22.00 (ISBN 0-915414-17-1). Inst Environ Sci.

Annual Technical Meeting of the Institute of Environmential Sciences, Fort Worth, Texas, April 1978. Combined Environments Technology Interrelations: Proceedings. LC 62-38584. (Illus.). 1978. pap. text ed. 22.00 (ISBN 0-915414-18-X). Inst Environ Sci.

Annual Technical Meeting of the Institute of Environmental Sciences, 26th, Philadelphia, May 1980. Life Cycle Problems & Environmental Technology: Proceedings. LC 62-38584. (Illus.). 1980. pap. text ed. 25.00 (ISBN 0-915414-20-1). Inst Environ Sci.

Annual West Coast Cancer Symposium, 10th, San Francisco, Calif., September 1974. Primary Bone Cancer: the Multidiscipline Disease: Proceedings. Vaeth, J., ed. (Frontiers of Radiation Therapy & Oncology: Vol. 10). viii, 243p. 1975. 40.50 (ISBN 3-8055-2185-5). S Karger.

Annual, 13th, San Francisco, Calif., March 1978. Combined Effects of Chemotherapy & Radiotherapy on Normal Tissue Tolerance. Vaeth, J. M., ed. (Frontiers of Radiation Therapy & Oncology: Vol. 13). (Illus.). 1979. 61.75 (ISBN 3-8055-2932-5). S Karger.

Anobile, Richard. The Book of Fame. Date not set. pap. 7.95 (ISBN 0-449-90044-4, Columbine). Fawcett.

--The Marx Brothers Scrapbook. (Illus.). 265p. pap. cancelled (ISBN 0-8119-0599-3). Fell.

Anobile, Richard & Anobile, Ulla. Freeform Marriage. 288p. 1981. pap. 2.95 (ISBN 0-523-41627-X). Pinnacle Bks.

Anobile, Richard, ed. Casablanca. (Film Classics Library Ser). (Illus.). 256p. 1974. pap. 5.95 (ISBN 0-380-00086-5, 21097-5, Flare). Avon.

--The General. (Illus.). 1972. pap. 6.45 (ISBN 0-380-00449-6, 25817-X, Flare). Avon.

--Psycho. (Film Classics Library). (Illus.). 256p. 1974. pap. 4.95 (ISBN 0-380-00085-7, 21063, Flare). Avon.

--Stagecoach. 1975. pap. 5.95 (ISBN 0-380-00291-4, 22913-7, Flare). Avon.

--Why a Duck? (Illus.). 288p. 1974. pap. 5.95 large-format (ISBN 0-380-00452-6, 40774-4). Avon.

Anobile, Richard J. Hooray for Captain Spaulding. (Illus.). 1975. pap. 4.95 (ISBN 0-380-00458-5, 25882-X). Avon.

--Outland: The Movie. (Illus., Orig.). 1981. pap. cancelled (ISBN 0-446-97829-9). Warner Bks.

Anobile, Richard J., ed. Alien: The Movie Novel. 1979. pap. 8.95 (ISBN 0-380-46631-7, 46631-7). Avon.

--A Flask of Fields. 1975. pap. 3.95 (ISBN 0-380-01189-1, 17533). Avon.

Anobile, Richard J, ed. Frankenstein. (Film Classics Library). (Illus.). 256p. 1974. pap. 4.95 (ISBN 0-380-01196-4, 19117, Flair). Avon.

Anobile, Richard J., ed. Godfrey Daniels. 1976. pap. 5.45 (ISBN 0-380-00614-6, 28628-1, Flare). Avon.

Anobile, Richard J, ed. The Maltese Falcon. (Film Classics Library). (Illus.). 256p. 1974. pap. 4.95 (ISBN 0-380-01485-8, 19109-1, Flare). Avon.

Anobile, Ulla, jt. auth. see Anobile, Richard.

Anolik, Alexander. The Law & the Travel Industry. Weiner, Kerry & Rattet, Zev, eds. LC 77-88827. (Orig.). 1978. 29.95 (ISBN 0-931290-00-7). Alchemy Bks.

--The Law & the Travel Industry, Vol. II. rev. ed. 300p. 1985. lift-ring binder 40.00 (ISBN 0-931290-94-5). Alchemy Bks.

Anolik, Ruth B., jt. auth. see Bienstock, June K.

Anon, jt. auth. see Abbott.

Anonym, Kenneth. Understanding the Recovering Alcoholic. 144p. 1980. pap. 4.95 (ISBN 0-89486-103-4). Hazelden.

--Understanding the Recovering Alcoholic. 139p. 1974. pap. 1.95 (ISBN 0-318-15357-2). Natl Coun Alcoholism.

Anonymous. Joy. 3.95 (ISBN 0-394-62287-1). Grove.

Anosike, Benji O. How to Adopt a Child Without a Lawyer. Rev. ed. LC 78-74123. 120p. (Orig.). 1984. pap. text ed. 10.95x (ISBN 0-932704-00-X). Do-It-Yourself Legal Pubs.

--How to Buy-Sell Your Own Home Without a Lawyer or Broker. 195p. (Orig.). 1985. pap. text ed. 14.95 (ISBN 0-932704-09-3). Do-It-Yourself Legal Pubs.

--How to Declare Your Personal Bankruptcy Without a Lawyer. LC 80-66445. 140p. 1983. pap. text ed. 10.95 (ISBN 0-932704-07-7). Do-It-Yourself Legal Pubs.

--How to Do Your Own Divorce Without a Lawyer. Rev. ed. LC 80-65725. 82p. (Orig.). 1980. pap. text ed. 9.95x (ISBN 0-932704-01-8). Do-It-Yourself Legal Pubs.

--How to Do Your Own Probate & Estate Settlement Without a Lawyer. LC 80-66446. 210p. (Orig.). 1984. pap. text ed. 12.95 (ISBN 0-932704-08-5). Do-It-Yourself Legal Pubs.

--How to Draw Up Your Legal Separation, Cohabitation, or Property Settlement Agreement Without a Lawyer. LC 80-66443. 120p. (Orig.). 1981. pap. text ed. 9.95x (ISBN 0-932704-04-2). Do-It-Yourself Legal Pubs.

--How to Draw up Your Own Will Without a Lawyer: Why You Can't Afford to Live--or Die--Without One! rev. ed. LC 80-966444. 108p. (Orig.). 1980. pap. text ed. 8.95x (ISBN 0-932704-05-0). Do-It-Yourself Legal Pubs.

--How to File For "Chapter II" Bankruptcy Relief from Your Business Debts, with or without A Lawyer. 140p. 1983. pap. text ed. 11.95 (ISBN 0-932704-14-X). Do-It-Yourself Pubns.

--How to Form Your Own Profit-Non-Profit Corporation Without a Lawyer. LC 80-66215. 130p. (Orig.). 1980. pap. text ed. 8.95x (ISBN 0-932704-03-4). Do-It-Yourself Legal Pubs.

--How to Legally Beat the Traffic Ticket Without a Lawyer. 90p. (Orig.). 1982. pap. text ed. 5.95x (ISBN 0-932704-12-3). Do-It-Yourself Legal Pubs.

--How to Legally Reduce Your Real Estate Taxes Without a Lawyer. 100p. (Orig.). 1982. pap. 8.95x (ISBN 0-932704-11-5). Do-It-Yourself Legal Pubs.

--How to Obtain Your U. S. Immigration Visa Without a Lawyer. 150p. 1981. pap. text ed. 9.95x (ISBN 0-932704-10-7). Do-It-Yourself Legal Pubs.

--How to Settle Your Own Auto Accident Claims Without a Lawyer. 120p. (Orig.). 1982. pap. 8.95 (ISBN 0-932704-13-1). Do-It-Yourself Legal Pubs.

--Win Your Legal Rights As a Tenant Without a Lawyer. LC 80-66213. (Illus., Orig.). 1980. pap. text ed. 8.95 (ISBN 0-932704-02-6). Do-It-Yourself Legal Pubs.

Anosov, D. V., ed. Twenty Lectures Delivered at the International Congress of Mathematicians in Vancouver, 1974. LC 77-9042. (Translation Ser. No. 2: Vol. 109). 129p. 1982. pap. 27.00 (ISBN 0-8218-3059-7, TRANS 2/109). Am Math.

Anosov, D. V., ed. see Steklov Institute of Mathematics, Academy of Sciences, U.S.S.R.

Anosov, D. V., et al. Twenty-Four Papers on Statistics & Probability: Twenty-Four Papers Statistics & Probability. LC 61-9803. (Selected Translations in Mathematical Statistics & Probability: Vol. 14). 296p. 1978. 38.00 (ISBN 0-8218-1464-8, STAPRO-14); institutional members 28.50; individual members 19.00. Am Math.

Anouilh, Jean. Alouette. 1963. pap. 3.95 (ISBN 0-685-10991-7, 1153). French & Eur.

--Alouette. Thomas, Merlin & Lee, Simon, eds. (Orig., Fr.,). 1975. pap. text ed. 12.95x incl. exercises (ISBN 0-89197-005-3). Irvington.

--Anouilh: Five Plays, Vol. 1. Incl. Romeo & Jeannette; Rehearsal; Ermine; Antigone; Eurydice. (Mermaid Dramabook Ser.). 340p. (Orig.). 1958. pap. 5.25 (ISBN 0-8090-0710-X). Hill & Wang.

--Antigone. 1975. pap. 5.50 (ISBN 0-685-11007-9). French & Eur.

--Ardele, Ou la Marguerite. 1970. pap. 3.95 (ISBN 0-685-11012-5). French & Eur.

--Becket. 1960. pap. 5.95 (ISBN 0-698-10031-X, Coward). Putnam Pub Group.

--Becket ou, l'Honneur de Dieu. 1973. pap. 5.50 (ISBN 0-685-11038-9, 1716). French & Eur.

--Le Boulanger, la Boulangere et le Petit Mitron. pap. 7.95 (ISBN 0-685-37157-3). French & Eur.

--Cecile ou, l'Ecole des Peres. 1954. pap. 6.50 (ISBN 0-685-11069-9). French & Eur.

--Cher Antoine ou L'amour Rote. 12.95 (ISBN 0-685-37158-1). French & Eur.
--Chers Zoiseaux. 1977. pap. 14.95 (ISBN 0-686-51895-0). French & Eur.
--Colombe. 1963. pap. 2.95 pocket ed. (ISBN 0-685-11094-X, 1049). French & Eur.
--Dear Antoine. Hill, Lucienne, tr. from Fr. 96p. 1971. 4.95 (ISBN 0-8090-3784-X). Hill & Wang.
--Le Directeur de l'Opera. 1972. pap. 7.95 (ISBN 0-686-51896-9). French & Eur.
--Eurydice. Incl. Romeo et Juliette. pap. 3.95 (ISBN 0-685-37159-X). French & Eur.
--Eurydice & Medee. Freeman, E., ed. (French Texts Ser.). 160p. (Fr.). 1984. pap. 9.95x (ISBN 0-631-13692-4). Basil Blackwell.
--Fables. 1966. 20.95 (ISBN 0-685-11179-2). French & Eur.
--Fables. 1973. pap. 3.95 (ISBN 0-686-51897-7). French & Eur.
--Foire D'Empoigne. 1962. pap. 3.95 (ISBN 0-685-11193-8). French & Eur.
--La Grotte. 1961. pap. 3.95 (ISBN 0-685-11225-X). French and Eur.
--L' Hurluberlu; ou, le Reactionnaire Amoureux. 1959. pap. 3.95 (ISBN 0-685-11239-X). French & Eur.
--Invitation Au Chateau. 1962. pap. 3.95 (ISBN 0-685-11255-1). French & Eur.
--Lark. Fry, Christopher, tr. 1956. 10.95x (ISBN 0-19-500393-4). Oxford U Pr.
--Leocadia. Knapp, Bettina L. & Della Fazia, Alba, eds. LC 66-17601. (Illus., Fr.). 1965. pap. text ed. 4.95x (ISBN 0-89197-273-0). Irvington.
--Medee. 1967. pap. 4.50 (ISBN 0-685-11355-8). French & Eur.
--Monsieur Barnett, Avec l'orchestre. 1975. pap. 12.95 (ISBN 0-686-51898-5). French & Eur.
--Ne Reveillez Pas Madame. 5.95 (ISBN 0-685-37160-3). French & Eur.
--Nouvelles Pieces Grincantes. Incl. L' Hurluberlu; La Grotte; L' Orchestre; Les Poissons Rouges; Le Boulanger; La Boulangere et le Petit Mitron. 19.95 (ISBN 0-685-37154-9). French & Eur.
--Nouvelles Pieces Noires. Incl. Jezabel; Antigone; Romeo et Juliette; Medee. 21.95 (ISBN 0-685-37155-7). French & Eur.
--Ornifle Ou le Courant D'air. 1974. pap. 3.95 (ISBN 0-685-11471-6). French & Eur.
--Pauvre Bitos, Ou, le Diner De Tetes. 1973. pap. 3.95 (ISBN 0-685-11481-3). French & Eur.
--Pieces Baroques. Incl. Cher Antoine; Ne Reveillez Pas, Madam; Le Directeur de l'Opera. 1974. 21.95 (ISBN 0-686-50202-7). French & Eur.
--Pieces Brillantes. Incl. L' Invitation au Chateau; Colombe; La Repetition ou L'amour Puni; Cecile ou L'ecole des Peres. 18.95 (ISBN 0-685-37149-2). French & Eur.
--Pieces Costumees: L'alouette, Becket, la Foire D'empoigne. 18.95 (ISBN 0-685-37150-6). French & Eur.
--Pieces Grincantes. Incl. Ardele ou la Marguerite; La Valse des Toreadors; Ornifle Ou le Courant D'air; Pauvre Bitos Ou le Diner De Tetes. 18.95 (ISBN 0-685-37151-4). French & Eur.
--Pieces Noires. Incl. L' Hermine; La Sauvage; Le Voyageur sans Bagage; Eurydice. 18.95 (ISBN 0-685-37152-2). French & Eur.
--Pieces Roses. Incl. Humulus le Monet; Le Bal des Voleurs; Le Rendez-vous de Senlis; Leocadia. 18.95 (ISBN 0-685-37153-0). French & Eur.
--Pieces Secretes. Incl. Tu estais Si Gentil Quand Tu Etais Petit; L' Arrestation; Le Scenario. 1977. 23.95 (ISBN 0-686-52219-2). French & Eur.
--Les Poissons Rouges. (Coll. Folio). pap. 3.95 (ISBN 0-685-37161-1). French & Eur.
--Le Rendez-Vous De Senlis. pap. 3.95 (ISBN 0-685-37162-X). French & Eur.
--La Repetition ou l'Amour Puni. pap. 3.95 (ISBN 0-685-23917-9, 2383, Pub. by Livre de poche). French & Eur.
--Repetition ou l'amour puni. (Documentation thematique). (Illus., Fr.). pap. 2.95 (ISBN 0-685-14066-0, 1). Larousse.
--Le Sauvage. Bd. with Invitation au Chateau. (Coll. Folio). 1961. pap. 4.95 (ISBN 0-685-23887-3, 748). French & Eur.
--Le Scenario. 1976. 13.95 (ISBN 0-686-51892-6). French & Eur.
--Theatre Complet, 9 tomes. Set. 175.00 (ISBN 0-685-11593-3). French & Eur.
--Tu Etais Si Gentil Quand Tu etais Petit. 1973. pap. 5.95 (ISBN 0-686-50126-8). French & Eur.
--Le Voyageur sans Bagages. Bd. with Le Bal des Voleurs. (Coll. Folio). 1961. pap. 3.95 (ISBN 0-685-23888-1, 678). French & Eur.
Anouilh, Jean see Moon, Samuel.
Anouilh, Jean, et al. Le Voyageur sans Bagage. (Fr.). 1973. text ed. 14.95 (ISBN 0-03-088529-9). HR&W.
Anoyianakis, Phoibos. Greek Folk Musical Instruments. (Illus.). 400p. 1979. 90.00x (ISBN 0-89241-082-5, Pub by Natl. Bank of Greece). Caratzas.
Anozie, S. O. Christopher Okigbo: Creative Rhetoric. LC 77-182593. (Modern African Writers Ser.). 225p. 1972. text ed. 19.50x (ISBN 0-8419-0086-8, Africana); pap. 9.75x (ISBN 0-8419-0117-1, Africana). Holmes & Meier.
Anozie, S. O., ed. Language Systems in Africa. (Studies in African Semiotics Ser.). 1973. 15.00 (ISBN 0-914970-06-2); pap. 10.00 (ISBN 0-914970-07-0). Conch Mag.
--Structuralism & African Folklore. (Studies in African Semiotics Ser.). 1970. pap. 7.00 (ISBN 0-914970-05-4). Conch Mag.
Anozie, Sunday O. Structural Models & African Poetics: Towards a Pragmatic View of Literature. 220p. 1981. 37.50x (ISBN 0-7100-0467-2). Routledge & Kegan.
Anozie, Sunday O., et al. Phenomenology in Modern African Studies, No. 5. (Studies in African Semiotics). 1982. 25.00 (ISBN 0-914970-69-0); pap. text ed. 12.95 (ISBN 0-914970-70-4). Conch Mag.
Anpilogova, B., et al. Essential Russian English Dictionary. 235p. (Rus. & Eng.). 1980. 2.95 (ISBN 0-8285-0596-9, Pub. by Progress Pubs USSR). Imported Pubns.
Anpilogova, B. G., et al. Foundation Dictionary of Russian: Three Thousand High Semantic Frequency Words. Orig. Title: Essential Russian-English Dictionary. (Rus. & Eng.). (YA) (gr. 9-12). 1967. pap. 4.50 (ISBN 0-486-21860-0). Dover.
Anquandah, James. Rediscovering Ghana's Past. LC 82-111384. (Illus.). 208p. (Orig.). 1982. pap. text ed. 9.95x (ISBN 0-582-64309-0). Longman.
Anquetil-Duperron, A. H. Zend-Avesta, Ouvrage de Zoroastre. Feldman, Burton & Richardson, Robert, eds. LC 78-60878. (Myth & Romanticism Ser.). 1984. lib. bdg. 240.00 (ISBN 0-8240-3550-X). Garland Pub.
Anquillare, John, jt. auth. see Joyce, Joan.
Anrais, David. Man & the Zodiac. LC 74-16328. 1970. pap. 5.95 (ISBN 0-87728-014-2). Weiser.
Anrep, G. V., ed. see Pavlov, Ivan P.
Anrep, G. V., tr. see Pavlov, Ivan P.
Anrias, David. Through the Eyes of the Masters. 1972. pap. 7.95 (ISBN 0-87728-116-5). Weiser.
Anrod, Barbara, jt. auth. see Fishman, Joan.
Anrooij, Francien Van see Van Anrooij, Francien, et al.
Ansah, Paul. Rural Journalism in Africa. (Reports & Papers on Mass Communication: No. 88). 35p. 1981. pap. 5.00 (ISBN 92-3-101752-7, U1098, UNESCO). Unipub.
Ansal, Kusum. Sing Me No Songs: A Novel. (Vikas Library of Modern Indian Writing: No. 22). 1982. text ed. 17.95x (ISBN 0-7069-1771-5, Pub. by Vikas India). Advent NY.
--Travelling with a Sunbeam: A Novel. (Vikas Library of Modern Indian Writing: No. 29). vi, 138p. 1983. text ed. 17.95x (ISBN 0-7069-2219-0, Pub. by Vikas India). Advent NY.
Ansaldi, Richard. Souvenirs from the Roadside West. (Illus.). 1978. 3.98 (ISBN 0-517-53338-3); pap. 1.98 (ISBN 0-517-53339-1). Crown.
Ansari, Aftab A. & De Serres, Frederick, eds. Single-Cell Mutation Monitoring Systems: Methodologies & Applications. (Topics in Chemical Mutagenesis Ser.: Vol. 2). 308p. 39.50x (ISBN 0-306-41537-2, Plenum Pr). Plenum Pub.
Ansari, Asloob A. Arrows of Intellect. LC 76-49659. 1976. Repr. of 1965 ed. lib. bdg. 27.50 (ISBN 0-8414-2988-X). Folcroft.
Ansari, F. R. Beyond Death. pap. 1.00 (ISBN 0-686-18473-4). Kazi Pubns.
--The Existence of the Soul. pap. 1.00 (ISBN 0-686-18460-2). Kazi Pubns.
--Foundations of Faith. pap. 1.50 (ISBN 0-686-18472-6). Kazi Pubns.
--Islam & Christianity in the Modern World. pap. 14.95 (ISBN 0-686-18577-3). Kazi Pubns.
--Islam & the Western Civilization. pap. 1.50 (ISBN 0-686-18533-1). Kazi Pubns.
--Philosophy of Worship in Islam. pap. 1.00 (ISBN 0-686-18603-6). Kazi Pubns.
--Through Science & Philosophy to Religion. pap. 1.25 (ISBN 0-686-18536-6). Kazi Pubns.
--What Is Islam? pap. 1.25 (ISBN 0-686-18478-5). Kazi Pubns.
Ansari, Javed. The Political Economy of International Economic Organisation. 300p. 1986. PLB 29.50x (ISBN 0-931477-42-5). Lynne Rienner.
Ansari, Javed, jt. auth. see Singer, Hans.
Ansari, Khwajih Abd Ansari see Abd Allah Ansarti, Khwajih.
Ansari, M. A. Administrative Documents of Mughal India. 139p. 1984. text ed. 25.00x (ISBN 0-86590-294-1, Pub. by B R Pub Corp India). Apt Bks.
--Muslims & the Congress: Correspondence of Dr. M. A. Ansari. Hasan, M., ed. 1979. 18.50 (ISBN 0-8364-0381-9). South Asia Bks.
Ansari, M. A., tr. from Persian. Man & His Destiny. 124p. 1985. pap. 5.00 (ISBN 0-941724-39-5). Islamic Seminary.
Ansari, M. A., tr. see Al-Sadr, Ayatullah B.
Ansari, M. A., tr. see Al Sadr, Muhammad B.
Ansari, M. A., tr. see Behishti, Ayatullah.
Ansari, M. A., tr. see Mutahhery, Murtaza.
Ansari, M. A., tr. see Nutanhhery, Murtaza.
Ansari, M. A., tr. see Sadr, Muhammad B.
Ansari, M. A., tr. see Sadr, Muhhammad B.
Ansari, Mary B. & Amaral, Anne. Gold & Silver Prospecting Books in Print. 23p. (Orig.). 1984. pap. 4.50 (ISBN 0-318-03520-0). Sierra NV Chapter.
Ansari, Mary B. & Newman, Linda P. Nevada Directory of Maps & Aerial Photo Resources. LC 83-26068. (Western Association of Map Libraries: Occasional Paper: No.11). 164p. 1984. pap. 15.00 (ISBN 0-939112-13-2). Western Assn Map.
Ansari, Masud. Modern Hypnosis: Theory & Practice. 232p. (gr. 5). 1982. pap. 6.95 (ISBN 0-9607984-0-4). MAS-Pr.
Ansari, S. A. Some Aspects of the Geography of Manipur. (Illus.). 131p. 1985. text ed. 20.00x (ISBN 0-86590-583-5, Pub. by B R Pub Corp Delhi). Apt Bks.
Ansari, Zafar I., jt. auth. see Ahmad, Khurshid.
Ansay, T. & Dessemontet, F. Introduction to Swiss Law. 1984. lib. bdg. 49.00 (ISBN 90-654-4020-8, Pub. by Kluwer Law Netherlands). Kluwer Academic.
Ansay, T. & Dessemontet, F., eds. Introduction to Swiss Law. 300p. 1983. 53.00 (ISBN 90-65-4402-08). Kluwer Academic.
Ansay, T., et al. Recueil Des Cours De L'academie De Droit International De la Haye: Collected Courses of the Hague Academy of Int'l Law, Vol. 156 (1977-III) 482p. 1980. 40.00x (ISBN 90-286-0650-7). Sijthoff & Noordhoff.
Ansay, Tugrul. American-Turkish Private International Law. LC 66-17535. 115p. 1966. 15.00 (ISBN 0-379-11416-X). Oceana.
--Introduction to Turkish Law. 2nd ed. 267p. 1978. 22.00 (ISBN 0-379-20332-4). Oceana.
Ansbacher, Heinz L. Alfred Adler Revisited. (Praeger Special Studies). 400p. 86. 24.95x (ISBN 0-03-045266-X). Praeger.
Ansbacher, Heinz L., ed. see Adler, Alfred.
Ansbacher, Max. How to Profit from the Coming Bull Market. 226p. 1982. pap. 6.95 (ISBN 0-13-429373-8). P-H.
Ansbacher, Max G. The New Options Market. rev. ed. LC 78-58600. (Illus.). 1979. 17.95 (ISBN 0-8027-0584-7). Walker & Co.
--The New Stock-Index Market, Strategies for Profit in Stock-Index Futures & Options. LC 83-6525. 192p. 1983. 16.95 (ISBN 0-8027-0733-5). Walker & Co.
Ansbacher, Rowena R., ed. see Adler, Alfred.
Ansbro, John J. Martin Luther King, Jr. The Making of a Mind. LC 82-6408. 368p. (Orig.). 1984. 17.95 (ISBN 0-88344-333-3); pap. 11.95 (ISBN 0-88344-346-5). Orbis Bks.
Anschel, Eugene. Homer Lea, Sun Yat-Sen, & the Chinese Revolution. LC 84-15999. 288p. 1984. 36.95 (ISBN 0-03-000063-7). Praeger.
Anschel, Eugene, ed. American Appraisals of Soviet Russia: 1917-1977. LC 78-5920. 404p. 1978. 22.00 (ISBN 0-8108-1135-9). Scarecrow.
Anscombe, E., ed. see Wittgenstein, Ludwik.
Anscombe, E., tr. see Wittgenstein, Ludwik.
Anscombe, Elizabeth, ed. see Descartes, Rene.
Anscombe, Elizabeth, tr. see Descartes, Rene.
Anscombe, Elizabeth, et al. Philosophical Writings: Descartes. 1971. pap. text ed. write for info. (ISBN 0-02-303600-1). Macmillan.
Anscombe, F. Computing in Statistical Science Through APL. (Springer Series in Statistics). 416p. 1981. 29.50 (ISBN 0-387-90549-9). Springer-Verlag.
Anscombe, G. E. Collected Philosophical Papers, 3 vols. 1981. Set. 85.00x (ISBN 0-8166-1084-3); Set. pap. 32.85x (ISBN 0-8166-1085-1). U of Minn Pr.
--Collected Philosophical Papers: Ethics, Religion & Politics, Vol. 3. LC 81-4315. 192p. 1981. 27.50x (ISBN 0-8166-1082-7); pap. 10.95x (ISBN 0-8166-1083-5). U of Minn Pr.
--Collected Philosophical Papers: From Parmenides to Wittgenstein, Vol. I. LC 81-4317. 160p. 1981. 25.00x (ISBN 0-8166-1078-9); pap. 9.95 (ISBN 0-8166-1079-7). U of Minn Pr.
--Collected Philosophical Papers: Metaphysics & the Philosophy of Mind, Vol. 2. LC 81-4316. 288p. 1981. 32.50x (ISBN 0-8166-1080-0); pap. 11.95x (ISBN 0-8166-1081-9). U of Minn Pr.
--Intention. 2nd ed. 102p. (Orig.). 1963. pap. text ed. 8.95x (ISBN 0-8014-9803-1). Cornell U Pr.
--Introduction to Wittgenstein's Tractatus. 1971. pap. 9.95x (ISBN 0-8122-1019-0). U of Pa Pr.
Anscombe, G. E., ed. see Wittgenstein, Ludwig.
Anscombe, G. E., tr. see Wittgenstein, Ludwig.
Anscombe, G. E. M., ed. see Wittgenstein, Ludwig.
Anscombe, G. E. M, tr. see Wittgenstein, Ludwig.
Anscombe, Isabelle. Boobies, Boojums & Snarks: The Ceramic Curiosities of the Martin Brothers, 1880-1914. 59p. (Orig.). 1981. pap. 45.00 (ISBN 0-942410-04-1). Jordan-Volpe Gall.
--Omega & After. LC 81-52311. (Illus.). 176p. 1985. pap. 12.95 (ISBN 0-500-27362-6). Thames Hudson.
--Omega & After: Bloomsbury & the Decorative Arts. LC 81-52311. (Illus.). 176p. 1982. 24.95 (ISBN 0-500-23337-3). Thames Hudson.
--A Woman's Touch. (Nonfiction Ser.). 216p. 1985. pap. 12.95 (ISBN 0-14-008100-3). Penguin.
Ansel, Howard C. Introduction to Pharmaceutical Dosage Forms. 4th ed. LC 84-9732. (Illus.). 405p. 1985. text ed. 29.75 (ISBN 0-8121-0956-2). Lea & Febiger.
Ansel, Howard C., jt. auth. see Stoklosa, Mitchell J.
Ansel, Walter. Hitler & the Middle Sea. LC 77-132026. pap. 131.50 (ISBN 0-317-29049-5, 2023757). Bks Demand UMI.
Ansel, William H., Jr. Frontier Forts along the Potomac & Its Tributaries. Date not set. price not set. McClain.
Ansel, Willits D. Restoration of the Smack Emma C. Berry. LC 72-95937. (Illus.). 94p. 1973. pap. 7.00 (ISBN 0-913372-08-0). Mystic Seaport.
--The Whaleboat: A Study of Design, Construction & Use. (Illus.). 147p. 1978. pap. 12.00 (ISBN 0-913372-40-4). Mystic Seaport.
Ansel, Willits D., jt. auth. see Blair, Carvel H.
Ansell, B M. Rheumatism & the Psyche. 52p. 1975. 35.00 (ISBN 3-456-80378-8, Pub. by Holdan Bk Ltd UK). State Mutual Bk.
Ansell, B. M., jt. ed. see Arden, G. P.
Ansell, Barbara M. Rheumatic Disorders in Children. LC 80-40275. (Postgraduate Paediatrics Ser.). (Illus.). 344p. 1980. text ed. 79.95 (ISBN 0-407-00186-7). Butterworth.
Ansell, George S., et al, eds. Oxide Dispersion Strengthening: Proceedings of a Symposium, Bolton Landing, New York, June 27-29, 1966. LC 67-26577. (Metallurgical Society Conference Ser.: Vol. 47). pap. 160.00 (ISBN 0-317-10618-X, 2001535). Bks Demand UMI.
Ansell, I. D. Atlas of Male Reproductive System Pathological. (Current Histopathology Ser.). 1985. lib. bdg. 77.00 (ISBN 0-85200-327-7, Pub. by MTP Pr England). Kluwer Academic.
Ansell, Jack. Dynasty of Air. LC 74-187807. 1974. 6.95 (ISBN 0-87795-094-6). Arbor Hse.
--Giants. LC 75-11149. 1975. 9.95 (ISBN 0-87795-111-X). Arbor Hse.
--Gospel. LC 72-82169. 1973. 7.95 (ISBN 0-87795-038-5). Arbor Hse.
--The Shermans of Mannerville. LC 77-139295. 1971. 6.95 (ISBN 0-87795-008-3). Arbor Hse.
--Summer. LC 73-82179. 1973. 7.95 (ISBN 0-87795-063-6). Arbor Hse.
Ansell, M. F. Rodd's Chemistry of Carbon Compounds, Suppl. Vol 3F, (Partial) G. 2nd ed. 1984. 86.75 (ISBN 0-444-42269-2, I-479-83). Elsevier.
--Rodd's Chemistry of Carbon Compounds-Heterocyclic Compounds: Part A-3, 4, 5 Membered Compounds. 1984. Vol. 4A, Supplement. 140.75 (ISBN 0-444-42397-4). Elsevier.
Ansell, M. F. & Pattenden, G. Saturated Heterocyclic Chemistry, Vols. 2-5. LC 72-83454. Vol. 2 1974. 47.00 (ISBN 0-85186-532-1); Vol. 3 1975. 1973 literature 43.00 (ISBN 0-85186-562-3); Vol. 4 1977. 1974 literature 77.00 (ISBN 0-85186-592-5); Vol. 5 1978. 66.00 (ISBN 0-85186-622-0). Am Chemical.
Ansell, M. F., ed. Rodd's Chemistry of Carbon Compounds, 2 pts. in 1, Suppl. Vol. 1 C & D. (Pt. A: Monocarbonyl Derivatives, Pt. 2: Dihydric Alcohols). 1973. 102.25 (ISBN 0-444-41072-4). Elsevier.
--Rodd's Chemistry of Carbon Compounds, 2 pts. in 1, Suppl. Vol. 1 A & B. (Pt. A: Hydrocarbons, Pt. B: Monohydric Alcohols). 1975. 76.75 (ISBN 0-444-40972-6). Elsevier.
--Rodd's Chemistry of Carbon Compounds, 3 pts. in 1, Suppl. Vol. 2, Pts. C-E. 1974. 85.00 (ISBN 0-444-41135-6). Elsevier.
--Rodd's Chemistry of Carbon Compounds, 2 pts. in 1, Suppl. Vol. 2 A & B. 1974. 102.25 (ISBN 0-444-41133-X). Elsevier.
--Rodd's Chemistry of Carbon Compounds, Suppl. Vols. 3 B & C. 1981. 91.50 (ISBN 0-444-42017-7). Elsevier.
--Rodd's Chemistry of Carbon Compounds, Suppl. Vols. 3, Pts. D-F. 1983. 110.75 (ISBN 0-444-42088-6). Elsevier.
--Rodd's Chemistry of Carbon Compounds: Aromatic Compounds, Part A, Vol. 3, Pt. A. 2nd ed. 1983. 110.75 (ISBN 0-444-42150-5). Elsevier.
--Supplement to the Second Edition of Rodd's Chemistry of Carbon Compounds, Vol. 1, Pts F & G. 404p. 1983. 115.00 (ISBN 0-444-42183-1). Elsevier.
--Supplements to the Second Edition of Rodd's Chemistry of Carbon Compounds; Supplement to Vol. IV: Heterocyclic Compounds, Part B: Five-membered Heterrocyclic Compounds with a Single Hetero-Atom in the Ring; Alkaloids, Dyes & Pigments. 320p. 1985. 98.25 (ISBN 0-444-42485-7). Elsevier.
--Supplements to the 2nd Edition of Rodd's Chemistry of Carbon Compounds; Supplement to Vol. 1: Aliphatic Compounds; Part E: Unsaturated Acyclic Hydrocarbons, Trihydric Alcohols, Their Oxidation Products & Derivatives. 510p. 1983. 144.75 (ISBN 0-444-42236-6). Elsevier.
Ansell, M. O., jt. auth. see Arif, I. M.
Ansell, M. O., jt. auth. see Arif, T. M.
Ansell, M. P. Jumping. 14.50x (ISBN 0-392-08278-0, SpS). Sportshelf.
Ansell, Mary. Dogs & Men. facs. ed. LC 70-142257. (Short Story Index Reprint Ser). 1924. 14.00 (ISBN 0-8369-3741-4). Ayer Co Pubs.
Ansell, Meredith O., jt. auth. see Arif, T. M.
Ansell, Thomas. The Many-Coloured Mantle. 10.00 (ISBN 0-89253-452-4); flexible cloth 4.80 (ISBN 0-89253-453-2). Ind-US Inc.
Anselm & Shizuko. Social Organization of Medical Work. LC 84-23995. (Illus.). 1985. lib. bdg. 25.00x (ISBN 0-226-77707-3). U of Chicago Pr.

Anselm, A. Introduction to Semiconductor Theory. (Illus.). 646p. 1982. 42.95 (ISBN 0-13-496034-3). P-H.

Anselm, Saint. The De Grammatico of St. Anselm: The Theory of Paronymy. LC 64-17066. (Notre Dame, University Publications in Mediaeval Studies Ser.: No. 18). pap. 47.00 (ISBN 0-317-08123-3, 2022069). Bks Demand UMI.

Anselm, St. Saint Anselm: Basic Writings. 2nd ed. Deane, Sidney M., tr. Incl. Proslogium; Monologium; Gaunilo's "In Behalf of the Fool"; Cur Deus Homo. LC 74-3309. 371p. 1974. 22.95 (ISBN 0-87548-108-6); pap. 9.25 (ISBN 0-87548-109-4). Open Court.

Anselme, Jean-Pierre, ed. N-Nitrosamines. LC 79-12461. (ACS Symposium Ser.: No. 101). 1979. 26.95 (ISBN 0-8412-0503-5). Am Chemical.

Anselme, Michel. Freedom & Morality: A Nonsubjective Moral Code. Wald, Susan, tr. from Fr. 1983. 15.00 (ISBN 0-8022-2414-8). Philos Lib.

Anselment, Carol & Gibson, Donald B., eds. Black & White Stories in American Life. (Orig.). 1971. pap. 0.95 (ISBN 0-671-47839-7). WSP.

Anselmi, Angelo T. Isotta Fraschini. (Illus.). 1978. 49.95 (ISBN 0-87938-052-7, Pub. by Milani Italy). Motorbooks Intl.

Anselm Of Canterbury. Anselm of Canterbury: Vol. I, Monologion, Proslogion, Debate with Gaunilo, & a Meditation on Human Redemption. Hopkins, Jasper & Richardson, Herbert, trs. LC 74-19840. 161p. 1974. 39.95x (ISBN 0-88946-000-0). E Mellen.

--Anselm of Canterbury: Vol. II, Philosophical Fragments; De Grammatico; on Truth; Freedom of Choice; the Fall of the Devil; the Harmony of the Foreknowledge, the Predestination, & the Grace of God with Free Choice. Hopkins, Jasper & Richardson, Herbert, trs. LC 74-19840. 237p. 1976. 49.95x (ISBN 0-88946-250-X). E Mellen.

--Anselm of Canterbury: Vol. III, Two Letters Concerning Roscelin; the Incarnation of the Word; Why God Became a Man; the Virgin Conception & Original Sin; the Procession of the Holy Spirit; Three Letters on the Sacraments. Hopkins, Jasper & Richardson, Herbert, trs. LC 74-19840. 265p. 1976. 39.95x (ISBN 0-88946-350-6). E Mellen.

--Anselm of Canterbury: Why God Became Man. Hopkins, Jasper & Richardson, Herbert, eds. 105p. 1980. soft cover 7.95x (ISBN 0-88946-009-4). E Mellen.

--Why God Became Man & the Virgin Conception & Original Sin. Colleran, Joseph M., tr. from Latin. & intro. by. LC 71-77166. 256p. (Orig.). 1982. pap. text ed. 4.95x (ISBN 0-87343-025-5). Magi Bks.

Anselone, P. M. Nonlinear Integral Equations. LC 64-17771. (U. S. Army Mathematics Research Center Publication Ser.: No. 11). pap. 97.50 (ISBN 0-317-08601-4, 2010205). Bks Demand UMI.

Ansen, Alan. Disorderly Houses. LC 61-14240. (Wesleyan Poetry Program Ser.: Vol. 11). (Orig.). 1962. 15.00x (ISBN 0-8195-2011-X); pap. 6.95 (ISBN 0-8195-1011-4). Wesleyan U Pr.

Ansermet, Ernest. Stravinsky. Guiney, Louise, tr. (Illus.). 1982. 20.00 (ISBN 0-933806-08-6). Black Swan CT.

Ansfield, Fred J. Chemotherapy of Malignant Neoplasms. 2nd ed. (Illus.). 328p. 1973. photocopy ed. 39.50x (ISBN 0-398-02570-3). C C Thomas.

Ansfield, Joseph G. The Adopted Child. 78p. 1971. 9.75x (ISBN 0-398-00050-6). C C Thomas.

Ansheim, Lester, jt. auth. see Berelson, Bernard.

Anshen, Frank, jt. auth. see Frank, Francine.

Anshen, Melvin. Corporate Strategies for Social Performance. LC 79-7888. (Studies of the Modern Corporation). 1980. 21.95 (ISBN 0-02-900730-5). Macmillan.

Anshen, Melvin, ed. Managing the Socially Responsible Corporation. LC 73-13364. (Studies of the Modern Corporation). (Illus.). 288p. 1974. 19.95 (ISBN 0-02-900680-5). Macmillan.

Anshen, Melvin & Bach, George Leland, eds. Management & Corporations 1985. LC 75-4938. 253p. 1975. Repr. of 1960 ed. lib. bdg. 15.00 (ISBN 0-8371-8051-1, ANMC). Greenwood.

Anshen, Ruth N. Anatomy of Evil. Orig. Title: The Reality of the Devil. (Illus.). 200p. 1985. pap. 8.95 (ISBN 0-918825-15-6). Moyer Bell Ltd.

Anshen, Ruth N., ed. Beyond Victory. facsimile ed. LC 75-156605. (Essay Index Reprint Ser). Repr. of 1943 ed. 18.00 (ISBN 0-8369-2303-0). Ayer Co Pubs.

--Mid-East-World Center: Yesterday, Today & Tomorrow. LC 78-20183. (Science & Culture Ser.). xiv, 386p. 1975. Repr. of 1956 ed. lib. bdg. 27.50 (ISBN 0-8154-0508-1). Cooper Sq.

--Our Emergent Civilization. facs. ed. LC 70-134048. (Essay Index Reprint Ser). 1947. 20.00 (ISBN 0-8369-2101-1). Ayer Co Pubs.

Anshen, Ruth N., ed. see Cavalieri, Liebe F.

Anshen, Ruth N., ed. see Chomsky, Noam.

Anshen, Ruth N., ed. see Delgado, Jose M.

Anshen, Ruth N., ed. see Glass, Bentley.

Anshen, Ruth N., ed. see Lovell, Bernard.

Anshen, Ruth N., ed. see Lovell, Bernard & Bank, Jodrell.

Anshen, Ruth N., ed. see Mayeroff, Milton.

Anshen, Ruth N., ed. see Mead, Margaret.

Anshen, Ruth N., ed. see Newell, Norman D.

Anshen, Ruth N., ed. see Salk, Jonas.

Anshen, Ruth N., ed. see Sperry, Roger.

Anshen, Ruth N., ed. see Tillich, Paul.

ANSI Accredited. Safety in Welding & Cutting: Z49. 1-83. (Illus.). 30p. (Orig.). 1983. pap. text ed. 20.00 (ISBN 0-87171-236-9); member 15.00. Am Welding.

Anski, S; see Landis, Joseph C.

Ansky, S. The Dybbuk. Engel, S. Morris, tr. from Yiddish. LC 79-63047. (Illus.). 1979. pap. 5.95 (ISBN 0-89526-904-X). Regnery-Gateway.

Ansley, Clive. The Heresy of Wu Han: His Play "Hai Jui's Dismissal" & Its Role on China's Cultural Revolution. LC 73-24463. pap. 33.30 (ISBN 0-317-10102-1, 2014112). Bks Demand UMI.

Ansley, Delight. Good Ways. rev. ed. LC 59-14674. (Illus.). (gr. 7-11). 1959. 10.95 (ISBN 0-690-33757-4). Crowell Jr Bks.

Ansley, F. Vice Versa. LC 85-42968. 302p. 1985. pap. 2.25 (ISBN 0-14-035067-5, Puffin). Penguin.

Ansley, Margene. One Woman's Feelings. 1981. pap. text ed. 5.00 (ISBN 0-939476-13-4, Pub. by Biblio Pr GA). Prosperity & Profits.

--The Thrift Book: A Directory. LC 80-70871. pap. text ed. 14.95 (ISBN 0-939476-09-6, Pub. by Biblio Pr GA). Prosperity & Profits.

Ansley, Margene, ed. The Thrift Book Index. LC 82-70344. 100p. 1982. pap. text ed. 8.95 (ISBN 0-939476-45-2, Pub. by Biblio Pr GA). Prosperity & Profits.

Ansley, Norman & Abrams, Stanley. The Polygraph Profession. pap. 20.00 (ISBN 0-317-27137-7, 2024681). Bks Demand UMI.

Ansley, Norman, ed. Legal Admissibility of the Polygraph. (Illus.). 348p. 1975. 43.00x. C C Thomas.

Ansley, Robert E., Jr. Discrimination in Housing. (CPL Bibliographies: No. 13). 75p. 1979. pap. 10.00 (ISBN 0-86602-013-6). CPL Biblios.

Anslinger, H. J. & Tompkins, William F. The Traffic in Narcotics. Grob, Gerald N., ed. LC 80-1211. (Addiction in America Ser.). 1981. Repr. of 1953 ed. lib. bdg. 30.00x (ISBN 0-405-13567-X). Ayer Co Pubs.

Ansoff. Understanding & Managing Strategic Change. 1982. 38.50 (ISBN 0-444-86405-9, I-344-82). Elsevier.

Ansoff, H. Igor. Strategic Management. LC 78-23402. 236p. 1979. 37.95x (ISBN 0-470-26585-X). Halsted Pr.

Ansoff, H. Igor, et al. Acquisition Behavior of United States Manufacturing Firms, 1946-1965. LC 79-163771. (Illus.). 1971. 9.95x (ISBN 0-8265-1174-0). Vanderbilt U Pr.

Ansoff, Igor, et al, eds. From Strategic Planning to Strategic Management. LC 74-20598. 259p. 1976. 57.95x (ISBN 0-471-03223-9, Pub. by Wiley-Interscience). Wiley.

Anson, Barbara. God Made Them Superstars. 1976. pap. 1.50 (ISBN 0-685-73454-4, LB405, Leisure Bks). Dorchester Pub Co.

--Golem. (Inflation Fighters Ser.). 192p. 1982. pap. 1.50 (ISBN 0-8439-1095-X, Leisure Bks). Dorchester Pub Co.

Anson, Barry & Donaldson, James A. Surgical Anatomy of the Temporal Bone. 3rd ed. (Illus.). 500p. 1981. 79.00 (ISBN 0-7216-1292-X). Saunders.

Anson, Barry J., jt. auth. see Bast, Theodore H.

Anson, Bert. Miami Indians. LC 74-108793. (Civilization of the American Indian Ser.: Vol. 103). (Illus.). Repr. of 1970 ed. 90.80 (ISBN 0-8357-9735-X, 2016191). Bks Demand UMI.

Anson, Doris C., tr. see Maritain, Jacques.

Anson, Edward, et al. Perceptions of Reality: A Sourcebook for the Social History of Western Civilization. LC 80-81665. 240p. 1980. pap. text ed. 11.95 (ISBN 0-8403-2224-0). Kendall-Hunt.

Anson, Edward M. A Civilization Primer. 121p. 1985. text ed. 5.95 spiral bdg. (ISBN 0-15-507595-0, HC). HarBraceJ.

Anson, Jay. The Amityville Horror. 1978. pap. 3.50 (ISBN 0-553-22634-7). Bantam.

--Six Sixty-Six. 1982. pap. 3.50 (ISBN 0-671-83126-7). PB.

Anson, Joan. Before the Trees Turn Gray. Perrin, Arnold, ed. 65p. (Orig.). 1981. pap. 4.95 (ISBN 0-939736-22-5). Wings ME.

Anson, John. Seasons & Surroundings, Pt. 2. 20p. 1984. pap. 4.00 (ISBN 0-941150-28-3). Barth.

Anson, John S. Sessions & Surroundings, Pt. 3. 24p. (Orig.). 1984. pap. 4.00 (ISBN 0-941150-32-1). Barth.

Anson, Lord. A Voyage Round the World in the Years 1740-1744. Rhys, Ernest, ed. 384p. 1981. Repr. lib. bdg. 20.00 (ISBN 0-89984-003-5). Century Bookbindery.

Anson, Robert S. Exile: The Unquiet Oblivion of Richard M. Nixon. 352p. 1984. 17.95 (ISBN 0-671-44021-7). S&S.

--The Yellow River. LC 80-52503. (Rivers of the World Ser.). 68p. (gr. 4 up). PLB 13.96 (ISBN 0-382-06371-6). Silver.

Anson, Ronald J., jt. auth. see Rist, Ray C.

Anson, W. S. Mottoes & Badges of Families, Regiments, Schools, Colleges, States, Towns, Livery Companies, Societies, Etc. LC 74-14502. 192p. 1975. Repr. of 1904 ed. 43.00x (ISBN 0-8103-4055-0). Gale.

Anson, W. S., ed. see MacDowall, M. W.

Anson, W. S., ed. see Wagner, W.

Anson, William R. The Law & Custom of the Constitution, 2 Vols. Repr. of 1892 ed. Set. 65.00 (ISBN 0-384-01603-0). Johnson Repr.

Anson, William R. & Guest, Anthony G. Anson's Law of Contract. 26th ed. LC 84-9703. 1984. 37.50x (ISBN 0-19-876148-1). Oxford U Pr.

Ansorge, Peter. Disrupting the Spectacle: Five Years of Experimental & Fringe Theatre in Britain. 1975. 15.00x (ISBN 0-273-00351-8); pap. 7.00 (ISBN 0-273-00255-4). Wesleyan U Pr.

Ansorge, R. & Toernig, W., eds. Numerical Treatment of Differential Equations in Applications: Proceedings, Oberwolfach, Germany, Dec. 1977. LC 78-11883. (Lecture Notes in Mathematics: Vol. 679). 1978. pap. 15.00 (ISBN 0-387-08940-3). Springer-Verlag.

Ansorge, R., et al, eds. Iterative Solution of Nonlinear Systems of Equations, Oberwolfach, FRG, 1982: Proceedings. (Lecture Notes in Mathematics: Vol. 953). 202p. 1982. pap. 14.00 (ISBN 0-387-11602-8). Springer-Verlag.

--Numerische Behandlung von Differentialbleichungen, 2 vols. (International Series of Numerical Mathematics: Nos. 27 & 31). (Ger.). Vol. 1, 1975, 335p. 44.95x (ISBN 0-8176-0771-4); Vol. 2, 1976, 276p. pap. 37.95x (ISBN 0-8176-0853-2). Birkhauser.

--Numerische Mathematik: Symposium on the Occasion of the Retirement of L. Collatz. (International Series of Numerical Mathematics: No. 49). 207p. (Ger.). 1979. 32.95x (ISBN 0-8176-1099-5). Birkhauser.

Anspach, Charles L. A Voice Speaks: Addresses & Prologues. (Illus.). xix, 394p. 1976. 10.00 (ISBN 0-916699-07-2). Clarke His.

Anspacher, Abraham S. Tiglath Pileser Third. LC 70-158263. (Columbia University. Contributions to Oriental History & Philology: No. 5). Repr. of 1912 ed. 12.50 (ISBN 0-404-50535-X). AMS Pr.

Anspacher, Louis K. Shakespeare As Poet & Lover. LC 73-9528. (Studies in Shakespeare, No. 24). 1973. Repr. of 1944 ed. lib. bdg. 29.95x (ISBN 0-8383-1701-4). Haskell.

Anspaugh, David & Ezell, Gene. Teaching Today's Health. 512p. 1983. text ed. 21.95 (ISBN 0-675-20025-3). Additional supplements may be obtained from publisher. Merrill.

Anspaugh, David, jt. auth. see Hamrick, Michael.

Ansted, A. A Dictionary of Sea Terms. 3rd ed. (Illus.). 360p. 1985. 24.50x (ISBN 0-85174-481-8, Pub. by Brown Son & Ferguson). Sheridan.

Anstein Holtet, Jan & Egeland, Alv, eds. The Polar Cusp. (NATO ASI C: Mathematical & Physical Sciences Ser.). 1985. lib. bdg. 55.00 (ISBN 90-277-1923-3, Pub. by Reidel Holland). Kluwer Academic.

Ansteinsson. English-Norse, Norse-English Technical Dictionary. 45.00 (ISBN 0-317-19060-1, N433). Vanous.

--Norse-English, English Norse Technical Dictionary. 38.00 (ISBN 0-317-19059-8, N432). Vanous.

Ansteinsson, ed. English-Norsk Technical Dictionary. Vol. 1. rev. ed. 542p. (Eng. & Norwegian.). 1983. 45.00 (ISBN 0-317-18981-6, N433). Vanous.

--Norsk-English Technical Dictionary, Vol. II. 328p. (Norwegian & Eng.). 1980. 38.00 (ISBN 0-317-18984-0, N432). Vanous.

Ansteinsson, J. Norwegian Technical Dictionary: English-Norwegian Oil Supplement, Vol. 1. 3rd. ed. (Norwegian & Eng.). 1983. 45.00x (ISBN 8-2702-8007-0, N433). Vanous.

Ansteinsson, J. & Andreassen, A. T. Norwegian-English, English-Norwegian Technical Dictionary, 2 Vols. (Norwegian & Eng.). Set. 65.00 (ISBN 8-2702-8007-0). Heinman.

Ansteinsson, J., ed. Norwegian Technical Dictionary: Norwegian-English, Vol. 2. rev. 4th ed. (Norwegian & Eng.). 1980. 38.00x (ISBN 82-702-8006-2, N432). Vanous.

Anstel, Edgar. Shots in the Dark: Films of 1949-1951. 1976. lib. bdg. 59.95 (ISBN 0-8490-2601-6). Gordon Pr.

Anstensen, Ansten. Proverb in Ibsen: Proverbial Sayings & Citations As Elements in His Style. LC 74-158264. (Columbia University. Germanic Studies, New Ser.: No. 1). Repr. of 1936 ed. 27.00 (ISBN 0-404-50451-5). AMS Pr.

Anstey, Edgar. Shots in the Dark. Kupelnick, Bruce S., ed. LC 76-52088. (Classics of Film Literature Ser.). 1978. lib. bdg. 22.00 (ISBN 0-8240-2864-3). Garland Pub.

Anstey, F., pseud. The Pariah, 3 vols. in 2. LC 79-8228. Repr. of 1889 ed. Set. 84.50 (ISBN 0-404-61757-3). AMS Pr.

Anstey, Henry, ed. Munimenta Academica, or Documents Illustrative of Academical Life & Studies at Oxford, 2 vols. (Rolls Ser.: No. 50). Repr. of 1868 ed. Set. 88.00 (ISBN 0-317-16697-2). Kraus Repr.

Anstey, Lavinia M., jt. ed. see Temple, Richard.

Anstey, N. A. Seismic Prospecting Instruments: Vol. 1: Signal Characteristics & Instrument Specifications. new, 2nd ed. (Geoexploation Monographs: Ser., No. 3). (Illus.). 154p. lib. bdg. 23.80x (ISBN 3-443-13303-7). Lubrecht & Cramer.

Anstey, Nigel A. Seismic Exploration for Sandstone Reservoirs. LC 80-82135. (Illus.). 138p. 1980. text ed. 36.00 (ISBN 0-934634-04-1). Intl Human Res.

--Seismic Interpretation: The Physical Aspects. LC 77-86312. (Illus.). 625p. 1977. text ed. 62.00 (ISBN 0-934634-01-7); pap. text ed. 36.00 (ISBN 0-934634-18-1). Intl Human Res.

Anstey, Robert L. Environments Through Time: A Laboratory Manual in Historical Geology. 2nd ed. 1979. pap. 14.95x (ISBN 0-8087-0050-2). Burgess.

Anstey, Roger. Britain & the Congo in the Nineteenth Century. LC 81-20224. (Illus.). viii, 260p. 1982. Repr. of 1962 ed. lib. bdg. 28.50x (ISBN 0-313-23366-7, ANBC). Greenwood.

Anstey, Sandra, ed. Critical Writings on R. S. Thomas: Select Bibliography of Critical Material on R. S. Thomas's Writings. 162p. 1982. 19.00 (ISBN 0-907476-11-2). Dufour.

Anstey, Sandra, ed. see Thomas, R. S.

Anstey, Vera. The Economic Development of India. Wilkins, Mira, ed. LC 76-29760. (European Business Ser.). (Illus.). 1977. Repr. of 1952 ed. lib. bdg. 52.00x (ISBN 0-405-09775-1). Ayer Co Pubs.

Anstice, R. H. Satan of Milton. LC 72-191957. 1910. lib. bdg. 10.00 (ISBN 0-8414-0289-2). Folcroft.

Anstie, Francis E. Stimulants & Narcotics: Their Mutual Relations. Grob, Gerald N., ed. LC 80-1212. (Addiction in America Ser.). 1981. Repr. of 1865 ed. lib. bdg. 35.00x (ISBN 0-405-13568-8). Ayer Co Pubs.

Anstis, Stuart. Write Your Own Apple Games. (Illus.). 174p. 1983. 12.95 (ISBN 0-916688-49-6, 2W). Creative Comp.

Anstruther, Gilbert. Look, Dad, They're Hanging Grandpa. (Illus.). 11.50 (ISBN 0-392-06966-0, AUS67-2366, ABC). Sportshelf.

Anstruther, Godfrey. The Seminary Priests: A Dictionary of the Secular Clery of England & Wales, 1558-1800. LC 76-441910. 1977. Vol. 4, 1716-1800. text ed. 27.50x (ISBN 0-8401-0074-4). A R Allenson.

--The Seminary Priests: A Dictionary of the Secular Clery of England & Wales, 1558 to 1800. Incl. Vol. 1. Elizabethan 1558-1603. 1969. text ed. 21.50x (ISBN 0-8401-0071-X); Vol. 2. Early Stuarts 1603-1659. 1975. text ed. 21.50x (ISBN 0-8401-0072-8); Vol. 3. 1660-1715. 1976. text ed. 27.50x (ISBN 0-8401-0073-6). LC 76-441910. A R Allenson.

--The Seminary Priests: A Dictionary of the Secular Clergy of England & Wales, 1558-1850, 4 vols. Incl. Vol. 1. Elizabethan, 1558-1603. 1968 (ISBN 0-87921-059-1); Vol. 2. Early Stuarts, 1603-1659. 1975 (ISBN 0-85597-082-0); Vol. 3 Paperback. 660-1715. 1976 (ISBN 0-85597-116-9); Vol. 4 Paperback. 1716-1800. 1977 (ISBN 0-85597-118-5). text ed. 18.50x ea. Attic Pr.

Anstruther, Ian. Oscar Browning: A Biography. 219p. 1984. 18.00 (ISBN 0-7195-4078-X, Pub. by Salem Hse Ltd). Merrimack Pub Cir.

Anstruther, Robert, ed. see Niger, Ralph.

Anstruther, Roberto, ed. see Herbert de Losinga.

Anstruther, Sir William. Essays, Moral & Divine. LC 74-170474. (The English Stage Ser.: Vol. 40). lib. bdg. 61.00 (ISBN 0-8240-0623-2). Garland Pub.

Anstruther-Thomson, Clementina. Art & Man. facsimile ed. LC 74-93314. (Essay Index Reprint Ser.). 1924. 25.50 (ISBN 0-8369-1270-5). Ayer Co Pubs.

--Art & Man: Essays & Fragments. LC 74-93314. (Essay Index Reprint Ser.). 371p. Repr. of 1924 ed. lib. bdg. 21.00 (ISBN 0-8290-0470-X). Irvington.

Anszky, K., jt. auth. see Csaki, F.

Antaki, Charles, ed. The Psychology of Ordinary Explanations of Social Behavior. (European Monographs in Social Psychology: No. 23). 352p. 1981. 49.50 (ISBN 0-12-058960-5). Acad Pr.

Antaki, Charles & Brewin, Chris, eds. Attributions & Psychological Change: Application of Attributional Theories to Clinical & Educational Practice. LC 81-71575. (Illus.). 1982. 33.00 (ISBN 0-12-058780-7). Acad Pr.

Antal, David, tr. see Glaeser, Bernhard.

Antal, Frederick. Florentine Painting & Its Social Background. LC 48-10125. 1956. Repr. 89.00x (ISBN 0-403-07218-2). Somerset Pub.

Antal, Laslo. Competitive Pistol Shooting. 196p. 1982. 30.00x (ISBN 0-7158-0787-0, Pub. by EP Pub England). State Mutual Bk.

--Competitive Pistol Shooting. (Illus.). 196p. 1983. 12.95 (ISBN 0-7158-0787-0, Pub by EP Publishing England). Sterling.

Antal, Paul, tr. see Lagarce, Jean-Luc.

Antaloczy, Z. Electrocardiology, 1981: Proceedings of the 8th International Congress, Budapest, Hungary, Sept. 1-4, 1981. Preda, I., ed. (International Congress Ser.: No. 586). 620p. 1982. 98.00 (ISBN 0-444-90295-3, I-328-82). Elsevier.

Antcak, Edward, jt. auth. see Shea, Peter.

Antcliff, A. J. Major Wine Grape Varieties of Australia. 1980. 25.00x (ISBN 0-643-02517-0, Pub. by CSIRO Australia). State Mutual Bk.

--Major Wine Grape Varieties of Australia. 62p. 1979. pap. 6.50 (ISBN 0-643-02517-0, C012, CSIRO). Unipub.

--Some Wine Grape Varieties for Australia. 50p. 1976. pap. 6.00 (ISBN 0-643-00180-8, C009, CSIRO). Unipub.

Antczak, D. F., jt. auth. see Kristensen, F.

Antczak, Edward & Shea, Peter. Vermont Lakes In Depth. LC 82-80500. 85p. (Orig.). 1982. pap. 4.95 (ISBN 0-9606738-1-4). NCI.

Antczak, Frederick J. Thought & Character: The Rhetoric of Democratic Education. 250p. 1985. text ed. 24.95 (ISBN 0-8138-1781-1). Iowa St U Pr.

Antczak, Janice. Science Fiction: The Myths of a New Romance. Hannigan, Jane Anne, ed. (Diversity & Direction in Children's Literature Ser.). 233p. 1985. 24.95 (ISBN 0-918212-43-X). Neal-Schuman.

Ante-Nicene Fathers. Writings of the Ante-Nicene Fathers, 10 vols. Roberts, A. & Donaldson, J., eds. 1951. Set. 169.50 (ISBN 0-8028-8097-5); 16.95 ea. Eerdmans.

Antek, Samuel & Hupka, Robert. This Was Toscanini. LC 63-15196. (Illus.). 196p. 1963. 25.00 (ISBN 0-8149-0018-6). Vanguard.

Antelava, H. G. Abbreviated Turkish-Russian Dictionary of New Words. 95p. (Turkish & Rus.). 1978. pap. 7.95 (ISBN 0-686-97387-9, M-9054). French & Eur.

Antell, Gerson. Economics: Institutions & Analysis. (gr. 10-12). 1970. 7.58 (ISBN 0-87720-609-0). AMSCO Sch.

Antell, Gerson & Harris, Walter. Current Issues in American Democracy. (Orig.). (gr. 10-12). 1975. pap. text ed. 8.58 (ISBN 0-87720-605-8). AMSCO Sch.

--Economics for Everybody. (Orig.). (gr. 11-12). 1973. text ed. 12.50 (ISBN 0-87720-621-X); pap. text ed. 7.67 (ISBN 0-87720-610-4). AMSCO Sch.

--Western Civilization. (Orig.). (gr. 10-12). 1982. text ed. 20.00 (ISBN 0-87720-632-5); pap. text ed. 15.42 (ISBN 0-87720-631-7). AMSCO Sch.

Antell, Steven. Backpacker's Recipe Book. LC 80-7569. (Illus.). 1980. pap. 6.50 (ISBN 0-87108-549-6). Pruett.

Antell, Will. William Warren. LC 72-91157. (Story of an American Indian Ser.). (Illus.). (gr. 5 up). 1973. PLB 7.95 (ISBN 0-87518-056-6). Dillon.

Antelman, Marvin S. & Harris, Franklin J., Jr. The Encyclopedia of Chemical Electrode Potentials. 286p. 1982. text ed. 42.50x (ISBN 0-306-40903-8, Plenum Pr). Plenum Pub.

Antelminelli, F. Castracane Degli see Castracane Degli Antelminelli, F.

Antes, H. W. see Hausner, H. H., et al.

Antes, Richard L., jt. auth. see Hopkins, Charles D.

Antes, Richard S., et al. Federal Income Taxation of Life Insurance Companies, 3 vols. 1984. Updates avail. looseleaf 225.00 (ISBN 0-317-09761-X, 693). Bender.

Antesberger, H. German Shepherds. (Pet Care Ser.). 80p. Date not set. pap. 3.95 (ISBN 0-8120-2982-8). Barron.

Antezana, Jorge Garcia see Garcia-Antezana, Jorge.

Antheil, George. Bad Boy of Music. (Illus.). 378p. 1981. lib. bdg. 39.50 (ISBN 0-306-76084-3). Da Capo.

Anthes, Earl W., et al, eds. The Nonprofit Board Book: Strategies for Organizational Success. rev. ed. (Illus.). 240p. 1985. pap. 24.50 (ISBN 0-916721-04-3). Ind Comm Con.

Anthes, Richard & Miller, Albert. Meteorology. 5th, rev. ed. 192p. Date not set. pap. text ed. 9.95 (ISBN 0-675-20411-9). Merrill.

Anthes, Richard, et al. The Atmosphere. 3rd ed. (Illus.). 384p. 1981. text ed. 27.95 (ISBN 0-675-08043-6). Additional supplements may be obtained from Publisher. Merrill.

Anthes, Richard A. Weather Around Us. (Physical Science Ser.). 1976. pap. text ed. 9.95 (ISBN 0-675-08635-3); Set of 4. cassettes & filmstrips o.p. 135.00 (ISBN 0-675-08634-5). Merrill.

Anthes, Rudolf, et al. Mit Rahineh, 1955. (University Museum Monographs: No. 16). (Illus.). vi, 93p. 1958. soft bound 12.00x (ISBN 0-934718-09-1). Univ Mus of U PA.

--Mit Rahineh, 1956. (University Museum Monographs: No. 27). (Illus.). x, 170p. 1965. soft bound 11.25x (ISBN 0-934718-19-9). Univ Mus of U PA.

Anthimos. The Reply of the Orthodox Church to Roman Catholic Overtures on Reunion. 1977. pap. 1.00 (ISBN 0-913026-15-8). St Nectarios.

Anthimus & Holy Synod of the Ecumenical Patriarchate. The Reply of the Orthodox Church to Roman Catholic Overtures on Reunion. Orthodox Christian Educational Society, ed. (Orig., Hellenic.). 1978. pap. 0.50x (ISBN 0-938366-35-1). Orthodox Chr.

Anthoine, Robert, ed. Tax Incentives for Private Investment in Developing Countries, 1979: Published Under the Auspices of the Tax Committee of the Section of Business Law of the International Bar Association. 286p. 1980. lib. bdg. 44.00 (ISBN 90-200-0587-1, Pub. by Kluwer Law Netherlands). Kluwer Academic.

Anthologia Graeca Selections. Poems from the Greek Anthology, in English Paraphrase. Fitts, Dudley, tr. LC 78-13574. 1978. Repr. of 1956 ed. lib. bdg. 24.75x (ISBN 0-313-21017-9, AGPG). Greenwood.

Anthony. Management Accounting. 3rd ed. (Plaid Ser.). 1980. 9.95 (ISBN 0-256-01277-6). Dow Jones-Irwin.

Anthony & Lehman. The Quiltmaker's Big Book of Ten Inch Patterns. 14.95 (ISBN 0-942786-23-8). Leone Pubns.

Anthony, Albert S., jt. ed. see Brinton, Daniel G.

Anthony, Alberta P., jt. auth. see Kahananui, Dorothy M.

Anthony And Company. Illustrated Catalogue of Photographic Equipment & Material for Amateurs. Orig. Title: Illustrated Photographic Catalogue. 1970. pap. 7.95 (ISBN 0-87100-016-4). Morgan.

Anthony, Arthur B. Economic & Social Problems of the Machine Age. LC 30-24166. 40p. 1984. Repr. of 1930 ed. lib. bdg. 19.95x (ISBN 0-89370-860-7). Borgo Pr.

Anthony, Barry T., jt. auth. see Bontrager, Kenneth L.

Anthony, C. The Biochemistry of Methylotrophs. 1982. 57.50 (ISBN 0-12-058820-X). Acad Pr.

Anthony, C. & Anthony, R. There Is a Safe Place to Hide. 1950. pap. 2.95 (ISBN 0-910140-01-4). C & R Anthony.

Anthony, Carol K. Guide to the I Ching. 2nd ed. 184p. 1982. pap. 5.95 (ISBN 0-9603832-3-9). Anthony Pub Co.

--The Philosophy of the I Ching. LC 81-69537. 160p. 1981. pap. 6.50 (ISBN 0-9603832-1-2). Anthony Pub Co.

Anthony, Catherine P. & Thibodeau, Gary A. Anatomy & Physiology Laboratory Manual. 10th ed. LC 78-11927. (Illus.). 1979. pap. text ed. 11.95 (ISBN 0-8016-0270-X). Mosby.

--Basic Concepts in Anatomy & Physiology: A Programmed Presentation. 4th ed. LC 79-19392. (Illus.). 1979. pap. text ed. 13.95 (ISBN 0-8016-0260-2). Mosby.

--Structure & Function of the Body. 7th ed. (Illus.). 374p. 1984. pap. text ed. 14.95 (ISBN 0-8016-0296-3). Mosby.

--Textbook of Anatomy & Physiology. 11th ed. LC 82-12555. (Illus.). 887p. 1983. text ed. 28.95 (ISBN 0-8016-0289-0). Mosby.

Anthony, D. M. Metrology. 1986. write for info. (ISBN 0-08-028682-8); pap. write for info. (ISBN 0-08-028683-6). Pergamon.

Anthony, D. W., tr. see Morishima, M.

Anthony, David. The Mayor, the Commissioner & the Metropolitan Administration (Bombay) 274p. 1984. text ed. 32.50x (ISBN 0-7069-2531-9, Pub. by Vikas India). Advent NY.

Anthony, Diana. Out of a Dream. (Orig.). 1983. pap. 2.95 (ISBN 0-671-46728-X). PB.

Anthony, Dick, jt. ed. see Robbins, Thomas.

Anthony, Don. Field Athletics. (Competitive Sports Ser.). (Illus.). 64p. (YA) (gr. 7-12). 1982. 10.95 (ISBN 0-7134-4281-6, Pub. by Batsford England). David & Charles.

--A Strategy for British Sport. 1980. 21.50x (ISBN 0-7735-0531-8). McGill-Queens U Pr.

Anthony, Dorothy M. World of Bells, No.1. (Illus.). 50p. 1980. Repr. of 1971 ed. mechanical bdg. 8.95 (ISBN 0-9607944-1-7). Anthony D M.

--World of Bells, No. 2. (Illus.). 50p. 1980. Repr. of 1974 ed. mechanical bdg. 8.95 (ISBN 0-9607944-2-5). Anthony D M.

--World of Bells, No.4. (Illus.). 50p. 1980. mechanical bdg. 7.95 (ISBN 0-9607944-0-9). Anthony D M.

--World of Bells, Vol. 5. (Illus.). 24p. 1984. mechanical bdg. 8.95 (ISBN 0-9607944-3-3). Anthony D M.

--The World of Bells, No. 3. 1978. pap. 6.95 (ISBN 0-87069-183-X). Wallace-Homestead.

Anthony, Douglas. Do It In Bed: An Exercise Program. LC 82-90978. (Illus.). 96p. 1983. pap. 5.95 (ISBN 0-911433-00-7). HealthRight.

--Never Say Old. (Illus.). 96p. (Orig.). 1984. pap. 6.95 (ISBN 0-911433-03-1). HealthRight.

Anthony, E., jt. auth. see Snelling, Henry H.

Anthony, E. James & Chiland, Colette. The Child in His Family: Children in Turmoil, Tomorrow's Parents, Vol. 7. LC 82-8421. (Yearbook of the International Association of Child & Adolescent Psychiatry & Allied Professions Ser.). 328p. 1982. 44.95x (ISBN 0-471-86873-6, Pub. by Wiley-Interscience). Wiley.

Anthony, E. James, ed. Explorations in Child Psychiatry. LC 75-2308. 519p. 1975. 32.50x (ISBN 0-306-30819-3, Plenum Pr). Plenum Pub.

Anthony, E. James & Benedek, Therese, eds. Depression & Human Existence. 568p. 1975. 26.95 (ISBN 0-316-04371-0). Little.

--Parenthood: Its Psychology & Psychopathology. LC 75-112005. 650p. 1970. 28.50 (ISBN 0-316-04370-2). Little.

Anthony, E. James & Koupernik, Cyrille, eds. The Child in His Family: The International Yearbook for Child Psychiatry & Allied Disciplines, Vol. 1. LC 78-31654. 525p. 1979. Repr. of 1970 ed. lib. bdg. 28.50 (ISBN 0-88275-863-2). Krieger.

Anthony, E. James, et al. The Child in His Family. Incl. Vol. 2. The Impact of Disease & Death. 1973; Vol. 3. Children at Psychiatric Risk. LC 74-6169. 1974; Vol. 4. Vulnerable Children. LC 78-120701. 1978; Vol. 5. Children & Their Parents in a Changing World. LC 78-120701. 1978. 45.95x (ISBN 0-471-04432-6); Vol. 6. Preventative Child Psychiatry in an Age of Transition. 645p. 1980. 48.95x (ISBN 0-471-08403-4, 80-21022). LC 72-11702. (International Association for Child Psychiatry & Allied Professions Yearbook, Pub. by Wiley-Interscience). Wiley.

Anthony, Earl & Taylor, Dawson. Earl Anthony's Championship Bowling. (Illus.). 224p. (Orig.). 1983. pap. 7.95 (ISBN 0-8092-5490-5). Contemp Bks.

--Winning Bowling. LC 77-75718. (Winning Ser.). (Illus.). 194p. 1977. pap. 8.95 (ISBN 0-8092-7791-3). Contemp Bks.

Anthony, Ed. Information Sources in Engineering. 2nd ed. (Illus.). 560p. 1985. text ed. 75.95 (ISBN 0-408-11475-4). Butterworth.

Anthony, Edgar W. Early Florentine Architecture & Decoration. LC 78-143335. (Illus.). 1975. Repr. of 1927 ed. 35.00 (ISBN 0-87817-055-3). Hacker.

--History of Mosaics. LC 68-9000. (Illus.). 1968. Repr. of 1935 ed. 40.00 (ISBN 0-87817-001-4). Hacker.

--Romanesque Frescoes. LC 76-112320. (Illus.). 208p. Repr. of 1951 ed. lib. bdg. 26.25x (ISBN 0-8371-4707-7, ANRF). Greenwood.

Anthony, Elwyn J., et al, eds. The Child in His Family, Vol. 4. pap. 160.00 (ISBN 0-317-28589-0, 2055181). Bks Demand UMI.

Anthony, Evans E. Handbook of Tritium NMR Spectroscopy & Applications. LC 84-15273. 1985. 39.95 (ISBN 0-471-90583-6). Wiley.

Anthony, Evelyn. Albatross. LC 82-20456. 240p. 1983. 14.95 (ISBN 0-399-12773-9, Putnam). Putnam Pub Group.

--Albatross. Large Print ed. LC 83-17905. 452p. 1983. Repr. of 1983 ed. 16.95 (ISBN 0-89621-484-2). Thorndike Pr.

--Albatross. 1984. pap. 3.95 (ISBN 0-515-07644-9). Jove Pubns.

--The Company of Saints. LC 83-23019. 240p. 1984. 15.95 (ISBN 0-399-12895-6, Putnam). Putnam Pub Group.

--The Company of Saints. large print ed. LC 84-8605. 437p. 1984. Repr. of 1983 ed. 14.95 (ISBN 0-89621-555-5). Thorndike Pr.

--The Defector. 1982. pap. 3.95 (ISBN 0-451-13588-1, AE1765, Sig). NAL.

--The Janus Imperative. 1981. pap. 2.95 (ISBN 0-451-09890-0, E9890, Sig). NAL.

--Voices on the Wind. 288p. 1985. 16.95 (ISBN 0-399-13067-5). Putnam Pub Group.

Anthony, George. The Road to Deadman Cove Selected Poems. LC 77-91127. (Open Places Poets Ser.: No. 4). 1978. 7.00x (ISBN 0-913398-03-9). Open Places.

Anthony, Geraldine. Gwen Pharis Ringwood. (World Authors Ser.). 1981. lib. bdg. 16.95 (ISBN 0-8057-6444-5, Twayne). G K Hall.

Anthony, Gloria M. Echoes in a Shell. LC 74-77317. 1974. pap. 2.95 (ISBN 0-913748-04-8). Orovan Bks.

Anthony, Irvin. Paddle Wheels & Pistols. 329p. 1980. Repr. of 1929 ed. lib. bdg. 30.00 (ISBN 0-8495-0075-3). Arden Lib.

--Raleigh & His World. 1934. Repr. 20.00 (ISBN 0-8274-3237-2). R West.

--Revolt at Sea: A Narration of Many Mutinies. Repr. of 1937 ed. 25.00 (ISBN 0-686-19878-6). Ridgeway Bks.

Anthony, Ivan. Past Reflections. 1982. 7.95 (ISBN 0-533-05274-2). Vantage.

Anthony, J. Joseph Paxton. (Clarendon Biography Ser.). (Illus.). 1973. pap. 3.50 (ISBN 0-912728-70-1). Newbury Bks.

Anthony, J. Garner. Hawaii under Army Rule. 213p. 1975. pap. 3.95 (ISBN 0-8248-0377-9). UH Pr.

Anthony, James E. & Gilpin, Doris C., eds. Three Further Clinical Faces of Childhood. (Illus.). 340p. 1981. text ed. 35.00 (ISBN 0-89335-110-5). SP Med & Sci Bks.

Anthony, James R. French Baroque Music. (Illus.). 468p. 1981. pap. 8.95 (ISBN 0-393-00967-X). Norton.

--Michel-Richard Delalande's "De Profundis": Grand Motet for Soloists, Chorus, Woodwinds, Strings, & Continuo. LC 79-29740. (Early Musical Masterworks Ser.). viii, 173p. 1981. 23.00x (ISBN 0-8078-1439-3). U of NC Pr.

Anthony, James T., et al. Basic Geography: A Manual of Exercises. 1975. pap. 3.50 (ISBN 0-910042-16-0). Allegheny.

Anthony, John. Collecting Greek Coins. LC 82-9947. (Illus.). 256p. (Orig.). 1983. 14.95 (ISBN 0-582-50310-8). Longman.

--Collecting Greek Coins. 1984. pap. 12.95. Caroline Hse.

--Derbyshire & the Peak District. (Shire County Guide Ser.: No. 6). (Orig.). 1985. pap. 4.95 (ISBN 0-85263-739-X, Pub. by Shire Pubns England). Seven Hills Bks.

--Discovering Period Gardens. (Discovering Ser.: No. 129). 1985. pap. 4.95 (ISBN 0-85263-724-1, Pub. by Shire Pubns England). Seven Hills Bks.

--Joseph Paxton. (Shire Lifelines Ser.: No. 21). 1985. pap. 4.95 (ISBN 0-85263-208-8, Pub. by Shire Pubns England). Seven Hills Bks.

--Vanbrugh. (Lifelines Ser.: No. 42). (Illus., Orig.). 1983. pap. 3.50 (ISBN 0-85263-339-4, Pub. by Shire Pubns England). Seven Hills Bks.

Anthony, John D. Historical & Cultural Dictionary of the Sultanate of Oman & the Emirates of Eastern Arabia. LC 76-42216. (Historical & Cultural Dictionaries of Asia Ser.: No. 9). 144p. 1976. 17.50 (ISBN 0-8108-0975-3). Scarecrow.

--U. S. - Arab Relations: The Iran-Iraq War & the Gulf Cooperation Council, No. 12. (Orig.). 1984. pap. 2.00 (ISBN 0-916729-10-9). Natl Coun Arab.

Anthony, John D., ed. The Middle East: Oil, Politics & Development. LC 75-29689. (Conference Proceedings Ser). 1975. 12.25 (ISBN 0-8447-2067-4); pap. 5.25 (ISBN 0-8447-2066-6). Am Enterprise.

Anthony, John W., et al. Mineralogy of Arizona. rev. ed. LC 75-44670. 255p. 1982. 27.50x (ISBN 0-8165-0765-1); pap. 14.95 (ISBN 0-8165-0764-3). U of Ariz Pr.

Anthony, Julie & Bollettieri, Nick. A Winning Combination. (Illus.). 272p. 1982. pap. 6.95 (ISBN 0-684-17637-8, ScribT); encore ed o.p. 4.95 (ISBN 0-684-17583-5). Scribner.

Anthony, Katharine. Margaret Fuller: Phychological Biography. LC 72-195019. 1920. lib. bdg. 17.50 (ISBN 0-8414-0288-4). Folcroft.

--Queen Elizabeth. 1979. Repr. of 1929 ed. lib. bdg. 22.50 (ISBN 0-8482-0024-1). Norwood Edns.

Anthony, Katharine S. Louisa May Alcott. LC 77-2388. 1977. Repr. of 1938 ed. lib. bdg. 27.50 (ISBN 0-8371-9552-7, ANLMA). Greenwood.

Anthony, Katherine. The Lambs: A Study of Pre-Victorian England. 1978. Repr. of 1948 ed. lib. bdg. 20.00 (ISBN 0-8495-0299-3). Arden Lib.

--Queen Elizabeth. 1978. Repr. of 1929 ed. lib. bdg. 22.50 (ISBN 0-8495-0148-2). Arden Lib.

Anthony, Katherine S. Margaret Fuller: A Psychological Biography. 1978. Repr. of 1920 ed. lib. bdg. 25.00 (ISBN 0-8495-0020-6). Arden Lib.

Anthony, Kenneth R., et al. Agricultural Change in Tropical Africa. LC 78-58039. (Illus.). 304p. 1978. 32.50x (ISBN 0-8014-1159-9). Cornell U Pr.

Anthony, Lillian S., jt. auth. see Sieben, J. Kenneth.

Anthony, Luean E., jt. auth. see Taylor, Keith B.

Anthony, M. L., ed. Space Flight Mechanics Symposium. (Science & Technology Ser.: Vol. 11). 1966. 45.00 (ISBN 0-87703-039-1, Pub. by Am Astronaut). Univelt Inc.

Anthony, Michael. All That Glitters. (Caribbean Writers Ser.: No. 25). 202p. (Orig.). 1983. pap. text ed. 5.00x (ISBN 0-435-98034-3). Heinemann Ed.

--All That Glitters: The Caribbean. 224p. 1981. 14.95 (ISBN 0-233-97369-9). Andre Deutsch.

--All That Glitters: The Caribbean. 224p. 1981. 14.95 (ISBN 0-233-97369-9, Pub. by A Deutsch England). David & Charles.

--Cricket in the Road. (Caribbean Writers Ser.). 1973. pap. text ed. 4.00x (ISBN 0-435-98032-7). Heinemann Ed.

--The Games Were Coming. (Caribbean Writers Ser.). 1977. pap. text ed. 4.00x (ISBN 0-435-98033-5). Heinemann Ed.

--The Games Were Coming: The Caribbean. 224p. 1963. 9.95 (ISBN 0-233-95646-8). Andre Deutsch.

--Green Days by the River. (Caribbean Writers Ser.). 192p. (Orig.). 1973. pap. text ed. 4.50x (ISBN 0-435-98030-0). Heinemann Ed.

--Handbook of Small Business Advertising. 192p. 1981. text ed. 24.95 (ISBN 0-201-00086-5). Addison-Wesley.

--Sandra Street & Other Stories. (Heinemann Secondary Readers Ser.). 1973. pap. text ed. 3.00x (ISBN 0-435-92512-1). Heinemann Ed.

--The Year in San Fernando. (Caribbean Writers Ser.). 1970. pap. text ed. 4.00x (ISBN 0-435-98031-9). Heinemann Ed.

Anthony, P. J. America, the Hope of the Ages. LC 59-6919. 297p. (gr. 11-12). 1959. 7.50 (ISBN 0-911876-03-0). Greenvale.

Anthony, P. P. & MacSween, Run, eds. Recent Advances in Histopathology. (No. 11). (Illus.). 1981. pap. text ed. 37.50 (ISBN 0-443-02386-7). Churchill.

Anthony, Peter. John Ruskin's Labour: A Study of Ruskin's Social Theory. LC 83-8803. 224p. 1984. 37.50 (ISBN 0-521-25233-4). Cambridge U Pr.

Anthony, Philip K., jt. auth. see Vinson, Donald E.

Anthony, Piers. Anthonology. 384p. 1985. 14.95 (ISBN 0-312-93027-5). Tor Bks.

--Apprentice Adept, 3 vols. Boxed Set. pap. 8.85 (ISBN 0-317-12490-0, Del Rey). Ballantine.

--Battle Circle. 1978. pap. 3.95 (ISBN 0-380-01800-4, 67009-5). Avon.

--Bio of a Space Tyrant, Vol. 3: Politician. 352p. 1985. pap. 2.95 (ISBN 0-380-89685-0). Avon.

--Blue Adept. 368p. 1981. 10.95 (ISBN 0-345-29384-3, Del Rey). Ballantine.

--Blue Adept. 336p. 1983. pap. 2.95 (ISBN 0-345-31424-7, Del Rey). Ballantine.

--Castle Roogna. 1979. pap. 2.50 (ISBN 0-345-29421-1, Del Rey Bks). Ballantine.

--Centaur Isle. 304p. (Orig.). 1982. pap. 2.75 (ISBN 0-345-29770-9, Del Rey). Ballantine.

--Chaining the Lady. (The Cluster Ser. 2). 1978. pap. 2.95 (ISBN 0-380-01779-2, 61614-9). Avon.

--Chthon. (Orig.). 1984. pap. 2.95 (ISBN 0-425-07982-1). Berkley Pub.

--Cluster. (The Cluster Ser.: No. 1). 256p. 1985. pap. 2.95 (ISBN 0-380-01755-5). Avon.

--Crewel Lye: A Caustic Yarn. LC 84-90936. 320p. (Orig.). 1985. pap. 3.50 (ISBN 0-345-31309-7, Del Rey). Ballantine.

--Dragon on a Pedestal. 320p. (Orig.). 1983. pap. 2.95 (ISBN 0-345-31107-8, Del Rey). Ballantine.

--Faith of Tarot. 256p. (Orig.). 1984. pap. 2.95 (ISBN 0-425-07371-8). Berkley Pub.

--God of Tarot. (Orig.). 1983. pap. 2.95 (ISBN 0-425-07038-7). Berkley Pub.

--Hasan. LC 77-24589. (Illus.). 1977. lib. bdg. 12.95x (ISBN 0-89370-115-7); pap. 4.95x (ISBN 0-89370-215-3). Borgo Pr.
--Hasan. 192p. 1977. pap. 4.95 (ISBN 0-87877-215-4). Newcastle Pub.
--Hasan. 256p. 1986. pap. 2.95 (ISBN 0-8125-3112-4, Dist. by Warner Pub Services & St. Martin). Tor Bks.
--Juxtaposition. 1982. 13.50 (ISBN 0-345-30196-X, Del Rey). Ballantine.
--Juxtaposition. 352p. 1983. pap. 2.95 (ISBN 0-345-28215-9, Del Rey). Ballantine.
--Kirlian Quest. (The Cluster Ser. 3). 1978. pap. 2.95 (ISBN 0-380-01778-4, 60191-5). Avon.
--Macroscope. 1969. pap. 3.95 (ISBN 0-380-00209-4, 81992-9). Avon.
--The Magic of Xanth, 3 vols. 1982. pap. 8.65 (ISBN 0-345-30073-4, Del Rey). Ballantine.
--Mercenary. (Bio of a Space Tyrant Ser.: Vol. II). 400p. 1984. pap. 2.95 (ISBN 0-380-87221-8, 87221-8). Avon.
--More Magic of Xanth, 3 vols. Boxed Set. pap. 8.85 (ISBN 0-345-32057-3, Del Rey). Ballantine.
--Mute. 448p. 1981. pap. 3.95 (ISBN 0-380-77578-6, 84772-8). Avon.
--Night Mare. LC 82-90817. (Magic of Zanith Ser.). 320p. 1983. pap. 2.95 (ISBN 0-345-30456-X, Del Rey). Ballantine.
--Ogre, Ogre. LC 82-6659. (Magic of Zanith Ser.). 320p. (Orig.). 1982. pap. 2.95 (ISBN 0-345-30187-0, Del Rey). Ballantine.
--Omnivore. 1978. pap. 2.95 (ISBN 0-380-40527-X, 82362-4). Avon.
--On a Pale Horse. (Incarnations of Immortality Ser.: Bk. 1). 288p. 12.95 (ISBN 0-345-30924-3, Del Rey). Ballantine.
--On a Pale Horse. (Incarnations of Immortality Ser.: Bk. 1). 336p. 1984. pap. 2.95 (ISBN 0-345-30518-3, Del Rey). Ballantine.
--Orn. 1975. pap. 2.95 (ISBN 0-380-00266-3, 85324-8). Avon.
--Ox. 1976. pap. 2.95 (ISBN 0-380-00461-5, 60097-8). Avon.
--Phthor. 208p. 1984. pap. 2.95 (ISBN 0-425-07485-4). Berkley Pub.
--Race Against Time. 256p. 1985. pap. 2.95 (ISBN 0-8125-3110-8, Dist. by Pinnacle Bks, Warner Pub Services & St. Martin). Tor Bks.
--Refugee. (Bio of a Space Tyrant Ser.: Vol. I). 320p. 1983. pap. 2.95 (ISBN 0-380-84194-0, 84194). Avon.
--Rings of Ice. 1974. pap. 1.50 (ISBN 0-380-00039-3, 38166). Avon.
--The Source of Magic. 1979. pap. 2.25 (ISBN 0-345-28765-7, Del Rey Bks). Ballantine.
--A Spell for Chameleon. LC 77-1666. 1977. pap. 2.25 (ISBN 0-345-28766-5). Ballantine.
--Split Infinity. 368p. 1981. pap. 2.50 (ISBN 0-345-28213-2, Del Rey). Ballantine.
--Split Infinity. 1981. 9.95 (ISBN 0-345-28645-6, Del Rey). Ballantine.
--Steppe. 256p. 1985. 13.95 (ISBN 0-312-93748-2, Dist. by St. Martin). Tor Bks.
--Thousandstar. (Cluster Ser.: No. 4). 304p. 1980. pap. 2.95 (ISBN 0-380-75556-4, 60248-2). Avon.
--Viscous Circle. (Cluster Ser. No. 5). 272p. 1982. pap. 2.95 (ISBN 0-380-79897-2, 60247-4). Avon.
--Vision of Tarot. 272p. 1984. pap. 2.95 (ISBN 0-425-07490-0). Berkley Pub.
--With a Tangled Skein. (Incarnations of Immortality Ser.: Bk. 3). 1985. 14.95 (ISBN 0-345-31884-6, Del Ray). Ballantine.
Anthony, Piers & Hall, Frances. Pretender. LC 79-317. (Illus.). 1979. lib. bdg. 12.95x (ISBN 0-89370-130-0); pap. 4.95x (ISBN 0-89370-230-7). Borgo Pr.
--Pretender. 288p. 1985. pap. 3.50 (ISBN 0-8125-3108-6). Tor Bks.
--Pretender. 160p. 1979. pap. 4.95 (ISBN 0-87877-230-8). Newcastle Pub.
Anthony, R., jt. auth. see Anthony, C.
Anthony, Raymond G., jt. auth. see Holland, Charles D.
Anthony, Rebecca & Roe, Gerald. Educators' Passport to International Jobs: How to Find & Enjoy Employment Abroad. 196p. 1984. pap. 9.95 (ISBN 0-87866-271-5). Petersons Guides.
--Finding a Job in Your Field: A Handbook for Ph.D.'s & M.A.'s. 144p. (Orig.). 1985. pap. 8.95 (ISBN 0-87866-278-2). Petersons Guides.
--From Contact to Contract. LC 82-17837. 96p. 1983. 6.95 (ISBN 0-910328-37-4). Carroll Pr.
Anthony, Richard. How to Perform Your Own Urinalysis Without a Doctor for Under Fifty Cents. (Illus.). pap. 10.00 (ISBN 0-916976-00-9). P I Industries.
Anthony, Richard, et al. The New Religious Movements: Conversion, Coercion & Commitment. 352p. 19.50 (ISBN 0-8245-0484-4); pap. 9.95 (ISBN 0-686-83096-2). Crossroad NY.
Anthony, Robert. Essentials of Accounting. 3rd ed. LC 81-17557. (Accounting Ser.). (Illus.). 192p. 1982. pap. text ed. 16.95 (ISBN 0-201-00006-7). Addison-Wesley.
--Put Your Money Where Your Mouth Is: How to Make a Fortune from Public Speaking. 176p. 1985. pap. 3.50 (ISBN 0-425-08030-7). Berkley Pub.
--The Ultimate Secrets of Total Self-Confidence. 240p. 1984. pap. 3.50 (ISBN 0-425-07010-7). Berkley Pub.
Anthony, Robert & Young, David. Management Control in Nonprofit Organizations. 3rd ed. 1984. 34.95x (ISBN 0-256-02960-1). Irwin.
Anthony, Robert, et al. Management Control Systems. 5th ed. 1984. 34.95x (ISBN 0-256-02961-X). Irwin.
Anthony, Robert N. Financial Accounting in Nonbusiness Organizations: An Exploratory Study of Conceptual Issues. LC 78-58734. (The Financial Accounting Standards Board Research Report). (Illus.). 205p. (Orig.). 1978. pap. 5.00 (ISBN 0-910065-02-0). Finan Acct.
--Future Directions for Financial Accounting. LC 84-70261. 250p. 1984. 22.50 (ISBN 0-87094-551-3). Dow Jones-Irwin.
--Teach Yourself Essentials of Accounting on the IBM PC. incl. documentation & four disks for the IBM PC 129.95 (ISBN 0-201-15328-9); incl. documentation & four disks for the Apple II, II Plus & IIe 79.95. Addison-Wesley.
--Teach Yourself Essentials of Accounting on the IBM PC. 80p. 1983. write for info. (ISBN 0-201-15329-7); write for info. incl. disk (ISBN 0-201-15328-9); write for info. incl. disk (ISBN 0-201-15331-9). Addison-Wesley.
--Tell It Like It Was: A Conceptual Framework for Financial Accounting. LC 83-81733. (Anthony-Graham Series in Accounting). 313p. 1983. pap. 14.95x (ISBN 0-256-03090-1). Irwin.
Anthony, Robert N. & Graham-Walker, Ross. Essentials of Accounting: A Reference Guide. LC 84-6469. 1985. pap. text ed. 12.95 (ISBN 0-201-10234-X). Addison-Wesley.
Anthony, Robert N. & Reece, James S. Accounting Principles. 5th ed. 1983. 29.95x (ISBN 0-256-02785-4). Irwin.
--Accounting: Text & Cases. 7th ed. 1983. 33.95x (ISBN 0-256-02787-0). Irwin.
Anthony, Robert N., jt. auth. see Reece, James S.
Anthony, Robert N., et al. Fundamentals of Management Accounting. 4th ed. 1985. 31.95x (ISBN 0-256-02962-8). study guide 12.95x (ISBN 0-256-02963-6). Irwin.
Anthony, Sally, jt. ed. see McCabe, Robert.
Anthony, Susan B. An Account of the Proceedings on the Trial of Susan B. Anthony on the Charge of Illegal Voting at the Presidential Election in Nov. 1872. LC 74-3923. (Women in America Ser). 220p. 1974. Repr. of 1874 ed. 19.00x (ISBN 0-405-06072-6). Ayer Co Pubs.
--Geraldine Ferraro Coloring Book. 1984. pap. 3.95 (ISBN 0-943084-20-2). Turnbull & Willoughby.
--Survival Kit: Triumph over Suffering Break Through to Serenity with These Life-Saving Tools. rev. ed. LC 81-9771. 1981. pap. 7.95 (ISBN 0-89638-050-5). CompCare.
Anthony, T. M. The Way Out. LC 82-72166. (Illus.). 141p. (Orig.). 1982. pap. 5.95 (ISBN 0-89305-042-3). Anna Pub.
Anthony, Travis D. Climbing the Mountain. 122p. 1980. 8.95 (ISBN 0-9604686-0-9). T D Anthony.
Anthony, Travis D., ed. Sunshine & Shadows. LC 81-70847. (Illus.). 223p. 1981. 12.95x (ISBN 0-9604686-1-7). T D Anthony.
Anthony, William. Bible Stories. LC 77-71655. (Illus., Orig.). pap. 5.00 (ISBN 0-912330-25-2, Dist. by Inland Bk). Jargon Soc.
Anthony, William A. The Art of Health Care. LC 75-40867. 104p. 1976. pap. text ed. 10.00x (ISBN 0-914234-25-0). Human Res Dev Pr.
--Principles of Psychiatric Rehabilitation. LC 78-59285. 284p. 1979. pap. 7.00 (ISBN 0-8391-1658-6). Pro Ed.
--Psychiatric Rehabilitation Practice Series: Instructor's Guide. 200p. 1980. pap. 7.00 (ISBN 0-8391-1578-4). Pro Ed.
--The Skills of Career Counseling. LC 79-29688. 112p. 1980. pap. 7.00 (ISBN 0-8391-1579-2). Pro Ed.
--The Skills of Career Placement. LC 79-29689. 112p. 1980. pap. 7.00 (ISBN 0-8391-1577-6). Pro Ed.
--The Skills of Community Service Coordination. LC 79-29693. 128p. 1980. pap. 7.00 (ISBN 0-8391-1575-X). Pro Ed.
--The Skills of Diagnostic Planning. LC 79-29629. 192p. 1980. pap. 7.00 (ISBN 0-8391-1574-1). Pro Ed.
--The Skills of Professional Evaluation. LC 79-29690. 96p. 1980. pap. 7.00 (ISBN 0-8391-1576-8). Pro Ed.
--The Skills of Rehabilitation Programming. LC 79-29687. 128p. 1980. pap. 7.00 (ISBN 0-8391-1573-3). Pro Ed.
Anthony, William A., ed. Rehabilitating the Person with A Psychiatric Disability: The State of the Art. 1980. 4.00 (ISBN 0-686-36379-5, 70524W34). Am Assn Coun Dev.
Anthony, William B. Managing Your Boss. LC 83-45212. 224p. 1983. 17.95 (ISBN 0-8144-5773-8); pap. 10.95 members (ISBN 0-8144-7597-3). AMACOM.
Anthony, William E., jt. auth. see Hill, Richard T.
Anthony, William P. Management: Competencies & Incompetencies. LC 79-25171. 604p. 1981. text ed. 16.95 (ISBN 0-201-00085-7). Addison-Wesley.
--Managing Incompetence. 256p. 1982. 17.95 (ISBN 0-8144-5672-3). AMACOM.
--Participative Management. LC 77-83035. 1978. pap. text ed. 11.95 (ISBN 0-201-00253-1). Addison-Wesley.
Anthony, William P., jt. auth. see Hodge, B. J.
Anthony of Sourozh. God & Man. 2nd ed. 125p. 1983. pap. text ed. 3.95 (ISBN 0-88141-024-1). St Vladimirs.
Anthraquinone Symposium, Buergenstock-Luzern, September, 1978. Natural Anthraquinone Drugs. Fairbairn, J. W., ed. (Pharmacology Journal: Vol. 20, Suppl. 1). (Illus.). 140p. 1980. pap. 17.25 (ISBN 3-8055-0683-X). S Karger.
Anthropos Institute. Studia, Vols. 1-11. 375.00 (ISBN 0-384-01655-3). Johnson Repr.
Anti-Defamation League of B'nai Brith. The Holocaust & Genocide: A Search for Conscience, An Anthology for Students. 217p. 9.95 (ISBN 0-317-03375-1). ADL.
--The Holocaust & Genocide: A Search for Conscience, A Curriculum Guide. 184p. 12.00 (ISBN 0-317-03374-3). ADL.
Anti-Sabbath Convention, Melodeon, Boston. Proceedings. Parkhurst, Henry M., ed. LC 79-122662. 1971. Repr. of 1848 ed. 13.50x (ISBN 0-8046-1311-7, Pub. by Kennikat). Assoc Faculty Pr.
Antia, K. K. & Bhattacharya, S. S. Botany Practicals: Including General Biology. 120p. 1981. 29.00x (ISBN 0-86125-641-7, Pub. by Orient Longman India). State Mutual Bk.
Antia, K. K., jt. auth. see Bhattacharya, S. S.
Anticaglia, Elizabeth. A Housewife's Guide to Women's Liberation. LC 72-85889. 229p. 1972. 18.95 (ISBN 0-911012-69-9). Nelson-Hall.
--Twelve American Women. LC 74-23229. (Illus.). 272p. 1975. 23.95x (ISBN 0-88229-102-5); pap. 11.95x (ISBN 0-88229-758-9). Nelson-Hall.
Anticancer-Symposium Held in Connection with the 10th International Congress of Chemotherapy, Zurich, September 1977. Application of Cancer Chemotherapy: Proceedings. Schoenfeld, H., et al, eds. (Antibiotics & Chemotherapy: Vol. 24). (Illus.). 1978. 31.50 (ISBN 3-8055-2831-0). S Karger.
--Fundamentals in Cancer Chemotherapy: Proceedings. (Antibiotics & Chemotherapy: Vol. 23). (Illus.). 1978. 37.50 (ISBN 3-8055-2830-2). S Karger.
Antieau, C. J., et al. Current Constitutional Issues: A Symposium. LC 77-153885. (Symposia on Law & Society Ser.). 1971. Repr. of 1967 ed. lib. bdg. 25.00 (ISBN 0-306-70154-5). Da Capo.
Antieau, Chester J. Adjudicating Constitutional Issues. LC 85-3056. 441p. 1985. lib. bdg. 35.00 (ISBN 0-379-20844-X). Oceana.
--Constitutional Construction. LC 82-1250. 255p. 1982. lib. bdg. 30.00 (ISBN 0-379-20682-X). Oceana.
--Federal Civil Rights Acts: Civil Practice, 2 vols. LC 74-148243. 1980. Set. 129.00 (ISBN 0-686-14507-0); Suppl. 1984. 22.00; Suppl. 1983. 20.00. Lawyers Co-Op.
--Modern Constitutional Law, 2 vols. LC 69-19951. 1969. 129.00 (ISBN 0-686-14506-2). Lawyers Co-Op.
--State Rights under Federal Constitutions. LC 83-13276. 169p. 1984. lib. bdg. 30.00 (ISBN 0-379-20845-8). Oceana.
Antill, James M. & Woodhead, Ronald. Critical Path Methods in Construction Practice. 2nd ed. LC 79-121902. pap. 81.40 (ISBN 0-8357-9870-4, 2019295). Bks Demand UMI.
Antill, James M. & Woodhead, Ronald W. Critical Path Methods in Construction Practice. 3rd. ed. LC 81-19713. 425p. 1982. 42.95x (ISBN 0-471-86612-1, Pub. by Wiley-Interscience). Wiley.
Antin, David. Talking. pap. 3.50 (ISBN 0-686-09756-4). Kulchur Foun.
--Talking at the Boundaries. LC 76-15374. 1976. 11.95 (ISBN 0-8112-0559-2); pap. 3.95 (ISBN 0-8112-0560-6, NDP388). New Directions.
--Tuning. LC 84-3446. 288p. (Orig.). 1984. pap. 12.50 (ISBN 0-8112-0894-X, NDP570). New Directions.
Antin, David, tr. see Dorrie, Heinrich.
Antin, David, et al. Coherence. Wellman, Don, ed. Waldrop, Rosmarie, tr. (Illus.). 208p. 1981. pap. 6.95 (ISBN 0-942030-01-X). O ARS.
Antin, Eleanor. Being Antinova. LC 83-72104. (Illus.). 88p. 1983. limited edition 25.00 (ISBN 0-937122-12-2); pap. 10.00 (ISBN 0-937122-11-4). Astro Artz.
Antin, Eleanor, et al. Dialogue-Discourse-Research. LC 79-54783. (Orig.). 1979. pap. 17.50x (ISBN 0-89951-033-7). Santa Barb Mus Art.
Antin, Mary. From Plotzk to Boston. LC 74-104404. Repr. of 1899 ed. lib. bdg. 14.50 (ISBN 0-8398-0060-6). Irvington.
--From Plotzk to Boston. Sarna, Jonathan D., ed. (Masterworks of Modern Jewish Writing Ser.). 140p. 1985. pap. 6.95 (ISBN 0-910129-51-7). Wiener Pub Inc.
--The Promised Land. Baxter, Annette K., ed. LC 79-8768. (Signal Lives Ser.). 1980. Repr. of 1969 ed. lib. bdg. 24.00x (ISBN 0-405-12818-5). Ayer Co Pubs.
--The Promised Land: The Autobiography of a Russian Immigrant. LC 84-42936. 400p. 1985. 35.00x (ISBN 0-691-04722-7); pap. 12.50x (ISBN 0-691-00598-2). Princeton U Pr.
Antinori, Romualdo. Is the United States Able to Win a War? (Illus.). 123p. 1984. 115.75x (ISBN 0-86722-075-9). Inst Econ Pol.
Antinozzi, M. A. The Practical Resume: A Writer's Guide. LC 83-51320. 160p. (Orig.). 1983. pap. 5.95 (ISBN 0-915543-00-1). Writers Workshp.
Antinucci, F., jt. auth. see Parisi, D.
Antioch Review. Antioch Review Anthology. facs. ed. Bixler, Paul, ed. LC 79-117752. (Essay Index Reprint.). 1953. 25.00 (ISBN 0-8369-1782-0). Ayer Co Pubs.
Antiquarian Catalogues. Prints & Illustrated Books Six Centuries. (Illus.). 56p. 1974. 5.00 (ISBN 0-915346-21-4). A Wofsy Fine Arts.
Antique Airplane Association. Classic Airplanes of the Thirties - Aircraft of the Roaring Twenties. Gilbert, James, ed. LC 79-7238. (Flight: Its First Seventy-Five Years Ser.). (Illus.). 1979. Repr. of 1965 ed. lib. bdg. 17.00x (ISBN 0-405-12153-9). Ayer Co Pubs.
Antique Collector's Club. Britten's Old Clock & Watches & Their Makers. 3rd ed. (Illus.). 517p. 1978. Repr. of 1911 ed. 49.50 (ISBN 0-902028-69-3). Antique Collect.
--The Dictionary of British Artists: 1880-1940. 567p. 1976. 59.50 (ISBN 0-902028-36-7). Antique Collect.
Antique Collectors' Club. The Royal Society of British Artists: 1824-1893. 620p. 1975. 79.50 (ISBN 0-902028-35-9). Antique Collect.
Antitrust Law Sect. American Bar Association. Handbook on Antitrust Grand Jury Investigations. LC 77-60755. 169p. 1978. pap. 15.00 (ISBN 0-686-47782-0, 503-0022). Amer Bar Assn.
Antitrust Law Section. Antitrust Discovery Handbook Supplement. 1983. pap. 19.00 (ISBN 0-317-16871-1); incl. handbook 45.00. Amer Bar Assn.
--Antitrust Law Developments: Student Edition. 2nd ed. 516p. 1984. pap. 20.00 (ISBN 0-317-16873-8). Amer Bar Assn.
Antitrust Law Section Members. Criminal Antitrust Litigation Manual. LC 83-71753. 655p. 1983. 35.00 (ISBN 0-89707-107-7). Amer Bar Assn.
--Franchise Law Bibliography. LC 84-70162. 119p. 1984. pap. 20.00 (ISBN 0-89707-135-2). Amer Bar Assn.
--Merger Case Digest 1982. 756p. 1984. write for info. (ISBN 0-317-16855-X). Amer Bar Assn.
--Refusals to Deal & Exclusive Distributorships. 64p. 1983. pap. 10.00 (ISBN 0-317-16856-8). Amer Bar Assn.
Antl, Boris. Currency Risk. 194p. 1980. 88.00x (ISBN 0-8002-3417-0). Intl Pubns Serv.
Antl, Moris, jt. auth. see Ensor, Richard.
Antle, Nancy. The Good Bad Cat. Gregorich, Barbara, ed. (Start to Read! Ser.). (Illus.). 16p. (Orig.). (gr. k-2). 1985. pap. 1.95 (ISBN 0-88743-012-0, 06012). Sch Zone Pub Co.
Antler. Factory. LC 80-25727. (Pocket Poets Ser.: No. 38). (Orig.). 1980. 8.50 (ISBN 0-87286-123-6); pap. 3.00 (ISBN 0-87286-122-8). City Lights.
Antler, Stephen, ed. Child Abuse & Child Protection: Policy & Practice. LC 82-80767. 164p. (Orig.). 1982. pap. text ed. 12.95 (ISBN 0-87101-091-7). Natl Assn Soc Wkrs.
Antler, Steven D., jt. auth. see Miller, Roger L.
Antler, Steven D., ed. see Miller, Roger L.
Antman, Elliot M., jt. auth. see Stone, Peter H.
Antognetti, P. Power-Integrated Circuits: Physics, Design & Applications. 576p. 1985. price not set (ISBN 0-07-002129-5). McGraw.
Antognetti, P., et al, eds. see Computer Design Aids for VLSI Circuits, Urbino, Italy, July 1980.
Antognetti, Paolo, ed. Process & Device Simulation for MOS-VLSI Circuits. 1983. lib. bdg. 78.50 (ISBN 90-2472-824-X, Pub. by Martinus Nijhoff Netherlands). Kluwer Academic.
Antognetti, Paolo, jt. ed. see Tsividis, Yannis.
Antoine, Andre. Memories of the Theatre-Libre. Albright, H. D., ed. Carlson, Marvin, tr. LC 64-8734. (Bks of the Theatre: No. 5). (Illus.). 1964. 12.95x (ISBN 0-87024-034-X). U of Miami Pr.
Antoine, Jacques C. Jean Price-Mars & Haiti. (Illus.). 224p. 1981. 20.00 (ISBN 0-914478-55-9); pap. 10.00 (ISBN 0-914478-56-7). Three Continents.
Antoine, Jean-Pierre & Tirapegui, Enrique, eds. Functional Integration: Theory & Application. LC 80-21935. 365p. 1980. 55.00x (ISBN 0-306-40573-3, Plenum Pr). Plenum Pub.
Antoine, Robert. Rama & the Bards: Epic Memory in the Ramayana. (Greybird Book). 114p. 1975. 12.00 (ISBN 0-88253-821-7); pap. 6.75 (ISBN 0-88253-822-5). Ind-US Inc.
Antoine, Robert, tr. see Kalidasa.
Antoine, Valerie. Guidance for Using Metric System (SI Version) 39p. 1976. pap. 8.00 (ISBN 0-914548-23-9). Soc Tech Comm.
Antoine Le, Roux De Lincy see Leroux De Lincy, Antoine J.
Antokoletz, Elliott. The Music of Bela Bartok: A Study of Tonality & Progression in Twentieth Century Music. LC 82-17352. (Illus.). 472p. 1984. lib. bdg. 38.50x (ISBN 0-520-04604-8). U of Cal Pr.
Antolinez, Crescencio. Fachworterbuch Fur Recht und Verwaltung. (Span. & Ger.). 1970. leatherette 35.00 (ISBN 3-452-17065-9, M-7398, Pub. by Carl Heymanns Verlag KG). French & Eur.

Antolini, Renzo, et al, eds. Transport in Biomembranes: Model Systems & Reconstitution. 288p. 1982. text ed. 42.00 (ISBN 0-89004-868-1). Raven.

Antomarchi, D., tr. see Sabatier, Leopold.

Anton, Ferdinand, et al. Primitive Art: Pre-Columbian, North American Indian, African, Oceanic. (Illus.). 1979. 37.50 (ISBN 0-8109-1459-X). Abrams.

Anton, H. Calculus: With Analytic Geometry. brief, 2nd ed. 738p. 1984. 32.95 (ISBN 0-471-88817-6); student's manual 10.95 (ISBN 0-471-80732-X). Wiley.

--Elementary Linear Algebra. 2nd ed. 386p. (Arabic.). 1982. pap. 16.50 (ISBN 0-471-06389-4). Wiley.

Anton, Haberkamp De see Haensch, G. & De Anton, Haberkamp G.

Anton, Hans H. Studien Zu Den Klosterprivilegien der Paepste Im Fruehen Mittelalter Unter Besonderer Beruecksichti der Privilegierung Von St. Maurice D'agaune. (Beitraege Zur Geschichte und Quellenkunde Des Mittelalters Ser.: Vol. 4). 1975. pap. 39.60x (ISBN 3-11-004686-5). De Gruyter.

Anton, Hector R., et al. Contemporary Issues in Cost & Managerial Accounting: A Discipline in Transition. 3rd ed. LC 77-74383. (Illus.). 1978. pap. text ed. 29.95 (ISBN 0-395-25435-3). HM.

Anton, Howard. Calculus with Analytic Geometry. LC 79-11469. 1220p. 1980. 40.45 (ISBN 0-471-03248-4); solution manual 11.95 (ISBN 0-471-04498-9). Wiley.

--Calculus with Analytic Geometry. 2nd ed. LC 83-19778. 1239p. 1984. text ed. 40.45 (ISBN 0-471-08271-6); write for info. solution manual (ISBN 0-471-86901-5); pap. 15.95 students solution manual (ISBN 0-471-86902-3). Wiley.

--Elementary Linear Algebra. 4th ed. LC 83-27382. 464p. 1984. 27.45 (ISBN 0-471-09890-6); student solutions manual 8.95x (ISBN 0-471-87976-2). Wiley.

Anton, Howard & Kolman, Bernard. Applied Finite Mathematics. 3rd ed. LC 81-66947. 1982. 22.50i (ISBN 0-12-059566-4); instrs' manual 2.50i (ISBN 0-12-059571-0); study guide 6.50i (ISBN 0-12-059570-2). Acad Pr.

Anton, Howard & Rorres, Chris. Applications of Linear Algebra. 3rd ed. 364p. 1985. pap. text ed. 16.95x (ISBN 0-471-86800-0). Wiley.

Anton, Howard & Kolman, B., eds. Mathematics with Applications for the Management, Life & Social Sciences. 2nd ed. LC 81-66947. 851p. 1982. text ed. 22.50i (ISBN 0-12-059561-3); instr's. manual 2.50i (ISBN 0-12-059563-X); study guide 6.50i (ISBN 0-12-059562-1). Acad Pr.

Anton, John. Critical Humanism As a Philosophy of Culture: The Case of E. P. Papanoutos. Stavrou, Theofanis G., intro. by. (Modern Greek History & Culture Ser.). 1981. 10.00 (ISBN 0-935476-07-5). Nostos Bks.

Anton, John P., ed. Naturalism & Historical Understanding: Essays on the Philosophy of John Herman Randall, Jr. LC 67-63753. 1967. 39.50x (ISBN 0-87395-021-6). State U NY Pr.

--Science & the Sciences in Plato. LC 78-13418. 1980. 25.00x (ISBN 0-88206-301-4). Caravan Bks.

Anton, John P. & Kustas, George L., eds. Essays in Ancient Greek Philosophy, Vol. 1. LC 69-14648. 1971. 44.50x (ISBN 0-87395-050-X). State U NY Pr.

Anton, John P. & Preus, Anthony, eds. Essays in Ancient Greek Philosophy, Vol.2. 1983. 44.50x (ISBN 0-87395-623-0); pap. 19.95x (ISBN 0-87395-624-9). State U NY Pr.

Anton, John P., ed. see Papanoutsos, Evangelos P.

Anton, John P., jt. ed. see Walton, Craig.

Anton, John P., tr. see Papanoutsos, Evangelos P.

Anton, Liz & Dooley, Beth. Recipes from Massachusetts with Love. (Illus.). 250p. (Orig.). 1985. pap. 4.50 comb bd. (ISBN 0-913703-07-9). New Boundary Design.

Anton, Michael. From Humbug to Heaven. 1972. 2.15 (ISBN 0-89536-070-5). CSS of Ohio.

--The Night That Was. 1972. 2.25 (ISBN 0-89536-164-7). CSS of Ohio.

--What Are We Going to Do with the King? 1972. 3.00 (ISBN 0-89536-287-2). CSS of Ohio.

Anton, Michael J. Good News for Now. 1976. pap. 4.50 (ISBN 0-89536-087-X). CSS of Ohio.

Anton, Peter J. Naturalism & Historical Understanding: Essays on the Philosophy of John Hermann Randall, Jr. LC 67-63753. pap. 44.70 (ISBN 0-317-09035-6, 2010957). Bks Demand UMI.

Anton, Thomas. Occupational Safety & Health Management. 1979. text ed. 34.00 (ISBN 0-07-002106-6). McGraw.

Anton, Thomas J. Administered Politics: Elite Political Culture in Sweden. 1980. lib. bdg. 19.95 (ISBN 0-89838-025-1, Pub. by Martinus Nijhoff Netherlands). Kluwer Academic.

--Federal Aid to Detroit. LC 82-74099. 80p. 1983. pap. 5.95 (ISBN 0-8157-0437-2). Brookings.

--Governing Greater Stockholm: A Study of Policy Development & System Change. LC 79-94447. (Institute of Governmental Studies, U. C. Berkeley, & Lane Studies in Regional Government). 1974. 38.50x (ISBN 0-520-02718-3). U of Cal Pr.

Anton, Thomas J., et al. Moving Money: An Empirical Analysis of Federal Expenditure Patterns. LC 80-21700. 288p. 1980. text ed. 35.00 (ISBN 0-89946-066-6). Oelgeschlager.

Antonacci, Gary. Optional Commodity Investing. 1983. 35.00 (ISBN 0-318-00212-4). Windsor.

Antonacci, R. J. & Lockhart, B. B. Tennis for Young Champions. 192p. 1982. 9.95 (ISBN 0-07-002145-7). Mcgraw.

Antonacci, Robert J. Basketball for Young Champions. 2nd ed. LC 78-8029. (Young Champions Ser.). (Illus.). (gr. 4-6). 1979. 10.95 (ISBN 0-07-002141-4). McGraw.

--Soccer for Young Champions. 7th ed. (Young Champions Ser.). (Illus.). (gr. 4-6). 1978. 10.95 (ISBN 0-07-002147-3). McGraw.

Antonacci, Robert J. & Barr, Jene. Football for Young Champions. 2nd ed. LC 75-10825. (Illus.). 160p. (gr. 4-6). 1976. PLB 10.95 (ISBN 0-07-002154-6). McGraw.

Antonaccio, Michael J., ed. Cardiovascular Pharmacology. rev., 2nd ed. 606p. 1984. text ed. 48.00 (ISBN 0-89004-872-X). Raven.

Antone, E. H., ed. see Braddy, Haldeen.

Antone, E. H., ed. see Murphy, Lawrence R.

Antonelli, P. L., et al. Concordance-Homotopy Groups of Geometric Automorphism Groups. LC 73-171479. (Lecture Notes in Mathematics: Vol. 215). 1971. pap. 11.00 (ISBN 0-387-05560-6). Springer-Verlag.

Antonellis, Costanzo J. Saint of Ardent Desires. (Orig.). 1965. 4.00 (ISBN 0-8198-0137-2). Dghtrs St Paul.

--The Story of Peter Donders. 115p. 3.50 (ISBN 0-8198-6834-5, BI0217); pap. 2.50 (ISBN 0-8198-6835-3). Dghtrs St Paul.

Antonetti, Vincent. The Computer Diet. LC 73-80174. (Illus.). 284p. 1973. 6.95 (ISBN 0-87131-122-4). M Evans.

--The Dell Gas Mileage Guidebook. (Orig.). 1980. pap. 1.95 (ISBN 0-440-12021-7). Dell.

Antonetti, Vincent W. Fitness Management. LC 76-42583. (Illus., Orig.). 1976. pap. 6.95x (ISBN 0-918278-01-5). Fitness.

Antongini, Tom. D'Annunzio. facsimile ed. LC 75-37327. (Select Bibliographies Reprint Ser). Repr. of 1938 ed. 31.00 (ISBN 0-8369-6676-7). Ayer Co Pubs.

--D'Annunzio. 1938. 18.50 (ISBN 0-8274-2129-X). R West.

Anton-Guirgis, Hoda, jt. auth. see Lynch, Henry T.

Antoni, Carlo. From History to Sociology: The Transition in German Historical Thinking. White, Hayden V., tr. LC 76-40127. (Ital.). 1976. Repr. of 1959 ed. lib. bdg. 22.50 (ISBN 0-8371-9282-X, ANFH). Greenwood.

Antoni, F. & Staub, M., eds. Tonsils: Structure, Immunology & Biochemistry. 1978. 17.00 (ISBN 0-9960011-5-8, Pub. by Akademiai Kaido Hungary). Heyden.

Antoni, Manfred. Arbeit Als Betriebswirtschaftlicher Grundbegriff. (European University Studies Section 5: Vol. 369). vii, 286p. (Ger.). 1982. 35.25 (ISBN 3-8204-5798-4). P Lang Pubs.

Antonia, Fraser. Oxford Blood: A Jemima Shore Mystery. 1985. 13.95 (ISBN 0-393-02229-3). Norton.

Antoniades, Anthony C. Architecture & Allied Design: An Environmental Design Perspective. (Illus.). 384p. (Orig.). 1980. pap. text ed. 19.50 (ISBN 0-8403-2154-6). Kendall-Hunt.

--Introduction to Environmental Design. LC 76-20696. (Illus.). 360p. 1976. pap. text ed. 8.95x (ISBN 0-8422-0543-8). Irvington.

Antoniades, Harry N., ed. Hormones in Human Blood: Detection & Assay. 1976. 60.00x (ISBN 0-674-40635-4, ANHH). Harvard U Pr.

Antoniades, John, ed. Uncommon Malignant Tumors. LC 82-6610. (Masson Cancer Management Ser.). (Illus.). 408p. 1982. 68.00 (ISBN 0-89352-046-2). Masson Pub.

Antoniak, Peter, jt. auth. see Tymes, Elna.

Antonick, Michael. The Corvette Black Book, 1953-1984. 1984. 9.95. Motorbooks Intl.

--Illustrated Corvette Buyer's Guide. (Buyer's Guide Ser.). (Illus.). 156p. 1983. pap. 13.95 (ISBN 0-87938-160-4). Motorbooks Intl.

Antonick, Mike. Illustrated Camaro Buyer's Guide. (Buyer's Guide Ser.). (Illus.). 156p. 1985. pap. 13.95 (ISBN 0-87938-187-6). Motorbooks Intl.

Antonides, Harry. Multinationals & the Peaceable Kingdom. 248p. 4.95 (ISBN 0-7720-1196-6). Chr Labour.

Antonini, Eraldo, jt. ed. see Colowick, Sidney.

Antonini, Gustavo A., et al. Population & Energy: A Systems Analysis of Resource Utilization in the Dominican Republic. LC 75-2495. (University of Florida Latin American Monographs: No. 14). 166p. 1975. 15.00 (ISBN 0-8130-0502-7). U Presses Fla.

Antoninus, Bro. Robinson Jeffers: Fragments of an Older Fury. 1970. 7.50 (ISBN 0-685-04672-9). Oyez.

Antonio, Angelo Di see Di Antonio, Angelo.

Antonio, Diana. Once a Lover. 1983. pap. 3.50 (ISBN 0-671-42183-2). PB.

Antonio, Emile de see De Antonio, Emile & Tuchman, Mitch.

Antonio, Robert J. & Glassman, Ronald M., eds. A Weber-Marx Dialogue. 352p. 1985. 29.95x (ISBN 0-7006-0265-8). U Pr of KS.

Antonio, T. De Nicolas see Lincoln, Victoria.

Antonioni, Michelangelo. Blow-Up. (Lorrimer Classic Screenplay Ser.). (Illus.). pap. 6.95 (ISBN 0-8044-6007-8). Ungar.

--That Bowling Alley on the Tiber: Tales of a Director. Arrowsmith, William, tr. 258p. 1985. 18.95 (ISBN 0-19-503676-X). Oxford U Pr.

Antonio-Tristan, Regina. My Children & I. LC 84-51431. 104p. 1984. 6.95 (ISBN 0-938232-53-3). Winston-Derek.

Antoniou, Andreas. Digital Filters: Analysis & Design. (Electrical Engineering Ser.). (Illus.). 1979. text ed. 46.00 (ISBN 0-07-002117-1). McGraw.

Antoniou, J. Environmental Management: Planning for Traffic. 1972. 39.95 (ISBN 0-07-094222-6). McGraw.

Antoniou, Jim. Greece. LC 75-44871. (Countries Ser.). (Illus.). (gr. 6 up). 1976. PLB 13.96 (ISBN 0-382-06104-7). Silver.

--Islamic Cities & Conservation. (Illus.). 109p. 1982. pap. 17.00 (ISBN 92-3-101919-8, U1247, UNESCO). Unipub.

Antoniou, Mary. Welfare Activities among the Greek People in Los Angeles: Thesis. LC 74-7650. 1974. Repr. of 1939 ed. soft bdg. 10.95 (ISBN 0-88247-283-6). R & E Pubs.

Antonio y Bas Peired, Carlos, jt. auth. see Jonch, Cuspinera.

Antonius, George. The Arab Awakening. 1976. lib. bdg. 75.00 (ISBN 0-8490-1444-1). Gordon Pr.

--The Arab Awakening. 22.00x (ISBN 0-86685-000-7). Intl Bk Ctr.

Antoniv, V. F., jt. auth. see Pogosov, V. S.

Antonopulos, Barbara. The Abominable Snowman. LC 77-21387. (Great Unsolved Mysteries Ser.). (Illus.). (gr. 4-5). 1977. PLB 14.25 (ISBN 0-8172-1053-9). Raintree Pubs.

--The Abominable Snowman. LC 77-21387. (Great Unsolved Mysteries Ser.). (Illus.). 48p. (gr. 4up). 1983. pap. 9.27 (ISBN 0-8172-2151-4). Raintree Pubs.

Antonov, A. N. Physiology & Pathology of the Newborn. (SRCD.M). 1945. 21.00 (ISBN 0-527-01535-0). Kraus Repr.

Antonov, N. R. Khram Bozhij i Tserkovnija Sluzhbi. 300p. 1983. pap. text ed. 10.00 (ISBN 0-317-30284-1). Holy Trinity.

Antonova, K. A History of India, Book Two. 342p. 1979. 10.80 (ISBN 0-8285-1629-4, Pub. by Progress Pubs USSR). Imported Pubns.

Antonova, K., et al. History of India, Vol. 1. 264p. 1976. 10.80 (ISBN 0-8285-1628-6, Pub. by Progress Pubs USSR). Imported Pubns.

--History of India, Vol. 2. 342p. 1976. 10.80 (ISBN 0-8285-1629-4, Pub. by Progress Pubs USSR). Imported Pubns.

--A History of India, Book One. 264p. 1979. 10.80 (ISBN 0-8285-1628-6, Pub. by Progress Pubs USSR). Imported Pubns.

Antonova, X. Tretyakov Gallery. 375p. 1983. 75.00 (ISBN 0-8285-2662-1, Pub. by Aurora Pubs USSR). Imported Pubns.

Antonovich, Michael P. User's Guide to the Apple II Computer. LC 80-70465. (WSI's How to Use Your Personal Computer Ser.). 350p. (gr. 10-12). 1985. pap. 13.95 (ISBN 0-938862-03-0). Weber Systems.

Antonov-Ovseyeneko, Anton. The Time of Stalin: Portrait of a Tyranny. LC 80-8681. 376p. 1983. pap. 8.61i (ISBN 0-06-039027-1, CN1040, CN). Har-Row.

Antonov-Ovseyenko, A. V. The Time of Stalin: Portrait of a Tyranny. LC 80-8681. (Illus.). 384p. 1981. 21.10i (ISBN 0-06-010148-2, HarpT). Har-Row.

Antonovskii, M. Ja, et al. Topological Semifields & Their Applications to General Topology. LC 77-11046. (Translation Ser. No 2: Vol. 106). 142p. 1979. pap. 23.00 (ISBN 0-8218-3056-2, TRAN 2/106). Am Math.

Antonovsky, Aaron. Health, Stress, & Coping: New Perspectives on Mental & Physical Well-Being. LC 79-83566. (Social & Behavioral Science Ser.). 1979. 19.95x (ISBN 0-87589-412-7). Jossey-Bass.

Antonovsky, Aaron & Katz, Abraham D. From the Golden to the Promised Land: Americans in Israel. 231p. 1985. Repr. of 1985 ed. lib. bdg. 30.00 (ISBN 0-8414-4125-1). Folcroft.

Antonovsky, Helen F., et al. Adolescent Sexuality: A Study of Attitudes & Behavior. LC 80-8337. 176p. 1980. 24.50x (ISBN 0-669-04030-4). Lexington Bks.

Antonovych, Marc, ed. see Mijakovs'kyj, Volodymyr.

Antonson, Joan M. & Hanable, William S. Alaska's Heritage, 2 vols. LC 84-72718. (Alaska Historical Commission Studies in History: No. 133). (Illus., Orig.). Date not set. Set. text ed. 25.00 (ISBN 0-943712-18-1); Vol. I. pap. text ed. 12.50 (ISBN 0-943712-16-5); Vol. II. pap. text ed. 12.50 (ISBN 0-943712-17-3). Alaska Hist.

Antonson, Joan M., jt. ed. see Liljeblad, Sue E.

Antonucci, T., ed. see Symposium of the American Psychological Association, New Orleans, 1974.

Antony, Arthur. Guide to Basic Information Sources in Chemistry. LC 79-330. (Information Resources Ser.). 219p. 1979. 24.95x (ISBN 0-470-26587-6). Halsted Pr.

Antony, Judith. Where Time Becomes Space. 1978. 8.95 (ISBN 0-8199-0699-9). Franciscan Herald.

Antony, Richard, et al, eds. Spiritual Choices. Date not set. price not set. Paragon Hse.

Antopol, Justine & Kusnet, Jack, eds. Modern Banking Forms: Cumulative Supplementation, 3 vols. 3rd ed. 1981. Set. 145.00 (ISBN 0-88262-549-7). Warren.

Antopol, Justine T. & Kusnet, Jack. Modern Banking Checklists: Cumulative Supplementation. 3rd ed. 1981. 96.00 (ISBN 0-88262-608-6). Warren.

Antosiewicz, H. A., ed. International Conference on Differential Equation: Proceedings. 1975. 76.50 (ISBN 0-12-059650-4). Acad Pr.

Antosik, P. & Schwartz, C. Matrix Methods in Analysis. (Lecture Notes in Mathematics: Vol.1113). iv, 114p. 1985. pap. 9.80 (ISBN 0-387-15185-0). Springer-Verlag.

Antosik, Stanley J. The Question of Elites: An Essay on the Cultural Elitism of Nietzche, George & Hesse. (New York University Ottendorfer Series, Neue Folge: Vol. 11). 204p. 1978. 22.75 (ISBN 3-261-03102-6). P Lang Pubs.

Antoun, Richard. Low-Key Politics: A Case Study of Local Level Leadership & Change in the Middle East. LC 77-19018. (Illus.). 1979. 35.50x (ISBN 0-87395-373-8). State U NY Pr.

Antoun, Richard T. Arab Village: A Social Structural Study of a Transjordanian Peasant Community. LC 70-633555. (Indiana University Social Science Ser.: Vol. 29). pap. 52.00 (ISBN 0-317-27951-3, 2056022). Bks Demand UMI.

Antreasian, Garo Z. & Adams, Clinton. Tamarind Book of Lithography: Art & Techniques. LC 76-121328. 27.50 (ISBN 0-8109-9017-2). Abrams.

Antreassian, Alice. Armenian Recipes: The 40 Days of Lent. (Illus.). 150p. 1985. spiral 10.00 (ISBN 0-935102-16-7). Ashod Pr.

Antreassian, Alice & Jebejian, Mariam. Classic Armenian Recipes: Cooking Without Meat. LC 81-10961. 350p. 1981. text ed. 16.00 looseleaf binder (ISBN 0-935102-05-1). Ashod Pr.

--Classic Armenian Recipes: Cooking Without Meat. LC 81-10961. (Illus.). 350p. 1983. pap. 10.00 (ISBN 0-935102-11-6). Ashod Pr.

Antreassian, Antranig. The Cup of Bitterness & Other Stories. Antreassian, Jack, tr. from Armenian. LC 79-21572. 1979. pap. 4.95 (ISBN 0-935102-01-9). Ashod Pr.

Antreassian, Jack. The Confessions of Kitchoonie. LC 79-23979. (Orig.). 1979. pap. 3.95 (ISBN 0-935102-02-7). Ashod Pr.

Antreassian, Jack, tr. see Antreassian, Antranig.

Antreassian, Jack, tr. see Baronian, Hagop.

Antreassian, Jack, tr. see Charents, Eghishe.

Antreassian, Jack, tr. see Zohrab, Krikor.

Antrei, A. C., ed. A Topical History of Sanpete County Utah, 1849-1983. (Illus.). 500p. 1983. 22.50 (ISBN 0-914740-26-1). Western Epics.

Antrei, Albert C., et al, eds. see Sanpete County Commission.

Antrich, J. & Usher, S. Xenophon: The Persian Expedition. 200p. 1978. 29.00x (ISBN 0-906515-11-4, Pub. by Bristol Classical Pr). State Mutual Bk.

Antrim, Craig. Color Consciousness: Seven Los Angeles Artists. (Illus.). 12p. 1978. 2.00 (ISBN 0-915478-39-0). Galleries Coll.

Antrim, Harry T. T. S. Eliot's Concept of Language: A Study of its Development. LC 76-634405. (University of Florida Humanities Monographs: No. 35). 75p. 1971. pap. 3.50 (ISBN 0-8130-0326-1). U Presses Fla.

Antrim, William. Advertising. 2nd ed. Dorr, Eugene L., ed. (Occupational Manuals & Projects in Marketing). (Illus.). (gr. 11-12). 1978. pap. text ed. 8.68 (ISBN 0-07-002114-7). McGraw.

Antrobus, Edmund. Britain Nineteen Eighty-Five. Fisher, Robert C., ed. (Fisher Annotated Travel Guides Ser.). 320p. 1984. 12.95 (ISBN 0-8116-0069-6). NAL.

--London, 1985. Fisher, Robert C., ed. (Fisher Annotated Travel Guides Ser.). 128p. 1984. pap. 8.95 (ISBN 0-8116-0018-1). NAL.

Antrobus, John. Hitler in Liverpool & Other Plays. 1984. pap. 7.95 (ISBN 0-7145-3898-1). Riverrun NY.

--Ronnie & the Great Knitted Robbery. LC 83-61282. (Illus.). 56p. (gr. 8-10). 1984. 7.50 (ISBN 0-88186-351-3). Parkwest Pubns.

--Ronnie & the Haunted Rolls Royce. (Illus.). 56p. (gr. 3). 1985. 7.50 (ISBN 0-88186-352-1). Parkwest Pubns.

Antrobus, Molly. District Nursing: The Nurse, the Patients & the Work. LC 85-5226. (Illus.). 250p. (Orig.). 1985. pap. 9.95 (ISBN 0-571-13651-6). Faber & Faber.

Antropov, L. Theoretical Electrochemistry. (Illus.). 568p. 1972. 21.00x (ISBN 0-8464-1143-1). Beekman Pubs.

--Theoretical Electrochemistry. 568p. 1972. 8.95 (ISBN 0-8285-0667-1, Pub. by Mir Pubs USSR). Imported Pubns.

Antsey, Nigel A. Simple Seismics. LC 82-80267. (Short Course Handbooks). (Illus.). 168p. 1982. text ed. 29.00 (ISBN 0-934634-37-8); pap. text ed. 21.00 (ISBN 0-934634-43-2). Intl Human Res.

Antsiferov, Alexis N., et al. Russian Agriculture During the War: Rural Economy; The Land Settlement. (Economic & Social History of the World War, Russian Ser.). 1930. 19.50x (ISBN 0-317-27551-8). Elliots Bks.

Antsyferov, M. S., ed. Seismo-Acoustic Methods in Mining. LC 65-26634. 134p. 1966. 34.50x (ISBN 0-306-10752-X, Consultants). Plenum Pub.

Anttila. Analogy. (Trends in Linguistics: No. 10). 1977. 18.00 (ISBN 9-0279-7975-8). Mouton.

Anttila, Elizabeth K. English Oral Production. 1980. pap. 7.50 (ISBN 0-8477-3333-5). U of PR Pr.

--English Structure Exercises. pap. 1.85 (ISBN 0-8477-3300-9). U of PR Pr.

Anttila, Raimo & Brewer, Warren A. Analogy: A Basic Bibliography. (Library & Information Sources in Linguistics Ser: No.1). xiv, 50p. 1977. 16.00x (ISBN 90-272-0992-8). Benjamins North Am.

Antunes, Antonio L. South of Nowhere. Lowe, Elizabeth, tr. 1983. 11.95 (ISBN 0-394-52574-4). Random.

Antwerp, Emily S. Van see Van Antwerp, Emily S.

Antwerp, Margaret A. Van see Van Antwerp, Margaret A.

Antwerp, William C. Van see Van Antwerp, William C.

Antzak, R. Denny Davis. (Illus.). (ps-3). 1.75 (ISBN 0-8198-0196-8). Dghtrs St Paul.

Anuchin, V. A. Theoretical Problems of Geography. Fuchs, Roland J. & Demko, George J., eds. Shabad, Steven, tr. LC 77-8437. 339p. 1977. 16.00x (ISBN 0-8142-0221-7). Ohio St U Pr.

Anugraham, Catherine E. No Time for Tears. 160p. 1981. 7.95 (ISBN 0-89962-222-4). Todd & Honeywell.

Anuman, Rajadhon Phraya. Life & Ritual in Old Siam: Three Studies of Thai Life & Customs. Gedney, William J., ed. LC 78-23833. (Illus.). 1979. Repr. of 1961 ed. lib. bdg. 24.75x (ISBN 0-313-21193-0, ARLF). Greenwood.

Anurag, Ma Yoga, ed. see Rajneesh, Bhagwan Shree.

Anurag, Ma yoga, ed. see Rajneesh, Bhagwan Shree.

Anurag, Ma Yoga, ed. see Rajneesh, Bhagwan Shree.

Anurag, Ma yoga, ed. see Rajneesh, Bhagwan Shree.

Anurag, Ma Yoga, ed. see Rajneesh, Bhagwan Shree.

Anurag, Ma yoga, ed. see Rajneesh, Bhagwan Shree.

Anurag, Ma YOga, ed. see Rajneesh, Bhagwan Shree.

Anuskiewicz, J. Michael. How to Survive Our Savage Society: A Self-Help Guide to Smart Living. LC 78-55863. 1978. pap. 4.95 (ISBN 0-9601690-1-6). Gemini Pr.

Anuta, Larry. The Complete Mail Sales Promotion. LC 76-19677. (Illus.). 1977. pap. 15.00 (ISBN 0-917302-00-1). Surevelation.

--The Information Game. LC 76-19676. (Illus.). 1977. pap. 15.00 (ISBN 0-917302-01-X). Surevelation.

Anvari, Moshen. Cash Management Techniques. 320p. 86. 22.95x (ISBN 0-03-059007-8). Praeger.

Anvil, Christopher. The Steel, the Mist & the Blazing Sun. 288p. 1983. pap. 2.75 (ISBN 0-441-78571-9). Ace Bks.

Anwander, Erna. Pseudoklassizistisches und Romantisches in Thomson's Seasons. 12.00 (ISBN 0-384-01665-0). Johnson Repr.

Anwar, Doreen. We Live & Remember. 144p. 1978. 5.95 (ISBN 977-247-513-8). Diotima Bks.

Anwar, Khaidir. Indonesian: The Development & Use of a National Language. LC 82-95008. (Illus.). viii, 205p. 1980. pap. 9.50x (ISBN 0-8214-0770-8). Ohio U Pr.

Anwar, Mohammed S. Be An Equational Sentences in Egyptian Colloguial Arabic. (Studies in Language Companion Ser.: No. 2). vi, 128p. 1979. 15.00x (ISBN 90-272-3001-3, SLCS 2). Benjamins North Am.

Anwar, Muhammad. The Myth of Return: Pakistanis in Britain. LC 80-450770. 1979. text ed. 27.50x (ISBN 0-435-82022-2). Gower Pub Co.

Anwar, Mumtaz A., ed. see Al-Nahari, Abdulaziz M.

Anwar, Rebecca A., ed. Emergency Medicine Residencies. (Emergency Health Services Quarterly: Vol. 1, No. 1). 129p. 1981. pap. text ed. 15.00 (ISBN 0-917724-57-7, B57). Haworth Pr.

Anwar, S. A. The European Community & Indo-British Trade Relations. 168p. 1983. text ed. 33.00 (ISBN 0-566-00574-3). Gower Pub Co.

Anwarali, Maulana, ed. see Rizvi, Allama S.

Anway, Carol. Family Enrichment Book. 1979. pap. 8.00 (ISBN 0-8309-0247-3). Herald Hse.

Anwyl, Edward. Celtic Religion: In Prechristian Times. 1977. lib. bdg. 59.95 (ISBN 0-8490-1590-1). Gordon Pr.

Anyan, Walter R. Adolescent Medicine in Primary Care. LC 78-16772. 387p. 1978. 34.00x (ISBN 0-471-03976-4, Pub. by Wiley Medical). Wiley.

Anyan, Walter R., jt. auth. see Schowalter, John E.

Anyanwu, K. C. The African Experience in the American Marketplace: A Comparative Study of Cultural Philosophy. 128p. 1983. pap. 5.00 (ISBN 0-682-49976-5, University). Exposition Pr FL.

Anyanwu, Nze E. Higher Education in Nigeria: Its Philosophy, Structure & Organization. 200p. 1984. 19.50 (ISBN 0-914970-39-9); pap. text ed. 12.50 (ISBN 0-914970-40-2). Conch Mag.

Anyidoho, Kofi. Harvest of Our Dreams with Elegy for the Revolution. (African Writers Ser.: No. 261). vi, 90p. (Orig.). 1984. pap. text ed. 7.50x (ISBN 0-435-90261-X). Heinemann Ed.

Anyidoho, Kofi, et al, eds. Interdisciplinary Dimensions of African Literature. LC 84-51448. (African Literature Association Annuals Ser.: No. 8). 223p. (Eng. & Fr.). 1985. 22.00 (ISBN 0-89410-456-X); pap. 14.00 (ISBN 0-89410-457-8). Three Continents.

Anylan, William G, jt. ed. see Yaggy, Duncan.

Anyon, George J. Entrepreneurial Dimensions of Management. LC 73-622. 1973. text ed. 9.95 (ISBN 0-915180-12-X). Harrowood Bks.

Anyon, Roger & LeBlanc, Steven A. The Galaz Ruin: A Prehistoric Mimbres Village in Southwestern New Mexico. LC 83-27403. (Illus.). 520p. 1984. pap. 24.95 (ISBN 0-8263-0748-5). U of NM Pr.

Anza, Frank see De Anza, Frank.

Anzaldua, Mike. Mexican American Literature: A Preliminary Bibliography of Literary Criticism. (Latin American Curriculum Units for Junior & Community Colleges Ser.). vii, 29p. (Orig.). 1980. pap. text ed. 3.95x (ISBN 0-86728-004-2). U TX Inst Lat Am Stud.

Anzaldua, Mike M., Jr. & Pierce, James A. First Steps: Grammar & Guided Composition for Basic Writing Students. 200p. 1980. pap. text ed. 9.95x wkbk. (ISBN 0-89641-034-X). American Pr.

Anzalone, Joan, ed. Good Works: A Guide to Careers in Social Change. 3rd, expanded ed. LC 84-23902. 1985. 25.00 (ISBN 0-934878-55-2); pap. 14.50 (ISBN 0-934878-56-0). Dembner Bks.

Anzalone, Joseph T., jt. auth. see Phillips, Celeste R.

Anzalone, Stephen & McLaughlin, Stephen. Making Literacy Work: The Specific Literacy Approach. (Illus.). 73p. 1983. pap. 4.00 (ISBN 0-932288-73-1). Ctr Intl Ed U of MA.

Anzar, Naosherwan. The Beloved: The Life & Work of Meher Baba. rev. ed. LC 83-13540. (Illus.). 160p. 1983. 15.00 (ISBN 0-913078-50-6); pap. 9.95 (ISBN 0-913078-47-6). Sheriar Pr.

Anzar, Naosherwan, ed. The Best of the Glow: A Fifteen Year Retrospective, Vol. 1. LC 84-23518. 208p. (Orig.). 1984. pap. 8.95 (ISBN 0-913078-54-9). Sheriar Pr.

Anzelewky, Fedja. Durer: His Art & Life. 276p. 1983. 175.00x (ISBN 0-86092-068-2, Pub. by Fraser Bks). State Mutual Bk.

Anzelon, Robyn. The Forever Spell. (Superromances Ser.). 384p. 1983. pap. 2.50 (ISBN 0-373-70049-0, Pub. by Worldwide). Harlequin Bks.

--The Goblin Tree. (Harlequin Category Romances Ser.). 224p. 1983. pap. 2.25 (ISBN 0-373-33002-2). Harlequin Bks.

--Sous le Signe de la Licorne. (Harlequin Seduction Ser.). 332p. 1984. pap. 3.25 (ISBN 0-373-45036-2). Harlequin Bks.

Anzia, Joan & Durkin, Mary. Maritial Intimacy: A Catholic Perspective. 81p. pap. 6.95. Loyola.

Anzieu, D. Freud's Self-Analysis & the Discovery of Psychoanalysis, Vols. 1 & 2. 1984. Set. text ed. write for info. (ISBN 0-8236-2045-X). Vol. I (ISBN 0-8236-2046-8). Vol. 2 (ISBN 0-8236-2046-8). Intl Univs Pr.

Anzieu, Didier. The Group & the Unconscious. Kiborne, Benjamin, tr. from Fr. (International Library of Group Psychotherapy & Group Process). 288p. 1984. 45.00X (ISBN 0-7100-0693-4). Routledge & Kegan.

Anzilotti, Gloria Italiano. Four English-Italian Stories: Experiments in Translation. LC 84-23351. (Edward Sapir Monograph Series in Language, Culture & Cognition: No. 11). viii, 84p. (Orig., Ital. & Eng.). 1984. pap. 8.00x (ISBN 0-933104-16-2). Jupiter Pr.

Anzul, Dario. The Paintings of Mysticism & Violence in Full Colours of Dario Anzul. (Illus.). 97p. 1983. 225.75x (ISBN 0-86650-073-1). Gloucester Art.

Aodha, Michael O. The Weaver's Grave. (The New Abbey Theatre Ser.). 1985. pap. 2.95x (ISBN 0-912262-81-8). Proscenium.

AOG Systems Corp. Draft Proposed American National Standard Information Resource Dictionary System. 1985. write for info. QED Info Sci.

Aoki, Haruo. Nez Perce Grammar. (California Library Reprint: No. 41). 1974. 34.50x (ISBN 0-520-02524-5). U of Cal Pr.

--Nez Perce Texts. LC 77-91776. (Publications in Linguistics: Vol. 90). 1979. 20.00x (ISBN 0-520-09593-6). U of Cal Pr.

Aoki, Hiroyuki. Shintaido: An Art of Movement & Life Expression. Thompson, Michael & Ito, Haruyoshi, trs. from Japanese. LC 82-80496. (Illus.). 120p. 1982. pap. 8.95 (ISBN 0-942634-00-4). Shintaido.

Aoki, Hisako & Gantschev, Ivan. Santa's Favorite Story. LC 82-60895. (Illus.). 28p. 1982. 9.95 (ISBN 0-907234-16-X, Pub. by Picture Bk Studio USA). Neugebauer Pr.

Aoki, Hisako, tr. see Sugita, Yotaka.

Aoki, K., et al, eds. Animal Behavior. 274p. 1984. 42.00 (ISBN 0-387-13046-2). Springer Verlag.

--Cancer Prevention in Developing Countries: Proceedings of the First UICC Conference on Cancer Prevention in Developing Countries. (Illus.). 628p. 1982. text ed. 62.00x (ISBN 4-930689-02-3, Pub. by Japan Sci Soc Pr Japan). Intl Spec Bk.

Aoki, Katsutada, jt. auth. see Shimizu, Akinao.

Aoki, M. Economic Analysis of the Japanese Firm. (Contributions to Economic Analysis Ser.: Vol. 151). 1984. 48.00 (ISBN 0-444-86822-4, I-463-83). Elsevier.

--Notes on Economic Times Series Analysis: System Theoretic Perspectives. (Lecture Notes in Economics & Mathematical Systems Ser.: Vol. 220). 249p. 1983. pap. 19.00 (ISBN 0-387-12696-1). Springer-Verlag.

--Optimal Control & System Theory in Dynamic Economic Analysis. (Dynamic Economics Ser.: Vol. 1). 402p. 1976. 56.00 (ISBN 0-444-00176-X, North-Holland). Elsevier.

Aoki, Masahiko. The Co-Operative Game Theory of the Firm. (Illus.). 1985. 29.95x (ISBN 0-19-828485-3). Oxford U Pr.

Aoki, Masanao. Dynamic Analysis of Open Economies. LC 80-2763. 1981. 45.00 (ISBN 0-12-058940-0). Acad Pr.

--Optimization of Stochastic Systems. (Mathematics in Science & Engineering Ser: Vol. 32). 1967. 68.50 (ISBN 0-12-058850-1). Acad Pr.

Aoki, Masanao & Marzollo, Angelo, eds. New Trends in Dynamic System Theory & Economics. LC 78-27701. 1979. 41.50 (ISBN 0-12-058860-9). Acad Pr.

Aoki, Michiko Y. & Dardess, Margaret B., eds. As the Japanese See It: Past & Present. LC 81-11526. 324p. 1981. text ed. 17.50x o. p. (ISBN 0-8248-0759-6); pap. text ed. 7.95x (ISBN 0-8248-0760-X). UH Pr.

Aoki, T., et al, eds. Manipulation of Host Defence Mechanisms. (International Congress Ser.: Vol. 576). 282p. 1982. 50.75 (ISBN 0-444-90245-7). Elsevier.

Aonghusa, Proinsias Mac see Mac Aonghusa, Proinsias.

Aoothill, Eric, jt. auth. see Fairhurst, Alan.

Aoun, Joseph. A Grammar of Anaphora. (Illus.). 192p. (Orig.). 1985. text ed. 25.00x (ISBN 0-262-01075-5); pap. text ed. 15.00 (ISBN 0-262-51033-2). MIT Pr.

Aoyagi, Akiko, jt. auth. see Shurtleff, William.

Aoyama, Y., jt. ed. see Kawamura, A., Jr.

APA Commission on Psychiatric Therapies. The Psychosocial Therapies. Karasu, Toksoz B., ed. LC 84-3058. 616p. 1984. pap. text ed. 25.00x (ISBN 0-89042-103-X, 42-103-X). Am Psychiatric.

--The Somatic Therapies. Karasu, Toksoz B., ed. LC 84-3048. 360p. 1984. pap. text ed. 17.50x (ISBN 0-89042-104-8, 42-104-8). Am Psychiatric.

APA Commission on Psychotherapies. Psychotherapy Research: Methodological & Efficacy Issues. LC 82-8763. (Illus.). 280p. 1982. pap. 15.00x Report (ISBN 0-89042-101-3, 42-101-3). Am Psychiatric.

Apa, Ma Prem, ed. see Rajneesh, Bhagwan S.

APA Office of Public Affairs. Economic Fact Book for Psychiatry. 152p. 1983. pap. text ed. 15.00x (ISBN 0-88048-152-8, 48-152-8). Am Psychiatric.

APA Task Force on Nomenclature & Statistics. Desk Reference to the Diagnostic Criteria from DSM-III. (Illus.). 233p. 1982. spiral bound 15.00x (ISBN 0-89042-046-7, 42-046-7). Am Psychiatric.

Apache Jim. Apache Jim: Stories from his Private Files on Treasures. (Illus.). 107p. 1973. pap. 4.00 (ISBN 0-941620-00-X). H G Carson Ent.

Apadeva. Mimansa Nyaya Prakasa. Edgerton, Franklin, tr. 1929. 75.00x (ISBN 0-685-69815-7). Elliots Bks.

Apalin, G. & Mityayev, U. Militarism in Peking's Policies. 1980. pap. 6.95 (ISBN 0-8285-1937-4, Pub. by Progress Pubs USSR). Imported Pubns.

Apar, Bruce. The Home Video Book. (Illus.). 144p. (Orig.). 1982. 14.95 (ISBN 0-8174-3990-0, Amphoto); pap. 8.95 (ISBN 0-8174-3991-9). Watson-Guptill.

Aparicio, Frances, tr. see Paoli, Francisco Matos.

Aparis, Fina, tr. see Clymer, R. Swinburne.

Apartment Life Editors. The New Apartment Book. (Illus.). 1979. 14.98 (ISBN 0-517-55045-8). Crown.

Apartment Life Staff, ed. The New Apartment Book. rev. ed. 27.50 (ISBN 0-517-55045-8, Harmony). Crown.

Apaulding, J. G., jt. auth. see Pollock, T. C.

Apblett, William R., Jr., ed. Shell & Tube Heat Exchangers. 1982. 67.00 (ISBN 0-87170-145-6). ASM.

Apczynski, John. Foundations of Religious Literacy. LC 83-4453. (College Theology Society Annual Publications Ser.). 188p. 1983. pap. 10.50 (ISBN 0-89130-621-8, 34 10 82). Scholars Pr GA.

Apczynski, John V. Doers of the Word. LC 76-51640. (American Academy of Religion. Dissertation Ser.). 1977. pap. 10.50 (ISBN 0-89130-128-3, 010118). Scholars Pr GA.

Apel, J. R., jt. ed. see Seeber, G.

Apel, K. O. Analytic Philosophy of Language & the Geisteswissenschaften. (Foundations of Languages Supplementary Ser: No. 4). 63p. 1967. 13.00 (ISBN 90-277-0022-2, Pub. by Reidel Holland). Kluwer Academic.

Apel, Karl O. Understanding & Explanation: A Transcendental Pragmatic Perspective. Warnke, Georgia, tr. from Ger. (Studies in Contemporary German Social Thought). 320p. 1984. text ed. 25.00x (ISBN 0-262-01079-8). MIT Pr.

Apel, Karl-Otto. Charles Sanders Peirce: From Pragmatism to Pragmaticism. Krois, John M., tr. from Ger. LC 81-3337. Orig. Title: Der Denkweg Von Charles Sanders Peirce. 288p. 1981. lib. bdg. 22.50x (ISBN 0-87023-177-4). U of Mass Pr.

--Towards a Transformation of Philosophy. (International Library of Phenomenology & Moral Sciences). 1980. 30.00x (ISBN 0-7100-0403-6). Routledge & Kegan.

Apel, Max & Luds, Peter. Philosophiches Woerterbuch. 6th ed. (Sammlung Goeschen: 2202). (Ger.). 1980. pap. 5.10x (ISBN 3-11-006729-3). De Gruyter.

Apel, Willi. French Secular Music of the Late 14th Century. 1962. Repr. of 1950 ed. 18.00x (ISBN 0-910956-29-4). Medieval Acad.

--Gregorian Chant. LC 57-10729. (Illus.). 544p. 1958. 35.00x (ISBN 0-253-32650-8). Ind U Pr.

--Harvard Dictionary of Music. rev., enl. ed. LC 68-21970. (Illus.). 1969. 25.00 (ISBN 0-674-37501-7, Belknap Pr). Harvard U Pr.

--The History of Keyboard Music to 1700. Tischler, Hans, tr. LC 79-135015. 896p. 1972. 39.50x (ISBN 0-253-32795-4). Ind U Pr.

--Masters of the Keyboard: A Brief Survey of Pianoforte Music. LC 47-12245. (Illus.). 1947. 25.00 (ISBN 0-674-55300-4). Harvard U Pr.

--Notation of Polyphonic Music, 900-1600. 5th ed. LC 61-12067. 1961. 20.00x (ISBN 0-910956-15-4). Medieval Acad.

Apel, Willi & Daniel, Ralph T., eds. The Harvard Brief Dictionary of Music. 348p. 1968. pap. 3.95 (ISBN 0-671-43475-6). WSP.

Apel, Willi, jt. ed. see Davison, Archibald T.

Apel, William D. Witnesses Before Dawn. 1984. pap. 9.95 (ISBN 0-8170-1031-9). Judson.

Apelblat, A. Tables of Definite & Infinite Integrals. (Physical Sciences Data Ser.: Vol. 13). 458p. 1983. 106.50 (ISBN 0-444-42151-3, I-470-82). Elsevier.

Apeldoorn, G. Jan Van see Van Apeldoorn, G. Jan.

Apeldoorn, Jo V. Pratiques de la Description. (Faux Titre Ser.: No. 11). 299p. (Fr.). 1982. pap. text ed. 28.25x (ISBN 90-6203-814-X, Pub. by Rodopi Holland). Humanities.

Apelian, D. & Brody, H., eds. Modeling of Casting & Welding Processes: Proceedings, Rindge, New Hampshire, 1980. (Illus.). 540p. 40.00 (ISBN 0-89520-380-4); members 25.00 (ISBN 0-317-36252-6); student members 14.00 (ISBN 0-317-36253-4). ASM.

Apelian, D., jt. ed. see Szekely, J.

Apelman, Maja, tr. see Brecht, Bertolt.

Apelt, H. P. Reading Knowledge in German for Art Historians & Archaeologists: An English-German Course in Art History & Archaeology. 1975. pap. 11.50x (ISBN 3-503-00799-7). Adlers Foreign Bks.

Apelt, H. P., jt. auth. see Apelt, Mary L.

Apelt, M. German-English Dictionary: Art History-Archaeology. 1982. 25.00 (ISBN 3-503-01619-8). Heinman.

Apelt, Mary L. & Apelt, H. P. Reading Knowledge in German: A Course for Art Historians & Archaeologists (1975) pap. 12.50 (ISBN 3-503-00799-7). Heinman.

Apelt, Otto. Platonis Sophista: Recentsuit, Prolegomenis et Commentariis Instruxit. Taran, Leonardo, ed. LC 78-66612. (Ancent Philosophy Ser.: Vol. 1). 225p. lib. bdg. 26.00 (ISBN 0-8240-9611-8). Garland Pub.

--Platonische Aufsatze. facsimile ed. LC 75-13251. (History of Ideas in Ancient Greece Ser.). (German.). 1976. Repr. of 1912 ed. 19.00x (ISBN 0-405-07288-0). Ayer Co Pubs.

Aperjis, Dimitri. The Oil Market in the Nineteen Eighties: OPEC Oil Policy & Economic Development. LC 81-15050. 240p. 1982. Prof. Ref. 35.00x (ISBN 0-88410-903-8). Ballinger Pub.

Aperyan, V. A. Manpower Resources & Population Under Socialism. 198p. 1979. 4.95 (ISBN 0-8285-1607-3, Pub. by Progress Pubs USSR). Imported Pubns.

Apes, William. Eulogy on King Philip. Dexter, Lincoln A., ed. Date not set. pap. 4.50x (ISBN 0-9601210-3-X). L A Dexter.

--Indian Nullification of the Unconstitutional Laws of Massachusetts, Relative to the Marshpee Tribe: Or, the Pretended Riot Explained. (American Indians at Law Ser.). 1980. Repr. of 1835 ed. text ed. 17.50 (ISBN 0-930576-34-9). E M Coleman Ent.

Ap Evans, Humphrey. Falconry. LC 73-80791. (Illus.). 160p. 1974. 15.00 (ISBN 0-668-03339-8). Arco.

Apfel, Necia. Astronomy & Plantology: Projects for Young Scientists. (Illus.). 128p. (gr. 9up). PLB 9.90 (ISBN 0-531-04668-0). Watts.

Apfel, Necia H. Astronomy Projects for Young Scientists. (Illus.). 128p. 1984. pap. 5.95 (ISBN 0-668-06006-9, 6006-9). Arco.

--Calendars. (First Bk.). (Illus.). 96p. (gr. 5-8). 1985. PLB 9.40 (ISBN 0-531-10034-0). Watts.

--It's All Elementary: From Atoms to the Quantum World of Quarks, Leptons, & Gluons. LC 84-9718. (Illus.). 160p. (gr. 4 up). 1985. PLB 11.88 (ISBN 0-688-04093-4); pap. 7.25 (ISBN 0-688-04092-6). Lothrop.

--It's All Relative: Einstein's Theory of Relativity. LC 80-28188. (Illus.). 144p. (gr. 5 up). 1981. 12.25 (ISBN 0-688-41981-X); PLB 11.76 (ISBN 0-688-51981-4). Lothrop.

--It's All Relative: Einstein's Theory of Relativity. LC 84-21819. (Illus.). 144p. (gr. 4 up). 1985. pap. 7.25 (ISBN 0-688-04301-1). Lothrop.

--The Moon & Its Exploration. (First Bks). (Illus.). 72p. (gr. 4 up). 1982. PLB 8.90 (ISBN 0-531-04385-1). Watts.

--Stars & Galaxies. (First Bks). (Illus.). 72p. (gr. 4 up). 1982. PLB 8.90 (ISBN 0-531-04389-4). Watts.

Apfel, Roberta J. & Fisher, Susan M. To Do No Harm: DES & the Dilemmas of Modern Medicine. LC 84-5089. (Illus.). 192p. 1984. 15.95x (ISBN 0-300-03192-0). Yale U Pr.

Apfelbaum, H. Jack & Ottesen, Walter O. Basic Engineering Sciences & Structural Engineering for Engineer-in-Training Examinations. Hollander, Lawrence J., ed. (Professional Engineering Examinations Ser.). (Illus.). 1970. 23.95 (ISBN 0-8104-5712-1). Hayden.

Apfelbaum, John D., jt. auth. see Lidman, David.

Apfelbeck, Alma, et al, eds. Favorite Recipes of the Nebraska Czechs. 1968. pap. 5.95 (ISBN 0-8220-1615-X). Cliffs.

Apffel, Helmut, et al. Die Verfassungsdebatte bei Herodot & Politisches Denken bei Herodot & Frauenimuncipation in Athen, 3 vols. in one. Vlastos, Gregory, ed. LC 78-14603. (Morals & Law in Ancient Greece Ser.). 1979. Repr. of 1900 ed. lib. bdg. 19.00x (ISBN 0-405-11574-1). Ayer Co Pubs.

Apgar, Kathryn & Callahan, Betsy N. Stress Management. 128p. 1982. 13.95 (ISBN 0-87304-189-5). Family Serv.

Apgar, Kathryn & Riley, Donald P. Life Education in the Workplace: How to Design, Lead & Market Employee Seminars. 184p. 1982. 19.95 (ISBN 0-87304-197-6). Family Serv.

Apgar, Kathryn, jt. auth. see Callahan, Betsy N.

Apgar, William C., Jr., jt. auth. see Kain, John F.

Apicius. Cookery & Dining in Imperial Rome. Vehling, Joseph D., ed. & tr. from Latin. LC 77-89410. Orig. Title: Apicius De Re Coquinaria. 1977. pap. 6.00 (ISBN 0-486-23563-7). Dover.

APICS. Management Seminar: Proceedings. 104p. 1982. 6.00 (ISBN 0-935406-15-8). Am Prod & Inventory.

--Master Planning Seminar: Proceedings. 84p. 1982. 6.00 (ISBN 0-935406-13-1). Am Prod & Inventory.

--Planning & Control Seminar: Proceedings. 156p. 1982. 8.50 (ISBN 0-935406-14-X). Am Prod & Inventory.

APICS Annual Conference, 25th. Proceedings. LC 79-640341. 590p. 1982. 30.00 (ISBN 0-935406-20-4). Am Prod & Inventory.

APICS Bucks-Mont Cnapter. Material Requirements Planning Training Aid. 62p. 1979. 37.50 (ISBN 0-935406-10-7). Am Prod & Inventory.

APICS Cirriculum & Certification Program Council Committee, ed. Shop Floor Controls Reprints. 165p. 1973. 13.50 (ISBN 0-935406-17-4). Am Prod & Inventory.

APICS Curricula & Certification Council, Capacity Management Subcommittee. Capacity Management Reprints. LC 84-70311. 129p. 1984. pap. 13.00 (ISBN 0-935406-45-X, 40645). Am Prod & Inventory.

APICS Curricula & Certification Council Inventory Management Subcommittee, ed. Inventory Management Reprints. LC 84-70312. 534p. 1984. pap. 20.00 (ISBN 0-935406-46-8, 40646). Am Prod & Inventory.

APICS Curriculum & Certification Program Council Planning & Control Committee, ed. Capacity Planning & Control Reprints. 110p. 1975. 10.50 (ISBN 0-935406-16-6). Am Prod & Inventory.

APICS Curriculum & Certification Program Council Inventory Planning Subcommittee, ed. Inventory Planning Reprints. 212p. 1978. pap. 15.00 (ISBN 0-935406-27-1). Am Prod & Inventory.

APICS Milwaukee Chapter. Shop Floor Control Training Aid. 30p. 1979. 27.00 (ISBN 0-935406-08-5). Am Prod & Inventory.

APICS Repetitive Manufacturing Group see Hall, Robert W.

APICS 24th Annual Conference, 1981. Proceedings. 458p. 1981. pap. 30.00 (ISBN 0-935406-05-0). Am Prod & Inventory.

Apilado, Vincent P. & Morehart, Thomas B. Personal Financial Management. (Illus.). 650p. 1980. text ed. 26.95 (ISBN 0-8299-0327-5); instrs.' manual avail. (ISBN 0-8299-0457-3); study guide 7.50 (ISBN 0-8299-0308-9). West Pub.

Apilado, Vincent P., et al. Cases in Financial Management. 2nd ed. (Illus.). 250p. 1981. pap. text ed. 13.95 (ISBN 0-314-63152-6). West Pub.

Apisson, Barbara, jt. auth. see McQueen-Williams, Morvyth.

Apjohn, Lewis. The Earl of Beaconsfield: His Life & Work. 296p. 1981. Repr. of 1884 ed. lib. bdg. 50.00 (ISBN 0-89984-005-1). Century Bookbindery.

Apkarian, P. A., jt. ed. see Spekreijse, H.

Apker, Wes, et al. A Dialogue on Teacher Evaluation. LC 78-45888. 1975. 6.00 (ISBN 0-939630-03-6). Inst Qual Hum Life.

Apker, Wesley L. Reflections with Dream Songs & Other Tales. 80p. 1982. 6.00 (ISBN 0-682-49798-3). Exposition Pr FL.

Apker, Westley, et al. A Dialogue on the Selection of Educators. 1977. 6.00 (ISBN 0-939630-05-2). Inst Qual Hum Life.

Aplan, F. F. & Pernichele, A. D., eds. Solution Mining Symposium. 469p. 1974. 15.00 (ISBN 0-317-35843-X, 025-2); members 10.00 (ISBN 0-317-35844-8); student members 6.00 (ISBN 0-317-35845-6). Soc Mining Eng.

Aplan, F. F., et al, eds. Solution Mining Symposium, 1974: Proceedings of a Symposium, 103rd AIME Annual Meeting, Dallas, Texas, Feb. 25-27, 1974. LC 73-94005. pap. 119.80 (ISBN 0-317-29727-9, 2017422). Bks Demand UMI.

Apley, J., ed. see O'Donohue, Niall F.

Apley, John. Care of the Handicapped Child: A Festschrift for Ronald Mac Keith. (Clinics in Developmental Medicine Ser.: Vol. 67). 145p. 1978. text ed. 22.00 (ISBN 0-433-00710-9, Pub. by Spastics Intl England). Lippincott.

--Paediatrics: Concise Medical Textbook. 2nd ed. (Illus.). 1979. pap. text ed. 14.95 (ISBN 0-7216-0702-0, Pub. by Bailliere-Tindall). Saunders.

APLIC International. Proceedings of the Thirteenth Annual Conference. Burns, Adele B., ed. LC 76-643241. 157p. 1980. pap. 13.00 (ISBN 0-933438-05-2). APLIC Intl.

Apling, A. J., et al. Air Pollution from Oxides of Nitrogen, Carbon Monoxide & Hydrocarbons, 1979. 1981. 59.00x (ISBN 0-686-97009-8, Pub. by W Spring England). State Mutual Bk.

--Air Pollution in Homes: Validation of Diffusion Tube Measurements of Nitrogen Dioxide, 1979. 1981. 40.00x (ISBN 0-686-97013-6, Pub. by W Spring England). State Mutual Bk.

Aplon, Roger. By Dawn's Early Light at One Hundred Twenty Miles Per Hour. 1983. 12.95 (ISBN 0-931848-58-X); pap. 4.95 (ISBN 0-931848-57-1). Dryad Pr.

--Stiletto. 1976. 12.00 (ISBN 0-931848-13-X); pap. 4.50 (ISBN 0-931848-14-8). Dryad Pr.

Apodaca, Rudy S. The Waxen Image. LC 77-73631. 1977. 9.50 (ISBN 0-9603314-0-9). Titan Pub Co.

Apol, Ekbal. Feel Yourself. (Illus.). 128p. 1979. 28.00 (ISBN 0-7156-1147-X, Pub. by Duckworth England); pap. 10.95 (ISBN 0-7156-1148-8, Pub. by Duckworth England). Biblio Dist.

Apolinsky. Tax Planning for Professionals. 1985. 78.00 (ISBN 0-88712-375-9). Warren.

Apollinaire, Guillaume. Alcools. 1971. pap. 3.95 (ISBN 0-685-10983-6). French & Eur.

--Alcools. deluxe ed. 500.00 (ISBN 0-685-37177-8). French & Eur.

--Alcools. Greet, Anne Hyde, tr. & annotations by. LC 65-20148. 1966. pap. 8.95 (ISBN 0-520-00029-3, CAL121). U of Cal Pr.

--Alcools. Rees, Garnet, ed. (French Poets Ser.). 181p. (Fr.). 1975. pap. 14.95 (ISBN 0-485-12708-3, Pub. by Athlone Pr Ltd). Longwood Pub Group.

--Anecdotiques. pap. 8.95 (ISBN 0-685-37164-6). French & Eur.

--Le Bestaire ou Cortege d'Orphee. Shakely, Lauren, tr. from Fr. LC 77-23500. (Illus.). 1977. 8.95 (ISBN 0-87099-165-5). Metro Mus Art.

--Le Bestiaire. (Coll. Les Peintres du Livre). (Illus.). deluxe ed. 24.95 (ISBN 0-685-37178-6). French & Eur.

--Bestiary, or the Parade of Orpheus. Karmel, Pepe, tr. from Fr. LC 80-66191. (Illus.). 80p. 1980. 12.95; pap. 5.95 (ISBN 0-87923-359-1). Godine.

--Calligrammes. (Coll. Soleil). 1964. 9.95 (ISBN 0-685-11057-5); pap. 3.95 (ISBN 0-686-66415-9). French & Eur.

--Calligrammes. Greet, Anne H., tr. LC 73-149946. 600p. (Fr. & Eng.). 1980. 19.95 (ISBN 0-520-01968-7). U of Cal Pr.

--Calligrams. 2nd ed. Greet, Anne H., tr. LC 69-13012. (Unicorn French Ser). (Eng. & Fr.). 1973. 15.00 (ISBN 0-87775-010-6); pap. 5.00 (ISBN 0-87775-068-8). Unicorn Pr.

--Couleur du Temps. pap. 3.95 (ISBN 0-685-37166-2). French & Eur.

--Les Diables Amoureux. 7.50 (ISBN 0-685-37167-0). French & Eur.

--L' Enchanteur Pourrissant. Burgos, ed. (Coll. Paralogue). 36.65 (ISBN 0-685-37168-9). French & Eur.

--La Femme Assise. pap. 4.95 (ISBN 0-685-37169-7). French & Eur.

--Le Flaneur des Deux Rives. pap. 3.95 (ISBN 0-685-37170-0). French & Eur.

--Le Guetteur Melancolique. 7.95 (ISBN 0-685-37171-9). French & Eur.

--L' Heresiarque et Cie. 8.95 (ISBN 0-685-37172-7). French & Eur.

--Lettres a sa Marraine (1915-1918) pap. 3.95 (ISBN 0-685-37173-5). French & Eur.

--Oeuvres Completes, 8 vols. Decaudin, ed. Set. deluxe ed. 550.00 (ISBN 0-685-37179-4). French & Eur.

--Oeuvres Poetiques Completes. Adema & Decaudin, eds. (Bibl. de la Pleiade). 1957. 45.00 (ISBN 0-685-11459-7). French & Eur.

--Les Onze Mille Virges. Rootes, Nina, tr. from Fr. LC 78-24595. 1979. 7.95 (ISBN 0-8008-2384-2). Taplinger.

--Poems a Low. Decaudin, ed. Bd. with Il y a. (Coll. Poesie). pap. 5.50 (ISBN 0-685-37174-3). French & Eur.

--Poesies Libres. 1978. 16.95 (ISBN 0-686-51899-3). French & Eur.

--The Poet Assassinated & Other Stories. Padgett, Ron, tr. from Fr. 160p. 1984. pap. 12.50 (ISBN 0-86547-151-7). N Point Pr.

--Le Poete Asassine. 12.50 (ISBN 0-685-37175-1). French & Eur.

--Selected Writings of Apollinaire. rev. ed. Shattuck, Roger, tr. from Fr. LC 72-145928. 1971. pap. 8.95 (ISBN 0-8112-0003-5, NDP310). New Directions.

--Tendre comme le Souvenir. 11.95 (ISBN 0-685-37176-X). French & Eur.

Apollinaire, Guillaume & Guillaume, Paul. Sculptures Negres. Bd. with Sculptures D'Afrique, D'Amerique, D'Oceanie. Breton, Andre & Eluard, Paul.. LC 71-143336. (Fr.). 1973. Repr. of 1917 ed. 40.00 (ISBN 0-87817-056-1). Hacker.

Apollodorus. Library, 2 Vols. (Loeb Classical Library: No. 121, 122). 12.50x ea. Vol. 1, Bks. 1-3 (ISBN 0-674-99135-4). Vol. 2 (ISBN 0-674-99136-2). Harvard U Pr.

Apolloni, Tony & Cooke, Thomas P., eds. A New Look at Guardianship: Protective Services that Support Personalized Living. LC 83-23936. 360p. 1984. text ed. 24.95 (ISBN 0-933716-37-0, 370). P H Brookes.

Apollonio, Umbro, ed. Futurist Manifestos. (Documents of 20th Century Art Ser.). (Illus.). 256p. 1973. 17.95 (ISBN 0-670-33338-7). Viking.

Apollonius, Rhodius. The Argonautica of Apollonius Rhodius, Bk. III. Connor, W. R., ed. LC 78-18578. (Greek Texts & Commendtaries Ser.). (Greek & Eng.). 1979. Repr. of 1928 ed. lib. bdg. 17.00x (ISBN 0-405-11421-4). Ayer Co Pubs.

Apollonius Rhodius. Argonautica. (Loeb Classical Library: No. 1). 12.50x (ISBN 0-674-99001-3). Harvard U Pr.

Aponte, Barbara B. Alfonso Reyes & Spain: His Dialogue with Unamuno, Valle-Inclan, Ortega y Gasset, Jimenez, & Gomez de la Serna. 216p. 1972. 15.00x (ISBN 0-292-70300-7). U of Tex Pr.

Aponte, Barbara B., tr. see Marques, Rene.

Aponte, Gladys, et al. Curso Individualizado de Matematicas Basicas: Aritmetica, Algebra Elemental & Algebra Intermedia. LC 84-20838. 356p. (Span.). 1984. pap. text ed. 15.00 (ISBN 0-8477-2638-X). U of PR Pr.

Apostel, L. African Philosophy-Myth or Reality. (Philosophy & Anthropology Ser.: Vol. 2). 428p. 1981. pap. text ed. 45.50x (ISBN 90-6439-183-1, Pub. by E. Story Belgium). Humanities.

Apostel, L., ed. Religious Atheism? (Philosophy & Anthropology Ser.: Vol. 3). 180p. 1981. pap. text ed. 26.75x (ISBN 90-6439-272-2, Pub. by E. Story Belgium). Humanities.

Apostle, H. G., tr. see Aristotle.

Apostle, Hippocrates G., tr. see Aristotle.

Apostle, Richard A. & Glock, Charles Y. The Anatomy of Racial Attitudes. LC 82-4867. 277p. 1983. 30.00x (ISBN 0-520-04719-2). U of Cal Pr.

Apostol, ed. Topics in Modern Operator Theory. (Operator Theory, Advances & Applications Ser.: 2). 335p. 1981. text ed. 32.95x (ISBN 0-8176-1244-0). Birkhauser.

Apostol, C., et al. Approximation of Hilbert Space Operators, Vol. 2. (Research Notes in Mathematics: No. 102). 544p. 1984. pap. text ed. 29.95 (ISBN 0-273-08641-3). Pitman Pub MA.

Apostol, T. M. Calculus: Multi-Variable Calculus & Linear Algebra with Application, Vol. 2. 2nd ed. LC 67-14605. 673p. 1969. 44.00 (ISBN 0-471-00007-8); student solution 15.95 (ISBN 0-471-04498-9); calculus companion 12.95 (ISBN 0-471-88614-9). Wiley.

--Calculus: One-Variable Calculus with an Introduction to Linear Algebra, Vol. 1. 2nd ed. LC 73-20899. 666p. 1967. text ed. 44.00x (ISBN 0-471-00005-1); 15.95 (ISBN 0-471-86902-3); calculus companion 16.95 (ISBN 0-471-09230-4). Wiley.

Apostol, Tom, ed. Selected Papers in Precalculus. LC 77-792000079. (Raymond W. Brink Selected Mathematical Papers: Vol. 1). 21.00 (ISBN 0-88385-201-2). Math Assn.

Apostol, Tom, et al, eds. Selected Papers in Calculus. LC 76-102902. (Brink Selected Mathematical Papers: Vol. 2). 397p. 1969. 21.00 (ISBN 0-88385-202-0). Math Assn.

Apostol, Tom M. Introduction to Analytic Number Theory. (Undergraduate Texts in Mathematics Ser.). (Illus.). 370p. 1976. text ed. 29.80 (ISBN 0-387-90163-9). Springer-Verlag.

--Mathematical Analysis: A Modern Approach to Advanced Calculus. 2nd ed. LC 72-11473. 1974. text ed. 32.95 (ISBN 0-201-00288-4, Med-Nurse). Addison-Wesley.

Apostola, Nicholas K., tr. see Lungu, N., et al.

Apostolakis, G., et al, eds. Synthesis & Analysis Methods for Safety & Reliability Studies. LC 79-21315. 474p. 1980. 69.50x (ISBN 0-306-40316-1, Plenum Pr). Plenum Pub.

Apostolic Fathers. Works of Apostolic Fathers, 2 vols. Incl. Vol. 1. Clement, Ignatius, Polycarp, Didache, Barnabas (ISBN 0-674-99027-7); Vol. 2. Shepherd of Hermas, Martyrdom of Polycarp, Epistle to Diognetus (ISBN 0-674-99028-5). (Loeb Classical Library: No. 24-25). 12.50x ea. Harvard U Pr.

Apostolic Oblates Of Stanton Calif, tr. see Giaquinta, Guglielmo.

Apostolico, A. & Galil, Z., eds. Combinatorial Algorithms on Words. (NATO ASI Ser.: Series F, Vol. 12). viii, 361p. 1985. 48.50 (ISBN 0-387-15227-X). Springer-Verlag.

Apostoliti, Carmelina. The Love Story of Lisa & Snowball, Two Beloved Pets. (Illus.). 64p. 1981. 5.00 (ISBN 0-682-49815-7). Exposition Pr FL.

Apostolon, Billy. Evangelistic Sermon Outlines. (Sermon Outline Ser.). pap. 2.50 (ISBN 0-8010-0144-7). Baker Bk.

--Preach the Word. (Sermon Outline Ser.). 1978. pap. 2.25 (ISBN 0-8010-0039-4). Baker Bk.

--Special Days & Occasions. (Sermon Outline Ser). 1978. pap. 2.45 (ISBN 0-8010-0007-6). Baker Bk.

Apostolos-Cappadona, Diane, ed. Art, Creativity & the Sacred: An Anthology in Religion & Art. (Illus.). 352p. 1983. pap. 15.95 (ISBN 0-8245-0609-X). Crossroad NY.

Apostolos-Cappadona, Diane, tr. see Eliade, Mircea.

Apotheker, Nan, tr. see Garaudy, Roger.

App, August J. Lancelot in English Literature. LC 65-21392. (Arthurian Legend & Literature Ser., No. 1). 1969. Repr. of 1929 ed. lib. bdg. 49.95x (ISBN 0-8383-0504-0). Haskell.

App, Austin J. The Curse of Anti-Semitism. 1984. lib. bdg. 79.95 (ISBN 0-87700-595-8). Revisionist Pr.

--German-American Voice for Truth & Justice: The Autobiography of Austin J. App. 1984. lib. bdg. 79.95 (ISBN 0-87700-518-4). Revisionist Pr.

--History's Most Terrifying Peace. 1984. lib. bdg. 79.95 (ISBN 0-87700-524-9). Revisionist Pr.

--Hitler-Himmler Order on the Jews. 1984. lib. bdg. 79.95 (ISBN 0-87700-516-8). Revisionist Pr.

--Holocaust: Sneak Attack on Christianity. 1984. lib. bdg. 79.95 (ISBN 0-87700-517-6). Revisionist Pr.

--Morgenthau Era Letters. 1984. lib. bdg. 79.95 (ISBN 0-87700-520-6). Revisionist Pr.

--Power & Propaganda in American Politics & Foreign Policy. 1984. lib. bdg. 79.95 (ISBN 0-87700-515-X). Revisionist Pr.

--Ravishing the Women of Conquered Europe. 1984. lib. bdg. 79.95 (ISBN 0-87700-522-2). Revisionist Pr.

--The Six Million Swindle. 1984. lib. bdg. 79.95 (ISBN 0-87700-519-2). Revisionist Pr.

--A Straight Look at the Third Reich. 1984. lib. bdg. 79.95 (ISBN 0-87700-521-4). Revisionist Pr.

--The Sudeten-German Tragedy. (Illus.). 84p. (Orig.). 1979. pap. 3.00x (ISBN 0-911038-66-3, Inst Hist Rev). Noontide.

--The Sudeten German Tragedy. 1984. lib. bdg. 79.95 (ISBN 0-87700-523-0). Revisionist Pr.

App, Timothy, intro. by. Karl Benjamin, Recent Paintings. (Illus.). 10p. 1978. 3.00 (ISBN 0-915478-37-4). Galleries Coll.

Appadorai, A. Domestic Roots of India's Foreign Policy: Nineteen Forty-Seven to Nineteen Seventy-Two. 1982. 16.95x (ISBN 0-19-561144-6). Oxford U Pr.

Appadorai, A., ed. Status of Women in South Asia. LC 75-38654. 1976. Repr. of 1954 ed. 17.95 (ISBN 0-89201-026-6). Zenger Pub.

Appadorai, Angadipuram. Select Documents on India's Foreign Policy & Relation, 1947-72, Vol. 1. 1982. 42.00x (ISBN 0-19-561309-0). Oxford U Pr.

Appadorai, Angadipuram, ed. Select Documents on India's Foreign Policy & Relations: 1984, Vol. 2. 800p. 1984. 42.00x (ISBN 0-19-561496-8). Oxford U Pr.

Appadurai, Arjun. Worship & Conflict Under Colonial Rule: A South India Case. (Cambridge South Asian Studies: No. 27). (Illus.). 282p. 1981. 49.50 (ISBN 0-521-23122-1). Cambridge U Pr.

Appalachian Land Ownership Task Force. Who Owns Appalachia? Landownership & Its Impact. LC 82-40173. (Illus.). 272p. 1983. 25.00x (ISBN 0-8131-1476-4). U Pr of Ky.

Apparao, K. M. Composition of Cosmic Radiation. (Topics in Astrophysics & Space Physics Ser.). 96p. 1975. 37.25 (ISBN 0-677-03770-8). Gordon.

Appasamy, Jaya. Introduction to Modern Indian Sculpture. (Illus.). 1973. 7.50x (ISBN 0-686-20261-9). Intl Bk Dist.

--Tanjavur Painting of the Maratha Period. 121p. 1981. text ed. 42.50x (ISBN 0-391-02235-0, Pub. by Abhinav India). Humanities.

Appaswamy, J. An Introduction to Modern Indian Sculpture. 1970. 9.50 (ISBN 0-89684-540-0). Orient Bk Dist.

Appel, Alfred. Nabokov's Dark Cinema. (Illus.). 1974. 27.50x (ISBN 0-19-501834-6). Oxford U Pr.

Appel, Alfred, Jr Signs of Life. LC 83-47960. (Illus.). 202p. 1983. 30.00 (ISBN 0-394-50773-8); pap. 16.95 (ISBN 0-394-72112-8). Knopf.

Appel, Alfred, Jr., ed. see De Forest, John W.

Appel, Alfred, Jr., jt. ed. see Karlinsky, Simon.

Appel, Alfred, Jr., ed. see Nabokov, Vladimir.

Appel, Allan. Judah. 1976. pap. 1.75 (ISBN 0-685-74570-8, LB418KK, Leisure Bks). Dorchester Pub Co.

Appel, Allan P. Portfolio of Estate Planning Tools. LC 83-8717. 212p. 1983. 34.50 (ISBN 0-13-687434-7, Busn). P-H.

Appel, Allen. Time after Time. 420p. (Orig.). 1985. 17.95 (ISBN 0-88184-182-X). Carroll & Graf.

--Vengeance Valley. 1979. pap. 1.75 (ISBN 0-505-51448-6, Pub. by Tower Bks). Dorchester Pub Co.

--Vengeance Valley. 240p. 1985. pap. 2.25 (ISBN 0-8439-2193-5, Leisure Bks). Dorchester Pub Co.

Appel, Benjamin. Hell's Kitchen: A Novel. LC 76-44014. (YA) 1977. 7.95 (ISBN 0-394-83236-1). Pantheon.

--The People Talk. Repr. of 1940 ed. 37.00 (ISBN 0-384-01780-0). Johnson Repr.

--Shepherd of the Sun. (Illus.). (gr. 5 up). 1961. 5.95 (ISBN 0-8392-3033-8). Astor-Honor.

Appel, Brian E., ed. ALI-ABA Course of Study on Defense of Drug Cases. 406p. 1971. pap. 11.55 (ISBN 0-317-30871-8, B187). Am Law Inst.

Appel, Carl. Provenzalische Chrestomathie, Mit Abriss der Formenlehre & Glossar. 6th ed. LC 71-38488. Repr. of 1930 ed. 15.00 (ISBN 0-404-08345-5). AMS Pr.

Appel, Carl L. Provenzalische Lautlehre: Mit Einer Karte. LC 80-2165. (Provenzalische Chrestomathie Ser.). Repr. of 1918 ed. 30.00 (ISBN 0-404-19027-8). AMS Pr.

--Die Singweisen Bernarts Von Ventadorn nach den Handschriften mitgeteilt. LC 80-2171. Repr. of 1934 ed. 17.50 (ISBN 0-404-19002-2). AMS Pr.

--Der Trobador Uc Brunec Oder Brunenc in: Abhandlungen Herrn Prof. Adolf Tobler. LC 80-2177. 1981. Repr. of 1895 ed. 15.00 (ISBN 0-404-19003-0). AMS Pr.

Appel, David, jt. ed. see Worrall, John D.

Appel, David H., ed. An Album for Americans. 9.98 (ISBN 0-517-54374-5). Crown.

Appel, Frederic C. Encyclopedie De la Femme, 2: Son Corps. 144p. (Fr.). 14.95 (ISBN 0-686-56896-6, M-6006). French & Eur.

Appel, G. The Concise Code of Jewish Law: Daily Prayers & Religious Observances in the Life-Cycle of the Jew, Vol. 1. 11.95 (ISBN 0-87068-298-9). Ktav.

Appel, Gabriela, et al. A Selected Bibliography on Temporal Variables in Speech. (Tuebinger Beitrage Zur Linguistik Ser.: No. 138). 211p. (Orig.). 1980. pap. 15.00x (ISBN 3-87808-138-3). Benjamins North Am.

Appel, Georgius. De Romanorum Precationibus. facsimile ed. LC 75-10628. (Ancient Religion & Mythology Ser.). 1976. Repr. of 1909 ed. 18.00x (ISBN 0-405-07004-7). Ayer Co Pubs.

Appel, Gerald & Hitschler, Fred. Stock Market Trading Systems: A Guide to Investment Strategy for the 80's. LC 79-55228. 218p. 1980. 40.00 (ISBN 0-87094-195-X). Dow Jones-Irwin.

Appel, Gersion. A Philosophy of Mizvot. 20.00x (ISBN 0-87068-250-4). Ktav.

--Samuel K. Mirsky Memorial Volume. 1970. 25.00x (ISBN 0-87068-084-6). Ktav.

Appel, H. see Hellwege, K. H.

Appel, Jeanette, jt. auth. see Keller, Clifton.

Appel, John J. Immigrant Historical Societies in the United States, 1880-1950. Cordasco, Francesco, ed. LC 80-838. (American Ethnic Groups Ser.). 1981. lib. bdg. 43.00x (ISBN 0-405-13402-9). Ayer Co Pubs.

Appel, Joseph H. Africa's White Magic. 1978. Repr. of 1928 ed. lib. bdg. 25.00 (ISBN 0-8492-0089-X). R West.

--Business Biography of John Wanamaker. Repr. of 1930 ed. lib. bdg. 32.50 (ISBN 0-404-00365-6). AMS Pr.

Appel, Karen W. America's Changing Families: A Guide for Educators. LC 84-62989. (Fastback Ser.: No. 219). 50p. 1985. pap. 0.75 (ISBN 0-87367-219-4). Phi Delta Kappa.

Appel, Kenneth I., et al, eds. Contributions to Group Theory. LC 84-18454. (Contemporary Mathematics Ser.: Vol. 33). 42.00 (ISBN 0-8218-5035-0). Am Math.

Appel, L. Lexique des Fruits et Legumes. 133p. (Fr. & Eng.). Date not set. pap. 9.95 (ISBN 0-686-97410-7, M-9238). French & Eur.

Appel, Libby. Mask Characterization: An Acting Process. LC 81-9157. 136p. (Orig.). 1982. pap. 12.95x (ISBN 0-8093-1039-2). S Ill U Pr.

Appel, Libby & Flachmann, Michael. Shakespeare's Lovers: A Text for Performance & Analysis. LC 82-5444. 156p. 1982. pap. 5.95x (ISBN 0-8093-1072-4). S Ill U Pr.

Appel, Louise. Lexique Anglais-Francais Des Fruits et Legumes. rev. ed. 128p. (Eng. & Fr.). 1974. pap. 9.95 (ISBN 0-686-56897-4, M-6007). French & Eur.

Appel, M., jt. auth. see Cetron, M.

Appel, M. H. & Goldberg, L., eds. Equilibration: Theory, Research & Application. LC 77-5010. (Illus.). 234p. 1977. 32.50x (ISBN 0-306-33001-6, Plenum Pr). Plenum Pub.

Appel, M. J. & Gillespie, J. H. Canine Distemper Virus. Bd. with Marburg Virus. Siegert, R. LC 2-79603. (Virology Monographs: Vol. 11). (Illus.). 159p. 1972. 27.00 (ISBN 0-387-81059-5). Springer-Verlag.

Appel, Marcia, jt. auth. see Cetron, Marvin.

Appel, Marsha C. Illustration Index. 4th ed. LC 79-26091. 468p. 1980. lib. bdg. 28.50 (ISBN 0-8108-1273-8). Scarecrow.

--Illustration Index V: 1977-1981. LC 83-15201. 421p. 1984. 27.50 (ISBN 0-8108-1656-3). Scarecrow.

Appel, Martin, jt. auth. see Munson, Thurman.

Appel, Martin, jt. auth. see Seaver, Tom.

Appel, Odette M, jt. auth. see Sobieszek, Robert.

Appel, Odette M., jt. auth. see Sobieszek, Robert A.

Appel, Paul P. Sacco-Vanzetti Case: A Transcript of the Record of the Trial of Nicola Sacco & Bartolomeo Vanzetti in the Courts of Massachusetts & Subsequent Proceedings, 1920-27, 6 Vols. 2nd ed. (Illus.). 1969. Set. 250.00x (ISBN 0-911858-01-6). Appel.

Appel, Paul P., ed. Homage to Sherwood Anderson. LC 77-105304. 1970. lib. bdg. 12.00x (ISBN 0-911858-02-4). Appel.

Appel, Richard G. The Music of the Bay Psalm Book: Ninth Edition (1698) LC 75-34880. (I.S.A.M. Monographs: No. 5). 44p. (Orig.). 1975. pap. 4.00 (ISBN 0-914678-04-3). Inst Am Music.

Appel, Robert. The Rebound System. LC 9-10240. (Illus.). 144p. 1982. pap. 8.61i (ISBN 0-06-091024-0, CN1024, CN). Har-Row.

Appel, Theodore. Life & Work of John Williamson Nevin. LC 71-83409. (Religion in America, Ser. 1). 1969. Repr. of 1889 ed. 30.00 (ISBN 0-405-00203-3). Ayer Co Pubs.

Appel, Willa. Cults in America: Programmed for Paradise. LC 82-15538. 212p. 1985. pap. 7.95 (ISBN 0-03-004997-0, Owl Bks.). HR&W.

Appel, William. The Watcher Within. 1983. pap. 2.50 (ISBN 0-449-12548-3, GM). Fawcett.

--Water World. 224p. (Orig.). 1983. pap. 2.75 (ISBN 0-449-12537-8, GM). Fawcett.

--The White Jaguar. 224p. 1985. 16.95 (ISBN 0-931933-02-1). Richardson & Steirman.

Appelbaum, Arlene, ed. see Ilse, Sherokee.

Appelbaum, Eileen. Back to Work: Determinants of Women's Successful Re-entry. 160p. 1981. 23.00 (ISBN 0-86569-076-6). Auburn Hse.

Appelbaum, Elie, jt. auth. see Scheffman, David T.

Appelbaum, Judith & Evans, Nancy. How to Get Happily Published: A Complete & Candid Guide. 288p. 1982. pap. 6.95 (ISBN 0-452-25475-2, Z5475, Plume). NAL.

Appelbaum, Neil. Is There a Hole in Your Head? (Illus.). (gr. k-3). 1963. 6.95 (ISBN 0-8392-3012-5). Astor-Honor.

Appelbaum, Richard P. Theories of Social Change. LC 81-80801. 1970. pap. text ed. 14.50 (ISBN 0-395-30558-6). HM.

Appelbaum, Robert H. Geological & Engineering Mapping of the Subsurface. (Illus.). 225p. 1985. price not set lab manual (ISBN 0-88746-066-6). Intl Human Res.

Appelbaum, S., ed. see Wurts, Richard.

Appelbaum, Samuel, et al. The Way They Play, Bk. 13. (Illus.). 288p. (gr. 9-12). 12.95 (ISBN 0-86622-009-7, Z-76). Paganiniana Pubns.

Appelbaum, Stanley. The Chicago World's Fair of Eighteen Ninety-Three: A Photographic Record. (Illus.). 144p. (Orig.). 1980. pap. 6.00 (ISBN 0-486-23990-X). Dover.

--The Chicago World's Fair of Eighteen Ninety-Three: A Photographic Record. (Illus.). 16.50 (ISBN 0-8446-5729-8). Peter Smith.

--The Hollywood Musical: A Picture Quiz Book. (Illus., Orig.). 1974. pap. 4.50 (ISBN 0-486-23008-2). Dover.

--Silent Movies: A Picture Quiz Book. 1974. pap. 3.50 (ISBN 0-486-23054-6). Dover.

Appelbaum, Stanley & Camner, James. Stars of the American Musical Theater in Historic Photographs: 361 Portraits from the 1860s to 1950. (Illus.). 176p. 1981. pap. 9.95 (ISBN 0-486-24209-9). Dover.

Appelbaum, Stanley & Cirker, Hayward. The Movies: A Picture Quiz Book. (Illus.). 128p. (Orig.). 1972. pap. 4.95 (ISBN 0-486-20222-4). Dover.

Appelbaum, Stanley, ed. French Satirical Drawings from "L'Assiette au Beurre". LC 77-84742. (Illus.). 1978. pap. 7.95 (ISBN 0-486-23583-1). Dover.

--Great Actors & Actresses of the American Stage in Historic Photographs: 331 Protraits from 1850-1950. (Performing Arts: Drama, Film & Dance Ser.). 144p. (Orig.). 1984. pap. 9.95 (ISBN 0-486-24555-1). Dover.

--The New York Stage: Famous Productions in Photographs. LC 75-14558. (Illus.). 160p. (Orig., 148 photos, 1883-1939). 1976. pap. 8.95 (ISBN 0-486-23241-7). Dover.

--Scenes from the Nineteenth-Century Stage in Advertising Woodcuts. (Pictorial Archive Ser.). (Illus.). 176p. 1977. pap. 6.95 (ISBN 0-486-23434-7). Dover.

--Scenes from the Nineteenth-Century Stage in Advertising Woodcuts. 13.25 (ISBN 0-8446-5552-X). Peter Smith.

--Show Songs from 'The Black Crook' to 'The Red Mill' (Illus.). 320p. 1974. 9.95 (ISBN 0-486-23085-6). Dover.

Appelbaum, Stanley, ed. & tr. from Ger. Simplicissimus: One-Hundred Eighty Satirical Drawings from the Famous German Weekly. LC 74-79171. (Illus.). 192p. 1975. 14.95 (ISBN 0-486-23099-6); pap. 8.95 (ISBN 0-486-23098-8). Dover.

Appelbaum, Stanley & Kelly, Richard, eds. Great Drawings & Illustrations from Punch Eighteen Forty-One to Nineteen Hundred-One: One Hundred Ninety-Two Works by Leech, Keene, du Maurier, May & 21 Others. (Illus.). 144p. (Orig.). 1981. pap. 6.95 (ISBN 0-486-24110-6). Dover.

Appelbaum, Stanley, ed. see Grandville, J. J.

Appelbaum, Stanley, ed. see Posada, Jose G.

Appelbaum, Stanley, tr. see Amman, Jost & Sachs, Hans.

Appelbaum, Stanley, tr. see Beveridge, June.

Appelbaum, Stanley, tr. see Brahms, Johannes.

Appelbaum, Stanley, tr. see Braque, Georges.

Appelbaum, Stanley, tr. see Cocteau, Jean.

Appelbaum, Stanley, tr. see Durer, Albrecht.

Appelbaum, Stanley, tr. see Grosz, George.

Appelbaum, Stanley, tr. see Schubert, Franz.

Appelbaum, Stanley, tr. see Schumann, Robert.

Appelbaum, Stanley, tr. see Seurat, Georges.

Appelbaum, Stephen. Effecting Change in Psychotherapy. LC 81-65786. 240p. 1981. 25.00 (ISBN 0-87668-452-5). Aronson.

Appelbaum, Stephen, ed. The Anatomy of Change. LC 77-5382. (Illus.). 334p. 1977. 29.50x (ISBN 0-306-31002-3, Plenum Pr). Plenum Pub.

Appelbaum, Steven. Stress Management for Health Care Professionals. LC 80-25213. 487p. 1981. text ed. 29.95 (ISBN 0-89443-332-6). Aspen Systems.

Appelbaum, Steven & Rohrs, Walter F. Time Management for Health Care Professionals. LC 81-3512. 260p. 1981. text ed. 29.50 (ISBN 0-89443-378-4). Aspen Systems.

Appelfeld, Aharon. The Age of Wonders. Bilu, Dalya, tr. from Hebrew. LC 81-47318. 224p. 1981. 12.95 (ISBN 0-87923-402-4). Godine.

--The Age of Wonders. 1983. pap. 3.95 (ISBN 0-671-45858-2). WSP.

--Badenheim Nineteen Thirty-Nine. (General Ser.). 1981. lib. bdg. 11.95 (ISBN 0-8161-3205-4, Large Print Bks). G K Hall.

--Badenheim, Nineteen Thirty-Nine. Bilu, Dalya, tr. from Hebrew. LC 80-66192. 160p. 1980. 12.95 (ISBN 0-87923-342-7). Godine.

--Badenheim Nineteen Thirty-Nine. Bilu, Dalya, tr. 208p. 1981. pap. 3.50 (ISBN 0-671-43592-2). WSP.

--The Retreat. Bilu, Dalya, tr. 164p. 1984. 12.95 (ISBN 0-525-24237-6, 01258-370). Dutton.

--The Retreat. (Penguin Fiction Ser.). 176p. 1985. pap. 5.95 (ISBN 0-14-007660-3). Penguin.

--Tzili: The Story of a Life. 192p. 1984. pap. 4.95 (ISBN 0-14-007058-3). Penguin.

Appelgate, Ray D., ed. Trolleys & Streetcars on American Picture Postcards. LC 78-64854. (Illus.). 1979. pap. 5.00 (ISBN 0-486-23749-4). Dover.

Appelhof, Mary. Nomad Shelves. (Illus.). 14p. (Orig.). 1977. pap. 3.50 (ISBN 0-942256-02-6). Flower Pr.

--Vermicomposting: Selected Articles. 32p. 1982. 10.00x (ISBN 0-942256-04-2). Flower Pr.

--Workshop on the Role of Earthworms in the Stabilization of Organic Residues: Proceedings, Vol. I. LC 81-65289. 340p. 1981. pap. 25.00x (ISBN 0-939294-07-9). Flower Pr.

--Workshop on the Role of Earthworms in the Stabilization of Organic Residues, Vol. 1. (Orig.). pap. 25.00 (TD-772-W6). Beech Leaf.

--Worms Eat My Garbage. LC 82-242012. (Illus., Orig.). 1982. pap. 6.95 (ISBN 0-942256-03-4). Flower Pr.

Appell, Allen. A Practical Approach to Human Behavior to Business. 1984. text ed. 24.95 (ISBN 0-675-20087-3). Additional supplements may be obtained from publisher. Merrill.

Appell, G. N. Ethical Dilemmas in Anthropological Inquiry: A Case Book. 1978. 15.00 (ISBN 0-918456-24-X, Crossroads). African Studies Assn.

Appell, G. N. & Wright, Leigh R. The Status of Social Science Research in Borneo. (Data Papers: No. 109). 131p. 1979. pap. 5.75 (ISBN 0-87727-109-7). Cornell SE Asia.

Appell, G. N., ed. The Societies of Borneo: Explorations in the Theory of Cognatic Social Structure. 1976. pap. 4.00 (ISBN 0-686-36568-2). Am Anthro Assn.

Appell, Paul, et al. Theorie Des Fonctions Algebriques et Leurs Integrales, Vol. 1. 3rd ed. LC 72-114210. 1977. text ed. 29.50 (ISBN 0-8284-0285-X). Chelsea Pub.

--Theorie Des Fonctions Algebriques et Leurs Integrales: Volume II. LC 72-114210. text ed. 25.00 (ISBN 0-8284-0299-X). Chelsea Pub.

Appelman, D. Ralph. Science of Vocal Pedagogy: Theory & Application. LC 67-10107. (Illus.). 448p. 1967. 27.50x (ISBN 0-253-35110-3); companion cassettes of 3 tapes 17.50 (ISBN 0-253-35115-4); Tape 1. 6.95 (ISBN 0-253-35112-X); Tape 2. 6.95 (ISBN 0-253-35113-8); Tape 3. 6.95 (ISBN 0-253-35114-6). Ind U Pr.

Appelman, Henry D. Pathology of the Esophagus, Stomach & Duodenum. (Contemporary Issues in Surgical Pathology Ser.: Vol. 4). (Illus.). 287p. 1984. text ed. 49.50 (ISBN 0-443-08219-7). Churchill.

Appelman, Hyman. Appelman's Outlines & Illustrations. (Pocket Pulpit Library). 128p. 1981. pap. 2.95 (ISBN 0-8010-0072-6). Baker Bk.

--Seeds for Sermons. (Sermon Outline Ser.). 1980. pap. 1.95 (ISBN 0-8010-0026-2). Baker Bk.

--Sermon Outlines on Key Bible Themes. (Sermon Outline Ser.). pap. 1.95 (ISBN 0-8010-0003-3). Baker Bk.

--Sermons on Evangelism. (Pocket Pulpit Library). 96p. 1981. pap. 1.95 (ISBN 0-8010-0068-8). Baker Bk.

Appelqvist, L. A. & Ohlson, R., eds. Rapeseed. 391p. 1973. 104.25 (ISBN 0-444-40892-4). Elsevier.

Appels, A. & Falger, P., eds. The Role of Psychosocial Factors in the Pathogenesis of Coronary Heart Disease, 1980. (Journal: Psychotherapy & Psychosomatics: Vol. 34, No. 2-3). (Illus.). iv, 160p. 1981. pap. 17.50 (ISBN 3-8055-2286-X). S Karger.

Appelt, Douglas E. Planning English Sentences. (Studies in Natural Language Processing). 200p. Date not set. price not set (ISBN 0-521-30115-7). Cambridge U Pr.

Appelt, T. C., compiled by. Vest Pocket German Dictionary. rev. ed. 344p. pap. 2.95 (ISBN 0-317-19727-4). New Century.

Appenzeller, Herb. From the Gym to the Jury. (Illus.). 1970. 18.50 (ISBN 0-87215-068-2). Michie Co.

--The Right to Participate: The Law & Individuals with Handicapping Conditions in Physical Education & Sports. 421p. 1983. 25.00 (ISBN 0-87215-620-6). Michie Co.

Appenzeller, Herb & Appenzeller, Thomas. Sports & the Courts. 423p. 1980. 18.50 (ISBN 0-87215-243-X). Michie Co.

Appenzeller, Herb, et al. Sports & the Law. (Illus.). 200p. 1984. pap. text ed. 4.95 (ISBN 0-314-79386-0). West Pub.

--Sports & the Law. 100p. 1984. write for info. tchr's. resource guide avail. (ISBN 0-314-79387-9). West Pub.

Appenzeller, Herbert. Athletics & the Law. 270p. 1975. 18.50 (ISBN 0-87215-179-4). Michie Co.

--Physical Education & the Law. 185p. 1978. 18.50 (ISBN 0-87215-210-3). Michie Co.

Appenzeller, O. Autonomic Nervous System. 3rd ed. 524p. 1982. 110.75 (ISBN 0-444-80392-0). Elsevier.

Appenzeller, O., ed. Health Aspects of Endurance Training. (Medicine & Sport: Vol. 12). 1978. 20.50 (ISBN 3-8055-2960-0). S Karger.

Appenzeller, Otto, jt. auth. see Raskin, Neil H.

Appenzeller, Otto & Atkinson, Ruth A., eds. Sports Medicine: Fitness, Training, Injuries. 2nd ed. LC 83-3471. (Illus.). 460p. 1983. pap. text ed. 24.50 (ISBN 0-8067-0132-3). Urban & S.

Appenzeller, Otto, tr. see Mumenthaler, Marco.

Appenzeller, Thomas, jt. auth. see Appenzeller, Herb.

Appere, Guy. Dialogue with God. LC 81-83729. 72p. 1982. pap. 1.95 (ISBN 0-8361-1984-3). Herald Pr.

Apperson, G. Jane Austen Dictionary. LC 68-24894. (Studies in Fiction, No. 34). 1969. Repr. of 1932 ed. lib. bdg. 49.95x (ISBN 0-8383-0909-7). Haskell.

Apperson, G. L. English Proverbs & Proverbial Phrases. 59.95 (ISBN 0-8490-0116-1). Gordon Pr.

--Jane Austen Dictionary. LC 73-15997. 1932. lib. bdg. 17.50 (ISBN 0-8414-2922-7). Folcroft.

Appert, Robert. New Century World Wide German Dictionary. LC 82-81061. (Ger.). 1966. pap. 5.95 (ISBN 0-8329-9687-4); 9.95 (ISBN 0-8329-0144-X). New Century.

Appia, Adolphe. Music & Art of the Theatre. Hewitt, Barnard, ed. LC 62-20172. (Bks. in the Theatre: No. 3). 1962. pap. 20.00 (ISBN 0-87024-018-8). U of Miami Pr.

Appia, Adolpho. The Work of Living Art & Man is the Measure of All Things. 1962. 15.00x (ISBN 0-87024-305-5). U of Miami Pr.

Appiah, Anthony. Assertion & Conditionals. (Cambridge Studies in Philosophy). 250p. Date not set. price not set (ISBN 0-521-30411-3). Cambridge U Pr.

Appiah, Peggy. Tales of An Ashanti Father. LC 80-2697. (Illus.). 160p. (gr. 2-7). 1981. 8.95 (ISBN 0-233-95927-0). Andre Deutsch.

Appiah-Kubi, Kofi. Man Cures, God Heals: Religion & Medical Practice Among the Akans of Ghana. LC 81-65019. (Illus.). 188p. 1981. text ed. 18.95x (ISBN 0-86598-011-X). Allanheld.

--Man Cures, God Heals: Religion & Medical Practice Among the Akans of Ghana. (Orig.). 1981. pap. 10.95 (ISBN 0-377-00114-7). Friend Pr.

Appiah-Kubi, Kofi & Torres, Sergio, eds. African Theology En Route: Papers from the Pan-African Conference of Third World Theologians, December 17-23, 1977, Accra, Ghana. LC 78-10604. 184p. (Orig.). 1978. pap. 9.95 (ISBN 0-88344-010-5). Orbis Bks.

Appian. Roman History, 4 Vols. (Loeb Classical Library: No. 2-5). 12.50x ea. Vol. 1 (ISBN 0-674-99002-1). Vol. 2 (ISBN 0-674-99004-8). Vol. 3 (ISBN 0-674-99005-6). Vol. 4 (ISBN 0-674-99006-4). Harvard U Pr.

Appice, Carmine. The Updated Realistic Rock Drum Method. (Illus.). 76p. (Orig.). 1979. pap. 7.95 (ISBN 0-89705-012-6). Almo Pubns.

Appignanesi, Lisa. Femininity & the Creative Imagination: A Study of Henry James, Robert Musil & Marcel Proust. 1973. 12.95x (ISBN 0-8464-0407-9). Beekman Pubs.

Appignanesi, Lisa, tr. see Bielski, Nella.

Appignanesi, Richard. Lenin for Beginners. LC 78-20408. (Illus.). 1979. pap. 3.95 (ISBN 0-394-73715-6). Pantheon.

Appignanesi, Richard & Zarate, Oscar. Freud for Beginners. LC 79-1891. 1979. pap. 4.95 (ISBN 0-394-73800-4). Pantheon.

Appignanesi, Richard, jt. auth. see Wesker, Arnold.

Appignesi, Richard. Italia Perversa. (Stalin's Orphans Ser.: Pt. 1). 296p. 1983. cancelled (ISBN 0-906495-46-6). Writers & Readers.

Appius & Virginia. Appius & Virginia. LC 70-133632. (The Tudor Facsimile Texts. Old English Plays: No. 47). Repr. of 1908 ed. 49.50 (ISBN 0-404-53347-7). AMS Pr.

Applbaum, Ronald & Hart, Roderick. MASSCOM: Modules in Mass Communication Comparative Broadcasting Systems. (Orig.). 1984. pap. text ed. 3.95 (ISBN 0-574-22603-6, 13-5603). SRA.

--MASSCOM: Modules in Mass Communication-Careers in Mass Media. (Orig.). 1984. pap. text ed. 3.95 (ISBN 0-574-22604-4, 13-5604). SRA.
--MASSCOM: Modules in Mass Communication-History of Mass Media. (Orig.). 1984. pap. text ed. 3.95 (ISBN 0-574-22607-9, 13-5607). SRA.
--MASSCOM: Modules in Mass Communication-Mass Media & Future Technologies. (Orig.). 1984. pap. text ed. 3.95 (ISBN 0-574-22606-0, 13-5606). SRA.
--MASSCOM: Modules in Mass Communication-Mass Media & Popular Culture. (Orig.). 1984. pap. text ed. 3.95 (ISBN 0-574-22602-8, 13-5602). SRA.
--Masscom: Modules in Mass Communication-Mass Media Criticism. LC 13-5601. 1984. pap. text ed. 3.95 (ISBN 0-574-22601-X). SRA.
--MASSCOM: Modules in Mass Communication-Mass Media Law. (Orig.). 1984. pap. text ed. 3.95 (ISBN 0-574-22605-2, 13-5605). SRA.
--MODCOM: Business & Professional Speech. Rev. ed. (Orig.). 1984. pap. text ed. 3.50 (ISBN 0-574-22595-1, 13-5595). SRA.
--Modcom: Communication & Conflict. 2nd ed. LC 13-5588. 1984. pap. text ed. 3.25 (ISBN 0-574-22586-2). SRA.
--MODCOM: Nature of Human Communications. 2nd ed. 1984. SRA.
--Modcom: Orientations to Organizational Communication. LC 13-5533. 1984. pap. text ed. 3.25 (ISBN 0-574-22533-1). SRA.
--MODCOM: Speech Criticism. 2nd ed. 1984. pap. text ed. 3.25 (ISBN 0-574-22599-4, 13-5599). SRA.
Applbaum, Ronald, ed. see Campbell, John A.
Applbaum, Ronald, ed. see Chesebro & Hamsher.
Applbaum, Ronald, ed. see Frandsen & Benson.
Applbaum, Ronald, ed. see Leathers.
Applbaum, Ronald, ed. see Measell.
Applbaum, Ronald, ed. see Motley.
Applbaum, Ronald, ed. see Osborn.
Applbaum, Ronald, et al. The Process of Group Communication. 2nd ed. LC 78-18501. 352p. 1979. text ed. 19.95 (ISBN 0-574-22710-5, 13-5710); instr's guide avail. (ISBN 0-574-22711-3, 13-5711). SRA.
Applbaum, Ronald L. & Anatol, Karl W. Effective Oral Communication in Business & the Professions. 352p. 1982. 21.95 (ISBN 0-574-22590-0, 13-5591); tchr's guide avail. (ISBN 0-574-22591-9). SRA.
Apple Computer, Inc. Staff. Apple IIe Technical Reference Manual. 1985. write for info. (ISBN 0-201-17720-X). Addison-Wesley.
--The Applesoft Tutorial. 1985. 29.95 (ISBN 0-201-17724-2). Addison-Wesley.
--BASIC Programming with ProDOS. 1985. 29.95 (ISBN 0-201-17721-8). Addison-Wesley.
Apple, David F. & Cantwell, John D. Medicine for Sport. (Illus.). 1980. 28.95 (ISBN 0-8151-1422-2). Year Bk Med.
Apple, David J. & Rabb, Maurice F. Clinicopathologic Correlation of Ocular Disease: A Text & Stereoscopic Atlas. 2nd ed. LC 78-15635. 1979. text ed. 116.00 (ISBN 0-8016-0272-6). Mosby.
Apple, J. Lawrence & Smith, Ray F., eds. Integrated Pest Management. LC 76-17549. (Illus.). 213p. 1976. 32.50x (ISBN 0-306-30929-7, Plenum Pr). Plenum Pub.
Apple, J. M. Plant Layout & Materials Handling. 3rd ed. LC 77-75127. (Illus.). 600p. 1977. 40.95x (ISBN 0-471-07171-4). Wiley.
Apple, James M. Material Handling Systems Design. (Illus.). 656p. 1972. 51.50 (ISBN 0-471-06652-4, Pub. by Wiley-Interscience). Wiley.
Apple, Jody L. Hermeneutical Agnosticism: A Critique of Subjectivism in Biblical Interpretation. LC 84-62067. 195p. (Orig.). 1985. pap. 7.95 (ISBN 0-931247-00-4). New Testament Christ Pr.
Apple, Max. Free Agents. LC 83-48810. 224p. 1984. 13.94 (ISBN 0-06-015282-6, HarpT). Har-Row.
--Free Agents. LC 83-48810. 224p. 1985. pap. 5.72i (ISBN 0-06-091140-9, CN 1140, CN). Har-Row.
--The Oranging of America & Other Stories. 1981. pap. 4.95 (ISBN 0-14-005849-4). Penguin.
--The Oranging of America & Other Stories. 1976. 10.95 (ISBN 0-670-52801-3, Grossman). Viking.
--Three Stories. 1983. signed limited ed. 55.00 (ISBN 0-939722-11-9). Pressworks.
Apple, Max, et al. Studies in English. (Rice University Studies: Vol. 61, No. 1). 150p. (Orig.). 1975. pap. 10.00x (ISBN 0-89263-223-2). Rice Univ.
Apple, Michael. Education & Power. 226p. 1985. pap. 7.95 (ISBN 0-7448-0030-7, Ark Paperbacks). Routledge & Kegan.
Apple, Michael W. Education & Power: Reproduction & Contradiction in Education. LC 81-19920. 218p. 1982. 26.95x (ISBN 0-7100-0977-1). Routledge & Kegan.
--Ideology & Curriculum. (Routledge Education Bks.). 212p. 1979. 21.95x (ISBN 0-7100-0136-3); pap. 9.95x (ISBN 0-7100-0686-1). Routledge & Kegan.
--Ideology & Curriculum. (Education Bks.). 1979. 18.00x (ISBN 0-7100-0136-3). Routledge & Kegan.
Apple, Michael W., ed. Cultural & Economic Reproduction in Education. (Routledge Educaton Bks.). 350p. 1982. 27.95x (ISBN 0-7100-0845-7); pap. 12.95x (ISBN 0-7100-0846-5). Routledge & Kegan.
Apple, Michael W., jt. ed. see Haubrich, Vernon F.
Apple, Michael W., et al. Educational Evaluation: Analysis & Responsibility. LC 73-17611. 1974. 24.25x (ISBN 0-8211-0011-4); 10 or more copies 22.25x ea. McCutchan.
Apple, Peg, jt. auth. see Apple, Russ.
Apple, Russ & Apple, Peg. Land, Lili'uokalani & Annexation. 1979. pap. 4.95 (ISBN 0-914916-40-8). Topgallant.
Apple, Victor, II. Tom Swift the Astral Fortress. 13.95 (ISBN 0-88411-461-9, Pub. by Aeonian Pr). Amereon Ltd.
Apple, W. Michael & Weis, Lois, eds. Ideology & Practice in Schooling. 320p. 1983. 34.95 (ISBN 0-87722-295-9); pap. 12.95 (ISBN 0-87722-313-0). Temple U Pr.
Applebaum, Edward L. & Bruce, David L. Tracheal Intubation. LC 75-19837. (Illus.). 130p. 1976. text ed. 13.95 (ISBN 0-7216-1311-X). Saunders.
Applebaum, Edward L., ed. Reader in Technical Services. LC 72-87717. 284p. 1973. 28.50 (ISBN 0-313-24048-5, ZRP/). Greenwood.
Applebaum, Eleanor G. & Firestein, Stephen, eds. A Genetic Counseling Casebook. LC 82-48605. 320p. 1983. 19.95 (ISBN 0-02-900860-3). Free Pr.
Applebaum, Herbert. Blue Chips. LC 85-70680. 180p. 1985. 14.95 (ISBN 0-931494-68-0); pap. 7.95 (ISBN 0-931494-67-2). Brunswick Pub.
Applebaum, Herbert, ed. Work in Market & Industrial Societies. (Anthropology of Work Ser.). 352p. 1984. 39.50x (ISBN 0-87395-810-1); pap. 10.95x (ISBN 0-87395-811-X). State U NY Pr.
--Work in Non-Market & Transitional Societies. LC 83-4970. (Anthropology of Work Ser.). 398p. 1983. 39.50x (ISBN 0-87395-774-1); pap. 10.95x (ISBN 0-87395-775-X). State U NY Pr.
Applebaum, Herbert A. Royal Blue: The Culture of Construction Workers. LC 80-18487. 1981. pap. text ed. 9.95 (ISBN 0-03-057309-2, HoltC). HR&W.
Applebaum, Irwyn. The World According to Beaver: The Official Guide. LC 83-46004. (Illus.). 1984. pap. 7.95 (ISBN 0-553-34095-6). Bantam.
Applebaum, Paul, jt. auth. see Gutheil, Thomas.
Applebaum, Ronald & Hart, Roderick. MODCOM: Persuasive Speaking. 2nd ed. 1984. pap. text ed. 3.25 (ISBN 0-574-22566-8, 13-5513). SRA.
Applebaum, S., tr. see Tcherikover, Victor.
Applebaum, Sada, jt. auth. see Applebaum, Samuel.
Applebaum, Samuel & Applebaum, Sada. Way They Play, Bk. 1. (Illus.). 380p. 1972. 12.95 (ISBN 0-87666-437-0, Z-1). Paganiniana Pubns.
--The Way They Play, Bk. 2. (Illus.). 384p. 1983. 12.95 (ISBN 0-87666-438-9, Z-4). Paganiniana Pubns.
--The Way They Play, Bk. 3. (Illus.). 320p. 1975. 12.95 (ISBN 0-87666-447-8, Z-7). Paganiniana Pubns.
--Way They Play, Bk. 4. (Illus.). 320p. 1975. 12.95 (ISBN 0-87666-448-6, Z-8). Paganiniana Pubns.
Applebaum, Samuel & Roth, Henry. The Way They Play, Bk. 5. (Illus.). 320p. 1978. 12.95 (ISBN 0-87666-449-4, Z-11). Paganiniana Pubns.
--Way They Play, Bk. 6. (Illus.). 352p. 1978. 12.95 (ISBN 0-87666-615-2, Z-29). Paganiniana Pubns.
--The Way They Play, Bk. 7. (Illus.). 288p. 1980. 12.95 (ISBN 0-87666-619-5, Z-33). Paganiniana Pubns.
--The Way They Play, Bk. 8. (Illus.). 288p. 1980. 12.95 (ISBN 0-87666-622-5, Z-34). Paganiniana Pubns.
--The Way They Play, Bk. 9. (Illus.). 285p. (gr. 9-12). 1981. 12.95 (ISBN 0-87666-586-5, Z-56). Paganiniana Pubns.
--The Way They Play, Bk. 10. (Illus.). 253p. (YA) (gr. 9-12). 1982. 12.95 (ISBN 0-87666-595-4, Z-65). Paganiniana Pubns.
Applebaum, Samuel, et al. The Way They Play, Bk. 11. (Illus.). 253p. 1983. 12.95 (ISBN 0-87666-799-X, Z-74). Paganiniana Pubns.
--The Way They Play, Bk. 12. (Illus.). 283p. 1983. 12.95 (ISBN 0-87666-798-1, Z-75). Paganiniana Pubns.
Applebaum, Samuel B. Demineralization by Ion Exchange. LC 68-18653. 1968. 76.00 (ISBN 0-12-058950-8). Acad Pr.
Applebaum, Sharon, jt. auth. see Hirshmann, Linda.
Applebaum, Shimon. Jews & Greeks in Ancient Cyrene. (Illus.). 367p. 1980. text ed. 64.50x (ISBN 90-04-05970-9). Humanities.
Applebaum, Stan & Cox, Victoria. Going My Way? LC 76-8492. (Let Me Read Ser.). (Illus.). (gr. k-3). 1976. pap. 1.65 (ISBN 0-15-231126-2, VoyB). HarBraceJ.
Applebaum, Stanley, ed. Show Songs from the Black Crook to the Red Mill: Original Sheet Music for 60 Songs from 50 Shows, 1866-1906. (Illus.). 15.25 (ISBN 0-8446-5152-4). Peter Smith.
Applebaum, Stanley & Camner, James, eds. Stars of the American Musical Theater in Historic Photographs. 1983. 16.50 (ISBN 0-8446-5933-9). Peter Smith.
Applebaum, Stanley, tr. see Revault, Jacques.
Applebaum, Stanley, tr. see Schumann, Robert.
Applebaum, Steven H., jt. auth. see Certo, Samuel C.
Applebee, Arthur. Contexts for Learning to Write. Farr, Marcia, ed. LC 84-6428. (Writing Research Ser.). 224p. 1984. text ed. 28.50 (ISBN 0-89391-225-5); pap. text ed. 17.95 (ISBN 0-89391-283-2). Ablex Pub.
Applebee, Arthur N. The Child's Concept of Story: Ages Two to Seventeen. LC 77-8309. (Illus.). 1978. lib. bdg. 18.00x (ISBN 0-226-02117-3); pap. 7.00x (ISBN 0-226-02118-1). U of Chicago Pr.
--Tradition & Reform in the Teaching of English: A History. LC 74-82650. 298p. (Orig.). 1974. pap. 10.00 (ISBN 0-8141-5501-4). NCTE.
--Writing in the Secondary School: English & the Content Areas. LC 81-18799. (Research Report Ser.: No. 21). 130p. 1981. pap. 8.50 (ISBN 0-8141-5884-6). NCTE.
Applebee, Jackie. Low-Fat & No-Fat Cooking. (Cooking for Special Diets Ser.). 128p. (Orig.). 1984. pap. 3.95 (ISBN 0-7225-0826-3). Thorsons Pubs.
Applebee, Roger K., jt. auth. see Squire, James R.
Appleberg, Marilyn. I Love New York Guide. 2nd ed. Levine, Charles, ed. (Illus.). 288p. 1985. pap. 7.95 (ISBN 0-02-097230-X, Collier). Macmillan.
Appleberg, Marilyn, compiled by. The I Love New York Guide, 1981. (Illus.). 208p. 1981. pap. 5.95 (ISBN 0-02-097220-2, Collier). Macmillan.
Appleberg, Marilyn J. I Love Boston Guide. (Illus.). 160p. 1983. pap. 6.95 (ISBN 0-02-097300-4, Collier). Macmillan.
--I Love Chicago Guide. (Illus.). 160p. 1982. pap. 4.95 (ISBN 0-02-097190-7, Collier). Macmillan.
--I Love Washington Guide. (Illus.). 160p. 1982. pap. 4.95 (ISBN 0-02-097290-3, Collier). Macmillan.
Appleberg, Marilyn J., ed. I Love Los Angeles Guide. 224p. 1984. 7.95 (ISBN 0-02-097240-7). Macmillan.
Applebury, T. R. Moments with the Master. 1974. pap. 1.50 (ISBN 0-89900-115-7). College Pr Pub.
Appleby. Famine in Tudor & Stuart England. 262p. 1982. 50.00x (ISBN 0-85323-014-5, Pub. by Liverpool Univ England). State Mutual Bk.
Appleby, Andrew B. Famine in Tudor & Stuart England. LC 77-76151. 1978. 20.00x (ISBN 0-8047-0956-4). Stanford U Pr.
Appleby, B. L. Elsevier's Dictionary of Commercial Terms & Phrases: In English, German, Spanish, French & Swedish. 1984. 181.50 (ISBN 0-444-42270-6, I-251-84). Elsevier.
Appleby, David P. The Music of Brazil. (Illus.). 223p. 1983. text ed. 25.00x (ISBN 0-292-75068-4). U of Tex Pr.
Appleby, Derek. Horary Astrology: An Introduction to the Astrology of Time. 160p. 1985. pap. 8.95 (ISBN 0-85030-380-X). Newcastle Pub.
Appleby, Ellen, illus. The Three Billy-Goats Gruff. (Easy to Read Folk Tales Ser.). (Illus.). 32p. (gr. k-2). 1985. pap. 1.95 (ISBN 0-590-33449-2); incl. cassette 5.95. Scholastic Inc.
Appleby, Harrison, jt. auth. see Donovan, Michael.
Appleby, Joyce. Capitalism & a New Social Order: The Republican Version of the 1790's. (Anson G. Phelps Lectureship on Early American History Ser.). 132p. 1984. pap. 10.00 (ISBN 0-8147-0583-9). NYU Pr.
--Capitalism & a New Social Order: The Republican Vision of the 1790s. 120p. 1984. pap. 10.00x (ISBN 0-8147-0583-9). NYU Pr.
Appleby, Joyce O. Economic Thought & Ideology in Seventeenth-Century England. LC 77-85527. 1978. text ed. 35.00x (ISBN 0-691-05265-4); pap. 9.95x (ISBN 0-691-00779-9). Princeton U Pr.
Appleby, Judith A. Training Programs & Placement Services. LC 78-17901. (Vocational Education for the Handicapped Ser.). 1978. text ed. 16.95x (ISBN 0-913420-77-8). Olympus Pub Co.
Appleby, Paul H. Citizens As Sovereigns. LC 62-10727. pap. 56.00 (ISBN 0-317-29314-1, 2022378). Bks Demand UMI.
--Policy & Administration. LC 49-9327. 128p. 1975. pap. 5.95 (ISBN 0-8173-4803-4). U of Ala Pr.
Appleby, Robert C. & Burstinger, Irving. The Essential Guide to Management. 161p. 1981. 16.95 (ISBN 0-13-286211-5); pap. 7.95 (ISBN 0-13-286203-4). P-H.
Appleby, William & Fowler, Frederick, eds. Songs for Choirs: A Collection for Mixed Voices. 1972. pap. 6.00 (ISBN 0-19-330158-X). Oxford U Pr.
Appleduck, Chef Cosmo. Chocolate Has No Natural Enemies. 1985. pap. 6.95 (ISBN 0-911505-20-2). Lifecraft.
Applegarth, Albert C. Quakers in Pennsylvania. LC 78-63813. (Johns Hopkins University. Studies in the Social Sciences. Tenth Ser. 1892: 8-9). Repr. of 1892 ed. 11.50 (ISBN 0-404-61076-5). AMS Pr.
--Quakers in Pennsylvania. pap. 9.00 (ISBN 0-384-01765-7). Johnson Repr.
Applegate, jt. auth. see Waldhart.
Applegate & Hanselka. La Junta de los Rios del Norte y Conchos. (Southwestern Studies Ser.: No. 41). (Eng.). 1974. pap. 3.00 (ISBN 0-87404-147-3). Tex Western.
Applegate, Bergen, tr. see Verlaine, Paul.
Applegate, Dorothy. HHH Helpful Homemaker Hints. Applegate, William G., ed. LC 79-55468. (Illus.). 1979. softcover 2.95 (ISBN 0-9602122-3-X). Apple-Gems.
--Mission A-Go-Go. LC 78-73043. (Illus.). 1979. 9.95 (ISBN 0-9602122-2-1). Apple-Gems.
Applegate, Frank G. Indian Stories from the Pueblos: Tales of New Mexico & Arizona. (Beautiful Rio Grande Classics Ser.). 198p. 12.00 (ISBN 0-87380-076-1); pap. 4.00 (ISBN 0-87380-138-5). Rio Grande.
Applegate, Gary. Happiness; It's Your Choice: The Skill Development Theory for Successful Change. 1985. 15.00 (ISBN 0-9614987-0-6). Berringer Pub.
Applegate, Howard G. Environmental Problems of the Borderlands. 1979. pap. 8.00 (ISBN 0-87404-063-9). Tex Western.
Applegate, Howard G. & Bath, C. Richard, eds. Air Pollution along the United States-Mexico Border. LC 74-80108. 1974. 6.00 (ISBN 0-87404-051-5). Tex Western.
Applegate, James L., jt. auth. see Sypher, Howard E.
Applegate, Joseph R. An Outline of the Structure of Shila. LC 58-13941. viii, 71p. 1971. pap. 3.00x (ISBN 0-87950-252-5). Spoken Lang Serv.
Applegate, Kay. The Breakfast Book. LC 75-17486. 1975. 11.95 (ISBN 0-89016-016-3); pap. 3.95 (ISBN 0-89016-015-5). Lightning Tree.
--The Little Book of Baby Foods. LC 78-54220. (Span. & Eng.). 1978. pap. 2.50 (ISBN 0-89016-042-2). Lightning Tree.
Applegate, Minerva & Entrekin, Nina. Case Studies for Students: A Companion to Teaching Ethics in Nursing. 48p. (Orig.). 1984. pap. text ed. 5.95 (ISBN 0-88737-107-8). Natl League Nurse.
--Teaching Ethics in Nursing: A Handbook for Use of the Case Study Approach. 88p. (Orig.). 1984. pap. text ed. 14.95 (ISBN 0-88737-094-2, 41-1963). Natl League Nurse.
Applegate, Rex. Kill or Get Killed. (Illus.). 400p. 1976. 19.95 (ISBN 0-87364-084-5). Paladin Pr.
Applegate, William G., ed. see Applegate, Dorothy.
Applegath, John. Working Free: Practical Alternatives to the Nine to Five Job. 192p. 1982. 13.95 (ISBN 0-8144-5658-8). AMACOM.
Appleman, Jean. The Midas Touch: Dynamics of Market Investment. LC 75-18229. 260p. 1975. pap. 9.95 (ISBN 0-916036-00-6). Am Pub.
Appleman, Jean, jt. auth. see Mirza, Jerome.
Appleman, John A. How to Increase Your Money-Making Power in the 80's. 4th rev. ed. LC 81-66409. 320p. 1981. 12.95 (ISBN 0-8119-0433-4). Fell.
--Insurance Law & Practice. write for info. West Pub.
--Military Tribunals & International Crimes. LC 76-152589. (Illus.). 421p. 1972. Repr. of 1954 ed. lib. bdg. 28.50x (ISBN 0-8371-6022-7, APMT). Greenwood.
Appleman, Milo D. Epitaph for Planet Earth: How to Survive the Approaching End of the Human Species. LC 81-70329. 240p. 1982. 14.95 (ISBN 0-8119-0447-4). Fell.
Appleman, Philip. Darwin's Ark. LC 83-49412. (Illus.). 96p. 1984. 15.00 (ISBN 0-253-11594-9). Ind U Pr.
--Summer Love & Surf: Poems. LC 68-9290. 1968. 7.95 (ISBN 0-8265-1124-4). Vanderbilt U Pr.
Appleman, Philip, ed. Darwin. 2nd ed. (Norton Critical Edition). (Illus.). 1979. 24.95x (ISBN 0-393-01192-5); pap. 8.95x (ISBN 0-393-95009-3). Norton.
Appleman, Philip, ed. see Darwin, Charles.
Appleman, Philip, ed. see Malthus, Thomas R.
Appleman, Solomon. The Jewish Woman in Judaism: Women's Status in Religious Culture. 1979. 7.50 (ISBN 0-682-49431-3). Exposition Pr FL.
Applequist, Douglas E., et al. Introduction to Organic Chemistry. 3rd ed. LC 81-14694. 384p. 1982. 31.50 (ISBN 0-471-05641-3, Pub by Wiley); pap. 8.50 solutions 81p (ISBN 0-471-09416-1). Wiley.
Applequist, Harry A., jt. auth. see Means, Louis E.
Appleton, A. D. Superconducting D. C. Machines. 1984. write for info. Elsevier.
Appleton, A. S., jt. auth. see Bodsworth, Colin.
Appleton, B. R. & Cellar, G. K., eds. Laser & Electron-Beam Interactions with Solids. (Materials Research Society Symposia Ser.: Vol. 4). 812p. 1982. 109.00 (ISBN 0-444-00693-1). Elsevier.
Appleton, D. R., et al. Cell Proliferation in the Gastrointestinal Tract. 428p. text ed. cancelled (ISBN 0-272-79597-6, Pub. by Pitman Bks Ltd UK). Pitman Pub MA.
Appleton, George. Prayers from a Troubled Heart. LC 83-48010. 64p. 1983. pap. 3.50 (ISBN 0-8006-1711-8, 1-1711). Fortress.
--The Quiet Heart: Prayers & Meditations for Each Day of the Year. LC 84-6019. 480p. 1984. pap. 7.95 (ISBN 0-8006-1789-4). Fortress.
Appleton, George, et al, eds. The Oxford Book of Prayer. 1985. 19.95 (ISBN 0-19-213222-9). Oxford U Pr.
Appleton, George A. The Louvre Complete Treatise in Charcoal Drawing with the Lessons by M. Allonge. (The Promotion of the Arts Library Bk.). (Illus.). 139p. 1983. Repr. of 1880 ed. 79.75 (ISBN 0-89901-098-9). Found Class Reprints.
Appleton, I., ed. Leisure, Research & Policy. 1974. 15.00x (ISBN 0-7073-0193-9, Pub. by Scottish Academic Pr Scotland). Columbia U Pr.
Appleton, J., jt. auth. see Goose, D. H.
Appleton, J. D. Labour Economics. 3rd ed. 250p. 1982. pap. text ed. 16.95x (ISBN 0-7121-2703-8). Trans-Atlantic.
Appleton, Jane & Appleton, William. How Not to Split up. LC 77-89874. 1978. 7.95 (ISBN 0-385-13201-8). Doubleday.
Appleton, Jay H. The Experience of Landscape. LC 73-20899. 293p. 1975. 63.95x (ISBN 0-471-03256-5, Pub. by Wiley-Interscience). Wiley.

Appleton, Jon H. & Perera, Ronald C., eds. The Development & Practice of Electronic Music. LC 74-12478. (Illus.). 288p. 1975. 28.95 (ISBN 0-13-207605-5). P-H.

Appleton, Leroy. American Indian Design & Decoration. Orig. Title: Indian Art of the Americas. (Illus.). 1971. pap. 7.95 (ISBN 0-486-22704-9). Dover.

Appleton, Leroy H. American Indian Design & Decoration. Orig. Title: Indian Art of the Americans. (Illus.). 16.75 (ISBN 0-8446-0007-5). Peter Smith.

Appleton, Lilla E. A Comparative Study of the Play Activities of Adult Savages & Civilized Children. LC 75-35062. (Studies in Play & Games). 1976. Repr. of 1910 ed. 14.00x (ISBN 0-405-07913-3). Ayer Co Pubs.

Appleton, Marguerite. A Portrait Album of Four RI Leaders. 1978. 8.95 (ISBN 0-932840-00-0). RI Hist Soc.

Appleton, Marion B., ed. Index of Pacific Northwest Portraits. LC 70-38982. (Pacific Northwest Library Association, Reference Division). 220p. 1972. 20.00x (ISBN 0-295-95179-6). U of Wash Pr.

Appleton, Nicholas & Benevento, Nicole. Cultural Pluralism in Education: Theoretical Foundations. LC 82-12741. (Illus.). 288p. (Orig.). 1983. pap. text ed. 14.95x (ISBN 0-582-28233-0). Longman.

Appleton, Sheldon. Eternal Triangle? Communist China, the United States & the United Nations. 1961. 5.95 (ISBN 0-87013-061-7). Mich St U Pr.

Appleton, Victor. Chaos on Earth. (Tom Swift Ser.: No. 12). (gr. 2-7). 1984. 3.95 (ISBN 0-671-53230-8). Wanderer Bks.

--The Invisible Force. Barish, Wendy, ed. (Tom Swift Ser.: No. 10). 192p. (Orig.). (gr. 3-8). 1983. 8.95 (ISBN 0-671-43958-8); pap. 3.50 (ISBN 0-671-43959-6). Wanderer Bks.

--Planet of Nightmares. Schwartz, Betty, ed. (Tom Swift Ser.: No. 11). 176p. (gr. 3-7). 1984. pap. 3.95 (ISBN 0-671-49924-6). Wanderer Bks.

--Tom Swift: Ark Two. (Tom Swift Ser.: No. 7). (Illus.). 192p. (gr. 3-7). 1982. 8.95 (ISBN 0-671-43952-9); pap. 2.95 (ISBN 0-671-43953-7). Wanderer Bks.

--Tom Swift: Crater of Mystery. Barish, Wendy, ed. (Tom Swift Ser.: No. 8). 192p. (gr. 3-7). 1983. 8.95 (ISBN 0-671-43954-5); pap. 3.95 (ISBN 0-671-43955-3). Wanderer Bks.

--Tom Swift: Gateway to Doom. Barish, Wendy, ed. (Tom Swift Ser.: No. 9). 192p. (gr. 8-10). 1983. 8.95 (ISBN 0-671-43956-1); pap. 3.95 (ISBN 0-671-43957-X). Wanderer Bks.

--The Tom Swift Gift Set, 3 vols. Boxed Set. pap. 7.95 (ISBN 0-317-12430-7). Wanderer Bks.

--Tom Swift: The Alien Probe. (Tom Swift Ser.: No. 3). 192p. (Orig.). (gr. 3-7). 1981. 8.95 (ISBN 0-671-42538-2); pap. 2.95 (ISBN 0-671-42578-1). Wanderer Bks.

--Tom Swift: The City in the Stars. (Tom Swift Ser.: No. 1). 192p. (Orig.). (gr. 3-7). 1981. 8.95 (ISBN 0-671-41120-9); pap. 3.95 (ISBN 0-671-41115-2). Wanderer Bks.

--Tom Swift: The Rescue Mission. (Tom Swift Ser.: No. 6). 192p. (gr. 3-7). 1981. 8.95 (ISBN 0-671-43370-9); pap. 2.95 (ISBN 0-671-43386-5). Wanderer Bks.

--Tom Swift: The Space Fortress. (Tom Swift Ser.: No. 5). 192p. (gr. 3-7). 1981. 8.95 (ISBN 0-671-43369-5); pap. 3.95 (ISBN 0-671-43385-7). Wanderer Bks.

--Tom Swift: The War in Outer Space. (Tom Swift Ser.: No. 4). 192p. (Orig.). (gr. 3-7). 1981. 8.95 (ISBN 0-671-42539-0); pap. 2.95 (ISBN 0-671-42579-X). Wanderer Bks.

Appleton, Victor, II. Tom Swift & His Electronic Electroscope. 13.95 (ISBN 0-88411-462-7, Pub. by Aeonian Pr). Amereon Ltd.

--Tom Swift & His Space Solatron. 13.95 (ISBN 0-88411-457-0, Pub. by Aeonian Pr). Amereon Ltd.

--Tom Swift & His Triphibian Atomicar. 13.95 (ISBN 0-88411-459-7, Pub. by Aeonian Pr). Amereon Ltd.

--Tom Swift Terror on the Moons of Jupiter. 13.95 (ISBN 0-88411-460-0, Pub. by Aeonian Pr). Amereon Ltd.

--Tom Swift the Alien Probe. 13.95 (ISBN 0-88411-464-3, Pub. by Aeonian Pr). Amereon Ltd.

--Tom Swift the City in the Stars. 13.95 (ISBN 0-88411-463-5, Pub. by Aeonian Pr). Amereon Ltd.

--Tom Swift the Rescue Mission. 13.95 (ISBN 0-88411-458-9, Pub. by Aeonian Pr). Amereon Ltd.

--Tom Swift the Water in Outer Space. 12.95 (ISBN 0-88411-465-1, Pub. by Aeonian Pr). Amereon Ltd.

Appleton, William, jt. auth. see Appleton, Jane.

Appleton, William S. Fathers & Daughters. 224p. 1984. pap. 3.50 (ISBN 0-425-06837-4). Berkley Pub.

Appleton, William W. Beaumont & Fletcher: A Critical Study. LC 74-22014. 1974. Repr. of 1956 ed. lib. bdg. 15.00 (ISBN 0-8414-2982-0). Folcroft.

--Cycle of Cathay. 1979. Repr. of 1951 ed. lib. bdg. 18.50x (ISBN 0-374-90277-1). Octagon.

--Madame Vestris & the London Stage. LC 73-10106. (Illus.). 230p. 1974. 25.00x (ISBN 0-231-03794-5). Columbia U Pr.

Appleton, William W., ed. see Cibber, Colley.

Appleton, William W., ed. see Fielding, Henry.

Appleton, William W., ed. see Hill, Aaron & Popple, William.

Appleton, Zuhr R. Ion Beam & Surface Analysis in Plasma Edge Studies. (Nuclear Science Applications Ser.: Section B). 60p. 1984. 21.00 (ISBN 3-7186-0200-8). Harwood Academic.

Applewhite, D., tr. see Villarejo, F. J.

Applewhite, E. J. Washington Itself: An Informal Guide to the Capital of the United States. LC 81-47484. 384p. 1981. 15.50 (ISBN 0-394-51157-3); pap. 8.95 (ISBN 0-394-74875-1). Knopf.

Applewhite, Edgar J., jt. auth. see Fuller, R. Buckminster.

Applewhite, Fuller. A Synergetics Dictionary, 2 vols. 1985. lib. bdg. 450.00 (ISBN 0-8240-8729-1). Garland Pub.

Applewhite, James. Following Gravity. LC 80-21578. 1980. 9.95x (ISBN 0-8139-0885-X). U Pr of Va.

--Forseeing the Journey: Poems. LC 82-17165. 56p. 1983. text ed. 13.95x (ISBN 0-8071-1079-5); pap. 5.95 (ISBN 0-8071-1080-9). La State U Pr.

--Seas & Inland Journeys: Landscape & Consciousness from Wordsworth to Roethke. LC 85-1165. 224p. 1986. text ed. 25.00 (ISBN 0-8203-0795-5). U of Ga Pr.

Applewhite, Karen M. On the Road to Nowhere: A History of Greer, Arizona, 1879-1979. LC 79-54966. (Illus., Orig.). 1979. pap. text ed. 6.95 (ISBN 0-9603472-0-8). Applewhite.

Applewhite, Philip B. Molecular Gods: How Molecules Determine Our Behavior. LC 80-22834. (Illus.). 288p. 1981. 10.95 (ISBN 0-13-599530-2). P-H.

Applewhite, Steven R., et al, eds. Genetic Screening & Counseling-A Multidisciplinary Perspective. (Illus.). 260p. 1981. 19.50x (ISBN 0-398-04080-X). C C Thomas.

Applewhite, Thomas H., ed. Bailey's Industrial Oil & Fat Products, Vol. 3. 448p. 1985. 55.00 (ISBN 0-471-80951-9). Wiley.

Appley, Dee G. & Winder, Alvin E. T-Groups & Therapy Groups in a Changing Society. LC 73-10934. (Jossey-Bass Behavioral Science Ser.). Repr. of 1973 ed. 58.00 (ISBN 0-8357-9350-8, 2013913). Bks Demand UMI.

Appley, Lawrence A. & Irons, Keith L. Manager Manpower Planning: A Professional Management System. 128p. 1981. 16.95 (ISBN 0-8144-5707-X). AMACOM.

Appley, M. H. Adaptation-Level Theory: A Symposium. 1971. 58.00 (ISBN 0-12-059250-9). Acad Pr.

Appleyard, Bryan. The Culture Club: A Crisis in the Arts. 128p. 1984. pap. 6.95 (ISBN 0-571-13279-0). Faber & Faber.

Appleyard, Donald. Planning a Pluralist City: Conflicting Realities in Ciudad Guayana. LC 75-40026. 350p. 1976. text ed. 37.50x (ISBN 0-262-01044-5). MIT Pr.

Appleyard, Donald & Gerson, M. S. Livable Streets. LC 78-54789. 382p. 1981. 27.50 (ISBN 0-520-03689-1, CAL 580); pap. 14.95 (ISBN 0-520-04769-9). U of Cal Pr.

Appleyard, Donald, ed. Conservation of European Cities. (Illus.). 1979. 39.95x (ISBN 0-262-01057-7). MIT Pr.

Appleyard, H. M. Guide to the Identification of Animal Fibres. 124p. 1982. 60.00x (ISBN 0-686-87161-8). State Mutual Bk.

Appleyard, John. De Luna. 1977. lib. bdg. 5.95 (ISBN 0-686-22981-9). Appleyard Agency.

Appleyard, R. T. & Manford, Toby. The Beginning. 239p. 1980. 17.95x (ISBN 0-85564-146-0, Pub. by U of W Austral Pr). Intl Spec Bk.

Appleyard, R. T., ed. Man & His Environment: Octagon Lectures, 1969. 1970. pap. 6.50x (ISBN 0-85564-042-1, Pub. by U of W Austral Pr). Intl Spec Bk.

Appleyard, Rollo. Pioneers of Electrical Communication. facs. ed. LC 68-54322. (Essay Index Reprint Ser). 1930. 24.50 (ISBN 0-8369-0156-8). Ayer Co Pubs.

Appleyard, S. F. Marine Electronic Navigation. (Illus.). 256p. 1980. 34.95X (ISBN 0-7100-0533-4). Routledge & Kegan.

Application Engineering Corporation. Engineering & Application Manual for AEC Companies: Material Handling Division. 214p. 1982. 80.00 (ISBN 0-910447-02-0). Application Eng Corp.

--Engineering & Application Manual for AEC Companies: Water Division. 165p. 1981. 80.00 (ISBN 0-910447-00-4). Application Eng Corp.

Applied Psychology Research Unit. Human Factors in Telephony. 1961. pap. 20.00 (ISBN 0-686-37971-3). Info Gatekeepers.

Applied Research & Development Inc. Staff & Shaffer. Electric Art Gallery. 1985. pap. 29.95 incl. disk (ISBN 0-912677-68-6). Ashton-Tate Bks.

Applied Research Staff & Shaffer. BASIC Booster Library: Apple. 250p. 1985. pap. 29.95 incl. disk (ISBN 0-912677-26-0). Apple IIc-IIe (ISBN 0-912677-51-1). Ashton-Tate Bks.

--Special Effects Library. 1985. Commodore 64 version. pap. 29.95 incl. disk (ISBN 0-912677-27-9). IIc-IIe version (ISBN 0-912677-52-X). Ashton-Tate Bks.

Applied Science Publishers Ltd. London, ed. Biodegradation of Polymers & Synthetic Polymers: Sessions of the 3rd International Biodegradation Symposium. (Illus.). 1976. 26.00x (ISBN 0-85334-708-5, Pub. by Applied Science). Burgess-Intl Ideas.

Appollinaire, Guillaume. Alcools. Pilkington, A. E., ed. (French Text Ser.). 224p. (Fr.). 1970. pap. 9.95 (ISBN 0-631-00710-5). Basil Blackwell.

--Alcools. (Documentation Thematique). (Illus., Fr.). pap. 2.95 (ISBN 0-685-13795-3, 2). Larousse.

--Les Exploits d'un Jeune Don Juan. 1970. 9.95 (ISBN 0-686-51894-2). French & Eur.

Appolloni, et al. La Dori, l'Equisto overo Chi soffre speri, l'erul cinese, Eurodica Ippolito ed Aricia. LC 76-20993. (Italian Opera Ser.: No. II). 400p. 1983. lib. bdg. 83.00 (ISBN 0-8240-4834-2). Garland Pub.

Appollonius of Rhodes. Voyage of Argo. Rieu, Emil V., tr. (Classics Ser.). (Orig.). 1959. pap. 3.95 (ISBN 0-14-044085-2). Penguin.

Apprey, Maurice, jt. auth. see Stein, Howard F.

Apps. Forty Educational Games for the BBC Micro. (Illus.). 204p. (Orig.). 1984. pap. 11.95 (ISBN 0-246-12317-6, Pub. by Granada England). Sheridan.

Apps, D. K., jt. auth. see Ottaway, J. H.

Apps, Jerold. Study Skills for Adults Returning to School. 2nd ed. 240p. 1982. 14.95x (ISBN 0-07-002165-1). McGraw.

Apps, Jerold W. Adult Learner on Campus. 264p. 29.27 (ISBN 0-8428-2206-2). Cambridge Bk.

--Barns of Wisconsin. LC 77-5472. (Illus.). 1977. pap. 10.00 (ISBN 0-915024-14-4). Tamarack Pr.

--Improving Your Writing Skills: A Learning Plan for Adults. 219p. 23.33 (ISBN 0-8428-2203-8). Cambridge Bk.

--Problems in Continuing Education. 1979. text ed. 24.95 (ISBN 0-07-002159-7). McGraw.

--Toward a Working Philosophy of Adult Education. LC 73-7425. (Occassional Papers Ser.). 65p. 1973. pap. 5.00 (ISBN 0-87060-059-1, OCP 36). Syracuse U Cont Ed.

Apps, Jerry. Breweries of Wisconsin, 1840-1980: The Growth & Decline of the Beer Industry. (Illus.). 192p. (Orig.). 1986. pap. 19.95 (ISBN 0-88361-093-0). Stanton & Lee.

--Mills of Wisconsin. LC 80-24684. (Illus., Orig.). 1980. pap. 12.50 (ISBN 0-915024-22-5). Tamarack Pr.

--Skiing into Wisconsin: A Celebration of Winter. (Illus.). 270p. (Orig.). 1985. pap. 10.95 (ISBN 0-9606240-7-4). Pearl-Win.

--The Wild Oak. 204p. (Orig.). 1985. pap. 9.95 (ISBN 0-88361-094-9). Stanton & Lee.

Apps, Patricia. A Theory of Inequality & Taxation. LC 81-3881. (Illus.). 160p. 1982. 37.50 (ISBN 0-521-23437-9). Cambridge U Pr.

Apps, R. L., jt. auth. see Milner, D. R.

Apps, Vince. The Commodore 64 Program Book. 122p. 1984. pap. 12.95 (ISBN 0-946576-06-8, Pub. by Phoenix Pub). David & Charles.

--The MSX Program Book. (Illus.). 144p. 1984. pap. 12.95 (ISBN 0-946576-22-X, Pub. by Phoenix Pub). David & Charles.

--The Texas Program Book: TI 99-4A. 104p. 1984. pap. 12.95 (ISBN 0-946576-00-9, Pub. by Phoenix Pub). David & Charles.

APR Industries Division of Aero Products Research, Inc., ed. The Complete CB Dictionary. 1977. pap. 2.98 (ISBN 0-912682-17-5). Aero Products.

APR Industries Division of Aero Products Research, Inc. FCC Rules & Regulations 1977: Part 95, Citizens Radio Service. 1977. pap. 2.98 (ISBN 0-912682-16-7). Aero Products.

--Official CB Crossword Puzzles for Big Dummy's. (Illus.). (gr. 8 up). 1977. pap. 1.98 (ISBN 0-912682-18-3). Aero Products.

Apraxine, Pierre. Haitian Painting: The Naive Tradition. new ed. (Illus.). 68p. 1973. pap. text ed. 3.75 (ISBN 0-685-56733-8). Am Fed Arts.

Apresjan, Ju. D. Principles & Methods of Contemporary Structural Linguistics. Crockett, Dina B., tr. from Dutch. LC 72-94441. (Janua Linguarum, Ser. Minor: No. 144). (Illus.). 349p. (Orig.). 1973. pap. text ed. 26.00x (ISBN 90-2792-386-8). Mouton.

Apresjan, Yuri D. Lexical Semantics. Lehrman, Alexander, tr. from Rus. (Linguistica Extranea: Studia: No. 13). 450p. 1985. 35.00 (ISBN 0-89720-039-X); pap. 22.50 (ISBN 0-89720-040-3). Karoma.

Apresyan, Y. D., et al. English-Russian Dictionary of Synonyms. 543p. (Eng. & Rus.). 1980. 11.00 (ISBN 0-8285-1973-0, Pub. by Rus Lang Pubs USSR). Imported Pubns.

Aprieto, Virginia L. Fishery Management & Extended Maritime Jurisdiction: The Philippine Tuna Fishery Situation. LC 81-3262. (East-West Environment & Policy Institute Research Report: No. 4). vi, 78p. (Orig.). 1981. pap. text ed. 3.00 (ISBN 0-86638-026-4). E W Center HI.

April, Ernest W., jt. auth. see PreTest Service Inc.

Aprison, M. H., jt. auth. see Agranoff, Bernard W.

Aprison, M. H., jt. ed. see Agranoff, B. W.

Aprison, M. H., jt. ed. see Haber, Bernard.

Apsche, Jack see Axelrod, Saul.

Apsey, Lawrence S. Transforming Power for Peace. (FGC). 86p. 1964. 0.75 (ISBN 0-318-14158-2). Friends Genl Conf.

Apsimon, Hugh. Mathematical Byways: In Ayling, Beeling, & Ceiling. (Recreations in Mathematics Ser.). (Illus.). 1984. 9.95x (ISBN 0-19-853201-6). Oxford U Pr.

Apsimon, J. W. The Total Synthesis of Natural Products, Vol. 5. 550p. 1983. 64.00 (ISBN 0-471-09808-6). Wiley.

Apsimon, John. The Total Synthesis of Natural Products, Vol. 6. LC 72-4075. 291p. 1984. 44.00 (ISBN 0-471-09900-7, Pub. by Wiley-Interscience). Wiley.

Apsimon, John W., ed. The Total Synthesis of Natural Products, 3 vols. LC 72-4075. 1973. Vol. 1, 603p. 59.95x (ISBN 0-471-03251-4); Vol. 2, 754p. 64.50x (ISBN 0-471-03252-2); Vol. 3, 566p. 64.50x (ISBN 0-471-02392-2, Pub. by Wiley-Interscience). Wiley.

--The Total Synthesis of Natural Products, Vol. 4. LC 72-4075. (The Total Synthesis of Natural Products Ser.). 610p. 1981. 71.95x (ISBN 0-471-05460-7, Pub. by Wiley-Interscience). Wiley.

Apsler, Alfred. Sie Kamen aus Deutschen Landen. (Orig., Ger.). 1962. pap. text ed. 4.95x (ISBN 0-89197-408-3). Irvington.

Apstein, C. Die Pyrocysteen der Plankton-Expedition der Humboldt-Stiftung. 1971. Repr. of 1909 ed. 7.00 (ISBN 3-7682-0807-9). Lubrecht & Cramer.

Apstein, C., jt. ed. see Brandt, K.

Apt, K. R., ed. Logics & Models of Concurrent Systems. (NATO ASI Ser.: Series F, Vol. 13). viii, 498p. 1985. 52.00 (ISBN 0-387-15181-8). Springer-Verlag.

Apt, Patricia, ed. Higher Education & the Older Learner: A Special Issue of AHE, Vol. 5, No. 1. 86p. 1980. pap. 9.95 (ISBN 0-89885-063-0). Human Sci Pr.

Apte, Mahadev L. Humor & Laughter: An Anthropological Approach. LC 84-15618. 320p. 1985. text ed. 32.50x (ISBN 0-8014-1720-1); pap. text ed. 14.95x (ISBN 0-8014-9307-2). Cornell U Pr.

Apte, Robert Z., jt. auth. see Friedlander, Walter A.

Apte, Stuart C. Stu Apte's Fishing in the Florida Keys & Flamingo. 3rd ed. LC 76-360969. (Illus.). 96p. 1982. pap. 4.95 (ISBN 0-89317-006-2). Windward Pub.

--Stu Apte's Fishing in the Florida Keys & Flamingo. 3rd ed. (Illus.). 1982. pap. 4.95 (ISBN 0-89317-019-4). Windward Pub.

Apte, V. S. Practical Sanskrit-English Dictionary. rev. ed. (Sanskrit & Eng.). 1978. Repr. 43.50x (ISBN 0-89684-294-0). Orient Bk Dist.

--Sanskrit-English, English-Sanskrit Student's Dictionary, 2 vols. (Sanskrit & Eng.). 45.00 (ISBN 0-685-36176-4). Heinman.

--The Student's English-Sanskrit Dictionary. (Eng. & Sanskrit.). 1974. Repr. 14.00 (ISBN 0-8426-0507-X). Orient Bk Dist.

Apte, Y. S. Linear Multivariable Control Theory. 1981. 9.00 (ISBN 0-07-451512-8). McGraw.

Aptecker, George. Beyond Despair. (Illus.). 72p. 1980. 25.00 (ISBN 0-9604286-0-7). Kahn & Kahan.

Apted, F. I., jt. ed. see Manson-Bahr, P. E.

Apted, M. R., et al, eds. Ancient Monuments & Their Interpretation: Essays Presented to A. J. Taylor. (Illus.). 371p. 1977. 45.00x (ISBN 0-8476-1493-X). Rowman.

Aptekar, Herbert. Anjea. Infanticide, Abortion & Contraception in Savage Society. LC 79-2929. 192p. 1981. Repr. of 1931 ed. 19.25 (ISBN 0-8305-0097-9). Hyperion Conn.

Aptekar, Herbert H. Basic Concepts in Social Case Work. ix, 201p. 1941. 17.50 (ISBN 0-8078-0367-7). U of NC Pr.

Aptekar, Jane. Icons of Justice: Iconography & Thematic Imagery in Book Five of the Faerie Queen. LC 79-79189. (Illus.). 218p. 1969. 30.00x (ISBN 0-231-03246-3). Columbia U Pr.

Apter, D. E. Ghana in Transition. 1972. pap. 12.50x (ISBN 0-691-02166-X). Princeton U Pr.

Apter, David. Politics of Modernization. LC 65-24421. 1965. pap. 2.95 (ISBN 0-226-02347-8, P281, Phoen). U of Chicago Pr.

Apter, David E. Ghana in Transition. 2nd, rev. ed. LC 63-3161. (Illus.). pap. 115.50 (ISBN 0-317-11327-5, 2010013). Bks Demand UMI.

--Introduction to Political Analysis. 1977. text ed. 21.95 (ISBN 0-316-04930-1). Little.

--Political Change. 245p. 1973. 24.50x (ISBN 0-7146-2941-3, BHA 02941, F Cass Co); pap. 9.95x (ISBN 0-7146-4012-3, BHA 00097, F Cass Co). Biblio Dist.

Apter, David E. & Sawa, Nagayo. Against the State: Politics & Social Protest in Japan. LC 83-15338. (Illus.). 1984. 22.50 (ISBN 0-674-00920-7). Harvard U Pr.

Apter, David E., ed. Ideology & Discontent. LC 64-20305. 1964. 24.95 (ISBN 0-02-900760-7). Free Pr.

Apter, Evelyn. Pas de Vacanes pour le Commissaire. LC 82-9670. (Illus.). 40p. (Fr.). (gr. 7-12). 1982. pap. text ed. 1.95 (ISBN 0-88436-908-0, 40285); cassette 12.00. EMC.

Apter, Judith, jt. auth. see Klinghoffer, Arthur J.

Apter, Michael, ed. The Experience of Motivation: The Theory of Psychological Reversals. LC 81-66676. 392p. 1982. 37.50 (ISBN 0-12-058920-6). Acad Pr.

Apter, Michael J. & Westby, George. The Computer in Psychology. LC 72-5711. 309p. 1973. 48.95x (ISBN 0-471-03260-3, Pub. by Wiley-Interscience). Wiley.

Apter, Ronnie. Digging for the Treasure: Translation after Pound. LC 84-47778. (American University Studies IV (English Language & Literature): Vol. 13). 232p. (Orig.). 1985. text ed. 26.00 (ISBN 0-8204-0135-8). P Lang Pubs.

Apter, Steven J. & Conoley, Jane C. Childhood Behavior Disorders & Emotional Disturbance: An Introduction to Teaching Troubled Children. (Illus.). 352p. 1984. 26.95 (ISBN 0-13-130799-1). P-H.

Apter, Steven J., ed. Focus on Prevention: The Education of Children Labeled Emotionally Disturbed. 1978. pap. 5.00x (ISBN 0-8156-8100-3). Syracuse U Pr.

--Troubled Children - Troubled Systems. rev. ed. (Pergamon General Psychology Ser.: No. 104). 285p. 1982. 31.00 (ISBN 0-08-027167-7); pap. 13.95 (ISBN 0-08-027166-9). Pergamon.

Apter, Steven J. & Goldstein, Arnold P., eds. Youth Violence: Programs & Prospects. (Pergamon General Psychology Ser.). (Illus.). 400p. 1985. 35.00 (ISBN 0-08-031922-X, Pub. by P P I). Pergamon.

Apter, T. E. Fantasy Literature: An Approach to Reality. LC 82-47794. 176p. 1982. 20.00x (ISBN 0-253-32101-8). Ind U Pr.

--Thomas Mann: The Devil's Advocate. LC 78-61134. 1979. 25.00x (ISBN 0-8147-0566-9). NYU Pr.

--Virginia Woolf: A Study of Her Novels. LC 78-78175. (The Gotham Library). 1979. Cusa. 27.00x (ISBN 0-8147-0568-5); Cusa. pap. 13.50x (ISBN 0-8147-0569-3). NYU Pr.

Apter, Terri. Why Women Don't Have Wives: Professional Success & Motherhood. 1985. 21.00 (ISBN 0-8052-3958-8). Schocken.

Aptheker, Bettina. The Academic Rebellion in the United States. 256p. 1972. 7.95 (ISBN 0-8065-0288-6). Citadel Pr.

--Big Business & the American University. 1966. pap. 0.40 (ISBN 0-87898-009-1). New Outlook.

--The Morning Breaks: The Trial of Angela Davis. LC 75-1268. 300p. 1975. pap. 3.75 (ISBN 0-7178-0459-3). Intl Pubs Co.

--Woman's Legacy: Essays on Race, Sex, & Class in American History. LC 81-23137. 192p. 1982. pap. 9.50x (ISBN 0-87023-365-3). U of Mass Pr.

Aptheker, Bettina, ed. see Aptheker, Herbert.

Aptheker, Herbert. American Foreign Policy & the Cold War. 1962. 24.00 (ISBN 0-527-02771-5). Kraus Repr.

--American Negro Slave Revolts. LC 77-10450. 1978. Repr. of 1974 ed. 24.00 (ISBN 0-527-03000-7). Kraus Repr.

--American Negro Slave Revolts. 5th ed. LC 83-7063. 416p. 1983. pap. 4.95 (ISBN 0-7178-0605-7). Intl Pubs Co.

--American Revolution, Seventeen Sixty-Three to Seventeen Eighty-Three, Vol. 2. LC 60-9948. (A History of the American People Ser.). 340p. 1960. pap. 3.25 (ISBN 0-7178-0005-9). Intl Pubs Co.

--Annotated Bibliography of the Published Writings of W. E. B. Du Bois. LC 73-13805. 1973. 54.00 (ISBN 0-527-02750-2). Kraus Intl.

--Colonial Era, Vol. 1. 2nd ed. LC 59-11215. (History of the American People Ser.). 158p. 1966. pap. 2.25 (ISBN 0-7178-0033-4). Intl Pubs Co.

--Czechoslovakia & Counter-Revolution: Why the Socialist Countries Intervened. 1969. pap. 0.35 (ISBN 0-87898-032-6). New Outlook.

--A Documentary History of the Negro People in the United States from Colonial Times to 1910. 15.00 (ISBN 0-8065-0346-7). Citadel Pr.

--A Documentary History of the Negro People in the United States, Vol. 3: 1932-1945. 640p. 1974. 17.50 (ISBN 0-8065-0438-2). Citadel Pr.

--Early Years of the Republic, 1783-1793. LC 76-40213. (A History of the American People Ser.: Vol. 3). 177p. (Orig.). 1976. pap. 2.75 (ISBN 0-7178-0471-2). Intl Pubs Co.

--Essays in the History of the American Negro. 2nd ed. 216p. 1964. pap. 2.25 (ISBN 0-7178-0061-X). Intl Pubs Co.

--The Nature of Democracy, Freedom & Revolution. 2nd ed. LC 67-20076. 128p. (Orig.). 1981. pap. 1.95 (ISBN 0-7178-0137-3). Intl Pubs Co.

--The Negro People in America. LC 46-8650. 1946. pap. 10.00 (ISBN 0-527-02770-7). Kraus Repr.

--To Be Free: Studies in American Negro History. LC 48-5693. pap. 64.00 (ISBN 0-317-28070-8, 2025544). Bks Demand UMI.

--The Truth about Hungary. LC 57-2931. 1976. Repr. of 1957 ed. 21.00 (ISBN 0-527-03001-5). Kraus Repr.

--The Unfolding Drama: Studies in U. S. History by Herbert Aptheker. Aptheker, Bettina, ed. LC 78-21025. 188p. 1979. 11.00 (ISBN 0-7178-0560-3); pap. 3.50 (ISBN 0-7178-0501-8). Intl Pubs Co.

--The Urgency of Marxist - Christian Dialogue. LC 73-109081. 1976. Repr. of 1970 ed. 18.00 (ISBN 0-527-03002-3). Kraus Repr.

--The World of C. Wright Mills. LC 60-50975. 1976. Repr. of 1960 ed. 10.00 (ISBN 0-527-03003-1). Kraus Repr.

Aptheker, Herbert, ed. Contributions by W. E. B. Du Bois in Government Publications & Proceedings. LC 80-13063. (The Complete Published Works of W. E. B. Du Bois). 1981. lib. bdg. 70.00 (ISBN 0-527-25292-1). Kraus Intl.

--Documentary History of the Negro People in the United States: Vol. 1 - from Colonial Times Through the Civil War. 1962. pap. 9.95 (ISBN 0-8065-0168-5, 109). Citadel Pr.

--Documentary History of the Negro People in the United States: Vol. 2 - from the Reconstruction Years to the Founding of the National Association for the Advancement of Colored People, 1910. 1964. pap. 9.95 (ISBN 0-8065-0167-7, 160). Citadel Pr.

--A Documentary History of the Negro People in the United States: 1910-1932. 832p. 1973. 17.50 (ISBN 0-8065-0355-6). Citadel Pr.

--Marxism & Democracy. (AIMS Monographs: No. 1). 1965. 6.50x (ISBN 0-391-00435-2). Humanities.

--Nat Turner's Slave Rebellion: Together with the Full Text of the So-Called "Confessions" of Nat Turner Made in Prison in 1831. (AIMS Historical Ser: No. 2). 1966. text ed. 10.45x (ISBN 0-391-00437-9). Humanities.

Aptheker, Herbert, intro. by. Newspaper Columns by W. E. B. Du Bois. (The Complete Published Works of W. E. B. Du Bois Ser.). 1986. lib. bdg. price not set (ISBN 0-527-25347-2). Kraus Intl.

Aptheker, Herbert, ed. Writings by W. E. B. Du Bois in Non-Periodical Literature Edited by Others. LC 81-18607. (The Complete Published Works of W. E. B. Du Bois Ser.). (Orig.). 1982. lib. bdg. 55.00 (ISBN 0-527-25344-8). Kraus Intl.

--Writings by W. E. B. Du Bois in Periodicals Edited by Others, 4 vols. LC 81-17186. (The Complete Published Works of W. E. B. Du Bois). 1982. Set. lib. bdg. 270.00 (ISBN 0-527-25343-X). Kraus Intl.

--Writings in Periodicals Edited by W. E. B. Du Bois: Selections from Phylon. LC 80-13721. (The Complete Published Works of W. E. B. Du Bois Ser.). 1980. lib. bdg. 65.00 (ISBN 0-527-25353-7). Kraus Intl.

--Writings in Periodicals Edited by W. E. B. Du Bois: Selections from The Brownies' Book. LC 80-14063. (The Complete Published Works of W. E. B. Du Bois Ser.). 1980. lib. bdg. 20.00 (ISBN 0-527-25345-6). Kraus Intl.

--Writings in Periodicals Edited by W. E. B. Du Bois: Selections from "The Crisis". LC 82-49048. (The Complete Published Works of W. E. B. Du Bois Ser.). (Orig.). 1983. lib. bdg. 125.00 (ISBN 0-527-25351-0). Kraus Intl.

Aptheker, Herbert, ed. see Du Bois, W. E.

Aptheker, Herbert, ed. see Du Bois, W. E. B.

Aptheker, Herbert, ed. see DuBois, W. E. B.

Aptheker, Herbert, ed. & intro. by see Du Bois, W. E. B.

Aptheker, Herbert, ed. see Du Bois, William E.

Aptheker, Herbert C. Afro-American History: The Modern Era. 1971. 7.95 (ISBN 0-8065-0228-2); pap. 2.95 (ISBN 0-8065-0362-9). Citadel Pr.

Apthorp, Stephen P. Alcohol & Substance Abuse. 288p. 1985. pap. 16.95 (ISBN 0-8192-1372-1). Morehouse.

Apthorp, W. F. Musicians & Music Lovers. 59.95 (ISBN 0-8490-0684-8). Gordon Pr.

--The Opera, Past & Present. 59.95 (ISBN 0-8490-0770-4). Gordon Pr.

Apthorp, William F. Musicians & Music-Lovers: And Other Essays. LC 74-39633. (Essay Index Reprint Ser.). Repr. of 1894 ed. 20.00 (ISBN 0-8369-2736-2). Ayer Co Pubs.

--Musicians & Music-Lovers & Other Essays. LC 78-58194. 1978. Repr. of 1894 ed. lib. bdg. 35.00 (ISBN 0-89341-433-6). Longwood Pub Group.

--Musicians & Music-Lovers & Other Essays. 1979. Repr. of 1894 ed. lib. bdg. 30.00 (ISBN 0-8492-0095-4). R West.

--Opera, Past & Present. LC 72-4148. (Select Bibliographies Reprint Ser.). 1972. Repr. of 1901 ed. 19.00 (ISBN 0-8369-6870-0). Ayer Co Pubs.

--The Opera Past & Present. LC 78-58193. 1978. Repr. of 1930 ed. lib. bdg. 25.00 (ISBN 0-89341-432-8). Longwood Pub Group.

Apthorp, William F., jt. auth. see Berlioz, Hector.

Apthorp, William F., tr. see Berlioz, Hector & Apthorp, William F.

Apthorpe, Raymond, ed. People Planning & Development Studies: Some Reflections on Social Planning. 168p. 1970. 29.50x (ISBN 0-7146-2582-5, BHA 02582, F Cass Co). Biblio Dist.

Aptowitzer, V. & Schwarz, A. Z. Abhandlungen zur Erinnerung an Hirsch Perez Chajes. LC 7-7163. (Jewish Philosophy, Mysticism & History of Ideas Ser.). 1980. Repr. of 1933 ed. lib. bdg. 60.00x (ISBN 0-405-12237-3). Ayer Co Pubs.

Aptowitzer, Victor. Das Schriftwort in der Rabbinischen Literatur. rev. ed. (Library of Biblical Studies Ser). 1970. 45.00x (ISBN 0-87068-005-6). Ktav.

Apuleius. Apuleius on the God of Socrates. Taylor, Thomas, tr. (Latin.). 1984. pap. 3.95 (ISBN 0-916411-25-7, Pub. by Alexandrian Pr). Holmes Pub.

--Cupid & Psyche. Balme, M. G. & Morwood, J. H., eds. (Illus.). 1976. pap. 6.95x (ISBN 0-19-912047-1). Oxford U Pr.

--Golden Ass. (Loeb Classical Library: No. 44). 12.50x (ISBN 0-674-99049-8). Harvard U Pr.

--The Golden Ass. Lindsay, Jack, tr. LC 62-1610. (Midland Bks.: No.36). 256p. 1962. pap. 5.95x (ISBN 0-253-20036-9). Ind U Pr.

--The Story of Cupid & Psyche As Related by Apuleius. Purser, Louis C., ed. (College Classical Ser.). cviii, 155p. 1982. lib. bdg. 25.00x (ISBN 0-89241-359-X); pap. text ed. 12.50x (ISBN 0-89241-111-2). Caratzas.

Apuleius, Lucius. The Most Delectable Jests from Lucius Apuleius' the Golden Ass. (Essential Library of the Great Philosophers Ser.). (Illus.). 125p. 1983. 69.75 (ISBN 0-89266-398-7). Am Classical Coll Pr.

Apuleius, Madaurensis. Apologia & Florida of Apuleius of Madaura. Butler, H. E., tr. LC 72-95084. Repr. of 1909 ed. lib. bdg. 18.75 (ISBN 0-8371-3066-2, APAF). Greenwood.

--Golden Ass of Apuleius. Adlington, William, tr. LC 78-158265. (The Tudor Translations: No. 4). Repr. of 1893 ed. 45.00 (ISBN 0-404-51851-6). AMS Pr.

Apurvananda, Swami. Acharya Shankara. 362p. 1985. pap. 7.95 (ISBN 0-87481-529-0, Pub. by Ramakrishna Math Madras India). Vedanta Pr.

Aputis, J. The Glade with Life-Giving Water. 431p. 1981. 12.00 (ISBN 0-8285-2025-9, Pub. by Progress Pubs USSR). Imported Pubns.

APWA Research Foundation. Street Cleaning Practice. 3rd ed. (Illus.). 1978. text ed. 28.00x (ISBN 0-917084-27-6). Am Public Works.

Apy, Deborah. Beauty & the Beast. LC 83-4395. (Illus.). 72p. (gr. 1-5). 1983. 12.95 (ISBN 0-03-064076-8). HR&W.

Aqua Group. Contract Administration for Architects & Quantity Surveyors. 5th ed. 87p. 1979. pap. text ed. 17.25x (ISBN 0-258-97139-8, Pub. by Granada England). Brookfield Pub Co.

--Fire & Building: Guide for the Design Team. 190p. 1984. pap. 26.00x (ISBN 0-246-11878-4, Pub by Granada England). Sheridan.

--Pre-Contract Practice for Architects & Quality Surveyors. 6th ed. 101p. 1980. pap. text ed. 12.50x (ISBN 0-246-11338-3, Pub. by Granada England). Brookfield Pub Co.

--Pre-Contract Practice for Architects & Quantity Surveyors. 6th ed. 100p. 1980. pap. 12.00x (ISBN 0-246-11338-3, Pub. by Granada England). Sheridan.

--Tenders & Contracts for Building. 110p. 1982. 12.00x (ISBN 0-246-11838-5, Pub by Granada England). Sheridan.

Aquadro, Charles, et al. Canoeing the Brandywine: A Naturalist's Guide. 1980. 1.50x (ISBN 0-940540-00-2). Brandywine Conserv.

Aquessy, W., et al. Time & the Philosophies. (At the Crossroads of Culture Ser.). (Illus.). 1977. pap. 17.25 (ISBN 92-3-101396-3, U821, UNESCO). Unipub.

Aquila, Frank D. Title IX: Implications for Education of Women. LC 81-80014. (Fastback Ser.: No. 156). 1981. pap. 0.75 (ISBN 0-87367-156-2). Phi Delta Kappa.

Aquila, Mirella. Selected Poems. 120p. 1981. pap. 5.00 (ISBN 0-682-49666-9). Exposition Pr FL.

Aquila, Richard E. Intentionality: A Study of Mental Acts. LC 76-15160. 1977. 22.50x (ISBN 0-271-01228-5). Pa St U Pr.

--Representational Mind: A Study of Kant's Theory of Knowledge. LC 83-47918. (Studies in Phenomenology & Existential Philosophy Ser.). 256p. 1983. 22.50x (ISBN 0-253-35005-0). Ind U Pr.

--Rhyme or Reason: A Limerick History of Philosophy. LC 81-40013. 126p. (Orig.). 1981. lib. bdg. 14.00 (ISBN 0-8191-1562-2); pap. text ed. 5.75 (ISBN 0-8191-1563-0). U Pr of Amer.

Aquilano, Nicholas J., jt. auth. see Chase, Richard B.

Aquilar, et al. Palabra Nueva: Cuentos Chicanos. LC 84-50576. 1984. pap. 9.00 (ISBN 0-87404-088-4). Tex Western.

Aquilar, Nona. The New No Pill, No Risk Birth Control. (Illus.). 256p. 1986. 12.95 (ISBN 0-89256-299-4); pap. 6.95 (ISBN 0-89256-300-1). Rawson Assocs.

Aquilon, Jeff & Aquilon, Nancy D. One on One: Exercising Together, the Sensual Way to Superbly Conditioned Bodies. (Illus.). 160p. 1984. 16.95 (ISBN 0-671-50399-5). S&S.

Aquilon, Nancy D., jt. auth. see Aquilon, Jeff.

Aquinas, St. Thomas. Political Ideas of St. Thomas Aquinas: A Selection from His Writings. 1973. pap. 9.95x (ISBN 0-317-30522-0). Free Pr.

--Summa Theologica, 5 vols. 3057p. 1982. 195.00 (ISBN 0-87061-063-5); pap. 125.00 (ISBN 0-87061-069-4). Chr Classics.

Aquinas, Saint Thomas. Summer Theologiae: Pt. 1, Vol. 1. Gilby, Thomas, ed. LC 70-84399. 1969. pap. 4.95 (ISBN 0-385-02768-0, Im). Doubleday.

Aquinas, Thomas. Aquinas on Politics & Ethics. Sigmund, Paul e., ed. (Norton Critical Edition Ser.). pap. write for info. (ISBN 0-393-95243-6). Norton.

--The Pocket Aquinas. Bourke, V., ed. pap. 3.95 (ISBN 0-671-47354-9). WSP.

--St. Thomas Aquinas: Philosophical Texts. Gilby, Thomas, ed. xxiv, 406p. 1982. pap. 12.50x (ISBN 0-939464-06-3). Labyrinth Pr.

--St. Thomas Aquinas: Theological Texts. Gilby, Thomas, ed. 444p. 1982. pap. 12.50x (ISBN 0-939464-01-2). Labyrinth Pr.

--Treatise on the Virtues. Oesterle, John A., tr. LC 84-10691. 171p. 1984. pap. text ed. 7.95 (ISBN 0-268-01855-3, 85-18557). U of Notre Dame Pr.

Aquinas, Thomas see Aquinas, Saint Thomas.

Aquinas, Thomas see Thomas Aquinas, Saint.

Aquinas, Saint Thomas. Commentary on St. Paul's Epistle to the Ephesians. Lamb, M. L., tr. LC 66-19307. (Aquinas Scripture Ser.). 1966. Vol. 2. 10.00x (ISBN 0-87343-022-0). Magi Bks.

--Commentary on St. Paul's Epistle to the Galatians. Larcher, F. R., tr. LC 66-19306. (Aquinas Scripture Ser.). 1966. Vol. 1. 10.00x (ISBN 0-87343-021-2). Magi Bks.

--Commentary on Saint Paul's Epistle to the Philippians & First Thessalonians. LC 66-19306. (Aquinas Scripture Ser.: Vol. 3). 1969. lib. bdg. 10.00x (ISBN 0-87343-047-6); pap. 6.00x (ISBN 0-87343-028-X). Magi Bks.

--Commentary on the Gospel of St. John. Weisheipl, James A., ed. Larcher, Fabian R., tr. from Lat. LC 66-19306. (Aquinas Scripture Ser.: Vol. 4, Pt. 1). (Illus.). 512p. 1980. 35.00x (ISBN 0-87343-031-X). Magi Bks.

--Commentary on the Posterior Analytics of Aristotle. LC 73-132009. 1969. lib. bdg. 12.95x (ISBN 0-87343-042-5). Magi Bks.

Aquinas, St. Thomas. On Kingship. Phelan, Gerald B., tr. LC 78-14098. 1979. Repr. of 1949 ed. 17.75 (ISBN 0-88355-772-X). Hyperion Conn.

Aquin De Chateau-Lyon, Pierre-Louis. Siecle litteraire de Louis XV; ou, lettres sur les hommes celebres, 2 vols. in 1. LC 76-43913. (Music & Theatre in France in the 17th & 18th Centuries). Repr. of 1754 ed. 39.00 (ISBN 0-404-60156-1). AMS Pr.

Aquin de Chateau-Lyon, Pierre Louis d' see Aquin De Chateau-Lyon, Pierre-Louis.

Aquino, John. Fantasy in Literature. 64p. 1977. pap. 5.95 (ISBN 0-8106-1817-6). NEA.

--Film in the Language Arts Classes. 56p. 1976. 5.95 (ISBN 0-8106-1811-7). NEA.

--Science Fiction As Literature. 64p. 1976. pap. 5.95 (ISBN 0-8106-1804-4). NEA.

Aquino, John T. Artists As Teachers. LC 78-61316. (Fastback Ser.: No. 113). 1978. pap. 0.75 (ISBN 0-87367-113-9). Phi Delta Kappa.

Aquino, Valentin R. The Filipino Community in Los Angeles: Thesis. LC 74-76502. 1974. Repr. of 1952 ed. soft bdg. 9.95 (ISBN 0-88247-272-0). R & E Pubs.

Aquistapace, Jean-Noel. Diccionario de la Politica. 2nd ed. 344p. (Span.). 1969. pap. 7.95 (ISBN 84-265-7047-X, S-21237). French & Eur.

Aqvist, Lennart. New Approachs to the Logical Theory of Interrogatives. 2nd ed. (Tuebinger Beitrage Zur Linguistik Ser.: No. 65). 184p. 1975. pap. 15.00x (ISBN 3-87808-065-4). Benjamins North Am.

Arab Federation for Engineering Industries. Aluminium in Arab World. (Proceedings of the 1st International Arab Aluminium Conference). 731p. 1984. pap. text ed. 114.00 (ISBN 0-9911001-3-1, Pub. by Aluminium W Germany). Heyden.

Arab Horse Society. The Arab Horse Stud Book: Containing the Entries of Arab Stallions & Mares, 6 vols. 1976. lib. bdg. 634.95 (ISBN 0-8490-1445-X). Gordon Pr.

Arab, L., et al. Ernaehrung und Gesundheit. (Beitraege zu Infusionstherapie und Klinische Ernaehrung: Band 7). (Illus.). xii, 204p. 1981. pap. 14.25 (ISBN 3-8055-2384-X). S Karger.

--Nutrition & Health. (Illus.). xviii, 244p. 1982. pap. 20.50 (ISBN 3-8055-3465-5). S Karger.

Arab Office, London. The Future of Palestine. LC 75-12167. (The Rise of Jewish Nationalism & the Middle East Ser). 166p. 1976. Repr. of 1947 ed. 16.50 (ISBN 0-88355-229-9). Hyperion Conn.

Arab Petroleum Research Center. Arab Oil & Gas Directory: 1985. 450p. 1980. 175.00x (ISBN 0-686-64697-5, Pub. by Graham & Trotman England). State Mutual Bk.

Arab World Business Guides. Nineteen Eighty Businessman's Guide to the Arab World & Iran: 1980. 1980. pap. 30.00 (ISBN 0-931000-13-0). Guides Multinatl Busn.

Arabi, Ibn. Journey to the Lord of Power: A Sufi Manual on Retreat. Harris, Rabia, tr. from Arab. (Illus.). 144p. 1981. pap. 8.95 (ISBN 0-89281-018-1). Inner Tradit.

Arabinda, Ray. The Manager Beyond the Organization. 1980. 9.50x (ISBN 0-8364-0636-2, Pub. by Macmillan India). South Asia Bks.

Arab-Ogly, E. In the Forecaster's Maze. 224p. 1975. 3.95 (ISBN 0-8285-0236-6, Pub. by Progress Pubs USSR). Imported Pubns.

Arac, Johnathan, et al, eds. The Yale Critics: Deconstruction in America. LC 83-1127. (Theory & History of Literature Ser.: Vol. 6). 259p. 1983. 29.50x (ISBN 0-8166-1201-3); pap. 12.95 (ISBN 0-8166-1206-4). U of Minn Pr.

Arac, Jonathan. Commissioned Spirits: The Shaping of Social Motion in Dickens, Carlyle, Melville, & Hawthorne. 1979. 20.00 (ISBN 0-8135-0874-6). Rutgers U Pr.

Arad, Miriam, tr. see Megged, Aharon.

Arad, Ruth, et al. The Economics of Peacemaking: Focus on the Egyptian-Israeli Situation. LC 83-4569. 260p. 1983. 25.00 (ISBN 0-312-23441-4). St Martin.
Arad, Yitzhak. Ghetto in Flames. 1980. 22.50x (ISBN 0-87068-753-0). Ktav.
--Ghetto in Flames. LC 80-50198. (Illus.). 500p. 1982. pap. 9.95 (ISBN 0-89604-043-7). Holocaust Pubns.
--The Partisan. LC 78-71299. (Illus.). 288p. 1979. 12.95 (ISBN 0-317-06371-5); pap. 8.95 (ISBN 0-89604-011-9). Holocaust Pubns.
--The Partisan: From the Valley of Death to Mount Zion. LC 78-71299. 1979. 9.95 (ISBN 0-8052-5011-5, Pub. by Holocaust Library); pap. 4.95 (ISBN 0-8052-5010-7, Pub. by Holocaust Library). Schocken.
--The Partisan: From the Valley of Death to Mount Zion. (Illus.). 288p. pap. 4.95 (ISBN 0-686-95079-8). ADL.
Arad, Z. & Herzog, M., eds. Products of Conjugacy Classes in Groups. (Lecture Notes in Mathematics: Vol. 1112). v, 244p. 1985. pap. 14.40 (ISBN 0-387-13916-8). Springer-Verlag.
Aragno, Anna. The Story of Felicity. (Illus.). 64p. 1980. 5.00 (ISBN 0-682-49633-2). Exposition Pr FL.
Arago, M. Historical Eloge of James Watt. LC 74-26247. (History, Philosophy & Sociology of Science Ser.). 1975. Repr. of 1839 ed. 21.00x (ISBN 0-405-06577-9). Ayer Co Pubs.
Aragon, George A. A Manager's Complete Guide to Financial Techniques. 1982. 15.95 (ISBN 0-02-900820-4). Free Pr.
Aragon, George A., jt. auth. see Viscione, Jerry A.
Aragon, Hilda, illus. My First Nursery Rhyme Book. 28p. (Orig.). (ps-7). 1981. pap. 3.75 (ISBN 0-915347-07-5). Pueblo Acoma Pr.
--A Pueblo Village. (Illus.). 8p. (Orig.). (ps-7). 1982. pap. 4.00 (ISBN 0-915347-17-2). Pueblo Acoma Pr.
Aragon, Louis & Cocteau, Jean. Conversations on the Dresden Gallery. Scarfe, Francis, tr. from Fr. LC 81-6640. (Illus.). 288p. 1982. text ed. 49.50x (ISBN 0-8419-0730-7). Holmes & Meier.
Aragon, Ray J. De. The Legend of La Llorona. LC 79-52953. (Illus.). 1980. pap. 5.95 (ISBN 0-932906-02-8). Pan-Am Publishing Co.
--Santeros & Curanderas. (Shield Non-Fiction Ser.). (Illus.). 1984. pap. 7.95 (ISBN 0-932906-12-5). Pan-Am Publishing Co.
Aragon, Ray J. De see De Aragon, Ray J.
Aragon, Ray J. De see Sanchez, Pedro.
Aragone, C., ed. Relativity, Cosmology, Topological Mass & Supergravity: Proceedings of the Silarg Symposium on Gravity, Gauge Theories & Supergravity, USB Campus, Caracas, Dec. 5-11, 1982. 400p. 1984. 44.00x (ISBN 9971-950-95-2, Pub. by World Sci Singapore). Taylor & Francis.
Aragones, Juan E. Veinte Anos de Teatro Espanol: 1960-1980. 280p. 1985. pap. 35.00 (ISBN 0-89295-043-9). Society Sp & Sp-Am.
Aragones, Sergio. Incurably Mad. (Illus.). 1977. pap. 1.75 (ISBN 0-446-94393-2). Warner Bks.
--Mad as a Hatter. (Illus.). 192p. (Orig.). 1981. pap. 2.25 (ISBN 0-446-30426-3). Warner Bks.
--Mad Marginals. (Illus.). 192p. 1974. pap. 1.75 (ISBN 0-446-94284-7). Warner Bks.
--Mad Menagerie. (Illus.). 192p. (Orig.). 1983. pap. 1.95 (ISBN 0-446-90900-9). Warner Bks.
--Mad's Sergio Aragones on Parade. (Illus.). 160p. (Orig.). 1979. pap. 5.95 (ISBN 0-446-37369-9). Warner Bks.
--More Mad Marginals. 192p. (Orig.). 1985. pap. 2.50 (ISBN 0-446-30853-6). Warner Bks.
--Shootin' Mad. (Mad Ser.). (Illus.). 192p. (Orig.). 1979. pap. 1.95 (ISBN 0-446-30430-1). Warner Bks.
--Viva Mad. (Illus.). 192p. 1975. pap. 1.95 (ISBN 0-446-30431-X). Warner Bks.
Arai, Hisao, ed. Biology of the Tapeworm Hymenolepis Diminuta. 1980. 66.00 (ISBN 0-12-058980-X). Acad Pr.
Arai, Toshikazu, tr. see Sakakibara, Tokuso, et al.
Arai, Tsuru. Mental Fatigue. LC 70-176521. (Columbia University. Teachers College. Contributions to Education: No. 54). Repr. of 1912 ed. 22.50 (ISBN 0-404-55054-1). AMS Pr.
Araico, Susana H. La Ironia en Tragedias de Calderon. 1984. 25.00 (ISBN 0-916379-18-3). Scripta.
Arakawa & Gins, Madeline H. Arakawa: The Mechanism of Meaning. (Art Bks. by Artists). (Illus.). 1979. o. p. 20.00; pap. 12.50 (ISBN 0-8109-2165-0). Abrams.
Arakawa, H., ed. Climates of Northern & Eastern Asia. (World Survey of Climatology Ser.: Vol. 8). 248p. 1970. 102.25 (ISBN 0-444-40704-9). Elsevier.
Arakawa, H., jt. ed. see Takahashi, K.
Arakawa, Hirokazu. The GO Collection of Netsuke, Tokyo National Museum. LC 82-48791. (Illus.). 216p. 1983. 125.00 (ISBN 0-87011-566-9). Kodansha.
Arakeri, H. R. & Donahue, Roy. Principles of Soil Conservation & Water Management. LC 83-27044. 266p. 1984. 30.50x (ISBN 0-8476-7350-2); tables incl. Rowman & Allanheld.
Araki, et al, eds. Group Theoretical Methods in Physics: Proceedings, Istanbul, Turkey, 1982. (Lecture Notes in Physics: Vol. 180). 569p. 1983. pap. 32.00 (ISBN 0-387-12291-5). Springer-Verlag.
Araki, Chiyo. Origami for Christmas. LC 82-80736. (Illus.). 148p. 1983. 14.95 (ISBN 0-87011-538-3). Kodansha.
--Origami in the Classroom, 2 vols. LC 65-13412. (Illus.). (gr. 1 up). 1965-68. bds. 8.95 ea. Vol. 1 (ISBN 0-8048-0452-4). Vol. 2 (ISBN 0-8048-0453-2). C E Tuttle.
Araki, H. & Effros, E. G., eds. Geometric Methods in Operator Algebras. (Research Notes in Mathematics Ser.: No. 123). 400p. 1985. pap. text ed. write for info. (ISBN 0-273-08683-9). Pitman Pub MA.
Araki, H., et al, eds. Operator Algebras & Their Connections with Topology & Ergodic Theory. (Lecture Notes in Mathematics: Vol. 1132). vi, 594p. 1985. pap. 35.50 (ISBN 0-387-15643-7). Springer-Verlag.
Araki, J., tr. see Inoue, Yasushi.
Araki, James T. The Ballad-Drama of Medieval Japan. LC 76-50314. 1977. pap. 4.25 (ISBN 0-8048-1279-9). C E Tuttle.
Araki, James T., tr. see Yamasaki, Toyoko.
Araki, Nancy K. & Horii, Jane. Matsuri! Festival! Japanese American Celebrations & Activities. (Illus., Orig.). 1985. pap. 8.95 (ISBN 0-89346-019-2). Heian Intl.
Arakin, T. English-Russian Dictionary. 988p. (Eng. & Rus.). 1980. 35.00x (ISBN 0-569-00013-0, Pub. by Collets). State Mutual Bk.
Arakin, V. D. English-Russian Dictionary. (Eng. & Rus.). 1980. leatherette 19.95 (ISBN 0-686-97371-2, M-9107). French & Eur.
Araldo, Josephine. French Country Cooking. Kelly, Orly & Witkin, Robin, eds. (Illus.). 240p. (Orig.). 1986. pap. 9.95 (ISBN 0-89407-046-0). Strawberry Hill.
Aram, Dorothy M. & Nation, James E. Child Language Disorders. LC 81-14063. (Illus.). 302p. 1982. text ed. 22.95 (ISBN 0-8016-0288-2). Mosby.
Aram, Dorothy M., jt. auth. see Nation, James E.
Aram, John D. Dilemmas of Administrative Behavior. 144p. 1976. Ref. Ed. 16.95 (ISBN 0-13-214247-3). P-H.
--Managing Business & Public Policy. (Pitman Series in Business Management & Organizational Behavior). 600p. 1982. text ed. 29.95 (ISBN 0-273-01656-3). Pitman Pub MA.
Aram, M. Peace in Nagaland: Eight Year Story, 1964-72. LC 74-902035. 335p. 1974. 13.00x (ISBN 0-88386-527-0). South Asia Bks.
Aramaki, S. & Kushiro, I., eds. Arc Volcanism: Selected Papers from the International Symposium on "Arc Volcanism" Held in Tokyo & Hakone & Sponsored by the Volcanological Society of Japan & the International Association of Volcanology & Chemistry of the Earth's Interior, Aug. 31-Sept. 5, 1981. (Developments in Volcanology Ser.: Vol. 2). 634p. 1984. Repr. 88.50 (ISBN 0-444-42234-X, I-307-83). Elsevier.
Arams, Frank R., ed. Infrared-to-Millimeter Wavelength Detectors. LC 78-189396. (Modern Frontiers in Applied Science Ser.). (Illus.). 290p. 1973. pap. 12.00x (ISBN 0-89006-012-6). Artech Hse.
Arana, Alice see Knorre, Marty, et al.
Arana, Oswaldo see Knorre, Marty, et al.
Aranadez, Richard, tr. see Masseron, Alexandre.
Arana Soto, Salvador. Diccionario de Temas Regionalistas En la Poesia Puertorriquena. (Span.). 12.50 (ISBN 0-686-56649-1, S-5220). French & Eur.
Arand, Louis A., tr. see Kuasten, J. & Plumpe, J.
Aranda, Charles. Dichos: Sayings & Proverbs from the Spanish. rev. ed. LC 77-78611. 32p. (Eng. & Span.). 1983. pap. 4.95 (ISBN 0-913270-47-4). Sunstone Pr.
Aranda, Francisco. Luis Bunuel: A Critical Biography. Robinson, David, ed. LC 76-7621. 1976. lib. bdg. 29.50 (ISBN 0-306-70754-3); pap. 6.95 (ISBN 0-306-80028-4). Da Capo.
Aranda, J. V., jt. ed. see Vert, P.
Araneta, Salvador. America's Double Cross of the Philippines: A Democratic Ally in 1899-1946. Date not set. 5.70 (ISBN 0-686-20847-1); pap. 3.70 (ISBN 0-686-20848-X). Philam Bk.
--The Effective Democracy for All. 1977. 9.90 (ISBN 0-686-20498-0); pap. 7.90 (ISBN 0-686-20499-9). Philam Bk.
Arangio-Ruis, V. & Olivieri, A. Insciptiones Graecae Sicilae et Infimae Italiae Ad Ius Pertinentes. 289p. 1980. 25.00 (ISBN 0-89005-321-9). Ares.
Arangio-Ruiz, G. U. N. Declaration on Friendly Relations & the System of Sources of International Law. 354p. 1979. 27.50x (ISBN 90-286-0149-X). Sijthoff & Noordhoff.
Arango, Tony, tr. Armonias Corales, Vol. 1. 144p. (Orig., Span.). 1977. pap. 4.75 (ISBN 0-89922-082-7). Edit Caribe.
Aranha, Jose P. Canaan. Lorente, Mariano J., tr. 1977. lib. bdg. 59.95 (ISBN 0-8490-1566-9). Gordon Pr.
Aranibar, A., jt. auth. see Lechner, H.
Aranibar, A., jt. ed. see Lechner, H.
Arano, Luisa C. see Ratti, Oscar & Westbrook, Adele.
Arano, Luisa C., intro. by. The Medieval Health Handbook: Tacuinum Sanitatis. LC 75-21725. (Illus.). 1981. 15.00 (ISBN 0-8076-1026-7). Braziller.
Aranovich, Felix. Nadgrobie Antokolskogo. LC 82-3030. (Illus.). 182p. (Rus.). 1982. pap. 9.00 (ISBN 0-938920-16-2). Hermitage.
Aranow, Edward R. & Einhorn, Herbert A. Tender Offers for Corporate Control. LC 72-10557. 352p. 1972. 55.00x (ISBN 0-231-03671-X). Columbia U Pr.
Aranow, Edward R., et al. Developments in Tender Offers for Corporate Control, 1973-76. LC 77-4235. 411p. 1977. 68.00x (ISBN 0-231-04170-5). Columbia U Pr.
Aranson, Peter H. American Government: Strategy & Choice. 1981. text ed. 24.95 (ISBN 0-316-04940-9); tchr's ed. avail. (ISBN 0-316-04941-7). Little.
Aranson, Peter H., ed. see Law & Economics Center of Emory University.
Arant, Olive G., illus. Magic: The Cookbook of the Junior League of Birmingham. 3rd ed. LC 81-85953. (Illus.). 348p. 1982. 10.95 (ISBN 0-9607810-0-5). Jr League Birm.
Arant, Patricia M. Russian for Reading. 214p. 1981. pap. text ed. 11.95 (ISBN 0-89357-086-9). Slavica.
Arany, A. Laszlo. Phonological System of a Hungarian Dialect: An Introduction to Structural Dialectology. LC 67-63039. (Uralic & Altaic Ser: Vol. 85). (Hun). 1967. pap. text ed. 7.50x (ISBN 0-87750-034-7). Res Ctr Lang Semiotic.
Arany, Cornel. Have Fun Playing Piano. (Music for Millions Ser.: Vol. 33). 1960. pap. 6.95 (ISBN 0-8256-4033-4). Music Sales.
Aranya, Hariharananda. Samkhya-Sutras of Pancasikha & the Samkhyatattvalcka. 1977. 11.25 (ISBN 0-89684-313-0, Pub. by Motilal Banarsidass India); pap. 6.95 (ISBN 0-89684-346-7). Orient Bk Dist.
Aranya, S. Hariharananda. Yoga Philosophy of Patanjali: Containing His Yoga Aphorisms with Vyasa's Commentary in Sanskrit & a Translation with Annotations Containing Many Suggestions for the Practice of Yoga. Mukerji, P. N., tr. from Sanskrit. 510p. 1983. 39.50x (ISBN 0-87395-728-8); pap. 10.95x (ISBN 0-87395-729-6). State U NY Pr.
Aranyi, Laszlo & Goldman, Larry L. Design of Long-Term Care Facilities. 240p. 1980. 37.95 (ISBN 0-442-26120-9). Van Nos Reinhold.
Aranza, Jacob. Backward Masking Unmasked: Backward Satanic Messages of Rock & Roll Exposed. LC 83-80043. 118p. (Orig.). (gr. 8-12). 1983. pap. 4.95 (ISBN 0-910311-04-8). Huntington Hse Inc.
--More Rock, Country & Backward Masking. 1985. pap. 4.95 (ISBN 0-910311-30-7). Huntington Hse Inc.
Aranza, Jacob & Lamson, Theresa. A Reasonable Reason to Wait. 101p. (Orig.). 1984. pap. 4.95 (ISBN 0-910311-21-8). Huntington Hse Inc.
Araoz, A., ed. Consulting & Engineering Design in Developing Countries. 140p. 1981. pap. 10.00 (ISBN 0-88936-278-5, IDRC161, IDRC), Unipub.
Araoz, Daniel L. Hypnosis & Sex Therapy. LC 82-4128. 200p. 1982. 25.00 (ISBN 0-87630-299-1). Brunner-Mazel.
--The New Hypnosis. 240p. 1985. 25.00 (ISBN 0-87630-387-4). Brunner-Mazel.
Araoz, Daniel L. & Bleck, Robert T. Hypnosex: Sexual Joy Through Self-Hypnosis. 1983. 5.95 (ISBN 0-87795-466-6, Pub. by Priam). Arbor Hse.
Arapoff, Nancy. Writing Through Understanding. LC 78-106600. 1970. pap. text ed. 10.95 (ISBN 0-03-076670-2, HoltC). HR&W.
Arapoff-Cramer, Nancy. The Writing Process. 1985. pap. text ed. 14.95 (ISBN 0-88377-287-6). Newbury Hse.
Arapura, J. G. Religion As Anxiety & Tranquillity: An Essay in Comparative Phenomenology of the Spirit. (Religion & Reason Ser.: No. 5). 1973. 14.40x (ISBN 90-2797-180-3). Mouton.
Arasaki, Seibin & Arasaki, Teruko. Vegetables from the Sea. LC 79-91516. (Illus.). 176p. (Orig.). 1983. pap. 13.95 (ISBN 0-87040-475-X). Japan Pubns USA.
Arasaki, Teruko, jt. auth. see Arasaki, Seibin.
Arasteh, A. R. Creativity in the Life Cycle, 2 vols. Incl. Vol. 1. An Annotated Bibliography; Vol. 2. An Interpretative Account of Creativity in Childhood, Adolescence & Adulthood. 1968. Set. 75.00 (ISBN 0-685-22604-2). Heinman.
--Education & Social Awakening in Iran, 1850-1968. rev. & enl. ed. 1969. 40.00 (ISBN 0-685-12010-4). Heinman.
--Faces of Persian Youth: A Sociological Study. 1970. 30.00 (ISBN 0-685-00395-7). Heinman.
--Man & Society in Iran. 1970. 35.00 (ISBN 0-685-12031-7). Heinman.
--Rumi the Persian. 1965. pap. 15.00 (ISBN --7100-7859-5). Heinman.
--Rumi the Persian: Rebirth in Creativity & Love. 1970. 6.00x (ISBN 0-87902-043-1). Orientalia.
--Teaching Through Research. 1966. 30.00 (ISBN 0-685-12048-1). Heinman.
Arasteh, A. Reza. Anxious Search: The Way to Universal Self. xiii, 293p. (Orig.). 1984. pap. 12.50 (ISBN 0-317-27429-5, Pub. by Inst Perspective Analsis M D). Heinman.
--Growth to Selfhood: The Sufi Contribution to Islam. (Orig.). 1980. pap. 7.95 (ISBN 0-7100-0355-2). Routledge & Kegan.
Arata, Esther S. More Black American Playwrights: A Bibliography. LC 78-15231. 335p. 1978. lib. bdg. 22.50 (ISBN 0-8108-1158-8). Scarecrow.
Arata, Luis O. The Festive Play of Fernando Arrabal. LC 81-51020. (Studies in Romance Languages: No. 25). 112p. 1982. 11.00x (ISBN 0-8131-1451-9). U Pr of Ky.
Arathorn, D. W. Kamal. 448p. 1983. pap. 3.95 (ISBN 0-380-65482-2, 65482). Avon.
Arato, Andrew & Gebhardt, Eike, eds. The Essential Frankfurt School Reader. LC 82-8063. 590p. 1982. pap. 16.95 (ISBN 0-8264-0194-5). Continuum.
Arato, Andrew, tr. see Konrad, George & Szelenyi, Ivan.
Arato, M. Linear Stochastic Systems with Constant Coefficients: A Statistical Approach. (Lecture Notes in Control & Information Sciences: Vol. 45). 309p. 1982. pap. 17.50 (ISBN 0-387-12090-4). Springer-Verlag.
Arato, M. & Varga, L., eds. Mathematical Models in Computer Science. 1982. 39.50 (ISBN 0-9960072-0-2, Pub. by Akademiai Kaido Hungary). Heyden.
Arato, M., et al. Twenty Papers on Statistics & Probability. (Selected Transactions in Mathematics Statistics & Probability Ser.: Vol. 13). 1973. 55.00 (ISBN 0-8218-1463-X, STAPRO 13). Am Math.
--Thirty-Two Papers on Statistics & Probability. LC 61-9803. (Selected Translations in Mathematical Statistics & Probability Ser.: Vol. 10). 1972. 36.00 (ISBN 0-8218-1460-5, STAPRO-10). Am Math.
Arato, M., et al, eds. Performance of Computer Systems. 566p. 1979. 81.00 (ISBN 0-444-85332-4). Elsevier.
--Stochastic Differential Systems: Proceedings. (Lecture Notes in Control & Information Sciences Ser.: Vol. 36). 230p. 1981. pap. 19.50 (ISBN 0-387-11038-0). Springer-Verlag.
Aratus see Callimachus.
Araujo, Aloisio & Gine, Evarist. The Central Limit Theorem for Real & Banach Valued Random Variables. LC 79-28274. (Series in Probability & Mathematical Statistics). 233p. 1980. 46.95x (ISBN 0-471-05304-X, Pub. by Wiley-Interscience). Wiley.
Araujo, Virginia De see Andrade, Carlos D.
Arauz, Nicomedes S., et al, trs. see Alifano, Roberto.
Araya, G. De Garcillaso a Garcia Lorca: Ocho Estudios Sobre Letras Espanolas. (Bhea Ser.: No.2). 215p. 1983. pap. text ed. 21.75x (ISBN 90-6203-505-1, Pub. by Rodopi Holland). Humanities.
Araya, G., et al, eds. Las Constantes Esteticas de la 'Comedia' del Siglo de Oro. (Dialogos Hispanicos de Amsterdam: No. 2). 137p. 1981. pap. text ed. 17.75x (ISBN 90-6203-583-3, Pub. by Rodopi Holland). Humanities.
--Los Cliticos en el Espanol Actual. (Dialogos Hispanicos De Amsterdam: No. 1). 123p. 1981. pap. text ed. 14.75x (ISBN 90-6203-901-4, Pub. by Rodopi Holland). Humanities.
Arazy, J. & Friedman, Y. Contractive Projections in C Sub 1 & C to Infinity. LC 77-28610. (Memoirs Ser: No. 200). 165p. 1978. pap. 14.00 (ISBN 0-8218-2200-4, MEMO-200). Am Math.
Arb, Sondra Von see Von Arb, Sondra.
Arban, Jean B. Complete Conservatory Method for Trumpet (Cornet) or E-Flat Alto, B-Flat Tenor, Baritone, Euphonium & B-Flat Bass in Treble Clef. Goldman, Edwin F. & Smith, Walter M., eds. 350p. (Orig.). 1936. pap. 14.95 (ISBN 0-8258-0010-2, 021). Fischer Inc NY.
Arbarello, E., et al. Geometry of Algebraic Curves, Vol. 1. (Grundlehren der Mathematischen Wissenschaften Ser.: Vol. 267). (Illus.). xvi, 387p. 1985. 34.00 (ISBN 0-387-90997-4). Springer-Verlag.
Arbatov, G. The War of Ideas in Contemporary International Relations. 313p. 1973. 5.45 (ISBN 0-8285-0325-7, Pub. by Progress Pubs USSR). Imported Pubns.
Arbaugh, George B., jt. auth. see Arbaugh, George E.
Arbaugh, George E. & Arbaugh, George B. Kierkegaard's Authorship: A Guide to the Writings of Kierkegaard. LC 68-2512. (Augustana College Library Ser.: No. 32). 431p. 1968. 6.95x (ISBN 0-910182-32-9). Augustana Coll.
Arbeau, T. Orchesography. Evans, Mary S., tr. 13.75 (ISBN 0-8446-1540-4). Peter Smith.
Arbeau, Thoinot. Orchesography. Sutton, Julia, ed. Evans, Mary S., tr. (Illus.). 1966. pap. 6.00 (ISBN 0-486-21745-0). Dover.
Arbeit, Eleanor W. Mrs. Cat Hides Something. (Illus.). 56p. (ps up). 1985. 10.95 (ISBN 0-87905-205-8). Gibbs M Smith.
Arbeit, Lorenzo. Chasin' the Blues Away: Instant Relief for Depression & Anxiety. (Illus.). 176p. 1984. pap. write for info. Prema Bks.
Arbeit, Sidney R., et al. Differential Diagnosis of the Electrocardiogram. 2nd ed. LC 74-2706. (Illus.). 208p. 1975. 17.95x (ISBN 0-8036-0241-3). Davis Co.
Arbeit, Wendy. What Are Fronds For? (Illus.). 128p. (Orig.). 1985. pap. 9.95 (ISBN 0-8248-0999-8). UH Pr.
Arbeiter, Jean. No Matter How You Slice It, It's Still Baloney: A Collection of Outrageous Quotes. LC 83-13687. (Illus.). 192p. (Orig.). 1984. pap. 5.95 (ISBN 0-688-01368-6). Morrow.

Arbeiter, Jean & Cirino, Linda D. Permanent Addresses: A Guide to the Resting Places of Famous Americans. LC 83-1618. (Illus.). 288p. 1983. pap. 7.95 (ISBN 0-87131-402-9). M Evans.
Arbeiter, Jean S., jt. ed. see Katz, Marjorie P.
Arbeiter, Solomon, jt. auth. see Ferrin, Richard I.
Arbeiter, Solomon, et al. Forty Million Americans in Career Transition: The Need for Information. 64p. 1978. pap. 4.50 (ISBN 0-87447-050-1, 237403). College Bd.
Arbeitman, Yoel L. & Bomhard, Allan R., eds. Bono Homini Donum: Essays in Historical Linguistics in Memory of J. Alexander Kerns, 2 vols. (Current Issues in Linguistic Theory: No. 16). 1981. Set. 110.00x (ISBN 90-272-3507-4). Benjamins North Am.
Arbeitsgemeinschaft Ausseruniversitarer Historischer Forschungseinrichtungen. Jarbucher der Historischen Forschung in der Bundesrepublik Deutschland 1983. Dertschland, Bundesrepublik, tr. 1984. lib. bdg. 95.00 (ISBN 3-598-20083-8). K G Saur.
Arbeitsgruppe Deutsch als Fremdsprache, Bielefeld. Als Auslandischer Student an einer Deutschen Hochschule: Unterrichtsvorschlage zur ersten Orientierung. 138p. (Ger.). 1983. 15.25. P Lang Pubs.
Arbel, Arie F. Analog Signal Processing & Instrumentation. LC 79-13461. (Illus.). 1980. 87.50 (ISBN 0-521-22469-1). Cambridge U Pr.
--Analog Signal Processing & Instrumentation. (Illus.). 246p. 1984. pap. 24.95 (ISBN 0-521-31866-1). Cambridge U Pr.
Arbel, Avner. How to Beat the Market with High-Performance Generic Stocks: Your Broker Won't Tell You about. LC 85-2886. 224p. 1985. 16.95 (ISBN 0-688-04371-2). Morrow.
Arbena, Joseph, et al. Regionalism & the Musical Heritage of Latin America. (Latin American Curriculum Units for Junior & Community Colleges Ser.). v, 84p. (Orig.). 1980. pap. text ed. 4.95x (ISBN 0-86728-006-9). U TX Inst Lat Am Stud.
Arbenz, K. & Martin, J. C. Mathematical Methods for Information Transmission. Orig. Title: Transmission de l'iformation Methodes Mathematiques. 1985. text ed. 50.00 (ISBN 0-89006-165-3). Artech Hse.
Arber, A. The Gramineae: A Study of Cereal, Bamboo & Grass. (Illus.). 1973. Repr. of 1934 ed. 28.00 (ISBN 3-7682-0276-3). Lubrecht & Cramer.
--Monocotyledons: A Morphological Study. (Illus.). 1961. Repr. of 1925 ed. 28.00 (ISBN 3-7682-0074-4). Lubrecht & Cramer.
Arber, Agnes. Manifold & the One. 1967. pap. 1.45 (ISBN 0-8356-0018-1, Quest). Theos Pub Hse.
--The Mind & the Eye. (Cambridge Science Classics Ser.). 150p. Date not set. pap. price not set (ISBN 0-521-31331-7). Cambridge U Pr.
--National Philosophy of Plant Form. LC 84-3606. 1970. Repr. of 1950 ed. 15.95x (ISBN 0-02-840360-6). Hafner.
--Water Plants: Study of Aquatic Angiosperms. (Illus.). 1963. Repr. of 1920 ed. 28.00 (ISBN 3-7682-0157-0). Lubrecht & Cramer.
Arber, Edward. The Goldsmith Anthology. 1900. 20.00 (ISBN 0-8274-2430-2). R West.
--An Introductory Sketch to the Martin Marprelate Controversy, 1558-90. 2nd ed. 1964. Repr. of 1895 ed. 19.50 (ISBN 0-8337-0077-4). B Franklin.
--The Milton Anthology Sixteen Hundred Thirty-Eight to Sixteen Hundred Seventy-Four. 1899. Repr. 20.00 (ISBN 0-8274-2736-0). R West.
--The Pope Anthology: Selections from the English Poets. 1901. Repr. 20.00 (ISBN 0-8274-3184-8). R West.
Arber, Edward, ed. The Cowper Anthology: 1775-1800 A.D. 335p. 1980. Repr. of 1901 ed. lib. bdg. 30.00 (ISBN 0-8495-0152-0). Arden Lib.
--The Dunbar Anthology, Fourteen Hundred & One to Fifteen Hundred & Eight A. D. (British Anthologies Ser.). 312p. Date not set. Repr. of 1901 ed. lib. bdg. 39.00 (ISBN 0-932051-23-5). Am Repr Serv.
--English Reprints, 8 Vols. LC 71-158266. Repr. of 1871 ed. Set. 385.00 (ISBN 0-404-00420-2). AMS Pr.
--English Scholar's Library of Old & Modern Works, 5 vols. in 4. LC 75-158267. Repr. of 1884 ed. Set. 235.00 (ISBN 0-404-00430-X). AMS Pr.
--The Rehearsal, 1671, 1672. large type ed. 132p. 1983. pap. 15.00 (ISBN 0-686-89438-3). Saifer.
--The Term Catalogues, 1668-1709 A. D, 3 Vols. Set. 150.00 (ISBN 0-384-01850-5). Johnson Repr.
--Transcripts of the Registers of the Company of Stationers of London: 1554-1640, 5 vols. Incl. Transcript of the Registers of the Worshipful Company of Stationers, London: From 1640-1708, 3 vols. Set Of 8 Vols. 190.00 (ISBN 0-8446-1449-1); 24.00 ea. Peter Smith.
Arber, Edward, ed. see Addison, Joseph.
Arber, Edward, ed. see Ascham, Roger.
Arber, Edward, ed. see Dryden, John.
Arber, Edward, ed. see Earle, John.
Arber, EDward, ed. see Gascoigne, George.
Arber, Edward, ed. see Googe, Barnabe.
Arber, Edward, ed. see Greene, Robert.
Arber, Edward, ed. see James Sixth of Scotland.
Arber, Edward, ed. see Latimer, Hugh.
Arber, Edward, ed. see Lyly, John.
Arber, Edward, ed. see Naunton, Robert.
Arber, Edward, ed. see Selden, John.
Arber, Edward, ed. see Sidney, Philip.
Arber, Edward, ed. see Smith, John.
Arber, Edward, ed. see Udall, Nicholas.
Arber, EDward, ed. see Villiers, George.
Arber, Edward, ed. see Webbe, William.
Arber, Edward, tr. see Habington, William.
Arber, Edward, tr. see Howell, James.
Arber, W., ed. Current Topics in Microbiology & Immunology, Vol. 72. LC 15-12910. (Illus.). 200p. 1976. 50.00 (ISBN 0-387-07564-X). Springer-Verlag.
--Current Topics in Microbiology & Immunology, Vol. 78. LC 15-12910. (Illus.). 1977. 56.00 (ISBN 0-387-08499-1). Springer-Verlag.
Arber, W., et al. Current Topics in Microbiology & Immunology, Vol. 75. LC 15-12910. (Illus.). 1976. 54.00 (ISBN 3-540-08013-9). Springer-Verlag.
--Current Topics in Microbiology & Immunology, Vol. 79. LC 15-12910. 1978. 63.00 (ISBN 0-387-08587-4). Springer-Verlag.
Arber, W., et al, eds. Current Topics in Microbiology & Immunology, Vols. 40-55. Incl. Vols. 40-50 & 52-55. Chronic Infections Neuropathic Agents & Other Slow Virus Infections. Brody, J. A., et al, eds. (Illus.). vii, 74p. 1967; Vol. 41. (Illus.). iv, 183p. 1967. 49.00 (ISBN 0-387-03755-1); Vol. 42. Insect Viruses. Maramorosch, K., ed. (Illus.). viii, 192p. 1968. 31.00 (ISBN 0-387-04071-4); Vol. 43. (Illus.). iii, 233p. (Incl. 32 pp. in German). 1968. 52.00 (ISBN 0-387-04072-2); Vol. 44. (Illus.). iii, 175p. 1968. 52.00 (ISBN 0-387-04073-0); Vol. 45. (Illus.). iii, 237p. (Incl. 61 pp. in German). 1968. 52.00 (ISBN 0-387-04074-9); Vol. 46. (Illus.). iii, 203p. (Incl. 90 pp. in German). 1968. 57.90 (ISBN 0-387-04075-7); Vol. 47. (Illus.). iii, 222p. (Incl. 29 pp. in German). 1969. 55.50 (ISBN 0-387-04445-0); Vol. 48. (Illus.). iii, 206p. 1969. 55.50 (ISBN 0-387-04446-9); Vol. 49. (Illus.). iii, 250p. 1969. 55.50 (ISBN 0-387-04447-7); Vol. 50. (Illus.). iii, 238p. 1969. 55.50 (ISBN 0-387-04448-5); Vol. 52. (Illus.). iv, 197p. 1970. 55.50 (ISBN 0-387-04787-5); Vol. 53. (Illus.). 236p. 1970. 58.50 (ISBN 0-387-05069-8); Vol. 54. (Illus.). 230p. 1971. 58.50 (ISBN 0-387-05289-5); Vol. 55. Arthropod Cell Cultures & Their Application to the Study of Viruses: Arthropod Cell Cultures & Their Application to the Study of Viruses. Weiss, E., ed. (Illus.). 340p. 1971. 58.00 (ISBN 0-387-05451-0). (Illus., Eng. & Ger.). Springer-Verlag.
--Current Topics in Microbiology & Immunology, Vol. 62. LC 73-17985. (Illus.). 170p. 1973. 43.00 (ISBN 0-387-06598-9). Springer-Verlag.
--Current Topics in Microbiology & Immunology, Vol. 63. LC 73-20915. (Illus.). 230p. 1974. 50.00 (ISBN 0-387-06599-7). Springer-Verlag.
--Current Topics in Microbiology & Immunology, Vol. 64. LC 74-3541. (Illus.). 190p. 1974. 48.00 (ISBN 0-387-06713-2). Springer-Verlag.
--Current Topics in Microbiology & Immunology, Vol. 65. LC 15-12910. (Illus.). 165p. 1974. 47.00 (ISBN 0-387-06774-4). Springer-Verlag.
--Current Topics in Microbiology & Immunology, Vol. 66. LC 15-12910. (Illus.). 130p. 1974. 36.00 (ISBN 3-540-06831-7). Springer-Verlag.
--Current Topics in Microbiology & Immunology, Vol. 67. LC 15-12910. (Illus.). iv, 162p. 1974. 46.00 (ISBN 3-540-06838-4). Springer-Verlag.
--Current Topics in Microbiology & Immunology, Vol. 76. LC 15-12910. (Illus.). 1977. 54.00 (ISBN 3-540-08238-7). Springer-Verlag.
--Current Topics in Microbiology & Immunology, Vol. 77. LC 15-12910. (Illus.). 1977. 51.00 (ISBN 0-387-08401-0). Springer-Verlag.
--Current Topics in Microbiology & Immunology, Vol. 82. LC 15-12910. (Illus.). 1978. 43.00 (ISBN 0-387-08981-0). Springer-Verlag.
--Current Topics in Microbiology & Immunology, Vol. 83. LC 15-12910. (Illus.). 1978. 45.00 (ISBN 0-387-09034-7). Springer-Verlag.
--Current Topics in Microbiology & Immunology, Vol. 85. (Illus.). 1979. 57.00 (ISBN 0-387-09410-5). Springer-Verlag.
--Current Topics in Microbiology & Immunology, Vols. 86-87. (Illus.). 1980. Vol. 86. 45.00 (ISBN 0-387-09432-6); Vol. 87. 42.00 (ISBN 0-387-09433-4). Springer-Verlag.
--Current Topics in Microbiology & Immunology, Vol. 90. (Illus.). 147p. 1980. 58.00 (ISBN 0-387-10181-0). Springer-Verlag.
--Current Topics in Microbiology & Immunology, Vol. 91. (Illus.). 250p. 1981. 59.00 (ISBN 0-387-10722-3). Springer-Verlag.
Arber, Werner, et al. Genetic Manipulation: Impact on Man & Society. LC 83-26166. 250p. 1984. 34.50 (ISBN 0-521-26417-0). Cambridge U Pr.
Arberry, A. J. Catalogue of the Library of the India office: Vol. 2 (Oriental Languages) Pt. 6, Persian Books. 574p. 1937. 18.00 (ISBN 0-317-30604-9, Pub. by British Lib). Longwood Pub Group.
--Doctrine of the Sufis. 12.95 (ISBN 0-686-18608-7). Kazi Pubns.
--The Doctrine of the Sufis. 1966. 7.25x (ISBN 0-87902-195-0). Orientalia.
--Sufism: An Account of the Mystics of Islam. (Unwin Paperback Ser.). 1979. pap. 5.50 (ISBN 0-04-297037-7). Allen Unwin.
Arberry, A. J., ed. Rubaiyat of Omar Khayyam. 1977. pap. 2.50x (ISBN 0-460-01996-1, Evman). Biblio Dist.
--The Rubaiyat of Omar Khayyam & Other Persian Poems. 1972. Repr. of 1954 ed. 8.95 (ISBN 0-460-00996-6, Evman). Biblio Dist.
Arberry, A. J., ed. see Hafiz.
Arberry, A. J., tr. see Al-Mutanabbi & Abu al-Tayyib Ahmad ibn al-Husan.
Arberry, A. J., tr. see Attar, Farid.
Arberry, A. J., tr. see Ibn-Hazm, Ali ibn Ahmad.
Arberry, A. J., tr. see Rumi, Jalal A.
Arberry, Arthur J. Aspects of Islamic Civilization As Depicted in the Original Texts. LC 77-673. 1977. Repr. of 1964 ed. lib. bdg. 29.25 (ISBN 0-8371-9494-6, ARAI). Greenwood.
--Aspects of Islamic Civilization as Depicted in the Original Text. 1967. pap. 9.95 (ISBN 0-472-06130-5, 130, AA). U of Mich Pr.
--Fitzgerald's Salaman & Absal. (Cambridge Oriental Ser.: No. 2). 1956. 37.50 (ISBN 0-521-05011-1). Cambridge U Pr.
--FitzGerald's Salaman & Absal: A Study. LC 57-6828. (University of Cambridge Oriental Studies). pap. 54.00 (ISBN 0-317-26126-6, 2024406). Bks Demand UMI.
--Koran Interpreted. 1964. pap. 12.95 (ISBN 0-02-083260-5). Macmillan.
--Modern Arabic Poetry. (Cambridge Oriental Ser: No. 1). 1967. 37.50 (ISBN 0-521-07050-3). Cambridge U Pr.
--Religion in the Middle East, 2 Vols. LC 68-21187. (Illus.). 1969. Set. 99.50 (ISBN 0-521-07400-2). Vol. 1. 62.50 (ISBN 0-521-20543-3); Vol. 2. 59.50 (ISBN 0-521-20544-1). Cambridge U Pr.
--Revelation & Reason in Islam. LC 80-1936. (BCL: Series I & II). Repr. of 1957 ed. 20.00 (ISBN 0-404-18952-0). AMS Pr.
--Shiraz, Persian City of Saints & Poets. LC 60-8752. (Centers of Civilization Ser.: No.2). (Illus.). pap. 47.80 (ISBN 0-317-11173-6, 2016192). Bks Demand UMI.
Arberry, Arthur J., ed. Arabic Poetry: A Primer for Students. LC 65-11206. pap. 45.80 (ISBN 0-317-26121-5, 2024405). Bks Demand UMI.
--Immortal Rose: An Anthology of Persian Lyrics. 1976. lib. bdg. 59.95 (ISBN 0-8490-2039-5). Gordon Pr.
Arberry, Arthur J., ed. see Dun Karm.
Arberry, Arthur J., tr. see Avicenna.
Arberry, Arthur J., tr. see Kalabadhi, Muhammed.
Arberry, Arthur John. A Maltese Anthology. LC 75-8831. 200p. 1975. Repr. of 1960 ed. lib. bdg. 22.50x (ISBN 0-8371-8112-7, ARMA). Greenwood.
Arberry, J. A. A Sufi Martyr: The Aplogia of Ain-Al-Qudat-Al-Hamadhani. 1969. text ed. 10.95x (ISBN 0-04-297020-2). Allen Unwin.
Arbetman, Lee & Roe, Richard L. Great Trials in American History: Civil War to the Present. (Illus.). 200p. (Orig.). 1984. pap. 10.95 (ISBN 0-314-80461-7). West Pub.
Arbetman, Lee, et al. Street Law: A Course in Practical Law. 2nd ed. 383p. 1980. pap. text ed. 8.75 (ISBN 0-8299-1031-X). West Pub.
Arbetman, Lee P. & Mcmahon, Edward T. New York State Supplement to Street Law: A Course in Practical Law. 2d ed. 80p. (gr. 9-12). 1983. pap. text ed. 4.95 (ISBN 0-314-73470-8). West Pub.
--Street Law: New York Supplement. 2nd ed. (Illus.). (gr. 9-12). 1982. write for info. (ISBN 0-314-72084-7). West Pub.
Arbetman, Lee P., et al. Law & the Consumer. (Illus.). 175p. 1982. pap. text ed. write for info. (ISBN 0-314-65092-X). West Pub.
--Street Law: A Course in Practical Law, with Florida Supplement. 2nd ed. (Illus.). 80p. pap. text ed. write for info. (ISBN 0-314-63413-4). West Pub.
Arbib, M. A., jt. auth. see Alagic, S.
Arbib, M. A., jt. auth. see Anderson, B. D.
Arbib, M. A., jt. ed. see Amari, S.
Arbib, M. A., et al. A Basis for Theoretical Computer Science. (Computer Science Texts & Monographs). (Illus.). 224p. 1981. 21.00 (ISBN 0-387-90573-1). Springer-Verlag.
Arbib, Michael. Computers & the Cybernetic Society. 2nd ed. 1984. 17.00i (ISBN 0-12-059046-8); instr's. manual 10.00i (ISBN 0-12-059047-6). Acad Pr.
--The Metaphorical Brain: An Introduction to Cybernetics As Artificial Intelligence & Brains Theory. LC 72-2490. (Illus.). 243p. 1972. 36.95x (ISBN 0-471-03249-2, Pub. by Wiley-Interscience). Wiley.
Arbib, Michael A. Algebraic Theory of Machines, Languages & Semigroups. LC 68-18654. 1968. 76.00 (ISBN 0-12-059050-6). Acad Pr.
--In Search of the Person: Philosophical Explorations in Cognitive Science. LC 85-14152. 160p. (Orig.). 1985. lib. bdg. 20.00x (ISBN 0-87023-499-4); pap. 9.95 (ISBN 0-87023-500-1). U of Mass Pr.
Arbib, Michael A., jt. auth. see Padulo, Louis.
Arbib, Michael A. & Manes, Ernest G., eds. Arrows, Structures & Functors: The Categorical Imperative. 1975. 33.50 (ISBN 0-12-059060-3). Acad Pr.
Arbib, Michael A., et al. Neural Models of Language Processes. LC 81-20520. (Perspectives in Neurolinguistic, Neuropsychology & Pscholinguistics Ser.). 1982. 54.50 (ISBN 0-12-059780-2). Acad Pr.
Arbib, Robert & Soper, Tony. Hungry Bird Book: How to Make Your Garden Their Haven on Earth. LC 75-122251. (Illus.). 1970. 8.95 (ISBN 0-8008-4020-8). Taplinger.
Arbib, Robert S., Jr. Lord's Woods. LC 73-139373. 1971. 6.95 (ISBN 0-393-08639-9). Norton.
Arbingast, Stanley A. & Hezlep, William L. Atlas of Central America. LC 78-64336. (Illus., Orig.). 1979. pap. 18.00 (ISBN 0-87755-262-2). Bureau Busn UT.
Arbingast, Stanley A., jt. auth. see Wright, Rita J.
Arbingast, Stanley A., et al. Atlas of Texas. LC 76-24780. (Illus.). 1979. pap. 29.95 (ISBN 0-87755-261-4). Bureau Busn UT.
--Atlas of Mexico. rev. ed. LC 75-11269. (Illus.). 1975. pap. 20.00 (ISBN 0-87755-187-1). Bureau Busn UT.
Arbit Books, ed. Toledoteinu: Finding Your Own Roots. Tarachow, Mike, tr. (Illus.). 1978. pap. text ed. 2.50 (ISBN 0-930038-10-X). Arbit.
Arbit, Bruce, jt. ed. see Berliant, Howard M.
Arbit, Naomi & Turner, June. Ground Meat Cookbook. (Illus.). 64p. (Orig.). 1981. pap. 3.50 (ISBN 0-8249-3005-3). Ideals.
--Pies & Pastries. (Illus.). 64p. pap. 3.50 (ISBN 0-8249-3011-8). Ideals.
--Soup, Salad, Sandwich Cookbook. (Illus.). 64p. (Orig.). 1981. pap. 3.50 (ISBN 0-8249-3001-0). Ideals.
Arbit, Nomi & Turner, June. The Gourmet Touch. Kuse, James & Luedtke, D. Ralph, eds. 1978. pap. 3.50 (ISBN 0-89542-610-2). Ideals.
Arbiter, N., jt. ed. see Somasundaran, P.
Arbiter, N. Nathaniel. Discussions Digest. 92p. 1968. 45.25 (ISBN 0-677-11630-6). Gordon.
Arbiter, N. Nathaniel, ed. Milling Methods in the Americas. 625p. 1965. 125.00x (ISBN 0-677-10690-4). Gordon.
Arbiter, Nathaniel, ed. Seventh International Mineral Processing Congress: Proceedings, 1965. 625p. 1965. 144.50x (ISBN 0-677-10690-4). Gordon.
Arbitman, Dena C., jt. auth. see Safford, Philip L.
Arblaster, Anthony. The Rise & Decline of Western Liberalism. 450p. 1984. 34.95x (ISBN 0-85520-765-5). Basil Blackwell.
Arblay, Frances. The Early Diary of Frances Burney, 1768-1778, 2 vols. 1913. 39.50 (ISBN 0-8274-2210-5). R West.
Arblay, Frances B. Fanny Burney & Her Friends: Select Passages from Her Diary & Other Writings. LC 75-76135. 1969. Repr. of 1890 ed. 35.00x (ISBN 0-8103-3896-3). Gale.
--Fanny Burney & Her Friends: Select Passages from Her Diary & Other Writings. 1890. Repr. 9.50 (ISBN 0-8274-3819-2). R West.
Arblay, Frances D' Memoirs of Dr. Burney, Arranged from His Own Manuscripts, from Family Papers, & from Personal Recollections, 3 vols. LC 78-37680. Repr. of 1832 ed. Set. 115.00 (ISBN 0-404-56704-5). AMS Pr.
Arbo, Jane. Invisible Wife. 192p. 1982. pap. 1.50 (ISBN 0-373-02467-3). Harlequin Bks.
Arbogast, Karen K. Exchange Lists & Diet Patterns. 352p. 1980. 17.95 (ISBN 0-442-25655-8). Van Nos Reinhold.
Arbona, Fred L., Jr. Mayflies, the Angler, & the Trout. LC 79-14092. (Illus.). 224p. 1980. 27.95 (ISBN 0-8329-2994-8, Pub. by Winchester Pr). New Century.
Arbona, Guillermo, et al. Health Objectives for the Developing Society: Responsibility of Individual, Physician, & Community. Long, E. Croft, ed. LC 65-19451. pap. 44.80 (ISBN 0-317-20454-8, 2023421). Bks Demand UMI.
Arbor, Jane. Au Palais a Venise. (Harlequin Romantique Ser.). 192p. 1983. pap. 1.95 (ISBN 0-373-41207-X). Harlequin Bks.
--La Baie des Nuages. (Harlequin Romantique Ser.). 192p. 1983. pap. 1.95 (ISBN 0-373-41198-7). Harlequin Bks.
--Dans les Heures Pales de L'Aube. (Collection Harlequin Ser.). 192p. 1983. pap. 1.95 (ISBN 0-373-49351-7). Harlequin Bks.
--The Feathered Shaft, Wildfire Quest: The Flower on the Rock. (Harlequin Romances Ser.). 576p. 1982. pap. 3.50 (ISBN 0-373-20056-0). Harlequin Bks.
--Handmaid to Midas. (Harlequin Romances Ser.). 192p. 1983. pap. 1.75 (ISBN 0-373-02545-9). Harlequin Bks.
--Une Moisson de Fleurs. (Collection Harlequin Ser.). 192p. 1983. pap. 1.95 (ISBN 0-373-49356-8). Harlequin Bks.
--The Price of Paradise. (Harlequin Romances Ser.). 192p. 1982. pap. 1.50 (ISBN 0-373-02509-2). Harlequin Bks.
--Roman Summer. (Nightingale Paperbacks (Large Print) Ser.). 1985. pap. 9.95 (ISBN 0-8161-3872-9). G K Hall.
Arbor, John H. Joe Broderick's Woman. 1978. pap. 1.50 (ISBN 0-532-15323-5). Woodhill.
Arbor, Marilyn. Tools & Trades of America's Past: The Mercer Collection. 1981. 116p. 6.95 (ISBN 0-910302-12-X). Bucks Co Hist.

Arbour, Basil. The Final Gift: A New Way of the Cross. (Illus.). 64p. 1981. pap. 2.95 (ISBN 0-86683-647-0). Winston Pr.
--Time Out: Prayers for Busy People. 96p. 1984. pap. 3.95 (ISBN 0-86683-828-7). Winston Pr.
Arbroath Abbey. Liber S. Thome De Aberbrothoc, 2 Vols. Innes, Cosmo & Chalmers, Patrick, eds. LC 79-158268. (Bannatyne Club, Edinburgh. Publications: No. 86). Repr. of 1856 ed. Set. 95.00 (ISBN 0-404-52815-5). AMS Pr.
Arbuckle, Elisabeth S., ed. Harriet Martineau's Letters to Fanny Wedgwood. LC 81-50783. 360p. 1983. 29.50x (ISBN 0-8047-1146-1). Stanford U Pr.
Arbuckle, Gwendolyne & Wolcott, Carolyn. Paul: Adventurer for Christ. 96p. (Orig.). 1984. pap. 5.50 (ISBN 0-687-30487-3). Abingdon.
Arbuckle, J. Gorden & Frick, G. William. Environmental Law Handbook. 8th ed. LC 76-41637. 586p. 1985. write for info. (ISBN 0-86587-122-1). Gov Insts.
Arbuckle, John T. Singing Words. LC 78-52243. 1978. 7.00 (ISBN 0-918626-04-8). Word Serv.
Arbuckle, Robert D. John Nicholson, 1757-1800: Pennsylvania Speculator & Patriot. LC 74-3446. (Illus.). 276p. 1975. 24.95x (ISBN 0-271-01168-8). Pa St U Pr.
Arbuckle, Wendell S. Ice Cream. 3rd ed. (Illus.). 1977. lib. bdg. 42.50 (ISBN 0-87055-256-2). AVI.
Arbur, Rosemarie. Leigh Brackett, Marion Zimmer Bradley, & Anne McCaffrey: A Primary & Secondary Bibliography. 1982. lib. bdg. 34.50 (ISBN 0-8161-8120-9, Hall Reference). G K Hall.
--Reader's Guide to Marion Zimmer Bradley. Schlobin, Roger C., ed. (Starmont Reader's Guide to Contemporary Science Fiction & Fantasy Authors Ser.: Vol. 27). (Illus., Orig.). 1985. 15.95x (ISBN 0-916732-96-7); pap. text ed. 7.95x (ISBN 0-916732-95-9). Starmont Hse.
Arbur, Rosemary. Marion Zimmer Bradley. (Starmont Reader's Guides Ser.: No. 27). 96p. 1985. Repr. lib. bdg. 15.95x (ISBN 0-89370-954-9). Borgo Pr.
Arbus, Diane, jt. auth. see Southall, Thomas W.
Arbus, Loreen. Test Your Own I. Q. 64p. 1986. 4.95 (ISBN 0-399-51120-2). Putnam Pub Group.
Arbuthmot, John. The History of John Bull. Bower, Alan W. & Erickson, Robert A., eds. (Oxford English Texts Ser.). (Illus.). 1976. 69.00x (ISBN 0-19-812719-7). Oxford U Pr.
Arbuthnot, jt. auth. see Burton.
Arbuthnot, Charles W., ed. see Tourn, Giorgio.
Arbuthnot, George, ed. Vestry Minute Book of the Parish of Stratford-on-Avon from 1617 to 1699. LC 72-142244. Repr. of 1899 ed. 11.50 (ISBN 0-404-00366-4). AMS Pr.
Arbuthnot, Jack & Faust, David. Teaching Moral Reasoning: Theory & Practice. (Illus.). 289p. 1980. text ed. 23.45 scp (ISBN 0-06-040321-7, HarpC). Har-Row.
Arbuthnot, John. Tables of Ancient Coins, Weights & Measures: 1754 Edition. 1981. write for info. (ISBN 0-08-027640-7, HE 085); microfiche 35.00 (ISBN 0-686-79357-9). Pergamon.
Arbuthnot, May H. & Root, Shelton L., Jr. Time for Poetry. 3rd ed. 1968. text ed. 17.95 (ISBN 0-673-05549-3). Scott F.
Arbuthnot, May H., et al. Childrens Books Too Good to Miss: 1979. LC 79-53812. (Illus.). 125p. 1980. 8.95 (ISBN 0-8295-0287-4). UPB.
Arbuthnott, Hugh & Edwards, Geoffrey, eds. A Common Man's Guide to the Common Market. 213p. 1982. text ed. 27.50 (ISBN 0-8419-5053-9); pap. text ed. 14.50x (ISBN 0-8419-5054-7). Holmes & Meier.
Arbuthnott, J. P., jt. ed. see Smith, Harry.
Arbuzo, Grigory, jt. auth. see Sarabyanov, Dmitry.
Arbuzov, Alexei see Weiss, Samuel A.
Arc, Kathleen. The Big Cat. LC 56-806. (Windings & Purrs & Tails Ser.). (Illus.). 20p. (gr. 3-6). 1981. pap. 2.97 (ISBN 0-9607074-0-9). ANURA Pub.
Arca, Emil & Pamel, Gregory J., eds. The Triumph of the American Spirit: The Presidential Speeches of Ronald Reagan. price not set. Natl Repro Corp.
Arca, Julie, jt. auth. see Waite, Mitch.
Arca, Julie A. Practical WordStar Uses. LC 83-72250. (Illus.). 303p. 1983. pap. 17.95 (ISBN 0-89588-107-1). SYBEX.
Arca, Julie A. & Pirro, Charles F. InfoPower: Practical InfoStar Uses. 275p. 16.95 (ISBN 0-89599-108-X). SYBEX.
--Introduction to InfoStar. 250p. 1984. pap. cancelled (ISBN 0-89588-108-X). SYBEX.
Arcambault, Paul J., tr. see Mustacchi, Marianna M. & Archambault, Paul J.
Arcamone, Federico. Doxorubicin: Anticancer Antibiotics. LC 80-1106. (Medicinal Chemistry Ser.). 1981. 70.00 (ISBN 0-12-059280-0). Acad Pr.
Arcana, Judith. Every Mother's Son. LC 82-12912. 336p. 1983. 16.95 (ISBN 0-385-15640-5, Anchor Pr). Doubleday.
--Our Mothers' Daughters. 1979. pap. 4.95 (ISBN 0-915288-38-9). Shameless Hussy.
Arcangeli, G. & Mauro, F., eds. Hyperthermia in Radiation Oncology. (Illus.). 299p. 1980. flexicover-Medical 41.50 (ISBN 0-89352-116-7, Masson Italia Editori). Masson Pub.
Arcangelis, Mario de. Electronic Warfare. (Illus.). 312p. 1985. 19.95 (ISBN 0-7137-1501-4, Pub. by Blandford Pr England). Sterling.
Arcario, Paul, jt. auth. see Glass, Elliot.
Arcaro, A., et al. Selected Readings for Casework Supervisors in Public Agencies. 1970. pap. text ed. 7.95x (ISBN 0-8290-1187-0). Irvington.
Arce, Gallego. Arrigoitia: Lecturas Puertorriquenas-Poesia. 1966. 14.95 (ISBN 0-87751-006-7, Pub by Troutman Press). E Torres & Sons.
Arce, Hector. The Secret Life of Tyrone Power. LC 79-51789. (Illus.). 1979. 9.95 (ISBN 0-688-03484-5). Morrow.
Arce, Julio G. see Ulica, Jorge, pseud.
Arce, Wilfredo F. & Alvarez, Gabrqel C., eds. Population Change in Southeast Asia. 499p. 1984. text ed. 58.50x (ISBN 9971-902-56-7, Pub. by Inst Southeast Asian Stud). Gower Pub Co.
Arce De Vazquez, et al. Lecturas Puertorriquenas - Prosa. 1966. 14.95 (ISBN 0-87751-011-3, Pub by Troutman Press). E Torres & Sons.
Arce de Vazquez, Margot. Garcilaso De la Vega: Contribucion Al Estudio De la Lirica Espanola Del Siglo XVI. 4th ed. (UPREX, E. Literarios: No. 43). pap. 1.85 (ISBN 0-8477-0043-7). U of PR Pr.
Arce de Vazquez, Margot, ed. see Pales Matos, Luis.
Arceivala. Wastewater Treatment & Disposal. (Pollution Engineering & Technology Ser.: Vol. 15). 920p. 1981. 99.50 (ISBN 0-8247-6973-2). Dekker.
Arcenaux, Claude, ed. see Electron Microscopy Society.
Arceneaux, Marc. Cars. (E-Z Color & Fold Bks.). (Illus.). (gr. 1-4). 1983. pap. 2.50 (ISBN 0-448-11056-3, G&D). Putnam Pub Group.
--City Vehicles. (E-Z Color & Fold Bks.). (Illus.). (gr. 1-4). 1983. pap. 2.50 (ISBN 0-448-11054-7, G&D). Putnam Pub Group.
--Country Vehicles. (E-Z Color & Fold Books). (Illus.). (gr. 1-4). 1983. pap. 2.50 (ISBN 0-448-11055-5, G&D). Putnam Pub Group.
--Paper Airplanes. (Illus.). 32p. 1974. pap. 3.95 (ISBN 0-8431-1703-6, 40-X). Troubador Pr.
--Space Base Vehicles. (E-Z Color & Fold Books). (Illus.). (gr. 1-4). 1983. pap. 2.50 (ISBN 0-448-11052-0, G&D). Putnam Pub Group.
--Trucks & Trailers. (E-Z Color & Fold Bks.). (gr. 1-4). 1983. pap. 2.50 (ISBN 0-448-11053-9, G&D). Putnam Pub Group.
Arceneaux, Marc, illus. The Little Big Rig. (Beep Beep Board Bks.). (Illus.). 14p. 1984. 2.95 (ISBN 0-671-47339-5, Little Simon). S&S.
--The Little Cement Mixer. (Beep Beep Board Bks.). (Illus.). 14p. 1984. 2.95 (ISBN 0-671-47340-9, Little Simon). S&S.
--The Little Fire Engine. (Beep Beep Board Bks.). (Illus.). 14p. 1984. 2.95 (ISBN 0-671-47338-7, Little Simon). S&S.
--The Little Garbage Truck. (Beep Beep Board Bks.). (Illus.). 14p. 1984. 2.95 (ISBN 0-671-47341-7, Little Simon). S&S.
Arceneaux, Thelma H. Reaching for the Unreachable. 53p. 1971. pap. 2.95 (ISBN 0-9600870-2-8). T H Arceneaux.
--They Emerged from the Shade. LC 74-86408. (Illus.). 253p. 1975. 6.95 (ISBN 0-9600870-1-X). T H Arceneaux.
Arceneaux, William. Acadian General: Alfred Mouton & the Civil War. (U. S. L. History Ser.). 220p. 1981. 10.95 (ISBN 0-940984-00-8). U of SW LA Ctr LA Studies.
Arceri, Gene, jt. auth. see LaGuardia, Robert.
Arch, John C. Income Tax Guide for Teachers: NEA Federal. 1983. pap. 5.95 (ISBN 0-8106-1386-7). NEA.
--NEA Federal Income Tax Guide for Teachers: 1984 Handbook. LC 83-121386. 158p. pap. 5.95. NEA.
Arch, Joseph. The Story of His Life, Told by Himself. LC 83-48472. (The World of Labour-English Workers 1850-1890 Ser.). 412p. 1984. lib. bdg. 50.00 (ISBN 0-8240-5700-7). Garland Pub.
Arch, Marjorie S., jt. auth. see Bishop, Edna B.
Archa, Amos & Landau, Eli. Phoenix. 340p. 1982. 20.00x (ISBN 0-7278-0599-1, Pub. by Severn Hse). State Mutual Bk.
Archaeological Textiles. Irene Emery Roundtable on Museum Textiles: 1974 Proceedings. Fiske, Patricia, ed. LC 75-21585. (Illus.). 312p. 1975. pap. 10.00 (ISBN 0-87405-005-7). Textile Mus.
Archambault, John, jt. auth. see Martin, Bill.
Archambault, Paul. Seven French Chroniclers: Witnesses to History. LC 73-16652. 224p. 1974. 12.00x (ISBN 0-8156-0099-2). Syracuse U Pr.
Archambault, Paul J., jt. ed. see Mustacchi, Marianna M.
Archambault, Reginald D., ed. & intro. by see Dewey, John.
Archambeault, Betty J., jt. auth. see Archambeault, William G.
Archambeault, James, photos by. Kentucky. LC 81-86037. (Illus.). 160p. (Text by Thomas D. Clark). 1982. 35.00 (ISBN 0-912856-74-2). Graphic Arts Ctr.
Archambeault, William G. & Archambeault, Betty J. Computers for Criminal Justice Administration & Management. 186p. 1984. pap. 12.95 (ISBN 0-932930-65-4). Pilgrimage Inc.
--Correctional Supervisory Management: Principles of Organization, Policy & Law. (Prentice Hall Series in Criminal Justice). (Illus.). 448p. 1982. reference 24.95 (ISBN 0-13-178269-X). P-H.
Archambeault-Jones, Claudella, jt. auth. see Feller, Irving.
Archard, David. Consciousness & the Unconscious. 136p. (Orig.). 1984. pap. 11.95 (ISBN 0-87548-435-2). Open Court.
Archard, Geoffrey C., tr. see Arifov, Ubai A.
Archard, Geoffrey D., tr. see Sirota, N. N.
Archard, Peter. Vagrancy & Alcoholism. (Illus.). 1979. text ed. 33.00x (ISBN 0-333-23190-2). Humanities.
Archbishop Bergan Mercy Hospital. Comprehensive Cardiac Rehabilitation Program. LC 80-13599. 62p. 1980. pap. 8.00 (ISBN 0-87125-063-2). Cath Health.
Archbishop of York, et al. More Points of View. facs. ed. LC 69-18933. (Essay Index Reprint Ser). 1930. 14.00 (ISBN 0-8369-0048-0). Ayer Co Pubs.
Archbishop Athanasius Martos. Religioznaya Tchuvstvo, Promisl Bozhil i Dukovnoje Prizvanije. 30p. 1983. pap. 2.00 (ISBN 0-317-29069-X). Holy Trinity.
Archbishop Averky Taushev. O Monashistvje. 46p. pap. 2.00 (ISBN 0-317-29064-9). Holy Trinity.
--Provozvjestnik Karl Bozhijej Russkomy Narodu. 30p. 1968. pap. 1.00 (ISBN 0-317-29066-5). Holy Trinity.
--Rukovodstvo k Izuchjeniju Svjashchennago Pisanija Novago Zavjeta-Tchetvjerojevangelija. 345p. 1974. pap. text ed. 12.00 (ISBN 0-317-29299-4). Holy Trinity.
--Rukovodstvo po Gomiletikje. 110p. 1961. pap. text ed. 5.00 (ISBN 0-317-30276-0). Holy Trinity.
--Visokopreosvjashennij Theofan, Arkhiepiskop Poltavsky i Perejaslavsky. 88p. 1974. pap. 5.00 (ISBN 0-317-29284-6). Holy Trinity.
Archbishop Joseph Raya & Baron Jose de Vinck. Byzantine Daily Worship. (Illus.). 1036p. 48.75 (ISBN 0-911726-08-X). Alleluia Pr.
Archbishop Konstantine Zaitsev. Pamjati Igumena Fillimona. 58p. 1954. pap. 2.00 (ISBN 0-317-29287-0). Holy Trinity.
Archbishop Metodies. O Znamjenii Obnovlenija Svatykh Ikon. 82p. 1963. pap. 3.00 (ISBN 0-317-29041-X). Holy Trinity.
Archbishop Nikon Rklitsky, ed. Zhizneopisanie i Tvorenije Blazhennejshago Antonia, Mitropolita Kievskago i Galitzkago, v 17 tomakh, 17 vols. 6000p. 1971. pap. 200.00 (ISBN 0-317-29015-0). Holy Trinity.
Archbishop of York. Palmer's Bible Atlas (Facsimile Edition) 84p. 1982. 14.95 (ISBN 0-686-43010-7, Carta Pub Isreal). Hippocrene Bks.
Archbishop Vitaly Maximenko. Motivi Moijej Zhizni. 205p. 1955. pap. 7.00 (ISBN 0-317-29054-1). Holy Trinity.
Archbold, Lawrence. Style & Structure in the Praeludia of Dietrich Buxtehude. Buelow, George, ed. LC 85-1064. (Studies in Musicology: No. 82). 358p. 1985. 49.95 (ISBN 0-8357-1646-5). UMI Res Pr.
Archbold, Richard & Rand, Austin L. New Guinea Expedition, Fly River Area, 1936-1937. LC 75-32797. (Illus.). Repr. of 1940 ed. 30.00 (ISBN 0-404-14100-5). AMS Pr.
Archbold, William A., ed. Twentieth-Century Essays & Addresses. facs. ed. LC 78-128202. (Essay Index Reprint Ser). 1927. 18.00 (ISBN 0-8369-1861-4). Ayer Co Pubs.
Archdall, Mervyn, ed. see Lodge, John.
Archdeacon, H. C. & Ellsworth, Ken, eds. Track Cyclopedia 1985. 10th ed. (Illus.). 1985. price not set (ISBN 0-911382-02-X). Simmons Boardman.
Archdeacon, Thomas J. Becoming American: An Ethnic History. LC 82-48691. 320p. 1983. 17.95 (ISBN 0-02-900830-1); pap. 7.95x (ISBN 0-02-900980-4). Free Pr.
--New York City, 1664-1710: Conquest & Change. LC 75-22893. 224p. 1976. 22.50x (ISBN 0-8014-0944-6). Cornell U Pr.
Archdiocese of Baltimore. Partners in Catechesis. 96p. 1984. pap. 9.95 (ISBN 0-697-02016-9). Wm C Brown.
Archdiocese of Dubuque. R. C. I. A. Foundations of Christian Initiation. 96p. 1982. wire coil 7.95 (ISBN 0-697-01781-8). Wm C Brown.
Archdiocese of Newark. Growing in Faith with Your Child. Ivory, Thomas P., ed. 48p. (Orig.). pap. 2.50 (ISBN 0-697-01693-5). Wm C Brown.
Archdiocese of Newark, Office of Pastoral Renewal. Renew, Leadership Book. 1980. 10.00 (ISBN 0-8091-9195-4). Paulist Pr.
--Renew, Parish Book. 1980. 75.00 (ISBN 0-8091-9191-1). Paulist Pr.
--Renew, Participant Book: Empowerment by the Spirit. 1980. 3.00 (ISBN 0-8091-9194-6). Paulist Pr.
--Renew, Participant Book: Our Response. 1980. 2.50 (ISBN 0-8091-9193-8). Paulist Pr.
--Renew, Participant Book: The Lord's Call. 1980. 2.00 (ISBN 0-8091-9192-X). Paulist Pr.
--Renew, Pastoral Staff Book. 1980. 3.50 (ISBN 0-8091-9196-2). Paulist Pr.
Archdiocese of San Francisco. Great Misconceptions: People with Disabilities. 48p. 1982. saddle stitched 4.95 (ISBN 0-8403-2674-2). Kendall-Hunt.
Archenhold, W. F., jt. auth. see Treloar, L. R.
Archenhold, W. F., et al. School Science Laboratories: A Handbook of Design, Management & Organization. 303p. 1980. 35.00x (ISBN 0-7195-3436-4, Pub. by Murray Pubs England). State Mutual Bk.
Archer. Bacterial Transformation. 1973. 65.00 (ISBN 0-12-059450-1). Acad Pr.
Archer, B. J., ed. Follies: Architecture for the Late Twentieth Century Landscape. LC 83-42958. (Illus.). 112p. 1983. pap. 19.95 (ISBN 0-8478-0510-7). Rizzoli Intl.
Archer, Beth, tr. see Chastel, Andre.
Archer, Beth, tr. see Valensi, Lucette.
Archer, C., tr. see Bojer, Johan.
Archer, Carol R. Atlas of Computed Tomography of the Larynx. (Illus.). 200p. 1985. 27.50 (ISBN 0-87527-240-1). Green.
Archer, Charles. William Archer: Life, Works & Friendships. 1931. 49.50x (ISBN 0-685-89793-1). Elliots Bks.
Archer, Christon, jt. ed. see Travers, Timothy.
Archer, Clive. International Organizations. (Key Concepts in International Relations: No. 1). 160p. (Orig.). 1983. text ed. 24.50x (ISBN 0-04-320156-3); pap. text ed. 9.95x (ISBN 0-04-320157-1). Allen Unwin.
Archer, Clive & Maxwell, Stephen. The Nordic Model: Studies in Public Policy Innovation. 176p. 1980. text ed. 36.50x (ISBN 0-566-00341-4). Gower Pub Co.
Archer, Clive & Main, John, eds. Scotland's Voice in International Affairs. 160p. 1980. 21.50x (ISBN 0-7735-0512-1). McGill-Queens U Pr.
Archer, Dane. How to Expand Your S. I. Q. (Social Intelligence Quotient) LC 79-19568. (Illus.). 176p. 1980. pap. 5.95 (ISBN 0-87131-296-4). M Evans.
Archer, Dane & Gartner, Rosemary. Violence & Crime in Cross National Perspective. LC 83-21700. 416p. 1984. 31.00x (ISBN 0-300-03149-1). Yale U Pr.
Archer, Dave. Beyond the X's & O's. (Illus.). 113p. (Orig.). 1981. pap. 6.50 (ISBN 0-9607372-0-0). Motiv Aids.
Archer, Denis, ed. Jane's Pocket Book of Pistols & Submachine Guns. (Jane's Pocket Book Ser.). 1977. pap. 8.95 (ISBN 0-02-079970-5, Collier). Macmillan.
Archer, Denis, ed. see Jane's Pocket Books.
Archer, E. C. & Pemberton, LeRoy A. Typing Skill Drills. 1973. pap. text ed. 4.35 (ISBN 0-89420-103-4, 143000). Natl Book.
Archer, Eric, jt. auth. see Rosenberg, Ron.
Archer, F. C. & Stewart, J. R. Model Office Practice Set. 2nd ed. 1975. text ed. 9.00 (ISBN 0-07-002306-9). McGraw.
Archer, F. C., et al. General Office Procedures. 4th ed. (Illus.). 512p. (gr. 9-12). 1975. text ed. 18.80 (ISBN 0-07-002161-9). McGraw.
--Office Cashiering Practice Set. 1969. text ed. 9.00 (ISBN 0-07-002167-8). McGraw.
--Stock Control Practice Set. 1969. text ed. 9.00 (ISBN 0-07-002176-7). McGraw.
--Accounts Payable Practice Set. 1969. text ed. 8.96 (ISBN 0-07-002196-1). McGraw.
--Accounts Receivable Practice Set. 1970. text ed. 8.96 (ISBN 0-07-002195-3). McGraw.
Archer, Francis Bisset. Gambia Colony & Protectorate: An Official Handbook. 342p. 1967. Repr. of 1906 ed. 30.00x (ISBN 0-7146-1139-5, BHA 01139, F Cass Co). Biblio Dist.
Archer, Fred. Sir Lionel. (Illus.). 339p. 1980. 12.95 (ISBN 0-86595-005-9). Gift Pubns.
Archer, Gleason L. Big Business & Radio. LC 76-161133. (History of Broadcasting: Radio to Television Ser). 1971. Repr. of 1939 ed. 36.50 (ISBN 0-405-03558-6). Ayer Co Pubs.
--The Encyclopedia of Bible Difficulties. 352p. 1982. 16.95 (ISBN 0-310-43570-6). Zondervan.
--Ethical Obligations of the Lawyer. 367p. 1981. Repr. of 1910 ed. lib. bdg. 27.50x (ISBN 0-8377-0207-0). Rothman.
--History of Radio to 1926. LC 72-161132. (History of Broadcasting: Radio to Television Ser). (Illus.). 1971. Repr. of 1938 ed. 28.00 (ISBN 0-405-03557-8). Ayer Co Pubs.
--Resena Critica de una Introduccion al Antiguo Testamento. Orig. Title: Survey of Old Testament Introduction. 564p. (Span.). 1981. pap. 13.95 (ISBN 0-8254-1033-9). Kregel.
--Resena Critica De Uno (Survey of Old Testament Introduction) Sipowicz, Edwin & Lieuanor, M. Francisco, trs. from Eng. 507p. (Sp.). 1982. pap. 13.95 (ISBN 0-8254-1033-9). Kregel.
--A Survey of Old Testament Introduction. LC 64-20988. 582p. 1973. 19.95 (ISBN 0-8024-8446-8). Moody.
Archer, Gleason L. & Chirichigno, G. C. Old Testament Quotations in the New Testament: A Complete Survey. 1983. 21.95 (ISBN 0-8024-0236-4). Moody.
Archer, Gleason L., jt. auth. see Hill, Gary.
Archer, Gleason L., tr. see Ahmanson, John.
Archer, Gleason L., Jr. The Book of Job: God's Answer to the Problem of Undeserved Suffering. 128p. (Orig.). 1983. pap. 5.95 (ISBN 0-8010-0190-0). Baker Bk.
Archer, Gleason L., Jr., et al. The Rapture. LC 83-126250. 256p. (Orig.). 1984. 7.95 (ISBN 0-310-44741-0, Pub. by Academie Bks). Zondervan.
Archer, Horace R., ed. Rare Book Collections: Some Theoretical & Practical Suggestions for Use by Librarians & Students. LC 81-13311. (ACRL Monograph: No. 27). viii, 128p. 1982. Repr. of 1965 ed. lib. bdg. 24.75x (ISBN 0-313-23226-1, ARRB). Greenwood.
Archer, Ian, jt. ed. see Royle, Trevor.

Archer, J. & Birke, L. Exploration in Humans & Animals. 1983. 47.95 (ISBN 0-442-30527-3). Van Nos Reinhold.
Archer, James, jt. auth. see Conway, Richard.
Archer, James, Jr. Managing Anxiety & Stress. LC 81-68413. 232p. 1982. pap. text ed. 12.95x (ISBN 0-915202-32-8). Accel Devel.
Archer, Jane. Rebellious Rapture. 448p. (Orig.). 1980. pap. 2.50 (ISBN 0-345-28262-0). Ballantine.
--Spring Dreams. 304p. (Orig.). 1983. pap. 3.25 (ISBN 0-440-08110-6, Emerald). Dell.
Archer, Jeffrey. First among Equals. 1984. 16.95 (ISBN 0-671-50406-1, Linden Pr). S&S.
--First among Equals. 1985. pap. 4.50 (ISBN 0-671-50468-1). PB.
--First among Equals. (General Ser.). 1984. lib. bdg. 17.95 (ISBN 0-8161-3758-7, Large Print Bks); pap. 10.95 (ISBN 0-8161-3778-1). G K Hall.
--Kane & Abel. 480p. 1982. pap. 3.75 (ISBN 0-449-24376-1, Crest). Fawcett.
--Not a Penny More, Not a Penny Less. 256p. 1981. pap. 2.95 (ISBN 0-449-24428-8, Crest). Fawcett.
--The Prodigal Daughter. (General Ser.). 1983. lib. bdg. 21.50 (ISBN 0-8161-3499-5, Large Print Bks). G K Hall.
--The Prodigal Daughter. 1985. pap. 4.50 (ISBN 0-671-60407-4). PB.
--A Quiver Full of Arrows. 1985. pap. 3.95. PB.
--Shall We Tell the President? 228p. 1985. pap. 3.95 (ISBN 0-449-20806-0, Crest). Fawcett.
--Willie Visits the Square World. (Illus.). 48p. (gr. 5 up). 6.95 (ISBN 0-7064-1200-1, Rutledge Pr). Smith Pubs.
Archer, Jerome W. & Schwartz, A. Reader for Writers. 3rd ed. 1971. text ed. 28.95 (ISBN 0-07-002193-7). McGraw.
Archer, John. Animals under Stress. (Studies in Biology: No. 108). 64p. 1979. pap. text ed. 8.95 (ISBN 0-7131-2737-6). E Arnold.
--The Literature of British Domestic Architecture 1715-1842. LC 84-880. (Illus.). 1078p. 1985. text ed. 100.00x (ISBN 0-262-01076-3). MIT Pr.
--Winning at Poker: An Expert's Guide. 1978. 5.00 (ISBN 0-87980-362-2). Wilshire.
--Winning at Twenty-One. 1977. pap. 5.00 (ISBN 0-87980-328-2). Wilshire.
Archer, John & Lloyd, Barbara. Sex & Gender. (Illus.). 228p. 1985. 32.50 (ISBN 0-521-26497-9); pap. 10.95 (ISBN 0-521-31921-8). Cambridge U Pr.
Archer, John, jt. auth. see Lydenberg, Harry M.
Archer, John, jt. ed. see Lloyd, Barbara.
Archer, John B; see Bottiglia, William F.
Archer, John C. Faiths Men Live by. facsimile ed. LC 79-156606. (Essay Index Reprint Ser). Repr. of 1934 ed. 25.50 (ISBN 0-8369-2266-2). Ayer Co Pubs.
--Mystical Elements in Mohammed. LC 80-26396. (Yale Oriental Ser. Researches: No. 11 Pt. 1; All Published). Repr. of 1924 ed. 22.50 (ISBN 0-404-60281-9). AMS Pr.
Archer, John C. & Taylor, Peter J. Section & Party: A Political Geography of American Presidential Elections from Andrew Jackson to Ronald Reagan. (Geographical Research Studies Press Ser.). 271p. 1981. 59.95x (ISBN 0-471-10014-5, Pub. by Res Stud Pr). Wiley.
Archer, John H. Art & Architecture in Victorian Manchester. LC 84-17132, (Illus.). 352p. 1985. 55.00 (ISBN 0-7190-0957-X, Pub. by Manchester Univ pr). Longwood Pub Group.
Archer, Jules. China in the Twentieth Century. LC 73-6050. (Illus.). 240p. (gr. 7 up). 1974. 10.95 (ISBN 0-02-705620-1, 70562). Macmillan.
--From Whales to Dinosaurs: The Story of Roy Chapman Andrews. LC 76-10541. (Illus.). (YA) 1976. 6.95 (ISBN 0-312-30870-1). St Martin.
--Hunger on Planet Earth. LC 76-3603. (Illus.). (gr. 8 up). 1977. 15.34i (ISBN 0-690-01126-1). Crowell Jr Bks.
--Jungle Fighters: A GI War Correspondent's Experience in the New Guinea Campaign. (Illus.). 192p. (gr. 7 up). 1985. 9.29 (ISBN 0-671-46058-7). Messner.
--Legacy of the Desert: Understanding the Arabs. (gr. 7-12). 1976. 8.95 (ISBN 0-316-04965-4). Little.
--Police State: Could It Happen Here? LC 76-58720. 192p. (gr. 7 up). 1977. PLB 12.89 (ISBN 0-06-020154-1). HarpJ.
--Washington vs. Main Street: The Struggle Between Federal & Local Power. LC 74-8623. (Illus.). 256p. (gr. 7 up). 1974. Crowell Jr Bks.
--Watergate: America in Crisis. LC 74-5567. (Illus.). (gr. 7 up). 1975. Crowell Jr Bks.
--Who's Running Your Life: A Look at Young People's Rights. (Illus.). (YA) (gr. 7 up). 1979. PLB 7.95 (ISBN 0-15-296058-9, HJ). HarBraceJ.
--Winners & Losers: How Elections Work in America. LC 83-18368. (Illus.). 240p. (gr. 7-12). 1984. 13.95 (ISBN 0-15-297945-X, HJ). HarBraceJ.
--You Can't Do That to Me: Famous Fights for Human Rights. LC 79-5127. 204p. (gr. 6 up). 1980. 10.95 (ISBN 0-02-705600-7, 70560). Macmillan.
Archer, K., et al. Industrial Democracy: Ways Forward in Britain & West Germany. 101p. 1979. 25.00x (ISBN 0-905492-15-3, Pub. by Anglo-German Found England). State Mutual Bk.
Archer, Laird. Athens Journal Nineteen Forty-Nineteen Forty-One: The Graeco-Italian & the Graeco-German Wars & the German Occupation. 599p. 1983. pap. 18.00x (ISBN 0-89126-122-2). MA-AH Pub.
Archer, M. An Introduction to Canadian Business. 4th ed. 1982. 23.95 (ISBN 0-07-548449-8). McGraw.
Archer, M. & Dakin, C. Introductory Business Management Simulation: Guide for Participants. 2nd ed. 144p. 1982. 10.95 (ISBN 0-07-548540-0). McGraw.
Archer, M. & Lightbown, R. India Observed: British Artists in India 1760-1860. (Illus.). 160p. 1982. pap. text ed. 10.40x (ISBN 0-86294-024-9, Pub. by Trefoil Bks Ltd UK). Humanities.
Archer, Margaret, jt. auth. see Vaughan, Michalina.
Archer, Margaret, ed. The Sociology of Educational Expansion: Take-Off, Growth, & Inflation in Educational Systems. (Sage Studies in International Sociology: Vol. 27). (Illus.). 320p. 1982. 25.00 (ISBN 0-8039-9773-6). Sage.
Archer, Margaret S. Social Origins of Educational Systems. LC 77-84072. (Illus.). 815p. 1979. 27.50 (ISBN 0-8039-9876-7). Sage.
Archer, Margaret S., jt. ed. see Giner, Salvador.
Archer, Margaret S., tr. see Sullerot, Evelyne.
Archer, Marguerite. Jean Anouilh. LC 70-136495. (Essays on Modern Writers Ser.: No. 55). 48p. 1971. 2.50 (ISBN 0-231-03346-X). Columbia U Pr.
Archer, Marion F. see Laughlin, Mildred.
Archer, Michael & Morgan, Brian. Fair As China Dishes: English Delftware. LC 77-83716. (Illus.). 128p. 1977. pap. 11.50 (ISBN 0-88397-003-1, Pub. by Intl Exhibit Foun). C E Tuttle.
Archer, Michael, ed. see Lipski, Louis L.
Archer, Mildred. British Drawings in the India Office Library, 2 vols. (Illus.). 712p. 1969. Set. 90.00x (ISBN 0-11-880416-2, Pub. by Sotheby Pubns England). Biblio Dist.
--Company Drawings in the India Office Library. (Illus.). 298p. 1972. 45.00x (ISBN 0-11-880422-7, Pub. by Sotheby Pubns England). Biblio Dist.
--Early Views of India: The Picturesque Journeys of Thomas & William Daniell 1788-1793. (Illus.). 240p. 1980. 37.50 (ISBN 0-500-01238-5). Thames Hudson.
--India & British Portraiture Seventeen Seventy to Eighteen Twenty-Five. (Illus.). 536p. 1979. 105.00x (ISBN 0-85667-054-5, Pub by Sotheby Pubns England). Biblio Dist.
--Natural History Drawings in the India Office Library. (Illus.). 116p. 1962. 25.00x (ISBN 0-85667-082-0, Pub. by Sotheby Pubns England). Biblio Dist.
--Tippoo's Tiger. (Illus.). 48p. (Orig.). 1984. pap. 7.95 (ISBN 0-905209-53-2, Pub. by Victoria & Albert Mus UK). Faber & Faber.
Archer, Mildred & Lightbown, Ronald. India Observed: India as Viewed by British Artists 1760-1860. (Orig.). 1984. pap. 10.95 (ISBN 0-905209-18-4, Pub. by Victoria & Albert Mus UK). Faber & Faber.
Archer, Mildred, jt. auth. see Falk, Toby.
Archer, Mildred, ed. see Archer, William G.
Archer, Peter & Lord Reay. Freedom at Stake. LC 67-15647. (Background Ser.). 1967. 7.95 (ISBN 0-8023-1118-0). Dufour.
Archer, R. L. Secondary Education in the 19th Century. 363p. 1966. Repr. of 1921 ed. 26.00x (ISBN 0-7146-1446-7, BHA 01446, F Cass Co). Biblio Dist.
Archer, R. L., tr. from Fr. & see Rousseau, Jean-Jacques.
Archer, R. W. Land Pooling by Local Government for Planned Urban Development in Perth. (Lincoln Institute Monograph: No. 80-4). (Illus.). 69p. 1980. pap. 5.00 (ISBN 0-686-29508-0, Australian Institute of Urban Studies). Lincoln Inst Land.
Archer, Raymond L. Muhammadan Mysticism in Sumatra. LC 77-87487. (Royal Asiatic Society, Malayan Branch. Journal: Vol. 15). Repr. of 1937 ed. 16.50 (ISBN 0-404-16695-4). AMS Pr.
Archer, Richard P. Concept Spelling Student Workbook, No. 4. 69p. 1979. 10.00 (ISBN 0-935276-00-9). Concept Spelling.
--Concept Spelling's: Language Awareness Workbook. (Concept Spelling Ser.). 56p. (Orig.). (gr. 4-12). 1982. 10.00 (ISBN 0-935276-06-8). Concept Spelling.
--Concept Spelling's: The Secrets of Spelling-Cassette-Workbook. (Concept Spelling Ser.). 30p. (gr. 5-12). 1982. Wkbk. 20.00 (ISBN 0-935276-07-6). Concept Spelling.
--Introduction to Concept Spelling Teacher's Guide. 48p. (Orig.). 1980. tchrs. guide 5.00 (ISBN 0-935276-02-5); 10.00 (ISBN 0-935276-01-7). Concept Spelling.
--The Shortcut to Reading. 29p. 1983. 10.00 (ISBN 0-317-02255-5). Concept Spelling.
Archer, Richard P., ed. Concept Spelling Teacher's Manual. 132p. 1979. 50.00 (ISBN 0-935276-03-3). Concept Spelling.
Archer, Robert & Bouillon, Antoine. The South African Game: Sport & Racism. 368p. 1982. 25.00x (ISBN 0-86232-066-6, Pub. by Zed Pr England); pap. 9.95x (ISBN 0-86232-082-8, Pub. by Zed Pr England). Biblio Dist.
Archer, Robert F. The Lehigh Valley Railroad. LC 77-85753. (Illus.). 1977. 30.00 (ISBN 0-8310-7113-3). Howell-North.
Archer, S. H., et al. Financial Management: An Introduction. 2nd ed. LC 82-23890. 764p. 1983. 35.50x (ISBN 0-471-09001-8); study guide avail. (ISBN 0-471-87248-2). Wiley.
Archer, Sarah E. & Fleshman, Ruth P. Community Health Nursing. 3rd ed. LC 84-29105. (Nursing Ser.). 650p. 1984. text ed. 21.75 pub net (ISBN 0-534-04344-5). Wadsworth Health.
Archer, Sarah E. & Goehner, Patricia A. Nurses: A Political Force. 1982. pub net 15.25 (ISBN 0-8185-0513-3, 81-16206). Brooks-Cole.
Archer, Sarah Ellen, et al. Implementing Change for Communities: A Collaborative Process. (Illus.). 256p. 1984. pap. text ed. 21.95 (ISBN 0-8016-0300-5). M Evans.
Archer, Sellers G. Soil Conservation. LC 56-6002. (Illus.). 1969. Repr. of 1956 ed. 16.95x (ISBN 0-8061-0346-9). U of Okla Pr.
Archer, Stanley. Richard Hooker. (English Authors Ser.). 93p. 1983. lib. bdg. 14.50 (ISBN 0-8057-6836-X, Twayne). G K Hall.
Archer, Stephen H. & D'Ambrosie, Charles A. Theory of Business Finance: A Book of Readings. rev. ed. (Illus.). 1976. text ed. write for info. (ISBN 0-02-303820-9). Macmillan.
Archer, Stephen H., jt. auth. see Francis, Clark.
Archer, Stephen M. How Theatre Happens. 2nd ed. 304p. 1983. text ed. write for info. (ISBN 0-02-303750-4). Macmillan.
Archer, Stephen M., ed. American Actors & Actresses: A Guide to Information Sources. (Performing Arts Information Guide Ser.: Vol. 8). 350p. 1983. 60.00x (ISBN 0-8103-1495-9). Gale.
Archer, Stephen N. & D'Ambrosio, Charles A. The Theory of Business Finance: A Book of Readings. 3rd ed. 720p. 1983. pap. write for info. (ISBN 0-02-304150-1). Macmillan.
Archer, T. A. The Crusades. 1894. 15.00 (ISBN 0-8482-7265-X). Norwood Edns.
Archer, Thomas. The Highway of Letters & Its Echoes of Famous Footsteps. 1979. Repr. of 1893 ed. lib. bdg. 30.00 (ISBN 0-8495-0209-8). Arden Lib.
--The Highway of Letters & Its Echoes of Famous Footsteps. 1973. Repr. of 1893 ed. 30.00 (ISBN 0-8274-1548-6). R West.
--The Pauper, the Thief & the Convict: Sketches of Some of Their Homes, Haunts & Habits. LC 84-48264. (The Rise of Urban Britain Ser.). 239p. 1985. 35.00 (ISBN 0-8240-6266-3). Garland Pub.
--William Ewart Gladstone & His Contemporaries: Fifty Years of Social & Political Progress, 4 vols. Repr. Set. 150.00 (ISBN 0-685-43663-2). Norwood Edns.
Archer, Thomas A. The Crusade of Richard I, 1189-92. LC 76-29828. Repr. of 1889 ed. 52.50 (ISBN 0-404-15408-5). AMS Pr.
Archer, Thomas A. & Kingsford, Charles L. The Crusades: The Story of the Latin Kingdom of Jerusalem. LC 76-29833. Repr. of 1900 ed. 39.50 (ISBN 0-404-15409-3). AMS Pr.
Archer, Tod. Simplifying Microcomputer-Based Product Design With Special Development Equipment. (Illus.). 192p. 1982. lib. bdg. 26.95 (ISBN 0-13-810796-3); pap. text ed. 18.95 (ISBN 0-13-810788-2). P-H.
Archer, Trevor, jt. ed. see Nilsson, L. G.
Archer, W. G. Blue Grove. LC 72-7219. (Select Bibliographies Reprint Ser.). 1972. Repr. of 1940 ed. 22.00 (ISBN 0-8369-6920-0). Ayer Co Pubs.
--Indian Paintings from the Punjab Hills: A Survey & History of Pahari Miniature Painting, 2 vols. (Illus.). 840p. 1973. Set. 180.00x (ISBN 0-85667-002-2, Pub. by Sotheby Pubns England). Biblio Dist.
--Tribal Law & Justice. 700p. 1984. 39.50x (ISBN 0-391-03087-6, Pub. by Concept India). Humanities.
--Visions of Courtly India. (Illus.). 128p. 1977. 34.00x (ISBN 0-85667-032-4, Pub. by Sotheby Pubns England). Biblio Dist.
Archer, W. G., ed. The Kama Sutra: The Richard Burton Classic Translation. (Unwin Paperbacks). 295p. 1981. pap. 4.95 (ISBN 0-04-891048-1). Allen Unwin.
Archer, W. Harry. Oral & Maxillofacial Surgery, 2 vols. 5th ed. LC 73-89931. (Illus.). 1859p. 1975. Vol. 1. text ed. 54.00 (ISBN 0-7216-1362-4). Saunders.
Archer, William. English Dramatists of To-Day. (Works of William Archer Ser.). 387p. Date not set. Repr. of 1882 ed. 39.00 (ISBN 0-932051-64-2). Am Repr Serv.
--English Dramatists of Today. 1976. Repr. of 1882 ed. 39.00 (ISBN 0-403-06038-9, Regency). Scholarly.
--Henry Irving, Actor & Manager. LC 70-107156. 1970. Repr. of 1883 ed. 17.00 (ISBN 0-403-00468-3). Scholarly.
--Henry Irving; Actor & Manager: A Critical Study. (Works of William Archer Ser.). 108p. Repr. lib. bdg. 29.00 (ISBN 0-932051-21-9). Am Repr Serv.
--Life, Trial & Death of Francisco Ferrer. 59.95 (ISBN 0-8490-0540-X). Gordon Pr.
--The Old Drama & the New: An Essay in Re-Valuation. 396p. 1983. Repr. of 1923 ed. lib. bdg. 85.00 (ISBN 0-89760-070-3). Telegraph Bks.
--Play Making: A Manual for Craftsmanship. 1913. 45.00 (ISBN 0-8482-3255-0). Norwood Edns.
--Poets of the Younger Generation. LC 76-120572. (BCL: Series I). Repr. of 1902 ed. 12.50 (ISBN 0-404-00367-2). AMS Pr.
--Poets of the Younger Generation. LC 72-8574. 564p. 1902. Repr. 12.00 (ISBN 0-403-00240-0). Scholarly.
--Real Conversations. LC 72-195438. 1904. lib. bdg. 20.00 (ISBN 0-8414-1199-9). Folcroft.
--Theatrical World of Eighteen Ninety-Seven. LC 77-82818. Repr. of 1898 ed. 22.00 (ISBN 0-405-08211-8, Pub. by Blom). Ayer Co Pubs.
--Theatrical World of Eighteen Ninety-Three. LC 77-82818. Repr. of 1894 ed. 22.00 (ISBN 0-405-08210-X, Pub. by Blom). Ayer Co Pubs.
--Through Afro-America. (The Works of William Archer). xvi, 295p. Repr. of 1910 ed. 39.00 (ISBN 0-932051-75-8). Am Repr Serv.
--Through Afro-America, an English Reading on the Race Problem. LC 76-132074. Repr. of 1910 ed. cancelled (ISBN 0-8371-0429-7). Greenwood.
Archer, William & Barker, H. Granville, eds. National Theatre: Scheme & Estimates. LC 78-102845. 1970. Repr. of 1907 ed. 22.50x (ISBN 0-8046-0749-4, Pub. by Kennikat). Assoc Faculty Pr.
Archer, William, ed. see Hazlitt, William.
Archer, William, ed. see Ibsen, Henrik.
Archer, William, tr. see Kielland, Alexander L.
Archer, William G. Songs for The Bride: Wedding Rites of Rural India. Miller, Barbara S. & Archer, Mildred, eds. (Studies in Oriental Culture). 224p. 1985. 22.50x (ISBN 0-317-18769-4). Brooklyn Coll Pr.
Archer-Hind, R. D., ed. see Plato.
Archetti, F. & Cugiani, M. Numerical Techniques for Stochastic Systems. 406p. 1980. 85.00 (ISBN 0-444-86000-2). Elsevier.
Archibald, Carol, jt. auth. see Moser, Kenneth M.
Archibald, Claudia J. Noise Control Directory. pap. 24.50 (ISBN 0-915586-14-2). Fairmont Pr.
Archibald, David J. A Study of Mammalia & Geology Across the Cretaceous-Tertiary Boundary in Garfield County, Montana. (Publications in Geological Sciences: Vol. 122). 1982. pap. 36.00x (ISBN 0-520-09639-8). U of Cal Pr.
Archibald, Douglas. The Story of the Earth's Atmosphere. 1904. 15.00 (ISBN 0-686-17416-X). Ridgeway Bks.
--Yeats. (Irish Studies). 296p. 1983. 25.00x (ISBN 0-8156-2263-5). Syracuse U Pr.
Archibald, Douglas N. John Butler Yeats. LC 71-125792. (Irish Writers Ser.). 103p. 1974. 4.50 (ISBN 0-8387-7759-7); pap. 1.95 (ISBN 0-8387-7733-3). Bucknell U Pr.
Archibald, E. H. Dictionary of Sea Painters. (Illus.). 453p. 1980. 79.50 (ISBN 0-902028-84-7). Antique Collect.
--Dictionary of Sea Painters. (Illus.). 1979. 79.50 (ISBN 0-902028-84-7). Apollo.
--The Fighting Ship in the Royal Navy: 897-1984. (Illus.). 424p. 1984. 29.95 (ISBN 0-7137-1348-8, Pub. by Blandford Pr England). Sterling.
Archibald, J. & Catcott, E. J., eds. Canine & Feline Surgery, Vol. I: Abdomen. LC 83-72264. (Illus.). 550p. 1984. 45.00 (ISBN 0-939674-01-7). Am Vet Pubns.
Archibald, J., et al, eds. Management of Trauma in Dogs & Cats. LC 81-66269. (Illus.). 480p. 1981. 65.00 (ISBN 0-939674-09-2). Am Vet Pubns.
Archibald, J. A., et al, eds. The Contribution of Laboratory Animal Science to the Welfare of Man & Animals. 450p. 1985. lib. bdg. 67.50 (ISBN 0-89574-203-9, Pub. by Gustav Fisher Verlag). VCH Pubs.
Archibald, Jim, ed. see Schacht, Wilhelm.
Archibald, John & Darisse, Alan. A Guide to Multilingual Publishing. 10p. 1982. pap. 6.00 (ISBN 0-914548-36-0). Soc Tech Comm.
Archibald, Katherine. Wartime Shipyard: A Study in Social Disunity. LC 76-7621. (FDR & the Era of the New Deal Ser.). 1976. Repr. of 1947 ed. 27.50 (ISBN 0-306-70802-7). Da Capo.
--Wartime Shipyard: Study in Social Disunity. Stein, Leon, ed. LC 77-70478. (Work Ser.). (Illus.). 1977. Repr. of 1947 ed. lib. bdg. 23.50x (ISBN 0-405-10152-X). Ayer Co Pubs.
Archibald, Leon, jt. ed. see Schwartz, Betty A.
Archibald, Liliana, tr. see Klyuchevsky, Vasili.
Archibald, Norman. Heaven High, Hell Deep: Nineteen Seventeen to Nineteen Eighteen. Gilbert, James, ed. LC 79-7231. (Flight: First Seventy-Five Years Ser.). 1979. Repr. of 1935 ed. lib. bdg. 28.50x (ISBN 0-405-12147-4). Ayer Co Pubs.
Archibald, R. E. M. The Diatoms of the Sundays & Great Fish Rivers in the Eastern Cape Province of South Africa. (Bibliotheca Diatomologica: Vol.1). 432p. 1983. text ed. 42.00 (ISBN 3-7682-1365-X). Lubrecht & Cramer.
Archibald, Raymond. Carlyle's First Love. LC 72-3374. (English Literature Ser., No. 33). (Illus.). 1972. Repr. of 1910 ed. lib. bdg. 56.95x (ISBN 0-8383-1535-6). Haskell.
Archibald, Raymond C. Outline of the History of Mathematics. 6th ed. pap. 7.00 (ISBN 0-384-01880-7). Johnson Repr.
--A Semicentennial History of the American Mathematical Society: Eighteen Hundred Eighty-Eight to Nineteen Hundred Thirty-Eight; with Biographies & Bibliographies Odents, 2 vols. Cohen, I. Bernard, ed. LC 79-7947. (Three Centuries of Science in America Ser.). (Illus.). 1980. Repr. of 1938 ed. Set. lib. bdg. 55.00x (ISBN 0-405-12528-3). Ayer Co Pubs.

--Alfred Hitchcock & the Three Investigators in the Secret of Shark Reef. Hitchcock, Alfred, ed. (Three Investigators Ser.: No. 30). (Illus.). (gr. 4-7). 1979. PLB 5.39 (ISBN 0-394-94249-3); pap. 1.95 (ISBN 0-394-84249-9). Random.
--Alfred Hitchcock & the Three Investigators in the Secret of Phantom Lake. Hitchcock, Alfred, ed. (Three Investigators Ser.: No. 19). (Illus.). (gr. 4-7). 1973. (BYR); PLB 5.39 (ISBN 0-394-92651-X); pap. 1.95 (ISBN 0-394-84257-X). Random.
--The Mystery of the Dancing Devil. Hitchcock, Alfred, ed. LC 80-29350. (Three Investigators Ser.). 144p. (gr. 4-7). 1981. pap. 1.95 (ISBN 0-394-86425-5). Random.
--The Mystery of the Deadly Double. LC 79-29638. (Alfred Hitchcock & the Three Investigators Ser.). 160p. (gr. 4-7). 1981. pap. 1.95 (ISBN 0-394-84491-2). Random.
--The Mystery of the Headless Horse. Hitchcock, Alfred, ed. LC 80-29259. (Three Investigators Ser.). 160p. (gr. 4-7). 1981. pap. 1.95 (ISBN 0-394-84861-6). Random.
--The Mystery of the Purple Pirate. LC 82-372. (The Three Investigators Mystery Ser.: No. 33). (Illus.). 192p. (gr. 4-7). 1982. PLB 5.99 (ISBN 0-394-94951-X); pap. 1.95 (ISBN 0-394-84951-5). Random.
--The Mystery of the Smashing Glass. LC 83-26984. (The Three Investigators Mystery Ser.: No. 38). (Illus.). 192p. (gr. 4-7). 1984. pap. 1.95 (ISBN 0-394-86550-2, Pub. by BYR); lib. bdg. 5.99 GLB (ISBN 0-394-96550-7). Random.

Arden-Close, Charles F. Early Years of the Ordnance Survey. LC 69-12830. (Illus.). Repr. of 1926 ed. 22.50x (ISBN 0-678-05509-2). Kelley.

Ardener, Shirley. Women & Space: Ground Rules & Social Maps. 1981. 25.00 (ISBN 0-312-88733-7). St Martin.

Ardener, Shirley, ed. Defining Females: The Nature of Women in Society. LC 78-16867. 227p. 1978. 28.95x (ISBN 0-470-26465-9). Halsted Pr.
--Perceiving Women. 192p. 1982. pap. text ed. 9.95x (ISBN 0-460-12536-2, BKA 04659, Pub. by J M Dent England). Biblio Dist.

Ardener, Shirley, jt. ed. see Callan, Hilary.

Arder, F., jt. ed. see Allgower, M.

Ardery, Julia S., ed. see Garland, Jim.

Ardery, Philip. Bomber Pilot: A Memoir of World War Two. LC 77-92919. (Illus.). 280p. 1978. 18.00 (ISBN 0-8131-1379-2). U Pr of Ky.

Ardery, Mrs. William B. Kentucky (Court & Other) Records, Vol. 1. LC 65-24115. 206p. 1981. Repr. of 1926 ed. 12.50 (ISBN 0-8063-0005-1). Genealog Pub.
--Kentucky Court & Other Records, Vol. 2: Wills, Deeds, Orders, Suits, Church Minutes, Marriages, Old Bibles & Tombstone Inscriptions. LC 65-24115. 257p. 1984. Repr. of 1932 ed. 15.00 (ISBN 0-8063-0510-X). Genealog Pub.

Ardila, Alfredo. The Neurology & Neuropsychology of the Right Hemisphere. (Neuroscience Monographs: Vol. 1). 200p. 1984. 58.00 (ISBN 0-677-06320-2). Gordon.

Ardila, Alfredo & Ostosky-Solis, Peggy. The Right Hemisphere: Neurology & Neuropsychology. (Monographs in Neuroscience). 294p. 1984. text ed. 58.00 (ISBN 2-88124-103-4). Gordon.

Ardiles, Osvaldo. Ossie: My Life in Football. (Illus.). 208p. 1983. 14.95 (ISBN 0-283-98872-X, Pub. by Sidgwick & Jackson). Merrimack Pub Cir.

Arditi, Luigi. My Reminiscences. LC 77-5500. (Music Reprint Ser.). (Illus.). 1977. Repr. of 1896 ed. lib. bdg. 35.00 (ISBN 0-306-77417-8). Da Capo.

Arditti, Joseph. Orchid Biology: Reviews & Perspectives, Vol I. (Illus.). 1977. 45.00x (ISBN 0-8014-1040-1). Comstock.

Arditti, Joseph, ed. Orchid Biology, No. III. LC 76-25648. (A Comstock Bk.). (Illus.). 416p. 1983. 49.50x (ISBN 0-8014-1512-8). Cornell U Pr.
--Orchid Biology: Reviews & Perspectives, I. LC 76-25648. (Illus.). 328p. 1977. 45.00x (ISBN 0-8014-1040-1). Cornell U Pr.
--Orchid Biology: Reviews & Perspectives, II. LC 76-25648. (Illus.). 400p. 1982. 45.00x (ISBN 0-8014-1276-5). Cornell U Pr.
--Orchid Biology: Reviews & Perspectives, Vol. III. (Illus.). 416p. 1983. 49.50x (ISBN 0-8014-1512-8). Comstock.

Arditti, M., jt. auth. see Cromwell, Leslie.

Arditti, Rita, et al, eds. Test-Tube Women: What Future for Motherhood? Klein, Renate D. & Minden, Shelley. 350p. (Orig.). 1984. pap. 8.95 (ISBN 0-86358-030-0, Pandora Pr). Routledge & Kegan.
--Science & Liberation. LC 79-64087. (Illus.). 398p. 1980. 15.00 (ISBN 0-89608-023-4); pap. 10.00 (ISBN 0-89608-022-6). South End Pr.

Arditty, H. J., jt. ed. see Ezekiel, S.

Ardizzone. Tim & Charlotte. pap. 4.95 (ISBN 0-19-272118-6, Pub. by Oxford U Pr Childrens). Merrimack Pub Cir.
--Tim & Ginger. pap. 4.95 (ISBN 0-19-272113-5, Pub. by Oxford U Pr Childrens). Merrimack Pub Cir.
--Tim in Danger. pap. 4.95 (ISBN 0-19-272106-2, Pub. by Oxford U Pr Childrens). Merrimack Pub Cir.
--Tim to the Lighthouse. pap. 4.95 (ISBN 0-19-272107-0, Pub. by Oxford U Pr Childrens). Merrimack Pub Cir.
--Tim's Friend Towser. pap. 4.95 (ISBN 0-19-272112-7, Pub. by Oxford U Pr Childrens). Merrimack Pub Cir.

Ardizzone, D. A Bibliography of African Freshwater Fish: Supplement 1, 1968-1975. (Commission for Inland Fisheries of Africa (CIFA): Technical Papers: No. 5). 52p. (Eng. & Fr.). 1976. pap. 7.50 (ISBN 92-5-000092-8, F737, FAO). Unipub.

Ardizzone, Edward. Indian Diary, Nineteen Fifty-Two to Nineteen Fifty-Three. (Illus.). 160p. 1984. text ed. 24.95 (ISBN 0-370-30525-6, Pub. by the Bodley Head). Merrimack Pub Cir.
--Little Tim & Brave Sea. (Illus.). 48p. (ps-3). 1983. pap. 3.95 (ISBN 0-14-050175-4, Puffin). Penguin.
--Tim & Charlotte. (Illus.). (ps-3). 1979. Repr. of 1951 ed. 11.95 (ISBN 0-19-279562-7). Oxford U Pr.

Ardizzone, Edward, compiled by. Ardizzone's Hans Andersen: Fourteen Classic Tales. Corrin, Stephen, tr. LC 78-18908. (Illus.). (gr. 3 up). 1979. 10.95 (ISBN 0-689-50128-5, McElderry Bk). Atheneum.

Ardizzone, Edward, ed. see Daudet, Alphonse.

Ardizzone, Edward, illus. Ardizzone's Hans Andersen: Fourteen Classic Tales. Corrin, Stephen, tr. LC 85-71251. (Illus.). 78p. (ps up). 1985. 10.95 (ISBN 0-233-97306-0). Andre Deutsch.
--Ardizzone's Kilvert: Selections from the Diary of the Rev. Francis Kilvert 1870-79. abr. ed. (Illus.). 176p. (gr. 5-7). 1980. 7.95 (ISBN 0-224-01276-2, Pub. by Jonathan Cape). Merrimack Pub Cir.

Ardizzone, G. D., jt. auth. see Zeisler, R.

Ardley, Bridget. The Austerity Cookbook. 160p. 1985. pap. 8.95 (ISBN 0-8052-8247-5, Pub. by Allison & Busby England). Schocken.

Ardley, Bridget & Ardley, Neil. The Arco Book of One-Thousand One Questions & Answers. LC 83-26614. (Illus.). 160p. (YA) (gr. 7 up). 1984. 8.95 (ISBN 0-668-06161-8, 6161-8). Arco.

Ardley, G. The Common Sense Philosophy of James Oswald. 112p. 1980. 21.50x (ISBN 0-08-025717-8, Pub. by Aberdeen Pr Scotland). Humanities.

Ardley, Neil. Air & Flight. LC 83-51441. (Action Science Ser.). (Illus.). 32p. (gr. 4-8). 1984. PLB 8.90 (ISBN 0-531-03775-4). Watts.
--At School, Work & Play. (World of Tomorrow Ser.). (Illus.). 40p. (gr. 4 up). 1982. PLB 8.90 (ISBN 0-531-04361-4). Watts.
--Atoms & Energy. rev. ed. (Modern Knowledge Library). (Illus.). 48p. (gr. 5 up). 1982. PLB 9.90 (ISBN 0-531-01200-X, Warwick). Watts.
--Computers. (Illus.). 80p. (gr. 5 up). PLB 10.90 (ISBN 0-531-09219-4). Watts.
--Discovering Electricity. (Action Science Ser.). (Illus.). 32p. (gr. 4-6). 1984. PLB 9.90 (ISBN 0-531-03770-3). Watts.
--Exploring Magnetism. (Action Science Ser.). 32p. (gr. 4-6). 1984. lib. bdg. 8.90 (ISBN 0-531-04617-6). Watts.
--Fact or Fantasy. LC 82-50059. (The World of Tomorrow Ser.). (Illus.). 40p. (gr. 4 up). 1982. PLB 9.90 (ISBN 0-531-04473-4). Watts.
--Force & Strength. (Action Science Ser.). (Illus.). 32p. (gr. 4-6). 1985. lib. bdg. 9.90 (ISBN 0-531-03777-0). Watts.
--Future War & Weapons. (World of Tomorrow Ser.). (Illus.). 40p. (gr. 4 up). 1982. PLB 8.90 (ISBN 0-531-04359-2). Watts.
--Health & Medicine. LC 82-50060. (The World of Tomorrow Ser.). (Illus.). 40p. (gr. 4 up). 1982. PLB 8.90 (ISBN 0-531-04474-2). Watts.
--Hot & Cold. (Action Science Ser.). (Illus.). 32p. (gr. k-3). 1983. PLB 8.90 (ISBN 0-531-04614-1). Watts.
--How Things Work. (Illus.). 127p. 1984. lib. bdg. 9.79 (ISBN 0-317-11494-8). Messner.
--Know Your Underwater Exploration. LC 77-76217. (Illus.). (gr. 3-7). 1978. pap. 1.95 (ISBN 0-528-87019-X). Rand.
--Making Metric Measurements. (Action Science Ser.). 32p. (gr. 4-6). 1984. lib. bdg. 8.90 (ISBN 0-531-04615-X). Watts.
--Making Things Move. (Action Science Ser.). (Illus.). 32p. (gr. 4-6). 1984. PLB 9.90 (ISBN 0-531-03771-1). Watts.
--Our Future Needs. (World of Tomorrow Ser.). (Illus.). 40p. (gr. 4 up). 1982. PLB 8.90 (ISBN 0-531-04360-6). Watts.
--Out into Space. (The World of Tomorrow Ser.). (Illus.). 40p. (gr. 4 up). 1981. lib. bdg. 8.90 (ISBN 0-531-04345-2). Watts.
--Simple Chemistry. (Action Science Ser.). (Illus.). 32p. (gr. 4-6). 1985. PLB 9.90 (ISBN 0-531-03778-9). Watts.
--Sound & Music. LC 83-51441. (Action Science Ser.). (Illus.). 32p. (gr. 4-8). 1984. PLB 9.90 (ISBN 0-531-03776-2). Watts.
--Sun & Light. (Action Science Ser.). 32p. (gr. k-3). 1983. PLB 8.90 (ISBN 0-531-04616-8). Watts.
--Tomorrow's Home. (World of Tomorrow Ser.). (Illus.). 40p. (gr. 4 up). 1982. PLB 8.90 (ISBN 0-531-04362-2). Watts.
--Transport on Earth. (The World of Tomorrow Ser.). (Illus.). 40p. (gr. 4 up). 1981. lib. bdg. 8.90 (ISBN 0-531-04346-0). Watts.
--Using the Computer. (Action Science Ser.). 32p. (gr. 4-6). 1983. PLB 8.90 (ISBN 0-531-04518-8). Watts.
--Why Things Are. (Illus.). 127p. 1984. lib. bdg. 9.79 (ISBN 0-671-49993-9). Messner.
--Working with Water. (Action Science Ser.). 32p. (gr. 4-6). 1983. PLB 8.90 (ISBN 0-531-04519-6). Watts.

Ardley, Neil, jt. auth. see Ardley, Bridget.

Ardman, Harvey. Endgame. (Orig.). 1975. pap. 1.75 (ISBN 0-380-00352-X, 24299). Avon.
--Normandie: Her Life & Times. 432p. 1985. 22.50 (ISBN 0-531-09784-6). Watts.
--On a Scale of One to Ten. 64p. 1981. pap. 3.95 (ISBN 0-671-42484-X, Wallaby). S&S.
--The Woman's Day Book of Weddings. LC 82-4236. 1982. 14.95 (ISBN 0-672-52729-4). Bobbs.

Ardman, Harvey & Ardman, Perri. The Complete Apartment Guide: Everything You Should Know About Selecting & Utilizing Your Living Space. (Illus.). 320p. 1982. 19.95 (ISBN 0-02-500110-8, Collier); pap. 9.95 (ISBN 0-02-079020-1). Macmillan.

Ardman, Harvey, jt. auth. see Ardman, Perri.

Ardman, Perri & Ardman, Harvey. The Woman's Day Book of Fund Raising. 320p. 1982. pap. 7.95 (ISBN 0-312-88650-0). St Martin.

Ardman, Perri, jt. auth. see Ardman, Harvey.

Ardoin, Birthney, jt. auth. see Frair, John.

Ardoin, John. Stages of Menotti. LC 82-45316. (Illus.). 256p. 1985. 40.00 (ISBN 0-385-14938-7). Doubleday.

Ardoin, Robert B. Louisiana Census Records, Vol. 1: Avoyelles & St. Landry Parishes, 1810 & 1820. LC 71-134170. (Illus.). 102p. 1970. 12.00 (ISBN 0-8063-0446-4). Genealog Pub.
--Louisiana Census Records, Vol. 2: Iberville, Natchitoches, Pointe Coupee, & Rapides Parishes, 1810 & 1820. LC 71-134170. (Illus.). 187p. 1972. 15.00 (ISBN 0-8063-0507-X). Genealog Pub.

Ardoin, Robert B., compiled by. Louisiana Census Records: Ascension, Assumption, T. Charles, St. Bernard, St. John the Baptist, St. James, East & West Baton Rouge, 1810-1820, Vol. III. 1977. 20.00 (ISBN 0-686-10449-8). Polyanthos.

Ardolino, Frank. Thomas Kyd's Mystery Play: Myth & Ritual in the Spanish Tragedy. (American University Studies IV (English Language & Literature): Vol. 29). 194p. text ed. 24.60 (ISBN 0-8204-0232-X). P Lang Pubs.

Ardrey, Robert. The Social Contract: A Personal Inquiry into the Evolutionary Source of Order & Disorder. LC 73-124967. (Illus.). 1970. 10.00 (ISBN 0-689-10347-6). Atheneum.
--The Territorial Imperative: A Personal Inquiry into the Animal Origins of Property & Nations. LC 66-23572. (Illus.). 1966. 10.95 (ISBN 0-689-10015-9). Atheneum.

Ardrey, Robert L. American Agricultural Implements, a Review of Invention & Development in the Agricultural Implement Industry of the United States: Pt. 1 - General History of Invention & Improvement, Pt. 2 - Pioneer Manufacturing Centers, 2 pts. LC 72-5028. (Technology & Society Ser.). (Illus.). 240p. 1972. Repr. of 1894 ed. 20.00 (ISBN 0-405-04681-2). Ayer Co Pubs.

Ardura, Ernesto. America en el Horizonte: Una Perspectiva Cultural. LC 79-54965. (Coleccion De Estudios Hispanicos: Hispanic Studies Collection). (Illus.). 161p. (Orig., Span.). 1981. pap. 10.95 (ISBN 0-89729-240-5). Ediciones.

Ardus, D. A., jt. auth. see McQuillin, R.

Ardzrooni, Leon, ed. see Veblen, Thorstein B.

ARE Editorial Department. An Edgar Cayce Health Anthology. 198p. (Orig.). 1979. pap. 5.95 (ISBN 0-87604-119-5). ARE Pr.

Are, Ennio T., tr. see Gumina, Deanna P.

Are, Thomas L. Faithsong: A New Look at the Ministry of Music. LC 81-4789. 96p. 1981. pap. 6.95 (ISBN 0-664-24375-4). Westminster.
--The Gospel for the Clockaholic. 128p. 1985. pap. 7.95 (ISBN 0-8170-1075-0). Judson.
--Heaven Knows, Kate. LC 84-60625. 110p. (Orig.). 1984. pap. 4.95 (ISBN 0-8192-1347-0). Morehouse.

Arecchi, F. T. & Aussenegg, F. R. Current Trends in Optics. LC 81-7046. 190p. 1981. pap. 39.95x (ISBN 0-470-27278-3). Halsted Pr.

Arecchi, F. T. & Aussenegg, F. R., eds. Current Trends in Optics. 200p. 1981. pap. cancelled (ISBN 0-85066-222-2). Taylor & Francis.

Arecchi, F. T. & Schulz-Dubois, E. D., eds. Laser Handbook, 2 vols. LC 73-146191. 1947p. 1973. Set. 213.00 (ISBN 0-444-10379-1, North-Holland). Elsevier.

Arecchi, F. T., et al, eds. Coherence in Spectroscopy & Modern Physics. LC 78-14474. (NATO ASI Series B, Physics: Vol. 37). 410p. 1978. 62.50x (ISBN 0-306-40050-2, Plenum Pr). Plenum Pub.

Arechiga, H., jt. ed. see Valverde-Rodriguez, C.

Arednt, Hannah. On Revolution. 14.25 (ISBN 0-8446-6147-3). Peter Smith.

Areeda, Phillip. Antitrust Analysis: Problems, Text, Cases. 3rd ed. LC 80-84032. 1418p. 1981. text ed. 34.00 (ISBN 0-316-05056-3). Little.
--Antitrust Analysis, 1984 Supplement: Cases & Materials. LC 80-84032. 100p. 1984. pap. text ed. 8.95 (ISBN 0-316-05038-5). Little.

Areeda, Phillip & Turner, Donald. Antitrust Law: An Analysis of Antitrust Law Principles & their Application. lawyers ed. 1980. Vol. I-VII. text ed. 295.00 set (ISBN 0-316-05052-0). Little.
--Antitrust Law: Vol. I & III Lawyer's Supplement. LC 77-15710. 300p. 1982. 50.00 (ISBN 0-316-05039-3). Little.

Areen, Judith. Family Law, Cases & Materials on: 1983 Supplement. (University Casebook Ser.). 393p. 1982. pap. text ed. 8.95 (ISBN 0-88277-107-8). Foundation Pr.
--Standards Relating to Youth Service Agencies. LC 77-14496. (IJA-ABA Juvenile Justice Standards Project Ser.). 140p. 1980. prof ref 22.50 (ISBN 0-88410-756-6); pap. 12.50 (ISBN 0-88410-804-X). Ballinger Pub.
--Standards Relating to Youth Service Agencies. LC 77-14496. (Juvenile Justice Standards Project Ser.). 22.50 (ISBN 0-88410-756-6); pap. 12.50 (ISBN 0-88410-804-X). Ballinger Pub.

Areen, Judith, et al. Law, Science & Medicine. LC 84-8181. (University Casebook Ser.). 1494p. 1984. text ed. 34.50 (ISBN 0-88277-179-5). Foundation Pr.

Areen, Judith C. Family Law: Cases & Materials. 2nd ed. LC 85-6928. 1985. write for info. (ISBN 0-88277-238-4). Foundation Pr.

Arellanes, Audrey S., ed. Bookplates: A Selected, Annotated Bibliography of the Periodical Literature. LC 71-123720. 1971. 36.00x (ISBN 0-8103-0340-X). Gale.

Arellano, Richard G. & Allen, Alexandra. Export Potential: Mexico Special Research Study. 31p. 1979. 10.00 (ISBN 0-942286-02-2). Intl Mktg.

Arem, Joel E. Color Encyclopedia of Gemstones. (Illus.). 1977. 42.50 (ISBN 0-442-20333-0). Van Nos Reinhold.
--Gemology. write for info. (ISBN 0-442-25632-9). Van Nos Reinhold.
--Man-Made Crystals. LC 73-8695. (Illus.). 122p. 1973. pap. 9.95x (ISBN 0-87474-141-6). Smithsonian.

Aremu, Odaleye, jt. auth. see Stevick, E. W.

Aremu, Olaleye, jt. auth. see Stevick, Earl W.

Arena, James W., jt. auth. see Hardin, James W.

Arena, Jay M. Poisoning: Toxicology, Symptoms, Treatments. 4th ed. (Illus.). 864p. 1979. 49.00x (ISBN 0-398-03767-1). C C Thomas.

Arena, Jay M. & Bachar, Miriam. Child Safety Is No Accident: A Parents' Handbook of Emergencies. LC 77-80346. 296p. 1978. 14.00 (ISBN 0-8223-0390-6). Duke.

Arena, Jay M., jt. auth. see Echols, Barbara E.

Arena, Jay M. & Drew, Richard H., eds. Poisoning: Toxicology, Symptoms, Treatments. 5th ed. (Illus.). 1416p. 1986. 84.50x (ISBN 0-398-05143-7). C C Thomas.

Arena, Jay M., ed. see Davidson, Wilburt C.

Arena, John, ed. see Boggs, Edward.

Arena, Louis A. Linguistics & Composition: A Method to Improve Expository Writing Skills. LC 75-34100. 202p. 1975. pap. 4.95 (ISBN 0-87840-162-8). Georgetown U Pr.

Arenas, Bibi Armas De see Armas de Arenas, Bibi.

Arenas, Reinaldo. El Central. 96p. 1984. pap. 3.50 (ISBN 0-380-86934-9, 86934, Bard). Avon.
--Farewell to the Sea. 1985. 18.95 (ISBN 0-670-52960-5). Viking.
--Hallucinations: Being an Account of the Life & Adventures of Friar Servando Teresa de Mier. Brotherston, Gordon, tr. LC 78-156559. (Span.). 1971. 15.00 (ISBN 0-06-010124-5). Ultramarine Pub.

Arenas, Rosa M. She Said Yes. 26p. 1980. pap. 3.00x (ISBN 0-931598-09-5). Fallen Angel.

Arenberg, Gerald S., et al. Preventing Missing Children. 128p. (Orig.). 1984. pap. 6.95 (ISBN 0-936320-21-4). Compact Bks.

Arend, Anthony C., jt. ed. see Coll, Alberto R.

Arends, Jane H., jt. auth. see Arends, Richard I.

Arends, Mark. Product Rendering with Markers. (Illus.). 180p. 1985. 35.00 (ISBN 0-442-20952-5). Van Nos Reinhold.

Arends, Richard I. & Arends, Jane H. Systems Change Strategies in Educational Settings. Walz, Garry R. & Benjamin, Libby, eds. LC 77-22315. (New Vistas in Counseling Ser.: Vol. III). 120p. 1977. 16.95 (ISBN 0-87705-310-3). Human Sci Pr.

Arends, T., et al, eds. see Symposium On Hemoglobin - 1st Inter-American - Caracas - 1969.

Arendson. Living & Leaving It. 385p. (Orig.). 1982. 12.50. P Arendson.

Arendson, Peter. The Vision. 348p. (Orig.). 1982. 12.50. P Arendson.

Arendt, Hanna. On Revolution. LC 82-6266. viii, 343p. 1982. Repr. of 1963 ed. lib. bdg. 35.00x (ISBN 0-313-23493-0, AROR). Greenwood.

Arendt, Hannah. Antisemitism. LC 66-22273. Orig. Title: Origins of Totalitarianism, Pt. 1. 1968. pap. 3.95 (ISBN 0-15-607810-4, HB131, Harv). HarBraceJ.
--Between Past & Future. 1983. 12.50 (ISBN 0-8446-5976-2). Peter Smith.
--Between Past & Future: Eight Exercises in Political Thought. enl. ed. 1977. pap. 5.95 (ISBN 0-14-004662-3). Penguin.
--Crises of the Republic. LC 72-187703. 1972. pap. 5.95 (ISBN 0-15-623200-6, Harv). HarBraceJ.
--Eichman in Jerusalem. 1983. 14.25 (ISBN 0-8446-5977-0). Peter Smith.
--Eichmann in Jerusalem: A Report of the Banality of Evil. rev ed. 1977. pap. 6.95 (ISBN 0-14-004450-7). Penguin.
--Human Condition. LC 58-5535. 1970. pap. 11.95 (ISBN 0-226-02593-4, P361, Phoen). U of Chicago Pr.

--The Psychology of Interpersonal Behavior. Rev. ed. (Pelican Ser.). 336p. 1985. pap. 5.95 (ISBN 0-14-022483-1). Penguin.
--The Scientific Study of Social Behaviour. LC 73-13021. (Illus.). 239p. 1974. Repr. of 1957 ed. lib. bdg. 17.75x (ISBN 0-8371-7108-3, ARSS). Greenwood.
--Social Interaction. 1973. pap. 15.95x (ISBN 0-422-75480-3, Pub. by Tavistock England, NO. 2840). Methuen Inc.
Argyle, Michael & Beit-Hallahmi, Benjamin. Social Psychology of Religion. 1975. 25.00x (ISBN 0-7100-7997-4); pap. 10.95X (ISBN 0-7100-8043-3). Routledge & Kegan.
Argyle, Nolan J. The Bridge at Kilometer 575. (Orig.). 1979. pap. 1.75 (ISBN 0-532-17244-2). Woodhill.
Argyle, R. W. & Webb Society. Webb Society Deep-Sky Observer's Handbook, Volume 1: Double Stars. rev. ed. Jones, Kenneth G., ed. (Illus.). 192p. 1985. pap. 12.95x (ISBN 0-89490-122-2). Enslow Pubs.
Argyll, Archibald C. Letters from Archibald, Earl of Argyll, to John, Duke of Lauderdale. Sinclair, George & Sharpe, C. K., eds. LC 75-38489. (Bannatyne Club, Edinburgh: Publications: No. 33). Repr. of 1829 ed. 17.50 (ISBN 0-404-52739-6). AMS Pr.
Argyris, C. The Applicability of Organizational Sociology. (Illus.). 138p. 1974. 27.95 (ISBN 0-521-08448-2); pap. 11.95 (ISBN 0-521-09894-7). Cambridge U Pr.
Argyris, Chris. Behind the Front Page: Organizational Self-Renewal in Metropolition Newspapers. LC 73-22558. (Social & Behavioral Science Ser.). 1974. 21.95x (ISBN 0-87589-223-X). Jossey-Bass.
--Increasing Leadership Effectiveness. LC 83-14874. 304p. 1983. Repr. of 1976 ed. 21.50 (ISBN 0-89874-666-3). Krieger.
--Inner Contradictions of Rigorous Research. LC 79-6792. (Organizational & Occupational Psychology Ser.). 1980. 23.50 (ISBN 0-12-060150-8). Acad Pr.
--Integrating the Individual & the Organization. LC 64-13209. pap. 85.50 (ISBN 0-317-09905-1, 2019296). Bks Demand UMI.
--Intervention Theory & Method: A Behavioral Science View. LC 79-114331. (Business Ser). 1970. text ed. 33.95 (ISBN 0-201-00342-2). Addison-Wesley.
--Organization of a Bank: Study of the Nature of Organization & the Fusion Process. Stein, Leon, ed. LC 77-70479. (Work Ser.). 1977. Repr. of 1954 ed. lib. bdg. 26.50x (ISBN 0-405-10153-8). Ayer Co Pubs.
--Reasoning, Learning, & Action: Individual & Organizational. LC 81-48662. (Management Ser.). 1982. text ed. 22.95x (ISBN 0-87589-524-7). Jossey-Bass.
--Strategy, Change & Defensive Routines. 384p. 1985. text ed. 23.95 (ISBN 0-273-02329-2). Pitman Pub MA.
Argyris, Chris & Cyert, Richard M. Leadership in the Eighties: Essays on Higher Education. LC 80-80425. 100p. 1980. pap. text ed. 5.95x (ISBN 0-934222-01-0). Inst Ed Manage.
Argyris, Chris & Harrison, Roger. Interpersonal Competence & Organizational Effectiveness. LC 62-11287. (The Irwin-Dorsey Series in Behavioral Science). pap. 76.00 (ISBN 0-317-09045-3, 2001087). Bks Demand UMI.
Argyris, Chris & Schon, Donald A. Organizational Learning: A Theory of Action Perspective. LC 77-81195. 1978. text ed. 23.95 (ISBN 0-201-00174-8). Addison-Wesley.
--Theory in Practice: Increasing Professional Effectiveness. LC 74-3606. (Higher Education Ser.). 218p. 1974. 16.95x (ISBN 0-87589-230-2). Jossey-Bass.
Argyris, J. H. Introduction to the Finite Element Method. 1984. write for info. (North-Holland). Elsevier.
Argyris, J. H. & Kelsey, S. Energy Theorems & Structural Analysis. 85p. 1960. 22.50x (ISBN 0-306-30664-6, Plenum Pr). Plenum Pub.
Arhangelsky, A. V., et al. Eleven Papers on Topology. LC 51-5559. (Translations Ser.: No. 2, Vol. 78). 1968. 33.00 (ISBN 0-8218-1778-7, TRANS 2-78). Am Math.
Arhem, Kaj. Makuna Social Organization: A Study in Descent, Alliance & the Formation of Corporate Groups in the North-Western Amazon. (Uppsala Studies in Cultural Anthropology Ser.: No. 4). 379p. 1981. pap. text ed. 30.75x (ISBN 91-554-1116-9, Pub. by Almquist & Wiksell Sweden). Humanities.
Arhin, Kwame, et al. Marketing Boards in Tropical Africa. (Monographs from African Studies). (Illus.). 350p. 1985. 59.95x (ISBN 0-7103-0109-X, Kegan Paul International). Routledge & Kegan.
Arhipov, G. I. see Steklov Institute of Mathematics.
Ari, Thorgilsson. Book of the Icelanders. (Islandica Ser: Vol. 20). Repr. of 1930 ed. 12.00 (ISBN 0-527-00350-6). Kraus Repr.
Arian, Alan. The Choosing People: Voting Behavior in Israel. LC 72-7828. (Illus.). 276p. 1973. 20.00 (ISBN 0-8295-0249-1). UPB.
Arian, Asher. The Elections in Israel: Nineteen Seventy-Seven. 290p. 1980. pap. 19.95 (ISBN 0-87855-996-5). Transaction Bks.
--The Elections in Israel: Nineteen Seventy-Three. 311p. 1973. 19.95 (ISBN 0-87855-238-3). Transaction Bks.
--The Elections in Israel: Nineteen Sixty-Nine. 311p. 1969. 13.95 (ISBN 0-87855-237-5). Transaction Bks.
--Politics in Israel: The Second Generation. LC 84-29300. (Illus.). 304p. 1985. 25.00 (ISBN 0-934540-38-1); pap. text ed. 12.95x (ISBN 0-934540-37-3). Chatham Hse Pubs.
Arian, Asher, ed. The Elections in Israel: Nineteen Hundred Eighty-One. 300p. 1984. pap. 19.95 (ISBN 0-87855-995-7). Transaction Bks.
--Israel: A Developing Society. 456p. 1980. pap. text ed. 14.75x (ISBN 90-232-1710-1). Humanities.
Arian, Edward. Bach, Beethoven & Bureaucracy: The Case of the Philadelphia Orchestra. LC 75-169494. x, 158p. 1971. 11.50 (ISBN 0-8173-4815-8). U of Ala Pr.
--Bach, Beethoven, & Bureaucracy: The Case of the Philadelphia Orchestra. LC 75-169494. pap. 32.00 (ISBN 0-317-10094-7, 2010130). Bks Demand UMI.
Arian, Philip, jt. auth. see Eisenberg, Azriel.
Arian, Phillip & Eisenberg, Azriel. The Story of the Prayer Book. (gr. 7-9). 1971. pap. 5.95x (ISBN 0-87677-017-0). Prayer Bk.
Ariana. Sleeping Beauty Retold: For Those Who Can't Wait 100 Years for a Happy Ending. (Faerytales Retold Ser.). (Illus.). 22p. (Orig.). (gr. 1-6). 1983. pap. 3.50 (ISBN 0-916549-00-3). Ariana Prods.
Ariane. Small Cloud. LC 83-14029. (Illus.). 24p. (ps-1). 1984. 10.95 (ISBN 0-525-44085-2, 01063-320, Unicorn). Dutton.
Arias, Arnold. The Iridescent Dimension. 1976. 2.50 (ISBN 0-9602374-0-2). Dimensionist Pr.
Arias, Esther & Arias, Mortimer. El Clamor de Mi Pueblo. Martinez, Ana E., tr. from English. (Illus., Orig., Span.). 1981. pap. 2.95 (ISBN 0-377-00105-8). Friend Pr.
--Cry of My People. (Orig.). 1980. pap. 2.95 (ISBN 0-377-00095-7). Friend Pr.
Arias, Harmodio. Panama Canal: A Study in International Law & Diplomacy. LC 79-111707. (American Imperialism: Viewpoints of United States Foreign Policy, 1898-1941). 1970. Repr. of 1911 ed. 16.00 (ISBN 0-405-02001-5). Ayer Co Pubs.
Arias, I. M. & Frenkel, M., eds. The Liver Annual, Vol. 2, 1982. (Liver Ser.: Vol. 2). 474p. 1982. 81.00 (ISBN 0-444-90241-4). Elsevier.
Arias, I. M., et al, eds. The Liver Annual, 1984, Vol. 4. 520p. 1984. 70.00 (ISBN 0-444-90346-1, I-275-84). Elsevier.
--The Liver: Annual 1. (Liver Ser.: Vol. 1). 380p. 1981. 81.00 (ISBN 0-444-90196-5). Elsevier.
Arias, Irwin, et al, eds. The Liver: Biology & Pathobiology. 928p. 1982. text ed. 119.00 (ISBN 0-89004-575-5). Raven.
Arias, Jorge R., jt. auth. see Penny, Norman D.
Arias, M. M., jt. auth. see Lubian, Rafael.
Arias, Mortimer. Announcing the Reign of God: Evangelization & the Subversive Memory of Jesus. LC 83-5696. 176p. 1984. pap. 8.95 (ISBN 0-8006-1712-6, 1-1712). Fortress.
Arias, Mortimer, jt. auth. see Arias, Esther.
Arias, Ron. The Road to Tamazunchale. 110p. 1978. pap. 5.00 (ISBN 0-915596-12-1). West Coast.
Arias, Toby & Frassanito, Elaine. Fiesta Mexicana. (Illus.). 90p. 1982. pap. 6.95 (ISBN 0-9609942-0-3). T & E Ent.
Ariav, Gadi & Clifford, James. New Directions in Database Systems. Ginzberg, Michael, ed. (Computer-Based Systems in Information Management Ser.). 304p. 1985. text ed. 35.00 (ISBN 0-89391-344-8). Ablex Pub.
Arichea, D. C. & Nida, E. A. Translator's Handbook on the First Letter from Peter. LC 81-108426. (Helps for Translators Ser.). 190p. 1980. pap. 3.20x (ISBN 0-8267-0152-3, 08624, Pub. by United Bible). Am Bible.
Arichea, D. C., Jr. & Nida, E. A. Translator's Handbook on Paul's Letter to the Galatians. LC 79-115359. (Helps for Translators Ser.). 176p. Repr. of 1976 ed. soft cover 2.60x (ISBN 0-8267-0142-6, 08527, Pub. by United Bible). Am Bible.
Arick, Martin R. Data Communications Concepts & Systems. LC 84-62291. (Orig.). Date not set. pap. price not set (ISBN 0-89435-150-8, AC 1508). QED Info Sci.
Arico, D., ed. see Metos, Thomas H.
Arico, Diane, ed. see Crocker, Chris.
Arico, Diane, ed. see Dixon, Franklin W.
Arico, Diane, ed. see Dolan, Edward F., Jr.
Arico, Diane, ed. see Hope, Laura L.
Arico, Diane, ed. see Kaye, Annene.
Arico, Diane, ed. see Keene, Carolyn.
Arico, Diane, ed. see Keene, Carolyn & Dixon, Franklin W.
Arico, Diane, ed. see McGee, Eddie.
Arico, Diane, ed. see Martin, Nancie S.
Arico, Diane, ed. see Matthews, Gordon.
Arico, Diane, ed. see Milton, Hilary.
Arico, Diane, ed. see Rotsler, William.
Arico, Diane, ed. see Russell, Kate.
Arico, Diane, ed. see Sullivan, George.
Aridas, Chris. Discernment: Seeking God in Every Situation. 120p. (Orig.). 1981. pap. 3.50 (ISBN 0-914544-37-3). Living Flame Pr.
Aridas, Christopher. Soundings: A Thematic Guide for Daily Scripture Prayer. LC 83-16509. 224p. 1984. pap. 4.50 (ISBN 0-385-19157-X, Im). Doubleday.
--Your Catholic Wedding: A Complete Plan-Book. LC 81-43250. (Illus.). 192p. 1982. pap. 2.95 (ISBN 0-385-17731-3, Im). Doubleday.
Aridjis, Homero. Exaltation of Light. Weinberger, Eliot, tr. (New American Translation Ser.: No. 2). 12.00 (ISBN 0-918526-28-0); pap. 6.00 (ISBN 0-918526-29-9). Boa Edns.
Aridrade, Mario de see De Andrade, Mario.
Arie, Staal. Hawthorne's Narrative Art. 1976. lib. bdg. 79.95 (ISBN 0-87700-250-9). Revisionist Pr.
Arief, Sritua. A Test of Leser's Model of Household Consumption Expenditure in Malaysia & Singapore. 35p. (Orig.). 1980. pap. text ed. 7.50x (ISBN 9971-902-03-6, Pub. by Inst Southeast Asian Stud). Gower Pub Co.
Ariel, Frederick. The Classical Guitar. (Illus., Orig.). 1976. pap. 7.95 (ISBN 0-8256-9952-5, Noad). Music Sales.
Ariel, Irving, ed. Progress in Clinical Cancer, Vols. 2, 4-7. Incl. Vol. 2. (Illus.). 392p. 1966. 69.50 (ISBN 0-8089-0014-5); Vol. 4. (Illus.). 424p. 1970. 96.50 (ISBN 0-8089-0016-1); Vol. 5. (Illus.). 296p. 1973. 97.00 (ISBN 0-8089-0777-8, 790185); Vol. 6. 240p. 1975. 92.50 (ISBN 0-8089-0906-1, 790186); Vol. 7. 288p. 1977. 71.50 (ISBN 0-8089-1087-6, 790187). LC 64-24793. Grune.
--Progress in Clinical Cancer, Vol. 8. 368p. 1982. 83.50 (ISBN 0-8089-1430-8, 790188). Grune.
Arielli, A. D. Grisons. (Panorama Bks). (Illus.). 62p. (Fr.). 4.95 (ISBN 0-685-23347-2). French & Eur.
Arienda, Roger & Roque, Marichelle. Libre Dentro de la Carcel. 176p. (Span.). 1984. pap. 4.50 (ISBN 0-311-46102-6). Casa Bautista.
Arienda, Roger & Roque-Lutz, Marichelle. Free Within Prison Walls. 157p. 1984. pap. 4.75x (ISBN 971-10-0143-8, Pub. by New Day Philippines). Cellar.
Ariens, C. U., et al. The Comparative Anatomy of the Nervous System of Vertebrates Including Man, 3 vols. 2nd ed. (Illus.). 1845p. 1936. Set. 97.50x (ISBN 0-02-840400-9). Hafner.
Ariens, E. J. Drug Design. (Medicinal Chemistry Ser.: Vol. 11). Vol. 1 1971. 88.00 (ISBN 0-12-060301-2); Vol. 2 1972. 88.00 (ISBN 0-12-060302-0); Vol.3 1972. 85.50 (ISBN 0-12-060303-9); Vol 4. 1973. 85.50 (ISBN 0-12-060304-7); Vol. 5 1975. 82.50 (ISBN 0-12-060305-5); Vol. 6 1975. 82.50 (ISBN 0-12-060306-3); Vol. 7 1976. 80.00 (ISBN 0-12-060307-1); Vol. 8, 1978. 74.50 (ISBN 0-12-060308-X). Acad Pr.
Ariens, E. J. & Soudjin, W. Stereochemistry & Biological Activity of Drugs. (Illus.). 204p. 1983. 37.00x (ISBN 0-632-01155-6). Blackwell Pubns.
Ariens, E J., ed. Drug Design, Vol. 9. LC 72-127678. (Medicinal Chemistry Ser.). 1980. 55.00 (ISBN 0-12-060309-8). Acad Pr.
Ariens, E. J., ed. Drug Design, Vol. 10. (Medicinal Chemistry Ser.). 1980. 66.00 (ISBN 0-12-060310-1). Acad Pr.
--Molecular Pharmacology: The Mode of Action of Biologically Active Compounds, 2 vols. 1964. Vol. 1. 85.50 (ISBN 0-12-060401-9); Vol. 2. 67.00 (ISBN 0-12-060402-7). Acad Pr.
Ariens-Kappers, J. & Pevet, P., eds. The Pineal Gland of Vertebrates Including Man. (Progress in Brain Research Ser.: Vol. 52). 534p. 1980. 116.25 (ISBN 0-444-80114-6). Elsevier.
Aries, A. B., tr. see Fridman, A. M. & Polyachenko, V. I.
Aries, A. B., tr. see Fridman, A. M. & Polyachenko, V. L.
Aries, A. B., tr. see Ibragimov, I. A. & Rozanov, Y. A.
Aries, A. B., tr. see Liptser, R. S. & Shiryayev, A. N.
Aries, A. B., tr. see Morozov, V. A.
Aries, A. B., tr. see Shiryayev, A. N.
Aries, Philippe. Centuries of Childhood: A Social History of Family Life. 1965. pap. 6.95 (ISBN 0-394-70286-7, V286, Vin). Random.
--The Hour of Our Death. LC 79-2227. (Illus.). 800p. 1981. 20.00 (ISBN 0-394-41074-2). Knopf.
--Images of Man & Death. Lloyd, Janet, tr. from Fr. (Illus.). 288p. 1985. 35.00 (ISBN 0-674-44410-8); pre-Jan. 1986 29.95 (ISBN 0-317-20021-6). Harvard U Pr.
--Western Attitudes toward Death: From the Middle Ages to the Present. Ranum, Patricia, tr. from Fr. LC 73-19340. (Symposia in Comparative History Ser). (Illus.). 122p. 1974. text ed. 7.50x (ISBN 0-8018-1566-5); pap. 4.95x (ISBN 0-8018-1762-5). Johns Hopkins.
Aries, Philippe & Bejin, Andre. Western Sexuality. 224p. 1985. 24.95x (ISBN 0-631-13476-X). Basil Blackwell.
Aries, Phillippe. The Hour of Our Death. Weaver, Helen, tr. from Fr. LC 81-52266. Orig. Title: L' Homme Devant la Mort. (Illus.). 704p. 1982. pap. 9.95 (ISBN 0-394-75156-6, Vin). Random.
Aries, S. J. Dictionary of Telecommunications. 336p. 1981. 39.95 (ISBN 0-408-00328-6). Butterworth.
Arieti, James A., jt. ed. see Stump, Donald V.
Arieti, James A. & Crossett, John M., trs. Longinus: On the Sublime. LC 84-25435. (Studies in Art & Religious Interpretation: Vol. 5). 275p. 1985. 49.95x (ISBN 0-88946-554-1). E Mellen.
Arieti, Silvano. Abraham & the Contemporary Mind. LC 80-68187. 187p. 1981. 13.50 (ISBN 0-465-00005-3). Basic.
--Creativity: The Magic Synthesis. LC 75-36374. (Illus.). 450p. 1980. pap. 10.95 (ISBN 0-465-01444-5, CN-5054). Basic.
--Interpretation of Schizophrenia. 2nd ed. LC 73-91078. 1974. 37.50x (ISBN 0-465-03429-2). Basic.
--Understanding & Helping the Schizophrenic: A Guide for Family & Friends. 1981. pap. 7.75 (ISBN 0-671-41252-3, Touchstone Bks). S&S.
Arieti, Silvano & Bemporad, Jules. Severe & Mild Depression. LC 78-53811. 1978. text ed. 26.95x (ISBN 0-465-07693-9). Basic.
Arieti, Silvano & Chrzanowski, Gerard, eds. New Dimensions in Psychiatry: A World View. LC 74-16150. pap. 87.40 (ISBN 0-317-07912-3, 2011951). Bks Demand UMI.
Arieti, Silvano, et al, eds. American Handbook of Psychiatry, 7 vols. 2nd, rev. ed. Incl. Vol. 1-The Foundations of Psychiatry. 1974. text ed. 48.00x (ISBN 0-465-00147-5); Vol. 2-Child & Adolescent Psychiatry, Sociocultural & Community Psuchiatry. 1974. text ed. 47.00x (ISBN 0-465-00148-3); Vol. 3-Adult Clinical Psychiatry. 1974. text ed. 48.00x (ISBN 0-465-00149-1). LC 72-89185. Basic.
Arieti, Silvano H. & Brodie, Keith H., eds. American Handbook of Psychiatry, Vol. 7: Advances & New Directions, 7 vols, Vols. 1-7. LC 80-68960. (American Handbook of Psychiatry Ser.). 784p. 1981. 295.00 set (ISBN 0-465-00158-0). Basic.
Ariew, Robert, jt. auth. see Bragger, Jeannette.
Ariew, Roger, tr. see Duhem, Pierre.
Ariew, Roger, tr. see Gueroult, Martial.
Arif, Abu A., jt. auth. see Ali, Syed A.
Arif, I. M. & Ansell, M. O. Libyan Civil Code. (Libya Past & Present Ser.: Vol. 4). 45.00 (ISBN 0-902675-00-1). Oleander Pr.
--Libyan Revolution: A Sourcebook of Legal & Historical Documents, Vol. 1, Sept. 1, 1969 to Aug. 30, 1970. (Libya Past & Present Ser.: Vol. 1). 1971. 25.00 (ISBN 0-902675-10-9). Oleander Pr.
Arif, T. M. & Ansell, M. O. The Libyan Revolution: A Source-Book of Legal & Historical Documents. 1981. 150.00x (ISBN 0-902675-10-9, Pub. by Oleander Pr). State Mutual Bk.
Arif, T. M. & Ansell, Meredith O. The Libyan Civil Code. 1981. 190.00x (Pub. by Oleander Pr). State Mutual Bk.
Arif Al-Arif. Bedouin Love, Law & Legend, Dealing Exclusively with the Badu of Beersheba. LC 79-180318. (Mid-East Studies). (Illus.). Repr. of 1944 ed. 19.00 (ISBN 0-404-56213-2). AMS Pr.
Ariff, Mohamed. Malaysia & Asian Economic Cooperation. 177p. (Orig.). 1981. pap. text ed. 20.00x (ISBN 9971-902-07-9, Pub. by Inst Southeast Asian Stud). Gower Pub Co.
Arifov, U. A. Interaction of Atomic Particles with a Solid Surface. LC 79-76223. 374p. 1969. 45.00x (ISBN 0-306-10831-3, Consultants). Plenum Pub.
Arifov, Ubai A., ed. Secondary Emission & Structural Properties of Solids. Archard, Geoffrey C., tr. from Russian. LC 78-157931. pap. 38.50 (ISBN 0-317-08295-7, 2020683). Bks Demand UMI.
Ariga, Eiko, tr. see Okura, Nagatsune.
Ariga, Shinobu. Who Has the Yellow Hat? (Surprise Bks.). 22p. 1982. 4.95 (ISBN 0-8431-0638-7). Price Stern.
Arijon, Daniel. Grammar of the Film Language. (Illus.). 650p. 1976. 51.95 (ISBN 0-240-50779-7). Focal Pr.
Arikha, Avigdor. Nicolas Poussin: The Rape of the Sabines. LC 82-60726. (Illus.). 68p. (Orig.). 1982. pap. 9.95 (ISBN 0-295-96132-5, Pub. by Museum of Fine Arts, Houston). U of Wash Pr.
Arillano, E. Ramirez de see De Arrillano, E. Ramirez & Sundararaman, D.
Arima, M., et al, eds. The Developing Brain & Its Disorders: Proceedings of the 4th Annual Symposium on Development Disabilities, "Biological Aspects in the Pathogenesis of Developmental Disabilities," November 3-5, 1983, Tokyo. (Illus.). viii, 314p. 1985. 68.25 (ISBN 3-8055-4010-8). S Karger.
Arima, Masataka, et al, eds. The Developing Brain & its Disorders. 316p. 1985. 96.00. Transaction Bks.
Arima, Tatsuo. The Failure of Freedom: A Portrait of Modern Japanese Intellectuals. LC 74-82292. (Harvard East Asian Ser.: No. 39). pap. 78.80 (ISBN 0-317-08153-5, 2006428). Bks Demand UMI.
Ariman, T., ed. Earthquake Behavior & Safety of Oil & Gas Storage Facilities, Buried Pipelines & Equipment, Vol. 77. 478p. 1983. pap. text ed. 70.00 (ISBN 0-317-02615-1, H00263). ASME.
Ariman, T., jt. ed. see Shibata, H.
Ariman, T., et al, eds. Lifeline Earthquake Engineering: Buried Pipelines, Seismic Risk & Instrumentation. PYP, Vol. 34. 292p. 1979. 40.00 (ISBN 0-317-33560-X, H00148); Members 20.00 (ISBN 0-317-33561-8). ASME.
Arimany Coma, Miguel. Diccionari Catala General Usual. 4th ed. 1418p. (Catalan.). 1976. 35.95 (ISBN 84-7211-097-4, S-50049). French & Eur.
--Diccionari Escolar Catala Arimany. 4th ed. 310p. (Catalan.). 1978. pap. 7.95 (ISBN 84-7211-117-2, S-50050). French & Eur.
--Diccionari Manual Castella-Catala. 2nd ed. 413p. (Castella & Catalan.). 1975. 8.75 (ISBN 84-7211-084-2, S-50358). French & Eur.

--Diccionari Manual Catala-Castella. 2nd ed. 535p. (Catalan & Castella.). 1975. 8.75 (ISBN 84-7211-078-8, S-50357). French & Eur.

--Diccionari Manual Catala-Castella i Castella-Catala. 9th ed. 956p. (Catalan & Castella.). 1976. 16.50 (ISBN 84-7211-088-5, S-50360). French & Eur.

--Diccionari Practic Castella-Catala, Catala-Castella. 3rd ed. 456p. (Castella & Catalan.). 1976. 9.95 (ISBN 84-7211-087-7, S-50356). French & Eur.

--Diccionari Practic Catala-Frances. 2nd ed. 256p. (Catalan & Span.). 1977. pap. 5.25 (ISBN 84-7211-048-6, S-50413). French & Eur.

--Diccionari Usual Catala-Castella i Castella-Catala. 7th ed. 958p. (Catalan & Castella.). 1976. 23.95 (ISBN 84-7211-080-X, S-50361). French & Eur.

Arimany Coma, Miquel. Diccionari Basic Catala-Castella, Castella-Catala. 9th ed. 390p. (Catala & Span.). 1975. pap. 3.95 (ISBN 84-7211-085-0, S-50359). French & Eur.

Arinc Research Corporation. Reliability Engineering. 1964. ref. ed. 45.00 (ISBN 0-13-773127-2). P-H.

--Thirty Twenty GHz Communications Satellite Trunking Network Study. 1981. 100.00 (ISBN 0-686-37982-9). Info Gatekeepers.

Aring, Charles D. Understanding Physician: Writings of Charles D. Aring, M.D. LC 73-143469. 228p. 1971. Repr. text ed. 8.95x (ISBN 0-8143-1440-6). Wayne St U Pr.

Aringhi, Paolo. The Catacombs of Rome, 2 vols. (Printed Sources of Western Ser.). (Illus., Latin.). 1981. pap. 120.00 slipcase (ISBN 0-915346-61-3). A Wofsy Fine Arts.

Arintero, John G. Mystical Evolution, 2 vols. Aumann, Jordan, tr. from Sp. LC 78-62254. Orig. Title: La Evolucion Mistica. 1979. Set. pap. 24.00 (ISBN 0-89555-071-7); Vol. I. pap. (ISBN 0-89555-072-5); Vol. II. pap. (ISBN 0-89555-073-3). TAN Bks Pubs.

Arioglu, E., jt. auth. see Biron, C.

Ariosti, Attilio. Vespasiano. Brown, Howard M., ed. LC 76-21078. (Italian Opera 1640-1770 Ser.). 1978. lib. bdg. 77.00 (ISBN 0-8240-2625-X). Garland Pub.

Ariosto. Orlando Furioso. 1983 ed. Hough, ed. Harington, tr. 90.00x (ISBN 0-900000-39-2, Pub. by Centaur Pr England). State Mutual Bk.

Ariosto, L. Orlando Furioso. Waley, P., ed. (Italian Texts Ser.). 272p. (Ital.). 1972. pap. text ed. 6.50 (ISBN 0-7190-0498-5, Pub. by Machester Univ Pr). Longwood Pub Group.

Ariosto, Ludovico. Ariostos Seven Planets Governing Italie, or His Satyrs. LC 76-57350. (English Experience Ser.: No. 770). 1977. Repr. of 1611 ed. lib. bdg. 11.50 (ISBN 90-221-0770-1). Walter J Johnson.

--Orlando Furioso. Waldman, Guido, tr. (The World's Classics Ser.). 1983. pap. 12.95 (ISBN 0-19-281636-5, WC). Oxford U Pr.

--Orlando Furioso: An English Translation with Introductions, Notes & Index by Allan Gilbert, 2 vols. 1954. 45.00x set (ISBN 0-913298-31-X). S F Vanni.

--Orlando Furioso in English Heroical Vers. LC 77-25638. (English Experience Ser.: No. 259). (Illus.). 424p. Repr. of 1591 ed. 51.00 (ISBN 90-221-0259-9). Walter J Johnson.

--Orlando Furioso: Vol. Two. Reynolds, Barbara, tr. from It. (Classics Se.). 1977. pap. 14.95 (ISBN 0-14-044310-X). Penguin.

Ariotti, Piero, ed. see Bronowski, Jacob.

Aripul, Samuel B. Sefer Sar Shalom: Commentary on the Book of Song of Songs, Safed 1579. 31.00 (ISBN 0-405-11954-2). Ayer Co Pubs.

Aris, M. Bhutan: The Early History of a Himalayan Kingdom. 344p. 1979. text ed. 44.50x (ISBN 0-85668-082-6, Pub. by Aris & Phillips England); pap. text ed. 26.75x (ISBN 0-85668-199-7, Pub. by Aris & Phillips England). Humanities.

Aris, M. & San Suu, Aung, eds. Tibetan Studies in Honour of Hugh Richardson. 348p. 1981. pap. text ed. 42.50x (ISBN 0-85668-190-3, Pub. by Aris & Phillips England). Humanities.

Aris, Michael. Views of Medieval Bhutan: The Diary Drawings of Samuel Davis, 1783. (Illus.). 124p. 1982. 35.00 (ISBN 0-87474-210-2, Pub. by Serindia Pubs London). Smithsonian.

Aris, Pepita. The Sauce Book. 176p. 1984. 15.95 (ISBN 0-07-002189-9). McGraw.

Aris, R. & Strieder, W. C. Variational Methods Applied to Problems of Diffusion & Reaction. (Springer Tracts in Natural Philosophy: Vol. 24). (Illus.). 120p. 1973. 25.00 (ISBN 0-387-06311-0). Springer-Verlag.

Aris, Reinhold. History of Political Thought in Germany, 1789-1815. 414p. 1965. Repr. 30.00x (ISBN 0-7156-1646-3, F Cass Co). Biblio Dist.

Aris, Rutherford. Mathematical Modeling Techniques. (Research Notes in Mathematics Ser.: No. 24). 191p. 1978. pap. text ed. 24.95 (ISBN 0-273-08413-5). Pitman Pub MA.

--The Mathematical Theory of Diffusion & Reaction in Permeable Catalysts, 2 vols. Incl. Vol. 1. Theory of the Steady State. 65.00x (ISBN 0-19-851931-1); Vol. 2. Questions of Uniqueness, Stability, & Transient Behaviour. 45.00x (ISBN 0-19-851942-7). (Illus.). 1975. 98.00x set (ISBN 0-19-519829-8). Oxford U Pr.

Aris, Rutherford & Davis, H. Ted, eds. Springs of Scientific Creativity: Essays on Founders of Modern Science. LC 82-23715. (Illus.). 352p. 1983. 32.50x (ISBN 0-8166-1087-8). U of Minn Pr.

Aris, Rutherford & Varma, Arvind, eds. The Mathematical Understanding of Chemical Engineering Systems: Selected Papers of Neal R. Amundson. LC 79-40686. (Illus.). 1980. 155.00 (ISBN 0-08-023836-X). Pergamon.

Aris, Stephen. Going Bust: Inside the Bankruptcy Business. 194p. 1985. 16.95 (ISBN 0-233-97693-0, Pub. by A Deutsch England). David & Charles.

Arishima, Takeo. A Certain Woman. Strong, Kenneth, tr. & intro. by. 382p. 1978. 25.00 (ISBN 0-86008-237-7, Pub. by U of Tokyo Japan). Columbia U Pr.

Arisian, Khoren. The New Wedding: Creating Your Own Marriage Ceremony. 1973. 13.50 (ISBN 0-394-48334-0). Knopf.

--The New Wedding: Creating Your Own Marriage Ceremony. 160p. 1973. 13.50 (ISBN 0-394-48334-0, Vin); pap. 8.95 (ISBN 0-394-71919-0). Random.

Ariste, Paul. Grammar of the Votic Language. Keerdoga, Liina, tr. LC 66-64931. (Uralic & Altaic Ser: Vol. 68). 1968. pap. text ed. 9.50x (ISBN 0-87750-024-X). Res Ctr Lang Semiotic.

Aristides. Aristides, Vol. 1. Behr, C. A., tr. (Loeb Classical Library: No. 458). 1973. text ed. 12.50x (ISBN 0-674-99505-8). Harvard U Pr.

--Aristides Quintilianus on Music: In Three Books. Matheiesen, Thomas J., tr. LC 82-20244. (Music Theory Translation Ser.). 232p. 1983. text ed. 28.00x (ISBN 0-300-02893-8). Yale U Pr.

Ariston, H. J. Decide! LC 83-80421. (Illus.). 56p. (Orig.). 1983. pap. 5.95 (ISBN 0-935344-01-2). Jupiter Bks.

--Reality. LC 83-80423. 60p. (Orig.). 1983. pap. 5.95 (ISBN 0-935344-03-9). Jupiter Bks.

--Win! LC 83-80422. 80p. (Orig.). 1983. pap. 5.95 (ISBN 0-935344-02-0). Jupiter Bks.

Aristophanes. Acharnians. Sommerstein, Alan H., ed. 215p. 1980. 24.50x (ISBN 0-318-04782-9); pap. 12.00x (ISBN 0-318-04783-7). Bolchazy Carducci.

--The Acharnians of Aristophanes. Connor, W. R., ed. LC 78-18610. (Greek Text & Commentaries Ser.). (Gr. & Eng.). 1979. Repr. of 1909 ed. lib. bdg. 27.50x (ISBN 0-405-11450-8). Ayer Co Pubs.

--Aristophanes Plutos, with Commentary. Connor, W. R., ed. LC 78-18582. (Greek Texts & Commentaries Ser.). (Illus., Ger.). 1979. Repr. of 1940 ed. lib. bdg. 27.50x (ISBN 0-405-11425-7). Ayer Co Pubs.

--The Birds. Arnott, Peter D., ed. & tr. Bd. with The Brothers Menaechmus. Plautus. LC 58-12716. (Crofts Classics Ser.). 1958. pap. text ed. 3.75x (ISBN 0-88295-004-5). Harlan Davidson.

--The Clouds. Arnott, Peter D., ed. & tr. Bd. with The Pot of Gold. Plautus. LC 67-17194. (Crofts Classics Ser.). 1967. pap. text ed. 3.75x (ISBN 0-88295-005-3). Harlan Davidson.

--Clouds. abr. ed. Dover, K. J., ed. 1970. pap. 9.95x (ISBN 0-19-912009-9). Oxford U Pr.

--Clouds. Dover, K. J., ed. 1968. 32.50x (ISBN 0-19-814174-2). Oxford U Pr.

--Clouds. Sommerstein, Alan H., ed. 232p. 1892. 24.50x (ISBN 0-318-04784-5); pap. 12.00x (ISBN 0-318-04785-3). Bolchazy Carducci.

--Clouds, Women in Power, Knights. McLeish, K., tr. LC 78-51680. (Translations from Greek & Roman Authors). 1980. 29.95 (ISBN 0-521-22900-6); pap. 9.95 (ISBN 0-521-29707-9). Cambridge U Pr.

--Commodiae, 2 Vols. Hall, F. W. & Geldart, W. M., eds. (Oxford Classical Texts Ser). Vol. 1. 14.95x (ISBN 0-19-814504-7); Vol. 2. 14.95x (ISBN 0-19-814505-5). Oxford U Pr.

--Comoediae, 2 vols. Bergk, Theodorus, ed. 658p. 1985. Set. 30.00 (ISBN 0-89005-413-4). Ares.

--Four Comedies: Lysistrata, the Congresswomen, the Acharnians, the Frogs. Arrowsmith, William, ed. (Illus.). 432p. 1969. pap. 8.95 (ISBN 0-472-06152-6, 152, AA). U of Mich Pr.

--Four Major Plays. new ed. Incl. The Acharnians; The Birds; The Clouds; Lysistrata. (Classics Ser.). (gr. 11 up). 1968. pap. 1.50 (ISBN 0-8049-0189-9, CL-189). Airmont.

--The Frogs. Murray, Gilbert, tr. 1908. pap. text ed. 3.95x (ISBN 0-04-882021-0). Allen Unwin.

--Frogs & Other Plays. Barrett, David, tr. Incl. Wasps; Poet & the Women. (Classics Ser.). (Orig.). 1964. pap. 2.95 (ISBN 0-14-044152-2). Penguin.

--Knights. Sommerstein, Alan H., ed. 220p. 1981. 24.50x (ISBN 0-318-04786-1). Bolchazy Carducci.

--Lysistrata. Sutherland, Donald, tr. (Orig.). 1961. pap. 4.50 scp (ISBN 0-8102-0031-7, HarpC). Har-Row.

--Lysistrata. Webb, Robert H., tr. 106p. 1963. 5.95 (ISBN 0-8139-0010-7). U Pr of Va.

--Lysistrata & Other Plays. Sommerstein, A. H., tr. (Classics Ser.). 1974. pap. 3.95 (ISBN 0-14-044287-1). Penguin.

--Lysistrate. Parker, Douglass, tr. 1970. pap. 2.50 (ISBN 0-451-62367-3, Ment). NAL.

--Peace. Webb, Robert H., tr. LC 64-22630. 99p. 1964. pap. 3.95x (ISBN 0-8139-0013-1). U Pr of Va.

--Peace. Sommerstein, Alan H., ed. 225p. 1985. 24.50x (ISBN 0-318-04790-X); pap. 12.00x (ISBN 0-318-04791-8). Bolchazy Carducci.

--Three Comedies: The Birds, the Clouds, the Wasps. Arrowsmith, William, ed. (Illus.). 400p. 1969. pap. 8.95 (ISBN 0-472-06153-4, 153, AA). U of Mich Pr.

--Wasps. MacDowell, Douglas M., ed. 1971. text ed. 21.50x (ISBN 0-19-814182-3). Oxford U Pr.

--Wasps. Sommerstein, Alan H., ed. 248p. 1983. 24.50x (ISBN 0-318-04788-8); pap. 12.00x (ISBN 0-318-04789-6). Bolchazy Carducci.

--Works. Incl. Acharnians, Clouds, Knights, Wasps (ISBN 0-674-99197-4); Peace, Birds, Frogs (ISBN 0-674-99198-2); Lysistrata, Thesmophoriazusae, Ecclesiazusae, Plutus (ISBN 0-674-99199-0). (Loeb Classical Library: No. 178-180). 12.50x ea. Harvard U Pr.

Aristophanes see Fitts, Dudley.

Aristophanes see Hadas, Moses.

Aristophanes see Lind, Levi R.

Aristophanes see Oates, Whitney J. & O'Neill, Eugene, Jr.

Aristophanes see Robinson, Charles A., Jr.

Aristos. Diccionario Ilustrado De la Lengua Espanola. 640p. (Span.). 10.95 (ISBN 84-303-0048-1, S-12234). French & Eur.

Aristoteles. Aristotle's Art of Poetry: A Greek View of Poetry & Drama. LC 83-45409. Repr. of 1940 ed. 20.00 (ISBN 0-404-20007-9). AMS Pr.

Aristoteles, Seudo. Poridat de las Poridades. Kasten, Lloyd, ed. 94p. 1957. pap. 4.00x (ISBN 0-942260-00-7). Hispanic Seminary.

Aristotelian Society For The Systematic Study Of Philosophy. Knowledge & Foreknowledge: Proceedings, Supplementary Vol. 16. 16.00 (ISBN 0-384-29990-3); pap. 11.00 (ISBN 0-384-29991-1). Johnson Repr.

--Knowledge, Experience & Realism: Proceedings, Supplementary Vol. 9. 11.00 (ISBN 0-384-29993-8); pap. 6.00 (ISBN 0-384-29994-6). Johnson Repr.

--Life & Finite Individuality: Proceedings, Supplementary Vol. 1. 14.00 (ISBN 0-685-92697-4); pap. 9.00 (ISBN 0-384-32653-6). Johnson Repr.

--Logic & Reality: Proceedings, Supplmentary Vol. 20. 16.00 (ISBN 0-384-33395-8); pap. 11.00 (ISBN 0-384-33396-6). Johnson Repr.

--Logical Positivism & Ethics: Proceedings, Supplementary Vol. 22. 15.00 (ISBN 0-685-02190-4); pap. 10.00 (ISBN 0-384-33402-4). Johnson Repr.

--Men & Machines: Proceedings, Supplementary Vol. 26. 17.00 (ISBN 0-384-38120-0); pap. 12.00 (ISBN 0-384-38121-9). Johnson Repr.

--Mind, Matter & Purpose: Proceedings, Supplementary Vol. 8. 11.00 (ISBN 0-384-39030-7); pap. 6.00 (ISBN 0-384-39031-5). Johnson Repr.

--Mind, Objectivity & Fact: Proceedings, Supplementary Vol. 7. 13.00 (ISBN 0-384-39034-X); pap. 8.00 (ISBN 0-384-39035-8). Johnson Repr.

--Modern Tendencies in Philosophy: Proceedings, Supplementary Vol. 13. 16.00 (ISBN 0-384-39380-2); pap. 11.00 (ISBN 0-384-39381-0). Johnson Repr.

--Phenomenology: Proceedings, Supplementary Vol. 11. 15.00 (ISBN 0-384-46215-4); pap. 10.00 (ISBN 0-384-46216-2). Johnson Repr.

--Philosophy & Metaphysics: Proceedings, Supplementary Vol. 5. 11.00 (ISBN 0-384-46398-3); pap. 6.00 (ISBN 0-384-46399-1). Johnson Repr.

--Politics, Psychology & Art: Proceedings, Supplementary Vol. 23. 14.00 (ISBN 0-384-47122-6); pap. 9.00 (ISBN 0-384-47123-4). Johnson Repr.

--Problems in Psychotherapy & Jurisprudence: Proceedings, Supplementary Vol. 29. 16.00 (ISBN 0-384-47979-0); pap. 11.00 (ISBN 0-384-47980-4). Johnson Repr.

--Problems of Science & Philosophy: Proceedings, Supplementary Vol. 2. 15.00 (ISBN 0-384-47981-2); pap. 10.00 (ISBN 0-384-47982-0). Johnson Repr.

--Proceedings, New Series: Vols. 1-61, 1900-1961. Set. 825.00 (ISBN 0-685-02211-0); Set. pap. 650.00 (ISBN 0-685-02212-9). Johnson Repr.

--Proceedings, Old Series: Vols. 1-3, 1887-1896. Set. 75.00 (ISBN 0-685-02209-9); Set. pap. 60.00 (ISBN 0-685-02210-2). Johnson Repr.

--Psychical Research, Ethics & Logic: Proceedings, Supplementary Vol. 24. 16.00 (ISBN 0-685-92690-7); pap. 11.00 (ISBN 0-384-48086-1). Johnson Repr.

--Relativity, Logic & Mysticism: Proceedings, Supplementary Vol. 3. 14.00 (ISBN 0-384-50269-5); pap. 9.00 (ISBN 0-384-48086-1). Johnson Repr.

--Science History & Theology: Proceedings, Suppl. 14. 13.00 (ISBN 0-384-54410-X); pap. 8.00 (ISBN 0-384-54411-8). Johnson Repr.

Aristotelian Society For The Systematics Study Of Philosophy - London. What Can Philosophy Determine: Proceedings, Suppl. 15. 15.00 (ISBN 0-384-67815-7); pap. 10.00 (ISBN 0-384-67816-5). Johnson Repr.

Aristotle. An Analysis of the Soul of Man. (The Most Meaningful Classics in World Culture Ser.). (Illus.). 129p. 1983. 67.85 (ISBN 0-89920-052-4). Am. Inst Psych.

--Analytica Priora et Posteriora. Ross, Sir David, ed. (Oxford Classical Texts Ser.). 1964. text ed. 14.95x (ISBN 0-19-814562-4). Oxford U Pr.

--Aristole De Anima. facsimile ed. Hicks, Robert D., tr. & intro. by. LC 75-13252. (History of Ideas in Ancient Greece Ser.). 1976. Repr. of 1907 ed. 43.00x (ISBN 0-405-07289-9). Ayer Co Pubs.

--Aristote: Traite de l'ame, 2 vols. Rodier, G., tr. (Classical Studies). (Fr. & Gr.). Repr. of 1900 ed. lib. bdg. 76.00x set (ISBN 0-89197-662-0); lib. bdg. 39.50x ea. Vol. 1 (ISBN 0-697-00045-1). Vol. 2 (ISBN 0-697-00046-X). Irvington.

--Aristotle de Sensu & de Memoria. Ross, George R., tr. LC 72-9301. (The Philosophy of Plato & Aristotle Ser.). (Gr. & Eng.). Repr. of 1906 ed. 19.00 (ISBN 0-405-04856-4). Ayer Co Pubs.

--Aristotle, Metaphysics: Books Zeta, Eta, Theta, Iota (or 7-10) Furth, Montgomery, tr. from Greek. 156p. 1985. lib. bdg. 17.50 (ISBN 0-915145-89-8); pap. text ed. 7.50 (ISBN 0-915145-90-1). Hackett Pub.

--Aristotle Nicomachaen Ethics, Bk. 6. Greenwood, L. H., tr. LC 72-9290. (The Philosophy of Plato & Aristotle Ser.). (Gr. & Eng.). Repr. of 1909 ed. 16.00 (ISBN 0-405-04842-4). Ayer Co Pubs.

--Aristotle on Education: Extracts from Ethics & Politics. Burnet, John, ed. 1968. pap. 9.95 (ISBN 0-521-09443-7, 443). Cambridge U Pr.

--Aristotle on His Predecessors. 2nd ed. Taylor, A. E., tr. from Gr. 159p. 1969. 16.00 (ISBN 0-87548-001-2); pap. 4.95 (ISBN 0-87548-002-0). Open Court.

--Aristotle: Selected Works. Apostle, H. G. & Gerson, L. P., trs. from Greek. LC 82-62715. 705p. (Orig.). 1983. text ed. 24.00x (ISBN 0-911589-00-7); pap. 12.00x (ISBN 0-911589-01-5). Peripatetic.

--Aristotle's Categories & Propositions (De Interpretatione) Apostle, H. G., tr. LC 80-80777. (Apostle Translations of Aristotle's Works Ser.: Vol. 3). 157p. (Orig.). 1980. text ed. 13.60x (ISBN 0-9602870-4-3); pap. text ed. 6.80x (ISBN 0-9602870-5-1). Peripatetic.

--Aristotle's Constitution of Athens. 2nd rev. & enl. ed. LC 78-155630. (BCL Ser.: No. 1). Repr. of 1912 ed. 18.00 (ISBN 0-404-00368-0). AMS Pr.

--Aristotle's Constitution of Athens. rev. 2nd ed. LC 72-9302. (The Philosophy of Plato & Aristotle Ser.). (Gr. & Eng.). Repr. of 1912 ed. 23.00 (ISBN 0-405-04857-2). Ayer Co Pubs.

--Aristotle's Eudemian Ethics, Bks. I, II & VIII. Woods, M. J., ed. (Clarendon Aristotle Ser.). 1982. O.P. 29.95x (ISBN 0-19-872060-2); pap. 13.95x (ISBN 0-19-872061-0). Oxford U Pr.

--Aristotle's Metaphysics. Apostle, H. G., tr. from Gr. LC 79-88598. (Apostle Translations of Aristotle's Works Ser.: Vol. 1). 498p. 1979. text ed. 21.60x (ISBN 0-9602870-0-0); pap. text ed. 10.80x (ISBN 0-9602870-1-9). Peripatetic.

--Aristotle's Nicomachean Ethics. 2nd ed. Apostle, H. G., tr. from Greek. LC 84-60009. (Apostle Translations of Aristotle: Vol. 6). 372p. 1984. pap. text ed. 12.00x (ISBN 0-911589-03-1). Peripatetic.

--Aristotle's On the Soul (De Anima) Apostle, H. G., tr. LC 81-86481. (Apostle Translations of Aristotle's Works Ser.: No. 5). 225p. (Orig.). 1982. text ed. 18.00x (ISBN 0-9602870-8-6); pap. text ed. 9.00x (ISBN 0-9602870-9-4). Peripatetic.

--Aristotle's Physics. Apostle, H. G., tr. from Gr. LC 80-80037. (Apostle Translations of Aristotle's Works Ser.: Vol. 2). 386p. 1980. text ed. 21.60x (ISBN 0-9602870-2-7); pap. text ed. 10.80x (ISBN 0-9602870-3-5). Peripatetic.

--Aristotle's Physics. Hope, Richard, tr. LC 61-5498. xiv, 242p. 1961. pap. 6.25x (ISBN 0-8032-5093-2, BB 122, Bison). U of Nebr Pr.

--Aristotle's Poetics. Butcher, S. H., tr. from Greek. (Drama Book Ser.). 118p. (Orig.). 1961. pap. 3.95 (ISBN 0-8090-0527-1). Hill & Wang.

--Aristotle's Poetics. Kirkwood, G. M., ed. Hutton, James. 120p. 1982. text ed. 15.95x (ISBN 0-393-01599-8); pap. text ed. 4.95x (ISBN 0-393-95216-9). Norton.

--Aristotle's Posterior Analytics. Apostle, H. G., tr. LC 81-80233. (Apostle Translations of Aristotle's Works Ser.: Vol. 4). 328p. (Orig.). 1981. text ed. 21.60x (ISBN 0-9602870-6-X); pap. text ed. 10.80x (ISBN 0-9602870-7-8). Peripatetic.

--Aristotle's Psychology. facsimile ed. LC 75-13253. (History of Ideas in Ancient Greece Ser.). (Greek & English.). 1976. Repr. of 1882 ed. 27.50x (ISBN 0-405-07290-2). Ayer Co Pubs.

--Aristotles's Physics, Bks. 1 & 2. Charlton, W., ed. (Clarendon Aristotle Ser.). 1970. 12.95x (ISBN 0-19-872026-2). Oxford U Pr.

--Ars Rhetorica. Ross, W. David, ed. (Oxford Classical Texts). 1959. 16.95x (ISBN 0-19-814557-8). Oxford U Pr.

--Art of Rhetoric. (Loeb Classical Library: No. 193). 12.50 (ISBN 0-674-99212-1). Harvard U Pr.

--Athenian Constitution. Bd. with Eudemian Ethics, Bks 1-3, 7 & 8; Virtues & Vices. (Loeb Classical Library: No. 285). 12.50x (ISBN 0-674-99315-2). Harvard U Pr.

--The Athenian Constitution. Rhodes, P. J., tr. Hurlimann, Martin. (Classics Ser.). 208p. 1984. pap. 4.95 (ISBN 0-14-044431-9). Penguin.

--Atheniensium Respublica. Kenyon, F. G., ed. (Oxford Classical Texts Ser). 1920. 9.95x (ISBN 0-19-814506-3). Oxford U Pr.

--Basic Works of Aristotle. McKeon, Richard P., ed. 1941. boxed 27.95 (ISBN 0-394-41610-4). Random.

--Categories. Bd. with On Interpretation; Prior Analytics, Bks. 1 & 2. (Loeb Classical Library: No. 325). (Gr. & Eng.). 12.50x (ISBN 0-674-99359-4). Harvard U Pr.

--Categories & De Interpretatione. Ackrill, J. L., tr. (Clarendon Aristotle Ser.). 1963. pap. 11.95x (ISBN 0-19-872086-6). Oxford U Pr.

--Categories Et Liber De Interpretatione. Minio-Paluello, L., ed. (Oxford Classical Texts Ser). 1949. 14.95x (ISBN 0-19-814507-1). Oxford U Pr.

--The Complete Works of Aristotle: The Revised Oxford Translation, 2 Vols, No. 2. Barnes, Jonathan, ed. LC 82-5317. (Bollingen Ser.: LXXI). 3762p. 1984. 75.00x set (ISBN 0-691-09950-2). Princeton U Pr.

--Constitution of Athens & Related Texts. (Library of Classics Ser.: No. 13). pap. text ed. 9.95x (ISBN 0-02-840420-3). Hafner.

--Constitution of Athens & Related Texts. 1974. pap. 9.95x (ISBN 0-317-30525-5). Free Pr.

--De Anima. Ross, W. David, ed. (Oxford Classical Texts Ser). 1956. 12.50x (ISBN 0-19-814508-X). Oxford U Pr.

--De Anima, Bks. 2 & 3. Hamlyn, D. W., tr. & intro. by. (Clarendon Aristotle Ser). (With certain passages from bk. 1). 1975. pap. 11.95x (ISBN 0-19-872076-9). Oxford U Pr.

--De Arte Poetica. Kassel, Rudolf V., ed. (Oxford Classical Texts Ser.). 1965. 10.50x (ISBN 0-19-814564-0). Oxford U Pr.

--Ethica Nicomachea. Bywater, Ingram, ed. (Oxford Classical Texts Ser). 1890. 16.95x (ISBN 0-19-814511-X). Oxford U Pr.

--Ethics. Warrington, John, tr. 1975. Repr. of 1963 ed. 12.95x (ISBN 0-460-00547-2, Evman). Biblio Dist.

--The Ethics of Aristotle. Burnet, John, ed. LC 72-9282. (The Philosophy of Plato & Aristotle Ser.). (Gr. & Eng.). Repr. of 1900 ed. 33.00 (ISBN 0-405-04833-5). Ayer Co Pubs.

--The Ethics of Aristotle, 2 vols. in 1. 4th ed. LC 72-9289. (The Philosophy of Plato & Aristotle Ser.). (Gr. & Eng.). Repr. of 1885 ed. 58.50 (ISBN 0-405-04839-4). Ayer Co Pubs.

--The Fifth Book of the Nicomachaen Ethics of Aristotle. Jackson, Henry, ed. LC 72-9294. (The Philosophy of Plato & Aristotle Ser.). (Gr. & Eng.). Repr. of 1879 ed. 12.00 (ISBN 0-405-04845-9). Ayer Co Pubs.

--Fragmenta Selecta. Ross, W. David, ed. (Oxford Classical Texts Ser). 1955. 13.95x (ISBN 0-19-814512-8). Oxford U Pr.

--Generation of Animals. (Loeb Classical Library: No. 366). 1943. 12.50x (ISBN 0-674-99403-5). Harvard U Pr.

--Historia Animalium, Bks. 1-3. (Loeb Classical Library: No. 437). (Gr. & Eng.). 12.50x ea. Harvard U Pr.

--Introduction to Aristotle. McKeon, Richard, ed. (Modern Library College Editions). 1965. pap. text ed. 5.00 (ISBN 0-394-30973-1, T73, RanC). Random.

--Metaphysica. Jaeger, Werner, ed. (Oxford Classical Texts Ser). 1957. 19.95x (ISBN 0-19-814513-6). Oxford U Pr.

--Metaphysics. Warrington, John, tr. 1976. Repr. of 1956 ed. 9.95x (ISBN 0-460-01000-X, Evman). Biblio Dist.

--Metaphysics, 2 Vols. rev. ed. Ross, W. David, ed. 1924. Set. 89.00x (ISBN 0-19-814107-6). Oxford U Pr.

--Metaphysics. Hope, Richard, tr. 1960. pap. 8.95 (ISBN 0-472-06042-2, 42, AA). U of Mich Pr.

--Metaphysics, Bks. 1-9. (Loeb Classical Library: No. 271). 12.50x (ISBN 0-674-99299-7). Harvard U Pr.

--Metaphysics, Bks. 4-6. Kirwan, Christopher, tr. (Clarendon Aristotle Ser.). 1971. 16.95x (ISBN 0-19-872027-0). Oxford U Pr.

--Metaphysics, Bks. 10-14. Bd. with Oeconomica, Bks 1-3; Magna Moralia, Bks 1 & 2. (Loeb Classical Library: No. 287). 12.50x (ISBN 0-674-99317-9). Harvard U Pr.

--Metaphysics: Books M & N. Annas, Julia, ed. (Clarendon Aristotle Ser.). 1976. 29.95x (ISBN 0-19-872085-8). Oxford U Pr.

--Meteorologica. (Loeb Classical Library: No. 397). 1952. 12.50x (ISBN 0-674-99436-1). Harvard U Pr.

--Minor Works. (Loeb Classical Library: No. 307). 1936. 12.50x (ISBN 0-674-99338-1). Harvard U Pr.

--Nicomachean Ethics. Ostwald, Martin, tr. LC 62-15690. (Orig.). 1962. pap. 6.65 scp (ISBN 0-672-60256-3, LLA75). Bobbs.

--Nicomachean Ethics. (Loeb Classical Library: No. 73). 12.50x (ISBN 0-674-99081-1). Harvard U Pr.

--The Nicomachean Ethics. Apostle, Hippocrates G., tr. LC 75-5871. (Synthese Historical Library: No. 13). 372p. 1975. lib. bdg. 71.00 (ISBN 90-277-0569-0, Pub. by Reidel Holland). Kluwer Academic.

--The Nicomachean Ethics. Ross, W. D., tr. (World's Classics Ser.). 1980. pap. 4.95 (ISBN 0-19-281518-0). Oxford U Pr.

--On Poetry & Style. Grube, G. M., tr. LC 58-13827. 1958. pap. 5.99 scp (ISBN 0-672-60244-X, LLA68). Bobbs.

--On Sophistical Refutations, on Coming-To-Be & Passing-Away, on the Cosmos. (Loeb Classical Library: No. 400). 12.50x (ISBN 0-674-99441-8). Harvard U Pr.

--On the Art of Poetry. Bywater, Ingram, tr. 1920. pap. 5.50x (ISBN 0-19-814110-6). Oxford U Pr.

--On the Art of Poetry with a Supplement on Music. 2nd ed. Nahm, Milton C., ed. Butcher, S. H., tr. 1956. pap. 3.56 scp (ISBN 0-672-60168-0, LLA 6). Bobbs.

--On the Heavens. (Loeb Classical Library: No. 338). 12.50x (ISBN 0-674-99372-1). Harvard U Pr.

--On the Soul, Parva Naturalia, on Breath. (Loeb Classical Library: No. 288). 12.50x (ISBN 0-674-99318-7). Harvard U Pr.

--Parts of Animals. Bd. with Movement of Animals; Progression of Animals. (Loeb Classical Library: No. 323). (Gr. & Eng.). 12.50x (ISBN 0-674-99357-8). Harvard U Pr.

--Physica. Ross, W. David, ed. (Oxford Classical Texts Ser). 1950. 17.50x (ISBN 0-19-814514-4). Oxford U Pr.

--Physics, 2 Vols. (Loeb Classical Library: No. 228, 255). 12.50x ea. Bks. 1-4 (ISBN 0-674-99251-2). Bks. 5-8 (ISBN 0-674-99281-4). Harvard U Pr.

--Physics. rev. ed. Ross, W. David, ed. 1936. 67.50x (ISBN 0-19-814109-2). Oxford U Pr.

--Physics, 2 vols, Vols. I & II. Charlton, ed. 1983. Set. 12.95x (ISBN 0-317-06326-X). Oxford U Pr.

--The Pocket Aristotle. Kaplan, Justin, ed. 400p. 1983. pap. 5.95 (ISBN 0-671-46377-2). WSP.

--Poetics. 1978. Repr. of 1963 ed. 8.95x (ISBN 0-460-00901-X, Evman). Biblio Dist.

--Poetics. Bd. with On the Sublime. Longinus; On Style. Demetrius. (Loeb Classical Library: No. 199). 12.50x (ISBN 0-674-99219-9). Harvard U Pr.

--Poetics. 1968. 19.95x (ISBN 0-19-814024-X). Oxford U Pr.

--Poetics. Else, Gerald F., tr. LC 67-11980. 1967. pap. 5.95 (ISBN 0-472-06166-6). U of Mich Pr.

--Poetics. 1970. pap. 5.95 (166, AA). U of Mich Pr.

--The Poetics of Aristotle. Epps, Preston H., tr. xii, 70p. 1967. pap. 4.00x (ISBN 0-8078-4017-3). U of NC Pr.

--Politica. Ross, W. David, ed. (Oxford Classical Texts). 1957. 18.95x (ISBN 0-19-814515-2). Oxford U Pr.

--Politics. (Loeb Classical Library: No. 264). 1932. 12.50x (ISBN 0-674-99291-1). Harvard U Pr.

--Politics. Barker, Ernest, tr. (YA) (gr. 9 up). 1946. pap. 8.95x (ISBN 0-19-500306-3). Oxford U Pr.

--The Politics. Lord, Carnes, tr. from Gr. LC 84-215. (Illus.). 352p. 1985. lib. bdg. 35.00x (ISBN 0-226-02667-1); pap. 9.95 (ISBN 0-226-02669-8). U of Chicago Pr.

--Politics: Aristotle. rev. ed. (Classics Ser.). 1981. pap. 4.95 (ISBN 0-14-044421-1). Penguin.

--The Politics of Aristotle, 4 vols. LC 72-9297. (The Philosophy of Plato & Aristotle Ser.). (Gr. & Eng.). Repr. of 1902 ed. Set. 154.00 (ISBN 0-405-04848-3); 38.50 ea. Vol.1 (ISBN 0-405-04849-1). Vol.2 (ISBN 0-405-04850-5). Vol.3 (ISBN 0-405-04851-3). Vol.4 (ISBN 0-405-04852-1). Ayer Co Pubs.

--The Politics of Aristotle. facsimile ed. LC 75-13363. (History of Ideas in Ancient Greece Ser.: Bks. 1-5). (Greek & English.). 1976. Repr. of 1894 ed. 39.00x set (ISBN 0-405-07291-0). Ayer Co Pubs.

--Posterior Analytics. Barnes, Jonathan, ed. (Clarendon Aristotle Ser.). 1975. pap. 14.95x (ISBN 0-19-872067-X). Oxford U Pr.

--Posterior Analytics, Bks. 1 & 2. Bd. with Topica, Bks. 1-8. (Loeb Classical Library: No. 391). (Gr. & Eng.). 12.50x (ISBN 0-674-99430-2). Harvard U Pr.

--Prior & Posterior Analytics. Warrington, John, tr. 1964. 12.95x (ISBN 0-460-00450-6, Evman). Biblio Dist.

--Problems, Bks. 1-21. (Loeb Classical Library: No. 316). 12.50x (ISBN 0-674-99349-7). Harvard U Pr.

--Problems, Bks 22-38. Bd. with Rhetorica ad Alexandrum. (Loeb Classical Library: No. 317). 12.50x (ISBN 0-674-99350-0). Harvard U Pr.

--The Rhetoric & Poetics. LC 54-9971. 1954. 6.95 (ISBN 0-394-60425-3). Modern Lib.

--The Rhetoric & Poetics of Aristotle. (Modern Library College Editions). 250p. 1984. pap. text ed. 4.95 (ISBN 0-394-33924-X, MLCE). Random.

--The Rhetoric of Aristotle, 2 vols. in 1. Sandys, John E., ed. LC 72-9304. (The Philosophy of Plato & Aristotle Ser.). (Gr. & Eng.). Repr. of 1877 ed. 55.00 (ISBN 0-405-04858-0). Ayer Co Pubs.

--Secreta Secretorum. Copland, Robert, tr. LC 71-26095. (English Experience Ser.: No. 220). 72p. Repr. of 1528 ed. 11.50 (ISBN 90-221-0220-3). Walter J Johnson.

--Topica Et Sophistici Elenchi. Ross, W. David, ed. (Oxford Classical Texts Ser.). 1958. 17.50x (ISBN 0-19-814516-0). Oxford U Pr.

--Works, Vol. 7, Problems - Problemata. Ross, David, ed. Beare, J. I., tr. 1927. text ed. 28.00x (ISBN 0-19-824207-7). Oxford U Pr.

--Works, Vol. 9, Ethics, Ethica NicoMachea, Magna Moralia & Ethica Eudemia. Ross, David, ed. Beare, J. I., tr. 1925. text ed. 32.50x (ISBN 0-19-824209-3). Oxford U Pr.

Aristotle see Dorsch, T. S.

Aristotle, Pseudo. Aragonese Version of the Secreto Secretorum. (Dialect Ser.: No. 3). 1985. 12.00x (ISBN 0-942260-30-9). Hispanic Seminary.

Ariyadasa, K. D. Management of Educational Reforms in Sri Lanka. (Experiments & Innovations in Education: No. 25). 41p. 1976. pap. 5.00 (ISBN 92-3-101372-6, U365, UNESCO). Unipub.

Ariyama, Joe, et al. Radiology in Disorders of the Liver, Biliary Tract & Pancreas. LC 81-82117. (Illus.). 208p. 1981. text ed. 37.50 (ISBN 0-89640-059-X). Igaku-Shoin.

Ariyan, Stephan. The Hand Book. 2nd ed. 290p. 1983. lib. bdg. 24.00 (ISBN 0-683-00252-X). Williams & Wilkins.

Ariyoshi, Sawako. The Doctor's Wife. Hironaka, Wakako & Kostant, Ann S., trs. from Japanese. LC 80-85380. 184p. pap. 4.25 (ISBN 0-87011-465-4). Kodansha.

--The Doctor's Wife. Hironaka, Wakako & Kostant, Ann S., trs. from Japanese. LC 78-55080. 1978. 12.95x (ISBN 0-87011-337-2). Kodansha.

--The River Ki. Tahara, Mildred, tr. from Japanese. LC 79-66240. 243p. 1982. pap. 5.25 (ISBN 0-87011-514-6). Kodansha.

--The River Ki. Tahara, Mildred, tr. from Japanese. LC 79-66240. 1980. 14.95x (ISBN 0-87011-385-2). Kodansha.

--The Twilight Years. Tahara, Mildred, tr. from Japanese. LC 84-47687. 216p. 1984. 14.95 (ISBN 0-87011-677-0). Kodansha.

Arizaga, Lavora S. Exercising Your Legal Rights. (Orig.). 1983. pap. text ed. 2.00x (ISBN 0-915757-01-X). League Women Voters TX.

--Women Under Texas Law. 32p. (Orig.). 1982. pap. text ed. 2.00x (ISBN 0-915757-00-1). League Women Voters TX.

Arizona & West Publishing Company. Arizona Revised Statutes, Annotated: Prepared Under Legislative Authority, Laws 1956, Chapter 129. LC 57-26. Date not set. cancelled. West Pub.

Arizona ASBO, ed. Warehousing & Distributing Guidelines. 0.69 (ISBN 0-685-05645-7). Assn Sch Busn.

Arizona State University Library. Solar Energy Index. 1980. 175.00 (ISBN 0-08-023888-2). Pergamon.

--Solar Energy Index: Supplement I. 250p. 1982. 105.00 (ISBN 0-08-028832-4). Pergamon.

Arizona University, Mechanical & Energy Systems Engineering Dept. Simplified Design Guide for Estimating Photovoltaic Flat Array & System Performance. 175p. 1982. pap. 29.95x (ISBN 0-89934-168-3, P-047). Solar Energy Info.

Arjani, K. A. Structured Programming Flowcharts. 1978. pap. text ed. 6.95 (ISBN 0-89669-000-8). Collegium Bk Pubs.

Arje, Frances B., et al. Psychiatric-Mental Health Nursing. 3rd ed. (Nursing Examination Review Book: Vol. 2). 1972. spiral bdg. 7.50 (ISBN 0-87488-502-7). Med Exam.

Arjmand, Mihdi. Gulshan-i Haqayiq. 320p. (Persian.). 1982. Repr. 12.95 (ISBN 0-933770-15-4). Kalimat.

Arjomand, Said A. The Shadow of God & the Hidden Iman: Religion, Political Order & Societal Change in Shi'ite Iran from the Beginning to 1890. LC 83-27196. (Publications of the Center for the Middle Eastern Studies: No. 17). (Illus.). 344p. 1984. lib. bdg. 28.00x (ISBN 0-226-02782-1). U of Chicago Pr.

Arjomand, Said A., ed. From Nationalism to Revolutionary Islam: Essays on Social Movements in the Contemporary Near & Middle East. 272p. 1984. 39.50x (ISBN 0-87395-870-5); pap. 15.95x (ISBN 0-87395-871-3). State U NY Pr.

Arjona, Carlos V., jt. auth. see Arjona, Doris K.

Arjona, Doris K. & Arjona, Carlos V. Quince Cuentos de las Espanas. LC 71-135971. 256p. (Span.). 1971. pap. text ed. price not set (ISBN 0-02-301200-5, Pub. by Scribner). Macmillan.

Arjona, Doris K., jt. ed. see Helman, Edith F.

Ark Publishing, ed. The Book of Bible Knowledge. 296p. 1981. 40.00x (ISBN 0-686-75527-8, Pub. by Ark Pub England). State Mutual Bk.

Arkadie, Brian Von see Van Arkadie, Brian.

Arkangeliskii, A. V. & Ponomarev, V. I. Fundamentals of General Topology. 1984. lib. bdg. 69.00 (ISBN 90-277-1355-3, Pub. by Reidel Holland). Kluwer Academic.

Arkansas Dept. of Planning. Arkansas Natural Area Plan. (Illus.). xvii, 248p. (Orig.). 1974. pap. 10.95 (ISBN 0-912456-07-8). Ozark Soc Bks.

Arkansas Supreme Court Committee on Criminal Jury Instructions. Arkansas Model Criminal Jury Instructions. (State Practice Publications Ser.). 389p. 1979. Incl. hardcover binder & 1982 supplement. looseleaf 65.00 (ISBN 0-672-83758-7); Nineteen Eighty-Two supplement only. 25.00 (ISBN 0-87215-628-1). Michie Co.

Arkava, Morton & Russell, John. Coping with Smoking. (Personal Adjustment Ser.). 144p. 1984. lib. bdg. 8.97 (ISBN 0-8239-0614-0). Rosen Group.

Arkava, Morton L. Beginning Social Work Research. 300p. 1983. pap. 19.29 scp (ISBN 0-205-07815-X, 817815). Allyn.

--Hiking Trails of the Bitterroot Mountains. (Illus.). 120p. (Orig.). 1983. pap. 6.95 (ISBN 0-87108-650-6). Pruett.

--Kick the Smoking Habit. LC 82-83982. 120p. (Orig.). 1984. pap. text ed. 4.95 (ISBN 0-88247-704-8). R & E Pubs.

Arkava, Morton L. & Snow, Mark. Psychological Tests & Social Work Practice: An Introductory Guide. (Illus.). 112p. 1978. spiral 16.75x (ISBN 0-398-03832-5). C C Thomas.

Arkell, Anthony J. A History of the Sudan: From the Earliest Times to 1821. LC 73-13413. (Illus.). 252p. 1974. Repr. of 1961 ed. lib. bdg. 16.00 (ISBN 0-8371-7129-6, ARHS). Greenwood.

Arkell, Claudia, jt. auth. see Van Etten, Glen.

Arkell, David. Looking for Laforgue: An Informal Biography of Jules Laforgue. LC 79-89449. 1979. 20.00 (ISBN 0-89255-042-2). Persea Bks.

Arkell, Reginald. Richard Jefferies. 294p. 1983. Repr. of 1933 ed. text ed. 45.00 (ISBN 0-89984-020-5). Century Bookbindery.

Arkell, W. J. The Ammonites of the English Corallian Beds, Vols. 1-14. Set. 160.00 (ISBN 0-384-02010-0). Johnson Repr.

--The Corallian Lamellibranchia, Vols. 1-10. Set. 110.00 (ISBN 0-384-02030-5). Johnson Repr.

--The English Bathonian Ammonities, Vols. 1-6. Set. 54.00 (ISBN 0-384-02040-2). Johnson Repr.

Arkell, W. J., jt. auth. see Sandford, Kenneth S.

Arkenbout Schokker, J. C., et al. The Design of Merchant Ships. 600p. 1959. 250.00x (ISBN 0-85950-086-1, Pub. by Stam Pr England). State Mutual Bk.

Arkes, Hadley. Bureaucracy, the Marshall Plan, & the National Interest. LC 78-166360. 404p. 1973. 40.00x (ISBN 0-691-04607-7). Princeton U Pr.

--The Philosopher in the City: The Moral Dimensions of Urban Politics. LC 80-8536. 496p. 1981. 35.00x (ISBN 0-691-09356-3); pap. 9.95x (ISBN 0-691-02822-2). Princeton U Pr.

Arkes, Hal R. & Garske, John P. Psychological Theories of Motivation. 2nd ed. LC 81-10057. (Psychology Ser.). 400p. 1981. text ed. 22.75 pub net (ISBN 0-8185-0465-X). Brooks-Cole.

Arkharov, A. Theory & Design of Cryogenic Systems. 430p. 1981. 11.60 (ISBN 0-8285-1974-9, Pub. by Mir Pubs USSR). Imported Pubns.

Arkharov, V. I., ed. Surface Interactions Between Metals & Gases. LC 65-23067. 163p. 1966. 35.00x (ISBN 0-306-10738-4, Consultants). Plenum Pub.

Arkhurst, Joyce C. The Adventures of Spider. (Illus.). (gr. 2-6). 1964. 9.70 (ISBN 0-316-05106-3). Little.

Arkin, Alan. Halfway Through the Door: First Steps on a Path of Enlightenment. LC 83-48415. 112p. 1984. pap. 5.72 (ISBN 0-06-250035-X, CN 4094, HarpR). Har-Row.

--The Lemming Condition. LC 75-6296. (Illus.). 64p. (gr. 4 up). 1976. 9.57i (ISBN 0-06-020133-9); PLB 10.89 (ISBN 0-06-020134-7). HarpJ.

Arkin, Arthur M. Sleep-Talking: Psychology & Psychophysiology. LC 81-3300. (Illus.). 640p. 1982. text ed. 55.00x (ISBN 0-89859-031-0). L Erlbaum Assocs.

Arkin, Arthur M., et al, eds. The Mind in Sleep: Psychology & Psychophysiology. LC 78-6025. 653p. 1978. 29.95x (ISBN 0-470-26369-5). Halsted Pr.

Arkin, Frieda. The Cook's Companion: The Dictionary of Culinary Tips & Terms. 160p. 1972. pap. 2.95 (ISBN 0-380-01120-4, 12799). Avon.

--More Kitchen Wisdom. LC 81-7188. (Illus.). 176p. 1982. pap. 5.95 (ISBN 0-03-071056-1). HR&W.

Arkin, G. F. & Taylor, H. M., eds. Modifying the Root Environment to Reduce Crop Stress. LC 81-69116. 420p. 1981. text ed. 34.50 (ISBN 0-916150-40-2); text ed. 24.95 members. Am Soc Ag Eng.

Arkin, H. & Arkin, R. Statistical Sampling Software for Auditing & Accounting. 160p. 1985. 275.00 (ISBN 0-07-079119-8). McGraw.

--Statistical Sampling Software for Auditing & Accounting, IBM Version. 160p. 1985. 295.00 (ISBN 0-07-852135-1). McGraw.

Arkin, Herbert. Handbook of Sampling for Auditing & Accounting. 526p. 1984. 52.50 (ISBN 0-07-002245-3). McGraw.

--Sampling Methods for the Auditor: An Advanced Treatment. LC 81-2735. (Illus.). 288p. 1982. 32.95 (ISBN 0-07-002194-5). McGraw.

Arkin, Herbert & Colton, Raymond R. Statistical Methods. 5th ed. 344p. (Orig.). 1971. pap. 5.95 (ISBN 0-06-460027-0, CO 27, COS). Har-Row.

--Tables for Statisticians. 2nd ed. (Illus.). 168p. 1971. pap. 4.50 (ISBN 0-06-460075-0, CO 75, COS). Har-Row.

Arkin, Marian. Tutoring ESL Students. 80p. 1982. pap. 4.95x (ISBN 0-582-28230-6). Longman.

Arkin, Marian & Shollar, Barbara. The Tutor Book. LC 81-13697. (Illus.). 352p. (Orig.). 1982. pap. text ed. 14.95x (ISBN 0-582-28233-0); tutor supplements o.p. 4.95x (ISBN 0-686-32740-3). Longman.

--The Writing Tutor. 80p. 1982. pap. 4.95x (ISBN 0-582-28232-2). Longman.

Arkin, R., jt. auth. see Arkin, H.

Arkin, Stanley S. & Dudley, Earl C. Business Crime: Criminal Liability of the Business Community, 6 vols. 1981. Updates avail. looseleaf 450.00 (265); looseleaf 1983 160.00; looseleaf 1984 185.00. Bender.

Arkin, Stephen, ed. see Weiss, Daniel.

Arkin, V. I. & Evstigneev, J. V. Stochastic Models of Control & Economic Dynamics. Date not set. 49.00 (ISBN 0-12-062080-4). ACad Pr.

Arkin, William, jt. auth. see Cochran, Thomas.

Arkin, William, jt. auth. see Pringle, Peter.

Arkin, William M. Research Guide to Current Military & Strategic Affairs. 232p. 1981. 19.95 (ISBN 0-89758-032-X); pap. 9.95 (ISBN 0-89758-025-7). Inst Policy Stud.

Arkin, William M. & Fieldhouse, Richard. Nuclear Battlefields: Global Links in the Arms Race. LC 84-24236. 352p. 1985. 28.00x (ISBN 0-88730-021-9); pap. 14.95 (ISBN 0-88730-002-2). Ballinger Pub.

Arkinstall, William, jt. auth. see Janzen, John M.

Arkoff. Psychology & Personal Growth. 2nd ed. 1980. text ed. 24.27 (ISBN 0-205-06822-7, 7968221) (ISBN 0-205-06855-3). Allyn.

Arkow, Phil, ed. Dynamic Relationships in Practice: Animals in the Helping Professions. (Illus.). 500p. (Orig.). 1984. pap. 15.95 (ISBN 0-931735-00-9). Latham Found Pubn.

Arkowitz, Hal & Messer, Stanley, eds. Psychoanalytic Therapy & Behavior Therapy: Is Integration Possible? 369p. 1984. 34.50x (ISBN 0-306-41578-X, Plenum Pr). Plenum Pub.

Arkowitz, M. & Curjel, C. R. Groups of Homotopy Classes: Rank Formulas & Homotopy - Commutativity. 2nd ed. (Lecture Notes in Mathematics: Vol. 4). (Orig.). 1967. pap. 10.70 (ISBN 0-387-03900-7). Springer-Verlag.

Arksey, Laura & Pries, Nancy, eds. American Diaries: An Annotated Bibliography of Published American Diaries & Journals to 1980, 2 vols. Incl. Vol. 1. Diaries Written from 1492 to 1844 (ISBN 0-8103-1800-8); Vol. 2. Diaries Written from 1845 to 1980 (ISBN 0-8103-1801-6). 600p. vol. 1 in print, vol. 2 due Feb '86 90.00x ea. Gale.

Arkus, Leon A. & McSwigan, Marie. John Kane, Painter. Incl. Sky Hooks: The Autobiography of John Kane. LC 72-134488. (Illus.). 1971. 29.95 (ISBN 0-8229-3217-2). U of Pittsburgh Pr.

Arkush, Allan, tr. see Mendelssohn, Moses.

Arkush, R. David. Fei Ziaotong & Sociology in Revolutionary China. (Harvard East Asian Monographs: No. 98). 400p. 1981. text ed. 22.50x (ISBN 0-674-29815-2). Harvard U Pr.

Arkwright, G. E. P., ed. Old English Edition, 25 vols. Incl. Vol. 1. Masque in Honor of the Marriage of Lord Hayes, 1607. Campion, Thomas, et al. (ISBN 0-8450-1601-6); Vol. 2. Six Songs. Arne, Thomas A (ISBN 0-8450-1602-4); Vol. 3. Six Madrigals to Four Voices, 1597. Kirbye, George (ISBN 0-8450-1603-2); Vol. 4. Twelve Madrigals to Five Voices, 1597. Kirbye, George (ISBN 0-8450-1604-0); Vol. 5. Six Madrigals to Six Voices, 1597. Kirbye, George (ISBN 0-8450-1605-9); Vol. 6. Songs of Sundry Natures, 1589: Fourteen Songs to Three Voices. Byrd, William (ISBN 0-8450-1606-7); Vol. 7. Songs of Sundry Natures, 1589: Nine Songs to Four Voices. Byrd, William (ISBN 0-8450-1607-5); Vol. 8. Songs of Sundry Natures, 1589: Twelve Songs to Five Voices. Byrd, William (ISBN 0-8450-1608-3); Vol. 9. Songs of Sundry Natures, 1589: Ten Songs to Six Voices. Byrd, William (ISBN 0-8450-1609-1); Vol. 10. Mass to Six Voices, Euge Bone. Tye, Christopher (ISBN 0-8450-1610-5); Vol. 11. Nine Madrigals to Five Voices from Musica Transalpina, 1588. Ferrabosco, Alfonso. only as part of set avail. (ISBN 0-8450-1611-3); Vol. 12. Five Madrigals to Six Voices from Musica Transalpina, 1588. Ferrabosco, Alfonso (ISBN 0-8450-1612-1); Vol. 13. Eight Ballets & Madrigals, 1598. Weelkes, Thomas (ISBN 0-8450-1613-X); Vol. 14. Eight Ballets & Madrigals, 1598. Weelkes, Thomas (ISBN 0-8450-1614-8); Vol. 15. Eight Ballets & Madrigals, 1598. Weelkes, Thomas. only as part of set avail. (ISBN 0-8450-1615-6); Vol. 16. Airs or Fantastic Spirits, 1608. Weelkes, Thomas (ISBN 0-8450-1616-4); Vol. 17. Airs or Fantastic Spirits, 1608. Weelkes, Thomas (ISBN 0-8450-1617-2); Vol. 18. The First Book of Songs or Airs of Four Parts, 1605. Pilkington, Francis (ISBN 0-8450-1618-0); Vol. 19. The First Book of Songs or Airs of Four Parts, 1605. Pilkington, Francis (ISBN 0-8450-1619-9); Vol. 20. The First Book of Songs or Airs of Four Parts, 1605. Pilkington, Francis (ISBN 0-8450-1620-2); Vol. 21. Anthems & Motets. White, Robert, et al. (ISBN 0-8450-1621-0); Vol. 22. Six Anthems. Milton, John (ISBN 0-8450-1622-9); Vol. 23. Six Songs from Amphion Anglicus, 1700. Blow, John (ISBN 0-8450-1623-7); Vol. 24. Six Songs from the Orpheus Britannicus. Purcell, Henry (ISBN 0-8450-1624-5); Vol. 25. Venus & Adonis. Blow, John (ISBN 0-8450-1625-3). 1970. pap. 475.00 (ISBN 0-8450-1600-8); pap. 20.00x ea. Broude.

Arkwright, Richard. The Queen Anne's Gate Mystery: A Novel, 2 vols. in 1. LC 75-32733. (Literature of Mystery & Detection). 1976. Repr. of 1889 ed. 37.50x (ISBN 0-405-07863-3). Ayer Co Pubs.

Arlacchi, Pino. Mafia, Peasants & Great Estates: Society in Traditional Calabria. Steinberg, Jonathan, tr. LC 82-19929. (Illus.). 208p. 1983. 27.95 (ISBN 0-521-25136-2). Cambridge U Pr.

Arland, ed. see De Marivaux, Pierre C.

Arland, ed. see Marivaux, Pierre C.

Arland, Marcel & Mouton, Jean, eds. Entretiens Sur Andre Gide: Decades Du Centre Culturel International De Cerisy-la-Salle. (Nouvelle Ser.: No. 3). 1967. pap. 14.00x (ISBN 90-2796-014-3). Mouton.

Arlay, Stephen B. The Price of Silence. 270p. 1984. 16.95 (ISBN 0-241-10986-8, Pub. by Hamish Hamilton England). David & Charles.

Arledge, Byron W. Laugh with Your Teenager. 128p. 1985. pap. 4.95 (ISBN 0-8423-2102-0). Tyndale.

Arlen, Gary H. & Adler, Richard, eds. Videotex-Teleservices Directory, Nineteen Eighty-Five. 272p. (Orig.). 1985. pap. text ed. 80.00 (ISBN 0-9609768-1-7). Arlen Comm Inc.

Arlen, Leslie. Fate & Dreams. (Borodins Ser.: No. 3). 384p. (Orig.). 1982. pap. 3.50 (ISBN 0-515-06898-5). Jove Pubns.

--Fortune & Fury. (The Borodins Ser.: No. 6). 336p. (Orig.). 1984. pap. 3.50 (ISBN 0-515-07869-7). Jove Pubns.

--Hope & Glory. (The Borodins Ser.: Bk. 4). (Orig.). 1982. pap. 3.25 (ISBN 0-515-06041-0). Jove Pubns.

--Love & Honor. 384p. 1980. pap. 2.75 (ISBN 0-515-05480-1). Jove Pubns.

--War & Passion. (The Borodins Ser.: No. 2). 368p. (Orig.). 1981. pap. 2.75 (ISBN 0-515-05481-X). Jove Pubns.

Arlen, Michael. Ghost Stories. Reginald, R. & Menville, Douglas, eds. LC 75-46249. (Supernatural & Occult Fiction Ser.). 1976. Repr. of 1932 ed. lib. bdg. 14.00x (ISBN 0-405-08109-X). Ayer Co Pubs.

--The Green Hat. 244p. 1983. pap. text ed. 7.95 (ISBN 0-85115-209-0, Pub. by Boydell & Brewer). Academy Chi Pubs.

--London Venture. Van Thal, Herbert, ed. 1920-1968. pap. 3.95 (ISBN 0-304-92614-0). Dufour.

Arlen, Michael J. The Camera Age: Essays on Television. LC 80-28710. 337p. 1981. 13.95 (ISBN 0-374-11822-1). FS&G.

--The Camera Age: Essays on Television. 1982. pap. 5.95 (ISBN 0-14-006107-X). Penguin.

--Exiles. 232p. 1970. 6.95 (ISBN 0-374-15096-6). FS&G.

--Living-Room War. 256p. 1982. pap. 5.95 (ISBN 0-14-006081-2). Penguin.

--Passage to Ararat. 293p. 1975. 8.95 (ISBN 0-374-22989-9). FS&G.

--Passage to Ararat & Exiles. 1982. pap. 8.95 (ISBN 0-14-006311-0). Penguin.

--Say Goodbye to Sam. LC 84-48378. 231p. 1984. 12.95 (ISBN 0-374-25409-5). FS&G.

--Say Goodbye to Sam. (Contemporary American Fiction Ser.). 240p. 1985. pap. 5.95 (ISBN 0-317-19385-6). Penguin.

--Thirty Seconds. LC 80-10801. 211p. 1980. 9.95 (ISBN 0-374-27576-9). FS&G.

--Thirty Seconds. 224p. 1981. pap. 4.95 (ISBN 0-14-005810-9). Penguin.

--The View from Highway One: Essays on Television. LC 76-24900. 293p. 1976. 8.95 (ISBN 0-374-28371-0). FS&G.

Arlen, R., jt. auth. see Woltz, P.

Arlen, Richard T., jt. auth. see Woltz, Phebe M.

Arley, Catherine. Dead Man's Bay. 160p. 1980. pap. 1.95 (ISBN 0-441-14149-8, Pub. by Charter Bks). Ace Bks.

Arlin, M., et al. Music Sources: A Collection of Excerpts & Complete Movements. 1979. pap. 27.95 (ISBN 0-13-607168-6). P-H.

Arlin, Marian T. The Science of Nutrition. 2nd ed. (Illus.). 352p. 1977. text ed. write for info. (ISBN 0-02-303840-3, 30384). Macmillan.

Arling, Emanie S. The Terrible Siren: Victoria Woodhull (1838-1927) LC 72-2587. (American Women Ser: Images & Realities). (Illus.). 478p. 1972. Repr. of 1928 ed. 26.50 (ISBN 0-405-04474-7). Ayer Co Pubs.

Arlingaus, Bruce E. Military Development in Africa: Political & Economic Risks of Arms Transfers. (Special Studies on Africa). 175p. 1984. lib. bdg. 23.50x (ISBN 0-86531-434-9). Westview.

Arlinghaus, Bruce, ed. Africa Security Issues: Sovereignty, Stability, & Solidarity. (Western Special Studies on Africa). 200p. 1984. 28.50x (ISBN 0-86531-607-4). Westview.

Arlinghaus, Bruce & Baker, Pauline, eds. African Armies: Force Modernization & Defense Policymaking in the Developing World. 180p. 1985. 31.50x (ISBN 0-86531-757-7). Westview.

Arlinghaus, Bruce E., ed. Arms for Africa: Military Assistance & Foreign Policy in the Developing World. LC 81-48668. 256p. 1982. 28.50x (ISBN 0-669-05527-1). Lexington Bks.

Arlington County Genealogical Society. Graveyards of Arlington County, Virginia. 124p. 1985. pap. text ed. write for info. (ISBN 0-915156-54-7). Natl Genealogical.

Arlington, Lewis C. Chinese Drama. LC 65-19614. (Illus.). Repr. of 1930 ed. 42.00 (ISBN 0-405-08212-6). Ayer Co Pubs.

Arlington, R. Rene, jt. auth. see Murphy, Paul I.

Arliss, G. Picturegoers Who's Who & Encyclopedia of the Screen. 608p. 1976. lib. bdg. 95.00 (ISBN 0-8490-0837-9). Gordon Pr.

Arliss, Peter. Who's Who of Golf. LC 83-11047. (Illus.). 381p. 1983. 24.95 (ISBN 0-13-958497-8, Busn); pap. 14.95 (ISBN 0-13-958489-7). P-H.

Arlitt, A. H. see Dearborn, George Van Ness.

Arlitt, Ada H. Psychology of Infancy & Early Childhood. 1979. Repr. of 1946 ed. lib. bdg. 30.00 (ISBN 0-8495-0200-4). Arden Lib.

Arlott & Fitter. The Complete Guide to British Wildlife. pap. 18.95 (ISBN 0-00-219212-8, Collins Pub England). Greene.

Arlott, jt. auth. see Williams.

Arlott, J., jt. auth. see Hamilton, G.

Arlott, John, compiled by. Wine. (Small Oxford Bks.). 1984. 9.95 (ISBN 0-19-214146-5). Oxford U Pr.

Arlott, John, et al. County Champions. 224p. 1982. 19.95 (ISBN 0-434-98024-2, Pub. by W Heinemann Ltd). David & Charles.

Arlott, Norman. Bird Paintings. (Illus.). 64p. 1983. 26.50 (ISBN 0-437-00630-1, Pub. by Worlds Work). David & Charles.

Arlotti, John, et al. Island Camera: The Isles of Scilly in the Photography of the Gibson Family. (Illus.). 110p. 1983. pap. 14.95 (ISBN 0-7153-8391-4). David & Charles.

Arlotto, Anthony. Introduction to Historical Linguistics. LC 80-6309. 284p. 1981. lib. bdg. 25.25 (ISBN 0-8191-1459-6); pap. text ed. 11.00 (ISBN 0-8191-1460-X). U Pr of Amer.

Arlow, Jacob A. Legacy of Sigmund Freud. LC 56-9746. 1956. text ed. 20.00 (ISBN 0-8236-2980-5). Intl Univs Pr.

Arlow, Jacob A. & Brenner, Charles. Psychoanalytic Concepts & the Structural Theory. LC 64-16190. (Journal of the American Psychoanalytic Association Monograph Ser.: No. 3). 216p. (Orig.). 1964. text ed. 25.00 (ISBN 0-8236-5060-X). Intl Univs Pr.

Arlow, Jacob A., ed. & intro. by. Selected Writings of Bertram D. Lewin, M. D. LC 72-94802. (Illus.). 608p. 1973. 25.00 (ISBN 0-911194-02-9). Psych Qtly.

Arlt, Gustave O., ed. see Werfel, Franz.

Arlt, Lenelis, jt. auth. see Kruse, Lenelis.

Arlt, Roberto. The Seven Madmen. Lindstrom, Naomi, tr. LC 83-48518. 288p. 1984. 14.95 (ISBN 0-87923-492-X). Godine.

Arlt, W., jt. auth. see Sorensen, J. M.

Arlt, W., jt. auth. see Sorenson, J. M.

Arluck, Mary S., ed. Papers of the American Association for Labor Legislation, 1905-1943: Guide to the Microfilm Edition. 73p. 1974. 25.00 (ISBN 0-667-00527-7). Microfilming Corp.

Arluke, Arnold, jt. auth. see Gritzer, Glenn.

Armacost. The Structure of Locally Compact Abelian Groups. 152p. 1981. 45.00 (ISBN 0-8247-1507-1). Dekker.

Armacost, George H. High School Principals' Annual Reports. LC 78-176523. (Columbia University. Teachers College. Contributions to Education Ser.: No. 807). Repr. of 1940 ed. 22.50 (ISBN 0-404-55807-0). AMS Pr.

Armacost, Michael H. Politics of Weapons Innovation: The Thor-Jupiter Controversy. LC 70-90213. (Institute on War & Peace Studies). 304p. 1969. 30.00x (ISBN 0-231-03206-4). Columbia U Pr.

Armah, Ayi. Two Thousand Seasons. LC 74-980017. 1980. 8.95 (ISBN 0-88378-084-4); pap. 6.95 (ISBN 0-88378-046-1). Third World.

Armah, Ayi K. The Beautyful Ones Are Not Yet Born. (African Writers Ser.: No. 43). 224p. 1969. pap. text ed. 5.00x (ISBN 0-435-90043-9). Heinemann Ed.

Armajani, Yahya. Middle East-Past & Present. (Illus.). 1969. text ed. 27.95 (ISBN 0-13-581579-7). P-H.

Armajani, Yahya & Ricks, Thomas. The Middle East: Past & Present. 2nd ed. (Illus.). 544p. 1986. text ed. 26.95 (ISBN 0-13-581554-1). P-H.

Armajani, Yahya, tr. see Elder, John.

Armalinsky, Mikhail, pseud. Majatnik. 2nd ed. LC 84-90582. 130p. 1984. pap. 6.50 (ISBN 0-916201-01-5). M I P Co.

--Muskulistaya Smert: Raskazi. 150p. (Orig., Rus.). 1984. pap. 9.50 (ISBN 0-916201-00-7, 83-63508). M I P Co.

Armalinsky, Mikhail. Posle Proshlogo. LC 82-18523. 110p. (Orig., Rus.). 1982. pap. 5.50 (ISBN 0-938920-30-8). Hermitage.

Arman, David & Arman, Linda. First Supplement to Historical Staffordshire: An Illustrated Check List. (Illus.). 1977. pap. 15.00 (ISBN 0-915438-01-1). Arman Ent.

--Historical Staffordshire: Illustrated Checklist. LC 74-18756. (Illus.). 258p. 1975. 30.00 (ISBN 0-915438-00-3). Arman Ent.

Arman, Florence & Wooldridge, Glen. The Rogue: A River to Run. LC 81-52732. (Illus.). 1982. pap. 11.95 (ISBN 0-9607260-0-4). Wildwood Pr.

Arman, Linda, jt. auth. see Arman, David.

Arman, Mike. Motorcycle Electrics Without Pain. (Illus.). 1980. pap. 8.00 (ISBN 0-933078-03-X). M Arman.

Arman, Mike & Bolender, John. Unauthorised Flat Rate Schedule for Harley Davidson Motorcycles 1984. looseleaf 5.00x (ISBN 0-317-18200-5, H-D FLATRATE BOOK). M Arman.

Arman, Mike & Heinrichs, Kurt. Harley Davidson Special Tools: Where to Get Them, How to Use Them. (Illus.). 64p. 1982. pap. text ed. 5.00 (ISBN 0-933078-07-2). M Arman.

--What Fits What on Harley Davidson Nineteen Thirty-Six to Nineteen Eighty-Three. 6th ed. (Illus.). 1983. pap. 5.00 (ISBN 0-933078-11-0). M Arman.

Arman, Mike & McClanahan, Carl. V-Twin Thunder. (Illus.). 56p. (Orig.). 1984. pap. 8.00 (ISBN 0-933078-12-9). M Arman.

Arman, Mike, ed. see Geokan, Mike.

Arman, Mike, ed. see Shenton, Stan.

Armand, Barton L. The Roots of Horror in the Fiction of H.P. Lovecraft. (Illus.). 1977. 12.50 (ISBN 0-911499-04-0, Pub. by Dragon Pr). Ultramarine Pub.

Armand, Octavio. With Dusk. Maier, Carol, tr. from Span. 48p. (Orig.). 1984. ltd. ed.o.p. 24.00 (ISBN 0-937406-31-7); pap. 3.50 (ISBN 0-937406-30-9). Logbridge-Rhodes.

Armand De, Quatrefages De Breau see Quatrefages de Breau, Armand de.

Armandi, Barry R. Organizational Structure & Efficiency. LC 80-69049. 276p. 1981. lib. bdg. 23.25 (ISBN 0-8191-1610-6); pap. text ed. 12.50 (ISBN 0-8191-1611-4). U Pr of Amer.

Armandi, Barry R. & Barbera, John J. Organizational Behavior: Classical & Contemporary Readings. 368p. 1982. pap. text ed. 16.95 (ISBN 0-8403-2807-9). Kendall-Hunt.

Armanet, J. & Becquer, A. Annales des Mines: Lexique Technique Allemand-Francais. 344p. (Ger. & Fr.). 1951. 8.95 (ISBN 0-686-56901-6, M-6011). French & Eur.

Armani, Frank H., jt. auth. see Alibrandi, Tom.

Armanino, Dominic C. Dominoes: Five-up & Other Games. LC 59-12264. 194p. 1972. pap. 4.95 (ISBN 0-679-14009-3). McKay.

--Dominoes, Popular Games, Rules & Strategy. 1977. 3.95 (ISBN 0-346-12302-X). Cornerstone.

Armantrout, Neil B., ed. Acquisition & Utilization of Aquatic Habitat Inventory Information. 376p. 1982. pap. 22.00 (ISBN 0-913235-19-9). Am Fisheries Soc.

Armantrout, Rae. Extremities. 1978. 2.50 (ISBN 0-685-59023-2); signed ed. 7.50 (ISBN 0-686-67238-0). Figures.

--Precedence. 48p. 1985. 15.00 (ISBN 0-930901-23-1); pap. 5.00 (ISBN 0-930901-24-X). Burning Deck.

Armarego, W. Stereochemistry of Heterocyclic Compounds: Part II-Oxygen; Sulfur; Mixed N, O, & S; & Phosphorus Heterocycles. LC 76-26023. 512p. 1977. 66.50 (ISBN 0-471-03322-7). Krieger.

Armas, Frederick A. De see DeArmas, Frederick A.

Armas, Frederick de see De Armas, Frederick, et al.

Armas, Jose, ed. see Menendez, Enrique C.

Armas, Jose, jt. ed. see Ramos, Luis A.

Armas, Jose, ed. see Vento, Arnold C.

Armas, Jose R. De see De Armas, Jose R. & Steele, Charles W.

Armas, Linda M., ed. see Martin, Patricia.

Armas de Arenas, Bibi. Luces y Sombras De un Destierro. 166p. 1979. pap. 6.95 (ISBN 0-686-65594-X). Ediciones.

Armatas, James P., jt. auth. see Lundberg, Donald E.

Armato, Rosario P. & Spalek, John M., eds. Medieval Epic to the Epic Theater of Brecht. LC 68-29169. (University of Southern California Studies in Comparative Literature Ser.: No. 1). 1968. 7.95x (ISBN 0-912158-00-X). Hennessey.

Armbrecht, H. J., et al, eds. Nutritional Intervention in the Aging Process. (Illus.). 330p. 1984. 42.50 (ISBN 0-387-96025-2). Springer-Verlag.

Armbruster, C. H. Dongolese Nubian: A Grammar. 1965. text ed. 175.00 (ISBN 0-521-04050-7). Cambridge U Pr.

--Dongolese Nubian, a Lexicon. 1965. text ed. 145.00 (ISBN 0-521-04051-5). Cambridge U Pr.

Armbruster, Carl, ed. see Liszt, Franz.

Armbruster, David L., jt. ed. see Zenkovsky, Serge A.

Armbruster, Frank. United States Energy Needs Through the Year 2000. (Research Memorandum: No. 42). 73p. 1977. 25.00 (ISBN 0-318-14359-3, HI-2712-P). Hudson Inst.

Armbruster, Greg, jt. ed. see Dorter, Tom.

Armbruster, Joan M. & Miller, Maurice H. Getting the Most Out of Your Hearing Aid. LC 81-68720. 40p. 1981. pap. 2.00 (ISBN 0-88200-148-5, M7046). Alexander Graham.

Armbruster, Karl, jt. auth. see Rembold, Ulrich.

Armbruster, Maxim. The Presidents of the United States & Their Administrations from Washington to the Present. 7th ed. (Illus.). 400p. 1981. 15.95 (ISBN 0-8180-0812-1). Horizon.

Armbruster, Virginia B., jt. auth. see Cook, Ruth E.

Armbruster, Wally. A Bag of Noodles. (Illus.). (YA) 1973. pap. 3.95 (ISBN 0-570-03158-3, 12-2543). Concordia.

--Let Me Out: I'm a Prisoner in a Stained Glass Jail. LC 85-11561. 1985. pap. 6.95 (ISBN 0-88070-111-0). Multnomah.

--Noodles du Jour. LC 75-42818. (Illus.). 192p. 1976. pap. 5.50 (ISBN 0-570-03729-8, 12-2631). Concordia.

Armbruster, Walter, et al, eds. Federal Marketing Programs in Agriculture: Issues & Options. (Illus.). 326p. 1983. pap. text ed. 9.75x (ISBN 0-8134-2292-2). Interstate.

Arme, C., et al. Studies in Parasitology in Memory of Clark P. Read. Byram, J. E. & Stewart, George, eds. (Rice University Studies: Vol. 62, No. 4). 236p. 1977. pap. 10.00x (ISBN 0-89263-230-5). Rice Univ.

Arme, Christopher, ed. A Biology of the Eucestoda, Vol. 1. Pappas, Peter. 1984. 60.00 (ISBN 0-12-062101-0). Acad Pr.

Arme, Christopher & Pappas, Peter, eds. Biology of the Eucestoda, Vol. 2. 1983. 65.00 (ISBN 0-12-062102-9). Acad Pr.

Armedia Consultants. Las Vegas Survival Guide. rev. ed. LC 81-71218. 200p. 1984. pap. 6.95 (ISBN 0-9607626-0-4). Armedia Con.

Armeding, Carl E. The Old Testament & Criticism. 144p. 1983. pap. 6.95 (ISBN 0-8028-1951-6). Eerdmans.

Armelagos, George, jt. auth. see Farb, Peter.

Armelagos, George J., jt. ed. see Cohen, Mark N.

Armen, H. & Stiansen, S. Computational Methods for Offshore Structures. (AMD: Vol. 37). 161p. 1980. 24.00 (ISBN 0-686-69845-2, G00170). ASME.

Armen, Harry, ed. Applications of Numerical Methods to Forming Processes: AMD, Vol. 28. Jones, R. F., Jr. 208p. 1978. 30.00 (ISBN 0-685-66790-1, H00111). ASME.

Armendares, S. & Lisker, R. Human Genetics. (International Congress Ser.: No. 411). 1978. 98.00 (ISBN 0-444-15252-0, Excerpta Medica). Elsevier.

Armengaud, Andre. Les Populations De L'est-Aquitain Au Debut De L'epoque Contempoaine: Recherche Sur une Region Moins Developpee, 1845-1871. (Societe, Mouvements Sociaux et Ideologis, Etudes: No. 3). 1961. pap. 34.80x (ISBN 90-2796-236-7). Mouton.

Armengol, Joseph, et al, eds. English-Spanish Guide for Medical Personnel. (Eng. & Span.). 1966. pap. 7.50 (ISBN 0-87488-721-6). Med Exam.

Armenini, Giovanni B. On the True Precepts of the Art of Painting. 1977. 25.00 (ISBN 0-89102-054-3); pap. 9.95 (ISBN 0-89102-100-0). B Franklin.

Armens, Sven M. John Gay, Social Critic. 1966. lib. bdg. 21.50x (ISBN 0-374-90285-2). Octagon.

Armentani, Andy & Donatelli, Gary. The Monday Night Football Cookbook & Restaurant Guide. LC 82-71965. (Illus.). 160p. 1982. pap. 9.95 (ISBN 0-8019-7270-1). Chilton.

Armentano, Dominick T. Antitrust & Monopoly: Anatomy of a Policy Failure. LC 81-16440. 292p. 1982. 28.95x (ISBN 0-471-09931-7, Pub. by Wiley-Interscience); pap. 14.95x (ISBN 0-471-09930-9). Wiley.

--Antitrust & Monopoly: Anatomy of a Policy Failure. 304p. 1982. 22.95 (ISBN 0-686-98110-3). Telecom Lib.

Armentrout, Donald S., ed. see DuBose, William P.

Armentrout, Fred & Barrett, Dean. Images of Hong Kong. (Illus.). 144p. (Orig.). 1984. pap. 14.95 (ISBN 962-7035-08-4, Pub. by Salem Hse Ltd). Merrimack Pub Cir.

Armentrout, Fred, ed. see CEP & Komanoff, Charles.

Armentrout, Frederick S., jt. auth. see Cannon, James S.

Armentrout, J. Michael, jt. auth. see Doman, Glenn.

Armentrout, John M., ed. Pacific Northwest Cenozoic Biostratigraphy. LC 80-82937. (Special Paper: No. 184). (Illus., Orig.). 1981. pap. 26.00 (ISBN 0-8137-2184-9). Geol Soc.

Armentrout, Steve. Cellular Decompositions of Three-Manifolds that Yield Three-Manifolds. LC 52-42839. (Memoirs). 72p. 1971. pap. 9.00 (ISBN 0-8218-1807-4, MEMO-107). Am Math.

Armentrout, Winfield D., jt. auth. see Wrinkle, William L.

Armer, Alan A. Directing Television & Film. 350p. 1985. text ed. write for info. (ISBN 0-534-05202-9). Wadsworth Pub.

Armer, F. K., jt. auth. see Garas, G. S.

Armer, G. S. T., jt. ed. see Garas, F. K.

Armer, Laura A. Waterless Mountain. (Illus.). (gr. 5-8). 1931. 10.95 (ISBN 0-679-20233-1). McKay.

Armer, Michael. African Social Psychology: Review & Annotated Bibliography. LC 74-23711. (African Bibliography Ser.: No. 2). 400p. 1975. text ed. 45.00x (ISBN 0-8419-0164-3, Africana). Holmes & Meier.

Armerding, Hudson T. A Word to the Wise. 1980. pap. 3.95 (ISBN 0-8423-0099-6). Tyndale.

Armes, Alice. English Smocks. (Illus.). 50p. 1980. pap. 4.00 (ISBN 0-85219-027-1, Pub. by Batsford England). David & Charles.

Armes, Ethel. The Story of Coal & Iron in Alabama. LC 73-1988. (Big Business; Economic Power in a Free Society Ser.). (Illus.). Repr. of 1910 ed. 40.00 (ISBN 0-405-05072-0). Ayer Co Pubs.

Armes, Ethel, ed. Nancy Shippen: Her Journal. LC 68-21204. 1968. 22.00 (ISBN 0-405-08213-4, Pub. by Blom). Ayer Co Pubs.

Armes, Keith, tr. see Solzhenitsyn, Aleksandr.

Armes, Roy. A Critical History of British Cinema. LC 77-73893. (Illus.). 1978. 27.50x (ISBN 0-19-520043-8). Oxford U Pr.

--The Films of Alain Robbe-Grillet. (Purdue University Monographs in Romance Languages: Vol. 6). 216p. 1981. 28.00x (ISBN 90-272-1716-5). Benjamins North Am.

--French Cinema. 1985. 25.00 (ISBN 0-19-520471-9); pap. 10.95 (ISBN 0-19-520472-7). Oxford U Pr.

--Patterns of Realism. LC 82-49216. (Cinema Classics Ser.). 226p. 1985. lib. bdg. 60.00 (ISBN 0-8240-5750-3). Garland Pub.

Armfield, Diana. The Simon & Schuster Pocket Guide to Drawings. 1982. 8.25 (ISBN 0-671-42474-2). S&S.

--The Simon & Schuster Pocket Guide to Painting in Oils. 1982. 8.25 (ISBN 0-671-42473-4). S&S.

Armfield, W. A., Jr. Investment in Subsidized Housing: Opportunities & Risks. LC 78-15544. 64p. 1979. pap. 10.00 (ISBN 0-87576-072-4). Pilot Bks.

Armi, Anna M., tr. see Petrarca, Francesco.

Armi, C. Edson. Masons & Sculptors in Romanesque Burgundy: The New Aesthetic of Cluny III, 2 Vols. LC 82-42784. (Illus.). 384p. 1984. 87.50x (ISBN 0-271-00338-3). Pa St U Pr.

Armide & Lully, Jean-Baptiste. Oper von ihren ersten Anfaengen bis zur Mitte des 18. Jahrhunderts: III. Theil. Eitner, Robert, ed. (Publikation aelterer praktischer und theoretischer Musikwerke Ser.: Vol. XIV). (Ger., Fr., It.). 1967. Repr. of 1885 ed. write for info. (ISBN 0-8450-1714-4). Broude.

Armijo, Moses A., jt. auth. see Harcharik, Kathleen.

Armijos, Jack, jt. ed. see Severns, Rudy.

Armin, Robert. The Collected Works of Robert Armin, 2 vols. xxviii, 460p. 70.00 (ISBN 0-384-01950-1). Johnson Repr.

--Two Maids of Moreclacke. LC 77-133634. (Tudor Facsimile Texts. Old English Plays: No. 127). Repr. of 1913 ed. 49.50 (ISBN 0-404-53427-9). AMS Pr.

Armingeat, Jacqueline see Porzio, Domenico, et al.

Armington, R. Q. & Ellis, William D. More: The Rediscovery of American Common Sense. 280p. 1984. 12.95 (ISBN 0-89526-605-9). Regnery-Gateway.

Armington, R. Q. & Ellis, William D., eds. This Way Up: The Local Official's Handbook for Privatization & Contracting Out. LC 84-14371. 168p. (Orig.). 1985. pap. 6.95 (ISBN 0-89526-824-8). Regnery-Gateway.

Armington, Stan. Exploring Nepal. (Illus.). 1976. pap. text ed. 3.50 (ISBN 0-910856-62-1). La Siesta.

--Trekking in the Himalayas. 3rd ed. (Lonely Planet Travel Ser.). 224p. 1982. pap. 6.95 (ISBN 0-908086-06-7, Pub. by Lonely Planet Australia). Hippocrene Bks.

Armisen, Pedro, tr. see Malgorn, Guy.

Armistead, Charles. In Search of the Golden Rainbow. Van Dolson, Bobbie J., ed. (gr. 5-9). 1981. pap. 5.95 (ISBN 0-8280-0086-7). Review & Herald.

Armistead, J. M. Four Restoration Playwrights: A Reference Guide to Thomas Shadwell, Aphra Behn, Nathaniel Lee, & Thomas Otway. (Reference Guides to Literature Ser.). 1984. lib. bdg. 65.00 (ISBN 0-8161-8289-2, Hall Reference). G K Hall.

--Nathaniel Lee. (English Authors Ser.). 1979. 15.95 (ISBN 0-8057-6748-7, Twayne). G K Hall.

Armistead, Jack M. The First English Novelists: Essays in Understanding. LC 85-3153. (Tennessee Studies in Literature Ser.). 320p. 1985. text ed. 24.95x (ISBN 0-87049-468-6). U of Tenn Pr.

Armistead, Lew. Building Confidence in Education: A Practical Approach for Principals. Bruce, C., ed. 64p. (Orig.). 1982. pap. 4.00 (ISBN 0-88210-131-5, 2108101). Natl Assn Principals.

Armistead, Samuel G. & Silverman, Joseph H. Folk-Literature of the Sephardic Jews, Vol. 1. The Judeo-Spanish Ballad Chapbooks of Yacob Abraham Yona. LC 71-78565. 1971. 60.00x (ISBN 0-520-01648-3). U of Cal Pr.

Armistead, Samuel G. & Silverman, Joseph H., eds. Judeo-Spanish Ballads from Bosnia. LC 76-131487. (Folklore & Folklife, Haney Ser.). (Illus.). pap. 26.50 (ISBN 0-8357-9747-3, 2019420). Bks Demand UMI.

--Judeo-Spanish Ballads from New York: Collected by Mair Jose Bernardete. LC 80-28174. 1981. 19.95x (ISBN 0-520-04348-0). U of Cal Pr.

Armistead, W. S. Negro Is a Man. facs. ed. LC 74-89427. (Black Heritage Library Collection Ser). 1903. 20.25 (ISBN 0-8369-8505-2). Ayer Co Pubs.

Armistead, Wilson. Five Hundred Thousand Strokes for Freedom. facs. ed. LC 77-83953. (Black Heritage Library Collection Ser). 1853. 19.25 (ISBN 0-8369-8504-4). Ayer Co Pubs.

--Tribute for the Negro. facs. ed. (Black Heritage Library Collection Ser). 1848. 27.50 (ISBN 0-8369-8503-6). Ayer Co Pubs.

--Tribute for the Negro. LC 70-89026. Repr. of 1848 ed. cancelled (ISBN 0-8371-1925-1). Greenwood.

Armistead, Wilson, pref. by. Five Hundred Thousand Strokes for Freedom. LC 71-90105. (Illus.). Repr. of 1853 ed. 17.50x (ISBN 0-8371-2014-4, FHS&, Pub. by Negro U Pr). Greenwood.

Armitage. Principles of Modern Biology. (gr. 9-12). 1972. pap. text ed. 9.00 each incl. 9 texts (ISBN 0-8449-0450-3); tchrs' manual 4.00; test 3.00. Learning Line.

Armitage, Angus. The World of Copernicus. 1972. pap. 7.95x (ISBN 0-8464-0979-8). Beekman Pubs.

Armitage, D. A. Inorganic Rings & Cages. LC 72-76951. 387p. 1972. 52.50x (ISBN 0-8448-0004-X). Crane-Russak Co.

Armitage, David, jt. auth. see Armitage, Ronda.

Armitage, F. B. & Burley, J. Pinus Kesiya. 1980. 39.00x (ISBN 0-85074-030-4, Pub. by For Lib Comm England). State Mutual Bk.

Armitage, George T. A Brief History of Hawaii. 1973. soft bdg. 2.50 (ISBN 0-930492-04-8). Hawaiian Serv.

Armitage, J. G. Jubilee Conference on the Helium-4: Proceedings of the 75th Meeting, St. Andrew, Scotland, Aug.1-5, 1983. 232p. 1983. 26.00x (ISBN 9971-966-23-9, Pub. by World Sci Singapore). Taylor & Francis.

Armitage, J. V., ed. Journees Arithmetiques Nineteen Eighty. LC 81-18032. (London Mathematical Society Lecture Ser.: No. 56). 350p. 1982. pap. 32.50 (ISBN 0-521-28513-5). Cambridge U Pr.

Armitage, John. History of Brazil, from the Period of the Arrival of the Braganza Family in 1808, to the Abdication of Don Pedro the First in 1831, 2 Vols. LC 78-128438. 1836. Set. 49.50 (ISBN 0-404-00440-7). AMS Pr.

Armitage, Jonathan G. & Farquhar, Ian E., eds. The Helium Liquid. (A NATO Advanced Study Institute). 1976. 89.50 (ISBN 0-12-062550-4). Acad Pr.

Armitage, Kenneth B. Investigations in General Biology. 1970. text ed. 15.00i (ISBN 0-12-062460-5). Acad Pr.

Armitage, M. M. & Mason, R. A. Air Power in the Nuclear Age. 2nd ed. LC 82-17551. (Illus.). 264p. 1985. pap. 10.95x (ISBN 0-252-01231-3). U of Ill Pr.

Armitage, Merle. Dance Memoranda. facs. ed. Corle, Edwin, ed. LC 78-76890. (Essay Index Reprint Ser). 1947. 40.00 (ISBN 0-8369-0001-4). Ayer Co Pubs.

--Dance Memoranda. Corle, Edwin, ed. (Essay Index Reprint Ser.). (Illus.). 200p. 1982. Repr. of 1946 ed. lib. bdg. 35.00 (ISBN 0-8290-0836-5). Irvington.

--George Gershwin, Man & Legend. facsimile ed. LC 75-117324. (Biography Index Reprint Ser). 1958. 26.50 (ISBN 0-8369-8016-6). Ayer Co Pubs.

--Igor Stravinsky. facs. ed. Corle, Edwin, ed. LC 77-84295. (Essay Index Reprint Ser). 1949. 31.25 (ISBN 0-8369-1120-2). Ayer Co Pubs.

Armitage, Merle, ed. Martha Graham: The Early Years. LC 78-17608. (Series in Dance). (Illus.). 1978. lib. bdg. 22.50 (ISBN 0-306-79504-3); pap. 7.95 (ISBN 0-306-80084-5). Da Capo.

--Schoenberg: Articles by Arnold Schoenberg, Erwin Stein & Others, 1929-1937. LC 79-106709. 1977. Repr. of 1937 ed. lib. bdg. 19.50 (ISBN 0-8371-3439-0, ARSC); fiche 11.80 (ISBN 0-8371-9600-0); fiche & cloth 20.65 (ISBN 0-8371-9599-3). Greenwood.

--Schoenberg: 1929-1937. facsimile ed. LC 77-157360. (Select Bibliographies Reprint Ser.). Repr. of 1937 ed. 21.00 (ISBN 0-8369-5783-0). Ayer Co Pubs.

Armitage, Merle, ed. see Schmitz, Elie R.

Armitage, P. Statistical Methods in Medical Research. 509p. 1971. 37.95x (ISBN 0-471-03320-0). Halsted Pr.

Armitage, Paul. The Common Market. LC 78-61095. (Countries Ser.). (Illus.). 1978. PLB 13.96 (ISBN 0-382-06199-3). Silver.

Armitage, Philip. Laboratory Safety: A Science Teacher's Source Book. 1977. pap. text ed. 6.50x (ISBN 0-435-57050-1). Heinemann Ed.

Armitage, Richard, et al. Beginning Spanish: A Cultural Approach. 4th ed. (Illus.). 1979. 24.95 (ISBN 0-395-27507-5); exercise bk. 10.50 (ISBN 0-395-27508-3); recordings-13 reels 280.00 (ISBN 0-395-27510-5). HM.

--Fundamentals of Spanish Grammar. 1975. pap. text ed. 10.50 (ISBN 0-395-19865-8). HM.

Armitage, Ronda. The Bossing of Josie. LC 79-8656. (Illus.). 32p. (ps-2). 1980. 8.50 (ISBN 0-233-97231-5). Andre Deutsch.

--Ice Creams for Rosie. (Illus.). 32p. (ps-2). 1982. 9.95 (ISBN 0-233-97361-3). Andre Deutsch.

--Lighthouse Keeper's Lunch. (Illus.). (ps-2). 1979. 9.95 (ISBN 0-233-96868-7). Andre Deutsch.

--One Moonlit Night. (Illus.). 32p. (ps-2). 1983. 9.95 (ISBN 0-233-97540-3). Andre Deutsch.

Armitage, Ronda & Armitage, David. Grandma Goes Shopping. (Illus.). 32p. (ps-2). Date not set. 9.95 (ISBN 0-233-97627-2). Andre Deutsch.

Armitage, Thomas. A History of the Baptists, 2 vols. (Illus.). 1009p. 1980. Repr. of 1890 ed. Set. 26.00 (ISBN 0-937136-00-X). Vol. 1 (ISBN 0-937136-01-8). Vol. 2 (ISBN 0-937136-02-6). Maranatha Baptist.

Armitage, Yvonne N., et al. Ei Nei, Do You Remembah? LC 93-21243. (Illus.). 96p. (Orig.). 1983. pap. 4.95 (ISBN 0-916630-38-2). Pr Pacifica.

Armitage-Smith, George. Free-Trade Movement & Its Results. LC 77-95061. (Select Bibliographies Reprint Ser). 1903. 26.50 (ISBN 0-8369-5063-1). Ayer Co Pubs.

Armogathe, J. R. Theologia Cartesiana. (International Archives of the History of Ideas Ser: No. 84). 1977. lib. bdg. 42.00 (ISBN 90-247-1869-4, Pub. by Martinus Nijhoff Netherlands). Kluwer Academic.

Armon, Cheryl see Commons, Michael L.

Armond, Dale De see De Armond, Dale.

Armond, Dale de see De Armond, Dale.

Armond, Robert N. De see Pierce, W. H.

Armond Marchant, Alexander N. De see De Armond Marchant, Alexander N.

Armor, D. J. & Couch, A. S. Data-Text Primer. LC 78-165564. 1972. pap. text ed. 15.95 (ISBN 0-02-901020-9). Free Pr.

Armor, David J. The American School Counselor: A Case Study in the Sociology of Professions. LC 68-58127. 228p. 1969. 10.00x (ISBN 0-87154-069-X). Russell Sage.

Armor, David J., jt. auth. see Polich, J. Michael.

Armor, David J., et al. Alcoholism & Treatment. LC 77-17421. (Personality Processes Ser.). 348p. 1978. 37.50x (ISBN 0-471-02558-5, Pub. by Wiley-Interscience). Wiley.

Armor, Reginald. Ernest Holmes: The Man. 128p. 1977. pap. 6.50 (ISBN 0-911336-66-4). Sci of Mind.

Armor, William. Lives of the Governors of Pennsylvania with the... 500p. Date not set. Repr. of 1872 ed. lib. bdg. 59.00 (ISBN 0-932051-37-5). Am Repr Serv.

Armorer, Harry. Africa & Her Children: An Introduction to the Origin of Civilization. 64p. 1979. 6.00 (ISBN 0-682-49356-2). Exposition Pr FL.

Armour. The Door of Purgatory: A Study of Multiple Symbolism in Dante's Purgatorio. 1983. 29.95x (ISBN 0-19-815787-8). Oxford U Pr.

Armour & Company Kitchens. The Quick & Easy Armour Cookbook. LC 80-66316. (Orig.). 5.95 (ISBN 0-87502-082-8). Benjamin Co.

Armour, Andrew J., ed. Asia & Japan: The Search for Modernization & Identity. LC 85-9029. 220p. 1985. 36.00 (ISBN 0-485-11261-2, Pub. by Athlone Pr Ltd). Longwood Pub Group.

Armour, Audrey, jt. auth. see Lang, Reg.

Armour, David. Fort Michilimackinac Sketch Book. (Illus.). 48p. (Orig.). 1975. pap. 1.50 (ISBN 0-911872-16-7). Mackinac Island.

Armour, David, ed. Treason at Michilimackinac. LC 67-81179. (Illus.). 103p. 1967. pap. 2.50 (ISBN 0-911872-32-9). Mackinac Island.

Armour, David A. & Widder, Keith R. At the Crossroads: Michilimackinac During the American Revolution. (Illus.). 249p. 1978. 12.50 (ISBN 0-911872-24-8). Mackinac Island.

--Michilimackinac: A Handbook to the Site. 1st ed. (Illus.). 48p. (Orig.). 1980. pap. 1.50 (ISBN 0-911872-39-6). Mackinac Island.

Armour, David A., ed. Attack at Michilimackinac, 1763: Alexander Henry's Travels & Adventures in Canada & the Indian Territories Between the Years 1760 & 1764. (Illus.). 131p. 1971. pap. 2.50 (ISBN 0-911872-37-X). Mackinac Island.

Armour, David A., ed. see Dunnigan, Brian L.

Armour, David A., ed. see Hamilton, T. M.

Armour, David A., ed. see Heldman, Donald P. & Minnerly, William L.

Armour, David A., ed. see Peterson, Eugene T.

Armour, David A., ed. see Porter, Phil.

Armour, David A., ed. see Stone, Lyle M.

Armour, David A., ed. see Widder, Keith R.

Armour, Graham. Super Profile: Lotus Elan. 56p. 9.95 (ISBN 0-85429-330-2, F330). Haynes Pubns.

Armour, Leslie. The Concept of Truth. 1979. text ed. 29.50x (ISBN 90-232-0728-9). Humanities.

--The Idea of Canada: And the Crisis of Community. (Illus.). 180p. 1981. 15.50x (ISBN 0-88791-026-2, Pub. by Steel Rail Canada). Humanities.

Armour, Leslie & Bartlett, Edward T., 3rd. The Conceptualization of the Inner Life: A Philosophical Exploration. 1981. text ed. 18.00x (ISBN 0-391-01759-4). Humanities.

Armour, Leslie & Trott, Elizabeth. The Faces of Reason: An Essay on Philosophy & Culture in English Canada 1850-1950. 500p. 1981. text ed. 27.75x (ISBN 0-88920-107-2, Pub. by Wilfrid Laurier U Pr). Humanities.

Armour, Margaret. The Fall of the Nibelungs. 1897. Repr. 10.00 (ISBN 0-8274-2329-2). R West.

--The Home & Early Haunts of Robert Louis Stevenson. 1973. Repr. of 1895 ed. 15.00 (ISBN 0-8274-1211-8). R West.

Armour, Philip K. The Cycles of Social Reform: Mental Health Policy Making in the United States, England, & Sweden. LC 80-6187. 374p. (Orig.). 1982. lib. bdg. 29.00 (ISBN 0-8191-2033-2); pap. text ed. 15.50 (ISBN 0-8191-2034-0). U Pr of Amer.

Armour, R. American Lit Relit. 1970. pap. 2.95 (ISBN 0-07-002283-6). McGraw.

--It All Started with Nudes: An Artful History of Art. 1977. pap. 7.95 (ISBN 0-07-002271-2). McGraw.

--Twisted Tales from Shakespeare. pap. 4.95 (ISBN 0-07-002251-8). McGraw.

Armour, Richard. Anyone for Insomnia? A Playful Look at Sleeplessness. LC 82-9996. 128p. (Orig.). 1982. pap. 4.95 (ISBN 0-912800-69-0). Woodbridge Pr.

--Armoury of Light Verse. (Orig.). 1962. pap. 2.50 (ISBN 0-8283-1424-1, 25, IPL). Branden Pub Co.

--Educated Guesses: Light-Serious Suggestions for Parents & Teachers. LC 82-17670. 192p. (Orig.). 1983. 9.95 (ISBN 0-88007-126-5); pap. 5.95 (ISBN 0-88007-127-3). Woodbridge Pr.

--English Lit Relit. 1969. 5.95 (ISBN 0-07-002224-0). McGraw.

--Going Like Sixty: A Lighthearted Look at the Later Years. LC 73-13783. (McGraw-Hill Paperbacks). 1976. pap. 4.95 (ISBN 0-07-002292-5). McGraw.

--Golf Is a Four-Letter Word: The Intimate Confessions of a Hooked Slicer. (Illus.). 1964. pap. 3.95 (ISBN 0-07-002259-3). McGraw.

--Have You Ever Wished You Were Something Else? LC 82-17102. (Easy Reading Picture Bks.). (Illus.). 48p. (gr. k-3). 1983. PLB 11.25 (ISBN 0-516-03475-8). Childrens.

--Our Presidents. rev. ed. LC 82-23762. (Illus.). 96p. 1983. 9.95 (ISBN 0-88007-133-8); pap. 5.95 (ISBN 0-88007-134-6). Woodbridge Pr.

--Satirist Looks at the World. (William K. McInally Memorial Lecture Ser.: 2nd). 1967. pap. 1.00 (ISBN 0-87712-146-X). U Mich Busn Div Res.

--Strange Monsters of the Sea. LC 78-11263. (Illus.). 1979. 10.95 (ISBN 0-07-002294-1). McGraw.

Armour, Richard & Galdone, P. Insects All Around Us. 1981. 9.95 (ISBN 0-07-002266-6). McGraw.

Armour, Richard & Gurney, Eric. Richard Armour's Punctured Poems: Famous First & Infamous Second Lines. LC 82-10989. (Illus.). 96p. 1982. pap. 3.95 (ISBN 0-912800-55-0). Woodbridge Pr.

Armour, Richard, ed. Pieces of Posthumorous Prose. 224p. 1985. pap. 9.95 (ISBN 0-88007-149-4). Woodbridge Pr.

Armour, Richard W. & Howes, Raymond F. Coleridge the Talker. (English Literary Reference Ser). Repr. of 1940 ed. 28.00 (ISBN 0-384-02060-7). Johnson Repr.

Armour, Richard W., intro. by see Cornwall, Barry.

Armour, Robert A. Film: A Reference Guide. LC 79-6566. (American Popular Culture). xxiv, 251p. 1980. lib. bdg. 29.95 (ISBN 0-313-22241-X, AFR/). Greenwood.

Armour, Rollin S. Anabaptist Baptism. LC 66-19026. (Study in Anabaptist & Mennonite History No. 11). 1966. 12.95x (ISBN 0-8361-1178-8). Herald Pr.

Armour, Tommy. How to Play Your Best Golf All the Time. 1971. pap. 5.95 (ISBN 0-671-21150-1, Fireside). S&S.

--How to Play Your Best Golf all the Time. 10.95 (ISBN 0-89190-272-4, Pub. by Am Repr). Amereon Ltd.

Armour, William J. The Football (Soccer) Association Guide to the Treatment & Rehabilitation of Injuries in Sports. (Illus.). 224p. 1984. 24.95 (ISBN 0-434-02751-0, Pub. by W Heinemann Ltd). David & Charles.

Armour, William J., jt. auth. see Colson, John H.

Armroyd, George. Connected View of the Whole Internal Navigation of the United States. LC 77-146133. (American Classics in History & Social Science Ser.: No. 204). 1971. Repr. of 1830 ed. lib. bdg. 40.50 (ISBN 0-8337-0064-2). B Franklin.

Arms Control Association & International Institute for Strategic Studies. Approaches to East-West Arms Control. 114p. 1979. 4.00 (ISBN 0-317-33391-7); members free. Arms Control.

Arms, George. The Fields Were Green: A New View of Bryant, Whittier, Holmes, Lowell & Longfellow, with a Selection of Their Poems. 1953. 20.00x (ISBN 0-8047-0443-0). Stanford U Pr.

Arms, George, jt. auth. see Gibson, William M.

Arms, George, ed. Selected Letters of W. D. Howells, Vol. 2: 1873-1881. (Critical Editions Program Ser.). lib. bdg. 31.50 (ISBN 0-8057-8528-0, Twayne). G K Hall.

Arms, George, jt. ed. see Gibson, William M.

Arms, George, ed. see Howells, William D.

Arms, George, et al, eds. The Writer's World: Readings for College Composition. LC 77-86290. 1978. pap. text ed. 13.95x (ISBN 0-312-89433-3); instr's manual avail. St Martin.

Arms, George, et al, eds. see Howells, W. D.

Arms, George A., jt. auth. see Gibson, William M.

Arms, Karen & Camp, Pamela S. Biology. 2nd ed. 1982. text ed. 36.95 (ISBN 0-03-059961-X, CBS C); instr's manual 13.95 (ISBN 0-03-059962-8); study guide 13.95 (ISBN 0-03-059966-0). SCP.

Arms, Karen, jt. auth. see Camp, Pamela.

Arms, Richard W., Jr. Volume Cycles in the Stock Market. LC 82-73619. 200p. 1983. 35.00 (ISBN 0-87094-405-3). Dow Jones-Irwin.

Arms, Suzanne. Immaculate Deception: A New Look at Women & Childbirth. (Illus.). 1984. 22.95 (ISBN 0-89789-060-4); pap. 6.95 (ISBN 0-89789-061-2); pap. text ed. 9.95 (ISBN 0-89789-062-0). Bergin & Garvey.

--To Love & Let Go. LC 83-47938. (Illus.). 240p. 1983. 14.95 (ISBN 0-394-50319-8). Knopf.

Armsby, Leonora W. Musicians Talk. facsimile ed. LC 76-99679. (Essay Index Reprint Ser). 1935. 19.00 (ISBN 0-8369-1338-8). Ayer Co Pubs.

Armson, K. A. Forest Soils: Properties & Processes. 1977. 27.50 (ISBN 0-8020-2265-0). U of Toronto Pr.

Armstead, H. C. Geothermal Energy: Its Past, Present & Future Contributions to the Energy Needs to Man. 2nd ed. LC 83-337. 1983. 53.00 (ISBN 0-419-12220-6, NO. 6824, Pub. by E & FN Spon). Methuen Inc.

Armstead, H. Christopher. Geothermal Energy. 2nd ed. LC 83-337. (Illus.). 404p. 1983. 55.00 (ISBN 0-419-12220-6, NO. 6824). Methuen Inc.

Armstead, H. Christopher, ed. Geothermal Energy: Review of Research & Development. (Earth Sciences Ser.: No. 12). 186p. (3rd Imprint 1977). 1973. pap. 24.25 (ISBN 92-3-101063-8, U265, UNESCO). Unipub.

Armstead, Lloyd D. Whitewater Rafting in Eastern America. LC 81-17345. (Illus.). 150p. (Orig.). 1982. pap. 6.95 (ISBN 0-914788-52-3). East Woods.

Armstong, Ray. X-Ray Astronomy, Including a Catalogue & Bibliography of Galactic X-Ray Sources: Proceedings of the 21st Plenary Meeting, Innsbruck, Austria, 1978. Baity, W. A. & Peterson, L. E., eds. (Illus.). 1979. text ed. 69.00 (ISBN 0-08-023418-6). Pergamon.

Armstong, Robert G. One Too Many Mornings. 1982. 8.95 (ISBN 0-533-05021-9). Vantage.

Armstrog, William H. Minister Heal Thyself. 64p. (Orig.). 1985. pap. 4.95 (ISBN 0-8298-0551-6). Pilgrim NY.

Armstron, H., jt. auth. see Trew, A. J.

Armstrong. Crosby, Stills & Nash. (Rock 'n Pop Stars Ser.). (Illus.). 32p. (gr. 4-12). PLB 7.95 (ISBN 0-317-31124-7). Creative Ed.

--Fleetwood Mac. (Rock 'n Pop Stars Ser.). (Illus.). 32p. (gr. 4-12). PLB 7.95 (ISBN 0-317-31127-1). Creative Ed.

--Long-Range Forecasting. 2nd ed. 600p. 1985. 42.50 (ISBN 0-471-82360-0); pap. 22.95 (ISBN 0-471-82260-4). Wiley.

--ORACLS: A Design System for Linear Multivariable Control. (Control & Systems Theory Ser.: Vol. 10). 256p. 1980. 45.50 (ISBN 0-8247-1239-0). Dekker.

--The Rolling Stones. (Rock 'n Pop Stars Ser.). (Illus.). 32p. (gr. 4-12). PLB 7.95 (ISBN 0-317-31147-6). Creative Ed.

Armstrong, ed. see Pike & Buckley.

Armstrong, A. H. An Introduction to Ancient Philosophy. 3rd ed. LC 81-3731. (Quality Paperback Ser.: No. 418). 260p. 1981. pap. 5.95 (ISBN 0-8226-0418-3). Littlefield.

--An Introduction to Ancient Philosophy. 3rd ed. 250p. 1981. Repr. of 1957 ed. 27.50x (ISBN 0-8476-6017-6). Rowman.

Armstrong, A. Hilary. Plotinian & Christian Studies. 384p. 1979. 60.00x (ISBN 0-86078-047-3, Pub. by Variorum). State Mutual Bk.

Armstrong, A. N. History of Oregon. enl. ed. 1969. Repr. of 1857 ed. 9.95 (ISBN 0-87770-002-8). Ye Galleon.

Armstrong, A. W. How to Use Lotus 1-2-3 for Productive Business Applications. (Professional Development Programs Ser.). 256p. 1985. pap. 75.00 (ISBN 0-471-80689-7). Wiley.

Armstrong, Alan. Maori Customs & Crafts. 60p. 1973. pap. 2.50 (ISBN 0-85467-009-2, Pub. by Viking New Zealand). Intl Spec Bk.

--Say It in Maori. 60p. 1968. (Pub. by Viking New Zealand). Intl Spec Bk.

Armstrong, Alfredlene, ed. see Bice, David A., et al.

Armstrong, Alice, jt. auth. see Place, Irene.

Armstrong, Alison. The Joyce of Cooking. 240p. 1983. 12.95 (ISBN 0-930794-85-0). Station Hill Pr.

--The Joyce of Cooking: Irish Food & Drink from James Joyce's Dublin. (Illus.). 240p. 1985. 16.95 (ISBN 0-930794-85-0). Station Hill Pr.

Armstrong, Allen. Belief, Truth & Knowledge. LC 72-83586. 240p. 1973. 42.50 (ISBN 0-521-08706-6); pap. 13.95 (ISBN 0-521-09737-1). Cambridge U Pr.

Armstrong, Alvie. Collected Short Stories. LC 83-91452. 65p. 1984. 7.95 (ISBN 0-533-06049-4). Vantage.

Armstrong, Anne. Unconditional Surrender. LC 73-22633. 304p. 1974. Repr. of 1961 ed. lib. bdg. 35.00 (ISBN 0-8371-7042-7, ARUS). Greenwood.

Armstrong, Anne see Armstrong, Terry R.

Armstrong, Anthony, et al. Thee Second Century of Humor. 30.00 (ISBN 0-8495-6264-3). Arden Lib.

Armstrong, Barbra K. Index to the 1800 Census of New York. LC 83-83026. 432p. 1984. 30.00 (ISBN 0-8063-1070-7). Genealog Pub.

Armstrong, Barry L. & Murphy, James B. The Natural History of Mexican Rattlesnakes. Wiley, E. O. & Collins, Joseph T., eds. (U of KS Museum of Nat. Hist. Special Publication: No. 5). (Illus.). 88p. (Orig.). 1979. pap. 6.00 (ISBN 0-89338-010-5). U of KS Mus Nat Hist.

Armstrong, Barry L., jt. auth. see Murphy, James B.

Armstrong, Ben. Media with a Message. 180p. 1985. 9.95 (ISBN 0-8407-5451-5). Nelson.

Armstrong, Betsy, jt. auth. see Williams, Knox.

Armstrong, Bev. Comprehension Collection. (Skill Builder Ser.). (Illus.). 32p. (gr. 4-7). 1979. wkbk. 3.95 (ISBN 0-88160-070-9). Learning Wks.

--Dinosaur Detective. (Skill Builder Ser.). (Illus.). 32p. (gr. k-3). 1979. 3.95 (ISBN 0-88160-075-X). Learning Wks.

--Have Fun Following Directions. (Skill Builder Ser.). (Illus.). 32p. (gr. k-3). 1979. wkbk. 3.95 (ISBN 0-88160-077-6). Learning Wks.

--Lively Listening. (Skill Builder Ser.). (Illus.). 32p. (gr. 4-6). 1981. wkbk. 3.95 (ISBN 0-88160-080-6). Learning Wks.

--Math a la Mode. (Math Ser.). (gr. 3-4). 1979. pap. 5.50 (ISBN 0-88160-064-4). Learning Wks.

--Math Mascots. (Math Ser.). (gr. 3-4). 1979. pap. 5.50 (ISBN 0-88160-063-6). Learning Wks.

--The Subtraction Submarine. (gr. 1-2). 1979. pap. 5.50 (ISBN 0-88160-062-8). Learning Wks.

--Who's Following Directions? (Skill Builder Ser.). (Illus.). 32p. (gr. 4-7). 1979. wkbk. 3.95 (ISBN 0-88160-072-5). Learning Wks.

--Who's Listening? (Skill Builders Ser.). (Illus.). 32p. (gr. 1-3). 1981. wkbk. 3.95 (ISBN 0-88160-079-2). Learning Wks.

Armstrong, Beverly. All Occasion Pages. (Teacher Time-Savers Ser.). 32p. (gr. 1-6). 1982. 3.95 (ISBN 0-88160-014-8, LW 117). Learning Wks.

--Awards Galore. (Teacher Time-Savers Ser.). 48p. (gr. 1-6). 1981. 4.95 (ISBN 0-88160-040-7, LW 225). Learning Wks.

--Outrageous Pages. (Teacher Time-Savers Ser.). 32p. (gr. 1-6). 1982. 3.95 (ISBN 0-88160-013-X, LW 116). Learning Wks.

--Punctuation Passport. (Language Arts Ser.). 38p. (gr. 4-7). 1979. 4.95 (ISBN 0-317-14735-8, LW 214). Learning Wks.

Armstrong, Beverly, jt. auth. see Renfro, Nancy.

Armstrong, Blair M., ed. Arizona Anthem. (The Mnemosyne Series of Poetry). (Illus.). 608p. (Poetic & Pictorial History of Arizona). 1982. 75.00 (ISBN 0-686-30562-0). Mnemosyne.

Armstrong, Brian G. Calvinism & the Amyraut Heresy: Protestant Scholasticism & Humanism in Seventeenth-Century France. LC 72-84949. (Illus.). 350p. 1969. 30.00 (ISBN 0-299-05490-X). U of Wis Pr.

Armstrong, Bruce. Sable Island. LC 80-2745. (Illus.). 256p. 1981. 19.95 (ISBN 0-385-13113-5). Doubleday.

Armstrong, C. The Charlotte Armstrong Treasury. 23.95 (ISBN 0-88411-576-3, Pub. by Aeonian Pr). Amereon Ltd.

Armstrong, C. A. England, France & Burgundy in the Fifteenth Century. (No. 16). 450p. 1983. 40.00 (ISBN 0-907628-13-3). Hambledon Press.

Armstrong, C. A., jt. ed. see Allmand, C. T.

Armstrong, C. F. Hymns for Little Children. 1977. lib. bdg. 59.95 (ISBN 0-8490-2030-1). Gordon Pr.

Armstrong, C. J. & Large, J. A. A Microcomputer Teaching Package for On-Line Bibliographic Searching: Complete Package. (R&D Report: No. 5741). (Illus., Orig.). 1984. manual, wkbk, floppy discs 90.00 (ISBN 0-7123-3023-2, Pub. by Croom Helm Ltd); pap. text ed. 10.50 wkbk. only (ISBN 0-7123-3024-0). Longwood Pub Group.

Armstrong, Carolyn T. Leather & Lace, No. 6: Honeysuckle Love. 1983. pap. 2.50 (ISBN 0-686-82614-0). Zebra.

Armstrong, Cecil F. A Century of Great Actors 1750-1850. 1912. 15.00 (ISBN 0-8482-7263-3). Norwood Edns.

--Shakespeare to Shaw. LC 70-95402. (BCL Ser.: No. 1). Repr. of 1913 ed. 15.00 (ISBN 0-404-00383-4). AMS Pr.

--Shakespeare to Shaw: Studies in the Life's Work of Six Dramatists of the English Stage. facs. ed. LC 68-8435. (Essay Index Reprint Ser). 1913. 21.50 (ISBN 0-8369-0157-6). Ayer Co Pubs.

Armstrong, Charles, jt. auth. see Drowatzky, John.

Armstrong, Charles W. The Survival of the Unfittest. 59.95 (ISBN 0-8490-1163-9). Gordon Pr.

Armstrong, Charlotte. A Dram of Poison. Repr. lib. bdg. 11.95 (ISBN 0-88411-565-8, Pub. by Aeonian Pr). Amereon Ltd.

--The Turret Room. Repr. lib. bdg. 11.95x (ISBN 0-88411-566-6, Pub. by Aeonian Pr). Amereon Ltd.

--The Unsuspected. Repr. lib. bdg. 12.95x (ISBN 0-88411-567-4, Pub. by Aeonian Pr). Amereon Ltd.

Armstrong, Christa, tr. see Von Lang, Jochen & Sibyll, Claus.

Armstrong, Christopher. Evelyn Underhill: Eighteen Seventy-Five to Nineteen Forty-One: An Introduction to Her Life & Writing. LC 75-33401. Repr. of 1976 ed. 81.80 (ISBN 0-8357-9127-0, 2012859). Bks Demand UMI.

--The Politics of Federalism: Ontario's Relations with the Federal Government 1867-1942. (Ontario Historical Studies). 316p. 1981. 18.95 (ISBN 0-8020-2434-3). U of Toronto Pr.

Armstrong, Constance H. Senior Adult Camping. Job, Glenn T., ed. (Illus.). 46p. 1978. pap. 4.95 (ISBN 0-87603-042-8). Am Camping.

Armstrong, D., et al. The Old Church Slavonic Translation of the Andron Hagion Biblos in the Edition of Nikolas Van Wijk. Van Schooneveld, C. H., ed. (Slavistic Printings & Reprintings Ser: No. 1). 310p. 1975. text ed. 67.20x (ISBN 90-2793-196-8). Mouton.

--Ceroid Liposfucsinosis: Batten's Disease. 422p. 1982. 99.75 (ISBN 0-444-80329-7). Elsevier.

Armstrong, D. M. Cambridge History of Later Greek & Early Medieval Philosophy. 1967. 82.50 (ISBN 0-521-04054-X). Cambridge U Pr.

--Materialist Theory of the Mind. (International Library of Philosophy & Scientific Method). 1968. text ed. 27.00x (ISBN 0-7100-3634-5). Humanities.

--The Nature of Mind & Other Essays. LC 80-68117. 188p. 1981. 24.50x (ISBN 0-8014-1353-2). Cornell U Pr.

--Universals & Scientific Realism: Vol. 1, Nominalism & Realism. LC 77-80824. 165p. 1980. pap. 10.95 (ISBN 0-521-28033-8). Cambridge U Pr.

--Universals & Scientific Realism: Vol. 1, Nominalism & Realism. LC 77-80824. 1978. 34.50 (ISBN 0-521-21741-5). Cambridge U Pr.

--Universals & Scientific Realism: Vol. 2, A Theory of Universals. LC 77-80824. 200p. 1980. pap. 10.95 (ISBN 0-521-28032-X). Cambridge U Pr.

--Universals & Scientific Realism: Vol. 2, a Theory of Universals. LC 77-80824. 1978. 32.50 (ISBN 0-521-21950-7). Cambridge U Pr.

--What Is a Law of Nature? LC 83-5130. (Cambridge Studies in Philosphy). 180p. 1983. 32.50 (ISBN 0-521-25343-8). Cambridge U Pr.

--What Is a Law of Nature? (Cambridge Studies in Philosophy). 190p. 1985. pap. 9.95 (ISBN 0-521-31481-X). Cambridge U Pr.

Armstrong, D. Wade. Evangelistic Growth in Acts One & Two. LC 83-70375. (Orig.). 1983. pap. 4.95 (ISBN 0-8054-6242-2). Broadman.

Armstrong, Daniel, tr. see Polivanov, E. D.

Armstrong, David. Political Anatomy of the Body: Medical Knowledge in Britain in the Twentieth Century. LC 82-9546. 176p. 1983. 32.50 (ISBN 0-521-24746-2). Cambridge U Pr.

--The Rise of International Organization. LC 82-16767. (Making of the 20th Century Ser.). 180p. 1983. 22.50x (ISBN 0-312-68427-4). St Martin.

--A Trumpet to Arms: Alternative Media in America. 350p. 1984. pap. 9.00 (ISBN 0-89608-193-1). South End Pr.

Armstrong, David & Malcolm, Norman. Consciousness & Causality. (Great Debates in Philosophy Ser.). 200p. 1984. 24.95x (ISBN 0-631-13212-0); pap. 9.95x (ISBN 0-631-13433-6). Basil Blackwell.

Armstrong, David A. Bullets & Bureaucrats: The Machine Gun & the United States Army, 1861-1916. LC 81-7226. (Contributions in Military History Ser.: No. 29). (Illus.). xv, 239p. 1982. lib. bdg. 29.95 (ISBN 0-313-23029-3, ABU). Greenwood.

Armstrong, David G. Social Studies in Secondary Education. (Illus.). 1980. text ed. write for info. (ISBN 0-02-303980-9). Macmillan.

Armstrong, David G. & Savage, Tom V. Secondary Education: An Introduction. 1st ed. 576p. 1983. write for info. (ISBN 0-02-304070-X). Macmillan.

Armstrong, David G., et al. Instructional Skills Handbook. LC 77-25986. (Illus.). 320p. 1978. 27.95 (ISBN 0-87778-102-8). Educ Tech Pubns.

--Education: An Introduction. 2nd ed. 544p. 1985. text ed. write for info. (ISBN 0-02-304100-5); write for info. instr's. manual (ISBN 0-02-304110-2). Macmillan.

Armstrong, David M. Perception & the Physical World. (International Library of Philosophy & Scientific Method). 1961. text ed. 25.25x (ISBN 0-7100-3603-5). Humanities.

Armstrong, David M., ed. see Berkeley, George.

Armstrong, Don. The Lloyd Shaw Foundation Recreational Dance Program. 133p. 1985. pap. text ed. 20.00 (ISBN 0-915213-01-X). L Shaw Found.

Armstrong, Donald. Book Publishing: A Working Guide. 1979. 10.00 (ISBN 0-918464-20-X). D Armstrong.

Armstrong, Donald, jt. auth. see Lindeman, John.

Armstrong, Donald, jt. ed. see Brown, Arthur E.

Armstrong, Donald, jt. ed. see Ma, Pearl.

Armstrong, Donald, et al, eds. Free Radicals in Molecular Biology, Aging, & Disease. (Aging Ser.: vol 27). 432p. 1984. text ed. 76.50 (ISBN 0-88167-048-0). Raven.

Armstrong, Donald R. Strategies for Success in Small Business. (Illus.). 1977. text ed. 10.00 (ISBN 0-918464-15-3). D Armstrong.

--Texas Schools of Business Administration. (Texas College & Career Guide Ser.). 1978. 14.00 (ISBN 0-685-05984-7); pap. 8.00 (ISBN 0-918464-18-8). D Armstrong.

--Texas Senior Colleges & Universities. (Texas College & Career Guide Ser.). (Illus.). 1977. pap. 8.00 (ISBN 0-918464-09-9). D Armstrong.

Armstrong, E. The Emperor Charles V, 2vols. 1976. Set. lib. bdg. 250.00 (ISBN 0-8490-1762-9). Gordon Pr.

Armstrong, E. F. & Armstrong, Sara. In a Copper Kettle. 15th ed. (Illus.). 1958. pap. 4.95x (ISBN 0-87315-019-8). Golden Bell.

Armstrong, Earl, ed. see National Board of YMCA.

Armstrong, Edward. Discovering Bird Courtship. (Discovering Ser.: No. 236). (Illus., Orig.). 1978. pap. 3.50 (ISBN 0-85263-415-3, Pub. by Shire Pubns England). Seven Hills Bks.

--The Emperor Charles V, 2 Vols. LC 83-45652. Date not set. Repr. of 1902 ed. Set. 85.00 (ISBN 0-404-19800-7). AMS Pr.

--Italian Studies. facs. ed. Ady, C. M., ed. LC 67-30172. (Essay Index Reprint Ser). 1934. 20.00 (ISBN 0-8369-0158-4). Ayer Co Pubs.

Armstrong, Edward, ed. see Penn, William.

Armstrong, Edward A. The Life & Lore of the Bird. lib. bdg. 7.98 (ISBN 0-486-23719-2). Dover.

--St. Francis, Nature Mystic: The Derivation & Significance of the Nature Stories in the Franciscan Legend. LC 74-149949. (Hermeneutics: Studies in the History of Religions). 1973. 38.50x (ISBN 0-520-01966-0, CAL 314); pap. 5.95 (ISBN 0-520-03040-0). U of Cal Pr.

--Shakespeare's Imagination: A Study of the Psychology of Association & Inspiration. Landmark ed. LC 63-8165. vi, 230p. 1963. 22.95x (ISBN 0-8032-1005-1). U of Nebr Pr.

Armstrong, Edward C. Authorship of the Vengement Alixandre & of the Venjance Alixandre. (Elliott Monographs: Vol. 19). 1926. pap. 15.00 (ISBN 0-527-02622-0). Kraus Repr.

--French Metrical Versions of Barlaam & Josaphat. (Elliott Monographs: Vol. 10). 1922. 11.00 (ISBN 0-527-02614-X). Kraus Repr.

--Marshall Elliot, a Retrospect. (Elliott Monographs: Vol. 15). 1923. pap. 15.00 (ISBN 0-527-02618-2). Kraus Repr.

Armstrong, Elizabeth H. Crisis of Quebec, Nineteen Fourteen to Nineteen Eighteen. LC 77-158270. (BCL Ser.: No. 2). Repr. of 1937 ed. 17.50 (ISBN 0-404-00384-2). AMS Pr.

Armstrong, Emma P. see Pryor, Harold.

Armstrong, Eric & Lucas, Rosemary. Improving Industrial Relations: The Advisory Role of ACAS. LC 85-6638. 256p. 1985. 29.00 (ISBN 0-7099-0554-8, Pub. by Croom Helm Ltd). Longwood Pub Group.

Armstrong, Este & Falk, Dean, eds. Primate Brain Evolution: Methods & Concepts. LC 81-21150. 346p. 1982. text ed. 42.50 (ISBN 0-306-40914-3, Plenum Pr). Plenum Pub.

Armstrong, F. W. The Changing. 320p. (Orig.). 1985. pap. 3.50 (ISBN 0-8125-2754-2, Dist. by Pinnacle Books). Tor Bks.

Armstrong, Fiona & Baum, Myra. Getting Ready for the World of Work. (Illus.). 1980. pap. text ed. 7.95 (ISBN 0-07-002517-7). McGraw.

--A Realistic Job Search. (Lifeworks Ser.). (Illus.). 1980. pap. 7.95 (ISBN 0-07-002518-5). McGraw.

Armstrong, Fiona, et al. The Reality of Work & Promotion. (Illus.). 208p. 1980. pap. text ed. 7.96 (ISBN 0-07-002519-3). McGraw.

--Realizing What's Available in the World of Work. (Lifeworks Ser.). (Illus.). 1980. pap. text ed. 7.96 (ISBN 0-07-002516-9). McGraw.

--You & the World of Work. (Lifeworks Ser.). (Illus.). 1980. pap. text ed. 7.96 (ISBN 0-07-002515-0). McGraw.

Armstrong, Frank B. Biochemistry. 2nd ed. (Illus.). 1983. 29.95x (ISBN 0-19-503109-1). Oxford U Pr.

Armstrong, Fred C. The Business of Economics. 200p. 1986. pap. text ed. 9.56 (ISBN 0-314-85316-2). West Pub.

--Our Economic Predicament in Perspective. LC 77-91219. 1978. 6.95 (ISBN 0-87212-100-3). Libra.

Armstrong, Frederick H., et al. Bibliography of Canadian Urban History: Part IV: Ontario. (Public Administration Ser.: Bibliography P-541). 68p. 1980. pap. 7.50 (ISBN 0-88066-077-5). Vance Biblios.

--Bibliography of Canadian Urban History: Part V: Western Canada. (Public Adminstration Ser.: Bibliography P-542). 72p. 1980. pap. 7.50 (ISBN 0-88066-078-3). Vance Biblios.

Armstrong, Gail & Friis, Robert. Stress-Heart Disease Connection. 60p. (Orig.). 1981. pap. 14.95 (ISBN 0-939552-05-1, 007). Human Behavior.

Armstrong, Garner T. The Real Jesus. 1978. pap. 2.25 (ISBN 0-380-40055-3, 40055-3). Avon.

Armstrong, George. Zionist Wall Street. 1982. lib. bdg. 69.95 (ISBN 0-87700-380-7). Revisionist Pr.

--The Zionists. 1982. lib. bdg. 69.95 (ISBN 0-87700-341-6). Revisionist Pr.

Armstrong, George D. Christian Doctrine of Slavery. LC 69-16595. Repr. of 1857 ed. 15.00x (ISBN 0-8371-0892-6, ARC&, Pub. by Negro U Pr). Greenwood.

--A Discussion on Slaveholding. LC 72-6454. (Black Heritage Library Collection). 1972. Repr. of 1858 ed. 13.25 (ISBN 0-8369-9155-9). Ayer Co Pubs.

Armstrong, George M., Jr. Louisiana Landlord & Tenant. 1988. price not set; price not set looseleaf with binder (ISBN 0-409-25148-8). Butterworth TX.

--The Soviet Law of Property. 1984. lib. bdg. 30.00 (ISBN 90-247-2864-9, Pub. by Martinus Nijhoff Netherlands). Kluwer Academic.

Armstrong, George P., jt. auth. see Darst, Paul W.

Armstrong, George R., jt. auth. see Guthrie, John A.

Armstrong, George W. The Rothschild Money Trust. lib. bdg. 75.00 (ISBN 0-87700-370-X). Revisionist Pr.

Armstrong, H. & Taylor, J. Regional Economic Policy & Its Analysis. 335p. 1982. pap. text ed. 21.50x (ISBN 0-86003-116-0, Pub. by Allan Pubs England). Humanities.

Armstrong, H. C. Grey Wolf: Mustafa Kemal: An Intimate Study of a Dictator. LC 72-8397. (Select Bibliographies Reprint Ser.). 1972. Repr. of 1932 ed. 23.50 (ISBN 0-8369-6962-6). Ayer Co Pubs.

Armstrong, H. C. & Lewis, C. V. Practical Boiler Firing. 4th ed. 387p. 1954. 10.95x (ISBN 0-85264-065-X, Pub. by Griffin England). State Mutual Bk.

Armstrong, Hamilton F. The Calculated Risk. 1947. 1.50 (ISBN 0-911090-02-9). Pacific Bk Supply.

Armstrong, Hamilton F., jt. auth. see Dulles, Allen W.

Armstrong, Harold C. Gray Wolf: Mustafa Kemal, an Intimate Study of a Dictator. LC 75-180317. (Mid-East Studies). Repr. of 1933 ed. 23.50 (ISBN 0-404-56212-4). AMS Pr.

Armstrong, Helen, jt. ed. see Armstrong, O. V.

Armstrong, Isobel. Language As Living Form in Nineteenth Century Poetry. LC 82-6694. 234p. 1982. text ed. 28.50x (ISBN 0-389-20293-2, 07128). B&N Imports.

Armstrong, Isobel, ed. Victorian Scrutinies: Reviews of Poetry, 1830-1870. 344p. 1972. text ed. 38.50 (ISBN 0-485-11131-4, Pub. by Athlone Pr Ltd). Longwood Pub Group.

--Writers & Their Background: Robert Browning. LC 72-96846. (Writers & Their Background Ser). xxvi, 365p. 1975. 20.00x (ISBN 0-8214-0131-9, 82-81347); pap. 10.00x (ISBN 0-8214-0132-7, 82-81354). Ohio U Pr.

Armstrong, J. D. Revolutionary Diplomacy: Chinese Foreign Policy & the United Front Doctrine. LC 76-14315. 259p. 1977. 36.00x (ISBN 0-520-03251-9, CAMPUS 268); pap. 7.95x (ISBN 0-520-04273-5). U of Cal Pr.

Armstrong, J. Scott. Long-Range Forecasting: From Crystal Ball to Computer. LC 77-25176. 612p. 1978. 47.50x (ISBN 0-471-03002-3, Pub. by Wiley-Interscience). Wiley.

Armstrong, James. The Nation Yet to Be: Christian Mission & the New Patriotism. (Orig.). 1975. pap. 2.25 (ISBN 0-377-00023-X). Friend Pr.

Armstrong, James A. From the Underside: Evangelism from a Third World Vantage Point. LC 81-9509. 112p. (Orig.). 1981. pap. 4.95 (ISBN 0-88344-146-2). Orbis Bks.

Armstrong, James W., jt. auth. see Sarafino, Edward P.

Armstrong, Jane. A National Assessment of Achievement & Participation of Women in Mathematics: Final Report. 236p. 1979. avail. (10-MA-60). Natl Assessment.

Armstrong, Jane & Kahl, Stuart. A National Assessment of Performance & Participation of Women in Mathematics. annual 60p. 1978. avail. (ED 176 961, Natl Assessment Ed Progress-ERIC). Ed Comm States.

Armstrong, Janice G., jt. auth. see Pike, Martha V.

Armstrong, Joe E. Tales of a Fledging Homestead. LC 84-25389. (Illus.). 110p. (Orig.). 1985. pap. 7.95 (ISBN 0-317-28576-9). Misty Hill Pr.

Armstrong, John. All about Signals. (Illus.). 26p. 1967. pap. 2.50 (ISBN 0-89024-502-9). Kalmbach.

--The Art of Preserving Health: A Poem. Kastenbaum, Robert, ed. LC 78-22185. (Aging & Old Age Ser.). 1979. Repr. of 1744 ed. lib. bdg. 14.00x (ISBN 0-405-11803-1). Ayer Co Pubs.

--Creative Layout Design. Schafer, Mike, ed. LC 78-71457. 1978. pap. 11.95 (ISBN 0-89024-538-X). Kalmbach.

--The Idea of Holiness & the Humane Response: A Study of the Concept of Holiness & Its Social Consequences. 177p. 1982. 16.95 (ISBN 0-04-200042-4). Allen Unwin.

--Track Planning for Realistic Operation. rev. ed. LC 63-5732. (Illus.). 100p. (gr. 6). 1979. pap. 7.95 (ISBN 0-89024-504-5). Kalmbach.

Armstrong, John A. The European Administrative Elite. 400p. 1973. 43.00 (ISBN 0-691-07551-4); pap. 17.50 L.P.E. (ISBN 0-691-10016-0). Princeton U Pr.

--Nations Before Nationalism. LC 81-12988. xxxvi, 411p. 1982. 26.00x (ISBN 0-8078-1501-2). U of NC Pr.

--Ukrainian Nationalism. 2nd ed. LC 79-25529. 361p. 1980. Repr. of 1963 ed. 30.00 (ISBN 0-87287-193-2). Libs Unl.

Armstrong, John A., ed. Soviet Partisans in World War Two. (Illus.). 812p. 1964. 45.00x (ISBN 0-299-03060-1). U of Wis Pr.

Armstrong, John H. Eighteen Tailor-Made Model Railroad Track Plans. Hayden, Bob, ed. (Illus.). 80p. (Orig.). 1984. pap. 10.95 (ISBN 0-89024-040-X). Kalmbach.

Armstrong, John M., ed. see Michigan University, Institute of Science & Technology, Industrial Development Division.

Armstrong, John R., jt. ed. see Sawyer, Stephen W.

Armstrong, John W. The Water of Life. 136p. 1971. pap. 4.75x (ISBN 0-8464-1060-5). Beekman Pubs.

--The Water of Life. 1980. 17.50x (ISBN 0-85032-194-8, Pub. by Daniel Co England). State Mutual Bk.

--The Water of Life: A Treatise on Urine Therapy. 2nd ed. 136p. 1957. pap. text ed. 7.95 (ISBN 0-88697-016-4). Life Science.

Armstrong, Juliet. Orange Blossom Island, the Flowering Valley, the Tideless Sea. (Harlequin Romances Ser.). 576p. 1982. pap. 3.50 (ISBN 0-373-20066-8). Harlequin Bks.

Armstrong, Karen. Through the Narrow Gate. 288p. 1981. 12.95 (ISBN 0-312-80383-4). St Martin.

Armstrong, Kathleen. Joys & Teardrops. 1976. pap. 2.95 (ISBN 0-917578-02-3). Eternal Ent.

Armstrong, Larry. Disaster & Deliverance. LC 79-88400. 1979. pap. 3.75 (ISBN 0-933350-22-8). Morse Pr.

Armstrong, Lee H., jt. auth. see Pettofrezzo, Anthony J.

Armstrong, Leroy & Denny, J. O. Financial California: An Historical Review of the Beginnings & Progess of Banking in the State. Bruchey, Stuart, ed. LC 80-1131. (The Rise of Commercial Banking Ser.). 1981. Repr. of 1916 ed. lib. bdg. 26.00x (ISBN 0-405-13632-3). Ayer Co Pubs.

Armstrong, Leslie & Morgan, Roger. Space for Dance: An Architectural Design Guide. Lipske, Mike, ed. LC 84-4919. (Illus.). 192p. (Orig.). 1984. 19.50 (ISBN 0-89062-189-6); pap. 14.50 (ISBN 0-89062-190-X). Pub Ctr Cult Res.

Armstrong, Lilian. Renaissance Miniature Painters & Classical Imagery: The Master of the Putti & His Venetian Workshop. (Harvey Miller Publications). (Illus.). 1981. 55.00x (ISBN 0-19-921023-3). Oxford U Pr.

Armstrong, Lindsay. Enter My Jungle. (Harlequin Presents Ser.). 192p. 1983. pap. 1.95 (ISBN 0-373-10607-6). Harlequin Bks.

--Melt a Frozen Heart. (Harlequin Presents Ser.). 192p. 1983. pap. 1.75 (ISBN 0-373-10559-2). Harlequin Bks.

--My Dear Innocent. (Harlequin Romances Ser.). 192p. 1982. pap. 1.50 (ISBN 0-373-02497-5). Harlequin Bks.

--Perhaps Love. (Harlequin Romances Ser.). 192p. 1983. pap. 1.75 (ISBN 0-373-02582-3). Harlequin Bks.

--Un Voeu Trop Secret. (Harlequin Romantique Ser.). 192p. 1983. pap. 1.95 (ISBN 0-373-41222-3). Harlequin Bks.

Armstrong, Louise. The Home Front: Notes from the Family War Zone. (Paperbacks Ser.). 276p. 1984. pap. 6.95 (ISBN 0-07-002347-6). McGraw.

--How to Turn War into Peace: A Child's Guide to Conflict Resolution. LC 79-11797. (A Let-Me-Read Bk.). (Illus.). 32p. (ps-3). 1979. pap. 1.95 (ISBN 0-15-642206-9, VoyB). HarBraceJ.

--Saving the Big-Deal Baby. LC 79-22838. (Illus.). (gr. 7 up). 1980. 7.95 (ISBN 0-525-38805-2, Skinny Book). Dutton.

Armstrong, Louise V. We Too Are the People. LC 78-137155. (Poverty U.S.A. Historical Record Ser.). 1971. Repr. of 1938 ed. 28.00 (ISBN 0-405-03093-2). Ayer Co Pubs.

--We Too Are the People. LC 74-168679. (FDR & the Era of the New Deal Ser.). 1972. Repr. of 1938 ed. lib. bdg. 55.00 (ISBN 0-306-70367-X). Da Capo.

Armstrong, M. The Canadian Economy & Its Problems. 2nd ed. 1977. pap. 13.95 (ISBN 0-13-113076-5). P-H.

--George Borrow. LC 74-6381. (English Literature Ser., No. 33). 1974. lib. bdg. 46.95x (ISBN 0-8383-1963-7). Haskell.

Armstrong, M. A. Basic Topology. Rev. ed. (Undergraduate Texts in Mathematics). (Illus.). 250p. 1983. Repr. of 1983 ed. 22.00 (ISBN 0-387-90839-0). Springer-Verlag.

Armstrong, M. C. Practical Ship Handling. 112p. 1980. 19.50x (ISBN 0-85174-387-0). Sheridan.

Armstrong, Mrs. M. & Ludlow, Helen W. Hampton & Its Students. facs. ed. Fenner, Thomas P., ed. LC 75-149862. (Black Heritage Library Collection Ser). 1874. 16.00 (ISBN 0-8369-8744-6). Ayer Co Pubs.

Armstrong, Margaret. Trelawny, a Man's Life. 1977. lib. bdg. 20.00 (ISBN 0-8495-0000-1). Arden Lib.

Armstrong, Margaret A. Learning FORTH: A Self-Teaching Guide. 223p. 1985. pap. 16.95 (ISBN 0-471-88245-3, Pub. by Wiley Pr). Wiley.

Armstrong, Margaret E., jt. ed. see Howe, Jeanne.

Armstrong, Marsha F., jt. auth. see Cohen, Stanley N.

Armstrong, Martha, jt. auth. see Fenner, Peter.

Armstrong, Martin. Jeremy Taylor: A Selection from His Works. 1973. lib. bdg. 15.00 (ISBN 0-8414-1165-4). Folcroft.

--Lady Hester Stanhope. (Women Ser.). 1928. 17.50 (ISBN 0-8482-7275-7). Norwood Edns.

--Laughing. Priestley, J. B., ed. 1975. Repr. of 1928 ed. 10.00 (ISBN 0-8274-4067-7). R West.

Armstrong, Martin D. Bazaar & Other Stories. facsimile ed. LC 71-106242. (Short Story Index Reprint Ser.). 1924. 18.00 (ISBN 0-8369-3278-1). Ayer Co Pubs.

--Puppet Show. facsimile ed. LC 71-163020. (Short Story Index Reprint Ser.). Repr. of 1923 ed. 13.00 (ISBN 0-8369-3934-4). Ayer Co Pubs.

--Sir Pompey & Madame Juno: And Other Tales. facsimile ed. LC 75-163021. (Short Story Index Reprint Ser.). Repr. of 1927 ed. 17.00 (ISBN 0-8369-3935-2). Ayer Co Pubs.

Armstrong, Mary F. & Ludlow, Helen W. Hampton & Its Students. LC 71-132385. 256p. Repr. of 1874 ed. 11.00 (ISBN 0-404-07234-8). AMS Pr.

--Hampton & Its Students by Two of Its Teachers, with Fifty Cabin & Plantation Songs. LC 77-99332. 1969. Repr. of 1874 ed. lib. bdg. 12.75 (ISBN 0-8411-0003-9). Metro Bks.

Armstrong, Michael. Be a Better Manager: Improve Performance, Profits, & Productivity. 256p. 1984. pap. 7.95 (ISBN 0-88908-597-8, 9533, Pub. by Intl Self-Counsel Pr). TAB Bks.

--Case Studies in Personnel Management Practice. 1979. 32.50x (ISBN 0-85038-243-2). Nichols Pub.

--Closely Observed Children: The Diary of a Primary Classroom. (Chameleon Education Ser.). (Illus.). 224p. (Orig.). 1981. 12.95 (ISBN 0-906495-04-0, Pub. by Writers & Readers); pap. 5.95 (ISBN 0-906495-21-0). Writers & Readers.

--Handbook of Personnel Management Practice. 1977. 29.50x (ISBN 0-85038-111-8). Nichols Pub.

--How to Be a Better Manager. 250p. 1984. 25.00 (ISBN 0-89397-180-4). Nichols Pub.

Armstrong, Michael & Lorentzen, John. A Handbook of Personnel Management Practice. (Illus.). 420p. 1982. 17.95 (ISBN 0-13-380790-8); pap. 8.95 (ISBN 0-13-380782-7). P-H.

Armstrong, Michael & Murlis, Helen. Handbook of Salary Administration. 246p. 1982. 32.50 (ISBN 0-85038-369-2). Nichols Pub.

Armstrong, Michael, ed. Personnel & Training Databook 1983 (UK) 2nd Edition. x2nd ed. Orig. Title: Personnel & Training Management Yearbook & Directory. (Illus.). 417p. 1982. 40.00x (ISBN 0-85038-567-9). Intl Pubns Serv.

Armstrong, Michael, jt. ed. see Pinch, Alan.

Armstrong, Michael, frwd. by. The Knapp Commission Report on Police Corruption. LC 73-76969. 1973. pap. 5.95 (ISBN 0-8076-0689-8). Braziller.

Armstrong, Michael L. Electrocardiograms. 5th ed. (Illus.). 336p. 1985. 20.00 (ISBN 0-7236-0793-1). PSG Pub Co.

Armstrong, Mimi. Calligraphic Designs. (International Design Library). (Illus.). 48p. (Orig.). 1983. pap. 3.50 (ISBN 0-88045-031-2). Stemmer Hse.

Armstrong, Morris D., III. The Treasure: The World's First One-Step Guide to Success, Prosperity & Happiness. 136p. 1984. 8.95 (ISBN 0-8059-2951-7). Dorrance.

Armstrong, Moses K. Early Empire Builders of the Great West. LC 72-2557. (Select Bibliographies Reprint Ser.). 1972. Repr. of 1901 ed. 29.00 (ISBN 0-8369-6846-8). Ayer Co Pubs.

--History & Resources of Dakota, Montana & Idaho. 62p. 1967. 4.95 (ISBN 0-87770-104-0); pap. 3.00 (ISBN 0-87770-031-1). Ye Galleon.

Armstrong, Nancy. The Book of Fans. (Illus.). 1979. 12.95 (ISBN 0-8317-0952-9, Mayflower Bks). Smith Pubs.

--Fans. 174p. 1985. 24.95 (ISBN 0-285-62591-8, Pub. by Souvenir Pr Ltd UK). Seven Hills Bks.

--Navajo Children. (Indian Culture Ser.). (gr. 2-6). 1975. 1.95 (ISBN 0-89992-037-3). Coun India Ed.

--Navajo Long Walk. (gr. 4-9). 1983. pap. 4.95 (ISBN 0-89992-083-7). Coun India Ed.

Armstrong, Nancy, et al. The Heritage. (gr. 3-6). 1977. 1.95 (ISBN 0-89992-065-9). Coun India Ed.

Armstrong, Nell & Wakat, Diane. The Energetic Diabetic: A Personal Fitness Guide. (Illus.). 304p. 1985. pap. 14.95 (ISBN 0-89303-437-1). Brady Comm.

Armstrong, O. V., compiled by. Comfort for Those Who Mourn. LC 77-17182. pap. 20.00 (ISBN 0-8357-9003-7, 2016353). Bks Demand UMI.

Armstrong, O. V. & Armstrong, Helen, eds. Prayer Poems. facsimile ed. LC 72-86793. (Granger Index Reprint Ser). 1942. 16.00 (ISBN 0-8369-6094-7). Ayer Co Pubs.

Armstrong, Pat & Dawson, Chris. People in Organisations. 1982. 40.00x (ISBN 0-9505828-2-4, Pub by ELM Pubns England). State Mutual Bk.

Armstrong, Patrick. Changing Landscape. (Illus.). 1979. 20.00 (ISBN 0-900963-53-0, Pub. by Terence Dalton England). State Mutual Bk.

--Discovering Geology. (Discovering Ser.: No. 189). (Illus., Orig.). 1983. pap. 3.95 (ISBN 0-85263-409-9, Pub. by Shire Pubns England). Seven Hills Bks.

Armstrong, Paul B. The Phenomenology of Henry James. LC 82-24713. xiii, 242p. 1983. 26.00 (ISBN 0-8078-1556-X). U of NC Pr.

Armstrong, Paul W. & Baigrie, Ronald S. Hemodynamic Monitoring in the Critically Ill. (Illus.). 250p. 1980. text ed. 18.95 (ISBN 0-06-140268-0, 14-02684, Harper Medical). Lippincott.

Armstrong, Peg. I-Openers. LC 81-82584. (Illus., Orig.). 1981. pap. 6.95 (ISBN 0-686-35731-0). Guadalupe River Pr.

Armstrong, Perry A. The Sauks & the Black Hawk War. LC 76-43643. (Illus.). Repr. of 1887 ed. 47.50 (ISBN 0-404-15478-6). AMS Pr.

Armstrong, Peter. Critical Problems in Diagnostic Radiology. (Illus.). 304p. 1983. text ed. 38.75 (ISBN 0-397-50496-9, 65-06406, Lippincott Medical). Lippincott.

Armstrong, R. Personal Income Tax Practice Set: 1983 Edition. 1983. 7.60 (ISBN 0-07-002525-8). McGraw.

--Personal Income Tax Practice Set: 1985 Edition. 1985. 8.95 (ISBN 0-07-002527-4). McGraw.

Armstrong, R. D., ed. Solid Ionic & Ionic-Electronic Conductors. LC 77-747. 1977. text ed. 37.00 (ISBN 0-08-021592-0). Pergamon.

Armstrong, R. D., ed. see International Meeting on Solid Electrolytes, 2nd, University of St. Andrews, Sep. 20-22, 1978.

Armstrong, R. D., et al. Robust Estimation Procedures & Visual Display Techniques in a Two-Way Classification Model. (Research Report Ser.: 1978-2). (Illus.). 1978. pap. 4.00 (ISBN 0-87755-229-0). Bureau Busn UT.

Armstrong, R. F., tr. see Gruber, U. F.

Armstrong, R. W. & Lewis, H. T., eds. Human Ecology: North Kohala Studies. (Social Science & Linguistics Institute Special Publications). (Illus.). 144p. 1972. pap. 8.00x (ISBN 0-8248-0247-0). UH Pr.

Armstrong, Ray L. The Poems of James Shirley. 108p. 1980. Repr. of 1941 ed. lib. bdg. 27.50 (ISBN 0-8495-0062-1). Arden Lib.

--Poems of James Shirley. LC 73-1692. 1941. lib. bdg. 20.00 (ISBN 0-8414-1713-X). Folcroft.

Armstrong, Regina B. Regional Accounts: Structure & Performance of the New York Region's Economy in the Seventies. LC 79-3659. 296p. 1980. 25.00x (ISBN 0-253-17965-3). Ind U Pr.

Armstrong, Regina B. & Simmer, Bill, eds. Economic Development & Public Intrastructure in the New York Urban Region. 72p. 1982. 15.00 (ISBN 0-318-17805-2). Regional Plan Assn.

Armstrong, Regis J. & Brady, Ignatius C., eds. Francis & Clare: The Complete Works. (Classics of Western Spirituality Ser.). 1983. 11.95 (ISBN 0-8091-0330-3); pap. 7.95 (ISBN 0-8091-2446-7). Paulist Pr.

Armstrong, Richard. Kim MacConnel: Collection Applied Design. 1976. 2.00x (ISBN 0-686-99808-1). La Jolla Mus Contemp Art.

--The Modern Chair: Its Origins & Evolution. LC 77-84973. (Illus.). 62p. 1977. pap. 7.00x (ISBN 0-934418-05-5). La Jolla Mus Contemp Art.

--Out to Change the World: A Life of Father James Keller of the Christophers. LC 84-9494. 224p. 1984. 15.95. Crossroad NY.
--Richard Anuszkiewicz. (Illus.). 40p. 1976. 10.00 (ISBN 0-686-99811-1). La Jolla Mus Contemp Art.
--Sculpture in California Nineteen Seventy-Five to Nineteen-Eighty. LC 80-51414. (Illus.). 96p. 1982. pap. 10.00 (ISBN 0-295-95917-7, Pub. by San Diego Museum Art). U of Wash Pr.
Armstrong, Richard, et al. Richard Artschwager's Themes. (Illus.). 104p. 1979. pap. 12.00 (ISBN 0-934418-00-4). La Jolla Mus Contemp Art.
Armstrong, Richard A. Agnosticism & Theism in the Nineteenth Century. 1977. lib. bdg. 59.95 (ISBN 0-8490-1406-9). Gordon Pr.
--Faith & Doubt in the Century's Poets. 1898. lib. bdg. 10.00 (ISBN 0-8414-2914-6). Folcroft.
Armstrong, Richard S. The Pastor As Evangelist. LC 84-10359. 202p. 1984. pap. 9.95 (ISBN 0-664-24556-0). Westminster.
--Service Evangelism. LC 78-26701. 198p. 1979. pap. 8.95 (ISBN 0-664-24252-9). Westminster.
Armstrong, Robert. The Coaches. (Stars of the NBA Ser.). (Illus.). (gr. 4-12). 1977. PLB 7.95 (ISBN 0-87191-566-9). Creative Ed.
--Dramatic Interpretation of Shakespeare's Tragedies. 59.95 (ISBN 0-8490-0060-2). Gordon Pr.
--Personal Income Tax Practice Set. 1976. 4.50x (ISBN 0-916060-02-0). Math Alternatives.
--Rick Barry. (Sports Superstars Ser.). (Illus.). (gr. 3-9). 1977. pap. 3.95 (ISBN 0-89812-185-X). Creative Ed.
Armstrong, Robert & Shenk, Janet. El Salvador: The Face of Revolution. 260p. 1982. 20.00 (ISBN 0-89608-138-9); pap. 7.50 (ISBN 0-89608-137-0). South End Pr.
Armstrong, Robert & Wheaton, Philip. Reform & Repression: U. S. Policy in El Salvador. (Illus.). 14p. 1983. pap. 1.50 (ISBN 0-942638-01-8, 14L). Solidarity.
Armstrong, Robert C. Just Before the Dawn: Life & Work of Ninomiya Sontoku. LC 78-72370. Repr. of 1912 ed. 32.50 (ISBN 0-404-17217-2). AMS Pr.
--Light from the East: Studies in Japanese Confucianism. lib. bdg. 79.95 (ISBN 0-87968-134-9). Krishna Pr.
Armstrong, Robert D. Nevada Printing History: A Bibliography of Imprints & Publications, 1858-1880. LC 81-7422. (Illus.). 421p. 1982. 35.00x (ISBN 0-87417-063-X). U of Nev Pr.
Armstrong, Robert H. & Alaska Magazine Editors. Guide to the Birds of Alaska. LC 80-20882. 309p. 1983. pap. 16.95 (ISBN 0-88240-254-4). Alaska Northwest.
Armstrong, Robert L. Metaphysics & British Empiricism. LC 78-109602. xviii, 169p. 1970. 15.50x (ISBN 0-8032-0750-6). U of Nebr Pr.
Armstrong, Robert P. The Affecting Presence: An Essay in Humanistic Anthropology. LC 75-107090. (Illus.). 235p. 1971. 18.95x (ISBN 0-252-00104-4). U of Ill Pr.
--The Powers of Presence: Consciousness, Myth, & Affecting Presence. LC 81-51136. (Illus.). 224p. 1981. 25.50x (ISBN 0-8122-7804-6). U of Pa Pr.
--Wellspring: On the Myth & Source of Culture. LC 73-85781. (Illus.). 100p. 1975. 27.50x (ISBN 0-520-02571-7). U of Cal Pr.
Armstrong, Roger. Beginning Jewelry: A Notebook for Design & Technique. (Illus.). 1979. pap. text ed. 8.95x (ISBN 0-89863-018-5). Star Pub CA.
--Wax & Casting: A Notebook of Process & Technique. (Illus.). 160p. 1985. pap. 8.95 (ISBN 0-89863-038-X). Star Pub CA.
Armstrong, Roger, et al. Laboratory Chemistry: A Life Science Approach. (Illus.). 1980. pap. text ed. write for info. (ISBN 0-02-303920-5). Macmillan.
Armstrong, Ronald M., jt. auth. see Steele, Marion A.
Armstrong, Russ, jt. auth. see Hemingway, Joan.
Armstrong, Russell M. Modular Programming in COBOL. LC 73-4030. (Business Data Processing Ser.). 224p. 1973. 49.95x (ISBN 0-471-03325-1, Pub. by Wiley-Interscience). Wiley.
Armstrong, Ruth. Enchanted Trails. Tryk, Sheila & King, Scottie, eds. 260p. Date not set. text ed. 7.95 (ISBN 0-937206-01-6). New Mexico Mag.
Armstrong, Ruth & New Mexico Magazine. Enchanted Trails. Tryk, Sheila & King, Scottie, eds. LC 80-82644. (Illus.). vi, 249p. (Orig.). 1980. pap. 5.95 (ISBN 0-937206-01-6, Pub. by NM Magazine). U of NM Pr.
Armstrong, Ruth G. Sisters under the Sari. LC 63-22164. pap. 127.00 (ISBN 0-317-11036-5, 2022765). Bks Demand UMI.
Armstrong, Sara, jt. auth. see Armstrong, E. F.
Armstrong, Sarah. Blood Red Roses. (Twilight Ser.: No. 8). (Orig.). (YA) (gr. 5 up). 1982. pap. 1.95 (ISBN 0-440-90314-9, LFL). Dell.
Armstrong, Scott, jt. auth. see Woodward, Bob.
Armstrong, Stephen. The Clay Courts of Norwich. (Illus.). 200p. 1984. 12.50 (ISBN 0-682-40184-6). Exposition Pr FL.
Armstrong, Steve W. & Frith, Greg H. Practical Self-Help Monitoring for Classroom Use: An Introductory Text. (Illus.). 168p. 1984. 19.75x (ISBN 0-398-04961-0). C C Thomas.
Armstrong, Sue. Who Do You Think You Are. 1983. 24.00x (ISBN 0-86334-046-6, Pub. by Macdonald Pub UK). State Mutual Bk.
Armstrong, Terence E. The Russians in the Arctic. LC 71-177485. (Illus.). 182p. 1972. Repr. of 1958 ed. lib. bdg. 22.50 (ISBN 0-8371-6272-6, ARRA). Greenwood.
Armstrong, Terence I. Ten Contemporaries. 1978. Repr. of 1933 ed. lib. bdg. 27.50 (ISBN 0-88305-244-X). Norwood Edns.
Armstrong, Terrence, et al. The Circumpolar North: A Political & Economic Geography of the Arctic & Sub-Artic. 1978. 16.95x (ISBN 0-416-16930-9, NO.6010); pap. 16.95x (ISBN 0-416-85430-3, NO.6011). Methuen Inc.
Armstrong, Terry, et al. Reader's Hebrew-English Lexicon of the Old Testament, Vol. 3. 208p. 1985. 12.95 (ISBN 0-310-37010-8, Pub. by Regency Ref Lib). Zondervan.
Armstrong, Terry, et al, eds. A Reader's Hebrew-English Lexicon of the Old Testament: Genesis-II Kings. (Hebrew & Eng.). 1982. 16.95 (ISBN 0-310-37040-X). Zondervan.
Armstrong, Terry R. & Cinnamon, Kenneth M. Power & Authority in Law Enforcement. 208p. 1976. 21.75x (ISBN 0-398-03571-7). C C Thomas.
Armstrong, Terry R., ed. Planning to Stay Together. Armstrong, Anne. 1980. pap. 4.00 (ISBN 0-8309-0308-9). Herald Hse.
Armstrong, Thomas. Creating Classroom Structure: A Practical Guide for the Special Educator. (Illus.). 96p. (Orig.). 1984. pap. text ed. 8.50 (ISBN 0-87562-081-7). Spec Child.
--The Radiant Child. LC 85-40409. 220p. (Orig.). 1985. pap. 6.75 (ISBN 0-8356-0600-7, Quest). Theos Pub Hse.
Armstrong, Thomas H. & Barnes, Caren M. Dental Hygiene Examination Review. LC 82-8760. (Illus.). 320p. 1982. pap. 14.95 (ISBN 0-668-05483-2). ACC.
Armstrong, Tim. The Moving Pattern Book. 56p. (Orig.). 1983. pap. 4.95 (ISBN 0-8431-0744-8). Price Stern.
Armstrong, Tom. Echoes from Silence. (Illus.). 1977. with jacket 6.95 (ISBN 0-9604246-0-1). Jemta Pr.
--Love in Being. (Illus.). 64p. 1981. 5.95 (ISBN 0-9604246-1-X). Jemta Pr.
--Marvin: A Star Is Born. LC 82-40388. (Field Enterprises Ser.). (Illus.). 96p. 1982. 3.95 (ISBN 0-89480-237-2, 496). Workman Pub.
--Marvin Explains the Facts of Life. LC 83-40045. (Illus.). 96p. 1983. pap. 3.95 (ISBN 0-89480-603-3, 603). Workman Pub.
Armstrong, Tom see Lipman, Jean.
Armstrong, Tory. Does God Still Bless America. (Illus.). 96p. 1980. 5.95 (ISBN 0-935378-00-6). Seashell Pr.
--Does God Still Bless America? (Illus.). 112p. 1979. 5.95 (ISBN 0-935378-00-6). Comm Creat.
Armstrong, Troy. Restitution: A Guidebook for Juvenile Justice Practitioners. LC 83-188220. (Juvenile Justice Textbook Ser.: No. 450). (Illus.). xii, 92p. 1983. 7.50 (ISBN 0-318-00254-X). Natl Juv & Family Ct Judges.
Armstrong, Virginia I., ed. I Have Spoken: American History Through the Voices of the Indians. LC 74-150755. xxii, 206p. 1971. pap. 7.95 (ISBN 0-8040-0530-3, 82-72684, SB). Ohio U Pr.
Armstrong, Virginia W. Gone Away with the Winmills. 1977. 17.85 (ISBN 2-902704-01-1, Pub. by V W Armstrong Switzerland). A Robinson.
--Notre Livre de Science. Borle, Marie, tr. from Eng. (Illus.). 27p. (gr. k). 1982. pap. 6.00x (ISBN 2-88089-001-2). A Robinson.
Armstrong, Virginia W. L. Guest of China: English-Chinese Phrase Book. (Illus.). 120p. 1982. pap. 10.00x (ISBN 2-88089-000-4). A Robinson.
Armstrong, W. Prayer-Hymns: A New & Different Hymnal for Church & Home. LC 73-101347. pap. write for info. (ISBN 0-686-08988-X). Gonzaga U Pr.
Armstrong, W. G. A Record of the Opera in Philadelphia. LC 74-27327. Repr. of 1884 ed. 22.50 (ISBN 0-404-12853-X). AMS Pr.
Armstrong, Wallace E. Rossel Island: An Ethnological Study. LC 75-32798. Repr. of 1928 ed. 27.50 (ISBN 0-404-14101-3). AMS Pr.
Armstrong, Walt. Beep-Beep! Here Comes Trucker Bard. Hakes, Thomas L., ed. (Cartoon Panel Ser.). 20p. 1985. pap. 2.75 (ISBN 0-915020-48-3). Bardic.
Armstrong, Walter. Art in Great Britain & Ireland. 332p. 1980. Repr. of 1913 ed. lib. bdg. 65.00 (ISBN 0-8492-3206-6). R West.
--Lawrence. LC 70-100531. (BCL Ser.: No. 2). (Illus.). Repr. of 1913 ed. 18.50 (ISBN 0-404-00385-0). AMS Pr.
Armstrong, Walter, ed. see Muntz, Eugene.
Armstrong, Walter, ed. see Perrot, Georges.
Armstrong, Walter, tr. see Perrot, Charles & Chipiez, Charles.
Armstrong, Sir Walter. Art in Great Britain & Ireland. Repr. of 1913 ed. 40.00 (ISBN 0-8482-7256-0). Norwood Edns.
Armstrong, Warwick & McGee, Terence. Theatres of Accumulation: Studies in Asian & Latin America Urbanization. 320p. 1985. text ed. 39.95 (ISBN 0-416-78570-0, 9527); pap. text ed. 16.95 (ISBN 0-416-39800-6, 9528). Methuen Inc.
Armstrong, Wayne. Camping Basics. (Illus.). 48p. (gr. 3-7). 1985. 10.95 (ISBN 0-13-112657-1). P-H.
Armstrong, William. Better Tools for the Job: Specifications for Hand Tools & Equipment. (Illus.). 43p. (Orig.). 1980. pap. 7.75x (ISBN 0-903031-71-X, Pub. by Intermediate Tech England). Intermediate Tech.
--Hospital Humor Cartoons. 2nd ed. (Armstrong Cartoon Ser.). (Illus.). 48p. (Orig.). 1972. pap. 1.00 (ISBN 0-913452-06-8). Jesuit Bks.
--Romantic World of Music. facs. ed. LC 71-90602. (Essay Index Reprint Ser). 1922. 19.00 (ISBN 0-8369-1271-3). Ayer Co Pubs.
Armstrong, William, ed. see King, Cecil.
Armstrong, William A. The Elizabethan Private Theatres. LC 76-52989. 1977. Repr. of 1958 ed. lib. bdg. 10.00 (ISBN 0-8414-2955-3). Folcroft.
Armstrong, William A., ed. see Bacon, Francis.
Armstrong, William C. Pioneer Families of Northwestern New Jersey. 1979. lib. bdg. 25.00 (ISBN 0-912606-04-5). Hunterdon Hse.
Armstrong, William E. Purser's Handbook. LC 65-21748. 287p. 1966. 10.00x (ISBN 0-87033-086-1). Cornell Maritime.
Armstrong, William H. Sounder. LC 70-85030. (Illus.). 128p. (gr. 6 up). 1969. 9.57i (ISBN 0-06-020143-6); PLB 10.89 (ISBN 0-06-020144-4). HarpJ.
--Sounder. 1969. pap. 3.37i (ISBN 0-06-080379-7, P379, PL). Har-Row.
--Sounder. LC 70-85030. (Illus.). 116p. (gr. 6 up). 1972. pap. 2.50 (ISBN 0-06-440020-4, Trophy). HarpJ.
--Sour Land. LC 70-135783. (gr. 7 up). 1971. PLB 10.89 (ISBN 0-06-020142-8). HarpJ.
--Sour Land. 128p. (gr. 7 up). 1976. pap. 2.95 (ISBN 0-06-440074-3, Trophy). HarpJ.
--Study Is Hard Work. 2nd ed. LC 67-10074. 1967. 8.95i (ISBN 0-06-000220-4, HarpT). Har-Row.
--Study Tactics. 272p. (gr. 10-12). 1983. pap. text ed. 5.50 (ISBN 0-8120-2590-3). Barron.
--Study Tips: How to Study Effectively & Get Better Grades. 2nd ed. (gr. 9-12). 1983. pap. text ed. 3.95 (ISBN 0-8120-2366-8). Barron.
--Study Tips: How to Study Effectively & Get Better Grades. 2nd ed. LC 75-16482. (gr. 7-12). 1983. pap. text ed. 3.95 (ISBN 0-8120-2366-8). Barron.
--Through Troubled Waters: A Young Father's Struggles with Grief. 96p. (Orig.). 1983. pap. 3.35 (ISBN 0-687-41895-X, Festival). Abingdon.
--Warrior in Two Camps: Ely S. Parker, Union General & Seneca Chief. (Illus.). 14.95x (ISBN 0-8156-0143-3). Syracuse U Pr.
--Word Power in Five Easy Lessons: A Self-Help Workbook for Elementary School Pupils. rev. ed. LC 68-25868. (gr. 3-6). 1969. pap. text ed. 5.95 (ISBN 0-8120-0317-9). Barron.
Armstrong, William H., ed. see Smith, Edward P.
Armstrong, William M. E. L. Godkin: A Biography. LC 77-12918. 1978. 49.50x (ISBN 0-87395-371-1). State U NY Pr.
--E. L. Godkin & American Foreign Policy: 1865-1900. LC 77-9534. 1977. Repr. of 1957 ed. lib. bdg. 22.50x (ISBN 0-8371-9711-2, ARGA). Greenwood.
Armstrong, William M., ed. The Gilded Age Letters of E. L. Godkin. LC 74-6462. (Illus.). 1974. 49.50x (ISBN 0-87395-246-4). State U NY Pr.
Armstrong, William N. Around the World with a King. LC 76-434070. (Illus.). 1977. pap. 5.75 (ISBN 0-8048-1215-2). C E Tuttle.
Armstrong, William P., ed. Calvin & the Reformation: Four Studies. (Twin Brooks Ser.). 1980. pap. 6.95 (ISBN 0-8010-2901-5). Baker Bk.
Armstrong, Wm. The Angels Must Have Smiled. 2nd ed. LC 70-101346. (Illus.). 144p. (Orig.). 1969. pap. 1.00 (ISBN 0-913452-01-7). Jesuit Bks.
--Las Aventuras De Pepito. Igartua, Arturo & Armstrong, Wm., trs. (Armstrong Cartoon Ser., Spanish Cartoons, Vol. 1). (Illus.). 48p. (Orig., Span. & Eng.). (gr. 1-10). 1973. pap. 1.00 (ISBN 0-913452-23-8). Jesuit Bks.
--Benedictine Cartoons. (Armstrong Cartoon Ser.). (Illus., Orig.). 1973. pap. 1.00 (ISBN 0-913452-25-4). Jesuit Bks.
--Clerical Cartoons. 2nd ed. (Armstrong Cartoon Ser.). (Illus.). 48p. (Orig.). 1971. pap. 1.00 (ISBN 0-913452-02-5). Jesuit Bks.
--Ecclesiastical Cartoons. 2nd ed. (Armstrong Cartoon Ser.). (Illus.). 48p. (Orig.). 1972. pap. 1.00 (ISBN 0-913452-08-4). Jesuit Bks.
--Family Fun Cartoons. 2nd ed. (Armstrong Cartoon Ser.). (Illus.). 48p. (Orig.). 1971. pap. 1.00 (ISBN 0-913452-03-3). Jesuit Bks.
--Franciscan Cartoons. (Armstrong Cartoon Ser.). (Illus., Orig.). 1974. pap. 1.00 (ISBN 0-913452-24-6). Jesuit Bks.
--I Ate the Whole Thing. (Armstrong Cartoon Ser.). (Illus.). 48p. (Orig.). 1973. pap. 1.00 (ISBN 0-913452-21-1). Jesuit Bks.
--Prayer-Poems. 3rd ed. LC 79-100082. (Illus.). 50p. (Orig.). 1968. pap. 1.00 (ISBN 0-913452-00-9). Jesuit Bks.
--Senior Citizens' Cartoons. 2nd ed. (Armstrong Cartoon Ser.). (Illus.). 48p. (Orig.). 1971. pap. 1.00 (ISBN 0-913452-12-2). Jesuit Bks.
--Summer Cabin Cartoons. 2nd ed. (Armstrong Cartoon Ser.). (Illus.). 48p. (gr. 1-6). 1972. pap. 1.00 (ISBN 0-913452-11-4). Jesuit Bks.
--Tavern Cartoons. 2nd ed. (Armstrong Cartoon Ser.). (Illus.). 48p. (Orig.). 1972. pap. 1.00 (ISBN 0-913452-09-2). Jesuit Bks.
--TV Cartoons. 2nd ed. (Armstrong Cartoon Ser.). (Illus.). 48p. (Orig.). 1972. pap. 1.00 (ISBN 0-913452-31-9). Jesuit Bks.
--Waiting Room Cartoons. 2nd ed. (Armstrong Cartoon Ser.). (Illus.). 48p. 1971. pap. 1.00 (ISBN 0-913452-10-6). Jesuit Bks.
Armstrong, Wm., tr. see Armstrong, Wm.
Armstrong, Zella. Notable Southern Families. 1976. lib. bdg. 59.95 (ISBN 0-8490-2355-6). Gordon Pr.
--Some Tennessee Heroes of the Revolution. LC 75-21541. 162p. 1975. Repr. of 1933 ed. 12.50 (ISBN 0-8063-0684-X). Genealog Pub.
--Twenty-Four Hundred Tennessee Pensioners: Revolution & War of 1812. LC 75-971. 121p. 1981. pap. 7.50 (ISBN 0-8063-0665-3). Genealog Pub.
Armytage, W. H. Civil Universities: Aspects of a British Tradition. LC 76-55207. (The Academic Profession Ser.). (Illus.). 1977. Repr. of 1955 ed. lib. bdg. 25.50x (ISBN 0-405-10031-0). Ayer Co Pubs.
--Four Hundred Years of English Education. 2nd ed. LC 78-85709. pap. 91.30 (ISBN 0-317-07967-0, 2051488). Bks Demand UMI.
Armytage, W. H. & Peel, John, eds. Perimeter of Social Repair. 1978. 41.50 (ISBN 0-12-062750-7). Acad Pr.
Armytage, W. H., et al. Changing Patterns of Sexual Behavior. LC 79-42830. 1980. 37.50 (ISBN 0-12-062650-0). Acad Pr.
Arn, E. A. Group Technology: An Integrated Planning & Implementation Concept for Small & Medium Batch Production. (Illus.). vi, 200p. 1975. pap. 31.90 (ISBN 0-387-07505-4). Springer-Verlag.
Arn, Winfield, jt. auth. see McGavran, Donald.
Arn, Winfield C., jt. auth. see McGavran, Donald A.
Arnade, Charles W. Siege of St. Augustine. LC 59-63743. (Illus.). 100p. (Orig.). 1959. pap. 3.95 (ISBN 0-917553-00-4). St Augustine Hist.
ARnakis, G. G. Stillman: American Consul in a Cretan War. rev. ed. 146p. 1966. 10.00 (ISBN 0-318-12222-7); pap. 8.00 (ISBN 0-318-12223-5). Ad Council.
Arnakis, G. G., ed. Howe: A Historical Sketch of the Greek Revolution, Pts. 1 & 2. 251p. 1966. 10.00 (ISBN 0-317-34059-X); pap. 8.00 (ISBN 0-317-34060-3). Ctr Neo Hellenic.
--Return to Mount Athos. 171p. 1968. 9.00 (ISBN 0-317-34062-X); pap. 6.00 (ISBN 0-317-34063-8). Ctr Neo Hellenic.
--Stillman: Articles & Despatches from Crete. LC 76-9149. 138p. 1976. 10.00 (ISBN 0-317-34064-6); pap. 7.00 (ISBN 0-317-34065-4). Ctr Neo Hellenic.
Arnakis, G. G. & Demetracopoulou, E., eds. Jarvis: His Journal & Related Documents. 282p. 1965. 8.00 (ISBN 0-317-34061-1). Ctr Neo Hellenic.
Arnakis, G. G. & Demetracopoulou, E., eds. Historical Texts of the Greek Revolution from the Papers of George Jarvis. 98p. 1967. 10.00 (ISBN 0-317-34057-3); pap. 6.00 (ISBN 0-317-34058-1). Ctr Neo Hellenic.
Arnakis, George & Vucinish. History of the Near East in Modern Times, 3 vols. Incl. Vol. 1. The Ottoman Empire & the Balkan States to 1900. (Illus.). 452p (ISBN 0-8363-0046-7); Vol. 2. Forty Crucial Years: 1900-1940 (ISBN 0-8363-0047-5). 15.00 ea. Jenkins.
Arnakis, George G. & Proussis, Costas M., eds. Neo-Hellenika III. 1978. pap. 25.00 (ISBN 0-932242-00-6). Ctr Neo Hellenic.
Arnaktauyok, Germaine, illus. Stories from Pangirtung. (Illus.). 100p. 1976. 5.95 (ISBN 0-295-95972-X, Pub. by Hurtig Pubs). U of Wash Pr.
Arnal, Oscar L. Ambivalent Alliance: The Catholic Church & the Action Francaise, 1899-1939. LC 84-21961. 270p. 1985. 24.95x (ISBN 0-8229-3812-X). U of Pittsburgh Pr.
Arnaldi De Olmeda, Cecilia. Concha Melendez: Vida y Obra. 4.35 (ISBN 0-8477-3107-3); pap. 3.10 (ISBN 0-8477-3108-1). U of PR Pr.
--La Individualizacion De la Ensenanza: Consideraciones y Proceso. LC 76-1904. (Illus.). 124p. (Orig.). 1976. pap. 3.75 (ISBN 0-8477-2733-5). U of PR Pr.
Arnall, Franklin M. The Padlock Collector. 4th ed. LC 82-74067. (Illus.). 140p. 1982. pap. 8.95 (ISBN 0-914638-03-3). Collector.
Arnall, L. & Keymer, I. F. Bird Diseases: 'An Introduction to the Study of Birds in Health & Disease' (Illus.). 1975. 34.95 (ISBN 0-87666-950-X, H-964). TFH Pubns.
Arnandez, Richard, tr. see De Lubac, Henri.
Arnandez, Richard, tr. see Leclerc, Eloi.
Arnandez, Richard, tr. see Manteau-Bonamy, H. M.
Arnason, Barry G. W. Clinical Immunology of the Nervous System. (Clinical Neurology & Neurosurgery Monographs). (Illus.). text ed. write for info. (ISBN 0-443-08002-X). Churchill.
Arnason, H. H. History of Modern Art: Painting, Sculpture, & Architecture. rev. ed. LC 68-26863. (Illus.). 1977. 40.00 (ISBN 0-8109-0181-1). Abrams.
Arnason, H. H. & Diamonstein, Barbaralee. Robert Motherwell: New & Revised. (Illus.). 252p. 1982. 75.00 (ISBN 0-8109-1333-X). Abrams.
Arnason, H. H., jt. auth. see Lipchitz, Jacques.
Arnason, H. Horvard. History of Modern Art. 2nd ed. (Illus.). 1976. 32.95 (ISBN 0-13-390351-6). P-H.

Arnason, J. Icelandic Legends, 2 vols. Powell, G. E., tr. LC 78-67683. (The Folktale). (Illus.). Repr. of 1866 ed. Set. 75.00 (ISBN 0-404-16050-6). AMS Pr.

Arnason, K. Quantity in Historical Phonology. LC 79-41363. (Cambridge Studies in Linguistics: No. 30). (Illus.). 256p. 1980. 52.50 (ISBN 0-521-23040-3). Cambridge U Pr.

Arnason, Wayne. Follow the Gleam. 1980. pap. 3.50 (ISBN 0-933840-07-1). Unitarian Univ.

Arnau, Frank. Universal Film Lexicon. 69.95 (ISBN 0-8490-1246-5). Gordon Pr.

Arnau, J. Sanchez, ed. Debt & Development. LC 82-431. 348p. 1982. 38.95x (ISBN 0-03-061904-1). Praeger.

Arnaud, A. A. Investment Trusts Explained. 2nd ed. 145p. 1983. 22.50 (ISBN 0-85941-243-1). Woodhead-Faulkner.

Arnaud, Bonnevierre, jt. auth. see Gardner, Horace J.

Arnaud, J. A. Beam & Fiber Optics. (Quantum Electronics Ser.). 1976. 76.50 (ISBN 0-12-063250-0). Acad Pr.

Arnaud, Jean F. Diccionario de la Electronica. 3rd ed. 368p. (Span.). 1976. pap. 5.25 (ISBN 84-01-90304-1, S-14211). French & Eur.

Arnaud, Noel, ed. see Jarry, Alfred.

Arnaud, Pierre, jt. ed. see Barredo-Carneiro, Paulo E. De.

Arnaud, Pierre, jt. ed. see Berredo Carneiro, Paulo E.

Arnaud, Rene. Second Republic & Napoleon Third. LC 70-158271. Repr. of 1930 ed. 30.00 (ISBN 0-404-50799-9). AMS Pr.

Arnaudet, Martin & Barrett, Mary E. Approaches to Academic Reading & Writing. (Illus.). 288p. 1984. pap. text ed. 10.95 (ISBN 0-13-043679-8). P-H.

Arnaudet, Martin L. & Barrett, Mary E. Paragraph Development: A Guide for Students of English As a Second Language. (ESL Ser.). (Illus.). 160p. 1981. pap. text ed. 11.95 (ISBN 0-13-648618-5). P-H.

Arnaudon, Jean-Claude. Dictionnaire du Blues. 296p. (Fr.). 1978. 35.50 (ISBN 0-686-56868-0, M-6646). French & Eur.

Arnauld, Antoine. The Arrainment of the Whole Societie of Jesuites in Fraunce: Holden-the Twelfth & Thirteenth of July, 1594. LC 79-84084. (English Experience Ser.: No. 904). 68p. 1979. Repr. of 1594 ed. lib. bdg. 8.00 (ISBN 0-686-71069-X). Walter J Johnson.

Arnbal, Carl A. & Crawford, Joe V. Problems in Engineering Graphics. 208p. 1982. pap. text ed. 11.95 (ISBN 0-8403-2646-7). Kendall-Hunt.

Arnberger, Leslie P. Flowers of the Southwest Mountains. 6th ed. Jackson, Earl, ed. LC 74-84444. (Popular Ser.: No. 7). 1974. pap. 7.50 (ISBN 0-911408-00-2). SW Pks Mnmts.

--Flowers of the Southwest Mountains. rev. ed. Priehs, T. J., ed. Dodson, Carolyn. LC 81-86380. 1983. pap. 7.95 (ISBN 0-911408-61-4). SW Pks Mnmts.

Arndt, Bonnie, ed. see Zieman, Nancy.

Arndt, Christian O., ed. Community Education. LC 59-751. (National Society for the Study of Education Yearbooks Ser: No. 58, Pt. 1). 1959. 7.00x (ISBN 0-226-60048-3); pap. text ed. 4.50x (ISBN 0-226-60049-1). U of Chicago Pr.

Arndt, Christian O. & Everett, Samuel, eds. Education for a World Society: 11th Yearbook of John Dewey Society. LC 72-142603. (Essay Index Reprint Ser.). Repr. of 1951 ed. 20.00 (ISBN 0-8369-2383-9). Ayer Co Pubs.

Arndt, Diether. Manganese Compounds As Oxidizing Agents in Organic Chemistry. Muller, Eugen, ed. Lee, Donald G., tr. from Ger. 368p. 1981. 45.00x (ISBN 0-87548-355-0). Open Court.

Arndt, Elise. A Mother's Touch. 156p. 1983. pap. 4.95 (ISBN 0-88207-101-7). Victor Bks.

Arndt, H. W. Economic Lessons of the Nineteen Thirties. new ed. 314p. 1963. 30.00x (ISBN 0-7146-1204-9, BHA 01204, F Cass Co). Biblio Dist.

--The Rise & Fall of Economic Growth: A Study in Contemporary Thought. LC 83-24185. vi, 162p. 1984. pap. 6.95x (ISBN 0-226-02717-1). U of Chicago Pr.

Arndt, Hana J. West Germany: Politics of Non-Planning. LC 66-17524. (National Planning Ser.: No. 8). pap. 46.50 (ISBN 0-317-28999-3, 2020394). Bks Demand UMI.

Arndt, Hans W. Methodo Scientifica pertractatum: Mos geometricus und Kalkuelbegriff in der Philosophischen Theorienbildung des 17. und 18. (Quellen und Studien Zur Philosophie Ser.: Vol. 4). 1971. 35.60x (ISBN 3-11-003942-7). De Gruyter.

Arndt, Heinz W. & Blackert, Wesley J. The Australian Trading Banks. 5th ed. 1977. pap. 13.00x (ISBN 0-522-84126-0, Pub. by Melbourne U Pr). Intl Spec Bk.

Arndt, Helmut. Economic Theory vs. Economic Reality. 224p. 1983. 17.95 (ISBN 0-87013-235-0). Mich St U Pr.

--Economic Theory vs. Economic Reality. LC 83-60727. 210p. 1984. 17.95 (ISBN 0-87013-235-0). Wayne St U Pr.

Arndt, Herman. Why Did Jesus Fast? 87p. 1962. pap. 4.95 (ISBN 0-88697-039-3). Life Science.

Arndt, K. A., et al. Cutaneous Laser Therapy: Principles & Methods. LC 82-17379. 241p. 1983. 47.00 (ISBN 0-471-87751-4, Pub. by Wiley Med). Wiley.

Arndt, K. A., et al, eds. Cutaneous Laser Therapy: Principles & Methods. 241p. 1983. 50.00x (ISBN 0-471-90075-3). Wiley.

Arndt, Karl J. A Documentary History of the Indiana Decade of the Harmony Society 1814-1824, Vol. I. 837p. 1975. 17.50 (ISBN 0-317-14594-0); pap. 8.00 (ISBN 0-317-14595-9). Harmony Soc.

--A Documentary History of the Indiana Decade of the Harmony Society 1814-1824, Vol. II 1820-1824. 978p. 1978. 17.50 (ISBN 0-317-14598-3); pap. 8.00 (ISBN 0-317-14599-1). Harmony Soc.

--Economy on the Ohio, 1826-1834. The Harmony Society During the Period of Its Greatest Power & Influence & Its Messianic Crisis. LC 84-648. (Illus.). 1056p. (Eng. & Ger.). 1984. 50.00 (ISBN 0-937640-03-4). Harmony Soc.

--George Rapp's Separatists: 1700-1803. LC 80-82896. (Illus.). 480p. (Ger. & Eng.). 1980. bilingual ed. 30.00x (ISBN 0-937640-00-X). Harmony Soc.

--George Rapp's Successors & Material Heirs: 1847-1916. LC 76-147268. (Illus.). 445p. 1972. 45.00 (ISBN 0-8386-7889-0). Fairleigh Dickinson.

--Harmony on the Connoquenessing: George Rapp's First American Harmony: 1803-1815. LC 80-10828. (Documentary History of Rapp's Harmony Society, 1700-1916 Ser.). (Illus.). 1021p. (Eng. & Ger.). 1981. 38.00x (ISBN 0-937640-01-8). Harmony Soc.

Arndt, Karl J., ed. Harmony On the Wabash in Transition 1824-1826: Transitions to Rapp's Divine Economy on the Ohio & Robert Owen's New Moral World. LC 82-80176. 876p. 1982. 40.00 (ISBN 0-937640-02-6). Harmony Soc.

Arndt, Karl J. & Olson, May E., eds. The German Language Press of the Americas, 3 Vols. Incl. Vol. 1. History & Bibliography 1732-1968: U. S. A. 3rd rev. & enl. ed. 845p. 1976. lib. bdg. 60.00 (ISBN 3-7940-3422-8); History & Bibliography 1732-1968: Argentina, Bolivia, Brasilia, Chile, Costa Rica, Dominican Republic, Ecuador, Guatemala, Guyana, Canada, Columbia, Cuba, Mexico, Paraguay, Peru, Uruguay, Venezuela, United States of America. (Illus.). 709p. 1973. lib. bdg. 77.00 (ISBN 3-7940-3421-X); German American Press Research from the American Revolution to the Bicentennial. 816p. 1980. lib. bdg. 100.00 (ISBN 3-598-10152-X). K G Saur.

Arndt, Karl J. K. The Annotated & Enlarged Edition of Ernst Steiger's Precentennial Bibliography; "The Periodical Literature of the United States of America". LC 79-25836. 1980. lib. bdg. 60.00 (ISBN 0-527-03668-4). Kraus Intl.

Arndt, Karl J. R. George Rapp's Harmony Society: 1785-1847. rev. ed. LC 72-147267. (Illus.). 713p. 1972. 45.00 (ISBN 0-8386-7888-2). Fairleigh Dickinson.

Arndt, Kenneth A. Manual of Dermatologic Therapeutics. Third ed. (Little, Brown SPIRAL Manual Series). 1983. 16.95 (ISBN 0-316-05181-0). Little.

Arndt, N. T. & Nisbet, E. G., eds. Komatiites. (Illus.). 544p. 1982. text ed. 75.00x (ISBN 0-04-552019-4). Allen Unwin.

Arndt, Paul. Gesellschaftliche Verhaltnisse der Ngadha. Repr. of 1954 ed. 46.00 (ISBN 0-384-02114-X). Johnson Repr.

--Religion Auf Ostflores, Adonare und Solor. 28.00 (ISBN 0-384-02115-8). Johnson Repr.

Arndt, R. E., jt. ed. see Billet, M. L.

Arndt, R. E., jt. ed. see Swift, W. L.

Arndt, Richard. Safe at Home. 1979. pap. 3.95 (ISBN 0-570-03619-4, 39-1061). Concordia.

Arndt, Rick. Athletes Afire. LC 85-71182. 1985. pap. 3.50 (ISBN 0-88270-590-3). Bridge Pub.

--Winning with Christ. 1982. pap. 4.95 (ISBN 0-570-03627-5, 39-1073). Concordia.

Arndt, Robert J. & Rabenhorst, James F. Cost Accounting for Law Firms. 76p. pap. 25.00 (ISBN 0-89707-127-1). Chicago Review.

Arndt, Roger E., ed. see American Society of Mechanical Engineers, et al.

Arndt, Rolf & Gold, Richard. Clinical Arthrography. 2nd ed. 250p. 1985. 45.00 (ISBN 0-683-00256-2). Williams & Wilkins.

Arndt, Sven W., ed. Political Economy of Austria. 1982. 16.95 (ISBN 0-8447-2241-3); pap. 8.95 (ISBN 0-8447-2240-5). Am Enterprise.

Arndt, Sven W., et al, eds. Exchange Rates, Trade & the U. S. Economy: An American Enterprise Institute Book. 320p. 1985. Prof. ref. 39.95x (ISBN 0-88410-948-8). Ballinger Pub.

Arndt, Thomas. Encyclopedia of Conures: The Aratingas. (Illus.). 176p. 1982. 29.95 (ISBN 0-87666-873-2, H-1042). TFH Pubns.

Arndt, Thomas M., et al, eds. Resource Allocation & Productivity in National & International Agricultural Research. LC 76-44064. (Illus.). 1977. 32.50x (ISBN 0-8166-0805-9). U of Minn Pr.

Arndt, U. W. & Wonacott, A. J. The Rotation Method in Crystallography. 276p. 1977. 70.25 (ISBN 0-7204-0594-7, Biomedical Pr). Elsevier.

Arndt, Ulrich W. & Willis, B. T. Single Crystal Diffractometry. LC 66-13637. (Cambridge Monographs on Physics). pap. 88.80 (ISBN 0-317-26117-7, 2024404). Bks Demand UMI.

Arndt, W. Does the Bible Contradict Itself? 192p. 1976. pap. 4.95 (ISBN 0-570-03721-2, 12-2623). Concordia.

Arndt, Walter, ed. see Akhmatova, Anna.

Arndt, Walter, ed. see Busch, William.

Arndt, Walter, tr. see Busch, Wilhelm.

Arndt, Walter, tr. see Goethe, Johann W. Von.

Arndt, Walter, tr. see Grass, Gunter.

Arndt, Walter, tr. see Harman, Mark.

Arndt, Walter, tr. see Pasternak, Boris, et al.

Arndt, Walter, tr. see Pushkin, Alexander.

Arndt, Walter W., jt. auth. see Friederich, Werner P.

Arndt, Walter W., et al, eds. Studies in Historical Linguistics in Honor of George Sherman Lane. (Studies in the Germanic Languages & Literatures Ser.: No. 58). xx, 241p. 1967. 20.00 (ISBN 0-8078-8058-2). U of NC Pr.

Arndt, William. Fundamental Christian Beliefs. pap. text ed. 3.25 (ISBN 0-570-06324-8, 22-1144); pap. 3.75 guide (ISBN 0-570-06325-6, 22-1146); pap. tests 1.25 (ISBN 0-570-06362-0, 22-1145). Concordia.

Arndt, William F. Bible Difficulties. 1981. 4.25 (ISBN 0-570-03120-6, 12-2357). Concordia.

Arndt, William F., tr. see Bauer, Walter, et al.

Arndts, Gary. How to Market the Smaller Industrial Company. (Illus.). 134p. 1984. ring binder 65.00 (ISBN 0-9612342-0-2). Datafax.

Arne, Thomas A see Arkwright, G. E. P.

Arneil, G. C. & Metcoff, J., eds. Pediatric Nutrition. (BIMR Pediatrics Ser.: Vol. 3). 320p. 1985. text ed. 69.95 (ISBN 0-407-02310-0). Butterworth.

Arneil, Gavin C., jt. auth. see Forfar, John O.

Arneil, Steve & Dowler, Bryan. Better Karate: The Key to Better Technique. (Better Bks.). (Illus.). 98p. 1980. text ed. 17.95x (ISBN 0-7182-1444-7, SpS). Sportshelf.

--Modern Karate. (Illus.). 1984. text ed. 19.50x (ISBN 0-7182-1093-X, SpS). Sportshelf.

--Modern Karateys. 7.95 (ISBN 0-8092-8256-9). Contemp Bks.

Arnell, Diane & Browns, Freda. A Guide to the Selection & Use of Reading Instructional Materials. LC 81-68722. (Illus.). 112p. 1981. pap. 11.95 (ISBN 0-88200-147-7, D2161). Alexander Graham.

Arnell, Peter & Bickford, Ted. Charles Gwathmey & Robert Siegel, Architects. LC 84-47554. (Illus.). 304p. 1984. 48.08i (ISBN 0-06-433285-3, Icon Edns). Har-Row.

Arnell, Peter & Bickford, Ted, eds. A Center for the Visual Arts: The Ohio State University Competition. LC 83-63329. (Illus.). 152p. 1984. pap. 17.50 (ISBN 0-8478-0528-X). Rizzoli Intl.

--Frank O. Gehry: Buildings & Projects 1954-1984. LC 84-42646. (Illus.). 304p. 1985. 45.00 (ISBN 0-8478-0542-5); pap. 29.95 (ISBN 0-8478-0543-3). Rizzoli Intl.

--James Stirling: Buildings & Projects. LC 82-50500. (Illus.). 342p. 1985. 45.00 (ISBN 0-8478-0448-8); pap. 29.95 (ISBN 0-8478-0449-6). Rizzoli Intl.

--Mississauga City Hall: A Canadian Competition. LC 83-61685. (Illus.). 120p. 1984. pap. 14.95 (ISBN 0-8478-0516-6). Rizzoli Intl.

--Southwest Center: The Houston Competition. (Illus.). 120p. 1983. pap. 14.95 (ISBN 0-8478-0488-7). Rizzoli Intl.

Arnell, Peter, ed. see Andrews, Mason.

Arnell, Peter, ed. see Stern, Robert A.

Arnell, Peter, jt. ed. see Wheeler, Karen.

Arnell, Peter, et al, eds. see Venturi, Robert & Brown, Denise S.

Arner, George B. Consanguineous Marriages in the American Population. LC 74-77992. (Columbia University, Studies in the Social Sciences Ser.: No. 83). Repr. of 1908 ed. 12.50 (ISBN 0-404-51083-3). AMS Pr.

Arnesen. The Medieval Japanese Daimyo. 1979. text ed. 27.00x (ISBN 0-300-02341-3). Yale U Pr.

Arneson, Ben A. The Democratic Monarchies of Scandinavia. LC 74-4728. (Illus.). 294p. 1975. Repr. of 1949 ed. lib. bdg. 20.50x (ISBN 0-8371-7485-6, ARDM). Greenwood.

Arneson, D. J. First Cowboy Comedy. (Political Satire Ser.). 1985. pap. 4.25 (ISBN 0-89319-017-9). Andor Pub.

--Friend Indeed. LC 80-23062. (gr. 4 up). 1981. PLB 7.90 (ISBN 0-531-04257-X). Watts.

--The Official Computer Hater's Handbook. (Orig.). 1983. pap. 3.95 (ISBN 0-440-56619-3, Dell Trade Pbks). Dell.

--The Original Preppy Cookbook. (Orig.). 1981. pap. 3.95 (ISBN 0-440-56614-2, Dell Trade Pbks). Dell.

--The Original Preppy Jokebook. 192p. (Orig.). 1981. pap. 3.95 (ISBN 0-440-56694-0, Dell Trade Pbks). Dell.

--Sometimes in the Dead of Night. Schneider, Meg, ed. (Chiller Ser.). (gr. 3-7). 1983. pap. 3.95 (ISBN 0-671-45593-1). Wanderer Bks.

--There He Goes Again. (Political Satire Ser.). 1985. pap. 4.95 (ISBN 0-89319-019-5). Andor Pub.

Arneson, D. J. & Brett, Bernard. Sometimes in the Dead of Night. LC 82-10514. (Chiller Ser.). 128p. (gr. 8-12). 1983. PLB 8.79 (ISBN 0-671-46782-4). Messner.

Arneson, Donald. Arnie, Knight of the Day. LC 79-18491. (Illus.). (gr. 5-8). 1979. lib. bdg. 4.00 (ISBN 0-934778-01-9). Bookmaker.

--Doing Something Nice, Inc. & Other Short Plays for Kids. (Illus.). 72p. (Orig.). (gr. 3-6). 1978. pap. 4.00 (ISBN 0-934778-00-0). Bookmaker.

Arnett, Alex M. Populist Movement in Georgia: A View of the Agrarian Crusade in the Light of Solid-South Politics. LC 74-158272. (Columbia University Studies in the Social Sciences: No. 235). Repr. of 1922 ed. 20.00 (ISBN 0-404-51235-6). AMS Pr.

Arnett, Benjamin H., jt. auth. see Ashley, James M.

Arnett, Bishop, ed. see Bell, James M.

Arnett, Caroline. Christina. (Coventry Romance Ser.: No. 65). 224p. 1980. pap. 1.75 (ISBN 0-449-50096-9, Coventry). Fawcett.

--Clarissa. 1980. pap. 1.75 (ISBN 0-449-50059-4, Coventry). Fawcett.

Arnett, Carroll. Come. 1973. 16.00 (ISBN 0-685-38495-0). Elizabeth Pr.

--Earlier. 1972. 16.00 (ISBN 0-685-27705-4); pap. 8.00 (ISBN 0-685-27706-2). Elizabeth Pr.

--Like a Wall. 1969. 5.00 (ISBN 0-685-00983-1). Elizabeth Pr.

--Not Only That. 1967. 3.00 (ISBN 0-685-00982-3). Elizabeth Pr.

--South Line. 1979. 12.00 (ISBN 0-686-26666-8, Pub. by Elizabeth Pr); pap. 5.00 (ISBN 0-686-26667-6). Elizabeth Pr.

--Then. 1965. pap. 3.00 (ISBN 0-685-00981-5). Elizabeth Pr.

--Through the Woods. 1971. 10.00 (ISBN 0-685-00984-X); pap. 5.00 (ISBN 0-685-00985-8). Elizabeth Pr.

--Tsalagi. 1976. pap. 5.00 (ISBN 0-685-79197-1). Elizabeth Pr.

Arnett, David W. & Truran, James W., eds. Nucleosynthesis: Challenges & New Developments. LC 85-1160. (Illus.). x, 308p. 1985. 36.00x (ISBN 0-226-02787-2); pap. 18.00 (ISBN 0-226-02788-0). U of Chicago Pr.

Arnett, Edward M. & Kent, Allen, eds. Computer Based Chemical Information. (Bks. in Library & Information Science: Vol. 4). 232p. 1973. 49.75 (ISBN 0-8247-6045-X). Dekker.

Arnett, Ethel S. Mrs. James Madison: The Incomparable Dolley. LC 78-183987. (Illus.). 240p. 1972. 10.95 (ISBN 0-911452-00-1). Straughan.

--O. Henry from Polecat Creek. LC 63-16928. (Illus.). 1962. 5.95x (ISBN 0-911452-01-X). Straughan.

--William Swaim, Fighting Editor: The Story of O. Henry's Grandfather. LC 63-11676. (Illus.). 1963. 6.95x (ISBN 0-911452-02-8). Straughan.

Arnett, Harold & Danos, Paul. CPA Firm Viability: A Study of Major Environmental Factors Affecting Firms of Various Sizes & Characteristics. LC 79-18672. (Illus., Orig.). 1979. pap. 6.50 (ISBN 0-87712-199-0). U Mich Busn Div Res.

Arnett, Harold E. Proposed Funds Statements for Managers & Investors. 137p. pap. 15.95 (ISBN 0-86641-019-8, 79114). Natl Assn Accts.

Arnett, Harold E. & Smith, Donald L. Metal Finishing Industry: Framework for Success. (Michigan Business Reports: No. 60). (Illus.). 1977. pap. 5.50 (ISBN 0-87712-182-6). U Mich Busn Div Res.

Arnett, Harold E. & Smith, Donald N. The Tool & Die Industry: Problems & Prospects. (Michigan Business Reports, New Ser.: No. 1). (Illus.). 109p. (Orig.). 1975. pap. 6.00 (ISBN 0-87712-173-7). U Mich Busn Div Res.

Arnett, John A. Bibliopegia; or, the Art of Bookbinding in All Its Branches. Bidwell, John, ed. LC 78-74390. (Nineteenth-Century Book Arts & Printing History Ser.: Vol. 5). (Illus.). 1980. lib. bdg. 33.00 (ISBN 0-8240-3879-7). Garland Pub.

Arnett, Mary E., jt. auth. see Arnett, Ross H.

Arnett, Mary E., jt. ed. see Arnett, Ross H., Jr.

Arnett, Peter & MacLear, Michael. The Ten Thousand Day War: Vietnam 1945-1975. LC 81-8841. (Illus.). 368p. 1981. 16.95 (ISBN 0-312-79094-5). St Martin.

Arnett, R. & Jacques, R., Jr. S&S Guide to Insects. 1981. pap. 9.95 (ISBN 0-671-25014-0). S&S.

Arnett, R. H., Jr., ed. Bibliography of Cooleoptera of North America North of Mexico: Seventeen Fifty-Eight to Nineteen Forty-Seven. 1978. pap. 17.50 (ISBN 0-916846-07-5). World Natural Hist.

--Catalog of the Coleoptera of the World, 35 vols. (Coleopterorum Catalogus (New Series)). 8000p. 1985. Set. pap. write for info. (ISBN 0-916846-24-5). Flora & Fauna.

Arnett, R. H., Jr., ed. see Udayagiri, Susjaya & Wadhi, Sukhdev R.

Arnett, Ronald C. Dwell in Peace. 156p. (Orig.). 1980. pap. 5.95 (ISBN 0-87178-199-9). Brethren.

Arnett, Ross. American Insects: A Handbook of the Insects of America North of Mexico. (Illus.). 850p. 1985. 79.50 (ISBN 0-442-20866-9). Van Nos Reinhold.

Arnett, Ross H. & Arnett, Mary E. The Naturalists' Directory & Almanac (International), 1985. 44th ed. 160p. 1985. pap. 15.50 (ISBN 0-916846-33-4). Flora & Fauna.

Arnett, Ross H. & Jacques, Richard L. Insect Life: A Field Entomology Manual for the Amateur Naturalist. (Illus.). 384p. 1985. 25.95 (ISBN 0-13-467259-3); pap. 12.95 (ISBN 0-13-467242-9). P-H.

Arnett, Ross H., Jr. Checklist of the Beetles of North & Central America & the West Indies: Introduction. 26p. 1983. with 3-post 4" binder 15.00x (ISBN 0-916846-29-6). Flora & Fauna.

--Checklist of the Beetles of North & Central America & the West Indies, Vol. 10: Bibliography. 240p. 1985. pap. 25.00x (ISBN 0-916846-27-X). Flora & Fauna.
--Checklist of the Beetles of North & Central America & the West Indies: Ground Beetles, Water Beetles, & Related Groups, Vol. 1. 135p. 1983. 15.00x (ISBN 0-916846-12-1). Flora & Fauna.
--Checklist of the Beetles of North & Central America & the West Indies: The Rove Beetles & Related Groups, Vol. 2. 258p. 1983. looseleaf with binder 28.00x (ISBN 0-916846-13-X). Flora & Fauna.
--Checklist of the Beetles of North & Central America & the West Indies: The Scarab Beetles, Buprestid Beetles, & Related Groups, Vol. 3. 254p. 1983. 27.00x (ISBN 0-916846-14-8). Flora & Fauna.
--Checklist of the Beetles of North & Central America & the West Indies: The Click Beetles, Fireflies, Checkered Beetles, & Related Groups, Vol. 4. 215p. 1983. 23.00x (ISBN 0-916846-17-2). Flora & Fauna.
--Checklist of the Beetles of North & Central America & the West Indies: The Ladybird Beetles & Related Group, Vol. 5. 129p. 1983. 15.00 (ISBN 0-916846-18-0). Flora & Fauna.
--Checklist of the Beetles of North & Central America & the West Indies: The Darkling Beetles, Strepsiptera, & Related Groups, Vol. 6. 221p. 1983. 24.00x (ISBN 0-916846-19-9). Flora & Fauna.
--Checklist of the Beetles of North & Central America & the West Indies: The Fungus Weevils, Bark Beetles, Weevils & Related Groups, Vol. 9. 453p. 1983. 40.00x (ISBN 0-916846-21-0). Flora & Fauna.
--Entomological Information Storage & Retrieral. 210p. 1970. 4.95 (ISBN 0-916846-00-8). Flora & Fauna.
--Entomological Information Storage & Retrieval. LC 70-140434. 1970. 7.95 (ISBN 0-916846-00-8). World Natural Hist.
Arnett, Ross H., Jr. & Samuelson, G. Allan. The Insect & Spider Collections of the World. 368p. 1985. pap. price not set (ISBN 0-916846-30-X). Flora & Fauna.
Arnett, Ross H., Jr., jt. auth. see Blackwelder, Richard E.
Arnett, Ross H., Jr., jt. auth. see Wilcox, John A.
Arnett, Ross H., Jr., ed. The Naturalists' Directory & Almanac: International Supplement, 1980-1981. 43rd ed. 310p. (Orig.). 1980. pap. 5.00x (ISBN 0-916846-11-3). Flora & Fauna.
Arnett, Ross H., Jr. & Arnett, Mary E., eds. The Naturalists' Directory of Insect Collectors & Identifiers, International, Pt. I. 44th ed. (The Naturalists' Directory (International) Ser.). 96p. (Orig.). 1985. pap. cancelled (ISBN 0-916846-15-6). Flora & Fauna.
--The Naturalists' Directory of Plant Collectors & Identifiers, International, Pt. II, No. 4. 4th ed. (Naturalists' Directory (International) Ser.). 96p. (Orig.). 1985. pap. cancelled (ISBN 0-916846-16-4). Flora & Fauna.
Arnett, Ross H., Jr., et al. Checklist of the Beetles of North & Central America & the West Indies, 10 vols. 2092p. 1983. Set 250.00x (ISBN 0-916846-26-1). Flora & Fauna.
--How to Know the Beetles. 2nd ed. (Pictured Key Nature Ser.). 384p. 1980. write for info. wire coil (ISBN 0-697-04776-8). Wm C Brown.
Arnett, W. B., et al, eds. Nucleosynthesis. LC 67-28241. 282p. 1968. 80.95 (ISBN 0-677-11580-6). Gordon.
Arnett, W. David, jt. ed. see Schramm, David N.
Arnett, W. E. Santayana & the Sense of Beauty. 1984. 12.00 (ISBN 0-8446-0458-5). Peter Smith.
Arnett, Willard E. Religion & Judgment: An Essay on the Method & Meaning of Religion. LC 66-11680. (Century Philosophy Ser.). 1966. 37.50x (ISBN 0-89197-377-X). Irvington.
Arnett, Willard E., ed. Modern Reader in the Philosophy of Religion. LC 66-20470. (Century Philosophy Ser.). 1966. 39.50x (ISBN 0-89197-482-2); pap. text ed. 19.95x (ISBN 0-89197-483-0). Irvington.
Arnett, William S. The Predynastic Origin of Egyptian Hieroglyphs: Evidence for the Development of Rudimentary Forms of Hieroglyphs in Upper Egypt in the Fourth Millennium B.C. LC 82-17562. (Illus.). 176p. (Orig.). 1983. lib. bdg. 21.75 (ISBN 0-8191-2775-2); pap. text ed. 9.25 (ISBN 0-8191-2776-0). U Pr of Amer.
Arnette, Grigsby. I Just Can't Lie No More. (Illus.). 224p. 1984. 12.95 (ISBN 0-89962-426-X). Todd & Honeywell.
Arney, William R. Power & the Profession of Obstetrics. LC 82-8410. (Illus.). 280p. 1983. lib. bdg. 25.00x (ISBN 0-226-02728-7). U of Chicago Pr.
--Power & the Profession of Obstetrics. LC 82-8410. (Illus.). xii, 290p. 1985. pap. 10.95 est. (ISBN 0-226-02729-5). U of Chicago Pr.
Arney, William R. & Bergen, Bernard J. Medicine & the Management of Living: Taming the Last Great Beast. LC 83-24380. (Illus.). 192p. 1984. 19.95 (ISBN 0-226-02792-9). U of Chicago Pr.
Arnez, John A. Slovenci V New Yorku: (Slovenians in New York) LC 67-119909. (Studia Slovenica, Special Series). 268p. (Slovenian.). 1966. 6.00 (ISBN 0-686-28387-2). Studia Slovenica.
--Slovenia in European Affairs: Reflections on Slovenian Political History. LC 58-12797. 204p. 1958. 6.00 (ISBN 0-686-28373-2). Studia Slovenica.
--A Slovenian Community in Bridgeport, Conn. LC 73-170467. (Studia Slovenica, Special Series). 96p. 1971. 5.00 (ISBN 0-686-28388-0). Studia Slovenica.
--Slovenian Lands & Their Economies, 1848-1873. LC 83-116220. (Studia Slovenica Ser.: No. 15). 321p. 1983. soft cover 16.00 (ISBN 0-938616-16-1). Studia Slovenica.
Arnez, John A., intro. by. Slovenian Letters by Missionaries in America, 1851-1874. (Studia Slovenica Special Ser.: No.4). 230p. 1984. pap. 11.00 (ISBN 0-318-01454-8). Studia Slovenica.
Arnez, Nancy L. The Besieged School Superintendent: A Case Study of School Superintendent-School Board Relations in Washington, D. C. 1973-75. LC 80-69044. (Illus.). 815p. (Orig.). 1981. lib. bdg. 35.75 (ISBN 0-8191-1634-3); pap. text ed. 26.25 (ISBN 0-8191-1635-1). U Pr of Amer.
--Moll Flanders Notes. (Orig.). 1969. pap. text ed. 3.50 (ISBN 0-8220-0854-8). Cliffs.
Arngart, O. see Malone, Kemp & Schibsbye, Knud.
Arngart, Olof. The Middle English Genesis & Exodus: Re-edited from Manuscript C.C.C.C.444. (Lund Studies in English: Vol. 36). 1968. pap. 30.00 (ISBN 0-317-16428-7). Kraus Repr.
Arnhart, Larry. Aristotle on Political Reasoning: A Commentary on the "Rhetoric". LC 81-11330. 230p. 20.00 (ISBN 0-87580-080-7). N Ill U Pr.
Arnheim, Daniel D. Dance Injuries: Their Prevention & Care. 2nd ed. LC 79-24526. (Illus.). 246p. 1980. pap. 14.95 (ISBN 0-8016-0311-0). Mosby.
Arnheim, Daniel D. & Sinclair, William A. The Clumsy Child: A Program of Motor Therapy. 2nd ed. LC 78-2. (Illus.). 320p. 1979. pap. 16.95 (ISBN 0-8016-0310-2). Mosby.
--Physical Education for Special Populations: A Developmental, Adapted & Remedial Approach. (Illus.). 512p. 1985. text ed. 26.95 (ISBN 0-13-668245-6). P-H.
Arnheim, Daniel D., jt. auth. see Klafs, Carl E.
Arnheim, Louise & Webb, Lee, eds. A Health Care Agenda for the States. 150p. 1985. 9.95 (ISBN 0-89788-083-8). Conf Alt State & Local.
Arnheim, Michael. Is Christianity True? LC 84-42861. (The Skeptic's Bookshelf Ser.). 198p. 1984. 19.95 (ISBN 0-87975-262-9). Prometheus Bks.
Arnheim, Rudolf. Art & Visual Perception: A Psychology of the Creative Eye, the New Version. 2nd, rev. & enl. ed. LC 73-87587. 1974. 28.50 (ISBN 0-520-02327-7, CAL 285); pap. 10.95 (ISBN 0-520-02613-6). U of Cal Pr.
--Dynamics of Architectural Form. LC 76-19955. (Illus.). 1977. 26.50 (ISBN 0-520-03305-1, CAL 376); pap. 10.95 (ISBN 0-520-03551-8). U of Cal Pr.
--Entropy & Art: An Essay on Disorder & Order. LC 71-128585. (Illus.). 1971. pap. 4.95 (ISBN 0-520-02617-9). U of Cal Pr.
--Film As Art. LC 57-10496. 1957. pap. 4.95 (ISBN 0-520-00035-8, CAL 6). U of Cal Pr.
--The Genesis of a Painting: Picasso's Guernica. LC 62-20637. (Illus.). 1980. 36.50x (ISBN 0-520-00037-4); pap. 10.95 (ISBN 0-520-04266-2, CAL 485). U of Cal Pr.
--Kunst und Sehen: Eine Psychologie Des Schopeferischen Auges. 2nd ed. (Illus.). 1978. 19.20x (ISBN 3-11-006682-3). De Gruyter.
--The Power of the Center: A Study of Composition in the Visual Arts. rev. ed. LC 83-10332. (Illus.). 256p. 1984. 18.95 (ISBN 0-520-05014-2); pap. 8.95 (ISBN 0-520-05015-0, CAL 639). U of Cal Pr.
--Radio. LC 73-161151. (History of Broadcasting: Radio to Television Ser). (Illus.). 1971. Repr. of 1936 ed. 25.50 (ISBN 0-405-03570-5). Ayer Co Pubs.
--Radio: The Psychology of an Art of Sound. LC 73-164504. (Cinema Ser). 1972. Repr. of 1936 ed. lib. bdg. 35.00 (ISBN 0-306-70291-6). Da Capo.
--Toward a Psychology of Art: Collected Essays. LC 66-10692. 1966. 29.95x (ISBN 0-520-00038-2); pap. 7.95 (ISBN 0-520-02161-4, CAL242). U of Cal Pr.
--Visual Thinking. LC 71-76335. (Illus.). 1980. 27.50x (ISBN 0-520-01378-6); pap. 10.95 (ISBN 0-520-01871-0, CAL 229). U of Cal Pr.
Arnikar, H. J. & Kulharni, R. A. Topics in Physical Chemistry. 246p. 1981. 30.00x (ISBN 0-86125-417-1, Pub. by Orient Longman India). State Mutual Bk.
Arnikar, H. J. & Kulkarni, R. A. A Course in Physical Chemistry. 126p. 1981. 30.00x (ISBN 0-86125-404-X, Pub. by Orient Longman India). State Mutual Bk.
Arnikar, Hari J. Essentials of Nuclear Chemistry. LC 81-6818. 335p. 1982. 19.95 (ISBN 0-470-27176-0). Halsted Pr.
Arnim & Mayor. Seeing the Real New York. 2nd ed. 1982. pap. 8.95 (ISBN 0-8120-2561-X). Barron.
Arnim, Christian von see Steiner, Rudolf.
Arnim, Faye. Fur Craft: How to Glamorize Your Wardrobe with Fur. pap. 2.50 (ISBN 0-87497-056-3). Assoc Bk.
Arnim, Hans von see Von Arnim, Hans F.
Arnim, J. Von. Stoicorum Veterum Fragmenta, 4 vols. (Classical Studies Ser.). (Lat. & Gr.). Repr. of 1903 ed. Vol. 1. lib. bdg. 62.00x (ISBN 0-697-00024-9); Vol. 2. lib. bdg. 64.00x (ISBN 0-697-00025-7); Vol. 3. lib. bdg. 60.00x (ISBN 0-697-00026-5); Vol. 4. lib. bdg. 60.00x (ISBN 0-697-00027-3). Irvington.
Arnink, Donna J. Creative Theatrical Makeup. 240p. 1984. 22.95 (ISBN 0-13-191313-1); pap. 14.95 (ISBN 0-13-191305-0). P-H.
Arnison, Jim. The Million Pound Strike. 86p. 1971. pap. 5.00x (ISBN 0-8464-0631-4). Beekman Pubs.
Arnitage, R. O., et al, eds. Guide to New Zealand Fish Species. LC 83-15132. (Illus.). 1984. Repr. of 1981 ed. 55.00x (ISBN 0-943738-10-5). Osprey Bks.
Arno, Andrew & Dissanayake, Wimal. The News Media in National & International Conflict. LC 84-50130. (Special Study). 250p. 1984. pap. 25.00x (ISBN 0-86531-776-3). Westview.
Arno, J. An Atlas of Lymph Node Pathology. (Current Histopathology Ser.: Vol. 1). (Illus.). 1980. text ed. 45.00 (ISBN 0-397-50451-9, Lippincott Medical). Lippincott.
Arno, Michael, jt. auth. see Moore, Michael.
Arno, Peter. Man in the Shower. (Illus.). 128p. 1976. 13.50 (ISBN 0-7156-1149-6, Pub. by Duckworth England). Biblio Dist.
--Sizzling Platter. (Illus.). 128p. 1977. 13.50 (ISBN 0-7156-1269-7, Pub. by Duckworth England). Biblio Dist.
Arno Press & Silk, Leonard, eds. The Poetry of Industry: Two Literary Reactions to the Industrial Revolution 1755-1757. LC 70-38474. (The Evolution of Capitalism Ser.). 1972. Repr. of 1755 ed. 19.00 (ISBN 0-405-04131-4). Ayer Co Pubs.
--Religious Attitudes Toward Usury: Two Early Polemics. LC 79-38471. (The Evolution of Capitalism Ser.). 1972. 25.50 (ISBN 0-405-04135-7). Ayer Co Pubs.
Arno, Roger. The Story of Space & Rockets. (Illus.). 1978. pap. 2.95 (ISBN 0-88388-063-6). Bellerophon Bks.
Arno, Stephen F. Discovering Sierra Trees. (Discovering Sierra Ser.). 89p. (Orig.). 1973. pap. 2.95 (ISBN 0-939666-04-9). Yosemite Natl Hist.
--Northwest Trees. LC 77-82369. (Illus.). 1977. pap. 8.95 (ISBN 0-916890-50-3). Mountaineers.
--Timberline: Mountain & Arctic Forest Frontiers. (Illus.). 304p. (Orig.). 1984. pap. 9.95 (ISBN 0-89886-085-7). Mountaineers.
Arnobius, Afer. Adversvs Nationes Libri Seven, Bk. 7. (Corpus Scriptorum Ecclesiasticorum Latinorum, Vol. 4). 31.00 (ISBN 0-384-02120-4). Johnson Repr.
Arnof, Dorothy, jt. auth. see Davis, Bertha.
Arnoff, M. J. Power & Ritual in the Israel Labor Party: A Study in Political Anthropology. (Illus., Orig.). 1977. pap. text ed. 23.75x (ISBN 90-232-1453-6). Humanities.
Arnold. Beyond Politics. 1974. pap. text ed. 3.00 (ISBN 0-8442-5194-1). Natl Textbk.
--Lectures & Essays in Criticism. Super, R. H., ed. 1980. 19.95. U of Mich Pr.
--Selected Poems & Prose. 1978. 12.95x (ISBN 0-460-10951-0, Evman); pap. 3.50x (ISBN 0-460-11951-6, Evman). Biblio Dist.
Arnold & Burton. A Field Guide to Reptiles & Amphibians of Britain & Europe. 29.95 (ISBN 0-00-219318-3, Collins Pub England). Greene.
Arnold & Luke. Riders of the Range. 8.95 (ISBN 0-392-09348-0, SpS). Sportshelf.
Arnold, et al. Singularities of Differentiable Maps: Vol. 1. (Monographs in Mathematics). 1984. text ed. write for info. (ISBN 0-8176-3187-9). Birkhauser.
Arnold, A. Pearls of the Faith. pap. 3.50 (ISBN 0-686-18468-8). Kazi Pubns.
Arnold, A. J. Paul Valery & His Critics. LC 72-12808. (Studies in French Literature, No. 45). 1972. Repr. of 1970 ed. lib. bdg. 68.95x (ISBN 0-8383-1590-9). Haskell.
Arnold, A. James. Modernism & Negritude: The Poetry & Poetics of Aime Cesaire. LC 80-29007. 368p. 1981. text ed. 25.00x (ISBN 0-674-58057-5). Harvard U Pr.
Arnold, A. S. General Insurance Principles. rev. ed. LC 83-6959. (Illus.). 542p. 1983. lib. bdg. 33.75 (ISBN 0-8191-3202-0); pap. text ed. 19.50 (ISBN 0-8191-3203-9). U Pr of Amer.
--The Story of Thomas Carlyle. 1973. Repr. of 1903 ed. 20.00 (ISBN 0-8274-1549-4). R West.
Arnold, Adele. Red Son Rising. LC 74-17283. (Illus.). (gr. 5 up). 1974. 6.95 (ISBN 0-87518-077-9). Dillon.
Arnold, Alan. Once Upon a Galaxy: A Journal of the Making of the Empire Strikes Back. 1980. pap. 2.75 (ISBN 0-345-29075-5, Del Rey Bks). Ballantine.
Arnold, Allyn, et al. Secondary Programs for the Gifted-Talented. 67p. 10.95 (ISBN 0-318-02148-X). NSLTIGT.
Arnold, Allyn, jt. auth. see Arnold, Lee.
Arnold, Alvin. Real Estate Investor's Deskbook: Annual Supplement. 1982. 64.00 (ISBN 0-88262-732-5). Warren.
--Real Estate Syndication Manual. 1984. 84.00 (ISBN 0-317-17510-6). Warren.
Arnold, Alvin L. Modern Real Estate & Mortgage Forms: Cumulative Supplementation. 2nd. ed. (Modern Real Estate & Mortgage Ser: Vol. 1). 1970. 64.00 (ISBN 0-88262-204-8, 78-50305). Warren.
Arnold, Alvin L. & Kusnet, Jack. The Arnold Encyclopedia of Real Estate. 1978. 65.00 (ISBN 0-88262-239-0, 78-67783). Warren.
Arnold, Alvin L. & Smith, Owen T. Modern Ownership & Investment Forms: Annual Supplement. 2nd. ed. 1976. 64.00 (ISBN 0-88262-026-6). Warren.
Arnold, Alvin L., jt. auth. see Kusnet, Jack.
Arnold, Alvin L., et al. Modern Real Estate & Mortgage Forms Checklists: Annual Supplement. LC 79-50553. 1979. 72.00 (ISBN 0-88262-280-3). Warren.
Arnold, Annemarie. Youth Movement to Bruderhof: Letters & Diaries of Annemarie Arnold (Nee Wachter) Brethren, Hutterian & Bruderhof, Woodcrest, eds. (Illus.). 220p. (Orig.). 1985. pap. 5.95 (ISBN 0-87486-183-7). Plough.
Arnold, Annemarie, jt. auth. see Arnold, Heini.
Arnold, Anthony. Afghanistan: The Soviet Invasion in Perspective. rev., 2nd ed. (Publication Ser.: No. 321). (Illus.). xliv, 168p. (Orig.). 1985. pap. 10.95x (ISBN 0-8179-8212-4). Hoover Inst Pr.
--Afghanistan's Two-Party Communism: Parcham & Khalq. (Publication Ser.: No. 279). 260p. 1983. pap. 10.95 (ISBN 0-8179-7792-9). Hoover Inst Pr.
Arnold, Armin. Casar Von Arx: Briefe An Den Vater. 182p. (Ger.). 1982. write for info. (ISBN 3-261-05000-4). P Lang Pubs.
--Friedrich Durrenmatt. LC 78-178169. (Literature and Life Ser.). 128p. 1972. 12.95 (ISBN 0-8044-2000-9). Ungar.
Arnold, Arnold. The Crowell Book of Arts & Crafts for Children. LC 75-2333. (Illus.). 356p. (YA) 1975. 12.45i (ISBN 0-690-00567-9). T Y Crowell.
--Pictures & Stories from Forgotten Children's Books. (Illus., Orig.). (gr. k-6). 1970. pap. 5.95 (ISBN 0-486-22041-9). Dover.
Arnold, Arnold, ed. Antique Paper Dolls: Nineteen Fifteen to Nineteen Twenty. LC 75-3822. 1975. pap. 3.50 (ISBN 0-486-23176-3). Dover.
Arnold, Augusta F. Sea-Beach at Ebb-Tide. LC 68-20554. (Illus.). 1968. pap. 7.95 (ISBN 0-486-21949-6). Dover.
Arnold, Barbara J., ed. see Conference on Periodical Publishing in Wisconsin, May 11-12, 1978, et al.
Arnold, Benjamin W. History of the Tobacco Industry in Virginia from 1860 to 1894. LC 78-63855. (Johns Hopkins University. Studies in the Social Sciences. Fifteenth Ser. 1897: 1-2). Repr. of 1897 ed. 11.50 (ISBN 0-404-61111-7). AMS Pr.
Arnold, Benjamin W., Jr. History of the Tobacco Industry in Virginia from 1860 to 1894. Repr. of 1894 ed. 11.00 (ISBN 0-384-02120-4). Johnson Repr.
Arnold, Beverly, jt. auth. see Keppie, Lawrence.
Arnold, Bion J. Report on the Improvement & Development of the Transportation Facilities of San Francisco. LC 73-11900. (Metropolitan America Ser.). (Illus.). 510p. 1974. Repr. 46.50 (ISBN 0-405-05383-5). Ayer Co Pubs.
Arnold, Bob. Back Road Caller. (Jumiper Bk.: No. 48). 1985. pap. 6.00 (ISBN 0-317-26493-1). Juniper Pr WI.
--Discount America Guide's Craft & Records Directory. 1983. pap. text ed. 3.00 (ISBN 0-942528-12-3). Discount America.
--Discount America Guide's Directory of Discount Computer Supplies. 1983. pap. text ed. 3.50 (ISBN 0-942528-05-0). Discount America.
--Discount America Guide's Directory of Sporting Goods Discounts. 1983. pap. text ed. 3.25 (ISBN 0-942528-10-7). Discount America.
--Discount America Guide's Special Budget Travel Edition. 1983. pap. text ed. 3.50 (ISBN 0-942528-11-5). Discount America.
--Self-Employed. (Illus., Orig.). 1983-84. pap. 10.00 ltd. signed ed. (ISBN 0-937596-08-6). Pentagram.
Arnold, Bruce. The Muted Swan. 288p. 1982. 14.95 (ISBN 0-241-10687-7, Pub. by Hamish Hamilton England). David & Charles.
--Orpen: Mirror to an Age. (Illus.). 448p. 1982. 49.95 (ISBN 0-224-01581-8, Pub. by Jonathan Cape). Merrimack Pub Cir.
--A Singer at the Wedding. 285p. 1980. 17.95 (ISBN 0-241-89825-0, Pub. by Hamish Hamilton England). David & Charles.
--The Song of the Nightingale. 256p. 1980. 19.95 (ISBN 0-241-10497-1, Pub. by Hamish Hamilton England). David & Charles.
--What Kind of Country: Modern Irish Politics, Nineteen Sixty-Eight to Nineteen Eighty-Three. (Illus.). 320p. 1984. 17.95 (ISBN 0-224-02046-3, Pub. by Jonathan Cape); pap. 7.95 (ISBN 0-224-02971-1, Pub. by Jonathan Cape). Merrimack Pub Cir.
Arnold, C. B. Could There Be a Medical Basis for the Declining SAT Scores? 1977. 2.00 (ISBN 0-87447-025-0, 251704). College Bd.
Arnold, C. D. The Dinosaur Plays. LC 83-8446. (Gay Play Script Ser.). (Illus.). 80p. 1984. pap. 5.95 (ISBN 0-935672-09-5). JH Pr.
Arnold, C. J. The Anglo-Saxon Cemeteries of the Isle of Wight. 208p. 1982. 99.00x (ISBN 0-7141-1359-X, Pub. by Brit Mus Pubns England). State Mutual Bk.

--Roman Britain to Saxon England. LC 84-47813. (Illus.). 192p. 1984. 22.50x (ISBN 0-253-35017-4). Ind U Pr.

Arnold, C. P., jt. auth. see Arrillaga, J.

Arnold, Carol B., ed. see Hardy, George.

Arnold, Caroline. Animals that Migrate. LC 82-1253. (On My Own Bks.). (Illus.). 56p. (gr. 1-4). 1982. lib. bdg. 8.95g (ISBN 0-87614-194-7). Carolrhoda Bks.

--The Biggest Living Thing. LC 83-1860. (Carolrhoda On My Bks.). (Illus.). 48p. (gr. k-4). 1983. PLB 8.95g (ISBN 0-87614-245-5). Carolrhoda Bks.

--Electric Fish. LC 80-12479. (Illus.). 64p. (gr. 4-6). 1980. 10.00 (ISBN 0-688-22237-4); PLB 10.88 (ISBN 0-688-32237-9). Morrow.

--How Do We Communicate? (Easy-Read Community Bks.). (Illus.). 32p. (gr. k-3). 1983. PLB 7.90 (ISBN 0-531-04505-6). Watts.

--How Do We Have Fun? (Easy-Read Community Bks.). (Illus.). 32p. (gr. k-3). 1983. PLB 7.90 (ISBN 0-531-04506-4). Watts.

--How Do We Travel? (Easy-Read Community Bks.). (Illus.). 32p. (gr. k-3). 1983. PLB 7.90 (ISBN 0-531-04507-2). Watts.

--Land Masses: Fun, Facts, & Activities. (Easy-Read Geography Activities Bk.). (Illus.). 32p. (gr. k-3). 1985. lib. bdg. 9.40 (ISBN 0-531-04897-7). Watts.

--Music Lessons for Alex. LC 85-4090. (Illus.). 64p. (gr. 1-5). 1985. 12.95 (ISBN 0-89919-328-5, Clarion). HM.

--My Friend from Outer Space. (Easy-Read Story Bks). (Illus.). 32p. (gr. k-3). 1981. 8.60 (ISBN 0-531-04192-1). Watts.

--Natural Resources: Fun, Facts, & Activities. Carter, Penny, tr. (Easy-Read Geography Activity Book Ser.). (Illus.). 32p. (gr. k-3). 1985. lib. bdg. 9.40 (ISBN 0-531-04898-5). Watts.

--Pets Without Homes. LC 83-2106. (Illus.). 48p. (gr. k-3). 1983. PLB 10.95 (ISBN 0-89919-191-6, Clarion). HM.

--Saving the Peregrine Falcon. LC 84-15576. (Carolrhoda Nature Watch Bks.). (Illus.). 48p. (gr. 2-5). 1985. PLB 12.95 (ISBN 0-87614-225-0). Carolrhoda Bks.

--Sex Hormones: Why Males & Females Are Different. LC 81-38388. (Illus.). 128p. (YA) (gr. 7-9). 1981. 11.25 (ISBN 0-688-00696-5); PLB 11.88 (ISBN 0-688-00697-3). Morrow.

--The Summer Olympics. (Easy-Read Sports Bks.). (Illus.). 48p. (gr. 2-4). 1983. PLB 8.60 (ISBN 0-531-04622-2). Watts.

--Sun Fun. (Easy-Read Activity Bks.). (Illus.). 32p. (gr. 1-3). 1981. lib. bdg. 8.90 (ISBN 0-531-04312-6). Watts.

--Too Fat? Too Thin? Do You Have a Choice? LC 83-23841. 112p. (gr. 5 up). 1984. PLB 8.59 (ISBN 0-688-02780-6); pap. 5.00 (ISBN 0-688-02779-2). Morrow.

--What Is a Community? (Easy-Read Community Bks.). (Illus.). 32p. (gr. 1-3). 1982. lib. bdg. 7.90 (ISBN 0-531-04444-0). Watts.

--What Is Pain? (Illus.). 96p. (gr. 3-7). 1986. 12.50 (ISBN 0-688-05710-1); PLB 12.88 (ISBN 0-688-05711-X). Morrow.

--What Will We Buy? (Easy-Read Community Bks.). (Illus.). 32p. (gr. k-3). 1983. PLB 7.90 (ISBN 0-531-04508-0). Watts.

--Where Do You Go to School? (Easy-Read Community Bks.). (Illus.). 32p. (gr. 1-3). 1982. lib. bdg. 7.90 (ISBN 0-531-04442-4). Watts.

--Who Keeps Us Healthy? (Easy-Read Community Bks.). (Illus.). (gr. 1-3). 1982. lib. bdg. 7.90 (ISBN 0-531-04440-8). Watts.

--Who Keeps Us Safe? (Easy-Read Community Bks.). (Illus.). 32p. (gr. 1-3). 1982. lib. bdg. 7.90 (ISBN 0-531-04441-6). Watts.

--Who Works Here? (Easy-Read Community Bks.). (Illus.). 32p. (gr. 1-3). 1982. lib. bdg. 7.90 (ISBN 0-531-04443-2). Watts.

--Why Do We Have Rules? (Easy-Read Community Bks.). (Illus.). 32p. (gr. k-3). 1983. PLB 7.90 (ISBN 0-531-04509-9). Watts.

--The Winter Olympics. (Easy-Read Sports Bks.). (Illus.). 48p. (gr. 2-4). 1983. PLB 8.60 (ISBN 0-531-04623-0). Watts.

Arnold, Caroline & Silverstein, Herma. Anti-Semitism: A Modern Perspective. (Illus.). 224p. (gr. 7 up). 1985. 10.79 (ISBN 0-671-49850-9). Messner.

Arnold, Carolyn. Charts & Graphs: Fun, Facts & Activities. LC 84-7569. (Easy Read Geography Bks.). (Illus.). 32p. (gr. k-4). PLB 9.40 (ISBN 0-531-04719-9). Watts.

--Maps & Globes: Fun, Facts, & Activities. LC 84-7595. (Easy Read Geography Bk.). (Illus.). 32p. (gr. k-4). 1984. PLB 9.40 (ISBN 0-531-04720-2). Watts.

--Measurements: Fun, Facts & Activities. LC 84-7555. (Easy Read Geography Activity Bks.). (Illus.). 32p. (gr. k-4). 1984. lib. bdg. 9.40 (ISBN 0-531-04721-0). Watts.

Arnold, Carroll C. & Bowers, John W. Handbook of Rhetorical & Communication Theory. 1984. text ed. 67.51 (ISBN 0-205-08057-X, 488057). Allyn.

Arnold, Carroll C., jt. auth. see Wilson, John F.

Arnold, Channing & Frost, F. J. The American Egypt: A Record of Travel in the Yucatan. (Yucatan Ser.). 1979. lib. bdg. 69.95 (ISBN 0-8490-2863-9). Gordon Pr.

Arnold, Charles A. Folklore, Manners & Customs of the Mexicans in San Antonio, Texas. LC 71-166049. 1970. pap. 9.95 (ISBN 0-88247-141-4). R & E Pubs.

Arnold, Charles B., et al. Advances in Disease Prevention, Vol. I. 1981. text ed. 35.00 (ISBN 0-8261-2830-0). Springer Pub.

Arnold, Charles G. Aquatic Safety & Lifesaving Program. 2nd ed. pap. text ed. 6.95x (ISBN 0-88035-017-2). Human Kinetics.

--Aquatic Safety & Lifesaving Program. (Illus.). 128p. 6.95x (ISBN 0-88035-017-2, 475). YMCA USA.

Arnold, Charlotte. Group Readings for the Church. (Paperback Program Ser.). (Orig.). 1975. pap. 1.95 (ISBN 0-8010-0065-3). Baker Bk.

Arnold, Christopher & Reitherman, Robert. Building Configuration & Seismic Design: The Architecture of Earthquake Resistance. 296p. 1982. 45.95 (ISBN 0-471-86138-3). Wiley.

Arnold, Corliss R. Organ Literature: A Comprehensive Survey, 2 vols. 2nd ed. LC 83-20075. 1984. Set. 43.50; Vol. I, Historical Survey 320 pg. 19.50 (ISBN 0-8108-1662-8); Vol. II, Biographical Catalog 620 pg. 29.50 (ISBN 0-8108-1663-6). Scarecrow.

Arnold, Curtis M. Your Personal Computer Can Make You Rich in Stocks & Commodities. LC 83-51498. (Illus.). 300p. 34.95 (ISBN 0-9613048-0-4). M D Weiss Pub.

--Your Personal Computer Can Make You Rich in Stocks & Commodities. 310p. 1985. 19.95 (ISBN 0-89526-596-6). Regnery-Gateway.

Arnold, D. M., et al, eds. Abelian Group Theory: Proceedings of the 2nd New Mexico State University Bicentennial Conference on Abelian Group, Held at Las Cruces, New Mexico, Dec. 9-12 1976. (Lecture Notes in Mathematics: Vol. 616). 1977. pap. text ed. 26.00 (ISBN 0-387-08447-9). Springer-Verlag.

Arnold, D. R., et al. Photochemistry: An Introduction. 1974. 45.00 (ISBN 0-12-063350-7). Acad Pr.

Arnold, Danny, jt. auth. see Cockran, Daniel S.

Arnold, Danny R., et al. Strategic Retail Management. LC 82-8852. 752p. 1983. text ed. 33.95 (ISBN 0-201-10085-1); instr's. manual 25.00 (ISBN 0-201-10086-X). Addison-Wesley.

Arnold, Darlene B. & Doyle, Kenneth O., Jr. Education-Psychology Journals: A Scholar's Guide. LC 74-23507. 143p. 1975. 15.00 (ISBN 0-8108-0779-3). Scarecrow.

Arnold, David. The Age of Discovery: 1400-1600. (Lancaster Pamphlets Ser.). 50p. 1984. pap. 3.95 (ISBN 0-416-36040-8, NO. 3982). Methuen Inc.

--The Congress in Tamiland: Nationalist Politics in South India, Nineteen Nineteen to Nineteen Thirty-Seven. 1977. 12.00x (ISBN 0-88386-958-6). South Asia Bks.

Arnold, David & Cortesi, David. Hey Junior! Using IBM's Home Computer. (The IBM PCjr Home Computer Ser.). 250p. 1984. pap. 14.95 (ISBN 0-03-071772-8). HR&W.

Arnold, David & PC World Staff. Getting Started with the IBM PC & XT. 256p. 1984. pap. 14.95 (ISBN 0-671-49277-2, Pub. by Computer Bks). S&S.

Arnold, David A., ed. see Lowenstein, Bill.

Arnold, David M. Finite Rank Torsion Free Abolian Groups & Rings. (Lecture Notes in Mathematics Ser.: Vol. 931). 191p. 1982. pap. 13.00 (ISBN 0-387-11557-9). Springer-Verlag.

Arnold, David S., et al, eds. Effective Communication: Getting the Message Across. LC 83-289. (Municipal Management Ser.). (Illus.). 230p. (Orig.). 1983. pap. text ed. 26.00 (ISBN 0-87326-029-5). Intl City Mgt.

Arnold, Dean A. American Economic Enterprises in Korea, 1895-1939. Bruchey, Stuart & Bruchey, Eleanor, eds. (American Business Abroad Ser.). (Illus.). 1976. 43.00x (ISBN 0-405-09264-4). Ayer Co Pubs.

Arnold, Dean E. Ceramic Theory & Cultural Process. LC 83-23223. (New Studies in Archaeology). (Illus.). 256p. 1985. 37.50 (ISBN 0-521-25262-8). Cambridge U Pr.

Arnold, Dean E., jt. auth. see Neuenswander, Helen L.

Arnold, Denis. Bach. (Past Masters Ser.). 1984. pap. 3.95 (ISBN 0-19-287554-X). Oxford U Pr.

--Bach. (Past Masters Ser.). (Illus.). 1984. 12.95x (ISBN 0-19-287555-8). Oxford U Pr.

--The Baroque Operatic Arias, Book 1: Gionabbi Bononcini; Arias from the Vienna Opera. Ford, Anthony, ed. 1971. 13.10x (ISBN 0-19-713412-2). Oxford U Pr.

--Giovanni Gabrieli & the High Renaissance. (Illus.). 1979. text ed. 69.00x (ISBN 0-19-315232-0); pap. 12.95x (ISBN 0-19-315247-9). Oxford U Pr.

--Monteverdi. (Master Musicians: No. M153). (Illus.). 1975. pap. 7.95 (ISBN 0-8226-0716-6). Littlefield.

--Monteverdi. rev. ed. (The Master Musicians Ser.). 224p. 1975. 13.50x (ISBN 0-460-03155-4, Pub. by J. M. Dent England). Biblio Dist.

--Monteverdi Church Music. LC 81-71298. (BBC Music Guides Ser.). 64p. (Orig.). 1983. pap. 4.95 (ISBN 0-295-95923-1). U of Wash Pr.

--Monteverdi Madrigals. LC 75-80511. (BBC Music Guides Ser.: No. 7). (Illus.). 61p. 1969. pap. 4.95 (ISBN 0-295-95021-8, BBC7). U of Wash Pr.

Arnold, Denis, pref. by. The New Oxford Companion to Music, 2 vols. (Illus.). 1983. Set. 95.00x (ISBN 0-19-311316-3). Oxford U Pr.

Arnold, Denis, ed. Ten Venetian Motets. 1981. text ed. 10.75x (ISBN 0-19-353035-X). Oxford U Pr.

Arnold, Denis & Fortune, Nigel, eds. Beethoven Reader. LC 77-139374. (Illus.). 1971. 25.00x (ISBN 0-393-02149-1). Norton.

--The New Monteverdi Companion. rev. ed. LC 85-6845. (Illus.). 386p. 1985. 39.95 (ISBN 0-571-13148-4); pap. 19.95 (ISBN 0-571-13357-6). Faber & Faber.

--The New Monteverdi Companion. LC 85-6845. (Illus.). 386p. 1985. 39.95 (ISBN 0-571-13148-4); pap. 19.95 (ISBN 0-571-13357-6). Faber & Faber.

Arnold, Denis, ed. see Lassus, Orlandus.

Arnold, Denis, ed. see Marenzio, Luca.

Arnold, Denis, et al. The New Grove Italian Baroque Masters. Sadie, Stanley, ed. (New Grove Composer Biography Ser.). 1984. 17.95 (ISBN 0-393-01690-0); pap. 9.95 (ISBN 0-393-30094-3). Norton.

Arnold, Denis V. The Management of the Information Department. 144p. 1976. 20.00x (ISBN 0-233-96652-8, 05767-3, Pub. by Gower Pub Co England). Lexington Bks.

Arnold, Dieter. The Temple of Mentuhotep at Dier El Bahari. (Publications of the Metropolitan Museum of Art Egyptian Expedition: Vol. XXI). (Illus.). 1979. 60.00 (ISBN 0-87099-163-9). Metro Mus Art.

Arnold, Don E. Legal Considerations in the Administration of Public School Physical Education & Athletic Programs. 372p. 1983. 33.75x (ISBN 0-398-04518-6). C C Thomas.

Arnold, Dorothy M. Where is the Light. 244p. 32.00x (ISBN 0-85335-236-4, Pub. by W Maclellan Scotland). State Mutual Bk.

Arnold, Douglas R. Congress & the Bureaucracy: A Theory of Influence. LC 78-65493. (Sudies in Political Science: No. 28). (Illus.). 250p. 1980. 31.00x (ISBN 0-300-02345-6, Y-367); pap. 7.95x (ISBN 0-300-02592-0). Yale U Pr.

Arnold, Duane W. & Fry, C. George. The Way, the Truth, & the Life: An Introduction to Lutheran Christianity. (Illus.). 204p. (Orig.). 1982. pap. 9.95 (ISBN 0-8010-0189-7). Baker Bk.

Arnold, E. Pearls of the Faith: Islam's Rosary. pap. 3.25x (ISBN 0-87902-044-X). Orientalia.

Arnold, E. V. Vedic Metre in Its Historical Development. 1967. Repr. 25.00 (ISBN 0-89684-338-6). Orient Bk Dist.

Arnold, E. Vernon. Roman Stoicism: Being Lectures. Repr. of 1911 ed. 35.00 (ISBN 0-8274-4331-5). R West.

Arnold, Eberhard. Children's Education in Community: The Basis of Bruderhof Education. Mow, Merrill, ed. LC 76-27728. 1976. pap. 3.25 (ISBN 0-87486-164-0). Plough.

--The Early Anabaptists. 1984. pap. 2.95 (ISBN 0-87486-192-6). Plough.

--Early Christians: After the Death of the Apostles. 1979. pap. 8.95 (ISBN 0-8010-0142-0). Baker Bk.

--Early Christians: After the Death of the Apostles. LC 70-115839. (Illus.). 1970. 13.95 (ISBN 0-87486-110-1); pap. 8.95 (ISBN 0-686-66330-6). Plough.

--Eberhard Arnold: A Testimony to the Church Community from His Life & Writings. 2nd ed. LC 73-11605. 107p. 1973. 3.95 (ISBN 0-87486-112-8). Plough.

--Foundation & Orders of Sannerz & the Rhon Bruderhof: Introductory History: The Basis for Our Orders, Vol. 1. LC 76-5856. 1976. pap. 2.50 (ISBN 0-87486-162-4). Plough.

--Gemeinsames Leben und Kindererziehung: Grundlagen Der Bruderhoferziehung. Mow, Merrill, ed. LC 76-56452. 60p. (Ger.). 1977. pap. 3.25 (ISBN 0-87486-165-9). Plough.

--God's Revolution: The Witness of Eberhard Arnold. Yoder, John H., ed. Hutterian Society of Brothers, tr. LC 83-62952. 230p. 1984. pap. 8.95 (ISBN 0-8091-2609-5, Pub. by Paulist Pr). Plough.

--Innenland: Ein Wegweiser In Die Seele Der Bibel und In Den Kampf Um Die Wirklichkeit. 492p. (Ger.). 1936. 12.95 (ISBN 0-87486-150-0). Plough.

--Inner Land: A Guide into the Heart & Soul of the Bible. LC 74-30356. 608p. 1976. 12.95 (ISBN 0-87486-152-7). Plough.

--The Inner Land, Vol. 1: The Inner Life. LC 74-18434. 1975. postpaid 3.50 (ISBN 0-87486-153-5). Plough.

--The Inner Land, Vol. 2: The Struggle of the Conscience. LC 75-1335. 1975. 3.50 (ISBN 0-87486-154-3). Plough.

--The Inner Land, Vol. 3: The Experience of God. LC 75-9720. 1975. 3.50 (ISBN 0-87486-155-1). Plough.

--The Inner Land, Vol. 4: Light & Fire & the Holy Spirit. LC 75-16303. 1975. 3.50 (ISBN 0-87486-156-X). Plough.

--The Inner Land, Vol. 5: The Living Word. LC 75-33241. 1975. 3.50 (ISBN 0-87486-157-8). Plough.

--Living Churches: The Essence of Their Life - Love to Christ & Love to the Brothers, Vol. 1. LC 73-21273. 1974. pap. 2.50 (ISBN 0-87486-116-0). Plough.

--Living Churches: The Essence of Their Life - the Meaning & Power of Prayer Life, Vol. 2. LC 75-42829. 1976. pap. 2.50 (ISBN 0-87486-159-4). Plough.

--Love & Marriage in the Spirit. LC 64-24321. 1965. 6.95 (ISBN 0-87486-103-9). Plough.

--Salt & Light: Talks & Writings of the Sermon on the Mount. 1977. pap. 4.95 (ISBN 0-87486-170-5). Plough.

--Salt & Light: Talks & Writings on the Sermon on the Mount. LC 67-18009. 1967. 7.95 (ISBN 0-87486-105-5). Plough.

--Sendbrief from the Alm Bruderhof to the Rhoen Bruderhof. LC 74-23145. 1974. pap. 2.50 (ISBN 0-87486-148-9). Plough.

--Why We Live in Community. 1976. pap. 1.50 (ISBN 0-87486-168-3). Plough.

Arnold, Eberhard & Arnold, Emmy. Seeking for the Kingdom of God: Origins of the Bruderhof Communities. LC 74-6317. 200p. 1974. 6.50 (ISBN 0-87486-133-0). Plough.

Arnold, Eberhard, et al. Else Von Hollander. LC 72-96191. 1973. 4.50 (ISBN 0-87486-111-X). Plough.

--When the Time Was Fulfilled: Talks & Writings on Advent & Christmas. LC 65-17599. 1965. 6.95 (ISBN 0-87486-104-7). Plough.

--The Heavens Are Opened. LC 73-20715. (Illus.). 190p. 1974. 7.95 (ISBN 0-87486-113-6). Plough.

Arnold, Edmund C. Arnold's Ancient Axioms: Typography for Publications Editors. (Illus., Orig.). 1978. pap. 12.50 (ISBN 0-931368-02-2). Ragan Comm.

--Designing the Total Newspaper. LC 80-8788. (Illus.). 320p. 1981. 25.00i (ISBN 0-06-014836-5, HarpT). Har-Row.

--Editing the Organizational Publication. LC 82-60043. (Communications Library). 284p. (Orig.). 1982. pap. 25.00 (ISBN 0-931368-09-X); pap. text ed. 18.75 (ISBN 0-686-82102-5). Ragan Comm.

--F. F. & B.: Producing Flyers, Folders & Brochures Producing. 64p. (Orig.). 1984. pap. 20.00 (ISBN 0-931368-16-2). Ragan Comm.

--Modern Newspaper Design. LC 69-15294. (Illus.). 1969. 13.95i (ISBN 0-06-030241-0, HarpT). Har-Row.

--Student Journalist & Editing the Yearbook. LC 72-94929. (YA) (gr. 7-12). 1973. PLB 9.66 (ISBN 0-8239-0279-X). Rosen Group.

Arnold, Edmund C. & Krieghbaum, Hillier. Handbook of Student Journalism: A Guide for Staff & Advisors. LC 75-27047. 335p. 1976. 28.50x (ISBN 0-8147-0557-X). NYU Pr.

Arnold, Edward, ed. see Hitopadesa.

Arnold, Edward V. Rigveda. LC 73-139172. (Popular Studies in Mythology, Romance & Folklore: No. 9). Repr. of 1900 ed. 5.50 (ISBN 0-404-53509-7). AMS Pr.

--Roman Stoicism. facsimile ed. LC 76-169750. (Select Bibliographies Reprint Ser). Repr. of 1911 ed. 27.50 (ISBN 0-8369-5970-1). Ayer Co Pubs.

--Roman Stoicism. LC 76-169750. 468p. Repr. of 1911 ed. 24.00x (ISBN 0-8290-0494-7). Irvington.

Arnold, Edwin. Light of Asia. LC 79-4436. 1969. pap. 4.50 (ISBN 0-8356-0405-5, Quest). Theos Pub Hse.

--The Light of Asia or, the Great Renunciation (Mahabhinishkramana) Being the Life & Teaching of Gautama, Prince of India, Founder of Buddhism. x, 176p. 1972. pap. 5.00 (ISBN 0-7100-7006-3). Routledge & Kegan.

--The Light of Asia: The Life & Teaching of Gautama Buddha. xi, 238p. 1977. 5.00 (ISBN 0-938998-17-X). Theosophy.

--Poets of Greece. LC 70-39680. (Essay Index Reprint Ser.). Repr. of 1869 ed. 16.00 (ISBN 0-8369-2738-9). Ayer Co Pubs.

--Song Celestial. 1971. pap. 1.50 (ISBN 0-8356-0418-7, Quest). Theos Pub Hse.

--Wandering Words. LC 75-39660. (Essay Index Reprint Ser.). (Illus.). Repr. of 1894 ed. 28.00 (ISBN 0-8369-2739-7). Ayer Co Pubs.

Arnold, Edwin, tr. The Light of Asia & the Indian Song of Songs: Gita Govinda. 1949. pap. 2.00 (ISBN 0-88253-115-8). Ind-US Inc.

Arnold, Edwin, tr. from Sanskrit. Song Celestial: Bhagavad-Gita. 1977. 2.95 (ISBN 0-87612-210-1). Self Realization.

Arnold, Edwin, tr. The Song Celestial or Bhaggvad-Gita: From the Mahabharata, Being a Discourse Between Arjuna, Prince of India, & the Supreme Being Under the Form of Krishna. 1967. pap. 5.00 (ISBN 0-7100-6268-0). Routledge & Kegan.

Arnold, Edwin L. Lepidus the Centurion: A Roman of Today. Reginald, R. & Melville, Douglas, eds. LC 77-84196. (Lost Race & Adult Fantasy Ser.). 1978. Repr. of 1901 ed. lib. bdg. 26.50x (ISBN 0-405-10954-7). Ayer Co Pubs.

--Lieut. Gulliver Jones: His Vacation. LC 74-15947. (Science Fiction Ser). 304p. 1975. Repr. 23.50x (ISBN 0-405-06273-7). Ayer Co Pubs.

--Phra the Phoenician. (Forgotten Fantasy Library: Vol. 11). (Illus.). 1977. pap. 4.95 (ISBN 0-87877-110-7, F-110). Newcastle Pub.

--The Wonderful Adventures of Phra the Phoenician. Reginald, R. & Menville, Douglas, eds. LC 80-19173. (Newcastle Forgotten Fantasy Library Ser.: Vol. 11). 329p. 1980. Repr. of 1977 ed. lib. bdg. 14.95x (ISBN 0-89370-510-1). Borgo Pr.

Arnold, Edwin P. Gulliver of Mars. 1976. lib. bdg. 12.95x (ISBN 0-89968-173-5). Lightyear.

--Phra the Phoenician. 1976. lib. bdg. 12.95x (ISBN 0-89968-174-3). Lightyear.

Arnold, Edwin T., ed. see Perry, Benjamin F.

Arnold, Elliot. The Commandos. 304p. pap. 2.75 (ISBN 0-8439-2009-2, Kable Bks). Dorchester Pub Co.

Arnold, Elliott. Blood Brother. LC 78-26788. x, 454p. 1979. pap. 8.95 (ISBN 0-8032-5901-8, BB 706, Bison). U of Nebr Pr.

--The Time of the Gringo. 626p. Repr. of 1970 ed. lib. bdg. 23.95x (ISBN 0-88411-180-6, Pub. by Aeonian Pr). Amereon Ltd.

Arnold, Emily. A Craving. 256p. 1982. pap. 2.95 (ISBN 0-380-79442-X, 79442, Bard). Avon.

--Life Drawing. 1986. 15.95 (ISBN 0-318-11921-8). Delacorte.

Arnold, Emmy. Gegen Den Strom. 200p. (Ger.). 1983. pap. 4.95 (ISBN 3-87067-206-4, Pub. by Brendow-Verlag, West Germany). Plough.

--Torches Together: The Beginning & Early Years of the Bruderhof Communities. LC 63-23426. 1971. 8.95 (ISBN 0-87486-109-8). Plough.

--Torches Together: The Beginning & Early Years of the Bruderhof Communities. Society of Brothers, tr. from Ger. (Illus.). 1976. pap. 4.95 (ISBN 0-87486-171-3). Plough.

Arnold, Emmy, jt. auth. see Arnold, Eberhard.

Arnold, Emmy, ed. Inner Words for Every Day of the Year. LC 77-164915. 1963. 3.50 (ISBN 0-87486-101-2). Plough.

Arnold, Emmy. Ein Inneres Wort Fur Jeden Tag Des Jahres. LC 76-10987. 192p. 1976. 3.50 (ISBN 0-87486-166-7). Plough.

Arnold, Eric & Loeb, Jeff. Lights Out! Kids Talk about Summer Camp. (Illus.). (gr. 3 up). 1985. 13.95 (ISBN 0-316-05184-5); pap. 4.95 (ISBN 0-317-29254-4). Little.

Arnold, Eugene L., ed. Helping Parents Help Their Children. LC 77-24520. 1978. 27.50 (ISBN 0-87630-146-4). Brunner-Mazel.

--Parents, Children & Change. (Illus.). 224p. 1984. 21.00x (ISBN 0-669-09567-2); pap. text ed. 9.95x (ISBN 0-669-09822-1). Lexington Bks.

Arnold, Eunice. Teach Yourself Torchon Lace: Six Basic Lessons in Bobbin Lace with Workcards. 1980. 9.95 (ISBN 0-686-27276-5). Robin & Russ.

Arnold, Eve. Flashback! The 50's. LC 78-54901. (Illus.). 1978. 12.95 (ISBN 0-394-50043-1). Knopf.

--In America. LC 83-48023. 1983. 35.00 (ISBN 0-394-52235-4). Knopf.

--In China. LC 80-7626. (Illus.). 204p. 1980. 40.00 (ISBN 0-394-50901-3). Knopf.

Arnold, Eve, et al. Portrait of a Film: The Making of "White Nights". (Illus.). 176p. 1985. 35.00 (ISBN 0-8109-1484-0). Abrams.

Arnold, F. C. Gesammelte Lichenologische Schriften. Incl. Vol. 3. Lichenologische Ausfluege in Tirol, 30 pts. & register. 80.00 (ISBN 3-7682-0707-2). 1971. 70.00. Lubrecht & Cramer.

Arnold, F. T. Art of Accompaniment from a Thorough-Bass, 2 Vols. (Illus.). Set. 29.00 (ISBN 0-8446-1551-X). Peter Smith.

Arnold, Francena. Road Winds On. 1970. pap. 3.95 (ISBN 0-8024-0066-3). Moody.

--Straight Down a Crooked Lane. (gr. 9-12). 1959. pap. 3.95 (ISBN 0-8024-0041-8). Moody.

Arnold, Francena H. Brother Beloved. 1967. pap. 3.95 (ISBN 0-8024-0050-7). Moody.

--Not My Will. 1946. pap. 3.95 (ISBN 0-8024-3805-9). Moody.

--Then Am I Strong. 1969. pap. 3.95 (ISBN 0-8024-0060-4). Moody.

--Three Shall Be One. (Orig.). (gr. 9-12). 1966. pap. 3.95 (ISBN 0-8024-0085-X). Moody.

Arnold, Franck T. Art of Accompaniment from a Thorough-Bass: As Practised in the 17th & 18th Centuries, 2 Vols. 1965. 7.50 ea.; Vol. 1. (ISBN 0-486-21442-7). Dover.

Arnold, Frazer see Carroll, John M.

Arnold, Fred & Cochrane, Susan H. Economic Motivation vs. City Lights: Testing Hypotheses about Inter-Changwat Migration in Thailand. (Working Paper: No. 416). 41p. 1980. pap. 3.00 (ISBN 0-686-39756-8, WP-0416). World Bank.

Arnold, Fred & Shah, Nasra M., eds. Asian Labor Migration: Pipeline to the Middle East. 275p. 1985. pap. 22.50 (ISBN 0-8133-7084-1). Westview.

Arnold, Fred, et al. The Value of Children: A Cross-National Study. Incl. Vol. 1. Introduction & Comparative Analysis. Arnold, Fred, et al. 120p. pap. 5.00x (ISBN 0-8248-0383-3); Vol. 2. Philippines. Bulatao, Rodolfo A. 230p. pap. 5.00x (ISBN 0-8248-0384-1); Vol. 3. Hawaii. Arnold, Fred & Fawcett, James T. 160p. pap. 5.00x (ISBN 0-8248-0382-5). 1975. pap. (Eastwest Ctr). UH Pr.

Arnold, Frederick. Turning Points in Life. LC 72-4480. (Essay Index Reprint Ser.). Repr. of 1873 ed. 22.00 (ISBN 0-8369-2934-9). Ayer Co Pubs.

Arnold, Frederick C. College English: A Silent Way Approach. 214p. 1981. pap. 7.50 (ISBN 0-933704-19-4). Dawn Pr.

--Stepping into College English. 264p. 1984. pap. 9.50 (ISBN 0-933704-48-8). Dawn Pr.

Arnold, Fredric. Door Knob Five Two. (Illus.). 274p. 1984. 14.95 (ISBN 0-914961-00-4). Maxwell Pub Co.

--Kohn's War. 1985. pap. 3.95 (ISBN 0-451-13997-6, Sig). NAL.

Arnold, G. H., jt. ed. see Prins, W. H.

Arnold, G. W. & Dudzinski, M. L. Ethology of Free Ranging Domestic Animals. (Developments in Animal & Veterinary Sciences Ser.: Vol. 2). 198p. 1979. 57.50 (ISBN 0-444-41700-1). Elsevier.

Arnold, Gary J. The Washington Cladden Collection: An Inventory to the Microfilm Edition. 235p. 1972. 3.00 (ISBN 0-318-03209-0). Ohio Hist Soc.

Arnold, Genevieve. Progressive Sound Game. 1973. text ed. 3.00 (ISBN 0-686-09405-0). Expression.

--Sound & Articulation Game. 1973. text ed. 3.00 (ISBN 0-686-09406-9). Expression.

--Sound Ladder Game. 1973. text ed. 3.00 (ISBN 0-686-09404-2). Expression.

--Speech-O, a Phonetic Game. 1973. text ed. 4.25 (ISBN 0-686-09407-7). Expression.

Arnold, Glen, jt. auth. see Ziefe, Helmut.

Arnold, Godfrey E., jt. auth. see Luchsinger, Richard.

Arnold, Grant. Creative Lithography & How to Do It. (Illus.). 1941. pap. 4.95 (ISBN 0-486-21208-4). Dover.

--Creative Lithography & How to Do It. (Illus.). 12.50 (ISBN 0-8446-1552-8). Peter Smith.

Arnold, Guy. Aid in Africa. 250p. 1979. 29.50 (ISBN 0-89397-062-X). Nichols Pub.

--Coal. (Energy Today Ser.). (Illus.). 32p. (gr. 1-3). 1985. lib. bdg. 9.40 (ISBN 0-531-03486-0). Watts.

--Datelines of World History. (Illus.). 96p. (gr. 5up). PLB 12.90 (ISBN 0-531-09212-7). Watts.

--Modern Kenya. (Illus.). 156p. (Orig.). 1981. pap. text ed. 10.95x (ISBN 0-582-64287-6). Longman.

--The Unions. 224p. 1981. 25.00 (ISBN 0-241-10107-7, Pub. by Hamish Hamilton England). David & Charles.

Arnold, Guy & Weiss, Ruth. Strategic Highways of Africa. LC 76-53953. (Illus.). 1977. 20.00 (ISBN 0-312-76431-6). St Martin.

Arnold, H. J. Photographer of the World: A Biography of Herbert Ponting. LC 75-156270. (Illus.). 176p. 1972. 18.50 (ISBN 0-8386-7959-5). Fairleigh Dickinson.

Arnold, H. J., jt. ed. see Wefelscheid, H.

Arnold, Harry L. Poisonous Plants of Hawaii. LC 68-15017. (Illus.). (YA) (gr. 9 up). 1968. 5.95 (ISBN 0-8048-0474-5). C E Tuttle.

Arnold, Harry L., Jr. & Fasal, Paul. Leprosy: Diagnosis & Management. 2nd ed. (Illus.). 108p. 1973. photocopy ed. 19.50x (ISBN 0-398-02681-5). C C Thomas.

Arnold, Harry L., Jr., jt. auth. see Domonkos, Anthony N.

Arnold Harvey Associates. Anatomy of an Art Auction. LC 75-185400. 84p. 1972. pap. 2.98 (ISBN 0-913014-01-X). A Harvey.

Arnold, Heini. Freedom from Sinful Thoughts: Christ Alone Breaks the Curse. LC 73-20199. 130p. 1973. 3.50 (ISBN 0-87486-115-2). Plough.

--Freiheit Von Gedankensunden Nur Christus Bricht Den Fluch. LC 73-20198. 118p. (Ger.). 1973. text ed. 3.50 (ISBN 0-317-07744-9). Plough.

--In the Image of God: Marriage & Chastity in Christian Life. LC 76-53542. 1977. pap. 3.50 (ISBN 0-87486-169-1). Plough.

--Man, the Image of God & Modern Psychology. 14p. 1973. pap. 1.25 (ISBN 0-87486-176-4). Plough.

Arnold, Heini & Arnold, Annemarie. Living in Community: A Way to True Brotherhood. 26p. 1974. pap. 1.50 (ISBN 0-87486-121-7). Plough.

--The Purity of Childhood. 10p. 1974. pap. 1.25 (ISBN 0-87486-118-7). Plough.

Arnold, Heini & Blough, Dwight. Christmas Night, O Night of Nights. 1976. pap. 1.25 (ISBN 0-87486-120-9). Plough.

Arnold, Helen K. An Emily Dickinson Year Book. 1978. lib. bdg. 20.00 (ISBN 0-8492-3430-1). R West.

Arnold, Henri & Lee, Bob. Jumble Book, No. 1. 128p. 1984. pap. 1.95 (ISBN 0-425-05982-0). Berkley Pub.

--Jumble Book, No. 7. 128p. 1984. pap. 2.25 (ISBN 0-425-07034-4). Berkley Pub.

--Jumble Book, No. 24. 128p. 1983. Berkley Pub.

--Jumble Book, No. 30. 128p. 1984. pap. 2.25 (ISBN 0-425-07198-7). Berkley Pub.

--Jumble Book, No. 31. 128p. 1984. pap. 2.25 (ISBN 0-425-07391-2). Berkley Pub.

--Jumble: That Scrambled Word Game, No. 10. (Orig.). 1976. pap. 1.75 (ISBN 0-451-11683-6, AE1683, Sig). NAL.

--Jumble: That Scrambled Word Game, No. 11. (Orig.). 1977. pap. 1.50 (ISBN 0-451-11588-0, AW1588, Sig). NAL.

--Jumble: That Scrambled Word Game, No. 13. (Orig.). 1978. pap. 1.50 (ISBN 0-451-09831-5, W9831, Sig). NAL.

--Jumble: That Scrambled Word Game, No. 15. (Orig.). 1980. pap. 1.50 (ISBN 0-451-11322-5, Sig). NAL.

--Jumble: That Scrambled Word Game, No. 16. 128p. (Orig.). 1980. pap. 1.75 (ISBN 0-451-11331-4, AE1331, Sig). NAL.

--Jumble: That Scrambled Word Game, No. 18. (Orig.). 1981. pap. 1.50 (ISBN 0-451-09740-8, W9240, Sig). NAL.

--Jumble: That Scrambled Word Game, No. 20. 1981. pap. 1.95 (ISBN 0-451-12319-0, AJ2319, Sig). NAL.

--Jumble: That Scrambled Word Game, No. 19. (Orig.). 1981. pap. 1.95 (ISBN 0-451-12170-8, AJ2170, Sig). NAL.

Arnold, Henri & Lee, Bob, eds. Jumble: That Scrambled Word Game, No. 2. (Orig.). pap. 1.25 (ISBN 0-451-08378-4, Y8378, Sig). NAL.

Arnold, Henry H. Global Mission. LC 70-169404. (Literature & History of Aviation Ser). 1972. Repr. of 1949 ed. 34.00 (ISBN 0-405-03750-3). Ayer Co Pubs.

Arnold, Herbert, tr. see Scheurig, Bodo.

Arnold, Horace L. The Complete Cost-Keeper: Some Original Systems of Shop Cost-Keeping or Factory Accounting Together with an Exposition of the Advantages of Account Keeping by Means of Cards. Chandler, Alfred D., ed. LC 79-7530. (History of Management Thought & Practice Ser.). 1980. Repr. of 1901 ed. lib. bdg. 37.00x (ISBN 0-405-12313-2). Ayer Co Pubs.

Arnold, Horace L. & Faurote, Fay L. Ford Methods & the Ford Shops. LC 72-5029. (Technology & Society Ser.). (Illus.). 450p. 1972. Repr. of 1915 ed. 38.50 (ISBN 0-405-04682-0). Ayer Co Pubs.

Arnold, Howard P. European Mosaic. LC 72-39709. (Essay Index Reprint Ser.). Repr. of 1864 ed. 18.00 (ISBN 0-8369-2740-0). Ayer Co Pubs.

--The Washington Medal. 1976. 3.00 (ISBN 0-89073-040-7). Boston Public Lib.

Arnold, Hugh. Stained Glass of the Middle Ages in England & France. LC 83-45692. (Illus.). Repr. of 1939 ed. 84.50 (ISBN 0-404-20008-7). AMS Pr.

Arnold, Hugh J., jt. auth. see Feldman, Daniel.

Arnold, Isaac N. History of Abraham Lincoln: And Overthrow of Slavery. facs. ed. LC 72-154069. (Black Heritage Library Collection). 1866. 33.50 (ISBN 0-8369-8780-2). Ayer Co Pubs.

--The Life of Benedict Arnold. Kohn, Richard H., ed. LC 78-22373. (American Military Experience Ser.). 1979. Repr. of 1880 ed. lib. bdg. 30.50x (ISBN 0-405-11851-1). Ayer Co Pubs.

Arnold, J., jt. auth. see Leben, J.

Arnold, J., et al, eds. Topics in Management Accounting. 300p. 1981. text ed. 38.50x (ISBN 0-86003-508-5, Pub. by Allan Pubs England); pap. text ed. 19.50x (ISBN 0-86003-609-X). Humanities.

Arnold, J. Barto & Weddle, Robert. The Nautical Archeology of Padre Island: The Spanish Shipwrecks of 1554. (Studies in Archeology Ser.). 1978. 68.00 (ISBN 0-12-063650-6). Acad Pr.

Arnold, J. C., jt. auth. see Milton, J. S.

Arnold, J. M. Loligo Pealei. LC 74-77352. 1974. pap. 6.00x (ISBN 0-685-52859-6). Marine Bio.

Arnold, James. All Drawn by Horses. LC 79-51087. (Illus.). 1985. 24.00 (ISBN 0-7153-7682-9). David & Charles.

--Farm Waggons & Carts. LC 76-57081. 1977. 18.95 (ISBN 0-7153-7330-7). David & Charles.

Arnold, James N. Vital Record of Cranston, Johnston & North Providence, Rhode Island. (Vital Record of Rhode Island Ser.: Vol. 2, Pts. 2, 3 & 4). 138p. 1983. Repr. of 1892 ed. lib. bdg. 14.00 (ISBN 0-912606-12-6). Hunterdon Hse.

--Vital Record of Warwick, Rhode Island. (Vital Record of Rhode Island Ser.: Vol. 1, Pt. 1). 234p. 1983. Repr. of 1891 ed. lib. bdg. 16.00 (ISBN 0-912606-11-8). Hunterdon Hse.

Arnold, James T. Simplified Digital Automation with Microprocessors. LC 78-51242. 1979. 44.50 (ISBN 0-12-063750-2). Acad Pr.

Arnold, Janet. A Handbook of Costume. (Illus.). 336p. (Orig.). 1980. pap. text ed. 14.95x (ISBN 0-87599-231-5). S G Phillips.

--Patterns of Fashion: Eighteen Sixty to Nineteen Forty, Vol. 2. 3rd rev. ed. LC 76-189820. (Illus.). 88p. 1977. text ed. 15.00x (ISBN 0-89676-027-8). Drama Bk.

--Patterns of Fashion: Fifteen Sixty to Sixteen Twenty. 1985. text ed. 20.00x (ISBN 0-89676-083-9). Drama Bk.

--Patterns of Fashion: Sixteen Sixty to Eighteen Sixty, Vol. 1. 3rd rev. ed. LC 76-189820. (Illus.). 76p. 1977. text ed. 15.00x (ISBN 0-89676-026-X). Drama Bk.

Arnold, Jay. A Chord Guide to Pop Music. 1967. pap. 6.95 (ISBN 0-8256-4167-5). Music Sales.

Arnold, Jerry & Holder, William. Economic Impact of Statement 52. 1985. price not set. Finan Exec.

Arnold, Jerry L. & Diamond, Michael A. The Market for Compilation, Review & Audit Services. (Auditing Research Monographs: No. 4). 111p. 1981. pap. 9.00 (ISBN 0-686-84303-7). Am Inst CPA.

Arnold, Jim, jt. auth. see Leben, Joe.

Arnold, Joan, ed. see Plaskow, Judith.

Arnold, Joan H. & Buschman-Gemma, Penelope R. A Child Dies: A Portrait of Family Grief. LC 83-7132. 184p. 1983. 26.00 (ISBN 0-89443-816-6). Aspen Systems.

Arnold, John & Harmer, Jeremy. Advanced Writing Skills. (English As a Second Language Bk.). 1978. pap. text ed. 7.50x (ISBN 0-582-55481-0). Longman.

Arnold, John, jt. auth. see Waterson, D. B.

Arnold, John D. The Art of Decision-Making: Seven Steps to Achieving More Effective Results. Orig. Title: Make up Your Mind. 1980. pap. 8.95 (ISBN 0-8144-7537-X). AMACOM.

--Make up Your Mind! The Seven Building Blocks to Better Decisions. LC 78-16253. (Illus.). 1979. 13.95 (ISBN 0-8144-5479-8). AMACOM.

--Trading Up: A Career Guide. LC 82-45554. 160p. 1984. pap. 7.95 (ISBN 0-385-18390-9, Anchor Pr). Doubleday.

Arnold, John D. & Tompkins, Bert. How to Make the Right Decisions. 180p. 1982. pap. 5.95 (ISBN 0-915134-82-9). Mott Media.

Arnold, John D. & Tompkins, Burt. How to Make the Right Decisions. 192p. 1985. pap. 2.95 (ISBN 0-345-32558-3). Ballantine.

Arnold, Joseph L. Maryland: Old Line to New Prosperity. 256p. 1985. 24.95 (ISBN 0-89781-147-X). Windsor Pubns Inc.

--The New Deal in the Suburbs: A History of the Greenbelt Town Program, 1935-1954. LC 74-141494. 286p. 1971. 10.00 (ISBN 0-8142-0153-9). Ohio St U Pr.

Arnold, Jud. The Illustrated Encyclopedia of House Plants. (Illus.). 224p. 1983. pap. 11.95 (ISBN 0-396-08251-3). Dodd.

Arnold, Judd. A Grace Peculiar: Ben Jonson's Cavalier Heroes. (Penn State Studies: No. 35). 1972. pap. text ed. 4.95 (ISBN 0-271-00518-1). Pa St U Pr.

Arnold, Judith M., jt. auth. see Jacob, Diane B.

Arnold, Julean & Myers, Ramon H. Commerical Handbook of China, 2 vols. LC 78-24800. (Modern Chinese Economy Ser.: Vol. 16). (Illus.). 1979. Set. lib. bdg. 133.00 (ISBN 0-8240-4264-6). Garland Pub.

Arnold, Julius. Student's Guide to Basic French. 2nd ed. 184p. (gr. 9-11). 1980. pap. text ed. 7.50x (ISBN 0-88334-021-6). Ind Sch Pr.

Arnold, Katrin. Anna Joins in. 28p. (gr. 6 up). 1983. text ed. 9.95 (ISBN 0-687-01530-8). Abingdon.

Arnold, Kenneth J., jt. auth. see Beck, James V.

Arnold, Klaves, ed. Johannes Trithemius: In Praise of Scribes. Behrendt, Roland, tr. 125p. 1974. 7.50x (ISBN 0-87291-066-0). Coronado Pr.

Arnold, L. & Kotelenz, P., eds. Stochastic Space-Time Models & Limit Theories. (Mathematics & its Applications Ser.). 1985. lib. bdg. 44.00 (ISBN 90-277-2038-X, Pub. by Reidel Holland). Kluwer-Academic.

Arnold, L. & Lefever, R., eds. Stochastic Nonlinear Systems. (Springer Series in Synergetics: Vol. 8). (Illus.). 237p. 1981. 33.00 (ISBN 0-387-10713-4). Springer-Verlag.

Arnold, L., tr. see Hackmack, Adolf.

Arnold, L. E., ed. Preventing Adolescent Alienation: An Interprofessional Approach. LC 82-48532. 160p. 1983. 21.50x (ISBN 0-669-06269-3). Lexington Bks.

Arnold, L. Eugene & Estreicher, Donna G. Parent-Child Group Therapy: Building Self-Esteem in a Cognitive-Behavioral Group. LC 84-40723. 288p. 1985. 25.00x (ISBN 0-669-09934-1). Lexington Bks.

Arnold, Lee & Arnold, Allyn. Secondary Programs for the Gifted-Talented. 67p. 10.95 (ISBN 0-318-16020-X, 30). NSLTIGT.

Arnold, Lee E., Jr. Commercial-Investment Real Estate: Marketing & Management. Gerth, Dawn M., ed. LC 82-62949. (Illus.). 250p. text ed. 19.95 (ISBN 0-913652-53-9, BK 161). Realtors Natl.

Arnold, Linda. A Very Special Christmas Tree. (Stick-On Activity & Coloring Bks.). 16p. (gr. k-3). 1983. pap. 1.50 (ISBN 0-87239-685-1, 2365). Standard Pub.

Arnold, Lionel K. Introduction to Plastics. (Illus.). 1968. pap. 8.95x (ISBN 0-8138-1272-0). Iowa St U Pr.

Arnold, Lois B. Four Lives in Science: Women's Education in the Nineteenth Century. LC 83-42716. (Illus.). 192p. 1983. 14.95 (ISBN 0-8052-3865-4). Schocken.

--Preparing Young Children for Science: A Book of Activities. LC 79-26119. (Illus.). 128p. (Orig.). 1980. text ed. 11.95x (ISBN 0-8052-3740-2); pap. 6.95 (ISBN 0-8052-0641-8). Schocken.

Arnold, Ludwig. Stochastic Differential Equations: Theory & Applications. LC 73-22256. 228p. 1974. 48.50x (ISBN 0-471-03359-6, Pub. by Wiley-Interscience). Wiley.

Arnold, Luis. Frederic the Cat & the Spanish Idioms. (Books by Frederic the Cat). (Illus.). 60p. (Orig.). 1983. pap. 6.50 (ISBN 0-9610434-0-7). L Arnold.

--Gatto Federico El Proverbi Italiani, Vol. II. (Books by Frederic the Cat). (Illus.). 200p. (Orig.). 1983. pap. 6.50 (ISBN 0-9610434-1-5). L Arnold.

Arnold, Luis, ed. Flamenco Styling for the Latin American Dances. (Ballroom Dance Ser.). 1985. lib. bdg. 79.95 (ISBN 0-87700-871-X). Revisionist Pr.

Arnold, M. B. Feelings & Emotions: The Loyola Symposium. (Personality & Psychopathology Ser.: Vol. 7). 1970. 59.00 (ISBN 0-12-063550-X). Acad Pr.

Arnold, M. H. Agricultural Research for Development. 368p. 1976. 67.50 (ISBN 0-521-21051-8). Cambridge U Pr.

Arnold, M. H., ed. Agricultural Research for Development: The Hamulonge Contribution. LC 75-31400. pap. 93.80 (ISBN 0-317-26071-5, 2024411). Bks Demand UMI.

Arnold, Magda B. Memory & the Brain. 544p. 1983. text ed. 49.95 (ISBN 0-89859-290-9). L Erlbaum Assocs.

Arnold, Margaret. Profiles: Real Arkansas Characters. LC 80-65465. (Illus.). 47p. (Orig.). 1980. pap. 2.95 (ISBN 0-935304-16-9). August Hse.

Arnold, Margot. Affairs of State. 352p. 1983. pap. 3.50 (ISBN 0-449-12384-7, GM). Fawcett.
--The Cape Cod Caper. LC 79-90922. (Murder Mystery Ser.). 192p. 1982. pap. 2.50 (ISBN 0-86721-206-3). Jove Pubns.
--Death of a Voodoo Doll. 224p. (Orig.). 1982. pap. 2.50 (ISBN 0-86721-114-8). Jove Pubns.
--Death on the Dragon's Tongue. LC 82-80216. 224p. (Orig.). 1982. pap. 2.50 (ISBN 0-86721-150-4). Jove Pubns.
--Exit Actors, Dying. LC 79-65196. 176p. 1982. pap. 2.50 (ISBN 0-86721-181-4). Jove Pubns.
--Lament for a Lady Laird. LC 81-86251. 224p. (Orig.). 1982. pap. 2.50 (ISBN 0-86721-132-6). Jove Pubns.
--Love among the Allies. 320p. (Orig.). 1985. pap. 3.50 (ISBN 0-449-12685-4, GM). Fawcett.
--Zadok's Treasure. LC 80-80980. 192p. (Orig.). 1980. pap. 2.50 (ISBN 0-86721-228-4). Jove Pubns.
Arnold, Marilyn, ed. Willa Cather's Short Fiction. LC 83-13269. xvi, 198p. 1984. 22.95x (ISBN 0-8214-0721-X, 82-84903). Ohio U Pr.
Arnold, Mark, jt. ed. see Windling, Terry.
Arnold, Mark A., jt. auth. see Windling, Terri.
Arnold, Mark A., jt. ed. see Windling, Terri.
Arnold, Marti. Alaska, Uncle Jim & Me. Lesko, Marian, ed. (Illus.). 146p. (Orig.). (gr. 6 up). 1983. pap. 5.95 (ISBN 0-912683-00-7). Fireweed.
Arnold, Mary E. & Reed, Mabel. In the Land of the Grasshopper Song: Two Women in the Klamath River Indian Country in 1908-09. LC 80-12556. (Illus.). iv, 329p. 1980. 24.50x (ISBN 0-8032-1804-4); pap. 6.95 (ISBN 0-8032-6703-7, BB 740, Bison). U of Nebr Pr.
Arnold, Matthew. Arnold: Poems. (Penguin Poetry Library). 256p. 1985. pap. 4.95 (ISBN 0-14-058509-5). Penguin.
--Arnold: Selected Poems. Brown, E. K., ed. LC 51-6752. (Crofts Classics Ser.). 1951. pap. text ed. 3.95x (ISBN 0-88295-007-X). Harlan Davidson.
--Bitter Knowledge" & "Unconquerable Hope". Fryman, Erik, ed. LC 72-194436. 1966. lib. bdg. 15.00 (ISBN 0-8414-3077-2). Folcroft.
--Civilization in the United States, First & Last Impressions. 59.95 (ISBN 0-87968-874-2). Gordon Pr.
--The Complete Prose Works of Matthew Arnold, 11 vols. Super, R. H., ed. Incl. Vol. 1. On the Classical Tradition. 282p. 1960. 19.95x (ISBN 0-472-11651-7); Vol. 2. Democratic Education. 430p. 1962. 19.95x (ISBN 0-472-11652-5); Vol. 3. Lectures & Essays in Criticism. 586p. 1962. 19.95x (ISBN 0-472-11653-3); Vol. 4. Schools & Universities on the Continent. 446p. 1964. 19.95x (ISBN 0-472-11654-1); Vol. 5. Culture & Anarchy. 580p. 1965. 19.95x (ISBN 0-472-11655-X); Vol. 6. Dissent & Dogma. 624p. 1967. 19.95x (ISBN 0-472-11656-8); Vol. 7. God & the Bible. 604p. 1970. 19.95x (ISBN 0-472-11657-6); Vol. 8. Essays Religious & Mixed. 576p. 1972. 19.95x (ISBN 0-472-11658-4); Vol. 9. English Literature & Irish Politics. 1973. 19.95x (ISBN 0-472-11659-2); Vol. 10. Philistinism in England & America. 1974. 19.95x (ISBN 0-472-11660-6); Vol. 11. The Last Word. 1976. 19.95x (ISBN 0-472-11661-4). LC 60-5018. U of Mich Pr.
--Discourses in America. LC 76-131610. 1970. Repr. of 1896 ed. 25.00 (ISBN 0-403-00497-7). Scholarly.
--Essays in Criticism: Third Series. LC 74-13264. 1974. Repr. of 1910 ed. lib. bdg. 25.00 (ISBN 0-8414-2991-X). Folcroft.
--Four Essays on Life & Letters. Brown, E. K., ed. LC 47-4419. (Crofts Classics Ser.). 1947. pap. text ed. 1.25x (ISBN 0-88295-006-1). Harlan Davidson.
--God & the Bible: A Review of Objections to "Literature & Dogma". LC 75-129382. Repr. of 1875 ed. 15.00 (ISBN 0-404-00386-9). AMS Pr.
--God & the Bible: A Review of Objections to Literature & Dogma. 1973. Repr. of 1875 ed. 14.75 (ISBN 0-8274-1704-7). R West.
--John Keats in "Essays in Criticism". Second Series. Repr. 15.00 (ISBN 0-8274-2625-9). R West.
--Letters of Matthew Arnold, 1848-1888, 2 Vols. Russell, Goerge W., ed. LC 4-13997. 1969. Repr. Set. 59.00 (ISBN 0-403-00141-2). Scholarly.
--Literature & Dogma. Repr. of 1873 ed. lib. bdg. 20.00 (ISBN 0-8414-3076-4). Folcroft.
--Literature & Dogma. Livingston, James C., ed. LC 79-107032. (Milestones of Thought Ser). 1970. 8.50 (ISBN 0-8044-2008-4); pap. 3.45 (ISBN 0-8044-6011-6). Ungar.
--Literature & Dogma: An Essay Towards a Better Apprehension of the Bible. LC 78-126650. 1970. Repr. of 1883 ed. 15.00 (ISBN 0-404-00387-7). AMS Pr.
--Matthew Arnold & the Education of the New Order: A Selection of Arnold's Writings on Education. Smith, Peter & Summerfield, Geoffrey, eds. LC 69-10433. (Cambridge Texts & Studies in the History of Education). pap. 67.00 (ISBN 0-317-20802-0, 2024533). Bks Demand UMI.
--On the Study of Celtic Literature & Other Essays. 1976. 12.95x (ISBN 0-460-00458-1, Evman). Biblio Dist.
--On Translating Homer. LC 78-136411. (BCL Ser.: No. 2). Repr. of 1905 ed. 16.25 (ISBN 0-404-00388-5). AMS Pr.
--Poems. 1965. 12.95x (ISBN 0-460-00334-8, Evman). Biblio Dist.
--Poetical Works. Tinker, C. B. & Lowry, H. F., eds. (Standard Authors Ser). 1950. 35.00 (ISBN 0-19-254110-2). Oxford U Pr.
--The Poetical Works of Matthew Arnold. 1978. Repr. of 1893 ed. lib. bdg. 30.00 (ISBN 0-8495-0018-4). Arden Lib.
--Poetry & Criticism of Matthew Arnold. Culler, A. D., ed. LC 61-19991. (Riverside Editions). (YA) (gr. 9 up). 1961. pap. 6.50 (ISBN 0-395-05152-5, RivEd). HM.
--Selected Poems of Matthew Arnold. 1878. 15.00 (ISBN 0-932062-06-7). Sharon Hill.
--Selected Prose. Keating, P. J., ed. (Penguin Classics Ser.). 480p. 1971. pap. 6.95 (ISBN 0-14-043058-X). Penguin.
--Unpublished Letters of Matthew Arnold. LC 77-24248. 1977. Repr. of 1923 ed. lib. bdg. 17.00 (ISBN 0-8414-9490-8). Folcroft.
--The Works of Matthew Arnold, 15 vols. LC 72-113544. (BCL Ser.: No. 1). Repr. of 1904 ed. deluxe ed. 425.00. Set (ISBN 0-404-00450-4). AMS Pr.
--Works of Matthew Arnold, 15 Vols. LC 70-107157. 1970. Repr. of 1903 ed. Set. 395.00x (ISBN 0-403-00201-X); 40.00 ea. Scholarly.
Arnold, Matthew, ed. see Burke, Edmund.
Arnold, Mildred. Taking a Look at My Faith. 80p. 1982. pap. 5.95 (ISBN 0-8170-0966-3). Judson.
Arnold, Millard, ed. see Biko, Steve.
Arnold, Morris L. Soliloquies of Shakespeare: A Study in Technic. LC 78-58273. Repr. of 1911 ed. 19.50 (ISBN 0-404-00389-3). AMS Pr.
Arnold, Morris S. Unequal Laws unto a Savage Race: European Legal Traditions in Arkansas, 1686-1836. LC 84-168. (Illus.). 240p. 1985. 23.00 (ISBN 0-938626-33-7). U of Ark Pr.
Arnold, Norman R. & Frumker, Sanford C. Occlusal Treatment: Preventive & Corrective Occlusal Adjustment. LC 75-1306. (Illus.). 163p. 1976. text ed. 13.50 (ISBN 0-8121-0526-5). Lea & Febiger.
Arnold O. Beckman Conference in Clinical Chemistry, 1st & Young, Donald. Clinician & Chemist: The Relationship of the Laboratory to the Physician. LC 78-72880. 375p. 1979. 35.00 (ISBN 0-915274-08-6); members 25.00. Am Assn Clinical Chem.
Arnold O. Beckman Conference in Clinical Chemical. Human Nutrition: Clinical & Biochemical Aspects: Proceedings. Garry, Philip J., ed. LC 81-65736. 405p. 1981. 35.00 (ISBN 0-915274-15-9); members 25.00. Am Assn Clinical Chem.
Arnold, Oren. Aim for a Job in Cattle Ranching. LC 78-153810. (Aim High Vocational Guidance Ser.). (Illus.). (gr. 7 up). 1972. PLB 8.97 (ISBN 0-8239-0245-5). Rosen Group.
--Arnold's Sourcebook of Family Humor. LC 79-92503. 1972. 4.95 (ISBN 0-8254-2106-3). Kregel.
--A Boundless Privilege. LC 74-81628. 192p. 1974. 10.00 (ISBN 0-89052-007-0). Madrona Pr.
--Junior Saints: The Rich Rare Humor of Kids in Church. LC 75-12108. (Illus.). 1976. pap. 3.50 (ISBN 0-8254-2117-9). Kregel.
--Marvels of the U. S. Mint. LC 70-141860. (Illus.). (gr. 1 up). 1972. PLB 11.89 (ISBN 0-200-71798-7, 254701, AbS-J). Har-Row.
--Pancho Villa: The Mexican Centaur. LC 76-29143. 1979. 7.50 (ISBN 0-916620-06-9). Portals Pr.
--The Sacred Ninety Minutes: Popular History of the Service Club Movement. LC 75-15283. (Illus.). 1975. 10.00 (ISBN 0-916620-00-X). Portals Pr.
--Snappy Steeple Stories. LC 79-128150. (Church Humor Series). 1970. pap. 1.95 (ISBN 0-8254-2107-1). Kregel.
--Wit of the West. 1979. 2.95 (ISBN 0-685-59275-8). Eakin Pubns.
Arnold, Oren & Hale, John P. Hot Irons. LC 71-188637. 242p. 1972. Repr. of 1940 ed. lib. bdg. 19.50 (ISBN 0-8154-0416-6). Cooper Sq.
Arnold, Oren, ed. More Steeple Stories. LC 77-76437. (Church Humor Series). 1969. pap. 1.95 (ISBN 0-8254-2105-5). Kregel.
Arnold, Oren W. Thunder in the Southwest: Echoes from the Wild Frontier. LC 52-4324. pap. 61.50 (ISBN 0-317-28707-9, 2055508). Bks Demand UMI.
Arnold, P., et al, eds. Marker Proteins in Inflammation: Proceedings of the Second Symposium, Lyon, France, June 27-30, 1983, Vol. 2. LC 84-9462. (Illus.). xix, 687p. 1984. 98.00x (ISBN 3-11-009872-5). De Gruyter.
Arnold, Pauline & White, Percival. How We Named Our States. LC 65-24208. (Illus.). (gr. 5-9). 1965. 13.41 (ISBN 0-200-71911-4, 339010, AbS-J). Har-Row.
Arnold, Peter. Education, Physical Education & Personality Development. 1968. pap. text ed. 10.00x (ISBN 0-435-80035-3). Heinemann Ed.
--Meaning in Movement, Sport & Physical Education. LC 80-670037. 1980. text ed. 29.95x (ISBN 0-435-80033-7); pap. text ed. 15.95x (ISBN 0-435-80034-5). Heinemann Ed.
Arnold, Peter & Pendagast, Edward, Jr. Emergency Handbook: A First Aid Manual for Home & Travel. LC 81-11146. (Mosby Medical Library). 250p. 1982. pap. 5.95 (ISBN 0-452-25372-1, 0347-1). Mosby.
Arnold, Peter, jt. auth. see Germann, Richard.
Arnold, Peter, jt. auth. see Percelay, Bruce A.
Arnold, Peter, jt. auth. see Wallach, Ellen J.
Arnold, R. M. The Golden Years of the Great Northern Railway; Part 1: Belafast, Portadown, Londonderry, Enniskillen. 170p. 1983. pap. 11.95 (ISBN 0-85640-300-8, Pub. by Blackstaff Pr). Longwood Pub Group.
Arnold, Rhodes. The Republic F-Eighty-Four: From "Lead Sled" to "Super Hawg". (Illus.). 128p. pap. 12.95 cancelled (ISBN 0-89404-054-5). Aztex.
Arnold, Richard. Better Ice Skating. (Better Ser.). (Illus.). (gr. 7 up). 17.95x (ISBN 0-7182-1442-0, SpS). Sportshelf.
--Better Ice Skating. (Illus.). 96p. 1980. 9.95 (ISBN 0-7182-1442-0, Pub. by Kaye & Ward). David & Charles.
--Better Roller Skating. (Illus.). 96p. 1984. pap. 9.95 (ISBN 0-7182-1479-X, Pub. by Kaye & Ward). David & Charles.
--Better Sport Skating. (Illus.). 96p. 1983. 9.95 (ISBN 0-7182-1468-4, Pub. by Kaye & Ward). David & Charles.
--Dancing on Skates. (Illus.). 128p. 1985. 11.95 (ISBN 0-312-18209-0). St Martin.
Arnold, Richard A. Ecological Studies of Six Endangered Butterflies, (Lepidoptera, Lycaenidae) Island Biogeography, Patch Dynamics & the Design of Habitat Preserves. (University of California Publications in Entomology: Vol. 99). 1983. pap. 15.00x (ISBN 0-520-09671-1). U of Cal Pr.
Arnold, Richard D. Letters of Richard D. Arnold, M. D., 1808-1876. Shryock, Richard H., ed. LC 71-115999. (Duke University. Trinity College Historical Society. Historical Papers: Nos. 18-19). Repr. of 1929 ed. 24.50 (ISBN 0-404-51768-4). AMS Pr.
Arnold, Richard L. Scene Technology. (Illus.). 352p. 1985. text ed. 27.95 (ISBN 0-13-791765-1). P-H.
Arnold, Rist. I Like Birds. LC 76-58705. (Illus.). (ps-1). 1977. 2.95 (ISBN 0-88776-043-0). Tundra Bks.
Arnold, Rita E., jt. auth. see Cannatella, Mary M.
Arnold, Robert. Dismal Swamp & Lake Drummond. (Illus.). 1969. Repr. 7.50 (ISBN 0-930230-07-8). Johnson NC.
Arnold, Robert D. Alaska Native Land Claims. rev. ed. (Illus.). 1978. 15.95 (ISBN 0-686-25002-8). Books AK.
Arnold, Robert H. A Rock & A Fortress. LC 78-75365. 1979. 6.95 (ISBN 0-686-25996-3). Blue Horizon.
Arnold, Robert R., et al. Modern Data Processing. 3rd ed. LC 77-14941. 435p. 1978. 35.00x (ISBN 0-471-03361-8); wkbk. o.p. 11.95 (ISBN 0-471-03362-6); avail. tchrs. manual (ISBN 0-471-03405-3). Wiley.
Arnold, Roland, ed. Bibliographie der Veroffentlichungen von S. B. Liljegren. (Essays & Studies on English Language & Literature: Vol. 16). pap. 13.00 (ISBN 0-317-16356-6). Kraus Repr.
--Bibliographie II der Veroffentlichungen von S. B. Liljegren. (Essays & Studies on English Language & Literature Ser.: Vol. 22). pap. 13.00 (ISBN 0-317-16373-6). Kraus Repr.
--Bibliographie III der Veroffentlichungen von S. B. Liljegren. (Essays & Studies on English Language & Literature: Vol. 26). pap. 15.00 (ISBN 0-317-16387-6). Kraus Repr.
Arnold, Roslyn, ed. Timely Voices. 1983. 16.95x (ISBN 0-19-554363-7). Oxford U Pr.
Arnold, Sam, jt. auth. see Smart, L. Edwin.
Arnold, Samuel G. An Historical Sketch of Middletown, Rhode Island: From Its Organization in 1743 to the Centennial Year, 1876. (Illus.). 66p. 1976. pap. 6.50 (ISBN 0-917012-58-5). RI Pubns Soc.
--History of the State of Rhode Island & Providence Plantations, 2 vols. LC 79-120136. (Illus.). 1970. Repr. of 1859 ed. 12.50 ea. Vol. 1 (ISBN 0-87152-057-5). Vol. 2 (ISBN 0-87152-058-3). Set. 25.00 (ISBN 0-87152-307-8). Reprint.
Arnold, Stanley. I Ran Against Jimmy Carter. (Orig.). 1979. pap. 2.25 (ISBN 0-532-22173-7). Woodhill.
Arnold, Stephen, ed. African Literature Studies: The Present State - L'Etat Present. LC 84-51447. (African Literature Association Annuals Ser.). 317p. 26.00 (ISBN 0-89410-435-7); pap. 16.00 (ISBN 0-89410-436-5). Three Continents.
Arnold, Stephen, jt. ed. see Parker, Carolyn.
Arnold, Steven F. The Theory of Linear Models & Multivariate Analysis. LC 80-23017. (Probability & Math Statistics Ser.). 475p. 1981. 47.50x (ISBN 0-471-05065-2). Wiley.
Arnold, Steven H. Implementing Development Assistance European Approaches to Basic Needs. (Replica Edition Ser.). (Illus.). 190p. 1982. softcover 23.00x (ISBN 0-86531-904-9). Westview.
Arnold, Susan. Eggshells to Objects. LC 79-4328. (Illus.). (gr. 6 up). 1979. 7.95 (ISBN 0-03-043981-7). HR&W.
Arnold, T. Preaching of Islam. 1968. 25.00x (ISBN 0-87902-045-8). Orientalia.
Arnold, T. K., tr. see Hengstenberg, E. W.
Arnold, T. W. The Old & New Testaments in Muslim Religious Art. (British Academy, London, Schweidr Lectures in Biblical Archaeology Series, 1928). pap. 19.00 (ISBN 0-317-15825-2). Kraus Repr.
--Preaching of Islam. 32.50 (ISBN 0-686-18455-6). Kazi Pubns.
--The Preachings of Islam. 467p. 1984. Repr. of 1913 ed. text ed. 50.00x (ISBN 0-86590-250-X, Pub. by Renaissance New Delhi). Apt Bks.
Arnold, T. W. & Guillaume, A. The Legacy of Islam. 1976. lib. bdg. 75.00 (ISBN 0-8490-2141-3). Gordon Pr.
Arnold, Terrell E., jt. ed. see Livingstone, Neil C.
Arnold, Thomas. A History of Islam. 1983. cancelled (ISBN 0-86304-037-3, Pub. by Octagon Pr England). Ins Study Human.
--A Manual of English Literature: Historical & Critical: with an Appendix on English Metres. 1979. Repr. of 1873 ed. lib. bdg. 50.00 (ISBN 0-8495-0147-4). Arden Lib.
--Miscellaneous Works of Thomas Arnold. D.D. 1979. Repr. of 1874 ed. lib. bdg. 50.00 (ISBN 0-8495-0149-0). Arden Lib.
--Observations on the Nature, Kinds, Causes, & Prevention of Insanity: Containing Observations on the Nature, & Various Kinds of Insanity & the Appearances on Dissection, 2 vols. in 1. 2nd ed. LC 75-16680. (Classics in Psychiatry Ser.). 1976. Repr. of 1806 ed. 51.00x (ISBN 0-405-07412-3). Ayer Co Pubs.
Arnold, Thomas, ed. Henrici Huntendunensis Historia Anglorum: The History of the English by Henry, Archdeacon of Huntingdon, from 55-1154, 8 bks. (Rolls Ser.: No. 74). Repr. of 1879 ed. 44.00 (ISBN 0-317-16797-9). Kraus Repr.
--Memorials of St. Edmund's Abbey, 3 vols. (Rolls Ser.: No. 96). Repr. of 1896 ed. Set. 132.00 (ISBN 0-317-16819-3). Kraus Repr.
--Symeonis Monachi Opera Omnia, 2 vols. Incl. Vol. 1. Historia Ecclesiae Dunelmensis; Vol. 2. Historia Regum. (Rolls Ser.: No. 75). Repr. of 1885 ed. Set. 88.00 (ISBN 0-317-16799-5). Kraus Repr.
Arnold, Thomas W. Painting in Islam. (Illus.). 16.25 (ISBN 0-8446-1553-6). Peter Smith.
--Painting in Islam: A Study of the Place of Pictorial Art in Muslim Culture. (Illus.). 1928. pap. 7.95 (ISBN 0-486-21310-2). Dover.
--The Preaching of Islam: A History of Propagation of the Muslim Faith. LC 72-180319. (Mid-East Studies). Repr. of 1913 ed. 27.50 (ISBN 0-404-56214-0). AMS Pr.
Arnold, Thurman W. The Bottlenecks of Business. LC 72-2363. (FDR & the Era of the New Deal Ser.). 352p. 1973. Repr. of 1940 ed. lib. bdg. 42.50 (ISBN 0-306-70470-6). Da Capo.
--The Folklore of Capitalism. LC 79-26573. 1980. Repr. of 1937 ed. lib. bdg. 32.50x (ISBN 0-313-22199-5, ARFC). Greenwood.
Arnold, Thurman W., et al. Future of Democratic Capitalism. facsimile ed. LC 77-142631. (Essay Index Reprint Ser). Repr. of 1950 ed. 12.00 (ISBN 0-8369-2395-2). Ayer Co Pubs.
Arnold, Tom & Vaden, Frank S. Invention Protection for Practicing Engineers. LC 73-133266. 1971. 13.95 (ISBN 0-8436-0312-7); pap. 9.95 (ISBN 0-8436-0313-5). Van Nos Reinhold.
Arnold, Tom, jt. auth. see Goldscheider, Robert.
Arnold, Ulli. Strategische Beschaffungspolitik. (European University Studies: No. 5, Vol. 380). 311p. (Ger.). 1982. 35.80 (ISBN 3-8204-5842-5). P Lang Pubs.
Arnold, V. I. Catastrophe Theory. Thomas, R. K., tr. (Illus.). 80p. 1984. pap. 9.80 (ISBN 0-387-12859-X). Springer-Verlag.
--Geometrical Methods in the Theory of Ordinary Differential Equations. (Grundlehren der Mathematischen Wissenschaften: Vol. 250). (Illus.). 384p. 1983. 39.50 (ISBN 0-387-90681-9). Springer-Verlag.
--Mathematical Methods in Classical Mechanics. (Graduate Texts in Mathematics Ser.: Vol. 60). (Illus.). 1978. 32.00 (ISBN 0-387-90314-3). Springer-Verlag.
--Ordinary Differential Equations. Silverman, Richard A., tr. from Rus. (Illus.). 270p. 1973. pap. 13.75x (ISBN 0-262-51018-9). MIT Pr.
--Singularity Theory. LC 81-6091. (London Mathematical Society Lecture Notes Ser.: No. 53). (Illus.). 280p. 1981. pap. 34.50 (ISBN 0-521-28511-9). Cambridge U Pr.
Arnold, V. I., et al. Eleven Papers on Analysis. LC 51-5559. (Translations, Ser.: No. 2, Vol. 53). 1966. 36.00 (ISBN 0-8218-1753-1, TRANS 2-53). Am Math.
Arnol'd, V. I., et al. Fourteen Papers on Functional Analysis & Differential Equations. LC 51-5559. (Translations Ser.: No. 2, Vol. 61). 1967. 38.00 (ISBN 0-8218-1761-2, TRANS 2-61). Am Math.
--Seventeen Papers on Analysis. (Translations Ser.: No. 2, Vol. 28). 1963. 27.00 (ISBN 0-8218-1728-0, TRANS 2-28). Am Math.
--Thirteen Papers on Functional Analysis & Differential Equations. LC 51-5559. (Translations Ser.: No. 2, Vol. 79). 1968. 35.00 (ISBN 0-8218-1779-5, TRANS 2-79). Am Math.
Arnold, Victor L., ed. Alternatives to Confrontation: National Policy Toward Regional Change. LC 79-2374. 400p. 1980. 37.50x (ISBN 0-669-03165-8). Lexington Bks.
Arnold, W. D. Oakfield: Or, Fellowship in the East. xi, 442p. Repr. of 1855 ed. 49.00 (ISBN 0-932051-74-X). Am Repr Serv.
Arnold, W. H. Ventures in Book Collecting. 59.95 (ISBN 0-8490-1257-0). Gordon Pr.
Arnold, W. T. Roman Provincial Administration. 298p. 1974. 15.00 (ISBN 0-89005-027-9). Ares.

Arnold, Walter, jt. ed. see Ozaki, Robert S.
Arnold, Wendy. The Historic Country Hotels of England: A Select Guide. 1985. 19.95 (ISBN 0-03-004132-5); pap. 11.95 (ISBN 0-03-004133-3). HR&W.
Arnold, Wesley E. Amplenomics Ample for All Can Be Created: Workable Solutions & Practical Insights into the Problems of Our Time. 224p. (Orig.). 1984. pap. 6.00 (ISBN 0-915935-00-7); pap. text ed. 10.00 (ISBN 0-915935-01-5). Intl Better Life.
Arnold, Wesley Edward. The International Language. 80p. (Orig.). 1985. pap. 2.00 (ISBN 0-915935-02-3). Intl Better Life.
Arnold, Wesley F. & Cardy, Wayne C. Fun with Next to Nothing: Handicraft Projects for Boys & Girls. LC 62-8039. (Illus.). 96p. (gr. 2-6). 1962. PLB 11.89 (ISBN 0-06-020146-0). HarpJ.
Arnold, Wilfred N., ed. Yeast Cell Envelopes: Biochemistry, Biophysics, & Ultrastructure, Vols. I & II. 1981. Vol. I, 144p. 56.00 (ISBN 0-8493-5965-1); Vol. Ii, 192p. 71.50 (ISBN 0-8493-5966-X). CRC Pr.
Arnold, Willard B. Essays on Honesty, Morality, & Competition. 136p. 1985. 10.00 (ISBN 0-682-40235-4). Exposition Pr FL.
Arnold, William. China Gate. LC 83-48073. 448p. 1983. 15.95 (ISBN 0-394-53373-9, Pub. by Villard Bks). Random.
--China Gate. 512p. 1984. pap. 3.95 (ISBN 0-345-30850-6). Ballantine.
--The Compaq Portable Computer: Use, Applications & BASIC. LC 84-19219. 1985. pap. text ed. 18.45 (ISBN 0-03-064119-5). HR&W.
Arnold, William & Brungardt, Terrence. Juvenile Misconduct & Delinquency. LC 82-82284. 512p. 1983. pap. text ed. 22.95 (ISBN 0-395-32562-5); instrs.' manual 2.00 (ISBN 0-395-32563-3). HM.
Arnold, William D. Oakfield; Or, Fellowship in the East, 1854. 2nd ed. Wolff, Robert L., ed. LC 75-1522. (Victorian Fiction Ser.). 1975. lib. bdg. 73.00 (ISBN 0-8240-1594-0). Garland Pub.
Arnold, William E. Crisis Communication. (Illus.). 90p. (Orig.). 1980. pap. text ed. 9.50x (ISBN 0-89787-302-5). Gorsuch Scarisbrick.
Arnold, William H. French Diction for Singers & Speakers. LC 74-27328. Repr. of 1912 ed. 14.50 (ISBN 0-404-12854-8). AMS Pr.
Arnold, William J. Nebraska Symposium on Motivation, 1970. (Current Theory & Research in Motivation: Vol. 18). pap. 72.00 (ISBN 0-317-26228-9, 2055618). Bks Demand UMI.
Arnold, William J., ed. Nebraska Symposium on Motivation, 1968. LC 53-11655. (Nebraska Symposia on Motivation Ser.: Vol. 16). x, 337p. 1968. 25.50x (ISBN 0-8032-0610-0); pap. 6.50x (ISBN 0-8032-5616-7). U of Nebr Pr.
--Nebraska Symposium on Motivation, 1975: Conceptual Foundations of Psychology. LC 53-11655. (Nebraska Symposium on Motivation Ser.: Vol. 23). xxviii, 586p. 1976. 37.50x (ISBN 0-8032-0618-6); pap. 11.95x (ISBN 0-8032-5624-8). U of Nebr Pr.
Arnold, William J. & Page, Monte M., eds. Nebraska Symposium on Motivation, 1970. LC 53-11655. (Nebraska Symposium on Motivation Ser.: Vol. 18). xiv, 288p. 1971. 21.50x (ISBN 0-8032-0612-7); pap. 5.95x (ISBN 0-8032-5618-3). U of Nebr Pr.
Arnold, William R. Ephod & Ark. LC 17-18713. (Harvard Theological Studies Ser.). 1917. 11.00 (ISBN 0-527-01003-0). Kraus Repr.
Arnold, William R. & Bowie, John S. Artificial Intelligence: A Personal Commonsense Journey. (Illus.). 224p. 1986. text ed. 24.95 (ISBN 0-13-048877-1). P-H.
Arnold, William T. The Roman System of Provincial Adminstration: To the Accession of Constantine the Great. facsimile & 3rd ed. Bouchier, E. S., ed. LC 79-179501. (Select Bibliographies Reprint Ser). Repr. of 1914 ed. 23.50 (ISBN 0-8369-6630-9). Ayer Co Pubs.
Arnold, William V. Introduction to Pastoral Care. LC 81-16092. 222p. 1982. pap. 10.95 (ISBN 0-664-24400-9). Westminster.
--The Power of Your Perceptions. LC 83-26089. (Potentials: Guides for Productive Living Ser.,: Vol. 6). 118p. (Orig.). 1984. pap. 7.95 (ISBN 0-664-24524-2). Westminster.
--When Your Parents Divorce, Vol. 1. LC 79-20055. (Christian Care Books). 118p. 1980. pap. 6.95 (ISBN 0-664-24294-4). Westminster.
Arnold, William V., et al. Divorce: Prevention or Survival. LC 77-22066. 1977. pap. 5.95 (ISBN 0-664-24142-5). Westminster.
Arnold, Willus J. The Black Nazi. LC 81-20526. 1984. 15.95 (ISBN 0-87949-198-1). Ashley Bks.
Arnold, Winifred H. Glossary of a Thousand & One Terms Used in Conchology. 1965. 4.50 (ISBN 0-913792-05-5). Shell Cab.
Arnold-Forster, Mark. The World at War. LC 83-42965. (Illus.). 384p. pap. 9.95 (ISBN 0-8128-6202-3). Stein & Day.
--The World at War. 384p. (Orig.). 1984. pap. 3.95 (ISBN 0-8128-8057-9). Stein & Day.
Arnold-Forster, Nigel, jt. auth. see Hull, Peter.
Arnold-Foster, Mark. World at War. (YA) (RL 8). 1974. pap. 3.95 (ISBN 0-451-12733-1, AE2733, Sig). NAL.
Arnoldi, Mary Jo, jt. auth. see Anderson, Martha G.
Arnolds, Edward B. & Carroll, William K. Eyewitness Testimony. (Trial Publications). 368p. 1984. write for info. (Pub. By Shepard's-McGraw). McGraw.
Arnolds, Eef. Ecology & Coenology of Macrofungi in Grasslands & Moist Heathlands in Drenthe, the Netherlands: Pt. 1: Introduction & Synecology. (Bibliotheca Mycologica: Vol. 83). (Illus.). 410p. 1981. text ed. 48.00x (ISBN 3-7682-1314-5). Lubrecht & Cramer.
--Ecology & Coenology of Macrofungi in Grasslands & Moist Heathlands in Drenthe, the Netherlands. (Illus.). 510p. (Orig.). 1982. Pt. 3 Taxonomy. lib. bdg. 70.00 (ISBN 3-7682-1346-3). Lubrecht & Cramer.
Arnoldson, Torild W. Parts of the Body in Older Germanic & Scandinavian. LC 71-158274. (Chicago. University. Germanic Studies: No. 2). Repr. of 1915 ed. 26.00 (ISBN 0-404-50282-2). AMS Pr.
Arnon, I. Modernization of Agriculture in Developing Countries: Resources, Potentials & Problems. LC 80-41588. (Environmental Monographs & Symposia: A Series in Environmental Science). 592p. 1981. 89.95x (ISBN 0-471-27928-5, Pub. by Wiley-Interscience). Wiley.
--The Planning & Programming of Agricultural Research. 122p. (2nd Printing 1978). 1975. pap. 7.50 (ISBN 92-5-100850-7, F320, FAO). Unipub.
Arnon, Isaac. Organisation & Administration of Agricultural Research. 342p. 1971. 39.00 (ISBN 0-444-20028-2, Pub. by Elsevier Applied Sci England). Elsevier.
Arnon, R., jt. ed. see Spreafico, F.
Arnon-Ohanna, Yuval, jt. auth. see Yodfat, Aryeh.
Arnonowitz, Eugene & Bromberg, Eleanor M., eds. Mental Health & Long-Term Physical Illness. 96p. 1984. pap. 6.95 (ISBN 0-88135-001-X, Pub. by N Watson). Watson Pub Intl.
Arnopoulos, Sheila M. Voices from French Ontario. 216p. 1982. 17.50x (ISBN 0-7735-0405-2); pap. 7.95 (ISBN 0-7735-0406-0). McGill-Queens U Pr.
Arnopoulos, Sheila M. & Clift, Dominique. The English Fact in Quebec. 2nd ed. LC 84-98406. 296p. 1984. 30.00x (ISBN 0-7735-0413-3); pap. 9.95 (ISBN 0-7735-0414-1). McGill-Queens U Pr.
Arnorld, Benjamin. German Knighthood One Thousand-Fifty to Thirteen Hundred. 400p. 1985. cloth 34.50 (ISBN 0-19-821960-1). Oxford U Pr.
Arnosky, Jim. Drawing from Nature. LC 82-15327. (Illus.). 64p. (gr. 5 up). 1982. 11.75 (ISBN 0-688-01295-7). Lothrop.
--Drawing Life in Motion. LC 83-25129. (Illus.). 48p. (gr. 6 up). 1984. 11.75 (ISBN 0-688-03803-4). Lothrop.
--Flies in the Water, Fish in the Air. LC 84-29684. (Illus.). 128p. 1986. 11.75 (ISBN 0-688-05834-5). Lothrop.
--Mouse Numbers & Letters. LC 81-13305. (Illus.). 48p. (ps-3). 1982. 10.95 (ISBN 0-15-256022-X, HJ). HarBraceJ.
--Mouse Writing. LC 83-4298. (Illus.). 48p. (ps-3). 1983. PLB 10.95 (ISBN 0-15-256028-9, HJ). HarBraceJ.
--Secrets of a Wildlife Watcher. LC 82-24920. (Illus.). 64p. (gr. 5 up). 1983. 10.25 (ISBN 0-688-02079-8); lib. bdg. 9.88 (ISBN 0-688-02081-X). Lothrop.
--Watching Foxes. LC 84-20157. (Illus.). 24p. (ps-3). 1984. PLB 11.88 (ISBN 0-688-04260-0); 11.75 (ISBN 0-688-04259-7). Lothrop.
Arnot, Frederick L. Collision Processes in Gases. 4th ed. LC 50-12768. (Methuen's Monographs on Physical Subjects). pap. 29.00 (ISBN 0-317-08481-X, 2013148). Bks Demand UMI.
Arnot, Frederick S. Garenganze or Seven Years' Pioneer Mission Work in Central Africa. 2nd, rev. ed. (Illus.). 276p. 1969. 29.50x (ISBN 0-7146-1860-8, BHA 01860, F Cass Co). Biblio Dist.
Arnot, Madeleine, jt. ed. see Whitelegg, Elizabeth.
Arnot, Phil & Monroe, Elvira. Exploring Point Reyes: A Guide to Point Reyes National Seashore. Rev. ed. LC 82-51259. (Illus.). 160p. 1983. pap. 5.95 (ISBN 0-933174-16-0). Wide World-Tetra.
--Run for Your Life. 1977. pap. 3.95 (ISBN 0-933174-01-2). Wide World-Tetra.
Arnot, R. Page. Bernard Shaw & William Morris. 1978. Repr. of 1957 ed. lib. bdg. 10.00 (ISBN 0-8495-0027-3). Arden Lib.
--Bernard Shaw & William Morris. LC 73-4396. 1973. lib. bdg. 9.50 (ISBN 0-8414-1725-3). Folcroft.
--The Impact of the Russian Revolution in Britain. 191p. 1972. 9.00x (ISBN 0-8464-0504-0). Beekman Pubs.
--The Miners: One Union, One Industry: A History of the National Union of Mineworkers 1939-46. (Illus.). 1979. text ed. 30.00x (ISBN 0-04-331074-5). Allen Unwin.
Arnot, R. Page, tr. see Varga, Eugen.
Arnot, Robert. The Complete Manual of Fitness & Well-Being. LC 84-40259. (Illus.). 312p. 1984. 25.00 (ISBN 0-670-23431-1). Viking.
--The Miners: One Union, One Industry, A History of the National Union of Mineworkers, 1939-46. LC 78-40603. pap. 60.00 (ISBN 0-317-20059-3, 2023306). Bks Demand UMI.
Arnot, Robert & Gaines, Charles. Sportselection: Test, Choose & Training for the Sport That's Right for You. LC 83-47929. (Illus.). 288p. 1984. 17.95 (ISBN 0-670-66467-7). Viking.
--SportsTalent. 320p. 1986. pap. 8.95 (ISBN 0-14-007790-1). Penguin.
Arnot, Robert & Bourget, Paul, eds. The Life Work of Henri Rene Guy De Maupassami, 17 vols. 1983. Repr. of 1903 ed. Set. lib. bdg. 550.00 (ISBN 0-89987-181-X). Darby Bks.
Arnot, Robert, ed. see Mendes, H. Pereira.
Arnot, Robert P. General Strike, May Nineteen Twenty-Six: Its Origin & History. LC 67-20085. Repr. of 1926 ed. 25.00x (ISBN 0-678-00254-1). Kelley.
--The Miners: A History of the Miners' Federation of Great Britain, 3 Vols. Incl. Vol. 1. 1889-1910; Vol. 2. Years of Struggle from 1910 Onwards. 1953. 35.00x (ISBN 0-678-06031-2); Vol. 3. In Crisis and War, from 1930 Onwards. (Illus.). 1949-1961. Kelley.
--The Miners in Crisis & War: A History of The Miner's Federation of Great Britain from 1930 Onwards. (Illus.). 451p. 1961. lib. bdg. 27.50x (ISBN 0-678-08024-0). Kelley.
--William Morris, the Man & the Myth. LC 76-107. 131p. 1976. Repr. of 1964 ed. lib. bdg. 15.00 (ISBN 0-8371-8652-8, ARWM). Greenwood.
Arnot, William. The Lesser Parables of Our Lord. LC 80-8066. 464p. 1981. 10.95 (ISBN 0-8254-2121-7). Kregel.
--The Parables of Our Lord. LC 80-8065. 532p. 1981. 12.95 (ISBN 0-8254-2119-5). Kregel.
--Studies in Acts: The Church in the House. LC 78-59141. 1978. 11.95 (ISBN 0-8254-2120-9). Kregel.
Arnott, Anna L. People Speak. 64p. (Orig.). 1982. pap. 4.50 (ISBN 0-682-49857-2). Exposition Pr FL.
Arnott, Brian. Towards a New Theatre: Edward Gordon Craig & Hamlet. (Illus.). 1975. pap. 7.50X (ISBN 0-88884-305-4, 56521-1, Pub. by Natl Gallery Canada). U of Chicago Pr.
Arnott, Catherine M. & Trussler, Simon, eds. Tennessee Williams on File. (Writers on File Ser.). 96p. 1985. pap. 6.50 (ISBN 0-413-54280-7, 9388). Methuen Inc.
Arnott, D. G. Our Nuclear Adventure. 1958. 6.00 (ISBN 0-8022-0040-0). Philos Lib.
Arnott, James F. & Robinson, John W. English Theatrical Literature, Fifteen Fifty-Nine to Nineteen Hundred: A Bibliography Incorporating Robert W. Lowe's a Bibliographical Account of English Theatrical Literature, Published in 1888. 50.00 (ISBN 0-384-02125-5). Johnson Repr.
Arnott, Kathleen. Dragons, Ogres, & Scary Things: Two African Folktales. LC 74-9876. (Venture Ser.). (Illus.). 64p. (gr. 2). 1974. PLB 7.68 (ISBN 0-8116-6978-5). Garrard.
--Spiders, Crabs, & Creepy Crawlers: Two African Folktales. LC 78-1057. (Imagination Ser.). (Illus.). (gr. k-6). 1978. PLB 7.47 (ISBN 0-8116-4412-X). Garrard.
Arnott, Marilyn S., et al, eds. Molecular Interrelations of Nutrition & Cancer. (M. D. Anderson Symposium on Fundamental Cancer Research Ser.: 34th Annual). 490p. 1982. text ed. 83.50 (ISBN 0-89004-701-4). Raven.
Arnott, Peter. Romans & Their World. LC 79-119015. (Illus.). 1970. pap. 11.95 (ISBN 0-312-69160-2). St Martin.
--The Theater in Its Time: An Introduction. 1981. text ed. 21.95 (ISBN 0-316-05194-2). Little.
Arnott, Peter, jt. auth. see Reinert, Otto.
Arnott, Peter, jt. ed. see Reinert, Otto.
Arnott, Peter D. Greek Scenic Conventions in the Fifth Century B.C. LC 78-5950. 1978. Repr. of 1962 ed. lib. bdg. 24.75x (ISBN 0-313-20401-2, ARGS). Greenwood.
--An Introduction to the French Theatre. 164p. 1977. 18.75x (ISBN 0-87471-949-6). Rowman.
Arnott, Peter D., ed. & tr. see Aeschylus.
Arnott, Peter D., ed. & tr. see Aristophanes.
Arnott, Peter D., ed. & tr. see Sophocles.
Arnott, Struther, et al, eds. Molecular Biophysics of the Extracellular Matrix. LC 84-6640. (Molecular Biology & Biophysics Ser.). 224p. 1984. 39.50 (ISBN 0-89603-051-2). Humana.
Arnou, X. B., jt. auth. see Benveniste, J.
Arnoudt, Peter J. The Imitation of the Sacred Heart of Jesus. LC 79-112463. 1974. pap. 10.00 (ISBN 0-89555-012-1). TAN Bks Pubs.
Arnould, Arthur. Histoire populaire et parlementaire de la Commune de Paris. LC 75-158275. Repr. of 1878 ed. 29.00 (ISBN 0-404-07117-1). AMS Pr.
Arnould, Dominique. Guerre et Paix Dans la Poesie Greque. rev. ed. Connor, W. R., ed. LC 80-2639. (Monographs in Classical Studies). 1981. lib. bdg. 45.00 (ISBN 0-405-14027-4). Ayer Co Pubs.
Arnould, E. F., ed. see Beaumarchais, Pierre-Augustin.
Arnould, E. J., ed. see Beaumarchais, Pierre.
Arnould, E. J., ed. see Henry Duke Of Lancaster.
Arnould, Louis. Racan Mille Cinq Cent Quatre-Vingt-Neuf a Mille Six Cent Soixante-Dix: Histoire Anecdotique et Critique de Sa Vie et de Ses Oeuvres, 2 Vols. LC 70-132532. (Research & Source Works Ser: No. 553). (Fr). 1970. Repr. of 1896 ed. Set. 43.00 (ISBN 0-8337-0093-6). B Franklin.
Arnould, M. & Zubini, F. English-French Petroleum Dictionary. 267p. (Eng. & Fr.). 1982. 75.00x (ISBN 0-86010-374-9, Pub. by Graham & Trotman England). State Mutual Bk.
Arnould, Michel & Zubini, Fabio. English-French Petroleum Dictionary. 267p. (Eng. & Fr.). 1983. pap. 37.00x (ISBN 0-8448-1432-6). Crane-Russak Co.
Arnout, Susan. The Frozen Lady. LC 81-71662. 581p. 1983. 15.95 (ISBN 0-87795-368-6). Arbor Hse.
--The Frozen Lady. 1984. pap. 3.95 (ISBN 0-8217-1338-8). Zebra.
Arnov, Boris. Water: Experiments to Understand It. LC 79-24297. (Illus.). (gr. 5 up). 1980. 10.00 (ISBN 0-688-41927-5); PLB 10.88 (ISBN 0-688-51927-X). Lothrop.
Arnove, Robert F., ed. Philanthropy & Cultural Imperialism: The Foundations at Home & Abroad. 1980. lib. bdg. 26.00 (ISBN 0-8161-8259-0, Univ Bks). G K Hall.
--Philanthropy & Cultural Imperialism: The Foundations at Home & Abroad. LC 82-48055. (Midland Bks.: No. 303). 488p. 1982. pap. 10.95x (ISBN 0-253-20303-1). Ind U Pr.
Arnow, E. Earle. Food Power: A Doctor's Guide to Common Sense Nutrition. LC 75-185419. (Illus.). 305p. 1972. 19.95x (ISBN 0-911012-37-0). Nelson-Hall.
Arnow, Harriet. The Dollmaker. 608p. 1972. pap. 3.95 (ISBN 0-380-00947-1, 64345-6). Avon.
Arnow, Harriette. The Dollmaker. LC 85-40073. 560p. 1985. 30.00. U Pr of KY.
--Hunter's Horn. (YA) 1979. pap. 2.50 (ISBN 0-380-42283-2, 42283-2). Avon.
Arnow, Harriette S. Flowering of the Cumberland. LC 82-40458. (Illus.). 464p. 1984. 28.00 (ISBN 0-8131-1488-8); pap. 13.00 (ISBN 0-8131-0147-6). U Pr of KY.
--Mountain Path. LC 85-40073. 384p. 1985. 24.00 (ISBN 0-8131-1550-7). U Pr of Ky.
--Old Burnside. LC 77-73699. (Kentucky Bicentennial Bookshelf Ser). (Illus.). 148p. 1977. 6.95 (ISBN 0-8131-0208-1). U Pr of Ky.
--Seedtime on the Cumberland. LC 82-40464. (Illus.). 480p. 1983. 28.00 (ISBN 0-8131-1487-X); pap. 13.00 (ISBN 0-8131-0146-8). U Pr of Ky.
Arnow, Jan. Louisville Slugger: The Making of a Baseball Bat. LC 84-7049. (Photo Essay Ser.). (Illus.). 48p. (gr. 3-7). 1984. 11.95 (ISBN 0-394-86297-X, Pant Bks Young); PLB 11.99 (ISBN 0-394-96297-4). Pantheon.
Arnow, Murray. The Apple CP-M Book. LC 85-2393. 164p. 1985. pap. 12.95 (ISBN 0-673-18068-9). Scott F.
Arnsdorff, Edward F. How to Install & Repair Your Telephone. 2nd ed. (Illus.). 47p. 1983. pap. 3.50 (ISBN 0-9612878-0-2). T A P.
Arnson, Cynthia. El Salvador: A Revolution Confronts the United States. (Illus.). 120p. 1982. pap. 5.95 (ISBN 0-89758-036-2). Inst Policy Stud.
Arnson, Cynthia, jt. auth. see Klare, Michael T.
Arnspiger, Varney C. Measuring the Effectiveness of Sound Pictures As Teaching Aids. LC 71-176524. (Columbia University. Teachers College. Contributions to Education: No. 565). Repr. of 1933 ed. 22.50 (ISBN 0-404-55565-9). AMS Pr.
Arnst, Dennis & Katz, Jack, eds. Central Auditory Assessment: The SSW Test. LC 81-17987. (Illus.). 538p. 1982. pap. 32.50 (ISBN 0-933014-66-X). College-Hill.
Arnstein. When a Parent Is Mentally Ill: What to Say to Your Child. rev. ed. 1974. 1.25 (ISBN 0-87183-245-3). Child Study.
Arnstein, Helene S. Between Mothers-in-Law & Daughters-in-Law: Achieving a Successful & Caring Relationship. 224p. 1985. 14.95 (ISBN 0-396-08557-1). Dodd.
--Billy & Our New Baby. LC 73-7951. (Illus.). 32p. (ps-3). 1973. 10.95 (ISBN 0-87705-093-7). Human Sci Pr.
--When a Parent Is Mentally Ill: What to Say to Your Child. 36p. 1974. pap. 1.50 (ISBN 0-686-12282-8). Jewish Bd Family.
Arnstein, Joel. The International Dictionary of Graphic Symbols. LC 84-40180. 240p. 1984. pap. 9.95 (ISBN 0-394-71277-3, Vin). Random.
Arnstein, Walter, ed. The Past Speaks: Sources & Problems in British History Since 1688. 448p. 1981. pap. text ed. 10.95 (ISBN 0-669-02919-X). Heath.
Arnstein, Walter L. The Bradlaugh Case: Atheism, Sex, & Politics among the Late Victorians. LC 83-6814. (Illus.). 384p. 1984. text ed. 30.00x; pap. text ed. 13.50x (ISBN 0-8262-0417-1). U of Mo Pr.
--A History of England, Vol. IV: Britain Yesterday & Today 1830 to Present. Smith, Lacey B., ed. 304p. 1983. pap. text ed. 12.95 (ISBN 0-669-04380-X). Heath.
--Protestant vs. Catholic in Mid-Victorian England: Mr. Newdegate & the Nuns. LC 81-11451. 272p. text ed. 20.00x (ISBN 0-8262-0354-X). U of Mo Pr.
Arnstein, Walter L. see Smith, Lacey B.
Arnstein, Walter L., jt. auth. see Willcox, William B.
Arnstein, William E. & Gilabert, Frank. Direct Costing. LC 79-54827. pap. 72.00 (ISBN 0-317-10203-6, 2022615). Bks Demand UMI.
Arnston, L. Joyce. Word-Information Processing: Concepts & Procedures. LC 82-18020. write for info. (ISBN 0-534-01346-5). Kent Pub Co.
Arntson, Herbert E. Caravan to Oregon. LC 57-13207. (Illus.). (gr. 7-11). 1957. 4.50 (ISBN 0-8323-0164-7). Binford.

Arntson, L. Joyce. Word-Information Processing: Applications, Skills & Procedures. LC 82-18009. write for info. (ISBN 0-534-01345-7). Kent Pub Co.

Arntz, Mary L. Richard Rolle & the Holy Boke Gratia Dei. (Salzburg - Studies in English Literature: No. 92). 207p. 1981. pap. text ed. 25.50x (ISBN 0-391-02672-0, Pub. by Salzburg Austria). Humanities.

Arntzen, Etta & Rainwater, Robert. Guide to the Literature of Art History. LC 78-31711. 634p. 1981. 75.00x (ISBN 0-8389-0263-4). ALA.

Arntzen, Helmnt, et al, eds. Literatur Wissenschaft und Geschichtsphilosophie: Festschrift Fuer Wilhelm Emrich. 602p. 1975. 96.00x (ISBN 3-11-005726-3). De Gruyter.

Arntzen, Sonja. Ikkyu Sojun: A Zen Monk & His Poetry. LC 73-620051. (Occasional Papers: Vol. 4). (Illus.). 171p. 1973. microfiche 1.00 (ISBN 0-914584-99-5). West Wash Univ.

Arntzen, Sonya. Ikkyu & the Crazy Cloud Anthology. 230p. 1984. 20.00x (ISBN 0-86008-340-3, Pub. by U of Tokyo Japan). Columbia U Pr.

Arny, Linda Ray. The Search for Data in the Physical & Chemical Sciences. LC 83-20376. 160p. 1984. pap. 17.00 (ISBN 0-87111-308-2). SLA.

Arny, Thomas, jt. auth. see Pananides, Nicholas A.

Aroca, J. M., et al, eds. Algebraic Geometry, La Rabida, Spain 1981: Proceedings. (Lecture Notes in Mathematics Ser.: Vol. 961). 500p. 1982. pap. 27.00 (ISBN 0-387-11969-8). Springer-Verlag.

Arojan, Lois A. & Mitchell, Richard P. The Modern Middle East & Northern Africa. 496p. 1984. text ed. write for info. (ISBN 0-02-304200-1). Macmillan.

Arom, Simha, jt. auth. see Dournon, Genevieve.

Aron & Aron. Dr. Aron's Guide to Apple IIc. 1985. 16.95 (ISBN 0-8104-6755-0). Hayden.

--Dr. Aron's Guide to the Care, Feeding & Training of Your IBM PCjr. 320p. 1984. 16.95 (6368). Hayden.

Aron, Art. Beginner's Guide to the Commodore 64. 256p. 12.95 (6450). Hayden.

--Dr. Aron's Guide to the Care, Feeding, & Training of Your Commodore 64. 1983. 12.95 (ISBN 0-317-04671-3). Hayden.

Aron, Arthur. Free Ourselves: Forgotten Goals of the Revolution. (Illus.). 64p. (Orig.). 1972. pap. 1.35 (ISBN 0-87810-018-0). Times Change.

Aron, Arthur & Aron, Elaine. Love & the Expansion of Self. (Clinical & Community Psychology Ser.). 420p. 1985. text ed. 29.95 (ISBN 0-89116-394-8). Hemisphere Pub.

--Using Appleworks. LC 85-60693. 400p. 1985. pap. 16.95 (ISBN 0-88022-161-5, 181). Que Corp.

Aron, Elaine, jt. auth. see Aron, Arthur.

Aron, Jean P., et al. Anthropologie Du Conscrit Francais D'apres les Comptes Numeriques et Sommaires Du Recrutement De L'armee, 1819-1826: Presentation Cartographique. (Civilisation et Societes: No. 28). 1972. 28.40 (ISBN 90-2797-167-6). Mouton.

Aron, Jean-Paul. The Office. Ward, Matthew & Ilton, Irene, trs. from Fr. (Ubu Repertory Theater Publications Ser.: No. 4). 131p. (Orig.). 1983. pap. text ed. 6.25 (ISBN 0-913745-03-0, Dist. by Publishing Center for Cultural Resources). Ubu Repertory.

Aron, Joan B. The Quest for Regional Cooperation: A Study of the New York Metropolitan Regional Council. LC 69-16738. (California Studies in Urbanization & Environmental Design). 1969. 36.50x (ISBN 0-520-01505-3). U of Cal Pr.

Aron, Joel D. Program Development Process, Pt. I: The Individual Programmer. (IBM Systems Programming Ser.). (Illus.). 280p. 1974. text ed. 27.95 (ISBN 0-201-14451-4). Addison-Wesley.

--The Program Development Process: Pt. II: The Programming Team. LC 74-2847. (Illus.). 704p. 1983. text ed. 32.95 (ISBN 0-201-14463-8). Addison-Wesley.

Aron, Jon, jt. auth. see Linsley, Leslie.

Aron, Karl. Into the Wild Blue Yonder. Soskinsky, Sergei, tr. 32p. 1984. pap. 3.95 (ISBN 0-8285-2824-1, Pub. by Raduga Pubs USSR). Imported Pubns.

Aron, Milton. Ideas & Ideals of the Hassidim. 1969. 7.95 (ISBN 0-8065-0319-X). Citadel Pr.

--Ideas & Ideals of the Hassidim. 1980. pap. 5.95 (ISBN 0-8065-0722-5). Citadel Pr.

Aron, R. M. & Dineen, S., eds. Vector Space Measures & Applications I: Proceedings, Dublin, June 26-July 2, 1977. (Lecture Notes in Mathematics Ser.: Vol. 644). 1978. pap. 25.00 (ISBN 0-387-08668-4). Springer-Verlag.

--Vector Space Measures & Applications II: Proceedings, Dublin, June 26-July 2, 1977. (Lecture Notes in Mathematics: Vol. 645). 1978. pap. 16.00 (ISBN 0-387-08669-2). Springer-Verlag.

Aron, Raymond. The Century of Total War. LC 81-40. 379p. 1981. Repr. of 1954 ed. lib. bdg. 28.75x (ISBN 0-313-22852-3, ARCT). Greenwood.

--The Century of Total War. 380p. 1985. pap. text ed. 14.50 (ISBN 0-8191-4563-7). U Pr of Amer.

--Clausewitz: Philosopher of War. LC 84-26569. 418p. 1985. 24.95 (ISBN 0-13-136342-5). P H.

--German Sociology. Coser, Lewis A. & Powell, Walter W., eds. Bottomore, Mary & Bottomore, Thomas, trs. LC 79-6983. (Perennial Works in Sociology Ser.). 1979. Repr. of 1964 ed. lib. bdg. 13.00x (ISBN 0-405-12083-4). Ayer Co Pubs.

--German Sociology. Bottomore, Mary & Bottomore, Thomas, trs. LC 78-13596. 1979. Repr. of 1957 ed. lib. bdg. 18.75 (ISBN 0-313-21027-6, ARGE). Greenwood.

--The Great Debate: Theories of Nuclear Strategy. Pawel, Ernst, tr. from Fr. LC 81-495. ix, 265p. 1981. Repr. of 1965 ed. lib. bdg. 32.50x (ISBN 0-313-22851-5, ARGR). Greenwood.

--The Great Debate: Theories of Nuclear Strategy. Pawel, Ernst, tr. from Fr. 278p. 1985. pap. text ed. 13.25 (ISBN 0-8191-4564-5). U Pr of Amer.

--History, Truth, Liberty: Selected Writings of Raymond Aron. Draus, Franciszek, ed. Krance, Charles, tr. LC 85-8590. 416p. 1986. lib. bdg. price not set (ISBN 0-226-02800-3). U of Chicago Pr.

--The Imperial Republic: The United States & the World 1945-1973. Jellinek, Frank, tr. from Fr. LC 81-40938. Orig. Title: Republique Imperiale; les Etats-Unis Dans le Monde, 1945-1972. 378p. 1982. lib. bdg. 29.00 (ISBN 0-8191-2101-0); pap. text ed. 14.75 (ISBN 0-8191-2102-9). U Pr of Amer.

--In Defense of Decadent Europe. Cox, Stephen, tr. from Fr. LC 78-74438. 1979. 14.95 (ISBN 0-89526-686-5). Regnery-Gateway.

--In Defense of Decadent Europe. 308p. 1984. pap. text ed. 10.25 (ISBN 0-8191-3316-7). U Pr of Amer.

--Main Currents in Sociological Thought: Durkhelm, Pareto & Weber, Vol. 2. LC 68-14142. 1970. pap. 5.95 (ISBN 0-385-01976-9, Anch). Doubleday.

--Main Currents in Sociological Thought: Montesquieu, Comte, Marx, Tocqueville, the Sociologists, & the Revolution of 1848, Vol. 1. LC 68-14142. 1968. pap. 5.95 (ISBN 0-385-08804-3, Anch). Doubleday.

--On War. Kilmartin, Terence, tr. 1968. pap. 3.45x (ISBN 0-393-00107-5, Norton Lib). Norton.

--On War. Kilmartin, Terence, tr. 164p. 1985. pap. text ed. 10.50 (ISBN 0-8191-4565-3). U Pr of Amer.

--The Opium of the Intellectuals. Kilmartin, Terence, tr. from Fr. LC 77-7400. 1977. lib. bdg. 24.25 (ISBN 0-8371-9672-8, AROI). Greenwood.

--The Opium of the Intellectuals. Kilmartin, Terence, tr. from Fr. 344p. 1985. pap. text ed. 14.25 (ISBN 0-8191-4566-1). U Pr of Amer.

--Peace & War: A Theory of International Relations. LC 81-14296. 838p. 1981. Repr. of 1966 ed. 46.50 (ISBN 0-89874-391-5). Krieger.

--Politics & History. Conant, Miriam B., ed. 304p. 1984. pap. 12.95 (ISBN 0-87855-944-2). Transaction Bks.

--Politics & History: Selected Essays. Conant, Miriam B., ed. LC 78-54122. 1978. 24.95 (ISBN 0-02-901000-4). Free Pr.

--War & Industrial Society. Bottomore, Mary, tr. from Fr. LC 80-19002. (Auguste Comte Memorial Trust Lecture Ser.: No. 3). 63p. 1980. Repr. of 1958 ed. lib. bdg. 18.75 (ISBN 0-313-22512-5, ARWI). Greenwood.

Aron, Raymond & Heckscher, August. Diversity of Worlds. LC 72-12631. 178p. 1973. Repr. of 1957 ed. lib. bdg. 22.50 (ISBN 0-8371-6686-1, ARDW). Greenwood.

Aron, Raymond, et al. The Tanner Lectures on Human Values, Vol. II: 1981. 272p. 1981. 20.00x (ISBN 0-87480-193-1). U of Utah Pr.

Aronald, Carolyn. Bodies of Water: Fun, Facts, & Activities. (Easy-Read Geography Activity Bk.). (Illus.). 32p. (gr. 4up). 1985. lib. bdg. 9.40 (ISBN 0-531-04896-9). Watts.

Aronberg, Jerome M. Caring for Your Skin with Over-the-Counter Drugs. (Illus.). 96p. pap. 2.50 (ISBN 0-8326-2256-7, 7061). Delair.

Aron-Brunetiere, R. Beauty & Medicine. Kilmartin, Joanna, tr. (Illus.). 200p. 1980. 12.95 (ISBN 0-224-01449-8, Pub. by Jonathan Cape). Merrimack Pub Cir.

Aronian, Sona, ed. Alexei Remizov: Selected Prose. Date not set. 25.00 (ISBN 0-317-20389-4). Ardis Pubs.

Aronian, Sona, intro. by see Remizov, Alexei.

Aronica, Lou, jt. auth. see Silverberg, Robert.

Aronica, Paul, tr. see Bosco, St. John.

Aronin, Ben. The Secret of the Sabbath Fish. LC 78-63437. (Illus.). (gr. k-4). 1979. 5.95 (ISBN 0-8276-0110-7, 433). Jewish Pubns.

Aronin, J. Climate & Architecture. 2nd ed. 1984. write for info. (ISBN 0-442-28267-2); pap. write for info. (ISBN 0-442-28266-4). Van Nos Reinhold.

Aronis, Christine, ed. Annotated Bibliography of ESL Materials. 243p. 1983. 12.00 (ISBN 0-318-18069-3); members 10.50 (ISBN 0-318-18070-7). Tchrs Eng Spkrs.

Aronld, Guy. Gas. (Energy Today Ser.). (Illus.). 32p. (gr. 1-3). 1985. lib. bdg. 9.40 (ISBN 0-531-03487-9). Watts.

Aronoff, Craig. Business & the Media. LC 78-10394. 1979. text ed. 27.10x case ed. (ISBN 0-673-16071-8). Scott F.

Aronoff, Craig & Baskin, Otis W. Interpersonal Communication in Organizations. 1979. text ed. 19.05 (ISBN 0-673-16090-4); pap. text ed. 14.70x (ISBN 0-673-16091-2). Scott F.

Aronoff, Craig, et al. Getting Your Message Across: A Practical Guide to Business Communication. (Illus.). 500p. 1981. text ed. 25.95 (ISBN 0-8299-0362-3). West Pub.

Aronoff, Craig E. & Ward, John, eds. The Future of Private Enterprise: Challenges & Responses. 150p. 1984. 15.95 (ISBN 0-88406-164-7). Ga St U Busn Pub.

Aronoff, Frances W. Move with the Music: Songs & Activities for Young Children, A Teacher-Parent Preparation Workbook Including Keyboard Explorations. LC 81-24070. 133p. 1982. looseleaf bd. 12.95x (ISBN 0-9602590-1-5); perfect bd. 12.95 (ISBN 0-9602590-2-3). Turning Wheel Pr.

--Music & Young Children: Expanded Edition. LC 72-75917. 224p. 1979. pap. text ed. 8.95x (ISBN 0-9602590-0-7). Turning Wheel Pr.

Aronoff, Gerald M., ed. Evaluation & Treatment of Chronic Pain. (Illus.). 728p. 1985. text ed. 65.00 (ISBN 0-8067-0151-X). Urban & S.

Aronoff, Joel & Wilson, John P. Personality in the Social Process. 408p. 1985. text ed. 39.95 (ISBN 0-89859-526-6). L Erlbaum Assocs.

Aronoff, Mark. Word Formation in Generative Grammar. (Linguistic Inquiry Monographs). 134p. 1976. pap. text ed. 13.50x (ISBN 0-262-51017-0). MIT Pr.

Aronoff, Mark & Kean, Mary-Louise, eds. Juncture. (Studia Linguistica et Philologica: Vol. 7). 144p. 1980. pap. 25.00 (ISBN 0-915838-46-X). Anma Libri.

Aronoff, Mark, et al, eds. Language Sound & Structure. (Illus.). 360p. 1984. text ed. 35.00x (ISBN 0-262-01074-7). MIT Pr.

Aronoff, Myron J., ed. Cross Currents in Israeli Culture & Politics. (Political Anthropology Ser.: Vol. IV). 115p. 1984. text ed. 29.95x (ISBN 0-88738-010-7); pap. text ed. 12.95 (ISBN 0-87855-811-X). Transaction Bks.

--Culture & Political Change. LC 79-92197. (Political Anthropology Ser.: Vol. II). 224p. 1982. 29.95 (ISBN 0-87855-434-3). Transaction Bks.

--The Frailty of Authority. (Political Anthropology Ser.: Vol. 5). 221p. (Orig.). 1985. 29.95 (ISBN 0-88738-091-3); pap. text ed. 12.95x (ISBN 0-88738-634-2). Transaction Bks.

--Ideology & Interest: The Dialectic of Politics. LC 79-92197. (Political Anthropology Ser.: Vol. 1). 217p. 1980. text ed. 29.95 (ISBN 0-87855-371-1). Transaction Bks.

--Political Anthropplogy: Cross Currents in Israeli Culture & Politics, Vol. 5. 217p. 1984. 29.95 (ISBN 0-88738-010-7). Transaction Bks.

--Religion & Politics. (Political Anthropology Ser.: Vol. III). 145p. 1983. 24.95 (ISBN 0-87855-459-9); pap. 12.95 (ISBN 0-87855-977-9). Transaction Bks.

Aronoff, S., ed. Phloem Transport. LC 75-15501. (NATO ASI Series A: Life Sciences: Vol. 4). 646p. 1975. 79.50x (ISBN 0-306-35604-X, Plenum Pr). Plenum Pub.

Aronofsky, et al, eds. Energy Policy, Vol. 10. (TIMS Studies in the Management Sciences). 262p. 29.25 (ISBN 0-318-14455-7). Inst Mgmt Sci.

Aronofsky, J. S., et al, eds. Energy Policy. (TIMS Studies in the Management Sciences: Vol. 10). 260p. 1979. 32.50 (ISBN 0-444-85238-7, North Holland). Elsevier.

Aronofsky, Julius S., jt. auth. see Greynolds, Elbert B.

Aronofsky, Julius S., et al. Managerial Planning with Linear Programming: In Process Industry Operations. LC 78-2848. (Illus.). pap. 98.00 (ISBN 0-317-10743-7, 2055399). Bks Demand UMI.

--Programmable Calculators Business Applications. 203p. 1978. pap. 11.95 (ISBN 0-317-06593-9). Tex Instr Inc.

--Programmable Calculators: Business Applications. (Illus.). 1978. pap. text ed. 11.95 (ISBN 0-07-002317-4). McGraw.

Aronovici, Carol. Housing the Masses. 21.25 (ISBN 0-8369-7128-0, 7962). Ayer Co Pubs.

Aronow, Edward & Reznikoff, Marvin. Rorschach Content Interpretation. LC 76-25544. 384p. 1976. 49.50 (ISBN 0-8089-0961-4, 790200). Grune.

Aronow, Edward & Reznikoff, Marvin, eds. A Rorschach Introduction: Content & Perceptual Approaches. 160p. 1982. 18.00 (ISBN 0-8089-1516-9, 790201). Grune.

Aronow, Sara. Seven Days of Creation. (Bible Stories in Rhymes Ser.: Vol. 1). (Illus.). 32p. (ps-2). 1985. 4.95 (ISBN 0-87203-119-5). Hermon.

Aronowicz, Annette, et al, trs. see Dumezil, Georges.

Aronowitz, Dennis S. Legal Aspects of Arms Control Verification in the United States. LC 65-26174. 224p. 1965. 15.00 (ISBN 0-379-00279-5). Oceana.

Aronowitz, Eugene, ed. Prevention Strategies for Mental Health. LC 82-24133. 1982. pap. 9.95 (ISBN 0-88202-139-7, Prodist). Watson Pub Intl.

Aronowitz, Stanley. The Crisis in Historical Materialism: Class, Politics & Culture in Marxist Theory. 376p. 1981. 29.95x (ISBN 0-686-76469-2); pap. 12.95x (ISBN 0-686-86216-3). Bergin & Garvey.

--The Crisis in Historical Materialism: Class, Politics, & Culture in Marxist Theory. LC 80-29488. 372p. 1981. 37.95x (ISBN 0-03-059031-0); pap. 16.95x 1982 (ISBN 0-03-062026-0). Praeger.

--False Promises: The Shaping of American Working-Class Consciousness. LC 73-5679. 480p. 1973. pap. 5.95 (ISBN 0-07-002316-6). McGraw.

--Honor America: The Nature of Fascism, Historic Struggles Against It & a Strategy for Today. (Orig.). 1971. pap. 0.75 (ISBN 0-87810-011-3). Times Change.

--Working Class Hero: A New Strategy for Labor. LC 84-11018. 248p. 1984. pap. 12.95 (ISBN 0-915361-13-2, Dist. by Watts). Adama Pubs Inc.

--Working Class Hero: Evolution of the American Labor Movement. 320p. 1983. 18.95 (ISBN 0-8298-0653-9). Pilgrim NY.

Aronowitz, Stanley & Giroux, Henry A. Education under Siege: The Conservative, Liberal & Radical Debate over Schooling. 256p. (Orig.). 1985. 27.95 (ISBN 0-89789-067-1); pap. 12.95 (ISBN 0-89789-068-X). Bergin & Garvey.

Aronowitz, Stanley, ed. see Larkin, Ralph & Foss, Daniel A.

Aronowitz, Stanley, ed. see Lichten, Eric.

Aron-Rosa, Daniele, ed. Pulsed Yag Laser Surgery. LC 83-60475. 224p. 1983. 49.50 (ISBN 0-943432-03-0, 278). Slack Inc.

Arons, Arnold. The Various Language: An Inquiry Approach to the Physical Sciences. (Illus.). 1977. 19.95x (ISBN 0-19-502147-9). Oxford U Pr.

Arons, Harry. Handbook of Self-Hypnosis. rev. ed. pap. 5.95 (ISBN 0-87505-284-3). Borden.

--Hypnosis in Criminal Investigation. pap. 11.00 (ISBN 0-398-00054-9). Borden.

--New Master Course in Hypnotism. 16.00 (ISBN 0-87505-264-9). Borden.

--Speed Hypnosis. pap. 3.00 (ISBN 0-87505-299-1). Borden.

Arons, Harry & Bubeck, Marne F. H. Handbook of Professional Hypnosis. 1976. pap. 15.00 (ISBN 0-87505-288-6). Borden.

Arons, Raymond A. New Economic Health Care: Drugs Case Mix & Patients' Length of Stay. LC 84-6831. 256p. 1984. 34.95 (ISBN 0-03-071663-2). Praeger.

Arons, S. Compelling Belief: The Culture of American Schooling. 256p. 19.95 (ISBN 0-07-002326-3). McGraw.

Aronsberg, E., tr. see Platonov, Sergei F.

Aronsfeld, C. C. The Text of the Holocaust: A Documentation of the Nazis' Extermination Propaganda from 1919-45. 1985. 16.00 (ISBN 0-916288-17-X); pap. 10.00 (ISBN 0-916288-18-8). Micah Pubns.

Aronsohn, Alan J. Partnership Taxation. 7th ed. 1984. text ed. 35.00 (J4-3552). PLI.

Aronsohn, Richard B. Your Looks: Younger & Better Through Cosmetic Surgery. 1981. pap. text ed. 8.95 (ISBN 0-935236-17-1). Nurseco.

Aronson, Alex. Music & the Novel: A Study in Twentieth Century Fiction. 267p. 1980. 22.50x (ISBN 0-8476-6170-9). Rowman.

Aronson, Arnold. American Set Design. 182p. 1985. cloth 25.95 (ISBN 0-930452-38-0); pap. 16.95 paper (ISBN 0-930452-39-9). Theatre Comm.

--The History & Theory of Environmental Scenography. Beckerman, Bernard, ed. LC 81-11677. (Theater & Dramatic Studies: No. 3). 296p. 1981. 44.95 (ISBN 0-8357-1224-9). UMI Res Pr.

Aronson, Arnold E. Clinical Voice Disorders. 2nd ed. (Illus.). 432p. 1985. text ed. 30.00 (ISBN 0-86577-127-8). Thieme Stratton.

--Psychogenic Voice Disorders: An Interdisciplinary Approach to Detention Diagnosis & Therapy. 1973. pap. 4.95 (ISBN 0-7216-9846-8); tapes & booklet 75.00 (ISBN 0-7216-9842-5). Saunders.

Aronson, Carl E., ed. Veterinary Pharmaceuticals & Biologicals, 1982-1983. 650p. 1982. write for info., cloth (ISBN 0-471-89591-1). Wiley.

Aronson, Charles N. The Big House. LC 74-81876. (Illus.). 288p. 1974. 20.00 (ISBN 0-915736-04-7). C N Aronson.

--Eagle in a Butterfly Net. LC 74-22641. (Eagle Ser.: No. 1). (Illus.). 652p. 1975. 16.00 (ISBN 0-915736-05-5); pap. 10.00 (ISBN 0-915736-06-3). C N Aronson.

--Free Enterprise. LC 78-73546. (Eagle Ser.: No. 5). (Illus.). 1979. 25.00 (ISBN 0-915736-15-2); pap. 18.00 (ISBN 0-915736-16-0). C N Aronson.

--In the Labor Pool. LC 77-78227. (Eagle Ser.: No. 4). (Illus.). 1977. 12.00 (ISBN 0-915736-13-6); pap. 8.00 (ISBN 0-915736-14-4). C N Aronson.

--Into Man. new ed. LC 76-44030. (Eagle Ser.: No. 3). 1977. 18.00x (ISBN 0-915736-11-X); pap. 12.00x (ISBN 0-915736-12-8). C N Aronson.

--Mud & Dust. new ed. LC 76-5966. (Eagle Ser: No. 2). (Illus.). 1976. 16.00 (ISBN 0-915736-09-8); pap. 10.00 (ISBN 0-915736-10-1). C N Aronson.

--Positioneering. (Illus.). 347p. 1969. 20.00 (ISBN 0-915736-01-2). C N Aronson.

--Regimen for Weight Control in Retired Couples & Others Who Want to Control Weight Happily. LC 73-88985. (Illus.). 1973. 5.00 (ISBN 0-915736-03-9). C N Aronson.

--Sculptured Hyacinths. (Illus.). 1973. 20.00 (ISBN 0-915736-02-0). C N Aronson.

--The Writer Publisher. LC 75-36854. 1976. 10.00 (ISBN 0-915736-07-1); pap. 7.00 (ISBN 0-915736-08-X). C N Aronson.

Aronson, D., jt. ed. see Galaty, J. G.

Aronson, Dan R. The City Is Our Farm: Seven Migrant Ijebu Yoruba Families. 2nd ed. 224p. 1978. pap. text ed. 9.95 (ISBN 0-87073-563-2). Schenkman Bks Inc.

Aronson, David. Jewish Way of Life. 1957. 5.00x (ISBN 0-8381-1107-6). United Syn Bk.

Aronson, E., jt. auth. see Lindzey, Gardner.
Aronson, E. A., et al. Satellites & Forecasting of Solar Radiation. Bahm, Raymond E., ed. LC 80-70943. (International Solar Energy Society, American Section, Workshop Ser.). 1982. pap. text ed. 32.50x (ISBN 0-89553-026-0). Am Solar Energy.
Aronson Editorial Board see Langs, Robert.
Aronson, Elliot. The Social Animal. (Illus.). 320p. 1972. 7.95 (ISBN 0-670-65513-9). Viking.
--The Social Animal. 3rd ed. LC 79-27721. (Psychology Ser.). (Illus.). 377p. 1980. text ed. 19.95 (ISBN 0-7167-1229-6); pap. text ed. 9.95 (ISBN 0-7167-1230-X); test & study questions avail. W H Freeman.
--The Social Animal. 4th ed. 440p. 1984. text ed. 20.95 (ISBN 0-7167-1605-4); pap. text ed. 14.95 (ISBN 0-7167-1606-2). W H Freeman.
Aronson, Elliot, jt. auth. see Lindzey, Gardner.
Aronson, Elliot, ed. Readings about the Social Animal. 3rd ed. LC 80-18208. (Psychology Ser.). (Illus.). 457p. 1981. text ed. 23.95 (ISBN 0-7167-1267-9); pap. text ed. 11.95 (ISBN 0-7167-1268-7). W H Freeman.
--Readings about the Social Animal. 4th ed. pap. 12.95; pap. text ed. 20.95. W H Freeman.
Aronson, Elliot, jt. ed. see Lindzey, Gardner.
Aronson, Elliot, tr. see Peterkops, Raimonds.
Aronson, Elliot, et al. The Jigsaw Classroom. LC 78-583. (A Sageview Edition). (Illus.). 197p. 1978. 17.50 (ISBN 0-8039-0997-7). Sage.
Aronson, Elliott, jt. ed. see Lindzey, Garner.
Aronson, Elyse, jt. auth. see LaFray-Young, Joyce.
Aronson, Geoffrey. From Sideshow to Center Stage: U. S. Policy Toward Egypt 1946-1956. 170p. 1985. PLB 17.50x (ISBN 0-931477-39-5). Lynne Rienner.
Aronson, Harvey, jt. auth. see Sullivan, Gerard.
Aronson, Harvey B. Love & Sympathy in Theravada Buddhism. cancelled (ISBN 0-8364-0627-3, Pub. by Motilal Banarsidass). South Asia Bks.
Aronson, Howard I. Georgian: A Reading Grammar. (Illus.). 526p. 1982. 25.95 (ISBN 0-89357-100-8). Slavica.
Aronson, J. Hugo & Brockmann, L. O. Galloping Swede. LC 71-122313. (Illus.). 180p. 1970. 8.50 (ISBN 0-87842-013-4). Mountain Pr.
Aronson, J. K., jt. auth. see Grahame-Smith, D. G.
Aronson, J. Richard. The Scorecard. 1979. Set of 5. pap. 12.95x (ISBN 0-7216-1409-4). Dryden Pr.
Aronson, J. Richard, jt. auth. see Maxwell, James A.
Aronson, J. Richard & Schwartz, Eli, eds. Management Policies in Local Government Finance. rev., 2nd ed. LC 81-2934. (Municipal Management Ser.). (Illus.). 493p. 1981. text ed. 37.50 (ISBN 0-87326-022-8). Intl City Mgt.
Aronson, Jake. Two Hundred Eighty-Nine Most Asked Questions on Condominiums Answered. 224p. 1984. pap. 4.95 (ISBN 0-913428-39-6). Landfall Pr.
Aronson, James, jt. auth. see Belfrage, Cedric.
Aronson, Jerrold R. A Realist Philosophy of Science. LC 82-22956. 278p. 1984. 25.00 (ISBN 0-312-66474-5). St Martin.
Aronson, Jonathan D. Money & Power: Banks & the World Monetary System. LC 78-6630. (Sage Library of Social Research: No. 66). 216p. 1978. 24.00 (ISBN 0-8039-0998-5); pap. 12.00 (ISBN 0-8039-1046-0). Sage.
Aronson, Jonathan D., ed. Debt & the Less Developed Countries. (Special Studies in National Security & Defense Policy). 1979. 35.00x (ISBN 0-89158-370-X); text ed. 13.50. Westview.
--Profit & the Pursuit of Energy: Markets & Regulations. Cowhey, Peter F. LC 82-13424. (Special Studies in Economics). 200p. 1983. 28.50x (ISBN 0-86531-216-8). Westview.
Aronson, Joseph. Encyclopedia of Furniture. rev. ed. (Illus.). (YA) (gr. 9 up). 1965. 17.95 (ISBN 0-517-03735-1). Crown.
Aronson, Lester R., et al, eds. Development & Evolution of Behavior, Essays in Memory of T. C. Schneirla. LC 76-84600. (Illus.). 656p. 1970. text ed. 41.95 (ISBN 0-7167-0921-X). W H Freeman.
Aronson, Marvin L., jt. ed. see Wolberg, Lewis R.
Aronson, Mike, jt. auth. see Shumaker, Terence M.
Aronson, Miriam K. & Bennett, Ruth, eds. The Acting-Out Elderly: Issues for Helping Professionals. LC 82-23430. (Advanced Models & Practice in Aged Care Ser.: No. 1). 132p. 1983. text ed. 24.95 (ISBN 0-917724-76-3, B76). Haworth Pr.
Aronson, R. Public Finance. 576p. 1985. 29.95 (ISBN 0-07-002362-X). McGraw.
Aronson, Robert H. & Weckstein, Donald T. Professional Responsibility in a Nutshell. LC 80-15007. (Nutshell Ser.). 399p. 1980. pap. text ed. 8.95 (ISBN 0-8299-2095-1). West Pub.
Aronson, Robert H., et al. Professional Responsibility, Problems, Cases & Materials. LC 84-27029. (American Casebook Ser.). 702p. 1985. pap. text ed. 27.95 (ISBN 0-314-87537-9). West Pub.
Aronson, Robert L., jt. auth. see Adams, Leonard P.
Aronson, Robert L., ed. The Localization of Federal Manpower Planning. LC 73-620149. 112p. 1973. pap. 4.50 (ISBN 0-87546-053-4); special hard bdg. 8.50 (ISBN 0-87546-283-9). ILR Pr.
Aronson, Ronald. The Dialectics of Disaster: A Preface to Hope. 328p. 1984. 25.00 (ISBN 0-8052-7169-4, Pub. by NLB England); pap. 11.50 (ISBN 0-8052-7170-8). Schocken.
--Jean Paul Sartre: Philosophy in the World. 320p. 1980. 19.50x (ISBN 0-8052-7045-0, Pub by NLB England); pap. 9.95 (ISBN 0-8052-7085-X). Schocken.
Aronson, S. M. & Volk, B. W., eds. Cerebral Sphingolipidoses: A Symposium on Tay-Sach's Disease & Allied Disorders. 1962. 82.50 (ISBN 0-12-064450-9). Acad Pr.
--Inborn Disorders of Sphingolipid Metabolism. 1967. 76.00 (ISBN 0-08-012038-5). Pergamon.
Aronson, S. M., jt. ed. see Volk, Bruno W.
Aronson, Sara P. Communicable Disease Nursing. (Nursng Outline Ser.). 1978. pap. 13.25 (ISBN 0-87488-387-3). Med Exam.
Aronson, Shlomo. The Beginnings of the Gestapo System. 80p. 1969. Casebound 5.95x (ISBN 0-87855-203-0). Transaction Bks.
--Conflict & Bargaining in the Middle East: An Israeli Perspective. LC 77-10967. 1978. text ed. 35.00x (ISBN 0-8018-2046-4). Johns Hopkins.
Aronson, Stephen & Mascia, Michael. The Stress Management Workbook: An Action Plan For Taking Control of Your LIfe & Health. (Appleton Consumer Health Guides Ser.). (Illus.). 164p. 1981. pap. 8.95 (ISBN 0-8385-8696-1). ACC.
Aronson, Steven M. Hype. LC 82-21679. 410p. 1983. 15.95 (ISBN 0-688-01228-0). Morrow.
Aronson, Steven M., jt. auth. see Robins, Natalie.
Aronson, Theo. Grandmama of Europe: The Crowned Descendants of Queen Victoria. (Illus.). 368p. 1984. pap. 11.95 (ISBN 0-7195-4139-5, Pub. by Salem Hse Ltd). Merrimack Pub Cir.
--Royal Ambassadors: British Royalties in Southern Africa, 1860-1947. (Illus.). 144p. 1975. 14.00x (ISBN 0-8476-2392-0). Rowman.
--Royal Family: Years of Transition. (Illus.). 272p. 1984. 19.95 (ISBN 0-7195-4084-4, Pub. by Salem Hse Ltd). Merrimack Pub Cir.
Aronson, Trudy. English Grammar Digest. 256p. 1984. pap. 11.95 (ISBN 0-13-281014-X). P-H.
Aronson, V., jt. auth. see Stare, F. J.
Aronson, Virginia. The Dietetic Technician: Effective Nutrition Counseling. (Illus.). 1985. text ed. 29.50 (ISBN 0-87055-474-3). AVI.
--The Joy of Being Thin. 128p. 1981. pap. 2.00 (ISBN 0-936320-08-7). Compact Bks.
--Thirty Days to Better Nutrition. LC 84-10264. (Illus.). 240p. 1984. pap. 10.95 (ISBN 0-385-19418-8). Doubleday.
Aronson, Virginia & Fitzgerald, Barbara. Guidebook for Nutrition Counselors. 484p. 1980. 19.50 (ISBN 0-8158-0387-7). Chris Mass.
Aronson, Virginia & Stare, Fredrick. RX Executive Diet. 1985. 9.75 (ISBN 0-8158-0424-5). Chris Mass.
Aronson, Virginia, jt. auth. see Stare, Frederick J.
Aronson, Virginia, jt. auth. see Stare, Fredrick J.
Aronsson, Bertil & Lundstrohm, Torsten. Borides, Silicides, & Phosphides: A Critical Review of Their Preparation, Properties & Crystal Chemistry. LC 65-8351. pap. 34.50 (ISBN 0-317-08693-6, 2013149). Bks Demand UMI.
Aronstein, Claude S., ed. The International Handbook on Contracts of Employment. International Bar Association & Labour Law Committee of the Section on Business Law of the International Bar Association. 334p. 1976. 40.00 (ISBN 90-312-0096-4, Pub. by Kluwer Law, Netherlands). Kluwer Academic.
Aronstein, Claude Serge, ed. International Handbook on Contracts of Employment. xxxv, 297p. 1976. text ed. 34.00x (ISBN 90-312-0030-1, Pub. by Kluwer). Rothman.
Aronszajn, N. & Creese, T. M. Polyharmonic Functions. (Mathematical Monographs). 1983. 59.00x (ISBN 0-19-853906-1). Oxford U Pr.
Arora, David. Mushrooms Demystified. LC 79-8513. (Illus.). 680p. 1979. 18.95 (ISBN 0-89815-010-8). Ten Speed Pr.
Arora, Jasbir S., jt. auth. see Haug, Edward J.
Arora, M. N. A Textbook of Cost Accountancy. 750p. 1984. text ed. 45.00x (ISBN 0-7069-2538-6, Pub. by Vikas India); (Pub. by Vikas India). Advent NY.
Arora, R. K., jt. auth. see Khan, A.
Arora, Raj K. Historical & Cultural Data from the Bhavisya Purana. LC 72-900674. 340p. 1972. 13.50x (ISBN 0-89684-399-8). Orient Bk Dist.
Arora, Ramesh K. Comparative Public Administration. 1972. 12.00 (ISBN 0-686-20203-1). Intl Bk Dist.
Arora, Renu. Cooking With Curry. (Illus.). 96p. 1982. pap. 9.95 (ISBN 4-07-973079-9, Pub. by Shufunotomo Co. Ltd. Japan). C E Tuttle.
Arora, S. K. Chemistry & Biochemistry of Legumes. 400p. 1983. text ed. 49.50 (ISBN 0-7131-2854-2). E Arnold.
Arora, S. P. Office Organization & Management. 2nd ed. xi, 570p. 1982. text ed. 37.50x (ISBN 0-7069-1796-0, Pub. by Vikas India). Advent NY.
Arora, Shirley. Proverbial Comparisons & Related Expressions in Spanish: Recorded in Los Angeles, California. LC 75-46053. (University of California Publications, Folklore Studies: No. 29). pap. 132.50 (ISBN 0-317-29033-9, 2021208). Bks Demand UMI.
Aros, Andrew A. Actor's Guide to the Talkies, Nineteen Sixty-Five to Nineteen Seventy-Four. LC 77-21589. 781p. 1977. 42.50 (ISBN 0-8108-1052-2). Scarecrow.
--Broadway & Hollywood Too. LC 80-67670. 60p. 1980. pap. 6.50 (ISBN 0-932352-04-9). Applause Pubns.
--Elvis Presley: His Films, & Music. LC 79-55876. (Vinyl Gold Ser.: No. 1). 75p. (Orig.). 1980. pap. 6.50 (ISBN 0-932352-01-4). Applause Pubns.
--The Latin Music Handbook. LC 78-59987. (Illus.). 1978. pap. 6.50 (ISBN 0-932352-00-6). Applause Pubns.
--The Latin Music Yearbook: 1980. (Vinyl Gold Ser.: No. 2). (Orig.). 1980. pap. 6.50 (ISBN 0-932352-02-2). Applause Pubns.
--A Title Guide to the Talkies, Nineteen Sixty-Four to Nineteen Seventy-Four. LC 76-40451. 344p. 1977. 23.00 (ISBN 0-8108-0976-1). Scarecrow.
Aros, Andrew A., jt. auth. see Pearson, John C.
Arosio, G. Enciclopedia de la Construccion. 1004p. (Espn.). 1970. 58.00 (ISBN 84-224-0560-1, S-50541). French & Eur.
Aroskar, Mila A., jt. auth. see Davis, Anne J.
Arotsky, J. & Glassbrook, D. W. An Introduction to Microcomputing with the PET. 288p. 1983. pap. text ed. 16.95 (ISBN 0-7131-3475-5). E Arnold.
Aroul, G., et al, trs. see Paz, Octavio.
Arp, Bill, pseud. Bill Arp, So Called: Side Show of the Southern Side of the War. LC 72-158277. (Illus.). Repr. of 1866 ed. 25.00 (ISBN 0-404-00213-7). AMS Pr.
--Bill Arp's Peace Papers. LC 79-158276. (Illus.). Repr. of 1873 ed. 27.50 (ISBN 0-404-00405-9). AMS Pr.
Arp, Claudia. Almost Thirteen. 160p. 1985. 9.95 (ISBN 0-8407-5493-0). Nelson.
Arp, Claudia, jt. auth. see Arp, Dave.
Arp, Claudia, jt. auth. see Dillow, Linda.
Arp, Dave & Arp, Claudia. Ten Dates for Mates. LC 83-3954. 176p. 1983. pap. 6.95 (ISBN 0-8407-5845-6). Nelson.
Arp, Gerald. Tropical Gardening Along the Gulf Coast. LC 78-53815. (Illus.). 96p. (Orig.). 1978. pap. 6.95x (ISBN 0-88415-883-7, Pub. by Pacesetter Pr). Gulf Pub.
Arp, Hans, jt. auth. see Lissitsky, El.
Arp, Hans, et al, eds. Plastique, Nos. 1-5. LC 74-91379. (Contemporary Art Ser). Repr. of 1939 ed. 16.00 (ISBN 0-405-00725-6). Ayer Co Pubs.
Arp, Jean, jt. auth. see Museum of Modern Art, New York Staff.
Arp, Thomas R., jt. auth. see Perrine, Laurence.
Arpaci, Vedat S. Conduction Heat Transfer. 1966. 38.95 (ISBN 0-201-00359-7). Addison-Wesley.
Arpaci, Verdat S. & Larsen, Paul S. Convection Heat Transfer. (Illus.). 544p. 1984. text ed. 47.95 (ISBN 0-13-172346-4). P-H.
Arpad, Joseph J. & Lincoln, Kenneth R. Buffalo Bill's Wild West. LC 73-106990. (Wild & Woolly West Ser, No. 19). (Illus., Orig.). 1971. 8.00 (ISBN 0-910584-22-2); pap. 1.50 (ISBN 0-910584-62-1). Filter.
Arpad, Joseph J., ed. see Crockett, David.
Arpad, Susan S., ed. Sam Curd's Diary: The Diary of a True Woman. LC 83-22082. viii, 172p. 1984. 24.95x (ISBN 0-8214-0730-9, 82-84994). Ohio U Pr.
Arpan, Jeffery S. & Radebaugh, Lee. H. International Accounting & Multinational Enterprises. 2nd ed. 370p. 32.95 (ISBN 0-471-88231-3). Wiley.
Arpan, Jeffrey S. & AlHashim, Dhia D. International Dimensions of Accounting. Ricks, David A., ed. LC 83-18747. (International Dimensions of Business Ser.). 240p. 1983. write for info. (ISBN 0-534-01467-4). Kent Pub Co.
Arpan, Jeffrey S. & Radebaugh, Lee H. International Accounting & Multinational Enterprises. LC 80-26070. 400p. 1982. 36.45 (ISBN 0-471-87746-8); tchr's manual avail. (ISBN 0-471-89512-1). Wiley.
Arpan, Jeffrey S. & Ricks, David A., eds. Directory of Foreign Manufacturers in the United States. 2nd ed. LC 79-4146. 1979. lib. bdg. 34.95 (ISBN 0-88406-128-0). Ga St U Busn Pub.
--Directory of Foreign Manufacturers in the United States. 3rd ed. 400p. 1985. 45.00 (ISBN 0-88406-163-9). Ga St U Busn Pub.
Arpan, Jeffrey S., et al. The U. S. Apparel Industry: International Challenge - Domestic Response. LC 88-6647. (Research Monograph: No. 88). 1982. pap. 20.00 (ISBN 0-88406-141-8). Ga St U Busn Pub.
Arpe, Curt. Das Ti Nv Eivai Bei Aristoteles. Bd. with Logische Regeln der Platonischen Schule in der Aristotelischen Topik. Hambruch, Ernst. LC 75-13254. (History of Ideas in Ancient Greece Ser.). (Ger.). 1976. Repr. of 1974 ed. 10.00x (ISBN 0-405-07292-9). Ayer Co Pubs.
Arpe, H-J., jt. auth. see Weissermel, K.
Arpee, Leon. The Armenian Awakening. (Works of Leon Arpee Ser.). xi, 234p. Date not set. Repr. of 1909 ed. 34.00 (ISBN 0-932051-67-7). Am Repr Serv.
Arpel, Adrien. How to Look Ten Years Younger. (Illus.). 1981. pap. 9.95 (ISBN 0-446-37706-6). Warner Bks.
Arpel, Adrien & Ebenstein, Ronnie S. Adrien Arpel's Eight Hundred Fifty-One Fast Beauty Fixes & Facts. (Illus.). 256p. 1985. 17.95 (ISBN 0-399-13016-0, Putnam). Putnam Pub Group.
--Adrien Arpel's Three-Week Crash Makeover-Shapeover Beauty Program. 1982. pap. 3.95 (ISBN 0-671-45928-7). PB.
Arpin, Gary Q. John Berryman: A Reference Guide. 1976. lib. bdg. 20.50 (ISBN 0-8161-7804-6, Hall Reference). G K Hall.
Arps, G. F. see Hull, Clark L.
Arps, Louisa W. Denver in Slices. LC 83-11058. (Illus.). 268p. 1983. 17.95 (ISBN 0-8040-0840-X, 82-76123, Swallow); pap. 9.95 (ISBN 0-8040-0841-8, 82-76131). Ohio U Pr.
Arpy, Jim. Magnificent Mississippi. rev. ed. LC 84-153332. (Illus.). 136p. (Orig.). write for info. (ISBN 0-910381-08-9); pap. 10.95 (ISBN 0-910381-07-0). Sutherland IA.
Arquembourg, P. C. Immunoelectrophoresis Theory, Methods, Identification, Interpretation. 2nd rev. ed. (Illus.). ix, 104p. 1975. 26.00 (ISBN 3-8055-2136-7). S Karger.
Arquette, Mardiningsih. She Child. (Illus.). 32p. (Orig.). 1982. pap. 4.00 (ISBN 0-9605594-1-8). Monkey Man.
Arquilla, Edward R., jt. ed. see Volk, Bruno W.
Arquin, Florence. Diego Rivera, the Shaping of An Artist, 1889-1921. LC 71-108795. (Illus.). pap. 42.80 (ISBN 0-317-10469-1, 2016193). Bks Demand UMI.
Arr, Billy, jt. auth. see Sadler, Barry.
Arrabal, Fernando. L' Architecte et l'Empereur d'Assyrie. 9.95 (ISBN 0-686-54447-1). French & Eur.
--L' Architecte et l'Empereur d'Assyrie. 320p. 1971. pap. 4.95 (ISBN 0-686-54448-X). French & Eur.
--Baal Babylone. 172p. 9.95 (ISBN 0-686-54449-8). French & Eur.
--Burial of the Sardine. 1980. pap. 4.95 (ISBN 0-7145-0147-6). Riverrun NY.
--Ceremonie Pour une Chevre Sur un Nuage. 24p. 1966. 17.95 (ISBN 0-686-54450-1). French & Eur.
--Le Cimetiere des Voitures. 192p. 1972. 4.95 (ISBN 0-686-54451-X). French & Eur.
--L' Enterrement de la Sardine. 200p. 1970. 9.95 (ISBN 0-686-54452-8); pap. 4.95 (ISBN 0-686-54453-6). French & Eur.
--Fetes et Rites De la Confusion. 172p. 1974. 5.95 (ISBN 0-686-54454-4). French & Eur.
--Guernica. 192p. 1975. 5.95 (ISBN 0-686-54455-2). French & Eur.
--Guernica & Other Plays. Wright, Barbara, tr. from Fr. Incl. Labyrinth; Tricycle; Picnic on the Battlefield. 1969. pap. 4.95 (ISBN 0-394-17318-X, E521, Ever). Grove.
--Jeunes Barbares de'aujourd'hui. 48p. 1975. 5.95 (ISBN 0-686-54456-0). French & Eur.
--Lettre Au General Franco. 192p. 1972. 5.95 (ISBN 0-686-54457-9). French & Eur.
--Lettre Aux Communistes Espagnols. 176p. 1978. 9.95 (ISBN 0-686-54446-3). French & Eur.
--Le New York d'Arrabal. 1973. 14.95 (ISBN 0-686-54458-7). French & Eur.
--La Panique: Inedit. 320p. 1973. 5.95 (ISBN 0-686-54459-5). French & Eur.
--La Pierre De la Folie: Poemes. 1970. 17.00 (ISBN 0-686-54460-9); pap. 5.95 (ISBN 0-686-54461-7). French & Eur.
--Sur Fischer: Initiation Aux Echecs. (Illus.). 180p. 1973. 14.95 (ISBN 0-686-54462-5). French & Eur.
--Sur le Fil ou la Ballade du Train Fantome. 118p. 1974. 6.95 (ISBN 0-686-54463-3). French & Eur.
--Theatre: Avec: Le Ciel et la Mer, La Grande Revue du 20e Siecle, Vol. 9. 261p. 1969. 9.95 (ISBN 0-686-54468-4). French & Eur.
--Theatre: Avec: Le Grand Ceremonial, Ceremonie Pour un Noir Assassine, Dieu est-il Devenu Fou, Vol. 3. 221p. 1968. 9.95 (ISBN 0-686-54465-X). French & Eur.
--Theatre: Avec: Le Jardin des Delices, Bestialite Erotique, Une Torture Nommee Dostoievsky, Vol. 6. 192p. 1969. 9.95 (ISBN 0-686-54466-8). French & Eur.
--Theatre: Avec: Operas Paniques, Ars Amandi, Dieu Tente par le Mathematiques, Vol. 8. 192p. 1970. 9.95 (ISBN 0-686-54467-6). French & Eur.
--Theatre Bouffe, Vol. 12. 240p. 1978. 14.95 (ISBN 0-686-54470-6). French & Eur.
--Theatre 1970: Theatre en Mange. 208p. 1970. 9.95 (ISBN 0-686-54473-0). French & Eur.
--Theatre 1971: Les Monstres. 9.95 (ISBN 0-686-54474-9). French & Eur.
--Theatre 1972: Bob Wilson. 9.95 (ISBN 0-686-54475-7). French & Eur.
--La Tour de Babel, Vol. 11. 120p. 1976. 9.95 (ISBN 0-686-54476-5). French & Eur.
--Viva la Muerta (Baal Babylone) 4.95 (ISBN 0-686-54477-3). French & Eur.
--Viva la Muerte. 111p. 1971. 10.95 (ISBN 0-686-54478-1). French & Eur.
Arraj, Jim, jt. auth. see Arraj, Tyra.
Arraj, Tyra & Arraj, Jim. A Tool for Understanding Human Differences: How to Discover & Develop Your Type According to Dr. C. G. Jung & Dr. William Sheldon. LC 83-91430. (Illus.). 180p. 1985. pap. 7.95 (ISBN 0-914073-00-1). Tools for Inner.
Arrandale, Thomas. The Battle for Natural Resources. Congressional Quarterly Inc., ed. LC 83-20939. 230p. 1983. pap. 10.50 (ISBN 0-87187-263-3). Congr Quarterly.
Arrants, Cheryl. Sew Wonderful Gourmet Garments. St. Amant, Kristi, ed. (Illus.). 96p. (Orig.). 1982. pap. text ed. 6.95 (ISBN 0-943704-01-4). Arrants & Assoc.

Arrants, Cheryl & Arrants, Dennis. Thimbelina & the Notion Parade. (Sew Young Ser.). (Illus.). 32p. (Orig.). (gr. k-4). 1983. pap. text ed. 2.50 (ISBN 0-943704-03-0). Arrants & Assoc.

Arrants, Cheryl & Asbjornsen, Jan. Sew Wonderful Silk. rev. ed. Amant, Kristi, ed. (Illus.). 128p. 1981. pap. text ed. 5.95 (ISBN 0-943704-02-2). Arrants & Assoc.

Arrants, Dennis, jt. auth. see Arrants, Cheryl.

Arras, John & Hunt, Robert. Ethical Issues in Modern Medicine. 2nd ed. LC 82-61239. 574p. 1983. pap. 19.95 (ISBN 0-87484-574-2). Mayfield Pub.

Arrasjid, Dorine, jt. auth. see Arrasjid, Harun.

Arrasjid, Harun & Arrasjid, Dorine. Media: A Pocket Guide. 250p. 1972. pap. text ed. 6.95x (ISBN 0-8422-0255-2). Irvington.

Arrastia, Cecilio. Itinerario De la Pasion: Meditaciones De la Semana Santa. 1981. pap. 2.95 (ISBN 0-311-43036-8). Casa Bautista.

Arrathoon, Leigh A., ed. see Fleming, John, et al.

Arrathoon, Leigh A., ed. see Haidu, Peter, et al.

Arredondo, Larry. How to Choose & Successfully Use a Microcomputer: A Personal Computer, a Small Business Computer, a Professional Computer, a Desktop Computer, a Home Computer, a Portable Computer, etc. (Orig.). 1982. pap. text ed. write for info. (ISBN 0-936648-16-3, Pub. by Comp Know Ctr). Telecom Lib.

Arredondo, Larry A. Getting Started in Telecommunications Management. 1980. softcover 30.00 (ISBN 0-936648-04-X). Telecom Lib.

--Telecommunications Management for Business & Government. Newton, Harry, ed. 280p. 1981. 30.00 (ISBN 0-936648-07-4). Telecom Lib.

Arrens, Christa, tr. see Bielfeld, Horst & Heidenreich, Manfred.

Arreola, Allysia J. Elephant Eater. Kamei, Marlene, ed. 12p. (Orig.). 1977. pap. 2.00 (ISBN 0-935684-00-X). Plumbers Ink Bks.

Arreola, Juan J. Confabulario & Other Inventions. Schade, George D., tr. LC 64-13315. (Texas Pan American Ser.). (Illus.). 263p. 1964. 14.95x (ISBN 0-292-73196-5); pap. 7.95 (ISBN 0-292-71030-5). U of Tex Pr.

--The Fair. Upton, John, tr. from Span. LC 76-48981. (Texas Pan American Ser.). (Illus.). 164p. 1977. 12.95 (ISBN 0-292-72417-9). U of Tex Pr.

Arrhenius, G., jt. auth. see Alfven, H.

Arriaga, Eduardo E. Mortality Decline & Its Demographic Effects in Latin America. LC 76-4852. (Population Monograph Ser.: No. 6). (Illus.). 1976. Repr. of 1970 ed. lib. bdg. 55.00x (ISBN 0-8371-8827-X, ARLT). Greenwood.

--New Life Tables for Latin American Populations in the Nineteenth & Twentieth Centuries. LC 76-4841. (Population Monograph Ser.: No. 3). (Illus.). 1976. Repr. of 1968 ed. lib. bdg. 55.00 (ISBN 0-8371-8827-X, ARLT). Greenwood.

Arrian. Alexander the Great: Selections from Arrian. Lloyd, J. Gordon, tr. LC 81-9453. (Translations from Greek & Roman Authors Ser.). 112p. 1982. pap. 5.95 (ISBN 0-521-28195-4). Cambridge U Pr.

--Anabasis of Alexander, Indica, 2 Vols. (Loeb Classical Library: No. 236, 269). 12.00x ea. Vol. 1, Bks. 1-4 (ISBN 0-674-99260-1). Vol. 2, Bks. 5-7 (ISBN 0-674-99297-0). Harvard U Pr.

--The Campaigns of Alexander. De Selincourt, Aubrey, tr. (Classics Ser). 1976. pap. 5.95 (ISBN 0-14-044253-7). Penguin.

Arrick, Fran. Chernowitz! LC 81-7712. 176p. (gr. 7 up). 1981. 9.95 (ISBN 0-02-705720-8). Bradbury Pr.

--Chernowitz. 1983. pap. 2.50 (ISBN 0-451-13717-5, Sig Vista). NAL.

--God's Radar. LC 83-2666. 224p. (gr. 7 up). 1983. 10.95 (ISBN 0-02-705710-0). Bradbury Pr.

--God's Radar. (gr. k-6). 1985. pap. 2.95 (ISBN 0-440-92960-1, LFL). Dell.

--Nice Girl from Good Home. LC 84-11002. 160p. (gr. 7 up). 1984. 11.95 (ISBN 0-02-705840-9). Bradbury Pr.

--Steffie Can't Come Out to Play. LC 78-4423. 192p. (YA) (gr. 8 up). 1978. 9.95 (ISBN 0-02-705800-X). Bradbury Pr.

--Steffie Can't Come Out to Play. 160p. (gr. 7 up). pap. 2.50 (ISBN 0-317-00569-3, LFL). Dell.

--Tunnel Vision. LC 79-25939. 192p. (YA) (gr. 8 up). 1980. 9.95 (ISBN 0-02-705810-7). Bradbury Pr.

--Tunnel Vision. 176p. (gr. 7 up). 1981. pap. 2.50 (ISBN 0-440-98579-X, LE); tchr's. guide by Lou Stanek 0.50. Dell.

Arridge, jt. auth. see SIPRI Staff.

Arrighi, Frances E., et al, eds. see M. D. Anderson Symposia on Fundamental Cancer Research, 33rd.

Arrighi, Giovanni. The Geometry of Imperialism. 2nd ed. 160p. 1983. 14.50 (ISBN 0-8052-7005-1, Pub. by NLB England); pap. 5.95 (ISBN 0-8052-7138-4). Schocken.

Arrighi, Giovanni & Saul, John S. Essays on the Political Economy of Africa. LC 72-81772. 416p. 1973. pap. 6.50 (ISBN 0-85345-250-4). Monthly Rev.

Arrighi, Mel. Manhattan Gothic. 240p. 1985. 14.95 (ISBN 0-312-51281-3). St Martin.

Arrighini, G. P. Intermolecular Forces & Their Evaluation by Perturbation Theory. (Lecture Notes in Chemistry Ser.: Vol. 25). 243p. 1981. pap. 18.60 (ISBN 0-387-10866-1). Springer-Verlag.

Arrigo, Joseph A. The French Quarter & Other New Orleans Scenes. (Illus.). 96p. (Orig.). 1981. pap. 4.95 (ISBN 0-88289-301-7, 455-2). Pelican.

--Mississippi Gulf Coast Scenes. (Illus.). 96p. (Orig.). 1981. pap. 3.95 (ISBN 0-88289-302-5). Pelican.

Arrigo, Joseph A. & Batt, Cara M. Plantations: Forty-Four of Louisiana's Most Beautiful Antebellum Plantation Houses. (Illus.). 96p. (Orig.). 1983. pap. 6.95 (ISBN 0-938530-19-4, 19-4). Lexikos.

Arrigoni, Edward. A Nature Walk to Ka'ena Point. 1978. pap. 3.95 (ISBN 0-914916-30-0). Topgallant.

Arrigoni, Enrico. The Totalitarian Nightmare. 280p. pap. 4.00 (ISBN 0-686-35963-1). West World Pr.

Arrigoni, Patricia. Making the Most of Marin. LC 81-5145. (Illus.). 286p. (Orig.). 1981. pap. 7.95 (ISBN 0-89141-108-9). Presidio Pr.

Arrillaga. Power System Harmonics. LC 84-22097. 1985. 39.95 (ISBN 0-471-90640-9). Wiley.

Arrillaga, J. High Voltage Direct Current Transmission. (IEE Power Engineering Ser.: No. 6). 245p. 1983. casebound 66.00 (ISBN 0-906048-97-4, PO006, Pub. by Peregrinus England). Inst Elect Eng.

Arrillaga, J. & Arnold, C. P. Computer Modeling of Electrical Power Systems. LC 82-2664. 423p. 1983. 63.95 (ISBN 0-471-10406-X, Pub. by Wiley-Interscience). Wiley.

Arrillaga-Torrens, Rafael. Filosofia Griega: Introduccion Al Pensamiento Moderno. 2nd ed. 1978. 9.35 (ISBN 84-292-5103-0). U of PR Pr.

Arrillaga Torrens, Rafael. Sonar y Hacer. LC 76-56437. (Coleccion Mente y Palabra). 1977. 6.25 (ISBN 0-8477-0546-3); pap. 5.00 (ISBN 0-8477-0547-1). U of PR Pr.

Arrington, Fred. History of Dickens County: Ranches & Rolling Plains. 19.95 (ISBN 0-685-48795-4). Eakin Pubns.

Arrington, French. Maintaining the Foundations. 1983. pap. 4.95 (ISBN 0-8010-0192-7). Baker Bk.

Arrington, French L. Ministry of Reconciliation: A Study of Two Corinthians. LC 80-68770. 176p. (Orig.). 1980. pap. 3.95 (ISBN 0-8010-0162-5). Baker Bk.

Arrington, L. R. Introductory Laboratory Animal Science: The Breeding, Care & Management of Experimental Animals. 2nd ed. LC 77-78419. (Illus.). 211p. 1978. 15.65 (ISBN 0-8134-1963-8, 1963); text ed. 11.75x. Interstate.

Arrington, L. R. & Kelley, Kathleen C. Domestic Rabbit Biology & Production. LC 76-10173. 1976. 10.00 (ISBN 0-8130-0537-X). U Presses Fla.

Arrington, Leonard J. Beet Sugar in the West: A History of the Utah-Idaho Sugar Company, 1891-1966. LC 66-28453. (Illus.). 248p. 1966. 20.00x (ISBN 0-295-74037-X). U of Wash Pr.

--Brigham Young: American Moses. LC 84-48685. (Illus.). 544p. 1985. 24.95 (ISBN 0-394-51022-4). Knopf.

--Great Basin Kingdom: An Economic History of the Latter-Day Saints, 1830-1900. LC 58-12961. (Illus.). xx, 534p. 1966. pap. 8.95 (ISBN 0-8032-5006-1, BB 342, Bison). U of Nebr Pr.

Arrington, Leonard J. & Bitton, Davis. The Mormon Experience: A History of the Latter-Day Saints. LC 78-20561. (Illus.). 1979. 17.50 (ISBN 0-394-46566-0). Knopf.

--The Mormon Experience: A History of the Latter-Day Saints. LC 80-11843. (Illus.). 404p. 1980. pap. 5.95 (ISBN 0-394-74102-1, Vin). Random.

--Saints Without Halos: The Human Side of Mormon History. 168p. 1981. 10.95 (ISBN 0-941214-01-X). Signature Bks.

Arrington, Leonard J. & Cluff, Anthony T. Federally Financed Industrial Plants Constructed in Utah During World War Two. 72p. (Orig.). 1969. pap. 3.50 (ISBN 0-87421-035-6). Utah St U Pr.

Arrington, Leonard J. & Hansen, Gary B. The Richest Hole on Earth: A History of the Bingham Copper Mine. 103p. (Orig.). 1963. pap. 4.50 (ISBN 0-87421-028-3). Utah St U Pr.

Arrington, Leonard J., jt. auth. see Cornwall, Rebecca.

Arrington, R. E. see Wolf, Ralph R.

Arrington, Renee, et al. Voices of Inspiration. 34p. 1982. pap. 3.50 (ISBN 0-939296-04-7). Bond Pub Co.

Arrington, Veneta B. Daughters of the American Colonists in Oklahoma: Our Book of Memories. LC 84-61836. (Illus.). 1984. 24.95 (ISBN 0-913507-02-4). New Forums.

Arrington, Veneta B; see Mitchell, Alvan.

Arriola, Gus, ed. & illus. Gordo's Cat. LC 81-9563. (Illus.). 128p. (Orig.). 1981. pap. 6.95 (ISBN 0-916392-84-8). Oak Tree Pubns.

Arriola, Lewis. Vengeance of the God. 206p. 1981. 9.50 (ISBN 0-682-49687-1). Exposition Pr FL.

Arrivi, Francisco. Via Poetica. LC 77-25892. 1978. 6.25 (ISBN 0-8477-3222-3); pap. text ed. 5.00 (ISBN 0-8477-3223-1). U of PR Pr.

Arrom, Jose J. Historia De la Literatura Dramatica Cubana. LC 73-38491. (Yale Romanic Studies: No. 23). Repr. of 1944 ed. 24.00 (ISBN 0-404-53223-3). AMS Pr.

Arrom, Silvia M. The Women of Mexico City, 1790-1857. LC 83-51324. 400p. 1985. 42.50x (ISBN 0-8047-1233-6). Stanford U Pr.

Arronet, Nikola'i I. Motile Muscle & Cell Models. LC 72-88884. (Studies in Soviet Science). pap. 50.50 (ISBN 0-317-28729-X, 2020685). Bks Demand UMI.

Arrons, Edward S. Nightmare. 160p. 1974. pap. 0.95 (ISBN 0-532-95363-0). Woodhill.

Arrons, J., et al, eds. Particle Acceleration Mechanics in Astrophysics. LC 79-55844. (AIP Conference Proceedings: No. 56). (Illus.). 425p. lib. bdg. 22.00 (ISBN 0-88318-155-X). Am Inst Physics.

Arros, Jean D' see Jean D'Arras.

Arrow, G. J. Coleoptera: Clavicornia, Erotylidae, Languriidae & Endomychidae. (Fauna of British India Ser.). (Illus.). xvi, 416p. 1976. Repr. of 1910 ed. 25.00 (ISBN 0-88065-016-8, Pub. by Messers Today & Tomorrows Printers & Publishers India). Scholarly Pubns.

--Coleoptera: Lamellicornia, Cetoniinae, & Dynastinae. (Fauna of British India Ser.). (Illus.). xiv, 328p. 1976. Repr. of 1925 ed. 25.00 (ISBN 0-88065-017-6, Pub. by Messers Today & Tomorrows Printers & Publishers India). Scholarly Pubns.

--Coleoptera: Lamellicornia, Coprinae, Pt. III. (Fauna of British India Ser.). (Illus.). xii, 452p. 1977. Repr. of 1931 ed. 25.00 (ISBN 0-88065-019-2, Pub. by Messers Today & Tomorrows Printers & Publishers India). Scholarly Pubns.

--Coleoptera: Lamellicornia, Rutelinae, Desmonoycinae & Euchirinae. (Fauna of British India Ser.). (Illus.). xiv, 400p. 1974. Repr. of 1917 ed. 15.00 (ISBN 0-88065-018-4, Pub. by Messers Today & Tomorrows Printers & Publishers India). Scholarly Pubns.

Arrow, John. J. C. Squire & D. H. Lawrence. 1973. 8.50 (ISBN 0-8274-1547-8). R West.

Arrow, K. J. & Hahn, F. H. General Competitive Analysis. (Advance Textbooks in Economics: Vol. 12). 452p. 1977. 39.50 (ISBN 0-7204-0750-8, North Holland). Elsevier.

Arrow, K. J. & Hurwicz, L., eds. Studies in Resource Allocation Process. LC 76-9171. (Illus.). 1977. 59.50 (ISBN 0-521-21522-6). Cambridge U Pr.

Arrow, K. J. & Intriligator, M. D., eds. Handbook of Mathematical Economics, 3 vols. (Handbooks in Economics Ser.: No. 1). 1981. Set. 150.00 (ISBN 0-444-86054-1); Vol. 1. 65.00 (ISBN 0-444-86126-2); Vol. 2. 65.00 (ISBN 0-444-86127-0); Vol. 3. 65.00 (ISBN 0-444-86128-9). Elsevier.

Arrow, Kenneth & Honkapohja, Seppo, eds. Frontiers of Economics. 300p. 1985. 39.95x (ISBN 0-631-13408-5). Basil Blackwell.

Arrow, Kenneth, et al, eds. Applied Research for Social Policy: The United States & the Federal Republic of Germany Compared. LC 78-74781. 1979. text ed. 24.00 (ISBN 0-89011-519-2). Abt Bks.

Arrow, Kenneth J. Collected Papers of Kenneth J. Arrow: Applied Economics, Vol. 6. (Illus.). 280p. 1985. text ed. 22.50x (ISBN 0-674-13778-7, Belknap Pr). Harvard U Pr.

--Collected Papers of Kenneth J. Arrow: Production & Capital, Vol. 5. (Illus.). 496p. 1985. text ed. 29.50x (ISBN 0-674-13777-9, Belknap Pr). Harvard U Pr.

--Collected Papers of Kenneth J. Arrow: Vol. 1, Social Choice & Justice; Vol. 2, General Equilibrium. 1983. Vol. 1. text ed. 20.00x (ISBN 0-674-13760-4, Belnap Pr); Vol. 2. text ed. 25.00x (ISBN 0-674-13761-2). Harvard U Pr.

--The Economics of Information. (Collected Papers of Kenneth J. Arrow: Vol. 4). (Illus.). 288p. 1984. text ed. 22.50x (ISBN 0-674-13763-9, Belknap Pr). Harvard U Pr.

--Individual Choice under Certainty & Uncertainty. (Collected Papers of Kenneth J. Arrow: Vol. 3). (Illus.). 296p. 1984. text ed. 25.00x (ISBN 0-674-13762-0, Belknap Pr). Harvard U Pr.

--The Limits of Organization. (Fels Center of Government Ser.). 86p. 1974. pap. 3.95x (ISBN 0-393-09323-9). Norton.

--Social Choice & Individual Values. 2nd ed. (Cowles Foundation Monograph: No. 12). 1970. pap. 5.95x (ISBN 0-300-01364-7, Y233). Yale U Pr.

Arrow, Kenneth J. & Kalt, Joseph P. Petroleum Price Regulation: Should We Decontrol? 1979. pap. 4.25 (ISBN 0-8447-3359-8). Am Enterprise.

Arrow, Kenneth J. & Kurz, Mordecai. Public Investment, the Rate of Return, & Optimal Fiscal Policy. LC 73-108380. (Resources for the Future Ser.). 236p. 1970. 20.00x (ISBN 0-8018-1124-4). Johns Hopkins.

Arrow, Kenneth J., et al. Studies in Linear & Non-Linear Programming. (Illus.). 1958. pap. 18.50x (ISBN 0-8047-0562-3). Stanford U Pr.

--Studies in the Mathematical Theory of Inventory & Production. 1958. 27.50x (ISBN 0-8047-0541-0). Stanford U Pr.

Arrow, Kenneth J., et al, eds. Studies in Applied Probability & Management Science. 1962. 22.50x (ISBN 0-8047-0099-0). Stanford U Pr.

--Applied Research for Social Policy: The United States & the Federal Republic of Germany Compared. 332p. 1984. Repr. of 1979 ed. lib. bdg. 37.50 (ISBN 0-8191-4094-5). U Pr of Amer.

Arrow, Kenneth J., et al, eds. see First Stanford Symposium.

Arrow, Kenneth V., jt. auth. see Lind, Robert C.

Arrow Pub Staff, ed. Arrow Street Guide of Berkshire County. 1976. pap. 2.25 (ISBN 0-913450-29-4). Arrow Pub.

Arrow Pub. Staff, ed. Arrow Street Guide of Cincinnati. 1975. 2.75 (ISBN 0-913450-25-1). Arrow Pub.

--Arrow Street Guide of Cleveland. 1983. 3.95 (ISBN 0-913450-28-6). Arrow Pub.

Arrow Pub Staff, ed. Arrow Street Guide of Greater Hartford. 1976. pap. 4.25 (ISBN 0-913450-90-1). Arrow Pub.

--Arrow Street Guide of the North Shore. 1976. pap. 2.50 (ISBN 0-913450-30-8). Arrow Pub.

Arrowood, Charles F. The Taxation of the United Kingdom. (Works of Charles Flinn Arrowood Ser.). vi, 180p. Date not set. Repr. of 1869 ed. lib. bdg. 29.00 (ISBN 0-932051-59-6). Am Repr Serv.

--Thomas Jefferson & Education in a Republic. (Works of Charles Flinn Arrowood Ser.). vii, 184p. Date not set. Repr. of 1930 ed. lib. bdg. 29.00 (ISBN 0-932051-59-6). Am Repr Serv.

Arrowood, Charles F., jt. auth. see Eby, Frederick.

Arrowood, Charles F., ed. Thomas Jefferson & Education in a Republic. LC 79-136406. (BCL Ser.: No. 1). Repr. of 1930 ed. 12.00 (ISBN 0-404-00406-7). AMS Pr.

--Thomas Jefferson & Education in a Republic. LC 70-131611. 1970. Repr. of 1930 ed. 11.00 (ISBN 0-403-00498-5). Scholarly.

Arrowood, Clinton, jt. auth. see Elliott, Donald.

Arrowood, Clinton L., jt. auth. see Elliott, Donald.

Arrowsmith, et al, eds. Four Plays by Aristophanes: The Clouds, The Frogs, The Birds, Lysistrata. 1984. pap. 5.95 (ISBN 0-452-00717-8, Mer). NAL.

Arrowsmith, D. K. & Place, C. M. Ordinary Differential Equations. LC 81-14003. 1982. 43.00 (ISBN 0-412-22600-6, NO. 6618, Pub. by Chapman & Hall); pap. 19.95 (ISBN 0-412-22610-3, NO. 6617). Methuen Inc.

Arrowsmith, Don. Princess's Birthday Party. (Illus.). (gr. 2-4). 1975. pap. 2.95 (ISBN 0-913270-46-6). Sunstone Pr.

Arrowsmith, John P. Art of Instructing the Infant Deaf & Dumb: Including de l'Epee's Method of Educating Mutes. (Contributions to the History of Psychology B, Psychometrics & Educational Psychology Ser.). 1983. Repr. of 1819 ed. 30.00 (ISBN 0-89093-319-7). U Pubns Amer.

Arrowsmith, Nancy. A Field Guide to the Little People. 296p. 1977. 10.00 (ISBN 0-8090-4450-1). Hill & Wang.

Arrowsmith, Richard S. The Prelude to the Reformation: A Study of English Church Life from the Age of Wycliffe to the Breach with Rome. LC 83-45573. Date not set. Repr. of 1923 ed. 30.00 (ISBN 0-404-19891-0). AMS Pr.

Arrowsmith, William, ed. Hard Labor: Poems by Cesare Pavese. LC 79-2371. 272p. 1979. 9.95 (ISBN 0-8018-2180-0). Johns Hopkins.

Arrowsmith, William, ed. see Aeschylus.

Arrowsmith, William, ed. see Aristophanes.

Arrowsmith, William, ed. see Euripides.

Arrowsmith, William, tr. The Storm & Other Poems. 250p. 1984. 20.00 (ISBN 0-8180-1582-9); pap. 9.95 (ISBN 0-8180-1585-3). Horizon.

Arrowsmith, William, tr. see Antonioni, Michelangelo.

Arrowsmith, William, tr. see Euripides.

Arrowsmith, William see Euripides.

Arrowsmith, William, tr. see Montale, Eugenio.

Arrowsmith, William, tr. see Petronius.

Arroyo, Anita. America en Su Literatura. 2nd ed. LC 77-3041. (Illus.). 1978. 15.00 (ISBN 0-8477-3175-8); pap. text ed. 12.00 (ISBN 0-8477-3182-0). U of PR Pr.

--El Grillo Grunon: Cuentos para Chicos y Grandes. LC 84-13199. (Ninos y Letras Ser.). (Illus.). 122p. (Orig., Span.). (gr. 1-6). 1984. pap. 5.50 (ISBN 0-8477-3527-3). U of PR Pr.

--Narrativa Hispanoamericana Actual: America y Sus Problemas. LC 79-19468. (Mente y Palabra Ser.). v, 517p. 1980. 20.00 (ISBN 0-8477-0562-5); pap. 15.00 (ISBN 0-8477-0563-3). U of PR Pr.

Arroyo, Mary T. The Systematics of the Legume Genus Harpalyce: Leguminoseae. Lotoideae. Incl. A Monographs of the Genus Hamelia: Rubiaceae. Elias, Thomas S. LC 66-6394. (Memoirs of the New York Botanical Garden: Vol. 26, No. 4). 1976. pap. 16.00x (ISBN 0-89327-001-6). NY Botanical.

Arroyo, Santana. Bright Glows the Dawn. 384p. 1985. pap. 3.75 (ISBN 0-8439-2270-2, Leisure Bks). Dorchester Pub Co.

--Hustle into Death. 1977. pap. 1.50 (ISBN 0-532-15289-1). Woodhill.

--Witchfires. (Orig.). 1981. pap. 2.75 (ISBN 0-505-51707-8, Pub. by Tower Bks). Dorchester Pub Co.

Arroyo, Stephen. Astrology, Karma & Transformation: The Inner Dimensions of the Birthchart. LC 76-21588. (Illus.). 249p. 1978. 17.95x (ISBN 0-916360-04-0); pap. 9.95 (ISBN 0-916360-03-2). CRCS Pubns NV.

--Astrology, Psychology & the Four Elements. LC 75-27828. 208p. (Orig.). 1975. 14.95x (ISBN 0-916360-02-4); pap. 7.95 (ISBN 0-916360-01-6). CRCS Pubns NV.

--The Practice & Profession of Astrology: Rebuilding Our Lost Connections with the Cosmos. 200p. (Orig.). 1984. pap. 7.95 (ISBN 0-916360-15-6). CRCS Pubns NV.

--Relationships & Life Cycles: Modern Dimensions of Astrology. LC 79-53979. 1979. pap. 7.95 (ISBN 0-916360-12-1). CRCS Pubns NV.

Arroyo, Stephen & Greene, Liz. The Jupiter-Saturn Conference Lectures. LC 82-45632. (Lectures on Modern Astrology). 1983. pap. 8.95 (ISBN 0-916360-16-4). CRCS Pubns NV.

Arroyo De La Cuesta, Felipe. Grammar of the Mutsun Language Spoken at the Mission of San Juan Bautista Alta California. LC 76-158278. (Library of American Linguistics: Vol. 4). Repr. of 1861 ed. 28.50 (ISBN 0-404-50984-3). AMS Pr.

--Vocabulary or Phrase Book of the Mutsun Language of Alta California. (Library of American Linguistics: Vol. 8). (Catalan.). Repr. of 1862 ed. 28.50 (ISBN 0-404-50988-6). AMS Pr.

Arrubla, Gerardo, jt. auth. see Henao, Jesus M.

Arruda, ed. Mathematical Logic: Proceedings of the First Brazilian Conference. (Lecture Notes in Pure & Applied Mathematics Ser.: Vol. 39). 1978. 55.00 (ISBN 0-8247-6772-1). Dekker.

Arruda, A. L., et al, eds. Mathematical Logic in Latin America. (Studies in Logic & the Foundations of Mathematics: Vol. 99). 392p. 1980. 64.00 (ISBN 0-444-85402-9, North Holland). Elsevier.

Arruda, J. A. & Kurtzman, N. A., eds. Disorders of Tubular Transport: Physiologic & Clinical Correlations. (Journal: Mineral & Electrolyte Metabolism: Vol. 5, 2-4). (Illus.). 144p. 1981. pap. 44.75 (ISBN 3-8055-2515-X). S Karger.

Arrupe, Pedro. Challenge to Religious Life Today: Selected Letters & Addresses--1. Aixala, Jerome, ed. LC 79-87603. 310p. 1979. 7.00 (ISBN 0-912422-45-9); pap. 6.00 smyth sewn (ISBN 0-912422-44-0). Inst Jesuit.

--In Him Alone Is Our Hope: Texts on the Heart of Christ (1966-1983) Aixala, Jerome, ed. Ganss, G. E., et al, trs. from Span. LC 83-80037. (Selected Letters & Addresses of: IV). xvi, 180p. 1984. pap. 7.00 Smyth sewn (ISBN 0-912422-85-8); pap. 6.00 (ISBN 0-912422-87-4). Inst Jesuit.

--Justice with Faith Today: Selected Letters & Addresses--II. Aixala, Jerome, ed. LC 80-81055. 336p. 1980. 8.00 (ISBN 0-912422-51-3); pap. 7.00 smyth sewn (ISBN 0-912422-50-5). Inst Jesuit.

--Pedro Arrupe Other Apostolates Today: Selected Letters & Addresses - III. Aixala, Jerome, ed. LC 81-80741. 380p. 1981. 9.00 (ISBN 0-912422-81-5); pap. 8.00 smyth sewn (ISBN 0-912422-80-7). Inst Jesuit.

Arrupe, Pedro S. J. One Jesuit's Spiritual Journey: Autobiographical Conversations with Jean-Claude Dietsch, S. J. Ganss, George E., frwd. by. Bradley, Ruth, tr. LC 84-81990. Orig. Title: Pedro Arrupe. Itineraire d'um Jesuite.Entretiens avec Jean-Claude Dietsch, S. J. 190p. 1985. smyth-sewn 10.00 (ISBN 0-912422-69-6); pap. 8.00 (ISBN 0-912422-68-8). Inst Jesuit.

Ars Ceramica, Ltd. The Markham Pottery Book & Catalogue. (Illus.). 1979. 8.00 (ISBN 0-89344-028-0). Ars Ceramica.

--The Story of Teco. (Illus.). 6.00 (ISBN 0-686-53148-5). Ars Ceramica.

--Teco Art Pottery. (Illus.). 1.50 (ISBN 0-89344-029-9). Ars Ceramica.

Ars Edition Staff. The Littlest Book for a Friend. (Illus.). 28p. 1984. 2.95 (ISBN 0-86724-070-9). Ars Edition.

--The Littlest Book for a New Mother. (Illus.). 28p. 1984. 2.95 (ISBN 0-86724-060-1). Ars Edition.

--The Littlest Book for Mother's Day. 28p. 1984. 2.95 (ISBN 0-86724-065-2). Ars Edition.

--The Littlest Book for the Heart. 28p. 1984. 2.95 (ISBN 0-86724-069-5). Ars Edition.

--The Littlest Book for Your Birthday. (Illus.). 28p. 1984. 2.95 (ISBN 0-86724-071-7). Ars Edition.

--The Littlest Book Just for You. (Illus.). 28p. 1984. 2.95 (ISBN 0-86724-062-8). Ars Edition.

--The Littlest Book of Birds. (Illus.). 28p. 1984. 2.95 (ISBN 0-86724-072-5). Ars Edition.

--The Littlest Book of Joy. (Illus.). 28p. 1984. 2.95 (ISBN 0-86724-068-7). Ars Edition.

--The Littlest Book of Kittens. (Illus.). 28p. 1984. 2.95 (ISBN 0-86724-073-3). Ars Edition.

--The Littlest Book of Life. (Illus.). 28p. 1984. 2.95 (ISBN 0-86724-064-4). Ars Edition.

--The Littlest Book of Roving. (Illus.). 30p. 1984. 2.95 (ISBN 0-86724-076-8). Ars Edition.

--The Littlest Book of Seasons. (Illus.). 28p. 1984. 2.95 (ISBN 0-86724-063-6). Ars Edition.

Ars Edition Staff, ed. see Ars Sacra.

Ars Edition Staff, ed. see Keussen, Gudrun.

ARS Enterprises. Directory of Collectors & Suppliers: Including Phonograph & TV Collectors. 8th ed. (Orig.). 1982. pap. 4.00 (ISBN 0-938630-02-4). ARS Enterprises.

Ars Sacra. The Hummel. Ars Edition Staff, ed. (Illus.). 78p. 1981. 15.00 (ISBN 0-86724-031-8). Ars Edition.

Arsac, Jacques. Foundations of Programming. Duncan, Fraser, tr. (APIC Studies in Data Processing Monographs: No. 20). 1985. 29.50 (ISBN 0-12-064460-6). Acad Pr.

Arsan, Emmanuelle. Emmanuelle One. Bair, Lowell, tr. from Fr. LC 78-139255. 1980. pap. 3.95 (ISBN 0-394-17657-X, B439, BC). Grove.

--Emmanuelle Two. Hollo, Anselm, tr. from Fr. LC 74-24995. 1981. 4.50 (ISBN 0-394-17891-2, B453, BC). Grove.

Arsanes. Orations of Arsanes Agaynst Philip: Of the Embassadors of Venice. LC 70-26068. (English Experience Ser.: No. 233). 164p. Repr. of 1560 ed. 14.00 (ISBN 90-221-0233-5). Walter J Johnson.

Arsanjani, Mahnoush H. International Regulation of Internal Resources: A Study of Law & Policy. LC 80-21169. 558p. 1981. 37.50x (ISBN 0-8139-0879-5). U Pr of Va.

Arsapada, see Gotama.

Arscott, et al. Remedial Mathematics for Science & Engineering. 152p. 1983. pap. text ed. 8.95 (ISBN 0-8403-3068-5). Kendall-Hunt.

Arscott-Berry. Introduction to Applied Mathematics: Summary Notes. 296p. 1983. pap. text ed. 11.95 (ISBN 0-8403-3086-3). Kendall-Hunt.

Arsdale, May B. Van see Van Arsdale, May B. & Emellos, Ruth P.

Arsdale, Robert S. Van see Van Arsdale, Robert S.

Arsdell, Paul M. van see Van Arsdell, Paul M.

Arsenault, J. E. & Roberts, J. A., eds. Reliability & Maintainability of Electronic Systems. LC 79-10543. (Computer Software Engineering Ser.). (Illus.). 584p. 1980. text ed. 41.95 (ISBN 0-914894-24-2). Computer Sci.

Arsenault, Raymond. The Wild Ass of the Ozarks: Jeff Davis & the Social Bases of Southern Politics. LC 83-5103. 618p. 1984. 34.95 (ISBN 0-87722-326-2). Temple U Pr.

Arsene, et al. Spectral Theory of Linear Operators & Related Topics. (Operator Theory Ser.: No. 14). 1985. text ed. 39.95x (ISBN 0-317-18422-9). Birkhauser.

Arsene, Gr., ed. Invariant Subspaces & Other Topics. (Operator Theory: Advances & Applications Ser.: No. 6). 229p. 1983. 28.95x (ISBN 0-8176-1360-9). Birkhauser.

Arsene, Grigore, ed. Dilation Theory, Toeplitz Operators, & Other Topics. (Operators Theory: Vol. II). 400p. 1983. text ed. 39.95 (ISBN 3-7643-1516-4). Birkhauser.

Arsen'ev, Nicolai S. We Beheld His Glory. Ewer, Mary A., tr. LC 76-113545. Repr. of 1936 ed. 18.00 (ISBN 0-404-00407-5). AMS Pr.

Arsenian, Seth. Bilingualism & Mental Development. LC 75-176525. (Columbia University. Teachers College. Contributions to Education: No. 712). Repr. of 1937 ed. 22.50 (ISBN 0-404-55712-0). AMS Pr.

Arseniev, Nicholas. Mysticism & the Eastern Church. 173p. 1979. pap. 6.95 (ISBN 0-913836-55-9). St Vladimirs.

--Revelation of Life Eternal: An Introduction to the Christian Message. 144p. 1964. pap. 5.95 (ISBN 0-913836-00-1). St Vladimirs.

--Russian Piety. 143p. 1964. pap. 4.95 (ISBN 0-913836-21-4). St Vladimirs.

Arseniew, Nicholas. Mysticism & the Eastern Church. 1977. lib. bdg. 59.95. Gordon Pr.

Arsenijevic, N. S. German-Serbocroatian Electrotechnical Dictionary. 150p. (Ger. & Serbocroatian.). 1971. Leatherette 24.95 (ISBN 0-686-92462-2, M-963X3). French & Eur.

Arson, I. S., et al. Eighteen Papers on Logic & Theory of Functions. LC 51-5559. (Translations Ser.: No. 2, Vol. 83). 1969. 33.00 (ISBN 0-8218-1783-3, TRANS 2-83). Am Math.

Arsove, Maynard & Leutwiler, Heinz. Algebraic Potential Theory. LC 79-24384. (Memoirs of the American Mathematical Society Ser.: Vol. 226). 130p. 1983. pap. 11.00 (ISBN 0-8218-2226-8, MEMO 226). Am Math.

Arsove, Maynard G. & Johnson, Guy, Jr. Conformal Mapping Technique for Infinitely Connected Regions. (Memoirs: No. 91). 56p. 1970. pap. 9.00 (ISBN 0-8218-1291-2, MEMO-91). Am Math.

Arstila, A. U., jt. ed. see Trump, Benjamin F.

Arstila, Antti U., jt. ed. see Trump, Benjamin F.

Arsuaga De Vila, Maria. Manual De Espanol. rev. ed. LC 80-36752. 253p. 1980. Set. 12.50 (ISBN 0-8477-3177-4); Vol. 1, Pt. 1. 6.25 (ISBN 0-8477-3195-2); Vol. 1, Pt. 2. 6.25 (ISBN 0-8477-3196-0); Vol. 2. 6.25 (ISBN 0-8477-3165-0). U of PR Pr.

Art Address Verlag. The International Directory of the Arts, 1985-86, 2 vols. 2000p. 1985. 120.00 set (ISBN 3-921529-04-2). Bowker.

Art & Antiques Magazines Editors, ed. Nineteenth Century Furniture: Innovation, Revival & Reform. (Illus.). 160p. 1982. 25.00 (ISBN 0-8230-8004-8, Art & Antiques). Watson-Guptill.

Art Direction Magazine Editors, intro. by. Creativity, One. LC 59-14827. (Creativity Ser., Vol. 1). (Illus.). 288p. 1972. 22.50 (ISBN 0-910158-02-9). Art Dir.

Art Direction Staff, jt. ed. see Barron, Don.

Art Directors Club of New York. Art Directors Annual, 62nd. Solomon, Miriam L., ed. (Illus.). 816p. 1984. 39.95 (ISBN 0-937414-03-4). R Silver.

--The Sixty-First Art Directors Annual. Solomon, Miriam L., ed. (Illus.). 672p. 1982. 39.95 (ISBN 0-937414-02-6). ADC Pubns.

--Sixty-Second Art Directors Annual. Solomon, Miriam L., ed. (Illus.). 816p. 1983. 39.95 (ISBN 0-937414-03-4). ADC Pubns.

--Sixty-Third Art Directors Annual. Soloman, Miriam L., ed. (Illus.). 516p. 1984. 39.95 (ISBN 0-937414-04-2, Dist. by R Silver). ADC Pubns.

Art Directors Club of Tokyo. Annual of Advertising Art in Japan, 1983. 27th ed. LC 61-66515. 420p. (Japenese.). 1983. 92.00x (ISBN 0-8002-3127-9). Intl Pubns Serv.

Art Directors Club of Tokyo, ed. Annual of Advertising Art in Japan, 1980. 24th ed. LC 61-66515. (Illus.). 343p. (Eng. & Japanese.). 1980. 72.50x (ISBN 0-8002-2886-3). Intl Pubns Serv.

Art Directors Club, 3rd Communications Conference, New York. Creativity: An Examination of the Creative Process. facsimile ed. Smith, Paul, ed. LC 77-167306. (Essay Index Reprint Ser). Repr. of 1959 ed. 32.00 (ISBN 0-8369-2578-5). Ayer Co Pubs.

Art Directors Club, 4th Communications Conference, New York. Symbology: The Use of Symbols in Visual Communications. facsimile ed. Whitney, Elwood, ed. LC 70-167307. (Essay Index Reprint Ser). Repr. of 1960 ed. 36.00 (ISBN 0-8369-2579-3). Ayer Co Pubs.

Art Flicks. Art Flicks New Streamside Guide to Naturals & Them Imitations. LC 83-5744. (Illus.). 176p. 1983. pap. 7.95 (ISBN 0-8329-0331-0, Pub. by Winchester Pr). New Century.

Art Gallery California State University, Fullerton & McAlpine, Barbara. Emerson Woelffer: Profile of the Artist 1947-1981. (Orig.). 1982. pap. write for info. (ISBN 0-935314-00-8). CSU Art Gallery.

Art, Henry W. A Garden of Wildflowers: One Hundred One Native Species & How to Grow Them. LC 85-45163. (Illus.). 304p. 1986. 22.50 (ISBN 0-88266-404-2); pap. 12.95 (ISBN 0-88266-405-0). Garden Way Pub.

Art Institute of Chicago. Twenty-Four Full-Color Postcards of Great Impressionist & Post-Impressionist Paintings. pap. 3.50 (ISBN 0-486-24616-7). Dover.

Art Institute of Chicago & Joachim, Harold. French Drawings & Sketchbooks of the Nineteenth Century, 2 vols. LC 78-23641. 1979. (Chicago Visual Lib); Vol. 1. 5 color fiches 75.00 (ISBN 0-226-68796-1, CVL 25); Vol. 2. color fiches 100.00 (ISBN 0-226-68798-8, CVL 26). U of Chicago Pr.

--French Drawings of the Sixteenth & Seventeenth Centuries. LC 77-9417. 1977. 1 color fiche incl. 23.50 (ISBN 0-226-68794-5, Chicago Visual Lib). U of Chicago Pr.

--Italian Drawings of the Eighteenth & Nineteenth Centuries: Spanish Drawings of the Seventeenth Through Nineteenth Centuries. LC 79-19721. (Illus.). 1980. text-fiche 45.00 (ISBN 0-226-68803-8). U of Chicago Pr.

--Italian Drawings of the Fifteenth, Sixteenth, & Seventeenth Centuries. LC 79-14276. (Chicago Visual Library: No. 31). (Illus.). 1979. text ed. 80.00 incl. microfiche (ISBN 0-226-68801-1). U of Chicago Pr.

Art Institute of Chicago & Speyer, A. James. Twentieth Century European Paintings. LC 80-18785. (Illus.). 112p. 1981. incl fiche 60.00 (ISBN 0-226-68804-6). U of Chicago Pr.

Art Institute of Chicago & Rizzoli International Publications & Rubin, Rebecca. Chicago Architects Design. LC 82-60339. (Illus.). 174p. 1982. pap. 25.00 (ISBN 0-8478-0466-6). Art Inst Chi.

Art Institute of Chicago, Ryerson Library. Index to Art Periodicals, 11 Vols. 1962. Set. 1030.00 (ISBN 0-8161-0627-4, Hall Library). G K Hall.

--Index to Art Periodicals, 1st Supplement. 1975. lib. bdg. 110.00 (ISBN 0-8161-0727-0, Hall Library). G K Hall.

Art-Journal. Crystal Palace Exhibition Illustrated Catalogue: London, 1851. Orig. Title: Art-Journal Illustrated Catalogue. (Illus.). 1970. pap. 11.95 (ISBN 0-486-22503-8). Dover.

Art Libraries Society of North America. AACR2 Goes Public. (Occasional Papers: No. 1). 64p. (Orig.). 1982. pap. 5.00 (ISBN 0-942740-00-9). Art Libs Soc.

--Current Issues in Fine Arts Collection Development. (Occasional Papers: 3). 36p. (Orig.). 1984. pap. 7.50 (ISBN 0-942740-03-3). Art Libs Soc.

Art Research Libraries of Ohio. Union List of Periodicals & Serials in Ohio Art Research Libraries. LC 74-620198. 1975. 5.00x (ISBN 0-88215-040-5). Ohio St U Lib.

Art, Robert J. & Jervis, Robert. International Politics: Anarchy, Force, Political Economy, & Decision-Making. 2nd ed. 1984. pap. text ed. 16.95 (ISBN 0-316-05239-6). Little.

Art, Robert J. & Jervis, Robert, eds. International Politics: Anarchy, Force, Imperialism. 1973. pap. text ed. 15.95 (ISBN 0-316-05244-2). Little.

Art, Robert J. & Waltz, Kenneth N., eds. The Use of Force: International Politics & Foreign Policy. 2nd ed. 674p. 1983. lib. bdg. 30.00 (ISBN 0-8191-3424-4); pap. text ed. 13.75 (ISBN 0-8191-3425-2). U Pr of Amer.

Art, Robert J., et al, eds. Reorganizing America's Defense: Leadership in War & Peace. (Illus.). 400p. 1985. 27.00 (ISBN 0-08-031973-4, Pub. by Aberdeen Scotland); pap. 14.95 (ISBN 0-08-031972-6, Pub. by Aberdeen Scotland). Pergamon.

Artaega, Robert F. Building of the Arch. 28p. 1967. pap. 2.00 (ISBN 0-686-95726-1). Jefferson Natl.

Artal, Raul & Wiswell, Robert. Exercise in Pregnancy: Experimental & Clinical Management. (Illus.). 263p. 1985. pap. 32.00 (ISBN 0-683-00257-0). Williams & Wilkins.

Artandi, Susan B. An Introduction to Computers in Information Science. 2nd ed. LC 72-1136. (Illus.). 190p. 1972. 13.00 (ISBN 0-8108-0485-9). Scarecrow.

Artaud, Antonin. Anthology. 2nd rev. ed. Hirschman, Jack, ed. LC 65-12730. 1965. pap. 6.95 (ISBN 0-87286-000-0). City Lights.

--Artaud: Four Texts. Eshleman, Clayton, tr. from Fr. (Illus.). 100p. 1982. 14.95 (ISBN 0-915572-57-5); pap. 6.95 (ISBN 0-915572-56-7). Panjandrum.

--The Death of Satan. Hamilton, Alastair, tr. from Fr. 1980. 9.95 (ISBN 0-7145-0979-5); pap. 3.95 (ISBN 0-7145-1085-8). Riverrun NY.

--Oeuvres Completes, Vol. 1, Pt. 2. 312p. 1976. 22.50 (ISBN 0-686-53827-7). French & Eur.

--Oeuvres Completes, Vol. 10. 328p. 1974. 18.50 (ISBN 0-686-53828-5). French & Eur.

--Oeuvres Completes, Vol. 11. 368p. 1974. 19.95 (ISBN 0-686-53829-3). French & Eur.

--Oeuvres Completes: Avec: Le Momo, Cigit, La Culture Indienne, Lettre a Peter Watson, Vol. 12. 352p. 1974. 19.95 (ISBN 0-686-53830-7). French & Eur.

--Oeuvres Completes: Avec: Van Gogh, Pour en Finir avec le Jugement de Dieu, Le Theatre de la Cruante, Vol. 13. 400p. 1974. 22.50 (ISBN 0-686-53831-5). French & Eur.

--Oeuvres Completes: Supplement Au Tome 1. 248p. 1970. 7.95 (ISBN 0-686-53826-9). French & Eur.

--Oeuvres Completes: Suppots et Supplications, Vol. 14, Pt. 1. 321p. 1978. 25.00 (ISBN 0-686-53832-3). French & Eur.

--Oeuvres Completes: Suppots et Supplications, Vol. 14, Pt. 2. 310p. 1978. 25.00 (ISBN 0-686-53833-1). French & Eur.

--L' Ombilic de Limbes: Avec: Correspondance avec Jacques Riviere, Le Pese-Nerfs, Fragments d'un Journal d'enfer, L'Art et la Mot, Etc. 256p. 1968. 4.95 (ISBN 0-686-53834-X). French & Eur.

--Poete Noir et Autres Textes. 64p. 1966. 5.95 (ISBN 0-686-53835-8). French & Eur.

--A Second Artaud Anthology. Hirschman, Jack, ed. & tr. 1972. tabloid 5.00 (ISBN 0-88031-004-9). Invisible-Red Hill.

--Selected Writings of Artaud. Sontag, Susan, ed. Weaver, Helen, tr. from Fr. LC 79-143303. 661p. 1976. 20.00 (ISBN 0-374-26048-6); pap. 9.95 (ISBN 0-374-51399-6). FS&G.

--Les Tarahumaras. 217p. 1963. 19.95 (ISBN 0-686-53837-4). French & Eur.

--Les Tarahumaras. 160p. 1974. 3.95 (ISBN 0-686-53838-2). French & Eur.

--Theater & Its Double. Richards, Mary C., tr. from Fr. (Illus.). 1958. pap. 6.95 (ISBN 0-394-17213-2, E127, Ever). Grove.

--Le Theatre et Son Double. 256p. 1971. 3.95 (ISBN 0-686-53839-0). French & Eur.

Artaud, Antonin & Gonzague-Frick, Louis de. Probetes et Prophetes. 1976. 6.95 (ISBN 0-686-53836-6). French & Eur.

Artaud, Yvonne, jt. auth. see Joshi, Kireet.

Artedi, P. Genera Piscium: Emendata & Aucta. 1967. Repr. of 1792 ed. 42.00 (ISBN 3-7682-0190-2). Lubrecht & Cramer.

--Ichthyolgia. Linnaeus, C., ed. 1961. Repr. of 1738 ed. 35.00 (ISBN 3-7682-0082-5). Lubrecht & Cramer.

Artel, Linda & Wengraf, Susan. Positive Images: A Guide to 400 Non-Sexist Films for Young People. LC 75-46089. 1976. pap. 10.00x (ISBN 0-912932-03-1). Booklegger Pr.

Artells, Eduard. Vocabulari Castella-Catala. 3rd ed. 224p. (Catalan & Span.). 1958. 5.95 (ISBN 84-7226-344-4, S-50355). French & Eur.

--Vocabulari Catala-Castella. 3rd ed. 465p. (Catalan & Span.). 1961. 5.25 (ISBN 84-7226-345-2, S-50354). French & Eur.

Artemiadis, Nicolas. Real Analysis. LC 75-29189. 594p. 1976. 15.00x (ISBN 0-8093-0727-8). S Ill U Pr.

Arter, David. The Nordic Parliaments: A Comparative Analysis. LC 84-9803. 432p. 1985. 30.00 (ISBN 0-312-57767-2). St Martin.

Arter, Elisabeth. The Salad Garden. 190p. 1984. 15.00 (ISBN 0-7099-0530-0, Pub. by Croom Helm Ltd). Longwood Pub Group.

Arter, Jared M. Echoes from a Pioneer Life. facsimile ed. LC 72-170688. (Black Heritage Library Collection). Repr. of 1922 ed. 14.50 (ISBN 0-8369-8877-9). Ayer Co Pubs.

Arterburn, S. Write English, Bk. 6. (Speak English Ser.). (Illus.). 64p. (Orig.). 1983. pap. text ed. 4.95 (ISBN 0-88499-689-1). Inst Mod Lang.

Arterburn, Stephen, jt. auth. see Timmons, Tim.

Arterburn, Yvonne. The Loom of Interdependence: Silkweaving Cooperatives in Kanchipuram. (Studies in Sociology & Social Anthropology). 220p. 1982. text ed. 14.25x (ISBN 0-391-02749-2, Pub. by Hindustan India). Humanities.

Arterton, Christopher F. Media Politics: The News Strategies of Presidential Campaigns. LC 83-48735. 240p. 1984. 27.00x (ISBN 0-669-07504-3). Lexington Bks.

Artes, Dorothy B. Bits & Pieces about Maryland. 120p. pap. text ed. 5.00 (ISBN 0-686-73104-2). Maryland Hist.

Arth, Marvin & Ashmore, Helen. The Newsletter Editor's Desk Book. 3rd ed. LC 81-83398. 188p. 1984. pap. 10.00 (ISBN 0-938270-03-6). Parkway Pr Ltd.

Arth, Michael E. Michael E. Arth Introspective Nineteen Seventy-Two to Nineteen Eighty-Two. LC 83-80162. (Illus.). 256p. 1983. 29.95 (ISBN 0-912467-00-2); special edition 295.00 (ISBN 0-912467-01-0). Linnaea.

--Palms: Anatomy of a Passion. (Illus.). 104p. (gr. 6-12). 1986. 19.95 (ISBN 0-912467-02-9); Leather bound 250.00 (ISBN 0-912467-03-7). Linnaea.

Arthanari, Subramanvam & Dodge, Yadolah. Mathematical Programming in Statistics. LC 80-21637. (Probability & Math Statistics Ser.: Applied Probability & Statistics). 413p. 1981. 45.95x (ISBN 0-471-08073-X, Pub. by Wiley-Interscience). Wiley.

Arthaud, Gaston. The Fully Illustrated Artistic Guide to the Treasures of Versailles. (Illus.). 118p. 1984. Repr. of 1935 ed. 88.85 (ISBN 0-89901-171-3). Found Class Reprints.

Arther, Richard O. The Scientific Investigator. (Illus.). 248p. 1976. photocopy ed. 19.75x (ISBN 0-398-00055-7). C C Thomas.

Arthos, John. The Art of Shakespeare. LC 76-45420. 1976. lib. bdg. 25.00 (ISBN 0-8414-2994-4). Folcroft.

--Dante, Michelangelo, & Milton. LC 78-32053. 1979. Repr. of 1963 ed. lib. bdg. 22.50x (ISBN 0-313-20979-0, ARDA). Greenwood.

--Language of Natural Description in Eighteenth Century Poetry. 1966. lib. bdg. 34.50x (ISBN 0-374-90304-2). Octagon.

--On the Poetry of Spenser & the Form of Romances. facs. ed. LC 77-119951. (Select Bibliographies Reprint Ser). 1956. 17.00 (ISBN 0-8369-5394-0). Ayer Co Pubs.

--Shakespeare's Use of Dream & Vision. 208p. 1977. 16.50x (ISBN 0-87471-912-7). Rowman.

--The Status of the Humanities. LC 80-84732. 256p. 1981. 12.50 (ISBN 0-8022-2377-X). Philos Lib.

Arthritis Foundation. Understanding Arthritis: What It Is, How It's Treated, How to Cope with It. (Illus.). 308p. 1985. 18.95 (ISBN 0-684-18199-1, ScribT). Scribner.

Arthur. Application of On-Line Analytical Instrumentation to Process Control. LC 82-70694. (Activated Sludge Process Control Ser.). 222p. 1982. 39.95 (ISBN 0-250-40539-3). Butterworth.

--New Concepts & Practices in Activated Sludge Process Control. LC 81-69767. (Activated Sludge Process Control Ser.). 125p. 1982. 34.95 (ISBN 0-250-40525-8). Butterworth.

Arthur & Kernion. Old Families of Louisiana. 1971. 13.50 (ISBN 0-87511-141-6). Claitors.

Arthur, A. S., tr. see Gladkov, F. V.

Arthur Andersen & Co. Interest Rate Futures: The Corporate Decision. LC 82-82392. 1982. 8.00 (ISBN 0-910586-46-2). Finan Exec.

--Tolley's UK-US Double Tax Treaty. 1982. 75.00x (ISBN 0-510-49421-8, Pub. by Tolley Pub England). State Mutual Bk.

Arthur Andersen & Co. Staff. Interpretation of FASB Statement No. 80: Accounting for Interest Rate Futures & Options, a Supplement to the Interest Rate Futures Hedging Course. 36p. (Orig.). 1985. pap. 9.95 (ISBN 0-915513-13-7). Ctr Futures Ed.

Arthur Andersen Company Staff. The First Fifty Years, Nineteen Thirteen to Nineteen Sixty-Three. LC 83-49117. (Accounting History & the Development of a Profession Ser.). 140p. 1984. lib. bdg. 20.00 (ISBN 0-8240-6317-1). Garland Pub.

--Tax Shelters: The Basics. LC 82-74373. (Illus.). iii, 147p. 1985. 15.95 (ISBN 0-318-11685-5). A Andersen.

Arthur, Anthony. Critical Essays on Wallace Stegner. (Critical Essays on American Literature Ser.). 1982. lib. bdg. 30.00 (ISBN 0-8161-8487-9, Twayne). G K Hall.

--Deliverence at Los Banos: The Dramatic True Story of Survival & Triumph in a Japanese Internment Camp. (Illus.). 1985. 15.95 (ISBN 0-312-19185-5). St Martin.

Arthur, Anthony, jt. ed. see Brier, Peter A.

Arthur, Bev & Arthur, Martin. Mama's Boy. (Illus.). 240p. (Orig.). 1986. pap. 9.95 (ISBN 0-89407-054-1). Strawberry Hill.

Arthur, Bonnie. Unicorns in Soft Sculpture, Bk. 1. (Illus., Orig.). 1982. pap. 3.50 (ISBN 0-941284-14-X). Deco Design Studio.

Arthur, Budd & Arthur, Burt. Brothers of the Range. (Orig.). 1980. pap. text ed. 1.75 (ISBN 0-505-51550-4, Pub. by Tower Bks). Dorchester Pub Co.

Arthur, Budd, jt. auth. see Arthur, Burt.

Arthur, Burt. The Black Rider. 1978. pap. 1.25 (ISBN 0-505-51258-0, Pub. by Tower Bks). Dorchester Pub Co.

--The Drifter. (Illus.). 192p. 1975. pap. 1.25 (ISBN 0-532-12359-X). Woodhill.

--Empty Saddles. 1976. pap. 1.25 (ISBN 0-532-12383-2). Woodhill.

--Flaming Guns. 1978. pap. 1.25 (ISBN 0-505-51278-5, Pub. by Tower Bks). Dorchester Pub Co.

--Gunsmoke in Nevada. 1976. pap. 1.25 (ISBN 0-532-12390-5). Woodhill.

--Gunsmoke in Paradise. 1978. pap. 1.25 (ISBN 0-505-51246-7, Pub. by Tower Bks). Dorchester Pub Co.

--Lead Hungry Lobos. 1978. pap. 1.25 (ISBN 0-505-51255-6, Pub. by Tower Bks). Dorchester Pub Co.

--Outlaw Fury. 1976. pap. 0.95 (ISBN 0-685-72359-3, LB385NK, Leisure Bks). Dorchester Pub Co.

--Return of the Texan. 1975. pap. 0.95 (ISBN 0-685-61048-9, LB321, Leisure Bks). Dorchester Pub Co.

--Trouble at Moon Pass. 1978. pap. 1.25 (ISBN 0-505-51257-2, Pub. by Tower Bks.). Dorchester Pub Co.

Arthur, Burt & Arthur, Budd. Canavan's Trail. 192p. 1984. pap. 2.25 (ISBN 0-8439-2149-8, Leisure Bks). Dorchester Pub Co.

--Ride a Crooked Trail. 1979. pap. 1.25 (ISBN 0-505-51389-7, Pub. by Tower Bks). Dorchester Pub Co.

--The Saga of Denny McCune. 1979. pap. 1.25 (ISBN 0-505-51397-8, Pub. by Tower Bks). Dorchester Pub Co.

--Three Guns North. 1979. pap. 1.25 (ISBN 0-505-51349-8, Pub. by Tower Bks). Dorchester Pub Co.

--Westward the Wagons. 1979. pap. 1.25 (ISBN 0-505-51396-X, Pub. by Tower Bks). Dorchester Pub Co.

Arthur, Burt, jt. auth. see Arthur, Budd.

Arthur, C. J., ed. see Marx, Karl & Engels, Friedrich.

Arthur Campbell Inc. Staff. How to Make Your Own Liqueurs. (Illus., Orig.). 1982. pap. 2.95 (ISBN 0-932775-02-0). Campbell Inc.

--I Want You to Eat Soup. (Illus.). 60p. (Orig.). 1985. pap. 3.95 (ISBN 0-932775-01-2). Campbell Inc.

--Outrageous Fish Recipes. (Illus.). 60p. (Orig.). 1985. pap. 3.95 (ISBN 0-932775-02-0). Campbell Inc.

Arthur, Catherine. My Sister's Silent World. LC 78-13140. (Social Values Ser.). (Illus.). 32p. (gr. 3). 1979. PLB 10.35 (ISBN 0-516-02022-6); pap. 3.95 (ISBN 0-516-42022-4). Childrens.

Arthur, Chris, intro. by see Pashukanis, Evgeny.

Arthur, Chris, ed. see Pashukanis, Evgeny.

Arthur D. Inc. Evaluation of LNG Vapor Control Methods. 150p. 1974. pap. 7.00 (ISBN 0-318-12609-5, M19875). Am Gas Assn.

Arthur D. Little. Electronic Document Delivery. 233p. 1983. 45.00 (ISBN 0-317-00234-1). Learned Info.

Arthur D. Little, Inc. Financial Reporting Requirements of Small Publicly Owned Companies. LC 84-80985. 1984. 10.00 (ISBN 0-910586-54-3). Finan Exec.

--Health Care Cost Containment: Challenge to Industry. LC 80-6830. 1980. 8.00 (ISBN 0-910586-34-9). Finan Exec.

--Nuclear Environment Information-Resources & Action Plans: AIF-NESP-001. (National Environmental Studies Project: NESP Reports). 1974. 10.00 (ISBN 0-318-02230-3). Atomic Indus Forum.

Arthur D. Little, Inc., et al. Civil Aviation Development: A Policy & Operation Analysis. LC 70-185656. (Special Studies in U.S. Economic, Social & Political Issues). 1980. Repr. of 1972 ed. 39.50x (ISBN 0-89197-697-3). Irvington.

Arthur, David S. The Oasis Project. LC 80-54845. (Illus.). 448p. 1981. 12.95 (ISBN 0-939086-00-X). Sword & Stone.

--The Oasis Project. 1983. pap. 3.50 (ISBN 0-8217-1296-9). Zebra.

Arthur, Donald, tr. see Sevela, Efraim.

Arthur, Elizabeth. Beyond the Mountain. LC 83-47551. 224p. 1983. 12.45i (ISBN 0-06-015189-7, HarpT). Har-Row.

Arthur, Eric & Ritchie, Thomas. Iron: Cast & Wrought Iron in Canada from the Seventeenth Century to the Present. (Illus.). 256p. 1982. 27.50 (ISBN 0-8020-2429-7). U of Toronto Pr.

Arthur, Frank. Another Mystery In Suva. Barzun, J. & Taylor, W. H., eds. LC 81-47382. (Crime Fiction 1950-1975 Ser.). 223p. 1982. lib. bdg. 18.00 (ISBN 0-8240-4989-6). Garland Pub.

Arthur, G. H., et al. Veterinary Reproduction & Obstetrics. 5th ed. (Illus.). 512p. 1982. 48.00 (ISBN 0-7216-0778-0, Pub. by Bailliere-Tindall). Saunders.

Arthur, George. From Phelps to Gielgud. LC 77-91472. Repr. of 1936 ed. 20.00 (ISBN 0-405-08214-2, Pub. by Blom). Ayer Co Pubs.

Arthur, George, tr. see Poincare, Raymond.

Arthur, George C. From Phelps to Gielgud: Reminiscences of the Stage Through Sixty-Five Years. facs. ed. LC 67-23174. (Essay Index Reprint Ser). 1967. Repr. of 1936 ed. 18.00 (ISBN 0-8369-0160-6). Ayer Co Pubs.

Arthur, Griscom, jt. ed. see Griscom, Morgan.

Arthur, J. Morality & Moral Controversies. 1981. pap. 21.95 (ISBN 0-13-601278-7). P-H.

Arthur, J. & Russell, T. The British Educational Software Directory. 398p. (Orig.). 1985. pap. 30.00 (ISBN 0-7121-0452-6). Trans Atlantic.

Arthur, Jett C., ed. Cellulose & Fiber Science Developments: A World View. LC 77-22540. (American Chemical Society Symposium Ser.: No. 50). pap. 74.00 (ISBN 0-317-08900-5, 2019941). Bks Demand UMI.

Arthur, Jett C., Jr., ed. Polymers or Fibers & Elastomers. LC 84-14635. (Symposium Ser.: No. 260). 434p. 1984. lib. bdg. 69.95x (ISBN 0-8412-0859-X). Am Chemical.

Arthur, Jett C, Jr., ed. Textile & Paper Chemistry & Technology. LC 77-7938. (ACS Symposium Ser.: No. 49). 1977. 27.95 (ISBN 0-8412-0377-6). Am Chemical.

Arthur, Jett C., Jr., ed. see Symposium on International Developments in Cellulose, Paper & Textiles.

Arthur, Jett C., Jr., ed. see Symposium on International Developments in Cellulose, Papers, & Textiles (1976: New York).

Arthur, John. Realist Drawings & Watercolors: Contemporary American Works on Paper. 144p. 1980. 34.00i (ISBN 0-8212-1102-1, 736376); pap. 17.00 (ISBN 0-8212-1527-2, 736384). NYGS.

--Realists at Work: Studio Interviews & Working Methods of 10 Leading Comtemporary Painters. (Illus.). 160p. 1983. 27.50 (ISBN 0-8230-4510-2). Watson-Guptill.

Arthur, John & Shaw, William. Readings in Philosophy of Law. 640p. 1984. text ed. 29.95 (ISBN 0-13-761628-7). P-H.

Arthur, John, ed. Morality & Moral Controversies. 2nd ed. 640p. 1986. pap. text ed. 20.95 (ISBN 0-13-601287-6). P-H.

Arthur, John & Shaw, William, eds. Justice & Economic Distribution. 1978. pap. text ed. 18.95 (ISBN 0-13-514166-4). P-H.

Arthur, John P. Western North Carolina: A History from 1730 to 1913. LC 73-1945. (Illus.). 710p. 1973. Repr. of 1914 ed. 35.00 (ISBN 0-87152-126-1). Reprint.

Arthur, Kay. How Can I Be Blessed? 256p. (Orig.). 1984. pap. 6.95 (ISBN 0-317-06624-2, Power Bks). Revell.

--How Can I Live. 528p. (Orig.). 1981. pap. 6.95 (ISBN 0-8007-5077-2, Power Bks). Revell.

--Lord, I Want to Know You. 192p. (Orig.). 1984. pap. 6.95 (ISBN 0-8007-5159-0, Power Bks). Revell.

--Teach Me How to Live. 384p. (Orig.). 1983. pap. 6.95 (ISBN 0-8007-5125-6, Power Bks). Revell.

Arthur, Lee. The Mer-Lion. 624p. (Orig.). 1982. pap. 3.50 (ISBN 0-446-90044-3). Warner Bks.

Arthur, Lindsay G. & Gauger, William. Disposition Hearings: The Heartbeat of the Juvenile Court. 85p. 1974. 3.50 (ISBN 0-318-15764-0, T400). Natl Juv & Family Ct Judges.

Arthur, Lowell J. Programmer Productivity: Myths, Methods & Murphy's Law. 288p. 1984. pap. 17.95 (ISBN 0-471-81493-8, Pub. by Wiley-Interscience). Wiley.

--Programmer Productivity: Myths, Methods & Murphy's Law & Murphology-A Guide for Managers, Analysts & Programmers. LC 82-13417. 288p. 1983. 26.95 (ISBN 0-471-86434-X, Pub. by Wiley-Interscience). Wiley.

--Software Metrics Users Guide. LC 84-13176. 292p. 1985. 33.95 (ISBN 0-471-88713-7, Pub. by Wiley-Interscience). Wiley.

Arthur, Martin, jt. auth. see Arthur, Bev.

Arthur, Michael B., et al. Working with Careers: Understanding What We Apply & Applying What We Understand. 1983. text ed. 22.50 (ISBN 0-914383-00-0); pap. text ed. 17.50 (ISBN 0-914383-01-9). Columbia U Res.

Arthur, Mildred H. God, Why Am I So Miserable? (gr. 3-6). 1979. pap. 3.50 (ISBN 0-570-03623-2, 39-1065). Concordia.

Arthur, Pat. Calvin Crocker in a Very Busy Day. (Illus.). 22p. (ps-3). 1983. 2.50 (ISBN 0-89954-212-3). Antioch Pub Co.

--Dracula's Castle. (Illus.). 12p. (ps-4). 1982. pap. 2.95 (ISBN 0-89954-204-2). Antioch Pub Co.

Arthur, Paul. Government & Politics of Northern Ireland. 2nd ed. (Political Realities Ser.). (Illus.). 168p. 1985. pap. text ed. 7.95 (ISBN 0-582-35480-3). Longman.

--The People's Democracy, 1968-1973. 159p. 1974. 15.95 (ISBN 0-85640-021-1, Pub. by Blackstaff Pr). Longwood Pub Group.

Arthur, Richard. Engineer's Guide to Better Communication. (PROCOM Ser.). 1984. pap. 9.95 (ISBN 0-673-15554-4). Scott F.

Arthur, Richard L., tr. see Arthur, Rose H.

Arthur, Robert. Alfred Hitchcock & the Three Investigators in the Mystery of the Green Ghost. Hitchcock, Alfred, ed. (Three Investigators Ser.: No. 4). (Illus.). (gr. 4-8). 1965. (BYR); PLB 5.99 (ISBN 0-394-91228-4); pap. 1.95 (ISBN 0-394-84258-8). Random.

--Alfred Hitchcock & the Three Investigators in the Mystery of the Screaming Clock. Hitchcock, Alfred, ed. LC 68-23676. (Three Investigators Ser.: No. 9). (Illus.). (gr. 4-7). 1968. (BYR); pap. 1.95 (ISBN 0-394-86409-3). Random.

--Alfred Hitchcock & the Three Investigators in the Mystery of the Stuttering Parrot. Hitchcock, Alfred, ed. (Three Investigators Ser.: No. 1). (Illus.). (gr. 4-8). 1964. (BYR); pap. 1.95 (ISBN 0-394-83767-3). Random.

--Alfred Hitchcock & the Three Investigators in the Mystery of the Talking Skull. Hitchcock, Alfred, ed. LC 69-20274. (Three Investigators Ser.: No. 11). (Illus.). (gr. 4-7). 1969. (BYR); pap. 1.95 (ISBN 0-394-86411-5). Random.

--Alfred Hitchcock & the Three Investigators in the Mystery of the Vanishing Treasure. Hitchcock, Alfred, ed. (Three Investigators Ser.: No. 5). (Illus.). (gr. 4-8). 1966. (BYR); pap. 1.95 (ISBN 0-394-86405-0). Random.

--Alfred Hitchcock & the Three Investigators in the Mystery of the Whispering Mummy. Hitchcock, Alfred, ed. (Three Investigators Ser.: No. 3). (Illus.). (gr. 4-8). 1965. (BYR); pap. 1.95 (ISBN 0-394-83768-1). Random.

--Alfred Hitchcock & the Three Investigators in the Mystery of the Fiery Eye. LC 77-28860. (Three Investigators Ser.: No. 7). (Illus.). (gr. 4-8). 1967. (BYR); pap. 1.95 (ISBN 0-394-86407-7). Random.

--Alfred Hitchcock & the Three Investigators in the Mystery of the Silver Spider. (Three Investigators Ser.: No. 8). (Illus.). (gr. 4-8). 1967. (BYR); PLB 5.39 (ISBN 0-394-91663-8); pap. 1.95 (ISBN 0-394-83771-1). Random.

--Alfred Hitchcock & the Three Investigators in the Secret of Skeleton Island. Hitchcock, Alfred, ed. (Three Investigators Ser.: No. 6). (Illus.). (gr. 4-9). 1966. (BYR); PLB 5.39 (ISBN 0-394-91552-6); pap. 1.95 (ISBN 0-394-83769-X). Random.

--Alfred Hitchcock & the Three Investigators in the Secret of Terror Castle. Hitchcock, Alfred, ed. (Three Investigators Ser.: No. 2). (Illus.). (gr. 4-8). 1964. (BYR); PLB 5.39 o.s.i (ISBN 0-394-91241-1); pap. 1.95 (ISBN 0-394-83766-5). Random.

--His Other Half. LC 84-60762. 400p. 1985. 15.95 (ISBN 0-915677-07-5). Roundtable Pub.

Arthur, Robert, ed. Spies & More Spies. (gr. 7-11). 1967. PLB 5.39 (ISBN 0-394-91673-5, BYR). Random.

Arthur, Robert P., jt. auth. see Weinstock, E. B.

Arthur, Rose H. The Wisdom Goddess: Feminine Motifs in Eight Nag Hammadi Documents. Arthur, Richard L., tr. (Illus.). 256p. (Orig.). 1984. lib. bdg. 23.75 (ISBN 0-8191-4171-2); pap. text ed. 13.25 (ISBN 0-8191-4172-0). U Pr of Amer.

Arthur, Ruth. A Candle in Her Room. (Illus.). (gr. 4-8). 1972. pap. 1.95 (ISBN 0-689-70315-5, A-18, Aladdin). Atheneum.

--Requiem for a Princess. (YA) (gr. 6 up). 1976. pap. 1.95 (ISBN 0-689-70419-4, A-50, Aladdin). Atheneum.

Arthur, Ruth M. A Candle in Her Room. (Illus.). Date not set. 12.00 (ISBN 0-8446-6194-5). Peter Smith.

Arthur, Stanley C. Famous New Orleans Drinks & How to Mix'em. (Illus.). 1977. pap. 3.50 (ISBN 0-88289-132-4). Pelican.

--Index to the Archives of Spanish West-Florida, 1782-1810. 1975. 17.50 (ISBN 0-686-20873-0). Polyanthos.

Arthur, Stanley C., compiled by. Index to the Dispatches of Spanish Governors of Louisiana: 1766-1792. 1975. 12.50 (ISBN 0-686-20876-5). Polyanthos.

Arthur, Terry. The Moped Handbook. (Illus.). 1977. (Harmony); pap. 1.00 Outlet (ISBN 0-517-53107-0). Crown.

--Ninety-Five Per-Cent Is Crap: A Plain Man's Guide to British Politics. (Illus.). 1976. 12.95 (ISBN 0-905004-01-9). Libertarian Bks.

Arthur, Timothy S. The Hand but Not the Heart. LC 78-104405. Repr. of 1858 ed. lib. bdg. 14.75 (ISBN 0-8398-0061-4). Irvington.

--Hidden Wings & Other Stories. facs. ed. LC 72-137719. (American Fiction Reprint Ser.). Repr. of 1864 ed. 17.00 (ISBN 0-8369-7018-7). Ayer Co Pubs.

--Riches Have Wings: A Tale for the Rich & Poor. facs. ed. LC 77-137720. (American Fiction Reprint Ser). Repr. of 1847 ed. 17.00 (ISBN 0-8369-7019-5). Ayer Co Pubs.

--Sowing the Wind & Other Stories. facs. ed. LC 77-137721. (American Fiction Reprint Ser). Repr. of 1864 ed. 17.00 (ISBN 0-8369-7020-9). Ayer Co Pubs.

--Sunshine at Home & Other Stories. facs. ed. LC 77-137722. (American Fiction Reprint Ser). Repr. of 1864 ed. 18.00 (ISBN 0-8369-7021-7). Ayer Co Pubs.

Arthur, Wallace. Mechanisms of Morphological Evolution: A Combined Genetic, Developmental & Ecological Approach. LC 83-16993. 288p. 1984. 36.00x (ISBN 0-471-90347-7, Pub. by Wiley Interscience). Wiley.

Arthur, William. Etymological Dictionary of Family & Christian Names. LC 68-17911. 1969. Repr. of 1857 ed. 40.00x (ISBN 0-8103-3107-1). Gale.

--An Etymological Dictionary of Family & Christian Names. 59.95 (ISBN 0-8490-0135-8). Gordon Pr.

--Italy in Transition. 469p. 1980. Repr. of 1860 ed. lib. bdg. 50.00 (ISBN 0-89760-005-3). Telegraph Bks.

Arthur, William J. A Financial Planning Model for Private Colleges: A Research Report. LC 72-92879. pap. 33.00 (2017807). Bks Demand UMI.

Arthur Young & Co., jt. auth. see Jenkins, Michael D.

Arthur Young & Company, jt. auth. see Association of the Bar of the City of New York; Committee on the Corporate Law Departments.

Arthur Young & Company Staff. The Arthur Young Tax Guide 1986. Bernstein, Peter W., ed. (Orig.). 1986. pap. 8.95 (ISBN 0-345-31702-5). Ballantine.

Arthur-Lynch, Maureen. To Lift Your Heart. (Orig.). 1985. pap. 5.00 (ISBN 0-915541-05-X). Star Bks Inc.

Arthurs, A. M. Complementary Variational Principles. 2nd ed. (Mathematical Monographs). 1980. 49.00x (ISBN 0-19-853532-5). Oxford U Pr.

Arthurs, A. M. & Bhagavan, M. R., eds. Functional Integration & Its Applications. 1975. 68.00x (ISBN 0-19-853346-2). Oxford U Pr.

Arthurs, E., jt. auth. see Stuck, B. W.

Arthurs, H. W. Collective Bargaining by Public Employee Unions in Canada: Five Models. LC 70-634394. (Comparative Studies in Public Employment Labor Relations Ser.). 1971. 9.00x (ISBN 0-87736-005-7); pap. 4.50x (ISBN 0-87736-006-5). U of Mich Inst Labor.

Arthurs, H. W., et al. Labour Law & Industrial Relations in Canada. 292p. 1982. cancelled 18.00 (ISBN 90-312-0139-1, Pub. by Kluwer Law Netherlands). Kluwer Academic.
--Labour Law & Industrial Relations in Canada. 2nd ed. LC 84-14375. 1984. write for info. (ISBN 9-06-544190-5); write for info. (ISBN 0-409-81185-8). Kluwer Academic.
Arthurs, Peter. With Brendan Behan. (Illus.). 320p. 1981. 16.95 (ISBN 0-312-88471-0). St Martin.
Arthus, Gothard. Dialogues in the English & Malaiane Languages. Spalding, A., tr. LC 74-80160. (English Experience Ser.: No. 640). 1974. Repr. of 1614 ed. 8.00 (ISBN 90-221-0640-3). Walter J Johnson.
Arthus-Bertrand, Yann, photos by. Tender Killers. Bougrain-Dubourg, Allain. (Illus.). 116p. 1985. 27.50 (ISBN 0-86565-054-3). Vendome.
Artibise, A. F. Winnipeg: A Social History of Urban Growth, 1874-1914. (Illus.). 400p. 1975. 23.00x (ISBN 0-7735-0202-5). McGill-Queens U Pr.
Artic-Waters, Edward, ed. Graffiti du Jour: The Graffiti of Iowa. LC 80-67883. 52p. (Orig.). 1980. pap. 12.95 (ISBN 0-935954-09-0). Gormezano Ref.
Artigas, J. Llorens & Corredor-Mathéos, J. Spanish Folk Ceramics. (Illus.). 235p. 1982. 35.00 (ISBN 84-7031-362-2, Pub. by Editorial Blume Spain). Intl Spec Bk.
Artigas, Joaquin T. The Spanish Educational Reform & Lifelong Education. (Experiments & Innovations in Education Ser.: No. 31). 112p. 1979. pap. 5.25 (ISBN 92-3-101434-X, U868, UNESCO). Unipub.
Artin, E. Algebraic Numbers & Algebraic Functions. 364p. 1967. pap. 41.75 (ISBN 0-677-00635-7). Gordon.
--Geometric Algebra: Pure & Applied Mathematics. (A Wiley-Interscience Ser. of Texts, Monographs & Tracts). 224p. 1952. 37.95x (ISBN 0-470-03432-7, Pub. by Wiley-Interscience). Wiley.
Artin, Emil. Collected Papers. Lang, S. & Tate, J. T., eds. (Illus.). 576p. 1982. 32.00 (ISBN 0-387-90686-X). Springer-Verlag.
--Galois Theory. (Mathematical Lectures Ser.: No. 2). (Orig.). 1966. pap. 3.95 (ISBN 0-268-00108-1). U of Notre Dame Pr.
Artin, Emil & Tate, J. Class Field Theory. (Math Lecture Notes Ser.: No. 6). 259p. 1967. pap. text ed. 30.95 (ISBN 0-8053-0291-3). Benjamin-Cummings.
Artin, M. & Tate, John, eds. Arithmetic, Vol. 1. (Progress in Mathematics Ser.). 350p. 1983. 29.95 (ISBN 0-8176-3132-1). Birkhauser.
Artin, M. see Zariski, Oscar.
Artin, Michael & Mumford, David, eds. Contributions to Algebraic Geometry in Honor of Oscar Zariski. 1979. text ed. 40.00x (ISBN 0-8018-2307-2). Johns Hopkins.
Artin, Michael & Tate, John, eds. Geometry: Papers Dedicated to I. R. Shafarevich on the Occasion of His Sixtieth Birthday, Vol. 2. (Progress in Mathematics). 450p. 1983. write for info (ISBN 0-8176-3133-X). Birkhauser.
Artin, Tom. The Allegory of Adventure: Reading Chretien's "Erec & Yvain". LC 73-687. 264p. 1974. 18.00 (ISBN 0-8387-1257-6). Bucknell U Pr.
Artin, Y. Contes populaires du Soudan Egyptien. LC 78-20143. (Collection de contes et de chansons populaires: Vol. 34). Repr. of 1909 ed. 21.50 (ISBN 0-404-60384-X). AMS Pr.
Artinian, Artine, jt. auth. see Artinian, Robert W.
Artinian, Robert W. & Artinian, Artine. Maupassant Criticism: A Centennial Bibliography, 1880-1979. LC 82-80724. 200p. 1982. lib. bdg. 29.95x (ISBN 0-89950-046-3). McFarland & Co.
Artino, jt. auth. see Barro-Neto.
Artino, Ralph A. & Gaglione, Anthony M. Contest Problem Book IV: Annual High School Examinations 1973-1982. LC 82-51076. (New Mathematical Library Ser.: No. 29). 200p. 1982. pap. 11.00 (ISBN 0-88385-629-8, 82-0151-076). Math Assn.
Artis, M. J. & Lewis, M. K. Monetary Control in the United Kingdom. 156p. 1981. text ed. 23.75x (ISBN 0-86003-040-7, Pub. by Phillip Allan England); pap. text ed. 12.25x (ISBN 0-86003-137-3). Humanities.
Artis, M. J., ed. Essays in Economic Analysis. Nobay, A. R. LC 75-46207. (Illus.). 422p. 1976. 57.50 (ISBN 0-521-21154-9). Cambridge U Pr.
Artis, M. J. & Miller, M. H., eds. Essays in Fiscal & Monetary Economics. 1981. 42.00x (ISBN 0-19-829001-2). Oxford U Pr.
Artis, M. J., et al. Demand Management Supply Constraints & Inflation. LC 81-16373. 256p. 1982. pap. 23.95x (ISBN 0-470-27287-2). Halsted Pr.
Artis, Michael. Macroeconomics. (Illus.). 1984. 24.95x (ISBN 0-19-877106-1); pap. 11.95 (ISBN 0-19-877107-X). Oxford u Pr.
Artis, Michael J. & Nobay, A. R., eds. Contemporary Economic Analysis: Papers Presented at the Conference of the Association of University Teachers of Economics April 1977. 448p. 1978. 29.00x (ISBN 0-85664-802-7, Pub. by Croom Helm). Longwood Pub Group.
Artis, Vicki K. Pajama Walking. (Illus.). (gr. k-3). 1981. PLB 6.95 (ISBN 0-395-30343-5). HM.
Artisien, Patrick F. Joint Ventures in Yugoslav Industry. 240p. 1985. text ed. 34.95x (ISBN 0-566-00762-2). Gower Pub Co.
Artiss, David. Theodor Storm: Studies in Ambivalence. (German Language & Literature Monographs: No. 5). xix, 215p. 1978. 26.00x (ISBN 90-272-0965-0). Benjamins North Am.
Artiss, Kenneth. The Brain: In Wisdom, Loving & Hating. 1985. text ed. 37.50x (ISBN 0-8290-1362-8). Irvington.
Artists Foundation, Inc. Money Business: Grants & Awards for Creative Artists. 1982. pap. 6.00 (ISBN 0-932246-01-X). Artists Found.
Artken, J. Conversations: The Diary of a Worried Journalist's Trek Across a Divided & Threatened Canada. 1978. pap. 7.95 (ISBN 0-13-172056-2). P-H.
Artley, Alexandra, ed. Artist, Architect & Patron. (Illus.). 96p. 1980. 22.50 (ISBN 0-85139-075-7). Eastview.
Artley, Bob. Memories of a Former Kid. (Illus.). 1978. 8.95 (ISBN 0-8138-1070-1). Iowa St U Pr.
Artley, Sterl. Inventory of Teacher Knowledge of Reading. (Lucas Text Ser). text ed. 1.35x saddle stitched (ISBN 0-87543-102-X). Lucas.
--Word Perception for Teachers. 3rd ed. (Lucas Text Ser.). 1978. text ed. 2.75x saddle stitched (ISBN 0-87543-141-0). Lucas.
Artman, Charles E. Food Costs & City Consumers. LC 70-76687. (Columbia University Studies in the Social Sciences: No. 280). Repr. of 1926 ed. 16.50 (ISBN 0-404-51280-1). AMS Pr.
Artman, John. Cowboys: An Activity Book. (gr. 4-8). 1982. 5.95 (ISBN 0-86653-068-1, GA 417). Good Apple.
--Good Apple & Grammar Fun. (Illus.). 144p. (gr. 3-7). 1983. wkbk. 9.95 (ISBN 0-86653-128-9, GA 466). Good Apple.
--Good Apple & Reading Fun. (gr. 3-7). 1981. 9.95 (ISBN 0-86653-046-0, GA 278). Good Apple.
--Indians: An Activity Book. (gr. 4-8). 1981. 5.95 (ISBN 0-86653-012-6, GA 240). Good Apple.
--Slanguage. (gr. 4-8). 1980. 6.95 (ISBN 0-916456-60-9, GA 175). Good Apple.
--Slanguage II. 80p. (gr. 4-8). 1983. wkbk. 6.95 (ISBN 0-86653-146-7, GA 474). Good Apple.
Artner, Stephen J. A Change of Course: The West German Social Democrats & NATO, 1957-1961. LC 84-15786. (Contributions in Political Science Ser.: No. 127). xvii, 242p. 1985. lib. bdg. 35.00 (ISBN 0-313-24701-3, ACC/). Greenwood.
Artobolevsky, I. Mechanism in Modern Engineering Design, Vol. V. (Illus.). 1101p. 1980. 15.00 (ISBN 0-8285-3012-2, Pub. by Mir Pubs USSR). Imported Pubns.
--Mechanisms in Modern Engineering Design, Vol. II. (Illus.). 1059p. 1979. 15.00 (ISBN 0-8285-0687-6, Pub. by Mir Pubs USSR). Imported Pubns.
--Mechanisms in Modern Engineering Design, Vol. III. (Illus.). 663p. 1977. 10.00 (ISBN 0-8285-0688-4, Pub. by Mir Pubs USSR). Imported Pubns.
--Mechanisms in Modern Engineering Design, Vol. IV. (Illus.). 663p. 1977. 9.45 (ISBN 0-8285-0689-2, Pub. by Mir Pubs USSR). Imported Pubns.
--Mechanisms in Modern Engineering Design, Vol. I. (Illus.). 631p. 1979. 7.45 (ISBN 0-8285-0686-8, Pub. by Mir Pubs USSR). Imported Pubns.
Artos, Allen. Arthur: The King & His Court. 100p. 1986. pap. 5.00 (ISBN 0-934852-29-4). Lorien Hse.
--Jonah. 52p. (Orig.). 1984. 10.00 (ISBN 0-934852-00-6); pap. 3.50 (ISBN 0-934852-24-3). Lorien Hse.
Artos, John, ed. see Keats, John.
Arts & Antiques Magazines Editors, ed. Americana: Folk & Decorative Art. (Illus.). 160p. 1982. 25.00 (ISBN 0-8230-8005-6, Art & Antiques). Watson-Guptill.
Arts Council, ed. Arts Council Collection Catalogue. 264p. 1984. 79.00x (ISBN 0-7287-0212-6, Pub. by Arts Coun England). State Mutual Bk.
--The Hungarian Avant Garde. 128p. 1981. 37.50x (ISBN 0-7287-0230-4, Pub. by Arts Coun England). State Mutual Bk.
--Pier & Ocean. 160p. 1981. 35.00x (ISBN 0-7287-0239-8, Pub. by Arts Coun England). State Mutual Bk.
--Pissarro. 264p. 1981. 50.00x (ISBN 0-7287-0261-4, Pub. by Arts Coun England). State Mutual Bk.
Arts Council Of Great Britain. Pictorial History of Shakespearean Production in England, 1576-1946. facsimile ed. Byrne, M. St. Clare, ed. LC 70-109640. (Select Bibliographies Reprint Ser). 1948. 11.00 (ISBN 0-8369-5249-9). Ayer Co Pubs.
Arts, Herwig. With Your Whole Soul: On the Christian Experience of God. LC 82-61419. 192p. 1983. pap. 7.95 (ISBN 0-8091-2517-X). Paulist Pr.
Artsibasov, A. In Disregard for the Law. 268p. 1985. pap. 2.95 (ISBN 0-8285-2997-3, Pub. by Progress Pubs USSR). Imported Pubns.
Artsimovich, L. A Physicist's ABC on Plasma. 1978. pap. 3.95 (ISBN 0-8285-5196-0, Pub. by Mir Pubs USSR). Imported Pubns.
Artsimovich, L. A. & Lukyanov, S. Y. Motion of Charged Particles in Electric & Magnetic Fields. 1980. 8.95 (ISBN 0-8285-1871-8, Pub. by Mir Pubs USSR). Imported Pubns.
Artsimovich, L. A., et al, eds. Controlled Thermonuclear Reactions. (Illus.). 422p. 1964. 112.25 (ISBN 0-677-20020-X). Gordon.
Artsruni, Thomas. History of the House of the Artsrunik' Thomson, Robert W., tr. from Armenian. LC 85-1045. (Byzantine Texts in Translation). 372p. 1985. 30.00 (ISBN 0-8143-1784-7). Wayne St U Pr.
Artsybashev, Mikhail P. Millionaire. facsimile ed. Pinkerton, Percy, tr. LC 78-103491. (Short Story Index Reprint Ser.). 1915. 18.00 (ISBN 0-8369-3233-1). Ayer Co Pubs.
Artucio, Alejandlo, jt. auth. see Fragoso, Heleno C.
Arturo del Hoyo, Asesor, ed. see Sainz de Robles, Federico C.
Artusi, Pellegrino. Italianissimo: Italian Cooking at Its Best. Abbott, Elisabeth, tr. from It. 552p. 1975. 12.50 (ISBN 0-87140-596-2). Liveright.
Artusio, Joseph F., jt. ed. see Yao, Fun-Sun F.
Artwick, B. Microcomputer Interfacing. 1980. 37.95 (ISBN 0-13-580902-9). P-H.
Artwick, Bruce. Applied Concepts in Microcomputer Graphics. (Illus.). 400p. 1984. text ed. 34.95 (ISBN 0-13-039322-3). P-H.
Artwick, Bruce A. Microcomputer Displays, Graphics, & Animation. LC 84-61429. (Illus.). 384p. 1985. pap. text ed. 18.95 (ISBN 0-13-580226-1). P-H.
Artyushkov, E. V. Geodynamics. (Developments in Geotectonics: Vol. 18). 312p. 1984. 74.50 (ISBN 0-444-42162-9, I-397-83). Elsevier.
Artz, Curtis P., et al. Burns-A Team Approach. LC 76-50146. (Illus.). 1979. text ed. 44.00 (ISBN 0-7216-1418-3). Saunders.
Artz, F. B. Intellectual History of Europe from St. Augustine to Marx: A Guide. 59.95 (ISBN 0-8490-0412-8). Gordon Pr.
Artz, Frederick B. Enlightenment in France. LC 68-21503. 176p. 1968. pap. 4.75x (ISBN 0-87338-032-0). Kent St U Pr.
--France under the Bourbon Restoration, 1814-1830. LC 63-11027. (Illus.). 1963. Repr. of 1931 ed. 22.00x (ISBN 0-8462-0380-4). Russell.
--From the Renaissance to Romanticism: Trends in Style in Art, Literature, & Music 1300-1830. LC 62-20021. 1962. 23.00x (ISBN 0-226-02837-2); pap. 10.00x (ISBN 0-226-02838-0). U of Chicago Pr.
--The Mind of the Middle Ages: An Historical Survey: A. D. 200-1500. 3rd rev. ed. LC 79-16259. 1980. pap. 15.95 (ISBN 0-226-02840-2, P859, Phoen). U of Chicago Pr.
--Reaction & Revolution: 1814-1832. Langer, William L., ed. (Rise of Modern Europe Ser.). 1977. pap. 6.95xi (ISBN 0-06-133034-5, TB 3034, Torch). Har-Row.
Artz, Robert J. Experimental Chemistry: An Introduction. 1982. 11.95 (ISBN 0-316-05278-7); pap. avail. instrs' manual (ISBN 0-316-05279-5). Little.
Artz, Robert J. & Walker, J. Robert. Solar Energy. 1984. text ed. 26.95 (ISBN 0-8359-7017-5); instr's. manual avail. (ISBN 0-8359-7018-3). Reston.
Artz, Thomas & Haley, Ruth M. Helping Your Child Appreciate the Mass & the Sacraments. LC 80-82779. 144p. (Orig.). 1980. pap. 2.95 (ISBN 0-89243-132-6). Liguori Pubns.
Artz, Thomas, jt. auth. see Farrell, Christopher.
Artzberger, William, Jr. Corvair: A History & Restoration Guide. (Illus.). 240p. 1984. pap. 19.95 (ISBN 0-89404-079-0). Aztex.
Artzibashev, Michael. The Doctor. Goldberg, Isaac, ed. Pinkerton, Percy, tr. (International Pocket Library). pap. 3.00 (ISBN 0-8283-1450-0). Branden Pub Co.
Artzner, James H. The Black Minute. 342p. (Orig.). 1980. 14.95 (ISBN 0-938936-00-X); pap. 8.95 (ISBN 0-938936-01-8). Daring Bks.
Artzy, R. & Vaisman, I., eds. Geometry & Differential Geometry. (Lecture Notes in Mathematics: Vol. 792). 443p. 1980. pap. 28.00 (ISBN 0-387-09976-X). Springer-Verlag.
Aruego, Ariane, jt. auth. see Aruego, Jose.
Aruego, Jose. Look What I Can Do. LC 73-158880. (Illus.). (gr. k-1). 1971. reinforced bdg. o. s. i. 6.95 (ISBN 0-684-12493-9, ScribJ); pap. 2.95 (ISBN 0-684-16215-6, ScribJ). Scribner.
Aruego, Jose & Aruego, Ariane. Crocodile's Tale. (gr. k-3). 1976. pap. 1.95 (ISBN 0-590-09899-3). Scholastic Inc.
Aruego, Jose & Dewey, Ariane. We Hide, You Seek. LC 78-13638. (Illus.). 32p. (gr. k-3). 1979. 13.00 (ISBN 0-688-80201-X); PLB 11.88 (ISBN 0-688-84201-1). Greenwillow.
Aruego, Jose & Dewey, Ariane, illus. Mushroom in the Rain. LC 72-92438. 32p. (ps-1). 1974. pap. 3.95x (ISBN 0-02-043270-4). Macmillan.
Aruego, Jose, jt. auth. see Addams, Charles.
Aruguelles, Ivan. Manicomio. Moody, Rodger, et al, eds. (Illus.). 32p. 1984. 3.00 (ISBN 0-9610508-2-9). Silverfish Rev Pr.
Arum, Nancy. Ice Cream & Ices. Stein, Margery, ed. LC 81-68842. (Great American Cooking Schools Ser.). (Illus.). 84p. 1981. pap. 5.95 (ISBN 0-941034-07-0). I Chalmers.
--Ice Cream & Ices. LC 82-48653. (Great American Cooking School Ser.). (Illus.). 80p. 1983. 8.61i (ISBN 0-06-015148-X, HarpT). Har-Row.
Arundale, G. S. You. LC 73-4783. 156p. 1973. pap. 1.75 (ISBN 0-8356-0434-9, Quest). Theos Pub Hse.
Arundale, George S. Kundalini. 1972. 3.50 (ISBN 0-8356-7102-X). Theos Pub Hse.
Arundel, Honor. The Longest Weekend. 1980. pap. 1.50 (ISBN 0-448-17146-5, Pub. by Tempo). Ace Bks.
Arundel, Jocelyn. Land of the Zebra. Bourne, Russell & Rifkin, Natalie S., eds. LC 74-80050. (Ranger Rick's Best Friends Ser.). (Illus.). 32p. (gr. 1-6). 1974. 2.00 (ISBN 0-912186-13-5). Natl Wildlife.
Arundell, Dennis. The Critic at the Opera: Contemporary Comments on Opera in London Over Three Centuries. (Music Reprint Ser.: 1980). (Illus.). 1980. Repr. of 1957 ed. lib. bdg. 37.50 (ISBN 0-306-76026-6). Da Capo.
--The Story of Sadler's Wells, Sixteen Eighty-Three to Nineteen Seventy-Seven. 2nd ed. (Illus.). 352p. 1978. 16.50x (ISBN 0-8476-6138-5). Rowman.
Arundell, Dennis D. Henry Purcell. facsimile ed. LC 72-109614. (Select Bibliographies Reprint Ser.). 1927. 12.00 (ISBN 0-8369-5223-5). Ayer Co Pubs.
--Henry Purcell. LC 72-114454. (Illus.). 1971. Repr. of 1927 ed. lib. bdg. 15.00 (ISBN 0-8371-4752-2, ARHP). Greenwood.
Arup, H. & Parkins, R. N. Stress Corrosion Research, No. 30. (NATO Advanced Study Institute Ser.). 279p. 1979. 30.00x (ISBN 90-286-0647-5). Sijthoff & Noordhoff.
Arup, Jens see Ibsen, Henrik.
Arup, Jens, tr. see Ibsen, Henrik.
Aruri, N. & Moughrabi, F. Reagan & the Middle East. (Monograph: No. 17). 95p. (Orig.). 1983. pap. text ed. 5.50 (ISBN 0-937694-59-2). Assn Arab-Amer U Grads.
Aruri, Naseer. The Sinai Accord As a Phase of the U. S. Containment Policy. (Occasional Papers: No. 2). 7p. 1976. pap. 1.00 (ISBN 0-937694-41-X). Assn Arab-Amer U Grads.
Aruri, Naseer & Shoufani, Elias. Arab Areas Occupied by Israel in June, 1967. (Information Papers: No. 2). 37p. (Orig.). pap. text ed. 2.75 (ISBN 0-937694-18-5). Assn Arab-Amer U Grads.
Aruri, Naseer, ed. Middle East Crucible: Studies on the Arab-Israeli War of October 1973. (Monograph Ser.: No. 6). 447p. 1975. 15.00 (ISBN 0-914456-10-5); pap. 7.95 (ISBN 0-914456-11-3). ASsn Arab-Amer U Grads.
--Occupation: Israel over Palestine. 480p. cancelled (ISBN 0-86232-361-4, Pub. by Zed Pr England); pap. cancelled (ISBN 0-86232-362-2, Pub. by Zed Pr England). Biblio Dist.
Aruri, Naseer H. The Middle East on the U. S. Campus. (Information Papers: No. 26). (Orig.). 1985. pap. 3.95 (ISBN 0-937694-67-3). Assn Arab-Amer U Grads.
Aruri, Naseer H., ed. Middle East Crucible. (Monograph Ser.: No. 6). 479p. 1975. 15.00 (ISBN 0-914456-10-5); pap. 7.95 (ISBN 0-914456-11-3). Medina Pr.
--Occupation: Israel over Palestine. (Monograph: No. 18). (Illus.). 467p. (Orig.). 1983. 30.00 (ISBN 0-937694-65-7); pap. 13.50 (ISBN 0-937694-64-9). Assn Arab Amer U Grads.
Arvanitis, Jim. Mu Tau: The Modern Greek Karate. (Illus.). 272p. (Orig.). 1979. pap. 15.00 (ISBN 0-89962-001-9). Todd & Honeywell.
Arveson, W. An Invitation to C-Algebras. LC 76-3656. 1976. 22.00 (ISBN 0-387-90176-0). Springer-Verlag.
Arveson, William. Ten Lectures on Operator Algebras. LC 84-9222. (CBMS Regional Conference Series in Mathematics: Vol. 55). 104p. 1984. pap. 14.00 (ISBN 0-8218-0705-6). Am Math.
Arvetis, Chris. Just Ask Series. Incl. Why Does It Rain (ISBN 0-528-82073-7); Why Does It Float (ISBN 0-528-82399-X); What Is a Volcano (ISBN 0-528-82434-1); What Is a Rainbow (ISBN 0-528-82433-3); Why Does It Fly (ISBN 0-528-82074-5); Why Is It Dark (ISBN 0-528-82075-3). 32p. (ps-3). 1984. 3.95 ea. Rand.
Arvetis, Chris & Palmer, Carole. Why Is the Grass Green? Bd. with Why Does It Thunder & Lightning? 3.95 (ISBN 0-528-82671-9). (Just Ask Ser.). 32p. (ps-3). 1985. 3.95 (ISBN 0-528-82670-0). Rand.
Arvey, M. Dale. A Check-list of the Birds of Idaho. (Museum Ser.: Vol. 1, No. 10). 24p. 1947. pap. 1.50 (ISBN 0-317-04582-2). U of KS Mus Nat Hist.
--Phylogeny of the Waxwings & Allied Birds. (Museum Ser.: Vol. 3, No. 3). 58p. 1951. pap. 3.00 (ISBN 0-317-04583-0). U of KS Mus Nat Hist.
Arvey, Richard D. Fairness in Selecting Employees. LC 78-74678. 1979. pap. text ed. 10.95 (ISBN 0-201-00070-9). Addison-Wesley.
Arvey, Verna. In One Lifetime. LC 83-24226. (Illus.). 263p. 1984. 16.00x (ISBN 0-938626-31-0); pap. 9.95 (ISBN 0-938626-36-1). U of Ark Pr.
Arvidson, Lucy. Alaawich. 1978. 2.00 (ISBN 0-939046-01-6). Malki Mus Pr.
Arvin, Evelyn F. Ante-Bellum Homes of Lunenburg. LC 72-119595. (Illus.). 177p. 1969. 12.50x (ISBN 0-685-65055-3). Va Bk.
Arvin, Jack. The Footsteps of Jesus. (Ser. Outlines). 4.95 (ISBN 0-89315-053-3). Lambert Bk.
Arvin, Neil C. Eugene Scribe & the French Theatre, 1815-1860. LC 67-13422. 1924. 18.00 (ISBN 0-405-08216-9, Pub. by Blom). Ayer Co Pubs.
Arvin, Newton. Herman Melville. LC 72-7818. (Illus.). 316p. 1973. lib. bdg. 24.75x (ISBN 0-8371-6524-5, ARHM); pap. 5.95 (ISBN 0-8371-8952-7, ARH:). Greenwood.

--Longfellow: His Life & Work. LC 77-1342. 1977. Repr. of 1963 ed. lib. bdg. 65.00 (ISBN 0-8371-9505-5, ARLO). Greenwood.
--Whitman. LC 68-27047. 1969. Repr. of 1938 ed. 13.00x (ISBN 0-8462-1191-2). Russell.
Arvin, Newton, ed. see Hawthorne, Nathaniel.
Arvine, K. Cyclopedia of Anecdotes of Literature & the Fine Arts. 75.00 (ISBN 0-87968-982-X). Gordon Pr.
Arvine, Kazlitt. Cyclopedia of Anecdotes of Literature. LC 67-14020. 1967. Repr. of 1851 ed. 46.00x (ISBN 0-8103-3296-5). Gale.
Arvon, Henri. Marxist Esthetics. Lane, Helen, tr. from Fr. LC 72-12405. 149p. 1973. pap. 5.95x (ISBN 0-8014-9142-8, CP142). Cornell U Pr.
Arwas, Victor. Art Deco. (Illus.). 316p. 1980. 49.50 (ISBN 0-686-62692-3, 0691-0). Abrams.
--Art Deco. (Illus.). 316p. 1985. 49.50 (ISBN 0-8109-0691-0). Abrams.
--Art Deco Sculpture. (Illus.). 116p. 1985. pap. 11.95 (ISBN 0-312-05251-0). St Martin.
Arwood, Ellyn L. Pragmaticism: Theory & Application. LC 83-9982. 312p. 1983. 30.50 (ISBN 0-89443-885-9). Aspen Systems.
Arx, J. A. von. The Genera of Fungi Sporulating in Pure Culture. 3rd rev. ed. (Illus.). 410p. 1981. lib. bdg. 42.00x (ISBN 3-7682-0693-9). Lubrecht & Cramer.
--Pilzkunde: Ein Kurzer Abriss der Mykologie Unter Besonderer Beruecksichtigung der Pilze in Reinkultur. 3rd ed. (Illus.). 1976. 10.50 (ISBN 3-7682-1067-7). Lubrecht & Cramer.
Arx, J. A. Von see Von Arx, J. A.
Arx, Jeffery P. von see Von Arx, Jeffery P.
Ary, Donald & Jacobs, Lucy C. Introduction to Statistics: A Systems Approach. LC 75-38831. 1976. text ed. 28.95 (ISBN 0-03-088412-8, HoltC). HR&W.
Ary, Sheila & Gregory, Mary. Oxford Book of Wild Flowers. (Illus.). 1960. 35.00x (ISBN 0-19-910001-2). Oxford U Pr.
Arya, Atam P. Elementary Modern Physics. new ed. LC 73-1466. 1974. text ed. 24.95 (ISBN 0-201-00304-X). Addison-Wesley.
--Introductory College Physics. (Illus.). 1979. text ed. 31.95 (ISBN 0-02-304000-9); instrs'. manual avail.; student study guide avail. Macmillan.
Arya, J. C. & Lardner, R. W. Algebra & Trigonometry with Applications. (Illus.). 272p. 1983. text ed. 29.95 (ISBN 0-13-021675-5). P-H.
--College Algebra with Applications. (Illus.). 560p. 1983. text ed. 29.95 (ISBN 0-13-140699-X). P-H.
--Mathematics for the Biological Sciences. (Illus.). 1979. 34.95 (ISBN 0-13-562439-8). P-H.
Arya, Jagdish C. & Lardner, Robin. Mathematical Analysis for Business & Economics. 2nd ed. (Illus.). 704p. 1985. text ed. 31.95 (ISBN 0-13-561101-6); study guide 9.95 (ISBN 0-13-561176-8). P-H.
Arya, Jagdish C. & Lardner, Robin W. Applied Calculus for Business & Economics. (Illus.). 528p. 1981. text ed. 31.95 (ISBN 0-13-039255-3). P-H.
Arya, O. P., et al. Tropical Venereology. (Medicine in the Tropics Ser.). (Illus.). 234p. 1980. pap. text ed. 20.00 (ISBN 0-443-01467-1). Churchill.
Arya, P. L. Social Accounting for Developing Countries. 1976. 11.00x (ISBN 0-333-90092-8). South Asia Bks.
Arya, Pandit U. Philosophy of Hatha Yoga. 2nd ed. LC 84-19790. 120p. 1985. pap. 5.95 (ISBN 0-89389-088-X). Himalayan Pubs.
--Superconcious Meditation. 2nd ed. LC 78-102982. 132p. 1978. pap. 5.95 (ISBN 0-89389-035-9). Himalayan Pubs.
Arya, Pandit U. & Litt, D. Yoga-Sutras of Patanjali with the Exposition of Vyasa: A Translation & Commentary. 600p. 1985. price not set (ISBN 0-89389-092-8). Himalayan Pubs.
Arya, Suresh C., et al. Design of Structures & Foundations for Vibrating Machines. LC 78-56171. 190p. 1979. 37.95x (ISBN 0-87201-294-8). Gulf Pub.
Arya, Usharbudh. God. LC 79-88824. 162p. (Orig.). 1979. pap. 6.95 (ISBN 0-89389-060-X). Himalayan Pubs.
--Meditation & the Art of Dying. LC 78-78252. 179p. 1979. pap. 6.95 (ISBN 0-89389-056-1). Himalayan Pubs.
Arya, Usharbudh & Litt, D. Mantra & Meditation. LC 81-84076. 237p. (Orig.). 1981. pap. 7.95 (ISBN 0-89389-074-X). Himalayan Intl.
Arya, V. K. & Aggarwal, J. K., eds. Deconvolution of Seismic Data. LC 81-6311. (Benchmark Papers in Electrical Engineering & Computer Science Ser.: Vol. 24). 336p. 1982. 49.95 (ISBN 0-87933-406-1). Van Nos Reinhold.
Aryal, Krishna R. Education for the Development of Nepal. 166p. 1971. 8.00 (ISBN 0-318-12872-1, 1). Am-Nepal Ed.
Aryan, K. The Cultural Heritage of Punjab (3000 B.C.-1947 A.D.) 149p. 1983. text ed. 40.50x (ISBN 0-391-03015-9, Pub. by R Prakashan India). Humanities.
--Folk Bronzes of North-Western India. (Illus.). 124p. 1979. text ed. 19.75x (ISBN 0-391-03017-5, Pub. by R Prakashan India). Humanities.
--Hanuman in Art & Mythology. (Illus.). 1976. text ed. 40.50x (ISBN 0-391-03014-0, Pub. by R Prakashan India). Humanities.
--Himachal Embroidery. (Illus.). 84p. 1976. text ed. 19.75x (ISBN 0-391-03016-7, Pub. by R Prakashan India). Humanities.
--Indian Decorative Designs. 51p. 1983. pap. text ed. 5.25x (ISBN 0-391-03020-5, Pub. by R Prakashan India). Humanities.
--The Little Goddesses. (Illus.). 150p. 1980. text ed. 19.75x (ISBN 0-391-03013-2, Pub. by R Prakashan India). Humanities.
--Punjab Murals. (Illus.). 100p. 1977. text ed. 32.50x (ISBN 0-391-03018-3, Pub. by R Prakashan India). Humanities.
Aryan, K. C. Basis of Decorative Element in Indian Art. 141p. 1981. text ed. 48.00x (ISBN 0-391-02659-3). Humanities.
Aryan, K. C. & Aryan, S. Rural Art of the Western Himalaya. (Illus.). 99p. 1985. text ed. 66.50x (ISBN 0-391-03327-1, Pub. by R Prakashan India). Humanities.
Aryan, S., jt. auth. see Aryan, K. C.
Aryanpur-Kashani, Abbas & Aryanpur-Kashani, Manoochehr. The Combined New Persian-English & English-Persian Dictionary. 688p. 1985. lib. bdg. 49.95x (ISBN 0-939214-28-8); pap. text ed. 36.00x (ISBN 0-939214-29-6). Mazda Pubs.
Aryanpur-Kashani, Manoochehr, jt. auth. see Aryanpur-Kashani, Abbas.
Arya-Sura. The Gatnkamala: Or, Garland of Birth-Stories. Muller, F. Max, ed. Speyer, J. C., tr. from Sanskrit. LC 78-72371. Repr. of 1895 ed. 37.50 (ISBN 0-404-17218-0). AMS Pr.
Aryasura. The Marvelous Companion: Life Stories of the Buddha. (Illus.). 250p. 1983. 25.00 (ISBN 0-913546-88-7). Dharma Pub.
Aryu, P. L., jt. auth. see Kpedekpo, G. M.
Arzaga, Jim, jt. auth. see Layne, Lisa.
Arzans de Orsua y Vela, Bartolome. Historia de la Villa Imperial de Potosi, 3 vols. Mendoza, Gunnar & Hanke, Lewis, eds. LC 63-13533. (Illus.). 1680p. 1965. Set. 130.00x (ISBN 0-87057-097-8). U Pr of New Eng.
--Tales of Potosi. Padden, R. C., ed. LC 74-6574. 245p. 1975. 18.01053605x (ISBN 0-87057-144-3). U Pr of New Eng.
Arzel, P. Traditional Management of Seaweeds in the District of Leon. (Fisheries Tehnical Papers). 49p. 1985. pap. 7.50 (ISBN 92-5-102144-9, F2738, FAO). Unipub.
Arzelies, H. Relativistic Point Dynamics. LC 72-142173. 416p. 1972. text ed. 72.00 (ISBN 0-08-015842-0). Pergamon.
Arzoomanian, Raffi. Four Plays. LC 80-13309. 1980. 12.50 (ISBN 0-933706-18-9); pap. 5.95 (ISBN 0-933706-19-7). Ararat Pr.
Arzooni, O. G. The Israeli Film: Social & Cultural Influences 1912-1973. Jowett, Garth S., ed. LC 81-48345. (Dissertations on Film Ser.). 387p. 1983. lib. bdg. 55.00 (ISBN 0-8240-5102-5). Garland Pub.
Arzt, Max. Joy & Remembrance. LC 79-63435. 1979. 10.00 (ISBN 0-686-37150-X). Hartmore.
Arzt, Max, jt. auth. see Silverman, Morris.
Asa, Donald L. Introduction to Trucking. (Illus.). 1978. pap. text ed. 7.95x (ISBN 0-685-08729-8). D & A Pub.
Asad, Talal, ed. Anthropology & the Colonial Encounter. LC 73-12199. 1979. pap. text ed. 10.45x (ISBN 0-391-00391-7). Humanities.
Asad, Talal & Owen, Roger, eds. The Middle East. LC 83-42527. (Sociology of "Developing Societies" Ser.). 240p. 1983. 20.00 (ISBN 0-85345-636-4); pap. 8.00 (ISBN 0-85345-637-2). Monthly Rev.
Asada, Bin. Earthquake Prediction Techniques. 317p. 1982. 34.50x (ISBN 0-86008-290-3, Pub. by U of Tokyo Japan). Columbia U Pr.
Asada, Y., et al, eds. Plant Infection: The Physiological & Biochemical Basis. 362p. 1982. 58.00 (ISBN 0-387-11873-X). Springer-Verlag.
Asada, Yohoji, et al. Fishery Management in Japan. (Fisheries Technical Papers: No. 238). 26p. (Orig.). 1984. pap. text ed. 7.50 (ISBN 92-5-101392-6, F2532, FAO). Unipub.
Asafiev. A Book about Stravinsky. Brown, Malcolm, ed. French, Richard F., tr. from Rus. LC 82-4810. (Studies in Russian Music: No. 5). 316p. 1982. 44.95 (ISBN 0-8357-1320-2). UMI Res Pr.
Asahina & Shibata. Chemistry of Lichen Substances. (Illus.). 1972. 26.75 (ISBN 90-6123-218-X). Lubrecht & Cramer.
Asahina, K. & Shigiya, R., eds. Physiological Adaptability & Nutritional Status of the Japanese (B, Vol. 4. (Japan International Biological Program Synthesis Ser.). 250p. 1975. 32.50x (ISBN 0-86008-214-8, Pub. by U of Tokyo Japan). Columbia U Pr.
Asai, Kazuhiko. Miracle Cure: Organic Germanium. LC 79-91512. (Illus.). 256p. 1980. 12.95 (ISBN 0-87040-474-1). Japan Pubns USA.
Asakawa, K. The Russo-Japanese Conflict: Its Causes & Issues. (Illus.). 399p. 1972. Repr. of 1904 ed. 35.00x (ISBN 0-7165-2048-6, BBA 02211, Pub. by Irish Academic Pr Ireland). Biblio Dist.
Asakawa, Kanichi, ed. & tr. The Documents of Iriki, Illustrative of the Development of the Feudal Institutions of Japan. LC 77-136514. (Yale Historical Publications Ser.). (Illus.). xvi, 584p. Repr. of 1929 ed. lib. bdg. 44.00x (ISBN 0-8371-5432-4, ASDI). Greenwood.
Asakura, Sho, jt. auth. see Oosawa, Fumio.
Asalache, Khadambi. Calabash of Life. (Orig.). 1967. pap. text ed. 5.45x (ISBN 0-582-64001-6). Humanities.
Asals, Frederick. Flannery O'Connor: The Imagination of Extremity. LC 81-10513. 288p. 1982. 20.00x (ISBN 0-8203-0592-8). U of Ga Pr.
Asals, Heather, jt. auth. see Stanwood, Paul G.
Asals, Heather A. Equivocal Predication: George Herbert's Way to God. 152p. 1981. 30.00x (ISBN 0-8020-5536-2). U of Toronto Pr.
Asamani, J. O. Index Africanus. new ed. LC 76-187266. (Bibliographical Ser., No. 53). 452p. 1975. 30.00x (ISBN 0-8179-2531-7). Hoover Inst Pr.
Asano, Hachiro. Hands: The Complete Book of Palmistry. (Illus.). 224p. (Orig.). 1985. pap. 12.95 (ISBN 0-87040-633-7). Japan Pubns USA.
Asano, Osamu & Ishiwata, Mutsuko, eds. The Japanese Press, 1982. 34th ed. Henshu-sha, Century Eibun & Higashi, Shinbu, trs. LC 49-25552. (Illus.). 192p. 1982. pap. 28.50x (ISBN 0-8002-3022-1). Intl Pubns Serv.
Asano, Shuzo, ed. Structure of the Transition Zone. (Advances in Earth & Planetary Sciences Ser.: No. 8). 184p. 1980. lib. bdg. 26.50 (ISBN 90-277-1149-6, Pub. by D. Reidel). Kluwer Academic.
Asano, Takashi. Artificial Recharge of Groundwater. 800p. 1985. text ed. 69.95 (ISBN 0-250-40549-0). Butterworth.
Asano, Takashi, jt. auth. see Pettygrove, G. Stuart.
Asante, Kariamu W., jt. auth. see Asante, Molefi K.
Asante, Molefi K. Afrocentricity: The Theory of Social Change. 156p. (Orig.). 1980. pap. text ed. 7.95 (ISBN 0-936360-00-3). Amulefi.
Asante, Molefi K. & Asante, Kariamu W. African Culture: The Rhythms of Unity. LC 84-9015. (Contributions in Afro-American & African Studies: No. 81). (Illus.). 288p. 1985. lib. bdg. 35.00 (ISBN 0-313-24404-9, ASA/). Greenwood.
Asante, Molefi K. & Vandi, Abdulai S., eds. Contemporary Black Thought: Alternative Analyses in Social & Behavioral Science. LC 80-15186. (Sage Focus Editions Ser.: Vol. 26). (Illus.). 302p. 1980. 28.00 (ISBN 0-8039-1500-4). Sage.
--Contemporary Black Thought: Alternative Analyses in Social & Behavioral Science. LC 80-15186. (Sage Focus Editions: Vol. 26). (Illus.). 302p. 1980. pap. 14.00 (ISBN 0-8039-1501-2). Sage.
Asante, Molefi K., et al, eds. Handbook of Intercultural Communication. LC 78-2468. 1979. 35.00 (ISBN 0-8039-0954-3); pap. 17.50 (ISBN 0-8039-1074-6). Sage.
Asante, S. K. Pan-African Protest: West Africa & the Italo-Ethiopian Crisis, 1934-1941. LC 78-312713. (Legon History Ser.). pap. 65.00 (ISBN 0-317-27780-4, 2025231). Bks Demand UMI.
Asantewa, Doris. Two Make a Team. LC 76-20192. 1976. pap. 2.95 (ISBN 0-917336-01-1). Pambili Bks.
Asanuma, Hiroshi, ed. & pref. by. Intergration in the Nervous System. LC 79-84783. (Illus.). 357p. 1979. 52.50 (ISBN 0-89640-033-6). Igaku-Shoin.
Asanuma, T. Flow Visualization. 1979. 69.50 (ISBN 0-07-002378-6). McGraw.
Asao, Hirokazu & Kiichi, Oji. Hepatocerebral Degeneration. (Illus.). 96p. 1968. photocopy ed. 12.75x (ISBN 0-398-00056-5). C C Thomas.
Asare, Bediako. Rebel. (African Writers Ser.). 1969. pap. text ed. 4.00x (ISBN 0-435-90059-5). Heinemann Ed.
Asari, V. Gopalakrishnan. Technological Change for Rural Development in India. ix, 236p. 1985. text ed. 37.50x (ISBN 0-86590-600-9, Pub. by B R Pub Corp Delhi). Apt Bks.
Asaria, Gerald. Challenge: Lone Sailors of the Atlantic. LC 79-10041. (Illus.). 1979. 19.95 (ISBN 0-8317-1242-2, Mayflower Bks). Smith Pubs.
Asaria, Gerald, jt. auth. see Vann, Peter.
Asay, J. R., et al, eds. Shock Waves in Condensed Matter, 1983: Proceedings of the American Physical Society, Topical Conference, Conference, Sante Fe, Mexico, July 18-21, 1983. 670p. 1985. 68.75 (ISBN 0-444-86904-2, North-Holland). Elsevier.
Asay, Karol & Carroll, John M., eds. Camp Talk: The Very Private Letters of Captain Frederick W. Benteen of the 7th U. S. Calvalry to His Wife, 1871-1888. (Illus.). 1985. 29.95 (ISBN 0-8488-0001-X, Pub. by J M C & Co). Amereon Ltd.
Asbell, Bernard. The Senate Nobody Knows. LC 80-8928. 480p. 1981. pap. text ed. 9.95x (ISBN 0-8018-2620-9). Johns Hopkins.
Asbell, Bernard, jt. auth. see Amster, Gerald.
Asberg, M. & Stern, W. T., eds. Linnaeus's Oland & Gotland Journey, 1741: Casebound Edition of Biological Journal of the Linnean Society, Vol. 5, No's 1 & 2. 1974. 41.50 (ISBN 0-12-064750-8). Acad Pr.
Asbjornsen & Moe. A Time for Trolls. (Tanum of Norway Tokens Ser). 1982. pap. 10.00x (ISBN 82-518-0081-1, N431). Vanous.
Asbjornsen, Jan, jt. auth. see Arrants, Cheryl.
Asbjornsen, P. C. & Moe, J. The Runaway Pancake. Tate, Joan, tr. from Danish. LC 80-80439. (Illus.). 32p. (ps-8). 1980. 9.95 (ISBN 0-88332-137-8, 8067). Larousse.
Asbjornsen, P. Chr. & Moe, Jorgen. Norwegian Folk Tales. (Illus.). 188p. 1978. 20.00x (ISBN 82-09-01603-2, N449). Vanous.
Asbjornsen, Peter C. Tales from the Fjeld. Dasent, George W., tr. LC 69-13232. (Illus.). 1969. Repr. of 1896 ed. 20.00 (ISBN 0-405-08217-7). Ayer Co Pubs.
Asbjornsen, Peter C. & Moe, Jorgen. Norwegian Folk Tales. 1982. pap. 5.95 (ISBN 0-394-71054-1). Pantheon.
ASBO Management Techniques Research Committee. Control Points in School Business Management. 1979. 3.00 (ISBN 0-910170-10-X). Assn Sch Busn.
ASBO's Maintenance & Operations Research Committee. Custodial Methods & Procedures Manual. 1981. 10.50 (ISBN 0-910170-19-3). Assn Sch Busn.
ASBO's Management Techniques Research Committee. Compendium of Management Techniques. 1982. 5.00 (ISBN 0-910170-23-1). Assn Sch Busn.
ASBO's Negotiations Research Committee. Negotiations & the Manager in Public Education. 1980. 27.50 (ISBN 0-910170-16-9). Assn Sch Busn.
ASBO's Purchasing & Supply Management Research Committee. Cooperative Purchasing Guidelines. 1979. 5.00 (ISBN 0-910170-09-6). Assn Sch Busn.
ASBO's School Facilities Council Division Staff. Schoolhouse Planning. 1980. 8.50 (ISBN 0-910170-12-6). Assn Sch Busn.
Asbraf, Mary. Political Verse & Song from Britain & Ireland. 1976. 9.95x (ISBN 0-8464-0731-0). Beekman Pubs.
Asbrook, Joseph. Astronomical Scrapbook-One. (Illus.). text ed. 19.95 (ISBN 0-933346-24-7). Sky Pub.
Asbury, A. J. ABC of Computing. 69p. 1984. 14.00 (ISBN 0-7279-0160-5, Pub. by British Med Assoc UK). Taylor & Francis.
Asbury, A. K., jt. ed. see Gilliatt, R. W.
Asbury, Arthur K. & Johnson, Peter C. Pathology of Peripheral Nerve. LC 77-11328. (Major Problems in Pathology Ser.: No. 9). (Illus.). 1978. pap. text ed. 33.95 (ISBN 0-7216-1426-4). Saunders.
Asbury, Carolyn H. Orphan Drugs: Medical vs. Market Value. LC 84-47648. (Illus.). 240p. 1985. 27.00 (ISBN 0-669-08389-5). Lexington Bks.
Asbury, Francis. Heart & Church. pap. 4.95 (ISBN 0-686-23583-5). Schmul Pub Co.
--Journal & Letters of Francis Asbury, 3 Vols. Clark, Elmer T., et al, eds. 1958. Set. 50.00 (ISBN 0-687-20580-8); 18.00 ea. Vol. I (ISBN 0-687-20581-6). Vol. II (ISBN 0-687-20582-4). Vol. III (ISBN 0-687-20583-2). Abingdon.
Asbury, Herbert. The French Quarter. 1981. pap. 2.95 (ISBN 0-89176-028-8, 6028). Mockingbird Bks.
--Great Illusion: An Informal History of Prohibition. LC 68-8051. (Illus.). 1968. Repr. of 1950 ed. lib. bdg. 65.00x (ISBN 0-8371-0008-9, ASGI). Greenwood.
--Suckers Progress: An Informal History of Gambling in America from the Colonies to Canfield. LC 69-14909. (Criminology, Law Enforcement, & Social Problems Ser.: No. 51). (Illus.). 1969. Repr. of 1938 ed. 17.50x (ISBN 0-87585-051-0). Patterson Smith.
Asbury, Taylor, jt. auth. see Vaughan, Daniel.
Ascani, Sparky. Commune's Child. (Orig.). 1981. pap. 2.25 (ISBN 0-505-51681-0, Pub. by Tower Bks). Dorchester Pub Co.
--Ransomed Heart. 208p. 1983. pap. 2.95 (ISBN 0-380-83287-9). Avon.
Ascarrunz de Gilman, Graciela & Sugano, Marian Z. Horizontes Gramaticales. 368p. 1984. pap. 17.50 scp (ISBN 0-06-042314-5); pap. text ed. 10.50 scp wkbk. (ISBN 0-06-042313-7); inst. manual avail. (ISBN 0-06-362366-8); scp paper reader 16.50 (ISBN 0-06-042311-0); scp cassette tapes or reel-to-reel tapes 295.00 (ISBN 0-06-047445-9). Har-Row.
ASCD Committee on Research & Theory & Brookover, Wilbur B. Measuring & Attaining the Goals of Education. 105p. (Orig.). 1980. pap. text ed. 6.50 (ISBN 0-87120-102-X). Assn Supervision.
ASCD 1973 Yearbook Committee. Education for Peace: Focus on Mankind. Henderson, George, ed. LC 44-6213. (Yearbook Ser. 1973). (Illus., Orig.). 1973. 7.50 (ISBN 0-87120-017-1, 17946). Assn Supervision.
ASCE, jt. auth. see Water Pollution Control Federation.
ASCE Committee on Engineering Management, Aug. 1976. Civil Engineer's Role in Productivity in the Construction Industry, 2 vols. 402p. 1976. Set. pap. 17.75x (ISBN 0-87262-075-1). Am Soc Civil Eng.
ASCE Committee on Seismic Analysis. Seismic Response of Buried Pipes & Structural Components. 58p. 1983. pap. 11.75x (ISBN 0-87262-368-8). Am Soc Civil Eng.
ASCE Conference, Aerospace Division, 1980. Civil Engineering Applications of Remote Sensing. Kiefer, Ralph W., ed. LC 80-67879. 199p. 1980. pap. 19.50x (ISBN 0-87262-253-3). Am Soc Civil Eng.
ASCE Conference, Construction Division, 1979. Construction Risks & Liability Sharing, 2 vols. LC 80-65819. 427p. 1979. pap. 42.00x (ISBN 0-87262-048-4). Am Soc Civil Eng.

ASCE Conference, Environment Engineering Division, 1980. Environmental Engineering. Saukin, Walter, ed. LC 80-66954. 719p. 1980. pap. 52.00x (ISBN 0-87262-249-5). Am Soc Civil Eng.

ASCE Conference, Hydraulics Division, 1980. Computer & Physical Modeling in Hydraulic Engineering. Ashton, George, ed. LC 80-67878. 500p. 1980. pap. 36.00x (ISBN 0-87262-252-5). Am Soc Civil Eng.

--Urban Stormwater Management in Coastal Areas. Kuo, Chin Y., ed. LC 80-66949. 442p. 1980. pap. 32.00x (ISBN 0-87262-247-9). Am Soc Civil Eng.

ASCE Conference, Irrigation & Drainage Division, 1980. Irrigation & Drainage-Today's Challenges. Eggleston, Jerry, ed. LC 80-66950. 502p. 1980. pap. 38.50x (ISBN 0-87262-251-7). Am Soc Civil Eng.

--Watershed Management 1980: Proceedings of the ASCE Conference, 2 vols. LC 80-66952. 1122p. 1980. Set. pap. 68.00x (ISBN 0-87262-250-9). Am Soc Civil Eng.

ASCE Conference on Environmental Engineering, New York, July, 1980. The Hazardous Waste Dilemma: Issues & Solutions. Saukin, Walter, ed. LC 81-65627. 334p. 1981. pap. 24.75x (ISBN 0-87262-266-5). Am Soc Civil Eng.

ASCE Conference, San Francisco, May 1978. Coastal Zone '78: 1978, 4 vols. 3195p. 1978. Set. pap. 118.00x (ISBN 0-87262-134-0). Am Soc Civil Eng.

ASCE Conference, Surveying & Mapping Division, 1980. The Planning & Engineering Interface with a Modernized Land Data System. Marks, G. Warren, ed. LC 80-66123. 269p. 1980. pap. 26.50x (ISBN 0-87262-243-6). Am Soc Civil Eng.

ASCE Conference, Urban Transportation Division, 1980. Transportation & the 1977 Clean Air Act Amendments. LC 80-66291. 440p. pap. 33.50x (ISBN 0-87262-242-8). Am Soc Civil Eng.

ASCE Conference, Urban Transportation Division, 1979. Urban Transportation Financing. LC 80-66290. 312p. 1980. pap. 25.50x (ISBN 0-87262-241-X). Am Soc Civil Eng.

ASCE Conference, Waterway, Port, Coastal & Ocean Division, 1980. Ports '80. Mascenik, John, ed. LC 80-65719. 849p. 1980. pap. 50.00x (ISBN 0-87262-108-1). Am Soc Civil Eng.

ASCE Geotechnical Engineering Division, New York, 1981. Recent Developments in Geotechnical Engineering for Hydro Projects: Embankment Dam Instrumentation Performance, Engineering Geology Aspects, Rock Mechanics Studies. Kulhavy, Fred, ed. LC 81-66345. 253p. 1981. pap. 17.00x (ISBN 0-87262-269-X). Am Soc Civil Eng.

ASCE Hydraulics Division, Univ. of Minnesota, June, 1980. Surface Water Impoundments, 2 vols. Stefan, H., ed. LC 81-67445. 1724p. 1981. Set. pap. 115.00x (ISBN 0-87262-271-1). Am Soc Civil Eng.

ASCE National Convention, Environmental Analysis Research Council, Atlanta, 1979. Appropriate Technology in Resource Conservation & Recovery. Gunnerson, Charles G. & Kalbermatten, John M., eds. LC 80-65304. 218p. 1979. pap. 19.50x (ISBN 0-87262-035-2). Am Soc Civil Eng.

ASCE Pipeline Division, New Orleans, March, 1981. Underground Plastic Pipe. Schrock, B. J., ed. LC 81-65630. 553p. 1981. pap. 37.50x (ISBN 0-87262-265-7). Am Soc Civil Eng.

ASCE Professional Activities Committee Conference, March 1977. Ethics, Professionalism, & Maintaining Competence. American Society of Civil Engineers, compiled By. 357p. 1977. pap. 18.50x (ISBN 0-87262-076-X). Am Soc Civil Eng.

ASCE Task Committee on Hydrographic Investigations. Measurement of Hydrographic Parameters in Large Sand-Bed Streams from Boats. 84p. 1983. pap. 13.50x (ISBN 0-87262-354-8). Am Soc Civil Eng.

ASCE Technical Council on Cold Regions Engineering, Seattle, April 1981. The Northern Community: A Search for a Quality Environment. Vinson, Ted, ed. LC 81-65629. 794p. 1981. pap. 49.75x (ISBN 0-87262-267-3). Am Soc Civil Eng.

ASCE, Technical Council on Computer Practices, 1980. Computing in Civil Engineering 1980. Schelling, David R., ed. LC 80-66141. 739p. 1980. pap. 34.00x (ISBN 0-87262-246-0). Am Soc Civil Eng.

ASCE Technical Council on Computer Practices, New York, May, 1981. International Conference on Computing in Civil Engineering. LC 81-66346. 1222p. 1981. pap. 75.50x (ISBN 0-87262-270-3). Am Soc Civil Eng.

ASCE Technical Council on Ocean Engineering, Dec. 1969. Civil Engineering in the Oceans II. 1280p. 1970. 38.00x (ISBN 0-87262-018-2). Am Soc Civil Eng.

ASCE Urban Transportation Division, May 1973. Environmental Impact. American Society of Civil Engineers, compiled By. 399p. 1973. pap. 16.00x (ISBN 0-87262-063-8). Am Soc Civil Eng.

ASCE Urban Water Resources Research Council Conference, Nov. 1976. Guide for Collection, Analysis, & Use of Urban Stormwater Data. 128p. 1977. pap. 5.75x (ISBN 0-87262-077-8). Am Soc Civil Eng.

ASCE Waterway, Port Coastal & Ocean Division Conference, Charleston, Nov. 1977. Coastal Sediments: 1977. American Society of Civil Engineers, compiled By. 1143p. 1977. pap. 47.00x (ISBN 0-87262-090-5). Am Soc Civil Eng.

Asch, Berta & Mangus, A. R. Farmers on Relief & Rehabilitation. LC 78-165678. (Research Monograph). 1971. Repr. of 1937 ed. lib. bdg. 27.50 (ISBN 0-306-70340-8). Da Capo.

Asch, David C. Cost Accounting & Budgeting. (Illus.). 288p. 1983. pap. text ed. 22.95x (ISBN 0-7121-0474-7). Trans-Atlantic.

Asch, David L. The Middle Woodland Population of the Lower Illinois Valley. LC 82-101264. (Scientific Papers: No. 1). (Illus.). 112p. 1976. 15.00 (ISBN 0-942118-00-6); pap. 9.00 (ISBN 0-942118-01-4). Ctr Amer Arche.

Asch, Frank. Bear Shadow. (Illus.). 32p. (gr. k-8). 1985. 11.95 (ISBN 0-13-071580-8). P-H.

--Bear's Bargain. (Illus.). 32p. (gr. k-3). 1985. 11.95 (ISBN 0-13-071606-5). P-H.

--Bread & Honey. LC 81-16893. (Illus.). 48p. (ps-3). 1982. 5.95 (ISBN 0-8193-1077-8); PLB 5.95 (ISBN 0-8193-1078-6). Parents.

--City Sandwich. LC 77-18902. (Illus.). 48p. (gr. 1-4). 1978. 10.25 (ISBN 0-688-80156-0); PLB 10.88 (ISBN 0-688-84156-2). Greenwillow.

--Country Pie. LC 78-14837. (Illus.). 32p. (gr. 1-3). 1979. 11.75 (ISBN 0-688-80188-9); PLB 11.88 (ISBN 0-688-84188-0). Greenwillow.

--George's Store. LC 82-22298. (Illus.). 48p. (ps-3). 1983. 5.95 (ISBN 0-8193-1101-4); PLB 5.95 (ISBN 0-8193-1102-2). Parents.

--Good Night, Horsey. (Illus.). 32p. (gr. k-3). 1984. pap. 4.95 (ISBN 0-13-360363-6). P-H.

--Goodnight, Horsey. (Illus.). (ps-3). 1981. 9.95 (ISBN 0-13-360461-6). P-H.

--Happy Birthday, Moon. (Illus.). 32p. (ps-3). 1982. 9.95x (ISBN 0-13-383687-8). P-H.

--Happy Birthday, Moon. (Illus.). 32p. (gr. k-3). 1985. pap. 4.95 (ISBN 0-13-383696-7). P-H.

--Just Like Daddy. (ps-3). 1981. 10.95x (ISBN 0-13-514042-0). P-H.

--Just Like Daddy. (Illus.). 32p. (ps-3). 1984. pap. 4.95 (ISBN 0-13-514035-8, Pub. by Treehouse). P-H.

--The Last Puppy. (Illus.). 30p. (ps-3). 1983. pap. 3.95 (ISBN 0-13-524041-7). P-H.

--Macgooses' Grocery. LC 77-86270. (Pied Piper Book). (Illus.). 32p. (ps-2). 1980. pap. 1.95 (ISBN 0-8037-5328-4). Dial Bks Young.

--Milk & Cookies. LC 82-7962. (Illus.). 48p. (ps-3). 1982. 5.95 (ISBN 0-8193-1087-5); PLB 5.95 (ISBN 0-8193-1088-3). Parents.

--Mooncake. (Illus.). 28p. (ps-3). 1983. 9.95 (ISBN 0-13-601013-X). P-H.

--Moongame. (Illus.). 32p. (gr. k-3). 1984. 10.95 (ISBN 0-13-600503-9). P-H.

--Pearl's Promise. LC 83-17153. (Illus.). 160p. (gr. 4-6). 1984. 12.95 (ISBN 0-385-29325-9); PLB 12.95 (ISBN 0-385-29321-6). Delacorte.

--Pearl's Promise. 160p. (gr. 1-4). 1984. pap. 2.25 (ISBN 0-440-46863-9, YB). Dell.

--Popcorn. LC 79-216. (Illus.). 48p. (ps-3). 1979. 5.95 (ISBN 0-686-86568-5). Parents.

--Rebecka. LC 72-765222. (Illus.). 32p. (ps-3). 1972. PLB 8.89 (ISBN 0-06-020150-9). HarpJ.

--Sand Cake. LC 78-11183. (Illus.). 48p. (ps-3). 1979. 5.95 (ISBN 0-686-86571-5). Parents.

--Skyfire. LC 83-16165. (Illus.). 32p. 1984. 10.95 (ISBN 0-13-812389-6). P-H.

--Turtle Tale. LC 78-51328. (Pied Piper Bk.). (Illus.). 32p. (gr. 3-7). 1980. pap. 2.75 (ISBN 0-8037-8785-5). Dial Bks Young.

Asch, Frank & Asch, Jan. Running with Rachel. LC 78-72471. (Illus.). (gr. 3-6). 1979. PLB 9.89 (ISBN 0-8037-7553-9); pap. 3.95 (ISBN 0-8037-7552-0). Dial Bks Young.

Asch, Jan, jt. auth. see Asch, Frank.

Asch, Peter. Economic Theory & the Antitrust Dilemma. LC 83-19947. 426p. 1984. Repr. of 1970 ed. 33.95 (ISBN 0-89874-699-X). Krieger.

--Industrial Organization & Antitrust Policy. rev. ed. LC 82-20012. 399p. 1983. 33.95 (ISBN 0-471-09762-4). Wiley.

Asch, Ricardo H., jt. auth. see Smith, Carol G.

Asch, Shalom. Mother. Ausubel, Nathan, tr. LC 73-114047. (BCL Ser.: No. 1). Repr. of 1930 ed. 12.50 (ISBN 0-404-00408-3). AMS Pr.

--Mottke the Thief. LC 73-98807. Repr. of 1935 ed. lib. bdg. 27.50 (ISBN 0-8371-2953-2, ASMO). Greenwood.

--Sabbatai Zevi. Whyte, Florence & Noyes, George R., trs. LC 74-3622. (Illus.). 131p. 1974. Repr. of 1930 ed. lib. bdg. 18.75 (ISBN 0-8371-7449-X, ASSZ). Greenwood.

Asch, Sholem. Apostle. 804p. 1985. pap. 10.95 (ISBN 0-88184-167-6). Carroll & Graf.

--Children of Abraham. (Short Story Index Reprint Ser.). 433p. 1982. Repr. of 1942 ed. lib. bdg. 24.00 (ISBN 0-8290-0827-6). Irvington.

--Children of Abraham: The Short Stories of Sholem Asch. facsimile ed. Samuel, Maurice, tr. LC 74-152934. (Short Story Index Reprint Ser.). Repr. of 1942 ed. 27.50 (ISBN 0-8369-3792-9). Ayer Co Pubs.

--East River. 448p. 1983. pap. 8.95 (ISBN 0-88184-014-9, Publishers Group West). Carroll & Graf.

--In the Beginning: Stories from the Bible. Cunningham, Caroline, tr. LC 66-24907. (Illus.). 1966. 6.00 (ISBN 0-8052-3109-9). Schocken.

--In the Beginning: Stories from the Bible. Cunningham, Caroline, tr. from Yiddish. LC 66-24907. (Illus.). (gr. 3-6). 1979. pap. 3.95 (ISBN 0-8052-0626-4). Schocken.

--Mary. 436p. 1985. pap. 10.95 (ISBN 0-88184-141-2). Carroll & Graf.

--The Nazarene. 702p. 1984. 21.95 (ISBN 0-88184-072-6); pap. 10.95 (ISBN 0-88184-048-3). Carroll & Graf.

--Tales of My People. facs. ed. Levin, Meyer, tr. LC 75-128752. (Short Story Index Reprint Ser). 1948. 20.00 (ISBN 0-8369-3609-4). Ayer Co Pubs.

--Three Cities. 899p. pap. 10.50 (ISBN 0-88184-009-2, Publishers Group West). Carroll & Graf.

--A Trilogy: The Nazarene, the Apostle, Mary. 1985. Boxed set. pap. 32.85 cancelled (ISBN 0-88184-142-0). Carroll & Graf.

Asch, Sholem see Landis, Joseph C.

Asch, Sholom. Kiddush Ha-Shem: An Epic of 1648. facsimile ed. Learsi, Rufus, tr. LC 74-27960. (Modern Jewish Experience Ser.). 1975. Repr. of 1926 ed. 21.00x (ISBN 0-405-06691-0). Ayer Co Pubs.

Asch, Solomon E., ed. see Kohler, Wolfgang.

Aschaffenburg, Gustav. Crime & Its Repression. Albrecht, Adalbert, tr. LC 68-55767. (Criminology, Law Enforcement, & Social Problems Ser.: No. 11). 1968. Repr. of 1913 ed. 20.00x (ISBN 0-87585-011-1). Patterson Smith.

Ascham, Anthony. Of the Confusions & Revolutions of Governments. LC 75-33731. 226p. 1975. lib. bdg. 35.00x (ISBN 0-8201-1161-9). Schol Facsimiles.

Ascham, Roger. Scholemaster. Mayor, J. E., ed. LC 75-161717. Repr. of 1863 ed. 14.00 (ISBN 0-404-00409-1). AMS Pr.

--The Scholemaster. Arber, Edward, ed. LC 76-13152. Repr. of 1870 ed. lib. bdg. 17.00 (ISBN 0-8414-2976-6). Folcroft.

--The Scholemaster: Or, Plaine & Perfite Way of Teachyng Children the Latin Tong. LC 68-54609. (English Experience Ser.: No. 15). 134p. 1968. Repr. of 1570 ed. 14.00 (ISBN 90-221-0015-4). Walter J Johnson.

--Schoolmaster (1570) Ryan, Lawrence V., ed. (Paperback Ser). 1978. 7.90x (ISBN 0-918016-64-9). Folger Bks.

--Taxophilus, the Schole of Shootinge, 2 bks. LC 75-76431. (English Experience Ser.: No. 79). 184p. 1969. Repr. of 1545 ed. 25.00 (ISBN 90-221-0079-0). Walter J Johnson.

--Toxophilus, 1545. Arber, Edward, ed. LC 73-131612. 1971. Repr. of 1895 ed. 29.00 (ISBN 0-403-00499-3). Scholarly.

--Whole Works, 3 vols. in 4 pts. Giles, J. A., ed. LC 70-121837. Repr. of 1865 ed. Set. 145.00 (ISBN 0-404-00490-3). AMS Pr.

Aschan, Gunnar, et al. Nystagmography, Recording of Nystagmus in Clinical Neuro-Otological Examinations. 12.00 (ISBN 0-384-02165-4). Johnson Repr.

Aschbacher, Michael. The Finite Simple Groups & Their Classifications. LC 79-20927. (Yale Mathematical Monograph: No. 7). (Orig.). 1980. pap. text ed. 8.95x (ISBN 0-300-02449-5). Yale U Pr.

Aschbacher, Michael, et al, eds. Future Directions in Finite Group Theory. 400p. 1984. 39.50 (ISBN 0-521-26493-6). Cambridge U Pr.

Aschenbrener, Thomas D. & Mosan, Paul. Physicians Assistant Examination Review. LC 78-26893. 144p. 1980. pap. 13.95 (ISBN 0-668-04026-2). ACC.

Aschenbrenner, Erich. Oriental Rugs: Persian, Vol. 2. (Illus.). 272p. 1981. 49.50 (ISBN 0-907462-12-X). Antique Collect.

Aschenbrenner, George. A God for a Dark Journey. 1984. pap. 5.95 (ISBN 0-87193-211-3). Dimension Bks.

Aschenbrenner, Joyce. Lifelines: Black Families in Chicago. (Illus.). 146p. 1983. pap. text ed. 6.95x (ISBN 0-88133-023-X). Waveland Pr.

Aschenbrenner, K. The Concepts of Value: Foundations of Value Theory. LC 70-159651. (Foundations of Language Supplementary Ser: No. 12). 462p. 1971. 58.00 (ISBN 90-277-0185-7, Pub. by Reidel Holland). Kluwer Academic.

Aschenbrenner, Karl. Analysis of Appraisive Characterization. 1983. lib. bdg. 48.00 (ISBN 90-277-1452-5, Pub. by Reidel Holland). Kluwer Academic.

--A Companion to Kant's Critique of Pure Reason: Transcendental Aesthetic & Analytic. LC 83-6889. 334p. (Orig.). 1983. lib. bdg. 27.00 (ISBN 0-8191-3229-2); pap. text ed. 13.25 (ISBN 0-8191-3230-6). U Pr of Amer.

--The Concepts of Criticism. LC 74-80523. (Foundations of Language, Supplementary Ser: No. 20). 540p. 1974. lib. bdg. 79.00 (ISBN 90-277-0482-1, Pub. by Reidel Holland). Kluwer Academic.

Aschenbrenner, Karl, tr. see Bochenski, Innocentius.

Aschenbrenner, S. E., jt. ed. see Rapp, George R., Jr.

Ascher & Straus. Red Moon-Red Lake. 32p. (Orig.). 1984. pap. 3.00 (ISBN 0-917061-21-7). Top Stories.

Ascher & Russell, eds. Numerical Boundary Value ODE's. (Progress in Scientific Computing: No. 6). 1985. text ed. write for info. (ISBN 0-8176-3302-2). Birkhauser.

Ascher, Abraham. Pavel Axelrod & the Development of Menshevism. LC 72-78423. (Russian Research Center Studies: No. 70). 610p. 1972. 25.00x (ISBN 0-674-65905-8). Harvard U Pr.

Ascher, Amalie A. The Complete Flower Arranger. 1977. pap. 12.95 (ISBN 0-671-22774-2, Fireside). S&S.

Ascher, Carol. Simone De Beauvoir: A Life of Freedom. LC 80-70361. 1982. pap. 9.95 (ISBN 0-8070-3241-7). Beacon Pr.

Ascher, Carol, et al, eds. Between Women. LC 83-70651. 292p. 1984. 29.95x (ISBN 0-8070-6712-1); pap. 11.95 (ISBN 0-8070-6713-X, BP676). Beacon Pr.

Ascher, Karl W. The Aqueous Veins: Biomicroscopic Study of the Aqueous Humor Elimination. (Illus.). 294p. 1961. photocopy ed. 29.50x (ISBN 0-398-00057-3). C C Thomas.

Ascher, L., jt. auth. see Turner, Ralph.

Ascher, Marcia & Ascher, Robert. Code of the Quipu: A Study of Media, Mathematics, & Culture. (Illus.). 176p. 1981. pap. 8.95 (ISBN 0-472-06325-1). U of Mich Pr.

Ascher, R. E., tr. see Bashear, Vokom M.

Ascher, Robert, jt. auth. see Ascher, Marcia.

Ascher, Scott & Shadburne, William. Scuba Handbook for Humans. 2nd ed. LC 75-3832. (Illus.). 1977. pap. text ed. 8.95 (ISBN 0-8403-1126-5). Kendall-Hunt.

Ascher, Sheila & Straus, Dennis. Letter to an Unknown Woman. (Treacle Story Ser.: No. 6). (Illus.). 48p. 1979. signed 8.00x (ISBN 0-914232-21-5); pap. 2.50 (ISBN 0-914232-20-7). McPherson & Co.

--The Menaced Assassin. LC 82-2866. 160p. 1982. 8.95 (ISBN 0-914232-49-5); pap. 4.95 (ISBN 0-914232-48-7); ltd. signed 25.00 (ISBN 0-914232-50-9). McPherson & Co.

Ascher, Steven, jt. auth. see Pincus, Edward.

Ascher, William. Forecasting: An Appraisal for Policy-Makers & Planners. LC 77-21423. (Illus.). 256p. 1978. pap. 7.95x (ISBN 0-8018-2273-4). Johns Hopkins.

--Scheming for the Poor: The Politics of Redistribution in Latin America. LC 83-12866. (Illus.). 360p. 1984. text ed. 25.00x (ISBN 0-674-79085-5). Harvard U Pr.

Ascher, William & Overholt, William H. Strategic Planning & Forecasting: Political Risk & Economic Opportunity. 311p. 1983. 32.50 (ISBN 0-471-87342-X, Pub by Wiley-Interscience). Wiley.

Aschermann, Arla. Beds for Rest: Pueblo's Hotels from Stagestop to Motel. (Orig.). 1986. pap. write for info. (ISBN 0-915617-11-0). Pueblo Co Hist Soc.

--Winds in the Cornfields of Early Pueblo County. (Illus.). 52p. 1982. pap. 3.50x (ISBN 0-915617-04-8). Pueblo Co Hist Soc.

Aschermann, Kurt, jt. auth. see O'Shea, Gerard P.

Ascherson, N. The Polish August: The Self-Limiting Revolution. 320p. pap. 6.00 (ISBN 0-317-36698-X). Kosciuszko.

Ascherson, Neal. The Polish August: The Self Limiting Revolution. LC 81-52150. (Illus.). 351p. 1982. 14.95 (ISBN 0-670-56305-6). Viking.

Ascherson, Neal, et al. The Nazi Legacy: Klaus Barbie & the International Fascist Connection. 351p. 1984. pap. 17.95 (ISBN 0-03-069303-9). HR&W.

Aschheim, Barbara, et al. Development of Special Mental Health Technical Assistance Materials for Self-Help Groups in Particular Populations. 57p. 1978. pap. 2.60 (ISBN 0-89785-000-9). Am Inst Res.

Aschheim, Joseph & Ching-Yao Hsieh. Macroeconomics: Income & Monetary Theory. LC 80-5519. 279p. 1980. pap. text ed. 13.00 (ISBN 0-8191-1128-7). U Pr of Amer.

Aschheim, Steven E. Brothers & Strangers: The East European Jew in German & German Jewish Consciousness, 1800-1923. LC 81-69812. 350p. 1982. text ed. 25.00x (ISBN 0-299-09110-4). U of Wis Pr.

Aschiero, Hipolito F. Diccionario de Homofonos Castellaros. 120p. (Span.). 1975. 15.95 (ISBN 0-686-56712-9, S-33053). French & Eur.

Aschinger, G. A. Stabilitatsaussagen uber Klassen Von Matrizen mit Verschwindenden Zeilensummen. (Lecture Notes in Economics & Mathematical Systems: Vol. 113). 112p. 1975. pap. 13.00 (ISBN 0-387-07414-7). Springer-Verlag.

Aschkenasy, Nehama, jt. auth. see Hirsch, David H.

Aschman Associates Inc. Shared Parking. LC 83-51648. 86p. (Orig.). 1983. pap. 48.00 (ISBN 0-87420-652-9, S-22); pap. 36.00 members. Urban Land.

Aschmann, Herman P. Vocabulario Totonaco de la Sierra: Castellano-Totonaco, Totonaco-Castellano. (Vocabularios Indigenas Ser.: No. 7). 171p. (Span.). 1962. pap. 10.20x (ISBN 0-88312-666-4); 2.25 (ISBN 0-88312-568-4). Summer Inst Ling.

Aschmann, Homer. Central Desert of Baja California: Demography & Ecology. LC 66-29636. (Illus.). 1967. lib. bdg. 69.50x (ISBN 0-910950-01-6). Ransom Dist Co.

Aschner, Bernard. Arthritis Can Be Cured. 1968. pap. 2.50 (ISBN 0-668-01764-3). Arco.

Aschner, Katherine. The Word Processing Handbook. pap. 8.95 (9530). TAB Bks.

--The Word Processing Handbook: A Step-by-Step Guide to Automating the Office. 200p. 1983. pap. 19.95 (ISBN 0-442-21076-0). Van Nos Reinhold.

--The Word Processing Handbook: A Step-by-Step Guide to Automating Your Office. LC 82-3. (Information & Comunications Management Guides Ser.). (Illus.). 193p. 1982. 32.95 (ISBN 0-86729-017-X, 705-BW); pap. 22.95 (ISBN 0-86729-018-8). Knowledge Indus.
--Word Processing Handbook: A Step-by-Step Guide to Automating Your Office. 2nd ed. 1983. pap. 8.95 (ISBN 0-88908-913-2). Self Counsel Pr.
Aschner, Katherine, ed. Managing Your Office Records & Files. 199p. 1984. 14.95 (ISBN 0-88908-588-9). Schocken.
--Taking Control of Your Office Records: A Manager's Guide. LC 83-6133. (Information & Communications Management Guides Ser.). (Illus.). 264p. 1983. professional 32.95 (ISBN 0-86729-057-9, 704-BW); pap. 22.95 professional (ISBN 0-86729-058-7). Assn Inform & Image Mgmt.
--Taking Control of Your Office Records: A Manager's Guide. (Illus.). 264p. 1984. pap. text ed. 22.95x (ISBN 0-471-81860-7). Wiley.
Aschoff, Angelus G. The Negotiation Between Chu-Yung & Lagrene: Eighteen Fourty-Four to Eighteen Fourty-Six. (Missiology Ser.). 1950. Franciscan Inst.
Aschoff, J., et al, eds. Vertebrate Circadian Systems: Structure & Physiology. (Proceedings in Life Sciences). (Illus.). 340p. 1982. 58.00 (ISBN 0-387-11664-8). Springer-Verlag.
Aschoff, Jurgen, ed. Handbook of Behavioral Neurobiology, Vol. 4: Biological Rhythms. 582p. 1981. 55.00x (ISBN 0-306-40585-7, Plenum Pr). Plenum Pub.
Aschwanden, Charles, ed. see Aschwanden, Maria.
Aschwanden, Charles R., ed. see Aschwanden, Richard J. & Aschwanden, Maria.
Aschwanden, Maria. Challenged by a Woman. Aschwanden, Richard & Aschwanden, Charles, eds. 125p. (Orig.). 1986. pap. 4.95 (ISBN 0-913071-03-X). Rama Pub Co.
--Congratulations, America. 184p. 1982. 8.50 (ISBN 0-682-49800-9). Exposition Pr FL.
--If Men Were Men. Aschwanden, Richard & Aschwanden, Charles, eds. 127p. (Orig.). 1984. pap. 4.95 (ISBN 0-913071-02-1). Rama Pub Co.
Aschwanden, Maria, jt. auth. see Aschwanden, Richard.
Aschwanden, Maria, jt. auth. see Aschwanden, Richard J.
Aschwanden, Richard & Aschwanden, Maria. Escaping Collusion. 90p. (Orig.). 1983. pap. 4.20x (ISBN 0-913071-01-3). Rama Pub Co.
Aschwanden, Richard, ed. see Aschwanden, Maria.
Aschwanden, Richard J. & Aschwanden, Maria. A Time of Personal Regeneration. Aschwanden, Charles R., ed. 60p. 1984. pap. 3.40x (ISBN 0-913071-00-5, TX1-202-40). Rama Pub Co.
Asclepiodotus see Aeneas Tacticus.
Ascoli. Crisis & Evasion in the Orlando Furioso. 37.50 (ISBN 0-317-14199-6). Princeton U Pr.
Ascoli, Max, ed. see Reporter.
Ascombe, Isabelle. A Woman's Touch: Women in Design from 1860 to the Present Day. (Illus.). 210p. 1984. 20.00 (ISBN 0-670-77825-7, Elizabeth Sifton Bks). Viking.
Ascroft, Winifred. The Quickening Flame. (Basic Bible Study). 60p. 1985. pap. 2.95 (ISBN 0-932305-20-2, 521020). Aglow Pubns.
Asefa, Sisay, ed. Economic Decision Making: Public & Private Decisions. 112p. 1985. pap. text ed. 8.50x (ISBN 0-8138-0111-7). Iowa St U Pr.
ASEI Magazine Staff see Marier, Donald & Stoiaken, Larry.
Aseltine, Gwen P. Letters to Virgins. LC 79-65034. 1979. pap. 3.95 (ISBN 0-917182-13-8). Triumph Pub.
Aseltine, J. A. Transform Method in Linear System Analysis. (Electrical & Electronic Eng. Ser). 1958. 48.00 (ISBN 0-07-002389-1). McGraw.
Aseltine, Lorraine, et al. I'm Deaf, & It's Okay. (Concept Bks.). (Illus.). 40p. (gr. 1-4). 1985. 10.25 (ISBN 0-8075-3472-2). A Whitman.
Asencio, Diego & Asencio, Nancy. Our Man Is Inside. 288p. 1983. 17.00 (ISBN 0-316-05294-9, Pub. by Atlantic Monthly Pr). Little.
Asencio, Nancy, jt. auth. see Asencio, Diego.
Asenjo, Alfonso. Neurosurgical Techniques. (Illus.). 360p. 1963. photocopy ed. 30.75x (ISBN 0-398-00058-1). C C Thomas.
Asenjo, Federico. Fiestas of San Juan. (Puerto Rico Ser.). 1979. lib. bdg. 59.95 (ISBN 0-8490-2917-1). Gordon Pr.
Aseshananda, Swami. Glimpses of a Great Soul: The Life of Swami Saradananda. 320p. (Orig.). 1982. pap. 7.95 (ISBN 0-87481-039-6). Vedanta Pr.
Asfahl, C. Ray. Robots & Manufacturing Automation. 490p. 1985. 32.95 (ISBN 0-471-80212-3). Wiley.
Asfahl, Ray. Industrial Safety & Health Management. rev. ed. (Illus.). 416p. 1984. text ed. 35.95 (ISBN 0-13-463141-2). P-H.
Asfaw, Girma-Selassie, et al, eds. The Ampharic Letters of Emperor Theodore of Ethiopia. (Oriental Documents-British Academy Ser.). 1979. pap. 27.50x (ISBN 0-19-725988-X). Oxford U Pr.
Asfour, Edmund Y. Syria: Development & Monetary Policy. LC 59-13357. (Middle Eastern Monographs Ser: No. 1). (Illus.). 1959. pap. 5.95x (ISBN 0-674-86190-6). Harvard U Pr.
Asgar Ali Engineer. Islamic State. 192p. 1981. text ed. 17.95x (ISBN 0-89891-002-1, Pub. by Vikas India). Advent NY.
ASGE Engineering Management Division Conference Held at Chicago, April 1981. Effective Management of Engineering Design. LC 81-65628. 175p. 1981. pap. 18.00x (ISBN 0-87262-268-1). Am Soc Civil Eng.
Asghar, Syed S., jt. auth. see Cormane, Rudi H.
Asgill, John. Several Assertions Proved in Order to Create Another Species of Money. Repr. of 1696 ed. 15.00 (ISBN 0-384-02180-8). Johnson Repr.
Ash, et al. Communication Storage & Retrieval of Chemical Information. 1985. 45.00 (ISBN 0-470-20145-2). Wiley.
--Headwaters: Tales of the Wilderness. LC 78-78296. (Illus.). 1979. pap. 6.00 (ISBN 0-933280-00-9). Island CA.
Ash, A., et al. Smooth Compactification of Locally Symmetric Varieties. LC 75-38142. (Lie Groups: History, Frontiers & Applications Ser.: No. 4). 340p. 1975. 19.00 (ISBN 0-915692-12-0, 991600061). Math Sci Pr.
Ash, Anthony L. Decide to Love. LC 80-80294. (Journey Books). 140p. (Orig.). 1980. pap. 2.95 (ISBN 0-8344-0116-9). Sweet.
--The Word of Faith. Thomas, J. D., ed. LC 73-89757. (Twentieth Century Sermons Ser.). 1973. 11.95 (ISBN 0-89112-308-3). Bibl Res Pr.
Ash, Brian. Faces of the Future: The Lessons of Science Fiction. LC 74-21697. 224p. 1975. 8.95 (ISBN 0-8008-2583-7). Taplinger.
--The Visual Encyclopedia of Science Fiction. (Illus.). 1977. 17.95 (ISBN 0-517-53174-7, Harmony); pap. 3.98 Outlet (ISBN 0-517-53175-5). Crown.
--Who's Who in H. G. Wells. 1979. 22.50 (ISBN 0-241-89597-9, Pub. by Hamish Hamilton England). David & Charles.
--Who's Who in Science Fiction. LC 76-11667. 1978. pap. 4.95 (ISBN 0-8008-8279-2). Taplinger.
Ash, Carol, jt. auth. see Ash, Robert.
Ash, Cay Van see Van Ash, Cay.
Ash, Cay Van see Van Ash, Cay & Rohmer, Elizabeth S.
Ash Deposit & Corrosion from Impurities in Combustion Gases Symposium, June 26-July 1, 1977, New England College, Henniker, New Hampshire. Ash Deposits & Corrosion Due to Impurities in Combustion Gases: Proceedings. Bryers, R. W., ed. LC 78-7001. (Illus.). 691p. 1978. text ed. 89.95 (ISBN 0-89116-074-4). Hemisphere Pub.
Ash, Edward A. In the Country of Kings. LC 80-82570. 150p. (Orig.). 1982. pap. 6.95 (ISBN 0-686-31318-6). Arbor Pr CA.
Ash, Edward C. Dogs: Their History & Development, 2 vols. LC 72-79945. Set. 50.00x (ISBN 0-405-08218-5, Pub. by Blom); 27.50 ea.; Vol. 1. 25.00 (ISBN 0-405-08219-3). Vol. 2 (ISBN 0-405-08220-7). Ayer Co Pubs.
Ash, Eric, ed. Scanned Image Microscopy. LC 80-41580. 1981. 49.50 (ISBN 0-12-065180-7). Acad Pr.
Ash, Eric A. & Hill, C. R., eds. Acoustical Imaging, Vol. 12. LC 69-12533. 790p. 1983. 110.00x (ISBN 0-306-41247-0, Plenum Press). Plenum Pub.
Ash, Fenton. A Trip to Mars. LC 74-15948. (Science Fiction Ser). (Illus.). 326p. 1975. Repr. of 1909 ed. 24.50x (ISBN 0-405-06274-5). Ayer Co Pubs.
Ash, I., jt. auth. see Ash, M.
Ash, James L., Jr. Protestantism & the American University: An Intellectual Biography of William Warren Sweet. (Illus.). 180p. 1982. 15.95 (ISBN 0-87074-183-7). SMU Press.
Ash, John. The Branching Stairs. 159p. 1985. pap. 7.50 (ISBN 0-85635-501-1). Carcanet.
--The Goodbyes. 64p. pap. 7.00 (ISBN 0-85635-423-6). Carcanet.
--Grammatical Institutes. LC 79-15248. (American Linguistics Ser.). 216p. 1979. Repr. of 1785 ed. 40.00x (ISBN 0-8201-1339-5). Schol Facsimiles.
Ash, Lawrence R., jt. auth. see Garcia, Lynne S.
Ash, Lawrence R., et al. Atlas of Human Parasitology. 2nd ed. LC 83-21514. (Illus.). 212p. 1984. text ed. 70.00 (ISBN 0-89189-179-X, 16-7-003-00). Am Soc Clinical.
Ash, Lee. Serial Publications Containing Medical Classics. 2nd ed. 1979. 30.00 (ISBN 0-9603990-0-3). Antiquarium.
--Subject Collections, 2 vols. 6th ed. 2144p. 1985. 165.00 (ISBN 0-8352-1917-8). Bowker.
Ash, Lee, et al. Who's Who in Library Service: A Biographical Directory of Professional Librarians in the United States & Canada. 4th ed. 776p. 1966. 37.50 (ISBN 0-208-00598-6). Shoe String.
Ash, M. & Ash, I. Encyclopedia of Industrial Chemical Additives, Vol. 2, G-O. 1984. 75.00 (ISBN 0-8206-0308-2). Chem Pub.
--Encyclopedia of Industrial Chemical Additives, Vol. 3, P-Z. 1984. 75.00 (ISBN 0-8206-0309-0). Chem Pub.
--Encyclopedia of Industrial Chemical Additives, Vol. 1, A-F. 1984. 75.00 (ISBN 0-8206-0299-X). Chem Pub.
--Encyclopedia of Plastics, Polymers & Resins Vol. 1, A-G. 1981. 75.00 (ISBN 0-8206-0290-6). Chem Pub.
--Encyclopedia of Plastics, Polymers & Resins Vol. 2, H-O. 1982. 75.00 (ISBN 0-8206-0296-5). Chem Pub.
--Encyclopedia of Plastics, Polymers & Resins Vol. 3, P-Z. 1983. 75.00 (ISBN 0-8206-0303-1). Chem Pub.
--Encyclopedia of Surfactants, Vol. IV. 1985. 75.00 (ISBN 0-8206-0317-1). Chem Pub.
--Encyclopedia of Surfactants, Vol. 1, A-F. 1980. 75.00 (ISBN 0-8206-0249-3). Chem Pub.
--Encyclopedia of Surfactants, Vol. 2, G-O. 1981. 75.00 (ISBN 0-8206-0287-6). Chem Pub.
--Encyclopedia of Surfactants, Vol. 3, P-Z. 1981. 75.00 (ISBN 0-8206-0289-2). Chem Pub.
--Formulary of Adhesives & Sealants. 1985. 35.00 (ISBN 0-8206-0297-3). Chem Pub.
--Formulary of Cosmetic Preparations. 1977. text ed. 35.00 (ISBN 0-8206-0218-3). Chem Pub.
--Formulary of Detergents & Other Cleaning Agents. 1980. 35.00 (ISBN 0-8206-0247-7). Chem Pub.
--Formulary of Paints & Other Coatings, Vol. 1. 1978. 35.00 (ISBN 0-8206-0248-5). Chem Pub.
--Formulary of Paints & Other Coatings Vol. 2. 1982. 35.00 (ISBN 0-8206-0292-2). Chem Pub.
--Thesaurus of Chemical Products: Generic-to-Tradename, Vol. 1. 1985. 145.00 (ISBN 0-8206-0315-5). Chem Pub.
--Thesaurus of Chemical Products: Tradename-to-Generic, Vol. 2. 1985. 145.00 (ISBN 0-8206-0316-3). Chem Pub.
Ash, M., Jr., jt. auth. see Kerr, Donald A.
Ash, McKinley, Jr., jt. auth. see Ramfjord, Sigurd.
Ash, Major M. Wheeler's Dental Anatomy, Physiology & Occlusion. 6th ed. (Illus.). 464p. 1984. 25.00 (ISBN 0-7216-1429-9). Saunders.
Ash, Major M., Jr. Wheeler's Atlas of Tooth Form. 5th ed. (Illus.). 158p. 1984. spiral bound 19.95 (ISBN 0-7216-1277-6). Saunders.
Ash, Major M., Jr. & Ramfjord, Sigurd P. An Introduction to Functional Occlusion. LC 81-5275. (Illus.). 240p. 1982. 15.95 (ISBN 0-7216-1428-0). Saunders.
Ash, Major M., Jr., jt. auth. see Ramfjord, Sigurd P.
Ash, Marshall J., ed. Studies in Harmonic Analysis. LC 76-16431. (MAA Studies Ser.: No. 13). 319p. 1976. 21.00 (ISBN 0-88385-113-X). Math Assn.
Ash, Martha C. Grandmother's Visit with Sam. Andrews, M. Doris, ed. LC 85-71540. (Illus.). 48p. (Orig.). (gr. 3-5). 1985. pap. 4.25 (ISBN 0-933865-00-7, 002). Doris Pubns.
Ash, Mary K. Mary Kay. (Illus.). 228p. 1984. pap. 4.76i (ISBN 0-06-464804-4, BN 4804). B&N NY.
--Mary Kay on People Management. 208p. 1984. text ed. 15.50 (ISBN 0-446-51314-8). Warner Bks.
--Mary Kay on People Management. 208p. 1985. pap. 3.95 (ISBN 0-446-32974-6). Warner Bks.
--Mary Kay: The Success Story of America's Most Dynamic Business Woman. LC 81-47219. (Illus.). 256p. 1981. 11.49i (ISBN 0-06-014878-0, HarpT). Har-Row.
Ash, Milton. Optimal Shutdown Control of Nuclear Reactors. (Mathematics in Science and Engineering Ser.: Vol. 26). 1966. 49.50 (ISBN 0-12-065150-5). Acad Pr.
Ash, Milton S. Nuclear Reactor Kinetics. 2nd ed. (Illus.). 1979. text ed. 75.00 (ISBN 0-07-002380-8). McGraw.
Ash, Norma C. Sheza Joy. 1985. 6.95 (ISBN 0-533-06563-1). Vantage.
Ash, Peter F. & Robinson, Edward E. Basic College Mathematics: A Calculator Approach. LC 80-15352. (Illus.). 544p. 1981. 23.95 (ISBN 0-201-00091-1); instrs' manual 3.00 (ISBN 0-201-00092-X). Addison-Wesley.
Ash, Philip. Meeting Civil Rights Requirements in Your Selection Programs. 1974. 4.00 (ISBN 0-87373-288-X, PR 742). Intl Personnel Mgmt.
Ash, Philip, ed. Volunteers for Mental Health. LC 73-10368. 1973. 28.00x (ISBN 0-8422-5121-9); pap. text ed. 7.95x (ISBN 0-8422-0322-2). Irvington.
Ash, Raymond H., jt. auth. see Deshpande, Pradeep B.
Ash, Raymond H., jt. ed. see Deshpande, Pradeep B.
Ash, Rene L. The Motion Picture Film Editor. LC 74-4072. 193p. 1974. 16.50 (ISBN 0-8108-0718-1). Scarecrow.
Ash, Robert & Ash, Carol. The Calculus Tutoring Book. 1985. write for info. (ISBN 0-87942-183-5, PC01776). Inst Electrical.
Ash, Robert B. Real Analysis & Probability. (Probability & Mathematical Statistics Ser.). 476p. 1972. 22.50i (ISBN 0-12-065201-3). solutions to problems 2.50i (ISBN 0-12-065240-4). Acad Pr.
Ash, Russell. The Pig Book. (Illus.). 96p. 1986. 5.95 (ISBN 0-87795-751-7). Arbor Hse.
Ash, Sarah. Moment in Time. 80p. 1972. 4.00 (ISBN 0-8233-0173-7). Golden Quill.
--Slack Water. LC 77-8210. 70p. 1977. 5.00 (ISBN 0-8233-0263-6). Golden Quill.
Ash, Steve & Thornhill, Jerry, eds. Handbook of Animal Models of Renal Failures. 304p. 1985. 99.50 (ISBN 0-8493-2975-2). CRC Pr.
Ash, Timothy G. The Polish Revolution: Solidarity. 384p. 1984. 17.95 (ISBN 0-684-18114-2, ScribT). Scribner.
--The Polish Revolution: Solidarity. 1985. 10.95 (ISBN 0-394-72907-2, Vin). Random.
Ash, William. The Way to Write Radio Drama. 160p. 1985. 16.95 (ISBN 0-241-11445-4, Pub. by Hamish Hamilton England); pap. 9.95 (ISBN 0-241-11446-2, Pub. by Hamish Hamilton England). David & Charles.
Asha, Ma Prem, ed. see Rajneesh, Bhagwan Shree.
Ashabranner, Brent. Dark Harvest: Migrant Farmworkers in America. (Illus.). 160p. (gr. 7 up). 1985. PLB 14.95 (ISBN 0-396-08624-1). Dodd.
--Gavriel & Jemal: Two Boys of Jerusalem. LC 84-8135. (Illus.). 96p. (gr. 4-7). 1984. PLB 11.95 (ISBN 0-396-08455-9). Dodd.
--Morning Star, Black Sun: The Northern Cheyenne Indians & America's Energy Crisis. (Illus.). 160p. (gr. 7 up). 1982. PLB 10.95 (ISBN 0-396-08045-6). Dodd.
--The New Americans: Changing Patterns in U. S. Immigration. LC 82-45999. (Illus.). 160p. (gr. 7 up). 1983. 13.95 (ISBN 0-396-08140-1). Dodd.
--To Live in Two Worlds: American Indian Youth Today. LC 83-25405. (Illus.). 149p. (gr. 8 up). 1984. PLB 12.95 (ISBN 0-396-08321-8). Dodd.
Ashall, C. & Ellis, P. E. Studies on Numbers & Mortality in Field Populations of the Desert Locust (Schistocerca Gregaria Forskal) 1962. 35.00x (ISBN 0-85135-004-6, Pub. by Centre Overseas Research). State Mutual Bk.
Ashall, C., jt. auth. see Clark, D. P.
Ashani, Y., jt. auth. see Green, B. S.
Ashanti, B. J. Nubiana, Vol. 1. 48p. 1977. pap. 2.00x (ISBN 0-917886-01-1). Shamal Bks.
Ashbaugh, Carolyn. Lucy Parsons, American Revolutionary. LC 75-23909. (Illus.). 288p. 1976. 19.95 (ISBN 0-88286-014-3); pap. 6.95 (ISBN 0-88286-005-4). C H Kerr.
--Lucy Parsons: American Revolutionary. 288p. 5.95 (ISBN 0-317-06695-1). Indus Workers World.
Ashbaugh, Don. Nevada's Turbulent Yesterday. LC 63-16925. (Illus.). 349p. 14.00 (ISBN 0-87026-024-3). Westernlore.
Ashbee, C. B. An Endeavor Towards the Teaching of John Ruskin & William Morris. LC 73-7761. Repr. of 1901 ed. lib. bdg. 10.00 (ISBN 0-8414-2854-9). Folcroft.
Ashbee, C. R., tr. see Cellini, Benvenuto.
Ashbee, Charles R., ed. Parish of Bromley-By-Bow. LC 73-138270. (London County Council. Survey of London: No. 1). Repr. of 1900 ed. 74.50 (ISBN 0-404-51651-3). AMS Pr.
Ashbee, F., tr. see Shingarev, A. I.
Ashbee, F., tr. see Zhdanov, Andrei.
Ashbee, Paul. The Ancient British. 314p. 1980. 19.55 (ISBN 0-86094-015-2, Pub. by GEO Abstracts England); pap. 14.95 (ISBN 0-86094-014-4, Pub. by GEO Abstracts England). State Mutual Bk.
Ashbery, J., et al. ZZZZZ, Vol. 5. Elmslie, Kenward, ed. (Illus.). 1977. pap. 5.00 (ISBN 0-915990-08-3). Z Pr.
Ashbery, John. As We Know. (Poet Ser.). 1979. pap. 7.95 (ISBN 0-14-042274-9). Penguin.
--As We Know. 1979. 12.50 (ISBN 0-670-13780-4). Viking.
--The Double Dream of Spring. LC 75-34557. (The American Poetry Ser: Vol 8). 95p. 1976. 7.95 (ISBN 0-912946-30-X); pap. 4.95 (ISBN 0-912946-27-X). Ecco Pr.
--Houseboat Days. 1977. pap. 3.95 (ISBN 0-14-042202-1). Penguin.
--Houseboat Days. 1977. 9.95 (ISBN 0-670-38035-0). Viking.
--Rivers & Mountains. LC 76-46176. (American Poetry Ser: Vol. 12). 1977. pap. 4.95 (ISBN 0-912946-38-5). Ecco Pr.
--Self-Portrait in a Convex Mirror. (Poets Ser.). 1976. pap. 5.95 (ISBN 0-14-042201-3). Penguin.
--Self-Portrait in a Convex Mirror. LC 75-1095. 83p. 1975. 9.95 (ISBN 0-670-63283-X). Viking.
--Self-Portrait in a Convex Mirror. (Illus.). 40p. 1984. 2500.00 (ISBN 0-910457-03-4). Arion Pr.
--Shadow Train. 64p. 1981. 8.95 (ISBN 0-670-63786-6). Viking.
--Shadow Train: Fifty Lyrics. (Poets Ser.). 1981. pap. 4.95 (ISBN 0-14-042288-9). Penguin.
--Some Trees. 1970. Repr. of 1956 ed. 6.50 (ISBN 0-87091-066-3). Corinth Bks.
--Some Trees. LC 56-5946. (American Poetry Ser: No. 14). 1978. pap. 4.95 (ISBN 0-912946-47-4). Ecco Pr.
--The Tennis Court Oath. 94p. 1962. pap. 7.95 (ISBN 0-8195-1013-0). Wesleyan U Pr.
--Three Plays. 1978. 15.00 (ISBN 0-915990-12-1); pap. 7.50 (ISBN 0-915990-13-X). Z Pr.
--A Wave. LC 83-40217. 112p. 1984. 14.95 (ISBN 0-670-75176-6). Viking.
--A Wave. (Poetry Ser.). 96p. 1985. pap. 7.95 (ISBN 0-14-042343-5). Penguin.
Ashbery, John & Myers, John B. Fairfield Porter. (Illus.). 108p. 1983. 34.00 (ISBN 0-87846-211-2, 273260). NYGS.
Ashbery, John & Schuyler, James. A Nest of Ninnies. LC 75-28625. 191p. (Orig.). 1976. pap. 5.00 (ISBN 0-915990-02-4). Z Pr.
Ashbery, John & Shannon, Joe. Kitaj: Paintings, Drawings, Pastels. LC 82-84467. (Illus.). 1983. pap. 15.95f (ISBN 0-500-27303-0). Thames Hudson.
Ashbery, John, ed. see Marcus, Bruce.
Ashbery, John, ed. see Snow, Richard.
Ashbery, John, et al. Apparitions. 60p. ltd. signed ed. 50.00 (ISBN 0-935716-10-6). Lord John.
--Fairfield Porter. (Illus.). 108p. 1983. pap. 25.00 (ISBN 0-87846-211-2). Mus Fine Arts Boston.
Ashbery, John, et al, trs. see Jacob, Max.
Ashbrook, A. W., jt. auth. see Ritcey, G. M.

Ashbrook, Debra L. & Solley, Linda C. Women & Heroin Abuse: A Survey of Sexism in Drug Abuse Administration. LC 78-68461. 1979. perfect bdg. 10.00 (ISBN 0-88247-556-8). R & E Pubs.

Ashbrook, Frank G. Butchering, Processing & Preservation of Meat. (Illus.). 336p. 1955. pap. 9.95 (ISBN 0-442-20377-2). Van Nos Reinhold.

--Silver-Fox Farming. facs. ed. (Shorey Lost Arts Ser.). 68p. pap. 5.95 (ISBN 0-8466-6047-4, U47). Shorey.

Ashbrook, James B. The Human Mind & the Mind of God: Theological Promise in Brain Research. (Illus.). 408p. (Orig.). 1985. lib. bdg. 27.75 (ISBN 0-8191-4225-5); pap. text ed. 17.50 (ISBN 0-8191-4226-3). U Pr of Amer.

Ashbrook, Joseph. The Astronomical Scrapbook: Skywatchers, Pioneers & Seekers in Astronomy. (Illus.). 384p. 1985. 19.95 (ISBN 0-521-30045-2). Cambridge U Pr.

Ashbrook, Marguerite L., jt. auth. see Sumption, Lois L.

Ashbrook, R. L., ed. Rapid Solidification Technology: Source Book. 1983. 54.00 (ISBN 0-87170-162-6). ASM.

Ashbrook, William. Donizetti & His Operas. LC 81-12235. (Illus.). 720p. 1982. 42.50 (ISBN 0-521-23526-X). Cambridge U Pr.

--Donizetti & His Operas. LC 81-12235. 752p. 1983. pap. 18.95 (ISBN 0-521-27663-2). Cambridge U Pr.

--The Operas of Puccini. LC 84-72674. 288p. (Orig.). 1985. 29.95x (ISBN 0-8014-9309-9); pap. 9.95 (ISBN 0-8014-9309-9). Cornell U Pr.

Ashburn, Frank D., ed. see Ashburn, Percy M.

Ashburn, Percy M. A History of the Medical Department of the United States Army. LC 75-23675. Repr. of 1929 ed. 38.50 (ISBN 0-404-13228-6). AMS Pr.

--The Ranks of Death: A Medical History of the Conquest of America. Ashburn, Frank D., ed. LC 80-24672. (Perspectives in Latin American History Ser.: No. 2). xix, 298p. 1981. Repr. of 1947 ed. lib. bdg. 25.00x (ISBN 0-87991-599-4). Porcupine Pr.

Ashburn, Richie. Richie Ashburn's Phillies Trivia. LC 83-3335. (Illus.). 164p. (Orig.). (gr. 5 up). 1983. lib. bdg. 12.90 (ISBN 0-89471-220-9); pap. 4.95 (ISBN 0-89471-219-5). Running Pr.

Ashburn, Robert R. Selected Spanish Stories of the Nineteenth & Twentieth Centuries. Repr. of 1943 ed. 25.00 (ISBN 0-89987-095-3). Darby Bks.

Ashburn, Shirley, jt. auth. see Schuster, Clara.

Ashburner, M. & Novitski, E., eds. The Genetics & Biology of Drosophila. Incl. Vol. 1, 3 pts. 1976. Pt. A. 82.50 (ISBN 0-12-064901-2); Pt. B. 75.00 (ISBN 0-12-064902-0); Pt. C. 89.50 (ISBN 0-12-064903-9); Vol. 2, 5 pts. 1978-79. Pt. A. 90.00 (ISBN 0-12-064940-3); Pt. B. 90.00 (ISBN 0-12-064941-1); Pt. C. 89.50 (ISBN 0-12-064942-X); Pt. D. 99.00 (ISBN 0-12-064943-8); Pt. E. write for info. (ISBN 0-12-064944-6). Acad Pr.

Ashburner, M., et al. The Genetics & Biology of Drosophilia, Vol. 3D. 1984. 95.00 (ISBN 0-12-064948-9). Acad Pr.

Ashburner, M., et al, eds. The Genetics & Biology of Drosophila, Vol. 3B. 1982. 88.50 (ISBN 0-12-064946-2). Acad Pr.

--The Genetics of Drosphila, Vol. 3, Pt. A. Carson, H. L. 1981. 86.50 (ISBN 0-12-064945-4). Acad Pr.

--The Genetics & Biology of Drosophila. Date not set. price not set (ISBN 0-12-064949-7). Acad Pr.

--The Genetics & Biology of Drosophilia, Vol. 3C. 1983. 86.00 (ISBN 0-12-064947-0). Acad Pr.

Ashby, Bernice M. Shenandoah County, Virginia: Marriage Bonds 1772-1850. LC 66-14986. 418p. 1967. write for info. (ISBN 0-685-65056-1). Va Bk.

Ashby, C. Plain Song: Collected Poems. 220p. 1985. text ed. 21.50x (ISBN 0-85635-562-3, Pub. by Carcanet New Pr England). Humanities.

Ashby, Cliff. Lies & Dreams. 95p. 1980. pap. text ed. 7.45x (ISBN 0-85635-297-7, Pub. by Carcanet New Pr England). Humanities.

Ashby, Clifford & May, Suzanne D. Trouping Through Texas: Harley Sadler & His Tent Show. LC 81-82503. 194p. 1982. 14.95 (ISBN 0-87972-184-7); pap. 8.95 (ISBN 0-87972-185-5). Bowling Green Univ.

Ashby, Elizabeth. Above the Clouds. 196p. 1979. 12.00 (ISBN 0-88428-046-2); pap. 8.50 (ISBN 0-88428-047-0). Parchment Pr.

Ashby, Eric. Adapting Universities to a Technological Society. LC 73-22555. (Jossey-Bass Series in Higher Education). pap. 44.00 (ISBN 0-317-08568-9, 2021083). Bks Demand UMI.

--Any Person, Any Study: An Essay on Higher Education in the United States. LC 73-144765. pap. 31.30 (ISBN 0-317-29025-8, 2020877). Bks Demand UMI.

--Reconciling Man with the Environment. LC 77-91909. 1978. 10.00x (ISBN 0-8047-0986-6); pap. 3.95 (ISBN 0-8047-1041-4, SP-155). Stanford U Pr.

--The Structure of Higher Education: A World View. (Occasional Paper of ICED). 1973. pap. 1.00 (ISBN 0-89192-153-2). Interbk Inc.

Ashby, Eric & Anderson, Mary. The Politics of Clean Air. (Monographs on Science, Technology, & Society). 1981. 36.50x (ISBN 0-19-858330-3). Oxford U Pr.

--Portrait of Haldane at Work on Education. xvi, 202p. 1974. 19.50 (ISBN 0-208-01463-2, Archon). Shoe String.

--Rise of the Student Estate in Britain. 1970. 12.50x (ISBN 0-674-77290-3). Harvard U Pr.

Ashby, Eric, et al. The Tanner Lectures on Human Values, Vol. I: 1980. 1980. 20.00x (ISBN 0-87480-178-8). U of Utah Pr.

Ashby, F. Gregory, jt. auth. see Townsend, James T.

Ashby, G. F. Pre-School Theories & Strategies. (The Second Century in Australian Education Ser.: Vol. 6). 80p. 1972. pap. 8.50x (ISBN 0-522-84027-2, Pub. by Melbourne U Pr). Intl Spec Bk.

Ashby, Gene, ed. see Micronesian Community College Students.

Ashby, Gwynneth. Take a Trip to Japan. LC 80-52719. (Take a Trip Ser.). (gr. 1-3). 1981. PLB 8.40 (ISBN 0-531-00990-4). Watts.

Ashby, Helena. Ramp Creek Rhythms: A Book of Poems. LC 85-90773. 54p. 1985. 8.00 (ISBN 0-9614781-0-1); pap. 4.00 (ISBN 0-9614781-1-X). H Ashby Bks.

Ashby, J., et al, eds. Evaluation of Short-Term Tests for Carcinogens: Report of the International Program on Chemical Safety Collaborative Study on In Vitro Assays. (Progress in Mutation Research Ser.: Vol. 5). 762p. 1985. 139.00 (ISBN 0-444-80615-6). Elsevier.

Ashby, LeRoy. Saving the Waifs: Reformers & Dependent Children, 1890-1917. (American Civilization Ser.). 336p. 1984. 37.95 (ISBN 0-87722-337-8). Temple U Pr.

--The Spearless Leader: Senator Borah & the Progressive Movement in the 1920s. LC 74-170963. 84.00 (ISBN 0-8357-9698-1, 2011733). Bks Demand UMI.

Ashby, Lloyd W. Effective School Board Member. LC 68-9492. (Illus.). 120p. 1968. pap. text ed. 3.50x (ISBN 0-8134-1053-3, 1053). Interstate.

Ashby, Lloyd W., ed. Man in the Middle: The Superintendent of Schools. LC 68-8369. 1968. pap. text ed. 3.50x (ISBN 0-8134-1054-1, 1054). Interstate.

--Student Activism in the Secondary Schools. LC 72-120819. 1970. pap. 2.50x (ISBN 0-8134-1176-9, 1176). Interstate.

Ashby, Lloyd W., et al, eds. Common Sense in Negotiations in Public Education. LC 78-170850. 145p. 1972. pap. text ed. 3.95x (ISBN 0-8134-1421-0, 1421). Interstate.

Ashby, Lynn. As I Was Saying. Lubeck, Scott, ed. 272p. 1984. 14.95 (ISBN 0-932012-29-9). Texas Month Pr.

--As Your Acknowledged Leader: The Best of Lynn Ashby. Rodriguez, Barbara, ed. 281p. 1983. 12.95 (ISBN 0-932012-64-7). Texas Month Pr.

Ashby, M. F. & Jones, D. R. Engineering Materials: An Introduction to Their Properties & Applications. (International Ser. on Materials Science & Technology: Vol. 34). (Illus.). 120p. 1980. 43.00 (ISBN 0-08-026139-6); pap. 14.75 (ISBN 0-08-026138-8). Pergamon.

Ashby, M. F. & Brown, L. M., eds. Perspectives in Creep Fracture. 180p. 1983. 35.00 (ISBN 0-08-030541-5). Pergamon.

Ashby, M. F., jt. auth. see Frost, H. J.

Ashby, M. F., et al, eds. Dislocation Modeling of Physical Systems: Proceedings of the International Conference, Gainesville, Florida USA, June 22-27, 1980. LC 80-41473. (Illus.). 640p. 1981. 83.00 (ISBN 0-08-026724-6). Pergamon.

Ashby, M. K. Joseph Ashby of Tysoe Eighteen Fifty-Nine to Nineteen Nineteen: A Study of English Village Life. 303p. 1979. pap. 10.95 (ISBN 0-85036-180-X). Dufour.

Ashby, Mabel K. Joseph Ashby of Tysoe: Eighteen Fifty-Nine to Nineteen Nineteen. 302p. Repr. of 1961 ed. lib. bdg. 27.50x (ISBN 0-678-08055-0). Kelley.

Ashby, N. B. The Riddle of the Sphinx. LC 75-300. (The Radical Tradition in America Ser.). 474p. 1975. Repr. of 1890 ed. 31.25 (ISBN 0-88355-205-1). Hyperion Conn.

Ashby, Nora. Gone from Breezy Hill. 336p. 1985. pap. 3.50 (ISBN 0-425-07672-5). Berkley Pub.

Ashby, Philip H. Modern Trends in Hinduism. (Lectures in the History of Religions Ser.: No. 10). 143p. 1974. 21.00x (ISBN 0-231-03768-6). Columbia U Pr.

Ashby, Susan. The Fiji Tea Trader. LC 83-50266. 110p. (Orig.). 1983. pap. 5.95 (ISBN 0-938232-33-9, Dist. by Baker & Taylor). Winston-Derek.

--Granny's Muffin House. 1983. pap. 8.95 (ISBN 0-930440-18-8). Royal Hse.

--Pancakes from Vinegar Hill Farm. LC 82-62909. (Illus.). 100p. 1984. 5.95 (ISBN 0-938232-26-6). Winston-Derek.

--The Shadow Hill Book of Mix Easy Cakes. (Illus.). 64p. (Orig.). 1984. pap. 3.95 (ISBN 0-912661-05-4). Woodsong Graph.

--The Shadow Hill Book of Squares, Bars & Brownies. LC 84-52106. (Illus.). 144p. 1984. pap. 7.95 (ISBN 0-912661-03-8). Woodsong Graph.

Ashby, Sylvia. Professor Zuccini's Traveling Tales. 44p. 1983. pap. 2.50x (ISBN 0-88680-208-3). I E Clark.

Ashby, Thomas. The Roman Campagna in Classical Times. LC 78-12509. (Illus.). 1979. Repr. of 1970 ed. lib. bdg. 24.75x (ISBN 0-313-21115-9, ASRC). Greenwood.

Ashby, Thomas A. Life of Turner Ashby. 1985. Repr. of 1914 ed. 17.50 (ISBN 0-686-73904-3). Pr of Morningside.

Ashby, W. R. Design for a Brain: The Origin of Adaptive Behavior. 2nd ed. 286p. 1966. pap. 12.95x (ISBN 0-412-20090-2, NO.6012, Pub. by Chapman & Hall England). Methuen Inc.

Ashby, W. Ross. Introduction to Cybernetics. 1964. pap. 12.95 (ISBN 0-416-68300-2, NO. 2064). Methuen Inc.

--Mechanisms of Intelligence: Ashby's Writings on Cybernetics. Conant, Roger, ed. (Systems Inquiry Ser.). 394p. (Orig.). 1981. pap. text ed. 16.95x (ISBN 0-914105-04-3). Intersystems Pubns.

Ashby, Warren. Frank Porter Graham: A Southern Liberal. LC 80-23370. (Illus.). 1980. 24.95 (ISBN 0-89587-009-6). Blair.

Ashby, William, et al. Romanitas: Studies in Romance Linguistics, Vol. 4. Pulgram, Ernst, ed. (Michigan Romance Studies). 272p. (Orig.). 1984. pap. 8.00 (ISBN 0-939730-03-0). Mich Romance.

Ashby, William M. Redder Blood. LC 73-18570. Repr. of 1915 ed. 17.00 (ISBN 0-404-11380-X). AMS Pr.

Ashby-Davis, Claire, jt. auth. see Cicchelli, Terry.

Ashby-Davis, Claire & Francks, Olive R., eds. Tapestry: The Interrelationships of the Arts in Reading & Language Development. 1979. pap. text ed. 9.50 (ISBN 0-686-62268-5). Collegium Bk Pubs.

Ashcraft, Keith W., jt. auth. see Holder, Thomas M.

Ashcraft, Morris. Christian Faith & Beliefs. LC 83-71872. 1984. 8.95 (ISBN 0-8054-1603-X). Broadman.

--Rudolf Bultmann. Patterson, Bob E., ed. LC 74-188059. (Makers of the Modern Theological Mind Ser.). 128p. 1972. 5.95 (ISBN 0-87680-252-8, 80252). Word Bks.

--The Will of God. LC 80-65714. 1980. pap. 4.75 (ISBN 0-8054-1620-X). Broadman.

Ashcroft, Edward A., jt. auth. see Wadge, William W.

Ashcroft, G. L., jt. auth. see Hanks, R. J.

Ashcroft, J., et al. Programming with FORTRAN 77. 304p. 1981. pap. 18.50x (ISBN 0-246-11573-4, Pub. by Granada England). Sheridan.

Ashcroft, J. Barrie, jt. auth. see Owens, R. Glynn.

Ashcroft, J. Robert. The Sequence of the Supernatural. 80p. 1972. pap. 1.00 (ISBN 0-88243-748-8, 02-0748). Gospel Pub.

Ashcroft, Neil W. & Mermin, N. David. Solid State Physics. LC 74-9772. 1976. text ed. 46.95 (ISBN 0-03-083993-9, CBS C). SCP.

Ashcroft, Tony, jt. auth. see Watson, Elizabeth A.

Ashcroft-Nowicki, Dolores. First Steps in Ritual: Safe, Effective Techniques for Experiencing the Inner Worlds. 96p. 1983. pap. 6.95 (ISBN 0-85030-314-1). Newcastle Pub.

--The Shining Paths: An Experimental Journey Through the Tree of Life. 240p. 1984. pap. 9.95 (ISBN 0-85030-347-8). Newcastle Pub.

Ashdown. Color Atlas of the Ruminants. (Illus.). 240p. 1983. text ed. 75.00 (ISBN 0-8391-1760-4). Univ Park.

Ashdown, Charles H. Armour & Weapons in the Middle Ages. (Illus.). 22.00 (ISBN 0-87556-603-0). Saifer.

Ashdown, Inez. Stories of Old Lahaina. soft bdg. 1.50 (ISBN 0-930492-12-9). Hawaiian Serv.

Ashdown, Inez M. Kahoolawe: Recollections of Kahoolawe. 1979. pap. 5.95 (ISBN 0-914916-48-3). Topgallant.

Ashdown, John, jt. auth. see Kersting, Anthony F.

Ashdown, Paul, ed. see Agee, James.

Ashdown, Peter. Caribbean History in Maps. (Illus.). 84p. 1979. pap. text ed. 6.95x (ISBN 0-582-76541-2). Longman.

Ashe & Dunleavy, eds. Processing & Testing of Reaction Injection Molding Urethanes - STP 788. 95p. 1982. pap. 13.95 (ISBN 0-8031-0779-X, 04-788000-20). ASTM.

Ashe, Amy E., jt. auth. see Bossone, Richard M.

Ashe, Arthur. Arthur Ashe's Tennis Clinic. LC 80-84951. (Illus.). 144p. 1981. 12.95 (ISBN 0-914178-44-X, A Tennis Mag. Bk). Golf Digest.

Ashe, Arthur, et al. Mastering Your Tennis Strokes. Sheehan, Larry, ed. LC 75-41854. 1976. 12.95 (ISBN 0-689-10718-8); pap. 12.95 (ISBN 0-689-70562-X). Atheneum.

Ashe, Dora J., compiled by. Four Hundred Years of Virginia, Fifteen Eighty-Four to Nineteen Eighty-Four: An Anthology. 234p. (Orig.). 1985. lib. bdg. 22.50 (ISBN 0-8191-4481-9); pap. text ed. 9.75 (ISBN 0-8191-4482-7). U Pr of Amer.

Ashe, Dora J., ed. see Beaumont, Francis & Fletcher, John.

Ashe, Geoffrey. A Guidebook to Arthurian Britain. (Longman Travellers Ser.). (Illus.). 1983. text ed. 13.95x (ISBN 0-582-50282-9). Longman.

--Kings & Queens of Early Britain. 224p. 1984. 16.95 (ISBN 0-413-47920-X, NO. 9166). Methuen Inc.

--The Quest for Arthur's Britain. (Illus.). 238p. 1980. pap. 8.95 (ISBN 0-586-08044-9, Granada Publishing Limited). Academy Chi Pubs.

Ashe, Geoffrey & Debretts, Peerage. The Discovery of King Arthur. LC 83-45168. (Illus.). 240p. 1985. 18.95 (ISBN 0-385-19032-8, Anchor Pr). Doubleday.

Ashe, Jeffrey. Assessing Rural Needs: A Manual for Practitioners. 127p. 1978. 5.95, softcover (ISBN 0-86619-075-9, 11058-BK). Vols Tech Asst.

Ashe, John. Highlights of History. 1981. 10.00x (ISBN 0-7223-1358-6, Pub. by Stockwell Bk). State Mutual Bk.

Ashe, Kaye. Today's Woman, Tomorrow's Church. 1983. 12.95 (ISBN 0-88347-145-0). Thomas More.

--Today's Woman, Tomorrow's Church. 200p. 1984. pap. 7.95 (ISBN 0-88347-168-X). Thomas More.

Ashe, Laura. All You Wanted to Know about Vending. (Illus.). 1985. pap. 5.95 (ISBN 0-933381-03-4). Green Apple.

--Cartooning for Fun & Profit. (Illus.). 1985. lib. bdg. 24.95 (ISBN 0-933381-02-6). Green Apple.

--Inlanders Guide to Seafood Cooking. (Illus.). 1985. pap. 3.00 (ISBN 0-933381-01-8). Green Apple.

Ashe, Marjorie D. The Princess & the Enchanted Wood & Other Fairy Tales. (Illus.). 80p. 1982. 5.50 (ISBN 0-682-49842-4). Exposition Pr FL.

Ashe, Megan. A Mountain Man. (Rapture Romance Ser.: No. 46). 192p. 1984. pap. 1.95 (ISBN 0-451-12631-9, Sig). NAL.

Ashe, Robert P. Chronicles of Uganda. 480p. 1971. Repr. of 1894 ed. 32.50x (ISBN 0-7146-1861-6, BHA 01861, F Cass Co). Biblio Dist.

--Two Kings of Uganda: Or, Life by the Shores of Victoria Nyanza. (Illus.). 354p. 1970. Repr. of 1889 ed. 30.00x (ISBN 0-7146-1862-4, BHA 01862, F Cass Co). Biblio Dist.

Ashe, Rosalind. Literary Houses. 144p. 1982. 17.95x (ISBN 0-87196-676-X). Facts on File.

--More Literary Houses. (Illus.). 144p. 17.95 (ISBN 0-87196-422-8). Facts on File.

Ashe, Rosalind & Avigdor, Albert. Brazilian-Portuguese Frasograf. 7.50 (ISBN 0-8044-0026-1). Ungar.

Ashe, Rosalind & Tuttle, Lisa. Children's Literary Houses. LC 84-10143. (Illus.). (gr. 7 up). 17.95 (ISBN 0-87196-971-8). Facts on File.

Ashe, Samuel A. History of North Carolina, 2 vols. LC 72-149340. (Illus.). 1971. Repr. of 1908 ed. Vol. 1. 35.00 (ISBN 0-87152-059-1); Vol. 2. 40.00 (ISBN 0-87152-060-5); Set. 75.00 (ISBN 0-87152-323-X). Reprint.

Ashe, Susan, tr. see Deledda, Grazia.

Ashe, T., ed. see Coleridge, Samuel Taylor.

Asheervath, Jeyanthi & Blevins, Dorothy. Handbook of Clinical Nursing Practice. (Illus.). 512p. 1986. text ed. 21.95 (ISBN 0-13-376765-5). P-H.

Asheim, Lester, ed. Forum on the Public Library Inquiry. LC 76-106680. Repr. of 1950 ed. lib. bdg. 18.75 (ISBN 0-8371-3351-3, ASPL). Greenwood.

--Persistent Issues in American Librarianship: Proceedings of the 25th Annual Conference of the Graduate Library School. (University of Chicago Studies in Library Science). 1961. PLB 7.00x (ISBN 0-226-02960-3). U of Chicago Pr.

Asheim, Lester & Fenwick, Sara I., eds. Differentiating the Media. (Studies in Library Science). vi, 74p. 1975. 10.00x (ISBN 0-226-02964-6). U of Chicago Pr.

Asheim, Lester, ed. see Conference on Library Manpower.

Asheim, Lester, et al. Reading & Successful Living: The Family-School Partnership. xx, 161p. 1983. pap. 11.50x (ISBN 0-208-02004-7, Lib Prof Pubns). Shoe String.

Asheim, Lester E. The Humanities & the Library: Problems in the Interpretation, Evaluation, & Use of Library Materials. LC 56-12395. pap. 74.50 (ISBN 0-317-29360-5, 2024204). Bks Demand UMI.

Ashelford, Jane. The Visual History of Costume: The Sixteenth Century. LC 83-14120. (The Visual History of Costume Ser.). (Illus.). 144p. 1983. text ed. 17.95x (ISBN 0-89676-076-6). Drama Bk.

Ashem, Beatrice A. & Poser, Ernest G., eds. Adaptive Learning: Behavior Modification with Children. LC 72-156903. 460p. 1975. pap. 16.50 (ISBN 0-08-017683-6). Pergamon.

Ashendorf, Jeffrey, jt. auth. see Older, Jack S.

Ashenfelter, Orley & Rees, Albert, eds. Discrimination in Labor Markets. LC 72-4037. 136p. 1974. 22.00 (ISBN 0-691-04170-9). Princeton U Pr.

Ashenfelter, Orley, jt. ed. see Bowen, William G.

Ashenhurst, Harry J. Divorce & Beyond. 1984. pap. 7.75 (ISBN 0-8309-0385-2). Herald Hse.

Ashenhurst, Robert L., jt. auth. see AFIPS Taxonomy Committee.

Ashenhust, Paul H. Police & the People. 216p. 1956. 16.50x (ISBN 0-398-04194-6). C C Thomas.

Asher, Asher. PB: Moral Choices. (A Religious Perspective by Rabbi Joseph Asher Ser.). 50p. (Orig.). 1984. pap. write for info. (ISBN 0-936434-14-7). Zellerbach F F.

Asher, Cash. Bacteria, INC. 1981. 5.95x (ISBN 0-911238-14-X). B Of A.

Asher, Don. Honeycomb. LC 78-75155. (Illus.). 1979. 3.95 (ISBN 0-89395-021-1). Cal Living Bks.

Asher, Don, jt. auth. see Gold, Herbert.

Asher, Don, jt. auth. see Hawes, Hampton.

Asher, Evelyn W. Urteil ohne Richter: Psychishe Integration oder Charakterentfaltung im Werke Franz Kafkas. LC 83-45168. (Stanford German Studies: Vol. 20). 139p. (Ger.). 1984. pap. text ed. 14.75 (ISBN 0-8204-0062-9). P Lang Pubs.

Asher, Frederick, ed. Indian Epigraphy-Its Bearing on the History of Art. 288p. 1984. text ed. 40.50x (ISBN 0-391-03051-5). Humanities.

Asher, Frederick & Gai, G. S., eds. Indian Epigraphy: Its Bearing on the History of Art. 1985. 48.50x (ISBN 0-8364-1356-3, Pub. by Oxford IBH). South Asia Bks.

Asher, Frederick M. The Art of Eastern India, Three Hundred-Eight Hundred. LC 80-10352. (Illus.). 1980. 35.00x (ISBN 0-8166-0975-6). U of Minn Pr.

Asher, George M., ed. Henry Hudson the Navigator. (Hakluyt Soc: First Ser.: No. 27). (Illus.). 1964. Repr. of 1613 ed. 32.00 (ISBN 0-8337-0098-7). B Franklin.

Asher, Gerald. On Wine. 1982. 15.95 (ISBN 0-394-52737-2). Random.

Asher, Gloria J. Izmirli Proverbs & Songs from the Bronx. 10p. 1976. softcover 1.25 (ISBN 0-686-74365-2). ADELANTRE.

Asher, Harry. Photographic Principles & Practices. 224p. 1975. 11.95 (ISBN 0-13-665539-4, Spec); pap. text ed. write for info. (ISBN 0-13-665497-5, Spec). P-H.

Asher, Herbert. Presidential Elections & American Politics: Voters, Candidates & Campaigns since 1952. 3rd ed. 1984. pap. 18.00x (ISBN 0-256-03034-0). Dorsey.

Asher, Herbert A., et al. Political Participation. 243p. (Orig.). 1984. pap. text ed. 15.00 (ISBN 0-317-28641-2, Pub. by Campus Verlag W. Germany). Transnatl Pubs.

Asher, Herbert B. Causal Modeling. LC 76-25696. (University Papers). 1976. 5.00 (ISBN 0-8039-0654-4). Sage.

Asher, Herbert B., et al, eds. Theory Building & Data Analysis in the Social Sciences. LC 83-3458. 464p. 1984. text ed. 34.95x (ISBN 0-87049-398-1); pap. text ed. 14.95x (ISBN 0-87049-399-X). U of Tenn Pr.

Asher, Inez. Family Sins. 256p. (Orig.). 1983. pap. 2.75 (ISBN 0-523-41186-3). Pinnacle Bks.

Asher, J. A. Amis et Amiles: An Exploratory Survey. 1978. Repr. of 1952 ed. lib. bdg. 10.00 (ISBN 0-8482-0120-5). Norwood Edns.

Asher, J. William. Educational Research & Evaluation Methods. 1976. 21.95 (ISBN 0-316-05390-2); tchr's manual avail. (ISBN 0-316-05391-0). Little.

Asher, Jane. Jane Asher's Fancy Dress. (Illus.). 142p. 1984. 15.95 (ISBN 0-88162-069-6, Pub. by Salem Hse Ltd). Merrimack Pub Cir.

--Jane Asher's Party Cakes. (Illus.). 112p. 1984. 14.95 (ISBN 0-7207-1412-5). Merrimack Pub Cir.

--Silent Night for You & Your Baby. (Illus.). 112p. 1985. 9.95 (ISBN 0-7207-1548-2, Pub. by Michael Joseph). Merrimack Pub Cir.

Asher, Jeremiah. Incidents in the Life of the Rev. J. Asher. facsimile ed. LC 74-168506. (Black Heritage Library Collection). Repr. of 1850 ed. 12.00 (ISBN 0-8369-8860-4). Ayer Co Pubs.

Asher, John A. Amis et Amiles: An Exploratory Survey. 26p. 1980. Repr. of 1952 ed. lib. bdg. 10.00 (ISBN 0-8492-3433-6). R West.

--Amis et Amis: An Exploratory Survey. LC 77-21930. Repr. of 1952 ed. lib. bdg. 8.50 (ISBN 0-8414-1704-0). Folcroft.

--Short Descriptive Grammar of Middle High German. 1967. pap. 9.95x (ISBN 0-19-647410-8). Oxford U Pr.

Asher, Kenneth. Compugraphic Confidential. (Compugraphic Confidential Ser.). (Illus.). 104p. 1984. pap. 50.00 (ISBN 0-89288-099-6). Maverick.

--Flea Market Almanac. (Illus.). 120p. (Orig.). 1985. pap. 5.95 (ISBN 0-89288-079-1). Maverick.

--Living Relics: Oregon's Old Hotels. (Illus.). 120p. (Orig.). 1982. pap. 5.95 cancelled (ISBN 0-89288-077-5). Maverick.

Asher, M. J. & Shipton, P. J., eds. Biology & Control of Take-All. LC 80-42280. 1982. 89.50 (ISBN 0-12-065320-6). Acad Pr.

Asher, Marty. Fifty-Seven Reasons Not to Have a Nuclear War. (Illus.). 120p. (Orig.). 1984. pap. 4.95 (ISBN 0-446-38167-5). Warner Bks.

--Shelter. 1986. price not set (ISBN 0-87795-772-X). Arbor Hse.

Asher, Michael. In Search of the Forty Days Road. 1984. text ed. 19.95 (ISBN 0-582-78364-X). Longman.

Asher, Mukul & Osborne, Susna, eds. Issues in Public Finance in Singapore. 1981. 22.95x (ISBN 9971-69-007-1, 82-93656, Pub. by Singapore U Pr); pap. 14.00x (ISBN 9971-69-023-3, 82-93755, Pub. by Singapore U Pr). Ohio U Pr.

Asher, Mukul G. Revenue Systems of ASEAN Countries: An Overview. 76p. 1980. pap. 5.00x (ISBN 0-8214-0546-2, 82-93565, Pub. by Singapore U Pr). Ohio U Pr.

Asher, Mukul G. see Wadhva, Charan D.

Asher, R. E. Tamil. (Descriptive Grammars Ser.). 280p. 1982. 40.00 (ISBN 0-7099-0563-7, Pub. by Croom Helm Ltd). Longwood Pub Group.

Asher, R. E. & Radharkrishnan, R. Tamil Prose Reader. LC 73-93705. 1971. text ed. 42.50 (ISBN 0-521-07214-X). Cambridge U Pr.

Asher, R. E. & Henderson, Eugenie, eds. Towards a History of Phonetics. 330p. 50.00x (ISBN 0-85224-374-X, Pub. by Edinburgh Univ England). State Mutual Bk.

Asher, R. E., tr. see Pillai, Thakazhi S.

Asher, Robert E., jt. auth. see Mason, Edward S.

Asher, Ross. Discovery Two Thousand One. LC 78-51727. Date not set. 9.95 (ISBN 0-931662-00-1). Photo-Go Pr.

Asher, Sandy. Daughters of the Law. LC 80-20400. 160p. (gr. 7 up). 1980. 7.95 (ISBN 0-8253-0006-1). Beaufort Bks NY.

--Daughters of the Law. 160p. (YA) (gr. 7 up). 1983. pap. 1.95 (ISBN 0-440-92098-1, LFL). Dell.

--Just Like Jenny. LC 82-70315. 160p. (gr. 5-9). 1984. pap. 2.50 (ISBN 0-440-94289-6). Dell.

--Just Like Jenny. LC 82-70315. (gr. 4-6). 1982. 12.95 (ISBN 0-385-28496-9). Delacorte.

--Just Like Jenny. 160p. (gr. 5-9). pap. 2.50 (ISBN 0-440-94289-6, LFL). Dell.

--Just Like Jenny. 160p. (gr. 5-9). pap. 2.50 (ISBN 0-440-94289-6). Dell.

--Missing Pieces. LC 83-14381. 144p. (gr. 7 up). 1984. 12.95 (ISBN 0-385-29318-6). Delacorte.

--Teddy Teabury's Fabulous Facts. (Illus., Orig.). (gr. k-6). 1985. pap. 2.50 (ISBN 0-440-48576-2, YB). Dell.

--Things Are Seldom What They Seem. LC 82-72819. 144p. (gr. 7up). 1983. 13.95 (ISBN 0-385-29250-3). Delacorte.

--Things Are Seldom What They Seem. 144p. (gr. k-12). 1985. pap. 2.25 (ISBN 0-440-98713-X, LFL). Dell.

Asher, Shirley J., jt. ed. see Bloom, Bernard L.

Asher, Spring, jt. ed. see Chambers, Wicke.

Asher, Steven & Gottman, John, eds. The Development of Children's Friendships. LC 80-25920. (Cambridge Studies in Social & Emotional Development). (Illus.). 336p. 1981. 42.50 (ISBN 0-521-23103-5); pap. 16.95 (ISBN 0-521-29806-7). Cambridge U Pr.

Asher, W. L., ed. Treating the Obese. LC 74-3289. 265p. 1974. pap. 25.50 (Pub. by W & W). Krieger.

Asher, W. Michael, jt. auth. see Leopold, George R.

Asher, William L., Jr. Seven Steps to Effective Prayer. 36p. (Orig.). 1978. pap. 2.00 (ISBN 0-915235-01-3). United Res.

--Siete Pasos a las Oracion Efectiva. 44p. (Orig., Span.). 1982. pap. 2.00 (ISBN 0-915235-07-2). United Res.

Asher-Greve, Julia M. Frauen in Altsumerischer Zeit. (Bibliotheca Mesopotomica Ser.: Vol. 18). 252p. 1985. 55.00 (ISBN 0-89003-161-4); pap. 45.00 (ISBN 0-89003-162-2). Undena Pubns.

Asheri, Michael. Living Jewish. enl. deluxe ed. 1980. 12.00 (ISBN 0-89696-003-X, An Everest House Book). Dodd.

--Living Jewish: The Lore & the Law of the Practicing Jew. 446p. 1983. pap. 9.95 (ISBN 0-396-08263-7). Dodd.

Asheron, Sara. Will You Come to My Party. (Easy Readers Ser.). (Illus.). (gr. k-3). 1.50 (ISBN 0-8431-4305-3). Wonder.

Ashery, R. E., jt. ed. see Sereni, Ezo H.

Ashery, Rebecca Sager & Basen, Michele Margolin. Parents with Careers Workbook. LC 83-7110. 160p. 1983. pap. 6.95 (ISBN 0-87491-601-1). Acropolis.

Ashfield, Helen. Garnet. 192p. 1985. 12.95 (ISBN 0-312-31727-1). St Martin.

--The Loving Highwayman. 192p. 1983. 10.95 (ISBN 0-312-49973-6). St Martin.

--The Loving Highwayman. 208p. 1985. pap. 2.50 (ISBN 0-449-20873-7, Crest). Fawcett.

--The Marquis & Miss Jones. LC 82-5550. 192p. 1982. 9.95 (ISBN 0-312-51547-2). St Martin.

--The Michaelmas Tree. 176p. 1982. 9.95 (ISBN 0-312-53225-3). St Martin.

--Midsummer Morning. 192p. 1984. 10.95 (ISBN 0-312-53186-9). St Martin.

--Pearl. 1985. 12.95 (ISBN 0-312-59968-4). St Martin.

--Regency Rogue. LC 81-23177. 168p. 1982. 9.95 (ISBN 0-312-66900-3). St Martin.

--Ruby. LC 84-13027. 128p. 1984. 10.95 (ISBN 0-312-69537-3). St Martin.

Ashford, Ann. If I Found a Wistful Unicorn. LC 78-59094. (Illus.). 1978. 10.95 (ISBN 0-931948-00-2). Peachtree Pubs.

Ashford, Bob, jt. auth. see Gibbons, Robert.

Ashford, David, jt. auth. see Clark, Alan.

Ashford, Douglas. Financing Urban Government in the Welfare State. LC 80-12166. 1980. 30.00 (ISBN 0-312-28985-5). St Martin.

Ashford, Douglas, ed. Comparative Policy Studies. 1977. pap. 8.00 (ISBN 0-918592-24-0). Policy Studies.

Ashford, Douglas E. British Dogmatism & French Pragmatism: Central-Local Policy Making in the Welfare State. (New Local Government Ser.: No. 22). (Illus.). 432p. 1982. text ed. 40.00x (ISBN 0-04-352096-0). Allen Unwin.

--Morocco-Tunisia: Politics & Planning. LC 65-25988. pap. 21.30 (ISBN 0-317-29003-7, 2020395). Bks Demand UMI.

--National Development & Local Reform: Political Participtíon in Morocco, Tunisia, & Pakistan. 1967. 43.00 (ISBN 0-691-07510-7). Princeton U Pr.

--Policy & Politics in Britain: The Limits of Consensus. (Policy & Politics in Industrial States Ser.). 330p. 1980. 34.95 (ISBN 0-87722-194-4); pap. text ed. 12.95 (ISBN 0-87722-195-2). Temple U Pr.

--Policy & Politics in France: Living with Uncertainty. LC 82-5771. (Policy & Politics in Industrial States Ser.). 365p. 1982. 34.95 (ISBN 0-87722-261-4); pap. text ed. 12.95x (ISBN 0-87722-262-2). Temple U Pr.

Ashford, Douglas E., et al, eds. Comparative Public Policy: A Cross-National Bibliography. LC 77-25371. pap. 69.00 (ISBN 0-317-29671-X, 2021922). Bks Demand UMI.

Ashford, Gerald. Everyday Publicity. LC 73-132372. 90p. 1970. 6.95x (ISBN 0-88238-051-6). Law-Arts.

--Spanish Texas: Yesterday & Today. LC 72-157044. (Illus.). 1971. 12.50 (ISBN 0-8363-0090-4). Jenkins.

Ashford, Jane. Cachet. 288p. (Orig.). 1984. pap. 2.95 (ISBN 0-449-12681-1, GM). Fawcett.

--First Season. (Regency Romance Ser.). 224p. 1984. pap. 2.25 (ISBN 0-451-12678-5, Sig). NAL.

--The Headstrong Ward. (Regency Romance Ser.). 1983. pap. 2.25 (ISBN 0-451-12267-4, Sig). NAL.

--Impetuous Heiress. 1984. pap. 2.25 (ISBN 0-451-12968-7, Sig). NAL.

--The Irresolute Rivals. 1985. pap. 2.50 (ISBN 0-451-13519-9, Sig). NAL.

--The Marchington Scandal. 1982. pap. 2.25 (ISBN 0-451-11623-2, AE1623, Sig). NAL.

--A Radical Arrangement. 1983. pap. 2.25 (ISBN 0-451-12515-0, Sig). NAL.

--The Repentant Rebel. 1984. pap. 2.50 (ISBN 0-451-13195-9, Sig). NAL.

--The Three Graces. 1982. pap. 2.25 (ISBN 0-451-11418-3, AE1418, Sig). NAL.

Ashford, Janet I., ed. Birth Stories: The Experience Remembered. LC 84-17017. (Birth Ser.). (Illus.). 208p. (Orig.). 1984. 18.95 (ISBN 0-89594-150-3); pap. 7.95 (ISBN 0-89594-149-X). Crossing Pr.

--The Whole Birth Catalog: A Sourcebook for Choices in Childbirth. LC 83-838. (Illus.). 300p. (Orig.). 1983. 32.95 (ISBN 0-89594-108-2); pap. 15.95 (ISBN 0-89594-107-4). Crossing Pr.

Ashford, Jeffery. Loss of the Cullion. (Walker British Paperback Mysteries Ser.). 192p. 1985. pap. 2.95 (ISBN 0-8027-3136-8). Walker & Co.

Ashford, Jeffrey. Consider the Evidence. (Orig.). 1985. pap. 2.95 (ISBN 0-8027-3114-7). Walker & Co.

--Guilt with Honor. 1982. 11.95 (ISBN 0-8027-5476-7). Walker & Co.

--The Hands of Innocence. (British Mysteries Ser.). 1984. pap. 2.95 (ISBN 0-8027-3049-3). Walker & Co.

--Hostage To Death. 1985. pap. 2.95 (ISBN 0-8027-3102-3). Walker & Co.

--The Loss of the Cullion. 1981. 9.95 (ISBN 0-8027-5445-7). Walker & Co.

--Presumption of Guilt. 192p. 1985. 13.95 (ISBN 0-8027-5619-0). Walker & Co.

--Recipe for Murder. 152p. 1980. 8.95 (ISBN 0-8027-5423-6). Walker & Co.

--A Recipe for Murder. LC 80-51721. (British Mystery Ser.). 175p. 1984. Repr. of 1980 ed. pap. 2.95 (ISBN 0-8027-3059-0). Walker & Co.

--A Sense of Loyalty. LC 83-40400. 192p. 1984. 12.95 (ISBN 0-8027-5586-0). Walker & Co.

--Slow Down the World. 186p. 1983. pap. 2.95 (ISBN 0-8027-3015-9). Walker & Co.

--Three Layers of Guilt. 185p. 1983. pap. 2.95 (ISBN 0-8027-3016-7). Walker & Co.

Ashford, John. Statistics for Management. 2nd ed. (Illus.). 458p. (Orig.). 1980. pap. text ed. 25.00x (ISBN 0-85292-271-X). Intl Pubns Serv.

Ashford, Nicholas A. Crisis in the Workplace: Occupational Disease & Injury - (A Report to the Ford Foundation) LC 75-28424. 1976. 35.00x (ISBN 0-262-01045-3). MIT Pr.

Ashford, Norman & Stanton, H. P. Airport Operations. LC 83-10371. 475p. 1984. 49.95x (ISBN 0-471-89613-6, Pub. by Wiley-Interscience). Wiley.

Ashford, Norman & Wright, Paul H. Airport Engineering. 2nd ed. LC 83-23494. 433p. 1984. 38.95 (ISBN 0-471-86568-0, Pub. by Wiley-Interscience). Wiley.

Ashford, Norman, et al, eds. Mobility & Transport for Elderly & Handicapped Persons. (Transportation Studies: Vol. 2). 383p. 1982. 57.50 (ISBN 0-677-16380-0). Gordon.

Ashford, Ray. The Surrender & the Singing: Happiness Through Letting Go. 168p. (Orig.). 1985. pap. 7.95 (ISBN 0-86683-964-X, AY8546, Pub. by Seabury). Winston Pr.

Ashford, Theodore H. A Programmed Introduction to the Fundamentals of Music. 3rd ed. 300p. 1980. pap. text ed. write for info. (ISBN 0-697-03440-2). Wm C Brown.

Ashforth, Albert. Murder after the Fact. 208p. 1984. 13.95 (ISBN 0-312-55278-5). St Martin.

Ashida, K. & Frisch, K. C., eds. International Progress in Urethanes, Vol. 3. LC 77-71704. 260p. 1982. pap. 35.00 (ISBN 0-87762-303-1). Technomic.

Ashida, T. & Hall, Sydney, eds. Methods & Applications in Crystallographic Computing. (Illus.). 500p. 1984. 32.50x (ISBN 0-19-855190-8). Oxford U Pr.

Ashihara, Eiryo. The Japanese Dance. LC 79-7749. (Dance Ser.). (Illus.). 1980. Repr. of 1964 ed. lib. bdg. 14.00x (ISBN 0-8369-9276-8). Ayer Co Pubs.

Ashihara, Hideyuki. Fighting Karate 1. LC 85-50353. (Illus.). 160p. (Orig.). 1985. pap. 7.95 (ISBN 0-87011-742-4). Kodansha.

Ashihara, Yoshinobu. The Aesthetic Townscape. Riggs, Lynne E., tr. from Japanese. (Illus.). 196p. 1983. 24.75 (ISBN 0-262-01069-0); pap. 9.95 (ISBN 0-262-51031-6). MIT Pr.

--The Aesthetic Townscape. (Illus.). 196p. 1984. pap. 9.95 (ISBN 0-262-51031-6). MIT Pr.

Ashim Kumar Roy, et al. Homage to Jaipur. LC 80-901924. (Illus.). 102p. 1979. 17.50x (ISBN 0-89684-409-9). Orient Bk Dist.

Ashish, Sri Madhava. Man, Son of Man. LC 79-98267. 1970. 8.50 (ISBN 0-8356-0011-4). Theos Pub Hse.

Ashish, Sri Madhava, jt. auth. see Prem, Sri K.

Ashit, Paul. Woodcut Prints of Nineteenth Century Calcutta. 1984. 34.00x (ISBN 0-317-05024-9, Pub. by Seagull Bks India). South Asia Bks.

Ashkar, F., et al, eds. A Study Guide in Nuclear Medicine. (Illus.). 488p. 1975. photocopy ed. spiral 54.75x (ISBN 0-398-03029-4). C C Thomas.

Ashkar, Fuad S. Radiobioassays, 2 vols. 1983. Vol. I. 77.00 (ISBN 0-8493-6029-3); Vol. II. 73.00 (ISBN 0-8493-6030-7). CRC Pr.

Ashkar, Fued, ed. Practical Nuclear Medicine. LC 73-13794. 217p. 1974. 25.00 (ISBN 0-8463-0126-1, Pub. by W & W). Krieger.

Ashken, M. H., ed. Urinary Diversion. (Clinical Practice in Urology Ser.). (Illus.). 143p. 1982. pap. 48.00 (ISBN 0-387-11273-1). Springer-Verlag.

Ashkenazy, Vladimir, jt. auth. see Parrott, Jasper.

Ashlag, R. Yehuda. A Gift of the Bible. 160p. 1984. pap. 9.95 (ISBN 0-943688-22-1). Res Ctr Kabbalah.

Ashlag, Yehuda. An Entrance to the Tree of Life of Rabbi Isaac Luria. Berg, Philip S., ed. 1977. 12.95 (ISBN 0-943688-05-1). Res Ctr Kabbalah.

--An Entrance to the Zohar. Berg, Philip S., ed. 1974. 12.95 (ISBN 0-943688-04-3). Res Ctr Kabbalah.

--Etz Chaim: Hebrew Text. condensed ed. 40.00 (ISBN 0-943688-18-3). Res Ctr Kabbalah.

--Ten Luminous Emanations, Vol. 1. 1970. 11.95 (ISBN 0-943688-08-6); pap. 9.95 (ISBN 0-943688-29-9). Res Ctr Kabbalah.

--Ten Luminous Emanations, Vol. 2. Berg, Philip S., ed. 1972. 11.95 (ISBN 0-943688-09-4); pap. 9.95 (ISBN 0-943688-25-6). Res Ctr Kabbalah.

Ashleigh, C., tr. see Gladkov, F. V.

Ashley. CICS-VS Command Level Programming, Bk. 3. (Data Processing Training Ser.). 1985. pap. price not set (ISBN 0-471-82367-8). Wiley.

--CICS-VS Command Level Programming Introduction, Bk. 1. (Data Processing Training Ser.). 1985. pap. write for info. (ISBN 0-471-82366-X). Wiley.

--Command Level Programming Using Maps & Files, Vol. 2. (Data Processing Training Ser.). 1984. pap. write for info. (ISBN 0-471-82365-1). Wiley.

--Hospitals, Paternalism & the Role of the Nurse. pap. text ed. 9.95 (ISBN 0-8077-2471-8, Lippincott Nursing). Lippincott.

Ashley, Alma. Love's Raging Torment. 1978. pap. 2.25 (ISBN 0-505-51250-5, Pub. by Tower Bks). Dorchester Pub Co.

--Love's Raging Torment. 352p. 1984. pap. 3.50 (ISBN 0-8439-2175-7, Leisure Bks). Dorchester Pub Co.

Ashley, Alta. Time Before the Boat. (Illus.). 306p. (Orig.). 1985. pap. 8.95 (ISBN 0-9614592-1-2). Grey Gull Pubns.

Ashley, April, jt. auth. see Fallowell, Duncan.

Ashley, Benedict M. Theologies of the Body: Humanist & Christian. 770p. (Orig.). Date not set. pap. 20.95 (ISBN 0-935372-15-6). Pope John Ctr.

Ashley, Benedict M. & O'Rourke, Kevin D. Health Care Ethics: A Theological Analysis. 2nd ed. LC 81-17973. 1982. 25.00 (ISBN 0-87125-075-6); pap. 16.00 (ISBN 0-87125-070-5). Cath Health.

Ashley, Bernard. All My Men. LC 78-12683. (gr. 6 up). 1978. 10.95 (ISBN 0-87599-228-5). S G Phillips.

--A Break in the Sun. (Illus.). 186p. (gr. 6 up). 1980. 10.95 (ISBN 0-87599-230-7). S G Phillips.

--Dodgem. (gr. 7 up). 1982. lib. bdg. 9.90 (ISBN 0-531-04363-0, MacRae). Watts.

--High Pavement Blues. (Julia Macrae BKs). (Illus.). 176p. (gr. 6 up). PLB 9.50 (ISBN 0-531-04607-9). Watts.

--A Kind of Wild Justice. LC 78-10899. (Illus.). (gr. 7 up). 1979. 10.95 (ISBN 0-87599-229-3). S G Phillips.

--Linda's Lie. (Julia MacRae Blackbird Bks.). (Illus.). 48p. (gr. k-3). 1983. 5.95 (ISBN 0-531-04576-5, MacRae). Watts.

--Terry on the Fence. LC 76-39898. (Illus.). (gr. 5-9). 1977. 10.95 (ISBN 0-87599-222-6). S G Phillips.

--Your Guess Is As Good As Mine. (Redwing Bks.). 48p. (gr. 7-11). 1984. 6.95 (ISBN 0-531-03765-7, Macrae). Watts.

Ashley, C. C. & Campbell, A. K. Measurement of Free Calcium in Cells. 1980. 81.00 (ISBN 0-444-80185-5). Elsevier.

Ashley, Clara, jt. auth. see Gambill, Sandra.

Ashley, Clifford W. Ashley Book of Knots. (Illus.). 1944. 24.95 (ISBN 0-385-04025-3). Doubleday.

Ashley, David & Orenstein, David M. Sociological Theory: Classical Statements. 1984. pap. text ed. 20.65 (ISBN 0-205-08249-1, 818249). Allyn.

Ashley, David J. Evan's Histological Appearances of Tumours, 2 vols. 3rd ed. (Illus.). 900p. 1978. text ed. 125.00 (ISBN 0-443-01762-X). Churchill.

Ashley, Elizabeth & Firestone, Ross. Actress: Postcards from the Road. 1980. pap. 2.25 (ISBN 0-449-24104-1, Crest). Fawcett.

--Actress: Postcards from the Road. LC 78-172718. (Illus.). 256p. 1978. 10.00 (ISBN 0-87131-264-6). M Evans.

Ashley, Faye. Blue Wildfire. 320p. 1983. pap. 3.25 (ISBN 0-8439-2018-1, Leisure Bks). Dorchester Pub Co.

Ashley, Franklin. James Dickey: A Checklist. (Illus.). 15.00 (ISBN 0-685-77421-X). Gale.

Ashley, Franklin, jt. auth. see Fox, William P.

Ashley, Holt & Landahl, Marten. Aerodynamics of Wings & Bodies. 288p. 1985. pap. 6.95 (ISBN 0-486-64899-0). Dover.

Ashley, Holt, jt. auth. see Bisplinghoff, Raymond L.

Ashley, Holt, et al, eds. Energy & the Environment, a Risk-Benefit Approach. 1976. text ed. 31.00 (ISBN 0-08-020873-8). Pergamon.

Ashley, Howard J. Accurate Perspective Simplified. LC 73-89328. (Illus.). 224p. 1974. text ed. 16.00 (ISBN 0-914214-01-2). Abak Pr.

Ashley, Jacqueline. Hunting Season. (American Romance Ser.). 256p. 1984. pap. 2.25 (ISBN 0-373-16040-2). Harlequin Bks.

--Love's Revenge. (Harlequin American Romance Ser.). 256p. 1983. pap. 2.25 (ISBN 0-373-16020-8). Harlequin Bks.

Ashley, James M. & Arnett, Benjamin H. Duplicate Copy of the Souvenir from the Afro-American League of Tennessee to Hon. James M Ashley, of Ohio. 41.75 (ISBN 0-8369-9218-0, 9073). Ayer Co Pubs.

Ashley, Jo Ann. Hospitals, Paternalism, & the Role of the Nurse. LC 76-7908. 1976. pap. 8.50x (ISBN 0-8077-2470-X). Tchrs Coll.

Ashley, L. R. George Peele. LC 68-17242. 256p. 1970. text ed. 24.00x (ISBN 0-8290-0175-1). Irvington.

Ashley, Laura. Laura Ashley Home Furnishings Catalog 1984. (Illus.). 1984. pap. 3.50 (ISBN 0-517-55245-0, Harmony). Crown.

--Laura Ashley Home Furnishings Catalog: 1985. 1985. pap. 4.00 (ISBN 0-517-55582-4, Harmony). Crown.

Ashley, Laurence M. Laboratory Anatomy of the Turtle. (Laboratory Anatomy Ser.). 50p. 1982. write for info. wire coil (ISBN 0-697-04601-X). Wm C Brown.

Ashley, Laurence M. & Chiasson, Robert B. Laboratory Anatomy of the Shark. 4th ed. (Laboratory Anatomy Ser.). 80p. 1982. write for info wire coil bdg (ISBN 0-697-04731-8). Wm C Brown.

Ashley, Leonard R. Names in British Fact & Folklore. (The International Library of Names). 400p. 1984. text ed. 29.50 (ISBN 0-8290-1216-8). Irvington.

--The Wonderful World of Superstition, Prophecy & Luck. LC 83-23182. (Illus.). 192p. (Orig.). 1984. pap. 8.95 (ISBN 0-934878-33-1). Dembner Bks.

Ashley, Leonard R. N. Names & American Slang. (The International Library of Names Ser.). 200p. Date not set. text ed. price not set (ISBN 0-8290-1225-7). Irvington.

Ashley, Liza. Thirty Years at the Mansion. LC 84-73313. (Illus.). 208p. 1985. 18.95 (ISBN 0-935304-88-6). August Hse.

Ashley, Margaret, tr. see Fustel De Coulanges, Numa D.

Ashley, Maurice. Charles II. (Illus.). 368p. 1981. pap. 5.95 (ISBN 0-586-03805-1, Pub. by Granada England). Academy Chi Pubs.

--England in the Seventeenth Century. new ed. 275p. 1980. 26.50x (ISBN 0-686-70947-0, 06319); pap. 9.95 (ISBN 0-686-70948-9, 06320). B&N Imports.

--Financial & Commercial Policy under Cromwellian Protectorate. 2nd ed. 190p. 1962. Repr. of 1934 ed. 28.50x (ISBN 0-7146-1265-0, BHA 01265, F Cass Co). Biblio Dist.

--The House of Stuart: It's Rise & Fall. (Illus.). 237p. 1980. 22.50 (ISBN 0-460-04458-3, Pub. by J M Dent England). Biblio Dist.

--James II. (Illus.). 1978. 19.50x (ISBN 0-8166-0826-1). U of Minn Pr.

--Louis the Fourteenth & the Greatness of France. 1965. pap. 11.95 (ISBN 0-02-901080-2). Free Pr.

--Magna Carta in the Seventeenth Century. LC 65-23456. (Illus.). 62p. (Orig.). 1965. pap. 3.95x (ISBN 0-8139-0014-X). U Pr of Va.

--The People of England: A Short Social & Economic History. LC 82-84225. (Illus.). 214p. 1983. text ed. 22.50x (ISBN 0-8071-1105-8). La State U Pr.

Ashley, Maurice P. Mr. President: An Introduction to American History. LC 79-38317. (Biography Index Reprint Ser). Repr. of 1948 ed. 23.50 (ISBN 0-8369-8115-4). Ayer Co Pubs.

Ashley, Meg. Danger on the Quarry Path. (A Boarding House Adventure Ser.). (gr. 6-9). 1985. pap. 3.95 (ISBN 0-8307-1034-5, 5900139). Regal.

--The Deserted Rooms. LC 84-11493. (A Boarding House Adventure Ser.). 160p. (gr. 6-9). 1984. pap. 3.95 (ISBN 0-8307-0973-8, 5900111). Regal.

--Lights in the Lake. LC 83-10980. (A Boarding HouseAdventure). 1983. pap. 3.95 (ISBN 0-8307-0846-4, 5900021). Regal.

--Meg. LC 83-1332. 128p. 1983. pap. text ed. 2.95 (ISBN 0-88449-101-3, A324581). Vision Hse.

--The Secret of the Old House. LC 82-13158. (A Boarding House Adventure Ser.). 1982. pap. 3.95 (ISBN 0-8307-0845-6, 5900014). Regal.

Ashley, Merrill & Kaplan, Larry. Dancing for Balanchine. (Illus.). 256p. 1984. 29.95 (ISBN 0-525-24280-5, 02908-870). Dutton.

Ashley, Michael. Fantasy Readers Guide to Ramsey Campbell. LC 80-22744. 64p. 1980. Repr. lib. bdg. 14.95x (ISBN 0-89370-098-3). Borgo Pr.

--The Work of R. Lionel Fanthorpe: An Annotated Bibliography & Guide. (Bibliographies of Modern Authors: No. 11). 144p. 1985. lib. bdg. 19.95x (ISBN 0-89370-390-7); pap. text ed. 9.95x (ISBN 0-89370-490-3). Borgo Pr.

Ashley, Mike. The Illustrated Book of Science Fiction Lists. (Orig.). 1983. pap. 7.95 (ISBN 0-346-12628-2, Cornerstone). S&S.

--Who's Who in Horror & Fantasy Fiction. LC 77-4608. 1978. pap. 4.95 (ISBN 0-8008-8278-4). Taplinger.

Ashley, Mike, jt. ed. see Parnell, Frank H.

Ashley, Nancy. Create Your Own Reality: A Seth Workbook. 144p. 1984. 15.95 (ISBN 0-13-189135-9); pap. 6.95 (ISBN 0-13-189127-8). P-H.

Ashley, Nova. Call Me Grandma! (Illus.). 48p. 1984. 6.95 (ISBN 0-8378-5063-0). Gibson.

Ashley, P. P. Oh Promise Me But Put It in Writing: Living Together Agreements Without, Before, During & After Marriage. 1980. pap. 3.95 (ISBN 0-07-002414-6). McGraw.

Ashley, Paul. You & Your Will. 1985. pap. 3.50 (ISBN 0-451-62415-7, Ment). NAL.

Ashley, Pauline. The Money Problems of the Poor: A Literature Review. (SSRC-DHSS Studies in Deprivation & Disadvantage: No. 11). xiii, 226p. 1983. pap. text ed. 18.50x (ISBN 0-435-82024-9). Gower Pub Co.

Ashley, Percy W. Modern Tariff History: Germany, the United States & France. 1980. lib. bdg. 75.50 (ISBN 0-8490-3124-9). Gordon Pr.

Ashley, Perry. American Newspaper Journalists, Nineteen Twenty-Six to Nineteen Fifty. (The Dictionary of Literary Biograhy: Vol. 29). 550p. 1984. 88.00x (ISBN 0-8103-1707-9). Gale.

Ashley, Perry, ed. Dictionary of Literary Biography Documentary Series, Vol. 4. 426p. 1984. 92.00x (ISBN 0-8103-1113-5). Gale.

Ashley, Perry J., ed. American Newpaper Journalists, 1690-1872, Vol. 43. (The Dictionary of Literary Biography Ser.). 500p. 1985. 88.00x (ISBN 0-8103-1721-4). Gale.

--American Newspaper Journalists, Eighteen Seventy-Three-Nineteen Hundred. (Dictionary of Literary Biography Ser.: Vol. 23). 392p. 1984. 85.00x (ISBN 0-8103-1145-3). Gale.

--American Newspaper Journalists, Nineteen Hundred-Nineteen Twenty-Five. (Dictionary of Literary Biography Ser.: Vol. 25). (Illus.). 400p. 1983. 85.00x (ISBN 0-8103-1704-4). Gale.

Ashley, R. Background Math for a Computer World. 2nd ed. LC 80-11562. (Wiley Self-Teaching Guides Ser.). 308p. 1980. pap. text ed. 10.95 (ISBN 0-471-08086-1, Pub. by Wiley Pr). Wiley.

--Wilkie Collins. LC 75-30887. (Studies in Fiction, No. 34). 1975. lib. bdg. 39.95x (ISBN 0-8383-2095-3). Haskell.

Ashley, R., jt. auth. see Fernandez, J. N.

Ashley, Rebecca. A Season of Surprises. (Orig.). 1981. pap. 1.50 (ISBN 0-440-18281-6). Dell.

Ashley, Richard. Cocaine: Its History, Uses & Effects. 240p. 1976. pap. 3.95 (ISBN 0-446-30500-6). Warner Bks.

Ashley, Richard & Duggal, Heidi. Dictionary of Nutrition. 1983. pap. 3.50 (ISBN 0-671-49407-4). PB.

Ashley, Richard K. Political Economy of War & Peace. 320p. 1980. 35.00 (ISBN 0-89397-087-5). Nichols Pub.

Ashley, Robert. Wilkie Collins. LC 74-6031. Repr. of 1952 ed. lib. bdg. 12.50 (ISBN 0-8414-2975-8). Folcroft.

Ashley, Robert, tr. A Comparison of the English & Spanish Nation: Composed by a French Gentleman Against Those of the League. LC 72-38141. (English Experience Ser.: No. 467). 52p. 1972. Repr. of 1589 ed. 8.00 (ISBN 90-221-0467-2). Walter J Johnson.

Ashley, Roy. Matchstick Modelling. (Illus.). 80p. 1980. 10.95 (ISBN 0-7207-1150-9, Pub. by Michael Joseph). Merrimack Pub Cir.

Ashley, Ruth. ANS COBOL. 2nd ed. LC 78-27717. (Self-Teaching Guide Ser.). 265p. 1979. pap. text ed. 10.95 (ISBN 0-471-05136-5). Wiley.

--Human Anatomy. LC 76-65. (Self-Teaching Guides Ser.). 274p. 1976. pap. text ed. 8.95 (ISBN 0-471-03508-4, Pub. by Wiley Pr). Wiley.

--PC-DOS: Using IBM-PC Operating System. LC 82-24720. (IBM Personal Computer Ser.: No. 1646). 225p. 1983. pap. text ed. 16.95 (ISBN 0-471-89718-3, Pub. by Wiley Pr). Wiley.

--Structured COBOL. LC 79-27340. (Self-Teaching Guides Ser.: No. 1-581). 295p. 1980. pap. text ed. 12.95 (ISBN 0-471-05362-7, Pub. by Wiley Pr). Wiley.

Ashley, Ruth & Fernandez, Judi. COBOL for Microcomputers. LC 83-6914. (Self-Teaching Guide Ser.: I-581). 326p. 1983. pap. text ed. 15.95 (ISBN 0-471-87241-5, Pub by Wiley Pr). Wiley.

Ashley, Ruth & Fernandez, Judi N. Essential Framework: A Self-Teaching Guide. 1985. pap. 19.95 (ISBN 0-471-82048-2). Wiley.

--Introduction to Structured COBOL, Bk. 1. LC 83-21591. (Data Processing Training Ser.: No. 1-615). 342p. 1984. pap. 49.95x (ISBN 0-471-87025-0). Wiley.

--Job Control Language. 2nd ed. (Wiley Self Teaching Guides Ser.: No. 1581). 154p. 1984. pap. 12.95 (ISBN 0-471-79983-1, Pub. by Wiley Pr). Wiley.

--PC-DOS: A Self-Teaching Guide. 2nd ed. 1985. pap. 16.95 (ISBN 0-471-82471-2). Wiley.

--Using Structured COBOL, Bk. 2. LC 84-17206. (Data Processing Training Ser.: No. 1-615). 256p. 1984. pap. text ed. 49.95x spiral bd. (ISBN 0-471-87185-0). Wiley.

Ashley, Ruth, jt. auth. see Fernandez, Judi.

Ashley, Ruth, jt. auth. see Fernandez, Judi N.

Ashley, Ruth, jt. auth. see Tabler, Donna.

Ashley, Ruth & Fernandez, Judi N., eds. Tape & Disk Files, COBOL 3. (Data Processing Training Ser.). 250p. 1985. pap. text ed. 49.95x spiral bd. (ISBN 0-471-87184-2). Wiley.

Ashley, Ruth, et al. WordStar Without Tears: A Self-Teaching Guide. LC 84-17314. 224p. 1984. pap. 14.95 (ISBN 0-471-80540-8, Pub. by Wiley Pr). Wiley.

Ashley, Sally. Connecting: A Handbook for Housewives Returning to Paid Work. 224p. 1982. pap. 5.95 (ISBN 0-380-79251-6, 79251-6). Avon.

Ashley, Sarah. Cherished Moments. (Second Chance at Love Ser.: No. 133). 192p. 1983. pap. 1.95 (ISBN 0-515-07221-4). Jove Pubns.

Ashley, Stephen S. Bad Faith Actions-Liability & Damages. LC 84-28489. 1984. 75.00 (ISBN 0-317-17768-0). Callaghan.

Ashley, Steven. The Last Brigade. 320p. 1982. pap. 2.95 (ISBN 0-515-05559-X). Jove Pubns.

--Love Out of Time. 272p. 1985. pap. 3.50 (ISBN 0-425-07967-8). Berkley Pub.

Ashley, William, ed. see Mill, John S.

Ashley, William H. British Establishments on the Columbia & the State of the Fur Trade. 60p. 1981. 9.95 (ISBN 0-87770-255-1). Ye Galleon.

Ashley, William J. The Economic Organization of England: An Outline History. LC 83-45574. Date not set. Repr. of 1935 ed. 32.50 (ISBN 0-404-19892-9). AMS Pr.

--An Introduction to English Economic History & Theory, 2 vols. in 1. Incl. Pt. 1. The Middle Ages. Repr. of 1888 ed; Pt. 2. The End of the Middle Ages. Repr. of 1893 ed. LC 65-26358. 45.00x (ISBN 0-678-00167-7). Kelley.

--Surveys: Historic & Economic. LC 66-21366. Repr. of 1900 ed. 37.50x (ISBN 0-678-00170-7). Kelley.

--Tariff Problem. 4th ed. LC 68-30515. Repr. of 1920 ed. 27.50x (ISBN 0-678-00433-1). Kelley.

Ashley, William J., ed. see Mill, John S.

Ashley, William J., tr. see Turgot, A. Robert.

Ashley, William L. Occupational Information Resources: A Catalog of Data Bases & Classification Schemes. 353p. 1977. 18.20 (ISBN 0-318-15521-4, IN104). Natl Ctr Res Voc Ed.

Ashley, William L. & Laitman-Ashley, Nancy M. Occupational Adaptability - Perspectives on Tomorrow's Careers Symposium: Proceedings, 1979. 62p. 4.50 (ISBN 0-318-15540-0, IN189). Natl Ctr Res Voc Ed.

Ashley, William L. & Laitman-Ashley, Nancy M., eds. Occupational Adaptability: Perspectives on Tomorrow's Careers - A Symposium. 62p. 1979. 4.50 (ISBN 0-318-15520-6, IN189). Natl Ctr Res Voc Ed.

Ashley Montagu. The Biosocial Nature of Man. LC 72-11331. 123p. 1973. Repr. of 1956 ed. lib. bdg. 15.00 (ISBN 0-8371-6658-6, MOBN). Greenwood.

--Darwin: Competition & Cooperation. LC 72-11332. 148p. 1973. Repr. of 1952 ed. lib. bdg. 24.75 (ISBN 0-8371-6657-8, MODC). Greenwood.

--Education & Human Relations. LC 72-11333. 191p. 1973. Repr. of 1958 ed. lib. bdg. 15.00 (ISBN 0-8371-6659-4, MOEH). Greenwood.

--The Elephant Man: A Study in Human Dignity. rev. ed. (Illus.). 1979. pap. 5.95 (ISBN 0-525-47617-2, 0558-370). Dutton.

--Growing Young. (Illus.). 1981. 12.95 (ISBN 0-07-042841-7); pap. 6.95 (ISBN 0-07-042844-1). McGraw.

--Man & Aggression. 2nd ed. 1973. pap. 7.95 (ISBN 0-19-501680-7, 250, GB). Oxford U Pr.

--Man, His First Two Million Years: A Brief Introduction to Anthropology. LC 80-15749. (Illus.). vi, 262p. 1980. Repr. of 1969 ed. lib. bdg. 27.50x (ISBN 0-313-22600-8, MOMH). Greenwood.

--The Natural Superiority of Women. rev. ed. 1974. pap. 4.95 (ISBN 0-02-096080-8, Collier). Macmillan.

--The Nature of Human Aggression. LC 75-32360. (Illus.). 1976. 16.95x (ISBN 0-19-501822-2); pap. 8.95 (ISBN 0-19-502373-0, GB535, GB). Oxford U Pr.

--On Being Human. (gr. 9-12). 1967. pap. 3.50 (ISBN 0-8015-5514-0, Hawthorn). Dutton.

--On Being Intelligent. LC 72-11742. 236p. 1973. Repr. of 1951 ed. lib. bdg. 18.75 (ISBN 0-8371-6704-3, MOOB). Greenwood.

--The Practice of Love. 1975. pap. 2.95 (ISBN 0-13-694463-9, Spec). P-H.

--Statement on Race. 3rd ed. 1972. pap. 8.95 (ISBN 0-19-501531-2, GB). Oxford U Pr.

--Statement on Race: An Annotated Elaboration & Exposition of the Four Statements on Race Issued by the United Nations Educational, Scientific & Cultural Organization. 3rd ed. LC 80-27835. xii, 278p. 1981. Repr. of 1972 ed. lib. bdg. 27.50x (ISBN 0-313-22739-X, MOSR). Greenwood.

--Touching: The Human Significance of Skin. 2nd, rev. ed. 1978. pap. 7.21i (ISBN 0-06-090630-8, CN 630, CN). Har-Row.

--Touching: The Human Significance of the Skin. 2nd, rev. ed. LC 77-3762. 384p. 1978. 10.53i (ISBN 0-06-012979-4, HarpT). Har-Row.

Ashley Montagu & Matson, Floyd. The Human Connection. 228p. 1981. pap. 4.95 (ISBN 0-07-042842-5). McGraw.

--The Human Connection. 1979. 10.95 (ISBN 0-07-042840-9). McGraw.

Ashley Montagu & Rowe, David N. Great Issues 76: A Forum on Important Questions Facing the American Public, Vol. 8. LC 77-85525. 9.95x (ISBN 0-916624-11-0). Troy State Univ.

Ashley Montagu, jt. auth. see Steen, Edwin B.

Ashley Montagu, ed. The Concept of Race. LC 80-21682. xviii, 270p. 1980. Repr. of 1964 ed. lib. bdg. 32.50x (ISBN 0-313-22721-7, MOCR). Greenwood.

--Culture & Human Development: Insights into Growing Human. LC 74-18338. 192p. 1974. 8.95 (ISBN 0-13-195578-0, Spec); (Spec). P-H.

--Learning Non-Aggression: The Experience of Non-Literate Societies. (Illus.). 1978. 19.95x (ISBN 0-19-502342-0). Oxford U Pr.

--Learning Non-Aggression: The Experience of Non-Literate Societies. (Illus.). 1978. pap. 6.95 (ISBN 0-19-502343-9, GB525, GB). Oxford U Pr.

--Meaning of Love. LC 72-11335. 248p. 1974. Repr. of 1953 ed. lib. bdg. 16.25x (ISBN 0-8371-6656-X, MOML). Greenwood.

--Science & Creationism. LC 82-14173. (Galaxy Bks.). 1984. 24.95 (ISBN 0-19-503252-7); pap. 10.95x (ISBN 0-19-503253-5, GB). Oxford U Pr.

--Sociobiology Examined. 1980. 22.50x (ISBN 0-19-502711-6); pap. 7.95 (ISBN 0-19-502712-4, GB602). Oxford U Pr.

Ashley Montagu, M. F. Anthropology & Human Nature. pap. 5.00 (ISBN 0-910294-00-3). Brown Bk.

--Anthropology & Human Nature. (Extending Horizons). 390p. 1957. 6.00 (ISBN 0-87558-030-0). Porter Sargent.

--The Reproductive Development of the Female: A Study in the Comparative Physiology of the Adolescent Organism. 3rd ed. LC 78-55285. (Illus.). 252p. 1979. 26.00 (ISBN 0-88416-218-4). PSG Pub Co.

Ashley Montagu, M. F., ed. Studies & Essays in the History of Science & Learning. LC 74-26275. (History, Philosophy & Sociology of Science Ser). (Illus.). 1975. Repr. of 1944 ed. 47.50x (ISBN 0-405-06603-1). Ayer Co Pubs.

--Toynbee & History. (Extending Horizons Ser). 385p. 1956. 7.00 (ISBN 0-87558-026-2). Porter Sargent.

Ashlock, Patrick & Grant, Sister Marie. Educational Therapy Materials from the Ashlock Learning Center. (Illus.). 440p. 1976. spiral 34.50x (ISBN 0-398-02218-6). C C Thomas.

Ashlock, Patrick & Stephen, Alberta. Educational Therapy in the Elementary School: An Educational Approach to the Learning Problems of Children. (Illus.). 120p. 1970. spiral 14.75x (ISBN 0-398-00060-3). C C Thomas.

Ashlock, Robert. Error Patterns in Computation. 3rd ed. 208p. 1982. pap. text ed. 10.95 (ISBN 0-675-09880-7). Merrill.

Ashlock, Robert B. & Humphrey, James H. Teaching Elementary School Mathematics Through Motor Learning. 168p. 1976. 16.25x (ISBN 0-398-03578-4). C C Thomas.

Ashlock, Robert B. & Johnson, Martin L. Guide Each Child's Learning of Mathematics: A Diagnostic Approach to Instruction. 612p. 1983. text ed. 23.95 (ISBN 0-675-20023-7). Additional supplements may be obtained from publisher. Merrill.

Ashlock, Wilma J. Love, Laughter & Tears. 1983. 6.95 (ISBN 0-8062-2020-1). Carlton.

Ashman, Adrian & Laura, Ronald, eds. Education & Training of the Mentally Retarded. 300p. 1985. 23.95 (ISBN 0-89397-217-7). Nichols Pub.

Ashman, Adrian F., jt. ed. see Laura, Ronald S.

Ashman, Bernie. Twelve Astrological Chords. (Orig.). 1986. pap. 9.95 (ISBN 0-917086-74-0). A C S Pubns Inc.

Ashman, Charles & Sobel, Rebecca. The Strange Disappearance of Jimmy Hoffa. 224p. 1976. pap. 1.50 (ISBN 0-532-15179-8). Woodhill.

Ashman, Chuck. The Gospel According to Billy. 1977. 8.95 (ISBN 0-8184-0251-2). Lyle Stuart.

Ashman, Iain. Make This Model Castle. (Illus.). (gr. 4-9). 1983. pap. 5.95 (ISBN 0-13-545947-8, Pub. by Treehouse). P-H.

--Make This Model Village. (Illus.). (gr. 4-9). 1983. pap. 5.95 (ISBN 0-13-545954-0, Pub. by Treehouse). P-H.

Ashman, Sandra & George, Alan. Study & Learn. (Illus.). 200p. (Orig.). 1982. pap. 12.50 (ISBN 0-434-90080-X, Pub. by W Heinemann Ltd). David & Charles.

Ashmanskas, Donald C., et al. Local Government. rev. ed. LC 82-62722. 1983. 97.50. OR Bar CLE.

Ashmead, Ann H. & Phillips, Kyle M., Jr. Catalog of the Classical Collection: Vases. LC 76-45537. (Illus.). 1976. 10.00 (ISBN 0-686-17937-4). Mus of Art RI.

Ashmead, DeWayne. Chelated Mineral Nutrition. 186p. (Orig.). 1981. pap. 5.95 (ISBN 0-86664-002-9). Intl Inst Nat Health.

--Chelated Mineral Nutrition in Plants, Animals, & Man. (Illus.). 346p. 1982. 38.75x (ISBN 0-398-04603-4). C C Thomas.

Ashmead, H. DeWayne, et al. Intestinal Absorbtion of Metal Ions & Chelates. (Illus.). 262p. 1985. 26.50x (ISBN 0-398-05047-3). C C Thomas.

--Intestinal Absorption of Metal Ions& Chelates. 26.50 (ISBN 0-317-29017-7). C C Thomas.

Ashmead, W. H., et al. Insects, 2 pts. (Harriman Alaska Expedition, 1899). 1910. Pt. 1. pap. 24.00 (ISBN 0-527-38168-3); Pt. 2. pap. 24.00 (ISBN 0-527-38169-1). Kraus Repr.

Ashmead-Bartlett, Ellis. Passing of the Shereefian Empire. LC 78-109314. (Illus.). Repr. of 1910 ed. cancelled (ISBN 0-8371-3565-6). Greenwood.

Ashmole, Bernard. Architect & Sculptor in Classical Greece. LC 72-76019. (The Wrightsman Lectures Ser.). (Illus.). 218p. 1972. 45.00x (ISBN 0-8147-0553-7). NYU Pr.

Ashmole, Bernard, jt. auth. see Groenewegen Frankfort, Mrs. H.

Ashmole, Elias. Institution, Laws & Ceremonies of the Most Noble Order of the Garter. LC 78-147882. (Illus.). 720p. 1971. Repr. of 1672 ed. 50.00 (ISBN 0-8063-0467-7). Genealog Pub.

--Theatrum Chemicum Britannicum. 33.00 (ISBN 0-384-02185-9). Johnson Repr.

Ashmolean Museum, ed. Edgar Degas, 1834-1917. 87p. 1983. 30.00x (ISBN 0-317-20324-X, Pub. by Ashmolean Mus UK). State Mutual Bk.

--Samuel Palmer: A Vision Recaptured. 88p. 1978. 40.00x (ISBN 0-317-20346-0, Pub. by Ashmolean Mus UK). State Mutual Bk.

Ashmore, Anne R. & Library of Congress Law Library. Presidential Proclamations Concerning Public Lands, January 24, 1791-March 19, 1936: Numerical List & Index. LC 81-600031. 1981. write for info. Lib Congress.

Ashmore, Harry. Arkansas: A History. (States & the Nation Ser.). (Illus.). 1984. pap. 7.95 (ISBN 0-393-30177-X). Norton.

--Hearts & Minds: The Anatomy of Racism from Roosevelt to Reagan. 1982. pap. 15.95 (ISBN 0-07-002456-1). Mcgraw.

Ashmore, Harry S. Arkansas. (States & the Nation Ser.). (Illus.). 1978. 14.95 (ISBN 0-393-05669-4, Co-Pub by AASLH). Norton.

Ashmore, Helen, jt. auth. see Arth, Marvin.

Ashmore, Jerome. Santayana, Art, & Aesthetics. LC 66-16889. pap. 38.30 (ISBN 0-317-08999-4, 2001348). Bks Demand UMI.

Ashmore, Lewis. The Modesto Messiah. LC 77-72716. 1977. pap. 1.95 (ISBN 0-918950-01-5). Universal Pr.

Ashmore, Owen. Industrial Archaeology of Lancashire. LC 68-18643. 1969. 24.95x (ISBN 0-678-05529-7). Kelley.

--The Industrial Archaeology of North-West England. (Illus.). 272p. 25.00 (ISBN 0-7190-0820-4, Pub. by Manchester Univ Pr). Longwood Pub Group.

Ashmore, Philip G., et al, eds. Photochemistry & Reaction Kinetics. LC 67-105417. pap. 98.50 (ISBN 0-317-26113-4, 2024403). Bks Demand UMI.

Ashmore, Richard D. & Brodzinsky, David M., eds. Thinking about the Family: Views of the Parents of Children. 350p. 1986. Set. text ed. 36.00 (ISBN 0-89859-693-9). L Erlbaum Assocs.

Ashmore, Richard D. & Del Boca, Frances K., eds. The Social Psychology of Female-Male Relations: A Critical Analysis of Central Concepts. Date not set. price not set (ISBN 0-12-065280-3). Acad Pr.

Ashmore, Wendy, ed. Lowland Maya Settlement Patterns. (School of American Research Advanced Seminar Ser.). 464p. 1981. 32.50x (ISBN 0-8263-0556-3). U of NM Pr.

Ashmore, Wendy, ed. see Ashmore, Wendy, et al.

Ashmore, Wendy, et al. Quirigua Reports, Vol. I, Papers 1-5. Sharer, Robert J. & Ashmore, Wendy, eds. (University Museum Monographs: No. 37). (Illus.). ix, 73p. (Orig.). 1979. pap. 15.00x (ISBN 0-934718-26-1). Univ Mus of U PA.

Ashmore, Wendy A., jt. auth. see Sharer, Robert J.

Ashmun, Jehudi, ed. see Bacon, Samuel.

Ashmun, Margaret. The Singing Swan: An Account of Anna Seward & Her Acquaintance with Dr. Johnson, Etc. 1931. Repr. 20.00 (ISBN 0-8274-3417-0). R West.

--The Singing Swan: An Account of Anne Seward & Her Acquaintance with Dr. Johnson, Boswell, & Others of Their Time. 1931. 15.50x (ISBN 0-686-51310-X). Elliots Bks.

Ashmun, Margaret E. Singing Swan: An Account of Anna Seward & Her Acquaintance with Doctor Johnson, Boswell & Others of Their Time. LC 68-57589. (Illus.). 1969. Repr. of 1931 ed. lib. bdg. 19.75x (ISBN 0-8371-0287-1, ASSS). Greenwood.

Ashmun, Richard, jt. auth. see Ernest, John.

Ashner, S. Shapiro, jt. auth. see Christensen, J. Ippolito.

Ashokananda, Swami, tr. see Dattatreya.

Ashour, Said, et al, eds. Computer Simulation in Design Applications. (SCS Simulation Ser.: Vol. 3, No. 1). 1976. 30.00 (ISBN 0-686-36662-X). Soc Computer Sim.

Ashour, Y., jt. auth. see Wardhaugh, K.

Ashraf. Lessons in Islams, 5. 8.50 (ISBN 0-686-18391-6). Kazi Pubns.

Ashraf, Ali & Sharma, L. N. Political Sociology: A New Grammar of Politics. 224p. 1983. pap. text ed. 8.95x (ISBN 0-86131-439-5, Pub. by Orient Longman Ltd. India). Apt Bks.

Ashraf, Mujeeb. Muslim Attitudes Toward British Rule & Western Culture in India. 1983. 19.00x (ISBN 0-8364-1076-9, Pub. by Idarah). South Asia Bks.

Ashri, A., et al. Sesame - Status & Improvement: Proceedings of Expert Consultation, Rome, Italy, Dec. 1980. (Plant Production & Protection Papers: No. 29). 203p. 1981. pap. 14.75 (ISBN 92-5-101122-2, F2259, FAO). Unipub.

Ashtiany, J. The Arabic Documents in the Archives of the British Political Agency, Kuwait, 1904-1949. 372p. (Orig.). 1982. pap. 32.25 (ISBN 0-903359-32-4, Pub. by British Lib). Longwood Pub Group.

Ashton & Denton Publishing Co., ed. Know Jersey Nineteen Eighty-One. 300p. 1981. 25.00x (ISBN 0-686-32131-6, Pub. by Ashton & Denton). State Mutual Bk.

Ashton, Ann. The Lovely & the Lonely. LC 83-25375. (Starlight Romance Ser.). 192p. 1984. 11.95 (ISBN 0-385-19355-6). Doubleday.

--The Passion Allegro. LC 84-18788. (Starlight Romance Ser.). 192p. 1985. 11.95 (ISBN 0-385-19773-X). Doubleday.

Ashton, Brad. How to Write Comedy. (Illus.). 160p. 1983. 19.95 (ISBN 0-241-11045-9, Pub. by Hamish Hamilton England); pap. 12.95 (ISBN 0-241-11092-0, Pub. by Hamish Hamilton England). David & Charles.

Ashton, D. L., jt. auth. see McPherson, E.

Ashton, David. Boardroom Issues. 1980. 90.00x (ISBN 0-86176-007-7, Pub. by MCB Pubns). State Mutual Bk.

Ashton, David, et al. Auditing Management Development. 1978. 89.00x (ISBN 0-905440-73-0, Pub. by MCB Pubns). State Mutual Bk.

Ashton, Dore. About Rothko. LC 83-2268. (Illus.). 1983. 19.95 (ISBN 0-19-503348-5). Oxford U Pr.

--American Art since Nineteen Forty-Five. (Illus.). 1982. 25.00 (ISBN 0-19-520359-3). Oxford U Pr.

--Bonevardi. (Illus., Eng. & Span.). 1980. pap. 3.00 (ISBN 0-89192-336-5, Pub. by Ctr Inter-Am Rel). Interbk Inc.

--A Fable of Modern Art. (Illus.). 1980. 17.95 (ISBN 0-500-23301-2). Thames Hudson.

--Isamu Noguchi: New Sculpture, 1983. LC 83-8059. (Illus.). 36p. (Orig.). 1983. pap. text ed. 10.00 (ISBN 0-938608-18-5). Pace Gallery Pubns.

--The New York School: A Cultural Reckoning. (Illus.). 1979. pap. 6.95 (ISBN 0-14-005263-1). Penguin.

--The New York School: A Cultural Reckoning. 14.25 (ISBN 0-8446-6176-7). Peter Smith.

--A Reading of Modern Art. LC 68-19064. (Illus.). pap. 63.80 (ISBN 0-317-10195-1, 2002261). Bks Demand UMI.

Ashton, Dore & Flam, Jack. Robert Motherwell. LC 83-3859. (Illus.). 176p. 1983. 35.00 (ISBN 0-89659-387-8). Abbeville Pr.

Ashton, Dore & Marter, Jean M. Jose de Rivera Constructions. LC 79-56553. (Illus.). 254p. 1983. 85.00 (ISBN 0-8390-0311-0). Abner Schram Ltd.

Ashton, Dore, jt. auth. see Delehanty, Suzanne.

Ashton, Dore, et al. Jean Cocteau & the French Scene. Peters, Arthur, ed. LC 83-73421. (Illus.). 240p. 1984. 19.95 (ISBN 0-89659-412-2). Abbeville Pr.

Ashton, E. B., jt. auth. see Pauli, Hertha.

Ashton, E. B., ed. see Benn, Gottfried.

Ashton, E. B., tr. see Adorno, Theodor W.

Ashton, E. B., tr. see Jaspers, Karl.

Ashton, E. B., tr. see Saner, Hans.

Ashton, E. H. & Holmes, R. L., eds. Perspectives in Primate Biology. (Symposia of the Zoological Society of London Ser.: No. 46). 1981. 68.50 (ISBN 0-12-613346-8). Acad Pr.

Ashton, E. O. Swahili Grammar. 2nd ed. 1976. pap. text ed. 6.50x (ISBN 0-582-62701-X). Longman.

Ashton, E. T., jt. auth. see Young, Agnes F.

Ashton, Eliyahu. Studies on the Levantine Trade in the Middle Ages. 372p. 1980. 60.00x (ISBN 0-86078-020-1, Pub. by Variorum England). State Mutual Bk.

Ashton, Elizabeth. La Plus Douce Des Musiques. (Harlequin Romantique Ser.). 192p. 1983. pap. 1.95 (ISBN 0-373-41189-8). Harlequin Bks.

--White Witch. (Harlequin Romances Ser.). 192p. 1982. pap. 1.50 (ISBN 0-373-02503-3). Harlequin Bks.

Ashton, Floyd M. & Crafts, Alden S. Mode of Action of Herbicides. 2nd ed. LC 80-23077. 525p. 1981. 58.95x (ISBN 0-471-04847-X, Pub. by Wiley-Interscience). Wiley.

Ashton, Floyd M., jt. auth. see Klingman, Glenn C.

Ashton, Frances. The Breaking of the Seals. Stine, Hank, ed. LC 82-2386. (Illus.). 174p. 1982. pap. 6.95 (ISBN 0-89865-200-6). Donning Co.

Ashton, Geoffrey. Giselle. (Stories of the Ballets Ser.). (Illus.). 48p. 1985. 7.95 (ISBN 0-8120-5673-6). Barron.

--Petrushka. (Stories of the Ballets Ser.). (Illus.). 48p. 1985. 7.95 (ISBN 0-8120-5671-X). Barron.

Ashton, George, ed. see ASCE Conference, Hydraulics Division, 1980.

Ashton, Gordon C. & McMillan, Ian. A Medley of Statistical Techniques for Researchers. 64p. 1981. pap. 7.25 (ISBN 0-8403-2341-7). Kendall-Hunt.

Ashton, H. A Preface to Moliere. LC 73-15535. Repr. of 1927 ed. lib. bdg. 32.50 (ISBN 0-8414-2916-2). Folcroft.

Ashton, Heather & Stepney, Rod. Smoking: Psychology & Pharmacology. LC 81-18829. 250p. 1982. (Pub. by Tavistock); pap. 8.95 (ISBN 0-422-77710-2, NO. 3836). Methuen Inc.

Ashton, Helen. I Had a Sister. LC 74-13304. 1974. Repr. of 1937 ed. lib. bdg. 22.50 (ISBN 0-8414-2989-8). Folcroft.

--Parson Austen's Daughter. 352p. 1982. Repr. lib. bdg. 40.00 (ISBN 0-89987-034-1). Darby Bks.

--Parson Austen's Daughter. 337p. lib. bdg. 30.00 (ISBN 0-8495-0155-5). Arden Lib.

Ashton, Horace, jt. auth. see Gassette, Grace.

Ashton, J. The Devil in Britain & America. 75.00 (ISBN 0-87968-450-X). Gordon Pr.

--Humor, Wit & Satire of the Seventeenth Century. 59.95 (ISBN 0-8490-0377-6). Gordon Pr.

--Modern Street Ballads. 59.95 (ISBN 0-8490-0653-8). Gordon Pr.

Ashton, Jean. Harriet Beecher Stowe: A Reference Guide. 1977. lib. bdg. 22.00 (ISBN 0-8161-7833-X, Hall Reference). G K Hall.

Ashton, John. Adventures & Discourses of Captain John Smith. LC 76-78108. (Illus.). 1969. Repr. of 1883 ed. 35.00x (ISBN 0-8103-3565-4). Gale.

--Century of Ballads. LC 67-23925. 1968. Repr. of 1887 ed. 40.00x (ISBN 0-8103-3406-2). Gale.

--Curious Creatures in Zoology. LC 68-57297. 1968. Repr. of 1890 ed. 45.00x (ISBN 0-8103-3525-5). Gale.

--The Dawn of the Nineteenth Century in England: A Social Sketch of the Times. (Victorian Age Ser.). 1936. Repr. 20.00 (ISBN 0-8482-7266-8). Norwood Edns.

--Dawn of the Nineteenth Century in England. LC 67-23941. (Social History Reference Ser.). 1968. Repr. of 1886 ed. 34.00x (ISBN 0-8103-3247-7). Gale.

--The Devil in Britain & America. LC 80-19692. 363p. 1980. Repr. of 1972 ed. lib. bdg. 15.95x (ISBN 0-89370-608-6). Borgo Pr.

--Eighteenth Century Waifs. facsimile ed. LC 71-38741. (Essay Index Reprint Ser). Repr. of 1887 ed. 23.50 (ISBN 0-8369-2634-X). Ayer Co Pubs.

--Eighteenth Century Waifs. LC 68-58971. 1968. Repr. of 1887 ed. 40.00x (ISBN 0-8103-3517-4). Gale.

--English Caricature & Satire on Napoleon 1st. LC 68-25953. (Illus.). 1968. Repr. of 1888 ed. 27.50 (ISBN 0-405-08222-3, Pub. by Blom). Ayer Co Pubs.

--English Caricature & Satire on Napoleon 1st. LC 67-24349. (Social History Reference Ser.). 1968. Repr. of 1888 ed. 40.00x (ISBN 0-8103-3248-5). Gale.

--Fleet: Its River, Prison, & Marriages. LC 68-21753. 1969. Repr. of 1888 ed. 43.00x (ISBN 0-8103-3414-3). Gale.

--Gossip in the First Decade of Victoria's Reign. LC 67-23942. 1968. Repr. of 1903 ed. 30.00x (ISBN 0-8103-3249-3). Gale.

--History of English Lotteries. LC 67-23945. (Illus.). 1969. Repr. of 1893 ed. 40.00x (ISBN 0-8103-3250-7). Gale.

--History of Gambling in England. 1969. Repr. of 1899 ed. 15.00 (ISBN 0-8337-0099-5). B Franklin.

--History of Gambling in England. LC 68-21520. 1968. Repr. of 1899 ed. 30.00x (ISBN 0-8103-3501-8). Gale.

--History of Gambling in England. LC 69-14910. (Criminology, Law Enforcement, & Social Problems Ser.: No. 73). 1969. Repr. of 1898 ed. 10.00x (ISBN 0-87585-073-1). Patterson Smith.

--Humor, Wit & Satire of the Seventeenth Century. 12.00 (ISBN 0-8446-1557-9). Peter Smith.

--Humour, Wit & Satire of the Seventeenth Century. LC 72-114821. (Research & Source Works Ser: No. 431). 1970. Repr. of 1883 ed. text ed. 14.00 (ISBN 0-8337-0100-2). B Franklin.

--Humour, Wit & Satire of the Seventeenth Century. LC 67-24350. (Social History Reference Ser.). 1968. Repr. of 1883 ed. 30.00x (ISBN 0-8103-3251-5). Gale.

--Humour, Wit & Satire of the Seventeenth Century. 454p. 1983. Repr. of 1883 ed. lib. bdg. 50.00 (ISBN 0-8495-0233-0). Arden Lib.

--Modern Street Ballads. LC 67-23926. (Illus.). 1968. Repr. of 1888 ed. 34.00x (ISBN 0-8103-3407-0). Gale.

--Modern Street Ballads. 1973. Repr. of 1888 ed. 10.75 (ISBN 0-8274-1303-3). R West.

--Old Times. LC 67-23944. (Illus.). 1969. Repr. of 1885 ed. 35.00x (ISBN 0-8103-3252-3). Gale.

--Righte Merrie Christmasse. LC 68-56543. (Illus.). 1968. Repr. of 1894 ed. 15.00 (ISBN 0-405-08225-8, Pub. by Blom). Ayer Co Pubs.

--Romances of Chivalry. 1978. Repr. of 1887 ed. lib. bdg. 65.00 (ISBN 0-8482-0122-1). Norwood Edns.

--Romances of Chivalry Told & Illustrated in Facsimile. LC 78-63486. Repr. of 1887 ed. 33.50 (ISBN 0-404-17135-4). AMS Pr.

--Social England under the Regency. LC 67-23940. 1968. Repr. of 1899 ed. 30.00x (ISBN 0-8103-3253-1). Gale.

--Social Life in the Reign of Queen Anne. (Works of John Ashton Ser.). xix, 474p. Date not set. Repr. 59.00 (ISBN 0-932051-24-3). Am Repr Serv.

--Varia. LC 68-9573. (Illus.). 1968. Repr. of 1894 ed. 35.00x (ISBN 0-8103-3502-6). Gale.

--When William Fourth Was King. LC 67-23943. (Social History Reference Ser.). 1968. Repr. of 1896 ed. 35.00x (ISBN 0-8103-3255-8). Gale.

Ashton, John, jt. auth. see Mew, James.

Ashton, John, ed. Chap-Books of the Eighteenth Century. LC 68-25953. (Illus.). 1882. 17.00 (ISBN 0-405-08221-5, Pub. by Blom). Ayer Co Pubs.

--Chapbooks of the Eighteenth Century. LC 70-11202. Repr. of 1882 ed. lib. bdg. 37.50x (ISBN 0-678-08011-9). Kelley.

--Modern Street Ballads. LC 68-58949. (Illus.). 1968. Repr. of 1888 ed. 20.00 (ISBN 0-405-08223-1, Pub. by Blom). Ayer Co Pubs.

--Real Sailor-Songs. LC 78-160612. (Illus.). Repr. of 1891 ed. 27.50 (ISBN 0-405-08224-X, Pub. by Blom). Ayer Co Pubs.

Ashton, John R. Everyday Psychiatry. 136p. 1980. 40.00x (ISBN 0-906141-12-5, Pub. by MTP Pr). State Mutual Bk.

Ashton, John W., ed. Types of English Drama. Repr. of 1940 ed. 79.00x (ISBN 0-403-07209-3). Somerset Pub.

Ashton, Leila. Checks from God. (My Church Teaches Ser.). 32p. (ps-1). 1981. pap. 1.95 (ISBN 0-8127-0314-6). Review & Herald.

Ashton, Leila M. It's Sabbath. (My Church Teaches Ser.). (Illus.). 1978. pap. 1.95 (ISBN 0-8127-0177-1). Review & Herald.

--My "Feel Good" Secrets. (My Church Teaches Ser.). (Illus.). 1978. pap. 1.50 (ISBN 0-8127-0178-X). Review & Herald.

--Today Is Friday. (My Church Teaches Ser.). (Illus.). (ps-1). 1978. pap. 1.954 (ISBN 0-8127-0176-3). Review & Herald.

Ashton, M. & Christie, B. Yakshagana: A Dance Drama of India. (Illus.). 136p. 1977. text ed. 36.00x (ISBN 0-391-03298-4, Pub. by Abhinav India). Humanities.

Ashton, M. L. Mind at Ease. 1961. pap. 2.95 (ISBN 0-87508-902-X). Chr Lit.

Ashton, Martha B. Yakshagana: A Dance Drama of India. 1977. 35.00x (ISBN 0-88386-972-1). South Asia Bks.

Ashton, Marvin J. What Is Your Destination? LC 78-14982. 1978. 7.95 (ISBN 0-87747-719-1). Deseret Bk.

--Ye Are My Friends. 151p. 1982. 6.95 (ISBN 0-87747-934-8). Deseret Bk.

Ashton, Mollie. Debt of Honor. (Harlequin Category Romances Ser.). 224p. 1983. pap. 2.25 (ISBN 0-373-31001-3). Harlequin Bks.

--The Noble Impostor. (Regency Romance Ser.). 224p. 1984. pap. 2.25 (ISBN 0-451-12915-6, Sig). NAL.

Ashton, P. S. Ecological Studies in the Mixed Dipterocarp Forests of Brunei State. 1964. 45.00x (ISBN 0-686-45497-9, Pub. by For Lib Comm England). State Mutual Bk.

Ashton, Patricia M. E., et al. Teacher Education in the Classroom: Initial & In-Service. 144p. 1983. 21.50 (ISBN 0-7099-1248-X, Pub. by Croom Helm Ltd). Longwood Pub Group.

Ashton, Patricia S., jt. auth. see Ashton, Ray E., Jr.

Ashton, Peter M. & Underwood, Richard C., eds. Non-Point Sources of Water Pollution: Proceedings of Southeastern Regional Conference Conducted on May 1, 1975, Blacksburg, Va. pap. 79.50 (ISBN 0-317-10937-5, 2005128). Bks Demand UMI.

Ashton, R. The City & the Court: Sixteen Hundred Three to Sixteen Forty-Three. LC 78-67296. 1979. 39.50 (ISBN 0-521-22419-5). Cambridge U Pr.

Ashton, R. K., ed. UK Financial Accounting Standards: A Descriptive & Analytical Approach. 208p. 1983. pap. 19.95 (ISBN 0-85941-202-4). Bradford Mtn Bk.

Ashton, Ray E., Jr. & Ashton, Patricia S. Handbook of Reptiles & Amphibians of Florida: Lizards, Turtles & Crocodilians, Part 2. LC 81-51066. (Illus.). 192p. 1985. pap. 16.95 (ISBN 0-89317-036-4). Windward Pub.

--Handbook of Reptiles & Amphibians of Florida: The Snakes, Vol. 1. LC 81-51066. (Handbook of Reptiles & Amphibians of Florida Ser.). (Illus.). 176p. (Orig.). 1981. pap. 12.95 (ISBN 0-89317-033-X). Windward Pub.

Ashton, Raymond K. U. K. Financial Accounting Standards: A Descriptive & Analytical Approach. 234p. 1983. 25.00 (ISBN 0-85941-201-6); pap. 16.50 (ISBN 0-85941-202-4). Woodhead Faulkner.

Ashton, Rick J., et al. Genealogy Beginner's Manual. 28p. 1977. pap. 1.50 (ISBN 0-911028-14-5). Newberry.

Ashton, Robert. The English Civil War: Conservatism & Revolution, 1603-1649. 464p. 1979. pap. avail. (ISBN 0-393-01207-7); pap. text ed. 7.95x (ISBN 0-393-95202-9). Norton.

--Reformation & Reformation: 1558-1660. (Paladin History of England Ser.). 503p. 1985. pap. 9.95 (ISBN 0-586-08449-5, Pub. by Granada England). Academy Chi Pubs.

--Reformation & Revolution, 1558-1660. (The Paladin History of England Ser.). 1984. 39.95x (ISBN 0-19-520444-1). Oxford U Pr.
--Reformation & Revolution 1558-1660. 503p. pap. 9.95 (ISBN 0-586-08449-5). Academy Chi Pubs.
Ashton, Robert & Stuart, Jozefa. Images of American Indian Art. LC 77-78131. 1977. 11.95 (ISBN 0-8027-0577-4); pap. 6.95 (ISBN 0-8027-7116-5). Walker & Co.
Ashton, Robert H. Human Information Processing in Accounting, Vol. 17. (Studies in Accounting Research). 215p. 1982. 9.00 (ISBN 0-86539-038-X); members 6.00. Am Accounting.
Ashton, Robert H., ed. The Evolution of Behavioral Accounting Research: An Overview. LC 83-49435. (Accounting History & the Development of a Profession Ser.). 117p. 1984. lib. bdg. 20.00 (ISBN 0-8240-6302-3). Garland Pub.
--Some Early Contributions to the Study of Audit Judgment. LC 83-49436. (Accounting History & the Development of a Profession Ser.). 170p. 1984. lib. bdg. 20.00 (ISBN 0-8240-6303-1). Garland Pub.
Ashton, Rosemary. George Eliot. (Past Masters Ser.). 1983. 12.95x (ISBN 0-19-287627-9); pap. 3.95 (ISBN 0-19-287626-0). Oxford U Pr.
--The German Idea. LC 78-75254. 1980. 37.50 (ISBN 0-521-22560-4). Cambridge U Pr.
Ashton, S. R. British Policy Towards the Indian States, 1905-1939. 240p. 1981. 30.00x (ISBN 0-7007-0146-X, Pub. by Curzon England). State Mutual Bk.
Ashton, Sylvia, ed. see Able, James E.
Ashton, Sylvia, ed. see Baker, Robert H.
Ashton, Sylvia, ed. see Bassett, Steve.
Ashton, Sylvia, ed. see Bierman, Elenore C.
Ashton, Sylvia, ed. see Bolotoff, George P.
Ashton, Sylvia, ed. see Brosten, Olga.
Ashton, Sylvia, ed. see Carter, Frank B., Jr.
Ashton, Sylvia, ed. see Cassity, Joan.
Ashton, Sylvia, ed. see Cole, Bruce.
Ashton, Sylvia, ed. see Curzon, Daniel.
Ashton, Sylvia, ed. see Donnelly, Hugh.
Ashton, Sylvia, ed. see Duc, Robert.
Ashton, Sylvia, ed. see Duncan, John D., Jr.
Ashton, Sylvia, ed. see Farrar, Kenneth G.
Ashton, Sylvia, ed. see Fineberg, Robert G.
Ashton, Sylvia, ed. see Fischer, Max.
Ashton, Sylvia, ed. see Fucci, Marie.
Ashton, Sylvia, ed. see Gay, Kathlyn & Barnes, Ben E.
Ashton, Sylvia, ed. see Gestwicki, Ronald.
Ashton, Sylvia, ed. see Goodman, Marguerite.
Ashton, Sylvia, ed. see Gray, Juanita & De Felice, Louise.
Ashton, Sylvia, ed. see Healy, John.
Ashton, Sylvia, ed. see Jacobson, James R.
Ashton, Sylvia, ed. see Jessep, Al.
Ashton, Sylvia, ed. see Keith, Jeff.
Ashton, Sylvia, ed. see King, Kris.
Ashton, Sylvia, ed. see Kizilos, Tolly.
Ashton, Sylvia, ed. see Miller, Alan C., et al.
Ashton, Sylvia, ed. see Montgomery, Elizabeth.
Ashton, Sylvia, ed. see Park, Evelyn.
Ashton, Sylvia, ed. see Peskin, Dean B.
Ashton, Sylvia, ed. see Peterson, Knut D.
Ashton, Sylvia, ed. see Plunkett, Marion.
Ashton, Sylvia, ed. see Ruthel.
Ashton, Sylvia, ed. see Samuels, Carl, et al.
Ashton, Sylvia, ed. see Zerkle, Keith.
Ashton-Tate, ed. see Expert Systems Staff.
Ashton-Tate, ed. see Forefront Corporation Staff.
Ashton, Thomas L., ed. Byron's Hebrew Melodies. LC 70-165921. 250p. 1971. 16.95x (ISBN 0-292-70141-1). U of Tex Pr.
--Heath Ten Short Novels. 704p. 1978. pap. text ed. 8.95 (ISBN 0-669-01029-4). Heath.
--Heath's Ten Short Novels. 1978. pap. text ed. 8.95x (ISBN 0-669-01029-4). Heath.
Ashton, Thomas S. Economic & Social Investigations in Manchester, 1833-1933. LC 77-3570. Repr. of 1934 ed. 25.00x (ISBN 0-678-08067-4). Kelley.
--An Economic History of England: The Eighteenth Century. 270p. 1972. pap. 13.95x (ISBN 0-416-57360-6, NO.2065). Methuen Inc.
--Industrial Revolution: 1760-1830. 1948. pap. 4.95x (ISBN 0-19-500252-0). Oxford U Pr.
--Iron & Steel in the Industrial Revolution. LC 74-555. Repr. of 1924 ed. 29.50x (ISBN 0-678-06751-1). Kelley.
Ashton, Violet. Love by Fire. 256p. (Orig.). 1980. pap. 2.25 (ISBN 0-449-14360-0, GM). Fawcett.
Ashton, W. D. The Logit Transformation. 1972. pap. 9.75 (ISBN 0-02-840570-6). Hafner.
Ashton, Warren T. Hatchie, the Guardian Slave. facsimile ed. LC 72-539. (Black Heritage Library Collection). Repr. of 1852 ed. 20.50 (ISBN 0-8369-8976-7). Ayer Co Pubs.
Ashton, Winifred. Legend. LC 78-17053. 1978. Repr. of 1919 ed. lib. bdg. 22.50x (ISBN 0-313-20572-8, ASLE). Greenwood.
--Regiment of Women. LC 78-17055. 1979. Repr. of 1966 ed. lib. bdg. 24.75x (ISBN 0-313-20582-5, ASRW). Greenwood.
Ashton, Winifred see Dane, Clemence, pseud.
Ashton, Winifred see Dane, Clemens, pseud.
Ashton-Gwatkin, Frank T., jt. ed. see Toynbee, Arnold J.
Ashton-Warner, Sylvia. I Passed This Way. LC 79-2133. (Illus.). 1979. 15.95 (ISBN 0-394-42612-6). Knopf.
Ashtor, E. A Social & Economic History of the Near East in the Middle Ages. LC 74-29800. (Near Eastern Center Series, UCLA). 1976. 45.00x (ISBN 0-520-02962-3). U of Cal Pr.
Ashtor, Eliyahu. The Jews of Moslem Spain, Vol. III. Klein, Aaron & Klein, Jenny M., trs. from Hebrew. 380p. 1985. 19.95 (ISBN 0-8276-0237-5). Jewish Pubns.
--The Jews of Moslem Spain, Vol. 1. Machlowitz Klein, Aaron, tr. from Heb. LC 73-14081. (Illus.). 469p. 1974. 12.00 (ISBN 0-8276-0017-8, 352). Jewish Pubns.
--The Jews of Moslem Spain, Vol. 2. 381p. 1978. 12.00 (ISBN 0-8276-0100-X, 411). Jewish Pubns.
--Levant Trade in the Later Middle Ages. LC 83-42545. 640p. 1984. 60.00x (ISBN 0-691-05386-3). Princeton U Pr.
--The Medieval Near East: Social & Economic History. 362p. 1978. 60.00x (ISBN 0-86078-025-2, Pub. by Variorum). State Mutual Bk.
Ashurst, Henry F. A Many-Colored Toga: The Diary of Henry Fountain Ashurst. Sparks, George, ed. LC 62-10625. (Illus.). 416p. 1962. 7.50 (ISBN 0-8165-0056-8). U of Ariz Pr.
Ashvin, ed. Himalaya: Encounters with Eternity. LC 84-51199. (Illus.). 1985. 35.00 (ISBN 0-500-24119-8). Thames Hudson.
Ashwal, Stephen, jt. auth. see Swaiman, Kenneth.
Ashwal, Stephen, jt. auth. see Swaiman, Kenneth F.
Ashwell, D. G., ed. see Conference on Finite Elements Applied to Thin Shells & Curved Members (1974: University College, Cardiff, Wales).
Ashwin, Clive. Drawing & Education in German-Speaking Europe, 1800-1900. Kuspit, Donald, ed. LC 81-14705. (Studies in the Fine Arts: Art Theory: No. 7). 284p. 1981. 49.95 (ISBN 0-8357-1239-7). UMI Res Pr.
--Encyclopedia of Drawing. (Illus.). 264p. 1983. 22.50 (ISBN 0-7134-0133-8, Pub by Batsford England). North Light Pub.
--History of Graphic Design & Communications: A Sourcebook. (Pembridge History of Design Ser.). 290p. 1983. 29.50 (ISBN 0-86206-005-2, Pub. by Pembridge Pr UK). Shoe String.
Ashwin, E. A., tr. see Guazzo, Francesco M.
Ashwood, M. J. & Farrant, Smith J. Low Temperature Preservation in Medicine & Biology. 336p. 1980. text ed. 42.00 (ISBN 0-8391-1492-3). Univ Park.
Ashworth, Andrew. Sentencing & Penal Policy. (Law in Context Ser.). xx, 500p. 1983. 30.00x (ISBN 0-297-78236-3, Pub. by Weidenfeld & Nicholson England). Rothman.
Ashworth, B. & Saunders, M. Management of Neurological Disorders. 2nd ed. 336p. 1985. pap. text ed. 24.95 (ISBN 0-407-00310-X). Butterworth.
Ashworth, Ben. The Last Days of Steam in Gloucestershire. 140p. 1983. text ed. 17.25x (ISBN 0-86299-057-2, Pub. by Alan Sutton England). Humanities.
Ashworth, Bryan & Isherwood, Ian. Clinical Neuro-Ophthalmology. 2nd. ed. (Illus.). 360p. 1981. text ed. 72.50 (ISBN 0-632-00593-9, B 0371-4). Mosby.
Ashworth, David R. & Smith, David R., eds. Thermal Conductivity; No. 18: Proceedings of an International Conference Held in Rapid City, South Dakota, October 3-5, 1983. 764p. 1985. 125.00x (ISBN 0-306-41918-1, Plenum Pr). Plenum Pub.
Ashworth, E. J. Language & Logic in the Post Medieval Period. LC 74-76478. (Synthese Historical Library: No. 12). 350p. 1974. lib. bdg. 53.00 (ISBN 90-277-0464-3, Pub. by Junk Pubs Netherlands). Kluwer Academic.
Ashworth, E. M. Toronto Hydro Recollections. (Illus.). pap. 61.50 (ISBN 0-317-09137-9, 2014116). Bks Demand UMI.
Ashworth, Georgina. World Minorities in the Eighties. 190p. 29.00x (ISBN 0-905898-11-7, Pub. by Quartermaine England). State Mutual Bk.
Ashworth, Georgina & Bonnerjea, Lucy. The Invisible Decade: U. K. Women in the United Nations Decade 1976-1985. 220p. (Orig.). 1985. pap. text ed. 32.95 (ISBN 0-566-00895-5). Gower Pub Co.
Ashworth, Georgina, ed. World Minorities, Vol. 1. 189p. 1981. 49.00x (ISBN 0-905898-00-1, Pub. by Quartermaine England). State Mutual Bk.
--World Minorities, Vol. 2. 172p. 1981. 49.00x (ISBN 0-905898-01-X, Pub. by Quartermaine England). State Mutual Bk.
Ashworth, Gregory, jt. auth. see Riley, R. C.
Ashworth, H., jt. auth. see Shacklette, L.
Ashworth, Harry A., jt. ed. see Ewing, Galen.
Ashworth, J. H. Catalogue of the Chaetopoda in the British Museum (Natural History) A. Polychaeta: Part I Arenicolidae. (Illus.). xii, 175p. 1912. 17.50x (ISBN 0-565-00102-7, Pub. by British Mus Nat Hist England). Sabbot-Natural Hist Bks.
Ashworth, J. M. Cell Differentiation. 1973. pap. 6.50x (ISBN 0-412-11760-6, NO.6013, Pub. by Chapman & Hall). Methuen Inc.
Ashworth, J. R., ed. Migmatites. 288p. 1985. text ed. 49.95 (ISBN 0-412-00841-6, 9352, Pub. by Chapman & Hall England). Methuen Inc.
Ashworth, J. Stuart, ed. Product Liability Casebook. 1984. 60.00 (ISBN 1-85044-015-8). Lloyds London Pr.
Ashworth, John. Agrarians & Aristocrats. (Royal Historical Society, Studies in History: No. 37). 327p. 1983. text ed. 42.50x (ISBN 0-391-02926-6, Pub. by Swiftbks England). Humanities.
Ashworth, John H. The Helper & American Trade Unions. LC 78-63953. (Johns Hopkins University. Studies in the Social Sciences, Thirty-Third Ser. 1915: 3). Repr. of 1915 ed. 24.50 (ISBN 0-404-61201-6). AMS Pr.
Ashworth, Kenneth H. American Higher Education in Decline. LC 78-21780. 117p. 1979. 9.95 (ISBN 0-89096-074-7). Tex A&M Univ Pr.
Ashworth, M. J. Feedback Design of Systems with Significant Uncertainty. LC 82-1929. 246p. 1982. 44.95x (ISBN 0-471-10213-X, Pub. by Research Studies Pr). Wiley.
Ashworth, M. R. Analytical Methods for Glycerol. 1979. 61.00 (ISBN 0-12-065050-9). Acad Pr.
--The Determination of Sulphur-Containing Groups. (The Analysis of Organic Materials & International Series of Monographs, No. 2). Vol. 1 1973. 45.00 (ISBN 0-12-065001-0); Vol. 2 1976. 55.00 (ISBN 0-12-065002-9); Vol. 3 1977. 55.00 (ISBN 0-12-065003-7). Acad Pr.
Ashworth, M. R., tr. see Fischer, Helmut A. & Werner, Gottfried.
Ashworth, M. R., tr. see Stahl, E.
Ashworth, Mae H. Candles in the Dark. LC 83-70253. 1983. 6.50 (ISBN 0-8054-5256-7). Broadman.
--Six Times True. 48p. (Orig.). (gr. 7-9). 1973. pap. 1.95 (ISBN 0-377-03601-3). Friend Pr.
Ashworth, Mary & Wakefield, Patricia. Teaching the Non-English-Speaking Child: Grades K-2. (Language in Education Ser.: No. 45). 60p. (Orig.). 1982. pap. 3.95x (ISBN 0-15-599002-0). Ctr Appl Ling.
Ashworth, Mary W., jt. auth. see Carroll, John A.
Ashworth, Mary W. see Freeman, Douglas S.
Ashworth, P. D. Social Interaction & Consciousness. LC 78-27252. 227p. 1979. 53.95x (ISBN 0-471-27567-0, Pub. by Wiley-Interscience). Wiley.
Ashworth, Philip A., tr. see Gneist, Rudolph.
Ashworth, V., ed. Corrosion-Industrial Problems, Treatment & Control Techniques: Proceedings of the 1st Arabian Conference on Corrosion, Kuwait, 1984. (Kuwait Foundation for the Advancement of Science Ser.: Vol. 2). (Illus.). 450p. 1986. 75.00 (ISBN 0-08-032576-9, Pub. by Aberdeen Scotland). Pergamon.
Ashworth, V. & Grant, W. A., eds. Ion Implantation into Metals: Proceedings of the 3rd International Conference on Modification of Surface Properties of Metals by Ion Implantation, Held UMIST, Manchester, UK, June 23-26, 1981. LC 82-5293. 383p. 1982. 77.00 (ISBN 0-08-027625-3). Pergamon.
Ashworth, Wilfred. Special Librarianship. (Outlines of Modern Librarianship Ser.). 120p. 1979. 12.00 (ISBN 0-85157-277-4, Pub. by Bingley England). Shoe String.
Ashy, Peter J. Arabic Language for Self-Study. 2nd ed. LC 76-17407. 212p. 1976. 20.00x (ISBN 0-686-17436-4). Furman U Bkstr.
Asia Pacific Centre. Survey Research Group Ltd. Malaysia. cancelled (ISBN 0-87196-585-2). Singapore (ISBN 0-87196-584-4). Thailand (ISBN 0-87196-586-0). Set (ISBN 0-87196-596-8). Facts on File.
Asian Coalition of Human Rights Organizations (ACHRO) Staff, ed. Human Rights Activism in Asia: Some Perspectives, Problems & Approaches. 79p. (Orig.). 1984. pap. 8.00x (ISBN 0-936876-19-0). Learn Res Intl Stud.
Asian Cultural Center for UNESCO. Folk Tales from Asia for Children Everywhere, Bk. 2. LC 74-82605. (Illus.). (gr. 3-6). 1975. 6.50 (ISBN 0-8348-1033-6). Weatherhill.
--Folk Tales from Asia for Children Everywhere, Bk. 5. LC 74-82605. (Illus.). (gr. 3-6). 1977. 6.50 (ISBN 0-8348-1036-0). Weatherhill.
--Folk Tales from Asia for Children Everywhere, Bk. 6. LC 74-82605. (Illus.). 1978. 6.50 (ISBN 0-8348-1037-9). Weatherhill.
--Folktales from Asia for Children Everywhere, Bk. 1. LC 74-82605. (Illus.). 56p. (gr. 1-4). 1975. 6.50 (ISBN 0-8348-1032-8). Weatherhill.
--Stories from Asia Today: A Collection for Young Readers, Bk 2. LC 74-82605. 192p. 1980. pap. 8.95 (ISBN 0-8348-1040-9). Weatherhill.
Asian Cultural Center for UNESCO, ed. Folk Tales from Asia for Children Everywhere, Bk. 3. LC 74-82605. (Illus.). 64p. (gr. 3-6). 1976. 6.50 (ISBN 0-8348-1034-4). Weatherhill.
--Folk Tales from Asia for Children Everywhere, Bk. 4. LC 74-82605. (gr. 2-5). 1976. 6.50 (ISBN 0-8348-1035-2). Weatherhill.
Asian Cultural Centre for Unesco, compiled by. More Festivals in Asia. LC 75-34740. (Illus.). 68p. (gr. 9-12). 1975. 8.25 (ISBN 0-87011-273-2). Kodansha.
Asian Development Bank. Asian Agricultural Survey. 795p. 1969. 50.00x (ISBN 0-295-97866-X); pap. 25.00x (ISBN 0-295-78585-3). U of Wash Pr.
Asian Development Bank Staff. Asian Energy Problems. LC 81-84610. 304p. 1982. 39.95x (ISBN 0-03-061566-6). Praeger.
Asian Development Bank Staff, ed. Key Indicators of Developing Members of the Asian Development Bank. 368p. Date not set. text ed. 60.00x (ISBN 0-8147-1776-4). NYU Pr.
Asian-Pacific Congress of Cardiology - 4th. Cardiology: Current Topics & Progress. Eliakim, M. & Neufeld, Henry M., eds. 1970. 61.00 (ISBN 0-12-237802-4). Acad Pr.
Asian-Pacific Congress Of Cardiology. Proceedings, Pt. 1. Eliakim, M., ed. 1970. 80.50 (ISBN 0-12-237801-6). Acad Pr.
Asian Programme of Educational Innovation for Development. Curriculum Development: Linking Science Education to Life: Report of a Sub-regional Workshop on Designing & Development Innovative Science Curriculum & Instructional Materials, Bangkok, December 8-20, 1980. 74p. 1981. pap. 7.00 (ISBN 0-686-81860-1, UB104, UB). Unipub.
--Distance Learning for Teacher Education: Report of a Technical Working Group Meeting, Islamabad, Pakistan, November 4-16, 1981. Incl. Vol. 1. Current Status, Programmes, Practices. 29p; Vol. 2. Guidelines on Development of Materials. 203p; Vol. 3. Exemplar Materials. 1981. Set. pap. 20.75 (ISBN 0-686-81859-8, UB102, UB). Unipub.
--Social Change & New Profiles of Educational Personnel: National Studies: India, Nepal, Philippines, Republic of Korea. 44p. 1981. pap. 5.00 (ISBN 0-686-81854-7, UB100, UB). Unipub.
--Vocational & Technical Education - Development for Curricula, Instructional Materials, Physical Facilities and Teacher Training, with Focus on Electrical & Electronic Subjects: Report of a Technical Working Groups Meeting, Adelaide, Australia, October 6-18, 1980. 97p. 1981. pap. 5.25 (ISBN 0-686-81850-4, UB110, UNESCO). Unipub.
Asian Regional Conference, 7th, Teheran, 1971. Agenda for Asia: The Social Perplexities of the Second Development Decade. 48p. 1971. 2.30 (ISBN 92-2-100103-2). Intl Labour Office.
Asian Regional Team for Employment Promotion, Bangkok. Employment Expansion Through Local Resource Mobilisation: Papers & Poceedings of a Workshop, Comilla, Bangladesh, 1-3 July 1981. iv, 45p. 1981. 5.00 (ISBN 92-2-102696-5). Intl Labour Office.
Asiatic Exclusion League, 1907-1913. Proceedings. Grob, Gerald, ed. LC 76-46064. (Anti-Movements in America Ser). 1977. Repr. of 1907 ed. lib. bdg. 59.50x (ISBN 0-405-09939-8). Ayer Co Pubs.
Asiatic Research Center, Korea University CSIS. Northeast Asia: Prosperity & Vulnerability, Vol. I. LC 79-65209. (Significant Issues Ser.: No. 2). 89p. 1979. 5.95 (ISBN 0-89206-008-5). CSI Studies.
Asiedu, E. S., ed. Public Administration in English-Speaking West Africa: An Annotated Bibliography. 1977. lib. bdg. 57.50 (ISBN 0-8161-7811-9, Hall Reference). G K Hall.
Asiegbu, J. U. Nigeria & Its British Invaders. LC 83-62253. (Illus.). 409p. 1984. 27.95 (ISBN 0-88357-101-3); pap. 12.95 (ISBN 0-88357-102-1). NOK Pubs.
Asiegbu, Johnson U. Slavery & the Politics of Liberation, 1787-1861: A Study of Liberated African Emigration & British Anti-Slavery Policy. LC 70-94838. 224p. 1970. text ed. 35.00x (ISBN 0-8419-0027-2, Africana). Holmes & Meier.
Asifi, Allama M. Al-Salat. 1983. pap. 4.00 (ISBN 0-941724-10-7). Islamic Seminary.
--Children's Guide to Islam. 112p. 1983. pap. 5.00 (ISBN 0-941724-11-5). Islamic Seminary.
Asihene, E. V. Introduction to Traditional Art of Western Africa. LC 72-195063. (Illus.). pap. 24.00 (ISBN 0-317-10526-4, 2019380). Bks Demand UMI.
Asihene, Emmanuel V. Understanding the Traditional Art of Ghana. (Illus.). 100p. 1978. 18.50 (ISBN 0-8386-2130-9). Fairleigh Dickinson.
Asimakopulos, A. An Introduction to Economic Theory: Microeconomics. (Illus.). 1978. text ed. 18.95x (ISBN 0-19-540281-2). Oxford U Pr.
Asimor, Isaac. The Adventures of Science Fiction, Vol. 3. 16.95 (ISBN 0-88411-587-9, Pub. by Aeonian Pr). Amereon Ltd.
Asimor, Issac. Marvels of Science Fiction, Vol. 2. 16.95 (ISBN 0-88411-586-0, Pub. by Aeonian Pr). Amereon Ltd.
Asimov & Greenberg. Isaac Asimov Presents the Great Science Fiction Stories, No. 13. 1985. pap. 3.50 (ISBN 0-88677-058-0). DAW Bks.
Asimov, et al. Spells. (Issac Asimov's Ser.: No. 4). 352p. 1985. pap. 3.95 (ISBN 0-451-13578-4, Sig). NAL.
Asimov, Isaac. Alpha Centauri, the Nearest Star. LC 76-29037. (Illus.). 224p. (gr. 7 up). 1976. PLB 12.88 (ISBN 0-688-51779-X). Lothrop.
--Asimov on Astronomy. LC 73-80946. (Illus.). 288p. 1975. pap. 5.50 (ISBN 0-385-06881-6, Anch). Doubleday.
--Asimov on Chemistry. LC 73-15322. (Illus.). 288p. 1974. 8.95 (ISBN 0-385-04100-4); (Anch). Doubleday.
--Asimov on Numbers. 1983. pap. 3.95 (ISBN 0-671-49404-X). PB.
--Asimov on Physics. 1978. pap. 3.95 (ISBN 0-380-41848-7, 63602-6, Discus). Avon.
--Asimov on Science Fiction. 320p. 1982. pap. 2.95 (ISBN 0-380-58511-1, 58511-1, Discus). Avon.

--Asimov on Science Fiction. LC 80-2246. 288p. 1981. 14.95 (ISBN 0-385-17443-8). Doubleday.

--Asimov's Annotated Paradise Lost. LC 73-81424. 720p. 1974. 16.95 (ISBN 0-385-07992-3). Doubleday.

--Asimov's Biographical Encyclopedia of Science & Technology. 2nd. rev. ed. LC 81-47861. (Illus.). 984p. 1982. 29.95 (ISBN 0-385-17771-2). Doubleday.

--Asimov's Guide to Halley's Comet. (Illus.). 61p. 1985. 12.95 (ISBN 0-8027-0836-6); pap. cancelled (ISBN 0-8027-7281-1). Walker & Co.

--Asimov's Guide to Halley's Comet. 1985. pap. 5.95 (ISBN 0-440-50434-1, Dell Trade Pbks). Dell.

--Asimov's Guide to the Bible: The New Testament. 640p. 1971. pap. 8.95 (ISBN 0-380-01031-3, 60255-5). Avon.

--Asimov's Guide to the Bible: The Old Testament. 720p. 1971. pap. 8.95 (ISBN 0-380-01032-1, 65748-1). Avon.

--Asimov's Mysteries. LC 68-10573. (Science Fiction Ser.). 1968. 6.95 (ISBN 0-385-09063-3). Doubleday.

--Asimov's Mysteries. 1979. pap. 1.95 (ISBN 0-449-24011-8, Crest). Fawcett.

--Asimov's New Guide to Science. rev. ed. LC 83-46093. (Illus.). 940p. 1984. 29.95 (ISBN 0-465-00473-3). Basic.

--Asimov's Sherlockian Limericks. LC 77-92791. 1978. 7.50 (ISBN 0-89296-039-6). Mysterious Pr.

--Banquets of the Black Widowers. LC 84-1592. 216p. 1984. 13.95 (ISBN 0-385-19541-9). Doubleday.

--Before the Golden Age. LC 73-10965. 1008p. 1974. 19.95 (ISBN 0-385-02419-3). Doubleday.

--Before the Golden Age, Vol. 1. 1978. pap. 1.95 (ISBN 0-449-22913-0, Crest). Fawcett.

--The Beginning & the End. 1983. pap. 3.50 (ISBN 0-671-47644-0). PB.

--The Best of Isaac Asimov. 320p. 1978. pap. 2.50 (ISBN 0-449-23653-6, Crest). Fawcett.

--The Bicentennial Man & Other Stories. LC 76-2749. 216p. 1976. 9.95 (ISBN 0-385-12198-9). Doubleday.

--The Bicentennial Man & Other Stories. 1978. pap. 2.25 (ISBN 0-449-24110-6, Crest). Fawcett.

--The Bicentennial Man: And Other Stories. 224p. 1985. pap. 2.95 (ISBN 0-345-32071-9, Del Rey). Ballantine.

--Bloodstream: River of Life. rev. ed. 221p. (Orig.). 1961. pap. 3.95 (ISBN 0-02-091150-5, Collier). Macmillan.

--Buy Jupiter & Other Stories. 1978. pap. 1.95 (ISBN 0-449-23828-8, Crest). Fawcett.

--Casebook of the Black Widowers. LC 79-7812. (Crime Club Ser.). (Illus.). 1980. 10.95 (ISBN 0-385-15704-5). Doubleday.

--Casebook of the Black Widowers. 256p. 1981. pap. 2.50 (ISBN 0-449-24384-2, Crest). Fawcett.

--The Caves of Steel. 1983. pap. 2.95 (ISBN 0-345-31389-5, Del Rey). Ballantine.

--Chemicals of Life. pap. 3.95 (ISBN 0-451-62418-1, MJ2037, Ment). NAL.

--A Choice of Catastrophes. 384p. 1981. pap. 6.95 (ISBN 0-449-90048-7, Columbine). Fawcett.

--Clock We Live On. rev. ed. LC 65-12072. (Illus.). (gr. 7 up). 1965. (AbS-J). Har-Row.

--The Collapsing Universe: The Story of Black Holes. LC 76-53639. (Illus.). 256p. 1977. 14.95 (ISBN 0-8027-0486-7). Walker & Co.

--The Complete Robot. LC 81-43134. 576p. 1982. 19.95 (ISBN 0-385-17724-0). Doubleday.

--Counting the Eons. LC 82-45068. 192p. 1983. 13.95 (ISBN 0-385-17976-6). Doubleday.

--Counting the Eons. 224p. 1984. pap. 3.95 (ISBN 0-380-67090-9, 67090, Discus). Avon.

--Currents of Space. 1983. pap. 2.95 (ISBN 0-345-31195-7, Del Rey). Ballantine.

--The Disappearing Man & Other Mysteries. 64p. (gr. 3-5). 1985. 9.95 (ISBN 0-8027-6578-5); reinforced 9.95 (ISBN 0-8027-6602-1). Walker & Co.

--Early Asimov, Bk. 1. 1978. pap. 2.25 (ISBN 0-449-23873-3, Crest). Fawcett.

--The Early Asimov, Bk. 2. 304p. 1978. pap. 2.25 (ISBN 0-449-23700-1, Crest). Fawcett.

--Earth Is Room Enough. 1979. pap. 2.50 (ISBN 0-449-24125-4, Crest). Fawcett.

--Earth: Our Crowded Spaceship. 1978. pap. 1.95 (ISBN 0-449-23172-0, Crest). Fawcett.

--The Edge of Tomorrow. 480p. 1985. 15.95 (Dist. by St. Martin). Tor Bks.

--Egyptians. 288p. (YA) (gr. 7 up). 1967. 11.95 (ISBN 0-395-06572-0). HM.

--Eight Stories from the Rest of the Robots. 192p. 1983. pap. 2.75 (ISBN 0-425-06119-1). Berkley Pub.

--Enciclopedia Biografica De Ciencia y Tecnologia. 2nd ed. 800p. (Espn.). 1974. 47.95 (ISBN 84-292-7004-3, S-50544). French & Eur.

--End of Eternity. 1978. pap. 2.25 (ISBN 0-449-23704-4, Crest). Fawcett.

--The End of Eternity. 192p. 1984. pap. 2.95 (ISBN 0-345-31832-3, Del Rey). Ballantine.

--Environments Out There. LC 67-16837. (Illus.). (gr. 5-10). 1967. 13.50i (ISBN 0-200-00059-4, B22680, AbS-J). Har-Row.

--The Exploding Suns: The Secrets of the Supernovas. LC 84-21077. (Truman Talley Bk.). (Illus.). 288p. 1985. 18.95 (ISBN 0-525-24323-2, 01840-550). Dutton.

--Extraterrestrial Civilizations. 1979. 10.00 (ISBN 0-517-53075-9). Crown.

--Extraterrestrial Civilizations. 1980. pap. 5.95 (ISBN 0-449-90020-7, Columbine). Fawcett.

--Eyes on the Universe: A History of the Telescope. LC 75-15830. 288p. 1975. 8.95 (ISBN 0-395-19427-X). HM.

--Fact & Fancy. (Illus.). 208p. 1972. pap. 1.25 (ISBN 0-380-01174-3, 10306). Avon.

--Fantastic Voyage. (YA) (gr. 7 up). pap. 2.95 (ISBN 0-553-24794-8). Bantam.

--Fantastic Voyage. 226p. (gr. 8 up). 1966. 11.95 (ISBN 0-395-07352-9). HM.

--Foundation. 1963. 10.95 (ISBN 0-385-05047-X). Doubleday.

--Foundation. 256p. 1984. pap. 2.95 (ISBN 0-345-30899-9, Del Rey). Ballantine.

--Foundation & Empire. 1963. 6.95 (ISBN 0-385-05045-3). Doubleday.

--Foundation & Empire. 256p. 1983. pap. 2.95 (ISBN 0-345-31799-8, Del Rey). Ballantine.

--Foundation Trilogy. 1974. pap. 7.95 (ISBN 0-380-00101-2, 54403-2). Avon.

--Foundation Trilogy. LC 82-19919. (Science Fiction Ser.). 684p. 1982. 19.95 (ISBN 0-385-18830-7). Doubleday.

--The Foundation Trilogy, 3 vols. 528p. 1983. pap. 8.95 (ISBN 0-345-31205-8). Ballantine.

--Foundation's Edge. LC 82-45450. 384p. 1982. 14.95 (ISBN 0-385-17725-9). Doubleday.

--Foundation's Edge. signed & numbered ed. 1982. leather spine 51.00x (ISBN 0-918372-10-0). Whispers.

--Foundation's Edge. 1983. pap. 3.95 (ISBN 0-345-30898-0, Del Rey). Ballantine.

--The Gods Themselves. 288p. 1978. pap. 2.50 (ISBN 0-449-23756-7, Crest). Fawcett.

--The Golden Door: The United States from 1865 to 1918. LC 77-21385. 288p. (gr. 7 up). 1977. 10.95 (ISBN 0-395-25798-0). HM.

--Great Ideas of Science. LC 70-82476. (Illus.). 144p. (gr. 7 up). 1969. 6.95 (ISBN 0-395-06580-1). HM.

--Greeks: A Great Adventure. (Illus.). 320p. (gr. 7 up). 1965. 13.95 (ISBN 0-395-06574-7). HM.

--The History of Physics. LC 83-6478. (Illus.). 720p. 1984. 29.95 (ISBN 0-8027-0751-3). Walker & Co.

--How Did We Find Out about Antarctica? (Illus.). 64p. 1981. pap. 1.95 (ISBN 0-380-53421-5, Camelot). Avon.

--How Did We Find Out about Antarctica? (How Did We Find Out Ser.). (Illus.). (gr. 5-8). 1979. 6.95 (ISBN 0-8027-6370-7); PLB 6.85 (ISBN 0-8027-6371-5). Walker & Co.

--How Did We Find Out about Atoms. LC 75-3910. (How Did We Find Out Ser.). 64p. (gr. 5-8). 1976. PLB 8.85 (ISBN 0-8027-6248-4). Walker & Co.

--How Did We Find Out about Atoms? 64p. (gr. 9-12). 1982. pap. 1.95 (ISBN 0-380-59576-1, 59576-1, Camelot). Avon.

--How Did We Find Out about Black Holes? LC 73-4320. (How Did We Find Out Ser.). (Illus.). (gr. 5 up). 1978. 8.95 (ISBN 0-8027-6336-7); PLB 9.85 (ISBN 0-8027-6337-5). Walker & Co.

--How Did We Find Out about Coal? LC 80-50448. (History of Science (How Did We Find Out About...?) Ser.). (Illus.). 64p. (gr. 5-8). 1980. 6.95 (ISBN 0-8027-6400-2); PLB 7.85 (ISBN 0-8027-6401-0). Walker & Co.

--How Did We Find Out about Comets? (Illus.). 64p. 1981. pap. 1.95 (ISBN 0-380-53454-1, 53454-1, Camelot). Avon.

--How Did We Find Out about Comets? LC 74-78115. (How Did We Find Out Ser.). (Illus.). 64p. (gr. 5-8). 1975. lib. bdg. 8.85 (ISBN 0-8027-6204-2). Walker & Co.

--How Did We Find Out about Computers? LC 83-40401. (How Did We Find Out about Ser.). (Illus.). 64p. 1984. lib. bdg. 8.85 (ISBN 0-8027-6533-5). Walker & Co.

--How Did We Find Out about Dinosaurs. LC 72-95793. (How Did We Find Out Ser.). PLB 8.85 (ISBN 0-8027-6134-8). Walker & Co.

--How Did We Find Out about Dinosaurs? 64p. (gr. 5-7). 1982. pap. 1.95 (ISBN 0-380-59584-2, 59584-2, Camelot). Avon.

--How Did We Find Out about DNA? (How Did We Find Out about Ser.). 64p. (gr. 4-7). 1985. 9.95 (ISBN 0-8027-6596-3); PLB 9.85 (ISBN 0-8027-6604-8). Walker & Co.

--How Did We Find Out about Earthquakes? (Illus.). 64p. 1981. pap. 1.95 (ISBN 0-380-53462-2, 53462-2, Camelot). Avon.

--How Did We Find Out about Earthquakes? LC 77-78984. (gr. 6 up). 1978. PLB 8.85 (ISBN 0-8027-6306-5). Walker & Co.

--How Did We Find Out about Energy? (Illus.). 64p. (gr. 5-7). 1981. pap. 1.95 (ISBN 0-380-53447-9, 53447-9, Camelot). Avon.

--How Did We Find Out about Germs? (Illus.). 64p. (gr. 4-7). 1981. pap. 1.95 (ISBN 0-380-53439-8, 53439-8, Camelot). Avon.

--How Did We Find Out about Life in the Deep Sea? (gr. 4-7). 1981. 7.95 (ISBN 0-8027-6427-4); lib. bdg. 8.85 (ISBN 0-8027-6428-2). Walker & Co.

--How did We Find Out about Life in the Deep Sea? 64p. (gr. 2-7). 1982. pap. 1.95 (ISBN 0-380-59592-3, 59592-3, Camelot). Avon.

--How Did We Find Out about Nuclear Power? LC 76-12067. (How Did We Find Out Ser.). (Illus.). (gr. 4 up). 1976. PLB 8.85 (ISBN 0-8027-6266-2). Walker & Co.

--How Did We Find Out about Oil? (History of Science Ser.). (Illus.). 64p. (gr. 5-8). 1980. 6.95 (ISBN 0-8027-6380-4); PLB 8.85 (ISBN 0-8027-6381-2). Walker & Co.

--How Did We Find Out about Our Genes? LC 83-1211. (Illus.). 64p. (gr. 5-8). 1983. 8.95 (ISBN 0-8027-6499-1); PLB 9.85 (ISBN 0-8027-6500-9). Walker & Co.

--How Did We Find Out about Our Human Roots? (How Did We Find Out Ser.). (Illus.). (gr. 4-8). 1979. 6.95 (ISBN 0-8027-6360-X); PLB 8.85 (ISBN 0-8027-6361-8). Walker & Co.

--How Did We Find Out about Our Human Roots? 64p. (gr. 9-12). 1982. pap. 1.95 (ISBN 0-380-59600-8, 59600-8, Camelot). Avon.

--How Did We Find Out about Outer Space? (Illus.). 64p. (gr. 9-12). 1981. pap. 1.95 (ISBN 0-380-53413-4, 53413-4, Camelot). Avon.

--How Did We Find Out About Outer Space? 64p. 1977. PLB 8.85 (ISBN 0-8027-6284-0). Walker & Co.

--How Did We Find Out about Robots? (How Did We Find Out about Ser.). (Illus.). 64p. (gr. 4-7). 1984. PLB 9.85 (ISBN 0-8027-6563-7). Walker & Co.

--How Did We Find Out about Solar Power? (History of Science Ser.). (Illus.). 64p. (gr. 4-7). 1981. 7.95 (ISBN 0-8027-6422-3); PLB 8.85 (ISBN 0-8027-6423-1). Walker & Co.

--How Did We Find Out about Solar Power? 64p. (gr. 2-7). 1982. pap. 1.95 (ISBN 0-380-59618-0, 59618-0, Camelot). Avon.

--How Did We Find Out about the Atmosphere? (How Did We Find Out about Ser.). 64p. (gr. 4 up). 1985. 9.95 (ISBN 0-8027-6588-2); reinforced 9.85 (ISBN 0-8027-6580-7). Walker & Co.

--How Did We Find Out about the Beginning of Life? LC 81-71196. (History of Science Ser.). (Illus.). 64p. (gr. 4-7). 1982. 7.95 (ISBN 0-8027-6447-9); PLB 8.85 (ISBN 0-8027-6448-7). Walker & Co.

--How Did We Find Out about the Universe? LC 82-42531. (How Did We Find Out Ser.). (Illus.). 64p. (gr. 5-8). 1983. 7.95 (ISBN 0-8027-6476-2); PLB 9.85 (ISBN 0-8027-6477-0). Walker & Co.

--How Did We Find Out about Volcanoes? (History of Science Ser.). (Illus.). 64p. (gr. 4-7). 1981. 7.95 (ISBN 0-8027-6411-8); PLB 8.85 (ISBN 0-8027-6412-6). Walker & Co.

--How did We Find Out about Volcanoes? 64p. (gr. 2-7). 1982. pap. 1.95 (ISBN 0-380-59626-1, 59626-1, Camelot). Avon.

--How Did We Find Out the Earth Is Round? Selsam, Millicent, ed. LC 72-81378. (How Did We Find Out Ser.). (Illus.). 64p. (gr. 5-8). 1972. PLB 5.85 (ISBN 0-8027-6122-4). Walker & Co.

--The Hugo Winners, Vol. 1. 320p. 1977. pap. 2.25 (ISBN 0-449-23917-9, Crest). Fawcett.

--Human Body. (Illus.). 1964. pap. 3.95 (ISBN 0-451-62358-4, Ment). NAL.

--Human Brain: Its Capacities & Functions. pap. 4.95 (ISBN 0-451-62363-0, Ment). NAL.

--I, Robot. LC 63-6943. 6.95 (ISBN 0-385-05048-8). Doubleday.

--I, Robot. 1984. pap. 2.95 (ISBN 0-345-32140-5). Ballantine.

--I, Robot. Date not set. pap. 2.95 (ISBN 0-345-31390-9, Del Rey). Ballantine.

--In Joy Still Felt: Autobiography of Isaac Asimov 1954-1978. 1981. pap. 9.95 (ISBN 0-380-53025-2, 53025-2). Avon.

--In Joy Still Felt: The Autobiography of Isaac Asimov, 1954-1978. LC 79-3685. (Illus.). 1980. 24.95 (ISBN 0-385-15544-1). Doubleday.

--In Memory Yet Green: The Autobiography of Isaac Asimov 1920-1954. LC 78-55838. (Illus.). 1979. 19.95 (ISBN 0-385-13679-X). Doubleday.

--In Memory Yet Green: The Autobiography of Isaac Asimov, 1920-1954, Vol. 1. 1980. pap. 7.95 (ISBN 0-380-75432-0, 75432-0). Avon.

--Inside the Atom. rev. ed. LC 74-5458. (Illus.). (gr. 7 up). 1974. 13.50i (ISBN 0-200-00061-6, B43260, AbS-J). Har-Row.

--Is Anyone There. LC 67-12879. 1967. 6.95 (ISBN 0-385-08401-3). Doubleday.

--Isaac Asimov. 1983. Boxed set. 6.75 (ISBN 0-380-56440-8). Avon.

--Isaac Asimov's Adventures in Science Fiction. 288p. 1980. 9.95 (ISBN 0-385-27172-7, Dial). Doubleday.

--Isaac Asimov's Fantasy. McCarthy, Shawna, ed. LC 78-60795. 348p. 1985. 12.95 (ISBN 0-385-23017-6, Dial). Doubleday.

--Isaac Asimov's Limericks for Children. LC 83-23987. (Illus.). 48p. 1984. 9.95 (ISBN 0-89845-239-2, B2393); PLB 10.45 (ISBN 0-89845-240-6, B2406). Caedmon.

--Isaac Asimov's Near Futures & Far. (Illus.). 288p. 1981. 10.95 (ISBN 0-385-27205-7, Dial). Doubleday.

--Isaac Asimov's Space of Her Own. McCarthy, Shawna, ed. LC 78-60795. 288p. 1984. 12.95 (ISBN 0-385-27953-1, Dial). Doubleday.

--Isaac Asimov's Treasury of Humor. 1979. pap. 8.95 (ISBN 0-395-28412-0). HM.

--It's Such a Beautiful Day. Redpath, Ann, ed. (Classic Short Stories Ser.). (Illus.). 32p. (gr. 7 up). 1985. PLB 8.95 (ISBN 0-88682-008-1). Creative Ed.

--The Key Word & Other Mysteries. (Illus.). 56p. (gr. 2-6). 1979. pap. 1.95 (ISBN 0-380-43224-2, 63776-6, Camelot). Avon.

--Land of Canaan. LC 70-155557. (Illus.). (gr. 7 up). 1971. 5.95 (ISBN 0-395-12572-3). HM.

--Lecherous Limericks. LC 75-7922. (Illus.). 96p. 1975. pap. 3.95 (ISBN 0-8027-7096-7). Walker & Co.

--Life & Energy. 384p. 1972. pap. 4.50 (ISBN 0-380-00942-0, 60007-2, Discus). Avon.

--Life & Time. LC 78-62644. 1978. 9.95 (ISBN 0-385-14645-0). Doubleday.

--Lucky Starr & the Big Sun of Mercury. (Lucky Starr Ser.). 1978. pap. 1.95 (ISBN 0-449-23492-4, Crest). Fawcett.

--Lucky Starr & the Oceans of Venus. (Lucky Starr Ser.). 1978. pap. 2.25 (ISBN 0-449-23461-4, Crest). Fawcett.

--Lucky Starr & the Rings of Saturn. (Lucky Starr Ser.). 1978. pap. 2.25 (ISBN 0-449-23462-2, Crest). Fawcett.

--Lucky Starr & the Rings of Saturn. 176p. 1984. pap. 1.95 (ISBN 0-345-31830-7, Del Rey). Ballantine.

--Mars, the Red Planet. LC 77-24151. (Illus.). (gr. 7 up). 1977. PLB 12.88 (ISBN 0-688-51812-5). Lothrop.

--The Martian Way. 224p. 1985. pap. 2.95 (ISBN 0-345-32587-7, Del Ray). Ballantine.

--The Martian Way & Other Stories. LC 81-15009. 224p. 1982. Repr. of 1955 ed. 12.50x (ISBN 0-8376-0463-X). Bentley.

--The Martian Way & Other Stories. 1978. pap. 2.25 (ISBN 0-449-23783-4, Crest). Fawcett.

--The Measure of the Universe. LC 82-48654. (Illus.). 224p. 1983. 15.34 (ISBN 0-06-015129-3, HarpT). Har-Row.

--More Tales of the Black Widowers. LC 76-2750. (Crime Club Ser.). 1976. 10.95 (ISBN 0-385-11176-2). Doubleday.

--More Tales of the Black Widowers. 1978. pap. 2.25 (ISBN 0-449-23806-7, Crest). Fawcett.

--Murder at the ABA. 1978. pap. 1.75 (ISBN 0-449-23202-6, Crest). Fawcett.

--The Naked Sun. 1979. pap. 2.25 (ISBN 0-449-24243-9, Crest). Fawcett.

--The Naked Sun. 1983. pap. 2.95 (ISBN 0-345-31390-9). Ballantine.

--The Naked Sun. pap. 2.95 (ISBN 0-317-14135-X, Del Rey). Ballantine.

--Nightfall & Other Stories. LC 77-78711. (Science Fiction Ser.). 1969. 7.95 (ISBN 0-385-08104-9). Doubleday.

--Nightfall & Other Stories. 1978. pap. 2.25 (ISBN 0-449-23672-2, Crest). Fawcett.

--Nightfall & Other Stories. 352p. 1984. pap. 3.50 (ISBN 0-345-31091-8, Del Rey). Ballantine.

--Nine Tomorrows. 1978. pap. 2.25 (ISBN 0-449-24084-3, Crest). Fawcett.

--Nine Tomorrows. 224p. 1985. pap. 2.95 (ISBN 0-345-32072-7, Del Rey). Ballantine.

--One Hundred Great Fantasy Short Short Stories. Carr, Terry & Greenberg, Martin H., eds. LC 82-45097. 288p. 1984. 15.95 (ISBN 0-385-18165-5). Doubleday.

--Opus Three Hundred. 1984. 18.95 (ISBN 0-395-36108-7). HM.

--Opus Two Hundred. 432p. (gr. 7 up). 1980. pap. 2.50 (ISBN 0-440-16666-7). Dell.

--Our Federal Union: The United States from 1816-1865. LC 74-32378. (Illus.). 304p. (gr. 7 up). 1975. 8.95 (ISBN 0-395-20283-3). HM.

--Pebble in the Sky. LC 81-15516. 224p. 1982. Repr. of 1950 ed. 12.50x (ISBN 0-8376-0462-1). Bentley.

--Pebble in the Sky. 1978. pap. 2.25 (ISBN 0-449-23423-1, Crest). Fawcett.

--The Planet That Wasn't. LC 75-40710. 216p. 1976. 8.95 (ISBN 0-385-11687-X). Doubleday.

--The Planet That Wasn't There. 1977. pap. 1.75 (ISBN 0-380-01813-6, 35709-7, Discus). Avon.

--Please Explain. LC 73-7908. (Illus.). 224p. (gr. 7 up). 1973. 5.95 (ISBN 0-395-17517-8). HM.

--Prisoners of the Stars: The Collected Fiction of Isaac Asimov, Vol. 2. LC 77-25576. 1979. 12.95 (ISBN 0-385-13270-0). Doubleday.

--Quasar, Quasar, Burning Bright. 1979. pap. 2.25 (ISBN 0-380-44610-3, 44610-3, Discus). Avon.

--Quasar, Quasar, Burning Bright. LC 77-82613. (Illus.). 1978. 7.95 (ISBN 0-385-13464-9). Doubleday.

--Quick & Easy Math. (gr. 7 up). 1964. 10.95 (ISBN 0-395-06573-9). HM.

--Realm of Algebra. 144p. 1981. pap. 2.50 (ISBN 0-449-24398-2, Crest). Fawcett.

--Realm of Algebra. (Illus.). (gr. 7 up). 1961. 10.95 (ISBN 0-395-06563-1). HM.

--Realm of Measure. (Illus.). (gr. 8 up). 1960. 8.95 (ISBN 0-395-06564-X). HM.

--Realm of Numbers. 144p. 1981. pap. 2.50 (ISBN 0-449-24399-0, Crest). Fawcett.

--The Road to Infinity. 256p. 1981. pap. 2.75 (ISBN 0-380-54155-6, 54155-6, Discus). Avon.

--The Road to Infinity. LC 78-22362. 1979. 10.95 (ISBN 0-385-14962-X). Doubleday.

--Robots & Empire. LC 85-1600. 360p. 1985. 16.95 (ISBN 0-385-19092-1). Doubleday.

--Robots of Dawn. LC 83-8960. 432p. 1983. 15.95 (ISBN 0-385-18400-X). Doubleday.
--The Robots of Dawn, Vol. 3. 416p. Date not set. pap. 3.95 (ISBN 0-345-31571-5, Del Rey). Ballantine.
--The Roving Mind. LC 83-60203. 348p. 1983. 19.95 (ISBN 0-87975-201-7). Prometheus Bks.
--The Roving Mind. 350p. 1985. 19.95 (ISBN 0-317-19994-3); pap. 10.95 (ISBN 0-87975-315-3). Prometheus Bks.
--Satellites in Outer Space. rev. ed. (Gateway Ser.: No. 16). (Illus.). (gr. 3-5). 1964. PLB 5.99 (ISBN 0-394-90116-9, BYR). Random.
--Second Foundation. 1963. 5.95 (ISBN 0-385-05044-5). Doubleday.
--Second Foundation. 256p. 1983. pap. 2.75 (ISBN 0-345-30901-4, Del Rey). Ballantine.
--The Shaping of France. LC 72-75604. (Illus.). 288p. (gr. 7 up). 1972. 5.95 (ISBN 0-395-13891-4). HM.
--The Shaping of North America: From Earliest Times to 1763. LC 72-7931. (Illus.). 272p. (gr. 7-12). 1973. 5.95 (ISBN 0-395-15493-6). HM.
--A Short History of Biology. LC 80-15464. (American Museum Science Bks.). (Illus.). ix, 189p. 1980. Repr. of 1964 ed. lib. bdg. 32.50x (ISBN 0-313-22583-4, ASSB). Greenwood.
--A Short History of Chemistry. LC 78-25789. (Illus.). 1979. Repr. of 1965 ed. lib. bdg. 29.50x (ISBN 0-313-20769-0, ASSH). Greenwood.
--The Solar System & Back. 256p. 1972. pap. 1.50 (ISBN 0-380-01444-0, 36012, Discus). Avon.
--Stars, Like Dust. 1978. pap. 2.25 (ISBN 0-449-23595-5, Crest). Fawcett.
--The Subatomic Monster. LC 84-28655. 240p. 1985. 16.95 (ISBN 0-385-19659-8). Doubleday.
--The Sun Shines Bright. LC 80-2039. 312p. 1981. 13.95 (ISBN 0-385-17145-5). Doubleday.
--The Sun Shines Bright. 256p. 1983. pap. 2.95 (ISBN 0-380-61390-5, 61390-5, Discus). Avon.
--Tales of the Black Widowers. 224p. 1978. pap. 1.95 (ISBN 0-449-23788-5, Crest). Fawcett.
--Tales of the Black Widowers. 14.95 (ISBN 0-89190-278-3, Pub. by Am Repr). Amereon Ltd.
--Those Amazing Electronic Thinking Machines. 160p. (gr. 7up). PLB 10.90 (ISBN 0-531-04667-2). Watts.
--To the Ends of the Universe. new ed. LC 75-10524. 144p. 1976. PLB 7.85 (ISBN 0-8027-6235-2). Walker & Co.
--Today & Tomorrow &... LC 72-89619. 360p. 1973. 8.95 (ISBN 0-385-03247-1). Doubleday.
--Today & Tomorrow &... 1983. pap. 3.50 (ISBN 0-440-15933-4). Dell.
--The Tragedy of the Moon. 1974. pap. 3.50 (ISBN 0-440-18999-3). Dell.
--Understanding Physics: Light, Magnetism & Electricity. (Signet Science Ser). 1969. pap. 3.95 (ISBN 0-451-62304-5, ME2304, Ment). NAL.
--Understanding Physics: Motion, Sound & Heat. (Signet Science Ser.). 1969. pap. 4.50 (ISBN 0-451-62365-7, ME2202, Ment). NAL.
--Understanding Physics: The Electron, Proton & Neutron. (Signet Science Ser). 1969. pap. 4.50 (ISBN 0-451-62402-5, ME2190, Ment). NAL.
--Union Club Mysteries. LC 82-45974. 216p. 1983. 13.95 (ISBN 0-385-18806-4). Doubleday.
--The Union Club Mysteries. 224p. 1985. pap. 2.95 (ISBN 0-449-20525-8, Crest). Fawcett.
--Universe. 1980. 15.95 (ISBN 0-8027-0655-X). Walker & Co.
--The Universe: From Flat Earth to Quasar. 1976. pap. 3.95 (ISBN 0-380-01596-X, 62208-4, Discus). Avon.
--Venus, Near Neighbor of the Sun. LC 80-26700. (Illus.). 224p. (gr. 5 up). 1981. 11.75 (ISBN 0-688-41976-3); PLB 11.88 (ISBN 0-688-51976-8). Lothrop.
--View from a Height. 1975. pap. 2.25 (ISBN 0-380-00356-2, 45336-3, Discus). Avon.
--Visions of the Universe. 29.95 (ISBN 0-939540-01-0). Cosmos Store.
--What Makes the Sun Shine? (Illus.). (gr. 4-6). 1971. 5.95 (ISBN 0-316-05462-3, Pub. by Atlantic Monthly Pr.). Little.
--Where Do We Go from Here? 1977. pap. 1.75 (ISBN 0-449-22849-5, X2849, Crest). Fawcett.
--A Whiff of Death. 1979. pap. 1.95 (ISBN 0-449-23660-9, Crest). Fawcett.
--The Winds of Change & Other Stories. LC 81-43912. 288p. 1983. 15.95 (ISBN 0-385-18099-3). Doubleday.
--The Winds of Change: And Other Stories. 1984. pap. 2.95 (ISBN 0-345-31188-4, Del Rey). Ballantine.
--Words from the Myths. (Illus.). 224p. (gr. 5-10). 1961. 12.95 (ISBN 0-395-06568-2). HM.
--Words from the Myths. (Illus.). 144p. (RL 6). 1969. pap. 1.95 (ISBN 0-451-12377-8, Sig). NAL.
--Words on the Map. (Illus.). 288p. (gr. 7 up). 1962. 9.95 (ISBN 0-395-06569-0). HM.
--World of Carbon. rev. ed. 1962. pap. 4.95 (ISBN 0-02-091350-8, Collier). Macmillan.
--Worlds Within Worlds: The Story of Nuclear Energy. 1980. 10.95 (ISBN 0-89875-000-8, Pub. by U Pr Pacific); pap. 7.95 (ISBN 0-89875-001-6, Pub by U Pr Pacific). Intl Spec Bk.
--X Stands for Unknown. LC 83-45019. (Illus.). 224p. 1984. 13.95 (ISBN 0-385-18915-X). Doubleday.
--X Stands for Unknown. 224p. 1985. pap. 3.95 (ISBN 0-380-69847-1, Discus). Avon.

Asimov, Isaac & Asimov, Janet. Norby's Other Secret. LC 83-40417. 128p. 1984. 9.95 (ISBN 0-8027-6525-4). Walker & Co.

Asimov, Isaac & Ciardi, John. A Grossery of Limericks. 1981. 9.95 (ISBN 0-393-01483-5). Norton.
--Limericks: Too Gross. 1978. 9.95 (ISBN 0-393-04522-6). Norton.
--Limericks: Too Gross. 128p. 1985. pap. 4.95 (ISBN 0-393-04530-7). Norton.

Asimov, Isaac & Frenkel, Karen A. Robots: Machines in Man's Image. LC 84-22758. 19.95 (ISBN 0-517-55110-1, Harmony). Crown.

Asimov, Isaac & Greenberg, Martin H. Dragon Tales. 320p. 1982. pap. 2.95 (ISBN 0-686-98388-2, Crest). Fawcett.

Asimov, Isaac & Jeppson, J. O. Laughing Space. (Illus.). 512p. 1982. 17.95 (ISBN 0-395-30519-5). HM.

Asimov, Isaac, jt. auth. see Asimov, Janet.

Asimov, Isaac see French, Paul, pseud.

Asimov, Isaac, ed. The Annotated Gulliver's Travels. (Illus.). 416p. 1980. 9.98 (ISBN 0-517-53949-7, C N Potter Bks). Crown.
--The Hugo Winners, Vol. III, Bk. I. 1979. pap. 2.25 (ISBN 0-449-23841-5, Crest). Fawcett.
--The Hugo Winners, Vol. 3. LC 73-180538. 1977. 14.95 (ISBN 0-385-12218-7). Doubleday.
--The Hugo Winners, 1976-1979, Vol. 4. LC 84-18735. 384p. 1985. 18.95 (ISBN 0-385-18934-6). Doubleday.
--Isaac Asimov Presents Living in the Future. (Illus.). 288p. 1985. 19.95 (ISBN 0-8253-0225-0). Beaufort Bks NY.
--Isaac Asimov Presents the Great Science Fiction Stories, 1950: 1950, No. 12. 1984. pap. 3.50 (ISBN 0-87997-953-4). DAW Bks.
--Isaac Asimov Presents the Great Science Fiction: Ten. 1983. pap. 3.50 (ISBN 0-87997-854-6). DAW Bks.
--Isaac Asimov Presents the Great SF 1947, No. 9. 368p. 1983. pap. 3.50 (ISBN 0-87997-802-3). Daw Bks.
--More Stories from the Hugo Winners, Vol. 2. 1979. pap. 2.25 (ISBN 0-449-23883-0, Crest). Fawcett.
--Space Mail. 416p. (Orig.). 1980. pap. 2.50 (ISBN 0-449-24312-5, Crest). Fawcett.
--Stories from the Hugo Winners, Vol. II. 1978. pap. 1.95 (ISBN 0-449-23791-5, Crest). Fawcett.

Asimov, Isaac & Conklin, Groff, eds. Fifty Short Science Fiction Tales. 1963. pap. 3.95 (ISBN 0-02-016390-8, Collier). Macmillan.

Asimov, Isaac & Greenberg, Martin, eds. Isaac Asimov Presents the Great Science Fiction Stories, No. 4. pap. 2.50 (ISBN 0-87997-570-9). DAW Bks.
--The Last Man on Earth. (Orig.). 1982. pap. 2.95 (ISBN 0-449-24531-4, Crest). Fawcett.
--Mutants. LC 81-1738. (Science Fiction Shorts). (Illus.). (gr. 5-7). 1982. PLB 15.15 (ISBN 0-8172-1734-7). Raintree Pubs.

Asimov, Isaac & Greenberg, Martin H., eds. Amazing Stories: Sixty Years of the Best Science Fiction. (Illus.). 240p. (Orig.). 1985. pap. 7.95 (ISBN 0-88038-216-3, 8112). TSR Inc.
--Election Day Twenty Eighty-Four: Science Fiction Stories about the Politics of the Future. LC 84-42794. 301p. 1984. 19.95 (ISBN 0-87975-258-0); pap. 11.95 (ISBN 0-87975-270-X). Prometheus Bks.
--Isaac Asimov Presents the Golden Years of Science Fiction. 784p. 1983. 6.98 (ISBN 0-517-40147-9, Bonanza). Outlet Bk Co.
--Isaac Asimov Presents the Golden Years of Science Fiction: Second Series. 720p. 1983. 6.98 (ISBN 0-517-41367-1, Bonanza). Outlet Bk Co.
--Isaac Asimov Presents the Great Science Fiction Stories, No. 11: 1949. 320p. 1984. pap. 3.50 (ISBN 0-87997-918-6). DAW Bks.
--Isaac Asimov Presents the Great SF Stories, No. 1. (Science Fiction Ser.). 1979. pap. 2.95 (ISBN 0-87997-700-0, UE1700). DAW Bks.
--Isaac Asimov Presents the Great SF Stories, No. 2. (DAW Science Fiction Ser.). (Orig.). 1979. pap. 2.25 (ISBN 0-87997-483-4, UE1483). Daw Bks.
--Isaac Asimov Presents the Great SF Stories, No. 3. 1980. pap. 3.50 (ISBN 0-87997-870-8, UE1870). Daw Bks.
--Isaac Asimov Presents the Great SF Stories, No. 5. 1981. pap. 2.75 (ISBN 0-87997-604-7, UE1604). Daw Bks.
--Isaac Asimov Presents the Great SF Stories, No. 6. (Science Fiction Ser.). 1981. pap. 2.95 (ISBN 0-87997-670-5, U E 1670). DAW Bks.
--Isaac Asimov Presents the Great SF Stories, No. 7. 368p. 1982. pap. 3.50 (ISBN 0-87997-746-9, UE1746). DAW Bks.
--Isaac Asimov's Wonderful World of Science Fiction: The Science Fictional Olympics. (No. 2). 1984. pap. 3.50 (ISBN 0-451-12976-8, Sig). NAL.
--Miniature Mysteries: One Hundred Malicious Little Mystery Stories. LC 80-28667. 1983. pap. 9.95 (ISBN 0-8008-5252-4). Taplinger.
--Science Fiction A to Z. 22.95 (ISBN 0-395-31285-X). HM.

Asimov, Isaac & Laurance, Alice, eds. Speculations. 312p. 1982. 13.95 (ISBN 0-395-32065-8). HM.

Asimov, Isaac & Martin, George R., eds. The Science Fiction Weightloss Book. 1983. 3.98 (ISBN 0-517-54978-6). Crown.

Asimov, Isaac & Waugh, Charles G., eds. Isaac Asimov Presents the Best Science Fiction of the 19th Century. LC 80-27721. (Isaac Asimov Presents Anthologies). 326p. 1981. 15.95 (ISBN 0-8253-0038-X). Beaufort Bks NY.

Asimov, Isaac, ed. see Fisher, Ken.

Asimov, Isaac, jt. ed. see Greenberg, Martin H.

Asimov, Isaac, et al. Work in the Twenty-First Century: An Anthology of Writings. 132p. (Orig.). 1984. 14.95 (ISBN 0-88254-939-1); pap. 5.95 (ISBN 0-939900-06-8). Hippocrene Bks.
--Giants. (Isaac Asimov's Magical Worlds of Fantasy Ser.: No. 5). 1985. pap. 3.95 (ISBN 0-451-13922-4, Sig). NAL.
--Bug Awful. LC 83-21309. (Science Fiction Shorts Ser.). (Illus.). 48p. (gr. 4-12). 1984. PLB 15.15 (ISBN 0-8172-1739-8). Raintree Pubs.
--Children of the Future. LC 83-21316. (Science Fiction Shorts Ser.). (Illus.). 48p. (gr. 4-12). 1984. PLB 15.15 (ISBN 0-8172-1740-1). Raintree Pubs.
--The Future in Question. (Orig.). 1980. pap. 2.50 (ISBN 0-449-24266-8, Crest). Fawcett.
--The Immortals. LC 83-21315. (Science Fiction Shorts Ser.). (Illus.). 48p. (gr. 4-12). 1984. PLB 15.15 (ISBN 0-8172-1741-X). Raintree Pubs.
--Time Warps. LC 83-22888. (Science Fiction Shorts Ser.). (Illus.). 48p. (gr. 4-12). 1984. PLB 15.15 (ISBN 0-8172-1742-8). Raintree Pubs.
--Flying Saucers. 352p. 1982. pap. 2.95 (ISBN 0-449-24503-9, Crest). Fawcett.
--Fantastic Reading: Stories & Activities for Grade 5-8. 1984. pap. 11.95 (ISBN 0-673-15936-1). Scott F.

Asimov, Isaac, et al, eds. Isaac Asimov Presents the Best Horror & Supernatural Stories of the 19th Century. LC 82-20794. 368p. 1983. 16.95 (ISBN 0-8253-0128-9). Beaufort Bks NY.
--One Hundred Great Fantasy Short Short Stories. 336p. 1985. pap. 2.95 (ISBN 0-380-69917-6). Avon.
--After the End. LC 81-8520. (Science Fiction Shorts). (Illus.). 48p. (gr. 5-7). 1981. PLB 15.15 (ISBN 0-8172-1729-0). Raintree Pubs.
--Earth Invaded. LC 81-19170. (Science Fiction Shorts). (Illus.). 48p. (gr. 5-7). 1982. PLB 15.15 (ISBN 0-8172-1732-0). Raintree Pubs.
--Fantastic Creatures. LC 81-10412. 160p. (gr. 7 up). 1981. lib. bdg. 9.90 (ISBN 0-531-04342-8). Watts.
--Mad Scientists. LC 81-17739. (Science Fiction Shorts Ser.). (Illus.). 48p. (gr. 5-7). 1982. PLB 15.15 (ISBN 0-8172-1733-9). Raintree Pubs.
--One Hundred Great Science Fiction Short Short Stories. 1980. pap. 2.95 (ISBN 0-380-50773-0, 60483-3). Avon.
--The Seven Deadly Sins & Cardinal Virtues of Science Fiction, 2 vols. 672p. 1982. 6.98 set (ISBN 0-517-38595-3, Bonanza). Outlet Bk Co.
--Thinking Machines. LC 81-8662. (Science Fiction Shorts). (Illus.). 48p. (gr. 5-7). 1981. PLB 15.15 (ISBN 0-8172-1727-4). Raintree Pubs.
--Tomorrow's TV. LC 81-1737. (Science Fiction Shorts). (Illus.). 48p. (gr. 5-7). 1982. PLB 15.15 (ISBN 0-8172-1735-5). Raintree Pubs.
--Travels Through Time. LC 81-8521. (Science Fiction Shorts Ser.). (Illus.). 48p. (gr. 5-7). 1981. PLB 15.15 (ISBN 0-8172-1726-6). Raintree Pubs.
--Wild Inventions. LC 81-8511. (Science Fiction Shorts Ser.). (Illus.). 48p. (gr. 5-7). 1981. PLB 15.15 (ISBN 0-8172-1728-2). Raintree Pubs.
--Young Extraterrestrials. LC 83-49489. 224p. (YA) (gr. 6-9). 1984. PLB 10.89g (ISBN 0-06-020168-1); pap. 7.64i (ISBN 0-06-020167-3). HarpJ.
--Young Monsters. LC 84-48352. 224p. (YA) (gr. 6-9). 1985. PLB 11.89g (ISBN 0-06-020170-3); pap. 7.64i (ISBN 0-06-020169-X). HarpJ.
--Young Mutants. LC 83-48444. 224p. (YA) (gr. 6-9). 1984. 10.89g (ISBN 0-06-020157-6); pap. 7.64i (ISBN 0-06-020156-8). HarpJ.
--Catastrophes. 416p. (Orig.). 1981. pap. 2.50 (ISBN 0-449-24425-3, Crest). Fawcett.
--Caught in the Organ Draft: Biology in Science Fiction. LC 82-15756. 276p. (gr. 6 up). 1983. 12.95 (ISBN 0-374-31228-1). FS&G.
--Computer Crimes & Capers. Waugh, Charles G. 242p. (Orig.). 1983. 17.95 (ISBN 0-89733-082-X); pap. 7.95 (ISBN 0-89733-087-0). Academy Chi Pubs.
--Cosmic Knights. (Isaac Asimov's Magical Worlds of Fantasy Ser.: No. 3). 1985. pap. 3.95 (ISBN 0-451-13342-0, Sig). NAL.
--Great Science Fiction Stories by the World's Great Scientists. LC 84-73519. 416p. 1985. 18.95 (ISBN 0-917657-26-8). D I Fine.
--Hallucination Orbit: Psychology in Science Fiction. LC 82-21107. 279p. (gr. 6 up). 1983. 12.95 (ISBN 0-374-32835-8). FS&G.
--Intergalactic Empires. (Isaac Asimov's Wonderful World of Science Fiction Ser.: No. 1). 303p. (Orig.). pap. 2.95 (ISBN 0-451-12624-6, Sig). NAL.
--Microcosmic Tales: One Hundred Wondrous Science Fiction Short-Short Stories. LC 79-66641. 1980. 12.95 (ISBN 0-8008-5238-9). Taplinger.
--The Science Fictional Solar System. LC 78-20198. (Illus.). 1979. 11.95i (ISBN 0-06-010152-0, HarpT). Har-Row.
--The Seven Cardinal Virtues of Science Fiction. 1981. pap. 2.50 (ISBN 0-449-24440-7, Crest). Fawcett.
--Sherlock Holmes Through Time & Space. LC 84-18580. (Illus.). 320p. 1984. 14.95 (ISBN 0-312-94400-4). Bluejay Bks.
--Supermen. (Isaac Asimov's Wonderful Worlds of Science Fiction Ser.: No. 3). 1984. pap. 3.50 (ISBN 0-451-13201-7, Sig). NAL.
--TV: Two Thousand. 352p. 1982. pap. 2.95 (ISBN 0-449-24493-8, Crest). Fawcett.
--Witches. (Isaac Asimov's Magical Worlds of Fantasy Ser.: No. 2). 304p. 1984. pap. 3.95 (ISBN 0-451-12882-6, Sig). NAL.
--Wizards. (Isaac Asimov's Magical Worlds of Fantasy: No. 1). 1983. pap. text ed. 3.50 (ISBN 0-451-12542-8, Sig). NAL.
--Young Ghosts. LC 85-42644. 224p. (YA) (gr. 7 up). 1985. 11.49i (ISBN 0-06-020171-1); PLB 11.89g (ISBN 0-06-020172-X). HarpJ.
--Starships: Stories Beyond the Boundaries of the Universe. 352p. (Orig.). 1983. pap. 3.50 (ISBN 0-449-20126-0, Crest). Fawcett.
--One Hundred Great Science Fiction Short Short Stories. LC 77-76221. 1978. 8.95 (ISBN 0-385-13044-9). Doubleday.
--Machines That Think: The Best Science Fiction Stories about Robots & Computers. LC 83-245. 562p. 1983. 22.95 (ISBN 0-03-061498-8). HR&W.
--Isaac Asimov Presents the Best Fantasy of the Nineteenth Century. 357p. 1982. 15.95 (ISBN 0-8253-0099-1). Beaufort Bks NY.
--Isaac Asimov Presents the Best Science-Fiction Firsts. 1984. 17.95 (ISBN 0-8253-0184-X). Beaufort Bks NY.
--The Seven Deadly Sins of Science Fiction. 1980. pap. 2.50 (ISBN 0-449-24349-4, Crest). Fawcett.

Asimov, Isaac. Masters of Science Fiction, Vol. I. 16.95 (ISBN 0-88411-585-2, Pub. by Aeonian Pr). Amereon Ltd.

Asimov, Janet & Asimov, Isaac. Norby & the Invaders. (Norby Ser.). 128p. (gr. 4-7). 1985. 10.95 (ISBN 0-8027-6599-8); PLB 10.85 (ISBN 0-8027-6607-2). Walker & Co.
--Norby & the Lost Princess. 160p. (gr. 4-8). 1985. 10.95 (ISBN 0-8027-6583-1); reinforced 10.85 (ISBN 0-8027-6593-9). Walker & Co.
--Norby, the Mixed up Robot. LC 82-25173. 96p. (gr. 5-7). 1983. cancelled (ISBN 0-8027-6495-9); PLB 10.85 (ISBN 0-8027-6496-7). Walker & Co.

Asimov, Janet, jt. auth. see Asimov, Isaac.

Asimow, L. & Ellis, A. J. Convexity, Theory & Its Application in Functional Analysis. LC 80-40648. (London Mathematical Society Monographs: No. 16). 1981. 70.00 (ISBN 0-12-065340-0). Acad Pr.

Asinger, F., et al. Chemistry, Physics & Application of Surface Active Substances, 3 vols. 3004p. 1967. Set. 708.25 (ISBN 0-677-10510-X). Gordon.

Asinof, Eliot. Eight Men Out. (Autographed Sports Classics Ser.). 1981. Repr. of 1963 ed. 17.95 (ISBN 0-941372-00-6). Holtzman Pr.

Asinof, Eliot, et al. Ten-Second Jailbreak. 1979. pap. 1.75 (ISBN 0-532-17118-7). Woodhill.

ASIS Annual Meeting, 43rd, 1980. Communicating Information: Proceedings of the 43rd ASIS Annual Meeting, Vol. 17. Benenfeld, Alan R., ed. LC 64-8303. (Illus.). 417p. 1980. professional ed. 19.50x (ISBN 0-914236-73-3, 319-BW). Knowledge Indus.

Asiwaju, A. I. Partitioned Africans: Ethnic Relations Across Africa's International Boundaries, 1884-1984. LC 84-18002. 350p. 1985. 29.95 (ISBN 0-312-59753-3). St Martin.
--Western Yorubaland under European Rule 1889-1945. LC 76-10146. (Ibadan History Ser). 1976. text ed. 17.50x (ISBN 0-391-00605-3). Humanities.

Asiwaju, A. I., ed. see Tarikh, et al.

Asiwaju, A. I., ed. see Tarikh.

Asiwaju, A. I., ed. see Tarikh, et al.

Asiwaju, A. I., ed. see Tarikh.

ASJA Publications Committee. American Society of Journalists & Authors, 1984: A Listing of Professional Free-Lance Writers. 84p. 1983. pap. 40.00 (ISBN 0-9612200-0-7). Am Soc Jrnl & Auth.

Ask, Robert W. High on a Hill. Jacobson, William C. & Reitz, Robert, eds. (Cedar Rapids Local History Ser.). (Illus.). 182p. (Orig.). 1984. pap. 12.00 (ISBN 0-9614227-0-X). Jefferson High.

Aska, Warabe. Who Goes to the Park. (Illus.). 32p. 1984. 17.95 (ISBN 0-88776-162-3). Tundra Bks.

Askari, Hasan, jt. auth. see Hick, John.

Askari, Hossein & Cummings, John T. Agricultural Supply Response: A Survey of the Econometric Evidence. LC 76-23376. 464p. 1976. 59.95x (ISBN 0-275-23260-3). Praeger.
--Middle East Economies in the 1970's: A Comparative Approach. LC 76-25351. (Illus.). 620p. 1976. text ed. 49.95 (ISBN 0-275-23130-5). Praeger.
--Oil, OECD, & the Third World: A Vicious Triangle? (Center for Middle Easternn Studies Monographs: No. 5). 151p. 1978. pap. text ed. 6.95x (ISBN 0-292-76011-6, Pub. by Ctr. for Middle Eastern Studies). U of Tex Pr.

Askari, Hossein & Glover, Michael C. Military Expenditures & the Level of Economic Development. (Studies in International Business: No. 3). 1977. pap. 4.00 (ISBN 0-87755-272-X). Bureau Busn UT.

Askari, S. Husan, ed. see Khan, Zain.

Aske, James. Elizabetha Triumphans: Conteyning the Damned Practizes Used Ever Sithence Her Highnesse First Comming to the Crowne. LC 73-6111. (English Experience Ser.: No. 78). 36p. 1969. Repr. of 1588 ed. 9.50 (ISBN 9-0221-0078-2). Walter J Johnson.

Askeland, Donald R. The Science & Engineering of Materials. alt. ed. 1985. text ed. write for info. (ISBN 0-534-05034-4, 21R7100, Pub. by PWS Engineering). PWS Pubs.

Askenasy, Alexander. Attitudes Toward Mental Patients. (New Babylon, Studies in the Social Sciences). 1974. text ed. 23.20x (ISBN 90-2797-891-3). Mouton.

Askenasy, Hans. Are We All Nazis? 1978. 8.95 (ISBN 0-8184-0248-2). Lyle Stuart.

--Hitler's Secret. (Illus.). 360p. (Orig.). 1984. pap. 8.95 (ISBN 0-9613497-0-0). H Askenasy.

Asker, jt. auth. see Hauglid.

Asker, Randi. Rose Painting in Norway. 2nd, rev. ed. (Illus.). 56p. 1971. pap. 20.00x (ISBN 82-09-00382-8, N390). Vanous.

Askevold, Gerald, jt. auth. see Vallee, Jacques.

Askew, A. J., et al, eds. Logistics & Benefits of Using Mathematical Models of Hydrologic & Water Resource Systems: Selected Papers from an International Symposium, IIASA Laxenburg, Austria. 270p. 1981. 55.00 (ISBN 0-08-025662-7). Pergamon.

Askew, G. Coins of Roman Britain. (Illus.). 1981. pap. 12.00 (ISBN 0-686-45246-1, Pub. by B A Seaby England). S J Durst.

Askew, Gilbert. The Coinage of Roman Britain. 2nd ed. 1980. 12.00 (ISBN 0-686-35923-2). Numismatic Fine Arts.

Askew, Neil. City Slicker Slaughter & Other Stories. Date not set. 4.95 (ISBN 0-8062-2354-5). Carlton.

Askew, Pamela, ed. Claude Lorrain, 1600-1682: A Symposium. (Studies in the History of Art: Vol. 14). (Illus.). 91p. (Orig.). 1984. pap. 17.50x (ISBN 0-89468-076-5). U Pr of New Eng.

Askew, Stella. How to Use the Pendulum. 1981. pap. 8.95x (ISBN 0-317-07322-2, Regent House). B of A.

Askew, Thomas A., Jr. & Spellman, Peter W. The Churches & the American Experience. 205p. 1984. pap. 9.95 (ISBN 0-8010-0199-4). Baker Bk.

Askew, William C., jt. ed. see Wallace, Lillian P.

Askey, Arthur. Before Your Very Eyes: An Autobiography. (Illus.). 192p. 1975. 13.50x (ISBN 0-7130-0134-8, Woburn Pr, England). Biblio Dist.

Askey, Donald E., et al. Nordic Area Studies in North America: A Survey & Directory of the Human & Material Resources. LC 75-21996. 153p. 1975. pap. text ed. 7.95x (ISBN 0-89067-056-0). Am Scandinavian.

Askey, R., ed. The Collected Papers of Gabor Szego, 3 vols. 1982. text ed. 180.00x (ISBN 0-8176-3063-5). Birkhauser.

--The Collected Papers of Gabor Szego, Vol. I. 872p. 1982. text ed. 60.00x (ISBN 0-8176-3056-2). Birkhauser.

--The Collected Papers of Gabor Szego, Vol. 2. 894p. 1982. text ed. 60.00x (ISBN 0-8176-3060-0). Birkhauser.

--The Collected Papers of Gabor Szego, Vol. 3. 892p. 1982. text ed. 60.00x (ISBN 0-8176-3061-9). Birkhauser.

Askey, R. A., et al, eds. Special Functions: Group Theoretical Aspects & Applications. 1984. lib. bdg. 49.50 (ISBN 90-277-1822-9, Pub. by Reidel Holland). Kluwer Academic.

Askey, Richard. Orthogonal Polynomials & Special Functions. (CBMS-NSF Regional Conference Ser.: No. 21). vii, 110p. (Orig.). 1975. pap. text ed. 16.00 (ISBN 0-89871-018-9). Soc Indus-Appl Math.

Askey, Richard & Ismail, Mourad. Recurrence Relations, Continued Fractions & Orthogonal Polynomials. LC 84-3075. (Memoirs of the American Mathematical Society: No. 300). 110p. 1984. pap. 11.00 (ISBN 0-8218-2301-9). Am Math.

Askey, Richard A., ed. see Advanced Seminar, the University of Wisconsin, Madison, March-April, 1975.

Askh, Upendranath. Sorrow of the Snows. Ratan, Jai, tr. (Translated from Hindi). 9.00 (ISBN 0-89253-639-X); flexible cloth 6.75 (ISBN 0-89253-640-3). Ind-US Inc.

Askham, Anthony. A Little Herball of the Properties of the Herbes. LC 77-6848. (English Experience Ser.: No. 843). 1977. Repr. of 1561 ed. lib. bdg. 11.50 (ISBN 90-221-0843-0). Walter J Johnson.

Askham, Janet. Fertility & Deprivation. LC 75-2718. (Papers in Sociology Ser.: No. 5). (Illus.). 192p. 1975. 32.50 (ISBN 0-521-20795-9). Cambridge U Pr.

--Identity & Stability in Marriage. LC 83-26150. 250p. 1984. 39.50 (ISBN 0-521-25996-7). Cambridge U Pr.

Askill, John. Tracer Diffusion Data for Metals, Alloys, & Simple Oxides. LC 73-95202. 107p. 1970. 37.50x (ISBN 0-306-65147-5, IFI Plenum). Plenum Pub.

Askim, P. Norwegian-English, English-Norwegian Maritime-Technical Dictionary, 2 vols. X ed. (Norwegian & Eng.). Set. 35.00 (ISBN 82-504-0612-5). Heinman.

Askin, Frederic, jt. auth. see Katzenstein, Anna-Louise.

Askin, Julian, jt. auth. see Moore, Robin.

Askins, A. L. F., ed. Cancioneiro de Corte e de Magnates: MSCXIV 2-2 da Biblioteca Publica e Arquivo Distrital de Evora. LC 68-66887. (U. C. Publ. in Modern Philology: Vol. 84). Repr. of 1968 ed. 115.90 (ISBN 0-8357-9627-2, 2013807). Bks Demand UMI.

Askins, Arthur. The Hispano-Portuguese Cancionero of the Hispanic Society of America. (Studies in the Romance Languages & Literatures: No. 144). 247p. 1974. pap. 13.50x (ISBN 0-8078-9144-4). U of NC Pr.

Askins, Arthur L. F., jt. auth. see Schoberlin, Melvin H.

Askins, Arthur L-F., jt. auth. see Schoberlin, Melvin.

Askins, Bill, ed. see Askins, Charles.

Askins, Charles. Askins on Pistols & Revolvers. Bryant, Ted & Askins, Bill, eds. 144p. 1980. text ed. 25.00 (ISBN 0-935998-22-5); pap. 8.95 (ISBN 0-935998-21-7). Natl Rifle Assn.

Askland, Carl L., jt. auth. see Lyons, Jerry L.

Askling, Lawrence, jt. auth. see Craft, John L.

Askov & Kamm. Study Skills in te Content Areas. 1985. 21.43 (ISBN 0-205-07743-9, 237743). Allyn.

Askov, Eunice & Otto, Wayne. Meeting the Challenge: Corrective Reading Instruction in the Classroom. 480p. 1985. text ed. 22.95 (ISBN 0-675-20303-1). Additional supplements may be obtained from publisher. Merrill.

Askov, Eunice N. & Kamm, Karlyn. Study Skills in the Content Areas. 288p. 1982. pap. text ed. 21.43 (ISBN 0-205-07743-9, 2377438). Allyn.

Askwith, Betty. Keats. 288p. 1980. Repr. of 1924 ed. lib. bdg. 25.00 (ISBN 0-8495-0072-9). Arden Lib.

--Keats. LC 76-43959. 1976. lib. bdg. 25.00 (ISBN 0-8414-2892-1). Folcroft.

Askwith, George R. Industrial Problems & Disputes. facsimile ed. LC 72-179502. (Select Bibliographies Reprint Ser). Repr. of 1920 ed. 26.50 (ISBN 0-8369-6631-7). Ayer Co Pubs.

Aslakson, Sarah Z., ed. see Conference on Book Publishing in Wisconsin, May 6, 1977, et al.

Aslam, Abukamil Shuja Ibn see Shuja Ibn Aslam, Abukamil.

Aslam, Mohd. Social Implications of Technological Change in Rural Kashmir. 147p. 1981. text ed. 17.00x (ISBN 0-391-02377-2, Pub. by Concept India). Humanities.

Aslanapa, Oktay. Turkish Art & Architecture. 1971. 57.95 (ISBN 0-571-08781-7). Faber & Faber.

Aslani, Marilyn. Harrods Cookery Book. (Illus.). Date not set. 25.00 (ISBN 0-87795-736-3). Arbor Hse.

Aslanian, Carol B. & Brickell, Henry M. Americans in Transition: Life Changes as Reasons for Adult Learning. 160p. 1980. 6.50 (ISBN 0-87447-127-3, 001273). College Bd.

Aslanian, Carol B., ed. Improving Educational Evaluation Methods: Impact on Policy. (Sage Research Progress Ser. in Evaluation: Vol. 12). (Illus.). 160p. 1981. 20.00 (ISBN 0-8039-1729-5); pap. 9.95 (ISBN 0-8039-1730-9). Sage.

Aslanian, Carol B., jt. ed. see Schmelter, Harvey B.

Aslet, C. & Powers, A. National Trust Book of English Houses. 1985. 20.00 (ISBN 0-670-80175-5). Viking.

Aslet, Clive. The Last Country Houses. LC 82-50439. (Illus.). 1982. 35.00x (ISBN 0-300-02904-7). Yale U Pr.

--The Last Country Houses. LC 82-50439. (Illus.). 352p. 1985. pap. 13.95 (ISBN 0-300-03474-1, Y-550). Yale U Pr.

Aslett, Don. Clutter's Last Stand. LC 84-3683. 288p. 1984. pap. 8.95 (ISBN 0-89879-137-5). Writers Digest.

--Do I Dust or Vacuum First. LC 82-13488. 183p. (Orig.). 1982. pap. 6.95 (ISBN 0-89879-094-8). Writers Digest.

--Is There Life after Housework? LC 81-11666. (Illus.). 192p. (Orig.). 1985. pap. 7.95 (ISBN 0-89879-165-0). Writers Digest.

Aslin, Richard, ed. Advances in Neural & Behavioral Development. (Advances in Neural & Behav. Devel. Ser.). 296p. 1985. text ed. 34.50 (ISBN 0-89391-223-9). Ablex Pub.

Aslin, Richard, et al. The Development of Perception: Psychobiological Perspectives: Vol. 1, Audition, Somatic Perception & the Chemical Senses. LC 81-7946. (Behavioral Biology Ser.). 1982. 43.50 (ISBN 0-12-065301-X). Acad Pr.

--The Development of Perception: Psychobiological Perspectives, Vol. 2: The Visual Systems. LC 81-7946. (Behavioral Biology Ser.). 1981. 47.50 (ISBN 0-12-065302-8). Acad Pr.

Asloan, John. The Asloan Manuscript: A Miscellany of Prose & Verse Written by John Asloan in the Reign of James the Fifth, 2 vols. Craigie, W. A., ed. Repr. Set. 57.00 (ISBN 0-384-02191-3). Johnson Repr.

Aslund, Anders. Private Enterprise in Eastern Europe: The Non-Agricultural Private Sector in Poland & the GDR, 1945-83. LC 84-40388. 320p. 1984. 29.95 (ISBN 0-312-64706-9). St Martin.

ASM International Conference on Production, Fabrication, Properties, & Application of Ferretic Steels for High-Temperature Applications, Warren, Pennsylvania, 6-8 October 1981. Ferritic Steels for High-Temperature Applications: Proceedings. LC 82-73608. write for info. Metal Prop Coun.

Asmal, Kadmar & Chairman of Inquiry Commission, eds. Shoot to Kill. 173p. (Orig.). 1985. pap. 8.95 (ISBN 0-85342-743-7, Pub. by Mercier Pr Ireland); pap. text ed. 8.95 (ISBN 0-317-29176-9). Irish Bks Media.

Asmal, Louise, tr. see Hadjinicolaou, Nicos.

Asman, David & Meyerson, Adam, eds. The Wall Street Journal on Management: The Best of the Manager's Journal. 200p. 1985. 19.95 (ISBN 0-87094-685-4). Dow Jones-Irwin.

Asmann, Lynn & Sprague, Jane. Baby Basics. (Illus.). (gr. 5 up). 1980. pap. 4.95 (ISBN 0-938416-00-6). BCS Educ Aids.

ASME-ASLE Lubrication Conference, Washington, DC, Oct. 1982. Advances in Computer-Aided Bearing Design. Chang, C. M. & Kennedy, F. E., eds. 156p. 1982. 30.00 (G00220). ASME.

ASME Design Engineering Conference, New York, 1967. Designing for High Impact Technology: Papers Presented at the Design Engineering Conference, New York City, May 15-18, 1967. LC 77-20859. (Illus.). pap. 20.00 (ISBN 0-317-12978-3, 2011323). Bks Demand UMI.

ASME Winter Annual Meeting, Phoenix, Ariz., Nov. 1982. Robotics Research & Advanced Applications. Book, Wayne J., ed. 287p. 1982. 50.00 (H00236). ASME.

Asmis, Elizabeth. Epicurus' Scientific Method. LC 83-45133. 400p. 1983. 49.50x (ISBN 0-8014-1465-2). Cornell U Pr.

Asmundsson, Doris R. Georg Brandes: Aristocratic Radical. LC 81-3324. pap. 105.00 (ISBN 0-317-19891-2). Bks Demand UMI.

Asmus, E. Barry, jt. auth. see Billings, Donald B.

Asmussen, E. Biomechanics. (Illus.). 1978. VI-A, 592p. text ed. 48.00 (ISBN 0-8391-1242-4); VI-B, 390p. text ed. 48.00 (ISBN 0-8391-1243-2). Univ Park.

Asmussen, E., ed. International Calibration Study of Traffic Conflict Techniques. (NATO ASI Series, Series F Computer & Systems Sciences: No. 5). 229p. 1984. 36.60 (ISBN 0-387-12716-X). Springer Verlag.

Asmussen, Jes P., compiled by. Manichaean Literature: Representative Texts, Chiefly from Middle Persian & Parthian Writings. LC 74-22063. (Unesco Collection of Representative Works, Oriental Ser.). 160p. 1975. lib. bdg. 30.00x (ISBN 0-8201-1141-4). Schol Facsimiles.

Asmussen, Patricia D. Simplified Recipes for Day Care Centers. LC 74-222. 224p. 1973. spiral bdg. 14.95 (ISBN 0-8436-0590-1). Van Nos Reinhold.

Asmussen, Soren & Hering, Heinrich. Branching Processes. (Progress in Probability & Statistics Ser.: Vol. 3). 468p. 1983. text ed. 34.95 (ISBN 0-8176-3122-4). Birkhauser.

Asner, Michael. Up Your Computer: A Survival Handbook for Executives. 1984. text ed. 28.95 (ISBN 0-8359-8084-7); pap. text ed. 18.95 (ISBN 0-8359-8083-9). Reston.

Asnes, Fred. These Little Worlds. Taylor, Chuck, ed. (Illus.). 82p. (Orig.). 10.95 (ISBN 0-941720-23-3); pap. 4.95 (ISBN 0-941720-22-5). Slough Pr Tx.

Asnin, Scott. A Cold Wind from Orion. 288p. (Orig.). 1980. pap. 2.25 (ISBN 0-345-28498-4). Ballantine.

Asoka, King of Magadha. The Edicts of Asoka. LC 78-72372. Repr. of 1909 ed. 24.00 (ISBN 0-404-17219-9). AMS Pr.

Asolon, Karel B., ed. The Phantom of Devil's Bridge & the Tale of Bufalo Castle. (Maravian Tales, Legends, Myths Ser.). (Illus.). 41p. (Orig.). (gr. 4). 1985. pap. 16.00 (ISBN 0-930329-04-X). Kabel Pubs.

ASP. Technical Papers, 1985: ASP 51st Annual Meeting, March 1985, 2 vols. 883p. 1985. pap. 15.50 (ISBN 0-937294-62-4). ASP & RS.

Asp, C. Elliott, jt. auth. see Garbarino, James.

Asp, Carolyn. A Study of Thomas Middleton's Tragicomedies. (Salzburg Studies in English Literature, Jacobean Drama Studies: No. 28). 282p. 1974. pap. text ed. 25.50x (ISBN 0-391-01303-3). Humanities.

Asp, William G., et al. Continuing Education for the Library Information Professions. 256p. (Orig.). 1985. lib. bdg. 25.00 (ISBN 0-208-01897-2, Lib Prof Pubns); pap. text ed. 18.50 (ISBN 0-208-01898-0). Shoe String.

ASPA Foundation. Fear of Firing: A Legal & Personnel Analysis of Employment at Will. 1984. pap. 9.95 (ISBN 0-939900-07-6). Am Soc Personnel.

Aspaturian, Vernon V. Soviet Union in the World Communist System. LC 66-15085. (Studies Ser.: No. 13). 1966. pap. 5.95x (ISBN 0-8179-3132-5). Hoover Inst Pr.

--The Union Republics in Soviet Diplomacy: A Study of Soviet Federalism in the Service of Soviet Foreign Policy. LC 83-22696. 228p. 1984. Repr. of 1960 ed. lib. bdg. 29.75x (ISBN 0-313-24368-9, ASUP). Greenwood.

Aspaturian, Vernon V., et al, eds. Eurocommunism between East & West. LC 80-7489. (Midland Bks.: No. 248). 384p. 1980. 32.50x (ISBN 0-253-32346-0). Ind U Pr.

Aspden, Bryan. News of the Changes. 42p. (Orig.). 1985. pap. 8.25 (Pub. by Poetry Wales Pr UK). Dufour.

Aspe, Pedro & Sigmund, Paul E., eds. The Political Economy of Income Distribution in Mexico. (The Political Economy of Income Distribution in Developing Countries Ser.). 562p. 1984. text ed. 85.00x (ISBN 0-8419-0907-5). Holmes & Meier.

Aspe-Armella, Pedro & Dornbusch, Rudiger. Financial Policies & The World Capital Market: The Problem of Latin American Countries. LC 82-24820. 304p. 1983. lib. bdg. 36.00X (ISBN 0-226-02996-4). U of Chicago Pr.

Aspel, Geoff. Suzuki. LC 83-73616. (Illus.). 64p. (Orig.). 1984. 7.95 (ISBN 0-668-06164-2); pap. 3.95 (ISBN 0-668-06171-5). Arco.

Aspell, A. L. Catholics: A Celebration. 1986. pap. price not set (ISBN 0-940518-05-8). Guildhall Pubs.

Aspen Art Museum. American Paintings Nineteen Seventy-Five to Nineteen Eighty-Five: Selections from the Collection of Aron & Phyllis Katz. 60p. 1985. pap. write for info. (ISBN 0-934324-08-5). Aspen Art.

Aspen Institute for Humanistic Studies, jt. auth. see Foundation Center.

Aspen Institute for Humanistic Studies & Bohen, Halycone H. Corporate Employment Policies Affecting Families & Children: The United States & Europe. LC 83-72997. (Illus.). vi, 174p. cancelled (ISBN 0-89843-052-6). Aspen Systems.

Aspen, Marvin E., jt. auth. see Inbau, Fred E.

Aspen Systems Corporation. National Directory of Health-Medicine Organizations, 1982-83. 234p. 1982. 42.50 (ISBN 0-89443-691-0). Aspen Systems.

Aspenstrom, Werner. You & I & the World. Barkan, Stanley H., ed. Cedering, Siv, tr. from Swedish & Eng. (Cross-Cultural Review Chapbook 5: Swedish Poetry 1). 40p. pap. 3.50 (ISBN 0-89304-803-8). Cross Cult.

Asperheim, Mary K. Pharmacology: An Introduction Text. 5th ed. (Illus.). 272p. 1981. pap. text ed. 14.95 (ISBN 0-7216-1446-9). Saunders.

Asperheim, Mary K. & Eisenhauer, Laurel A. The Pharmacologic Basis of Patient Care. 4th ed. (Illus.). 624p. 1981. text ed. 24.50 (ISBN 0-7216-1438-8). Saunders.

Aspey, Wayne P. & Lustick, Sheldon I., eds. Behavioral Energetics: The Cost of Survival in Vertebrates. LC 82-12512. (Ohio State Univ. Biosciences Colloquia: No. 7). 312p. 1983. 27.50x (ISBN 0-8142-0332-9). Ohio St U Pr.

Aspilden, C., jt. auth. see Rainey, R. C.

Aspillera, Paraluman S. Basic Tagalog for Foreigners & Non-Tagalogs. LC 69-13503. 1969. Repr. of 1956 ed. bds. 10.50 (ISBN 0-8048-0058-8). C E Tuttle.

Aspin, B. Terry. Workshop Practice Series, No. 4: Foundrywork for the Amateur. rev ed. (Illus.). 96p. 1984. pap. 9.95 (ISBN 0-85242-842-1). Aztex.

Aspin, Chris. The Cotton Industry. (Album Ser.: No. 63). (Illus.). 32p. 1984. pap. 2.95 (ISBN 0-85263-545-1, Pub. by Shire Pubns England). Seven Hills Bks.

--The Woolen Industry. (Shire Album Ser.: No. 81). (Illus.). 32p. 1985. pap. 3.50 (ISBN 0-85263-598-2, Pub. by Shire Pubns England). Seven Hills Bks.

Aspin, Isabel S., ed. Anglo-Norman Political Songs. 30.00 (ISBN 0-384-02201-4); pap. 24.00 (ISBN 0-384-02202-2). Johnson Repr.

Aspin, Robert. Myth Directions. Stine, Hank, ed. LC 82-12776. (Myth Ser.: Vol. 3). (Illus.). 176p. (Orig.). 1982. pap. 6.95 (ISBN 0-89865-250-2, Starblaze). Donning Co.

Aspinall, Algernon. Guide to the West Indies. 1978. lib. bdg. 59.95 (ISBN 0-8490-1924-9). Gordon Pr.

Aspinall, Algernon E. West Indian Tales of Old. LC 69-18650. (Illus.). Repr. of 1915 ed. 22.50x (ISBN 0-8371-4977-0, ASW&). Greenwood.

Aspinall, Arthur. Lord Brougham & the Whig Party. LC 78-179576. (Illus.). 322p. 1972. Repr. of 1927 ed. 24.50 (ISBN 0-208-01240-0, Archon). Shoe String.

Aspinall, Arthur & Smith, E. Anthony, eds. English Historical Documents: 1783-1832, Vol. 11. 1959. 75.00x (ISBN 0-19-519508-6). Oxford U Pr.

Aspinall, D., ed. The Microprocessor & Its Application. LC 78-54572. (Illus.). 402p. 1980. pap. 19.95 (ISBN 0-521-29798-2). Cambridge U Pr.

--The Microprocessor & Its Application. LC 78-54572. (Illus.). 1978. 52.50 (ISBN 0-521-22241-9). Cambridge U Pr.

Aspinall, D., jt. ed. see Paleg, L. G.

Aspinall, David, jt. auth. see Dagless, Erik L.

Aspinall, David & Dagless, Erik, eds. Introduction to Microprocessors. 1977. 29.50 (ISBN 0-12-064550-5). Acad Pr.

Aspinall, G. O., ed. The Polysaccharides, Vol. 1. (Molecular Biology Ser.). 330p. 1982. 55.00 (ISBN 0-12-065601-9). Acad Pr.

--The Polysaccharides, Vol. 2. LC 82-6689. (Molecular Biology Ser.). 1983. 70.00 (ISBN 0-12-065602-7). Acad Pr.

--The Polysaccharides, Vol. 3. (Molecular Biology Ser.). 1985. 85.00 (ISBN 0-12-065603-5). Acad Pr.

Aspinall, K. W. First Steps in Veterinary Science. (Illus.). 224p. 1976. pap. 6.50 (ISBN 0-7216-0783-7, Pub. by Bailliere-Tindall). Saunders.

Aspinall, Mary Jo. Aortic Arch Surgery. (Continuing Education in Cardiovascular Nursing Ser.). (Illus.). 105p. 1980. pap. 6.95x (ISBN 0-8385-0171-0). ACC.

Aspinall, Richard. Radio Programme Production: A Manual for Training. 151p. (3rd Printing 1977). 1971. pap. 9.25 (ISBN 92-3-101030-1, U516, UNESCO). Unipub.

Aspinall, Richard D., jt. auth. see Stradley, William E.

Aspinwall, B. Portable Utopia: Glasgow & the U.S. 1820-1920. 363p. 1984. text ed. 35.75x (ISBN 0-08-028447-7, Pub by Aberdeen Pr Scotland). Humanities.

Aspinwall, Dorothy. Modern Verse Translations from French. 220p. 1981. 9.95 (ISBN 0-89962-020-5). Todd & Honeywell.

Aspinwall, Dorothy, tr. see Aspinwall, Dorothy B. & Reda, Jacques.

Aspinwall, Dorothy B. & Reda, Jacques. Recitatif. Aspinwall, Dorothy, tr. (Fr. & Eng.). 1983. 10.00x (ISBN 0-936968-05-2). Intl Bk Ctr.

Aspinwall, Margaret, jt. auth. see Lipman, Jean.

Aspinwall, Margaret, ed. see Mathews, Zena P.

Aspinwall, Margaret, ed. see Nickel, Helmut, et al.

Aspinwall, Richard C. & Eisenbeis, Robert A., eds. Handbook for Banking Strategy: Professional Banking & Finance Ser. LC 84-19487. 880p. 1985. 49.95 (ISBN 0-471-89314-5, Pub. by Wiley-Interscience). Wiley.

ASPIRA of New York, tr. see Fernandez, Happy.

ASPIRA of New York, tr. see Fernandez, Happy & NCCE.

Aspiran, Robert. Myth Conceptions. 208p. 1985. pap. 2.95 (ISBN 0-441-55519-5). Ace Bks.

Aspital, A., ed. see Latham, Robert.

Aspiz, Harold. Walt Whitman & the Body Beautiful. LC 79-28280. 304p. 1980. 19.95x (ISBN 0-252-00799-9). U of Ill Pr.

Aspland, Clifford W., ed. A Medieval French Reader. 1979. text ed. 42.00x (ISBN 0-19-872035-1); pap. text ed. 21.50x (ISBN 0-19-815761-4). Oxford U Pr.

Aspler, Tony, jt. auth. see Pape, Gordon.

Aspley, John. Speculum Nauticum: A Looking Glasse, for Sea-Men. LC 77-6849. (English Experience Ser: No. 844). 1977. Repr. of 1624 ed. lib. bdg. 9.50 (ISBN 90-221-0844-9). Walter J Johnson.

Asplund, Gisele, jt. auth. see Asplund, Goran.

Asplund, Goran & Asplund, Gisele. An Integrated Development Strategy. LC 81-14822. 136p. 1982. 32.95x (ISBN 0-471-10075-7, Pub. by Wiley-Interscience). Wiley.

Asplund, John. The Annual Register of the Baptist Denomination in North America to 1970. 1979. Repr. 10.00 (ISBN 0-317-01254-1). Church History.

--The Universal Register of the Baptist Denomiation in North America for the Years 1790, 1791, 1792, 1793, & Part of 1794. Gaustad, Edwin S., ed. LC 79-52581. (The Baptist Tradition Ser.). 1980. Repr. of 1794 ed. lib. bdg. 14.00x (ISBN 0-405-12448-1). Ayer Co Pubs.

Asprey, Robert B. The First Battle of the Marne. LC 78-10667. 1979. Repr. of 1962 ed. lib. bdg. 22.50x (ISBN 0-313-21229-5, ASFB). Greenwood.

Aspril, Elizabeth. As Battles Raged. (Illus., Orig.). 1981. 12.95 (ISBN 0-9604750-1-X); pap. 7.95 (ISBN 0-9604750-0-1). E Keys.

Asprin, Robert. Another Fine Myth. Freas, Polly & Freas, Kelly, eds. LC 78-2630. (Myth Ser.: Vol. 1). (Illus.). 1978. pap. 6.95 (ISBN 0-915442-54-X, Starblaze). Donning Co.

--Another Fine Myth. 208p. 1984. pap. 2.75 (ISBN 0-441-02359-2). Ace Bks.

--Another Fine Myth. 1985. pap. 2.95 (ISBN 0-441-02360-6). Ace Bks.

--The Bug Wars. 1980. pap. 2.25 (ISBN 0-440-10806-3). Dell.

--Hit or Myth. Reynolds, Kay, ed. LC 83-16496. (Myth Ser.: No. 4). (Illus.). 172p. (Orig.). 1983. lib. bdg. 12.95 (ISBN 0-89865-339-8, Starblaze); pap. 6.95 (ISBN 0-89865-331-2). Donning Co.

--Hit or Myth. 176p. 1985. pap. 2.95 (ISBN 0-441-33850-X). Ace Bks.

--Mirror Friend, Mirror Foe. 224p. 1985. pap. 2.75 (ISBN 0-441-53380-9). Ace Bks.

--Myth Conceptions. Freas, Polly & Freas, Kelly, eds. LC 79-9216. (Illus.). 1980. pap. 6.95 (ISBN 0-915442-94-9, Starblaze). Donning Co.

--Myth Conceptions. 1985. pap. 2.95 (ISBN 0-441-55519-5). Ace Bks.

--Myth Directions. 208p. 1985. pap. 2.95 (ISBN 0-441-55525-X). Ace Bks.

--Myth Directions. 1985. pap. 2.95 (ISBN 0-441-55525-X). Ace Bks.

--Myth-ing Persons. Reynolds, Kay, ed. LC 84-13824. (Myth Ser.: No. 5). 224p. 1984. 12.95 (ISBN 0-89865-380-0); pap. 6.95 (ISBN 0-89865-379-7); limited ed. 35.00 (ISBN 0-89865-381-9). Donning Co.

Asprin, Robert, jt. auth. see Takei, George.

Asprin, Robert, ed. Storm Season. 1982. pap. 2.95 (ISBN 0-441-78710-X, Pub. by Ace Science Fiction). Ace Bks.

Asprin, Robert L. Shadows of Sanctuary. (Thieves' World Ser.: No. 3). 352p. 1984. pap. 2.95 (ISBN 0-441-76030-9, Pub. by Ace Science Fiction). Ace Bks.

--Storm Season. (Thieves' World Ser.: No. 4). 320p. 1984. pap. 2.95 (ISBN 0-441-78712-6, Pub. by Ace Science Fiction). Ace Bks.

--Tales from the Vulgar Unicorn. (Thieves' World Ser.: No. 2). 320p. 1984. pap. 2.95 (ISBN 0-441-79579-X, Pub. by Ace Science Fiction). Ace Bks.

--Tambu. 1985. pap. 2.75 (ISBN 0-441-79744-X, Pub. by Ace Science Fiction). Ace Bks.

--Theive's World. 1982. pap. 2.95 (ISBN 0-441-80581-7). Ace Bks.

--Thieve's World. 320p. 1985. pap. 2.95 (ISBN 0-441-80583-3). Ace Bks.

--Thieves World. Abbey, Lynn, ed. (Thieves World: No. 1). 1985. pap. 2.95 (ISBN 0-441-80583-3) (ISBN 0-317-31894-2). Ace Bks.

Asprin, Robert L. & Abbey, Lynn. Face of Chaos. (Thieves' World Ser.: No. 5). 1985. pap. 2.95 (ISBN 0-441-22550-0) (ISBN 0-317-31750-4). Ace Bks.

--Shadows of Sanctuary. (Thieves World Ser.: No. 3). 1985. pap. 2.95 (ISBN 0-441-76031-7) (ISBN 0-317-31876-4). Ace Bks.

--Storm Season. (Thieves' World: No. 4). 1985. pap. 2.25 (ISBN 0-441-78713-4) (ISBN 0-317-31885-3). Ace Bks.

--Tales from the Vulgar Unicorn. (Thieves World Ser.: No. 2). 1985. pap. 2.95 (ISBN 0-441-79580-3). Ace Bks.

--Wings of Omen. (Thieves' World: No. 6). 1985. pap. 2.95 (ISBN 0-441-80594-9) (ISBN 0-317-31902-7). Ace Bks.

Asprin, Robert L., ed. Shadows of Sanctuary. 320p. (Orig.). 1983. pap. 2.95 (ISBN 0-441-76029-5, Pub. by Ace Science Fiction). Ace Bks.

--Thieves World. 320p. 1982. pap. 2.95 (ISBN 0-441-80581-7, Pub. by Ace Science Fiction). Ace Bks.

Asprin, Robert L. & Abbey, L., eds. The Dead of Winter. (Thieve's World Ser.: No. 7). 272p. 1985. pap. 2.95 (ISBN 0-441-14089-0). Ace Bks.

Asprin, Robert L. & Abbey, Lynn, eds. Wings of Omen. (Thieves' World Ser.: No. 6). 1984. pap. 2.95 (ISBN 0-441-80593-0). Ace Bks.

--Wings of Omen. (Thieves' World Ser.: No. 6). 304p. 1984. pap. 2.95 (ISBN 0-317-12645-8). Ace Bks.

Aspurz-Iriarte, Lazaro De see De Aspurz-Iriarte, Lazaro.

Aspy, D. N., et al, eds. The Third Century in American Education. 158p. 1984. pap. text ed. 25.00 (ISBN 0-914234-67-6). Human Res Dev Pr.

Aspy, David & Roebuck, Flora. Kids Don't Learn from People They Don't Like. 297p. (Orig.). 1977. pap. text ed. 15.00x (ISBN 0-914234-85-4). Human Res Dev Pr.

Aspy, David N. The Best & the Brightest. 91p. 1984. pap. 10.00 (ISBN 0-914234-76-5). Human Res Dev Pr.

Asquith, Cynthia. The Duchess of York. 1977. 15.00 (ISBN 0-8274-4287-4). R West.

--Married to Tolstoy. 1964. 7.95 (ISBN 0-251-15039-9). Dufour.

--Portrait of Barrie. LC 74-156172. 230p. 1972. Repr. of 1954 ed. lib. bdg. 18.75 (ISBN 0-8371-6115-0, ASPB). Greenwood.

--Portrait of Barrie. 1973. Repr. of 1954 ed. 20.00 (ISBN 0-8274-1702-0). R West.

Asquith, Cynthia, compiled by. The Black Cap. 318p. 1981. Repr. lib. bdg. 35.00 (ISBN 0-89987-008-2). Darby Bks.

Asquith, George. Log Analysis by Microcomputer. 104p. 1980. 39.95x (ISBN 0-87814-118-9). Pennwell Bks.

Asquith, George B. Subsurface Carbonate Depositional Models. 121p. 1979. 39.95x (ISBN 0-87814-104-9). Pennwell Bks.

Asquith, Glenn H. Church Officers at Work. pap. 3.95 (ISBN 0-8170-0048-8). Judson.

--Living Creatively As an Older Adult. LC 75-22590. 180p. 1975. pap. 1.95 (ISBN 0-8361-1780-8). Herald Pr.

--Mature Faith: A Spiritual Pilgrimage. LC 84-12890. 120p. (Orig.). 1984. pap. 6.95 (ISBN 0-8361-3366-8). Herald Pr.

--Preaching According to Plan. (Orig.). 1968. pap. 1.95 (ISBN 0-8170-0390-8). Judson.

--Renewed Power for Preaching. 128p. 1983. pap. 6.95 (ISBN 0-8170-1003-3). Judson.

Asquith, H. H. Some Aspects of the Victorian Age. LC 74-13333. 1918. lib. bdg. 10.00 (ISBN 0-8414-2997-9). Folcroft.

Asquith, Herbert H. The Genesis of the War. LC 71-39714. (Select Bibliographies Reprint Ser). 1972. Repr. of 1923 ed. 19.75 (ISBN 0-8369-9926-6). Ayer Co Pubs.

--Occasional Addresses, Eighteen Ninety-Three-Nineteen Sixteen. facsimile ed. LC 76-99715. (Essay Index Reprint Ser.). Repr. of 1918 ed. 18.00 (ISBN 0-8369-1368-X). Ayer Co Pubs.

Asquith, Herbert H., jt. auth. see Oxford.

Asquith, Nan. The Garden of Persephone, The Girl from Rome, Time May Change. (Harlequin Romances (3-in-1) Ser.). 576p. 1984. pap. 3.95 (ISBN 0-373-20081-1). Harlequin Bks.

Asquith, P. D., ed. see Philosophy of Science Association, Biennial Meeting, 1976.

Asquith, Pamela. Truffles & Other Chocolate Confections. LC 83-18650. 128p. 1984. 12.95 (ISBN 0-03-063356-7). HR&W.

Asquith, Pamella. Pamella Asquith's Ultimate Chocolate Cake Book. (Illus.). 256p. 1985. pap. 8.95 (ISBN 0-345-31929-X). Ballantine.

--Pamella Z. Asquith's Ultimate Chocolate Cake Book. LC 83-41. (Illus.). 240p. 1983. 16.95 (ISBN 0-03-062196-8). HR&W.

--The Quintessential Croissant. (Illus.). 1982. pap. 5.95 (ISBN 0-89087-336-4). Celestial Arts.

Asquith, Pamella Z. The Joy of Pizza. 1984. pap. 5.95 (ISBN 0-394-71322-2, Vin). Random.

--Pamella Z. Asquith's Fruit Tart Cookbook. LC 81-23773. 192p. 1982. 12.95 (ISBN 0-517-54621-3, Harmony). Crown.

Asquith, Peter. Immunology of the Gastrointestinal Tract. (Illus.). 1979. text ed. 69.00 (ISBN 0-443-01589-9). Churchill.

Asquith, Peter D. & Giere, Ronald, eds. PSA 1980, 2 Vols. 1980. Vol. I. 9.50 (ISBN 0-917586-14-X); pap. 7.50 (ISBN 0-917586-13-1); Vol. II, 678P. 1982. 23.75 (ISBN 0-917586-16-6). Philos Sci Assn.

Asquith, Peter D. & Kitcher, Philip, eds. PSA, 1984, Vol. 1. 223p. 1984. 15.50 (ISBN 0-917586-21-2); pap. 13.50 (ISBN 0-917586-20-4). Philos Sci Assn.

Asquith, Peter D. & Kyburg, Henry E., Jr., eds. Current Research in Philosophy of Science. LC 78-61267. 533p. 1979. 12.50 (ISBN 0-917586-08-5); pap. 10.50 (ISBN 0-917586-07-7). Philos Sci Assn.

Asquith, Peter D. & Nickles, Thomas, eds. PSA 1982, 2 Vols. 414p. 1982. Vol. I. 21.00 (ISBN 0-917586-18-2); pap. 19.00 (ISBN 0-917586-17-4); Vol. II, 730P. 1983. 25.00 (ISBN 0-917586-19-0). Philos Sci Assn.

Asquith, R. S., ed. Chemistry of Natural Protein Fibers. LC 76-52636. (Illus.). 417p. 1977. 65.00x (ISBN 0-306-30898-3, Plenum Pr). Plenum Pub.

Asquith, Stewart. Children & Justice. 258p. 1982. 26.00x (ISBN 0-85224-429-0, Pub. by Edinburgh U Pr Scotland); pap. 17.50x (ISBN 0-85224-466-5). Columbia U Pr.

Asquith, Stewart, jt. auth. see Clark, Chris L.

Asquith, Stewart, jt. ed. see Adler, Michael.

Asrani, C. H., jt. auth. see Baxi, Nilesh.

Asratian, E. A. Compensatory Adaptations, Reflex Activity & the Brain. 1965. text ed. 44.00 (ISBN 0-08-010591-2). Pergamon.

Asratyan, E. Learning Brain. 222p. 1983. 7.45 (ISBN 0-8285-2336-3, Pub. by Mir Pubs USSR). Imported Pubns.

Assad, Mike, jt. auth. see Duffy, Neil.

Assadi, Amir H. Finite Group Actions on Simply-Connected Manifolds & CW Complexes. LC 81-19104. (Memoirs: No. 257). 117p. 1982. pap. 9.00 (ISBN 0-8218-2257-8, MEMO-257). Am Math.

Assael, H., ed. see Rogers, Jason.

Assael, Henry. Consumer Behavior & Marketing Action. 2nd ed. LC 83-22197. 720p. 1983. text ed. write for info. (ISBN 0-534-02990-6); write for info. instr's. manual. Kent Pub Co.

--Marketing Management: Strategy & Action. LC 84-23534. 816p. 1985. text ed. write for info. (ISBN 0-534-04788-2). Kent Pub Co.

Assael, Henry, ed. A Century of Marketing Series, 33 bks. (Illus.). 1978. lib. bdg. 1157.50x set (ISBN 0-405-11156-8). Ayer Co Pubs.

--The Collected Works of C. C. Parlin: An Original Anthology. LC 78-260. (Century of Marketing Ser.). (Illus.). 1978. lib. bdg. 22.00x (ISBN 0-405-11159-2). Ayer Co Pubs.

--Early Development & Conceptualization of the Field of Marketing: An Original Anthology. LC 78-278. (Century of Marketing Ser.). 1978. lib. bdg. 21.00x (ISBN 0-405-11188-6). Ayer Co Pubs.

--A Pioneer in Marketing: L. D. H. Weld. an orginal anthology ed. LC 78-283. (Century of Marketing Ser.). 1978. lib. bdg. 40.00x (ISBN 0-405-11157-6). Ayer Co Pubs.

Assael, Henry, ed. see Alderson, Wroe.

Assael, Henry, ed. see Bartels, Robert.

Assael, Henry, ed. see Blankenship, Albert B.

Assael, Henry, ed. see Borden, Neil H.

Assael, Henry, ed. see Breyer, Ralph F.

Assael, Henry, ed. see Calkins, Earnest E. & Holden, Ralph.

Assael, Henry, ed. see Clark, Fred E.

Assael, Henry, jt. ed. see Clark, Lincoln H.

Assael, Henry, ed. see Coles, Jessie V.

Assael, Henry, ed. see Collins, Virgil D.

Assael, Henry, ed. see Converse, Paul D.

Assael, Henry, ed. see Copeland, Melvin T.

Assael, Henry, ed. see Dichter, Ernest.

Assael, Henry, ed. see Frederick, John H.

Assael, Henry, ed. see Frederick, Justus G.

Assael, Henry, ed. see Hower, Ralph M.

Assael, Henry, ed. see Leachman, Harden B.

Assael, Henry, ed. see Lockwood, R. Bigelow.

Assael, Henry, ed. see Longman, Donald R.

Assael, Henry, ed. see Lyon, Leverett S.

Assael, Henry, ed. see Northwestern University School of Commerce.

Assael, Henry, ed. see Nystrom, Paul H.

Assael, Henry, ed. see Reilly, William J.

Assael, Henry, ed. see Revzan, David A.

Assael, Henry, jt. ed. see Rosenberg, Larry J.

Assael, Henry, ed. see Scott, Walter D.

Assael, Henry, ed. see Sorenson, Helen.

Assael, Henry, ed. see Starch, Daniel.

Assael, Henry, ed. see Terry, Samuel H.

Assael, Henry, ed. see Tosdal, Harry R.

Assael, Henry, ed. see White, Percival.

Assael, Henry, ed. see Woodward, Helen.

Assael, Michael. Moneysmarts. LC 81-83255. 288p. (Orig.). 1982. pap. 3.25 (ISBN 0-86721-009-5). Jove Pubns.

Assaf, Karen & Assaf, Said. Handbook of Mathematical Calculations: For Science Students & Researchers. (Illus.). 310p. 1974. text ed. 6.50x (ISBN 0-8138-1135-X). Iowa St U Pr.

Assaf, Said, jt. auth. see Assaf, Karen.

Assagioli, Roberto. Act of Will. 1974. pap. 5.95 (ISBN 0-14-003866-3). Penguin.

--Psychosynthesis. 1971. pap. 4.95 (ISBN 0-14-004263-6). Penguin.

Assai, T., jt. ed. see Agee, E. M.

Assaiante, Paul, ed. Championship Tennis by the Experts. LC 80-83978. (Illus.). 208p. (Orig.). 1981. pap. text ed. 6.95 (ISBN 0-918438-23-3). Leisure Pr.

As-Said, Labib. Recited Koran: A History of the First Recorded Version. Weiss, Bernard, ed. LC 73-20717. (Illus.). 156p. 1975. 10.00 (ISBN 0-87850-024-3). Darwin Pr.

Assal. International Diabetes Federation: Abstracts of the 11th Congress, Nairobi, Kenya, November 10-17, 1982. (International Congress Ser.: Vol. 577). 284p. 1983. 53.25 (ISBN 0-444-90253-8). Elsevier.

Assal, J. P., et al, eds. Diabetes Education: How to Improve Patient Education. (International Congress Ser.: No. 624). 336p. 1984. 90.50 (ISBN 0-444-90338-0, Excerpta Medica). Elsevier.

Assali, N. S. Biology of Gestation, 2 Vols. 1968. Vol. 1. 75.00 (ISBN 0-12-065401-6); Vol. 2. 72.00 (ISBN 0-12-065402-4). Acad Pr.

Assali, N. S., ed. Pathophysiology of Gestational Disorders. Incl. Vol. 1. Maternal Disorders. 1972. 77.50 (ISBN 0-12-065501-2); Vol. 2. Fetal-Placental Disorders. 1972. 68.00 (ISBN 0-12-065502-0); Vol. 3. Fetal & Neonatal Disorders. 1973. 78.00 (ISBN 0-12-065503-9). 1972. Acad Pr.

As-Samarra'i, Ibrahim. Al Fara'id: Gems from the Arabic Classical Dictionaries. (Arabic.). 1984. 18.00x (ISBN 0-86685-357-X). Intl Bk Ctr.

Assar, M. M. Guide to Sanitation in Natural Disasters. (Illus.). 135p. 1971. pap. 7.20 (ISBN 92-4-154011-7, 442). World Health.

Assarsson-Rizzi, Kerstin & Bohrn, Harold. Gunnar Myrdal: A Bibliography, 1919-1981. (Reference Library of Social Science). 240p. 1984. lib. bdg. 33.00 (ISBN 0-8240-9256-2). Garland Pub.

Assaykeen, Tatiana A., ed. Control of Renin Secretion. LC 76-185044. (Advances in Experimental Medicine & Biology Ser.: Vol. 17). 302p. 1972. 42.50x (ISBN 0-306-39017-5, Plenum Pr). Plenum Pub.

Asscher. Nephro-Urology. (Intergrated Clinical Science Ser.). 1984. pap. 19.95 (ISBN 0-8151-0305-0). Year Bk Med.

Asscher, et al. Nephrology Illustrated: An Integrated Text & Color Atlas. 230p. 1982. text ed. 90.00 (ISBN 0-7216-1447-7). Saunders.

Asscher, A. W. The Challenge of Urinary Tract Infections. 218p. 1980. 41.50 (ISBN 0-8089-1268-2, 790220). Grune.

Asscher, A. W., ed. see Symposium on Urinary Tract Infection, London, England, Sept. 23-24, 1974.

Asscher, A. W., et al. Nephrology Illustrated: An Integrated Text & Colour Atlas. (Pergamon Medical Publications Ser.). (Illus.). 256p. 1982. 105.00 (ISBN 0-08-028851-0). Pergamon.

Asseal, Henry, ed. see George P. Rowell & Staff.

Assecuranz & Compass. Year Book for International Insurance. 88th ed. 1751p. 1982. 305.00x. Intl Pubns Serv.

Assefi, Touraj. Stochastic Processes & Estimation Theory with Applications. LC 79-17872. 291p. 1979. 37.50x (ISBN 0-471-06454-8, Pub. by Wiley-Interscience). Wiley.

Assel, Henry, ed. see Frederick, J. George.

Assel, Henry, ed. see Lucas, Darrell B. & Britt, Steuart H.

Asselain, Jean-Charles. Planning & Profit in Socialist Economies. (International Library of Economics). 256p. 1984. 35.00x (ISBN 0-7102-0257-1). Routledge & Kegan.

Asselin, Cheryl, et al. Teacher Study Group Leader's Manual. 1975. pap. 5.00x (ISBN 0-918560-10-1). A Adler Inst.

Asselin, Claudette, tr. see Risso, Giuseppe.

Asselin, E. Donald. New England Laughs. (Orig.). 1963. pap. 2.95 (ISBN 0-911570-01-2). Vermont Bks.

--Portuguese-American Cookbook. LC 66-20571. 1966. pap. 3.95 (ISBN 0-8048-0480-X). C E Tuttle.

Asselin, John T. The Connecticut Workers' Compensation Practice Manual. 354p. 1985. 75.00 (ISBN 0-910051-03-8). CT Law Trib.

Asselineau, Roger. Edgar Allan Poe. LC 72-629875. (Pamphlets on American Writers Ser: No. 89). (Orig.). 1970. pap. 1.25x (ISBN 0-8166-0561-0, MPAW89). U of Minn Pr.

--Evolution of Walt Whitman: The Creation of a Book. LC 60-13297. Repr. of 1962 ed. 76.00 (ISBN 0-8357-9159-9, 2014651). Bks Demand UMI.

--Literary Reputation of Mark Twain from 1910-1950. LC 73-98744. Repr. of 1954 ed. lib. bdg. 18.75 (ISBN 0-8371-3069-7, ASLR). Greenwood.

--Studies in the House of Seven Gables. LC 73-146037. 1971. pap. text ed. 6.95x (ISBN 0-675-09246-9). Merrill.

--The Transcendentalist Constant in American Literature. (The Gotham Library). 1981. 27.00x (ISBN 0-8147-0572-3); pap. 13.50x (ISBN 0-8147-0573-1). NYU Pr.

Asselt, Jeannie Van see Murat, Ines.

Assemblee de la Societe Suisse d'ophtalmologie, 63rd, Lausanne, 1970, jt. auth. see Colloque du Club Jules Gonin, 7th.

Assembly of Behavioral & Social Sciences, National Research Council. Ability Testing of Handicapped People: Dilemma for Government, Science & the Public. 242p. 1982. pap. text ed. 13.50 (ISBN 0-309-03240-7). Natl Acad Pr.

Assembly of Behavioral & Social Sciences. Deterrence & Incapacitation: Estimating the Effects of Criminal Sanctions on Crime Rates. 1978. pap. 16.75 (ISBN 0-309-02649-0). Natl Acad Pr.

Assembly of Behavioral & Social Sciences, National Research Council. Knowledge & Policy in Manpower: A Study of the Manpower, Research & Development Program in the Department of Labor. LC 75-37384. xi, 171p. 1975. pap. 7.75 (ISBN 0-309-02439-0). Natl Acad Pr.

Assembly of Behavioral & Social Sciences. Knowledge & Policy: The Uncertain Connection. 1978. pap. 9.75 (ISBN 0-309-02732-2). Natl Acad Pr.

Assembly of Behavioral & Social Sciences, National Research Council. Making Policies for Children: A Study of the Federal Process. 265p. 1982. pap. text ed. 13.95 (ISBN 0-309-03241-5). Natl Acad Pr.

--Neither Angels Nor Thieves: Studies in Deinstitutionalization of Status Offenders. 949p. 1982. 29.95 (ISBN 0-309-03192-3). Natl Acad Pr.

Assembly of Behavioral & Social Sciences. Noise Abatement: Policy Alternatives for Transportation. 1977. pap. 9.50 (ISBN 0-309-02648-2). Natl Acad Pr.

Assembly of Behavioral & Social Sciences, National Research Council. Toward a National Policy for Children & Families. LC 76-56640. 143p. 1976. pap. 8.95 (ISBN 0-309-02533-8). Natl Acad Pr.

Assembly of Elementary Schools. A Journey Through the Inner School. 61p. 6.00 (ISBN 0-318-14819-6, AES 2); for members 3.00 (ISBN 0-318-14820-X). Mid St Coll & Schl.

--Judgement by the Profession. 80p. 6.00 (ISBN 0-318-14821-8, AES 3); for members 3.00 (ISBN 0-318-14822-6). Mid St Coll & Schl.

--The Unseen Hand. 87p. 6.50 (ISBN 0-318-14824-2, AES 4); members 3.50 (ISBN 0-318-14825-0). Mid St Coll & Schl.

Assembly of Engineering, Institute of Medicine, National Research Council. Medical Technology & the Health Care System: A Study of the Diffusion of Equipment-Embodied Technology. 1979. pap. text ed. 12.25 (ISBN 0-309-02865-5). Natl Acad Pr.

Assembly of Life Sciences, National Research Council. Alternatives to the Current Use of Nitrite in Foods. 280p. 1982. pap. text ed. 12.95 (ISBN 0-309-03277-6). Natl Acad Pr.

--Drinking Water & Health, Vol. 4. 1982. pap. text ed. 15.95 (ISBN 0-309-03198-2). Natl Acad Pr.

--Ecological Aspects of Development in the Humid Tropics. 1982. pap. text ed. 14.50 (ISBN 0-309-03235-0). Natl Acad Pr.

--Seriously Handicapping Orthodontic Conditions. LC 76-16344. 1976. pap. 6.75 (ISBN 0-309-02501-X). Natl Acad Pr.

Assembly of Mathematical & Physical Sciences, National Research Council. Long-Term Worldwide Effects of Multiple Nuclear-Weapons Detonations. LC 75-29733. xvi, 213p. 1975. pap. 14.95 (ISBN 0-309-02418-8). Natl Acad Pr.

Assembly on University Goals & Governance. The Students Themselves. 320p. 1974. text ed. 15.95x (ISBN 0-87073-432-6). Schenkman Bks Inc.

Assendelft, Marion M. van see Van Assendelft, Marion M.

Assendelft, Van & England, J. M. Advances in Hematological Methods: The Blood Count. 272p. 1982. 74.00 (ISBN 0-8493-6596-1). CRC Pr.

Asseng, Rolf E. When Jesus Comes Again: What the Bible Says. LC 83-72118. 96p. (Orig.). 1984. pap. 4.95 (ISBN 0-8066-2062-5, 10-7070). Augsburg.

Assenheim, Harry M. Introduction to Electron Spin Resonance. LC 67-21449. (Monographs of Electron Spin Resonance Ser.). 200p. 1967. 27.50x (ISBN 0-306-30306-X, Plenum Pr). Plenum Pub.

Assenmacherm, I. & Farner, D. S., eds. Environmental Endocrinology: Proceedings of an International Symposium Held in Montpellier (France), July 11-15, 1977. (Proceedings in Life Sciences). (Illus.). 1978. 45.00 (ISBN 0-387-08809-1). Springer-Verlag.

Assfalg, Julius & Krueger, P. Kleines Woerterbuch Des Christlichen Orients. 1st ed. (Ger.). 1975. 52.00 (ISBN 3-447-01707-4, M-7514, Pub. by Harrassowitz). French & Eur.

Assheton, Nicholas. The Journal of Nicholas Assheton of Downham Esq., in the County of Lancaster, for Part of the Year 1617. (Chetham Society Ser: Vol. 14). 20.00 (ISBN 0-384-02205-7). Johnson Repr.

Assiac. Opening Preparation. 1982. 15.90 (ISBN 0-08-024095-X); pap. 8.95 (ISBN 0-08-024096-8). Pergamon.

Assimakopoulos, Pat. Search for Sanity. 176p. 1985. pap. 2.95 (ISBN 0-345-32638-5). Ballantine.

Assimeng, J. M., ed. Traditional Life, Culture and Literature in Ghana. (Africa in Transition Ser.). 200p. 1976. 17.50 (ISBN 0-914970-26-7). Conch Mag.

Assimil. Assimil Language Course: For French Speaking People Who Want to Learn Latin - le Latin Sans Peine. 11.95 (ISBN 0-686-56090-6); accompanying records & tapes 75.00 (ISBN 0-686-56091-4). French & Eur.

--Assimil Language Course: For French Speaking People Who Want to Learn Advanced Dutch - la Pratique du Neerlandais. 13.95 (ISBN 0-686-56100-7); accompanying records & tapes 75.00 (ISBN 0-686-56101-5). French & Eur.

--Assimil Language Courses: English for Children - Assimil Junior. 15.95 (ISBN 0-686-56110-4); accompanying records & tapes 99.50 (ISBN 0-686-56111-2). French & Eur.

--Assimil Language Courses: For Dutch Speaking People Who Want to Learn English - Engels Zonder Moeite. 12.95 (ISBN 0-686-56170-8); accompanying records & tapes 75.00 (ISBN 0-686-56171-6). French & Eur.

--Assimil Language Courses: For Dutch Speaking People Who Want to Learn German - Duits Zonder Moeite. 12.95 (ISBN 0-686-56172-4); accompanying records & tapes 75.00 (ISBN 0-686-56173-2). French & Eur.

--Assimil Language Courses: For Dutch Speaking People Who Want to Learn Spanish - Spaans Zonder Moeite. 12.95 (ISBN 0-686-56174-0); accompanying records & tapes 75.00 (ISBN 0-686-56175-9). French & Eur.

--Assimil Language Courses: For Dutch Speaking People Who Want to Learn Italian - Italiaans Zonder Moeite. 12.95 (ISBN 0-686-56176-7); accompanying records & tapes 75.00 (ISBN 0-686-56177-5). French & Eur.

--Assimil Language Courses: For Dutch Speaking People Who Want to Learn French - Frans Zondar Moeite. 12.95 (ISBN 0-686-56180-5); accompanying records & tapes 75.00 (ISBN 0-686-56181-3). French & Eur.

--Assimil Language Courses: For English Speaking People Who Want to Learn German - German Without Toil. 11.95 (ISBN 0-686-56142-2); accompanying records & tapes 75.00 (ISBN 0-686-56143-0). French & Eur.

--Assimil Language Courses: For English Speaking People Who Want to Learn Spanish - Spanish Without Toil. 11.95 (ISBN 0-686-56144-9); accompanying records & tapes 75.00 (ISBN 0-686-56145-7). French & Eur.

--Assimil Language Courses: For English Speaking People Who Want to Learn Italian - Italian Without Toil. 11.95 (ISBN 0-686-56146-5); accompanying records & tapes 75.00 (ISBN 0-686-56147-3). French & Eur.

--Assimil Language Courses: For English Speaking People Who Want to Learn Russian - Russian Without Toil. 11.95 (ISBN 0-686-56148-1); accompanying records & tapes 75.00 (ISBN 0-686-56149-X). French & Eur.

--Assimil Language Courses: For English Speaking People Who Want to Learn French - French Without Toil. 11.95 (ISBN 0-686-56150-3); accompanying records & tapes 75.00 (ISBN 0-686-56151-1). French & Eur.

--Assimil Language Courses: For English Speaking People Who Want to Learn French - Let's Learn French. 15.95 (ISBN 0-686-56152-X); accompanying records & tapes 75.00 (ISBN 0-686-56153-8). French & Eur.

--Assimil Language Courses: For French Speaking People Who Want to Learn English - l'Anglais Sans Peine. 13.95 (ISBN 0-686-56070-1); accompanying records & tapes 75.00 (ISBN 0-686-56071-X). French & Eur.

--Assimil Language Courses: For French Speaking People Who Want to Learn German - l'Allemand Sans Peine. 11.95 (ISBN 0-686-56072-8); accompanying records & tapes 75.00 (ISBN 0-686-56073-6). French & Eur.

--Assimil Language Courses: For French Speaking People Who Want to Learn Spanish - l'Espagnol Sans Peine. 11.95 (ISBN 0-686-56074-4); accompanying records & tapes 75.00 (ISBN 0-686-56075-2). French & Eur.

--Assimil Language Courses: For French Speaking People Who Want to Learn Greek - Le Grec sans Peine. 11.95 (ISBN 0-686-56076-0); accompanying records & tapes 75.00 (ISBN 0-686-56077-9). French & Eur.

--Assimil Language Courses: For French Speaking People Who Want to Learn Italian - l'Italien sans Peine. 11.95 (ISBN 0-686-56078-7); accompanying records & tapes 75.00 (ISBN 0-686-56079-5). French & Eur.

--Assimil Language Courses: For French Speaking People Who Want to Learn Dutch - le Neerlandais sans Peine. 13.95 (ISBN 0-686-56080-9); accompanying records & tapes 85.00 (ISBN 0-686-56081-7). French & Eur.

--Assimil Language Courses: For French Speaking People Who Want to Learn Portuguese - le Poertugais sans Peine. 11.95 (ISBN 0-686-56082-5); accompanying records & tapes 75.00 (ISBN 0-686-56083-3). French & Eur.

--Assimil Language Courses: For French Speaking People Who Want to Learn Russian - le Russe sans Peine. 11.95 (ISBN 0-686-56084-1); accompanying records & tapes 95.00 (ISBN 0-686-56085-X). French & Eur.

--Assimil Language Courses: For French Speaking People Who Want to Learn Esperanto - l'Esperanto sans Peine. 12.95 (ISBN 0-686-56088-4); accompanying records & tapes 95.00 (ISBN 0-686-56089-2). French & Eur.

--Assimil Language Courses: For French Speaking People Who Want to Learn Advanced English - la Pratique de l'Anglais. 11.95 (ISBN 0-686-56096-5); accompanying records & tapes 75.00 (ISBN 0-686-56097-3). French & Eur.

--Assimil Language Courses: For French Speaking People Who Want to Learn Advanced Spanish - la Pratique de l'Espagnol. 11.95 (ISBN 0-686-56098-1); accompanying records & tapes 75.00 (ISBN 0-686-56099-X). French & Eur.

--Assimil Language Courses: For French Speaking People Who Want to Learn Corsican - le Corse Sans Peine. 13.95 (ISBN 0-686-56102-3); accompanying records & tapes 75.00 (ISBN 0-686-56103-1). French & Eur.

--Assimil Language Courses: For French Speaking People Who Want to Learn Occitan - l'Occitan Sans Peine. 13.95 (ISBN 0-686-56108-2); accompanying records & tapes 75.00 (ISBN 0-686-56109-0). French & Eur.

--Assimil Language Courses: For French Speaking People Who Want to Learn Yugoslavian - le Serboc-Croate Sans Peine (Yougoslave) 16.95 (ISBN 0-686-56086-8); accompanying records & tapes 95.00 (ISBN 0-686-56087-6). French & Eur.

--Assimil Language Courses: For French Speaking People Who Want to Learn Arabic - l'Arabe sans Peine, Tome 1. 15.95 (ISBN 0-686-56092-2); accompanying records & tapes 75.00 (ISBN 0-686-56093-0). French & Eur.

--Assimil Language Courses: For French Speaking People Who Want to Learn Breton - le Breton Sans Peine, Vol. 1. 13.95 (ISBN 0-686-56104-X); accompanying records & tapes 75.00 (ISBN 0-686-56105-8). French & Eur.

--Assimil Language Courses: For French Speaking People Who Want to Learn Arabic - l'Arabe sans Peine, Tome 2. 18.95 (ISBN 0-686-56094-9); accompanying records & tapes 75.00 (ISBN 0-686-56095-7). French & Eur.

--Assimil Language Courses: For German Speaking People Who Want to Learn English - Englisch ohne Muhe. 11.95 (ISBN 0-686-56130-9); accompanying records & tapes 75.00 (ISBN 0-686-56131-7). French & Eur.

--Assimil Language Courses: For German Speaking People Who Want to Learn Spanish - Spanisch ohne Muhe. 11.95 (ISBN 0-686-56132-5); accompanying records & tapes 75.00 (ISBN 0-686-56133-3). French & Eur.

--Assimil Language Courses: For German Speaking People Who Want to Learn Italian - Italeinisch ohne Muhe. 11.95 (ISBN 0-686-56134-1); accompanying records & tapes 75.00 (ISBN 0-686-56135-X). French & Eur.

--Assimil Language Courses: For German Speaking People Who Want to Learn Portuguese - Portugiesisch ohne Muhe. 11.95 (ISBN 0-686-56136-8); accompanying records & tapes 75.00 (ISBN 0-686-56137-6). French & Eur.

--Assimil Language Courses: For German Speaking People Who Want to Learn Russian - Russisch ohne Muhe. 11.95 (ISBN 0-686-56138-4); accompanying records & tapes 95.00 (ISBN 0-686-56139-2). French & Eur.

--Assimil Language Courses: For German Speaking People Who Want to Learn French - Franzosisch ohne Muhe. 11.95 (ISBN 0-686-56140-6); accompanying records & tapes 75.00 (ISBN 0-686-56141-4). French & Eur.

--Assimil Language Courses: For Greek Speaking People Who Want to Learn German. 11.95 (ISBN 0-686-56178-3); accompanying records & tapes 75.00 (ISBN 0-686-56179-1). French & Eur.

--Assimil Language Courses: For Italian Speaking People Who Want to Learn English - l'Inglese senza Sforzo. 11.95 (ISBN 0-686-56154-6); accompanying records & tapes 75.00 (ISBN 0-686-56155-4). French & Eur.

--Assimil Language Courses: For Italian Speaking People Who Want to Learn English - Let's Start Inglese. 18.95 (ISBN 0-686-56156-2); accompanying records & tapes 75.00 (ISBN 0-686-56157-0). French & Eur.

--Assimil Language Courses: For Italian Speaking People Who Want to Learn German - il Tedesco senza Sforzo. 11.95 (ISBN 0-686-56158-9); accompanying records & tapes 75.00 (ISBN 0-686-56159-7). French & Eur.

--Assimil Language Courses: For Italian Speaking People Who Want to Learn Spanish - lo Spagnolo senza Sforzo. 11.95 (ISBN 0-686-56160-0); accompanying records & tapes 75.00 (ISBN 0-686-56161-9). French & Eur.

--Assimil Language Courses: For Italian Speaking People Who Want to Learn French -il Francese senza Sforzo. 11.95 (ISBN 0-686-56162-7); accompanying records & tapes 75.00 (ISBN 0-686-56163-5). French & Eur.

--Assimil Language Courses: For Portuguese Speaking People Who Want to Learn English - o Ingles sem Custo. 11.95 (ISBN 0-686-56124-4); accompanying records & tapes 75.00 (ISBN 0-686-56125-2). French & Eur.

--Assimil Language Courses: For Portuguese Speaking People Who Want to Learn German - Alemao sem Custo. 11.95 (ISBN 0-686-56126-0); accompanying records & tapes 75.00 (ISBN 0-686-56127-9). French & Eur.

--Assimil Language Courses: For Portuguese Speaking People Who Want to Learn French - o Frances sem Custo. 11.95 (ISBN 0-686-56128-7); accompanying records & tapes 75.00 (ISBN 0-686-56129-5). French & Eur.

--Assimil Language Courses: For Spanish Speaking People Who Want to Learn English - el Ingles sin Esfuerzo. 11.95 (ISBN 0-686-56112-0); accompanying records & tapes 75.00 (ISBN 0-686-56113-9). French & Eur.

--Assimil Language Courses: For Spanish Speaking People Who Want to Learn English - Let's Start Ingles. 15.95 (ISBN 0-686-56114-7); accompanying records & tapes 75.00 (ISBN 0-686-56115-5). French & Eur.

--Assimil Language Courses: For Spanish Speaking People Who Want to Learn English - Let's Get Better Ingles. 15.95 (ISBN 0-686-56116-3); accompanying records & tapes 75.00 (ISBN 0-686-56117-1). French & Eur.

--Assimil Language Courses: For Spanish Speaking People Who Want to Learn German - el Aleman sin Esfuerzo. 11.95 (ISBN 0-686-56118-X); accompanying records & tapes 75.00 (ISBN 0-686-56119-8). French & Eur.

--Assimil Language Courses: For Spanish Speaking People Who Want to Learn French - el Frances sin Esfuerzo. 11.95 (ISBN 0-686-56120-1); accompanying records & tapes 75.00 (ISBN 0-686-56121-X). French & Eur.

--Assimil Language Courses: For Spanish Speaking People Who Want to Learn Russian - el Russo sin Esfuerzo. 14.95 (ISBN 0-686-56122-8); accompanying records & tapes 95.00 (ISBN 0-686-56123-6). French & Eur.

--Assimil Language Courses: For Yugoslav Speaking People Who Want to Learn English - Engleski bez Muke. 12.95 (ISBN 0-686-56164-3); accompanying records & tapes 75.00 (ISBN 0-686-56165-1). French & Eur.

--Assimil Language Courses: For Yugoslav Speaking People Who Want to Learn German - Nemacki bez Muke. 12.95 (ISBN 0-686-56166-X); accompanying records & tapes 75.00 (ISBN 0-686-56167-8). French & Eur.

--Assimil Language Courses: For Yugoslav Speaking People Who Want to Learn French - Francuski bez Muke. 12.95 (ISBN 0-686-56168-6); accompanying records & tapes 75.00 (ISBN 0-686-56169-4). French & Eur.

Assimil, ed. French Without Toil. 1957. 9.50x (ISBN 2-7005-0028-8); 3 cassettes 70.00 (ISBN 0-686-09278-3); 12 records 70.00x (ISBN 0-686-28531-X); bk. & cassettes 79.00x (ISBN 0-686-28532-8). Intl Learn Syst.

Assiouly, E. Banking & Financial Dictionary: English-French-Arabic. 338p. (Eng., Fr. & Arabic.). 1980. pap. 75.00 (ISBN 0-686-92351-0, M-9767). French & Eur.

Assis, Joaquim M. The Attendant's Confession, the Fortune Teller, & Life. Goldberg, Isaac, ed. & tr. (International Pocket Library). pap. 4.00 (ISBN 0-8283-1426-8). Branden Pub Co.

--Hand & the Glove. Bagby, Albert I., Jr., tr. LC 74-111502. (Studies in Romance Languages: No. 2). 144p. 1970. 12.00x (ISBN 0-8131-1211-7). U Pr of Ky.

--The Heritage of Quincas Borba. 1977. lib. bdg. 59.95 (ISBN 0-8490-1946-X). Gordon Pr.

--Iaia Garcia. Bagby, Albert I., Jr., tr. LC 76-24338. (Studies in Romance Languages: No. 17). 192p. 1977. 18.00x (ISBN 0-8131-1353-9). U Pr of Ky.

Assis, Joaquim M. Machado De see Machado de Assis, Joaquim M.

Assis, Machada de see De Assis, Machado.

Assis, Machado De see De Assis, Machado.

Assis, Machado de see De Assis, Machado.

Assmann, David, et al. Clinical Simulations for Respiratory Care Practitioners. (Orig.). 1979. pap. 34.95 (ISBN 0-8151-0318-2). Year Bk Med.

Assmann, Heinz-Dieter. The Broker-Dealer's Liability for Recommendations: Under U. S. Securities Laws & the Suitability Rules of Self-Regulatory Organizations. (European University Studies: No. 2, Vol. 305). 122p. 1982. pap. 13.15 (ISBN 3-8204-7153-7). P Lang Pubs.

Assn Ed Comm Tech, ed. see Frederick, Franz J.

Asso, Doreen. The Real Menstrual Cycle. 214p. 1983. 42.95x (ISBN 0-471-90043-5, Pub by Wiley Interscience); pap. 16.95x (ISBN 0-471-90175-X). Wiley.

Associaiton for Information & Image Management. Microfilm Readers: ANSI-AIIM MS20-1979. 1979. 6.00 (ISBN 0-89258-061-5); member 5.25. Assn Inform & Image Mgmt.

Associated Advertisers Services Staff. Associated Advertisers Services Reference Pages. 20p. pap. 1.00 (ISBN 0-686-40867-5). Nunciata.

Associated Business Press, ed. The Marketing of Generic Drugs. 224p. 1982. 75.00x (ISBN 0-85227-268-5, Pub. by Assoc Bus Pr England). State Mutual Bk.

Associated Features Inc. Dan Fouts, Ken Anderson, Joe Theismann, & Other All-Time Great Quarterbacks. LC 83-4543. (Sports Library). (Illus.). 128p. (gr. 5-9). 1983. pap. 2.50 (ISBN 0-394-85805-0). Random.

--Home Run: Baseball's Greatest Hits & Hitters. Hollander, Zander, ed. LC 83-19200. (Random House Sports Library). (Illus.). 144p. (gr. 5-9). 1984. pap. 2.50 (ISBN 0-394-86488-3, BYR). Random.

--The Masked Marvels: Baseball's Great Catchers. LC 81-12182. (Random House Sports Library). (Illus.). 144p. (gr. 5-9). 1982. pap. 1.95 (ISBN 0-394-85013-0). Random.

--Winners Under Twenty-One: America's Spectacular Young Sports Champions. LC 81-13786. (Random House Sports Library). (Illus.). 144p. (gr. 5-9). 1982. pap. 1.95 (ISBN 0-394-85015-7). Random.

Associated Grantmakers of Massachusetts, Inc. Massachusetts Foundation Directory Supplement: Sources of Private Support for Individuals. LC 84-71466. 117p. (Orig.). 1984. pap. 12.00 (ISBN 0-912427-02-7). Assoc Grant.

--Massachusetts Foundation Directory: 1983 Edition. LC 83-70670. 136p. (Orig.). 1983. pap. text ed. 15.00 (ISBN 0-912427-00-0). Assoc Grant.

Associated Press. The Associated Press Stylebook. 1977. 12.95 (ISBN 0-89328-016-X). Lorenz Pr.

--The Associated Press Stylebook & Libel Manual. 288p. 1982. pap. 8.95 (ISBN 0-201-10091-6). Addison-Wesley.

Associated Press & Currier, Chet. The Investor's Encyclopedia. 480p. 1985. 24.95 (ISBN 0-531-09586-X). Watts.

Associated Press, jt. auth. see Esper, George.

Associated Press, jt. auth. see Goldstein, Norm.

Associated Press, ed. The Associated Press Sunday Crossword Puzzle Book. (Illus.). 96p. (Orig.). 1983. pap. 4.95 spiral bdg. (ISBN 0-8092-5573-1). Contemp Bks.

Associated Press Editors. The Associated Press Sunday Crossword Puzzle Book 2. (Illus.). 96p. 1985. spiral 4.95 (ISBN 0-8092-5319-4). Contemp Bks.

Associated Press Editors & Varoga, Chuck. It's a Fact. (Illus.). 256p. (Orig.). 1983. pap. 6.95 (ISBN 0-8092-5576-6). Contemp Bks.

Associated Press Editors, jt. auth. see Groves, Seli.

Associated Press Editors, jt. auth. see Perkes, Dan.

Associated Press Editors, jt. auth. see Simonet, Tom.

Associated Press Staff & Cappon, Rene J., eds. The Associated Press Guide to Good Writing. 196p. 1982. pap. 7.95 (ISBN 0-201-10320-6). Addison-Wesley.

Associated Women's Organization, Mars Hill Bible School. Something Special. Simpson, Peggy & Stanley, Linda, eds. 1977. pap. 4.95 (ISBN 0-89137-408-6). Quality Pubns.

--What Are We Doing Here? 1972. pap. 4.95 (ISBN 0-89137-404-3). Quality Pubns.

Associated Writing Programs Staff, ed. Intro Thirteen. (Intro Ser.). 224p. (Orig.). 1982. pap. 7.95x (ISBN 0-936266-03-1). Assoc Writing Progs.

Associates for James Knuppe, jt. auth. see Siegel, Robert L.

Associates of Price Pottinger Nutrition Foundation, jt. auth. see Connolly, Pat.

Association Europeene D'etudes Juridiques et Fiscales see Strom, Paul.

Association Europpeene D'etudes Juridiques et Fiscales. Business Law in Europe: Legal, Tax & Labour Aspects of Business Operations in the Ten European Community Countries & Switzerland. Ellis, Maarten J., et al, eds. 622p. 1982. 92.00 (ISBN 90-654-4040-2, Pub. by Kluwer Law Netherlands). Kluwer Academic.

Association for Advancement of Medical Instrumentation. Cardiac Monitoring in a Complex Patient Care Environment. 96p. (Orig.). 1982. pap. text ed. 35.00 (ISBN 0-910275-09-2); members 25.00. Assn Adv Med Instrs.

Association for Asian Studies. Cumulative Bibliography of Asian Studies, 1966-1970. Incl. Author Bibliography, 3 vols. 1973. lib. bdg. 415.00 (ISBN 0-8161-0959-1); Subject Bibliography, 3 vols. 1972. lib. bdg. 415.00 (ISBN 0-8161-0235-X). Hall Library). G K Hall.

--Cumulative Bibliography of Asian Studies, 1941-1965, Author Bibliography, 4 Vols. 1969. Set. 405.00 (ISBN 0-8161-0805-6, Hall Library). G K Hall.

--Cumulative Bibliography of Asian Studies, 1941-1965, Subject Bibliography, 4 Vols. 1970. Set. 415.00 (ISBN 0-8161-0127-2, Hall Library). G K Hall.

Association for Biology Laboratory Education Staff. Tested Studies for Laboratory Teaching: Proceedings of the Third Workshop-Conference of Association for Biology Laboratory Education. 240p. 1984. text ed. 19.95 (ISBN 0-8403-3178-9). Kendall-Hunt.

Association for Childhood Education International. Migrant Children: Their Education. Sunderlin, Sylvia, ed. LC 74-162482. pap. 20.00 (ISBN 0-317-28803-2, 2020631). Bks Demand UMI.

Association for Counselor Education & Supervision Committee on Accreditation. Standards for Preparation in Counselor Education. 22p. 1979. 2.50 (ISBN 0-911547-69-X, 72128W34). Am Assn Coun Dev.

Association for Educational Communications & Technology & Association of Media Producers. Copyright & Educational Media: A Guide to Fair Use & Permissions Procedures. 1977. pap. 2.95 members (ISBN 0-89240-004-8). Assn Ed Comm Tech.

Association for Educational Communications & Technology. Task Force on Definition & Terminology. Educational Technology: A Glossary of Terms. Silber, Kenneth, ed. LC 79-53125. 1979. pap. text ed. 21.00 (ISBN 0-89240-007-2); pap. text ed. 18.00 members. Assn Ed Comm Tech.

Association for Educational Communications & Technology. Evaluation of Instructional Materials. 1979. soft cover 5.00 (ISBN 0-89240-033-1); members 4.00. Assn Ed Comm Tech.

Association for Eye Research, 18th, Bonn, July 1977. Gerontological Aspects of Eye Research: Selected Papers. (Interdisciplinary Topics in Gerontology: Vol. 13). (Illus.). 1978. 55.00 (ISBN 3-8055-2877-9). S Karger.

Association for Holistic Health Staff. The National Directory of Holistic Health Professionals. 3rd ed. (Illus.). 270p. 1984. pap. 7.95 (ISBN 0-915407-00-0). Assn Holistic.

Association for Information & Image Management. AIIM Buying Guide. McAllister, Douglas & Plunka, Gene, eds. (Consumer Ser.). 193p. 1985. pap. 25.00 (ISBN 0-317-06202-6, C183); pap. 18.75 member. Assn Inform & Image Mgmt.

--All about Microfilm Cameras. (Consumer Ser.: No. C106). (Illus.). 24p. 1977. 5.00 (ISBN 0-89258-047-X, C106); member 3.75. Assn Inform & Image Mgmt.

--Alphanumeric COM Quality Test Slide: MS 28-1983. rev. ed. 8p. 1983. pap. 6.00 (ISBN 0-89258-081-X, M028); pap. 5.25 member. Assn Inform & Image Mgmt.

--Dimensions & Operational Constraints for Double Core (Bi-Axial) Cassette for 16mm Processed Microfilm: ANSI-AIIM MS16-1981. (Standards & Recommended Practices Ser.). 6p. 1981. pap. 6.00 (ISBN 0-89258-074-7, M016). Assn Inform & Image Mgmt.

--Dimensions & Operational Constraints for Single-Core Cartridge for 16mm Processed Microfilm: ANSI-AIIM MS15-1977. (Standards & Recommended Practices Ser.). 10p. 1977. pap. 6.00 (ISBN 0-89258-008-9, M015). Assn Inform & Image Mgmt.

--Document Mark (BLIP) Used in Image Mark Retrieval Systems: ANSI-AIIM MS8-1979. Rev. ed. (Standards & Recommended Practices). 1980. 6.00 (ISBN 0-89258-060-7, M008); member 5.25. Assn Inform & Image Mgmt.

--Format & Coding for Computer Output Microfilm: ANSI-AIIM MS2-1978. (Standards & Recommended Practices). 1978. 6.00 (ISBN 0-89258-054-2, M002); member 5.25. Assn Inform & Image Mgmt.

--Identification of Microforms: ANSI-AIIM MS19-1978. (Standards & Recommended Practices). 1978. 6.00 (ISBN 0-89258-051-8, M019). Assn Inform Image.

--Measuring COM Recording Speeds: AIIM MS21-1979. (Standards & Recommended Practices). 1979. 6.00 (ISBN 0-89258-058-5, M021); member 5.25. Assn Inform & Image Mgmt.

--Method for Measuring the Screen Luminance, Contrast, & Reflectance of Microform Readers: ANSI-AIIM MS12-1977. (Standards & Recommended Practices Ser.). 1977. pap. 6.00 (M012); pap. 5.25 member. Assn Inform & Image Mgmt.

--Method for Measuring Thickness of Buildup Area on Unitized Microfilm Carriers (Aperture, Camera, Copy & Image Cards) ANSI-AIIM MS9-1973 (R1977) (Standards & Recommended Practices Ser.). 8p. 1973. pap. 6.00 (ISBN 0-89258-007-0, M009); pap. 5.25 member. Assn Inform & Image Mgmt.

--Metric Conversion Recommendations: AIIM TR1-1979. (Technical Reports Ser.). 1979. pap. text ed. 10.00 (ISBN 0-89258-063-1, T001); pap. text ed. 7.75 member. Assn Inform & Image Mgmt.

--Microfilm Package Labeling: ANSI-AIIM MS6-1981. (Standards & Recommended Practices Ser.). 2p. pap. 6.00 (ISBN 0-89258-009-7, M006); pap. 5.25 member. Assn Inform & Image Mgmt.

--Microfilming Newspapers: ANSI-AIIM MS111-1977. 1978. 6.00 (ISBN 0-89258-050-X); member 5.25. Assn Inform & Image Mgmt.

--Practice for Operational Practices-Inspection & Quality Control for Alphanumeric Computer-Output Microforms: ANSI-AIIM MS1-1981. 15p. 1980. pap. 6.00 (ISBN 0-89258-064-X, M001); pap. 5.25 member. Assn Inform & Image Mgmt.

--Practice for Operational Procedures: Inspection & Quality Control of First-Generation Silver-Gelatin Microfilm of Documents (ANSI-AIIM MS23-1983) rev. ed. 1979. pap. text ed. 12.50 (ISBN 0-89258-067-4); pap. text ed. 10.75 member. Assn Inform & Image Mgmt.

--Practice for Uniform Product Disclosure for Unitized Microform Readers (Microfiche, Jackets & Image Cards) ANSI/AIIM MS22-1981. (Standards & Recommended Practices). 1981. 6.00 (ISBN 0-89258-057-7, M021); member 5.25. Assn Inform & Image Mgmt.

--Recommended Practice for Microfilming Newspapers: ANSI-AIIM MS111-1977. (Standards & Recommended Practices Ser.). 9p. 1977. pap. 6.00 (ISBN 0-89258-010-0, M111). Assn Inform & Image Mgmt.

--Silver Recovery Techniques: AIIM TR4-1982. (Technical Ser.). 12p. (Orig.). 1982. pap. 10.00 (ISBN 0-89258-077-1, T004); pap. 7.75 member. Assn Inform & Image Mgmt.

--Specifications for Sixteen & Thirty-Five Millimeter Microfilms in Roll Form: ASNI-AIIM MS14-1978. (Standards & Recommended Practices). 1978. 6.00 (ISBN 0-89258-052-6, M014). Assn Inform Image.

--Test Chart for Rotary Microfilm Cameras: ANSI-AIIM MS17-1983. (Standards & Recommended Practices Ser.). 10p. 1983. pap. 6.00 (ISBN 0-317-06197-6, M017); pap. 5.25 member. Assn Inform & Image Mgmt.

--Test Target for Use in Microrecording Engineering Graphics on 35-MM Microfilm. (Standards Ser.). 1980. pap. 6.00 (ISBN 0-89258-068-2, AIIM MS24-1980); pap. 5.25 member. Assn Inform & Image Mgmt.

--Thermally Processed Silver Microfilm: AIIM TR3-1981. (Technical Reports Ser.). 5p. 1981. pap. 10.00 (ISBN 0-89258-073-9, T003); pap. 7.75 member. Assn Inform & Image Mgmt.

--Uniform Product Disclosure for Roll Film Readers: AIIM MS27-1982. (Standards & Recommended Practices Ser.). 4p. 1982. pap. 6.00 (ISBN 0-89258-078-X, M027); pap. 5.25 member. Assn Inform & Image Mgmt.

Association for Library Service to Children. Let's Read Together: Books for Family Enjoyment. 4th ed. LC 80-39957. 124p. 1981. pap. 5.00x (ISBN 0-8389-3253-3). ALA.

Association for Library Service to Children & Young Adult Services Division. Selecting Materials for Children & Young Adults: A Bibliography of Bibliographies & Review Sources. LC 80-12374. 80p. 1980. pap. 7.00x (ISBN 0-8389-3241-X). ALA.

Association for Library Service to Children. Sex & Youth: A Symposium. 53p. (Reprint from Top of the News, Winter 1978). 1978. 2.00 (ISBN 0-8389-5541-X, ALSC). ALA.

Association for Programmed Learning & Educational Technology Conference, 1979. Aspects of Educational Technology, Vol. XIII: Educational Technology Twenty Years On. Page, G. Terry & Whitlock, Quentin, eds. 1979. 36.00 (ISBN 0-85038-247-5). Nichols Pub.

Association for Radiation Research, Winter Meeting Jan. 3-5, 1979. Radiation Biology & Chemistry: Research Developments: Proceedings. Edwards, H. E., et al, eds. LC 79-15532. (Studies in Physical & Theoretical Chemistry Ser.: Vol. 6). 505p. 1979. 93.75 (ISBN 0-444-41821-0). Elsevier.

Association for Research & Enlightenment, Readings Research Dept., compiled by. Attitudes & Emotions Pt. I. (Library: Vol. 13). 445p. 1981. 11.95 (ISBN 0-87604-138-1). ARE Pr.

--Attitudes & Emotions, Pt. II. (Library: Vol. 14). 393p. 1982. 11.95 (ISBN 0-87604-140-3). ARE Pr.

--Christ Consciousness. (Library: Vol. 11). 277p. 1980. 10.95 (ISBN 0-87604-124-1). ARE Pr.

--Daily Living. (Library: Vol. 12). 241p. 1981. 10.95 (ISBN 0-87604-133-0). ARE Pr.

--Dreams & Dreaming, 2 parts. (Library: Vols. 4-5). 1976. 25.00 set (ISBN 0-87604-100-4). Vol. 4 592 pp (ISBN 0-87604-087-3). Vol. 5 1176 pp (ISBN 0-87604-088-1). ARE Pr.

Association for Research & Enlightement, Readings Research Dept., compiled by. The Early Christian Epoch. (Library: Vol. 6). 593p. 1976. 10.95 (ISBN 0-87604-089-X). ARE Pr.

--The Expanded Search for God: Pts. 1 & 2. (Library: Vol.16 & 17). Pt. 1 479pgs. 11/1983. 12.95 (ISBN 0-87604-153-5); Pt. 2 662pgs. 12/1983. 14.95 (ISBN 0-87604-154-3). ARE Pr.

Association for Research & Enlightenment, Readings Research Dept., compiled by. Jesus the Pattern: Library. (Vol. 10). 336p. 1980. 10.95 (ISBN 0-87604-123-3). ARE Pr.

--Meditation, 1: Healing, Prayer, & the Revelation. (Library: Vol. 2). 306p. 1974. 10.95 (ISBN 0-87604-072-5). ARE Pr.

Association for Research & Enlightenment, Readings Research Dept., ed. Meditation, 2: Meditation, Endocrine Glands, Prayer, & Affirmations. (Library: Vol. 3). 274p. 1975. 10.95 (ISBN 0-87604-082-2). ARE Pr.

Association for Research & Enlightenment, Readings Reasearch Dept., compiled by. On Life & Death: The Edgar Cayce Readings. (Library: Vol. 1). 188p. 1973. 8.95 (ISBN 0-87604-065-2). ARE Pr.

Association for Research & Enlightenment, Inc. Virginia Beach, Va. Study Groups, et al, eds. Search for God: Nineteen Forty-Two to Nineteen Fifty, 2 Bks. 1942-1950. 4.95 ea. Bk. 1 (ISBN 0-87604-000-8). Bk. 2 (ISBN 0-87604-001-6). ARE Pr.

Association for Research in Nervous & Mental Disease. Biology of the Major Psychoses: A Comparative Analysis. Freedman, D. X., ed. LC 75-14571. (Research Publications: Vol. 54). 384p. 1975. 45.50 (ISBN 0-89004-034-6). Raven.

--Brain Dysfunction in Metabolic Disorders, Vol. 53. Plum, Fred, ed. LC 74-79190. 336p. 1974. 50.50 (ISBN 0-911216-81-2). Raven.

Association for Supervision & Curriculum Development. Evaluation. 80p. 2.00 (ISBN 0-317-33681-9, 611-80182). Assn Supervision.

Association For Supervision And Curriculum Development. Life Skills in School & Society. LC 44-6213. 1969. pap. 5.50 (ISBN 0-87120-039-2, 610-17786). Assn Supervision.

Association for Supervision & Curriculum Development. Linguistics & the Classroom Teacher. LC 67-27469. 1967. pap. 2.75 (ISBN 0-87120-040-6, 611-17720). Assn Supervision.

--Supervision: Emerging Profession. LC 75-94523. 1969. pap. 5.00 (ISBN 0-87120-060-0, 611-17796). Assn Supervision.

--Supervision: Perspectives & Propositions. LC 67-29804. 1967. pap. 2.00 (ISBN 0-87120-062-7, 611-17732). Assn Supervision.

Association for the Advancement of Medical Instrumentation. Inhospital Sterility Assurance: Current Perspectives. (Illus.). 80p. (Orig.). 1982. pap. 35.00 (ISBN 0-910275-14-9); pap. 25.00 members. Assn Adv Med Instrs.

Association for the Anthropological Study of Play. The Paradoxes of Play: Papers. Loy, John J., ed. 224p. (Orig.). 1981. pap. text ed. 14.95 (ISBN 0-88011-001-5). Leisure Pr.

Association for the Improvement of the Conditions of the Poor. Housing Conditions in Baltimore: Report of a Special Committee of the Assoc. for the Improvement of the Condition of the Poor and the Charity Organization Society. LC 73-11915. (Metropolitan America Ser.). (Illus.). 104p. 1974. Repr. of 1907 ed. 12.00 (ISBN 0-405-05384-3). Ayer Co Pubs.

Association for University Business & Economic Research-AUBER. Readings in Business & Economic Research Management: Execution & Enterprise, Vol. 1. 1980. pap. 7.50 (ISBN 0-86603-000-X). Bur Busn Wis.

Association International du Droit d'Assurance. New Trends in Automobile Insurance in Europe. 1979. pap. 31.50 (ISBN 90-6321-014-0, Pub. by Kluwer Law Netherlands). Kluwer Academic.

Association of American Colleges & Howe, Florence. Liberal Education & the New Scholarship on Women: Issues & Constraints in Institutional Change. vi, 56p. (Orig.). 1982. pap. 3.50 (ISBN 0-911696-12-1). Assn Am Coll.

Association of American Geographers. Field Trip Guide, 1984. 1984. 2.00 (ISBN 0-89291-180-8). Assn Am Geographers.

--Program Abstracts, 1984. write for info. (ISBN 0-89291-176-X). Assn Am Geographers.

Association of American Geologists & Naturalists at Philadelphia, 1840 & 1841. Proceedings. Albritton, Claude C., ed. LC 77-6507. (History of Geology Ser.). Repr. of 1843 ed. lib. bdg. 46.50x (ISBN 0-405-10430-8). Ayer Co Pubs.

Association of American Law Schools. Law Books Recommended for Libraries. (Compilation of 46 subject lists complete in ten binders). 1967-70. loose leaf 475.00x, with 1974-1976 suppl. (ISBN 0-8377-0201-1). Rothman.

Association of American Publishers. The Accidental Profession. 103p. 1977. 6.50 (ISBN 0-317-32065-3, 7). AAP.

--Wholesale Textbook Industry Study. (Illus.). 130p. 500.00 (ISBN 0-317-32067-X, 43); members 395.00 (ISBN 0-317-32068-8). AAP.

Association of American University Presses, ed. One Book-Five Ways: The Publishing Procedures of Five University Presses. LC 78-9505. (Illus.). 349p. 1978. 19.95x (ISBN 0-913232-53-X); pap. 12.95x (ISBN 0-913232-54-8). W Kaufmann.

Association Of Assistant Masters In Secondary Schools. Teaching of Economics in Secondary Schools. (Illus.). 1971. 15.95 (ISBN 0-521-08010-X). Cambridge U Pr.

Association of College & Research Libraries & American Library Association. Books for College Libraries, 6 vols. 2nd ed. LC 74-13743. 2000p. 1975. pap. 80.00x set (ISBN 0-8389-0178-6). ALA.

Association of College & Research Libraries. Eighteenth Century English Books: Considered by Librarians & Booksellers, Bibliographers & Collectors. pap. 25.80 (ISBN 0-317-26559-8, 2023945). Bks Demand UMI.

Association of College & Research Libraries & Council on Postsecondary Accreditation. Libraries & Accreditation in Institutions of Higher Education: Proceedings of the Association of College & Research Libraries & the Council on Postsecondary Accreditation Invitational Conference, June 26-28, 1980. Virgo, Julie C. & Yuro, David A., eds. 176p. 1981. 19.00 (ISBN 0-317-32213-3); members 15.00 (ISBN 0-317-32214-1). ALA.

Association of Commonwealth Universities, ed. Awards for Commonwealth University Staff, 1978-80. 4th ed. 1977. pap. 8.50x (ISBN 0-85143-049-X). Intl Pubns Serv.

Association of Commonwealth Universities(London), ed. Awards for Commonwealth University Staff, 1981-1983. 5th ed. 210p. (Orig.). 1980. pap. 17.50x (ISBN 0-85143-068-6). Intl Pubns Serv.
Association of Commonwealth Universities, ed. Commonwealth Universities Yearbook, 1982, 4 vols. 58th ed. LC 59-24175. 2650p. (Orig.). 1982. Boxed Set. pap. 155.00x (ISBN 0-85143-076-7). Intl Pubns Serv.
Association of Desk & Derrick Clubs of America. D & D Standard Oil Abbreviator. 2nd ed. LC 72-96172. 230p. 14.95 (ISBN 0-87814-017-4). Pennwell Bks.
Association of Educational Data Systems. Capitolizing on Computers in Education: Proceedings. Martin, C. Dianne, ed. LC 84-7084. 1984. 35.95 (ISBN 0-88175-019-0). Computer Sci.
Association of Energy Engineers. Advances in Energy Cost Savings for Industry & Buildings. Payne, F. William, ed. (Illus.). 500p. 1983. text ed. 45.00 (ISBN 0-915586-78-9); pap. text ed. 30.00 (ISBN 0-915586-79-7). Fairmont Pr.
--Advances in Energy Utilization Technology. 1982. text ed. 45.00 (ISBN 0-915586-62-2); pap. text ed. 30.00 (ISBN 0-915586-61-4). Fairmont Pr.
--AEE Directory of Energy Professionals, 1982-83. rev. ed. 1982. text ed. 28.00 (ISBN 0-915586-58-4). Fairmont Pr.
--Energy Audit Source Book. 1982. text ed. 28.00 (ISBN 0-915586-42-8). Fairmont Pr.
--New Directions in Energy Technology. LC 84-81176. 500p. 1984. text ed. 45.00 (ISBN 0-915586-87-8); pap. text ed. 30.00 (ISBN 0-915586-88-6). Fairmont Pr.
Association of Energy Engineers Staff. Strategic Planning for Cogeneration & Energy Management. 600p. 1985. 45.00; pap. 30.00. Van Nos Reinhold.
--Strategic Planning for Cogenteration & Energy Management. Payne, F. William, ed. LC 85-80321. 600p. 1985. text ed. 45.00 (ISBN 0-88173-008-4); pap. text ed. 30.00 (ISBN 0-88173-009-2). Fairmont Pr.
Association of Hospital & Institution Libraries, Hospital Library Standards Committee. Standards for Library Services in Health Care Institutions. LC 74-124576. pap. 20.00 (ISBN 0-317-27838-X, 2024220). Bks Demand UMI.
Association of Insurance & Risk Managers in Industry & Commerce, ed. Company Insurance Handbook. LC 83-20738. 360p. 1984. text ed. 47.50x (ISBN 0-566-02299-0). Gower Pub Co.
Association of Licensed Automobile Manufacturers. Handbook of Gasoline Automobiles, 1904 to 1906. (Illus.). 9.00 (ISBN 0-8446-4705-5). Peter Smith.
Association of Mental Health Librarians. Directory of Mental Health Libraries & Information Centers. Epstein, Barbara A. & Detlefsen, Ellen G., eds. LC 84-21582. 312p. 1984. 20.00x (ISBN 0-88048-047-5, 48-047-5). Am Psychiatric.
Association of Muslim Scientists & Engineers. The Educational Guide: A Handbook for Foreign Muslim Applicats to U.S. & Canadian Universities. rev. ed. 114p. pap. 7.00 (ISBN 0-916581-00-4). Assn Muslim Sci.
Association of National Advertisers, jt. auth. see Booz, Allen & Hamilton.
Association of Noise Consultants, jt. auth. see Institution of Chemical Engineers, London & South-Eastern Branch.
Association of Operative Millers. Cereal Miller's Handbook. 1963. 25.00 (ISBN 0-686-00364-0). AG Pr.
--Technical Bulletins: 1944-1974, Vol. 3. 1975. 25.00 (ISBN 0-686-00376-4). AG Pr.
--Technical Bulletins: 1944-1975, Vol. 4. 1977. 25.00 (ISBN 0-686-00375-6). AG Pr.
Association of Orthodox Jewish Scientists. Proceedings, 2 vols. Set. 3.95 (ISBN 0-87306-072-5); Vol. 1. 4.95 (ISBN 0-686-67018-3). Vol. 2 (ISBN 0-87306-073-3). Feldheim.
--Proceedings, Vol. 5. Rosner, Fred, ed. 1978. pap. 6.95 (ISBN 0-87306-150-0). Feldheim.
Association of Pacific Coast Geographers. Yearbook of the Association of Pacific Coast Geographers: Vol. 37, 1975. (Illus.). 144p. pap. 7.00 (ISBN 0-87071-237-3). Oreg St U Pr.
--Yearbook of the Association of Pacific Coast Geographers: Vol. 38, 1976. LC 37-13376. (Illus.). pap. 7.00x (ISBN 0-87071-238-1). Oreg St U Pr.
--Yearbook of the Association of Pacific Coast Geographers: Vol. 39, 1977. LC 37-13376. (Illus.). pap. 7.00x (ISBN 0-87071-239-X). Oreg St U Pr.
--Yearbook of the Association of Pacific Coast Geographers: Vol. 45, 1983. LC 37-13376. (Illus.). 144p. pap. 7.00x (ISBN 0-87071-245-4). Oreg St U Pr.
--Yearbook of the Association of Pacific Coast Geographers: Vol. 40, 1978. LC 37-13376. (Illus.). pap. 7.00x (ISBN 0-87071-240-3). Oreg St U Pr.
--Yearbook of the Association of Pacific Coast Geographers: Vol. 41, 1979. Monahan, Robert, ed. LC 37-13376. (Illus.). 180p. 1981. pap. 7.00x (ISBN 0-87071-241-1). Oreg St U Pr.
--Yearbook of the Association of Pacific Coast Geographers: Vol. 42, 1980. Scott, James, ed. LC 37-13376. (Illus.). 172p. 1981. pap. 7.00x (ISBN 0-87071-242-X). Oreg St U Pr.
--Yearbook of the Association of Pacific Coast Geographers: 1981, Vol. 43. Scott, James, ed. LC 37-13376. (Illus.). 176p. 1982. pap. 7.00x (ISBN 0-87071-243-8). Oreg St U Pr.
--Yearbook of the Association of Pacific Coast Geographers: 1982, Vol. 44. Scott, James, ed. LC 37-13376. (Illus.). 144p. 1983. pap. 7.00x (ISBN 0-87071-244-6). Oreg St U Pr.
--Yearbooks of the Association of Pacific Coast Geographers, Vol. 1-36. Incl. Vols. 1-19. 1935-1957. pap. 5.00x ea.; Vol. 20-27. 1958-1965. pap. 5.00x ea.; Vols. 28, 29, 31. 1966-1967, 1969. pap. 5.00x ea.; Vol. 30, 1968. 8.00x (ISBN 0-87071-230-6); Vols. 32-36. 1970-1974. pap. 7.00x ea.. LC 37-13376. Oreg St U Pr.
Association of Pediatric Oncology. Nursing Care of the Child With Cancer. 1982. text ed. 22.50 (ISBN 0-316-04884-4). Little.
Association of Physical Plant Administrators of Universities & Colleges. Comparative Costs & Staffing Report for College & University Facilities: 1982-1983. 35.00 (ISBN 0-913359-25-4). Assn Phys Plant Admin.
Association of Physicians. The Cholera Bulletin. LC 77-180564. (Medicine & Society in America Ser). 198p. 1972. Repr. of 1832 ed. 19.00 (ISBN 0-405-03942-5). Ayer Co Pubs.
Association of Research Libraries, Office of Management Studies. New York State Library Conference on Planning for Collection Development. 1982. 5.00 (ISBN 0-318-03472-7, ED225 568). Assn Res Lib.
Association of Research Libraries Staff. The Future of Card Catalogs. 1975. write for info. Assn Res Lib.
Association of Research Libraries, Systems & Procedures Exchange Center Staff. The Assistant-Associate Director Position. (SPEC Kit & Flyer Ser.: No. 103). 100p. 1984. 20.00 (ISBN 0-318-03453-0); 10.00. Assn Res Lib.
Association of Research Libraries, Systems & Procedures Exchange Center. Branch Libraries. (SPEC Kit & Flyer Ser.: No. 99). 101p. 1983. (10.00 for ARL members) 20.00 (ISBN 0-318-03457-3). Assn Res Lib.
--Building Renovation. (SPEC Kit & Flyer Ser.: No. 97). 99p. 1983. (10.00 for ARL members) 20.00 (ISBN 0-318-03459-X). Assn Res Lib.
--Collection Security. (SPEC Kit & Flyer Ser.: No. 100). 115p. 1984. (10.00 for ARL members) 20.00 (ISBN 0-318-03456-5). Assn Res Lib.
--Copyright Policies. (SPEC Kit & Flyer Ser.: No. 102). 98p. 1984. 20.00 (ISBN 0-318-03454-9); members 10.00. Assn Res Lib.
--Corporate Use of Research Libraries. (SPEC Kit & Flyer Ser.: No. 88). 101p. 1982. (10.00 for ARL members) 20.00 (ISBN 0-318-03467-0). Assn Res Lib.
--Fund Raising. (SPEC Kit & Flyer Ser.: No. 94). 103p. 1983. (10.00 for ARL members) 20.00 (ISBN 0-318-03462-X). Assn Res Lib.
--Integrated Library Information Systems. (SPEC Kit & Flyer Ser.: No. 90). 88p. 1983. (10.00 for ARL members) 20.00 (ISBN 0-318-03465-4). Assn Res Lib.
--Interlibrary Loan. (SPEC Kit & Flyer Ser.: No. 92). 98p. 1983. for ARL members 10.00 (ISBN 0-318-03463-8). Assn Res Lib.
--Library Materials Cost Studies. (SPEC Kit & Flyer Ser.: No. 95). 121p. 1983. 20.00 (ISBN 0-318-03461-1); members 10.00. Assn Res Lib.
--Online Catalogs. (SPEC Kit & Flyer Ser.: No. 96). 97p. 1983. 20.00 (ISBN 0-318-03460-3); members 10.00. Assn Res Lib.
--Professional Development. (SPEC Kit & Flyer Ser.: No. 86). 105p. 1982. (10.00 for ARL members) 20.00 (ISBN 0-318-03468-9). Assn Res Lib.
--Public Services Goals & Objectives. (SPEC Kit & Flyer Ser.: No. 84). 108p. 1982. (10.00 for ARL members 20.00 (ISBN 0-318-03470-0). Assn Res Lib.
--Student Assistants in ARL Libraries. (SPEC Kit & Flyer Ser.: 91). 98p. 1983. (10.00 for ARL members) 20.00 (ISBN 0-318-03464-6). Assn Res Lib.
--Telecommunications. (SPEC Kit & Flyer Ser.: No. 98). 129p. 1983. 20.00 (ISBN 0-318-03458-1). Assn Res Lib.
--User Studies. (SPEC Kit & Flyer Ser.: No. 101). 115p. 1984. (10.00 for ARL members) 20.00 (ISBN 0-318-03455-7). Assn Res Lib.
Association of Scottish District Salmon Fishery Boards. Salmon Fisheries of Scotland. (Illus.). 80p. 1978. pap. 11.00 (ISBN 0-85238-091-7, FN67, FNB). Unipub.
Association of Specialized & Cooperative Library Agencies. Revised Standards & Guidelines of Service for the Library of Congress Network of Libraries for the Blind & Physically Handicapped 1984. LC 84-6356. 55p. 1984. pap. text ed. 6.50x (ISBN 0-8389-3306-8). ALA.
Association of Specialized & Cooperative Library Agencies. Subcommittee on Standards for Library Functions at the State Level. Standards for Library Functions at the State Level. rev. ed. LC 85-1372. 48p. 1985. pap. 6.75x (ISBN 0-8389-3317-3). ALA.
Association of Student International Law Societies & American Society of International Law, ed. see Jessup, Philip C.
Association of Student International Law Societies, American Society of International Law. Phillip C. Jessup International Law Moot Court Competition, 1960-1983, 16 vols. LC 80-85091. 1984. lib. bdg. 735.00 (ISBN 0-89941-094-4). W S Hein.
Association of Teachers of Management. Breaking down Barriers. Garratt, Bob & Stopford, John, eds. 352p. text ed. 41.00x (ISBN 0-566-02122-6). Gower Pub Co.
Association Of Teachers Of Mathematics. Mathematical Reflections. (Illus.). 1970. 27.50 (ISBN 0-521-07260-3); pap. 12.95 (ISBN 0-521-09582-4, 582). Cambridge U Pr.
--Notes on Mathematics for Children. LC 76-14026. (Illus.). 1977. 28.95 (ISBN 0-521-20970-6); pap. 10.95 (ISBN 0-521-29015-5). Cambridge U Pr.
Association of Teachers of Social Studies in the City of New York Staff. A Handbook for the Teaching of Social Studies. 333p. 1985. 24.95x (ISBN 0-205-08149-5, Pub. by Longwood Div). Allyn.
Association of the Bar of the City of New York, jt. auth. see Medina, H. R.
Association of The Bar of The City of N.Y. Benjamin N. Cardozo Memorial Lectures, 2 Vols. 1970. 16.25 ea.; 35.00 set. Bender.
Association of the Bar of the City of New York; Committee on the Corporate Law Departments & Arthur Young & Company. National Survey of Corporate Law Compensation & Organization Practices. 6th ed. (Illus.). Date not set. Set. price not set. Assn Bar NYC.
Association of the Bar of the City of New York, ed. Professional Responsibility of the Lawyer: The Murky Divide Between Right & Wrong. LC 76-5391. 170p. 1976. lib. bdg. 38.00 (ISBN 0-379-00775-4); pap. 8.50 (ISBN 0-379-00776-2). Oceana.
Association of the Bar of the City of New York. Report of the Special Committee on the Federal Loyalty Security Program. LC 74-6494. (Civil Liberties in American History Ser.). 301p. 1974. Repr. of 1956 ed. lib. bdg. 39.50 (ISBN 0-306-70596-6). Da Capo.
Association of Theatrical Artists & Craftspeople. The New York Theatrical Sourcebook, 1985-86. 550p. 1985. pap. 25.00 (ISBN 0-911747-04-4). Broadway Pr.
Association of Trial Lawyers of America. Education Fund. Medical Negligence & Hospital Liability. LC 84-71194. 91p. Date not set. price not set (ISBN 0-941916-14-6). Assn Trial Ed.
Association of Trial Lawyers of America Education Fund Staff. Toxic Tort Reference Materials. 543p. 1985. pap. write for info. (ISBN 0-941916-23-5). Assn Trial Ed.
Association of Trial Lawyers of America Education Fund. Using Expert Witnesses. LC 83-71596. (Illus.). 86p. 1983. write for info. (ISBN 0-941916-11-1). Assn Trial Ed.
Association of University Evening College Convention. Inter-Association Cooperation Reconsidered. 1964. 2.50 (ISBN 0-87060-017-6, OCP 10). Syracuse U Cont Ed.
Association of Voluntary Agency for Rural Development, India. Block-Level Planning. 134p. 1980. pap. 12.50x (ISBN 0-7069-1063-X, Pub by Vikas India). Advent NY.
Associations for Research & Enlightenment, Readings Research Dept., compiled by. Psychic Awareness. (Library: Vol. 9). 1979. 9.95 (ISBN 0-87604-109-8). ARE Pr.
--Psychic Development. (Library: Vol. 8). 327p. 1978. 10.95 (ISBN 0-87604-108-X). ARE Pr.
Associations of Orthodox Jewish Scientists. Proceedings, Vol. 3 & 4. Rosner, Fred, ed. 248p. 1976. pap. 7.95 (ISBN 0-87306-074-1). Feldheim.
Assocition for Research & Enlightenment, Readings Research Dept., compiled by. The Study Group Readings. (Library: Vol. 7). 545p. 1977. 10.95 (ISBN 0-87604-094-6). ARE Pr.
Assonyi, Cs. & Richter, R. The Continuum Theory of Rock Mechanics. Balkay, B., tr. from Hungarian. (Rock & Soil Mechanics Ser.). (Illus.). 1979. 58.00x (ISBN 0-87849-027-2). Trans Tech.
Assorodobraj-Kula, N., et al, eds. Studies in Economic Theory & Practice: Essays in Honor of Edward Lipinski. 252p. 1981. 64.00 (ISBN 0-444-86010-X). Elsevier.
Ast, Friedrich. Lexicon Platonicum, 3 vols. (Lat.). 1969. Set. 89.00 (ISBN 0-8337-0105-3). B Franklin.
Astafiev, V. Horse with the Pink Mane. 336p. 1978. pap. 3.95 (ISBN 0-8285-0943-3, Pub. by Progress Pubs USSR). Imported Pubns.
--Queen Fish. 444p. 1982. 12.95 (ISBN 0-8285-2523-4, Pub. by Progress Pubs USSR). Imported Pubns.
Astaire, Fred. Steps in Time. (Series in Dance). 1979. Repr. of 1959 ed. 26.00 (ISBN 0-306-79575-2). Da Capo.
--Steps in Time. (Quality Paperbacks Ser.). (Illus.). 327p. 1981. pap. 7.95 (ISBN 0-306-80141-8). Da Capo.
Astaire, Mark, jt. auth. see Hunter, Allan.
Astanin, L. P. & Blagosklonov, K. N. Conservation of Nature. 149p. 1983. 5.95 (ISBN 0-8285-2602-8, Pub. by Progress Pubs USSR). Imported Pubns.
Astapovich, A. Z. Strategy of Transnational Corporations. 288p. 1983. pap. 3.95 (ISBN 0-8285-2601-X, Pub. by Progress Pubs USSR). Imported Pubns.
Astarita, G. & Nicolais, L., eds. Polymer Processing & Properties. 464p. 1984. 69.50x (ISBN 0-306-41728-6, Plenum Pr). Plenum Pub.
Astarita, Gianni, et al. Gas Treating with Chemical Solvents. LC 82-11016. 493p. 1983. 54.95 (ISBN 0-471-05768-1, Pub. by Wiley-Interscience). Wiley.
Astarita, Giovanni, et al, eds. Rheology, 3 vols. Incl. Vol. 1: Principles. 437p. 69.50x (ISBN 0-306-40465-6); Vol. 2: Fluids. 702p. 95.00x (ISBN 0-306-40466-4); Vol. 3: Applications. 702p. 99.50x (ISBN 0-306-40467-2). LC 80-16929. 1980. 225.00 set (ISBN 0-686-64855-2, Plenum Pr). Plenum Pub.
Astarte. Astrology Made Easy. pap. 3.00 (ISBN 0-87980-009-7). Wilshire.
Astavakra. Ashtavakra Samhita. Nityaswarupananda, Swami, tr. (Sanskrit & Eng.). pap. 4.50 (ISBN 0-87481-165-1). Vedanta Pr.
Astbury, Leigh. The Heidelberg School & Rural Mythology. (Illus.). 204p. 1985. 45.00 (ISBN 0-19-554501-X). Oxford U Pr.
Astbury, N. F., et al. Experimental Gas Explosions: Report of Further Tests at Potters Marston. 1972. 25.00x (ISBN 0-900910-17-8, Pub. by Brit Ceramic Soc England). State Mutual Bk.
--Gas Explosions in Load-Bearing Brick Structures. 1970. 10.00x (ISBN 0-900910-09-7, Pub. by Brit Ceramic Soc England). State Mutual Bk.
Astbury, Peter, tr. see Amaldi, Ginestra.
Aste, Mario. Two Novels of Pirandello: An Essay. 1979. pap. text ed. 9.25 (ISBN 0-8191-0735-2). U Pr of Amer.
Astell-Burt, Caroline. Puppetry for the Mentally Handicapped. 198p. 1981. 15.95 (ISBN 0-285-64933-7, Pub. by Souvenir Pr). Brookline Book.
Asten, Dietrich V. Sacramental & Spiritual Communion. Glas, Werner, ed. (Orig.). 1984. pap. 2.50 (ISBN 0-88010-121-0). Anthroposophic.
Asten, H. Keller-von. Encounters with the Infinite: Geometrical Experiences Through Active Contemplation. Juhr, Gerald, tr. from Germ. (Illus.). 364p. 1971. 19.95 (ISBN 0-88010-040-0, Pub. by Verlag Walter Keller Switzerland). Anthroposophic.
Asten, M., ed. see Alperovitch, I. M., et al.
Aster, Sidney. British Foreign Policy, Nineteen Eighteen to Nineteen Forty-Five: A Guide to Research & Research Materials. LC 84-5339. 324p. 1984. 20.00 (ISBN 0-8420-2176-0). Scholarly Res Inc.
Asterita, Mary F. Mind over Fatter. (Illus.). 64p. (Orig.). pap. 5.95 (ISBN 0-933019-01-7). Aster Pub Co.
Asterita, Mary F. & Macchia, Donald D. Physiology of Stress. Didelot, Mary, ed. 1985. incl. tapes & slides 140.00 (ISBN 0-933019-00-9). Aster Pub Co.
Astesiano, E. & Boehm, C., eds. CAAP 1981 Trees in Algebra & Programming: Proceedings. (Lecture Notes in Computer Science Ser: Vol. 112). 364p. 1981. pap. 22.00 (ISBN 0-387-10828-9). Springer-Verlag.
Asthana, Rama K. Henry James: A Study in the Aesthetics of the Novel. 130p. 1980. Repr. of 1936 ed. text ed. 12.25x (ISBN 0-391-02180-X). Humanities.
Asthana, S. C. & Misra, C. P. An Introduction to Business Management. 250p. 1982. text ed. 22.50 (ISBN 0-7069-1823-1, Pub by Vikas India). Advent NY.
Asthma & Allergy Foundation of America & Norback, Craig T., eds. The Allergy Encyclopedia. (Mosby Medical Library). 256p. 1982. pap. 7.95 (ISBN 0-452-25345-4, 3717-1). Mosby.
--The Allergy Encylopedia. (Mosby Medical Library). (Illus.). 1981. pap. 8.95 (ISBN 0-452-25629-1, Z5629, Plume). NAL.
Astier, Pierre. Eduardo Arroyo. (QLP Art Ser.). pap. 9.95 (ISBN 0-517-54868-2). Crown.
Astin, Alan E. Cato the Censor. 1978. text ed. 57.00x (ISBN 0-19-814809-7). Oxford U Pr.
Astin, Alexander W. Academic Gamesmanship: Student-Oriented Change in Higher Education. LC 76-12520. (Illus.). 224p. 1976. text ed. 31.95x (ISBN 0-275-56720-6). Praeger.
--Achieving Educational Excellence: A Critical Assessment of Priorities & Practices in Higher Education. LC 84-43025. (Higher Education Ser.). 1985. text ed. 18.95x (ISBN 0-87589-636-7). Jossey-Bass.
--Four Critical Years: Effects of College on Beliefs, Attitudes, & Knowledge. LC 76-57308. (Higher Education Ser.). 1977. text ed. 18.95x (ISBN 0-87589-346-5). Jossey-Bass.
--Minorities in American Higher Education: Recent Trends, Currect Prospects, & Recommendations. LC 81-48663. (Higher Education Ser.). 1982. 18.95x (ISBN 0-87589-523-9). Jossey-Bass.
--Preventing Students from Dropping Out: A Longitudinal, Multi-Institutional Study of College Dropouts. LC 74-28915. (Higher Education Ser.). 288p. 1975. 17.95x (ISBN 0-87589-255-8). Jossey-Bass.
Astin, Alexander W. & Scherrei, Rita A. Maximizing Leadership Effectiveness: Impact of Administrative Style on Faculty & Students. LC 79-9665. (Higher Education Ser.). 1980. text ed. 18.95x (ISBN 0-87589-454-2). Jossey-Bass.

Astin, Majorie. Mary Russell Mitford: Her Circle & Her Books. 1930. Repr. 15.00 (ISBN 0-8274-2685-2). R West.

Astiz, Carlos A., ed. Latin American International Politics: Ambitions, Capabilities & the National Interests of Mexico, Brazil & Argentina. LC 68-30668. 1969. 19.95 (ISBN 0-268-00323-8). U of Notre Dame Pr.

Astiz, Carlos A., tr. see Ciria, Alberto.

Astiz, Carlos A., tr. see De Imaz, Jose L.

Astle, Thomas. Origin & Progress of Writing. 2nd ed. LC 76-161701. Repr. of 1803 ed. lib. bdg. 60.00 (ISBN 0-404-00413-X). AMS Pr.

Astley, H. J. Biblical Anthropology. 1977. Repr. of 1929 ed. 32.50 (ISBN 0-685-82796-8). Sharon Hill.

Astley, John. The Art of Riding: Set Forthe in a Breefe Treatise. LC 68-54610. (English Experience Ser.: No. 10). 80p. 1968. Repr. of 1584 ed. 13.00 (ISBN 90-221-0010-3). Walter J Johnson.

Astley, Juliet. The Fall of Midas. (General Ser.). 1979. 14.50 (ISBN 0-8161-6727-3, Large Print Bks). G K Hall.

Astley, Thea. The Acolyte. 158p. 1980. pap. 7.25x (ISBN 0-7022-1540-6). U of Queensland Pr.

--A Boat Load of Home Folk. 224p. (Orig.). 1983. pap. 4.95 (ISBN 0-14-006743-4). Penguin.

--A Descant for Gossips. (UQP Paperbacks Ser.). 259p. (Orig.). Date not set. pap. 7.95 (ISBN 0-7022-1843-X). U of Queensland Pr.

--An Item from the Late News. LC 82-11177. 200p. 1983. 12.95 (ISBN 0-7022-1702-6). U of Queensland Pr.

--An Item from the Late News. 208p. 1984. pap. 4.95 (ISBN 0-14-006948-8). Penguin.

Astley, Thomas. New General Collection of Voyages & Travels, 1745-1747, 4 vols. (Illus.). 1968. Repr. Set. 350.00x (ISBN 0-7146-1786-5, F Cass Co). Biblio Dist.

ASTM Committee B-10. Refractory Metals & Their Industrial Applications-STP 849. Smallwood, Robert E., ed. LC 84-70136. (Illus.). 115p. 1984. pap. text ed. 19.00 (ISBN 0-8031-0203-8, 04-849000-05). ASTM.

ASTM Committee C-11 on Gypsum. The Chemistry & Technology of Gypsum. Kuntze, Richard A., ed. LC 84-70880. (Special Technical Publication Ser.: No. 861). 208p. 1984. text ed. 29.00 (ISBN 0-8031-0219-4, 04-861000-07). ASTM.

ASTM Committee D-18 on Soil & Rock. Laterally Loaded Deep Foundations: Analysis & Performance. Langer, J. A., et al, eds. LC 83-72942. (Special Technical Publication Ser.: No. 835). 250p. 1984. text ed. 34.00 (ISBN 0-8031-0207-0, 04-835000-38). ASTM.

ASTM Committee D-19 on Water. Ecological Assessment of Macrophyton: Collection, Use, & Meaning of Data. Dennis, W. M. & Isom, W. G., eds. LC 83-73513. (Special Technical Publications Ser.: No. 843). (Illus.). 120p. 1984. pap. text ed. 20.00 (ISBN 0-8031-0204-6, 04-843000-16). ASTM.

--Statistics in the Environmental Sciences - STP 845. Gertz, Steven M. & London, M. D., eds. LC 83-73439. 115p. 1984. pap. 24.00 (ISBN 0-8031-0206-2, 04-845000-16). ASTM.

ASTM Committee E-24 on Fracture Testing. Fracture Mechanics: Fifteenth Symposium - STP 833. Sanford, R. J., ed. LC 83-72816. 750p. 1984. text ed. 74.00 (ISBN 0-8031-0208-9, 04-833000-30). ASTM.

ASTM Committee E-29 on Particle Size. Liquid Particle Size Measurement Techniques. Tichkoff, J. M., et al, eds. LC 83-73515. (Special Technical Publication Ser.: No. 848). 200p. 1984. text ed. 37.00 (ISBN 0-8031-0227-5, 04-848000-41). ASTM.

ASTM Committee F-20, Division on Hazardous Materials Spill Response, ed. A Guide to the Safe Handling of Hazardous Materials Accidents- STP 825-A. LC 83-71801. 55p. 1983. pap. text ed. 15.00 (ISBN 0-8031-0261-5, 04-825000-31). ASTM.

ASTM Committee G-1 on Corrosion of Metals. Environmental-Sensitive Fracture: Evaluation & Comparison of Test Methods. Dean, S. W., et al, eds. LC 83-70260. (Special Technical Publications Ser.: No. 821). 554p. 1984. text ed. 59.00 (ISBN 0-8031-0264-X, 04-821000-27). ASTM.

ASTM Committees D-22 & E-34. Definitions for Asbestos & Other Health-Related Silicates - STP 834. Levadie, Benjamin, ed. LC 83-72557. (Illus.). 205p. 1984. pap. text ed. 30.00 (ISBN 0-8031-0209-7, 04-834000-17). ASTM.

ASTM Committees D-30 & EO9. Effects of Defects in Composite Materials. LC 83-73441. (Special Technical Publications Ser.: No. 836). (Illus.). 280p. 1984. 39.00 (ISBN 0-8031-0218-6, 04-836000-33). ASTM.

ASTM Committees E-17 on Skid Resistance & F-9 on Tires, ed. Frictional Interaction of Tire & Pavement. LC 82-72886. (Special Technical Publications Ser.: No. 793). 330p. 1983. text ed. 30.00 (ISBN 0-8031-0231-3, 04-793000-37). ASTM.

ASTM Standardization News, September, 1983. The Metal Properties Council Grows Up. write for info. Metal Prop Coun.

Astolfi, Douglas. Teaching the Ancient World. LC 82-10831. (Scholars Press General Ser.). 194p. 1983. pap. 14.25 (ISBN 0-89130-590-4, 00 03 05). Scholars Pr GA.

Aston. History of Esmeralda County. facsimile ed. (Shorey Historical Ser.). 48p. pap. 3.95 (ISBN 0-8466-0175-3, S175). Shorey.

Aston, Athina. How to Play with Your Baby. LC 83-48037. (Your Learning Child Ser.: Vol. 1). (Illus.). 120p. 1983. pap. 7.95 (ISBN 0-914788-73-6). East Woods.

--Toys That Teach Your Child: From Birth to Two. Emerson, William A., ed. LC 84-48038. (Illus.). 128p. 1984. pap. 8.95 (ISBN 0-88742-015-X). East Woods.

Aston, Bryan & Duncan, Peter. Making Mead. (Illus.). 70p. Date not set. pap. 4.95 (ISBN 0-900841-07-9, Pub. by Aztex Corp). Argus Bks.

Aston, Clive C. A Contemporary Crisis: Political Hostage-Taking & the Experience of Western Europe. LC 82-6165. (Contributions in Political Science Ser.: No. 84). xiv, 217p. 1982. lib. bdg. 29.95 (ISBN 0-313-23289-X, ASP/). Greenwood.

Aston, George, ed. The Study of War for Statesmen & Citizens. LC 72-89260. 216p. 1973. Repr. of 1927 ed. 21.50x (ISBN 0-8046-1762-7, Pub. by Kennikat). Assoc Faculty Pr.

Aston, Hugh see Buck, P. C. & Fellowes, E. H.

Aston, John. Social England under the Regency, Vol. I. (Illus.). 1976. 25.00x (ISBN 0-7158-1110-X). Charles River Bks.

Aston, Margaret. The Fifteenth Century: The Prospect of Europe. (Library of World Civilization). (Illus.). 1979. pap. 7.95x (ISBN 0-393-95097-2). Norton.

--Lollards & Reformers: Images & Literacy in Late Medieval Religion. 405p. 1984. 30.00 (ISBN 0-907628-03-6). Hambledon Press.

Aston, Melba. Developing Sentence Skills. (English Ser.). 24p. (gr. 4-7). 1980. wkbk. 5.00 (ISBN 0-8209-0182-2, E-10). ESP.

--Learning to Outline & Organize: Grades 7-12. (Language Arts Ser.). 24p. 1977. wkbk. 5.00 (ISBN 0-8209-0321-3, LA-7). ESP.

--Understanding Punctuation: Grades 7-12. (English Ser.). 24p. (gr. 7-12). 1977. wkbk. 5.00 (ISBN 0-8209-0184-9, E12). ESP.

Aston, Norman. Leicestershire Watermills. 1982. 40.00x (ISBN 0-905837-02-9, Pub. by Sycamore Pr England). State Mutual Bk.

Aston, P., jt. auth. see Paynter, J.

Aston, Paul, tr. see Konrad, George.

Aston, S. C. Peirol, Troubadour of Auvergne. LC 80-2185. Repr. of 1953 ed. 35.00 (ISBN 0-404-19012-X). AMS Pr.

Aston, S. R. Silicon Geochemistry & Biogeochemistry. 1983. 44.50 (ISBN 0-12-065620-5). Acad Pr.

Aston, T. H. & Philpin, C. H., eds. The Brenner Debate: Agrarian Class Structure & Economic Development in Pre-Industrial Europe. (Past & Present Publications Ser.). 250p. Date not set. price not set (ISBN 0-521-26817-6). Cambridge U Pr.

Aston, T. H., jt. ed. see Hilton, R. H.

Aston, Trevor, ed. Crisis in Europe, Fifteen Sixty to Sixteen Sixty: Essays from "Past & Present". 376p. 1983. pap. 9.95X (ISBN 0-7100-6889-1). Routledge & Kegan.

Aston, Trevor, et al. Social Relations & Ideas. LC 82-9727. (Past & Present Publications). 352p. 1983. 44.50 (ISBN 0-521-25132-X). Cambridge U Pr.

Aston, W. G. History of Japanese Literature. LC 73-157264. 1971. pap. 6.50 (ISBN 0-8048-0997-6). C E Tuttle.

--History of Japanese Literature. 30.00 (ISBN 0-384-02240-5). Johnson Repr.

--A History of Japanese Literature. lib. bdg. 79.95 (ISBN 0-87968-471-2). Krishna Pr.

--A History of Japanese Literature: Works of W. G. Aston. (Works of W. G. Aston Ser.). vi, 410p. Date not set. Repr. of 1899 ed. 49.00 (ISBN 0-932051-69-3). Am Repr Serv.

--Shinto: The Ancient Religion of Japan. 83p. 1982. lib. bdg. 25.00 (ISBN 0-89760-018-5). Telegraph Bks.

--Shinto, the Way of the Gods. lib. bdg. 75.00 (ISBN 0-87968-076-8). Krishna Pr.

Aston, William G. Nihongi: Chronicles of Japan from the Earliest Times to A.D. 697. LC 70-152110. (Illus.). 1971. pap. 10.50 (ISBN 0-8048-0984-4). C E Tuttle.

Astone, Nicholas A., jt. auth. see Martin, Julian A.

Astor, Brooke. Footprints. large print ed. LC 81-8589. 609p. 1981. Repr. of 1980 ed. 13.95 (ISBN 0-89621-296-3). Thorndike Pr.

Astor, Gerald. The Disease Detectives: Deadly Medical Mysteries & the People Who Solve Them. 250p. 1983. 14.95 (ISBN 0-453-00429-6). NAL.

--The Disease Detectives: Deadly Medical Mysteries & the People Who Solved Them. LC 82-22554. 224p. 1984. pap. 6.95 (ISBN 0-452-25540-6, Plume). NAL.

--The Last Nazi: The Life & Times of Dr. Joseph Mengele. LC 85-80251. 384p. 1985. 18.95 (ISBN 0-917657-46-2). D I Fine.

Astor, Michael & Rowley, Trevor. Landscape Archaeology: An Introduction to Fieldwork Techniques on Post Roman Landscapes. 1975. 8.50 (ISBN 0-7153-6670-X). David & Charles.

Astor, Saul D. Loss Prevention: Controls & Concepts. LC 77-28164. 1978. 21.95 (ISBN 0-913708-29-1); instr's manual avail. Butterworth.

Astor, Stephen. Babies. 257p. (Orig.). 1983. pap. 6.35 (ISBN 0-915001-00-4). Two A's.

--Doctor Fabers's Test Tube Babies. 257p. (Orig.). 1983. pap. 6.35 (ISBN 0-915001-03-9). Two A's.

--What's New in Allergy. (What's New in Medicine Ser.). 128p. (Orig.). 1985. pap. 6.50 (ISBN 0-915001-02-0). Two A's.

Astor, Susan. Dame. LC 80-11966. (Contemporary Poetry Ser.). 88p. 1980. pap. 5.95 (ISBN 0-8203-0522-7). U of Ga Pr.

Astrakhan. Brave New World (Huxley) (Book Notes Ser.). 1984. pap. 2.50 (ISBN 0-8120-3405-8). Barron.

Astrand, Per-Olof & Rodahl, Kaare. Textbook of Work Physiology: Physiological Basis of Exercisers. 2nd ed. (McGraw-Hill Series in Health, Physical Education & Recreation). 1977. text ed. 44.95 (ISBN 0-07-002406-5). McGraw.

Astro Numeric Service. Tables of Houses Campanus. 208p. 1977. 12.00 (ISBN 0-86690-054-3, 2005-05). Am Fed Astrologers.

--Tables of Houses Koch. 208p. 1977. 12.00 (ISBN 0-86690-251-1, 2006-05). Am Fed Astrologers.

--Tables of Houses Placidus. 208p. 1977. 12.00 (ISBN 0-86690-252-X, 2007-05). Am Fed Astrologers.

Astro Publishers. Military Competency Test, with Explanations. 1979. pap. 8.95 (ISBN 0-686-70926-8, Pub. by Astro). Aviation.

Astro, Richard. Edward F. Ricketts. LC 76-46147. (Western Writers Ser.: No. 21). 1976. pap. 2.00x (ISBN 0-88430-020-X). Boise St Univ.

Astro, Richard & Benson, Jackson J., eds. The Fiction of Bernard Malamud. LC 77-23232. 1977. text ed. 12.95x (ISBN 0-87071-446-5). Oreg St U Pr.

--Hemingway in Our Time: Published Record of a Literary Conference Devoted to a Study of the Work of Ernest Hemingway Held at Oregon State University on April 26-27, 1973. LC 73-18428. pap. 55.50 (ISBN 0-317-28801-6, 2020634). Bks Demand UMI.

Astro, Richard & Hayashi, Tetsumaro, eds. Steinbeck: The Man & His Work. LC 76-632182. (Illus.). 1971. pap. text ed. 9.95x (ISBN 0-87071-443-0). Oreg St U Pr.

Astro, Richard, jt. ed. see Nagel, James.

Astroff, Milton T. & Abbey, James R. Convention Sales & Services. 464p. 1978. text ed. write for info. (ISBN 0-697-08408-6). Wm C Brown.

Astrol, D. F., jt. auth. see Geddes, Sheila.

Astrom, K. J. Introduction to Stochastic Control Theory. (Mathematics in Science & Engineering Ser.: Vol. 70). 1970. 60.00 (ISBN 0-12-065650-7). Acad Pr.

Astrom, Karl J. & Wittenmark, Bjorn. Computer Controlled Systems: Theory & Design. (Illus.). 432p. 1984. text ed. 38.95 (ISBN 0-13-164319-3). P-H.

Astrom, P., et al. Hala Sultan Tekke: Excavations 1971-79. (Studies in Mediterranean Archaeology: Vol. 8). 253p. 1983. pap. text ed. 69.50x (ISBN 91-86098-04-7, Pub. by Paul Astroms Sweden). Humanities.

Astrom, Paul. Cuirass Tomb & Other Finds at Dendra: Pt. 2, Excavations in the Cemeteries the Lower Town & the Citadel. (Studies in Mediterranean Archaeology: Vol. IV: 2). 94p. 1983. pap. text ed. 35.50x (ISBN 91-86098-13-6, Pub. by Paul Astroms Sweden). Humanities.

--Excavations at Kalopsidha & Ayios Lakovos in Cyprus. (Studies in Mediterranean Archaeology Ser.: No. II). (Illus.). 1966. pap. text ed. 37.75x (ISBN 91-85058-01-7). Humanities.

Astrom, Paul, jt. auth. see Gullberg, Elsa.

Astrom, Paul, et al. Studies in Aegean Chronology. (Studies in Mediterranean Archaeology Pocketbks.: No. 25). 119p. 1984. pap. text ed. 30.50x (ISBN 91-86098-15-2, Pub. by Paul Astroms Sweden). Humanities.

Astroms, P. & Eriksson, A. Fingerprints & Archaeology. (Studies in Mediterranean Archaeology Ser.: Vol. XXVIII). 88p. 1981. pap. text ed. 45.50x (Pub. by Paul Astroms Sweden). Humanities.

Astronomy Survey Committee, National Research Council. Challenges to Astronomy & Astrophysics: Working Documents of the Astronomy Survey Committee. 296p. 1983. pap. text ed. 14.50 (ISBN 0-309-03335-7). Natl Acad Pr.

Astrop, John. John Astrop's Ghastly Games. 24p. (ps-3). 1983. pop-up bk. 9.95 (ISBN 0-385-29307-0). Delacorte.

Astrophysics & Space Science. The Scientific Satellite Programmed During the International Magnetospheric Study: Proceedings, Vol. 57. Knott, K. & Battrick, B., eds. LC 75-44353. 1976. lib. bdg. 58.00 (ISBN 90-277-0688-3, Pub. by Reidel Holland). Kluwer Academic.

Astrov, N. J., jt. auth. see Gronsky, Paul P.

Astrow, Andre. Zimbabwe: A Revolution That Lost Its Way? (Illus.). 270p. 1983. 26.25x (ISBN 0-86232-140-9, Pub. by Zed Pr England); pap. 9.25 (ISBN 0-86232-141-7). Biblio Dist.

Astruc, Jean. A Treatise of the Venereal Disease. Barrowby, William, ed. LC 83-48590. (Marriage, Sex & the Family in England Ser.). 1015p. 1985. lib. bdg. 110.00 (ISBN 0-8240-5914-X). Garland Pub.

--A Treatise on All the Diseases Incident to Women. LC 83-48603. (Marriage, Sex & the Family in England Ser.). 480p. 1985. lib. bdg. 60.00 (ISBN 0-8240-5927-1). Garland Pub.

Astrup, Christian. The Chronic Schizophrenias. (Orig.). 1979. pap. 18.00x (ISBN 82-00-01810-5, Dist. by Columbia U. Pr.). Universitet.

--Pavlovian Psychiatry: A New Synthesis. 180p. 1965. 18.75x (ISBN 0-398-00061-1). C C Thomas.

--Schizophrenia: Conditional Reflex Studies. (Illus.). 368p. 1962. 32.50x (ISBN 0-398-00062-X). C C Thomas.

Astrup, Christian, et al. Prognosis in Functional Psychoses: Clinical, Social & Genetic Aspects. (Illus.). 224p. 1963. 17.50x (ISBN 0-398-00063-8). C C Thomas.

Asturias, Miguel. Guatemalan Sociology. Ahern, Maureen, tr. LC 77-8270. 122p. 1977. pap. 7.95x (ISBN 0-87918-037-4). ASU Lat Am St.

Asturias, Miguel & Partridge, Frances. El Senor Presidente. LC 64-10908. 1975. pap. text ed. 5.95x (ISBN 0-689-70521-2, 211). Atheneum.

Asturias, Miguel A. Leyendas De Guatemala. (Easy Readers, C). 1977. pap. text ed. 4.25 (ISBN 0-88436-290-6, 70272). EMC.

--Mulata. 352p. 1982. pap. 3.50 (ISBN 0-380-58552-9, 58552-9, Bard). Avon.

Astwood, E. B. see Laurentian Hormone Conferences.

Astwood, William, jt. auth. see Neuhaus, Edmund C.

Asua, L. Jimenez de see Jimenez de Asua, L., et al.

Asvaghosa. The Principle & Practice of Mahayana Buddhism: An Interpretation of Professor Suzuki's Translation of Ashvaghosa's Awakening of Faith. Goodard, Dwight, ed. LC 78-72373. Repr. of 1933 ed. 18.00 (ISBN 0-404-17223-7). AMS Pr.

Asvaghosha, B. Asvaghosha's Discourse on the Awakening of Faith in the Mahayana. lib. bdg. 79.95 (ISBN 0-87968-472-0). Krishna Pr.

--A Life of Buddha. lib. bdg. 79.95 (ISBN 0-87968-473-9). Krishna Pr.

Asvaishch, B., et al. Hermitage. 355p. 1977. 60.00 (ISBN 0-8285-0872-0, Pub. by Aurora Pubs USSR). Imported Pubns.

A. S. Van, Der Woude see Van Hartingsveld, L.

A. S. Van, Der Woude see Van Selms, A.

Asvarishch, B. & Kosareva, N. Western European Art in the Hermitage: Paintings, Drawings, Sculpture. 1977. 110.00x (ISBN 0-317-14333-6, Pub. by Collet's). State Mutual Bk.

Aswad, Barbara C. Arabic Speaking Communities in American Cities. LC 73-88936. (Illus.). 215p. 1974. pap. text ed. 9.95x (ISBN 0-913256-12-9). Ctr Migration.

--Property Control & Social Strategies: Settlers on a Middle Eastern Plain. (Anthropological Papers: No. 44). 1971. pap. 4.00x (ISBN 0-932206-42-5). U Mich Mus Anthro.

Aswad, Betsy. Family Passions. LC 84-25989. 360p. 1985. 16.95 (ISBN 0-385-19346-7, Dial). Doubleday.

--Winds of the Old Days. 256p. 1983. pap. 2.95 (ISBN 0-523-41820-5). Pinnacle Bks.

Aswell, James, jt. auth. see Writers Program, Tennessee.

Aswell, James R., ed. Native American Humor. facs. ed. LC 76-117753. (Essay Index Reprint Ser). 1947. 25.50 (ISBN 0-8369-1862-2). Ayer Co Pubs.

Aswell, James R., et al. God Bless the Devil! Liars' Bench Tales. facsimile ed. LC 84-22054. (Tennesseana Editions Ser.). (Illus.). 288p. (Orig.). 1985. lib. bdg. 19.95x (ISBN 0-87049-457-0); pap. 9.95 (ISBN 0-87049-475-9). U of Tenn Pr.

Aszalos, Adorjan, ed. Antitumor Compounds of Natural Origin. 216p. 1981. vol. 1, 256 pgs. 79.50 (ISBN 0-8493-5520-6); vol. 2, 224 pgs. 69.00, (ISBN 0-8493-5521-4). CRC Pr.

Atack, Jeremy. The Estimation of Economies of Scale in Nineteenth Century United States Manufacturing. Bruchey, Stuart, ed. LC 84-48303. (American Economic History Ser.). 225p. 1985. lib. bdg. 35.00 (ISBN 0-8240-6651-0). Garland Pub.

Atack, Sally M. Art Activities for the Handicapped. 144p. 1980. 30.00x (ISBN 0-285-64905-1, Pub. by Souvenir Pr); pap. 20.00x (ISBN 0-285-64904-3, Pub. by Souvenir Pr). State Mutual Bk.

--Art Activities for the Handicapped Child: A Guide for Parents & Teachers. LC 82-5282. (Illus.). 131p. 1982. 13.95 (ISBN 0-13-046995-5); pap. 6.95 (ISBN 0-13-046987-4). P-H.

Ataka, Toshihiro, tr. see Koshimura, Shinzaburo.

Atal, C. K., et al, eds. see Survey & Cultivation of Edible Mushrooms in India, First National Symposium, Srinagar, 1976.

Atal, Yogesh. Building a Nation: Essays on India. 1982. 20.00x (ISBN 0-8364-0843-8, Pub. By Abhinav India). South Asia Bks.

Atal, Yogesh & Pieris, Ralph. Asian Rethinking on Development. 1976. 9.00x (ISBN 0-88386-829-6). South Asia Bks.

Atal, Yogesh, ed. Social Sciences in Asia. 1974. 14.50 (ISBN 0-88386-552-1). South Asia Bks.

Atallah & Shilling. A Practical Guide to Arabic for the Businessman. 1978. 100.00 (ISBN 0-916400-08-5). Inter Crescent.

Atanasijevi'c, I. Selected Exercises in Galactic Astronomy. (Astrophysics & Space Science Library: No.26). 144p. 1971. lib. bdg. 21.00 (ISBN 90-277-0198-9, Pub. by Reidel Holland). Kluwer Academic.

Atanasijevie, Ksenija. The Metaphysical & Geometrical Doctrine of Bruno. Tomashevich, George V., tr. from Fr. LC 76-155339. 151p. 1972. 12.50 (ISBN 0-87527-081-6). Green.

Atanassova, T., et al. Bulgarian-English Dictionary. 2nd ed. 1050p. (Bulgarian & Eng.). 1980. 55.00x (ISBN 0-569-08665-5, Pub. by Collets). State Mutual Bk.

Atanda, J. A. The New Oyo Empire: A Study of British Indirect Rule in Oyo Province 1894-1934. (Ibadan History Ser.). (Illus.). 332p. 1973. text ed. 13.00x (ISBN 0-391-00252-X). Humanities.

AT&T Bell Laboratories Staff. A History of Engineering & Science in the Bell System: Electronics Technology (1925-1975) Smits, F. M., ed. LC 84-73157. (Illus.). 400p. 1985. write for info (ISBN 0-932764-07-X, 500-472). Bell Telephone.

AT&T Bell Laboratories Technical Staff. A History of Science & Engineering in the Bell System Communications Sciences, 1925-1980. Millman, S., ed. LC 84-72181. (Illus.). 544p. 1984. write for info (ISBN 0-932764-06-1). Bell Telephone.

AT&T Computer Information Systems, Inc. Staff. AT&T Computer Software Guide. 1985. 19.95 (ISBN 0-8359-9276-4). Reston.

AT&T Information Systems Inc. Staff. AT&T Computer Software Guide PC 6300. 1985. pap. 19.95 (ISBN 0-8359-9279-9). Reston.

--AT&T Computer Software Guide 3B2. 1985. pap. 19.95 (ISBN 0-8359-9279-9). Reston.

--AT&T Computer Software Guide 3B5-3B20. 1985. pap. 19.95 (ISBN 0-8359-9277-2). Reston.

AT&T Technologies Staff. The UNIX System V Software Catalog. 1985. 19.95 (ISBN 0-8359-8068-5). Reston.

AT&T Technology Systems. The C Programmer's Handbook. 88p. 1985. pap. 14.95 (ISBN 0-13-110073-4). P-H.

Atangana, Engelbert, jt. auth. see Bahoken, J. C.

Atassi, M. Z., ed. Immunochemistry of Proteins, 3 vols. LC 76-2596. (Illus.). Vol. 1, 501p, 1977. 59.50x (ISBN 0-306-36221-X, Plenum Pr); Vol. 2, 458p, 1977. 59.50x (ISBN 0-306-36222-8); Vol. 3, 339p, 1979. 45.00x (ISBN 0-306-40131-2). Plenum Pub.

Atassi, M. Z. & Benjamini, E., eds. Immunobiology of Proteins & Peptides II. (Advances in Experimental Medicine & Biology: Vol. 150). 238p. 1982. 35.00x (ISBN 0-306-41110-5, Plenum Pr). Plenum Pub.

Atassi, M. Z. & Stavitsky, A. B., eds. Immunobiology of Proteins & Peptides I. LC 78-5083. (Advances in Experimental Medicine & Biology Ser.: Vol. 98). 523p. 1978. 59.50x (ISBN 0-306-32698-1, Plenum Pr). Plenum Pub.

Atcheson, Daniel B. Estimating Earthwork Quantities. 2nd ed. LC 84-62802. (Illus.). 216p. 1985. pap. 25.95 (ISBN 0-9613202-3-0). Norseman Pub.

Atcheson, Jean, ed. see Johner, Martin & Goldberg, Gary.

Atcheson, Jean, ed. see Sass, Lorna J.

Atcheson, Jean, ed. see Sax, Richard.

Atcheson, Jean, ed. see Taylor, Suzanne.

Atcheson, Mack & Mills, John. ECONOCALC (TM)-Project & Venture Economics & Analysis. LC 85-7648. 200p. 1985. incl. floppy disk 495.00x (ISBN 0-87201-239-5). Gulf Pub.

Atcheson, Marguerite. Mouse Who Didn't Believe. LC 80-69472. (Illus.). 60p. (Orig.). (gr. k-3). 1980. pap. 3.50x (ISBN 0-9603118-6-6). Davenport.

--The Mouse Who Didn't Believe. (Illus.). 60p. 1980. 2.50 (ISBN 0-9603118-6-6). MD Bks.

Atcheson, Richard, ed. see Dupree, Nathalie.

Atcheson, Richard, ed. see Middione, Carlo.

Atcheson, Richard, ed. see Urvater, Michele.

Atchinson, Joseph E. Nonwood Plant Fiber Pulping Progress Report. LC 82-80290. (No. 13). 148p. 1983. pap. 48.95 (ISBN 0-89852-404-0, 01 01 R104). TAPPI.

Atchison, Evelyn, jt. auth. see Glass, Marion.

Atchison, Joseph, ed. Nonwood Plant Fiber Pulping, No. 14. (Illus.). 1985. pap. 49.95 (ISBN 0-89852-416-4). TAPPI.

Atchison, Joseph E. Nonwood Plant Fiber Pulping, Progress Report, No. 10. (TAPPI PRESS Reports). (Illus.). 125p. 1979. pap. 38.95 (ISBN 0-89852-381-8, 01-01-R081). TAPPI.

Atchison, Joseph E., ed. Nonwood Plant Fiber Pulping, Progress Report, No. 1. compiled by D. L. Miller ed. (TAPPI PRESS Reports). 140p. 1975. 28.95 (ISBN 0-317-36017-5, 01-01-R034). TAPPI.

Atchison, Joseph E., compiled by. Nonwood Plant Fiber Pulping, Progress Report, No. 6. (TAPPI PRESS Reports). 108p. 1975. 18.95 (ISBN 0-317-36018-3, 01-01-R058). TAPPI.

Atchison, Joseph E., ed. Nonwood Plant Fiber Pulping, Progress Report, No. 8. (TAPPI PRESS Reports). 93p. 1977. 28.95 (ISBN 0-317-36019-1, 01-01-R071). TAPPI.

Atchison, Joseph E., et al, eds. Nonwood Plant Fiber Pulping, 13 Vols. 1835p. 1983. soft cover 297.95 (ISBN 0-686-98535-4, 01-01-NPFS). TAPPI.

Atchity, John K. Denise Lervertov: An Interview. (New London Interviews). 1980. signed ltd. ed 10.00 (ISBN 0-89683-031-4); pap. 3.95 (ISBN 0-89683-030-6). New London Pr.

Atchity, Kenneth. A Writer's Time: A Guide to the Creative Process, From Vision Through Revision. 1986. 12.95 (ISBN 0-393-02235-8). Norton.

Atchity, Kenneth J. Homer's Iliad: The Shield of Memory. LC 77-17065. (Literary Structures Ser.). 367p. 1978. 17.50x (ISBN 0-8093-0809-6). S Ill U Pr.

--Sleeping with an Elephant. LC 77-93163. 1978. pap. 3.95 (ISBN 0-912760-62-1). Valkyrie Pub Hse.

Atchity, Kenneth J., ed. Eterne in Mutabilitie: The Unity of "The Faerie Queen". LC 70-147174. xxvii, 209p. 1972. 21.00 (ISBN 0-208-01202-8, Archon). Shoe String.

Atchity, Kenneth J., jt. ed. see Rimanelli, Giose.

Atchley. Social Forces & Aging: An Introduction to Social Gerontology. 4th ed. 510p. 1985. write for info. (ISBN 0-534-04338-0). Wadsworth Pub.

Atchley, W. R. & Bryant, E. H. Multivariate Statistical Methods: Among-Groups Covariation. LC 75-9893. (Benchmark Papers in Systematic & Evolutionary Biology: Vol. 1). 480p. 1975. 66.00 (ISBN 0-12-786085-1). Acad Pr.

Atchley, W. R. & Woodruff, David S., eds. Evolution & Speciation: Essays in Honor of M. J. D. White. (Illus.). 496p. 1981. 70.00 (ISBN 0-521-23823-4). Cambridge U Pr.

Atchley, William R., jt. auth. see Wirth, Willis W.

Atchley, William R., et al. Bibliography & Keyword-in-Context Index of the Ceratopogonidae (Diptera) from Seventeen Fifty-Eight to Nineteen Seventy-Three. 330p. (Orig.). 1975. pap. 4.00 (ISBN 0-89672-052-7). Tex Tech Pr.

Atcom Editorial Staff. Helpful Hints on How You Can Sell Your Home: The Do's & Dont's by Sally Seller. LC 76-15144. 1976. 18.45 (ISBN 0-915260-03-4). Atcom.

--Hospitality & Foodservice Management Directory 1985. 224p. 1985. pap. 37.50 (ISBN 0-915260-19-0). Atcom.

--Inside the Used Car Business. 52p. 1985. pap. 37.50 (ISBN 0-915260-17-4). Atcom.

Atelier, Johnson, jt. auth. see Elsen, Albert.

Aten, A. & Innes, R. F. Flaying & Curing of Hides & Skins as a Rural Industry. (Agricultural Development Papers: No. 49). 136p. (3rd Printing 1978). 1955. pap. 4.50 (ISBN 92-5-100476-5, F1463, FAO). Unipub.

Aten, A., jt. auth. see Dowson, V. H.

Aten, James. The Denver Auditory Phoneme Sequencing Test. LC 79-651. (Illus.). 310p. 1979. clinical test 65.00 (ISBN 0-933014-51-1). College-Hill.

Aten, Jerry. Americans, Too! (gr. 4-8). 1982. 6.95 (ISBN 0-86653-099-1, GA 444). Good Apple.

--Community Friends. (Illus.). 64p. (ps-2). 1983. wkbk. 5.95 (ISBN 0-86653-127-0, GA 477). Good Apple.

--Good Apple & Math Fun. (gr. 3-7). 1981. 9.95 (ISBN 0-86653-023-1, GA 279). Good Apple.

--Maptime... U. S. A. (gr. 4-8). 1982. 5.95 (ISBN 0-86653-093-2, GA 422). Good Apple.

--A Part of Something Great. (gr. 4-8). 1981. 5.95 (ISBN 0-916456-97-8, GA 226). Good Apple.

--Prime Time Life Skills. (Illus.). 64p. (gr. 2-5). 1983. wkbk. 5.95 (ISBN 0-86653-126-2, GA 487). Good Apple.

--Prime Time Maps. (Illus.). 64p. (gr. 2-5). 1983. wkbk. 5.95 (ISBN 0-86653-108-4, GA 470). Good Apple.

Aten, Lawrence. Indians of the Upper Texas Coast. LC 82-13828. (New World Archaeological Record Ser.). 338p. 1983. 40.00 (ISBN 0-12-065740-6). Acad Pr.

Aten, Marilyn J. & McAnarney, Elizabeth R. A Behavioral Approach to the Care of Adolescents. LC 81-1959. 179p. 1981. pap. text ed. 13.95 (ISBN 0-8016-3201-3). Mosby.

Ater, Malcolm W., Jr. Success Through Handwriting Analysis. 1985. pap. 4.95 (ISBN 0-8283-1900-6). Branden Pub Co.

Atha, Anthony. A Scottish Naturalist: The Sketches & Notes of Charles St. John, 1809-1856. (Illus.). 192p. 1982. 21.95 (ISBN 0-233-97390-7, Pub. by Salem Hse Ltd). Merrimack Pub Cir.

Athanasiev, D., jt. auth. see Archpriest Michael Kheraskov.

Athanasius. Contra Gentes & De Incarnatione. Thomas, Robert W., ed. (Oxford Early Christian Texts Ser). 1971. 42.50x (ISBN 0-19-826801-7). Oxford U Pr.

Athanasius, Saint The Life of St. Anthony the Great. pap. 2.95 (ISBN 0-686-16367-2). Eastern Orthodox.

--On the Incarnation of the Word. pap. 2.95 (ISBN 0-686-25556-9). Eastern Orthodox.

Athanasius, St. Select Treatises of St. Athanasius in Controversy with the Arians, 2 vols. 5th ed. Newman, John H., tr. LC 77-84694. (Heresies of the Early Christian & Medieval Era Ser.). Repr. of 1890 ed. 52.00 set (ISBN 0-404-16100-6). AMS Pr.

Athanasopoulos, C. N. Corporate Productivity Atlas. 2nd ed. LC 82-150492. 220p. 1983. pap. 30.00 (ISBN 0-916987-00-0). Delphi Res.

Athanasopulos, Christos G. Contemporary Theater: Evolution & Design. LC 82-17508. 368p. 1983. 64.95x (ISBN 0-471-87319-5, Pub. by Wiley-Interscience). Wiley.

Athanasoulis, C. A., et al, eds. Therapeutic Angiography. (Illus.). 128p. 1981. pap. 27.00 (ISBN 0-387-10526-3). Springer-Verlag.

Athanasoulis, Christos A., et al. Interventional Radiology. LC 77-11329. (Illus.). 806p. 1982. text ed. 98.00 (ISBN 0-7216-1448-5). Saunders.

Athanassakis, Apostolos N. The Life of Pachomius. LC 84-4046. (Society of Biblical Literature. Texts & Translation-Early Christian Literature Ser.). 216p. 1975. pap. 14.25 (ISBN 0-89130-065-1, 06 02 07). Scholars Pr GA.

Athanassakis, Apostolos N., tr. from Gr. The Homeric Hymns. LC 75-40305. 128p. 1976. 12.00x (ISBN 0-8018-1791-9); pap. 5.95x (ISBN 0-8018-1792-7). Johns Hopkins.

Athanassakis, Apostolos N., tr. see Hesiod.

Athanassiadi-Fowden, Polymnia. Julian & Hellenism: An Intellectual Biography. 1981. 52.00x (ISBN 0-19-814846-1). Oxford U Pr.

Athanassoglou, Nina M. French Images from the Greek War of Independence (1821-1830) Art & Politics under the Restoration. (Illus.). 256p. 45.00 (ISBN 0-89241-382-4). Caratzas.

Athanassoula, E. Internal Kinematics & Dynamics of Galaxies. 1983. lib. bdg. 49.50 (ISBN 90-277-1546-7, Pub. by Reidel Holland). Kluwer Academic.

--International Kinematics & Dynamics of Galaxies. 1983. 49.50 (ISBN 90-2771-546-7, Pub. by Reidel Holland); pap. 26.00 (ISBN 90-2771-547-5). Kluwer Academic.

Athanassova, Theodora, tr. see Panayotova, Dora.

Athans, Michael & Falb, P. Optimal Controls. 1966. 58.00 (ISBN 0-07-002413-8). McGraw.

Athappilly, Kuriakose K. Programming & Problem Solving with VAX-11 BASIC. LC 85-3161. (Illus.). 434p. 1985. pap. text ed. write for info. (ISBN 0-534-04926-5). Wadsworth Pub.

Athay, R. G. Radiation Transport in Spectral Lines. LC 72-188002. (Geophysics & Astrophysics Monographs: No. 1). 266p. 1972. lib. bdg. 39.50 (ISBN 90-277-0228-4, Pub. by Reidel Holland); pap. 21.50 (ISBN 90-277-0241-1, Pub. by Reidel Holland). Kluwer Academic.

--The Solar Chromosphere & Corona: Quiet Sun. LC 75-33385. (Astrophysics & Space Science Library: No. 53). 540p. 1975. lib. bdg. 79.00 (ISBN 90-277-0244-6). Kluwer Academic.

Athay, R. G., ed. see I.A.U. Symposium No. 56, Surfer's Paradise, Queensland, Australia, September 3-7, 1973.

Athayde, Roberto. Miss Margarida's Way. 1979. pap. 1.95 (ISBN 0-380-40568-7, Bard). Avon.

Athearn, Furden. How to Divorce Your Wife. 1977. pap. 1.95 (ISBN 0-8439-0503-4, LB503, Leisure Bks). Dorchester Pub Co.

Athearn, James L. Risk & Insurance. 4th ed. (Illus.). 512p. 1981. text ed. 26.95 (ISBN 0-8299-0298-8); student guide 9.50 (ISBN 0-8299-0364-X). West Pub.

Athearn, James L. & Pritchett, S. Travis. Risk & Insurance. 5th ed. (Illus.). 550p. 1984. text ed. 29.95 (ISBN 0-314-77828-4); instrs.' manual avail. (ISBN 0-314-77833-0). West Pub.

Athearn, Robert G. The Coloradans. LC 76-21528. (Illus.). 1982. pap. 12.95 (ISBN 0-8263-0623-3). U of NM Pr.

--The Denver & Rio Grande Western Railroad: Rebel of the Rockies. LC 76-30296. (Illus.). xvi, 395p. 1977. 27.95x (ISBN 0-8032-0920-7); pap. 10.95 (ISBN 0-8032-5861-5, BB 641, Bison). U of Nebr Pr.

--Forts of the Upper Missouri. LC 67-24466. (Illus.). xii, 339p. 1972. pap. 7.50 (ISBN 0-8032-5762-7, BB 555, Bison). U of Nebr Pr.

--High Country Empire: The High Plains & Rockies. LC 60-8822. (Illus.). x, 358p. 1965. pap. 6.50 (ISBN 0-8032-5008-8, BB 314, Bison). U of Nebr Pr.

--In Search of Canaan: Black Migration to Kansas, 1879-80. LC 78-2343. (Illus.). 1978. 25.00x (ISBN 0-7006-0171-6). U Pr of KS.

--Thomas Francis Meagher: An Irish Revolutionary in America. LC 76-6321. (Irish Americans Ser.). (Illus.). 1976. Repr. of 1949 ed. 15.00 (ISBN 0-405-09318-7). Ayer Co Pubs.

--Union Pacific Country. LC 75-11707. (Illus.). 480p. 1976. 26.50x (ISBN 0-8032-0858-8); pap. 11.95 (ISBN 0-8032-5829-1, BB 610, Bison). U of Nebr Pr.

--Westward the Briton. (Illus.). 10.75 (ISBN 0-8446-5710-7). Peter Smith.

Atheling, William, Jr., pseud. Issue at Hand. LC 65-2533. 1964. 8.00 (ISBN 0-911682-09-0); pap. 4.00 (ISBN 0-911682-17-1). Advent.

--More Issues at Hand. LC 72-115400. vi, 154p. 1970. 8.00 (ISBN 0-911682-10-4); pap. 4.00 (ISBN 0-911682-18-X). Advent.

Athelstan, Gary T., jt. auth. see Crewe, Nancy M.

Athenaeus. Deipnosophists, 7 vols. Incl. Vol. 1. Bks. 1-3, 106e: Ser. No. 204 (ISBN 0-674-99224-5); Vol. 2. Bks. 3, 106e-5: Ser. No. 208 (ISBN 0-674-99229-6); Vol. 3. Bks. 6 & 7: Ser. No. 224 (ISBN 0-674-99247-4); Vol. 4. Bks. 8-10: Ser. No. 235 (ISBN 0-674-99259-8); Vol. 5. Bks. 11 & 12: Ser. No. 274 (ISBN 0-674-99302-0); Vol. 6. Bks. 13-14, 653b: Ser. No. 327 (ISBN 0-674-99361-6); Vol. 7. Bks. 14, 653b-15: Ser. No. 345 (ISBN 0-674-99380-2). (Loeb Classical Library: No. 204, 208, 224, 235, 274, 327, 345). 12.50x ea. Harvard U Pr.

Athenagoras. Legatio & De Resurrectione. Schoedel, William R., ed. (Oxford Early Christian Texts Ser). 1972. 32.50x (ISBN 0-19-826808-4). Oxford U Pr.

Athenais, Louis see Mourier, Athenais, pseud.

Atherley, G. R. Occupational Health & Safety Concepts: Chemical Processing Hazards. (Illus.). 408p. 1978. 74.00 (ISBN 0-85334-742-5, Pub. by Elsevier Applied Sci England); pap. 37.00 (ISBN 0-85334-848-0, Pub. by Elsevier Applied Sci England). Elsevier.

Atherley, Gordon R. Occupational Health & Safety Concepts: Chemical & Processing Hazards. (Popular Edition Ser.). (Illus.). 1978. 22.50x (ISBN 0-85334-848-0, Pub. by Applied Science). Burgess-Intl Ideas.

Atherton, Alexine L., ed. International Organizations: A Guide to Information Sources. LC 73-17502. (International Relations Guide Ser.: Vol. 1). 1976. 60.00x (ISBN 0-8103-1324-3). Gale.

Atherton, Charles P., jt. auth. see Prigmore, Charles S.

Atherton, Charles R. & Klemmack, David L. Methods of Social Work Research. 496p. 1982. text ed. 20.95 (ISBN 0-669-03473-8). Heath.

Atherton, D. Nonlinear Control Engineering. 1982. pap. 26.95 (ISBN 0-442-30486-2). Van Nos Reinhold.

Atherton, D. P., ed. see IFAC International Symposium, 4th, Fredericton, NB, Canada, July 1977.

Atherton, Derek P. Stability of Nonlinear Systems. LC 80-40947. (Control Theory & Applications Studies Ser.). 244p. 1981. 54.95x (ISBN 0-471-27856-4, Pub. by Research Studies Pr). Wiley.

Atherton, Gertrude. American Wives & English Husbands: A Novel. 339p. 1984. Repr. of 1901 ed. lib. bdg. 35.00 (ISBN 0-89987-974-8). Darby Books.

--The Bell in the Fog & Other Stories. 1972. Repr. of 1905 ed. 28.00 (ISBN 0-8422-8003-0). Irvington.

--California: An Intimate History. facsimile & rev ed. LC 74-152969. (Select Bibliographies Reprint Ser). Repr. of 1927 ed. 29.00 (ISBN 0-8369-5721-0). Ayer Co Pubs.

--California: An Intimate History. 1914. 30.00 (ISBN 0-8482-7262-5). Norwood Edns.

--California: An Intimate History. 330p. 1982. Repr. of 1914 ed. lib. bdg. 45.00 (ISBN 0-89760-014-2). Telegraph Bks.

--California: An Intimate History. 330p. 1983. Repr. of 1914 ed. lib. bdg. 65.00 (ISBN 0-89987-041-4). Darby Bks.

--The Californians. LC 68-23712. (Americans in Fiction Ser.). lib. bdg. 19.00 (ISBN 0-8398-0063-0); pap. text ed. 6.95x (ISBN 0-89197-689-2). Irvington.

--The Conqueror. 25.95 (ISBN 0-88411-588-7, Pub. by Aeonian Pr). Amereon Ltd.

--The Doomswoman. 375p. 1977. Repr. lib. bdg. 15.50x (ISBN 0-89966-281-1). Buccaneer Bks.

--The Doomswoman: An Historical Romance of Old California. LC 71-104406. Repr. of 1892 ed. lib. bdg. 14.00 (ISBN 0-8398-0064-9). Irvington.

Atherton, Gertrude F. Adventures of a Novelist. Baxter, Annette K., ed. LC 79-8769. (Signal Lives Ser.). 1980. Repr. of 1932 ed. lib. bdg. 62.00x (ISBN 0-405-12819-3). Ayer Co Pubs.

--The Aristocrats. LC 68-20003. (Americans in Fiction Ser.). lib. bdg. 14.00 (ISBN 0-8398-0062-2); pap. text ed. 4.95x (ISBN 0-89197-661-2). Irvington.

--Can Women Be Gentlemen? facsimile ed. LC 70-117754. (Essay Index Reprint Ser). Repr. of 1938 ed. 18.00 (ISBN 0-8369-1692-1). Ayer Co Pubs.

--Los Cerritos. LC 68-23711. (Americans in Fiction Ser.). 1977. lib. bdg. 15.00 (ISBN 0-8398-0065-7); pap. text ed. 5.50x (ISBN 0-89197-695-7). Irvington.

--Foghorn. facs. ed. LC 78-116928. (Short Story Index Reprint Ser). 1934. 18.00 (ISBN 0-8369-3430-X). Ayer Co Pubs.

--Patience Sparhawk. LC 75-104407. Repr. of 1897 ed. lib. bdg. 16.50 (ISBN 0-8398-0066-5). Irvington.

--Rezanov. LC 78-96873. Repr. of 1906 ed. lib. bdg. 15.00 (ISBN 0-8398-0067-3). Irvington.

--Senator North. LC 67-29258. (Americans in Fiction Ser.). Repr. of 1900 ed. lib. bdg. 14.00 (ISBN 0-8398-0068-1). Irvington.

--The Splendid Idle Forties. LC 68-20004. (Americans in Fiction Ser.). (Illus.). lib. bdg. 19.50 (ISBN 0-8398-0069-X); pap. text ed. 7.95x (ISBN 0-89197-947-6). Irvington.

Atherton, Henry V. & Newlander, John A. Chemistry & Testing of Dairy Products. 4th ed. (Illus.). 1977. text ed. 23.50 (ISBN 0-87055-253-8). AVI.

Atherton, Herbert M. Political Prints in the Age of Hogarth: A Study of the Ideographic Representation of Politics. (Illus.). 1974. 59.00x (ISBN 0-19-827188-3). Oxford U Pr.

Atherton, J. C. & Mumphrey, Anthony. Essential Aspects of Career Planning & Development. 2nd ed. LC 75-39156. 376p. (gr. 10-12). 1977. text ed. 13.25x (ISBN 0-8134-1786-4, 1786). Interstate.

Atherton, J. G. & Holmes, I. R. ICTV Code for the Description of Virus Characters. (Monographs in Virology: Vol. 14). vi, 154p. 1983. 41.75 (ISBN 3-8055-3769-7). S Karger.

Atherton, J. S. The Books at the Wake: A Study of Literary Allusions in James Joyce's "Finnegans Wake". rev. ed. 15.00x (ISBN 0-911858-26-1). Appel.

Atherton, James S. The Books at the Wake: A Study of Literary Allusions in James Joyce's "Finnegans Wake". LC 74-5407. (Arcturus Books Paperbacks). 308p. 1974. pap. 7.95 (ISBN 0-8093-0687-5). S Ill U Pr.

Atherton, Judith. Management of Professional Information Services. 1978. 90.00x (ISBN 0-905440-32-3, Pub. by MCB Pubns). State Mutual Bk.

--Quantitative Techniques in Financial Decision-Making. 1978. 70.00x (ISBN 0-905440-74-9, Pub. by MCB Pubns). State Mutual Bk.

Atherton, Larry, jt. auth. see Schreib, Larry.

Atherton, Lewis. The Cattle Kings. LC 61-13722. (Illus.). xii, 342p. 1972. pap. 8.95 (ISBN 0-8032-5759-7, BB 552, Bison). U of Nebr Pr.

--The Cattle Kings. LC 84-9143. (Illus.). 308p. 1984. Repr. of 1967 ed. lib. bdg. 39.75x (ISBN 0-313-24460-X, ATCK). Greenwood.

--Main Street on the Middle Border. LC 54-7970. (Illus.). 464p. (Orig.). 1984. 25.00x (ISBN 0-253-33655-4); pap. 10.95x (ISBN 0-253-20329-5). Ind U Pr.

Atherton, Lewis E. Frontier Merchant in Mid-America. LC 70-155845. 184p. 1971. 15.00x (ISBN 0-8262-0530-5). U of Mo Pr.

--The Pioneer Merchant in Mid-America. LC 75-77700. (American Scene Ser.). 1969. Repr. of 1939 ed. 24.50 (ISBN 0-306-71338-1). Da Capo.

Atherton, M. A. & Lawrence, James K. An Experimental Introduction to Reaction Kinetics. LC 72-575245. (Longman Concepts in Chemistry Ser.). pap. 44.00 (ISBN 0-317-09836-5, 2004556). Bks Demand UMI.

Atherton, M. P. & Gribble, C. D., eds. Migmatites, Melting & Metamorphism. 200p. 1982. 60.00x (ISBN 0-906812-26-7, Pub. by Shiva Pub England); pap. 40.00x (ISBN 0-906812-25-9). State Mutual Bk.

--Migmatites, Melting & Metamorphism. 200p. 1983. text ed. 39.95 (Pub. by Shiva Pub Ltd.); pap. text ed. 19.95 (Pub. by Shiva Pub Ltd.). Birkhauser.

Atherton, M. P. & Tarney, J., eds. Origin of Granite Batholiths: Geochemical Evidence. 150p. (Orig.). 1981. pap. text ed. 11.95x (ISBN 0-906812-00-3). Birkhauser.

Atherton, Mary K., et al. Touch with Your Eyes! (Illus.). 48p. (Orig.). (gr. k-8). 1982. pap. 4.50 (ISBN 0-9613069-0-4). Orinda Art Coun.

Atherton, Pauline. Handbook for Information Systems & Services. (Illus.). 259p. (2nd Printing 1980). 1977. pap. 21.75 (ISBN 92-3-101457-9, U790, UNESCO). Unipub.

--Putting Knowledge to Work. 1973. 6.00 (ISBN 0-7069-0264-5). Intl Bk Dist.

Atherton, Roy. Structured BASIC for Acorn Computers. 207p. (Orig.). 1983. pap. 15.95 (ISBN 0-471-80600-5, Pub. by Wiley Pr). Wiley.

--Structured Programming with COMAL. (Computers & Their Applications Ser.). 266p. 1982. 58.95x (ISBN 0-470-27318-6); pap. 26.95 (ISBN 0-470-27359-3). Halsted Pr.

Atherton, Sarah H. Mark's Own. LC 74-26207. (The Labor Movement in Fiction & Non-Fiction Ser.). Repr. of 1941 ed. 29.50 (ISBN 0-404-58404-7). AMS Pr.

Atherton, Toni-Lee. The Man in the Tree. (Readers' Theatre Exercises Ser.: No. 1). (Illus.). 1977. pap. text ed. 2.95 (ISBN 0-912484-07-1). Joseph Nichols.

--Woman Within. (Readers' Theatre Editions Ser.). (Illus.). 1978. pap. text ed. 2.95 (ISBN 0-912484-10-1). Joseph Nichols.

Atherton, W., et al. Power Plant Fitting & Testing, 2 vols. (Illus.). 492p. 1981. Repr. of 1981 ed. spiral 89.95x (ISBN 0-85083-445-7). Intl Ideas.

Atherton, W. A. From Compass to Computer: A History of Electrical & Electronics Engineering. (Illus.). 1983. 30.00 (ISBN 0-911302-48-4); pap. 12.50 (ISBN 0-911302-49-2). San Francisco Pr.

Atherton, Wallace N. Theory of Union Bargaining Goals. LC 72-14017. 160p. 1973. 21.50x (ISBN 0-691-04199-7). Princeton U Pr.

Athey, Jackie, jt. auth. see Meintjes, Ria.

Athey, Jackie, ed. see Hasegawa, Hideo.

Athey, Jackie, ed. see Smuts, Margie.

Athey, Margaret & Hotchkiss, Gwen. Complete Handbook of Music Games & Activities for Early Childhood. LC 82-2289. 218p. 1982. 15.50 (ISBN 0-13-161083-X). P-H.

--A Galaxy of Games for the Music Class. 1975. 15.95x (ISBN 0-13-346064-9, Parker). P-H.

Athey, Margaret, jt. auth. see Hotchkiss, Gwen.

Athey, Patricia A. & Hadlock, Frank P. Ultrasound in Obstetrics & Gynecology. LC 81-4646. (Illus.). 283p. 1981. text ed. 51.95 (ISBN 0-8016-0374-9). Mosby.

Athey, Patricia A. & McClendon, Linda. Diagnostic Ultrasound for Radiographers. LC 83-13203. (Illus.). 121p. (Orig.). 1983. pap. 12.95x (ISBN 0-940122-09-X). Multi Media CO.

Athey, Thomas H. Systematic Systems Approach: An Integrated Method for Solving Systems Problems. (Illus.). 416p. 1982. text ed. 31.95 (ISBN 0-13-880914-3). P-H.

Athey, Thomas H. & Zmud, Robert W. Introduction to Computers & Information Systems. 1986. text ed. 24.95x (ISBN 0-673-15961-2). Scott F.

--Introduction to Computers & Information Systems with BASIC. 1986. text ed. 26.95x (ISBN 0-673-18185-5). Scott F.

Athill, Diana. Instead of a Letter. 224p. 1984. 15.95 (ISBN 0-88184-040-8); pap. 7.95 (ISBN 0-88184-046-7). Carroll & Graf.

Athill, Diana, tr. see De Pougy, Liane.

Athletic Institute, ed. Archery: A Sport for Everyone. LC 82-74329. (Illus.). 96p. (Orig.). 1984. pap. 6.95 (ISBN 0-87670-086-5, Dist. by Sterling). Athletic Inst.

--Youth League Soccer: Coaching & Playing. LC 81-70308. (Athletic Institute Bk.). (Illus.). 160p. (Orig.). (gr. 3 up). 1983. pap. 7.95 (ISBN 0-8069-7734-5). Sterling.

Athletic Institute Editors. Youth League Football: Coaching & Playing. (Illus.). 128p. (Orig.). (gr. 2 up). 1984. pap. 6.95 (ISBN 0-87670-081-4). Athletic Inst.

Athletic Institute Editors, ed. Youth League Basketball: Coaching & Playing. (Illus.). 128p. (Orig.). 1984. pap. 6.95 (ISBN 0-87670-092-X). Athletic Inst.

Athletic Training Council Editorial Committee Staff. Tips on Training. (Illus.). 99p. (Orig.). 1983. pap. 10.45x (ISBN 0-88314-231-7). AAHPERD.

Atholl, Katherine. Conscription of a People. LC 73-161703. Repr. of 1931 ed. 17.00 (ISBN 0-404-00414-8). AMS Pr.

Athos, A. & Gabarro, J. Interpersonal Behavior. 1978. 29.95 (ISBN 0-13-475004-7). P-H.

Athos, Anthony G., jt. auth. see Pascale, Richard T.

Athos Monasteries. Catalogue of the Greek Manuscripts in the Library of the Laura on Mt. Athos, with Notices from Other Libraries. (Harvard Theological Studies Ser.). 1925. 51.00 (ISBN 0-527-01012-X). Kraus Repr.

--Catalogue of the Greek Manuscripts in the Library of the Monastery of Vatopedi on Mt. Athos. (Harvard Theological Studies Ser.). 1924. 24.00 (ISBN 0-527-01011-1). Kraus Repr.

Athreya, Balu M. & Silverman, Benjamin K. Pediatric & Neonatal Physical Diagnosis. 1985. write for info. (ISBN 0-8385-7797-0). ACC.

Athreya, K. B. & Ney, P. E. Branching Processes. LC 72-75819. (Die Grundlehren der Mathematischen Wissenshaften: Vol. 196). 300p. 1972. 39.00 (ISBN 0-387-05790-0). Springer-Verlag.

Ati, H. A. Islam in Focus. pap. 9.50 (ISBN 0-686-18504-8). Kazi Pubns.

Atichison, Diane, et al. Aldine: Our District & Its Community, Study Book. new ed. Hawke, Sharrly D., ed. 1984. pap. 4.50 (ISBN 0-87746-008-6). Graphic Learning.

Atienza, Loretta J. VTR Workshop: Small Format Video. (Monographs on Communication Technology & Utilization: No. 4). (Illus.). 114p. (2nd Printing 1979). 1977. pap. text ed. 5.00 (ISBN 92-3-101467-6, U748, UNESCO). Unipub.

Atik, Anne. Words in Hock. 1974. wrappers 3.50 (ISBN 0-685-46792-9, Pub. by Enitharmon Pr); 4.75 (ISBN 0-685-46793-7); special edition 150.00 (ISBN 0-685-46794-5). Small Pr Dist.

Atil, Esin. Brush of the Masters: Drawings from Iran & India. LC 78-70427. (Illus.). 1978. pap. 20.00x (ISBN 0-934686-29-7). Freer.

--Kalila Wa Dimna: Fables from a Fourteenth Century Arabic Manuscript. LC 81-607053. (Illus.). 96p. (Orig.). 1981. 17.50 (ISBN 0-87474-216-1); pap. 9.95 (ISBN 0-87474-215-3). Smithsonian.

--Renaissance of Islam: Art of the Mamluks. LC 80-607866. (Illus.). 288p. (Orig.). 1981. 47.50 (ISBN 0-87474-214-5); pap. 22.50 (ISBN 0-87474-213-7). Smithsonian.

--Turkish Art of the Ottoman Period. (Illus.). 1973. pap. 5.00x (ISBN 0-934686-26-2). Freer.

Atil, Esin, ed. Turkish Art. LC 79-22171. (Illus.). 386p. 1981. 65.00 (ISBN 0-87474-218-8). Smithsonian.

Atil, Esin, et al. Islamic Metalwork in the Freer Gallery of Art. LC 85-40502. (Illus.). 288p. (Orig.). 1985. pap. 17.50 (ISBN 0-87474-249-8, ATIMP). Smithsonian.

Atimono, Emiko. Law & Diplomacy in Commodity Economics. 400p. 1981. text ed. 55.00x (ISBN 0-8419-5080-6). Holmes & Meier.

Atis, Sarah M. Semantic Structuring in the Modern Turkish Short Story: An Analysis of the Dreams of Abdullah Efendi & Other Short Stories by Tanpinar. (Social, Economic & Political Studies of the Middle East: No. 34). 200p. 1983. text ed. 24.50x (ISBN 90-04-07117-2, Pub. by E J Brill). Humanities.

Atisa. A Lamp for the Path & Commentary. Sherburne, Richard, tr. (Wisdom of Tibet: No. 5). 240p. 1983. text ed. 27.50 (ISBN 0-04-294124-5); pap. text ed. 12.50 (ISBN 0-04-294125-3). Allen Unwin.

Atiya, Aziz S. The Crusade: Historiography & Bibliography. LC 75-22640. 1976. lib. bdg. 18.75 (ISBN 0-8371-8364-2, ATTC). Greenwood.

--The Crusade of Nicopolis. LC 76-29829. (Illus.). Repr. of 1934 ed. 23.50 (ISBN 0-404-15410-7). AMS Pr.

--History of Eastern Christianity. LC 80-232. 1980. Repr. lib. bdg. 52.00 (ISBN 0-527-03703-6). Kraus Repr.

Atiya, Nayra. Khul-Khaal: Five Egyptian Women Tell Their Stories. LC 82-5773. (Contemporary Issues in the Middle East Ser.). (Illus.). 216p. 1982. text ed. 20.00x (ISBN 0-8156-0177-8); pap. 11.95X (ISBN 0-8156-0181-6). Syracuse U Pr.

Atiyah, Edward. The Arabs. (Arab Background Ser.). 1968. pap. 7.95x (ISBN 0-86685-001-5). Intl Bk Ctr.

Atiyah, Edward S. An Arab Tells His Story; a Study in Loyalties. LC 79-3071. (Illus.). 229p. 1981. Repr. of 1946 ed. 21.50 (ISBN 0-8305-0023-5). Hyperion Conn.

Atiyah, M. F. Elliptic Operators & Compact Groups. (Lecture Notes in Mathematics Ser.: Vol. 401). v, 93p. 1974. pap. 13.00 (ISBN 3-540-06855-4). Springer-Verlag.

Atiyah, M. F., et al. Representation Theory of Lie Groups. LC 78-73820. (London Mathematical Society Lecture Note: No. 34). 1980. pap. 37.50 (ISBN 0-521-22636-8). Cambridge U Pr.

Atiyah, Michael F. & Macdonald, I. G. Introduction to Commutative Algebra. 1969. text ed. 24.95 (ISBN 0-201-00361-9). Addison-Wesley.

Atiyah, P. S. Accidents, Compensation & the Law. 3rd ed. (Law in Context Ser.). xxiv, 695p. 1980. 47.00x (ISBN 0-297-77754-8, Pub. by Weidenfeld & Nicolson England). Rothman.

--Law & Modern Society. (Oxford Paperbacks University Ser.). 1983. 22.00x (ISBN 0-19-219166-7); pap. 7.95x (ISBN 0-19-289152-9). Oxford U Pr.

--Promises, Morals, & Law. 1981. 35.00x (ISBN 0-19-825377-X); pap. 15.95x (ISBN 0-19-825479-2). Oxford U Pr.

--The Rise & Fall of Freedom of Contract. LC 85-10515. 800p. 1985. pap. 19.95 (ISBN 0-19-825527-6). Oxford U Pr.

Atiyah, P. S., jt. auth. see Kaplan, Benjamin.

Atiyah, Patrick S. An Introduction to the Law of Contract. 3rd ed. (Claredon Law Ser.). 1981. pap. 39.95x (ISBN 0-19-876140-6); pap. text ed. 15.95x (ISBN 0-19-876141-4). Oxford U Pr.

--The Rise & Fall of Freedom of Contract. 1979. 65.00x (ISBN 0-19-825342-7). Oxford U Pr.

Atiyeh, George, ed. Arab & American Cultures. 1977. 15.25 (ISBN 0-8447-2116-6); pap. 7.25 (ISBN 0-8447-2115-8). Am Enterprise.

Atiyeh, George N., compiled by. The Contemporary Middle East, Nineteen Forty-Eight to Nineteen Seventy-Three: An Selective & Annotated Bibliography. 775p. 1975. lib. bdg. 57.50 (ISBN 0-8161-1085-9, Hall Reference). G K Hall.

Atiyeh, Wadeeha. Fourth Wise Man. (gr. 4 up). 1959. pap. 3.00 (ISBN 0-8315-0038-7). Speller.

Atkeson, Mary. A Study of the Local Literature of the Upper Ohio Valley: With Especial Reference to the Early Pioneer & Indian Tales, 1820-1840. LC 74-7917. (Ohio State University, Columbus Contributions to English: No. 2). Repr. of 1921 ed. 11.50 (ISBN 0-404-11800-3). AMS Pr.

Atkeson, Mira, photos by. The World of Mira Atkeson. LC 77-77012. (Illus.). 120p. (Text by Luella O'Conner). 1977. 19.50 (ISBN 0-912856-36-X). Graphic Arts Ctr.

Atkeson, Ray. Washington & Oregon in Color. (Illus.). 1954. pap. 1.00 (ISBN 0-8323-0077-2). Binford.

Atkeson, Ray, photos by. The Oregon Coast. LC 75-188295. (Belding Imprint Ser.). (Illus.). 128p. (Text by Archie Satterfield). 1972. 32.50 (ISBN 0-912856-06-8). Graphic Arts Ctr.

--Oregon II. LC 74-75124. (Belding Imprint Ser.). (Illus.). 192p. (Text by Archie Satterfield). 1974. 32.50 (ISBN 0-912856-15-7). Graphic Arts Ctr.

--Portrait of California. LC 79-55978. (Portrait of America Ser.). (Illus.). 80p. (Orig., Text by Lee Foster). 1980. pap. 5.95 (ISBN 0-912856-54-8). Graphic Arts Ctr.

--Portrait of Oregon. LC 79-91507. (Portrait of America Ser.). (Illus.). 80p. (Orig., Text by Tom Barr). 1980. pap. 7.50 (ISBN 0-912856-52-1). Graphic Arts Ctr.

--Portrait of Washington. LC 79-55977. (Portrait of America Ser.). (Illus.). 80p. (Orig., Text by Tom Barr). 1980. pap. 7.50 (ISBN 0-912856-53-X). Graphic Arts Ctr.

--Washington II. LC 70-81401. (Belding Imprint Ser.). (Illus.). 128p. (Text by Archie Satterfield). 1973. 32.50 (ISBN 0-912856-12-2). Graphic Arts Ctr.

Atkey, Ronald G., jt. ed. see Lyon, J. Noel.

Atkin, Abraham. Chelkeinu. 200p. text ed. 5.00 (ISBN 0-914131-09-5, A16). Torah Umesorah.

--Darkeinu Aleph & Bais: In One Volume. pap. text ed. 3.00 (ISBN 0-686-33046-3, A13). Torah Umesorah.

--Darkeinu Daled. text ed. 3.00 (ISBN 0-914131-13-3, A15). Torah Umesorah.

Atkin, E. The Applalachian Indian Frontier: The Edmond Atkin Report & Plan of 1775. Jacobs, Wilbur R., ed. (Illus.). 11.25 (ISBN 0-8446-1561-7). Peter Smith.

--The Metric Theory of Banach Manifolds. LC 78-14728. (Lecture Notes in Mathematics: Vol. 662). 1978. pap. 19.00 (ISBN 0-387-08915-2). Springer-Verlag.

Atkin, Edith. In Praise of Marriage. LC 81-16324. 352p. 1982. 14.95 (ISBN 0-8149-0854-3). Vanguard.

Atkin, Edith & Rubin, Estelle. Part-Time Father. LC 75-25146. 192p. 1976. 12.95 (ISBN 0-8149-0766-0). Vanguard.

Atkin, Edmond. Appalachian Indian Frontier: The Edmond Atkin Report & Plan of 1755. Jacobs, Wilbur R., ed. LC 54-12059. (Illus.). xxxviii, 108p. 1967. pap. 3.95x (ISBN 0-8032-5011-8, BB 374, Bison). U of Nebr Pr.

Atkin, J. K. Computer Science. 2nd ed. (Illus.). 224p. (Orig.). 1980. pap. 14.95x (ISBN 0-7121-0396-1). Trans-Atlantic.

Atkin, Jane. A Moment's Enchantment. (Candlelight Ecstasy Ser.: No. 404). (Orig.). 1986. pap. 2.25 (ISBN 0-440-15792-7). Dell.

Atkin, John. Practical Small Boat Designs. LC 82-48618. (Illus.). 192p. 1983. pap. 14.95 (ISBN 0-87742-160-9, P577). Intl Marine.

Atkin, John, jt. auth. see Atkin, William.

Atkin, John Michael. British Overseas Investment: 1918-1931. Bruchey, Stuart, ed. LC 77-81821. (Dissertations in European Economic History Ser.). (Illus.). 1977. lib. bdg. 37.50x (ISBN 0-405-10774-9). Ayer Co Pubs.

Atkin, M. J., ed. ICCH Commodities & Financial Futures Yearbook, 1983-84. 424p. 1983. 52.50 (ISBN 0-7099-0536-X, Pub. by Croom Helm Ltd). Longwood Pub Group.

Atkin, Muriel. Russia & Iran, Seventeen Eighty to Eighteen Twenty-Eight. LC 80-10391. (Illus.). 1980. 20.00x (ISBN 0-8166-0924-1). U of Minn Pr.

Atkin, N. B. Cytogenetic Aspects of Malignant Transformation. Wolsky, A, ed. (Experimental Biology & Medicine: Vol. 6). (Illus.). 200p. 1976. 31.50 (ISBN 3-8055-2330-0). S Karger.

Atkin, R. H. Mathematical Structures in Human Affairs. LC 73-93383. 218p. 1974. 27.50x (ISBN 0-8448-0319-7). Crane-Russak Co.

Atkin, R. K., jt. auth. see Goodenough, P. W.

Atkin, R. K., jt. ed. see Day, W.

Atkin, Ron. Multidimensional Man. 1982. pap. 6.95 (ISBN 0-14-005478-2). Penguin.

Atkin, Ronald & McCabe, Eamonn. The Book of Wimbledon. (Illus.). 96p. (Orig.). 1982. 19.95 (ISBN 0-434-98011-0, Pub. by W Heinemann Ltd); pap. 12.50 (ISBN 0-434-98028-5). David & Charles.

Atkin, Samuel, ed. see Rosen, Victor.

Atkin, William. Of Yachts & Men. (Illus.). 320p. 1984. Repr. of 1949 ed. 22.50 (ISBN 0-911378-51-0). Sheridan.

Atkin, William & Atkin, John. The Book of Boats. LC 76-25311. (Illus.). 1976. Repr. of 1948 ed. 10.95 (ISBN 0-87742-081-5). Intl Marine.

Atkin, William W. Architectural Presentation Techniques. 196p. 1982. pap. 10.95 (ISBN 0-442-21074-4). Van Nos Reinhold.

Atkins. Highway Materials: Soils & Concrete. 2nd ed. LC 82-20526. 1983. text ed. 28.95 (ISBN 0-8359-2829-2). Reston.

Atkins, jt. auth. see Spence.

Atkins, A. G., jt. ed. see Alsmeyer, D.

Atkins, Abraham. Darkeinu Gimel. (gr. 4 up). text ed. 3.00 (ISBN 0-686-33046-3, A14). Torah Umesorah.

Atkins, Annette. Harvest of Grief: Grasshopper Plagues & Public Assistance in Minnesota, 1873-78. LC 84-10855. 147p. 1984. 12.95 (ISBN 0-87351-171-9). Minn Hist.

Atkins, Anthony C., jt. auth. see Felbeck, David K.

Atkins, Anthony G. & Mai, Y. W. Elastic & Plastic Fracture. (Mechanical Engineering Ser.). Date not set. 112.95 (ISBN 0-470-20195-9). Halsted Pr.

Atkins, B. & Glick, H., eds. Prisons, Protest & Politics. 1972. pap. 2.95 (ISBN 0-13-710798-6, Spec, Spec). P-H.

Atkins, Beryl, jt. auth. see McArthur, Tom.

Atkins, Burton & Pogrebin, Mark. Invisible Justice System: Discretion & the Law. 1978. text ed. 13.95 (ISBN 0-87084-709-0). Anderson Pub Co.

Atkins, Burton, jt. auth. see Pogrebin, Mark.

Atkins, Dale V. Sisters. 140p. 1984. 15.95 (ISBN 0-87795-597-2). Arbor Hse.

Atkins, Dorothy. George Eliot & Spinoza. (Salzburg Studies in English Literature: Romantic Reassessment Ser.: No. 78). 1979. pap. text ed. 25.50x (ISBN 0-391-01302-5). Humanities.

Atkins, E. Wulstan. The Elgar-Atkins Friendship. (Illus.). 510p. 1984. 32.00 (ISBN 0-7153-8583-6). David & Charles.

Atkins, Edwin F. Sixty Years in Cuba: Reminiscences of Edwin F. Atkins. Bruchey, Stuart, ed. LC 80-555. (Multinational Corporations Ser.). (Illus.). 1980. Repr. of 1926 ed. lib. bdg. 44.00x (ISBN 0-405-13352-9). Ayer Co Pubs.

Atkins, Elizabeth. The Poet's Poet. LC 74-9902. 1922. lib. bdg. 25.00 (ISBN 0-8414-2981-2). Folcroft.

--Treasures of the Medranos. 1957. 4.25 (ISBN 0-395-27666-7). HM.

Atkins, Frank. The Devil-Tree of el Dorado: A Novel. Reginald, R. & Melville, Douglas, eds. LC 77-84196. (Lost Race & Adult Fantasy Ser.). (Illus.). 1978. Repr. of 1897 ed. lib. bdg. 33.00x (ISBN 0-405-10955-5). Ayer Co Pubs.

--King of the Dead: A Weird Romance. Reginald, R. & Melville, Douglas, eds. LC 77-84197. (Lost Race & Adult Fantasy Ser.). 1978. Repr. of 1903 ed. lib. bdg. 26.50x (ISBN 0-405-10956-3). Ayer Co Pubs.

Atkins, G. Douglas. The Faith of John Dryden: Change & Continuity. LC 80-12890. 208p. 1980. 19.00x (ISBN 0-8131-1401-2). U Pr of Ky.

--Reading Deconstruction-Deconstructive Reading. LC 83-10308. 168p. 1983. 18.00x (ISBN 0-8131-1493-4); pap. 7.00 (ISBN 0-8131-0165-4). U Pr of Ky.

Atkins, G. Douglas & Johnson, Michael L., eds. Writing & Reading Differently: Deconstruction & the Teaching of Literature & Composition. 208p. 1985. 25.00x (ISBN 0-7006-0282-8); pap. text ed. 12.95x (ISBN 0-7006-0283-6). U Pr of KS.

Atkins, G. L. Multicompartment Models for Biological Systems. 1974. pap. 9.95x (ISBN 0-412-21180-7, NO. 6014, Pub. by Chapman & Hall). Methuen Inc.

Atkins, G. Pope. Arms & Politics in the Dominican Republic. (Special Studies on Latin America & the Caribbean). 158p. 1981. 23.50x (ISBN 0-86531-112-9). Westview.

--Latin America in the International Political System. LC 76-20882. 1977. 24.95 (ISBN 0-02-901060-8). Free Pr.

Atkins, Gaius. Modern Religious Cults & Movements. LC 74-126684. Repr. of 1923 ed. 26.50 (ISBN 0-404-00415-6). AMS Pr.

Atkins, Gaius G. Pilgrims of the Lonely Road. facs. ed. LC 67-28741. (Essay Index Reprint Ser). 1913. 18.00 (ISBN 0-8369-0162-2). Ayer Co Pubs.

--Resources for Living. facs. ed. LC 77-117756. (Essay Index Reprint Ser). 1938. 19.00 (ISBN 0-8369-1741-3). Ayer Co Pubs.

Atkins, Gaius G., ed. see Maclaren, Alexander.

Atkins, Guy & Anderson, Troels. Asger Jorn: The Final Years, 1965-73. 256p. 1980. 150.00x (ISBN 0-85331-438-1, Pub. by Lund Humphries England). State Mutual Bk.

Atkins, Guy, jt. auth. see Anderson, Troels.

Atkins, H. G. Johann Wolfgang Goethe. 180p. 1981. Repr. of 1904 ed. lib. bdg. 35.00 (ISBN 0-8495-0077-X). Arden Lib.

Atkins, Harold & Cotes, Peter. The Barbirollis: A Musical Marriage. (Illus.). 238p. 1985. text ed. 17.50x (ISBN 0-87663-394-7). Universe.

Atkins, Harold L. Pulmonary Nuclear Medicine. (Lung Biology in Health & Diseases Ser.). 344p. 1984. 69.75 (ISBN 0-8247-7233-4). Dekker.

Atkins, Hazel. The Receptionist. 112p. 1981. pap. 14.95x (ISBN 0-7131-0580-1). Intl Ideas.

Atkins, Henry G., jt. auth. see Kastner, L. E.

Atkins, Irene K. Source Music in Motion Pictures. LC 81-65338. (Illus.). 192p. 1983. 22.50 (ISBN 0-8386-3076-6). Fairleigh Dickinson.

Atkins, Ivor A. The Early Occupants of the Office of Organist & Master of the Choristers of the Cathedral Church of Christ & the Blessed Virgin Mary, Worcester. LC 74-27329. Repr. of 1913 ed. 24.50 (ISBN 0-404-12855-6). AMS Pr.

Atkins, J. Walter De la Mare: An Exploration. LC 75-22359. (Studies in Poetry, No. 38). 1975. lib. bdg. 46.95x (ISBN 0-8383-2105-4). Haskell.

Atkins, J. W. Literary Criticism in Antiquity: A Sketch of Its Development, 2 vols. 1978. Repr. of 1952 ed. Set. lib. bdg. 65.00 (ISBN 0-8495-0138-5). Arden Lib.

Atkins, Jeannette see Levy, Harold L.

Atkins, John. The British Spy Novel. 1984. 19.95 (ISBN 0-7145-3997-X). Riverrun NY.

--George Orwell. 1981. 14.95 (ISBN 0-7145-0715-6); pap. 8.95 (ISBN 0-7145-0716-4). Riverrun NY.

--Graham Greene. 1979. Repr. of 1957 ed. lib. bdg. 35.00 (ISBN 0-8495-0139-3). Arden Lib.

--Graham Greene. 2nd rev. ed. 1970. text ed. 16.50x (ISBN 0-7145-0262-6). Humanities.

--Graham Greene. 240p. 1980. Repr. lib. bdg. 30.00 (ISBN 0-8492-3447-6). R West.

--Graham Greene. 1982. 14.95 (ISBN 0-7145-0262-6). Riverrun NY.

--J. B. Priestley: The Last of the Sages. 1981. 25.00 (ISBN 0-7145-3804-3); pap. 13.95 (ISBN 0-7145-3950-3). Riverrun NY.

--Sex in Literature, Vol. 2. 1980. 15.95 (ISBN 0-7145-0919-1); pap. 6.95 (ISBN 0-7145-1138-2). Riverrun NY.

--Sex in Literature, Vol. 1. 1981. pap. 12.95 (ISBN 0-7145-0522-6). Riverrun NY.

--Sex in Literature, Vol. 4: The Eighteenth Century. 400p. 1982. 24.95 (ISBN 0-7145-3756-X); pap. 12.95 (ISBN 0-7145-3977-5). Riverrun NY.

--Six Novelists Look at Society. 1980. 11.95 (ISBN 0-7145-3535-4); pap. 7.95 (ISBN 0-7145-3863-9). Riverrun NY.

--A Voyage to Guinea, Brasil, & the West Indies, with Remarks on the Gold, Ivory & Slave Trade. LC 70-99333. 265p. 1972. Repr. of 1735 ed. lib. bdg. 16.50 (ISBN 0-8411-0004-7). Metro Bks.

--Voyage to Guinea, Brazil & the West Indies in H.M.S. "Swallow" & "Weymouth". 258p. 1970. Repr. of 1735 ed. 27.50x (ISBN 0-7146-1787-3, F Cass Co). Biblio Dist.

--Walter De la Mare. LC 73-16197. 1973. lib. bdg. 8.50 (ISBN 0-8414-2931-6). Folcroft.

Atkins, John A. Walter De la Mare: An Exploration. LC 76-47035. 1976. Repr. of 1947 ed. lib. bdg. 12.00 (ISBN 0-8482-0059-4). Norwood Edns.

Atkins, John F. The Paper Machine Wet Press Manual. LC 79-6366. (TAPPI PRESS Books). (Illus.). 120p. 1979. 14.95 (ISBN 0-89852-042-8, 01-02 B042). TAPPI.

Atkins, John W. English Literary Criticism: The Medieval Phase. 12.00 (ISBN 0-8446-1032-1). Peter Smith.

--Literary Criticism in Antiquity, 2 vols. Incl. Vol. 1. Greek. 10.75 (ISBN 0-8446-1033-X); Vol. 2. Graeco-Roman. 11.75 ea.. Peter Smith.

Atkins, John W., ed. & tr. Owl & the Nightingale. LC 77-139898. 1971. Repr. of 1922 ed. 16.00x (ISBN 0-8462-1530-6). Russell.

Atkins, Ken & Rainey, Ron. Winning Basketball Drills. LC 84-22674. 217p. 1984. 18.95 (ISBN 0-13-960618-1). Parker Pub OR.

Atkins, Kenneth R., et al. Essentials of Physical Science. LC 77-12507. 546p. 1978. text ed. 35.95 (ISBN 0-471-03617-X); study guide 13.45 (ISBN 0-471-03551-3); avail. tchrs. manual (ISBN 0-471-03552-1). Wiley.

Atkins, M. Atlas of Continuous Cooling Transformation Diagrams for Engineering Steels. 1980. 102.00 (ISBN 0-87170-093-X). ASM.

Atkins, M. H. & Lowe, J. F. Case Studies in Pollution Control in the Textile Dyeing & Finishing Industries: A Study in Non-Technical Language of Essential Information on the Economics of Control, the Problems & Their Solutions. 1979. 53.00 (ISBN 0-08-022457-1). Pergamon.

--Economics of Pollution Control in the Non-Ferrous Metals Industry. (Illus.). 1979. 53.00 (ISBN 0-08-022458-X). Pergamon.

--Pollution Control Costs in Industry: An Economic Study. pap. text ed. 14.75 (ISBN 0-08-021841-5). Pergamon.

Atkins, Marguerite H. Also My Journey. 160p. 1985. 12.95 (ISBN 0-8192-1362-4). Morehouse.

Atkins, Michael D. Insects in Perspectives. (Illus.). 1978. text ed. write for info. (ISBN 0-02-304500-0). Macmillan.

Atkins, P. W. The Creation. LC 81-5578. (Illus.). 132p. 1981. 11.95 (ISBN 0-7167-1350-0). W H Freeman.

--Molecular Quantum Mechanics. 2nd ed. (Illus.). 1983. pap. 27.95x (ISBN 0-19-855170-3). Oxford U Pr.

--Molecular Quantum Mechanics: Solutions Manual. (Illus.). 1983. pap. 14.95x (ISBN 0-19-855180-0). Oxford U Pr.

--Physical Chemistry. 2nd ed. LC 81-15260. (Illus.). 1095p. 1982. text ed. 35.95 (ISBN 0-7167-1381-0); solutions manual 10.95. W H Freeman.

--Physical Chemistry. LC 77-21208. (Illus.). 1008p. 1978. text ed. 29.95x (ISBN 0-7167-0187-1); solutions manual o.p. 7.95x (ISBN 0-7167-1071-4). W H Freeman.

--Quanta: A Handbook of Concepts. (Oxford Chemistry Ser.). (Illus.). 1977. pap. 26.00x (ISBN 0-19-855494-X). Oxford U Pr.

--The Second Law. LC 84-5377. 230p. 1984. 27.95 (ISBN 0-7167-5004-X). W H Freeman.

Atkins, P. W., jt. ed. see Muus, L. T.

Atkins, Peter W. Physical Chemistry. 3rd ed. LC 85-7048. (Illus.). 528p. 1985. text ed. write for info. (ISBN 0-7167-1749-2). W H Freeman.

Atkins, Robert. Dr. Atkins Diet Revolution. 336p. 1981. pap. 3.95 (ISBN 0-553-20729-6). Bantam.

--Nutrition Breakthrough. 1979. 12.95x (ISBN 0-688-03644-9); pap. 3.50x (ISBN 0-553-20279-0). Cancer Control Soc.

--Super Energy Diet. 1981. 18.95 (ISBN 0-686-76750-0). B Of A.

Atkins, Robert & Linde, Shirley M. Dr. Atkins' Superenergy Diet. 1978. pap. 3.95 (ISBN 0-553-20758-X). Bantam.

Atkins, Robert, et al. Dr. Atkins Super-Energy Cookbook. (Orig.). 1978. pap. 3.95 (ISBN 0-451-12176-7, AE2176, Sig). NAL.

Atkins, Robert C. Dr. Atkins Nutrition Breakthrough: How to Treat Your Medical Condition Without Drugs. 1982. pap. 3.50 (ISBN 0-553-20279-0). Bantam.

Atkins, Robert C., ed. Peritonial Dialysis. (Illus.). 426p. 1981. 62.50 (ISBN 0-443-02394-8). Churchill.

Atkins, Russell. Here in The. (Cleveland Poets Ser.: No. 13). 52p. 1976. pap. 4.50 (ISBN 0-914946-03-X). Cleveland St Univ Poetry Ctr.

Atkins, Ruth. The Government of the Australian Capital Territory. (Governments of Australian States & Territories Ser.). (Illus.). 1979. 30.00x (ISBN 0-7022-1424-8); pap. 19.95x (ISBN 0-7022-1430-2). U of Queensland Pr.

Atkins, Ruth E. The Measurement of the Intelligence of Young Children by an Object-Fitting Test. LC 75-12673. (Univ. of Minnesota Institute of Child Welfare Monograph: No. 5). (Illus.). 89p. 1975. Repr. of 1931 ed. lib. bdg. 18.75 (ISBN 0-8371-8083-X, CWAI). Greenwood.

Atkins, Stanley & McConnell, Theodore, eds. Churches on the Wrong Road. 150p. (Orig.). 1985. pap. 7.95 (ISBN 0-89526-803-5). Regnery-Gateway.

Atkins, Stuart. The Name of your Game: Four Game Plans for Success at Home & at Work. LC 81-71849. (Illus.). 1982. 16.95 (ISBN 0-686-39188-8); pap. 4.95. Ellis & Stewart Pub.

Atkins, Stuart, ed. & tr. Faust I & II. LC 82-16999. 330p. (Ger. & Eng.). 1984. 29.95 (ISBN 3-518-03055-8). Suhrkamp.

Atkins, Susan & Hoggett, Brenda. Women & the Law. 224p. 1985. 24.95x (ISBN 0-85520-181-9); pap. 8.95x (ISBN 0-85520-180-0). Basil Blackwell.

Atkins, Susan & Slosser, Bob. Child of Satan, Child of God. LC 77-81947. 1977. (Pub. by Logos); pap. 2.95 (ISBN 0-88270-276-9). Bridge Pub.

Atkins, Thomas R., ed. Sexuality in the Movies. LC 74-17564. (Illus.). Repr. of 1975 ed. cancelled (ISBN 0-8357-9241-2, 2017607). Bks Demand UMI.

--Sexuality in the Movies. (Quality Paperbacks Ser.). (Illus.). 244p. 1984. pap. 12.95 (ISBN 0-306-80220-1). Da Capo.

Atkins, Thomas V. & Langstaff, Eleanor D. Access to Information Library Research Methods. 1979. pap. text ed. 10.95 (ISBN 0-686-62264-2). Collegium Bk Pubs.

Atkins, Thomas V., ed. Cross Reference Index, 1 vol. 2nd ed. 368p. Date not set. 49.95x (ISBN 0-8352-1918-6). Bowker.

Atkinson. Data Design, 2 vols. (Infotech Computer State of the Art Reports). 600p. 1980. Set. 310.00 (ISBN 0-08-028535-X). Pergamon.

--Database. (Infotech Computer State of the Art Reports). 623p. 1982. 130.00 (ISBN 0-08-028561-9). Pergamon.

Atkinson, A. B. The Economics of Inequality. 2nd ed. (Illus.). 1983. 29.95x (ISBN 0-19-877209-2); pap. text ed. 9.95x (ISBN 0-19-877208-4). Oxford U Pr.

--Social Justice & Public Policy. 480p. 1982. 40.00x (ISBN 0-262-01067-4). MIT Pr.

Atkinson, A. B. & Harrison, A. J. Distribution of Personal Wealth in Britain. LC 77-2715. 1978. 47.50 (ISBN 0-521-21735-0). Cambridge U Pr.

Atkinson, A. B., ed. Wealth, Income, & Inequality. 2nd ed. (Illus.). 1980. pap. 24.00x (ISBN 0-19-877144-4). Oxford U Pr.

Atkinson, A. B., et al. Parents & Children: Incomes in Two Generations. (DHSS Studies in Deprivation & Disadvantage: No. 10). 224p. 1983. text ed. 30.00x (ISBN 0-435-82097-4). Gower Pub Co.

--Wealth & Personal Incomes. LC 77-30556. 1978. text ed. 44.00 (ISBN 0-08-022450-4). Pergamon.

Atkinson, A. C. & Fienberg, S. E., eds. A Celebration of Statistics. (Illus.). 608p. 1985. 39.00 (ISBN 0-387-96111-9). Springer Verlag.

Atkinson, Alex. Exit Charlie. Barzun, J. & Taylor, W. H., eds. LC 81-47402. (Crime Fiction 1950-1975 Ser.). 221p. 1982. lib. bdg. 18.00 (ISBN 0-8240-4970-5). Garland Pub.

Atkinson, Alexander. Social Order & the General Theory of Strategy. LC 81-17906. 305p. (Orig.). 1982. pap. 17.50x (ISBN 0-7100-0907-0). Routledge & Kegan.

Atkinson, Alice M. The European Beginnings of American History. 1912. 17.50 (ISBN 0-8482-7269-2). Norwood Edns.

Atkinson, Allen, illus. The Cat & the Fiddle & Other Favorites. (Mother Goose Ser.). (Illus.). 64p. (Orig.). (gr. k). 1985. pap. 2.50 (ISBN 0-553-15321-8). Bantam.

--Humpty Dumpty & Other Favorites. (Mother Goose Ser.). (Illus.). 64p. (Orig.). (gr. k). 1985. pap. 2.50 (ISBN 0-553-15340-4). Bantam.

--Little Boy Blue & Other Favorites. (Mother Goose Ser.). 64p. (Orig.). (gr. k). 1985. pap. 2.50 (ISBN 0-553-15320-X). Bantam.

--Mary Had a Little Lamb & Other Favorites. (Mother Goose Ser.). (Illus., Orig.). (gr. k). 1985. pap. 2.50 (ISBN 0-553-15319-6). Bantam.

--Mother Goose. (Illus.). 1985. price not set. Bantam.

--Mother Goose's Nursery Rhymes. LC 83-48846. (Illus.). (gr. k up). 1984. PLB 13.95 (ISBN 0-394-53699-1). Knopf.

Atkinson, Alta. Volume Feeding Menu Selector. Blair, Eulalia, ed. LC 78-145861. 185p. 1971. 17.95 (ISBN 0-8436-0528-6). Van Nos Reinhold.

Atkinson, Anthony & Stiglitz, Joseph. Lectures on Public Economics. (McGraw-Hill Economics Handbook Ser.). 640p. 1980. text ed. 38.95 (ISBN 0-07-084105-5). McGraw.

Atkinson, Anthony B. Poverty in Britain & the Reform of Social Security. LC 76-85711. (University of Cambridge, Dept. of Applied Economics, Occasional Paper: 18). pap. 56.00 (ISBN 0-317-26110-X, 2024402). Bks Demand UMI.

Atkinson, Arthur J., Jr. & Ambre, John J. Kalman & Clark's Drug Assay: The Strategy of Therapeutic Drug Monitoring. 2nd ed. (Illus.). 200p. 1984. text ed. 29.50 (ISBN 0-89352-216-3). Masson Pub.

Atkinson, B. & Mavituna, F. Biochemical Engineering & Biotechnology Handbook. 1982. 105.00x (ISBN 0-943818-02-8, Nature Pr). Groves Dict Music.

Atkinson, B., jt. ed. see Cooper, P. F.

Atkinson, B. F. Biochemical Reactors. (Advanced Biochemistry Ser.). 264p. 1974. 22.50x (ISBN 0-85086-042-3, NO.2945, Pub. by Pion England). Methuen Inc.

Atkinson, B. G. & Walden, S. B., eds. Changes in Gene Expression in Response to Environmental Stress. 1985. 65.00 (ISBN 0-12-066290-6). Acad Pr.

Atkinson, B. W. Meso-Scale Atmospheric Circulations. LC 81-66386. 1981. 55.00 (ISBN 0-12-065960-3). Acad Pr.

Atkinson, B. W., ed. Dynamical Meteorology: An Introductory Selection. LC 80-41675. 250p. 1981. pap. 13.95x (ISBN 0-416-73840-0, NO.3462). Methuen Inc.

Atkinson, Benjamin P., jt. ed. see Waite, Harlow O.

Atkinson, Betty J. The Medical Assistant: Clinical Practice. LC 76-5301. 1976. pap. 13.80 (ISBN 0-8273-0351-3). Delmar.

Atkinson, Brooks. Broadway. (Illus.). 572p. 1985. pap. 13.95 (ISBN 0-87910-047-8). Limelight Edns.

--Sean O'Casey: From Times Past. Lowery, Robert G., ed. 186p. 1982. 28.50x (ISBN 0-389-20005-0, 06782). B&N Imports.

Atkinson, Brooks & Hirschfeld, Al. The Lively Years: Nineteen Twenty to Nineteen Seventy-Three. (Quality Paperbacks Ser.). (Illus.). 312p. 1985. pap. 9.95 (ISBN 0-306-80234-1). Da Capo.

Atkinson, Brooks, ed. see Emerson, Ralph Waldo.

Atkinson, Brooks, ed. see Thoreau, Henry D.

Atkinson, Brooks, ed. & intro. by see Thoreau, Henry David.

Atkinson, C. T., jt. auth. see Johnson, Arthur H.

Atkinson, Caroline P., ed. Letters of Susan Hale. 472p. 1981. lib. bdg. 40.00 (ISBN 0-89760-339-7). Telegraph Bks.

Atkinson, Carroll. The Show Must Go On -- Even for Children. (Illus.). 224p. 1977. 7.50 (ISBN 0-682-48769-4). Exposition Pr FL.

Atkinson, Charles F., tr. see Spengler, Oswald.

Atkinson, Charles M. Jeremy Bentham, His Life & Work. (BCL Ser.: No. 1). Repr. of 1905 ed. 8.50 (ISBN 0-404-00416-4). AMS Pr.

--Jeremy Bentham: His Life & Work. LC 78-98208. Repr. of 1905 ed. lib. bdg. 15.00 (ISBN 0-8371-3243-6, ATJB). Greenwood.

Atkinson, Christine. Making Sense of Piaget: The Philosophical Roots. 200p. 1984. 24.95X (ISBN 0-7100-9580-5). Routledge & Kegan.

Atkinson, Christopher T. A History of Germany, 1715-1815. LC 70-114456. (Illus.). xx, 732p. Repr. of 1908 ed. lib. bdg. 34.25x (ISBN 0-8371-4807-3, ATHG). Greenwood.

Atkinson, Clarissa W. Mystic & Pilgrim: The Book & the World of Margery Kempe. LC 82-22219. (Illus.). 240p. 1983. 22.50x (ISBN 0-8014-1521-7). Cornell U Pr.

--Mystic & Pilgrim: The Book & the World of Margery Kempe. LC 82-22219. 248p. (Orig.). 1985. 25.00x (ISBN 0-8014-1521-7); pap. text ed. 8.95x (ISBN 0-8014-9895-3). Cornell U Pr.

Atkinson, Clarissa W., et al, eds. Immaculate & Powerful: The Female in Sacred Image & Social Reality. LC 85-70448. (Harvard Women's Studies in Religion Ser.: Vol. 1). 272p. 1985. 19.95 (ISBN 0-8070-6724-5). Beacon Pr.

Atkinson, Clifford W. A Lay Reader's Guide to the Book of Common Prayer. 1981. pap. 2.95 (ISBN 0-8192-1222-9). Morehouse.

Atkinson, D., jt. auth. see Grossbard, E.

Atkinson, Daniel E. Cellular Energy Metabolism & Its Regulation. 1977. 39.50 (ISBN 0-12-066150-0). Acad Pr.

Atkinson, David. Homosexuals in the Christian Fellowship. 128p. (Orig.). 1981. pap. 4.95 (ISBN 0-8028-1890-0). Eerdmans.

--Hotel & Catering French: A New Approach for Advanced Students & Practitioners. (Illus.). 1980. pap. text ed. 11.50 (ISBN 0-08-023730-4). Pergamon.

--Menu French. (International Ser. in Hospitality Management). (Illus.). 96p. 1980. 16.50 (ISBN 0-08-024309-6); pap. 7.50 (ISBN 0-08-024308-8). Pergamon.

--The Message of Ruth. LC 82-25847. (Bible Speaks Today Ser.). 128p. 1983. pap. 4.95 (ISBN 0-87784-294-9). Inter-Varsity.

Atkinson, Donald R. & Morten, George. Counseling American Minorities: A Cross-Cultural Perspective. 2nd ed. 304p. 1982. pap. text ed. write for info. (ISBN 0-697-06652-5). Wm C Brown.

Atkinson, Donald T. Magic, Myth & Medicine. LC 72-8510. (Essay Index Reprint Ser.). 1972. Repr. of 1956 ed. 19.00 (ISBN 0-8369-7316-X). Ayer Co Pubs.

Atkinson, Dorothy. The End of the Russian Land Commune, 1905-1930. LC 81-84457. 472p. 1983. 29.50x (ISBN 0-8047-1148-8). Stanford U Pr.

Atkinson, Dorothy, et al, eds. Women in Russia. LC 75-39333. 1977. 30.00x (ISBN 0-8047-0910-6); pap. 9.95 (ISBN 0-8047-0920-3, SP-157). Stanford U Pr.

Atkinson, Dorothy F. Edmund Spenser: Bibliographical Supplement. LC 67-30806. (Studies in Spenser, No. 26). 1969. Repr. of 1937 ed. lib. bdg. 49.95x (ISBN 0-8383-0705-1). Haskell.

Atkinson, Earl. Ballroom Polka. (Ballroom Dancing Ser.). 1983. lib. bdg. 79.95 (ISBN 0-87700-476-5). Revisionist Pr.

--Ballroom Terminology. (Ballroom Dancing Ser.). 1983. lib. bdg. 79.95 (ISBN 0-87700-480-3). Revisionist Pr.
--Bolero-Rumba. (Ballroom Dancing Ser.). 1983. lib. bdg. 79.95 (ISBN 0-87700-488-9). Revisionist Pr.
--Cha Cha Cha. (Ballroom Dancing Ser.). 1983. lib. bdg. 79.95 (ISBN 0-87700-478-1). Revisionist Pr.
--Fox Trot. (Ballroom Dancing Ser.). 1983. lib. bdg. 79.95 (ISBN 0-87700-471-4). Revisionist Pr.
--Hustle, Advanced. (Ballroom Dancing Ser.). 1983. lib. bdg. 79.95 (ISBN 0-87700-485-4). Revisionist Pr.
--Hustle & Disco. (Ballroom Dancing Ser.). 1983. lib. bdg. 79.95 (ISBN 0-87700-482-X). Revisionist Pr.
--Latin Ballroom Dancing. (Ballroom Dancing Ser.). 1983. lib. bdg. 79.95 (ISBN 0-87700-481-1). Revisionist Pr.
--Mambo Combinations. (Ballroom Dancing Ser.). 1983. lib. bdg. 79.95 (ISBN 0-87700-475-7). Revisionist Pr.
--Merengue. (Ballroom Dancing Ser.). 1983. lib. bdg. 79.95 (ISBN 0-87700-472-2). Revisionist Pr.
--Paso Doble. (Ballroom Dancing Ser.). 1983. lib. bdg. 79.95 (ISBN 0-87700-489-7). Revisionist Pr.
--Peabody Steps. 1983. lib. bdg. 79.95 (ISBN 0-87700-484-6). Revisionist Pr.
--Rumba Combinations. (Ballroom Dancing Ser.). 1983. lib. bdg. 79.95 (ISBN 0-87700-477-3). Revisionist Pr.
--Samba. (Ballroom Dancing Ser.). 1983. lib. bdg. 79.95 (ISBN 0-87700-473-0). Revisionist Pr.
--Swing. (Ballroom Dancing Ser.). 1983. lib. bdg. 79.95 (ISBN 0-87700-470-6). Revisionist Pr.
--Tango. (Ballroom Dancing Ser.). 1983. lib. bdg. 79.95 (ISBN 0-87700-490-0). Revisionist Pr.
--The Waltz (American) (Ballroom Dancing Ser.). 1983. lib. bdg. 79.95 (ISBN 0-87700-479-X). Revisionist Pr.
--Waltz (Viennese) 1983. lib. bdg. 79.95 (ISBN 0-87700-486-2). Revisionist Pr.

Atkinson, Earl, ed. Bossa Nova. (Ballroom Dancing Ser.). 1983. lib. bdg. 79.95 (ISBN 0-87700-487-0). Revisionist Pr.

Atkinson, Edward. The Industrial Progress of the Nation. LC 73-1989. (Big Business; Economic Power in a Free Society Ser.). Repr. of 1889 ed. 24.00 (ISBN 0-405-05073-9). Ayer Co Pubs.

Atkinson, Edwin F. Notes on the History of Religion in the Himalaya of the N.W.P., India. LC 78-72374. Repr. of 1883 ed. 37.50 (ISBN 0-404-17224-5). AMS Pr.

Atkinson, F. V. Discrete & Continuous Boundary Problems. (Mathematics in Science & Engineering Ser.: Vol. 8). 1964. 80.00 (ISBN 0-12-065850-X). Acad Pr.
--Multiparameter Eignevalue Problems: Matrices & Compact Operators. (Mathematics in Science & Engineering Ser.). 1972. Vol. 1. 55.00 (ISBN 0-12-065801-1); Vol. 2. write for info. (ISBN 0-12-065802-X). Acad Pr.

Atkinson, Francis, jt. auth. see Locatis, Craig.

Atkinson, Frank. Fiction Librarianship. (Outlines of Modern Librarianship Ser.). 108p. 1981. 12.00 (ISBN 0-85157-293-6, Pub. by Bingley England). Shoe String.

Atkinson, Fred & Hall, Stephen. Oil & the British Economy. LC 83-11044. 200p. 1983. 32.50 (ISBN 0-312-58295-1). St Martin.

Atkinson, G. Origin & Chemistry of Petroleum: Proceedings of the Third Annual Karcher Symposium, Oklahoma, 1979. Zuckerman, J. J., ed. (Illus.). 120p. 1981. 33.00 (ISBN 0-08-026179-5). Pergamon.

Atkinson, G. B., ed. Developments in Economics: An Annual Review, Vol. 1. (Illus.). 186p. 1985. loose leaf binder 50.00x (ISBN 0-946183-15-5, Pub. by Causeway Pr Ltd England). Sheridan.

Atkinson, G. F. Studies of American Fungi: Mushrooms, Edible, Poisonous, Etc. (Illus.). 1961. Repr. of 1903 ed. 24.95x (ISBN 0-02-840600-1). Hafner.

Atkinson, Gary M. & Moraczewski, Albert S. Genetic Counseling, the Church & the Law. LC 79-92084. xvii, 259p. (Orig.). 1980. pap. 9.95 (ISBN 0-935372-06-7). Pope John Ctr.
--A Moral Evaluation of Contraception & Sterilization: A Dialogical Study. LC 79-90971. viii, 115p. (Orig.). 1979. pap. 4.95 (ISBN 0-935372-05-9). Pope John Ctr.

Atkinson, Geoffrey. The Creation Memos. 128p. (Orig.). 1983. pap. 5.95 (ISBN 0-8431-1031-7). Price Stern.
--Extraordinary Voyage in French Literature, 2 vols. Incl. Vol. 1. Before 1700; Vol. 2. 1700-1720. Repr. of 1920 ed. Set. 33.00 (ISBN 0-8337-0115-0). B Franklin.
--Relations de voyages du Dixieme siecle a l'evolution des idees. LC 79-166450. (Research & Source Works Ser.: No. 785). 1971. Repr. of 1924 ed. lib. bdg. 22.50 (ISBN 0-8337-3948-4). B Franklin.

Atkinson, Geoffroy. Extraordinary Voyage in French Literature Before 1700. LC 70-161705. (Columbia University. Studies in Romance Philology & Literature: No. 26). Repr. of 1920 ed. 18.00 (ISBN 0-404-50626-7). AMS Pr.
--Litterature geographique francaise de la Renaissance, 2 vols. in 1. LC 68-7028. (Bibliography & Reference Ser.: No. 213). (Illus.). 1968. Repr. of 1927 ed. with supplement 45.50 (ISBN 0-8337-0113-4). B Franklin.
--The Sentimental Revolution: French Writers of 1690-1740. Keller, Abraham C., ed. LC 64-18424. 200p. 1966. 20.00x (ISBN 0-295-74024-8). U of Wash Pr.

Atkinson, Geoffroy & Keller, Abraham C. Prelude to the Enlightenment: French Literature, 1690-1740. LC 70-114416. 221p. 1971. 20.00x (ISBN 0-295-95082-X). U of Wash Pr.

Atkinson, George & Bengtsson, Hans. Orienteering for Sport & Pleasure. LC 75-41872. (Environmental Sports Ser.). (Illus.). 1977. pap. 9.95 (ISBN 0-8289-0270-4). Greene.

Atkinson, George H., ed. Time-Resolved Vibrational Spectroscopy (Symposium) LC 83-9928. 1983. pap. 47.50 (ISBN 0-12-066280-9). Acad Pr.

Atkinson, Gerald M. Arab Banks & the Financial Leadership of the World. (The Great Currents of History Library Bk.). (Illus.). 137p. 1983. 97.85x (ISBN 0-86722-029-5). Inst Econ Pol.

Atkinson, Grace & Hudson, Betty M. Fundamentals of Writing. 160p. (Orig.). 1980. pap. 9.95 (ISBN 0-89529-111-8). Avery Pub.

Atkinson, H. J., jt. auth. see Lee, Donald Lewis.

Atkinson, Herbert. Cockfighting & Game Fowl. (Illus.). 288p. 1977. 24.95 (ISBN 0-904558-23-1). Saiga.
--The Old English Game Fowl. 1981. 16.50 (ISBN 0-904558-99-1). Saiga.

Atkinson, Holly. Women & Fatigue: Effective Solutions to this Very Real Problem. (Illus.). 320p. 1986. 17.95 (ISBN 0-399-13050-0). Putnam Pub Group.

Atkinson, Hugh C., ed. Theodore Dreiser: A Checklist. LC 77-626231. (Serif Ser.: No. 15). 104p. 1971. 10.00x (ISBN 0-87338-048-7). Kent St U Pr.

Atkinson, I. Construction Management. 150p. 1971. 13.00 (ISBN 0-85334-016-X, Pub. by Elsevier Applied Sci England). Elsevier.
--The Viking Ships. LC 77-17510. (Cambridge Introduction to the History of Mankind Ser.). 1979. 4.50 (ISBN 0-521-21951-5). Cambridge U Pr.

Atkinson, Ian. The Viking Ships. LC 80-11690. (Cambridge Topic Books). (Illus.). (gr. 5-10). 1980. PLB 7.95 (ISBN 0-8225-1221-1). Lerner Pubns.

Atkinson, J., tr. see Nizami.

Atkinson, J., et al. Gear Cutting. (Illus.). 171p. 1979. spiral 47.50x (ISBN 0-85083-459-7). Trans-Atlantic.

Atkinson, J. Brooks. Broadway Scrapbook. LC 71-104221. Repr. of 1947 ed. lib. bdg. 19.75x (ISBN 0-8371-3331-9, ATBS). Greenwood.
--Henry Thoreau: A Cosmic Yankee. 1978. Repr. of 1927 ed. lib. bdg. 25.00 (ISBN 0-8495-0051-6). Arden Lib.

Atkinson, J. E. A Commentary on Q. Curtius' Historiae Alexandri Magni. (London Studies in Classical Philology: No. 3). 1980. text ed. 69.00x (ISBN 90-70265-61-3). Humanities.

Atkinson, J. H. Foundations & Slopes: An Introduction to Applications of Critical State Soil Mechanics. 382p. 1981. pap. 34.95x (ISBN 0-470-27246-5). Halsted Pr.

Atkinson, J. Maxwell. Order in Court: The Organization of Verbal Interaction in Judicial Settings. (Oxford Sociolegal Studies). 1979. text ed. 30.50x (ISBN 0-391-01025-5). Humanities.

Atkinson, J. Maxwell & Heritage, John, eds. Structures of Social Action: Studies in Conversation Analysis. 480p. 1985. 49.50 (ISBN 0-521-24815-9); pap. 18.95 (ISBN 0-521-31862-9). Cambridge U Pr.

Atkinson, J. W. & Feather, N. T., eds. Theory of Achievement Motivation. LC 74-7064. 404p. 1974. Repr. of 1966 ed. 23.50 (ISBN 0-88275-166-2). Krieger.

Atkinson, Jack H. Export Marketing Manual: A Results-Oriented Guide for the Eighties. 267p. 1981. loose leaf bdg. 49.95 (ISBN 0-931094-00-3). Mackenzie-Koch.

Atkinson, Jacquiline M. Schizophrenia: A Guide for Sufferers, Family & Friends. 144p. (Orig.). 1985. pap. 6.95 (ISBN 0-85500-216-6, Pub. by Turnstone Pr England). Sterling.

Atkinson, James. An Account of the State of Agriculture & Grazing in New South Wales. (Illus.). 184p. 1975. Repr. of 1826 ed. 21.00x (ISBN 0-424-06960-1, Pub by Sydney U Pr). Intl Spec Bk.
--Martin Luther & the Birth of Protestantism. LC 81-82356. 348p. 1981. pap. 5.25 (ISBN 0-8042-0941-3). John Knox.
--Martin Luther: Prophet to the Catholic Church. 224p. (Orig.). 1983. pap. 7.95 (ISBN 0-8028-1260-0). Eerdmans.

Atkinson, James, ed. & tr. Customs & Manners of the Women of Persia. xvi, 93p. Date not set. Repr. lib. bdg. price not set. Am Repr Serv.

Atkinson, James, ed. Luther: Early Theological Works. LC 62-12358. (Library of Christian Classics). 376p. 1980. pap. 9.95 (ISBN 0-664-24166-2). Westminster.
--The Prince: Machaivelli. 1976. pap. text ed. write for info. (ISBN 0-02-304270-2). Macmillan.

Atkinson, James, jt. ed. see Lehmann, Helmut T.

Atkinson, James, ed. see Machiavelli, Niccolo.

Atkinson, James, tr. see Firdawsi.

Atkinson, James, tr. see Kulsan, Nah'Nah.

Atkinson, James B., ed. see Machiavelli, Niccolo.

Atkinson, Jennifer, ed. see O'Neill, Eugene.

Atkinson, Jennifer M. Eugene O'Neill: A Descriptive Bibliography. LC 73-13312. (Pittsburgh Series in Bibliography). (Illus.). 1974. 49.00x (ISBN 0-8229-3279-2). U of Pittsburgh Pr.

Atkinson, Jeremy. Clogs & Clogmaking. (Shire Album Ser.: No. 113). (Illus.). 32p. (Orig.). 1984. pap. 2.95 (ISBN 0-85263-665-2, Pub. by Shire Pubns England). Seven Hills Bks.
--Clogs & Clogmaking. 3.25 (ISBN 0-913714-67-4). Legacy Bks.

Atkinson, Jim, jt. auth. see Bloom, John.

Atkinson, John & Azar, Maliha. Flight. (Heinman Science & Technical Reorders). 1980. pap. text ed. 2.95x (ISBN 0-435-29000-2). Heinemann Ed.

Atkinson, John W. Personality, Motivation & Action: Selected Papers. Spielberger, Charles D., ed. (Centennial Psychology Ser.). 446p. 1983. 35.95 (ISBN 0-03-060541-5). Praeger.

Atkinson, John W. & Raynor, Joel O. Personality, Motivation & Achievement. abr. ed. LC 77-24985. 272p. 1978. Repr. of 1974 ed. text ed. 10.95x (ISBN 0-470-99336-7). Halsted Pr.

Atkinson, John W., et al. Motivation & Achievement. LC 73-21754. (Illus.). pap. 122.80 (ISBN 0-317-10283-4, 2050707). Bks Demand UMI.

Atkinson, Joseph D., Jr. & Shafritz, Jay M. The Real Stuff: A History of NASA's Astronaut Recruitment Policy. LC 85-9460. 192p. 1985. pap. 11.95 (ISBN 0-03-005188-6); 36.95 (ISBN 0-03-005187-8). Praeger.

Atkinson, Julia. Eleven Out of Twelve: A Bibliography. 95p. (Orig.). 1980. pap. 4.00x (ISBN 0-931040-03-5). Independ Unltd.
--Emergence. 360p. 1974. pap. 9.00 ltd. ed. (ISBN 0-931040-02-7). Independ Unltd.
--Seeing Is Perceiving. 312p. 1978. pap. 5.00 (ISBN 0-931040-02-7). Independ Unltd.

Atkinson, K. B., ed. Developments in Close Range Photogrammetry, Vol. 1. (Illus.). 220p. 1982. 44.50 (ISBN 0-85334-882-0, Pub. by Elsevier Applied Sci England). Elsevier.

Atkinson, Kathleen M. Ancient Sparta, a Re-Examination of the Evidence. LC 73-114457. (Illus.). xv, 527p. Repr. of 1949 ed. lib. bdg. 22.50x (ISBN 0-8371-4709-3, ATAS). Greenwood.

Atkinson, Kendall E. Elementary Numerical Analysis. LC 84-11974. 416p. 1985. 31.95 (ISBN 0-471-89733-7). Wiley.
--An Introduction to Numerical Analysis. LC 78-6706. 587p. 1978. text ed. 40.00x (ISBN 0-471-02985-8). Wiley.
--A Survey of Numerical Methods for the Solution of Fredholm Integral Equations of the Second Kind. LC 75-28900. vii, 230p. (Orig.). 1976. pap. text ed. 27.00 (ISBN 0-89871-034-0). Soc Indus-Appl Math.

Atkinson, L. Hit & Run. 1981. 8.90 (ISBN 0-531-04265-0). Watts.

Atkinson, L. E., jt. ed. see Sairam, M. R.

Atkinson, L. J. & Kohn, M. J. Berry & Kohn's Introduction to Operating Room Technique. 1978. pap. text ed. 30.00 (ISBN 0-07-002540-1). McGraw.

Atkinson, L. J. & Kohn, M. L. Berry & Kohn's Introduction to Operating Room Techniques. 6th ed. 640p. 1986. price not set (ISBN 0-07-002541-X). McGraw.

Atkinson, L. V. & Harley, P. J. An Introduction to Numerical Methods with Pascal. 1982. pap. text ed. 17.95 (ISBN 0-201-13788-7). Addison-Wesley.

Atkinson, Laurence. Pascal Programming. LC 80-40126. (Computing Ser.). 428p. 1980. 58.95x (ISBN 0-471-27773-8); pap. 19.95 (ISBN 0-471-27774-6). Wiley.

Atkinson, Leroy & Lake, Austen. Famous American Athletes of Today, Third Series. facsimile ed. LC 70-93348. (Essay Index Reprint Ser: Famous Leaders Ser). Repr. of 1932 ed. 24.50 (ISBN 0-8369-2580-7). Ayer Co Pubs.

Atkinson, Leroy, et al. Famous American Athletes of Today, Fifth Series. facsimile ed. LC 70-93348. (Essay Index Reprints - Famous Leaders Ser). Repr. of 1937 ed. 24.00 (ISBN 0-8369-2480-0). Ayer Co Pubs.

Atkinson, Leslie D. & Murray, Mary E. Understanding the Nursing Process. 2nd ed. (Illus.). 155p. 1983. pap. text ed. write for info. (ISBN 0-02-304580-9). Macmillan.

Atkinson, Linda. Have We Lived Before? (High Interest, Low Vocabulary Ser.). (Illus.). 112p. (gr. 4 up). 1982. PLB 8.95 (ISBN 0-396-07999-7). Dodd.
--In Kindling Flame: The Story of Hannah Senesh 1921-1944. LC 83-24392. 256p. (gr. 9 up). 1985. 13.50 (ISBN 0-688-02714-8). Lothrop.
--Mother Jones: The Most Dangerous Woman in America. LC 77-15863. (Illus.). (gr. 7 up). 1978. 2.98 (ISBN 0-517-53201-8). Crown.
--Women in the Martial Arts: A New Spirit Rising. LC 83-16302. (Illus.). 181p. (gr. 6 up). 1983. 13.95 (ISBN 0-396-08223-8); pap. 7.95 (ISBN 0-396-08297-1). Dodd.
--Your Legal Rights. LC 82-6963. (Triumph Ser.). (Illus.). 96p. (gr. 7). 1982. lib. bdg. 8.90 (ISBN 0-531-04495-5). Watts.

Atkinson, Lloyd C. Economics: The Science of Choice. (Student Guide by Dennis Sullivan). 1982. 29.95x (ISBN 0-256-02486-3); student guide 11.95x (ISBN 0-256-02487-1). Irwin.

Atkinson, Lucy. Recollections of Tartar Steppes & Their Inhabitants. 351p. 1972. Repr. of 1863 ed. 32.50x (ISBN 0-7146-1531-5, F Cass Co). Biblio Dist.

Atkinson, M. J., ed. A Commentary on Plotinus: Emnead. (Classical & Philosophical Monographs: Vol. 1). 1983. 47.50x (ISBN 0-19-814719-8). Oxford U Pr.

Atkinson, M. Jourdan & Giles, Eugene V. Kingdom Come! Kingdom Go! (Illus.). 200p. 1980. 11.95 (ISBN 0-89015-243-8). Eakin Pubns.

Atkinson, Margaret E. August Wilhelm Schlegel As a Translator of Shakespeare. LC 76-51367. (Studies in Shakespeare, No. 24). 1977. lib. bdg. 46.95x (ISBN 0-8383-2135-6). Haskell.

Atkinson, Martin. Explanations in the Study of Child Language Development. LC 81-10015. (Cambridge Studies in Linguistics: No. 35). (Illus.). 350p. 1982. 44.50 (ISBN 0-521-24302-5); pap. 14.95 (ISBN 0-521-28593-3). Cambridge U Pr.

Atkinson, Martin, et al. Foundations of General Linguistics. (Illus.). 384p. 1982. text ed. 35.00x (ISBN 0-04-410003-5); pap. text ed. 12.95x (ISBN 0-04-410004-3). Allen Unwin.

Atkinson, Mary D. Abstracts: Willbook IA, 1815-1836, Tyler County, West Virginia. LC 80-67523. 220p. 1980. pap. text ed. 15.00 (ISBN 0-937436-03-8). Atkinson.
--Cemetary Records: Vol. II, Centerville District, Tyler County, West Virginia. LC 80-67522. 225p. 1980. pap. text ed. 18.00 (ISBN 0-937436-02-X). Atkinson.
--Cemetary Records: Vol. 1, Tyler & Pleasants Counties, West Virginia. LC 80-123889. 269p. (Orig.). 1980. pap. text ed. 18.00 (ISBN 0-937436-00-3). Atkinson.
--Tyler County, West Virginia, Marriage Records: 1815-1852. LC 80-67521. 73p. 1980. pap. text ed. 10.00 (ISBN 0-937436-01-1). Atkinson.

Atkinson, Mary W. Johnny Smith Goes to His Speech Pathologist. 32p. (gr. k-6). 1982. pap. 7.95 (ISBN 0-88450-734-3, 2084-B). Communication Skill.

Atkinson, Max. Our Masters' Voices: The Language & Body-Language of Politics. (Illus.). 176p. 1984. pap. 9.95 (ISBN 0-416-37700-9, NO. 9085); 22.00 (ISBN 0-416-37690-8, NO. 9265). Methuen Inc.

Atkinson, Michael, ed. Computational Group Therapy. 1984. 60.00 (ISBN 0-12-066270-1). Acad Pr.

Atkinson, Michael M. & Chandler, Marsha A., eds. The Politics of Canadian Public Policy. 296p. 1983. 30.00x (ISBN 0-8020-2485-8); pap. 12.50 (ISBN 0-8020-6517-1). U of Toronto Pr.

Atkinson, Oriana. Big Eyes: A Story of the Catskill Mountains. 1980. pap. 4.95 (ISBN 0-686-64342-9). Hope Farm.

Atkinson, P. Feedback Control Systems for Engineers. LC 68-31674. 425p. 45.00x (ISBN 0-306-30363-9, Plenum Pr). Plenum Pub.

Atkinson, P., jt. ed. see Heath, C.

Atkinson, Paul. The Clinical Experience. 148p. 1981. text ed. 34.25x (ISBN 0-566-00413-5). Gower Pub Co.

Atkinson, Paul, jt. auth. see Hammersley, Martyn.

Atkinson, Paul, jt. auth. see Rees, Teresa L.

Atkinson, Peter & Woodcock, John. Doppler Ultrasound & Its Use in Clinical Measurement. (Medical Physics Ser.: Vol. 5). 1982. 55.00 (ISBN 0-12-066260-4). Acad Pr.

Atkinson, Phillip S. & Clement, John. Medical Office Practice: Simulation. 1984. 11.75 (ISBN 0-538-11170-4, K17). SW Pub.

Atkinson, R. C. The Federal Role in Unemployment Compensation Administration: A Report Prepared for the Committee on Social Security. LC 77-74927. (American Federalism-the Urban Dimension). 1978. Repr. of 1941 ed. lib. bdg. 17.00x (ISBN 0-405-10476-6). Ayer Co Pubs.

Atkinson, R. F. Knowledge & Explanation in History: An Introduction to the Philosophy of History. LC 77-90896. 239p. 1978. pap. 8.95x (ISBN 0-8014-9171-1). Cornell U Pr.

Atkinson, R. L. Tin & Tin Mining. (Shire Album Ser.: No. 139). (Orig.). 1985. pap. 3.50 (ISBN 0-85263-733-0, Pub. by Shire Pubns England). Seven Hills Bks.

Atkinson, R. S. Handbook of Intensive Care. (Illus.). 386p. 1981. 46.50 (ISBN 0-8151-0338-7). Year Bk Med.

Atkinson, R. S. & Rushman, G. B. A Synopsis of Anaesthesia. 9th ed. (Illus.). 976p. 1982. pap. text ed. 37.00 (ISBN 0-7236-0621-8). PSG Pub Co.

Atkinson, R. S. & Hewer, C. Langton, eds. Recent Advances in Anaesthesia & Analgesia, No. 14. (Illus.). 1982. pap. text ed. 29.00 (ISBN 0-443-02571-1). Churchill.

Atkinson, Raymond C., et al. Public Employment Service in the United States. LC 72-69. (Select Bibliographies Reprint Ser). 1972. Repr. of 1938 ed. 22.50 (ISBN 0-8369-9950-9). Ayer Co Pubs.

Atkinson, Rhonda & Longman, Debbie. Reading Enhancement & Development. (Illus.). 375p. 1985. pap. text ed. 14.95 (ISBN 0-314-85215-8). West Pub.

Atkinson, Richard. White Sands, of Wind, Sand & Time. LC 76-57523. (Popular Ser.: No. 21). (Illus.). 1977. pap. 3.00 (ISBN 0-911408-46-0). SW Pks Mnmts.

Atkinson, Richard C., jt. auth. see Suppes, Patrick.

Atkinson, Richard C., ed. Studies in Mathematical Psychology. 1964. 30.00x (ISBN 0-8047-0181-4). Stanford U Pr.

Atkinson, Richard J. Field Archeology. LC 78-58999. (Illus.). 1980. Repr. of 1953 ed. 22.50 (ISBN 0-88355-675-8). Hyperion Conn.

Atkinson, Rita L., intro. by. Mind & Behavior: Readings from Scientific American. LC 80-15307. (Illus.). 289p. 1980. text ed. 21.95 (ISBN 0-7167-1215-6); pap. text ed. 12.95 (ISBN 0-7167-1216-4). W H Freeman.

Atkinson, Rita L., et al. Introduction to Psychology. 8th ed. 701p. 1983. text ed. 27.95 (ISBN 0-15-543677-5, HC); study guide 9.95 (ISBN 0-15-543679-1); instr's manual avail. (ISBN 0-15-543678-3); test item file avail. (ISBN 0-15-543680-5). HarBraceJ.

Atkinson, Robert, ed. The Book of Ballymote. LC 78-72618. (Celtic Language & Literature: Goidelic & Brythonic). Repr. of 1887 ed. 130.00 (ISBN 0-404-17535-X). AMS Pr.

--The Book of Leinster. LC 78-72619. (Celtic Language & Literature: Goidelic & Brythonic). Repr. of 1880 ed. 135.00 (ISBN 0-404-17536-8). AMS Pr.

Atkinson, Robert, tr. The Passions & the Homilies from Leabhar Breac. LC 78-72680. (Royal Irish Academy. Todd Lecture Ser.: Vol. 2). Repr. of 1887 ed. 72.50 (ISBN 0-404-60562-1). AMS Pr.

Atkinson, Robert, intro. by. The Yellow Book of Lecan. LC 78-72657. (Celtic Language & Literature: Goidelic & Brythonic). Repr. of 1896 ed. 125.00 (ISBN 0-404-17616-X). AMS Pr.

Atkinson, Roland M. Alcohol & Drug Abuse in Old Age. LC 84-6271. (Clinical Insights Monograph). 96p. 1984. pap. text ed. 12.00x (ISBN 0-88048-050-5, 48-050-5). Am Psychiatric.

Atkinson, Ron. Looking for My Name. 1973. pap. 4.00 (ISBN 0-912846-06-2). Bookstore Pr.

Atkinson, Ross, ed. Back to the Books: Bibliographic Instruction & the Theory of Information Sources. 76p. 1983. 15.00 (ISBN 0-8389-6587-3); members 12.00 (ISBN 0-317-36630-0). Assn Coll & Res Libs.

Atkinson, Ruth A., jt. ed. see Appenzeller, Otto.

Atkinson, Ruth M., jt. auth. see Keator, Glenn.

Atkinson, Sallyanne. Brisbane Guide. 2nd ed. (Illus.). 126p. 1985. pap. 7.95 (ISBN 0-7022-1845-6). U of Queensland Pr.

Atkinson, Sam F., et al. Saltwater Intrusion. (Illus.). 433p. 1985. 39.95 (ISBN 0-87371-054-1). Lewis Pubs Inc.

Atkinson, Scott & Sharpe, Fred. Wild Plants of the San Juan Islands. (Illus.). 176p. (Orig.). 1985. pap. 7.95 (ISBN 0-89886-104-7). Mountaineers.

Atkinson, Stephen. Discoverie & Historie of the Gold Mynes in Scotland. LC 77-38492. (Bannatyne Club, Edinburgh. Publications: No. 14). Repr. of 1825 ed. 24.50 (ISBN 0-404-52714-0). AMS Pr.

Atkinson, Susan & Rattiner, Dan. It's All Her Fault. LC 83-63246. (Illus.). 64p. (Orig.). 1984. pap. 4.95 (ISBN 0-932966-43-8). Permanent Pr.

--It's All His Fault. (Illus.). 64p. 1984. pap. 4.95 (ISBN 0-932966-42-X). Permanent Pr.

Atkinson, T., ed. see Royal Society Discussion Meeting, June 16-17, 1982.

Atkinson, T. R. Pattern of Financial Asset Ownership: Wisconsin Individuals, 1949, Vol. 7. (National Bureau of Economic Research). 1956. 22.00x (ISBN 0-691-04155-5). Princeton U Pr.

Atkinson, Terry & Cerf, Martin. Billy Squier: An Illustrated History. (Illus.). 48p. (Orig.). 1983. pap. 6.95 (ISBN 0-89524-174-9, 8615). Cherry Lane.

Atkinson, Thomas E. Wills. 2nd ed. (Hornbook Ser.). 975p. 1953. 19.95 (ISBN 0-317-00049-7). West Pub.

Atkinson, Thomas R. Pattern of Financial Asset Ownership: Wisconsin Individuals, 1949. (Financial Research Program Ser.). 194p. 1956. 20.00 (ISBN 0-691-04155-5, Dist. by Princeton U Pr). Natl Bur Econ Res.

Atkinson, Thomas W. Oriental & Western Siberia: A Narrative of Seven Years' Explorations & Adventures in Siberia, Mongolia, the Kirghissteppes, Chinese Tartary & Part of Central Asia. LC 75-115504. (Russia Observed, Ser., No. 1). 1970. Repr. of 1858 ed. 25.50 (ISBN 0-405-03002-9). Ayer Co Pubs.

Atkinson, Mrs. Thomas W. Recollections of Tartar Steppes & Their Inhabitants. LC 71-115503. (Russia Observed, Ser., No. 1). 1970. Repr. of 1863 ed. 25.50 (ISBN 0-405-03003-7). Ayer Co Pubs.

Atkinson, William. Working at Home: Is It for You? LC 85-70192. 1985. 10.95 (ISBN 0-87094-630-7). Dow Jones-Irwin.

--The Writer's Tax & Recordkeeping Handbook: Including Everything You Can Legally Deduct. LC 83-10110. 128p. 1983. pap. 7.95 (ISBN 0-8092-5539-1). Contemp Bks.

Atkinson, William & DeSanctis, Paul. Introduction to VSAM. 168p. 14.50 (5159). Hayden.

Atkinson, William C., tr. see De Cameens, Luis Vaz.

Atkinson, William W. Memory Culture. 92p. 1976. Repr. of 1903 ed. 6.00 (ISBN 0-911662-61-8). Yoga.

--Mental Influence. pap. 1.00 (ISBN 0-911662-42-1). Yoga.

--Mind Power: The Secret of Mental Magic. limited ed. limited ed. 8.00 (ISBN 0-911662-27-8). Yoga.

--Practical Mind Reading. pap. 1.00 (ISBN 0-911662-43-X). Yoga.

--Psychomancy & Crystal Gazing. pap. 1.00 (ISBN 0-911662-41-3). Yoga.

--Reincarnation & Law of Karma. 7.00 (ISBN 0-911662-26-X). Yoga.

Atkinson, Wilmer. Autobiography. (American Newspapermen Ser., 1790-1933). (Illus.). 375p. 1974. Repr. of 1920 ed. 21.50x (ISBN 0-8464-0032-4). Beekman Pubs.

Atkisson, A. A., jt. auth. see Petak, W. J.

Atkyns, Richard & Gwyn, John. The Civil War. Young, Peter & Tucker, Norman, eds. (Military Memoirs Ser). xi, 129p. 1967. 15.00 (ISBN 0-208-00632-X, Archon). Shoe String.

Atlan, Henri, et al. Laying Down a Path in Walking: Essays for a New Philosophy of Biology. LC 83-82697. 96p. (Orig.). pap. 7.50postponed (ISBN 0-940262-05-3). Lindisfarne Pr.

Atlan, Liliane. Modern Literatures Annual: Theatre Pieces, an Anthology. Knapp, Bettina L., ed. Feitlowitz, Marguerite, tr. from Fr. (Modern Literatures Annual Ser.). 225p. 1985. lib. bdg. 15.00 (ISBN 0-913283-03-7). Penkevill.

Atlanta Town Committee of the National Society of Colonial Dames of America. Abstracts of Colonial Wills of the State of Georgia 1733-1777. LC 81-17745. 158p. 1982. Repr. of 1962 ed. 17.50 (ISBN 0-87152-357-4). Reprint.

Atlanta University. Atlanta University Publications: Nos. 1, 2, 4, 8, 9, 11, & 13-18. LC 68-28965. (American Negro: His History & Literature, Ser. No. 1). 1968. Repr. of 1897 ed. Set. 37.50 (ISBN 0-405-01804-5). Ayer Co Pubs.

--Atlanta University Publications: Nos. 3, 5-7, 10, 12, 19 & 20. LC 68-28985. (The American Negro: History & Literature, Ser. No. 3). 1970. Repr. of 1898 ed. Set. 49.50 (ISBN 0-405-01914-9). Ayer Co Pubs.

Atlantic Council's Special Committee on Intergovernmental Organization & Reorganization. Beyond Diplomacy. 81p. 1975. pap. text ed. 4.50 (ISBN 0-87855-744-X). Transaction Bks.

Atlantic Council's Working Group on Western Interest & U. S. Policy Options in the Caribbean Basin. Western Interests & U. S. Policy Options in the Caribbean Basin. Greene, James R. & Scowcroft, Brent, eds. LC 84-3571. 290p. 1984. text ed. 30.00 (ISBN 0-89946-181-6); pap. 12.50 (ISBN 0-89946-183-2). Oelgeschlager.

Atlantic Institute. Partnership for Progress: A Program for Transatlantic Action. Uri, Pierre, ed. LC 78-27575. 1979. Repr. of 1963 ed. lib. bdg. 18.75x (ISBN 0-313-20901-4, AIPP). Greenwood.

Atlantic Monthly. Atlantic Harvest: Memoirs of the Atlantic. Sedgwick, Ellery, ed. LC 83-45694. Repr. of 1947 ed. 57.50 (ISBN 0-404-20010-9). AMS Pr.

Atlas, Alan. The Cappella Giulia Chansonnier. (Wissenschaftliche Abhandlungen-Musicological Studies Ser.: Vol. 27). 220p. 1976. Pt. 1. lib. bdg. 55.00 (ISBN 0-912024-23-2); Pt. lib. bdg. 45.00 (ISBN 0-912024-24-0). Inst Mediaeval Mus.

Atlas, Allan. Music at the Aragonese Court of Naples. 280p. Date not set. price not set (ISBN 0-521-24828-0). Cambridge U Pr.

Atlas, Allan, ed. see Morton, Robert.

Atlas, Allan W., ed. Music in the Classic Period: Essays in Honor of Barry S. Brook. (Festschrift Ser.: No. 5). 400p. 1985. lib. bdg. 48.00x (ISBN 0-918728-37-1). Pendragon NY.

Atlas, James. Delmore Schwartz: The Life of an American Poet. 418p. 1977. 15.00 (ISBN 0-374-13761-7). FS&G.

--Delmore Schwartz: The Life of an American Poet. LC 85-5501. (Illus.). 432p. 1985. pap. 10.95 (ISBN 0-15-625272-4, Harv). HarBraceJ.

Atlas, James, ed. see Schwartz, Delmore.

Atlas, Nava. Vegetariana. LC 83-10103. (Illus.). 224p. 1984. pap. 12.95 (ISBN 0-385-27910-8, Dial). Doubleday.

Atlas, Ronald M. Basic Microbiology: Fundamentals & Applications. 1986. text ed. price not set (ISBN 0-02-304350-4). Macmillan.

--Instructor's Manual-Microbiology: Fundamentals & Applications. 144p. 1984. write for info. (instr's manual) (ISBN 0-02-304560-4). Macmillan.

Atlas, Ronald M. & Bartha, Richard. Microbial Ecology: Fundamentals & Applications. (Life Sciences Ser.). 500p. 1981. 36.95 (ISBN 0-201-00051-2). Addison-Wesley.

Atlas, Ronald M. & Browm, Alfred E. Experimental Microbiology. 400p. 1984. pap. write for info. (ISBN 0-02-304530-2). Macmillan.

Atlas, Ronald M., ed. Petroleum Microbiology. 500p. 1984. text ed. 55.00 (ISBN 0-02-949000-6). Macmillan.

Atlas, S. M., jt. auth. see Lewin, Menachem.

Atlas, Stephen L. Parents Without Partners Sourcebook: The World's Largest Organization for Single Parents Gives You Positive, Practical Solutions to the Questions & Challenges of Single Parenting. LC 84-13435. 192p. (Orig.). 1984. pap. 8.95 (ISBN 0-89471-269-1); lib. bdg. 19.80 (ISBN 0-89471-270-5). Running Pr.

--Single Parenting: A Practical Resource Guide. 256p. 1981. 12.95 (ISBN 0-13-810622-3, Spec); pap. 5.95 (ISBN 0-13-810614-2). P-H.

Atlas, Yehuda. It's Me! Lacks, Roslyn, tr. LC 85-1239. (Illus.). 48p. 1985. 9.95 (ISBN 0-915361-20-5, Dist. by Watts). Adama Pubs Inc.

Atlee, Barber A. & Barber, Adwin A. The Collector's Manual in Anglo-American Pottery. (Illus.). 187p. 1984. Repr. of 1897 ed. 87.45x (ISBN 0-89901-148-9). Found Class Reprints.

Atlee, H. B. Acute & Chronic Iliac Pain in Women: A Problem in Diagnosis. 2nd ed. (Illus.). 208p. 1966. photocopy ed. 16.75x (ISBN 0-398-00067-0). C C Thomas.

--Natural Childbirth. (Illus.). 96p. 1956. spiral 9.75x (ISBN 0-398-04195-4). C C Thomas.

Atleson, James B. Values & Assumptions in American Labor Law. LC 82-21993. 256p. 1983. pap. 12.50x (ISBN 0-87023-390-4). U of Mass Pr.

Atleson, James B. & Labor Law Group (U.S.) Collective Bargaining in Private Employment: With 1982 Supplement. 2nd ed. LC 84-1767. (Labor Relations & Social Problems: A Course Book: Unit 1). 856p. 1984. 26.00 (ISBN 0-87179-424-1). BNA.

Atleson, James B., et al see Labor Law Group.

Atluri, S. N. & Gallagher, R. H. Hybrid & Mixed Finite Element Methods. LC 82-8615. (Numerical Methods in Engineering Ser.). 582p. 1983. 94.95x (ISBN 0-471-10486-8, Pub. by Wiley-Interscience). Wiley.

Atluri, S. N., jt. ed. see Perrone, N.

Atluri, Satya & Perrone, Nicholas, eds. Computer Methods for Nonlinear Solids & Structural Mechanics. 264p. 1983. pap. text ed. 50.00 (ISBN 0-317-02562-7, G00224). ASME.

Atmaprana, Pravrajika. Story of Sister Nivedita. pap. 1.95 (ISBN 0-87481-109-0). Vedanta Pr.

Atmore, A., jt. auth. see Oliver, Roland.

Atmore, Anthony & Stacey, Gillian. Black Kingdoms, Black Peoples. (Illus.). 128p. 1985. 20.00 (ISBN 0-85613-303-5, Pub. by Salem Hse Ltd). Merrimack Pub Cir.

Atmore, Anthony, jt. ed. see Marks, Shula.

Atnassova, T., et al. Bulgarian-English Dictionary. 1050p. (Bulgarian & Eng.). 1980. 65.00 (ISBN 0-686-97393-3, M-9829). French & Eur.

Atomic Industrial Forum. Positive Experiences in Constructing & Operating Nuclear Power Plants Worldwide. (Technical & Economic Reports: Construction). 76p. 1984. 100.00 (ISBN 0-318-02250-8). Atomic Indus Forum.

Atomic Industrial Forum Staff. Industry's Role in Development of Fusion Power: Set of Papers. (Technical & Economic Reports: Fusion). 1984. 375.00 (ISBN 0-318-02241-9). Atomic Indus Forum.

--An Overview of Decommissioning Nuclear Power Plants. (Technical & Economic Reports: Decommissioning). 1983. 30.00 (ISBN 0-318-02246-X). Atomic Indus Forum.

--Radiation Education Notebook. (Public Affairs & Information Program: General). 1983. 15.00 (ISBN 0-318-02249-4). Atomic Indus Forum.

--Radiation Issues for the Nuclear Industry: Set of Papers from AIF Conference on Radiation. (Technical & Economic Reports: Radiation Protection & Environmental Considerations). 1982. 150.00 (ISBN 0-318-02244-3). Atomic Indus Forum.

--Use of Potassium Iodide in Emergency Planning for Nuclear Power Plants: Selected Technical Papers from Radiation Issues. (Technical & Economic Reports: Radiation Protection & Environmental Considerations). 1982. 15.00 (ISBN 0-318-02243-5). Atomic Indus Forum.

Ator, Nancy, jt. auth. see Henningfield, Jack E.

Atre, S. Data Base: Structured Techniques for Designs, Performance & Management. 442p. 1980. members 31.95 (ISBN 0-318-17046-9); (W1) 33.95 (ISBN 0-318-17047-7). Data Process Mgmt.

Atre, Shaku. Database Management Systems for the Eighties. LC 83-60769. 600p. 1983. 95.00 (ISBN 0-89435-053-6). QED Info Sci.

Atre, Shakuntala. Data Base Structured Techniques for Design, Performance, & Management: With Case Studies. LC 80-14808. (Business Data Processing Ser.). 442p. 1980. 36.95x (ISBN 0-471-05267-1, Pub. by Wiley-Interscience). Wiley.

Atrek, E., et al. Optimum Structural Design: New Concepts & Software Systems. Gallagher, R. H. & Ragsdell, K. M., eds. (Numerical Methods in Engineering Ser.). 727p. 1984. text ed. 100.00x (ISBN 0-471-90291-8, 1405, Pub. by Wiley-Interscience). Wiley.

Atrens, Andrejs, jt. ed. see Speidel, Markus O.

Atrens, D. M. & Curthoys, J. S., eds. Neuroscience & Behavior: An Introduction. 2nd ed. 214p. 1982. 9.00i (ISBN 0-12-066850-5). Acad Pr.

Atreya, B. L. Deification of Man: Its Methods & Stages According to the Yoga Vasistha Including a Translation of the Essence of Vasistha's Teachings. 116p. 1980. pap. 4.50 (ISBN 0-935548-02-5). Santarasa Pubns.

Atreya, S. K. & Caldwell, J. J., eds. Planetary Aeronomy & Astronomy. (Advances in Space Research Ser.: Vol. 1, No.9). (Illus.). 216p. 1981. pap. 31.00 (ISBN 0-08-028385-3). Pergamon.

Atria, Arturo. Endocrine Function Tests. (Illus.). 144p. 1970. 19.75x (ISBN 0-398-00069-7). C C Thomas.

Atroshenko, V. S., et al. Calculation of the Brightness of Light in the Case of Anisotropic Scattering, Pt. 2. LC 60-8720. (Institute of Physics of the Atmosphere Ser.: No. 2). 226p. 1963. 27.50x (ISBN 0-306-17002-7, Consultants). Plenum Pub.

Atschul, bj, ed. see LaFray, Joyce.

Atshul, B. J., ed. see LaFray, Joyce & Baldwin, Barbie.

Atsumi, Ikuko, jt. tr. see Rexroth, Kenneth.

Atsumi, K., ed. New Frontiers in Laser Medicine & Surgery. (International Congress Ser.: No. 609). 528p. 1983. 100.00 (ISBN 0-444-90305-4, I-205-83, Excerpta Medica). Elsevier.

Atsumi, K, et al, eds. Progress in Artificial Organs: Proceedings, Fourth International Society for Artificial Organs, Kyoto, 1983. 110.00 (ISBN 0-936022-17-5); pap. 100.00 (ISBN 0-936022-16-7). Intl Soc Artifical Organs.

Atsumi, Kazuhiko, ed. Medical Thermography. 380p. 1973. 40.00x (ISBN 0-86008-076-5, Pub. by U of Tokyo Japan). Columbia U Pr.

Atsuta, Toshio, jt. auth. see Chen Wai-Fah.

Atta, Jacob K., jt. auth. see El Mallakh, Ragai.

Atta, Marian Van. Wild Edibles, Identification for Living off the Land. rev. ed. LC 84-62805. (Living off the Land Ser.). (Illus.). 64p. 1985. pap. text ed. 4.95 (ISBN 0-938524-01-1). Geraventure.

Atta, Robert E. Van see Van Atta, Robert E.

Atta, Winfred Van see Van Atta, Winfred.

Attal, Pierre & Muller, Claude, eds. Actes du Colloque de Linquistique de Rennes, Nov. 17-19, 1979. (Lingvisticae Investigationes Supplementa Ser.: 8). 389p. (Fr.). 1983. 40.00x (ISBN 9-02723-118-4). Benjamins North Am.

Attali, Jacques. Noise. Massumi, Brian, tr. (Theory & History of Literature Ser.: Vol. 16). Date not set. 29.50 (ISBN 0-8166-1286-2); pap. 12.95 (ISBN 0-8166-1287-0). U of Minn Pr.

Attali, Marc, jt. auth. see Mallet-Joris, Francois.

Attalides, Michael A. Cyprus: Nationalism & International Politics. LC 79-1388. 1979. 10.95 (ISBN 0-312-18057-8). St Martin.

Attanasio, A. A. Beastmarks. LC 84-52083. (Illus.). 120p. 1984. 13.95 (ISBN 0-9612970-2-6); ed. signed 25.00. Ziesing Mark.

--In Other Worlds. LC 84-4652. 224p. 1984. 12.95 (ISBN 0-688-03990-1). Morrow.

--Radix. LC 81-2612. 544p. 1981. pap. 8.95 (ISBN 0-688-00508-X). Morrow.

Attanasio, Salvator, tr. see Danielou, Jean.

Attanasio, Salvator, tr. see Gabrieli, Francesco.

Attanasio, Salvator, tr. see Godechot, Jacques.

Attanasio, Salvator, tr. see Lohfink, Gerhard.

Attanasio, Salvator, tr. see Rustow, Alexander.

Attanasio, Salvator, tr. see Wohlstein, Herman.

Attanasio, Salvatore, tr. see Pedraz, Juan L.

Attar. Conference of the Birds. 5.95 (ISBN 0-87728-117-3). Weiser.

Attar, Chand. Non-Aligned Nations: Arms Race & Disarmaments. 375p. 1983. 39.95 (ISBN 0-317-12422-6, Pub. by U D H Pubs India). Asia Bk Corp.

Attar, Farid. Muslim Saints & Mystics: Episodes from the Tadhkirat Al-Auliya (Memorial of the Saints) Arberry, A. J., tr. from Persian. (Persian Heritage Ser.). 1979. pap. 8.95 (ISBN 0-7100-0169-X). Routledge & Kegan.

Attar, Farid Ud-Din. The Conference of the Birds: A Sufi Fable. Nott, C. S., tr. (Clear Light Ser). (Illus.). 147p. (Orig.). 1971. pap. 6.95 (ISBN 0-87773-031-8, 73001-1). Shambhala Pubns.

Attar, Farid-ud-Din. The Divine Book. Orig. Title: Ilahi-Nama. 1983. cancelled 22.95 (ISBN 0-86304-030-6, Pub. by Octagon Pr England). Ins Study Human.

Attar, Samar. The Intruder in Modern Drama. (European University Studies: Series 1,German Language & Literature, Vol. 354). 237p. 1980. pap. 31.85 (ISBN 3-8204-6722-X). P Lang Pubs.

Attardi, Guiseppe, et al. Animal Ribosomes: Experimental Studies of the Last Five Years. 200p. 1972. text ed. 22.50x (ISBN 0-8422-7012-4). Irvington.

Atta-Ur-Rahman & Basha, Anwar. Biosynthesis of Indole Alkaloids. (International Series of Monographs on Chemistry). (Illus.). 1983. 49.00x (ISBN 0-19-855610-1). Oxford U Pr.

Attaway, John, jt. ed. see Nagy, Steven.

Attaway, William. Blood on the Forge. 279p. 1969. Repr. of 1941 ed. 8.95x (ISBN 0-911860-00-2). Chatham Bkseller.

--Let Me Breathe Thunder. 267p. 1969. Repr. of 1939 ed. 8.95x (ISBN 0-911860-01-0). Chatham Bkseller.

Attea, Mary. Turning Students on Through Creative Writing. (Illus.). 40p. (Orig.). (gr. 3-9). 1973. text ed. 4.50 (ISBN 0-914634-08-9). DOK Pubs.

Atteberry, Pat H. Power Mechanics. LC 80-20581. (Illus.). 112p. 1980. text ed. 6.40 (ISBN 0-87006-307-3). Goodheart.

Atteberry, William. Modern Real Estate Finance. 3rd ed. LC 79-24627. (Finance & Real Estate Ser.). 392p. 1980. text ed. 34.45 (ISBN 0-471-84147-1, Pub. by Grid). Wiley.

Atteberry, William, et al. Real Estate Law. 3rd ed. LC 83-14704. 378p. 1984. 31.95 (ISBN 0-471-87170-2); write for info tchr's manual (ISBN 0-471-87171-0). Wiley.

Attebery, Brian. The Fantasy Tradition in American Literature: From Irving to Le Guin. LC 80-7670. 256p. 1980. 17.50x (ISBN 0-253-35665-2). Ind U Pr.

Attebery, Louie W., ed. Idaho Folklife: Homesteads to Headstones. (Illus.). 288p. (Orig.). 1985. pap. 19.95 (ISBN 0-87480-240-7). U of Utah Pr.

Attebery, Paul. Guide to Brittany. (Illus.). 1985. pap. 5.95 (ISBN 0-318-04739-X). Merrimack.

Attebury, Jean E., ed. Project Plans for All Around the House from the Pages of Better Homes & Gardens. LC 84-80185. (Illus.). 128p. (Orig.). 1984. pap. 3.95 (ISBN 0-938708-09-0). L F Garlinghouse Co.

--Project Plans for Outdoor Living from the Pages of Better Homes & Gardens. LC 84-80186. (Illus.). 128p. (Orig.). 1984. pap. 3.95 (ISBN 0-938708-08-2). L F Garlinghouse Co.

--Project Plans to Build for Children from the Pages of Better Homes & Gardens. LC 84-80184. (Illus.). 128p. (Orig.). 1984. pap. 3.95 (ISBN 0-938708-07-4). L F Garlinghouse Co.

Atteia, M., et al. Nonlinear Problems of Analysis in Geometry & Mechanics. LC 80-21647. (Research Notes in Mathematics: No. 46). 288p. (Orig.). 1981. pap. text ed. 27.00 (ISBN 0-273-08493-3). Pitman Pub MA.

Attenborough, David. Journeys to the Past. (Illus.). 384p. 1983. 21.95 (ISBN 0-7188-2507-1, Pub. by Salem Hse Ltd). Merrimack Pub Cir.

--Journeys to the Past: Travels in New Guinea, Madagascar, & the Northern Territory of Australia. 352p. 1983. pap. 4.95 (ISBN 0-14-006413-3). Penguin.

--The Living Planet: A Portrait of the Earth. (Illus.). 1985. 25.00 (ISBN 0-316-05748-7). Little.

--Tribal Encounters. 96p. 1981. 26.00x (ISBN 0-85022-101-3, Pub. by Leicestershire). State Mutual Bk.

--The Zoo Quest Expeditions. 1983. pap. 4.95 (ISBN 0-14-005765-X). Penguin.

--The Zoo Quest Expeditions. (Illus.). 384p. 1983. 21.95 (ISBN 0-7188-2465-2, Pub. by Salem Hse Ltd). Merrimack Pub Cir.

Attenborough, John. The Priest's Story. 192p. 1984. 16.95 (ISBN 0-340-34935-2, Pub. by Hodder & Stoughton UK). David & Charles.

Attenborough, Keith & Pollitt, C., eds. Pollution: The Professionals & the Public. 216p. 1977. pap. 11.00x (ISBN 0-335-00037-1, Pub. by Open Univ Pr). Taylor & Francis.

Attenborough, Richard, intro. by. The Words of Gandhi. LC 82-14403. (Illus.). 112p. 1982. 9.95 (ISBN 0-937858-14-5). Newmarket.

Atteraas, L., et al, eds. Underwater Technology-Offshore Petroleum: Proceedings of the International Conference, Bergen, Norway, April 14-16 1980. LC 80-40414. 450p. 1980. 78.00 (ISBN 0-08-026141-8). Pergamon.

Atterbury, Anson P. Islam in Africa. LC 73-91254. Repr. of 1899 ed. 22.50x (ISBN 0-8371-2064-0, ATI&, Pub. by Negro U Pr). Greenwood.

Atterbury, P., jt. auth. see Philip, P.

Atterbury, Paul. English Rivers & Canals. (Illus.). 1984. 15.95 (ISBN 0-393-01829-6). Norton.

--The History of Porcelain. LC 82-2275. (Illus.). 256p. 1982. 35.00 (ISBN 0-688-01402-X). Morrow.

Atterbury, Paul, ed. Antiques: An Encyclopedia of the Decorative Arts. LC 79-13548. (Illus.). 1980. 35.00 (ISBN 0-7064-0711-3, Mayflower Bks). Smith Pubs.

Atterbury, Paul J., ed. European Pottery & Porcelain. (Illus.). 1979. pap. 7.95 (ISBN 0-8317-3056-0, Mayflower Bks). Smith Pubs.

Atterbury, Rowley S. The Contributors. (Illus.). 15.00 (ISBN 0-913720-03-8, Sandstone). Beil.

Atterbury, T. J., et al. Measurements of Secondary Stresses in Pipeline: Report 1, Additional Data. 80p. 1959. softcover 3.00 (ISBN 0-318-12653-2, L00220). Am Gas Assn.

Attewell, P. B. & Taylor, A. K., eds. Ground Movements & Their Effects on Structures. 288p. 1984. 59.95 (ISBN 0-412-00391-0, 5048, Pub. by Chapman & Hall England). Methuen Inc.

Attewell, Paul A. Radical Political Economy since the Sixties: A Sociology of Knowledge Analysis. LC 83-24650. 1984. text ed. 30.00 (ISBN 0-8135-1053-8). Rutgers U Pr.

Attfield, C. L. E., et al. Rational Expectation in Macroeconomics. 232p. 1985. 39.95x (ISBN 0-631-13963-X); pap. 16.95x (ISBN 0-631-13964-8). Basil Blackwell.

Attfield, Harlan H. D. Raising Rabbits. 90p. (Avail. in Fr.). 1977. prfct. bnd. 5.50 (ISBN 0-86619-060-0, 11040-BK); in French 4.35 (ISBN 0-86619-061-9, 19040-BK). Vols Tech Asst.

Attfield, J. & Williams, S., eds. Nineteen Thirty-Nine: The Communist Party & the War. 200p. 1984. text ed. 19.50x (ISBN 0-85315-582-8, Pub. by Lawrence & Wishart Ltd). Humanities.

Attfield, Robin. The Ethics of Environmental Concern. 215p. 1983. 26.00x (ISBN 0-231-05802-0); pap. 13.00x (ISBN 0-231-05798-9). Columbia U Pr.

Atthill, Catherine, tr. see Zanetti, Adriano.

Atthill, Robin. Mendip: A New Study. LC 76-45509. (Illus.). 1977. 28.00 (ISBN 0-7153-7297-1). David & Charles.

--The Somerset & Dorset Railway. (Illus.). 224p. 1985. 18.95 (ISBN 0-7153-8692-1); pap. 10.95 (ISBN 0-7153-8693-X). David & Charles.

Atthill, William L., ed. Documents Relating to the Foundation & Antiquities of the Collegiate Church of Middleham in the County of York. LC 70-161702. (Camden Society, London. Publications, First Ser.: No. 38). Repr. of 1847 ed. 19.00 (ISBN 0-404-50138-9). AMS Pr.

--Documents Relating to the Foundation & Antiquities of the Collegiate Church of Middleham, County of York. (Camden Society Ser.: Vol. 38). 19.00 (ISBN 0-384-02270-7). Johnson Repr.

Atti, C. Ciofi & De Sanctis, E., eds. Few Body Systems & Electromagnetic Interaction: Proceedings of the Workshop Held in Frascati (Italy) March 7-10, 1978. (Lecture Notes in Physics: Vol. 86). 1978. pap. 25.00 (ISBN 0-387-09095-9). Springer-Verlag.

Attia, E. L., jt. auth. see Marshall, Kenneth G.

Attia, Zizo. A Flower Veils the Sun. (Illus.). 68p. 1979. 7.50 (ISBN 0-682-49418-6). Exposition Pr FL.

Attie, Joseph N. & Khafif, Rene A. Melanotic Tumors: Biology, Pathology & Clinical Features. (Illus.). 364p. 1964. photocopy ed. 36.50x (ISBN 0-398-00070-0). C C Thomas.

Attig, Thomas, jt. auth. see Scherer, Donald.

Attig, Thomas, et al, eds. Social Policy & Conflict Resolution. (Studies in Applied Philosophy: Vol. VI). 200p. 1984. 15.00 (ISBN 0-935756-07-8). BGSU Dept Phil.

Attig, Thomas W., jt. ed. see Miller, Fred D., Jr.

Attikiouzel. Pascal for Electronic Engineers. 1984. 22.50 (ISBN 0-442-30596-6). Van Nos Reinhold.

Attinelli, E. J. A Bibliography of American Numismatic Auction Catalogues, 1828-1875. LC 75-32394. (Illus.). 1976. Repr. of 1875 ed. 25.00x (ISBN 0-88000-072-4). Quarterman.

Attinello, Lauren. Wintertime in Fraggle Rock. (Illus.). 48p. (gr. k-1). 1985. 0.99 (ISBN 0-03-005633-0). HR&W.

Attinger, E. O., ed. Global Systems Dynamics. 353p. 1970. 42.95 (ISBN 0-471-03640-4). Halsted Pr.

Attinger, E. O., ed. see International Symposium, Charlottesville, Va. 1969.

Attir, Mustafa O., et al, eds. Directions of Change: Modernization Theory, Research, & Realities. (Special Study Ser.). 300p. (Orig.). 1981. pap. 11.95x (ISBN 0-86531-274-5). Westview.

Attiret, Jean D. & Shenstone, William. A Particular Account of the Emperor of China's Gardens Near Peking with Unconnected Thoughts on Gardening & Other Items: An Essay on Design in Gardening. Hunt, John D., ed. LC 79-56989. (The English Landscape Garden Ser.). 194p. 1982. lib. bdg. 26.00 (ISBN 0-8240-0165-6). Garland Pub.

Attitude Research Conference. Attitude Research Enters the '80s. Olshavsky, Richard W., ed. LC 80-20621. (American Marketing Association, Proceedings Ser.). pap. 51.50 (ISBN 0-317-20073-9, 2023355). Bks Demand UMI.

--Attitude Research Plays for High Stakes. Maloney, John C. & Silverman, Bernard, eds. LC 78-14033. (American Marketing Association, Proceedings Ser.). pap. 71.80 (ISBN 0-317-20067-4, 2023349). Bks Demand UMI.

--Attitude Research under the Sun. Eighmey, John, ed. LC 78-13992. (American Marketing Association, Proceedings Ser.). pap. 56.30 (ISBN 0-317-20066-6, 2023348). Bks Demand UMI.

--A Look Back, A Look Ahead. Hafer, George B., ed. LC 80-10370. (American Marketing Association, Proceedings Ser.). pap. 54.30 (ISBN 0-317-20074-7, 2023356). Bks Demand UMI.

Attix, F. & Roesch, William. Radiation Dosimetry, 3 vols. 2nd ed. Incl. Vol. 1. Fundamentals. 1968. 69.50 (ISBN 0-12-066401-1); Vol. 2. Instrumentation. 1967. 69.50 (ISBN 0-12-066402-X); Vol. 3. Sources, Field Measurements & Applications. Attix, F. & Tochilin, E., eds. 1969. 113.50 (ISBN 0-12-066403-8); Suppl. 1. Topics in Radiation Dosimetry. 1972. 77.00 (ISBN 0-12-066501-8). Acad Pr.

Attix, Frank H., ed. Luminescence Dosimetry: Proceedings. LC 67-60038. (AEC Symposium Ser.). 532p. 1967. pap. 21.25 (ISBN 0-87079-263-6, CONF-650637); microfiche 4.50 (ISBN 0-87079-264-4, CONF-650637). DOE.

Attiyate, Y. H. & Shah, R. Dictionary of Microelectronics & Microcomputed Technology: German-English, English-German. 460p. 1984. 31.00 (ISBN 0-9907001-0-0, Pub. by VDI Verlag Gmbh Dusseldorf). Heyden.

Attiyeh, R., et al. Basic Economics: Theory & Cases. 2nd ed. 1977. pap. 20.95 (ISBN 0-13-059030-4). P-H.

Attiyeh, Richard & Lumsden, Keith. Macroeconomics: A Programmed Book. 4th ed. 256p. 1982. pap. text ed. 18.95 (ISBN 0-13-542704-5). P-H.

Attkisson, C. Clifford, Jr., et al, eds. Evaluation of Human Service Programs. 1978. 44.00 (ISBN 0-12-066350-3). Acad Pr.

Attkisson, Franklin. How to Cut Your Energy Bill Thirty per-Cent to Fifty per-Cent. rev. ed. 56p. (Orig.). 1977. pap. 3.00x (ISBN 0-686-30559-0). Energy Pub.

Attlee, Rosemary. William's Story: A Mother's Account of Her Son's Struggle Against Cancer. 160p. 1984. pap. 2.95 (ISBN 0-87788-927-9). Shaw Pubs.

Attman, Arthur. Dutch Enterprise in the World Bullion Trade 1550-1800. (No. 23). 113p. 1983. pap. text ed. 17.50x (ISBN 91-8525-233-6, Pub. by Goteborg). Humanities.

Attman, Artu. The Struggle for Baltic Markets: Powers in Conflict 1558-1618. (Acta Regiae Societatis Scientiarum et Litterarum, Goteborg, Humaniora: No. 14). (Illus.). 1980. pap. text ed. 22.50x (ISBN 91-85252-15-8). Humanities.

Attman, Artur. The Bullion Flow: Between Europe & the East 1000-1750. (Goteborg - Acta Humaniora Ser.: No. 20). 149p. 1981. pap. text ed. 18.50x (ISBN 91-85252-27-1, Pub. by Goteborg Sweden). Humanities.

Attneave, Carolyn L., jt. ed. see Kelso, Dianne R.

Attneave, Carolyn L., jt. ed. see Tulipan, Alan B.

Attner, Paul. The Terrapins: Maryland Football. LC 75-12204. (College Sports Ser.). 1975. 9.95 (ISBN 0-87397-066-7). Strode.

Attner, Paul, jt. auth. see Denlinger, Ken.

Attner, Raymond F., jt. auth. see Plunkett, Warren R.

Attner, Raymond F., jt. auth. see Straub, Joseph.

Attoch, jt. auth. see Ahuma, S. R.

Attoe, Wayne. Architecture & Critical Imagination. 188p. 1978. 44.95x (ISBN 0-471-99574-6, Pub. by Wiley-Interscience). Wiley.

--Skylines: Understanding & Molding Urban Silhouettes. LC 80-41684. 128p. 1981. 48.95x (ISBN 0-471-27940-4, Pub. by Wiley-Interscience). Wiley.

Atton, H. & Holland, H. H. King's Customs: An Account of Maritime Revenue & Contraband Traffic, 2 vols. (Illus.). 1968. Repr. of 1908 ed. Set. 75.00x (ISBN 0-7146-1266-9, F Cass Co). Biblio Dist.

Atton, Henry & Holland, Henry H. King's Customs, 2 Vols. LC 67-21884. Repr. of 1908 ed. Set. 87.50x (ISBN 0-678-00272-X). Kelley.

Attonito, Joan K. A Science Lab. 72p. (gr. 4-6). 1982. 5.95 (ISBN 0-88047-009-7, 8212). DOK Pubs.

Attorney General's Committee Report see Timberg, Sigmund & Zaidins, Earle W.

Attorney General's Department, Australia. International Trade Law Seminars: Nineteen Hundred Seventy-Four to Nineteen Hundred Eighty-Three, 5 bks. 1985. Repr. of 1974 ed. lib. bdg. write for info. (ISBN 0-89941-454-0). W S Hein.

Attouch, H. & Universite de Paris-Sud. Variational Convergence for Functions & Operators. (Applicable Math Ser.). 304p. 1984. pap. text ed. 29.95 (ISBN 0-273-08583-2). Pitman Pub MA.

Attridge, D. Well-Weighed Syllables. LC 74-80362. (Illus.). 280p. 1975. pap. 15.95 (ISBN 0-521-29722-2). Cambridge U Pr.

Attridge, Derek & Ferrer, Daniel, eds. Post-Structuralist Joyce: Essays from the French. 200p. 1985. 34.50 (ISBN 0-521-26636-X); pap. 12.95 (ISBN 0-521-31979-X). Cambridge U Pr.

Attridge, G. G., jt. auth. see Walls, H. J.

Attridge, Geoffrey. Photographic Developing in Practice. (Illus.). 152p. 1984. 22.50 (ISBN 0-7153-8407-4). David & Charles.

Attridge, Harold W. First-Century Cynicism in the Epistles of Heraclitus. LC 76-20736. (Harvard Theological Review. Harvard Theological Studies: No. 29). 1976. pap. 9.00 (ISBN 0-89130-111-9, 020029). Scholars Pr GA.

Attridge, Harold W. & Oden, Robert A. De Dea Syria. LC 76-135. (Society of Biblical Literature. Texts & Translations Ser.). 1976. pap. 9.25 (ISBN 0-89130-073-2, 060209). Scholars Pr GA.

Attridge, Harold W. & Oden, Robert A., Jr. Philo of Byblos: Phoenician History. LC 80-25781. (Introdution, Critical Text, Translations, Notes: No. 9). x, 110p. 1981. pap. 3.50 (ISBN 0-915170-08-6). Catholic Biblical.

Attridge, Harold W. see Comstock, Susan T., et al.

Attwater, Donald. Golden Book of Eastern Saints. facsimile ed. LC 72-156607. (Essay Index Reprint Ser). Repr. of 1938 ed. 18.00 (ISBN 0-8369-2267-0). Ayer Co Pubs.

--Names & Name-Days: A Dictionary of Catholic Christian Names in Alphabetical Order with Origins & Meanings. LC 68-30595. 1968. Repr. of 1939 ed. 45.00x (ISBN 0-8103-3108-5). Gale.

--The Penguin Dictionary of Saints. rev. ed. John, Catherine R., rev. by. 352p. 1984. pap. 5.95 (ISBN 0-14-051123-7). Penguin.

Attwater, Donald, ed. Modern Christian Revolutionaries. facsimile ed. LC 76-156608. (Essay Index Reprint Ser). Repr. of 1947 ed. 23.00 (ISBN 0-8369-2304-9). Ayer Co Pubs.

Attwater, Donald, tr. see Lawrence, Brother.

Attwater, Donald, tr. see Solovyev, Vladimir.

Attwater, Thurston, ed. see Butler, Alban.

Attwater, W. A. The Technique of Leathercraft. (Illus.). 144p. 1983. 19.95 (ISBN 0-7134-2345-5, Pub. by Batsford England). David & Charles.

Attwell, Arthur A. The School Psychologist's Handbook. rev ed. LC 76-182925. (Professional Handbk Ser). 75p. 1976. pap. text ed. 17.50x (ISBN 0-87424-122-7). Western Psych.

Attwell, Arthur A. & Clabby, D. A. The Retarded Child: Answers to Questions Parents Ask. LC 72-182924. 139p. 1975. pap. 13.95x (ISBN 0-87424-120-0). Western Psych.

Attwell, Peter & Farmer, Ian. Principles of Engineering Geology. 1976. 93.00 (ISBN 0-412-11280-9, NO. 6016, Pub. by Chapman & Hall). Methuen Inc.

Attwood, Anna C. The Disputed Territory. 1982. 8.50 (ISBN 0-8062-1962-9). Carlton.

Attwood, D. & Florence, A. T. Surfactant Systems: Their Chemistry, Pharmacy & Biology. 1982. 99.00x (ISBN 0-412-14840-4, 6714, Pub. by Chapman & Hall). Methuen Inc.

Attwood, D., jt. auth. see Florence, A. T.

Attwood, D. T. & Henke, B. L., eds. Low Energy X-Ray Diagnostics: Monterey, 1981. (AIP Conference Proceedings: No. 75). 394p. 1981. lib. bdg. 44.00 (ISBN 0-88318-174-6). Am Inst Physics.

Attwood, George H. The Prowler of Mount Hebrew. 48p. 1985. 6.95 (ISBN 0-89962-458-8). Todd & Honeywell.

Attwood, John. A Roof over My Head. LC 84-90089. 107p. 1985. 8.95 (ISBN 0-533-06170-9). Vantage.

Attwood, Les T. Management Development in British Companies. 1979. 90.00x (ISBN 0-86176-039-5, Pub. by MCB Pubns). State Mutual Bk.

Attwood, P., ed. Crop Protection Handbook: Cereals. 85.00x (ISBN 0-901436-72-0, Pub. by CAB Bks England). State Mutual Bk.

Attwood, Stanley B. Length & Breadth of Maine. 1973. pap. 5.95 (ISBN 0-89101-027-0). U Maine Orono.

Attwood, William. Making It Through Middle Age: Notes While in Transit. LC 81-69157. (Illus.). 256p. 1982. 12.95 (ISBN 0-689-11268-8). Atheneum.

Attwood, William, tr. see Vadim, Roger.

Attwooll, Elspeth, ed. Perspectives in Jurisprudence. 240p. 1977. 50.00x (ISBN 0-85261-134-X, Pub. by U of Glasgow Pr Scotland). State Mutual Bk.

Atulananda, Swami. Atman Alone Abides: Conversations with Swami Atulananda. Vidyatmananda, Swami, ed. 1978. pap. 5.50 (ISBN 0-87481-480-4). Vedanta Pr.

Atwan, R., jt. auth. see Wright, J.

Atwan, Robert & Forer, Bruce. Bedside Hollywood. (Illus.). 1985. 24.95 (ISBN 0-918825-11-3). Moyer Bell Ltd.

Atwan, Robert & Vesterman, William. One Hundred Major Modern Writers: Essays for Composition. 704p. 1984. pap. text ed. write for info. (ISBN 0-02-304910-3). Macmillan.

Atwan, Robert, jt. auth. see McQuade, Donald.

Atwan, Robert & Vesterman, William, eds. One Hundred Major Modern Writers: Essays for Composition. 704p. 1984. pap. text ed. 13.15 scp (ISBN 0-672-61602-5); scp instr's guide 7.33 (ISBN 0-672-61603-3). Bobbs.

Atwan, Robert, jt. ed. see McQuade, Donald.

Atwan, Robert, et al. American Mass Media. 2nd ed. 426p. 1982. pap. text ed. 15.00 (ISBN 0-394-32668-7). Random.

--American Mass Media: Industries & Issues. 3rd ed. 458p. 1986. pap. text ed. 15.95 (ISBN 0-394-34033-7, RanC). Random.

Atwater, Caleb. Description of the Antiquities Discovered in the State of Ohio & Other Western States. LC 72-4997. (Harvard University. Peabody Museum of Archaeology & Ethnology. Antiquities of the New World: No. 1). (Illus.). 27.50 (ISBN 0-404-57301-0). AMS Pr.

--Remarks Made on a Tour to Prairie du Chien: Thence to Washington City in 1829. fascimile ed. LC 75-82. (Mid-American Frontier Ser.). 1975. Repr. of 1831 ed. 25.50x (ISBN 0-405-06851-4). Ayer Co Pubs.

Atwater, Constance. Baton Twirling: The Fundamentals of an Art & a Skill. LC 64-22749. (Illus.). (YA) (gr. 9 up). 1965. 15.00 (ISBN 0-8048-0060-X). C E Tuttle.

--Tap Dancing: Techniques, Routines, Terminology. LC 75-158799. (Illus.). (YA) (gr. 9 up). 1971. 13.50 (ISBN 0-8048-0671-3). C E Tuttle.

Atwater, Dorothea. First Aid for Your Apple II-IIe. 144p. (Orig.). 1985. pap. 6.95 (ISBN 0-345-31942-7). Ballantine.

--First Aid for Your Commodore 64. 1985. pap. 7.95 (ISBN 0-345-31944-3). Ballantine.

--First Aid for Your IBM PC. 144p. (Orig.). 1985. pap. 6.95 (ISBN 0-345-31943-5). Ballantine.

Atwater, Eastwood. I Hear You: Listening Skills to Make You a Better Manager. 127p. 1982. 12.95 (ISBN 0-13-450684-7); pap. 5.95 (ISBN 0-13-450676-6). P-H.

--Psychology of Adjustment: Personal Growth in a Changing World. 2nd ed. (Illus.). 448p. 1983. 24.95 (ISBN 0-13-734855-X). P-H.

Atwater, Elton. American Regulation of Arms Exports. 287p. 37.00 (ISBN 0-384-02308-8). Johnson Repr.

Atwater, Florence, jt. auth. see Atwater, Richard.

Atwater, George P. The Episcopal Church: Its Message for Today. rev ed. 1978. pap. 4.95 (ISBN 0-8192-1244-X). Morehouse.

Atwater, Harry A. Introduction to Microwave Theory. rev ed. LC 80-28674. 1981. lib. bdg. 21.00 (ISBN 0-89874-192-0). Krieger.

Atwater, James D., jt. auth. see Ford Foundation.

Atwater, Lynn. The Extramaritial Connection: Sex, Intimacy & Identity. LC 82-6561. 272p. 1982. 19.50 (ISBN 0-8290-0460-2); pap. 9.95 (ISBN 0-8290-0549-8). Irvington.

Atwater, Mary M. Design & the Handweaver. LC 61-4138. (Shuttle Craft Guild Monograph: No. 3). (Illus.). 26p. 1961. pap. 6.45 (ISBN 0-916658-03-1). HTH Pubs.

--Guatemala Visited. LC 47-24720. (Shuttle Craft Guild Monograph: No. 15). (Illus.). 46p. 1965. pap. 7.45 (ISBN 0-916658-15-5). HTH Pubs.

--Handwoven Rugs. LC 76-24018. (Shuttle Craft Guild Monograph: No. 29). (Illus.). 28p. 1948. pap. 7.45 (ISBN 0-916658-29-5). HTH Pubs.

Atwater, Richard & Atwater, Florence. Mr. Popper's Penguins. (Illus.). 144p. (gr. 3-7). 1978. pap. 2.95 (ISBN 0-440-45934-6, YB). Dell.

--Mr. Popper's Penguins. (Illus.). (gr. 3 up). 1938. 10.45 (ISBN 0-316-05842-4). Little.

Atwater, Richard, tr. see Procopius.

Atwater, W. Eastwood. Adolescence. (Illus.). 448p. 1983. pap. 23.95 (ISBN 0-13-008631-2). P-H.

--Human Relations. (Illus.). 400p. 1986. pap. text ed. 19.95 (ISBN 0-13-445727-7). P-H.

Atwater, Wilbur O., jt. auth. see Billings, John S.

Atwell, Anthony, Jr. Dia por Dia. LC 85-2691. 96p. (Orig.). 1985. pap. 16.95 (ISBN 0-86534-058-7). Sunstone Pr.

Atwell, Charles A. & Sullins, Robert. Curricular Comprehensiveness in Small Rural Community Colleges. (Horizons Issues Monograph: No. 24). 68p. (Orig.). 1984. pap. 5.00 (ISBN 0-87117-138-4). Am Assn Comm Jr Coll.

Atwell, David. Cathedrals of the Movies: A History of British Cinemas & Their Audiences. LC 82-11020. 192p. 1981. pap. text ed. 17.50 (ISBN 0-85139-773-5). Nichols Pub.

Atwell, Lee. G. W. Pabst. (Filmmakers Ser.). 1977. lib. bdg. 13.50 (ISBN 0-8057-9251-1, Twayne). G K Hall.

Atwell, Lionel. The Official Survival Game Manual. (Illus.). 1983. pap. 6.95 (ISBN 0-671-47395-6). PB.

Atwell, Lucie. Lucie Atwell's Goodnight Stories. (Illus.). 1985. 3.98 (ISBN 0-517-46903-0). Outlet Bk Co.

Atwell, Margaret A., et al. Learning in College: Integrating Information. 88p. 1983. pap. text ed. 8.95 (ISBN 0-8403-2854-0). Kendall-Hunt.

Atwell, Robert H., et al. The Money Game: Financing Collegiate Athletics. 72p. 1980. 10.00 (ISBN 0-02-901010-1). ACE.

Atwell, Susan, ed. see Petit, Ronald E.

Atwill, A. C., jt. auth. see Blake, S. F.

Atwood, Ann. Haiku: The Mood of the Earth. LC 70-162737. (Illus.). (gr. 3 up). 1971. PLB 9.95 o.s.i (ISBN 0-684-12494-7, ScribJ); pap. 4.95 (ISBN 0-684-16214-8, ScribJ). Scribner.

--Haiku Vision: In Poetry & Photography. LC 76-42287. (Illus.). (gr. 3 up). 1977. reinforced bdg. 7.95 (ISBN 0-684-14858-7, ScribJ). Scribner.

Atwood, Ann, tr. see Klinge, Gunther.

Atwood, Bagby E., jt. auth. see Babington, Mima.

Atwood, Beth S. Building Independent Learning Skills. LC 74-16807. (Learning Handbooks Ser.). 1974. pap. 6.50 (ISBN 0-8224-1973-4). Pitman Learning.

Atwood, Charles. A Doughnut on the Nose Is Better than Mustard on the Toes. LC 83-70117. 96p. (Orig.). 1983. pap. 3.95 (ISBN 0-89815-088-4). Ten Speed Pr.

Atwood, E. Bagby. The Regional Vocabulary of Texas. 1962 ed ed. LC 62-9784. (Illus.). 286p. 1969. pap. 7.95 (ISBN 0-292-77008-1). U of Tex Pr.

Atwood, Evangeline. Frontier Politics: Alaska's James Wickersham. LC 79-71140. (Illus.). 1979. 14.95 (ISBN 0-8323-0317-8). Binford.

Atwood, Evangeline & De Armond, Robert N.compiled by. Who's Who in Alaskan Politics: A Biographical Dictionary of Alaskan Political Personalities, 1884-1974. LC 77-76025. 1977. 10.00 (ISBN 0-8323-0287-2). Binford.

Atwood, George E. & Stolorow, Robert D. Structures of Subjectivity: Explorations in Psychoanalytic Phenomenology, Vol. 4. (Psychoanalytic Inquiry Book Ser.). 144p. 1984. 19.95 (ISBN 0-88163-012-8). Analytic Pr.

Atwood, George E., jt. auth. see Stolorow, Robert D.

Atwood, H. L., jt. ed. see Bliss, Dorothy.

Atwood, Harold, jt. ed. see Bliss, Dorothy.

Atwood, Harry. Constitution Explained. 5.00 (ISBN 0-685-08800-6). Destiny.

--Our Republic. 5.00 (ISBN 0-685-08812-X). Destiny.

Atwood, Jerry L., et al. Inclusion Compounds, Vol. 1. 1984. 70.00 (ISBN 0-12-067101-8). Acad Pr.

--Inclusion Compounds, Vol. 2. 1984. 72.00 (ISBN 0-12-067102-6). Acad Pr.

--Inclusion Compounds, Vol. 3. 1985. 98.00 (ISBN 0-12-067103-4). Acad Pr.

Atwood, Jerry W. The Systems Analyst: How to Design Computer-Based Systems. 1977. text ed. 14.50x (ISBN 0-8104-5102-6). Hayden.

--The Systems Analyst: How to Design Computer-Based Systems. 240p. 17.50 (5102). Hayden.

Atwood, Jesse H., et al. Thus Be Their Destiny: The Personality Development of Negro Youth in Three Communities. LC 71-155631. Repr. of 1941 ed. 12.50 (ISBN 0-404-00135-1). AMS Pr.

Atwood, Jim D. Inorganic & Organometallic Reaction Mechanisms. LC 84-19904. (Chemistry Ser.). 325p. 1985. text ed. 26.75 pub net (ISBN 0-534-03777-1). Brooks-Cole.

Atwood, Joan. Making Contact with Human Sexuality. (Illus.). 96p. (Orig.). pap. 6.95 (ISBN 0-942494-66-0). Coleman Pub.

Atwood, June, jt. auth. see Cronan, Marion.

Atwood, Kathryn. Renegade Lady. 352p. 1982. pap. 3.25 (ISBN 0-515-06045-3). Jove Pubns.

Atwood, L. Erwin, jt. auth. see Schramm, Wilbur.

Atwood, L. Erwin, et al, eds. International Perspectives on News. LC 82-3273. 215p. 1982. 15.95x (ISBN 0-8093-1069-4). S Ill U Pr.

Atwood, Lyman, jt. auth. see Marshall, Samuel.

Atwood, Margaret. Bodily Harm. 1983. pap. 3.95 (ISBN 0-553-23289-4). Bantam.

--Bodily Harm. 1982. 15.00 (ISBN 0-671-44153-1). Ultramarine Pub.

--The Circle Game. (House of Anansi Poetry Ser.: No. 3). 1967. (Pub. by Hse Anansi Pr Canada); pap. 4.95 (ISBN 0-88784-070-1). U of Toronto Pr.

--Dancing Girls: And Other Stories. 1982. 14.95 (ISBN 0-671-24249-0). S&S.

--Dancing Girls & Other Stories. 1985. 8.95 (ISBN 0-553-34115-4). Bantam.

--The Edible Woman. 288p. 1983. pap. 3.50 (ISBN 0-446-31105-7). Warner Bks.

--The Handmaids's Tale. 1986. price not set. S&S.

--Journals of Susanna Moodie: Poems. 1970. pap. 5.95x (ISBN 0-19-540169-7). Oxford U Pr.

--Lady Oracle. 1977. pap. 3.95 (ISBN 0-380-01799-7, 64758-3, Bard). Avon.

--Life Before Man. 304p. 1983. pap. 3.95 (ISBN 0-446-31331-9). Warner Bks.

--Power Politics. LC 73-146455. (House of Anansi Poetry Ser.: No. 20). 56p. 1971. (Pub. by Hse Anansi Pr Canada); pap. 4.95 (ISBN 0-88784-020-5). U of Toronto Pr.

--Second Words: Selected Critical Prose. 448p. 1982. 17.95 (ISBN 0-88784-095-7, Pub. by Hse Anansi Pr Canada). U of Toronto Pr.

--Second Words: Selected Critical Prose. LC 83-71983. 1984. 18.95x (ISBN 0-8070-6358-4); pap. 9.95 (ISBN 0-8070-6359-2, BP669). Beacon Pr.

--Surfacing. 224p. 1983. pap. 3.50 (ISBN 0-446-31107-3). Warner Bks.

--Survival: A Thematic Guide to Canadian Literature. LC 72-91501. 287p. (Orig.). 1972. pap. 6.95 (ISBN 0-88784-613-0, Pub. by Hse Anansi Pr Canada). U of Toronto Pr.

--True Stories. 1982. 13.50 (ISBN 0-671-45271-1); pap. 4.95 (ISBN 0-671-45971-6). S&S.

--Two-Headed Poems. 1981. (Touchstone Bks); pap. 6.95 (ISBN 0-671-25373-5). S&S.

Atwood, Margaret, ed. The New Oxford Book of Canadian Verse in English. 1982. 25.00 (ISBN 0-19-540396-7). Oxford U Pr.

Atwood, Mary A. Hermetic Philosophy & Alchemy. LC 79-8592. Repr. of 1960 ed. 57.50 (ISBN 0-404-18446-4). AMS Pr.

--A Suggestive Inquiry into the Hermetic Mystery. LC 75-36825. (Occult Ser.). 1976. Repr. of 1920 ed. 51.00x (ISBN 0-405-07938-9). Ayer Co Pubs.

Atwood, Mary Anne. A Suggestive Inquiry into the Hermetic Mystery. 597p. 1976. Repr. of 1918 ed. 15.50 (ISBN 0-911662-64-2). Yoga.

Atwood, Rodney. The Hessians: Mercenaries from Hessen Kassel in the American Revolution. LC 79-20150. 1980. 37.50 (ISBN 0-521-22884-0). Cambridge U Pr.

Atwood, Seth, jt. auth. see Andrewes, William.

Atwood, Stephen J. A Doctor's Guide to Feeding Your Child: Complete Nutrition for Healthy Growth. (Illus.). 288p. 1982. 12.95 (ISBN 0-02-504400-1). Macmillan.

Atwood, Thomas. History of the Island of Dominica. 286p. 1971. Repr. of 1791 ed. 29.50x (ISBN 0-7146-1929-9, F Cass Co). Biblio Dist.

Atwood, Valerie D. Drug Withdrawal Symptoms: A Medical Subject Analysis & Research Index with Bibliography. LC 83-70087. 149p. 1985. 29.95 (ISBN 0-941864-88-X); pap. 21.95 (ISBN 0-941864-89-8). ABBE Pubs Assn.

Atwood, W. B. & Bjorken, J. D. Lectures on Lepton Nucleon Scattering & Quantum Chromo-Dynamics. (Progress in Physics Ser.: Vol. 4). 1982. 34.95 (ISBN 0-8176-3079-1). Birkhauser.

Atwood, William G. The Lioness & the Little One. LC 80-11288. (Illus.). 352p. 1980. 24.00x (ISBN 0-231-04942-0). Columbia U Pr.

Atyeo, Henry C. The Excursion As a Teaching Technique. LC 79-176526. (Columbia University. Teachers College. Contributions to Education: No. 761). Repr. of 1939 ed. 22.50 (ISBN 0-404-55761-9). AMS Pr.

Atyeo, Marilyn, jt. auth. see Uhde, Anna.

Au, Kathryn, jt. auth. see Mason, Jana.

Au, Tung. Engineering Economics for Capital Investment Analysis. 600p. 1983. scp 36.39 (ISBN 0-205-07911-3, 277911); write for info. solutions manual (ISBN 0-205-07912-1). Allyn.

Au, Wanda K. How I Made Millions in Hawaii's Real Estate. LC 83-70355. 160p. 1983. 6.95 (ISBN 0-935848-18-5). Bess Pr.

Au, William A. The Cross, the Flag, & the Bomb: American Catholics Debate War & Peace, 1960-1983. LC 84-25290. (Contributions to the Study of Religion Ser.: No. 12). 256p. 1985. lib. bdg. 29.95 (ISBN 0-313-24754-4, AUC/). Greenwood.

Aub, Joseph C. & Hapgood, Ruth K. Pioneer in Modern Medicine: David Linn Edsall of Harvard. LC 78-145896. (Illus.). 1970. 22.50x (ISBN 0-674-66875-8). Harvard U Pr.

Aubart & Pobe. L' Art monumental roman en France: Coll. Art et Geoge. 21.95 (ISBN 0-685-38374-1). French & Eur.

Auber, Daniel F. Gustave ou le Bal Masque, 2 vols. LC 76-49212. (Early Romantic Opera Ser.: Vol. 31). 1980. lib. bdg. 198.00 (ISBN 0-8240-2930-5). Garland Pub.

--La Muette De Portici, 2 vols. Grossett, Philip & Rosen, Charles, eds. LC 76-49211. (Early Romantic Opera Ser.: Vol. 30). 1980. Set. lib. bdg. 198.00 (ISBN 0-8240-2929-1). Garland Pub.

Auber, Peter. Analysis of the Constitution of the East-India Company & of the Laws Passed by the Parliament for the Government of Their Affairs, at Home & Abroad, 2 vols. (With suppl). 1966. Repr. of 1828 ed. Set. 57.50 (ISBN 0-8337-0121-5). B Franklin.

Auberlen, Eckhard. The Commonwealth of Wit: The Writer's Image & His Strategies of Self-Representation in Elizabethan Literature. (Studies & Texts in English: No. 5). 296p. (Orig.). 1984. pap. write for info. (Pub. by G N Verlag Germany). Benjamins North Am.

Auberon, Reginald. The Nineteen Hundreds. 1979. Repr. of 1922 ed. lib. bdg. 35.00 (ISBN 0-8492-0096-2). R West.

Aubert & Goubet. Cathedrales Abbatiales, Collegiales et Prieures Romans en France. 153.25 (ISBN 0-685-34010-4). French & Eur.

--Cathedrales et Tresors Gothiques en France. 153.25 (ISBN 0-685-34011-2). French & Eur.

Aubert, Alvin. Against the Blues. pap. 2.00 (ISBN 0-910296-73-1). Broadside.

Aubert, Charles. Art of Pantomime. LC 68-56484. (Illus.). 1969. Repr. of 1927 ed. 20.00 (ISBN 0-405-08226-6, Pub. by Blom). Ayer Co Pubs.

Aubert, Claude & Frapa, Pierre. Hunger & Health. 192p. 1985. 14.95 (ISBN 0-87857-549-9). Rodale Pr Inc.

Aubert, H. & Pinta, M. Trace Elements in Soils. (Developments in Soil Science: Vol. 7). 396p. 1977. 89.50 (ISBN 0-444-41511-4). Elsevier.

Aubert, Henri. Diccionario de Mitologia. 238p. (Span.). 1961. 14.95 (ISBN 0-686-56710-2, S-33055). French & Eur.

Aubert, J. J., jt. ed. see Preparata, G.

Aubert, Jim. Baker's Dozen. 12p. 1983. pap. 1.00 (ISBN 0-686-46859-7). Samisdat.

Aubert, K. E., ed. see Scandinavian Congress - 15th - Oslo - 1968.

Aubert, Louis. Reconstruction of Europe. 1925. 39.50x (ISBN 0-686-83724-X). Elliots Bks.

Aubert, Maitre. Bolshevism's Terrible Record: An Indictment. 1976. lib. bdg. 59.95 (ISBN 0-8490-1524-3). Gordon Pr.

Aubert, Roger. Christian Centuries: Church in a Secularized Society, Vol. 5. LC 78-53496. 820p. 1978. 19.95 (ISBN 0-8091-0244-7). Paulist Pr.

--Le Problem de L'acte de Foi: Donnees Traditionnelles et Resultants des Controverses Recentes. 1978. Repr. of 1958 ed. lib. bdg. 85.00 (ISBN 0-8492-0092-X). R West.

--Prophets in the Church. LC 68-57877. (Concilium Ser.: Vol. 37). 160p. 1964. 6.95 (ISBN 0-8091-0120-3). Paulist Pr.

--Sacralization & Secularization. LC 76-96949. (Concilium Ser.: Vol. 47). 190p. 6.95 (ISBN 0-8091-0128-9). Paulist Pr.

Aubert, Roger & Van Cauwenberg. Dictionnaire d'Histoire et du Geographie Ecclesiastiques, 16 vols. (Fr.). Set. pap. 1795.00 (ISBN 0-686-56903-2, M-6014). French & Eur.

Aubert, Roger, ed. Historical Investigations. LC 66-29260. (Concilium Ser.: Vol. 17). 196p. 1966. 6.95 (ISBN 0-8091-0063-0). Paulist Pr.

--Historical Problems of Church Renewal. LC 65-26792. (Concilium Ser.: Vol. 7). 196p. 1965. 6.95 (ISBN 0-8091-0064-9). Paulist Pr.

--Progress & Decline in the History of Church Renewal. LC 67-30136. (Concilium Ser.: Vol. 27). 191p. 1967. 6.95 (ISBN 0-8091-0119-X). Paulist Pr.

Aubert, Vilhelm. The Hidden Society. LC 80-18939. (Social Science Classics Ser.). 359p. 1982. pap. 12.95 (ISBN 0-87855-730-X). Transaction Bks.

--In Search of Law. 186p. 1983. 27.50 (ISBN 0-318-02909-X). Biblio Dist.

--In Search of Law: Sociological Approaches to Law. LC 82-24491. 186p. 1983. text ed. 28.50 (ISBN 0-389-20385-8, 07260). B&N Imports.

Aubert De Gaspe, Philippe J. Memoires par Philippe A. De Gaspe: Auteur des Anciens Canadiens. 35.00 (ISBN 0-384-02310-X). Johnson Repr.

Aubert de la Chenaye-Desbois, Francais. Dictionnaire de la Noblesse, 10 vols. 9800p. (Fr.). 1978. Set. 155.00 (ISBN 0-686-56904-0, M-6015). French & Eur.

Aubery, Ronald. A Royal Chef's Notebook. 160p. 1980. 29.00x (ISBN 0-905418-28-X, Pub. by Gresham England). State Mutual Bk.

Aubignac, Francois H. The Whole Art of the Stage. LC 68-21218. 33.00 (ISBN 0-405-08227-4, Pub. by Blom). Ayer Co Pubs.

Aubigne, Theodore A., jt. auth. see Merimee, Proper.

Aubin, tr. see De Liguori, Alphonse.

Aubin, Albert K., ed. The French in Rhode Island: A History. (Ethnic Heritage Ser.). (Illus.). 52p. (Orig.). 1981. pap. 3.00 (ISBN 0-917012-54-2). RI Pubns Soc.

Aubin, E. Morocco of Today. 1977. lib. bdg. 59.95 (ISBN 0-8490-2283-5). Gordon Pr.

Aubin, J. P. Explicit Methods of Optimization. 300p. 1984. 44.00 (ISBN 0-9912000-0-4, Pub. by Gauthier-Villars FR). Heyden.

--Mathematical Methods of Game & Economic Theory. 2nd ed. (Studies in Mathematics & Its Applications: Vol. 7). 616p. 1982. 98.00 (ISBN 0-444-85184-4, North-Holland). Elsevier.

Aubin, J. P. & Cellina, A. Differential Inclusions: Set-Valued Maps & Viability Theory. LC 84-1327. (Grundlehren der Mathematischen Wissenschaften: Vol. 264). (Illus.). 350p. 1984. 44.00 (ISBN 0-387-13105-1). Springer-Verlag.

Aubin, J. P. & Vinter, R. B. Convex Analysis & Optimization. (Research Notes in Mathematics Ser.: No. 57). 240p. 1982. pap. text ed. 22.95 (ISBN 0-273-08547-6). Pitman Pub MA.

Aubin, J. P., et al, eds. Annals of the CEREMADE: Mathematical Techniques of Optimization, Control, & Decision. 223p. 1982. text ed. 27.00x (ISBN 0-8176-3032-5). Birkhauser.

Aubin, Jean-Pierre. Applied Abstract Analysis. LC 77-2382. (Pure & Applied Mathematics Ser.). 263p. 1977. 47.50x (ISBN 0-471-02146-6, Pub. by Wiley-Interscience). Wiley.

--Applied Functional Analysis. LC 78-20896. (Pure & Applied Mathematics Ser.). 423p. 1979. 48.50x (ISBN 0-471-02149-0, Pub. by Wiley-Interscience). Wiley.

--Approximation of Elliptic Boundary-Value Problems. LC 79-26276. 386p. 1980. Repr. of 1972 ed. lib. bdg. 26.00 (ISBN 0-89874-077-0). Krieger.

Aubin, Jean-Pierre & Ekeland, Ivar. Applied Nonlinear Analysis. (Pure & Applied Mathematics Ser.: 1237). 518p. 1984. 47.50x (ISBN 0-471-05998-6, Pub. by Wiley-Interscience). Wiley.

Aubin, Michel & Picard, Philippe. Homeopathy for Doctor & Patient. 224p. 1982. 32.00x (ISBN 0-906798-21-3, Pub. by Ashgrove Pr England). State Mutual Bk.

Aubin, Penelope see Haywood, Eliza.

Aubin, Pierre & Cotter, George. Agencies for Project Assistance: Sources of Support for Small Church & or Lag Sponsored Projects in Africa, Asia, Latin America & the Pacific. 2nd ed. (Illus.). 330p. 1984. pap. 50.00 (ISBN 0-913671-03-7). Mission Proj Serv.

Aubin, Robert A. Topographical Poetry in Eighteenth Century England. (MLA Rev. Fund Ser.). 1936. 32.00 (ISBN 0-527-03800-8). Kraus Repr.

Aubin, T. Nonlinear Analysis on Manifolds: Monge-Ampere Equations. (Grundlehren der mathematischen Wiszenschaften: Vol. 252). 204p. 1983. 37.50 (ISBN 0-387-90704-1). Springer-Verlag.

Aublet, Henri, jt. auth. see Marcenac, Louis N.

Aublet, J. B. Histoire des Plantes de la Guiane Francaise, 4 vols. bd. in one. (Historia Naturalis Classica Ser.: No. 100). 1977. Repr. of 1775 ed. lib. bdg. 175.00x (ISBN 3-7682-1105-3). Lubrecht & Cramer.

Auboyer, J., et al. Buddha: A Pictorial History of His Life & Legend. (Illus.). 55.00 (ISBN 0-89410-500-0, Pub. by UBSPD India). Three Continents.

Auboyer, Jeannine. Buddha: A Pictorial History of His Life & Legacy. Marans, Nelly, tr. from Fr. LC 83-10140. (Illus.). 272p. 1983. 100.00 (ISBN 0-8245-0588-3). Crossroad NY.

Aubrey, Angelo C. Sketches of Travel in Oregon & Idaho. Date not set. Repr. of 1866 ed. price not set. Ye Galleon.

Aubrey, Crispin, ed. Nukespeak: The Media & the Bomb. 1982. 35.00x (ISBN 0-906890-27-6, Pub. by Comedia England); pap. 25.00x (ISBN 0-906890-26-8). State Mutual Bk.

Aubrey, Crispin, et al. Here is the Other News: Challenges to the Local Commercial Press. 30.00x (ISBN 0-686-45536-3, Pub. by Comedia England). State Mutual Bk.

Aubrey, Edmund. The Case of the Murdered President: In Which Sherlock Holmes Applies His Famed Powers of Detection to History's Greatest Unsolved Crime-the Assassination of John F. Kennedy. 224p. 1983. pap. 8.95 (ISBN 0-312-92083-0). Congdon & Weed.

Aubrey, Frank. A Queen of Atlantis: Romance of the Caribbean Sea. LC 74-15949. (Science Fiction Ser). 394p. 1975. Repr. of 1899 ed. 30.00x (ISBN 0-405-06275-3). Ayer Co Pubs.

Aubrey, Henry G. Coexistence: Economic Challenge & Response. LC 75-28675. 323p. 1976. Repr. of 1961 ed. lib. bdg. 22.50x (ISBN 0-8371-8471-1, AUCO). Greenwood.

--The Dollar in World Affairs: An Essay in International Financial Policy. LC 82-6086. xii, 295p. 1982. Repr. of 1964 ed. lib. bdg. 35.00x (ISBN 0-313-23577-5, AUDW). Greenwood.

Aubrey, John. Aubrey's Brief Lives. Dick, Oliver L., ed. 1982. pap. 6.95 (ISBN 0-14-043079-2). Penguin.
--Brief Lives. (Bookmarks). 332p. 1983. pap. text ed. 8.95 (ISBN 0-85115-206-6, Pub. by Boydell & Brewer). Academy Chi Pubs.
--Brief Lives & Other Selective Writings. Powell, Anthony, intro. by. 1981. Repr. of 1949 ed. lib. bdg. 30.00 (ISBN 0-89987-027-9). Darby Bks.
--Brief Lives (Modern English Version) Barber, Richard, ed. LC 82-24416. 336p. 1983. text ed. 25.00x (ISBN 0-389-20366-1, 07239). B&N Imports.
--Monumenta Britannica. Fowles, John, ed. 1982. 125.00 (ISBN 0-316-05908-0). Little.
--Remaines of Gentilisme & Judaisme, Sixteen Hundred Eighty-Six to Eighty-Seven. Britten, James, ed. (Folk-Lore Society, London, Monograph Ser.: Vol. 4). pap. 29.00 (ISBN 0-317-16394-9). Kraus Repr.
--Three Prose Works. Buchanan-Brown, John, ed. Incl. Miscelanies; Remaines of Gentilisme & Judaisme; Observations. LC 77-183306. (Centaur Classics Ser.). 624p. 1972. 35.00x (ISBN 0-8093-0567-4). S Ill U Pr.
--Three Prose Works. Buchanan & Brown, eds. 1983. 70.00x (ISBN 0-900000-21-X, Pub. by Centaur Pr England). State Mutual Bk.
Aubrey, John, jt. auth. see Washburn, W-Ilcomb E.
Aubrey, Paul & Chiltern, Crispin, eds. Nineteen-Eighty-Four in 1984: Autonomy, Control & Communication. (Comedia Social Issues Ser.). 160p. 1984. pap. 7.95 (ISBN 0-906890-43-8, Dist. by Scribner); 15.00 (ISBN 0-906890-42-X). M Boyars.
Aubrey, Philip. The Defeat of James Stuart's Armada, 1692. (Illus.). 192p. 1979. 17.50x (ISBN 0-8476-6156-3). Rowman.
Aubrey, Roger F. Career Development Needs of Thirteen-Year Olds. 82p. 1978. pap. text ed. 5.80 (ISBN 0-911547-11-8, 72216W34). Am Assn Coun Dev.
Aubrey, Vickey. Chinese Brush Painting for Beginners. LC 81-19651. (Illus.). 64p. (gr. 2 up). 1982. 9.95 (ISBN 0-8149-0851-9). Vanguard.
Aubrey, Wilson, jt. auth. see Stacey, Nicholas A.
Aubry, Arthur S., Jr. The Officer in the Small Department. (Illus.). 416p. 1961. photycopy ed. 40.50x (ISBN 0-398-00071-9). C C Thomas.
Aubry, Arthur S., Jr. & Caputo, Rudolph R. Criminal Interrogation. 3rd ed. 464p. 1980. 45.75x (ISBN 0-398-03978-X). C C Thomas.
Aubry, Joseph. The Renewal of Our Salesian Life, 2 vols. Bedard, Paul & Whitehead, Kenneth, trs. from Ital. Orig. Title: Rinnovare la Nostra Vita Salesiana. 426p. 1984. pap. text ed. write for info. (ISBN 0-89944-071-1); Vol. I:The Active Apostolate. pap. 5.00; Vol. II:The Salesian Community & Family. pap. 5.50 (ISBN 0-89944-077-0). Don Bosco Multimedia.
--Savio: A Study Guide. Boenzi, Joe, tr. from Ital. LC 79-50460. (Orig.). 1979. pap. 2.75 (ISBN 0-89944-038-X). Don Bosco Multimedia.
Aubry, Joseph, ed. The Spiritual Writings of St. John Bosco. Caselli, Joseph, tr. from Italian. LC 83-71820. 412p. 1984. pap. 12.95 (ISBN 0-89944-049-5). Don Bosco Multimedia.
Aubry, M. P. Handbook of Cenozoic Calcareous Nannoplankton, 7 vols. 1983. 50.00 ea. Am Mus Natl Hist.
Aubry, Pierre. Cent Motets du XIIIe siecle, 3 vols. (Illus.). 540p. (Fr.). 1964. pap. 125.00x (ISBN 0-8450-0001-2). Broude.
--Trouveres & Troubadours: A Popular Treatise. Aveling, Claude, tr. LC 68-59029. Repr. of 1914 ed. 20.00 (ISBN 0-8154-0265-1). Cooper Sq.
Aubry, Pierre, et al. Melanges de Musicologie Critique, 4 vols. Incl. Vol. 1. La Musicologie Medievale, Histoire et Methodes. pap. 32.50x (ISBN 0-8450-2511-2); Vol. 2. Adam de Saint-Victor, les Proses Texte et Musique. pap. 42.50x (ISBN 0-8450-2512-0); Vol. 3. Lais et Descorts Francais du XIIIe Siecle, Texte et Musique. pap. 35.00x (ISBN 0-8450-2513-9); Vol. 4. Les Plus Anciens Monuments de la Musique Francaise. pap. 32.50x (ISBN 0-8450-2514-7). (Illus., Repr. of 1900-1905 ed). 1969. pap. 142.50x set (ISBN 0-8450-2510-4). Broude.
Auburn, F. M. Antarctic Law & Politics. LC 81-48081. (Illus.). 384p. 1982. 35.00x (ISBN 0-253-30749-X). Ind U Pr.
Auburn, Mark S. Sheridan's Comedies: Their Contexts & Achievements. LC 77-7205. x, 221p. 1977. 18.50x (ISBN 0-8032-0914-2). U of Nebr Pr.
Auburn, Mark S., ed. see Dryden, John.
Aubyn, Fiona St. see St. Aubyn, Fiona & Wagenvoord, James.
Aubyn, G. R. St. see Barker, W. A. & St. Aubyn, G. R.
Aubyn, Giles St. see St. Aubyn, Giles.
Aucamp, A. J. Bilingual Education & Nationalism with Special Reference to South Africa. Cordasco, Francesco, ed. LC 77-90405. (Bilingual-Bicultural Education in the U. S. Ser.). 1978. Repr. of 1926 ed. lib. bdg. 24.50x (ISBN 0-405-11074-X). Ayer Co Pubs.
Auch, Ron. Prayer Can Change Your Marriage. Dudley, Cliff, ed. LC 84-61916. 120p. (Orig.). 1985. pap. 5.95 (ISBN 0-89221-118-0). New Leaf.
Auchampaugh, Philip C. James Buchanan & His Cabinet on the Eve of Secession. 1965. Repr. of 1926 ed. 10.00x (ISBN 0-910324-01-8). Canner.
Auchard, John, jt. ed. see Leary, Lewis.
Auchincloss, Louis. The Book Class. 224p. 1984. 14.95 (ISBN 0-395-36138-9). HM.
--The Cat & the King. 192p. 1981. 10.95 (ISBN 0-395-30225-0). HM.
--The Country Cousin. 1978. 8.95 (ISBN 0-395-26687-4). HM.
--The Dark Lady. 1977. 8.95 (ISBN 0-395-25402-7). HM.
--Ellen Glasgow. LC 64-63338. (University of Minnesota Pamphlets on American Writers Ser.: No. 33). pap. 20.00 (ISBN 0-317-29467-9, 2055929). Bks Demand UMI.
--Embezzler. 1966. 5.95 (ISBN 0-395-07362-6). HM.
--Exit Lady Masham. 169p. 1983. 13.95 (ISBN 0-395-34388-7). HM.
--False Dawn: Women in the Age of the Sun King. LC 82-45620. 192p. 1984. 14.95 (ISBN 0-385-18021-7). Doubleday.
--Henry Adams. (Pamphlets on American Writers Ser.: No. 93). (Orig.). 1971. pap. 1.25x (ISBN 0-8166-0596-3, MPAW93). U of Minn Pr.
--Honorable Men. 288p. 1985. 15.95 (ISBN 0-395-38812-0). HM.
--The House of the Prophet. (General Ser.). 1980. lib. bdg. 14.95 (ISBN 0-8161-3133-3, Large Print Bks). G K Hall.
--The House of the Prophet. 1981. pap. 3.95 (ISBN 0-395-30520-9). HM.
--The House of the Prophet. 1980. 10.95 (ISBN 0-395-29084-8). HM.
--Narcissa & Other Fables. 1983. 13.95 (ISBN 0-395-33114-5). HM.
--The Partners. 1974. 6.95 (ISBN 0-395-18279-4). HM.
--Pioneers & Caretakers: A Study of Nine American Women Novelists. LC 65-17016. 1965. 13.95x (ISBN 0-8166-0344-8). U of Minn Pr.
--Pioneers & Caretakers: A Study of Nine American Women Novelists. (Non-Fiction Ser.). 216p. 1985. pap. 7.95 (ISBN 0-8398-2882-9, Gregg). G K Hall.
--Quotations from Henry James. LC 84-10428. 176p. 1985. text ed. 30.00x (ISBN 0-8139-1037-4). U Pr of Va.
--The Rector of Justin. 1980. pap. 3.95 (ISBN 0-395-29179-8). HM.
--Reflections of a Jacobite. LC 74-156968. Repr. of 1961 ed. lib. bdg. 22.50x (ISBN 0-678-03571-7). Kelley.
--Romantic Egoists. LC 73-106666. Repr. of 1954 ed. lib. bdg. 24.75 (ISBN 0-8371-3418-8, AUEG). Greenwood.
--Sybil. LC 75-108840. 284p. 1972. Repr. of 1952 ed. lib. bdg. 24.75x (ISBN 0-8371-3728-4, AUSY). Greenwood.
--Three "Perfect Novels" - & What They Have in Common. 1981. ltd. ed. 10.00 (ISBN 0-89723-025-6). Bruccoli.
--Watchfires. 368p. 1982. 13.95 (ISBN 0-395-31546-8). HM.
--Writer's Capital. 1979. pap. 4.95 (ISBN 0-395-28518-6). HM.
Auchincloss, William S. Slide Value & Link Motions. 1983. pap. 9.95 (ISBN 0-917914-13-9). Lindsay Pubns.
Auchinleck, Gilbert. A History of the War of 1812. (Americana Ser.). (Illus.). 1972. 11.95 (ISBN 0-916988-00-7). Pendragon Ltd.
Auchmuty, A. C., ed. Economics & Philosophy of Henry George. 109p. 1980. pap. 1.00 (ISBN 0-911312-23-4). Schalkenbach.
Auchmuty, J. Lecky: A Biographical & Critical Essay. 59.95 (ISBN 0-8490-0494-2). Gordon Pr.
Auchmuty, James A., Jr. Brothers of the Bible. LC 84-17510. 1985. pap. 4.50 (ISBN 0-8054-2254-4). Broadman.
Auchmuty, Margaret W. Churchill Fellows of Australia, 1966-1977. 93p. (Orig.). 1980. pap. text ed. 5.00 (ISBN 0-7081-1012-6, 1585, Pub. by ANUP Australia). Australia N U P.
Auchter, Terri. Almost Coping. LC 83-61876. (Illus.). 160p. 1983. pap. 2.95 (ISBN 0-931762-20-0). Phunn Pubs.
Auchterlonie, Paul & Safadi, Yasin H., eds. Union Catalogue of Arabic Serials & Newspapers in British Libraries. 164p. 1977. 26.00 (ISBN 0-7201-0636-2). Mansell.
Auciello, O. & Kelly, R. Modification of Surfaces. 1984. write for info. Elsevier.
Auciello, O. & Kelly, R., eds. Ion Bombardment Modification of Surfaces: Fundamentals & Applications. (Beam Modification of Materials Ser.: No. 1). 468p. 1984. 94.50 (ISBN 0-444-42365-6, I-308-84). Elsevier.
Auckett, Amelia D. Baby Massage: Parent-Child Bonding Through Touching. LC 82-2172. (Illus.). 128p. (Orig.). 1982. pap. 6.95 (ISBN 0-937858-07-2). Newmarket.
Auckland Art Gallery. Raymond McIntyre: A New Zealand Painter. (Illus.). 112p. 1984. 21.75 (ISBN 0-86863-051-9, Pub. by Heinemann Pub New Zealand). Intl Spec Bk.
Aucoin, James. Water in Nebraska: Use, Politics, Policies. LC 83-12512. (Illus.). xvi, 157p. 1984. 15.95 (ISBN 0-8032-1013-2). U of Nebr Pr.
Aucoin, Peter. The Politics & Management of Restraint in Government. 254p. 1981. pap. text ed. 17.95x (ISBN 0-920380-32-8, Pub. by Inst Res Pub Canada). Brookfield Pub Co.
Audacious Abby & Salutary Sam. Twenty-One Graceful Ways to Find Out If Your Partner Has Herpes. (Illus.). 32p. (Orig.). 1984. pap. 4.25 (ISBN 0-914597-00-0). Juno-West.
Audah, A. Q. Islam Between Ignorant Followers & Incapable Scholars. pap. 4.50 (ISBN 0-686-18505-6). Kazi Pubns.
Audah, Abdul Q. Al-Islam bain Jahl 'Abna'ihi wa Ajz Ulama'ihi. 79p. (Orig., Arabic.). 1980. pap. 1.55x (ISBN 0-939830-12-4, Pub. by IIFSO Kuwait). New Era Pubns MI.
Audah, Adbul Q. Islam Between Ignorant Followers & Incapable Scholars. 115p. (Orig.). pap. 2.50x (ISBN 0-939830-01-9, Pub. by IIFSO Kuwait). New Era Pubns MI.
Audax & Adams, Vyvyon. Men in Our Time. facs. ed. LC 70-99680. (Essay Index Reprint Ser). 1940. 20.00 (ISBN 0-8369-1389-2). Ayer Co Pubs.
Aude, Sapere, ed. The Chaldean Oracles. LC 78-58111. 1978. 10.00 (ISBN 0-935214-02-X). Heptangle.
Audebert, et al. Microsurgery in Infertility. (Illus.). 162p. (Eng. & Fr.). 1980. text ed. 55.00 (ISBN 88-212-0860-5, Pub. by Piccin Italy). J K Burgess.
Audebert, A., jt. ed. see Emperaire, J. C.
Audebert, A. J., jt. ed. see Hafez, E. S.
Audefroi Le Bastard. Die Lieder und Romanzen Des Audefroi le Bastard. LC 80-2159. Repr. of 1914 ed. 26.50 (ISBN 0-404-19021-9). AMS Pr.
Audemars, Pierre. And One for the Dead. 1981. 9.95 (ISBN 0-8027-5440-6). Walker & Co.
--And One for the Dead. (Scene of the Crime: No. 56). 1983. pap. 2.50 (ISBN 0-440-10442-4). Dell.
--The Bitter Path of Death. 1983. 11.95 (ISBN 0-8027-5484-8). Walker & Co.
--Now Dead Is Any Man. 184p. 1980. 9.95 (ISBN 0-8027-5422-8). Walker & Co.
--Now Dead Is Any Man. (British Mysteries Ser.). 1983. pap. 2.95 (ISBN 0-8027-3036-1). Walker & Co.
--Slay Me a Sinner. 188p. 1980. 9.95 (ISBN 0-8027-5417-1). Walker & Co.
--Slay Me a Sinner. (Scene of the Crime Ser.: No. 62). 1983. pap. 2.95 (ISBN 0-440-18191-7). Dell.
Auden, ed. see MacNeice, Louis.
Auden, C. How to Finance Your Company. 1977. 18.00x (ISBN 0-8464-0491-5). Beekman Pubs.
Auden, H. W. Greek Phrase Book: Based on the Writings of Thucydides, Xenophon, Demosthenes Plato. 122p. 1981. pap. text ed. 10.95x (ISBN 0-7156-1468-1, Pub. by Duckworth England). Biblio Dist.
Auden, W. H. City Without Walls. 1969. 7.95 (ISBN 0-394-40322-3). Random.
--The Double Man. LC 79-4323. 1979. Repr. of 1941 ed. lib. bdg. 27.50x (ISBN 0-313-21073-X, AUDM). Greenwood.
--Dyer's Hand & Other Essays. 1968. pap. 4.95 (ISBN 0-394-70418-5, V-418, Vin). Random.
--The Enchafed Flood. viii, 151p. 1979. 9.95x (ISBN 0-8139-0827-2); pap. 4.95x (ISBN 0-8139-0820-5). U Pr of Va.
--Epistle to a Godson & Other Poems. 1972. 10.95 (ISBN 0-394-48203-4). Random.
--Forewords & Afterwords. 1973. 19.95 (ISBN 0-394-48359-6). Random.
--Forewords & Afterwords. 1973. pap. 2.95 (ISBN 0-394-71887-9, Vin). Random.
--Homage to Clio. 1960. 15.00 (ISBN 0-394-40364-9). Random.
--The Platonic Blow & My Epitaph. 8p. 1985. pap. 5.00 (ISBN 0-914061-04-6). Orchises Pr.
--Secondary Worlds. 127p. 1985. pap. 6.95 (ISBN 0-571-13221-9). Faber & Faber.
--Selected Poems of W. H. Auden. Mendelson, Edward, ed. LC 78-55719. 1979. pap. 5.95 (ISBN 0-394-72506-9, V-506, Vin). Random.
--Thank You, Fog: Last Poems. LC 74-9049. 1974. 8.95 (ISBN 0-394-49496-2). Random.
Auden, W. H. & Garrett, John. The Poet's Tongue. 222p. 1981. Repr. of 1948 ed. lib. bdg. 35.00 (ISBN 0-89760-008-8). Telegraph Bks.
Auden, W. H. & Isherwood, Christopher. Journey to a War. LC 78-185634. (Illus.). 302p. 1972. Repr. of 1939 ed. lib. bdg. 21.50x (ISBN 0-374-90315-8). Octagon.
Auden, W. H. & Kallman, Chester. An Elizabethan Song Book. Greenberg, Noah, ed. 240p. 1968. pap. 8.95 (ISBN 0-571-08602-0). Faber & Faber.
Auden, W. H. & Kronenberger, Louis. The Viking Book of Aphorisms: A Personal Selection. 442p. 1981. pap. 6.95 (ISBN 0-14-005966-0). Penguin.
Auden, W. H., ed. The Oxford Book of Light Verse. 1979. pap. 8.95 (ISBN 0-19-881331-7, GB 401, GB). Oxford U Pr.
--Portable Greek Reader. (Viking Portable Library: No. 39). 1977. pap. 7.95 (ISBN 0-14-015039-0, P39). Penguin.
--The Selected Poetry & Prose of Byron. 1983. pap. 7.95 (ISBN 0-452-00658-9, Mer). NAL.
Auden, W. H. & Garrett, John, eds. The Poet's Tongue. LC 75-161942. 222p. 1935. Repr. 29.00x (ISBN 0-403-01326-7). Scholarly.
Auden, W. H. & Pearson, Norman H., eds. Poets of the English Language, Vol. 4: Romantic Poets. (Viking Portable Library: No. 52). 1977. pap. 7.95 (ISBN 0-14-015052-8, P52). Penguin.
Auden, W. H., ed. see Campion, Thomas.
Auden, W. H., jt. ed. see Greenberg, Noah.
Auden, W. H., ed. see Smith, Sydney.
Auden, W. H., tr. see Brecht, Bertolt.
Auden, W. H., tr. see Lagerkvist, Par.
Auden, W. H., tr. see Von Goethe, Johann W.
Auden, W. H., et al. Authors Take Sides on the Spanish Civil War. 59.95 (ISBN 0-87968-680-4). Gordon Pr.
--What I Believe. Booth, Mark, ed. 182p. 1984. 16.95 (ISBN 0-8245-0676-6); pap. 8.95 (ISBN 0-8245-0677-4). Crossroad NY.
Auden, W. H., et al, trs. St. John Perse: Collected Poems, Complete Bilingual Edition. rev. ed. LC 82-47633. (Bollingen Ser., No. 87). 1982. 60.00 (ISBN 0-691-09949-9). Princeton U Pr.
Auden, W. H., et al, trs. see Voznesensky, Andrei.
Auden, Wystan H. Look, Stranger! LC 83-45406. Repr. of 1936 ed. 19.00 (ISBN 0-404-20011-7). AMS Pr.
--Making, Knowing, & Judging: An Inaugural Lecture Delivered Before the University of Oxford on 11 June 1956. LC 83-45407. Repr. of 1956 ed. 16.00 (ISBN 0-404-20012-5). AMS Pr.
--The Orators: An English Study. LC 77-131613. 116p. 1932. Repr. 29.00x (ISBN 0-403-00500-0). Scholarly.
Auden, Wysten H. & Isherwood, Christopher. On the Frontier: A Melodrama in Three Acts. LC 75-41011. (BCL Ser.: No. 2). Repr. of 1938 ed. 12.50 (ISBN 0-404-14638-4). AMS Pr.
Audesirk, Gerald J. & Audesirk, Teresa E. Biology: Life on Earth. 1985. text ed. write for info. (ISBN 0-02-304690-2). Macmillan.
Audesirk, Teresa E., jt. auth. see Audesirk, Gerald J.
Audet, Thelma & Dreizen, Laverne. Medical Assistant's Examination Review. 3rd ed. 1984. pap. text ed. 14.95 (ISBN 0-87488-490-X). Med Exam.
Audette, Vicki. Vicki Audette's Bargain Hunter's Guide to the Twin Cities. 197p. (Orig.). 1984. pap. 6.95 (ISBN 0-931674-06-9). Waldman Hse Pr.
Audi, Michael. The Interpretation of Quantum Mechanics. LC 73-78663. pap. 53.50 (ISBN 0-317-08073-3, 2019953). Bks Demand UMI.
Audiberti, Jacques. L' Abhumanisme. 232p. 1955. 3.95 (ISBN 0-686-54479-X). French & Eur.
--Ange Aux Entrailles. 164p. 1964. 7.95 (ISBN 0-686-54480-3). French & Eur.
--Le Cavalier Seul. 246p. 1955. 9.95 (ISBN 0-686-54481-1). French & Eur.
--Cent Jours. 288p. 1950. 4.95 (ISBN 0-686-54482-X). French & Eur.
--Coeur a Cuivre. 288p. 1950. 5.95 (ISBN 0-686-54483-8). French & Eur.
--Dimanche m'attend. 296p. 1965. 7.95 (ISBN 0-686-54484-6). French & Eur.
--L' Empire et la Trappe. 192p. 1969. 9.95 (ISBN 0-686-54485-4). French & Eur.
--Les Enfants Naturels. 126p. 1956. 6.95 (ISBN 0-686-54486-2). French & Eur.
--Entretiens Avec Georges Charbonnier. 176p. 1965. 5.95 (ISBN 0-686-54487-0). French & Eur.
--La Hobereaute. 9.95 (ISBN 0-686-54488-9). French & Eur.
--Les Jardins et les Fleuves. 400p. 1954. 6.95 (ISBN 0-686-54490-0). French & Eur.
--La Logeuse. 9.95 (ISBN 0-686-54491-9). French & Eur.
--Le Maitre de Milan. 264p. 1950. 6.95 (ISBN 0-686-54492-7). French & Eur.
--Marie Dubois. 288p. 1952. 4.95 (ISBN 0-686-54493-5). French & Eur.
--Les Medecins de Snot pas des Plombiers. 200p. 1949. 12.95 (ISBN 0-686-54494-3). French & Eur.
--Moliere. 144p. 1973. 7.95 (ISBN 0-686-54495-1). French & Eur.
--Monorail. 344p. 1964. 9.95 (ISBN 0-686-54496-X). French & Eur.
--L' Opera du Monde. 360p. 1947. 8.95 (ISBN 0-686-54497-8). French & Eur.
--L' Ouvre-Boite: Colloque Abhumaniste. 4.95 (ISBN 0-686-54498-6). French & Eur.
--Poesies, 1934-1943: La Pluie sur les Boulevards, Des Tonnes de Semences, Toujours. 266p. 1976. 19.95 (ISBN 0-686-54499-4). French & Eur.
--La Poupee. 112p. 1969. 3.95 (ISBN 0-686-54500-1). French & Eur.
--Quoat-Quoat. 9.95 (ISBN 0-686-54501-X). French & Eur.
--Race des Hommes: Avec: L'Empire et la Trappe. 224p. 1968. 4.95 (ISBN 0-686-54502-8). French & Eur.
--Rempart. 144p. 1953. 3.95 (ISBN 0-686-54503-6). French & Eur.
--Theatre, Vol. 4. 14.95 (ISBN 0-686-54507-9). French & Eur.
--Theatre: Avec: La Logeuse, Opera Parle, Le Oullou, Aetanima, Vol. 3. 264p. 1956. 6.95 (ISBN 0-686-54506-0). French & Eur.
--Theatre: Avec: Pucelle, La Fete Noire, Les Naturels du Borelais, Vol. 2. 312p. 1970. 8.95 (ISBN 0-686-54505-2). French & Eur.
--Theatre: Avec: Quoat-Quoat, L'Ampelour, Les Femmes de Boeuf, La Mal Court, Vol. 1. 200p. 1970. 6.95 (ISBN 0-686-54504-4). French & Eur.

--Les Tombeaux Ferment Mal. 240p. 1963. 5.95 (ISBN 0-686-54509-5). French & Eur.

--Le Victorieux. 242p. 1947. 4.95 (ISBN 0-686-54510-9). French & Eur.

Audiganne, Armand. Les Populations ouvrieres et les industries de la France, 2 Vols. 2nd ed. (Research & Source Works Ser., History, Economics & Social Science). 1971. Repr. of 1860 ed. lib. bdg. 48.00 (ISBN 0-8337-0124-X). B Franklin.

Audio-Forum. Learner's Guide for Laer at Tale Dansk. 46p. 1984. pap. 95.00x plus 6, 1 hour audio cassettes (ISBN 0-88432-127-4, DA40). J Norton Pubs.

Audio-Forum, et al. Learner's Guide for Norsk for Utlendinger 1. 126p. (Orig.). 1985. pap. 5.95 (ISBN 0-88432-128-2, NW99). J Norton Pubs.

Audit Bureau of Circulations. Scientific Space Selection. LC 75-22798. (America in Two Centuries Ser). 1976. Repr. of 1921 ed. 15.00x (ISBN 0-405-07669-X). Ayer Co Pubs.

Audouard, Yvan, jt. auth. see Pagnol, Marcel.

Audouin-Dubreuil, Louis, jt. auth. see Haardt, Georges M.

Audoux, Marguerite. Valserine & Other Stories. facsimile ed. LC 73-110178. (Short Story Index Reprint Ser.). 1912. 18.00 (ISBN 0-8369-3329-X). Ayer Co Pubs.

Audouze, J., et al, eds. Diffuse Matter in Galaxies. 1983. lib. bdg. 39.50 (ISBN 90-277-1626-9, Pub. by Reidel Holland). Kluwer Academic.

Audouze, Jean & Tran Thanh Van, Jean. Formation & Evolution of Galaxies & Large Structures in the Universe. 1984. lib. bdg. 58.00 (ISBN 90-277-1685-4, Pub. by Reidel Holland). Kluwer Academic.

Audouze, Jean & Vauclair, Sylvie. An Introduction to Nuclear Astrophysics: The Formation & Evolution of Matter in the Universe. (Geophysics & Astrophysics Monographs: No. 18). 1980. lib. bdg. 39.50 (ISBN 90-277-1012-0, Pub. by Reidel Holland); pap. 21.00 (ISBN 90-277-1053-8, Pub. by Reidel Holland). Kluwer Academic.

Audouze, Jean, ed. CNO Isotopes in Astrophysics. (Astrophysics & Space Science Lib. Ser.: No. 67). 1977. lib. bdg. 29.00 (ISBN 90-277-0807-X, Pub. by Reidel Holland). Kluwer Academic.

Audouze, Jean & Israel, Guy, eds. The Cambridge Atlas of Astronomy. (Illus.). 432p. 1985. 75.00 (ISBN 0-521-26369-7). Cambridge U Pr.

Audra, E. La Influence Francaise Dans L'oeuvre de Pope. (Fr.). 1973. Repr. of 1931 ed. 75.00 (ISBN 0-8274-1795-0). R West.

--Les Traductions Francaises De Pope. (1717-1825) Etude De Bibliographie. 1979. Repr. of 1931 ed. lib. bdg. 65.00 (ISBN 0-8495-0201-2). Arden Lib.

Audra, R. Ashley, tr. see Bergson, Henri.

Audretsch, David B. The Effectiveness of Antitrust Policy Towards Horizontal Mergers. Bateman, Fred, ed. LC 83-6985. (Research in Business Economics & Public Policy Ser.: No. 1). 164p. 1983. 39.95 (ISBN 0-8357-1434-9). UMI Res Pr.

Audretsch, David B., jt. ed. see Kindleberger, Charles P.

Audretsch, H. Supervision in European Community Law: Observance by the Member States of Their Treaty Obligations - A Treatise on International & Supranational Supervision. 304p. 1978. 61.75 (ISBN 0-444-85037-6, North-Holland). Elsevier.

Audsley, G., jt. auth. see Audsley, W.

Audsley, G. A. Duo-Art Aeolian Pipe-Organ. (Illus.). 1921. pap. 7.50x (ISBN 0-913746-16-9). Organ Lit.

--Organ-Stops & Their Artistic Registration. LC 77-94542. 1978. Repr. of 1921 ed. lib. bdg. 30.00 (ISBN 0-89341-400-X). Longwood Pub Group.

Audsley, George A. The Art of Organ Building, 2 vols. Incl. Vol. 1. Proem. (Illus.). x, 600p. 19.95 (ISBN 0-486-21314-5); Vol. 2. Specifications of Organs. (Illus.). iv, 750p. 19.95 (ISBN 0-486-21315-3). Dover.

--Art of Organ Building, 2 vols. (Illus.). Set. 32.00 (ISBN 0-8446-1034-8). Peter Smith.

--Temple of Tone. LC 79-108119. (BCL Ser.: No. 1). (Illus.). 1970. Repr. of 1925 ed. lib. bdg. 19.50 (ISBN 0-404-00417-2). AMS Pr.

Audsley, W. & Audsley, G. Designs & Patterns from Historic Ornament. Orig. Title: Outlines of Ornament in the Leading Styles. 1968. pap. 5.00 (ISBN 0-486-21931-3). Dover.

Audubon, John J. Audubon & His Journals, 2 vols. Audubon, Maria R., ed. LC 75-38340. (Select Bibliographies Reprint Ser.). 1897. Set. 56.50 (ISBN 0-8369-6660-0). Ayer Co Pubs.

--Audubon & His Journals, 2 Vols. Audubon, Maria, ed. (Illus.). Set. 32.00 (ISBN 0-8446-1566-8). Peter Smith.

--Audubon's Birds of America Coloring Book. 48p. 1974. pap. 2.25 (ISBN 0-486-23049-X). Dover.

--Birds of America. (Illus.). (gr. 5 up). 1947. 29.95 (ISBN 0-02-504440-0). Macmillan.

--Birds of America, 7 vols. (Illus.). Repr. of 1840 ed. Set. 73.50 (ISBN 0-8446-1567-6); 10.50ea. Peter Smith.

--The Birds of America. 468p. 1985. 39.95 (ISBN 0-02-504450-8). MacMillan.

--Delineations of American Scenery & Character. LC 70-125730. (American Environmental Studies). 1970. Repr. of 1926 ed. 24.50 (ISBN 0-405-02655-2). Ayer Co Pubs.

--The Eighteen Twenty-Six Journal of John James Audubon. Ford, Alice, ed. (Illus.). 1967. 22.95x (ISBN 0-8061-0731-6). U of Okla Pr.

--Synopsis of the Birds of North America. Repr. of 1839 ed. 22.00 (ISBN 0-384-02343-6). Johnson Repr.

Audubon, John J. & Bachman, John. The Quadrupeds of North America, 3 vols. LC 73-17796. (Natural Sciences of America Ser.). (Illus.). 1406p. 1974. Repr. Set. 99.00x (ISBN 0-405-05706-7); Vol. 1. 33.00x (ISBN 0-405-05707-5); Vol. 2. 33.00x (ISBN 0-405-05708-3); Vol. 3. 33.00x (ISBN 0-405-05709-1). Ayer Co Pubs.

Audubon, John Woodhouse. Audubon's Western Journal, 1849-1850. LC 83-17860. (Illus.). 249p. 1984. 22.50x (ISBN 0-8165-0840-2); pap. 8.50 (ISBN 0-8165-0841-0). U of Ariz Pr.

Audubon, Maria, ed. see Audubon, John J.

Audubon, Maria R., ed. see Audubon, John J.

Audubon Society. The Audubon Society Field Guide to North American Wildflowers. Incl. Eastern Region. LC 78-20383. 13.50 (ISBN 0-394-50432-1); Western. LC 78-20384. 13.50 (ISBN 0-394-50431-3). (Illus.). 1979. Knopf.

--Encyclopedia of Animal Life. Farrand, John, Jr., ed. (Illus.). 1982. 45.00 (ISBN 0-517-54657-4, C N Potter Bks). Crown.

Audubon Society & Bull, John. The Audubon Society Guides to North American Birds: Eastern Region. 1977. 13.50 (ISBN 0-394-41405-5). Knopf.

Audubon Society & Chesterman, Charles W. The Audubon Society Field Guide to North American Rocks & Minerals. LC 78-54893. (Illus.). 1979. 13.50 (ISBN 0-394-50269-8). Knopf.

Audubon Society & King, F. Wayne. The Audubon Society Field Guide to North American Reptiles & Amphibians. LC 79-2217. (Illus.). 1979. flexible bdg. 13.50 (ISBN 0-394-50824-6). Knopf.

Audubon Society & Lawrence, Susannah. The Audubon Society Field Guide to the Natural Places of the Mid-Atlantic States: Coastal, Vol. I. LC 83-21417. (Illus.). 330p. 1984. pap. 9.95 (ISBN 0-394-72279-5). Knopf.

--The Audubon Society Field Guide to the Natural Places of the Mid-Atlantic States: Inland, Vol. II. LC 83-21417. (Illus.). 355p. 1984. pap. 9.95 (ISBN 0-394-72280-9). Knopf.

Audubon Society & Lincoff, Gary H. The Audubon Society Field Guide to North American Mushrooms. LC 81-80827. (Illus.). 864p. 1981. 13.50 (ISBN 0-394-51992-2). Knopf.

Audubon Society & Little, Elbert L., Jr. Audubon Field Guide to North American Trees. Western ed. 1980. 13.50 (ISBN 0-394-50761-4). Knopf.

--Audubon Field Guide to North American Trees: Eastern Edition. 1980. 13.50 (ISBN 0-394-50760-6). Knopf.

Audubon Society & Meinkoth, Norman A. The Audubon Society Field Guide to North American Seashore Creatures. LC 81-80828. (Illus.). 1981. 13.50 (ISBN 0-394-51993-0). Knopf.

Audubon Society & Milne, Lorus. The Audubon Society Field Guide to North American Insects & Spiders. LC 80-7620. (Illus.). 1008p. 1980. 13.50 (ISBN 0-394-50763-0). Knopf.

Audubon Society & Pyle, Robert M. The Audubon Society Field Guide to North American Butterflies. LC 80-84240. (Illus.). 864p. 1981. 13.50 (ISBN 0-394-51914-0). Knopf.

Audubon Society & Rehder, Harrold A. The Audubon Society Field Guide to North American Seashells. LC 80-84239. 1981. 13.50 (ISBN 0-394-51913-2). Knopf.

Audubon Society & Thompson, Ida. The Audubon Society Field Guide to North American Fossils. LC 81-84772. (Illus.). 1982. 13.50 (ISBN 0-394-52412-8). Knopf.

Audubon Society & Udvardy, M. D. Audubon Society Guide to North American Birds: Western Region. 1977. 13.50 (ISBN 0-394-41410-1). Knopf.

Audubon Society & Whitaker, John O., Jr. The Audubon Field Guide to North American Mammals. LC 79-3525. (Illus.). 752p. 1980. 13.50 (ISBN 0-394-50762-2). Knopf.

Audubon Society, et al. The Audubon Society Field Guide to North American Fishes, Whales, & Dolphins. LC 83-47962. (Illus.). 848p. 1983. 13.50 (ISBN 0-394-53405-0). Knopf.

Audus, L. J., ed. Herbicides: Physiology, Biochemistry Ecology. 2nd ed. Vol. 1, 1976. 95.00 (ISBN 0-12-067701-6); Vol. 2, 1977. 90.00 (ISBN 0-12-067702-4). Acad Pr.

Audy, Robert. Tap Dancing: How to Teach Yourself to Tap. 1976. pap. 4.95 (ISBN 0-394-71644-2, Vin). Random.

Audy dos Santos, Joyce see Dos Santos, Joyce A.

Aue, A. E., tr. see Wittgenstein, Ludwig.

Aue, Hartmann Von see Hartmann Von Aue.

Aue, Maximilian A. E., tr. see Wittgenstein, Ludwig.

Auel, Jean. The Valley of Horses. 1983. pap. 4.95 (ISBN 0-553-25053-1). Bantam.

Auel, Jean M. Clan of the Cave Bear. 512p. 1981. pap. 4.95 (ISBN 0-553-25042-6). Bantam.

--The Clan of the Cave Bear. 480p. 1980. 15.95 (ISBN 0-517-54202-1). Crown.

--The Mammoth Hunters. (Earth's Children Ser.). 480p. 1986. 19.95 (ISBN 0-517-55627-8). Crown.

--The Valley of Horses: Earth's Children. 512p. 1982. 15.95 (ISBN 0-517-54489-X). Crown.

Auel, R. And Then I Remember When. 1983. 13.50 (ISBN 0-934860-33-5). Adventure Pubns.

Auer, Eric. Splinters of Light. LC 75-46407. 56p. 1977. pap. 5.00x (ISBN 0-940580-00-4). Green River.

Auer, J. Jeffery. Essentials of Parliamentary Procedure. 3rd ed. (Orig.). 1959. pap. 10.95 (ISBN 0-13-283788-9). P-H.

Auer, J. Jeffery & Ewbank, Henry L. Handbook for Discussion Leaders. rev. ed. LC 74-6782. 153p. 1974. Repr. of 1954 ed. lib. bdg. 15.00 (ISBN 0-8371-7565-8, AUDL). Greenwood.

Auer, J. Jeffery, ed. Antislavery & Disunion, Eighteen Fifty-Eight to Eighteen Sixty-One: Studies in the Rhetoric of Compromise & Conflict. 11.75 (ISBN 0-8446-0464-X). Peter Smith.

Auer, J. Jeffery & Jenkinson, Edward B., eds. On Teaching Speech in Elementary & Junior High Schools. LC 73-138412. (Indiana University English Curriculum Study Ser.). Repr. of 1971 ed. 36.50 (ISBN 0-8357-9228-5, 2015464). Bks Demand UMI.

Auer, James E. The Postwar Rearmament of Japanese Maritime Forces, 1945-1971. LC 72-83564. (Special Studies in International Politics & Government). 1973. 34.50x (ISBN 0-275-28633-9). Irvington.

Auer, Jim. For Teens Only: Straight Talk about Parents - Life - Love. 64p. 1985. pap. 1.50 (ISBN 0-89243-228-4). Liguori Pubns.

--Sorting It out with God. 64p. 1982. pap. 1.95 (ISBN 0-89243-163-6). Liguori Pubns.

Auer, John J. An Introduction to Research in Speech. LC 77-5311. 1977. Repr. of 1959 ed. lib. bdg. 24.75 (ISBN 0-8371-9581-0, AUIR). Greenwood.

Auer, Joseph & Harris, Charles E. Computer Contract Negotiations. 423p. 1981. 39.50 (ISBN 0-442-20369-1). Van Nos Reinhold.

--Major Equipment Procurement. 448p. 1983. 44.50 (ISBN 0-442-20870-7). Van Nos Reinhold.

Auer, L. The Pathogenesis of Hypertensive Encephalography. (Acta Neurochirurgica: Supplementum 27). (Illus.). 1978. pap. 44.90 (ISBN 0-387-81490-6). Springer-Verlag.

Auer, L. M. & Loew, F., eds. The Cerebral Veins. (Illus.). 380p. 1983. 67.00 (ISBN 0-387-81767-0). Springer-Verlag.

Auer, L. M., et al, eds. Prolactinomas: An Interdisiplinary Approach. (Illus.). x, 439p. 1985. 59.20x (ISBN 3-11-010153-X). De Gruyter.

Auer, Leopold. Graded Course of Violin, Bk. 1. (Illus.). 64p. 1926. pap. 7.00 (ISBN 0-8258-0251-2, 0-1416). Fischer Inc NY.

--Violin Masterworks & Their Interpretation. LC 78-66897. (Encore Music Editions Ser.). (Illus.). 1979. Repr. of 1925 ed. 19.00 (ISBN 0-88355-724-X). Hyperion Conn.

--Violin Playing As I Teach It. 1980. pap. 2.75 (ISBN 0-486-23917-9). Dover.

--Violin Playing As I Teach It. LC 75-35022. (Illus.). 99p. 1976. Repr. of 1960 ed. lib. bdg. 15.00 (ISBN 0-8371-8573-4, AUVP). Greenwood.

Auer, Leopold, ed. see Bach, J. S.

Auer, Leopold, ed. see Corelli, A.

Auer, Leopold, ed. see Handel, Georg F.

Auer, Marilyn M., ed. see Chirgotis, William G.

Auer, Marilyn M., ed. see Jones, Robert E. & Burch, Monte.

Auer, Marilyn M., ed. see Philbin, Tom.

Auer, Marilyn M., ed. see Russell, James E.

Auer, P. L., ed. Advances in Energy Systems & Technology. LC 78-4795. 1979. Vol. 1. 65.00 (ISBN 0-12-014901-X); Vol. 2. 50.00 (ISBN 0-12-014902-8). Acad Pr.

Auer, P. L., ed. see Kirkwood, John G.

Auer, Peter, ed. Energy & the Developing Nations: Proceedings of the Electric Power Research Institute (EPRI) Workshop on Energy & the Developing Nations, Hoover Institution, Stanford University, March 18-20, 1980. LC 80-29586. (Pergamon Policy Studies on Energy). (Illus.). 528p. 1981. 65.00 (ISBN 0-08-027527-3). Pergamon.

Auer, Peter L., ed. Advances in Energy Systems & Technology, Vol. 3. 308p. 1982. 55.00 (ISBN 0-12-014903-6). Acad Pr.

Auer, Peter L. & Douglas, David, eds. Advances in Energy Systems & Technology, Vol. 4. (Serial Publication Ser.). 1983. 55.00 (ISBN 0-12-014904-4). Acad Pr.

Auerbach, ed. Best Computer Papers, 1979. (Annual Computer Papers). 334p. 1980. 60.00 (ISBN 0-444-00350-9). Elsevier.

--Best Computer Papers, 1980. (Annual Computer Papers). 412p. 1980. 71.75 (ISBN 0-444-00447-5). Elsevier.

Auerbach, A. J. & Feldstein, M. Handbook of Public Economics, Vol. 1. Date not set. write for info. (ISBN 0-444-87612-X). Elsevier.

Auerbach, A. J. & Feldstein, M., eds. Handbook of Public Economics, 2 vols. (Handbook in Economics: No. 4). 474p. 1985. Set. 130.00 (ISBN 0-444-87667-7, North-Holland). Elsevier.

Auerbach, Alan J. The Taxation of Capital Income. (Harvard Economic Studies: Vol. 153). 144p. 1983. 17.50x (ISBN 0-674-86845-5). Harvard U Pr.

Auerbach, Aline B. How to Give Your Child a Good Start. 1961. pap. 0.75 (ISBN 0-87183-040-X). Child Study.

--How to Give Your Child a Good Start. rev. ed. 12p. 1961. pap. 1.00 (ISBN 0-686-12270-4). Jewish Bd Family.

--The Why & How of Discipline. rev. ed. LC 70-78184. 1974. pap. 1.25 (ISBN 0-87183-085-X). Child Study.

Auerbach, Aline B., jt. auth. see Wolf, Katherine M.

Auerbach, Arthur H., jt. auth. see Gottschalk, Louis A.

Auerbach, Barbara & Snyder, Beth. Paragraph Patterns. 147p. 1983. pap. text ed. 8.95 (ISBN 0-15-567983-X, HC). HarBraceJ.

Auerbach, Berthold. Black Forest Village Stories. facsimile ed. Goepp, Charles, tr. LC 70-101791. (Short Story Index Reprint Ser.). 1869. 20.00 (ISBN 0-8369-3179-3). Ayer Co Pubs.

Auerbach, Carl & Zinnes, Joseph L. Psychological Statistics: A Case Approach. 1979. text ed. 21.50 scp (ISBN 0-397-47376-1, HarpC); avail.instr. manual (ISBN 0-06-379301-6); scp student wkbk. 7.85 (ISBN 0-397-47398-2). Har-Row.

Auerbach, Charlotte. Mutation Research: Problems, Results & Perspectives. 1976. 53.00 (ISBN 0-412-11280-9, NO. 6017, Pub. by Chapman & Hall). Methuen Inc.

--Notes for Introductory Courses in Genetics. rev. ed. 1965. pap. 2.25 (ISBN 0-910824-02-9). Kallman.

Auerbach, Debbie, jt. ed. see Satterlee, Sarah.

Auerbach, Doris. Sam Shepard, Arthur Kopit, & the Off-Broadway Theater. (United States Authors Ser.). 1982. lib. bdg. 14.50 (ISBN 0-8057-7371-1, Twayne). G K Hall.

Auerbach, E., ed. Experimental & Clinical Amblyopia. (Documenta Ophthalmologica Proceedings: Vol. 11). 1975. lib. bdg. 31.50 (ISBN 90-6193-151-7, Pub. by Junk Pubs. Netherlands). Kluwer Academic.

Auerbach, Elias. Moses. Lehman, Israel O. & Barclay, R. A., trs. from Ger. LC 72-6589. 255p. 1975. text ed. 13.95x (ISBN 0-8143-1491-0). Wayne St U Pr.

Auerbach, Erich. Literary Language & Its Public in Late Latin Antiquity & in the Middle Ages. Manheim, R., tr. LC 73-7397. (Bollingen Ser.: No. 74). Repr. of 1965 ed. cancelled (ISBN 0-8357-9503-9, 2011976). Bks Demand UMI.

--Mimesis: The Representation of Reality in Western Literature. Trask, W. R., tr. 1953. 35.00x (ISBN 0-691-06078-9); pap. 8.95x (ISBN 0-691-01269-5, 124). Princeton U Pr.

--Scenes from the Drama of European Literature: Six Essays. 11.50 (ISBN 0-8446-5834-0). Peter Smith.

--Scenes from the Drama of European Literature. LC 83-12549. (Theory & History of Literature Ser.: Vol. 9). 272p. 1984. 25.00x (ISBN 0-8166-1242-0); pap. 9.95 (ISBN 0-8166-1243-9). U of Minn Pr.

Auerbach, Jerold S. Justice Without Law? (Galaxy Bks.). (Illus.). 208p. 1983. 16.95 (ISBN 0-19-503175-X); pap. 6.95 (ISBN 0-19-503447-3, GB 762). Oxford U Pr.

--Labor & Liberty: The La Follette Committee & the New Deal. LC 66-28233. 1966. 18.50x (ISBN 0-672-51153-3). Irvington.

--Unequal Justice. 1976. 29.95x (ISBN 0-19-501939-3). Oxford U Pr.

--Unequal Justice: Lawyers & Social Change in Modern America. LC 75-7364. 1976. pap. 9.95 (ISBN 0-19-502170-3, 490, GB). Oxford U Pr.

Auerbach, Jessica. Winter Wife. LC 83-5079. 204p. 1983. 13.95 (ISBN 0-89919-194-0). Ticknor & Fields.

Auerbach, Jill. One-to-One Lipreading Lessons for Adults. (Illus.). 88p. 1984. spiral 13.75x (ISBN 0-398-04924-6). C C Thomas.

--One-to-One Lipreading Lessons for Kids, 7-12. (Illus.). 82p. 1983. pap. 13.75x spiral (ISBN 0-398-04797-9). C C Thomas.

--One-to-One Lipreading Lessons for Teenagers. (Illus.). 96p. 1981. spiral 13.75x (ISBN 0-398-04477-5). C C Thomas.

Auerbach, Marc & Eager, James L. Playing & Winning Racquetball. 225p. 1982. (Parker); pap. 5.95 (ISBN 0-13-683102-8, Parker). P-H.

Auerbach, Melissa, jt. auth. see Sarath, Maria.

Auerbach, Nina. Communities of Women: An Idea in Fiction. LC 77-21213. 1978. 15.00x (ISBN 0-674-15168-2). Harvard U Pr.

--Romantic Imprisonment: Women & Other Glorified Outcasts. 328p. 1985. 25.00x (ISBN 0-231-06004-1). Columbia U Pr.

--Woman & the Demon: The Life of a Victorian Myth. (Illus.). 256p. 1982. text ed. 17.50x (ISBN 0-674-95406-8). Harvard U Pr.

--Woman & the Demon: The Life of a Victorian Myth. 272p. 1984. pap. 6.95 (ISBN 0-674-95407-6). Harvard U Pr.

Auerbach, Paul & Budassi, Susan, eds. Cardiac Arrest & CPR: Assessment, Planning & Intervention. 2nd ed. LC 82-16382. 230p. 1982. 36.00 (ISBN 0-89443-841-7). Aspen Systems.

Auerbach, Paul S. Medicine for the Outdoors: A Guide to Emergency Medical Procedures & First Aid for Wilderness Travelers. (Illus.). 1986. 24.95 (ISBN 0-316-05928-5); pap. 12.95 (ISBN 0-316-05929-3). Little.

Auerbach, Paul S. & Geehr, Edward C., eds. Management of Wilderness & Environmental Emergencies. 1983. write for info. (ISBN 0-02-304630-9). Macmillan.

Augustine, Saint City of God Against the Pagans, 7 vols. (Loeb Classical Library: No. 411-417). 12.50x ea. Harvard U Pr.

Augustine, St. Commentary on the Lord's Sermon on the Mount with Seventeen Related Sermons. Bd. with Related Sermons. LC 63-18827. (Fathers of the Church Ser.: Vol. 11). 382p. 1951. 21.95x (ISBN 0-8132-0011-3). Cath U Pr.

--Confessions. LC 66-20310. (Fathers of the Church Ser.: Vol. 21). 481p. 1953. 25.95x (ISBN 0-8132-0021-0). Cath U Pr.

Augustine, Saint Confessions, 2 Vols. (Loeb Classical Library: No. 26-27). 1912. 12.50x ea. Vol. 1 (ISBN 0-674-99029-3). Vol. 2 (ISBN 0-674-99030-7). Harvard U Pr.

--Confessions. Pine-Coffin, R. S., tr. (Classics Ser.). (Orig.). 1961. pap. 3.95 (ISBN 0-14-044114-X). Penguin.

--Confessions of Saint Augustine. (Classics Ser). (gr. 11 up). 1968. pap. 1.95 (ISBN 0-8049-0190-2, CL-190). Airmont.

--Confessions of Saint Augustine. Pusey, Edward B., tr. 1961. pap. 2.95 (ISBN 0-02-064230-X, Collier). Macmillan.

--Confessions of Saint Augustine. Warner, Rex, tr. pap. 3.95 (ISBN 0-451-62188-3, ME2188, Ment). NAL.

Augustine, St. Eighty-Three Different Questions. LC 81-2546. (Fathers of the Church Ser.: Vol. 70). 257p. 1982. 29.95x (ISBN 0-8132-0070-9). Cath U Pr.

Augustine, Saint Enchiridion on Faith, Hope & Love. Paolucci, Henry, ed. 177p. 1961. pap. 4.95 (ISBN 0-89526-938-4). Regnery-Gateway.

Augustine, St. Essays by Various Writers. 12.00 (ISBN 0-8446-5239-3). Peter Smith.

Augustine, Saint The Essential Augustine. Bourke, Vernon J., commentary by. 274p. 1973. 15.00 (ISBN 0-915144-08-5); pap. text ed. 4.95 (ISBN 0-915144-07-7). Hackett Pub.

Augustine, St. The Happy Life & Other Works. (Fathers of the Church Ser.: Vol. 5). 450p. 1948. 22.95x (ISBN 0-8132-0005-9). Cath U Pr.

--Immortality of the Soul. (Fathers of the Church Ser.: Vol. 4). 489p. 1947. 29.95x (ISBN 0-8132-0004-0). Cath U Pr.

--Letters, Nos. 1-82. LC 64-19948. (Fathers of the Church Ser.: Vol. 12). 420p. 1951. 22.95x (ISBN 0-8132-0012-1). Cath U Pr.

--Letters, Nos. 131-164. (Fathers of the Church Ser.: Vol. 20). 398p. 1953. 29.95x (ISBN 0-8132-0020-2). Cath U Pr.

--Letters, Nos. 83-130. LC 64-19948. (Fathers of the Church Ser.: Vol. 18). 401p. 1953. 29.95x (ISBN 0-8132-0018-0). Cath U Pr.

--Letters: 165-203. (Fathers of the Church Ser.: Vol. 30). 421p. 1955. 21.95x (ISBN 0-8132-0030-X). Cath U Pr.

--Letters: 204-270. (Fathers of the Church Ser.: Vol. 32). 317p. 1956. 17.95x (ISBN 0-8132-0032-6). Cath U Pr.

Augustine, Saint On Christian Doctrine. Robertson, D. W., Jr., tr. LC 58-9956. 1958. pap. 7.20 scp (ISBN 0-672-60262-8). Bobbs.

--On Free Choice of the Will. Benjamin, A. S. & Hackstaff, L. H., trs. LC 63-16932. (Orig.). 1964. pap. 7.20 scp (ISBN 0-672-60368-3, LLAS150). Bobbs.

--Political Writings of St. Augustine. Paolucci, Henry, ed. 358p. pap. 5.95 (ISBN 0-89526-941-4). Regnery-Gateway.

--Presdestinacion of Saintes. Bd. with Perserveraunce Unto Thende. LC 68-54611. (English Experience Ser.: No. 32). Repr. of 1556 ed. 20.00 (ISBN 90-221-0032-4). Walter J Johnson.

Augustine, St. Retractations. (Fathers of the Church Ser.: Vol. 60). 451p. 1968. 17.95x (ISBN 0-8132-0060-1). Cath U Pr.

--St. Augustine on the Psalms, Vol. 1. Quasten, J. & Burghardt, W. J., eds. Hebgin, Scholastica & Corrigan, Felicitas, trs. LC 60-10722. (Ancient Christian Writers Ser.: No. 29). 360p. 1960. 12.95 (ISBN 0-8091-0104-1). Paulist Pr.

--St. Augustine, Sermons for Christmas & Epiphany. Quasten, J. & Plumpe, J., eds. Lawler, Thomas, tr. LC 78-62464. (Ancient Christian Writers Ser.: No. 15). 250p. 1952. 10.95 (ISBN 0-8091-0137-8). Paulist Pr.

--St. Augustine, the First Catechetical Instruction. Quasten, J. & Plumpe, J., eds. Christopher, Joseph P., tr. LC 78-62449. (Ancient Christian Writers Ser.: No. 2). 170p. 1946. 10.95 (ISBN 0-8091-0047-9). Paulist Pr.

--St. Augustine: The Greatness of the Soul, Vol. 9. Quasten, J. & Plumpe, J., eds. Colleran, Joseph M., tr. LC 78-62455. (Ancient Christian Writers Ser.: No. 9). 255p. 1950. 11.95 (ISBN 0-8091-0060-6). Paulist Pr.

Augustine, Saint Select Letters. (Loeb Classical Library: No. 239). 12.50x (ISBN 0-674-99264-4). Harvard U Pr.

Augustine, St. Sermons on the Liturgical Seasons. (Fathers of the Church Ser.: Vol. 38). 1959. 29.95x (ISBN 0-8132-0038-5). Cath U Pr.

--The Teacher, The Free Choice of the Will, Grace & Free Will. Bd. with Two Works on Free Will. LC 67-30350. (Fathers of the Church Ser.: Vol. 59). 232p. 1968. 17.95x (ISBN 0-8132-0059-8). Cath U Pr.

--Treatises on Marriage & Other Subjects. LC 73-75002. (Fathers of the Church Ser.: Vol. 27). 456p. 1955. 29.95x (ISBN 0-8132-0027-X). Cath U Pr.

--Treatises on Various Moral Subjects. LC 65-18319. (Fathers of the Church Ser.: Vol. 16). 479p. 1952. 24.95x (ISBN 0-8132-0016-4). Cath U Pr.

--The Trinity. LC 63-72482. (Fathers of the Church Ser.: Vol. 45). 539p. 1963. 27.95x (ISBN 0-8132-0045-8). Cath U Pr.

Augustine, St. see St. Augustine.

Augustine of Hippo. Augustine of Hippo: Selected Writings. Clark, Mary T., tr. (Classics of Western Spirituality Ser.). 544p. 1984. 15.95 (ISBN 0-8091-0348-6); pap. 12.95 (ISBN 0-8091-2573-0). Paulist Pr.

Augustinian Educational Conferences. Augustinian Studies: Papers Read at Recent Augustinian Educational Conferences. facs. ed. LC 67-22052. (Essay Index Reprint Ser.). 1937. 16.00 (ISBN 0-8369-0163-0). Ayer Co Pubs.

Augustinos, Gerasimos. Consciousness & History: Nationalist Critics of Greek Society, 1897-1914. (East European Monographs: No. 32). 182p. 1977. 20.00x (ISBN 0-914710-25-7). East Eur Quarterly.

Augustinus, Aurelius. Contra Felicem De Natura Boni Epistula Secundini, Contra Secundinum, Pt. 2. Bd. with De Natura Boni Epistula Secundini; Contra Secundinum. (Corpus Scriptorum Ecclesiasticorum Latinorum Ser: Vol. 25). (Lat.). Repr. of 1892 ed. unbound 50.00 (ISBN 0-384-02365-7). Johnson Repr.

--De Peccatorum Meritis et Remissione et de Baptismo Parvulorum, Ad Marcellinum Libri Tres, Bk. 3. Urba, C. F. & Zycha, I., eds. (Corpus Scriptorum Ecclesiasticorum Latinorum Ser: Vol. 60). 50.00 (ISBN 0-384-02490-4). Johnson Repr.

--De Perfectione Ivstitiae Hominis, De Gestis Pelagii, De Gratia Christi et De Peccato Originali Libri Duo. (Corpus Scriptorum Ecclesiasticorum Latinorum Ser: Vol. 42). Repr. of 1902 ed. 50.00 (ISBN 0-384-02495-5). Johnson Repr.

--De Utilitate Credendi, Pt. 1. Bd. with De Duabus Animabus; Contra Fortunatem; Contra Adimantum. (Corpus Scriptorum Ecclesiasticorum Latinorum Ser: Vol. 25). Repr. of 1891 ed. 50.00 (ISBN 0-384-02364-9). Johnson Repr.

Augustinus, St. Aurelius. Contra Academicos Libri Tres De Beata Vita Liber Unus De Ordine Libri Duo. Bd. with De Beata Vita Liber Unus; De Ordine Libri Duo. (Corpus Scriptorum Ecclesiasticorum Latinorum Ser: Vol. 63). (Lat.). pap. 50.00 (ISBN 0-384-02360-6). Johnson Repr.

Augustinus, Saint Aurelius. De Civitate Dei Libri 22: Sec. 5, 2 pts, Pts. 1 & 2. (Corpus Scriptorum Ecclesiasticorum Latinorum Ser: Vol. 40). Repr. of 1899 ed. 50.00 ea. (ISBN 0-384-02370-3). Johnson Repr.

--De Consensu Evangelistarum Libri 4, Bk. 4. Weihrich, F., ed. (Corpus Scriptorum Ecclesiasticorum Latinorum Ser: Vol. 43). 40.00 (ISBN 0-384-02480-7). Johnson Repr.

--De Fide et Symbolo, De Fide et Operibus, De Agone Christiano, Pt. 3. (Corpus Scriptorum Ecclesiasticorum Latinorum Ser: Vol. 41). 65.00 (ISBN 0-384-02385-1). Johnson Repr.

--De Genesi Ad Litteram Libri Duodecim Eiusdem Libri Capitula, Pt. 1. (Corpus Scriptorum Ecclesiasticorum Latinorum Ser: Vol. 28). 50.00 (ISBN 0-384-02485-8). Johnson Repr.

--Epistulae. (Corpus Scriptorum Ecclesiasticorum Latinorum Ser: Vols. 34, 44, 57, 58). 180.00 (ISBN 0-384-02358-4). Johnson Repr.

--Liber Qvi Appellatvr Specvlvm et Liber De Divinis Scriptvris. (Corpus Scriptorum Ecclesiasticorum Latinorum Ser: Vol. 12). 50.00 (ISBN 0-384-02505-6). Johnson Repr.

--Quaestionum in Heptateuchum Libri 7, Adnotationum in Iob Liber Unus. (Corpus Scriptorum Ecclesiasticorum Latinorum Ser: Vol. 38, Pt. 2). 50.00 (ISBN 0-384-02515-3). Johnson Repr.

--Retractationum Libri Duo. (Corpus Scriptorum Ecclesiasticorum Latinorum Ser: Vol. 36). 34.00 (ISBN 0-384-02357-6). Johnson Repr.

--Spurious & Doubtful Works, Pseudo-Augustini Quaestiones Veteris et Novi Testamenti CXXVII. Souter, A., ed. (Corpus Scriptorum Ecclesiasticorum Latinorum Ser: Vol. 50). 40.00 (ISBN 0-384-02575-7). Johnson Repr.

Augustinus, Saint Scripta Contra Donatistas, 3 Vols, Pts. 3. (Corpus Scriptorum Ecclesiasticorum Latinorum Ser: Vols. 51, 52, 53). Set. 130.00 (ISBN 0-384-02553-6). Johnson Repr.

Augustithis, S. S. Atlas of the Textural Patterns of Basalts & Their Genetic Significance. 324p. 1978. 102.25 (ISBN 0-444-41566-1). Elsevier.

--Atlas of the Textural Patterns of Basic & Ultrabasic Rocks & Their Genetic Significance. 1979. 102.00x (ISBN 3-11-006571-1). De Gruyter.

--Atlas of the Textural Patterns of Granites, Gneisses & Associated Rock Types. 378p. 1973. 113.00 (ISBN 0-444-40977-7). Elsevier.

Augustus. Res Gestae Divi Augusti. Brunt, P. A. & Moore, J. M., eds. 1967. pap. 6.95x (ISBN 0-19-831772-7). Oxford U Pr.

Augustus, Betty. Handbook of Agency Procedures. 10.00 (ISBN 0-942326-59-8, 30183). Rough Notes.

Augustus, John. John Augustus, First Probation Officer. LC 79-129308. (Ser. in Criminology, Law Enforcement & Social Problems: No. 130). (Illus.). 10.00x (ISBN 0-87585-130-4). Patterson Smith.

Augustyn, James. The Solar Cat Book. enl. ed. 112p. 1982. pap. 4.95 (ISBN 0-89815-071-X). Ten Speed Pr.

Augustyniak, J., ed. Biological Implications of Protein-Nucleic Acid Interactions. 668p. 1981. 81.00 (ISBN 0-444-80292-4). Elsevier.

Aukee, Waino E., et al, eds. Inside the Management Team. 102p. 1973. pap. text ed. 2.00x (ISBN 0-8134-1571-3, 1571). Interstate.

Auken, John Van see Van Auken, John.

Aukerman, Dale. Darkening Valley. 1981. pap. 8.95 (ISBN 0-8164-2295-8, Pub. by Seabury). Winston Pr.

Aukerman, Dale, jt. auth. see Pritchett, Reuel B.

Aukerman, Louise R., jt. auth. see Aukerman, Robert C.

Aukerman, Robert C. Approaches to Beginning Reading. 2nd ed. LC 83-23423. 656p. 1984. text ed. 28.95 (ISBN 0-471-03692-7); pap. text ed. 19.95 (ISBN 0-471-03693-5). Wiley.

--The Basal Reader Approach to Reading. LC 80-28174. 339p. 1981. pap. text ed. 18.95 (ISBN 0-471-09066-2). Wiley.

--Reading in the Secondary School Classroom. (Illus.). 425p. 1972. text ed. 30.95 (ISBN 0-07-002483-9). McGraw.

Aukerman, Robert C. & Aukerman, Louise R. How Do I Teach Reading? LC 80-23380. 543p. 1981. text ed. 30.95 (ISBN 0-471-03687-0). Wiley.

Aukerman, Robert C., ed. Some Persistent Questions on Beginning Reading. LC 73-190454. (Convention Publications Ser). 1972. 6.00 (ISBN 0-87207-451-X). Intl Reading.

Aulakh, H. S. Changing Foodgrain Market Structure in India. 312p. 1983. text ed. 37.50x (ISBN 0-86590-121-X). Apt Bks.

Aulard, Francois V. Paris Pendant la Reaction Thermidorienne et sous le Directoire, 5 vols. LC 70-161713. (Collection de documents relatifs a l'histoire de Paris pendant la Revolution francaise). Repr. of 1902 ed. Set. 350.00 (ISBN 0-404-52570-9); 70.00 ea. AMS Pr.

--Paris sous le Consulat, 4 vols. LC 74-161714. (Collection de documents relatifs a l'histoire de Paris pendant la Revolution francaise). Repr. of 1909 ed. Set. 280.00 (ISBN 0-404-52580-6); 70.00 ea.; Vol. 1. (ISBN 0-404-52581-4); Vol. 2. (ISBN 0-404-52582-2); Vol. 3. 1.00 (ISBN 0-404-52583-0); Vol. 4. (ISBN 0-404-52584-9). AMS Pr.

--Paris sous le Premier Empire, 3 vols. LC 74-161706. (Collection de documents relatifs a l'histoire de Paris pendant la Revolution francaise). Repr. of 1923 ed. Set. 210.00 (ISBN 0-404-52576-8); 70.00 ea.; Vol. 1. (ISBN 0-404-52577-6); Vol. 2. (ISBN 0-404-52578-4); Vol. 3. (ISBN 0-404-52579-2). AMS Pr.

Aulard, Francois V., tr. Societe des Jacobins, 6 Vols. LC 78-161707. (Collection de documents relatifs a l'histoire de Paris pendant la Revolution francaise). Repr. of 1897 ed. Set. 420.00 (ISBN 0-404-52560-1); 70.00 ea. AMS Pr.

Aulard, Francois V., et al. Collection de Documents Relatifs a l'Histoire de Paris Pendant la Revolution Francaise, 16 titles in 54 vols. Repr. of 1888 ed. Set. 3780.00 (ISBN 0-404-52550-4); 70.00 ea. AMS Pr.

Aulbach, B. Continuous & Discrete Dynamics near Manifolds of Equilibria. (Lecture Notes in Mathematics Ser.: Vol. 1058). ix, 142p. 1984. pap. 11.00 (ISBN 0-387-13329-1). Springer-Verlag.

Aulbach, Robert E. Energy Management. Newton, Karen, ed. 243p. 1984. text ed. 34.95 (ISBN 0-86612-019-X). Educ Inst Am Hotel.

Auld, A. Graeme. Joshua, Judges, & Ruth. LC 84-22076. (The Daily Study Bible-Old Testament). 290p. 1985. 15.95 (ISBN 0-664-21809-1); pap. 8.95 (ISBN 0-664-24576-5). Westminster.

Auld, D. A. Issues in Government Expenditure Growth. (Illus.). 59p. 1976. 3.00 (ISBN 0-88806-020-3). Inst C D Howe.

Auld, Douglas & Bannock, Graham. The American Dictionary of Economics. 352p. 1983. 17.95x (ISBN 0-87196-532-1). Facts on File.

Auld, Douglas A. L. The Government Sector in the Nineteen Seventies: Economic Context for a Tax System, 05, Vol. 1. (The White Paper on Taxation Ser.). (Illus.). 61p. 1971. 2.00 ea. (ISBN 0-88806-103-X); 8.00 set (ISBN 0-317-34270-3). Inst C D Howe.

Auld, Janice L. Cut & Paste Phonics: Extra Help for Troublesome Letter Combinations. (gr. 1-3). 1985. pap. 5.95 (ISBN 0-8224-5540-4). Pitman Learning.

Auld, John. Marijuana Use: A Social Control. 1981. 38.00 (ISBN 0-12-068280-X). Acad Pr.

Auld, William, ed. Pasoj Al Plena Posedo. 4th ed. (Esperanto.). 1974. pap. text ed. 8.25x (ISBN 8-4499-4305-1, 1052). Esperanto League North Am.

Auld, William M. Christmas Traditions. LC 68-58167. 1968. Repr. of 1931 ed. 40.00x (ISBN 0-8103-3353-8). Gale.

--Christmas Traditions. 1977. lib. bdg. 59.95 (ISBN 0-8490-1619-3). Gordon Pr.

Auleb, Ann W., jt. auth. see Auleb, Leigh.

Auleb, Leigh & Auleb, Ann W. Laboratory Exercises for Human Biology. (Illus.). 104p. 1983. lab manual 6.95x (ISBN 0-917962-81-8). Peek Pubns.

Aulen, Gustaf. The Faith of the Christian Church. rev. ed. Wahlstrom, Eric H., tr. from Swedish. LC 61-5302. 416p. 1973. pap. 8.95 (ISBN 0-8006-1655-3, 1-1655). Fortress.

Aulen, Gustaf E. Reformation & Catholicity. Wahlstrom, Eric H., tr. from Swedish. LC 78-25981. 1979. Repr. of 1961 ed. lib. bdg. 22.50x (ISBN 0-313-20809-3, AURC). Greenwood.

Aulen, Gustav. Christus Victor. (Orig.). 1969. pap. 4.95 (ISBN 0-02-083400-4). Macmillan.

Auletta, Ken. The Art of Corporate Success. LC 83-17749. 1984. 15.95 (ISBN 0-399-12930-8, Putnam). Putnam Pub Group.

--The Art of Corporate Success. (Penguin Nonfiction Ser.). 192p. 1985. pap. 6.95 (ISBN 0-14-007950-5). Penguin.

--Greed & Glory on Wall Street: The Fall of the House of Lehman. 1986. 19.95 (ISBN 0-394-54410-2). Random.

--The Streets Were Paved with Gold: The Decline of New York--An American Tragedy. LC 79-22305. 1980. pap. 4.95 (ISBN 0-394-74355-5, V-355, Vin). Random.

--The Underclass. 1982. 17.50 (ISBN 0-394-52343-1). Random.

--The Underclass. LC 82-40433. 368p. 1983. pap. 6.95 (ISBN 0-394-71388-5, Vin). Random.

Auletta, Richard. Two Hundred One Swedish Verbs Fully Conjugated in All Tenses. LC 74-9748. 1975. pap. 6.95 (ISBN 0-8120-0528-7). Barron.

Aulger, Sam V. Logic Thinking. 1985. write for info. Carlton.

Aulin-Ahmavaara, Arvid. Cybernetic Laws of Social Progress: Towards a Critical Social Philosophy & a Criticism of Marxism. (Systems Science & World Order Library). (Illus.). 224p. 1981. 50.00 (ISBN 0-08-025782-8). Pergamon.

Aull. Rings of Continuous Function. (Lecture Notes in Pure & Applied Mathematics Ser.: Vol. 95). 336p. 1985. 65.00 (ISBN 0-8247-7144-3). Dekker.

Aulls, Mark. Developing Readers in Today's Elementary School. 650p. (gr. k-6). 1982. scp 34.29 (ISBN 0-205-07722-6, 237722). Allyn.

Aulock, Wilhelm H. Von see Von Aulock, Wilhelm H.

Aulson, Nan & Aulson, Pam. Fun 'n Festive Holiday Trimmers. (Illus.). 1983. pap. 3.50 (ISBN 0-9601896-6-1). Patch as Patch.

Aulson, Pam. Crafty Ideas with Placemats. (Illus.). 24p. 1979. pap. 3.00 (ISBN 0-9601896-3-7). Patch As Patch.

--No-Sew Patchwork. (Illus.). 1984. pap. 3.00 (ISBN 0-9601896-7-X). Patch as Patch.

--Placemat Pets 'n Playmates. (Illus.). 24p. 1980. pap. 3.50 (ISBN 0-9601896-2-9). Patch As Patch.

--Placement Plus & Plenty More. (Illus.). 64p. 1982. pap. 3.50 (ISBN 0-9601896-5-3). Patch As Patch.

--Pretty as a Picture: Fabric Frames. (Illus.). 24p. 1981. pap. 3.00 (ISBN 0-9601896-4-5). Patch As Patch.

Aulson, Pam, jt. auth. see Aulson, Nan.

Aulson, Pam, ed. Seventy-Six Great Gifts. (Illus.). 96p. (Orig.). 1979. pap. 2.00 (ISBN 0-918178-16-9). Simplicity.

--Timeless Fashions. (Illus.). 72p. (Orig.). 1981. pap. 2.00 (ISBN 0-918178-25-8). Simplicity.

Aulson, Pam, jt. ed. see Randolph, Elizabeth.

Ault, Addison. Techniques & Experiments for Organic Chemistry. 4th ed. 1983. text ed. 35.72 (ISBN 0-205-07920-2, 6879209). Allyn.

Ault, Addison & Ault, Margaret R. A Handy & Systematic Catalog of NMR Spectra: Instruction Through Examples. LC 79-57227. 425p. 1980. 24.00x (ISBN 0-935702-00-8). Univ Sci Bks.

Ault, Addison & Dudek, Gerald. An Introduction to Proton NMR Spectroscopy. LC 75-26286. 141p. 1976. pap. text ed. 12.95x (ISBN 0-8162-0331-8). Holden-Day.

Ault, D. S., tr. see Dollinger, Philippe.

Ault, Donald. Narrative Unbound. 414p. (Orig.). 1986. price not set (Pub. by Clinamen Studies); pap. price not set. Station Hill Pr.

--Visionary Physics: Blake's Response to Newton. LC 73-77128. (Midway Reprint Ser). 1976. pap. 9.50x (ISBN 0-226-03226-4). U of Chicago Pr.

Ault, G. M., jt. ed. see Hehemann, R. F.

Ault, G. M., et al, eds. High Temperature Materials II: Proceedings of a Technical Conference, Cleveland, Ohio, April 26-27, 1961. LC 62-18703. (Metallurgical Society Conference: Vol. 18). pap. 160.00 (ISBN 0-317-10351-2, 2001506). Bks Demand UMI.

Ault, Gary L., et al. Three Papers on Quality of Urban Environment. 55p. 1967. pap. 2.00 (ISBN 0-318-00016-4, EDA 5). Inst for Urban & Regional.

Ault, Hugh J., jt. auth. see McDaniel, Paul R.

Ault, Hugh J. & Radler, Albert J., trs. from Ger. German Corporation Tax Reform Law 1977. 117p. 1976. pap. text ed. 15.00x (ISBN 3-7875-5261-8, Pub. by Kluwer). Rothman.

Ault, Karuna, ed. see Hari Dass, Baba.

Ault, Karuna K., ed. see Hari Dass, Baba.

Ault, Leonard, jt. ed. see Smith, W. Novis.

Ault, Leslie H. The Chess Tutor: Elements of Combinations. 352p. 1976. pap. 6.95 (ISBN 0-452-25557-0, Z5557, Plume). NAL.

Ault, Margaret R., jt. auth. see Ault, Addison.

Ault, Nelson A., jt. auth. see Magill, Lewis M.

Ault, Norman. Life in Ancient Britain. LC 70-39667. (Select Bibliographies Reprint Ser). 1972. Repr. of 1920 ed. 16.50 (ISBN 0-8369-9927-4). Ayer Co Pubs.

--The Poets' Life of Christ. 30.00 (ISBN 0-686-17669-3). Quaker City.

--Poets's Life of Christ. LC 72-2513. (Select Bibliographies Reprint Ser). 1972. Repr. of 1922 ed. 22.00 (ISBN 0-8369-6847-6). Ayer Co Pubs.

--Pope's Own Miscellany: Being A Reprint of Poems on Several Occasions 1717 Containing New Poems by Alexander Pope & Others. LC 73-1492. 1973. lib. bdg. 25.00 (ISBN 0-8414-1710-5). Folcroft.

--The Treasury of Unfamiliar Lyrics. 1938. 30.00 (ISBN 0-686-17670-7). Quaker City.

Ault, Norman, ed. Elizabethan Lyrics from the Original Texts. 3rd ed. Repr. of 1949 ed. 69.00x (ISBN 0-686-02251-3). Somerset Pub.

Ault, Phil. Whistles Round the Bend: Travel on America's Waterways. (Illus.). 192p. (gr. 7 up). 1982. PLB 10.95 (ISBN 0-396-08036-7). Dodd.

Ault, Rosalie S. BASIC Programming for Kids. LC 83-12773. (Illus.). 192p. (gr. 5 up). 1983. 10.95; pap. 7.95 (ISBN 0-395-34920-6). HM.

Ault, Ruth L. Children's Cognitive Development: Piaget's Theory & the Process Approach. 2nd ed. (Illus.). 1983. 19.95x (ISBN 0-19-503183-0); pap. 7.95x (ISBN 0-19-503184-9). Oxford U Pr.

Ault, Stephen, tr. see Hoetink, Harry.

Ault, Stephen K., tr. see Warman, Arturo.

Ault, Warren O. Open-Field Farming in Medieval England. (Historical Problems; Studies & Documents). 1972. text ed. 18.95x (ISBN 0-04-942104-2); pap. text ed. 8.95x (ISBN 0-04-942105-0). Allen Unwin.

--Private Jurisdiction in England. LC 80-1998. Repr. of 1923 ed. 41.00 (ISBN 0-404-18550-9). AMS Pr.

--Private Jurisdiction in England. Helmholz, R. H. & Reams, Bernard D., Jr., eds. LC 80-84955. (Historical Writings in Law & Jurisprudence Ser.: No. 25, Bk. 39). 370p. 1981. Repr. of 1923 ed. lib. bdg. 35.00 (ISBN 0-89941-091-X). W S Hein.

Aultman, Dick, jt. auth. see Golf Digest Editors.

Aultman, Dick, jt. auth. see Grout, Jack.

Aultman, Dick, jt. auth. see Runyan, Paul.

Aultman, Dick, jt. auth. see Toski, Bob.

Aultman, Donald S. Contemporary Christian Education. 122p. 1968. 4.95 (ISBN 0-87148-159-6); pap. 3.95 (ISBN 0-87148-160-X). Pathway Pr.

--Guiding Youth. 1977. pap. 3.95 (ISBN 0-87148-358-0). Pathway Pr.

--Learning Christian Leadership. 1960. 4.95 (ISBN 0-87148-501-X). Pathway Pr.

--The Ministry of Christian Teaching. 111p. 1966. 4.95 (ISBN 0-87148-554-0); pap. 3.95 (ISBN 0-87148-555-9). Pathway Pr.

Aultman, Donald S., jt. auth. see Conn, Charles P.

Auluck, Sunita V. Intracity Residential Mobility in an Industrial City: A Case Study of Ludhiana. 180p. 1980. text ed. 11.25x (ISBN 0-391-02134-6). Humanities.

Aumann, Francis R. Changing American Legal System: Some Selected Phases. LC 79-92625. (Law, Politics, & History Ser). 1969. Repr. of 1940 ed. 39.50 (ISBN 0-306-71762-X). Da Capo.

Aumann, Jordan & Urs von Baltlasar, Hans. Dedicated to St. Teresa of Avila. LC 82-10795. (Word & Spirit Ser.: Vol. IV). 1983. pap. 7.00 (ISBN 0-932506-19-4). St Bedes Pubns.

Aumann, Jordan, tr. see Arintero, John G.

Aumann, Jordan, tr. see John Paul, Pope, II.

Aumann, Jordan, tr. see Louis Of Granada.

Aumann, R. J. & Shapley, L. S. Values of Non-Atomic Games. (A Rand Corporation Research Study). 300p. 1972. 35.00x (ISBN 0-691-08103-4). Princeton U Pr.

Aumann, R. J. & Harsanyi, J. C., eds. Essays in Game Theory & Mathematical Economics. 196p. 1981. pap. text ed. 21.95x (ISBN 3-411-01609-4). Birkhauser.

Auma-Osolo, Agola. Cause-Effects of Modern African Nationalism on the World Market. LC 83-14615. (Illus.). 232p. (Orig.). 1984. lib. bdg. 22.50 (ISBN 0-8191-3475-9); pap. text ed. 12.00 (ISBN 0-8191-3476-7). U Pr of Amer.

Aumiaux, M. Microprocessor Systems. Starza, Arletta, tr. (Wiley Series in Computing). 218p. 1982. 29.95 (ISBN 0-471-10129-X). Wiley.

--The Use of Microprocessors. Hutt, Annel, tr. LC 79-42904. (Wiley Series in Computing). 198p. 1980. 34.95 (ISBN 0-471-27689-8, Pub. by Wiley Interscience). Wiley.

Aumiller, Dr. Jochen. You Don't Have to Be Next. 1980. pap. 5.95 (ISBN 0-8065-0683-0). Citadel Pr.

Aumonier, Stacy. Overheard. LC 72-3289. (Short Story Index Reprint Ser). 1972. Repr. of 1924 ed. 18.00 (ISBN 0-8369-4142-X). Ayer Co Pubs.

Aumonier, Stacy & Belcher, George F. Odd Fish. facs. ed. LC 71-116929. (Short Story Index Reprint Ser). 1923. 13.00 (ISBN 0-8369-3431-8). Ayer Co Pubs.

Aumra. As of a Trumphet. 1968. 4.95 (ISBN 0-686-27649-3). Cole-Outreach.

Aumueller, G. Prostate Gland & Seminal Vesicle. (Handbuch der Mikroskopischen Anatomie Des Menschen: Vol. 7, Pt. 6). (Illus.). 1979. 176.00 (ISBN 0-387-09191-2). Springer-Verlag.

Aune, A. B. & Vlietstra, J. Automation for Safety in Shipping & Off-Shore Petroleum Operations. (Computer Applications in Shipping & Shipbuilding Ser.: Vol. 8). 426p. 1980. 98.00 (ISBN 0-444-85498-3). Elsevier.

Aune, B. A. Knowledge, Mind & Nature. 1979. lib. bdg. 24.00x (ISBN 0-917930-27-4); pap. text ed. 8.50x (ISBN 0-917930-07-X). Ridgeview.

Aune, Bruce. Kant's Theory of Morals. LC 79-17938. 1980. 25.00 (ISBN 0-691-07238-8). Princeton U Pr.

--Reason & Action. (Studies in Philosophy: No. 9). 1977. lib. bdg. 31.50 (ISBN 90-277-0805-3, Pub. by Reidel Holland); pap. 16.00 (ISBN 90-277-0851-7, Pub. by Reidel Holland). Kluwer Academic.

Aune, Bruce A. Rationalism, Empiricism & Pragmatism: An Introduction. 1970. pap. text ed. 9.00x (ISBN 0-394-30017-3, RanC). Random.

Aune, David E. Jesus & the Synoptic Gospels: A Bibliographic Study Guide. Branson, Mark L., ed. (TSF - IBR Bibliographic Study Guides Ser.). 99p. (Orig.). 1981. pap. 2.95 (ISBN 0-8308-5498-3). Inter-Varsity.

--Prophecy in Early Christianity & the Ancient Mediterranean World. 400p. 1983. 29.95 (ISBN 0-8028-3584-8). Eerdmans.

Aunger, Edmund A. In Search of Political Stability: A Comparative Study of New Brunswick & Northern Ireland. 238p. 1981. 25.00x (ISBN 0-7735-0366-8). McGill-Queens U Pr.

Aungier, George J., ed. The French Chronicle of London. Incl. LC 77-161712. (Camden Society First Ser.: No. 28). (Eng. & Fr.). Repr. of 1844 ed. 19.00 (ISBN 0-404-50128-1). AMS Pr.

Aung San Suu Kyi. Aung San. (Leaders of Asia Ser.). 1984. pap. 4.95 (ISBN 0-318-12096-8). U of Queensland Pr.

Aung-Thwin, Michael. Pagan: The Origins of Modern Burma. 288p. 1985. text ed. 25.00x. UH Pr.

Aunt Naomi, pseud. Jewish Fairy Tales & Legends. 16.95 (ISBN 0-89190-314-3, Pub. by Am Repr). Amereon ltd.

Aupetit, Bernard. Complex Approximation, Proceedings, Quebec, Canada. (Progress in Mathematics Ser.: No. 4). 128p. 1980. pap. 12.50x (ISBN 0-8176-3004-X). Birkhauser.

Auphan, Gabriel & Mordal, Jacques. The French Navy in World War Two. Sabalot, Captain, tr. LC 75-38376. (Illus.). 413p. 1976. Repr. of 1959 ed. lib. bdg. 29.50x (ISBN 0-8371-8660-9, AUFN). Greenwood.

Auping, M., et al. Art of Our Time: The Saatchi Collection, Vol. 4. 144p. 1985. pap. 27.50 (ISBN 0-8478-0577-8). Rizzoli Intl.

Auping, Michael. Common Ground: Five Artists in the Florida Landscape, Hamish Fulton, Helen & Newton Harriston, Michael Singer, Alan Sonfist. LC 82-81122. (Illus.). 152p. 1982. pap. 16.00 (ISBN 0-916758-09-5). Ringling Mus Art.

--Francesco Clemente. (Contemporary Artists Ser.). (Illus.). 192p. 1985. 35.00 (ISBN 0-8109-0772-0). Abrams.

--Jess: Pasteups Nineteen Fifteen to Nineteen Eighty-Three. LC 83-82281. (Illus.). 155p. 1983. 30.00 (ISBN 0-916758-14-1). Ringling Mus Art.

--John Chamberlain: Wall Reliefs 1960-1983. LC 82-83513. (Illus.). 85p. (Orig.). 1983. pap. 15.00 (ISBN 0-916758-10-9). Ringling Mus Art.

--Judy Pfaff: Installation, Collages & Drawings. LC 81-82511. (Illus.). 16p. (Orig.). 1981. pap. 3.50 (ISBN 0-916758-06-0). Ringling Mus Art.

--Marcel Duchamp: Works from the John & Mable Ringling Museum of Art Collection. LC 83-81504. (Illus.). 50p. (Orig.). 1983. pap. 9.00 (ISBN 0-916758-13-3). Ringling Mus Art.

--Philip Pearlstein: Paintings & Watercolors. LC 81-51324. (Illus.). 16p. 1981. pap. 3.50 (ISBN 0-916758-05-2). Ringling Mus A.

--Stephen Shore Photographs. LC 81-83669. (Illus.). 20p. 1981. pap. 3.50 (ISBN 0-916758-07-9). Ringling Mus Art.

Auquier, Antoine A. French Industry's Reaction to the European Common Market. LC 80-8616. (Outstanding Dissertations in Economics Ser.). 650p. 1984. lib. bdg. 52.00 (ISBN 0-8240-4173-9). Garland Pub.

Auran, John H. Skiing Is a Family Sport. LC 68-31329. 4.95 (ISBN 0-910294-33-X). Brown Bk.

Aurand, A. Monroe, Jr., ed. see Church, Jeremiah.

Aurand, Harold W. From the Molly Maguires to the United Mine Workers: The Social Ecology of an Industrial Union, 1869-97. LC 73-157737. 1971. 29.95 (ISBN 0-87722-006-9). Temple U Pr.

Aurand, L. W., jt. auth. see Woods, A. E.

Aurandt, Paul. Destiny & One Hundred Two Other Real-Life Mysteries. 256p. 1984. pap. 3.50 (ISBN 0-553-24364-0). Bantam.

--Destiny: From Paul Harvey's "The Rest of the Story". LC 83-61567. 256p. 1983. FPT 10.95 (ISBN 0-688-02205-7). Morrow.

--More of Paul Harvey's the Rest of the Story. 208p. 1981. pap. 3.50 (ISBN 0-553-24842-1). Bantam.

--Paul Harvey's the Rest of the Story. 1978. pap. 3.50 (ISBN 0-553-24782-4). Bantam.

Aurbach, Joseph, jt. ed. see Stevens, Cj.

Aureli. Italian Opera Librettos, Vol. V. Brown, Howard M. & Weimer, Eric, eds. (Italian Opera Ser., 1640-1770). 77.00 (ISBN 0-8240-2654-3). Garland Pub.

Aureli, et al. Pompeo Magno in Cilicia, la Rosaura, Semiramide Riconosciuta, lo Spirito di Contraddizione, il Trinfo di Clelia. LC 76-20993. (Italian Opera Ser.: No. II). 382p. 1983. lib. bdg. 83.00 (ISBN 0-8240-4836-9). Garland Pub.

Aurelia, Joseph C. Aphasia Therapy Manual. 2nd ed. 86p. 1980. pap. text ed. 3.95x (ISBN 0-8134-2112-8, 2112). Interstate.

Aurelio, John. The Beggars' Christmas. LC 79-65893. (Illus.). 96p. 1979. pap. 3.95 (ISBN 0-8091-2221-9). Paulist Pr.

--The Boy Who Stole the Christmas Star. LC 81-9714. (Illus.). 64p. (Orig.). (gr. 4-7). 1981. pap. 3.95 (ISBN 0-8245-0079-2). Crossroad NY.

--Gather Round: Christian Fairy Tales for All Ages. LC 81-84389. 128p. (Orig.). 1982. pap. 4.95 (ISBN 0-8091-2444-0). Paulist Pr.

Aurelio, John R. Story Sunday: Christian Fairy Tales for Children, Parents & Educators. LC 78-51587. 104p. 1978. pap. 3.95 (ISBN 0-8091-2115-8). Paulist Pr.

Aurelius, Marcus. Meditations. (Loeb Classical Library: No. 58). 12.00x (ISBN 0-674-99064-1). Harvard U Pr.

--Meditations. Staniforth, Maxwell, tr. (Classics Ser.). (Orig.). (YA) (gr. 9 up). 1964. pap. 3.95 (ISBN 0-14-044140-9). Penguin.

--Meditations. Grube, G. M. A., ed. & tr. LC 83-22722. (HPC Philosophical Classics Ser.). 170p. 1984. lib. bdg. 15.00 (ISBN 0-915145-78-2); pap. text ed. 4.95 (ISBN 0-915145-79-0). Hackett Pub.

--The Most Meaningful Writings by Marcus Aurelius. (Illus.). 155p. 1982. 69.65 (ISBN 0-89266-352-9). Am Classical Coll Pr.

Aurelius Antoninus, Marcus. The Commentaries of the Emperor Marcus Antoninus: Containing His Maxims of Science & Rules of Life, Wrote for His Own Use & Address'd to Himself. LC 77-158297. Repr. of 1747 ed. 28.00 (ISBN 0-404-54103-8). AMS Pr.

Aurell, Tage. Rose of Jericho & Other Stories. Allwood, Martin S., tr. from Swedish. (Nordic Translation Ser). Orig. Title: Smarre besattelser & Nya bersattelser. 152p. 1968. 15.00x (ISBN 0-299-04701-6); pap. 6.00x (ISBN 0-299-04704-0). U of Wis Pr.

Aureneche, Olivier. Dictionnaire Illustre Multilinque De L'architecture du Procher-Orient Ancien. 392p. (Fr.). 1978. 125.00 (ISBN 0-686-56729-3, M-6017). French & Eur.

Aureon, pseud. Anybody's Instant Power Formula. LC 84-70874. 75p. (Orig.). 1984. pap. 6.95 (ISBN 0-9613386-0-1). Aureon Pub.

Auricchio, Father John. Future of Theology. Therese, Sr. Eloise, ed. LC 69-15853. 1970. 6.95 (ISBN 0-8189-0055-5). Alba.

Auriche, M. & Burke, J., eds. Drug Safety: Proceeding of the Fourth International Congress of Pharmaceutical Physicians by the Association des Medecins de l'Industrie Pharmaceutique (AMPI) under the Auspices of the International Federation of the Association of the Pharmaceutical Physicians (IFAPP) in Paris, April 1981. 320p. 1982. cancelled 60.50; pap. 40.00 (ISBN 0-08-027074-3). Pergamon.

Aurigemma, Ann & Bohny, Barbara. Dosage Calculation: Method & Workbook. 160p. 1984. pap. text ed. 12.95 (ISBN 0-88737-116-7). Natl League Nurse.

Aurner, Nellie S. Hengest: A Study in Early English Hero Legend. 1978. lib. bdg. 25.00 (ISBN 0-8495-0044-3). Arden Lib.

Aurner, Nellis S. Hengest: A Study in Early English Hero Legend. LC 74-19126. 1973. lib. bdg. 25.00 (ISBN 0-8414-3002-0). Folcroft.

Aurobindo. Glossary of Terms in Sri Aurobindo's Writings. 1979. 14.00 (ISBN 0-89744-980-0, Pub. by Sri Aurobindo Ashram Trust India); pap. 7.50 (ISBN 0-89744-981-9, Pub. by Sri Aurobindo Ashram Trust India). Auromere.

--Letters on Yoga, 3 vols. 1979. Vol. 1. 11.25 (ISBN 0-89071-236-0); Vol. 2. 12.50 (ISBN 0-89071-238-7); Vol. 3. 14.50 (ISBN 0-89071-240-9); Vol. 1. pap. 10.00 (ISBN 0-89071-237-9); Vol. 2. pap. 11.25 (ISBN 0-89071-239-5); Vol. 3. pap. 12.50 (ISBN 0-89071-241-7). Matagiri.

--Life Companion Paperback Supplement Series. (Life Companion Ser.). 1339p. (Orig.). 1984. pap. 39.25 (ISBN 0-89744-013-7, Pub. by Madanlal Himatsinghlea). Auromere.

--The Mother. 62p. 1977. pap. 1.00 (ISBN 0-89071-243-3). Matagiri.

--The Problem of Rebirth. 186p. 1978. 7.50 (ISBN 0-89071-235-2); pap. 5.50 (ISBN 0-89071-234-4). Matagiri.

--Sri Aurobindo Life Companion Library. (Life Companion Ser.). 4522p. 1984. Repr. of 1979 ed. 111.85 (ISBN 0-317-19956-0, Pub. by Mandanlal Himatsinghlea). Auromere.

Aurobindo & Alfassa, Mira. Sri Aurobindo & the Mother on Education. 168p. 1973. pap. 3.50 (ISBN 0-89071-249-2). Matagiri.

--Sri Aurobindo & the Mother on Love. Saint-Hilaire, P. B., ed. & intro. by. 49p. 1973. pap. 2.00 (ISBN 0-89071-275-1). Matagiri.

Aurobindo, tr. from Fr. Prayers & Meditations. rev. ed. 380p. (Orig.). 1979. pap. 16.00 (ISBN 0-89744-998-3, Sri Aurobindo Ashram Trust India); text ed. 21.00 (ISBN 0-89744-219-9). Auromere.

Aurobindo, Sri. Bande Mataram: Early Political Writings. 1979. pap. 14.00 (ISBN 0-89744-900-2); 18.00 (ISBN 0-686-85667-8). Auromere.

--Bankim-Tilak-Dayanand. 49p. Date not set. 2.00 (ISBN 0-317-17425-8). Auromere.

--Bases of Yoga. 108p. 1983. pap. 3.50 (ISBN 0-89744-012-9). Auromere.

--Bhagavad Gita in Light of Sri Aurobindo. Maheshwar, ed. 1979. 20.00 (ISBN 0-89744-902-9); pap. 15.00 (ISBN 0-89744-903-7). Auromere.

--Collected Poems. 1979. 20.00 (ISBN 0-89744-904-5). Auromere.

--Dictionary of Sri Aurobindo's Yoga. Pandit, Sri M., ed. 1979. Repr. of 1966 ed. 7.50 (ISBN 0-941524-04-3). Lotus Light.

--The Durga Stotra. 31p. (Orig.). 1982. pap. 5.00 (ISBN 0-89744-235-0). Auromere.

--Essays on the Gita. 1979. 20.00 (ISBN 0-89744-907-X); lib. bdg. 30.00 (ISBN 0-89744-906-1); pap. 16.00 (ISBN 0-89744-908-8). Auromere.

--Evolution. 28p. Date not set. 2.50 (ISBN 0-317-17430-4). Auromere.

--Foundations of Indian Culture. 1979. Repr. of 1953 ed. 18.00 (ISBN 0-89744-909-6). Auromere.

--The Future Poetry & Letters on Poetry, Literature, Art. 1979. 22.00 (ISBN 0-89744-919-3). Auromere.

--The Gita with Text, Translation & Sri Aurobindo's Comments. rev. ed. Jhunjhunwala, Shyam S., ed. 270p. 1974. 9.45 (ISBN 0-89071-207-7); pap. 4.50 (ISBN 0-89071-200-X). Matagiri.

--Hymns to the Mystic Fire. Aurobindo, Sri, tr. Date not set. 18.00 (ISBN 0-89744-918-5). Auromere.

--Ideal of the Karmayogin. 170p. Date not set. 7.00 (ISBN 0-317-17429-0). Auromere.

--Letters on Yoga, Vol. I. 502p. 1979. 16.00 (ISBN 0-89744-984-3, Pub. by Sri Aurogindo Ashram Trust); pap. 12.00 (ISBN 0-89744-985-1). Auromere.

--Letters on Yoga, Vol. III. 720p. 1979. 22.00 (ISBN 0-89744-988-6, Pub. by Sri Aurobindo Ashram Trust); pap. 19.00 (ISBN 0-89744-989-4). Auromere.

--Letters on Yoga, Vol. II. 587p. 1979. 19.00 (ISBN 0-89744-986-X, Pub. by Sri Arobindo Ashram Trust); pap. 16.00 (ISBN 0-89744-987-8). Auromere.

--Letters on Yoga, 2 vols. (Life Companion Library Bible Paper Ser.). 1984p. 40.00 (ISBN 0-89744-014-5). Auromere.

--Life Divine. (Life Companion Library Bible Paper Ser.). 1112p. 1983. Repr. of 1949 ed. deluxe ed. 24.95 (ISBN 0-89744-008-0); write for info. Auromere.

--The Life Divine: A Commentary on Isha Upanished. 108p. (Orig.). 1981. pap. 7.50 (ISBN 0-89744-230-X, Pub. by Sri Aurobindo Ashram Trust India). Auromere.

--The Message of the Gita: With Text, Translation & Notes. Roy, Anilbaran, ed. (Sanskrit & Eng.). 1979. (Pub. by Sri Aurobindo Ashram Trust India); pap. 9.00 (ISBN 0-89744-977-0, Pub. by Sri Aurobindo Ashramtrust India). Auromere.

--More Lights on Yoga. 1979. pap. 3.50 (ISBN 0-89744-950-9). Auromere.

--Practical Guide to Integral Yoga. 7th ed. Manibhai, ed. 1979. pap. 9.00 (ISBN 0-89744-942-8). Auromere.

--Santan Dharma Ka Mahatva: (Uttarpara Speech) 14p. 3.00 (ISBN 0-317-17480-0). Auromere.

--Savitri: A Legend & a Symbol. 1976. 12.50 (ISBN 0-89071-266-2). Matagiri.

--The Secret of the Veda. (Sanskrit & Eng.). 1979. oversize ed. 40.00 (ISBN 0-89744-975-4, Pub. by Sri Aurobindo Ashram Trust India); pap. 30.00. Auromere.

--Sri Aurobindo Birth Centenary Library: Complete Writings of Sri Aurobindo, 30 vols. 1979. Set. 300.00x (ISBN 0-89744-964-9); lib. bdg. 400.00x (ISBN 0-89744-965-7). Auromere.

--Sri Aurobindo on the Tantra. Pandit, Sri M. P., compiled by. 47p. (Orig.). 1979. pap. 2.00 (ISBN 0-941524-17-5). Lotus Light.

--The Synthesis of Yoga. 899p. 1981. 12.50 (ISBN 0-89071-293-X, Pub. by Sri Aurobindo Ashram India); pap. 10.95 (ISBN 0-89071-292-1). Matagiri.

--Synthesis of Yoga. 6th ed. 1979p. 36.00 (ISBN 0-89744-931-2). Auromere.

--Synthesis of Yoga. 1979p. 30.00 (ISBN 0-89744-932-0). Auromere.

--Synthesis of Yoga. (Life Companion Bible Bks.). 1984p. 24.95 (ISBN 0-89744-017-X). Auromere.

--The Upanishads. 466p. (Sanskrit & Eng.). 1981. 40.00 (ISBN 0-89744-026-9, Pub. by Sri Aurobindo Ashram Trust India); pap. 30.00 (ISBN 0-89744-025-0). Auromere.

--The Upanishads: Texts, Translations & Commentaries, Pt. 1. 466p. 1981. 12.50 (ISBN 0-89071-295-6, Pub. by Sri Aurobindo Ashram India); pap. 9.50 (ISBN 0-89071-294-8). Matagiri.

Aurobindo, Sri & Sri Aurobindo Ashram Publications Dept. On Women. 126p. (Orig.). Date not set. pap. 6.00 (ISBN 0-89744-236-9, Pub. by Sri Aurobindo Ashram Trust India). Auromere.

Aurobindo, Sri, tr. see Pandit, M. P.

Aurobindo, Sri, tr. see Sri Aurobindo.

Aurora Art Publishers. The Hermitage. (Illus.). 191p. 1980. text ed. 11.25x (ISBN 0-391-02811-1, Pub. by Heinemann India). Humanities.

Aurora Art Publishing. The Russian Museum Painting. (Illus.). 211p. 1979. text ed. 11.25 (ISBN 0-391-02812-X, Pub. by Heinemann India). Humanities.

Aurousseau, M., ed. The Letters of F. W. Ludwig Leichhardt, 3 vols. 424p. 1968. Set. 45.00x (ISBN 0-686-79458-3, Pub. by Hakluyt Soc England). State Mutual Bk.

Aurousseau, Marcel. The Rendering of Geographical Names. LC 73-21258. (Illus.). 148p. 1975. Repr. of 1957 ed. lib. bdg. 15.00 (ISBN 0-8371-6133-9, AUGN). Greenwood.

Aurthur, Jonathan. Socialism in the Soviet Union. LC 77-5727. 1977. pap. 5.95 (ISBN 0-917348-14-1). Workers Pr.

Aus, Roger, jt. auth. see Hultgren, Arland J.

Ausband, John R., ed. Ear, Nose and Throat Disorders: Essentials of Primary Care. 2nd ed. 1982. spiral bdg. 12.00 (ISBN 0-87488-705-4); pap. 26.00. Med Exam.

Ausband, Stephen C. Myth & Meaning, Myth & Order. LC 83-5478. 137p. 1983. 10.45x (ISBN 0-86554-089-6). Mercer Univ Pr.

Ausberger, Carolyn. Syntax One: Syntactic Skills Development. 112p. 1982. 3-ring binder 37.50 (ISBN 0-88450-675-4, 3018-B). Communication Skill.

--Syntax Two: Interaction with 'WH' Questions. 208p. 1980. 3-ring binder 37.50 (ISBN 0-88450-717-3, 4000-B). Communication Skill.

Ausberger, Carolyn & Martin, Margaret J. Learning to Talk is Child's Play. 120p. 1982. pap. text ed. 11.95 (ISBN 0-88450-826-9, 3000-B). Communication Skill.

Ausberger, Carolyn & Mullica, Karyn. Group Games Galore: Wkbk. (Worksheets Unlimited Ser.). 120p. (gr. k-7). wkbk. 29.95 (ISBN 0-686-84661-3, 2074-B). Communication Skill.

--How to Use Reproducible Illustrations in Language Remediation. 224p. (Orig.). 1983. pap. text ed. 17.95 (ISBN 0-318-03003-9). Syndactics.

--My Own Notebook: Wkbk. (Worksheets Unlimited Ser.). 120p. (gr. k-8). 1982. wkbk. 29.95 (ISBN 0-88450-840-4, 2075-B). Communication Skill.

Ausberger, Carolyn, jt. auth. see Martin, Margaret J.

Ausbrook, Perry C., jt. auth. see Zeidman, Philip F.

Ausdle, Stephen Van see Van Ausdle, Stephen.

Ausdle, Steven Van see Van Ausdle, Steven.

Ausebel, J. & Biswas, A. K. Climatic Constraints & Human Activities. LC 80-41073. (IIASA Proceedings: Vol. 10). (Illus.). 215p. 1980. 35.00 (ISBN 0-08-026721-1). Pergamon.

Auser, Cortland P. Nathaniel P. Willis. (Twayne's United States Authors Ser.). 1969. pap. 5.95x (ISBN 0-8084-0009-6, T132, Twayne). New Coll U Pr.

Ausfeld, Margaret L., jt. auth. see Mecklenburg, Virginia.

Ausfeld, Margaret L., ed. see Willett, E. Henry & Brackner, Joey.

Ausiello, G. & Boehm, C., eds. Automata, Languages & Programming '78. (Lecture Notes in Computer Science Ser.: Vol. 62). 1978. pap. 28.00 (ISBN 0-387-08860-1). Springer-Verlag.

Ausiello, G. & Lucertini, M., eds. Analysis & Design of Algorithms for Combinational Problems. (Mathematical Studies: Vol. 109). 1985. 48.25 (ISBN 0-444-87699-5, North-Holland). Elsevier.

--Analysis & Design of Algorithms in Combinatorial Optimization. (CISM International Centre for Mechanical Sciences Ser.: Vol. 266). 209p. 1981. pap. 26.00 (ISBN 0-387-81626-7). Springer-Verlag.

Ausiello, G. & Protasi, M., eds. CAAP 1983. (Lecture Notes in Computer Science: Vol. 159). 416p. (Eng. & Fr.). 1983. pap. 20.00 (ISBN 0-387-12727-5). Springer-Verlag.

Ausiello, G., et al, eds. Algorithm Design for Computer System Design. (CISM International Centre for Mechanical Sciences Courses & Lectures: No. 284). (Illus.). vii, 236p. 1984. pap. 18.30 (ISBN 0-387-81816-2). Springer-Verlag.

Ausikaitis, J. P., jt. ed. see Ma, Y. H.

Ausin, R. G. The Inch High Kid. (Which Way Secret Door Bks.). (Illus.). 64p. (Orig.). (gr. 1 up). 1983. pap. 1.95 (ISBN 0-671-46984-3). Archway.

Auslander, et al. Introduction to Dynamic Systems & Control. (Illus.). 400p. 1974. text ed. 47.00 (ISBN 0-07-002491-X). McGraw.

Auslander, D. M., ed. Case Studies in Computer Control. 87p. 1978. 18.00 (ISBN 0-685-66791-X, H00117). ASME.

Auslander, David & Sagues, Paul. Microprocessors for Measurement & Control. 310p. (Orig.). 1981. pap. 15.99 (ISBN 0-07-931057-5, 57-5). Osborne-McGraw.

Auslander, J. & Hill, F. E. Winged Horse: The Story of the Poets & Their Poetry. LC 68-24959. (Studies in Poetry, No. 38). 1968. Repr. of 1928 ed. lib. bdg. 49.95x (ISBN 0-8383-0328-5). Haskell.

Auslander, L. Lecture Notes on Nil-Theta Functions. LC 77-16471. (Conference Board of the Mathematical Sciences Ser.: No. 34). 96p. 1984. pap. 10.00 (ISBN 0-8218-1684-5, CBMS34). Am Math.

Auslander, L. & Tolimieri, R. Abelian Harmonic Analysis, Theta Functions & Functional Analysis on a Nilmanifold. (Lecture Notes in Mathematics Ser.: Vol. 436). v, 99p. 1975. pap. 13.00 (ISBN 0-387-07134-2). Springer-Verlag.

Auslander, Louis & Mackenzie, Robert E. Introduction to Differentiable Manifolds. 1977. pap. 4.50 (ISBN 0-486-63455-8). Dover.

Auslander, Louis & Markus, Lawrence. Flat Lorentz Three Manifolds. LC 52-42839. (Memoirs: No. 30). 60p. 1959. pap. 11.00 (ISBN 0-8218-1230-0, MEMO-30). Am Math.

Auslander, Louis & Moore, C. C. Unitary Representations of Solvable Lie Groups. LC 52-42839. (Memoirs: No. 62). 199p. 1971. pap. 12.00 (ISBN 0-8218-1262-9, MEMO-62). Am Math.

Auslander, Louis, et al. Mathematics Through Statistics. LC 79-9749. 224p. 1979. pap. 13.50 (ISBN 0-88275-949-3). Krieger.

Auslander, M. & Bridger, M. Stable Module Theory. LC 52-42839. (Memoirs: No. 94). 146p. 1969. pap. 10.00 (ISBN 0-8218-1294-7, MEMO-94). Am Math.

Auslander, M. & Lluis, E., eds. Representations of Algebras, Mexico Nineteen Eighty: Proceedings. (Lecture Notes in Mathematics Ser.: Vol. 903). 371p. 1981. pap. 22.00 (ISBN 0-387-11179-4). Springer-Verlag.

--Representations of Algebras, Workshopnotes, Puebla, Mexico 1980. (Lecture Notes in Mathematics: Vol. 944). 258p. 1982. pap. 16.00 (ISBN 0-387-11577-3). Springer-Verlag.

Auslender, A., ed. see Conference, Murat-le-Quaire, March 1976.

Auslender, A., et al, eds. Optimization & Optimal Control: Proceedings. (Lecture Notes in Control & Information Sciences Ser.: Vol. 30). 254p. 1981. pap. 18.00 (ISBN 0-387-10627-8). Springer-Verlag.

Auslin, Myra S. Back Off. 72p. (gr. 5-12). 1984. pap. text ed. 4.95 (ISBN 0-86575-543-4). Dormac.

--Sticky Fingers. 72p. 1983. pap. text ed. 4.95 (ISBN 0-86575-434-9). Dormac.

Ausloos, M & Elliot, R. J., eds. Magnetic Phase Transitions. (Springer Series in Solid-State Sciences: Vol. 48). (Illus.). 269p. 1983. 32.00 (ISBN 0-387-12842-5). Springer Verlag.

Ausloos, P., ed. Kinetics of Ion-Molecule Reactions. LC 79-367. (NATO ASI Ser. B, Physics: Vol. 40). 516p. 1979. 75.00x (ISBN 0-306-40153-3, Plenum Pr). Plenum Pub.

Ausloos, Pierre, ed. Interactions Between Ions & Molecules. LC 74-31389. (NATO ASI Series B; Physics: Vol. 6). 690p. 1975. 95.00x (ISBN 0-306-35706-2, Plenum Pr). Plenum Pub.

Ausman, Robert K. Intravascular Infusion Systems Principles & Practice. 300p. 1984. lib. bdg. 41.25 (ISBN 0-85200-727-2, Pub. by MTP Pr England). Kluwer Academic.

Ausmus, Harry J. The Polite Escape: On the Myth of Secularization. LC 81-16924. xii, 189p. 1982. lib. bdg. 22.95x (ISBN 0-8214-0650-7, 82-84192). Ohio U Pr.

Ausonius. Poems, 2 Vols. (Loeb Classical Library: No. 96, 115). 12.50x ea. Vol. 1 (ISBN 0-674-99107-9). Vol. 2 (ISBN 0-674-99127-3). Harvard U Pr.

Auspitz, Katherine. The Radical Bourgeoisie: The Ligue de l'Enseignement & the Origins of the Third Republic. LC 81-15462. 320p. 1982. 34.50 (ISBN 0-521-23861-7). Cambridge U Pr.

Aussenegg, F. R., jt. auth. see Arecchi, F. T.

Aussenegg, F. R., jt. ed. see Arecchi, F. T.

Aussenegg, F. R., et al, eds. Surface Studies with Lasers. (Springer Series in Chemical Physics: Vol. 33). (Illus.). 270p. 1983. 29.00 (ISBN 0-387-12598-1). Springer-Verlag.

Aust, W. The Conservative Management of Squint. Bedwell, C. H. & Obstfeld, H., trs. (Illus.). 152p. 1970. 12.00 (ISBN 3-8055-0752-6). S Karger.

Austen, A. D., ed. see International Labour Organisation Staff.

Austen, Brian. English Provincial Posts, Sixteen Thirty-Three to Eighteen Forty: A Study Based on Kent Examples. (Illus.). 192p. 1978. 21.00x (ISBN 0-8476-2308-4). Rowman.

Austen, D. E. & Rhymes, I. L. A Laboratory Manual of Blood Coagulation. (Illus.). 160p. 1976. 19.95 (ISBN 0-632-00781-8, B 0376-5, Blackwell). Mosby.

Austen, E. E. Bombylidae of Palestine. (Illus.). 188p. 1937. 17.50x (ISBN 0-565-00108-6, Pub. by Brit Mus Nat Hist England). Sabbot-Natural Hist Bks.

Austen, Ernest E. Handbook of the Tsetse-Flies. 16.00 (ISBN 0-384-02585-4). Johnson Repr.

--Illustrations of African Blood-Sucking Flies Other Than Mosquitoes & Tsetse-Flies. 28.00 (ISBN 0-384-02590-0). Johnson Repr.

--Monograph of the Tsetse-Flies. 35.00 (ISBN 0-384-02595-1). Johnson Repr.

Austen, Jane. Charades. LC 74-13339. Repr. of 1926 ed. lib. bdg. 25.00 (ISBN 0-8414-2993-6). Folcroft.

--Charades. 1977. 16.50 (ISBN 0-685-81153-0). Porter.

--Charades & C: Written a Hundred Years Ago. 1978. Repr. of 1895 ed. lib. bdg. 27.50 (ISBN 0-8495-0042-7). Arden Lib.

--The Complete Novels of Jane Austen. Incl. Vol. 1. Sense & Sensibility, Pride & Prejudice, Mansfield Park. pap. 6.95 (ISBN 0-394-71891-7, V-891); Vol. 2. Emma, Northanger Abbey, Persuasion (ISBN 0-394-71892-5, V-892). (YA) 1976. pap. 4.95 ea. (Vin). Random.

--The Complete Novels of Jane Austen. LC 83-5473. 10.95 (ISBN 0-394-60436-9). Modern Lib.

--Complete Novels of Jane Austen. 1376p. 1983. pap. 8.95 (ISBN 0-14-009002-9). Penguin.

--Emma. (Classics Ser). (gr. 9 up). pap. 1.95 (ISBN 0-8049-0102-3, CL-102). Airmont.

--Emma. Lodge, David, ed. LC 76-127565. (Casebook Ser). 1970. pap. text ed. 2.50 (ISBN 0-87695-036-5). Aurora Pubs.

--Emma. (Bantam Classics Ser.). 446p. (gr. 9-12). 1981. pap. 1.95 (ISBN 0-553-21159-5). Bantam.

--Emma. (Illus.). 1976. pap. 3.50x (ISBN 0-460-01024-7, Evman). Biblio Dist.

--Emma. lib. bdg. 16.95 (ISBN 0-89966-242-0). Buccaneer Bks.

--Emma. Trilling, Lionel, ed. 1957. pap. 5.95 (ISBN 0-395-05115-0, RivEd). HM.

--Emma. (The Zodiac Press Ser.). 520p. 1978. 9.95 (ISBN 0-7011-1232-8, Pub. by Chatto & Windus). Merrimack Pub Cir.

--Emma. 1964. pap. 2.25 (ISBN 0-451-51941-8, CJ1524, Sig Classics). NAL.

--Emma. Parrish, Stephen, ed. (Norton Critical Editions). 430p. 1972. pap. 7.95x (ISBN 0-393-09667-X). Norton.

--Emma. Kinsley, James & Lodge, David, eds. (World's Classics Ser.). 1980. pap. 2.50 (ISBN 0-19-281504-0). Oxford U Pr.

--Emma. Blythe, Ronald, ed. (English Library Ser). 1966. pap. 2.50 (ISBN 0-14-043010-5). Penguin.

--Emma. abr. ed. Sen, Manju S., ed. (Sangam Abridged Texts). 144p. 1983. pap. 3.95x (ISBN 0-86131-322-4, Pub. by Orient Longman India). Apt Bks.

--Five Letters from Jane Austen to Her Niece Fanny Knight. 1978. Repr. of 1924 ed. lib. bdg. 15.00 (ISBN 0-8495-0031-1). Arden Lib.

--Fragment of a Novel. Repr. of 1925 ed. lib. bdg. 15.00 (ISBN 0-8414-1676-1). Folcroft.

--Jane Austen & Lyme Regis. LC 76-12354. 1973. lib. bdg. 12.50 (ISBN 0-8414-2971-5). Folcroft.

--The Jane Austen Library. Chapman, R. W., ed. (The Jane Austen Library Ser.). 152p. 1984. 18.00 (ISBN 0-8052-3937-5). Schocken.

--The Jane Austen Library: Lady Susan, Vol. I. Chapman, R. W., ed. LC 83-40456. 576p. 1984. 20.00x (ISBN 0-8052-3894-8). Schocken.

--Jane Austen's Letters to Her Sister Cassandra & Others. 2nd ed. Chapman, R. W., ed. 716p. (Orig.). 1979. Repr. of 1952 ed. 39.00x (ISBN 0-19-212102-2). Oxford U Pr.

--Lady Susan-the Watsons-Sanditon. Drabble, Margaret, ed. (English Library Ser.). 1975. pap. 3.95 (ISBN 0-14-043102-0). Penguin.

--Love & Friendship. 2.95 (ISBN 0-7043-3823-8, Pub. by Quartet England). Charles River Bks.

--Mansfield Park. (Classics Ser). (gr. 10 up). pap. 1.95 (ISBN 0-8049-0131-7, CL-131). Airmont.

--Mansfield Park. (Illus.). 1980. 12.95x (ISBN 0-460-00023-3, Evman); pap. 3.75x (ISBN 0-460-01023-9, Evman). Biblio Dist.

--Mansfield Park. lib. bdg. 16.95 (ISBN 0-89966-244-7). Buccaneer Bks.

--Mansfield Park. (The Zodiac Press Ser.). 352p. 1978. 9.95 (ISBN 0-7011-1233-6, Pub. by Chatto & Windus). Merrimack Pub Cir.

--Mansfield Park. 1964. pap. 3.50 (ISBN 0-451-51752-0, CE1752, Sig Classics). NAL.

--Mansfield Park. Kinsley, James & Lucas, John, eds. (The World's Classics Ser.). 1981. pap. 3.50 (ISBN 0-19-281526-1). Oxford U Pr.

--Mansfield Park. Tanner, Tony, ed. (English Library Ser.). 1966. pap. 3.50 (ISBN 0-14-043016-4). Penguin.

--Mansfield Park. (Bantam Classics Ser.). 400p. 1983. pap. 3.50 (ISBN 0-553-21121-8). Bantam.

--The Manuscript Chapters of Persuasion. Chapman, R. W., ed. LC 85-6174. (The Jane Austen Library: Vol. 3). (Illus.). 94p. 1985. Repr. of 1926 ed. 18.95 (ISBN 0-485-10502-0, Pub. by Athlone Pr Ltd). Longwood Pub Group.

--Northanger Abbey. 1980. 12.95x (ISBN 0-460-00893-5, Evman); pap. 2.95x (ISBN 0-460-01893-0, Evman). Biblio Dist.

--Northanger Abbey. Clay, N. L., ed. (The Guide Novel Ser.). pap. text ed. 4.50x (ISBN 0-435-16042-7). Heinemann Ed.

--Northanger Abbey. (The Zodiac Press Ser.). 240p. 1978. 9.95 (ISBN 0-7011-1234-4, Pub. by Chatto & Windus). Merrimack Pub Cir.

--Northanger Abbey. pap. 2.50 (ISBN 0-451-51834-9, CE1834, Sig Classics). NAL.

--Northanger Abbey. (World's Classics Ser.). 296p. Date not set. 8.95 (ISBN 0-19-250355-3). Oxford U Pr.

--Northanger Abbey. Davie, John, ed. Bd. with Lady Susan; The Watsons; Sandition. (The World's Classics Ser.). 1981. pap. 2.50 (ISBN 0-19-281525-3). Oxford U Pr.

--Northanger Abbey. Ehrenpries, Anne, ed. (English Library Ser.). 1972. pap. 2.50 (ISBN 0-14-043074-1). Penguin.

--Northanger Abbey & Persuasion. 1974. Repr. of 1906 ed. 12.95x (ISBN 0-460-00025-X, Evman). Biblio Dist.

--Persuasion. (Classics Ser). (gr. 10 up). pap. 1.50 (ISBN 0-8049-0107-4, CL-107). Airmont.

--Persuasion. 1976. pap. 2.95x (ISBN 0-460-01894-9, Evman). Biblio Dist.

--Persuasion. Clay, N. L., ed. (The Guide Novel Ser.). pap. text ed. 4.50x (ISBN 0-435-16040-0). Heinemann Ed.

--Persuasion. (The Zodiac Press Ser.). 248p. 1978. 9.95 (ISBN 0-7011-1235-2, Pub. by Chatto & Windus). Merrimack Pub Cir.

--Persuasion. pap. 2.95 (ISBN 0-451-51715-6, CE1715, Sig Classics). NAL.

--Persuasion. Davie, John, ed. (The World's Classics Ser.). 1981. pap. 2.95 (ISBN 0-19-281546-6). Oxford U Pr.

--Persuasion. Harding, D. W., ed. (English Library Ser.). 1967. pap. 2.95 (ISBN 0-14-043005-9). Penguin.

--Persuasion. (Bantam Classics Ser.). 240p. 1984. pap. 2.95 (ISBN 0-553-21137-4). Bantam.

--Plan of a Novel. 1979. 28.50 (ISBN 0-685-94338-0). Porter.

--Plan of a Novel According to Hints from Various Quarters. LC 72-188492. 1973. lib. bdg. 17.50 (ISBN 0-8414-1677-X). Folcroft.

--Pride & Prejudice. (Classics Ser). (gr. 10 up). pap. 1.95 (ISBN 0-8049-0001-9, CL-1). Airmont.

--Pride & Prejudice. (Literature Ser). (gr. 7-12). 1969. pap. text ed. 4.92 (ISBN 0-87720-711-9). AMSCO Sch.

--Pride & Prejudice. (Bantam Classics Ser.). 304p. (gr. 9-12). 1981. pap. 1.75 (ISBN 0-553-21154-4). Bantam.

--Pride & Prejudice. Kendrick, Walter, ed. (Mcdonald Classics Ser.). 410p. 1980. deluxe ed. 14.95 (ISBN 0-8464-1071-0). Beekman Pubs.

--Pride & Prejudice. 1978. (Evman); pap. 2.95x (ISBN 0-460-01022-0, DEL-04305, Evman). Biblio Dist.

--Pride & Prejudice. lib. bdg. 16.95x (ISBN 0-89966-243-9). Buccaneer Bks.

--Pride & Prejudice. (Reader's Request Ser.). 1980. lib. bdg. 13.95 (ISBN 0-8161-3076-0, Large Print Bks). G K Hall.

--Pride & Prejudice. Clay, N. L., ed. (The Guide Novel Ser.). pap. text ed. 4.50x (ISBN 0-435-16041-9). Heinemann Ed.

--Pride & Prejudice. Schorer, Mark, ed. LC 56-13877. (YA) (gr. 9 up). 1956. pap. 5.50 (ISBN 0-395-05101-0, RivEd). HM.

--Pride & Prejudice. (The Zodiac Press Ser.). 248p. 1978. 10.95 (ISBN 0-7011-1236-0, Pub. by Chatto & Windus). Merrimack Pub Cir.

--Pride & Prejudice. 1962. pap. 1.75 (ISBN 0-451-51916-7, Sig Classics). NAL.

--Pride & Prejudice. Gray, Donald, ed. (Critical Editions). (Annotated). 1966. pap. text ed. 6.95x (ISBN 0-393-09668-8, NortonC). Norton.

--Pride & Prejudice. Kinsley, James & Bradbrook, F. W., eds. (World's Classics). 1980. pap. 2.95 (ISBN 0-19-281503-2). Oxford U Pr.

--Pride & Prejudice. (Enriched Classic Ser.). (YA) (gr. 9-12). 1978. pap. 2.95 (ISBN 0-671-44389-5). PB.

--Pride & Prejudice. Tanner, Tony, ed. (English Library Ser.). 1972. pap. 1.95 (ISBN 0-14-043072-5). Penguin.

--Pride & Prejudice. LC 81-5215. (Raintree Short Classics). (Illus.). 48p. (gr. 4 up). 1981. PLB 15.15 (ISBN 0-8172-1673-1). Raintree Pubs.

--Pride & Prejudice. 464p. 1982. pap. 2.95 (ISBN 0-671-44389-5). WSP.

--Pride & Prejudice. Stewart, Diana, adapted by. LC 81-5215. (Raintree Short Classics). (Illus.). 48p. (gr. 4-12). 1983. pap. 9.27 (ISBN 0-8172-2018-6). Raintree Pubs.

--Pride & Prejudice. (The Illustrated Junior Library). (Illus.). 384p. (gr. 4 up). 1984. 10.95 (ISBN 0-448-06032-9, G&D). Putnam Pub Group.

--Pride & Prejudice. (Illus.). 304p. 1985. 11.95 (ISBN 0-396-08536-9). Dodd.

--Pride & Prejudice. LC 84-60894. (Illus.). 368p. 1984. 12.95 (ISBN 0-89577-198-5). RD Assn.

--Sanditon: A Facsimile of the Manuscript. 1975. 35.00x (ISBN 0-19-812556-9). Oxford U Pr.

--Sanditon, the Watsons, Lady Susan, & Other Miscellanea. 1978. Repr. of 1934 ed. 9.95x (ISBN 0-460-00004-7, Evman). Biblio Dist.

--Selected Letters, Seventeen Ninety-Six to Eighteen Seventeen. Chapman, R. W., ed. 240p. 1985. pap. 6.95 (ISBN 0-19-281485-0). Oxford U Pr.

--Sense & Sensibility. (Classics Ser). (gr. 10 up). pap. 1.50 (ISBN 0-8049-0058-2, CL-58). Airmont.

--Sense & Sensibility. (Literature Ser). (gr. 10-12). 1970. pap. text ed. 5.00 (ISBN 0-87720-738-0). AMSCO Sch.

--Sense & Sensibility. 1978. 12.95x (ISBN 0-460-00021-7, Evman); pap. 2.95x (ISBN 0-460-01021-2, Evman). Biblio Dist.

--Sense & Sensibility. 544p. 1981. Repr. lib. bdg. 19.95x (ISBN 0-89966-287-0). Buccaneer Bks.

--Sense & Sensibility. (The Zodiac Press Ser). 280p. 1978. 10.95 (ISBN 0-7011-1237-9, Pub. by Chatto & Windus). Merrimack Pub Cir.

--Sense & Sensibility. pap. 2.25 (ISBN 0-451-51826-8, CE1826, Sig Classics). NAL.

--Sense & Sensibility. Kinsley, James & Lamont, Claire, eds. (World's Classics Ser.). 1980. pap. 2.95 (ISBN 0-19-281501-6). Oxford U Pr.

--Sense & Sensibility. Tanner, Tony, ed. (English Library Ser.). 1969. pap. 2.95 (ISBN 0-14-043047-4). Penguin.

--Sense & Sensibility. (Bantam Classics Ser.). 352p. (YA) (gr. 9-12). 1983. pap. 2.50 (ISBN 0-553-21110-2). Bantam.

--Three Evening Prayers. LC 77-7349. lib. bdg. 15.00 (ISBN 0-8414-1727-X). Folcroft.

--Two Chapters of Persuasion. LC 76-50133. Repr. of 1926 ed. lib. bdg. 15.00 (ISBN 0-8414-2867-0). Folcroft.

--The Watsons. LC 72-9808. 318p. 1973. Repr. of 1958 ed. lib. bdg. 27.50x (ISBN 0-8371-6598-9, AUTW). Greenwood.

--The Watsons. Chapman, R. W., ed. (The Jane Austen Library: vol. 4). 160p. 1985. Repr. of 1927 ed. 18.95 (ISBN 0-485-10503-9, Pub. by Athlone Pr Ltd). Longwood Pub Group.

Austen, Jane & Bell, Harriet. Love & Friendship & Other Early Works. (Illus.). 128p. 1981. 8.95 (ISBN 0-517-54459-8, Harmony); pap. 3.95 (ISBN 0-517-54372-9). Crown.

Austen, Jane & Hemmant, Lynette. Pride & Prejudice. 1980. 14.95 (ISBN 0-437-24575-6, Pub. by World's Work). David & Charles.

Austen, Jane see Eyre, A. G.

Austen, Jane see Swan, D. K.

Austen, Jane see Walpole, Horace.

Austen, Jillian. Way of the Dragon. LC 81-85172. 400p. (Orig.). 1982. pap. 3.50 (ISBN 0-86721-073-7). Jove Pubns.

Austen, K. F. & Lichtenstein, L. M., eds. Asthma-Physiology, Immunopharmacology & Treatment. 1974. 60.00 (ISBN 0-12-068450-0). Acad Pr.

Austen, Leigh J. A Memoir of Jane Austen. LC 79-11013. 1979. Repr. of 1882 ed. lib. bdg. 25.00 (ISBN 0-8414-2930-8). Folcroft.

Austen, Michael. Love-Act. 192p. 1982. Outlet 1.98 (ISBN 0-517-54674-4, Harmony). Crown.

Austen, Peter. The Country Antique Dealer. LC 81-67011. (Illus.). 192p. 1982. 17.50 (ISBN 0-7153-8223-3). David & Charles.

Austen, Ralph, jt. auth. see Lawson, William.

Austen, Terence. The Managerial Wisdom of Benjamin Franklin. (Illus.). 165p. 1983. 63.45x (ISBN 0-89266-402-9). Am Classical Coll Pr.

Austen, W. Gerald, jt. auth. see Behrendt, Douglas M.

Austen-Leigh, Emma. Jane Austen & Bath. LC 76-30698. Repr. of 1939 ed. lib. bdg. 10.00 (ISBN 0-8414-2967-7). Folcroft.

--Jane Austen & Steventon. 1978. Repr. of 1937 ed. lib. bdg. 20.00 (ISBN 0-8495-0047-8). Arden Lib.

Austen-Leigh, Mary A. Personal Aspects of Jane Austen. 1978. Repr. of 1920 ed. lib. bdg. 25.00 (ISBN 0-8495-0057-5). Arden Lib.

--Personal Aspects of Jane Austen. LC 74-5080. Repr. of 1920 ed. lib. bdg. 20.00 (ISBN 0-8414-2972-3). Folcroft.

Auster, Albert. Actresses & Suffragists: Women in the American Theatre, 1890-1920. LC 83-19253. 192p. 1984. text ed. 22.95 (ISBN 0-03-069778-6). Praeger.

Auster, Albert, jt. auth. see Quart, Leonard.

Auster, Ethel, ed. Managing Online Reference Services. 300p. 1986. pap. text ed. 35.00 (ISBN 0-918212-93-6). Neal-Schuman.

Auster, Henry. Local Habitations: Regionalism in the Early Novels of George Eliot. LC 74-116734. 1970. 15.00x (ISBN 0-674-53676-2). Harvard U Pr.

Auster, Louis, jt. auth. see Krantz, Morris.

Auster, Paul. City of Glass. (New American Fiction Ser.: No. 4). 208p. 1985. 13.95 (ISBN 0-940650-52-5); ltd., signed ed. 30.00 (ISBN 0-940650-53-3). Sun & Moon MD.

--Facing the Music. 1980. pap. 2.50 (ISBN 0-930794-29-X). Station Hill Pr.

--The Invention of Solitude. LC 82-16757. (Illus.). 174p. (Orig.). 1982. pap. 8.00 (ISBN 0-915342-37-5). SUN.

--The Invention of Solitude. 192p. 1985. pap. 3.95 (ISBN 0-380-69845-5, Discus). Avon.

--Wall Writing. 1976. signed ed. 10.00 (ISBN 0-685-79213-7); pap. 3.00 (ISBN 0-685-79214-5). Figures.

--White Spaces. 1980. pap. 3.50 (ISBN 0-930794-27-3). Station Hill Pr.

Auster, Paul, ed. The Random House Book of Twentieth Century French Poetry. LC 82-17342. 688p. 1984. pap. 11.95 (ISBN 0-394-71748-1, Vin). Random.

--The Random House Book of Twentieth-Century French Poetry: With Translations by American & British Poets. LC 82-280. 746p. 1982. 25.00 (ISBN 0-394-52197-8). Random.

Auster, Paul, ed. & tr. see Joubert, Joseph.

Auster, Paul, tr. see Blanchot, Maurice.

Auster, Paul, tr. see Chesneaux, Jean, et al.

Auster, Paul, tr. see Chesneaux, Jean.

Auster, Paul, tr. see Friedlander, Saul & Hussein, Mahmoud.

Auster, Paul, tr. see Mallarme, Stephane.

Auster, Paul, tr. see Petit, Philippe.

Auster, Paul, tr. see Sartre, Jean-Paul.

Auster, Richard D. & Silver, Morris. The State As a Firm. (Studies in Public Choice: Vol. 3). 1979. lib. bdg. 17.25 (ISBN 0-89838-000-6, Pub. by Martinus Hijhoff Netherlands). Kluwer Academic.

Auster, Rolf. Tax Strategies: Making the Right Decision. 308p. 1983. 27.50 (ISBN 0-317-04234-3, 4935). Commerce.

Austerman, Miriam. Animals: Unique Moments. LC 77-11699. 1977. lib. bdg. 10.00x (ISBN 0-916004-06-6); pap. 4.95 (ISBN 0-916004-05-8). Theorex.

Austerman, Wayne R. Sharps Rifles & Spanish Mules: The San Antonio-El Paso Mail, 1851-1881. LC 84-40557. (Illus.). 336p. 1985. 29.50 (ISBN 0-89096-220-0). Tex A&M Univ Pr.

Austermann, Winnefred. A Legislator's Guide to Oversight of Federal Funds. (Legislative Finance Paper Ser.). 100p. 1980. 5.00 (ISBN 0-317-36349-2). Natl Conf State Legis.

Austern, Norman. Direct Nuclear Reaction Theories. LC 78-100327. (Interscience Monographs & Texts in Physics & Astronomy: Vol. 25). pap. 100.00 (ISBN 0-317-08487-9, 2006343). Bks Demand UMI.

Austgen, Robert J. Natural Motivation in the Pauline Epistles. rev. ed. 1969. 10.95 (ISBN 0-268-00374-2). U of Notre Dame Pr.

Austin. Aeneid. 1984. 11.95 (ISBN 0-317-14013-2). Oxford U Pr.

Austin & Howard. Born to Sing: Voice Training Course. 120p. pap. 39.95 incl. 4 cassettes (ISBN 0-934419-03-5). Cherry Lane.

Austin & Jeffreys. The Manufacture of Methyl-Ethyl-Ketone from 2 Butanol: A Worked Solution to a Problem in Chemical Engineering. 221p. 1981. 54.00x (ISBN 0-85295-115-9, Pub. by Inst Chem Eng England). State Mutual Bk.

Austin, jt. auth. see Burns.

Austin, A. The Autobiography of Alfred Austin, Poet Laureate. Repr. of 1911 ed. 36.00 (ISBN 0-527-03880-6). Kraus Repr.

Austin, A. Everett, Jr. A Director's Taste & Achievement. (Illus.). 92p. 1958. pap. 2.50 (ISBN 0-317-13586-4). Wadsworth Atheneum.

Austin, Aleine. Matthew Lyon: "New Man" of the Democratic Revolution, 1749-1822. LC 80-281. (Illus.). 208p. 1980. 22.50x (ISBN 0-271-00262-X). Pa St U Pr.

Austin, Alfred. Autobiography of Alfred Austin, Poet Laureate, 1835-1910, 2vols. in 1. LC 79-148744. (Illus.). Repr. of 1911 ed. 34.50 (ISBN 0-404-08717-5). AMS Pr.

--Bridling of Pegasus: Prose Papers on Poetry. facs. ed. LC 67-22053. (Essay Index Reprint Ser). 1910. 18.00 (ISBN 0-8369-0164-9). Ayer Co Pubs.

--Haunts of Ancient Peace. Repr. of 1902 ed. 20.00 (ISBN 0-8492-9991-8). R West.

--Lamia's Winter Quarters. Repr. of 1898 ed. 20.00 (ISBN 0-8492-9988-8). R West.

--The Poetry of the Period. (Victoria Muse Ser.). 300p. 1985. lib. bdg. 40.00 (ISBN 0-8240-8600-7). Garland Pub.

Austin, Alicia. The Illustrated Night Before Christmas. (Illus.). 96p. (gr. k-5). 1983. pap. 1.95 (ISBN 0-448-14151-5, Pub. by Tempo). Ace Bks.

Austin, Allan D. African Muslims in Antebellum America: A Sourcebook. LC 80-9045. 500p. 1981. lib. bdg. 83.00 (ISBN 0-8240-9317-8). Garland Pub.

Austin, Althea. First Impressions: From the Diary of Althea Austin. 1984. 6.95 (ISBN 0-533-05806-6). Vantage.

Austin, Ann E. & Gamson, Zelda F. Academic Workplace: New Demands, Heightened Tensions. Fife, Jonathan D., ed. LC 84-219871. (ASHE-ERIC Higher Education Research Report Ser.: No. 10, 1983). 120p. (Orig.). 1984. pap. 7.50 (ISBN 0-913317-09-8). Assn Study Higher Ed.

Austin, Anne L. The Woolsey Sisters of New York: A Family's Involvement in the Civil War & a New Profession. LC 78-161991. (Memoirs Ser.: Vol. 85). (Illus.). 1971. pap. 6.00 (ISBN 0-87169-085-3). Am Philos.

Austin, Arthur D. Complex Litigation Confronts the Jury System: A Case Study. 120p. 1984. 20.00 (ISBN 0-89093-484-3). U Pubns Amer.

--In Stalin's Secret Service. (Foreign Intelligence Bks.). 320p. 1985. Repr. of 1939 ed. 24.00 (ISBN 0-89093-549-1). U Pubns Amer.

Austin, Barbara, jt. auth. see Wardell, Judy.

Austin, Ben. The Forty Year Cycle. (Illus.). 405p. 1980. 10.00 (ISBN 0-937982-00-8). Kilmarnock Pr.

--Goodbye, Dolly. Date not set. price not set. Kilmarnock Pr.

--How to Handle the Spoilers. LC 83-90320. 172p. 1983. pap. 3.95 (ISBN 0-317-02513-9). Kilmarnock Pr.

Austin, Bertram & Lloyd, W. Francis. The Secret of High Wages. Chandler, Alfred D., ed. LC 79-7529. (History of Management Thought & Practice Ser.). 1980. Repr. of 1926 ed. lib. bdg. 12.00x (ISBN 0-405-12314-0). Ayer Co Pubs.

Austin, Bill. How to Get What You Pray For. LC 83-50970. 160p. 1984. pap. 4.95 (ISBN 0-8423-1473-3); leader's guide 2.95 (ISBN 0-8423-1474-1). Tyndale.

Austin, Bill R. Austin's Topical History of Christianity. 527p. 1983. 14.95 (ISBN 0-8423-0096-1). Tyndale.

Austin, Bruce. Current Research in Film, Vol. 1. Voigt, Melvin J., ed. (Communication & Information Science Ser.). 232p. 1985. text ed. 29.50 (ISBN 0-89391-269-7). Ablex Pub.

Austin, Bruce A. The Film Audience: An International Bibliography of Research. LC 83-3316. (Illus.). 224p. 1983. 16.50 (ISBN 0-8108-1622-9). Scarecrow.

Austin, C. The Cow & the Coronary: Diary of Discovery, Nineteen Forty-Eight to Nineteen Seventy-Eight. (Illus.). 1979. 10.00 (ISBN 0-682-49327-9). Exposition Pr FL.

Austin, C., jt. ed. see Kassel, R.

Austin, C. K. Formwork to Concrete: Basic Design Principles & Construction Methods. 3rd ed. (Illus.). 1978. text ed. 43.50x (ISBN 0-7114-3602-9). Intl Ideas.

Austin, C. R. & Edwards, U. R., eds. Mechanisms of Sex Differentiation in Animals & Man. LC 81-66380. 1981. 89.00 (ISBN 0-12-068540-X). Acad Pr.

Austin, C. R. & Short, R. V., eds. Artificial Control of Reproduction. LC 70-185569. (Reproduction in Mammals Ser.: Bk. 5). (Illus.). 1973. 32.50 (ISBN 0-521-08505-5); pap. 9.95 (ISBN 0-521-09713-4). Cambridge U Pr.

--Embryonic & Fetal Development. 2nd ed. LC 81-18060. (Reproduction in Mammals Ser.: Bk. 2). (Illus.). 200p. 1983. 32.50 (ISBN 0-521-24786-1); pap. 12.95 (ISBN 0-521-28962-9). Cambridge U Pr.

--The Evolution of Reproduction. LC 76-8170. (Reproduction in Mammals Ser.: Bk. 6). (Illus.). 1975. pap. 9.95 (ISBN 0-521-29085-6). Cambridge U Pr.

--Germ Cells & Fertilization. 2nd ed. LC 81-18060. (Reproduction in Mammals Ser.: No. 1). (Illus.). 180p. 1982. 29.95 (ISBN 0-521-24628-8); pap. 12.95 (ISBN 0-521-28861-4). Cambridge U Pr.

--Hormonal Control of Reproduction. 2nd ed. LC 81-18060. (Reproduction of Mammals Ser.: No. 3). 170p. 1984. 42.50 (ISBN 0-521-25637-2); pap. 16.95 (ISBN 0-521-27594-6). Cambridge U Pr.

--Hormones in Reproduction. LC 73-178279. (Reproduction in Mammals Ser.: Bk. 3). (Illus.). 1972. Cambridge U Pr.

--Human Sexuality. LC 78-18959. (Reproduction in Mammals Ser.: Bk. 8). (Illus.). 110p. 1980. 32.50 (ISBN 0-521-22361-X); pap. 10.95 (ISBN 0-521-29461-4). Cambridge U Pr.

--Mechanisms of Hormone Action. LC 79-16287. (Reproduction in Mammals Ser.: Bk. 7). (Illus.). 1980. 42.50 (ISBN 0-521-22945-6); pap. 11.95 (ISBN 0-521-29737-0). Cambridge U Pr.

--Reproductive Fitness. (Reproduction in Mammals Ser.: Bk. 4). (Illus.). 225p. 1985. 39.50 (ISBN 0-521-26649-1); pap. 14.95 (ISBN 0-521-31984-6). Cambridge U Pr.

--Reproductive Patterns. LC 78-189597. (Reproduction in Mammals Ser.: Bk. 4). (Illus.). 120p. 1973. 32.50 (ISBN 0-521-08578-0); pap. 9.95 (ISBN 0-521-09616-2). Cambridge U Pr.

Austin, Cathrine, jt. auth. see MacKay, Harry.

Austin, Cedric. One Hundred Winemaking Problems Answered. 84p. Date not set. pap. 3.95 (ISBN 0-900841-41-9, Pub. by Aztex Corp). Argus Bks.

Austin, Charles J. Information Systems for Hospital Administration. 2nd ed. LC 83-8495. (Illus.). 340p. 1983. text ed. 28.00x (ISBN 0-914904-91-4). Health Admin Pr.

--The Politics of National Health Insurance: An Interdisciplinary Research Study. LC 75-14975. (Trinity Univ. Health Services Research Ser.). 109p. 1975. 7.50 (ISBN 0-911536-60-4). Trinity U Pr.

Austin, Colinus, ed. Comicorum Graecorum Fragmenta in papyris reperta (1838-1971) 1973. 158.00x (ISBN 3-11-004046-8). De Gruyter.

Austin, Cyril K. Formwork to Concrete. 3rd ed. LC 78-315629. pap. 81.80 (ISBN 0-317-27850-9, 2025255). Bks Demand UMI.

Austin, D. G. Chemical Engineering Drawing Symbols. 96p. 1979. 27.95x (ISBN 0-470-26601-5). Halsted Pr.

Austin, Daniel J., jt. auth. see Smith, Brian R.

Austin, David, et al. Reading Rights for Boys: Sex Role & Development in Language Experiences. LC 71-130790. (Orig.). 1971. pap. text ed. 3.95x (ISBN 0-89197-369-9). Irvington.

Austin, David, et al, illus. Deep Digs: Cartoons of the Miners' Strike. (Illus.). 128p. (Orig.). 1985. pap. 4.50 (ISBN 0-7453-0088-X, Pub. by Pluto Pr). Longwood Pub Group.

Austin, David R. Therapeutic Recreation Processes & Techniques. 241p. 1982. text ed. 24.45 (ISBN 0-471-08666-5). Wiley.

Austin, Dee. Reckless Heart. (Dawn of Love Ser.: No. 1). 1985. pap. 2.25 (ISBN 0-317-19327-9). Archway.

Austin, Dennis. Britain & South Africa. LC 81-4550. (Illus.). viii, 191p. 1981. Repr. of 1966 ed. lib. bdg. 22.50x (ISBN 0-313-22994-5, AUBS). Greenwood.

--Ghana Observed: Essays on the Politics of a West African Republic. LC 76-15398. 200p. 1976. text ed. 32.50x (ISBN 0-8419-0278-X, Africana). Holmes & Meier.

--Malta & the End of the Empire. (Illus.). 144p. 1971. 22.50x (ISBN 0-7146-2774-7, F Cass Co). Biblio Dist.

--Politics in Africa. 2nd ed. LC 83-40053. (Illus.). 199p. 1984. text ed. 16.00x (ISBN 0-87451-272-7); pap. text ed. 8.95x (ISBN 0-87451-278-6). U Pr of New Eng.

--South Africa & Its Neighbours. (Chatham House Papers). 296p. 1985. pap. 10.95x (ISBN 0-7102-0620-8). Routledge & Kegan.

Austin, Dennis & Lucuham, Robin, eds. Politicians & Soldiers in Ghana, 1966-1972. (Studies in Commonwealth Politics & History: No. 3). 332p. 1975. 32.50x (ISBN 0-7146-3049-7, F Cass Co); pap. 9.95x (ISBN 0-7146-4019-0, F Cass Co). Biblio Dist.

Austin, Diana J. The Maker. 1983. 4.95 (ISBN 0-8062-1995-5). Carlton.

Austin, Diane J. Australian Sociologies. 202p. 1984. 25.00 (ISBN 0-86861-512-9, 3390); pap. 9.95 (ISBN 0-86861-520-X). Allen Unwin.

--Urban Life in Kingston, Jamaica. (Caribbean Studies: Vol. 3). 312p. 1984. 48.50. Gordon.

Austin, Don. Portable City. 149p. (Orig.). 1983. pap. 7.95 (ISBN 0-317-14859-1). Left Bank.

Austin, Donald F. & Werner, S. Benson. Epidemiology for the Health Sciences: A Primer on Epidemiologic Concepts & Their Uses. (Illus.). 88p. 1982. pap. 8.75x (ISBN 0-398-02949-0). C C Thomas.

Austin, Dorothea. The Name Book: 1200 Names-Their Meanings, Origin, & Significance. 352p. (Orig.). 1982. pap. 6.95 (ISBN 0-87123-412-2, 210412). Bethany Hse.

Austin, Douglas V. & Fishman, Jay A. Corporations in Conflict... the Tender Offer. LC 75-94688. 1970. 15.95 (ISBN 0-912164-08-5). Masterco Pr.

Austin, Douglas V., et al. Modern Banking: A Practical Guide to Managing Deregulated Financial Institutions. LC 84-21754. (Bankers Management Ser.). 406p. 1985. 46.50 (ISBN 0-87267-053-8). Bankers.

Austin, E. L. Gift of Christmas. pap. 3.95 (ISBN 0-8010-0149-8). Baker Bk.

Austin, E. L. & Hauser, Odell. The Sesqui-Centennial International Exposition. LC 75-24109. (America in Two Centuries Ser). 1976. Repr. of 1929 ed. 53.00x (ISBN 0-405-07670-3). Ayer Co Pubs.

Austin, E. L. C. Earth's Greatest Day. 96p. (Orig.). 1980. pap. 3.95 (ISBN 0-8010-0163-3). Baker Bk.

Austin, E. V. A House by the Side of the Road. Wilcox, Patricia, ed. LC 75-31566. 105p. (Orig.). 1975. pap. 4.00 (ISBN 0-916078-01-9); pap. 6.00 signed (ISBN 0-916078-10-8). Iris Pr.

Austin, Ellis H. Drilling Engineering Handbook. (Short Course Handbooks). (Illus.). 288p. 1983. text ed. 36.00 (ISBN 0-934634-46-7); pap. text ed. 26.00 (ISBN 0-934634-54-8). Intl Human Res.

Austin, Emily. Mormonism: Or Life Among the Mormons. LC 74-134388. 1972. Repr. of 1882 ed. 21.50 (ISBN 0-404-08480-X). AMS Pr.

--Raven McCord. 1980. pap. 2.75 (ISBN 0-8439-0837-8, Pub. by Nordon Pubns). Dorchester Pub Co.

--Raven McCord. 432p. pap. 3.75 (ISBN 0-8439-2290-7, Leisure Bks). Dorchester Pub Co.

Austin, Evelyn. Secretarial Services. 208p. 1982. pap. text ed. 12.95x (ISBN 0-7121-1984-1). Trans-Atlantic.

--Senior Secretarial Duties & Office Organisation. 3rd ed. 432p. (Orig.). 1983. pap. text ed. 22.95x (ISBN 0-7121-1983-3). Trans-Atlantic.

Austin, Frederick B. Red Flag. facsimile ed. LC 72-37258. (Short Story Index Reprint Ser.). Repr. of 1934 ed. 21.50 (ISBN 0-8369-4069-5). Ayer Co Pubs.

--Saga of the Sea. facsimile ed. LC 76-116930. (Short Story Index Reprint Ser.). Repr. of 1929 ed. 19.00 (ISBN 0-8369-3432-6). Ayer Co Pubs.

--Saga of the Sword. facsimile ed. LC 75-106243. (Short Story Index Reprint Ser.). 1929. 19.00 (ISBN 0-8369-3279-X). Ayer Co Pubs.

--When Mankind Was Young. facs. ed. LC 71-125201. (Short Story Index Reprint Ser). 1927. 17.00 (ISBN 0-8369-3568-3). Ayer Co Pubs.

Austin, G. R. Early Childhood Education: An International Perspective. (Educational Psychology Ser.). 1976. 45.00 (ISBN 0-12-068550-7). Acad Pr.

Austin, Gabriel. The Library of Jean Grolier. LC 78-85855. (Illus.). viii, 137p. 1971. 10.00x (ISBN 0-8139-0458-7, Grolier Club). U Pr of Va.

--Library of Jean Grolier: A Preliminary Catalogue. LC 78-85855. (Illus.). 137p. 1971. 10.00x (ISBN 0-8139-0458-7, Dist. by U Pr of Va). Grolier Club.

Austin, Gary. Bibliography on Deafness. 1976. pap. 4.00 (ISBN 0-913072-20-6). Natl Assn Deaf.

Austin, Gary F., jt. auth. see Neyhus, Arthur I.

Austin, George. The Spinal Cord. 3rd ed. LC 82-15523. (Illus.). 848p. 1983. monograph 86.00 (ISBN 0-89640-079-4). Igaku-Shoin.

--Spinal Cord: Basic Aspects & Surgical Considerations. 2nd ed. (Illus.). 780p. 1972. photocopy ed. 61.50x (ISBN 0-398-02219-4). C C Thomas.

Austin, George L. Henry Wadsworth Longfellow. LC 73-12138. 1888. 40.00 (ISBN 0-8414-2889-1). Folcroft.

--Henry Wadsworth Longfellow: His Life, His Works & His Friendships. 419p. 1980. Repr. of 1888 ed. lib. bdg. 35.00 (ISBN 0-8492-3249-X). R West.

--Henry Wadsworth Longfellow: His Life, His Works, His Friendship. 1980. Repr. of 1888 ed. lib. bdg. 35.00 (ISBN 0-8495-0153-9). Arden Lib.

--Life & Times of Wendell Phillips. LC 74-99334. 1969. Repr. of 1884 ed. lib. bdg. 21.00 (ISBN 0-8411-0005-5). Metro Bks.

--The Life of Franz Schubert. LC 74-27330. Repr. of 1873 ed. 17.50 (ISBN 0-404-12856-4). AMS Pr.

Austin, George M. Microneurosurgical Anastomoses for Cerebral Ischemia. (Illus.). 392p. 1976. photocopy ed. 54.75x (ISBN 0-398-03436-2). C C Thomas.

Austin, Gerard. Anointing with the Spirit. (Reformed Rites of the Catholic Church Ser.: Vol. 2). 192p. (Orig.). 1985. pap. 10.95 (ISBN 0-916134-70-9). Pueblo Pub Co.

Austin, Gilbert. Chironomia: Or, a Treatise on Rhetorical Delivery. Robb, Mary M. & Thonssen, Lester, eds. LC 66-17967. (Landmarks in Rhetoric & Public Address Ser). (Illus.). 658p. 1966. 12.50x (ISBN 0-8093-0229-2). S Ill U Pr.

Austin, Gilbert & Garber, Herbert. The Rise & Fall of National Test Scores. LC 81-17668. (Educational Psychology Ser.). 1981. 30.00 (ISBN 0-12-068580-9). Acad Pr.

Austin, Glenn. Parents' Medical Manual. LC 78-2759. (Illus.). 1978. (Spec); pap. 8.95 (ISBN 0-13-650309-8). P-H.

Austin, Glenn, ed. The Parents' Guide to Child Raising. LC 77-28168. (Illus.). 1978. 15.95 (ISBN 0-13-650028-5, Spec); (Spec). P-H.

Austin, Gregory A. Alcohol in Western Society: From Antiquity to 1800; A Chronological History. 467p. 1985. lib. bdg. 60.00 (ISBN 0-87436-418-3). ABC-Clio.

Austin, Gregory A., et al. Drug Use & Abuse: A Guide to Research Findings, 2 vols. LC 84-3015. 1984. Vol. 1: Adults, 443p. lib. bdg. 55.00 (ISBN 0-87436-412-4); Vol. 2: Adolescence, 510p. lib. bdg. 65.00 (ISBN 0-87436-413-2); Set. lib. bdg. 110.00 (ISBN 0-87436-414-0). ABC-Clio.

Austin, Howard, jt. auth. see Howard, Elisabeth.

Austin, J. L. How to Do Things with Words. 2nd ed. Urmsson, J. O. & Sbisa, Marina, eds. 1975. 4.95x (ISBN 0-674-41152-8). Harvard U Pr.

Austin, J. L., tr. see Frege, Gottlob.

Austin, Jacqueline & Isern, Margarita. Arithmetic. 432p. 1984. pap. text ed. write for info. (ISBN 0-02-304720-8). Macmillan.

--Technical Mathematics. 3rd ed. LC 82-60533. 1983. pap. text ed. 25.95 (ISBN 0-03-061234-9); instr's manual 20.00 (ISBN 0-03-061236-5). HR&W.

Austin, James, jt. ed. see Krisberg, Barry.

Austin, James C. American Humor in France: Two Centuries of French Criticism of the Comic Spirit in American Literature. 1978. text ed. 10.50x (ISBN 0-8138-1920-2). Iowa St U Pr.

--Artemus Ward. (Twayne's United States Authors Ser.). 1964. pap. 5.95x (ISBN 0-8084-0055-X, T51, Twayne). New Coll U Pr.

--Bill Arp. LC 68-24308. (United States Authors Ser.). 1969. lib. bdg. 8.95 (ISBN 0-89197-678-7); pap. text ed. 4.95x (ISBN 0-8290-0081-X). Irvington.

--Fields of the Atlantic Monthly: Letters to an Editor, 1861-1870. LC 53-12551. 445p. 1953. 8.50 (ISBN 0-87328-007-5). Huntington Lib.

--Petroleum V. Nasby. (Twayne's United States Authors Ser). 1965. pap. 5.95x (ISBN 0-8084-0242-0, T89, Twayne). New Coll U Pr.

--The Significant Name in Terence. pap. 9.00 (ISBN 0-384-02605-2). Johnson Repr.

Austin, James E. Agroindustrial Project Analysis. LC 80-550. (World Bank Ser.). (Illus.). 224p. 1981. text ed. 20.00x (ISBN 0-8018-2412-5); pap. text ed. 7.50x (ISBN 0-8018-2413-3). Johns Hopkins.

--Confronting Urban Malnutrition: The Design of Nutrition Programs. LC 79-3705. (World Bank Occasional Paper). 1980. pap. 6.50x (ISBN 0-8018-2261-0). Johns Hopkins.

Austin, James E. & Hitt, Christopher. Nutrition Intervention in the United States: Cases & Concepts. LC 79-14494. 416p. 1979. prof ref 35.00 (ISBN 0-88410-370-6). Ballinger Pub.

Austin, James E., ed. Nutrition Programs in the Third World: Cases & Readings. LC 80-21083. 480p. 1981. text ed. 35.00 (ISBN 0-89946-024-0). Oelgeschlager.

Austin, James E. & Zeitlin, Marian F., eds. Nutrition Intervention in Developing Countries: An Overview. LC 80-29223. (Nutrition Intervention in Developing Countries Ser.). 256p. 1981. text ed. 35.00 (ISBN 0-89946-077-1). Oelgeschlager.

Austin, James H. Chase, Chance, & Creativity. LC 77-23011. 236p. 1978. 24.00x (ISBN 0-231-04294-9). Columbia U Pr.

--Chase, Chance, & Creativity: The Lucky Art of Novelty. 237p. 1985. pap. 11.95 (ISBN 0-231-04295-7). Columbia U Pr.

Austin, James T. The Life of Elbridge Gerry, 2 Vols. LC 77-99470. (American Public Figures Ser). 1970. Repr. of 1828 ed. Set. lib. bdg. 89.50 (ISBN 0-306-71841-3). Da Capo.

Austin, Jane. David Alden's Daughter, & Other Stories of Colonial Times. facsimile ed. LC 71-98556. (Short Story Index Reprint Ser.). 1892. 19.00 (ISBN 0-8369-3130-0). Ayer Co Pubs.

Austin, Jeanette H. Georgia Bible Records. LC 84-70998. 538p. 1985. 30.00 (ISBN 0-8063-1125-8). Genealog Pub.

--The Georgians: Genealogies of Pioneer Families. LC 84-80783. 479p. 1984. 30.00 (ISBN 0-8063-1081-2). Genealog Pub.

--Index to Georgia Wills. LC 84-73074. 169p. 1985. Repr. of 1976 ed. 17.50 (ISBN 0-8063-1112-6). Genealog Pub.

Austin, Jim, jt. auth. see Krisberg, Barry.

Austin, Joan B. & Fuller, Charlene. Fitness for All Ages. 192p. 1984. 14.95 (ISBN 0-8119-0533-0). Fell.

Austin, John. Lectures on Jurisprudence, or the Philosophy of Positive Law. 1976. 79.00x (ISBN 0-403-06116-4, Regency); pap. 59.00. Scholarly.

Austin, John & Brown, W. Jethro. The Austinian Theory of Law: Being an Edition of Lectures I, V, & VI of Austin's "Jurisprudence," & of Austin's "Essay on the Uses of the Study of Jurisprudence" with Critical Notes & Excursus. LC 83-22935. xv, 383p. 1983. Repr. of 1906 ed. lib. bdg. 37.50x (ISBN 0-8377-0342-5). Rothman.

Austin, John C. Chelsea Porcelain at Williamsburg. LC 76-49537. (Williamsburg Decorative Art Ser.). (Illus.). 227p. 1977. 30.00x (ISBN 0-87935-023-7). U Pr of Va.

Austin, John L. Philosophical Papers. 3rd ed. Urmson, James & Warnock, Geoffrey, eds. (Oxford Paperbacks Ser.). 1979. text ed. 22.00x (ISBN 0-19-824627-7); pap. text ed. 7.95x (ISBN 0-19-283021-X). Oxford U Pr.

--Sense & Sensibilia. Warnock, Geoffrey J., ed. 1962. pap. 6.95x (ISBN 0-19-500307-1). Oxford U Pr.

Austin, John O. Genealogical Dictionary of Rhode Island: Comprising Three Generations of Settlers Who Came Before 1690. LC 68-56072. 496p. 1982. Repr. of 1887 ed. 35.00 (ISBN 0-8063-0006-X). Genealog Pub.

--One Hundred & Sixty Allied Families. LC 77-71317. 288p. 1982. Repr. of 1893 ed. 28.50 (ISBN 0-8063-0763-3). Genealog Pub.

Austin Junior Forum, Inc. Lone Star Legacy: A Texas Cookbook. (Illus.). 368p. 1981. comb binding 14.95 (ISBN 0-9607152-0-7). Austin Junior.

Austin, Karen O., tr. see Galdos, Benito P.

Austin, Karl L., tr. see Dexeus, Santiago, Jr., et al.

Austin, L. Allan & Cheek, Logan M. Zero-base Budgeting: A Decision Package Manual. LC 79-12657. pap. 54.30 (ISBN 0-317-20402-5, 2023505). Bks Demand UMI.

Austin, L. G., et al. Process Engineering of Size Reduction: Ball Milling. (Illus.). 561p. 1984. text ed. 70.00x (ISBN 0-89520-421-5). Soc Mining Eng.

Austin, Larry M. & Burns, James R. Management Science. 608p. 1985. text ed. write for info. (ISBN 0-02-304840-9). Macmillan.

Austin, Lawrence & Jeffrey, Peter L., eds. Molecular Aspects of Neurological Disorders. 373p. 1983. 45.00 (ISBN 0-12-068420-9). Acad Pr.

Austin, Lettie, et al. College Reading Skills. (Orig.). 1966. pap. text ed. 12.00x (ISBN 0-394-30021-1, KnopfC). Knopf.

Austin, Lewis, ed. Japan: The Paradox of Progress. LC 75-18163. (Illus.). pap. 86.00 (ISBN 0-317-09754-7, 2021975). Bks Demand UMI.

Austin, Lou. The Little Me & the Great Me. 5.00 (ISBN 0-934538-26-3); pap. 3.00 (ISBN 0-934538-21-2). Partnership Foundation.

--A Lou Austin Anthology. 1983. 12.00; pap. 6.50. Partnership Foundation.

--My Secret Power. (gr. 1-6). 5.00 (ISBN 0-934538-22-0); pap. 3.00 (ISBN 0-934538-27-1). Partnership Foundation.

--Why & How Was I Born. (gr. 1-6). 5.00 (ISBN 0-934538-28-X); pap. 3.00 (ISBN 0-934538-23-9). Partnership Foundation.

--You Are Greater Than You Know. 7.50 (ISBN 0-934538-16-6); pap. 4.50 (ISBN 0-934538-11-5). Partnership Foundation.

--Your Perfect Partnership. 8.75 (ISBN 0-934538-17-4); pap. 4.50 (ISBN 0-934538-12-3). Partnership Foundation.

Austin, M. M. The Hellenistic World from Alexander to the Roman Conquest: A Selection of Ancient Sources in Translation. LC 81-6136. (Illus.). 504p. 1981. 68.50 (ISBN 0-521-22829-8); pap. 21.95 (ISBN 0-521-29666-8). Cambridge U Pr.

Austin, M. M. & Vidal-Naquet, P. Economic & Social History of Ancient Greece. 1978. 40.00x (ISBN 0-520-02658-6, CAL 465); pap. 8.95 (ISBN 0-520-04267-0). U of Cal Pr.

Austin, M. P. & Cocks, K. D. Land Use on the South Coast of New South Wales. 129p. 1981. 40.00x (ISBN 0-643-00248-0, Pub. by CSIRO Australia). State Mutual Bk.

--Land Use on the South Coast of New South Wales, 4 vols. Incl. Vol. 1. General Report. (Illus.). 129p (ISBN 0-643-00248-0); Vol. 2. Bio-Physical Background Studies. 119p (ISBN 0-643-00249-9); Vol. 3. Socio-Economic Background Studies. 107p (ISBN 0-643-00250-2); Vol. 4. Land Function Studies. 209p (ISBN 0-643-00251-0). 1978. Set. pap. 72.00 (ISBN 0-643-00247-2, C022, CSIRO). Unipub.

--Land Use on the South Coast of New South Wales: Bio-Physical Background Studies, Vol. 2. 119p. 1981. 40.00x (ISBN 0-643-00249-9, Pub. by CSIRO Australia). State Mutual Bk.

--Land Use on the South Coast of New South Wales: Land Function Studies, Vol. 4. 209p. 1981. 50.00x (ISBN 0-643-00251-0, Pub. by CSIRO Australia). State Mutual Bk.

--Land Use on the South Coast of New South Wales: Socio-Economic Background Studies, Vol. 3. 107p. 1981. 40.00x (ISBN 0-643-00250-2, Pub. by CSIRO Australia). State Mutual Bk.

Austin, Margaret F. & Vines, Harriet M. Bridges to Success: Finding Jobs & Changing Careers. LC 82-20107. (General Trade BKs.). (Illus.). 301p. 1983. 15.95 (ISBN 0-471-87062-5, Pub. by Wiley Pr); pap. text ed. 10.95 (ISBN 0-471-86577-X). Wiley.

Austin, Margot. Churchkitten Stories & More Kitten Tales. (Illus.). 80p. (ps-3). 1984. pap. 1.95 (ISBN 0-440-41282-X, YB). Dell.

--Churchmouse Stories. (Illus.). 112p. (ps-3). 1984. pap. 1.95 (ISBN 0-440-41284-6, YB). Dell.

Austin, Marilyn. Blackwater Bayou. (Orig.). 1979. pap. 1.75 (ISBN 0-532-17211-6). Woodhill.

--A Dream for Tomorrow. (YA) 1980. 8.95 (ISBN 0-686-73927-2, Avalon). Bouregy.

--Karen Connors, Family Therapist. (YA) 1978. 8.95 (ISBN 0-685-19059-5, Avalon). Bouregy.

--Stolen Secrets. (Orig.). 1981. pap. 1.95 (ISBN 0-8439-8045-1, Tiara Bks). Dorchester Pub Co.

Austin, Martha & Lynch, Regina. Saad Ahaah Sinil: Dual Language. 41p. 1983. 5.00 (ISBN 0-936008-18-0). Navajo Curr.

Austin, Mary. Acupuncture Therapy. 1983. 20.00 (ISBN 0-943358-17-5, Pub. by Aurora Pr). Weiser.

--American Rhythm: Studies & Reexpression of Amer-Indian Songs. LC 72-141890. 1971. Repr. of 1930 ed. lib. bdg. 18.50 (ISBN 0-8154-0367-4). Cooper Sq.

--Experiences Facing Death. Kastenbaum, Robert, ed. LC 76-19557. (Death and Dying Ser.). 1977. Repr. of 1931 ed. lib. bdg. 23.50x (ISBN 0-405-09553-8). Ayer Co Pubs.

--The Flock. LC 73-83228. (Illus.). 266p. 1973. Repr. of 1906 ed. 17.50 (ISBN 0-88307-509-1). Gannon.

--Isidro. LC 79-104408. (Illus.). Repr. of 1905 ed. lib. bdg. 14.00 (ISBN 0-8398-0070-3). Irvington.

--The Land of Journey's Ending. LC 83-1217. 459p. 1983. PLB 24.50x (ISBN 0-8165-0807-0); pap. 12.50 (ISBN 0-8165-0808-9). U of Ariz Pr.

--Land of Little Rain. (Illus.). 12.00 (ISBN 0-8446-0465-8). Peter Smith.

--The Land of Little Rain. LC 74-84233. (Zia Bks). (Illus.). 171p. 1974. pap. 6.95 (ISBN 0-8263-0358-7). U of NM Pr.

--The Textbook of Acupuncture Therapy. rev. 2nd ed. LC 72-78147. (Illus.). 280p. 1975. text ed. 20.00 (ISBN 0-88231-003-8). ASI Pubs Inc.

--A Woman of Genius. 320p. 1985. pap. 8.95 (ISBN 0-935312-44-7). Feminist Pr.

--The Young Woman Citizen. LC 18-21835. 1976. pap. 4.95x (ISBN 0-686-17163-2). Designs Three.

Austin, Mary & Jenkins, Esther. Promoting World Understanding Through Literature, K-8. 254p. 1983. lib. bdg. 22.50 (ISBN 0-87287-356-0). Libs Unl.

Austin, Mary, jt. auth. see Adams, Ansel.

Austin, Mary C., jt. auth. see Morrison, Coleman.

Austin, Mary C., et al. The First R: The Harvard Report on Reading in Elementary Schools. LC 77-13883. (Illus.). 1978. Repr. of 1963 ed. lib. bdg. 21.25x (ISBN 0-8371-9877-1, AUFR). Greenwood.

Austin, Mary H. Arrow-Maker. rev. ed. LC 70-90082. (BCL Ser.: No. 2). Repr. of 1915 ed. 12.50 (ISBN 0-404-00419-9). AMS Pr.

--The Basket. 1973. lib. bdg. 59.95 (ISBN 0-87968-710-X). Gordon Pr.

--Basket Woman. 1969. Repr. of 1904 ed. 14.00 (ISBN 0-404-00429-6). AMS Pr.

--Basket Woman: A Book of Indian Tales for Children. LC 4-27247. 1904. 10.00 (ISBN 0-403-00001-7). Scholarly.

--Isidro. 1973. lib. bdg. 59.95 (ISBN 0-8490-0427-6). Gordon Pr.

--Land of Journey's Ending. LC 70-86831. (BCL Ser.: No. I). (Illus.). 1969. Repr. of 1924 ed. 27.50 (ISBN 0-404-00435-0). AMS Pr.

--The Land of Little Rain. 1973. lib. bdg. 69.95 (ISBN 0-87968-182-9). Gordon Pr.

--A Woman of Genius. LC 76-51663. (Recovered Fiction by American Women Ser.). 1977. Repr. of 1912 ed. lib. bdg. 30.00x (ISBN 0-405-10043-4). Ayer Co Pubs.

Austin, Mary S. Philip Freneau, the Poet of the Revolution. Vreeland, Helen K., ed. LC 67-23885. 1968. Repr. of 1901 ed. 35.00x (ISBN 0-8103-3040-7). Gale.

Austin, Melanie, jt. auth. see Rodabaugh, Barbara J.

Austin, Michael J. Management Simulations for Mental Health & Human Services Administration. LC 78-12172. 436p. 1978. pap. 16.95 wkbk. (ISBN 0-917724-07-0, B7). Haworth Pr.

--Professionals & Paraprofessionals. LC 77-26273. 295p. 1977. text ed. 26.95 (ISBN 0-87705-305-7). Human Sci Pr.

--Supervisory Management for the Human Services. (P-H Ser. in Social Work Practices). 352p. 1981. text ed. 27.95 (ISBN 0-13-877068-9). P-H.

Austin, Michael J. & Cox, Gary. Evaluating Your Agency's Programs. (Sage Human Services Guides: Vol. 29). 192p. 1982. pap. 9.95 (ISBN 0-8039-0989-6). Sage.

Austin, Michael J., jt. auth. see Giddan, Norman S.

Austin, Michael J. & Hershey, William E., eds. Handbook on Mental Health Administration. (Social & Behavioral Science Ser.). 1982. text ed. 29.95x (ISBN 0-87589-544-1). Jossey Bass.

Austin, Michael J., et al. Managing Staff Development Programs. LC 84-6887. 252p. 1984. text ed. 23.95x (ISBN 0-8304-1104-6); pap. text ed. 12.95x (ISBN 0-88229-823-2). Nelson-Hall.

Austin, Mildred C. Woman's Divine Destiny. LC 78-21274. 1979. 7.95 (ISBN 0-87747-733-7). Deseret Bk.

Austin, Mrs., ed. A Memoir of the Reverend Sydney Smith by His Daughter, Lady Holland, 2 vols. 1973. Repr. of 1855 ed. 45.00 set (ISBN 0-8274-1210-X). R West.

Austin, Nancy, jt. auth. see Phelps, Stanlee.

Austin, Nancy K., jt. auth. see Peters, Thomas J.

Austin, Neal F. Biography of Thomas Wolfe. (Illus.). 1968. 15.85 (ISBN 0-911796-00-2). Beacham.

Austin, Norman. Archery at the Dark of the Moon: Poetic Problems in Homer's Odyssey. LC 73-9442. 311p. 1975. 32.50x (ISBN 0-520-02713-2, CAMPUS 302); pap. 9.95x (ISBN 0-520-04790-7). U of Cal Pr.

Austin, O. L., ed. Antarctic Bird Studies. LC 68-61438. (Antarctic Research Ser.: Vol. 12). (Illus.). 262p. 1968. 21.00 (ISBN 0-87590-112-3). Am Geophysical.

Austin, Oliver L., Jr. Birds of the World. (Illus.). 320p. 1983. 24.95 (ISBN 0-307-46645-0, 46645, Golden Pr). Western Pub.

--Families of Birds. Rev. ed. (Golden Field Guide Ser.). (Illus.). (gr. 9 up). 1985. pap. 7.95 (ISBN 0-307-24015-0, Golden Pr). Western Pub.

--Families of Birds: Golden Field Guides Ser. rev. ed. (Illus.). 200p. 1985. pap. 7.95 (ISBN 0-307-13669-8, 13669, Golden Pr). Western Pub.

Austin, P. A Grammar of Diyari, South Australia. (Cambridge Studies in Linguistics Monographs: No. 32). (Illus.). 230p. 1981. 85.00 (ISBN 0-521-22849-2). Cambridge U Pr.

Austin, P. B. Life & Songs of Carl Michael Bellman. 1967. 12.95x (ISBN 0-89067-048-X). Am Scandinavian.

Austin, Paul, jt. auth. see Lindfors, Viveca.

Austin, Paul B., tr. see Delblanc, Sven.

Austin, Paul B., tr. see Friis, Erik J., et al.

Austin, Phil. Capturing Mood in Watercolor. LC 84-6004. (Illus.). 192p. 1984. 21.95 (ISBN 0-89134-069-6, North Light). Writers Digest.

Austin, Philip R. Design & Operation of Clean Rooms. rev. ed. LC 79-103628. (Illus.). 462p. 1970. 59.95 (ISBN 0-912524-00-6). Busn News.

Austin, Phylis A. & Thrash, Agatha M. More Natural Remedies. (Illus.). 1984. pap. write for info. (ISBN 0-942658-06-X). Yuchi Pines.

--Natural Remedies: A Manual. 283p. (Orig.). 1983. pap. 6.95 (ISBN 0-942658-05-1). Thrash Pubns.

Austin, Phylis A., jt. auth. see Thrash, Agatha M.

Austin, Phylis A., et al, illus. Food Allergies Made Simple. 1985. pap. write for info. (ISBN 0-942658-08-6). Yuchi Pines.

Austin, R. B. Decision Making in the Practice of Crop Protection. 250p. 1982. 70.00x (ISBN 0-901436-71-2, Pub. by CAB Bks England). State Mutual Bk.

Austin, R. B., ed. Decision Making in the Practice of Crop Protection. (Illus.). 238p. 1983. pap. text ed. 28.00x (ISBN 0-901436-71-2, Pub. by B C P C England). Intl Spec Bk.

Austin, R. G. The Black Box. (Which Way Bks.). 1983. pap. 1.95. Archway.

--Brontosaurus Moves In. (Which Way Secret Door Ser.: No. 10). 64p. (Orig.). (gr. 1-3). 1984. pap. 1.95 (ISBN 0-671-47571-1). Archway.

--The Castle of No Return. (Which Way Bks.: No. 1). (Illus.). (gr. 3-6). 1982. pap. 1.95. Archway.

--Cosmic Encounters. (Which Way Bks.: No. 8). (Orig.). (gr. 3-6). 1982. pap. 1.95 (ISBN 0-671-45097-2). Archway.

--Crazy Computers. (Which Way Secret Door Ser.: No. 12). 64p. (Orig.). (gr. 1-3). 1984. pap. 1.95 (ISBN 0-671-47573-8). Archway.

--Creatures of the Dark. (Which Way Bks.: No. 9). (Illus., Orig.). (gr. 3-6). 1982. pap. 1.95 (ISBN 0-671-52449-6). Archway.

--Creatures of the Deck. (Which Way Bk.: No. 9). (gr. 6). 1982. pap. 1.95 (ISBN 0-671-46021-8). Archway.

--Curse of the Sunken Treasure. (Which Way Bks.: No. 7). (Illus.). (gr. 3-6). 1982. pap. 1.95 (ISBN 0-671-52447-X). Archway.

--The Enchanted Forest. (Which Way Secret Door Ser.: No. 11). 64p. (Orig.). (gr. 1-3). 1984. pap. 1.95 (ISBN 0-671-47572-X). Archway.

--Famous & Rich. (Which Way Bks.: No. 4). (Illus.). (gr. 3-6). 1982. pap. 1.95 (ISBN 0-671-43920-0). Archway.

--Giants, Elves & Scary Monsters. (Which Way Secret Door Bks.). (Illus.). (gr. 1-3). 1983. pap. 1.95 (ISBN 0-671-46980-0). Archway.

--Happy Birthday to You. (Which Way Secret Door Bks.). (Illus., Orig.). (gr. 1-3). 1983. pap. 1.95 (ISBN 0-671-47657-X). Archway.

--The Haunted Castle. (Which Way Secret Door Bks.). (Illus., Orig.). (gr. 1-3). 1983. pap. 1.95 (ISBN 0-671-46981-9). Archway.

--The Invasion of the Black Slime: And Other Tales of Horror. (Which Way Bks.). (Illus.). (gr. 8-12). 1983. pap. 1.95 (ISBN 0-686-44315-2). Archway.

--Islands of Terror. (Orig.). (gr. 3-6). 1985. pap. 1.95. Archway.

--Lost in a Strange Land. (Which Way Bks.: No. 5). (Illus.). (gr. 3-6). 1982. pap. 1.95 (ISBN 0-671-44110-8). Archway.

--The Magic Carpet. (Which Way Secret Door Bks.). (Illus.). 64p. (Orig.). (gr. 1-3). 1983. pap. 1.95 (ISBN 0-671-47568-1). Archway.

--The Monster Family. (Which Way Secret Door Ser.: No. 9). (gr. 1-3). 1984. pap. 1.95 (ISBN 0-671-47570-3). Archway.

--Poltergeists, Ghosts & Other Weird Stuff. (Which Way Bks.: No. 14). 128p. (Orig.). (gr. 3-6). 1984. pap. 1.95 (ISBN 0-671-46977-0). Archway.

--The Secret Life of Toys. (Which Way Secret Door Bks.). (Illus.). (gr. 1-3). 1983. pap. 1.95 (ISBN 0-671-46982-7). Archway.

--The Shadow Stealers. (Which Way Bk.: No. 16). 128p. (Orig.). (gr. 3-6). 1984. pap. 1.95 (ISBN 0-671-52635-9). Archway.

--The Spell of the Black Raven. (Which Way Bks.: No. 3). (Illus.). (gr. 3-6). 1982. pap. 1.95 (ISBN 0-686-85653-8). Archway.

--Trapped in the Black Box. (A Which Way Bks.: No. 12). (Orig.). (gr. 3-6). 1983. pap. 1.95 (ISBN 0-671-46731-X). Archway.

--Vampires, Spies & Alien Beings. (Which Way Bks.: No. 2). (Illus.). (gr. 3-6). 1982. pap. 1.75 (ISBN 0-686-85654-6). Archway.

--The Visitors from Outer Space. (Which Way Secret Door Bks.: No. 5). (Illus.). 64p. (Orig.). (gr. 3 up). 1983. pap. 1.95 (ISBN 0-671-46983-5). Archway.

--Wow! You Can Fly. (Which Way Secret Door Bks.). (Illus.). (gr. 1-3). 1983. pap. 1.95. Archway.

Austin, R. G., ed. see Cicero.

Austin, R. G., ed. see Virgil.

Austin, R. G., jt. ed. see Virgil, P.

Austin, R. M., et al. Seal Users Handbook. 2nd ed. 1979. text ed. 65.00x (ISBN 0-900983-90-6, Dist. by Air Science Co.). BHRA Fluid.

Austin, R. T., jt. auth. see Pearson, J. R.

Austin, R. W. Sufis of Andalusia: The Ruh Al-Quds & Al-Durrat Al-Fakhirah of Ibn 'Arabi. Austin, R. W., tr. LC 77-165230. (California Library Reprint: Vol. 91). 1978. Repr. of 1971 ed. 30.00x (ISBN 0-520-03553-4). U of Cal Pr.

Austin, R. W., ed. Ibn Al Arabi: The Bezels of Wisdom. LC 80-83892. (The Classics of Western Spirituality Ser.). 320p. 1980. 11.95 (ISBN 0-8091-0313-3); pap. 10.95 (ISBN 0-8091-2331-2). Paulist Pr.

Austin, Reginald P. The Stoichedon Style in Greek Inscriptions. LC 72-7884. (Greek History Ser). Repr. of 1938 ed. 19.00 (ISBN 0-405-04778-9). Ayer Co Pubs.

Austin, Reid, jt. auth. see Vargas, Alberto.

Austin, Richard. Designing the Natural Landscape. 165p. 1984. 21.95 (ISBN 0-442-20978-9); pap. 14.95 (ISBN 0-442-20977-0). Van Nos Reinhold.

--The Guardians. 240p. 1985. pap. 2.75 (ISBN 0-515-07980-4). Jove Pubns.

--The Guardian's: Night of the Phoenix, No. 4. 224p. 1985. pap. 2.75 (ISBN 0-317-26569-5); pap. text ed. 3.25. Jove Pubns.

--Report Graphics: Writing the Design Report. 176p. 1984. 25.95 (ISBN 0-442-20886-3). Van Nos Reinhold.

--Thunder of Hell. (The Guardian Ser.: No. 3). 224p. 1985. pap. 2.75 (ISBN 0-515-08327-5). Jove Pubns.

--Trial by Fire. (The Guardians Ser.: No. 2). 240p. 1985. pap. 2.75 (ISBN 0-515-08184-1). Jove Pubns.

Austin, Richard L. Site Graphics. (Illus.). 128p. 1984. text ed. 19.95 (ISBN 0-442-21077-9). Van Nos Reinhold.

Austin, Richard L., et al. Yearbook of Landscape Architecture: Historic Preservation. 1983. 32.50 (ISBN 0-442-20885-5). Van Nos Reinhold.

Austin, Richard L., et al, eds. Yearbook of Landscape Architecture: The Issues of Energy. (Illus.). 160p. 1985. 35.00 (ISBN 0-442-20987-8). Van Nos Reinhold.

--The Yearbook of Landscape Architecture: Private Spaces in the Landscape. (Illus.). 208p. 1984. 32.50 (ISBN 0-442-21075-2). Van Nos Reinhold.

Austin, Robert & Ueda, Koichiro. Bamboo. LC 70-96051. (Illus.). 216p. 1970. 27.50 (ISBN 0-8348-0048-9). Weatherhill.

Austin, Roger, jt. ed. see Kedward, H. R.

Austin, S. M., ed. The Two-Body Force in Nuclei. Crawley, G. M. LC 72-76009. 390p. 1972. 55.00x (ISBN 0-306-30598-4, Plenum Pr). Plenum Pub.

Austin, Stephanie. The Preppy Problem. 1984. pap. 1.95 (ISBN 0-449-70036-4, Juniper). Fawcett.

Austin, Stephen F. Establishing Austin's Colony: The First Book Printed in Texas, with the Laws, Orders, & Contracts of Colonization. Gracy, David B., 2nd, ed. (Illus.). 9.50 (ISBN 0-8363-0031-9). Jenkins.

Austin, T., ed. Two Fifteenth-Century Cookery-Books. (EETS OS Ser.: Vol. 91). Repr. of 1888 ed. 18.00 (ISBN 0-317-16317-5). Kraus Repr.

Austin, Thomas J. A Practical Account of General Paralysis, Its Mental & Physical Symptoms, Statistics, Causes, Seat, & Treatment. LC 75-16681. (Classics in Psychiatry Ser.). 1976. Repr. of 1859 ed. 18.00x (ISBN 0-405-07413-1). Ayer Co Pubs.

Austin, Timothy R. Language Crafted: A Linguistic Theory of Poetic Syntax. LC 83-48933. (Illus.). 192p. 1984. 22.50x (ISBN 0-253-33197-8). Ind U Pr.

Austin, Tony. Technical Training & Development in Papua 1894-1941. (Australian National University, Canberra Development Studies Centre Pacific Research Monograph: No. 1). 1978. pap. 8.00 (ISBN 0-7081-1003-7, Pub by ANUP Australia). Australia N U P.

Austin, Tricia & Long, John V., eds. Menus of the Valley's Finest Restaurants, 1985-86. 176p. 1985. pap. 5.95 (ISBN 0-930380-16-9). Quail Run.

Austin, Vincent. Rural Project Management. 1984. 32.00 (ISBN 0-7134-4416-9, Pub. by Batsford England). David & Charles.

Austin-Walker Sales Co. Apache Beadwork: Instructions & Designs. (Illus.). pap. 4.95 (ISBN 0-8466-4078-3, 178). Shorey.

Austin, William. Bill Austin's Freshwater Fishing Digest. (Illus.). 224p. 1983. pap. 9.95 (ISBN 0-911007-02-4). Prairie Hse.

--Music in the Twentieth Century. (Illus.). 1966. 24.95x (ISBN 0-393-09704-8, NortonC). Norton.

--Peter Rugg, the Missing Man. LC 72-104409. Repr. of 1824 ed. lib. bdg. 14.00 (ISBN 0-8398-0071-1). Irvington.

Austin, William, tr. see Dahlhaus, Carl.

Austin, William H. The Relevance of Natural Science to Theology. LC 75-43222. (Library of Philosophy & Religion). 132p. 1976. text ed. 28.50x (ISBN 0-06-490240-4, 06321). B&N Imports.

Austin, William M., ed. Papers in Linguistics in Honor of Leon Dostert. (Janua Linguarum, Ser. Major: No. 25). 1967. text ed. 23.20x (ISBN 90-2790-616-5). Mouton.

Austin, William W., ed. New Looks at Italian Opera: Essays in Honor of Donald J. Grout. LC 76-1010. (Illus.). 290p. 1976. Repr. of 1968 ed. lib. bdg. 21.75 (ISBN 0-8371-8761-3, AUNL). Greenwood.

Austin, William W., ed. see Debussy, Claude.

Austing, Richard H., et al. Advanced Placement Test in Computer Science (Pascal) 160p. 1985. pap. 8.95 (ISBN 0-668-06095-6). Arco.

Auston, D. H. & Eisenthal, K. B., eds. Ultrafast Phenomena IV. (Chemical Physics Ser.: Vol. 38). (Illus.). xvi, 509p. 1984. 29.00 (ISBN 0-387-13834-X). Springer-Verlag.

Australia Bureau of Census & Statistics. The Mathematical Theory of Population, of Its Character & Fluctuations, & of the Factors Which Influence Them. LC 75-38132. (Demography Ser.). (Illus.). 1976. Repr. of 1917 ed. 40.00x (ISBN 0-405-07985-0). Ayer Co Pubs.

Australia Bureau of Statistics. Yearbook Australia 1981. 65th ed. LC 9-6317. (Illus.). 843p. (Orig.). 1981. pap. 30.00x (ISBN 0-8002-3012-4). Intl Pubns Serv.

--Yearbook Australia, 1982. 66th ed. LC 9-6317. (Illus.). 843p. (Orig.). 1982. pap. 45.00 (ISBN 0-8002-2975-4). Intl Pubns Serv.

Australian Academy of Science, ed. see Commonwealth Scientific & Industrial Research Institute.

Australian Conference on Combinational Mathematics, Sixth, Armidale, Australia, August 1978. Combinatorial Mathematics VI: Proceedings. Horadam, A. F. & Wallis, W. D., eds. (Lecture Notes in Mathematics: Vol. 748). 1979. pap. 17.00 (ISBN 0-387-09555-1). Springer-Verlag.

Australian Conference on Combinatorial Mathematics. Proceedings. Holton, D. A., ed. (Lecture Notes in Mathematics Ser.: Vol. 403). viii, 148p. 1974. pap. 13.00 (ISBN 3-540-06903-8). Springer-Verlag.

Australian Conference, 3rd, Queensland, 1974. Combinatorial Mathematics Three: Proceedings. Street, A. P. & Wallis, W. D., eds. (Lecture Notes in Mathematics Ser.: Vol. 452). ix, 233p. 1975. pap. 16.00 (ISBN 0-387-07154-7). Springer-Verlag.

Australian Group for the Scientific Study of Mental Deficiency, ed. Beyond Normalisation: Philosophy, Theory & Practice in Services for the Intellectually Handicapped in Australia, Vol. 1. (Beyond Normalisation Ser.). (Illus.). 408p. (Orig.). 1983. pap. 40.25x (ISBN 0-9595220-2-6, Pub. by U of W Austral Pr). Intl Spec Bk.

--Beyond Normalisation: Philosophy, Theory & Practice in Services for the Intellectually Handicapped in Australia, Vol. 2. (Beyond Normalisation Ser.). (Illus.). 414p. (Orig.). 1983. pap. 40.25x (ISBN 0-9595220-3-4, Pub. by U of W Austral Pr). Intl Spec Bk.

Australian Information Service. Australia Handbook, 1982-83. 21st ed. LC 70-7283. (Illus.). 160p. (Orig.). 1982. pap. 15.00x (ISBN 0-642-07106-3). Intl Pubns Serv.

Australian Institute of Aboriginal Studies Biennial General Meeting, May, 1974, jt. auth. see Linguistic Symposium, Part B.

Australian Institute Of International Affairs. Australia & the Pacific. facsimile ed. LC 70-106405. (Essay Index Reprint Ser.). 1944. 19.00 (ISBN 0-8369-1443-0). Ayer Co Pubs.

Australian Military Forces. Ambush & Counter Ambush. (Illus.). 80p. 1965. pap. 5.00 (ISBN 0-87364-098-5). Paladin Pr.

Australian Museum Trust. The Wrens & Warblers of Australia. 376p. 1982. 125.00x (ISBN 0-207-14480-X, Pub. by Angus & Robertson). State Mutual Bk.

Australian National University. People & Places in a Landscape: Canberra Companions. new ed. 1979. pap. text ed. 3.25 (ISBN 0-7081-1004-5, Pub. by ANUP Australia). Australia N U P.

Australian National University Library. How to Locate Australian Theses: A Guide to Theses in Progress or Completed at Australian Universities & the University of Papua New Guinea. (Orig.). 1980. pap. text ed. 6.00 (ISBN 0-909775-06-0, 0539, Pub. by ANUP Australia). Australia N U P.

--The Sacred Texts of Buddhism - A Catalogue. LC 81-69251. (Bibliographical Ser.: No. 1). (Orig.). 1981. pap. text ed. 9.00 (ISBN 0-909775-08-7, 1029, Pub. by ANUP Australia). Australia N U P.

Australian Society. Animal Production: Proceedings of the Australian Society of Animal Production 13th Biennial Conference, Perth, August 1980. (Illus.). 544p. 1980. 79.00 (ISBN 0-08-024812-8). Pergamon.

Australian Society of Animal Production 14th Biennial Conference, Brisbane, Queensland, May 1982. Animal Production in Australia: Proceeding. (Illus.). 708p. 1982. 59.50 (ISBN 0-08-024836-5); pap. 40.00 (ISBN 0-08-024837-3). Pergamon.

Austrian, Geoffrey D. Herman Hollerith. LC 81-7752. (Illus.). 242p. 1982. 24.00x (ISBN 0-231-05146-8). Columbia U Pr.

--Herman Hollerith: Forgotten Giant of Information Processing. 418p. 1982. 25.00 (ISBN 0-231-05146-8, EY-00020-DP). Digital Pr.

--Herman Hollerith: Forgotten Giant of Information Processing. LC 81-7752. 418p. 1985. pap. 12.95 (ISBN 0-231-05147-6). Columbia U Pr.

Austrian Institute. Humanizing Prisons: Experiences from the Austrian Model. 1982. 6.45 (ISBN 0-318-02053-X). Natl Coun Crime.

Austrian, Robert. Notes from the Bedside, Laboratory, & Library. LC 85-1001. (Illus.). 160p. 1985. 25.00 (ISBN 0-8122-7977-8). U of Pa Pr.

Austrian Society for Geomechanics, 18th Colloquium. Stability of Rock Slopes & Underground Excavations. Mueller, L., ed. (Illus.). 1970. 33.70 (ISBN 0-387-80958-9). Springer-Verlag.

Austridan, Y., ed. Diccionario Hebreo-Castellano: Castellano-Hebreo. 390p. (Hebrew & Span.). 1979. pap. 40.00 (ISBN 0-686-92419-3, S-37819). French & Eur.

Austrin, Miriam G. Young's Learning Medical Terminology Step by Step: Textbook & Workbook. 5th ed. LC 82-14110. (Illus.). 387p. 1983. pap. 17.95 (ISBN 0-8016-5662-1). Mosby.

Austrom, Douglas R. The Consequences of Being Single. LC 83-49354. (American University Studies XI (Anthropology & Sociology): Vol. 6). 190p. (Orig.). 1983. pap. text ed. 24.70 (ISBN 0-8204-0095-5). P Lang Pubs.

Aust-Schminke, Janith. From Mary's Side: Summons for Change. 160p. (Orig.). Date not set. price not set (ISBN 0-916865-00-2); pap. price not set (ISBN 0-916865-01-0). Sansper.

Ausubel, David P. Drug Addiction: Physiological, Psychological, & Sociological Aspects. LC 58-8012. (Orig.). 1958. pap. text ed. 6.00 (ISBN 0-394-30877-8, RanC). Random.

--Ego Development & the Personality Disorders. LC 52-2222. 576p. 1953. 55.00 (ISBN 0-8089-0023-4, 790270). Grune.

--The Fern & the Tiki. 1977. pap. 8.95 (ISBN 0-8158-0359-1). Chris Mass.

--Maori Youth. 1978. pap. 8.95 (ISBN 0-8158-0358-3). Chris Mass.

--Psychology of Meaningful Verbal Learning: An Introduction to School Learning. LC 63-13252. 272p. 1963. 37.00 (ISBN 0-8089-0025-0, 790272). Grune.

--What Every Well-Informed Person Should Know about Drug Addiction. LC 79-16961. 1980. 18.95x (ISBN 0-88229-566-7); pap. 9.95 (ISBN 0-88229-721-X). Nelson-Hall.

Ausubel, David P. & Kirk, Daniel, eds. Ego Psychology & Mental Disorder: A Developmental Approach to Psychopathology. 368p. 1977. 43.50 (ISBN 0-8089-1004-3, 790275). Grune.

Ausubel, David P., et al. Theory & Problems of Adolescent Development. 2nd ed. 576p. 1977. 37.00 (ISBN 0-8089-1031-0, 790279). Grune.

--Theory & Problems of Child Development. 3rd ed. LC 79-93284. 688p. 1980. 38.00 (ISBN 0-8089-1183-X, 790280). Grune.

Ausubel, Herman. In Hard Times: Reformers among the Late Victorians. LC 72-9826. 403p. 1973. Repr. of 1960 ed. lib. bdg. 22.50x (ISBN 0-8371-6600-4, AUHT). Greenwood.

Ausubel, Nathan. Book of Jewish Knowledge. (Illus.). 1962. 22.95 (ISBN 0-517-09746-X). Crown.

--Pictorial History of the Jewish People: From Biblical Times to Our Own Day Throughout the World. rev ed. (Illus.). 1984. 19.95 (ISBN 0-517-55283-3). Crown.

--Pictorial History of the Jewish People. (Illus.). 1953. 19.95 (ISBN 0-517-09757-5). Crown.

Ausubel, Nathan, ed. Treasury of Jewish Folklore. 1948. 14.95 (ISBN 0-517-50293-3). Crown.

--Treasury of Jewish Humor. LC 51-10639. 1951. 17.95 (ISBN 0-385-04499-2). Doubleday.

Ausubel, Nathan, tr. see Asch, Shalom.

Auten, James H. Training in the Small Department. 144p. 1973. 16.50x (ISBN 0-398-02719-6). C C Thomas.

Autenrieth, Georg. Homeric Dictionary. Keep, Robert, tr. (Illus.). 366p. 1985. pap. 10.95x (ISBN 0-7156-1773-7, Pub. by Duckworth England). Biblio Dist.

--A Homeric Dictionary for Schools & Colleges. Flagg, Isaac, ed. Keep, Robert P., tr. (Illus.). 318p. (YA) (gr. 9 up). 1979. pap. 8.95x (ISBN 0-8061-1289-1). U of Okla Pr.

Auteroche, Jean Chappe D' see Chappe d'Auteroche, Jean.

Autery & Holl. Help I Need a Bulletin Board. pap. 5.50 (ISBN 0-89137-621-6). Quality Pubns.

Auteur, Hillary. The Carnal Confessions of Catherine the Great. (The Courtesans Ser.). 320p. 1984. pap. 3.95 (ISBN 0-523-42141-9). Pinnacle Bks.

--The Erotic Memoirs of Lucrezia Borgia. (The Courtesans Ser.). 320p. (Orig.). 1984. pap. 3.75 (ISBN 0-523-42142-7). Pinnacle Bks.

--The Erotic Memoirs of Marie Antoinette. (The Courtesans Ser.). 320p. (Orig.). 1984. pap. 3.75 (ISBN 0-523-42139-7). Pinnacle Bks.

Autgaerden, S., jt. ed. see Thomas, A.

Auth, Joanne B. Deskbook of Math Formulas & Tables. 208p. 19.95 (ISBN 0-442-20813-8); pap. 14.45 (ISBN 0-442-21106-6). Van Nos Reinhold.

Auth, Susan H. Ancient Glass at the Newark Museum. LC 76-47222. 1977. 15.95 (ISBN 0-932828-02-7); pap. 9.95 (ISBN 0-932828-08-6). Newark Mus.

Authier, Jerry, jt. auth. see Ivey, Allen E.

Author Aid-Research Associates International. Freelancers of North America, 1984-1985 Marketplace: Editors, Ghostwriters-Collaborators, Speechwriters, Business-Technical-Medical-Writers. 316p. 1984. pap. 32.95 (ISBN 0-911085-01-7). Author Aid.

Author Aid-Research Associates International, ed. Literary Agents of North America: 1984-85 Marketplace. 144p. (Orig.). 1984. pap. 16.95 (ISBN 0-911085-00-9, 0082-1). Author Aid.

Authur Andersen & Co., ed. see Blackman, Maurice.

Authur Andersen & Company. Book Distribution in the United States: Issues & Perceptions. (Illus.). 187p. 1982. pap. 60.00 (ISBN 0-940016-12-5); pap. 20.00. Bk Indus Study.

Autocar Editors, ed. see Garnier.

AUTOFACT Five Conference on Computer Integrated Manufacturing & the Automated Factory, Detroit, Mich., Nov. 1983. Autofact Five: Proceedings. xvi, 1048p. 1983. pap. 60.00 (ISBN 0-87263-127-3). SME.

Autofact Five Conference on Computer-Integrated Manufacturing & the Automated Factory, Detroit, Mich., Nov. 1983. Autofact Five: Proceedings. xvi, 1048p. 1983. 60.00 (ISBN 0-444-86820-8). Elsevier.

Autofact Four Conference on Computer-Integrated Manufacturing & the Automated Factory, Philadelphia, Pa., Nov.-Dec. 1982. Autofact Four: Proceedings. 688p. 1983. 60.00 (ISBN 0-87263-093-5). Elsevier.

Automated Design & Engineering for Electronics. Automated Design & Engineering for Electronics: Proceedings of the Technical Sessions, February 26-28, 1985, Anaheim, CA. pap. 97.30 (ISBN 0-317-26163-0, 2025191). Bks Demand UMI.

Automated Education Center. Analysis & Synthesis of a Learning Teaching System. LC 79-121255. 19.00 (ISBN 0-403-04450-2). Scholarly.

--An Annotated Bibliography of Biomedical Computer Applications. LC 79-120081. 19.00 (ISBN 0-403-04451-0). Scholarly.

--Annotated Bibliography of Human Factors Laboratory Reports (1945-1968) LC 72-121256. 29.00 (ISBN 0-403-04452-9). Scholarly.

--Automated Data Processing for Education-Curricular Implications. LC 79-119433. 29.00 (ISBN 0-403-04453-7). Scholarly.

--Automated School Administration. 19.00 (ISBN 0-403-04454-5). Scholarly.

--Automatic Language Processing. 19.50 (ISBN 0-403-04455-3). Scholarly.

--Automatic Program Analysis. 19.00 (ISBN 0-403-04456-1). Scholarly.

--A Computation Model with Data Flow Sequencing. 19.00 (ISBN 0-403-04457-X). Scholarly.

--Computer-Assisted Instructions. LC 76-121257. 25.00 (ISBN 0-403-04458-8). Scholarly.

--Computerized Educational Technology, Vol. 1. LC 79-119433. 25.00 (ISBN 0-403-04459-6). Scholarly.

--Computers in Education: Their Use & Cost. LC 78-119891. 25.00 (ISBN 0-403-04460-X). Scholarly.

--Data Display Programming. LC 77-118118. 275p. 29.00 (ISBN 0-403-04461-8). Scholarly.

--Data Processing for Guidance & Counseling Handbook. LC 67-22802. 19.00 (ISBN 0-403-04462-6). Scholarly.

--The Decision Module Compiler. LC 78-120097. 29.00 (ISBN 0-403-04463-4). Mgmt Info Serv.

--Design of Digital Control Systems. LC 70-120079. 19.00 (ISBN 0-403-04464-2). Scholarly.

--Digital Computer Graphics, 2 vols. 69.00 (ISBN 0-403-04465-0). Scholarly.

--Disc File Applications. LC 64-23108. 19.00 (ISBN 0-403-04466-9). Scholarly.

--Establishing an Educational Data Processing Center. 29.00 (ISBN 0-403-04467-7). Scholarly.

--Guide to PL-1, 2 vols. 740p. 49.00 (ISBN 0-403-04468-5). Scholarly.

--Hybrid Computer Application to Mathematical Models of Physical Systems. LC 70-125998. 19.00 (ISBN 0-403-04469-3). Scholarly.

--Information System Program Planning. LC 74-88620. 20.00 (ISBN 0-403-04470-7). Scholarly.

--Innovations in Teaching & Training. 19.00 (ISBN 0-403-04471-5). Scholarly.

--Management Guide to Computer Programming. 1969. 25.00 (ISBN 0-403-04472-3). Scholarly.

--Management of On Line Systems. 1969. 19.00 (ISBN 0-403-04473-1). Scholarly.

--Management Systems & Programming. LC 78-79912. 17.50 (ISBN 0-403-04474-X). Scholarly.

--On Line Computing Systems. LC 65-21221. 19.00 (ISBN 0-403-04475-8). Scholarly.

--On the Feedback Complexity of Automata. LC 75-120080. 19.00 (ISBN 0-403-04476-6). Scholarly.
--Records Management Handbook. 600p. looseleaf binder 95.00 (ISBN 0-403-04477-4). Scholarly.
--Simulation of a Production Control System. LC 71-118564. 259p. 1969. 29.00 (ISBN 0-403-04478-2). Scholarly.
--Source Data Automation. LC 72-125996. 1969. 29.00 (ISBN 0-403-04479-0). Scholarly.
--Studies in Indexing & Cataloging. LC 78-120543. 29.00 (ISBN 0-403-04480-4). Scholarly.
--A System Study of Abstracting & Indexing. LC 78-118563. 228p. 1969. 29.00 (ISBN 0-403-04480-4). Scholarly.
--Time Sharing. 1969. 15.00 (ISBN 0-403-04482-0). Scholarly.
--Total Systems. LC 62-14778. 19.00 (ISBN 0-403-04483-9). Scholarly.
--A User's Guide to the Adam System. LC 76-125997. 1969. 19.00 (ISBN 0-403-04484-7). Scholarly.

Automated Systems, NEMA. Automation User Survey. 15.00 (ISBN 0-318-18039-1). Natl Elec Mfrs.
--Strategic Justification of Flexible Automation. 10.00 (ISBN 0-318-18040-5). Natl Elec Mfrs.

Automatic Control in Electricity Supply Staff. Symposium on Automatic Control in Electricity Supply, 29-31 March, 1966 in Manchester, England. (IEE Conference Publication Ser.: No. 16, Pt. 1). (Illus.). pap. 98.00 (ISBN 0-317-09932-9, 2051588). Bks Demand UMI.

Automation Technology Symposium, 3rd, Monterey, Calif., Sept. 1981. Automation Technology for Management & Productivity Advancements Through CAD-CAM & Engineering Data Handling: Proceedings. Wang, Peter C., ed. (Illus.). 336p. 1983. text ed. 36.95 (ISBN 0-13-054593-7). P-H.

Automobile Association. AA Ireland: Where to Go, What to Do. (Illus.). 208p. 1981. pap. 8.95 (ISBN 0-86145-035-3, Pub. by Auto Assn-British Tourist Authority England). Merrimack Pub Cir.
--AA The Motorists' Atlas of Western Europe. (Illus.). 1982. 14.95 (ISBN 0-86145-029-9, Pub. by Auto Assn-British Tourist Authority England). Merrimack Pub Cir.
--AA Touring Map of Western Europe. (Illus.). 1981. pap. 4.95 (ISBN 0-86145-001-9). Merrimack Pub Cir.

Automobile Association & British Tourist Authority. A-Z Visitors' London Atlas & Guide. (Illus.). 96p. 1981. pap. 4.95 (ISBN 0-85039-107-5, Pub. by Auto Assn-British Tourist Authority England). Merrimack Pub Cir.
--AA-BTA Where to Go in Britain. (Illus.). 224p. 1981. 18.95 (ISBN 0-86145-028-0, Pub. by Auto Assn-British Tourist Authority England). Merrimack Pub Cir.
--AA Great Britain Road Atlas. (Illus.). 314p. 1982. pap. 34.95 (ISBN 0-86145-033-7, Pub. by Auto Assn-British Tourist Authority England). Merrimack Pub Cir.

Automobile Association British Tourist Authority. A-Z London Map. (Illus.). 1981. pap. 4.95 (ISBN 0-85039-021-4, Pub. by Auto Assn-British Tourist Authority England). Merrimack Pub Cir.

Automobile Association of England. Book of British Villages: A Guide to Seven Hundred of the Most Interesting & Attractive Villages in Britain. (Automobile Association of England Series on Motorist Travelling in England). (Illus.). 448p. 1981. 27.95 (ISBN 0-393-01501-7). Norton.
--Illustrated Guide to Britain. (Illus.). 1979. 24.95 (ISBN 0-393-01227-1). Norton.
--New Book of the Road. rev. ed. (Illus.). 1979. 22.95 (ISBN 0-393-01229-8). Norton.

Automobile Association of England, ed. Treasures of Britain. 3rd ed. (Illus.). 1976. 24.95 (ISBN 0-393-08743-3). Norton.

Automobile Association of England Staff. Discovering Britain. (Illus.). 1983. 24.95 (ISBN 0-393-01741-9). Norton.

Automobile Association of Great Britain & British Broadcasting Company. The Breakaway Guide to Trouble-Free Travel: The Agony & Ecstacy of Going Places Abroad. (Orig.). 1984. pap. 11.95 (ISBN 0-86145-192-9, Pub. by Auto Assn-British Tourist Authority England). Merrimack Pub Cir.

Automobile Association of Great Britain. New Motorists' Atlas of Britain. (Illus.). 128p. (Orig.). 1984. pap. 11.95 (ISBN 0-86145-227-5, Pub. by Auto Assn-British Tourist Authority England). Merrimack Pub Cir.
--The Touring Book of Britain. (Illus.). 320p. 1984. 34.95 (ISBN 0-86145-202-X, Pub. by Auto Assn-British Tourist Authority England). Merrimack Pub Cir.

Automobile Association of Great Britain & Littlewood, Barbara. Travellers' Guide to France, 1984: Best Places to Stay in France. (Illus.). 112p. (Orig.). 1984. pap. 7.95 (ISBN 0-86145-223-2, Pub. by Auto Assn-British Tourist Authority England). Merrimack Pub Cir.

Automobile Club of Italy. World Cars, 1972. Orig. Title: World Car Catalogue. (Illus.). 440p. 1972. 85.00 (ISBN 0-910714-04-5). Herald Bks.
--World Cars 1982. LC 74-643381. (Illus.). 440p. 1982. 45.00 (ISBN 0-910714-14-2). Herald Bks.
--World Cars, 1983. LC 74-643381. (Illus.). 440p. 1983. 41.75 (ISBN 0-910714-15-0). Herald Bks.
--World Cars, 1984. LC 74-643381. (Illus.). 440p. 1984. 45.95 (ISBN 0-910714-16-9). Herald Bks.

Automobile Club of Italy, ed. World Car Catalogue, 1971. (Illus.). 1971. 36.00 (ISBN 0-910714-03-7). Herald Bks.
--World Cars 1973. LC 73-3055. (Illus.). 440p. 1973. 75.00 (ISBN 0-910714-05-3). Herald Bks.
--World Cars 1974. LC 74-3055. (Illus.). 440p. 1974. 75.00 (ISBN 0-910714-06-1). Herald Bks.
--World Cars, 1975. annual LC 74-643381. (Illus.). 440p. 1975. 95.00 (ISBN 0-910714-07-X). Herald Bks.
--World Cars 1977. LC 7-643381. (Illus.). 1977. 45.00 (ISBN 0-910714-09-6). Herald Bks.
--World Cars 1978. LC 74-643381. (Illus.). 1978. 50.00 (ISBN 0-910714-10-X). Herald Bks.
--World Cars 1979. LC 7-643381. (Illus.). 1979. 50.00 (ISBN 0-910714-11-8). Herald Bks.
--World Cars 1981. LC 74-643381. (Illus.). 1981. 75.00 (ISBN 0-910714-13-4). Herald Bks.

Automobile Panel of the Committee on Technology & International Economic & Trade Issues, National Academy of Engineering, National Research Council. The Competitive Status of the U. S. Auto Industry: A Study of the Influences of Technology in Determining International Industrial Competitive Advantage. 203p. 1982. pap. text ed. 13.95 (ISBN 0-309-03289-X). Natl Acad Pr.

Automobile Quartely Staff. Corvette! Thirty Years of Great Advertising, the Collection of William & Sharon Landis. LC 82-73577. (Marque Reference Ser.). (Illus.). 176p. 1983. 21.95 (ISBN 0-915038-38-2). Auto Quarterly.

Automobile Quarterly. General Motors, the First 75 Years. (Illus.). 224p. 1983. 24.95 (ISBN 0-915038-41-2). Auto Quarterly.

Automobile Quarterly Magazine, ed. General Motors: The First Seventy-Five Years. LC 83-14318. (Illus.). 223p. 1983. 24.95 (ISBN 0-517-55169-1). Crown.

Auton, Graeme P., jt. auth. see Hanrieder, Wolfram.

Autor, Anne, ed. Pathology of Oxygen. 360p. 1982. 70.00 (ISBN 0-12-068620-1). Acad Pr.

Autore, Donald D., jt. auth. see Beakley, George C.

Autorentaem. Management Enzyklopaedie, 7 vols, Vols. 1-7. (Ger.). 1973. Set. 1295.00 (ISBN 0-686-56647-5, M-7091). French & Eur.

Autorenteam. Management Enzyklopaedie, 10 vols, Vols. 1-10. 3200p. (Ger.). 1975. Set. pap. 225.00 (ISBN 0-686-56648-3, M-7092). French & Eur.

Autrum, H., ed. Comparative Physiology & Evolution of Vision in Invertebrates: A: Invertebrate Photoreceptors. LC 78-21470. (Handbook of Sensory Physiology: Vol. 7, Pt. 6A). (Illus.). 1979. 187.00 (ISBN 0-387-08837-7). Springer-Verlag.
--Comparative Physiology & Evolution of Vision in Invertebrates B: Invertebrate Visual Centers & Behavior I. (Handbook of Sensory Physiology: Vol. VII, Pt. 6B). (Illus.). 650p. 1980. 161.00 (ISBN 0-387-08703-6). Springer-Verlag.
--Comparative Physiology & Evolution of Vision in Invertebrates C: Invertebrate Visual Centers & Behavior II. (Handbook of Sensory Physiology Ser.: Vol. VII-6c). (Illus.). 660p. 1981. 161.00 (ISBN 0-387-10422-4). Springer-Verlag.

Autrum, H., et al. Progress in Sensory Physiology, Vol. 2. (Illus.). 190p. 1981. 39.00 (ISBN 0-387-10923-4). Springer Verlag.

Autrum, H., et al, eds. Handbook of Sensory Physiology, 8 vols. Incl. Vol. 1. Principles of Receptor Physiology. Loewenstein, W. R., ed. 1971. 76.00 (ISBN 0-387-05144-9); Vol. 2. Somatosensory System. Iggo, A., ed. 1973. 158.00 (ISBN 0-387-05941-5); Vol. 3, Pt. 1. Enteroceptors. Neil, E., ed. 1972. 39.50 (ISBN 0-387-05523-1); Vol. 3, Pt. 2. Muscle Receptors. Hunt, C. C., et al. 1974. 78.00 (ISBN 0-387-06891-0); Vol. 4. Chemical Sense. Beidler, L. M., ed. 1971. Pt. 1 Olfaction. 63.00 (ISBN 0-387-05291-7); Pt. 2. Taste. 58.00 (ISBN 0-387-05501-0); Vol. 5, Pt. 1. Auditory System. 152.00 (ISBN 0-387-06676-4); Vol. 6, Pt. 1. Vestibular System. Kornhuber, H. H., ed. 148.00 (ISBN 0-387-06889-9); Vol. 7, Pt. 1. Photochemistry of Vision. Dartnall, H. J., ed. 1972. 93.00 (ISBN 0-387-05145-7); Vol. 7, Pt. 2. Physiology of Photoreceptor Organs. Fuortes, M. G., ed. 1972. 115.00 (ISBN 0-387-05743-9); Vol. 7, Pts. 3A & 3B. Central Processing of Vision Information. Jung, R., ed. LC 70-190496. 1973. Pt. A. 149.00 (ISBN 0-387-05769-2); Pt. B. 137.00 (ISBN 0-387-06056-1). Pt. B; Vol. 7, Pt. 4. Visual Psychophysics. Jameson, D. & Hurvich, L. M., eds. 1972. 125.00 (ISBN 0-387-05146-5); Vol. 8. Perception. Teuber, H. L., ed. 155.00 (ISBN 0-387-08300-6). Springer-Verlag.

Autrum, H., et al, eds. see Symposium On Animal Orientation - Garmisch-Partenkirchen - 1962.

Autrup, Herman & Williams, Gary M., eds. Experimental Colon Carcinogenesis. 320p. 1983. 87.50 (ISBN 0-8493-5543-5). CRC Pr.

Autrup, Herman N., jt. ed. see Harris, Curtis C.

Autry, Ewart A. & Autry, Lola M. Bible Puppet Plays. (Paperback Program Ser.). pap. 3.95 (ISBN 0-8010-0032-7). Baker Bk.

Autry, George. Much Obliged! A Limited & Loose Collection of Gratitude & Bias, Tales & Sensations. Greer, Mary A., ed. LC 76-42053. (Illus.). 1977. 15.00x (ISBN 0-9601890-0-9); pap. 7.00 (ISBN 0-9601890-1-7). King & Mary.

Autry, Gloria D. & Allen, T. Diener. The Color-Coded Allergy Cookbook. LC 82-17826. 400p. 1983. 19.95 (ISBN 0-672-52746-4). Bobbs.

Autry, James A. Nights under a Tin Roof. 12.95 (ISBN 0-916242-26-9). Yoknapatawpha.

Autry, Jarry, jt. auth. see Lindsay, Gordon.

Autry, Lola M., jt. auth. see Autry, Ewart A.

Autry, Raz. The Adventures of Bad Sam. (Illus.). 100p. (gr. 7-10). 1985. 7.95 (ISBN 0-934145-00-8). Leigh-Newcomb.

Autry, William O., Jr. Archaeological Investigations at the Tennessee Valley Authority Hartsville Nuclear Plants Off-Site Borrow Areas: The Taylor Tract. (T.A.R.A. Reports: No. 2). (Illus.). 125p. (Orig.). 1984. pap. 10.00x (ISBN 0-940148-03-X). Anthro Research.

Autry, William O., Jr. & Hinshaw, Jane S. A Cultural Resource Reconnissance of the Tennessee National Wildlife Refuge with Archaeological Survey of Selected Areas, 2 vols. (T.A.R.A. Report: No. 1). (Illus.). viii, 268p. (Orig.). 1981. Anthro Research.

Autumn, Violeta. Flavors of Northern Italy. LC 80-83215. (Illus.). 168p. (Orig.). 1980. pap. 6.95 (ISBN 0-89286-164-9). One Hund One Prods.

Auty, Martyn & Roddick, Nick. British Cinema Now. (British Film Institute Bks.). (Illus.). 172p. 1985. 21.95x (ISBN 0-85170-130-2); pap. 10.95 (ISBN 0-85170-131-0). U of Ill Pr.

Auty, R. & Lewitter, L R, eds. A Garland of Essays for E. M. Hill. (Publications of the Modern Humanities Research Association: Vol.2). x, 321p. 1970. avail. Modern Humanities Res.

Auty, R. & Obolensky, D., eds. Companion to Russian Studies: An Introduction to Russian Art & Architecture. LC 75-10691. (Illus.). 196p. 1981. pap. 18.95 (ISBN 0-521-28384-1). Cambridge U Pr.
--Companion to Russian Studies: An Introduction to Russian Art & Architecture, Vol. 3. LC 75-10691. (Illus.). 1980. 42.50 (ISBN 0-521-20895-5). Cambridge U Pr.
--Companion to Russian Studies: An Introduction to Russian History. LC 75-10688. 403p. 1981. pap. 18.95 (ISBN 0-521-28038-9). Cambridge U Pr.
--Companion to Russian Studies: An Introduction to Russian History, Vol. 1. LC 75-10688. 1976. 52.50 (ISBN 0-521-20893-9). Cambridge U Pr.
--Companion to Russian Studies: An Introduction to Russian Language & Literature. LC 75-10688. 300p. 1981. pap. 18.95 (ISBN 0-521-28039-7). Cambridge U Pr.
--Companion to Russian Studies: An Introduction to Russian Language & Literature, Vol. 2. LC 75-10691. (Illus.). 1977. Cambridge U Pr.

Auty, R., ed. see Unbegaun, Boris O.

Auty, R., et al, eds. Oxford Slavonic Papers: New Series, Vol.11. (Oxford Slavonic Papers Ser.: Vol. XI). (Illus.). 1978. 28.00x (ISBN 0-19-815653-7). Oxford U Pr.

Auty, Robert. Handbook of Old Church Slavonic, Pt. 2: Texts & Glossary. (London East European Ser.). 148p. 1977. pap. 48.50 (ISBN 0-485-17518-5, Pub. by Athlone Pr Ltd). Longwood Pub Group.

Auty, Robert, et al, eds. Oxford Slavonic Papers. (Oxford Slavonic Papers Ser.). 1975. Vol. 8. 19.95x (ISBN 0-19-815649-9). Oxford U Pr.

Auty, Susan G. The Comic Spirit of Eighteenth Century Novels. (National University Publications Literary Criticism Ser.). 200p. 1975. 18.00x (ISBN 0-8046-9120-7, Pub. by Kennikat). Assoc Faculty Pr.

Auvenshine, Charles D. & Noffsinger, Anne-Russell L. Counseling: An Introduction for the Health & Human Services. LC 83-6498. (Illus.). 322p. 1984. text ed. 21.00 (ISBN 0-8391-1793-0). Pro Ed.

Auvenshine, Martha & Enriquez, Martha. Maternity Nursing. LC 84-27035. (Nursing Ser.). 1000p. 1985. text ed. 28.75 pub net (ISBN 0-534-04368-2). Wadsworth Health.

Auvil, D. L. Calculus with Applications. LC 81-14914. 1982. text ed. 32.95 (ISBN 0-201-10063-0); student supplement 9.95 (ISBN 0-201-10064-9). Addison-Wesley.

Auvil, Daniel L. Intermediate Algebra. LC 78-18643. (Illus.). 1979. text ed. 24.95 (ISBN 0-201-00135-7); student supplement 3.95 (ISBN 0-201-00136-5). Addison-Wesley.

Auvil, Daniel L. & Poluga, Charles. Elementary Algebra. 2nd ed. (Illus.). 1984. 26.95 (ISBN 0-201-11030-X); pap. 6.95 student supplment (ISBN 0-201-11031-8). Addison-Wesley.

Auvil, Kenneth W. Serigraphy: Silk Screen Techniques for the Artist. (Illus., Orig.). 1965. 16.95 (ISBN 0-13-807164-0). P-H.

Auvine, Brian, et al. A Manual for Group Facilitators. 2nd ed. 90p. pap. text ed. 6.80 (ISBN 0-941492-00-1). Ctr Conflict Resol.

Auvinen, Jewell S. Ringer the Kitten Learns to Read. (Illus.). 22p. (ps-3). 1982. pap. 2.95 (ISBN 0-9610158-0-2). J S Auvinen.

Auvray, J. & Fourrier, M. Problems in Electronics. LC 73-7617. 444p. 1974. text ed. 54.00 (ISBN 0-08-016982-1); pap. text ed. 17.50 (ISBN 0-08-017871-5). Pergamon.

Auvray, Louis, jt. auth. see De La Chavignerie, Emile B.

Auw, Alvin Von see Von Auw, Alvin.

Auwera, Johan van der see Van Der Auwera, Johan.

Auxentios, Hieromonk, jt. auth. see Chrysostomos, Archimandrite.

Auxentios, Hieromonk, tr. see Cavarnos, Constantine.

Auxier, Jane. Marriage & Family Law in British Columbia. 5th ed. 145p. 1982. 6.95 (ISBN 0-88908-148-4). Self Counsel Pr.

Auxier, John A. Ichiban: Radiation Dosimetry for the Survivors of the Bombings of Hiroshima & Nagasaki. LC 76-30780. (ERDA Critical Review Ser.). 128p. 1977. pap. 11.25 (TID-27080); microfiche 4.50 (ISBN 0-87079-244-X, TID-27080). DOE.

Auxter, Thomas. Kant's Moral Teleology. LC 82-7838. 209p. 1982. 16.95x (ISBN 0-86554-022-5). Mercer Univ Pr.

Au-Yang, M. K., ed. Flow-Induced Vibration of Power Plant Components. (PVP: No. 41). 176p. 1980. 24.00 (ISBN 0-686-69851-7, H00168). ASME.

Au-Yang, M. K. & Brown, S. J., Jr., eds. Fluid-Structure Interaction Phenomena in Pressure Vessel & Piping Systems, Series PVP-PB-026. 1977. pap. text ed. 16.00 (ISBN 0-685-86866-4, G00130). ASME.

Au-Yang, M. K. & Moody, F. J., eds. Interactive-Fluid-Structural Dynamic Problems in Power Engineering. (PVP Ser.: vol. 46). 177p. 1981. 30.00 (ISBN 0-686-34516-9, H00182). ASME.

Au-Yang, M. K., jt. ed. see Lin, C.

Au-Yang, M. K., jt. ed. see Shin, Y. S.

Au-Yang, M. K., et al, eds. Dynamics of Fluid-Structure Systems in the Energy Industry. (PVP-39). (Orig.). 1979. 30.00 (ISBN 0-685-96305-5, H00153). ASME.

Au-Yeung, Cecilia. Dim Sum. (Chopsticks Recipes Ser.). (Illus.). 128p. (Orig., Eng. & Chinese.). 1985. pap. 4.95 (ISBN 9-627-01802-3). Parkwest Pubns.
--Traditional Dishes. (Chpsticks Recipes Ser.). (Illus.). 128p. (Orig., Eng. & Chinese.). 1985. pap. 4.95 (ISBN 9-627-01803-1). Parkwest Pubns.

Au-Yeung, Cecilia J. Bean Products. (Chopsticks Recipes Ser.). (Illus.). 128p. (Orig., Eng. & Chinese.). 1985. pap. 4.95 (ISBN 0-317-30498-4). Parkwest Pubns.
--Budget Meals. (Chopsticks Recipes Ser.). (Illus.). 128p. (Orig., Eng. & Chinese.). 1985. pap. 4.95 (ISBN 9-627-01809-0). Parkwest Pubns.
--Cakes & Bread. (Chopsticks Recipes Ser.). (Illus.). 128p. (Orig., Eng. & Chinese.). 1985. pap. 4.95 (ISBN 9-627-01806-6). Parkwest Pubns.
--Chinese Casseroles. (Chopsticks Recipes Ser.). (Illus.). 128p. (Orig., Eng. & Chinese.). 1985. pap. 4.95 (ISBN 9-627-01810-4). Parkwest Pubns.
--Chopsticks Introduction Recipes. rev. ed. (Chopsticks Recipes Ser.). (Illus.). 128p. (Orig.). 1985. pap. 4.95 (ISBN 9-627-01813-9). Parkwest Pubns.
--Chopsticks Introduction Recipes. (Chopsticks Recipes Ser.). (Illus.). 128p. (Orig., Eng. & Chinese.). 1985. pap. 4.95 (ISBN 9-627-01801-5). Parkwest Pubns.
--Cookeries for Beginners. (Illus.). 96p. (Eng. & Chinese.). 1985. pap. 3.95 (ISBN 9-627-01881-3). Parkwest Pubns.
--Dim Sum Two. (Chopsticks Recipes Ser.). (Illus.). 128p. (Orig., Eng. & Chinese.). 1985. pap. 4.95 (ISBN 9-627-01808-2). Parkwest Pubns.
--Everyday Menu. (Chopsticks Recipes Ser.). (Illus.). 128p. (Orig., Eng. & Chinese.). 1985. pap. 4.95 (ISBN 9-627-01805-8). Parkwest Pubns.
--Quick Meals. (Chopsticks Recipes Ser.). (Illus.). 128p. (Orig., Eng. & Chinese.). 1985. pap. 4.95 (ISBN 9-627-01804-X). Parkwest Pubns.
--Vegetable Carvings. (Chopsitks Recipes Ser.). (Illus.). 128p. (Orig., Eng. & Chinese.). 1985. pap. 4.95 (ISBN 0-317-30502-6). Parkwest Pubns.
--Vegetarian Dishes. (Chopsticks Recipes Ser.). (Illus.). 128p. (Orig., Eng. & Chinese.). 1985. pap. 4.95 (ISBN 9-627-01807-4). Parkwest Pubns.
--Wok Miracles. (Chopsticks Wok Ser.). (Illus.). 128p. (Eng. & Chinese.). 1985. pap. 5.95 (ISBN 9-627-01851-1). Parkwest Pubns.

Auzas, Pierre M., jt. auth. see Merimee, Prosper.

Avadhuta. Avadhuta Gita: The Song of the Ever-Free. Chetanananda, tr. from Sanskrit. 138p. 1985. text ed. 3.50 (ISBN 0-87481-224-0, Pub. by Advaita Ashram India). Vedanta Pr.

Avakian, Arra, ed. see Sheohmelian, O.

Avakian, Arra S. The Armenians in America. LC 77-73739. (In America Bks). (Illus.). (gr. 5 up). 1977. PLB 7.95 (ISBN 0-8225-0228-3). Lerner Pubns.

Avakian, Bob. Charting the Uncharted Course Questions of Revolutionary Strategy for the 1980s: Strategic Outlook & Alliances, No. 1. 279p. 1983. 5.00 (ISBN 0-89851-058-9). RCP Pubns.
--Charting the Uncharted Course: Questions of Revolutionary Strategy for the 1980s: Leadership, No. 2. 306p. 1983. 5.00 (ISBN 0-89851-059-7). RCP Pubns.
--For a Harvest of Dragons: On the "Crisis of Marxism" & the Power of Marxism, Now More Than Ever. LC 83-13715. 160p. (Orig.). 1983. 13.95 (ISBN 0-89851-066-X); pap. 6.95 (ISBN 0-89851-065-1). RCP Pubns.
--A Horrible End, Or An End to the Horror. LC 84-18215. 216p. (Orig.). 1984. pap. 6.95 (ISBN 0-89851-070-8). RCP Pubns.

--Leadership. Incl. If There is to be Revolution, There Must be a Revolutionary Party. 74p. 1982. 2.00 (ISBN 0-89851-056-2); Anarchism. Avakian, Bob. 1982. 2.25 (ISBN 0-89851-068-6); Bob Avakian Speaks on the Mao Defendants' Railroad & the Historic Battles Ahead. 69p. 1981. 1.50 (ISBN 0-89851-047-3); Summing Up the Black Panther Party. 1980. 0.60 (ISBN 0-89851-042-2); Communists are Rebels. 1980. 0.50 (ISBN 0-686-82474-1); Important Struggles in Building the RCP. 55p. 1978. 1.00 (ISBN 0-89851-018-X); New Constitution of the RCP, U. S. A. 1981. 0.75 (ISBN 0-89851-064-3). 5.00 (ISBN 0-89851-059-7). RCP Pubns.

--The Loss in China & the Revolutionary Legacy of Mao Tsetung. (Illus.). 1978. pap. 2.00 (ISBN 0-89851-017-1). RCP Pubns.

--Mao Tsetung's Immortal Contributions. 1978. 12.95 (ISBN 0-89851-020-1); pap. 4.95 (ISBN 0-89851-021-X). RCP Pubns.

Avakian, Lindy, jt. auth. see Watanabe, Jiichi.

Avakumovic, I., jt. auth. see Woodcock, G.

Avalle-Arce, J. B. El Cronista Pedro de Escavias: Una Vida del Siglo XV. (Studies in the Romance Languages & Literatures: No. 127). 240p. 1973. pap. 12.50x (ISBN 0-8078-9127-4). U of NC Pr.

--Las Memorias de Gonzalo Fernandez de Oviedo, Vol. 1. (Studies in the Romance Languages & Literatures: No. 154). 391p. 1974. pap. 16.50x (ISBN 0-8078-9154-1). U of NC Pr.

--Las Memorias de Gonzalo Fernandez de Oviedo, Vol. 2. (Studies in the Romance Languages & Literatures: No. 155). 340p. 1974. pap. 15.50x (ISBN 0-8078-9155-X). U of NC Pr.

--Los Narradores Hispanoamericanos de Hoy. (Studies in the Romance Languages & Literatures: No. 157). 100p. 1973. pap. 7.00x (ISBN 0-8078-9157-6). U of NC Pr.

Avallone, Michael. Cannonball Run. 1981. pap. 2.50 (ISBN 0-8439-0993-5, Pub. by Nordon Pubns). Dorchester Pub Co.

--Five-Minute Mysteries: Cases from Files of Ed Noon. (gr. 7 up). 1978. pap. 1.95 (ISBN 0-590-05368-X). Scholastic Inc.

--A Woman Called Golda. 272p. 1982. pap. 2.95 (ISBN 0-8439-1114-X, Leisure Bks). Dorchester Pub Co.

Avallone, Paul. Reason, Religion, & Kindness. 3rd, rev. ed. LC 77-83952. 1977. pap. 4.75 (ISBN 0-89944-030-4). Don Bosco Multimedia.

Avallone, Paul P. The Consecrated Woman: A Guide to the Don Bosco Volunteers. (Salesian Family Ser.). 27p. 1983. pap. 3.00 (ISBN 0-89944-075-4). Don Bosco Multimedia.

Avalon, A., jt. auth. see Vidyaratna, T.

Avalon, Arthur, pseud. Mahanirvana Tantra. 473p. (Sanskrit.). 1982. text ed. 28.00 (ISBN 0-89744-237-7). Auromere.

Avalon, Arthur. The Serpent Power. LC 74-75259. (Illus.). 1974. pap. 8.50 (ISBN 0-486-23058-9). Dover.

--Shakti & Shakta. 1978. pap. 8.95 (ISBN 0-486-23645-5). Dover.

--Tantra of the Great Liberation. (Illus.). 512p. 1913. pap. 8.50 (ISBN 0-486-20150-3). Dover.

Avalon, Arthur & Shastri, Lakshmana. Tantraraja Tantra. 740p. (Sanskrit.). 1982. text ed. 52.00 (ISBN 0-89744-238-5). Auromere.

Avalon, Arthur, ed., pseud. Prapanchasara Tantra. 617p. (Sanskrit.). 1982. text ed. 48.00 (ISBN 0-89744-239-3). Auromere.

Avalos, B. & Haddad, W. A Review of Teacher Effectiveness Research in Africa, India, Latin America, Middle East, Malaysia, Philippines, & Thailand: Synthesis of Results. 128p. (Eng. & Span.). 1981. pap. 10.00 (ISBN 0-88936-272-6, IDRCTS23, IDRC). Unipub.

Avalov, Zurab D. The Independence of Georgia in International Politics, 1918-1920. LC 79-2890. 286p. 1981. Repr. of 1940 ed. 23.50 (ISBN 0-8305-0059-6). Hyperion Conn.

A. Van, Der Heijden see Besseling, J. F. & Van Der Heijden, A. M.

Avanesov, G. Principles of Criminology. 344p. 1982. 7.95 (ISBN 0-8285-2511-0, Pub. by Progress Pubs USSR). Imported Pubns.

Avanesova, R. I. Orthoepic Russian Dictionary. 703p. (Rus.). 1983. 14.95 (ISBN 0-8285-2663-X, Pub. by Rus Lang Pubs USSR). Imported Pubns.

Avant, D. A. Like a Straight Pine Tree: Stories of Reconstruction Days in Alabama & Florida 1855-1971. (Illus.). 124p. 1971. 7.95x (ISBN 0-914570-03-X). L'Avant Studios.

--Like a Straight Pine Tree: Stories of Reconstruction Days in Alabama & Florida 1885-1971. LC 73-184128. (Illus.). 134p. 7.95 (ISBN 0-317-03286-0). L'Avant Studios.

Avant, David A., III. Professional Raccoon Trapping. 3rd, rev. ed. LC 78-57404. (Illus.). 61p. pap. 4.95 (ISBN 0-317-03287-9). L'Avant Studios.

Avant, David A., Jr. Some Southern Colonial Families, Vol. 1. LC 81-84670. 528p. buckram 35.00 (ISBN 0-914570-04-8). L'Avant Studios.

Avant, Fenton G. The Davis-Wood Family of Gadsden County, Florida & Their Forebears. LC 79-189245. (Illus.). 535p. 35.00 (ISBN 0-317-03284-4). L'Avant Studios.

--My Tallahassee. LC 81-85398. (Illus.). 246p. 16.95 (ISBN 0-914570-05-6). L'Avant Studios.

Avant-Garde Creations. The Creativity Life Dynamic Book. (Illus.). 84p. 1980. pap. 9.95 (ISBN 0-930182-07-3); pkg. including book, 2 drawing cards & program disk 24.95 (ISBN 0-930182-08-1). Avant Garde Pub.

Avant, Kay C., jt. auth. see Walker, Lorraine O.

Avante-Garde Publishing Corporation Staff, et al. Getting Graphic on the Apple. 204p. 1985. pap. 14.95 (ISBN 0-13-354044-8). P-H.

--Getting Graphic on the Commodore 64. (Illus.). 208p. 1985. pap. 14.95 (ISBN 0-13-354051-0). P-H.

Avante-Garde Publishing Corporation Staff & Thiel, James R. Getting Graphic on the IBM-PC. 192p. 1985. pap. 14.95 (ISBN 0-13-354069-3). P-H.

Avary, Myrta. Dixie After the War. LC 73-94473. (Illus.). Repr. of 1906 ed. 21.50x (ISBN 0-8371-2368-2, AVD&, Pub. by Negro U Pr). Greenwood.

Avary, Myrta L. Dixie After the War. facs. ed. LC 76-124224. (Select Bibliographies Reprint Ser). 1906. 27.50 (ISBN 0-8369-5412-2). Ayer Co Pubs.

--Dixie After the War: An Exposition of Social Conditions Existing in the South, During the 12 Years Succeeding the Fall of Richmond. LC 79-77701. (American Scene Ser). (Illus.). 1970. Repr. of 1937 ed. 49.50 (ISBN 0-306-71339-X). Da Capo.

Avary, Myrta L., ed. Recollections of Alexander H. Stephens: His Diary Kept When a Prisoner at Fort Warren, Boston Harbor, 1865. LC 76-124914. (American Public Figures Ser). 1971. Repr. of 1910 ed. lib. bdg. 69.50 (ISBN 0-306-71984-3). Da Capo.

Avary, Myrta L., ed. see Chesnut, Mary B.

Avasthi, A. & Rao, S. P., eds. Crisis Administration in India. 1983. text ed. 27.50x (ISBN 0-86590-161-9). Apt Bks.

Avatar, Ram. Theory of Indian Music. (Illus.). 160p. 1980. 29.95 (ISBN 0-940500-13-2, Pub. by Punkaj India). Asia Bk Corp.

Avato, Rose, jt. ed. see Foy, Felician A.

Avato, Rose M., jt. ed. see Foy, Felician A.

Avchenassoglou-Kollmeyer, Nina. The Soul of Indonesia: A Cultural Journey. (Illus.). 156p. 1985. 22.50 (ISBN 0-8071-1241-0). La State U Pr.

Avdoian, Nancy M. Alpha Books to Color Presents Color Me Armenian. (Alpha Books to Color: No. 3). (Illus.). (gr. k-7). 1983. pap. 5.00 (ISBN 0-912507-03-9, VA 118-448). Three Star Ent.

Avduyevsky, V. S. Scientific Foundations of Space Manufacturing. 173p. 1985. pap. 5.95 (ISBN 0-8285-2949-3, Pub. by Mir Pubs USSR). Imported Pubns.

Ave, Mario P. Characteristics of Filipino Organizations in Los Angeles: Thesis. LC 74-76500. 1974. soft bdg. 10.95 (ISBN 0-88247-248-8). R & E Pubs.

Avebury. The Dread & the Love of Nature. (Illus.). 1980. Repr. of 1909 ed. deluxe ed. 60.75 deluxe binding (ISBN 0-89901-012-1). Found Class Reprints.

Avebury, John L. Essays & Addresses, Nineteen Hundred to Nineteen Hundred Three. facsimile ed. LC 67-22069. (Essay Index Reprint Ser). 1903. 20.00 (ISBN 0-8369-0165-7). Ayer Co Pubs.

--Origin of Civilisation & the Primitive Condition of Man. LC 72-1280. (Select Bibliographies Reprint Ser.). 1972. Repr. of 1912 ed. 29.00 (ISBN 0-8369-6819-0). Ayer Co Pubs.

Avebury, Lord. The Search for Happiness. (Illus.). 117p. (YA) 1982. 67.85 (ISBN 0-89920-041-9). Am Inst Psych.

Aved, Joe. Ami. LC 81-51961. 192p. 1981. 10.00 (ISBN 0-88400-077-X). Shengold.

Aved, Thomas G. Toomas, the Little Armenian Boy: Childhood Reminiscence of Turkish-Armenia. LC 79-90192. 10.95 (ISBN 0-914330-28-4, Pub by Pioneer Pub Co). Panorama West.

Avedeyenko, Y. Wild Hop Leaf. 372p. 1979. pap. 6.45 (ISBN 0-8285-0944-1, Pub. by Progress Pubs USSR). Imported Pubns.

Avedichian, Gabriel, tr. see Migne, J. P.

Avedon, Elliott M. Socio-Recreative Programming for the Retarded: A Handbook for Sponsoring Groups. LC 64-15576. (Orig.). 1964. pap. 3.50x (ISBN 0-8077-1041-5). Tchrs Coll.

Avedon, Elliott M. & Sutton-Smith, Brian. The Study of Games. LC 79-21194. 544p. 1979. Repr. of 1971 ed. lib. bdg. 32.50 (ISBN 0-89874-045-2). Krieger.

Avedon, John F. In Exile from the Land of Snows: The First Full Account of the Dalai Lama & the Tibetans since the Chinese Conquest. LC 83-48848. (Illus.). 384p. 1984. 18.95 (ISBN 0-394-51817-9). Knopf.

--An Interview with the Dalai Lama. LC 80-83015. (Illus.). 83p. (Orig.). 1980. pap. 6.95 (ISBN 0-937896-00-4). Littlebird.

Avedon, Luciana & Molli, Jeanne. Luciana Avedon's Body Book. LC 76-15189. (Illus.). 208p. 1976. 12.95 (ISBN 0-87131-211-5). M Evans.

Avedon, Richard. In the American West: Richard Avedon-Photographs, 1979-1984. (Illus.). 184p. 1985. 40.00 (ISBN 0-8109-1105-1). Abrams.

Avedon, Richard, et al. Aperture 101: The Human Street. Date not set. price not set. Aperture.

Ave-Lallemant, E., jt. auth. see Spiegelberg, H.

Aveline, Claude & Duffet, Michel. Bourdelle & the Dance. 25.00 (ISBN 0-8283-1366-0). Branden Pub Co.

Aveline, Claude, jt. auth. see France, Anatole.

Aveline, Claude see Otten, Anna.

Aveling, Claude, tr. see Aubry, Pierre.

Aveling, Edward, ed. see Marx, Karl.

Aveling, Edward, tr. see Engels, Frederick.

Aveling, Edward, tr. see Marx, Karl.

Aveling, Edward, tr. see Tikhomirov, Lev A.

Aveling, Edward B. & Aveling, Eleanor M. Working Class Movement in America. LC 78-89716. (American Labor, from Conspiracy to Collective Bargaining Ser., No. 1). 239p. 1969. Repr. of 1891 ed. 14.00 (ISBN 0-405-02102-X). Ayer Co Pubs.

Aveling, Eleanor, ed. see Marx, Karl.

Aveling, Eleanor M., jt. auth. see Aveling, Edward B.

Aveling, Eleanor M., ed. see Marx, Karl.

Aveling, Eleanor M., tr. see Plekhanov, Georgii V.

Aveling, Eleanor Marx, tr. see Bernstein, Edward.

Aveling, Francis. Personality & Will. 1978. Repr. of 1931 ed. lib. bdg. 27.50 (ISBN 0-8492-0070-9). R West.

Aveling, Harry. Contemporary Indonesian Poetry. (Asian & Pacific Writing Ser.). 1975. 14.95x (ISBN 0-7022-0931-7); pap. 8.50x (ISBN 0-7022-0932-5). U of Queensland Pr.

Aveling, Harry, ed. & tr. Contemporary Indonesian Poetry. LC 85-1034. 261p. (Eng. & Indonesian.). 1985. pap. 10.95 (ISBN 0-7022-0932-5). U of Queensland Pr.

Aveling, Harry, ed. The Development of Indonesian Society. LC 79-11452. 1980. 30.00 (ISBN 0-312-19661-X). St Martin.

Aveling, Harry, ed. & tr. From Surabaya to Armageddon: Indonesian Short Stories. (Writing in Asia Ser.). 1976. pap. text ed. 5.50x (ISBN 0-686-60434-2, 00209). Heinemann Ed.

Aveling, Harry, tr. Arjuna in Meditation. 1976. flexible cloth 8.00 (ISBN 0-89253-800-7). Ind-US Inc.

Aveling, Harry, tr. see Ahmad, Shahnon.

Aveling, Harry, tr. see Danarto.

Aveling, Harry, tr. see Kayam, Umar.

Aveling, Harry, tr. see Muhammad, Ishak H.

Aveling, Harry, tr. see Said, A Samad.

Aveling, Harry, tr. see Shahnon Ahmad.

Aveling, Harry, tr. see Simatupang, Iwan.

Aveling, J. C. The Jesuits. LC 81-40482. 396p. 1982. 19.95 (ISBN 0-8128-2838-0). Stein & Day.

Aveling, J. C., et al. Rome & The Anglicans: Historical & Doctrinal Aspects of Anglican-Roman Catholic Relations. Haase, Wolfgang, ed. 301p. 1982. 55.20 (ISBN 3-11-008267-5). De Gruyter.

Aveling, James H. The Chamberlens & the Midwifery Forceps. LC 75-23677. Repr. of 1882 ed. 19.00 (ISBN 0-404-13230-8). AMS Pr.

--English Midwives: Their History & Prospects. LC 75-23678. Repr. of 1872 ed. 16.00 (ISBN 0-404-13231-6). AMS Pr.

Aveling, Marian, ed. Westralian Voices: Documents in Western Australian Social History. 384p. 1980. 30.00x (ISBN 0-85564-158-4, Pub. by U of Australia Press). Intl Spec Bk.

Avellani, Pamela B., jt. auth. see Vandergoot, David.

Avellani, Pamela B., jt. auth. see Jacobsen, Richard J.

Aven, Mrs. Del. Anna's Tree Swing. LC 81-65799. (gr. k-3). 1981. bds. 5.95 (ISBN 0-8054-4268-5, 4242-68). Broadman.

Aven, Russell E. Devotions for Layman... by a Layman. LC 81-67751. 1982. pap. 5.95 (ISBN 0-8054-5185-4). Broadman.

Avena, M. R. Tatlong Dula. 198p. (Orig., Tagalog.). 1983. pap. 8.50x (ISBN 971-10-0062-8, Pub. by New Day Phillipines). Cellar.

Avenarius, Ferdinand. Das Bild Als Naar. LC 70-147679. (Library of War & Peace; Artists on War). 1972. lib. bdg. 42.00 (ISBN 0-8240-0436-1). Garland Pub.

Avendano, Fausto. El Corrido de California. LC 79-89. 1979. pap. 6.00 (ISBN 0-915808-35-8). Editorial Justa.

Avendano, Jorge, et al, eds. Workers' Self-Management & Participation: Bangladesh, Malta, Peru, Yugoslavia, Vol. I. xxiv, 455p. (Orig.). 1980. 20.00x (ISBN 92-9038-012-8, Pub. by Intl Ctr Pub Yugoslavia). Kumarian Pr.

Avenel, Georges D' see D'Avenel, Georges.

Avenell, Donne & Romero, Enrique. Axa. (First American Edition Ser.). (Illus.). 64p. 1981. pap. 5.95 (ISBN 0-912277-04-1). K Pierce Inc.

--Axa Four. (First American Edition Ser.). (Illus.). 64p. 1983. pap. 5.95 (ISBN 0-912277-01-7). K Pierce Inc.

--Axa Three. (First American Edition Ser.). (Illus.). 64p. 1983. pap. 5.95 (ISBN 0-912277-06-8). K Pierce Inc.

--Axa Two. (First American Edition Ser.). (Illus.). 64p. 1982. pap. 5.95 (ISBN 0-912277-05-X). K Pierce Inc.

--AXA 5. (First American Edition Ser.). (Illus.) 64p. 1984. pap. 5.95 (ISBN 0-912277-21-1). K Pierce Inc.

--AXA 6. (First American Edition Ser.). (Illus.) 64p. 1984. pap. 5.95 (ISBN 0-912277-22-X). K Pierce Inc.

--AXA 7. (First American Edition Ser.). (Illus.). 64p. 1985. pap. 5.95 (ISBN 0-912277-29-7). K Pierce Inc.

Aveney, Brian & Butler, Brett, eds. Online Catalogs, Online Reference: Converging Trends. LC 84-11023. (Library & Information Technology Ser.: No. 2). 212p. 1984. pap. text ed. 20.00x (ISBN 0-8389-3308-4). ALA.

Avenhaus, R., jt. ed. see Argentesi, F.

Avenhaus, Rudolf & Huber, Reiner K., eds. Quantitative Assessment in Arms Control: Mathematical Modeling & Simulation in the Analysis of Arms Control Problems. 488p. 1984. 65.00x (ISBN 0-306-41818-5, Plenum Pr). Plenum Pub.

Aveni, A. F., ed. Archaeoastronomy in the New World: American Primitive Astronomy. LC 82-1344. 230p. 1982. 34.50 (ISBN 0-521-24731-4). Cambridge U Pr.

Aveni, Anthony F. Skywatchers of Ancient Mexico. (Texas Pan American Ser.). (Illus.). 369p. 1980. text ed. 30.00x (ISBN 0-292-77557-1). U of Tex Pr.

--Skywatchers of Ancient Mexico. (Texas Pan American Ser.). (Illus.). 369p. 1983. pap. 17.50 (ISBN 0-292-77578-4). U of Tex Pr.

Aveni, Anthony F., ed. Native American Astronomy. LC 76-53569. (Illus.). 304p. 1977. text ed. 18.95x (ISBN 0-292-75511-2). U of Tex Pr.

Avenoso, Frank, ed. see DeSanto, et al.

Avens, John, jt. auth. see Moreng, Robert.

Avens, Roberts. Imaginal Body: Para-Jungian Reflections on Soul, Imagination & Death. LC 81-43814. 264p. (Orig.). 1982. lib. bdg. 26.00 (ISBN 0-8191-2411-7); pap. text ed. 13.00 (ISBN 0-8191-2412-5). U Pr of Amer.

--Imagination Is Reality. rev. ed. Severson, R. & Bedford, G., eds. 127p. 1980. pap. 11.50 (ISBN 0-88214-311-5). Spring Pubns.

--The New Gnosis: Heidegger, Hillman, & Angels. LC 84-5297. 155p. (Orig.). 1984. 18.50 (ISBN 0-88214-328-X); pap. 11.50 (ISBN 0-88214-327-1). Spring Pubns.

Avensand, Anthony F., ed. Ethnoastronomy & Archaeoastronomy in the American Tropics, Vol. 385. 365p. 1982. 77.00x (ISBN 0-89766-160-5); pap. 77.00x (ISBN 0-89766-161-3). NY Acad Sci.

Avent, Sue. Spells, Chants, & Potions. LC 77-22779. (Myth, Magic & Superstition). (Illus.). (gr. 4-5). 1977. PLB 14.25 (ISBN 0-8172-1035-0). Raintree Pubs.

Avento, Genarro P. The Church's Moral Teaching, Bk. III. pap. 3.95 (ISBN 0-941850-08-0). Sunday Pubns.

Averbach, Albert. Handling Accident Cases: 1963-73, 8 vols. in 8 bks. LC 58-4149. 1973. Set. 440.00 (ISBN 0-686-14528-3); Vols. 1-2. 129.00 (ISBN 0-686-31708-4); Vols. 3a-3b. 64.50 ea.; Vols. 4-5. 129.00 (ISBN 0-686-31709-2); Vols. 6-7. 129.00 (ISBN 0-686-31710-6); Suppl. 1984. 53.00; Suppl. 1983. 48.00. Lawyers Co-Op.

Averbach, Bonnie & Chein, Orin. Mathematics: Problem Solving Through Recreational Mathematics. LC 80-11989. (Mathematical Sciences Ser.). (Illus.). 400p. 1980. text ed. 22.95 (ISBN 0-7167-1124-9); instrs'. guide avail.; solutions manual avail. W H Freeman.

Averbakh, Y. Chess Endings: Essential Knowledge. (Pergamon Chess Ser.). (Illus.). 1966. pap. 6.50 (ISBN 0-08-011822-4). Pergamon.

Averbakh, Y. & Checkover, V. Comprehensive Chess Endings: Bishop Endings & Knight Endings, Vol. 1. Neat, K. P., tr. from Rus. (Russian Chess Ser.). 232p. 1983. 24.95 (ISBN 0-08-026900-1). Pergamon.

Averbakh, Yuri. Bishop Endings. 1977. 21.00 (ISBN 0-7134-0096-X, Pub. by Batsford England). David & Charles.

--Bishop V. Knight Endings. 1977. 21.00 (ISBN 0-7134-3179-2, Pub. by Batsford England). David & Charles.

--Queen V. Rook Minor Piece Endings. 1978. 21.00 (ISBN 0-7134-0866-9, Pub. by Batsford England). David & Charles.

Averbakh, Yuri & Chekhover, V. Knight Endings. 1977. 21.00 (ISBN 0-7134-0552-X, Pub. by Batsford England). David & Charles.

Averbhh, V. I., et al. Transactions of the Moscow Mathematical Society, Vol. 27 (1972) LC 65-7413. 1974. 62.00 (ISBN 0-8218-1627-6, MOSCOW-27). Am Math.

Averbuch, Gloria. The Woman Runner: Free to Be the Complete Athlete. LC 84-9528. (Illus.). 192p. 1984. 9.95 (ISBN 0-346-12644-4). Cornerstone.

Averbuh, V. I., et al. Transactions of the Moscow Mathematical Society, Vol. 24 (1971) LC 65-7413. 1974. 71.00 (ISBN 0-8218-1624-1, MOSCOW-24). Am Math.

Averch, Harvey A. A Strategic Analysis of Science & Technology Policy. LC 84-47961. 232p. 1985. text ed. 20.00x (ISBN 0-8018-2467-2). Johns Hopkins.

Averch, Harvey A., et al. How Effective Is Schooling? A Critical Review of Research. LC 74-2165. 280p. 1974. 27.95 (ISBN 0-87778-071-4). Educ Tech Pubns.

Averch, Koehler, et al. Matrix of Policy in the Philippines. LC 70-154989. (Rand Corporation Research Study Ser.). (Illus.). 1972. text ed. 35.00 (ISBN 0-691-07541-7). Princeton U Pr.

Averchenko, Arkadii. Salat Iz Bulavok. LC 82-60958. 230p. 1982. pap. 9.95 (ISBN 0-89830-064-9). Russica Pubs.

Averell, P. R., ed. see Streuli, C. A.

Averett, Joy & Smith, Donna. Bible Handwork Ideas for Twos & Threes. 1983. pap. 2.95 (ISBN 0-89137-613-5). Quality Pubns.

Averett, Sarah E. Striking Courage. 1983. 4.95 (ISBN 0-8062-1976-9). Carlton.

Averett, Tanner F. Basic Drama Projects. 4th ed. (Illus.). 286p. 1982. pap. text ed. 8.34 (ISBN 0-931054-06-0). Clark Pub.

--Creative Communication. rev. ed. (Illus.). 379p. 1985. pap. text ed. 10.25 (ISBN 0-931054-09-5). Clark Pub.

Averill, C. F. Sprinkler Systems Design: Past, Present & Future. 1979. 2.50 (TR 79-3). Society Fire Protect.

Averill, Charles V., et al. Placer Mining for Gold in California. (Illus.). 357p. 1981. Repr. text ed. 24.95 (ISBN 0-89632-011-1). Del Oeste.

Averill, Deborah M. The Irish Short Story from George Moore to Frank O'Connor. LC 81-40188. 338p. (Orig.). 1982. lib. bdg. 27.50 (ISBN 0-8191-2133-9); pap. text ed. 14.25 (ISBN 0-8191-2134-7). U Pr of Amer.

Averill, E. W. Elements of Statistics. LC 72-4352. 268p. 1972. 16.00 (ISBN 0-471-03840-7, Pub. by Wiley). Krieger.

Averill, Esther. Cartier Sails the St. Lawrence. LC 56-5159. (Illus.). (gr. 4 up). 1956. HarpJ.

--Fire Cat. LC 60-10234. (I Can Read Bk.). (Illus.). 64p. (gr. k-3). 1960. PLB 9.89 (ISBN 0-06-020196-7). HarpJ.

--The Fire Cat. LC 60-10234. (A Trophy I Can Read Bk.). (Illus.). 64p. (gr. k-3). 1983. pap. 2.84i (ISBN 0-06-444038-9, Trophy). HarpJ.

--Hotel Cat. LC 74-77941. (Illus.). (gr. k-3). pap. 2.95 (ISBN 0-06-440057-3, Trophy). HarpJ.

--Jenny's Birthday Book. LC 54-6589. (Illus.). 32p. (gr. k-3). 1954. PLB 11.89 (ISBN 0-06-020251-3). HarpJ.

--Jenny's Moonlight Adventure. 32p. (Orig.). 1982. pap. 1.95 (ISBN 0-553-15328-5). Bantam.

Averill, Gerald. Ridge Runner. LC 79-14339. (Illus.). 1979. pap. 5.95 (ISBN 0-89621-030-8). Thorndike Pr.

Averill, James, ed. see Wordsworth, William.

Averill, James H. Wordsworth & the Poetry of Human Suffering. LC 79-21783. 320p. 1980. 27.50x (ISBN 0-8014-1249-8). Cornell U Pr.

Averill, James R. Anger & Aggression: An Essay on Emotion. (Springer Series in Social Psychology). (Illus.). 402p. 1982. 34.00 (ISBN 0-387-90719-X). Springer-Verlag.

--Patterns of Psychological Thought: Readings in Classical & Contemporary Texts. LC 76-4901. (Series in Clinical & Community Psychology). 603p. 1976. 22.50x (ISBN 0-470-15070-X). Halsted Pr.

Averill, L. H. Estate Valuation Handbook: 1984 Supplement. (Tax Library). 53p. 1984. pap. 23.00 (ISBN 0-471-81833-X). Wiley.

Averill, L. W. Estate Valuation Handbook. (Wiley Tax Library Ser.). 424p. 1983. Annual supplements avail. 75.00 (ISBN 0-471-89859-7). Wiley.

Averill, Lawrence H. Uniform Probate Code. (Nutshell Ser.). 425p. 1978. pap. 7.95 (ISBN 0-317-00050-0). West Pub.

Averill, Lloyd J. Learning to Be Human: A Vision for the Liberal Arts. LC 83-8840. 267p. 1983. 22.50x (ISBN 0-8046-9323-4, Natl U). Assoc Faculty Pr.

Averill, Peg, ed. Eighty Years of Political Art in the U.S. 1980 Peace Calendar. 128p. spiralbound 2.50 (ISBN 0-317-36142-2, 1510). War Res League.

Averintsev, Sergei. Religya i Literatura: Religion & Literature. LC 81-4115. 140p. (Rus.). 1981. pap. 7.00 (ISBN 0-938920-02-2). Hermitage.

Averitt, Max W. Boatwatch. (Encore Edition). (Illus., Orig.). 1979. pap. 1.95 (ISBN 0-684-17689-0, SL854, ScribT). Scribner.

Averitt, Robert T. Dual Economy. 1968. pap. 6.95x (ISBN 0-393-09781-1, NortonC). Norton.

Averitt-Taylor, Ann. Popcorn & Firecrackers. (Illus.). 64p. 1985. 6.95 (ISBN 0-89962-477-4). Todd & Honeywell.

Averley, G., jt. ed. see Jolliffe, J. W.

Avernikov, Y. Whose Is the Sun? 16p. 1973. pap. 0.99 (ISBN 0-8285-1270-1, Pub. by Progress Pubs USSR). Imported Pubns.

Averoff-Tossizza, Evangelos. By Fire & Axe: The Communist Party & the Civil War in Greece, 1944-49. Rigos, Sarah A., tr. LC 77-91603. (Modern Greek History Ser.: No. 1). (Illus.). 438p. 1978. 15.00 (ISBN 0-89241-078-7). Caratzas.

--The Call of the Earth. Michalopoulos, Andre, tr. from Greek. 300p. 1980. 11.95 (ISBN 0-89241-134-1). Caratzas.

--Lost Opportunities: The Cyprus Question, 1950-1963. Cullen, Timothy & Kyriakides, Susan, trs. from Modern Greek. 456p. 1985. 30.00 (ISBN 0-89241-389-1). Caratzas.

Averroes. Averroes' Destructio Destructionum Philosophiae Algazelis in the Latin Version of Calo Calonymos. Zedler, Beatrice H., ed. 1961. 14.95 (ISBN 0-87462-421-5). Marquette.

--Averroes: Epitome of Parva Naturalia. Blumberg, Harry, tr. LC 58-3296. 1961. 9.60x (ISBN 0-910956-45-6). Medieval Acad.

--Averroes on Aristotle's De Generatione et Corruptione: Middle Commentary & Epitome. Kurland, Samuel, tr. LC 50-1421. 1958. 11.20x (ISBN 0-910956-41-3). Medieval Acad.

--Averrois Cordubensis Commentarium Magnum in Aristotelis De Anima Libros, Lat. Ed. Crawford, F. S., ed. LC 53-9617. 1953. 32.00 (ISBN 0-910956-33-2). Medieval Acad.

--Averrois Cordubensis Commentarium Medium in Aristotelis De Generatione et Corruptione Libros, Lat. Ed. Fobes, F. H. & Kurland, Samuel, eds. LC 50-1421. 1956. 12.80x (ISBN 0-910956-39-1). Medieval Acad.

--Averrois Cordubensis Commentarium Medium in Porphyrii Isagogen et Aristotelis Categorias, Heb. Ed. Davidson, Herbert A., ed. LC 68-24426. 1969. 20.00x (ISBN 0-910956-52-9). Medieval Acad.

--Averrois Cordubensis Compendia Librorum Aristotelis Qui Parva Naturalia Vocantur, Heb. Ed. Blumberg, Harry, ed. LC 50-1421. 1954. 11.20x (ISBN 0-910956-36-7). Medieval Acad.

--Averrois Cordubensis Compendia Librorum Aristotelis Qui Parva Naturalia Vocantur. Blumberg, Harry, ed. LC 78-108420. (Arabic.). 1972. 20.00x (ISBN 0-910956-54-5). Medieval Acad.

--Averrois Cordubensis Compendia Librorum Aristotelis Qui Parva Naturalia Vocantur, Lat. Ed. Shields, E. L. & Blumberg, Harry, eds. 1949. 19.20x (ISBN 0-910956-28-6). Medieval Acad.

Averrois. Averroes: Middle Commentary on Porphyry's Isagoge. Davidson, Herbert A., ed. LC 68-24427. 1969. 9.60x (ISBN 0-910956-53-7). Medieval Acad.

--Averrois Cordubensis Commentarium Medium et Epitome in Aristotelis De Generatione et Corruptione Libros, Heb Ed. Kurland, Samuel, ed. LC 50-1421. 1958. 16.00x (ISBN 0-910956-40-5). Medieval Acad.

Avers, Charlotte J. Biology of Sex. LC 74-1021. pap. 73.30 (ISBN 0-317-28753-2, 2055487). Bks Demand UMI.

--Genetics. 2nd ed. 700p. 1984. text ed. write for info (ISBN 0-87150-779-X, 4541, Pub. by Willard Grant Pr). PWS Pubs.

Avery, Andrews D., III. Studies in the Syntax of Relative & Comparative Clauses. Hankamer, Jorge, ed. (Outstanding Dissertations in Linguistics Ser.). 200p. 1985. 25.00 (ISBN 0-8240-5419-9). Garland Pub.

Avery Architectural & Fine Arts Library, Columbia University. Avery Index to Architectural Periodicals, 1979-1982. (Library Reference-Supplements Ser.). 1985. 295.00 (ISBN 0-8161-0384-4). G K Hall.

Avery, Arthur C. A Modern Guide to Foodservice Equipment. LC 79-20831. (Illus.). 560p. 1980. text ed. 29.95 (ISBN 0-8436-2179-6). Van Nos Reinhold.

Avery, Benedict R., tr. see Gregorius I.

Avery, Burniece. Walk Quietly Through the Night & Cry Softly. new ed. LC 77-2891. (Illus.). 1977. 7.00 (ISBN 0-913642-08-8). Balamp Pub.

Avery, C. The New Century Classical Handbook. 1962. 29.95 (ISBN 0-13-611905-0, Spec). P-H.

--The New Century Handbook of Leaders of the Classical World. 1972. 8.95 (ISBN 0-13-612002-4, Spec). P-H.

Avery, C. Louise. An Exhibition of Early New York Silver. LC 77-168417. (Metropolitan Museum of Art Publications in Reprint). (Illus.). 92p. 1972. Repr. of 1931 ed. 17.00 (ISBN 0-405-02255-7). Ayer Co Pubs.

Avery, Charles & Lang, Alastair. Fingerprints of the Artist: European Terra-Cotta Sculpture from the Arthur M. Sackler Collections. (Illus.). 290p. 1980. text ed. 150.00x (ISBN 0-674-30202-8); pap. text ed. 75.00x slip case (ISBN 0-674-30203-6). Harvard U Pr.

Avery, Charles, et al. The Isabella Stewart Gardner Museum. LC 78-61640. (Illus.). 80p. 1978. Repr. 15.00 (ISBN 0-914660-05-5). I S Gardner Mus.

Avery, Connie, jt. ed. see Brown, Alan R.

Avery, Constance & Cembuna, Al. Garnier Bottles. 1970. pap. 4.95 (ISBN 0-87505-221-5). Borden.

--Luxardo Bottles. 1968. pap. 4.75 (ISBN 0-686-85727-5). Borden.

Avery, Constance & Cimbuna, Al. Bischoff Kord & Kamotsuru Bottles. 1969. pap. 4.75 (ISBN 0-87505-276-2). Borden.

Avery, Constance, jt. auth. see Cembura, Al.

Avery, Craig, ed. see Portland Cement Association.

Avery, David R., jt. auth. see McDonald, Ralph E.

Avery, Don. Transcendental Americana. Galef, Jack, ed. LC 82-82852. (Unpublished Poets Ser.). 80p. (Orig.). 1983. pap. 6.95 (ISBN 0-910323-00-3). Elizabeth St Pr.

Avery, Donna, ed. see Keillor, Garrison.

Avery, Emmett L. London Stage, Seventeen Hundred to Seventeen Twenty-Nine: A Critical Introduction, Pt. 2. LC 60-6539. (Arcturus Books Paperbacks). (Illus.). 199p. 1968. pap. 5.95x (ISBN 0-8093-0337-X). S Ill U Pr.

Avery, Emmett L., ed. see Congreve, William.

Avery, Evelyn. Rebels & Victims: The Fiction of Richard Wright & Bernard Malamud. (National Univ. Pubns. Literary Criticism Ser.). 1979. 11.50x (ISBN 0-8046-9234-3, Pub. by Kennikat). Assoc Faculty Pr.

Avery, G. S., ed. see Milner, G.

Avery, G. S., Jr., ed. Survey of Biological Progress, Vols. 2-4. Incl. Vol. 2. 1952. 49.50 (ISBN 0-12-609802-6); Vol. 3. Glass, Bentley, ed. 1957. 48.00 (ISBN 0-12-609803-4); Vol. 4. 1962. 57.50 (ISBN 0-12-609804-2). Acad Pr.

Avery, Gillian, ed. & intro. by. Victorian Doll Stories. Incl. Victoria-Bess. Brenda; Aunt Sally's Life. Gatty, Mrs.; Racketty-Packetty House. Burnett, Frances H. LC 69-14797. (Victorian Revival Ser). (Illus.). 140p. (gr. 4 up). 1969. pap. 2.95 (ISBN 0-8052-0224-2). Schocken.

Avery, Gordon B. Neonatology. 2nd ed. (Illus.). 129p. 1981. text ed. 89.50 (ISBN 0-397-50429-2, 65-05762, Lippincott Medical). Lippincott.

Avery, Graeme S. Drug Treatment. 3rd ed. 1342p. 1985. 54.00 (ISBN 0-683-11008-X). Williams & Wilkins.

Avery, Isaac W. History of the State of Georgia from 1850-1881. LC 75-161709. Repr. of 1881 ed. 49.50 (ISBN 0-404-04571-5). AMS Pr.

Avery, J., ed. Membrane Structure & Mechanisms of Biolological Energy Transduction. LC 72-95064. 608p. 1974. 57.50x (ISBN 0-306-30718-9, Plenum Pr). Plenum Pub.

Avery, J. H. & Nelkon, M. Mathematics of Physics. 3rd ed. 1973. text ed. 13.50x (ISBN 0-435-68045-5). Heinemann Ed.

Avery, James R. & Null, Roberta L. Environmental Design Laboratory Guide. 3rd ed. (Illus.). 1978. pap. text ed. 8.95 (ISBN 0-8403-1077-3). Kendall-Hunt.

Avery, James S., jt. auth. see Marlin, John T.

Avery, Jean. The Adventures of Wally Dolphin. 1985. 6.95 (ISBN 0-533-06598-4). Vantage.

Avery, Jeanne. Astrological Aspects: Your Inner Dialogues. LC 84-21086. 384p. 1985. pap. cancelled (ISBN 0-385-18857-9, Dolp). Doubleday.

--Rising Sign: Your Astrological Mask. LC 77-16894. (Illus.). 480p. 1982. pap. 9.95 (ISBN 0-385-13278-6, Dolp). Doubleday.

Avery, John, jt. ed. see Dahl, Jens P.

Avery, Kevin Quinn. The Numbers of Life. LC 76-45969. 354p. 1977. pap. 8.95 (ISBN 0-385-12629-8, Dolp). Doubleday.

Avery, Laurence G., ed. see Anderson, Maxwell.

Avery, Lois, jt. auth. see Debnam, Betty.

Avery, Mary E. & Litwack, Georgia. Born Early: The Story of a Premature Baby. (Illus.). 160p. 1983. 15.45i (ISBN 0-316-05865-3). Little.

Avery, Mary E. & Taeusch, H. William, Jr. Schaffer's Diseases of the Newborn. 5th ed. (Illus.). 104p. 1984. 70.00 (ISBN 0-7216-1458-2). Saunders.

Avery, Mary E., et al. The Lung & Its Disorders in the Newborn Infant. 4th ed. (Major Problems in Clinical Pediatrics: Vol. 1). (Illus.). 560p. 1981. text ed. 39.95 (ISBN 0-7216-1462-0). Saunders.

Avery, Mary W. Government of Washington State. rev. ed. LC 73-13937. (Illus.). 288p. (gr. 7-12). 1973. text ed. 25.00x (ISBN 0-295-95256-3). U of Wash Pr.

--Washington: A History of the Evergreen State. LC 61-8211. (Illus.). 374p. 1965. 20.00x (ISBN 0-295-95126-5). U of Wash Pr.

Avery, Maurine & Imdieke, Bonnie. Medical Records in Ambulatory Care. LC 83-11836. 256p. 1983. 29.95 (ISBN 0-89443-940-5). Aspen Systems.

Avery, Michael & Rudovsky, David. Police Misconduct: Law & Litigation. 2nd ed. LC 80-23165. 1980. looseleaf 67.50 (ISBN 0-87632-112-0). Boardman.

Avery, Michael, et al. Do Your Own Divorce in Connecticut. 1981. pap. 10.00 (ISBN 0-89166-014-3). Cobblesmith.

Avery, Michel, et al. Building United Judgment: A Handbook for Consensus Decision Making. 124p. (Orig.). 1981. pap. text ed. 7.30 (ISBN 0-941492-01-X). Ctr Conflict Resol.

Avery, Nancy C., jt. auth. see Wayne, Julianne.

Avery, P. & Heath-Stubbs, eds. Ruba'lyat of Omar Khayyam. (Penguin Classic Ser.). 1981. pap. 3.95 (ISBN 0-14-044384-3). Penguin.

Avery, Peter, tr. see Khayyam, Omar.

Avery, R. America's Triumph at Panama. 1976. lib. bdg. 59.95 (ISBN 0-8490-1420-4). Gordon Pr.

Avery, Rachel R. LOGO & the Apple. (Illus.). 224p. 1985. pap. 16.95 (ISBN 0-13-539933-5). P-H.

--LOGO & the IBM PC. (Illus.). 240p. 1985. pap. 16.95 (ISBN 0-13-539941-6). P-H.

Avery, Robert, et al, eds. Turkish-English, English-Turkish Dictionary (The Redhouse Portable Dictionary) (Turkish & Eng.). 17.50 (ISBN 0-685-80306-6). Heinman.

Avery, Robert K. & Pepper, Robert. The Politics of Interconnection: A History of Public Television at the National Level. 66p. 1979. pap. 3.00 (ISBN 0-686-77630-5, Pub Telecom). NAEB.

Avery, Robert K., et al. Research Index of NAEB Journals, 1957 to 1979. 169p. 1980. pap. 13.50 (ISBN 0-686-70303-0). NAEB.

Avery, Robert S. Experiment in Management: Personnel Decentralization in the Tennessee Valley Authority. LC 54-11202. pap. 56.00 (ISBN 0-317-09065-8, 2022211). Bks Demand UMI.

Avery, Samuel P. The Diaries, Eighteen Hundred & Seventy-One to Eighteen Hundred & Eighty-Two, of Samuel P Avery, Art Dealer. Fidell-Beaufort, Madeleine, et al, eds. 66.00 (ISBN 0-405-11517-2). Ayer Co Pubs.

Avery, Thomas E. & Berlin, Graydon L. Interpretation of Aerial Photographs. 4th ed. (Illus.). 428p. 1985. text ed. write for info. (ISBN 0-8087-0096-0). Burgess.

Avery, Thomas E. & Burkhart, Harold E. Forest Measurements. 3rd ed. (McGraw-Hill Ser. in Forest Measurements). (Illus.). 384p. 1983. text ed. 37.95 (ISBN 0-07-002503-7). McGraw.

Avery, Valeen T., jt. auth. see Newell, Linda K.

Avery, Virginia. Big Book of Applique. (Illus.). 176p. 1982. 17.50 (ISBN 0-684-15623-7, ScribT); pap. 12.95 (ISBN 0-684-17422-7). Scribner.

--Quilts to Wear. (Illus.). 160p. 1983. pap. 14.95 (ISBN 0-684-18034-0, ScribT). Scribner.

Avery, William & Rapkin, David P., eds. America in a Changing World Political Economy. LC 81-12377. (Illus.). 256p. 1982. pap. text ed. 13.50x (ISBN 0-582-28270-5). Longman.

Avery, William P., et al, eds. Rural Change & Public Policy: Eastern Europe, Latin America & Australia. (Pergamon Policy Studies). 1980. 43.00 (ISBN 0-08-023109-8). Pergamon.

Avery Jones, J. F., ed. Tax Havens & Measures Against Tax Evasion & Avoidance in the EEC. xiv, 144p. 1974. text ed. 25.00x (ISBN 0-85227-027-5). Rothman.

Averyt, Anne C., jt. auth. see Brobeck, Steven.

Averyt, William F., Jr. Agropolitics in the European Community: Interest Groups & the Common Agricultural Policy. LC 77-10619. 144p. 1977. 31.95x (ISBN 0-03-039666-2). Praeger.

Aves, Diane & Anderson, Debra. Planning Your Job Search: Making the Right Moves. 84p. 9.75 (ISBN 0-88440-036-0, 716P). Sis Kenny Inst.

Avesta. The Hymns of Zarathustra. Henning, M., tr. LC 78-20446. 1980. Repr. of 1952 ed. 16.00 (ISBN 0-88355-826-2). Hyperion Conn.

Avesta, English. Zend-Avesta, 3 Vols. LC 68-30997. 1880-87. Repr. lib. bdg. 49.00x (ISBN 0-8371-3070-0, AVZE). Greenwood.

Avestruz, Fred S. Risk & Technology Choice in Developing Countries: The Case of Philippine Sugar Factories. (Illus.). 192p. (Orig.). 1985. lib. bdg. 19.75 (ISBN 0-8191-4774-5); pap. text ed. 10.75 (ISBN 0-8191-4775-3). U Pr of Amer.

Avett, Elizabeth M. Today's Business Letter Writing. LC 76-22687. (Illus.). 1977. pap. 17.95 (ISBN 0-13-924027-6). P-H.

Avey, Elijah. Capture & Execution of John Brown. LC 78-99335. 1969. Repr. of 1906 ed. lib. bdg. 8.50 (ISBN 0-8411-0006-3). Metro Bks.

Avez, A. & Blaquiere, A. Dynamical Systems & Microphysics: Symposium. 465p. 1982. 44.00 (ISBN 0-12-068720-8). Acad Pr.

Avi. Bright Shadow. LC 85-5719. 144p. (gr. 5-7). 1985. 11.95 (ISBN 0-02-707750-0). Bradbury Pr.

--Devil's Race. LC 84-47636. (A Lippincott Page-Turner). 160p. (YA) (gr. 7 up). 1984. 10.10i (ISBN 0-397-32094-9); PLB 9.89g (ISBN 0-397-32095-7). Lipp Jr Bks.

--Emily Upham's Revenge. LC 77-13739. (gr. 5-8). 1978. PLB 6.99 (ISBN 0-394-93506-3). Pantheon.

--Encounter at Easton. LC 79-9439. (gr. 5-8). 1980. PLB 6.99 (ISBN 0-394-94342-2). Pantheon.

--The Fighting Ground. LC 82-47719. (Illus.). 160p. (gr. 4-7). 1984. 11.06i (ISBN 0-397-32073-6); PLB 11.89g (ISBN 0-397-32074-4). Lipp Jr Bks.

--The History of Helpless Harry: To Which Is Added a Variety of Amusing & Entertaining Adventures. (Illus.). 1980. 8.99 (ISBN 0-394-94505-0). Pantheon.

--Man from the Sky. LC 79-26909. (Capers Ser.). (Illus.). 128p. (gr. 3-6). 1980. pap. 1.95 (ISBN 0-394-84468-8). Knopf.

--Night Journeys. LC 78-10151. (Illus.). (gr. 5-9). 1979. 6.99g (ISBN 0-394-94116-0). Pantheon.

--A Place Called Ugly. LC 80-23326. (Illus.). 224p. (YA) (gr. 7-9). 1981. PLB 8.99 (ISBN 0-394-94755-X). Pantheon.

--A Place Called Ugly. 144p. (gr. 7 up). 1982. pap. 1.95 (ISBN 0-590-32447-0, Vagabond). Scholastic Inc.

--Shadrach's Crossing. LC 82-19008. 192p. (gr. 5 up). 1983. PLB 10.99 (ISBN 0-394-95816-0). Pantheon.

--Snail Tale: The Adventures of a Rather Small Snail. (Illus.). (gr. 2-4). 1972. PLB 6.99 (ISBN 0-394-92443-6). Pantheon.

--Sometimes I Think I Hear My Name. LC 81-38421. 160p. (gr. 7 up). 1982. 9.95 (ISBN 0-394-85048-3); PLB 9.99 (ISBN 0-394-95048-8). Pantheon.

--Sometimes I Think I Hear My Name. 144p. 1983. pap. 1.95 (ISBN 0-451-12151-1, Sig). NAL.

--S.O.R. Losers. LC 84-11022. 112p. (gr. 5-7). 1984. 9.95 (ISBN 0-02-793410-1). Bradbury Pr.

--Who Stole the Wizard of Oz? LC 81-884. (A Capers Bk.). (Illus.). 128p. (gr. 3-6). 1981. PLB 6.99 (ISBN 0-394-94644-8); pap. 1.95 (ISBN 0-394-84644-3). Knopf.

Aviad, Janet. Return to Judaism: Religious Renewal in Israel. LC 82-17663. 208p. 1985. lib. bdg. 20.00x (ISBN 0-226-03236-1); pap. 8.95 (ISBN 0-226-03235-3). U of Chicago Pr.

Aviad, Janet, jt. auth. see Elazar, Daniel J.

Aviad, Janet O., jt. auth. see O'Dea, Thomas F.

Aviation Book Company, ed. see Federal Aviation Administration.

Aviation Book Company Editors, jt. auth. see Federal Aviation Administration.

Aviation Book Company Staff, ed. see Federal Aviation Administration.

Aviation Language School Inc. Air Traffic Control Communications for V.F.R. Pilots. 138p. 1979. pap. text ed. 15.95 (ISBN 0-941456-02-1). Aviation Lang Sch.

--Intermediate Aeronautical Language Manual. 124p. 1978. pap. text ed. 15.95 (ISBN 0-941456-01-3). Aviation Lang Sch.

--Primary Aeronautical Language Manual. 201p. 1980. pap. text ed. 29.95 (ISBN 0-941456-00-5). Aviation Lang Sch.

Aviation Maintenance Foundation. Aircraft Hydraulics Systems. Crane, Dale, ed. (Aviation Technician Training Ser.). (Illus.). 87p. 1975. pap. text ed. 5.95 (ISBN 0-89100-058-5, EA-AH-1). Aviation Maint.

--Aircraft Ignition & Electrical Systems. Crane, Dale, ed. LC 76-47110. (Aviation Technician Training Ser.). (Illus.). 76p. 1977. pap. 5.95 (ISBN 0-89100-063-1, EA-IGS). Aviation Maint.

Aviation Maintenance Publishers. Aircraft Batteries: Lead Acid & Nickel Cadmium. Crane, Dale, ed. (Aviation Technician Training Ser.). 32p. 1975. pap. 3.95 (ISBN 0-89100-052-6, EA-AB-1). Aviation Maint.

--Aircraft Instrument Systems. Crane, Dale, ed. (Aviation Technician Training Ser.). (Illus.). 81p. 1976. pap. 5.95 (ISBN 0-89100-062-3, EA-AIS). Aviation Maintenance.

--Aircraft Logbook. 74p. 1975. pap. 4.95 (ISBN 0-89100-190-5, EA-AFL-1). Aviation Maintenance.

--Engine Logbook. 74p. 1975. pap. 4.95 (ISBN 0-89100-187-5, EA-EFL-1). Aviation Maintenance.

--Pilot Logbook. 70p. 1979. text ed. 2.50 (ISBN 0-89100-112-3, EA-PLO-2). Aviation Maintenance.

--Radio Logbook. 64p. 1974. pap. 3.95 (ISBN 0-89100-186-7, EA-ARL-1). Aviation Maintenance.

--Radio Logbook. 64p. 1974. text ed. 4.95 (ISBN 0-89100-195-6, EA-ARL-2). Aviation Maintenance.

Aviation Maintenance Publishers & & Crane, Dale. Aircraft Bonded Structure. (Aviation Technician Training Ser.). (Illus.). 45p. 1977. pap. 3.95 (ISBN 0-89100-065-8, EA-NMR). Aviation Maint.

Aviation Publications. Comprehensive Reference Guide to Airfoil Sections for Light Aircraft. (Illus.). 168p. 1982. pap. 19.95 (ISBN 0-87994-038-7). Aviat Pub.

Aviation Supplies & Academics. Flight Engineer Test Prep Program. 1978. 3-ring binder 49.95 (ISBN 0-940732-26-2, Pub. by ASA). Aviation.

Avicenna. Avicenna on Theology. Arberry, Arthur J., tr. LC 78-59000. 1979. Repr. of 1951 ed. 15.00 (ISBN 0-88355-676-6). Hyperion Conn.

--Avicenna's Psychology. Rahman, F., ed. LC 79-2848. 127p. 1981. Repr. of 1952 ed. 15.25 (ISBN 0-8305-0024-3). Hyperion Conn.

--A Treatise on the Canon of Medicine of Avicenna. LC 73-12409. Repr. of 1930 ed. 45.00 (ISBN 0-404-11231-5). AMS Pr.

Avidar, Yosef. The Party & the Army in the Soviet Union. 340p. 1983. text ed. 30.50x (ISBN 965-223-495-8, Pub. by Magnes Israel). Humanities.

--The Party & the Army in the Soviet Union. LC 84-43066. 348p. 1985. 24.95x (ISBN 0-271-00393-6). Pa St U Pr.

Aviel, Joanne F. Resource Shortages & World Politics. 162p. 1977. pap. text ed. 10.00 (ISBN 0-8191-0263-6). U Pr of Amer.

Aviel, S. David. The Politics of Nuclear Energy. LC 81-40875. (Illus.). 274p. (Orig.). 1982. lib. bdg. 26.25 (ISBN 0-8191-2201-7); pap. text ed. 13.00 (ISBN 0-8191-2202-5). U Pr of Amer.

Aviel, S. David, jt. auth. see Duncan, Doris G.

Avienus, Lucius Festus. Ora Maritima. Murphy, J. P., ed. (Ancient Greek & Roman Writers Ser.). 1977. 15.00 (ISBN 0-89005-175-5). Ares.

Avigad, Nahman. Discovering Jerusalem. (Illus.). 268p. 1983. 24.95 (ISBN 0-8407-5299-7). Nelson.

Avigdor, Albert, jt. auth. see Ashe, Rosalind.

Avi-hai, Avraham. Ben Gurion: State Builder. 365p. 1974. casebound 12.95x (ISBN 0-87855-156-5). Transaction Bks.

Avi-Itzhak, Benjamin. Developments in Operations Research, 2 vols. LC 78-141897. (Illus.). 652p. 1971. Set. 157.25 (ISBN 0-677-30510-9); Vol. 1,308p. 80.95 (ISBN 0-677-30830-2); Vol 2.,344p. 93.75 (ISBN 0-677-30840-X). Gordon.

Avi-Itzhak, Benjamin, jt. auth. see Vardi, Joseph.

Avila, jt. auth. see Combs, Arthur W.

Avila, et al. The Helping Relationship Sourcebook. 2nd ed. 1985. 20.00 (ISBN 0-205-05843-4, 245843). Allyn.

Avila, Charles. Ownership: Early Christian Teaching. LC 83-8330. 256p. (Orig.). 1981. pap. 9.95 (ISBN 0-88344-384-8). Orbis Bks.

Avila, Crucita B. see Diaz Zayas, Carmen E. & Benitez de Avila, Crucita.

Avila, Kay, et al. Harian Creative Awards - I: Featuring the Gospel According to Everyman by Baron Mikan. Barba, Harry, ed. 220p. 1981. lib. bdg. 8.95 (ISBN 0-911906-09-6); pap. 4.95 (ISBN 0-911906-16-9). Harian Creative.

Avila, Penny, et al. Between Raindrops. LC 85-60471. (Illus., Orig.). 1985. 20.00x (ISBN 0-931321-01-8); pap. 6.95x (ISBN 0-931321-02-6). Mica Pub Co.

Avila, Rafael. Worship & Politics. Neely, Alan, tr. LC 81-38356. 144p. (Orig.). 1981. pap. 6.95 (ISBN 0-88344-714-2). Orbis Bks.

Avila, Wanda. Jean Stafford: A Comprehensive Bibliography. LC 82-49127. 200p. 1985. lib. bdg. 32.00 (ISBN 0-8240-9210-4). Garland Pub.

Aviles, J. J. Ecuador. 1977. lib. bdg. 59.95 (ISBN 0-8490-1749-1). Gordon Pr.

Avilez, Alexander. Population Increases into Alta California in the Spanish Period, 1769-1821: Thesis. LC 74-76499. 1974. Repr. of 1955 ed. soft bdg. 10.95 (ISBN 0-88247-268-2). R & E Pubs.

Avillez, Martim, jt. auth. see Meyer, Susan E.

Avilova, Lidiia. Chekhov in My Life. Magarshack, David, tr. from Rus. LC 79-138198. (Illus.). 1971. Repr. of 1950 ed. lib. bdg. 22.50 (ISBN 0-8371-5551-7, AVCH). Greenwood.

Avina, Rose H. Spanish & Mexican Land Grants in California. Cortes, Carlos E., ed. LC 76-1231. (Chicano Heritage Ser.). (Illus.). 1976. 16.00x (ISBN 0-405-09483-3). Ayer Co Pubs.

Avineri. Varieties of Marxism. (Van Leer Jerusalem Foundation Ser.). 1977. lib. bdg. 30.00 (ISBN 90-247-2024-9, Pub by Martinus Nijhoff Netherland). Kluwer Academic.

Avineri, Shlomo. Hegel's Theory of the Modern State. LC 70-186254. (Cambridge Studies in the History & Theory of Politics). 266p. 1973. 39.50 (ISBN 0-521-08513-6); pap. 12.95 (ISBN 0-521-09832-7). Cambridge U Pr.

--The Making of Modern Zionism: Intellectual Origins of the Jewish State. LC 81-66102. 272p. 1981. 15.50 (ISBN 0-465-04328-3). Basic.

--The Making of Modern Zionism: The Intellectual Origins of the Jewish State. LC 81-66102. 244p. 1984. pap. 7.95 (ISBN 0-465-04330-5, CN 5113). Basic.

--Moses Hess: Prophet of Communism & Zionism. 300p. 1985. 22.50x (ISBN 0-8147-0584-7). NYU Pr.

--Social & Political Thought of Karl Marx. LC 68-12055. (Studies in the History & Theory of Politics). 1971. 42.50 (ISBN 0-521-04071-X); pap. 12.95 (ISBN 0-521-09619-7). Cambridge U Pr.

Avineri, Shlomo, jt. auth. see Sisco, Joseph J.

Avineri, Shlomo, ed. Marx's Socialism. (Controversy Ser.). 236p. 1973. 11.95x (ISBN 0-88311-004-0); pap. 5.95 (ISBN 0-88311-005-9). Lieber-Atherton.

Avins, Alfred. Penalties for Misconduct on the Job. LC 71-156375. (Legal Almanac Ser: No. 69). 124p. 1972. lib. bdg. 5.95 (ISBN 0-379-11075-X). Oceana.

Avins, Carol. Border Crossings: The West & Russian Identity in Soviet Literature, 1917-1934. LC 81-19729. 200p. 1983. 24.50x (ISBN 0-520-04233-6). U of Cal Pr.

Avio, K. L. & Clark, C. Scott. Property Crime in Canada: An Econometric Study. LC 76-925. (Ontario Economic Council Ser.). 1975. pap. 6.00 (ISBN 0-8020-3334-2). U of Toronto Pr.

Avioli, Louis V. The Osteoporotic Syndrome: Detection, Prevention, Treatment. 176p. 1983. 19.50 (ISBN 0-8089-1548-7, 790285). Grune.

Avioli, Louis V. & Krane, Stephen M., eds. Metabolic Bone Disease. LC 76-27431. 1977-78. Vol. 1. 75.00 (ISBN 0-12-068701-1); Vol. 2. 82.50 (ISBN 0-12-068702-X). Acad Pr.

Avioli, Louis V., et al, eds. Glucocorticoid Effects & Their Biological Consequences. (Advances in Experimental Medicine & Biology Ser.: Vol. 171). 432p. 1984. 57.50x (ISBN 0-306-41615-8, Plenum Pr). Plenum Pub.

Avirett, James B. The Memoirs of General Turner Ashby & His Compeers. 428p. 1984. Repr. of 1867 ed. 28.50 (ISBN 0-913419-04-4). Butternut Pr.

Avirgan, Tony & Honey, Martha. War in Uganda: The Legacy of Idi Amin. 348p. 1982. 16.95 (ISBN 0-88208-136-5); pap. 9.95 (ISBN 0-88208-137-3). Lawrence Hill.

Avis, et al. Pharmaceutical Dosage Forms: Parenteral Medications, Vol. 1. 520p. 1984. 59.75 (ISBN 0-8247-7084-6). Dekker.

Avis, Kenneth E. & Akers, Michael J. Sterile Preparation for the Hospital Pharmacist: An Illustrated Manual of Procedures. LC 81-69246. 1982. pap. text ed. 19.95 (ISBN 0-250-40518-0). Butterworth.

Avis, Paul. Truth Beyond Words: Problems & Solutions for Anglican-Roman Catholic Unity. 160p. (Orig.). 1985. pap. 7.95 (ISBN 0-936384-26-3). Cowley Pubns.

Avis, Paul D. The Church in the Theology of the Reformers. Toon, Peter & Martin, Ralph, eds. LC 80-16186. (New Foundations Theological Library). 256p. 1981. 6.49 (ISBN 0-8042-3708-5); pap. 2.99 (ISBN 0-8042-3728-X). John Knox.

Avishai, Bernard. The Tragedy of Zionism: Revolution and Democracy in the Land fo Israel. LC 85-10235. (Illus.). 384p. 1985. 18.95 (ISBN 0-374-27863-6). FS&G.

Avison, D. E. Microcomputers & Their Commercial Applications. 112p. 1983. 9.95 (ISBN 0-632-01172-6). Computer Sci.

Avitabile, Alphonse, jt. auth. see Sammataro, Diana.

Avitable, Gunhild G. Cloisonne & Champleve, Fourteen Hundred to Nineteen Hundred. (Illus.). 272p. (Ger.). 1984. 45.00 (ISBN 0-317-28168-2, Pub. by Kunst & Antiquitaten West Germany). Seven Hills Bks.

Avital, Samuel. Mime Workbook. 2nd, rev. ed. Reed, Ken, ed. LC 77-84487. (Illus.). 176p. 1977. pap. 8.95 (ISBN 0-914794-30-2). Wisdom Garden.

--The Mime Workbook. 3rd ed. (Illus.). 158p. 1982. pap. 9.95 (ISBN 0-941524-19-1). Lotus Light.

Avitzur. Metal Forming. (Manufacturing, Engineering, & Materials Processing Ser.: Vol. 4). 224p. 1980. 39.75 (ISBN 0-8247-6847-7). Dekker.

Avitzur, B. & Van Tyne, C. J., eds. Production to Near Net Shape: Source Book. 1983. 54.00 (ISBN 0-87170-152-9). ASM.

Avitzur, Betzalel. Handbook of Metal Forming Processes. LC 82-17435. 1020p. 1983. 99.50x (ISBN 0-471-03474-6, Pub. by Wiley-Interscience). Wiley.

Avi-Yonah, M. Art in Ancient Palestine. (Illus.). 404p. 1981. 40.00 (ISBN 0-8390-0277-7). Abner Schram Ltd.

Avi-Yonah, Michael. Ancient Scrolls. LC 72-10792. (The Lerner Archaeology Ser.: Digging up the Past). (Illus.). 96p. (gr. 5 up). 1974. PLB 7.95g (ISBN 0-8225-0827-3). Lerner Pubns.

--The Art of Mosaics. LC 72-10793. (The Lerner Archaeology Ser.: Digging up the Past). (Illus.). 96p. 1975. PLB 7.95 (ISBN 0-8225-0828-1). Lerner Pubns.

--Encyclopedia of Archaeological Excavations in the Holy Land, Vol. 3. LC 73-14997. (Illus.). 1975. 25.00 (ISBN 0-13-275131-3). P-H.

--The Encyclopedia of Archaeological Excavations in the Holy Land, Vol. 4. 1975. 25.00 (ISBN 0-13-275149-6). P-H.

--The Jews under Roman & Byzantine Rule: A Political History of Palestine from the Bar-Kokhba War to the Arab Conquest. LC 84-5612. Orig. Title: The Jews of Palestine. (Illus.). 304p. 1984. Repr. 23.00x (ISBN 0-8052-3580-9). Schocken.

--Search for the Past: An Introduction to Archaeology. LC 72-10791. (The Lerner Archaeology Ser.: Digging up the Past). (Illus.). 96p. (gr. 5 up). 1974. PLB 7.95 (ISBN 0-8225-0826-5). Lerner Pubns.

Avi-Yonah, Michael, jt. auth. see Aharoni, Yohanon.

Avi-Yonah, Michael, jt. auth. see Mazar, Benjamin.

Avi-Yonah, Michael see Mazar, Benjamin & Avi-Yonah, Michael.

Avi-Yonah, Michael, ed. Encyclopedia of Archaeological Excavations in the Holy Land, Vol. 1. LC 73-14997. (Illus.). 1975. 25.00 (ISBN 0-13-275115-1). P-H.

--The Encyclopedia of Archaeological Excavations in the Holy Land, Vol. 2. LC 76-14997. (Illus.). 400p. 1975. 25.00 (ISBN 0-13-275123-2). P-H.

Avner, Sidney H. Introduction to Physical Metallurgy. 2nd ed. (Illus.). 672p. 1974. text ed. 35.50 (ISBN 0-07-002499-5). McGraw.

Avneri, Arieh L. The Claim of Dispossesion: Jewish Land Settlement & the Arabs, 1878-1948. 303p. 1982. pap. 9.95 (ISBN 0-87855-964-7). Transaction Bks.

Avnet, I. Duke. How to Prove Damages in Wrongful Personal Injury & Death Cases. 2nd ed. (Illus.). 1978. 34.95 (ISBN 0-13-429415-7, Busn). P-H.

Avni, Haim. Spain, the Jews & Franco. Shimoni, Emanuel, tr. from Hebrew. LC 80-39777. 320p. 1981. 19.95 (ISBN 0-8276-0188-3, 469). Jewish Pubns.

Avni, Ora. Tics, Tics & Tics: Figures, Syllogismes, Recit Dans les Chants de Maldoror. LC 84-81849. (French Forum Monographs: No. 54). 186p. 1984. pap. 12.50x (ISBN 0-917058-54-2). French Forum.

Avogaro, P., jt. ed. see Galli, C.

Avogaro, Pietro, et al, eds. Phospholipids & Atherosclerosis. 292p. 1983. text ed. 60.00 (ISBN 0-89004-842-8). Raven.

Avon, Dennis & Hawkins, Andrew. Photography: A Complete Guide to Technique. (Illus., Orig.). 1979. (Amphoto); pap. 16.95 (ISBN 0-8174-2191-2). Watson-Guptill.

Avon, Dennis & Tilford, Tony. Birds of Britain & Europe. (Illus.). 1975. 11.95 (ISBN 0-7137-0762-3, Pub by Blandford Pr England). Sterling.

Avon, Dennis, jt. auth. see Hawkins, Andrew.

Avondo-Bodino, G. Economic Applications of the Theory of Graphs. 126p. 1962. 37.25 (ISBN 0-677-00030-8). Gordon.

Avram, A., jt. auth. see Wilmarth, S. S.

Avram, C. & Anastasescu, D., eds. Space Structures. (Developments in Civil Engineering Ser.: Vol. 9). 378p. 1984. 73.00 (ISBN 0-444-99639-7, I-394-83). Elsevier.

Avram, C., et al. Concrete Strength & Strains. (Developments in Civil Engineering Ser.: Vol. 3). 558p. 1982. 100.00 (ISBN 0-444-99733-4). Elsevier.

Avram, M. M., ed. Prevention of Kidney Disease & Long-Term Survival. 344p. 1982. 35.00x (ISBN 0-306-40965-8, Plenum Med Bk). Plenum Pub.

Avram, Margareta & Mateescu, Gh. Infrared Spectroscopy: Applications in Organic Chemistry. LC 78-16322. 532p. 1978. Repr. of 1972 ed. lib. bdg. 33.00 (ISBN 0-88275-711-3). Krieger.

Avrameas, S., et al, eds. Immunoenzymatic Techniques: Proceedings of the Second International Symposium on Immunoenzymatic Techniques, Held in Cannes, France, 16-18 March, 1983. (Developments in Immunology Ser.: Vol. 18). 398p. 1983. 89.50 (ISBN 0-444-80515-X, I-334-83). Elsevier.

Avramovic, Dragoslav, ed. South-South Financial Cooperation. LC 83-6668. 250p. 1983. 27.50 (ISBN 0-312-74741-1). St Martin.

Avran, M. M., ed. see International Symposium on Parathyroid in Uremia, 1st, N.Y., May, 1979.

Avrett, Eugene, ed. Frontiers of Astrophysics. (Illus.). 1976. 32.50x (ISBN 0-674-32559-1); pap. text ed. 12.95x (ISBN 0-674-32660-1). Harvard U Pr.

Avrett, Robert. Timid Pup. (Illus.). (gr. 1-3). PLB 6.19 (ISBN 0-8313-0004-3). Lantern.

Avrett, Roz. Seventy-Second & Rodeo. 200p. 1984. 15.50 (ISBN 0-87795-535-2). Arbor Hse.

Avrich, Paul. An American Anarchist: The Life of Voltairine De Cleyre. LC 78-51153. (Illus.). 1978. text ed. 32.00x (ISBN 0-691-04657-3). Princeton U Pr.

--The Haymarket Tragedy. LC 83-26924. (Illus.). 553p. 1984. 29.50x (ISBN 0-691-04711-1). Princeton U Pr.

--Kronstadt Nineteen Twenty-One. 288p. 1974. pap. 5.95x (ISBN 0-393-00724-3, Norton Lib). Norton.

--The Modern School Movement: Anarchism & Education in the United States. LC 79-3188. (Illus.). 1980. 42.00 (ISBN 0-691-04669-7); LPE 16.00 (ISBN 0-691-10094-2). Princeton U Pr.

--The Russian Anarchists. LC 80-21590. (Studies of the Russian Institute, Columbia University). (Illus.). vii, 303p. 1980. Repr. of 1967 ed. lib. bdg. 32.50x (ISBN 0-313-22571-0, AVRA). Greenwood.

--Russian Rebels, 1600-1800. (Illus.). 1976. pap. 7.95 (ISBN 0-393-00836-3, Norton Lib). Norton.

Avrich, Paul, ed. The Anarchists in the Russian Revolution. LC 72-13386. (Documents of Revolution Ser.). 180p. 1973. pap. 7.95x (ISBN 0-8014-9141-X, CP141). Cornell U Pr.

Avrich, Paul, ed. see Dana, Charles A.

Avriel, M. & Dembo, R. S., eds. Engineering Optimization. (Mathematical Programming Ser.: Vol. 11). 207p. 1980. pap. 42.75 (ISBN 0-444-85399-5, North Holland). Elsevier.

Avriel, Mordecai. Nonlinear Programming: Analysis & Methods. (Illus.). 1976. 40.95 (ISBN 0-13-623603-0). P-H.

Avriel, Mordecai, ed. Advances in Geometric Programming. LC 79-20806. (Mathematical Concepts & Methods in Science & Engineering Ser.: Vol. 21). 470p. 1980. 55.00x (ISBN 0-306-40381-1, Plenum Pr). Plenum Pub.

Avriel, Mordecai & Amit, Raphael, eds. Perspectives on Resource Policy Modeling: Theory & Applications. LC 81-12697. 456p. 1982. prof ref 42.00x (ISBN 0-88410-837-6). Ballinger Pub.

Avril, Francois. Manuscript Painting at the Court of France. LC 77-78271. (Magnificent Paperback Ser.). (Illus.). 1978. 19.95 (ISBN 0-8076-0878-5); pap. 11.95 (ISBN 0-8076-0879-3). Braziller.

Avrin, Cookie, jt. auth. see Sassen, Georgia.

Avron, M., jt. ed. see Trebst, A.

Avruch, Kevin. American Immigrants in Israel: Social Identities & Change. LC 81-1291. (Illus.). 1981. lib. bdg. 25.00x (ISBN 0-226-03241-8). U of Chicago Pr.

AvRutick, Frances R. The Complete Passover Cookbook. LC 80-39633. 432p. 1981. 12.95 (ISBN 0-8246-0262-5). Jonathan David.

Avrutis, Raymond. How to Collect Unemployment Insurance: Complete Information for All 50 States. LC 83-870. 206p. 1983. 14.95 (ISBN 0-13-403832-0); pap. 5.95 (ISBN 0-13-403782-0). P-H.

Avsharian, Evelyn. Where Did the Sun Go? (Illus.). 24p. (Orig.). (ps-1). 1984. pap. 3.95 (ISBN 0-932229-01-8). Falling Water.

Avtgis, Alexander, jt. auth. see Villanucci, Robert.

Avtgis, Alexander W., jt. auth. see Villanucci, Robert S.

Avtorkhanov, Abdurakham, pseud. The Reign of Stalin. Smith, L. J., tr. from Fr. LC 74-10074. (Russian Studies: Perspectives on the Revolution Ser). 256p. 1974. Repr. of 1953 ed. 23.00 (ISBN 0-88355-182-9). Hyperion Conn.

Avvento, Gennaro. Sexuality: A Christian View, Toward Formation of Mature Values. 208p. 1982. pap. 7.95 (ISBN 0-89622-158-X). Twenty-Third.

Avyzius, J. The Lost Home. 544p. 1974. 7.45 (ISBN 0-8285-0945-X, Pub. by Progress Pubs USSR). Imported Pubns.

Aw, S. E. Chemical Evolution. LC 81-70575. 1982. pap. 9.95 (ISBN 0-89051-082-2). Master Bks.

Awad, A., jt. auth. see Abu-Salih, M.

Awad, A. G., et al. Evaluation of Quality of Care in Psychiatry: Proceedings of a Symposium Held at the Queen St. Mental Health Centre, Toronto, Canada, June 22, 1979. LC 80-94280. 140p. 1981. 23.00 (ISBN 0-08-025364-4). Pergamon.

Awad, A. G., et al, eds. Disturbed Behavior in the Elderly. LC 84-18016. 208p. 1985. text ed. price not set (ISBN 0-89335-215-2). SP Med & Sci Bks.

Awad, Elias M. Business Data Processing. 5th ed. (Illus.). 1980. text ed. 28.95 (ISBN 0-13-093807-6); student guide 9.95 (ISBN 0-13-093757-6). P-H.

--Introduction to Computers. 2nd ed. (Illus.). 496p. 1983. text ed. 25.95 (ISBN 0-13-479444-3). P-H.

--Systems Analysis & Design. 1979. 29.95x (ISBN 0-256-02091-4). Irwin.

Awad, Elias M., jt. auth. see Cascio, Wayne F.

Awad, Joseph. The Neon Distances. 1980. 5.50 (ISBN 0-8233-0320-9). Golden Quill.

Awad, Joseph F. The Power of Public Relations. LC 85-6258. 176p. 1985. 29.95 (ISBN 0-03-002884-1). Praeger.

Awad, Louis. The Literature of Ideas, Pt. I: Arabic Writing Today. LC 84-52207. (Studies in New Eastern Culture & Society). 300p. 1985. 35.00x (ISBN 0-89003-177-0); pap. 26.50x (ISBN 0-89003-176-2). Undena Pubns.
Awakawa, Yasuichi. Zen Painting. Bester, John, tr. from Japanese. LC 78-82660. (Illus.). 1978. pap. 18.75 (ISBN 0-87011-300-3). Kodansha.
Awan, Akhtar A. Equality, Efficiency, & Property Ownership in the Islamic Economic System. (Illus.). 122p. 1984. lib. bdg. 21.50 (ISBN 0-8191-3562-3); pap. text ed. 9.25 (ISBN 0-8191-3563-1). U Pr of Amer.
Awani, Alfred O. Data Processing Project Management. 1985. 24.95 (ISBN 0-89433-234-1). Petrocelli.
--Project Management Techniques. (Illus.). 192p. 22.95 (ISBN 0-89433-197-3). Petrocelli.
Awashti, D. D. Catalogue of the Lichens from India, Nepal, Pakistan & Ceylon. 1965. 14.00 (ISBN 3-7682-5417-8). Lubrecht & Cramer.
Awasthi, D. The Dawn of Modern Administration in India. 298p. 1981. 35.00x (ISBN 0-686-78832-X, Pub. by Bks India England). State Mutual Bk.
Awasthi, D. D. A Monograph of the Lichen Genus Dirinaria. 1975. 14.00 (ISBN 3-7682-0957-1). Lubrecht & Cramer.
Awasthi, Rajendra. The Red Soil. (Vikas Library of Modern Indian Writing: No.27). 136p. 1982. text ed. 17.95x (ISBN 0-7069-1961-0, Pub. by Vikas India). Advent NY.
Awasthy, Rajendra. Stories of Valour. (Nehru Library for Children). (Illus.). (gr. 1-9). 1979. pap. 2.00 (ISBN 0-89744-182-6). Auromere.
Awasthy, Rajendra, ed. Hindi Short Stories-an Anthology. (Vikas Library of Modern Indian Writing: No. 16). 175p. 1981. text ed. 17.95x (ISBN 0-7069-1312-4, Pub. by Vikas India). Advent NY.
Awbery, Gwen. The Syntax of Welsh. LC 76-11489. (Cambridge Studies in Linguistics: No. 18). 1977. 42.50 (ISBN 0-521-21341-X). Cambridge U Pr.
Awdeley, J. The Fraternitye of Vacabondes. Viles, E., ed. (EETS, ES Ser.: No. 9). Repr. of 1869 ed. 10.00 (ISBN 0-527-00223-2). Kraus Repr.
Awdry, Philip & Nicholls, C. S. Cataract. LC 84-25884. (Illus.). 250p. (Orig.). 1985. 14.95 (ISBN 0-571-13478-5); pap. 5.95 (ISBN 0-571-13425-4). Faber & Faber.
Awdry, W. V. & Cook, Chris, eds. A Guide to the Steam Railways of Great Britain. 312p. 1983. 19.95 (ISBN 0-7207-1417-6, Pub. by Michael Joseph). Merrimack Pub Cir.
Awerkamp, Don. Ethics & Politics: The Philosophy of Emanuel Lavinas. 1974. lib. bdg. 59.95 (ISBN 0-87700-235-5). Revisionist Pr.
Awevera, Johan Van der see Van der Awevera, Johan.
Awh, Robert Y. Exercises in Microeconomics: Theory & Applications. LC 75-38643. 492p. 1976. text ed. 38.95x (ISBN 0-471-03849-0); pap. text ed. 17.95x wkbk. (ISBN 0-471-03853-9); tchrs. manual avail. (ISBN 0-471-03854-7). Wiley.
Awiaka, Marilou. Rising Fawn & the Fire Mystery. Eassun, Roger R., ed. (A Child's Christmas in Memphis Ser.: Vol. 1). (Illus.). 48p. (Orig.). (gr. 5 up). 1984. lib. bdg. 9.95 (ISBN 0-918518-35-0); pap. 6.95 (ISBN 0-918518-29-6). St Luke TN.
Awoonor, Kofi. The Breast of the Earth: A Survey of the History, Culture & Literature of Africa South of the Sahara. 1983. 19.95x (ISBN 0-88357-102-1); pap. text ed. 7.95 (ISBN 0-88357-103-X). NOK Pubs.
--Fire in the Valley: Ewe Folktales. LC 73-88805. Date not set. 10.00x (ISBN 0-88357-079-3); pap. text ed. 3.95 (ISBN 0-88357-080-7). NOK Pubs.
--Guardians of the Sacred Word: Ewe Poetry. LC 73-85559. 104p. 1974. text ed. 11.95x (ISBN 0-88357-007-6). Nok Pubs.
--The House by the Sea. 1978. perfect bdg. 3.00 (ISBN 0-912678-33-X). Greenfld Rev Pr.
--This Earth, My Brother. (African Writers Ser.). 1972. pap. text ed. 5.00x (ISBN 0-435-90108-7). Heinemann Ed.
Awoonor, Kofi & Adali-Mortty, Adali, eds. Messages: Poems from Ghana. (African Writers Ser.). 1971. pap. text ed. 5.50x (ISBN 0-435-90042-0). Heinemann Ed.
Awoonor, Kofi, tr. see Akpalu, Vinoko.
Awoonor, Kofi, et al. There Is a Song, We Shall Sing It. (African Poetry Ser.). cancelled. Greenfld Rev Pr.
AWP Board of Directors. AWP Catalogue of Writing Programs. 4th ed. 120p. 1983. 10.00 (ISBN 0-936266-05-8). Assoc Writing Progs.
Awret, Irene. Days of Honey: The Tunisian Boyhood of Rafael Uzan. LC 84-5338. 256p. 1984. 18.95 (ISBN 0-8052-3923-5). Schocken.
AWS A2 Committee on Definitions & Symbols. Symbols for Welding & Nondestructive Testing: AWS A2.4-79. new ed. LC 78-74600. 80p. pap. text ed. 22.00 (ISBN 0-87171-170-2). Am Welding.
AWS Conference on Welding for the Aerospace Industry, October 1980. Welding Technology for the Aerospace Industry: Proceedings. (Welding Technology Ser.). 176p. 1981. 25.00 (ISBN 0-686-95643-5). Am Welding.
AWS Conference, 1979. Maintenance Welding in Nuclear Power Plants: Proceedings. 176p. 1980. 25.00 (ISBN 0-87171-191-5); member 18.75. Am Welding.
AWS Conference, 1980. Underwater Welding of Offshore Platforms & Pipelines, OPP: Proceedings. 189p. 1981. 25.00 (ISBN 0-87171-215-6). Am Welding.
AWS Pipeline Conference, 1980. Pipeline Welding & Inspection, PWI: Proceedings. 108p. 1980. 25.00 (ISBN 0-87171-199-0); member 18.75. Am Welding.
AWS-SAE Joint Committee on Automotive Welding. Standard for Automotive Resistance Spot Welding Electrodes, D8.6-77. (Illus.). 67p. 1977. pap. 20.00 (ISBN 0-87171-136-2). Am Welding.
AWS Structural Welding Committee. Structural Welding Code-Reinforcing Steel: AWS D1-1. (Illus.). 1979. 15.00 (ISBN 0-87171-125-7). Am Welding.
Awtrey, Amy & Markos, Carol. The Reading Program: Critical Reading, Bk. G. 2nd ed. 72p. 1982. pap. 3.75x (ISBN 0-88069-006-2). L A Meyer.
--The Reading Program: Essay Structure, Bk. F. 2nd ed. 72p. 1982. pap. 3.75 (ISBN 0-88069-005-4). L A Meyer.
--The Reading Program: Relationships, Bk. E. 3rd ed. 58p. 1982. pap. 3.75x (ISBN 0-88069-004-6). L A Meyer.
--The Reading Program: Sentence Structure, Bk. C. 2nd ed. 48p. 1982. pap. 3.75x (ISBN 0-88069-002-X). L A Meyer.
--The Reading Program: Signals, Bk. D. 2nd ed. 62p. 1982. pap. 3.75x (ISBN 0-88069-003-8). L A Meyer.
--The Reading Program: Vocabulary, Bk. B. 2nd ed. 48p. 1982. pap. 3.75x (ISBN 0-88069-001-1). L A Meyer.
--The Reading Program: Word Patterns, Bk. A. 3rd ed. 48p. 1982. pap. 3.75x (ISBN 0-88069-000-3). L A Meyer.
--Tests & Checkpoints for the Reading Program. (The Reading Program Ser.). 100p. (gr. 10-12). 1982. ring binder 10.00x (ISBN 0-88069-013-5). L A Meyer.
AWWA Research Foundation. Future of Water Reuse: Proceedings, Vols. 1, 2, 3. (Illus.). 1810p. (Orig.). 1985. pap. 50.00 (ISBN 0-915295-02-4, 90506). AWWA Res Found.
Awwad, Tawfiq Y. Death in Beirut. McLoughlin, Leslie, tr. from Arabic. 1978. o. p. 12.00 (ISBN 0-914478-86-9); pap. 8.00 (ISBN 0-914478-87-7). Three Continents.
Axcell, Claudia, jt. auth. see Kinmont, Vikki.
Axe, John. Collectible Dionne Quintuplets. Ruddell, Gary, ed. (Illus.). 154p. 1977. 9.95 (ISBN 0-87588-136-X). Hobby Hse.
--Collectible Sonja Henie. (Illus.). 48p. pap. 4.95 (ISBN 0-87588-146-7). Hobby Hse.
--The Encyclopedia of Celebrity Dolls. 420p. 1983. 29.95 (ISBN 0-87588-186-6). Hobby Hse.
--Tammy & Dolls You Love to Dress. (Illus.). 81p. pap. 9.95 (ISBN 0-87588-155-6). Hobby Hse.
Axe, John & Mandeville, Glenn A. Celebrity Doll Price Guide & Annual. 88p. (Orig.). 1984. pap. 5.95 (ISBN 0-87588-225-0). Hobby Hse.
Axe, John, ed. Collecting Modern Dolls. 64p. 1981. pap. 7.95 (ISBN 0-87588-178-5). Hobby Hse.
Axe, Ruth F., et al, eds. see Oak, Henry L.
Axel, Helen. Organizing & Managing for Energy Efficiency. (Report: No. 837). (Illus.). 54p. (Orig.). 1983. pap. 100.00 (ISBN 0-8237-0277-4); pap. 20.00 member. Conference Bd.
Axel, Helen, jt. auth. see Shaeffer, Ruth G.
Axel, Helen, ed. Regional Perspectives on Energy Issues. (Report Ser.: No. 825). (Illus.). vii, 63p. (Orig.). 1982. pap. 75.00 (ISBN 0-8237-0264-2); pap. 15.00 member. Conference Bd.
Axel, Helen, jt. ed. see Linden, Fabian.
Axel, Jan & McCready, Karen. Porcelain: Traditions & New Visions. (Illus.). 200p. 1981. 30.00 (ISBN 0-8230-4091-7). Watson-Guptill.
Axel, Larry E., ed. see Wieman, Henry Nelson.
Axel, Richard, et al, eds. Eucaryotic Gene Regulation: Icn-Ucla Symposia on Molecular & Cellular Biology, Vol. XIV. LC 79-23151. 1979. 50.00 (ISBN 0-12-068350-4). Acad Pr.
Axelgard, Fred. U. S. - Arab Relations: The Iraq Dimension, No. 5. 45p. (Orig.). 1985. pap. 4.00 (ISBN 0-916729-05-2). Natl Coun Arab.
Axel-Lute, Paul. New Jersey Legal Research Handbook. Suretsky, Harold, ed. xv, 378p. 1984. 25.00 (ISBN 0-318-02062-9); pap. 20.00 (ISBN 0-318-02063-7). NJ Inst CLE.
Axel-Nilsson, Christian. Type Studies: The Norstedt Collection of Matrices in the Typefoundry of the Royal Printing Office; A History & Catalogue. (Illus.). 199p. 1985. 87.50x (ISBN 0-8390-0350-1). Abner Schram Ltd.
Axelos, Christos. Die Ontologischen Grundlagen der Freiheitstheorie von Leibniz. LC 72-81544. 385p. 1973. 28.40x (ISBN 3-11-002221-4). De Gruyter.
Axelrad, Albert S. Call to Conscience. 1985. text ed. 25.00x (ISBN 0-88125-092-9); pap. 14.95x (ISBN 0-88125-081-3). Ktav.
--Meditations of a Maverick Rabbi. Whitfield, Stephen, ed. 256p. (Orig.). 1985. pap. 8.95 (ISBN 0-940646-12-9). Rossel Bks.
Axelrad, Allan M. History & Utopia. 231p. 1980. Repr. of 1978 ed. lib. bdg. 35.00 (ISBN 0-8414-2938-3). Folcroft.
--History & Utopia: A Study of the World View of James Fenimore Cooper. 1978. lib. bdg. 37.50 (ISBN 0-8482-0038-1). Norwood Edns.
Axelrad, D. R. Foundations of the Probabilistic Mechanics of Discrete Media. (Foundations & Philosophy of Science & Technology Ser.). (Illus.). 200p. 1984. 28.00 (ISBN 0-08-025234-6). Pergamon.
--Micromechanics of Solids. 1978. 64.00 (ISBN 0-444-99806-3). Elsevier.
Axelrad, D. R., ed. see CISM (International Center for Mechanical Sciences), Dept. of Mechanics of Solids.
Axelrad, E. Flexible Shells. (Applied Mathematics & Mechanics Ser.). 400p. 1984. write for info. (North-Holland). Elsevier.
Axelrad, E. L. & Emmerling, F. A., eds. Flexible Shells: Theory & Applications. (Illus.). 290p. 1984. 23.00 (ISBN 0-387-13526-X). Springer-Verlag.
Axelrad, Jacob. Patrick Henry: The Voice of Freedom. LC 75-23310. (Illus.). 318p. 1975. Repr. of 1947 ed. lib. bdg. 22.50x (ISBN 0-8371-8331-6, AXPH). Greenwood.
--Philip Freneau: Champion of Democracy. 492p. 1966. 20.00x (ISBN 0-292-73605-3). U of Tex Pr.
Axelrad, S., jt. ed. see Muensterberger, W.
Axelrad, Sidney, jt. auth. see Brody, Sylvia.
Axelrod, jt. auth. see Packard.
Axelrod, A. Reanimacion Sin Sensaciones. 155p. (Span.). 1977. pap. 2.95 (ISBN 0-8285-1699-5, Pub. by Mir Pubs USSR). Imported Pubns.
Axelrod, Alan. Charles Brockden Brown: An American Tale. 224p. 1983. text ed. 27.50x (ISBN 0-292-71076-3). U of Tex Pr.
Axelrod, Alan, ed. The Colonial Revival in America. (Winterthur Bk.). (Illus.). 1985. 29.95 (ISBN 0-393-01942-X). Norton.
Axelrod, Allan & Berger, Curtis J. Land Transfer & Finance. 2nd ed. 1978. 32.00 (ISBN 0-316-06032-1). Little.
Axelrod, C. Warren. Computer Effectiveness: Bridging the Management-Technology Gap. LC 79-53113. (Illus.). xi, 200p. 1979. text ed. 22.95 (ISBN 0-87815-028-5). Info Resources.
--Computer Productivity: A Planning Guide for Cost Effective Management. 254p. 1982. 29.95 (ISBN 0-471-07744-5). Wiley.
Axelrod, Charles D. Studies in Intellectual Breakthrough: Freud, Simmel, & Buber. LC 78-53177. 112p. 1979. lib. bdg. 10.00x (ISBN 0-87023-256-8). U of Mass Pr.
Axelrod, Daniel I. Contributions to the Neogene Paleobotany of Central California. (U. C. Publications in Geological Sciences Ser.: Vol. 121). 222p. 1981. pap. 24.50x (ISBN 0-520-09621-5). U of Cal Pr.
--History of the Maritime Closed-Cone Pines, Alta & Baja California. (U. C. Publications in Geological Sciences Ser.: Vol. 120). 1980. pap. 15.50x (ISBN 0-520-09620-7). U of Cal Pr.
--Middle Miocene Floras from the Middlegade Basin, West-Central Nevada: (Published in Geological Sciences, Vol. 129) 1985. 22.00x (ISBN 0-520-09695-9). U of Cal Pr.
--New Pleistocene Conifer Records: Coastal California. LC 83-6874. (Geological Sciences Ser.: Vol. 127). 120p. 1984. pap. text ed. 11.00x (ISBN 0-520-09707-6). U of Cal Pr.
--Role of Volcanism in Climate & Evolution. LC 81-80345. (Special Paper: No. 185). (Illus.). 1981. pap. 7.00 (ISBN 0-8137-2185-7). Geol Soc.
Axelrod, David, jt. auth. see Moss, Jeffrey.
Axelrod, David B. A Dream of Feet. LC 76-21123. (Poetry Ser.). (Illus.). 1976. o. p. 8.95x (ISBN 0-89304-004-5, CCC105); signed ltd. ed. 15.00 (ISBN 0-89304-042-8); pap. 3.95x (ISBN 0-89304-007-X). Cross Cult.
--The Man Who Fell in Love with a Chicken. Barkan, Stanley H., ed. (Cross-Cultural Review Chapbook 2: American Poetry 1). 16p. 1980. pap. 2.00 (ISBN 0-89304-801-1). Cross Cult.
--Meeting with David B. Axelrod & Gnazino Russo. Scammacca, Nat, ed. & tr. LC 79-90012. (Sicilian Antigruppo Ser.: No. 3). (Illus.). 1979. pap. 3.00x (ISBN 0-89304-507-1); signed ltd. ed. 6.00x (ISBN 0-89304-506-3). Cross Cult.
Axelrod, Diana, et al, eds. Personal Injury Newsletter. Gans, Alfred W. 1958. Updates avail. looseleaf incl. one year's subs. 90.00 (540); looseleaf 1983 75.00; looseleaf 1984 75.00. Bender.
Axelrod, Diana T., jt. ed. see Nates, Jerome H.
Axelrod, Donald C., et al. Micrographic Film Technology: Ro11-1983. 2nd ed. Bartoli, Renator, ed. LC 83-2222. (Reference Ser.). (Illus.). 123p. 1983. 12.50 (ISBN 0-89258-059-3, R011); member 10.50. Assn Inform & Image Mgmt.
Axelrod, H., et al. Exotic Tropical Fishes. rev. ed. (Illus.). 1302p. 1980. 39.95 (ISBN 0-87666-543-1, H-1028); looseleaf 49.95 (ISBN 0-87666-537-7, H-1028L). TFH Pubns.
Axelrod, Herbert & Shaw, Susan. Breeding Aquarium Fishes, Bk. 1. 1968. 16.95 (ISBN 0-87666-006-5, H-930). TFH Pubns.
Axelrod, Herbert & Vorderwinkler, William. Goldfish & Koi in Your Home. rev. ed. (Illus.). 224p. 1985. text ed. 12.95 (ISBN 0-86622-041-0, H-909). TFH Pubns.
Axelrod, Herbert, jt. auth. see Emmens, C. W.
Axelrod, Herbert, jt. auth. see Emmens, Clifford W.
Axelrod, Herbert R. African Cichlids of Lakes Malawi & Tanganyika. (Illus.). 224p. 1973. 19.95 (ISBN 0-87666-792-2, PS-703). TFH Pubns.
--Breeding Aquarium Fishes, Bk. 2. 1971. 16.95 (ISBN 0-87666-007-3, H-941). TFH Pubns.
--Breeding Aquarium Fishes, Bk. 4. (Illus.). 320p. 1976. 16.95 (ISBN 0-87666-451-6, H-963). TFH Pubns.
--Breeding Aquarium Fishes, Bk. 5. (Illus.). 1978. 16.95 (ISBN 0-87666-469-9, H-986). TFH Pubns.
--Breeding Aquarium Fishes, Bk.6. (Illus.). 288p. 1980. 16.95 (ISBN 0-87666-536-9, H-995). TFH Pubns.
--Koi of the World. (Illus.). 239p. 1973. 39.95 (ISBN 0-87666-092-8, H-947). TFH Pubns.
--The T.F.H. Book of Tropical Aquariums. (Illus.). 96p. 1982. 6.95 (ISBN 0-87666-800-7, HP 005). TFH Pubns.
--Tropical Fish. (Illus.). 1979. 4.95 (ISBN 0-87666-510-5, KW-020). TFH Pubns.
--Tropical Fish for Beginners. (Illus.). 1972. 7.95 (ISBN 0-87666-752-3, PS-304). TFH Pubns.
Axelrod, Herbert R. & Burgess, Lourdes. Breeding Aquarium Fishes, Bk. 3. 1973. 16.95 (ISBN 0-87666-025-1, H-946). TFH Pubns.
Axelrod, Herbert R. & Burgess, Warren. Pacific Marine Fishes, 7 bks. Incl. Book 1. (Illus.). 1972 (ISBN 0-87666-123-1, PS-697); Book 2. (Illus.). 1973 (ISBN 0-87666-124-X, PS-699). 29.95 ea. TFH Pubns.
--Pacific Marine Fishes, Bk. 6. (Illus.). 1976. text ed. 29.95 (ISBN 0-87666-128-2, PS-722). TFH Pubns.
--Pacific Marine Fishes, Bk. 7. (Illus.). 1976. text ed. 29.95 (ISBN 0-87666-129-0, PS723). TFH Pubns.
--Saltwater Aquarium Fishes. 12.95 (ISBN 0-87666-138-X, H-914). TFH Pubns.
Axelrod, Herbert R. & Burgess, Dr. Warren. Marine Fishes. (Illus.). 1979. 4.95 (ISBN 0-87666-513-X, KW-031). TFH Pubns.
Axelrod, Herbert R. & Burgess, Warren E. Freshwater Angelfish. (Illus.). 1979. 4.95 (ISBN 0-87666-516-4, KW-048). TFH Pubns.
Axelrod, Herbert R. & Schultz, Leonard P. Handbook of Tropical Aquarium Fishes. rev. ed. 736p. 1983. 8.95 (ISBN 0-87666-491-5, PS-663). TFH Pubns.
Axelrod, Herbert R. & Vorderwinkler, W. Encyclopedia of Tropical Fish. new ed. 1975. 14.95 (ISBN 0-87666-158-4, H-905). TFH Pubns.
Axelrod, Herbert R. & Whitern, Wilfred H. Guppies. (Orig.). pap. 2.95 (ISBN 0-87666-082-0, M-505). TFH Pubns.
Axelrod, Herbert R., jt. auth. see Burgess, Warren E.
Axelrod, Herbert R., jt. auth. see Sheppard, Leslie.
Axelrod, Herbert R., jt. auth. see Vriends, Matthew M.
Axelrod, Herbert R., ed. Heifetz. 2nd ed. (Illus.). 640p. 1981. 25.00 (ISBN 0-87666-600-4, Z-24). Paganiniana Pubns.
Axelrod, Herbert R., ed. see Anderson, Douglas P.
Axelrod, Herbert R., ed. see Ginsberg, Lev.
Axelrod, Herbert R., ed. see Ginsburg, L.
Axelrod, Herbert R., ed. see Ginsburg, Lev.
Axelrod, Herbert R., ed. see Neish, Gordon A. & Hughes, Gilbert C.
Axelrod, Herbert R., et al. Exotic Tropical Fishes. 19.95 (ISBN 0-87666-051-0, H-907); looseleaf 29.95 (ISBN 0-87666-052-9, H-907L). TFH Pubns.
--Dr. Axelrod's Atlas of Freshwater Aquarium Fishes. (Illus.). 780p. 1985. text ed. 49.95 (ISBN 0-86622-052-6, H-1077). TFH Pubns.
--Exotic Marine Fishes. (Illus.). 608p. 1973. 19.95 (ISBN 0-87666-102-9, H938); looseleaf bdg. 29.95 (ISBN 0-87666-103-7, H-938). TFH Pubns.
Axelrod, Herman C. Bilingual Background & Its Relation to Certain Aspects of Character & Responsibility of Elementary School Children. Cordasco, Francesco, ed. LC 77-90406. (Bilingual-Bicultural Education in the U. S. Ser.). 1978. lib. bdg. 20.00x (ISBN 0-405-11075-8). Ayer Co Pubs.
Axelrod, Jeanette, tr. see Ziem, Jochen.
Axelrod, Jennifer. Breeding Guinea Pigs. 1980. 4.95 (ISBN 0-87666-929-1, KW-073). TFH Pubns.
Axelrod, Joeseph see Sanford, R. Nevitt.
Axelrod, Joseph. The University Teacher As Artist: Toward an Aesthetics of Teaching with Emphasis on the Humanities. LC 73-3773. (Higher Education Ser). 256p. 1973. 18.95x (ISBN 0-87589-183-7). Jossey-Bass.
Axelrod, Joseph, et al. Search for Relevance: The Campus in Crisis. LC 72-75941. (Jossey-Bass Higher Education Ser.). Repr. of 1969 ed. 48.70 (ISBN 0-8357-9346-X, 2013946). Bks Demand UMI.
Axelrod, Julius. Lipids & the Transduction of Biological Signals Through Membranes. 60p. 15.00 (ISBN 0-318-13193-5). Am Soc Neuro.
Axelrod, M. Creative Timed Writings. 1975. 9.84 (ISBN 0-07-002610-6). McGraw.
Axelrod, Nathan. Selected Cases in Fashion Marketing, 2 vols. 3rd ed. 1968. pap. 13.50 ea.; Vol. 2. pap. 16.33 scp (ISBN 0-672-96038-9). Bobbs.
Axelrod, Nathan, jt. auth. see Packard, Sidney.
Axelrod, Paul. Scholars & Dollars: Politics, Economics, & the Universities of Ontario 1945-1980. (State & Economic Life Ser.). 388p. 1982. o. p. 35.00x (ISBN 0-8020-5609-1); pap. 12.50 (ISBN 0-8020-6492-2). U of Toronto Pr.

Axelrod, Regina. Conflict Between Energy & Urban Environment: Consolidated Edison Versus the City of New York. LC 80-67179. 214p. (Orig.). 1982. lib. bdg. 26.00 (ISBN 0-8191-2376-5); pap. text ed. 12.25 (ISBN 0-8191-2377-3). U Pr of Amer.

Axelrod, Regina S., ed. Environment, Energy, & Public Policy: Conflict & Resolution. LC 79-3523. (Conflict & Resolution). (Illus.). 1981. 26.00x (ISBN 0-669-03460-6). Lexington Bks.

Axelrod, Rise B. & Cooper, Charles R. The St. Martin's Guide to Writing. LC 84-51679. 700p. 1985. text ed. 18.95 (ISBN 0-312-69728-7); instrs. manual avail. St Martin.

Axelrod, Robert. The Evolution of Cooperation. LC 83-45255. 241p. 1984. 17.95 (ISBN 0-465-02122-0). Basic.

--Evolution of Cooperation. LC 83-45255. 252p. 1985. pap. 6.95 (ISBN 0-465-02121-2, CN 5145). Basic.

--The Structure of Decision: The Cognitive Maps of Political Elites. 375p. 1976. text ed. 42.00x (ISBN 0-691-07578-6); pap. 16.50x LPE (ISBN 0-691-10050-0). Princeton U Pr.

Axelrod, Saul. Behavior Modification for the Classroom Teacher. 2nd ed. (Illus.). 272p. 1983. pap. text ed. 19.95 (ISBN 0-07-002572-X). McGraw.

Axelrod, Saul, ed. The Effects of Punishment on Human Behavior. Apsche, Jack. LC 82-13892. 342p. 1982. 37.50 (ISBN 0-12-068740-2). Acad Pr.

Axelrod, Solomon J., jt. ed. see Donabedian, Avedis.

Axelrod, Steven G. Robert Lowell: Life of Art. LC 78-51155. (Illus.). 1978. text ed. 33.00 (ISBN 0-691-06363-X); pap. 11.95 (ISBN 0-691-01364-0). Princeton U Pr.

Axelrod, Steven G. & Deese, Helen. Robert Lowell: A Reference Guide. 460p. 1982. lib. bdg. 36.50 (ISBN 0-8161-7814-3, Pub by Hall Reference). G K Hall.

Axelrod, Valija, et al. Career Resource Centers. 112p. 1977. 6.75 (ISBN 0-318-15415-3, SN 15). Natl Ctr Res Voc Ed.

Axelrod, Warren C. Computer Productivity: A Planning Guide for Cost-Effective Management. 255p. 1982. members 22.95 (ISBN 0-318-17048-5); (W2) 24.95 (ISBN 0-318-17049-3). Data Process Mgmt.

Axelsen, J., jt. ed. see Vinterberg, L.

Axelsen, Nils H., ed. Handbook of Immunoprecipitation-in-Gel Techniques. (Illus.). 394p. 1983. text ed. 90.00x (ISBN 0-632-01057-6, Pub. by Blackwell Sci UK). Blackwell Pubns.

Axelson, David E. Solid State Nuclear Magnetic Resonance of Fossil Fuels. 320p. 1985. text ed. 56.00x (ISBN 0-919868-25-8, Pub. by Multisci Pubns Ltd). Brookfield Pub Co.

Axelson, E. V. South-East Africa, Fourteen Eighty Eight-Fifteen Thirty. Repr. of 1940 ed. 22.00 (ISBN 0-527-03950-0). Kraus Repr.

Axelson, John A. Counseling & Development in a Multicultural Society. LC 85-5920. (Counseling-Psychology Ser.). 450p. 1985. text ed. 23.00 pub. net (ISBN 0-534-04974-5). Brooks-Cole.

Axelson, R. Dean. Caring for Your Pet Bird. (Illus.). 168p. 1985. 12.95 (ISBN 0-7137-1438-7, Pub. by Blandford Pr England); pap. 6.95 (ISBN 0-7137-1538-3). Sterling.

Axelson, Roland G. The Psychological Influence of Street Gangs on School-Aged Youth: A Case Study in Hartford, Connecticut. 13p. 1984. 1.50 (ISBN 0-317-17788-5). I N Thut World Educ Ctr.

Axelsson, O., et al, eds. Analytical & Numerical Approaches to Asymptotic Problems in Analysis. (Mathematical Studies: Vol. 47). 382p. 1981. 64.00 (ISBN 0-444-86131-9). Elsevier.

Axelsson, R. A., jt. auth. see Oehman, R. L.

Axeman, Lois, illus. Holidays. LC 84-9429. (Shape of Poetry Ser.). (Illus.). 32p. (gr. k-3). 1984. PLB 7.45 (ISBN 0-89565-266-8). Childs World.

Axenrod, Theodore & Webb, Graham. Nuclear Magnetic Resonance Spectroscopy of Nuclei Other Than Protons. LC 80-27361. 424p. 1981. Repr. of 1974 ed. lib. bdg. 32.50 (ISBN 0-89874-290-0). Krieger.

Axford, E. C. Bodmin Moor. LC 75-26357. (British Topographical Ser.). (Illus.). 200p. 1976. 14.50 (ISBN 0-7153-6943-1). David & Charles.

Axford, Faye A. The Lure & Lore of Limestone County: Alabama Antebellum Houses & Families. LC 77-94486. (Illus.). 1978. 17.50 (ISBN 0-916620-16-6). Portals Pr.

Axford, Faye A., ed. The Journals of Thomas Hubbard Hobbs. LC 74-2819. 1976. 20.00 (ISBN 0-8173-5313-5). U of Ala Pr.

Axford, H. William. Gilpin County Gold: Peter McFarlane, 1848-1929 Mining Entrepreneur in Central City, Colorado. LC 76-115034. (Illus.). xii, 210p. 1976. 8.95 (ISBN 0-8040-0550-8, 82-72825, Pub. by Swallow). Ohio U Pr.

Axford, Lavonne, ed. English Language Cookbooks, Sixteen Hundred to Nineteen Seventy-Three. LC 76-23533. 1976. 90.00x (ISBN 0-8103-0534-8). Gale.

Axford, Lavonne B. An Index to the Poems of Ogden Nash. LC 72-7266. 145p. 1972. 20.00 (ISBN 0-8108-0547-2). Scarecrow.

Axford, Michael D. The Stick People & the Family Help a Wounded Deer. 1984. 5.95 (ISBN 0-8062-2306-5). Carlton.

Axford, Roger W. Adult Education: The Open Door to Lifelong Learning. rev. ed. 504p. 1980. pap. 12.50x (ISBN 0-935648-01-1). Halldin Pub.

--Black American Heroes. (Illus.). 164p. (Orig.). pap. 6.00 (ISBN 0-935648-09-7). Halldin Pub.

--Successful Recareering: How to Shift Gears Before You're over the Hill. (Illus.). 154p. 1983. pap. 12.95 (ISBN 0-939644-10-X). Media Prods & Mktg.

Axford, Wendy A. & McMurtrie, Douglas C. Handicapped Children in Britain: Their Problems & Education & Index Catalogue of A Library of Rehabilitation of the Disabled, 2 vols. in 1. Phillips, William R. & Rosenberg, Janet, eds. LC 79-6894. (Physically Handicapped in Society Ser.). 1980. Repr. of 1959 ed. lib. bdg. 17.00x (ISBN 0-405-13105-4). Ayer Co Pubs.

Axido, L., jt. auth. see Stratila, S.

Axinn, Donald E. The Hawk's Dream & Other Poems. LC 82-48002. (Poetry Ser.). 128p. 1982. pap. 5.95 (ISBN 0-394-62419-X, E812, Ever). Grove.

Axler, Bruce A. Foodservice: A Managerial Approach. LC 78-70714. 1979. text ed. 17.95 (ISBN 0-697-00079-6); student manual 32.50 (ISBN 0-317-18574-8). Wm C Brown.

Axler, Bruce H., jt. auth. see National Institute for Food Service Industry.

Axley, Jim. Oranges & Sweet Red Wines. LC 79-84632. (Lightning Tree Contemporary Poets Ser.: No. 3). 1979. 12.95 (ISBN 0-89016-049-X); pap. 4.95 (ISBN 0-89016-048-1). Lightning Tree.

Axline, Andrew W. Agricultural Policy & Collective Self-Reliance in the Caribbean. (A Westview Replica Ser.). 130p. 1985. pap. 16.00x (ISBN 0-86531-836-0). Westview.

Axline, Andrew W., jt. auth. see Stegenga, James A.

Axline, Virginia M. Dibs: In Search of Self. 224p. 1976. pap. 2.50 (ISBN 0-345-29536-6). Ballantine.

--Play Therapy. rev. ed. (Illus.). 1974. pap. 3.50 (ISBN 0-345-29592-7). Ballantine.

Axline, W. Andrew. Caribbean Integration: The Politics of Regional Negotiations. 233p. 1979. 29.50 (ISBN 0-89397-049-2). Nichols Pub.

--European Community Law & Organizational Development. LC 68-8917. 256p. 1968. 12.00 (ISBN 0-379-00356-2). Oceana.

Axman, Steve. Complete Handbook of Offensive Football Drills. 228p. 1982. 15.95 (ISBN 0-13-161166-6, Parker). P-H.

Axnick, Karen & Yarbrough, Mary. Infection Control: An Integrated Approach. LC 82-24933. (Illus.). 578p. 1983. text ed. 29.95 (ISBN 0-8016-0411-7). Mosby.

Axon, W. E. John Ruskin: A Biological Bibliography. 59.95 (ISBN 0-8490-0456-X). Gordon Pr.

Axon, William, ed. English Dialect Words of the Eighteenth Century: As Shown in the "Universal Etymological Dictionary" of Nathaniel Bailey. (English Dialect Society Publications Ser.: No. 41). pap. 25.00 (ISBN 0-317-15905-4). Kraus Repr.

Axon, William E. Folk Song & Folk-Speech of Lancashire. (Folklore Ser). 15.00 (ISBN 0-8482-7270-6). Norwood Edns.

--Shelley's Vegetarianism. LC 79-116789. (Studies in Shelley, No. 25). 1971. Repr. of 1890 ed. lib. bdg. 22.95x (ISBN 0-8383-1031-1). Haskell.

Axsom, R., et al. The Prints of Frank Stella: A Catalogue Raisonne. 1983. 50.00 (ISBN 0-912303-92-1); pap. 19.50 (ISBN 0-912303-25-5). Michigan Mus.

Axsom, Richard. Frank Stella: Prints Nineteen Sixty-Seven to Nineteen Eighty-Two. (Illus.). 300p. 1983. write for info (ISBN 0-902825-16-X). Petersburg Pr.

Axsom, Richard H. Parade: Cubism As Theater. LC 78-74361. (Outstanding Dissertations in the Fine Arts, Fourth Ser.). (Illus.). 1979. lib. bdg. 46.00 (ISBN 0-8240-3950-5). Garland Pub.

--The Prints of Frank Stella: A Catalogue Raisonne 1967-1982. LC 82-15729. (Illus.). 192p. 1983. 50.00 (ISBN 0-933920-40-7); pap. 19.50 for museum distribution only (ISBN 0-933920-41-5). Hudson Hills.

Axtell, Harold L. The Deification of Abstract Ideas in Roman Literature & Inscriptions. 100p. Repr. of 1907 ed. lib. bdg. 20.00 (ISBN 0-89241-159-7). Caratzas.

Axtell, James. The European & the Indian: Essays in the Ethnohistory of Colonial North America. (Illus.). 1981. 25.00x (ISBN 0-19-502903-8). Oxford U Pr.

--The European & the Indian: Essays in the Ethnohistory of Colonial North America. (Illus.). 1981. pap. 8.95 (ISBN 0-19-502904-6, GB643). Oxford U Pr.

--The Invasion Within: The Contest of Cultures in Colonial North America. (Illus.). 355p. 1985. 29.95 (ISBN 0-317-28541-6). Oxford U Pr.

--White Indians of Colonial America. 38p. pap. 3.00. Ye Galleon.

Axtell, James, ed. The Indian Peoples of Eastern America: A Documentary History of the Sexes. (Illus.). 1981. pap. text ed. 9.95x (ISBN 0-19-502741-8). Oxford U Pr.

Axtell, Susan, jt. auth. see Bethell, Jean.

Axthelm, Pete. The City Game: Basketball from the Garden to the Playgrounds. Schaap, Dick, ed. (Penguin Sports Library). 224p. 1982. pap. 4.95 (ISBN 0-14-006218-1). Penguin.

Axthelm, Peter M. The Modern Confessional Novel. LC 67-13428. (Yale Colllege Ser.: No. 6). pap. 50.30 (ISBN 0-317-09478-5, 2021976). Bks Demand UMI.

Axton, Marie. The Queen's Two Bodies: Drama & the Elizabethan Succession. (Royal Historical Society-Studies in History Ser.: Vol. 5). 174p. 1977. text ed. 29.00x (ISBN 0-901050-36-9, Pub. by Swiftbks England). Humanities.

Axton, Marie, ed. Three Tudor Classical Interludes: "Thersites", "Jacke Jugeler" & "Horestes". (Tudor Interludes Ser.: No. III). 246p. 1982. text ed. 47.50x (ISBN 0-8476-7193-3). Rowman.

Axton, Marie & Williams, R., eds. English Drama. LC 76-57099. 1977. 34.50 (ISBN 0-521-21588-9). Cambridge U Pr.

Axton, Richard. European Drama of the Early Middle Ages. LC 74-24680. 1975. 17.95x (ISBN 0-8229-3301-2). U of Pittsburgh Pr.

Axton, W. F., jt. auth. see Hewett, Edward W.

Axton, William F. Tobacco & Kentucky. LC 74-18929. (Kentucky Bicentennial Bookshelf Ser.). (Illus.). 160p. 1975. 6.95 (ISBN 0-8131-0207-3). U Pr of Ky.

Axum, Donna. How to Be & Look Your Best Every Day. LC 77-83345. 1978. 1.95 (ISBN 0-8499-4147-4). Word Bks.

Aya, R., jt. auth. see Miller, N.

Ayad, Foaud, tr. see Hazm, Imam Ibn.

Ayal, Eliezer B., ed. Micro Aspects of Development. LC 72-89641. (Special Studies in International Economics & Development). 1973. 49.50x (ISBN 0-275-28685-1); pap. text ed. 24.50x (ISBN 0-89197-846-1). Irvington.

--The Study of Thailand: Analyses of Knowledge. LC 79-4544. (Papers in International Studies: Southeast Asia Ser.: No. 54). 1979. pap. 13.50x (ISBN 0-89680-079-2, 82-90553, Ohio U Ctr Intl). Ohio U Pr.

Ayal, Igal, jt. auth. see Hempel, Donald J.

Ayal, Ora. Ugbu. Nakao, Naomi L., tr. from Hebrew. LC 79-1716. (Illus.). 32p. (ps-2). 1979. PLB 8.89 (ISBN 0-06-020308-0). HarpJ.

Ayal, Ora & Nakao, Naomi. The Adventures of Chester the Chest. LC 81-48642. (Illus.). 32p. (gr. k-3). 1982. PLB 8.89g (ISBN 0-06-020306-4). HarpJ.

Ayala. Evolutionary & Population Genetics: A Primer. 1982. 19.95 (ISBN 0-8053-0315-4). Benjamin-Cummings.

--Prairie Farmer Meat Cookbook. 1985. 10.95 (ISBN 0-87069-459-6). Wallace-Homestead.

Ayala, F. Evolutionary & Population Genetics: A Primer. 1982. text ed. 21.95. Addison-Wesley.

Ayala, F. J. Genetic Variation & Evolution. Head, J. J., ed. LC 81-67985. (Carolina Biology Readers Ser.). (Illus.). 16p. (gr. 10 up). 1983. pap. 1.60 (ISBN 0-89278-326-5, 45-9726). Carolina Biological.

--Origin of Species. Head, J. J., ed. LC 81-67980. (Carolina Biology Readers Ser.). (Illus.). 16p. (gr. 10 up). 1983. pap. 1.60 (ISBN 0-89278-269-2, 45-9669). Carolina Biological.

Ayala, F. J. & Kiger, J. A., Jr. Modern Genetics. 2nd ed. 1984. 36.95 (ISBN 0-8053-0316-2); solutions manual 4.95 (ISBN 0-8053-0317-0). Benjamin-Cummings.

Ayala, Felipe, jt. ed. see Sanchez-Camara, Florencio.

Ayala, Francisco. El Problema de Liberalismo. 2nd ed. pap. 4.35 (ISBN 0-8477-2402-6). U. of PR Pr.

Ayala, Francisco & Dobzhansky, Theodosius, eds. Studies in the Philosophy of Biology: Reduction & Related Problems. LC 73-90656. 1974. 38.50x (ISBN 0-520-02649-7). U of Cal Pr.

Ayala, Francisco J. & Valentine, James W. Evolving: The Theory & Processes of Organic Evolution. 1979. text ed. 30.95 (ISBN 0-8053-0310-3). Benjamin-Cummings.

Ayala, Mitzi. Prairie Farmer Poultry Cookbook. LC 85-51023. (Prairie Farmer Cookbooks). 272p. 1985. pap. 10.95 (ISBN 0-87069-457-X). Wallace-Homestead.

Ayala, Ramon P. De see De Ayala, Ramon P.

Ayala, Ramon Perez De see Perez de Ayala, Ramon.

Ayalon, David. Gunpowder & Firearms in the Mamluk Kingdom: A Challenge to Mediaeval Society. 2nd ed. 154p. 1978. 25.00x (ISBN 0-7146-3090-X, F Cass Co). Biblio Dist.

--The Mamluk Military Society. 364p. 1980. 70.00x (ISBN 0-86078-049-X, Pub. by Variorum England). State Mutual Bk.

--Studies on the Mamluks of Egypt. 360p. 1980. 60.00x (ISBN 0-86078-006-6, Pub. by Variorum England). State Mutual Bk.

Ayalon, O., et al. The Holocaust & Its Perseverance. (SANAI Ser.: No. 2). 64p. 1983. pap. text ed. 9.75x (Pub. by Van Gorcum). Humanities.

Ayalti, Hanan J., ed. Yiddish Proverbs. LC 49-11135. (Illus., Bilingual). 1963. pap. 4.75 (ISBN 0-8052-0050-9). Schocken.

Ayanaba, A. & Dart, P. J., eds. Biological Nitrogen Fixation in Farming Systems of the Tropics. LC 77-1304. 377p. 1978. 86.95x (ISBN 0-471-99499-5, Pub. by Wiley-Interscience). Wiley.

Ayandele, E. A. African Historical Studies. 314p. 1979. 30.00x (ISBN 0-7146-2942-1, F Cass Co). Biblio Dist.

--Holy Johnson, Pioneer of African Nationalism: 1836-1917. (Illus.). 417p. 1970. 29.50x (ISBN 0-7146-1743-1, F Cass Co). Biblio Dist.

--Holy Johnson: Pioneer of African Nationalism, 1836-1917. (Africana Modern Library: No. 13). 1970. text ed. 18.00x (ISBN 0-391-00041-1). Humanities.

--Nigerian Historical Studies. 305p. 1979. 30.00x (ISBN 0-7146-3113-2, F Cass Co). Biblio Dist.

Ayandele, E. A., et al. Making of Modern Africa, Vol. 2: The Late 19th Century to the Present Day. (Growth of African Civilization Ser.). (Orig.). 1971. pap. text ed. 9.25x (ISBN 0-391-00149-3). Humanities.

Ayandele, Emmanuel A. Missionary Impact on Modern Nigeria, 1842-1914. (Ibadan History Ser.). 1967. pap. text ed. 15.75x (ISBN 0-582-64512-3). Humanities.

Ayany, Samuel G. A History of Zanzibar: A Study in Constitutional Development, 1934-1964. (Illus.). 208p. 1970. 9.50x (ISBN 0-87471-212-2). Rowman.

Ayars, Albert L. & Ryan, John M. The Teenager & the Law. 1978. pap. 8.95 (ISBN 0-8158-0369-9). Chris Mass.

Ayars, Christine M. Contributions to the Art of Music in America by the Music Industries of Boston: 1640-1936. 27.00 (ISBN 0-384-02825-X). Johnson Repr.

Ayarslan, Solmaz D. A Dynamic Stochastic Model for Current Asset & Liability Management of a Multinational Corporation. Bruchley, Stuart, ed. LC 80-565. (Multinational Corporations Ser.). (Illus.). 1980. lib. bdg. 25.00x (ISBN 0-405-13362-6). Ayer Co Pubs.

Ayatey, Siegfried B. Elementary FORTRAN IV Microeconomics Programs. LC 84-5155. 238p. (Orig.). 1984. pap. text ed. 12.00 (ISBN 0-8191-3950-5). U Pr of Amer.

--Essentials of Economic Analysis: Vol. 1, Microeconomics. LC 79-66234. 1979. pap. text ed. 13.00 (ISBN 0-8191-0803-0). U Pr of Amer.

--Essentials of Economic Analysis: Vol. 2, Macroeconomics. LC 79-66234. 1979. pap. text ed. 11.25 (ISBN 0-8191-0804-9). U Pr of Amer.

Ayati, Ibrahim. A Probe into the History of Ashura. 234p. 1985. pap. 9.00 (ISBN 0-941724-41-7). Islamic Seminary.

Ayatullah Al-Khu'i. Islamic Practical Law, Pts. I & II. Shaikh Muhammad Sarwar, tr. from Arabic. 1981. 15.00 (ISBN 0-941724-08-5); pap. 10.00 (ISBN 0-941724-01-8). Islamic Seminary.

--Rules of HAJJ. Shaikh Muhammad Sarwar, tr. from Arabic. 50p. 1981. pap. 3.00 (ISBN 0-941724-02-6). Islamic Seminary.

Ayckbourn, Alan. Confusions. (Methuen Student Editions). (Illus.). 128p. 1983. pap. 3.95 (ISBN 0-413-53270-4, NO. 3968). Methuen Inc.

--The Norman Conquests: Table Manners, Living Together, Round & Round the Garden. LC 78-73051. 1979. pap. 6.95 (ISBN 0-394-17082-2, B422, BC). Grove.

--Sisterly Feelings Taking Steps. 256p. 1981. 30.00x (ISBN 0-7011-2561-6, Pub. by Chatto Bodley Head England). State Mutual Bk.

--Three Plays: Absurd Person Singular, Absent Friends, & Bedroom Farce. LC 78-20339. 1979. pap. 3.95 (ISBN 0-394-17083-0, B423, BC). Grove.

Aycoberry, Pierre. The Nazi Question: An Essay on the Interpretations of National Socialism (1922-1975) Hurley, Robert, tr. 1981. 15.95 (ISBN 0-394-50948-X); pap. 6.95 (ISBN 0-394-74841-7). Pantheon.

Aycock, Alan, jt. auth. see Leach, Edmund.

Aycock, Dale. Stardrifter. 1981. pap. 1.95 (ISBN 0-8439-0855-6, Leisure Bks). Dorchester Pub Co.

--Starspinner. 240p. 1981. pap. 2.25 (ISBN 0-8439-0973-0, Leisure Bks). Dorchester Pub Co.

Aycock, Don, ed. Preaching with Purpose & Power: Selected E. Y. Mullins Lectures on Preaching. LC 81-22388. 320p. 1982. 15.95x (ISBN 0-86554-027-6). Mercer Univ Pr.

Aycock, Don M. The E. Y. Mullins Lectures on Preaching with Reference to the Aristotelian Triad. LC 79-6080. 113p. 1980. text ed. 20.50 (ISBN 0-8191-0981-9); pap. text ed. 9.25 (ISBN 0-8191-0982-7). U Pr of Amer.

--Heralds to a New Age: Preaching for the Twenty-First Century. 228p. 1985. 11.95 (ISBN 0-87178-352-5). Brethren.

Aycock, Shirley. About Frogs. 28p. 1981. stapled chapbook 1.00 (ISBN 0-942432-03-7). M O P Pr.

--The Bus Stop. 20p. 1981. 1.25 (ISBN 0-942432-04-5). M O P Pr.

--Comma. 50p. 1982. stapled chapbook 3.25 (ISBN 0-942432-05-3). M O P Pr.

--Diet-Notes. 32p. 1985. stapled chapbook 2.75 (ISBN 0-942432-07-X). M O P Pr.

--Of Chimes & Wind. 24p. 1981. stapled chapbook 1.00 (ISBN 0-942432-02-9). M O P Pr.

--Ripcord. 24p. 1978. stapled chapbook 2.25 (ISBN 0-942432-00-2). M O P Pr.

--Winging It. 24p. 1979. stapled chapbook 1.25 (ISBN 0-942432-01-0). M O P Pr.

Aycock, Wendell M., ed. Shakespeare's Art from a Comparative Perspective. LC 80-54322. (Proceedings of the Comparitive Literature Symposium, No. 12). (Illus.). 197p. (Orig.). 1981. pap. 17.50 (ISBN 0-89672-081-0). Tex Tech Pr.

--The Teller & the Tale: Aspects of the Short Story. LC 81-52254. (Proceedings Comparative Literature Symposium Ser.: Vol. 13). 156p. 1982. pap. 18.95 (ISBN 0-89672-100-0). Tex Tech Pr.

Aycock, Wendell M. & Cravens, Sydney P., eds. Calderon de la Barca at the Tercentenary: Comparative Views. LC 82-80309. (Proceedings of the Comparative Literature Symposium: Vol. 14). 195p. 1982. pap. 24.95 (ISBN 0-89672-101-9). Tex Tech Pr.

Aycock, Wendell M. & Klein, Theodore M., eds. Classical Mythology in Twentieth-Century Thought & Literature. (Proceedings of the Comparative Literature Symposium, Vol. XI). (Illus.). 221p. (Orig.). 1980. pap. 12.00 (ISBN 0-89672-079-9). Tex Tech Pr.

Aycock, Wendell M., jt. ed. see Hopkins, Patricia M.

Aycock, Wendell M., jt. ed. see Zyla, Wolodymyr T.

Aycock, Wendell M., tr. see Zilyns'Kyj, Ivan.

Aycock, William B. & Wurfel, Seymour W. Military Law Under the Uniform Code of Military Justice. LC 72-6929. (Illus.). 430p. 1973. Repr. of 1955 ed. lib. bdg. 29.50 (ISBN 0-8371-6507-5, AYML). Greenwood.

Aycox, Frank. Games We Should Play in School: A Revealing Analysis of the Social Forces in the Classroom & a Practical Approach to Understanding & Shaping Them Including over 55 Dynamic & Fun Social Games. Alexander, Frank, ed. (Illus.). 103p. (Orig.). (gr. 1-12). 1985. pap. 6.95 (ISBN 0-915256-16-9). Front Row.

Ayd, Frank, et al, eds. Affective Disorders Reassessed, 1983. 250p. (Orig.). 1983. text ed. 35.00 (ISBN 0-931858-05-4). Ayd Medical Comm.

Ayd, Frank J., ed. Medical, Moral & Legal Issues in Mental Health Care. LC 74-11375. 220p. 1974. 14.00 (ISBN 0-683-00295-3, Pub. by W & W). Krieger.

Aydelotte, Frank. Elizabethan Rogues & Vagabonds. 187p. 1980. Repr. of 1913 ed. lib. bdg. 22.50 (ISBN 0-8495-0151-2). Arden Lib.

--Elizabethan Rogues & Vagabonds. new ed. (Illus.). 187p. 1967. 25.00x (ISBN 0-7146-1099-2, F Cass Co). Biblio Dist.

--Elizabethan Rogues & Vagabonds. LC 73-15966. 1971. Repr. of 1913 ed. lib. bdg. 25.00 (ISBN 0-8414-2933-2). Folcroft.

--Oxford Stamp, & Other Essays. facs. ed. LC 67-26712. (Essay Index Reprint Ser). 1917. 17.00 (ISBN 0-8369-0166-5). Ayer Co Pubs.

Aydelotte, W. O. Bismarck & British Colonial Policy: The Problem of South West Africa, 1883-1885. LC 76-120225. 1970. Repr. lib. bdg. 18.50x (ISBN 0-374-90325-5). Octagon.

Aydelotte, William O. Bismarck & British Colonial Policy: The Problem of South West Africa, 1883-1885. LC 71-111563. 1937. Repr. of 1937 ed. 17.50x (ISBN 0-8371-4584-8, ABB&, Pub. by Negro U Pr). Greenwood.

--History of Parliamentary Behavior. LC 76-24290. (Quantative Studies in History). 1977. text ed. 37.50 (ISBN 0-691-05242-5); pap. 13.50 LPE (ISBN 0-691-10046-2). Princeton U Pr.

Aydelotte, William O., et al, eds. Dimensions of Quantitative Research in History. LC 72-736. (Quantitative Studies in History Ser). 420p. 1972. pap. 18.00 LPE (ISBN 0-691-10045-4, 45). Princeton U Pr.

Ayden, Erje. Sadness at Leaving: A Novel of Espionage. 110p. (Orig.). 1972. pap. 7.50 (ISBN 0-89366-005-1). Ultramarine Pub.

Aydt, Deborah. How Can We Talk? 144p. (Orig.). (gr. 7 up). 1982. pap. 1.95 (ISBN 0-590-32282-6, Wishing Star Bks). Scholastic Inc.

--I Don't Want to Be Your Shadow. 144p. (Orig.). (gr. 7 up). 1981. pap. 1.95 (ISBN 0-590-31719-9, Wishing Star Bks). Scholastic Inc.

--Katie. (Orig.). (gr. 7 up). 1980. pap. 1.95 (ISBN 0-590-32202-8, Wishing Star Bks). Scholastic Inc.

--Love Games. 176p. (Orig.). (gr. 7 up). 1984. pap. 1.95 (ISBN 0-590-32431-4, Wildfire). Scholastic Inc.

--Secrets. 160p. (Orig.). (gr. 7 up). 1981. pap. 1.95 (ISBN 0-590-32518-3, Wishing Star Bks). Scholastic Inc.

Aye, John. Humour in the Theatre. 1975. Repr. 20.00 (ISBN 0-8274-4101-0). R West.

Ayed, Sabine L., tr. see Cranefield, Paul F.

Ayelrod, Todd M. Collecting Historical Documents: A Guide to Owning History. (How To... Ser.). (Illus.). 192p. 1984. 29.95 (ISBN 0-86622-008-9, HT-1002). TFH Pubns.

Ayeni, Bola. Concepts & Techniques in Urban Analysis. LC 78-19219. 1979. 32.50 (ISBN 0-312-16044-5). St Martin.

Ayeni, Bola & Moboguunje, Akin L. Political Processes & Regional Development Planning in Nigeria. (Working Papers Ser.: No. 82-7). 33p. 1982. pap. 6.00 (ISBN 0-686-43301-7, CRD144, UNCRD). Unipub.

Ayensu, E. S. see Metcalfe, C. R.

Ayensu, Edward. Jungles. (Illus.). 208p. 1980. 35.00 (ISBN 0-517-54136-X). Crown.

Ayensu, Edward S. Medicinal Plants of the West Indies. Irvine, Keith, ed. LC 80-54714. (Medicinal Plants of the World Ser.: No. 2). (Illus.). 1981. 39.95 (ISBN 0-917256-12-3). Ref Pubns.

--Medicinal Plants of West Africa. Irvine, Keith, ed. LC 78-3110. (Medicinal Plants of the World Ser.: No. 1). (Illus.). 1978. 39.95 (ISBN 0-917256-07-7). Ref Pubns.

--Rhythms of Life. (Illus.). 208p. 1982. 35.00 (ISBN 0-517-54523-3). Crown.

Ayensu, Edward S. & DeFilipps, Robert A. Endangered & Threatened Plants of the United States. LC 77-25138. (Illus.). 403p. 1978. 35.00x (ISBN 0-87474-222-6). Smithsonian.

Ayensu, Edward S., jt. auth. see Duke, James A.

Ayensu, Edward S., ed. see Boulos, Loutfy.

Ayensu, Edward S., et al. Our Green & Living World: The Wisdom to Save It. (Illus.). 256p. 1984. 24.95 (ISBN 0-521-26842-7). Cambridge U Pr.

--Our Green & Living World: The Wisdom to Save It. Goodwin, Joseph, ed. LC 84-600181. (Illus.). 256p. 1984. 25.00 (ISBN 0-89599-016-4, Dist. by Cambridge). Smithsonian Bks.

Ayer, jt. auth. see Barbato.

Ayer, A. J. Freedom & Morality & Other Essays. 1984. 19.95x (ISBN 0-19-824731-1). Oxford U Pr.

--Hume. (Past Masters Ser.). 1980. pap. 3.95 (ISBN 0-19-287528-0). Oxford U Pr.

--Logical Positivism. 1966. pap. 14.95x (ISBN 0-317-30526-3). Free Pr.

--Philosophy in the Twentieth Century. LC 83-47822. 304p. pap. 7.95 (ISBN 0-394-71655-8, Vin). Random.

--Wittgenstein: The Man & His Philosophy. Date not set. 17.95. Random.

Ayer, Adelaide M. Some Difficulties in Elementary School History. LC 72-176527. (Columbia University. Teachers College. Contributions to Education: No. 212). Repr. of 1926 ed. 17.50 (ISBN 0-404-55212-9). AMS Pr.

Ayer, Alfred J. Language, Truth & Logic. 2nd ed. 1936. pap. 2.75 (ISBN 0-486-20010-8). Dover.

--Language, Truth & Logic. 13.50 (ISBN 0-8446-1571-4). Peter Smith.

--Logical Positivism. LC 78-6321. 1978. Repr. of 1959 ed. lib. bdg. 32.50 (ISBN 0-313-20462-4, AYLP). Greenwood.

--Metaphysics & Common Sense. LC 79-89830. 267p. 1970. text ed. 8.00x (ISBN 0-87735-507-X). Freeman Cooper.

--Origins of Pragmatism: Studies in the Philosophy of Charles Sanders Peirce & William James. LC 68-21669. 1968. 12.50x (ISBN 0-87735-501-0). Freeman Cooper.

--Philosophical Essays. LC 79-24852. 289p. 1980. Repr. of 1954 ed. lib. bdg. 27.50x (ISBN 0-313-20902-2, AYPE). Greenwood.

--Probability & Evidence. LC 71-185572. (John Dewey Lecture Ser). 144p. 1979. 19.50x (ISBN 0-231-03650-7); pap. 10.00x (ISBN 0-231-04767-3). Columbia U Pr.

--Problem of Knowledge. (Orig.). 1957. pap. 4.95 (ISBN 0-14-020377-X, Pelican). Penguin.

--Russell & Moore: The Analytical Heritage. LC 77-133216. (William James Lectures Ser: 1970). 1971. 16.50x (ISBN 0-674-78103-1). Harvard U Pr.

Ayer, Eleanor, jt. ed. see Jende-Hagan Bookcorp.

Ayer, Eleanor, ed. see Thumhart, Suzanne.

Ayer, Frederick, Jr. Before the Colors Fade; Portrait of a Soldier: George Patton. LC 64-18329. (Illus.). 266p. 1971. 16.95 (ISBN 0-910220-61-1). Berg.

Ayer, Frederick W. Woman at Apocalypse. 1981. pap. 5.00 (ISBN 0-682-49809-2). Exposition Pr FL.

Ayer, Harriet H. Harriet Hubbard Ayer's Book: A Complete & Authentic, Treatise on the Laws of Health & Beauty. LC 74-3927. (Women in America Ser). (Illus.). 546p. 1974. Repr. of 1902 ed. 41.00x (ISBN 0-405-06074-2). Ayer Co Pubs.

Ayer, Harry. Time for it All. 64p. 1984. 5.95 (ISBN 0-8059-2924-X). Dorrance.

Ayer, Hilary. Variations on the Hermit. 64p. 1973. pap. 2.00 (ISBN 0-87924-025-3). Membrane Pr.

Ayer, James C. Some of the Usages & Abuses in the Management of Our Manufacturing Corporations. LC 75-126399. (Research & Source Works Ser.: No. 435). 1971. Repr. of 1863 ed. wrappers 11.00 (ISBN 0-8337-0140-1). B Franklin.

Ayer, Joseph C. Sourcebook of Ancient Church History. LC 70-113536. Repr. of 1913 ed. lib. bdg. 24.50 (ISBN 0-404-00436-9). AMS Pr.

Ayer, Jules A. Part of My Life. (Illus.). 1978. pap. 7.95 (ISBN 0-19-281245-9, GB). Oxford U Pr.

Ayer, M. Jane, jt. auth. see Fennema, Elizabeth.

Ayer Press Staff. Ayer Fund-Raising Dinner Guide: 1974. 1974. 8.90x (ISBN 0-910190-03-8). IMS Pr.

Ayer, Sam & Alaszewski, Andy. Community Care & the Mentally Handicapped: Services for Mothers & Their Mentally Handicapped Children. LC 84-45289. 262p. 1984. 25.00 (ISBN 0-7099-0533-5, Pub. by Croom Helm Ltd). Longwood Pub Group.

Ayer, Steve J. Documenting PC Systems. (Illus., Orig.). 1986. pap. text ed. 39.50 (ISBN 0-9611694-9-4). Tech Comm Assoc.

Ayer, Steve J. & Patrinostro, Frank S. Software Configuration Management Documentation. LC 85-51305. (Software Development Documentation Ser.: Vol. 6). (Illus., Orig.). 1985. pap. 49.50 (ISBN 0-9611694-7-8). Tech Comm Assoc.

--Software Development Analysis Documentation. LC 85-51301. (Software Development Documentation Ser.: Vol. 2). (Orig.). 1985. pap. 55.00 (ISBN 0-9611694-4-3). Tech Comm Assoc.

--Software Development Design Documentation. LC 85-51302. (Software Development Documentation Ser.: Vol. 3). (Illus., Orig.). 1985. pap. 60.00 (ISBN 0-317-19586-7). Tech Comm Assoc.

--Software Development Documentation, 6 vols. (Software Development Documentation Ser.). (Illus., Orig.). Date not set. Set. pap. 314.00 (ISBN 0-9611694-8-6). Tech Comm Assoc.

--Software Development Planning & Management Documents. (Software Development Documentation Ser.: Vol. 1). (Illus., Orig.). 1985. pap. 49.50 (ISBN 0-9611694-2-7). Tech Comm Assoc.

--Software Implementation Documentation. LC 85-51304. (Software Development Documentation Ser.: Vol. 5). (Illus., Orig.). 1985. pap. 65.00 (ISBN 0-9611694-6-X). Tech Comm Assoc.

--Software Program & Test Documentation. LC 85-51303. (Software Development Documentation Ser.: Vol. 4). (Illus., Orig.). 1985. pap. 35.00 (ISBN 0-9611694-5-1). Tech Comm Assoc.

--Systems Development Documentation: Forms Method. (Illus.). 430p. (Orig.). pap. 56.00 (ISBN 0-9611694-0-0). Tech Comm Assoc.

Ayer, W. R., ed. Some Social Aspects of Dentistry. 100p. 1981. pap. 16.25 (ISBN 0-08-028132-X). Pergamon.

Ayer, William A. & Hirschman, Richard D., eds. Psychology & Dentistry: Selected Readings. 208p. 1972. 21.75x (ISBN 0-398-02220-8). C C Thomas.

Ayeroff, Stan. Jazz Masters: Benny Goodman. 1980. pap. 6.95 (ISBN 0-8256-4092-X, Amsco Music). Music Sales.

--Jazz Masters: Charlie Christian. 72p. pap. 6.95 (ISBN 0-686-75680-0). Music Sales.

--Jazz Masters: Django Reinhardt. 72p. pap. 6.95 (ISBN 0-8256-4083-0). Music Sales.

Ayers, A. J. Philosophy in the Twentieth Century. LC 82-40131. 283p. 1982. 22.50 (ISBN 0-394-50454-2). Random.

Ayers, Alfred. The Verbalist. 1911. 12.50 (ISBN 0-8274-3669-6). R West.

Ayers, Donald M. Bioscientific Terminology. LC 74-163010. 325p. 1972. pap. 6.95x (ISBN 0-8165-0305-2). U of Ariz Pr.

--English Words from Latin & Greek Elements. LC 64-17264. 271p. 1965. pap. 4.95x (ISBN 0-8165-0403-2). U of Ariz Pr.

Ayers, Edward L. Vengeance & Justice: Crime & Punishment in the 19th Century American South. LC 83-17472. 354p. 1984. 24.95x (ISBN 0-19-503383-3). Oxford U Pr.

Ayers, Helge, tr. see Redeker, Hans.

Ayers, James. The Artist's Craft. (Illus.). 240p. 1985. 27.50 (ISBN 0-7148-2343-0, Pub. by Salem Hse Ltd). Merrimack Pub Cir.

Ayers, Jody & Rogers, Lynn H. A Changed Man. LC 72-94208. (Pic Epic Ser.). 172p. 1973. pap. 1.95 (ISBN 0-913562-00-9). Rocking Chair Pr.

Ayers, John. Chinese Ceramics in the Koger Collection. LC 85-50715. (Illus.). 180p. 1985. 35.00 (ISBN 0-85667-301-3, Pub. by P Wilson Pubs). Sotheby Pubns.

--Don Bosco Finds Mary in the Church. (Salesian Family Ser.). 43p. 1983. pap. 3.50 (ISBN 0-89944-074-6). Don Bosco Multimedia.

--Far Eastern Ceramics in the Victoria & Albert Museum. (Illus.). 174p. 1980. 110.00x (ISBN 0-85667-076-6, Pub. by Sotheby Pubns England). Biblio Dist.

--Japanese Ceramics. (The Baur Collection Ser.). (Illus.). 184p. 1983. 195.00 (Pub. by Baur Foundation Switzerland). Routledge & Kegan.

Ayers, John, jt. auth. see Howard, David.

Ayers, John, jt. auth. see Howard, David S.

Ayers, John, ed. see Krahl, Regina & Erbahar, Nurdan.

Ayers, Peter K., ed. see Ogali, Ogali.

Ayers, R., et al. Action for Clean Air. 77p. 1971. 2.00 (ISBN 0-318-15826-4). Natl Resources Defense Coun.

Ayers, Rachel. Nursing Service in Transition: A Description of Organization for Classification & Utilization of Nurse Practitioners. 124p. 1972. pap. 5.00 (ISBN 0-940876-03-5). City Hope.

Ayers, Rachel, et al. The Clinical Nurse Specialist: An Experiment in Role Effectiveness & Role Development. 75p. 1971. pap. 5.00 (ISBN 0-940876-02-7). City Hope.

Ayers, Ralph. Graphics for Television. 320p. 1984. pap. 19.95 (ISBN 0-13-363177-X). P-H.

Ayers, Robert H. Judaism & Christianity: Origins, Developments & Recent Trends. LC 83-3548. (Illus.). 478p. (Orig.). 1983. lib. bdg. 32.25 (ISBN 0-8191-3156-3); pap. text ed. 16.50 (ISBN 0-8191-3157-1). U Pr of Amer.

Ayers, Robert L. Banking on the Poor: The World Band & World Poverty. 296p. 1983. pap. 7.95 (ISBN 0-262-51028-6). MIT Pr.

Ayers, Robert U. & McKenna, Richard P. Alternatives to the Internal Combustion Engine. 340p. 27.50 (ISBN 0-8018-1369-7). Resources Future.

Ayers, Ronald. Case of the Deadly Triangle. (Orig.). 1975. pap. 2.25 (ISBN 0-87067-222-3, BH222). Holloway.

Ayers, Tim, ed. Art at Auction: The Year at Sotheby's 1981-82. (Illus.). 392p. 1982. text ed. 45.00 (ISBN 0-85667-165-7, Pub. by Sotheby Pubns England). Biblio Dist.

Ayers, William. Chang Chih-Tung & Educational Reform in China. LC 71-129121. (East Asian Ser: No. 54). 1971. 18.50x (ISBN 0-674-10762-4). Harvard U Pr.

Ayerst, David. Garvin of the OBSERVER. LC 84-23767. 314p. 1985. 29.95 (ISBN 0-7099-0560-2, Pub. by Croom Helm Ltd). Longwood Pub Group.

Ayerst, David & Fisher, A. T. Records of Christianity: Christendom. LC 77-70660. (Records of Christianity Ser.: Vol. 2). (Illus.). 329p. 1977. text ed. 27.50x (ISBN 0-06-490255-2, 06322). B&N Imports.

Ayerst, Peter, jt. auth. see Wilson, Derek.

Ayisi, Eric O. An Introduction to the Study of African Culture. 2nd ed. 1979. pap. text ed. 5.50x (ISBN 0-435-89051-4). Heinemann Ed.

Aykac, A. & Brumat, eds. New Developments in the Applications of Bayesian Methods: Proceedings of the CEDEP-INSEAD Conference, June 1976. (Contributions to Economic Analysis: Vol. 119). 386p. 1978. 74.50 (ISBN 0-444-85059-7, North-Holland). Elsevier.

Aykroyd, Peter. Modern Gymnastics: Skills & Techniques. (Illus.). 152p. 1985. 12.95 (ISBN 0-668-06458-7). Arco.

--Skills & Tactics of Gymnastics. LC 79-18629. (Skills & Tactics Ser.). (Illus.). 152p. 1983. Repr. of 1980 ed. 6.95 (ISBN 0-668-05887-0, 5887). Arco.

Aykroyd, W. R. Conquest of Deficiency Diseases: Achievements & Prospects. (Freedom from Hunger Campaign Basic Studies: No. 24). (Orig.). 1971. pap. 6.75 (ISBN 0-685-02916-6, F98, FAO). Unipub.

--Conquest of Deficiency Diseases: Achievements & Prospects. (Freedom from Hunger Campaign Basic Study Ser: No. 24). 98p. 1970. pap. 4.80 (ISBN 92-4-156018-5, 410). World Health.

Aykroyd, W. R. & Doughty, Joyce. Legumes in Human Nutrition. 2nd ed. (Food & Nutrition Papers: No. 20). 160p. (Eng., Fr. & Span.). 1982. pap. 11.75 (ISBN 92-5-101181-8, F2329, FAO). Unipub.

Aykroyd, Wallace R. Three Philosophers: Lavoisier, Priestley & Cavendish. LC 77-98808. Repr. of 1935 ed. lib. bdg. 18.75 (ISBN 0-8371-2890-0, AYTB). Greenwood.

Aykroyo, W. R. & Doughty, J. Legumes in Human Nutrition. (Nutritional Studies: No. 19). 138p. (5th Printing 1977). 1964. pap. 7.25 (ISBN 92-5-100440-4, F257, FAO). Unipub.

Aylen, Leo. The Greek Theater. LC 82-49313. (Illus.). 384p. 1985. 47.50 (ISBN 0-8386-3184-3). Fairleigh Dickinson.

--I, Odysseus. pap. text ed. cancelled (ISBN 0-8290-1301-6). Irvington.

--Red Alert: This is a God Warning. 1983. pap. text ed. cancelled (ISBN 0-8290-1304-0). Irvington.

--Return to Zululand. 1983. pap. text ed. cancelled (ISBN 0-8290-1302-4). Irvington.

--Sunflower. 1983. pap. text ed. cancelled (ISBN 0-8290-1300-8). Irvington.

Aylen, R., et al. Heavy Vehicle Fitting. (Illus.). 251p. 1980. spiral 49.95x (ISBN 0-85083-510-0). Intl Ideas.

Aylen, R., et al, eds. Light Vehicle Fitting. (Engineering Craftsmen Ser.: No. H32). (Illus.). 261p. 1981. wire-bound 52.50x (ISBN 0-85083-487-2). Intl Ideas.

--Vehicle Fitting. (Engineering Craftsmen: No. H8). (Illus.). 1978. spiral bdg. 39.95x (ISBN 0-89563-036-2). Intl Ideas.

Aylesworth, Jim. The Bad Dream. Fay, Ann, ed. (Concept Bks.). (Illus.). 32p. (ps-2). 1985. 10.25 (ISBN 0-8075-0506-4). A Whitman.

--Hush Up! LC 79-2137. (Illus.). 32p. (gr. k-2). 1980. 7.95 (ISBN 0-03-054841-1). HR&W.

--Mary's Mirror. LC 81-6917. (Illus.). 32p. (gr. k-3). 1982. 9.95 (ISBN 0-03-060392-7). HR&W.

--Shenandoah Noah. LC 84-22554. (Illus.). (gr. k-2). 1985. 11.95 (ISBN 0-03-003749-2). HR&W.

--Siren in the Night. Fay, Ann, ed. LC 83-3654. (Self-Starter Bks.). (Illus.). 32p. (ps-2). 1983. PLB 9.25 (ISBN 0-8075-7374-4). A Whitman.

--Tonight's the Night. Fay, Ann, ed. (Self-Starter Bks.). (Illus.). 32p. (ps-1). 1981. PLB 9.25 (ISBN 0-8075-8020-1). A Whitman.

Aylesworth, Owen R. Caleb Sheldon Butts Aylesworth, His Descendants. LC 82-90493. (Illus.). 287p. 1982. text ed. 25.00 (ISBN 0-9609312-0-1). O R Aylesworth.

Aylesworth, T. G. The Story of Werewolves. 1982. 9.95 (ISBN 0-07-002645-9). McGraw.

Aylesworth, Thomas. Animal Superstitions. 120p. (gr. 5-8). 1981. 7.95 (ISBN 0-07-002658-0). McGraw.

--Spoon Bending & Other Impossible Feats. LC 80-20901. (Monsters & Mysteries Ser.). (gr. 4-10). 1980. pap. 2.25 (ISBN 0-88436-767-3, 35290). EMC.

Aylesworth, Thomas G. Geological Disasters: Earthquakes & Volcanoes. (Impact Bks.). (Illus.). 1979. PLB 9.90 s&l (ISBN 0-531-02288-9). Watts.

--Monsters from the Movies. 160p. (gr. 4-6). 1981. pap. 2.50 (ISBN 0-553-15273-4, Skylark). Bantam.

--Movie Monsters. LC 75-12997. (Illus.). 80p. (gr. 1-3). 1975. 10.10i (ISBN 0-397-31639-9). Lipp Jr Bks.

--Science Looks at Mysterious Monsters. LC 82-2304. (gr. 5 up). 1982. PLB 9.79 (ISBN 0-671-43657-0). Messner.

--The Story of Dragons & Other Monsters. LC 79-21550. (Illus.). 96p. (gr. 5-8). 1980. 9.95 (ISBN 0-07-002646-7). McGraw.

Aylesworth, Thomas G. & Aylesworth, Virginia L. The Mount St. Helens Disaster: What We've Learned. (Impact Ser.). 96p. (gr. 7 up). 1983. PLB 9.90 (ISBN 0-531-04488-2). Watts.

Aylesworth, Virginia L., jt. auth. see Aylesworth, Thomas G.

Aylett, B. J. Fundamentals of Inorganic Chemistry: A Programmed Introduction. Billing, D. E., ed. pap. 27.00 (ISBN 0-317-29354-0, 2024006). Bks Demand UMI.

--Organometallic Compounds, Vol. 1, Pt. 2: Groups IV & V. 4th ed. 1979. 85.00 (ISBN 0-412-13020-3, NO. 6018, Pub. by Chapman & Hall). Methuen Inc.

Aylett, B. J. & Harris, M. M. Progress in Stereochemistry, Vol. 4. LC 54-12738. 389p. 1969. 35.00x (ISBN 0-306-30684-0, Plenum Pr). Plenum Pub.

Aylett, B. J. & Smith, B. C. Problems in Inorganic Chemistry. LC 66-18189. pap. 40.00 (ISBN 0-317-09068-2, 2007643). Bks Demand UMI.

Aylett, R. P. The Nature of Realism in Grimmelshausen's "Simplicissimus" Cycle of Novels. (European University Studies: Series 1, German Language & Literature: Vol. 479). 264p. 1981. pap. 29.55 (ISBN 3-261-04967-7). P Lang Pubs.

Aylett, Stanley. Surgeon at War. 186p. 1980. 25.00x (ISBN 0-86116-190-4, Pub. by New Horizon England). State Mutual Bk.

Ayliffe, G. A. & Taylor, L. J. Hospital-Acquired Infection: Principles & Prevention. (Illus.). 160p. 1982. pap. text ed. 17.50 (ISBN 0-7236-0608-0). PSG Pub Co.

Ayliffe, Jerry. American Premium Guide to Juke Boxes & Slot Machines. 2nd ed. (Illus.). 312p. 1985. pap. 10.95 (ISBN 0-89689-055-4, Pub. by Bks Americana). C E Tuttle.

--Collecting Juke Boxes & Slot Machines. 2nd ed. (Illus.). 392p. (Orig.). 1985. pap. 10.95 (ISBN 0-89689-055-4). Bks Americana.

Ayliffe-Jones, Noel. World Tanks & Reconnaissance Vehicles since 1945. (Illus.). 144p. 1984. 19.95 (ISBN 0-88254-978-2). Hippocrene Bks.

Ayling, Alan & Mackintosh, Duncan, trs. Further Collection of Chinese Lyrics. LC 73-112602. (Illus.). 1970. 14.95 (ISBN 0-8265-1150-3). Vanderbilt U Pr.

Ayling, Alan, et al, trs. Folding Screen Chinese Lyrics. (Writing in Asia Ser.). 1976. pap. text ed. 7.50x (ISBN 0-686-60433-4, 00204). Heinemann Ed.

Ayling, David E. Underwriting Decisions under Uncertainity: A Catastrophe Market. 240p. 1984. text ed. 36.95x (ISBN 0-566-00692-8). Gower Pub Co.

Ayling, Ronald. Continuity & Innovation in Sean O'Casey's Drama. (Salzburg Studies in English Literature Poetic Drama & Poetic Theory: No. 23). 1976. pap. 25.50x (ISBN 0-391-01304-1). Humanities.

Ayling, Ronald & Durkan, Michael J. Sean O'Casey: A Bibliography. LC 77-83181. 436p. 1978. 40.00x (ISBN 0-295-95566-X). U of Wash Pr.

Ayling, Ronald, ed. Sean O'Casey. LC 79-127563. (Modern Judgement Ser). 1970. pap. text ed. 2.50 (ISBN 0-87695-097-7). Aurora Pubs.

Ayling, Ronald, ed. see O'Casey, Sean.

Ayling, Stanley. John Wesley. 1983. 16.95 (ISBN 0-687-20376-7). Abingdon.

Ayling, Tony & Cox, Geoffrey J. The Collins Guide to the Sea Fishes of New Zealand. (Illus.). 384p. 1983. 19.95x (ISBN 0-00-216987-8, Pub. by W Collins New Zealand). Intl Spec Bk.

Ayllon, Candido & Smith, Paul. Spanish Composition Through Literature. 1968. text ed. 22.95 (ISBN 0-13-824052-3). P-H.

Ayllon, Ted, jt. auth. see Kandel, Henry J.

Ayllon, Teodoro. How to Set Up a Token Economy. 36p. 1982. 5.00 (ISBN 0-89079-069-8). Pro Ed.

Aylmer, G. E. & Cant, R. C., eds. A History of York Minster. (Illus.). 1977. 32.50x (ISBN 0-19-817199-4). Oxford U Pr.

Aylmer, G. E., ed. see Cooper, J. P.

Aylmer, John. An Harborowe for Faithfull & Trewe Subjects Agaynst the Late Blowne Blaste, Concerning the Government of Wemen. LC 76-38142. (English Experience Ser.: No. 423). 134p. 1972. Repr. of 1559 ed. 20.00 (ISBN 9-0221-0423-0). Walter J Johnson.

Aylock, S., ed. Tiotiscontology: Anthology. 28p. 1984. 2.00 (ISBN 0-942432-10-X). M O P Pr.

Aylsworth, Sandra. Apple LOGO for Apple II Plus, Apple IIe & IIc. (Computer Fun Ser.). (Illus.). 1984. pap. 3.95 (ISBN 0-86582-166-6, EN79252). Enrich.

Aylward. Little Woman - Gladys Aylward. 2.95 (ISBN 0-318-18161-4). WCTU.

Aylward, Gladys. La Pequena Gran Mujer en la China. Orig. Title: Little Woman in China. 160p. (Span.). 1974. pap. 3.25 (ISBN 0-8254-1048-7). Kregel.

Aylward, Gladys & Hunter, Christine. Gladys Aylward. 1970. pap. 2.95 (ISBN 0-8024-2986-6). Moody.

--La Pequena en la China - Little Woman in China. pap. 3.25 (ISBN 0-8254-1048-7). Kregel.

Aylward, Jim. Your Burro Is No Jackass. LC 81-4603. (Illus.). 64p. (gr. 4-7). 1981. 7.95 (ISBN 0-03-059527-4). HR&W.

--Your Burro is No Jackass: And over 100 Other Things No One Ever Told You. (Illus.). 64p. (gr. 3-7). pap. 2.25 (ISBN 0-380-63453-8, 63453-8, Camelot). Avon.

--You're Dumber in the Summer: And Over 100 Other Things No One Ever Told You. (Illus.). 64p. (gr. 3-7). pap. 2.25 (ISBN 0-380-57935-9, 57935-9, Camelot). Avon.

Aylwin, Susan. Structure in Thought & Feeling. 320p. 1985. 49.95 (ISBN 0-416-35990-6, 9466). Methuen Inc.

Aymar, Brandt & Sagarin, Edward. A Pictorial History of the World's Great Trials: From Socrates to Eichmann. updated ed. LC 84-27413. (Bonanza Bks.). 1985. 12.98 (ISBN 0-517-46793-3, Bonanza). Outlet Bk Co.

Aymar, Brandt, ed. see Willis, John.

Aymard, Leopold L. Les Tovareg. LC 77-87625. Repr. of 1911 ed. 21.00 (ISBN 0-404-16445-5). AMS Pr.

Ayme, Marcel. Aller Retour. 1927. pap. 3.95 (ISBN 0-686-51900-0). French & Eur.

--La Belle Image. 1972. pap. 3.95 (ISBN 0-686-51901-9). French & Eur.

--Le Boeuf Clandestin. (Illus.). deluxe ed. 61.25 (ISBN 0-685-37181-6). French & Eur.

--Brulebois. 1976. pap. 3.95 (ISBN 0-686-51910-8). French & Eur.

--Le Chemin des Ecoliers. 1946. pap. 3.95 (ISBN 0-685-23913-6, 1621). French & Eur.

--Clerambard. 1958. 8.95 (ISBN 0-685-23919-5, 306). French & Eur.

--Le Confort Intellectual. 1967. pap. 11.95 (ISBN 0-686-50129-2). French & Eur.

--Les Contes Bleues du Chat Perche. 1975. 7.95 (ISBN 0-686-51911-6). French & Eur.

--Les Contes du Chat Perche. 1964. 14.95 (ISBN 0-686-51912-4). French & Eur.

--Les Contes Rouge du Chat Perche. 1975. 7.95 (ISBN 0-686-50130-6). French & Eur.

--Derriere Chez Martin. 1973. pap. 3.95 (ISBN 0-686-51913-2). French & Eur.

--En Arriere. 1950. pap. 6.95 (ISBN 0-686-51914-0). French & Eur.

--Gustalin. 1938. pap. 3.95 (ISBN 0-686-51915-9). French & Eur.

--Jambees. 1967. pap. 4.95 (ISBN 0-686-50131-4). French & Eur.

--Jument Verte. (Coll. Soleil). 1960. 12.50 (ISBN 0-685-11282-9). French & Eur.

--La Jument Verte. (Illus.). deluxe ed. 61.25 (ISBN 0-685-37182-4). French & Eur.

--Louisiane. 1961. pap. 4.95 (ISBN 0-686-51902-7). French & Eur.

--Lucienne et le Boucher. 1955. 6.95 (ISBN 0-685-23920-9). French & Eur.

--Maison Basse. 1978. pap. 3.95 (ISBN 0-686-51903-5). French & Eur.

--Les Maxibules. 1978. pap. 3.95 (ISBN 0-686-51916-7). French & Eur.

--La Mouche Bleue. 1978. pap. 3.95 (ISBN 0-686-51917-5). French & Eur.

--La Moulin de la Sourdine. 1973. pap. 3.95 (ISBN 0-686-51918-3). French & Eur.

--La Nain. 1977. pap. 3.95 (ISBN 0-686-51919-1). French & Eur.

--Oeuvres Romanesques. 1977. 595.00 (ISBN 0-686-51920-5). French & Eur.

--Les Oiseaux de Lune. 1956. pap. 4.95 (ISBN 0-686-51921-3). French & Eur.

--Passe-Muraille. 1943. 6.95 (ISBN 0-685-11479-1). French & Eur.

--Le Passe-muraille. (Illus.). deluxe ed. 61.25 (ISBN 0-685-37183-2). French & Eur.

--Le Puits aux Images. 1932. pap. 4.95 (ISBN 0-686-50127-6). French & Eur.

--Les Quatres Verites. 1954. pap. 6.95 (ISBN 0-686-51904-3). French & Eur.

--La Rue sans Nom. 1930. pap. 6.95 (ISBN 0-686-50128-4). French & Eur.

--Shihouette du Scandale. 1973. pap. 7.95 (ISBN 0-686-51905-1). French & Eur.

--La Table aux Creves. 1929. pap. 12.95 (ISBN 0-686-51906-X). French & Eur.

--La Tete des Autres. 1956. pap. 3.95 (ISBN 0-685-23918-7, 180). French & Eur.

--Tiroirs De L'inconnu. (Coll. Soleil). 1960. 9.95 (ISBN 0-685-11600-X). French & Eur.

--Travelingue. (Coll. Soleil). 1965. 12.95 (ISBN 0-685-23912-8). French & Eur.

--Uranus. (Coll. Soleil). 1962. 13.50 (ISBN 0-685-11611-5). French & Eur.

--Le Vaurien. 1931. pap. 6.95 (ISBN 0-686-51907-8). French & Eur.

--Le Vin de Paris. 1947. pap. 6.95 (ISBN 0-686-51908-6). French & Eur.

--Vogue la Galere. 1944. pap. 7.95 (ISBN 0-686-51909-4). French & Eur.

--La Vouivre. 1959. 4.95 (ISBN 0-685-11625-5). French & Eur.

--La Vouivre. (Illus.). deluxe ed. 61.25 (ISBN 0-685-37184-0). French & Eur.

Aymes, Clement A. The Pictorial Language of Hieronymus Bosch. Frommer, Eva A., tr. from Ger. (Illus.). 124p. 1975. 22.00 (ISBN 0-88010-063-X, Pub. by Steinerbooks). Anthroposophic.

Aymes, Maria de la Cruz see De la Cruz Aymes, Maria, et al.

Aymes, Maria de la Maria see De la Cruz Aymes, Maria, et al.

Aynesworth, Hugh, jt. auth. see Michaud, Stephen.

Aynesworth, Hugh, jt. auth. see Michaud, Stephen G.

Aynsley, R. M., et al. Architectural Aerodynamics. (Illus.). 254p. 1977. 40.75 (ISBN 0-85334-698-4, Pub. by Elsevier Applied Sci England). Elsevier.

Aynsley-Green, A. Paediatric Endocrinology in Clinical Practice. 1984. lib. bdg. 47.50 (ISBN 0-85200-864-3, Pub. by MTP Pr England). Kluwer Academic.

Ayoade, J. O. Introduction to Climatology for the Tropics. LC 82-2648. 258p. 1983. 34.95x (ISBN 0-471-10349-7, Pub. by Wiley-Interscience); pap. 15.95 (ISBN 0-471-10407-8, Pub. by Wiley-Interscience). Wiley.

Ayoob, Mohammed. Conflict & Intervention in the Third World. 1980. 29.00 (ISBN 0-312-16228-6). St Martin.

--The Horn of Africa: Regional Conflict & Super Power Involvement. O'Neill, Robert, ed. (Canberra Papers on Strategy & Defence: No. 18). 1979. pap. text ed. 1.95 (ISBN 0-909851-19-0, 0526, Pub. by ANUP Australia). Australia N U P.

--The Politics of Islamic Reassertion. 1981. 27.50 (ISBN 0-312-62707-6). St Martin.

Ayoob, Mohammed, ed. The Middle East in World Politics. LC 80-22312. 224p. 1981. 26.00 (ISBN 0-312-53184-2). St Martin.

--The Middle East in World Politics. LC 81-169898. pap. 54.30 (ISBN 0-317-11221-X, 2019359). Bks Demand UMI.

Ayoub, M. Great Tiding: Thirtieth Part of Holy Quran. pap. 4.50 (ISBN 0-317-01597-4). Kazi Pubns.

Ayoub, Mahmoud. Redemptive Suffering in Islam. (Religion & Society Ser.: No. 10). 1978. 26.80 (ISBN 90-279-7948-0). Mouton.

Ayoub, Mahmoud M. The Qur'an & Its Interpreters, Vol. 1. LC 82-21713. 290p. 1984. 29.50x (ISBN 0-87395-727-X). State U NY Pr.

Ayoub, Raymond G. An Introduction to the Analytic Theory of Numbers. LC 63-11989. (American Mathematical Society Mathematical Surveys Ser.: Vol. 10). Repr. of 1963 ed. 98.30 (ISBN 0-317-11024-1, 2022249). Bks Demand UMI.

Ayraud, Steve & Thumann, Albert. Introduction to Efficient Electrical System Design. LC 83-49500. 300p. 1985. text ed. 29.95 (ISBN 0-915586-98-3). Fairmont Pr.

Ayrault, Evelyn W. Growing up Handicapped: A Guide to Helping the Exceptional Child. LC 77-13447. 1977. 9.95 (ISBN 0-8264-0110-4). Continuum.

--Sex, Love & the Physically Handicapped. 172p. 1981. 11.95 (ISBN 0-8264-0051-5). Continuum.

Ayre, J. Randolph. Corporate Legal Departments: Strategies for the 1980s. 225p. 1984. text ed. 50.00 (ISBN 0-317-14128-7, BI-1299). PLI.

Ayre, Jessica. Hard to Handle. (Harlequin Romances Ser.). 192p. 1984. pap. 1.75 (ISBN 0-373-02599-8). Harlequin Bks.

--Not to Be Trusted. (Harlequin Romances Ser.). 192p. 1982. pap. 1.50 (ISBN 0-373-02504-1). Harlequin Bks.

Ayre, Peter, ed. Finance in Developing Countries. 174p. 1977. 29.50x (ISBN 0-7146-3077-2, F Cass Co). Biblio Dist.

Ayres, A. Jean. Interpreting the Southern California Sensory Integration Tests. LC 76-46889. 58p. 1976. pap. 14.50x (ISBN 0-87424-130-8). Western Psych.

--Sensory Integration & Learning Disorders. LC 72-91446. 294p. 1973. 31.50x (ISBN 0-87424-303-3). Western Psych.

--Sensory Integration & the Child. LC 79-66987. 191p. 1979. pap. text ed. 14.95x (ISBN 0-87424-158-8). Western Psych.

Ayres, C. E. Science-the False Messiah. Bd. with Holier Than Thou; The Way of the Righteous. LC 71-130660. Repr. of 1927 ed. 37.50x (ISBN 0-678-00774-8). Kelley.

--The Theory of Economic Progress. 3rd ed. 1978. pap. 6.95 (ISBN 0-932826-03-2). New Issues MI.

--Toward a Reasonable Society: The Values of Industrial Civilization. 309p. 1961. pap. 8.95x (ISBN 0-292-78026-5). U of Tex Pr.

Ayres, Carter A. Soaring. 1985. 8.95 (ISBN 0-8225-0442-1). Lerner Pubns.

Ayres, Frank, Jr. Calculus. 2nd ed. (Schaum Outline Ser.). 1968. pap. 9.95 (ISBN 0-07-002653-X). McGraw.

--Differential Equations. (Schaum's Outline Ser). (Orig.). 1952. pap. 8.95 (ISBN 0-07-002654-8). McGraw.

--First-Year College Mathematics. (Schaum's Outline Ser). (Orig.). 1958. pap. 9.95 (ISBN 0-07-002650-5). McGraw.

--Mathematics of Finance. (Schaum's Outline Ser.). (Orig.). 1963. pap. 8.95 (ISBN 0-07-002652-1). McGraw.

--Matrices. (Schaum's Outline Ser.). (Orig.). 1968. pap. 7.95 (ISBN 0-07-002656-4). McGraw.

--Modern Algebra. (Schaum's Outline Ser). (Orig.). 1965. pap. 8.95 (ISBN 0-07-002655-6). McGraw.

--Projective Geometry. (Schaum's Outline Ser). (Orig.). 1967. pap. 7.95 (ISBN 0-07-002657-2). McGraw.

--Trigonometry. (Schaum's Outline Ser). (Orig.). 1954. pap. 8.95 (ISBN 0-07-002651-3). McGraw.

Ayres, Harry M. Mary of Nimmegen: A Facsimile Reproduction of the Copy of the English Version in the Huntington Library. LC 32-31585. (Huntington Library Publications Ser.). pap. 20.00 (ISBN 0-317-29236-6, 2055540). Bks Demand UMI.

Ayres, Harry M., tr. Dante Alighieri: La Divina Commedia, 3 vols. 1953. 35.00x set (ISBN 0-913298-29-8). S F Vanni.

Ayres, J. A., ed. Decontamination of Nuclear Reactors & Equipment. (Illus.). 825p. 1970. 85.50x (ISBN 0-471-06687-7, Pub. by Wiley-Interscience). Wiley.

Ayres, J. C., et al, eds. Chemical & Biological Hazards in Food. (Illus.). 1970. Repr. of 1962 ed. 17.95x (ISBN 0-02-840650-8). Hafner.

Ayres, Jak, jt. auth. see McLachlan, Dan H.

Ayres, James. British Folk Art. LC 76-57876. (Illus.). 144p. 1977. 37.95 (ISBN 0-87951-060-9). Overlook Pr.

Ayres, Jane. Une Merveilleuse Odyssee. (Harlequin Seduction Ser.). 332p. 1983. pap. 3.25 (ISBN 0-373-45019-2). Harlequin Bks.

Ayres, Janet. Odyssey of Love. (Superromances Ser.). 384p. 1982. pap. 2.50 (ISBN 0-373-70026-1, Pub. by Worldwide). Harlequin Bks.

Ayres, Joe & Miller, Janice. Effective Public Speaking. 320p. 1983. pap. text ed. write for info. (ISBN 0-697-04229-4); instrs.' manual avail. (ISBN 0-697-04230-8). Wm C Brown.

Ayres, John C. & Kirschman, John C., eds. Impact of Toxicology on Food Processing. (Institute of Food Technologists Basic Symposia Ser.). (Illus.). 1981. lib. bdg. 55.00 (ISBN 0-87055-387-9). AVI.

Ayres, John C., et al. Microbiology of Foods. LC 79-16335. (Food & Nutrition Ser.). (Illus.). 708p. 1980. text ed. 30.95x (ISBN 0-7167-1049-8). W H Freeman.

Ayres, Katherine S. Charcoal Sketches. LC 72-6512. (Black Heritage Library Collection). 1972. Repr. of 1927 ed. 13.50 (ISBN 0-8369-9156-7). Ayer Co Pubs.

Ayres, Leonard P. Cleveland School Survey: Summary Volume. LC 72-112539. (Rise of Urban America). (Illus.). 1970. Repr. of 1917 ed. 20.00 (ISBN 0-405-02433-9). Ayer Co Pubs.

--Turning Points in Business Cycles. LC 68-20527. Repr. of 1940 ed. 22.50x (ISBN 0-678-00453-6). Kelley.

--The War with Germany. Kohn, Richard H., ed. LC 78-22374. (American Military Experience Ser.). (Illus.). 1979. Repr. of 1919 ed. lib. bdg. 12.00x (ISBN 0-405-11852-X). Ayer Co Pubs.

Ayres, Linda & Myers, Jane. American Paintings, Watercolors & Drawings from the Collection of Rita & Daniel Fraad. LC 85-70941. (Illus.). 128p. 1985. pap. 12.95 (ISBN 0-88360-075-7). Amon Carter.

Ayres, P. G. Effects of Disease on the Physiology of the Growing Plant. LC 80-42175. (Society for Experimental Biology Symposium Ser.: No. 11). (Illus.). 200p. 1982. 54.50 (ISBN 0-521-23306-2); pap. 22.95 (ISBN 0-521-29898-9). Cambridge U Pr.

Ayres, Pat, ed. see Klapthor, Margaret & Lucas, Dione.

Ayres, Phillip J., ed. see Munday, Anthony.

Ayres, Quincy C. Soil Erosion & Its Control. LC 72-2832. (Use & Abuse of America's Natural Resources Ser). (Illus.). 382p. 1972. Repr. of 1936 ed. 30.00 (ISBN 0-405-04501-8). Ayer Co Pubs.

Ayres, R. L., jt. ed. see Mann, W. B.

Ayres, R. U. Resources, Environment, & Economics: Applications of the Materials-Energy Balance Principle. LC 77-20049. 207p. text ed. 40.00 (ISBN 0-471-02627-1). Krieger.

Ayres, Robert. Banking on the Poor: The World Bank's Antipoverty Work in Developing Countries. 384p. 1981. write for info. Overseas Dev Council.

Ayres, Robert U. The Next Industrial Revolution: Reviving Industry Through Innovation. LC 83-21394. 304p. 1984. prof. ref. 29.95x (ISBN 0-88410-885-6). Ballinger Pub.

--Uncertain Futures: Challenges for Decision-Makers. LC 78-10252. 429p. 1979. 45.95 (ISBN 0-471-04250-1, Pub. by Wiley-Interscience). Wiley.

Ayres, Robert U. & McKenna, Richard P. Alternatives to the Internal Combustion Engine: Impacts on Environmental Quality. LC 74-181555. (Resources for the Future Ser). 340p. 1972. 27.50x (ISBN 0-8018-1369-7). Johns Hopkins.

Ayres, Robert U. & Miller, Steven M. Robotics: Applications & Social Implications. LC 82-13881. 368p. 1982. prof ref 32.50x (ISBN 0-88410-891-0). Ballinger Pub.

--Robotics: Applications & Social Implications. 339p. 1983. text ed. 32.50scp (ISBN 0-88410-891-0, HarpC). Har-Row.

Ayres, Ronald F. VLSI: Silicon Compilation & the Art of Automatic Microchip Design. (Illus.). 496p. 1983. text ed. 56.95 (ISBN 0-13-942680-9). P-H.

Ayres, Ruby M. The Phantom Lover. 1975. lib. bdg. 14.85x (ISBN 0-89966-003-7). Buccaneer Bks.

--The Road That Bends. 1975. lib. bdg. 15.80x (ISBN 0-89966-004-5). Buccaneer Bks.

Ayres, Stephen, et al. Medical Resident's Manual. 4th ed. (Illus.). 667p. 1982. pap. 18.95 (ISBN 0-8385-6253-1). ACC.

Ayres, Stephen M., jt. auth. see Parrillo, Joseph E.

Ayres, William. The Warner Collector's Guide to American Toys. (Illus., Orig.). 1981. pap. 9.95 (ISBN 0-446-97632-6). Warner Bks.

Ayres, William S. The Main Street Pocket Guide to Toys. rev. ed. LC 84-15510. (Illus.). 256p. 1985. pap. 6.95 (ISBN 0-915590-54-9). Main Street.

Ayrey, Betty. Ferns: Facts & Fantasy. (Illus.). 1979. 6.95x (ISBN 0-85091-062-5, Pub. by Lothian). Intl Spec Bk.

Ayrey, G., jt. auth. see Chapman, J. M.

Ayrock, Don M. Symbols of Salvation. LC 81-70976. 1982. 4.50 (ISBN 0-8054-5190-0). Broadman.

Ayrout, Henry H. The Fellaheen. Wayment, Hilary, tr. LC 79-2849. 179p. 1981. Repr. of 1945 ed. 18.70 (ISBN 0-8305-0025-1). Hyperion Conn.

--Moeurs et coutumes des fellahs. 5th ed. LC 74-15009. (Illus.). Repr. of 1938 ed. 19.50 (ISBN 0-404-12004-0). AMS Pr.

Ayrton, Elisabeth. English Provincial Cooking. LC 79-2612. (Illus.). 1980. 17.26i (ISBN 0-06-010157-1, HarpT). Har-Row.

--Good Simple Cookery. LC 99-943989. (Illus.). 288p. 1984. 17.95 (ISBN 0-356-10169-X, Pub. by Salem Hse Ltd). Merrimack Pub Cir.

Ayruni, A. T. Theory & Practice of Mine Gas Control at Deep Levels. Cooley, W. C., ed. Peabody, A. L., tr. from Russian. (Illus.). 416p. 1984. 70.00x (ISBN 0-918990-10-6). Terraspace.

Ayscough, Florence. Chinese Women: Yesterday & Today. LC 74-32095. (China in the 20th Century Ser). (Illus.). xiv, 324p. 1975. Repr. of 1937 ed. lib. bdg. 42.50 (ISBN 0-306-70700-4). Da Capo.

Ayscough, Florence & Lowell, Amy, trs. from Chinese. Fir-Flower Tablets. LC 73-862. (China Studies: From Confucius to Mao Ser.). (Illus.). xcv, 227p. 1973. Repr. of 1921 ed. 23.50 (ISBN 0-88355-058-X). Hyperion Conn.

Ayscough, P. B., ed. Electron Spin Resonance, Vols. 1-5. Incl. Vol. 1. 1971-72 Literature. 1973. 36.00 (ISBN 0-85186-751-0); Vol. 2. 1972-73 Literature. 1974. 38.00 (ISBN 0-85186-761-8); Vol. 3. 1973-75 Literature. 1976. 45.00 (ISBN 0-85186-771-5); Vol. 4. 1975-76 Literature. 1977. 61.00 (ISBN 0-685-55713-8); Vol. 5. 1979. 77.00 (ISBN 0-85186-791-X, Pub. by Royal Soc Chem London). LC 72-95099. Am Chemical.

Ayscough, S. Index to the Remarkable Passages & Words Made Use of by Shakespeare. LC 74-135728. Repr. of 1790 ed. 27.50 (ISBN 0-404-00437-7). AMS Pr.

--An Index to the Remarkable Passages & Words Made Use of by Shakespeare. 59.95 (ISBN 0-8490-0395-4). Gordon Pr.

Aysha, Noor, jt. auth. see Khan, Mumtaz A.

Ayto, John, jt. ed. see Barratt, Alexandra.

Ayton, Angela & Morgan, Margaret. Photographic Slides in Language Teaching. (Practical Language Teaching: No. 6). (Orig.). 1981. pap. 6.95x (ISBN 0-435-28970-5). Heinemann Ed.

Ayton, Cyril. Manx Norton. (Super Profile Ser.). (Illus.). 56p. 1985. 9.95 (ISBN 0-85429-452-X, Pub. by G T Foulis Ltd). Interbook.

Ayton, Cyril, ed. World Motorcycles: Number One. (Illus.). 238p. 24.95 (ISBN 0-85429-360-4, F360). Haynes Pubns.

Ayton, Cyril, et al. The History of Motorcycling. (Illus.). 340p. 1985. 30.00 (ISBN 0-85613-517-8, Pub. by Salem Hse Ltd). Merrimack Pub Cir.

Ayton, Eric. Clay Tobacco Pipes. (Shire Album Ser.: No. 37). (Illus.). 32p. (Orig.). 1984. pap. 2.95 (ISBN 0-85263-450-1, Pub. by Shire Pubns England). Seven Hills Bks.

Aytoun, William E., et al. The Book of Ballads. Gautier, Bon, ed. (The Victorian Muse Ser.). 40.00 (ISBN 0-8240-8620-1). Garland Pub.

Ayub, Mahmood A. Made in Jamaica: The Development of the Manufacturing Sector. LC 80-27765. (World Bank Staff Occasional Papers: No. 31). 120p. (Orig.). 1981. pap. text ed. 6.50x (ISBN 0-8018-2568-7). Johns Hopkins.

Ayubi, Shaheen & Bissell, Richard E. Economic Sanctions in U. S. Foreign Policy. LC 82-13589. (Philadelphia Policy Papers). 1982. pap. 3.95 (ISBN 0-910191-01-8). For Policy Res.

Ayusawa, Iwao. A History of Labor in Modern Japan. LC 76-20683. 406p. 1976. Repr. of 1966 ed. lib. bdg. 29.50 (ISBN 0-8371-8991-8, AYHL). Greenwood.

Ayusawa, Iwao F. International Labor Leglislation. LC 75-82244. (Columbia University Studies in the Social Sciences: No. 208). Repr. of 1920 ed. 16.50 (ISBN 0-404-51208-9). AMS Pr.

Ayvazian, Arthur A. Armenian Victories at Khznavous & Sardarabad on May 23, 1918 & Program for Re-establishment of Independent & Neutral State of Armenia. (Illus.). 120p. 10.00 (ISBN 0-934728-15-1). D O A C.

Ayyad, A. T. Arabic: Teach Yourself. 8.95x (ISBN 0-86685-343-X). Intl Bk Ctr.

Ayyangar, N. R., et al. A Course in Industrial Chemistry, Pt. 1. 204p. 1981. 30.00x (ISBN 0-86125-687-5, Pub. by Orient Longman India). State Mutual Bk.

Ayyildiz, Judy. Smuggled Seeds. Kulikowski, M. Karl, ed. (Gusto Press Poetry Discovery Ser.). (Orig.). 1979. pap. 3.50 (ISBN 0-933906-09-9). Gusto Pr.

Ayyub, Abu S. Poetry & Truth: A Philosophical Essay on Modern Poetry. 1978. Repr. of 1970 ed. lib. bdg. 20.00 (ISBN 0-8482-7372-9). Norwood Edns.

--Poetry & Truth: A Philosophical Essay on Modern Poetry. 163p. 1983. lib. bdg. 40.00 (ISBN 0-89760-058-4). Telegraph Bks.

Azaad, Meyer. Half for You. LC 78-128813. (Illus.). (gr. k-5). 1971. PLB 4.95g (ISBN 0-87614-016-9). Carolrhoda Bks.

--The Tale of Ringy. Ghanoonparvar, Mohammad R. & Wilcox, Diane L., trs. from Persian. (Illus.). 24p. (Orig.). (gr. 3 up). 1983. pap. 4.95 (ISBN 0-686-43078-6). Mazda Pubs.

Azaad, Meyer, jt. auth. see Fardjam, Faridah.

Azaad, Meyer, jt. auth. see Farjam, Farideh.

Azad, A. K. Tarjaman-ul-Quran, 3 vols. Vol. 1. 16.50 (ISBN 0-686-18512-9); Vol. 2. 20.00 (ISBN 0-686-67787-0); Vol. 3. 20.00. Kazi Pubns.

Azad, Hardam S. Industrial Wastewater Management Handbook. 1976. 57.00 (ISBN 0-07-002661-0). McGraw.

Azadivar, Farhad. Design & Engineering of Production Systems. 630p. 1984. text ed. 28.95x (ISBN 0-910554-43-9). Engineering.

Azam, Salem. Concept of Islamic State. 42p. 1980. pap. 2.95x (ISBN 0-906041-13-9, Pub. by Islamic Council of Europe England). Intl Spec Bk.

Azami, M. M. Early Hadith Literature. LC 77-90341. 1978. 8.25 (ISBN 0-89259-012-2). Am Trust Pubns.

Azami, Mustafa. On Schacht's Origins of Muhammadan Jurisprudence. LC 84-2270. 500p. 1985. 28.00 (ISBN 0-471-89145-2). Wiley.

--Studies in Hadith Methodology & Literature. Beg, Anwer, ed. LC 77-90335. 1978. 8.25 (ISBN 0-89259-011-4). Am Trust Pubns.

Azana, Manuel. Vigil in Benicarlo. Stewart, Josephine & Stewart, Paul, eds. LC 81-65339. (Illus.). 136p. 1981. 16.50 (ISBN 0-8386-3093-6). Fairleigh Dickinson.

Azar, Betty S. Basic English Grammar. (Illus.). 304p. 1984. pap. text ed. 11.95 (ISBN 0-13-060434-8). P-H.

--Fundamentals of English Grammar. (Illus.). 304p. 1985. pap. text ed. 12.95 (ISBN 0-13-338500-0). P-H.

Azar, Edward E. & Ben-Dak, Joseph. Theory & Practice of Events Research. 328p. 1975. 65.95 (ISBN 0-677-15550-6). Gordon.

Azar, Edward E., et al. The Emergence of a New Lebanon: Fantasy or Reality? LC 84-15974. 302p. 1984. 32.95x (ISBN 0-03-070736-6). Praeger.

Azar, Henry A. & Potter, Michael. Multiple Myeloma & Related Disorders, Vol. 1. LC 72-13525. (Illus.). Repr. of 1973 ed. 83.60 (ISBN 0-8357-9426-1, 2013349). Bks Demand UMI.

Azar, Ines. Discurso Retorico y Mundo Pastoral En la 'egloga Segunda' De Garcilaso. (Purdue University Monographs in Romance Languages: Vol. 5). 172p. (Span.). 1981. 23.00x (ISBN 90-272-1715-7). Benjamins North Am.

Azar, J. J. Matrix Structural Analysis. 1972. text ed. 33.00 (ISBN 0-08-016781-0). Pergamon.

Azar, J. J., jt. auth. see Peery, D. J.

Azar, Maliha, jt. auth. see Atkinson, John.

Azar, Miguel M., jt. ed. see Schwartz, Lagar M.

Azar, U. N., ed. see Yaremchuk, A. P., et al.

Azara, Don Felix De see De Azara, Don Felix.

Azari, Farah, ed. Women of Iran. 225p. (Orig.). 1984. pap. 8.00 (ISBN 0-903729-95-4). Evergreen Dist.

Azariah, Isaiah. Lord Bentinck & Indian Education, Crime, & Status of Women. LC 78-64822. 1978. pap. text ed. 11.25 (ISBN 0-8191-0641-0). U Pr of Amer.

Azarian, Mary. A Farmer's Alphabet. LC 80-84938. 56p. (ps-2). 1981. 14.95 (ISBN 0-87923-394-X); pap. 7.95 (ISBN 0-87923-397-4). Godine.

--Farmers Alphabet Junior. LC 80-84938. 64p. 1985. pap. 6.95 (ISBN 0-87923-589-6). Godine.

--The Tale of John Barleycorn: Or From Barley to Beer. LC 82-3130. (Illus.). 32p. 1982. 12.95 (ISBN 0-87923-446-6); pap. 6.95 (ISBN 0-87923-447-4). Godine.

Azarian, Mary, illus. Mary Azarian Address Book. (Illus.). 112p. (gr. 3 up). 1983. spiral bdg. 9.95 (ISBN 0-87923-479-2). Godine.

Azarias. Phases of Thought & Criticism: Emerson, Dante, Newman. 273p. 1983. Repr. of 1892 ed. lib. bdg. 40.00 (ISBN 0-89987-046-5). Darby Bks.

Azarias, Brother. The Philosophy of Literature. (Illus.). 187p. 1984. Repr. of 1898 ed. 88.95 (ISBN 0-89901-164-0). Found Class Reprints.

Azarin, V. S., et al. Thirteen Papers on Functions of Real & Complex Variables. LC 51-5559. (Translations Ser.: No. 2, Vol. 80). 1969. 36.00 (ISBN 0-8218-1780-9, TRANS 2-80). Am Math.

Azarnoff, Daniel L. Steroid Therapy. LC 74-24511. pap. 88.00 (ISBN 0-317-29812-7, 2016651). Bks Demand UMI.

Azarnoff, Daniel L., ed. see Greenberger, Norton J., et al.

Azarnoff, Pat. Health, Illness & Disability: A Guide to Books for Children & Young Adults. 432p. 1983. 29.95 (ISBN 0-8352-1518-0). Bowker.

Azarnoff, Pat & Flegal, Sharon. A Pediatric Play Program: Developing a Therapeutic Play Program for Children in Medical Settings. (Illus.). 112p. 1980. pap. 12.75x spiral bound (ISBN 0-398-03272-6). C C Thomas.

Azarnoff, Pat & Hardgrove, Carol. The Family in Child Health Care. LC 80-26586. 247p. 1981. pap. 22.00x (ISBN 0-471-08663-0, Pub. by Wiley-Med). Wiley.

Azarnoff, Pat, ed. Preparation of Young Healthy Children for Possible Hospitalization: The Issues. LC 83-17168. 112p. (Orig.). 1983. pap. 12.00x (ISBN 0-912599-00-6). Pediatric Projects.

--Psychological Abuse of Pediatric Patients. (The Issues Ser.: No. 2). (Illus.). 101p. pap. text ed. 12.00 spiral bdg. (ISBN 0-912599-04-9). Pediatric Projects.

Azarnoff, Roy S. & Seliger, Jerome. Delivering Human Services. (Illus.). 288p. 1982. text ed. 26.95 (ISBN 0-13-198317-2). P-H.

Azaroff, Leonid V. Introduction to Solids. LC 75-20462. 474p. 1975. Repr. of 1960 ed. 28.00 (ISBN 0-88275-345-2). Krieger.

Azarov, Y. Book about Bringing Up Children. 319p. 1983. 7.95 (ISBN 0-8285-2562-5, Pub. by Progress Pubs USSR). Imported Pubns.

Azarova, E. G., jt. auth. see Tolkunova, V.

Azarpay, Guitty. Sogdian Painting: The Pictorial Epic in Oriental Art. (Illus.). 300p. 1981. 80.00x (ISBN 0-520-03765-0); pap. 25.00 (ISBN 0-520-05448-2). U of Cal Pr.

Azarya, Victor. Aristocrats Facing Change: The Fulbe in Guinea, Nigeria, & Cameroon. LC 77-15025. (Illus.). 1978. lib. bdg. 28.00x (ISBN 0-226-03356-2). U of Chicago Pr.

--The Armenian Quarter of Jerusalem: Urban Life Behind Monastery Walls. LC 83-47847. 224p. 1984. text ed. 22.50x (ISBN 0-520-04749-4). U of Cal Pr.

Azavedo, Carlos de see De Azavedo, Carlos.

Azbel, David. Chemical & Process Equipment Design: Vessel Design & Selection. LC 81-70863. 791p. 1982. 59.95 (ISBN 0-250-40478-8). Butterworth.

--Fundamentals of Heat Transfer for Process Engineering. LC 84-4213. (Illus.). 382p. 1984. 36.00 (ISBN 0-8155-0982-0). Noyes.

--Heat Transfer Applications in Process Engineering. LC 84-14781. (Illus.). 584p. 1985. 39.00 (ISBN 0-8155-0996-0). Noyes.

--Two Phase Flows in Chemical Engineering. LC 80-20936. (Illus.). 400p. 1981. 95.00 (ISBN 0-521-23772-6). Cambridge U Pr.

Azbel, David S., jt. auth. see Cheremisinoff, Nicholas P.

Azbel, David S., jt. ed. see Cheremisinoff, Nicholas P.

Azbelev, N. V., et al. Fifteen Papers on Differential Equations. LC 51-5559. (Translations Ser.: No. 2, Vol. 42). 1964. 25.00 (ISBN 0-8218-1742-6, TRANS 2-42). Am Math.

Azcar. How to Talk Directly with God. 51p. 1977. pap. 1.95 (ISBN 0-931865-05-0). Psychegenics.

Azcarate, P. De see De Azcarate, P.

Azcarate, Pablo de see De Azcarate, Pablo.

Azcarraga, J. A., ed. Topics in Quantum Field Theory & Gauge Theories: Proceedings of the VIII International Seminar on Theoretical Physics, Held by GIFT in Salamanca, June 13-19, 1977. (Lecture Notes in Physics Ser.: Vol. 77). 1978. pap. 20.00 (ISBN 0-387-08841-5). Springer-Verlag.

Azcuy, Lucila E. Poesias de Lucila E. Azcuy: Poesias de Ayer y de Hoy. Para Siempre... LC 81-69540. (Coleccion Espejo de Paciencia Ser.). (Illus.). 67p. (Orig., Span.). 1982. pap. 5.95 (ISBN 0-89729-267-7). Ediciones.

Azema, J. & Yor, M., eds. Seminaire de Probabilites XIX 1983-84. (Lecture Notes in Mathematics: Vol. 1123). iv, 504p. (Eng. & Fr.). 1985. pap. 32.80 (ISBN 0-387-15230-X). Springer-Verlag.

Azema, Jean-Pierre. From Munich to the Liberation, Nineteen Thirty-Eight to Nineteen Forty-Four. Lloyd, Janet, tr. (History of Modern France Ser.: No. 6). 356p. 1985. 39.50 (ISBN 0-521-25237-7); pap. 15.95 (ISBN 0-521-27238-6). Cambridge U Pr.

Azen, Stanley P., jt. auth. see Afifi, A. A.

Azencott, R. & Wilson, E. N. Homogenous Manifolds with Negative Curvature II. LC 76-44403. (Memoirs: No. 178). 102p. 1976. pap. 13.00 (ISBN 0-8218-2178-4, MEMO178). Am Math.

Azerrad, Jacob. Anyone Can Have a Happy Child. 240p. (Orig.). 1981. pap. 3.50 (ISBN 0-446-32284-9). Warner Bks.

--Anyone Can Have a Happy Child: The Simple Secret of Positive Parenting. LC 79-26959. 180p. 1980. 8.95 (ISBN 0-87131-141-0). M Evans.

Azevedo, Aluizio. A Brazilian Tenement. Brown, Harry W., tr. 1977. lib. bdg. 59.95 (ISBN 0-8490-1552-9). Gordon Pr.

Azevedo, J. M. Manual De Hidraulica. (Span.). 1976. pap. text ed. 17.00 (ISBN 0-06-310007-X, IntlDept). Har-Row.

Azevedo, M. T., jt. auth. see Bicudo, C. E.

Azevedo, Mario & Prater. Africa & Its People: An Interdisciplinary Survey of the Continent. 192p. (gr. 11-12). 1982. pap. text ed. 13.95 (ISBN 0-8403-2730-7). Kendall-Hunt.

Azevedo, Mario, ed. Cameroon & Its National Character. LC 84-80033. (Illus.). 105p. (Orig.). 1984. pap. text ed. 8.50 (ISBN 0-317-04155-X). Educ Awareness.

Azevedo, Milton M. A Contrastive Phonology of Portuguese & English. (Orig.). 1981. pap. text ed. 7.95 (ISBN 0-87840-082-6). Georgetown U Pr.

--Passive Sentences in English & Portuguese. 124p. 1980. pap. text ed. 7.95 (ISBN 0-87840-078-8). Georgetown U Pr.

Azevedo, Milton M. & Kerr, Herminia J. Self-Paced Exercises in Spanish. 176p. (Span.). 1982. pap. text ed. 14.00 (ISBN 0-8403-2803-6). Kendall-Hunt.

Azevedo, Milton M. & McMahon, Kathryn K. Lecturas Periodisticas. 2nd ed. 288p. 1981. pap. text ed. 10.95 (ISBN 0-669-04026-6). Heath.

Azevedo, Ross. Labor Economics: A Guide to Information Sources. LC 73-17568. (Economics Information Guide Ser.: Vol. 8). 1978. 60.00x (ISBN 0-8103-1297-2). Gale.

Azevedo, Ross E., jt. auth. see Mitchell, Daniel J.

Azevedo, Warren, ed. Washo Indians of California & Nevada. (Utah Anthropological Papers: No. 67). Repr. of 1963 ed. 22.50 (ISBN 0-404-60667-9). AMS Pr.

Azevedo, Warren L., ed. The Traditional Artist in African Societies. LC 79-160126. (Illus.). pap. 90.90 (ISBN 0-8357-9248-X, 2017615). Bks Demand UMI.

Azhar, A. Christianity in History. 12.50 (ISBN 0-686-18580-3). Kazi Pubns.

Azhary, M. S. see El Azhary, M. S.

Azif, Herbert B. China Trade: A Guide to Doing Business with the People's Republic of China. LC 80-84105. (Illus.). 131p. (Orig.). 1981. pap. 14.50 (ISBN 0-9605190-0-9). China Res.

Azikiwe, Nnamdi. Liberia in World Politics. LC 71-107503. Repr. of 1934 ed. 20.50 (ISBN 0-8371-3774-8, AZL&, Pub. by Negro U Pr). Greenwood.

--Renascent Africa. 314p. 1968. Repr. of 1937 ed. 29.50x (ISBN 0-7146-1744-X, F Cass Co). Biblio Dist.

--Renascent Africa. LC 79-94488. Repr. of 1937 ed. 17.50x (ISBN 0-8371-2365-8, AZR&). Greenwood.

Azima, Fern J. & Richmond, Lewis. Group Therapies for Adolescent. Date not set. price not set (BN#02255). Intl Univs Pr.

Aziz, A. Studies in Block Planning. 146p. 1983. text ed. 17.75x (ISBN 0-391-02843-X, Pub. by Concept India). Humanities.

Aziz, A. K., ed. The Mathematical Foundations of the Finite Element Method with Applications to Partial Differentail Equations. 1972. 84.00 (ISBN 0-12-068650-3). Acad Pr.

Aziz, A. K., et al, eds. Control Theory of Systems Governed by Partial Differential Equations. 1977. 41.50 (ISBN 0-12-068640-6). Acad Pr.

Aziz, Abdul. Organizing Agricultural Labourers in India. 1980. 7.50x (ISBN 0-8364-0651-6, Pub. by Minerva India). South Asia Bks.

Aziz, Ahmad, ed. Muslim Self-Statement in India & Pakistan 1857-1968. 1970. 60.00x (ISBN 3-447-00072-4). Intl Pubns Serv.

Aziz, Harry. Police Procedures & Defense Tactics Training Manual. Halet, Sydney S., ed. (Illus.). 1979. 20.95 (ISBN 0-87040-451-2). Japan Pubns USA.

Aziz, K. & Settari, A. Petroleum Reservoir Simulation. (Illus.). 475p. 1979. 89.00 (ISBN 0-85334-787-5, Pub. by Elsevier Applied Sci England). Elsevier.

Aziz, Khalid. Indian Cooking. (Illus.). 192p. 1983. pap. 9.95 (ISBN 0-399-50842-2, Perigee). Putnam Pub Group.

Aziz, Khalid, jt. auth. see Govier, George W.

Aziz, Madbool, ed. see James, Henry.

Aziz, Maqbool, ed. see James, Henry.

Aziz, Nasima. No Metaphor, Remember. flexible cloth 5.00 (ISBN 0-89253-647-0). Ind-US Inc.

--One More: Poems. (Redbird Bk). 43p. 1975. 8.00 (ISBN 0-88253-837-3); pap. 4.80 (ISBN 0-88253-838-1). Ind-US Inc.

Aziz, Nor L., et al. The Case of Malaysia. (Culture & Fertility Ser.). 92p. (Orig.). 1980. pap. text ed. 13.00x (ISBN 9971-902-15-X, Pub. by Inst Southeast Asian Stud). Gower Pub Co.

Aziz, Sartaj. Rural Development: Learning from China. LC 78-489. 201p. 1978. text ed. 36.50x (ISBN 0-8419-0371-9); pap. text ed. 17.50x (ISBN 0-8419-0372-7). Holmes & Meier.

Aziz, Sartaj, ed. Hunger, Politics & Markets: The Real Issues in the Food Crisis. LC 75-34674. 130p. 1975. pap. 9.50x (ISBN 0-8147-0560-X). NYU Pr.

Aziza, C. & Olivieri, C. Dictionnaire des Types et Charateres Litteraires. 208p. (Fr.). 1978. pap. 29.95 (ISBN 0-686-56866-4, M-6644). French & Eur.

Aziz Al-Azmeh. Ibn Khaldun: An Essay in Reinterpretation. 192p. 1982. 30.00x (ISBN 0-7146-3130-2, BHA 03130, F Cass Co). Biblio Dist.

Azizullah. Glimpses of Hadith, 3. pap. 6.50 (ISBN 0-686-18380-0). Kazi Pubns.

--Glimpses of the Holy Quran. pap. 6.50 (ISBN 0-686-18517-X). Kazi Pubns.

Azizur, Rahman Khan & Lee, Eddy. Agrarian Policies & Institutions in China After Mao. (Orig.). 1984. pap. 8.00 (ISBN 92-2-103281-7, ILO295, ILO). Unipub.

Azkue, Resurreccion M. Diccionario Vasco-Espanol-Frances, 2 vols. (Span. & Fr.). Set. leatherette 68.00 (ISBN 84-248-0015-X, S-12384). French & Eur.

Azmi, Sanaa, jt. auth. see Baccouche, Belkacem.

Aznar, J., ed. see International Congress on Thrombosis, 7th, Valencia, Spain, October, 1982.

Azorin, pseud. La Ruta de Don Quijote. Ramsden, H., intro. by. (Spanish Texts Ser.). 220p. (Orig., Span.). 1966. pap. text ed. 7.50 (ISBN 0-7190-0204-4, Pub. by Manchester Univ Pr). Longwood Pub Group.

Azorin. The Sirens & Others Stories. Wells, Warre B., tr. 1978. Repr. of 1931 ed. lib. bdg. 30.00 (ISBN 0-8492-0062-8). R West.

Azoy, G. Whitney. Buzkashi: Game & Power in Afghanistan.,LC 81-14679. (Symbol & Culture Ser.). (Illus.). 152p. 1982. 19.50x (ISBN 0-8122-7821-6). U of Pa Pr.

Azpadu, Dodici. Goat Song. 1984. pap. text ed. 6.50 (ISBN 0-317-17374-X). Aunt Lute Bk Co.

--Saturday Night in the Prime of Life. 1983. pap. 5.95 (ISBN 0-317-02244-X). Aunt Lute Bk Co.

Azrael. Wisdom for the New Age. LC 81-85815. 208p. (Orig.). 1982. pap. 6.95 (ISBN 0-87516-477-3). De Vorss.

Azrael, Jeremy R., ed. Soviet Nationality Policies & Practices. LC 77-83478. 408p. 1978. 47.95 (ISBN 0-03-041476-8). Praeger.

Azrael, Mary. Victorians. LC 81-84759. 76p. (Orig.). 1982. pap. 4.95 (ISBN 0-87376-039-5). Red Dust.

Azrin, Nathan & Besalel, Victoria B. Finding a Job. LC 82-50904. 160p. (Orig.). 1983. pap. 6.95 (ISBN 0-89815-049-3). Ten Speed Pr.

Azrin, Nathan & Fox, Richard M. Toilet Training in Less Than a Day. 1981. pap. 2.95 (ISBN 0-671-43660-0). PB.

Azrin, Nathan H. & Besalel, V. A. How to Use Overcorrection. 37p. 1980. 5.00 (ISBN 0-89079-047-7). Pro Ed.

Azrin, Nathan H. & Besalel, Victoria A. How to Use Positive Practice. 44p. 1981. 5.00 (ISBN 0-89079-060-4). Pro Ed.

--Job Club Counselor's Manual. LC 79-20865. (Illus.). 224p. 1979. pap. 17.00 (ISBN 0-8391-1535-0). Pro-Ed.

--A Parent's Guide to Bedwetting Control: A Step by Step Method. 1981. pap. 2.95 (ISBN 0-671-82774-X). PB.

Azrin, Nathan H., jt. auth. see Foxx, Richard M.

Azuela, Arturo. Shadows of Silence. Murray, Elena C., tr. LC 84-40361. 304p. 1985. text ed. 20.00 (ISBN 0-268-01716-6, 85-17161, Dist. by Har-Row). U of Notre Dame Pr.

Azuela, Mariano. Three Novels by Mariano Azuela. Hendricks, Frances K. & Berler, Beatrice, trs. from Span. LC 78-68663. 373p. 1979. 15.00 (ISBN 0-911536-78-7). Trinity U Pr.

--Two Novels of Mexico: The Flies & The Bosses. Simpson, Lesley B., tr. 1956. pap. 3.95 (ISBN 0-520-00053-6, CAL1). U of Cal Pr.

Azuelo, Mariano. Underdogs. Munguia, E., Jr., tr. (Orig.). pap. 2.95 (ISBN 0-451-51970-1, CE1741, Sig Classics). NAL.

Azuma, Hiroshi, et al. Child Development & Education in Japan. (Illus.). 400p. 1986. price not set (ISBN 0-7167-1740-9); pap. price not set (ISBN 0-7167-1741-7). W H Freeman.

Azumi, Koya. Higher Education & Business Recruitment in Japan. LC 71-81593. 1969. pap. 7.50x (ISBN 0-8077-1042-3). Tchrs Coll.

Azur, Betty S. Understanding & Using English Grammar. (Illus.). 416p. 1981. pap. text ed. 13.50 (ISBN 0-13-936492-7, Spec). P-H.

Azzalina, Claire E. The No Name Pet Name Guide. 68p. (Orig.). 1983. pap. 5.00 (ISBN 0-686-47046-X). Potpourri.

Azzam, Abd-Al-Rahman. Eternal Message of Muhammad. 1964. 9.50 (ISBN 0-8159-5401-8). Devin.

Azzam, R. M. & Bashara, N. M. Ellipsometry & Polarized Light. 530p. 1977. 113.00 (ISBN 0-444-10826-2, North-Holland). Elsevier.

--Ellipsometry & Polarized Light. xvii, 530p. 1977. 112.75 (ISBN 0-7204-0694-3, North-Holland). Elsevier.

Azzam, Salem. Islam & Contemporary Society. LC 82-253. 256p. 1982. 16.95x (ISBN 0-582-78323-2); pap. 7.95x (ISBN 0-582-78322-4). Longman.

Azzam, Salem, frwd. by. The Muslim World & the Future Economic Order. 383p. 1980. 29.95x (ISBN 0-906041-10-4, Pub. by Islamic Council of Europe England); pap. 14.95x (ISBN 0-906041-09-0). Intl Spec Bk.

Azzi, A. & Zahler, P., eds. Enzymes, Receptors & Carriers of Biological Membranes: A Laboratory Manual. (Illus.). 135p. 1984. pap. 12.00 (ISBN 0-387-13751-3). Springer-Verlag.

Azzi, A., et al, eds. Membrane Proteins: A Laboratory Manual. (Illus.). 250p. 1981. pap. 22.50 (ISBN 0-387-10749-5). Springer-Verlag.

Azzi, Abderrahmane. News Cross Culturally. 1981. 6.95 (ISBN 0-8062-1840-1). Carlton.

Azzolina, David S. Tale Type & Motif Indexes: An Annotated Bibliography. 250p. 1985. lib. bdg. 33.00 (ISBN 0-8240-8788-7). Garland Pub.

Azzolina, L. S., ed. Comparative Immunology: Proceedings of the Verona Workshop, 16-17 July 1980, Verona, Italy. (Illus.). 180p. 1982. pap. 28.00 (ISBN 0-08-028019-6). Pergamon.

Azzone, G. F., ed. Mechanisms in Bioenergetics. 1973. 70.00 (ISBN 0-12-068960-X). Acad Pr.

Azzone, G. F., ed. see Symposium on Biochemistry & Biophysics of Mitochondrial Membranes.

Azzopardi, John G. Problems in Breast Pathology. (Major Problems in Pathology Ser.: Vol. 11). (Illus.). 466p. 1979. 49.00 (ISBN 0-7216-1463-9). Saunders.

B

B., Bill. Compulsive Overeater. LC 80-70095. 1981. 12.95 (ISBN 0-89638-046-7). CompCare.

B, Bill. Maintenance: The Twelve-Step Way to Ongoing Recovery from Compulsive Overeating. 325p. 1985. 12.95 (ISBN 0-89638-091-2). CompCare.

B. E. S. T. Inventory Control with the Commodore 64. 128p. 1984. pap. cancelled (ISBN 0-88056-221-8). Dilithium pr.

B, Mary. The Adventures of Summer & Abby: A Collection of Stories. 1984. 6.95 (ISBN 0-533-05918-6). Vantage.

B., Mel. Is There Life After Sobriety? 130p. 1980. pap. 6.95 (ISBN 0-89486-101-8). Hazelden.

B, Mel. Pride. 24p. (Orig.). 1985. pap. 0.85 (ISBN 0-89486-267-7, 1397). Hazelden.

--Step Eleven: Maintaining the New Way of Life. 20p. (Orig.). 1982. pap. 0.70 (ISBN 0-89486-160-3). Hazelden.

--Step Ten: A Good Tenth Step. 20p. (Orig.). 1982. pap. 0.80 (ISBN 0-89486-153-0). Hazelden.

B. P. Foundation. Mail Order Operation. 2.00x (ISBN 0-685-22025-7). Wehman.

B-T Books, ed. see National Bureau of Standards, Automation Technology Branch.

Ba, Mallam A. Kaidara. Whitman, Daniel, tr. from French. LC 84-51200. (Illus.). 161p. 1985. 18.00 (ISBN 0-89410-137-4); pap. 8.00 (ISBN 0-89410-138-2). Three Continents.

Ba, Mariama. So Long a Letter. Thomas, Modupe Bode, tr. from Fr. (African Writers Ser.: No. 248). 96p. (Orig.). 1981. pap. text ed. 6.00x (ISBN 0-435-90248-2). Heinemann Ed.

Ba, Sylvia W. The Concept of Negritude in the Poetry of Leopold Sedar Senghor. LC 72-7797. 250p. 1973. 30.00x (ISBN 0-691-06251-X). Princeton U Pr.

Baa, Enid M., ed. Theses on Caribbean Topics, Seventeen Seventy-Eight to Nineteen Sixty-Eight. pap. 3.10 (ISBN 0-8477-2000-4). U of PR Pr.

Baack, Lawrence J. Christian Bernstorff & Prussia: Diplomacy & Reform Conservatism, 1818-1832. 1980. 32.00x (ISBN 0-8135-0884-3). Rutgers U Pr.

Baade, H. W., ed. Soviet Impact on International Law. LC 65-22170. (Library of Law & Contemporary Problems: Vol. 29, No. 4). 192p. 1965. 10.00 (ISBN 0-379-11505-0). Oceana.

Baade, Hans W. & Everett, Robinson O., eds. Academic Freedom: The Scholar's Place in Modern Society. LC 64-19353. (Library of Law & Contemporary Problems). 256p. 1964. 10.00 (ISBN 0-379-11504-2). Oceana.

--African Law, New Law for New Nations. LC 63-17558. (Library of Law & Contemporary Problems). 119p. 1963. 10.00 (ISBN 0-379-11503-4). Oceana.

Baade, Hans W., jt. ed. see Thomas, Norman C.

Baader, Horst, ed. Onze Etudes sur L'Esprit de la Satire. (Etudes Litteraires Francaise Ser.: No. 3). 219p. (Orig., Fr.). 1978. pap. 21.00x (ISBN 3-87808-882-5). Benjamins North Am.

Baadsgaard, Janene W. Is There Life After Birth? LC 83-5322. 99p. 1983. 5.95 (ISBN 0-87747-972-0). Deseret Bk.

--A Sense of Wonder. Knowles, Eleanor, ed. LC 84-71595. 140p. 1984. 7.95 (ISBN 0-87747-941-0). Deseret Bk.

Baak, J. J. van see Van Baak, J. J.

Baak, J. P. & Oort, J. A Manual of Morphometry in Diagnostic Pathology. (Illus.). 230p. 1983. 45.00 (ISBN 0-387-11431-9). Springer-Verlag.

Baaklini, Abdo I. Legislature & Political Development: Lebanon 1842-1972. LC 75-18369. 316p. 1976. 18.75 (ISBN 0-8223-0335-3). Duke.

Baaklini, Abdo I. & Heaphy, James J., eds. Comparative Legislative Reforms & Innovations. LC 77-4249. 1977. 33.50x (ISBN 0-87395-805-5). State U NY Pr.

Baal, J. van see Van Baal, J.

Ba'Alabaki, Munir. English-Arabic Pocket Dictionary: Al-Mawrid Al Quareb. (Eng. & Arabic.). 1980. pap. 5.95x (ISBN 0-86685-062-7). Intl Bk Ctr.

Ba'Albaki, Munir. English-Arabic Dictionary: Al-Mawrid. (Eng. & Arabic.). 1985. 48.00x (ISBN 0-86685-059-7). Intl Bk Ctr.

--English-Arabic Dictionary: Al-Mawrid Al-Waset. (Eng. & Arabic.). 25.00x (ISBN 0-86685-060-0). Intl Bk Ctr.

--English-Arabic Pocket Dictionary: Al Mawrid. (Arabic & Eng.). 1978. 4.00x (ISBN 0-86685-325-1). Intl Bk Ctr.

Baalen, Jan K. Van see Van Baalen, Jan K.

Baali, F. Ibn Khaldun's Science of Human Culture. 14.95 (ISBN 0-317-01604-0). Kazi Pubns.

Baali, Fuad. Relation of the People to the Land in Southern Iraq. LC 66-64914. (University of Florida Social Sciences Monographs: No. 31). 1966. 3.50 (ISBN 0-8130-0010-6). U Presses Fla.

Baal-Teshuva, Jacob. Mission of Israel. 1963. 10.95 (ISBN 0-8315-0046-8). Speller.

Baan, Jan, ed. see Ballistocardiographic Research Society 17th Meeting, Atlantic City, Apr, 1973.

Baan, Jan, et al, eds. Cardiac Dynamics: A Selection of Papers Presented at the Third International Conference on Cardiovascular System Dynamics Held at the Univ. of Leiden, the Netherlands, August 1978. (Developments in Cardiovascular Medicine Ser.: No. 2). 545p. 1980. lib. bdg. 81.50 (ISBN 90-247-2212-8). Kluwer Academic.

--Cardiovascular System Dynamics. 1978. 95.00x (ISBN 0-262-18078-2). MIT Pr.

Baar, C. A. Applied Salt Rock Mechanics, Vol. 1: The In-Situ Behavior of Salt Rocks. (Developments in Geotechnical Engineering Ser.: Vol. 16A). 296p. 1977. 68.00 (ISBN 0-444-41500-9). Elsevier.

Baar, Carl, jt. auth. see Millar, Perry S.

Baar, Charles A. Solstice Poems. 40p. (Orig.). 1983. pap. 3.00 (ISBN 0-934852-53-7). Lorien Hse.

Baarak, Erik & Sigurdson, Jon, eds. India-China Comparative Research: Technology & Science for Development. 1981. pap. 12.50x (ISBN 0-7007-0138-9, Pub. by Scandian Inst). South Asia Bks.

Baard, D. P. Hals. Stuyck, George, tr. (Library of Great Painters). (Illus.). 1981. 40.00 (ISBN 0-8109-1055-1). Abrams.

Baardman, Bob, jt. ed. see Gijlstra, D. J.

Baardseth, E. Synopsis of Biological Data on Kobbed Wrack: Ascophyllum Nodosum (Linnaeus) Le Jolis. (Fisheries Synopses: No. 38, Rev. 1). 41p. 1970. pap. 7.50 (ISBN 92-5-101895-2, F1825, FAO). Unipub.

Baark, Erik. Catalogue of Chinese Manuscripts in the Danish Archives: Chinese Diplomatic Correspondence from the Ch'ing Dynasty (1644-1911) (Studies on Asian Topics: No. 2). (Orig.). 1979. pap. text ed. 11.50x (ISBN 0-7007-0120-6). Humanities.

Baark, Erik & Sigurdson, Jon, eds. India-China Comparative Research: Technology & Science for Development. (Studies on Asian Topics: No. 3). 180p. 1980. pap. text ed. 11.00x (ISBN 0-7007-0138-9). Humanities.

Baarli, J., ed. Health & Medical Physics: Proceedings. (Enrico Fermi International Summer School of Physics Ser.: Vol. 66). 540p. 1978. 123.50 (ISBN 0-7204-0728-1, North-Holland). Elsevier.

Baars, Bernard J. The Cognitive Revolution in Psychology. xxx, 518p. 1985. text ed. write for info. (ISBN 0-89862-656-0). Guilford Pr.

Baars, Conrad. The Homosexual's Search for Happiness. (Synthesis Ser.). 1977. pap. 1.25 (ISBN 0-8199-0709-X). Franciscan Herald.

Baars, Conrad W. Born Only Once: The Miracle of Affirmation. 1977. pap. 4.00 (ISBN 0-8199-0700-6). Franciscan Herald.

--Feeling & Healing Your Emotions. LC 79-53629. 1979. pap. 5.95 (ISBN 0-88270-384-6, Pub. by Logos). Bridge Pub.

--How to Treat & Prevent the Crisis in the Priesthood. 1972. pap. 0.75 (ISBN 0-8199-0399-X). Franciscan Herald.

--A Priest for Now: Masculine & Celibate. LC 72-87091. (Synthesis Ser). 1972. pap. 1.25 (ISBN 0-8199-0375-2). Franciscan Herald.

Baars, Conrad W. & Terruwe, Anna A. Healing the Unaffirmed: Recognizing the Deprivation Neurosis. LC 76-7897. 214p. 1979. pap. 5.95 (ISBN 0-8189-0393-7). Alba.

--Psychic Wholeness & Healing: Using All the Powers of the Human Psyche. LC 81-4964. 245p. (Orig.). 1981. pap. 6.95 (ISBN 0-8189-0410-0). Alba.

Baars, Donald L. The Colorado Plateau: A Geologic History. rev. ed. LC 81-52050. 272p. 1983. 27.95 (ISBN 0-8263-0598-9); pap. 13.95 (ISBN 0-8263-0599-7). U of NM Pr.

Baas, Jacquelynn & Field, Richard. The Artistic Revival of the Woodcut in France, 1850-1900. (Illus.). 160p. 1984. pap. 15.00 (ISBN 0-912303-29-8). Michigan Mus.

Baas, Jacquelynn, et al. Treasures of the Hood Museum of Art, Dartmouth College. (Illus.). 160p. 1985. 35.00 (ISBN 0-933920-71-7); pap. 20.00 (ISBN 0-933920-72-5). Hudson Hills.

Baas, John H. History of Medicine, 2 vols. LC 70-154541. 1534p. 1971. Repr. of 1889 ed. Set. leather bdg. o.p. 90.00 (ISBN 0-88275-983-3); lib. bdg. 68.50 set (ISBN 0-88275-001-1). Krieger.

Baas, P. New Perspectives in Wood Anatomy. 1982. 54.00 (ISBN 90-247-2526-7, Pub. by Martinus Nijhoff Netherlands). Kluwer Academic.

Baase, Sara. Computer Algorithms: Introduction to Design & Analysis. LC 77-81197. 1978. text ed. 31.95 (ISBN 0-201-00327-9). Addison-Wesley.

--VAX-11 Assembly Language Programming. (Computer Science Ser.). (Illus.). 416p. 1983. text ed. 29.95 (ISBN 0-13-940957-2). P-H.

Baasel, W. D. Preliminary Chemical Engineering Plant Design. 2nd & rev. ed. 500p. 1984. write for info. (ISBN 0-444-00890-X). Elsevier.

Baasel, William D. Preliminary Chemical Engineering Plant Design. LC 74-19453. xiv, 490p. 1976. 44.50 (ISBN 0-444-00152-2). Elsevier.

Baasher, T. A., et al, eds. see WHO Seminar on the Organization of Mental Health Services, Addis Ababa, 1973.

Baatz, Charles A., ed. Philosophy of Education: A Guide to Information Sources. (Education Information Guide Ser.: Vol. 6). 1980. 60.00x (ISBN 0-8103-1452-5). Gale.

Baatz, Charles A. & Baatz, Olga K., eds. The Psychological Foundations of Education: A Guide to Information Sources. (Education Information Guide Ser.: Vol. 10). 350p. 1981. 55.00x (ISBN 0-8103-1467-3). Gale.

Baatz, Olga K., jt. ed. see Baatz, Charles A.

Baatz, Simon. Venerate the Plough: A History of the Philadelphia Society for Promoting Agriculture, 1785-1985. LC 84-26453. (Illus.). 124p. 1985. 25.00 (ISBN 0-9614267-0-5). Phila Soc Prom.

Baatz, Wilmer H., jt. ed. see Klotman, Phyllis R.

Bab. Selections from the Writings of the Bab. LC 79-670141. 1976. 10.95 (ISBN 0-85398-066-7, 105-050); pap. 6.00 (ISBN 0-85398-135-3). Baha'i.

Bab, Werner. The Uses of Psychology in Geriatric Ophthalmology. 104p. 1964. 11.75x (ISBN 0-398-00074-3). C C Thomas.

Baba, Bangali. The Yogasutra of Patanjali. 2nd rev. ed. 1979. pap. 9.95 (ISBN 0-8426-0916-4, Pub. by Motilal Banarsidass India). Orient Bk Dist.

Baba, Meher. Darshan Hours. Jessawala, Eruch & Chapman, Rick, eds. 80p. 1973. 5.95 (ISBN 0-940700-06-9); pap. 3.45 (ISBN 0-940700-05-0). Meher Baba Info.

--The Everything & the Nothing. 100p. (Orig.). 1963. pap. 3.45 (ISBN 0-940700-00-X). Meher Baba Info.

--The Everything & the Nothing. 1976. 70p. 4.95, (ISBN 0-913078-49-2, Pub. by R J Mistry India); pap. 2.95, 115p. (ISBN 0-913078-48-4). Sheriar Pr.

--The Face of God. (Illus.). 28p. pap. 1.75 (ISBN 0-913078-00-X). Sheriar Pr.

--The Narrow Lane. Le Page, William, ed. 148p. 1979. pap. 3.95 (ISBN 0-913078-39-5). Sheriar Pr.

--Not We but One: Meher Baba on Life, Living & Love. Le Page, William, ed. 148p. 1977. pap. 3.95 (ISBN 0-913078-33-6). Sheriar Pr.

--Sparks of the Truth: From the Dissertations of Meher Baba. Deshmukh, C. D., ed. (Illus.). 96p. (Orig.). 1971. pap. 2.95 (ISBN 0-913078-02-6). Sheriar Pr.

Baba, Meher, ed. God to Man & Man to God. 287p. 1984. 8.95 (ISBN 0-913078-27-1); pap. 6.95 (ISBN 0-913078-21-2). Sheriar Pr.

Baba, Meher, et al. Meher Baba Journal, Vol. 1, No. 11. Patterson, Elizabeth ed. (No. 11). (Illus.). 66p. 1974. pap. 2.50x (ISBN 0-913078-18-2). Sheriar Pr.

--Meher Baba Journal, Vol. 1, No. 6. Patterson, Elizabeth C., ed. (Illus.). 68p. 1972. pap. 2.50x (ISBN 0-913078-10-7). Sheriar Pr.

--Meher Baba Journal, Vol. 1, No. 7. Patterson, Elizabeth C., ed. (Illus.). 68p. 1972. pap. 2.50x (ISBN 0-913078-11-5). Sheriar Pr.

--Meher Baba Journal, Vol. 1, No. 9. Patterson, Elizabeth C., ed. (Illus.). 1973. pap. 2.50x (ISBN 0-913078-13-1). Sheriar Pr.

--Meher Baba Journal, Vol. 1, No. 10. Patterson, Elizabeth C., ed. (Illus.). 1973. pap. 2.50x (ISBN 0-913078-14-X). Sheriar Pr.

--Treasures from the Meher Baba Journals. Haynes, Jane B., ed. LC 79-92169. (Illus.). 246p. 1980. pap. 6.95 (ISBN 0-913078-37-9). Sheriar Pr.

Baba, N. New Topics in Learning Automata Theory & Applications. (Lecture Notes in Control & Information Sciences: Vol. 71). 150p. 1985. pap. 10.00 (ISBN 0-387-15613-5). Springer-Verlag.

Baba, Shigeaki, et al, eds. Diabetes Mellitus: Recent Knowledge on Aetiology, Complications & Treatment. 272p. 1984. 29.00 (ISBN 0-12-069450-6). Acad Pr.

Baba, V. V., jt. auth. see Kelly, Joe.

Bababunmi, E. A. & Smith, R. L. Toxicology in the Tropics. 280p. 1980. 37.50 (ISBN 0-85066-194-3, Pub. by Taylor & Francis England). J K Burgess.

Bababunmi, E. A., jt. ed. see Smith, R. L.

Babad, A., tr. see Ahnefeld, F. W., et al.

Babad, Elisha Y. & Birnbaum, Max. The Social Self: Group Influences on Personal Identity. LC 82-21553. (Sage Library of Social Research). (Illus.). 267p. 28.00 (ISBN 0-8039-1938-7); pap. 14.00 (ISBN 0-8039-1939-5). Sage.

Baba Hari Dass. Hariakhan Baba-Known, Unknown. LC 75-3838. (Illus.). 96p. (Orig.). 1975. pap. 2.50 (ISBN 0-918100-00-3). Sri Rama.

--Mystic Monkey. LC 81-51051. (Illus.). 64p. (Orig.). (gr. 4-8). 1984. pap. 7.95 (ISBN 0-918100-05-4). Sri Rama.

Babakina, V. S., ed. Grain & Pulse Crops. 255p. 1981. 60.00x (ISBN 0-686-76641-5, Pub. by Oxford & IBH India). State Mutual Bk.

Babalova, L. L., et al. Russian for Everybody: Recorded Supplement. 94p. 1983. 10.95 (ISBN 0-8285-2610-9, Pub. by Rus Lang Pubs USSR). Imported Pubns.

Babansky, Yuri K. & Bota, Liviu. UNESCO Yearbook on Peace & Conflict Studies: 1982. 269p. (Orig.). 1984. pap. 35.00 (ISBN 92-3-102119-2, U1339, UNESCO). Unipub.

Babar, Emperor of Hindustan. Babur-Nama in English: Memoirs of Babur, 2 Vols. Beveridge, Annette S., tr. LC 72-161719. (BCL Ser.: No. I). Repr. of 1922 ed. Set. 85.00 (ISBN 0-404-00510-1). AMS Pr.

Babary, J. P., jt. auth. see IFAC Symposium, 3rd, Toulouse, France, June-July 1982.

Babayan, E. A., et al, eds. Modern Approaches to the Treatment of Hypertension. 1976. 10.75 (ISBN 3-8055-2400-5). S Karger.

Babayan, Edward A. The Structure of Psychiatry in the USSR. 350p. 40.00 (ISBN 0-8236-6169-5). Intl Univs Pr.
--Textbook of Alcoholism & Drug Abuse. 1984. text ed. 30.00 (ISBN 0-8236-6470-8). Intl Univs Pr.
Babb, Emerson M. Purdue Grain Elevator Management Game. 1979. Repr. of 1973 ed. 6.25x (ISBN 0-933836-06-6). Simtek.
--Purdue Supermarket Chain Management Game. rev. ed. 1979. student's manual 6.25x (ISBN 0-933836-07-4). Simtek.
Babb, Henry C. & Wake Forest University. Continuing Legal Education. North Carolina Contract Practice Manual. LC 85-118032. (Illus.). Date not set. price not set. Wake Forest Law.
Babb, Hugh W. & Martin, Charles. Business Law. 3rd ed. 400p. (Orig.). 1981. pap. 6.50 (ISBN 0-06-460198-6, COS 198, COS). B&N NY.
Babb, Hugh W., tr. see Lenin, V. I., et al.
Babb, Hugh W., tr. see Petrazhitskii, Lev I.
Babb, Hugh W., tr. see Vyshinskii, Andrei I.
Babb, Janice B. & Dordick, B. F., eds. Real Estate Information Sources. LC 63-16246. (Management Information Guide Ser.: No. 1). 1963. 60.00x (ISBN 0-8103-0801-0). Gale.
Babb, Jewel & Taylor, Pat E. Border Healing Woman: The Story of Jewel Babb. (Illus.). 152p. 1981. text ed. 16.95x (ISBN 0-292-70729-0); pap. 7.95 (ISBN 0-292-70730-4). U of Tex Pr.
Babb, Kenneth R. Diesel Engine Service. 1984. text ed. 29.95 (ISBN 0-8359-1291-4). Reston.
Babb, L. The Physiological Concept of Love in the Elizabethan & Early Stuart Drama. 59.95 (ISBN 0-8490-0833-6). Gordon Pr.
Babb, Lawrence. Moral Cosmos of Paradise Lost. 1970. 7.50 (ISBN 0-87013-154-0). Mich St U Pr.
--Sanity in Bedlam: A Study of Robert Burton's "Anatomy of Melancholy". LC 77-13309. 1977. lib. bdg. 18.75 (ISBN 0-8371-9856-9, BBSB). Greenwood.
Babb, Lawrence A. The Divine Hierarchy: Popular Hinduism in Central India. (Illus.). 266p. 1975. 26.00x (ISBN 0-231-03882-8). Columbia U Pr.
Babb, Warren, tr. see Palisca, Claude V.
Babbage, C. Reflections on the Decline of Science in England & on Some of Its Causes. 256p. 1971. Repr. of 1830 ed. 25.00x (ISBN 0-7165-1578-4, BBA 02134, Pub. by Irish Academic Pr Ireland). Biblio Dist.
Babbage, Charles. Comparative View of the Various Institutions for the Assurance of Lives. LC 67-18568. Repr. of 1826 ed. 25.00x (ISBN 0-678-00335-1). Kelley.
--Ninth Bridgewater Treatise Fragment. 270p. 1967. Repr. of 1837 ed. 27.50x (ISBN 0-7146-1106-9, F Cass Co). Biblio Dist.
--On the Economy of Machinery & Manufactures. 4th ed. LC 74-22019. Repr. of 1835 ed. 39.50x (ISBN 0-678-00001-8). Kelley.
--Passages from the Life of a Philosopher. LC 67-30854. Repr. of 1864 ed. 45.00x (ISBN 0-678-00479-X). Kelley.
--Reflections on the Decline of Science in England. LC 77-115928. Repr. of 1830 ed. 27.50x (ISBN 0-678-00645-8). Kelley.
Babbage, Charles, et al. Charles Babbage: On the Principle & Development of the Calculator & Other Seminal Writings. 400p. 1984. pap. 7.95 (ISBN 0-486-24691-4). Dover.
Babbage, Henry. Babbage's Calculating Engines. (Charles Babbage Institute Reprint for the History of Computing Ser.: Vol. 2). (Illus.). 390p. 1984. Repr. of 1889 ed. text ed. 55.00x (ISBN 0-262-02200-1). MIT Pr.
--Babbage's Calculating Machines. (Charles Babbage Reprint Ser.). (Illus.). 390p. 1984. 55.00x. MIT Pr.
Babbage, Henry P., ed. Babbage's Calculating Engines. (The Charles Babbage Institute Reprint Series for the History of Computing: Vol. 2). (Illus.). 1983. Repr. of 1889 ed. 55.00x (ISBN 0-938228-04-8). Tomash Pubs.
Babbage, Ross. Rethinking Australia's Defence. (Illus.). 312p. 1981. text ed. 30.25x (ISBN 0-7022-1486-8). U of Queensland Pr.
Babbage, Ross, et al. The Development of Australian Army Officers for the 1980s. (Canberra Papers on Strategy & Defence: No. 17). 1979. pap. text ed. 2.50 (ISBN 0-909851-35-2, Pub. by ANUP Australia). Australia N U P.
Babbage, Stuart B. Puritanism & Richard Bancroft. LC 63-2799. (Church Historical Society Ser.: No. 84). 1962. 20.00x (ISBN 0-8401-5084-9). A R Allenson.
--Sex & Sanity: A Christian View of Sexual Morality. rev. ed. LC 67-11492. 1967. Westminster.
Babbidge, Homer D. & Rosenzweig, Robert M. The Federal Interest in Higher Education. LC 74-25991. 214p. 1975. Repr. of 1962 ed. lib. bdg. 15.50x (ISBN 0-8371-7882-7, BAFI). Greenwood.
Babbidge, Homer D., jt. auth. see Watney, Bernard M.
Babbidge, Homer D., intro. by see Dodge, Marshall & Bryan, Robert.
Babbie. Procedures Disk for Apple LOGO for Teachers. 1984. write for info. (ISBN 0-317-14709-9). Wadsworth Pub.
Babbie, Earl. You Can Make a Difference: The Heroic Potential Within Us All. 224p. 1985. 14.95 (ISBN 0-312-89673-5). St Martin.
Babbie, Earl R. The Practice of Social Research. 4th ed. 600p. 1985. text ed. write for info. (ISBN 0-534-05658-X). Wadsworth Pub.
--Social Research for Consumers. 400p. 1982. text ed. write for info. (ISBN 0-534-01125-X). Wadsworth Pub.
--Sociology: An Introduction. 3rd ed. 736p. 1983. pap. write for info. (ISBN 0-534-01366-X). Wadsworth Pub.
--Survey Research Methods: A Cookbook & Other Fables. 320p. 1973. write for info. (ISBN 0-534-00224-2). Wadsworth Pub.
--Understanding Sociology: A Context for Action. 464p. 1981. pap. text ed. write for info. (ISBN 0-534-01024-5). Wadsworth Pub.
Babbin, Kenneth & Oleksy, Walter. Reach for the Stars: Helping Yourself With Personal Astrology. 1982. pap. 4.95 (ISBN 0-686-97517-0, Reward). P-H.
Babbin, Toni, jt. auth. see Horne, Ross.
Babbington, Bruce & Evans, Peter. Blue Skies & Silver Linings: Aspects of the Hollywood Musical. LC 84-25046. 1985. 19.00 (ISBN 0-7190-1739-4, Pub. by Manchester Univ Pr). Longwood Pub Group.
Babbini, Barbara E. Manual Communication: Fingerspelling & the Language of Signs. LC 72-94999. (Illus.). 203p. 1974. instructor's manual 17.50x (ISBN 0-252-00334-9); student manual 12.00x (ISBN 0-252-00333-0). U of Ill Pr.
Babbit, Colette O. Medical Mass Screening for Health & Disease: Research Survey Index with Reference Bibliography. 1985. 29.95 (ISBN 0-88164-370-X); pap. 21.95 (ISBN 0-88164-371-8). ABBE Pubs Assn.
Babbit, Harold W., jt. auth. see Gotherman, John E.
Babbit, Irving. The New Laokoon. 259p. 1980. Repr. of 1910 ed. lib. bdg. 40.00 (ISBN 0-89760-049-5). Telegraph Bks.
Babbitt, Bruce. Grand Canyon: An Anthology. LC 78-58470. (Illus.). 1978. 15.95 (ISBN 0-87358-180-6). Northland.
--Grand Canyon: An Anthology. LC 78-58470. (Illus.). 276p. 1980. pap. 8.95 (ISBN 0-87358-275-6). Northland.
Babbitt, Edmond H. Pastor's Pocket Manual for Hospital & Sickroom. 1949. 6.95 (ISBN 0-687-30265-X). Abingdon.
Babbitt, Edwin D. Principles of Light & Color. (Illus.). 578p. Date not set. 27.00 (ISBN 0-89540-060-X, SB-060). Sun Pub.
Babbitt, Edwin S. The Principles of Light & Color. 1980. pap. text ed. 7.95 (ISBN 0-8065-0748-9). Citadel Pr.
Babbitt, Ellen. Granny's Blackie. (Envelope Bks.). (Illus.). 1982. pap. 2.50 (ISBN 0-88138-007-5). Green Tiger Pr.
Babbitt, Elwood & Hapgood, Charles. The God Within: A Testament of Vishnu; A Handbook for the Spiritual Renaissance. LC 82-83874. (Orig.). 1982. 12.95 (ISBN 0-913917-02-8); pap. 6.95 (ISBN 0-913917-03-6). Fine Line.
Babbitt, Harold E. Plumbing. 3rd ed. 1959. 61.50 (ISBN 0-07-002688-2). McGraw.
Babbitt, Irving. Democracy & Leadership. LC 78-11418. 1979. 9.00 (ISBN 0-913966-54-1, Liberty Clas); pap. 4.00 (ISBN 0-913966-55-X). Liberty Fund.
--Irving Babbitt: Representative Writings. Panichas, George A., ed. LC 81-2968. xl, 316p. 1981. 23.95x (ISBN 0-8032-3655-7). U of Nebr Pr.
--Literature & the American College: Essays in Defense of the Humanities. LC 74-138537. 263p. Repr. of 1908 ed. lib. bdg. 25.00x (ISBN 0-678-03561-X). Kelley.
--The Master of Modern French Criticism. LC 76-56408. 1977. Repr. of 1912 ed. lib. bdg. 27.50x (ISBN 0-8371-9415-6, BAMF). Greenwood.
--The Masters of Modern French Criticism. 426p. 1981. Repr. of 1912 ed. lib. bdg. 40.00 (ISBN 0-8495-0469-4). Arden Lib.
--Rousseau & Romanticism. LC 75-28989. (BCL Ser.: No. II). 1976. Repr. of 1919 ed. 26.50 (ISBN 0-404-14000-9). AMS Pr.
--Spanish Character, & Other Essays: With a Bibliography of His Publications & an Index to His Collected Works. Manchester, Frederick, et al, eds. LC 83-45695. Repr. of 1940 ed. 29.50 (ISBN 0-404-20013-3). AMS Pr.
Babbitt, Irving, tr. see Buddha, Gautama.
Babbitt, Katharine M. Janet Montgomery: Hudson River Squire. LC 75-9600. 60p. 1975. pap. text ed. 3.45 (ISBN 0-912526-18-1). Lib Res.
Babbitt, Lucy C. The Oval Amulet. LC 83-49479. 224p. (YA) (gr. 7 up). 1985. 12.98i (ISBN 0-06-020299-8); PLB 13.89g (ISBN 0-06-020301-3). HarpJ.
Babbitt, Natalie. The Devil's Storybook. LC 74-5488. (Illus.). 112p. (ps up). 1974. 3.45 (ISBN 0-374-41708-3). FS&G.
--The Devil's Storybook. (Illus.). (gr. 6 up). pap. 3.45 (ISBN 0-317-13268-7). FS&G.
--The Eyes of the Amaryllis. LC 77-11862. 160p. (gr. 3 up). 1977. 9.95 (ISBN 0-374-32241-4). FS&G.
--Goody Hall. LC 73-149221. (Illus.). 92p. (gr. 4 up). 1971. 10.95 (ISBN 0-374-32745-9). FS&G.
--Herbert Rowbarge. LC 82-18274. 216p. (gr. 9 up). 1982. 11.95 (ISBN 0-374-32959-1); pap. 3.95 (ISBN 0-374-51852-1). FS&G.
--Knee-Knock Rise. (gr. 3-6). 1974. pap. 1.50 (ISBN 0-380-00849-1, 44875, Camelot). Avon.
--Kneeknock Rise. LC 79-105622. (Illus.). 118p. (gr. 3 up). 1970. 9.95 (ISBN 0-374-34257-1); pap. 3.45 (ISBN 0-374-44260-6). FS&G.
--Phoebe's Revolt. LC 68-13679. (Illus.). 40p. (ps-3). 1977. pap. 9.95 (ISBN 0-374-35907-5). FS&G.
--The Search for Delicious. (gr. 3-7). 1974. pap. 1.50 (ISBN 0-380-01541-2, 42085, Camelot). Avon.
--The Search for Delicious. LC 69-20374. (Illus.). 176p. (gr. 3 up). 1969. 10.95 (ISBN 0-374-36534-2); pap. 3.45 (ISBN 0-374-46536-3). FS&G.
--The Something. (Illus.). 32p. (gr. k-2). 1980. pap. 1.50 (ISBN 0-440-49050-2, YB). Dell.
--The Something. LC 70-125143. 40p. (ps-3). 1970. 6.95 (ISBN 0-374-37137-7). FS&G.
--Tuck Everlasting. LC 75-33306. 144p. (gr. 3 up). 1975. 10.95 (ISBN 0-374-37848-7); pap. 3.45 (ISBN 0-374-48009-5). FS&G.
Babbitt, Susan. Oresme's Livre de Politiques & the France of Charles V. LC 84-71076. (Transaction Ser.: Vol. 75, Pt. 1). 156p. 1985. 15.00 (ISBN 0-87169-751-3). Am Philos.
Babbitt, Theodore. Cronica De Veinte Reyes. LC 74-38494. (Yale Romanic Studies: No. 13). Repr. of 1936 ed. 24.00 (ISBN 0-404-53213-6). AMS Pr.
--Cronica de Veinte Reyes. 1936. 13.50x (ISBN 0-686-83515-8). Elliots Bks.
Babbush, Charles A. Surgical Atlas of Dental Implant Techniques. LC 78-65373. (Illus.). 280p. 1980. text ed. 49.00 (ISBN 0-7216-1474-4). Saunders.
Babbush, H. Edward & Bormann, Allen G. College Relations & Recruiting: A Guide for Developing an Effective Program. LC 82-71184. 1982. 11.95 (ISBN 0-913936-18-9). Coll Placement.
Babby, Leonard H. Existential Sentences & Negation in Russian. (Linguistica Extranea: Studia: No. 8). 199p. 1980. 12.50 (ISBN 0-89720-013-6); pap. 7.50 (ISBN 0-89720-014-4). Karoma.
--A Transformational Grammar of Russian Adjectives. LC 73-83929. (Janua Linguarum, Ser. Practica: No. 235). 242p. 1975. pap. text ed. 39.20x (ISBN 90-2793-022-8). Mouton.
Babco, Eleanor L., jt. ed. see Vetter, Betty M.
Babcock, Arthur E. Portraits of Artists: Reflexivity in Gidean Fiction, 1902-1936. 127p. 1981. 14.95 (ISBN 0-917786-26-2). Summa Pubns.
Babcock, Barbara, jt. auth. see Carrington, Paul.
Babcock, Barbara A. & Freedman, Ann. E. Sex Discrimination & the Law (1975) Causes & Remedies. 1092p. 1975. 33.00 (ISBN 0-316-07420-9); Suppl., 1978. pap. 7.95 (ISBN 0-316-07421-7). Little.
Babcock, C. Merton. Some Expressions from Herman Melville. Bd. with A Word-Finder List for Whiz Mob. Maurer, David W; Louis Pound: In Memoriam. (Publications of the American Dialect Society: No. 31). 41p. 1959. pap. 4.20 (ISBN 0-8173-0631-5). U of Ala Pr.
--A Word-List from Zora Neale Hurston. Bd. with To As Preposition of Location in Linguistic Atlas Materials. McDavid, Virginia; The Nineteen Hundred Sixty-One Conference on Dialectology. McDavid, Raven I. & Larsen, Vernon S.. (Publications of the American Dialect Society: No. 40). 38p. 1963. pap. 3.95 (ISBN 0-8173-0640-4). U of Ala Pr.
Babcock, C. Merton, ed. Ideas in Process. LC 72-113343. (Essay & General Literature Index Reprint Ser). 1971. Repr. of 1958 ed. 29.50x (ISBN 0-8046-1397-4, Pub. by Kennikat). Assoc Faculty Pr.
Babcock, Charlotte M., et al, eds. Windsingers. 125p. (Orig.). 1984. pap. text ed. write for info. (ISBN 0-917557-01-8). Wyo Writers.
Babcock, Clarence L. Silicate Glass Technology Methods. LC 84-27821. 336p. 1985. Repr. of 1977 ed. lib. bdg. write for info. (ISBN 0-89874-831-3). Krieger.
--Silicate Glass Technology Methods. LC 76-30716. (Wiley Series in Pure & Applied Optics). pap. 84.00 (ISBN 0-317-28068-6, 2055768). Bks Demand UMI.
Babcock, David, jt. auth. see Gruenberger, Fred.
Babcock, Denise L. NFPA Fire Protection Reference Directory, 1979. 4th ed. 1980. pap. 8.00. Natl Fire Prot.
Babcock, Dennis & Boyd, Preston. Careers in the Theater. LC 74-11907. (Early Career Bks.). (Illus.). 36p. (gr. 2-5). 1975. PLB 5.95 (ISBN 0-8225-0324-7). Lerner Pubns.
Babcock, Dorothy E. Introduction to Growth, Development & Family Life. 3rd ed. 192p. 1972. pap. text ed. 7.50x (ISBN 0-8036-0541-2). Davis Co.
Babcock, Dorothy E. & Keepers, Terry D. Raising Kids O. K. 1977. pap. 1.95 (ISBN 0-380-00937-4, 31989-6). Avon.
Babcock, Emily A., ed. see William, Archbishop of Tyre.
Babcock, Havilah. I don't want to Shoot an Elephant & other Stories. LC 58-7636. 184p. 1985. 19.95 (ISBN 0-318-12127-1); limited handbound 200.00 (ISBN 0-318-12128-X). Gunnerman Pr.
--Jaybirds go to Hell on Friday & other Stories. LC 64-21917. 149p. 1985. Repr. of 1964 ed. 19.95 (ISBN 0-318-12125-5); limited handbound 200.00 (ISBN 0-318-12126-3). Gunnerman Pr.
--My Health Is Better in November: Thirty-Five Stories of Hunting & Fishing in the South. (Illus.). 284p. 1985. 19.95 (ISBN 0-87249-440-3). U of SC Pr.
--Tails of Quails n' Such. (Illus.). 237p. 1985. Repr. of 1951 ed. 19.95 (ISBN 0-87249-441-1). U of SC Pr.
Babcock, Henry. Appraisal Principles & Procedures. 289p. 1980. pap. text ed. 20.00 (ISBN 0-937828-19-X). Am Soc Appraisers.
Babcock, James C., tr. & intro. by see Huysmans, J. K.
Babcock, James C., et al, eds. Gorostiza's Contigo Pan y Cebolla. LC 49-8551. (Graded Spanish Readers, Bk. 3). (Span). (gr. 10-11). 1953. pap. text ed. 6.50 (ISBN 0-395-04126-0). HM.
--Marmol's Amalia. LC 49-8551. (Graded Spanish Readers Ser.: Bk. 1). (Span). (gr. 10-11). 1949. pap. text ed. 6.95 (ISBN 0-395-04124-4). HM.
Babcock, Judy & Kennedy, Judy. The Spa Book: A Guided, Personal Tour of Health Resorts & Beauty Spas for Men & Women. LC 82-18249. (Illus.). 288p. 1983. 14.95 (ISBN 0-517-54950-6). Crown.
Babcock, K. W. Rise of American Nationality 1811-1819. LC 68-24970. (American History & Americana Ser., No. 47). 1969. Repr. of 1906 ed. lib. bdg. 49.95x (ISBN 0-8383-0910-0). Haskell.
Babcock, Kendric C. Scandinavian Element in the United States. LC 69-18757. (American Immigration Collection Ser., No. 1). 1969. Repr. of 1914 ed. 10.00 (ISBN 0-405-00505-9). Ayer Co Pubs.
--The Scandinavian Element in the United States. 15.00 (ISBN 0-384-02915-9). Johnson Repr.
Babcock, Maltbie D. Letters from Egypt & Palestine. Davis, Moshe, ed. LC 77-70662. (America & the Holy Land Ser.). (Illus.). 1977. Repr. of 1902 ed. lib. bdg. 19.00x (ISBN 0-405-10223-2). Ayer Co Pubs.
Babcock, Molly, jt. auth. see Tiger, Peggy.
Babcock, Nicolas. Billy's Army. LC 81-69129. (Illus.). 256p. 1982. 14.95 (ISBN 0-689-11242-4). Atheneum.
Babcock, Richard F. Billboards, Glass Houses, & the Law, & Other Land Use Fables. LC 76-58488. 1977. pap. 7.95 (ISBN 0-07-002801-X, Shepards-McGraw). McGraw.
--Zoning Game: Municipal Practices & Policies. (Illus.). 218p. 1966. 20.00x (ISBN 0-299-04091-7); pap. 9.50x (ISBN 0-299-04094-1). U of Wis Pr.
Babcock, Richard F. & Banta, John S. New Zoning Techniques for Inner-City Areas. (PAS Reports: No. 297). 60p. 1973. 6.00 (ISBN 0-318-13036-X). Am Plan Assn.
Babcock, Richard F. & Bosselman, Fred P. Exclusionary Zoning: Land-Use Regulation & Housing in the 1970s. 210p. 1973. pap. 5.95 (ISBN 0-318-12982-5). Am Plan ASsn.
Babcock, Richard F., jt. auth. see Weaver, Clifford L.
Babcock, Robert H. Gompers in Canada: A Study in American Continentalism Before the First World War. LC 74-78507. pap. 75.50 (ISBN 0-317-27774-X, 2055958). Bks Demand UMI.
Babcock, Robert T. A Long-Time Cowboy. (Illus.). 1978. 7.50 (ISBN 0-685-42183-X). Word Serv.
Babcock, Robert W. The Genesis of Shakespeare Idolatry, 1766-1799. LC 75-28990. Repr. of 1931 ed. 24.50 (ISBN 0-404-14001-7). AMS Pr.
Babcock, Rufus, ed. see Peck, John M.
Babcock, Sandra S. Syntax of Spanish Reflexive Verbs: The Parameters of the Middle Verb. LC 74-106468. (Janua Linguarum, Ser. Practica: No. 105). (Orig.). 1970. pap. text ed. 12.80 (ISBN 90-2790-742-0). Mouton.
Babcock, U. C., ed. see Eoff, Sherman, et al.
Babcock, Weston. Hamlet: A Tragedy of Errors. 134p. 1984. Repr. of 1961 ed. lib. bdg. 45.00 (ISBN 0-89760-174-2). Telegraph Bks.
Babcock, William H. Early Norse Visits to North America. 1976. lib. bdg. 59.95 (ISBN 0-8490-1742-4). Gordon Pr.
--Legendary Islands of the Atlantic. (Illus.). 196p. 1984. Repr. of 1922 ed. photocopy 12.95 (ISBN 0-915554-17-8). Sourcebook.
--Legendary Islands of the Atlantic: Study in Medieval Geography. LC 72-8459. (Select Bibliography Reprint Ser.). 1972. Repr. of 1922 ed. 18.00 (ISBN 0-8369-6963-4). Ayer Co Pubs.
Babcock, Winifred. Jung, Hesse, Harold: Contributions of C. G. Jung, Hermann Hesse, and Preston Harold to Spiritual Psychology. LC 83-12945. 1983. 14.95 (ISBN 0-396-08082-0); pap. 8.95 (ISBN 0-396-08113-4). Dodd.
Babcox, Neil. A Search for Charismatic Reality: One Man's Pilgrimage. LC 84-25506. 160p. 1985. pap. 5.95 (ISBN 0-88070-085-8). Multnomah.
Babe, R. E. Cable Television & Telecommunications in Canada: An Economic Analysis. LC 75-620061. 338p. 1975. pap. 7.50 (ISBN 0-87744-129-4). Mich St U Pr.
Babe, Thomas. Fathers & Sons. pap. 3.35x (ISBN 0-686-69574-7). Dramatists Play.
Babe Winkelman. The Comprehensive Guide to Fish Locators. Babe Winkelman Production Staff, ed. (Illus., Orig.). pap. 19.95 (ISBN 0-915405-02-4). B Winkelman Prods.
--The Comprehensive Guide to Walleye Patterns. Grooms, Steve, ed. (Illus.). 319p. (Orig.). 1985. pap. 11.95 (ISBN 0-915405-01-6). B Winkelman Prods.

Babe Winkelman Production Staff, ed. see Babe Winkelman.

Babeau, Albert A. La Province Sous l'Ancien Regime, 2 vols. LC 77-161720. Date not set. 65.00 set (ISBN 0-404-07506-1). AMS Pr.

--Le Village Sous L'Ancien Regime. 3rd rev. & enl. ed. LC 70-161721. Repr. of 1882 ed. 26.00 (ISBN 0-404-07509-6). AMS Pr.

--Ville sous l'ancien regime, 2 Vols. 2nd ed. Repr. of 1884 ed. Set. 65.00 (ISBN 0-404-07516-9). Vol. 1 (ISBN 0-404-07517-7). Vol. 2 (ISBN 0-404-07518-5). AMS Pr.

Babel, Isaac. Collected Stories. Morison, Walter, ed. & tr. pap. 7.95 (ISBN 0-452-00667-8, F667, Mer). NAL.

--A Letter. Goldberg, Isaac, ed. Deutsch, Babette, tr. (International Pocket Library). pap. 3.00 (ISBN 0-8283-1450-0). Branden Pub Co.

--You Must Know Everything. Babel, Nathalie, ed. Hayward, Max, tr. from Rus. 283p. 1969. 10.95 (ISBN 0-374-29408-9); pap. 6.95 (ISBN 0-374-51580-8). FS&G.

--You Must Know Everything. Hayward, Max, tr. 304p. 1984. pap. 8.95 (ISBN 0-88184-027-0). Carroll & Graf.

Babel, Isaac see Goldberg, Isaac.

Babel, Isaak. Bluzhdaiushchie Zvezdy. 1981. pap. 6.00 (ISBN 0-686-74657-0). Ardis Pubs.

--Konarmiia. (Rus.). 1982. 16.00 (ISBN 0-88233-846-3). Ardis Pubs.

Babel, Isaak E. Benia Krik: A Film Novel. Montagu, Ivor & Nalbandov, Sergei, trs. from Rus. LC 72-90292. (Soviet Literature in English Translation Ser.). 95p. 1973. Repr. of 1935 ed. 15.00 (ISBN 0-88355-000-8). Hyperion Conn.

--Istoriia Moei Golubiatni. (Rus.). 1978. pap. 3.00 (ISBN 0-933884-03-6). Berkeley Slavic.

Babel, Issac & Yarmolinsky, Avraham. Benya Krik, the Gangster & Other Stories. 128p. 1985. pap. 4.95 (ISBN 0-8052-0244-7). Schocken.

Babel, John S., jt. auth. see Gunstream, Stanley E.

Babel, Nathalie, ed. see Babel, Isaac.

Babelon, E. Origines de La Monnaie a Athenes. 1985. Repr. of 1905 ed. 20.00 (ISBN 0-89005-406-1). Ares.

Babelon, Ernest. Introduction Generale a l'etude des Monnaies de l'antiquite. Finley, Moses, ed. LC 79-4960. (Ancient Economic History). (Fr.). 1980. Repr. of 1901 ed. lib. bdg. 34.50x (ISBN 0-405-12348-5). Ayer Co Pubs.

--Les Origines De la Monnaie a Athenes. (Illus.). 92p. (Fr.). 1979. Repr. of 1905 ed. 20.00 (ISBN 0-916710-59-9). Obol Intl.

Babelon, Ernest C. Origines de la monnaie considerees au point de vue economique et historique. LC 77-129030. (Research & Source Works Ser.: No. 530). (Fr). 1970. Repr. of 1897 ed. lib. bdg. 29.00 (ISBN 0-8337-0142-8). B Franklin.

Babelon, Jean. Histoire de l'Art: L'Europe Medievale, Vol. 2. (Historique Ser.). 1760p. 63.50 (ISBN 0-686-56451-0). French & Eur.

--Histoire de l'Art: Renaissance, Baroque, Romantisme, Vol. 3. (Historique Ser.). 1712p. 63.50 (ISBN 0-686-56452-9). French & Eur.

Babenko, K. I. On the Theory of Extremal Problems for Univalent Functions of Class S. (Proceedings of the Steklov Institute of Mathematics: No. 101). 1974. 90.00 (ISBN 0-8218-3001-5, STEKLO-101). Am Math.

Babenko, K. I., et al. Twelve Papers on Approximations & Integrals. LC 51-5559. (Translations Ser.: No. 2, Vol. 44). 1966. Repr. of 1965 ed. 24.00 (ISBN 0-8218-1744-2, TRANS 2-44). Am Math.

Baber, Alfred W. Handbook of Hi-Fi Audio Systems & Projects. 235p. 1981. 18.95 (ISBN 0-13-378307-3, Parker). P-H.

Baber, Asa. Tranquillity Base & Other Stories. LC 79-89138. 140p. 1979. pap. 5.00 (ISBN 0-931362-01-6). Fiction Intl.

Baber, Bob H., ed. Time Is an Eight Ball. 88p. 1984. pap. 6.00 (ISBN 0-940510-08-1). Tooth of Time.

Baber, Colin & Jeffrey, Henry B. The Co-Operative Republic of Guyana: Politics, Economics & Society. Szajkowski, Bogdan, ed. LC 84-62669. (Marxist Regimes Ser.). (Illus.). 160p. 1986. lib. bdg. 22.50x (ISBN 0-931477-23-9); pap. text ed. 10.95x (ISBN 0-931477-24-7). Lynne Rienner.

Baber, Elizabeth A., jt. auth. see Adler, Anne G.

Baber, Frank, illus. The Adventures of Brer Rabbit. (Illus.). 96p. (ps-5). 1980. 9.95 (ISBN 0-528-82300-0). Rand.

Baber, Lina G. Office Practices & Procedures. 544p. 1982. text ed. 23.95 (ISBN 0-675-09846-7); practice set 9.95 (ISBN 0-675-20007-5). Additional supplements may be obtained from publisher. Merrill.

--Word-Information Processing: Concepts & Applications. (Illus.). 352p. 1984. Additional supplements may be obtained from publisher. text ed. 23.95 (ISBN 0-675-20095-4). Merrill.

Baber, Lucy H. & Williamson, Hazel L. Marriages of Campbell County, Virginia, 1782-1810. LC 79-56412. (Illus.). 185p. 1980. Repr. of 1971 ed. 15.00 (ISBN 0-8063-0879-6). Genealog Pub.

Baber, Lucy H., et al. Marriages & Deaths from Lynchburg, Virginia Newspapers, 1794-1836. LC 79-55836. 266p. 1980. pap. 15.00 (ISBN 0-8063-0874-5). Genealog Pub.

Baber, Robert L. Software Reflected: The Socially Responsible Programming of Computers. 192p. 1982. 29.95 (ISBN 0-444-86372-9). Elsevier.

Baber, Shirley G. Survival in Your Own Backyard. LC 82-99943. (First Edition). (Illus.). 60p. (Orig.). 1982. pap. 10.00 (ISBN 0-686-42957-5). Shirleys Pub.

Baber, Walter F. Organizing the Future: Matrix Models for the Postindustrial Polity. (Illus.). 133p. 1983. text ed. 16.50 (ISBN 0-8173-0123-2). U of Ala Pr.

Baberi, Susan, tr. see Sato, Masahiko.

Babic, S. Serbo-Croat for Foreigners I. rev. 6th ed. 1981. 18.50 (ISBN 0-89918-702-1, Y702). Vanous.

--Serbo-Croat Reading Passages. 1975. 7.50 (ISBN 0-89918-732-3, Y732). Vanous.

--Serbo-Croatian for Foreigners, Vol. 1. Rev. & enl. ed. (Illus.). 1981. pap. 25.00 (ISBN 0-686-64047-0). Heinman.

--Serbo-Croatian Reading Passages, with Comments Exercises, Vocabulary. 207p. 1975. pap. text ed. 11.50 (ISBN 0-317-26231-9, Pub. by Kolarcev Narodni Yugoslavia). Heinman.

Babic, Slavna. Serbo Croat for Foreigners: Vocabulary & Grammar. 6th ed. (Illus.). 233p. 1981. pap. text ed. 18.50x (ISBN 0-89918-702-1, Y702). Vanous.

Babic, V. M. & Kirpichnikova, N. Y. The Boundary-Layer Method in Diffraction Problems. (Springer Series in Electrophysics: Vol. 3). (Illus.). 1979. 23.00 (ISBN 0-387-09605-1). Springer-Verlag.

Babic, V. M., ed. see Steklov Institute of Mathematics, Academy of Sciences, U S S R, No. 115.

Babich, Betsy & Thompson, Cecelia. Learning Centers: A Personalized Approach to Mainstreaming. 1983. 4.00 (ISBN 0-318-00041-5, A261-08458). Home Econ Educ.

Babich, Mary L. Hospitals & the News Media: A Guide to Good Media Relations. (Illus.). 56p. (Orig.). 1985. pap. 16.00 (ISBN 0-939450-40-2, 166130). Am Hospital.

Babich, V. M., ed. Mathematical Problems in Wave Propagation Theory, Pt. II. LC 69-12506. (Seminars in Mathematics Ser.: Vol. 15). 119p. 1971. 27.50x (ISBN 0-306-18815-5, Plenum Pr). Plenum Pub.

--Mathematical Problems in Wave Propagation Theory, Pt. III. LC 79-13851. (Seminars in Mathematics Ser.: Vol. 17). 139p. 1972. 27.50x (ISBN 0-306-18817-1, Plenum Pr). Plenum Pub.

--Mathematical Problems in Wave Propagation Theory, Pt. 1. LC 77-103945. (Seminars in Mathematics Ser.: Vol. 9). 107p. 1970. 27.50x (ISBN 0-306-18809-0, Consultants). Plenum Pub.

Babics, Walter V. Assimilation of Yugoslavs in Franklin County, Ohio. LC 73-155330. 1972. Repr. of 1964 ed. softcover 8.00 (ISBN 0-686-61035-0). Ragusan Pr.

Babiiha, Thaddeo K. The James-Hawthorne Relation: Biographical Essays. 1980. lib. bdg. 23.00 (ISBN 0-8161-8431-3, Hall Reference). G K Hall.

Babin, A. E., jt. auth. see Capesius, P.

Babin, Claude. Elements of Palaeontology. LC 79-1323. 446p. 1980. 72.95 (ISBN 0-471-27577-8, Pub. by Wiley-Interscience); pap. 31.95x (ISBN 0-471-27576-X). Wiley.

Babin, Edith H. & Cordes, Carole V. TOEFL (Test of English as a Foreign Language) 3rd ed. LC 82-22809. 352p. 1983. pap. 8.95 (ISBN 0-668-05446-8); cassette 7.95 (ISBN 0-668-05743-2). Arco.

Babin, Lawrence J. Agony in the Garden. LC 75-158476. 1971. deluxe ed. 3.00x (ISBN 0-912492-25-2); pap. 1.00 (ISBN 0-912492-00-7). Pyquag.

--And Heaven Cried. 1971. deluxe ed. 3.00x (ISBN 0-685-02597-7); pap. 1.00x (ISBN 0-912492-01-5). Pyquag.

--Cecilia of Rome. 1977. 4.00x (ISBN 0-912492-09-0). Pyquag.

--Library Media Center in the Public School. 1979. deluxe ed. 8.95 (ISBN 0-912492-12-0). Pyquag.

--Oldtime Schooldays. 1975. deluxe ed. 3.00x (ISBN 0-686-57764-7); pap. 1.00x (ISBN 0-912492-10-4). Pyquag.

--Pyquag Poetry. 1971. pap. 1.00x (ISBN 0-912492-02-3). Pyquag.

--Teacher: Twenty-Five Years Later. 1981. pap. 1.00x (ISBN 0-912492-26-0). Pyquag.

--Trouble in Tampa. 1971. pap. 1.00x (ISBN 0-912492-03-1). Pyquag.

Babin, Maria T. Estudios Lorquianos. LC 76-1827. (Coleccion Mente y Palabra). 480p. (Span.). 1976. 7.50 (ISBN 0-8477-0528-5); pap. 6.25 (ISBN 0-8477-0529-3). U of PR Pr.

Babineau, Edmour J. Love of God & Social Duty in the Ramcaritmanas. 1979. 13.95 (ISBN 0-89684-050-6, Pub. by Motilal Banarsidass India). Orient Bk Dist.

Babinger, Franz. Mehmed the Conqueror & His Time. Hickman, William C., ed. Manheim, Ralph, tr. from Ger. LC 77-71972. (Bollingen Ser.: No. 96). (Illus.). 1978. 54.00x (ISBN 0-691-09900-6). Princeton U Pr.

Babington, Anthony. For the Sake of Example: Capital Courts-Martial, 1914-1920. LC 83-40288. 244p. 1984. 21.95 (ISBN 0-312-29816-1). St Martin.

Babington, Audrey. Creative Wall-Hangings & Panels. LC 82-1834. (Illus.). 192p. 1982. 19.95 (ISBN 0-668-05603-7, 5603). Arco.

Babington, B. G., ed. see Von Feuchtersleben, Ernst F.

Babington, B. G., tr. see Hecker, J. F.

Babington, B. G., tr. see Hecker, Justus F.

Babington, Caroline H. Parenting & the Retarded Child. (Illus.). 196p. 1981. 16.95x (ISBN 0-398-04539-9). C C Thomas.

Babington, Churchill & Lumby, Joseph R., eds. Polychronicon Ranulphi Higden, Monachi Cestrensis, Together with the English Translation of John of Trevisa & of an Unknown Writer in the 15th Century, 9 vols. (Rolls Ser.: No. 41). Repr. of 1886 ed. Set. 396.00 (ISBN 0-317-16688-3). Kraus Repr.

Babington, Churchill, ed. see Peacock, Reginald.

Babington, J. A. Reformation. LC 71-118513. 1971. Repr. of 1901 ed. 26.75x (ISBN 0-8046-1135-1, Pub. by Kennikat). Assoc Faculty Pr.

Babington, John. A Short Treatise of Geometrie. LC 76-25837. (English Experience Ser.: No. 296). 200p. Repr. of 1635 ed. 35.00 (ISBN 90-221-0296-3). Walter J Johnson.

Babington, K. G. The Kremlin Cat & the Bomb. 159p. 1983. 14.95x (ISBN 0-85362-203-5, Oriel). Routledge & Kegan.

Babington, Mima & Atwood, Bagby E. Lexical Usage in Southern Louisiana. Bd. with Word List of Construction Terms. Lish, T. G. (Publications of the American Dialect Society: No. 36). 31p. 1961. pap. 3.20 (ISBN 0-8173-0636-6). U of Ala Pr.

Babington, Percy L. Bibliography of the Writings of John Addington Symonds. 1967. Repr. of 1925 ed. 24.50 (ISBN 0-8337-0143-6). B Franklin.

--Browning & Calverley. LC 74-13383. 1925. lib. bdg. 10.00 (ISBN 0-8414-3261-9). Folcroft.

--Browning & Calverley, or Poem & Parody. 1978. Repr. of 1925 ed. lib. bdg. 10.00 (ISBN 0-8495-0387-6). Arden Lib.

Babington Smith, V. International Directory of Exhibiting Artists 1983. Incl. Vol. 1. Painters, Printmakers, Draughtsmen, & Collagists. 525p. lib. bdg. 44.75 (ISBN 0-903450-76-3); Vol. 2. Sculptors, Photographers, Performance Artists, & Others. 401p. lib. bdg. 28.75 (ISBN 0-903450-77-1); Set. lib. bdg. 65.00 (ISBN 0-903450-75-5). 1983. ABC-Clio.

Babinski, Hubert F. The Mazeppa Legend in European Romanticism. LC 74-6152. 164p. 1974. 22.00x (ISBN 0-231-03825-9). Columbia U Pr.

Babior, Bernard M., ed. Cobalamin: Biochemistry & Pathophysiology. LC 74-32499. pap. 122.30 (ISBN 0-317-07781-3, 2017398). Bks Demand UMI.

Babister, A. W. Aircraft Dynamic Stability & Response. (Illus.). 230p. 1980. pap. 19.50 (ISBN 0-08-024768-7). Pergamon.

Babkin, Boris P. Pavlov: A Biography. LC 49-11887. xiv, 366p. 1975. pap. 4.25x (ISBN 0-226-03373-2, P621, Phoen). U of Chicago Pr.

Babladelis, Georgia. The Study of Personality. 400p. 1984. text ed. 29.95 (ISBN 0-03-063662-0). HR&W.

Babler, E. B., tr. see Plockinger, Erwin & Etterich, Otto.

Babler, P. E., tr. see Plockinger, Erwin & Etterich, Otto.

Bablet, Denis. Revolutions of Stage Design in the Twentieth Century. (Illus.). 1976. 100.00 (ISBN 0-8148-0652-X). L Amiel Pub.

--The Theatre of Edward Gordon Craig. Woodward, D., tr. LC 66-23134. Orig. Title: Edward Gordon Craig. (Illus.). 1966. pap. 7.25 (ISBN 0-87830-581-5). Theatre Arts.

Bablet, Dennis & Bablet, Marie-Louise. Adolpha Appia. Melnik, Burton, tr. from Fr. (Illus.). 96p. (Orig.). 1982. pap. 8.00 (ISBN 0-7145-3964-3). Riverrun NY.

Bablet, Marie-Louise, jt. auth. see Bablet, Dennis.

Babloyantz. Molecules, Dynamics & Life: An Introduction to Self-Organization of Matter. (Nonequilibrium Problems in the Physical Sciences & Biology Ser.). 1986. price not set (ISBN 0-471-82380-5). Wiley.

Baboian, Robert, jt. ed. see Haynes, G. S.

Babor, Daryl, jt. auth. see Marten, Gerald G.

Babor, Thomas. Alcohol: Customs & Rituals. (Encyclopedia of Psychoactive Drugs Ser.). (Illus.). 1985. PLB 15.95x (ISBN 0-87754-763-7). Chelsea Hse.

Babris, Janina. The Covenant of Love. pap. 6.95 (ISBN 0-686-74587-6, 101-25). Prow Bks-Franciscan.

--Draudziba Uz Sparna. (Illus.). 80p. 1975. 4.75 (ISBN 0-89023-006-4). Res Publs.

--Friendship on the Wing. LC 74-25969. (Illus.). 80p. 1975. 5.95 (ISBN 0-89023-005-6). Res Publs.

--In Human Touch. 17p. 1976. 5.95 (ISBN 0-912414-20-0). Lumen Christi.

Babris, Peter J. Baltic Youth Under Communism. LC 67-16896. 1967. 7.95 (ISBN 0-911252-01-0). Res Publs.

--Silent Churches: Persecution of Religions in Soviet Dominated Areas. LC 78-52811. 1978. 19.50 (ISBN 0-911252-02-9). Res Publs.

Babrius. Babrius & Phaedrus. Perry, B. E., tr. (Loeb Classical Library: No. 436). 1965. 12.50x (ISBN 0-674-99480-9). Harvard U Pr.

Babrius, Valerius. Aesop's Fables. Hull, Denison B., tr. from Gr. LC 60-14237. 112p. 1974. pap. 2.95 (ISBN 0-226-03384-8, P577, Phoen). U of Chicago Pr.

Babson, J. H. Disease Costing. 1973. 11.00 (ISBN 0-7190-0524-8, Pub. by Manchester Univ Pr). Longwood Pub Group.

Babson, John J. History of the Town of Gloucester, (Mass.) Cape Ann: Including the Town of Rockport. (Illus.). 15.00 (ISBN 0-8446-0014-8). Peter Smith.

Babson, Marian. Bejewelled Death. 173p. 1982. 10.95 (ISBN 0-8027-5467-8). Walker & Co.

--Bejewelled Death. 1985. pap. 2.95 (ISBN 0-8027-3127-9). Walker & Co.

--Cruise of a Deathtime. LC 83-40415. 192p. 1984. 12.95 (ISBN 0-8027-5588-7). Walker & Co.

--Dangerous to Know. LC 80-54820. 1981. 9.95 (ISBN 0-8027-5442-2). Walker & Co.

--Dangerous to Know. 168p. 1983. pap. 2.95 (ISBN 0-8027-3029-9). Walker & Co.

--Death Beside the Sea. 176p. 1983. 12.95 (ISBN 0-8027-5490-2). Walker & Co.

--Death Swap. 160p. 1985. 12.95 (ISBN 0-8027-5616-6). Walker & Co.

--Death Warmed Up. 1982. 11.95 (ISBN 0-8027-5479-1). Walker & Co.

--Death Warmed Up. 1984. pap. 2.95 (ISBN 0-8027-3109-0). Walker & Co.

--A Fool for Murder. LC 83-42731. (Mysteries Ser.). 192p. 1984. 12.95 (ISBN 0-8027-5571-2). Walker & Co.

--Line up for Murder. 200p. 1981. 9.95 (ISBN 0-8027-5453-8). Walker & Co.

--The Lord Mayor of Death. 193p. 1983. pap. 2.95 (ISBN 0-8027-3026-4). Walker & Co.

--Murder, Murder, Little Star. (Scene of the Crime Ser.: No. 40). 1982. pap. 2.25 (ISBN 0-440-16226-2). Dell.

--Murder, Murder, Little Star. 192p. 1980. 9.95 (ISBN 0-8027-5416-3). Walker & Co.

--A Trail of Ashes. 1985. 12.95 (ISBN 0-8027-5607-7). Walker & Co.

--Twelve Deaths of Christmas. 180p. 1980. 10.95 (ISBN 0-8027-5426-0). Walker & Co.

--The Twelve Deaths of Christmas. (Walker British Paperback Mysteries Ser.). 1985. pap. 2.95 (ISBN 0-8027-3140-6). Walker & Co.

Babson, Marion. Line up for Murder. 1984. pap. 2.95 (ISBN 0-8027-3091-4). Walker & Co.

--Lord Mayor of Death. (Walker Mystery Ser.). 1979. 7.95 (ISBN 0-8027-5415-5). Walker & Co.

--The Twelve Deaths of Christmas. 192p. 1985. pap. 3.25 (ISBN 0-440-19183-1). Dell.

Babson, Roger W. The Folly of Installment Buying. LC 75-39241. (Getting & Spending: the Consumer's Dilemma). 1976. Repr. of 1938 ed. 20.00x (ISBN 0-405-08006-9). Ayer Co Pubs.

--Washington & the Revolutionists: A Characterization of Recovery Policies & of the People Who Are Giving Them Effect. facsimile ed. LC 76-111812. (Essay Index Reprint Ser). Repr. of 1934 ed. 21.50 (ISBN 0-8369-1642-5). Ayer Co Pubs.

Babson, S. Gorham, et al. Diagnosis & Management of the Fetus & Neonate at Risk: A Guide for Team Care. 4th ed. LC 79-16957. (Illus.). 344p. 1979. text ed. 37.95 (ISBN 0-8016-0415-X). Mosby.

Babson, Stanley M., Jr. Fringe Benefits: The Depreciation, Obsolescence & Transience of Man: Cost, Strategies & Trends for Financial Managers, Personnel Directors & General Management. LC 74-13767. (Systems & Controls for Financial Management Ser.). Repr. of 1974 ed. 34.60 (ISBN 0-8357-9894-1, 2012596). Bks Demand UMI.

Babson, Steve. Working Detroit: The Making of a Union Town. LC 84-11019. (Illus.). 256p. 1984. 19.95 (ISBN 0-915361-01-9, Dist. by Watts). Adama Pubs Inc.

Babst, Earl D. & Vander Velde, Lewis G., eds. Michigan & the Cleveland Era: Sketches of University of Michigan Staff Members & Alumni Who Served the Cleveland Administrations, 1885-89,1893-97. facsimile ed. LC 70-179724. (Biography Index Reprint Ser). Repr. of 1948 ed. 27.50 (ISBN 0-8369-8092-1). Ayer Co Pubs.

Babu, Mohammed. African Socialism. 224p. (Orig.). 1981. 20.00x (ISBN 0-905762-19-3, Pub. by Zed Pr England); pap. 9.95x (ISBN 0-905762-39-8, Pub. by Zed Pr England). Biblio Dist.

Babuel-Peyrissac, Jean-Paul. Equations Cinetiques des Fluides & des Plasmas. (Cours & Documents de Mathematiques & de Physique Ser.). 306p. 1975. 129.50 (ISBN 0-677-50630-9). Gordon.

Babula, William. Shakespeare in Production, Nineteen Thirty-Five to Nineteen Seventy-Eight: A Catalogue. 1981. lib. bdg. 61.00 (ISBN 0-8240-9814-5). Garland Pub.

--Wishes Fall Out As They're Willed: Shakespeare & the Tragicomic Archetype. (Salzburg Studies in English Literature, Elizabethan & Renaissance Studies Ser.: No. 48). 133p. 1975. pap. text ed. 25.50x (ISBN 0-391-01305-X). Humanities.

Babunakis, Michael. Budget Reform for Government: A Comprehensive Allocation & Management System (CAMS) LC 82-354. xviii, 231p. 1982. lib. bdg. 35.00 (ISBN 0-89930-016-2, BBG/, Quorum). Greenwood.

--Budgets: An Analytical & Procedural Handbook for Government & Non-Profit Organizations. LC 76-5323. (Illus.). 257p. 1976. lib. bdg. 35.00x (ISBN 0-8371-8900-4, BBP). Greenwood.

Babuscio, Jack & Dunn, Richard M. European Political Facts, 1648-1789. 400p. 1984. 24.95x (ISBN 0-87196-992-0). Facts On File.
Babushkin, V. I., et al. Thermodynamics of Silicates. Frenkel, B. N. & Terentyev, V. A., trs. from Rus. (Illus.). 470p. (Eng.). 1985. 98.00 (ISBN 0-387-12750-X). Springer Verlag.
Babusis, Vytautas, ed. see Love, Richard H.
Babuska, I., et al, eds. Adaptive Computational Methods for Partial Differential Equations. LC 83-51382. xii, 251p. 1984. text ed. 25.50 (ISBN 0-89871-191-6). Soc Indus-Appl Math.
Baby, R. A Hopewell Human Bone Whistle. (Illus.). 2p. 1961. pap. 0.50 (ISBN 0-318-00847-5). Ohio Hist Soc.
--Unique Hopewellian Mask-Headdress. (Illus.). 2p. 1956. pap. 0.50 (ISBN 0-318-00853-X). Ohio Hist Soc.
Baby, Raymond. Hopewell Cremation Practices. (Illus.). 7p. 1954. pap. 0.50 (ISBN 0-318-00846-7). Ohio Hist Soc.
Baby, Raymond & Potter, Martha. Exploration of the O.C. Voss Mound. (Illus.). 34p. 1966. pap. 3.50 (ISBN 0-318-00844-0). Ohio Hist Soc.
Baby, Raymond, jt. auth. see Webb.
Babyonyshev, Alexander, ed. On Sakharov. LC 82-40034. 224p. 1982. pap. 6.95 (ISBN 0-394-71033-9, Vin). Random.
Baca. Los Angeles in Your Pocket. 2nd ed. (Barron's City in Your Pocket Ser.). 1984. pap. 2.95 (ISBN 0-8120-2746-9). Barron.
Baca, Jimmy S. Immigrants in Our Own Land. LC 79-9812. 72p. 1979. 13.95x (ISBN 0-8071-0572-4); pap. 4.95 (ISBN 0-8071-0573-2). La State U Pr.
--What's Happening. LC 82-5089. 36p. (Orig.). 1982. pap. 4.50 (ISBN 0-915306-27-1). Curbstone.
Baca, Leonard & Bransford, Jim. An Appropriate Education for Handicapped Children of Limited English Proficiency. 1982. 4.00 (ISBN 0-86586-157-9). Coun Exc Child.
Baca, Leonard & Cervantes, Hermes. The Bilingual Special Education Interface. (Illus.). 512p. 1984. text ed. 28.95 (ISBN 0-8016-0425-7). Mosby.
Baca, M. Carlota & Stein, Ronald H. Ethical Principles, Practices, & Problems in Higher Education. 290p. 1983. 27.50x (ISBN 0-398-04865-7). C C Thomas.
Baca, Murtha, tr. see Pignatti, Terisio.
Baca Fabiola, Cabeza de see Cabeza de Baca, Fabiola.
Baca Gilbert, Fabiola Cabeza de see De Baca Gilbert, Fabiola C.
Bacal, Azril, tr. see Jackins, HarTey.
Bacal, Azril, tr. see Jackins, Harvey.
Bacall, Aaron, et al. Chemistry. LC 83-26624. (Regents Review Ser.). 272p. (Orig.). (gr. 9-12). 1984. pap. 3.95 (ISBN 0-668-05975-3). Arco.
Bacall, Lauren. Lauren Bacall by Myself. 1984. pap. 3.50 (ISBN 0-345-31793-9). Ballantine.
--Lauren Bacall by Myself. LC 78-54902. (Illus.). 1978. 12.95 (ISBN 0-394-41308-3). Knopf.
Bacardi, Amalia E., tr. see Santa Cruz, Mercedes.
Bacardi, Emilio. Via Cruis, 2 pts. Incl. Pt. 1 Paginas De Ayer; Pt. 2 Magdalena. LC 77-128478. (Cuban Reprint Ser). 475p. 15.00 (ISBN 0-685-58251-5). Mnemosyne.
Bacarisse, S., et al, eds. What's Past Is Prologue. 208p. 1984. 15.00x (ISBN 0-7073-0344-3, Pub. by Scottish Academic Pr Scotland). Columbia U Pr.
Bacarisse, Salvador. Contemporary Latin American Fiction. 120p. 1980. 10.00x (ISBN 0-7073-0255-2, Pub. by Scottish Academic Pr Scotland). Columbia U Pr.
Baccelli, F. & Fayolle, G., eds. Modelling & Performance Evaluation Methodology: Proceedings of the International Seminar, Paris, France, January 24-26, 1983. (Lecture Notes in Control & Information Sciences: Vol. 60). (Illus.). vii, 653p. (Fr. & Eng.). 1984. pap. 34.50 (ISBN 0-387-13288-0). Springer-Verlag.
Baccetti, Baccio, ed. Comparative Spermatology. 1971. 98.50 (ISBN 0-12-069950-8). Acad Pr.
Bacchi, Carol L. Liberation Deferred? The Ideas of the English-Canadian Suffragists, 1877-1918. (Social History of Canada Ser.). 222p. 1983. 25.00x (ISBN 0-8020-2455-6); pap. 9.95 (ISBN 0-8020-6466-3). U of Toronto Pr.
Bacchus, Alban N. Personal Wellness & Self-Realization. 224p. pap. cancelled (ISBN 0-916207-03-X). Oryn Pubns Inc.
Bacchus, Habeeb. Metabolic & Endocrine Emergencies: Recognition & Management. 2nd ed. LC 83-23591. (Illus.). 272p. 1984. pap. text ed. 25.00 (ISBN 0-8391-1970-4, 20699). Univ Park.
Bacchus, William I. Foreign Policy & the Bureaucratic Process: The State Department's Country Director System. LC 73-16759. 352p. 1974. 37.00 (ISBN 0-691-07565-4). Princeton U Pr.
--Inside the Legislative Process: The Passage of the Foreign Service Act of 1980. (Replica Editon). 150p. 1983. softcover 16.00x (ISBN 0-86531-800-X). Westview.
--Staffing for Foriegn Affairs: Personnel Systems for the 1980's & 1990's. LC 83-42546. 272p. 1983. 25.00x (ISBN 0-691-07660-X). Princeton U Pr.
Bacchylides. Bacchylides: Complete Poems. Fagles, Robert, tr. LC 75-14595. 1976. Repr. of 1961 ed. lib. bdg. 18.75 (ISBN 0-8371-8221-2, BACP). Greenwood.
Bacci, Judy L. The Second Coming: Why Jesus Christ Became a Carpenter Instead of an Electrician. 110p. (Orig.). 1981. pap. 5.95 (ISBN 0-940002-00-0). Studio J Pub.
Bacckman, Earl. Approaches to International Education. 352p. 1984. 19.95 (ISBN 0-02-901360-7). ACE.
Baccouche, Belkacem & Azmi, Sanaa. Conversations in Modern Standard Arabic. LC 84-40188. (Language Ser.). 432p. 1984. text ed. 35.00x (ISBN 0-300-03219-6); pap. 11.95x (ISBN 0-300-03274-9). Yale U Pr.
Baccus, Jim. I'm Thinking It Over: Spectator Columns, 1974-1984. 188p. (Orig.). Date not set. pap. price not set (ISBN 0-911042-31-8). N Dak Inst.
Bacetti, B. & Afzelius, B. The Biology of the Sperm Cell. (Monographs in Developmental Biology: Vol. 10). (Illus.). 250p. 1976. 54.25 (ISBN 3-8055-2204-5). S Karger.
Bach, Alice. A Father Every Few Years. LC 76-24303. 144p. (gr. 7 up). 1977. 12.45i (ISBN 0-06-020342-0). HarpJ.
--Grouchy Uncle Otto. 48p. (gr. k-3). 1978. pap. 0.95 (ISBN 0-440-43208-1, YB). Dell.
--Grouchy Uncle Otto. LC 76-24304. (Illus.). 48p. (gr. k-4). 1977. PLB 11.89 (ISBN 0-06-020345-5). HarpJ.
--He Will Not Walk with Me. LC 85-4570. (Illus.). 192p. (gr. 7 up). 1985. 15.95 (ISBN 0-385-29410-7). Delacorte.
--The Meat in the Sandwich. 176p. (gr. 5 up). pap. 2.25 (ISBN 0-440-95618-8, LFL). Dell.
--Millicent the Magnificent. (Illus.). 48p. (gr. k-3). 1981. pap. 1.25 (ISBN 0-440-45456-5, YB). Dell.
--Millicent the Magnificent. LC 77-11840. (Illus.). 48p. (gr. k-3). 1978. PLB 9.57i (ISBN 0-06-020309-9). HarpJ.
--Mollie Make-Believe. LC 73-14334. 160p. (gr. 7 up). 1974. PLB 11.89 (ISBN 0-06-020316-1). HarpJ.
--The Most Delicious Camping Trip Ever. LC 76-2956. (Illus.). 48p. (gr. k-3). 1976. PLB 9.57i (ISBN 0-06-020338-2). HarpJ.
--The Smartest Bear & His Brother Oliver. (Illus.). 48p. (gr. k-3). 1976. pap. 0.95 (ISBN 0-440-48697-1, YB). Dell.
--The Smartest Bear & His Brother Oliver. LC 74-29348. (Illus.). 48p. (gr. k-4). 1975. PLB 9.89 (ISBN 0-06-020335-8). HarpJ.
--They'll Never Make a Movie Starring Me. LC 72-12240. 208p. (gr. 7 up). 1973. 11.89 (ISBN 0-06-020323-4). HarpJ.
--Waiting for Johnny Miracle. LC 79-2813. 256p. (YA) (gr. 7 up). 1980. 10.53i (ISBN 0-06-020348-X); PLB 11.89 (ISBN 0-06-020349-8). HarpJ.
--Warren Weasel's Worse Than Measles. (gr. 1-4). 1982. pap. 1.25 (ISBN 0-440-49399-4, YB). Dell.
--When the Sky Began to Roar. 176p. (gr. 7 up). 1984. 11.95 (ISBN 0-395-36071-4). HM.
Bach, Alice, tr. see Belves, Pierre & Mathey, Francois.
Bach, Bob & Mercer, Ginger. Our Huckleberry Friend: The Life, Times & Lyrics of Johnny Mercer. 256p. 1982. 24.95 (ISBN 0-8184-0331-4). Lyle Stuart.
Bach, C. Microeconomics: Analysis & Applications. 2nd ed. 1980. pap. 20.95 (ISBN 0-13-581298-4). P-H.
Bach, C. P. Collection of Sonatas Published in Bach's Lifetime. Berg, Darrell, ed. 250p. 1985. 70.00 (ISBN 0-8240-6450-X). Garland Pub.
Bach, Carl P. Collections of Sonatas & Other Works Published in Bach's Lifetime. Berg, Darrell, ed. (Carl Phillip Emanuel Bach Collected Works for Solo Keyboard Ser.). 320p. 1985. 85.00 (ISBN 0-8240-6451-8). Garland Pub.
--Essay on the True Art of Playing Keyboard Instruments. Mitchell, William J., ed. (Illus.). 1948. 19.95x (ISBN 0-393-09716-1, NortonC). Norton.
--Great Keyboard Sonatas: Series I & II. (Music Scores to Play & Study Ser.). 192p. 1985. Series I. pap. 6.95 (ISBN 0-486-24853-4); Series II. pap. 6.95 (ISBN 0-486-24854-2). Dover.
--Sonatas & Other Multi-Movement Works Unpublished in Bach's Lifetime. Berg, Darrell, ed. (Carl Phillip Emanuel Bach 1714-1788, Collected Works for Solo Keyboard Ser.). 285p. 1985. 75.00 (ISBN 0-8240-6453-4). Garland Pub.
Bach, Cile M. & Tonelli, Edith A. Frank Mechau: Artist of Colorado. Yenawine, Philip, ed. (Illus.). 100p. 1981. 10.00 (ISBN 0-934324-02-6). Aspen Ctr Visual Arts.
Bach, Edward. The Bach Flower Remedies. LC 79-87679. 1979. 6.95 (ISBN 0-87983-192-8); pap. 6.95 (ISBN 0-87983-193-6). Keats.
--Heal Thyself. 1980. pap. 4.95x (ISBN 0-317-07341-9, Regent House). B of A.
--Twelve Healers. 1980. pap. 4.95x (ISBN 0-317-07340-0, Regent House). B of A.
Bach, Emmon. Syntactic Theory. LC 81-40918. 310p. 1982. pap. text ed. 14.25 (ISBN 0-8191-2258-0). U Pr of Amer.
Bach, Eric. Analytic Methods in the Analysis & Design of Number Theoretic Algorithms. (ACM Distinguished Dissontation Award Ser.). 50p. 1985. text ed. 15.00x (ISBN 0-262-02219-2). MIT Pr.
Bach, Fritz H., ed. Clinical Immunobiology, Vol. 4. 1980. 33.00 (ISBN 0-12-070004-2). Acad Pr.
--Immunobiology of Transplantation: The Histocompatibility Systems. LC 74-2019. Orig. Title: Transplantation Proceedings, December G & S Journal. 400p. 1974. 92.50 (ISBN 0-8089-0840-5, 790310). Grune.
Bach, Fritz H. & Good, Robert A., eds. Clinical Immunobiology. (Illus.). Vol. 1 1972. 55.00 (ISBN 0-12-070001-8); Vol. 2 1974. 55.00 (ISBN 0-12-070002-6); Vol. 3 1976. 70.00 (ISBN 0-12-070003-4). Acad Pr.
Bach, Fritz H., et al, eds. see ICN-UCLA Symposia on Molecular & Cellular Biology, 1979.
Bach, George & Goldberg, Herb. Creative Aggression: The Art of Assertive Living. LC 82-45621. 432p. 1983. pap. 8.95 (ISBN 0-385-18442-5, Anch). Doubleday.
Bach, George & Torbet, Laura. A Time for Caring. 1981. 15.95 (ISBN 0-385-29059-4). Delacorte.
Bach, George L. Macroeconomics: Analysis & Applications. 2nd ed. 1980. pap. text ed. 20.95 (ISBN 0-13-542712-6). P-H.
Bach, George Leland, jt. ed. see Anshen, Melvin.
Bach, George R. & Deutsch, Ronald M. Pairing. 1971. pap. 3.95 (ISBN 0-380-00394-5, 65367-6). Avon.
--Stop! You're Driving Me Crazy. 1985. pap. 3.95 (ISBN 0-425-07988-0). Berkley Pub.
Bach, George R. & Torbet, Laura. The Inner Enemy: How to Fight Fair with Yourself. LC 82-14397. 224p. 1983. 11.95 (ISBN 0-688-01557-3). Morrow.
Bach, George R. & Wyden, Peter. The Intimate Enemy: How to Fight Fair in Love & Marriage. 384p. 1981. pap. 3.95 (ISBN 0-380-00392-9, 65086-X). Avon.
Bach, H. & Florant, J. Luftartsteknisk Ordbog Engelsk-Dansk. 255p. (Eng. & Danish.). 1968. 35.00 (ISBN 0-686-92484-3, M-1280). French & Eur.
Bach, H. I. The German Jew: A Synthesis of Judaism & Western Civilization, 1730-1930. (Litman Library of Jewish Civilization). 256p. 1985. 24.95x (ISBN 0-19-710033-3). Oxford U Pr.
Bach, Hans. Jean Pauls Hesperus. 27.00 (ISBN 0-384-02935-3); pap. 22.00 (ISBN 0-685-02214-5). Johnson Repr.
Bach, Heinrich. Die Thuringisch-Sachsische Kanzleisprache Bis 1325, Miteiner Neven Einleitung Von Richard K. Seymour, 2 Vols. 40.00 (ISBN 0-384-02945-0). Johnson Repr.
Bach, I. S. Two Part Inventions, 3 bks. (Quality Edition Classics Ser.). 32p. 1983. Bk. I. pap. text ed. 2.95 (ISBN 0-935474-12-9); Bk.II. pap. text ed. 2.95 (ISBN 0-935474-11-0); Bk.III. pap. 2.95 (ISBN 0-935474-13-7). Carousel Pub Corp.
Bach, I. W., et al, eds. Carbon Dioxide: Current Views & Developments in Energy-Climate Research. 1983. lib. bdg. 72.00 (ISBN 90-2771-485-1, Pub. by Reidel Holland). Kluwer Academic.
Bach, Ira J. Chicago's Famous Buildings: A Photographic Guide to the City's Architectural Landmarks & Other Notable Buildings. 3rd, rev. & enl. ed. LC 79-23365. (Illus.). 1980. lib. bdg. 15.00x (ISBN 0-226-03395-3); pap. 6.95 (ISBN 0-226-03396-1). U of Chicago Pr.
Bach, Ira J. & Gray, Mary L. A Guide to Chicago's Public Sculpture. LC 82-20214. (Illus.). 384p. 1983. lib. bdg. 20.00x (ISBN 0-226-03398-8); pap. 8.95 (ISBN 0-226-03399-6). U of Chicago Pr.
Bach, Ira J. & Wolfson, Susan. A Guide to Chicago's Historic Suburbs on Wheels & on Foot. LC 81-9516. (Illus.). xvi, 726p. 1981. 19.95 (ISBN 0-8040-0374-2, 82-75216, Pub. by Swallow); pap. 9.95 (ISBN 0-8040-0384-X, 82-75224, Pub. by Swallow). Ohio U Pr.
--A Guide to Chicago's Train Stations: Past & Present. 300p. 1985. 32.95 (ISBN 0-8040-0869-8, Pub. by Swallow). Ohio U Pr.
Bach, J. S. Fifteen Three-Part Inventions for Piano. Czerny, Carl, ed. (Carl Fischer Music Library: No. 255). (Illus.). 63p. 1912. pap. 4.95 (ISBN 0-8258-0099-4). Fischer Inc NY.
--Fifteen Two Part Inventions for Piano. Czerny, Carl, ed. (Carl Fischer Music Library: No. 254). (Illus.). 1903. pap. 4.95 (ISBN 0-8258-0098-6). Fischer Inc NY.
--Keyboard Music. 312p. 1970. pap. 7.95 (ISBN 0-486-22360-4). Dover.
--Organ Music. 357p. 1970. pap. 8.95 (ISBN 0-486-22359-0). Dover.
--Short Preludes & Fugues for Piano. (Carl Fischer Music Library: No. 516). 1914. pap. 3.50 (ISBN 0-8258-0132-X, L516). Fischer Inc NY.
--Six Sonatas for Unaccompanied Violin. Auer, Leopold, ed. (Carl Fischer Music Library: No. 788). 1917. pap. 7.00 (ISBN 0-8258-0088-9, L788). Fischer Inc NY.
--Two & Three-Part Inventions for Piano. Czerny, Carl, ed. (Carl Fischer Music Library: No. 304). 63p. (Eng & Ger.). 1903. pap. 6.50 (ISBN 0-8258-0102-8, L 304). Fischer Inc NY.
Bach, Jean. Collecting German Dolls. (Illus.). 192p. 1983. 20.00 (ISBN 0-8184-0333-0). Lyle Stuart.
--The Main Street Dictionary of Doll Marks. (Illus.). 288p. 1985. 14.95 (ISBN 0-915590-57-3). Main Street.
--Main Street Pocket Guide to Dolls. rev. ed. LC 83-61593. (Illus.). 256p. 1983. pap. 6.95 (ISBN 0-915590-36-0). Main Street.
Bach, Jean-Francois, et al, eds. Immunology. 2nd ed. LC 81-11503. 1014p. 1982. 80.00 (ISBN 0-471-08044-6, Pub. by Wiley Med). Wiley.
Bach, Johan C., jt. auth. see Abel, Carl F.
Bach, Johann. Harpsichord Music. (Bach-Gesellschaft ed.). 11.50 (ISBN 0-8446-0467-4). Peter Smith.
Bach, Johann C. Adriano in Siria. LC 83-48734. (Johann Christian Bach: The Collected Works Ser.). 550p. 1984. lib. bdg. 90.00 (ISBN 0-8240-6050-4). Garland Pub.
--Alessandro nell'Indie. (Johann Christian Bach: The Collected Works Ser.). 600p. 1984. lib. bdg. 120.00 (ISBN 0-8240-6052-0). Garland Pub.
--Keyboard Concertos I. (Johann Christian Bach: The Collected Works). 250p. 1984. lib. bdg. 50.00 (ISBN 0-8240-6081-4). Garland Pub.
--Libretti II. (Johann Christian Bach: The Collected Works Ser.). 325p. 1984. lib. bdg. 40.00 (ISBN 0-8240-6093-8). Garland Pub.
--Music for Vespers II. (Johann Christian Bach: The Collected Works). 400p. 1984. lib. bdg. 60.00 (ISBN 0-8240-6072-5). Garland Pub.
--Symphonies I. LC 83-48727. (Johann Christian Bach: The Collected Works Ser.). 300p. 1984. lib. bdg. 45.00 (ISBN 0-8240-6075-X). Garland Pub.
--Symphonies II. Warburton, Ernest, ed. (Johann Christian Bach: The Collected Works Ser.). 330p. 1984. lib. bdg. 75.00 (ISBN 0-8240-6076-8). Garland Pub.
Bach, Johann Christian. Endimione. LC 83-48730. (The Collected Works Ser.). 440p. 1984. lib. bdg. 65.00 (ISBN 0-8240-6063-6). Garland Pub.
Bach, Johann S. Bach Cantata No. 140. Herz, Gerhard, ed. (Critical Score Ser.). (Illus.). 1972. 10.00x (ISBN 0-393-02154-8); pap. 6.95x (ISBN 0-393-09555-X). Norton.
--Bach Cantata No. 4. Herz, Gerhard, ed. (Critical Score Ser.). (Illus., Orig.). 1967. pap. 6.95x (ISBN 0-393-09761-7, NortonC). Norton.
--Clavier-Buchlein Vor Wilhelm Friedmann Bach. (Music Reprint Ser.). 1979. Repr. of 1959 ed. 25.00 (ISBN 0-306-79558-2). Da Capo.
--Eleven Great Cantatas in Full Vocal & Instrumental Score. 352p. 1976. pap. 10.95 (ISBN 0-486-23268-9). Dover.
--Eleven Great Cantatas in Full Vocal & Instrumental Score from the Bach-Gesellschaft Edition. 16.50 (ISBN 0-8446-5459-0). Peter Smith.
--The Four-Part Chorals of J. S. Bach. Terry, Charles S., ed. LC 74-27331. Repr. of 1929 ed. 49.50 (ISBN 0-404-12857-2). AMS Pr.
--Neue Ausgabe Saemtlicher Werke. write publisher for info. (ISBN 0-685-37398-3). Adlers Foreign Bks.
--The Six Brandenburg Concertos & the Four Orchestral Suites in Full Score. 273p. 1976. pap. 7.95 (ISBN 0-486-23376-6). Dover.
--Six Great Secular Cantatas in Full Score. 288p. (Orig.). 1980. pap. 10.95 (ISBN 0-486-23934-9). Dover.
--Two & Three Part Inventions (Fifteen Inventions & Fifteen Symphonies) Simon, Eric, ed. LC 68-11918. (Facsimile Series of Musical Manuscripts). (Orig.). 1969. pap. 5.50 (ISBN 0-486-21982-8). Dover.
--The Well-Tempered Clavier: Bks I & II Complete. (Music Ser.). 208p. (Orig.). 1984. pap. 6.95 (ISBN 0-486-24532-2). Dover.
--Works for Violin: The Complete Sonatas & Partitas for Unaccompanied Violin & the Six Sonatas for Violin & Clavier. 1978. pap. 5.95 (ISBN 0-486-23683-8). Dover.
Bach, Johann Sebastian. Chorale Preludes of the Bach Circle: A Facsimilie Edition. 184p. 1985. text ed. 16.00x (ISBN 0-300-03510-1). Yale U Pr.
--Complete Preludes & Fugues for Organ. (Music Scores to Play & Study Ser.). 168p. 1985. pap. 6.95 (ISBN 0-486-24816-X). Dover.
--Johann Sebastian Bach: Chorale Preludes from the Yale Manuscript, LM 4708, First Edition. Wolff, Christoph, ed. 96p. 1985. 18.50 (ISBN 0-300-03509-8). Yale U Pr.
Bach, Jovanka, jt. auth. see McLure, Nicola.
Bach, Kent & Harnish, Robert M. Linguistic Communication & Speech Acts. (Illus.). 1979. text ed. 30.00x (ISBN 0-262-02136-6). MIT Pr.
--Linguistic Communication & Speech Acts. 1979. pap. text ed. 9.95x (ISBN 0-262-52078-8). MIT Pr.
Bach, Laurence & Goolrich, Robert. Paros Dream Book. LC 82-51223. (Artists' Bk.). 72p. (Orig.). 1983. pap. write for info. Visual Studies.
Bach, Marcus. Major Religions of the World. 128p. 1984. pap. 4.95 (ISBN 0-87516-543-5). De Vorss.
--Make It an Adventure. LC 75-32232. 206p. 1975. pap. 6.95 (ISBN 0-918936-01-2). Astara.
--The Power of Perception. LC 73-5535. 156p. 1983. pap. 5.95 (ISBN 0-87516-523-0). De Vorss.
--The Power of Total Living. 1978. pap. 2.50 (ISBN 0-449-23747-8, Crest). Fawcett.
--The Power of Total Living: A Holistic Approach to the Coming of the New Person for the New Age. (Illus.). 224p. 1984. pap. 7.95 (ISBN 0-396-08351-X). Dodd.
--Strange Sects & Curious Cults. LC 76-52474. Repr. of 1962 ed. lib. bdg. 18.75x (ISBN 0-8371-9457-1, BASS). Greenwood.
--The Unity Way. LC 82-50085. 387p. 1982. 4.95 (ISBN 0-87159-164-2). Unity School.
--The Will to Believe. 186p. 1973. pap. 7.50 (ISBN 0-911336-46-X). Sci of Mind.
--The World of Serendipity. 167p. 1980. pap. 4.95 (ISBN 0-87516-398-X). De Vorss.

Bach, Matthew G. Wieland's Attitude Toward Woman & Her Cultural & Social Relations. LC 71-159988. (Columbia University. Germanic Studies, Old Ser.: No. 26). Repr. of 1922 ed. 11.50 (ISBN 0-404-50426-4). AMS Pr.

Bach, Michael K., ed. Immediate Hypersensitivity: Modern Concepts & Developments. (Immunology Ser.: Vol. 7). 1978. 95.00 (ISBN 0-8247-6602-4). Dekker.

Bach, Orville E., Jr. Hiking the Yellowstone Backcountry. LC 72-96121. (Totebook Ser.). (Illus.). 240p. 1973. pap. 8.95 (ISBN 0-87156-078-X). Sierra.

Bach, Othello. Hector McSnector & the Mail Order Christmas Witch. LC 84-740001. (Illus.). 40p. (ps-4). 1985. pap. 7.95 (ISBN 0-89845-264-3); incl. read-along cassette 9.95. Caedmon.

--Lilly, Willy & the Mail-Order Witch. LC 83-7422. (Illus.). 48p. (ps-4). 1983. 12.95 (ISBN 0-89845-161-2, B1612); PLB 13.45 (ISBN 0-89845-048-9, B0489). Caedmon.

--Whoever Heard of a Fird? LC 83-23985. (Illus.). 64p. 1984. 14.95 (ISBN 0-89845-160-4); PLB 15.45 (ISBN 0-89845-047-0, B0470); pap. 5.95 (ISBN 0-89845-363-1, B363). Caedmon.

Bach, Othello, jt. auth. see D'Addio, Janie.

Bach, P. H., et al. Nephrotoxicity: Assessment & Pathogensis. (Series of Monographs in Applied Toxicology). 528p. 1982. 58.95 (ISBN 0-471-26212-9, Pub. by Wiley Heyden). Wiley.

Bach, Pedro & Bach, Rita. The Works of Pere Torroella: A Catalan Writer of the Fifteenth Century. 332p. 2.80 (ISBN 0-318-14319-4); pap. text ed. 2.00 (ISBN 0-318-14320-8). Hispanic Inst.

Bach, Peter, ed. Collector's Treasury of Antique Slot Machines from Contemporary Advertising 1925-1950. LC 80-82463. (Illus.). 480p. 1980. 24.95 (ISBN 0-911160-61-2). Post-Era.

Bach, Pieter, ed. Textile, Costume & Doll Collections: In the United States & Canada. LC 81-9022. 69p. 1981. pap. 4.95 (ISBN 0-914046-01-2). R L Shep.

Bach, Ricardo, ed. Lithium: Current Applications in Science, Medicine & Technology. 448p. 1985. 80.00 (ISBN 0-471-80073-2). Wiley.

Bach, Richard. Biplane. (Illus.). 176p. 1983. 12.95 (ISBN 0-02-504670-5). Macmillan.

--The Bridge Across Forever. 1986. 3.95 (ISBN 0-440-10826-8). Dell.

--The Bridge Across Forever: A True Love Story. LC 84-4654. 320p. 1984. 16.95 (ISBN 0-688-03917-0). Morrow.

--A Gift of Wings. (Illus.). 352p. 1974. 8.95 (ISBN 0-385-28365-2, E Friede). Delacorte.

--Gift of Wings. 1979. pap. 3.95 (ISBN 0-440-34571-5). Dell.

--Illusions: The Adventures of a Reluctant Messiah. 1977. 11.95 (ISBN 0-385-28501-9, E Friede). Delacorte.

--Illusions: The Adventures of a Reluctant Messiah. 192p. (gr. 7 up). 1979. pap. 3.50 (ISBN 0-440-34319-4). Dell.

--Jonathan Livingston Seagull. (YA) 1973. pap. 2.95 (ISBN 0-380-01286-3, 60100-1). Avon.

--Jonathan Livingston Seagull. LC 75-119617. (Illus.). 93p. 1970. 9.95 (ISBN 0-02-504540-7). Macmillan.

--Jonathan Livingston Seagull. 182p. 1985. pap. 5.95 large print ed. (ISBN 0-8027-2469-8). Walker & Co.

--Nothing By Chance: A Gypsy Pilot's Adventures in Modern America. (Illus.). 194p. 1983. 12.95 (ISBN 0-02-504690-X). Macmillan.

--Stranger to the Ground. (Illus.). 192p. 1983. 12.95 (ISBN 0-02-504520-2). Macmillan.

--There's No Such Place As Far Away. (Illus.). 1979. 6.95 (ISBN 0-385-29038-1, E Friede). Delacorte.

Bach, Rita, jt. auth. see Bach, Pedro.

Bach, Robert L., jt. auth. see Portes, Alejandro.

Bach, Sheldon. Narcissistic State & the Therapeutic Process. 250p. 1985. 25.00 (ISBN 0-317-15105-3). Aronson.

Bach, Shirley J., jt. auth. see Binkin, Martin.

Bach, Stanley & Sulzner, George T. Perspectives on the Presidency. 1974. pap. text ed. 9.95x (ISBN 0-669-85613-4). Heath.

Bach, Steven. Final Cut: Dreams & Disasters in the Making of Heaven's Gate. LC 85-4983. 1985. 19.95 (ISBN 0-688-04382-8). Morrow.

Bach, W., ed. Interactions of Food & Climate. 1982. 58.50 (ISBN 90-277-1353-7, Pub. by Reidel Holland); pap. 28.50 (ISBN 90-277-1354-5, Pub. by Reidel Holland). Kluwer Academic.

Bach, W., et al, eds. Renewable Energy Prospects: Proceedings of the Conference on Non-Fossil Fuel & Non-Nuclear Fuel Energy Strategies, Honolulu, USS, January 1979. 340p. 1980. 26.00 (ISBN 0-08-024252-9). Pergamon.

Bach, Wilfrid. Our Threatened Climate. 1983. lib. bdg. 29.00 (ISBN 90-277-1680-3, Pub. by Reidel Holland). Kluwer Academic.

Bach, Wilfrid, et al, eds. Interactions of Energy & Climate. 568p. 1980. lib. bdg. 58.00 (ISBN 90-277-1179-8, Pub. by Reidel Holland); pap. 26.50 (ISBN 90-277-1177-1, Pub. by Reidel Holland). Kluwer Academic.

Bacha, Edmar L. & Diaz Alejandro, Carlos F. International Financial Intermediation: A Long & Tropical View. LC 82-3096. (Essays in International Finance Ser.: No. 147). 1982. pap. text ed. 2.50x (ISBN 0-88165-054-4). Princeton U Int Finan Econ.

Bachar, J. M. & Hadwin, D. W., eds. Hilbert Space Operators: Proceedings, University of California Long Beach, LB CA, June 20-24, 1978. (Lecture Notes in Mathematics Ser.: Vol. 693). 1978. pap. 15.00 (ISBN 0-387-09097-5). Springer-Verlag.

Bachar, Miriam, jt. auth. see Arena, Jay M.

Bacharach, A. L. & Pearce, J. R., eds. The Musical Companion. (Illus.). 800p. 1982. Repr. of 1977 ed. 24.95 (ISBN 0-575-02263-9, Pub by Gollancz England). David & Charles.

Bacharach, A. L., jt. ed. see Laurence, D. R.

Bacharach, Alfred L., ed. Lives of the Great Composers. LC 72-276. (Essay Index Reprint Ser.). Repr. of 1935 ed. 30.00 (ISBN 0-8369-2783-4). Ayer Co Pubs.

Bacharach, Jere L. A Middle East Studies Handbook. rev. ed. LC 84-2225. (Illus.). 172p. 1984. 20.00x (ISBN 0-295-96138-4); pap. 9.95x (ISBN 0-295-96144-9). U of Wash Pr.

Bacharach, Jere L., jt. ed. see Kouymjian, Dickran K.

Bacharach, M. O., jt. ed. see Malinvaud, E.

Bacharach, S. L., et al. Electricity & Electronic Fundamentals, 3 vols. (Illus.). 1971. Set. loseleaf 150.00x (ISBN 0-87683-316-4); Vol. 1. 60.00x (ISBN 0-87683-317-2); Vol. 2; lab. manual; 270p. looseleaf 50.00x (ISBN 0-87683-318-0); Vol. 3; solutions manual; 270p. losseleaf 45.00x (ISBN 0-87683-319-9); Lesson Plans; 320p. looseleaf 1500.00x (ISBN 0-87683-321-0); Transparencies. looseleaf 1500.00x (ISBN 0-87683-322-9). G P Courseware.

Bacharach, Samuel. Research in the Sociology of Organizations, Vol. 3. 1984. 47.50 (ISBN 0-89232-450-3). Jai Pr.

Bacharach, Samuel B. Organizational Behavior in Schools & School Districts. LC 81-5138. 544p. 1981. 42.50 (ISBN 0-03-057669-5). Praeger.

Bacharach, Samuel B. & Lawler, Edward J. Bargaining: Power, Tactics & Outcomes. LC 81-8197. (Social & Behavioral Science Ser.). 1981. text ed. 19.95x (ISBN 0-87589-498-4). Jossey-Bass.

--Power & Politics in Organizations: The Social Psychology of Conflict, Coalitions, & Bargaining. LC 79-92460. (Social & Behavioral Science Ser.). 1980. text ed. 19.95x (ISBN 0-87589-458-5). Jossey-Bass.

Bacharach, Samuel B., ed. Research in the Sociology of Organizations, Vol. 1. 350p. 1981. 40.00 (ISBN 0-89232-170-9). Jai Pr.

Bacharach, Samuel B., jt. ed. see Hammer, Tove H.

Bacharach, Samuel B., et al. Paying for Better Teaching: Merit Pay & Its Alternatives. LC 84-1096. (OAP Monograph). 72p. (Orig.). 1984. pap. 14.50 (ISBN 0-930475-00-3). Organizational.

Bachardy, Don. Seventyxl. (Illus.). 80p. 1984. 45.00 (ISBN 0-89807-028-7); pap. 25.00 (ISBN 0-89807-029-5); signed & numbered 150.00 (ISBN 0-317-13030-7). Illuminati.

Bachardy, Don, jt. auth. see Isherwood, Christopher.

Bache, Constance, tr. see Liszt, Franz.

Bache, Constance, tr. see Von Buelow, Hans.

Bache, Constance, tr. see Von Bulow, Marie.

Bache, David H. & MacAskill, Ian A. Vegetation in Civil & Landscape Engineering. (Illus.). 320p. 1984. text ed. 40.00x (ISBN 0-246-11507-6, Pub. by Granada England). Sheridan.

Bache, William B. Measure for Measure As Dialectical Art. LC 69-16057. 70p. (Orig.). 1969. pap. 2.50 (ISBN 0-911198-18-0). Purdue U Pr.

Bachelard, Gaston. The New Scientific Spirit. Goldhammer, Arthur, tr. from Fren. LC 84-14609. 214p. 1985. 22.95 (ISBN 0-8070-1501-6). Beacon Pr.

--Poetics of Reverie: Childhood, Language & the Cosmos. 1971. pap. 7.95x (ISBN 0-8070-6413-0, BP375). Beacon Pr.

--Poetics of Space. Jolas, Maria, tr. 1969. pap. 6.95 (ISBN 0-8070-6439-4, BP330). Beacon Pr.

--Psychoanalysis of Fire. Ross, A. C., tr. 1964. pap. 5.95x (ISBN 0-8070-6461-0, BP277). Beacon Pr.

--Water & Dreams: An Essay on the Imagination of Matter. Farrell, Edith R., tr. from Fr. 213p. 22.00 (ISBN 0-317-04708-6). Pegasus Found.

Bachelard, H. S. Brain Biochemistry. 2nd ed. 1981. pap. 7.50 (ISBN 0-412-23470-X, NO.6490, Pub. by Chapman & Hall). Methuen Inc.

Bachelard, Suzanne. Study of Husserl's Formal & Transcendental Logic. Embree, Lester E., tr. LC 68-15330. (Studies in Phenomenology & Existential Philosophy Ser). 1968. 15.95 (ISBN 0-8101-0028-2). Northwestern U Pr.

Bachelder, John. A.D. 2050 Electrical Development at Atlantis: By a Former Resident of "The Hub". LC 76-42717. Repr. of 1890 ed. 12.50 (ISBN 0-404-60052-2). AMS Pr.

Bachelder, Joseph E., jt. auth. see Chadwick, William J.

Bachelder, Louise. Christmas Tidings. 2nd ed. LC 84-60961. 64p. 1984. Repr. of 1969 ed. 4.95 (ISBN 0-88088-088-0, 880880). Peter Pauper.

Bachelder, Louise, ed. The Gift of Music. 1975. 4.95 (ISBN 0-88088-218-2). Peter Pauper.

Bachelder, Robert S. Between Dying & Birth. 1983. 4.75 (ISBN 0-89536-623-1). CSS of Ohio.

--Mystery & Miracle. 1983. 3.00 (ISBN 0-89536-606-1, 1340). CSS of Ohio.

Bachelet, Joel, jt. auth. see Carpentier, Didier.

Bachelis, Faren, ed. see Davis, Hilarie.

Bachelis, Faren, ed. see Draze, Dianne.

Bachelis, Faren, ed. see Keene, Donna & Keene, Dathy.

Bachelis, Faren, ed. see Neff, Carolyn & Verett, Dotty.

Bacheller, Franklin. Listening & Recall. (Illus.). 160p. 1986. pap. text ed. 11.95 (ISBN 0-13-537481-2). P-H.

Bacheller, Irving. Eben Holden, a Tale of the North Country. LC 74-128934. (BCL Ser.: No. I). Repr. of 1903 ed. 18.50 (ISBN 0-404-00439-3). AMS Pr.

--Eben Holden: A Tale of the North Country. LC 3-32793. 1969. Repr. of 1903 ed. 16.00x (ISBN 0-403-00142-0). Scholarly.

Bacheller, Martin A., ed. Ambassador World Atlas. New census rev. ed. LC 84-675155. (Illus.). 500p. 1984. 39.95 (ISBN 0-8437-1251-1). Hammond Inc.

--Citation World Atlas: New World Census Edition. rev. ed. LC 84-675154. (Hammond World Atlas Ser.). (Illus.). 364p. 1984. 22.95 (ISBN 0-8437-1254-6); pap. 15.95 lexotone cover (ISBN 0-8437-1255-4). Hammond Inc.

--Medallion World Atlas: New Census Edition. rev. ed. LC 84-675070. (Hammond World Atlas Ser.). (Illus.). 672p. 1984. 65.00 (ISBN 0-8437-1250-3). Hammond Inc.

--The Whole Earth Atlas: New Census Edition. LC 82-83211. (Illus.). 256p. 1983. pap. 8.95 (ISBN 0-8437-2499-4). Hammond Inc.

Bachellis, F., ed. see Powell, Carolyn.

Bachelor, A. & Haley, J. Practice of English Fundamentals: V. Form. 1945. pap. text ed. 12.95. P-H.

Bachelor, Evelyn, et al, eds. Teen Conflicts. (Orig.). (YA) 1972. pap. 7.95 (ISBN 0-87297-007-8). Diablo.

Bachem, A., et al, eds. Bonn Workshop on Combinatorial Optimization. (Mathematics Studies: Vol. 66). 312p. 1982. pap. 51.00 (ISBN 0-444-86366-4, I-320-82, North Holland). Elsevier.

--Mathematical Programming - Bonn 1982: The State of the Art. (Illus.). 660p. 1983. 57.00 (ISBN 0-387-12082-3). Springer-Verlag.

Bachem, Michael. Heimito von Doderer. (World Authors Ser.). 1981. lib. bdg. 15.95 (ISBN 0-8057-6437-2, Twayne). G K Hall.

Bacher, J. M., et al, eds. Radical Banach Algebras & Automatic Continuity: Long Beach, California, 1981, Proceedings. (Lecture Notes in Mathematics: Vol. 975). 470p. 1983. pap. 26.00 (ISBN 0-387-11985-X). Springer-Verlag.

Bacher, June M. Echoes from the Past. (Rhapsody Romance Ser.). 192p. (Orig.). 1985. pap. 2.95 (ISBN 0-89081-463-5). Harvest Hse.

--Echoes from the Past. (Mystery-Romance Ser.). (Orig.). 1985. pap. 4.95 (ISBN 0-89081-461-9). Harvest Hse.

--The Grandmother Book. 128p. 1982. 6.95 (ISBN 0-8010-0821-2). Baker Bk.

--Great Gifts of Christmas Joy. LC 83-70005. 96p. 1983. pap. 4.95 (ISBN 0-8054-5707-0). Broadman.

--The Heart That Lingers. (Rhapsody Romance Ser.). 192p. (Orig.). 1983. pap. 2.95 (ISBN 0-89081-398-1). Harvest Hse.

--Journey to Love. (Pioneer Romance Ser.). (Orig.). 1985. pap. 4.95 (ISBN 0-89081-453-8). Harvest Hse.

--Kitchen Delights. LC 82-81649. 176p. 1982. 7.95 (ISBN 0-89081-358-2). Harvest Hse.

--Love Is a Gentle Stranger. LC 82-83839. 160p. (YA) (gr. 10 up). 1983. pap. 4.95 (ISBN 0-89081-374-4). Harvest Hse.

--Love Leads Home. (Pioneer Romance Ser.). 1984. pap. 4.95 (ISBN 0-89081-425-2). Harvest Hse.

--Love's Silent Song. LC 83-80875. (Pioneer Romance Ser.). 176p. (Orig.). 1983. pap. 4.95 (ISBN 0-89081-378-7, 3787). Harvest Hse.

--A Mother's Joy. 1984. pap. 6.95 (ISBN 0-8010-0852-2). Baker Bk.

--Quiet Moment: For Women a Daily Devotional. LC 79-84722. 1979. pap. 6.95 (ISBN 0-89081-187-3). Harvest Hse.

--Until There Was You. (Rhapsody Romance Ser.). 192p. 1984. 2.95 (ISBN 0-89081-419-8). Harvest Hse.

--When Love Shines Through. (Rhapsody Romance Ser.). 1984. pap. 2.95 (ISBN 0-89081-430-9). Harvest Hse.

Bacher, June Masters. Diary of a Loving Heart. LC 83-82322. (Pioneer Romance Ser.). 176p. 1984. pap. 4.95 (ISBN 0-89081-377-9). Harvest Hse.

--A Mother's Joy. 128p. 1984. pap. 6.95 6x (ISBN 0-89081-415-5). Harvest Hse.

--With All My Heart. (Rhapsody Romance Ser.). 192p. 1983. 2.95 (ISBN 0-89081-410-4). Harvest Hse.

Bacher, L. The Mobile Mise En Scene: A Critical Analysis of the Theory & Practice of Long Take Camera Movement in the Narrative Film. LC 77-22904. (Dissertations on Film Ser.). 1978. lib. bdg. 24.50x (ISBN 0-405-10750-1). Ayer Co Pubs.

Bacher, Wilhelm. Abraham Ibn Esra Als Grammatiker: Ein Beitrag zur Geschichte der Hebraischen Sprachwissenschaft. Katz, Steven, ed. LC 79-7125. (Jewish Philosophy, Mysticism & History of Ideas Ser.). 1980. Repr. of 1882 ed. lib. bdg. 16.00x (ISBN 0-405-12239-X). Ayer Co Pubs.

--Die Anfaenge der Hebraeischen Grammatik (1895) Together with Die Hebraeische Sprachwissenschaft Vom 10. Bis Zum 16. Jahrhundert (1892) (Studies in the History of Linguistics Ser.: 4). xix, 235p. 1974. pap. 38.00x (ISBN 90-272-0895-6). Benjamins North Am.

Bachert, Russel E., Jr., ed. Hundreds of Ideas for Outdoor Education. 152p. 1979. pap. text ed. 8.50x (ISBN 0-8134-2095-4). Interstate.

Bachhofer, Ludwig. A Short History of Chinese Art. LC 83-45695. Repr. of 1946 ed. 47.50 (ISBN 0-404-20014-1). AMS Pr.

Bachhuber, Thomas D. When Your Son or Daughter Plans for the Future. LC 78-73014. (When Bk). (Illus.). 1978. pap. 2.45 (ISBN 0-87029-144-0, 20230-9). Abbey.

Bachhuber, Thomas D., jt. auth. see Van Roden, Albert C.

Bachi, Roberto. Graphical Rational Patterns: A New Approach to Graphical Presentation of Statistics. 264p. 1968. casebound 27.95x (ISBN 0-87855-201-4). Transaction Bks.

Bachinsky, M., et al. Practical Guide to Geriatric Medication. 1980. pap. 15.95 (ISBN 0-87489-205-8). Med Economics.

Bachman, Ben. Upstream: A Voyage on the Connecticut River. 1985. 15.95 (ISBN 0-395-34389-5). HM.

Bachman, Christian G. Radar Targets. LC 81-48003. 256p. 1982. 31.50x (ISBN 0-669-05232-9). Lexington Bks.

Bachman, George & Narici, Lawrence. Functional Analysis. 1966. text ed. 25.00i (ISBN 0-12-070250-9). Acad Pr.

Bachman, George K. Pipefitters & Plumbers Vest Pocket Reference Book. 214p. 1983. pap. 6.95 (ISBN 0-13-676262-X). P-H.

Bachman, George W. & Meriam, Lewis. The Issue of Compulsory Health Insurance. LC 75-17203. (Social Problems & Social Policy Ser.). (Illus.). 1976. Repr. of 1948 ed. 21.00x (ISBN 0-405-07475-1). Ayer Co Pubs.

Bachman, James E. Capitalization Requirements for Multiple Line Property Liability Insurance Companies. LC 78-57297. (S. S. Huebner Foundation Monographs: No. 6). (Illus.). 94p. 1978. pap. 11.50 (ISBN 0-918930-06-5). Huebner Foun Insur.

Bachman, Jerald C., jt. auth. see Johnston, Jerome.

Bachman, Jerald G. The Impact of Family Background & Intelligence on Tenth-Grade Boys. LC 79-630045. (Michigan University. Survey Research Center. Youth in Transition Ser.: Vol. 2). pap. 76.80 (ISBN 0-317-08277-9, 2005424). Bks Demand UMI.

Bachman, Jerald G., jt. auth. see Herzog, A. Regula.

Bachman, Jerald G., et al. Youth in Transition. Incl. Vol. 3. Dropping Out-- Problem or Symptom? LC 67-66009. 263p. 1971. 14.00x (ISBN 0-87944-111-9); Vol. 5. Young Men & Military Service. LC 67-66009. 260p. 1972. cloth 12.00x (ISBN 0-87944-119-4); pap. 8.00x (ISBN 0-87944-118-6); Vol. 6. Adolescence to Adulthood--Change & Stability in the Lives of Young Men. 350p. 1978. 18.00x (ISBN 0-87944-224-7). Inst Soc Res.

--The All-Volunteer Force: A Study of Ideology in the Military. LC 77-5631. 1977. text ed. 13.95x (ISBN 0-472-08095-4); pap. 7.95x (ISBN 0-472-08096-2). U of Mich Pr.

--Blueprint for a Longitudinal Study of Adolescent Boys. LC 72-610663. (Michigan University Survey Research Center Youth in Transition Ser.: Vol. 1). pap. 71.30 (ISBN 0-317-08278-7, 2005413). Bks Demand UMI.

Bachman, John, jt. auth. see Audubon, John J.

Bachman, John W. Faith That Makes a Difference. LC 83-70508. 128p. (Orig.). 1983. pap. 5.50 (ISBN 0-8066-2014-5, 10-2193). Augsburg.

--Media-Wasteland Or Wonderland: Opportunities & Dangers for Christians in the Electronic Age. 176p. (Orig.). 1984. pap. 7.95 (ISBN 0-8066-2116-8, 10-4307). Augsburg.

Bachman, Judith. City Size & the Quality of Life. (gr. 11 up). 1985. pap. 5.95 (ISBN 0-89420-060-7, 480041); cassette recordings 101.30 (ISBN 0-89420-134-4, 480020). Natl Book.

--A History of Indian Policy: Syllabus. 1978. pap. text ed. 5.75 (ISBN 0-89420-038-0, 333020); cassette recordings 146.10 (ISBN 0-89420-149-2, 333000). Natl Book.

Bachman, Kelly L., jt. auth. see Derrick, Sara M.

Bachman, Lyle F. Reading English Discourse: Business, Economics, Law & Political Science. 280p. 1986. pap. text ed. 11.95 (ISBN 0-13-755844-9). P-H.

Bachman, Mae G. The Silver Feather. 144p. (Orig.). 1981. pap. 2.50 (ISBN 0-87178-787-3). Brethren.

Bachman, Mary. Choosing Is Fun. LC 81-86704. (Happy Day Bks.). (Illus.). 24p. (Orig.). (ps-3). 1982. pap. 1.39 (ISBN 0-87239-534-0, 3580). Standard Pub.

--God's World of Colors. (A Happy Day Book). (Illus.). 24p. (gr. k-2). 1980. 1.39 (ISBN 0-87239-408-5, 3640). Standard Pub.

Bachman, Paul W. Research for Profit: The Problem, the Solution, a Case History. LC 78-75633. (Illus.). pap. 50.50 (ISBN 0-317-09730-X, 2012403). Bks Demand UMI.

Bachman, Richard. The Long Walk. 1979. pap. 3.50 (ISBN 0-451-13539-3, J8754, Sig). NAL.

Bachman, Richard, pseud. Thinner. 256p. 1984. 12.95 (ISBN 0-453-00468-7). NAL.

--Thinner. 1985. pap. 3.95 (ISBN 0-451-13796-5, Sig). NAL.

Bachman, Van Cleaf. Peltries or Plantations: The Economic Policies of the Dutch West India Company in New Netherland, 1623-1639. LC 74-91336. (Studies in Historical & Political Science: Eighty-Seventh Series). 292p. 1970. 27.50x (ISBN 0-8018-1064-7). Johns Hopkins.

Bachman, W. Bryant, Jr., tr. from Old Icelandic. Four Old Icelandic Sagas & Other Tales. 252p. (Orig.). 1985. lib. bdg. 21.00 (ISBN 0-8191-4703-6); pap. text ed. 12.50 (ISBN 0-8191-4704-4). U Pr of Amer.

Bachmann. A Beginner's Guide to the ISU Vax Computer. 112p. 1985. pap. text ed. 7.95 (ISBN 0-8403-3538-5). Kendall-Hunt.

Bachmann, Alberto. An Encyclopedia of the Violin. Weir, Albert E., ed. Martens, Frederick H., tr. from Ger. LC 65-23406. (Music Ser.). 1966. Repr. of 1925 ed. lib. bdg. 39.50 (ISBN 0-306-70912-0). Da Capo.

--An Encyclopedia of the Violin. Wier, Albert E., ed. Martens, Frederick H., tr. from Ger. LC 74-20867. (Music Reprint Ser). (Illus.). xiv, 470p. 1975. pap. 9.95 (ISBN 0-306-80004-7). Da Capo.

Bachmann, Barbara & Strickland, Walter N. Neurospore Bibliography & Index. LC 65-12538. pap. 58.50 (ISBN 0-317-10246-X, 2021977). Bks Demand UMI.

Bachmann, Bertha. Memories of Kazakhstan. Duin, Edgar C., tr. from Ger. LC 83-73393. 160p. (YA) (gr. 7-12). 1984. pap. text ed. 7.00 (ISBN 0-914222-12-0). Am Hist Soc Ger.

Bachmann, Diana. Beyond the Sunset. 384p. 1985. pap. 3.95 (ISBN 0-449-12772-9, GM). Fawcett.

Bachmann, Donna G. & Piland, Sherry. Women Artists: An Historical, Contemporary & Feminist Bibliography. LC 78-19182. 353p. 1978. 22.50 (ISBN 0-8108-1149-9). Scarecrow.

Bachmann, E. Theodore, tr. see Bornkamm, Heinrich.

Bachmann, F., et al, eds. International Congress on Fibrinolysis, 6th, Lausanne, July 1982: Abstracts. (Journal: Haemostasis, Vol. 11, Suppl. 1, 1982). iv, 108p. 1982. pap. 15.00 (ISBN 3-8055-3590-2). S Karger.

Bachmann, George K. Pipefitter's & Plumber's Vest Pocket Reference Book. 213p. 1960. 6.95 (ISBN 0-13-676312-X). P-H.

Bachmann, Heinz. Der Weg der Mathematischen Grundlagenforschung. 240p. (Ger.). 1983. 20.00 (ISBN 3-261-05089-6). P Lang Pubs.

Bachmann, Hugo. Partial Prestressing of Concrete Structures. (IBA Ser.: No. 95). 20p. 1979. pap. text ed. 9.95x (ISBN 0-8176-1150-9). Birkhauser.

Bachmann, I. New Writing & Writers, No. 14. (New Writing & Writers Ser.). 1980. pap. 6.00 (ISBN 0-7145-3553-2); 12.95 (ISBN 0-7145-3562-1). Riverrun NY.

Bachmann, Jul & Von Moos, Stanislaus. New Directions in Swiss Architecture. LC 72-78052. (New Directions in Architecture Ser). (Illus., Orig.). 1969. 7.95 (ISBN 0-8076-0525-5); pap. 3.95 (ISBN 0-8076-0529-8). Braziller.

Bachmann, K., jt. ed. see Kimmich, H. P.

Bachmann, P., et al, eds. MIRDAB: Microbiological Resource Databank Catalog, 1985. 612p. 1985. 83.50 (ISBN 0-444-90387-9). Elsevier.

Bachmann, Paul. Niedere Zahlentheorie, 2 Vols. in 1. LC 66-20395. 902p. (Ger). 1968. Repr. of 1902 ed. text ed. 24.00 (ISBN 0-8284-0217-5). Chelsea Pub.

--Zahlentheorie, 5 vols. (Nos. 15-20). (Ger). Repr. Set. 175.00 (ISBN 0-384-02990-6). Johnson Repr.

Bachmann, Peter A., ed. Biological Products for Viral Diseases: Munich Symposia on Microbiology. (Illus.). 268p. 1981. pap. text ed. 26.00 (ISBN 0-85066-226-5, Pub. by Taylor & Francis England). J K Burgess.

--Leukaemias, Lymphomas & Papillomas: Comparative Aspects. (Munich Symposia on Microbiology). (Illus.). 273p. (Orig.). 1980. pap. text ed. 26.00 (ISBN 0-85066-213-3, Pub. by Taylor & Francis England). J K Burgess.

Bachmann, Robert. Hand of a Thousand Rings: And Other Chinese Stories. facsimile ed. LC 76-178435. (Short Story Index Reprint Ser.). Repr. of 1924 ed. 15.00 (ISBN 0-8369-4035-0). Ayer Co Pubs.

Bachmann, Theodore & Lehmann, Helmut T., eds. Luther's Works: Word & Sacrament I, Vol. 35. LC 55-9893. 426p. 1960. 16.95 (ISBN 0-8006-0335-4, 1-335). Fortress.

Bachmann, W. & Mehnert, H., eds. Kombinationstherapie Insulin-Sulfonylharhstoff. (Illus.). viii, 208p. 1984. 27.75 (ISBN 3-8055-3850-2). S Karger.

Bachmann, W., et al, eds. Mental Load & Stress in Activity. 136p. 1983. 34.00 (ISBN 0-444-86349-4, I-107-82). Elsevier.

Bachmat, Y., jt. auth. see Bredehoeft, John.

Bachmayer, H., jt. ed. see Laver, W. G.

Bachmeyer, jt. auth. see Hauenstein.

Bachmeyer, T. J., jt. auth. see Everett, William W.

Bachner, John P. & Khosla, Naresh K. Marketing & Promotion for Design Professionals. LC 81-6002. 368p. 1981. Repr. of 1977 ed. lib. bdg. 22.00 (ISBN 0-89874-362-1). Krieger.

--Marketing & Promotion for Design Professionals. LC 76-57975. (Illus.). pap. 92.00 (ISBN 0-317-10554-X, 2014902). Bks Demand UMI.

Bachner, Susan. Picture This: An Illustrated Guide to Complete Dinners. (Illus.). 72p. 1984. 22.50 (ISBN 0-9613439-0-7). Spec Addns.

Bachofen, J. J. Myth, Religion, & Mother Right: Selected Writings of Johann Jakob Bachofen. Manheim, Ralph, tr. LC 67-22343. (Bollingen Series, No. 84). 368p. 1967. 34.50 (ISBN 0-691-09799-2); pap. 9.50 (ISBN 0-691-01797-2, 303). Princeton U Pr.

Bachofen, R. & Mislin, H., eds. New Trends in Research & Utilization of Solar Energy Through Biological Systems. (Experientia Supplementum: Vol. 43). 156p. 1982. text ed. 26.95 (ISBN 0-8176-1335-8). Birkhauser.

Bachorik, Joan E., et al. Internal Medicine Case Studies. 1984. pap. text ed. write for info (ISBN 0-87488-225-7). Med Exam.

Bachrach, A. G. Sir Constantine Huygens & Britain: 1597-1619, Vol. 1. (Publications of the Sir Thomas Browne Institute Ser: No. 1). 1962. 26.00 (ISBN 90-6021-059-X, Pub. by Leiden Univ Holland). Kluwer Academic.

Bachrach, A. G. H., ed. see Huygens, L., et al.

Bachrach, A. L. & Pearce, J. R., eds. The Musical Companion. 800p. 1984. pap. 13.95 (ISBN 0-15-662321-8, Harv). HarBraceJ.

Bachrach, Ann, et al. Developmental Therapy for Young Children with Autistic Characteristics. LC 77-16370. (Illus.). 200p. 1978. pap. 14.00 (ISBN 0-936104-61-9). Pro Ed.

Bachrach, Arthur J. Psychological Research: An Introduction. 4th ed. 205p. 1981. pap. text ed. 6.95 (ISBN 0-394-32288-6, RanC). Random.

Bachrach, B. S., ed. The Medieval Church: Success or Failure? LC 76-162863. (European Problem Ser.). 120p. 1972. pap. text ed. 5.95 (ISBN 0-03-085185-8, Pub. by HR&W). Krieger.

Bachrach, Bernard S. Jews in Barbarian Europe. 1977. 7.50x (ISBN 0-87291-088-1). Coronado Pr.

Bachrach, Bernard S., ed. Liber Historae Francorum. 123p. 1973. 5.00x (ISBN 0-87291-058-X). Coronado Pr.

Bachrach, Christine A., et al. National Survey of Family Growth, Cycle III: Sample Design, Weighting, & Variance Estimation (PHS) 85-1372. Olmstead, Mary, ed. (Series 2: No. 98). 28p. 1985. pap. text ed. 2.50 (ISBN 0-8406-0316-9). Natl Ctr Health Stats.

Bachrach, Judy & DeMonte, Claudia. The Height Report: A Tall Woman's Handbook. 72p. 1983. pap. 3.95 (ISBN 0-8362-6406-1). Andrews McMeel Parker.

Bachrach, Max. Fur - a Practical Treatise: Geography of the Fur World. 1977. lib. bdg. 75.00 (ISBN 0-8490-1873-0). Gordon Pr.

Bachrach, Peter. The Theory of Democratic Elitism: A Critique. LC 80-5747. 125p. 1980. lib. bdg. 19.75 (ISBN 0-8191-1184-8); pap. text ed. 8.00 (ISBN 0-8191-1185-6). U Pr of Amer.

Bachrach, Peter & Baratz, Morton S. Power & Poverty: Theory & Practice. 1970. pap. text ed. 6.95x (ISBN 0-19-500819-7). Oxford U Pr.

Bachrach, Peter, ed. Political Elites in a Democracy. (Controversy Ser.). 175p. 1971. text ed. 11.95x (ISBN 0-88311-003-2). Lieber-Atherton.

Bachrach, Susan. Dames Employees: The Feminization of Postal Work in Nineteenth-Century France. LC 83-22879. (Women & History Ser.: No. 8). 134p. 1984. text ed. 20.00 (ISBN 0-86656-205-2, B205). Haworth Pr.

Bachrach, Uriel. Function of Naturally Occuring Polyamines. 1973. 49.00 (ISBN 0-12-070650-4). Acad Pr.

Bachrach, Uriel, et al, eds. Advances in Polyamine Research, Vol. 4. 832p. 1983. text ed. 76.00 (ISBN 0-89004-890-8). Raven.

Bachrach, Yehoshua. Mother of Royalty. Oschry, Leonard, tr. 1973. 7.95 (ISBN 0-87306-018-0). Feldheim.

Bachrack, Stanley D. The Committee of One Million: "China Lobby" Politics, 1953-1971. LC 76-18117. 1976. 30.00x (ISBN 0-231-03933-6). Columbia U Pr.

Bachrich, Jack L. Dry Kiln Handbook. (Illus.). 373p. 1980. 50.00 (ISBN 0-87930-087-6, Pub. by H A Simons Intl Canada). Miller Freeman.

Bachtin, Michail. Fomalny Metod v Literaturovedenu: The Formal Method in Literary. 2nd ed. Kurtanovich, Konstantin, ed. (Illus.). 236p. (Orig., Russian.). pap. 12.50 (ISBN 0-940294-14-1). Silver Age Pub.

Bach-Y-Rita, Paul, jt. auth. see Levy, Joseph V.

Bach-Y-Rita, Paul, ed. Recovery of Function. (Illus.). 278p. 1980. pap. text ed. 29.95 (ISBN 0-8391-4111-4). Univ Park.

--Recovery of Function: Theoretical Considerations for Brain Injury Rehabilitation. (Illus.). 278p. (Orig.). 1980. pap. text ed. 23.50 (ISBN 3-456-80836-4, Pub. by Hans Huber Switzerland). J K Burgess.

Bach-Y-Rita, Paul & Collins, C. C., eds. Brain Mechanisms in Sensory Substitution. 1972. 40.00 (ISBN 0-12-071040-4). Acad Pr.

Bacig, Tom, jt. auth. see Thompson, Fred.

Bacigal, Ronald J. Virginia Criminal Procedure. 289p. incl. latest pocket part supplement 59.95 (ISBN 0-686-91021-4); Separate pocket part supplement 1984. 15.95. Harrison Co GA.

Bacigalupa, Drew. A Good & Perfect Gift. LC 78-60727. (ps-3). 1978. 4.95 (ISBN 0-87973-352-7). Our Sunday Visitor.

--The Song of Guadalupana. LC 79-88028. (ps up). 1979. pap. 4.95 (ISBN 0-87973-357-8). Our Sunday Visitor.

Bacigalupo, Leonard F. The American Franciscan Missions in Central America. LC 80-68205. 483p. (Orig.). 1980. 19.50 (ISBN 0-933402-20-1); pap. 9.95 (ISBN 0-933402-21-X). Charisma Pr.

Bacigalupo, Massimo, ed. The Formed Trace: The Later Poetry of Ezra Pound. LC 79-12877. 371p. 1980. 44.00x (ISBN 0-231-04456-9). Columbia U Pr.

Bacik, James J. Apologetics & the Eclipse of Mystery: Mystagogy According to Karl Rahner. LC 80-123. 192p. 1980. 15.00 (ISBN 0-268-00592-3); pap. 6.95 (ISBN 0-268-00593-1). U of Notre Dame Pr.

Bacila, Metry, et al, eds. Biochemistry & Genetics of Yeasts: Pure & Applied Aspects. LC 78-21898. 1978. 60.00 (ISBN 0-12-071250-4). Acad Pr.

Baciu, Nicolae. Sell-Out to Stalin: The Tragic Errors of Churchill & Roosevelt. LC 84-90004. 1984. lib. bdg. 13.50 (ISBN 0-533-06096-6). Vantage.

Baciu, Stefan, compiled by. Antologia de la Poesia Latinoamericana, 1950-1970, 2 vols. LC 73-37514. 1974. Set. pap. 23.50x (ISBN 0-87395-077-1). State U NY Pr.

Back, Brian. The Keewaydin Way: A Portrait, 1893-1983. (Illus.). 206p. (Orig.). 1983. pap. 17.00 (ISBN 0-9691378-1-8). Keewaydin Camp.

Back, D. H. L., jt. auth. see Neal, W. Keith.

Back, George R. & Torbet, Laura. The Inner Enemy: How to Fight Fair with Yourself. 224p. 1985. pap. 3.50 (ISBN 0-425-07706-3). Berkley Pub.

Back, Gloria G. Are You Still My Mother? 246p. 1985. pap. 7.95 (ISBN 0-446-38195-0). Warner Bks.

Back, H. The Synonyms for "Child", "Boys", "Girl" in Old English: An Etymological-Semiasiological Investigation. (Lund Studies in English: Vol. 2). pap. 30.00 (ISBN 0-317-16731-6). Kraus Repr.

Back, Harry, et al, eds. Polec: Dictionary of Politics & Economics. 2nd, rev. & enl. ed. (Ger., Eng. & Fr.). 1967. 28.40x (ISBN 3-11-000892-0). De Gruyter.

Back, Joe. Horses, Hitches & Rocky Trails. 1959. 9.95 (ISBN 0-933472-06-4). Johnson Bks.

Back, Kate, jt. auth. see Back, Ken.

Back, Ken & Back, Kate. Assertiveness at Work: A Practical Guide to Handling Awkward Situations. (Illus.). 176p. 1982. 23.95 (ISBN 0-07-084576-X). McGraw.

Back, Kurt W. Beyond Words: The Story of Sensitivity Training & the Encounter Movement. LC 73-182935. 266p. 1972. 9.95x (ISBN 0-87154-077-0). Russell Sage.

--Slums, Projects & People. LC 73-19572. 123p. 1974. Repr. of 1962 ed. lib. bdg. 22.50 (ISBN 0-8371-7289-6, BASL). Greenwood.

Back, Kurt W., ed. Life Course: Integrative Theories & Exemplary Populations. (AAAS Selected Symposium: No. 41). 160p. 1980. lib. bdg. 24.50x (ISBN 0-89158-777-2). Westview.

--Social Psychology. LC 76-30835. pap. 127.30 (ISBN 0-317-09548-X, 2055188). Bks Demand UMI.

Back, Mary. Seven Half-Miles from Home. (Illus.). 200p. 1985. pap. 9.95 (ISBN 0-933472-90-0). Johnson Bks.

Back, N. & Sicuteri, F., eds. Vasopeptides: Chemistry, Pharmocology & Pathophysiology. LC 78-190395. (Advances in Experimental Medicine & Biology Ser.: Vol. 21). 519p. 1972. 65.00x (ISBN 0-306-39021-3, Plenum Pr). Plenum Pub.

Back, N., jt. ed. see Mirand, E. A.

Back, Nathan, jt. auth. see Spector, Sydney.

Back, Nathan, jt. ed. see Bertelli, Aldo.

Back, Nathan, et al, eds. Kinins I: Pharmacodynamics & Biological Roles. LC 76-7006. (Advances in Experimental Medicine & Biology Ser.: Vol. 70). 409p. 1976. 55.00x (ISBN 0-306-39070-1, Plenum Pr). Plenum Pub.

--Pharmacology of Hormonal Polypeptides & Proteins. LC 68-19184. (Advances in Experimental Medicine & Biology Ser.: Vol. 2). 671p. 1968. 55.00x (ISBN 0-306-39002-7, Plenum Pr). Plenum Pub.

Back, Peg. Crickets & Corn. 1985. 2.95 (ISBN 0-377-00152-X). Friend Pr.

--Crickets & Corn: Leader's Guide. 1985. 4.95 (ISBN 0-317-17381-2). Friend Pr.

Back, Philippa. Choosing, Planting & Cultivating Herbs. LC 76-58770. (Living with Herbs Ser.: Vol. 2). (Illus.). 100p. 1977. pap. 2.50 (ISBN 0-87983-149-9). Keats.

Back, Philippa, jt. auth. see Huxley, Alyson.

Back, Philippa, jt. auth. see Loewenfeld, Claire.

Back, Philippa, jt. auth. see Lowenfeld, Claire.

Back, R. P. The Runes Are Cast. 1981. 15.00x (ISBN 0-7223-1368-3, Pub. by Stockwell). State Mutual BK.

Back, W. & Letolle, R., eds. Geochemistry of Groundwater: Proceedings of thd 26th International Geological Congress, Paris, France-July 1980. (Developments in Water Science Ser.: Vol. 16). 370p. 1982. 64.00 (ISBN 0-444-42036-3). Elsevier.

Back, W. & Stephenson, D. A., eds. Contemporary Hydrogeology: The George Burke Maxey Memorial. (Developments in Water Science Ser.: Vol. 12). 570p. 1980. Repr. 85.00 (ISBN 0-444-41848-2). Elsevier.

Back, W., jt. ed. see Freeze, R. A.

Back, William R. & Freeze, Allan, eds. Chemical Hydrogeology. LC 81-11853. (Benchmark Papers in Geology Ser.: Vol. 73). 416p. 1983. 49.00 (ISBN 0-87933-440-1). Van Nos Reinhold.

Backauskas, Anne L. Computer Capers. (Illus.). 32p. (Orig.). 1983. pap. 2.95 (ISBN 0-913405-00-0). ALB Assocs.

Backe, Torild, et al. Concise Swedish-English Glossary of Legal Terms. 164p. (Swedish & Eng.). 1973. text ed. 13.50x (ISBN 0-8377-0305-0). Rothman.

Backer, Barbara, jt. auth. see Larkin, Patricia.

Backer, Barbara A., et al. Psychiatric Mental Health Nursing: Contemporary Readings. 2nd ed. LC 84-29937. (Contemporary Readings Ser.). 300p. 1985. pap. text ed. 13.75 pub net (ISBN 0-534-04644-4). Wadsworth Health.

--Death & Dying: Individuals & Institutions. 332p. 1981. 18.50 (ISBN 0-471-08715-7, Pub. by Wiley Medical). Wiley.

Backer, Desaix. La Terrine de Sang. Gaujean, Gerard, ed. 1974. 5.00 (ISBN 0-685-39191-4). Haitian Soc.

Backer, Dorothy. The Parma Legacy. 1978. 10.95 (ISBN 0-393-08817-0). Norton.

Backer, John H. The Decision to Divide Germany: American Foreign Policy in Transition. LC 77-84614. 215p. 1978. 18.75 (ISBN 0-8223-0391-4). Duke.

--Priming the German Economy: American Occupational Policies, 1945-1948. LC 70-142289. pap. 55.50 (ISBN 0-317-28970-5, 2023758). Bks Demand UMI.

Backer, Morton. Current Value Accounting. LC 73-84374. 1973. 18.00 (ISBN 0-317-02341-1). Finan Exec.

Backer, Morton & Gosman, Martin L. Financial Reporting & Business Liquidity. 305p. pap. 24.95 (ISBN 0-86641-020-1, 78110). Natl Assn Accts.

Backer, S., et al. Textile Fabric Flammability. LC 75-23061. 400p. 1976. text ed. 32.50x (ISBN 0-262-02117-X). MIT Pr.

Backer, Thomas E., jt. auth. see Farmer, Helen S.

Backer-Grondahl, Agathe. Piano Music. (Women Composers Ser.: No. 9). 145p. 1983. lib. bdg. 26.50 (ISBN 0-306-76133-5). Da Capo.

Backett, E. Maurice. Domestic Accidents. (Public Health Papers Ser.: No. 26). 137p. (Eng, Fr, Rus, Span.). 1965. pap. 2.80 (ISBN 92-4-130026-4). World Health.

Backett, Katheryn C. Mothers & Fathers: Studies of Negotiation of Parental Behavior. LC 81-14343. 240p. 1982. 29.00x (ISBN 0-312-54934-2). St Martin.

Backhaut, Bernard, jt. auth. see Spiegel, Allen D.

Backhouse, Constance & Cohen, Leah. Sexual Harassment on the Job: How to Avoid the Working Woman's Nightmare. 240p. 1981. 12.95 (ISBN 0-13-807545-X, Spec); pap. 5.95 (ISBN 0-13-807537-9). P-H.

Backhouse, E. T. & Bland, J. O. Annals & Memoirs of the Court of Peking. LC 75-108118. (BCL Ser.: No. I). (Illus.). Repr. of 1914 ed. 24.50 (ISBN 0-404-00438-5). AMS Pr.

Backhouse, Gerry. Old Trade Handcarts. (Shire Album Ser.: No. 86). (Illus.). 32p. pap. 2.95 (ISBN 0-85263-608-3, Pub. by Shire Pubns England). Seven Hills Bks.

Backhouse, James. Narrative of a Visit to the Australian Colonies. 50.00 (ISBN 0-384-02995-7). Johnson Repr.

Backhouse, Janet. Books of Hours. (Illus.). 80p. (Orig.). 1985. pap. 8.95 (ISBN 0-7123-0052-X, Pub. by British Lib). Longwood Pub Group.

--The Lindisfarne Gospels. LC 81-65990. (Cornell Phaidon Bks.). (Illus.). 96p. 1981. 29.95 (ISBN 0-8014-1354-0). Cornell U Pr.

Backhouse, Janet, et al see Kren, Thomas.

Backhouse, Janet, et al, eds. The Golden Age of Anglo-Saxon Art, Nine Sixty-Six to Ten Sixty-Six. (Illus.). 256p. (Orig.). 1985. 32.50 (ISBN 0-253-13326-2); pap. 20.00 (ISBN 0-253-21268-5). Ind U Pr.

Backhouse, K. M. Color Atlas of Rheumatoid Hand Surgery. 1981. 104.50 (ISBN 0-8151-0371-9). Year Bk Med.

Backhouse, R. Syntax of Programming Languages Theory & Practice. 1979. 35.95 (ISBN 0-13-879999-7). P-H.

Backhouse, Roger. Information Services to Trade Unionists. 1982. 30.00x (ISBN 0-9505828-4-0, Pub by ELM Pubns England). State Mutual Bk.

Backhurst, J., jt. auth. see Harker, J. H.

Backhurst, J. R. & Harker, J. H. Process Plant Design. LC 72-12561. 411p. 1973. 46.95 (ISBN 0-444-19566-1). Elsevier.

Backhurst, J. R. see Coulson, J. M. & Richardson, J. F.

Backhuys, W. Land & Fresh Water Molluscs of the Azores. (Illus.). 1975. pap. 60.00 (ISBN 90-04-06447-8). Heinman.

Backiel, T. & Zawisza, J. Synopsis of Biological Data on the Bream: Abramis Brama (Linnaeus, 1758) (Fisheries Synopses: No. 36). 110p. 1968. pap. 8.00 (ISBN 0-686-93027-4, F1763, FAO). Unipub.

Backler, Alan & Hanvey, Robert. Global Geography. 352p. (gr. 7-10). 1986. pap. text ed. 15.95x (ISBN 0-8077-6103-6); 6.95x (ISBN 0-8077-6104-4). Tchrs Coll.

Backman, Ben. Shopping at Home for Camping & Outdoor Equipment. 192p. 1982. 15.95 (ISBN 0-87196-541-0); pap. 9.95 (ISBN 0-87196-535-6). Facts on File.

Backman, Carl A., jt. ed. see Smith, Seaton E.

Backman, Carl A., jt. ed. see Smith, Seaton E., Jr.

Backman, Eugene L. Religious Dances in the Christian & in Popular Medicine. Classen, E., ed. LC 77-8069. 1977. Repr. of 1952 ed. 32.00x (ISBN 0-8371-9678-7, BARD). Greenwood.

Backman, Jules. Business Problems of the Eighties. (ITT Key Issues Lecture Ser.). 1980. pap. 10.28 scp (ISBN 0-672-97499-1). Bobbs.

--Entrepreneurship & the Outlook for America. 1982. text ed. 12.95 (ISBN 0-02-922940-5). Free Pr.

--Regulation & Deregulation. (ITT Key Issues Lecture Ser.). 188p. (Orig.). 1981. pap. text ed. 8.40 scp (ISBN 0-672-97879-2). Bobbs.

Backman, Jules, jt. auth. see Czepiel, John.

Backman, Jules, ed. Advertising & Competition. 239p. (J). 1967. 5.00 (ISBN 0-318-13453-5, 4). Assn Natl Advertisers.

--Economic Growth or Stagnation. LC 78-10874. (ITT Key Issue Lecture Ser.). 1979. text ed. 14.47 scp (ISBN 0-672-97323-5); pap. text ed. 7.87 scp (ISBN 0-672-97322-7). Bobbs.

Backman, Milton V., Jr. Christian Churches of America. rev. ed. 288p. 1984. 17.95 (ISBN 0-684-17992-X, ScribT); pap. 12.95 (ISBN 0-684-17995-4). Scribner.

--Christian Churches of American Origins & Beliefs. rev. ed. 278p. 1983. pap. text ed. write for info. (ISBN 0-02-305090-X, Pub. by Scribner). Macmillan.

--The Heavens Resound: A History of the Latter-Day Saints in Ohio 1830-1838. LC 83-12882. (Illus.). 480p. 1983. 13.95 (ISBN 0-87747-973-9). Deseret Bk.

Backman, Pat. Journey with Matthew. (Orig.). 1984. tchr's. ed. 5.50 (ISBN 0-317-18415-6). LuraMedia.

Backman, Robert L. Take Charge of Your Life. LC 83-70332. 168p. 1983. 7.95 (ISBN 0-87747-970-4). Deseret Bk.

Backman, S. & Kjellmer, G., eds. Papers on Language & Literature. (Gothenburg Studies in English Ser.: No. 60). 399p. 1985. pap. text ed. 30.00x (ISBN 91-7346-155-5, Pub. by Acta-Universitatis Sweden). Humanities.

Backmen, Richard J. & Nerheim, Steven J. Toward a Healing Ministry: Exploring & Implementing a Congregational Ministry. 72p. (Orig.). 1985. pap. 5.95 (ISBN 0-8066-2176-1, 12-2022). Augsburg.

Backofen, Walter A. Deformation Processing. LC 71-132054. (Engineering Science Ser.). 1972. text ed. 29.95 (ISBN 0-201-00388-0). Addison-Wesley.

Backofen, Walter A., et al, eds. Fundamentals of Deformation Processing. LC 64-12568. (Sagamore Army Materials Research Conference Proceedings Ser.: Vol. 9). 435p. 1964. 35.00x (ISBN 0-306-34509-9, Plenum Pr). Plenum Pub.

Backpacker Editors, jt. auth. see Kemsley, William.

Backpacker Magazine, ed. see Bunnelle, Hasse R.

Backpacker Magazine Editors, jt. auth. see Kemsley, William.

Backpacking Journal Editors, jt. auth. see Schreiber, Lee.

Backscheider, ed. see Centlivre, Susanna.

Backscheider, P. R., ed. see Boaden, James.

Backscheider, P. R., ed. see Johnson, Samuel.

Backscheider, P. R., jt. ed. see Kenny, Shirley S.

Backscheider, P. R., jt. ed. see Liesenfeld, Vincent J.

Backscheider, P. R., ed. see Pix, Mary & Trotter, Catherine.

Backscheider, Paula R. A Being More Intense: A Study of the Prose Works of Bunyan, Swift, & Defoe. LC 83-45274. (Studies in the Eighteenth Century: No. 7). 222p. 1984. 29.50 (ISBN 0-404-61473-6). AMS Pr.

Backscheider, Paula R. & Nussbaum, Felicity A. Annotated Bibliography of Twentieth Century Critical Studies of Women & Literature, 1660-1800. LC 76-24746. (Reference Library of the Humanities Ser.: Vol. 64). 1977. lib. bdg. 43.00 (ISBN 0-8240-9934-6). Garland Pub.

Backscheider, Paula R., ed. The Plays of Samuel Foote, 3 vols. LC 78-66659. (Eighteenth Century English Drama Ser.). 1982. Set. lib. bdg. 218.00 (ISBN 0-8240-3589-5). Garland Pub.

--Probability, Time & Space in Eighteenth-Century Literature. LC 78-20850. (AMS Studies in the Eighteenth Century: No. 3). 1979. 29.50 (ISBN 0-404-16046-8). AMS Pr.

Backscheider, Paula R., ed. see Dennis, John.

Backscheider, Paula R., ed. see Gildon, Charles.

Backscheider, Paula R., ed. see Hoole, John.

Backscheider, Paula R., ed. see Inchbald, Elizabeth.

Backscheider, Paula R., ed. see Jephson, Robert.

Backscheider, Paula R., jt. ed. see Malek, James S.

Backscheider, Paula R., ed. see Murphy, Arthur.

Backscheider, Paula R., ed. see Thomson, James.

Backsheider, P. R., ed. see Thompson, Edward.

Backstrand, G. Resources, Society & Future. 1980. 47.00 (ISBN 0-08-023266-3); pap. 18.00 (ISBN 0-08-023267-1). Pergamon.

Backstrom, Charles H. & Hursch-Cesar, Gerald. Survey Research. 2nd ed. LC 81-1738. 436p. 1981. text ed. 23.95x (ISBN 0-471-02543-7). Wiley.

Backstrom, Philip N. Christian Socialism & Co-Operation in Victorian England: Edward Vansittart Neale & the Co-Operative Movement. 238p. 1974. 19.50x (ISBN 0-87471-582-2). Rowman.

Backus, Charles. The Nan-Chao Kingdom & T'ang China's Southwestern Frontier. LC 81-6138. (Cambridge Studies in Chinese History, Literature & Institutions). (Illus.). 200p. 1982. 42.50 (ISBN 0-521-22733-X). Cambridge U Pr.

Backus, David. European Recipes for American Fish & Game. 1978. pap. 4.50 (ISBN 0-932558-09-7). Willow Creek.

Backus, Harriet F. Tomboy Bride. LC 79-80764. (Illus.). 1977. pap. 7.50 (ISBN 0-87108-512-7). Pruett.

Backus, Harry. Designing Restaurant Interiors: A Guide for Restaurant Owners & Operators. (Illus.). 1977. 13.95 (ISBN 0-86730-212-7). Lebhar Friedman.

Backus, Henny, jt. auth. see Backus, Jim.

Backus, Irena. The Reformed Roots of the English New Testament: The Influence of Theodore Beza on the English New Testament. (Pittsburgh Theological Monographs: No. 28). 1980. pap. 12.75 (ISBN 0-915138-36-0). Pickwick.

Backus, Isaac. The Diary of Isaac Backus, 3 vols. McLoughlin, William G., ed. LC 76-12018. (Illus.). 1834p. 1979. Set. 120.00x (ISBN 0-87057-148-6). U Pr of New Eng.

--History of New England. LC 76-83410. (Religion in America, Ser. 1). 1969. Repr. of 1871 ed. 54.00 (ISBN 0-405-00231-9). Ayer Co Pubs.

Backus, Jean L., ed. Letters from Amelia: An Intimate Portrait of Amelia Earhart. LC 81-68356. (Illus.). 262p. 1982. 16.95x (ISBN 0-8070-6702-4); pap. 10.95 (ISBN 0-8070-6703-2, BP 655). Beacon Pr.

Backus, Jim & Backus, Henny. Backus Strikes Back. LC 83-40357. (Illus.). 192p. 1984. 14.95 (ISBN 0-8128-2962-X). Stein & Day.

Backus, John. Acoustical Foundations of Music. 2nd ed. LC 68-54957. (Illus.). 1977. 17.95x (ISBN 0-393-09096-5, NortonC); wkbk., questions & problems avail. Norton.

Backus, Richard H., jt. auth. see Lineaweaver, Thomas H., 3rd.

Backus, Richard H., jt. auth. see Lineweaver, Thomas H., III.

Backus, Richard H., ed. see Coastal Research Center.

Backus, Rob. Fire Music: A Political History of Jazz. (Illus.). 104p. (Orig.). 1977. pap. 3.95 (ISBN 0-917702-00-X). Vanguard Bks.

Backus, Robert L., tr. from Japanese. The Riverside Counselor's Stories: Vernacular Fiction of Late Heian Japan. LC 84-40446. 272p. 1985. 35.00x (ISBN 0-8047-1260-3). Stanford U Pr.

Backus, Sharron. Inside Softball for Women. 1979. pap. 6.95 (ISBN 0-8092-7490-6). Contemp Bks.

Backus, Truman. The Outlines of Literature, English & American. 59.95 (ISBN 0-8490-0791-7). Gordon Pr.

Backus, William. Telling Each Other the Truth. 250p. (Orig.). 1985. pap. 6.95 (ISBN 0-87123-852-7). Bethany Hse.

--Telling the Truth to Troubled People. 256p. (Orig.). 1985. pap. 6.96 (ISBN 0-87123-811-X). Bethany Hse.

Backus, William & Chapian, Marie. Telling Yourself the Truth. LC 80-10136. 41p. (Orig.). 1980. pap. 4.95 (ISBN 0-87123-562-5, 210562); study guide 1.95 (ISBN 0-87123-567-6, 210567). Bethany Hse.

--Why Do I Do What I Don't Want to Do? LC 84-6336. 144p. 1984. pap. 4.95 (ISBN 0-87123-625-7). Bethany Hse.

Backus, William & Chaplan, Marie. Digase la Verdad. 1983. 3.25 (ISBN 0-88113-049-4). Edit Betania.

Backus, William & Malte, Paul. Perspective. pap. 5.95 (ISBN 0-933350-06-6). Morse Pr.

Backus, William & Malte, Paul R. Crossroad. pap. 5.95 (ISBN 0-933350-03-1); tchrs' ed. 3.00 (ISBN 0-933350-53-8). Morse Pr.

Backus, William, et al. Adventuring in the Church. pap. 5.95 (ISBN 0-933350-08-2); tchrs' ed. 3.00 (ISBN 0-933350-58-9). Morse Pr.

Backwell, H. Occupation of Hausaland: Nineteen Hundred to Nineteen Hundred Four. 80p. 1969. Repr. of 1927 ed. 32.50x (ISBN 0-7146-1631-1, F Cass Co). Biblio Dist.

Baclarce, Alberto. The Long Night of Death. 185p. 1983. 15.95 (ISBN 0-88795-023-X). W W Pro Inter.

Baclawski, K., ed. see Kac, Mark.

Bacmeister, Arnold. Das Grosse Lexikon der Fischwaid. (Ger.). 1969. 65.00 (ISBN 3-87372-001-9, M-7324, Pub. by Jfland). French & Eur.

Bacon. The Advancement of Learning, 2 vols. (Illus.). 427p. 1984. Repr. of 1901 ed. Set. 165.50 (ISBN 0-89901-168-3). Found Class Reprints.

Bacon see White, Frederic R.

Bacon, A. Japanese Girls & Women. 69.95 (ISBN 0-87968-253-1). Gordon Pr.

Bacon, Albion F. Beauty for Ashes. Baxter, Annette K., ed. LC 79-8770. (Signal Lives Ser.). (Illus.). 1980. Repr. of 1914 ed. lib. bdg. 45.00x (ISBN 0-405-12820-7). Ayer Co Pubs.

Bacon, Ann, tr. see Jewel, John.

Bacon, Banjamin W. Non-Resistance: Christian or Pagan. 1918. pap. 19.50x (ISBN 0-686-83649-9). Elliots Bks.

Bacon, Benjamin W. Christianity, Old & New. 1914. 29.50x (ISBN 0-686-83503-4). Elliots Bks.

--Is Mark a Roman Gospel? (Harvard Theological Studies: Vol. 7). 1919. 11.00 (ISBN 0-527-01007-3). Kraus Repr.

Bacon, C. Paediatric Emergencies. 1982. 17.50 (ISBN 0-433-01051-7). Heinman.

Bacon, Corinne. Prison Reform: Together with a Discussion of the Prison of the Future by Thomas M. Osborne. LC 70-38659. Repr. of 1917 ed. 22.50 (ISBN 0-404-09147-4). AMS Pr.

Bacon, D. H. BASIC Thermodynamics & Heat Transfer. (BASIC Ser.). (Illus.). 160p. 1983. pap. text ed. 15.95 (ISBN 0-408-01312-5). Butterworth.

Bacon, Daniel W. From Faith to Faith. 1984. pap. 5.95 (ISBN 9971-972-03-4). OMF Bks.

Bacon, David & Maslov, Norman. The Beatles' England: There Are Places I'll Remember. LC 81-82555. (Illus.). 144p. 1982. pap. 12.95 (ISBN 0-9606736-1-X). Nine Hundred-Ten Pr.

Bacon, Delia S. Philosophy of the Plays of Shakspeare Unfolded. LC 73-113547. Repr. of 1857 ed. 34.50 (ISBN 0-404-00443-1). AMS Pr.

Bacon, Dolores, ed. Hymns That Every Child Should Know. 203p. 1980. Repr. of 1907 ed. lib. bdg. 25.00 (ISBN 0-89984-063-9). Century Bookbindery.

Bacon, E. M. Principles of Wheel Alignment. 3rd ed. 304p. 1984. 20.55 (ISBN 0-07-002857-5). McGraw.

Bacon, E. M., ed. Acts & Laws, of the Commonwealth of Massachusetts, 1780-1797: With Supplements 1780-1784, 13 vols. LC 74-19617. Repr. of 1896 ed. Set. 790.00 (ISBN 0-404-12439-9). AMS Pr.

Bacon, Edgar M. Chronicles of Tarrytown & Sleepy Hollow. Repr. 20.00 (ISBN 0-8274-2060-9). R West.

--Notes on Nassau: The Capital of the Bahamas. 1976. lib. bdg. 59.95 (ISBN 0-8490-2358-0). Gordon Pr.

Bacon, Edmund N. Design of Cities. rev ed. (Illus.). 336p. 1976. pap. 22.95 (ISBN 0-14-004236-9). Penguin.

Bacon, Edward. The Great Archaeologists. 1981. 50.00x (ISBN 0-436-03100-0, Pub. by Secker & Warburg England). State Mutual Bk.

Bacon, Edwin M. The Connecticut River & the Valley of the Connecticut: Three Hundred Fifty Miles from Mountain to Sea. (Rediscovering America Ser). 30.00 (ISBN 0-384-03005-X). Johnson Repr.

--Literary Pilgrimages in New England. 1973. Repr. of 1902 ed. 15.00 (ISBN 0-8274-1485-4). R West.

--Literary Pilgrimages in New England: To the Homes of Famous Makers of American Literature & Among Their Haunts & the Scenes of Their Writings. 532p. 1983. Repr. of 1902 ed. lib. bdg. 50.00 (ISBN 0-89987-962-4). Darby Bks.

Bacon, Edwin M., jt. ed. see Weeks, Lyman H.

Bacon, Elizabeth E. Central Asians under Russian Rule: A Study in Culture Change. (Illus.). 291p. 1980. pap. 7.95x (ISBN 0-8014-9211-4). Cornell U Pr.

--Obok: A Study of Social Structure in Eurasia. 14.00 (ISBN 0-384-03010-6). Johnson Repr.

Bacon, Ernest W. Bunyan Pilgrim & Dreamer: John Bunyan - His Life & Work. 186p. 1984. pap. 5.95 (ISBN 0-8010-0869-7). Baker Bk.

--Pilgrim & Dreamer: John Bunyan: His Life & Work. 176p. pap. text ed. 8.95 cancelled (ISBN 0-85364-309-1). Attic Pr.

--Spurgeon. (Christian Biography Ser.). 184p. 1982. pap. 3.95 (ISBN 0-8010-0823-9). Baker Bk.

Bacon, Ernst. Fifty Songs. (Living Composers' Library Ser.). pap. 5.00 (ISBN 0-686-05636-1). Dragons Teeth.

--Notes on the Piano. LC 63-13887. 1963. 19.95x (ISBN 0-8156-0030-5). Syracuse U Pr.

--Notes on the Piano. LC 63-13887. (Illus.). 175p. 1968. pap. 6.95x (ISBN 0-295-74028-0, WP35). U of Wash Pr.

--Words on Music. LC 73-427. 183p. 1973. Repr. of 1960 ed. lib. bdg. 45.00 (ISBN 0-8371-6768-X, BAWM). Greenwood.

Bacon, Eugene H., jt. auth. see Bernardo, C. Joseph.

Bacon, Eugenia J. Lyddy. facsimile ed. LC 77-37582. (Black Heritage Library Collection). Repr. of 1898 ed. 19.50 (ISBN 0-8369-8958-9). Ayer Co Pubs.

Bacon, Eve. Oakland, the Early Years. LC 74-81080. Orig. Title: History of Oakland, Florida. (Illus.). 1974. 8.95 (ISBN 0-913122-04-1). Mickler Hse.

--Orlando, a Centennial History. Incl. Vol. 1. (Illus.). 1975. 17.76 (ISBN 0-913122-08-4); Vol. 2. (Illus.). 1977. 19.95 (ISBN 0-913122-10-6). LC 75-21374. 2 vol. set 35.00 (ISBN 0-913122-13-0). Mickler Hse.

Bacon, F., et al. Petit Lexique de la Manutentio n. Anglais-Francais. Chartrand, P., ed. 37p. (Eng. & Fr.). 1974. pap. 5.95 (ISBN 0-686-92075-9, M-9226). French & Eur.

Bacon, Francis. The Advancement of Learning. Kitchin, G. W., ed. (Rowman & Littlefield University Library). 246p. 1973. 13.00x (ISBN 0-87471-664-0); pap. 7.50x (ISBN 0-87471-665-9). Rowman.

--The Advancement of Learning. Kitchin, G. W., ed. 246p. 1981. 15.00 (ISBN 0-460-10719-4, DEL 05092, Evman); pap. 7.95 (ISBN 0-460-11719-X, DEL 05093, Evman). Biblio Dist.

--The Advancement of Learning: Bk. 1. Armstrong, William A., ed. (Athlone Renaissance Library). 153p. 1975. 29.50 (ISBN 0-485-13605-8, Pub. by Athlone Pr Ltd); pap. 14.95 (ISBN 0-485-12605-2). Longwood Pub Group.

--Apophthegmes New & Old. LC 73-38144. (English Experience Ser.: No. 424). 310p. 1972. Repr. of 1625 ed. 29.00 (ISBN 9-0221-0424-9). Walter J Johnson.

--Bacon's Essays. rev. 5th ed. LC 73-1147. (Essay Index Reprint Ser.). Repr. of 1861 ed. 29.50 (ISBN 0-518-10035-9). Ayer Co Pubs.

--Bacon's Novum Organum. Fowler, Thomas, ed. 1979. Repr. of 1889 ed. PLB 100.00 (ISBN 0-8495-1702-8). Arden Lib.

--Certaine Miscellany Works. LC 79-25440. (English Experience Ser.: No. 222). 166p. Repr. of 1629 ed. 21.00 (ISBN 90-221-0222-X). Walter J Johnson.

--The Charge of Sir F. Bacon Touching Duells. LC 68-27475. (English Experience Ser.: No. 7). 62p. Repr. of 1614 ed. 8.00 (ISBN 90-221-0007-3). Walter J Johnson.

--De Sapientia Veterum, Repr. Of 1609 Ed. Bd. with The Wisedome of the Ancients. Gorges, Arthur, tr. Repr. of 1619 ed. LC 75-27863. (Renaissance & the Gods Ser.: Vol. 20). (Illus.). 1976. lib. bdg. 88.00 (ISBN 0-8240-2068-5). Garland Pub.

--The Elements of the Common Lawes of England. LC 77-26477. (English Experience Ser.: No. 164). 104p. 1969. Repr. of 1630 ed. 25.00 (ISBN 90-221-0164-9). Walter J Johnson.

--Essays. LC 83-45408. Repr. of 1940 ed. 31.50 (ISBN 0-404-20015-X). AMS Pr.

--Essays. 1983. 13.50 (ISBN 0-460-10010-6, DEL-05223, Evman); pap. 5.95 (ISBN 0-460-11010-1, DEL-05090, Evman). Biblio Dist.

--Essays & Colours of Good & Evil. LC 72-56. (Select Bibliographies Reprint Ser.). 1972. Repr. of 1862 ed. 20.25 (ISBN 0-8369-9951-7). Ayer Co Pubs.

--The Essays or Counsels, Civill & Morall. Kiernan, Michael, ed. (Illus.). 544p. 1985. text ed. 30.00x (ISBN 0-674-31740-8). Harvard U Pr.

--Essays: Religious Meditations; Places of Perswasion & Disswasion. LC 68-54612. (English Experience Ser.: No. 17). Repr. of 1597 ed. 9.50 (ISBN 90-221-0017-0). Walter J Johnson.

--Francis Bacon: A Selection of His Works. Warhaft, Sidney, ed. LC 65-20259. (College Classics in English Ser). 1965. pap. 13.24 scp (ISBN 0-672-63011-7). Odyssey Pr.

--Francis Bacon-Essays. (Rowman & Littlefield University Library). 200p. 1972. 11.75x (ISBN 0-87471-666-7); pap. 5.25x (ISBN 0-87471-667-5). Rowman.

--Great Instauration & New Atlantis. Weinberger, J., ed. (Croft Classics Ser.). 1980. text ed. 12.95x (ISBN 0-88295-115-7); pap. text ed. 3.95x (ISBN 0-88295-113-0). Harlan Davidson.

--The Historie of Life & Death: Observations Naturall & Experimentall for the Prolonging of Life. Kastenbaum, Robert, ed. LC 76-19558. (Death and Dying Ser.). 1977. Repr. of 1638 ed. lib. bdg. 30.00x (ISBN 0-405-09554-6). Ayer Co Pubs.

--The Historie of Life & Death: With Observations Naturall & Experimentall. LC 68-54613. (English Experience Ser.: No.20). 324p. Repr. of 1638 ed. 21.00 (ISBN 90-221-0020-0). Walter J Johnson.

--The Life & Correspondence of Francis Bacon, 2 vols. Date not set. Repr. lib. bdg. 59.00 (ISBN 0-932051-83-9). Am Repr Serv.

--New Organon & Related Writings. Anderson, Fulton H., ed. LC 60-11682. 1960. pap. 9.63 scp (ISBN 0-672-60289-X, LLA97). Bobbs.

--Philosophical Works of Francis Bacon. facs. ed. LC 70-119952. (Select Bibliographies Reprint Ser). 1905. 38.00 (ISBN 0-8369-5395-9). Ayer Co Pubs.

--The Physical and Metaphysical Works of Lord Bacon, Including the Advancement of Learning & Novum Organum. 1976. Repr. 55.00 (ISBN 0-403-06143-1, Regency). Scholarly.

--Two Books...of the Proficience & Advancement of Learning. LC 70-25525. (English Experience Ser.: No. 218). 236p. Repr. of 1605 ed. 39.00 (ISBN 90-221-0218-1). Walter J Johnson.

--Wisedome of the Ancients. Gorges, A., tr. LC 68-54614. (English Experince Ser.: No. 1). 176p. 1968. Repr. of 1619 ed. 13.00 (ISBN 90-221-0001-4). Walter J Johnson.

--Works, 14 Vols. Spedding, J., et al, eds. 1858-74. Set. 1030.00x (ISBN 3-7728-0023-8). Adlers Foreign Bks.

--Works of Francis Bacon, 15 vols. Repr. Set. lib. bdg. 695.00x (ISBN 0-403-00003-3). Scholarly.

Bacon, Frank R., Jr. & Butler, Thomas W., Jr. Planned Innovation: A Dynamic Approach to Strategic Planning & the Successful Development of New Products. rev. ed. (Illus.). 243p. 1981. 25.00 (ISBN 0-938654-32-2). Indus Dev Inst Sci.

Bacon, Frater R. De Retardatione Accidentium Senectutis cum Aliis Opusculis de Rebus Medicinalibus. 268p. 1928. text ed. 41.40x (ISBN 0-576-99214-3, Pub. by Gregg Intl Pubs England). Gregg Intl.

Bacon, G. E. Architecture of Solids. LC 81-9762. (Wykeham Science Ser.: No. 58). 138p. 1981. pap. 16.50x (ISBN 0-8448-1397-4). Crane-Russak Co.

--The Architecture of Solids. (The Wykeman Science Ser.: No. 58). 140p. 1981. pap. cancelled (ISBN 0-85109-850-9). Taylor & Francis.

--Neutron Diffraction. 3rd ed. (Monographs on the Physics & Chemistry of Materials). (Illus.). 1975. 98.00x (ISBN 0-19-851353-4). Oxford U Pr.

--X-Ray & Neutron Diffraction. 1966. pap. text ed. 21.00 (ISBN 0-08-011998-0). Pergamon.

Bacon, G. E. & Noakes, G. R. Neutron Physics. (Wykeham Science Ser.: No. 2). 1969. 9.95x (ISBN 0-8448-1104-1). Crane-Russak Co.

Bacon, Gaspar G. The Constitution of the U. S. In Some of Its Fundamental Aspects. facsimile ed. LC 79-37328. (Select Bibliographies Reprint Ser). Repr. of 1928 ed. 18.00 (ISBN 0-8369-6673-2). Ayer Co Pubs.

Bacon, George B. Siam: The Land of the White Elephant, As It Was & Is. LC 77-87064. Repr. of 1873 ed. 26.50 (ISBN 0-404-16792-6). AMS Pr.

Bacon, George E. & Spencer, Martha L. A Practical Approach to Pediatric Endocrinology. 2nd ed. (Illus.). 1982. 37.95 (ISBN 0-8151-0404-9). Year Bk Med.

Bacon, Gershon C., jt. auth. see Hundert, Gershon D.

Bacon, Greg O. Winning in Business: Starting & Staying. James, Mary, ed. 184p. 1984. text ed. 15.95 (ISBN 0-932127-07-X). Inter-Sellf.

Bacon, Helen, tr. see Aeschylus.

Bacon, Jack, ed. Eros in Art. (Illus.). 1969. 10.00 (ISBN 0-910550-03-4). Elysium.

Bacon, James. Hollywood Is a Four Letter Town. 1977. pap. 1.95 (ISBN 0-380-01671-0, 33399). Avon.

--How Sweet It Is: The Jackie Gleason Story. (Illus.). 256p. 1985. 15.95 (ISBN 0-312-39621-X). St Martin.

Bacon, Jeremy. Corporate Directorship Practices: Compensation 1975. LC 75-43396. (Report Ser.: No. 678). (Illus.). 79p. 1975. pap. 30.00 (ISBN 0-8237-0112-3). Conference Bd.

--Corporate Directorship Practices: Compensation 1977. LC 78-54031. (Report Ser.: No. 740). (Illus.). 78p. 1978. pap. 30.00 (ISBN 0-8237-0174-3); pap. 10.00 member. Conference Bd.

--Corporate Directorship Practices: Role, Selection & Legal Status of the Board. (Report Ser.: No. 646). 161p. (Orig.). 1975. pap. 15.00 (ISBN 0-8237-0065-8); pap. 5.00 member. Conference Bd.

--Corporate Directorship Practices: The Audit Committee. LC 79-55954. (Report Ser.: No. 766). (Illus.). 71p. (Orig.). 1979. pap. 37.50 (ISBN 0-8237-0202-2); pap. 7.50 member. Conference Bd.

Bacon, Jeremy & Brown, James K. The Board of Directors: Perspectives & Practices in Nine Countries. LC 77-83235. (Report Ser.: No. 728). (Illus.). 141p. 1977. pap. 45.00 (ISBN 0-8237-0162-X); pap. 15.00 members. Conference Bd.

Bacon, Josephine. The Citrus Cookbook. 176p. 1983. 14.95 (ISBN 0-916782-43-3); pap. 8.95 (ISBN 0-916782-42-5). Harvard Common Pr.

--Cooking the Israeli Way. (Easy Menu Ethnic Cookbooks). (Illus.). 48p. (gr. 5 up). 1985. lib. bdg. 8.95 (ISBN 0-8225-0912-1). Lerner Pubns.

--Middle Aged Love Stories. facsimile ed. LC 74-169538. (Short Story Index Reprint Ser.). Repr. of 1903 ed. 18.00 (ISBN 0-8369-3285-4). Ayer Co Pubs.

Bacon, Josephine, tr. see Biber, Yehoash.

Bacon, Josephine, tr. see De Pomiane, Edouard.

Bacon, Josephine D. Her Fiance. facs. ed. LC 73-121520. (Short Story Index Reprint Ser). 1904. 14.00 (ISBN 0-8369-3476-8). Ayer Co Pubs.

--Imp & the Angel. facs. ed. LC 74-81260. (Short Story Index Reprint Ser.). 1901. 15.00 (ISBN 0-8369-3012-6). Ayer Co Pubs.

--In the Border Country. facsimile ed. LC 79-106244. (Short Story Index Reprint Ser.). 1909. 14.00 (ISBN 0-8369-3280-3). Ayer Co Pubs.

--Madness of Philip & Other Tales of Childhood. facsimile ed. LC 75-98557. (Short Story Index Reprint Ser.). 1902. 17.00 (ISBN 0-8369-3131-9). Ayer Co Pubs.

--Smith College Stories. facsimile ed. LC 70-94701. (Short Story Index Reprint Ser.). 1900. 19.00 (ISBN 0-8369-3079-7). Ayer Co Pubs.

--Whom the Gods Destroyed. facs. ed. LC 70-116931. (Short Story Index Reprint Ser.). 1902. 17.00 (ISBN 0-8369-3433-4). Ayer Co Pubs.

Bacon, L. W., jt. auth. see Morse, Philip M.

Bacon, Leonard. A Discourse Preached in the Center Church. facsimile ed. LC 78-168507. (Black Heritage Library Collection). Repr. of 1828 ed. 11.50 (ISBN 0-8369-8861-2). Ayer Co Pubs.

--The Genesis of the New England Churches. LC 74-38435. (Religion in America, Ser. 2). 510p. 1972. Repr. of 1874 ed. 32.00 (ISBN 0-405-04056-3). Ayer Co Pubs.

--The Luisiads of Luis De Camoes. 435p. 1983. Repr. of 1950 ed. lib. bdg. 150.00 (ISBN 0-89984-097-3). Century Bookbindery.

--Slavery Discussed in Occasional Essays, from 1833-1846. facsimile ed. LC 72-82167. (Anti-Slavery Crusade in America Ser). 1969. Repr. of 1846 ed. 14.50 (ISBN 0-405-00607-1). Ayer Co Pubs.

Bacon, Leonard, ed. The Song of Roland. 1919. 20.00 (ISBN 0-8274-3469-3). R West.

Bacon, Leonard, tr. from Port. The Lusiads of Luis de Camoes. (Illus.). 435p. 1980. pap. text ed. 4.50 (ISBN 0-87535-128-X). Hispanic Soc.

Bacon, M. Songs That Every Child Should Know. (ps-6). 59.95 (ISBN 0-8490-1086-1). Gordon Pr.

Bacon, M., jt. auth. see McQuillin, R.

Bacon, M. D. & Bull, G. M. Data Transmission. (Computer Monograph Ser.: Vol. 20). 148p. 1973. 29.50 (ISBN 0-444-19564-5). Elsevier.

Bacon, Mardges. Ernest Flagg: Beaux-Arts Architect & Urban Reformer. (Architectural History Foundations American Monograph Ser.: No. 6). (Illus.). 400p. 1985. text ed. 40.00x (ISBN 0-262-02222-2). MIT Pr.

Bacon, Margaret. The Kingdom of the Rose. 530p. 1982. 35.00x (ISBN 0-86188-117-6, Pub. by Judy Piatkus). State Mutual Bk.

Bacon, Margaret H. I Speak for My Slave Sister: The Life of Abby Kelley Foster. LC 74-4042. (gr. 5-12). 1974. 11.06i (ISBN 0-690-00515-6). Crowell Jr Bks.

--The Quiet Rebels: The Story of the Quakers in America. 250p. 1985. lib. bdg. 24.95 (ISBN 0-86571-058-9); pap. 8.95 (ISBN 0-86571-057-0). New Soc Pubs.

--Valiant Friend: The Life of Lucretia Mott. (Illus.). 320p. 1980. 14.95 (ISBN 0-8027-0645-2). Walker & Co.

--Valiant Friend: The Life of Lucretia Mott. 1982. pap. 8.95 (ISBN 0-8027-7190-4). Walker & Co.

Bacon, Margaret Hope. Lucretia Mott Speaking: Excerpts from the Sermons & Speeches of a Famous 19th Century Quaker Minister & Reformers. LC 80-84890. 31p. (Orig.). 1980. pap. 2.30x (ISBN 0-87574-234-3). Pendle Hill.

Bacon, Martha S. Puritan Promenade. LC 81-1913. (Illus.). 160p. 1981. Repr. of 1964 ed. lib. bdg. 22.50x (ISBN 0-313-22954-6, BAPUP). Greenwood.

Bacon, Nancy. Candles & Caviar. (Love & Life Romance Ser.). 176p. 1983. pap. 1.75 (ISBN 0-345-29761-X). Ballantine.

--Champagne & Roses. 1982. pap. 1.75 (ISBN 0-345-29758-X). Ballantine.

--Country Music. (Love & Life Romance Ser.). 160p. (Orig.). 1982. pap. 1.75 (ISBN 0-345-29759-8). Ballantine.

--Love & Dreams. 600p. 1980. pap. 2.75 (ISBN 0-345-28767-3). Ballantine.

Bacon, Natalie, jt. auth. see Bacon, Ralph.

Bacon, P. R., ed. see Cooper, St. G.

Bacon, Paul & Hadler, Norton M. BIMR Rheumatology Vol. 1: Kidney & Rheumatic Disease. 498p. 1982. text ed. 39.95 (ISBN 0-407-02352-6). Butterworth.

Bacon, Philip J., ed. Population Dynamics of Rabies in Wildlife. Date not set. price not set (ISBN 0-12-071350-0). Acad Pr.

Bacon, R. For Better Relations with Our Latin American Neighbors. 1976. lib. bdg. 59.95 (ISBN 0-8490-1855-2). Gordon Pr.

Bacon, R. L. & Niles, N. R. Medical Histology: A Text-Atlas with Introductory Pathology. (Illus.). 368p. 1983. 36.50 (ISBN 0-387-90734-3). Springer-Verlag.

Bacon, R. W. Spatial Consumer Theory. 1984. 23.95x (ISBN 0-19-828476-4). Oxford U Pr.

Bacon, Ralph & Bacon, Natalie. Love Talk: A Model of Erotic Communication. Merryman, Bill, ed. (Illus.). 280p. (Orig.). 1985. pap. 9.95 (ISBN 0-933211-00-7). Shakti Pr.

Bacon, Richard M. The Forgotten Art of Building & Using a Brick Bake Oven. LC 77-74809. (Forgotten Arts Ser.). (Illus.). 64p. (Orig.). 1977. pap. 4.95 (ISBN 0-911658-76-9). Yankee Bks.

--The Forgotten Arts, Bk. 1. LC 75-10770. (Forgotten Arts Ser.). (Illus.). 64p. (Orig.). 1975. pap. 4.95 (ISBN 0-911658-65-3). Yankee Bks.

--The Forgotten Arts, Bk. 2. LC 75-10770. (Forgotten Arts Ser.). (Illus.). 64p. (Orig.). 1975. pap. 4.95 (ISBN 0-911658-66-1). Yankee Bks.

--The Forgotten Arts, Bk. 3. LC 75-10770. (Forgotten Arts Ser.). (Illus.). 64p. 1976. pap. 4.95 (ISBN 0-911658-71-8). Yankee Bks.

--The Forgotten Arts: Growing, Gardening & Cooking with Herbs. LC 72-91864. (Forgotten Arts Ser.). (Illus.). 128p. (Orig.). 1972. pap. 6.95 (ISBN 0-911658-51-3). Yankee Bks.

Bacon, Robert & Eltis, Walter. Britain's Economic Problem: Too Few Producers. 2nd ed. LC 78-52386. 1978. 27.50 (ISBN 0-312-09941-X). St Martin.

Bacon, Robert, jt. auth. see Rubenstein, James.

Bacon, Robert, ed. see Root, Elihu.

Bacon, Robert L. Secrets of Professional Turf Betting. 1965. 10.00 (ISBN 0-685-13752-X). Landau.

Bacon, Roger. Experimental Science & the Law of Ethics in the Life of Men. (Illus.). 141p. 1984. 97.85 (ISBN 0-89266-489-4). Am Classical Coll Pr.

--Roger Bacon Essays: Contributed by Various Writers on the Occasion of the Commemoration of the Seventh Centenary of His Birth. Little, A. G., ed. LC 71-173549. 425p. 1972. Repr. of 1914 ed. 18.00x (ISBN 0-8462-1656-6). Russell.

--Roger Bacon's Letter Concerning the Marvelous Power of Art & of Nature & Concerning the Nullity of Magic. Davis, Tenney L., tr. from Lat. LC 79-8594. 80p. Repr. of 1923 ed. 19.50 (ISBN 0-404-18495-2). AMS Pr.

--Root of the World. pap. 2.95 (ISBN 0-916411-42-7). Alchemical Pr.

Bacon, Roy. BMW Twins & Singles. (Osprey Collector's Library). (Illus.). 191p. 1982. 19.95 (ISBN 0-85045-470-0, Pub. by Osprey England). Motorbooks Intl.

--Foreign Racing Motorcycles. 204p. pap. 16.95 (ISBN 0-85429-295-0, F244). Haynes Pubns.

Bacon, Samuel. Memoir of the Life & Character of the Rev. Samuel Bacon. facs. ed. Ashmun, Jehudi, ed. (Black Heritage Library Collection). 1822. 20.25 (ISBN 0-8369-8781-0). Ayer Co Pubs.

Bacon, Selden, jt. auth. see Straus, Robert.

Bacon, Susan, jt. auth. see Valencia, Pablo.

Bacon, Terry R. & Freeman, Lawrence H. Shipley Associates Style Guide. 3 ring binder 24.95 (ISBN 0-933427-00-X). Shipley.

--Shipley Associates Style Guide for Oil & Gas Professionals. Date not set. 24.95 (ISBN 0-933427-01-8). Shipley.

Bacon, Theo. D. Leonard Bacon: A Statesman in the Church. 1931. 49.50x (ISBN 0-685-69788-6). Elliots Bks.

Bacon, Tony. Rock Hardware. 224p. 1981. 14.98 (ISBN 0-517-54521-7, Harmony); pap. 12.95 (ISBN 0-517-54520-9, Harmony). Crown.

Bacon, Wallace A., ed. see Warner, W.

Bacon, Wallace A., jt. ed. see Thompson, David W.

Bacon, Walter M., Jr., ed. Behind Closed Doors: Secret Papers on the Failure of Romanian-Soviet Negotiations 1931-1932. LC 77-78050. (Archival Documentation Publications Ser.: No. 180). (Illus.). 228p. 1979. 17.50x (ISBN 0-8179-6801-6). Hoover Inst Pr.

Bacon-Foster, Corra. Early Chapters in the Development of the Patomac Route to the West. LC 70-146134. (Research & Source Works Ser: No. 718). 1971. Repr. of 1912 ed. lib. bdg. 22.50 (ISBN 0-8337-0144-4). B Franklin.

Baconthorpe, John. Quaestiones in Quatuor Libros Sentntiarum et Quodlibetales. 1582p. 1618. text ed. 372.60x (ISBN 0-576-99128-7, Pub. by Gregg Intl Pubs England). Gregg Intl.

Bacot, Jacques. Three Tibetan Mysteries: Tchrimekundan, Nansal, Djroazanmo, As Performed in the Tibetan Monasteries. Woolf, H. I., tr. from Fr. LC 78-72375. Repr. of 1924 ed. 28.50 (ISBN 0-404-17225-3). AMS Pr.

Bacote, Samuel W. Who's Who Among the Colored Baptists of the United States. Gaustad, Edwin S., ed. LC 79-52588. (The Baptist Tradition Ser.). (Illus.). 1980. Repr. of 1913 ed. lib. bdg. 28.50x (ISBN 0-405-12455-4). Ayer Co Pubs.

Bacourt, Pierre de & Cunliffe, J. W. French Literature During the Last Half-Century. 407p. 1983. Repr. of 1923 ed. lib. bdg. 50.00 (ISBN 0-89760-054-1). Telegraph Bks.

Bacovcin, Helen, tr. The Way of a Pilgrim: And the Pilgrim Continues His Way. LC 76-52000. 1978. pap. 3.95 (ISBN 0-385-12400-7, Im). Doubleday.

Bacow, Lawrence & Wheeler, Michael. Environmental Dispute Resolution. (Environment, Development, & Public Policy Ser.). 388p. 1984. 29.50x (ISBN 0-306-41594-1, Plenum Pr). Plenum Pub.

Bacow, Lawrence, jt. auth. see O'Hare, Michael.

Bacow, Lawrence S. Bargaining for Job Safety & Health. 208p. 1980. text ed. 30.00x (ISBN 0-262-02152-8); pap. 10.95x (ISBN 0-262-52079-6). MIT Pr.

Bacq, Z. M. Sulfur Containing Radio-Protective Agents. 344p. 1975. text ed. 110.00 (ISBN 0-08-016298-3). Pergamon.

Bacq, Z. M. & Alexander, P. Fundamentals of Radiobiology. 2nd ed. 1971. 37.00 (ISBN 0-08-009406-6). Pergamon.

Bacquet, Paul. Un Contemporain D'Elisabeth I; Thomas Sackville: L'Homme Et L'Oeuvre. 363p. Date not set. Repr. of 1966 ed. lib. bdg. 100.00 (ISBN 0-89984-028-0). Century Bookbindery.

Bacri, Nicole. Fonctionnement de la Negation: Etude Psycholinguistique D'un Probleme D'enonciation. (Connaissance et Langage: No. 5). (Illus., Fr.). 1977. pap. text ed. 12.00x (ISBN 90-2797-028-9). Mouton.

Bacry, Henri. Lecons Sur la Theorie des Groupes & les Symetries des Particules Elementaires. (Cours & Documents de Mathematiques & de Physique Ser.). 466p. (Orig.). 1967. 94.95 (ISBN 0-677-50190-0). Gordon.

--Lectures on Group Theory & Particle Theory. LC 72-78879. (Documents on Modern Physics Ser.). (Illus.). 598p. 1977. 132.95 (ISBN 0-677-30190-1). Gordon.

Bacskai, J. A., et al, eds. Bibliography of Fossil Vertebrates, 1973-1977. LC 80-70567. (Bibliography of Fossil Vertebrates Ser.). 576p. 1983. pap. 240.00 (ISBN 0-913312-68-1). Am Geol.

Bacsley, Howard L. Quantitative Research Methods for Business & Economics. pap. 9.95 (ISBN 0-686-23874-5). Preston.

Bacus, Jim. Utilization of Microorganisms in Meat Processing: A Handbook for Meat Plant Operators. (Innovation in Microbiology Ser.: 1-694). 170p. 1984. 49.95x (ISBN 0-471-90312-4, Pub by Res Stud Pr). Wiley.

Baczynsky, Mark. Camera Repair, Restoration & Adaptation. (Illus.). 52p. 1982. pap. 9.95 (ISBN 0-89816-009-X). Embee Pr.

--Creative Projects & Processes. (Illus.). 54p. 1982. pap. 9.95 (ISBN 0-89816-007-3). Embee Pr.

--Directory of Profitable Microcomputer Ventures. (Illus.). 42p. 1984. pap. 9.95 (ISBN 0-89816-011-1). Embee Pr.

--How I Make a Comfortable Living with My Computer. 1983. pap. 9.95 (ISBN 0-89816-010-3). Embee Pr.

--How I Make a Comfortable Living Writing & Publishing Short Mini-Guides. (Illus.). 1981. pap. 9.95 (ISBN 0-89816-003-0). Embee Pr.

--Making Custom Cameras & Equipment. (Illus.). 44p. 1982. pap. 9.95 (ISBN 0-89816-008-1). Embee Pr.

--Making Money with Photography. (Illus.). 86p. 1982. pap. 14.95 (ISBN 0-89816-006-5). Embee Pr.

--Photocrafts Book of Guides, Vol. 1. (Illus.). 100p. 1978. pap. 19.95 (ISBN 0-89816-001-4). Embee Pr.

--Photocrafts Book of Guides, Vol. 2. LC 78-70581. (Illus.). 104p. 1980. pap. 19.95 (ISBN 0-89816-002-2). Embee Pr.

--Writer's Guide to the Photographic Craft. (Illus.). 1982. pap. 4.95 (ISBN 0-89816-004-9). Embee Pr.

Baczynskyj, Boris, jt. auth. see Welsh, David E.

Badalamenti, Rosalyn T., jt. auth. see Erhardt, Tell.

Badalamenti, Rosalyn T., jt. auth. see Klein, Diane.

Badalato, Billy & Richards, Charlie R. Comedy Realm. 140p. (Orig.). (gr. 5-12). 1982. pap. 10.50 (ISBN 0-9609224-0-7). Comedy Writ.

Badaloni, Nicola. Pour le Communisme: Questions de Theorie. (Archontes: No. 9). 262p. (Orig.). 1976. pap. text ed. 22.40x (ISBN 90-2797-533-7). Mouton.

Badaracco, Joseph A. Loading the Dice: A Five-Country Study of Vinyl Chloride Regulation. 208p. 1985. 19.95 (ISBN 0-317-19560-3). Harvard Busn.

Badarayana. Brahma Sutra: The Philosophy of Spiritual Life. Radhakrishnan, S., tr. LC 68-21330. 1968. Repr. of 1960 ed. lib. bdg. 37.25x (ISBN 0-8371-0291-X, BABS). Greenwood.

--Brahma-Sutras (Vedanta-Sutras) Vireswarananda, Swami, tr. (Sanskrit & Eng.). 11.95 (ISBN 0-87481-076-0). Vedanta Pr.

Badasch, Shirley & Chesebro, Doreen. The Health Care Worker: An Introduction to Health Occupations. (Illus.). 288p. 1984. text ed. 16.95 (ISBN 0-89303-514-9); instr's. guide 9.95 (ISBN 0-89303-502-5); wkbk. 7.95 (ISBN 0-89303-503-3). Brady Comm.

Badash, Lawrence. Kapitza, Rutherford & the Kremlin. LC 84-11822. (Illus.). 144p. 1985. 20.00x (ISBN 0-300-01465-1). Yale U Pr.

--Radioactivity in America: Growth & Decay of a Science. LC 78-20525. 1979. text ed. 27.50x (ISBN 0-8018-2187-8). Johns Hopkins.

Badash, Lawrence & Broida, H. P., eds. Reminiscences of Los Alamos: 1943-1945. (Studies in the History of Modern Science: No. 5). 180p. 1980. lib. bdg. 26.50 (ISBN 90-277-1097-X); pap. 9.95 (ISBN 90-277-1098-8). Kluwer Academic.

Badash, Lawrence, ed. see Rutherford, Ernest & Boltwood, Bertram B.

Badauni, M. T. Seerat-un-Nabi: 2 Vols-Shibli Numani. 19.95 ea. (ISBN 0-686-18339-8). Kazi Pubns.

Badaway, M. K. Achieving Excellence in Managing Technical Professionals. 1986. price not set (ISBN 0-442-20480-9). Van Nos Reinhold.

Badawi, G. A. Polygamy in Islamic Law. pap. 1.00 (ISBN 0-686-18440-8). Kazi Pubns.

Badawi, Gamal. The Status of Woman in Islam. Al-Jarrahi, Abdussamad, ed. Bekkari, Muhammad, tr. from English. 20p. (Orig.). 1982. pap. 2.00 (ISBN 0-89259-036-X). Am Trust Pubns.

Badawi, Gamal A. The Status of Woman in Islam: (French Edition) Quinlan, Hamid, ed. LC 82-74127. (Illus.). 28p. 1983. pap. 0.75 (ISBN 0-89259-039-4). Am Trust Pubns.

Badawi, M. M., ed. An Anthology of Modern Arabic Verse. 1970. pap. 8.95x (ISBN 0-19-920032-7). Oxford U Pr.

Badawi, M. M., tr. see Mahfouz, Naguib.

Badawi, Muhammad M. Coleridge: Critic of Shakespeare. LC 72-86417. pap. 57.50 (ISBN 0-317-28014-7, 2025575). Bks Demand UMI.

Badawi, Zaki. Dictionary of Social Sciences: English-French-Arabic. 25.00x (ISBN 0-86685-115-1). Intl Bk Ctr.

Badawy, A. A., ed. Biomedical Aspects of Drug Dependence: International Biomedical Research Symposium on Drug Dependence, Tangier, Morocco, 11-15 October 1982. (Illus.). 120p. 1984. pap. 20.00 (ISBN 0-08-030785-X). Pergamon.

Badawy, Alexander. The Tomb of Nyhetep-Ptah at Giza & the Tomb of 'Ankhm' Ahor at Saqqara. (Occasional Papers Archaeology Ser.: Vol. 11). 1978. pap. 26.50x (ISBN 0-520-09575-8). U of Cal Pr.

--The Tombs of Iteti, Sekhem ankh-Ptah, & Kaemnofert at Giza. LC 75-620057. (University of California Publications, Occasional Papers: No. 9). pap. 26.30 (ISBN 0-317-29106-8, 2021386). Bks Demand UMI.

Badawy, Michael K. Developing Managerial Skills in Engineers & Scientists. (Managerial Skill Development in Engineering & Science Ser.). 480p. 1982. 31.50 (ISBN 0-442-20481-7). Van Nos Reinhold.

Badawy, Shawsky, ed. Reproductive Endocrinology & Infertility. 1980. 45.50 (ISBN 0-8151-0406-5). Year Bk Med.

Badayev, A. The Bolsheviks in the Tsarist Duma. 245p. 1975. pap. text ed. 3.95 (ISBN 0-89380-001-5). Proletarian Pubs.

Badayum, T. B. A Short Handbook of Fiqh. pap. 2.95 (ISBN 0-686-63895-6). Kazi Pubns.

Badcock, jt. auth. see Tingay.

Badcock, C. R. Levi-Strauss: Structuralism & Sociological Theory. LC 75-45308. 121p. 1976. text ed. 12.75x (ISBN 0-8419-0258-5). Holmes & Meier.

--Madness & Modernity: A Study of Social Psychoanalysis. 192p. 1984. 34.95x (ISBN 0-631-12535-3); pap. 9.95 (ISBN 0-631-14146-4). Basil Blackwell.

--The Psychoanalysis of Culture. 272p. 1980. 39.95x (ISBN 0-631-11701-6); pap. 12.95x (ISBN 0-631-13033-0). Basil Blackwell.

Badcock, Francis J. The History of the Creeds. 2nd ed. (Church Historical Society, London, Ser.: No. 35). pap. 23.00 (ISBN 0-317-16746-4). Kraus Repr.

Badcock, John, Jr. Slaves to Duty. LC 72-77199. (Libertarian Broadsides Ser: No. 2). 36p. 1972. pap. 0.85 (ISBN 0-87926-013-0). R Myles.

Badcock, W. & Reynolds, J. A New Touch-Stone for Gold & Silver Wares. 390p. 1970. Repr. of 1679 ed. 10.00x (ISBN 0-7165-0056-6, Pub. by Irish Academic Pr). Biblio Dist.

Baddeley. Favourite Australian Recipes. 58p. 1983. pap. 3.95 (ISBN 0-938400-08-8). Donahoe Pubs.

Baddeley, Alan. Your Memory: A User's Guide. 224p. 1984. pap. 9.95 (ISBN 0-02-075310-1, Collier). Macmillan.

Baddeley, Alan, jt. ed. see Long, John.

Baddeley, Allan. Your Memory: A Users Guide. LC 82-7226. (Illus.). 222p. 1982. 16.95 (ISBN 0-02-504660-8); pap. 7.95x (ISBN 0-02-075310-1). Macmillan.

Baddeley, Clinton. My Foe Outstretch'd Beneath the Tree. 1981. pap. 2.25 (ISBN 0-440-15685-8). Dell.

Baddeley, Hiram. Radiological Investigation: A Guide to the Use of Medical Imaging in Clinical Practice. LC 82-23777. 1984. 60.00 (ISBN 0-471-25589-0, Pub. by Wiley Med.). Wiley.

Baddeley, Hiram, et al. Radiologic Atlas of Biliary & Pancreatic Disease. (Illus.). 1979. 64.50 (ISBN 0-8151-0374-3). Year Bk Med.

Baddeley, John F. The Rugged Flanks of Caucasus, 2 vols. in 1. LC 73-6267. (The Middle East Ser.). Repr. of 1940 ed. 55.00 (ISBN 0-405-05321-5). Ayer Co Pubs.

--Russia, Mongolia & China, 2 vols. 1976. lib. bdg. 250.00 (ISBN 0-8490-2549-4). Gordon Pr.

--Russia, Mongolia, China, 2 Vols. 1964. Repr. of 1919 ed. Set. 133.00 (ISBN 0-8337-0147-9). B Franklin.

--Russian Conquest of the Caucasus. LC 78-75459. (Illus.). 518p. 1969. Repr. of 1908 ed. 17.50x (ISBN 0-8462-1331-1). Russell.

Baddeley, St. Clair & Gordon, L. D. Rome & Its Story. 1977. lib. bdg. 59.95 (ISBN 0-8490-2543-5). Gordon Pr.

Baddeley, Welbore S. A Cotteswold Manor, Being the History of Painswick. 261p. 1980. Repr. of 1929 ed. text ed. 27.50x (ISBN 0-904387-54-2, Pub. by Alan Sutton England). Humanities.

Baddiley, James & Abraham, E. P., eds. Penicillin Fifty Years After Fleming. 2nd ed. (Royal Society Ser.). 378p. 1980. lib. bdg. 62.00x (ISBN 0-85403-140-5, Pub. by Royal Soc London). Scholium Intl.

Baddiley, James, et al, eds. Cambridge Studies in Biotechnology. Date not set. price not set. Cambridge U Pr.

Baddock, B. Press Ahead: A Teacher's Guide to the Use of Newspapers in English Language Teaching. (Language Teaching Methodolgy Series (Teaching Techniques)). (Illus.). 96p. 1984. pap. 4.50 (ISBN 0-08-029441-3). Pergamon.

--Scoop! Newspaper Materials for English Language Practice. (Materials for Language Practice Ser.). (Illus.). 128p. 1983. pap. 4.50 (ISBN 0-08-028635-6). Pergamon.

Baddour, Charles, ed. Yesterday, Today, & Tomorrow Cookbook. 416p. (YA) 1979. pap. 8.95 (ISBN 0-918544-24-6). Wimmer Bks.

Baddour, Raymond F. & Timmins, Robert S., eds. Application of Plasmas to Chemical Processing. 1967. 32.50x (ISBN 0-262-02027-0). MIT Pr.

Bade, David, jt. auth. see Blakely, James.

Bade, Patrick. Femme Fatale. LC 78-11577. (Illus.). 1979. 15.00 (ISBN 0-8317-3250-4, Mayflower Bks); pap. 6.95 (ISBN 0-8317-3251-2). Smith Pubs.

Bade, Robin. Macroeconomics. 192p. 1984. wkbk. & study guide 11.95 (ISBN 0-13-542457-7). P-H.

Bade, W. G., et al. Multipliers of Radical Banach Algebras of Power Series, No. 303. LC 84-3070. (Memoirs: No. 303). 86p. 1984. pap. 10.00 (ISBN 0-8218-2304-3). Am Math.

Bade, W. G., et al see Scedrov, Andrej.

Bade, William F. Life & Letters of John Muir, 2 Vols. LC 77-153302. (BCL Ser.: No. I). Repr. of 1924 ed. Set. 65.00 (ISBN 0-404-00444-X); cancelled. Vol. 1 (ISBN 0-404-08001-4). Vol. 2 (ISBN 0-404-08002-2). AMS Pr.

Bade, William F., ed. see Muir, John.

Badea, F. Reaction Mechanisms in Organic Chemistry. 1977. 44.00 (ISBN 0-9961004-8-2, Pub. by Abacus England). Heyden.

Badeau, Adam. Grant in Peace: From Appomattox to Mount McGregor. LC 72-152971. (Select Bibliographies Reprint Ser.). 1972. Repr. of 1887 ed. 38.50 (ISBN 0-8369-5723-7). Ayer Co Pubs.

--Military History of Ulysses S. Grant, from April, 1861 to April, 1865. 72.00 (ISBN 0-8369-7150-7, 7982). Ayer Co Pubs.

Badeau, John S. The American Approach to the Arab World. LC 67-22494. (Policy Books of the Council on Foreign Relations Ser.). pap. 55.80 (ISBN 0-317-08855-6, 2002941). Bks Demand UMI.

--The Middle East Remembered. LC 83-61202. 271p. 1983. 25.00 (ISBN 0-916808-21-1). Mid East Inst.

Badecker, William J. & Harnek, Ronald F. SEC Accounting & Reporting Manual. 1000p. 1983. 245.00. Warren.

Badeer, H. S. Cardiovascular Physiology. (Karger Continuing Education Series: Vol. 6). (Illus.). xvi, 276p. 1984. 24.75 (ISBN 3-8055-3796-4). S Karger.

Badel, Julie, jt. auth. see Erf, Stephen.

Baden. The Greatest Gift Is Love. LC 59-1314. (Arch Bks.). 24p. (gr. k-4). 1985. pap. 0.99 (ISBN 0-570-06196-2). Concordia.

Baden, H. P. The Chemotherapy of Psoriasis. 80.00 (ISBN 0-08-029823-0). Pergamon.

Baden, H. P., jt. auth. see Soter, N. A.

Baden, Jeffrey M. & Brodsky, Jay B., eds. The Pregnant Surgical Patient. (Illus.). 272p. 1985. monograph 36.00 (ISBN 0-87993-238-4). Futura Pub.

Baden, John. Earth Day Reconsidered. LC 80-81670. 1980. 4.00 (ISBN 0-89195-028-1). Heritage Found.

Baden, John, jt. auth. see Stroup, Richard.

Baden, John, ed. The Vanishing Farmland Crisis: Critical Views of the Movement to Preserve Agricultural Land. LC 84-2004. (Studies in Government & Public Policy). 184p. 1984. 19.95x (ISBN 0-7006-0253-4). U Pr of KS.

Baden, John & Stroup, Richard L., eds. Bureaucracy vs. Environment: The Environmental Costs of Bureaucratic Governance. 248p. 1981. text ed. 15.00x (ISBN 0-472-10010-6). U of Mich Pr.

Baden, John, jt. ed. see Hardin, Garrett.

Baden, John A., jt. auth. see Stroup, Richard L.

Baden, Marian. Being in God's Family. (Concordia Weekday Ser. - Gr. 3-4. Bk. 4, 2-V). 1967. pap. text ed. 2.75 (ISBN 0-570-06658-1, 22-2028); manual 5.85 (ISBN 0-686-82886-0, 22-2029). Concordia.

Baden, Michael M., jt. auth. see Haberman, Paul W.

Baden, Michael M., jt. auth. see Hauberman, Paul.

Baden, Nancy T., ed. Social Responsibility & Latin America. (Proceedings of the Pacific Coast Council on Latin American Studies: Vol. 8). (Illus.). 190p. (Orig.). 1981. pap. 12.00 (ISBN 0-916304-53-1). SDSU Press.

Baden, R. Kramer, jt. auth. see Seltzer, M. Seligson.

Baden, Robert. Anna & the Christchild. 1982. pap. 0.99 (ISBN 0-570-06157-1, 59-1271). Concordia.

Baden-Fuller, A. J. Engineering Field Theory. 272p. 1973. pap. text ed. 18.00 (ISBN 0-08-017034-X). Pergamon.

--Engineering Field Theory: Text & Examples, 2 vols. pap. 19.50 (ISBN 0-08-029320-4). Pergamon.

--Microwaves. 2nd ed. 1979. text ed. 48.00 (ISBN 0-08-024228-6); pap. text ed. 18.00 (ISBN 0-08-024227-8). Pergamon.

Baden-Fuller, A. J., ed. Worked Examples in Engineering Field Theory. 1977. text ed. 50.00 (ISBN 0-08-018143-0); pap. text ed. 16.50 (ISBN 0-08-018142-2). Pergamon.

Baden-Powell, Baden H. The Land Systems of British India: Being a Manual of the Land-Tenures & of the Systems of Land-Revenue Administration Prevalent in the Several Provinces, 3 Vols. LC 8-13098. Repr. of 1892 ed. Set. lib. bdg. 160.00 (ISBN 0-384-03034-3). Johnson Repr.

--The Origin & Growth of Village Communities in India. LC 1-18996. (Landmarks in Anthropology Ser). Repr. of 1899 ed. 15.00 (ISBN 0-384-03035-1). Johnson Repr.

Baden-Powell, Charlotte. Fireplace Design & Construction. LC 83-5449. (Illus.). 224p. text ed. 40.00 (ISBN 0-7114-5619-4). Longman.

Baden-Powell, Robert S. The Downfall of the Prempeh: A Diary of Life with the Native Levy in Ashanti, 1895-96. LC 72-6481. (Black Heritage Library Collection Ser). 1972. Repr. of 1896 ed. 22.50 (ISBN 0-8369-9157-5). Ayer Co Pubs.

--Matabele Campaign, 1896. LC 79-109309. (Illus.). Repr. of 1897 ed. 24.75x (ISBN 0-8371-3566-4, BPM&, Pub. by Negro U Pr). Greenwood.

Bader, Barbara. American Picturebooks from Noah's Ark to the Beast Within. LC 72-93304. (Illus.). 624p. 1976. 45.00 (ISBN 0-02-708080-3, 70808). Macmillan.

Bader, Clarisse. Women in Ancient India: Moral & Literary Studies. LC 72-9617. (Human Sexual Behavior Ser.). Repr. of 1925 ed. 18.00 (ISBN 0-404-57408-4). AMS Pr.

Bader, Iva M., jt. auth. see Morris, Woodrow W.

Bader, Lois A. Bader Reading & Language Inventory. LC 99-943799. 224p. 1983. pap. text ed. 14.95 (ISBN 0-02-305110-8). Macmillan.

--Reading Diagnosis & Remediation in Classroom & Clinic. (Illus.). 1980. pap. text ed. write for info. (ISBN 0-02-305100-0). Macmillan.

Bader, Morton E. Practical Quality Management in the Chemical Process Industry. (Industrial Engineering Ser.: Vol. 7). (Illus.). 160p. 1983. 27.50 (ISBN 0-8247-1903-4). Dekker.

Bader, Oliver & Theret, Michel. Diccionario Enciclopedico de Metalurgia. 960p. (Span., Fr. & Eng.). 1975. 44.95 (ISBN 84-7146-054-8, S-50132). French & Eur.

Bader, Robert S. The Great Kansas Bond Scandal. LC 82-9056. (Illus.). xiv, 394p. 1982. 25.00x (ISBN 0-7006-0223-2); pap. 9.95 (ISBN 0-7006-0248-8). U Pr of KS.

Bader, William & Burt, Daniel S. Miller Analogies Test. LC 81-152. 160p. 1982. pap. 5.95 (ISBN 0-668-04990-1). Arco.

Bader, William B. Austria Between East & West, 1945-1955. 1966. 17.50x (ISBN 0-8047-0258-6). Stanford U Pr.

Bader, Wolfgang. Literatur und Kolonialismus I: Die Verarbeitung der Kolonialen Expansion in der Europaischen Literatur. Riesz, Janos, ed. 348p. (Ger.). 1983. 39.45 (ISBN 3-8204-7317-3). P Lang Pubs.

Baderman, Howard, et al. Admission of Patients to Hospital. 51p. 1974. 29.00x (ISBN 0-900889-35-7, Pub. by Kings Fund). State Mutual Bk.

Baderschneider, et al. The Collective Bargaining Process: Readings & Analysis. 1983p. pap. 17.95 (ISBN 0-256-02752-8). Business Pubns.

Baderschneider, Earl R. & Miller, Paul F., eds. Labor Arbitration in Health Care. 324p. 10.00 (ISBN 0-318-12383-5); members 7.50 (ISBN 0-318-12384-3). Am Arbitration.

Badescu, L. & Popescu, D., eds. Algebraic Geometry, Bucharest 1982: Proceedings of the International Conference, Held in Bucharest, Romania, August 2-7, 1982. (Lecture Notes in Mathematics Ser.: Vol. 1056). vii, 380p. 1984. 18.50 (ISBN 0-387-12930-8). Springer-Verlag.

Badescu, Mario. Mario Badescu's Skin Care Program for Men. 224p. 1981. 10.95 (ISBN 0-89696-032-3, An Everest House Book). Dodd.

Badger, Anthony J. Prosperity Road: The New Deal, Tobacco & North Carolina. LC 79-310. (Fred Morrison Series in Southern Studies). (Illus.). xviii, 295p. 1980. 25.00 (ISBN 0-8078-1367-2). U of NC Pr.

Badger, Carl B. Badger's Illustrated Catalogue of Cast-Iron Architecture. 1982. pap. 9.95 (ISBN 0-486-24223-4). Dover.

Badger, D. D. & Bogardus, James. Origins of Cast Iron Architecture in America. LC 68-25760. (Architecture & Decorative Art Ser.: Vol. 13). (Illus.). 1970. Repr. of 1856 ed. lib. bdg. 55.00 (ISBN 0-306-71039-0). Da Capo.

Badger, Daniel D. Badger's Illustrated Catalogue of Cast-Iron Architecture. 1983. 16.50 (ISBN 0-8446-5938-X). Peter Smith.

Badger, Dennis & Whitehead, Geoffrey. Elements of Cargo Insurance. (Elements of Overseas Trade Ser.). 154p. (Orig.). 1983. pap. 9.50 (ISBN 0-85941-227-X). Woodhead-Faulkner.

Badger, Geoffrey M. The Structures & Reactions of the Aromatic Compounds. LC 54-3317. pap. 117.50 (ISBN 0-317-08966-8, 2051390). Bks Demand UMI.

Badger, George P., jt. ed. see Ruzaik, Salil Ibn.

Badger, George P., intro. by see Varthema, Lodovico De.

Badger, George P., tr. see Ruzaik, Salil Ibn & Badger, George P.

Badger, John. The Arthuriad. 1972. 10.00 (ISBN 0-916988-02-3). Pendragon Ltd.

Badger, L. W., jt. auth. see Montroll, E. W.

Badger, R. Reid, jt. auth. see Clayton, Lawrence A.

Badger, Reid. The Great American Fair: The World's Columbian Exposition & American Culture. LC 79-11774. (Illus.). 1979. 34.95x (ISBN 0-88229-448-2). Nelson-Hall.

Badgley, F. I., et al. Profiles of Wind, Temperature, & Humidity Over the Arabian Sea. LC 70-129539. (International Indian Ocean Expedition Meteorological Monographs: No. 6). (Illus.). 1972. text ed. 20.00x (ISBN 0-8248-0101-6, Eastwest Ctr). UH Pr.

Badgley, P. C., ed. see Goddard Memorial Symposium, 3rd, Washington D. C., 1965.

Badham, Linda, jt. auth. see Badham, Paul.

Badham, Paul & Badham, Linda. Immortality or Extinction? LC 81-17595. (Library of Philosophy & Religion). 156p. 1982. text ed. 28.50x (ISBN 0-389-20251-7, 07055). B&N Imports.

Badham, W. A. Ablaut in the Modern Dialects of the South of England. (English Dialects Society Publications Ser.: No. 63). pap. 15.00 (ISBN 0-317-15984-4). Kraus Repr.

Bad Heart Bull, Amos & Blish, Helen H. Pictographic History of the Oglala Sioux. LC 66-13404. (Illus.). xxii, 530p. 1968. 31.50 (ISBN 0-8032-0002-1). U of Nebr Pr.

Badi, Joseph, ed. Fundamental Laws of the State of Israel. LC 61-8605. 451p. 1961. text ed. 42.00x (ISBN 0-8290-0174-3). Irvington.

Badia, Leonard F. Basic Catholic Beliefs for Today: The Creed Explained. LC 84-14632. 170p. (Orig.). 1984. pap. 7.95 (ISBN 0-8189-0469-0). Alba.

--Jesus: Insights into This Life & Teaching. 144p. (Orig.). 1985. pap. 7.95 (ISBN 0-8091-2689-3). Paulist Pr.

Badia, Leonard F. & Sarno, Ronald. Morality: How to Live It Today. LC 79-20498. 1980. pap. 7.95 (ISBN 0-8189-0391-0). Alba.

Badia, Pietro & Runyon, Richard P. Fundamentals of Behavioral Research. 432p. 1982. text ed. 22.95 (ISBN 0-394-34811-7, RanC). Random.

Badia-Margarit, A. M. Pronunciacion Espanola: Curvas de Entonacion - Trozos Escogidos. (Illus.). 1956. pap. text ed. 3.95 (ISBN 0-940630-11-7, T-7103). Playette Corp.

Badian, E. Publicans & Sinners: Private Enterprise in the Service of the Roman Republic, with a Critical Bibliography. 176p. (Orig.). 1983. pap. 5.95x (ISBN 0-8014-9241-6). Cornell U Pr.

--Roman Imperialism in the Late Republic. 2nd ed. 129p. 1971. pap. 5.95x (ISBN 0-8014-9109-6, CP109). Cornell U Pr.

Badian, E., ed. Foreign Clientelae, Two Hundred Sixty-Four to Seventy BC. 356p. 1985. Repr. of 1958 ed. 39.95x (ISBN 0-19-814204-8). Oxford U Pr.

Badian, E., ed. see Syme, Ronald.

Badie, Bertrand & Birnbaum, Pierre. The Sociology of the State. Goldhammer, Arthur, tr. from Fr. LC 82-20249. 1983. lib. bdg. 24.00x (ISBN 0-226-03548-4); pap. text ed. 10.95x (ISBN 0-226-03549-2). U of Chicago Pr.

Badii, L., jt. auth. see Oberhettinger, F.

Badillo, Pedro A., compiled by. Antologia De Filosofia Griega. 6th, rev. ed. pap. 6.25 (ISBN 0-8477-2800-5). U of PR Pr.

Badillo, Tony. Tithing: God's Command Or Man's Demand - Which? (Illus.). 102p. (Orig.). 1984. pap. 8.50 (ISBN 0-912977-00-0). Xavier Pr.

Badillo Gerena, Pedro. Ciceron y el Imperio. LC 76-10131. (Coleccion UPREX: Serie Humanidades No. 50). 143p. (Orig.). 1976. pap. 1.85 (ISBN 0-8477-0050-X). U of PR Pr.

Badin, E. J. Coal Combustion Chemistry: Correlation Aspects. (Coal Science & Technology Ser.: Vol. 6). 260p. 1984. 61.75 (ISBN 0-444-42318-4, I-132-84). Elsevier.

Badinter, Elisabeth. Mother Love: Myth & Reality. Gray, Francine, frwd. by. 384p. 1982. pap. 8.95 (ISBN 0-02-048350-3). Macmillan.

Badler, Scott, ed. see Cutler, Roger L.

Badley, J. H. Bedales: A Pioneer School. 1979. Repr. of 1923 ed. lib. bdg. 20.00 (ISBN 0-8482-3435-9). Norwood Edns.

Badley, John H. Form & Spirit. LC 77-113347. (Essay & General Literature Index Reprint Ser). 1971. Repr. of 1951 ed. 17.50x (ISBN 0-8046-1398-2, Pub. by Kennikat). Assoc Faculty Pr.

Badley, Michael. Practical Seismic Interpretation. (Illus.). 269p. 1985. 62.00 (ISBN 0-934634-88-2). Intl Human Res.

Badmaieff, Alexis & Davis, Don. How to Build Speaker Enclosures. LC 66-29405. (Illus., Orig.). 1966. pap. 6.95 (ISBN 0-672-20520-3, 20520). Sams.

Badner, Mino. A Possible Focus of Andean Artistic Influence in Mesoamerica. LC 72-90528. (Studies in Pre-Columbian Art & Archaeology: No. 9). (Illus.). 56p. 1972. pap. 5.00x (ISBN 0-88402-042-8). Dumbarton Oaks.

Bado, Jose L. The Monteggia Lesion. Ponseti, Ignacio V., tr. (Illus.). 96p. 1962. photocopy ed. 14.50x (ISBN 0-398-04196-2). C C Thomas.

Badoglio, Pietro. Italy in the Second World War: Memories & Documents. Currey, Muriel, tr. LC 75-28658. 1976. Repr. of 1948 ed. lib. bdg. 20.75 (ISBN 0-8371-8485-1, BAIT). Greenwood.

Bador, Bernard. Sea Urchin Harakiri. Eshleman, Clayton, tr. (Illus.). 120p. 1985. 15.95 (ISBN 0-915572-77-X); pap. 6.95 (ISBN 0-915572-76-1). Panjandrum.

Badough, Rose M., jt. ed. see Lilley, Dorothy B.

Badovici, Jean, ed. L' Architecture Vivante, 5 vols. LC 75-5874. (Architecture & Decorative Arts Ser.). (Illus.). 885p. 1975. 695.00 set (ISBN 0-306-70540-0). Da Capo.

Badr, Ahmed M. Education of the Palestinians: An Annotated Bibliography. (Bibliography Ser.: No. 3). 29p. (Orig.). 1977. pap. text ed. 2.50 (ISBN 0-937694-16-9). Assn Arab-Amer U Grads.

Badr, Albirt Y. & Siksek, Simon G. Manpower & Oil in Arab Countries. LC 79-2850. (Illus.). 270p. 1981. Repr. of 1959 ed. 24.75 (ISBN 0-8305-0026-X). Hyperion Conn.

Badr, Gamal M. State Immunity. 1984. pap. text ed. 46.00 (ISBN 90-247-2880-0, Pub. by Martinus Nijhoff Netherlands). Kluwer Academic.

Badra, Robert. Meditations for Spiritual Misfits. 93p. (Orig.). 1982. pap. 7.95 (ISBN 0-9610274-0-1). JCL Hse.

Badre, Albert & Shneiderman, Ben, eds. Directions in Human-Computer Interaction. LC 82-11575. (Human-Computer Interaction Ser.: Vol. 1). 240p. 1982. text ed. 36.50 (ISBN 0-89391-144-5). Ablex Pub.

Badrena, Ana Rita & Wood, Maria R. Dictation Manual, 2 vols. 2nd ed. pap. 7.50 (ISBN 0-8477-2632-0). U of PR Pr.

Badri, M. B. Islam & Alcoholism. LC 76-42173. 1976. 1.95 (ISBN 0-89259-005-X). Am Trust Pubns.

Badrig, Robert H. Florenz Ziegfeld: Twentieth Century Showman. Rahmas, D. Steve, ed. (Outstanding Personalities Ser.: No. 37). 32p. (Orig.). (gr. 7-12). 1972. lib. bdg. 3.50 incl. catalog cards (ISBN 0-87157-537-X); pap. 1.95 vinyl laminated covers (ISBN 0-87157-037-8). SamHar Pr.

Badrkhan & Larky. Electronic Principles & Applications. (gr. 9-12). 1984. text ed. 21.00 (ISBN 0-538-33530-0, IE53). SW Pub.

Badrud-Din, Abdul-Amir. The Bank of Lebanon: Central Banking in a Financial Centre & a Financial Entrepot. LC 83-43270. 230p. 1984. 37.50 (ISBN 0-86187-461-7). F Pinter Pubs.

Badskey, Lorin J. Unaccustomed As I Am. 2nd ed. 1974. pap. 7.95 (ISBN 0-686-81687-0). Loru Co.

Badt, Kurt. The Art of Cezanne. LC 84-82410. (Illus.). 346p. 1985. Repr. of 1965 ed. lib. bdg. 50.00 (ISBN 0-87817-302-1). Hacker.

--Eugene Delacroix Drawings: With an Introduction based on the Artist's Journal. LC 83-45697. 1984. Repr. of 1946 ed. 49.50 (ISBN 0-404-20016-8). AMS Pr.

--John Constable's Clouds. Godman, Stanley, tr. from Ger. (Illus.). 1971. Repr. 12.50x (ISBN 0-87556-017-2). Saifer.

Badt-Strauss, Bertha. White Fire: The Life & Works of Jessie Sampter. Davis, Moshe, ed. LC 77-70663. (America & the Holy Land Ser.). (Illus.). 1977. Repr. of 1956 ed. lib. bdg. 20.00x (ISBN 0-405-10224-0). Ayer Co Pubs.

Badura-Skoda, Eva & Badura-Skoda, Paul. Interpreting Mozart on the Keyboard. Black, Leo, tr. from Ger. (Music Reprint Ser.). (Illus.). 329p. 1985. Repr. of 1962 ed. lib. bdg. 32.50 (ISBN 0-306-76265-X). Da Capo.

Badura-Skoda, Eva & Branscombe, Peter, eds. Schubert Studies: Problems of Style & Chronology. LC 81-38528. (Illus.). 350p. 1982. 39.50 (ISBN 0-521-22606-6). Cambridge U Pr.

Badura-Skoda, Paul. A Living Master Lesson on Mozart Sonata In A. 1983. 16.00 (ISBN 0-943748-02-X). Ekay Music.

Badura-Skoda, Paul, jt. auth. see Badura-Skoda, Eva.

Badura-Skoda, Paul, ed. see Czerny, Carl.

Bady, Donald B. Colt Automatic Pistols. rev. ed. 1973. 18.50 (ISBN 0-87505-099-9). Borden.

Badzinski, S. Carpentry in Commercial Construction. 2nd ed. 1980. 23.95 (ISBN 0-13-115220-3). P-H.

Badzinski, S., Jr. Carpentry in Residential Construction. 1981. 23.95 (ISBN 0-13-115238-6). P-H.

--Stair Layout. (Illus.). 72p. 1971. pap. 9.75 (ISBN 0-8269-0700-8). Am Technical.

Badzinski, Stanley. Home Construction & Estimating. (Illus.). 1979. ref. 20.95 (ISBN 0-13-392654-0). P-H.

Badzinski, Stanley, Jr. House Construction: A Guide to Buying, Building, & Evaluating. 256p. 1975. 20.95 (ISBN 0-13-394767-X). P-H.

--Roof Framing. (Illus.). 1976. 12.95 (ISBN 0-13-782466-1); student ed. 12.95. P-H.

Badzyo, Yuriy. State of Seige: Ukraine's National Predicament. Senkus, Roman, ed. LC 81-67209. (Illus.). 130p. (Orig.). 1981. 9.95 (ISBN 0-86725-001-1); pap. 3.75 (ISBN 0-86725-000-3). ERUHG.

Bae, Yoong. Alien Starships. (Illus.). 32p. 1980. pap. 3.50 (ISBN 0-8431-4014-3). Troubador Pr.

--Paper Rockets. (Illus.). 32p. 1980. pap. 3.95 (ISBN 0-8431-1729-X). Troubador Pr.

--Paper UFO's. (Illus.). 32p. (gr. 1-12). 1981. pap. 3.95 (ISBN 0-8431-4080-1). Troubador Pr.

Bae, Young. Paper Starships. (Illus.). 32p. (Orig.). (gr. 1-12). 1979. pap. 3.95 (ISBN 0-8431-4099-2). Troubador Pr.

Baechler, Jean. Suicides. Cooper, Barry, tr. from Fr. LC 78-54505. 1979. 22.50x (ISBN 0-465-08335-8). Basic.

Baechtold, Marquerite & McKinney, Eleanor. Library Service for Families. 245p. (Orig.). 1983. 19.50 (ISBN 0-208-01856-5, Lib Prof Pubns). Shoe String.

Baeck, Leo. Essence of Judaism. rev. ed. LC 61-8992. 1961. pap. 8.25 (ISBN 0-8052-0006-1). Schocken.

Baeck, Paul L., ed. The General Civil Code of Austria. annotated & rev. ed. LC 72-6158. 293p. 1972. lib. bdg. 27.50 (ISBN 0-379-00025-3). Oceana.

Baeckler, Virginia. Sparkle: PR for Library Staff. LC 80-50566. (Illus.). 80p. (Orig.). 1980. pap. 5.00x (ISBN 0-9603232-1-X). Sources.

Baeckler, Virginia & Larson, Linda. Go, Pep, & Pop: Two Hundred Fifty Tested Ideas for Lively Libraries. LC 75-20328. 1976. pap. 4.50 (ISBN 0-916444-01-5); pap. 5.50. UNABASHED Lib.

Baeckler, Virginia Van W. PR for Pennies: Low-Cost Library Public Relations. LC 77-90578. (Illus.). 1978. pap. 4.00x (ISBN 0-9603232-0-1). Sources.

Baedeker. Baedecker's Italy. (Baedeker Travel Ser.). 1981. 19.95 (ISBN 0-13-055905-9); pap. 14.95 (ISBN 0-13-055897-4). P-H.

--Baedeker's Caribbean. (Illus.). 250p. 1983. pap. 14.95 (ISBN 0-13-056143-6). P-H.

--Baedeker's Egypt. (Illus.). 423p. 1984. pap. 15.95 (ISBN 0-13-056358-7). P-H.

--Baedeker's France. (The Baedeker Travel Ser.). 1981. 19.95 (ISBN 0-13-055822-2); pap. 14.95 (ISBN 0-13-055814-1). P-H.

--Baedeker's Germany. (The Baedeker Travel Ser.). 320p. 1981. 19.95 (ISBN 0-13-055848-6); pap. 14.95 (ISBN 0-13-055830-3). P-H.

--Baedeker's Great Britain. (The Baedeker Travel Ser.). 424p. 1981. 19.95 (ISBN 0-13-055863-X); pap. 14.95 (ISBN 0-13-055855-9). P-H.

--Baedeker's Greece. (Illus.). 200p. 1982. 19.95 (ISBN 0-13-056010-3); pap. 14.95 (ISBN 0-13-056002-2). P-H.

--Baedeker's Israel. (Baedeker Ser.). (Illus.). 286p. 1983. pap. 14.95 (ISBN 0-13-056176-2). P-H.

--Baedeker's Japan. (Illus.). 382p. 1984. pap. 15.95 (ISBN 0-13-056382-X). P-H.

--Baedeker's Jerusalem. Orig. Title: Palestine & Syria. (Illus.). 1978. Repr. of 1876 ed. 25.25x (ISBN 0-930038-04-5). Arbit.

--Baedeker's Mexico. (Illus.). 328p. 1982. 19.95 (ISBN 0-13-056077-4); pap. 14.95 (ISBN 0-13-056069-3). P-H.

--Baedeker's Netherlands, Belgium, & Luxembourg. (Illus.). 328p. 1982. 19.95 (ISBN 0-13-056036-7); pap. 14.95 (ISBN 0-13-056028-6). P-H.

--Baedeker's Rhine. (Illus.). 1985. pap. 9.95 (ISBN 0-13-056466-4). P-H.

--Baedeker's Scandinavia. (Illus.). 344p. 1982. 19.95 (ISBN 0-13-056093-6); pap. 14.95 (ISBN 0-13-056085-5). P-H.

--Baedeker's Spain. (The Baedeker Travel Ser.). 1981. 19.95 (ISBN 0-13-055921-0); pap. 14.95 (ISBN 0-13-055913-X). P-H.

--Baedeker's Switzerland. (Illus.). 328p. 1981. 19.95 (ISBN 0-13-056051-0); pap. 14.95 (ISBN 0-13-056044-8). P-H.

--Baedeker's Tuscany. (Illus.). 1985. pap. 9.95 (ISBN 0-13-056482-6). P-H.

--Baedeker's Yugoslavia. (Baedeker Ser.). (Illus.). 280p. 1983. pap. 14.95 (ISBN 0-13-056184-3). P-H.

--Beadeker's Loire. (Illus.). 1985. pap. 9.95 (ISBN 0-13-056375-7). P-H.

--Shell Spain-Portugal. 1985. pap. 4.95 (ISBN 0-13-808676-1). P-H.

Baedeker, Karl. Baedeker's Historical Palestine. (Baedeker's Handbooks for Traveler's Ser.). (Illus.). 240p. 1985. Repr. of 1930 ed. 19.95 (ISBN 0-88254-699-6). Hippocrene Bks.

--Baedeker's New York. (Baedeker's Handbook for Traveler's Ser.). (Illus.). 320p. 1985. 19.95 (ISBN 0-88254-859-X). Hippocrene Bks.

Baedeker, Karl, ed. Baedeker's United States. LC 76-77703. (American Scene Ser.). Orig. Title: The United States with an Excursion into Mexico. (Illus.). 520p. 1971. Repr. of 1893 ed. lib. bdg. 25.00 (ISBN 0-306-71341-1). Da Capo.

Baedeker Staff, jt. auth. see British Automobile Association Staff.

Baedeker's. Shell France. 1985. pap. 4.95 (ISBN 0-13-808544-7). P-H.

--Shell Germany. 1985. pap. 4.95 (ISBN 0-13-808551-X). P-H.

--Shell Great Britain. 1985. pap. 4.95 (ISBN 0-13-808569-2). P-H.

--Shell Greece. 1985. pap. 4.95 (ISBN 0-13-808577-3). P-H.

--Shell Italy. 1985. pap. 4.95 (ISBN 0-13-808601-X). P-H.

Baeder, John. Gas, Food, & Lodging. LC 81-5427. (Illus.). 132p. 1982. 29.95 (ISBN 0-89659-308-8). Abbeville Pr.

Baedi, Philip, ed. Papers from the Twelfth Linguistic Symposium on Romance Languages. (Current Issues in Linguistic Theory, (CLIT) Ser.: Vol. 26). xii, 611p. 1984. 68.00x (ISBN 90-272-3518-X). Benjamins North Am.

Baegert, Jacob. The Letters of Jacob Baegert 1749-1761. Schulz-Bischof, Elsbeth, et al, trs. 1982. 36.00 (ISBN 0-686-91821-5). Dawsons.

Baegert, Johann J. Observations in Lower California. Brandenburg, M. M. & Baumann, Carl L., trs. from Ger. (Library Reprint Ser.: No. 100). 1979. Repr. of 1952 ed. 28.50x (ISBN 0-520-03873-8). U of Cal Pr.

Baeher, Helen, ed. Women & Media. LC 80-41424. (Illus.). 150p. 1980. 19.00 (ISBN 0-08-026061-6). Pergamon.

Baehler, James R. The Book of Perks. LC 82-3027. 224p. 1983. 13.95 (ISBN 0-312-08985-6). St Martin.

--Book of Perks. 1984. pap. 7.95 (ISBN 0-03-071073-1). HR&W.

--The New Manager's Guide to Success. LC 80-19509. 160p. 1980. 27.95 (ISBN 0-03-058014-5). Praeger.

Baehr, Consuelo. Best Friends. 432p. 1981. pap. 2.95 (ISBN 0-440-10510-2). Dell.

Baehr, Consuelo S. Report from the Heart. 1976. pap. 1.75 (ISBN 0-380-01658-3, 33266). Avon.

Baehr, Dieter. Die Englische Sprache in Kanada: Eine Analyse Des 'Survey of Canadian English' (Tuebinger Beitrage Zur Linguistik Ser.: No. 165). 235p. (Orig., Ger.). 1980. pap. 27.00x (ISBN 3-87808-165-0, Pub. by Gunter Narr Verlag Germany). Benjamins North Am.

Baehr, H. D., et al, eds. Power Engineering & Technology: Energy Efficient Use of Working Fluids, Alternative Processes, Heat Pumps& Organic Rankine Cycle. 1984. 179.50 (ISBN 0-89116-448-0). Hemisphere Pub.

Baehr, Harry W., Jr. The New York Tribune Since the Civil War. LC 77-159164. xiii, 420p. 1972. Repr. of 1936 ed. lib. bdg. 29.00x (ISBN 0-374-90335-2). Octagon.

Baehr, Patricia. Always Faithful. (gr. 7 up). 1983. pap. 1.95 (ISBN 0-451-12463-4, Sig Vista). NAL.

--Faithfully, Tru. LC 84-5792. 240p. (gr. 7 up). 1984. 11.95 (ISBN 0-02-708100-1). Macmillan.

--Indian Summer. (Magic Moments Ser.: No. 4). 1984. pap. 1.95 (ISBN 0-451-13171-1, Sig Vista). NAL.

Baehr, Patricia G. The Way to Windra. LC 79-23272. (Illus.). (gr. 4-7). 1980. 7.95g (ISBN 0-7232-6179-2). Warne.

Baehr, Peter R. & Gordenker, Leon. The United Nations: Reality & Ideal. LC 84-3155. 192p. 1984. 28.95 (ISBN 0-03-062757-5). Praeger.

Baehr, Peter R. & Wittrock, Bijorn. Policy Analysis & Policy Innovation: Patterns, Problems & Potentials. LC 80-41079. (Sage Modern Politics Ser.: Vol. 5). 240p. 1981. 28.00 (ISBN 0-8039-9809-0); pap. 14.00 (ISBN 0-8039-9810-4). Sage.

Baehr, Russell. This Was Our Land. Reaves, Verne, ed. (Illus.). 250p. (Orig.). 1985. 15.95x (ISBN 0-89288-113-5); pap. 8.95x (ISBN 0-89288-108-9). Maverick.

Baehr, Tom. New Tunes-Old Friends. (Illus.). 40p. (Orig.). 1979. music book 4.95 (ISBN 0-9608842-0-3). Hogfiddle Pr.

--A Pleasant Addiction. (Illus.). 48p. (Orig.). 1982. music book 5.95 (ISBN 0-9608842-1-1). Hogfiddle Pr.

Bae Hrens, Aemilius. Poetae Latini Minores, Leipzig, 1879-1883, 5 vols. Commager, Steele, ed. LC 77-70775. (Latin Poetry Ser.). 1979. Set. lib. bdg. 206.00 (ISBN 0-8240-2950-X). Garland Pub.

Baelz, Peter. Does God Answer Prayer? (Illus.). 122p. (Orig.). 1983. pap. 6.95 (ISBN 0-87243-117-7). Templegate.

Baelz, Peter R. The Forgotten Dream. (Bampton Lectures Ser.). 1975. text ed. 17.00x (ISBN 0-8401-0103-1). A R Allenson.

--Prayer & Providence: A Background Study. LC 68-6128. (Hulsean Lectures). 1968. text ed. 10.00x (ISBN 0-8401-0104-X). A R Allenson.

Baen, James, ed. Destinies, Vol. 3, No. 1. (Destinies Ser.). 320p. (Orig.). 1981. pap. 2.50 (ISBN 0-441-14289-3). Ace Bks.

Baen, James P., ed. see Bradley, Marion Z.

Baen, Jim, jt. auth. see Cohen, Barney.

Baen, Jim, ed. Galaxy: The Best of My Years. 1980. pap. 2.25 (ISBN 0-441-27296-7). Ace Bks.

Baen, Jim, ed. see Anderson, Poul & Broxon, Mildred D.

Baen, Jim, ed. see De Camp, L. Sprague.

Baen, Jim, ed. see Dickson, Gordon R.

Baen, Jim, ed. see Ing, Dean.

Baen, Jim, ed. see Madsen, Axel.

Baen, Jim, ed. see Niven, Larry.

Baen, Jim, ed. see Norton, Andre.

Baen, John S., jt. auth. see Friedman, Jack P.

Baender, Margaret W. Shifting Sands. 276p. 1981. 10.00 (ISBN 0-8059-2792-1). Dorrance.

--Tail Waggings of Maggie. (Illus.). 64p. (gr. 8-10). 1982. pap. 6.00 (ISBN 0-88100-012-4). Philmar Pub.

Baender, Paul, intro. by. The Adventures of Tom Sawyer: A Facsimile Edition of Mark Twain's Complete Manuscript. 920p. 1982. lib. bdg. 120.00 (ISBN 0-89093-456-8, Aletheia Bks). U Pubns Amer.

Baender, Paul, ed. & intro. by see Twain, Mark.

Baer. Getting by in German. (Getting by Ser.). 72p. 1982. pap. 2.95 (ISBN 0-8120-2572-5); cassette 11.95 (ISBN 0-8120-2573-3); book & cassette 14.95 (ISBN 0-8120-7104-2). Barron.

Baer, Adela S. The Genetic Perspective. 1977. text ed. 24.95 (ISBN 0-7216-1471-X, CBS C). SCP.

--Heredity & Society: Readings in Social Genetics. 2nd ed. 352p. 1977. pap. text ed. write for info. (ISBN 0-02-305160-4, 30516). Macmillan.

Baer, Bernhard. Ganymed. (Orig.). pap. 5.95 (ISBN 0-905209-14-1, Pub. by Victoria & Albert Mus UK). Faber & Faber.

Baer, Betty L. & Federico, Ronald C., eds. Educating the Baccalaureate Social Worker: A Curriculum Development Reource Guide, Vol. II. LC 79-11681. 288p. 1979. prof ref 29.95 (ISBN 0-88410-674-8). Ballinger Pub.

--Educating the Baccalaureate Social Worker: Report of the Undergraduate Social Work Curriculum Development Project, Vol. I. LC 77-16189. 256p. 1978. prof ref 29.95 (ISBN 0-88410-666-7). Ballinger Pub.

Baer, C. J. & Ottaway, J. R. Electrical & Electronic Drawing. 5th ed. 560p. 1985. 31.50 (ISBN 0-07-003028-6). McGraw.

Baer, Charles J. & Ottaway, John R. Electrical & Electronics Drawing. 4th ed. LC 79-15837. (Illus.). 1980. text ed. 31.50 (ISBN 0-07-003010-3). McGraw.

Baer, Christopher T. Canals & Railroads of the Mid-Atlantic States, 1800-1860. 80p. 1981. pap. 15.00x (ISBN 0-914650-19-X). Eleutherian Mills-Hagley.

Baer, D. Richard. The Film Buff's Checklist: Motion Pictures 1986-87. (Illus.). 240p. 1985. pap. cancelled (ISBN 0-913616-05-2). Hollywd Film Arch.

Baer, D. Richard, ed. The Movie World Almanac Nineteen Eighty-Six to Nineteen Eighty-Seven. (Illus.). 360p. 1985. lib. bdg. 65.00 (ISBN 0-913616-06-0). Hollywd Film Arch.

Baer, Dale, jt. auth. see Baer, Jane.

Baer, Daniel M. & Dito, William R., eds. Interpretations in Therapeutic Drug Monitoring. LC 81-826. (Illus.). 388p. 1981. text ed. 35.00 (ISBN 0-89189-080-7, 45-9-009-00). Am Soc Clinical.

Baer, Dobh & Jacobs, Louis. On Ecstasy. 196p. 1982. pap. 8.95 (ISBN 0-940646-03-X). Rossel Bks.

Baer, Donald M. How to Plan for Generalization. 36p. 1981. 5.00 (ISBN 0-89079-061-2). Pro Ed.

Baer, Donald M., jt. auth. see Bijou, Sidney W.

Baer, Edith. A Frost in the Night: A Childhood on the Eve of the Third Reich. LC 79-27774. 224p. 1980. lib. bdg. 8.99 (ISBN 0-394-94364-3). Pantheon.

--Words Are Like Faces. LC 79-18007. (Illus.). 36p. (ps-2). 1980. 4.95 (ISBN 0-394-84028-3). Pantheon.

Baer, Edward C. & Winikoff, Beverly, eds. Breastfeeding: Program, Policy, & Research Issues. (Studies in Family Planning: Vol. 12, No. 4). 92p. (Orig.). 1981. pap. 2.50 (ISBN 0-318-01178-6). Population Coun.

Baer, Elizabeth, jt. ed. see Fowler, Laurence H.

Baer, Eric, ed. Engineering Design for Plastics. LC 75-1222. 1216p. 1975. Repr. of 1964 ed. 68.50 (ISBN 0-88275-281-2). Krieger.

Baer, Eva. Metalwork in Medieval Islamic Art. LC 81-23243. (Illus.). 371p. 1983. 39.50x (ISBN 0-87395-602-8). State U NY Pr.

Baer, Eva see Evans, Barrie, pseud.

Baer, Frank. Max's Gang. 324p. (gr. 7 up). 1983. 17.00i (ISBN 0-316-07517-5). Little.

Baer, Gabriel. Fellah & Townsman in the Middle East: Studies in Social History. 350p. 1982. 36.00x (ISBN 0-7146-3126-4, F Cass Co). Biblio Dist.

--Population & Society in the Arab East. Szoke, Hanna, tr. LC 76-16835. (Illus.). 1976. Repr. of 1964 ed. lib. bdg. 21.25x (ISBN 0-8371-8963-2, BAPSA). Greenwood.

--Studies in the Social History of Modern Egypt. Polk, William R., ed. LC 69-17537. (Publications of the Center for Middle Eastern Studies Ser.: No. 4). 1969. 20.00x (ISBN 0-226-03405-4). U of Chicago Pr.

Baer, Gabriel, jt. ed. see Cohen, Amnon.

Baer, Gene. Gene Baer's Wild & Wonderful Art Lessons. LC 83-8093. 222p. 1983. 16.50 (ISBN 0-13-347567-0). P-H.

--Imaginative Art Lessons for Kids & Their Teachers. LC 81-18764. 224p. 1982. 17.50 (ISBN 0-13-451351-7). P-H.

Baer, George M., ed. The Natural History of Rabies. 1975. Vol. 1. 85.50 (ISBN 0-12-072401-4); Vol. 2. 74.50 (ISBN 0-12-072402-2). Acad Pr.

Baer, George W. International Organizations, Nineteen Eighteen to Nineteen Forty-Five: A Guide to Research & Research Materials. Kimmich, Christoph M., ed. LC 80-53893. 261p. 1981. lib. bdg. 20.00 (ISBN 0-8420-2179-5). Scholarly Res Inc.

--Test Case: Italy, Ethiopia & the League of Nations. new ed. LC 76-20293. (Publications Ser.: No. 159). 384p. 1977. 15.95x (ISBN 0-8179-6591-2). Hoover Inst Pr.

Baer, Gerhard, et al. World Cultures, Arts & Crafts. 388p. (Eng., Fr., Ger.). 1979. 24.95 (ISBN 0-8176-0996-2). Birkhauser.

Baer, Gordon & Howell-Koehler, Nancy. Vietnam: The Battle Comes Home. LC 84-61115. (Illus.). 128p. (Orig.). 1984. pap. 16.95 (ISBN 0-87100-199-3, 2199). Morgan.

Baer, Hans A. The Black Spiritual Movement: A Religious Response to Racism. LC 83-14559. 232p. 1984. text ed. 18.95x (ISBN 0-87049-413-9). U of Tenn Pr.

Baer, Harold & Broder, Aaron J. How to Prepare & Negotiate Cases for Settlement. rev. ed. LC 72-80204. 240p. 1973. 17.50 (ISBN 0-88238-031-1). Law-Arts.

Baer, Herbert R. Admiralty Law of the Supreme Court. 3rd ed. 1029p. 1985. 60.00 (ISBN 0-87215-216-2); 1984 supplement 22.50 (ISBN 0-87215-771-7); 1985 supplement 22.50 (ISBN 0-87215-884-5). Michie Co.

Baer, J., jt. auth. see Fensterheim, H.

Baer, J. A. & Lowenhaupt, Cecile K. Dining In-St. Louis. (Orig.). pap. 7.95 (ISBN 0-89716-045-2). Peanut Butter.

Baer, Jane & Baer, Dale. The Easter Bunny Gang. (Ideals Read Aloud Storybks.). (Illus.). 32p. (gr. k-4). 1983. 10.60 (ISBN 0-516-09193-X). Childrens.

Baer, Jean. How to Be an Assertive (Not Aggressive) Woman in Life, in Love, & on the Job: The Total Guide to Self-Assertiveness. 1976. pap. 3.95 (ISBN 0-451-13444-3, Sig). NAL.
--The Self-Chosen: "Our Crowd" Is Dead--Long Live "Our Crowd". (Illus.). 1984. pap. 7.95 (ISBN 0-87795-536-0, Pub. by Priam). Arbor Hse.
--The Self-Chosen: Our Crowd Is Dead-Long Live Our Crowd! LC 81-66962. (Illus.). 345p. 1982. 15.95 (ISBN 0-87795-330-9). Arbor Hse.
Baer, Jean, jt. auth. see Fensterheim, Herbert.
Baer, Jean-Loup. Computer Systems Architecture. LC 72-27039. (Illus.). 626p. 1980. text ed. 34.95 (ISBN 0-914894-15-3). Computer Sci.
Baer, Joachim T. Vladimir Ivanovicdal Aș a Belletrist. LC 72-88190. (Slavistic Printings & Reprintings Ser: No. 276). 204p. 1972. text ed. 25.00x (ISBN 90-2792-334-5). Mouton.
Baer, Judith A. The Chains of Protection: The Judicial Response to Women's Labor Legislation. LC 77-82695. (Contributions in Women's Studies: No. 1). x, 238p. 1978. lib. bdg. 27.50x (ISBN 0-8371-9785-6, BCP/). Greenwood.
--Equality Under the Constitution: Reclaiming the Fourteenth Amendment. LC 83-6220. 304p. 1983. 39.95x (ISBN 0-8014-1555-1); pap. 18.95x (ISBN 0-8014-9888-0). Cornell U Pr.
Baer, Judy. The Girl Inside. (First Love Ser.). 155p. (YA) 1984. pap. 1.95 (ISBN 0-671-53411-4). PB.
--Tender Adversary. 192p. (Orig.). 1985. pap. 2.50 (ISBN 0-310-46772-1, Pub. by Serenade-Serenata). Zondervan.
Baer, Karl E. Von see Von Baer, Karl E.
Baer, Kathy, tr. see American Office of War Information, et al.
Baer, Katie. Government by the People. Rev. ed. 72p. 1982. 2.85 (ISBN 0-317-35465-5). New Readers.
Baer, Klaus. Rank & Title in the Old Kingdom: The Structure of the Egyptian Administration in the Fifth & Sixth Dynasties. (Midway Reprint Ser). 1974. pap. 7.50x (ISBN 0-226-03412-7). U of Chicago Pr.
Baer, Larry L. The Parker Gun. 29.95 (ISBN 0-88227-047-8). Gun Room.
Baer, Louis S. Better Health with Fewer Pills. LC 82-8394. 132p. 1982. pap. 5.95 (ISBN 0-664-24425-4). Westminster.
--Let the Patient Decide: A Doctor's Advice to Older Persons. LC 78-19014. 156p. 1978. pap. 5.95 (ISBN 0-664-24207-3). Westminster.
Baer, Melvyn J. Growth & Maturation: An Introduction to Physical Development. new ed. LC 72-81296. (Illus.). 224p. 1973. pap. text ed. 5.95x (ISBN 0-87299-016-8). Howard Doyle.
Baer, Melvyn J., et al. The Postnatal Development of the Rat Skull. LC 81-19837. 1983. text ed. 125.00x (ISBN 0-472-10011-4). U of Mich Pr.
Baer, Mervin. The Christian Home. 1976. 1.75 (ISBN 0-686-11147-8). Rod & Staff.
Baer, Mervin J. The Doctrine of Salvation. 1980. 2.90 (ISBN 0-686-30768-2). Rod & Staff.
--El Hogar Cristiano. (Span.). pap. 1.75 (ISBN 0-686-32324-6). Rod & Staff.
Baer, Michael, ed. Theory of Chemical Reaction Dynamics, 3 vols, Vols. II, III, & IV. 1985. Vol. II, 320 pgs. 80.00 (ISBN 0-8493-6115-X); Vol. III, 320 pgs. 99.00 (ISBN 0-8493-6116-8); Vol. IV, 272 pgs. 86.00 (ISBN 0-8493-6117-6). CRC Pr.
--Theory of Chemical Reaction Dynamics, Vol. 1. 240p. 1985. 86.00 (ISBN 0-8493-6114-1). CRC Pr.
Baer, Morley, et al. Adobes in the Sun. LC 72-85173. (Illus.). 144p. 1980. pap. 8.95 (ISBN 0-87701-168-0). Chronicle Bks.
--Painted Ladies: The Art of San Francisco's Victorian Houses. (Illus.). 1978. pap. 11.50 (ISBN 0-525-47523-0, 01117-330). Dutton.
Baer, Phil & Merrifield, William R. Two Studies on the Lacandones of Mexico. (Publications in Linguistics & Related Fields Ser.: No. 33). 272p. 1971. pap. 4.00x (ISBN 0-88312-035-6); microfiche 3.00 (ISBN 0-88312-435-1). Summer Inst Ling.
Baer, Randall N. & Vittitow-Baer, Vicki. Windows of Light: Quartz Crystals & Self-Transformation. LC 84-478823. 176p. 1984. pap. 7.64 (ISBN 0-06-060325-9, CN 4104, HarpR). Har-Row.
Baer, Reinhold. Linear Algebra & Projective Geometry. (Pure and Applied Mathematics Ser.: Vol. 2). 1952. 59.50 (ISBN 0-12-072250-X). Acad Pr.
Baer, Richard, jt. auth. see Douglass, Vonda.
Baer, Richard, jt. auth. see Sedjo, Karen.
Baer, Ruth. Ancient History, Bk. 1. (gr. 7). 1979. 9.50 (ISBN 0-686-30770-4); tchr's ed. avail. 3.85 (ISBN 0-686-30771-2). Rod & Staff.
Baer, Steve. Sunspots. LC 75-20779. 1977. pap. 6.95 (ISBN 0-686-21779-9). Zomeworks Corp.
Baer, Thais. Four Seasons, Five Senses. 1985. pap. 9.95 (ISBN 0-8163-0589-7). Pacific Pr Pub Assn.
Baer, W. S., et al. Cable Television: Franchising Considerations. LC 73-90818. (Rand Cable Television Ser.). 294p. 1974. 16.50x (ISBN 0-8448-0258-1). Crane-Russak Co.
Baer, Walt. Winning in Labor Arbitration. LC 82-70973. 192p. 1982. 21.95 (ISBN 0-87251-071-9). Crain Bks.
Baer, Walter E. The Operating Manager's Labor Relations Guidebook. 1978. pap. text ed. 10.95 (ISBN 0-8403-1936-3). Kendall Hunt.
Baer, Werner. The Brazilian Economy: Growth & Development. 2nd ed. 368p. 1983. 36.95x (ISBN 0-03-062029-5); pap. 14.95x (ISBN 0-03-062031-7). Praeger.
--Development of the Brazilian Steel Industry. LC 70-89474. 1969. 12.50x (ISBN 0-8265-1143-0). Vanderbilt U Pr.
Baer, Werner & Samuelson, Larry. Latin America in the Post-Import Substitution Era. 1977. pap. text ed. 23.00 (ISBN 0-08-021822-9). Pergamon.
Baer, William, jt. auth. see Banerjee, Tridib.
Baer, William K., ed. see Mid-America Spectroscopy Symposium (18th; 1967; Chicago. IL), et al.
Baer, William P. The Aphasic Patient: A Program for Auditory Comprehension & Language Training, (Clinician's Edition) (Illus.). 144p. 1977. spiral vinyl 13.75x (ISBN 0-398-03567-9). C C Thomas.
--The Aphasic Patient: A Program for Auditory Comprehension & Language Training (Patients Edition) (Illus.). 424p. 1977. spiral 24.75x (ISBN 0-398-03568-7). C C Thomas.
Baer, Yitzhak. History of the Jews in Christian Spain, 2 Vols. LC 61-16852. 1966. pap. 6.95 ea. (ISBN 0-8276-0115-8, 425). Jewish Pubns.
Baerends, Gerard, et al, eds. Function & Evolution in Behaviour. (Illus.). 1975. 69.00x (ISBN 0-19-857382-0). Oxford U Pr.
Baerg, G. The Supernatural in the Modern German Drama. 59.95 (ISBN 0-8490-1160-4). Gordon Pr.
Baerg, Harry J. Birds That Can't Fly. Van Dolson, Bobbie J., ed. LC 82-21535. (Illus., Orig.). 1983. pap. 4.50 (ISBN 0-8280-0149-9). Review & Herald.
Baerheim, S., jt. auth. see Verpoorte, R.
Baerheim-Svendsen, A. Chromatography of Alkaloids: Thin Layer Chromatography, Pt. A. (Journal of Chromatography Library: Vol. 23). 534p. 1983. 104.25 (ISBN 0-444-42145-9). Elsevier.
Baerjee, P. K. & Butterfield, R., eds. Development in Soil Mechanics & Foundation Engineering Two, Vol. 2. 296p. 1985. 54.00 (ISBN 0-85334-345-4, Pub. by Elsevier Applied Sci England). Elsevier.
Baerlein, Henry. March of the Seventy Thousand. LC 72-115506. (Russia Observed Ser). (Illus.). 1971. Repr. of 1926 ed. 20.00 (ISBN 0-405-03076-2). Ayer Co Pubs.
Baerlein, Richard. Shergar: The Story of the Aga Khan & His Racing Empire. (Illus.). 224p. 1985. 15.95 (ISBN 0-7181-2176-7, Pub. by Michael Joseph). Merrimack Pub Cir.
Baermann, Carl. Complete Method for Clarinet: First & Second Division. Langenus, Gustave, ed. (Illus.). 92p. 1918. pap. 7.00 (ISBN 0-8258-0170-2, 0-32). Fischer Inc NY.
--Complete Method for Clarinet: Third Division. (Illus.). 55p. 1917. pap. 7.00 (ISBN 0-8258-0215-6, 0-33). Fischer Inc NY.
Baernreither, Joseph M. English Associations of Working Men. Taylor, A., tr. LC 66-28040. 1966. Repr. of 1889 ed. 46.00x (ISBN 0-8103-3078-4). Gale.
Baerresen, Donald W., et al. Latin American Trade Patterns. LC 80-479. (Illus.). xix, 329p. 1980. Repr. of 1965 ed. lib. bdg. 32.50x (ISBN 0-313-22288-6, BALT). Greenwood.
Baert, A. L. Atlas of Computer Tomography: Volume Two, Abdominal Computer Tomography. (Illus.). 210p. 1980. 130.00 (ISBN 0-387-10093-8). Springer-Verlag.
Baert, A. L., jt. auth. see Bulcke, J. A.
Baert, A. L., et al. Frontier in European Radiology, Vol. 2. (Illus.). 110p. 1982. 32.00 (ISBN 0-387-11349-5). Springer-Verlag.
Baert, A. L., et al, eds. Frontiers in European Radiology, Vol. 1. (Illus.). 170p. 1982. 42.00 (ISBN 0-387-10753-3). Springer-Verlag.
Baert, Andre E., jt. ed. see Mednick, Sarnoff A.
Baerthlein, Karl. Transzendentalienlehre der alten Ontologie, Pt. 1: Transzendentalienlehre im Corpus Aristotelicum. 415p. 1972. 43.20x (ISBN 3-11-004021-2). De Gruyter.
Baertschi, A. J. & Dreifus, J. J., eds. Neuroendocrinology of Vasopressin Carticolberin & Opiomelanocortins. 1982. 39.50 (ISBN 0-12-072440-5). Acad Pr.
Baertschi, Hans-Peter. Industrialisierung, Eisenbahnschlachten und Staedtebau in Zuerich, Aussersihl. (Geschichte und Theorie der Architektur: Vol. 25). 528p. 1983. 39.95 (ISBN 0-8176-1312-9). Birkhauser.
Baerwald, H. H. Japan's Parliament: An Introduction. LC 73-90810. 200p. 1974. 32.50 (ISBN 0-521-20387-2). Cambridge U Pr.
Baerwald, Hans H. The Purge of Japanese Leaders under the Occupation. LC 77-22428. (University of California Publications in Political Science Ser.: No. 8). 1977. Repr. of 1959 ed. lib. bdg. 29.75 (ISBN 0-8371-9088-6, BAPJ). Greenwood.
Baerwald, Sara, jt. auth. see Handelsman, Judith.
Baes, Charles F., Jr. & Mesmer, Robert E. The Hydrolysis of Cations. LC 75-44393. 489p. 1976. 63.95x (ISBN 0-471-03985-3, Pub. by Wiley-Interscience). Wiley.
--The Hydrolysis of Cations. 512p. 1986. Repr. of 1976 ed. lib. bdg. price not set (ISBN 0-89874-892-5). Krieger.
Baesl, John L. As--with the Wind. 1984. 6.95 (ISBN 0-8062-2246-8). Carlton.
Baeslack, W. A. & Hasson, D. F., eds. Advances in Titanium Welding. avail. Metal Soc.
Baetjer, Anna M. Women in Industry: Their Health & Efficiency. Stein, Leon, ed. LC 77-70480. (Work Ser.). (Illus.). 1977. Repr. of 1946 ed. lib. bdg. 32.00x (ISBN 0-405-10154-6). Ayer Co Pubs.
Baetjer, Katharine. European Paintings in the Metropolitan Museum of Art, by Artists in or Before 1865: A Summary Catalogue. Shultz, Ellen, ed. LC 80-17747. 2450p. 1981. 75.00 (ISBN 0-87099-250-3). Metro Mus Art.
Baettig, K., ed. see International Workshop, Zurich, September 15-17, 1976.
Baetz, Albert, jt. ed. see Phillips, Marshall.
Baetz, Mary. The Human Imperative: Planning for People in the Electronic Office. LC 84-72804. 224p. 1985. 25.00 (ISBN 0-87094-652-8). Dow Jones-Irwin.
Baeuerle, D., ed. Laser Processing & Diagnostics. (Springer Series in Chemical Physics: Vol. 39). (Illus.). 560p. 1984. 34.00 (ISBN 0-387-13843-9). Springer-Verlag.
Baeumer, Max L., jt. ed. see Fink, Karl J.
Baeyens, Dennis A. Experimental Physiology. 96p. (Orig.). 1981. lab manual 8.95x (ISBN 0-89459-131-2). Hunter Textbks.
Baeyer, Hans C. von see Von Baeyer, Hans C.
Baez, Albert V. Innovation in Science Education World-Wide. 249p. 1984. pap. 15.00 (ISBN 92-3-101331-9, U1406, UNESCO). Unipub.
Baez, Tony, et al. Desegregation & Hispanic Students: A Community Perspective. LC 80-80311. 84p. (Orig.). 1980. pap. 5.25 (ISBN 0-89763-023-8). Natl Clearinghse Bilingual Ed.
Baeza, R. Quadratic Forms over Semilocal Rings. (Lecture Notes in Mathematics Ser.: Vol. 655). 1978. pap. 16.00 (ISBN 0-387-08845-8). Springer-Verlag.
Baez-Camargo, Gonzalo. Archaeological Commentary on the Bible: From Genesis to Revelation. LC 82-45473. (Illus.). 336p. 1984. 17.95 (ISBN 0-385-17968-5). Doubleday.
--Comentario Arqueologico de la Biblia. 339p. (Orig., Span.). 1979. pap. 7.95 (ISBN 0-89922-148-3). Edit Caribe.
Bafaro, Johanna & Freedman, Melvin H., eds. Entrepreneur's Information Sourcebook. 72p. (Orig.). 1985. pap. 10.00 (ISBN 0-911665-01-3, EN982). Entre Prods.
Bafaro, Johanna, ed. see Freedman, Melvin H. & Silver, Samuel M.
Bagadion, Benjamin. Law in the Mobilization & Participatory Organization of the Rural Poor: The Kagawasan Case. LC 81-186807. 72p. 1979. write for info. (Pub. by Ateneo de Manila U Pr Phillippines). Cellar.
Bagai, Eric & Bagai, Judith. System FORE Handbook. (System FORE Ser.: Vol. 1). 96p. (Orig.). 1979. pap. text ed. 7.00x (ISBN 0-943292-01-8). Foreworks.
Bagai, Eric & Bagai, Judith, eds. System FORE, 5 Vols. (Illus.). 1328p. 1979. 90.00x (ISBN 0-943292-00-X). Foreworks.
Bagai, Eric, ed. see Los Angeles Unified School District, et al.
Bagai, Eric, ed. see West Linn Unified School District.
Bagai, Judith, jt. auth. see Bagai, Eric.
Bagai, Judith, jt. ed. see Bagai, Eric.
Bagai, Judith, ed. see Los Angeles Unified School District, et al.
Bagai, Judith, ed. see West Linn Unified School District.
Bagai, Leona B. The East Indians & Pakistanis in America. rev. ed. LC 67-15680. (In America Bks.). (gr. 5-11). 1972. PLB 7.95 (ISBN 0-8225-0210-0). Lerner Pubns.
Bagaraj, D. Joseph, jt. auth. see Powell, Conway L.
Bagarozzi, Dennis, jt. auth. see Wodarski, John S.
Bagarozzi, Dennis, et al, eds. Marital & Family Therapy: New Perspectives in Theory, Research & Practice. (Illus.). 128p. 1982. text ed. 29.95x (ISBN 0-89885-069-X). Human Sci Pr.
Bagby, Albert I., Jr., tr. see Assis, Joaquim M.
Bagby, Albert M. Mammy Rosie. facsimile ed. LC 71-38638. (Black Heritage Library Collection). Repr. of 1904 ed. 18.25 (ISBN 0-8369-8996-1). Ayer Co Pubs.
Bagby, Daniel G. Transition & Newness. LC 81-52301. 1982. pap. 5.50 (ISBN 0-8054-5201-X). Broadman.
--Understanding Anger in the Church. LC 79-52000. 1979. 7.95 (ISBN 0-8054-2706-6). Broadman.
Bagby, English. The Psychology of Personality. Repr. of 1928 ed. 25.00 (ISBN 0-89987-040-6). Darby Bks.
--The Psychology of Personality. 236p. 1980. Repr. of 1928 ed. lib. bdg. 35.00 (ISBN 0-8492-3590-1). R West.
Bagby, Martha C. Consumer Economics & Personal Finance: Syllabus. 1974. pap. text ed. 7.75 (ISBN 0-89420-063-1, 100030); cassette recordings 224.55 (ISBN 0-89420-136-0, 100000). Natl Book.
Bagby, Philip. Culture & History. LC 76-3680. (Illus.). 244p. 1976. Repr. of 1963 ed. lib. bdg. 17.50x (ISBN 0-8371-8797-4, BACH). Greenwood.
Bagby, Sara A., jt. auth. see Cooney, Stephanie H.
Bagby, Wesley. The Road to Normalacy: The Presidential Campaign & Election of 1920. (John Hopkins University. Studies in Historical & Political Science: 80 No. 1). pap. 52.00 (ISBN 0-317-19867-X, 2023108). Bks Demand UMI.
Bagby, Wesley M. Contemporary American Economic & Political Problems. LC 80-22510. 300p. 1981. text ed. 19.95x (ISBN 0-88229-328-1); pap. text ed. 9.95x (ISBN 0-88229-765-1). Nelson-Hall.
--Contemporary American Social Problems. LC 81-9505. 300p. 1981. text ed. 19.95x (ISBN 0-88229-772-4); pap. text ed. 9.95x (ISBN 0-88229-773-2). Nelson-Hall.
--Contemporary International Problems. LC 82-12615. 248p. 1983. 21.95x (ISBN 0-88229-774-0); pap. text ed. 9.95x (ISBN 0-88229-775-9). Nelson-Hall.
--The Road to Normalcy: The Presidential Campaign & Election of 1920. LC 78-64237. (Johns Hopkins University. Studies in the Social Sciences. Eightieth Ser. 1962: 1). Repr. of 1962 ed. 11.50 (ISBN 0-404-61342-X). AMS Pr.
Bagchee, Moni. Ananda Coomaraswamy: A Study. 1977. 10.00x (ISBN 0-8364-0067-4). South Asia Bks.
Bagchi, A. Stackelberg Differential Games in Economic Models. (Lecture Notes in Control & Information Sciences Ser.: Vol. 64). viii, 203p. 1984. pap. 12.50 (ISBN 0-387-13587-1). Springer-Verlag.
Bagchi, A. & Jongen, H. T., eds. Systems & Optimization. (Lecture Notes in Control & Information Sciences Ser.: Vol. 66). x, 206p. 1985. pap. 13.00 (ISBN 0-387-15004-8). Springer-Verlag.
Bagchi, Amiya K. The Political Economy of Underdevelopment. LC 81-10237. (Modern Cambridge Economics Ser.). 304p. 1982. 42.50 (ISBN 0-521-24024-7); pap. 14.95 (ISBN 0-521-28404-X). Cambridge U Pr.
--Private Investment in India & Pakistan, 1900-1939. LC 79-152631. (South Asian Studies: No. 10). (Illus.). 1971. 54.50 (ISBN 0-521-07641-2). Cambridge U Pr.
Bagchi, Prabodh C. India & China: A Thousand Years of Cultural Relations. rev. enl. 2nd ed. LC 71-136053. (Illus.). 1971. Repr. of 1951 ed. lib. bdg. 15.00 (ISBN 0-8371-5203-8, BAIC). Greenwood.
Bagchi, T. S., jt. auth. see Bhattacharya, D. S.
Bagdan, Karen & Musty, Sherrill. The Five to Eighteen Book: The Chittenden County, Vermont Resource Directory for Young People. 1984. pap. 2.00 (ISBN 0-317-11943-5). Waterfront Bks.
Bagdanavicius, Vytautas. Cultural Wellsprings of Folktales. Zemkalnis, Jeronimas, tr. Orig. Title: Kulturines Gelmes Pasakose. (Lithuanian). 1970. 6.00 (ISBN 0-87141-030-3). Manyland.
Bagdasarian, Nicholas Der see Der Bagdasarian, Nicholas.
Bagdasarian, Ross, jt. auth. see Karman, Janice.
Bagder, George P. An English-Arabic Lexicon. 80.00x (ISBN 0-86685-064-3). Intl Bk Ctr.
Bagdikian, Ben H. Information Machines: Their Impact on Men & the Media. 1971. pap. 5.95xi (ISBN 0-06-131900-7, TB1900, Torch). Har-Row.
--The Information Machines: Their Impact on Man & the Media. 13.25 (ISBN 0-8446-5845-6). Peter Smith.
--The Media Monopoly. LC 82-72503. 320p. 1984. 16.95x (ISBN 0-8070-6162-X); pap. 8.95 (ISBN 0-8070-6163-8, BP672). Beacon Pr.
Bagdonas, A & Georg, J. c. Techniques of Frost Prediction & Methods of Frost & Cold Protection. (Technical Note Ser.: No. 157). x, 101p. 1978. pap. 37.00 (ISBN 92-63-10487-5, W403, WMO). Unipub.
Bage, Robert. Barham Downs, 2 vols. Paulson, Ronald, ed. LC 78-60850. (Novel 1720-1805 Ser.: Vol. 9). 1979. Set. lib. bdg. 75.00 (ISBN 0-8240-3658-1). Garland Pub.
--The Fair Syrian, 2 vols. LC 78-60845. (Novel 1720-1805 Ser.: Vol. 10). 1980. Set. lib. bdg. 75.00 (ISBN 0-8240-3659-X). Garland Pub.
--Hermsprong; or, Man As He Is Not, 3 vols. LC 78-60853. (Novel 1720-1805 Ser.: Vol. 13). 1980. Set. lib. bdg. 112.00 (ISBN 0-8240-3662-X). Garland Pub.
--Hermsprong, or Man As He Is Not. Faulkner, Peter, ed. (The World's Classics (Paperback)). 272p. 1985. pap. 4.95 (ISBN 0-19-281688-8). Oxford U Pr.
--Hermsprong: Or, Man As He Is Not: A Critical Edition. Tave, Stuart, ed. LC 81-83149. 380p. 1982. text ed. 28.50x (ISBN 0-271-00298-0). Pa St U Pr.
--James Wallace, 3 vols. Paulson, Ronald, ed. LC 78-60847. (Novel 1720-1805 Ser.: Vol. 11). 1979. 112.00 (ISBN 0-8240-3660-3). Garland Pub.
--Mount Henneth, 2 vols. Paulson, Ronald, ed. LC 78-60846. (Novel 1720-1805 Ser.: Vol. 8). 1980. Set. lib. bdg. 75.00 (ISBN 0-8240-3657-3). Garland Pub.
Bage, Robert & Paulson, Ronald. Man As He Is, 4 vols. LC 78-60853. (Novel 1720-1805 Ser.: Vol. 12). 1979. Set. lib. bdg. 150.00 (ISBN 0-8240-3661-1). Garland Pub.
Bageant, Robert A., jt. auth. see Heironimus, Terring W., 3rd.
Bagehot, Wakter. Economic Studies: The Works of Wakter Bagehot. 280p. Date not set. Repr. lib. bdg. 34.00 (ISBN 0-932051-97-9, Pub. by Am Repr Serv). Am Biog Serv.
Bagehot, Walter. Biographical Studies. Hutton, Richard H., ed. LC 75-111469. (BCL Ser.: No. I). Repr. of 1881 ed. 12.50 (ISBN 0-404-00445-8). AMS Pr.

--Biographical Studies. 1973. Repr. of 1895 ed. 15.00 (ISBN 0-8274-1486-2). R West.
--Biographical Studies. Hutton, Richard H., ed. LC 70-144862. vii, 368p. 1972. Repr. of 1889 ed. 12.00 (ISBN 0-403-00850-6). Scholarly.
--Collected Works of Walter Bagehot, Vols. 3 & 4. St. John Stevas, Norman, ed. LC 66-1165. 1968. Set. 70.00x (ISBN 0-674-14002-8). Harvard U Pr.
--Economic Studies. Hutton, Richard H., ed. 1976. Repr. 23.00x (ISBN 0-403-06161-X). Scholarly.
--The English Constitution. 320p. (Orig.). 1966. pap. 7.95x (ISBN 0-8014-9023-5, CP23). Cornell U Pr.
--Estimates of Some Englishmen & Scotchmen. 453p. 1980. Repr. of 1858 ed. lib. bdg. 47.50 (ISBN 0-89987-060-0). Darby Bks.
--Estimates of Some Englishmen & Scotchmen. LC 72-13529. 1974. Repr. of 1858 ed. lib. bdg. 45.00 (ISBN 0-8414-1221-9). Folcroft.
--Estimations in Criticism, 2 vols. 1978. Repr. of 1908 ed. lib. bdg. 60.00 set (ISBN 0-8495-0419-8). Arden Lib.
--Estimations in Criticism, 2 vols. LC 73-4485. 1973. lib. bdg. 50.00 (ISBN 0-8414-1756-3). Folcroft.
--Literary Studies (Miscellaneous Essays) Hutton, Richard H., ed. (The Works of Walter Bagehot, 1826-1877). 357p. Repr. of 1903 ed. lib. bdg. 39.00 (ISBN 0-318-03809-9). Am Repr Serv.
--Literary Studies with a Prefatory Memoir, 2 Vols. Hutton, Richard H., ed. LC 72-148745. (BCL Ser.: No. I). Repr. of 1879 ed. Set. 95.00 (ISBN 0-404-07235-6). Vol. 1 (ISBN 0-404-07236-4). Vol. 2 (ISBN 0-404-07237-2). AMS Pr.
--Lombard Street. Wilkins, Mira, ed. LC 78-3895. (International Finance Ser.). 1978. Repr. of 1917 ed. lib. bdg. 30.00x (ISBN 0-405-11201-7). Ayer Co Pubs.
--Lombard Street: A Description of the Money Market; with "The Currency Monopoly". Withers, Hartley, ed. 218p. 1984. pap. cancelled (ISBN 0-87991-252-9). Orion Ed.
--Lombard Street: A Description of the Money Market. LC 78-59001. (Illus.). 1979. Repr. of 1962 ed. 19.00 (ISBN 0-88355-677-4). Hyperion Conn.
--Physics & Politics. LC 73-716. 164p. 1973. Repr. of 1956 ed. lib. bdg. 15.00 (ISBN 0-8371-6781-7, BAPO). Greenwood.
--Physics & Politics. 1881. 30.00 (ISBN 0-932062-08-3). Sharon Hill.
--Shakespeare, the Man. LC 71-126678. Repr. of 1901 ed. 7.50 (ISBN 0-404-00446-6). AMS Pr.
--Shakespeare the Man: An Essay. 66p. 1980. Repr. of 1901 ed. lib. bdg. 10.00 (ISBN 0-8495-0396-5). Arden Lib.
--Shakespeare the Man: An Essay. LC 73-4015. 1973. lib. bdg. 15.00 (ISBN 0-8414-1765-2). Folcroft.

Bagel, Marilyn & Bagel, Tom. The Bagels' Bagel Book. LC 84-20334. (Illus.). 144p. (Orig.). 1985. pap. 6.95 (ISBN 0-87491-764-6). Acropolis.
Bagel, Tom, jt. auth. see Bagel, Marilyn.
Bagemihl, Frederick, tr. see Kamke, E.
Bagemihl, Frederick, tr. see Knopp, Konrad.
Bagenal, Philip H. The American Irish & Their Influence on Irish Politics. LC 74-145469. (The American Immigration Library). viii, 252p. 1971. Repr. of 1882 ed. lib. bdg. 14.95x (ISBN 0-89198-001-6). Ozer.
Bagenal, T. B. Ageing of Fish. 240p. 1982. 40.00 (ISBN 0-686-84445-9, Pub. by Gresham England). State Mutual Bk.
--EIFAC Fishing Gear Intercalibration Experiments. (European Inland Fisheries Advisory Commission (EIFAC): Technical Papers: No.34). (Illus.). 92p. (Eng. & Fr.). 1979. pap. 9.00 (ISBN 92-5-100864-7, F1954, FAO). Unipub.
Bagenal, T. B., et al. EIFAC Experiments on Pelagic Fish Stocks: Assessment by Acoustic Methods in Lake Konnevesi, Finland. (European Inland Fisheries Advisory Commission (EIFAC): Technical Papers: No. 14). 22p. 1982. pap. 7.50 (ISBN 92-5-101234-2, F2349, FAO). Unipub.
Bager, Torben. Marketing Cooperatives & Peasants in Kenya. (Centre for Development Research Ser.: No. 5). (Illus.). 116p. 1983. pap. text ed. 9.50x (ISBN 0-8419-9760-8, Africana). Holmes & Meier.
Bagert, Brod. If Only I Could Fly: Poems for Kids to Read Out Loud. (Illus.). 54p. (gr. k-6). 1984. 9.95x (ISBN 0-9614228-0-7). Juliahouse Pubs.
Bagford, Ballads. Bagford Ballads, 2 Vols. Ebsworth, J. W., ed. (Ballad Society, London. Publications Ser.: Nos. 14-17 & 20). (Illus.). Repr. of 1878 ed. Set. 115.00 (ISBN 0-404-50830-8). AMS Pr.
Bagg, Elma W. Cooking Without a Grain of Salt. 1972. pap. 3.95 (ISBN 0-553-23418-8). Bantam.
--Cooking Without a Grain of Salt. LC 64-13870. 1964. 10.95 (ISBN 0-385-05432-7). Doubleday.
Bagg, Lyman H. see Kron, Karl, pseud.
Bagg, Robert. Madonna of the Cello. 88p. 1961. 15.00x (ISBN 0-8195-2009-8); pap. 6.95 members (ISBN 0-8195-1009-2). Wesleyan U Pr.
--Scrawny Sonnets & Other Narratives. Poems. LC 72-93266. 54p. 1973. 10.00x (ISBN 0-252-00317-9); pap. 5.95 (ISBN 0-252-00330-6). U of Ill Pr.
Bagg, Robert, tr. see Euripides.
Bagg, Robert, tr. see Sophocles.
Bagga, Raaj K., tr. see Kabir.
Bagga, Raaj K., tr. see Singh, Ajaib.
Baggaley, Andrew R. Mathematics for Introductory Statistics: A Programmed Review. LC 69-19103. pap. 46.30 (ISBN 0-317-09324-X, 2055271). Bks Demand UMI.
Bagge, Dominique. Les Idees Politiques en France Sous la Restauration. Mayer, J. P., ed. LC 78-67327. (European Political Thought Ser.). 1979. lib. bdg. 34.50x (ISBN 0-405-11674-8). Ayer Co Pubs.
Bagge, U. & Born, G. V. White Blood Cells. 1982. 34.50 (ISBN 90-247-2681-6, Pub. by Martinus Nijhoff Netherlands). Kluwer Academic.
Bagger, Eugene S. Eminent Europeans. facs. ed. LC 71-121446. (Essay Index Reprint Ser). 1924. 24.50 (ISBN 0-8369-1693-X). Ayer Co Pubs.
Bagger, Jonathan, jt. auth. see Wess, Julius.
Baggett, jt. auth. see Plevyak.
Baggett, jt. auth. see Ristau.
Baggett, Glick. Dollhouse Kit & Dining Room Accessories. 30p. pap. 1.95 (ISBN 0-87588-150-5). Hobby Hse.
--Dollhouse Lamps & Chandeliers. 30p. pap. 1.95 (ISBN 0-87588-149-1). Hobby Hse.
Baggett, Lee. Utilice Su Casa Para Evangelizar. 32p. 1983. Repr. of 1980 ed. 1.35 (ISBN 0-311-13832-2). Casa Bautista.
Baggett, Nancy. The Sixty-Minute Bread Book: And Other Fast-Yeast Recipes You Can Make in 1/2 the Usual Time. LC 84-24756. 1985. 17.95 (ISBN 0-399-13020-9). Putnam Pub Group.
Baggett, Nancy, jt. auth. see Settel, Joanne.
Baggett, Nancy, et al. Don't Tell 'Em It's Good for 'Em. LC 83-40087. 307p. 1984. 14.95 (ISBN 0-8129-1099-0). Times Bks.
--Eat Your Vegetables. LC 85-40276. (Illus.). 352p. (Orig.). pap. 8.95 (ISBN 0-8129-1201-2). Times Bks.
Baggett, Richard C. Programmed Approach to Good Spelling! 160p. 1981. pap. text ed. 13.95 (ISBN 0-13-729764-5). P-H.
Baggett, W. Michael. Texas Foreclosure: Law & Practice. LC 84-5376. 500p. 1984. 75.00 (ISBN 0-07-003027-8, Shepards-McGraw). McGraw.
Baggiani, J. M. & Tewell, V. M. The Chess Set & Other Stories. (Illus.). 21p. (gr. 2-3). 1966. pap. 3.50 (ISBN 0-934329-07-9). Baggiani-Tewell.
--In the Country. (Illus.). 26p. (gr. 2-4). 1966. pap. 3.50 (ISBN 0-934329-08-7). Baggiani-Tewell.
--Read & Draw. (Illus.). 12p. (gr. 1-3). 1966. pap. 2.00 (ISBN 0-934329-06-0). Baggiani-Tewell.
Baggiolini, M., ed. Immunopathology & Immunopharmacology of the Lung. (Journal: International Archives of Allergy & Applied Immunology: Vol. 76, Suppl. 1). (Illus.). iv, 128p. 1985. pap. 19.25 (ISBN 3-8055-4057-4). S Karger.
Baggiolini, M., jt. ed. see Brune, K.
Baggish, Michael S. Basic & Advanced Laser Surgery in Gynecology. 448p. 1985. write for info. (ISBN 0-8385-0520-1). ACC.
Baggot, J. Desmond. Principles of Drug Disposition in Domestic Animals: The Basis of Veterinary Clinical Pharmacology. LC 76-54036. (Illus.). 1977. text ed. 18.00 (ISBN 0-7216-1473-6). Saunders.
Bagguley, William H., ed. Andrew Marvell, Sixteen Twenty-One to Sixteen Seventy-Eight: Tercentenary Tributes. LC 65-18787. (Illus.). 1965. Repr. of 1922 ed. 7.00x (ISBN 0-8462-0587-4). Russell.
Baghban, Marcia. How Can I Help My Child Learn to Read English as a Second Language? (Micromonograph Ser.). 1972. 0.50 (ISBN 0-87207-874-4). Intl Reading.
--Our Daughter Learns to Read & Write: A Case Study from Birth to Three. 1984. 9.00 (ISBN 0-87207-956-2). Intl Reading.
Bagherzadeh, Firouz, et al. Iran Bastan Museum, Teheran. LC 80-82645. (Oriental Ceramics Ser.: Vol. IV). (Illus.). 166p. 1981. 65.00 (ISBN 0-87011-443-3). Kodansha.
Baghio'o, Jean-Louis. The Blue Flame-Tree. Romer, Stephen, tr. from Fr. 142p. 1985. 14.95 (ISBN 0-85635-470-8); pap. 7.50 (ISBN 0-85635-631-X). Carcanet.
Baghli, Sid-Ahmed. Aspects of Algerian Cultural Policy. (Studies & Documents on Cultural Policies). (Illus.). 1978. pap. 5.00 (ISBN 92-3-101474-9, U832, UNESCO). Unipub.
Bagiackas, Joseph. The Future Glory. LC 83-70962. 130p. (Orig.). 1983. pap. 3.95 (ISBN 0-943780-02-0, 8020). Charismatic Ren Servs.
--Mighty in Spirit. LC 82-72094. 54p. (Orig.). 1982. pap. 2.45 (ISBN 0-943780-00-4, 8004). Charismatic Ren Servs.
Bagin, Donald, et al. Public Relations for Administrators. 64p. (Orig.). 1985. pap. write for info. (ISBN 0-87652-101-4). Am Assn Sch Admin.
Baginsky, M., jt. auth. see Stanley, S.
Baginsky, Mary. Alternatives to Prison. 1981. 35.00x (ISBN 0-7206-0522-9, Pub. by Owen England). State Mutual Bk.
Bagir, I., et al. Labour Markets in the Sudan. International Labour Office Staff, ed. x, 224p. 1984. pap. 15.70 (ISBN 92-2-103749-5). Intl Labour Office.
Bagis, A., jt. ed. see Hale, W.
Baglee & Morlee. More Street Jewellery. (Illus.). 96p. 1984. 15.00 (ISBN 0-904568-39-3, Pub. by New Cavendish England). Schiffer.
Bagley, Ayers, ed. The Professor of Education: An Assessment of Conditions. (SPE Monographs). 125p. 1975. 7.50 (ISBN 0-317-35949-5). Soc Profs Ed.
Bagley, Bruce & Alvarez, Roberto. Contadora & the Central American Peace Process: Selected Documents. (SAIS Papers in International Affairs: No. 8). 1985. softcover 25.00x (ISBN 0-8133-0198-X). Westview.
Bagley, Charles R. & Diller, George E. France d'autrefois et d'aujourd'hui. 2nd ed. LC 61-13001. (Fr., Fr). 1961. 14.95x (ISBN 0-89197-177-7); pap. text ed. 7.95x (ISBN 0-89197-178-5). Irvington.
Bagley, Christopher. Social Psychology of the Epileptic Child. LC 79-142199. (Illus.). 1971. 14.95x (ISBN 0-87024-188-5). U of Miami Pr.
Bagley, Christopher & Verma, Gajendra K. Multicultural Childhood. 224p. 1983. text ed. 33.00x (ISBN 0-566-00568-9). Gower Pub Co.
--Racial Prejudice, the Individual & Society. 1979. 22.00x (ISBN 0-566-00294-9, 03085-6, Pub. by Saxon Hse England). Lexington Bks.
Bagley, Christopher, et al. Personality, Self-Esteem & Prejudice. 1979. 20.00x (ISBN 0-566-00265-5, 02836-3, Pub. by Saxon Hse England). Lexington Bks.
Bagley, Clarence. The Acquisition & Pioneering of Old Oregon & In the Beginning. 181p. 1983. Repr. of 1924 ed. 12.00 (ISBN 0-87770-280-2). Ye Galleon.
Bagley, Clarence B. In the Beginning. Meeker, Ezra, ed. (Northwest Historical Classics Ser.). (Illus.). 88p. 1980. pap. 4.98 (ISBN 0-939806-00-2). Hist Soc Seattle.
--Indian Myths of the Northwest. (Shorey Indian Ser.). (Illus.). 145p. pap. 8.95 (ISBN 0-8466-4041-4, I41). Shorey.
Bagley, Constance E., jt. auth. see Moody, Graham B.
Bagley, Demetirus H., et al. Urologic Endoscopy: A Manual & Atlas. 336p. 1984. 95.00 (ISBN 0-316-07518-3). Little.
Bagley, Desmond. Bahama Crisis. 256p. 1983. 15.95 (ISBN 0-671-43453-5). Summit Bks.
--Bahamas Crisis. LC 84-48575. 256p. 1985. pap. 3.37i (ISBN 0-06-080755-5, P755, PL). Har-Row.
--The Enemy. 1979. pap. 1.95 (ISBN 0-449-23906-3, Crest). Fawcett.
--The Enemy. LC 85-42548. 256p. 1985. pap. 2.95 (ISBN 0-06-080772-5, P 772, PL). Har-Row.
--Flyaway. LC 85-42549. 320p. 1985. pap. 2.84i (ISBN 0-06-080771-7, P 771, PL). Har-Row.
--The Freedom Trap. LC 83-48316. 224p. 1984. pap. 2.84i (ISBN 0-06-080692-3, P 692, PL). Har-Row.
--The Golden Keel. LC 84-47663. 224p. 1984. pap. 2.95 (ISBN 0-06-080730-X, P 730, PL). Har-Row.
--Running Blind. LC 83-48317. 224p. 1984. pap. 2.84i (ISBN 0-06-080693-1, P 693, PL). Har-Row.
--The Snow Tiger. LC 83-48318. 256p. 1984. pap. 2.84i (ISBN 0-06-080691-5, P 691, PL). Har-Row.
--The Tightrope Men. LC 84-47662. 256p. 1984. pap. 3.37i (ISBN 0-317-06645-5, P731, PL). Har-Row.
--The Vivero Letter. LC 84-47661. 256p. 1984. pap. 2.84 (ISBN 0-06-080732-6, P732, PL). Har-Row.
--Windfall. LC 84-48576. 320p. 1985. pap. 3.37i (ISBN 0-06-080756-3, P756, PL). Har-Row.
Bagley, Edward B., jt. ed. see Peleg, Micha.
Bagley, F. R., ed. & tr. see Bamdad, Badr ol-Moluk.
Bagley, F. R., ed. see Chubak, Sadeq.
Bagley, F. R., tr. see Dashti, Ali.
Bagley, Helen G. Sand in My Shoe: Homestead Days in Twenty-Nine Palms. 2nd ed. Weight, Harold & Weight, Lucile, eds. LC 77-94990. (Illus.). 269p. 1980. Repr. of 1978 ed. 11.95 (ISBN 0-912714-08-5). Homestead Pub.
Bagley, J. A. & Finley, P. J., eds. Progress in Aerospace Sciences, Vol. 18, No. 1. LC 74-618347. 1977. pap. text ed. 32.00 (ISBN 0-08-022133-5). Pergamon.
Bagley, J. J. The Earls of Derby: Fourteen Eighty-Five to Nineteen Eighty-Five. (Illus.). 258p. 1985. 22.95 (ISBN 0-283-99152-6, Pub. by Sidgwick & Jackson). Merrimack Pub Cir.
--Medieval People. (People in Period Ser.). 1978. 14.95 (ISBN 0-7134-1046-9, Pub. by Batsford England). David & Charles.
Bagley, James R. The Alchemist & the Other Poems. 1980. 5.50 (ISBN 0-8233-0318-7). Golden Quill.
--Soul-Speak from the Matrix. 1985. 6.50 (ISBN 0-8233-0404-3). Golden Quill.
--The Star & Other Poems. LC 76-58026. 1977. 5.00 (ISBN 0-8233-0257-1). Golden Quill.
Bagley, John J. History of Lancashire. rev. ed. (County History Ser.). (Illus.). 1961. 14.95 (ISBN 0-85208-047-6). Dufour.
Bagley, Michael. The Plutonium Factor. 240p. 1985. 13.95 (ISBN 0-8052-8227-0, Pub. by Allison & Busby England). Schocken.
Bagley, Michael T. & Foley, Joyce P. Suppose the Wolf Were An Octopus: A Guide to Creative Questioning for Primary Grade Literature. 9.95 (ISBN 0-89824-087-5). Trillium Pr.
Bagley, Michael T., et al. Two Hundred Ways of Using Imagery in the Classroom: A Guide for Developing Imagination & Creativity in Elementary Students. (gr. 1-8). 15.00 (ISBN 0-89824-084-0). Trillium Pr.
Bagley, Peter. Making Silver Jewelry. (Illus.). 144p. 1983. 26.50 (ISBN 0-7134-2580-6, Pub. by Batsford England). David & Charles.
Bagley, Robert E. To Him That Overcometh: Decline & Fall of the Earth, Bk. I. LC 83-91023. 256p. (Orig.). 1984. pap. 6.50 (ISBN 0-915315-00-9). Sons Prophets Pr.
Bagley, Robert W. Shang Ritual Bronzes in the Arthur M. Sackler Collections. (Ancient Chinese Bronzes in the Arthur M. Sackler Collections Ser.: Vol. 1). (Illus.). 350p. 1982. text ed. 95.00x (ISBN 0-674-80525-9). Harvard U Pr.
Bagley, Val C. Mission Mania: A Cartoonist's View of the Best Two Years of Life. (Illus.). 98p. (Orig.). 1980. pap. 3.95 (ISBN 0-88290-140-0). Horizon Utah.
Bagley, Val. C. Newlywed Nonsense-a Cartoonist's View of the First Year of Marriage. (Illus.). 96p. (Orig.). 1980. pap. 3.95 (ISBN 0-88290-145-1, 2039). Horizon Utah.
Bagley, Val C. Puppy Love. (Illus.). 96p. 1981. pap. 3.95 (ISBN 0-88290-158-3, 2043). Horizon Utah.
--Special Delivery: A Cartoonist's View of Expected Parenthood. (Illus.). 96p. (Orig.). 1980. pap. 3.95 (ISBN 0-88290-154-0, 2041). Horizon Utah.
--Very Anxiously Engaged. (Illus.). 96p. (Orig.). 1981. pap. 3.95 (ISBN 0-88290-157-5, 2042). Horizon Utah.
Bagley, Vicky & Cohen, Rona. Dining In Washington, D. C. (Dining in Ser.). 252p. (Orig.). 1982. pap. 8.95 (ISBN 0-89716-038-X). Peanut Butter.
Bagley, Victor. La Fontaine's Fables in Modern Clothes. (Illus.). 96p. (gr. 3-5). 1985. 7.95 (ISBN 0-89962-449-9). Todd & Honeywell.
Bagley, W. C., jt. auth. see Keith, J. A.
Bagley, William C. Classroom Management: Its Principles & Technique. 1979. Repr. of 1921 ed. lib. bdg. 20.00 (ISBN 0-8495-0538-0). Arden Lib.
--Determinism in Education. LC 70-89146. (American Education: Its Men, Institutions & Ideas, Ser. 1). 1969. Repr. of 1925 ed. 16.00 (ISBN 0-405-01383-3). Ayer Co Pubs.
--The Educative Process. 1979. Repr. of 1922 ed. lib. bdg. 20.00 (ISBN 0-8495-0537-2). Arden Lib.
--The Educative Process. 1917. lib. bdg. 20.00 (ISBN 0-8482-9992-2). Norwood Edns.
Baglin, J. E., et al, eds. Thin Films & Interfaces II: Materials Research Society Symposia Proceedings, Nov., 1983, Boston, MA, Vol. 25. 690p. 1984. 85.00 (ISBN 0-444-00905-1, North-Holland). Elsevier.
Baglin, John E., ed. see Symposium on Thin Film Phenomena-Interfaces & Interactions (1977: Atlanta).
Baglini, Norman A. Global Risk Management: How U. S. International Corporations Manage Foreign Risks. (Illus.). 144p. 1983. pap. 15.00 (ISBN 0-937802-04-2). Risk Mgmt Soc.
--Global Risk Management: How US International Corporations Manage Foreign Risks. Epstein, Rita, ed. (Illus.). 144p. 1983. pap. 15.00 (ISBN 0-937802-04-2). Risk Management.
--Risk Management in International Corporations. 217p. (LC A710912). 1976. 7.95 (ISBN 0-937802-14-X). Risk Management.
Baglivo, Jenny A. & Graver, Jack E., eds. Incidence & Symmetry in Design & Architecture. LC 81-18160. (Cambridge Urban & Architectural Studies: No. 7). 400p. 1983. 57.50 (ISBN 0-521-23043-8); pap. 16.95 (ISBN 0-521-29784-2). Cambridge U Pr.
Bagma, B. T., jt. auth. see Bljach, I. S.
Bagnall, Jim, jt. auth. see Koberg, Don.
Bagnall, Oscar. Origin & Properties of the Human Aura. LC 74-84848. 1975. pap. 3.50 (ISBN 0-87728-284-6). Weiser.
Bagnall, Roger & Derow, Peter. Greek Historical Documents: The Hellenistic Period. LC 81-5604. (SBL Sources for Biblical Study Ser.). 1981. pap. text ed. 13.50 (ISBN 0-89130-496-7, 060316). Scholars Pr GA.
Bagnall, Roger & Lewis, Naphtali. Columbia Papyri Seven: Fourth Century Documents from Karanis. LC 78-31952. 1980. 45.00 (ISBN 0-89130-277-8, 31 00 20). Scholars Pr GA.
Bagnall, Roger, ed. Research Tools for the Classics. LC 80-25766. (APA Pamphlets). 1980. pap. 7.50 (ISBN 0-89130-452-5, 40-06-06). Scholars Pr GA.
Bagnall, Roger S. & Samuel, Alan E. Ostraka in the Royal Ontario Museum II. (American Society of Papyrology Ser.). 24.00 (ISBN 0-89130-787-7, 31-00-15). Scholars Pr GA.
Bagnall, Roger S. & Worp, K. A. Regnal Formulas in Byzantine Egypt. LC 79-1316. (Supplements to the Bulletin of American Society of Papyrologists). 1979. pap. 10.00 (ISBN 0-89130-280-8, 311102). Scholars Pr GA.
Bagnall, Roger S., et al. Proceedings of the Sixteenth International Congress of Papyrology. LC 81-9025. (American Studies in Papyrology). 1981. text ed. 67.50 (ISBN 0-89130-516-5, 31-00-23). Scholars Pr GA.
Bagnall, William R. Textile Industries of the United States: Vol. 1, 1639-1810. LC 68-22370. Repr. of 1893 ed. 45.00x (ISBN 0-678-00735-7). Kelley.
Bagnara, Joseph T., jt. auth. see Turner, C. Donnell.
Bagnasco, Erminio. Submarines of World War Two. LC 77-81973. Orig. Title: I Sommergibili. 256p. 1978. 29.95 (ISBN 0-87021-962-6). Naval Inst Pr.
--Submarines of World War Two. (Illus.). 256p. 1978. 29.95 (ISBN 0-87021-962-6); bulk rates avail. Naval Inst Pr.
Bagnasco, John J. Plants for the Home, Vol. 1. 1975. 15.00 (ISBN 0-918134-01-3). Nature Life.

Bagnato, Stephen J. & Neisworth, John T. Linking Developmental Assessment & Curricula: Prescription for Early Intervention. LC 81-3468. 345p. 1981. text ed. 31.50 (ISBN 0-89443-367-9). Aspen Systems.

Bagne, Conrad, jt. auth. see Bangs, Frank S., Jr.

Bagnold, Enid. Letters to Frank Harris & Other Friends. 116p. 1980. 100.00x (ISBN 0-904845-32-X, Pub. by Whittington England). State Mutual Bk.

--Loved & Envied. LC 75-110820. Repr. of 1951 ed. lib. bdg. 19.75x (ISBN 0-8371-2700-9, BALE). Greenwood.

--National Velvet. (gr. 7-9). 1971. pap. 2.50 (ISBN 0-671-46528-7). Archway.

--National Velvet. 293p. 1981. Repr. PLB 16.95x (ISBN 0-89966-359-1). Buccaneer Bks.

--National Velvet. 339p. 1981. Repr. PLB 12.95x (ISBN 0-89967-033-4). Harmony Raine.

--National Velvet. (Illus.). (gr. 7 up). 1949. Repr. of 1935 ed. 12.50 (ISBN 0-688-21422-3); PLB 12.88 (ISBN 0-688-31422-8). Morrow.

--National Velvet. LC 85-2982. (Illus.). 304p. (gr. 3 up). 1985. 12.50 (ISBN 0-688-05788-8, Morrow Junior Books). Morrow.

Bagnold, R. A. Physics of Blown Sand & Desert Dunes. 1941. 43.00 (ISBN 0-412-10270-6, NO. 6020, Pub. by Chapman & Hall). Methuen Inc.

Bagnole, John W. TEFL, Perceptions, & the Arab World. 50p. 2.00 (ISBN 0-318-18141-X). Tchrs Eng Spkrs.

Bagnuolo, Pete. Figure Drawing Through Angular Construction. 1982. perfect bdg. 9.95 (ISBN 0-88252-120-9). Paladin Hse.

Bagot, J., ed. see Canning, George.

Bagot, Richard. The Italian Lakes. 1977. lib. bdg. 59.95 (ISBN 0-8490-2086-7). Gordon Pr.

Bagotskii, V. S. & Vasil'ev, Yu B., eds. Fuel Cells: Their Electrochemical Kinetics. LC 64-66348. 121p. 1966. 30.00x (ISBN 0-306-10741-4, Consultants). Plenum Pub.

Bagotzky, V. S. & Sjundin, A. M. Chemical Power Sources. LC 80-40832. 1981. 67.50 (ISBN 0-12-072650-5). Acad Pr.

Bagozzi, Richard P. Casual Models in Marketing. LC 79-11622. (Theories in Marketing Ser.). 303p. 1980. text ed. 39.45 (ISBN 0-471-01516-4). Wiley.

Bagozzi, Richard P., ed. Advances in Communication & Marketing Research, Vol. 1. 1984. 40.00 (ISBN 0-89232-248-9). Jai Pr.

Bagozzi, Richard P. & Tybout, Alice M., eds. Advances in Consumer Research: Proceedings of the 1982 Conference, Vol. X. 712p. pap. 29.00 (ISBN 0-915552-10-8). Assn Consumer Res.

Bagozzi, Richard P., et al, eds. see Annual Educators Conference Chicago, Illinois, August, 1980.

Bagratashvili, V. N., et al. Multiple Photon Infrared Laser Photophysics & Photochemistry. 530p. 1985. text ed. 65.00 (ISBN 3-7186-0269-5). Harwood Academic.

Bagrial, Ashok K. Company Law. 494p. 1984. pap. text ed. 19.95x (ISBN 0-7069-2647-1, Pub. by Vikas India). Advent NY.

Bagrow, Leo & Skeleton, R. A. History of Cartography. 312p. 1985. Repr. of 1964 ed. 49.95 (ISBN 0-913750-33-6). Precedent Pub.

Bagrow, Leo & Skelton, R. A. History of Cartography. rev. enlarged ed. 1975. 49.95 (ISBN 0-913750-33-6). Transaction Bks.

Bagshaw, C. R. Muscle Contraction. 80p. 1982. pap. 7.50 (ISBN 0-412-13450-0, NO. 6432, Pub. by Chapman & Hall). Methuen Inc.

Bagshaw, Malcolm A. Cancer of the Prostate. (OncoLOGIC: 18). (Illus.). 260p. 1984. Vol. 18. pap. 100.00 (ISBN 0-08-027471-4). Pergamon.

Bagshaw, Norman E. Batteries on Ships. LC 82-10954. (Battery Applications Bk.Ser.). 203p. 1983. 59.95x (ISBN 0-471-90021-4, Res Stud Pr). Wiley.

Bagshaw, W. Worked Examples in Relative Radar Plotting. 1981. 60.00x (ISBN 0-85174-118-5, Pub. by Nautical England). State Mutual Bk.

--Worked Examples in Relative Radar Plotting. 1981. 45.00x (ISBN 0-85174-330-7, Pub. by Brown, Son & Ferguson). State Mutual Bk.

--Worked Examples in Relative Radar Plotting. 91p. 1979. 15.00x (ISBN 0-85174-330-7). Sheridan.

Bagshawe, L. E., tr. The Maniyadanabon of Shin Sandalinka. 152p. 1981. 7.00 (ISBN 0-87727-115-1, DP 115). Cornell SE Asia.

Bagshawe, Richard W. Roman Roads. (Shire Archaeology Ser.: No. 10). (Illus.). 1985. pap. 6.95 (ISBN 0-85263-458-7, Pub. by Shire Pubns England). Seven Hills Bks.

Bagster, Samuel. Bagster's Bible Handbook. Elwell, Walter, intro. by. 264p. 1983. Repr. 9.95 (ISBN 0-8007-1334-6). Revell.

--Bagster's Keyword Concordance. 96p. 1983. Repr. 5.95 (ISBN 0-8007-1335-4). Revell.

--Daily Light. 1985. Repr. of 1975 ed. 5.99 (ISBN 0-916441-09-1). Barbour & Co.

Baguelin, F., et al. The Pressuremeter & Foundation Engineering. (Rock & Soil Mechanics Ser.). (Illus.). 1978. 58.00x (ISBN 0-87849-019-1). Trans Tech.

Baguley, David. Bibliographie de la Critique Sur Emile Zola, 1971-1980. 242p. (Fr.). 1982. 37.50x (ISBN 0-8020-2456-4). U of Toronto Pr.

--Bibliographie de la Critique Sur Emile Zola, 1864-1970. LC 76-23320. 1976. 55.00x (ISBN 0-8020-5369-6). U of Toronto Pr.

--Fecondite D'Emile Zola: Roman a These, Evangile, Mythe. LC 70-185700. (Romance Ser.). (Illus.). 264p. 1973. 30.00x (ISBN 0-8020-5270-3). U of Toronto Pr.

Bagus, Paul, jt. ed. see Kay, Eric.

Bagwell, Beth. Oakland: The Story of a City. (Illus.). 304p. 1982. 16.95 (ISBN 0-89141-146-1). Presidio Pr.

Bagwell, Marilyn & Clements, Sallee. A Political Handbook for Health Professionals. 1985. pap. text ed. 15.95 (ISBN 0-316-07522-1). Little.

Bagwell, P. S. Industrial Relations in Nineteenth Century Britain. 106p. 1974. 20.00x (ISBN 0-7165-2215-2, BBA 02040, Pub. by Irish Academic Pr Ireland). Biblio Dist.

Bagwell, Philip. End of the Line? 224p. 1984. 22.50 (ISBN 0-8052-7221-6, Pub. by Verso, England); pap. 5.95 (ISBN 0-8052-7220-8). Schocken.

--Railway Clearing House in the British Economy 1842-1922. LC 71-355685. (Illus.). 1968. 27.50x (ISBN 0-678-06013-4). Kelley.

Bagwell, Philip S. The Railwaymen: The History of the National Union of Railwaymen. (Beeching Era & After Ser.: Vol. 2). (Illus.). 456p. 1982. text ed. 60.00x (ISBN 0-04-331084-2). Allen Unwin.

--The Transport Revolution, from Seventeen Seventy. 1974. 17.50 (ISBN 0-7134-1386-7, Pub. by Batsford England). David & Charles.

Bagwell, W. Ray. Property & Liability Insurance Management Model. 1972. 15.95 (ISBN 0-88406-118-3). Ga St U Busn Pub.

Baha, Abdu'L. Selections from the Letters of Abdu'l-Baha. 309p. (Persian.). 1980. 13.95 (ISBN 0-87743-157-4, 406-046); pap. 7.95 (ISBN 0-87743-158-2, 406-047). Baha'i.

Bahadur, Birendra. Liquid Crystal Displays. (Molecular Crystals & Liquid Crystals Ser.). 104p. 1984. pap. 39.00 (ISBN 0-677-06675-9). Gordon.

Bahadur, K. P. Folk Tales of Uttar Pradesh. (No. 10). 1972. 3.75x (ISBN 0-89684-390-4). Intl Pubns Serv.

--One Hundred Rural Songs of India. 1978. 15.95 (ISBN 0-89684-004-2, Pub. by Motilal Banarsidass India). Orient Bk Dist.

--The Wisdom of Nyaaya. LC 78-670087. (The Wisdom of India Ser.: Vol. 3). 246p. 1978. 9.25x (ISBN 0-89684-468-4). Orient Bk Dist.

--The Wisdom of Saankhya. LC 78-901698. (The Wisdom of India Ser.: Vol. 2). 222p. 1977. 9.25x (ISBN 0-89684-469-2). Orient Bk Dist.

--The Wisdom of Vaisheshika. (The Wisdom of India Ser.: Vol. 4). 207p. 1979. 10.50x (ISBN 0-89684-470-6). Orient Bk Dist.

--The Wisdom of Vedanta. (Wisdom of India Ser.: No. 6). 412p. 1985. text ed. 40.00x (ISBN 0-86590-725-0, Pub. by Sterling Pubs India). APT Bks.

--The Wisdom of Yoga. LC 77-985594. (The Wisdom of India Ser.: Vol. 1). 116p. 1977. 9.25x (ISBN 0-89684-471-4). Orient Bk Dist.

Bahadur, K. P., tr. Rasikapriya of Keshavadasa. 1972. 12.50 (ISBN 0-89684-303-3). Orient Bk Dist.

Bahadur, Lal. Indian Freedom Movement & Thought, 1919-1929. Johari, J. C., ed. 1983. text ed. 40.00x (ISBN 0-86590-158-9, Pub. by Sterling India). Apt Bks.

Bahadur, R. R. Some Limit Theorems in Statistics. (CBMS-NSF Regional Conference Ser.: No. 4). v, 42p. 1971. pap. text ed. 8.00 (ISBN 0-89871-175-4). Soc Indus-Appl Math.

Bahadur KC, Kaisher. Assessment of the Judicial Customs of Nepal. 303p. 1957. 10.00 (ISBN 0-318-12867-5, 22). Am-Nepal Ed.

Bahadur Singh, I., ed. Indians in Southeast Asia. 232p. 1982. 24.95 (ISBN 0-940500-53-1, Pub. by Sterling India). Asia Bk Corp.

Bahal, Indra, jt. auth. see Kaul, Mohini.

Ba Han, Maung. William Blake: His Mysticism. 1978. Repr. of 1924 ed. lib. bdg. 35.00 (ISBN 0-8495-0377-9). Arden Lib.

--William Blake: His Mysticism. LC 72-13650. 1974. Repr. of 1924 ed. lib. bdg. 30.00 (ISBN 0-8414-1234-0). Folcroft.

Bahar, Mehrdad. Bastoor. LC 70-128811. (Illus.). (gr. k-5). 1972. PLB 4.95g (ISBN 0-87614-015-0). Carolrhoda Bks.

--Bastoor. new & rev. ed. Jabbari, Ahmad, ed. Alyeshmreni, Mansoor, tr. from Persian. LC 83-60451. (Illus.). 32p. (Orig.). (gr. 1 up). 1983. pap. 4.95 (ISBN 0-939214-17-2). Mazda Pubs.

Baharav, Gene, tr. see Noy, Dov.

Baharav, I. D. Winds of April. LC 65-17184. 1965. 3.95 (ISBN 0-911184-04-X). Primary.

Bahat, Dan. Historical Atlas of Jerusalem. 1978. 12.50x (ISBN 0-930038-05-3). Arbit.

Bahat, S., tr. see Weinreich, Uriel.

Baha'u'llah. Epistle to the Son of the Wolf. rev. ed. Effendi, Shoghi, tr. LC 53-18798. 1976. 13.95 (ISBN 0-87743-048-9, 103-001). Baha'i.

--Gleanings from the Writings of Baha'u'llah. 2nd rev. ed. Shoghi Effendi, tr. from Persian. LC 76-45364. 346p. 1976. 17.95 (ISBN 0-87743-111-6, 103-003); pap. 12.95 (ISBN 0-87743-112-4, 103-004). Baha'i.

--Gleanings from the Writings of Baha'u'llah. Effendi, Shoghi, tr. from Persian. 346p. 1983. pap. 6.50 pocket size (ISBN 0-87743-187-6). Baha'i.

--The Hidden Words of Baha'u'llah. rev. ed. Effendi, Shoghi, tr. LC 54-7328. 1954. 6.95 (ISBN 0-87743-007-1, 103-005); pap. 3.95 (ISBN 0-87743-002-0, 103-006). Baha'i.

--The Kitab-i-Iqan: The Book of Certitude. 2nd ed. Effendi, Shoghi, tr. from Persian. LC 51-22838. 257p. 1950. 17.95 (ISBN 0-87743-022-5). pap. 6.50 pocket sized (ISBN 0-87743-189-2). Baha'i.

--Prayers & Meditations. Effendi, Shoghi, tr. LC 53-10767. 1938. 17.95 (ISBN 0-87743-024-1, 103-010). Baha'i.

--The Proclamation of Baha'u'llah. LC 72-237435. 1967. 9.95 (ISBN 0-87743-064-0, 103-012); pap. 4.95 (ISBN 0-87743-065-9, 103-013). Baha'i.

--Selected Writings of Baha'u'llah. LC 79-15136. 1979. 11.95 (ISBN 0-87743-133-7, 303-024); pap. 1.50 (ISBN 0-87743-077-2, 303-023). Baha'i.

--The Seven Valleys & the Four Valleys. 3rd rev. ed. Gail, Marzieh, tr. LC 77-23326. 1978. 8.00 (ISBN 0-87743-113-2, 103-015); pap. 3.95 (ISBN 0-87743-114-0, 103-016). Baha'i.

--Tablets of Baha'u'llah Revealed after the Kitab-i-Aqdas. Effendi, Shoghi & Taherzadeh, Habib, trs. LC 79-670079. 1978. 13.95 (ISBN 0-85398-077-2, 103-021, Pub. by Universal Hse. of Justice). Baha'i.

--Tablets of Baha'u'llah Revealed after the Kitab-i-Aqdas. 175p. (Persian.). 1980. 19.95x (ISBN 3-87037-903-0, P-18, Pub. by Baha'i Verlag). Kalimat.

Baha'u'llah & Abdu'l-Baha. Baha'i Prayers & Tablets for the Young. LC 77-2228. (Illus.). 1978. 5.95 (ISBN 0-87743-115-9, 315-054). Baha'i.

--Waging Peace: Selections from the Baha'i Writings on Universal Peace. 1985. pap. 7.95 (ISBN 0-933770-34-0). Kalimat.

Baha'u'llah, et al. The Pattern of Baha'i Life. 3rd ed. 1963. pap. 1.45 (ISBN 0-900125-15-2, 315-030-10). Baha'i.

Baha'u'llah, Bab & Abdu'l-Baha. Baha'i Prayers: A Selection of Prayers Revealed by Baha'u'llah, the Bab & Abdu'l-Baha. LC 82-11502. 1982. 8.95 (ISBN 0-87743-175-2, 115-070); pap. 5.00 (ISBN 0-87743-176-0, 115-071). Baha'i.

--The Glad Tidings of Baha'u'llah: Being Extracts from the Sacred Writings of the Baha'is. rev. ed. 122p. 1975. 6.95 (ISBN 0-85398-046-2, 315-051). G Ronald Pub.

Baha'u'llah, the Bab & Abdu'l-Baha. Communion with God. large-type ed. 1976. pap. 1.95 (ISBN 0-87743-110-8, 315-011). Baha'i.

--Baha'i Prayers. LC 54-10901. 6.95 (ISBN 0-87743-012-8, 315-005). Baha'i.

Bahbah, Bishara A. & Bulter, Linda. Military Dimension in Israeli-Latin American Relations. Neznek, Mary, ed. 200p. 1985. 9.95 (ISBN 0-88728-144-3). Inst Palestine.

Baher, H. Synthesis of Electrical Networks. 285p. 1984. 41.95x (ISBN 0-471-90399-X, Pub. by Wiley-Interscience). Wiley.

Baheri, Antti, et al, eds. Fibroblast Surface Protein. (Annals of the New York Academy of Sciences: Vol. 312). 456p. 1978. pap. 54.00x (ISBN 0-89072-068-1). NY Acad Sci.

Bahic, Sluna. Serbo-Croation Reading Passages. 210p. 1975. pap. 7.50x (ISBN 0-89918-732-3, Y-732). Vanous.

Bahill, A. Terry. Bioengineering: Biomedical, Medical, & Clinical Engineering. (Illus.). 336p. 1981. text ed. 41.95 (ISBN 0-13-076380-2). P-H.

Bahl, I. J. & Bhartia, P. Microstrip Antennas. (Illus.). 355p. 1980. 64.00 (ISBN 0-89006-098-3). Artech Hse.

Bahl, I. J., jt. auth. see Bhartia, P.

Bahl, Ida. Nurse among the Navajos. 215p. 1984. pap. 7.95 (ISBN 0-941152-10-3). Bearstone Shepherd Pub.

Bahl, J. K. England, My England: My Bread & Butter. 1985. 9.95 (ISBN 0-533-06585-2). Vantage.

Bahl, Kali C. Studies in the Semantic Structure of Hindi, Two. 1979. 17.50x (ISBN 0-8364-0513-7). South Asia Bks.

Bahl, Roy. Financing State & Local Government in the 1980's. (Illus.). 1984. text ed. 24.95x (ISBN 0-19-503305-1); pap. text ed. 11.95x (ISBN 0-19-503306-X). Oxford U Pr.

--Urban Government Finance: Emerging Trends. LC 80-39559. (Urban Affairs Annual Reviews, Vol. 20). 287p. 1981. 28.00 (ISBN 0-8039-1564-0); pap. 14.00 (ISBN 0-8039-1565-9). Sage.

Bahl, Roy, ed. The Fiscal Outlook for Cities: Implications of a National Urban Policy. 1978. 8.95x (ISBN 0-8156-2200-7); pap. 3.50x (ISBN 0-8156-0148-4). Syracuse U Pr.

Bahl, Roy, et al. Urban Growth & Local Taxes in Less Developed Countries. LC 83-16427. (Papers of the East-West Population Institute: No. 89). vi, 33p. (Orig.). 1983. pap. text ed. 1.25 (ISBN 0-86638-050-7). E W Center HI.

--Public Finance During the Korean Modernization Process. (Harvard East Asian Monographs: No. 107). 1985. text ed. 15.00x (ISBN 0-674-72233-7, Pub. by Coun East Asian Stud). Harvard U Pr.

Bahl, Roy W. Metropolitan City Expenditures: A Comparative Analysis. LC 68-12965. (Illus.). 152p. 1969. 14.00x (ISBN 0-8131-1173-0). U Pr of Ky.

--The Taxation of Urban Property in Less Developed Countries. LC 78-65018. (Illus.). 298p. 1979. 29.50x (ISBN 0-299-07860-4). U of Wis Pr.

Bahl, Roy W. & Burkhead, Jesse, eds. Public Employment & State & Local Government Finance. LC 79-23946. 360p. 1980. prof. ref. 32.50 (ISBN 0-88410-683-7). Ballinger Pub.

Bahlke, George W. The Later Auden: From New Year Letter to About the House. LC 74-98179. 208p. 1970. 17.50x (ISBN 0-8135-0663-8). Lib Soc Sci.

Bahlmann, J. & Brod, J., eds. Disturbances of Water & Electrolyte Metabolism. (Contributions to Nephrology: Vol. 21). (Illus.). 1980. soft cover 32.00 (ISBN 3-8055-0215-X). S Karger.

Bahlmann, J. & Liebau, H., eds. Stress & Hypertension. (Contributions to Nephrology: Vol. 30). (Illus.). xiv, 206p. 1982. pap. 38.50 (ISBN 3-8055-3450-7). S Karger.

Bahlsen, Leopold. The Teaching of Modern Languages. Evans, M. Blakemore, tr. from Ger. 97p. 1980. Repr. lib. bdg. 12.50 (ISBN 0-8495-0602-6). Arden Lib.

Bahm, Archie J. Axiology: The Science of Values. LC 80-66405. 168p. 1980. 15.00 (ISBN 0-911714-11-1). Bahm.

--Axiology: The Science of Values. abbreviated ed. LC 84-51726. 84p. 1984. pap. 3.00 (ISBN 0-911714-14-6, World Bks). Bahm.

--Comparative Philosophy: Western, Indian & Chinese Philosophies Compared. LC 76-10406. 112p. 1978. pap. 6.00 (ISBN 0-911714-10-3, World Bks). Bahm.

--Ethics: The Science of Oughtness. LC 80-66406. 260p. 1980. pap. 15.00 (ISBN 0-911714-12-X). Bahm.

--Ethics: The Science of Oughtness. abbreviated ed. LC 84-52234. 184p. 1984. 5.00 (ISBN 0-911714-15-4, World Bks.). Bahm.

--The Heart of Confucius. LC 76-83638. (Arcturus Books Paperbacks). (Illus.). 159p. 1977. pap. 5.95x (ISBN 0-8093-0828-2). S Ill U Pr.

--The Philosopher's World Model. LC 78-67569. (Contributions in Philosophy: No. 12). (Illus.). 1979. lib. bdg. 29.95x (ISBN 0-313-21198-1, BPW/). Greenwood.

--The Philosophy of the Buddha. 175p. 1982. text ed. 15.95x (ISBN 0-7069-2017-1, Pub. by Vikas India). Advent NY.

--Polarity, Dialectic, & Organicity. LC 77-81834. 293p. 1977. pap. 10.00 (ISBN 0-911714-09-X, World Bks). Bahm.

--The Specialist: His Philosophy, His Disease, His Cure. LC 76-16883. 126p. 1977. 7.50 (ISBN 0-911714-08-1, World Bks). Bahm.

--What Is Philosophy? 28p. 1984. pap. 1.00 (ISBN 0-911714-13-8, World Bks). Bahm.

--World's Living Religions. (Arcturus Books Paperbacks). 384p. 1971. pap. 10.95x (ISBN 0-8093-0529-1). S Ill U Pr.

Bahm, Archie J., ed. Directory of American Philosophers 2, 1964-65. LC 62-4947. 1964. 12.25x (ISBN 0-911714-02-2). Bahm.

--Directory of American Philosophers 4, 1968-69. LC 62-4947. 1968. 13.95x (ISBN 0-911714-04-9). Bahm.

--Directory of American Philosophers 5, 1970-71. LC 62-4947. 1970. 14.95x (ISBN 0-911714-05-7). Bahm.

--Interdependence. LC 76-4181. 1977. pap. 9.95 (ISBN 0-911714-06-5, World Bks). Bahm.

Bahm, Linda, et al. Fiestas of San Juan Nuevo: Ceremonial Art from Michoacan, Mexico. LC 83-42809. (Illus.). 70p. 1983. pap. 12.50 (ISBN 0-912535-00-8). Max Mus.

Bahm, Raymond E., ed. see Aronson, E. A., et al.

Bahmanyar, M. & Cavanaugh, D. C. Plague Manual. (Illus., Also avail. in French). 1976. 8.00 (ISBN 92-4-154051-6). World Health.

Bahme, Charles W. Fire Officers Guide to Dangerous Chemicals. (Get Ahead Ser.). 250p. 1972. 8.50 (ISBN 0-685-46048-7, FSP#36). Natl Fire Prot.

--Fire Officer's Guide to Dangerous Chemicals. Lyons, Paul R., ed. LC 77-76481. (Illus.). 1978. 10.50 (ISBN 0-87765-101-9, FSP-36A). Natl Fire Prot.

--Fire Officer's Guide to Disaster Control. Lyons, Paul R., ed. LC 77-76486. (Fire Officer's Guide Ser.). 1978. text ed. 16.50 (ISBN 0-87765-099-3, FSP-48A). Natl Fire Prot.

--Fire Officer's Guide to Emergency Action. 3rd ed. LC 73-89341. (Get Ahead Ser.). (Illus.). 1976. pap. 7.50 (ISBN 0-685-75458-8, FSP-38). Natl Fire Prot.

--Fire Officer's Guide to Extinguishing Systems. (Get Ahead Ser.). 104p. 1970. 5.00 (ISBN 0-685-46047-9, FSP-30). Natl Fire Prot.

--Fire Officer's Guide to Extinguishing Systems. Lyons, Paul R., ed. LC 76-53155. (Fire Officer's Guide Ser.). 1977. text ed. 7.50 (ISBN 0-87765-091-8, FSP-30A). Natl Fire Prot.

--Fire Service & the Law. McKinnon, Gordon P., ed. LC 76-26786. 1976. 15.50 (ISBN 0-87765-081-0, FSP-3A). Natl Fire Prot.

--Fireman's Law Book. 4th ed. 256p. 1967. 5.50 (ISBN 0-685-46051-7, FSP-3). Natl Fire Prot.

Bahmueller, Charles F. The National Charity Company: Jeremy Bentham's Silent Revolution. LC 80-20632. 272p. 1981. 30.00x (ISBN 0-520-03796-0). U of Cal Pr.

Bahn, Anita K. Basic Medical Statistics. LC 72-6822. (Illus.). 320p. 1972. text ed. 29.00 (ISBN 0-8089-0782-4, 790335). Grune.

Bahn, Anita K., jt. auth. see Mausner, Judith S.

Bahn, Gilbert S. Kinetics, Equilibria, & Performance of High Temperature Systems. 406p. 1963. 106.50 (ISBN 0-677-10030-2). Gordon.

Bahn, Gilbert S., ed. High Temperature Systems: Third Conference, 2 vols. Incl. Vol. 1. 280p. 1968. 80.95 (ISBN 0-677-10600-9); Vol. 2. 360p. 1969. 97.95 (ISBN 0-677-12960-2). Gordon.

--Reaction Rate Compilation for the H-O-N System. LC 68-20396. 254p. 1968. Repr. of 1967 ed. 74.25 (ISBN 0-677-12750-2). Gordon.

Bahn, P. Pyrenean Prehistory: A Paleoeconomic Survey of the French Sites. 511p. 1984. 59.50x (Pub. by Aris & Phillips England). Humanities.

Bahna, Sami L. & Heiner, Douglas C. Allergies to Milk. 224p. 1980. 35.00 (ISBN 0-8089-1256-9, 790340). Grune.

Bahne, Siegfried. Archives de Jules Humbert-Droz: Nineteen Twenty-Three to Nineteen Twenty-Seven, Vol. II. 1983. 120.00 (ISBN 90-277-1241-7, Pub. by Reidel Holland). Kluwer Academic.

Bahne, Siegfried, ed. see Humbert-Droz, J.

Bahnick, Karen R. The Determination of Stages in the Historical Development of the Germanic Languages by Morphological Criteria: An Evaluation. (Janua Linguarum Ser. Practica: No. 139). 1973. pap. text ed. 26.00x (ISBN 90-2792-389-2). Mouton.

Bahniuk, Margaret H., jt. auth. see Mansfield, Carmella E.

Bahniuk, Margaret H., jt. auth. see Rosen, Arnold.

Bahnsen, Greg L. By This Standard. 432p. 1985. pap. 4.95 (ISBN 0-930464-06-0). Inst Christian.

--Theonomy in Christian Ethics. exp. ed. 1984. 17.95 (ISBN 0-87552-117-7). Presby & Reformed.

Bahntge, M. A., jt. auth. see Baumann, M. A.

Bahntge, Mary A., jt. auth. see Baumann, Mary A.

Bahoken, J. C. & Atangana, Engelbert. Cultural Policies in the United Republic of Cameroon. (Studies & Documents on Cultural Policies). (Illus.). 91p. 1976. pap. 5.00 (ISBN 92-3-101316-5, U143, UNESCO). Unipub.

Bahr, A. J. & McGonnagle, Warren J. Microwave Nondestructive Testing Methods. (Nondestructive Monographs: Vol. 1). 102p. 1983. 24.50. Gordon.

Bahr, Alice H. Automated Library Circulation Systems, 1979-80. 2nd ed. LC 79-16189. (Professional Librarian Ser.). (Illus.). 105p. 1979. softcover 24.50x (ISBN 0-914236-34-2, 201-BW). Knowledge Indus.

--Microforms: The Librarians' View, 1978-79. 2nd ed. LC 78-10645. (Professional Librarian Ser.). 118p. 1978. pap. 24.50 professional (ISBN 0-914236-25-3, 222-BW). Knowledge Indus.

--Video in Libraries: A Status Report, 1979-80. 2nd ed. LC 79-25951. (Professional Librarian Ser.). (Illus.). 119p. 1980. softcover professional 24.50 (ISBN 0-914236-49-0, 229-BW). Knowledge Indus.

Bahr, Amy, ed. see Durrell, Julie.

Bahr, Amy, ed. see Tannenbaum, D. Leb.

Bahr, Don. Piman & Papago Ritual Oratory. 1975. pap. 4.50 (ISBN 0-685-64956-3). Indian Hist Pr.

Bahr, Donald M., et al. Piman Shamanism & Staying Sickness: Ka: cim Mumkidag. LC 72-92103. 332p. 1974. pap. 9.95 (ISBN 0-8165-0303-6). U of Ariz Pr.

Bahr, Ehrhard & Kunzer, Ruth G. Georg Lukacs. LC 70-190350. (Literature and Life Ser.). 1972. 12.95 (ISBN 0-8044-2014-9). Ungar.

Bahr, Ehrhard, et al, eds. Lessing Yearbook Supplement: Humanitat und Dialog. LC 81-16027. 380p. 1982. 25.00 (ISBN 0-686-86868-4). Wayne St U Pr.

Bahr, Gisela, ed. see International Brecht Society.

Bahr, Gunter F., jt. auth. see Wied, George.

Bahr, Howard M., jt. auth. see Harvey, Carol D.

Bahr, Howard M., et al. American Ethnicity. 1979. text ed. 19.95x (ISBN 0-669-05358-9). Heath.

--Life in Large Families: Views of Mormon Women. LC 82-45005. 264p. (Orig.). 1982. lib. bdg. 26.25 (ISBN 0-8191-2551-2); pap. text ed. 13.00 (ISBN 0-8191-2552-0). U Pr of Amer.

Bahr, Jerome. Five Novellas. LC 76-53357. 220p. 1977. 13.95 (ISBN 0-685-59469-6). Trempealeau.

--The Lonely Scoundrel: A Supplement to the Perishing Republic. LC 73-80240. 89p. 1974. 12.95 (ISBN 0-686-63592-2). Trempealeau.

--The Perishing Republic. LC 79-129182. 148p. 1971. 10.95 (ISBN 0-686-63593-0). Trempealeau.

Bahr, Robert. Blizzard at the Zoo. LC 80-22285. (Illus.). 32p. (ps-3). 1982. 11.75 (ISBN 0-688-00423-7); PLB 11.88 (ISBN 0-688-00424-5). Lothrop.

--Good Hands: Massage Techniques for Total Health. (Illus.). 288p. 1985. pap. 8.95 (ISBN 0-452-25608-9, Plume). NAL.

--The Great Blizzard. LC 78-64428. (Illus.). (gr. 1-4). 1979. 3.50 (ISBN 0-89799-107-9); pap. 1.50 (ISBN 0-89799-042-0). Dandelion Pr.

Bahr, Stephen J., ed. Economics & the Family. LC 79-47985. 208p. 1980. 25.50x (ISBN 0-669-03623-4). Lexington Bks.

Bahrain Society of Engineers. Engineering & Development in the Gulf. 228p. 1977. 27.00x (ISBN 0-86010-047-2, Pub. by Graham & Trotman England). State Mutual Bk.

Bahrang, Samuel. Little Black Fish. LC 74-128812. (Illus.). (gr. k-4). 1971. PLB 3.95g (ISBN 0-87614-013-4). Carolrhoda Bks.

Bahrdt, C. F. Handbuch der Moral Fur Den Burgerstand. Repr. of 1789 ed. 50.00 (ISBN 0-384-03070-X). Johnson Repr.

Bahre, Conrad J. Destruction of the Natural Vegetation of North-Central Chile. LC 78-50836. (Publications in Geography Ser.: Vol. 23). 1979. 17.50x (ISBN 0-520-09594-4). U of Cal Pr.

Bahree, Pat. Hinduism. (World Religions Ser.). (Illus.). 72p. (gr. 7-12). 1984. 14.95 (ISBN 0-7134-3654-9, Pub. by Batsford England). David & Charles.

Bahree, Patricia. The Hindu World. LC 83-50691. (Religions of the World Ser.). 48p. 1983. lib. bdg. 13.72 (ISBN 0-382-06718-5); 9.25 (ISBN 0-382-06931-5). Silver.

Bahrenberg, Gerhard, et al, eds. Recent Developments in Spatial Data Analysis: Methodology, Measurement, Models. 426p. 1984. text ed. 41.95x (ISBN 0-566-00685-5). Gower Pub Co.

Bahrenburg, Bruce. The Creation of Dino De Laurentis' King Kong. 1976. pap. 1.75 (ISBN 0-671-80796-X). WSP.

Bahri, Vijal S. Introductory Course in Spoken Punjabi. (Ser. in Indian Languages & Linguistics). 1977. 15.95 (ISBN 0-89684-254-1, Pub. by Bahri Pubns India); pap. 11.95 (ISBN 0-89684-255-X). Orient Bk Dist.

Bahri, Vijal S. & Jagannathan, V. R. Introductory Course in Spoken Hindi. (India Languages & Linguistics Ser.). 280p. 1978. 11.95 (ISBN 0-89684-253-3, Pub. by Bahri Pubns India). Orient Bk Dist.

Bahrin, Tunku S., et al, eds. A Colloquium on Southeast Asian Studies. 319p. 1981. text ed. 31.50x (ISBN 9971-902-33-8, Pub. by Inst Southeast Asian Stud). Gower Pub Co.

Bahro, Rudolf. From Red to Green. 208p. 1984. 26.50 (ISBN 0-8052-7171-6, Pub. by NLB England); pap. 9.50 (ISBN 0-8052-7172-4). Schocken.

--Socialism & Survival. 160p. (Orig.). 1982. 13.00 (ISBN 0-946097-02-X); pap. 6.50 (ISBN 0-946097-00-3). Heretic Bks.

--Socialism & Survival. (Heretic Bks.). 206p. 1982. 12.95 (ISBN 0-317-18664-7, Pub. by GMP England); pap. 6.50 (ISBN 0-317-18665-5). Alyson Pubns.

Bahro, Rudolph. The Alternative in Eastern Europe. 464p. 1981. 19.50 (ISBN 0-8052-7056-6, Pub. by NLB England); pap. 9.50 (ISBN 0-8052-7098-1). Schocken.

Bahti, Mark. Consumer Guide to Arts & Craft. 32p. 1975. pap. 3.00 (ISBN 0-317-20198-0). Treasure Chest.

--Southwest Indian Arts & Crafts. 2nd, Rev. ed. LC 82-83654. (Illus.). 48p. 1983. lib. bdg. 8.95 (ISBN 0-916122-92-1); pap. 3.75 (ISBN 0-916122-91-3). KC Pubns.

Bahti, Timothy, tr. see Jauss, Hans R.

Bahti, Tom. Southwestern Indian Ceremonials. LC 79-136004. (Illus.). 1970. 8.95 (ISBN 0-916122-27-1); pap. 3.75 (ISBN 0-916122-02-6). KC Pubns.

--Southwestern Indian Tribes. LC 68-31188. (Illus.). 1968. 8.95 (ISBN 0-916122-26-3); pap. 3.75 (ISBN 0-916122-01-8). KC Pubns.

Bahtin, I. A., et al. Eleven Papers on Differential Equations, Functional Analysis & Measure Theory. LC 51-5559. (Translations, Ser.: No. 2, Vol. 51). 1966. 39.00 (ISBN 0-8218-1751-5, TRANS 2-51). Am Math.

Bahya Ben Joseph Ibn Pakuda. The Book of Direction to the Duties of the Heart. Mansoor, Menahem, et al, trs. from Arabic. (LLJC Ser.). 480p. 1973. 43.00x (ISBN 0-19-710020-1). Oxford U Pr.

Baiardi, John C. & Ruggieri, George D., eds. Aquatic Sciences. (Annals of the New York Academy of Sciences: Vol. 245). 70p. 1974. 17.00x (ISBN 0-89072-759-7). NY Acad Sci.

Baiardi, Peter, jt. auth. see Altman, Irving.

Baibi, S. Y. At the Threshold of Premonition. 1984. pap. 3.50 (ISBN 0-913054-38-0). Poet Gal Pr.

Baibi, Soy. In Kafka Castle. 1973. pap. 3.50 (ISBN 0-913054-07-0). Poet Gal Pr.

--The Secretary. 1971. pap. 3.50 (ISBN 0-913054-04-6). Poet Gal Pr.

Baich, Paul von see Von Baich, Paul.

Baichelor. Existence et Imagination: Essai sur le Theatre de Montherlant. Laredu, tr. (Fr.). 14.50 (ISBN 0-685-37000-3). French & Eur.

Baid, L. Managing Performance. (St. Clair Series in Management & Organizational Behavior). 200p. 16.95 (ISBN 0-471-06243-X). Wiley.

Baidyuk, Bronislav V. Mechanical Properties of Rocks at High Temperatures & Pressures. LC 65-25221. 75p. 1967. 25.00x (ISBN 0-306-10778-3, Consultants). Plenum Pub.

Baier. Elements of Direct Marketing. 1985. text ed. 41.95 (ISBN 0-07-002986-5). McGraw.

Baier, Annette. Postures of the Mind: Essays on Mind & Morals. 322p. 1985. 29.50 (ISBN 0-8166-1326-5); pap. 14.95 (ISBN 0-8166-1327-3). U of Minn Pr.

Baier, Jane, jt. auth. see Hules, Virginia.

Baier, Joseph. Striking Clocks: A Hands-On Survey for the Clockmaker. 1983. write for info. (ISBN 0-918845-07-6). Am Watchmakers.

Baier, Joseph, et al. Questions & Answers of & for the Clockmaking Profession. 1982. (ISBN 0-918845-04-1). Am Watchmakers.

Baier, Lesley K. & Shestack, Alan. The Katharine Ordway Collection, Yale University Art Gallery. (Illus.). 128p. 1983. pap. 12.95x (ISBN 0-89467-025-5). Yale Art Gallery.

Baier, Leslie K., ed. see Field, Richard & Baughman, SaraL.

Baier, Patricia, et al. Self Teaching or Instructional Manual. (Illus.). 131p. 10.00 (ISBN 0-318-15081-6). Natl Archery.

Baier, Richard C. Legal Traps for the Unwary Agent: How to Avoid Liability. LC 83-226703. (A Market Builder Library Selection). xiv, 122p. 1983. pap. 7.95. R & R Newkirk.

Baier, Stephen. An Economic History of Central Niger. (OSAA Ser.). (Illus.). 1980. text ed. 52.00x (ISBN 0-19-822717-5). Oxford U Pr.

Baier, Sue & Zimmeth, Mary. Bed Number Ten. (Illus.). 320p. 1985. 16.95 (ISBN 0-03-002997-X). HR&W.

Baier, W. Crop Weather Models & Their Use in Yield Assessments. (Technical Note Ser.: No. 151). 48p. 1977. pap. 18.00 (ISBN 92-6-310458-1, W375, WMO). Unipub.

Baierlein, Ralph. Atoms & Information Theory: An Introduction to Statistical Mechanics. LC 71-116369. (Illus.). 486p. 1971. text ed. 30.95 (ISBN 0-7167-0332-7). W H Freeman.

--Newtonian Dynamics. (Illus.). 336p. 1983. text ed. 37.95 (ISBN 0-07-003016-2). McGraw.

Baig, M. A. Wisdom of Islamic Civilization. 9.95 (ISBN 0-317-01595-8). Kazi Pubns.

Baig, M. R. Muslim Dilemma in India. 1974. 7.50 (ISBN 0-7069-0311-0). Intl Bk Dist.

Baig, Tara A. India's Woman Power. 300p. 1976. text ed. 16.00x (ISBN 0-8426-0869-9). Verry.

Baigell, Matthew. Albert Bierstadt. (Illus.). 84p. 1981. 25.00 (ISBN 0-8230-0494-5). Watson-Guptill.

--A Concise History of American Paintings & Sculpture. LC 84-47555. (Illus.). 432p. 1984. 33.65 (ISBN 0-06-430350-0, Icon Edns). Har-Row.

--Dictionary of American Art. 390p. 1979. 17.95i (ISBN 0-06-433254-3, Icon Edns); pap. 8.95i (ISBN 0-06-430078-1, IN 78, Icon Edns). Har-Row.

--The Western Art of Frederic Remington. 1980. pap. 9.95 (ISBN 0-345-29026-7). Ballantine.

Baigent, Michael, et al. Mundane Astrology. (Illus.). 416p. (Orig.). 1984. pap. 12.95 (ISBN 0-85030-302-8, Pub. by Aquarian Pr England). Sterling.

--Holy Blood, Holy Grail. 1983. pap. 3.95 (ISBN 0-440-13648-2). Dell.

Baigentt, jt. auth. see Lincoln, Henry.

Baigrie, Ronald S., jt. auth. see Armstrong, Paul W.

Baijal, M. D., ed. Plastics Polymer Science & Technology. (SPE Monograph). (Illus.). 945p. 1982. 172.50 (ISBN 0-686-48131-3, 0815). T-C Pubns CA.

Baijal, Mahendra D., ed. Plastic Polymers Science & Technology. LC 31-13066. (Society of Plastic Engineers Monographs). 945p. 1982. 172.50x (ISBN 0-471-04044-4, Pub. by Wiley-Interscience). Wiley.

Baijal, S. K. Flow Behavior of Polymers in Porous Media. 116p. 1982. 49.95x (ISBN 0-87814-188-X). Pennwell Bks.

Baikie, James. The Charm of the Scott Country. Home, Gordan, tr. 128p. 1984. Repr. of 1927 ed. lib. bdg. 75.00 (ISBN 0-89987-964-0). Darby Bks.

--Egyptian Papyri & Papyrus-Hunting. facsimile ed. LC 76-152972. (Select Bibliographies Reprint Ser). (Illus.). Repr. of 1925 ed. 26.50 (ISBN 0-8369-5724-5). Ayer Co Pubs.

--A History of Egypt: From the Earliest Times to the End of the Eighteenth Dynasty, 2 vols. facsimile ed. LC 79-157323. (Select Bibliographies Reprint Ser.). Repr. of 1929 ed. Set. 66.00 (ISBN 0-8369-5782-2). Ayer Co Pubs.

Baikie, Kenneth R. Lazy Man's Guide to Better Bridge. rev., updated ed. LC 75-24166. (Illus.). 104p. 1979. pap. 6.50 (ISBN 0-9607790-0-0). K Baikie.

Baikie, W. B. Narrative of an Exploring Voyage up to the Rivers Kuora & Binue Commonly Known As the Niger & Tsadda in 1854. 456p. 1966. 36.00x (ISBN 0-7146-1788-1, F Cass Co). Biblio Dist.

Baikov, V. & Sigalov, E. Reinforced Concrete Structures, 2 vols. 664p. 1981. 14.50 (ISBN 0-8285-1975-7, Pub. by Mir Pubs USSR). Imported Pubns.

Baikova, I. Museums in & Around Moscow. 197p. 1985. 8.95 (ISBN 0-8285-2920-5, Pub. by Raduga Pubs USSR). Imported Pubns.

Baikow, V. E. Manufacture & Refining of Raw Cane Sugar. 2nd ed. (Sugar Ser.: Vol. 2). 588p. 1982. 159.75 (ISBN 0-444-41896-2). Elsevier.

Bail, Eli. From Railway to Freeway: Pacific Electric & the Motorbus. Sebree, Mac, ed. (Interurbans Special Ser.: No. 90). (Illus.). 200p. 1984. 29.95 (ISBN 0-916374-61-0). Interurban.

Bail, Joe P. Agricultural Education: Renewal & Rebirth. 10p. 1973. pap. text ed. 1.00x (ISBN 0-8134-1622-1, 1622). Interstate.

Bail, Murray. The Drover's Wife & Other Stories. (Paperbacks Ser.). Orig. Title: Contmporary Portraits. 183p. 1985. pap. 7.95 (ISBN 0-7022-1818-9). U of Queensland Pr.

Bailar, J. C., et al, eds. Comprehensive Inorganic Chemistry, 5 vols. Incl. Vol. 1: H, Noble Gases, Group 1A, Group 11A, Group 111B, C & Si. 215.00 (ISBN 0-08-016987-2); Vol. 2: Ge, Sn, Pb, Group VB, Group VIB, Group VIIB. 215.00 (ISBN 0-08-016988-0); Vol. 3: Lanthanides, Transition Metal Compounds. 215.00 (ISBN 0-08-016989-9); Vol. 4: Actinides, Master Index. 215.00 (ISBN 0-08-016990-2). 1973. Set. text ed. 900.00 (ISBN 0-08-017275-X). Pergamon.

Bailar, John C., Jr., et al. Chemistry. 2nd ed. 1984. 28.00i (ISBN 0-12-072855-9); instrs' manual 10.00i (ISBN 0-12-072857-5); student solutions manual 7.25i (ISBN 0-12-072858-3); study guide 9.25i (ISBN 0-12-072859-1); transparency masters 50.00i (ISBN 0-12-072860-5). Acad Pr.

Bailard, Thomas E., et al. Personal Money Management. 4th ed. 640p. 1983. text ed. 27.95 (ISBN 0-574-19525-4, 13-2525); instr's guide avail. (ISBN 0-574-19526-2, 13-2526); study guide 10.95 (ISBN 0-574-19527-0, 13-2527). SRA.

Bailbe. Agrippa D'Aubigne, Poete des Tragiques. (Publ. Fac. des Lettres et Sc. Hum. Universite de Caen). 36.65 (ISBN 0-685-34181-X). French & Eur.

Bailding, Kenneth, et al. Methodology in the Social Sciences. (Economics Institute Monograph: Vol. 2). 60p. 1984. 6.50 (ISBN 0-88036-002-X). Econ Inst.

Baildon, H. B. Homes Haunts of Famous Authors. 1979. Repr. of 1906 ed. lib. bdg. 25.00 (ISBN 0-8495-0542-9). Arden Lib.

Baildon, H. B., et al. Homes & Haunts of Famous Authors. 1973. 25.00 (ISBN 0-8274-1484-6). R West.

Baildon, Henry B. Ralph Waldo Emerson: Man & Teacher. LC 72-14362. Repr. of 1884 ed. lib. bdg. 10.00 (ISBN 0-8414-1340-1). Folcroft.

Baildon, John, jt. auth. see De Beau Chesne, John.

Baile De Laperriere, C. & Baile De Laperriere, S. Silver Auction Records, 1979-1980. 4th ed. (Illus.). 1979. 75.00 (ISBN 0-904722-03-1). Hilmarton Manor.

Baile De Laperriere, Charles & Baile De Laperriere, Sarah. Silver Auction Records 1978-79. (Silver Auction Records Ser.). (Illus.). 1978. 60.00 (ISBN 0-686-09898-6). Hilmarton Manor.

Baile De Laperriere, S., jt. auth. see Baile De Laperriere, C.

Baile De Laperriere, Sarah, jt. auth. see Baile De Laperriere, Charles.

Bailen, D. Weak Interactions. LC 75-34572. 480p. 1977. pap. 24.95x (ISBN 0-8448-0851-2). Crane-Russak Co.

Bailenson, Stewart L. Control Your Unemployment Compensation Costs. Orig. Title: How to Control the Cost of Unemployment Compensation Claims & Taxes on Your Business. (Illus.). 200p. pap. 25.00 (ISBN 0-318-00477-1). N Coast Assoc.

Bailer, Uri. The Shadow of the Bomber: The Fear of Air Attack & British Politics, 1932-1939. (Royal Historical Society Studies in History: Vol. 18). 166p. 1980. text ed. 35.50x (ISBN 0-901050-78-4, Pub. by Swiftbks England). Humanities.

Bailes, Carlton & Hudson, Danny L. A Guide to Texas Lakes. LC 82-83011. 212p. (Orig.). 1982. pap. 7.95x (ISBN 0-88415-416-5, Pub by Pacesetter Pr). Gulf Pub.

Bailes, Edith G. An Album of Fragrance: With Complete Instructions for Making Your Own Perfume, Potpourri, Sachet, Herbal Moth Repellant & Incense. (Illus.). 100p. (Orig.). 1983. pap. 9.95 (ISBN 0-9611118-0-1). Cardamom.

--But Will It Bite Me? A Reference Book of Insects for Children & Their Grownups. 128p. (Orig.). 1985. pap. price not set (ISBN 0-9611118-1-X). Cardamom.

Bailes, Frederick. Basic Principles of the Science of Mind. 3rd ed. Bailes, Mrs. Frederick, ed. 182p. 1980. pap. 8.95 (ISBN 0-87516-404-8). De Vorss.

--Getting What You Go After. 1972. pap. 1.00 (ISBN 0-87516-125-1). De Vorss.

--Healing Power of Balanced Emotions. 1972. pap. 2.95 (ISBN 0-87516-124-3). De Vorss.

--Healing the Incurable. 1972. pap. 1.00 (ISBN 0-87516-126-X). De Vorss.

--Help Answer Your Own Prayers. 1972. pap. 1.00 (ISBN 0-87516-127-8). De Vorss.

--How to Get Along with Troublesome People. 1972. pap. 1.00 (ISBN 0-87516-128-6). De Vorss.

--Is There a Cure for Frustration? 1972. pap. 1.00 (ISBN 0-87516-129-4). De Vorss.

--The Secret of Healing. pap. 1.00 (ISBN 0-87516-163-4). De Vorss.

--What Is This Power That Heals. pap. 1.00 (ISBN 0-87516-171-5). De Vorss.

--Your Emotions Can Kill or Cure You. 1972. pap. 1.00 (ISBN 0-87516-130-8). De Vorss.

--Your Mind Can Heal You. LC 78-128864. 206p. 1975. pap. 4.95 (ISBN 0-87516-201-0). De Vorss.

Bailes, Frederick W. Hidden Power for Human Problems. 1980. pap. 5.95 (ISBN 0-13-386979-2). P-H.

Bailes, Jack C. Management Budgeting for CETA. (Papers in Manpower Studies & Education: No. 1). 1975. pap. 2.00x (ISBN 0-87071-327-2). Oreg St U Pr.

Bailes, Kendall E. Technical Elites & Soviet Society under Lenin & Stalin. LC 77-85558. (Studies of the Russian Institute, Columbia University). 1978. 50.00x (ISBN 0-691-05260-3); pap. 17.00x LPE (ISBN 0-691-10063-2). Princeton U Pr.

Bailes, Kendall E., ed. Environmental History: Critical Issues in Comparative Perspective. 706p. (Orig.). 1985. lib. bdg. 41.50 (ISBN 0-8191-4376-6, Am Soc Environmental Hist); pap. text ed. 25.50 (ISBN 0-8191-4377-4). U Pr of Amer.

Bailes, Mary A. Ryme & Thought. 48p. (Orig.). 1981. pap. 2.95 (ISBN 0-938468-00-6). Marcella.

Bailes, N. J. & Brown, J. L., eds. Layman's Guide to Virginia Law. LC 77-81626. 373p. 1977. 14.50 (ISBN 0-87215-201-4). Michie Co.

Bailes, Tressie N. My Land & People-Of Thee I Sing. 176p. 1982. 7.95 (ISBN 0-89962-281-X). Todd & Honeywell.

Bailess, R. R., et al, eds. Vintage Vicksburg. 464p. 1985. 16.95 (ISBN 0-9614988-0-3). Vicksburg Jr Aux.

Bailey. Age: Colloquial Satire. (The Victorian Music Ser.). 1985. text ed. 30.00 (ISBN 0-8240-8622-8). Garland Pub.

--Annual Reports in Medicinal Chemistry, Vol. 19. 1984. 35.00 (ISBN 0-12-040519-9). Acad Pr.

--Prisoners of War. LC 81-9403. (World War II Ser.). lib. bdg. 22.60 (ISBN 0-8094-3392-3, Pub. by Time-Life). Silver.

Bailey, jt. auth. see Draper.

Bailey, jt. auth. see Miller.

Bailey, A. E., et al, eds. see Kaye, G. W. & Laby, T. H.

Bailey, A. Peter see Fields, Mike.

Bailey, A. R. & Hull, D. G. The Way Out. (Illus.). 85p. 1980. pap. text ed. 6.95x (ISBN 0-920380-62-X, Pub. by Inst Res Pub Canada). Brookfield Pub Co.

Bailey, Abigail. Memoirs of Mrs. Abigail Bailey Who Had Been the Wife of Major Asa Bailey Formerly of Landoff, N. H. Baxter, Annette K., ed. LC 79-5487. (Signal Lives Ser.). 1980. Repr. of 1815 ed. lib. bdg. 28.50x (ISBN 0-405-12821-5). Ayer Co Pubs.

Bailey, Adrian. Cooking of the British Isles. LC 69-19833. (Foods of the World Ser.). (Illus.). (gr. 7 up). 1969. lib. bdg. 19.94 (ISBN 0-8094-0065-0, Pub. by Time-Life). Silver.

--Cooks' Ingredients. Ortiz, Elisabeth L., ed. LC 80-81457. (Illus.). 256p. 1980. 24.95 (ISBN 0-688-03681-3). Morrow.

--Walt Disney's World of Fantasy. Ridgeway, Julie & Ridgeway, Steve, eds. LC 82-1547. (Illus.). 252p. 1982. 35.00 (ISBN 0-89696-117-6, An Everest House Book). Dodd.

Bailey, Adrian & Holloway, Adrian. The Book of Color Photography. LC 83-49190. (Illus.). 216p. 1984. pap. 12.95 (ISBN 0-394-72467-4). Knopf.

Bailey, Adrian & Hooloway, Adrian. The Book of Colour Photography. 160p. 1981. 45.00x (ISBN 0-85223-150-4, Pub. by Ebury Pr England). State Mutual Bk.

Bailey, Afred M. & Niedrach, Robert J. Stepping Stones Across the Pacific. (Museum Pictorial: No. 3). 1951. pap. 1.10 (ISBN 0-916278-32-8). Denver Mus Natl Hist.

Bailey, Albert E. Gospel in Hymns. (Illus.). 1950. lib. rep. ed. 45.00x (ISBN 0-684-15554-0, ScribT). Scribner.

--Notes on the Literary Aspects of Tennyson's Princess. LC 73-18307. Repr. of 1897 ed. lib. bdg. 9.50 (ISBN 0-8414-9897-0). Folcroft.

Bailey, Albina. Dressing Dolls in Nineteenth Century Fashions, Vol. II. (Illus.). 256p. pap. 14.95 (ISBN 0-87069-299-2). Wallace-Homestead.

--Dressing Dolls in Nineteenth Century Fashions. (Illus.). 200p. softbound 14.95 (ISBN 0-87069-275-5). Wallace-Homestead.

Bailey, Alfred G. The Conflict of European & Eastern Algonkian Cultures, 1504-1700: A Study in Canadian Civilization. 2nd ed. LC 78-434310. 1969. pap. 7.50 (ISBN 0-8020-6310-1). U of Toronto Pr.

Bailey, Alfred M. Field Work of a Museum Naturalist: Alaska Southeast, 1919-1921; Alaska Far North, 1921-1922. (Museum Pictorial: No. 22). 1971. pap. 2.25 (ISBN 0-916278-49-2). Denver Mus Natl Hist.

--Galapagos Islands. (Museum Pictorial: No. 9). 1970. pap. 1.50 (ISBN 0-916278-46-8). Denver Mus Natl Hist.

--The Hawaiian Monk Seal. (Museum Pictorial Ser.: No. 7). 1949. pap. 1.10 (ISBN 0-916278-36-0). Denver Mus Natl Hist.

--Laysan & Black Footed Albatrosses. (Museum Pictorial: No. 6). 1952. pap. 1.10 (ISBN 0-916278-35-2). Denver Mus Natl Hist.

--Nature Photography with Miniature Cameras. (Museum Pictorial Ser.: No. 1). 1951. pap. 1.10 (ISBN 0-916278-30-1). Denver Mus Natl Hist.

Bailey, Alfred M. & Sorenson, J. H. Subantarctic Campbell Island. (Proceedings: No. 10). 1962. 4.00 (ISBN 0-916278-62-X); pap. 2.00 (ISBN 0-916278-63-8). Denver Mus Natl Hist.

Bailey, Alfred M., et al. The Red Crossbills of Colorado. (Museum Pictorial: No. 9). 1953. pap. 1.10 (ISBN 0-916278-38-7). Denver Mus Natl Hist.

Bailey, Alice A. A Compilation on Sex. 160p. (Orig.). pap. 5.50 (ISBN 0-85330-136-0). Lucis.

--Consciousness of the Atom. 1972. 11.00 (ISBN 0-85330-001-1); pap. 5.00 (ISBN 0-85330-101-8). Lucis.

--Death: The Great Adventure. 1985. pap. 6.00 (ISBN 0-85330-138-7). Lucis.

--The Destiny of the Nations. 1968. 11.00 (ISBN 0-85330-002-X); pap. 5.00 (ISBN 0-85330-102-6). Lucis.

--Discipleship in the New Age, 2 Vols. Vol. 1, 1971. 13.50 (ISBN 0-85330-003-8); Vol. 2, 1968. 22.00 (ISBN 0-85330-004-6); Vol. 1. pap. 10.50 (ISBN 0-85330-103-4); Vol. 2. pap. 10.50 (ISBN 0-85330-104-2). Lucis.

--Education in the New Age. 1971. 11.00 (ISBN 0-85330-005-4); pap. 5.00 (ISBN 0-85330-105-0). Lucis.

--The Externalisation of the Hierarchy. 1968. 26.00 (ISBN 0-85330-006-2); pap. 10.50 (ISBN 0-85330-106-9). Lucis.

--From Bethlehem to Calvary. 1974. 9.50 (ISBN 0-85330-007-0); pap. 5.00 (ISBN 0-85330-107-7). Lucis.

--From Intellect to Intuition. 1972. 7.50 (ISBN 0-85330-008-9); pap. 5.00 (ISBN 0-85330-108-5). Lucis.

--Glamour: A World Problem. 1973. 11.00 (ISBN 0-85330-009-7); pap. 5.00 (ISBN 0-85330-109-3). Lucis.

--Initiation, Human & Solar. 1977. 11.25 (ISBN 0-85330-010-0); pap. 5.00 (ISBN 0-85330-110-7). Lucis.

--The Labors of Hercules: An Astrological Interpretation. 1982. pap. 7.25 (ISBN 0-85330-130-1). Lucis.

--Letters on Occult Meditation. 1973. 11.25 (ISBN 0-85330-011-9); pap. 5.50 (ISBN 0-85330-111-5). Lucis.

--The Light of the Soul. 1972. 12.50 (ISBN 0-85330-012-7); pap. 5.75 (ISBN 0-85330-112-3). Lucis.

--Ponder on This: A Compilation. 432p. 1980. pap. 7.00 (ISBN 0-85330-131-X). Lucis.

--Problems of Humanity. 1972. pap. 5.00 (ISBN 0-85330-113-1). Lucis.

--The Reappearance of the Christ. 1978. 12.00 (ISBN 0-85330-014-3); pap. 5.00 (ISBN 0-85330-114-X). Lucis.

--Serving Humanity: A Compilation. 1977. pap. 7.00 (ISBN 0-85330-133-6). Lucis.

--The Soul & Its Mechanism. 1971. 11.00 (ISBN 0-85330-015-1); pap. 5.00 (ISBN 0-85330-115-8). Lucis.

--The Soul, the Quality of Life. 1979. pap. 7.00 (ISBN 0-85330-132-8). Lucis.

--Telepathy & the Etheric Vehicle. 1971. 11.00 (ISBN 0-85330-016-X); pap. 5.00 (ISBN 0-85330-116-6). Lucis.

--Treatise on Cosmic Fire. 1973. 28.00 (ISBN 0-85330-017-8); pap. 15.00 (ISBN 0-85330-117-4). Lucis.

--A Treatise on the Seven Rays, 5 vols. Incl. Vol. 1. Esoteric Psychology. 1979. 17.00 (ISBN 0-85330-018-6); pap. 6.00 (ISBN 0-85330-118-2); Vol. 2. Esoteric Psychology. 1970. 26.00 (ISBN 0-85330-019-4); pap. 10.50 (ISBN 0-85330-119-0); Vol. 3. Esoteric Astrology. 1975. 26.00 (ISBN 0-85330-020-8); pap. 10.50 (ISBN 0-85330-120-4); Vol. 4. Esoteric Healing. 1978. 26.00 (ISBN 0-85330-021-6); pap. 10.50 (ISBN 0-85330-121-2); Vol. 5. The Rays & the Initiations. 1970. 26.00 (ISBN 0-85330-022-4); pap. 10.50 (ISBN 0-85330-122-0). pap. Lucis.

--Treatise on White Magic. 1979. 26.00 (ISBN 0-85330-023-2); pap. 10.50 (ISBN 0-85330-123-9). Lucis.

--Unfinished Autobiography. 1970. 11.00 (ISBN 0-85330-024-0); pap. 7.50 (ISBN 0-85330-124-7). Lucis.

Bailey, Allen A. & Wake Forest University. Continuing Legal Education. North Carolina Trial Book-Criminal: Master. LC 82-235375. 1985. 70.00. Wake Forest Law.

Bailey, Andrew D., jt. auth. see Anderson, Hershel M.

Bailey, Andrew D., Jr. Statistical Auditing: Review, Concepts & Problems. 308p. 1981. pap. text ed. 15.95 (ISBN 0-15-583758-3, HC); solutions manual avail. (ISBN 0-15-583759-1). HarBraceJ.

Bailey, Anita, ed. see Tozer, Aiden W.

Bailey, Anne M., ed. The Asiatic Mode of Production: Science & Politics. (Illus.). 1981. pap. 15.95x (ISBN 0-7100-0738-8). Routledge & Kegan.

Bailey, Anthony. America, Lost & Found. 1981. 10.95 (ISBN 0-394-51088-7). Random.

Bailey, Arthur W., jt. auth. see Wright, Henry A.

Bailey, B. Timmons. A Treatment Module for Alcoholism. 65p. 1984. 17.50 (ISBN 0-318-03776-9). Intl Univ Pr.

Bailey, Bailey. Methods of Social Research. 2nd ed. LC 81-67988. (Illus.). 544p. 1982. 21.95 (ISBN 0-02-901280-5). Free Pr.

Bailey, Barbara R. Main Street, Northeastern Oregon: The Founding & Development of Small Towns. LC 80-84483. (Illus.). 240p. 1982. 12.95 (ISBN 0-87595-105-8, Western Imprints); pap. 8.95 (ISBN 0-87595-073-6, Western Imprints). Oreg Hist Soc.

Bailey, Barry. Living with the Unexpected. 128p. 1984. 8.95 (ISBN 0-687-22366-0). Abingdon.

--Living with Your Feelings. LC 79-27889. (Illus.). 1980. 6.50 (ISBN 0-687-22380-6). Abingdon.

--We Are Not Alone: Sermons on the Presence of God. LC 78-10226. 1979. 7.50 (ISBN 0-687-44280-X). Abingdon.

--With Best Wishes. LC 81-20632. 1982. 7.50 (ISBN 0-687-45842-0). Abingdon.

Bailey, Belle. Makeover. (Wildfire Extra Ser.). (Illus.). 96p. (Orig.). (gr. 7 up). 1985. pap. 2.25 (ISBN 0-590-33480-8, Wildfire). Scholastic Inc.

Bailey, Bernadine. Wonders of the World of Bears. LC 74-15239. (Wonders Ser.). (gr. 3-7). 1975. PLB 9.95 (ISBN 0-396-07031-0). Dodd.

Bailey, Betty. Scampers. 1985. 15.00 (ISBN 0-682-40208-7). Exposition Pr FL.

Bailey, Betty, jt. auth. see Twitchett, John.

Bailey, Brian. The English Village Green. (Illus.). 208p. 1985. 17.95 (ISBN 0-7090-2339-1, Pub. by Salem Hse Ltd). Merrimack Pub Cir.

--Great Romantic Ruins of England & Wales. (Illus.). 1984. 25.00 (ISBN 0-517-55151-9). Crown.

--The Industrial Heritage of Britain. 208p. 1982. 45.00x (ISBN 0-85223-228-4, Pub. by Ebury Pr England). State Mutual Bk.

--Villages of England. (Illus.). 1984. 14.95 (ISBN 0-517-55343-0, Harmony). Crown.

Bailey, Brian J. Lakeland Walks & Legends. (Walks & Legends Ser.). (Illus.). 172p. 1982. pap. 4.95 (ISBN 0-583-13249-9, Pub. by Granada England). Academy Chi Pubs.

Bailey, Byron J. & Biller, Hugh F. Surgery of the Larynx. (Illus.). 650p. Date not set. price not set (ISBN 0-7216-1472-8). Saunders.

Bailey, C. A. Advanced Cryogenics. LC 77-119158. (International Cryogenics Monographs Ser.). 527p. 1971. 65.00x (ISBN 0-306-30458-9, Plenum Pr). Plenum Pub.

Bailey, C. J. Nineteenth Century German Drawings from the Ashmolean. 1982. 75.00x (ISBN 0-900090-96-0, Pub. by Ashmolean Mus UK). State Mutual Bk.

Bailey, Carol R. Treasures of My Heart. 1985. 5.95 (ISBN 0-317-28977-2). Vantage.

Bailey, Carolyn S. For the Story Teller, Story Telling & Stories to Tell. LC 74-23576. 1975. Repr. of 1913 ed. 48.00x (ISBN 0-8103-3802-5). Gale.

--Miss Hickory. LC 46-7275. (Illus.). (gr. 4-7). 1977. pap. 2.95 (ISBN 0-14-030956-X, Puffin). Penguin.

--Miss Hickory. (Illus.). (gr. 4-7). 1946. 12.95 (ISBN 0-670-47940-3). Viking.

--Stories for Every Holiday. LC 73-20149. 277p. 1974. Repr. of 1918 ed. 51.00x (ISBN 0-8103-3957-9). Gale.

Bailey, Carolyn S. & Lewis, Clara M. For the Children's Hour. LC 73-20186. (Illus.). 336p. 1974. Repr. of 1920 ed. 51.00x (ISBN 0-8103-3958-7). Gale.

Bailey, Carolyn S., ed. Plays for the Children's Hour: An American Childhood Presentation. LC 77-94332. (One-Act Plays in Reprint Ser.). 1978. Repr. of 1931 ed. 21.50x (ISBN 0-8486-2032-1). Core Collection.

Bailey, Catherine T. The Measurement of Job Performance. 248p. 1983. text ed. 29.50x (ISBN 0-566-00619-7). Gower Pub Co.

Bailey, Charles, jt. auth. see Bridges, David.

Bailey, Charles H. Beyond the Present & the Particular: A Theory of Liberal Education. 288p. 1984. 34.95x (ISBN 0-7100-9897-9). Routledge & Kegan.

Bailey, Charles-James N. English Phonetic Transcription. LC 85-50101. (Summer Institute of Linguistics Publications in Linguistics Ser.: No. 74). 291p. (Orig.). 1985. 18.00 (ISBN 0-88312-000-3). Summer Inst Ling.

--On the Yin & Yang Nature of Language. viii, 120p. 1982. pap. 7.50 (ISBN 0-89720-060-8). Karoma.

--Variation & Linguistic Theory. LC 73-84648. 162p. 1973. pap. 9.95 (ISBN 0-15-599003-9). Ctr Appl Ling.

Bailey, Charles-James N., jt. ed. see Shuy, Roger W.

Bailey, Charles R. French Secondary Education, 1763-1790: The Secularization of Ex-Jesuit Colleges. LC 78-56730. (Transactions Ser.: Vol. 68, Pt. 6). 1978. pap. 15.00 (ISBN 0-87169-686-X). Am Philos.

Bailey, Charles W., jt. auth. see Knebel, Fletcher.

Bailey, Christina A., jt. auth. see Bailey, Philip S.

Bailey, Clinton. Jordan's Palestinian Challenge, 1948-1983: A Political History. (Leonard Davis Institute Studies in International Politics). 165p. 1985. pap. 12.95x (ISBN 0-8133-0047-9). Westview.

Bailey, Conner. Broker, Mediator, Patron, & Kinsman: An Historical Analysis of Key Leadership Roles in a Rural Malaysian District. LC 75-620141. (Papers in International Studies: Southeast Asia Ser.: No. 38). (Illus.). 1976. pap. 7.00x (ISBN 0-89680-024-5, 82-90397, Ohio U Ctr Intl). Ohio U Pr.

--Small-Scale Fisheries of San Miguel Bay, Philippines: Occupational & Geographical Mobility. (ICLARM Technical Reports: No. 10). (Illus.). 57p. (Orig.). 1983. pap. 11.50x (ISBN 0-89955-396-6, Pub. by ICLARM Philippines). Intl Spec Bk.

Bailey, Conner, ed. Small-Scale Fisheries of San Miguel Bay, Philippines: Social Aspects of Production & Marketing. (ICLARM Technical Reports Ser.: No. 9). (Illus.). 57p. (Orig.). 1982. pap. text ed. 14.00x (ISBN 0-89955-397-4, Pub. by ICLARM Philippines). Intl Spec Bk.

Bailey, Connor. The Sociology of Production in Rural Malay Society. (EASSM Ser.). (Illus.). 1983. text ed. 32.50x (ISBN 0-19-582530-6). Oxford U Pr.

Bailey, Covert. Fit of Fat Target Diet. pap. 5.95 (ISBN 0-395-36139-7). HM.

--Fit or Fat? pap. 5.95 (ISBN 0-395-27162-2). HM.

--The Fit or Fat Target Diet. 1984. 11.95 (ISBN 0-395-35561-3); pap. 5.95 (ISBN 0-395-36139-7). HM.

Bailey, Covert & Bishop, Lea. Target Recipes: The Fit-or-Fat System. (Illus.). 169p. 1985. 11.95 (ISBN 0-395-37698-X); pap. 5.95 (ISBN 0-395-37699-8). HM.

Bailey, Cyril. Phases in the Religion of Ancient Rome. LC 75-114460. 340p. 1972. Repr. of 1932 ed. lib. bdg. 21.00x (ISBN 0-8371-4759-X, BARA). Greenwood.

Bailey, Cyril, ed. Legacy of Rome. (Illus.). 1923. 24.95x (ISBN 0-19-821906-7). Oxford U Pr.

Bailey, Cyril, ed. see Lucretius.

Bailey, Cyril, tr. see Epicurus.

Bailey, D. K. & MacDonald, R., eds. The Evolution of the Crystalline Rocks. 1977. 77.00 (ISBN 0-12-073450-8). Acad Pr.

Bailey, D. K., et al, eds. see Mineralogical Society Geochemistry Group, November 1 & 2, 1978.

Bailey, D. L. & Clayton, P. The Measurement of Suspended Particulate & Carbon Concentrations in the Atmosphere Using Standard Smoke Shade Methods, 1980. 1982. 45.00x (ISBN 0-686-97112-4, Pub. by W Spring England). State Mutual Bk.

Bailey, D. R. Cicero. (Classical Life & Letters Ser.). 302p. 1979. 40.50x (ISBN 0-7156-0574-7, BPA-02527, Pub. by Duckworth England); pap. 12.00x (ISBN 0-7156-1603-X, BPA-01031, Pub. by Duckworth England). Biblio Dist.

--Two Studies in Roman Nomenclature. (American Philological Association, American Classical Studies). 1976. pap. 9.00 (ISBN 0-89130-716-8, 400403). Scholars Pr GA.

Bailey, D. R., ed. see Cicero.

Bailey, D. R. Shakleton. Two Studies in Roman Nomenclature. 135p. 1976. 9.00 (ISBN 0-317-35738-7, 40-04-03). Scholars Pr GA.

Bailey, D. Shackleton see Cicero.

Bailey, D. Waylon & Strange, John O. Biblical Hebrew Grammar. LC 85-60960. 246p. 1985. 17.00 (ISBN 0-914520-23-7). Insight Pr.

Bailey, Dan A., jt. auth. see Knepper, William E.

Bailey, Dan E. WW II Wrecks of the Kwajalein & Truk Lagoons. LC 82-63006. (Illus.). 152p. 1983. pap. text ed. 15.95 (ISBN 0-911615-00-8). North Valley.

Bailey, Daniel E., jt. auth. see Tryon, Robert C.

Bailey, Daniel E., ed. Computer Science in Social & Behavioral Science Education. LC 77-25087. (Illus.). 520p. 1978. 32.95 (ISBN 0-87778-101-X). Educ Tech Pubns.

Bailey, David. How to Take Better Pictures. (Illus.). 212p. 1983. 29.50 (ISBN 0-937950-03-3). Xavier-Moreau.

--London NW1: Urban Landscapes. 59p. 1982. 34.95x (ISBN 0-460-04588-1, Pub. by J M Dent England). Biblio Dist.

Bailey, David & Castoro, Laura. Careers in Computers. (Illus.). 192p. (gr. 7 up). 1985. 9.79 (ISBN 0-671-49849-5). Messner.

Bailey, David, ed. Productivity Measurement: An International Review of Concepts, Techniques, Programmes & Current Issues. Hubert, Tony. 284p. 1981. text ed. 44.50x (ISBN 0-566-02230-3). Gower Pub Co.

Bailey, David, et al, photos by. Nine by Nine. (Illus.). 96p. 1984. pap. 12.95 (ISBN 0-912810-47-5). Lustrum Pr.

Bailey, David C. Viva Cristo Rey: The Cristero Rebellion & the Church-State Conflict in Mexico. (Illus.). 360p. 1974. 22.50x (ISBN 0-292-78700-6). U of Tex Pr.

Bailey, David H. & Gottlieb, Louise. Biblioteca Basica de Rotary. White, Willmon L. & Perlberg, Mark, eds. (Illus.). 506p. (Span.). 1982. 14.50 (ISBN 0-915062-15-1). Rotary Intl.

--Bibliotheque de Base du Rotary. White, Willmon L. & Perlberg, Mark, eds. (Illus.). 506p. (French.). 1982. 14.50 (ISBN 0-915062-10-0). Rotary Intl.

--Fondamenti del Rotary. White, Willmon L. & Perlberg, Mark, eds. (Illus.). 506p. (Italian.). 1982. 14.50 (ISBN 0-915062-12-7). Rotary Intl.

--Literature Basica de Rotary. White, Willmon L. & Perlberg, Mark, eds. (Illus.). 506p. (Portuguese.). 1982. 14.50 (ISBN 0-915062-14-3). Rotary Intl.

--Roatry Basic Library. White, Willmon L. & Perlberg, Mark, eds. (Illus.). 506p. (Japanese.). 1982. 14.50 (ISBN 0-915062-13-5). Rotary Intl.

--Roatrys Handbibliotek. White, Willmon L. & Perlberg, Mark, eds. (Illus.). 506p. (Swedish.). 1982. 14.50 (ISBN 0-915062-16-X). Rotary Intl.

--Rotary Basic Library, 7 vols. White, Willmon L. & Perlberg, Mark, eds. (Illus.). 506p. 1982. 14.50 (ISBN 0-915062-08-9). Rotary Intl.

--Rotaryn Peruskirjaston, 7 Vols. White, Willmon L. & Perlberg, Mark, eds. (Illus.). 506p. (Finnish.). 1982. 14.50 (ISBN 0-915062-09-7). Rotary Intl.

--Schlag Nach Uber Rotary. White, Willmon L. & Perlberg, Mark, eds. (Illus.). 506p. (German.). 1982. 14.50 (ISBN 0-915062-11-9). Rotary Intl.

Bailey, David S., et al. Therapeutic Approaches to the Care of the Mentally Ill. 2nd ed. LC 84-71007. 294p. 1984. pap. text ed. 12.95x (ISBN 0-8036-0551-X). Davis Co.

Bailey, David T. Shadow on the Church: Southwestern Evangelical Religion & the Issue of Slavery, 1783-1860. LC 84-45795. 264p. 1985. text ed. 24.95x (ISBN 0-8014-1763-5). Cornell U Pr.

Bailey, De Witt & Nie, Douglas A. English Gunmakers: The Birmingham & Provincial Gun Trade in the 18th & 19th Century. LC 77-29162. (Illus.). 1978. 18.95 (ISBN 0-668-04566-3, 4566). Arco.

Bailey, Deloros S. God's Country U. S. A. 1982. 17.95 (ISBN 0-913730-04-1). Robinson Pr.

Bailey, Denis M., jt. ed. see Chakrin, Lawrence W.

Bailey, Dennis, jt. auth. see Bischoff, David.

Bailey, Dennis R., jt. auth. see Bischoff, David F.

Bailey, Derek. Musical Improvisation. 154p. 1983. 14.95 (ISBN 0-13-607044-2); pap. 6.95 (ISBN 0-13-607051-5). P-H.

Bailey, Derrick S. The Mystery of Love & Marriage: A Study in the Theology of Sexual Relation. LC 77-3313. 1977. Repr. of 1952 ed. lib. bdg. 15.00 (ISBN 0-8371-9577-2, BAML). Greenwood.

Bailey, Don C. A Glossary of Japanese Neologisms. LC 62-17990. pap. 43.00 (ISBN 0-317-10176-5, 2055363). Bks Demand UMI.

Bailey, Don W. Laboratory Manual for Animal Physiology. 3rd ed. 1984. pap. 8.95x (ISBN 0-89917-383-7). TIS Inc.

Bailey, Donald & Wolery, Mark. Teaching Infants & Preschoolers with Handicaps. 1984. text ed. 28.50 (ISBN 0-675-20132-2). Merrill.

Bailey, E. B. Tectonic Essays, Mainly Alpine. 1935. 39.50x (ISBN 0-19-854368-9). Oxford U Pr.

Bailey, E., Sr. James Hutton: Founder of Modern Geology. 161p. 1971. 20.50 (ISBN 0-686-43854-X, Pub. by Elsevier Applied Sci England). Elsevier.

Bailey, Earl L. Product-Line Strategies. (Report Ser.: 816). (Illus.). vii, 76p. (Orig.). 1982. pap. text ed. 50.00 (ISBN 0-8237-0253-7); pap. text ed. 10.00 member. Conference Bd.

Bailey, Earl L., jt. auth. see Hopkins, David S.

Bailey, Earl L., ed. Pricing Practices & Strategies. LC 78-70226. (Report Ser.: No. 751). (Illus.). 68p. 1978. pap. 22.50 (ISBN 0-8237-0187-5); pap. 7.50 member. Conference Bd.

--Tomorrow's Marketing: A Symposium. (Report Ser: No. 623). 65p. (Orig.). 1974. pap. 5.00 (ISBN 0-8237-0053-4); pap. 2.00 member. Conference Bd.

Bailey, Edward, Jr. The Practical Writer: From Paragraph to Theme. 2nd ed. 1983. pap. text ed. 15.95 (ISBN 0-03-061739-1). HR&W.

--Writing Clearly. (No. 174). 160p. 1984. pap. text ed. 11.95 (ISBN 0-675-20269-8). Merrill.

Bailey, Edward, Jr., et al. Writing Research Papers: A Practical Guide. LC 80-25548. 218p. 1981. pap. text ed. 9.95 (ISBN 0-03-050626-3, HoltC). HR&W.

Bailey, Elizabeth. The Falling Place. (Orig.). 1981. pap. 1.95 (ISBN 0-8439-8040-0, Tiara Bks). Dorchester Pub Co.

Bailey, Elizabeth E., ed. Selected Economic Writings of William J. Baumol. LC 75-34649. 655p. 1976. 65.00x (ISBN 0-8147-1005-0). NYU Pr.

Bailey, Elizabeth E., et al. Deregulating the Airlines. (Regulating Economics Activity Ser.). (Illus.). 386p. 1985. text ed. 25.00x (ISBN 0-262-02213-3). MIT Pr.

Bailey, Elmer J. Novels of George Meredith. LC 75-163892. (Studies in George Meredith, No. 21). 1971. Repr. of 1908 ed. lib. bdg. 49.95 (ISBN 0-8383-1312-4). Haskell.

--Religious Thought in the Greater American Poets. facs. ed. LC 68-8436. (Essay Index Reprint Ser). 1968. Repr. of 1922 ed. 16.00 (ISBN 0-8369-0167-3). Ayer Co Pubs.

Bailey, Emma. Sold to the Lady in the Green Hat. rev. ed. 228p. 1969. 8.95 (ISBN 0-914960-01-6). Academy Bks.

Bailey, Eric. The Christmas Island Story. 88p. 1984. 29.00 (ISBN 0-905743-08-3, Pub. by Stacey Intl Pubs UK). State Mutual Bk.

--Domestic Poultry Keeper. (Illus.). 192p. 1985. 19.95 (ISBN 0-7137-1338-0, Pub. by Blandford Pr England). Sterling.

Bailey, Esther S., jt. auth. see Flexner, Abraham.

Bailey, Eva. Disease & Discovery. (History in Focus Ser.). (Illus.). 72p. (gr. 7-12). 1985. 14.95 (ISBN 0-7134-4633-1, Pub. by Batsford England). David & Charles.

--Music & Musicians. (History in Focus Ser.). (Illus.). 72p. (gr. 7-12). 1983. 14.95 (ISBN 0-7134-1310-7, Pub. by Batsford England). David & Charles.

Bailey, F. My Summer in a Mormon Village. 59.95 (ISBN 0-8490-0692-9). Gordon Pr.

Bailey, F. E. The Perfect Age. 1943. Repr. 15.00 (ISBN 0-8274-3121-X). R West.

Bailey, F. G. Stratagems & Spoils: A Social Anthropology of Politics. (Pavilion Ser.). 254p. 1969. pap. 12.95x (ISBN 0-631-11760-1). Basil Blackwell.

--The Tactical Uses of Passion: An Essay on Power, Reason & Reality. LC 82-22074. 277p. 1983. 33.50x (ISBN 0-8014-1556-X); pap. 10.95x (ISBN 0-8014-9884-8). Cornell U Pr.

Bailey, F. L. Some Sex Beliefs & Practices in a Navaho Community. (Harvard University Peabody Museum of Archaeology & Ethnology Papers Ser). 1950. 11.00 (ISBN 0-527-01300-5). Kraus Repr.

Bailey, F. Lee. The Defense Never Rests. pap. 3.95 (ISBN 0-451-12640-8, AE2640, Sig). NAL.

--The Defense Never Rests. (William K. McInally Memorial Lecture Ser.: 6th). 1971. pap. 1.00 (ISBN 0-87712-150-8). U Mich Busn Div Res.

--For the Defense. 1976. pap. 2.50 (ISBN 0-451-09050-0, E9050, Sig). NAL.

--How to Protect Yourself. 96p. 1984. pap. 2.95 (ISBN 0-8128-8022-6). Stein & Day.

--How to Protect Yourself Against Cops in California & Other Strange Places. LC 82-48516. 96p. 1983. 9.95 (ISBN 0-8128-2891-7). Stein & Day.

--To Be a Trial Lawyer. LC 82-19187. 215p. 1982. text ed. 39.95 leather bd. (ISBN 0-910287-01-5); pap. text ed. 14.95. TelShare Pub Co.

--To Be a Trial Lawyer. 240p. 1985. 40.00 (ISBN 0-471-82733-9); pap. 14.95 (ISBN 0-471-82734-7). Wiley.

Bailey, F. Lee & Marcy, Lynn P. What You Should Know about the Lie Detector. 200p. 1984. cancelled (ISBN 0-910287-03-1). TelShare Pub Co.

Bailey, F. Lee & Rothblatt, Henry. Cross-Examination in Criminal Trials, Vol. 1. LC 78-18628. 1978. 66.50 (ISBN 0-686-29231-6); Suppl. 1984. 19.00; Suppl. 1983. 17.00. Lawyers Co-Op.

Bailey, F. Lee & Rothblatt, Henry B. Complete Manual of Criminal Forms, 2 vols. 2nd ed. LC 74-17692. (Criminal Law Library). 1974. 129.00 (ISBN 0-686-14486-4); Suppl. 1984. 24.00; Suppl. 1983. 22.00. Lawyers Co-Op.

--Crimes of Violence: Homicide & Assault. LC 72-97625. (Criminal Law Library). 543p. 1973. 66.50 (ISBN 0-686-05455-5); Suppl. 1984. 21.50; Suppl. 1983. 19.50. Lawyers Co-Op.

--Crimes of Violence: Rape & Other Sex Crimes. LC 72-97625. (Criminal Law Library). 1973. 66.50 (ISBN 0-686-14500-3); Suppl. 1984. 21.50; Suppl. 1983. 19.50. Lawyers Co-Op.

--Defending Business & White Collar Crimes. 2nd ed. LC 84-80662. 1984. 129.00 (ISBN 0-318-01916-7). Lawyers Co-Op.

--Handling Juvenile Delinquency Cases, Vol. 1. LC 78-70828. (Criminal Law Library). 69.50; Suppl. 1984. 19.00; Suppl. 1983. 17.00. Lawyers Co-Op.

--Handling Narcotic & Drug Cases. LC 72-84855. (Criminal Law Library). 652p. 1972. 66.50 (ISBN 0-686-05452-0); Suppl. 1984. 21.50; Suppl. 1983. 19.50. Lawyers Co-Op.

--Investigation & Preparation of Criminal Cases, 1 vol. LC 71-118363. (Criminal Law Library). 1970. 66.50 (ISBN 0-686-14497-X); Suppl. 1984. 21.50; Suppl. 1983. 19.50. Lawyers Co-Op.

--Sucessful Techniques for Criminal Trials. 2nd ed. LC 84-82304. 1985. 66.50 (ISBN 0-318-04533-8). Lawyers Co-Op.

Bailey, Faith C. Adoniram Judson. (Golden Oldies Ser.). 128p. 1980. pap. 2.95 (ISBN 0-8024-0287-9). Moody.

--D. L. Moody. (Golden Oldies Ser.). 1959. pap. 2.95 (ISBN 0-8024-0039-6). Moody.

--George Mueller. 160p. 1980. pap. 2.95 (ISBN 0-8024-0031-0). Moody.

Bailey, Flora L. Some Sex Beliefs & Practices in a Navaho Community with Comparative Material from Other Navaho Areas. LC 52-8354. (Peabody Museum Papers: Vol. 40, No. 2). 1950. pap. 5.00x (ISBN 0-87365-118-9). Peabody Harvard.

Bailey, Florence H. Poems of Life & Living Things. 1984. 5.95 (ISBN 0-8062-2371-5). Carlton.

Bailey, Foster. Changing Esoteric Values. 2nd. rev. ed. 1974. pap. 2.50 (ISBN 0-85330-125-5). Lucis.

--Reflections. 1979. pap. 5.00 (ISBN 0-85330-134-4). Lucis.

--Running God's Plan. 190p. (Orig.). 1972. pap. 5.00 (ISBN 0-85330-128-X). Lucis.

--The Spirit of Masonry. rev. ed. 143p. 1979. pap. 5.00 (ISBN 0-85330-135-2). Lucis.

--Things to Come. 264p. (Orig.). 1974. pap. 5.00 (ISBN 0-85330-129-8). Lucis.

Bailey, Francis L. A Planned Study of Teachers for Vermont. LC 76-176528. (Columbia University. Teachers College. Contributions to Education Ser.: No. 771). Repr. of 1939 ed. 22.50 (ISBN 0-404-55771-6). AMS Pr.

Bailey, Frank A. Basic Mathematics. 1977. pap. 14.70x (ISBN 0-673-15064-X). Scott F.

--Basic Mathematics for Automotive Technology. 1977. pap. 9.75x (ISBN 0-673-15065-8). Scott F.

--Basic Mathematics for Drafting & Machine Shop. 1977. pap. 9.75x (ISBN 0-673-15066-6). Scott F.

--Basic Mathematics for Electricity & Electronics. 1977. pap. 9.75x (ISBN 0-673-15067-4). Scott F.

Bailey, Frank E. British Policy & the Turkish Reform Movement: A Study in Anglo-Turkish Relations, 1826-1853. LC 74-80519. 1970. Repr. of 1942 ed. 27.50x (ISBN 0-86527-019-8). Fertig.

Bailey, Fred, jt. auth. see Krause, John.

Bailey, Freddie & Regan, Mardee H. Aunt Freddie's Pantry: Southern-Style Jams, Jellies, Relishes, Sauces, Chutneys, & What Goes with Them. 1984. 7.95 (ISBN 0-517-55300-7, C N Potter Bks). Crown.

Bailey, Frederic W. Early Connecticut Marriages As Found on Ancient Church Records Prior to 1800. LC 68-18785. 994p. 1982. Repr. of 1896 ed. 40.00 (ISBN 0-8063-0007-8). Genealog Pub.

--The Heirloom Publication of Bailey's Photo-Ancestral Record: The Record of My Ancestory. 7th ed. 144p. 1982. 29.95 (ISBN 0-9609488-0-5); 34.95 (ISBN 0-9609488-1-3). Heirloom Pubns.

Bailey, Frederick E., Jr., ed. Initation of Polymerization. LC 83-2613. (ACS Symposium Ser.: No. 212). 498p. 1983. lib. bdg. 52.95x (ISBN 0-8412-0765-8). Am Chemical.

Bailey, Frederick G. Tribe, Caste & Nation. 1971. Repr. of 1960 ed. text ed. 21.75x (ISBN 0-7190-0250-8). Humanities.

Bailey, Frederick H., jt. auth. see Woods, Frederick S.

Bailey, G. M. The Mythology of Brahma. 1983. 24.95x (ISBN 0-19-561411-9). Oxford U Pr.

Bailey, Geoff, ed. Hunter-Gatherer Economy in Prehistory: A European Perspective. LC 82-9505. (New Directions in Archaeology Ser.). (Illus.). 250p. 1983. 52.50 (ISBN 0-521-23742-4). Cambridge U Pr.

Bailey, Geoffrey. Maverick: Succeeding As a Freelance Entrepreneur. 224p. 1982. 13.95 (ISBN 0-531-09869-9). Watts.

Bailey, Geoffrey, jt. auth. see Landau, Suzanne.

Bailey, George. Armageddon in Prime Time. 1984. pap. 3.95 (ISBN 0-380-89598-6). Avon.

--Germans: The Biography of an Obsession. 1974. pap. 4.50 (ISBN 0-380-00140-3, 64428-2, Discus). Avon.

Bailey, George, ed. Kontinent Four: Contemporary Russian Writers. 528p. 1982. pap. 4.95 (ISBN 0-380-81182-0, 81182-0, Bard). Avon.

Bailey, George G. The Patch Unit. (Orig.). 1981. pap. 1.95 (ISBN 0-505-51624-1, Pub. by Tower Bks). Dorchester Pub Co.

Bailey, George L., ed. Hemodialysis: Principles & Practice. 1972. 68.50 (ISBN 0-12-072950-4). Acad Pr.

Bailey, George W. Privacy & the Mental. (Elementa Ser.: No. 6). 1979. pap. text ed. 23.50x (ISBN 90-6203-862-X). Humanities.

Bailey, George W., jt. ed. see Schaller, Frank W.

Bailey, Gerald D. Teacher-Designed Student Feedback: A Strategy for Improving Classroom Instruction. 64p. 1983. 6.95 (ISBN 0-8106-1689-0). NEA.

--Teacher Self-Assessment: A Means for Improving Classroom Instruction. 72p. 1981. 5.95 (ISBN 0-8106-1687-4). NEA.

Bailey, Gerald E. The House of a Stranger. 1977. 6.95 (ISBN 0-87141-065-6). Manyland.

Bailey, Gilbert E. & Thayer, Paul S. California's Disappearing Coast: A Legislative Challenge. LC 74-170336. (Illus., Orig.). 1971. pap. 3.00x (ISBN 0-87772-083-5). Inst Gov Stud Berk.

Bailey, Guy. Bienvenue Chez Nous-Welcome to Our Town. (Illus.). 1978. 3.95 (ISBN 0-88776-111-9). Tundra Bks.

Bailey, Guy H., Jr., jt. auth. see Montgomery, Michael B.

Bailey, H. C. Mr. Fortune: Eight of His Adventures. LC 75-44958. (Crime Fiction Ser). 1976. lib. bdg. 21.00 (ISBN 0-8240-2352-8). Garland Pub.

--Mr. Fortune Speaking. 269p. 1977. Repr. lib. bdg. 12.95x (ISBN 0-89966-276-5). Buccaneer Bks.

Bailey, H. J., et al. Apple LOGO: Activities for Exploring Turtle Graphics. (Illus.). 256p. (gr. 5 up). 1984. pap. 14.95 (ISBN 0-89303-312-X). Brady Comm.

Bailey, H. W. Indo-Scythian Studies: Khotanese Texts, Vol. VII. 160p. 1985. 69.50 (ISBN 0-521-25779-4). Cambridge U Pr.

Bailey, Harold & Kerlin, Edward. Apple Graphics: Activities Handbook for the Beginner. LC 83-21406. 432p. 1984. 16.95 (ISBN 0-89303-308-1); bk. & diskette 36.95 (ISBN 0-89303-309-X); diskette 20.00 (ISBN 0-89303-310-3). Brady Comm.

--Commodore 64 Graphics: Activities Handbook. 14.95 (ISBN 0-89303-379-0). Brady Comm.

Bailey, Harold J., et al. Commodore LOGO: Activities for Exploring Turtle Graphics. (Illus.). 320p. (gr. 5-8). 1984. pap. 14.95 (ISBN 0-89303-376-6). Brady Comm.

Bailey, Harold W. Culture of the Sakas in Ancient Iranian Khotan. LC 82-1236. (Columbia Lectures on Iranian Studies). 1983. 25.00x (ISBN 0-88206-053-8). Caravan Bks.

--Dictionary of Khotan Saka. LC 77-80825. 1979. 235.00 (ISBN 0-521-21737-7). Cambridge U Pr.

--Khotanese Buddhist Texts. rev. ed. LC 80-41425. (University of Cambridge Oriental Publications Ser.: No. 31). 168p. 1981. 57.50 (ISBN 0-521-23717-3). Cambridge U Pr.

Bailey, Harry A., ed. Classics of the American Presidency. LC 80-61. (Classics Ser.). (Orig.). 1980. pap. 14.00 (ISBN 0-935610-10-3). Moore Pub IL.

Bailey, Harry P. The Weather of Southern California. (California Natural History Guides: No. 17). (Illus., Orig.). 1966. pap. 2.65 (ISBN 0-520-00062-5). U of Cal Pr.

Bailey, Helen M. & Nasatir, Abraham P. Latin America: The Development of Its Civilization. 3rd ed. (Illus.). 896p. 1973. ref. ed. 29.95 (ISBN 0-13-524264-9). P-H.

Bailey, Henry C. Mister Fortune Speaking. facs. ed. LC 78-140325. (Short Story Index Reprint Series). 1931. 18.00 (ISBN 0-8369-3717-1). Ayer Co Pubs.

Bailey, Henry J. Brady on Bank Checks: Cumulative Supplements. 5th ed. 1979. 68.00 (ISBN 0-88262-314-1, 79-65733). Warren.

Bailey, Henry J., jt. auth. see Hawkland, William.

Bailey, Henry J., jt. auth. see Hursh, Robert D.

Bailey, Henry J., III. Oregon Uniform Commercial Code, 2 vols, Vol. 1. 381p. 1982. 55.00 (ISBN 0-409-24954-8). Butterworth Legal Pubs.

--Oregon Uniform Commercial Code, 2 vols, Vol. 2. 571p. 1984. 65.00 (ISBN 0-409-20043-3). Butterworth Legal Pubs.

--Secured Transactions in a Nutshell. 2nd ed. LC 81-7404. (Nutshell Ser.). 391p. 1981. pap. text ed. 8.95 (ISBN 0-314-59846-4). West Pub.

Bailey, Henry J., III, jt. auth. see Clarke, John J.

Bailey, Herbert. Gerovital (GH3) Will It Keep You Young Longer. 3.95x (ISBN 0-553-14460-X). Cancer Control Soc.

--Vitamin E: Your Key to a Healthy Heart. 1.65x (ISBN 0-668-01514-4). Cancer Control Soc.

Bailey, Herbert S., Jr. The Art & Science of Book Publishing. 230p. 1980. pap. 8.95 (ISBN 0-292-70351-1). U of Tex Pr.

Bailey, Hilary. All the Days of My Life. 1985. 17.95 (ISBN 0-394-54446-3). Random.

Bailey, Hugh C. Edgar Gardner Murphy: Gentle Progressive. LC 68-29705. (Illus.). 1968. 10.95x (ISBN 0-87024-093-5). U of Miami Pr.

--Liberalism in the New South: Southern Social Reformers & the Progressive Movement. LC 78-81620. (Illus.). 1969. 14.95x (ISBN 0-87024-124-9). U of Miami Pr.

Bailey, I. E. Dansk-Engelsk Handels-og Fagordbog. 514p. (Danish & Eng.). 1973. 75.00 (ISBN 87-570-0533-8, M-8411). French & Eur.

Bailey, J. & Ollis, D. Biochemical Engineering Fundamentals. 2nd ed. (Chemical Engineering Ser.). 928p. 1986. price not set (ISBN 0-07-003212-2). McGraw.

Bailey, J. C. & Bedborough, D. R. Tests on the Efficiency of Odour Removal of a Pilot-Scale Boiler Incinerator at an Activated Carbon Plant, 1979. 1981. 40.00x (ISBN 0-686-97145-0, Pub. by W Spring England). State Mutual Bk.

Bailey, J. C. & Viney, N. J. Analysis of Odours by Gas Chromatography & Allied Techniques, 1979. 1981. 75.00x (ISBN 0-686-97023-3, Pub. by W Spring England). State Mutual Bk.

Bailey, J. D. History of Grindal Shoals. 86p. 1981. pap. 10.00 (ISBN 0-89308-233-3). Southern Hist Pr.

--Some Heroes of the American Revolution. LC 75-44664. 295p. 1976. Repr. of 1924 ed. 10.00 (ISBN 0-89308-002-0). Southern Hist Pr.

Bailey, J. M. & Layzell, A. D. Special Transport Services for Elderly & Disabled People. 360p. 1983. text ed. 44.00x (ISBN 0-566-00615-4). Gower Pub Co.

Bailey, J. O. Thomas Hardy & the Cosmic Mind: A New Reading of "the Dynasts". LC 77-24118. 1977. Repr. of 1956 ed. lib. bdg. 24.75x (ISBN 0-8371-9743-0, BATH). Greenwood.

Bailey, J. W. Veterinary Handbook for Cattlemen. 5th rev. ed. Rossoff, Irving S., ed. LC 79-16235. 1980. text ed. 35.95 (ISBN 0-8261-0285-9). Springer Pub.

Bailey, Jack. The British Co-operative Movement. LC 73-19302. (Illus.). 178p. 1974. Repr. of 1955 ed. lib. bdg. 17.75x (ISBN 0-8371-7116-4, BABC). Greenwood.

Bailey, Jack S. Inside a Mormon Mission. 190p. pap. 3.95 (ISBN 0-89036-076-6). Hawkes Pub Inc.

--Let Not Your Heart Be Troubled: Answers to the Problems of Human Suffering. LC 76-3988. 1976. 6.95 (ISBN 0-88290-060-9). Horizon Utah.

Bailey, James. Energy Systems: An Analysis for Engineers & Policy Makers. (Energy Power & Environment: Vol. 2). 1978. 34.50 (ISBN 0-8247-6713-6). Dekker.

--How to Select & Use an Electronic Flash. (Illus.). 1983. pap. 11.95 (ISBN 0-89586-144-5). H P Bks.

--Sermons from the Parables. 128p. (Orig.). 1981. pap. 2.95 (ISBN 0-8341-0730-9). Beacon Hill.

Bailey, James & Ollis, David F. Biochemical Engineering Fundamentals. (McGraw-Hill Chemical Engineering Ser.). (Illus.). 1977. text ed. 47.00 (ISBN 0-07-003210-6). McGraw.

Bailey, James, jt. auth. see Broyles, Frank.

Bailey, James, jt. auth. see Rowland, Desmond.

Bailey, James A. Principles of Wildlife Management. LC 83-19766. 373p. 1984. text ed. 30.95 (ISBN 0-471-01649-7). Wiley.

Bailey, James A., et al, eds. Readings in Wildlife Conservation. LC 74-28405. (Illus.). 722p. (Orig.). 1974. pap. 10.00 (ISBN 0-933564-02-3). Wildlife Soc.

Bailey, James E., jt. auth. see Bedworth, David D.

Bailey, James E., et al. Scheduling Computer Operations. 2nd ed. 1984. 26.95 (ISBN 0-89806-058-3). Inst Indus Eng.

Bailey, James J., jt. ed. see Pryor, T. Allan.

Bailey, James O. Pilgrims Through Space & Time: Trends & Patterns in Scientific & Utopian Fiction. LC 76-38126. 341p. 1972. Repr. of 1947 ed. lib. bdg. 32.50x (ISBN 0-8371-6323-4, BAPS). Greenwood.

Bailey, Jane. Tuning. LC 78-11150. 1978. pap. 4.00 (ISBN 0-918366-09-7). Slow Loris.

Bailey, Janet. Keeping Food Fresh. LC 84-14924. 384p. 1985. pap. 12.95 (ISBN 0-385-27675-3, Dial). Doubleday.

Bailey, Jean P. Sensor Perceptor. (Illus.). 1977. pap. 2.95 (ISBN 0-917200-19-5). ESPress.

Bailey, Jeffrey A., jt. auth. see Nishijima, Gudo W.

Bailey, Jennifer. Norman Mailer: Quick-Change Artist. LC 79-14282. 160p. 1980. text ed. 28.50x (ISBN 0-06-490284-6, 06324). B&N Imports.

Bailey, Jill. Eyes. LC 83-13883. (Animals of Course! Ser.). (Illus.). 14p. (gr. k-1). 1984. 3.95 (ISBN 0-399-21026-1, Putnam). Putnam Pub Group.

--Feet. LC 83-13863. (Animals of Course! Ser.). (Illus.). 14p. (gr. k-1). 1984. 3.95 (ISBN 0-399-21029-6, Putnam). Putnam Pub Group.

--Mouths. LC 83-13840. (Animals of Course! Ser.). (Illus.). 14p. (gr. k). 1984. 3.95 (ISBN 0-399-21028-8, Putnam). Putnam Pub Group.

--Noses. LC 83-13694. (Animals of Course! Ser.). (Illus.). 14p. (gr. k-1). 1984. 3.95 (ISBN 0-399-21027-X, Putnam). Putnam Pub Group.

Bailey, Jocelyn. The Village Blacksmith. (Shire Album Ser.: No. 24). (Illus.). 32p. 1985. pap. 3.50 (ISBN 0-85263-511-7, Pub. by Shire Pubns England). Seven Hills Bks.

--The Village Wheelwright & Carpenter. (Shire Album Ser.: No. 11). 1985. pap. 3.50 (ISBN 0-85263-394-7, Pub. by Shire Pubns England). Seven Hills Bks.

Bailey, Joe. Ideas & Intervention: Social Theory for Practice. 1980. 26.95x (ISBN 0-7100-0367-6). Routledge & Kegan.

Bailey, John. Dr. Johnson & His Circle. 1913. Repr. 15.00 (ISBN 0-8274-2198-2). R West.

--Milton. 1979. 32.50 (ISBN 0-685-94334-8). Porter.

--Shakespeare. LC 73-12901. 1978. Repr. of 1929 ed. lib. bdg. 20.00 (ISBN 0-8414-6331-X). Folcroft.

--Some Political Ideas & Persons. 1973. Repr. of 1921 ed. 10.00 (ISBN 0-8274-1488-9). R West.

--Some Political Ideas & Persons: Queen Victoria, Disraeli, Lord Grey. 252p. 1984. Repr. of 1921 ed. lib. bdg. 25.00 (ISBN 0-89760-971-9). Telegraph Bks.

--Walt Whitman. LC 74-131615. 1970. Repr. of 1926 ed. 11.00 (ISBN 0-403-00502-7). Scholarly.

Bailey, John & McLeish, Kenneth. Gods & Men: Myths & Legends from the World's Religions. (Illus.). 160p. 1982. 11.95 (ISBN 0-19-278020-4, Pub. by Oxford U Pr Childrens). Merrimack Pub Cir.

Bailey, John, ed. Great Cartoons of the World: Fifth Series. (Illus.). 144p. (YA) 1971. 5.95 (ISBN 0-517-50719-6). Crown.

--Shakespeare Engravings Taken from the Twenty Drawings by Henry William Bunbury. 1978. 425.00x (ISBN 0-686-79151-7, Pub. by Ariel Pr). State Mutual Bk.

Bailey, John A. & Deverall, Brian J. The Dynamics of Host Defence. LC 83-70713. 233p. 1983. 33.00 (ISBN 0-12-073460-5). Acad Pr.

Bailey, John A. & Mansfield, John W. Phytoalexins. LC 81-13192. 256p. 1982. 79.95x (ISBN 0-470-27291-0). Halsted Pr.

Bailey, John C. Claims of French Poetry: Nine Studies in the Greater French Poets. facs. ed. LC 67-30195. (Essay Index Reprint Ser). 1909. 18.00 (ISBN 0-8369-0168-1). Ayer Co Pubs.

--Continuity of Letters. facs. ed. LC 67-30173. (Essay Index Reprint Ser). 1923. 18.00 (ISBN 0-8369-0169-X). Ayer Co Pubs.

--Dr. Johnson & His Circle. LC 76-9063. 1976. Repr. of 1913 ed. lib. bdg. 15.00 (ISBN 0-8414-3338-0). Folcroft.

--English Elegies. 236p. 1980. Repr. of 1900 ed. lib. bdg. 30.00 (ISBN 0-8495-0451-1). Arden Lib.

--English Elegies. LC 76-14450. 1976. Repr. of 1900 ed. lib. bdg. 30.00 (ISBN 0-8414-3342-9). Folcroft.

--Introduction to Jane Austen. LC 74-13375. 1931. lib. bdg. 15.00 (ISBN 0-8414-3255-4). Folcroft.

--Introductions to Jane Austen. 147p. 1980. Repr. of 1931 ed. lib. bdg. 25.00 (ISBN 0-8495-0456-2). Arden Lib.

--Milton. 256p. 1980. Repr. of 1945 ed. lib. bdg. 20.00 (ISBN 0-8495-0463-5). Arden Lib.

--Milton. LC 73-12210. 1973. lib. bdg. 17.50 (ISBN 0-8414-3218-X). Folcroft.

--Poets & Poetry: Being Articles Reprinted from the Literary Supplement of 'The Times' facs. ed. LC 67-30196. (Essay Index Reprint Ser). 1911. 16.00 (ISBN 0-8369-0170-3). Ayer Co Pubs.

--Shakespeare. 208p. 1980. Repr. of 1929 ed. lib. bdg. 20.00 (ISBN 0-8482-3419-7). Norwood Edns.

--Shakespeare. 208p. 1980. Repr. of 1929 ed. lib. bdg. 15.00 (ISBN 0-8492-3584-7). R West.

Bailey, John K. San Francisco Insider's Guide: A Unique Guide to Bay Area Restaurants, Bars, Best Bets, Bargains, Sex & Sensuality & More... 224p. 1980. pap. 4.95 (ISBN 0-936816-00-7). Non Stop Bks.

--San Francisco Insider's Guide: A Unique Guide to Bay Area Restaurants, Bars, Best Bets, Bargains, the Outdoors & More... 2nd, rev. ed. LC 84-60548. 160p. 1984. pap. 4.95 (ISBN 0-936816-04-X). Non Stop Bks.

Bailey, John W. Pacifying the Plains: General Alfred Terry & the Decline of the Sioux, 1866-1890. LC 78-19300. (Contributions in Military History Ser.: No. 17). 1979. lib. bdg. 27.50x (ISBN 0-313-20625-2, BAT/). Greenwood.

Bailey, Joseph C. Seaman A. Knapp: Schoolmaster of American Agriculture. LC 73-165702. (American Education, Ser. 2). 1971. Repr. of 1945 ed. 17.00 (ISBN 0-405-03691-4). Ayer Co Pubs.

Bailey, Joyce & Dash, Michael. Picture the People of the Caribbean. (Illus., Orig.). 1977. pap. 2.95 (ISBN 0-377-00065-5). Friend Pr.

Bailey, Joyce W. Handbook of Latin American Art: The Colonial Period, Vol. 2. 800p. 1985. lib. bdg. 75.00 (ISBN 0-87436-389-6). ABC-Clio.

Bailey, Joyce W., et al, eds. Handbook of Latin American Art, Bibliographic Compilation: General References & Art of the 19th & 20th Centuries, North America, 2 pts, Vol. I, Pt. I. LC 83-26656. 579p. 1984. lib. bdg. 75.00 (ISBN 0-87436-384-5). ABC-Clio.

--Handbook of Latin American Art, Bibliographic Compilation: General References & Art of the 19th & 20th Centuries, South America 2 pts, Vol. 1, Pt 2. LC 83-26656. 616p. 1984. lib. bdg. 75.00 (ISBN 0-87436-385-3). ABC-Clio.

Bailey, June T. & Claus, Karen E. Decision Making in Nursing: Tools for Change. LC 74-28268. 168p. 1975. pap. text ed. 14.95 (ISBN 0-8016-0422-2). Mosby.

Bailey, June T., jt. auth. see Claus, Karen E.

Bailey, K. M. Christ's Coming & His Kingdom. LC 80-70733. 175p. 1981. pap. 4.95 (ISBN 0-87509-296-9); Leader's Guide. 2.95 (ISBN 0-87509-309-4). Chr Pubns.

Bailey, Katherine, jt. auth. see Mayer, Gloria G.

Bailey, Kathleen, et al, eds. Foreign Teaching Assistants in U. S. Universities. 144p. (Orig.). 1984. pap. text ed. 8.50 (ISBN 0-912207-03-5); members 5.50. Natl Assn Foreign Students.

Bailey, Keith M. Aprender a Vivir: Learning to Live. Bucher, Dorothy, tr. 125p. (Span.). 1980. 1.50 (ISBN 0-87509-299-3). Chr Pubns.

--As Many As Possible. 173p. 1979. 1.95 (ISBN 0-87509-260-8). Chr Pubns.

--The Children's Bread. LC 77-83941. 1977. kivar cover 4.95 (ISBN 0-87509-233-0). Chr Pubns.

--Learning to Live. 64p. (Orig.). 1978. pap. 0.95 (ISBN 0-87509-158-X). Chr Pubns.

--Servants in Charge. 123p. 1979. pap. 2.95 (ISBN 0-87509-160-1); Leader's Guide. 0.95 (ISBN 0-87509-261-6). Chr Pubns.

Bailey, Kenneth. The Cross & the Prodigal. LC 72-90957. 176p. 1973. pap. 5.25 (ISBN 0-570-03139-7, 12-2523). Concordia.

--Enciclopedia Infantil Molino. 234p. (Espn.). 1973. 53.95 (ISBN 84-272-5906-9, S-22860). French & Eur.

--Enciclopedia Juvenil Molino en Color, 5 vols. 510p. (Espn.). 1972. Set. leatherette 65.00 (ISBN 84-272-5900-X, S-22861). French & Eur.

Bailey, Kenneth D. Methods of Social Research. LC 77-6938. (Illus.). 1978. text ed. 17.95 (ISBN 0-02-901250-3). Free Pr.

Bailey, Kenneth E. Poet & Peasant. Bd. with Through Peasant Eyes. 448p. 1983. pap. 12.95 (ISBN 0-8028-1947-8). Eerdmans.

Bailey, Kenneth K. Southern White Protestantism in the Twentieth Century. 15.50 (ISBN 0-8446-1035-6). Peter Smith.

Bailey, L. H. The Cultivated Conifers in North America: Comprising the Pine Family & the Taxads. (Landmark Reprints in Plant Science). 1933. text ed. 27.00x (ISBN 0-86598-007-1). Allanheld.

Bailey, L. R. Indian Slave Trade in the Southwest: A Study of Slave-Taking & the Traffic in Indian Captives from 1700-1935. LC 66-2888. (Illus.). 9.95 (ISBN 0-87026-028-6). Westernlore.

Bailey, Larry J. Career Education for Teachers & Counselors: A Practical Approach. 1985. write for info. Carroll Pr.

Bailey, Leaonead P., ed. Broadside Authors & Artists. 1974. 9.95 (ISBN 0-685-42549-5). Broadside.

Bailey, Lee. Lee Bailey's City Food: Recipes for Good Food & Easy Living. (Illus.). 18.95 (ISBN 0-517-55154-3, C N Potter Bks). Crown.

--Lee Bailey's Country Flowers: Gardening & Bouquets from Spring to Fall. 176p. 1985. 19.95 (ISBN 0-517-55674-X). Crown.

--Lee Bailey's Country Weekends. 1983. 18.95 (ISBN 0-517-54880-1, C N Potter Bks). Crown.

Bailey, Lee, jt. ed. see Biklen, Douglas.

Bailey, Leo L. A Step-by-Step Guide to Landscaping & Gardening. LC 74-84421. 1974. 12.50 (ISBN 0-682-48084-3, Banner). Exposition Pr FL.

Bailey, Leslie. Honey Bee Pathology. LC 81-68981. 1982. 26.50 (ISBN 0-12-073480-X). Acad Pr.

Bailey, Leslie E., jt. ed. see Shibata, Shoji.

Bailey, Liberty H. Cyclopedia of American Horticulture, 6 vols. Set. lib. bdg. 600.00 (ISBN 0-87968-247-7). Gordon Pr.

--The Holy Earth. 59.95 (ISBN 0-8490-0369-5). Gordon Pr.

--The Holy Earth. LC 80-27854. (Illus.). 124p. 1980. pap. 4.95x (ISBN 0-9605314-6-7). NY St Coll Ag.

--Hortus Third: A Concise Dictionary of Plants Cultivated in the United States & Canada. (Illus.). 1976. 125.00 (ISBN 0-02-505470-8). Macmillan.

--How Plants Get Their Names. (Illus.). 1933. pap. 3.95 (ISBN 0-486-20796-X). Dover.

--How Plants Get Their Names. LC 73-30611. 1975. Repr. of 1933 ed. 30.00x (ISBN 0-8103-3763-0). Gale.

--How Plants Get Their Names. (Illus.). 12.75 (ISBN 0-8446-1574-9). Peter Smith.

--Manual of Cultivated Plants. rev. ed. 1949. 37.95 (ISBN 0-02-505520-8). Macmillan.

--Pruning Manual. Christopher, E. P., rev. by. 1954. 15.95 (ISBN 0-02-525420-0). Macmillan.

--Sketch of the Evolution of Our Native Fruits. LC 72-89072. (Rural America Ser.). 1973. Repr. of 1898 ed. 36.00 (ISBN 0-8420-1473-X). Scholarly Res Inc.

Bailey, Liberty H., et al, eds. Cyclopedia of American Agriculture: A Popular Survey of Agricultural Conditions, Practices & Ideals in the United States & Canada - Vol. 2, Crops Fourth Edition. facsimile ed. LC 74-30617. (American Farmers & the Rise of Agribusiness Ser.). (Illus.). 1975. Repr. of 1912 ed. 65.00x (ISBN 0-405-06762-3). Ayer Co Pubs.

Bailey, Linda J. How to Get Going When You Can Barely Get Out of Bed. 184p. 1984. 13.95 (ISBN 0-13-407312-6); pap. 6.95 (ISBN 0-13-407304-5). P-H.

Bailey, Lloyd R. The Pentateuch. LC 81-4495. (Interpreting Biblical Texts Ser.). 160p. (Orig.). 1981. pap. 8.75 (ISBN 0-687-30610-8). Abingdon.

--The Word of God: A Guide to English Versions of the Bible. LC 81-85335. 228p. 1982. 4.75 (ISBN 0-8042-0079-3). John Knox.

Bailey, Lloyd R., ed. see Fretheim, Terence E.

Bailey, Lloyd R., ed. see Murphy, Roland E.

Bailey, Lloyd R., Sr. Biblical Perspectives on Death, No. 5. Brueggemann, Walter & Donahue, John R., eds. LC 78-145661. (Overtures to Biblical Theology Ser.). 180p. 1978. pap. 8.95 (ISBN 0-8006-1530-1, 1-1530). Fortress.

Bailey, Lorraine H. Time to Spare. (Gregg-McGraw-Hill Series for Independent Living). 1978. pap. text ed. 9.60 (ISBN 0-07-003223-8). McGraw.

Bailey, Louise H. From Rockhill to Connemara: The Story Before Carl Sandburg. (Illus.). 48p. 1980. pap. 2.95 (ISBN 0-915992-14-0). Eastern Acorn.

Bailey, Lynn. Bisbee: Queen of the Copper Camps. (Illus.). 1983p. 1983. 20.00 (ISBN 0-87026-058-8). Westernlore.

Bailey, Lynn R. Bosque Redondo: A Study of Cultural Stress at the Navajo Reservation, 1863-1868. (Illus.). 275p. 8.50 (ISBN 0-87026-043-X). Westernlore.

--From Adze to Vermilion: A Bibliography of Writings on Historic Sites Archaeology. LC 68-29144. (Illus.). 250p. 12.00 (ISBN 0-686-74354-7). Westernlore.

--If You Take My Sheep... The Evolution & Conflicts of Navajo Pastoralism, 1630-1868. (Illus.). 304p. 12.00 (ISBN 0-87026-050-2). Westernlore.

--The Long Walk: A History of the Navajo Wars, 1846-1868. (Illus.). 300p. 1979. 9.95 (ISBN 0-87026-047-2). Westernlore.

Bailey, M. J. National Income & the Price Level: A Study in Macroeconomic Theory. 2nd ed. 1970. text ed. 43.95 (ISBN 0-07-003221-1). McGraw.

Bailey, M. R. British Railway Headcodes. pap. 4.00x (ISBN 0-392-15733-0, SpS). Sportshelf.

Bailey, M. Thomas. Reconstruction in Indian Territory. LC 77-189551. 1972. 18.50x (ISBN 0-8046-9022-7, PUb. by Kennikat). Assoc Faculty Pr.

Bailey, Margaret. Those Glorious Glamour Years. (Illus.). 384p. 1983. pap. 12.95 (ISBN 0-8065-0860-4). Citadel Pr.

Bailey, Margaret B., ed. Alcoholism & Family Casework Theory Practice. 176p. 1970. pap. 4.00 (ISBN 0-318-15287-8). Natl Coun Alcoholism.

Bailey, Margaret E. Wild Streak. facsimile ed. LC 72-106245. (Short Story Index Reprint Ser.). 1932. 18.00 (ISBN 0-8369-3281-1). Ayer Co Pubs.

Bailey, Margaret J. Those Glorious Glamour Years: The Great Hollywood Costume Designs of the Thirties. (Illus.). 352p. 1982. 25.00 (ISBN 0-8065-0784-5). Citadel Pr.

Bailey, Margaret L. Milton & Jakob Boehme. LC 65-15885. (Studies in Comparative Literature, No. 35). 1969. Repr. of 1914 ed. lib. bdg. 39.95x (ISBN 0-8383-0505-9). Haskell.

Bailey, Margery, ed. see Boswell, James.

Bailey, Marilyn. Index to Southern Wisconsin: A History of Old Crawford County, 1932. 59p. 1983. pap. 8.00 (ISBN 0-910255-41-5). Wisconsin Gen.

Bailey, Marilyn J. Index to "History of Southeastern Wisconsin-Old Milwaukee Country" 1932. 67p. 1984. pap. 8.50 (ISBN 0-910255-43-1). Wisconsin Gen.

Bailey, Marilyn J. & Wisconsin State Dept. of Transportation. Index to Racine: Belle City of the Lakes & Racine County, Wis., Ill., 1916. 33p. (Orig.). 1983. pap. text ed. 5.00 (ISBN 0-910255-40-7). Wisconsin Gen.

Bailey, Mark N. Electricity. LC 77-27324. (Read about Science Ser.). (Illus.). 48p. (gr. 2-5). 1983. pap. 9.27g (ISBN 0-8393-0293-2). Raintree Pubs.

Bailey, Mark W. Electricity. LC 77-27324. (Read About Science). (Illus.). (gr. k-3). 1978. PLB 13.31 (ISBN 0-8393-0085-9). Raintree Pubs.

Bailey, Martha J. The Special Librarian As a Supervisor or Middle Manager. LC 77-5021. (SLA State-of-the-Art Review Ser.: No. 6). 46p. 1977. pap. 6.00 (ISBN 0-87111-249-3). SLA.

--Supervisory & Middle Managers in Libraries. LC 80-23049. 218p. 1981. 15.00 (ISBN 0-8108-1400-5). Scarecrow.

Bailey, Martin. Union of Tanganyika & Zanzibar: A Study in Political Integration. (Foreign & Comparative Studies Program, Eastern African Ser.: No.9). 114p. 1973. pap. 5.50x (ISBN 0-915984-06-7). Syracuse U Foreign Comp.

Bailey, Martin J. Reducing Risks to Life: Measurement of the Benefits. 1980. pap. 4.25 (ISBN 0-8447-3346-6). Am Enterprise.

Bailey, Martin J., jt. ed. see Harberger, Arnold C.

Bailey, Mary Frances, jt. auth. see Bailey, Robert.

Bailey, Moses. The Prophetic Word: Ancient & Modern. (FGC). 109p. 1968. 0.75 (ISBN 0-318-14152-3). Friends Genl Conf.

Bailey, N. Louise, ed. Biographical Directory of the South Carolina House of Representatives, Vol. IV, 1791-1815. LC 73-13630. 800p. 1984. 24.95x (ISBN 0-87249-439-X). U of SC Pr.

Bailey, N. Louise & Cooper, Elizabeth I., eds. Biographical Directory of the South Carolina House of Representatives: 1775-1790, Vol. 3. 780p. 1981. text ed. 14.95x (ISBN 0-87249-406-3). U of SC Pr.

Bailey, N. Louise, jt. ed. see Edgar, Walter.

Bailey, N. T. J. The Biomathematics of Diseases: The Biomathematics of Malaria. (No. 1). 224p. 1982. 88.00x (ISBN 0-85264-266-0, Pub. by Griffin England). State Mutual Bk.

Bailey, Nathan. Universal Etymological English Dictionary. 1969. Repr. of 1721 ed. 100.00x (ISBN 3-4870-2625-2). Adlers Foreign Bks.

Bailey, Nevajac see Weikel, Bill.

Bailey, Ney. Faith Is Not a Feeling. LC 78-60077. 1979. pap. 4.95 (ISBN 0-918956-45-5). Campus Crusade.

Bailey, Norman & Feder, Stuart. Operational Conflict Analysis. 1973. 9.00 (ISBN 0-8183-0145-7). Pub Aff Pr.

Bailey, Norman T. Elements of Stochastic Processes with Applications to the Natural Sciences: Applied Probability & Statistics Section. LC 63-23220. (Probability & Mathematical Statistics Ser.). 249p. 1964. 45.95x (ISBN 0-471-04165-3, Pub. by Wiley-Interscience). Wiley.

--Mathematics, Statistics & Systems for Health. LC 77-1307. (Wiley Series Probability & Mathematical Statistics: Applied Probability & Statistics). 222p. 1977. 48.95x (ISBN 0-471-99500-2, Pub. by Wiley-Interscience). Wiley.

Bailey, Norman T. J., ed. Statistical Methods in Biology. 2nd ed. LC 80-15774. (Biological Science Text Ser.). 216p. 1981. pap. 12.95x (ISBN 0-470-27006-3). Halsted Pr.

Bailey, Patrick. Orkney. 2nd ed. (Islands Ser.). (Illus.). 248p. 1985. 18.95 (ISBN 0-7153-8655-7). David & Charles.

Bailey, Paul. City in the Sun: The Japanese Concentration Camp at Poston, Arizona. (Illus.). 1979. 8.95 (ISBN 0-87026-026-X). Westernlore.

--Ghost Dance Messiah: The Jack Wilson Story. LC 75-135152. 8.50 (ISBN 0-87026-025-1). Westernlore.

--Hawaii's Royal Prime Minister: The Life & Times of Walter Murray Gibson. (Illus.). 320p. 1980. 13.95 (ISBN 0-8038-3058-0). Hastings.

--Holy Smoke: A Dissertation on the Utah War. (Great West & Indian Ser.: Vol. 44). (Illus.). 1977. 8.95 (ISBN 0-87026-037-5). Westernlore.

--Polygamy Was Better Than Monotony: To My Grandfathers & Their Plural Wives. LC 72-83538. (Illus.). 8.95 (ISBN 0-87026-027-8). Westernlore.

--Those Kings & Queens of Old Hawaii: A Mele to Their Memory. LC 75-259. (Illus.). 381p. 1975. 20.00 (ISBN 0-87026-035-9). Westernlore.

--An Unnatural History of Death Valley: With Reflections on the Valley's Varmints, Virgins, Vandals & Visionaries. (Illus.). 1978. pap. 3.95 (ISBN 0-912494-31-X). Chalfant Pr.

--Vanishing Novelist. 1990. price not set (ISBN 0-670-80476-2). Viking.

Bailey, Paul B., et al. Nonlinear Two Point Boundary Value Problems. (Mathematics in Science & Engineering Ser.: Vol. 4). 1968. 49.50 (ISBN 0-12-073350-1). Acad Pr.

Bailey, Paul C., tr. see Rudin, Josef.

Bailey, Paul D. An Unnatural History of Death Valley. (Illus.). 84p. 1978. wrappers 3.95 (ISBN 0-912494-31-X). Death Valley Fortyniners.

Bailey, Paul J., tr. see Bastid, Marianne.

Bailey, Pearl. Duey's Tale. LC 74-22278. (Illus.). 59p. 1975. 8.95 (ISBN 0-15-126576-3). HarBraceJ.

--Pearl's Kitchen. LC 73-6624. 1973. 8.95 (ISBN 0-15-171600-5). HarBraceJ.

--The Raw Pearl. LC 67-11963. 1968. 9.50 (ISBN 0-15-175930-8). HarBraceJ.

--Talking to Myself. LC 78-153679. 233p. 1971. 7.95 (ISBN 0-15-187990-7). HarBraceJ.

Bailey, Percival. Intracranial Tumors. 2nd ed. (Illus.). 524p. 1948. photocopy ed. 50.50x (ISBN 0-398-04197-0). C C Thomas.

Bailey, Percival & Cushing, Harvey. Classification of the Tumors of the Glioma Group on a Histogenetic Basis with a Correlated Study of Prognosis. (Illus.). 1970. Repr. of 1926 ed. 15.00. Argosy.

Bailey, Percival, jt. auth. see Cushing, Harvey.

Bailey, Peter. Analysis with Ion-Selective Electrodes. 2nd ed. (Heyden International Topics in Science Ser.). 264p. 1980. 34.95 (ISBN 0-471-25590-4, Pub. by Wiley Heyden). Wiley.

Bailey, Peter J. Reading Stanley Elkin. LC 84-8735. 240p. 1985. 18.95x (ISBN 0-252-01172-4). U of Ill Pr.

Bailey, Philip, ed. Ozonation in Organic Chemistry: Nonolefinic Compounds, Vol. 2. LC 81-19096. 1982. 75.00 (ISBN 0-12-073102-9). Acad Pr.

Bailey, Philip S. Ozone Reactions with Organic Compounds: A Symposium Sponsored by the Division of Petroleum Chemistry at the 161st Meeting of the American Chemical Society, Los Angeles, California, March 29-30, 1971. LC 75-88560. (American Chemical Society Advances in Chemistry Ser.: Vol. 112). pap. 35.30 (ISBN 0-317-26313-7, 20204237). Bks Demand UMI.

Bailey, Philip S. & Bailey, Christina A. Organic Chemistry: A Brief Survey of Concepts & Applications. 3rd ed. 1985. text ed. 34.30 (ISBN 0-205-08195-9, 688195); net 14.29 (ISBN 0-205-08197-5, 688197); study guide avail. Allyn.

Bailey, Phillip. They Can Make Music. (Illus.). 1973. 8.95x (ISBN 0-19-311913-7). Oxford U Pr.

Bailey, Phyllis C. Fascinating Facts about the Spirit of Prophecy. 64p. pap. 2.95 (ISBN 0-317-01322-X). Review & Herald.

Bailey, R. The European Connection: Britain's Relationship with the European Community. (Illus.). 250p. 1983. 28.00 (ISBN 0-08-026775-0); pap. 12.50 (ISBN 0-08-026774-2). Pergamon.

Bailey, R., jt. auth. see Foren, R.

Bailey, R. A., et al. Introduction to the Chemistry of the Environment. 1979. 59.50 (ISBN 0-12-073050-2). Acad Pr.

Bailey, R. T., et al. Molecular Motion in High Polymers. (International Series of Monographs on Chemistry). (Illus.). 1981. text ed. 69.00x (ISBN 0-19-851333-X). Oxford U Pr.

Bailey, R. W., ed. Computing in the Humanities: Fifth International Conference on Computing in the Humanities, Ann Arbor, Michigan. 192p. 1982. 42.75 (ISBN 0-444-86423-7, I-298-82, North-Holland). Elsevier.

Bailey, R. W., jt. ed. see Butler, G. W.

Bailey, R. W., et al, eds. Sign: Semiotics Around the World. (Michigan Slavic Contributions Ser.: No. 9). 1980. 10.00 (ISBN 0-930042-39-5). Mich Slavic Pubns.

Bailey, Ralph, ed. House & Garden's Gardener's Day Book. LC 65-21771. (Illus.). 448p. 1965. 7.50 (ISBN 0-87131-008-2). M Evans.

Bailey, Ralph S. & McDonald, Elvin, eds. Good Housekeeping Basic Gardening Techniques. new ed. LC 74-79036. (Illus.). 320p. 1974. 10.95 (ISBN 0-87851-201-2). Hearst Bks.

Bailey, Raymond. Thomas Merton on Mysticism. LC 74-32570. 280p. 1976. pap. 1.95 (ISBN 0-385-12071-0, Im). Doubleday.

Bailey, Raymond C. Popular Influence upon Public Policy: Petitioning in Eighteenth-Century Virginia. LC 78-73792. (Contributions in Legal Studies Ser.: No. 10). (Illus.). xii, 203p. 1979. lib. bdg. 29.95x (ISBN 0-313-20892-1, BPP/). Greenwood.

Bailey, Rebecca A. & Burton, Elsie C. The Dynamic Self: Activities to Enhance Infant Development. LC 81-11220. (Illus.). 195p. 1982. pap. text ed. 14.95 (ISBN 0-8016-0438-9). Mosby.

Bailey, Richard. Energy: The Rude Awakening. LC 77-89057. 1978. 12.95 (ISBN 0-918998-03-4). Energy Educ.

Bailey, Richard B. Pilgrim-Possessions-Sixteen Twenty to Sixteen-Forty. (Pilgrim Society Notes Ser.: No. 7). 1957. 1.00 (ISBN 0-940628-29-5). Pilgrim Hall.

Bailey, Richard C. Heart of the Golden Empire: An Illustrated History of Bakersfield. (Illus.). 160p. 1984. 22.95 (ISBN 0-89781-065-1). Windsor Pubns Inc.

Bailey, Richard D. Estate Planning: A Workbook for Christians. LC 81-14907. 96p. (Orig.). 1982. pap. 6.95 (ISBN 0-687-12004-7). Abingdon.

Bailey, Richard M. Clinical Laboratories & the Practice of Medicine: An Economic Perspective. LC 78-70545. (Health Care Ser.). 1979. 23.00x (ISBN 0-8211-0132-3); text ed. 20.75x in ten or more copies. McCutchan.

Bailey, Richard W. & Robinson, Jay L. Varieties of Present-Day English. (Illus.). 416p. 1973. pap. text ed. write for info. (ISBN 0-02-305200-7, 30520). Macmillan.

Bailey, Richard W. & Fosheim, Robin M., eds. Literacy for Life: The Demand for Reading & Writing. 292p. 1983. 25.00 (ISBN 0-87352-130-7); pap. 14.00 (ISBN 0-87352-131-5). Modern Lang.

Bailey, Richard W. & Gorlach, Manfred, eds. English As a World Language. 480p. 1982. text ed. 29.95x (ISBN 0-472-10016-5); pap. text ed. 14.95x (ISBN 0-472-08048-2). U of Mich Pr.

Bailey, Robert & Bailey, Mary Frances. Coping with Stress in the Minister's Home. LC 79-51135. 1979. 6.95 (ISBN 0-8054-5266-4). Broadman.

Bailey, Robert, ed. Prelude & Transfiguration from Tristan & Isolde. 1985. 25.00x (ISBN 0-393-02207-2). Norton.

--Prelude & Transfiguration from Wagner's Tristan & Isolde. (Critical Scores Ser.). 1985. pap. text ed. 9.95x (ISBN 0-393-95405-6). Norton.

Bailey, Robert, Jr. Radicals in Urban Politics: The Alinsky Approach. LC 73-90938. xii, 188p. 1974. 16.00x (ISBN 0-226-03452-6). U of Chicago Pr.

--Radicals in Urban Politics: The Alinsky Approach. LC 73-90938. (Illus.). xii, 188p. 1976. pap. 3.95x (ISBN 0-226-03453-4, P674, Phoen). U of Chicago Pr.

Bailey, Robert L. The Career Education & Financial Aid Guide. LC 82-1696. 192p. 1982. 12.95 (ISBN 0-668-05289-9); pap. 7.95 (ISBN 0-668-05292-9). Arco.

--Disciplined Creativity for Engineers. 614p. 1982. pap. 19.95 (ISBN 0-250-40615-2). Butterworth.

--An Examination of Prime Time Network Television Special Programs: 1948-1966. Sterling, Christopher H., ed. LC 78-21716. (Dissertations in Broadcasting Ser.). (Illus.). 1979. lib. bdg. 27.50x (ISBN 0-405-11755-8). Ayer Co Pubs.

Bailey, Robert W. The Cervical Spine. LC 79-152020. pap. 67.80 (ISBN 0-317-07772-4, 2055676). Bks Demand UMI.

--The Crisis Regime: The M.A.C., the E.F.C.B. & the Political Impact of the New York City Financial Crisis. 336p. 1984. 39.50x (ISBN 0-87395-850-0); pap. 12.95x (ISBN 0-87395-851-9). State U NY Pr.

--Frost. (Orig.). 1983. pap. 2.75 (ISBN 0-671-45596-6, Timescape). PB.

--Human Error in Computer Systems. (Illus.). 160p. 1983. 21.95 (ISBN 0-13-445056-6). P-H.

--The Joy of Discipleship. LC 81-69402. 1982. pap. 5.95 (ISBN 0-8054-5188-9). Broadman.

--New Ways in Christian Worship. LC 81-65390. 1981. pap. 6.95 (ISBN 0-8054-2311-7). Broadman.

Bailey, Robert W. & Human Performance Associates. Human Performance Engineering: A Guide for System Designers. (Illus.). 672p. 1982. text ed. 44.95 (ISBN 0-13-445320-4); wkbk 9.95 (ISBN 0-13-445338-7). P-H.

Bailey, Robin. Skull Gate. 288p. (Orig.). 1985. pap. 2.95 (ISBN 0-8125-3139-6, Dist. by Warner Pub Services & St. Martin). Tor Bks.

Bailey, Roger B. Guide to Chinese Poetry & Drama. 1973. lib. bdg. 16.00 (ISBN 0-8161-1102-2, Hall Reference). G K Hall.

Bailey, Roger C. & Hankins, Norman E. Psychology of Effective Living. 2nd ed. (Illus.). 421p. 1984. pap. text ed. 15.95x (ISBN 0-88133-088-4). Waveland Pr.

Bailey, Roger C., jt. auth. see Hankins, Norman E.

Bailey, Ronald. The Air War in Europe. LC 78-2937. (World War II Ser.). (Illus.). (gr. 7 up). 1979. lib. bdg. 22.60 (ISBN 0-8094-2495-9, Pub. by Time-Life). Silver.

--Air War in Europe. (World War II Ser.). 1979. 14.95 (ISBN 0-8094-2494-0). Time-Life.

--Battles for Atlanta. (The Civil War Ser.). (YA) (gr. 7 up). 1986. lib. bdg. 19.94 (Pub. by Time-Life). Silver.

--The Bloodiest Day. LC 84-8871. (Civil War Ser.). (gr. 7 up). 1984. lib. bdg. 19.94 (ISBN 0-8094-4741-X, Pub. by Time-Life). Silver.

--The Home Front: U. S. A. LC 77-87556. (World War II Ser.). (Illus.). (gr. 7 up). 1977. lib. bdg. 22.60 (ISBN 0-8094-2479-7, Pub. by Time-Life). Silver.

--The Home Front: U. S. A. Time Life Books, ed. (World War II Ser.). (Illus.). 1978. 14.95 (ISBN 0-8094-2478-9). Time-Life.

--Partisans & Guerrillas. LC 78-2949. (World War II Ser.). (Illus.). 1978. lib. bdg. 22.60 (ISBN 0-8094-2491-6). Silver.

--Prisoners of War. 1982. 14.95 (ISBN 0-8094-3391-5). Time-Life.

Bailey, Ronald H. Forward to Richmond! (The Civil War Ser.). (Illus.). 176p. 1983. 14.95 (ISBN 0-8094-4720-7). Time Life.

--The Partisans & Guerrillas. Time-Life Books, ed. (World War II Ser.). 1978. 14.95 (ISBN 0-8094-2490-8). Time-Life.

Bailey, Rosemary E. & Grayshon, Jane. Obstetric & Gynaecological Nursing. 3rd ed. 344p. 1983. pap. 9.95 (ISBN 0-7216-0802-7, Pub. by Bailliere-Tindall). Saunders.

Bailey, Ross R. Single Dose Therapy of Tract Infection. 125p. 1983. pap. 18.00 (ISBN 0-683-10007-6). Williams & Wilkins.

Bailey, Roy & Brake, Mike, eds. Radical Social Work. LC 76-12937. 1976. reinforced bdg. 5.95 (ISBN 0-394-73265-0). Pantheon.

Bailey, Ruth. Shelley. LC 74-1442. 1934. lib. bdg. 12.50 (ISBN 0-8414-9910-1). Folcroft.

Bailey, S. W., ed. Micas. (Reviews in Mineralogy: Vol. 13). 584p. 1984. 13.00 (ISBN 0-939950-17-0). Mineralogical Soc.

Bailey, Samuel. Critical Dissertation on the Nature, Measure & Causes of Value. LC 65-26359. Repr. of 1825 ed. 45.00x (ISBN 0-678-00223-1). Kelley.

Bailey, Sandra B. Big Book of Baby Names & Announcements. 288p. 1983. pap. 4.95 (ISBN 0-89586-295-6). H P Bks.

Bailey, Saunders. The Life & Letters of James Macpherson. 1979. Repr. of 1894 ed. lib. bdg. 30.00 (ISBN 0-89760-814-3, Telegraph). Dynamic Learn Corp.

Bailey, Shackleton, ed. Harvard Studies in Classical Philology, Vol. 84. LC 44-32100. 1981. text ed. 30.00x (ISBN 0-674-37931-4). Harvard U Pr.

Bailey, Shackleton D., ed. Harvard Studies in Classical Philology, Vol. 89. 240p. 1985. text ed. 32.50x (ISBN 0-674-37936-5). Harvard U Pr.

Bailey, Sherwin. Canonical Houses of Wells. 192p. 1982. text ed. 21.75x (ISBN 0-904387-91-7, Pub. by Alan Sutton England). Humanities.

Bailey, Stephen. The Purposes of Education. LC 75-15300. (Foundation Monograph Ser.). xvii, 142p. 1976. 10.00 (ISBN 0-87367-408-1); pap. 5.00 (ISBN 0-87367-414-6). Phi Delta Kappa.

--The Purposes of Education. 142p. 1976. 10.00 (ISBN 0-87367-408-1); members 8.00 (ISBN 0-317-35578-3); 5.00, paper (ISBN 0-87367-414-6); members 4.00 (ISBN 0-317-35579-1). Phi Delta Kappa.

Bailey, Stephen K. Congress Makes a Law: The Story Behind the Employment Act of 1946. LC 80-12550. xii, 282p. 1980. Repr. of 1950 ed. lib. bdg. 27.50x (ISBN 0-313-22407-2, BACK). Greenwood.

Bailey, Stephen K. & Mosher, Edith K. ESEA: The Office of Education Administers a Law. LC 68-27692. 1968. text ed. 11.95x (ISBN 0-8156-2121-3). Syracuse U Pr.

Bailey, Stephen K., et al. Research Frontiers in Politics & Government. LC 72-7820. 240p. 1973. Repr. of 1947 ed. lib. bdg. 22.50 (ISBN 0-8371-6527-X, BARF). Greenwood.

Bailey, Sturges M. History of Columbia County, Wisconsin, Illnois, 1914: Index. 27p. (Orig.). 1982. pap. 5.00 (ISBN 0-910255-35-0). Wisconsin Gen.

Bailey, Sturges W. Index to a Standard History of Sauk County Wisconsin, 1918. (Illus.). 55p. (Orig.). 1983. pap. text ed. 8.00 (ISBN 0-910255-39-3). Wisconsin Gen.

--Index to Portrait & Biographical Album of Green Lake, Marquette, & Waushara Cos., Wis., 1890. (Illus.). 44p. (Orig.). 1983. pap. text ed. 6.50 (ISBN 0-910255-38-5). Wisconsin Gen.

Bailey, Sturges W., ed. see International Clay Conference, 1975.

Bailey, Sue, ed. see Polley, Louis E.

Bailey, Susan F. Women & the British Empire: An Annotated Guide to Sources. LC 82-49161. 200p. 1983. lib. bdg. 46.00 (ISBN 0-8240-9162-0). Garland Pub.

Bailey, Sydney D. British Parliamentary Democracy. 3rd ed. LC 77-18752. (Illus.). 1978. Repr. of 1971 ed. lib. bdg. 19.75x (ISBN 0-313-20195-1, BABR). Greenwood.

--The General Assembly of the United Nations: A Study of Procedure & Practice. rev. ed. LC 78-2810. (Carnegie Endowment for International Peace, United Nations Studies: No. 9). (Illus.). 1978. Repr. of 1964 ed. lib. bdg. 35.00x (ISBN 0-313-20336-9, BAGA). Greenwood.

--How Wars End: The United Nations & the Termination of Armed Conflict, 1946-1964, 2 vols. 400p. 1982. Vol. I, 89.00x (ISBN 0-19-827424-6); Vol. II, 98.00x (ISBN 0-19-827462-9). Oxford U Pr.

--The Making of Resolution 242. 1985. lib. bdg. 45.00 (ISBN 90-247-3073-2, Pub. by Martinus Nijhoff Netherlands). Kluwer Academic.

--The Procedure of the U. N. Security Council. (Illus.). 1975. 47.50x (ISBN 0-19-827199-9). Oxford U Pr.

--The Secretariat of the United Nations. LC 78-2880. (Carnegie Endowment for International Studies: No. 11). 1978. Repr. of 1964 ed. lib. bdg. 19.75 (ISBN 0-313-20338-5, BASU). Greenwood.

--Voting in the Security Council. LC 69-15990. Repr. of 1969 ed. 54.20 (ISBN 0-8357-9252-8, 2013017). Bks Demand UMI.

Bailey, Sydney D., ed. Political Parties & the Party System in Britain: A Symposium. LC 78-14099. 1979. Repr. of 1952 ed. 21.75 (ISBN 0-88355-773-8). Hyperion Conn.

Bailey, T. E. & Lundgaard, Kris. Program Design with Pseudocode. LC 82-17802. (Computer Science Ser.). 160p. 1983. pap. text ed. 10.00 pub net (ISBN 0-534-01361-9). Brooks-Cole.

--Program Design with Pseudocode. 2nd ed. 200p. 1985. pap. 13.50 (ISBN 0-534-05574-5). Brooks-Cole.

Bailey, T. Melville. Hamilton: Chronicle of a City. (Illus.). 184p. 1983. 24.95 (ISBN 0-89781-067-8). Windsor Pubns Inc.

Bailey, Temple. Contrary Mary. 1975. lib. bdg. 17.25x (ISBN 0-89966-009-6). Buccaneer Bks.

--Glory of Youth. 1975. lib. bdg. 15.30x (ISBN 0-89966-010-X). Buccaneer Bks.

--Radiant Tree, & Other Stories. facs. ed. LC 73-116932. (Short Story Index Reprint Ser). 1934. 19.00 (ISBN 0-8369-3434-2). Ayer Co Pubs.

--The Tin Soldier. 1975. lib. bdg. 19.10x (ISBN 0-89966-011-8). Buccaneer Bks.

Bailey, Terence. The Processions of Sarum & the Western Church. (Studies & Texts: No. 21). xvi, 208p. 1971. 22.00 (ISBN 0-88844-021-9). Pontifical Toronto.

Bailey, Thomas A. America Faces Russia. 1964. 11.75 (ISBN 0-8446-1037-2). Peter Smith.

--The American Pageant Revisited: Recollections of a Stanford Historian. LC 81-83069. (Publication Ser.: No. 263). 232p. 1982. 19.95 (ISBN 0-8179-7631-0). Hoover Inst Pr.

--The American Spirit: American History As Seen by Contemporaries, 2 vols. 5th ed. 1984. Vol. 1. pap. text ed. 12.95 (ISBN 0-669-05380-5); Vol. 2. pap. 912.95x (ISBN 0-669-05381-3). Heath.

--Art of Diplomacy: The American Experience. LC 68-11680. 1968. 27.50x (ISBN 0-89197-032-0); pap. text ed. 12.95x (ISBN 0-89197-033-9). Irvington.

--A Diplomatic History of the American People. 10th ed. (Illus.). 1980. text ed. 34.95 (ISBN 0-13-214726-2). P-H.

--Essays Diplomatic & Undiplomatic of Thomas A. Bailey. DeConde, Alexander & Rappaport, Armin, eds. LC 69-17917. (Illus.). 1969. 34.00x (ISBN 0-89197-151-3). Irvington.

--The Man in the Street: The Impact of American Public Opinion on Foreign Policy. 1964. 12.75 (ISBN 0-8446-0015-6). Peter Smith.

--The Marshall Plan Summer: An Eyewitness Report on Europe & the Russians in 1947. LC 77-2433. (Illus.). 250p. 1978. 11.95x (ISBN 0-8179-4201-7). Hoover Inst Pr.

--The Policy of the United States Towards the Neutrals, 1917-1918. 12.75 (ISBN 0-8446-1036-4). Peter Smith.

--Presidential Greatness: The Image & the Man from George Washington to the Present. LC 66-19996. 27.00x (ISBN 0-89197-356-7); pap. text ed. 12.95x (ISBN 0-89197-642-6). Irvington.

--Presidential Saints & Sinners. 288p. 1981. 17.95 (ISBN 0-02-901330-5). Free Pr.

--The Pugnacious Presidents: White House Warriors on Parade. LC 80-1646. (Illus.). 1980. 19.95 (ISBN 0-02-901220-1). Free Pr.

--Voices of America: The Nation's Story in Slogans, Sayings, & Songs. LC 76-8143. 1976. 24.95 (ISBN 0-02-901260-0). Free Pr.

Bailey, Thomas A. & Kennedy, David M. The American Pageant. 7th ed. 1983. lib. bdg. 25.95 case bd. 1020 p. (ISBN 0-669-05270-1); Vol. I, 592 p. lib. bdg. 17.95 (ISBN 0-669-05266-3); Vol. II, 512 p. lib. bdg. 17.95 (ISBN 0-669-05267-1). Heath.

Bailey, Thomas A. & Ryan, Paul B. Hitler vs. Roosevelt: The Undeclared Naval War. LC 78-73023. (Illus.). 1979. 19.95 (ISBN 0-02-901270-8). Free Pr.

--The Lusitania Disaster: An Episode in Modern Warfare & Diplomacy. LC 75-2806. (Illus.). 1975. 14.95 (ISBN 0-02-901240-6). Free Pr.

Bailey, Thomas P. Race Orthodoxy in the South & Other Aspects of the Negro Question. Repr. of 1914 ed. 15.00 (ISBN 0-404-00136-X). AMS Pr.

--Race Orthodoxy in the South, & Other Aspects of the Negro Question. LC 75-88422. Repr. of 1914 ed. 25.00x (ISBN 0-8371-1848-4, BAR&). Greenwood.

Bailey, Thoms A. Probing America's Past: A Critical Examination of Major Myths & Misconceptions, 2 vols. 1973. pap. text ed. 12.95x ea.; Vol. 1. (ISBN 0-669-84350-4); Vol. 2. (ISBN 0-669-84368-7). Heath.

Bailey, Trevor. History of Cricket. (Illus.). 1979. 14.95 (ISBN 0-04-796049-3). Allen Unwin.

Bailey, V. H. Magical City: Intimate Sketches of New York. 1977. lib. bdg. 59.95 (ISBN 0-8490-2196-0). Gordon Pr.

Bailey, Vernon. Animal Life of Yellowstone National Park. (Illus.). 232p. 1930. 19.75x (ISBN 0-398-04198-9). C C Thomas.

Bailey, Vicki, jt. ed. see Huisingh, Donald.

Bailey, Victor, ed. Policing & Punishment in Nineteenth Century Britain. (Crime, Law, & Deviance). 248p. 1981. 25.00x (ISBN 0-8135-0932-7). Rutgers U Pr.

Bailey, Victor B. & Tucker, Joanne. U. S. Foreign Trade Highlights, 1984. (Illus.). 173p. 1985. pap. 6.50 (ISBN 0-318-11741-X). Gov Printing Office.

Bailey, W. N. Generalized Hypergeometric Series. (Cambridge Tracts in Mathematics & Mathematical Physics Ser.: No. 32). 1972. Repr. of 1935 ed. 9.95x (ISBN 0-02-840760-1). Hafner.

Bailey, Walter. A Short Discourse of the Three Kindes of Peppers in Common Use. LC 77-38145. (English Experience Ser.: No. 425). 48p. Repr. of 1588 ed. 7.00 (ISBN 90-221-0425-7). Walter J Johnson.

--Two Treatises Concerning the Perservation of Eye-Sight. LC 74-28827. (English Experience Ser.: No. 709). 1975. Repr. of 1616 ed. 5.00 (ISBN 90-221-0709-4). Walter J Johnson.

Bailey, Walter B. Programmatic Elements in the Works of Schoenberg. Buelow, George, ed. LC 83-18310. (Studies in Musicology: No. 74). 200p. 1984. 39.95 (ISBN 0-8357-1480-2). UMI Res Pr.

Bailey, Waylon. As You Go. LC 81-47888. 118p. (Orig.). 1981. pap. 4.00 (ISBN 0-914520-15-6). Insight Pr.

Bailey, Wayne, jt. auth. see Brown, F. Martin.

Bailey, William. Man, Religion & Science: A Functional View. LC 80-65860. (Illus.). 242p. (Orig.). 1981. pap. 9.95 (ISBN 0-9604196-0-8). W Bailey Pub.

Bailey, William A., et al. Bill Bailey Came Home. LC 73-79904. 183p. 1973. 7.95 (ISBN 0-87421-061-5); pap. 5.95 (ISBN 0-87421-092-5). Utah St U Pr.

Bailey, William C., ed. Pediatric Burns. (Illus.). 1979. 39.95 (ISBN 0-8151-0453-7). Year Bk Med.

Bailey, William J. Managing Self-Renewal in Secondary Education. LC 74-13352. 208p. 1975. 26.95 (ISBN 0-87778-074-9). Educ Tech Pubn.

Bailey, William J. & Guynn, J. Bibliographic Index of Health Education Periodicals (BIHEP) 1980 Cumulative Edition. 428p. 1982. lib. bdg. 75.00x (ISBN 0-941636-00-3). IN U Dept Health.

Bailey, William J. & Guynn, Stephen J. Bibliographic Index of Health Education Periodicals (BIHEP) Vol. 2, 1981 Cumulative Edition. 650p. 1982. lib. bdg. 75.00x (ISBN 0-941636-01-1). IN U Dept Health.

Bailey, William J. & Tsuruta, Teiji, eds. Contemporary Topics in Polymer Science, Vol. 4. 1015p. 1983. 135.00x (ISBN 0-306-41248-9, Plenum Pr). Plenum Pub.

Bailey, William M., jt. auth. see Garrelick, Renee.

Bailey, Zeila, jt. auth. see Gross, Linda.

Bailie, Anne. In the Soul's Riptide. LC 82-4442. (Orig.). 1982. pap. 5.00 (ISBN 0-941608-02-6). Chantry Pr.

Bailie, Richard C. Energy Conversion Engineering. LC 78-11969. (Series of Graduate Textbooks, Monographs & Research Papers). (Illus.). 1978. text ed. 45.95 (ISBN 0-201-00840-8). Addison-Wesley.

Bailie, Victoria W. Bailie's Activities in China. LC 64-17671. (Illus.). 1964. 15.00x (ISBN 0-87015-128-2). Pacific Bks.

Bailie, William. Josiah Warren: The First American Anarchist, a Sociological Study. 69.95 (ISBN 0-87700-024-7). Revisionist Pr.

--Josiah Warren: The First American Anarchist. LC 78-172201. (Right Wing Individualist Tradition in America Ser.). (Illus.). 1972. Repr. of 1906 ed. 14.00 (ISBN 0-405-00411-7). Ayer Co Pubs.

Bailin, D. Weak Interactions. 1982. 26.50 (ISBN 0-9960023-1-6, Pub. by A Hilger England). Heyden.

Bailin, George. Collapsing Spaces, Tilting Times. (Poetry Ser.: No. 11). 48p. (Orig.). 1981. pap. 5.95x (ISBN 0-930020-10-3). Stone Country.

--Counterculture. Friedman, Eric, et al, eds. 1982. pap. 7.50 (ISBN 0-942856-00-7). Seaport Poets & Writers.

--Dead Reckoning. (Illus.). 64p. (Orig.). 1984. pap. 6.00 (ISBN 0-943120-00-4). Dragonsbreath.

Bai-Lin, Hao. Chaos. 586p. 1984. 56.00 (ISBN 9971-966-50-6, Pub. by World Sci Singapore); pap. 26.00x (ISBN 9971-966-51-4, Pub. by World Sci Singapore). Taylor & Francis.

Bailkey, Nels, ed. Readings in Ancient History: From Gilgamesh to Diocletian. 2nd ed. 1977. pap. text ed. 11.95x (ISBN 0-669-00249-6). Heath.

Baillet, Maurice, ed. Qumran Grotte Four, No. III. (Discoveries in the Judean Desert Ser.: Vol. 7). (Illus.). 1982. 140.00x (ISBN 0-19-826321-X). Oxford U Pr.

Bailleul, C. Dictionnaire Bambara-Francais - Francais-Bambara. (Bambara & Fr.). 95.00x (ISBN 0-686-79109-6, Pub. by Avebury Pub England). State Mutual Bk.

Bailleul, Charles. Petit Dictionnaire-Bambara-Francais Francais-Bambara. 339p. (Bambara & Fr.). 1981. text ed. 69.00x (ISBN 0-86127-220-X, Pub. by Avebury England). Humanities.

Bailleul, Pere C. Petit Dictionnaire Bambara-Francais Francais-Bambara. (Bambara & Fr.). 1981. 95.00x (ISBN 0-686-75433-6, 0-86127-220-X, Pub. by Avebury Pub England). State Mutual Bk.

Baillie, A. & Gilbert, R. J., eds. Automation, Mechanization & Data Handling in Microbiology. (Society for Applied Bacteriology Technical Ser.: No. 4). 1970. 41.50 (ISBN 0-12-073650-0). Acad Pr.

Baillie, D. C., jt. auth. see Sheppard, Norris E.

Baillie, Donald M. God Was in Christ. 232p. 1977. pap. 6.50 (ISBN 0-571-05685-7). Faber & Faber.

--God Was in Christ. 1948. (ScribT); lib. bdg. 20.00 lib. rep. ed. (ISBN 0-684-16470-1). Scribner.

--God Was in Christ. 230p. 1980. pap. text ed. price not set (ISBN 0-02-305440-9, Pub. by Scribner). Macmillan.

Baillie, G. H. Clocks & Watches, 2 Vols. 620p. 1981. Vol. 1, 1344-1800. 50.00 (ISBN 0-317-03737-4); Vol. 2, 1800-1899. 50.00 (ISBN 0-317-03738-2); Set. 100.00 (ISBN 0-87556-569-7). Saifer.

Baillie, George. Correspondence of George Baillie of Jerviswood. Earl Of Minto, ed. LC 76-161744. (Bannatyne Club, Edinburgh. Publications: No. 72). Repr. of 1842 ed. 40.00 (ISBN 0-404-52792-2). AMS Pr.

Baillie, Hugh. High Tension. facsimile ed. LC 79-90604. (Essay Index Reprint Ser.). 1959. 26.50 (ISBN 0-8369-1543-7). Ayer Co Pubs.

Baillie, J. B., tr. see Hegel, G. W.

Baillie, J. B., tr. see Hegel, Georg.

Baillie, J. B., tr. see Hegel, Georg W.

Baillie, James B. The Idealistic Construction of Experience. LC 83-48503. (The Philosophy of Hegel Ser.). 364p. 1984. lib. bdg. 45.00 (ISBN 0-8240-5626-4). Garland Pub.

--The Origin & Significance of Hegel's Logic. LC 83-48502. (The Philosophy of Hegel Ser.). 398p. 1984. lib. bdg. 50.00 (ISBN 0-8240-5625-6). Garland Pub.

Baillie, John. Diario de Oraciones Privada. pap. 2.75 (ISBN 0-8358-0412-7). Upper Room.

--A Diary of Private Prayer. 136p. 1984. 8.95 (ISBN 0-684-30997-1, ScribT). Scribner.

--A Diary of Private Prayer. 1979. pap. 3.50 (ISBN 0-684-16323-3, ScribT). Scribner.

--The Idea of Revelation in Recent Thought. LC 56-8158. (Bantam Lectures in America Ser.). 151p. 1956. 22.00x (ISBN 0-231-02142-9); pap. 9.50x (ISBN 0-231-08554-0). Columbia U Pr.

--The Interpretation of Religion: An Introductory Study of Theological Principles. LC 76-49990. Repr. of 1928 ed. lib. bdg. 25.00x (ISBN 0-8371-9038-X, BAIR). Greenwood.

Baillie, Katrine de see De Baillie, Katrine.

Baillie, Laureen, ed. The Catalogue of Printed Music in the British Library to 1980, 62 vols. (Illus.). 1980. Set. text ed. 10,400.00 (ISBN 0-86291-300-4). K G Saur.

Baillie, M. G. Tree-Ring Dating & Archeology. LC 81-16079. (Illus.). 1982. lib. bdg. 28.00 (ISBN 0-226-03630-8). U of Chicago Pr.

Baillie, N. A Digest of Muhammadan Law, 2 vols. 65.50 set (ISBN 0-686-18561-7). Kazi Pubns.

Baillie, N. B. Digest of Moohummudan Law, 2 Vols. 1965. 27.00x (ISBN 0-87902-048-2). Orientalia.

Baillie, Robert. Letters & Journals, 3 vols. Laing, David, ed. LC 70-161745. (Bannatyne Club, Edinburgh. Publications: No. 73). Repr. of 1842 ed. Set. 195.00 (ISBN 0-404-52800-7). AMS Pr.

Baillie, Thomas W., jt. ed. see De Boer, Jan.

Baillie, William M., ed. A Choice Ternary of English Plays: Gratiae Theatrales, 1662. LC 83-1915. (Medieval & Renaissance Texts & Studies: Vol. 26). 322p. 1984. 18.00 (ISBN 0-86698-054-7). Medieval & Renaissance NY.

Baillie-Grohman, F., ed. see Edward of Norwich.

Baillie-Grohman, William. Sport in Art. LC 69-18532. (Illus.). 66.00 (ISBN 0-405-08228-2, Pub. by Blom). Ayer Co Pubs.

Baillie-Grohman, William A., ed. see Edward of Norwich.

Baillif, Jean-Claude. Superpuzzles. LC 81-21112. (Illus.). 125p. 1982. 10.95 (ISBN 0-13-876201-5); pap. 4.95 (ISBN 0-13-876193-0). P-H.

Baillio, Joseph. Elisabeth Louise Vigee Le Brun, 1755-1842. LC 82-81554. (Illus.). 148p. 1983. 29.95 (ISBN 0-295-96012-4). U of Wash Pr.

Baillio, Joseph, jt. auth. see Zafran, Eric M.

Baillou, Jean, jt. auth. see Ronsard, Pierre de.

Bailly, Anatole. Dictionnaire Abrege Grec-Francais. 1012p. (Gr. & Fr.). 1969. pap. 39.95 (ISBN 0-686-56906-7, M-6019). French & Eur.

--Dictionnaire Grec-Francais. 2230p. (Gr.-Fr.). 1967. pap. 95.00 (ISBN 0-686-56907-5, M-6020). French & Eur.

Bailly, H. C. & De Borms, C. T. Materials Flow in the Post-Consumer Waste Stream of the EEC. 96p. 1977. 33.00x (ISBN 0-86010-080-4, Pub. by Graham & Trotman England). State Mutual Bk.

Bailor, Edwin M. Content & Form in Tests of Intelligence. LC 70-176529. (Columbia University. Teachers College. Contributions to Education: No. 162). Repr. of 1924 ed. 22.50 (ISBN 0-404-55162-9). AMS Pr.

Bails, Dale G. & Peppers, Larry C. Business Fluctuations: Forecasting Techniques & Applications. (Illus.). 480p. 1982. 33.95 (ISBN 0-13-098400-0). P-H.

Baily, Anthony. England, First & Last. 1985. 15.95 (ISBN 0-670-80404-5). Viking.

Baily, Auguste. Maeterlinck. LC 74-6385. (Studies in French Literature, No. 45). 1974. lib. bdg. 39.95x (ISBN 0-8383-1877-0). Haskell.

Baily, Charles M. Faint Praise: The Development of American Tanks & Tank Destroyers During World War II. (Illus.). 192p. 1983. 24.00 (ISBN 0-208-02006-3, Archon). Shoe String.

Baily, F. E. The Perfect Age. 187p. 1981. Repr. of 1946 ed. lib. bdg. 30.00 (ISBN 0-89987-064-3). Darby Bks.

--Six Great Victorian Novelists. LC 68-8221. 1969. Repr. of 1947 ed. 15.00x (ISBN 0-8046-0013-9, Pub.by Kennikat). Assoc Faculty Pr.

Baily, F. Lee & Rothblatt, Henry B. Fundamentals of Criminal Advocacy. LC 73-90861. 589p. 19.50. Lawyers Co-Op.

Baily, Francis. The Doctrine of Interest & Annuities: Analytically Investigated & Explained; Together with Several Useful Tables Connected with the Subject. Brief, Richard P., ed. LC 80-1470. (Dimensions of Accounting Theory & Practice Ser.). 1981. Repr. of 1908 ed. lib. bdg. 17.00x (ISBN 0-405-13500-9). Ayer Co Pubs.

Baily, James H. Motivation: The Holy Spirit. 1983. 5.50 (ISBN 0-89536-956-7). CSS of Ohio.

Baily, Keith M. Care of Converts. 95p. (Orig.). 1979. pap. 1.50 (ISBN 0-87509-156-3); leader's guide 0.75 (ISBN 0-87509-157-1). Chr Pubns.

Baily, Leslie. The Gilbert & Sullivan Book. 4th rev. ed. LC 75-181105. 475p. 1956. Repr. 59.00 (ISBN 0-403-01504-9). Scholarly.

Baily, Martin & Okun, Arthur M. Battle Against Unemployment & Inflation. 3rd ed. (Illus.). 1983. 19.50 (ISBN 0-393-01381-2); pap. 7.95x (ISBN 0-393-95055-7). Norton.

Baily, Martin N., ed. Workers, Jobs, & Inflation. LC 82-70891. 365p. 1982. 31.95 (ISBN 0-8157-0764-9); pap. 12.95 (ISBN 0-8157-0763-0). Brookings.

Baily, Mary A., ed. The Effects of Litigation on Health Care Costs. (Dialogue on Public Policy Ser.). 90p. 1985. pap. 9.95 (ISBN 0-8157-0757-6). Brookings.

Baily, Michael. Small Net in a Big Sea: The Redemptorists in the Philippines, 1905-1929. (Illus.). 7.25x (ISBN 0-686-24529-6, San Carlos Pubns); pap. 5.00x (ISBN 0-686-24530-X). Cellar.

Baily, P. J. Purchasing & Supply Management. 1978. pap. 18.50x (ISBN 0-412-15690-3, NO. 6021, Pub. by Chapman & Hall England). Methuen Inc.

Baily, Peter. Purchasing Systems & Records. 2nd ed. 127p. 1983. text ed. 42.00x (ISBN 0-566-02337-7). Gower Pub Co.

Baily, Peter & Farmer, David. Materials Management Handbook. 320p. 1982. text ed. 47.50x (ISBN 0-566-02272-9). Gower Pub Co.

Baily, R. Forward to Richmond. LC 83-5034. (Civil War Ser.). (gr. 7 up). 1983. lib. bdg. 19.94 (ISBN 0-8094-4721-5, Pub. by Time-Life). Silver.

Baily, Samuel L. Labor, Nationalism, & Politics in Argentina. 1967. 25.00x (ISBN 0-8135-0556-9). Rutgers U Pr.

Baily, T. E. & Lundgaard, Kris. Program Design with Pseudocode. 300p. 1983. pap. write for info. Wadsworth Pub.

Baily, Thelma F. & Baily, Walter H. Child Welfare Practice: A Guide to Providing Effective Services for Children & Families. LC 82-49034. (Social & Behavioral Science Ser.). 1983. text ed. 19.95x (ISBN 0-87589-558-1). Jossey-Bass.

Baily, Walter H., jt. auth. see Baily, Thelma F.

Baily, Walter L., Jr. Introductory Lectures on Automorphic Forms. LC 72-4034. (Publications of the Mathematical Society of Japan Series, No. 12). 272p. 1973. lib. bdg. 29.00 (ISBN 0-691-08123-9). Princeton U Pr.

Bailyn, Bernard. The Apologia of Robert Keane: The Self-Portrait of a Puritan Merchant. 10.25 (ISBN 0-8446-0470-4). Peter Smith.

--Education in the Forming of American Society. 160p. 1972. pap. 4.95 (ISBN 0-393-00643-3, Norton Lib). Norton.

--Education in the Forming of American Society: Needs & Opportunities for Study. (Institute of Early American History & Culture Ser.). xii, 147p. 1970. Repr. of 1960 ed. 13.50x (ISBN 0-8078-0797-4). U of NC Pr.

--Ideological Origins of the American Revolution. LC 67-13252. 1967. 18.50x (ISBN 0-674-44300-4, Belknap Pr); pap. 6.95x (ISBN 0-674-44301-2). Harvard U Pr.

--The New England Merchants in the Seventeenth Century. 1979. pap. 5.95x (ISBN 0-674-61280-9). Harvard U Pr.

--The Ordeal of Thomas Hutchinson. LC 73-76379. 458p. 1974. 25.00x (ISBN 0-674-64160-4, Belknap Pr); pap. 8.95x (ISBN 0-674-64161-2). Harvard U Pr.

--Origins of American Politics. LC 68-12665. 1970. pap. 4.95 (ISBN 0-394-70865-2, V604, Vin). Random.

--The Origins of American Politics. 1983. 12.00 (ISBN 0-8446-6034-5). Peter Smith.

Bailyn, Bernard & Garrett, N., eds. Pamphlets of the American Revolution, 1750-1776: Vol. 1, 1750-1765. (The John Harvard Library). 1965. 30.00x (ISBN 0-674-65250-9). Harvard U Pr.

Bailyn, Bernard & Hench, John B., eds. The Press & the American Revolution. LC 81-14207. 383p. 1981. text ed. 24.95 (ISBN 0-930350-32-4); pap. 9.95x (ISBN 0-930350-30-8). NE U Pr.

Bailyn, Bernard, jt. ed. see Fleming, Donald H.

Bailyn, Bernard, et al. The Great Republic: A History of the American People. 1977. 27.50 (ISBN 0-316-07672-4). Little.

--The Great Republic: A History of the American People. 2nd ed. 1008p. 1981. text ed. 25.95 (ISBN 0-669-02753-7); pap. text ed. 17.95 vol. 1 (ISBN 0-669-02754-5); pap. text ed. 17.95 vol. 2 (ISBN 0-669-02755-3); instr's guide 1.95 (ISBN 0-669-02757-X); student guide 7.95 (ISBN 0-669-02756-1). Heath.

Bain. Statistical Analysis of Reliability & Life Testing Models. (Statistics; Textbooks & Monographs Ser.: Vol. 24). 1978. 49.75 (ISBN 0-8247-6665-2). Dekker.

Bain, Alexander. Emotions & the Will. (Contributions to the History of Psychology Ser.: No. 5, Pt. a: Orientations). 1978. Repr. of 1859 ed. 30.00 (ISBN 0-89093-154-2). U Pubns Amer.

--James Mill: A Biography. LC 66-19689. Repr. of 1882 ed. 39.50x (ISBN 0-678-00214-2). Kelley.

--John Stuart Mill: A Criticism with Personal Recollections. LC 69-16521. Repr. of 1882 ed. 22.50x (ISBN 0-678-00468-4). Kelley.

--John Stuart Mill: A Criticism with Personal Recollections. 1973. Repr. of 1882 ed. 10.00 (ISBN 0-8274-1796-9). R West.

--Mental Science: A Compendium of Psychology & the History of Philosophy. LC 73-2958. (Classics in Psychology Ser.). Repr. of 1868 ed. 33.00 (ISBN 0-405-05132-8). Ayer Co Pubs.

--On the Study of Character, Including an Estimate of Phrenology. (Contributions to the History of Psychology Ser.: Pt. A, Vol. 14, Orientations). 1980. Repr. of 1861 ed. 30.00 (ISBN 0-89093-316-2). U Pubns Amer.

--Practical Essays. LC 72-4533. (Essay Index Reprint Ser.). Repr. of 1884 ed. 19.00 (ISBN 0-8369-2935-7). Ayer Co Pubs.

--Senses & the Intellect. (Contributions to the History of Psychology Ser.: No. 4, Pt. A Orientations). 1978. Repr. of 1855 ed. 30.00 (ISBN 0-89093-153-4). U Pubns Amer.

Bain, Alexander, ed. see Grote, George.

Bain, Barbara, et al. Texas Government Handbook. Russell, Donna, ed. (Illus.). 44p. (Orig.). 1982. pap. text ed. 3.00 (ISBN 0-915757-04-4). League Women Voters TX.

Bain, Bruce, ed. The Sociogenesis of Language & Human Conduct. 580p. 1983. 50.00x (ISBN 0-306-41041-9). Plenum Pub.

Bain, Carl, ed. Norton Introduction to Literature: Drama. 600p. 1973. pap. text ed. 13.95x (ISBN 0-393-09366-2). Norton.

Bain, Carl E., et al. Norton Introduction to Literature. 4th ed. 1986. pap. text ed. price not set (ISBN 0-393-95441-2); price not set classroom guide (ISBN 0-393-95443-9). Norton.

Bain, Carl E., et al, eds. The Norton Introduction to Literature. 3rd ed. 1536p. 1981. pap. text ed. 16.95x (ISBN 0-393-95146-4); classroom guide 2.95x (ISBN 0-393-95158-8). Norton.

--Writing Themes about Literature: A Guide to Accompany the Norton Introduction to Literature. 3rd ed. 1983. pap. 4.95x (ISBN 0-393-95350-5). Norton.

Bain, Carolyn. It's Easy to Become a Citizen. LC 68-28131. 1968. pap. 3.50 (ISBN 0-8015-4134-4, Hawthorn). Dutton.

Bain, Chester A. The Far East. 5th ed. Bain, June W., ed. (Quality Paperback: No. 44). (Orig.). 1972. pap. 3.95 (ISBN 0-8226-0044-7). Littlefield.

Bain, D. Heavy Current Fluidics. (CISM, International Centre for Mechanical Sciences: Vol. 45). (Illus.). 82p. 1970. pap. 10.00 (ISBN 0-387-81148-6). Springer-Verlag.

Bain, D., jt. ed. see Neu, H.

Bain, D. C. & Baker, P. J. A Technical & Market Survey of Fluidic Applications. 1969. text ed. 32.00x (ISBN 0-900983-02-7, Dist. by Air Science Co.). BHRA Fluid.

Bain, D. M. Menander, SAMIA. (BC-AP Classical Ser.). 200p. (Gr.). 1985. 24.50 (ISBN 0-86516-113-5); pap. 12.00 (ISBN 0-86516-114-3). Bolchazy-Carducci.

Bain, D. M., ed. Menander-Samia. 200p. 1983. text ed. 32.50x (ISBN 0-85668-224-1, Pub. by Aris & Phillips); pap. text ed. 15.00x (ISBN 0-85668-225-X, Pub. by Aris & Phillips). Humanities.

Bain, D. M., ed. see Menander.

Bain, David. Masters, Servants & Orders in Greek Tragedy: Some Aspects of Dramatic Technique & Convention. 84p. 1982. 15.00 (ISBN 0-7190-1296-1, Pub. by Manchester Univ Pr). Longwood Pub Group.

Bain, David, ed. see Le Duc, Simon & Saint-Georges, Le Chevalier de.

Bain, David H. Aftershocks: A Tale of Two Victims. 320p. 1980. 11.95 (ISBN 0-416-00681-7, NO.0179). Methuen Inc.

--Sitting in Darkness: Americans in the Philippines. LC 84-8945. (Illus.). 500p. 1984. 24.95 (ISBN 0-395-35285-1). HM.

Bain, David L. Productivity Prescription: A Practical Guide to Improving Productivity & Profits. (Illus.). 320p. 1982. 23.50 (ISBN 0-07-003235-1). McGraw.

Bain, Donald, jt. auth. see Stein, Gerald.

Bain, Donald, et al. Windy Landowner's Guide to Wind Farm Development. LC 84-51114. 175p. 1984. pap. 24.95 (ISBN 0-88016-035-7). Windbks.

Bain, E C. Pioneering in Steel Research. 1975. 7.00 (ISBN 0-686-95117-4). ASM.

Bain, Foster H. & Read, Thomas T. Ores & Industry in South America. Bruchey, Stuart & Bruchey, Eleanor, eds. LC 76-4767. (American Business Abroad Ser.). (Illus.). 1976. Repr. of 1934 ed. 32.00x (ISBN 0-405-09265-2). Ayer Co Pubs.

Bain, Francis W. Corner in Gold: Its History & Theory. LC 68-28615. 1968. Repr. of 1893 ed. lib. bdg. 22.50 (ISBN 0-8371-0292-8, BACG). Greenwood.

Bain, G. S. & Woolven, G. B. A Bibliography of British Industrial Relations. LC 76-53516. 1979. 130.00 (ISBN 0-521-21547-1). Cambridge U Pr.

Bain, George. Celtic Art. 168p. 1982. 40.00x (ISBN 0-85335-196-1, Pub. by W Maclellan Scotland). State Mutual Bk.

--Celtic Art: The Methods of Construction. (Illus.). 160p. 1973. pap. 6.00 (ISBN 0-486-22923-8). Dover.

--Celtic Art: The Methods of Construction. LC 73-75875. 1973. lib. bdg. 15.00x (ISBN 0-88307-590-3). Gannon.

--The Methods of Construction of Celtic Art. (Illus.). 15.50 (ISBN 0-8446-4706-3). Peter Smith.

Bain, George S. & Bennett, John. Bibliography of British Industrial Relations, 1971-1979. 250p. 64.50 (ISBN 0-521-26699-8). Cambridge U Pr.

Bain, George S. & Price, Robert. Profiles of Union Growth: A Comparative Statistical Portrait of Eight Countries. (Warwick Studies in Industrial Relations). (Illus.). 192p. 1981. 75.00x (ISBN 0-631-12633-3). Basil Blackwell.

Bain, George S., ed. Industrial Relations in Britain. (Warwick Studies in Industrial Relations). 500p. 1984. 45.00x (ISBN 0-631-13138-8); pap. 15.95x (ISBN 0-631-13295-3). Basil Blackwell.

Bain, Henry M. & Hecock, Donald S. Ballot Position & Voter's Choice. LC 72-9371. (Illus.). 108p. 1973. Repr. of 1957 ed. lib. bdg. 15.00 (ISBN 0-8371-6578-4, BABP). Greenwood.

Bain, Iain. Thomas Bewick: An Illustrated Record of His Life & Work. (Illus.). 112p. (Orig.). 1981. pap. 15.00 (ISBN 0-8390-0275-0). Abner Schram Ltd.

Bain, Ian. Mountains & Earth Movements. (Planet Earth Ser.). 48p. (gr. 5 up). lib. bdg. 9.40 (ISBN 0-531-03802-5, A Bookwright Press Bk). Watts.

--Mountains & People. LC 82-50392. (Nature's Landscape Ser.). PLB 15.96 (ISBN 0-382-06673-1). Silver.

Bain, J. & Hafez, E. S., eds. Diagnosis in Andrology. (Clinics in Andrology Ser.: No. 4). (Illus.). 255p. 1980. lib. bdg. 65.00 (ISBN 90-247-2365-5, Pub. by Martinus Nijhoff Netherlands). Kluwer Academic.

Bain, J., et al, eds. Treatment of Male Infertility. (Illus.). 330p. 1982. 70.00 (ISBN 0-387-10990-0). Springer-Verlag.

--Andrology: Basic & Clinical Aspects of Male Reproduction & Infertility. (Progress in Reproductive Biology: Vol. 3). (Illus.). 1978. 41.75 (ISBN 3-8055-2807-8). S Karger.

Bain, J. Kerr. The People of the Pilgrimage: An Expository Study of the "Pilgrim's Progress" As a Book of Character, 2 vols. 475p. 1981. Repr. of 1905 ed. Set. lib. bdg. 150.00 (ISBN 0-89984-071-X). Century Bookbindery.

Bain, J. Paul, ed. Rehabilitation & Handicapped Literature 1981 Update: A Bibliographic Guide to the Microfiche Collection. 38p. 1982. reference bk. 25.00 (ISBN 0-667-00678-8). Microfilming Corp.

Bain, J. S. & Jain, R. B., eds. Contemporary Political Theory. 300p. 1980. text ed. 14.50x (ISBN 0-391-01901-5). Humanities.

--Perspectives in Political Theory. 275p. 1980. text ed. 14.50x (ISBN 0-391-01900-7). Humanities.

Bain, James, ed. see Henry, Alexander.

Bain, James, ed. & illus. see Henry, Alexander.

Bain, Joe S. Economics of the Pacific Coast Petroleum Industry, 3 Vols. LC 69-10067. (Illus.). 1969. Repr. of 1947 ed. Set. lib. bdg. 44.25x (ISBN 0-8371-0293-6, BAPP). Greenwood.

--International Differences in Industrial Structure: Eight Nations in the 1950's. LC 80-14615. (Studies in Comparative Economics: No. 6). (Illus.). xiv, 209p. 1980. Repr. of 1966 ed. lib. bdg. 24.75x (ISBN 0-313-22408-0, BAID). Greenwood.

Bain, John, et al. A Colour Atlas of Mouth, Throat & Ear Disorders in Children. 1985. lib. bdg. 43.00 (ISBN 0-85200-767-1, Pub. by MTP Pr England). Kluwer Academic.

Bain, Joseph, ed. see Beaugue, Jean de.

Bain, Joseph, ed. see Maitland, Richard.

Bain, June W., ed. see Bain, Chester A.

Bain, Kenneth R. The March to Zion: United States Policy & the Founding of Israel. LC 79-7413. 256p. 1980. 18.50 (ISBN 0-89096-076-3). Tex A&M Univ Pr.

Bain, Linda L., jt. auth. see Jewett, Anne E.

Bain, Linda M. Evergreen Adventurer: The Real Frank Harris. 1975. 7.50 (ISBN 0-8283-1626-0). Branden Pub Co.

Bain, Sr. Mary A. Ancient Landmarks: A Social & Economic History of the Victoria District, Western Australia, 1839-1894. 1977. 25.00x (ISBN 0-85564-090-1, Pub. by U of W Austral Pr). Intl Spec Bk.

Bain, R. N. Hans Christian Andersen. 1895. 35.00 (ISBN 0-8274-2467-1). R West.

--Slavonic Europe: A Political History of Russia & Poland, 1447-1796. 1976. lib. bdg. 59.95 (ISBN 0-8490-2615-6). Gordon Pr.

Bain, R. Nisbet. Last King of Poland & His Contemporaries. LC 71-135789. (Eastern Europe Collection Ser). 1970. Repr. of 1909 ed. 24.50 (ISBN 0-405-02731-1). Ayer Co Pubs.

--More Tales from Tolstoi. 316p. 1981. Repr. of 1981 ed. lib. bdg. 30.00 (ISBN 0-89984-076-0). Century Bookbindery.

--Slavonic Europe: A Political History of Poland & Russia from 1447 to 1796. LC 76-135790. (Eastern Europe Collection Ser). 1970. Repr. of 1908 ed. 23.00 (ISBN 0-405-02732-X). Ayer Co Pubs.

Bain, R. Nisbet, tr. see Gorki, Maxim.

Bain, R. Nisbet, tr. see Jokai, Mor.

Bain, R. Nisbet, tr. see Tolstoi, Lev N.

Bain, R. V. Hemorrhagic Septicemia. 1963. pap. 4.75 (ISBN 0-685-36303-1, F231, FAO). Unipub.

Bain, R. V., et al. Haemorrhagic Septicaemia. (Animal Production & Health Papers: No. 33). 58p. 1982. pap. 7.50 (ISBN 92-5-101224-5, F2385, FAO). Unipub.

Bain, Richard C. & Parris, Judith H. Convention Decisions & Voting Records. 2nd ed. LC 73-1082. (Brookings Institution Studies in Presidential Selection Ser.). pap. 120.00 (ISBN 0-317-30178-0, 2025360). Bks Demand UMI.

Bain, Robert. H. L. Davis. LC 74-1969. (Western Writers Ser: No. 11). pap. 2.00x (ISBN 0-88430-010-2). Boise St Univ.

Bain, Robert N. Charles the Twelfth & the Collapse of the Swedish Empire: 1682-1719. LC 73-14432. (Heroes of the Nations Ser.). Repr. of 1895 ed. 30.00 (ISBN 0-404-58251-6). AMS Pr.

--Charles Twelfth & the Collapse of the Swedish Empire, 1682-1719. facsimile ed. LC 70-95062. (Select Bibliographies Reprint Ser). 1895. 33.00 (ISBN 0-8369-5064-X). Ayer Co Pubs.

--Daughter of Peter the Great. LC 72-136407. (BCL Ser.: No. II). Repr. of 1899 ed. 14.50 (ISBN 0-404-00447-4). AMS Pr.

--Daughter of Peter the Great. 1899. 13.00 (ISBN 0-403-00002-5). Scholarly.

--Peter Third, Emperor of Russia. 1902. 12.00 (ISBN 0-403-00465-9). Scholarly.

--Peter Third, Emperor of Russia: The Story of a Crisis & a Crime. LC 72-156962. (BCL Ser.: No. II). Repr. of 1902 ed. 14.50 (ISBN 0-404-00448-2). AMS Pr.

--The Pupils of Peter the Great. LC 76-27342. 1976. Repr. of 1897 ed. lib. bdg. 45.00 (ISBN 0-8414-3310-0). Folcroft.

Bain, Robert N., ed. Cossack Fairy Tales & Folk-Tales. LC 76-9882. (Children's Literature Reprint Ser.). (Illus.). (gr. 4-6). 1976. 18.75x (ISBN 0-8486-0200-5). Core Collection.

Bain, Robert N., ed. & tr. Cossack Fairy Tales & Folk-Tales. LC 11-132. Repr. of 1894 ed. 17.00 (ISBN 0-527-04404-0). Kraus Repr.

Bain, Willard S. Informed Sources. 144p. 1967. 7.50 (ISBN 0-571-09234-9); sewn in wrappers 3.50 (ISBN 0-571-09237-3). Small Pr Dist.

Bain, William & Watt, J. K. Essentials of Cardiovascular Surgery. 2nd ed. LC 74-19640. (Illus.). 160p. 1975. pap. text ed. 11.50x (ISBN 0-443-01254-7). Churchill.

Bain, Winifred E. An Analytical Study of Teaching in Nursery School, Kindergarten & First Grade. LC 74-176530. (Columbia University. Teachers College. Contributions to Education: No. 332). Repr. of 1928 ed. 22.50 (ISBN 0-404-55332-X). AMS Pr.

Bainbridge, A., jt. ed. see Scott, P. R.

Bainbridge, Beryl. Another Part of the Wood. LC 79-27297. 1980. 8.95 (ISBN 0-8076-0965-X). Braziller.

--The Bottle Factory Outing. LC 74-25294. 224p. 1975. 7.95 (ISBN 0-8076-0781-9). Braziller.

--English Journey: Or, The Road to Milton Keynes. 158p. 1984. 12.95 (ISBN 0-8076-1101-8). Braziller.

--Harriet Said. LC 73-76970. 1973. 5.95 (ISBN 0-8076-0687-1). Braziller.

--Injury Time: A Comedy of Middle-Aged Passion. LC 77-21051. 1978. 7.95 (ISBN 0-8076-0881-5). Braziller.

--A Quiet Life. LC 76-55837. 208p. 1977. 7.95 (ISBN 0-8076-0846-7). Braziller.

--The Secret Glass. LC 73-93608. 160p. 1974. 5.95 (ISBN 0-8076-0746-0). Braziller.

--Sweet William. LC 75-43672. 192p. 1976. 7.95 (ISBN 0-8076-0816-5). Braziller.

--Watson's Apology. 222p. 1985. 14.95 (ISBN 0-07-003254-8). McGraw.

--A Weekend with Claude. LC 81-17965. 152p. 1982. 10.95 (ISBN 0-8076-1031-3). Braziller.

--Winter Garden. LC 80-70841. 1981. 8.95 (ISBN 0-8076-1011-9). Braziller.

--Young Adolf. LC 78-26174. 208p. 1979. Repr. of 1978 ed. 7.95 (ISBN 0-8076-0910-2). Braziller.

Bainbridge, Brian W. The Genetics of Microbes. LC 80-15936. (Tertiary Level Biology Ser.). 193p. 1980. pap. 39.95x (ISBN 0-470-26995-2). Halsted Pr.

Bainbridge, Cyril. North Yorkshire & North Humberside. (Shire County Guide Ser.: No. 3). (Illus.). 56p. (Orig.). 1984. pap. 4.95 (ISBN 0-85263-683-0, Pub. by Shire Pubns England). Seven Hills Bks.

Bainbridge, Cyril, ed. One Hundred Years of Journalism: Social Aspects of the Press. 184p. 1985. 21.00 (ISBN 0-333-38451-2, Pub. by Salem Acad). Merrimack Pub Cir.

Bainbridge, David A. First Passive Solar Catalog. LC 78-78403. (Illus.). 1979. pap. 5.95 (ISBN 0-933490-00-3). Passive Solar.

--The Integral Passive Solar Water Heater Book. 1981. pap. 10.95 (ISBN 0-933490-03-8). Passive Solar.

--The Second Passive Solar Catalog. (Illus.). 110p. (Orig.). 1981. pap. 12.50 (ISBN 0-933490-02-X). Passive Solar.

--Waterglass. (Orig.). 1979. pap. 4.00 (ISBN 0-933490-01-1). Passive Solar.

Bainbridge, E. Gordon. The Old Rhinebeck Aerodrome. 1977. 8.95 (ISBN 0-682-48883-6, Banner). Exposition Pr FL.

Bainbridge, John. Astronomical Description of the Late Comet from the 18. of Novemb. 1618 to the 16. of December Following. LC 74-28828. (English Experience Ser.: No. 710). 1975. Repr. of 1619 ed. 6.00 (ISBN 90-221-0710-8). Walter J Johnson.

Bainbridge, John S. & Wood, Terry. The Study & Teaching of Law in Africa, with a Survey of Institutions of Legal Education in Africa. x, 342p. 1972. text ed. 12.50x (ISBN 0-8377-0304-2). Rothman.

Bainbridge, Marion S. Walk in Other Worlds with Dante. 1973. Repr. of 1914 ed. 9.45 (ISBN 0-8274-1188-X). R West.

Bainbridge, William S. Satan's Power: A Deviant Psychotherapy Cult. LC 77-80466. 1978. 30.00x (ISBN 0-520-03546-1). U of Cal Pr.

--The Space Flight Revolution: A Sociological Study. LC 82-21725. 304p. (Orig.). 1983. Repr. of 1976 ed. 24.50 (ISBN 0-89874-501-2). Krieger.

Bainbridge, William S., jt. auth. see Stark, Rodney.

Bainbrigge, Marion S. A Walk in Other Worlds in Dante. 253p. 1982. Repr. of 1914 ed. lib. bdg. 30.00 (ISBN 0-686-98149-9). Darby Bks.

--Walk in Other Worlds with Dante. LC 73-101024. 1969. Repr. of 1914 ed. 21.50x (ISBN 0-8046-0691-9, Pub. by Kennikat). Assoc Faculty Pr.

--A Walk in Other Worlds with Dante. 253p. 1982. Repr. of 1914 ed. lib. bdg. 40.00 (ISBN 0-89760-092-4). Telegraph Bks.

Baine, David. Instructional Design for Special Education. LC 81-9693. (Illus.). 320p. 1982. 27.95 (ISBN 0-87778-179-6). Educ Tech Pubns.

--Memory & Instruction. 340p. 1986. 37.95 (ISBN 0-87778-192-3). Educ Tech Pubns.

Baine, David, jt. auth. see Das, J. P.

Baine, Sean. Community Action & Local Government. 96p. 1975. pap. text ed. 8.75 (ISBN 0-7135-1842-1, Pub. by Bedford England). Brookfield Pub Co.

Bainer, Roy, jt. auth. see Kepner, R. A.

Baines, A. Research in the Chemical Industry: Environment Objective Strategy. (Illus.). 298p. 1971. 31.50 (ISBN 0-444-20035-5, Pub. by Elsevier Applied Sci England). Elsevier.

Baines, A., et al. Research in the Chemical Industry: The Environment, Objectives & Strategy. (Illus.). 1969. 33.60x (Pub. by Applied Science). Burgess-Intl Ideas.

Baines, Anthony. Brass Instruments: Their History & Development. 300p. 1981. 25.00 (ISBN 0-684-15229-0, ScribT); pap. 14.95 (ISBN 0-684-16668-2). Scribner.

Baines, Anthony, ed. Musical Instruments Through the Ages. LC 66-22505. (Illus.). 352p. 1975. 15.00 (ISBN 0-8027-0469-7); PLB 9.85 lib. bdg. (ISBN 0-8027-6234-4). Walker & Co.

Baines, Barbara. Fashion Revivals. (Illus.). 200p. 1981. text ed. 16.95x (ISBN 0-7134-1929-6). Drama Bk.

Baines, Barbara J. The Lust Motif in the Plays of Thomas Middleton. (Salzburg Studies in English Literature, Jacobean Drama Studies: No. 29). 160p. 1973. pap. text ed. 25.50x (ISBN 0-391-01306-8). Humanities.

--Thomas Heywood. (English Authors Ser.: No. 388). 1984. lib. bdg. 18.95 (ISBN 0-8057-6874-2, Twayne). G K Hall.

Baines, Edward. History of the Cotton Manufacture in Great Britain. 2nd ed. (Illus.). 544p. 1966. 36.00x (ISBN 0-7146-1386-X, F Cass Co). Biblio Dist.

--The Social, Educational & Religious State of the Manufacturing Districts: With Statistical Returns of the Means of Education & Religious Instruction. 2nd ed. (Social History of Education Ser.: First Ser. No. 1). 76p. 1969. Repr. of 1843 ed. 17.50x (ISBN 0-7130-0001-5, Pub. by Woburn Pr England). Biblio Dist.

--Social, Educational, & Religious State of the Manufacturing Districts. LC 75-5885. (Social History of Education). Repr. of 1843 ed. 15.00x (ISBN 0-678-08454-8). Kelley.

Baines, Gwendolyn L. People in the Web of Life. 1978. 5.00 (ISBN 0-682-48832-1). Exposition Pr FL.

Baines, Harry. Science of Photography. 3rd ed. LC 73-19208. 318p. 1969. 26.95x (ISBN 0-471-04340-0). Halsted Pr.

Baines, J. Fecundity Figures: Egyptian Personification & the Iconology of a Genre. 200p. 1982. text ed. 75.50x (ISBN 0-85668-087-7, 40651, Pub. by Aris & Phillips England). Humanities.

Baines, Jocelyn. Joseph Conrad: A Critical Biography. LC 75-17476. 507p. 1975. Repr. of 1961 ed. lib. bdg. 55.00x (ISBN 0-8371-8304-9, BAJOC). Greenwood.

Baines, John. Fecundity Figures: Egyptian Personification & the Iconology of a Genre. (Egyptology Ser.). (Illus.). 400p. (Orig.). 1985. pap. 48.00 (ISBN 0-86516-122-4). Bolchazy-Carducci.

--The Secret Science: For the Physical & Spiritual Transformation of Man--Hermetic Philosophy. (Bk. 1). 200p. 1980. pap. 5.95 (ISBN 0-87542-025-7). Llewellyn Pubns.

--The Stellar Man. Hipskind, Judith, ed. LC 84-48085. (Hermetic Science Ser.). (Illus.). 384p. (Orig.). 1985. pap. 9.95 (ISBN 0-87542-026-5, L-026). Llewellyn Pubns.

Baines, John & Malek, Jaromir. Atlas of Ancient Egypt. (Cultural Atlas Ser.). (Illus.). 240p. 1980. 35.00 (ISBN 0-87196-334-5). Facts on File.

Baines, John, jt. tr. see Hornung, Erik.

Baines, John, tr. see Schafer, Heinrich.

Baines, John M. Revolution in Peru: Mariategui & the Myth. LC 72-148690. 216p. 1972. 14.00 (ISBN 0-8173-4721-6). U of Ala Pr.

Baines, Lew. Cimarron & the Comancheros. (Cimarron Ser.: No. 17). 1985. pap. 2.75 (ISBN 0-451-13812-0, Sig). NAL.

Baines, M. J., jt. ed. see Morton, K. W.

Baines, Malory. Le Morte D'Arthur. 1962. pap. 4.50 (ISBN 0-451-62368-1, Ment). NAL.

Baines, Mary, jt. auth. see Saunders, Cicely.

Baines, Patricia. Flax & Linen: Shire Album Ser. (No. 133). (Orig.). 1985. pap. 3.50 (ISBN 0-85263-727-6, Pub. by Shire Pubns England). Seven Hills Bks.

--Spinning Wheels, Spinners & Spinning. 1980. pap. 10.95 (ISBN 0-686-27277-3). Robin & Russ.

--Spinning Wheels, Spinners & Spinning. new ed. pap. 10.95 (ISBN 0-686-37658-7). Robin & Russ.

Bains, G. S., et al. Power Systems Protection. 515p. 1981. 30.00x (ISBN 0-86125-205-5, Pub. by Orient Longman India). State Mutual Bk.

Bains, J. S. & Jain, R. B. Political Science in Transition. 1983. 22.00x (ISBN 0-8364-1025-4, Pub. by Gitanjali Prakashan). South Asia Bks.

Bains, J. S., jt. auth. see Schleicher, Charles P.

Bains, Malcolm A. Management Reform in English Local Government. (Centre for Research on Federal Financial Relations Research Monograph: No. 24). 1978. pap. 6.00 (ISBN 0-7081-1059-2, Pub by ANUP Australia). Australia N U P.

Bains, Rae. Abraham Lincoln. LC 84-2581. (Illus.). 32p. (gr. 2-6). 1985. PLB 7.59 (ISBN 0-8167-0146-6); pap. text ed. 1.95 (ISBN 0-8167-0147-4). Troll Assocs.

--Ancient Greece. LC 84-2685. (Illus.). 32p. (gr. 2-6). 1985. PLB 7.59 (ISBN 0-8167-0244-6); pap. text ed. 1.95 (ISBN 0-8167-0245-4). Troll Assocs.

--Babe Ruth. LC 84-2595. (Illus.). 32p. (gr. 2-6). 1985. PLB 7.59 (ISBN 0-8167-0144-X); pap. text ed. 1.95 (ISBN 0-8167-0145-8). Troll Assocs.

--Case of the Great Train Robbery. LC 81-7525. (Easy-To-Read Mystery Ser.). (Illus.). 48p. (gr. 2-4). 1982. PLB 8.59 (ISBN 0-89375-588-5); pap. text ed. 1.95 (ISBN 0-89375-589-3). Troll Assocs.

--Christopher Columbus. LC 84-2585. (Illus.). 32p. (gr. 2-6). 1985. lib. bdg. 7.59 (ISBN 0-8167-0150-4); pap. text ed. 1.95 (ISBN 0-8167-0151-2). Troll Assocs.

--Clara Barton: Angel of the Battlefield. LC 81-23123. (Illus.). 48p. (gr. 4-6). 1982. PLB 7.89 (ISBN 0-89375-752-7); pap. text ed. 1.95 (ISBN 0-89375-753-5). Troll Assocs.

--Discovering Electricity. LC 81-3339. (Illus.). 32p. (gr. 2-4). 1982. PLB 9.89 (ISBN 0-89375-564-8); pap. text ed. 1.95 (ISBN 0-89375-565-6). Troll Assocs.

--Europe. LC 84-8598. (Illus.). 32p. (gr. 2-6). 1985. PLB 7.59 (ISBN 0-8167-0304-3); pap. text ed. 1.95 (ISBN 0-8167-0305-1). Troll Assocs.

--Forests & Jungles. LC 84-8641. (Illus.). 32p. (gr. 2-6). 1985. PLB 7.59 (ISBN 0-8167-0312-4); pap. text ed. 1.95 (ISBN 0-8167-0313-2). Troll Assocs.

--Harriet Tubman: The Road to Freedom. LC 81-23145. (Illus.). 48p. (gr. 4-6). 1982. PLB 7.89 (ISBN 0-89375-760-8); pap. text ed. 1.95 (ISBN 0-89375-761-6). Troll Assocs.

--Health & Hygiene. LC 84-2627. (Illus.). 32p. (gr. 2-6). 1985. PLB 7.59 (ISBN 0-8167-0180-6); pap. text ed. 1.95 (ISBN 0-8167-0181-4). Troll Assocs.

--Hiccups, Hiccups. LC 81-4638. (Illus.). 32p. (gr. k-2). 1981. PLB 9.89 (ISBN 0-89375-537-0); pap. text ed. 2.50 (ISBN 0-89375-538-9). Troll Assocs.

--Indians of the Eastern Woodlands. LC 84-2664. (Illus.). 32p. (gr. 2-6). 1985. PLB 7.59 (ISBN 0-8167-0118-0); pap. text ed. 1.95 (ISBN 0-8167-0119-9). Troll Assocs.

--Indians of the Plains. LC 84-2645. (Illus.). 32p. (gr. 2-6). 1985. PLB 6.89 (ISBN 0-8167-0188-1); pap. text ed. 1.95 (ISBN 0-8167-0189-X). Troll Assocs.

--Indians of the West. LC 84-2600. (Illus.). 32p. (gr. 2-6). 1985. PLB 7.59 (ISBN 0-8167-0134-2); pap. text ed. 1.95 (ISBN 0-8167-0135-0). Troll Assocs.

--James Monroe, Young Patriot. LC 85-1071. (Illus.). 48p. (gr. 4-6). 1985. lib. bdg. 8.79 (ISBN 0-8167-0557-7); pap. text ed. 1.95 (ISBN 0-8167-0558-5). Troll Assocs.

--Light. LC 84-2719. (Illus.). 32p. (gr. 2-6). 1985. PLB 7.59 (ISBN 0-8167-0202-0); pap. text ed. 1.95 (ISBN 0-8167-0203-9). Troll Assocs.

--Louis Pasteur. LC 84-2748. (Illus.). 32p. (gr. 2-6). 1985. PLB 7.59 (ISBN 0-8167-0148-2); pap. text ed. 1.95 (ISBN 0-8167-0149-0). Troll Assocs.

--Martin Luther King. LC 84-2666. (Illus.). 32p. (gr. 2-6). 1985. PLB 7.59 (ISBN 0-8167-0160-1); pap. text ed. 1.95 (ISBN 0-8167-0161-X). Troll Assocs.

--Molecules & Atoms. LC 84-2712. (Illus.). 32p. (gr. 2-6). 1985. PLB 7.59 (ISBN 0-8167-0284-5); pap. text ed. 1.95 (ISBN 0-8167-0285-3). Troll Assocs.

--Pilgrims & Thanksgiving. LC 84-2686. (Illus.). 32p. (gr. 2-6). 1985. PLB 7.59 (ISBN 0-8167-0222-5); pap. text ed. 1.95 (ISBN 0-8167-0223-3). Troll Assocs.

--Prehistoric Animals. LC 84-2735. (Illus.). 32p. (gr. 2-6). 1985. PLB 7.59 (ISBN 0-8167-0296-9); pap. text ed. 1.95 (ISBN 0-8167-0297-7). Troll Assocs.

--Robert E. Lee, Brave Leader. LC 85-1092. (Illus.). 48p. (gr. 4-6). 1985. lib. bdg. 8.79 (ISBN 0-8167-0545-3); pap. text ed. 1.95 (ISBN 0-8167-0546-1). Troll Assocs.

--Rocks & Minerals. LC 84-8644. (Illus.). 32p. (gr. 2-6). 1985. PLB 7.59 (ISBN 0-8167-0186-5); pap. text ed. 1.95 (ISBN 0-8167-0187-3). Troll Assocs.

--Simples Machines. LC 84-2607. (Illus.). 32p. (gr. 2-6). 1985. PLB 7.59 (ISBN 0-8167-0166-0); pap. text ed. 1.95 (ISBN 0-8167-0167-9). Troll Assocs.

--Supreme Court. LC 84-2736. (Illus.). 32p. (gr. 2-6). 1985. PLB 7.59 (ISBN 0-8167-0272-1); pap. text ed. 1.95 (ISBN 0-8167-0273-X). Troll Assocs.

--Water. LC 84-2718. (Illus.). 32p. (gr. 2-6). 1985. PLB 7.59 (ISBN 0-8167-0194-6); pap. text ed. 1.95 (ISBN 0-8167-0195-4). Troll Assocs.

--Wonders of Rivers. LC 81-7423. (Illus.). 32p. (gr. 2-4). 1982. PLB 9.89 (ISBN 0-89375-570-2); pap. text ed. 1.95 (ISBN 0-89375-571-0). Troll Assocs.

Bainton, George, ed. The Art of Authorship. 355p. 1981. Repr. of 1890 ed. lib. bdg. 30.00 (ISBN 0-89987-066-X). Darby Bks.

Bainton, R. H. Hunted Heretic: The Life & Death of Michael Servetus. 11.25 (ISBN 0-8446-1580-3). Peter Smith.

Bainton, Roland. Erasmus of Christendom. (Crossroad Paperback Ser.). 320p. 1982. pap. 12.95 (ISBN 0-8245-0415-1). Crossroad NY.

--The Martin Luther Easter Book. LC 82-15996. 88p. 1983. pap. 3.95 (ISBN 0-8006-1685-5). Fortress.

--Reformation of the Sixteenth Century. 16.00 (ISBN 0-8446-1581-1). Peter Smith.

Bainton, Roland, jt. auth. see Brokering, Herb.

Bainton, Roland H. The Age of the Reformation. LC 83-25145. 192p. pap. 6.95 (ISBN 0-89874-736-8). Krieger.

--Christendom: A Short History of Christianity & Its Impact on Western Civilization, Vol. 1. rev. ed. (Illus.). pap. 6.95xi (ISBN 0-06-130131-0, TB131, Torch). Har-Row.

--Christendom: A Short History of Christianity & Its Impact on Western Civilization, Vol. 2. rev. ed. (Illus.). pap. 6.95xi (ISBN 0-06-130132-9, TB132, Torch). Har-Row.

--Christian Attitudes Toward War & Peace. LC 60-12064. 1979. pap. 7.75 (ISBN 0-687-07027-9). Abingdon.

--The Church of Our Fathers. (Illus.). 222p. 1978. pap. text ed. 9.95 (ISBN 0-02-305450-6, Pub. by Scribner). Macmillan.

--Concerning Heretics. 1965. Repr. lib. bdg. 27.50x (ISBN 0-374-90323-9). Octagon.

--Early Christianity. LC 83-25150. 188p. 1984. pap. text ed. 6.95 (ISBN 0-89874-735-X). Krieger.

--Erasmus of Christendom. LC 68-27788. (Illus.). 1969. 20.00 (ISBN 0-684-15380-7, ScribT). Scribner.

--George Lincoln Burr: His Life. Gibbons, Lois O., ed. LC 79-8223. Repr. of 1943 ed. 42.50 (ISBN 0-404-18402-2). AMS Pr.

--Here I Stand: A Life of Martin Luther. (Festival Books). 1978. pap. 4.95 (ISBN 0-687-16894-5, Co-Pub. with NAL). Abingdon.

--Here I Stand: A Life of Martin Luther. pap. 3.95 (ISBN 0-451-62404-1, ME2103, Ment). NAL.

--The Medieval Church. LC 78-11433. (Anvil Ser.). 192p. 1979. pap. 6.95 (ISBN 0-88275-786-5). Krieger.

--Reformation of the Sixteenth Century. LC 85-47516. (Illus.). 290p. 1985. pap. 9.95 (ISBN 0-8070-5695-2, BP69). Beacon Pr.

--Yesterday, Today, & What Next? Reflections on History & Hope. LC 78-52204. 1978. pap. 7.50 (ISBN 0-8066-1670-9, 10-7400). Augsburg.

Bainton, Roland H. & Gritsch, Eric W. Bibliography of the Continental Reformation: Materials Available in English. 2nd ed. ix, 220p. 1973. 24.50 (ISBN 0-208-01219-2, Archon). Shoe String.

Bainton, Roland H., tr. Martin Luther Christmas Book with Celebrated Woodcuts by His Contemporaries. LC 59-2930. 80p. 1948. pap. 3.95 (ISBN 0-8006-1843-2, 1-1843). Fortress.

Bainton, Roland H., tr. see Gedat, Gustav-Adolf.

Bainton, Roland H., tr. see Holborn, Hajo.

Bainton, Ronald H. The Church of Our Fathers. 1984. 16.00 (ISBN 0-8446-6120-1). Peter Smith.

Bainum, P. M., jt. ed. see Stoewer, H.

Bainum, Peter M., ed. Space in the Nineteen Eighties, & Beyond, the Seventeenth European Space Symposium. (Science & Technology Ser.: Vol. 53). (Illus.). 302p. 1981. lib. bdg. 40.00x (ISBN 0-87703-154-1, Pub. by Am Astronaut); pap. text ed. 30.00x (ISBN 0-87703-155-X). Univelt Inc.

Bainum, Peter M. & Koelle, Dietrich E., eds. Spacelab, Space Platforms & the Future. LC 57-43769. (Advances in the Astronautical Sciences Ser.: Vol. 49). (Illus.). 502p. (Orig.). 1982. lib. bdg. 55.00x (ISBN 0-87703-174-6, Pub. by Am Astronaut); pap. text ed. 45.00x (ISBN 0-87703-175-4); microfiche supplement 5.00. Univelt Inc.

Bainum, Peter M., jt. ed. see Adelman, Andrew.

Bainum, Peter M., jt. ed. see Carter, L. J.

Bainum, Peter M., jt. ed. see Stoewer, H.

Bainvel, S. J. Is There Salvation Outside the Catholic Church? LC 79-55461. 1979. pap. 1.50 (ISBN 0-89555-132-2). TAN Bks Pubs.

Bainville, Jacques. Napoleon. Miles, Hamish, tr. LC 74-112794. 1970. Repr. of 1932 ed. 35.00x (ISBN 0-8046-1061-4, Pub. by Kennikat). Assoc Faculty Pr.

Baiocchi, Claudio & Capelo, Antonio. Variational & Quasivariational Inequalities: Applications to Free Boundary Problems. 400p. 1984. 57.95x (ISBN 0-471-90201-2, Pub. by Wiley Interscience). Wiley.

Bair, Dierdre. Samuel Beckett: A Biography. LC 79-24485. (Illus.). 736p. 1980. pap. 7.95 (ISBN 0-15-679241-9, Harv). HarBraceJ.

Bair, Frank E. Handbook of the Nations. 4th ed. 300p. 1984. Repr. of 1983 ed. 68.00x (ISBN 0-8103-1647-1). Gale.

Bair, Frank E., ed. Countries of the World & Their Leaders Yearbook: 1985, 2 vols. 1500p. 1984. 100.00x (ISBN 0-8103-1642-0). Gale.

--Countries of the World & Their Leaders: Yearbook 1986, 2 vols. 1986ed ed. 1600p. 1985. 110.00x (ISBN 0-8103-2117-3). Gale.

--Countries of the World & Their Leaders Yearbook 1985: Supplement. 350p. 1985. pap. 50.00x (ISBN 0-8103-1120-8). Gale.

--International Marketing Handbook, Nineteen Eighty-Five. 2000p. 1985. 200.00x (ISBN 0-8103-2057-6). Gale.

--International Marketing Handbook, 1981, 2 vols. LC 80-28549. (Illus.). 2380p. 1981. Set. 190.00x (ISBN 0-8103-0544-5). Gale.

--International Marketing Handbook: 1983 Supplement. 1232p. 1982. 95.00x (ISBN 0-8103-0546-1). Gale.

Bair, Frank E. & Ruffner, James, eds. The Weather Almanac. 1979. pap. 7.95 (ISBN 0-380-43000-2, 52654-9). Avon.

Bair, Frank E., jt. ed. see Ruffner, James A.

Bair, Frederick H. The Social Understandings of the Superintendent of Schools. LC 78-176531. (Columbia University. Teachers College. Contributions to Education: No. 625). Repr. of 1934 ed. 22.50 (ISBN 0-404-55625-6). AMS Pr.

Bair, Frederick H. & Curtis, Virginia, eds. Planning Cities: Selected Writings on Principles & Practice. 499p. 1970. pap. 10.95 (ISBN 0-318-13048-3); pap. 8.95 members (ISBN 0-318-13049-1). Am Plan Assn.

Bair, Frederick H., Jr. Modular Housing, Including Mobile Homes: A Survey of Regulatory Practice & Planners' Opinions. (PAS Reports: No. 265). 52p. 1971. 6.00 (ISBN 0-318-13033-5). Am Plan Assn.

--Regulation of Modular Housing, with Special Emphasis on Mobile Homes. (PAS Reports: No. 271). 104p. 1971. 6.00 (ISBN 0-318-13072-6). Am Plan Assn.

--The Zoning Board Manual. LC 84-60300. 132p. 1984. 13.95 (ISBN 0-918286-32-8). Planners Pr.

Bair, Frieda A. Weathered Years. 96p. 1984. 4.95 (ISBN 0-8059-2940-1). Dorrance.

Bair, J. & Fourneau, R. Etude Geometrique des Espaces Vectoriels: Une Introduction. (Lecture Notes in Mathematics: Vol. 489). 185p. 1975. pap. 10.70 (ISBN 0-387-07413-9). Springer-Verlag.

Bair, J. H. see Jones, J. W.

Bair, Lillian, jt. auth. see Bair, Ray.

Bair, Lowell, ed. see Flaubert, Gustave.

Bair, Lowell, tr. see Arsan, Emmanuelle.

Bair, Lowell, tr. see Calic, Edouard.

Bair, Lowell, tr. see Delacorta.

Bair, Lowell, tr. see Dumas, Alexandre.

Bair, Lowell, tr. see Hugo, Victor.

Bair, Lowell, tr. see Voltaire.

Bair, Marjorie, jt. auth. see Bry, Adelaide.

Bair, Ray & Bair, Lillian. God's Managers. 48p. 1981. pap. 2.95 (ISBN 0-8361-1982-7). Herald Pr.

Bair, Robert, tr. see Munoz, Hector.

Bair, W G. & Linden, H R. Continuous Production of Natural Gas Supplements from Natural Gasoline & Petroleum Distillates in a Tube Furnace. (Research Bulletin Ser.: No.27). iv, 83p. (B). 1960. 5.00 (ISBN 0-317-34303-3). Inst Gas Tech.

Bair, W G., jt. auth. see Feldman, H F.

Bair, W. G., jt. auth. see Reid, J. M.

Bairacli Levy, Juliette de see De Bairacli Levy, Juliette.

Bairacli-Levy, Juliette De see De Bairacli-Levy, Juliette.

Baird. Power of Positive Self Image. 1983. 4.95 (ISBN 0-88207-316-8). Victor Bks.

Baird, et al. Physics Laboratory Manual. 2nd ed. 144p. 1984. pap. text ed. 13.95 (ISBN 0-8403-3209-2). Kendall Hunt.

Baird, A. Craig, ed. see Goodrich, Chauncey A.

Baird, A. Craig, et al. Essentials of General Speech Communication. 4th ed. (Speech Ser.). (Illus.). 288p. 1973. text ed. 36.95 (ISBN 0-07-003252-1). McGraw.

Baird, Ann. Little Tree. (Illus.). 16p. (ps). 1984. pap. 3.95 (ISBN 0-688-02421-1, Morrow Junior Books). Morrow.

--No Sheep. (Illus.). 16p. (ps). 1984. 3.95 (ISBN 0-688-02377-0, Morrow Junior Books). Morrow.

Baird, Anne. Baby Socks. (Illus.). 16p. (ps). 1984. pap. 3.95 (ISBN 0-688-02436-X, Morrow Junior Books). Morrow.

--Kiss, Kiss. (Illus.). 16p. (ps). 1984. pap. 3.95 (ISBN 0-688-02493-9, Morrow Junior Books). Morrow.

Baird, Arthur J., ed. see Parunak, Van Dyke H.

Baird, Arthur J., ed. see Radday, Yehuda & Levi, Yaakov.

Baird, Bil. Art of the Puppet. (Illus.). (YA) (gr. 9 up). 1966. 19.95 (ISBN 0-8238-0067-9). Plays.

Baird, Bruce F. The Technical Manager: How to Manage People & Make Decisions. (Illus.). 168p. 1983. 22.50 (ISBN 0-534-97925-4). Lifetime Learn.

Baird, C. Direlle, jt. auth. see Fluck, Richard C.

Baird, Charles. Rent Control: The Perennial Folly. LC 80-16317. (Cato Public Policy Research Cato Monograph: No. 2). 110p. (Orig.). 1980. pap. 5.00x (ISBN 0-932790-22-4). Cato Inst.

Baird, Charles W. Chronicle of a Border Town: History of Rye, Westchester County, New York, 1660-1870, including Harrison & White Plains till 1788. LC 74-6231. (Illus.). 1974. Repr. of 1871 ed. 35.00 (ISBN 0-916346-07-2). Harbor Hill Bks.

--History of the Huguenot Emigration to America, 2 Vols. in 1. LC 66-29569. (Illus.). 800p. 1985. Repr. of 1885 ed. 17.50 (ISBN 0-317-31632-X). Genealog Pub.

--John Bunyan: A Study in Narrative Technique. LC 76-53813. (National University Publications in Literary Criticism Ser.). 1977. 15.95x (ISBN 0-8046-9162-2, Pub. by Kennikat). Assoc Faculty Pr.

--Opportunity or Privilege: Labor Legislation in America. (Studies in Social Philosophy & Policy: No. 4). 97p. (Orig.). 1984. pap. 6.95 (ISBN 0-912051-02-7). Soc Phil Pol.

--Opportunity or Privilege: Labor Legislation in America. 97p. 1983. pap. 6.95 (ISBN 0-912051-02-7). Transaction Bks.

--Prices & Markets: Intermediate Microeconomics. 2nd ed. (Illus.). 396p. 1982. text ed. 25.95 (ISBN 0-314-63156-9). West Pub.

Baird, Charles W. & Cassuto, Alexander E. Macroeconomics: Monetary, Search & Income Theories. 2nd ed. 344p. 1981. text ed. 25.95 (ISBN 0-574-19400-2, 13-2400); instr's. guide avail. (ISBN 0-574-19401-0, 13-2401). SRA.

Baird, Chuck, et al. Encyclopedia for the TRS-80, Vol. 7. Putnam, Katherine & Comiskey, Kate, eds. 265p. 1982. 19.95 (ISBN 0-88006-042-5, EN8107); pap. 10.95 (ISBN 0-88006-043-3, EN8087). Green Pub Inc.

Baird, Coleen. Seven Days & Prayer. (gr. k-6). 1980. pap. 2.95 (ISBN 0-87747-802-3). Deseret Bk.

Baird, D. T., jt. auth. see Short, R. V.

Baird, David, jt. auth. see Baird, Ronald J.

Baird, David C. Experimentation: An Introduction to Measurement Theory & Experiment Design. 1962. text ed. 17.95 (ISBN 0-13-295345-5). P-H.

Baird, Don O. A Study of Biology Notebook Work in New York State. LC 71-176532. (Columbia University. Teachers College. Contributions to Education: No. 400). Repr. of 1929 ed. 22.50 (ISBN 0-404-55400-8). AMS Pr.

Baird, Douglas & Jackson, Thomas. Cases, Problems & Materials on Bankruptcy. LC 84-82546. 1985. text ed. write for info. (ISBN 0-316-07677-5). Little.

Baird, Douglas G. & Jackson, Thomas H. Cases, Problems, & Materials on Security Interests in Personal Property. LC 83-16400. (University Casebook Ser.). 935p. 1983. text ed. 29.00 (ISBN 0-88277-140-X). Foundation Pr.

--Cases, Problems, Materials on Security Interests in Personal Property: Teacher's Manual. (University Casebook Ser.). 153p. 1983. pap. text ed. write for info. (ISBN 0-88277-169-8). Foundation Pr.

Baird, Eric. The Clydesdale Horse. (Illus.). 160p. 1982. 24.00 (ISBN 0-7134-4041-4, Pub. by Batsford England). David & Charles.

Baird, Eva-Lee, jt. auth. see Wyler, Rose.

Baird, Floyd, ed. see Kyle, Robert C.

Baird, Forrest, jt. auth. see Rogers, Jack B.

Baird, Frank L., ed. Mexican Americans: Political Power, Influence, or Resource. (Graduate Studies: No. 14). (Illus.). 108p. (Orig.). 1977. pap. 7.00 (ISBN 0-89672-024-1). Tex Tech Pr.

Baird, George, et al, eds. Energy Performance of Buildings. 216p. 1984. 64.00 (ISBN 0-8493-5186-3). CRC Pr.

Baird, H. Gordon. Management Styles for The Nineties. 140p. (Orig.). 1982. 15.00 (ISBN 0-943000-00-9). Telstar Inc.

Baird, Henry C. Victorian Gothic & Renaissance Revival Furniture. (The Athenaeum Library of Nineteenth Century America). (Illus.). 1977. Repr. of 1868 ed. text ed. 20.00 (ISBN 0-89257-019-9). Am Life Foun.

Baird, Henry M. History of the Rise of the Huguenots of France, 2 Vols. LC 79-130236. Repr. of 1879 ed. Set. 90.00 (ISBN 0-404-00520-9); 45.00 ea. Vol. 1 (ISBN 0-404-00521-7). Vol. 2 (ISBN 0-404-00522-5). AMS Pr.

--Huguenots & Henry of Navarre, 2 Vols. LC 76-130987. Repr. of 1903 ed. Set. 74.50 (ISBN 0-404-00540-3). AMS Pr.

--The Huguenots & the Revocation of the Edict of Nantes, 2 vols. LC 76-161752. Repr. of 1895 ed. Set. 74.50 (ISBN 0-404-08003-0). AMS Pr.

--The Huguenots & the Revocation of the Edict of Nantes, 2 vols. 1977. lib. bdg. 250.00 (ISBN 0-8490-2025-5). Gordon Pr.

--Modern Greece: Narrative of a Residence & Travels in That Country. LC 77-87533. (Illus.). Repr. of 1856 ed. 30.00 (ISBN 0-404-16593-1). AMS Pr.

--Theodore Beza, The Counsellor of the French Reformation, 1519-1605. LC 76-121596. 1970. Repr. of 1899 ed. 25.50 (ISBN 0-8337-0151-7). B Franklin.

Baird, Henry S. Model-Based Image Matching Using Location. (Association for Computing Machinery Distinguished Dissertation Award Ser.: 1984). (Illus.). 115p. 1985. text ed. 25.00 (ISBN 0-262-02220-6). MIT Pr.

Baird, Henry W. & Gordon, Eleanora C. The Neurological Evaluation of Infants & Children. (Clinics in Developmental Medicine Ser.: Nos. 84-85). 260p. 1983. text ed. 29.75 (ISBN 0-433-01130-0). Lippincott.

Baird, J. A. & Ozelton, E. C. Timber Designer's Manual. 2nd ed. (Illus.). 656p. 1984. text ed. 75.00x (ISBN 0-246-12375-3, Pub. by Granada England). Sheridan.

Baird, J. A., jt. auth. see Ozelton, E. C.

Baird, J. Arthur. Audience Criticism & the Historical Jesus. 1969. 6.50 (ISBN 0-664-20846-0). Biblical Res Assocs.

--Rediscovering the Power of the Gospel: Jesus' Theology of the Kingdom. LC 82-83623. 1982. pap. 9.95 (ISBN 0-910789-00-2). Iona Pr.

Baird, J. Arthur, ed. see Morton, A. Q., et al.

Baird, J. Arthur, ed. see Morton, A. Q. & Michaelson, S.

Baird, J. Arthur, ed. see Morton, A. Q. & Michaelson, Sidney.

Baird, J. Arthur, ed. see Tyson, Joseph B. & Longstaff, Thomas R. W.

Baird, J. G. Private Letters of the Marquess of Dalhousie. (Illus.). 448p. 1984. Repr. of 1910 ed. text ed. 80.00x (ISBN 0-86590-374-3, Pub. by B R Pub Corp Delhi). Apt Bks.

Baird, J. G., ed. Private Letters of the Marquess of Dalhousie. (Illus.). 461p. 1972. Repr. of 1910 ed. 35.00x (ISBN 0-7165-2053-2, BBA 03051, Pub. by Irish Academic Pr). Biblio Dist.

Baird, J. L. & Kane, John R. La Querelle de la Rose: Letters & Documents. (Studies in the Romance Languages & Literatures: No. 199). 172p. 1978. pap. 11.00x (ISBN 0-8078-9199-1). U of NC Pr.

Baird, J. W. From Nuremberg to My Lai. (Problems in European Civilization Ser.). 1972. pap. text ed. 5.95x (ISBN 0-669-82081-4). Heath.

Baird, Jack, jt. auth. see Sopher, Charles.

Baird, James. The Dome & the Rock: Structure in the Poetry of Wallace Stevens. LC 68-19701. pap. 92.00 (ISBN 0-317-30116-0, 2025301). Bks Demand UMI.

Baird, James, et al see Kurtz, David L. & Boone, Louis E.

Baird, James W. Thunder over Scotland: George Wishart, Mentor of John Knox. LC 82-81516. (Illus.). 1982. text ed. 7.95 (ISBN 0-938462-04-0). Green Leaf CA.

Baird, Janet H., ed. These Harvest Years. facsimile ed. LC 74-167308. (Essay Index Reprint Ser). Repr. of 1951 ed. 18.00 (ISBN 0-8369-2581-5). Ayer Co Pubs.

Baird, Jo Ann. Using Media in the Music Program. (Classroom Music Enrichment Units Ser.). 1974. pap. 6.80x (ISBN 0-87628-211-7). Ctr Appl Res.

Baird, John. Make-Up. rev. ed. 132p. 1941. 5.00 (ISBN 0-573-69031-6). French.

Baird, John, jt. auth. see DeWelt, Don.

Baird, John A., Jr. Horn of Plenty. 1982. pap. 6.95 (ISBN 0-8423-1451-2). Tyndale.

--Profile of a Hero: Absalom Baird, His Family, & the American Military Tradition. 1977. 7.95 (ISBN 0-8059-2460-4). Dorrance.

Baird, John C. & Noma, Elliot. Fundamentals of Scaling & Psychophysics. LC 78-6011. (Behavior Ser.). 287p. 1978. 42.95x (ISBN 0-471-04169-6, Pub. by Wiley-Interscience). Wiley.

Baird, John C. & Lutkus, Anthony D., eds. Mind Child Architecture. LC 81-69937. (Illus.). 224p. 1982. text ed. 18.00x (ISBN 0-87451-233-6, Pub. by Dartmouth College). U Pr of New Eng.

Baird, John D. Fifteen Years in Hawken Lode. 17.95 (ISBN 0-88227-011-7). Gun Room.

--Hawken Rifles: The Mountain Man's Choice. 17.95 (ISBN 0-88227-010-9). Gun Room.

Baird, John D., ed. Editing Texts of the Romantic Period. (Conference on Editorial Problems Ser.). 1976. lib. bdg. 22.00 (ISBN 0-8240-2406-0). Garland Pub.

Baird, John D., ed. see Cowper, William.

Baird, John E. Corinthians Study Guide. (Search & Discover Bible Study). 104p. 1975. wkbk. 2.50 (ISBN 0-87239-024-1, 40016). Standard Pub.

--Matthew Study Guide. (Search & Discover Bible Study). 104p. 1975. wkbk. 2.50 (ISBN 0-87239-020-9, 40010). Standard Pub.

Baird, John E., Jr. Quality Circles: Leaders Manual. 256p. 1982. pap. 12.95 (ISBN 0-917974-88-3). Waveland Pr.

--Quality Circles: Participant's Manual. (Illus.). 192p. 1982. pap. text ed. 8.95x (ISBN 0-917974-79-4). Waveland Pr.

--Speaking for Results: Communication by Objectives. (Illus.). 301p. 1981. pap. text ed. 14.10 scp (ISBN 0-06-040457-4, HarpC); instr's. manual available (ISBN 0-06-360288-1). Har-Row.

Baird, John E., Jr. & Rittof, David J. Quality Circles: Facilitator's Manual. (Illus.). 247p. (Orig.). 1983. pap. 36.95X (ISBN 0-88133-010-8). Waveland Pr.

Baird, John E., Jr. & Weinberg, Sanford B. Group Communication: Essence of Synergy. 2nd ed. 270p. 1981. pap. text ed. write for info. (ISBN 0-697-04181-6); instrs.' manual avail. (ISBN 0-697-04187-5). Wm C Brown.

Baird, John E., Jr., jt. auth. see Bradley, Patricia H.

Baird, John W. & Stull, James B. Business Communication: Strategies & Solutions. LC 82-17228. (Illus.). 448p. 1983. text ed. 32.95 (ISBN 0-07-003281-5). McGraw.

Baird, Joseph A., Jr., jt. auth. see D'Emilio, Sandra.

Baird, Joseph A., Jr., et al. Sacred Places of San Francisco. (Illus.). 300p. 35.00 (ISBN 0-89141-192-5). Presidio Pr.

Baird, Joseph L. & Kane, John R. Rossignol. LC 78-38. 93p. 1978. 13.00x (ISBN 0-87338-211-0). Kent St U Pr.

Baird, Julia L., jt. auth. see Weaver, Donald B.

Baird, Leonard L. Using Self-Reports to Predict Student Performance. LC 76-4312. (Research Monographs: No. 7). 92p. 1976. pap. 5.00 (ISBN 0-87447-098-6, 251701). College Bd.

Baird, Leonard L. & Hartnett, Rodney T. Understanding Student & Faculty Life: Using Campus Surveys to Improve Academic Decision Making. LC 79-24863. (Higher Education Ser.). 1980. text ed. 19.95x (ISBN 0-87589-443-7). Jossey-Bass.

Baird, Lloyd, et al, eds. The Performance Appraisal Source Book. (Illus.). 256p. 1982. lib. bdg. 35.00x (ISBN 0-914234-56-0). Human Res Dev.

--The Training & Development Sourcebook. 381p. 1983. 35.00x (ISBN 0-914234-64-1). Human Res Dev Pr.

Baird, M. S., jt. auth. see McQuillin, F. J.

Baird, Macaran A., jt. auth. see Doherty, William J.

Baird, Mark. Uganda: Country Economic Memorandum. v, 161p. 1982. pap. 5.00 (ISBN 0-8213-0027-X). World Bank.

Baird, Martha. Nice Deity. LC 55-11012. 1955. 2.75 (ISBN 0-910492-04-2). Definition.

--Two Aesthetic Realism Papers: Opposites in the Drama; Opposites in Myself. LC 79-268159. 1971. pap. 2.50 (ISBN 0-910492-15-8). Definition.

Baird, Martha & Reiss, Ellen, eds. The Press Boycott of Aesthetic Realism: Documentation. LC 77-80498. 1978. pap. 2.00 (ISBN 0-910492-30-1). Definition.

Baird, Martha, ed. see Siegel, Eli, et al.

Baird, Martha, ed. see Siegel, Eli.

Baird, Michael. Weather Forecasting For Astronomy. LC 82-50215. (Illus.). 120p. (Orig.). 1982. pap. 12.95 (ISBN 0-9608278-0-3). Winmark Pr.

Baird, Michael G. Winmark I. Q. Scale. (Illus.). 1983. pap. 2.95 (ISBN 0-9608278-1-1). Winmark Pr.

Baird, Michael G., ed. Moonranch. (Illus.). 1984. pap. 24.00 (ISBN 0-9608278-2-X). Winmark Pr.

Baird, Nancy D. David Wendel Yandell: Physician of Old Louisville. LC 77-80461. (Kentucky Bicentennial Bookshelf Ser.). (Illus.). 132p. 1978. 6.95 (ISBN 0-8131-0245-6). U Pr of Ky.

--Luke Pryor Blackburn: Physician, Governor, Reformer. LC 79-888. (Kentucky Bicentennial Bookself Ser.). (Illus.). 136p. 1979. 6.95 (ISBN 0-8131-0248-0). U Pr of Ky.

Baird, Newton, et al. A Key to Fredric Brown's Wonderland: A Study & an Annotated Bibliographical Checklist. LC 81-52422. (Illus.). 64p. 1981. 15.00 (ISBN 0-686-78412-X); pap. 8.95 (ISBN 0-686-78413-8). Talisman Research.

Baird, P. Harmonic Maps with Symmetry, Harmonic Morphisms & Deformation of Metrics. (Research Notes in Mathematics Ser.: No. 87). 208p. 1983. pap. text ed. 17.95 (ISBN 0-273-08603-0). Pitman Pub MA.

Baird, Peter & McCaughan, Ed. Beyond the Border: Mexico & the U.S. Today. (Illus.). 205p. 1979. pap. 5.95 (ISBN 0-916024-37-7). NA Cong Lat Am.

Baird, R. N., et al. Human Disease for Dental Students. 352p. pap. text ed. cancelled (ISBN 0-272-79608-5). Pitman Pub MA.

Baird, R. N., et al, eds. Human Disease for Dental Students. 340p. 1981. pap. text ed. 29.95x (ISBN 0-8464-1217-9). Beekman Pubs.

Baird, R. W. Human Disease for Dental Students. 340p. 1981. 39.00x (ISBN 0-272-79608-5, Pub. by Pitman Bks England). State Mutual Bk.

Baird, Robert. Impressions & Experiences of the West Indies & North America in 1849. 17.25 (ISBN 0-8369-9216-4, 9072). Ayer Co Pubs.

--Religion in America: A Critical Abridgment. 11.25 (ISBN 0-8446-0471-2). Peter Smith.

--Religion in the U. S. A, 2 vols. (Works of Rev. Robert Baird Ser.). Date not set. Repr. Set. lib. bdg. 79.00 (ISBN 0-932051-57-X). Am Repr Serv.

--Religion in the United States of America. LC 70-83411. (Religion in America, Ser. 1). 1969. Repr. of 1844 ed. 38.50 (ISBN 0-405-00232-7). Ayer Co Pubs.

Baird, Robert D. Category Formation & the History of Religions. (Religion & Reason Ser: No. 1). 178p. 1971. text ed. 15.60x (ISBN 90-2796-889-6). Mouton.

Baird, Robert D. & Bloom, Alfred. Religion & Man: Indian & Far Eastern Religious Traditions. (Religion & Man: An Introduction, Pts. 2 & 3). 1972. pap. text ed. 13.45 scp (ISBN 0-06-040448-5, HarpC). Har-Row.

Baird, Robert D., ed. Methodological Issues in Religious Studies. LC 75-44170. (Orig.). 1976. lib. bdg. 14.95x (ISBN 0-914914-08-1); pap. text ed. 5.95x (ISBN 0-914914-07-3). New Horizons.

--Religion in Modern India. 1982. 36.00x (ISBN 0-8364-0826-8); 19.00x (ISBN 0-8364-0830-6). South Asia Bks.

Baird, Robert M., ed. The Philosophical Life: An Activity & an Attitude. LC 83-10226. 220p. (Orig.). 1983. pap. text ed. 9.50 (ISBN 0-8191-3354-X). U Pr of Amer.

Baird, Roger N. & Woodcock, John P., eds. Diagnosis & Monitoring in Arterial Surgery. (Illus.). 184p. 1980. pap. text ed. 23.50 (ISBN 0-7236-0556-4). PSG Pub Co.

Baird, Ronald J. Contemporary Industrial Teaching. LC 78-185957. (Illus.). 200p. 1972. text ed. 10.64 (ISBN 0-87006-130-5). Goodheart.

--Oxyacetylene Welding. LC 79-6555. (Illus.). 1980. pap. text ed. 7.00 (ISBN 0-87006-501-7). Goodheart.

Baird, Ronald J. & Baird, David. Industrial Plastics. LC 81-13514. (Illus.). 320p. 1982. 16.80 (ISBN 0-87006-402-9). Goodheart.

Baird, Ronald J., jt. auth. see Kicklighter, Clois E.

Baird, Ronald J., jt. auth. see Roth, Alfred C.

Baird, Ronald J., ed. see Kicklighter, Clois E.

Baird, Russell N., jt. auth. see Click, J. W.

Baird, Russell N., jt. auth. see Turnbull, Arthur T.

Baird, S. F., ed. see Copper, James G.

Baird, S. F., et al. Water Birds of North America, 2 vols. in one. (Natural Sciences in America Ser). (Illus.). 1974. 74.00 (ISBN 0-405-05716-4). Ayer Co Pubs.

--Birds of North America: The Descriptions of Species Based Chiefly on the Collections in the Museum of the Smithsonian Institution, 2 vols. in one. LC 73-17799. (Natural Sciences in America Ser). (Illus.). 1974. 73.00x (ISBN 0-405-05715-6). Ayer Co Pubs.

Baird, Samuel E. With Merrill's Cavalry. Annegan, Charles, ed. LC 80-69601. (Illus.). 51p. 1981. 12.00 (ISBN 0-9605200-0-7). C Annegan.

Baird, San F., ed. Scotish Feilde & Flodden Feilde: Two Flodden Poems. (Medieval Literature Ser.). 112p. 1982. lib. bdg. 24.00 (ISBN 0-8240-9449-2). Garland Pub.

Baird, Scott J., ed. see Fujiwara, Yoichi.

Baird, Spencer, et al. A History of North American Birds: Land Birds, 3 vols. LC 73-17798. (Natural Sciences in America Ser.). (Illus.). 1972p. 1974. Repr. Set. 132.00x (ISBN 0-405-05711-3); Vol. 1. 44.00x (ISBN 0-405-05712-1); Vol. 2. 44.00x (ISBN 0-405-05713-X); Vol. 3. 44.00x (ISBN 0-405-05714-8). Ayer Co Pubs.

Baird, Spencer F. Mammals of North America: The Descriptions of Species Based Chiefly on the Collections in the Museum of the Smithsonian Institution. LC 73-17797. (Natural Sciences in America Ser.). (Illus.). 844p. 1974. Repr. 58.50x (ISBN 0-405-05710-5). Ayer Co Pubs.

Baird, Susan. Junk Binge: Be a Junk Millionaire. LC 80-85023. (Illus.). 1984. pap. 8.95 (ISBN 0-913042-13-7). Holland Hse Pr.

Baird, Tate, ed. see McClure, Patricia.

Baird, Tate, ed. see Oana, Katherine.

Baird, Thomas. Finding Fever. LC 81-48646. 224p. (gr. 6 up). 1982. 11.06i (ISBN 0-06-020353-6); PLB 11.89g (ISBN 0-06-020354-4). HarpJ.

--Finding Out. 1979. pap. 1.95 (ISBN 0-380-44248-5, 44248). Avon.

--People Who Pull You Down. 1978. pap. 1.75 (ISBN 0-380-39339-5, 39339). Avon.

--Villa Aphrodite. 352p. 1984. 14.95 (ISBN 0-312-84679-7, J Kahn). St Martin.

--Walk Out a Brother. LC 82-48859. 288p. (YA) (gr. 7 up). 1983. 12.02i (ISBN 0-06-020355-2); PLB 12.89g (ISBN 0-06-020356-0). HarpJ.

Baird, Thomas B., jt. auth. see Hamblen, John W.

Baird, W. The Natural History of the British Entomostraca. 28.00 (ISBN 0-384-03080-7). Johnson Repr.

Baird, W. David. The Quapaw Indians: A History of the Downstream People. LC 79-4731. (Civilization of the American Indian Ser.: Vol. 152). (Illus.). 1980. 21.95 (ISBN 0-8061-1542-4). U of Okla Pr.

Baird, Wellesley. Guyana Gold: The Story of Wellesley Baird Guyana's Greatest Miner. Adams, Katherine, intro. by. LC 81-51666. 210p. (Orig.). 1982. 16.00x (ISBN 0-89410-192-7); pap. 7.00x (ISBN 0-89410-193-5). Three Continents.

Baird, William. General Wauchope. LC 72-4077. (Black Heritage Library Collection Ser.). Repr. of 1901 ed. 19.00 (ISBN 0-8369-9094-3). Ayer Co Pubs.

Baird, William see Hayes, John.

Baird, William, ed. see Bassler, Jouette M.

Baird, William, ed. see Fowler, Robert M.

Bairnsfather, Bruce. Best Fragments from France. Holt, Valmai & Holt, Tonie, eds. (Illus.). 1983. pap. 9.95 (ISBN 0-903852-40-3, Pub. by Milestone Pubns UK). Seven Hills Bks.

Bairoch, P. Working Population & Its Structure. 236p. 1969. 67.25 (ISBN 0-677-61130-7). Gordon.

Bairoch, Paul. Commerce Exterieur et Developpement Economique De L'europe Au X1Xe Siecle. (Civilisations et Societes: No. 53). 1976. pap. 26.40x (ISBN 90-2797-953-7). Mouton.

--The Economic Development of the Third World Since 1900. Postan, Cynthia, tr. LC 74-16706. (Illus.). 1975. pap. 10.50x (ISBN 0-520-03554-2). U of Cal Pr.

--Urban Unemployment in Developing Countries: The Nature of the Problem & Proposals for Its Solution. 2nd ed. 1976. 7.15 (ISBN 92-2-100998-X). Intl Labour Office.

Bairoch, Paul, ed. Disparities in Economic Development Since the Industrial Revolution. Levy-Leboyer, Maurice. 1981. 39.95x (ISBN 0-312-21271-2). St Martin.

Bairstow, Edward C. The Evolution of Musical Form. LC 72-80135. 119p. 1972. Repr. of 1943 ed. lib. bdg. 15.00 (ISBN 0-8154-0427-1). Cooper Sq.

Bairstow, Jeffrey. Four Season Camping. LC 82-40019. (Illus.). 288p. (Orig.). 1982. pap. 5.95 (ISBN 0-394-74783-6, Vin). Random.

Bairstow, Jeffrey & Brumfield, Charles. Off the Wall. 1978. pap. 8.95 (ISBN 0-385-27091-7, Dial). Doubleday.

Bairstow, Jeffrey, jt. auth. see Lott, George.

Bairstow, Jeffrey N. Camping Year Round. LC 82-20305. 164p. 1983. pap. 5.95 (ISBN 0-394-74783-6, Vin). Random.

Bairstow, John E. Practical & Decorative Woodworking Joints. LC 84-51838. (Illus.). 128p. 1985. 17.95 (ISBN 0-8069-5544-9); pap. 11.95 (ISBN 0-8069-7948-8). Sterling.

Bairstow, Linda. How to Stop Your Toddler from Driving You Crazy. 1985. 19.95 (ISBN 0-87949-243-0). AShley Bks.

Bairstow, Phillip J., jt. auth. see Laszlo, Judith I.

Baisden, C. Robert. The Office Practice Laboratory. 1985. pap. text ed. 30.00 (ISBN 0-8391-1997-6, 20982). Univ Park.

Baisden, Major J., Jr. The Dynamics of Homosexuality. LC 75-31. 199p. 1975. 6.95 (ISBN 0-912984-02-3). Allied Res Soc.

--The World of Rosaphrenia: The Sexual Psychology of the Female. LC 72-178852. 224p. 1971. 6.95 (ISBN 0-912984-01-5). Allied Res Soc.

Baise, Melanie. Inspection & Enforcement. (Your Rights in the Coalfields Ser.). (Illus.). 26p. 1983. pap. 3.00 (ISBN 0-943724-03-1). Illinois South.

Baishya, A. K. & Rao, R. R. Ferns & Fern-Allies of Meghalaya State, India. 161p. 1982. 40.00x (ISBN 0-686-45802-8, Pub. by United Bk Traders India). State Mutual Bk.

Baisier, Leon. Lapidaire Chretien: Its Composition, Its Influence, Its Sources. LC 71-94163. (Catholic University of America Studies in Romance Languages & Literatures Ser: No. 14). 1969. Repr. of 1936 ed. 20.00 (ISBN 0-404-50314-4). AMS Pr.

Baistow, Tom, tr. see Karol, K. S.

Baital, Jim see Greicus, Mike.

Baitch. Electrical Technology. 2nd ed. 1984. pap. write for info. (ISBN 0-471-33394-8). Wiley.

Baitsell, George A., ed. The Centennial of the Sheffield Scientific School (Yale University) 1950. 19.50x (ISBN 0-686-51350-9). Elliots Bks.

Baitsell, George A., ed. see Gamow, George, et al.

Baitsell, George A., ed. see Jewett, Frank B., et al.

Baitsell, George A., ed. see Lawrence, Ernest O.

Baitsell, George A., ed. see Miles, Walter R., et al.

Baitsell, George A., ed. see Patten, Bradley M., et al.

Baitsell, George A., ed. see Shapley, Harlow, et al.

Baitsell, George A., ed. see Smyth, H. D., et al.

Baitsell, George A., ed. see Snyder, Laurence H., et al.

Baitsell, George A., ed. see Stadler, L. J., et al.

Baity, Philip C. Religion in a Chinese Town. (Asian Folklore & Social Life Monographs: No. 64). 318p. 1975. 17.00 (ISBN 0-89986-059-1). Oriental Bk Store.

Baity, W. A., ed. see Armstong, Ray.

Baiulescu, G. E. & Ilie, A. V. Stationary Phases in Gas Chromatography. 1975. text ed. 65.00 (ISBN 0-08-018075-2). Pergamon.

Baiulescu, G. E., et al. Education & Teaching in Analytical Chemistry. (Series in Analytical Chemistry). 160p. 1982. 48.95x (ISBN 0-470-27283-X). Halsted Pr.

Baiz de Gelpi, Elsa. Meet the Essay. pap. 4.00 (ISBN 0-8477-3110-3). U of PR Pr.

--Meet the Short Story. pap. 4.00 (ISBN 0-8477-3111-1). U of PR Pr.

Baizer, Lund. Organic Electrochemistry. 2nd ed. 976p. 1983. 155.00 (ISBN 0-8247-6855-8). Dekker.

Baizerman, Suzanne & Searle, Karen. Finishes in the Ethnic Tradition. 1978. 7.50 (ISBN 0-932394-01-9). Dos Tejedoras.

--Latin American Brocades. 1976. Repr. 5.00 (ISBN 0-932394-02-7). Dos Tejedoras.

Bajada, E. & Colomb, F. R. Observations in the Twenty-One-CM Neutral Hydrogen Line. (Carnegie Institution of Washington Ser.: No. 632). pap. 20.00 (ISBN 0-317-09027-5, 2007900). Bks Demand UMI.

Bajaj & Singh. Cost-Effective Energy Management. LC 82-4243. (Illus.). 200p. 1982. 24.95x (ISBN 0-912524-22-7). Busn News.

Bajaj, J. S., jt. ed. see Foa, P. P.

Bajaj, K. K., et al, eds. Spectroscopy of Shallow Centers in Semiconductors: Selected Proceedings of the 1st International Conference, Berkeley, CA, USA, 2-3 Aug. 1984. 120p. 1985. pap. 25.00 (ISBN 0-08-032569-6, Pub. by PPL). Pergamon.

Bajaj, Satish K. Secondary Social Science Workbook. (Illus.). 236p. 1981. pap. text ed. 7.95x (ISBN 0-86131-271-6, Pub. by Orient Longman Ltd India). Apt Bks.

Bajaj, Y. P., jt. ed. see Reinert, J.

Bajandas, F. J., jt. ed. see Brooks, B. A.

Bajandas, Frank. Neuro-Ophthamology Board Review Manual. LC 80-50629. 143p. 1980. 19.50 (ISBN 0-913590-71-1). Slack Inc.

Bajaria, Hans J., ed. Quality Assurance: Methods, Management & Motivation. LC 81-50392. (Manufacturing Update Ser.). (Illus.). 265p. 1981. 32.00 (ISBN 0-87263-067-6). SME.

--Quality Assurance: Methods, Management, & Motivation. LC 81-50392. pap. 65.00 (ISBN 0-317-27736-7, 2024175). Bks Demand UMI.

Bajcar, A. Poland: A Tourist Guide. (Illus.). 1977. pap. 10.00 (ISBN 0-686-77959-2). Heinman.

Bajec, A. & Kalan, P. Dizionario Italian-Slovar. 843p. (Ital. & Slovene.). 1980. 49.95 (ISBN 0-686-97337-2, M-9692). French & Eur.

Bajema, Carl, jt. auth. see Hardin, Garrett.

Bajema, Carl J., ed. Artificial Selection & Development of Evolutionary Theory. LC 80-10784. (Benchmark Papers in Systematic & Evolutionary Biology: Vol. 4). 384p. 1982. 49.95 (ISBN 0-87933-369-3). Van Nos Reinhold.

--Eugenics: Then & Now. LC 75-43761. (Benchmark Papers in Genetics Ser: Vol. 5). 400p. 1976. 64.50 (ISBN 0-12-786110-6). Acad Pr.

--Natural Selection in Human Populations: The Measurement of Ongoing Genetic Evolution in Contemporary Societies. LC 76-50639. (Illus.). 416p. 1977. Repr. of 1971 ed. lib. bdg. 19.50 (ISBN 0-88275-476-9). Krieger.

--Natural Selection Theory: From the Speculations of the Greeks to the Quantitative Measurements of the Biometricians. LC 82-15633. (Benchmark Papers in Systematic and Evolutionary Biology: Vol. 5). 384p. 1983. 44.50 (ISBN 0-87933-412-6). Van Nos Reinhold.

Bajema, Clifford E. Abortion & the Meaning of Personhood. (Direction Bks). 1974. pap. 1.25 (ISBN 0-8010-0672-4). Baker Bk.

Bajer, Andrew S. see Bourne, G. H. & Danielli, J. F.

Bajic, B., et al. Technical-Economical Dictionary for Business Purposes. 1700p. (Eng., Fr., Ger. & Serbocroation.). 1973. 95.00 (ISBN 0-686-92638-2, M-9689). French & Eur.

Bajkai, Louis A. Teachers Guide to Overseas Teaching: A Complete & Comprehensive Guide of English-Language Schools & Colleges Overseas. 3rd, Rev. ed. LC 77-81788. (Illus.). 192p. 1983. pap. 19.95 (ISBN 0-9601550-2-3). Friends World Teach.

Bajpai, A. C. & Bond, R. M. Applied Math. 349p. 1983. pap. 15.95 (ISBN 0-471-86166-9). Wiley.

Bajpai, A. C., et al. Mathematics for Engineers & Scientists, 2 vols. LC 72-14009. (Series of Programs on Mathematics for Scientist & Technologist). 800p. 1973. Vol. 2, 661 Pgs. 26.95 (ISBN 0-471-04374-5, Pub. by Wiley-Interscience). Wiley.

--Numerical Methods for Engineers & Scientists. (Series of Programmes on Mathematics for Scientists & Technologists). 380p. 1977. 29.95x (ISBN 0-471-99542-8, Pub. by Wiley-Interscience). Wiley.

--Statistical Methods for Engineers & Scientists: A Students' Course Book. LC 78-2481. (Programmes on Mathematics for Scientists & Technologists Ser.). 444p. 1978. 32.95x (ISBN 0-471-99644-0). Wiley.

--Engineering Mathematics. LC 73-21230. 793p. 1974. pap. text ed. 29.95 (ISBN 0-471-04376-1, Pub. by Wiley-Interscience). Wiley.

--Specialist Techniques in Engineering Mathematics. LC 80-41274. 401p. 1980. 74.95 (ISBN 0-471-27907-2, Pub. by Wiley-Interscience); pap. 39.95 (ISBN 0-471-27908-0). Wiley.

Bajpai, Avi C. FORTRAN & Algol: A Programmed Course for Students of Science & Technology. LC 73-5712. pap. 51.90 (ISBN 0-317-08899-8, 2013981). Bks Demand UMI.

Bajpai, S. C. Kinnaur in the Himalayas: Mythology to Modernity. 250p. 1981. text ed. 14.75x (ISBN 0-391-02475-2, Pub. by Concept India). Humanities.

Bajpai, U. S., ed. Non-Alignment: Perspective & Prospects. 350p. 1983. text ed. 35.00x (ISBN 0-391-02923-1). Humanities.

Bajracharya, Surya B. Achievement Testing in Nepal. 61p. 1984. 6.50 (ISBN 0-318-04166-9). Am-Nepal Ed.

Bajura, R. A., ed. Polyphase Flow & Transport Technology. 270p. 1980. 40.00 (ISBN 0-686-69858-4, H00158). ASME.

Bajura, R. A. & Morrow, T. B., eds. Modeling of Environment Flow Systems. 88p. 1983. pap. text ed. 20.00 (ISBN 0-317-02634-8, H00281). ASME.

Bajusz, E. & Jasmin, C., eds. Nutritional Pathobiology. (Methods & Achievement in Experimental Pathology: Vol. 6). (Illus.). 1972. 51.25 (ISBN 3-8055-1343-7). S Karger.

Bajusz, E. & Jasmin, G., eds. Functional Morphology of the Heart. (Methods & Achievements in Experimental Pathology: Vol. 5). 1971. 84.25 (ISBN 3-8055-1209-0). S Karger.

Bajwa, Fauja S. Military System of the Sikhs (During the Period 1799-1899) (Illus.). 1964. 4.95 (ISBN 0-89684-280-0). Orient Bk Dist.

Bajwa, Joginer S. Bibliography of Panjabi Drama. 1985. 11.00x (ISBN 0-8364-1307-5, Pub. by Modern Library Prakashan). South Asia Bks.

Bajza, Charles C. & Schroeder, Mayme. At Home & Far Away. (Illus.). (gr. 3). 1966. text ed. 6.24 (ISBN 0-87443-049-6); tchr's ed. 4.68 (ISBN 0-87443-050-X); preprinted masters 4.95 (ISBN 0-87443-051-8). Benson.

Bajzer, Z., et al, eds. Applications of Physics to Medicine & Biology: Proceedings of the 2nd International Conference on the Applications of Physics to Medicine & Biology, Italy, November 1983. 664p. 1985. 60.00x (ISBN 9971-966-81-6, Pub. by World Sci Singapore). Taylor & Francis.

--Proceedings of the Second International Conference On Applications of Physics to Medicine & Biology. 664p. 1984. 86.00 (ISBN 9971-966-81-6). Taylor & Francis.

Bajzer, Z., jt. ed. see Alberi, G.

Bak, A. K-Theory of Forms. LC 80-7847. (Annals of Mathematics Studies: No. 98). 220p. 1981. 26.00x (ISBN 0-691-08274-X); pap. 10.50 (ISBN 0-691-08275-8). Princeton U Pr.

Bak, A., ed. see International Conference, Bielefeld, West Germany, July 26-30, 1982.

Bak, Janos, ed. The German Peasant War of Fifteen Twenty-Five. (The Library of Peasant Studies: No. 3). 135p. 1976. 26.00x (ISBN 0-7146-3063-2, F Cass Co). Biblio Dist.

Bak, Janos & Kiraly, Bela K., eds. War & Society in East Central Europe: Vol. 3, from Hunyadi to Rakoczi: War & Society in Late Medieval & Early Modern Hungary. (Brooklyn College Studies on Society in Change: No. 12). 600p. 1981. 30.00x (ISBN 0-930888-13-8). Brooklyn Coll Pr.

Bak, Janos, ed. see Szabo, Ervin.

Bak, Janos M. & Benecke, Gerhardt, eds. Religion & Rural Revolt. LC 83-18698. 464p. 1984. 45.00 (ISBN 0-7190-0990-1, Pub. by Manchester Univ Pr); pap. 9.95 (ISBN 0-7190-0991-X). Longwood Pub Group.

Bakacs, T., jt. ed. see Voino-Yasenetsky, M. V.

Bakal, Donald A. The Psychobiology of Chronic Headache. 176p. 1982. text ed. 17.95 (ISBN 0-8261-3890-X). Springer Pub.

--Psychology & Medicine: Psychobiological Dimensions of Health & Illness. LC 78-23439. 1979. text ed. 27.95 (ISBN 0-8261-2580-8); pap. text ed. 16.95 (ISBN 0-8261-2581-6). Springer Pub.

Bakalar, James B. & Grinspoon, Lester. Drug Control in a Free Society. 176p. 1985. 9.95 (ISBN 0-521-26572-X). Cambridge U Pr.

Bakalar, James B., jt. auth. see Brinspoon, Lester.

Bakalar, James B., jt. auth. see Grinspoon, Lester.

Bakalar, James B., jt. ed. see Grinspoon, Lester.

Bakalinsky, Adah. Stairway Walks in San Francisco. LC 82-81462. (Illus.). 128p. (Orig.). 1984. pap. 6.95 (ISBN 0-938530-10-0, 10-0). Lexikos.

Bakalis, Michael J. A Strategy for Excellence: Reaching for New Standards in Education. xvii, 252p. (Orig.). 1974. 22.50 (ISBN 0-208-01245-1, Linnet). Shoe String.

Bakalla, M. H. Arabic Culture: Through Its Language & Literature. 365p. (Orig.). 1984. pap. 11.95 (ISBN 0-7103-0027-1, Kegan Paul). Routledge & Kegan.

Bakalla, M. Hassan. The Morphological & Phonological Components of the Arabic Verb. (Spoken Meccan Arabic.). 1979. 25.00x (ISBN 0-86685-054-6). Intl Bk Ctr.

Bakalla, Muhammad. Dictionary of Modern Linguistic Terms: English-Arabic, Arabic-English. (Arabic & Eng.). 1975. 20.00x (ISBN 0-86685-304-9). Intl Bk Ctr.

Bakalla, Muhammad H. Arabic Linguistics: An Introduction & Bibliography. 600p. 1982. 64.00 (ISBN 0-7201-1583-3). Mansell.

Bakalla, Muhammed H., ed. see Ingham, Bruce.

Bakaly, Charles G., Jr. & Grossman, Joel M. Modern Law of Employment Contracts: Formation, Operation & Remedies for Breach. 357p. 1983. Supplements avail. 70.00 (ISBN 0-15-004288-4, H42884, Law & Business). HarBraceJ.

Bakan, David. Disease, Pain & Sacrifice: Toward a Psychology of Suffering. 1971. pap. 3.95x (ISBN 0-8070-2971-8, BP394). Beacon Pr.

--Duality of Human Existence: Isolation & Communion in Western Man. (Illus.). 1971. pap. 4.95x (ISBN 0-8070-2969-6, BP395). Beacon Pr.

--On Method: Toward a Reconstruction of Psychological Investigation. LC 67-28628. (Social & Behavioral Science Ser.). 1967. 19.95x (ISBN 0-87589-008-3). Jossey-Bass.

--Slaughter of the Innocents: A Study of the Battered Child Phenomenon. LC 78-155168. (Social & Behavioral Science Ser.). 1971. 19.95x (ISBN 0-87589-093-8). Jossey-Bass.

Bakay, Archie J. A Guide for Auditing of Maintainability & Maintenance. (Modern Concepts of Internal Auditing Ser.). (Illus.). 44p. 1982. pap. text ed. 9.50 (ISBN 0-89413-093-5). Inst Inter Aud.

Bakay, Louis. An Early History of Craniotomy: From Antiquity to the Napoleonic Era. 180p. 1985. 22.75x (ISBN 0-398-05115-1). C C Thomas.

--The Treatment of Head Injuries in the Thirty Years War (1618 to 1648) Joannis Scultetus & His Age. (Illus.). 120p. 1971. photocopy ed. 14.50x (ISBN 0-398-00082-4). C C Thomas.

Bakay, Louis, et al. Head Injury. 1980. text ed. 37.50 (ISBN 0-316-07774-7). Little.

Bake, William A. The Blue Ridge. (Illus.). 112p. 1984. pap. 12.45i (ISBN 0-8487-0631-5). Oxmoor Hse.

Bake, William A & Kilpatrick, James J. The American South: Four Seasons of the Land. LC 80-80754. (Illus.). 224p. 1980. 33.61i (ISBN 0-8487-0495-9). Oxmoor Hse.

Bake, William A., photos by. The American South: Towns & Cities. Kilpatrick, James J. LC 82-80593. (Illus.). 224p. 1982. 33.61i (ISBN 0-8487-0533-5). Oxmoor Hse.

Bakeless, John. Christopher Marlowe. LC 75-42103. (English Literature Ser., No. 33). 1974. lib. bdg. 56.95x (ISBN 0-8383-1881-9). Haskell.

--The Economic Causes of Modern War. 59.95 (ISBN 0-8490-0080-7). Gordon Pr.

--The Origin of the Next War. 59.95 (ISBN 0-8490-0777-1). Gordon Pr.

Bakeless, John, ed. Report of the Round Tables & General Conferences at the Twelfth Session (Institute of Politics, Williams College) 1932. 59.50x (ISBN 0-686-51301-0). Elliots Bks.

Bakeless, John, ed. see Lewis, Meriwether & Clark, William.

Bakeless, John E. The Tragicall History of Christopher Marlowe, 2 vols. LC 70-106681. (Illus.). Repr. of 1942 ed. lib. bdg. 37.50x (ISBN 0-8371-3352-1, BACM). Greenwood.

Bakelman, I. Ya. Inversions. Teller, Joan W. & Williams, Susan, trs. from Rus. LC 74-5727. (Popular Lectures in Mathematics Ser). 82p. 1975. pap. text ed. 4.50x (ISBN 0-226-03499-2). U of Chicago Pr.

Bakels, C. C. Analecta Praehistorica Leidensia: XI. 1978. pap. 42.00 (ISBN 90-6021-427-7, Pub. by Leiden Univ Holland). Kluwer Academic.

Bakely, Donald C. If, a Big Word With the Poor. new ed. LC 75-35305. (Illus.). 1976. 6.00 (ISBN 0-87303-343-4). Faith & Life.

Bakema, J. B. Thoughts about Architecture. Grey, Marianne, ed. (Academy Architecture Ser.). (Illus.). 160p. 1982. pap. 14.95 (ISBN 0-312-80190-4). St Martin.

Baken, Lenore. How to Camp Europe by Train. 4th ed. (Illus., Orig.). 1982. pap. 7.95 (ISBN 0-917656-04-0). Ariel Pubns.

Baken, R. J. Introduction to the Measurement of Speech. 32.95 (ISBN 0-471-88395-6). Wiley.

Baker. Baker's Ohio School Law Guide, 1980-1984. 483p. 1984. 120.00; 1984-85 incl.; 32.50. Anderson Pub Co.

--Bicycle Safety. (Safety First Ser.). (Illus.). 32p. (ps-3). 1979. 8.95 (ISBN 0-87191-738-6). Creative Ed.

--Explosion Hazards & Evaluation. (Fundamental Studies in Engineering: Vol. 5). 808p. 1983. 159.75 (ISBN 0-444-42094-0). Elsevier.

--Fire Safety. (Safety First Ser.). (Illus.). 32p. (ps-3). 1979. 8.95 (ISBN 0-87191-735-1). Creative Ed.

--Home Safety. (Safety First Ser.). (Illus.). 32p. (ps-3). 1979. 8.95 (ISBN 0-87191-739-4). Creative Ed.

--Lane Tech's Myrtle & the Gold: Memoirs of a 1922 Alumnus. LC 83-82891. (Illus.). 150p. 1984. pap. 5.95 (ISBN 0-87319-026-2). C Hallberg.

--Outdoor Safety. (Safety First Ser.). (Illus.). 32p. (ps-3). 1979. 8.95 (ISBN 0-87191-736-X). Creative Ed.

--School Safety. (Safety First Ser.). (Illus.). 32p. (ps-3). 1979. 8.95 (ISBN 0-87191-737-8). Creative Ed.

--Water Safety. (Safety First Ser.). (Illus.). 32p. (ps-3). 1979. 8.95 (ISBN 0-87191-740-8). Creative Ed.

Baker & Batten. Finite Geometrics. (Lecture Notes in Pure & Applied Mathematics). 392p. 1986. price not set (ISBN 0-8247-7488-4). Dekker.

Baker & Engel. Organic Chemistry: Problems & Solutions. 2nd ed. 1985. 12.69 (ISBN 0-205-07987-3, 687987). Allyn.

Baker, jt. auth. see Derick.

Baker, jt. auth. see McCullough.

Baker & Hostetler, eds. Hospital Contracts Manual. Semi-annually ed. LC 82-16344. 750p. 1982. looseleaf 235.00 (ISBN 0-89443-828-X). Aspen Systems.

Baker, A. Baptist Source Book. LC 66-22076. 1974. pap. 6.95 (ISBN 0-8054-6519-7). Broadman.

Baker, A. & Masser, D. W. Transcendence Theory & Its Applications. 1978. 49.50 (ISBN 0-12-074350-7). Acad Pr.

Baker, A., et al. Psychiatric Services & Architecture. (Public Health Papers Ser: No. 1). (Illus.). 59p. (Eng. & Span.). 1959. pap. 1.20 (ISBN 92-4-130001-9). World Health.

Baker, A. A., jt. auth. see Hyde, M. B.

Baker, A. B. & Baker, Lowell H., eds. Clinical Neurology, 4 vols. (Annual Revision Service Ser.). loose leaf 350.00 (ISBN 0-06-148006-1, Harper Medical); revision pages 45.00 (ISBN 0-686-97872-2). Lippincott.

Baker, A. D., jt. auth. see Brundle, C. R.

Baker, A. D., jt. ed. see Brundle, C. R.

Baker, A. D., III, tr. see Couhat, Jean L.

Baker, A. E. & Tennyson, Alfred. Concordance to the Devil & the Lady. Tennyson, Charles, ed. Repr. of 1931 ed. 15.00 (ISBN 0-527-04550-0). Kraus Repr.

Baker, A. E., ed. see Temple, William.

Baker, A. J. Examining British Politics. 2nd ed. 256p. 1984. pap. 6.95 (ISBN 0-09-156601-0, Pub. by Hutchinson Educ). Longwood Pub Group.

--Finite Element Computational Fluid Mechanics. 544p. 46.00 (ISBN 0-07-003465-6). McGraw.

Baker, A. J., et al. More Spectroscopic Problems in Organic Chemistry. 2nd ed. 139p. 1975. 35.95 (ISBN 0-471-25591-2, Wiley Heyden). Wiley.

Baker, A. S. Bibliography of the Helminth Parasites of New Zealand (1879-1971) 79p. 1973. 30.00x (ISBN 0-85198-265-4, Pub. by CAB Bks England). State Mutual Bk.

Baker, A. W. Death Is a Good Solution: The Convict Experience in Early Australia. LC 83-23556. (Scholar's Library). 223p. 1985. text ed. 37.50 (ISBN 0-7022-1685-2). U Of Queensland Pr.

Baker, Adelaide N. Return to Arcady. LC 73-80849. (Illus.). 192p. 1973. 8.95 (ISBN 0-88208-018-0). Lawrence Hill.

Baker, Adolph. Modern Physics & Anti-Physics. LC 74-109506. 1970. pap. 12.95 (ISBN 0-201-00485-2). Addison-Wesley.

Baker, Alan. Benjamin Bounces Back. (Illus.). (gr. k-2). 1978. 7.95i (ISBN 0-397-31809-X). Lipp Jr Bks.

--Benjamin's Book. LC 82-4605. (Illus.). 32p. (ps-1). 1983. 13.00 (ISBN 0-688-01697-9). Lothrop.

--Benjamin's Dreadful Dream. LC 79-5369. (Illus.). (ps-2). 1980. 9.95 (ISBN 0-397-31902-9); PLB 7.89 (ISBN 0-397-31903-7). Lipp Jr Bks.

--A Concise Introduction to the Theory of Numbers. (Illus.). 96p. 1985. 29.95 (ISBN 0-521-24383-1); pap. 9.95 (ISBN 0-521-28654-9). Cambridge U Pr.

Baker, Alan, jt. auth. see Terry, Len.

Baker, Alan J. Business Decision Making. 228p. 1981. 30.00 (ISBN 0-312-10902-4). St Martin.

--Investment, Valuation & the Managerial Theory of the Firm. 336p. 1978. text ed. 44.50x (ISBN 0-566-00192-6). Gower Pub Co.

Baker, Alan R. Transcendental Number Theory. LC 74-82591. 148p. 1975. 34.50 (ISBN 0-521-20461-5). Cambridge U Pr.

Baker, Alan R. & Billinge, Mark, eds. Period & Place: Research Methods in Historical Geography. LC 81-12266. (Cambridge Studies in Historical Geography: No. 1). (Illus.). 375p. 1982. Cambridge U Pr.

Baker, Alan R. & Butlin, R. A., eds. Studies of Field Systems in the British Isles. (Illus.). 728p. 1980. pap. 34.50 (ISBN 0-521-29790-7). Cambridge U Pr.

Baker, Alan R. & Gregory, Derek, eds. Explorations in Historical Geography: Interpretive Essays. LC 83-19003. (Studies in Historical Geography: No. 5). (Illus.). 264p. 1984. 49.50 (ISBN 0-521-24968-6). Cambridge U Pr.

Baker, Alan R. & Harley, J. B., eds. Man Made the Land: Essays in English Historical Geography. LC 73-5602. (Illus.). 208p. 1973. 23.50x (ISBN 0-87471-184-3). Rowman.

Baker, Albert E. Prophets for a Day of Judgment. facsimile ed. LC 72-90605. (Essay Index Reprint Ser). 1944. 17.00 (ISBN 0-8369-1390-6). Ayer Co Pubs.

Baker, Alice C. True Stories of New England Captives Carried to Canada During the Old French & Indian Wars. rev. ed. (Illus.). 412p. 1985. Repr. of 1897 ed. 25.00 (ISBN 0-917890-49-3). Heritage Bk.

Baker, Allen & Hamrick, Kathy. Conceptual Programming Using BASIC. (Illus.). 224p. 1984. pap. text ed. 18.95 (ISBN 0-13-166678-9). P-H.

Baker, Alonzo. My Sister Alma & I. (Daybreak Ser.). 1981. pap. 4.50 (ISBN 0-8163-0373-8). Pacific Pr Pub Assn.

Baker, Alton, jt. auth. see Sartain, Aaron.

Baker, Alton W. Personnel Management in Small Plants. (Illus.). 288p. 1955. 4.00x (ISBN 0-87776-076-4, R-76). Ohio St U Admin Sci.

Baker, Alton W. & Davis, Ralph C. Ratios of Staff to Line Employees & Stages of Differentiation of Staff Functions. 1954. pap. 1.00x (ISBN 0-87776-072-1, R72). Ohio St U Admin Sci.

Baker, Alvin L. Berkouwer's Doctrine of Election: Balance or Imbalance? 1981. pap. 5.95 (ISBN 0-87552-119-3). Presby & Reformed.

Baker, Amy, ed. see Kurtz, Bruce D.

Baker, Andrew & Goodman, Lori. Working with the Intermarried: A Practical Guide for Workshop Leaders. LC 85-71160. 36p. (Orig.). 1985. pap. 4.00 (ISBN 0-87495-071-6). Am Jewish Comm.

Baker, Andrew J., ed. Advances in Production of Forest Products. (AIChE Symposium Ser.: Vol. 79). 87p. 1983. pap. 30.00 (ISBN 0-8169-0247-X, S-223); pap. 15.00 (ISBN 0-317-03718-8). Am Inst Chem Eng.

Baker, Ann. Introducing English Pronunciation: A Teacher's Guide to Tree or Three? & Ship or Sheep. 1982. 8.95 (ISBN 0-521-28580-1). Cambridge U Pr.

--Ship or Sheep. (Cambridge English Learning Ser.). (Illus.). 1977. 6.50x (ISBN 0-521-28354-X). Cambridge U Pr.

Baker, Archibald G., ed. Short History of Christianity. LC 40-34185. (Midway Reprints Ser.). 1983. Repr. of 1940 ed. 11.00x (ISBN 0-226-03527-1). U of Chicago Pr.

Baker, Arthur. Arthur Baker's Copybook of Renaissance Calligraphy: Mercator's Italic Hand. (Illus.). 32p. (Orig.). 1981. pap. 2.00 (ISBN 0-486-24162-9). Dover.

--Arthur Baker's Historic Calligraphic Alphabets. (Pictorial Archive Ser.). (Illus.). 96p. (Orig.). 1980. pap. 3.95 (ISBN 0-486-24054-1). Dover.

--Arthur Baker's Historic Calligraphic Alphabets. 13.50 (ISBN 0-8446-5730-1). Peter Smith.

--Calligraphic Alphabets. LC 79-8223. (Pictorial Archive Ser.). (Illus.). 160p. (Orig.). 1974. pap. 4.95 (ISBN 0-486-21045-6). Dover.

--Calligraphic Alphabets. (Illus.). 15.75 (ISBN 0-8446-5154-0). Peter Smith.

--The Calligraphic Art of Arthur Baker. LC 82-42648. (Illus.). 64p. 1983. 10.95 (ISBN 0-684-17837-0, ScribT). Scribner.

--Calligraphic Cut-Paper Designs for Artists & Craftsmen. (Pictorial Archive Ser.). (Illus.). 80p. (Orig.). 1983. pap. 2.50 (ISBN 0-486-20306-9). Dover.

--Calligraphic Initials. LC 78-56108. (Illus.). 1978. 12.50 (ISBN 0-910158-44-4); pap. 8.95 (ISBN 0-910158-48-7). Art Dir.

--Calligraphic Swash Initials. (Illus.). 96p. (Orig.). (gr. 7 up). 1984. pap. 3.95 (ISBN 0-486-24427-X). Dover.

--Calligraphy. (Pictorial Archive Ser). (Illus.). 160p. (Orig.). 1973. pap. 6.00 (ISBN 0-486-22895-9). Dover.

--Calligraphy. (Illus.). 16.25 (ISBN 0-8446-4619-9). Peter Smith.

--Celtic Hand Stroke by Stroke (Irish Half-Uncial from "The Book of Kells") (An Arthur Baker Calligraphy Manual: Lettering, Calligraphy, Typography Ser.). (Illus.). 48p. (Orig.). 1983. pap. 2.50 (ISBN 0-486-24336-2). Dover.

--Chancery Cursive Stroke by Stroke: An Arthur Baker Calligraphy Manual. (Illus.). 64p. pap. 2.50 (ISBN 0-486-24278-1). Dover.

--Classic Roman Capitals Stroke by Stroke: An Arthur Baker Calligraphy Manual. (Illus.). 64p. (Orig.). (gr. 6 up). 1983. pap. 2.50 (ISBN 0-486-24450-4). Dover.

--Dance of the Pen. LC 78-56114. (Illus.). 1978. 12.50 (ISBN 0-910158-45-2); pap. 8.95 (ISBN 0-910158-49-5). Art Dir.

--The House Is Sitting. LC 74-68. (Illus.). 264p. 1974. Repr. of 1958 ed. lib. bdg. 15.75x (ISBN 0-8371-7364-7, BAHS). Greenwood.

--Mastering Italic Calligraphy. (Illus.). 128p. 1985. pap. 7.95 (ISBN 0-684-18214-9, ScribT). Scribner.

--New Calligraphic Ornaments & Flourishes. (Pictorial Archive Ser.). (Orig.). 1981. pap. 3.75 (ISBN 0-486-24095-9). Dover.

--The Roman Alphabet. LC 76-44477. (Illus.). 1977. 15.00 (ISBN 0-910158-23-1). Art Dir.

--The Script Alphabet. LC 78-56103. (Illus.). 1978. 12.50 (ISBN 0-910158-43-6); pap. 8.95 (ISBN 0-910158-47-9). Art Dir.

Baker, Arthur, illus. Brush Calligraphy. (Lettering, Calligraphy, Typography Ser.). 95p. (Orig.). 1984. pap. 4.95 (ISBN 0-486-24533-0). Dover.

Baker, Arthur E. Tennyson Dictionary. LC 67-30807. (Studies in Tennyson Ser., No. 27). 1916. Repr. of 1916 ed. lib. bdg. 49.95x (ISBN 0-8383-0706-X). Haskell.

Baker, Augusta & Greene, Ellin. Storytelling: Art & Technique. LC 77-16481. 1977. pap. 15.95 (ISBN 0-8352-0840-0). Bowker.

--Storytelling: Art & Technique. 142p. 8.95 (ISBN 0-318-15103-0, A101). Natl Assn Preserv & Perpet Storytelling.

Baker, B. Granville. The Walls of Constantinople. LC 72-178513. (Medieval Studies Ser.). Repr. of 1910 ed. 29.00 (ISBN 0-404-56509-3). AMS Pr.

Baker, B. N., jt. ed. see Williams, Theodore P.

Baker, B. R. Design of Active-Site Directed Irreversible Enzyme Inhibitors: The Organic Chemistry of the Enzymic Active-Site. LC 74-32255. 342p. 1975. Repr. of 1967 ed. 19.50 (ISBN 0-88275-259-6). Krieger.

Baker, Barton. History of the London Stage & Its Famous Players 1576-1903. LC 72-81971. (Illus.). Repr. of 1904 ed. 25.00 (ISBN 0-405-08231-2, Pub. by Blom). Ayer Co Pubs.

Baker, Benjamin S. Feeding the Sheep. 1985. pap. 5.95 (ISBN 0-8054-2544-6). Broadman.

--Shepherding the Sheep. LC 82-73531. 1983. 8.50 (ISBN 0-8054-2543-8). Broadman.

Baker, Bernard S., ed. Hydrocarbon Fuel Cell Technology: A Symposium. (Illus.). 1966. 89.50 (ISBN 0-12-074250-0). Acad Pr.

Baker, Betty. And Me, Coyote! LC 82-7134. (Illus.). 32p. (gr. k-4). 1982. 8.95 (ISBN 0-02-708280-6). Macmillan.

--Danby & George. LC 80-15707. (Illus.). 64p. (gr. 3-5). 1981. 11.75 (ISBN 0-688-80289-3); PLB 11.88 (ISBN 0-688-84289-5). Greenwillow.

--Dunderhead War. LC 67-18551. 192p. (gr. 5 up). 1967. PLB 11.89 (ISBN 0-06-020328-5). HarpJ.

--Latki & the Lightning Lizard. LC 79-11197. (Illus.). (gr. 1-3). 1979. 9.95 (ISBN 0-02-708210-5). Macmillan.

--Little Runner of the Longhouse. LC 62-8040. (I Can Read Bk.). 64p. (gr. k-3). 1962. PLB 10.89 (ISBN 0-06-020341-2). HarpJ.

--My Sister Says. LC 83-911. (Illus.). 32p. (ps-3). 1984. SBE 9.95 (ISBN 0-02-708160-5). Macmillan.

--The Night Spider Case. LC 83-22181. 120p. (gr. 5-8). 1984. 9.95 (ISBN 0-02-708170-2). Macmillan.

--Pig War. LC 69-10212. (I Can Read History Bk O). (Illus.). 64p. (gr. k-3). 1969. PLB 9.89 (ISBN 0-06-020333-1). HarpJ.

--Rat Is Dead & Ant Is Sad. LC 78-1943. (I Can Read Bk.). (Illus.). 64p. (gr. k-3). 1981. PLB 9.89g (ISBN 0-06-020347-1). HarpJ.

--Santa Rat. LC 79-24904. (Illus.). 64p. (gr. 3-5). 1980. 11.75 (ISBN 0-688-80262-1); PLB 11.88 (ISBN 0-688-84262-3). Greenwillow.

--Settlers & Strangers: Native Americans of the Desert Southwest & History As They Saw It. LC 77-4925. (Illus.). 96p. (gr. 3-7). 1977. 9.95 (ISBN 0-02-708220-2, 70822). Macmillan.

--Seven Spells to Farewell. LC 81-19305. 123p. (gr. 5-9). 1982. 8.95 (ISBN 0-02-708150-8). Macmillan.

--Spirit Is Willing. LC 73-8576. 128p. (gr. 5-8). 1974. 12.95 (ISBN 0-02-708270-9, 70827). Macmillan.

--The Turkey Girl. LC 82-17285. (Ready-to-Read Ser.). (Illus.). 64p. (gr. 1-4). 1983. 8.95 (ISBN 0-02-708260-1). Macmillan.

--Walk the World's Rim. LC 65-11458. 192p. (gr. 5 up). 1965. PLB 11.89 (ISBN 0-06-020381-1). HarpJ.

--Worthington Botts & the Steam Machine. LC 80-24627. (Ready-to-Read Ser.). (Illus.). 56p. (gr. 1-4). 1981. PLB 7.95 (ISBN 0-02-708190-7). Macmillan.

Baker, Betty S. A Study of Social Status, Personality Characteristics, & Motor Ability of Mentally Handicapped Girls. LC 74-28604. 1975. soft bdg. 10.95 (ISBN 0-88247-311-5). R & E Pubs.

Baker, Betty S. & Carter, Jo A. Dynamic Wellness Manual. (Illus.). 162p. (Orig.). 1983. pap. text ed. 8.95 (ISBN 0-88136-004-X). Jostens.

Baker, Bevan B. & Copson, E. T. The Mathematical Theory of Huygens Principle. 2nd ed. LC 50-8926. pap. 50.00 (ISBN 0-317-08620-0, 2051166). Bks Demand UMI.

Baker, Blanch M. Dramatic Bibliography. LC 68-20214. 1968. Repr. of 1933 ed. 22.00 (ISBN 0-405-08229-0, Pub. by Blom). Ayer Co Pubs.

--Theatre & Allied Arts. LC 66-12284. Repr. of 1953 ed. 43.50 (ISBN 0-405-08230-4, Pub. by Blom). Ayer Co Pubs.

Baker, Bob. Newsthinking: The Secret of Great Newswriting. LC 80-27833. 204p. 1981. 11.95 (ISBN 0-89879-043-3). Writers Digest.

Baker, Bonnie Jeanne. A Pear by Itself. LC 82-4430. (Rookie Readers Ser.). (ps-2). 1982. 8.65 (ISBN 0-516-02032-3); pap. 2.50 (ISBN 0-516-42032-1). Childrens.

Baker, Brian H. Fundamental Skills in Hematology. (Illus.). 508p. 1980. pap. 28.50x spiral (ISBN 0-398-04101-6). C C Thomas.

--Performing the Electrocardiogram. (Illus.). 232p. 1982. spiral bdg. 26.75x (ISBN 0-398-04651-4). C C Thomas.

Baker, Bruce, et al. Play Skills. LC 83-61811. (Illus.). 66p. 1983. pap. text ed. 10.95 (ISBN 0-87822-230-8). Res Press.

Baker, Bruce L. & Goldstein, Michael J. Readings in Abnormal Psychology. (Orig.). 1981. pap. text ed. 13.95 (ISBN 0-316-07830-1). Little.

Baker, Bruce L., et al. As Close As Possible. LC 77-81502. 1977. text ed. 13.95 (ISBN 0-316-07827-1); pap. text ed. 9.95 (ISBN 0-316-07829-8). Little.

Baker, C. Rothschilds Battle Rockefellers: The Bankers World Power Struggle. 1982. lib. bdg. 69.00 (ISBN 0-87700-435-8). Revisionist Pr.

Baker, C., tr. see Amman, J. C.

Baker, C. B. see Hopkin, John A., et al.

Baker, C. C. Introduction to Mathematics. LC 66-20198. (Illus.). 1966. pap. 1.65 (ISBN 0-668-01479-2). Arco.

Baker, C. F. Invertebrata Pacifica. 197p. 1969. Repr. of 1907 ed. 40.00x (ISBN 0-317-07103-3, Pub. by EW Classey UK). State Mutual Bk.

Baker, C. J. Beyond Death. 1977. 2.50 (ISBN 0-87813-953-2). Christian Light.

--The Politics of South India, 1920-1937. LC 75-2716. (Cambridge South Asian Studies: No. 17). (Illus.). 368p. 1976. 49.50 (ISBN 0-521-20755-X). Cambridge U Pr.

Baker, C. J. & Washbrook, D. A. South India: Political Institutions & Political Change 1880-1940. 1975. text ed. 27.50x (ISBN 0-8419-5016-4). Holmes & Meier.

Baker, C. L. Introduction to Generative-Transformational Syntax. 1977. text ed. 27.95 (ISBN 0-13-484410-6). P-H.

Baker, C. L. & McCarthy, John J., eds. The Logical Problem of Language Acquisition. (Cognitive Theory & Mental Representation Ser.). 358p. 1981. 37.50x (ISBN 0-262-02159-5). MIT Pr.

Baker, C. Lafayette. Authentic Stories of Spies, Traitors & Conspirators from the American Secret Service During the Civil War, 2 Vols. (Illus.). 377p. 1984. Repr. of 1894 ed. 239.50 (ISBN 0-89901-159-4). Found Class Reprints.

Baker, C. M., jt. auth. see Manwell, Clyde.

Baker, C. R. & Hayes, R. S. Lease Financing: A Practical Guide. LC 8-1576. 200p. 1981. 34.95 (ISBN 0-471-06040-2, Pub. by Wiley-Interscience). Wiley.

Baker, C. R., jt. auth. see Hayes, R. S.

Baker, Carlos. The Echoing Green: Romanticism, Modernism & Phenomena of Transference in Poetry. LC 83-43058. 392p. 1984. 32.50x (ISBN 0-691-06595-0). Princeton U Pr.

--Ernest Hemingway: A Life Story. 1980. pap. 6.95 (ISBN 0-380-50039-6, 69822-6, Discus). Avon.

--Ernest Hemingway: A Life Story. LC 68-57079. 1969. lib. rep. ed. 40.00 (ISBN 0-684-14740-8, ScribT). Scribner.

--Hemingway: The Writer As Artist. rev. 4th ed. 440p. 1972. 38.50 (ISBN 0-691-06231-5); pap. 10.95x (ISBN 0-691-01305-5, 86). Princeton U Pr.

--A Year & a Day. (Vanderbilt University Press Bks.). 64p. 1963. 7.95 (ISBN 0-8265-1064-7). U of Ill Pr.

--Year & A Day: Poems. LC 63-14645. 1963. 7.95 (ISBN 0-8265-1064-7). Vanderbilt U Pr.

Baker, Carlos, ed. Ernest Hemingway: Selected Letters 1917-1961. encore ed. 10.95 (ISBN 0-684-16765-4, ScribT); deluxe ed. 75.00 (ISBN 0-684-16961-4); pap. 12.95 (ISBN 0-684-17658-0). Scribner.

Baker, Carol, ed. The Book of Festivals in the Midwest, 1985 & 1986. (Illus.). 288p. (Orig.). 1985. pap. 10.95 (ISBN 0-89651-064-6). Icarus.

Baker, Carol, jt. ed. see Fingerhut, Astri.

Baker, Carroll. Baby Doll. 320p. 1985. pap. 3.95 (ISBN 0-440-10431-9). Dell.

--Baby Doll: An Autobiography. (Illus.). 1983. 15.95 (ISBN 0-87795-558-1). Arbor Hse.

--Love Italian Style. Date not set. D I Fine.

--A Roman Tale. 320p. 1986. 16.95 (ISBN 0-917657-53-5). D I Fine.

--To Africa with Love: A Romantic Adventure. 1986. price not set. D I Fine.

Baker, Charles. The Book of Bible History. 1980. lib. bdg. 59.95 (ISBN 0-8490-3159-1). Gordon Pr.

--Manual of Bible History: Reading Lessons, Explanations, Questions & Geographical Notes, 2 vols. 1980. lib. bdg. 195.95 (ISBN 0-8490-3117-6). Gordon Pr.

Baker, Charles E., jt. auth. see Hamlin, Paul M.

Baker, Charles, III, jt. ed. see Baker, Rosalie.

Baker, Charlotte & Battison, Robbin. Sign Language & the Deaf Community: Essays in Honor of William Stokoe. (Illus.). 267p. 1981. text ed. 14.00 (ISBN 0-913072-37-0); pap. text ed. 10.00 (ISBN 0-913072-36-2). Natl Assn Deaf.

Baker, Charlotte & Cokely, Dennis. American Sign Language: A Student Text, Units 10-18. 1981. Set. 18.95x (ISBN 0-932666-12-4); Set. pap. 14.95x (ISBN 0-932666-11-6). T J Pubs.

--American Sign Language: A Teacher's Resource Text on Grammar & Culture. 1980. 22.95x (ISBN 0-932666-07-8); pap. 18.95x (ISBN 0-932666-09-4). T J Pubs.

Baker, Charlotte & Padden, Carol. American Sign Language: A Look at Its History, Structure & Community. 1978. pap. 2.50x (ISBN 0-932666-01-9). T J Pubs.

Baker, Charlotte, jt. auth. see Cokely, Dennis.

Baker, Charlotte & Battison, Robbin, eds. Sign Language & the Deaf Community: Essays in Honor of William Stokoe. 1980. 13.00 (ISBN 0-317-05971-8); pap. 9.00 (ISBN 0-317-05972-6). Natl Assn Deaf.

Baker, Cherie. Naturally Delicious Desserts. 1985. pap. 8.95 (ISBN 0-345-30182-X). Ballantine.

Baker, Christopher J. An Indian Rural Economy, Eighteen Eighty to Nineteen Fifty-Five: The Tamilnad Countryside. (Illus.). 1984. 47.00x (ISBN 0-19-821572-X). Oxford U Pr.

Baker, Christopher T. The Numerical Treatment of Integral Equations. (Monographs on Numerical Analysis). (Illus.). 1977. text ed. 69.00x (ISBN 0-19-853406-X). Oxford U Pr.

Baker, Christopher T. & Miller, Geoffrey F. Treatment of Integral Equations by Numerical Methods. 1983. 45.00 (ISBN 0-12-074120-2). Acad Pr.

Baker, Christopher T. & Phillips, Chris. The Numerical Solution of Nonlinear Problems. (Illus.). 1981. 42.50x (ISBN 0-19-853354-3). Oxford U Pr.

Baker, Cindi, jt. auth. see Pestolesi, Robert A.

Baker, Clara B. Sing & Be Happy: Songs for the Young Child. LC 80-13421. (Illus.). 96p. 1980. pap. 7.95 spiral (ISBN 0-687-38547-4). Abingdon.

Baker, Cornelia D., ed. see Draves, Cornelia P.

Baker, Cory. Through the Kaleidoscope. LC 85-71412. (Illus.). 144p. 1985. write for info (ISBN 0-9608930-1-6). Beechcliff Bks.

Baker, Cozy. A Cozy Getaway: A Travel Guide to the Unusual. LC 76-15816. (Illus.). 150p. 1976. pap. 3.95 (ISBN 0-87491-063-3). Acropolis.

--Love Beyond Life. 64p. 1982. 8.00 (ISBN 0-9608930-0-8). Beechcliff Bks.

Baker, D. A. Transport Phenomena in Plants. (Outline Studies in Biology Ser.). 1978. pap. 7.50 (ISBN 0-412-15360-2, NO. 6022, Pub. by Chapman & Hall). Methuen Inc.

Baker, D. A., jt. auth. see Sutcliffe, J. F.

Baker, D. E., ed. see Cibber, Colley.

Baker, D. P. The Library Media Program & the School. 175p. 1984. lib. bdg. 19.50 (ISBN 0-87287-385-4). Libs Unl.

Baker, D. Phillip & Bender, David R. Library Media Programs & the Special Learner. 384p. 1981. 19.50 (ISBN 0-208-01852-2, Lib Prof Pubns); pap. text ed. 14.50x (ISBN 0-208-01846-8, Lib Prof Pubns). Shoe String.

Baker, Daisy. More Travels in a Donkey Trap. 1977. 9.95x (ISBN 0-285-62217-X, Pub. by Souvenir Pr). Intl Spec Bk.

Baker, Dan & Weisgerber, Bill. Television Production. Duane, James E., ed. LC 80-23479. (The Instructional Media Library: Vol. 15). (Illus.). 112p. 1981. 19.95 (ISBN 0-87778-175-3). Educ Tech Pubns.

Baker, Daniel, et al. Projects in Optical Properties of the Atmosphere, Upper Atmospheric Turbulence & Structure, Ionospheric Reflection Properties, Plasma Physics, Data Reduction & Perspective Drawing. LC 72-135075. 152p. 1970. 19.00 (ISBN 0-403-04485-5). Scholarly.

Baker, Darrell, illus. Monchhichi We Love Play School. (Golden Sturdy Shape Bks.). (Illus.). 14p. (ps). 1983. 2.95 (ISBN 0-307-12265-4, 12265, Golden Bks). Western Pub.

Baker, David. Conquest: A History of Space Achievements from Science Fiction to the Shuttle. (Illus.). 187p. 1985. pap. 12.95 (ISBN 0-947703-00-4, Pub by Salem Hse Ltd). Merrimack Pub Cir.

--History of Manned Space Flight. LC 81-3101. (Herbert Michelman Bks.). (Illus.). 512p. 1985. 19.95 (ISBN 0-517-54377-X). Crown.

--The Larousse Guide to Astronomy. LC 78-54635. (Illus.). 1980. 15.95 (ISBN 0-88332-094-0); pap. 9.95 (ISBN 0-88332-095-9). Larousse.

--Laws of the Land. 2nd ed. Burmaster, O., ed. LC 81-69224. (Modern & Contemporary Poetry of the West Ser.). 70p. (Orig.). 1981. pap. 3.00 (ISBN 0-916272-18-4). Ahsahta Pr.

--Shape of Wars to Come. LC 81-48447. 304p. 1982. 19.95 (ISBN 0-8128-2852-6). Stein & Day.

--The Shape of Wars to Come. LC 81-48447. (Illus.). 326p. 1984. pap. 10.95 (ISBN 0-8128-6221-X). Stein & Day.

Baker, David & Baker, Jeanne. Jazz Quiz Book. Baker, Lida, ed. 72p. (Orig.). 1984. pap. 2.95 (ISBN 0-89917-413-2). TIS Inc.

Baker, David E. Biographia Dramatica, 3 vols. Date not set. Repr. of 1812 ed. Set. lib. bdg. 149.00 (ISBN 0-318-04579-6). Am Repr Serv.

Baker, David E., et al. Biographia Dramatica, or Companion to the Playhouse, 4 pts. in 3 vols. LC 70-159990. (BCL Ser. I). Repr. of 1812 ed. Set. 110.00 (ISBN 0-404-00530-6). Vol. 1 (ISBN 0-404-00531-4). Vol. 2 (ISBN 0-404-00532-2). Vol. 3 (ISBN 0-404-00533-0). AMS Pr.

Baker, David N., et al. The Black Composer Speaks. LC 77-24146. 512p. 1978. 30.00 (ISBN 0-8108-1045-X). Scarecrow.

Baker, David R. Speculative High-Rise Dilemma: Fully Sprinklered or Hydraulic Fire Alarm. 4.35 (ISBN 0-318-03823-4). Society Fire Protect.

Baker, Dean. The Last Yoncalla: The Legend of Sam Fearn. LC 81-67395. (Illus.). 214p. (Orig.). (YA) 1981. pap. 6.50 (ISBN 0-940388-00-6). Blind John.

Baker, Denis, tr. see Roland, J. C. & Roland, F.

Baker, Dennis. Agricultural Prices & Marketing with Special Reference to the Hop Industry, North-East Kent 1680-1760. LC 84-45995. (British Economic History Ser.). 779p. 1985. lib. bdg. 80.00 (ISBN 0-8240-6675-8). Garland Pub.

Baker, Dennis, jt. auth. see Boone, Debby.

Baker, Dennis, jt. auth. see Sutcliffe, James.

Baker, Denys V., ed. A View From Land's End: Writers Against a Cornish Background. 1982. 39.00x (ISBN 0-686-82341-9, Pub. by W Kimber). State Mutual Bk.

Baker, Denys Val see Val Baker, Denys.

Baker, Derek. Religious Motivation: Biographical & Sociological Problems for the Church Historian. (Studies in Church History: Vol. 15). 516p. 1978. 45.00x (ISBN 0-631-19250-6). Basil Blackwell.

--Renaissance & Renewal in Christian History. (Studies in Church History: Vol. 14). 428p. 1977. 45.00x (ISBN 0-631-17780-9). Basil Blackwell.

--A Short History of Monasticism. (Illus., Orig.). 1982. pap. 10.00x (ISBN 0-85224-392-8, Pub. by Edinburgh U Pr Scotland). Columbia U Pr.

Baker, Derek, ed. The Church in Town & Countryside: Papers Read at the Seventeenth Summer Meeting & the Eighteenth Winter Meeting of the Ecclesiastical History Society. (Studies in Church History: Vol. 16). 502p. 1979. 45.00 (ISBN 0-631-11421-1). Basil Blackwell.

--Church Society & Politics. (Studies in Church History Ser.: Vol. 12). 440p. 1976. 45.00x (ISBN 0-631-16970-9). Basil Blackwell.

--Medieval Women. (Studies in Church History: Subsidia 1). (Illus.). 412p. 1979. 45.00x (ISBN 0-631-19260-3). Basil Blackwell.

--Medieval Women. (Studies in Church History: Subsidia 1). 412p. 1981. pap. 9.95x (ISBN 0-631-12539-6). Basil Blackwell.

--The Orthodox Churches & the West. (Studies in Church History Ser.: Vol. 13). 350p. 1976. 45.00x (ISBN 0-631-17180-0). Basil Blackwell.

--Reform & Reformation: England & the Continent c.1380-c.1750. (Studies in Church History: Subsidia 2). (Illus.). 336p. 1980. 45.00x (ISBN 0-631-19270-0). Basil Blackwell.

Baker, Derek & Wilks, Michael J., eds. The World of John of Salisbury. (Studies in Church History: Subsidia 3). 400p. 1985. text ed. 45.00x (ISBN 0-631-13122-1). Basil Blackwell.

Baker, Derek, jt. ed. see Sheils, W. J.

Baker, Don. Acceptance: Loosing the Webs of Personal Insecurity. LC 84-27246. 1985. pap. 5.95 (ISBN 0-88070-079-3). Multnomah.

--Beyond Choice: The Abortion Story No One Is Telling. LC 85-15295. 1985. 7.95 (ISBN 0-88070-127-7). Multnomah.

--Beyond Forgiveness: The Healing Touch of Church Discipline. LC 84-3417. 1984. 7.95 (ISBN 0-88070-054-8). Multnomah.

--Beyond Rejection: The Church, Homosexuality, & Hope. LC 85-8789. 1985. 7.95 (ISBN 0-88070-108-0). Multnomah.

--A Fresh Look at God. (Living Theology Ser.). 1986. pap. 6.95 (ISBN 0-88070-104-8). Multnomah.

--Pain's Hidden Purpose: Finding Perspective in the Midst of Suffering. LC 83-22135. 1984. pap. 5.95 (ISBN 0-88070-035-1). Multnomah.

--Philippians. (Lifebuilder Bible Studies). 60p. (Orig.). 1985. pap. text ed. 2.95 (ISBN 0-8308-1013-7). Inter-Varsity.

Baker, Don & Nester, Emery. Depression: Finding Hope & Meaning in Life's Darkest Shadow. LC 82-24609. (Critical Concern Ser.). 1983. 9.95 (ISBN 0-88070-011-4). Multnomah.

Baker, Don, jt. auth. see Needler, Marvin.

Baker, Donald. Fiber Optic Design & Application. 1985. text ed. 37.95 (ISBN 0-8359-1971-4). Reston.

Baker, Donald, et al. Fundamentals of Hearing & Speech Science. Hamlet, Sandra, ed. LC 72-92716. (Illus.). 160p. 1973. text ed. 5.95 (ISBN 0-88429-001-8). Collegiate Pub.

--Twenty-Second Annual Advanced Antitrust Seminar. LC 82-62189. (Corporate Law & Practice Course Handbook Ser.: No. 403). (Illus.). 792p. 1982. 35.00. PLI.

Baker, Donald C., jt. auth. see Ogilvy, J. D.

Baker, Donald C. & Chaucer, Geoffrey, eds. The Manciple's Tale. LC 83-14734. (A Variorum Edition of the Works of Geoffrey Chaucer: Vol. II, Pt. 10). (Illus.). 176p. 1984. 28.50x (ISBN 0-8061-1872-5). U of Okla Pr.

Baker, Donald C. & Murphy, J. L., eds. The Late Medieval Religious Plays of Bodleian Manuscripts Digby 133 & E Museo 160. (Early English Text Society Ser.). (Illus.). 1982. 37.50x (ISBN 0-19-722285-4). Oxford U Pr.

Baker, Donald G., ed. Race, Ethnicity & Power: A Comparative Study. 224p. 1983. 24.95x (ISBN 0-7100-9467-1). Routledge & Kegan.

Baker, Donald I., jt. auth. see Penney, Norman.

Baker, Donald R. Cooling Tower Performance. (Illus.). 1984. 40.00 (ISBN 0-8206-0300-7). Chem Pub.

Baker, Donald W. Formal Application. LC 81-71435. 64p. (Orig.). 1982. pap. 6.95 (ISBN 0-935306-14-5). Barnwood Pr.

--Lawyer's Basic Guide to Secured Transactions. 342p. 1983. text ed. 60.00 (ISBN 0-8318-0435-1). Am Law Inst.

--Unposted Letters. LC 83-173208. 64p. (Orig.). 1984. pap. 6.95 (ISBN 0-935306-23-4). Barnwood Pr.

Baker, Dora, tr. from Ger. see Steffen, Albert.

Baker, Dora, tr. see Steffen, Albert.

Baker, Dorothy. Young Man with a Horn. 1977. Repr. of 1938 ed. lib. bdg. 15.95x (ISBN 0-89244-025-2). Queens Hse.

Baker, Dorothy & Baker, Howard. The Ninth Day. (The Lost Play Ser.). Date not set. pap. 1.25x (ISBN 0-912262-05-2). Proscenium.

Baker, Dorothy, ed. see Masters, Roy.

Baker, Dorothy D. Trio. LC 77-5686. 1977. lib. bdg. 22.50x (ISBN 0-8371-9647-7, BATR). Greenwood.

Baker, Doug. River Place. LC 79-27119. 176p. 1980. pap. 7.95 (ISBN 0-917304-57-8). Timber.

Baker, Douglas. Alcoholism. 1982. 25.00x (ISBN 0-906006-06-6, Pub. by Baker Pubns England). State Mutual Bk.

--Bach Flower Remedy Repertoires, Pts. 1 & 2. 1982. Set. 50.00x (ISBN 0-686-45415-4, Pub. by Baker Pubns England); Pt. 1. 30.00 (ISBN 0-906006-60-0); Pt. 2. 30.00 (ISBN 0-906006-61-9). State Mutual Bk.

--Beyond the Intellect. 1982. 45.00x (ISBN 0-906006-45-7, Pub. by Baker Pubns England). State Mutual Bk.

--The Egoic Lotus. 1982. 30.00x (ISBN 0-906006-07-4, Pub. by Baker Pubns England). State Mutual Bk.

--Esoteric Astrology: Theory, Interpretation, & Practice, 10 vols. 1982. Set. 500.00x (ISBN 0-686-45417-0, Pub. by Baker Pubns England); vol. 55.00x ea. State Mutual Bk.

--Greek & Roman Mythology, Vols. D to L. 1982. Set. 40.00 (ISBN 0-906006-08-2, Pub. by Baker Pubns England). State Mutual Bk.

--Greek & Roman Mythology, Vol. M to Pom. 1982. 40.00x (ISBN 0-906006-13-9, Pub. by Baker Pubns England). State Mutual Bk.

--Greek & Roman Mythology, Vol. Pom to Z. 1982. 40.00x (ISBN 0-906006-15-5, Pub. by Baker Pubns England). State Mutual Bk.

--Greek & Roman Mythology, 4 vols. 1982. Set. 150.00x (ISBN 0-686-45418-9, Pub. by Baker Pubns England). State Mutual Bk.

--In the Steps of the Master. 1982. 40.00x (ISBN 0-9505502-4-8, Pub. by Baker Pubns England). State Mutual Bk.

--The Jewel in the Lotus. 1982. 40.00x (ISBN 0-9505502-8-0, Pub. by Baker Pubns England). State Mutual Bk.

--Karmic Laws. 1982. 25.00x (ISBN 0-906006-11-2, Pub. by Baker Pubns England). State Mutual Bk.

--Meditation, the Theory & Practice. 1982. 55.00x (ISBN 0-9505502-0-5, Pub. by Baker Pubns England). State Mutual Bk.

--Occult Glossary. 1982. 45.00x (ISBN 0-686-45419-7, Pub. by Baker Pubns England). State Mutual Bk.

--The Occult Significance of UFO's. 1982. 26.00x (ISBN 0-906006-43-0, Pub. by Baker Pubns England). State Mutual Bk.

--The Opening of the Third Eye. 128p. 1977. pap. 6.95 (ISBN 0-85030-140-8). Weiser.

--The Powers Latent in Man. (Illus.). 96p. (Orig.). 1977. pap. 6.95 (ISBN 0-85030-144-0, Pub. by Thorsons Pub). Weiser.

--The Practical Techniques of Astral Projection. (Illus.). 96p. (Orig.). 1977. pap. 6.95 (ISBN 0-85030-141-6, Pub. by Thorsons Pub). Weiser.

--Reincarnation-Why, Where & How We Have Lived Before. 1982. 20.00x (ISBN 0-906006-57-0, Pub. by Baker Pubns England). State Mutual Bk.

--The Seven Rays. 126p. (Orig.). 1977. pap. 6.95 (ISBN 0-85030-145-9, Pub. by Thorsons Pub). Weiser.

--Shakespeare, the True Authorship. 1982. 45.00x (ISBN 0-9505502-2-1, Pub. by Baker Pubns England). State Mutual Bk.

--The Spiritual Diary. 1982. 39.00x (ISBN 0-9505502-7-2, Pub. by Baker Pubns England). State Mutual Bk.

--Superconsciousness Through Meditation. 128p. 1979. pap. 3.95 (ISBN 0-87728-384-2). Weiser.

--The Third Eye. 1982. 29.00x (ISBN 0-906006-59-7, Pub. by Baker Pubns England). State Mutual Bk.

--The Wheel of Rebirth. 1982. 28.00x (ISBN 0-906006-16-3, Pub. by Baker Pubns England). State Mutual Bk.

Baker, Dwight C. T'ai Shan: An Account of the Sacred Eastern Peak of China. lib. bdg. 79.95 (ISBN 0-87968-474-7). Krishna Pr.

Baker, E., jt. auth. see Hess, Thomas B.

Baker, E., et al. Solar Heating & Cooling Systems: Design for Australian Conditions. (Illus.). 332p. 1984. pap. 33.50 (ISBN 0-08-029852-4). Pergamon.

Baker, E. C. Fighter Aces of the R. A. F., 1939-45. (Illus.). 1965. pap. 4.95 (ISBN 0-913076-00-7). Beachcomber Bks.

--Sir William Preece F. R. S. Victorian Engineer Extraordinary. (Illus.). 377p. 1976. 19.75x (ISBN 0-8476-1369-0). Rowman.

Baker, E. H., et al. Structural Analysis of Shells. LC 79-27250. 364p. 1981. Repr. of 1972 ed. lib. bdg. 42.50 (ISBN 0-89874-118-1). Krieger.

Baker, Edward W., jt. auth. see Tuttle, Donald M.

Baker, Elijah. Introduction to Steel Shipbuilding. 2nd ed. (Illus.). 1953. 34.45 (ISBN 0-07-003359-5). McGraw.

Baker, Elizabeth. Cherokee Country. LC 68-55990. (Illus.). 1968. pap. 2.95 (ISBN 0-8323-0178-7). Binford.

--Printers & Technology. LC 74-12847. (Illus.). 545p. 1974. Repr. of 1957 ed. lib. bdg. 32.50x (ISBN 0-8371-7763-4, BAPT). Greenwood.

--Protective Labor Legislation, with Special Reference to Women in the State of New York. LC 76-82239. (Columbia University Studies in the Social Sciences: No. 259). Repr. of 1925 ed. 20.00 (ISBN 0-404-51259-3). AMS Pr.

Baker, Elizabeth & Baker, Elton. Bandwagon to Health: The All Natural Way to Eat, Think & Exercise. (Illus.). 1984. pap. 6.95 (ISBN 0-937766-08-9). Drelwood Pubns.

--Bandwagon to Health: The All-Natural Way to Eat, Think & Exercise. 210p. 1984. pap. 6.95 (ISBN 0-937766-08-9). Comm Creat.

--Uncook Book: Raw Food Adventures to a New Health High. 210p. 1981. pap. 5.95 (ISBN 0-937766-05-4). Comm Creat.

--The Uncook Book: Raw Food Adventures to a New Health High. (Illus.). 198p. 1981. pap. 5.95 (ISBN 0-937766-05-4). Drelwood Pubns.

Baker, Elizabeth, et al. Plays of Today, Vol. 1. facs. ed. LC 76-132137. (Play Anthology Reprint Ser). 1925. 17.25 (ISBN 0-8369-8214-2). Ayer Co Pubs.

Baker, Elizabeth F. Displacement of Men by Machines: Effects of Technological Change in Commerical Printing. Stein, Leon, ed. LC 77-70481. (Work Ser.). (Illus.). 1977. Repr. of 1933 ed. lib. bdg. 26.50x (ISBN 0-405-10155-4). Ayer Co Pubs.

--Henry Wheaton: 1785-1848. LC 70-154698. (American Constitutional & Legal History Ser.). 1971. Repr. of 1937 ed. lib. bdg. 49.50 (ISBN 0-306-70152-9). Da Capo.

Baker, Elizabeth V. Chronicles of a Faith Life. (The Higher Christian Life Ser.). 270p. 1984. 35.00 (ISBN 0-8240-6403-8). Garland Pub.

Baker, Elsworth. Man in the Trap. LC 79-26675. 384p. 1980. pap. 5.95 (ISBN 0-02-083650-3, Collier). Macmillan.

Baker, Elton, jt. auth. see Baker, Elizabeth.

Baker, Eric & Blik, Tyler. Trademarks of the Twenties & Thirties. (Illus.). 144p. 1985. pap. 9.95 (ISBN 0-87701-360-8). Chronicle Bks.

Baker, Ernest A. Guide to Historical Fiction. LC 68-9157. 1968. Repr. of 1914 ed. 17.50 (ISBN 0-87266-001-X). Argosy.

--Guide to Historical Fiction. LC 68-58468. (Bibliography & Reference Ser: No. 253). 1969. Repr. of 1914 ed. 23.50 (ISBN 0-8337-0153-3). B Franklin.

--History in Fiction: A Guide to the Best Historical Romances, Sagas, Novels & Tales. 253p. 1983. Repr. of 1983 ed. lib. bdg. 40.00 (ISBN 0-89987-961-6). Darby Bks.

--History in Fiction: Guide to the Best Historical Romances, Sagas, Novels, & Tales. 1977. Repr. of 1907 ed. lib. bdg. 20.00 (ISBN 0-8495-0322-1). Arden Lib.

--A History of the English Novel, 11 vols. Incl. Vol. 1. The Age of Romance: From the Beginnings to the Renaissance. 336p. 1977. Repr. of 1924 ed. 22.50x (ISBN 0-06-480046-6, 06326); Vol. 2. The Elizabethan Age & After. 303p. 1966. Repr. of 1936 ed. 22.50x (ISBN 0-06-480047-4, 06327); Vol. 3. The Later Romances & the Establishment of Realism. 278p. 1969. Repr. of 1929 ed. 22.50x (ISBN 0-06-480048-2, 06328); Vol. 4. Intellectual Realism: From Richardson to Sterne. 297p. 1976. Repr. of 1936 ed. 22.50x (ISBN 0-06-480049-0, 06329); Vol. 5. The Novel of Sentiment & the Gothic Romance. 300p. 1975. Repr. of 1929 ed. 22.50x (ISBN 0-06-480050-4, 06330); Vol. 6. Edgeworth, Austen, Scott. 277p. 1979. Repr. of 1929 ed. 22.50x (ISBN 0-06-480051-2, 06331); Vol. 7. The Age of Dickens & Thackeray. 404p. 1968. Repr. of 1936 ed. 22.50x (ISBN 0-06-480052-0, 06332); Vol. 8. From the Brontes to Meredith: Romanticism in the English Novel. 411p. 1972. Repr. of 1936 ed. 22.50x (ISBN 0-06-480053-9, 06333); Vol. 9. The Day Before Yesterday. 364p. 1975. Repr. of 1936 ed. 22.50x (ISBN 0-06-480054-7, 06334); Vol. 10. Yesterday. 420p. 1976. Repr. of 1936 ed. 22.50x (ISBN 0-06-480055-5, 06335); Vol. 11. Yesterday & After. Stevenson, Lionel. 431p. 1975. Repr. of 1967 ed. 22.50x (ISBN 0-686-76930-9, 06336). Set. 247.50x (ISBN 0-686-66645-3). B&N Imports.

Baker, Ernest A., illus. The Novels of Mrs. Aphra Behn. 380p. Repr. of 1905 ed. lib. bdg. 75.00 (ISBN 0-918377-58-7). Russell Pr.

Baker, Eugene. At the Scene of the Crime. (Junior Detective Bks.). (Illus.). 32p. (gr. 2-6). 1980. PLB 9.25g (ISBN 0-516-06470-3). Childrens.

--At the Scene of the Crime. LC 80-14091. (Junior Detective Ser.). (Illus.). 32p. (gr. 2-5). 1980. PLB 6.95 (ISBN 0-89565-151-3). Childs World.

--In the Detective's Lab. LC 80-17787. (Junior Detective Bks.). (Illus.). 32p. (gr. 2-6). 1980. 9.25g (ISBN 0-516-06471-1). Childrens.

--In the Detective's Lab. LC 80-17787. (The Junior Detective Ser.). (Illus.). 32p. (gr. 2-5). 1980. PLB 6.95 (ISBN 0-89565-154-8). Childs World.

--Master of Disguise. LC 80-11297. (Junior Detective Bks.). (Illus.). 32p. (gr. 2-6). 1980. 9.25g (ISBN 0-516-06472-X). Childrens.

--Master of Disguise. LC 80-11297. (The Junior Detective Ser.). (Illus.). 32p. (gr. 2-5). 1980. PLB 6.95 (ISBN 0-89565-149-1). Childs World.

--Secret Writing-Codes & Messages. LC 80-11416. (Junior Detective Bks.). (Illus.). 32p. (gr. 2-6). 1980. 9.25g (ISBN 0-516-06473-8). Childrens.

--Secret Writing-Codes & Messages. LC 80-11416. (The Junior Detective Ser.). (Illus.). 32p. (gr. 2-5). 1980. PLB 6.95 (ISBN 0-89565-150-5). Childs World.

--Shadowing the Suspect. LC 80-13982. (The Junior Detective Ser.). (Illus.). 32p. (gr. 2-5). 1980. PLB 6.95 (ISBN 0-89565-152-1). Childs World.

--Spotting the Fakes-Counterfeits & Forgeries. LC 80-15998. (Junior Detective Ser.). (Illus.). 32p. (gr. 2-5). 1980. PLB 6.95 (ISBN 0-89565-153-X). Childs World.

--What's Right? Buerger, Jane, ed. LC 80-17552. (Illus.). 112p. 1980. 5.95 (ISBN 0-89565-175-0, 4932). Standard Pub.

--What's Right: A Handbook about Values. LC 80-17552. (Living the Good Life Ser.). (Illus.). 112p. (Orig.). (gr. 1-6). 1980. pap. 5.95 (ISBN 0-89565-175-0). Childs World.

--Your Manners Are Showing. Buerger, Jane, ed. (Illus.). 112p. 1980. 5.95 (ISBN 0-89565-178-5, 4935). Standard Pub.

Baker, Eugene H. What's Right? LC 81-16999. (Successful Living Ser.). (Illus.). 112p. (gr. 2-6). 1981. lib. bdg. 8.95 (ISBN 0-89565-208-0). Childs World.

--Your Manners Are Showing. LC 81-17051. (Successful Living Ser.). (Illus.). 112p. (gr. 2-6). lib. bdg. 8.95 (ISBN 0-89565-211-0). Childs World.

--Your Manners Are Showing: A Handbook about Etiquette. LC 80-17617. (Living the Good Life Ser.). (Illus.). 112p. (gr. 1-6). 1980. pap. 5.95 (ISBN 0-89565-178-5). Childs World.

Baker, Eugene W. Nothing Better Than This: The Biography of James Huckins, First Baptist Missionary to Texas. LC 85-70395. 175p. 1985. 11.95 (ISBN 0-933335-00-8). Baylor Univ Pr.

Baker, Eva, jt. auth. see Popham, James.

Baker, Eva, jt. auth. see Popham, W.

Baker, Eva L. & Quellmalz, Edys S., eds. Educational Testing & Evaluation: Design, Analysis, & Policy. LC 79-21678. (Sage Focus Editions: Vol. 15). 242p. 1980. 24.00x (ISBN 0-8039-1361-3); pap. 12.00 (ISBN 0-8039-1362-1). Sage.

Baker, Eve. Forest Willow. 112p. 1985. 7.95 (ISBN 0-89962-439-1). Todd & Honeywell.

Baker, F. C. The Fresh Water Mollusca of Wisconsin. 1973. Repr. of 1928 ed. lib. bdg. 70.00 (ISBN 3-7682-0764-1). Lubrecht & Cramer.

Baker, F. J. & Silverton, R. E. Introduction to Medical Laboratory Technology. 6th ed. 576p. 1985. pap. text ed. 25.00 (ISBN 0-407-73252-7). Butterworth.

Baker, F. Terry, jt. auth. see Basili, Victor R.

Baker, Fay. My Darling Darling Doctors. LC 74-25292. 224p. 1975. 6.95 (ISBN 0-8076-0774-6). Braziller.

Baker, Florence. Wedding Vows. Date not set. 5.95 (ISBN 0-8062-2398-7). Carlton.

Baker, Frances A. Keeper of the Idiom of the People: The Duquesne University Tamburitzans. LC 80-51690. (Illus.). 110p. 1981. perfect bound 10.00 (ISBN 0-918660-15-7). Ragusan Pr.

Baker, Frank. From Wesley to Asbury: Studies in Early American Methodism. LC 75-39454. 223p. 1976. 18.75 (ISBN 0-8223-0359-0). Duke.

Baker, Frank & Northman, John E. Helping: Human Services for the 80's. LC 80-27524. 241p. 1981. pap. text ed. 15.95 (ISBN 0-8016-0424-9). Mosby.

Baker, Frank, jt. auth. see Schulberg, Herbert C.

Baker, Frank, ed. The Heart of William Law. 2nd ed. 128p. 1985. pap. 5.95 (ISBN 0-310-39621-2, Pub. by F Asbury Pr). Zondervan.

Baker, Frank, jt. ed. see Schulberg, Herbert C.

Baker, Frank, ed. see Wesley, John.

Baker, Frank B. Computer Managed Instruction: Theory & Practice. LC 77-24006. (Illus.). 440p. 1978. 28.95 (ISBN 0-87778-099-4). Educ Tech Pubns.

Baker, Frank C. Life of the Pleistocene or Glacial Period. LC 74-80996. (BCL Ser. I). 1969. Repr. of 1920 ed. 37.50 (ISBN 0-404-00449-0). AMS Pr.

--The Molluscan Fauna of the Big Vermillion River, Illinois. 12.00 (ISBN 0-384-03095-5). Johnson Repr.

Baker, Frank H. Beef Cattle Science Handbook. (International Stockmen's School Handbooks: Vol. 20). 1000p. 1983. hardcover 44.50x (ISBN 0-86531-672-4, Published in Cooperation with Winrock International). Westview.

--Stud Manager's Handbook: International Stockmen's School Handbooks, Vol. 19. 500p. 1983. lib. bdg. 36.50X (ISBN 0-86531-675-9, Pub in cooperation with Winrock International). Westview.

Baker, Frank H. & Miller, Mason E. Emerging Technology & Management for Ruminants. (International Stockments School Proceedings, 1985 Ser.). 450p. 1985. 40.00x (ISBN 0-8133-0120-3). Westview.

Baker, Frank H., ed. Dairy Science Handbook: International Stockmen's School Handbooks, Vol. 15. 500p. Date not set. text ed. 36.50 (ISBN 0-86531-673-2). Westview.

--International Stockman's School Handbooks, 1984. Incl. Vol. 20. Beef Cattle Science Handbook. 1000p. 1983. 46.50x (ISBN 0-86531-672-4); Vol. 16. Dairy Science Handbook. 500p. 1983. 36.50x (ISBN 0-86531-673-2); Vol. iv. Sheep & Goat Handbook. 500p. 1983. 39.50x (ISBN 0-86531-674-0); Vol. 19. Stud Manager's Handbook. 500p. 1983. 36.50x (ISBN 0-86531-675-9). Westview.

Baker, Frank J. How to Make Your Camera Pay for Your Vacation. LC 81-10843. 1985. 15.95 (ISBN 0-87949-208-2). Ashley Bks.

--One Hundred One Ways to Make Money in Photography. 384p. 1980. pap. 7.95 (ISBN 0-8092-7042-0). Contemp Bks.

Baker, Fred. Ptolia, Bk. 1. LC 82-81453. 175p. (Orig.). 1982. pap. 3.95 (ISBN 0-914766-83-X, 0197). IWP Pub.

Baker, Frederick H., jt. auth. see Baker, Jeannine P.

Baker, G. Construction: Techniques. 1976. pap. 8.84 (ISBN 0-13-169409-X). P-H.

Baker, G., tr. see Simotta, George.

Baker, G., et al. Community Nursing: Research & Recent Developments. 240p. (Orig.). 1986. pap. 12.95 (ISBN 0-7099-4415-2, Pub. by Croom Helm Ltd). Longwood Pub Group.

Baker, G. B. & Coutts, R. T., eds. Evaluation of Analytic Methods in Biological Systems, Pt. A: Analysis of Biogenic Amines. (Techniques & Instrumentation in Analytical Chemistry Ser.: Vol. 4). 308p. 1982. 72.50 (ISBN 0-444-42110-6). Elsevier.

Baker, G. B., jt. ed. see Dewhurst, W. G.

Baker, G. P. Augustus: The Golden Age of Rome. 1937. 20.00 (ISBN 0-686-20084-5). Quality Lib.

--Charlemagne & the United States of Europe. 1976. lib. bdg. 59.95 (ISBN 0-8490-1595-2). Gordon Pr.

Baker, G. P. & Hacker, P. M. An Analytical Commentary on Wittgenstein's Philosophical Investigations. xxvi, 322p. 1985. pap. 13.95 (ISBN 0-317-28493-2). U of Chicago Pr.

--An Analytical Commentary on Wittgenstein's Philosophical Investigations. xxvi, 322p. 1983. pap. 12.95 (ISBN 0-226-03539-5). U of Chicago Pr.

--Frege: Logical Excavations. 1984. 39.95x (ISBN 0-19-503261-6). Oxford U Pr.

--Language, Sense & Nonsense: A Critical Investigation of Modern Theories of Language. 380p. 1984. 34.95x (ISBN 0-631-13519-7). Basil Blackwell.

--Scepticism: Rules & Language. 160p. 1984. 24.95x (ISBN 0-631-13614-2). Basil Blackwell.

--Wittgenstein: Meaning & Understanding: Essays on the Philosophical Investigations. xxvi, 374p. 1985. pap. 14.95 (ISBN 0-226-03540-9). U of Chicago Pr.

--Wittgenstein-Understanding & Meaning: An Analytical Commentary on the Philosophical Investigations, Vol. 1. LC 79-15740. 1980. lib. bdg. 60.00x (ISBN 0-226-03526-3). U of Chicago Pr.

Baker, Gary G., illus. There Once Was a Cook. (Illus.). Date not set. pap. 12.95 (ISBN 0-9614501-0-X). Wesley Inst.

Baker, Gayle C. & Montey, Vivian. Special Delivery: A Book for Kids About Cesarean & Vaginal Birth. Meyer, Linda D., ed. LC 81-67193. (Illus.). 70p. (Orig.). (ps-5). 1981. pap. 5.95 (ISBN 0-9603516-2-0). C Franklin Pr.

Baker, Geoffrey. Chronicon Galfridi le Baker De Swynebroke Temporibus Edwardi Secund et Edwardi Tertii. Giles, John A., ed. 1966. Repr. of 1847 ed. 24.00 (ISBN 0-8337-1343-4). B Franklin.

Baker, Geoffrey H. Le Corbusier: An Analysis of Form. 288p. 1984. pap. 14.95 (ISBN 0-442-30557-5). Van Nos Reinhold.

Baker, George. Mexico's Petroleum Sector. LC 83-4178. 312p. 1983. 49.95x (ISBN 0-87814-237-1, P-4332). Pennwell Bks.

--Oleum Magistrale. LC 72-171. (English Experience Ser.: No. 123). 104p. 1969. Repr. of 1574 ed. 16.00 (ISBN 9-0221-0123-1). Walter J Johnson.

Baker, George, jt. ed. see Needleman, Jacob.

Baker, George A., jt. ed. see Roueche, John E.

Baker, George A., Jr. Essentials of Pade Approximants in Theoretical Physics. 1975. 60.00 (ISBN 0-12-074855-X). Acad Pr.

--Point Lace & Diamonds. facsimile ed. LC 74-103080. (Granger Index Reprint Ser.). 1875. 14.00 (ISBN 0-8369-6095-5). Ayer Co Pubs.

Baker, George A., Jr. & Gammel, John L., eds. Pade Approximant in Theoretical Physics. (Mathematics in Science & Engineering Ser.: Vol. 71). 1970. 80.00 (ISBN 0-12-074850-9). Acad Pr.

Baker, George C., Jr. Introduction to the History of Early New England Methodism. LC 70-95393. 1969. Repr. of 1941 ed. 16.00 (ISBN 0-404-00466-0). AMS Pr.

Baker, George P. Charles Dickens & Maria Beadnell. LC 74-14754. 1974. Repr. of 1908 ed. lib. bdg. 35.00 (ISBN 0-8414-3285-6). Folcroft.

--Constantine the Great & the Christian Revolution. 351p. 1967. Repr. of 1931 ed. 11.50x (ISBN 0-87471-213-0). Rowman.

--Development of Shakespeare As a Dramatist. LC 71-160010. (BCL Ser. I). Repr. of 1907 ed. 24.50 (ISBN 0-404-00467-9). AMS Pr.

--Dramatic Technique. LC 77-77706. (Theatre, Film & the Performing Arts Ser.). 532p. 1971. Repr. of 1919 ed. lib. bdg. 45.00 (ISBN 0-306-71344-6). Da Capo.

--Dramatic Technique. LC 75-31999. (Theatre, Film & the Performing Arts Ser.). 1976. pap. 8.95 (ISBN 0-306-80030-6). Da Capo.

--Dramatic Technique. LC 74-100220. Repr. of 1919 ed. lib. bdg. 22.50x (ISBN 0-8371-3005-0, BADT). Greenwood.

--Dramatic Technique. 1975. Repr. of 1919 ed. 16.50 (ISBN 0-8274-4102-9). R West.

--Formation of the New England Railroad Systems: A Study of Railroad Combination in the Nineteenth Century. LC 68-8936. (Illus.). 1968. Repr. of 1937 ed. lib. bdg. 16.25x (ISBN 0-8371-0009-7, BANE). Greenwood.

--Modern American Plays. LC 73-4868. (Play Anthology Reprint Ser.). Repr. of 1920 ed. 28.25 (ISBN 0-8369-8247-9). Ayer Co Pubs.

--Sulla the Fortunate: The Great Dictator, Being an Essay on Politics in the Form of a Historical Biography. 320p. 1967. Repr. of 1927 ed. 11.50x (ISBN 0-87471-215-7). Rowman.

--Tiberius Caesar. 322p. 1967. Repr. of 1929 ed. 11.50x (ISBN 0-87471-216-5). Rowman.

Baker, George P., ed. see Goldsmith, Oliver.

Baker, George P., ed. see Lyly, John.

Baker, George T., jt. ed. see Rockstein, Morris.

Baker, Glenn, jt. auth. see Tester, Jerry.

Baker, Glenn A. The Beatles Down under. (Rock & Roll Remembrances Ser.: No. 7). 1985. write for info. Pierian.

Baker, Glenn A. & Cope, Stuart. The New Music. (Illus.). 1981. 14.95 (ISBN 0-517-54503-9, Harmony); pap. 6.95 (ISBN 0-517-54504-7, Harmony). Crown.

Baker, Glenn A., jt. auth. see Coupe, Stuart.

Baker, Glenn E. & Miller, Rex. Carpentry Fundamentals. (Contemporary Construction Ser.). (Illus.). 512p. (gr. 10-12). 1981. 28.00 (ISBN 0-07-003361-7). McGraw.

Baker, Glenn E. & Yeager, L. Dayle. Wood Technology. LC 72-83817. 1974. scp 30.85 (ISBN 0-672-97507-6); scp students manual 10.28 (ISBN 0-672-97107-0). Bobbs.

Baker, Gordon E. Rural Versus Urban Political Power: The Nature & Consequences of Unbalanced Representation. LC 78-12263. 1979. Repr. of 1955 ed. lib. bdg. 18.75x (ISBN 0-313-21223-6, BARV). Greenwood.

Baker, Gordon E., jt. ed. see Mason, Alpheus.

Baker, Gwendolyn C. Planning & Organizing for Multicultural Instruction. LC 82-8910. (Illus.). 288p. 1983. pap. text ed. 11.50 (ISBN 0-201-10188-2). Addison-wesley.

Baker, H. A. Black Literature in America. 1971. 25.95 (ISBN 0-07-003365-X). McGraw.

--Visions Beyond the Veil. 1973. pap. 3.50 (ISBN 0-88368-019-X). Whitaker Hse.

Baker, H. A., jt. auth. see Lerner, Joel V.

Baker, H. B. Zonitid Snails from Pacific Islands, 4 pts. in 3 vols. (BMB). Repr. of 1941 ed. Pt. 1. 19.00 (ISBN 0-527-02266-7); Pt. 2. 14.00 (ISBN 0-527-02273-X); Pt. 3. 22.00 (ISBN 0-527-02274-8). Kraus Repr.

Baker, H. F. Introduction to Plane Geometry. LC 70-141879. 1971. text ed. 18.50 (ISBN 0-8284-0247-7). Chelsea Pub.

Baker, H. G. & Stebbins, G. L., eds. The Genetics of Colonizing Species. 1965. 74.50 (ISBN 0-12-075150-X). Acad Pr.

Baker, Harry J. & Traphagen, Virginia. The Diagnosis & Treatment of Behavior-Problem Children. 1979. Repr. of 1936 ed. lib. bdg. 30.00 (ISBN 0-8492-3569-3). R West.

Baker, Harry T. The Contemporary Short Story: A Practical Manual. 271p. 1982. Repr. of 1916 ed. lib. bdg. 30.00 (ISBN 0-89984-080-9). Century Bookbindery.

Baker, Harvey, jt. auth. see Pegum, J. S.

Baker, Harvey W., jt. auth. see Wise, Robert A.

Baker, Hendrik. Stage Management & Theatrecraft. 3rd ed. LC 68-16449. (Illus.). 1981. pap. 15.95 (ISBN 0-87830-559-9). Theatre Arts.

Baker, Henry E. Colored Inventor: A Record of Fifty Years. LC 71-75851. (American Negro: His History & Literature, Ser. No. 2). 1969. pap. 1.00 (ISBN 0-405-01943-2). Ayer Co Pubs.

Baker, Henry F. Principles of Geometry, 6 vols. Incl. Vol. 1. Foundations. ix, 195p. 11.00 (ISBN 0-8044-4066-2); Vol. 2. Plane Geometry, Conics, Circles, Non-Euclidian Geometry. xix, 229p. 12.00 (ISBN 0-8044-4067-0); Vol. 3. Solid Geometry, Quadrics, Cubic Curves in Space, Cubic Surfaces. xv, 243p. 12.00 (ISBN 0-8044-4068-9); Vol. 4. Higher Geometry. 274p. 13.00 (ISBN 0-8044-4069-7); Vol. 5. Analytical Principles of the Theory of Curves. ix, 247p. 14.50 (ISBN 0-8044-4070-0); Vol. 6. Algebraic Surfaces. x, 308p. 13.00 (ISBN 0-8044-4071-9). LC 59-14676. Set. (ISBN 0-8044-4065-4). Ungar.

Baker, Henry J., et al, eds. The Laboratory Rat. LC 79-51688. (American College of Laboratory Animal Medicine Ser.). Vol. 1: Biology & Diseases 1979. 67.50 (ISBN 0-12-074901-7); Vol. 2: Research Applications 1980. 63.00 (ISBN 0-12-074902-5). Acad Pr.

Baker, Herbert. Cecil Rhodes. facs. ed. LC 77-102223. (Select Bibliographies Reprint Ser). 1938. 24.50 (ISBN 0-8369-5108-5). Ayer Co Pubs.

Baker, Herman & Frank, Oscar. Clinical Vitaminology: Methods & Interpretation. LC 68-24678. pap. 62.50 (ISBN 0-317-28628-5, 2051326). Bks Demand UMI.

Baker, Herschel. The Wars of Truth: Studies in the Decay of Christian Humanism in the Earlier 17th Century. 11.75 (ISBN 0-8446-0472-0). Peter Smith.

Baker, Herschel, jt. auth. see Rollins, Hyder E.

Baker, Herschel, ed. Four Essays on Romance. LC 77-152269. 1971. pap. 2.75x (ISBN 0-674-31475-1). Harvard U Pr.

Baker, Herschel, jt. ed. see Lumiansky, Robert M.

Baker, Herschel C. Hyder Edward Rollins: A Bibliography. LC 60-10032. (Illus.). 1960. 7.00x (ISBN 0-674-43001-8). Harvard U Pr.

--John Philip Kemble: The Actor in His Theatre. LC 76-90701. Repr. of 1942 ed. lib. bdg. 19.75x (ISBN 0-8371-2279-1, BAJK). Greenwood.

Baker, Houston. A Many Colored Coat: Countee Cullen. 1974. 5.00 (ISBN 0-685-42547-9); pap. 2.75 (ISBN 0-910296-36-7). Broadside.

Baker, Houston A. Singers of Daybreak: Studies in Black American Literature. LC 82-23280. 107p. 1975. 19.84 (ISBN 0-88258-017-5); pap. 6.95 (ISBN 0-88258-025-6). Howard U Pr.

Baker, Houston A., Jr. Blues, Ideology & Afro-American Literature: A Vernacular Theory. LC 84-2655. (Illus.). 288p. 1985. lib. bdg. 19.95x (ISBN 0-226-03536-0). U of Chicago Pr.

--Blues Journeys Home. LC 85-80142. 59p. (Orig.). 1985. pap. 5.00 (ISBN 0-916418-61-8). Lotus.

--The Journey Back: Issues in Black Literature & Criticism. LC 79-20861. 1980. lib. bdg. 12.95x (ISBN 0-226-03534-4); pap. 7.50x (ISBN 0-226-03535-2). U of Chicago Pr.

--Long Black Song: Essays in Black American Literature & Culture. LC 72-77261. 156p. 1972. 12.95x (ISBN 0-8139-0403-X). U Pr of Va.

--No Matter Where You Travel, You Still Be Black. LC 78-61608. 58p. 1979. pap. 3.00x perfect bdg. (ISBN 0-916418-18-9). Lotus.

--Spirit Run. LC 81-82664. 38p. 1982. pap. 3.00x (ISBN 0-916418-38-3). Lotus.

Baker, Houston A., Jr. see Fiedler, Leslie A.

Baker, Houston A., Jr., ed. Three American Literatures: Essays in Chicano, Native American, & Asian-American Literature for Teachers of American Literature. LC 82-63420. iii, 265p. 1982. 25.00x (ISBN 0-87352-353-9); pap. 12.50x (ISBN 0-87352-352-0). Modern Lang.

Baker, Houston A., Jr., ed. see Douglass, Frederick.

Baker, Howard. Howard Baker's Washington. (Illus.). 1982. 14.98 (ISBN 0-393-01562-9). Norton.

--Ode to the Sea & Other Poems. LC 66-20097. 77p. 1966. 5.95 (ISBN 0-8040-0228-2, 82-71561). Ohio U Pr.

--Persephone's Cave: Cultural Accumulations of the Early Greeks. LC 77-11162. 352p. 1979. 25.00 (ISBN 0-8203-0438-7). U of Ga Pr.

Baker, Howard, jt. auth. see Baker, Dorothy.

Baker, Howard H., Jr. No Margin for Error: America in the Eighties. 1980. 10.95 (ISBN 0-686-65902-3). Times Bks.

Baker, Hugh. Chinese Family & Kinship. LC 78-26724. 272p. 1979. 29.00x (ISBN 0-231-04768-1); pap. 11.00x (ISBN 0-231-04769-X). Columbia U Pr.

Baker, Hugh D. A Chinese Lineage Village: Sheung-Shui. (Illus.). 1968. 25.00x (ISBN 0-8047-0670-0). Stanford U Pr.

Baker, Ian F., ed. see Micklem, et al.

Baker, Imogene, jt. ed. see Fry, Timothy.

Baker, Ivan. Delicious Vegetarian Cooking. 168p. 1972. pap. 2.95 (ISBN 0-486-22834-7). Dover.

--Delicious Vegetarian Cooking. 11.25 (ISBN 0-8446-4505-2). Peter Smith.

Baker, J. & Cleaver, C., eds. Banach Spaces of Analytic Functions, Kent 1976: Proceedings of a Conference Held at Kent State University July 12-16, 1976. LC 77-11202. (Lecture Notes in Mathematics: Vol. 604). 1977. pap. text ed. 14.00 (ISBN 0-387-08356-1). Springer-Verlag.

Baker, J. & Nicholson, E. W., eds. The Commentary of Rabbi David Kimhi on Psalms 120-150. (Cambridge Oriental Publications Ser.: No. 22). 44.50 (ISBN 0-521-08670-1). Cambridge U Pr.

Baker, J., tr. see Eichrodt, Walther.

Baker, J. A., tr. see Von Campenhausen, Hans.

Baker, J. C. Baptist History of the North Pacific Coast. Gaustad, Edwin S., ed. LC 79-52589. (The Baptist Tradition Ser.). (Illus.). 1980. Repr. of 1912 ed. lib. bdg. 48.50x (ISBN 0-405-12456-2). Ayer Co Pubs.

Baker, J. E. Prisoner Participation in Prison Power. LC 85-8363. write for info. (ISBN 0-8108-1820-5). Scarecrow.

Baker, J. G. Flora of Mauritius & the Seychelles. 1971. Repr. of 1877 ed. 70.00 (ISBN 3-7682-0677-7). Lubrecht & Cramer.

--Handbook of the Amaryllideae: Including the Alstroemeriae & Agaveae. (Plant Monograph: No.7). 1972. Repr. of 1888 ed. 14.00 (ISBN 3-7682-0677-7). Lubrecht & Cramer.

--Handbook of the Bromeliaceae. (Plant Monograph: No.8). 1972. Repr. of 1889 ed. 14.00 (ISBN 3-7682-0752-8). Lubrecht & Cramer.

--Handbook of the Irideae. (Plant Monograph Ser.: No.9). 1972. Repr. of 1892 ed. 14.00 (ISBN 3-7682-0753-6). Lubrecht & Cramer.

Baker, J. H. The Legal Profession & the Common Law: Historical Essays. 450p. 1985. 40.00 (ISBN 0-907628-62-1). Hambledon Press.

--Legal Records & the Historian. (Royal Historical Society-Studies in History Ser.: Vol. 7). 233p. 1978. text ed. 24.50x (ISBN 0-901050-41-5, Pub. by Swiftbks Enland). Humanities.

--Manual of Law French. 208p. 1979. text ed. 31.00x (ISBN 0-86127-401-6, Pub. by Avebury England). Humanities.

--Manual of Law French. 1979. 95.00x (ISBN 0-86127-401-6, Pub. by Avebury Pub England). State Mutual Bk.

Baker, J. K. & Juergenson, E. M. Approved Practices in Swine Production. 6th ed. LC 79-142330. 438p. 1979. 18.60 (ISBN 0-8134-2038-5, 2038); text ed. 13.95x. Interstate.

Baker, J. N. History of Geographical Discovery & Exploration. LC 66-30785. 553p. 1937. Repr. of 1972 ed. 30.00 (ISBN 0-8154-0014-4). Cooper Sq.

Baker, J. Newton. Law of Disputed & Forged Documents. (Illus.). 1955. 35.00 (ISBN 0-87215-079-8). Michie Co.

Baker, J. R. Cytological Technique. 1966. pap. 7.95x (ISBN 0-412-20300-6, NO.6580, Pub. by Chapman & Hall). Methuen Inc.

--Julian Huxley: Scientist & World Citizen, 1887-1975: A Bibliographic Memoir. 184p. (Bibliography compiled by Jens-Peter-Green). 1978. pap. 7.00 (ISBN 92-3-101461-7, U894, UNESCO). Unipub.

Baker, J. R. & Brothwell, D. R. Animal Diseases in Archaeology. LC 79-42813. (Studies in Archaeological Science). 1980. 37.00 (ISBN 0-12-074150-4). Acad Pr.

Baker, J. R., ed. Advances in Parasitology, Vol. 24. Date not set. 60.00 (ISBN 0-12-031724-9). Acad Pr.

Baker, J. Stannard. Traffic Accident Investigation Manual. 346p. 1975. 35.00 (ISBN 0-912642-01-7). Traffic Inst.

Baker, J. Wayne. Heinrich Bullinger & the Covenant: The Other Reformed Tradition. LC 80-14667. xxvi, 300p. 1980. 24.95x (ISBN 0-8214-0554-3, 82-83475). Ohio U Pr.

Baker, J. Wayne, jt. auth. see Riede, David C.

Baker, Jack, et al. Basic Mathematics. 2nd ed. 1985. text ed. 24.95 (ISBN 0-03-071588-1, CBS C); instr's. manual 9.95 (ISBN 0-317-30070-9). SCP.

Baker, James. Eric Hoffer. (United States Authors Ser.). 1982. lib. bdg. 14.50 (ISBN 0-8057-7359-2, Twayne). G K Hall.

--Literary & Biographical Studies. 1973. Repr. of 1908 ed. 25.00 (ISBN 0-8274-1492-7). R West.

Baker, James, jt. auth. see Kearny, Mary Ann.

Baker, James C. & Ryans, John K., Jr., eds. Multinational Marketing: Dimensions in Strategy. LC 74-20370. (Grid Series in Marketing). pap. 88.50 (ISBN 0-317-27807-X, 2015239). Bks Demand UMI.

Baker, James F. Professional Resume Writing Techniques. (Illus.). 105p. 1984. 34.95x (ISBN 0-916780-26-0). CES.

Baker, James H., ed. Poems of Bishop Henry King. LC 60-8067. 138p. 1960. 5.95x (ISBN 0-8040-0249-5, 82-71710, Pub. by Swallow); (Pub. by Swallow). Ohio U Pr.

Baker, James K. & Greer, William J. Animal Health: A Layman's Guide to Disease Control. LC 78-62054. 404p. 1980. 26.00 (ISBN 0-8134-2053-9, 2053); text ed. 19.50x. Interstate.

Baker, James L. & Goodkind, Richard J. Theory & Practice of Precision Attachment Removable Partial Dentures. LC 81-2393. (Illus.). 282p. 1981. text ed. 56.95 (ISBN 0-8016-0427-3). Mosby.

Baker, James M., ed. Baldwin's Kentucky Practice, 4 Vols. 1310p. 1984. Incl. Annual Suppl. 190.00 (ISBN 0-8322-0056-5); 50.00 ea. Banks-Baldwin.

Baker, James R. & Siegler, Arthur B., Jr., eds. Lord of the Flies: Text, Notes & Criticism. casebook ed. 1964. pap. text ed. 4.95 (ISBN 0-399-50643-8, Putnam). Putnam Pub Group.

Baker, James T. Thomas Merton: Social Critic. LC 76-132827. 184p. 1971. 17.00x (ISBN 0-8131-1238-9). U Pr of Ky.

--Under the Sign of the Waterbearer: A Life of Thomas Merton. 1976. pap. 2.95 (ISBN 0-915216-15-9). Marathon Intl Pub Co.

Baker, James V. Sacred River: Coleridge's Theory of the Imagination. LC 73-90466. Repr. of 1957 ed. lib. bdg. 18.75 (ISBN 0-8371-2205-8, BASR). Greenwood.

Baker, James W. Illusions Illustrated: A Professional Magic Show for Young Performers. LC 83-19549. (Illus.). 120p. (gr. 6 up). 1984. PLB 10.95 (ISBN 0-8225-0768-4). Lerner Pubns.

Baker, Jan. The Church of England. 1978. pap. 3.20 (ISBN 0-08-021408-8). Pergamon.

--The Silent Bells. 1983. 14.95 (ISBN 0-686-34311-5). Bk Pools.

Baker, Jane & Ostmann, Barbara G., eds. Food Editors' Favorites Cookbook. LC 83-6199. 160p. 1983. pap. 8.95 (ISBN 0-8437-3396-9). Hammond Inc.

--Food Editors' Hometown Favorites Cookbook: American Regional & Local Specialties. LC 83-6199. 160p. (Orig.). 1984. pap. 8.95 (ISBN 0-8437-3398-5). Hammond Inc.

Baker, Janet. A.I.D.S. Everything You Must Know about Acquired Immune Defiency Syndrome - the Killer Epidemic of the 80's. LC 83-62309. (Illus.). 128p. 1983. 7.95 (ISBN 0-88247-700-5). R & E Pubs.

--Full Circle: An Autobiographical Journal. (Illus.). 224p. 1983. 19.95 (ISBN 0-531-09876-1). Watts.

Baker, Jarry. The Impatient Gardener. 288p. (Orig.). 1983. pap. 6.95 (ISBN 0-345-30949-9). Ballantine.

Baker, Jean H. Affairs of Party: The Political Culture of Northern Democrats in the Mid-19th Century. (Illus.). 368p. 1983. 39.50x (ISBN 0-8014-1513-6); pap. 14.95x (ISBN 0-8014-9883-X). Cornell U Pr.

--The Politics of Continuity: Maryland Political Parties from 1858 to 1870. LC 72-12354. (Goucher College Ser.). (Illus.). 254p. 1973. 24.00x (ISBN 0-8018-1418-9). Johns Hopkins.

Baker, Jeanne, jt. auth. see Baker, David.

Baker, Jeannie. Home in the Sky. LC 83-25379. (Illus.). 32p. (gr. k-3). 1984. 13.00 (ISBN 0-688-03841-7); PLB 11.96 (ISBN 0-688-03842-5). Greenwillow.

Baker, Jeannine P. & Baker, Frederick H. Conscious Conception: Elemental Journey Through the Sexual Labyrinth. (Illus.). 512p. (Orig.). 1985. pap. 16.95 (ISBN 0-914728-52-0). Wingbow Pr.

Baker, Jeffrey. Time & Mind in Wordsworth's Poetry. LC 80-11947. 212p. 1980. 16.95 (ISBN 0-8143-1655-7). Wayne St U Pr.

Baker, Jeffrey J. & Allen, Garland A. The Study of Biology. 4th ed. LC 81-17550. (Illus.). 1040p. 1982. text ed. 39.95 (ISBN 0-201-10180-7); instr's. manual 3.50 (ISBN 0-201-10181-5); study guide 13.95 (ISBN 0-201-10182-3). Addison-Wesley.

Baker, Jeffrey J. & Allen, Garland E. Course in Biology. 3rd ed. LC 78-67451. (Life Sciences Ser.). 1979. text ed. 24.95 (ISBN 0-201-00308-2). Addison-Wesley.

Baker, Jeffrey J. W. & Allen, Garland E. Matter, Energy, & Life: An Introduction to Chemical Concepts. 4th ed. LC 80-17946. (Life Sciences Ser.). 256p. 1981. 15.95 (ISBN 0-201-00169-1). Addison-Wesley.

Baker, Jennifer. Saddlery & Horse Equipment. LC 82-11468. (Illus.). 96p. 1985. 9.95 (ISBN 0-668-05633-9, 5633). Arco.

Baker, Jennifer L. & Mehalko, Laurie E. Storybook Quilting. LC 84-45699. 208p. (Orig.). 1985. pap. 15.95 (ISBN 0-8019-7528-X). Chilton.

Baker, Jennifer M., ed. see Institute of Petroleum.

Baker, Jenny. The Student's Cookbook. LC 85-1544. 144p. (Orig.). 1985. pap. 5.95 (ISBN 0-571-13522-6). Faber & Faber.

Baker, Jeremy. Tolstoy's Bicycle: Being an Amazing Compendium of All Human History & Mortal Achievement by Age, from Birth to Death. 560p. 1982. 24.95 (ISBN 0-312-80866-6); pap. 12.95 (ISBN 0-312-80867-4). St Martin.

Baker, Jerry. Jerry Baker's Fast, Easy Vegetable Garden. 1985. pap. 8.95 (ISBN 0-452-25670-4, Plume). NAL.

--Jerry Baker's Happy, Healthy House Plants. 1985. pap. 8.95 (ISBN 0-452-25734-4, Plume). NAL.

Baker, Jim. Benjamin Franklin: The Uncommon Man. (Illus.). 1976. pap. 1.00 (ISBN 0-914482-13-0). Ohio Hist Soc.

--For the Ohio Country. (Illus.). 1976. pap. 1.95 (ISBN 0-914482-12-2). Ohio Hist Soc.

--Forts in the Forest: Kentucky in the Year of the Bloody Sevens. LC 75-39915. (Illus.). 48p. (Orig.). 1975. pap. 1.95 (ISBN 0-914482-11-4). Ohio Hist Soc.

Baker, Joe. Coping with Drug Abuse: A Lifeline for Parents. LC 82-12723. (Illus.). 60p. 1982. pap. 7.95 (ISBN 0-943690-00-5). DARE.

Baker, John. Mauchline Ware & Associated Scottish Souventir Ware. (Shire Album Ser.: No. 140). (Illus.). 32p. (Orig.). 1985. pap. 3.50 (ISBN 0-85263-734-9, Pub. by Shire Pubns England). Seven Hills Bks.

Baker, John & Heyman, J. Plastic Design of Frames, 2 vols. Incl. Vol. 1. Fundamentals; Vol. 2. Applications. 47.50 (ISBN 0-521-07984-5). LC 69-19370. (Illus.). 1969-1971. Cambridge U Pr.

Baker, John, jt. ed. see Taylor, Angela.

Baker, John A. Peregrine. LC 67-23049. 1967. 10.00i (ISBN 0-06-070173-0, HarpT). Har-Row.

Baker, John A. & Collins, Mary S. Research on Administration of Physical Education & Athletics, 1971-1982: A Retrieval System. 88p. (Orig.). 1983. pap. 7.95 (ISBN 0-87881-107-9). Mojave Bks.

Baker, John A., tr. see Danielou, Jean.

Baker, John C. Directors & Their Functions. LC 73-1990. (Big Business; Economic Power in a Free Society Ser.). Repr. of 1945 ed. 10.00 (ISBN 0-405-05074-7). Ayer Co Pubs.

--Farm Broadcasting: The First Sixty Years. (Illus.). 342p. text ed. 17.95x (ISBN 0-8138-1485-5). Iowa St U Pr.

Baker, John C., jt. auth. see Berman, Robert P.

Baker, John F., et al. The Steel Skeleton, Vol. 2: Plastic Behaviour & Design. LC 54-3769. pap. 111.80 (ISBN 0-317-26067-7, 2024427). Bks Demand UMI.

Baker, John P., jt. auth. see Keith, T. B.

Baker, John R. The Biology of Parasitic Protozoa. (Studies in Biology: No. 138). 64p. 1982. pap. text ed. 8.95 (ISBN 0-7131-2837-2). E Arnold.

--Perspectives in Trypanosomiasis Research: Proceedings of the Twenty-First Trypanosomiasis Seminar: London 24 September 1981. (Tropical Medicine Research Studies). 105p. 1982. 34.95 (ISBN 0-471-10478-7, Pub. by Res Stud Pr). Wiley.

--Race. rev. ed. 625p. 1981. pap. 10.00 (ISBN 0-936396-01-6). Foun Human GA.

--Race. 1984. lib. bdg. 79.95 (ISBN 0-87700-637-7). Revisionist Pr.

Baker, John R. & Muller, Ralph. Advances in Parasitology, Vol. 23. LC 62-22124. (Serial Publication). 1985. 40.00 (ISBN 0-12-031723-0). Acad Pr.

Baker, John T., jt. auth. see Barnett, Nancy B.

Baker, Joseph E. Shelley's Platonic Answer to a Platonic Attack on Poetry. 72p. 1965. pap. 3.50x (ISBN 0-87745-006-4). U of Iowa Pr.

Baker, Joseph T. & Murphy, Vreni. Compounds from Marine Organisms, Vol. 2. (Section B, Handbook of Marine Science). 240p. 1981. 56.00 (ISBN 0-8493-0214-5). CRC Pr.

Baker, Joseph T. & Murphy, Vreni, eds. Handbook of Marine Science: Section B, Compounds from Marine Organisms, Vol. 1. 216p. 1976. 54.00 (ISBN 0-87819-391-X). CRC Pr.

Baker, Josephine & Bouillon, Jo. Josephine. LC 76-26212. (Illus.). 1977. 12.95i (ISBN 0-06-010212-8, HarpT). Har-Row.

Baker, Josephine T. The Literary Workshop. 1973. Repr. of 1918 ed. 8.50 (ISBN 0-8274-1487-0). R West.

Baker, Justine. Microcomputers in the Classroom. LC 82-60799. (Fastback Ser.: No. 179). 50p. 1982. pap. 1.50 (ISBN 0-87367-179-1). Phi Delta Kappa.

Baker, K. Wild Flowers of Western Australia. (Illus.). 1973. 6.00 (ISBN 0-912728-45-0). Newbury Bks.

Baker, K. & Fane, X. Understanding & Guiding Young Children. 3rd ed. LC 67-4932. 1975. 21.28 (ISBN 0-13-935825-0). P-H.

Baker, K. F. & Cook, R. J. Biological Control of Plant Pathogens. LC 82-70786. 433p. 1982. Repr. of 1974 ed. text ed. 32.50 (ISBN 0-89054-045-4); text ed. 27.50 members. Am Phytopathol Soc.

Baker, Karle W. Old Coins (Poetry) 1923. 24.50x (ISBN 0-686-83652-9). Elliots Bks.

Baker, Katherine R. Let's Play Outdoors. LC 66-10181. 45p. 1966. 2.50 (ISBN 0-912674-23-7, NAEYC 101). Natl Assn Child Ed.

Baker, Keith & Rubel, Tobert J. Violence & Crime in the Schools. LC 79-5325. 320p. 1980. 19.50x (ISBN 0-669-03389-8). Lexington Bks.

Baker, Keith A., ed. Bilingual Education: A Reappraisal of Federal Policy. Kenter, Adriana A. LC 82-48040. 272p. 1982. 24.50x (ISBN 0-669-05885-8). Lexington Bks.

Baker, Keith M. Condorcet: From Natural Philosophy to Social Mathematics. LC 74-5725. xiv, 538p. 1975. 27.50x (ISBN 0-226-03532-8). U of Chicago Pr.

--Condorcet: From Natural Philosophy to Social Mathematics. LC 74-5725. 538p. 1982. 17.00x (ISBN 0-226-03533-6). U of Chicago Pr.

Baker, Kendall L., et al. Germany Transformed: Political Culture & the New Politics. LC 80-18244. (Illus.). 384p. 1981. text ed. 25.00x (ISBN 0-674-35315-3). Harvard U Pr.

Baker, Kenneth. Chord & Progressions for Jazz & Popular Keyboards. 1983. pap. 8.95 (ISBN 0-8256-2286-7, Amsco Music). Music Sales.

--Fundamentals of Catholicism: Church, Grace, Sacraments & Eschatology or the Last Things, Vol. III. 1983. pap. 10.95 (ISBN 0-317-02736-0, Co-Pub. by Ignatius Pr-Catholic Polls). Guild Bks.

--Fundamentals of Catholicism: God, Trinity, Creation, Christ, Mary, Vol. II. LC 82-80297. 1983. pap. 10.95 (ISBN 0-89870-019-1, Co-Pub. by Ignatius Pr-Catholic Polls). Guild Bks.

--Fundamentals of Catholicism: Grace, the Church, the Sacraments, Eschatology, Vol. 3. LC 82-80297. 388p. (Orig.). 1983. pap. 11.95 (ISBN 0-89870-027-2). Ignatius Pr.

--Fundamentals of Catholicism: The Creed, the Commandments, Vol. 1. LC 82-80297. 282p. (Orig.). 1982. pap. 9.95 (ISBN 0-89870-017-5). Ignatius Pr.

--Fundamentals of Catholocism: The Creed, the Commandments, Vol. I. LC 82-80297. 1982. pap. 9.95 (ISBN 0-89870-017-5, Co-Pub. by Ignatius Pr-Catholic Polls). Guild Bks.

--Joan Snyder & Pat Steir. (Illus.). 1974. 2.00 (ISBN 0-910663-07-6). ICA Inc.

Baker, Kenneth & Chan, Paul. How to Order a Real Chinese Meal. 1976. pap. 1.25 (ISBN 0-685-78159-3). Guild Bks.

Baker, Kenneth F. & Cook, R. James. Biological Control of Plant Pathogens. LC 73-18420. (Biology of Plant Pathogens Books Ser.). pap. 111.80 (ISBN 0-317-29242-0, 2055548). Bks Demand UMI.

Baker, Kenneth F., jt. auth. see Cook, James R.

Baker, Kenneth F., et al, eds. Annual Review of Phytopathology, Vol. 11. LC 63-8847. (Illus.). 1973. text ed. 20.00 (ISBN 0-8243-1311-9). Annual Reviews.

--Annual Review of Phytopathology, Vol. 12. LC 63-8847. (Illus.). 1974. text ed. 20.00 (ISBN 0-8243-1312-7). Annual Reviews.

Baker, Kenneth G., jt. auth. see Udell, Gerald G.

Baker, Kenneth P., et al, eds. Annual Review of Phytopathology, Vol. 10. LC 63-8847. (Illus.). 1972. text ed. 20.00 (ISBN 0-8243-1310-0). Annual Reviews.

--Annual Review of Phytopathology, Vol. 13. LC 63-8847. (Illus.). 1975. text ed. 20.00 (ISBN 0-8243-1313-5). Annual Reviews.

--Annual Review of Phytopathology, Vol. 14. LC 63-8847. (Illus.). 1976. text ed. 20.00 (ISBN 0-8243-1314-3). Annual Reviews.

--Annual Review of Phytopathology, Vol. 15. LC 63-8847. (Illus.). 1977. text ed. 20.00 (ISBN 0-8243-1315-1). Annual Reviews.

Baker, Kenneth R. & Kropp, Dean H. Management Science: An Introduction to Decision Models. 650p. 1985. text ed. 33.95 (ISBN 0-471-87766-2). Wiley.

Baker, Kenneth S. Fundamentals of Catholicism: God, Trinity, Creation, Christ, Mary, Vol. 2. LC 82-80297. 387p. (Orig.). 1983. pap. 11.95 (ISBN 0-89870-019-1). Ignatius Pr.

Baker, Kent. Maryland Basketball: Red, White & Amen. LC 76-47353. (College Sports Ser.). (Illus.). 1980. 9.95 (ISBN 0-87397-079-9). Strode.

Baker, Kent H., et al. Financial Markets: Instruments & Concepts. 2nd ed. 1985. pap. text ed. 23.95 (ISBN 0-8359-2031-3). Reston.

Baker, Kitty, jt. auth. see Wagner, Jeannine.

Baker, Krystyna. Masks. 150p. 1981. pap. 20.00 (ISBN 0-89672-085-3); cloth, signed ltd. ed. 50.00 (ISBN 0-89672-086-1). Tex Tech Pr.

Baker, L. E., jt. auth. see Geddes, L. A.

Baker, L. R., ed. British Electro-Optics. 148p. 1977. cancelled (ISBN 0-85066-101-3). Taylor & Francis.

Baker, Lafayette C. History of the United States Secret Service. LC 70-156006. (Foundations of Criminal Justice Ser.). Repr. of 1868 ed. 32.50 (ISBN 0-404-09106-7). AMS Pr.

Baker, Larry N. Ethics in a Christian Perspective. LC 82-71441. Date not set. cancelled (ISBN 0-8054-6125-6). Broadman.

Baker, Laura N. The Friendly Beasts. (Illus.). 28p. (gr. k-3). 1957. Repr. 4.95 (ISBN 0-395-27662-4). HM.

Baker, Laurence H., ed. Soft Tissue Sarcomas. (Cancer Treatment & Research Ser.). 1983. lib. bdg. 36.00 (ISBN 0-89838-584-9, Pub. by Martinus Nijhoff Netherlands). Kluwer Academic.

Baker, Lawrence, et al. Biology & Therapy of Acute Leukemia. (Developments in Oncology Ser.). 1985. lib. bdg. 42.50 (ISBN 0-89838-728-0, Pub. by Martinus Nijhoff Netherlands). Kluwer Academic.

Baker, Leigh R. Development of University Libraries in Papua New Guinea. LC 80-26936. 410p. 1981. 22.00 (ISBN 0-8108-1393-9). Scarecrow.

Baker, Leighton L. Jim Baker: The Red Headed Shoshoni. Hughey, Roberta & Bason, M. L., eds. LC 83-51113. (Illus.). 425p. (Orig.). 1984. 22.50 (ISBN 0-9611028-2-9); pap. 13.95 (ISBN 0-9611028-3-7). Salt Warrior Pr.

Baker, Leonard. Brandeis & Frankfurter: A Dual Biography. LC 83-48319. (Illus.). 480p. 1984. 25.00 (ISBN 0-06-015245-1). Har-Row.

--Days of Sorrow & Pain: Leo Baeck & the Berlin Jews. (Illus.). 1980. pap. 9.95 (ISBN 0-19-502800-7, GB 611). Oxford U Pr.

--John Marshall: A Life in Law. 864p. 1981. 12.95 (ISBN 0-02-001700-6, Collier). Macmillan.

Baker, Leslie A. The Art Teacher's Resource Book. (Illus.). 1978. ref. 22.95 (ISBN 0-87909-022-7). Reston.

Baker, Lewis. The Percys of Mississippi: Politics & Literature in the New South. LC 83-7916. (Southern Biography Ser.). (Illus.). 288p. 1983. 19.95 (ISBN 0-8071-1102-3). La State U Pr.

Baker, Lida, ed. see Baker, David & Baker, Jeanne.

Baker, Lillian. The Concentration Camp Conspiracy: A Second Pearl Harbor. LC 82-147000615. (Illus.). 350p. 1983. 15.00 (ISBN 0-318-00818-1). AFHA Pubns.

Baker, Linda, jt. auth. see Derick, Mitch.

Baker, Liva. Miranda: Crime, Law & Politics. LC 81-69127. 480p. 1985. pap. 11.95 (ISBN 0-689-70692-8, 328). Atheneum.

Baker, Lowell H., jt. ed. see Baker, A. B.

Baker, Lucia, et al. Collage: An Intermediate French Program, 5 readers. 2nd ed. Incl. Reader 1. Grammar. pap. text ed. 16.95 (ISBN 0-394-33682-8); Reader 2. Literary Reader. pap. text ed. 10.00 (ISBN 0-394-33684-4); Reader 3. Cultural Reader. pap. text ed. 10.00 (ISBN 0-394-33683-6); Reader 4. Activities Manual. pap. text ed. 10.00 (ISBN 0-394-33685-2); Reader 5. Workbook. pap. text ed. 10.00 (ISBN 0-394-33686-0). 1985. pap. text ed. (RanC). Random.

Baker, Lynn S. The Fertility Fallacy: Sexuality in the Post Pill Age. LC 80-50715. 224p. 1981. 11.95 (ISBN 0-03-057656-3). HR&W.

Baker, M. Discovering London's Statues & Monuments. (Discovering Ser.: No. 42). 1979. pap. 3.95 (ISBN 0-85263-520-6, Pub. by Shire Pubns England). Seven Hills Bks.

Baker, M. C., jt. auth. see Winn, Charles S.

Baker, M. J., jt. auth. see Thoft-Christensen, P.

Baker, M. Jane, illus. Country Quilt Design Cut & Use Stencils. (Cut & Use Stencils Ser.). 64p. (Orig.). 1984. pap. 4.50 (ISBN 0-486-24525-X). Dover.

Baker, M. Joyce. Images of Women in Film: The War Years, 1941-1945. Berkhofer, Robert, ed. LC 80-39795. (Studies in American History & Culture: No. 21). 196p. 1981. 39.95 (ISBN 0-8357-1153-6). UMI Res Pr.

Baker, M. Pauline, jt. auth. see Hearn, D. Donald.

Baker, M. Pauline, jt. auth. see Hearn, Donald.

Baker, Madeline. Reckless Heart. 480p. (Orig.). 1985. pap. 3.95 (ISBN 0-8439-2255-9, Leisure Bks). Dorchester Pub Co.

Baker, Marcus. Alaskan Geographic Names. (Shorey Historical Ser.: No. 21). 20p. Shorey.

--Geographic Dictionary of Alaska. facsimile ed. (Shorey Historical Ser.). 75p. Repr. of 1906 ed. pap. 5.95 (ISBN 0-8466-0100-1, S100). Shorey.

Baker, Margaret. Discovering Christmas Customs & Folklore: A Guide to Seasonal Rites. 2.95 (ISBN 0-913714-56-9). Legacy Bks.

--Discovering Christmas Customs & Folklore. (Discovering Ser.: No. 32). (Illus.). 56p. (Orig.). 1985. pap. 3.50 (ISBN 0-85263-173-1, Pub. by Shire Pubns England). Seven Hills Bks.

--Discovering Statues in Southern England. (Discovering Ser.: No. 31). (Illus.). 1983. pap. 2.95 (ISBN 0-85263-059-X, Pub. by Shire Pubns England). Seven Hills Bks.

--Discovering the Folklore of Plants. (Discovering Ser.). (Illus.). 72p. (gr. 6 up). 1975. pap. 2.00 (ISBN 0-913714-04-6). Legacy Bks.

--Food & Cooking. (Junior Reference Ser.). (Illus.). 64p. (gr. 6 up). 1979. 8.95 (ISBN 0-7136-1465-X). Dufour.

Baker, Margret. Folklore of the Sea. (Illus.). 1979. 16.95 (ISBN 0-7153-7568-7). David & Charles.

Baker, Marguerite. And Then the Angels Came to the First Grade Children. 1964. pap. 1.50 (ISBN 0-685-79136-X). Summit Univ.

Baker, Mariam. Woman As Divine: Tales of the Goddess. (Illus., Orig.). 1982. pap. 8.95 (ISBN 0-9609916-0-3). Crescent Heart.

Baker, Marilyn. Encyclopedia of Packaging Technology. 99.50 (ISBN 0-471-80940-3). Wiley.

Baker, Marion L. On the Road to Unity: A Study-Action Guide. (Orig.). 1982. pap. 3.95 (ISBN 0-377-00116-3). Friend Pr.

Baker, Mark. Cops: Their Lives in Their Own Words. 320p. 1985. 16.95 (ISBN 0-671-49970-X). S&S.

--I Hate Videots. 1983. write for info. S&S.

--Nam. LC 80-26039. 288p. 1981. 12.95 (ISBN 0-688-00086-X). Morrow.

--NAM. 320p. 1984. pap. 3.50 (ISBN 0-425-07168-5). Berkley Pub.

--NAM: The Vietnam War in the Words of the Men & Women Who Fought There. LC 81-22674. 1982. 5.75 (ISBN 0-688-01224-8). Morrow.

Baker, Mark & Bassett, Libby. The World Environment Handbook: A Directory of Global Natural Resource Management Agencies & Non-Governmental Environment Organizations in 145 Countries. 2nd ed. 290p. 1984. pap. 29.50. Wiley.

Baker, Mark, et al. The World Environment Handbook: A Directory of Government Natural Resource Management Agencies & Non-Governmental Environment Organizations in 145 Countries. 2nd ed. 290p. 1984. pap. 29.50 (ISBN 0-910499-03-9). World Enviro.

Baker, Martha. How to Survive & Live in Heaven on Earth. rev. ed. LC 81-4234. 165p. 1981. pap. 4.95 (ISBN 0-86663-763-X). Ide Hse.

Baker, Mary J., jt. auth. see Cauvin, Jean-Pierre.

Baker, Mary L., jt. ed. see Mistic, Michael C.

Baker, Marybeth. The Adventures of Maynard, a Maine Moose. (Illus.). 44p. 1984. pap. 6.95 (ISBN 0-930096-60-6). G Gannett.

--Maynard Saves a Loon. 1985. pap. 6.95 (ISBN 0-930096-69-X). G Gannett.

Baker, Maryn. The Short Change Game: How to Stop the School from Depriving Your Retarded or Handicapped Child. LC 81-3653. 1985. 13.95 (ISBN 0-87949-211-2). Ashley Bks.

Baker, Maurice E., jt. ed. see Lawson, Merlin P.

Baker, Mervin S. The Century List. 1977. pap. 3.95 (ISBN 0-916608-04-2). Quill Pubns.

Baker, Michael. ECFMG - FMG Examination Review: Pt. I. 5th ed. 1983. pap. text ed. 16.95 (ISBN 0-87488-120-X). Med Exam.

--Our Three Selves: The Life of Radclyffe Hall. LC 85-7315. (Illus.). 384p. 1985. 17.95 (ISBN 0-688-04385-2). Morrow.

Baker, Michael A. Medical Examination Review: Medicine, Vol. 2. 8th ed. 1983. pap. text ed. 12.75. Med Exam.

Baker, Michael A., ed. Medicine. 7th ed. (Medical Examination Review Ser.: Vol. 2). 1980. pap. 12.75 (ISBN 0-87488-102-1). Med Exam.

Baker, Michael J., ed. Dictionary of Marketing & Advertising. 246p. 1985. 42.50 (ISBN 0-89397-206-1). Nichols Pub.

Baker, Michael K. The Sword. LC 84-90678. 303p. (gr. 5up). 1985. text ed. 8.00 (ISBN 0-932543-01-4); pap. 8.00 (ISBN 0-932543-00-6). M B Pub.

Baker, Muriel, ed. Scribner Book of Embroidery Designs. (Illus.). 1981. encore ed. o.p. 9.95 (ISBN 0-684-17570-3, ScribT); pap. 12.95 (ISBN 0-684-16944-4). Scribner.

Baker, Muriel L. Handbook of American Crewel Embroidery. LC 66-16722. (Illus.). 1966. 10.95 (ISBN 0-8048-0230-0). C E Tuttle.

Baker, N., jt. auth. see Turrent, d.

Baker, N. K., et al. Control of Leaf Growth. (Society for Experimental Biology Seminar Ser.: No. 27). 300p. Date not set. price not set (ISBN 0-521-30480-6). Cambridge U Pr.

Baker, N. R. & Barber, J., eds. Chloroplast Biogenesis. (Topics in Photosynthesis Ser.: Vol. 5). 380p. 1984. 96.00 (ISBN 0-444-80548-6). Elsevier.

Baker, Nancy C. Act Two: The Mid-Career Job Change & How to Make it. 256p. 1985. 12.95 (ISBN 0-8149-0833-0). Vanguard.

--Babyselling: The Scandal of Black-Market Adoption. LC 77-93231. 224p. 1978. 10.95 (ISBN 0-8149-0798-9). Vanguard.

--The Beauty Trap: Exploring Woman's Greatest Obsession. 288p. 1984. 16.95 (ISBN 0-531-09848-6). Watts.

--Cashing in on Cooking. 192p. 1982. pap. 8.95 (ISBN 0-8092-5873-0). Contemp Bks.

Baker, Nancy K., ed. see Koch, Heinrich C.

Baker, Newton D. Why We Went to War. LC 72-1278. (Select Bibliographies Reprint Ser). 1972. Repr. of 1936 ed. 12.00 (ISBN 0-8369-6820-4). Ayer Co Pubs.

Baker, Nina B. Garibaldi. (Illus.). (gr. 7-9). 1944. 10.95 (ISBN 0-8149-0264-2). Vanguard.

--He Wouldn't Be King: The Story of Simon Bolivar. (Illus.). (gr. 7-9). 1941. 10.95 (ISBN 0-8149-0262-6). Vanguard.

--Juarez, Hero of Mexico. (Illus.). (gr. 7-9). 1942. 10.95 (ISBN 0-8149-0261-8). Vanguard.

--Lenin. (Illus.). 257p. (gr. 7-9). 1945. 10.95 (ISBN 0-8149-0265-0). Vanguard.

--Peter the Great. 310p. (gr. 7 up). 1943. 10.95 (ISBN 0-8149-0263-4). Vanguard.

--Sun Yat-Sen. (Illus.). 247p. (gr. 4-6). 1946. 10.95 (ISBN 0-8149-0267-7). Vanguard.

Baker, Norman. The Way It Was in New City: An Informal History of New City. 1973. pap. 2.50 (ISBN 0-911183-09-4). Rockland County Hist.

--The Way It Was in North Rockland. 1973. pap. 3.50 (ISBN 0-911183-10-8). Rockland County Hist.

Baker, Norman B. Early Houses of New England. LC 67-11935. (Illus.). 1980. 29.50 (ISBN 0-8048-0154-1). C E Tuttle.

Baker, O. E., jt. auth. see Finch, Vernor C.

Baker, Olaf. Where the Buffaloes Begin. LC 80-23319. (Illus.). 48p. (gr. 2-5). 1981. 9.95g (ISBN 0-7232-6195-4); pap. 5.95 (ISBN 0-7232-6257-8). Warne.

--Where the Buffaloes Begin. LC 85-5682. (Illus.). 48p. (ps-4). 1985. pap. 5.95 (ISBN 0-14-050560-1, Puffin). Penguin.

Baker, Oneta M. History of the Town of Clarence. (Illus.). 640p. 1983. 35.00x (ISBN 0-932334-65-2). Heart of the Lakes.

Baker, Ovid, et al. Gas Liquid Two-Phase Flow in Pipelines: II-Design Manual. 53p. 1970. 3.00 (ISBN 0-318-12632-X, L20269). Am Gas Assn.

Baker, P. A., jt. ed. see Smith, E. G.

Baker, P. J. & Jacobs, B. E. Guide to Slurry Pipeline Systems. (Illus.). 58p. (Orig.). 1980. PLB 29.50x (ISBN 0-906085-38-1, Dist. by Air Science Co.). BHRA Fluid.

Baker, P. J., jt. auth. see Bain, D. C.

Baker, P. Randall. King Husain & the Kingdom of Hejaz. (Arabia Past & Present Ser.: Vol. 10). (Illus.). 1979. 29.95 (ISBN 0-900891-48-3). Oleander Pr.

Baker, P. T., ed. The Biology of High-Altitude Peoples. LC 76-50311. (International Biological Programme Ser.: No. 14). (Illus.). 1978. 79.50 (ISBN 0-521-21523-4). Cambridge U Pr.

Baker, P. T. & Little, Michael A., eds. Man in the Andes: A Multidisciplinary Study of High Altitude Quechua. LC 76-17025. 1976. 59.50 (ISBN 0-12-786115-7). Acad Pr.

Baker, Pat. Giving God What You Are. 1981. pap. 4.95 (ISBN 0-8054-5333-4). Broadman.

--Help! I've Just Given Birth to a Teenager. 128p. (Orig.). 1981. pap. 4.95 (ISBN 0-8010-0799-2). Baker Bk.

--I Now Pronounce You Parent: What Other Books Don't Tell You About Babies. 96p. (Orig.). 1983. pap. 4.95 (ISBN 0-8010-0850-6). Baker Bk.

Baker, Pat A. In This Moment. LC 76-28802. Repr. of 1977 ed. 23.50 (ISBN 0-8357-9012-6, 2016370). Bks Demand UMI.

--A Minute in the Morning: One Hundred & Fifty Devotionals for Women. 1984. pap. 4.95 (ISBN 0-8010-0864-6). Baker Bk.

--Mom, Take Time. 128p. 1976. pap. 3.95 (ISBN 0-8010-0857-3). Baker Bk.

Baker, Paul. Contemporary Christian Music: Where It Came from, Where It Is, Where It Is Going. rev. ed. 1985. pap. 8.95 (ISBN 0-89107-343-4, Crossway Bks). Good News.

--Integration of Abilities: Exercises for Creative Growth. (Illus.). 1977. pap. 10.00 (ISBN 0-87602-030-9). Anchorage.

Baker, Paul G. A Reassessment of D. H. Lawrence's "Aaron's Rod". Litz, Walton, ed. LC 83-9224. (Studies in Modern Literature: No. 31). 224p. 1983. 34.95 (ISBN 0-8357-1470-5). UMI Res Pr.

Baker, Paul J & Wilson, Everett K, eds. KAKN: Knowledge Available & Knowledge Needed to Improve Instruction in Sociology. 339p. 1979. 2.50 (ISBN 0-317-33280-5). Am Sociological.

Baker, Paul R. Atomic Bomb: The Great Decision. 2nd ed. LC 75-36668. 1976. pap. text ed. 12.95 (ISBN 0-03-089873-0, HoltC). HR&W.

--Richard Morris Hunt. (Illus.). 1980. 49.95x (ISBN 0-262-02139-0). MIT Pr.

Baker, Paul R., ed. see D'Arusmont, Frances W.

Baker, Pauline. Espanol Para Los Hispanos: A Guide to Spanish for Native Speakers. 128p. (Eng. & Span.). 1983. pap. 5.95 (ISBN 0-317-03424-3, 7116-3, Passport Bks.). Natl Textbk.

--Spanish Verb Drills. 136p. 1983. pap. 5.95 (ISBN 0-8442-7032-6, 7032-6, Passport Bks.). Natl Textbk.

Baker, Pauline, jt. ed. see Arlinghaus, Bruce.

Baker, Pauline H. Urbanization & Political Change: The Politics of Lagos, 1917-1967. LC 70-162001. 1975. 42.50x (ISBN 0-520-02066-9). U of Cal Pr.

Baker, Pearl. Robbers Roost Recollections. LC 76-4915. (Illus.). 194p. 1976. 7.95 (ISBN 0-87421-083-6). Utah St U Pr.

Baker, Peter. Mayday. 1976. in wrappers 2.00 (ISBN 0-686-18726-1, Pub. by Ferry Pr); signed 6.00 (ISBN 0-686-18727-X). Small Pr Dist.

Baker, Peter S. Animal War Heroes. 1933. 17.50 (ISBN 0-686-19921-9). Quest Edns.

Baker, Philip & Corne, Chris. Isle de France Creole: Affinities & Origins. viii, 299p. 23.50 (ISBN 0-89720-049-7); pap. 15.50 (ISBN 0-89720-048-9). Karoma.

Baker, Philip, ed. Residential Psychiatric Treatment of Children. (Illus.). 351p. 1974. text ed. 22.00x (ISBN 0-8464-1270-5). Beekman Pubs.

Baker, Philip J. Noel see Noel-Baker, Philip J.

Baker, Philip Noel see Noel Baker, Philip.

Baker Publications, ed. Esoteric Psychology-The Seven Rays. 1982. 40.00x (ISBN 0-906006-02-3, Pub. by Baker Pubns England). State Mutual Bk.

--The Psychology of Discipleship. 1982. 45.00x (ISBN 0-906006-05-8, Pub. by Baker Pubns England). State Mutual Bk.

Baker, R. & Holt, W. J. British Warship Design in World War II: Selected Papers from the Transactions of the Royal Institution of Naval Architects. (Illus.). 224p. 1983. 19.95 (ISBN 0-87021-921-9). Naval Inst Pr.

Baker, R., jt. ed. see Rudbach, B.

Baker, R. A. Compendio de la Historia Cristiana. Almanza, Francisco G., tr. Orig. Title: A Summary of Christian History. 372p. (Span.). 1981. pap. 9.50 (ISBN 0-311-15032-2). Casa Bautista.

Baker, R. J. Administrative Theory & Public Administration. 208p. 1972. pap. text ed. 8.75x (ISBN 0-09-110680-X, Hutchinson U Lib); (Hutchinson U Lib). Humanities.

Baker, R. Jerry, jt. auth. see Kuehne, Robert S.

Baker, R. Jerry, et al. Purchasing Factomatic. 1976. 54.95 (ISBN 0-13-742031-5, Busn). P-H.

Baker, R. L., et al. Russian for Everybody: Textbook. 496p. 1985. text ed. 8.95 (ISBN 0-8285-3001-7, Pub. by Rus Lang Pubns USSR); wkbk., 166 pg. 2.95 (ISBN 0-8285-3000-9). Imported Pubns.

Baker, R. Lisle & Wolfe, Norman H. Negotiated Development & Open Space Preservation. (Monograph: No. 84-1). (Illus.). 62p. 1984. pap. text ed. 10.00 (ISBN 0-318-01671-0). Lincoln Inst Land.

Baker, R. Lisle, jt. auth. see Schnidman, Frank.

Baker, R. P. A History of English-Canadian Literature. 59.95 (ISBN 0-8490-0324-5). Gordon Pr.

Baker, R. Ray. Red Brother. 1927. 2.95x (ISBN 0-685-21799-X). Wahr.

Baker, R. Robin. Bird Navigation: The Solution of a Mystery? 256p. 1984. text ed. 32.50x (ISBN 0-8419-0946-6); pap. text ed. 24.95x (ISBN 0-8419-0947-4). Holmes & Meier.

--The Evolutionary Ecology of Animal Migration. LC 78-34. (Illus.). 1024p. 1978. text ed. 135.00x (ISBN 0-8419-0368-9). Holmes & Meier.

--Migration: Paths Through Time & Space. (Illus.). 248p. 1983. pap. text ed. 15.95x (ISBN 0-8419-0822-2). Holmes & Meier.

Baker, R. S. Woodrow Wilson & the World Settlement, 3 vols. (Illus.). 1958. Set. 36.00 (ISBN 0-8446-1039-9). Peter Smith.

Baker, R. S., ed. see Wilson, Woodrow.

Baker, R. T., jt. ed. see Albright, Lyle F.

Baker, Ralph. Reality. 1983. 7.95 (ISBN 0-533-05434-6). Vantage.

Baker, Ralph, ed. Current Trends in the Management of Breast Cancer. LC 76-49094. pap. 43.80 (ISBN 0-317-19828-9, 2023079). Bks Demand UMI.

Baker, Ralph & Meyer, Fred, eds. Evaluating Alternative Law-Enforcement Policies. LC 79-1541. (Policy Studies Organization Bk.). (Illus.). 240p. 1979. 25.50x (ISBN 0-669-02898-3). Lexington Bks.

Baker, Ralph, jt. ed. see Meyer, Fred.

Baker, Ralph H. The National Bituminous Coal Commission Administration of the Bituminous Coal Act, 1937-1941. LC 78-64183. (Johns Hopkins University. Studies in the Social Sciences. Fifty-Ninth Ser. 1941: 3). (Illus.). 360p. Repr. of 1941 ed. 28.50 (ISBN 0-404-61291-1). AMS Pr.

Baker, Ralph L. & King, Glen. As Love Is My Witness. 370p. 1984. 14.95 (ISBN 0-915459-00-0); pap. 9.95 (ISBN 0-915459-01-9). Agape Pr.

Baker, Rance G. & Phillips, Billie R. The Sampler: Patterns for Composition. 1979. pap. text ed. 7.95x (ISBN 0-669-02267-5). Heath.

Baker, Randall. King Husain & the Kingdom of Hejaz. 1979. 92.00x (ISBN 0-900891-48-3, Pub. by Oleander Pr). State Mutual Bk.

Baker, Ray J. Japan Yesterdays. (Illus.). cancelled. Mutual Pub HI.

Baker, Ray J. see Ronck, Ronn.

Baker, Ray P. A History of English-Canadian Literature to the Confederation. 1973. Repr. of 1920 ed. 30.00 (ISBN 0-8274-1438-2). R West.

--Legacies of the Revolution. 1980. 10.95 (ISBN 0-89488-009-8). Shiver Mntn.

--War in the Revolution. 1976. 12.95 (ISBN 0-89488-001-2). Shiver Mntn.

Baker, Ray P., ed. see Haliburton, Thomas C.

Baker, Ray S. Following the Color Line. 314p. 1973. Repr. of 1908 ed. 15.00 (ISBN 0-87928-040-9). Corner Hse.

--New Industrial Unrest: Reasons & Remedies. LC 78-156402. (American Labor Ser., No. 2). 1971. Repr. of 1920 ed. 17.00 (ISBN 0-405-02912-8). Ayer Co Pubs.

--Woodrow Wilson: Life & Letters, 8 Vols. LC 68-8332. (Illus.). 1968. Repr. of 1939 ed. Set. lib. bdg. 222.00x (ISBN 0-8371-0010-0, BAWW). Greenwood.

Baker, Ray S. see Grayson, David, pseud.

Baker, Raymond W. Egypt's Uncertain Revolution Under Nasser & Sadat. LC 78-18356. 1978. 17.50x (ISBN 0-674-24154-1). Harvard U Pr.

Baker, Richard. Richard Baker's Music Guide. LC 79-52366. (Illus.). 144p. 1980. 12.50 (ISBN 0-7153-7782-5). David & Charles.

--Theatrum Redivivum. 154p. 25.00 (ISBN 0-384-03109-9). Johnson Repr.

Baker, Richard & Hayes, Rick S. Accounting for Small Manufacturers. LC 80-12001. (Wiley Series Small Business Management). 197p. 1980. 40.95 (ISBN 0-471-05704-5). Wiley.

Baker, Richard, jt. auth. see Hayes, Rick S.

Baker, Richard, ed. Controlled Release of Bioactive Materials. LC 80-198721. 1980. 55.00 (ISBN 0-12-074450-3). Acad Pr.

Baker, Richard & Miall, Antony, eds. Everyman's Book of Sea Songs. (Illus.). 288p. 1982. 24.95 (ISBN 0-460-04470-2, Pub. by Evman England). Biblio Dist.

Baker, Richard, jt. ed. see Keller, Charles.

Baker, Richard D. Judicial Review in Mexico: A Study of the Amparo Suit. (Latin American Monographs, No. 22). 318p. 1971. 13.50x (ISBN 0-292-70105-5). U of Tex Pr.

Baker, Richard E. The Killing Place. 65p. (Orig.). 1984. pap. 3.00 (ISBN 0-942648-04-8). Vardaman Pr.

--Shattered Visage. 103p. (Orig.). 1982. pap. 3.50 (ISBN 0-942648-01-3). Vardaman Pr.

--Shell Burst Pond. 1982. pap. 3.00 (ISBN 0-942648-02-1). Vardaman Pr.

Baker, Richard H. Building Your Business with Framework. 1985. pap. 16.95 (ISBN 0-8306-1908-9, 1908); 24.95 (ISBN 0-8306-0908-3). TAB Bks.

--How to Run Your Business with dBASE II. 26.95 (ISBN 0-8306-0918-0, 1918); pap. 16.95 (ISBN 0-8306-1918-6). TAB Bks.

--Scuttle the Computer Pirates: Software Protection Schemes. 208p. (Orig.). 1984. 21.95 (ISBN 0-8306-0718-8, 1718); pap. 15.50 (ISBN 0-8306-1718-3). TAB Bks.

Baker, Richard S. Dance of the Trees. Rateaver, Bargyla & Rateaver, Gylver, eds. (Conservation Gardening & Farming Ser). pap. write for info. (ISBN 0-685-61012-8). Rateavers.

Baker, Robert & Elliston, Frederick. Philosophy & Sex. rev. ed. 525p. 1984. pap. text ed. 14.95 (ISBN 0-87975-246-7). Prometheus Bks.

Baker, Robert, ed. The Stress Analysis of a Strapless Evening Gown. 192p. 1982. pap. 5.95 (ISBN 0-13-852608-7). P-H.

Baker, Robert A. Relations Between Northern & Southern Baptists. rev. ed. Gaustad, Edwin S., ed. LC 79-52590. (The Baptist Tradition Ser.). 1980. Repr. of 1954 ed. lib. bdg. 23.00x (ISBN 0-405-12457-0). Ayer Co Pubs.

--The Southern Baptist Convention & Its People. 17.95 (ISBN 0-8054-6516-2). Broadman.

--Summary of Christian History. (Illus.). 1959. 16.95 (ISBN 0-8054-6502-2). Broadman.

Baker, Robert A. & Craven, Paul J., Jr. Adventure in Faith: The First Three Hundred Years of First Baptist Church, Charleston, South Carolina. LC 82-71559. 1982. 10.95 (ISBN 0-8054-6563-4). Broadman.

Baker, Robert D., jt. auth. see Maxwell, Robert S.

Baker, Robert F. Handbook of Highway Engineering. LC 82-8922. 904p. 1982. Repr. of 1975 ed. lib. bdg. 62.50 (ISBN 0-89874-482-2). Krieger.

Baker, Robert H. The Suburbs. Ashton, Sylvia, ed. LC 77-82652. 1979. 14.95 (ISBN 0-87949-102-7). Ashley Bks.

Baker, Robert H., jt. auth. see Fredrick, Laurence W.

Baker, Robert H., jt. auth. see Zim, Herbert S.

Baker, Robert J. God Healed Me. LC 74-17801. 176p. 1974. pap. 1.75 (ISBN 0-8361-1755-7). Herald Pr.

--I'm Listening Lord, Keep Talking. LC 81-4278. 200p. 1981. pap. 6.95 (ISBN 0-8361-1953-3). Herald Pr.

--Insect Parables. LC 76-21398. 1976. pap. 1.95 (ISBN 0-8361-1337-3). Herald Pr.

Baker, Robert J., jt. auth. see Nyhus, Lloyd M.

Baker, Robert J., et al, eds. Biology of Bats of the New World Family Phyllostomatidae, Part III. (Special Publications: No. 16). (Illus.). 441p. (Orig.). 1979. pap. 20.00 (ISBN 0-89672-068-3). Tex Tech Pr.

--Biology of Bats of the New World Family Phyllostomatidae, Pt. I. (Special Publications: No. 10). (Illus.). 218p. (Orig.). 1976. pap. 8.00 (ISBN 0-89672-036-5). Tex Tech Pr.

--Biology of Bats of the New World Family Phyllostomatidae, Pt. II. (Special Publications: No. 13). (Illus.). 364p. (Orig.). 1977. pap. 16.00 (ISBN 0-89672-039-X). Tex Tech Pr.

Baker, Robert K. Doing Library Research: An Introduction for Community College Students. LC 80-22943. (Westview Guides to Library Research Ser.). 260p. 1981. 33.00x (ISBN 0-89158-778-0). Westview.

Baker, Robert L. The Best of Impact. LC 81-90543. (Illus.). 164p. 1982. pap. 17.50 (ISBN 0-9607474-0-0). Impact Pubns IL.

Baker, Robert L. & Mednick, Birgitte R. Influences on Human Development: A Longitudinal Perspective. 1984. lib. bdg. 36.95 (ISBN 0-89838-130-4). Kluwer Nijhoff.

Baker, Robert S. The Dark Historic Page: Social Satire & Historicism in the Novels of Aldous Huxley, 1921-1939. LC 81-70004. 264p. 1982. 27.00x (ISBN 0-299-08940-1). U of Wis Pr.

Baker, Robert T. Baker's Ohio School Law Handbook. 474p. 1985. pap. 32.50 (ISBN 0-317-30039-3). Anderson Pub Co.

Baker, Roger D., et al. Pathologic Anatomy of Mycoses. LC 25-11247. (Handbuch der Speziellen Pathologischen Anatomie: Vol. 3, Pt. 5). (Illus.). 1971. 318.60 (ISBN 0-387-05140-6). Springer-Verlag.

Baker, Roland. Liar's Manual. LC 83-4029. 280p. 1983. 22.95x (ISBN 0-8304-1010-4). Nelson-Hall.

Baker, Rollin H. Geographic Range of Peromyscus Melanophrys, with Description of New Subspecies. (Museum Ser.: Vol. 5, No. 18). 8p. 1952. pap. 1.25 (ISBN 0-317-04942-9). U of KS Mus Nat Hist.

--Mammals from Tamaulipas, Mexico. (Museum Ser.: Vol. 5, No. 12). 12p. 1951. pap. 1.25 (ISBN 0-317-04941-0). U of KS Mus Nat Hist.

--Mammals Taken Along the Alaskan Highway. (Museum Ser.: Vol. 5, No. 9). 31p. 1951. pap. 1.75 (ISBN 0-317-04940-2). U of KS Mus Nat Hist.

--Michigan Mammals. (Illus.). 666p. 1983. 60.00 (ISBN 0-87013-234-2). Mich St U Pr.

--A New Bat (Genus Pipistrellus) from Northeastern Mexico. (Museum Ser.: Vol. 7, No. 10). 4p. 1954. pap. 1.25 (ISBN 0-317-04950-X). U of KS Mus Nat Hist.

--A New Cottontail (Sylvilagus Floridanus) from Northeastern Mexico. (Museum Ser.: Vol. 7, No. 13). 4p. 1955. pap. 1.25 (ISBN 0-317-04952-6). U of KS Mus Nat Hist.

--The Pocket Gophers (Genus Thomomys) of Coahuila, Mexico. (Museum Ser.: Vol. 5, No. 28). 16p. 1953. pap. 1.25 (ISBN 0-317-04945-3). U of KS Mus Nat Hist.

--The Silky Pocket Mouse (Perognathus Flavus) of Mexico. (Museum Ser.: Vol. 7, No. 3). 9p. 1954. pap. 1.25 (ISBN 0-317-04946-1). U of KS Mus Nat Hist.

--Two New Moles (Genus Scalopus) from Mexico & Texas. (Museum Ser.: Vol. 5, No. 2). 8p. 1951. pap. 1.25 (ISBN 0-317-04938-0). U of KS Mus Nat Hist.

Baker, Rollin H. & Findley, James S. Mammals from Southeastern Alaska. (Museum Ser.: Vol. 7, No. 5). 5p. 1954. pap. 1.25 (ISBN 0-317-04948-8). U of KS Mus Nat Hist.

Baker, Rollin H. & Stains, Howard J. A New Long-Eared Myotis (Myotis Evotis) from Northeastern Mexico. (Museum Ser.: Vol. 7, No. 3). 4p. 1955. pap. 1.25 (ISBN 0-317-04954-2). U of KS Mus Nat Hist.

Baker, Rollin H., jt. auth. see Rainey, Dennis G.

Baker, Rollin H., jt. auth. see Russell, Robert J.

Baker, Ron. Oil & Gas: The Production Story. (Illus.). 91p. 1983. pap. text ed. 8.50 (ISBN 0-88698-002-X). PETEX.

--A Primer of Oilwell Drilling. 4th ed. Gerding, Mildred, ed. (Illus.). 94p. (Orig.). 1982. pap. text ed. 8.50 (ISBN 0-88698-116-6, 2.00040). Petex.

--Treating Oil Field Emissions. 2nd ed. Taylor, Lydia, ed. (Illus.). 112p. (Orig.). 1974. pap. text ed. 6.00 (ISBN 0-88698-121-2, 3.50030). Petex.

Baker, Ronald L. Folklore in the Writings of Rowland E. Robinson. 1973. 12.95 (ISBN 0-87972-038-7). Bowling Green Univ.

--Hoosier Folk Legends. LC 81-47568. 288p. (Orig.). 1982. 15.00 (ISBN 0-253-32844-6); pap. 7.95 (ISBN 0-253-20334-1). Ind U Pr.

Baker, Ronald L. & Carmony, Marvin. Indiana Place Names. LC 74-17915. 224p. 1976. pap. 7.95 (ISBN 0-253-28340-X). Ind U Pr.

Baker, Ronald L., ed. Names & Folklore: Selected Papers of the New York Folklore Society & The North East Names Institute. 1984 ed. (The International Library of Names). 400p. Date not set. text ed. price not set (ISBN 0-8290-1212-5). Irvington.

Baker, Rosalie & Baker, Charles, III, eds. Classical Calliope: 1981 Cumulative Edition, Vol. 1. (Illus.). 160p. (Orig.). (gr. 7-12). 1983. pap. 17.50 (ISBN 0-9607638-1-3). Cobblestone Pub.

--Classical Calliope: 1982 Cumulative Edition, Vol. 2. (Illus.). 160p. (Orig.). (gr. 7-12). 1983. pap. 17.50 (ISBN 0-9607638-2-1). Cobblestone Pub.

Baker, Roscoe. The American Legion & American Foreign Policy. LC 74-39. (Illus.). 329p. 1974. Repr. of 1954 ed. lib. bdg. 22.50x (ISBN 0-8371-7360-4, BAAL). Greenwood.

Baker, Ross & Pomper, Gerald. American Government. 704p. 1983. text ed. write for info. (ISBN 0-02-305400-X). Macmillan.

Baker, Ross K. Friend & Foe in the U. S. Senate. LC 79-7850. 1980. 14.95 (ISBN 0-02-901290-2). Free Pr.

Baker, Russell. All Things Considered. LC 81-6883. 213p. 1981. Repr. of 1965 ed. lib. bdg. 19.75x (ISBN 0-313-22875-2, BAAT). Greenwood.

--Growing Up. LC 82-12534. 256p. 1982. 15.00 (ISBN 0-312-92267-1). Congdon & Weed.

--Growing Up. LC 83-8213. 288p. 1983. 6.95 (ISBN 0-452-25550-3, Plume). NAL.

--Growing Up. 1984. pap. 3.95 (ISBN 0-451-13312-9, Sig). NAL.

--The Rescue of Miss Yaskell & Other Pipe Dreams. 304p. 1983. 14.95 (ISBN 0-312-92730-4). Congdon & Weed.

--The Rescue of Miss Yaskell & Other Pipe Dreams. Large Print ed. LC 83-18259. 473p. 1983. Repr. of 1983 ed. 15.95 (ISBN 0-89621-494-X). Thorndike Pr.

--Rescue of Miss Yaskell & Other Pipe Dreams. 1985. pap. 3.95 (ISBN 0-451-13472-9, Sig). NAL.

--So This Is Depravity. 336p. 1983. pap. 3.95 (ISBN 0-671-49656-5). WSP.

--So This Is Depravity & Other Observations. LC 80-67859. 1980. 10.95; deluxe signed, limited ed. 40.00 (ISBN 0-312-92783-5). Congdon & Weed.

Baker, Russell P. Marriages & Obituaries from the Tennessee Baptist, Eighteen Forty-Four to Eighteen Sixty-Two. 137p. 1979. 15.00 (ISBN 0-89308-127-2). Southern Hist Pr.

Baker, Ruth. Getting Rich in Real Estate Partnerships. LC 80-29162. 228p. (Orig.). 1981. 12.95 (ISBN 0-446-51222-2). Warner Bks.

--Rainbow Book of Poems. 1984. 3.95 (ISBN 0-89536-993-1). CSS of Ohio.

Baker, S. Hidden Manna. pap. 5.00 (ISBN 0-686-12875-3). Schmul Pub Co.

--Systematic Approach to Advertising Creativity. 288p. 1983. pap. 10.95 (ISBN 0-07-003353-6). McGraw.

Baker, S. Josephine. Fighting for Life. facsimile ed. LC 74-1664. (Children & Youth Ser.). (Illus.). 280p. 1974. Repr. of 1939 ed. 24.50x (ISBN 0-405-05945-0). Ayer Co Pubs.

Baker, S. K. Rail Atlas of Britain. 130p. 30.00x (ISBN 0-86093-106-4, Pub. by ORPC Ltd UK). State Mutual Bk.

Baker, Sally. Color Me Love. LC 75-27766. (Illus.). 1975. pap. 3.00 (ISBN 0-686-85871-9). Dennis-Landman.

Baker, Samm S. & Schur, Sylvia. The Delicious Quick-Trim Diet. 1985. 14.45 (ISBN 0-394-53431-X, Pub. by Villard Bks). Random.

--Delicious Quick-Trim Diet. 352p. 1985. pap. 3.95 (ISBN 0-345-30832-8). Ballantine.

Baker, Samm S., jt. auth. see Bellak, Leopold.

Baker, Samm S., jt. auth. see DeBetz, Barbara.

Baker, Samm S., jt. auth. see Miller, Mary S.

Baker, Samm S., jt. auth. see Stillman, Irwin M.

Baker, Samm S., jt. auth. see Tarnower, Herman.

Baker, Samuel W. Albert N'yanza, Great Basin of the Nile. 1869. 69.00 (ISBN 0-403-00464-0). Scholarly.

--In the Heart of Africa. LC 73-109310. Repr. of 1884 ed. 19.75x (ISBN 0-8371-3567-2, BHA&, Pub. by Negro U Pr). Greenwood.

--Ismailia: A Narrative of the Expedition to Central Africa for the Suppression of the Slave Trade, Organized by Ismail, Khedive of Egypt, 2 Vols. LC 77-79806. (Illus.). Repr. of 1874 ed. Set. 44.00x (ISBN 0-8371-1509-4, BAI&, Pub. by Negro U Pr). Greenwood.

--The Nile Tributaries of Abyssinia, & the Sword Hunters of the Hamran Arabs. 4th ed. Bd. with Sword Hunters of the Hamran Arabs. (Landmarks in Anthropology Ser). Repr. of 1867 ed. 58.00 (ISBN 0-384-03110-2). Johnson Repr.

--Wild Beasts & Their Ways. 45.00 (ISBN 0-686-19867-0). Ridgeway Bks.

Baker, Scott. Dhampire. 1982. pap. 2.95 (ISBN 0-671-44666-5, Timescape). PB.

--Nightchild. 256p. (Orig.). 1983. pap. 2.95 (ISBN 0-671-46931-2, Timescape). PB.

Baker, Sharon. Quarreling, They Met the Dragon. 288p. 1984. pap. 2.95 (ISBN 0-380-89201-4, 89201-4). Avon.

Baker, Sheridan. The Complete Stylist & Handbook. 3rd ed. 560p. 1984. text ed. 14.50 scp (ISBN 0-06-040442-6, HarpC); scp instr's manual 1.90 (ISBN 0-06-360302-0); scp diagnostic & ach. tests 2.50 (ISBN 0-06-360303-9). Har-Row.

--The Essayist. 4th ed. 334p. 1981. scp 12.50 (ISBN 0-06-040453-1, HarpC). Har-Row.

--The Practical Stylist. 5th ed. 206p. 1981. pap. text ed. 11.50 scp (ISBN 0-06-040454-X, HarpC); instructor's manual avail. (ISBN 0-06-360289-X). Har-Row.

--The Practical Stylist. 6th ed. 304p. 1985. pap. text ed. 10.95 scp (ISBN 0-06-040439-6, HarpC); instr's. manual avail. (ISBN 0-06-360286-5). Har-Row.

--The Practical Stylist with Readings. 430p. 1982. pap. text ed. 12.50 scp (ISBN 0-06-040461-2, HarpC); instr's. manual avail. (ISBN 0-06-360289-X). Har-Row.

Baker, Sheridan & Howard, C. Jeriel. The Essayist. 5th ed. 544p. 1985. pap. text ed. 11.85 scp (ISBN 0-06-040441-8, HarpC). Har-Row.

Baker, Sheridan, ed. see Fielding, Henry.

Baker, Sheridan, et al. The Practical Stylist. Canadian ed. Ledbetter, Ken & Gamache, Lawrence, eds. 209p. 1982. pap. text ed. 11.50 scp (ISBN 0-06-043889-4, HarpC); instr's. manual avail. (ISBN 0-06-360289-X). Har-Row.

Baker, Shirley R., ed. see American Family Records Association Staff.

Baker, Stephen. Executive Mother Goose. (Illus.). 96p. 1984. pap. 4.95 (ISBN 0-02-008180-4). MacMillan.

--How to Live with a Neurotic Cat. 128p. 1985. pap. 5.95 (ISBN 0-446-38191-8). Warner Bks.

--How to Live with a Neurotic Dog. (Illus.). 1960. 7.95 (ISBN 0-13-415463-0). P-H.

--How to Play Golf in the Low 120's. 1977. 7.95 (ISBN 0-13-428169-1, Reward); pap. 4.95 (ISBN 0-13-428151-9). P-H.

--The I Hate Meetings. (Illus.). 128p. 1983. 9.95 (ISBN 0-02-506370-7). Macmillan.

--The Systematic Approach to Advertising Creativity. 1979. 42.50 (ISBN 0-07-003352-8). McGraw.

Baker, Stephen R. & Elkin, Milton. Plain Film Approach to Abdominal Calcifications. (Saunders Monographs in Clinical Radiology: Vol. 21 c). (Illus.). 240p. 1983. 38.95 (ISBN 0-7216-1498-1). Saunders.

Baker, Steve J. California Co-op Directory & Resource Guide. 55p. pap. text ed. 5.50 (ISBN 0-910427-00-3). Calif Dept Co.

Baker, Steven J., jt. auth. see Purvis, Hoyt.

Baker, Stewart L., jt. auth. see Craig, Robert J.

Baker, Stuart E. Georges Feydeau & the Aesthetics of Farce. Beckerman, Bernard, ed. LC 81-16410. (Theater & Dramatic Studies: No. 9). 163p. 1981. 39.95 (ISBN 0-8357-1265-6). UMI Res Pr.

Baker, Susan P., et al. The Injury Fact Book. LC 82-49194. (An Insurance Institute for Highway Safety Bk.). 352p. 1984. 25.00x (ISBN 0-669-06426-2). Lexington Bks.

Baker, Susan R. Collaboration et Originalite Chez la Rochefoucauld. LC 79-21085. (University of Florida Humanities Monographs: No. 48). 135p. (Orig.). 1980. pap. 9.00 (ISBN 0-8130-0657-0). U Presses Fla.

Baker, Susan S. Radicals Beginnings: Richard Hofstadter & the 1930's. LC 84-27930. (Contributins in American History Ser.: No. 112). 296p. 1985. lib. bdg. 35.00 (ISBN 0-313-24713-7, BHO/). Greenwood.

Baker, T. F., ed. A History of the County of Middlesex, Vol. 7. (Victoria History of the Counties of England Ser.). (Illus.). 1982. 135.00 (ISBN 0-19-722756-2). Oxford U Pr.

--A History of the County of Middlesex, Vol. 8. (Victoria History of the Counties of England Ser.). (Illus.). 250p. 1985. 98.00x (ISBN 0-19-722762-7). Oxford U Pr.

--The Victoria History of the Counties of England: Middlesex, Vol. 6. (Illus.). 1980. 129.00x (ISBN 0-19-722750-3). Oxford U Pr.

Baker, T. Lindsay. The Early History of Panna Maria, Texas. (Graduate Studies: No. 9). (Illus.). 69p. (Orig.). 1975. pap. 4.00 (ISBN 0-89672-016-0). Tex Tech Pr.

--A Field Guide to American Windmills. LC 84-40272. (Illus.). 516p. 1985. 65.00 (ISBN 0-8061-1901-2). U of Okla Pr.

--The First Polish Americans: Silesian Settlements in Texas. LC 78-6373. 288p. 1979. 16.95 (ISBN 0-89096-060-7). Tex A&M Univ Pr.

--The Polish Texans. (Illus.). 120p. 1982. 8.95 (ISBN 0-933164-98-X); pap. 5.95 (ISBN 0-933164-99-8). U of Tex Inst Tex Culture.

Baker, T. N. Yield, Flow & Fracture of Polycrystals. (Illus.). 380p. 1984. 77.75 (ISBN 0-85334-225-3, Pub. by Elsevier Applied Sci England). Elsevier.

Baker, Th. Dictionary of Musical Terms: Containing an English-Italian Vocabulary for Composers & Students. (Eng. & Ital.). 35.00 (ISBN 0-87557-053-4, 053-4). Saphrograph.

Baker, Th., tr. see Bree, Malwine.

Baker, Theodore. Dictionary of Musical Terms. LC 75-124595. (BCL Ser.: No. 1). 1970. Repr. of 1923 ed. 8.00 (ISBN 0-404-00468-7). AMS Pr.

--Dictionary of Musical Terms. 1923. 10.95 (ISBN 0-02-870200-X). Schirmer Bks.

--A Dictionary of Musical Terms: With an English-Itlaian Vocabulary for Composers, 2 vols. (Illus.). 198p. 1986. 189.75 (ISBN 0-89266-542-4). Am Classical Coll Pr.

--On the Music of the North American Indians. Buckley, Ann, tr. from Ger. (Music Reprint Ser., 1977). 1978. lib. bdg. 22.50 (ISBN 0-306-70888-4). Da Capo.

--Schirmer Pronouncing Pocket Manual of Musical Terms. 4th ed. LC 77-5236. 1978. pap. 3.95 (ISBN 0-02-870250-6). Schirmer Bks.

--Uber die Musik der Nordamerikanischen Wilden. LC 71-38496. Repr. of 1882 ed. 15.00 (ISBN 0-404-08337-4). AMS Pr.

Baker, Theodore, tr. see D'Indy, Vincent.

Baker, Thomas & Ferrone, Frank. Liturgy Committee Basics: A No-nonsense Guide. (Orig.). 1985. pap. write for info. (ISBN 0-912405-11-2). Pastoral Pr.

Baker, Thomas B. War with Crime: Being a Selection of Reprinted Papers on Crime, Reformation, Etc. LC 83-49246. (Crime & Punishment in England, 1850-1922 Ser.). 299p. 1984. lib. bdg. 35.00 (ISBN 0-8240-6215-9). Garland Pub.

Baker, Thomas E. Another Such Victory. 1981. 2.95 (ISBN 0-915992-06-X). Eastern Acorn.

Baker, Thomas H. Memphis Commercial Appeal: The History of a Southern Newspaper. LC 74-165066. viii, 336p. 1971. 27.50x (ISBN 0-8071-0944-4). La State U Pr.

Baker, Tim & Heath, Tim. The Dragons at Marshmouldings. (Illus.). 72p. 1984. 8.95 (ISBN 0-8052-8196-7, Pub. by Allison & Busby England). Schocken.

Baker, Timothy. Assessment of Health Status & Needs. LC 77-85139. (International Health Perspectives Ser.: Vol. 2 of 5). 1977. pap. text ed. 5.00 (ISBN 0-8261-2492-5). Springer Pub.

Baker, Timothy D. & Perlman, Mark. Health Manpower in a Developing Economy: Taiwan, a Case Study in Planning. LC 67-22892. (The John Hopkins Monographs in International Health Ser.). pap. 54.80 (ISBN 0-317-19826-2, 2023081). Bks Demand UMI.

Baker, Tod A. & Steed, Robert P., eds. Religion & Politics in the South: Mass & Elite Perspectives. LC 83-21155. 208p. 1983. text ed. 25.95 (ISBN 0-03-069558-9). Praeger.

Baker, Toni. Mastering Machine Code on Your ZX-81. 176p. 1982. 18.41. P-H.

Baker, V. Historical Archaeology at Black Lucy's Garden, Andover Massachusetts: Ceramics from the Site of a 19th Century Afro-American, Vol. 8. 1978. 8.00 (ISBN 0-939312-09-3). Peabody Found.

Baker, V. R., ed. Catastrophic Flooding: The Origin of the Channeled Scabland. LC 79-22901. (Benchmark Papers in Geology: Vol. 55). 384p. 1981. 51.95 (ISBN 0-87933-360-X). Van Nos Reinhold.

Baker, Vaughan B., jt. ed. see Conrad, Glenn R.

Baker, Victor R. The Channels of Mars. (Illus.). 212p. 1982. text ed. 45.00x (ISBN 0-292-71068-2). U of Tex Pr.

Baker, Victor R., jt. auth. see Costa, John E.

Baker, W. M. Bell's Acrostic Dictionary. LC 77-141772. 1971. Repr. of 1927 ed. 35.00x (ISBN 0-8103-3379-1). Gale.

Baker, W. S. Bibliotheca Washingtoniana. 59.95 (ISBN 0-87968-746-0). Gordon Pr.

--Medallic Portraits of Washington. updated ed. (Illus.). 1983. lib. bdg. 45.00 (ISBN 0-915262-82-7). S J Durst.

Baker, Wallace H., ed. Grouting in Geotechnical Engineering. LC 81-71798. 1028p. 1982. pap. 69.00x (ISBN 0-87262-295-9). Am Soc Civil Eng.

Baker, Wilfred, et al. Similarity Methods in Engineering Dynamics: Theory & Practice of Scale Modeling. (Illus.). 1973. 22.95x (ISBN 0-8104-9214-8). Hayden.

Baker, Will. Backward: An Essay on Indians, Time, & Photography. (Illus.). 420p. 1983. 24.95 (ISBN 0-938190-13-X); pap. 12.95 (ISBN 0-938190-14-8). North Atlantic.

--Chip. LC 79-87510. (gr. 7 up). 1979. text ed. 7.95 (ISBN 0-15-217526-1, HJ). HarBraceJ.

Baker, William. George Eliot & Judaism: A Study of George Eliot's Interest & Knowledge of Judaism. (Salzburg Studies in English Literature, Romantic Reassessment Ser.: No. 45). 272p. 1975. pap. text ed. 25.50x (ISBN 0-391-01312-2). Humanities.

--George Eliot-George Henry Lewes Library: An Annotated Bibliography of Their Books at Dr. William's Library. LC 76-24744. (Reference Library of the Humanities Ser.: Vol. 67). 1977. lib. bdg. 55.00 (ISBN 0-8240-9931-1). Garland Pub.

--On Capital Punishment. rev. ed. 1985. pap. 5.95 (ISBN 0-8024-6060-7). Moody.

--Some George Eliot Notebooks: An Edition of the Carl H. Pforzheimer Library's George Eliot Holography Notebooks, Mss. 707, 5 vols. (Salzburg Studies in English Literature, Romantic Reassessment: No. 46). 332p. 1984. pap. text ed. 25.50x each (ISBN 0-391-01307-6). Humanities.

Baker, William & Kimber, John. F. R. & Q. D. Leavis: An Annotated Bibliography. LC 84-45398. 350p. 1985. lib. bdg. 47.00 (ISBN 0-8240-8894-8). Garland Pub.

Baker, William, jt. auth. see Smith, Harold.

Baker, William A. Maine Shipbuilding: A Bibliographical Guide. (Maine History Bibliographical Guide Ser.). 1974. pap. 4.00 (ISBN 0-915592-09-6). Maine Hist.

--The Mayflower & Other Colonial Vessels. LC 83-60472. (Illus.). 192p. 1983. 15.95 (ISBN 0-87021-843-3). Naval Inst Pr.

Baker, William D. Reading Skills. 2nd ed. LC 73-17161. (Illus.). 176p. 1974. pap. text ed. 12.95 (ISBN 0-13-762062-4). P-H.

Baker, William E. Jacques Prevert. LC 67-19347. (World Authors Ser.). 1967. lib. bdg. 15.95. Irvington.

Baker, William H., jt. auth. see Lewis, Philip V.

Baker, William H., ed. Diagnosis & Treatment of Carotid Artery Disease: With Special Emphasis on Noninvasive Diagnosis & Surgical Technique. LC 79-52753. (Illus.). 232p. 1980. 25.00 (ISBN 0-87993-123-X). Futura Pub.

Baker, William H., intro. by. Diagnosis & Treatment of Carotid Artery Disease. 2nd, rev. ed. (Illus.). 264p. 1985. 34.50 (ISBN 0-87993-224-4). Futura Pub.

Baker, William J. Beyond Port & Prejudice. 1981. 20.00 (ISBN 0-89101-032-7). U Maine Orono.

--Sports in the Western World. LC 82-3669. (Illus.). 368p. 1983. text ed. 25.50 (ISBN 0-8476-7075-9); pap. 9.50x (ISBN 0-8476-7194-1). Rowman.

Baker, William J. & Carroll, John M. Sports in Modern America. Broeg, Bob, ed. LC 81-51300. (Illus.). 192p. (Orig.). 1981. pap. 9.95x (ISBN 0-933150-30-X). River City MO.

Baker, William J. & Rog, James A., eds. Sports & the Humanities: A Symposium. LC 83-50027. 126p. (Orig.). 1983. pap. 8.95 (ISBN 0-89101-055-6). U Maine Orono.

Baker, William P. The English Village. LC 72-138199. 224p. 1972. Repr. of 1953 ed. lib. bdg. 15.00 (ISBN 0-8371-5552-5, BAEV). Greenwood.

Baker, William S. Bibliotheca Washingtoniana. LC 67-14022. 1967. Repr. of 1889 ed. 35.00x (ISBN 0-8103-3318-X). Gale.

--Itinerary of General George Washington from June 15, 1775, to December 23, 1783. 1970. Repr. of 1892 ed. lib. bdg. 12.00 (ISBN 0-912606-00-2). Hunterdon Hse.

--Itinerary of General Washington. 334p. Date not set. Repr. of 1892 ed. 39.00 (ISBN 0-932051-79-0). Am Repr Serv.

Baker, William W. Theft of a Nation. 164p. (Orig.). 1982. pap. 7.95 (ISBN 0-910643-00-8). Defenders Pubns.

--Thy Kingdom Came. 220p. (Orig.). 1985. pap. 9.00 (ISBN 0-910643-01-6). Defenders Pubns.

Baker, Yvonne. Guilt-Free Snacking. 160p. (Orig.). 1983. pap. 7.95 spiral bd. (comb) (ISBN 0-89636-106-3). Accent Bks.

--The Holiday Cookbook. (Orig.). 1981. pap. 6.95 deluxe (ISBN 0-89191-523-0, 55236). Cook.

Baker, Yvonne G. Guilt-Free Cooking. 1985. pap. 7.95 (ISBN 0-89636-179-9). Accent Bks.

--Guilt-Free Fast Foods. 176p. (Orig.). 1984. spiral bd. (comb) 7.95 (ISBN 0-89636-129-2). Accent Bks.

--Successfully Single. LC 85-7089. 1985. pap. 6.95 (ISBN 0-89636-163-2). Accent Bks.

Baker-Carr, Sally, ed. see Fregly, Bert.

Baker-Cassidy, Martha & Cassidy, David, eds. Werner Heisenberg: A Bibliography of His Writings. LC 82-60498. (Berkeley Papers in History of Science). 200p. (Orig.). 1984. pap. 10.00x (ISBN 0-918102-10-3). U Cal Hist Sci Tech.

Baker-Cohen, K. F. Comparative Enzyme Histochemical Observations on Submammalian Brains. Incl. Pt. 1: Striatal Structures in Reptiles & Birds; Pt. 2: Basal Structures of the Brainstem in Reptiles & Birds. (Advances in Anatomy: Vol. 40, Pt. 6). (Illus.). 70p. 1968. pap. 18.90 (ISBN 0-387-04090-0). Springer-Verlag.

Bakere, Jane. The Cornish Ordinalia: A Critical Study. 191p. 1980. text ed. 27.75x (ISBN 0-7083-0745-0, Pub. by Univ of Wales Pr England). Humanities.

Bakerman & De Marr. Adol Feminists Portraits. (Reference Ser.). 1985. text ed. 28.00 (ISBN 0-8240-9136-1). Garland Pub.

Bakerman, Jane S., jt. auth. see DeMarr, Mary Jean.

Bakerman, Jane S., ed. Murder X: Ten More Women of Mystery. (Illus.). 280p. 1983. write for info. Bowling Green Univ.

Bakerman, Seymour. Aging Life Processes. (Illus.). 204p. 1969. 17.50x (ISBN 0-398-00083-2). C C Thomas.

Bakerman, Theodore. Anthracite Coal: A Study in Advanced Industrial Decline. Bruchey, Stuart, ed. LC 78-22656. (Energy in the American Economy Ser.). (Illus.). 1979. lib. bdg. 23.00x (ISBN 0-405-11960-7). Ayer Co Pubs.

Baker of Windrush, Lord. Enterprise Versus Bureaucracy: The Development of Structural Air-Raid Precautions During the 2nd World War. LC 77-30397. 1978. text ed. 15.25 (ISBN 0-08-022149-1). Pergamon.

Bakescu, R., tr. see Klimontovich, Yu L.

Bakewell, Charles. Source Book in Ancient Philosophy. rev. ed. LC 75-148613. 1971. Repr. of 1939 ed. 15.00 (ISBN 0-87752-139-5). Gordian.

Bakewell, Charles M., ed. see Davidson, Thomas.

Bakewell, Dennis. The Black Experience in the United States: A Bibliography Based on Collections of the California State University, Northridge Library. 1970. 12.00 (ISBN 0-937048-11-9). CSUN.

Bakewell, Joan. The Complete Traveller. 1977. text ed. 14.95x (ISBN 0-8464-0269-6). Beekman Pubs.

Bakewell, K. G. How to Organise Information: A Manager's Guide to Techniques & Sources with a Checklist for Secretaries & Assistants. LC 84-10223. 225p. 1984. text ed. 33.95x (ISBN 0-566-02397-0). Gower Pub Co.

--A Manual of Cataloguing Practice. LC 73-171838. 312p. 1972. text ed. 59.00 (ISBN 0-08-016697-0). Pergamon.

Bakewell, K. G., jt. auth. see Hunter, Eric.

Bakewell, K. G., jt. auth. see Hunter, Eric J.

Bakewell, K. G., ed. Management Principles & Practice: A Guide to Information Sources. LC 76-16127. (Management Information Guide Ser.: No. 32). 1977. 60.00x (ISBN 0-8103-0832-0). Gale.

Bakewell, P. J. Silver Mining & Society in Colonial Mexico, Zacatecas, 1546-1700. LC 78-158553. (American Latin Studies: No. 15). (Illus.). 1972. 49.50 (ISBN 0-521-08227-7). Cambridge U Pr.

Bakewell, Peter. Miners of the Red Mountain: Indian Labor in Potosi, 1545-1650. LC 84-7582. (Illus.). 240p. 1984. text ed. 19.95x (ISBN 0-8263-0769-8). U of NM Pr.

Bakewell, Peter, et al, eds. Readings in Latin American History: The Formative Centuries, Vol. 1. (Illus.). 416p. 1985. 32.50 (ISBN 0-8223-0645-X); pap. 14.75 (ISBN 0-8223-0637-9). Duke.

Bakewell, Robert. An Introduction to Geology. Albritton, Claude C., Jr., ed. LC 77-6508. (History of Geology Ser.). 1978. Repr. lib. bdg. 40.00x (ISBN 0-405-10431-6). Ayer Co Pubs.

Bakhash, Shaul. The Politics of Oil & Revolution in Iran. LC 82-72116. 61p. 1982. pap. 5.95 (ISBN 0-8157-0781-9). Brookings.

--The Reign of the Ayatollahs: Iran & the Islamic Revolution. LC 83-46078. 246p. 1984. 18.95 (ISBN 0-465-06887-1). Basic.

Bakhit, Muhammad. Ottoman Province of Damascus in the Sixteenth Century. 1983. 48.00x (ISBN 0-86685-322-7). Intl Bk Ctr.

Bakhle, Y. S. & Vane, J. R., eds. Metabolic Functions of the Lung, Vol. 4. (Lung Biology in Health & Disease Ser.). 1977. 65.00 (ISBN 0-8247-6383-1). Dekker.

Bakht, B. & Jaeger, L. G. Bridge Analysis Simplified. 1985. 49.95 (ISBN 0-07-003020-0). McGraw.

Bakhtiar, Laleh, jt. auth. see Ardalan, Nader.

Bakhtiar, Laleh, tr. see Shariati, Ali.

Bakhtin, M. M. The Dialogic Imagination: Four Essays. Holquist, Michael, ed. Emerson, Caryl, tr. from Rus. LC 80-15450. (University of Texas Press Slavic Ser.: No. 1). 478p. 1981. pap. 12.95x (ISBN 0-292-71534-X). U of Tex Pr.

Bakhtin, M. M. & Medvedev, P. N. The Formal Method in Literary Scholarship: A Critical Introduction to Sociological Poetics. Wehrle, Albert J., tr. from Rus. 224p. 1985. pap. text ed. 8.95x (ISBN 0-674-30921-9). Harvard U Pr.

Bakhtin, M. M., jt. auth. see Medvedev, Pavel N.

Bakhtin, Mikhail. Problems of Dostoevsky's Poetics. Emerson, Caryl, ed. Emerson, Carl, tr. from Rus. LC 83-12348. (Theory & History of Literature Ser.: No. 8). 352p. 1984. 35.00x (ISBN 0-8166-1227-7); pap. 14.95 (ISBN 0-8166-1228-5). U of Minn Pr.

--Rabelais & His World. Iswolsky, Helene, tr. from Rus. LC 84-47792. 512p. 1984. 29.50x (ISBN 0-253-34830-7); pap. 10.95x (ISBN 0-253-20341-4, MB 341). Ind U Pr.

Bakhtin, V., ed. Selected Poems: Alexander Prokofiev. 277p. 1980. 6.45 (ISBN 0-8285-1982-X, Pub. by Progress Pubs USSR). Imported Pubns.

Bakhtine. L' Oeuvre de Francois Rabelais et la Culture Populaire au Moyen Age et sous Renaissance. Robel, tr. (Bibliotheque des Idees). 22.50 (ISBN 0-685-34193-3). French & Eur.

Baki, Heiman, jt. ed. see Schnitzer, Authur.

Bakir, A. Notes on Middle Egyptian Grammar. 2nd, rev. ed. 180p. 1984. pap. text ed. 21.50x (ISBN 0-85668-271-3, Pub. by Aris & Phillips England). Humanities.

Bakir, A. M. Notes on Late Egyptian Grammar: A Semitic Approach. 144p. 1983. pap. text ed. 28.50x (ISBN 0-85668-214-4, Pub. by Aris & Phillips England). Humanities.

Bakish, David. Richard Wright. LC 71-190353. (Literature & Life Ser.). 121p. 1973. 12.95 (ISBN 0-8044-2015-7). Ungar.

--Richard Wright. (Literature & Life Ser.). 121p. 1984. pap. 7.95 (ISBN 0-8044-6026-4). Ungar.

Bakish, David, jt. ed. see Margolies, Edward.

Bakish, R. see Winkler, O.

Bakish, Robert & White, S. S. Handbook of Electron Beam Welding. LC 64-7538. (Wiley Series on the Science & Technology of Materials). pap. 69.80 (ISBN 0-317-08643-X, 2007398). Bks Demand UMI.

Bakish, Robert, ed. see International Conference on Electron & Ion Beam Science & Technology (7th: 1976: San Francisco).

Bakish, Robert, ed. see International Conference on Electron & Ion Beam Science & Technology (8th: 1978: Seattle).

Bakish, Robert, ed. see International Conference on Electron & Ion Beam Science & Technology (4th: 1970: Los Angeles).

Bakish, Robert, ed. see International Conference on Electron & Ion Beam Science & Technology (6th: 1974: San Francisco).

Bakjian, Andy. Track Management. LC 81-51688. (Illus.). 96p. (Orig.). 1982. pap. 5.00 (ISBN 0-911521-01-1). Tafnews.

Bakke, E. Wight. Revolutionary Democracy: Challenge & Testing in Japan. x, 343p. 1968. 24.50 (ISBN 0-208-00627-3, Archon). Shoe String.

Bakke, E. Wight & Bakke, Mary S. Campus Challenge: Student Activism in Perspective. LC 77-150394. x, 573p. 1971. 32.50 (ISBN 0-208-01205-2, Archon). Shoe String.

Bakke, E. Wight, jt. auth. see Noland, William E.

Bakke, Mary S., jt. auth. see Bakke, E. Wight.

Bakken, Dick. Here I Am! (Orig.). 1979. pap. 4.00 (ISBN 0-932662-28-5). St Andrews NC.

Bakken, Gordon M. The Development of Law in Frontier California: Civil Law & Society, 1850-1890. LC 84-25202. (Contributions in Legal Studies: No. 33). (Illus.). 208p. 1985. lib. bdg. 29.95 (ISBN 0-313-24725-0, BFC/). Greenwood.

--The Development of Law on the Rocky Mountain Frontier: Civil Law & Society, 1850-1912. LC 82-10984. (Contributions in Legal Studies Ser.: No. 27). ix, 200p. 1983. lib. bdg. 29.95 (ISBN 0-313-23285-7, BDL). Greenwood.

Bakken, Harald. The Special String. (Illus.). (ps-3). 1982. 7.95 (ISBN 0-13-826370-1). P-H.

Bakken, Henry H. Basic Concepts, Principles, & Practices of Cooperation. 1963. 3.00 (ISBN 0-912084-05-7). Mimir.

--The Hills of Home-A Family History. 1976. 13.50 (ISBN 0-912084-11-1). Mimir.

Bakken, Kenneth. Call to Wholeness. Kelsey, Morton, intro. by. LC 84-23837. 128p. (Orig.). 1985. pap. 7.95 (ISBN 0-8245-0683-9). Crossroad NY.

Bakken, Lavolla J. Land of the North Umpquas: Peaceful Indians of the West. LC 73-84954. (Illus.). 32p. 1973. pap. 1.95 (ISBN 0-913508-03-9). Te Cum Tom.

Bakken, PAt, illus. One to Twenty Number Fun. (FunThinkers Ser.). (Illus.). 36p. (Basic Set includes: 8" x 10" activity book count-along book, 22 counters, zip-lock bag, parent's manual& box. Ensemble includes: Basic set plus 8 boxed regular crayons, scissors, paste stick & carrying case.). (ps-1). 1983. pap. 6.00 Basic Set (ISBN 0-88679-038-7, EI-5623); pap. 10.00 Ensemble (ISBN 0-88679-035-2, EI-5603). Educ Insights.

Bakken, Roger. The Coach's Pocket Planner. (Illus.). 68p. 1983. plastic comb 6.95 (ISBN 0-930097-00-9). Sportsrite Pub Co.

Bakken, Terry, jt. auth. see Monahan, Evelyn.

Bakker, A. R., jt. auth. see De Heere, R. F. Scheltema.

Bakker, Boudewijn. Amsterdam in Drawings Amsterdam Getekend. (Illus.). 1978. 30.00 (ISBN 90-247-2126-1). Heinman.

Bakker, Cornelis & Bakker-Rabdau, Marianne. No Trespassing! Explorations in Human Territoriality. LC 73-7326. 284p. 1973. pap. 9.95 (ISBN 0-88316-528-7). Chandler & Sharp.

Bakker, Dirk J., ed. Temporal Order in Disturbed Reading: Developmental & Neuropsychological Aspects in Normal & Reading-Retarded Children. (Modern Approaches to the Diagnosis & Instruction of Multi-Handicapped Children Ser.: Vol. 7). 100p. 1972. text ed. 16.00 (ISBN 90-237-4108-0, Pub. by Swets & Zeitlinger Netherlands). Hogrefe Intl.

Bakker, Dirk J. & Satz, Paul, eds. Specific Reading Disability: Advances in Theory & Method. (Modern Approaches to the Diagnosis & Instruction of Multi-Handicapped Children: Vol. 3). 166p. 1970. text ed. 16.00 (ISBN 90-237-4103-X, Pub. by Swets & Zeitlinger Netherlands). Hogrefe Intl.

Bakker, Dirk J., jt. ed. see Knights, Robert M.

Bakker, Dorothy, jt. auth. see Rigsbee, Ron.

Bakker, Dorothy F., jt. auth. see Hornbrook, John.

Bakker, Elna. An Island Called California: An Ecological Introduction to Its Natural Communities. 2nd, rev. & exp. ed. LC 82-17453. (Illus.). 400p. 1985. 29.95 (ISBN 0-520-04947-0). U of Cal Pr.

--An Island Called California: An Ecological Introduction to Its Natural Communities. 2nd. rev. ed. (Illus.). 400p. pap. 10.95 (ISBN 0-520-04948-9, CAL 641). U of Cal Pr.

Bakker, Elna S., jt. auth. see Cowles, Raymond B.

Bakker, F. Facets of Prayer. Pronk, Cornelis & Pronk, Fredericka, trs. from Dutch. (Summit Bks.). 96p. 1981. pap. 3.50 (ISBN 0-8010-0796-8). Baker Bk.

Bakker, H. De see De Bakker, H.

Bakker, J., jt. auth. see Riewald, J. G.

Bakker, J. J., jt. ed. see Politiek, R. D.

Bakker, J. W. & Leeuwen, J. Van, eds. Automata, Languages & Programming: Seventh Colloquium. (Lecture Notes in Computer Sciences: Vol. 85). 671p. 1980. pap. 36.00 (ISBN 0-387-10003-2). Springer-Verlag.

Bakker, James O. You Can Make It. 136p. (Orig.). 1983. pap. 4.95 (ISBN 0-912275-00-6). PTL Enterprises.

Bakker, Jan. Fiction As Survival Strategy. (Costerus New Ser.: Vol. XXXVII). 220p. 1983. pap. text ed. 23.00x (ISBN 9-062-03924-3, Pub. by Rodopi Holland). Humanities.

Bakker, Jan, jt. auth. see Butler, Francelia.

Bakker, Jan & Wilkinson, D. R., eds. From Cooper to Philip Roth: Essays on American Literature Presented to J. G. Riewald on the Occasion of His Seventieth Birthday. (Costerus New Ser.). 130p. 1980. pap. text ed. 14.75x (ISBN 90-6203-851-4). Humanities.

Bakker, Jim. Eight Keys to Success. LC 79-92249. 128p. 1980. pap. 2.50 (ISBN 0-89221-071-0). New Leaf.

--Survival-Unite to Live. LC 80-84504. 1980. 7.95 (ISBN 0-89221-081-8). New Leaf.

Bakker, Jim & Bakker, Tammy. How We Lost Weight & Kept It off. LC 79-90268. 1979. pap. 2.50 (ISBN 0-89221-070-2). New Leaf.

--Run to the Roar. LC 80-80656. 142p. 1982. pap. 2.95 (ISBN 0-89221-104-0). New Leaf.

Bakker, Tammy & Dudley, Cliff. Run to the Roar. LC 80-80656. 142p. 1980. 7.95 (ISBN 0-89221-073-7). New Leaf.

Bakker, Tammy, jt. auth. see Bakker, Jim.

Bakker, Tammy see Dudley, Cliff.

Bakker-Rabdau, Marianne, jt. auth. see Bakker, Cornelis.

Bakko, Darlene. Unusual Animals A to Z. LC 82-71047. (Illus.). 26p. (Orig.). (gr. k-5). 1982. color book spiral bound 2.50x (ISBN 0-943864-30-5). Davenport.

Baklanoff, Eric N., ed. Mediterranean Europe & the Common Market: Studies of Economic Growth & Integration. LC 75-19056. (Mediterranean Europe Ser.: No. 2). 255p. 1976. 20.00 (ISBN 0-8173-4605-8). U of Ala Pr.

Baklanov, Grigory, tr. from Rus. South of the Main Offensive. LC 64-25464. 1963. 9.95 (ISBN 0-8023-1006-0). Dufour.

Bako, Elemer. Guide to Hungarian Studies, 2 vols. LC 79-152422. (Bibliographical Ser.: No. 52). 1218p. 1973. PLB 45.00x (ISBN 0-8179-2521-X). Hoover Inst Pr.

Bakole Wa Ilunga. Paths of Liberation: A Third World Spirituality. O'Connell, Matthew J., tr. from Fr. LC 84-5177. 240p. (Orig.). 1984. pap. 12.95 (ISBN 0-88344-401-1). Orbis Bks.

Bakr, As-Sayyid. Studies in Arabic Philology. (Arabic.). 1969. 15.00x (ISBN 0-86685-055-4). Intl Bk Ctr.

Bakry, F. H., jt. auth. see Bakry, S. H.

Bakry, S. H. & Bakry, F. H. Introduction to Computers. (Arabic.). 1985. pap. 7.50 (ISBN 0-471-81337-0). Wiley.

Bakshi, Guha. Flora of Murshidaad District, West Bengal, India. 400p. 1982. 90.00x (ISBN 0-686-45803-6, Pub. by United Bk Traders India). State Mutual Bk.

Bakshi, S. R. Gandhi & Non-Cooperation Movement, 1920-22. 1983. 22.50x (ISBN 0-8364-1073-4, Pub. by Capital Pub). South Asia Bks.

--Jallianwala Bagh Tragedy. 1983. 15.00x (ISBN 0-8364-1074-2, Pub. by Capital Pub). South Asia Bks.

--Simon Commission & Indian Nationalism. 1977. 11.50x (ISBN 0-88386-966-7). South Asia Bks.

Bakshi, Trilochan S. & Naveh, Zev, eds. Environmental Education: Principles, Methods & Applications. LC 80-11837. (Environmental Science Research Ser.: Vol. 18). 300p. 1980. 42.50x (ISBN 0-306-40433-8, Plenum Pr). Plenum Pub.

Bakshy, Alexander. Theatre Unbound. LC 68-56535. 1968. Repr. of 1923 ed. 20.00 (ISBN 0-405-08232-0, Pub. by Blom). Ayer Co Pubs.

Bakshy, Alexander see Gorky, Maxim.

Bakshy, Alexander, tr. see Gorky, Maksim.

Bakshy, Alexander, tr. see Gorky, Maxim.

Bakst, Aaron. Arithmetic for the Modern Age. LC 60-53374. pap. 87.30 (ISBN 0-317-08507-7, 2007243). Bks Demand UMI.

Bakst, James. A History of Russian-Soviet Music. LC 76-55406. (Illus.). 1977. Repr. of 1966 ed. lib. bdg. 30.50 (ISBN 0-8371-9422-9, BARS). Greenwood.

Bakst, Leon. Decorative Art of Leon Bakst. LC 68-57183. (Illus.). 1969. Repr. of 1913 ed. 30.00 (ISBN 0-405-08234-7, Pub. by Blom). Ayer Co Pubs.

--The Decorative Art of Leon Bakst. Melvill, Harry, tr. LC 73-187844. (Illus.). 144p. 1973. pap. 6.00 (ISBN 0-486-22871-1). Dover.

--The Decorative Art of Leon Bakst. Melvill, Harry, tr. (Illus.). 13.25 (ISBN 0-8446-4620-2). Peter Smith.

--Designs of Leon Bakst for the Sleeping Princess. LC 68-56514. (Illus.). 1969. 33.00 (ISBN 0-405-08235-5, Pub. by Blom). Ayer Co Pubs.

Bakunin, Jack. Pierre Leroux & the Birth of Democratic Socialism. 1976. lib. bdg. 79.95 (ISBN 0-87700-221-5). Revisionist Pr.

Bakunin, M. A. Bakunin's Writings. Repr. of 1947 ed. 18.00 (ISBN 0-527-04600-0). Kraus Repr.

Bakunin, Michael. God & the State. facsimile ed. LC 78-148871. (Select Bibliographies Reprint Ser.). Repr. of 1916 ed. 12.00 (ISBN 0-8369-5643-5). Ayer Co Pubs.

--God & the State. LC 75-105664. 1970. pap. 3.50 (ISBN 0-486-22483-X). Dover.

Bakunin, Mikhail. From Out of the Dustbin: Articles & Speeches 1869-1871. Cutler, R., tr. from Rus. & intro. by. 212p. 1985. 22.50 (ISBN 0-88233-645-2). Ardis Pubs.

--Statism & Anarchy. Harrison, J. Frank, ed. 74. lib. bdg. 79.95 (ISBN 0-87700-219-3). Revisionist Pr.

Bakunin, Mikhail A. Political Philosophy of Bakunin. Maximoff, G. P., ed. 1964. pap. text ed. 14.95 (ISBN 0-02-901210-4). Free Pr.

Bakunts, A., et al. We of the Mountains. 246p. 1972. 4.95 (ISBN 0-8285-0946-8, Pub. by Progress Pubs USSR). Imported Pubns.

Bakur Weiner, Marcella & Teresi, Jeanne. Old People Are a Burden, but Not My Parents. LC 82-23034. 190p. 1983. 13.95 (ISBN 0-13-633818-6); pap. 6.95 (ISBN 0-13-633800-3). P-H.

Bakutis, Alice R. Nurse Anesthetists Continuing Education Review. 2nd ed. 1981. 21.00 (ISBN 0-87488-356-3). Med Exam.

--Self-Assessment of Current Knowledge for the Nurse Anesthetist. 3rd ed. 1981. 17.50 (ISBN 0-87488-715-1). Med Exam.

Bakvis, Herman. Catholic Power in the Netherlands. (Illus.). 254p. 1981. 26.50x (ISBN 0-7735-0361-7). McGill-Queens U Pr.

Bakwin, Harry & Bakwin, M. Behavior Disorders in Children. 4th ed. LC 75-173330. pap. 160.00 (ISBN 0-317-26426-5, 2024982). Bks Demand UMI.

Bakwin, M., jt. auth. see Bakwin, Harry.

Baky, John S., ed. Humans & Animals. (Reference Shelf Ser.). 1980. 8.00 (ISBN 0-8242-0647-9). Wilson.

Bal, L. Zoological Ripening of Soils. (Agricultural Research Reports: No.850). (Illus.). 382p. 1982. pap. 41.50 (ISBN 90-220-0615-8, PDC240, PUDOC). Unipub.

Bal, Sant S. George Orwell: The Ethical Imagination. 144p. 1981. text ed. 14.75x (ISBN 0-391-02202-4). Humanities.

Bala, M. S. Disciplinary Action in Industry: Including Banking Industry. 196p. 1979. pap. 18.95x (ISBN 0-86131-164-7, Pub by Orient Longman India). Apt Bks.

Bala, Nicholas C. & Clarke, Kenneth L. The Child & the Law. LC 81-179630. (Illus.). Date not set. price not set (ISBN 0-07-077868-X). McGraw.

Balaam, David N. & Carey, Michael J., eds. Food Politics: The Regional Conflict. LC 79-48097. 254p. 1981. text ed. 32.50x (ISBN 0-916672-52-2); pap. text ed. 9.50x (ISBN 0-86598-070-5). Allanheld.

Balaam, L. N. Fundamentals of Biometry. 259p. 1972. 32.95 (ISBN 0-470-04571-X). Halsted Pr.

Balaban, A., et al. Labelled Compounds & Radiopharmaceuticals Applied in Nuclear Medicine. 1985. 110.00 (ISBN 0-471-90458-9). Wiley.

Balaban, A. T. Chemical Applications of Graph Theory. 1976. 57.50 (ISBN 0-12-076050-9). Acad Pr.

Balaban, A. T., et al, eds. Steric Fit in Quantitative Structure-Activity Relations. (Lecture Notes in Chemistry: Vol. 15). (Illus.). 178p. 1980. pap. 21.00 (ISBN 0-387-09755-4). Springer-Verlag.

Balaban, John. After Our War. LC 73-13313. (Pitt Poetry Ser.). 1974. pap. 5.95 (ISBN 0-8229-5247-5). U of Pittsburgh Pr.

--Blue Mountain. LC 81-7505. 88p. 1982. 15.00 (ISBN 0-87775-143-9); pap. 6.00 (ISBN 0-87775-144-7). Unicorn Pr.

--Coming Down Again. 256p. 1985. 15.95 (ISBN 0-15-119519-6). HarBraceJ.

Balaban, John, ed. & tr. Ca Dao Vietnam: Bilingual Anthology of Vietnamese Folk Poetry. (Illus., Vietnamese & Eng.). 1980. 15.00 (ISBN 0-87775-128-5); pap. 6.00 (ISBN 0-87775-129-3). Unicorn Pr.

Balaban, M., ed. Molecular Structure & Dynamics. (Illus.). 368p. 1981. text ed. 35.00 (ISBN 0-86689-001-7, 992200148). Balaban Intl Sci Serv.

--Nucleic Acids & Nucleic Acid Complexes Viruses. (Structural Aspects of Recognition & Assembly of Biological Macromolecules Ser.: Vol. 2). 484p. 1981. 69.00 (ISBN 0-86689-003-3, 992200113). Balaban Intl Sci Serv.

--Proteins & Protein Complexes Fibrous Proteins. (Structural Aspects of Recognition & Assembly in Biological Macromolecules Ser.: Vol. 1). 494p. 69.00 (ISBN 0-86689-002-5, 992200205). Balaban Intl Sci Serv.

Balaban, M. & Eigen, M., eds. Molecular Mechanisms of Biological Recognition. 516p. 1980. 78.75 (ISBN 0-444-80130-8). Elsevier.

Balaban, Miriam. Biological Foundations & Human Nature. (Aharon Katzir-Katchalsky Lectures Ser.). 1984. 39.50 (ISBN 0-12-076150-5). Acad Pr.

Balaban, Miriam, ed. Scientific Information Transfer: The Editor's Role. 1978. lib. bdg. 37.00 (ISBN 90-277-0917-3, Pub. by Reidel Holland). Kluwer Academic.

Balaban, Nancy. Starting School: Separation, Independence, & the Preschool Experience. (Early Childhood Education Ser.). 160p. 1985. pap. text ed. 9.95x (ISBN 0-8077-2793-8). Tchrs Coll.

Balaban, Nancy, jt. auth. see Morey, G. B.

Balaban, T. On the Mixed Problem for a Hyperbolic Equation. LC 52-42839. (Memoirs: No. 112). 117p. 1971. pap. 9.00 (ISBN 0-8218-1812-0, MEMO-112). Am Math.

Balabanian, Norman. Fourier Series. 124p. 1976. pap. 6.95 (ISBN 0-916460-17-7). Matrix Pub.

Balabanian, Norman & Bickart, Theodore. Electrical Network Theory. LC 82-21224. 954p. 1983. Repr. of 1969 ed. lib. bdg. 59.50 (ISBN 0-89874-581-0). Krieger.

--Linear Network Theory: Analysis, Properties, Design & Synthesis. (Illus.). 648p. 1981. 34.95 (ISBN 0-916460-10-X). Matrix Pub.

Balabanis, Homer P. The American Discount Market. Bruchey, Stuart, ed. LC 80-1132. (The Rise of Commercial Banking Ser.). (Illus.). 1981. Repr. of 1935 ed. lib. bdg. 12.00x (ISBN 0-405-13633-1). Ayer Co Pubs.

Balabanoff, Angelica. My Life As a Rebel. LC 68-23270. 1968. Repr. of 1938 ed. lib. bdg. 32.75x (ISBN 0-8371-0011-9, BARB). Greenwood.

--My Life As a Rebel. LC 72-88914. (Classics in Russian Studies: No. 1). 336p. 1973. pap. 4.50x (ISBN 0-253-15485-5). Ind U Pr.

Balabkins, Nicholas. Germany under Direct Controls: Economic Aspects of Industrial Disarmament, 1945-1948. 1964. 27.00 (ISBN 0-8135-0449-X). Rutgers U Pr.

Balachandran, A. P. & Trahern, G. C. Lectures on Group Theory for Physicists. (Monographs & Textbooks on Physical Sciences). 110p. 1984. pap. text ed. 20.00x (ISBN 88-7088-088-5, Pub. by Bibliopolis, Italy). Humanities.

Balachandran, A. P., et al. Gauge Symmetries & Fibre Bundles. (Lecture Notes in Physics: Vol. 188). 140p. 1983. pap. 9.00 (ISBN 0-387-12724-0). Springer Verlag.

Balachandran, M. A Guide to Trade & Securities Statistics. LC 77-73818. 1977. 24.95 (ISBN 0-686-47059-1). Pierian.

Balachandran, M. & Balachandran, S. Subject Guide to Reference Books, 1970-1975. LC 79-83698. 1980. 60.00 (ISBN 0-87650-102-1). Pierian.

Balachandran, M., jt. auth. see Balachandran, S.

Balachandran, M., ed. A Guide to Trade & Securities Statistics. LC 77-73818. 1977. 29.50 (ISBN 0-87650-077-7). Pierian.

--Regional Statistics: A Guide to Information Sources. LC 80-14260. (Economics Information Guide Ser.: Vol. 13). 230p. 1980. 60.00x (ISBN 0-8103-1463-0). Gale.

Balachandran, M. & Balachandran, S., eds. Reference Book Review Index: 1973-1975. 1980. 60.00 (ISBN 0-87650-073-4). Pierian.

Balachandran, M., jt. ed. see Balachandran, S.

Balachandran, S. & Balachandran, M. Reference Sources: 1981. 1982. 75.00 (ISBN 0-686-47138-5). Pierian.

Balachandran, S., jt. auth. see Balachandran, M.

Balachandran, S. & Balachandran, M., eds. Reference Sources 1980. 1981. 75.00 (ISBN 0-87650-127-7). Pierian.

Balachandran, S., jt. ed. see Balachandran, M.

Balachandran, Sarojini. Airport Planning: Nineteen Sixty-Five to Nineteen Seventy-Five, No. 1140. 1976. 5.00 (ISBN 0-686-20412-3). CPL Biblios.

--Directory of Publishing Sources: The Researcher's Guide to Journals in Engineering & Technology. 386p. 1982. 39.95 (ISBN 0-471-09200-2, Pub. by Wiley-Interscience). Wiley.

--Employee Communication: A Bibliography. 1976. pap. 3.60 (ISBN 0-931874-04-1). Assn Busn Comm.

--Technical Writing: A Bibliography. 1977. pap. 4.60 (ISBN 0-931874-07-6). Assn Busn Comm.

Balachandran, Sarojini, ed. Energy Statistics: A Guide to Information Sources. LC 80-13338. (Natural World Information Guide Ser.: Vol. 1). 272p. 1980. 60.00x (ISBN 0-8103-1419-3). Gale.

--New Product Planning. LC 79-24046. (Management Information Guide Ser.: No. 38). 1980. 58.00x (ISBN 0-8103-0838-X). Gale.

Balado, J. L. The Story of Taize. (Illus.). 144p. (Orig.). 1981. pap. 4.95 (ISBN 0-8164-2321-0, Pub. by Seabury). Winston Pr.

Balado, Jose L. Stories of Mother Teresa: Her Smile & Her Words. Diaz, Olimpia, tr. from Span. 96p. 1983. pap. 2.50 (ISBN 0-89243-181-4). Liguori Pubns.

Balaguer, Joaquin. History of Dominican Literature. 1978. lib. bdg. 69.95 (ISBN 0-8490-1971-0). Gordon Pr.

Balaguer, Josemaria Escriva de see Escriva de Balaguer, Josemaria.

Balaguer, Miguel. Diccionario Griego-Espanol. 2nd ed. 940p. (Span. & Gr.). 1977. 17.95 (ISBN 84-216-0362-0, S-50344). French & Eur.

Balahura, Robert. Test Bank to Accompany General Chemistry. LW, LC & GLH, eds. 214p. 1984. pap. write for info. (ISBN 0-7167-1696-8). W H Freeman.

Balaji, K. P. Abhimanyu. 1978. 3.75x (ISBN 0-8364-0226-X); pap. 2.00x (ISBN 0-8364-0227-8). South Asia Bks.

--Abhimanyu. 216p. 1978. pap. 3.95x (ISBN 0-86131-000-4, Pub by Orient Longman India). Apt Bks.

Balajthy, Ernest. Microcomputers in Reading & Language Arts. (Illus.). 304p. 1986. pap. text ed. 16.95 (ISBN 0-13-580473-6). P-H.

Balakian, A. A., ed. The Symbolist Movement in the Literature of European Languages. (Comparative History of Literatures in European Language Ser.: Vol. 2). 732p. 1982. text ed. 63.50 (ISBN 963-05-2694-8, Pub. by Kultura Pr Hungary). Humanities.

Balakian, Anna. Andre Breton: Magus of Surrealism. LC 78-83006. 1971. 10.00x (ISBN 0-19-501298-4). Hawkshead Bk.

--The Symbolist Movement: A Critical Appraisal. LC 77-76044. 320p. 1977. pap. 15.00x (ISBN 0-8147-0994-X). NYU Pr.

Balakian, Anna & Guillen, Claudio, eds. Comparative Poetics. LC 84-48468. 600p. 1985. lib. bdg. 70.00 (ISBN 0-317-19425-9). Garland Pub.

Balakian, Anna & Valdes, M. J., eds. Inter-American Literary Relations. LC 84-48470. 306p. 1985. lib. bdg. 35.00 (ISBN 0-8240-4013-9). Garland Pub.

Balakian, Nona & Simmons, Charles. The Creative Present: Notes on Contemporary American Fiction. rev. ed. LC 77-189247. 302p. 1972. Repr. of 1963 ed. text ed. 12.50x (ISBN 0-87752-158-1). Gordian.

Balakian, Peter. Father Fisheye. LC 79-90840. 89p. 1980. 9.95 (ISBN 0-935296-08-5); pap. 4.95 (ISBN 0-935296-09-3). Sheep Meadow.

--Sad Days of Light. LC 82-10823. 72p. 1983. 13.95 (ISBN 0-935296-33-6); pap. 7.95 (ISBN 0-935296-34-4). Sheep Meadow.

Balakian, Peter & Smith, Bruce. Invisible Estate. (Illus.). 56p. 1984. 85.00 (ISBN 0-916375-01-3). Press Alley.

Balakrishman, V., et al. Genetic Diversity Among Australian Aborigines. (AIAS Research & Regional Ser.: No. 3). (Illus.). 1975. pap. text ed. 7.75x (ISBN 0-85575-043-X). Humanities.

Balakrishna, A. V., ed. Control Theory & the Calculus of Variations. LC 74-91431. 1969. 60.00 (ISBN 0-12-076953-0). Acad Pr.

Balakrishna, A. V. & Neustadt, Lucien W., eds. Computing Methods in Optimization Problems: Proceedings. 1964. 55.00 (ISBN 0-12-076950-6). Acad Pr.

--Mathematical Theory of Control: Proceedings. 1967. 70.00 (ISBN 0-12-076956-5). Acad Pr.

Balakrishna, A. V., et al, eds. see Symposium on Optimization, Nice, 1969.

Balakrishnan, A. V. Elements of State Space Theory of Systems. (University Series in Modern Engineering). ix, 187p. 1983. pap. 26.00 (ISBN 0-387-90904-4). Springer-Verlag.

--Kalman Filtering Theory. (University Series in Modern Engineering). xii, 222p. 1984. pap. 26.00 (ISBN 0-318-03102-7). Springer Verlag.

Balakrishnan, A. V. & Neustadt, L. W., eds. Techniques of Optimization. 1972. 65.00 (ISBN 0-12-076960-3). Acad Pr.

Balakrishnan, A. V., ed. see Yadrenko, Mikhail I.

Balakrishnan, T. R., et al. Fertility & Family Planning in a Canadian Metropolis. LC 75-332127. pap. 58.30 (ISBN 0-317-26449-4, 2023856). Bks Demand UMI.

Balan, C. A. In the Shadow of the Gallows. 1979. 3.25x (ISBN 0-8364-0569-2, Pub. by Sangam India). South Asia Bks.

Balan, Ion Dodu. Cultural Policy in Romania. (Studies & Documents on Cultural Policies). (Illus.). 70p. 1975. pap. 5.00 (ISBN 92-3-101188-X, U136, UNESCO). Unipub.

Balan, Jorge. Why People Move: Comparative Perspectives on the Dynamics of Internal Migration. (Illus.). 342p. 1981. pap. 28.25 (ISBN 92-3-101909-0, U1186, UNESCO). Unipub.

Balan, Jorge, et al. Men in a Developing Society: Geographic & Social Mobility in Monterrey, Mexico. LC 72-6282. (Latin American Monographs Ser.: No. 30). 404p. 1973. 20.00x (ISBN 0-292-75004-8). U of Tex Pr.

Balanchine, George & Mason, Francis. Balanchine's Complete Stories of the Great Ballets. LC 76-55684. (Illus.). 1977. 27.50 (ISBN 0-385-11381-1). Doubleday.

--One Hundred One Stories of the Great Ballets. LC 73-9140. 560p. 1975. pap. 7.95 (ISBN 0-385-03398-2, Dolp). Doubleday.

Balandin, R. Vladimir Vernadsky. 207p. 1982. pap. 4.95 (ISBN 0-8285-2465-3, Pub. by Mir Pubs USSR). Imported Pubns.

Balanis, Constantine A. Antenna Theory: Analysis & Design. 790p. 1982. text ed. 38.45 scp (ISBN 0-06-040458-2, HarpC); sol. manual avail. (ISBN 0-06-360410-8). Har-Row.

Balano. The Log of the Skipper's Wife. LC 79-52446. (Illus.). 1979. pap. 6.95 (ISBN 0-89272-062-X). Down East.

Balaquer, Josemaria Escriva de see Escriva de Balaguer, Josemaria.

Balaramiah, V. The Art of Deathlessness. (Illus.). 128p. 1980. pap. 4.95 (ISBN 0-937698-01-6). Golden Mean.

Balard, Michel. Genes et l'Outre-Mer: Les Actes de Caffa du Notaire Lamberto di Sambuceto, 1289-1290, Tome 1. (Documents et Recherches sur l'Economie des Pays Byzantins, Illamiques et Slaves et Leurs Relations Commerciales au Moyen-Age: No. 12). (Illus.). 1973. pap. 27.60x (ISBN 0-686-20914-1). Mouton.

Balas, Kornel, tr. see Sagvari, A.

Balas, P., ed. Angiology: New Developments. 1306p. 1984. 125.00x (ISBN 0-306-41349-3, Plenum Pr). Plenum Pub.

Balas, Robert & Rice, Donald. Qu'est-ce Qui Se Passe? Conversation Revision de Grammaire. 2nd ed. LC 83-82362. 448p. 1983. lab manual wkbk. 9.95 (ISBN 0-395-34448-4); instr's. ed. 22.95 (ISBN 0-395-34449-2); Cassettes 15.95 (ISBN 0-395-34453-0); reel to reel 200.00 (ISBN 0-395-34452-2); tapescript avail. (ISBN 0-395-34455-7). HM.

Balas, Robert S. Qu'est-ce Qui Se Passe? Conversation-Revision de Grammaire. 448p. 1979. pap. 22.95 (ISBN 0-395-30955-7); cahier d'exercises et de laboratoire 10.50 (ISBN 0-395-30957-3); recordings 200.00 (ISBN 0-395-30958-1). HM.

Balashov, Y. S. An Atlas of Ixodid Tick Ultrastructure. 289p. 1983. 18.00. Entomol Soc.

Balaskas, Arthur. Bodylife. (Illus.). 192p. 1985. pap. 12.95 (ISBN 0-283-98309-4, Pub. by Sidgwick & Jackson). Merrimack Pub Cir.

Balaskas, Arthur, jt. auth. see Balaskas, Janet.

Balaskas, Arthur S. & Stirk, John L. Soft Exercise. (Illus.). 160p. 1983. pap. 9.95 (ISBN 0-684-17508-8, ScribT). Scribner.

Balaskas, Janet. Active Birth. 1983. 14.95 (ISBN 0-07-003546-6); pap. 6.95 (ISBN 0-07-003545-8). McGraw.

--The Active Birth Partners Handbook. (Illus.). 192p. 1985. laminated boards 11.95 (ISBN 0-283-99038-4, Pub. by Sidgwick & Jackson). Merrimack Pub Cir.

Balaskas, Janet & Balaskas, Arthur. New Life: The Book of Exercises for Pregnancy & Childbirth. (Illus.). 144p. (Orig.). 1983. pap. 9.95 (ISBN 0-283-98997-1, Pub. by Sidgwick & Jackson). Merrimack Pub Cir.

Balasov, L. A., et al. Fourteen Papers on Series & Approximation. LC 51-5559. (Translations Ser.: No. 2, Vol. 77). 1968. 35.00 (ISBN 0-8218-1777-9, TRANS 2-77). Am Math.

Balassa, B. European Economic Integration. LC 74-76882. (Contributions to Economic Analysis: Vol. 89). 416p. 1975. 76.50 (ISBN 0-444-10649-9, North-Holland). Elsevier.

Balassa, B. & Nelson, R., eds. Economic Progress: Private Values & Public Policy. 340p. 1977. 68.00 (ISBN 0-7204-0515-7, North-Holland). Elsevier.

Balassa, Bela. Adjustment to External Shocks in Developing Economies. (Working Paper: No. 472). 31p. 1981. pap. 3.00 (ISBN 0-686-39760-6, WP-0472). World Bank.

--Change & Challenge in the World Economy. LC 85-1854. 400p. 1985. 29.95x (ISBN 0-312-12854-1). St Martin.

--Development Strategies in Semi-Industrial Economies. LC 81-15558. 416p. 1982. pap. text ed. 18.50x (ISBN 0-8018-2570-9); 39.95 (ISBN 0-8018-2569-5). Johns Hopkins.

--Economic Development & Integration. 157p. 1965. 2.50 (ISBN 0-317-33986-9, 308). Comm Econ Dev.

--The Hungarian Economic Reform, 1968-81. (Working Paper: No. 506). 31p. 1982. pap. 3.00 (ISBN 0-686-39675-8, WP-0506). World Bank.

--Industrial Prospects & Policies in the Developed Countries. (Working Paper: No. 453). 30p. 1981. pap. 3.00 (ISBN 0-686-39752-5, WP-0453). World Bank.

--The Newly Industrialized Countries in the World Economy. LC 80-20787. 450p. 1981. 30.00 (ISBN 0-08-026336-4). Pergamon.

--The Newly-Industrializing Developing Countries after the Oil Crisis. (Working Paper: No.437). 57p. 1980. 5.00 (ISBN 0-686-36173-3, WP-0437). World Bank.

--The Newly Industrializing Developing Countries after the Oil Crisis. (Working Paper: No. 437). 57p. 1980. pap. 3.00 (ISBN 0-686-39744-4, WP-0437). World Bank.

--The Policy Experience of Twelve Less Developed Countries, 1973-1978. (Working Paper: No. 449). 36p. 1981. pap. 3.00 (ISBN 0-686-39745-2, WP-0449). World Bank.

--Policy Reform in Developing Countries. 1977. text ed. 29.00 o. p. (ISBN 0-08-021477-0); pap. text ed. 16.25 (ISBN 0-08-021478-9). Pergamon.

--The Process of Industrial Development & Alternative Development Strategies. LC 81-1033. (Essays in International Finance Ser.: No. 141). 1980. pap. text ed. 2.50x (ISBN 0-88165-048-X). Princeton U Int Finan Econ.

--The Process of Industrial Development & Alternative Development Strategies. (Working Paper: No. 501). 127p. 1982. pap. 3.00 (ISBN 0-686-39754-1, WP-438). World Bank.

--Reforming the New Economic Mechanism in Hungary. (Working Paper: No. 534). 56p. 1982. pap. 3.00 (ISBN 0-8213-0048-2). World Bank.

--Structural Adjustment Policies in Developing Economies. (Working Paper: No. 464). 36p. 1981. pap. 3.00 (ISBN 0-686-39748-7, WP-0464). World Bank.

--Structural Change in Trade in Manufactured Goods Between Industrial & Developing Countries. (Working Paper: No. 396). 46p. 1980. pap. 3.00 (ISBN 0-686-39774-6, WP-0396). World Bank.

--Thailand: Industrial Development Strategy in Thailand. x, 59p. 1980. pap. 3.00 (ISBN 0-686-39672-3, RC-8012). World Bank.

--World Trade: Constraints & Opportunities in the 80's. (The Atlantic Papers Ser.: No. 36). 70p. 1979. 6.50x (ISBN 0-916672-76-X, Pub. by Atlantic Inst France). Allanheld.

Balassa, Bela & McCarthy, F. Desmond. Adjustment Policies in Developing Countries: An Update. (Staff Working Paper 675). 128p. 1985. 8.00 (ISBN 0-318-11906-4, WP 0675). World Bank.

Balassa, Bela, ed. Changing Patterns in Foreign Trade & Payments. (Problems of the Modern Economy Ser.). 1978. 12.95 (ISBN 0-393-05662-7); pap. 4.95x (ISBN 0-393-09138-4). Norton.

Balassa, Bela, et al. The Balance of Payments: Effects of External Shocks & of Policy Responses to These Shocks in Non-OPEC Developing Countries. 99p. (Orig.). 1981. pap. text ed. 11.00x (ISBN 92-64-12244-3). OECD.

Balassa, Bela A. The Theory of Economic Integration. LC 82-2971. (The Irwin Series in Economics). xiv, 304p. 1982. Repr. of 1961 ed. lib. bdg. 37.75x (ISBN 0-313-23543-0, BATY). Greenwood.

Balassa, Bela A. & Kreinin, M. E. Studies in Trade Liberalization: Problems & Prospects for the Industrial Countries. LC 67-22889. pap. 90.50 (ISBN 0-317-19827-0, 2023080). Bks Demand UMI.

Balassa, Bela & Associates. The Structure of Protection in Developing Countries. LC 77-147366. (World Bank Ser.). (Illus.). 384p. 1971. 34.50x (ISBN 0-8018-1257-7). Johns Hopkins.

Balassanian, Sonia. Portraits. (Illus.). 24p. (Orig.). 1983. pap. 10.00 (ISBN 0-9608388-1-3). S Balassanian.

--There Might Have Been An Insane Heart: Selected Poems In Armenian Language. 80p. (Orig., Armenian.). 1982. pap. 5.00 (ISBN 0-9608388-0-5). S Balassanian.

Balasubrahmanyam, V. Verse with Prose. 8.00 (ISBN 0-89253-559-8); flexible cloth 4.00 (ISBN 0-89253-560-1). Ind-US Inc.

Balasubrahmanyan, M. Business Communications. 1979. text ed. 12.50x (ISBN 0-7069-0753-1, Pub. by Vikas India). Advent NY.

Balasubrahomanyam, S. R. Early Chola Temples: Parantaka 1 to Rajaraja 1 (A.D. 907-985) 400p. 1981. 97.50x (ISBN 0-86125-048-6, Pub. by Orient Longman India). State Mutual Bk.

Balasubramaniam, A. S., jt. ed. see Yudhibir.

Balasubramanian, M. Nehru: A Study in Secularism. 120p. 1980. 14.95x (ISBN 0-940500-32-9). Asia Bk Corp.

Balasubramanian, N. V., et al. Differential Forms on Electromagnetic Networks. (Illus.). 1971. 17.25 (ISBN 0-8088-0040-X). Davey.

Bala Subramanian, V. Calcium Antagonists in Chronic Stable Angina Pectoris & Hypertension. (Current Clinical Practice Ser.: No. 5). x, 238p. 1983. 42.75 (ISBN 0-444-90322-4, I-243-83, Excerpta Medica). Elsevier.

Balasubramanyam, V. N. The Economy of India. 241p. 1985. 25.00 (ISBN 0-8133-0299-4). Westview.

--International Transfer of Technology to India. LC 73-163952. (Special Studies in International Economics & Development). 1973. 39.50x (ISBN 0-275-28245-7). Irvington.

Balasubramanyam, V. N., jt. auth. see MacBean, Alasdair.

Balasundaram, P. M. Kamaraj & His Secrets of Success. 1984. pap. 8.50x (ISBN 0-8364-1139-0, Pub. by D Poomphar Pubns). South Asia Bks.

Balasuriya, Tissa. The Eucharist & Human Liberation. LC 78-9160. 184p. (Orig.). 1979. pap. 6.95 (ISBN 0-88344-118-7). Orbis Bks.

--Planetary Theology. LC 83-19339. 352p. (Orig.). 1984. pap. 10.95 (ISBN 0-88344-400-3). Orbis Bks.

Balasz, Bela. Theory of the Film. 292p. 1981. 25.00x (ISBN 0-234-77659-5, Pub. by Dobson Bks England). State Mutual Bk.

Balatov, Ya., jt. auth. see Zamoshkin, Yu.

Balawyder, Aloysius. The Maple Leaf & the White Eagle: Canadian-Polish Relations, 1918-1978. (East European Monographs: No. 66). 300p. 1980. 30.00x (ISBN 0-914710-59-1). East Eur Quarterly.

Balawyder, Aloysius, ed. Cooperative Movements in Eastern Europe. LC 79-55001. (Illus.). 200p. 1980. text ed. 18.00x (ISBN 0-916672-45-X). Allanheld.

Balay, Maurice. Lexique Informatique. 128p. (Fr.). 1971. pap. 9.95 (ISBN 0-686-56908-3, M-6021). French & Eur.

Balaye, Simone, ed. see Stael, de.

Balaz, Joseph. After the Drought. 1985. pap. 20.00 (ISBN 0-914916-71-8). Topgallant.

Balazs, Andras, et al. Reproduction & Aging. 331p. 1974. text ed. 29.50x (ISBN 0-8422-7159-7). Irvington.

Balazs, B., jt. auth. see Ruprecht, J.

Balazs, Bela. Theory of the Film: Character & Growth of a New Art. LC 71-169347. (Arno Press Cinema Program). (Illus.). 312p. 1972. Repr. of 1952 ed. 24.50 (ISBN 0-405-03910-7). Ayer Co Pubs.

--Theory of the Film: Character & Growth of a New Art. LC 77-130963. 1971. pap. 6.50 (ISBN 0-486-22685-9). Dover.

Balazs, Endre A., jt. ed. see Jeanloz, Roger W.

Balazs, Etienne. Chinese Civilization & Bureaucracy: Variations on a Theme. Wright, Arthur F., ed. Wright, H. M., tr. LC 64-2909. (YA) (gr. 9-12). 1967. pap. 10.95x (ISBN 0-300-00013-8). Yale U Pr.

Balazs, Mary. The Stones Refuse Their Peace. (Poetry Chapbooks: No. 2). 32p. 1979. pap. 2.50 (ISBN 0-913282-16-2). Seven Woods Pr.

--The Voice of Thy Brother's Blood. LC 76-18590. 1976. pap. 3.00 (ISBN 0-936014-02-4). Dawn Valley.

Balazs, Mary W. & James, Nancy E., eds. Touching This Earth: Poems by Women. (Illus.). 1977. pap. 4.00 (ISBN 0-936014-03-2). Dawn Valley.

Balazs, Mary W., jt. ed. see James, Nancy E.

Balazs, Tibor. Cardiac Toxicology, Vol. I. 240p. 1981. 79.50 (ISBN 0-8493-5555-9). CRC Pr.

--Cardiac Toxicology, Vol. II. 240p. 1981. 79.50 (ISBN 0-8493-5556-7). CRC Pr.

--Cardiac Toxicology, Vol. III. 232p. 1981. 79.50 (ISBN 0-8493-5558-3). CRC Pr.

Balbach, M. K. & Bliss, L. C. Laboratory Manual for General Botany. 6th ed. LC 81-50369. 350p. 1982. 17.95 (ISBN 0-03-058514-7, HoltC). H&R&W.

Balbach, Margaret & Bliss, Lawrence C. General Botany: Laboratory Manual. 6th ed. 350p. 1982. pap. text ed. 19.95x (ISBN 0-03-058514-7). SCP.

Balbaki, M. Al-Mawrid: Dictionary. 65.00 (ISBN 0-686-18367-3). Kazi Pubns.

--Al-Mawrid: Pocket Size Dictionary. 5.95 (ISBN 0-686-18368-1). Kazi Pubns.

Balbani, Niccolo. Newes from Italy of a Second Moses or, the Life of Galeacius Carracciolus the Noble Marquese of Vico. Crashaw, W., tr. LC 79-84085. (English Experience Ser.: No. 905). 92p. 1979. Repr. of 1608 ed. lib. bdg. 10.00 (ISBN 90-221-0905-4). Walter J Johnson.

Balbert, Peter. D. H. Lawrence & the Psychology of Rhythm: The Meaning of Form in the Rainbow. (Studies in English Literature: No. 99). 1974. pap. 13.60x (ISBN 0-686-22634-8). Mouton.

Balbert, Peter & Marcus, Phillip L., eds. D. H. Lawrence: A Centenary Consideration. LC 84-45800. 256p. 1985. text ed. 25.00x (ISBN 0-8014-1596-9). Cornell U Pr.

Balbes, Raymond & Dwinger, Philip. Distributive Lattices. LC 73-94309. 320p. 1975. 25.00x (ISBN 0-8262-0163-6). U of Mo Pr.

Balbi, Adriano. Statistical Essay on the Libraries of Vienna & the World. Barr, Larry & Barr, Janet L., trs. LC 84-43235. 150p. 1985. lib. bdg. 25.95 (ISBN 0-89950-149-4). McFarland & Co.

Balbin, Julius. Strangled Cries. Barkan, Stanley H., ed. Rizzuto, Charlz, tr. (Cross-Cultural Review Chapbook 8: Esperanto Poetry 1). 24p. (Esperanto & Eng.). 1980. pap. 2.50 (ISBN 0-89304-807-0). Cross Cult.

Balbir Singh, ed. English-Punjabi Dictionary. 1984. 18.50x (ISBN 0-8364-1241-9, Pub. by Punjabi U India). South Asia Bks.

Balbkins, Nicholas. Indigenization & Economic Development: The Nigerian Experience, Vol. 33. Altman, Edward I. & Walter, Ingo, eds. LC 81-81654. (Contemporary Studies in Economic & Financial Analysis). 300p. 1981. 40.00 (ISBN 0-89232-227-6). Jai Pr.

Balbo, Count C. The Life & Times of Dante Alighieri, 2 vols. Bunbury, F. J., tr. 1973. Repr. of 1852 ed. 100.00 (ISBN 0-8274-1439-0). R West.

Balbo, G., jt. ed. see Bruell, S. C.

Balbo, Michael P., jt. auth. see Manhold, John H.

Balbo, P. J., jt. auth. see Bourgeron, J. P.

Balbus, Isaac D. The Dialectics of Legal Repression: Black Rebels Before the American Criminal Courts. LC 73-76762. 270p. 1973. 12.50x (ISBN 0-87154-081-9). Russell Sage.

--Marxism & Domination: A Neo-Hegelian, Feminist, Psychoanalytic Theory of Sexual, Political, & Technological Liberation. LC 82-47582. 464p. 1982. 44.00x (ISBN 0-691-07621-9); pap. 10.95 (ISBN 0-691-02210-0). Princeton U Pr.

Balbus, Issac D. The Dialectics of Legal Repression: Black Rebels Before the American Criminal Courts. new ed. LC 75-44825. (Law & Society Ser.). 269p. 1977. pap. text ed. 9.95x (ISBN 0-87855-609-5). Transaction Bks.

Balbus, Joannes. Catholicon. 746p. 1460. text ed. 186.30x (ISBN 0-576-72240-5, Pub. by Greggg Intl Pubs England). Gregg Intl.

Balcarres, Colin L. Memoirs Touching the Revolution in Scotland. LC 73-161754. (Bannatyne Club, Edinburgh. Publications: No. 71). Repr. of 1841 ed. 17.50 (ISBN 0-404-52791-4). AMS Pr.

Balcer, Jack. Sparda by the Bitter Sea: Imperial Interaction in Western Anatolia. (Brown Judaic Studies: No. 52). 616p. 1985. 39.95 (ISBN 0-89130-657-9, 14 00 52); pap. 29.95 (ISBN 0-89130-818-0). Scholars Pr GA.

Balcer, Nancy, et al. Zooplankton of the Great Lakes: A Guide to the Identification & Ecology of the Common Crustaceean Species. LC 83-27426. (Illus.). 256p. 1984. text ed. 35.00x (ISBN 0-299-09820-6). U of Wis Pr.

Balcerzak, Ann M. Hope for Young People with Alcoholic Parents. 20p. 1981. pap. 0.85 (ISBN 0-89486-137-9). Hazelden.

Balch & Milton. Cutaneous Melanoma. LC 65-7495. 1984. 69.00 (ISBN 0-397-50587-6, Lippincott Medical). Lippincott.

Balch, A. H. & Lee, Myung W. Vertical Seismic Profiling: Technique, Applications, & Case Studies. 512p. 1984. 58.00 (ISBN 0-934634-47-5). Intl Human Res.

Balch, C. C., jt. ed. see Pigden, W. J.

Balch, C. M., ed. Surgical Approaches to Cutaneous Melanoma. (Pigment Cell: Vol. 7). (Illus.). viii, 242p. 1985. 85.25 (ISBN 3-8055-4055-8). S Karger.

Balch, David. Let Wives Be Submissive: The Domestic Code in 1 Peter. LC 80-21203. (Society of Biblical Literature Monograph). 196p. 1981. pap. 21.00 (ISBN 0-89130-429-0). Scholars Pr GA.

Balch, Dianne. All Joy. LC 82-72303. 169p. 1982. pap. 5.95 (ISBN 0-86605-098-1). Here's Life.

Balch, Emily. Innocence Abroad. LC 74-2796. (Illus.). 270p. 1975. Repr. of 1931 ed. lib. bdg. 24.75x (ISBN 0-8371-7433-3, BAIB). Greenwood.

Balch, Emily G. Occupied Haiti. LC 75-14988. Repr. of 1927 ed. 15.00x (ISBN 0-8371-2785-8, BAL&, Pub. by Negro U Pr). Greenwood.

--Our Slavic Fellow Citizens. LC 69-18758. (American Immigration Collection Ser., No. 1). (Illus.). 1969. Repr. of 1910 ed. 26.50 (ISBN 0-405-00506-7). Ayer Co Pubs.

Balch, Emily G., ed. Occupied Haiti: Being the Report of a Committee of Six Disinterested Americans Representing Organizations Exclusively American. LC 79-147491. (Library of War & Peace; the Political Economy of War). lib. bdg. 46.00 (ISBN 0-8240-0284-9). Garland Pub.

Balch, Frederick H. Bridge of the Gods. LC 65-18447. (Illus.). 1985. pap. 9.95 (ISBN 0-8323-0433-6). Binford.

Balch, Glenn. Buck, Wild. LC 75-44168. (Illus.). (gr. 5 up). 1976. 10.53i (ISBN 0-690-01055-9). Crowell Jr Bks.

Balch, M. D., et al, eds. Essays on Economic Behavior under Uncertainty. (Contributions to Economic Analysis Ser.: Vol. 88). 436p. 1975. 76.75 (ISBN 0-444-10618-9, North-Holland). Elsevier.

Balch, Marston S. A Mad World, My Masters, & Three Farces & a Comedy of the 18th Centurty. Hogg, James, ed. (Jacobean Drama Ser.: No. 94). 91p. 1981. pap. text ed. 25.50x (ISBN 0-391-02431-0, Pub. by Inst Eng Lit Austria). Humanities.

--Middleton's a Trick to Catch the Old One & Massinger's New Way to Pay Old Debts, Vol. 2. (Salburg - Jacobean Drama Ser.: No. 94). 113p. 1981. pap. text ed. 25.50x (ISBN 0-391-02322-5, Pub. by Salzburg Austria). Humanities.

--Thomas Middleton's a Trick to Catch the Old One, a Mad World, My Masters & Aphra Behn's City Heiress, Vol. 3. Hogg, James, ed. (Salzburg - Jacobean Drama Studies: No. 94). 84p. 1981. pap. text ed. 25.50x (ISBN 0-391-02345-4, Pub. by Salzburg Austria). Humanities.

--Thomas Middleton's No Wit, No Help Like a Woman's & the Counterfeit Bridegroom (1677) & Further Adaptations. (Jacobean Drama Studies: No. 94). 1980. pap. text ed. 25.50x (ISBN 0-391-01921-X). Humanities.

Balch, Thomas. The French in America During the War of Independence of the United States, 2 vols. LC 72-8702. (American Revolutionary Ser.). Repr. of 1895 ed. Set. lib. bdg. 68.00x (ISBN 0-8398-0185-8). Irvington.

Balch, Thomas, ed. The Examination of Joseph Galloway, Esq., by a Committee of the House of Commons. LC 72-8749. (American Revolutionary Ser.). Repr. of 1855 ed. lib. bdg. 27.00x (ISBN 0-8398-0183-1). Irvington.
Balch, Thomas, ed. see Blanchard, Claude.
Balch, Thomas W. Alabama Arbitration. facsimile ed. LC 74-95063. (Select Bibliographies Reprint Ser.). 1900. 19.00 (ISBN 0-8369-5065-8). Ayer Co Pubs.
--A World Court in the Light of the United States Supreme Court. 165p. 1983. Repr. of 1918 ed. lib. bdg. 22.50x (ISBN 0-8377-0340-9). Rothman.
Balchem, R. F. Guide to Nuclear Energy. 5.00 (ISBN 0-685-28365-8). Philos Lib.
Balchin, John. Out of This World. 1986. pap. price not set (ISBN 0-89109-535-7). NavPress.
Balchin, John F. Understanding Scripture: What Is the Bible & How Does It Speak? LC 81-8271. 98p. (Orig.). 1981. pap. 2.95 (ISBN 0-87784-875-0). Inter-Varsity.
--What the Bible Teaches about the Church. 1979. pap. 3.95 (ISBN 0-8423-7883-9). Tyndale.
Balchin, N. C., ed. Manual Metal-Arc Welding. (Engineering Craftsmen: No. F24). (Illus.). 1977. 39.50x (ISBN 0-85083-395-7). Intl Ideas.
Balchin, N. C., et al, eds. Metal-Arc Gas Shielded Welding. (Engineering Craftsmen: No. F23). (Illus.). 1977. spiral bdg. 39.95x (ISBN 0-85083-385-X). Intl Ideas.
--Oxy-Acetylene Welding. (Engineering Craftsmen: No. F25). (Illus.). 1977. spiral bdg. 39.95x (ISBN 0-85083-396-5). Intl Ideas.
--Tungsten-Arc Gas Shielded Welding. (Engineering Craftsmen: No. F22). (Illus.). 1977. spiral bdg. 39.95x (ISBN 0-85083-394-9). Intl Ideas.
Balchin, Paul N. Housing Improvement & Social Inequality. 278p. 1979. text ed. 43.95x (ISBN 0-566-00274-4). Gower Pub Co.
--Housing Policy: An Introduction. LC 84-17668. 284p. 1984. 31.00 (ISBN 0-7099-3263-4, Pub. by Croom Held Ltd); pap. 13.95 (ISBN 0-7099-3282-0). Longwood Pub Group.
Balck, William. Tactics, 2 vols. 4th rev. ed. Krueger, Walter, tr. LC 70-84261. (West Point Military Library). 1977. Set. lib. bdg. 70.00x (ISBN 0-8371-9512-8, BATC); Vol. 1. lib. bdg. 70.00 (ISBN 0-8371-9513-6). Vol. 2 (ISBN 0-8371-9514-4). Greenwood.
Balckett, Ruth, et al. Berry Patch. Shreves, Kathey, ed. (Illus.). 104p. 1981. spiral binding 5.95 (ISBN 0-940158-02-7). Zucchini Patch.
Balckstock, Charity. The Foggy Foggy Dew. 192p. 1986. pap. 2.95 (ISBN 0-345-32801-9). Ballantine.
Balcolm, Kenneth C., III, jt. auth. see Angell, Tony.
Balcom, Mary G. The Catholic Church in Alaska. LC 78-97897. (Illus.). 1970. 2.50 (ISBN 0-685-47728-2). Balcom.
--Ghost Towns of Alaska. 7th ed. (Illus.). 1982. pap. 4.00 (ISBN 0-686-95259-6). Balcom.
--Ketchikan: Alaska's Totemland. 4th ed. (Illus.). 1980. pap. 4.50 (ISBN 0-686-59778-8). Balcom.
Balcomb, et al. Passive Solar Design Handbook: Vol. 2, Passive Solar Design Analysis. 428p. 1981. pap. 44.50x (ISBN 0-89934-128-4, A-015). Solar Energy Info.
Balcomb, D., jt. auth. see Los Alamos Scientific Laboratory, Solar Energy Group.
Balcomb, D., et al. Passive Solar Design Handbook: Passive Solar Design Analysis, Vol. 3. 668p. 1984. pap. 39.50x (ISBN 0-89934-203-5, A-923). Solar Energy Info.
--Passive Solar Design Handbook: Vol. 2, Passive Solar Design Analysis; Vol. 3, Passive Solar Design Analysis (Cont.) 1096p. (Vols. 2 & 3 in one binding). 1983. Repr. of 1982 ed. 89.50x (ISBN 0-89934-201-9, A-922). Solar Energy Info.
Balcomb, J. D., et al. Passive Solar Heating & Cooling: Proceedings of the Conference & Workshop, May 1976, Albuquerque, New Mexico. Keller, M. H., ed. 355p. pap. text ed. cancelled (ISBN 0-89553-108-9). Am Solar Energy.
Balcomb, J. Douglas, et al. Passive Solar Design Handbook. Jones, R., ed. (Passive Solar Design Handbook Ser.: Vol. 3, 1980). 668p. 1983. pap. text ed. 25.00x (ISBN 0-89553-106-2). Am Solar Energy.
Balcomb, Kenneth C. A Boy's Albuquerque, 1898-1912. LC 79-2774. (Illus.). 1980. 10.95 (ISBN 0-8263-0525-3). U of NM Pr.
Balcomb, Mary. Nicolai Fechin. LC 75-11161. (Illus.). 176p. 1975. 40.00 (ISBN 0-87358-374-4). Northland.
Balcomb, Mary N. William F. Reese. LC 83-72443. (Illus.). 176p. 1984. 60.00 (ISBN 0-916029-00-X); Ltd. Ed. 250.00 (ISBN 0-916029-01-8). Blue Raven Pub Co.
Balcombe, George. History of Building: Styles, Methods & Materials. (Mitchell's Building Ser.). (Illus.). 120p. 1985. pap. 16.95 (ISBN 0-7134-2186-X, Pub. by Batsford England); 26.00 (ISBN 0-7134-2187-8, Pub. by Batsford England). David & Charles.
Balcon, Michael, et al. Twenty Years of British Film: 1925-1945. LC 73-169326. (National Cinema Ser.). (Illus.). 120p. 1972. Repr. of 1947 ed. 18.00 (ISBN 0-405-03890-9). Ayer Co Pubs.
Bald, Marjory A. Women-Writers of the Nineteenth Century. LC 63-8356. 1963. Repr. of 1923 ed. 17.00x (ISBN 0-8462-0342-1). Russell.
Bald, R. C. Literary Friendships in the Age of Wordsworth. 1968. lib. bdg. 23.00 (ISBN 0-374-90342-5). Octagon.
Bald, R. C., ed. The Knave in Grain. LC 82-45712. Repr. of 1640 ed. 40.00 (ISBN 0-404-63112-6). AMS Pr.
Bald, R. C., ed. see Coleridge, Samuel T.
Bald, R. C., ed. see Shakespeare, William.
Bald, Robert C. Bibliographical Studies in the Beaumont & Fletcher Folio of Sixteen Forty-Seven. 1938. lib. bdg. 15.00 (ISBN 0-8414-1790-3). Folcroft.
--Donne's Influence in English Literature. 1932. 11.25 (ISBN 0-8446-1040-2). Peter Smith.
Bald, Robert C., ed. Six Elizabethan Plays. Incl. Tamburlaine, Pt. 1. Marlowe, Christopher; Shoemaker's Holiday. Dekker, Thomas; Knight of the Burning Pestle. Beaumont, Francis & Fletcher, John.; Epicoene. Jonson, Ben; Duchess of Malfi. Webster, John; Broken Heart. Ford, John. LC 63-4440. (YA) (gr. 9up). 1963. pap. 5.95 (ISBN 0-395-05135-5, RivEd). HM.
Bald, Robert C., ed. see Shakespeare, William.
Bald, S. Novelists & Political Consciousness: Literary Expression of Indian Nationalism 1919-1947. 175p. 1982. text ed. 18.00x (ISBN 0-391-02713-1). Humanities.
Bald, Suresht R. Novelists & Political Consciousness: Literary Expression of Indian Nationalism, 1919-1947. 1982. 17.50x (ISBN 0-8364-0921-3, Pub. by Chanakya). South Asia Bks.
Bald, Wolf-Dietrich & Ilson, Robert, eds. Studies in English Usage: The Resources of a Present-Day English Corpus for Linguistic Analysis. (Forum Linguisticum: Vol. 6). 230p. 1977. pap. 22.30 (ISBN 3-261-01701-5). P Lang Pubs.
Balda, Wesley. Heirs of the Same Promise: Using Acts as a Study Guide for Evangelizing Ethnic America. 1984. 3.50 (ISBN 0-912552-44-1). MARC.
Baldacchino, Joseph. Economics & the Moral Order. LC 84-62819. 43p. (Orig.). 1985. pap. 4.00 (ISBN 0-932783-00-7). Natl Human Inst.
Baldaia, Peter J., jt. auth. see Brockton Art Museum.
Baldamus, C. A. & Koch, K. M., eds. Biocompatibility in Hemodialysis. (Contributions to Nephrology: Vol. 36). (Illus.). viii, 140p. 1983. pap. 41.00 (ISBN 3-8055-3601-1). S Karger.
Baldassare, Mark. The Growth Dilemma: Residents' Views & Local Population Change in the United States. LC 81-1499. 224p. 1981. 27.50x (ISBN 0-520-04302-2). U of Cal Pr.
--Residential Crowding in Urban America. LC 77-83102. 1979. 25.00x (ISBN 0-520-03563-1). U of Cal Pr.
Baldassare, Mark, ed. Cities & Urban Living. LC 82-19875. 336p. 1983. 39.00x (ISBN 0-231-05502-1); pap. 13.00x (ISBN 0-231-05503-X). Columbia U Pr.
Baldassarre, John E. The New, Fully Illustrated Book of the Most Dramatic Paintings in the Vatican. (Illus.). 127p. 1982. 121.45 (ISBN 0-89266-323-5). Am Classical Coll Pr.
Baldasty, Richard. The Psychiatric Exam & Other Tales. 118p. (Orig.). 1975. pap. 2.25 (ISBN 0-915112-07-8). Seattle Bk.
Baldauf, Richard B. A Handy Guide to Grammar & Punctuation. (Programmed Instruction - Communications Skills Ser.). 160p. (Prog. Bk.). 1973. pap. text ed. 11.95 (ISBN 0-201-00382-1). Addison-Wesley.
Baldauski, Karen. The Cat Coloring Book. (Illus.). pap. 2.25 (ISBN 0-486-24011-8). Dover.
Baldausky, Karen, jt. auth. see Gos, Francois.
Baldegger, Markus & Mueller, Martin. Kontaktschwelle Deutsch als Fremdsprache. 504p. pap. 32.50 (ISBN 3-468-49450-5). Langenscheidt.
Baldensperger, Fernand. Mouvement des idees dans l'emigration francaise, 1789-1815, 2 vols. (Research & Source Works Ser: No. 178). 1968. Repr. of 1924 ed. Set. 47.00 (ISBN 0-8337-0157-6). B Franklin.
Balder, A. P. Mariner's Atlas: Long Island Sound, the South Shore & Southern New England, Vol. 1. (Illus.). 1984. pap. 24.95 (ISBN 0-317-11502-2). Chartcrafters Pubs.
--Mariner's Atlas: Maine. (Illus.). 1985. pap. 29.95 (ISBN 0-930151-05-4). Chartcrafters Pubs.
--Mariner's Atlas: New England. (Mariner's Atlas Ser.). (Illus.). 120p. (Orig.). 1985. pap. 29.95 (ISBN 0-930151-01-1). Chartcrafters Pubs.
--Mariner's Atlas: New Jersey, Delaware & Maryland. (Illus.). 1985. pap. 29.95 (ISBN 0-930151-04-6). Chartcrafters Pubs.
--Mariner's Atlas: South Florida. (Illus.). 1985. pap. 29.95 (ISBN 0-930151-02-X). Chartcrafters Pubs.
Balderas, Eduardo, tr. see Dean, Bessie.
Balderrama, Francisco E. In Defense of La Raza: The Los Angeles Mexican Consulate & Mexican Community, 1929-1936. LC 82-11121. 137p. 1982. pap. 7.95x (ISBN 0-8165-0787-2). U of Ariz Pr.
Balderson, Eileen & Goodlad, Douglas. Backstairs Life in a Country House. (Illus.). 128p. 1982. 14.95 (ISBN 0-7153-8021-4). David & Charles.
Balderson, J., jt. auth. see Rentz, D. C.
Balderson, John L., jt. auth. see Davis, Reba B.
Balderston, Daniel, tr. see Bianco, Jose.
Balderston, F. E. Regulation of Marketing & the Public Interest. 36.00 (ISBN 0-08-025563-9). Pergamon.
Balderston, Fred. Thrifts in Crisis: Structural Transformation of the Savings & Loan Industry. Rosen, Kenneth T., ed. (Real Estate Urban Economics Ser.). 216p. 1985. 29.95 (ISBN 0-88730-018-9). Ballinger Pub.
Balderston, Frederick E. Managing Today's University. LC 74-9111. (Higher Education Ser.). 272p. 1974. 18.95x (ISBN 0-87589-236-1). Jossey-Bass.
Balderston, Frederick E., et al. Proposition Thirteen, Property Transfers, & the Real Estate Markets. LC 79-10332. (Research Report: No. 79-1). 1979. pap. 3.00x (ISBN 0-87772-264-1). Inst Gov Stud Berk.
Balderston, Jack. Improving Office Operations: A Primer for Professionals. (Illus.). 350p. 1985. 34.95 (ISBN 0-442-21310-7). Van Nos Reinhold.
Balderston, Jack, et al. Modern Management Techniques in Engineers & R & D. 320p. 1984. 39.95 (ISBN 0-442-26436-4). Van Nos Reinhold.
Balderston, Judith & Wilson, Alan. Malnourished Children of the Rural Poor: The Web of Food, Health, Education, Fertility, & Agricultural Production. LC 81-3483. 204p. 1981. 24.95 (ISBN 0-86569-071-5). Auburn Hse.
Balderston, Katharine C. A Census of the Manuscripts of Oliver Goldsmith. 1978. Repr. lib. bdg. 15.00 (ISBN 0-8495-0375-2). Arden Lib.
--Collected Letters of Oliver Goldsmith. LC 75-42214. 1928. lib. bdg. 27.50 (ISBN 0-8414-3334-8). Folcroft.
Balderston, Katharine C. A Census of the Manuscripts of Oliver Goldsmith. LC 76-41731. 1976. lib. bdg. 16.50 (ISBN 0-8414-1789-X). Folcroft.
--The Collected Letters of Oliver Goldsmith. 189p. 1980. Repr. of 1928 ed. lib. bdg. 20.00 (ISBN 0-8492-3757-2). R West.
--The History & Sources of Percy's Memoir of Goldsmith, 1926. Bd. with Collected Letters. Goldsmith. 1928. 22.00 (ISBN 0-527-04700-7). Kraus Repr.
Balderston, Katherine G., ed. see Goldsmith, Oliver.
Balderston, Marion, ed. see Claypoole, James.
Baldeschwieler, John D., ed. Chemistry & Chemical Engineering in the People's Republic of China. LC 79-11217. 1979. pap. 12.95 (ISBN 0-8412-0502-7). Am Chemical.
Baldessari, John. Close-Cropped Tales. LC 81-50892. (Illus.). 88p. (Orig.). 1981. pap. 6.50 (ISBN 0-939784-00-9). CEPA Gall.
Baldessarini, Ross J. Biomedical Aspects of Depression & Its Treatment. LC 82-22659. (Illus.). 184p. 1983. casebound 19.50x (ISBN 0-88048-004-1, 48-004-1). Am Psychiatric.
--Chemotherapy in Psychiatry. 1977. 14.00x (ISBN 0-674-11380-2). Harvard U Pr.
--Chemotherapy in Psychiatry. rev. & enl. ed. (Illus.). 416p. 1985. text ed. 25.00x (ISBN 0-674-11383-7). Harvard U Pr.
Baldi, Philip. An Introduction to the Indo-European Languages. LC 82-19218. 208p. 1983. pap. 12.95x (ISBN 0-8093-1091-0). S Ill U Pr.
Baldi, Philip & Werth, Ronald N., eds. Readings in Historical Phonology: Chapters in the Theory of Sound Change. LC 77-13895. 1978. lib. bdg. 27.50x (ISBN 0-271-00525-4); pap. text ed. 12.50x (ISBN 0-271-00539-4). Pa St U Pr.
Baldi, Sergio see Muir, Kenneth.
Baldick, Chris. The Social Mission of English Criticism, Eighteen Forty-Eight to Nineteen Thirty-Two. (Oxford English Monographs). 1983. 37.50x (ISBN 0-19-812821-5). Oxford U Pr.
Baldick, Robert, tr. see Barrault, Jean-Louis.
Baldick, Robert, tr. see Flaubert, Gustave.
Baldick, Robert, tr. see Huysmans, Joris K.
Baldick, Robert, tr. see Manet, Eduardo.
Baldick, Robert, tr. see Villiers de l'Isle-Adam, P.
Baldinger, Kurt. Semantic Theory. 1980. 32.50 (ISBN 0-312-71258-8). St Martin.
Baldini, Baccio. Discorso Sopra la Mascherata Della Genealogia Delg'Iddei, Repr. Of 1565 Ed. Bd. with Discorso Sopra Li Dei De'Gentili. Zucchi, Jacopo. Repr. of 1602 ed. LC 75-27852. (Renaissance & the Gods Ser.: Vol. 10). (Illus.). 1976. lib. bdg. 88.00 (ISBN 0-8240-2059-6). Garland Pub.
Baldini, Gabriele. The Story of Giuseppe Verdi. Parker, Roger, tr. from Ital. LC 79-41376. 330p. 1980. 47.50 (ISBN 0-521-22911-1); pap. 13.95 (ISBN 0-521-29712-5). Cambridge U Pr.
Baldini, Mario & Ebbe, Shirley, eds. The Platelets: Production, Function, Transfusion, & Storage. LC 74-8749. (Illus.). 418p. 1974. 90.50 (ISBN 0-8089-0845-6, 790378). Grune.
Baldini, Massimo. La Semantica Generale. 352p. (Ital.). 1976. pap. 7.00 (ISBN 0-317-34320-3). Inst Gen Seman.
Baldini, Pier R., jt. auth. see Lebano, Edoardo A.
Baldini, Umberto. Toscana. Carpanini, Rudolf, tr. from It. (Illus.). 512p. 1976. 50.00 (ISBN 0-8390-0179-7). Abner Schram Ltd.
Baldinucci, Filippo. Vocabolario toscano dell'arte del disegno. (Documents of Art & Architectural History, Ser. 1: Vol. 5). (Ital.). 1980. Repr. of 1681 ed. 35.00x (ISBN 0-89371-105-5). Broude Intl Edns.
Baldisan, James R. A Manual of Sex & Sun Worship Rituals. (Illus.). 157p. 1983. 77.85x (ISBN 0-86650-065-0). Gloucester Art.
Baldner, Ralph W. Bibliography of Seventeenth-Century French Prose Fiction. xiv, 197p. 1967. 18.75x (ISBN 0-87352-016-5, Z3). Modern Lang.
Baldo-Ceolin, M. Weak Interactions. (Enrico Fermi Summer School Ser.: Vol. 71). 564p. 1980. 108.50 (ISBN 0-444-85286-7). Elsevier.
Baldock, Cora V. & Lally, James. Sociology in Australia & New Zealand: Theory & Methods. LC 72-778. (Contributions in Sociology: No. 16). (Illus.). 328p. 1975. lib. bdg. 29.95x (ISBN 0-8371-6126-6, BSA/). Greenwood.
Baldock, Cora V., jt. ed. see Cass, Bettina.
Baldock, G. R. & Bridgeman, T. The Mathematical Theory of Wave Motion. (Mathematics & Its Applications Ser.). 261p. 1983. pap. 32.95 (ISBN 0-470-27464-6). Halsted Pr.
Baldree, J. Martin. Sunday School Growth. 1971. 5.25 (ISBN 0-87148-761-6); pap. 4.25 (ISBN 0-87148-762-4). Pathway Pr.
Baldrick, Robert, tr. Pages from the Goncourt Journal. (Lives & Letters Ser.). 464p. 1985. pap. 8.95 (ISBN 0-14-057014-4). Penguin.
Baldridge, Alan, jt. auth. see Davis, John.
Baldridge, Ann, jt. auth. see Manthei, Howard.
Baldridge, C. Le Roy, jt. auth. see Bankhage, Hilman R.
Baldridge, Cyrus L., jt. auth. see Singer, Caroline.
Baldridge, J. V. Power & Conflict in the University: Research in the Sociology of Complex Organizations. LC 70-140548. Repr. of 1971 ed. 48.30 (ISBN 0-8357-9957-3, 2013113). Bks Demand UMI.
Baldridge, J. Victor. Sociology: A Critical Approach to Power, Conflict, & Change. 2nd ed. 547p. 1980. text ed. 29.50 (ISBN 0-471-04708-2); student action manual 14.95 (ISBN 0-471-07689-9); test avail. (ISBN 0-471-04568-3). Wiley.
Baldridge, J. Victor & Tierney, Michael L. New Approaches to Management: Creating Practical Systems of Management Information & Management by Objectives. LC 79-88105. (Higher Education Ser.). 1979. text ed. 18.95x (ISBN 0-87589-420-8). Jossey-Bass.
Baldridge, J. Victor, jt. auth. see Kemerer, Frank R.
Baldridge, J. Victor & Deal, Terrence, eds. The Dynamics of Organizational Change in Education. Rev. ed. LC 82-62033. 504p. 1983. 28.00x (ISBN 0-8211-0134-X); text ed. 25.50x ten or more copies. McCutchan.
Baldridge, J. Victor, et al. Policy Making & Effective Leadership: A National Study of Academic Management. LC 77-82909. (Higher Education Ser.). 1978. text ed. 18.95x (ISBN 0-87589-351-1). Jossey-Bass.
Baldridge, Letitia. Amy Vanderbilt Complete Book of Etiquette. rev. ed. LC 77-16896. 1978. 15.95 (ISBN 0-385-13375-8); thumb-indexed 17.95 (ISBN 0-385-14238-2). Doubleday.
Baldridge, Victor J., jt. ed. see Riley, Gary L.
Baldrige, Letitia. Letitia Baldrige's Complete Guide to Executive Manners. 640p. 1985. 22.95 (ISBN 0-89256-290-0). Rawson Assocs.
Baldry, George. The Rabbit Skin Cap. 256p. pap. 5.95 (ISBN 0-85115-226-0). Academy Chi Pubs.
--The Rabbitskin Cap. Haggard, Lilias R., ed. (Illus.). 258p. 1979. Repr. of 1939 ed. 12.75 (ISBN 0-85115-045-4, Pub. by Boydell & Brewer). Longwood Pub Group.
Baldry, H. C. The Greek Tragic Theatre. (Illus.). 160p. 1973. pap. 5.95x (ISBN 0-393-00585-2). Norton.
--Unity of Mankind in Greek Thought. 1965. 39.50 (ISBN 0-521-04091-4). Cambridge U Pr.
Baldry, J. C. General Equilibrium Analysis: An Introduction to the Two Sector Model. LC 80-82652. 228p. 1980. 39.95 (ISBN 0-470-27024-1, Pub. by Halsted Pr). Wiley.
Baldry, P. E. The Battle Against Bacteria: A Fresh Look. LC 76-639. (Illus.). 140p. 1976. 29.95 (ISBN 0-521-21268-5). Cambridge U Pr.
--The Battle Against Heart Disease: A Physician Traces the History of Man's Achievements in this Field for the General Reader. LC 75-108098. pap. 50.00 (ISBN 0-317-28415-0, 2022434). Bks Demand UMI.
Balducci, Carolyn. Is There a Life after Graduation, Henry Birnbaum? (Illus.). (gr. 7 up). 1971. 7.95 (ISBN 0-395-12749-1). HM.
Balducci Pegolotti, F. Practica Della Mercatura. Evans, Allan, ed. (MAA.P). 1936. 32.00 (ISBN 0-527-01695-0). Kraus Repr.
Balducelli, Roger, tr. see Galot, Jean.
Balduf, W. V. The Bionomics of Entomophagous Insects. (The Bionomics of Entomophagous Insects other than Coleoptera Ser.: Vol. 2). 338p. Repr. of 1974 ed. 60.00x (ISBN 0-317-07033-9, Pub. by EW Classey UK). State Mutual Bk.
Baldus, David C. & Cole, James W. Statistical Proof of Discrimination. (Illus.). 1979. 75.00x (ISBN 0-07-003470-2). McGraw.
Baldus, Harold, jt. auth. see Baldus, Phil.
Baldus, P. Homage to the Alphabet. 1986. pap. cancelled (ISBN 0-442-21274-7). Van Nos Reinhold.
Baldus, Phil & Baldus, Harold. Homage to the Alphabet: Over Fourteen Hundred Large-Format Complete Showings of Headline Typefaces. 2nd ed. LC 85-60114. (Illus.). 652p. 1985. pap. 30.00 (ISBN 0-933107-00-5). Phils Photo.

Baldwin. A Separate Peace (Knowles) (Book Notes Ser.). 1984. pap. 2.50 (ISBN 0-8120-3441-4). Barron.

Baldwin, A. The Coinages of Lapsakos. (Illus.). 111p. 1980. 30.00 (ISBN 0-916710-70-X). Obol Intl.

--Facing Heads on Ancient Greek Coins. (Illus.). 1982. pap. 6.00 (ISBN 0-942666-06-2). S J Durst.

Baldwin, A., et al. Sixteen-Bit Microprocessors. LC 81-50564. 352p. 1981. pap. 15.95 (ISBN 0-672-21805-4, 21805). Sams.

Baldwin, Agnes. The Electrum & Silver Coins of Chios, Issued During the Sixth, Fifth & Fourth Centuries B.C. A Chronological Study. (Illus.). 60p. 1979. Repr. of 1915 ed. 20.00 (ISBN 0-916710-61-0). Obol Intl.

--Symbolism on Greek Coins. LC 76-62839. (Illus.). 1977. Repr. of 1915 ed. lib. bdg. 15.00 (ISBN 0-915262-10-X). S J Durst.

Baldwin, Agnes L. First Settlers of South Carolina, 1670-1700. 264p. 1985. 25.00 (ISBN 0-89308-551-0); pap. 20.00 (ISBN 0-317-19610-3). Southern Hist Pr.

Baldwin, Alex. The Last Heroes: Men At War, Bk. 1. 1985. pap. 3.50 (ISBN 0-671-49778-2). PB.

Baldwin, Alfred L. Theories of Child Development. 2nd ed. LC 80-24517. 582p. 1980. text ed. 35.95 (ISBN 0-471-04583-7). Wiley.

Baldwin, Allen J. & Hess, Karen M. A Programmed Review of Engineering Fundamentals. 287p. 1978. pap. 18.95 (ISBN 0-442-21389-1). Van Nos Reinhold.

Baldwin, Andrew, jt. auth. see McCaffer, Ronald.

Baldwin, Anna P. The Theme of Government in "Piers Plowman". (Piers Plowman Studies: No. 1). 114p. 1981. 35.00x (ISBN 0-85991-073-3, BAB-03695, Pub. by Boydell & Brewer). Biblio Dist.

Baldwin, Anne N. A Little Time. LC 77-27764. (gr. 3-5). 1978. 8.95 (ISBN 0-670-43392-6). Viking.

Baldwin, B. Studies on Late Roman & Byzantine History, Literature & Language. (London Studies in Classical Philology: Vol. 12). 502p. 1984. text ed. 69.50x (ISBN 90-70265-56-7, Pub. by Gieben Holland). Humanities.

Baldwin, B. A., et al. Report on Research & Development in Relation to Farm Animal Welfare. (Animal Management Ser.). 92p. 1981. pap. 17.95x (ISBN 0-8176-1241-6). Birkhauser.

Baldwin, Barbara. Celebrate the Seasons. Sussman, Ellen, ed. (Illus.). 68p. (gr. 1-6). 1983. pap. text ed. 7.95 (ISBN 0-933606-23-0, MS-621). Monkey Sisters.

Baldwin, Barbie, jt. auth. see LaFray, Joyce.

Baldwin, Barry. The Philogelos or Laughter-Lover. (London Studies in Classical Philology Ser.: Vol. 10). 134p. 1983. text ed. 28.25x (ISBN 90-70265-45-1, Pub. by J C Gieben). Humanities.

--Studies in Aulua Gellius. 130p. 1975. 6.50x (ISBN 0-87291-071-7). Coronado Pr.

Baldwin, Barry, tr. Timarion. LC 84-10426. 161p. (Greek.). 1984. 18.95 (ISBN 0-8143-1771-5). Wayne St U Pr.

Baldwin, Betty C., ed. see American Family Records Association.

Baldwin, Bettye, jt. auth. see Gabriel, Joyce.

Baldwin, Bill. The Helmsman. 320p. (Orig.). 1985. pap. 2.95 (ISBN 0-445-20027-8, Pub. by Popular Lib). Warner Bks.

Baldwin, Bird T., et al. Farm Children: Investigation of Rural Child Life in Selected Areas of Iowa. LC 75-169372. (Family in America Ser). (Illus.). 1972. Repr. of 1930 ed. 22.00 (ISBN 0-405-03848-8). Ayer Co Pubs.

Baldwin, Bruce, jt. auth. see Burgess, Ann W.

Baldwin, Bruce A. It's All in Your Head: Lifestyle Management Strategies for Busy People! (Illus.). 270p. (Orig.). 1985. pap. 8.95 (ISBN 0-933583-00-1). Direction Dynamics.

Baldwin, C. & Paul, H. G., eds. English Poems. (Poetry Library). 416p. 1985. Repr. of 1908 ed. 39.50x (ISBN 0-89609-244-5). Granger Bk.

Baldwin, C. S. Medieval Rhetoric & Poetic to Fourteen Hundred. 1959. 11.25 (ISBN 0-8446-1043-7). Peter Smith.

--Renaissance Literary Theory & Practice. 1959. 11.25 (ISBN 0-8446-1042-9). Peter Smith.

Baldwin, C. Stephen, jt. auth. see Duza, M. Badrud.

Baldwin, Carol. The Buses Roll. Underhill, Linn, ed. (Illus.). 112p. 1974. pap. 4.95x (ISBN 0-393-05535-3). Norton.

Baldwin, Carol, jt. ed. see Wright, Jonathan V.

Baldwin, Charles. An Ambassador's Journey: An Exploration of People & Culture. (American Values Projected Abroad Ser.: Vol. XV). 148p. 1984. lib. bdg. 17.75 (ISBN 0-8191-3806-1); pap. text ed. 7.50 (ISBN 0-8191-3807-X). U Pr of Amer.

Baldwin, Charles C. Men Who Make Our Novels. facs. ed. rev. ed. LC 67-30174. (Essay Index Reprint Ser). 1924. 19.50 (ISBN 0-8369-0171-1). Ayer Co Pubs.

--Men Who Make Our Novels. 1924. 14.50 (ISBN 0-8274-2725-5). R West.

--Stanford White. LC 78-150512. (Architecture & Decorative Art Ser.: Vol. 39). 1971. Repr. of 1931 ed. lib. bdg. 45.00 (ISBN 0-306-70138-3). Da Capo.

--Stanford White. LC 75-31800. (Architectural & Decorative Art Ser.). 1976. pap. 6.95 (ISBN 0-306-80031-4). Da Capo.

Baldwin, Charles S. Ancient Rhetoric & Poetic. 1959. 10.25 (ISBN 0-8446-1041-0). Peter Smith.

--Ancient Rhetoric & Poetic, Interpreted from Representative Works. LC 77-90467. 1971. Repr. of 1924 ed. lib. bdg. 18.75 (ISBN 0-8371-3071-9, BAAR). Greenwood.

--Introduction to English Medieval Literature. LC 72-194018. 1922. lib. bdg. 20.00 (ISBN 0-8414-1663-X). Folcroft.

--Medieval Rhetoric & Poetic to Fourteen Hundred. LC 71-144865. xvii, 321p. 1972. Repr. of 1928 ed. 39.00 (ISBN 0-403-00852-2). Scholarly.

--Three Medieval Centuries of Literature in England, 1100-1400. LC 68-58890. 1968. Repr. of 1932 ed. 12.50x (ISBN 0-87753-003-3). Phaeton.

Baldwin, Christina. One to One: Self-Understanding Through Journal Writing. LC 76-58537. 204p. 1977. 8.95_o.p; pap. 5.95 (ISBN 0-87131-294-8). M Evans.

Baldwin, Christina, jt. auth. see Burmyn, Lynne.

Baldwin, Christopher. The Major Problems of the World at the End of the 20th Century & Possible Solutions to Avoid an Epochal Catastrophe. (Illus.). 149p. 1980. 69.75x (ISBN 0-930008-65-0). Inst Econ Pol.

Baldwin, Christopher C. Diary of Christopher Columbus Baldwin: Librarian of the American Antiquarian Society, 1829-1835. (Transactions & Collections of the American Antiquarian Society, Vol. 8). Repr. of 1901 ed. 35.00 (ISBN 0-384-03132-3). Johnson Repr.

Baldwin, Clare C. Organization & Administration of Substitute-Teaching Service in City-School Systems. LC 75-176533. (Columbia University. Teachers College. Contributions to Education: No. 615). Repr. of 1934 ed. 22.50 (ISBN 0-404-55615-9). AMS Pr.

Baldwin, Claudia. Nigerian Literature: A Bibliography of Criticism, 1952-1976. 1980. lib. bdg. 22.00 (ISBN 0-8161-8418-6, Hall Reference). G K Hall.

Baldwin, Clive, compiled by. Management: A Selected Annotated Bibliography. 1979. 125.00x (ISBN 0-905440-89-7, Pub. by MCB Pubns). State Mutual Bk.

Baldwin, D. C., jt. auth. see Broughton, L. N.

Baldwin, Dane L. & Broughton, L. N. Concordance to the Poems of John Keats. 1963. 48.00 (ISBN 0-8446-1044-5). Peter Smith.

Baldwin, Dave. Prescription for a Broken Heart: Leader's Guide. (Study & Grow Electives). 64p. 1985. pap. 3.95 (ISBN 0-8307-1017-5, 6102017). Regal.

Baldwin, David A. Economic Statecraft. LC 85-42672. 456p. 1985. text ed. 45.00x (ISBN 0-691-07687-1); pap. 12.50x (ISBN 0-691-10175-2). Princeton U Pr.

Baldwin, David A., ed. America in an Interdependent World: Problems of United States. LC 75-41909. pap. 93.00 (ISBN 0-317-20024-0, 2023232). Bks Demand UMI.

Baldwin, David M. Friendless American Male: Leader's Guide. 48p. 1984. pap. 3.95 (ISBN 0-8307-0991-6, 6101914). Regal.

Baldwin, Deirdra. Totemic. (Burning Deck Poetry Ser.). 32p. 1983. pap. 3.00 (ISBN 0-930901-13-4). Burning Deck.

Baldwin, Deirdra & Davis, Gene. Inside Outside. 40p. 1983. pap. 35.00 spec. signed ed. (ISBN 0-915380-17-X); unsigned 10.00. Word Works.

Baldwin, Deirdra B. Gathering Time. (Ser. One). 1975. pap. 2.00 (ISBN 0-931846-00-5). Wash Writers Pub.

Baldwin, Dorothy. Understanding Your Baby. 128p. 1982. 20.00x (ISBN 0-85223-156-3, Pub. by Ebury Pr England). State Mutual Bk.

--Understanding Your Baby. 144p. 1983. 8.00x (ISBN 0-7005-0621-7, Pub. by NFER Nelson UK). Taylor & Francis.

Baldwin, Dorothy & Lister, Claire. Your Heart & Lungs. LC 83-72784. (You & Your Body Ser.). (Illus.). 32p. (gr. 3-5). 1984. PLB 8.90 (ISBN 0-531-04801-2, Pub. by Bookwright Pr). Watts.

Baldwin, Ed. Makin' Things for Kids. LC 78-73845. 1980. soft cover 8.95 (ISBN 0-916752-33-X). Dorison Hse.

Baldwin, Ed & Baldwin, Stevie. Building Birdhouses & Bird-Feeders: Attract Birds to Your Backyard with Birdhouses & Feeders You've Built Yourself. LC 84-26050. (Family Workshop Bk.). (Illus.). 128p. 1985. 12.95 (ISBN 0-385-19712-8). Doubleday.

--The First Family Computer Book: A Commonsense Introduction. (A Family Workshop Bk.). (Illus.). 240p. 1984. pap. 12.95 (ISBN 0-8019-7498-4). Chilton.

--More Great Pantyhose Crafts. LC 84-22282. (Family Workshop Bk.). 128p. 1985. 16.95 (ISBN 0-385-19934-1). Doubleday.

--The Quilted Clothing Collection. LC 83-43304. 160p. (Orig.). 1984. pap. 10.95 (ISBN 0-8019-7507-7). Chilton.

--Riding Machines for Kids. LC 83-43300. 156p. 1984. pap. 10.95 (ISBN 0-8019-7506-9). Chilton.

--Scrap Fabric Crafts. (Illus.). 160p. 1982. pap. 7.95 (ISBN 0-89586-168-2). H P Bks.

--The Weepeeple: A Unique Adventure in Crafts in America. (Illus.). 160p. 1983. 17.95 (ISBN 0-399-12813-1, Putnam). Putnam Pub Group.

Baldwin, Ed & Baldwin, Stevie, eds. Old-Fashioned Wood Toys. 1984. 17.50 (ISBN 0-87851-306-X, Hearst Bk). Morrow.

Baldwin, Edward N., jt. auth. see Niebel, Benjamin W.

Baldwin, Elizabeth L., tr. see Groos, Karl.

Baldwin, Emily, jt. auth. see Glade, William P.

Baldwin, Ernest. An Introduction to Comparative Biochemistry. 4th ed. LC 64-21524. pap. 49.80 (ISBN 0-317-26096-0, 2024418). Bks Demand UMI.

Baldwin, Ethel M. & Benson, David V. Henrietta Mears & How She Did It. 352p. pap. 3.95 (ISBN 0-8307-0018-8, 5000505). Regal.

Baldwin, Ewart M. Geology of Oregon. 3rd ed. LC 76-4346. (Illus.). 1981. perfect bdg. 12.95 (ISBN 0-8403-2321-2). Kendall-Hunt.

Baldwin, Faith. Adam's Eden. 202p. Repr. of 1977 ed. lib. bdg. 12.95x (ISBN 0-88411-630-1, Pub. by Aeonian Pr). Amereon Ltd.

--Alimony. 1976. Repr. of 1928 ed. 16.95x (ISBN 0-88411-616-6, Pub. by Aeonian Pr). Amereon Ltd.

--American Family. 390p. Repr. of 1934 ed. lib. bdg. 16.95x (ISBN 0-88411-629-8, Pub. by Aeonian Pr). Amereon Ltd.

--Arizona Star. 1976. Repr. of 1945 ed. lib. bdg. 17.95x (ISBN 0-88411-601-8, Pub. by Aeonian Pr). Amereon Ltd.

--Blue Horizon. 1976. Repr. of 1941 ed. lib. bdg. 16.95 (ISBN 0-88411-618-2, Pub. by Aeonian Pr). Amereon Ltd.

--Breath of Life. 1976. Repr. of 1942 ed. lib. bdg. 16.95 (ISBN 0-88411-617-4, Pub. by Aeonian Pr). Amereon Ltd.

--Change of Heart. 1974. Repr. of 1944 ed. lib. bdg. 16.95 (ISBN 0-88411-606-9, Pub. by Aeonian Pr). Amereon Ltd.

--Face Towards the Spring. 219p. Repr. of 1956 ed. lib. bdg. 14.95 (ISBN 0-88411-628-X, Pub. by Aeonian Pr). Amereon Ltd.

--Garden Oats. 1976. Repr. of 1929 ed. lib. bdg. 16.95 (ISBN 0-88411-607-7, Pub. by Aeonian Pr). Amereon Ltd.

--Give Love the Air. 286p. Repr. of 1947 ed. lib. bdg. 16.95 (ISBN 0-88411-626-3, Pub. by Aeonian Pr). Amereon Ltd.

--Give Love the Air. 1981. pap. 2.50 (ISBN 0-671-83092-9). PB.

--He Married a Doctor. 1980. pap. 2.50 (ISBN 0-671-83093-7). PB.

--He Married a Doctor. Large Print ed. LC 83-17925. 418p. 1983. Repr. of 1943 ed. 12.95 (ISBN 0-89621-482-6). Thorndike Pr.

--The Heart Has Wings. 317p. Repr. of 1930 ed. lib. bdg. 17.95 (ISBN 0-88411-627-1, Pub. by Aeonian Pr). Amereon Ltd.

--The Heart Has Wings. 1981. pap. 2.75 (ISBN 0-671-83094-5). PB.

--The High Road. 1976. Repr. of 1939 ed. lib. bdg. 16.95 (ISBN 0-88411-608-5, Pub. by Aeonian Pr). Amereon Ltd.

--Hotel Hostess. 1976. Repr. of 1938 ed. lib. bdg. 16.95 (ISBN 0-88411-609-3, Pub. by Aeonian Pr). Amereon Ltd.

--Judy: A Story of Divine Corners. 1976. Repr. of 1930 ed. lib. bdg. 15.95 (ISBN 0-88411-619-0, Pub. by Aeonian Pr). Amereon Ltd.

--Letty & the Law. 1976. Repr. of 1940 ed. lib. bdg. 15.95 (ISBN 0-88411-610-7, Pub. by Aeonian Pr). Amereon Ltd.

--The Lonely Man. 1981. pap. 2.50 (ISBN 0-671-83095-3). PB.

--Look Out for Liza. 1976. Repr. of 1950 ed. lib. bdg. 15.95 (ISBN 0-88411-620-4, Pub. by Aeonian Pr). Amereon Ltd.

--Marry for Money. 1976. Repr. of 1948 ed. lib. bdg. 15.95 (ISBN 0-88411-621-2, Pub. by Aeonian Pr). Amereon Ltd.

--Men Are Such Fools. 1976. Repr. of 1936 ed. lib. bdg. 16.95 (ISBN 0-88411-611-5, Pub. by Aeonian Pr). Amereon Ltd.

--The Moon's Our Home. 1976. Repr. of 1936 ed. lib. bdg. 17.95 (ISBN 0-88411-602-6, Pub. by Aeonian Pr). Amereon Ltd.

--No Bed of Roses. 224p. 1981. pap. 2.50 (ISBN 0-671-83096-1). PB.

--No Private Heaven. 1976. Repr. of 1946 ed. lib. bdg. 14.95x (ISBN 0-88411-622-0). Amereon Ltd.

--The Office Wife. 1976. Repr. of 1930 ed. lib. bdg. 15.95x (ISBN 0-88411-603-4, Pub. by Aeonian Pr). Amereon Ltd.

--Rehearsal for Love. 1976. Repr. of 1940 ed. lib. bdg. 17.95x (ISBN 0-88411-612-3, Pub. by Aeonian Pr). Amereon Ltd.

--Skyscraper. 1976. Repr. of 1931 ed. lib. bdg. 17.95x (ISBN 0-88411-623-9, Pub. by Aeonian Pr). Amereon Ltd.

--Sleeping Beauty. 1976. Repr. of 1947 ed. lib. bdg. 15.95x (ISBN 0-88411-624-7, Pub. by Aeonian Pr). Amereon Ltd.

--Station Wagon Set. 1976. Repr. of 1939 ed. lib. bdg. 20.95x (ISBN 0-88411-604-2, Pub. by Aeonian Pr). Amereon Ltd.

--That Man Is Mine. 1976. Repr. of 1937 ed. lib. bdg. 17.95x (ISBN 0-88411-613-1, Pub. by Aeonian Pr). Amereon Ltd.

--Three Women. 1980. pap. 2.50 (ISBN 0-671-83098-8). PB.

--Twenty-Four Hours a Day. 1976. Repr. of 1937 ed. 17.95x (ISBN 0-88411-605-0, Pub. by Aeonian Pr). Amereon Ltd.

--White Collar Girl. 1976. Repr. of 1933 ed. lib. bdg. 17.95x (ISBN 0-88411-614-X, Pub. by Aeonian Pr). Amereon Ltd.

--White Magic. 1976. Repr. of 1939 ed. lib. bdg. 17.95x (ISBN 0-88411-615-8, Pub. by Aeonian Pr). Amereon Ltd.

--You Can't Escape. 1976. Repr. of 1943 ed. lib. bdg. 15.95x (ISBN 0-88411-625-5, Pub. by Aeonian Pr). Amereon Ltd.

Baldwin, Frances E. Sumptuary Legislation & Personal Regulation in England. LC 78-64119. (Johns Hopkins University. Studies in the Social Sciences. Forty-Fourth Ser. 1926: 1). Repr. of 1926 ed. 24.50 (ISBN 0-404-61233-4). AMS Pr.

Baldwin, Frank, ed. From Politics to Lifestyles: Japan in Print, Vol. I. (East Asia Papers: No. 35). 132p. 1984. 5.00 (ISBN 0-318-02247-8). Cornell China-Japan Pgm.

--From Politics to Lifestyles: Japan in Print II. Date not set. price not set. Cornell China-Japan Pgm.

--From Politics to Lifestyles: Japan in Print, I. (East Asia Papers: No. 35). 132p. 1984. 5.00 (ISBN 0-318-17868-0). Cornell China-Japan Pgm.

Baldwin, Frank, tr. see Ienaga, Saburo.

Baldwin, Frank, Jr., ed. see Noble, Harold J.

Baldwin, Fred D., et al. Conflicting Interests: Corporate-Governance Controversies. LC 83-48400. 224p. 1984. 24.50x (ISBN 0-669-07123-4). Lexington Bks.

Baldwin, Frederick C. & Watriss, Wendy V., photos by. Coming to Terms: The Texas German Hill Country. (Illus.). 160p. 1985. 24.95 (ISBN 0-940672-32-4). Shearer Pub.

Baldwin, George B. Beyond Nationalization: The Labor Problems of British Coal. LC 55-10966. (Wertheim Publications in Industrial Relations Ser). (Illus.). 1955. 20.00x (ISBN 0-674-06900-5). Harvard U Pr.

--Planning & Development in Iran. LC 67-18377. pap. 57.80 (ISBN 0-317-19825-4, 2023082). Bks Demand UMI.

Baldwin, George C. An Introduction to Nonlinear Optics. LC 69-16517. 155p. 1969. 27.50x (ISBN 0-306-30388-4, Plenum Pr); pap. 8.95 (ISBN 0-306-20004-X). Plenum Pub.

Baldwin, Gratia E. New Beatrice, or the Virtue That Counsels. LC 75-160011. Repr. of 1928 ed. 16.00 (ISBN 0-404-00469-5). AMS Pr.

Baldwin, H. A. Holiness & the Human Element. pap. 3.95 (ISBN 0-686-12876-1). Schmul Pub Co.

Baldwin, Hanson W. Tiger Jack. LC 78-61481. (Illus.). 1979. 12.95 (ISBN 0-88342-059-7). Old Army.

--World War One: An Outline History. (Illus.). 1962. 12.45i (ISBN 0-06-010190-3, HarpT). Har-Row.

Baldwin, Harriet & Ross-Larson, Bruce. The Developing World: Teaching Guide. (Toward a Better World Ser.). 1981. pap. 5.00 (ISBN 0-8213-0067-9). World Bank.

--Economic Summary: India. (Toward a Better World Ser.). 1981. pap. 1.00 (ISBN 0-8213-0068-7). World Bank.

--Economic Summary: Kenya. (Toward a Better World Ser.). 1981. pap. 1.00 (ISBN 0-8213-0071-7). World Bank.

--Economic Summary: Mexico. (Toward a Better World Ser.). (gr. 9-11). pap. 1.00 (ISBN 0-8213-0074-1). World Bank.

--The Rajasthan Canal Project. (Toward a Better World Ser.). 1981. pap. 3.00 (ISBN 0-8213-0069-5). World Bank.

--The Rajasthan Canal Project: Teaching Guide. (Toward a Better World Ser.). 1981. pap. 3.00 (ISBN 0-8213-0070-9). World Bank.

--Small-Scale Industries in Kenya. (Toward a Better World Ser.). 1981. pap. 3.00 (ISBN 0-8213-0072-5); teaching guide 3.00 (ISBN 0-8213-0073-3). World Bank.

--Tackling Poverty in Rural Mexico. (Toward a Better World Ser.). 1981. pap. 3.00 (ISBN 0-8213-0025-3). World Bank.

Baldwin, Harry G. & Holz, William B. Accounting for Value As Well As Original Cost: A Solution to the Appreciation Problem, 2 vols. in one. Brief, Richard P., ed. LC 77-87263. (Development of Contemporary Accounting Thought Ser). 1978. Repr. of 1931 ed. lib. bdg. 22.00x (ISBN 0-405-10892-3). Ayer Co Pubs.

Baldwin, Helen G., tr. see Binet, Alfred.

Baldwin, Helene L. Samuel Beckett's Real Silence. LC 80-21465. 184p. 1981. 19.95x (ISBN 0-271-00301-4). Pa St U Pr.

Baldwin, Henry. A General View of the Origin & Nature of the Constitution & Government of the United States. LC 72-118027. (American Constitutional & Legal History Ser). 1970. Repr. of 1837 ed. lib. bdg. 27.50 (ISBN 0-306-71944-4). Da Capo.

Baldwin, Huntley. Creating Effective TV Commercials. LC 81-66509. (Illus.). 200p. 1982. 24.95 (ISBN 0-87251-063-8). Crain Bks.

Baldwin, Ian & Stanley, John. The Garden Centre Manual. (Illus.). 250p. 1982. pap. text ed. 29.95 (ISBN 0-917304-19-5). Timber.

Baldwin, J. & Brand, Stewart, eds. Soft Tech. 1978. pap. 5.00 (ISBN 0-14-004806-5). Penguin.

Baldwin, J. N. Microprocessors for Industry. 144p. 1982. text ed. 19.95 (ISBN 0-408-00517-3). Butterworth.

Baldwin, Jackie, jt. auth. see Penny, Del Smith.

Baldwin, James. Amen Corner. 91p. 1968. 8.95 (ISBN 0-385-27002-X, Dial). Doubleday.

--Another Country. 1985. pap. 4.95 (ISBN 0-440-30200-5, LE). Dell.
--Blues for Mister Charlie. 1985. pap. 4.95 (ISBN 0-440-30637-X, LE). Dell.
--Devil Finds Work. 6.95 (ISBN 0-385-27260-X, Dial). Doubleday.
--The Evidence of Things Not Seen. 144p. 1985. 11.95 (ISBN 0-03-005529-6). HR&W.
--The Evidence of Things Not Seen: An Essay. LC 85-924. write for info. Amer Bar Assn.
--Fire Next Time. 1985. pap. 3.95 (ISBN 0-440-32542-0, LE). Dell.
--Giovanni's Room. 1985. pap. 4.95 (ISBN 0-440-32881-0, LE). Dell.
--Go Tell It on the Mountain. 224p. (gr. 9 up). 1985. pap. 4.95 (ISBN 0-440-33007-6, LE). Dell.
--Go Tell It on the Mountain. 256p. 1953. 13.95 (ISBN 0-385-27053-4, Dial). Doubleday.
--Going to Meet the Man. 1986. pap. 4.50 (ISBN 0-440-32931-0). Dell.
--If Beale Street Could Talk. 224p. 1974. 6.95 (ISBN 0-385-27066-6, Dial). Doubleday.
--If Beale Street Could Talk. (RL 10). 1975. pap. 3.95 (ISBN 0-451-13789-2, AE2743, Sig). NAL.
--If Beale Street Could Talk. 1986. pap. 4.50 (ISBN 0-440-34060-8, LE). Dell.
--Just above My Head. 1980. pap. 4.95 (ISBN 0-440-14777-8). Dell.
--Little Man, Little Man. 6.95 (ISBN 0-385-27305-3, Dial). Doubleday.
--No Name in the Street. 192p. 1972. 6.95 (ISBN 0-385-27328-2, Dial). Doubleday.
--No Name in the Street. 1986. pap. 3.95 (ISBN 0-440-36461-2, LE). Dell.
--Nobody Knows My Name. 242p. 1961. 7.95 (ISBN 0-385-27089-5, Dial). Doubleday.
--Nobody Knows My Name. 1986. pap. 3.95 (ISBN 0-440-36435-3, LE). Dell.
--Notes of a Native Son. LC 84-6396. 175p. 1984. pap. 6.95 (ISBN 0-8070-6431-9, BP39). Beacon Pr.
--Notes of a Native Son. 7.95 (ISBN 0-385-27329-0, Dial). Doubleday.
--The Price of the Ticket: Collected Nonfiction, 1948-1985. 704p. 1985. 29.95 (ISBN 0-312-64306-3, Pub. by Marek); deluxe ed. 100.00 ltd., signed ed. (ISBN 0-312-64307-1, Pub. by Marek). St Martin.
--The Story of Siegfried. 1898. Repr. 30.00 (ISBN 0-8274-3520-7). R West.
--Tell Me How Long the Train's Been Gone. 1986. pap. 4.95 (ISBN 0-440-38581-4, LE). Dell.

Baldwin, James E., Sr. Old Testament Tithing versus New Testament Giving. 1984. 6.95 (ISBN 0-317-03291-7). Vantage.

Baldwin, James F. The King's Council in England During the Middle Ages. 1965. 16.50 (ISBN 0-8446-1045-3). Peter Smith.

Baldwin, James M. Between Two Wars, Eighteen Sixty-One to Nineteen Twenty-One: Being Memories, Opinion & Letters Received by James Mark Baldwin, 2 vols. LC 75-3020. Repr. of 1926 ed. 48.50 set (ISBN 0-404-59013-6). AMS Pr.
--Darwin & the Humanities. LC 75-3021. Repr. of 1909 ed. 15.00 (ISBN 0-404-59016-0). AMS Pr.
--Development & Evolution: Including Psychophysical Evolution, Evolution by Orthoplasy & the Theory of Genetic Modes. LC 75-3022. (Philosophy in America Ser.). Repr. of 1902 ed. 42.50 (ISBN 0-404-59017-9). AMS Pr.
--Dictionary of Philosophy & Psychology, 3 vols. bound in 4. Incl. Vols. 1 & 2. 27.00 ea.; Vol. 1. (ISBN 0-8446-1047-X); Vol. 2. (ISBN 0-8446-1048-8); Vol. 3., 2 Pts. Bibliography of Philosophy, Psychology and Cognate Subjects. 24.00 ea.; Pt. 1. (ISBN 0-8446-1049-6); Pt. 2. (ISBN 0-8446-1050-X). Set. 102.00 (ISBN 0-8446-1046-1). Peter Smith.
--Fragments in Philosophy & Science: Being Collected Essays & Addresses. LC 75-3023. (Philosophy in America Ser.). Repr. of 1902 ed. 42.00 (ISBN 0-404-59018-7). AMS Pr.
--Genetic Theory of Reality. LC 75-3024. (Philosophy in America Ser.). Repr. of 1915 ed. 78.50 (ISBN 0-404-59019-5). AMS Pr.
--Handbook of Psychology, 2 vols. LC 75-3025. (Philosophy in America Ser.). Repr. of 1891 ed. 78.50 set (ISBN 0-404-59020-9). AMS Pr.
--The Individual & Society: Or, Psychology & Sociology. LC 75-3026. (Philosophy in America Ser.). Repr. of 1911 ed. 18.50 (ISBN 0-404-59023-3). AMS Pr.
--The Individual & Society: Psychology & Sociology. LC 73-14147. (Perspectives in Social Inquiry Ser.). 214p. 1974. Repr. 11.00x (ISBN 0-405-05492-0). Ayer Co Pubs.
--Social & Ethical Interpretations in Mental Development. 2nd ed. LC 73-2960. (Classics in Psychology Ser.). Repr. of 1899 ed. 36.50 (ISBN 0-405-05133-6). Ayer Co Pubs.
--Thought & Things: A Study of the Development & Meaning of Thought or Genetic Logic, 3 vols. LC 75-3029. (Philosopy in America Ser.). Repr. of 1911 ed. 97.00 set (ISBN 0-404-59025-X). AMS Pr.
--Thought & Things: Study of the Development & Meaning of Thought or Genetic Logic, 4 vols. in 2. LC 74-21397. (Classics in Child Development Ser). 1975. Repr. 94.00x (ISBN 0-405-06451-9). Ayer Co Pubs.

Baldwin, James M., et al. Dictionary of Philosophy & Psychology. 1977. lib. bdg. 395.00 (ISBN 0-8490-1721-1). Gordon Pr.

Baldwin, James W. The Social Studies Laboratory: A Study of Equipment & Teaching Aids for the Social Studies. LC 79-176534. (Columbia University. Teachers College. Contributions to Education: No. 371). Repr. of 1929 ed. 22.50 (ISBN 0-404-55371-0). AMS Pr.

Baldwin, Janice, jt. auth. see Baldwin, John D.

Baldwin, Janice I., jt. auth. see Baldwin, John D.

Baldwin, Jeduthan. Revolutionary Journal of Colonel Jeduthan Baldwin, 1775-1778. Baldwin, Thomas W., ed. LC 73-140853. (Eyewitness Accounts of the American Revolution Ser., No. 3). (Illus.). 1970. Repr. of 1906 ed. 14.00 (ISBN 0-405-01223-3). Ayer Co Pubs.

Baldwin, Jo G. Let's Make Ice Cream. 1977. 2.00 (ISBN 0-914208-02-0). Longhorn Pr.

Baldwin, John. Ice Pick. LC 82-14369. 228p. 1983. 12.50 (ISBN 0-688-00679-5). Morrow.
--Pre-Trial Justice: A Study of Case Reviews in Magistrates' Courts. LC 84-28303. 1985. 34.95x (ISBN 0-631-14064-6). Basil Blackwell.

Baldwin, John & McConville, Michael. Jury Trials. 1979. 19.95x (ISBN 0-19-825350-8). Oxford U Pr.

Baldwin, John D. Ancient America in Notes on America Archaeology. (The Works of John D. Baldwin Ser.). xii, 299p. Repr. of 1871 ed. lib. bdg. 34.00 (ISBN 0-932051-06-5, Pub. by Am Repr Serv). Am Biog Serv.
--Pre-Historic Nations. (The Works of John D. Baldwin Ser.). vii, 411p. Repr. of 1872 ed. lib. bdg. 49.00 (ISBN 0-932051-07-3, Pub. by Am Repr Serv). Am Biog Serv.

Baldwin, John D. & Baldwin, Janice. Behavior Principles in Everyday Life. 2nd ed. (Illus.). 352p. 1986. pap. text ed. 24.95 (ISBN 0-13-074238-4). P-H.

Baldwin, John D. & Baldwin, Janice I. Behavior Principles in Everyday Life. (Illus.). 336p. 1981. text ed. 24.95 (ISBN 0-13-072751-2). P-H.
--Beyond Sociobiology. LC 80-28032. x, 325p. 1981. lib. bdg. 35.00 (ISBN 0-444-99086-0, BBE/, Pub. by Elsevier North Holland, Inc.). Greenwood.

Baldwin, John E. Experimental Organic Chemistry. 2nd ed. LC 72-80966. pap. 51.30 (ISBN 0-317-08741-X, 2004352). Bks Demand UMI.

Baldwin, John H. Environmental Planning & Management. LC 84-2281. 1985. 42.50x (ISBN 0-86531-723-2); text ed. 19.95x (ISBN 0-8133-0063-0). Westview.

Baldwin, John R. A Formal Analysis of the Intonation of Modern Colloquial Russian. (Forum Phoneticum Ser.: No. 18). 230p. (Orig.). 1979. pap. text ed. 17.00x (ISBN 3-87118-391-1, Pub. by Helmut Buske Verlag Hamburg). Benjamins North AM.

Baldwin, John W. Masters, Princes, & Merchants: The Social Views & Reforms of Peter the Chanter & His Circle, 2 Vols. LC 69-18049. 1970. Set. 60.00x (ISBN 0-691-05178-X). Princeton U Pr.
--The Scholastic Culture of the Middle Ages: 1000-1300. LC 70-120060. (Civilization & Society Ser). 192p. 1971. pap. 8.95x (ISBN 0-669-62059-9). Heath.

Baldwin, Joseph. Flush Times of Alabama & Mississippi. 1959. 12.00 (ISBN 0-8446-1589-7). Peter Smith.

Baldwin, Joseph G. Party Leaders: Sketches of Thomas Jefferson, Alexander Hamilton, Andrew Jackson, Henry Clay, John Randolph of Roanoke; Including Notices of Many Other Distinguished American Statesmen. LC 72-39654. (Essay Index Reprint Ser.). Repr. of 1885 ed. 23.50 (ISBN 0-8369-2741-9). Ayer Co Pubs.

Baldwin, Joyce. Haggai, Zechariah, Malachi. LC 72-75980. (Tyndale Old Testament Commentary Ser.). 256p. 1972. 10.95 (ISBN 0-87784-908-0); pap. 6.95 (ISBN 0-87784-276-0). Inter-Varsity.

Baldwin, Joyce G. Daniel. Wiseman, D. J., ed. LC 78-18547. (Tyndale Old Testament Commentary Ser.). 1978. 10.95 (ISBN 0-87784-961-7); pap. 6.95 (ISBN 0-87784-273-6). Inter-Varsity.
--Esther. Wiseman, D. J., ed. LC 84-15670. (Tyndale Old Testament Commentaries Ser.). 122p. 1984. 10.95 (ISBN 0-87784-964-1); pap. 6.95 (ISBN 0-87784-262-0). Inter-Varsity.

Baldwin, Kenneth H. & Kirby, David K., eds. Individual & Community: Variations on a Theme in American Ficton. LC 74-75476. xvii, 222p. 1975. 16.75 (ISBN 0-8223-0319-1). Duke.

Baldwin, Leland D. The American Quest for the City of God. ix, 368p. 1981. 18.95x (ISBN 0-86554-016-0). Mercer Univ Pr.
--The Keelboat Age on Western Waters. LC 41-10342. (Illus.). 264p. 1980. pap. 5.95 (ISBN 0-8229-5319-6). U of Pittsburgh Pr.
--Pittsburgh: The Story of a City, 1750-1865. rev. ed. LC 73-104172. 1970. pap. 6.95 (ISBN 0-8229-5216-5). U of Pittsburgh Pr.
--Whiskey Rebels: The Story of a Frontier Uprising. LC 39-11763. (Illus.). 1968. pap. 6.95 (ISBN 0-8229-5151-7). U of Pittsburgh Pr.

Baldwin, Lewis V. Invisible Strands in African Methodism: A History of the African Union Methodist Protestant & Union American Methodist Episcopal Churches, 1805-1980. LC 83-15039. (ATLA Monographs: No. 19). (Illus.). 306p. 1983. 25.00 (ISBN 0-8108-1647-4). Scarecrow.

Baldwin Library of Childrens Literature, University of Florida, Gainesville. Index to Children's Literature in English Before 1900: Catalog of the Baldwin Library of the University of Florida at Gainesville. (Library Catalogs Supplements). 1981. lib. bdg. 340.00 (ISBN 0-8161-0370-4, Hall Library). G K Hall.

Baldwin-Lima-Hamilton Corporation. The Narrow-Gauge Locomotive: The Baldwin Catalog of 1877. LC 67-24619. pap. write for info (2016252). Bks Demand UMI.

Baldwin, Lindley. March of Faith: Samuel Morris. 96p. 1969. pap. 2.50 (ISBN 0-87123-360-6, 200360). Bethany Hse.
--Samuel Morris. 74p. 1980. 1.95 (ISBN 0-88113-319-1). Edit Betania.

Baldwin, Loammi. Thoughts on the Study of Political Economy. Bd. with Appendix: Drydocks. LC 66-22614. 105p. Repr. of 1809 ed. 22.50x (ISBN 0-678-00374-2). Kelley.

Baldwin, Louis. Edmond Halley & His Comet. (Illus.). 170p. (Orig.). 1985. 14.95 (ISBN 0-89288-115-1); pap. 7.95 (ISBN 0-89288-107-0). Maverick.
--The First American Revolution. 175p. (Orig.). 1985. 14.95x (ISBN 0-89288-114-3); pap. 7.95 (ISBN 0-89288-110-0). Maverick.
--Hon. Politician: Mike Mansfield of Montana. LC 79-10993. 362p. 1979. 14.95 (ISBN 0-87842-106-8). Mountain Pr.
--Jesus of Galilee. LC 79-11587. 1979. pap. 4.95 (ISBN 0-8170-0841-1). Judson.
--Oneselves: Multiple Personalities 1811-1981. LC 84-42603. 192p. 1984. lib. bdg. write for info. Univ. Microfilms (ISBN 0-89950-124-9). McFarland & Co.

Baldwin, Lydia W. A Yankee School-Teacher in Virginia. facsimile ed. LC 70-37583. (Black Heritage Library Collection). Repr. of 1884 ed. 15.50 (ISBN 0-8369-8959-7). Ayer Co Pubs.

Baldwin, Malcolm F. The Southwest Energy Complex: A Policy Evaluation. LC 73-79429. pap. 20.00 (ISBN 0-317-11229-5, 2015787). Bks Demand UMI.

Baldwin, Malcolm F., jt. auth. see Baldwin, Pamela L.

Baldwin, Margaret. The Boys Who Saved the Children. LC 81-14084. (A Jem Book Ser.). (Illus.). 64p. (gr. 2-3). 1981. PLB 9.29 (ISBN 0-671-43603-1); pap. 4.95 (ISBN 0-671-49470-8). Messner.
--Fortune Telling. (Illus.). 96p. (gr. 4-7). 1984. 9.29 (ISBN 0-671-46135-4). Messner.
--Kisses of Death: A World War II Escape Story. LC 82-42879. (Jem - High Interest-Low Reading Level Ser.). (Illus.). 64p. (gr. 7-9). 1983. PLB 9.29 (ISBN 0-671-43850-6). Messner.
--Thanksgiving. (First Bks.). (Illus.). 72p. (gr. 4 up). 1983. PLB 8.90 (ISBN 0-531-04532-3). Watts.

Baldwin, Margaret & Pack, Gary. Computer Graphics. (Computer-Awareness First Bk.). 96p. (gr. 6-8). 1984. lib. bdg. 8.90 (ISBN 0-531-04704-0). Watts.

Baldwin, Margaret & Peck, Gary. Robots & Robotics. (A Computer Awareness Bk.). 72p. 1984. lib. bdg. 8.90 (ISBN 0-531-04705-9). Watts.

Baldwin, Marilyn Austin, ed. see Howells, William Dean.

Baldwin, Marshall W. The Mediaeval Church. (Development of Western Civilization Ser). 124p. (Orig.). 1953. pap. 4.95x (ISBN 0-8014-9842-2). Cornell U Pr.
--The Mediaeval Church. LC 82-2992. (The Development of Western Civilization Ser.). xii, 124p. 1982. Repr. of 1953 ed. lib. bdg. 22.50x (ISBN 0-313-23554-6, BAME). Greenwood.
--Raymond III of Tripolis & the the Fall of Jerusalem: 1140-1187. LC 76-29830. Repr. of 1936 ed. 22.50 (ISBN 0-404-15411-5). AMS Pr.

Baldwin, Marshall W. see Setton, Kenneth M.

Baldwin, Marshall W., tr. see Erdmann, Carl.

Baldwin, Mary N. Times Winged Chariot. 80p. 1975. 5.00 (ISBN 0-8233-0218-0). Golden Quill.

Baldwin, Michael. The River & the Downs: Kent's Unsung Corner. (Illus.). 187p. 1984. 27.00 (ISBN 0-575-03463-7, Pub. by Gollancz England). David & Charles.
--The Way to Write Poetry. 96p. 1982. (Pub. by Hamish Hamilton England); pap. 9.95 (ISBN 0-241-10749-0, Pub. by Hamish Hamilton England). David & Charles.

Baldwin, Michael, ed. King Horn: Poems Written at Montolieu in Old Languedoc, 1969-1981. 118p. (Orig.). 1983. pap. 8.95x (ISBN 0-7100-9494-9). Routledge & Kegan.

Baldwin, Michelle, jt. auth. see Satir, Virginia.

Baldwin, Neil. To All Gentleness: William Carlos Williams, the Doctor-Poet. LC 83-15625. (Illus.). 224p. (gr. 7 up). 1984. 14.95 (ISBN 0-689-31030-7). Atheneum.

Baldwin, Nick. Farm Tractors. (Illus.). 64p. 1977. 10.95 (ISBN 0-7232-2060-3, Pub. by Warne Pubs England). Motorbooks Intl.
--Kaleidoscope of Farm Tractors. (Old Motor Kaleidoscopes Ser.). (Illus.). 1978. 16.50 (ISBN 0-906116-01-5, Pub. by Old Motor Magazine England). Motorbooks Intl.
--Kaliedoscope of Farm Tractors. 96p. 18.25 (ISBN 0-318-14877-3, G188). Midwest Old Settlers.
--Observer's Book of Commercial Vehicles 1981. (Illus.). 192p. 1980. 4.95 (ISBN 0-7232-1619-3, Pub. by Frederick Warne England). Motorbooks Intl.
--Trucks of the Sixties & Seventies. (Transport Library). (Illus.). 64p. 1980. 13.95 (ISBN 0-7232-2364-5, Pub. by Warne Pubs England). Motorbooks Intl.
--Vintage Tractor Album, No. 2. 96p. 1982. 40.00x (ISBN 0-7232-2895-7, Pub. by F Warne England). State Mutual Bk.

Baldwin, Norman F., jt. ed. see Seligman, Milton.

Baldwin, Pamela. How Small Grants Make a Difference: Examples from the Design Arts Program, National Endowment for the Arts. 2nd ed. (Illus.). 67p. (Orig.). 1980. pap. 3.50 (ISBN 0-941182-09-6). Partners Livable.

Baldwin, Pamela L. & Baldwin, Malcolm F. Onshore Planning for Offshore Oil: Lessons from Scotland. LC 75-606. (Illus.). 1975. pap. 5.00 (ISBN 0-89164-001-0). Conservation Foun.

Baldwin, Petie W. Winds of Imagination. LC 76-17537. 1976. pap. 5.00 (ISBN 0-917166-01-9). Creative Vent.

Baldwin, R. W. & Hanson, Gillian C. The Critically Ill Obstetric Patient. (Illus.). 569p. 1984. text ed. 39.93 (ISBN 0-397-58296-X, Lippincott Medical). Lippincott.

Baldwin, R. W., ed. Secondary Spread of Cancer. 1978. 47.50 (ISBN 0-12-076850-X). Acad Pr.

Baldwin, R. W. & Byers, Vera S., eds. Monoclonal Antibodies for Cancer Detection & Therapy. Date not set. price not set (ISBN 0-12-077020-2). Acad Pr.

Baldwin, Ralph. The Unity of the "Canterbury Tales". LC 75-155632. (BCL Ser. I). 112p. 1972. Repr. of 1955 ed. 14.00 (ISBN 0-404-00479-2). AMS Pr.
--Unity of the Canterbury Tales. LC 73-16142. 1955. lib. bdg. 17.50 (ISBN 0-8414-9885-7). Folcroft.

Baldwin, Ralph B. The Measure of the Moon. LC 62-20025. pap. 136.50 (ISBN 0-317-08505-0, 2020023). Bks Demand UMI.

Baldwin, Rebecca. The Dollar Duchess. 192p. (Orig.). 1982. pap. 1.50 (ISBN 0-449-50305-4, Coventry). Fawcett.
--The Matchmakers. 1980. pap. 1.75 (ISBN 0-449-50017-9, Coventry). Fawcett.
--A Matter of Honor. 176p. (Orig.). 1983. pap. 2.25 (ISBN 0-449-20102-3, Crest). Fawcett.
--Peerless Theodosia. 224p. (Orig.). 1980. pap. 1.75 (ISBN 0-449-50036-5, Coventry). Fawcett.
--A Season Abroad. 224p. 1981. pap. 1.50 (ISBN 0-449-50215-5, Crest). Fawcett.
--A Very Simple Scheme. (Coventry Romance Ser.: No. 173). 224p. 1982. pap. 1.50 (ISBN 0-449-50274-0, Coventry). Fawcett.

Baldwin, Richard. Divorce Guide for Oregon. 3rd ed. 119p. 1984. pap. write for info. (ISBN 0-88908-816-0). Self Counsel Pr.

Baldwin, Richard F. Operations Management in the Forest Products Industry. LC 84-61889. (Illus.). 264p. 1984. 59.50 (ISBN 0-87930-159-7); pap. 45.00 (ISBN 0-87930-160-0). Miller Freeman.
--Plywood Manufacturing Practices. 2nd rev. ed. LC 80-84894. (A Forest Industries Bk.). (Illus.). 344p. 1981. 42.50 (ISBN 0-87930-092-2). Miller Freeman.

Baldwin, Richard S. The Fungus Fighters: Two Women Scientists & Their Discovery. (Illus.). 184p. 1981. 18.95x (ISBN 0-8014-1355-9). Cornell U Pr.

Baldwin, Robert. Regulating the Airlines. 1985. 24.95x (ISBN 0-19-827515-3); pap. 14.95x (ISBN 0-317-14170-8). Oxford U Pr.

Baldwin, Robert C. & McPeek, James A. An Introduction to Philosophy Through Literature. LC 50-8252. 596p. 1950. 21.50 (ISBN 0-471-07000-9). Krieger.

Baldwin, Robert E. Economic Development & Growth. 2nd ed. LC 80-13597. 160p. 1980. pap. 8.50 (ISBN 0-89874-024-X). Krieger.
--The Inefficacy of Trade Policy. LC 82-23425. (Essays in International Finance Ser.: No. 150). 1982. pap. text ed. 2.50x (ISBN 0-88165-057-9). Princeton U Int Finan Econ.
--Multilateral Trade Negotiations: Toward Greater Liberalization? 1979. pap. 3.75 (ISBN 0-8447-1082-2). Am Enterprise.
--Nontariff Distortions of International Trade. LC 78-109436. pap. 55.50 (ISBN 0-317-28040-6, 2055779). Bks Demand UMI.

Baldwin, Robert E. & Richardson, David J. International Trade & Finance Readings. 2nd ed. 1981. pap. text ed. 15.95 (ISBN 0-316-07922-7). Little.

Baldwin, Robert E., jt. auth. see Anderson, Kym.

Baldwin, Robert E., jt. auth. see Meier, Gerald M.

Baldwin, Robert E. & Krueger, Anne O., eds. The Structure & Evolution of Recent U. S. Trade Policy. LC 84-2560. (NBER Conference Report). 504p. 1985. 50.00x (ISBN 0-226-03604-9). U of Chicago Pr.

Baldwin, Robert F. The End of the World: A Catholic View. LC 83-63166. 192p. 1984. pap. 5.95 (ISBN 0-87973-608-9, 608). Our Sunday Visitor.

Baldwin, Roger. Hawaii's Poisonous Plants. 112p. 1979. pap. 5.95 (ISBN 0-912180-34-X). Petroglyph.

--Inside a Cop: The Tensions in the Public & Private Lives of the Police. (Illus.). 1977. pap. 3.95 (ISBN 0-910286-55-8). Boxwood.

Baldwin, Roger & Paris, Ruth. The Book of Similes. (Illus.). 132p. 1982. 14.95x (ISBN 0-7100-9285-7); pap. 7.95 (ISBN 0-7100-9456-6). Routledge & Kegan.

Baldwin, Roger see Thomas, Norman.

Baldwin, Roger, ed. see Kropotkin, Peter.

Baldwin, Roger G. & Blackburn, Robert T., eds. College Faculty: Versatile Human Resources in a Period of Constraint. LC 82-84193. (Institutional Research Ser.: No. 40). 1983. pap. 8.95x (ISBN 0-87589-958-7). Jossey-Bass.

Baldwin, Roger N., ed. see Kropotkin, Peter.

Baldwin, Ruth M., ed. One Hundred Nineteenth-Century Rhyming Alphabets in English. LC 79-132482. (Illus.). 307p. 1972. 15.00x (ISBN 0-8093-0509-7). S Ill U Pr.

Baldwin, Sally. The Costs of Caring: Families with Disabled Children. (International Library of Social Policy). 224p. 1985. 34.95x (ISBN 0-7100-9882-0). Routledge & Kegan.

Baldwin, Sam, jt. auth. see Wyatt, Alan.

Baldwin, Scott. Art of Advocacy: Direct Examination (Release 1) 1983. write for info. (#036). Bender.

Baldwin, Scott, et al. The Preparation of a Products Liability Case. 1054p. 1981. 60.00 (ISBN 0-316-07925-1). Little.

--Preparation of a Product Liability Case: 1985 Supplement. 1985. pap. text ed. price not set. Little.

--The Preparation of a Product Liability Case: 1984 Supplement. LC 80-85201. 100p. 1984. pap. write for info. Little.

Baldwin, Shirley. First Aid for the Office & Workplace. (Illus.). 192p. 1985. 15.75 (ISBN 0-87527-258-4). Green.

Baldwin, Sidney. Poverty & Politics: The Rise & Decline of the Farm Security Administration. LC 68-18052. xvii, 438p. (Photos). 1968. 32.50 (ISBN 0-8078-1071-1). U of NC Pr.

Baldwin, Simeon E. Life & Letters of Simeon Baldwin. 1919. 75.00x (ISBN 0-685-89762-1). Elliots Bks.

Baldwin, Skip. A Province into Being. Anderson, Douglas, ed. (Illus.). 80p. (Orig.). 1984. pap. 6.95 (ISBN 0-912549-04-1). Bread and Butter.

Baldwin, Stan. Bruised But Not Broken. LC 85-2977. 1985. pap. 6.95 (ISBN 0-88070-080-7). Multnomah.

Baldwin, Stanley. On England, & Other Addresses. facsimile ed. LC 70-156609. (Essay Index Reprint Ser). Repr. of 1926 ed. 20.00 (ISBN 0-8369-2305-7). Ayer Co Pubs.

--This Torch of Freedom: Speeches & Addresses. facsimile ed. LC 73-157962. (Essay Index Reprint Ser). Repr. of 1935 ed. 20.00 (ISBN 0-8369-2213-1). Ayer Co Pubs.

Baldwin, Stanley C. How to Build Your Own Christian Character. 1982. pap. 3.95 (ISBN 0-88207-271-4). Victor Bks.

--A True View of You. LC 81-84569. 1982. pap. 5.95 (ISBN 0-8307-0779-4, 5414602). Regal.

--What Did Jesus Say about That? 224p. 1984. pap. 2.95 missal size (ISBN 0-89693-312-1). Victor Bks.

Baldwin, Stanley C., jt. auth. see Cook, Jerry.

Baldwin, Stanley C., jt. auth. see MacGregor, Malcolm.

Baldwin, Stanley C., jt. auth. see Mallory, James D.

Baldwin, Stanley G., jt. auth. see MacGregor, Malcolm.

Baldwin, Stevie, jt. auth. see Baldwin, Ed.

Baldwin, Stevie, jt. ed. see Baldwin, Ed.

Baldwin, Sue, ed. see Early Childhood Directors Association.

Baldwin, Summerfield. Business in the Middle Ages. LC 68-25172. (Berkshire Studies in European History Ser.). 1968. Repr. of 1937 ed. 15.00 (ISBN 0-8154-0015-2). Cooper Sq.

--Organization of Medieval Christianity. 11.25 (ISBN 0-8446-1051-8). Assn Inform & Image Mgmt.

Baldwin, T. W. On Act & Scene Division in the Shakespere First Folio. LC 64-20255. 190p. 1965. 6.50x (ISBN 0-8093-0153-9). S Ill U Pr.

--On the Compositional Genetics of The Comedy of Errors. LC 64-12251. 433p. 1965. 39.95x (ISBN 0-252-72585-9). U of Ill Pr.

--On the Literary Genetics of Shakespeare's Plays, 1592-1594. LC 58-6994. 571p. 1959. 39.95x (ISBN 0-252-72587-5). U of Ill Pr.

--Shakespeare's "Love's Labor's Won". LC 56-9515. 54p. 1957. 5.00x (ISBN 0-8093-0010-9). S Ill U Pr.

Baldwin, Thomas F. & McVoy, D. Stevens. Cable Communication. (Illus.). 432p. 1983. 31.95 (ISBN 0-13-110171-4). P-H.

Baldwin, Thomas W., ed. see Baldwin, Jeduthan.

Baldwin, Victor, jt. ed. see Campbell, Bob.

Baldwin, Victor L., et al. Isn't It Time He Outgrew This? or A Training Program for Parents of Retarded Children. (Illus.). 230p. 1980. 13.50x (ISBN 0-398-02636-X). C C Thomas.

Baldwin, W. W. The Price of Power. LC 76-990. (FDR & the Era of the New Deal Ser.). 361p. 1976. Repr. of 1948 ed. lib. bdg. 39.50 (ISBN 0-306-70803-5). Da Capo.

Baldwin, William. Beware the Cat. Holden, William P., ed. Bd. with The Funerals of King Edward Sixth. LC 62-21983. (Connecticut College Monograph: No. 8). 1963. 6.00 (ISBN 0-686-11997-5); pap. 4.50 (ISBN 0-686-11998-3). Conn Coll Bkshp.

--Suede Holloway. 1978. pap. 3.95 (ISBN 0-9602170-0-2). Ars Eterna.

--Treatise of Morall Philosophie. rev. ed. LC 67-10126. 1967. Repr. of 1620 ed. 50.00x (ISBN 0-8201-1003-5). Schol Facsimiles.

Baldwin, William H; see Brandt, Lilian.

Baldwin, William L. Antitrust & the Changing Corporation. LC 61-16905. pap. 78.80 (ISBN 0-317-28853-9, 2017879). Bks Demand UMI.

--Structure of the Defense Market, 1955-1964. LC 67-23730. Repr. of 1967 ed. 48.90 (2017880). Bks Demand UMI.

--The World Tin Market: Political Pricing & Economic Competition. LC 83-8888. (Duke Press Policy Studies). 440p. 1983. 45.00 (ISBN 0-8223-0505-4). Duke.

Bale, Don, Jr. Fabulous Investment Potential of Uncirculated Singles. 4th, rev. ed. 1980. pap. 5.00 (ISBN 0-686-70348-0). Bale Bks.

--Gold Mine in Gold. 4th, rev. ed. 1980. pap. 5.00 (ISBN 0-686-70349-9). Bale Bks.

--Gold Mine in Your Pocket. 4th, rev. ed. 1980. pap. 5.00 (ISBN 0-686-70350-2). Bale Bks.

--How to Find Valuable Old & Scarce Coins. 4th, rev. ed. 1980. pap. 3.00 (ISBN 0-686-70351-0). Bale Bks.

--How to Invest in Singles. 4th, rev. ed. 1980. pap. 5.00 (ISBN 0-686-70352-9). Bale Bks.

--How to Invest in Uncirculated Singles. 4th, rev. ed. 1980. pap. 5.00 (ISBN 0-686-70353-7). Bale Bks.

--Out of Little Coins, Big Fortunes Grow. 4th, rev. ed. 1980. pap. 5.00 (ISBN 0-686-70354-5). Bale Bks.

Bale, Don, Jr., ed. Fabulous Investment Potential of Liberty Walking Half Dollars. 4th, rev. ed. 1980. pap. 5.00 (ISBN 0-686-70346-4). Bale Bks.

Bale, John. Chief Promises of God. LC 70-133635. (Tudor Facsimile Texts. Old English Plays: No. 21). Repr. of 1908 ed. 49.50 (ISBN 0-404-53321-3). AMS Pr.

--The First Two Partes of the Acts or Unchaste Examples of the Englyshe Votaryes. LC 79-84086. (English Experience Ser.: No. 906). 540p. 1979. Repr. of 1560 ed. lib. bdg. 40.00 (ISBN 90-221-0906-2). Walter J Johnson.

--The Image of Bothe Curhces, After the Moste Wonderfull & Heavenly Revelation of Sainct John the Evangelist. LC 72-5965. (English Experience Ser.: No. 498). 872p. 1973. Repr. of 1548 ed. 51.00 (ISBN 90-221-0498-2). Walter J Johnson.

--John Bale's King Johan. Adams, Barry B., ed. LC 67-12048. 211p. 1969. 8.50 (ISBN 0-87328-039-3). Huntington Lib.

--King Johan. LC 82-45800. (Malone Society Reprint Ser.: No. 70). Repr. of 1931 ed. 40.00 (ISBN 0-404-63070-7). AMS Pr.

--Kynge Johan: A Play in Two Parts. Collier, J. Payne, ed. LC 79-160012. (Camden Society, London. Publications, First Ser.: No. 2). Repr. of 1838 ed. 19.00 (ISBN 0-404-50102-8). AMS Pr.

--Kynge Johan, a Play in Two Parts. 19.00 (ISBN 0-384-03130-7). Johnson Repr.

--Select Works of John Bale, Bishop of Ossory. 51.00 (ISBN 0-384-03135-8). Johnson Repr.

--Sport & Place: A Geography of Sport in England, Scotland & Wales. LC 82-5018. (Illus.). xvi, 187p. 1983. 15.95x (ISBN 0-8032-1180-5). U of Nebr Pr.

--Temptation of Christ. LC 74-133636. (Tudor Facsimile Texts. Old English Plays: No. 22). Repr. of 1909 ed. 49.50 (ISBN 0-404-53322-1). AMS Pr.

--Three Laws. LC 78-133637. (Tudor Facsimile Texts. Old English Plays: No. 23). Repr. of 1908 ed. 49.50 (ISBN 0-404-53323-X). AMS Pr.

Bale, Karen A. Distant Thunder. (Women at War Ser.: No. 14). 320p. (Orig.). 1983. pap. 3.25 (ISBN 0-440-01899-4, Emerald). Dell.

--The Forever Passion. (Orig.). 1980. pap. 3.50 (ISBN 0-8217-1315-9). Zebra.

--Little Flower's Desire. (Sweet Medicine's Prophecy: No. 2). (Orig.). 1982. pap. 2.95 (ISBN 0-89083-910-7). Zebra.

--Sweet Medicine's Propehcy: Sun Dancer's Passion. 1981. pap. 2.95 (ISBN 0-89083-776 7). Zebra.

--Sweet Medicine's Prophecy, No. 3: Winter's Love Song. 1983. pap. 3.50 (ISBN 0-8217-1154-7). Zebra.

Bale, Malcolm. Agricultural Trade & Food Policy: The Experience of Five Developing Countries. (Staff Working Paper No. 724). 56p. 1985. 5.00 (ISBN 0-318-11959-5, WP 0724). World Bank.

Bale, Malcolm D., jt. auth. see Koester, Ulrich.

Bale, Malcolm D., jt. auth. see Mutti, John H.

Bale, Peter. Wildlife Through the Camera. (Illus.). 224p. 1985. 24.95 (ISBN 0-88186-452-8). Parkwest Pubns.

Balek, J. Hydrology & Water Resources in Tropical Regions. (Developments in Water Science Ser.: Vol. 18). 272p. 1983. 70.25 (ISBN 0-444-99656-7, I-304-83). Elsevier.

Balek, Jaroslav. Hydrology & Water Resources in Tropical Africa. (Developments in Water Science Ser.: Vol. 8). 208p. 1977. 70.25 (ISBN 0-444-99814-4). Elsevier.

Balen, A. T. see Van Balen, A. T. & Houtman, W. A.

Balen, John Van see Van Balen, John.

Balent, Matthew. The Palladium Book of Exotic Weapons. Marciniszyn, Alex, ed. (Weapons Ser.: No. 6). (Illus.). 48p. (Orig.). 1984. pap. 5.95 (ISBN 0-916211-06-1). Palladium Bks.

--The Palladium Book of Weapons & Armour. 4th ed. Siembieda, Kevin, ed. (Weapon Ser.: No. 1). (Illus.). 48p. 1984. pap. 4.95 (ISBN 0-916211-07-X, 404). Palladium Bks.

--The Palladium Book of Weapons & Castles of the Orient. Marcinisyzn, Alex, ed. (Weapon Ser.: No. 4). (Illus.): 48p. (Orig.). 1984. pap. 4.95 (ISBN 0-916211-02-9, 407). Palladium Bks.

--Palladium Books of Weapons & Castles. 3rd ed. Korona, Robin, ed. (Weapons Ser.: No. 2). (Illus.). 48p. 1984. pap. 4.95 (ISBN 0-916211-08-8, 405). Palladium Bks.

Balent, Matthew & Marciniszyn, Alex. The Palladium Book of European Castles. (Weapons Ser.: No. 7). (Illus.). 48p. (Orig.). 1985. pap. 5.95 (ISBN 0-916211-11-8). Palladium Bks.

Balentine, J. Douglas. Pathology of Oxygen Toxicity. 346p. 1982. 55.00 (ISBN 0-12-077080-6). Acad Pr.

Balentine, Samuel E. The Hidden God: The Hiding of the Face of God in the Old Testament. (Oxford Theological Monographs). 1983. 32.00x (ISBN 0-19-826719-3). Oxford U Pr.

Balerdi, Susan. France: The Crossroads of Europe. (Discovering Our Heritage Ser.). (Illus.). 142p. (gr. 5-8). 1984. PLB 10.95 (ISBN 0-87518-248-8). Dillon.

Bales. Christ: The Fulfillment of the Law & Prophets. pap. 3.95 (ISBN 0-89315-009-6). Lambert Bk.

Bales, J. D. Communism & the Reality of Moral Law. 1969. pap. 3.75 (ISBN 0-934532-01-X). Presby & Reformed.

--The Holy Spirit & the Human Spirit. 5.95 (ISBN 0-89315-104-1). Lambert Bk.

--Restoration, Reformation or Revelation? 6.95 (ISBN 0-89315-236-6). Lambert Bk.

Bales, Jack, jt. auth. see Scharnhorst, Gary.

Bales, James. Biblical Doctrine of Christ. pap. 2.50 (ISBN 0-89315-020-7). Lambert Bk.

--Biblical Doctrine of God. pap. 2.50 (ISBN 0-89315-021-5). Lambert Bk.

--Communism Killed Kennedy but Did America Learn? 3.95 (ISBN 0-89315-015-0). Lambert Bk.

--Evangelism: Every Member, Every Day. pap. 2.50 (ISBN 0-89315-038-X). Lambert Bk.

--Jesus the Master Respondent. 2.50 (ISBN 0-89315-130-0). Lambert Bk.

--Romans. 2.50 (ISBN 0-89315-241-2). Lambert Bk.

--Two Worlds: Christianity & Communism. pap. 2.25 (ISBN 0-686-80419-8). Lambert Bk.

--You Believe. pap. 2.95 (ISBN 0-89315-425-3). Lambert Bk.

Bales, James & Teller, Woosey. Bales Teller Debate. pap. 4.95 (ISBN 0-89315-018-5). Lambert Bk.

Bales, James D. The Cross & the Church. pap. 1.95 (ISBN 0-89315-011-8). Lambert Bk.

--The Deacon & His Work. pap. 1.95 (ISBN 0-89315-025-8). Lambert Bk.

--The Faith Under Fire. 4.95 (ISBN 0-89315-050-9). Lambert Bk.

--The Finality of Faith. pap. 2.50 (ISBN 0-89315-051-7). Lambert Bk.

--The Holy Spirit & the Christian. pap. 3.95 (ISBN 0-89315-103-3). Lambert Bk.

--How Can Ye Believe? 4.95 (ISBN 0-89315-105-X). Lambert Bk.

--The Hub of the Bible. pap. 4.95 (ISBN 0-89315-107-6). Lambert Bk.

--Miracles or Mirages? 1956. 3.00 (ISBN 0-88027-010-1). Firm Foun Pub.

--Pentecostalism in the Church. pap. 2.95 (ISBN 0-89315-204-8). Lambert Bk.

--The Psalm for the Frightened & Frustrated Sheep. 1977. pap. 1.50 (ISBN 0-89315-216-1). Lambert Bk.

--Saul: From Persecutor to Persecuted. pap. 2.95 (ISBN 0-89315-252-8). Lambert Bk.

--Soils & Seeds of Sectarianism. 1977. pap. 4.50 (ISBN 0-89315-264-1). Lambert Bk.

--The Sower Goes Forth. 4.50 (ISBN 0-89315-259-5). Lambert Bk.

--Studies in Hebrews. pap. 3.95 (ISBN 0-89315-260-9). Lambert Bk.

Bales, Peter. The Art of Brachygraphie: That Is, to Write As Fast As a Man Speaketh Treatably, Writing but One Letter for a Word. LC 70-38146. (English Experience Ser.: No. 426). 120p. 1972. Repr. of 1597 ed. 11.50 (ISBN 90-221-0426-5). Walter J Johnson.

--The Writing Schoolmaster: Brachygraphie, Orthographie, Calygraphie. LC 70-26226. (English Experience Ser.: No. 194). 122p. 1969. Repr. of 1590 ed. 16.00 (ISBN 90-221-0194-0). Walter J Johnson.

Bales, Robert F. The Fixation Factor, in Alcohol Addition: An Hypothesis Derived from a Comparative Study of Irish-Jewish Social Norms. Zuckerman, Harriet & Merton, Robert K., eds. LC 79-8971. (Dissertations in Sociology Ser.). 1980. lib. bdg. 40.00x (ISBN 0-405-12948-3). Ayer Co Pubs.

--Interaction Process Analysis. (Midway Reprint Ser.). 1951. pap. 10.00x (ISBN 0-226-03618-9). U of Chicago Pr.

--Symlog Case Study Kit: With Instructions for a Group Self-Study. LC 79-7480. 1980. pap. text ed. 11.95 (ISBN 0-02-901310-0). Free Pr.

Bales, Robert F., et al. Symlog: A Manual for the Case Study of Groups. LC 79-7480. (Illus.). 1979. 29.95 (ISBN 0-02-901300-3). Free Pr.

Bales, W. I. Tso Tsung T'ang: Soldier & Statesman of Old China. lib. bdg. 79.95 (ISBN 0-87968-475-5). Krishna Pr.

Bales, William J. Facial Rejuvenation by Applied Pressure. (Illus.). 1977. pap. 9.95x (ISBN 0-9600560-1-7). Applied Press.

--Facial Rejuvenation by Applied Pressure. 3rd & rev. ed. (Illus.). 1978. pap. text ed. 9.95 (ISBN 0-9600560-1-7). Bales.

Balescu, Radu C. Equilibrium & Non-Equilibrium Statistical Mechanics. LC 74-20907. 742p. 1975. 67.95 (ISBN 0-471-04600-0, Pub. by Wiley-Interscience). Wiley.

Balesi, Charles J. From Adversaries to Comrades-in-Arms: West Africans & French Military, 1885-1918. 196p. 1979. pap. 12.00 (ISBN 0-918456-27-4, Crossroads). African Studies Assn.

Balestrino, Philip. Skeleton Inside You. LC 72-132290. (Crocodile Paperback Ser.). (gr. k-3). 1971. pap. 2.94 (ISBN 0-690-01263-2). Crowell Jr Bks.

--Skeleton Inside You. LC 72-132290. (A Let's-Read-and-Find-Out Science Bk). (Illus.). (gr. k-3). 1971. PLB 11.89 (ISBN 0-690-74123-5). Crowell Jr Bks.

Baley, B. A., jt. ed. see Jaeger, T. A.

Baley, James A. The Athlete's Guide: Increasing Strength, Power & Agility. 1982. pap. 5.95 (ISBN 0-13-049841-6, Reward). P-H.

Baley, James A. & Matthews, David L. Law & Liability in Athletics, Physical Education, & Recreation. LC 83-22492. 448p. 1984. 30.95x (ISBN 0-205-08115-0, 628115, Pub. by Longwood Div). Allyn.

Baley, James A., jt. auth. see Piscopo, John.

Baley, John D. Semi-Programmed Arithmetic for College Students. 144p. 1975. pap. text ed. 8.95x (ISBN 0-669-90886-X). Heath.

Baley, John D., et al. Basic Mathematics: A Program for Semi-Independent Study. 1978. pap. text ed. 19.95x (ISBN 0-669-01019-7); inst. resource bk. 1.95 (ISBN 0-669-01020-0); Set. cassette 150.00 (ISBN 0-669-01165-7); free tapescript (ISBN 0-669-01022-7). Heath.

Baley, Noel A. Where Is the Hope: The Baley Report. LC 80-68996. 171p. 1982. 8.95 (ISBN 0-533-04825-7). Vantage.

Baleyte, Jean, ed. see Quemner, T. A.

Balfe, Judith & Wyszomirski, Jane, eds. Art, Ideology & Politics. LC 84-26325. 384p. 1985. 39.95x (ISBN 0-03-000364-4). Praeger.

Balfoort, Dirk J. Antonius Stradivarius. LC 79-181106. 60p. 21.00 (ISBN 0-403-01505-7). Scholarly.

Balfour, A. & Marwick, D. H. Programming in Standard FORTRAN 77. LC 79-7450. (Heinemann Educational Bks.). 388p. 1979. 25.75 (ISBN 0-444-19465-7, North Holland). Elsevier.

Balfour, A. see Gunn, Hugh.

Balfour, A. J. Theism & Humanism. Repr. of 1915 ed. 24.00 (ISBN 0-527-04810-0). Kraus Repr.

Balfour, Arthur J. Essays & Addresses. LC 72-3422. (Essay Index Reprint Ser.). Repr. of 1893 ed. 18.00 (ISBN 0-8369-2890-3). Ayer Co Pubs.

--Essays, Speculative & Political. facsimile ed. LC 76-142604. (Essay Index Reprint Ser). Repr. of 1921 ed. 20.00 (ISBN 0-8369-2306-5). Ayer Co Pubs.

--Theism & Thought: A Study in Familiar Beliefs. LC 77-27208. (Gifford Lectures: 1922-23). Repr. of 1923 ed. 22.50 (ISBN 0-404-60469-2). AMS Pr.

Balfour, C. M. County Folklore Vol. IV: Printed Extracts No. 6, Examples of Printed Folklore Concerning Northumberland. Thomas, Northcote W., ed. (Folk-Lore Society, London, vol. 53). pap. 18.00 (ISBN 0-317-16283-7). Kraus Repr.

Balfour, Campbell, ed. Participation in Industry. 217p. 1973. 17.50x (ISBN 0-87471-429-X). Rowman.

Balfour, D., jt. ed. see Grant, W. A.

Balfour, D. J., ed. Nicotine & the Tobacco Smoking Habit. LC 83-21939. (International Encyclopedia of Pharmacology & Therapeutics Ser.: Section 114). (Illus.). 220p. 1984. 65.00 (ISBN 0-08-030779-5). Pergamon.

Balfour, David. Ancient Orkney Melodies. LC 73-14636. 1978. Repr. of 1885 ed. lib. bdg. 17.50 (ISBN 0-88305-071-4). Norwood Edns.

--Ancient Orkney Melodies. 1982. lib. bdg. 34.50. Porter.

--Saint Gregory the Sinaite: Discourse on he Transfiguration. 170p. 1985. Repr. lib. bdg. 19.95x (ISBN 0-89370-862-3). Borgo Pr.

Balfour, David, ed. Oppressions of the Sixteenth Century in the Islands of Orkney & Zetland: From Original Documents. (Maitland Club, Glasgow. Publications: No. 75). Repr. of 1859 ed. 17.50 (ISBN 0-404-53114-8). AMS Pr.

Balfour, E. B. The Living Soil & the Haughley Experiment. LC 75-27030. 384p. 1976. 20.00x (ISBN 0-87663-269-X). Universe.

Balfour, Frederic H. Taoist Texts. lib. bdg. 79.95 (ISBN 0-87968-191-8). Krishna Pr.

Balfour, Graham. Life of Robert Louis Stevenson, 2 vols. 1973. Repr. of 1901 ed. 40.00 (ISBN 0-8274-1440-4). R West.
--Life of Robert Louis Stevenson, 2 Vols. LC 1-25406. 1968. Repr. of 1901 ed. Set. 29.00x (ISBN 0-403-00143-9). Scholarly.
--The Life of Robert Louis Stevenson. 451p. 1983. Repr. of 1901 ed. lib. bdg. 45.00 (ISBN 0-89987-953-5). Darby Bks.
--The Life of Robert Louis Stevenson. 451p. 1983. lib. bdg. 30.00 (ISBN 0-89987-960-8). Darby Bks.
Balfour, Harold. Folk, Fish & Fun. (Illus.). 1979. 20.00x (ISBN 0-900963-85-9, Pub. by Terence Dalton England). State Mutual Bk.
Balfour, Henry. Natural History of the Musical Bow. LC 76-22326. (Illus.). 1976. Repr. of 1899 ed. lib. bdg. 12.50 (ISBN 0-89341-006-3). Longwood Pub Group.
Balfour, Henry, et al. Anthropological Essays Presented to Edward Burnett Tyler: In Honour of His 75th Birthday. LC 76-44683. (Festschrift). Repr. of 1907 ed. 39.00 (ISBN 0-404-15900-1). AMS Pr.
Balfour, Henry H., Jr. & Heussner, Ralph C. Herpes Diseases & Your Health. (Illus.). 150p. 1984. 14.95x (ISBN 0-8166-1335-4). U of Minn Pr.
--Herpes Diseases & Your Health. (Illus.). 1985. pap. 8.95 (ISBN 0-8166-1432-6). U of Minn Pr.
Balfour, I. B., ed. see De Bary, Anton.
Balfour, Issac B., tr. see Goebel, K.
Balfour, John. The Armoured Train. (Illus.). 168p. 1981. 29.00 (ISBN 0-7134-2547-4, Pub. by Batsford England). David & Charles.
Balfour, Michael. Britain & Joseph Chamberlain. 256p. 1985. text ed. 28.50x (ISBN 0-04-942191-3). Allen Unwin.
--The Kaiser & His Times. 560p. 1972. pap. 9.95x (ISBN 0-393-00661-1, Norton Lib). Norton.
--Magic Snake Shapes. 96p. 1981. pap. 1.95 (ISBN 0-671-45001-8). PB.
--West Germany: A Contemporary History. LC 81-21293. 1982. 25.00 (ISBN 0-312-86297-0). St Martin.
Balfour, Michael & Mair, John. Four Power Control in Germany & Austria, 1945-1946. Repr. of 1956 ed. 42.00 (ISBN 0-384-03138-2). Johnson Repr.
Balfour, Michael, et al, eds. Europe in the Eighties: An Encyclopedia of Contemporary European Politics, Economics & Culture. 400p. 1986. 59.95 (ISBN 0-943828-59-7). Karz-Cohl Pub.
Balfour-Browne, F. Water Beetles & Other Things (Half a Century's Work) 226p. 1962. 37.00x (ISBN 0-317-07182-3, Pub. by FW Classey UK). State Mutual Bk.
Balgopal, Pallassana R. & Vassil, Thomas V. Groups in Social Work: An Ecological Approach. 300p. 1983. text ed. write for info. (ISBN 0-02-305530-8). Macmillan.
Bali, Dev R. Modern Indian Thought from Ram Mohan Roy to M. N. Roy. 2nd ed. 1984. pap. text ed. 8.95x (ISBN 0-86590-310-7, Sterling Pubs India). Apt Bks.
Balian, Edward S. How to Design, Analyze, & Write Doctoral Research: The Practical Guidebook. LC 82-20164. (Illus.). 268p. (Orig.). 1983. lib. bdg. 25.75 (ISBN 0-8191-2879-1); pap. text ed. 13.25 (ISBN 0-8191-2880-5). U Pr of Amer.
Balian, Lorna. The Aminal. LC 74-186614. (Illus.). 48p. (ps-2). 1972. 9.95 (ISBN 0-687-01267-8). Abingdon.
--Bah! Humbug? LC 76-50625. (Illus.). (gr. k-3). 1982. 9.95 (ISBN 0-687-02345-9). Abingdon.
--Humbug Potion: An A B Cipher. 32p. 1984. 12.95 (ISBN 0-687-18021-X). Abingdon.
--Humbug Rabbit. rev. ed. LC 73-9555. (Illus.). 32p. (gr. k-2). 1974. 10.95 (ISBN 0-687-18046-5). Abingdon.
--Humbug Witch. (Illus.). (gr. k-2). 1965. 9.95 (ISBN 0-687-18023-6). Abingdon.
--Leprechauns Never Lie. LC 79-25950. (Illus.). 32p. (gr. k-3). 1980. 8.75 (ISBN 0-687-21371-1). Abingdon.
--Mother's Mother's Day. LC 81-10988. 32p. (ps-3). 1982. 9.95g (ISBN 0-687-27253-X). Abingdon.
--Sometimes It's Turkey, Sometimes It's Feathers. rev. ed. LC 72-3867. (Illus.). 32p. (gr. k-11). 1973. 9.95 (ISBN 0-687-39074-5). Abingdon.
--A Sweetheart for Valentine. rev. ed. LC 79-3957. (Illus.). 32p. (gr. k-3). 1979. 11.95 (ISBN 0-687-40771-0). Abingdon.
Balian, R. & Adam, J. G. Laser-Plasma Interactions. (Les Houches Summer School Ser.: Vol. 34). 808p. 1982. 159.75 (ISBN 0-444-86215-3, I-183-82). Elsevier.
Balian, R. & Adouse, J. Physical Cosmology. (Les Houches Summer School Ser.: Vol. 32). 668p. 1980. 115.00 (ISBN 0-444-85433-9). Elsevier.
Balian, R. & Llewellyn-Smith, C. H. Weak & Electromagnetic Interactions at High Energy: Proceedings at the Summer School on Weak & Electromagnetic Interactions at High Energy, Session XXIX, les Houches, July 5 - August 14. 1976. 670p. 1978. 117.00 (ISBN 0-7204-0742-7, North-Holland). Elsevier.
Balian, R. & Iagolnitzer, D., eds. Structural Analysis of Collision Amplitudes: Proceedings, les Houches June Institute of Physics, June 2-27, 1975. LC 76-17583. 1976. 95.75 (ISBN 0-7204-0506-8, North-Holland). Elsevier.
Balian, R. & Zinn-Justin, J., eds. Methods in Field Theory: Les Houches Session XXVIII. xx, 386p. 1981. pap. 21.00x (ISBN 9971-83-015-9, Pub. by World Sci Singapore). Taylor & Francis.
Balian, R., et al, eds. Claude Bloch Scientific Works, 2 vols. LC 74-84212. 1532p. 1975. Set. 234.00 (ISBN 0-444-10853-X, North-Holland). Elsevier.
--Atomic & Molecular Physics & the Interstellar Matter, 2 vols. LC 75-23253. (Les Houches Summer School Ser.: Vol. 26). 632p. 1975. Set. 115.00 (ISBN 0-444-10856-4, North-Holland). Elsevier.
--Physics of Defects: Proceedings of the Les Houches Summer School Session, XXXV. (Les Houches Summer Session Ser.: Vol. 35). 884p. 1982. 170.25 (ISBN 0-444-86225-0). Elsevier.
--Nuclear Physics with Heavy Ions & Mesons, 2 vols. (Les Houches Summer Session Ser.: No. 30). (Proceedings). 1979. Set. 172.50 (ISBN 0-444-85232-8); Vol. 1. 91.50 (ISBN 0-444-85122-4); Vol. 2. 115.00 (ISBN 0-444-85231-X). Elsevier.
Balian, R. M., et al, eds. Membranes & Intercellular Communication. (Les Houches Summer School Ser.: Vol. 33). 658p. 1981. 115.00 (ISBN 0-444-85469-X, North-Holland). Elsevier.
Balibar, Etienne, jt. auth. see Althusser, Louis.
Balicki, Stanislaw W., et al. Cultural Policy in Poland. LC 73-79494. (Studies & Documents on Cultural Policies). (Illus.). 67p. (Orig.). 1973. pap. 5.00 (ISBN 92-3-101067-0, U135, UNESCO). Unipub.
Baliga, B. J. & Chen, D. Y., eds. Power Transistors: Device Design & Applications. LC 84-19747. 1984. 51.95 (ISBN 0-87942-181-9, PC01750). Inst Electrical.
Baliga, R. R., jt. auth. see Negandhi, Anant R.
Balika, Susan S. Jesus Is My Special Friend. LC 81-86702. (Happy Day Bks.). (Illus.). 24p. (Orig.). (ps-3). 1982. pap. 1.39 (ISBN 0-87239-541-3, 3587). Standard Pub.
Balikci, Asen. Netsilik Eskimo. LC 71-114660. 1971. pap. 7.95 (ISBN 0-385-05766-0). Natural Hist.
Balin, Bobbi. Miss Raggedy Taggedy. LC 85-60793. (Illus.). 36p. (Orig.). (gr. 2-5). 1985. pap. 6.95 (ISBN 0-932967-02-7). Pacific Shoreline.
Balin, George. Afrika Korps. (Illus.). 64p. (Orig.). 1985. pap. 5.95 (ISBN 0-85368-692-0, Pub. by Arms & Armour). Sterling.
--D-Day Tank Battles: Beachhead to Breakout, No. 10. (Tanks Illustrated Ser.). (Illus.). 64p. 1984. pap. 7.95 (ISBN 0-85368-633-5, Pub. by Arms & Armour Pr). Sterling.
Balin, H. & Glasser, S., eds. Reproductive Biology. 1973. 74.50 (ISBN 0-444-15004-8, Excerpta Medica). Elsevier.
Balin, Peter. Flight of the Feathered Serpent. (Illus.). 184p. 1983. pap. 10.95 (ISBN 0-910261-01-6). Arcana Pub.
--Xultun Tarot. 2nd ed. (Illus., Orig.). 1981. 12.95 (ISBN 0-914794-33-7). Wisdom Garden.
--Xultun Tarot: A Maya Tarot Deck. 2nd ed. (Illus.). 78p. 1982. pap. 12.95 (ISBN 0-910261-00-8). Arcana Pub.
Balin, Peter & Delap, Richard. The Flight of Feathered Serpent. LC 78-64357. (Illus.). 184p. 1978. pap. 8.95 perfect bound (ISBN 0-914794-32-9). Wisdom Garden.
Balinkin, Ausma. The Central Women Figures in Carl Zuckmayer's Dramas. (European University Studies, German Language & Literature: Ser. 1, Vol. 235). 115p. 1978. pap. 13.25 (ISBN 3-261-03084-4). P Lang Pubs.
Balinski, M. L. & Hoffman, A. J. Polyhedral Combinatorics, Vol. 8. 234p. 1978. pap. 30.00 (ISBN 0-444-85196-8). Elsevier.
Balinski, M. L. & Lamarechal, C. Mathematical Programming in Use. 196p. 1978. pap. 30.00 (ISBN 0-444-85195-X). Elsevier.
Balinski, M. L. & Cottle, R. W., eds. Complementary & Fixed Point Problems. (Mathematical Programming Studies: Vol. 7). 184p. 1978. pap. 30.00 (ISBN 0-444-85123-2, North-Holland). Elsevier.
Balinski, Michel L. & Young, H. Peyton. Fair Representation: Meeting the Ideal of One Man, One Vote. LC 81-11518. (Illus.). 200p. 1982. 33.00x (ISBN 0-300-02724-9). Yale U Pr.
Balinsky, B. I. An Introduction to Embryology. 5th ed. 1981. text ed. 36.95 (ISBN 0-03-057712-8, CBS C). SCP.
Balinsky, Benjamin. Improving Personnel Selection Through Effective Interviewing: Essentials for Management. LC 77-94944. (Orig.). 1978. perfect bdg. 8.95 (ISBN 0-935198-04-0); pap. 8.50 saddle stitch (ISBN 0-935198-05-9). M M Bruce.
Balint, Andor. Physiological Genetics of Agricultural Crops. 167p. 15.00 (ISBN 9-63053-288-3, 991000439). Heyden.
Balint, G., jt. ed. see Varro, V.
Balint, Michael. The Basic Fault: Therapeutic Aspects of Regression. LC 79-15682. (Classics in Psychoanalysis: No. 5). 1979. Repr. of 1968 ed. 22.00 (ISBN 0-87630-219-3). Brunner-Mazel.
--The Doctor, His Patient & the Illness. 2nd ed. 395p. (Orig.). 1963. text ed. 32.50 (ISBN 0-8236-1380-1). Intl Univs Pr.
--Problems of Human Pleasure & Behavior. 1957. text ed. 8.95x (ISBN 0-87140-985-2). Liveright.
--Problems of Human Pleasure & Behavior. 1973. pap. 3.95 (ISBN 0-87140-279-3). Liveright.
--Thrills & Regressions. 148p. (Orig.). 1959. text ed. 17.50 (ISBN 0-8236-6540-2). Intl Univs Pr.
Balint, Michael, ed. see Ferenczi, Sandor.
Balint, Michael, et al. Treatment or Diagnosis: A Study of Repeat Prescriptions in General Practice. 208p. 1984. pap. text ed. 15.95 (ISBN 0-422-78770-1, 4004). Methuen Inc.
Balio, Tino. United Artists: The Company Built by the Stars. LC 75-12208. (Illus.). 344p. 1976. 22.50x (ISBN 0-299-06940-0); pap. 13.50x (ISBN 0-299-06944-3). U of Wis Pr.
Balio, Tino, ed. The American Film Industry. 2nd, rev. ed. LC 84-40143. (Illus.). 660p. 1984. text ed. 32.50x (ISBN 0-299-09870-2); pap. 14.95x (ISBN 0-299-09874-5). U of Wis Pr.
Balio, Tino & Gomery, Douglas, eds. High Sierra. LC 79-3961. (Wisconsin-Warner Bros. Screenplay Ser.). (Illus.). 200p. 1979. 17.50x (ISBN 0-299-07930-9); pap. 6.95t (ISBN 0-299-07934-1). U of Wis Pr.
Balio, Tino, jt. ed. see Behlmer, Rudy.
Balio, Tino, jt. ed. see Cripps, Thomas.
Baliozian, Ara. The Armenians. LC 80-19619. 250p. 1980. pap. 6.95 (ISBN 0-933706-22-7). Ararat Pr.
Baliozian, Ara, ed. see Pushkin, Alexander, et al.
Baliozian, Ara, tr. see Yessayan, Zabel.
Baliozian, Ara, tr. see Zarian, Gostan.
Balis, Andrea. What Are You Using: A Birth Control Guide for Teenagers. 111p. (YA) 1981. 2.95, ea. for 1-5 copies (ISBN 0-317-36544-4); 2.66, ea. for 6-25 copies (ISBN 0-317-36545-2); 2.36, ea. for 26 copies or more (ISBN 0-317-36546-0). Ed-U Pr.
Balis, Andrea & Reiser, Robert. P. J. 160p. (gr. 3-6). 1984. 10.95 (ISBN 0-395-36006-4, 5-81180). HM.
Balis, George U., jt. auth. see Reid, William H.
Balitas, Maggie, ed. see Ball, Jeff.
Balitas, Maggie, ed. see Wade, Herb.
Balitzer, Alfred. A Nation of Associations. 1981. pap. 15.00 (ISBN 0-88034-000-2). Am Soc Assn Execs.
Balitzer, Alfred, ed. A Time for Choosing: The Speeches of Ronald Reagan. Reagan, Ronald. LC 83-42905. 512p. 1983. pap. 9.95 (ISBN 0-89526-838-8). Regnery-Gateway.
Baliunas, S. L. & Hartmann, L., eds. Cool Stars, Stellar Systems, & the Sun: Proceedings of the Third Cambridge Workshop on Cool Stars, Stellar Systems, & the Sun, Held in Cambridge MA, October 5-7. (Lecture Notes in Physics Ser.: Vol. 193). vii, 364p. 1984. pap. 22.00 (ISBN 0-387-12907-3). Springer-Verlag.
Balizet, Carol. The Face of the Enemy. 384p. (Orig.). 1984. pap. 7.95 (ISBN 0-310-60801-5, 13050P, Pub. by Chosen Bks). Zondervan.
Balje, O. E. Turbomechanics: A Guide to Design, Selection & Theory. LC 80-21524. 513p. 1981. 64.95 (ISBN 0-471-06036-4, Pub. by Wiley-Interscience). Wiley.
Baljian-Gara, N. Noesis. (Contemporary Poets of Dorrance Ser.). 64p. 1982. 5.95 (ISBN 0-8059-2840-5). Dorrance.
Baljian-Gara, N. R. An Elegy, to Pace Upon a Plain. (Contemporary Poets of Dorrance Ser.). 80p. 1981. 3.95 (ISBN 0-8059-2800-6). Dorrance.
--Into the End. 52p. 1984. 5.95 (ISBN 0-8059-2926-6). Dorrance.
--The Mind Compelling. (Contemporary Poets of Dorrance Ser.). 1976. 2.95 (ISBN 0-8059-2336-5). Dorrance.
--Sonic Scotia. (Contemporary Poets of Dorrance Ser.). 53p. 1980. 3.50 (ISBN 0-8059-2751-4). Dorrance.
Baljo, Wallace, Jr. Cooking Frankly: Hot Dog Cuisine. (Illus.). 175p. (Orig.). pap. write for info. (ISBN 0-9606084-1-9). Clipboard.
--Grand Coulee: A Story of the Columbia River from Molten Lavas & Ice to Grand Coulee Dam. rev. ed. (Illus.). 80p. (gr. 4-6). pap. write for info. (ISBN 0-9606084-0-0). Clipboard.
Balk, Alfred. The Free List: Property Without Taxes. LC 78-129147. 276p. 1971. 9.95x (ISBN 0-87154-083-5). Russell Sage.
Balk, Alfred, ed. see Twentieth Century Fund. Task Force Report for a National News Council.
Balk, Christianne. Bindweed. Hecht, Anthony, ed. 64p. 1986. 13.95 (ISBN 0-02-627660-7); pap. 7.95 (ISBN 0-02-071220-0). MacMillan.
Balk, F., jt. auth. see Koeman, J. H.
Balk, H. Wesley. The Complete Singer-Actor: Training for Music Theatre. LC 77-83504. 1978. pap. 9.95x (ISBN 0-8166-0823-7). U of Minn Pr.
Balk, Melvin W. & Melby, Edward C., Jr. Importance of Laboratory Animal Genetics: Health & Environment in Biomedical Research. 1984. 28.00 (ISBN 0-12-489520-4). Acad Pr.
Balk, P., ed. The Si-Sio2 System. 1984. write for info. Elsevier.
Balk, Walter L., jt. auth. see Downey, Edward H.
Balkam, Jean & Moran, Cathleen. Pediatric Ambulatory Care Guidelines. LC 83-2684. 480p. 1983. pap. text ed. 21.95 (ISBN 0-89303-263-8). Brady Comm.
Balkan, Eric. The Directory of Software Publishers: How & Where to Sell Your Program. 320p. 1983. 24.95 (ISBN 0-442-21429-4). Van Nos Reinhold.
Balkan, Sheila & Berger, Ronald. Crime & Deviance in America. 416p. 1980. pap. text ed. write for info. (ISBN 0-534-00803-8). Wadsworth Pub.
Balkanski, M. & Moss, T. S. Handbook on Semiconductors: Optical Properties of Semiconductors, Vol. 2. 634p. 1980. 125.75 (ISBN 0-444-85273-5, North-Holland). Elsevier.
Balkanski, M. & Wallis, D. Many-Body Aspects of Optical Spectroscopy. Date not set. write for info. (ISBN 0-444-86829-1). Elsevier.
Balkay, B., tr. see Assonyi, Cs. & Richter, R.
Balkay, B., tr. see Csaki, Frigyes, et al.
Balke, S. T. Quantitative Column Liquid Chromatography: A Survey of Chemometric Methods. (Journal of Chromatography Library: Vol. 29). 1984. 61.00 (ISBN 0-444-42393-1). Elsevier.
Balke, William. Calvin & the Anabaptist Radicals. Heynen, William, tr. LC 81-12438. pap. 87.50 (ISBN 0-317-30132-2, 2025315). Bks Demand UMI.
Balke-Aurell, Gudrun. Changes in Ability as Related to Educational & Occupational Experience. (Goteborg Studies in Educational Science: No. 40). 203p. 1982. pap. text ed. 20.50x (ISBN 91-7346-107-5, Pub. by Goteborg Sweden). Humanities.
Balkema, John B., ed. Aging: A Guide to Resources. LC 83-9010. 232p. (Orig.). 1983. pap. 34.95 (ISBN 0-915794-48-9). Gaylord Prof Pubns.
Balkeslee, James R., jt. auth. see Yohn, David S.
Balkham, K. & Mills, R. Introductory Design Problems. 1979. pap. text ed. 7.50x (ISBN 0-435-75860-8). Heinemann Ed.
Balkin, Richard. How to Understand & Negotiate a Book Contract or Magazine Agreement. (Writer's Basic Bookshelf Ser.). 156p. 1985. 11.95 (ISBN 0-89879-190-1, 1417). Writers Digest.
--A Writer's Guide to Book Publishing. 2nd, rev. & expanded ed. 1981. pap. 10.95 (ISBN 0-317-17741-9, 01063-320, Hawthorn). Dutton.
Balkis, Marjory J. The Adventures of Boy Scouting. 1982. 5.95 (ISBN 0-533-05338-2). Vantage.
Balksus, Pat. Trailblazer for the Sacred Heart. (Encounter Ser.). 1976. 3.00 (ISBN 0-8198-0476-2). Dghtrs St Paul.
Balkuv-Ulutin, S., ed. see Gaffney, P. J.
Ball. Animal Farm (Orwell) (Book Notes). 1984. pap. 2.50 (ISBN 0-8120-3402-3). Barron.
--Architectural Drafting. (Illus.). 320p. 1980. text ed. 24.95 (ISBN 0-8359-0255-2). Reston.
--Light Construction Techniques: From Foundation to Finish. (Illus.). 416p. 1980. ref. ed. 23.95 (ISBN 0-8359-4035-7). Reston.
Ball, jt. auth. see Galloway.
Ball, A. The Price Guide to Pot-Lids & Other Underglaze Multicolour Prints on Ware. 2nd ed. (Price Guide Ser.). (Illus.). 320p. 1980. 44.50 (ISBN 0-902028-56-1). Antique Collect.
--Price Guide to Pot Lids & Other Underglaze Multicolor Prints on Ware. (Illus.). 1980. 44.50 (ISBN 0-902028-56-1). Apollo.
Ball, A. H., ed. see Ruskin, John.
Ball, A. R., tr. see Fitzpatrick, Edward A.
Ball, Adrian. The Last Day of the Old World. LC 77-18896. 1978. Repr. of 1963 ed. lib. bdg. 22.25x (ISBN 0-313-20202-8, BALD). Greenwood.
Ball, Adrian & Wright, Diana. SS Great Britain. (Illus.). 96p. 1981. 18.95 (ISBN 0-7153-8096-6). David & Charles.
Ball, Alan R. Modern Politics & Government. 4th ed. 320p. 1986. pap. 11.95x (ISBN 0-934540-45-4). Chatham Hse Pubs.
Ball, Albert. Incentive Reimbursement & Innovation in Health Care. 62p. 5.00 (ISBN 0-318-16284-9, E-9). Public Int Econ.
Ball, Ann. Modern Saints: Their Lives & Faces. LC 82-50357. (Illus.). 457p. 1983. pap. 10.00 (ISBN 0-89555-222-1). TAN Bks Pubs.
Ball, Armand B. & Ball, Beverly H. Basic Camp Management. 1979. pap. 9.00 (ISBN 0-87603-045-2). Am Camping.
Ball, Barbara. Coffee Talk: Sharing Christ Through Friendly Gatherings. LC 79-53980. 80p. 1980. pap. 5.50 (ISBN 0-934396-08-6). Churches Alive.
--The Hidden Heart. (Cadrice Romance Ser.: No. 34). 160p. 1984. pap. 1.95 (ISBN 0-441-32908-X). Ace Bks.
Ball, Ben. Careers Counseling in Practice. 175p. 1984. 25.00 (ISBN 0-905273-70-2, Pub. by Falmer Pr); pap. 15.00 (ISBN 0-905273-69-9, Pub. by Falmer Pr). Taylor & Francis.
Ball, Beverly H., jt. auth. see Ball, Armand B.
Ball, Bonnie S., compiled by. Scott County, Virginia: U.S. Census 1850. 182p. Repr. of 1963 ed. write for info. (ISBN 0-685-65085-5). Va Bk.
Ball, Brian. Death of a Low-Handicapped Man. LC 78-60749. (British Mystery Ser.). 175p. 1984. pap. 2.95 (ISBN 0-8027-3063-9). Walker & Co.
--Montenegrin Gold. (British Mysteries Ser.). 1984. pap. 2.95 (ISBN 0-8027-3050-7). Walker & Co.
--Space Guardians. (Space - 1999). 142p. 1975. lib. bdg. 5.95 (ISBN 0-88411-673-5, Pub. by Aeonian Pr). Amereon Ltd.
Ball, Bryan W. The English Connection: The Puritan Roots of Seventh-Day Adventist Belief. 252p. 1981. text ed. 15.95 (ISBN 0-227-67844-3). Attic Pr.
Ball, C. Slavery in the United States. 1836. 29.00 (ISBN 0-527-04850-X). Kraus Repr.
Ball, Charles. Fifty Years in Chains. 9.00 (ISBN 0-8446-0021-0). Peter Smith.

--Fifty Years in Chains: Or, the Life of an American Slave. facs. ed. LC 70-89426. (Black Heritage Library Collection Ser.). 1858. 17.50 (ISBN 0-8369-8507-9). Ayer Co Pubs.
--Fifty Years in Chains: Or the Life of an American Slave. LC 78-92413. 430p. 1859. Repr. 16.00x (ISBN 0-403-00149-8). Scholarly.
--Slavery in the United States: A Narrative of the Life & Adventures of Charles Ball, a Black Man. LC 68-55869. Repr. of 1837 ed. cancelled (ISBN 0-8371-4304-7). Greenwood.
--Slavery in the United States: A Narrative of the Life & Adventures of Charles Ball, a Black Man. LC 71-92414. 1970. Repr. of 1836 ed. 11.00 (ISBN 0-403-00178-1). Scholarly.
Ball, Charles E. Lafcadio Hearn: An Appreciation. LC 74-13639. 1926. lib. bdg. 17.00 (ISBN 0-8414-3251-1). Folcroft.
--Saddle up: The Farm Journal Book of Western Horsemanship. LC 71-11065. (Illus.). 1973. 12.45i (ISBN 0-397-00668-3); pap. 9.95i (ISBN 0-397-00990-9, LP-083). Har-Row.
Ball, Christopher, ed. Genetics & Breeding of Industrial Microorganisms. 240p. 1984. 72.00 (ISBN 0-8493-5672-5). CRC Pr.
Ball, Colin & Ball, Mary. Fit for Work? Youth, School & (un) Employment. 144p. pap. 5.95 (ISBN 0-906495-12-1). Writers & Readers.
Ball, Colin & Ball, Mog. Fit for Work? Youth, School & Unemployment. (Chameleon Education Ser.). 144p. (Orig.). 1981. pap. 5.95 (ISBN 0-686-30858-1). Writers & Readers.
Ball, David. Backwards & Forwards: A Technical Manual for Reading Plays. LC 82-19333. 128p. (Orig.). 1983. pap. 6.95x (ISBN 0-8093-1110-0). S Ill U Pr.
Ball, David, jt. auth. see Ross, Steven.
Ball, Derrick F., et al. Agglomeration of Iron Ores. LC 74-168614. pap. 102.00 (ISBN 0-317-10267-2, 2050890). Bks Demand UMI.
Ball, Desmond. Strategy & Defence: Australian Essays. 400p. 1983. text ed. 37.50x (ISBN 0-86861-316-9). Allen Unwin.
Ball, Desmond, ed. The Anzac Connection. (Illus.). 169p. 1985. text ed. 22.50x (ISBN 0-86861-503-X). Allen Unwin.
Ball, Desmond & Langtry, J. O., eds. Civil Defence & Australia's Security in the Nuclear Age. 350p. 1984. 18.50x (ISBN 0-86861-382-7). Allen Unwin.
Ball, Desmond J. Politics & Force Levels: The Strategic Missile Program of the Kennedy Administration. LC 78-57302. 400p. 1981. 40.00x (ISBN 0-520-03698-0). U of Cal Pr.
Ball, Doc. California Surfriders, 1946. 2nd ed. 116p. 1946. cloth 19.95 (ISBN 0-911449-05-1). Mountain Sea.
Ball, Don, Jr. America's Railroads: The Second Generation. (Illus.). 224p. 1980. 44.95 (ISBN 0-393-01416-9). Norton.
--Railroads. (Illus.). 1985. 37.50 (ISBN 0-393-02236-6). Norton.
--Rails. (Illus.). 1981. 24.95 (ISBN 0-393-01480-0). Norton.
Ball, Don, Jr. & Whitaker, Rogers E. Decade of the Trains: The Nineteen Forties. LC 75-37282. (Illus.). 1980. pap. 19.95 (ISBN 0-8212-0759-8, 178861). NYGS.
Ball, Donald & McCulloch, Wendell, Jr. International Business: Introduction & Essentials. 2nd ed. 1985. 28.95 (ISBN 0-256-03252-1). Business Pubns.
Ball, Donald W. Microecology: Social Situations & Intimate Space. pap. text ed. 3.95x (ISBN 0-8290-0328-2). Irvington.
Ball, Donna. Winners: A Love Story. 294p. 1982. 13.95 (ISBN 0-312-88229-7). St Martin.
Ball, Dorothy W. Don't Drive up a Dirt Road. LC 73-112653. (gr. 5-9). 1969. PLB 6.87 (ISBN 0-87460-144-4). Lion Bks.
Ball, Douglas. Victorian Publisher's Bindings. (Illus.). 204p. 1985. 32.50 (ISBN 0-916271-01-3). BkPr Ltd.
Ball, E. F., et al. The Middletown Photographs. Sargent, T. A., ed. (Illus.). 68p. (Orig.). 1984. pap. 5.00 (ISBN 0-915511-01-0). Ball State Art.
Ball, Eve. In the Days of Victorio: Recollections of a Warm Springs Apache. LC 73-101103. 222p. 1970. pap. 7.95 (ISBN 0-8165-0401-6). U of Ariz Pr.
--Indeh: An Apache Odyssey. LC 80-13186. (Illus.). 1980. 15.95 (ISBN 0-8425-1789-8). Brigham.
--Ma'am Jones of the Pecos. LC 68-9336. pap. 66.30 (ISBN 0-317-28057-0, 2025550). Bks Demand UMI.
Ball, Eve, ed. see Klasner, Lily.
Ball, F. Carlton. Decorating Pottery. 3.95 (ISBN 0-934706-05-0). Prof Pubns Ohio.
--Syllabus for Advanced Ceramics. LC 77-187486. pap. 3.95 (ISBN 0-935066-03-9). Keramos Bks.
Ball, F. Eddrington. Swift's Verse. LC 74-8049. 1974. Repr. of 1929 ed. lib. bdg. 35.00 (ISBN 0-8414-3196-5). Folcroft.
Ball, F. Erlington, ed. see Swift, Jonathan.
Ball, Francis E. Swift's Verse: An Essay. LC 70-120226. 1970. Repr. lib. bdg. 31.50 (ISBN 0-374-90365-4). Octagon.
Ball, Geoffrey V. Symptoms in Eye Examination. 154p. 1982. 49.95 (ISBN 0-407-00205-7). Butterworth.
Ball, George, et al. Conference on Foreign Direct Investment in the United States: Proceedings. (Orig.). pap. text ed. 10.00 (ISBN 0-935328-00-9). Intl Law Inst.
Ball, George E., ed. Taxonomy, Phylogeny & Zoogeography of Beetles & Ants. (Entomologica Ser.). 1985. lib. bdg. 105.00 (ISBN 90-6193-511-3, Pub. by Junk Pubs Netherlands). Kluwer Academic.
Ball, George W. The Past Has Another Pattern: Memoirs. LC 81-18924. (Illus.). 510p. 1982. 19.95 (ISBN 0-393-01481-9). Norton.
--The Past Has Another Pattern: Memoirs. (Illus.). 540p. 1983. pap. 9.95 (ISBN 0-393-30142-7). Norton.
Ball, George W., ed. see American Assembly Staff.
Ball, Gerald T., jt. auth. see Owens, Elisabeth A.
Ball, Geraldine. Innerchange Career Education Resource Set for Senior High. 1977. 95.00 (ISBN 0-86584-022-9). Palomares & Assoc.
--Innerchange Career Educational Resource Set for Junior High. 1977. 95.00 (ISBN 0-86584-027-X). Palomares & Assoc.
--Innerchange Conflict Management Resources Set for Sr. High. 95.00 (ISBN 0-86584-023-7). Palomares & Assoc.
--Innerchange Drug Abuse Prevention Resource Set for Jr. High. 95.00 (ISBN 0-86584-029-6). Palomares & Assoc.
--Innerchange Experiences: Reproducible Masters for Senior High. 1977. 29.95 (ISBN 0-86584-018-0). Palomares & Assoc.
--Innerchange for Junior High. 1977. 175.00 (ISBN 0-86584-021-0). Palomares & Assoc.
--Innerchange for Senior High. 1977. 175.00 (ISBN 0-86584-020-2). Palomares & Assoc.
--Innerchange Language Arts Resource Ser for Junior High. 1977. 95.00 (ISBN 0-86584-031-8). Palomares & Assoc.
--Innerchange Language Arts Resource Set for Senior High. 1977. 95.00 (ISBN 0-86584-026-1). Palomares & Assoc.
--Innerchange Leader's Manual. 1977. 14.95 (ISBN 0-86584-017-2). Palomares & Assoc.
Ball, Gerry. Circle of Warmth: Card Pack, Family Program. 1980. 12.00 (ISBN 0-86584-039-3). Palomares & Assoc.
--Circle of Warmth: Family Program. 1980. 34.95 (ISBN 0-86584-040-7). Palomares & Assoc.
--Circle of Warmth: Guided Journal, Family Program. 1980. 8.00 (ISBN 0-86584-038-5). Palomares & Assoc.
--Circle of Warmth: Sourcebook, Family Program. 1980. 14.95 (ISBN 0-86584-037-7). Palomares & Assoc.
--Grounds for Growth: Comprehensive Theory Manual. 1980. 14.95 (ISBN 0-86584-009-1). Palomares & Assoc.
--Innerchange Conflict Management Resource Set for Junior High. 95.00 (ISBN 0-86584-028-8). Palomares & Assoc.
--Innerchange Drug Abuse Prevention Resource Set for Sr. High. 95.00 (ISBN 0-86584-024-5). Palomares & Assoc.
--Innerchange Social Studies Resource Set for Jr. High. 95.00 (ISBN 0-86584-030-X). Palomares & Assoc.
--Innerchange Social Studies Resource Set for Sr. High. 95.00 (ISBN 0-86584-025-3). Palomares & Assoc.
Ball, Gerry, jt. auth. see Palomares, Uvaldo.
Ball, Gordon, ed. & intro. by see Ginsberg, Allen.
Ball, H. W., pref. By. British Palaeozoic Fossils. 4th ed. (Illus.). vi, 203p. 1975. pap. 10.50x (ISBN 0-686-27503-9, Pub. by Brit Mus Nat Hist). Sabbot-Natural Hist Bks.
Ball, Hal. How to Stop Snoring in Just Two Weeks. (Orig., Prog. Bk.). 1974. Repr. 10.00 (ISBN 0-686-05785-6). Relevant Pub.
Ball, Harry P. Of Responsible Command: A History of the U. S. Army War College. LC 84-70402. (Illus.). 534p. 1984. 18.50 (ISBN 0-9613301-0-4). Alumni Assn US.
Ball, Howard. Constitutional Powers: Cases on the Separation of Powers & Federalism. LC 80-12820. 355p. 1980. pap. text ed. 12.95 (ISBN 0-8299-2090-0). West Pub.
--Controlling Regulatory Sprawl: Presidential Strategies from Nixon to Reagan. LC 82-8541. (Contributions in Political Science: No. 105). xviii, 206p. 1984. 29.95 (ISBN 0-313-23525-2, BCF/). Greenwood.
--Courts & Politics: The Federal Judicial System. 1980. pap. text ed. 17.95 (ISBN 0-13-184655-8). P-H.
--Federal Administrative Agencies: Essays on Power & Politics. (Illus.). 384p. 1984. pap. text ed. 17.95 (ISBN 0-13-308445-0). P-H.
--Judicial Craftsmanship or Fiat? Direct Overturn by the United States Supreme Court. LC 77-91102. (Contributions in Political Science: No. 7). 160p. 1978. lib. bdg. 29.95x (ISBN 0-313-20035-1, BJC/). Greenwood.
--Justice Downwind: America's Atomic Testing Program in the 1950s. (Illus.). 288p. 1986. 19.95 (ISBN 0-19-503672-7). Oxford U Pr.
--No Pledge of Privacy: The Watergate Tapes Litigation, 1973-1974. (National University Pubns. Multi-Disciplinary Studies in the Law). 1977. 15.00x (ISBN 0-8046-9181-9, Pub. by Kennikat). Assoc Faculty Pr.
--Warren Court's Conceptions of Democracy: An Evaluation of the Supreme Court's Apportionment Opinions. LC 70-149826. 256p. 1971. 24.50 (ISBN 0-8386-7913-7). Fairleigh Dickinson.
Ball, Howard, et al. Compromised Compliance: Implementation of the 1965 Voting Rights Act. LC 81-6342. (Contributions in Political Science Ser.: No. 66). (Illus.). xi, 300p. 1982. lib. bdg. 29.95 (ISBN 0-313-22037-9, BCM/). Greenwood.
Ball, I. R. & Reynoldson, T. B. British Planarians. (Synopses of the British Fauna Ser.: No. 19). 120p. 1982. 34.50 (ISBN 0-521-23875-7). Cambridge U Pr.
Ball, Ian R., jt. ed. see Schockaert, Ernest R.
Ball, J. Dyer. Things Chinese: Or Notes Connected with China. rev. 5th ed. Werner, Chalmers, ed. LC 74-164085. (Tower Bks). 1971. Repr. of 1926 ed. 56.00x (ISBN 0-8103-3917-X). Gale.
Ball, J. M., ed. Systems of Nonlinear Partial Differential Equations. 1983. lib. bdg. 65.00 (ISBN 90-277-1629-3, Pub. by Reidel Holland). Kluwer Academic.
Ball, J. N. Merchants & Merchandise: The Expansion of Trade in Europe, 1500-1630. LC 77-74803. 1977. 23.00 (ISBN 0-312-53008-0). St Martin.
Ball, James, jt. auth. see Albert, Michel.
Ball, James D. Things Chinese: Or Notes Connected with China. lib. bdg. 79.95 (ISBN 0-87968-476-3). Krishna Pr.
Ball, Jeff. Jeff Ball's Sixty-Minute Garden. Balitas, Maggie, ed. (Illus.). 224p. 1985. 16.95 (ISBN 0-87857-572-3); pap. 9.95 (ISBN 0-87857-576-6). Rodale Pr Inc.
--The Self-Sufficient Suburban Gardener: A Step-by-Step Planning & Management Guide to Backyard Food Production. Halpin, Anne, ed. (Illus.). 256p. 1983. 14.95 (ISBN 0-87857-457-3, 01-083-0). Rodale Pr Inc.
Ball, Jerry, jt. auth. see Mick, Colin K.
Ball, John. Ananda: Where Yoga Lives. LC 82-82100. 240p. 1982. 15.95 (ISBN 0-87972-207-X); pap. 8.95 (ISBN 0-87972-208-8). Bowling Green Univ.
--Ananda: Where Yoga Lives. (Illus.). 232p. 1982. pap. 8.95 (ISBN 0-686-47068-0). Ananda.
--Cheif Tallon & the S.O.R. 196p. 1984. 11.95 (ISBN 0-396-08307-2). Dodd.
--The Cool Cottontail. LC 84-48136. 176p. (Orig.). 1985. pap. 3.37 (ISBN 0-06-080734-2, PL). Har-Row.
--The Eyes of Buddha: A Virgil Tibbs Mystery. LC 84-48577. 256p. pap. 3.37i (ISBN 0-06-080751-2, P751, PL). Har-Row.
--Five Pieces of Jade: A Virgil Tibbs Mystery. LC 84-48578. 288p. 1985. pap. 3.37i (ISBN 0-317-15870-8, P752, PL). Har-Row.
--In the Heat of the Night. LC 84-48135. 192p. 1985. pap. 3.37 (ISBN 0-06-080735-0, PL). Har-Row.
--Miss One Thousand Spring Blossoms. 1979. pap. 1.95 (ISBN 0-380-42325-1, 42325-1). Avon.
Ball, John, jt. auth. see McDonnell, Leo.
Ball, John A. Algorithms for RPN Calculators. LC 77-14977. 330p. 1977. 35.50 (ISBN 0-471-03070-8, Pub. by Wiley-Interscience). Wiley.
Ball, John C. Social Deviancy & Adolescent Personality. LC 72-12308. (Illus.). 119p. 1973. Repr. of 1962 ed. lib. bdg. 18.75 (ISBN 0-8371-6687-X, BASD). Greenwood.
Ball, John E. Architectural Drafting Fundamentals. (Illus.). 336p. 1980. text ed. 20.95 (ISBN 0-8359-0254-4). Reston.
--Carpenters & Builders Library. 5th ed. LC 82-133279. 1983. 39.95 set (ISBN 0-672-23369-X); 10.95 ea. Vol. 1 (ISBN 0-672-23365-7). Vol. 2 (ISBN 0-672-23366-5). Vol. 3 (ISBN 0-672-23367-3). Vol. 4 (ISBN 0-672-23368-1). Audel.
--Carpenters & Builders Library, 4 vols. 5th ed. 1982. 35.95 (ISBN 0-672-23244-8). G K Hall.
--Carpenters & Builders Library, Vol. 1. 5th ed. LC 82-1340. 1982. 10.95 (ISBN 0-672-23365-7). G K Hall.
--Carpenters & Builders Library, Vol. 2. 5th ed. LC 82-1341. 1982. 10.95 (ISBN 0-672-23366-5). G K Hall.
--Carpenters & Builders Library, Vol. 3. 5th ed. LC 82-1339. 1982. 10.95 (ISBN 0-672-23367-3). G K Hall.
--Carpenters & Builders Library, Vol. 4. 5th ed. LC 82-1332. 1982. 10.95 (ISBN 0-672-23368-1). G K Hall.
--Exterior & Interior Trim. LC 75-6060. 192p. 1975. pap. 13.00 (ISBN 0-8273-1120-6); instr.'s guide 2.25 (ISBN 0-8273-1121-4). Delmar.
--Practical Problems in Mathematics for Masons. LC 78-74431. (Mathematics - Construction Ser.). 200p. 1980. 7.80 (ISBN 0-8273-1283-0); instructor's guide 3.60 (ISBN 0-8273-1284-9). Delmar.
Ball, John M., et al. The Social Sciences & Geographic Education: A Reader. LC 73-140549. 329p. 1971. pap. 16.00 (ISBN 0-471-04631-0, Pub. by Wiley). Krieger.
Ball, John N., jt. auth. see Pearson, Ronald.
Ball, John S. Southern African Epiphytic Orchids. 1978. 200.00x (ISBN 0-86036-119-5, Pub. by Collins England). State Mutual Bk.
Ball, John W. Casting & Fishing the Artificial Fly. LC 79-140119. (Illus.). 1972. pap. 6.95 (ISBN 0-87004-217-3). Caxton.
Ball, Johnson. Paul & Thomas Sandby: Royal Academicians. (Illus.). 414p. 1985. 110.00x (ISBN 0-8390-0355-2). Abner Schram Ltd.
Ball, Joseph. Factorization & Model Theory for Contraction Operators with Unitary Part. LC 77-25161. (Memoirs Ser.: No. 198). 68p. 1978. pap. 12.00 (ISBN 0-8218-2198-9, MEMO-198). Am Math.
Ball, Joyce, ed. Foreign Statistical Documents: A Bibliography of General, International Trade & Agricultural Statistics, Including Holdings of the Stanford University Libraries. (Bibliographical Ser.: No. 28). 1967. pap. 7.95x (ISBN 0-8179-2282-2). Hoover Inst Pr.
Ball, K. P. & Fleming, J. Handbook of Cardiac Care. (Illus.). 288p. 1982. text ed. 28.00 (ISBN 0-85200-460-5, Pub. by MTP Pr England). Kluwer Academic.
Ball, Kenneth R., jt. auth. see Willcutt, J. Robert.
Ball, Larry A. Those Incomparable Bonanzas, 1944-1972. 1971. 24.95x (ISBN 0-911720-52-9, Pub. by Ball). Aviation.
Ball, Larry D. The United States Marshals of New Mexico & Arizona Territories, 1846 - 1912. (Illus.). 291p. 1982. pap. 9.95 (ISBN 0-8263-0617-9). U of NM Pr.
Ball, Larry D. & Clements, William M. Voices from State: An Oral History of Arkansas State University. Hawkins, Ruth, ed. 208p. 1985. 19.95 (ISBN 0-930677-00-5). Ark St Univ.
Ball, Les, ed. New England Directory for Computer Professionals, 1985. 128p. 1985. pap. 49.95 (ISBN 0-318-04766-7). Bradford Co.
Ball, Leslie D., et al. Information Systems Audit Review Manual. rev. ed. (Illus.). 334p. 1983. 23.95x (ISBN 0-912901-00-4). Leslie Pr.
Ball, Lola M. A Bathtub for Two. 32p. (gr. 1-3). 1984. 6.95 (ISBN 0-89962-409-X). Todd & Honeywell.
Ball, LuAnn see Smolen, Victor F.
Ball, LuAnn, jt. auth. see Smolen, Victor F.
Ball, LuAnn, jt. ed. see Smolin, Victor F.
Ball, Lyle V. & Laxalt, Paul, eds. The Art of Lyle V. Ball. (Illus.). 80p. 1984. deluxe ed. 250.00 signed ed. (ISBN 0-930083-01-6). Native Nevadan Pubns.
Ball, M., jt. auth. see Mattar, E. P.
Ball, M. A. Mathematics in the Social & Life Sciences: Theories, Models & Methods. (Mathematics & Its Applications Ser.). 1985. 49.95 (ISBN 0-470-20191-6). Halsted Pr.
Ball, M. Margaret. NATO & the European Union Movement. LC 74-9319. (Library of World Affairs, London, Institute of World Affairs Ser.: No. 45). (Illus.). 486p. 1974. Repr. of 1959 ed. lib. bdg. 22.50x (ISBN 0-8371-7642-5, BANA). Greenwood.
--Open Commonwealth. LC 78-171937. Repr. of 1971 ed. 75.00 (ISBN 0-8357-9113-0, 2017882). Bks Demand UMI.
Ball, Margaret. Sir Walter Scott As a Critic of Literature. LC 65-27125. 1907. Repr. 22.00x (ISBN 0-8046-0015-5, Pub. by Kennikat). Assoc Faculty Pr.
--Sunset & Dawn. (Orig.). 1985. pap. 3.50 (ISBN 0-523-42350-0). Pinnacle Bks.
Ball, Marion & Hannah, Kathryn. Using Computers in Nursing. 1984. text ed. 21.95 (ISBN 0-8359-8130-4); pap. text ed. 16.95 (ISBN 0-8359-8129-0). Reston.
Ball, Marion J. What Is a Computer. (Illus.). 92p. (gr. 4-12). 1972. pap. text ed. 8.88 (ISBN 0-395-13772-1). HM.
Ball, Marion J. & Charp, Sylvia. Be a Computer Literate. LC 78-52055. (Illus.). 61p. pap. 6.95 (ISBN 0-916688-08-9, 6H). Creative Comp.
Ball, Marion J., ed. How to Select a Computerized Hospital Information System. (Data Processing in Medicine: Vol. 2). (Illus.). 1973. 25.25 (ISBN 3-8055-1465-4). S Karger.
Ball, Martim, jt. auth. see Clutton Brock, Tim.
Ball, Martin & Jones, G., eds. Welsh Phonology. 296p. 1984. text ed. 40.50x (ISBN 0-7083-0861-9, Pub by Univ of Wales Pr England). Humanities.
Ball, Martin, jt. ed. see Code, Chris.
Ball, Mary, jt. auth. see Ball, Colin.
Ball, Maudette W. Nathan Oliveira Print Retrospective 1949-1980. (Illus.). 72p. (Orig.). 1980. pap. 12.50 (ISBN 0-936270-00-4). Art Mus Gall.
Ball, Max W., et al. This Fascinating Oil Business. LC 64-15660. (Illus.). 1979. pap. 11.95 (ISBN 0-672-52584-4). Bobbs.
Ball, Michael. Housing Policy & Economic Power: The Political Economy of Owner Occupation. LC 83-13070. 1983. pap. 17.95 (ISBN 0-416-35280-4, NO. 3967). Methuen Inc.
Ball, Michael, et al, eds. Land Rent, Housing & Urban Planning: A European Perspective. LC 84-17497. 228p. 1984. 34.50 (ISBN 0-7099-3240-5, Pub. by Croom Helm Ltd). Longwood Pub Group.
Ball, Milner S. Lying Down Together: Law, Metaphor & Theology. LC 85-40361. (Rhetoric of the Human Sciences Ser.). 224p. 1985. text ed. 24.00x (ISBN 0-299-10450-8). U of Wis Pr.

--The Promise of American Law: A Theological, Humanistic View of Legal Process. LC 81-4325. 214p. 1981. 17.00x (ISBN 0-8203-0572-3). U of Ga Pr.

Ball, Mog, jt. auth. see Ball, Colin.

Ball, Nicole. The Military in the Development Process: A Guide to Issues. LC 81-21009. (Guides to Contemporary Issues Ser.: No. 2). 124p. 1981. 16.50x (ISBN 0-941690-02-4); pap. 9.95x (ISBN 0-941690-03-2); pap. text ed. 6.95x. Regina Bks.

--World Hunger: A Guide to the Economic & Political Dimensions. LC 80-22504. (War-Peace Bibliography Ser.: No. 15). 386p. 1981. lib. bdg. 46.50 (ISBN 0-87436-308-X). ABC-Clio.

Ball, Nicole, jt. ed. see Leitenberg, Milton.

Ball, Patricia M. The Heart's Events: The Victorian Poetry of Relationships. 227p. 1976. 36.50 (ISBN 0-485-11163-2, Pub. by Athlone Pr Ltd). Longwood Pub Group.

Ball, R. J. Money & Employment. 450p. 1982. 29.95 (ISBN 0-470-27290-2). Halsted Pr.

Ball, Ray, et al, eds. Share Markets & Portfolio Theory: Readings & Australian Evidence. (Illus.). 369p. 1980. text ed. 48.50x (ISBN 0-7022-1426-4); pap. text ed. 24.25x (ISBN 0-7022-1427-2). U of Queensland Pr.

Ball, Richard. Mask of Aeschylus. LC 81-66410. 88p. (Orig.). 1981. pap. 3.00 (ISBN 0-940066-00-9). Dalmas & Ricour.

Ball, Richard & Campbell, Peter. Master Pieces: Making Furniture for Paintings. LC 83-81095. (Illus.). 144p. 1983. 22.95 (ISBN 0-688-02488-2, Hearst Bk). Morrow.

Ball, Richard & Cox, Paul. Low Tech: Fast Furniture for Next to Nothing. LC 83-2105. (Illus.). 224p. 1984. pap. 14.95 (ISBN 0-385-27905-1, Dial). Doubleday.

Ball, Richard, jt. auth. see Schartzman, Sylvan.

Ball, Richard E., jt. auth. see Schwartzman, Sylvan D.

Ball, Robert. Management Techniques & Quantitative Methods. (Illus.). 224p. 1985. pap. 19.95 (ISBN 0-434-90083-4, Pub. by W Heinemann Ltd). David & Charles.

Ball, Robert H., jt. auth. see Bowman, Walter P.

Ball, Robert J., ed. The Classical Papers of Gilbert Highet. 416p. 1984. 37.00x (ISBN 0-231-05104-2). Columbia U Pr.

Ball, Robert M. Social Security: Today & Tomorrow. LC 77-13713. 528p. 1978. 40.00x (ISBN 0-231-04254-X); pap. 15.00x (ISBN 0-231-04255-8). Columbia U Pr.

Ball, Robert R. Why Can't I Tell You Who I Really Am? 120p. 1984. 5.95 (ISBN 0-8499-3001-4, 3001-4). Word Bks.

Ball, Robert S. Great Astronomers. LC 74-994. (Essay Index Reprint Ser.). (Illus.). Repr. of 1895 ed. 22.50 (ISBN 0-518-10142-8). Ayer Co Pubs.

--Time & Tide: A Romance of the Moon. 1899. 15.00 (ISBN 0-686-17418-6). Ridgeway Bks.

Ball, Rouse W. An Essay on Newton's Principia. Repr. of 1893 ed. 32.00 (ISBN 0-384-03141-2, S155). Johnson Repr.

Ball, S. Beachside Comprehensive: A Case Study in Secondary Schooling. (Illus.). 280p. 1981. 59.50 (ISBN 0-521-23238-4); pap. 19.95 (ISBN 0-521-29878-4). Cambridge U Pr.

Ball, S. C. Jungle Fowls from Pacific Islands. (BMB). Repr. of 1933 ed. 21.00 (ISBN 0-527-02214-4). Kraus Repr.

Ball, S. C., jt. auth. see Fowler, H. W.

Ball, S. H. Mines of the Silver Peak Range, Kawich Range & Other Southernwestern Nevada Districts. 218p. pap. 14.95. Nevada Pubns.

Ball, Samuel. An Account of the Cultivation & Manufacture of Tea in China. LC 78-74309. (The Modern Chinese Economy Ser.). 382p. 1980. lib. bdg. 51.00 (ISBN 0-8240-4250-6). Garland Pub.

Ball, Samuel, jt. auth. see Anderson, Scarvia B.

Ball, Samuel, ed. Assessing & Interpreting Outcomes. LC 80-84296. (Program Evaluation Ser.: No. 9). (Orig.). 1981. pap. text ed. 8.95x (ISBN 0-87589-856-4). Jossey-Bass.

Ball, Stephen & Goodson, Ivan, eds. Teachers' Lives & Careers. 274p. 1985. text ed. 29.00x (ISBN 1-85000-030-1, Falmer Pr); pap. text ed. 17.00x (ISBN 1-85000-029-8, Falmer Pr). Taylor & Francis.

Ball, Stephen, jt. ed. see Goodson, Ivor.

Ball, Stephen J., ed. Comprehensive Schooling: A Reader. 296p. 1984. 34.00x (ISBN 0-905273-90-7, Pub. by Falmer Pr); pap. 19.00x (ISBN 0-905273-89-3, Pub. by Falmer Pr). Taylor & Francis.

Ball, Susan L. Ozenfant & Purism: The Evolution of a Style, 1915-1930. Foster, Stephen, ed. LC 81-15996. (Studies in the Fine Arts: Avant-Garde: No. 17). 224p. 1981. 39.95 (ISBN 0-8357-1235-4). UMI Res Pr.

Ball, Terence, ed. After Marx. Farr, James. LC 83-25237. 304p. 1984. 37.50 (ISBN 0-521-25702-6); pap. 11.95 (ISBN 0-521-27661-6). Cambridge U Pr.

--Political Theory & Praxis: New Perspectives. LC 77-73320. 1977. 16.75x (ISBN 0-8166-0816-4). U of Minn Pr.

Ball, Thomas. My Threescore Years & Ten. 2nd ed. LC 75-28884. (Art Experience in Late 19th Century America Ser.: Vol. 18). (Illus.). 1976. Repr. of 1892 ed. lib. bdg. 45.00 (ISBN 0-8240-2242-4). Garland Pub.

Ball, V., tr. see Tavernier, J. B.

Ball, Vic, ed. Ball Red Book. 1984. 26.95 (ISBN 0-8359-0382-6). Reston.

Ball, Victoria K. Architecture & Interior Design: A Basic History Through the Seventeenth Century. Vol. 1 ed. LC 79-21371. 448p. 1980. 65.00 (ISBN 0-471-05162-4, Pub. by Wiley-Interscience); pap. 37.50 (ISBN 0-471-08719-X). Wiley.

--Architecture & Interior Design: Europe & America from the Colonial Era to Today, 2 vols. set. LC 79-24851. 890p. 1980. Set. 75.50 (ISBN 0-471-08721-1, Pub. by Wiley-Interscience); Set. pap. 65.00 (ISBN 0-471-08720-3). Wiley.

--Architecture & Interior Design: Europe & America from the Colonial Era to Today. Vol. 2 ed. LC 79-24851. 442p. 1980. 65.00 (ISBN 0-471-05161-6, Pub. by Wiley-Interscience); pap. 37.50 (ISBN 0-471-08722-X). Wiley.

--The Art of Interior Design. 2nd ed. LC 82-2556. 273p. 1982. 29.95x (ISBN 0-471-09679-2, Pub. by Wiley-Interscience). Wiley.

--Opportunities in Interior Design. LC 76-51706. (VGM Career Bks.). (Illus.). (YA) (gr. 8 up). 1977. 7.95 (ISBN 0-8442-6335-4, 6335-4); pap. 5.95 (ISBN 0-8442-6336-2, 6336-2). Natl Textbk.

Ball, Virginia. A Summer Place. (Orig.). 1984. pap. 1.95 (ISBN 0-87067-206-1, BH206). Holloway.

Ball, W. E., jt. auth. see Brysch, O. P.

Ball, W. P., jt. ed. see Foote, G. W.

Ball, W. P., jt. auth. see Foote, G. W.

Ball, W. R; see Ball, W. Rouse, et al.

Ball, W. Rouse, et al, eds. String Figures & Other Monographs, 4 vols. in 1. Incl. String Figures. Ball, W. R; History of the Slide Rule. Cajori, F; Non Euclidean Geometry. Carslaw, Horatio S; Methods Geometrical Construction. Petersen, Julius. LC 59-11780. 15.95 (ISBN 0-8284-0130-6). Chelsea Pub.

Ball, W. W. Fun with String Figures. LC 76-173664. (Illus.). (gr. k-3). 1971. pap. 2.25 (ISBN 0-486-22809-6). Dover.

--Short Account of the History of Mathematics. 4th ed. 1908. pap. 7.50 (ISBN 0-486-20630-0). Dover.

--A Short Account of the History of Mathematics. LC 60-3187. 1960. lib. bdg. 16.50x (ISBN 0-88307-009-X). Gannon.

Ball, Wendy A., ed. Rare Afro-Americana: A Reconstruction of the Adger Library. 1981. 29.00 (ISBN 0-8161-8175-6, Hall Reference). G K Hall.

Ball, Wilfrid. Sussex. 1906. 20.00 (ISBN 0-686-17218-3). Scholars Ref Lib.

Ball, William. A Sense of Direction: Some Obervations on the Art of Directing. LC 84-8104. 208p. 1984. text ed. 17.95x (ISBN 0-89676-081-2); pap. text ed. 12.95x (ISBN 0-89676-082-0). Drama Bk.

Ball, William E. & Pollack, Seymour V. Guide to Structured Programming & Pascal. 450p. Date not set. text ed. price not set info. (ISBN 0-03-056844-7, HoltC). HR&W.

Ball, William M. Nationalism & Communism in East Asia. LC 75-30044. (Institute of Pacific Relations Ser.). Repr. of 1952 ed. 18.00 (ISBN 0-404-59502-2). AMS Pr.

Balla, D., jt. auth. see Zigler, E.

Balla, David A., jt. auth. see Lewis, Dorothy O.

Balla, Ignatius. Romance of the Rothschilds. 1981. lib. bdg. 75.00 (ISBN 0-87700-280-0). Revisionist Pr.

Balla, Mother Ignatius. Our Continuing Yes. 1973. pap. 2.00 (ISBN 0-8198-0243-3). Dghtrs St Paul.

Balla, J. I. The Diagnostic Process: Model for Clinical Teachers. (Illus.). 168p. Date not set. 39.50 (ISBN 0-521-30213-7). Cambridge U Pr.

Balla, M. J., jt. auth. see Podvesko, M. L.

Balla, Valentia D. The New Balance of Power in Europe. LC 78-64287. (Johns Hopkins University. Studies in the Social Sciences. Extra Volumes.: 17). Repr. of 1932 ed. 20.00 (ISBN 0-404-61387-X). AMS Pr.

Balla-Ach, S. M., jt. auth. see Berecz, E.

Ballabon, M., ed. Economics Selections, 2 vols. Incl. Vol. 1. 1954-1962. 378p. 1965. 103.95 (ISBN 0-677-01050-8); Vol. 2. 1963-1970. 402p. 121.50 (ISBN 0-677-01070-2). 1975. Gordon.

Ballabon, M. B., ed. Economic Perspectives: An Annual Survey of Economics, Vol. 1. (Economic Perspective Ser.). 280p. 1979. 49.95 (ISBN 3-7186-0001-3). Harwood Academic.

--Economic Perspectives: An Annual Survey of Economics, Vol. 2. 276p. 1981. lib. bdg. 64.95 (ISBN 3-7186-0036-6). Harwood Academic.

Ballabon, Maurice, ed. Economic Perspectives. (An Annual Survey of Economics Ser.: Vol. 3). 220p. 1984. text ed. 47.00 (ISBN 3-7186-0165-6). Harwood Academic.

Ballad Society. Publications of the Ballad Society, 14 vols, Nos. 1-38. (Ballad Society Ser.: Nos. 1-38). Repr. of 1899 ed. Set. 815.00 (ISBN 0-404-50820-0). AMS Pr.

Ballagh, J. C. White Servitude in the Colony of Virginia: A Study of the System of Indentured Labor in the American Colonies. 11.00 (ISBN 0-384-03146-3). Johnson Repr.

Ballagh, James C. A History of Slavery in Virginia. LC 78-64269. (Johns Hopkins University. Studies in the Social Sciences. Extra Volumes: 24). Repr. of 1902 ed. 11.50 (ISBN 0-404-61371-3). AMS Pr.

--History of Slavery in Virginia. (Basic Afro-American Reprint Library). Repr. of 1902 ed. 12.00 (ISBN 0-384-03145-5). Johnson Repr.

--White Servitude in the Colony of Virginia: A Study of the System of Indentured Labor in the American Colonies. LC 78-63840. (Johns Hopkins University. Studies in the Social Sciences. Thirteenth Ser. 1895: 6-7). Repr. of 1895 ed. 11.50 (ISBN 0-404-61098-6). AMS Pr.

--White Servitude in the Colony of Virginia. LC 71-101987. 1970. Repr. of 1898 ed. 15.00 (ISBN 0-8337-0158-4). B Franklin.

Ballagh, James C., ed. The Letters of Richard Henry Lee, 2 Vols. LC 79-107678. (Era of the American Revolution Ser). 1970. Repr. of 1914 ed. Set. 115.00 (ISBN 0-306-71894-4). Da Capo.

Ballagh, James H., ed. Employee Relations Outlook: Impact of Foreign & Domestic Competition. 52p. 1985. 4.00 (ISBN 0-89215-130-7). U Cal LA Indus Rel.

Ballagh, Robert. Dublin. (Illus.). 126p. 1981. 32.00 (ISBN 0-907085-15-6, Pub. by Ward River Pr Ireland); pap. 14.95 (ISBN 0-907085-40-7, Pub. by Ward River Pr Ireland). Irish Bks Media.

Ballagh, Robert, intro. by. & photos by Dublin. (Illus.). 126p. 1981. 35.00 (ISBN 0-907085-15-6, Pub. by Ward River Ireland); pap. 11.95 (lrge. format) (ISBN 0-686-40894-2). Irish Bk Ctr.

Ballam, John D. Shadows & the Crosses. LC 85-62907. 90p. (Orig.). 1985. pap. 5.95 (ISBN 0-938232-58-4). Winston-Derek.

Ballan, Dorothy. Feminism & Marxism. 68p. 1971. pap. 2.00 (ISBN 0-89567-006-2). WV Pubs.

--Feminism & Marxism. 68p. 1.50 (ISBN 0-89567-006-2). World View Pubns.

Ballance, Charles A. The Thomas Viceroy Lecture: A Glimpse into the History of Surgery of the Brain. LC 75-23679. Repr. of 1922 ed. 21.00 (ISBN 0-404-13232-4). AMS Pr.

Ballance, Peter F. & Reading, Harold G., eds. Sedimentation of Oblique-Slip Mobile Zones. (International Association of Sedimentologists & the Societ As Internationalis Limnological Symposium). 265p. 1980. pap. 69.95x (ISBN 0-470-26927-8). Halsted Pr.

Ballance, R., et al. The International Economy & Industrial Development: Trade & Investment in the Third World. 1982. 60.00x (ISBN 0-7108-0074-6, Pub. by Harvester Pr England). State Mutual Bk.

Ballance, Robert H. & Sinclair, Stuart W. Collapse & Survival: Industry Strategies in a Changing World. Walter, Ingo, ed. (World Industry Studies: No. 1). (Illus.). 224p. 1983. text ed. 25.00x (ISBN 0-04-338107-3); pap. text ed. 9.95x (ISBN 0-04-338108-1). Allen Unwin.

Ballance, Robert H., et al. The International Economy & Industrial Development: The Impact of Trade & Investment on the Third World. LC 82-6651. (Illus.). 338p. 1982. text ed. 34.95x (ISBN 0-86598-086-1). Allanheld.

Ballanger, Edgard G., et al, eds. see American Urological Association.

Ballanoff, Paul A., ed. Genetics & Social Structure: Mathematical Structuralism in Population Genetics & Social Theory. LC 73-20412. (Benchmark Papers in Genetics Ser.: Vol. 1). 504p. 1975. 53.50 (ISBN 0-87933-067-8). Van Nos Reinhold.

Ballantine, jt. auth. see Cargan.

Ballantine, Betty. Frazetta Four. 96p. 1980. pap. 12.95 (ISBN 0-553-34150-2). Bantam.

Ballantine, Betty, ed. The Fantastic Art of Frank Frazetta. 96p. (Orig.). 1975. pap. 12.95 (ISBN 0-553-34211-8, Peacock Pr). Bantam.

--Frank Frazetta: Book Three. 1978. pap. 11.95 (ISBN 0-553-34011-5, Peacock). Bantam.

Ballantine, Betty, ed. see Ballantine, Richard.

Ballantine, Christopher. Music & its Social Meanings. (Monographs on Musicology: Vol. 2). 220p. 1984. 29.95 (ISBN 0-677-06050-5). Gordon.

--Towards a Theory of the Twentieth Century Symphony: An Approach Through Symphonic History. 224p. 1981. 40.00x (ISBN 0-234-72042-5, Pub. by Dobson Bks England). State Mutual Bk.

Ballantine, David, jt. auth. see Haney, Robert.

Ballantine, Jeanne H. The Sociology of Education: A Systematic Analysis. (Illus.). 400p. 1983. 27.95 (ISBN 0-13-820860-3). P-H.

Ballantine, John W. The Human Side of Economics: Its Significance for Enterprise Management. (Illus.). 176p. 1973. text ed. 8.00 (ISBN 0-912084-08-1). Mimir.

Ballantine, Richard. Richard's Bicycle Book. 1982. pap. 7.95 (ISBN 0-345-30242-7). Ballantine.

--Richard's Bicycle Book, 1975. Ballantine, Betty, ed. 1976. pap. 5.95 (ISBN 0-345-29453-X). Ballantine.

Ballantine, Sergeant. Some Experiences of a Barrister's Life. Mersky, Roy M. & Jacobstein, J. Myron, eds. (Classics in Legal History Reprint Ser.: Vol. 13). 552p. 1972. Repr. of 1882 ed. lib. bdg. 36.00 (ISBN 0-89941-012-X). W S Hein.

Ballantine, Thomas. Passages Selected from the Writings of Thomas Carlyle: With a Biographical Memoir. 351p. 1984. Repr. of 1855 ed. lib. bdg. 40.00 (ISBN 0-918377-07-2). Russell Pr.

Ballantyne. Respiratory Protection. 1981. 49.95 (ISBN 0-8151-0415-4). Year Bk Med.

Ballantyne & Groves. Synopsis of Otolaryngology. 3rd ed. 614p. 1978. 41.50 (ISBN 0-7236-0460-6). PSG Pub Co.

Ballantyne & Shastri. Yoga-Sutras of Patanjali. Tailang, S. B., ed. Repr. of 1983 ed. 8.50 (ISBN 0-89684-474-9). Orient Bk Dist.

Ballantyne, Alexander, tr. see Tardy.

Ballantyne, Archibald. Voltaire's Visit to England, Seventeen Twenty-Six to Seventeen Twenty-Nine. (Works of Archibald Ballantyne Ser.). 338p. Date not set. Repr. of 1919 ed. lib. bdg. 39.00 (ISBN 0-932051-35-9). Am Repr Serv.

Ballantyne, D. L. & Converse, J. M. Experimental Skin Grafts & Transplantation Immunity. (Illus.). 196p. 1979. 39.00 (ISBN 0-387-90425-5). Springer-Verlag.

Ballantyne, Donald L. & Rosenberg, Benjamina B., eds. Organized Bibliography of Microsurgical Literature. 352p. 1985. pap. text ed. 63.00 (ISBN 0-8391-2049-4). Univ Park.

Ballantyne, Donald L., et al. Introduction to Microsurgical Technique: A Laboratory Manual. (Illus.). 128p. 1985. pap. text ed. 20.00 (ISBN 0-8391-2004-4, 21040). Univ Park.

Ballantyne, E. J., Jr., et al, eds. Manual of Geophysical Hand-Calculator Programs TI & HP Volumes. 1981. TI Vol. looseleaf 50.00 (ISBN 0-931830-20-6); HP Vol. 50.00 (ISBN 0-931830-17-6); Set, TI & HP. 90.00 (ISBN 0-317-12576-1). Soc Exploration.

Ballantyne, E. R. A Survey of Thermal Sensation in Port Moresby, Papua New Guinea. 1980. 20.00x (ISBN 0-643-00338-X, Pub. by CSJRO Australia). State Mutual Bk.

Ballantyne, G. H. The Signet Library Edinburgh & Its Librarians. 191p. 1982. 55.00x (ISBN 0-900649-18-6, Pub. by Scot Lib Scotland). State Mutual Bk.

Ballantyne, J. & Friedmann, T., eds. Ultrastructural Atlas of the Inner Ear. 1984. text ed. 130.00 (ISBN 0-407-00221-9). Butterworth.

Ballantyne, J. R., tr. & commentary by. Laghu Kaumudi of Varadaraja. 1976. Repr. 8.50 (ISBN 0-8426-0875-3). Orient Bk Dist.

Ballantyne, James R. Principles of Persian Calligraphy. 1977. lib. bdg. 59.95 (ISBN 0-8490-2480-3). Gordon Pr.

Ballantyne, Janet. Desserts from the Garden. Chesman, Andrea, ed. LC 82-2884. (Illus.). 144p. (Orig.). 1983. pap. 5.95 (ISBN 0-88266-322-4). Garden Way Pub.

--Garden Way's Red & Green Tomato Cookbook. LC 82-2884. (Illus.). 158p. 1982. pap. 5.95 (ISBN 0-88266-262-7). Garden Way Pub.

Ballantyne, Janet, et al. Garden Way's Joy of Gardening Cookbook. (Illus.). 336p. 1984. 25.00 (ISBN 0-88266-356-9); pap. 17.95 (ISBN 0-317-04556-3). Garden Way Pub.

Ballantyne, John. Deafness. 4th ed. LC 77-3104. (Illus.). 1984. pap. text ed. 13.00 (ISBN 0-443-02930-X). Churchill.

Ballantyne, John & Groves, John, eds. Scott Brown's Diseases of the Ear, Nose, & Throat. 4th ed. Incl. Vol. 1. Ear, Nose & Throat Diseases. 139.95 (ISBN 0-407-00147-6); Vol. 2. The Ear. 169.95 (ISBN 0-407-00148-4); Vol. 3. The Nose. 99.95 (ISBN 0-407-00149-2); Vol. 4. The Throat. 119.95 (ISBN 0-407-00150-6). LC 79-41008. (Illus.). 1979. Set. text ed. 499.95 (ISBN 0-407-00143-3). Butterworth.

Ballantyne, R. M. The Coral Island. (Children's Illustrated Classics). (Illus.). 348p. 1977. 9.95x (ISBN 0-460-05006-0, Pub. by J M Dent England). Biblio Dist.

Ballantyne, R. M; see Eyre, A. G.

Ballantyne, Robert M. Black Ivory: A Tale of Adventure among the Slavers of East Africa. LC 79-99338. 1969. Repr. of 1873 ed. lib. bdg. 20.00 (ISBN 0-8411-0009-8). Metro Bks.

--The Coral Island. 1985. pap. 2.25 (ISBN 0-14-035040-3). Penguin.

--Hudson Bay. 322p. Date not set. Repr. of 1857 ed. lib. bdg. 39.00 (ISBN 0-932051-89-8). Am Repr Serv.

--Martin Rattler. 1954. Repr. of 1907 ed. 8.95x (ISBN 0-460-00246-5, Evman). Biblio Dist.

Ballantyne, Sheila. Imaginary Crimes. (Contemporary American Ficton Ser.). 288p. 1983. pap. 4.95 (ISBN 0-14-006540-7). Penguin.

--Norma Jean the Termite Queen. (Contemporary American Fiction Ser.). 288p. 1983. pap. 5.95 (ISBN 0-14-006551-2). Penguin.

Ballantyne, Verne H. How & Where to Find Gold. 2nd ed. LC 82-13734. (Illus.). 176p. 1983. 12.95 (ISBN 0-668-05377-1); pap. 6.95 (ISBN 0-668-05385-2). Arco.

Ballantyne, W. M. Legal Development in Arabia: A Selection of Addresses & Articles. 148p. 1980. 40.00 (ISBN 0-86010-167-3, Pub. by Graham & Trotman England). State Mutual Bk.

Ballard, jt. auth. see Leroy.

Ballard, A. see Neilson, N.

Ballard, A. B. One More Day's Journey: The Story of a Family & a People. 320p. 1984. 17.95 (ISBN 0-07-003486-9). McGraw.

Ballard, Adolphus, ed. British Borough Charters, 1042-1216. LC 80-2236. Repr. of 1913 ed. 49.50 (ISBN 0-404-18750-1). AMS Pr.

Ballard, Charles L., et al. A General Equilibrium Model for Tax Policy Evaluation. LC 84-28096. (National Bureau of Economic Research-Monograph Ser.). (Illus.). 304p. 1985. lib. bdg. price not setx (ISBN 0-226-03632-4). U of Chicago Pr.

Ballard, Colin R. Napoleon: An Outline. facsimile ed. LC 76-179503. (Select Bibliographies Reprint Ser). Repr. of 1924 ed. 21.00 (ISBN 0-8369-6632-5). Ayer Co Pubs.

Ballard, D. Lee, et al. More on the Deep & Surface Grammar of Interclausal Relations. (Language Data, Asia-Pacific Ser: No. 1). 61p. 1971. pap. 2.50x (ISBN 0-88312-201-4); microfiche 1.93x (ISBN 0-88312-301-0). Summer Inst Ling.

Ballard, Dana H. & Brown, Christopher M. Computer Vision. (Illus.). 544p. 1982. text ed. 46.95 (ISBN 0-13-165316-4). P-H.

Ballard, Doris, jt. auth. see Jacobs, Muriel.

Ballard, Dorothy. Horseback Honeymoon. LC 75-15042. 1975. 8.95 (ISBN 0-89430-021-0). Palos Verdes.

Ballard, Edward B., et al, eds. A Technical Glossary of Horticultural & Landscape Terminology. LC 78-165521. 1971. text ed. 5.50 (ISBN 0-935336-00-1); tchr's. ed. 4.00 (ISBN 0-935336-00-1). Horticult Research.

Ballard, Edward G. Art & Analysis. (Works of Edward G. Ballard Ser.). xiv, 219p. Date not set. Repr. of 1857 ed. 29.00 (ISBN 0-932051-76-6). Am Repr Serv.

--Art & Analysis: An Essay Toward Theory in Aesthetics. 219p. 1957. Repr. 25.00x (ISBN 0-403-08903-4). Somerset Pub.

--Man & Technology: Toward the Measurement of a Culture. 1978. text ed. 15.50x (ISBN 0-391-00751-3); pap. text ed. 9.45x (ISBN 0-391-01048-4). Duquesne.

--Philosophy at the Crossroads. LC 72-130663. xii, 306p. 1971. 27.50x (ISBN 0-8071-0523-6). La State U Pr.

Ballard, Edward G, tr. see Ricoeur, Paul.

Ballard, Edward Goodwin. Principles of Interpretation. LC 83-4281. (Continental Thought Ser.: Vol. 5). xiv, 247p. 1983. text ed. 28.95x (ISBN 0-8214-0688-4, 82-84572); pap. 13.95x (ISBN 0-8214-0689-2, 82-84580). Ohio U Pr.

Ballard, F., et al, eds. Press Toolmaking. 2nd ed. (Engineering Craftsmen: No. H21). (Illus.). 1972. spiral bdg. 39.95x (ISBN 0-85083-168-7). Intl Ideas.

Ballard, Frederic L., Jr., jt. ed. see Strickler, Matthew M.

Ballard, G. A. The Black Battlefleet. 264p. 1980. 66.00x (ISBN 0-245-53030-4, Pub. by Nautical England). State Mutual Bk.

--The Influence of the Sea on the Political History of Japan. 312p. 1972. Repr. of 1921 ed. 25.00x (ISBN 0-7165-2049-4, BBA 02212, Pub. by Irish Academic Pr Ireland). Biblio Dist.

--Rulers of the Indian Ocean. 336p. 1983. Repr. text ed. 50.00x (ISBN 0-86590-204-6). Apt Bks.

Ballard, Gay, jt. auth. see Craig, Tracy.

Ballard, George. Memoirs of Several Ladies of Great Britain Who Have Been Celebrated for Their Writings or Skill in the Learned Languages, Arts & Sciences. Perry, Ruth, ed. LC 84-10385. 487p. 1985. 30.00 (ISBN 0-8143-1747-2). Wayne St U Pr.

Ballard, George A. The Influence of the Sea on the Political History of Japan. LC 74-136516. (Illus.). 311p. 1973. Repr. of 1921 ed. lib. bdg. 22.50x (ISBN 0-8371-5435-9, BAIS). Greenwood.

Ballard, Harlan. Adventures of a Librarian. 59.95 (ISBN 0-87968-579-4). Gordon Pr.

Ballard, Hoyt B. & Domhoff, G. William, eds. C. Wright Mills & "The Power Elite". LC 68-14705. 1969. pap. 6.95x (ISBN 0-8070-4185-8, BP334). Beacon Pr.

Ballard, J., jt. ed. see Hunt, G. E.

Ballard, J. A., ed. Policy-Making in a New State: Papua New Guinea 1972-77. (Illus.). 331p. 1981. text ed. 32.50x (ISBN 0-7022-1529-5). U of Queensland Pr.

Ballard, J. G. Empire of the Sun. 320p. 1984. 16.95 (ISBN 0-671-53051-8). S&S.

--Empire of the Sun. 1985. pap. 4.50. WSP.

--Re-Search: J. G. Ballard. Vale, V., ed. (Re-Search Ser.). (Illus.). 176p. 1984. pap. 8.95 (ISBN 0-940642-08-5). Re Search Media.

--The Unlimited Dream Company. 1985. pap. 4.50 (ISBN 0-318-04541-9). WSP.

Ballard, J. Z., ed. The Indian Captivity; or, the Long Lost Jackson Boy William Filley. LC 73-7044. (Illus.). 112p. 1971. pap. 5.50 (ISBN 0-912382-05-8). Black Letter.

Ballard, Jack S. The Shock of Peace: Military & Economic Demobilization After World War II. LC 82-24860. (Illus.). 270p. (Orig.). 1983. lib. bdg. 26.75 (ISBN 0-8191-3029-X); pap. text ed. 13.25 (ISBN 0-8191-3030-3). U Pr of Amer.

Ballard, James. Rolling All the Time (Stories) LC 76-13475. (Illinois Short Fiction Ser). 170p. 1976. 11.95x (ISBN 0-252-00613-5); pap. 5.95 (ISBN 0-252-00614-3). U of Ill Pr.

Ballard, Jerry. Never Say, "Can't". (Orig.). 1984. pap. 3.95 (ISBN 0-89265-091-5). Randall Hse.

Ballard, Jim. Boo! A Parable for Children Over & Under 21. LC 75-25393. (Mandala Ser. in Education). (Illus.). 1975. pap. 3.50 (ISBN 0-916250-08-3). Irvington.

--Circlebook: A Leader Handbook for Conducting Circletime - A Curriculum of Affect. LC 75-25396. (Mandala Ser. in Education). (Illus.). 60p. (Orig.). 1981. pap. 4.95 (ISBN 0-8290-0150-6). Irvington.

--Dibble & the Great Blob: A Parable for Children Over & Under 21. LC 75-25393. (Mandala Ser. in Education). 1975. pap. 3.50 (ISBN 0-916250-06-7). Irvington.

--Parables for Children Over & Under 21. Incl. Warm Snugglies & Cold Ouchies. pap. 3.50 (ISBN 0-916250-05-9); Dibble & the Great Blob. pap. 3.50 (ISBN 0-916250-06-7); Boo! pap. 3.50 (ISBN 0-916250-08-3); The Seeing Circle. pap. 3.50 (ISBN 0-916250-07-5). LC 75-25393. 100p. (Orig.). 1975. Set. pap. 14.00 (ISBN 0-916250-04-0). Irvington.

--Seeing Circle: A Parable for Children Over & Under 21. LC 75-25393. (Mandala Ser. in Education). 1975. pap. 3.50 (ISBN 0-916250-07-5). Irvington.

--Stop a Moment: A Group Leader's Handbook of Energizing Experiences. LC 77-81459. (Mandala Ser. in Education). (Illus.). 73p. 1982. pap. 5.95 (ISBN 0-8290-0981-7). Irvington.

--Stories with Holes: A Collection of Open-Ended Stories for Conducting Inquiry Training in the Classroom. LC 75-25392. (Mandala Series in Education). 32p. (Orig.). 1981. pap. 3.95 (ISBN 0-8290-0355-X). Irvington.

--Warm Snuggles & Cold Ouchies: A Parable for Children Over & Under 21. LC 75-25393. (Mandala Ser. in Education). 1975. pap. 3.50 (ISBN 0-916250-05-9). Irvington.

--Why Not? How to Be Doing What You Really Like...& Getting Paid. LC 76-14016. (Mandala Ser. in Education). 180p. (Orig.). 1976. pap. 8.95 (ISBN 0-916250-10-5). Irvington.

Ballard, Jim, jt. auth. see Timmermann, Tim.

Ballard, Jimmy & Quinn, Brennan. How to Perfect Your Golf Swing. LC 80-66691. (Illus.). 160p. (Orig.). 1981. 13.50 (ISBN 0-914178-38-5). Golf Digest.

Ballard, John. The Guide to End World Hunger. Ghose, Prema, ed. LC 84-63141. (MacBurnie King's Guides to End World Hunger Ser.). (Illus.). 72p. (Orig.). 1985. pap. 3.95 (ISBN 0-932279-25-2). New Hor Bk.

--Monsoon: A Novel to End World Hunger. Schorr, Andrew, ed. LC 84-62121. (MacBurnie King Adventure Ser.). (Illus.). 242p. (Includes 68 pg. supplement of India & world hunger.). 1985. 14.95 (ISBN 0-932279-00-7); pap. 9.95 (ISBN 0-932279-01-5). New Hor Bk.

Ballard, Joseph, et al, eds. Special Education in America: Its Legal & Governmental Foundations. 112p. 1982. pap. 16.50 (ISBN 0-86586-133-1). Coun Exc Child.

Ballard, Juliet B. The Art of Living. 251p. 1982. pap. 7.95 (ISBN 0-87604-144-6). ARE Pr.

--The Hidden Laws of Earth. 241p. (Orig.). 1979. pap. 7.95 (ISBN 0-87604-117-9). ARE Pr.

--Treasures from Earth's Storehouse. 311p. (Orig.). 1980. pap. 8.95 (ISBN 0-87604-128-4). ARE Pr.

Ballard, L. S., jt. auth. see Warren, Thomas B.

Ballard, Lois. Reptiles. LC 81-38525. (New True Bks.). (Illus.). 48p. 1982. PLB 10.60 (ISBN 0-516-01644-X); pap. 3.95 (ISBN 0-516-41644-8). Childrens.

Ballard, Lou, jt. auth. see Brown, Robert.

Ballard, Lou E., jt. auth. see Levie, Robert C.

Ballard, Martin. The Story of Teaching. (Illus.). 104p. 1972. 10.00 (ISBN 0-8022-2067-3). Philos Lib.

Ballard, Megan J. & Morales, Cecilio J., eds. A Survey of Press Freedom in Latin America 1984-1985. 50p. 1985. 6.95 (ISBN 0-318-17828-1). Coun Hemispheric Aff.

Ballard, Mignon F. Aunt Matilda's Ghost. (gr. 11 up). 1978. pap. 3.95 (ISBN 0-87695-211-2). Aurora Pubs.

Ballard, Patricia. Wine in Every Day Cooking. (Illus.). 128p. pap. 5.95 (ISBN 0-932664-20-2). Wine Appreciation.

Ballard, Peter, jt. auth. see Boughton, Brian.

Ballard, Philip B. Thought & Language. 1973. Repr. of 1934 ed. 14.50 (ISBN 0-8274-1291-6). R West.

Ballard, R. D. & Moore, J. G. Atlas of the Mid-Atlantic Ridge Rift Valley. (Illus.). 1977. 35.00 (ISBN 0-387-90247-3). Springer-Verlag.

Ballard, R. E. Photoelectron Spectroscopy & Molecular Orbital Theory. LC 78-40817. 192p. 1978. 74.95x (ISBN 0-470-26542-6). Halsted Pr.

Ballard, Ralph. Old Fort Saint Joseph. 1973. Repr. of 1949 ed. 3.50 (ISBN 0-915056-01-1). Hardscrabble Bks.

Ballard, Richard. Talking Dictionary. (Michigan Learning Modules Ser.: No. 21). 1978. write for info. (ISBN 0-914004-24-7). Ulrich.

Ballard, Richard, jt. auth. see Lamberg, Walter.

Ballard, Richard, jt. auth. see Lamberg, Walter J.

Ballard, Riley R. He Is Here. (Illus.). 80p. 1982. 5.50 (ISBN 0-682-49855-6). Exposition Pr FL.

Ballard, Robert D. Exploring Our Living Planet. Tourtellot, Jonathan B., ed. (Illus.). 366p. 1983. 19.95 (ISBN 0-87044-459-X); lib. bdg. 21.95 (ISBN 0-87044-397-6); deluxe edition 29.95 (ISBN 0-87044-460-3). Natl Geog.

Ballard, Ronn, jt. auth. see Sandbach, John.

Ballard, Steven C. & Devine, Michael D. Water & Western Energy: Impacts, Issues, & Choices. (Special Studies in Water Policy & Management). 350p. 1982. lib. bdg. 30.00x (ISBN 0-86531-332-6). Westview.

Ballard, Steven C. & James, Thomas E., Jr., eds. The Future of the Sunbelt: Managing Growth & Change. 268p. 1983. 28.95 (ISBN 0-03-063392-3). Praeger.

Ballard, Susan. Fairy Tales from Far Japan. lib. bdg. 79.95 (ISBN 0-87968-477-1). Krishna Pr.

Ballard, Todhunter. Applegate's Gold. 1973. pap. 0.75 (ISBN 0-380-01026-7, 17525). Avon.

--Fight or Die. Orig. Title: Westward the Monitors Roar. 1977. pap. 1.50 (ISBN 0-505-51184-3, Pub. by Tower Bks). Dorchester Pub Co.

--Gold in California. 320p. 1981. pap. 1.95 (ISBN 0-441-29743-9, Pub. by Charter Bks). Ace Bks.

Ballard, W. L. The Yuchi Green Corn Ceremonial. 81p. 1978. pap. 7.50 (ISBN 0-935626-27-1). U Cal AISC.

Ballardo, Victoria M. Count Me among the Living: The Story of My Wheelchair Liberation. 145p. 1983. 8.50 (ISBN 0-682-49945-5). Exposition Pr FL.

Ballare, Patricia. Wine in Everyday Cooking: Cooking with Wine for Family & Friends. 128p. pap. 5.95 (ISBN 0-932664-45-8). Wine Appreciation.

Ballarin, Eduard. Commercial Banks Amidst the Financial Revolution. 288p. 1986. prof. ref. 29.95x (ISBN 0-88730-081-2). Ballinger Pub.

Ballas, George C. & Hollas, Dave. The Making of an Entrepreneur: Keys to Your Success. (Illus.). 1980. (Spec); pap. 6.95 (ISBN 0-13-546770-5). P-H.

Ballas, Shimon. The Shoes of Tanboury. 40p. 1970. 4.95 (ISBN 0-88482-767-4). Hebrew Pub.

Ballast, Daniel L. & Shoemaker, Ronald L. Coactive Guidance: A Blueprint for the Future. 200p. 1980. 19.95x (ISBN 0-398-04089-3). C C Thomas.

--Guidance Program Development. (Illus.). 100p. 1978. 11.00x (ISBN 0-398-03744-2). C C Thomas.

Ballast, David K. The Architect's Handbook. LC 83-13795. 315p. 1984. 59.95 (ISBN 0-13-044677-7, Busn). P-H.

Ballato, Arthur, jt. ed. see Gerber, Eduard A.

Ballbach, Nathan A. The Gooseneck Tidings. LC 75-28578. 1977. 4.50 (ISBN 0-918808-01-4). Northlands MI.

Balle, Francis, jt. auth. see Rogers, Everett.

Ballem, John. Sacrifice Play. 256p. 1981. pap. 2.25 (ISBN 0-449-14381-3, GM). Fawcett.

Ballen, Roger. Boyhood. LC 79-11386. (Illus.). 96p. 1979. 12.95 (ISBN 0-87754-091-8). Chelsea Hse.

Ballenger, A. F. A Believer's Guide to Christian Maturity. LC 82-72493. 256p. 1982. pap. 4.95 (ISBN 0-87123-278-2, 210278). Bethany Hse.

Ballenger, Dean W. Maverick Gold. 1978. pap. 1.25 (ISBN 0-532-12532-0). Woodhill.

--The Money Hanging. 1978. pap. 1.25 (ISBN 0-532-12583-5). Woodhill.

Ballenger, James C. Biology of Agoraphobia. LC 84-6157. (Clinical Insights Monographs). 128p. 1984. pap. text ed. 12.00x (ISBN 0-88048-064-5). Am Psychiatric.

Ballenger, John J., ed. Diseases of the Nose, Throat, Ear, Head & Neck. 13th ed. LC 83-24903. (Illus.). 1432p. 1985. text ed. 110.00 (ISBN 0-8121-0909-0). Lea & Febiger.

Ballenger, Marcus, et al. Primary School Potpourri. Cohen, Monroe D., ed. LC 75-45119. (Illus.). 1980. Repr. of 1976 ed. 2.50 (ISBN 0-87173-072-3). ACEI.

Ballenger, Sally, jt. auth. see Taylor, Joyce.

Ballenger, Sharon M., ed. Respond, Vol. 6. 144p. 1980. pap. 7.95 (ISBN 0-8170-0880-2). Judson.

Ballentine, Henry A., jt. auth. see Sherman, Francis T.

Ballentine, J. Gregory. Equity, Efficiency & the U. S. Corporation Income Tax. 1980. pap. 5.25 (ISBN 0-8447-3366-0). Am Enterprise.

Ballentine, Jeanne A. Schools & Society: A Reader in Education & Sociology. 576p. (Orig.). 1985. pap. text ed. 16.95 (ISBN 0-87484-707-9). Mayfield Pub.

Ballentine, Martha. Himalayan Mountain Cookery: A Vegetarian Cookbook. LC 77-362033. (Illus.). 203p. (Orig.). 1976. spiral bdg. 6.95 (ISBN 0-89389-015-4). Himalayan Pubs.

Ballentine, R. Diet & Nutrition. LC 78-110274. 634p. 1978. text ed. 17.95 (ISBN 0-89389-022-7); pap. 12.95 (ISBN 0-89389-048-0). Himalayan Pubs.

Ballentine, Rudolph M., ed. see Himalayan International Institute.

Ballentyne, D. W. & Lovett, D. R. Dictionary of Named Effects & Laws in Chemistry, Physics & Mathematics. 4th ed. 1980. 19.95x (ISBN 0-412-22390-2, NO. 6780, Pub. by Chapman & Hall England). Methuen Inc.

Ballentyne, D. W. & Walker, L. E. Diccionario de Leyes y Efectos Cientificos En Quimica-Fisica Matematicas. 216p. (Span.). 14.95 (ISBN 0-686-56711-0, S-33054). French & Eur.

Baller, Eleazar, ed. Communism & Cultural Heritage. 267p. 1984. 7.95 (ISBN 0-8285-2809-8, Pub. by Progress Pubns USSR). Imported Pubns.

Baller, F. W. The Sacred Edict of K'ang Hsi. LC 79-89636. 18.00x (ISBN 0-915032-25-2); pap. 12.95x (ISBN 0-915032-28-7). Natl Poet Foun.

Baller, Scott, jt. auth. see Berkson, Larry.

Ballerini, Julia, jt. auth. see Castle, Ted.

Ballerini, Luigi. Che Figurato Muore. Harrison, Thomas, tr. from It. LC 78-58982. 1986. 7.95 (ISBN 0-915570-11-4). Oolp Pr.

Ballero, Mireille. My Village in India: Gopal & the Temples Secret. LC 85-2126. (Illus.). 48p. (gr. 4 up). PLB 12.95 (ISBN 0-382-09004-7). Silver.

Ballerstedt, Elke & Glatzer, Wolfgang. Soziologischer Almanach. 616p. (Ger.). 1982. text ed. 34.50x (ISBN 3-593-32419-9). Irvington.

Ballester, Gonzalo T. Don Juan. Lawrence, Sally, tr. 1981. 17.95 (ISBN 0-914366-10-6). Columbia Pub.

Ballesteros, Antonio M. Tres Farsas Contemporaneas y un Secuestro. Maroto, Angel R. & Whitehead, Charles E., eds. (Orig.). (gr. 10-12). 1980. pap. text ed. 4.50x (ISBN 0-88334-125-5). Ind Sch Pr.

Ballesteros, Luis W. Diccionario Tecnico De Electromecanica: Ingles-Espanol. 1976. pap. 13.50x (ISBN 968-18-0522-4). Intl Learn Syst.

Ballesteros, Octavio A. Behind Jail Bars. LC 78-61104. 1979. 14.95 (ISBN 0-8022-2233-1). Philos Lib.

--Bilingual-Bicultural Education: An Annotated Bibliography 1936-1982. LC 83-42884. 104p. 1983. pap. 15.95x (ISBN 0-89950-077-3). McFarland & Co.

Ballesteros, Otavio A. Mexican Proverbs: The Philosophy, Wisdom & Humor of a People. 1980. 6.95 (ISBN 0-89015-231-4). Eakin Pubns.

Ballesteros, Severiano & Doust, Dudley. Seve: The Young Champion. LC 83-83248. (Illus.). 156p. 1984. 14.95 (ISBN 0-914178-67-9). Golf Digest.

Ballestrem, K. G. Russian Philosophical Terminology. (Sovietica Ser: No. 19). 117p. (Eng., Fr., Ger. & Rus.). 1964. lib. bdg. 18.50 (ISBN 90-277-0036-2, Pub. by Reidel Holland). Kluwer Academic.

--Die Sowjetische Erkenntnismetaphysik und ihr Verhaeltnis zu Hegel. (Sovetica Ser.: No. 27). 189p. (Ger.). 1968. lib. bdg. 26.00 (ISBN 90-277-0037-0, Pub. by Reidel Holland). Kluwer Academic.

Ballew, Hunter. Teaching Children Mathematics. LC 73-75000. 1973. text ed. 22.95 (ISBN 0-675-08982-4). Merrill.

Ballew, Lynne. Straight & Circular: A Study of Imagery in Greek Philosophy. 1979. pap. text ed. 12.50x (ISBN 90-232-1676-8). Humanities.

Ballhatchet, K. & Harrison, J., eds. The City in South Asia. 1980. text ed. 16.25x (ISBN 0-391-01129-4). Humanities.

Ballhausen, C. J. & Gray, H. B. Molecular Orbital Theory. 1964. pap. text ed. 28.95 (ISBN 0-8053-0451-7, Adv Bk Prog). Benjamin-Cummings.

Ballian, R. & Maynard, R., eds. Ill-Condensed Matter: Les Houches Session XXXI. xxvi, 610p. 1983. 60.00x (ISBN 9971-950-59-6, Pub. by World Sci Singapore); pap. 28.00x (ISBN 9971-950-60-X, Pub. by World Sci Singapore). Taylor & Francis.

Balliet, Lee. Survey of Labor Relations. 208p. 1981. text ed. 14.00 (ISBN 0-87179-347-4); pap. text ed. 10.00 (ISBN 0-87179-351-2). BNA.

Balliett, Blue. The Ghosts of Nantucket: Twenty-Three True Accounts. (Illus.). 128p. 1984. o. p. 12.95; pap. 7.95 (ISBN 0-89272-191-X). Down East.

Balliett, G. Getting Started in Private Practice. 1978. 24.95 (ISBN 0-87489-134-5). Med Economics.

--How to Close a Medical Practice. 1978. 24.95 (ISBN 0-87489-142-6). Med Economics.

Balliett, Mrs. L. Don. Number Vibration in Question & Answer. 104p. 1983. pap. 5.50 (ISBN 0-89540-139-8, SB-139). Sun Pub.

--Vibration: A System of Numbers as Taught by Pythagoras. 80p. 1983. pap. 4.00 (ISBN 0-89540-138-X, SB-138). Sun Pub.

Balliett, Paul R. Parson's Parables. 1971. 4.75 (ISBN 0-89536-182-5). CSS of Ohio.

Balliett, Whitney. Alec Wilder & His Friends. (The Roots of Jazz Ser.). (Illus.). 205p. 1983. Repr. of 1974 ed. lib. bdg. 25.00 (ISBN 0-306-76153-X). Da Capo.

--American Singers. 1979. 19.95x (ISBN 0-19-502524-5). Oxford U Pr.

--Dinosaurs in the Morning: Forty-One Pieces on Jazz. LC 78-93. 1978. Repr. of 1962 ed. lib. bdg. 27.50 (ISBN 0-313-20283-4, BADI). Greenwood.

--Ecstasy at the Onion: Thirty-pieces on Jazz. LC 82-6249. 284p. 1982. Repr. of 1971 ed. lib. bdg. 29.75 (ISBN 0-313-22577-X, BAEO). Greenwood.

--Improvising: Sixteen Jazz Musicians & Their Art. LC 76-42635. 1977. 19.95x (ISBN 0-19-502149-5). Oxford U Pr.

--Jelly Roll, Jabbo & Fats: Nineteen Portraits in Jazz. (Galaxy Bks.). 1982. 17.95 (ISBN 0-19-503275-6); pap. 6.95 (ISBN 0-19-503425-2, GB 755). Oxford U Pr.

--New York Notes: A Journal of Jazz in the Seventies. LC 76-51396. (Quality Paperback Ser.). 1977. pap. 6.95 (ISBN 0-306-80037-3). Da Capo.

--Night Creature: A Journal of Jazz, 1975-1980. (Illus.). 1981. 19.95 (ISBN 0-19-502908-9). Oxford U Pr.

--The Sound of Surprise. LC 77-17852. (Roots of Jazz Ser.). 1978. Repr. of 1961 ed. lib. bdg. 25.00 (ISBN 0-306-77543-3). Da Capo.

Ballieux, Rudy, jt. ed. see Fauci, Anthony S.

Balling, Frederick J. Sister Carrie Notes. (Orig.). 1967. pap. 3.50 (ISBN 0-8220-1201-4). Cliffs.

Balling, L. Christian. A Game of Pawns. Brady, Upton, ed. LC 85-47785. 324p. 1985. 15.95 (ISBN 0-87113-024-6, Pub. by Atlantic Monthly Pr). Little.

Balling, Michael, ed. see Wagner, Richard.

Ballingall, James. A Taste of China. (Illus.). 208p. 1984. 13.95 (ISBN 0-531-09768-4). Watts.

Ballinger, Elizabeth. Training Your Dog: A Guide to a More Compatible Relationship. 120p. 1983. pap. write for info. Old Farm Ken.

Ballinger, J. Kenneth. Florida Real Estate Handbook. 400p. 1979. 35.00 (ISBN 0-87215-235-9). Michie Co.

Ballinger, James, ed. see Hildreth, Jean C.

Ballinger, James K. & Horton, Tonia L. Peter Hurd: Insight to a Painter. 84p. 1983. pap. 10.00x (ISBN 0-910407-02-9). Phoenix Art.

Ballinger, James K. & Rubinstein, Andrea. Visitors to Arizona 1846 to 1980. LC 80-82651. (Illus.). 207p. (Orig.). pap. 12.00 (ISBN 0-910407-07-X). Phoenix Art.

Ballinger, Lee. In Your Face! Sports for Love & Money. 151p. (Orig.). 1981. pap. 2.95 (ISBN 0-917702-12-3). Vanguard Bks.

Ballinger, Philip W. Merrill's Atlas of Radiographic Positions & Radiologic Procedures, 3 Vols. 5th ed. (Illus.). 950p. 1982. text ed. 99.95 (ISBN 0-8016-3408-3). Mosby.

Ballinger, R., ed. see Visigli, R.

Ballinger, Rex E., ed. see Usigli, Rodolfo.

Ballinger, Rex E., ed. see Zunzunegui, Juan A.

Ballinger, Richard A. A Treatise on the Property Rights of Husband & Wife, Under the Community or Ganancial System: Adapted to the Statutes & Decisions of Louisiana, Texas, California, Nevada, Washington, Idaho, Arizona & New Mexico. xiii, 543p. 1981. Repr. of 1895 ed. lib. bdg. 38.50x (ISBN 0-8377-0320-4). Rothman.

Ballinger, Royce E. & Lynch, John D. How to Know the Amphibians & Reptiles. (Pictured Key Nature Ser.). 240p. 1983. write for info. wire coil (ISBN 0-697-04786-5). Wm C Brown.

Ballinger, W. A. Alpha-Omega. 128p. 1982. 20.00x (ISBN 0-7278-0539-8, Pub. by Severn Hse). State Mutual Bk.

Ballinger, Walter F., ed. see American College of Surgeons.

Ballington, Rachel. Occasion of Sin. 1984. pap. 3.50 (ISBN 0-345-31515-4). Ballantine.

Ballio, Giulio & Mazzolani, Federico. Theory & Design of Steel Structures. 664p. 1983. 61.00x (ISBN 0-412-23660-5, NO. 6886, Pub. by Chapman & Hall England). Methuen Inc.

Ballistocardiograph Research Society, 16th Annual Meeting, Atlantic City, 1972. Ballistocardiography - Research & Computer Diagnosis: Proceedings. Franke, E. K., ed. (Bibliotheca Cardiologica: No. 32). (Illus.). 160p. 1973. pap. 18.00 (ISBN 3-8055-1376-3). S Karger.

Ballistocardiograph Research Society, 14th Annual Meeting, Atlantic City, 1970. Ballistocardiography & Clinical Studies: Proceedings. Harrison, W. K., ed. (Bibliotheca Cardiologica: No. 27). 1971. pap. 10.75 (ISBN 3-8055-1188-4). S Karger.

Ballistocardiograph Research Society, 15th Annual Meeting, Atlantic City, 1971. Circulatory Assist & Ballistocardiographic Studies: Proceedings. Jackson, D. H., ed. (Bibliotheca Cardiologica: No. 29). 1972. pap. 16.75 (ISBN 3-8055-1323-2). S Karger.

Ballistocardiographic Research Society 17th Meeting, Atlantic City, Apr, 1973. Ultrasound & Ballistocardiography in Cardiovascular Research: Proceedings. Baan, Jan, ed. (Bibliotheca Cardiologica: No. 34). (Illus.). 120p. 1974. 23.00 (ISBN 3-8055-1763-7). S Karger.

Ballistocardiography & Cardiovascular Dynamics Congress, 3rd World 9th European, Sofia, 1973. Ballistocardiographic Methods & Cardiovascular Dynamics: Proceedings. Talakov, A., ed. (Bibliotheca Cardiologica Ser.: No. 33). 300p. 1974. pap. 59.25 (ISBN 3-8055-1701-7). S Karger.

Ballmer, T. Logical Grammar. (Linguistic Ser.: Vol. 39). 378p. 1978. 59.75 (ISBN 0-444-85205-0, North Holland). Elsevier.

Ballmer, T. & Brennenstuhl, W. Speech Art Classification. (Springer Series in Language & Communication: Vol. 8). (Illus.). 274p. 1980. 31.50 (ISBN 0-387-10294-9). Springer-Verlag.

Ballmer, T. T., ed. Approaching Vagueness. (Linguistic Ser.: Vol. 50). 430p. 1983. 49.00 (ISBN 0-444-86745-7, I-252-83, North-Holland). Elsevier.

Ballmer, Thomas. Biological Foundations of Linguistic Communication: Towards a Biocybernetics of Language. (Pragmatics & Beyond: III-7). 161p. (Orig.). 1983. pap. 20.00 (ISBN 90-272-2520-6). Benjamins North Am.

Ballon, R. J., et al. Financial Reporting in Japan. LC 75-30179. (Illus.). 305p. 1976. 17.95x (ISBN 0-87011-269-4). Kodansha.

Ballon, Robert J., ed. Marketing in Japan. LC 73-79771. (Illus.). 200p. 1973. 16.95x (ISBN 0-87011-200-7). Kodansha.

Ballonoff, P. A., jt. ed. see Weiss, K. M.

Ballonoff, Paul A. Mathematical Foundations of Social Anthropology. (Publications of the Maison Des Sciences De L'homme Ser.). (Illus.). 131p. 1976. pap. text ed. 11.60x (ISBN 90-2797-934-0). Mouton.

Ballonoff, Paul A., ed. Genealogical Mathematics. 311p. 1975. pap. text ed. 31.20x (ISBN 90-2797-901-4). Mouton.

--Mathematical Models of Social & Cognitive Structures: Contributions to the Mathematical Development of Anthropology. LC 73-20082. (Studies in Anthropology Ser.: No. 9). (Illus.). 143p. 1974. pap. 8.95x (ISBN 0-252-00415-9). U of Ill Pr.

Ballot, Michael. Decision-Making Models in Production & Operations Management. LC 84-29740. 1985. lib. bdg. write for info. (ISBN 0-89874-825-9). Krieger.

Ballotti, Geno A. & Graubard, Stephen R., eds. The Embattled University. LC 71-128778. (Daedalus Library Ser). 1971. 6.95 (ISBN 0-8076-0581-6); pap. 3.95 (ISBN 0-8076-0580-8). Braziller.

Ballou, Adin. Autobiography of Adin Ballou 1803-1890. Heywood, William S., ed. LC 74-26603. (American Utopian Adventure Ser.). (Illus.). xviii, 586p. Repr. of 1896 ed. lib. bdg. 37.50x (ISBN 0-87991-033-X). Porcupine Pr.

--Christian Non-Resistance. LC 70-121104. (Civil Liberties in American History Ser). 1970. Repr. of 1910 ed. lib. bdg. 35.00 (ISBN 0-306-71980-0). Da Capo.

--Christian Non-Resistance in All Its Important Bearings, Illustrated & Defended. LC 76-137527. (Peace Movement in America Ser.). 240p. 1972. Repr. of 1846 ed. lib. bdg. 16.95x (ISBN 0-89198-054-7). Ozer.

--History of the Hopedale Community. Heywood, W. S., ed. LC 76-187467. (The American Utopian Adventure Ser.). 415p. 1973. Repr. of 1897 ed. lib. bdg. 27.50x (ISBN 0-87991-007-0). Porcupine Pr.

--History of the Hopedale Community, from Its Inception to Its Virtual Submergence in the Hopedale Parish. Heywood, William S., ed. LC 72-2935. (Communal Societies in America Ser.). Repr. of 1897 ed. 14.00 (ISBN 0-404-10701-X). AMS Pr.

--Practical Christian Socialism. LC 72-2936. (Communal Societies in America Ser.). Repr. of 1854 ed. 37.50 (ISBN 0-404-10702-8). AMS Pr.

--Practical Christian Socialism, 2 vols. 655p. Date not set. Repr. of 1854 ed. lib. bdg. 69.00 (ISBN 0-932051-86-3). Am Repr Serv.

Ballou, Ellen B. Building of the House: Houghton Mifflin's First Half Century. LC 69-15006. (Illus.). 1970. 12.50 (ISBN 0-395-07383-9). HM.

Ballou, F. W. The Appointment of Teachers in Cities. (Harvard Studies in Education: Vol. 2). 19.00 (ISBN 0-384-03155-2). Johnson Repr.

Ballou, Glen. Handbook for Sound Engineers. Date not set. 44.95 (ISBN 0-672-21983-2, 21983). Sams.

Ballou, Hosea. Treatise on Atonement. Cassara, Ernest, ed. 1985. pap. price not set (ISBN 0-933840-26-8). Unitarian Univ.

Ballou, John D. & Gorzelany, James A. Study Guide for Modern Real Estate Practice. 10th ed. (Illus.). 240p. (Orig.). 1985. pap. text ed. 9.95 (ISBN 0-88462-519-2, 1510-02, Real Estate Ed). Longman USA.

Ballou, John D., ed. see Real Estate Education Company.

Ballou, John E., ed. Radiation & the Lymphatic System: Proceedings. LC 75-38685. (ERDA Symposium Ser.). 264p. 1976. pap. 14.50 (ISBN 0-87079-030-7, CONF-740930); microfiche 4.50 (ISBN 0-87079-317-9, CONF-740930). DOE.

Ballou, Mary & Gabalac, Nancy W. A Feminist Position on Mental Health. 190p. 1985. 22.50x (ISBN 0-398-05040-6). C C Thomas.

Ballou, Maturin M. Aztec Land. 1976. lib. bdg. 59.95 (ISBN 0-87968-688-X). Gordon Pr.

--Due South, Cuba, Past & Present. LC 72-91661. Repr. of 1885 ed. 19.75x (ISBN 0-8371-2071-3, BAD&, Pub. by Negro U Pr). Greenwood.

--History of Cuba: Or Notes of a Traveler in the Tropics. LC 70-161756. (Illus.). Repr. of 1854 ed. 16.00 (ISBN 0-404-00488-1). AMS Pr.

Ballou, Patricia K. Women: A Bibliography of Bibliographies. 1980. lib. bdg. 18.00 (ISBN 0-8161-8292-2, Hall Reference). G K Hall.

Ballou, R. O., et al, eds. The Bible of the World. 1415p. 1980. pap. 5.50 (ISBN 0-380-01057-7, 17350). Avon.

Ballou, Ralph. Teaching Badminton. LC 81-68519. (Sport Teaching Ser.). 160p. (Orig.). 1982. pap. text ed. 8.95x (ISBN 0-8087-4068-7). Burgess.

Ballou, Richard. A Guide for Brass Bands in the Pacific. 1983. 6.95 (ISBN 0-939154-29-3). Inst Polynesian.

Ballou, Robert, ed. see James, William.

Ballou, Robert O. The Portable World Bible. (Viking Portable Library). 1977. pap. 6.95 (ISBN 0-14-015005-6). Penguin.

Ballou, Ronald H. Basic Business Logistics. (Illus.). 1978. ref. ed. 29.95 (ISBN 0-13-057364-7). P-H.

--Business Logistics Management: Planning & Control. 2nd ed. (Illus.). 688p. 1985. text ed. 34.95 (ISBN 0-13-104829-5). P-H.

Ballowe, James M. Trailer Park. 1981. 5.95 (ISBN 0-533-04783-8). Vantage.

Ball-Rokeach, Sandra & Grube, Joel W. The Great American Values Test: Influencing Behavior & Belief Through Television. LC 83-48468. 208p. 1983. 25.00x (ISBN 0-02-926850-8). Free Pr.

Ball-Rokeach, Sandra J., jt. auth. see DeFleur, Melvin.

Balls, Edward K. Early Uses of California Plants. (California Natural History Guides: No. 10). (Illus., Orig.). 1962. pap. 4.95 (ISBN 0-520-00072-2). U of Cal Pr.

Balls, M. & Billett, F. S., eds. The Cell Cycle in Development & Differentiation. (British Society for Developmental Biological Symposia Ser.). (Illus.). 450p. 1973. 80.00 (ISBN 0-521-20136-5). Cambridge U Pr.

Balls, M. & Monnickendam, Marjorie, eds. Organ Culture in Biomedical Research. LC 75-21034. (British Society for Cell Biology Symposium Ser.: No. 1). (Illus.). 600p. 1976. 99.00 (ISBN 0-521-21001-1). Cambridge U Pr.

Balls, M. & Wild, A. E., eds. The Early Development of Mammals. (British Society for Developmental Biology Symposium Ser). (Illus.). 500p. 1975. 99.00 (ISBN 0-521-20771-1). Cambridge U Pr.

Balls, M., jt. ed. see Newth, D. R.

Balls, Michael & Bownes, Mary, eds. Metamorphosis. (Illus.). 350p. 1985. 47.50 (ISBN 0-19-857183-6). Oxford U Pr.

Balls, Michael, et al. Animals & Alternatives in Toxicity Testing. 1983. 35.00 (ISBN 0-12-077480-1). Acad Pr.

Ballstadt, Carl, ed. The Search for English- Canadian Literature: An Anthology of Critical Articles from the Nineteenth & Early Twentieth Centuries. LC 75-15779. (Literature of Canada Ser.: No. 16). pap. 65.80 (ISBN 0-317-26829-5, 2023490). Bks Demand UMI.

--The Search for English-Canadian Literature: An Anthology of Critical Articles from the Nineteenth & Early Twentieth Centuries. LC 75-15779. 1975. pap. 8.50 (ISBN 0-8020-6263-6). U of Toronto Pr.

Ballve, Faustino. Essentials of Economics. 126p. 1969. pap. 3.00 (ISBN 0-910614-19-9). Foun Econ Ed.

Ballwebber, Edith. Group Instruction in Social Dancing. (Ballroom Dance Ser.). 1985. lib. bdg. 78.00 (ISBN 0-87700-829-9). Revisionist Pr.

Ballweber, Duane. Practical Applications in Basic Auto Body Repair. (Illus.). 288p. 1983. text ed. 24.95 (ISBN 0-13-689216-7). P-H.

Bally, A. W., et al, eds. Dynamics of Plate Interiors. LC 80-28968. (Geodynamics Series: Vol. 1). 168p. 1980. 20.00 (ISBN 0-87590-508-0, G00100). Am Geophysical.

Bally, Charles, ed. see De Saussure, Ferdinand.

Bally, G. V. & Greguss, P. Optics in Biomedical Sciences: Graz Austria 1981 Proceedings. (Springer Series in Optical Sciences: Vol. 31). (Illus.). 274p. 1982. 40.00 (ISBN 0-387-11666-4). Springer-Verlag.

Bally, G. Von see Von Bally, G.

Balmain, Aleksandr. Napoleon in Captivity: Reports of Count Balmain Russian Commissioner on the Island of St. Helena 1816-1820. facsimile ed. Park, Julian, ed. & tr. LC 72-160955. (Select Bibliographies Reprint Ser). Repr. of 1927 ed. 23.50 (ISBN 0-8369-5822-5). Ayer Co Pubs.

Balmain, K. G., jt. auth. see Jordan, Edward C.

Balman, F. E. & Dolan, A. G. Labour Employment in Private Forestry in England & Wales till 1976. 1983. 35.00x (ISBN 0-686-45528-2, Pub. by For Lib Comm England). State Mutual Bk.

Balmary, Marie. Psychoanalyzing Psychoanalysis: Freud & the Hidden Fault of the Father. Lukacher, Ned, tr. from Fr. LC 81-18568. 208p. 1982. text ed. 19.50x (ISBN 0-8018-2349-8). Johns Hopkins.

Balme, Joshua R. American States, Churches, & Slavery. LC 74-75529. Repr. of 1862 ed. 25.00x (ISBN 0-8371-1012-2, BAA&, Pub. by Negro U Pr). Greenwood.

Balme, M. G. Intellegenda: Comprehension Exercises in Latin Prose & Verse. 1970. pap. 6.95x (ISBN 0-19-831775-1). Oxford U Pr.

Balme, M. G. & Greenstock, M. C. Scrutanda. 1973. pap. 6.95x (ISBN 0-19-831777-8). Oxford U Pr.

Balme, M. G. & Warman, M. S. Aestimanda: Practical Criticism of Latin & Greek Poetry & Prose. 1965. pap. 6.95x (ISBN 0-19-831766-2). Oxford U Pr.

Balme, M. G., ed. see Apuleius.

Balmer, Edwin, jt. auth. see Wylie, Philip.

Balmer, James E. & Moes, Matthijs. The Portable Computer Book. 400p. 1984. 19.95 (ISBN 0-912003-36-7). Bk Co.

Balmer, Philip & Wylie, Edwin. When Worlds Collide. 192p. 1962. pap. 2.75 (ISBN 0-446-30539-1). Warner Bks.

Balmer, William T. History of the Akan Peoples of the Gold Coast. LC 79-76491. (Illus.). Repr. of 1925 ed. 17.50x (ISBN 0-8371-1089-0, BAP&, Pub. by Negro U Pr). Greenwood.

Balmes, Julie, jt. auth. see Balmes, Pat.

Balmes, Pat. Danger at the Flying Y. (Perspective I Novel Ser.). 48p. 1982. 2.50 (ISBN 0-87879-299-6, High Noon Books). Acad Therapy.

Balmes, Pat & Balmes, Julie. Danger in the Deep. (Perspectives II Ser.). (Illus.). 48p. (gr. 7-12). 1982. pap. 2.50 (ISBN 0-87879-320-8, High Noon Books). Acad Therapy.

Balmford, Rosemary. Learning about Australian Birds. (Illus.). 240p. 1982. 17.95x (ISBN 0-00-216440-X, Pub. by W Collins Australia). Intl Spec Bk.

Balmforth, C. K. & Cox, N. S., eds. Interface: Library Automation with Special Reference to Computing Activity. 1971. 27.50x (ISBN 0-262-02084-X). MIT Pr.

Balmforth, R. The Ethical & Religious Value of the Drama. 59.95 (ISBN 0-8490-0132-3). Gordon Pr.

--The Problem-Play. LC 76-52915. (Studies in Drama, No. 39). 1977. lib. bdg. 41.95x (ISBN 0-8383-2129-1). Haskell.

Balmori, Diana, et al. Beatrix Farrand's American Landscapes: Her Gardens & Campuses. LC 85-1969. (Illus.). 216p. 1985. 24.95 (ISBN 0-89831-003-2). SagaPr.

--Beatrix Farrand's American Landscapes: Her Gardens & Campuses. (Illus.). 216p. 1985. pap. 24.95. Wave Hill.

--Notable Family Networks in Latin America. LC 84-2423. (Illus.). 264p. 1984. lib. bdg. 27.00x (ISBN 0-226-03639-1). U of Chicago Pr.

Balmuth, Bernard. The Language of the Cutting Room. LC 81-84920. 90p. 1981. pap. text ed. 10.95 (ISBN 0-9607486-0-1). Rosallen Pubns.

Balmuth, Daniel. Censorship in Russia, Eighteen Sixty-Five to Nineteen Five. LC 79-52510. 1979. pap. text ed. 13.00 (ISBN 0-8191-0773-5). U Pr of Amer.

Balmuth, M. The Roots of Phonics: A Historical Introduction. LC 81-6041. 1982. 19.95 (ISBN 0-07-003490-7). McGraw.

Balner, H. Bone Marrow Transplantation & Other Treatment After Radiation Injury. 1977. pap. 21.00 (ISBN 90-247-2056-7, Pub. by Martinus Nijhoff Netherlands). Kluwer Academic.

Balner, Hans & Van Rood, J. J., eds. Transplantation Genetics of Primates. LC 72-1131. (Illus.). 148p. 1972. 56.00 (ISBN 0-8089-0770-0, 790395). Grune.

Balner, Hans, et al. Transplantation Today, Vol. I. LC 73-155314. 1000p. 1971. 110.00 (ISBN 0-8089-0704-2, 790391). Grune.

Balner, Jean V. Pebbles in the Wind. (Illus.). 52p. (Orig.). pap. 5.95 (ISBN 0-9615317-0-3). Baldner J V.

Balnpain, R. The OECD Guidelines for Multinational Enterprises & Labour Relations: Experience & Mid-Term Report, 1979-1982. 244p. 32.00 (ISBN 90-312-0194-4, Pub. by Kluwer Law, Netherlands). Kluwer Academic.

Baloff, Marsha. Crosswords for Nurses. Paquet, Judith B., ed. 120p. 1982. 9.95 (ISBN 0-913590-94-0). Slack Inc.

Balog, James. Wildlife Requiem. 1984. 30.00 (ISBN 0-933642-06-7); pap. 20.00 (ISBN 0-933642-07-5). Intl Ctr Photo.

Balog, Keesy, jt. auth. see Kievman, Beverly.

Balog, Paul. Umayyad, Abbasid & Tulunid Glass Weights & Vessel Stamps. (Numismatic Studies: No. 13). (Illus.). 322p. 1976. 60.00 (ISBN 0-89722-066-8). Am Numismatic.

Balogh, Barna, tr. see Lazlo, Gyula.

Balogh, F., jt. auth. see Ranyi-Vamos, F.

Balogh, F., jt. auth. see Renyi-Vamos, F.

Balogh, J. The Oribatid Genera of the World. (Illus.). 188p. (Orig.). 1972. 21.00 (ISBN 0-685-36757-6). Entomological Repr.

Balogh, J. & Mahunka, S., eds. Primitive Oribatids of the Palaearctic Region. (Soil Mites of the World Ser.: No. 1). 370p. 1983. 106.50 (ISBN 0-444-99655-9, I-301-83). Elsevier.

Balogh, Judy M., et al. Beyond a Dream: An Instructor's Guide for Small Business Exploration. 228p. 1985. 25.00 (ISBN 0-318-17848-6, LT 68). Natl Ctr Res Voc Ed.

Balogh, Mary. A Chance Encounter. 1985. pap. 2.50 (ISBN 0-451-14006-0, Sig). NAL.

--The Double Wager. 1985. pap. 2.50 (ISBN 0-451-13617-9, Sig). NAL.

--A Masked Deception. 1985. pap. 2.50 (ISBN 0-451-13405-2, Sig). NAL.

Balogh, Thomas. The Dollar Crisis, Causes & Cure. Wilkins, Mira, ed. LC 78-3896. (International Finance Ser.). 1978. Repr. of 1949 ed. lib. bdg. 26.50x (ISBN 0-405-11202-5). Ayer Co Pubs.

--Fact & Fancy in International Economic Relations: An Essay on International Monetary Reform. LC 73-7993. 132p. 1973. text ed. 23.00 (ISBN 0-08-017740-9). Pergamon.

--The Irrelevance of Conventional Economics. 1982. 18.95 (ISBN 0-87140-646-2). Liveright.

--Studies in Financial Organization. LC 82-48174. (Gold, Money, Inflation & Deflation Ser.). 332p. 1983. lib. bdg. 44.00 (ISBN 0-686-88530-9). Garland Pub.

Baloh, Robert W. Dizziness, Hearing Loss, & Tinnitus: The Essentials of Neurotology. LC 83-15241. (Illus.). 197p. 1983. text ed. 35.00x (ISBN 0-8036-0581-1). Davis Co.

Baloh, Robert W. & Honrubia, Vicente, eds. Clinical Neurophysiology of the Vestibular System. LC 78-15467. (Contemporary Neurology Ser.: No. 18). 1979. 40.00x (ISBN 0-8036-0580-3). Davis Co.

Baloian, James C. The Ararat Papers. LC 79-50729. 1979. 6.95 (ISBN 0-933706-06-5); pap. 3.95 (ISBN 0-933706-07-3). Ararat Pr.

Balokovic, Joyce B. Towards the Center. 1956. 3.95 (ISBN 0-910664-23-4). Gotham.

Balon, E. K. Early Life Histories of Fishes: Developmental, Ecological & Evolutionary Perspectives. (Developments in Environmental Biology of Fishes Ser.). 1985. lib. bdg. 75.00 (ISBN 90-6193-514-8, Pub. by Junk Pub Netherlands). Kluwer-Academic.

Balon, Eugene, ed. Charrs: Salmonid Fishes of the Genus Salvelinus. (Perspectives in Vertebrate Science: No. 1). (Illus.). 919p. 1980. lib. bdg. 210.50 (ISBN 90-6193-701-9, Pub. by Junk Pubs Netherlands). Kluwer Academic.

Balon, Eugene K. African Fishes of Lake Kariba Africa. (Illus.). 144p. 1974. 19.95 (ISBN 0-87666-073-1, PS-706). TFH Pubns.

Balon, Joseph. Etudes Franques, I: Aux Origines De la Noblesse. LC 80-2202. Repr. of 1963 ed. 21.50 (ISBN 0-404-18551-7). AMS Pr.

Balotti, R. Franklin & Finkelstein, Jesse A. The Delaware Law of Corporations & Business Organizations: Text, Forms, & Law, 3 vols. 1985. Supplements avail. 195.00 (ISBN 0-317-29371-0, #H43872). HarBraceJ.

Balough, Teresa. A Musical Genius from Australia. (Illus.). 161p. 1982. pap. 13.50x (ISBN 0-9599791-6-6, Pub. by U of W Austral Pr). Intl Spec Bk.

Balough, Teresa, ed. see Grainger, Percy.

Balows, Albert. Clinical Microbiology: How to Start & When to Stop. (Illus.). 104p. 1975. 13.50x (ISBN 0-398-03389-7). C C Thomas.

--Current Techniques for Antibiotic Susceptibility Testing. (Illus.). 170p. 1974. 24.75x (ISBN 0-398-02886-9). C C Thomas.

--Essays in Microbiology. LC 68-29639. Repr. of 1968 ed. 27.40 (ISBN 0-8357-9784-8, 2013514). Bks Demand UMI.

Balows, Albert & Isenberg, Henry. Biotyping in the Clinical Microbiology Laboratory. (Illus.). 128p. 1978. photocopy ed. 18.50x (ISBN 0-398-03806-6). C C Thomas.

Balows, Albert & Sonnenwirth, Alex C. Bacteremia: Laboratory & Clinical Aspects. (Illus.). 142p. 1983. 22.50x (ISBN 0-398-04807-X). C C Thomas.

Balows, Albert, et al. Anaerobic Bacteria: Role in Disease. (Illus.). 656p. 1975. photocopy ed. 76.75x (ISBN 0-398-03074-X). C C Thomas.

Baloyra, Enrique. El Salvador in Transition. LC 82-4815. xviii, 236p. 1982. 19.95x (ISBN 0-8078-1532-2); pap. 8.95 (ISBN 0-8078-4093-9). U of NC Pr.

Baloyra, Enrique A. & Martz, John D. Political Attitudes in Venezuela: Societal Cleavages & Political Opinion. LC 78-14241. (Texas Pan American Ser.). 323p. 1979. text ed. 22.50x (ISBN 0-292-76453-7). U of Tex Pr.

Baloyra, Enrique A., jt. auth. see Martz, John D.

BALPA Medical Study Group. Fit to Fly: A Medical Handbook for Pilots. 80p. 1980. pap. text ed. 5.50x (ISBN 0-246-11401-0, Pub. by Granada England). Brookfield Pub Co.

Balpe, Jean-Pierre. Le Bestiaire Fantastique. new ed. Barberis, Pierre & Jean, Georges, eds. (Textes pour aujourd'hui). (Illus.). 127p. (Fr.). 1974. pap. 4.50 (ISBN 2-03-038001-6). Larousse.

Balpinar, Belkis & Hirsch, Udo. Flatweaves of the Vakiflar Museum Istanbul. (Illus.). 294p. 1982. 95.00 (ISBN 3-923185-02-2, Pub. by Uta Hulsey). Textile Mus.

Balrow, Tani E. & Lowe, Donald M. Chinese Reflections: Americans Teaching in the People's Republic. (Illus.). 256p. 1985. 17.95 (ISBN 0-317-31495-5). Praeger.

Bals, H., jt. auth. see Logan, G.

Balsam, Alan, jt. auth. see Balsam, Rosemary M.

Balsam, Charles & Balsam, Elizabeth. Family Planning: A Guide for Exploring the Options. 32p. (Orig.). 1985. pap. 1.50 (ISBN 0-89243-238-1). Liguori Pubns.

Balsam, Elizabeth, jt. auth. see Balsam, Charles.

Balsam, M. S. & Sagarin, Edward, eds. Cosmetics: Science & Technology, 3 vols. 2nd ed. LC 75-177888. Set, 2083p. 268.00 (ISBN 0-471-04650-7); Vol. 1, 1972, 605 Pgs. 86.00 (ISBN 0-471-04646-9); Vol. 2, 1972, 691 Pgs. 86.00 (ISBN 0-471-04647-7); Vol. 3, 1974, 787 Pgs. 97.00 (ISBN 0-471-04649-3, Pub. by Wiley-Interscience). Wiley.

Balsam, Pearl. Kangaroo Girl. 45p. 1983. 5.95 (ISBN 0-533-05733-7). Vantage.

Balsam, Peter & Tomie, Arthur, eds. Context & Learning. 432p. 1984. text ed. 45.00 (ISBN 0-89859-442-1). L Erlbaum Assocs.

Balsam, Rosemary M. & Balsam, Alan. Becoming a Psychotherapist. LC 83-24301. xxii, 338p. 1984. lib. bdg. 30.00x (ISBN 0-226-03635-9); pap. 12.95x (ISBN 0-226-03636-7). U of Chicago Pr.

--Becoming a Psychotherapist: A Clinical Primer. LC 74-125. 270p. (Orig.). 1974. pap. text ed. 14.95 (ISBN 0-316-07980-4). Little.

Balsama, George D. The Politics of National Despair: French Royalism in the Post-Reformation Era. 1977. pap. text ed. 9.25 (ISBN 0-8191-0142-7). U Pr of Amer.

Balsdon, J. P. Roman Women. LC 82-48825. (Illus.). 354p. (gr. 11-12). 1983. pap. 6.68i (ISBN 0-06-464062-0, BN 4062). B&N NY.

--Romans & Aliens. LC 79-14471. x, 310p. 1980. 25.00x (ISBN 0-8078-1383-4). U of NC Pr.

Balsdon, John. Roman Women, Their History & Habits. LC 75-8718. (Illus.). 351p. 1975. Repr. of 1962 ed. lib. bdg. 45.00 (ISBN 0-8371-8040-6, BAROW). Greenwood.

Balsdon, John P. The Emperor Gaius (Caligula) LC 75-41014. (BCL Ser. II). Repr. of 1934 ed. 27.50 (ISBN 0-404-14503-5). AMS Pr.

--The Emperor Gaius (Caligula) LC 77-7328. (Illus.). 1977. Repr. of 1964 ed. lib. bdg. 24.00 (ISBN 0-8371-9074-6, BAEG). Greenwood.

Balse, Mayah. Mystics & Men of Miracles in India. (Illus.). 1976. 4.50 (ISBN 0-913244-10-4). Hapi Pr.

Balseiro, J. A., ed. see Casona, Alejandro.

Balseiro, Jose, ed. see Casona, Alejandro.

Balseiro, Jose A. Novelistas Espanoles Modernos. 8th, rev., enl. ed. LC 76-27662. (Span.). 1977. 9.00 (ISBN 0-8477-3173-1). U of PR Pr.

Balsekar, Ramesh s. Pointers from Nisargadatta Maharaj. LC 82-71505. xiv, 223p. 1983. Repr. of 1984 ed. 13.50 (ISBN 0-89386-004-2). Acorn NC.

Balser, A. & Zoeppritz, M., eds. Enduser Systems & Their Human Factors: Proceedings, Heidelberg, FRG, 1983. (Lecture Notes in Computer Science Ser.: Vol. 150). 138p. 1983. pap. 10.50 (ISBN 0-387-12273-7). Springer-Verlag.

Balser, Benjamin H., ed. Psychotherapy of the Adolescent: At Different Levels of Psychiatric Practice with Special Emphasis on the Role of the School. LC 57-9326. 270p. (Orig.). 1959. text ed. 27.50 (ISBN 0-8236-5400-1); pap. text ed. 9.95 (ISBN 0-8236-8249-8, 225400). Intl Univs Pr.

Balshin, M. Y. & Kiparisov, S. S. General Priciples of Powder Metallurgy. 1980. 8.45 (ISBN 0-8285-1834-3, Pub. by Mir Pubs USSR). Imported Pubns.

Balshone, Benjamin. Determined! 1984. 15.95 (ISBN 0-8197-0494-6). Bloch.

Balshone, Bruce L. & Deering, Paul L. Bicycle Transit: Its Planning Design. 186p. 1975. 17.95 (ISBN 0-318-13111-0); members & subscribers 16.95 (ISBN 0-318-13112-9). Am Plan Assn.

Balskus, Pat. Mary's Pilgrim. LC 68-58160. (Encounter Ser.). 3.00 (ISBN 0-8198-0279-4). Dghtrs St Paul.

Balslev, E., ed. Eighteenth Scandinavian Congress of Mathematicians. (Progress in Mathematics Ser.: No. 11). 528p. 1981. 35.00x (ISBN 0-8176-3040-6). Birkhauser.

Balsley, Betsy, ed. The Los Angeles Times California Cookbook. Los Angeles Times Food Staff. (Illus.). 528p. 1983. pap. 9.95 (ISBN 0-452-25448-5, Plume). NAL.

Balsley, Betsy, compiled by see Navarro, Dawn.

Balsley, Gene. Pentax MX & ME. (Amphoto Pocket Companion Ser.). (Illus.). 1980. pap. 4.95 (ISBN 0-8174-2183-1, Amphoto). Watson-Guptill.

Balsley, Howard L. Introduction to Statistical Method. (Quality Paperback: No. 82). 347p. (Orig.). 1977. pap. 1.50 (ISBN 0-8226-0082-X). Littlefield.

Balsley, Howard L., jt. auth. see Clover, Vernon T.

Balsley, Irol W. Century Twenty-One Shorthand: Theory & Practice. 1974. text ed. 11.24 (ISBN 0-317-05894-0, R70). SW Pub.

Balsley, Ronald D., jt. auth. see Birsner, E. Patricia.

Balsom, Denis & Burch, Martin. Political & Electoral Handbook for Wales: 1959-1979. 208p. 1980. text ed. 44.50x (ISBN 0-566-00236-1). Gower Pub Co.

Balson, Maurice. Understanding Classroom Behavior. 176p. 1983. 16.00x (ISBN 0-317-18054-1, Pub. by NFER Nelson UK). Taylor & Francis.

Balster, Robert L., jt. auth. see Seiden, Lewis S.

Balston, D. M., ed. Image Restoration & Enhancement: Proceedings Institution of Electrical Engineers Special Issue, Part E, Vol. 127, No. 5. 70p. 27.00 (ISBN 0-317-34287-8). Inst Elect Eng.

Balston, Thomas. James Whatman, Father & Son. Bidwell, John, ed. LC 78-74386. (Nineteenth-Century Book Arts & Printing History Ser.: Vol. 1). (Illus.). 1979. lib. bdg. 26.00 (ISBN 0-8240-3875-4). Garland Pub.

--Sitwelliana: 1915-1927. 1978. Repr. of 1928 ed. lib. bdg. 17.50 (ISBN 0-8482-3393-X). Norwood Edns.

--William Balston, Paper Maker, 1759-1849. Bidwell, John, ed. LC 78-74387. (Nineteenth-Century Book Arts & Printing History Ser.: Vol. 2). (Illus.). 1979. lib. bdg. 26.00 (ISBN 0-8240-3876-2). Garland Pub.

Balstrino, Philip. Fat & Skinny. LC 74-12306. (A Let's-Read-&-Find-Out Science Bk). (Illus.). (gr. k-3). 1975. o. p. 8.95i (ISBN 0-690-00454-0); PLB 11.89 (ISBN 0-690-00665-9). Crowell Jr Bks.

Balsys, Algis. Mamiya Ze & Ze-2: Amphoto Pocket Companion. (Illus.). 128p. 1981. pap. 4.95 (ISBN 0-8174-5530-2, Amphoto). Watson-Guptill.

Balta, E., jt. auth. see Balta, P.

Balta, P. & Balta, E. An Introduction to the Physical Chemistry of the Vitreous State. 1976. 39.00 (ISBN 0-9961001-4-8, Pub. by Abacus England). Heyden.

Baltake, Joe. The Films of Jack Lemmon. 1977. 14.95 (ISBN 0-8065-0560-5). Citadel Pr.

Baltaxe, Christiane A., tr. see Trubetzkoy, N. S.

Baltaxe, Harold A., et al. Coronary Angiography. (Illus.). 256p. 1976. 28.50x (ISBN 0-398-02709-9). C C Thomas.

Baltay, Charles & Rosenfeld, Arthur H., eds. Experimental Meson Spectroscopy. LC 78-137009. (Illus.). 664p. 1970. 50.00x (ISBN 0-231-03477-6). Columbia U Pr.

Baltay, Charles, ed. see AIP Conference, Philadelphia 1974.

Baltazar, Clare R. & Salazar, Nelia P. Philippine Insects: An Introduction. (Illus.). 1980. text ed. 17.00x (ISBN 0-8248-0675-1, Pub. by U of Philippines Pr); pap. text ed. 12.00x (ISBN 0-8248-0676-X). UH Pr.

Baltazzi, E. Kickboxing: Safe Sport, Deadly Defense. 6.50x (ISBN 0-685-70685-0). Wehman.

Baltazzi, Evan S. Basic American Self-Protection: For Fitness, for Sport, for Self Defense. LC 72-83542. (Illus.). pap. 6.00 (ISBN 0-918948-01-0). Evanel.

--Kickboxing: A Safe Sport - a Deadly Defense. LC 75-33439. (Illus.). 100p. 1976. pap. 6.95 (ISBN 0-8048-1171-7). C E Tuttle.

--Stickfighting: A Practical Guide for Self-Protection. LC 83-70808. (Illus.). 224p. 1983. 22.50 (ISBN 0-8048-1450-3). C E Tuttle.

Balter, Deborah J. Intermediate Aeronautical Language Manual. 1978. pap. 14.95 (ISBN 0-941456-01-3). Aviation.

--Primary Aeronautical Language Manual. 1980. pap. 30.95 (ISBN 0-941456-00-5). Aviation.

Balter, Harry G. Tax Fraud & Evasion: Annual Supplement. 5th ed. 1982. 84.00 (ISBN 0-88262-796-1, 76-10629). Warren.

Balter, Lawrence & Shreve, Anita. Dr. Balter's Baby Sense. 1985. 16.95 (ISBN 0-317-19267-1, Poseidon). PB.

--Dr. Balter's Child Sense: Understanding & Handling the Common Problems of Infancy & Early Childhood. 1985. 16.95 (ISBN 0-671-49627-1). S&S.

Baltes, H. P. & Hilf, E. R. Spectra of Finite Systems: A Review of Weyl's Problem--The Eigenvalue Distribution of the Wave Equation for Finite Domains & It Applications on the Physics of Small Systems. 116p. 1976. pap. 11.95x (ISBN 3-411-01491-1). Birkhauser.

Baltes, H. P., ed. Inverse Scattering Problems in Optics. (Topics in Current Physics: Vol. 20). (Illus.). 313p. 1980. 48.00 (ISBN 0-387-10104-7). Springer-Verlag.

--Inverse Source Problems in Optics. LC 78-12076. (Topics in Current Physics: Vol. 9). (Illus.). 1978. 28.00 (ISBN 0-387-09021-5). Springer-Verlag.

Baltes, Margaret M. & Baltes, Paul B., eds. The Psychology of Aging & Control. 496p. 1985. text ed. 49.95 (ISBN 0-89859-701-3). L Erlbaum Assocs.

Baltes, P. B. & Brim, O. C., Jr., eds. Life-Span Development & Behavior, Vol. 3. 1980. 47.50 (ISBN 0-12-431803-7). Acad Pr.

Baltes, Paul, ed. Life-Span Development & Behavior, Vol. 4. 362p. 1982. 39.50 (ISBN 0-12-431804-5). Acad Pr.

Baltes, Paul & Brim, Orville G., Jr., eds. Life-Span Development & Behavior, Vol.5. (Serial Publication). 1983. 43.00 (ISBN 0-12-431805-3). Acad Pr.

Baltes, Paul B. & Brim, Orville G., eds. Life Span Development & Behavior, Vol. 2. (Serial Publication). 1979. 39.00 (ISBN 0-12-431802-9). Acad Pr.

Baltes, Paul B. & Brim, Orville G., Jr., eds. Life-Span Development & Behavior, Vol. 6. 1984. 56.00 (ISBN 0-12-431806-1). Acad Pr.

Baltes, Paul B. & Schaie, K. Warner, eds. Life Span Developmental Psychology: Personality & Socialization. 1973. 39.50 (ISBN 0-12-077150-0). Acad Pr.

Baltes, Paul B., jt. ed. see Baltes, Margaret M.

Baltes, Paul B., jt. ed. see Goulet, L. R.

Baltes, Paul B., jt. ed. see Nesselroade, John R.

Baltes, Paul B., et al, eds. Life-Span Development & Behavior, Vol. 7. 328p. text ed. 34.95 (ISBN 0-89859-692-0). L Erlbaum Assocs.

Baltes, W., et al, eds. see Euro Food Chem.

Balthasar. Le Chretien Bernanos. 27.90 (ISBN 0-685-37226-X). French & Eur.

Balthasar, Hans U. von see Von Balthasar, Hans U.

Balthasar, Hans U. Von see Von Balthasar, Hans U.

Balthasar, Hans U. von see Von Balthasar, Hans U.

Balthasar, Hans Urs Von. A First Glance at Adrienne Von Speyr. Lawry, Antje & Englund, Sergia, trs. from Ger. LC 81-167170. Orig. Title: Erster Blick Auf Adrienne Von Speyr. 249p. (Orig.). 1981. pap. 9.95 (ISBN 0-89870-003-5). Ignatius Pr.

--The Glory of the Lord: A Theological Aesthetics-Seeing the Form, Vol. 1. LC 82-23553. 656p. (Orig.). 1983. 35.00x (ISBN 0-8245-0579-4). Crossroad NY.

Balthasar, Hans Urs von see Urs von Balthasar, Hans.

Balthasar, Hans Urs von see Von Balthasar, Hans Urs.

Balthasar, Hans von see Von Balthasar, Hans, et al.

Balthasas, Hans von see Von Balthasar, Hans U.

Balthasur, Hans Urs Von see Von Balthasar, Hans Urs.

Balthazar, Earl E. Training the Retarded: A Manual for Parents, Teachers, & Home Trainers. 48p. (Orig.). 1976. pap. 5.75x (ISBN 0-89106-010-3, 5188). Consulting Psychol.

Balthazar, Vera & Batista, Joao, eds. Dictionario Biblico Buckland. Orig. Title: Buckland Bible Dictionary. (Illus.). 453p. text ed. 6.50 (ISBN 0-8297-0836-7); pap. 4.50 (ISBN 0-686-97837-4). Life Pubs Intl.

Balthazart, J., jt. ed. see Gilles, R.

Balthazart, J., et al, eds. Hormones & Behavior in Higher Vertebrates. (Proceedings in Life Sciences Ser.). (Illus.). 500p. 1983. 57.00 (ISBN 0-387-12576-0). Springer-Verlag.

Baltimore Conference, 1975. Human Gene Mapping 3: Proceedings. Bergsma, D., ed. (Cytogenetics & Cell Genetics: Vol. 16, Nos. 1-5). (Illus.). 420p. 1976. pap. 47.00 (ISBN 3-8055-2345-9). S Karger.

Baltimore, H., ed. Nobel Lectures in Molecular Biology: 1933-1975. 534p. 1977. 30.00 (ISBN 0-444-00236-7). Elsevier.

Baltimore Museum of Art. American Prints, Eighteen Seventy to Nineteen Fifty. Johnson, Robert F., ed. LC 76-13195. 1976. 1 color fiche incl. 15.00 (ISBN 0-226-68824-0, Chicago Visual Lib). U of Chicago Pr.

Baltimore Plenary Council. Baltimore Catechism, No. 2. 1977. pap. 1.75 (ISBN 0-89555-008-3). TAN Bks Pubs.

Baltimore Plenary Council, 1885. Baltimore Catechism, No. 1. 1977. pap. 3.00 (ISBN 0-89555-010-5). TAN Bks Pubs.

Baltimore Plenary Council, 3rd. Baltimore Catechism: Cathechism of Christian Doctrine. 1974. pap. 3.50 (ISBN 0-89555-007-5, 147). TAN Bks Pubs.

Baltin, Mark R. Toward a Theory of Movement Rules. Hankamer, Jorge, ed. (Outstanding Dissertations in Linguistics Ser.). 204p. 1985. 25.00 (ISBN 0-8240-5420-2). Garland Pub.

Balton, Michael, ed. European Policing: The Law Enforcement News Interviews. (Orig.). 1978. pap. 2.95x (ISBN 0-89444-011-X). John Jay Pr.

Baltus, R. K. Personal Psychology for Life & Work. 2nd ed. 368p. 1983. 17.25 (ISBN 0-07-003594-6). McGraw.

Baltz, Frederick. Bible Readings for Farm Living. 112p. (Orig.). 1985. pap. 3.75 (ISBN 0-8066-2164-8, 10-0688). Augsburg.

Baltz, Howard B. Fundamentals of Inferential Statistics for Business Analysis. 2nd ed. 416p. 1980. pap. text ed. 18.95 (ISBN 0-8403-2217-8). Kendall-Hunt.

Baltz, Lewis. Park City. LC 80-65768. (Illus.). 252p. 1981. 75.00. Aperture.

Baltz, Lewis & Blaisdell, Gus. Park City. LC 80-65768. (Illus.). 252p. 1980. 75.00 (ISBN 0-9604140-0-2). Castelli-Artspace.

Baltzell, Catherine D. & Dentler, Robert A. Selecting American School Principals: A Sourcebook for Educators. 71p. 1983. pap. 2.50 (ISBN 0-318-11826-2). Gov Printing Office.

Baltzell, E. Digby. Philadelphia Gentlemen. rev. ed. LC 78-32123. (Illus.). 1979. pap. 14.95 (ISBN 0-8122-7765-1). U of Pa Pr.

--Puritan Boston & Quaker Philadelphia. LC 79-7581. (Illus.). 1980. 19.95 (ISBN 0-02-901320-8). Free Pr.

--Puritan Boston & Quaker Philadelphia. LC 81-70494. 585p. 1982. pap. 12.95 (ISBN 0-8070-5415-1, BP 638). Beacon Pr.

Baltzell, Edward D. Protestant Establishment: Aristocracy & Caste in America. 1966. pap. 4.95 (ISBN 0-394-70334-0, V334, Vin). Random.

Baltzell, Karin & Parsley, Terry. Living Without Salt. 208p. (Orig.). 1982. pap. 7.95 (ISBN 0-87178-539-0). Brethren.

Baltzell, Karin B. & Parsley, Terry M. Living Without Salt. 1982. pap. 7.95 (ISBN 0-686-34638-6). Caroline Hse.

Baltzer, Dieter. Ezechiel und Deuterojesaja: Beruehrungen in der Heilserwartung der beiden grossen Exilspropheten. (Beiheft 121 Zur Zeitschrift fuer die alttestamentliche Wissenschaft Ser.). 1971. 28.40x (ISBN 3-11-001756-3). De Gruyter.

Baltzer, Fritz. Theodor Boveri: The Life & Work of a Great Biologist, 1862-1915. Rudnick, Dorothea, tr. LC 67-21996. (Illus.). 1967. 34.00x (ISBN 0-520-00074-9). U of Cal Pr.

Baltzer, J., jt. ed. see Zander, J.

Baltzer, Klaus, ed. see Zimmerli, Walther.

Balukhaty, S. D., ed. see Stanislavski, Constantin.

Balukhatyi, Sergei D. Teoriia Literatury: Annotirovannaia Bibliografiia. 19.00 (ISBN 0-384-03170-6). Johnson Repr.

Baluses, Jane E. Legal Aspects of the Hospital's Role in Obtaining Organs for Transplantation. LC 84-621642. (Health Law Bulletin Ser.: No. 65). 1983. 2.00. U of NC Inst Gov.

Balutis, Alan P., jt. ed. see Honan, Joseph C.

Baluyut, E. A. Stocking & Introduction of Fish in Lakes & Reservoirs in the ASEAN Countries. (Fisheries Technical Paper Ser.: No. 236). 82p. (Orig.). 1984. pap. 7.50 (ISBN 92-5-101366-7, F2591, FAO). Unipub.

Baly, Denis & Rhodes, Royal W. The Faith of Christians. LC 84-47914. 256p. 1984. pap. 14.95 (ISBN 0-8006-1790-8). Fortress.

Baly, Dennis. God: History & the Old Testament. LC 76-9984. 256p. 1976. pap. 10.95x (ISBN 0-06-060369-0, RD 186, HarpR). Har-Row.

Baly, Monica E. Professional Responsibility. 2nd ed. 154p. 1984. pap. 13.00 (ISBN 0-471-26284-6, Pub. by Wiley Med). Wiley.

Baly, William, tr. see Mueller, Johannes.

Balyo, John G. Creation & Evolution. 24p. 1975. pap. 0.50 (ISBN 0-87227-025-4). Reg Baptist.

Balyoz, Harold. Signs of Christ. LC 79-64608. 1979. 18.00 (ISBN 0-9609710-0-9). Altai Pub.

Balys, Jonas, jt. auth. see Thompson, Stith.

Balyuzi, H. M. The Bab: The Herald of the Day of Days. (Illus.). 272p. 1973. 11.95 (ISBN 0-85398-048-9). G Ronald Pub.

--Baha'u'llah: The King of Glory. (Illus.). 552p. 1980. 24.00 (ISBN 0-85398-090-X). G Ronald Pub.

--Baha'u'llah: The Word Made Flesh. 134p. 1963. 8.95 (ISBN 0-85398-014-4); pap. 3.95 (ISBN 0-85398-001-2, 7-31-39). G Ronald Pub.

--Edward Granville Browne & the Baha'i Faith. (Illus.). 152p. 1970. 12.95 (ISBN 0-85398-023-3). G Ronald Pub.

--Khadijih Bagum: The Wife of the Bab. (Illus.). 52p. 5.95 (ISBN 0-85398-100-0). G Ronald Pub.

--Muhammad & the Course of Islam. (Illus.). 475p. 1976. 19.50 (ISBN 0-85398-060-8). G Ronald Pub.

Balz, Albert G. Descartes & the Modern Mind. xiv, 492p. 1967. Repr. of 1952 ed. 32.50 (ISBN 0-208-00023-2, Archon). Shoe String.

--Idea & Essence in the Philosophies of Hobbes & Spinoza. LC 70-161737. Repr. of 1918 ed. 17.00 (ISBN 0-404-00489-X). AMS Pr.

Balzac. Balzac: Selected Short Stories. Raphael, Sylvia, ed. & tr. (Classics Ser). 1977. pap. 3.95 (ISBN 0-14-044325-8). Penguin.

--Passion in the Desert. LC 83-71790. (Creative Classic Ser.). 32p. 1983. 8.95 (ISBN 0-87191-965-6). Creative Ed.

--Le Pere Goriot. (Easy Reader, D). pap. 4.25 (ISBN 0-88436-043-1, 40280). EMC.

Balzac, Honore de. Annette et le Criminel, ou Suite du Vicaire des Ardennes, 2 vols. facsimile ed. 496p. 1963. 50.00 ea. French & Eur.

--The Black Sheep. Adamson, Donald, tr. (Classics Ser.). 352p. 1976. pap. 5.95 (ISBN 0-14-044237-5). Penguin.

--Le Centenaire ou les Deux Beringheld, 2 vols. 468p. 1962. 50.00 ea. French & Eur.

--Cesar Birotteau. pap. 4.95 (ISBN 0-686-52230-3). French & Eur.

--Cesar Birotteau. Date not set. pap. price not set (ISBN 0-14-044347-9). Penguin.

--Chant Funebre. 3.95 (ISBN 0-686-53840-4). French & Eur.

--Le Chef - d'Oeuvre Inconnu. 443p. 1970. pap. 3.95 (ISBN 0-686-53841-2). French & Eur.

--Le Chef - d'Oeuvre Inconnu. (Illus.). 1966. 22.50 (ISBN 0-686-53842-0). French & Eur.

--Clotilde De Lusignan Ou le Beau Juif, 2 vols. facsimile ed. 628p. 1962. 50.00 ea. French & Eur.

--La Comedie Humaine: Avec: Contes Drolatiques, Vol. 11. 1744p. 54.95 (ISBN 0-686-53849-8). French & Eur.

--La Comedie Humaine: Avec: Etude de Moeurs, Scenes de la Vie Privee, Vol. 3. 1680p. 1976. 46.95 (ISBN 0-686-53845-5). French & Eur.

--La Comedie Humaine: Avec: La Fausse Maitresse, Vol. 2. 1176p. 1971. 45.00 (ISBN 0-686-53844-7). French & Eur.

--La Comedie Humaine: Avec: La Muse du Departement, Vol. 4. 1072p. 45.00 (ISBN 0-686-53846-3). French & Eur.

--La Comedie Humaine: Etudes de Moeurs (Scenes de la Vie Privee-1, Vol. 1. 1970. 19.95 (ISBN 0-686-53851-X). French & Eur.

--La Comedie Humaine: Etudes Philosophiques, Vol. 7. 1970. 19.95 (ISBN 0-686-53857-9). French & Eur.

--La Comedie Humaine: Scenes de la Vie de Province-2, Vol. 3. 1970. 19.95 (ISBN 0-686-53853-6). French & Eur.

--La Comedie Humaine: Scenes de la Vie Militaire, Scenes de la Vie de Campagne, Vol. 6. 1970. 19.95 (ISBN 0-686-53856-0). French & Eur.

--La Comedie Humaine: Scenes de la Vie Parisienne-1, Vol. 4. 1970. 19.95 (ISBN 0-686-53854-4). French & Eur.

--La Comedie Humaine: Scenes de la Vie Parisienne-2, Vol. 5. 1970. 19.95 (ISBN 0-686-53855-2). French & Eur.

--La Comedie Humaine: Scenes de la Vie Privee-2, Scenes de la Vie de Province-1, Vol. 2. 1970. 19.95 (ISBN 0-686-53852-8). French & Eur.

--Comment Fut Bati le Chateau d'Azay. 1975. 9.95 (ISBN 0-686-53858-7). French & Eur.

--Contes Drolatiques. 5.95 (ISBN 0-686-53859-5). French & Eur.

--Correspondance avec Zulma Carraud. 312p. 1951. 4.95 (ISBN 0-686-53860-9). French & Eur.

--Cousin Pons. Hunt, Herbert J., tr. (Classics Ser.). 1978. pap. 4.95 (ISBN 0-14-044205-7). Penguin.

--Un Debut Dans la Vie. 251p. 1950. 9.95 (ISBN 0-686-53861-7). French & Eur.

--Un Debut Dans la Vie: Avec: un Homme d'Affairs, Un Prince de la Boheme. pap. 3.95 (ISBN 0-686-53862-5). French & Eur.

--La Derniere Fee Ou la Nouvelle Lampe Merveilleuse, Paris, 1825. facsimile ed. 656p. 1976. 99.50 (ISBN 0-686-53863-3). French & Eur.

--Les Employes. 377p. 1970. 3.95 (ISBN 0-686-53865-X). French & Eur.

--Etudes de Femmes. 142p. 1971. 3.95 (ISBN 0-686-53867-6). French & Eur.

--Exposition Commemorative du 150e Anniversaire de la Mort de Balzac. (Illus.). 144p. 17.50 (ISBN 0-686-53870-6). French & Eur.

--Falthurne. 198p. 1950. 10.95 (ISBN 0-686-53872-2). French & Eur.

--La Fausse Maitresse. 5.95 (ISBN 0-686-53873-0). French & Eur.

--Gambara. 200p. 1964. 10.95 (ISBN 0-686-53875-7). French & Eur.

--Gosbeck: Maitre Cornelius, Facino Cane. 251p. 1969. 3.95 (ISBN 0-686-53876-5). French & Eur.

--Les Grandes Ecoles, Pourquoi Faire? 1973. pap. text ed. 5.95 (ISBN 0-686-53877-3). French & Eur.

--L' Heritier de Biraque, 2 vols. facsimile ed. 1961. 37.50 ea. French & Eur.

--L' Histoire de l'Empereur. facsimile ed. (Illus.). 1970. 29.95 (ISBN 0-686-53878-1). French & Eur.

--Honorine: Avec: Albert Savarus, La Fausse Maitresse. 3.95 (ISBN 0-686-53880-3). French & Eur.

--Jean-Louis Ou Lafille Trouvee, 2 vols. facsimile ed. 1961. 50.00 ea. French & Eur.

--The Letters of Honore De Balzac to Madame Hanska. 1976. lib. bdg. 59.95 (ISBN 0-8490-2152-9). Gordon Pr.

--Lost Illusions. Hunt, Herbert J., tr. (Classic Ser.). 1976. pap. 5.95 (ISBN 0-14-044251-0). Penguin.

--Lost Illusions. Date not set. pap. 8.95 (ISBN 0-394-60523-3). Modern Lib.

--Louis Lambert. 272p. (Edition critique). 1968. 10.95 (ISBN 0-686-53889-7). French & Eur.

--Louis Lambert: Avec: Le Proscrits, Jesus Christ en Flandre. 316p. 1968. pap. 3.95 (ISBN 0-686-53890-0). French & Eur.

--Mademoiselle du Vissard. 96p. 1950. 15.95 (ISBN 0-686-53891-9). French & Eur.

--La Maison du Chat-Qui-Pelote: Avec: La Vendetta, La Bourse, Le Bal de Sceaux. 3.95 (ISBN 0-686-53892-7). French & Eur.

--Massimilla Doni. 264p. 1964. 12.95 (ISBN 0-686-53893-5). French & Eur.

--Maximes et Pensees. 159p. 5.95 (ISBN 0-686-53894-3). French & Eur.

--Le Medecin de campagne. new ed. (Documentation thematique). (Illus.). 167p. (Orig., Fr.). 1975. pap. 2.95 (ISBN 0-685-54485-0, 116). Larousse.

--Memoires de Deux Jeunes Mariees. 380p. 1969. 3.95 (ISBN 0-686-53881-1). French & Eur.

--Modeste Mignon. 382p. 1967. 3.95 (ISBN 0-686-53882-X). French & Eur.

--Murky Business. (Penguin Classics Ser.). 1978. pap. 3.95 (ISBN 0-14-044271-5). Penguin.

--Oeuvres Completes: Cambara, La Recherche de l'Absolu, L'Enfant Maudit, Vol. 15. (Illus.). 1970. 50.00 (ISBN 0-686-53909-5). French & Eur.

--Oeuvres Completes: Contes Drolatiques, Vol. 18. (Illus.). 1970. 50.00 (ISBN 0-686-53912-5). French & Eur.

--Oeuvres Completes: Enquete sur la Politique des deux Ministeres, Ecrits et Articles Legitimistes, Enchantillon de Causerie Francaise, Vol. 23. (Illus.). 1971. 50.00 (ISBN 0-686-53917-6). French & Eur.

--Oeuvres Completes: Facino Cane, Sarrasine, Pierre Grassau, Vol. 9. (Illus.). 1969. 50.00 (ISBN 0-686-53903-6). French & Eur.

--Oeuvres Completes: Falthurne, Stenie, La Seconde Falthurne, Vol. 21. (Illus.). 1970. 50.00 (ISBN 0-686-53915-X). French & Eur.

--Oeuvres Completes: Ferragus, La Duchessa de Langeais, La Fille aux yeur d'Or, Vol. 8. (Illus.). 1969. 50.00 (ISBN 0-686-53902-8). French & Eur.

--Oeuvres Completes: La Femme Abandonee, Honorine, Beatrix, Vol. 3. (Illus.). 1968. 50.00 (ISBN 0-686-53897-8). French & Eur.

--Oeuvres Completes: La Maison du Chat-Qui-Pelote, Le Bal de Sceaux, Memoires de deux Jeunes Maries, Vol. 1. (Illus.). 1968. 50.00 (ISBN 0-686-53895-1). French & Eur.

--Oeuvres Completes: La Medicin de Capagne, Le Cure de Village, Les Paysans, Vol. 13. (Illus.). 1969. 50.00 (ISBN 0-686-53907-9). French & Eur.

--Oeuvres Completes: La Peau de Chagrin, Jesus-Christ en Flanders, Melmoth Reconcile, Vol. 14. (Illus.). 1969. 50.00 (ISBN 0-686-53908-7). French & Eur.

--Oeuvres Completes: La Pere Goriot, Le Colonel Chabert, la Messe de l'Athee, Vol. 4. (Illus.). 1968. 50.00 (ISBN 0-686-53898-6). French & Eur.

--Oeuvres Completes: L'Auberge Rouge, Sur Catherine de Medicis, L'Elexir de Longue Vie, Vol. 16. (Illus.). 1970. 50.00 (ISBN 0-686-53910-9). French & Eur.

--Oeuvres Completes: Le Cabinet des Antiques, Illusions Perdues, Vol. 7. (Illus.). 1968. 50.00 (ISBN 0-686-53901-X). French & Eur.

--Oeuvres Completes: Le Cousin Pons, Un Prince de la Boheme, Les Petits Boureois, Vol. 11. (Illus.). 1969. 50.00 (ISBN 0-686-53905-2). French & Eur.

--Oeuvres Completes: Le Cure de Tours, La Rabouilleuse, L'Illustre Gaudissart, Vol. 6. (Illus.). 1968. 50.00 (ISBN 0-686-53900-1). French & Eur.

--Oeuvres Completes: L'Epicier, La Femme comme Il Faut, Le Notaire, Vol. 24. (Illus.). 1971. 50.00 (ISBN 0-686-53918-4). French & Eur.

--Oeuvres Completes: Physiologie du Mariage, Petites Miseres de la Vie Conjugale, Vol. 17. (Illus.). 1970. 50.00 (ISBN 0-686-53911-7). French & Eur.

--Oeuvres Completes: Theatre, La Moratre, Le Faiseur, L'Ecole des Menages, Vol. 20. (Illus.). 1970. 50.00 (ISBN 0-686-53914-1). French & Eur.

--Oeuvres Completes: Theatre, Vautrin, Les Ressources de Quinola, Pamela Giraud, Vol. 19. (Illus.). 1970. 50.00 (ISBN 0-686-53913-3). French & Eur.

--Oeuvres Completes: Un Debut dans la Vie, Albert Savarus, La Vendetta, Vol. 2. (Illus.). 1968. 50.00 (ISBN 0-686-53896-X). French & Eur.

--Oeuvres Completes: Un Episode sous la Terrel, Une Tenebreuse Affaire, Le Depute d'Arcis, Les Chouans, Vol. 12. (Illus.). 1969. 50.00 (ISBN 0-686-53906-0). French & Eur.

--Oeuvres Completes: Un Homme d'Affaires, Les Employes, La Cousine Bette, Vol. 10. (Illus.). 1969. 50.00 (ISBN 0-686-53904-4). French & Eur.

--Oeuvres Completes: Ursule Mirouet, Eugenie Grandet, La Lys dans la Vallee, Vol. 5. (Illus.). 1968. 50.00 (ISBN 0-686-53899-4). French & Eur.

--Oeuvres Completes: Vie de Moliere, Vie de la Fontane, Souvenirs d'un Paria, Vol. 22. (Illus.). 1971. 50.00 (ISBN 0-686-53916-8). French & Eur.

--Old Goriot. Marriage, Ellen, tr. 1970. Repr. of 1948 ed. 12.95x (ISBN 0-460-00170-1, Evman). Biblio Dist.

--Old Goriot. Crawford, Marion A., tr. (Classics Ser.). (Orig.). 1951. pap. 3.95 (ISBN 0-14-044017-8). Penguin.

--Peau de Chagrin. 1973. 125.00 (ISBN 0-686-53922-2). French & Eur.

--Pere Goriot. Bd. with Eugenie Grandet. (Modern Library College Editions). 1950. pap. text ed. 5.00 (ISBN 0-394-30902-2, T2, RanC). Random.

--Physiologie du Mariage. Regard, Maurice, ed. 320p. 1968. 3.95 (ISBN 0-686-53923-0). French & Eur.

--Romans de Jeunesse: Avec: L'Heritiere de Biraque, Jean-Louis ou la Fille Trovee, Clotilde de Lusignan ou le beau Juif, Le Vicaire des Ardennes, 16 vols. facsimile ed. 1964. Set. 395.00 (ISBN 0-686-53925-7). French & Eur.

--Seraphita. facs. ed. LC 73-134961. (Short Story Index Reprint Ser). 1889. 18.00 (ISBN 0-8369-3691-4). Ayer Co Pubs.

--Seraphita. 303p. 1950. 3.95 (ISBN 0-686-53926-5). French & Eur.

--Une Tenebreuse Affaire. 1973. 3.95 (ISBN 0-686-53920-6). French & Eur.

--The Unknown Masterpiece. Neff, Michael, tr. from Fr. LC 82-73423. (Illus.). 84p. (Orig.). 1983. pap. 4.95 (ISBN 0-916870-55-3, A Donald S. Ellis Book). Creative Arts Bk.

--Ursule Mirouet. Adamson, Donald, tr. (Classics Ser). 1976. pap. 4.95 (ISBN 0-14-044316-9). Penguin.

--La Vieille Fille. 207p. 1966. 3.95 (ISBN 0-686-53921-4). French & Eur.

--The Wild Ass's Skin. Hunt, Herbert J., tr. (Classic Ser.). 1977. pap. 4.95 (ISBN 0-14-044330-4). Penguin.

--Works: With Introductions by George Saintsbury, 18 vols. facsimile ed. LC 78-150468. (Short Story Index Reprint Ser.). Repr. of 1901 ed. Set. 550.00 (ISBN 0-8369-3791-0). Ayer Co Pubs.

Balzac, Honore De & Castex, Pierre Georges. La Comedie Humaine: Etudes de Moeurs (Scenes de la Vie Parisienne, Vol. 6. 1577p. 1977. 47.50 (ISBN 0-686-53848-X). French & Eur.

--La Comedie Humaine: Etudes de Moeurs (Scenes de la Vie de Province, Vol. 5. 5th ed. 1574p. 1977. 46.95 (ISBN 0-686-53847-1). French & Eur.

--Histoire Des Treize: Avec: Ferragus, La Duchessa de Langeair, La Fille aux youx d'Or. (Illus.). 14.95 (ISBN 0-686-53879-X). French & Eur.

Balzac, Honore De & Charpak, A. Monsieur Vautrin. 46p. 1963. 9.95 (ISBN 0-686-53883-8). French & Eur.

Balzac, Honore De & Chollet, Roland. La Comedie Humaine, 10 vols. 1976. Set. 350.00 (ISBN 0-686-53850-1). French & Eur.

Balzac, Honore De & Citron, Pierre. Un Fille d'Eve. 3.95 (ISBN 0-686-53874-9). French & Eur.

--Pierrette. 3.95 (ISBN 0-686-53924-9). French & Eur.

Balzac, Honore De & Franck, Pierre. Le Faiseur. 46p. 1972. 9.95 (ISBN 0-686-53871-4). French & Eur.

Balzac, Honore De & Guyon, Bernard. L' Illustre Gaudissart: Avec: La Muse de Depatement. 576p. 1970. 15.95 (ISBN 0-686-53884-6). French & Eur.

Balzac, Honore De & Meininger, Anne-Marie. Les Celibataires: Avec: Le Cure de Tours, Pierrette. 1976. pap. 4.95 (ISBN 0-686-53869-2). French & Eur.

Balzac, Honore De & Pierrot, Roger. Lettres a Madame Hanska, 4 vols. (Edition critique). 1968-71. Vol. 1. 49.95 (ISBN 0-686-53885-4); Vol. 2, 1841-1845. 24.95 (ISBN 0-686-53886-2); Vol. 3, 1845-1847. 49.95 (ISBN 0-686-53887-0); Vol. 4, 1847-1850. 49.95 (ISBN 0-686-53888-9). French & Eur.

Balzac, Honore De & Pommier, J. L' Eglise. 108p. 1947. 6.95 (ISBN 0-686-53864-1). French & Eur.

Balzac, Honore De & Regard, Maurice. L' Envers de l'Histoire Contemporaine. 1959. 7.95 (ISBN 0-686-53866-8). French & Eur.

Balzac, Honore De & Richard, Marie Helene. Balzac En Sa Touraine. (Illus.). 68p. 1975. 8.95 (ISBN 0-686-53868-4). French & Eur.

Balzac, Honore de & Sacy, Samuel S. de. Les Paysans. 512p. 1975. 4.50 (ISBN 0-686-53919-2). French & Eur.

Balzac, Honore De see De Balzac, Honore.

Balzac, Honore de see De Balzac, Honore.

Balzac, Honore De see Peyrazat, Jean E.

Balzac, Honore De, et al. La Comedie Humaine: Avec: Etudes de Moeurs, Scenes de la Vie Privee, Vol. 1. 1574p. 1976. 49.95 (ISBN 0-686-53843-9). French & Eur.

Balzac, Irma, tr. see Beller, William S.

Balzano, Bill. Church of God & Roman Catholic Interfaith Marriage. (Truthway Ser.). 35p. (Orig.). 1981. pap. text ed. 1.25 (ISBN 0-87148-175-8). Pathway Pr.

Balzano, Michael P. Reorganizing the Federal Bureaucracy: The Rhetoric & the Reality. LC 77-84326. 1977. pap. 3.25 (ISBN 0-8447-3264-8). Am Enterprise.

Balzer, John A. Fabulous Freaky Fun Fill-Inns for Friday. (Illus.). 30p. (Orig.). 1979. pap. 3.95 (ISBN 0-914634-57-7). DOK Pubs.

Balzer, P., jt. auth. see Schoengrund, L.

Balzer, Richard. Clockwork: Life in & Outside an American Factory. LC 75-21209. 352p. 1976. 10.00 (ISBN 0-385-11036-7). Doubleday.

Balzer, Robert L. The Los Angeles Times Book of California Wines. LC 84-11067. (Illus.). 272p. 1984. 37.50 (ISBN 0-8109-1287-2). Abrams.

Balzer, Wolfgang, ed. & tr. from Eng. Zur Logik Empirischer Theorien. 331p. 1983. 31.20 (ISBN 3-11-008236-5); pap. 16.80 (ISBN 3-11-009711-7). De Gruyter.

Balzhiser, R. E., et al. Chemical Engineering Thermodynamics. (International Physical & Chemical Engineering Sciences Ser). (Illus.). 1972. ref. ed. 42.95 (ISBN 0-13-128603-X). P-H.

Balzola, A. & Parramon, J. M. Spring. (Exploring the Seasons Ser.). (Illus.). 32p. (ps-3). 1981. 10.60 (ISBN 0-516-02381-0). Childrens.

Balzola, Asun & Ma Parramon, Josep. Spring. (The Four Seasons Ser.). (Illus.). 32p. (ps-3). 2.95 (ISBN 0-8326-2616-3, 3630). Delair.

Baman Das Basu, ed. The Sacred Books of the Hindus, 47 vols. Repr. of 1937 ed. 1251.50 (ISBN 0-404-19548-2). AMS Pr.

Bambakidis, Gust, ed. Metal Hydrides. LC 81-17761. (NATO ASI Series B, Physics: Vol. 76). 393p. 1981. 65.00x (ISBN 0-306-40891-0, Plenum Pr). Plenum Pub.

Bambara, Toni C. Gorilla, My Love. 1972. 8.95 (ISBN 0-394-48201-8). Random.

--Gorilla, My Love. LC 81-51024. 192p. 1981. pap. 3.95 (ISBN 0-394-75049-7, Vin). Random.

--The Salt Eaters. LC 79-4806. 1980. 9.95 (ISBN 0-394-50712-6). Random.

--The Salt Eaters. LC 81-51023. 304p. 1981. pap. 4.95 (ISBN 0-394-75050-0, Vin). Random.

--The Sea Birds Are Still Alive. LC 82-40018. 224p. 1982. pap. 3.95 (ISBN 0-394-71176-9). Random.

Bambara, Toni C. & Wise, Leah, eds. Southern Black Utterances Today. (Southern Exposure Ser.). (Illus.). 120p. (Orig.). 1975. pap. 2.50 (ISBN 0-943810-04-3). Inst Southern Studies.

Bambas, L. L. Heterocyclic Compounds, Vol. 4. LC 52-6640. 416p. 1952. 58.50. Krieger.

Bambeck, Manfred. Goettliche Komoedie und Exegese. viii, 253p. 1975. pap. 38.00x (ISBN 3-11-004874-4). De Gruyter.

Bamber, C. J. Plants of the Punjab: A Descriptive Key to the Flora of the Punjab, Northwest Frontier Province & Kashmir. 1978. Repr. of 1916 ed. 56.25x (ISBN 0-89955-298-6, Pub. by Intl Bk Dist). Intl Spec Bk.

Bamber, Chrissie. Student & Teacher Absenteeism. LC 79-83631. (Fastback Ser.: No. 126). 1979. pap. 0.75 (ISBN 0-87367-126-0). Phi Delta Kappa.

Bamber, Greg. Managers in Unions: A Study of Union Growth & Industrial Relations in the Stell Industry. 170p. 1985. text ed. write for info. (ISBN 0-566-00987-0). Gower Pub Co.

Bamber, J. H. The Fears of Adolescents. 1979. 41.50 (ISBN 0-12-077550-6). Acad Pr.

Bamber, Linda. Comic Women, Tragic Men: A Study of Gender & Genre in Shakespeare. LC 81-51903. 224p. 1982. 20.00x (ISBN 0-8047-1126-7). Stanford U Pr.

Bamberg, Corona. Cost of Being Human. 7.95 (ISBN 0-87193-128-1). Dimension Bks.

Bamberg, G. & Spremann, A., eds. Risk & Capital: Proceedings of the 2nd Summer Workshop on Risk & Capital Held at the University of Ulm, West Germany, June 20-24, 1983. (Lecture Notes in Economics & Mathematical Systems Ser.: Vol. 227). 320p. 1984. pap. 20.00 (ISBN 0-387-12923-5). Springer Verlag.

Bamberg, Robert D., ed. see James, Henry.

Bamberger, Bernard J. Commentary on Leviticus. Plaut, W. Gunther, ed. (The Torah: a Modern Commentary Ser.). 1979. 20.00 (ISBN 0-8074-0011-4, 3816). UAHC.

--The Search for Jewish Theology. new ed. LC 77-28457. 1978. pap. 4.95x (ISBN 0-87441-300-1). Behrman.

--Story of Judaism. rev. 3rd ed. LC 64-16463. 1964. pap. 9.95 (ISBN 0-8052-0077-0). Schocken.

--Story of Judaism. rev. ed. 1970. 6.50 (ISBN 0-8074-0193-5, 959291). UAHC.

Bamberger, Bernard J., jt. auth. see Plaut, W. Gunther.

Bamberger, David. My People: Abba Eban's History of the Jews, Vol. II. (Illus.). 1979. pap. 6.95x (ISBN 0-87441-280-3); tchr's guide by Geoffrey Horn 12.50 (ISBN 0-87441-341-9). Behrman.

--My People: Abba Eban's History of the Jews, Vol. I. LC 77-10667. (Illus.). 1978. pap. text ed. 6.95x (ISBN 0-87441-263-3). Behrman.

--A Young Person's History of Israel. Mandelkern, Nicholas, ed. (Illus.). 150p. (Orig.). (gr. 5-7). 1985. pap. 6.95 (ISBN 0-87441-393-1). Behrman.

Bamberger, Eudes, jt. auth. see Abbot, John.

Bamberger, I. Nathan. The Viking Jews: The History of the Jews of Denmark. LC 83-50474. (Illus.). 160p. 1983. 10.95 (ISBN 0-88400-098-2). Shengold.

Bamberger, Jeanne S. & Brofsky, Howard. The Art of Listening: Developing Musical Perception. 4th ed. LC 78-20837. 1979. pap. text ed. 20.50 scp (ISBN 0-06-040943-6, HarpC); inst. manual avail. (ISBN 0-06-360966-5); Set Of 5 Records. scp 31.50 (ISBN 0-06-040981-9). Har-Row.

Bamberger, John E., tr. see Praktikos.

Bamberger, Michael & Gonzalez-Polio, Edgardo. Evaluation of Sites & Services Projects: The Evidence from El Salvador. (Working Paper: No. 549). 233p. 1982. pap. 10.00 (ISBN 0-8213-0116-0). World Bank.

Bamberger, Michael & Sanyal, Bishwapriya. Evaluation of Sites & Sevices Projects: The Experience from Lusaka, Zambia. (Working Paper: No. 548). 201p. 1982. pap. 10.00 (ISBN 0-8213-0115-2). World Bank.

Bamberger, Richard. Promoting the Reading Habit. (Reports & Papers on Mass Communication: No. 72). 52p. 1975. pap. 5.00 (ISBN 92-3-101218-5, U497, UNESCO). Unipub.

Bambiger, Michael. The Liberated Man's Natural Food Cookbook. Young, Billie, ed. LC 73-83920. 1974. 14.95 (ISBN 0-87949-013-6). Ashley Bks.

Bamboat, Zenobia. Les Voyageurs francais dans l'Inde aux XVIIe et XVIIIe siecles. LC 72-83617. (Bibliotheque d'histoire coloniale). 197p. (Fr.). 1972. Repr. of 1933 ed. lib. bdg. 22.50 (ISBN 0-8337-3964-6). B Franklin.

Bamborough, J. B. Ben Jonson. (English Literature Ser.). 1970. pap. text ed. 5.25x (ISBN 0-09-101691-6, Hutchinson U Lib). Humanities.

--Little World of Man: Elizabethan Psychological Theory. LC 72-191665. Repr. of 1952 ed. lib. bdg. 26.50 (ISBN 0-8414-0791-6). Folcroft.

Bambrey, Thomas E., jt. auth. see Lewis, Ann C.

Bambrough, J. R. Moral Scepticism & Moral Knowledge. LC 79-13540. (Studies in Philosophical Psychology). 1979. text ed. 15.75x (ISBN 0-391-01037-9). Humanities.

Bambrough, Renford. Reason, Truth & God. (Library Reprints Ser.). 174p. 1979. 45.00x (ISBN 0-416-72530-9, NO. 2823). Methuen Inc.

Bambrough, Renford, ed. New Essays on Plato & Aristotle. (International Library of Philosophy & Scientific Method). 1965. text ed. 15.00x (ISBN 0-391-00979-6). Humanities.

--Philosophy of Aristotle: A New Selection. (Orig.). pap. 3.95 (ISBN 0-451-62180-8, ME2180, Ment). NAL.

Bamburg, Ron. Run Your Race: Poems of An Athelete Who Became a Christian. 36p. 1982. 4.95 (ISBN 0-8059-2831-6). Dorrance.

Bamdad, Badr ol-Moluk. From Darkness into Light: Women's Emancipation in Iran. Bagley, F. R., ed. & tr. LC 76-50308. 1977. 8.00 (ISBN 0-682-48705-8, University). Exposition Pr FL.

Bame, E. Allen & Cummings, Paul. Exploring Technology. LC 79-53783. (Technology Series). (Illus.). 288p. 1980. text ed. 13.95 (ISBN 0-87192-112-X, 000-3); tchr's. guide 13.25 (ISBN 0-87192-114-6); activity manual 8.95 (ISBN 0-87192-113-8). Davis Mass.

Bame, Kwabena N. Come to Laugh: A Study of African Traditional Theatre in Ghana. LC 84-6259. (Illus.). 192p. 1985. text ed. 21.50x (ISBN 0-936508-07-8); pap. text ed. 10.00x (ISBN 0-936508-08-6). Barber Pr.

Bament, R. C., jt. auth. see Casimir, M.

Bamer, Donald. Applied Iridology & Herbology. pap. 12.95 (ISBN 0-89557-053-X). Bi World Indus.

Bamesberger, Velda C. An Appraisal of a Social Studies Course, in Terms of Its Effect upon the Achievement, Activities & Interests of Pupils. LC 72-176535. (Columbia University. Teachers College. Contributions to Education: No. 328). Repr. of 1928 ed. 22.50 (ISBN 0-404-55328-1). AMS Pr.

Bamford, C. & Tipper, C., eds. Comprehensive Chemical Kinetics: Complex Catalytic Processes, Vol. 20. 414p. 1978. 127.75 (ISBN 0-444-41651-X). Elsevier.

--Comprehensive Chemical Kinetics: Reactions in the Solid State, Vol. 22. 340p. 1980. 110.75 (ISBN 0-444-41807-5). Elsevier.

Bamford, C. G. & Robinson, H. Geography of the EEC: A Systematic Economic Approach. (Aspect Geographies Ser.). (Illus.). 296p. 1983. text ed. 24.50x (ISBN 0-7121-0745-2, Macdonald Evans); pap. text ed. 16.50x (ISBN 0-7121-0732-0). Sheridan.

--Geography of Transport. (Aspects Geography Ser.). (Illus.). 448p. 1983. pap. text ed. 19.95x (ISBN 0-7121-0730-4). Trans-Atlantic.

Bamford, C. H. & Tipper, C. F. Reactions of Solids with Gases. (Comprehensive Chemical Kinetics Ser.: Vol. 21). 1984. 79.75 (ISBN 0-444-42288-9, I-450-84). Elsevier.

--Simple Processes at the Gas-Solid Interface. (Comprehensive Chemical Kinetics Ser.: Vol. 19). 1984. 135.25 (ISBN 0-444-42287-0, I-147-84). Elsevier.

Bamford, C. H. & Tipper, C. F., eds. Comprehensive Chemical Kinetics, Vols. 1-18. Incl. Vol. 1. Practice of Kinetics. 450p. 1969. 102.25 (ISBN 0-444-40673-5); Vol. 2. Theory of Kinetics. 486p. 1969. 102.25 (ISBN 0-444-40674-3); Vol. 3. Formation & Decay of Excited Species: Formation & Decay of Excited Species. 300p. 1970. 87.25 (ISBN 0-444-40802-9); Vol. 4. Decomposition of Inorganic & Organometallic Compounds. 272p. 1972. 87.25 (ISBN 0-444-40936-X); Vol. 5. Decomposition & Isomerization of Organic Compounds. 779p. 1972. 149.00 (ISBN 0-444-40861-4); Vol. 6. Reactions of Non-Metallic Inorganic Compounds. 517p. 1972. 127.75 (ISBN 0-444-40944-0); Vol. 7. Reactions of Metallic Salts & Complexes & Organometallic Compounds. 615p. 1972. 136.25 (ISBN 0-444-40913-0); Vol. 8. Proton Transfer of Related Reactions. 262p. 1977. 87.25 (ISBN 0-444-41512-2); Vol. 9. Addition & Elimination Reactions of Aliphatic Compounds. 515p. 1973. 127.75 (ISBN 0-444-41051-1); Vol. 10. Ester Formation & Hydrolysis & Related Reactions. 309p. 1972. 87.25 (ISBN 0-444-40957-2); Vol. 12. Electrophilic Substitution at a Saturated Carbon Atom. 256p. 1973. 87.25 (ISBN 0-444-41052-X); Vol. 13. Reactions of Aromatic Compounds. 508p. 1972. 127.75 (ISBN 0-444-40937-8); Vol. 14. Degradation of Polymers. 564p. 1975. 136.25 (ISBN 0-444-41155-0); Vol. 14A. Free Radical Polymerization. 594p. 1977. 136.25 (ISBN 0-444-41486-X); Vol. 15. Nonradial Polymerization. 660p. 1976. 144.25 (ISBN 0-444-41252-2); Vol. 16. Liquid Phase Oxidation. 264p. 1980. 87.25 (ISBN 0-444-41860-1); Vol. 17. Gas Phase Combustion. 520p. 1977. 136.25 (ISBN 0-444-41513-0); Vol. 18. Selected Elementary Reactions. 486p. 1976. 136.25 (ISBN 0-444-41294-8). Elsevier.

--Comprehensive Chemical Kinetics, Vol. 11: Reactions of Carbonyl Compounds. Date not set. price not set (ISBN 0-685-84869-8). Elsevier.

--Modern Methods in Kinetics. (Comprehensive Chemical Kinetics Ser.: Vol. 24). 528p. 1983. 181.00 (ISBN 0-444-42028-2). Elsevier.

Bamford, C. H., et al. Kinetics & Chemical Technology. (Comprehensive Chemical Kinetics Ser.: Vol. 23). Date not set. write for info. (ISBN 0-444-42441-5). Elsevier.

Bamford, C. H., et al, eds. Comprehensive Chemical Kinetics, Vol. 25: Diffusion-Limited Reactions. 404p. 1985. 135.25 (ISBN 0-444-42354-0). Elsevier.

Bamford, C. R. Color Generation & Control in Glass. (Glass Science & Technology Ser.: Vol. 2). 1977. 64.00 (ISBN 0-444-41614-5). Elsevier.

Bamford, Don. Anchoring. LC 84-13935. (Illus.). 1985. 24.95 (ISBN 0-915160-64-1). Seven Seas.

Bamford, Francis, ed. see Oglander, John.

Bamford, Georgia L. Mystery of Jack London. LC 73-15997. 1931. lib. bdg. 30.00 (ISBN 0-8414-9856-3). Folcroft.

Bamford, James. The Puzzle Palace: A Report on America's Most Secret Agency. (Illus.). 436p. 1982. 16.95 (ISBN 0-395-31286-8). HM.

--The Puzzle Palace: A Report on America's Most Secret Agency. 656p. 1983. pap. 7.95 (ISBN 0-14-006748-5). Penguin.

Bamford, Joan. Collecting Antiques for the Future. (Illus.). 1976. 28.95x (ISBN 0-7188-7008-5). Intl Ideas.

Bamford, John, jt. ed. see Bench, John.

Bamford, Katherine, jt. auth. see Adams, Charles.

Bamford, Lawrence Von see Von Bamford, Lawrence.

Bamford, Nancy & Price, Anne. Successful Breastfeeding: A Complete Step-by-Step Guide to Nursing Your Baby. (Illus.). 192p. 1984. pap. cancelled (ISBN 0-88166-018-3). Meadowbrook.

Bamford, Paul W. Forests & French Sea Power: 1660-1789. LC 57-226. (Scholarly Reprint Ser.). pap. 62.30 (ISBN 0-317-09494-7, 2055455). Bks Demand UMI.

Bamford, Penny, jt. auth. see Bellack, Jan.

Bamford, Samuel. Autobiography. Chaloner, W. H., ed. 1967. Vol. 1, 364pgs. 25.00x (ISBN 0-7146-1055-0, F Cass Co); Vol. 2, 580pgs. 27.50x (ISBN 0-7146-1056-9, F Cass Co). Biblio Dist.

--The Autobiography of Samuel Bamford, 2 vols. Chaloner, W. H., ed. & intro. by. Incl. Vol. 1. Early Days. Repr. of 1849 ed; Vol. 2. Passages in the Life of a Radical. Repr. of 1844 ed. LC 67-23461. Set. 57.50x (ISBN 0-678-05025-2). Kelley.

--Passages in the Life of a Radical. (Oxford Paperback Bks.). 1984. pap. 7.95x (ISBN 0-19-281413-3). Oxford U Pr.

--Walks in South Lancashire & on Its Borders. LC 72-80019. 288p. Repr. of 1844 ed. lib. bdg. 35.00x (ISBN 0-678-08023-2). Kelley.

Bamford, Terry. Managing Social Work. 200p. 1983. 22.00 (ISBN 0-422-77960-1, NO. 3802, Tavistock). Methuen Inc.

Bamfylde, C. A., jt. auth. see Baring-Gould, Sabine.

Bamman, Henry A. & Brammer, Lawrence M. How to Study Successfully. rev. ed. LC 68-31290. (Orig.). 1969. 3.95 (ISBN 0-87015-177-0). Pacific Bks.

Bamman, Henry A., et al. Beyond Barriers. (Passport to Reading Ser.). (Illus., Orig.). (gr. 7-12). 1982. pap. 3.65 (ISBN 0-88436-723-1, 35675). EMC.

--Challenges. (Passport to Reading Ser.). (Illus.). 64p. (Orig.). (gr. 7-12). 1982. pap. 3.65 (ISBN 0-88436-725-8, 35676). EMC.

--Daredevils & Dreamers. (Passport to Reading Ser.). (Illus.). 64p. (Orig.). (gr. 7-12). 1982. pap. 3.65 (ISBN 0-88436-727-4, 35677). EMC.

--Extraordinary Episodes. (Passport to Reading Ser.). (Illus.). 64p. (Orig.). (gr. 7-12). 1982. pap. 3.65 (ISBN 0-88436-729-0, 35678). EMC.

--Fantastic Flights. (Passport to Reading Ser.). (Illus.). 64p. (gr. 7-12). 1982. pap. 3.65 (ISBN 0-88436-731-2, 35679). EMC.

Bamman, Henry S., et al. Amazing. (Passport to Reading Ser.). (Illus.). 64p. (Orig.). (gr. 7-12). 1982. pap. 3.65 (ISBN 0-88436-721-5, 35674). EMC.

Bammate, Haidar. Muslim Contribution to Civilization. Date not set. price not set (ISBN 0-89259-029-7). Am Trust Pubns.

Bammel, E & Barrett, C. K., eds. Donum Gentilicium: New Testament Studies in Honor of David Daube. 1978. 59.00x (ISBN 0-19-826629-4). Oxford U Pr.

Bammel, E. & Moule, C. F., eds. Jesus & the Politics of His Day. 320p. Date not set. pap. price not set (ISBN 0-521-31344-9). Cambridge U Pr.

Bammel, Ernst & Moule, C. F., eds. Jesus & the Politics of His Day. LC 77-95441. 420p. 1984. 69.50 (ISBN 0-521-22022-X). Cambridge U Pr.

Bammel, Gene & Bammel, Lei Lane Burrus. Leisure & Human Behavior. 384p. 1982. text ed. write for info. (ISBN 0-697-07183-9). Wm C Brown.

Bammel, Lei Lane Burrus, jt. auth. see Bammel, Gene.

Bammer, Kurt & Newberry, Benjamin H., eds. Stress & Cancer. 264p. (Orig.). 1981. pap. text ed. 19.00 (ISBN 0-88937-003-6). Hogrefe Intl.

Bamonte, Louis J. Your Faith: Leader's Guide. 1978. tchr's ed 2.95 (ISBN 0-89243-085-0). Liguori Pubns.

Bampflyde, Heather & Bampflyde, Zune. Gourmet Food Naturally. LC 83-48932. (Illus.). 176p. 1984. 19.95 (ISBN 0-88332-331-1, 8142). Larousse.

Bampflyde, Zune, jt. auth. see Bampflyde, Heather.

Ban, Arline J. Baptist Trailblazers. 48p. 1980. pap. 3.50 (ISBN 0-8170-0872-1). Judson.

--Children's Time in Worship. 128p. 1981. pap. 6.95 (ISBN 0-8170-0902-7). Judson.

--Teaching & Learning with Older Elementary Children. 1979. pap. 2.95 (ISBN 0-8170-0799-7). Judson.

Ban, Arline J. & Ban, Joseph D. The New Disciple: Church Membership Junior-Junior High. LC 75-35898. 96p. 1976. pap. 1.95 (ISBN 0-8170-0658-3). Judson.

--The New Disciple, Leader's Guide. 48p. 1976. pap. 1.50 (ISBN 0-8170-0706-7). Judson.

Ban, Arline J., jt. auth. see Harger, Grace B.

Ban, Arline J., jt. auth. see Lichtenwalner, Muriel E.

Ban, Carolyn, jt. ed. see Ingraham, Patricia W.

Ban, John & Ciminillo, Lewis. Violence & Vandalism. LC 77-87607. text ed. 6.95x (ISBN 0-8134-1981-6, 1981). Interstate.

Ban, Joseph D., jt. auth. see Ban, Arline J.

Ban, Joseph D., jt. ed. see Dekar, Paul R.

Ban, T., ed. see International Symposium, Montreal, October 1973.

Ban, T. A. & Hollender, M. H. Psychopharmacology for Everyday Practice. x, 198p. 1981. pap. 16.00 (ISBN 3-8055-2241-X). S Karger.

Ban, T. A. & Freyhan, F. A., eds. Drug Treatment of Sexual Dysfunction. (Modern Problems of Pharmacopsychiatry: Vol. 15). (Illus.). vi, 194p. 1980. 48.75 (ISBN 3-8055-2906-6). S Karger.

Ban, T. A., jt. ed. see Guy, W.

Ban, T. H., ed. Psychopharmacology for the Aged. xii, 216p. 1980. softcover 16.75 (ISBN 3-8055-1204-X). S Karger.

Ban, Thomas A. Psychopharmacology of Depression. (Illus.). vi, 130p. 1981. pap. 13.75 (ISBN 3-8055-1154-X). S Karger.

--Psychopharmacology of Thiothixene. LC 75-43191. 250p. 1978. 30.00 (ISBN 0-89004-108-3). Raven.

--Schizophrenia: A Psychopharmacological Approach. (Illus.). 144p. 1972. 24.50x (ISBN 0-398-02222-4). C C Thomas.

Ban, Thomas A. & Gonzalez, Rene. Prevention & Treatment of Depresssion. (Illus.). 320p. 1981. text ed. 31.50 (ISBN 0-8391-1674-8). Univ Park.

Ban, Thomas A., jt. auth. see Lehmann, Heinz E.

Banac, Ivo. Effects of World War I: The Class War after the Great War: The Rise of Communist Parties in East Central Europe, 1918-1921. (East European Monographs: No. 137). 277p. 1983. 28.50x (ISBN 0-88033-028-7). East Eur Quarterly.

--The National Question in Yugoslavia: Origins, History, Politics. LC 83-45931. (Illus.). 456p. 1984. 35.00x (ISBN 0-8014-1675-2). Cornell U Pr.

Banac, Ivo & Bushkovitch, Paul, eds. The Nobility in Russia & Eastern Europe. (Yale Russian & East European Publications Ser.: No. 3). 221p. 1983. 18.50 (ISBN 0-936586-02-8). Slavica.

--The Nobility in Russia & Eastern Europe, No. 3. (Yale Russian & East European Publications). xi, 221p. 1983. 18.50 (ISBN 0-936586-02-8). Yale Russian.

Banac, Ivo, et al, eds. Nation & Ideology. (East European Monographs: No. 95). 479p. 1981. 40.00x (ISBN 0-914710-89-3). East Eur Quarterly.

Banach, Jerzy, ed. Cracow. (Great Centers of Art Ser). (Illus.). 30.00 (ISBN 0-8390-0198-3, Allanheld & Schram). Abner Schram Ltd.

Banach, Stefan. Theorie Des Operations Lineaires. 2nd ed. LC 63-21849. (Fr). 10.95 (ISBN 0-8284-0110-1). Chelsea Pub.

Banachowski, Andy. Power Volleyball: The Woman's Game. LC 82-74326. (Illus.). 104p. (Orig.). 1983. pap. text ed. 6.95 (ISBN 0-87670-068-7). Athletic Inst.

Banahan, Mark & Rutter, Andy. The UNIX Book. LC 82-21853. 218p. 1983. pap. 16.95 (ISBN 0-471-89676-4, Pub. by Wiley Pr). Wiley.

Banai, E. & Ito, T. Algebraic Combinatorics I, Association Schemes. 1984. 41.95 (ISBN 0-8053-0490-8). Benjamin-Cummings.

Banaka, William H. Training in Depth Interviewing. 1971. pap. text ed. 12.85 scp (ISBN 0-06-040475-2, HarpC). Har-Row.

Bananas Child Care Information Referral & Support Service. The Bananas Guide. (Illus.). 250p. 1981. pap. 7.50 (ISBN 0-914728-33-4). Wingbow Pr.

Banani, Amin. The Modernization of Iran, 1921-1941. (Illus.). 1961. 17.50x (ISBN 0-8047-0050-8). Stanford U Pr.

Banard, Robert. A Little Local Murder. (Nightingale Large Print Ser.). 1985. pap. text ed. 9.95 (ISBN 0-8161-3798-6, Large Print Bks). G K Hall.

Banas & Goebel. Measures of Noncompactness in Banach Spaces. (Lecture Notes in Pure & Applied Mathematics Ser.: Vol. 60). 112p. 1980. 29.75 (ISBN 0-8247-1248-X). Dekker.

Banas, Jackie. Hope & the Purple Onion. (Illus.). 39p. (Orig.). 1984. wkbk. 3.95 (ISBN 0-9614014-1-9). Know Him Pr.

--Miracle in the Mirror, Success in Self Image. (Illus.). 36p. (Orig.). 1982. wkbk. 3.75 (ISBN 0-9614014-0-0). Know Him Pr.

--Reflections in Righteousness. (Illus.). 56p. (Orig.). 1985. 4.75 (ISBN 0-9614014-2-7). Know Him Pr.

Banas, Josef. The Scapegoats: The Exodus of the Remnants of Polish Jewry. Szafar, Tadeusz, tr. 221p. 1979. text ed. 18.50 (ISBN 0-8419-6303-7). Holmes & Meier.

Banas, N. & Willis, I. H. Prescriptive Teaching from the DTLA. 144p. (Orig.). 1980. pap. 6.00 (ISBN 0-87879-247-3). Acad Therapy.

Banas, Norma & Wills, I. H. H.E.L.P. LC 78-62104. 1979. pap. 7.95 (ISBN 0-89334-018-9). Humanics Ltd.

--Prescriptive Teaching: Theory into Practice. (Illus.). 314p. 1977. 30.75x (ISBN 0-398-03546-6). C C Thomas.

--WISC-R Prescriptions. LC 78-12881. 1978. pap. 5.00x (ISBN 0-87879-206-6). Acad Therapy.

Banaschewski, B., ed. Categorical Aspects of Topology & Analysis, Ottawa 1981: Proceedings. (Lecture Notes in Mathematics Ser.: Vol. 915). 385p. 1982. pap. 22.00 (ISBN 0-387-11211-1). Springer-Verlag.

Banaschewski, B. & Hoffmann, R. E., eds. Continuous Lattices: Proceedings. (Lecture Notes in Mathematics: Vol. 871). 413p. 1981. pap. 24.00 (ISBN 0-387-10848-3). Springer-Verlag.

Banasinski, A., jt. auth. see Lange, Oskar.

Banasinski, Antoni, ed. see Lange, Oskar.

Banaszak & Brennan. Teaching Economics: Content & Strategies. 256p. (Orig.). 1983. pap. 14.05 (ISBN 0-201-11012-1, Sch Div). Addison-Wesley.

Banat, Gabriel, ed. see Borghi, Luigi.

Banat, Gabriel, ed. see Cassanea de Mondonville, Jos.

Banat, Gabriel, ed. see Corrette, Michel.

Banat, Gabriel, ed. see De Saint-Georges, Chevalier.

Banat, Gabriel, ed. see Tessarini, Carlo.

Banat, Gabriel, ed. see Walther, Johann J.

Banathy, B. H., ed. Evolutionary Visions of the Future. (Illus.). 96p. 1985. pap. 16.50 (ISBN 0-08-032563-7, Pub. by PPL). Pergamon.

Banathy, Bela. Developing a Systems View of Education. (Systems Inquiry Ser.). 92p. (Orig.). 1980. pap. text ed. 9.95x (ISBN 0-914105-01-9). Intersystems Pubns.

Banathy, Bela H., ed. Systems Education: Perspectives, Programs, & Methods. (Systems Inquiry Ser.). 177p. 1983. pap. 15.95x (ISBN 0-914105-02-7). Intersystems Pubns.

Banay, R. S. Youth in Despair. Repr. of 1948 ed. 20.00 (ISBN 0-527-04960-3). Kraus Repr.

Banbery, Alan, jt. auth. see Huber, Martin.

Banbury, Gisela & Dewar, Angela. Embroidery for Fashion. Date not set. price not set. Larousse.

Bance, Alan. Theodor Fontane: The Major Novels. LC 81-21688. (Anglica Germanica Ser.: No. 2). 250p. 1982. 47.50 (ISBN 0-521-24532-X). Cambridge U Pr.

Bance, Alan, ed. Weimar Germany: Writers & Politics. 183p. 1983. pap. 16.00x (ISBN 0-7073-0291-9, Pub. by Scottish Academic Pr Scotland). Columbia U Pr.

Bance, Sandra, tr. see Deschner, Gunther.

Bancel, Daniel & Signore, Monique, eds. Problems of Collapse & Numerical Relativity. 1984. lib. bdg. 59.00 (ISBN 90-277-1816-4, Pub. by Reidel Holland). Kluwer Academic.

Banchek, Linda. Snake In, Snake Out. LC 78-51935. (Illus.). (ps-1). 1978. PLB 9.89 (ISBN 0-690-03853-4). Crowell Jr Bks.

Bancheri, Louis, et al. Biology. LC 82-20671. (Arco's Regents Review Ser.). 304p. (Orig.). 1983. pap. 3.95 (ISBN 0-668-05697-5, 5697). Arco.

Banchieri, Adriano. Conclusioni Nel Suono Dell'Organo. (Monuments of Music & Music Literature in Facsimile: Series II, Vol. 101). 78p. (It.). 1975. Repr. of 1609 ed. 30.00x (ISBN 0-8450-2301-2). Broude.

Banchoff, T. & Wermer, J. Linear Algebra through Geometry. (Undergraduate Texts in Mathematics). (Illus.). 257p. 1983. 24.00 (ISBN 0-387-90787-4). Springer-Verlag.

Banchoff, T., et al. Cusps of Gauss Mappings. (Research Notes in Mathematics Ser.: No. 55). 120p. (Orig.). 1981. pap. text ed. 15.95 (ISBN 0-273-08536-0). Pitman Pub MA.

Banci, Lewis. World in Morning. 1978. pap. 1.95 (ISBN 0-505-51229-7, Pub. by Tower Bks). Dorchester Pub Co.

Bancoast, Henry S. & Spaeth, John D., eds. Early English Poems. 548p. 1985. Repr. of 1911 ed. lib. bdg. 50.00 (ISBN 0-8482-5682-4). Norwood Edns.

Bancquart, ed. see De Maupassant, Guy.

Bancroft & Chein-Pai Han. Statistical Theory & Inference in Research. (Statistics: Textbooks & Monographs Ser.: Vol. 40). 432p. 1981. 45.00 (ISBN 0-8247-1400-8). Dekker.

Bancroft, Anne. The Buddhist World. LC 84-51193. (Religions of the World Ser.). (Illus.). 48p. (gr. 6 up). 1985. 9.25 (ISBN 0-382-06928-5); PLB 13.72 (ISBN 0-382-06747-9). Silver.

--The Luminous Vision: Six Medieval Mystics & Their Teachings. 194p. 1983. text ed. 18.50x (ISBN 0-04-189001-9). Allen Unwin.

--Zen: Direct Pointing to Reality. Purce, Jill, ed. LC 81-67702. (The Illustrated Library of Sacred Imagination). (Illus.). 96p. 1982. pap. 9.95 (ISBN 0-8245-0068-7). Crossroad NY.

Bancroft, August S. The Marvels of the Quattrocento in Italy. (The Art Library of the Great Masters of the World). (Illus.). 131p. 1982. Repr. of 1928 ed. 114.85 (ISBN 0-89901-072-5). Found Class Reprints.

Bancroft, Betsy B. Green Again. LC 74-175509. (Illus.). 52p. 1971. 5.95 (ISBN 0-911116-54-0). Pelican.

--Wild Honeysuckle. (Illus.). 20p. 1972. Repr. of 1966 ed. 5.95 (ISBN 0-911116-73-7). Pelican.

Bancroft, Caroline. Augusta Tabor: Her Side of the Scandal. 1955. pap. 1.75 (ISBN 0-933472-14-5). Johnson Bks.

--Colorado's Lost Gold Mines & Buried Treasures. 1961. pap. 3.00 (ISBN 0-933472-16-1). Johnson Bks.

--Colorful Colorado, Its Dramatic History. 1959. pap. 4.50 (ISBN 0-933472-13-7). Johnson Bks.

--Denver's Lively Past. 1959. pap. 3.00 (ISBN 0-933472-17-X). Johnson Bks.

--Estes Park & Trail Ridge. rev. ed. 1981. pap. 2.50 (ISBN 0-933472-18-8). Johnson Bks.

--Famous Aspen. 1967. pap. 3.00 (ISBN 0-933472-19-6). Johnson Bks.

--Grand Lake: From Utes to Yachts. (Bancroft Booklet Ser.). (Illus.). 40p. (Orig.). 1982. pap. 2.50 (ISBN 0-933472-68-4). Johnson Bks.

--Historic Central City. 1957. pap. 2.50 (ISBN 0-933472-20-X). Johnson Bks.

--Silver Queen: The Fabulous Story of Baby Doe Tabor. pap. 3.50 (ISBN 0-933472-21-8). Johnson Bks.

--Six Racy Madams of Colorado. 1965. pap. 3.00 (ISBN 0-933472-22-6). Johnson Bks.

--Tabor's Matchless Mine & Lusty Leadville. 1960. pap. 2.00 (ISBN 0-933472-23-4). Johnson Bks.

--Unique Ghost Towns & Mountain Spots. 1961. pap. 4.00 (ISBN 0-933472-24-2). Johnson Bks.

--Unsinkable Mrs. Brown. 1963. pap. 3.00 (ISBN 0-933472-25-0). Johnson Bks.

Bancroft, Emery. Christian Theology. Mayers, Ronald B., pref. by. 1976. 14.95 (ISBN 0-310-20440-2). Zondervan.

Bancroft, Emery & Mayers, Ronald B. Elemental Theology. 1977. 14.95 (ISBN 0-310-20460-7). Zondervan.

Bancroft, Frances, ed. see Elliott, Tom.

Bancroft, Frederic. Calhoun & the South Carolina Nullification Movement. 1966. 10.75 (ISBN 0-8446-1052-6). Peter Smith.

--A Sketch of the Negro in Politics, Especially in South Carolina & Mississippi. LC 70-160007. Repr. of 1885 ed. 14.50 (ISBN 0-404-00003-7). AMS Pr.

Bancroft, Frederic, ed. see Schurz, Carl.

Bancroft, G. Thomas & Woolfenden, Glen E. Molt of Scrub Jays & Blue Jays in Florida. 51p. 1982. 8.00 (ISBN 0-943610-29-X). Am Ornithologists.

Bancroft, George. History of the Formation of the Constitution of the United States of America, 2 vols. 1983. Repr. of 1882 ed. Set. lib. bdg. 85.00x (ISBN 0-8377-0339-5). Rothman.

--History of the Formation of the Constitution of the United States of America. 51.00 (ISBN 0-8369-7151-5, 7983). Ayer Co Pubs.

--History of the United States of America from the Discovery of the Continent. abr ed. Nye, Russel B., ed. LC 66-23683. (Orig.). 1966. pap. 3.45x (ISBN 0-226-03646-4, P235, Phoen). U of Chicago Pr.

--The Life & Letters of George Bancroft, 2 Vols. in 1. Howe, Mark D., ed. LC 78-106990. (American Public Figures Ser). 1970. Repr. of 1908 ed. lib. bdg. 79.50 (ISBN 0-306-71877-4). Da Capo.

--Literary & Historical Miscellanies. 19.75 (ISBN 0-8369-7208-2, 8007). Ayer Co Pubs.

--A Plea for the Constitution of the United States, Wounded in the House of Its Guardians. Saussy, F. Tupper, ed. LC 84-147576. 89p. 1982. pap. 5.00 (ISBN 0-911805-02-8). S Judd Pubs.

Bancroft, H. H. History of Utah: 1888. (Illus.). 1982. 25.00 (ISBN 0-913814-49-0). Nevada Pubns.

--Reproduction of Bancroft History of Nevada, 1888. (Illus.). 1982. 25.00 (ISBN 0-913814-44-X). Nevada Pubns.

--Resources & Development of Mexico. 1976. lib. bdg. 59.95 (ISBN 0-8490-2519-2). Gordon Pr.

Bancroft Hertiage Book Committee, ed. The Hertiage of Bancroft, Nebraska, 1884-1984, Vol. I. (Illus.). 315p. 1984. 40.00 (ISBN 0-88107-015-7). Natl ShareGraphics.

Bancroft, Hubert H. California Inter Pocula. LC 67-29422. (Works of Hubert Howe Bancroft Ser.). 1967. Repr. of 1888 ed. 25.00x (ISBN 0-914888-28-5). Bancroft Pr.

--Essays & Miscellany. LC 67-29422. (Works of Hubert Howe Bancroft Ser.). 1967. Repr. of 1888 ed. 25.00x (ISBN 0-914888-42-0). Bancroft Pr.

--History of California, 7 vols. LC 67-29422. Repr. of 1888 ed. Set. 150.00 (ISBN 0-914888-20-X). Bancroft Pr.

--History of California, 7 vols. facsimile ed. Repr. of 1880 ed. Set. 105.00 (ISBN 0-317-18708-2). U of Cal Pr.

--History of California Fifteen Forty-Two to Eighteen-Ninety, 7 vols. facsimile ed. 150.00 (ISBN 0-686-74339-3). Dawsons.

--History of Central America, 3 vols. LC 67-29422. (Works of Hubert Howe Bancroft Ser.). 1967. Repr. of 1888 ed. Set. 75.00x (ISBN 0-914888-06-4). Bancroft Pr.

--History of Mexico, 6 vols. LC 67-29422. (Works of Hubert Howe Bancroft Ser.). 1967. Repr. of 1888 ed. Set. 175.00x (ISBN 0-914888-10-2). Bancroft Pr.

--History of Mexico. 1976. lib. bdg. 59.95 (ISBN 0-8490-0336-9). Gordon Pr.

--History of Oregon, 2 vols. LC 67-29422. (Works of Hubert Howe Bancroft Ser.). 1967. Repr. of 1888 ed. 60.00x (ISBN 0-914888-34-X). Bancroft Pr.

--Literary Industries. LC 67-29422. (Works of Hubert Howe Bancroft Ser.). 1967. Repr. of 1888 ed. 25.00x (ISBN 0-914888-43-9). Bancroft Pr.

--The Native Races, 5 vols. LC 67-29422. (Works of Hubert Howe Bancroft Ser.). 1967. Repr. of 1888 ed. Set. 150.00x (ISBN 0-914888-00-5). Bancroft Pr.

--Popular Tribunals, 2 vols. LC 67-29422. (Works of Hubert Howe Bancroft Ser.). 1967. Repr. of 1888 ed. 50.00x (ISBN 0-914888-39-0). Bancroft Pr.

Bancroft, Iris. The Passionate Heart. 288p. (Orig.). 1983. pap. 2.95 (ISBN 0-523-41892-2). Pinnacle Bks.

Bancroft, John. Human Sexuality & Its Problems. LC 82-14719. 447p. 1983. pap. text ed. 24.95 (ISBN 0-443-01659-3). Churchill.

Bancroft, John C. Writing That Sells. (Illus.). 180p. 1975. pap. 10.95 (ISBN 0-686-11023-4). J C Bancroft.

Bancroft, John D. & Stevens, Alan, eds. Theory & Practice of Histological Techniques. 2nd ed. (Illus.). 662p. 1982. text ed. 79.00 (ISBN 0-443-02006-X). Churchill.

Bancroft, Keith. Amphoto Guide to Lenses. (Illus.). 169p. 1981. (Amphoto); pap. 7.95 (ISBN 0-8174-3527-1). Watson-Guptill.

Bancroft Library, University of California-Berkeley. Index to Printed Maps. 1964. lib. bdg. 79.00 (ISBN 0-8161-0704-1, Hall Library). G K Hall.

Bancroft Library, University of California, Berkeley. Index to Printed Maps, 1st Supplement. 1975. lib. bdg. 110.00 (ISBN 0-8161-1172-3, Hall Library). G K Hall.

Bancroft, Marie & Bancroft, Squire. Bancrofts: Recollections of Sixty Years. LC 70-87117. (Illus.). Repr. of 1909 ed. 33.00 (ISBN 0-405-08236-3, Blom Pubns). Ayer Co Pubs.

Bancroft, Mary. Autobiography of a Spy. LC 82-5384. (Illus.). 325p. 1983. 15.95 (ISBN 0-688-02019-4). Morrow.

Bancroft, Page, tr. see Barreda, Pedro.

Bancroft, Peter. Gem & Crystal Treasures. (Illus.). 488p. 1984. 60.00 (ISBN 0-9613461-1-6). Western Enter.

Bancroft, Richard. Dangerous Positions & Proceedings. LC 74-38147. (English Experience Ser.: No. 427). 192p. 1972. Repr. of 1593 ed. 28.50 (ISBN 90-221-0427-3). Walter J Johnson.

--A Survey of the Pretended Holy Dicipline. LC 78-38148. (English Experience Ser.: No. 428). 472p. 1972. Repr. of 1593 ed. 67.00 (ISBN 90-221-0428-1). Walter J Johnson.

Bancroft, Squire, jt. auth. see Bancroft, Marie.

Bancroft, T. A. Topics in Intermediate Statistical Methods, Vol. 1. 1968. 7.50x (ISBN 0-8138-0842-1). Iowa St U Pr.

Bancroft, T. A. & Brown, Susan A., eds. Statistical Papers in Honor of George W. Snedecor. LC 79-106603. (Illus.). 1972. 14.50x (ISBN 0-8138-1585-1). Iowa St U Pr.

Bancroft, William W. Joseph Conrad-His Philosophy of Life. LC 65-15867. (Studies in Conrad, No. 8). 1969. Repr. of 1933 ed. lib. bdg. 29.95x (ISBN 0-8383-0506-7). Haskell.

Bancroft-Hunt, Norman & Forman, Werner. People of the Totem: The Indians of the Pacific Northwest. (Echoes of the Ancient World Ser.). (Illus.). 128p. 1984. 20.00 (ISBN 0-85613-304-3, Pub. by Salem Hse Ltd). Merrimack Pub Cir.

Bancroft-Hunt, Norman & Werner, Forman. The Indians of the Great Plains. LC 81-85585. (Illus.). 128p. 1982. 25.00 (ISBN 0-688-01215-9). Morrow.

Band, Arnold. Nahman of Bratslav, the Tales. LC 78-53433. (Classics of Western Spirituality). 368p. 1978. o. p. 11.95 (ISBN 0-8091-0238-2); pap. 9.95 (ISBN 0-8091-2103-4). Paulist Pr.

Band, Arnold J. Nostalgia & Nightmare: A Study in the Fiction of S. Y. Agnon. LC 67-22714. (Near Eastern Center, UCLA). 1968. 42.50x (ISBN 0-520-00076-5). U of Cal Pr.

Band, Claire & Band, William. Two Years with the Chinese Communists. LC 75-36219. (Illus.). Repr. of 1948 ed. 30.00 (ISBN 0-404-14470-5). AMS Pr.

Band, Edward. Working His Purpose Out: The History of the English Presbyterian Mission, 1847-1947, CW-223. 1972. 16.85x (ISBN 0-89644-310-8, Pub. by Ch'eng Wen Taiwan). Chinese Materials.

Band, Ora, ed. see Bergman, Bella.

Band, Ora, et al. Hebrew: A Language Course, No. I. 256p. 1982. pap. text ed. 7.95x (ISBN 0-87441-331-1). Behrman.

Band, P. R., ed. Early Detection & Localization of Lung Tumors in High Risk Groups. (Recent Results in Cancer Research Ser.: Vol. 82). (Illus.). 210p. 1982. 48.00 (ISBN 0-387-11249-9). Springer-Verlag.

Band, Richard E. Contrary Investing: The Insider's Guide to Buying Low & Selling High. 1985. 16.95 (ISBN 0-07-003604-7). McGraw.

Band, Selah, Jr. Thoughts into Words. 41p. 1972. pap. 2.50 (ISBN 0-317-14998-9). Tech & Ed Ctr Graph Arts RIT.

Band, William, jt. auth. see Band, Claire.

Banda, Innocent O., et al. Nine Malawian Plays. Gibbs, James, ed. 171p. 1976. pap. 7.00x (ISBN 0-686-63460-8). Three Continents.

Banda, Tito. Sekani's Solution. (Malawian Writers Ser.). (Illus.). 112p. (Orig.). (gr. 9-12). 1979. pap. 6.00x (ISBN 0-686-63966-9). Three Continents.

Bandal, S. Kris, et al, eds. The Pesticide Chemist & Modern Toxicology. LC 81-10790. (ACS Symposium Ser.: No. 160). 1981. 49.95 (ISBN 0-8412-0636-8). Am Chemical.

Bandara, H. H. Cultural Policy in Sri Lanka. (Studies & Documents on Cultural Policies). (Illus.). 70p. (Orig.). 1972. pap. 5.00 (ISBN 9-231-01004-2, U138, UNESCO). Unipub.

Bandarage, Asoka. Colonialism in Sri Lanka: The Political Economy of the Kandyan Highlands, 1833-1886. LC 83-17274. (Studies in the Social Sciences: No. 39). xiv, 404p. 1983. 62.40x (ISBN 90-279-3080-5). Mouton.

Bandas, Rudolph G. Catholic Layman & Holiness. 1965. 8.95 (ISBN 0-8158-0046-0). Chris Mass.

Bandat, H. Von see Von Bandat, H.

Bande, Alexandre. The Vigilante Committees of the Attakapas. Edmonds, David C. & Gibson, Dennis, eds. Rogers, Hennietta G., tr. from Fr. (Illus.). 307p. 1981. Repr. of 1861 ed. 19.95 (ISBN 0-937614-02-5). Acadiana Pr.

Bandel, Betty. Sing the Lord's Song in a Strange Land: The Life of Justin Morgan. LC 78-73309. 264p. 1981. 24.50 (ISBN 0-8386-2411-1). Fairleigh Dickinson.

Bandel, Betty, ed. & compiled by. Walk into My Parlor. LC 76-158783. (gr. 6 up). 1972. 5.00 (ISBN 0-8048-0920-8). C E Tuttle.

Bandelier, A. F. The Gilded Man (el Dorado) & Other Pictures of the Spanish Occupancy of America. 1893. 27.50 (ISBN 0-932062-09-1). Sharon Hill.

--Islands of Titicaca & Koati. Repr. of 1910 ed. 36.00 (ISBN 0-527-04990-5). Kraus Repr.

--Scientist on the Trail. Hammond, George P., ed. LC 67-24721. (Quivira Society Publications, Vol. 10). 1967. Repr. of 1949 ed. 17.00 (ISBN 0-405-00084-7). Ayer Co Pubs.

Bandelier, A. F. & Hewett, Edgar L. On the Social Originization & Mode of Government of the Ancient Mexicans. 145p. 1975. Repr. of 1879 ed. lib. bdg. 18.50 (ISBN 0-8154-0504-9). Cooper Sq.

Bandelier, A. F., ed. see Nunez Cabeza de Vaca, Alvar.

Bandelier, Adolf F. The Delight Makers. 1979. Repr. of 1890 ed. lib. bdg. 50.00 (ISBN 0-8495-0536-4). Arden Lib.

--The Delight Makers. LC 70-28000. 1971. pap. 8.95 (ISBN 0-15-625264-3, Harv). HarBraceJ.

--Final Report of Investigations among the Indians of the Southwestern U. S, 2 vols. LC 74-7918. Repr. of 1892 ed. Set. 84.00 (ISBN 0-404-58054-8); index 17.00 (ISBN 0-404-58056-4). AMS Pr.

--Hemenway Southwestern Archaeological Expedition. LC 74-7922. Repr. of 1890 ed. 22.00 (ISBN 0-404-58057-2). AMS Pr.

--Historical Introduction to Studies Among the Sedentary Indians of New Mexico & a Report on the Ruins of the Pueblo at Pecos. LC 76-20788. Repr. of 1881 ed. 19.00 (ISBN 0-404-58051-3). AMS Pr.

--Pioneers in American Anthropology: The Bandelier-Morgan Letters, 1873-1883, 2 vols. White, Leslie A., ed. LC 74-7921. Repr. of 1940 ed. Set. 49.50 (ISBN 0-404-11806-2). AMS Pr.

--Report of an Archaeological Tour in Mexico in 1881. LC 76-24822. Repr. of 1884 ed. 35.00 (ISBN 0-404-58052-1). AMS Pr.

Bandelier, Adolf F. & Hewett, Edgar H. Indians of the Rio Grande Valley. LC 74-7920. Repr. of 1937 ed. 33.00 (ISBN 0-404-11805-4). AMS Pr.

Bandelier, Adolph F. The Discovery of New Mexico by the Franciscan Monk Friar Marcos de Niza in 1539. Rodack, Madeleine T., tr. from Fr. LC 80-25083. 135p. 1981. 14.95 (ISBN 0-8165-0717-1). U of Ariz Pr.

--Papers of the Archaeological Institute of America, 6 vols. (American Ser.). Repr. of 1891 ed. Set. with index 177.00 (ISBN 0-404-19502-4). AMS Pr.

--The Southwestern Journal of Adolph F. Bandelier, 1883. Lange, Charles H. & Riley, Carroll L., eds. LC 65-17862. pap. 140.50 (ISBN 0-317-26629-2, 2025431). Bks Demand UMI.

--The Southwestern Journals of Adolf F. Bandelier, 1880. Lange, Charles H. & Riley, Carroll L., eds. LC 65-17862. pap. 125.50 (ISBN 0-317-26625-X, 2025430). Bks Demand UMI.

--The Southwestern Journals of Adolph F. Bandelier, 1885. Lange, Charles H. & Riley, Carroll L., eds. LC 65-17862. pap. 160.00 (ISBN 0-317-26630-6, 2025432). Bks Demand UMI.

Bandelier, Adolph F. & Ten Kate, Herman F. An Outline of the Documentary History of the Zuni Tribe: Somatological Observations of Indians of the Southwest. LC 76-21219. (A Journal of American Ethnology & Archaeology: Vol. 3). Repr. of 1892 ed. 25.00 (ISBN 0-404-58043-2). AMS Pr.

Bandelier, Fanny, tr. see Nunez Cabeza de Vaca, Alvar.

Bandelier, Fanny, tr. see Sahagun, Fray B.

Bandello, Matteo. Certain Tragical Discourses of Bandello, 2 Vols. Fenton, Geffraie, tr. LC 73-160008. (Tudor Translations, First Ser.: Nos. 19-20). Repr. of 1898 ed. Set. 90.00 (ISBN 0-404-51900-8); 45.00 ea. Vol. 1 (ISBN 0-404-51901-6). Vol. 2 (ISBN 0-404-51902-4). AMS Pr.

Bandelow, Christoph. Inside Rubik's Cube & Beyond. (Illus.). 144p. 1982. pap. 7.95 (ISBN 0-8176-3078-3). Birkhauser.

Bandem, I. M. & De Boer, Frederick. Kaja & Kelod: Balinese Dance in Transition. (Illus.). 1981. 59.00x (ISBN 0-19-580469-4). Oxford U Pr.

Bander, David F., jt. auth. see Bander, Edward.

Bander, E. Mr. Dooley & Mr. Dunne. 150p. 1981. text ed. 14.50 (ISBN 0-87215-329-0). Michie Co.

Bander, E. J., jt. auth. see Marke, J. J.

Bander, E. J., ed. Mr. Dooley on the Choice of Law. 1963. 14.50 (ISBN 0-87215-004-6). Michie Co.

Bander, Edward & Bander, David F. Legal Research & Education Abridgment: A Manual for Law Students, Paralegals & Researchers. LC 78-2408. 240p. 1978. prof ref 27.50 (ISBN 0-88410-794-9). Ballinger Pub.

Bander, Edward J. Change of Name & Law of Names. LC 73-11060. (Legal Almanac Ser.: No. 34). 128p. 1973. lib. bdg. 5.95 (ISBN 0-379-11088-1). Oceana.

--Dictionary of Selected Legal Terms & Maxims, Vol. 58. 2nd ed. LC 79-19266. (Legal Almanac Ser.: No. 58). 154p. 1979. 5.95 (ISBN 0-379-11119-5). Oceana.

--Legal Research & Education Abridgement. 226p. 1978. 12.50 (ISBN 0-317-07350-8). Transnatl Pubs.

Bander, Edward J. & Wallach, Jeffrey J. Medical Legal Dictionary. LC 73-83743. 114p. 1970. lib. bdg. 7.50 (ISBN 0-379-14101-9). Oceana.

Bander, Edward J., jt. auth. see Marke, Julius J.

Bander, Edward J., ed. Corporation in a Democratic Society. (Reference Shelf Ser: Vol. 46, No. 6). 1974. 8.00 (ISBN 0-8242-0526-X). Wilson.

--Justice Holmes, Ex Cathedra. 1966. 14.50 (ISBN 0-87215-003-8). Michie Co.

--Turmoil on the Campus. (Reference Shelf Ser: Vol. 42, No. 3). 1970. 8.00 (ISBN 0-8242-0411-5). Wilson.

Bander, Edward J., jt. ed. see Julius, Marke J.

Bander, Edward J., et al. Researching the Law. 260p. 1985. lib. bdg. 30.00 (ISBN 0-941320-27-8). Transnatl Pubs.

Bander, M., et al, eds. see AIP Conference, Univ. of California at Irvine, Dec., 1971.

Bander, Peter. Carry on Talking: How Dead Are the Voices? 1972. text ed. 6.50x (ISBN 0-900675-66-7). Humanities.

--The Prophecies of St. Malachy. LC 74-125419. (Illus.). 1973. pap. 3.00 (ISBN 0-89555-038-5). TAN Bks Pubs.

--The Prophecies of St. Malachy & St. Columbkille. 3rd ed. 1979. pap. text ed. 6.50x (ISBN 0-901072-10-9). Humanities.

Bander, Robert G. American English Rhetoric. 3rd ed. 370p. 1983. pap. 14.95 (ISBN 0-03-061066-4). HR&W.

--From Sentence to Paragraph: A Writing Workbook in English As a Second Language. LC 79-2558. 248p. (Orig.). 1980. pap. text ed. 12.95 (ISBN 0-03-045641-X, HoltC). HR&W.

--Sentence Making: A Writing Workbook in English as a Second Language. 335p. 1982. pap. text ed. 14.95 (ISBN 0-03-050631-X). HR&W.

--Writing: Basics & Beyond. 1985. pap. text ed. 12.95x (ISBN 0-673-15596-X). Scott F.

Bandhauer, K. & Frick, J., eds. Disturbances in Male Fertility. (Encyclopedia of Urology: Vol. XVI). 500p. 1982. 132.00 (ISBN 0-387-05279-8). Springer-Verlag.

Bandholtz, Harry H. Undiplomatic Diary. LC 77-160009. Repr. of 1933 ed. 27.50 (ISBN 0-404-00494-6). AMS Pr.

Bandhyopadhyay, Samik, tr. see Chakraborty, Amalendu.

Bandhyopadhyay, Samik, tr. see Sircar, Badal.

Bandhyopadhyay, Samik, tr. see Tendulkar, Vijay.

Bandieramonte, Gaetano, jt. auth. see Bellina, Joseph H.

Bandinel, J. Some Account of the Trade in Slaves from Africa. 323p. 1968. Repr. of 1842 ed. 30.00x (ISBN 0-7146-1887-X, F Cass Co). Biblio Dist.

Band-Kuzmany, K. R. Glossary of the Theatre. 130p. (Eng., Fr., Ital. & Ger.). 1970. 32.00 (ISBN 0-444-40716-2). Elsevier.

Bandler, Richard. Magic in Action. LC 84-61646. 1985. 14.95 (ISBN 0-916990-14-1). Meta Pubns.

--Modulation of Sensorimotor Activity During Alterations in Behavioral States. LC 84-7952. (Neurology & Neurobiology Ser.: Vol. 12). 550p. 1984. 68.00 (ISBN 0-8451-2714-4). A R Liss.

--Using Your Brain: For a Change. Andreas, Connirae, ed. Andreas, Steve, tr. (Illus.). 159p. (Orig.). 1985. 10.00 (ISBN 0-911226-26-5); pap. 6.50 (ISBN 0-911226-27-3). Real People.

Bandler, Richard & Grinder, John. Frogs into Princes: Neuro Linguistic Programming. LC 79-13255. 1979. 10.00 (ISBN 0-911226-18-4); pap. 6.50 (ISBN 0-911226-19-2). Real People.

--Patterns of Hypnotic Techniques of Milton H. Erickson, M. D. LC 75-24584. 1975. pap. 8.95x (ISBN 0-916990-01-X). Meta Pubns.

--Reframing: Neuro-Linguistic Programming & the Transformation of Meaning. Andreas, Steve & Andreas, Connirae, eds. 215p. (Orig.). 1982. 10.00 (ISBN 0-911226-24-9); pap. 6.50 (ISBN 0-911226-25-7). Real People.

--Structure of Magic, Vol. 1. LC 75-12452. 1975. 8.95 (ISBN 0-8314-0044-7). Sci & Behavior.

Bandler, Richard, jt. auth. see Grinder, John.

Bandlow, Richard F., jt. auth. see Yehl, Joan K.

Bandlow, W. & Schweyen, R., eds. Mitochondria, 1977: Genetics & Biogenesis of Mitochondria. 1977. 80.00 (ISBN 3-11-007321-8). De Gruyter.

Bandlow, W., et al, eds. Genetics, Biogenetics & Bioenergetics of Mitochondria: Symposium, Sept. 1975, University of Munich, Germany. 1976. 56.00x (ISBN 3-11-006865-6). De Gruyter.

Bandman, Bertram. The Place of Reason in Education. LC 66-25169. (Studies in Educational Theory of the John Dewey Society: No. 4). 218p. 1967. 5.00 (ISBN 0-8142-0020-6). Ohio St U Pr.

Bandman, Bertram, jt. auth. see Bandman, Elsie L.

Bandman, Elsie L. & Bandman, Bertram. Bioethics & Human Rights. 1978. pap. text ed. 14.95 (ISBN 0-316-07998-7). Little.

--Nursing Ethics in the Life Span. 304p. (Orig.). 1984. pap. 19.95 (ISBN 0-8385-7026-7). ACC.

Bandman, M. K., ed. Regional Development in the USSR: Modelling the Formation of Soviet Territorial-Production Complexes. (Urban & Regional Planning Ser.). (Illus.). 332p. 1984. 49.50 (ISBN 0-08-023341-4). Pergamon.

Bandmann, H. J. & Breit, R., eds. Klinefelter's Syndrome. (Illus.). 250p. 1984. pap. 35.00 (ISBN 0-387-13267-8). Springer-Verlag.

Bandopadhyaya, J. North Over South: A NonWestern Perspective of International Relations. 1982. 26.00x (ISBN 0-8364-0894-2). South Asia Bks.

Bandopadhyaya, Manik. Padma River Boatman. (Asian & Pacific Writing Ser.). 1973. 14.95x (ISBN 0-7022-0833-7); pap. 8.50x (ISBN 0-7022-0834-5). U of Queensland Pr.

Bandrowski, Juliusz K., ed. Great Battle on the Vistula. LC 73-151603. (BCL Ser. I). Repr. of 1921 ed. 11.50 (ISBN 0-404-00495-4). AMS Pr.

Bandt, Jacques de see De Bandt, Jacques, et al.

Bandtock, John & Hanson, Paul. Success in Chemistry. (Success Studybooks Ser.). (Illus.). 380p. 1975. pap. 12.00 (ISBN 0-7195-2914-X). Transatlantic.

Bandura, A. Social Learning Theory. 1977. text ed. 22.95 (ISBN 0-13-816751-6); pap. text ed. 18.95 (ISBN 0-13-816744-3). P-H.

Bandura, A., jt. ed. see Ribes-Inesta, E.

Bandura, Albert. Aggression: A Social Learning Analysis. (P-H Social Learning Ser). (Illus.). 368p. 1973. ref. ed. 30.95 (ISBN 0-13-020743-8). P-H.

--The Social Foundations of Thought & Action: A Social Cognitive Theory. (Illus.). 544p. 1986. text ed. 32.95 (ISBN 0-13-815614-X). P-H.

Bandura, Albert & Walters, Richard H. Adolescent Aggression: A Study of the Influence of Child-Training Practices & Family Inter-Relationships. LC 59-12125. Repr. of 1959 ed. 93.00 (ISBN 0-8357-9518-7, 2012404). Bks Demand UMI.

Bandy, Anastasius. Ioannes Lydus on Powers or the Magistracies of the Roman State. LC 80-68491. (Memoirs Ser.: Vol. 149). 1983. 60.00 (ISBN 0-87169-149-3). Am Philos.

Bandy, Dale. Prentice-Hall Federal Tax Course 1984: Student Guide. (Illus.). 368p. 1983. pap. 10.95 (ISBN 0-13-312736-2). P-H.

--Prentice-Hall Federal Tax Course, 1983 Edition. (Illus.). 368p. 1982. pap. text ed. 9.95 Student Guide (ISBN 0-13-312637-4). P-H.

--Prentice-Hall Nineteen Eighty-Six Federal Tax Course: Student Guide. (Illus.). 352p. 1985. 11.95 (ISBN 0-13-312802-4). P-H.

--Prentice-Hall 1985 Federal Tax Course. 1985 ed. (Illus.). 368p. 1984. 11.95 (ISBN 0-13-312778-8). P-H.

Bandy, Dale & Swad, Randy. Federal Income Tax Procedures, 1982. 2nd ed. 800p. 1982. pap. text ed. 17.95 (ISBN 0-13-308494-9). P-H.

--Federal Income Tax Procedures, 1983. 320p. 1983. pap. text ed. 19.00 (ISBN 0-13-309104-X). P-H.

Bandy, Dale, jt. auth. see Hoffman, William.

Bandy, Franklin. The Blackstock Affair. 384p. (Orig.). 1980. pap. 2.50 (ISBN 0-441-06650-X, Pub. by Charter Bks). Ace Bks.

--The Farewell Party. 320p. (Orig.). 1980. pap. 2.50 (ISBN 0-441-22832-1, Pub. by Charter Bks). Ace Bks.

--The Shannonese Hustle. 1978. pap. 1.75 (ISBN 0-380-41327-2, 41327). Avon.

Bandy, Mary Lea, ed. Rediscovering French Film. (Illus.). 240p. 1982. pap. 15.00 (ISBN 0-87070-335-8, Pub. by Museum Mod Art). NYGS.

Bandy, Melanie. Mind Forg'd Manacles: Evil in the Poetry of Blake & Shelley. LC 80-18779. (Illus.). 210p. 1981. text ed. 19.95 (ISBN 0-8173-0046-5). U of Ala Pr.

Bandy, Patricia & Fritsche, Joellen, eds. Current Issues, 1985. LC 78-643561. 215p. 1986. 7.00 (ISBN 0-932765-01-7); 20 or more copies 5.25 ea. Close Up Foun.

Bandy, Patricia, ed. see Close Up Foundation.

Bandy, Way. Designing Your Face: An Illustrated Guide to Using Cosmetics. LC 77-5962. (Illus.). 112p. 1984. pap. 8.95 (ISBN 0-394-72758-4). Random.

Bandyk-Glander, Janice & Droge, Dennis. Woman's Day Book of Calligraphy. 96p. 1982. pap. 7.95 (ISBN 0-671-25019-1, Fireside). S&S.

Bandyopadhyay, Bholanath. The Political Ideas of Benoy Kumar Sarkar. 1985. 15.00x (ISBN 0-8364-1336-9, Pub. by KP Bagchi India). South Asia Bks.

Bandyopadhyay, Bimal. Metal Sculptures of Eastern India. (Illus.). 178p. 1981. text ed. 37.00x (ISBN 0-391-02658-5). Humanities.

Bandyopadhyay, Jayatanuja. Indian Nationalism Versus International Communism. 1966. 9.00x (ISBN 0-8364-1216-8, Pub. by K L Mukhopadhyay India). South Asia Bks.

Bandyopadhyay, P. K. Leadership Among the Mizos: An Emerging Dimension. (Illus.). 296p. 1985. text ed. 37.50x (ISBN 0-86590-719-6, Pub. by B R Pub Corp India). Apt Bks.

Bandyopadhyay, R. & Padwal, S. M. Introduction to Operational Research & Data Management. 400p. Date not set. text ed. price not set (ISBN 0-7069-1234-9, Pub. by Vikas India). Advent NY.

Bandyopadhyay, Samik, tr. see Sen, Mrinal.

Bandyopadhyay, Sukhamay. Temples of Birbhum. (Illus.). 180p. 1984. text ed. 75.00 (ISBN 0-86590-255-0, Pub. by B R Pub Corp India). Apt Bks.

Bandyopadhyaya, J. Climate & World Order. 180p. 1983. text ed. 17.75x (ISBN 0-391-02893-6). Humanities.

Bandyopadhyaya, Jayantanuja. The Making of India's Foreign Policy. 362p. 1980. 14.95x (ISBN 0-940500-35-3). Asia Bk Corp.

--Mao Tse-Tung & Gandhi: Perspectives on Social Transformation. 156p. 1973. 6.50x (ISBN 0-89684-432-3). Orient Bk Dist.

Bandyopadhyaya, Kalyani. Burma & Indonesia: Comparative Political Economy & Foreign Policy. LC 83-904372. vii, 250p. cancelled (ISBN 0-317-09862-4, Pub. by S Asian India). Humanities.

--Burma & Indonesia: Comparative Study of Political Economy & Foreign Policy. 260p. 1983. text ed. 18.75x (ISBN 0-391-02931-2). Humanities.

Bane, Bernard M. The Bane in Kennedy's Existence. LC 66-30557. 169p. 1967. soft bdg. 6.00 (ISBN 0-9600164-0-6). BMB Pub Co.

--Breaking Through. 63p. 1984. pap. 5.00 (ISBN 0-930924-18-5). BMB Pub Co.

--Controlled Brinkmanship. 8p. 1968. pap. 0.35 (ISBN 0-9600164-1-4). BMB Pub Co.

--The "Figure Eight" Schematic: Towards Codifying Bodily Functions. 100p. 1980. soft cover 4.00 (ISBN 0-930924-05-3). BMB Pub Co.

--The Grand Model of Mind. LC 62-13784. 73p. 1962. soft bdg. 5.00 (ISBN 0-9600164-2-2). BMB Pub Co.

--Guidelines to Authenticity Stepping Stones to Health. LC 77-87980. 60p. 1977. soft bdg. 3.00 (ISBN 0-9600164-6-5). BMB Pub Co.

--Is President John F. Kennedy Alive... & Well? LC 76-21807. 161p. 1981. pap. 7.50 (ISBN 0-930924-08-8). BMB Pub Co.

--On the Impact of Morality in Our Times. 113p. 1985. pap. 5.00 (ISBN 0-317-20545-5). BMB Pub Co.

--A Schematic Replica of the Cardiac Cycle. 45p. 1981. pap. 3.00 (ISBN 0-930924-11-8). BMB Pub Co.

--Tramp, Tramp, Tramp,the Girls are Marching: A Self-Styled Report on the Women's Liberation Movement. 80p. 1982. pap. 5.00 (ISBN 0-930924-15-0). BMB Pub Co.

--The Trilateral Template. 6p. 1982. pap. 0.25 (ISBN 0-930924-13-4). BMB Pub Co.

Bane, Charles A. The Electrical Equipment Conspiracies: The Treble Damage Actions. LC 73-75126. (Illus.). 554p. 1973. 17.50 (ISBN 0-87945-023-1). Fed Legal Pubns.

Bane, John J., Jr. Undercover on Fifth Avenue. LC 85-60453. (Illus.). 180p. 1986. 19.95 (ISBN 0-933341-06-7). Quinlan Pr.

Bane, Mary J. Here to Stay: American Families in the 20th Century. LC 76-44877. 1978. pap. 6.95x (ISBN 0-465-09726-X, TB-5039). Basic.

Bane, Mary J., jt. auth. see Carballo, Manuel.

Bane, Mary Jo, jt. auth. see Masnick, George.

Bane, Michael. Who's Who in Rock. 1981. 17.95 (ISBN 0-87196-465-1). Facts on File.

--Who's Who in Rock. (Illus.). 260p. 1982. pap. 10.95 (ISBN 0-89696-184-2, An Everest House Book). Dodd.

--Willie: A Biography of Willie Nelson. (Orig.). 1984. pap. 3.50 (ISBN 0-440-09290-6). Dell.

Bane, Michael & Moore, Ellen. Tampa: Yesterday, Today & Tomorrow. (Illus.). 180p. (Orig.). 1982. 19.95 (ISBN 0-9609530-0-0); pap. 12.95 (ISBN 0-9609530-2-7). King Co.

Bane, S., et al. Advanced Pipework. (Illus.). 213p. 1979. spiral 48.00 (ISBN 0-85083-450-3). Trans-Atlantic.

Baneham, Sam. The Cloud of Desolation. 302p. 1982. 13.95 (ISBN 0-905473-86-8, Pub. by Wolfhound Pr Ireland); pap. 6.95 (ISBN 0-905473-87-6). Irish Bks Media.

Banek, Reinhold & Scoville, Jon. Sound Designs: A Handbook of Musical Instrument Building. LC 80-65364. (Illus.). 224p. (Orig.). 1980. pap. 6.95 (ISBN 0-89815-011-6). Ten Speed Pr.

Banek, Yvette. Christmas Search-a-Picture Puzzles. (Puzzleback Ser.). (Illus.). 64p. (Orig.). (gr. 3-7). 1981. pap. 2.50 (ISBN 0-671-43365-2). Wanderer Bks.

Banel, Joseph. Lee Wong, Boy Detective. LC 72-1923. (Venture Ser.). (Illus.). 64p. (gr. 2). 1972. PLB 7.68 (ISBN 0-8116-6967-X). Garrard.

Banerian, James. Losers Are Pirates: A Close Look at the PBS Series "Vietnam: A Television History". rev. ed. LC 85-61423. 416p. 1985. pap. 14.95 (ISBN 0-932729-01-0). Sphinx Pub.

Banerja, J. R. Rhetoric & Prosody. 1973. Repr. of 1967 ed. 10.00 (ISBN 0-8274-1443-9). R West.

Banerjea, D. Coordination Chemistry: Twentieth International Conference on Coordination Chemistry, Calcutta, India, 10-14 Dec. 1979, Proceedings, Vol. 20. LC 80-41163. 286p. 1980. 88.00 (ISBN 0-08-023942-0). Pergamon.

Banerjea, Pramathanath. Public Administration in Ancient India. 316p. 1973. Repr. 18.75x (ISBN 0-89684-445-5). Orient Bk Dist.

Banerjee, A. C. English Law in India. 324p. 1984. text ed. 21.00x (ISBN 0-391-03008-6). Humanities.

--The Khalsa Raj. 1985. 17.50x (ISBN 0-8364-1355-5, Pub. by Abhinav India). South Asia Bks.

--The New History of Modern India: 1707-1947. 810p. 1983. 49.00x (ISBN 0-317-20272-3, Pub. by K P Bagchi & Co India). State Mutual Bk.

--Two Nations: The Philosophy of Muslim Nationalism. 268p. 1981. text ed. 16.75x (ISBN 0-391-02210-5, Pub. by Concept India). Humanities.

Banerjee, A. C., ed. see Chatterjee, Sunjeeb C.

Banerjee, Anil C. Annexation of Burma. LC 77-87007. Repr. of 1944 ed. 25.00 (ISBN 0-404-16793-4). AMS Pr.

Banerjee, G. C. Animal Nutrition. 576p. 1981. 45.00x (ISBN 0-686-72939-0, Pub. by Oxford & IBH India). State Mutual Bk.

--Poultry. 126p. 1981. 35.00x (ISBN 0-686-72961-7, Pub. by Oxford & IBH India). State Mutual Bk.

--A Textbook of Animal Husbandry. 4th ed. 1981. 35.00x (ISBN 0-686-72968-4, Pub. by Oxford & IBH India). State Mutual Bk.

Banerjee, Gauranga N. Hellenism in Ancient India. rev. ed. 276p. 1981. text ed. 20.50x (ISBN 0-391-02417-5, Pub. by Munshiram Manoharlal India). Humanities.

Banerjee, Himadri. Agrarian Society of the Punjab, 1849-1901. 1983. 24.00x (ISBN 0-8364-0968-X, Pub. by Manohar India). South Asia Bks.

Banerjee, J. India in Soviet Global Strategy. 1977. 12.50x (ISBN 0-88386-908-X). South Asia Bks.

Banerjee, K. India & Britain, 1947-1968. 1977. 14.00x (ISBN 0-88386-903-9). South Asia Bks.

--Regional Political Parties in India. 375p. 1984. text ed. 45.00x (ISBN 0-86590-293-3, Pub. by B R Pub Corp Indian). Apt Bks.

Banerjee, K. K., ed. Logic, Ontology & Action. (Jadavpur Studies in Philosophy: Vol. 1). 269p. 1982. text ed. 13.00x (ISBN 0-391-02490-6). Humanities.

--Logical Form, Predication & Ontology, Vol. 4. (Jadavpur Studies in Philosophy). 300p. 1983. text ed. 16.75x (ISBN 0-391-02837-5, Pub. by Macmillan India). Humanities.

--Mind, Language & Necessity. (Jadavpur Studies in Philosophy: Vol. 3). 275p. 1982. text ed. 13.00x (ISBN 0-391-02504-X). Humanities.

Banerjee, K. S. Cost of Living Index Numbers: Practice, Precision, & Theory. (Statistics: Textbooks & Monographs: Vol. 11). 200p. 1975. 35.00 (ISBN 0-8247-6266-5). Dekker.

Banerjee, M. L. & Thapa, B. B. Orchids of Nepal. (International Bioscience Ser.: No. 4). (Illus.). 150p. 1978. 9.00 (ISBN 0-88065-023-0, Pub. by Messers Today & Tomorrows Printers & Publishers India). Scholarly Pubns.

Banerjee, Malabika. The Nonaligned Movement. 1983. 16.00x (ISBN 0-8364-0956-6, Pub. by Mukhopadhyay India). South Asia Bks.

Banerjee, N. V. Buddhism & Marxism: A Study in Humanism. 152p. 1978. text ed. 15.00x (ISBN 0-86131-014-4, Pub by Orient Longman India). Apt Bks.

Banerjee, Nixmala. Women Workers in the Unorganized Sector: The Calcutta Experience. 208p. 1985. pap. text ed. 12.95x (ISBN 0-86131-492-1, Pub. by Sangam Bks India). Apt Bks.

Banerjee, P. K. Biophysical Chemistry Metal Ions DNA: Interactions. (International Bioscience Monographs: No. 8). 1979. 10.00 (ISBN 0-88065-022-2, Pub. by Messers Today & Tomorrows Printers & Publishers India). Scholarly Pubns.

Banerjee, P. K. & Butterfield, R. Boundary Element Methods in Engineering Science. 512p. 1982. text ed. 42.00 (ISBN 0-07-084120-9). McGraw.

Banerjee, P. K. & Mukherjee, S. Developments in Boundary Element Methods, Vol. 3. 328p. 1984. 70.50 (ISBN 0-85334-253-9, I-167-84, Pub. by Elsevier Applied Sci England). Elsevier.

Banerjee, P. K. & Butterfid, R. B., eds. Developments in Boundary Element Methods, Vol. 1. 292p. 1979. 72.25 (ISBN 0-85334-845-6, Pub. by Elsevier Applied Sci England). Elsevier.

Banerjee, P. K. & Butterfield, R., eds. Developments in Soil Mechanics & Foundation Engineering, Vol. 1. (Illus.). 266p. 1984. 59.25 (ISBN 0-85334-222-9, Pub. by Elsevier Applied Sci England). Elsevier.

Banerjee, P. K. & Shaw, R. P., eds. Developments in Boundary Element Methods, Vol. 2. (Illus.). 288p. 1982. 68.50 (ISBN 0-85334-112-5, Pub. by Elsevier Applied Sci England). Elsevier.

Banerjee, Pradeep, tr. Some Post-Independence Bengali Poems. (Translated from Bengali). 8.00 (ISBN 0-89253-606-3). Ind-US Inc.

Banerjee, Projesh. Indian Ballet Dancing. (Illus.). 170p. 1983. text ed. 45.50x (ISBN 0-391-02716-6). Humanities.

Banerjee, S. Deferred Hopes: Blacks in Contemporary America. 425p. 1983. text ed. 30.50x (ISBN 0-391-02800-6, Pub. by Radiant Pub India). Humanities.

Banerjee, S., ed. see International Heat Transfer Conference, 6th, Toronto, Aug. 1978.

Banerjee, S., ed. see Specialists Meeting on Transient Two-Phase Flow, Toronto, Canada, Aug. 3-4, 1976.

Banerjee, S. K., jt. auth. see Stacey, F. D.

Banerjee, S. P. & Moitra, Shefali, eds. Communication, Identity, & Self-Expression: Essays in Memory of S. N. Ganguly. 1984. 19.95x (ISBN 0-19-561683-9). Oxford U Pr.

Banerjee, Shibnath. The Chinese Government & Politics. 175p. 1980. 9.95 (ISBN 0-940500-04-3, Pub. by Bagchi India). Asia Bk Corp.

Banerjee, Sikhar N. Rehabilitation Management of Amputees. (RML). (Illus.). 456p. 1982. lib. bdg. 51.00 (ISBN 0-683-00470-0). Williams & Wilkins.

Banerjee, Srikumar. Critical Theories & Poetic Practice in the Lyrical Ballads. 1978. Repr. of 1931 ed. lib. bdg. 30.00 (ISBN 0-8495-0427-9). Arden Lib.

--Critical Theories & Poetic Practice in the Lyric Ballads. 1931. lib. bdg. 27.50 (ISBN 0-8414-9922-5). Folcroft.

Banerjee, Sumanta. Family Planning Communication: A Critique of the Indian Programme. (Illus.). 218p. 1980. text ed. 11.50x (ISBN 0-391-02169-9). Humanities.

--India's Simmering Revolution: The Naxalite Uprising. (Asia Ser.). 348p. (Orig.). 1984. pap. 12.25 (ISBN 0-86232-038-0, Pub. by Zed Pr England). Biblio Dist.

Banerjee, Tridib & Baer, William. Beyond the Neighborhood Unit: Residential Environments & Public Policy. LC 84-11619. (Environment, Development, & Public Policy. Environmental Policy & Planning Ser.). 1984. 29.50x (ISBN 0-306-41555-0, Plenum Pr). Plenum Pub.

Banerjee, Usha. Health Administration in a Metropolis. LC 76-900457. 1976. 16.00x (ISBN 0-88386-785-0). South Asia Bks.

Banerjee, Utpal. Information Management in Government. (Illus.). 400p. 1984. text ed. 19.00x (ISBN 0-391-03088-4, Pub. by Concept India). Humanities.

Banerjee, Utpal K. Management Perspectives. (Aima-Vikas Management Ser.). ix, 233p. 1984. pap. text ed. 13.95x (ISBN 0-7069-2610-2, Pub. by Vikas India). Advent NY.

--Operational Analysis & Indian Defence. 1980. text ed. 43.00x (ISBN 0-391-01839-6). Humanities.

Banerji. Palas of Bengal. 1973. 13.25 (ISBN 0-89684-491-9). Orient Bk Dist.

Banerji, Arun. Aspects of Indo-British Economic Relations, 1858-98. (Illus.). 1982. text ed. 24.95x (ISBN 0-19-561341-4). Oxford U Pr.

Banerji, Barenya K. Towards Quiescence & Immortality. LC 80-81693. 140p. 1981. 10.00 (ISBN 0-8022-2366-4). Philos Lib.

Banerji, Dilip & Raymond, Jacque. Elements of Microprogramming. (Illus.). 416p. 1982. text ed. 37.50 (ISBN 0-13-267146-8). P-H.

Banerji, Hiran K. Henry Fielding: Playwright, Journalist & Master of the Art of Fiction, His Life & Works. LC 62-13825. 1962. Repr. of 1929 ed. 9.50x (ISBN 0-8462-0116-X). Russell.

Banerji, M. L. Orchids of Nepal. (Illus.). 135p. (Orig.). 1982. text ed. 12.50 (ISBN 0-934454-95-7). Lubrecht & Cramer.

Banerji, M. L. & Pradhan, Prabha. The Orchids of Nepal Himalaya. (Illus.). 640p. 1983. lib. bdg. 189.00 (ISBN 3-7682-1366-8). Lubrecht & Cramer.

Banerji, P. Aesthetics of Indian Folk Dance. (Illus.). 1983. text ed. 33.50x (ISBN 0-391-02913-4). Humanities.

--Erotica in Indian Dance. 171p. 1983. text ed. 44.50x (ISBN 0-391-02951-7). Humanities.

--Kathak Dance Through Ages. 168p. 1982. text ed. 50.00x (ISBN 0-391-02915-0). Humanities.

Banerji, R., jt. ed. see Elithorn, A.

Banerji, R. B. Artificial Intelligence: A Theoretical Approach. 254p. 1980. 33.50 (ISBN 0-444-00334-7). Elsevier.

Banerji, Ranan, jt. auth. see Wood, Raquel.

Banerji, S. K., ed. see Symposium at the TMS-AIME Fall Meeting, Milwaukee, Wisconsin, Sept. 16-20, 1979.

Banerji, Sanat K. Sri Aurobindo & the Future of Man: A Study in Synthesis. 208p. 1974. 7.50 (ISBN 0-89071-204-2). Matagiri.

Banes, Charles H. History of the Philadelphia Brigade: 69th, 71st, 72nd, & 106th Penna Vols. 345p. 1984. Repr. of 1876 ed. 28.50X (ISBN 0-913419-11-7). Butternut Pr.

Banes, Daniel. A Chemist's Guide to Regulatory Drug Analysis. (Illus.). 134p. 1974. 12.00 (ISBN 0-935584-05-6). Assoc Official.

--The Provocative Merchant of Venice. LC 75-28622. 1975. 9.99 (ISBN 0-686-16724-4). Malcolm Hse.

--Shakespeare, Shylock & Kabbalah. LC 78-58912. 1978. 9.99 (ISBN 0-686-10284-3); pap. 3.60 (ISBN 0-686-10285-1). Malcolm Hse.

Banes, F. Dominico. Scholastica Commentaria in Primam Partem Summae Theologicae S. Thomae Aquinatis, De Deo Uno. Urbano, Luis, ed. (Medieval Studies Reprint Ser.). (Lat. & Sp.). Repr. of 1934 ed. lib. bdg. 45.00x (ISBN 0-697-00028-1). Irvington.

Banes, Noreen. Value Painting. (Illus., Orig.). 1974. pap. 6.50 (ISBN 0-917119-03-7, 45-1007). Priscillas Pubns.

Banes, Sally. Democracy's Body: Judson Dance Theater, 1962-1964. Foster, Stephen, ed. LC 83-15920. (Studies in the Fine Arts: The Avant-Garde: No. 43). 288p. 1983. 39.95 (ISBN 0-8357-1481-0). UMI Res Pr.

Banet, B., jt. auth. see Hohmann, M.

Banet, B. A. & Davis, J. R. Data Base Management Systems: The Desk-Top Generation. Seybold, P. B., ed. 208p. 1985. 15.95 (ISBN 0-07-056325-X). McGraw.

Banet, Barbara & Rozdilsky, Mary L. What Now? A Handbook for New Parents. LC 75-17669. (Illus.). 1975. (ScribT); pap. 4.95 (ISBN 0-684-14698-3, ScribT). Scribner.

Banff Conference on Theoretical Psychology, 1st: 1965. Toward Unification in Psychology: The First Banff Conference on Theoretical Psychology. Royce, Joseph R., ed. LC 72-505050. 1970. pap. 78.50 (ISBN 0-317-08093-8, 2014393). Bks Demand UMI.

Banfield, A. F. Mammals of Canada. LC 73-92298. (Illus.). 1974. 30.00 (ISBN 0-8020-2137-9). U of Toronto Pr.

Banfield, Beryle. Black Focus on Multicultural Education. 87p. 1979. pap. 5.95x (ISBN 0-914110-12-8). Blyden Pr.

Banfield, Beryle, jt. ed. see Meyers, Ruth S.

Banfield, Beryle, jt. ed. see Myers, Ruth S.

Banfield, Carolyn E., jt. ed. see Cauffield, Joyce V.

Banfield, E. C., jt. auth. see Meyerson, Martin.

Banfield, Edward C. The Democratic Muse: Visual Arts & the Public Interest. LC 83-45250. (Twentieth Century Fund Essay Ser.). 244p. 1984. 15.95 (ISBN 0-465-01598-0). Basic.

--Political Influence. LC 60-12182. 1965. pap. text ed. 12.95 (ISBN 0-02-901590-1). Free Pr.

--The Unheavenly City Revisited: A Revision of the Unheavenly City. 1974. pap. text ed. 11.95 (ISBN 0-316-08013-6). Little.

Banfield, Edward C. & Banfield, L. F. Moral Basis of a Backward Society. LC 58-9398. 1958. 12.95 (ISBN 0-02-901520-0); pap. text ed. 9.95 (ISBN 0-02-901510-3). Free Pr.

Banfield, Edward C. & Wilson, James Q. City Politics. LC 63-19134. (Joint Center for Urban Studies Publications Ser). (Illus.). 1963. 22.50x (ISBN 0-674-13250-5). Harvard U Pr.

Banfield, L. F., jt. auth. see Banfield, Edward C.

Banfield, Stephen. Sensibility & English Song: Critical Studies of the Early 20th Century, 2 vols. 1985. Vol. I, 336p. 54.50 (ISBN 0-521-23085-3); Vol. 2, 320p. 49.50 (ISBN 0-521-30360-5). Cambridge U Pr.

Banfield, Susan. De Gaulle. (World Leaders Past & Present Ser.). (Illus.). 112p. 1985. lib. bdg. 15.95x (ISBN 0-87754-551-0). Chelsea Hse.

--Joan of Arc. (World Leaders: Past & Present Ser.). (Illus.). 112p. 1985. lib. bdg. 15.95x (ISBN 0-87754-556-1). Chelsea Hse.

Banfield, Thomas C. Industry of the Rhine: Series 1-2, 2 Vols in 1. LC 68-55470. Repr. of 1848 ed. 45.00x (ISBN 0-678-00568-0). Kelley.

--Organization of Industry. 2nd ed. LC 68-55469. Repr. of 1848 ed. 25.00x (ISBN 0-678-00964-3). Kelley.

Banfill, P. F., jt. auth. see Tattersall, G. H.

Bang & Dahlstrom. Collins Guide to Animal Tracks & Signs. 29.95 (ISBN 0-00-219633-6, Collins Pub England). Greene.

Bang, Betsy. The Old Woman & the Rice Thief. LC 76-30671. (Illus.). 32p. (gr. k-3). 1978. 11.75 (ISBN 0-688-80098-X); PLB 11.88 (ISBN 0-688-84098-1). Greenwillow.

Bang, Betsy G. Functional Anatomy of the Olfactory System in 23 Orders of Birds. (Acta Anatomica: Suppl. 58, Vol. 79). 1971. pap. 9.50 (ISBN 3-8055-1193-0). S Karger.

Bang, Gustav. Crises in European History. 3rd ed. Petersen, Arnold, tr. 1974. pap. text ed. 0.75 (ISBN 0-935534-11-3). NY Labor News.

Bang, Herman. Tina. Christopherson, Paul, tr. LC 84-12286. 224p. 1984. 18.95 (ISBN 0-485-11254-X, Pub. by Athlone Pr Ltd). Longwood Pub Group.

Bang, Im & Ryuk, Yi. Korean Folk Tales: Imps, Ghosts & Fairies. Gale, James S., tr. LC 62-21538. 1962. pap. 4.95 (ISBN 0-8048-0935-6). C E Tuttle.

Bang, Kirsten. Yougga Finds Mother Teresa: Adventures of a Beggar Boy in India. Spink, Kathryn, tr. from Fr. LC 83-4267. 176p. (Orig.). 1983. pap. 3.95 (ISBN 0-8164-2469-1, Pub. by Seabury). Winston Pr.

Bang, M. Violin Method, Bk. 4. (Illus.). 96p. 1922. pap. 8.00 (ISBN 0-8258-0252-0, 0-45). Fischer Inc NY.

Bang, Molly. Dawn. LC 83-886. 32p. (gr. 4-7). 1983. 10.25 (ISBN 0-688-02400-9); PLB 10.88 (ISBN 0-688-02404-1). Morrow.

--The Paper Crane. LC 84-13546. (Illus.). 32p. (gr. k-3). 1985. 13.00 (ISBN 0-688-04108-6); lib. bdg. 12.88 (ISBN 0-688-04109-4). Greenwillow.

Bang, Molly G. Ten, Nine, Eight. LC 81-20106. (Illus.). 24p. (ps-1). 1983. 10.25 (ISBN 0-688-00906-9); PLB 10.88 (ISBN 0-688-00907-7). Greenwillow.

--Ten, Nine, Eight. 1985. pap. 3.95 (ISBN 0-14-050543-1). Penguin.

--Tye May & the Magic Brush. LC 80-16488. (Greenwillow Read-Alone Bks.). (Illus.). 56p. (gr. 1-3). 1981. 8.75 (ISBN 0-688-80290-7); PLB 8.88 (ISBN 0-688-84290-9). Greenwillow.

--Wiley & the Hairy-Man: Adapted from an American Folk Tale. LC 75-38581. (Ready-to-Read Ser.). (Illus.). 64p. (gr. 1-4). 1976. 7.95 (ISBN 0-02-708370-5, 70837). Macmillan.

Bang, Molly Garrett. Men from the Village in the Mountains: And Other Japanese Folktales. (Illus.). 96p. (gr. 3-6). 1973. 8.95x (ISBN 0-02-708350-0). Macmillan.

Bang, N. U. Thrombosis & Atherosclerosis. (Illus.). 466p. 1981. 69.50 (ISBN 0-8151-0413-8). Year Bk Med.

Bang, N. U., ed. Thrombosis & Bleeding Disorders: Theory & Methods. 1971. 60.00 (ISBN 0-12-077750-9). Acad Pr.

Bang, W., ed. Bale's King Johan: From MS in Chatsworth Collection. (Material for the Study of the Old English Drama Ser.: No. 1, Vol. 25). pap. 24.00 (ISBN 0-317-16737-5). Kraus Repr.

--The First Part of the Tragical Reign of Selimus. LC 82-45745. (Malone Society Reprint Ser.: No. 10). Repr. of 1908 ed. 40.00 (ISBN 0-404-63010-3). AMS Pr.

--The Obscure Beggar of Bednall Green, 1659. (Materials for the Old English Drama, Ser.: Vol. 1). pap. 11.00 (ISBN 0-317-16423-6). Kraus Repr.

--The Queen or the Excellency of Her Sex, 1655. (Material for the Study of the Old English Drama Ser.: No. 1, Vol. 13). pap. 11.00 (ISBN 0-317-16735-9). Kraus Repr.

Bang, W. & Brotanek, R., eds. The King & Queens Entertainment at Richmond, 1636. (Material for the Study of the Old English Drama Ser.: No. 1, Vol. 2). pap. 11.00 (ISBN 0-317-16732-4). Kraus Repr.

--Sir Gyles Goosecappe, 1606, Pt. 1. (Material for the Study of the Old English Drama Ser.: No. 1, Vol. 26). pap. 11.00 (ISBN 0-317-16738-3). Kraus Repr.

Bang, W. & McKerrow, R. B., eds. The Enterlude of Youth, with Fragments of the Playe of Lucres & Nature. (Material for the Study of the Old English Drama Ser.: No. 1, Vol. 12). pap. 14.00 (ISBN 0-317-16734-0). Kraus Repr.

Bang, W. see Ford, John.

Bang, W., ed. see Heywood, Thomas.

Bang, W., ed. see Jonson, Ben.

Banga, Indu. Agrarian System of the Sikhs Seventeen Fifty-Nine to Eighteen Forty-Nine. 1979. 18.50x (ISBN 0-88386-758-3). South Asia Bks.

Bangdel, Lain S. The Early Sculptures of Nepal. (Illus.). 183p. 1983. Set. text ed. 75.00x (ISBN 0-7069-1436-8, Pub. by Vikas India). Advent NY.

Bange, C. D., jt. auth. see Haynes, J. H.

Bange, David W., jt. auth. see Schelin, Charles W.

Bangel, Lain S. Early Sculptures of Nepal. 225p. 1982. 100.00x (ISBN 0-7069-1436-8, Pub. by Garlandfold England). State Mutual Bk.

Bangert, Albrecht. Kleinmobel aus drei Joahrhunderten: Typen-Stile-Meister. (Illus.). 152p. (Ger.). 1978. pap. 15.00 (ISBN 3-87405-106-4, Pub. by Keyser West Germany). Seven Hills Bks.

Bangert, Ethel. Child of the Wind. (Silver Bell Ser.). 192p. (Orig.). 1982. pap. 1.95 (ISBN 0-8439-1128-X, Leisure Bks). Dorchester Pub Co.

--The Haunting Fear. 1981. 8.95 (ISBN 0-686-84676-1, Avalon). Bouregy.

Bangert, Jeff, jt. auth. see Diedrich, William M.

Bangert, V. Nuclear Magnetic Resonance Tomography: NMR Scanner Techniques & the Theory of Image Reconstruction. 1982. 88.00 (ISBN 0-9961074-8-7, Pub. by VDI W Germany). Heyden.

Bangert, William. Claude Jay & Alfonso Salmeron: Two Early Jesuits. 1985. 12.95 (ISBN 0-8294-0459-7). Loyola.

Bangert, William V. A Bibliographical Essay on the History of the Society of Jesus. Ganss, George E., ed. LC 76-12667. (Study Aids on Jesuit Topics Ser.: No. 6). 72p. 1976. pap. 1.50 (ISBN 0-912422-16-5); Smyth Sewn. pap. 2.50 (ISBN 0-912422-21-1). Inst Jesuit.

Bangerter, Lowell A. The Bourgeois Proletarian: A Study of Anna Seghers. 1982. 36.00x (ISBN 3-416-01613-0, Pub. by Bouvier Verlag Ger). State Mutual Bk.

--The Bourgeois Proletarian: A Study of Anna Seghers. (Modern German Studies: Vol. 8). 207p. 1980. 24.00x (ISBN 3-416-01613-0, Pub. by Bouvier Verlag W Germany). Benjamins North Am.

--Hugo Von Hofmannsthal. LC 76-20408. (Literature and Life Ser.). 1977. 12.95 (ISBN 0-8044-2028-9). Ungar.

Bangham, Alec D., ed. The Lipsome Letters. 1983. 32.00 (ISBN 0-12-077780-0). Acad Pr.

Bangham, Mary D. When Jesus Was Four-or Maybe Five. (Illus., Orig.). (ps). 1968. pap. 3.95 (ISBN 0-8066-0824-2, 10-7058). Augsburg.

Bangham, Ralph V. A Resurvey of the Fish Parasites of Western Lake Erie. 1972. 1.00 (ISBN 0-86727-061-6). Ohio Bio Survey.

Bangham, William. Journey into Small Groups. 72p. 1.50 (ISBN 0-318-13662-7). Brotherhood Comm.

Bangley, Bernard. Growing in His Image. LC 82-19579. 155p. 1983. pap. 3.50 (ISBN 0-87788-328-9). Shaw Pubs.

Bangley, Bernard K. Bible BASIC: Bible Games for Personal Computers. LC 83-48461. 128p. (Orig.). 1983. pap. 9.57 (ISBN 0-06-250042-2, CN 4092, HarpR). Har-Row.

--Spiritual Treasure: Paraphrases of Spiritual Classics. LC 84-61026. 144p. (Orig.). 1985. pap. 6.95 (ISBN 0-8091-2646-X). Paulist Pr.

Bangor Public Library. Bibliography of the State of Maine. 1962. 100.00 (ISBN 0-8161-0636-3, Hall Library). G K Hall.

Bangs, Carl. Arminius. rev. ed. 384p. 1985. pap. 10.95 (ISBN 0-310-29481-9, Pub. by F Asbury Pr). Zondervan.

Bangs, Carol J. The Bones of the Earth. LC 83-12128. 64p. 1983. pap. 6.95 (ISBN 0-8112-0883-4, NDP563). New Directions.

--Irreconcilable Differences. 1979. pap. 3.00 (ISBN 0-917652-18-5). Confluence Pr.

Bangs, Frank S., Jr. & Bagne, Conrad. Transferable Development Rights. (PAS Reports: No. 304). 64p. 1975. 10.00 (ISBN 0-318-13090-4). Am Plan Assn.

Bangs, Frank S., Jr., jt. ed. see Heeter, David G.

Bangs, Frank S., Jr. see Heeter, David G. & Bangs, Frank S., Jr.

Bangs, Gail. Expenditures, Staff, & Salaries of Planning Agencies, 1974. (PAS Reports: No. 299). 60p. 1974. 6.00 (ISBN 0-318-12990-6). Am Plan Assn.

Bangs, Isaac. Journal of Lieutenant Isaac Bangs, April 1 to July 29, 1776. LC 67-29021. (Eyewitness Accounts of the American Revolution Ser.: No. 1). 1968. Repr. of 1890 ed. 13.00 (ISBN 0-405-01104-0). Ayer Co Pubs.

Bangs, John K. Booming of Acre Hill & Other Reminiscences of Urban & Suburban Life. facsimile ed. LC 79-98558. (Short Story Index Reprint Ser.). 1900. 18.00 (ISBN 0-8369-3132-7). Ayer Co Pubs.

--The Cheery Way: A Bit of Verse for Every Day. 1980. Repr. of 1910 ed. lib. bdg. 35.00 (ISBN 0-89984-075-2). Century Bookbindery.

--Dreamers, a Club. facsimile ed. LC 72-98559. (Short Story Index Reprint Ser.). 1899. 18.00 (ISBN 0-8369-3133-5). Ayer Co Pubs.

--The Enchanted Type-Writer. FAcsimile ed. LC 77-104410. lib. bdg. 11.00 (ISBN 0-8398-0150-5); pap. text ed. 5.95x (ISBN 0-89197-746-5). Irvington.

--Enchanted Typewriter. facsimile ed. LC 73-94702. (Short Story Index Reprint Ser.). 1899. 17.00 (ISBN 0-8369-3080-0). Ayer Co Pubs.

--Ghosts I Have Met. 1971. pap. 4.95 (ISBN 0-87877-005-4, P-5). Newcastle Pub.

--Ghosts I Have Met & Others. (The Works of John Kendrick Bangs Ser.). 191p. 1985. Repr. of 1902 ed. lib. bdg. 29.00 (ISBN 0-932051-12-X, Pub. by Am Repr Serv). Am Biog Serv.

--Ghosts I Have Met, & Some Others. LC 80-19172. 191p. 1980. Repr. of 1971 ed. lib. bdg. 14.95x (ISBN 0-89370-605-1). Borgo Pr.

--A House-Boat on the Styx. (The Works of John Kendrick Bangs Ser.). 171p. Repr. of 1895 ed. lib. bdg. 29.00 (ISBN 0-932051-13-8, Pub by Am Repr Serv). Am Biog Serv.

--A Houseboat on the Styx. Repr. lib. bdg. 12.95x (ISBN 0-89190-625-8, Pub. by River City Pr). Amereon Ltd.

--Houseboat on the Styx. LC 71-112788. (BCL Ser. II). 1970. Repr. of 1899 ed. 5.00 (ISBN 0-404-00496-2). AMS Pr.

--A Houseboat on the Styx. LC 78-131616. 171p. 1899. Repr. 4.00x (ISBN 0-403-00503-5). Scholarly.

--Little Book of Christmas. facs. ed. LC 77-116933. (Short Story Index Reprint Ser). (Illus.). 1912. 17.00 (ISBN 0-8369-3435-0). Ayer Co Pubs.

--Mantel-Piece Minstrels, & Other Stories. facs. ed. LC 78-85689. (Short Story Index Reprint Ser.). 1896. 13.00 (ISBN 0-8369-3030-4). Ayer Co Pubs.

--Mister Bonaparte of Corsica. LC 70-166657. (Illus.). 1971. Repr. of 1895 ed. 19.00 (ISBN 0-403-01416-6). Scholarly.

--Mister Munchausen. facs. ed. LC 78-81261. (Short Story Index Reprint Ser.). 1901. 17.00 (ISBN 0-8369-3013-4). Ayer Co Pubs.

--Over the Plum Pudding. facs. ed. LC 70-86136. (Short Story Index Reprint Ser.). 1901. 18.00 (ISBN 0-8369-3040-1). Ayer Co Pubs.

--Paste Jewels. facsimile ed. LC 70-96035. (Short Story Index Reprint Ser.). 1897. 17.00 (ISBN 0-8369-3081-9). Ayer Co Pubs.

--Pursuit of the House-Boat. LC 79-89550. Repr. of 1897 ed. 6.00 (ISBN 0-404-00497-0). AMS Pr.

--Pursuit of the Houseboat. Repr. lib. bdg. 13.95 (ISBN 0-89190-626-6, Pub. by River City Pr). Amereon Ltd.

--Pursuit of the Houseboat. 1897. 5.00x (ISBN 0-403-00474-8). Scholarly.

--R. Holmes & Co. Being the Remarkable Adventure of Raffles Holmes. LC 78-91073. (The American Humorists Ser.). Repr. of 1906 ed. lib. bdg. 37.50 (ISBN 0-8398-0151-3). Irvington.

--Rebellious Heroine. 1973. Repr. of 1896 ed. 12.50 (ISBN 0-8274-1491-9). R West.

--The Water Ghost & Others. 1972. lib. bdg. 24.00 (ISBN 0-8422-8005-7); pap. text ed. 8.95x (ISBN 0-8290-0677-X). Irvington.

Bangs, John K., ed. Potted Fiction: Being a Series of Extracts from the World's Best Sellers, Put up in Thin Slices for Hurried Consumers. facsimile ed. LC 70-178436. (Short Story Index Reprint Ser.). Repr. of 1908 ed. 12.00 (ISBN 0-8369-4036-9). Ayer Co Pubs.

Bangs, John K., ed. see Witherup, Anne W.

Bangs, Lester & Ochs, Michael. Rock Secrets. (Illus.). 192p. (Orig.). 1982. pap. 9.95 cancelled (ISBN 0-933328-45-1). Delilah Bks.

Bangs, Lester, jt. auth. see Nelson, Paul.

Bangs, Merwin, & Co., ed. Catalogue of Books on Hermetic Philosophy: The E. A. Hitchcock Collection. pap. 3.95 (ISBN 0-916411-33-8). Alchemical Pr.

Bangs, Richard & Kallen, Christian. Rivergods: Exploring the World's Great Wild Rivers. LC 85-2147. (Illus.). 224p. 1985. 37.50 (ISBN 0-87156-845-4). Sierra.

--Rivergods: Exploring the World's Great Wild Rivers. LC 85-2147. (Illus.). 224p. 1985. 37.50 (ISBN 0-87156-845-4). Sierra.

Bangs, Tina E. Language & Learning Disorders of the Pre-Academic Child: With Curriculum Guide. 2nd ed. (Illus.). 304p. 1982. 29.95 (ISBN 0-13-523001-2). P-H.

Bangura, Yusuf. Britain & Commonwealth Africa: The Politics of Economic Relations, 1951-75. LC 82-62265. 256p. 1983. 27.00 (ISBN 0-7190-0854-9, Pub. by Manchester Univ Pr). Longwood Pub Group.

Banham, Joanna & Harris, Jennifer, eds. William Morris & the Middle Ages. LC 84-15494. (Illus.). 240p. 1984. (Pub. by Manchester Univ Pr); pap. 10.50 (ISBN 0-7190-1721-1). Longwood Pub Group.

Banham, Katharine M., tr. see Chauvin, Remy.

Banham, Martin. African Theatre Today. 103p. 1976. pap. 8.50. Wesleyan U Pr.

Banham, Martin, jt. auth. see Hodgson, John.

Banham, Rayner. Los Angeles. 1973. pap. 6.95 (ISBN 0-14-021178-0, Pelican). Penguin.

Banham, Reyner. The Age of the Masters: A Personal View of Modern Architecture. LC 74-25276. (Icon Editions Ser.). (Illus.). 176p. 1975. 17.50i (ISBN 0-06-430369-1, HarpT); pap. 11.95 (ISBN 0-06-430064-1, IN-64). Har-Row.

--Architecture of the Well-Tempered Environment. LC 69-13119. (Illus.). 1969. 8.95x (ISBN 0-226-03695-2). U of Chicago Pr.

--Architecture of the Well-Tempered Environment. LC 69-13119. (Illus.). 296p. 1973. pap. 8.95 (ISBN 0-226-03696-0, P498, Phoen). U of Chicago Pr.

--The Architecture of the Well-Tempered Environment. 2nd, rev. ed. LC 84-156. (Illus.). 296p. 1984. lib. bdg. 30.00x (ISBN 0-226-03697-9); pap. 12.50 (ISBN 0-226-03698-7). U of Chicago Pr.

--The Architecture of Yorke Rosenberg Mardall 1944-1972. 128p. 1980. 40.00x (ISBN 0-85331-340-7, Pub. by Lund Humphries England). State Mutual Bk.
--Scenes in America Deserta. LC 82-3262. (Illus.). 228p. 1984. (Peregrine Smith); pap. 6.95 (ISBN 0-87905-095-0). Gibbs M Smith.
--Theory & Design in the First Machine Age. 340p. 1980. pap. 9.95 (ISBN 0-262-52058-3). MIT Pr.
Banham, Reyner, jt. auth. see Suzuki, Hiroyuki.
Banham, Reyner, et al. Buffalo Architecture: A Guide. (Illus.). 352p. 1981. 25.00 (ISBN 0-262-02172-2); pap. 9.95 (ISBN 0-262-52063-X). MIT Pr.
Banhidi, Zoltan, et al. Learn Hungarian. 1965. text ed. 22.00x (ISBN 963-17-0971-X). Intl Learn Syst.
Banica, Ronald J. Alaska Tokans. LC 78-54976. (Illus.). 208p. write for info. (ISBN 0-918492-03-3). TAMS.
Banik, Allan E. & Wade, Carlson. Your Water & Your Health. LC 81-81289. (Pivot Original Health Bks.). 128p. 1974. pap. 2.95 (ISBN 0-87983-073-5). Keats.
Banim, John & Banim, Michael. The Boyne Water: A Tale, 3 vols. in 2. LC 79-8229. Repr. of 1826 ed. 84.50 set (ISBN 0-404-61761-1). AMS Pr.
--The Croppy: A Tale of 1798, 3 vols. in 2. LC 79-8230. Repr. of 1828 ed. 84.50 set (ISBN 0-404-61765-4). AMS Pr.
Banim, Michael, jt. auth. see Banim, John.
Banin, A., ed. see Soil Chemistry, Soil Fertility & Soil Clay Mineralogy Commissions of the International Society of Soil Science, 13-18 July 1976, Jerusalem.
Banis, Carolyn S., jt. auth. see Shipley, Kenneth G.
Banis, V. J. The Earth & All It Holds. 416p. 1981. pap. 2.95 (ISBN 0-449-24459-8, GM). Fawcett.
--San Antone. 349p. 1985. 15.95 (ISBN 0-87795-683-9). Arbor Hse.
--This Splendid Earth. 1979. pap. 2.25 (ISBN 0-449-23835-0, Crest). Fawcett.
Banis, William J., jt. auth. see Krannich, Ronald L.
Banisadr, Abolhassan. The Fundamental Principles & Precepts of Islamic Government. Ghanoonparvar, Mohammed R., tr. from Persian. LC 81-82634. 120p. (Orig.). 1981. pap. 5.95 (ISBN 0-939214-01-6). Mazda Pubs.
Banish, Roslyn. I Want to Tell You About My Baby. LC 81-16489. (Illus.). 56p. (Orig.). (gr. k-3). 1982. pap. 5.95 (ISBN 0-914728-35-0). Wingbow Pr.
Banister, David. Rural Transport & Planning: A Bibliography with Abstracts. 446p. 1985. 50.00x (ISBN 0-7201-1692-9). Mansell.
--Transport Mobility & Deprivation in Inter-Urban Areas. 212p. 1980. text ed. 37.95x (ISBN 0-566-00307-4). Gower Pub Co.
Banister, David & Hall, Peter, eds. Transport & Public Policy Planning. (Illus.). 464p. 1981. 43.00x (ISBN 0-7201-1580-9). Mansell.
Banister, John. The Historie of Man. LC 74-26164. (English Experience Ser.: No. 122). (Illus.). 250p. 1969. Repr. of 1578 ed. 42.00 (ISBN 90-221-0122-3). Walter J Johnson.
--A Needfull, New & Necessarie Treatise of Chyrugerie. LC 73-171732. (English Experience Ser.: No. 300). 276p. Repr. of 1575 ed. 22.00 (ISBN 90-221-0300-5). Walter J Johnson.
Banister, Judith. China's Changing Population. 1986. price not set. Stanford U Pr.
Banister, Judith & Thapa, Shyam. The Population Dynamics of Nepal. LC 81-19444. (Papers of the East-West Population Institute Ser.: No. 78). vii, 119p. (Orig.). 1981. pap. text ed. 2.50 (ISBN 0-86638-013-2). E W Center HI.
--The Population Dynamics of Nepal. 120p. 1981. 12.00 (ISBN 0-318-17078-7, 49). Am-Nepal Ed.
--The Population Dynamics of Nepal: Extensive & Thorough. 120p. 1981. 12.00 (ISBN 0-318-04181-2). Am-Nepal Ed.
Banister, Manly. Making Picture Frames in Wood. LC 81-50985. (Home Craftsman Bk.). (Illus.). 128p. 1981. pap. text ed. 6.95 (ISBN 0-8069-7542-3). Sterling.
Banister, Richard. A Treatise of One Hundred & Thirteen Diseases of the Eyes. LC 79-37135. (English Experience Ser.: No. 297). 480p. Repr. of 1622 ed. 35.00 (ISBN 90-221-0297-1). Walter J Johnson.
Bank Administration Institute. Accounting & Reporting Practices of Community Banks. 40p. 1982. 30.00 (113). Bank Admin Inst.
--Acquisitions Guidelines for Small Computer Systems. 288p. 1982. 60.00 (264). Bank Admin Inst.
--An Analysis of Float in the Commercial Banking Industry. 96p. 1982. 36.00 (672). Bank Admin Inst.
--Consumer Requirements for Retail EFT in the Supermarket. 23p. 1977. 10.00 (642). Bank Admin Inst.
--The Costs & Benefits of Participation in the Treasury's Direct Deposit Program, 4 Vols. Incl. Vol. 1. Summary of the Study. 24p. 10.00 (675); Vol. 2. The Cost Difference Between Receiving a Social Security Check & a Direct Deposit Payment. 72p. 15.00 (676); Vol. 3. Customer Assessment of the Treasury's Direct Deposit Program & the Program's Effect on Account Balances. 88p. 15.00 (677); Vol. 4. Financial Institution Assessment of the Treasury's Direct Deposit Program. 72p. 15.00 (678). 1981. 45.00 (679). Bank Admin Inst.
--EDP Facility Accounting, 2 Vols. 1975. Vol. 1: Implementation; 205 pp. 50.00 (630); Vol. 2: Technical Foundations; 191 pp. 40.00 (631). Bank Admin Inst.
--Exception Item Recommendations. 56p. 1978. 14.00 (649). Bank Admin Inst.
--Internal Auditing in the Banking Industry, 3 vols. Incl. Vol. 1. Audit Principles & Methods. 136p. 1984 (237); Vol. 2. Auditing Basic Bank Functions, Assets. 126p. 1978 (238); Vol. 3. Auditing Basic Bank Functions--Liabilities & Other Specialized Services. 120p. 1979 (239). 20.00 ea. Bank Admin Inst.
--Security & Reliability in Electronic Systems for Payments. 108p. 1983. 20.00 (668). Bank Admin Inst.
Bank Administration Management. Contemporary Issues in Cash Management, 1980-1983. Set. 100.00 (722); member 60.00. Bank Admin Inst.
Bank, Adrianne, et al. A Practical Guide to Program Planning: A Teaching Models Approach. LC 81-959. (Orig.). 1981. pap. 16.95x (ISBN 0-8077-2641-9). Tchrs Coll.
Bank, B. & Guddat, J., eds. Non-Linear Parametric Optimization. 224p. 1983. 29.95 (ISBN 0-8176-1375-7). Birkhauser.
Bank, Caryl L., jt. auth. see Feingold, Barbara A.
Bank, David, ed. A Chronological & Occupational Index to the Dictionary of National Biography. 976p. 1985. 90.00 (ISBN 0-19-865209-7). Oxford U Pr.
Bank, Dena C. How Things Get Done: The Nitty-Gritty of Parliamentary Procedure. LC 79-1287. (Citizens' Handbook Ser.). 95p. 1984. 7.95 (ISBN 0-87249-378-4). U of SC Pr.
Bank, H., et al, eds. Patent Information & Documentation in Western Europe. 268p. 1981. lib. bdg. 34.00 (ISBN 3-598-10158-9). K G Saur.
Bank, Ira M. Community Careering Gamebook. 59p. (gr. 3-6). 1983. wkbk. 2.00 (ISBN 0-912578-15-7). Chron Guide.
--Community Careering Guidebook. new ed. 16p. 1974. pap. 3.00 (ISBN 0-912578-14-9). Chron Guide.
--Curriculum Careering Gamebook. (Illus.). 60p. (gr. 4-6). 1978. Repr. 2.00 (ISBN 0-912578-16-5). Chron Guide.
--Curriculum Careering Guidebook. 31p. (Orig.). (gr. 4-6). 1974. pap. 3.00 (ISBN 0-912578-17-3). Chron Guide.
--World of Workers. rev. ed. 80p. (gr. 2-3). 1981. pap. 2.75 (ISBN 0-912578-13-0). Chron Guide.
Bank, Jodrell, jt. auth. see Lovell, Bernard.
Bank, John. Outdoor Development for Managers. LC 84-18704. 196p. 1985. text ed. 35.50x (ISBN 0-566-02440-3). Gower Pub Co.
Bank, John & Jones, Ken. Worker Directors Speak. 102p. 1977. text ed. 19.50x (ISBN 0-566-02074-2). Gower Pub Co.
Bank, Mirra. Anonymous Was a Woman. 1979. 19.95 (ISBN 0-312-04185-3); pap. 10.95 (ISBN 0-312-04186-1). St Martin.
Bank of England. The Development & Oppurtunity of Monetary Policy. 1984. 29.95x (ISBN 0-19-877234-3); pap. 13.95 (ISBN 0-19-877233-5). Oxford U Pr.
--The Economics of Pension Arrangements: Papers Presented at the 20th Meeting of the Panel of Academic Consultants on 4 March, 1983. (Bank of England, Panel Paper Ser.: No. 20). pap. 20.00 (ISBN 0-317-28089-9, 2022521). Bks Demand UMI.
Bank of Ireland Centre for Co-op Studies, 1983, ed. see Linehan, Mary & Tucker, Vincent.
Bank, Stanley. Strange Creatures of the Desert. LC 83-60112. (Strange but True Ser.). 1983. 10.00 (ISBN 0-382-06692-8). Silver.
Bank, Stanley, jt. auth. see Swinburne, Laurence.
Bank, Stephen P. & Kahn, Michael D. The Sibling Bond. LC 81-68401. 1982. 16.95 (ISBN 0-465-07818-4). Basic.
--The Sibling Bond. LC 81-68401. 363p. 1983. pap. 10.95 (ISBN 0-465-07819-2, CN-5106). Basic.
Bank, Steven C. Winning the Battle of the Experts: An Expert Witness' Point of View. LC 83-151861. Date not set. price not set. Natl Prac Inst.
Bank Street College of Education. Animals, Animals, Animals: At Home - In the Circus - At the Zoo. (Bunny Bks.). (Illus.). 64p. (ps-k). 1985. pap. 2.95 (ISBN 0-8120-3610-7). Barron.
--One to Ten More Counting Fun. (Bunny Bks.). (Illus.). 64p. (ps-k). 1985. 2.95 (ISBN 0-8120-3614-X). Barron.
--Voyage of the Mimi. (Illus.). 160p. (gr. 4-7). 1984. 9.95 (ISBN 0-03-000753-4); pap. write for info. (ISBN 0-03-000943-X). HR&W.
Bank Street College of Education, jt. auth. see Brenner, Barbara.
Bank Street College of Education, jt. auth. see Oppenheim, Joanne F.
Bank Street College of Education, et al. Raising a Confident Child. LC 84-42706. 1985. pap. 7.95 (ISBN 0-394-72719-3). Pantheon.
Bank Street College of Education Editors. ABC Come Play with Me. (Bunny Bks.). (Illus.). 64p. (ps-k). 1985. 2.95 (ISBN 0-8120-3617-4). Barron.
--All Around the House. (Bunny Bks.). (Illus.). 64p. (ps-k). Date not set. 2.95 (ISBN 0-8120-3613-1). Barron.
--All Around the Neighborhood. (Bunny Bks.). (Illus.). 64p. (ps-k). 1985. 2.95 (ISBN 0-8120-3612-3). Barron.
--Get Ready to Read. (Bunny Bks.). (Illus.). 64p. (ps-k). 1985. 2.95 (ISBN 0-8120-3616-6). Barron.
--It's about Time: Play Time - Work Time - Learning Time. (Bunny Bks.). (Illus.). 64p. (ps-k). 1985. 2.95 (ISBN 0-8120-3611-5). Barron.
--One, Two, Three Come Count with Me. (Bunny Bks.). (Illus.). 64p. (ps-k). 1985. 2.95 (ISBN 0-8120-3615-8). Barron.
Bank, Ted, ed. Readings in Anthropology: People of the Bering Sea. 1971. pap. text ed. 6.95x (ISBN 0-8422-0137-8). Irvington.
Banka, Vidyas, jt. auth. see Helfant, Richard H.
Banker, B. Q., jt. auth. see Engel, A.
Banker, D. D. Modern Practice in Immunization. rev. 3rd ed. xii, 384p. 1980. pap. text ed. 12.95 (ISBN 0-86590-007-8, Pub. by Popular Prakashan India). Apt Bks.
Banker, G. & Rhodes, C. Modern Pharmaceutics. (Drugs & the Pharmaceutical Sciences Ser.: Vol. 7). 1979. 95.00 (ISBN 0-8247-6833-7). Dekker.
Banker, Gilbert S. & Chalmers, Robert K., eds. Pharmaceutics & Pharmacy Practice. (Illus.). 421p. 1981. text ed. 32.50 (ISBN 0-397-50483-7, 65-06240, Lippincott Medical). Lippincott.
Banker, John, et al. Bahnar Dictionary. 202p. (Orig., Bahnar.). 1979. pap. 9.00x (ISBN 0-88312-997-3); microfiche (3) 3.80 (ISBN 0-88312-933-7). Summer Inst Ling.
Banker, John, et al see Linguistic Circle of Saigon & Summer Institute of Linguistics.
Bankes, J. & Kerridge, E. The Early Records of the Bankes Family at Winstanley. 1973. 19.00 (ISBN 0-7190-1158-2, Pub. by Manchester Univ Pr). Longwood Pub Group.
Bankes, James L. Clinical Ophthalmology: A Text & Colour Atlas. LC 81-68264. (Illus.). 125p. 1983. pap. text ed. 17.50 (ISBN 0-443-02157-0). Churchill.
Bankhage, Hilman R. & Baldridge, C. Le Roy. I Was There! with the Yanks in France. LC 74-147680. (Library of War & Peace; Artists on War). 1972. lib. bdg. 46.00 (ISBN 0-8240-0437-X). Garland Pub.
Banki, Judith H. What Viewers Should Know about the Oberammergau Passion Play. 20p. 1980. pap. 1.50 (ISBN 0-87495-024-4). Am Jewish Comm.
Banki, L. Bioassay of Pesticides in the Laboratory. 1978. casebound 34.50 (ISBN 0-9960000-2-X, Pub. by Akademiai Kaido Hungary). Heyden.
Bankier, Joanna & Lashgari, Deirdre. Women Poets of the World. 416p. 1983. pap. text ed. write for info. (ISBN 0-02-305720-3). Macmillan.
Bankier, Joanna, et al, eds. The Other Voice. 1976. pap. 5.95 (ISBN 0-393-04421-1). Norton.
Banking Law Journal Editorial Board. Federal Income Taxation of Banks & Financial Institutions: Cumulative Supplementation. 5th ed. LC 77-29770. 1978. 96.00 (ISBN 0-88262-161-0). Warren.
Banking Law Journal Editors, ed. Banking Law Journal Digest: Annual Supplement, 2 vols. 7th ed. 1982. Set. 96.00 (ISBN 0-88262-752-X). Warren.
Banko, Winston E. The Trumpeter Swan: Its History, Habits, & Population in the United States. LC 80-12533. (Illus.). x, 214p. 1980. pap. 5.95 (ISBN 0-8032-6057-1, BB 731, Bison). U of Nebr Pr.
Bankoff, G. & Afgan, N. Heat Transfer in Nuclear Reactor. 1982. 95.00 (ISBN 0-07-003601-2). McGraw.
Bankoff, S. G., ed. Topics in Two-phase Heat Transfer & Flow: Presented at the Winter Annual Meeting of ASME, San Francisco, CA, Dec. 10-15, 1978. LC 78-68087. pap. 59.80 (ISBN 0-317-08175-6, 2013876). Bks Demand UMI.
Bankoff, S. G., jt. ed. see Chen, J. C.
Bankoff, S. G., jt. ed. see Jones, O. C., Jr.
Bankoff, S. George & Afgan, Naim H., eds. Heat Transfer in Nuclear Reactor Safety. (International Centre for Heat & Mass Transfer Ser.). (Illus.). 964p. 1982. text ed. 115.00 (ISBN 0-89116-223-2). Hemisphere Pub.
Bankowski, Zenon, jt. ed. see Mungham, Geoff.
Banks. Feminism & Family Planning in Victorian England. 154p. 1982. 39.00x (ISBN 0-85323-281-4, Pub. by Liverpool Univ England). State Mutual Bk.
--Killey's Fractures of the Middle Third of the Facial Skeleton. 4th ed. (Dental Practioner Handbook: No. 3). (Illus.). 104p. 1983. text ed. 14.50 (ISBN 0-7236-0625-0). PSG Pub Co.
--Multiethnic Education: Theory & Practice. 300p. 1981. text ed. 20.00 (ISBN 0-205-07293-3, 2373009); pap. text ed. 18.16 O.P. (ISBN 0-205-07300-X, 2372932). Allyn.
Banks, A. G. & Schofield, R. B. Brindley at Wet Earth Colliery. LC 68-8316. (Illus.). 1968. 19.95x (ISBN 0-678-05578-5). Kelley.
Banks, Ann. First-Person America. LC 80-7660. (Illus.). 320p. 1980. 13.95 (ISBN 0-394-41397-0). Knopf.
--First-Person America. LC 81-40092. (Illus.). 320p. 1981. pap. 5.95 (ISBN 0-394-74796-8, Vin). Random.
Banks, Ann & Evans, Nancy. Goodbye, House. (Illus.). 64p. (gr. 2-6). 1980. pap. 7.95 (ISBN 0-517-53907-1, Harmony). Crown.
Banks, Arthur. Atlas of Ancient & Medieval Warfare. rev. ed. (Illus.). 160p. 1982. 25.00 (ISBN 0-88254-698-8). Hippocrene Bks.
--A World Atlas of Military History: 1860-1945. LC 73-90857. (Illus.). 200p. 1978. 22.50 (ISBN 0-88254-454-3). Hippocrene Bks.
Banks, Arthur S. Cross-National Data Analysis. (CISE Learning Package Ser.: No. 3). (Illus.). 99p. (Orig.). 1974. pap. text ed. 4.00x (ISBN 0-936876-21-2). Learn Res Intl Stud.
--Political Handbook of the World: 1982-1983. 1983. 49.95 (ISBN 0-07-003631-4). McGraw.
Banks, Arthur S., ed. Political Handbook of the World: 1981. 407p. 1981. 49.95 (ISBN 0-07-003629-2). McGraw.
Banks, Arthur S., et al. Economic Handbook of the World: 1981. 608p. 1981. 49.95 (ISBN 0-07-003691-8). McGraw.
--Economic Handbook of the World: 1982. 640p. 1983. 49.95 (ISBN 0-07-003692-6). McGraw.
--Political Handbook of the World: 1984-1985. (Illus.). 768p. 1985. 79.95x (ISBN 0-933199-00-7). CSA Pubn.
Banks-Baldwin Law Publishing Company Staff. Kentucky Attorney General Opinions. 1985p. (Individual vols. 1968-1972, 85.00 ea.). Nineteen Eighty-Five subscription. 75.00 (ISBN 0-8322-0124-3); Prior years available. 45.00; Full set:1968-1985. 500.00; 1984 60.00 (ISBN 0-8322-0083-2); 1983 58.00 (ISBN 0-8322-0057-3); 1982 52.00 (ISBN 0-8322-0031-X); 1978-1979 65.00 (ISBN 0-8322-0127-8); Cumulative tables & index:1968-1979. 1976-1977 60.00 (ISBN 0-8322-0128-6); Cumulative tables & index:1956-1967. 25.00 (ISBN 0-317-12298-3). Banks-Baldwin.
Banks, Bill. Alive Again! 168p. (Orig.). 1977. pap. 3.95 (ISBN 0-89228-048-4). Impact Bks MO.
Banks, Bill & Banks, Sue. Ministering to Abortion's Aftermath. 144p. (Orig.). 1982. pap. 3.95 (ISBN 0-89228-057-3). Impact Bks MO.
Banks, Bruce & Kenny, Dick. Looking at Sails. (Illus.). 143p. 1979. 12.95 (ISBN 0-914814-21-4). Sail Bks.
--Looking at Sails. 144p. 1982. 29.00x (ISBN 0-333-32070-0, Pub. by Nautical England). State Mutual Bk.
Banks, C. H., jt. auth. see Von Fraunhofer, J. A.
Banks, Carolyn. The Girls on the Row. 256p. 1983. 12.95 (ISBN 0-517-55038-5). Crown.
--The Girls on the Row. 256p. 1984. pap. 2.95 (ISBN 0-449-20558-4, Crest). Fawcett.
Banks, Carolyn, ed. see Torres, Eliseo, et al.
Banks, Charles E. English Ancestry & Homes of the Pilgrim Fathers. LC 75-39986. 187p. 1984. Repr. of 1929 ed. 12.50 (ISBN 0-317-14559-2). Genealog Pub.
--The Planters of the Commonwealth: A Study of the Emigrants & Emigration in Colonial Times. LC 67-30794. (Illus.). 231p. 1984. Repr. of 1930 ed. 15.00 (ISBN 0-8063-0018-3). Genealog Pub.
--Topographical Dictionary of 2885 English Emigrants to New England, 1620-1650. LC 63-4154. (Illus.). 295p. 1981. Repr. of 1937 ed. 17.50 (ISBN 0-8063-0019-1). Genealog Pub.
--Winthrop Fleet of 1630: An Account of the Passengers. LC 68-57951. (Illus.). 119p. 1983. Repr. of 1930 ed. 12.00 (ISBN 0-8063-0020-5). Genealog Pub.
Banks, Charles W. The Life & Times of John Calvin: With an Earnest Appeal for the Adoption of Open-Air Preaching. LC 83-45599. Date not set. Repr. of 1891 ed. 21.50 (ISBN 0-404-19867-8). Ams Pr.
Banks, Cherry A., jt. auth. see Banks, James A.
Banks, David J. Malay Kinship. LC 82-2899. (Illus.). 210p. 1983. text ed. 32.50 (ISBN 0-89727-037-1). ISHI PA.
Banks, Edwin M. & Heisey, John A. Animal Behavior. (Programmed Biology Ser.). (Illus.). 1977. pap. text ed. 6.95 (ISBN 0-88462-026-3, Ed Methods). Longman USA.
Banks, Edwin M., ed. Vertebrate Social Organization. LC 76-26571. (Benchmark Papers in Animal Behavior: Vol. 8). 1977. 67.00 (ISBN 0-12-786130-0). Acad Pr.
Banks, Emma D., ed. Original Recitations with Lesson-Talks. enl. ed. LC 79-51959. (Granger Poetry Library). 1980. Repr. of 1908 ed. 17.50x (ISBN 0-89609-176-7). Granger Bk.
Banks, Enoch M. Economics of Land Tenure in Georgia. LC 68-56647. (Columbia University, Studies in the Social Sciences Ser.: No. 58). Repr. of 1905 ed. 16.50 (ISBN 0-404-51058-2). AMS Pr.
Banks, F. Coins of Bible Days. LC 84-71643. 1985. pap. 16.00 (ISBN 0-942666-41-0). S J Durst.
Banks, F. R. The Penguin Guide to London. (Handbooks Ser.). 608p. 1984. pap. 6.95 (ISBN 0-14-070419-1). Penguin.

Banks, Ferdinand E. Bauxite & Aluminum: An Introduction to the Economics of Non-Fuel Minerals. LC 78-24632. 208p. 1979. 26.00x (ISBN 0-669-02771-5). Lexington Bks.

--The Economics of Natural Resources. LC 76-25583. (Illus.). 267p. 1976. 27.50x (ISBN 0-306-30926-2, Plenum Pr). Plenum Pub.

--The Political Economy of Coal. LC 82-48522. 288p. 1984. 29.00x (ISBN 0-669-06169-7). Lexington Bks.

--The Political Economy of Oil. LC 79-3340. 256p. 1980. 29.00x (ISBN 0-669-03402-9). Lexington Bks.

--Resources & Energy: An Economic Analysis. LC 81-47967. 368p. 1983. 36.50x (ISBN 0-669-05203-5). Lexington Bks.

Banks, Frances. Teach Them to Live: A Study oF Education in English Prisons. 304p. 1958. text ed. 30.00x (ISBN 0-8236-6370-1). Intl Univs Pr.

Banks, H. T. Modelling & Control in the Biomedical Sciences. LC 75-25771. (Lecture Notes in Biomathematics: Vol. 6). v, 114p. 1975. pap. 13.00 (ISBN 0-387-07395-7). Springer-Verlag.

Banks, Hal N. An Introduction to Psychic Studies. LC 77-85576. 140p. (Orig.). 1980. pap. 9.95 (ISBN 0-89288-023-6). Maverick.

Banks, Herman J. & Romano, Anne T. Human Relations for Emergency Response Personnel. (Illus.). 286p. 1982. pap. 29.50x (ISBN 0-398-04555-0). C C Thomas.

Banks, Iain. The Wasp Factory. 184p. 1984. 13.95 (ISBN 0-395-36296-2). HM.

Banks, J. A. The Sociology of Social Movements. (Studies in Sociology). 1972. pap. text ed. 6.50x (ISBN 0-333-13433-8). Humanities.

--Victorian Values: Secularism & the Smaller Family. 288p. 1981. 26.95x (ISBN 0-7100-0807-4). Routledge & Kegan.

Banks, J. A. & Banks, Olive. Feminism & Family Planning in Victorian England. LC 63-18387. (Studies in the Life of Women). 154p. 1972. pap. 5.95 (ISBN 0-8052-0350-8). Schocken.

Banks, J. Houston, jt. auth. see Sobel, Max A.

Banks, James. Multiethnic Education: Practices & Promises. LC 76-57300. (Fastback Ser.: No. 87). 1977. pap. 0.75 (ISBN 0-87367-087-6). Phi Delta Kappa.

Banks, James A. Education in the Eighties: Multiethnic Education. 192p. 1981. 17.95 (ISBN 0-8106-3158-X); pap. 11.95 (ISBN 0-8106-3157-1). NEA.

--Teaching Strategies for Ethnic Studies. 3rd ed. 1983. text ed. 25.72 (ISBN 0-205-07973-3, 2379732). Allyn.

--Teaching Strategies for the Social Studies: Inquiry, Valuing & Decision Making. 3rd ed. LC 84-14388. 544p. 1985. text ed. 25.95x (ISBN 0-582-28570-4). Longman.

--Teaching the Black Experience: Methods & Materials. LC 74-126641. 1970. pap. 5.95 (ISBN 0-8224-6885-9). Pitman Learning.

Banks, James A. & Banks, Cherry A. March Toward Freedom: A History of Black Americans. rev., 2nd ed. LC 77-95084. (Illus.). (gr. 7-12). 1978. pap. text ed. 9.20 (ISBN 0-8224-4406-2). Pitman Learning.

Banks, James A. & Sebesta, Sam L. We Americans: Our History & People, 2 vols. (gr. 8-12). 1982. Vol. 1. pap. text ed. 14.64 (ISBN 0-205-07580-0, 7875800); Vol. 2. pap. text ed. 14.64 (ISBN 0-205-07584-3, 7875843); tchr's. ed. 13.20; avail; avail tests. Allyn.

Banks, James A., ed. Teaching Ethnic Studies: Concepts & Strategies, 43rd Yearbook. LC 73-75298. (Illus.). 300p. 1973. 8.25 (ISBN 0-87986-000-6, 490-15278); pap. 8.25 (ISBN 0-87986-036-7, 490-15276). Nat Coun Soc Studies.

Banks, James A., et al. Education for an Open Society: 1974 Yearbook. new ed. Della-Dora, Delmo & House, James E, eds. LC 73-92149. (Illus.). 244p. 1974. text ed. 8.00 (ISBN 0-87120-016-3, 610-74012). Assn Supervision.

Banks, James E. Alfred Packer's Wilderness Cookbook. LC 70-15764. (Wild & Woolly West Ser., No. 9). (Illus., Orig.). 1969. 8.00 (ISBN 0-910584-60-5); pap. 1.50 (ISBN 0-910584-09-5). Filter.

--Naming Organic Compounds: A Programmed Introduction to Organic Chemistry. 2nd ed. LC 75-291. 1976. pap. text ed. 18.95 (ISBN 0-7216-1536-8, CBS C). SCP.

--Uncle Jim's Book of Pancakes. 2ed ed. (Wild & Woolly West Ser., No. 3). (Illus., Orig.). 1979. 8.00 (ISBN 0-910584-58-3); pap. 1.50 (ISBN 0-910584-44-3). Filter.

Banks, James W. Two Hundred Years from Good Hope. 1983. write for info. (ISBN 0-9611582-0-4). McClain.

Banks, Jane, jt. auth. see Dong, Collin.

Banks, Jane, jt. auth. see Dong, Collin H.

Banks, Jane, jt. auth. see Dong, Collin J.

Banks, Jerry & Carson, John. Discrete Event System Simulation. (Illus.). 560p. 1984. professional 24.95 (ISBN 0-13-215582-6). P-H.

Banks, Jerry & Heikes, Russell. Handbook of Tables & Graphs for the Industrial Engineer. 1984. text ed. 39.95 (ISBN 0-8359-2764-4). Reston.

Banks, Jerry & Hohenstein, Charles L., Jr. Procurement & Inventory Ordering Tables. LC 77-8663. 1978. pap. text ed. 14.50 (ISBN 0-08-021945-4). Pergamon.

Banks, Jimmy. Gavels, Grit & Glory: The Story of Billy Clayton. 1981. 15.95 (ISBN 0-89015-310-8). Eakin Pubns.

Banks, Joseph & Lysaght, Averil. The Journal of Joseph Banks in the Endeavor, 2 vols. ltd. ed. (Illus.). 1980. Set. hand bound leather 460.00 (ISBN 0-904351-05-X). Vol. 1-544 pg. Vol. 2-706 pg. Genesis Pubns.

Banks, Lacy, jt. auth. see Carson, Julius M.

Banks, Louis A. Immortal Hymns & Their Story. LC 77-75198. 1977. Repr. of 1899 ed. lib. bdg. 30.00 (ISBN 0-89341-088-8). Longwood Pub Group.

Banks, Lynn R. The Writing on the Wall. LC 81-47796. (A Charlotte Zolotow Bk.). 256p. (YA) (gr. 7 up). 1982. 10.53i (ISBN 0-06-020388-9). HarpJ.

Banks, Lynne R. The Indian in the Cupboard. LC 80-2835. (Illus.). 192p. (gr. 4). 1981. 11.95 (ISBN 0-385-17051-3). Doubleday.

--The Indian in the Cupboard. (Illus.). 192p. (gr. 4-7). 1982. pap. 2.50 (ISBN 0-380-60012-9, 70013-1, Camelot). Avon.

--Letters to My Israeli Sons: The Story of Jewish Survival. 240p. 1980. 10.95 (ISBN 0-531-09934-2). Watts.

--My Darling Villain. LC 76-58718. 240p. (gr. 7 up). 1977. 10.95 (ISBN 0-06-020392-7); PLB 10.89 (ISBN 0-06-020393-5). HarpJ.

Banks, M. M. British Calendar Customs, Scotland, Vol. III: Fixed Festivals, June to December, Inclusive, Christmas, the Yules (Index to Vols. II & III) (Folk-Lore Society London Monographs: Vol. 108). Repr. of 1942 ed. 30.00 (ISBN 0-317-16723-5). Kraus Repr.

Banks, M. M., ed. Alphabetum Narrationum: An Alphabet of Tales. (EETS, OS: Nos. 126-7). Repr. of 1905 ed. 75.00 (ISBN 0-527-00122-8). Kraus Repr.

--British Calendar Customs, Orkney & Shetland. (Folk-Lore Society London Monographs: Vol. 112). Repr. of 1946 ed. 31.00 (ISBN 0-317-16724-3). Kraus Repr.

--British Calendar Customs, Scotland, Vol. II: Fixed Festivals, The Quarters, Hogmanay, January to March, Inclusive. (Folk-Lore Society, London, Monographs: Vol. 104). pap. 21.00 (ISBN 0-317-17936-5). Kraus Repr.

--British Calendar Customs, Scotland, Vol. I: Movable Festivals, Harvest, March Ridings & Wappynshaws, Wells, Fairs. (Folk-Lore Society, London, Monographs: Vol. 100). pap. 21.00 (ISBN 0-317-17934-9). Kraus Repr.

Banks, Martha. The Call of Jesus. (Aglow Bible Study: Bk. 9). 64p. 1976. 2.95 (ISBN 0-930756-19-3, 4220-9). Aglow Pubns.

Banks, Mary M., ed. see Robert Of Thornton.

Banks, Michael. Countdown: The Complete Guide to Model Rocketry. (Illus.). 224p. (Orig.). 1985. pap. 16.95 (ISBN 0-8306-1991-7, 1991). TAB Bks.

--Second Stage Advanced Model Rocketry. Angle, Burr, ed. (Illus., Orig.). 1985. pap. 8.50 (ISBN 0-89024-057-4). Kalmbach.

Banks, Michael, ed. Conflict in World Society: A New Perspective on International Relations. LC 84-4834. 256p. 1984. 27.50 (ISBN 0-312-16229-4). St Martin.

Banks, Michael A. Understanding Science Fiction. 180p. 1982. 10.20 (ISBN 0-382-29074-7). Silver.

Banks, Michael A., jt. auth. see Cannon, Robert L.

Banks, Mike. Mountain Climbing for Beginners. 1978. pap. 3.95 (ISBN 0-8128-2447-4). Stein & Day.

Banks, Natalie N. The Golden Thread. 1979. pap. 3.50 (ISBN 0-85330-127-1). Lucis.

Banks, Nathaniel P., jt. auth. see Shattuck, Lemuel.

Banks, Olive. The Biographical Dictionary of British Feminists, Vol. I: 1800-1930. 256p. text ed. 55.00x (ISBN 0-8147-1078-6). NYU Pr.

--Faces of Feminism: A Study of Feminism As a Social Movement. 1981. 25.00x (ISBN 0-312-27952-3). St Martin.

--The Sociology of Education: A Bibliography. 139p. 1978. 24.50x (ISBN 0-8476-2247-9). Rowman.

Banks, Olive, jt. auth. see Banks, J. A.

Banks, Oliver. The Caravaggio Obsession. 1984. 14.45i (ISBN 0-316-08022-5). Little.

--The Caravaggio Obsession. large print ed. LC 84-5977. 399p. 1984. Repr. of 1984 ed. 13.95 (ISBN 0-89621-538-5). Thorndike Pr.

--The Caravaggio Obsession. 1984. pap. 2.95 (ISBN 0-451-13277-7, Sig). NAL.

--The Rembrandt Panel. 288p. 1982. pap. 2.95 (ISBN 0-523-41621-0). Pinnacle Bks.

--Watteau & the North Studies in the Dutch & Flemish Baroque Influence on French Rocco Painting. LC 76-23602. (Outstanding Dissertations in the Fine Arts Ser.). 1977. lib. bdg. 76.00 (ISBN 0-8240-2676-4). Garland Pub.

Banks, P., et al. The Biochemistry of the Tissues. 2nd ed. LC 75-26739. 493p. 1976. (Pub. by Wiley-Interscience); pap. 35.95 (ISBN 0-471-01923-2, Pub. by Wiley-Interscience). Wiley.

Banks, P. M. & Kockarts, G. Aeronomy. Incl. Pt. A. 1973. 66.00 (ISBN 0-12-077801-7); Pt. B. 1973. 67.50 (ISBN 0-12-077802-5). Acad Pr.

Banks, Pam. Denver Nuggets. (NBA Today Ser.). (Illus.). 48p. 1984. PLB 9.95 (ISBN 0-87191-975-3). Creative Ed.

--Philadelphia Seventy-Sixers. (NBA Today Ser.). (Illus.). 48p. 1984. PLB 9.95 (ISBN 0-87191-985-0). Creative Ed.

Banks, Paul, ed. see Mitchell, Donald.

Banks, Paul N. Preservation of Library Materials. 1978. pap. 1.75 (ISBN 0-911028-20-X). Newberry.

--A Selective Bibliography on the Conservation of Research Library Materials. (Orig.). pap. 10.00 (ISBN 0-911028-26-9). Newberry.

--A Selective Bibliography on the Conservation of Research Library Materials. 150p. 1981. member 8.50 (ISBN 0-686-95761-X, 5003); non-member 10.00 (ISBN 0-686-99604-6). Soc Am Archivists.

Banks, Peter A. Pancreatitis. LC 78-11341. (Topics in Gastroenterology Ser.). (Illus.). 252p. 1979. 32.50x (ISBN 0-306-40116-9, Plenum Med. Bk.). Plenum Pub.

Banks, Peter A., ed. see National Foundation for Ileitis & Colitis.

Banks, R. E. Preparation Properties & Industrial Applications of Organofluorine Compounds. (Ellis Horwood Series in Chemical Science). 352p. 1982. 89.95 (ISBN 0-470-27526-X). Halsted Pr.

Banks, R. E., ed. Fluorocarbon & Related Chemistry, Vols. 1-3. Barlow, M. G. Incl. Vol. 1. 1969-70 Literature. 1971. 38.00 (ISBN 0-85186-504-6); Vol. 2. 1971-72 Literature. 1974. 49.00 (ISBN 0-85186-514-3); Vol. 3. 1973-74 Literature. 1976. 90.00 (ISBN 0-85186-524-0, Pub. by Royal Soc Chem London). LC 72-78530. Am Chemical.

Banks, Richard C., et al. Introductory Problems in Spectroscopy. 1980. 25.95 (ISBN 0-8053-0572-6). Benjamin-Cummings.

Banks, Robert. Paul's Idea of Community: The Early House Churches in the Historical Setting. 1980. pap. 5.95 (ISBN 0-8028-1830-7). Eerdmans.

--The Tyranny of Time. LC 84-28855. 265p. 1985. pap. 6.95 (ISBN 0-87784-338-4). Inter-Varsity.

Banks, Robert F. & Stieber, Jack, eds. Multinationals, Unions, & Labor Relations in Industrialized Countries. LC 77-4463. (International Report Ser.: No. 9). 208p. 1977. 10.00 (ISBN 0-87546-064-X). ILR Pr.

Banks, Ronald F. A History of Maine: A Collection of Readings on the History of Maine 1600-1976. 4th ed. (History Ser.). 1976. pap. text ed. 16.95 (ISBN 0-8403-0020-4). Kendall-Hunt.

--Maine During the Federal & Jeffersonian Period: A Bibliographical Guide. (Maine History Biblopgraphical Guide Ser.). 1974. pap. 4.00 (ISBN 0-915592-13-4). Maine Hist.

Banks, Rosemary. Black Jewels & White Pearls. 80p. 1984. 5.95 (ISBN 0-89962-372-7). Todd & Honeywell.

Banks, Russell. Continental Drift. LC 84-48137. 416p. 1985. 17.26 (ISBN 0-06-015383-0, HarpT). Harper Row.

--Family Life. (Orig.). 1975. pap. 2.95 (ISBN 0-380-00258-2, 22855). Avon.

--The New World: Tales. LC 78-10646. 144p. 1978. pap. 5.95 (ISBN 0-252-00722-0). U of Ill Pr.

--The Relation of My Imprisonment. LC 83-17873. (Contemporary Literature Ser.: No. 19). 128p. 1984. 12.95 (ISBN 0-940650-25-8); ltd. signed edition 20.00 (ISBN 0-940650-24-X). Sun & Moon MD.

--Searching for Survivors. LC 74-24911. 153p. 1975. 7.95 (ISBN 0-914590-07-3); pap. 3.95 (ISBN 0-914590-06-5). Fiction Coll.

--Snow. LC 74-20819. 22p. 1974. pap. 2.00 (ISBN 0-914102-03-6). Bluefish.

Banks, Russell, et al. Antaeus, No. 45-46: The Autobiographical Eye. LC 70-612646. (Illus.). 320p. 1982. 12.95 (ISBN 0-88001-003-7); pap. 8.00 (ISBN 0-88001-002-9). Ecco Pr.

Banks, S. P. State-Space & Frequency Domain Methods in the Control of Distributed Parameter Systems. (IEE Topics in Control Ser.). 125p. 1983. pap. 25.00 (ISBN 0-86341-000-6, TC003). Inst Elect Eng.

Banks, S. P., ed. see IFAC Symposium, 2nd, Coventry, UK, June 1977.

Banks, Sam W. & Laufman, Harold. Atlas of Surgical Exposures of the Extremities. LC 52-12872. (Illus.). 1973. 42.00 (ISBN 0-7216-1530-9). Saunders.

Banks, Sue, jt. auth. see Banks, Bill.

Banks, Sydney. Second Chance. 146p. 1983. pap. 6.95 (ISBN 0-89769-053-2, Dist. by Caroline Hse.). Pine Mntn.

Banks, Theodore H. Milton's Imagery. LC 69-19874. (BCL Ser. II). Repr. of 1950 ed. 17.00 (ISBN 0-404-00498-9). AMS Pr.

--Wild Geese. LC 73-144741. (Yale Ser. of Younger Poets: No. 7). Repr. of 1921 ed. 18.00 (ISBN 0-404-53807-X). AMS Pr.

Banks, Theodore H., ed. see Denham, John.

Banks, Theodore H., tr. see Sophocles.

Banks, Theodore M. Distribution Law for the Practitioner. write for info. Little.

Banks, Theodore R., jt. auth. see Molnar, J. J.

Banks, Velma. Adoption: A Self-Discovery Journey. Date not set. text ed. 24.50 (ISBN 0-8290-1363-6); pap. 12.95 (ISBN 0-8290-1364-4). Irvington.

Banks, W. H., ed. Advances in Printing Science & Technology, Vol. 17. 500p. 1984. 64.95 (ISBN 0-7273-0109-8, Pentech Press London). Bowker.

Banks, William. Questions You Have Always Wanted to Ask about Tongues, but... (Illus.). 1979. pap. 2.25 (ISBN 0-89957-526-9). AMG Pubs.

Banks, William J. Applied Veterinary Histology. (Illus.). 540p. 1981. 41.00 (ISBN 0-683-00410-7). Williams & Wilkins.

--Histology & Comparative Organology: A Text-Atlas. LC 79-24569. 296p. 1980. Repr. of 1974 ed. lib. bdg. 25.50 (ISBN 0-89874-084-3). Krieger.

Banks, William K., ed. see Lanzano, Susan & Abreu, Rosendo.

Bankson, Charles A. Central Solar Heating Plants with Seasonal Storage - Europe. 186p. Date not set. pap. 24.95 (ISBN 0-317-20244-8, I-072). Solar Energy Info.

Bankson, Marjory Z. Braided Streams: Esther & a Woman's Way of Growing. LC 85-50203. (Illus.). 184p. (Orig.). 1985. pap. 8.95 (ISBN 0-931055-05-9). LuraMedia.

Bankson, N. Bankson Language Screening Test. (Illus.). 78p. 1977. pap. text ed. 27.00 (ISBN 0-8391-1126-6). Univ Park.

Bankson, Nicholas W., jt. auth. see Bernthal, John E.

Bankwitz, Philip C. Alsatian Autonomist Leaders, 1919-1947. LC 77-10665. 1978. 22.50x (ISBN 0-7006-0160-0). U Pr of KS.

--Maxime Weygand & Civil-Military Relations in Modern France. LC 67-22860. (Historical Studies: No. 81). 1967. 27.50x (ISBN 0-674-55701-8). Harvard U Pr.

Bann, David. Print Production Handbook. (Illus.). 160p. 1985. 14.95 (ISBN 0-89134-160-9). North Light Pub.

Bann, Donald R. How to Lay Ceramic & Quarry Tile. LC 81-65040. 1981. pap. 7.95 (ISBN 0-87733-816-7). Easi-Bild.

Bann, Richard W., jt. auth. see Maltin, Leonard.

Bann, Stephen. The Clothing of Clio: A Study of the Representation of History in 19th Century Britain & France. LC 83-20909. 250p. 1984. 37.50 (ISBN 0-521-25616-X). Cambridge U Pr.

Bann, Stephen, jt. auth. see Finlay, Ian H.

Banna, M. Clinical Neuroradiology. (Illus.). Date not set. text ed. 50.00 (ISBN 0-8391-1809-0, 17523). Univ Park.

Banna, M., jt. auth. see Hankinson, John.

Banna, Mohamed M. Clinical Radiology of the Spine & the Spinal Cord. (Illus.). 544p. 1985. text ed. 125.00 (ISBN 0-8391-1917-8, 20303). Univ Park.

Bannan, John F. & Bannan, Rosemary S. Law, Morality, & Vietnam: The Peace Militants & the Courts. LC 73-16522. pap. 63.30 (ISBN 0-317-07958-1, 2015809). Bks Demand UMI.

Bannan, Rosemary S., jt. auth. see Bannan, John F.

Bannard, Darby & Johnson, Barbara. Scrimshaw. (Illus.). 288p. cancelled (ISBN 0-8038-6783-2). Hastings.

Bannasch, P. Cytoplasm of Hepatocytes During Carcinogenesis: Electron & Lightmicroscopial Investigations of the Nitrosomorphiline-Intoxicated Rat Liver. LC 69-18017. (Recent Results in Cancer Research: Vol. 19). (Illus.). 1968. 26.00 (ISBN 0-387-04308-X). Springer-Verlag.

Bannatyne, Alexander. Language, Reading & Learning Disabilities: Psychology, Neuropsychology, Diagnosis & Remediation. (Illus.). 800p. 1976. 81.00x (ISBN 0-398-02182-1). C C Thomas.

Bannatyne, Alexander & Bannatyne, Maryl. How Your Children Can Learn to Live a Rewarding Life: Behavior Modification for Parents & Teachers. (Illus.). 134p. 1973. 14.75x (ISBN 0-398-02572-X). C C Thomas.

Bannatyne Club. Adversaria. LC 78-158230. (Bannatyne Club, Edinburgh. Publications: No. 120). Repr. of 1867 ed. 17.50 (ISBN 0-404-52879-1). AMS Pr.

--Album of the Bannatyne Club. LC 72-160005. (Bannatyne Club, Edinburgh. Publications: No. 117). Repr. of 1867 ed. 15.00 (ISBN 0-404-52875-9). AMS Pr.

--Bannatyne Garlands. Nos. 1-10. LC 79-38498. (Bannatyne Club, Edinburgh. Publications: No. 118). 45.00 (ISBN 0-404-52877-5). AMS Pr.

--The Bannatyne Miscellany, 3 vols. Incl. Vol. 1. Scott, W., ed; Vols. 2-3. Laing, D., ed. LC 71-144412. (Bannatyne Club, Edinburgh. Publications: No. 19). Repr. of 1827 ed. 70.00 set (ISBN 0-404-52720-5). AMS Pr.

--Lists of Members & the Rules. LC 76-160006. (Bannatyne Club, Edinburgh. Publications: No. 116). Repr. of 1867 ed. 21.50 (ISBN 0-404-52874-0). AMS Pr.

--Publications of the Bannatyne Club, Nos. 1-120 & 8 Extra Vols. Repr. of 1875 ed. Set. write for info. (ISBN 0-404-52700-0). AMS Pr.

--Royal Letters, Charters, & Tracts. LC 78-174971. (Bannatyne Club, Edinburgh. Publications: No. 119). Repr. of 1867 ed. 31.00 (ISBN 0-404-52878-3). AMS Pr.

Bannatyne, George. Antient Scottish Poems. Dalrymple, David, ed. LC 78-67521. (Scottish Enlightenment Ser.). Repr. of 1770 ed. 38.50 (ISBN 0-404-17121-4). AMS Pr.

--The Bannatyne Manuscript, 4 vols. Ritchie, W. Tod, ed. Repr. of 1933 ed. Set. 120.00 (ISBN 0-384-03355-5). Johnson Repr.

--The Bannatyne Manuscript Written in Time of Pest, 4 Vols. Set. 155.00 (ISBN 0-384-03364-4). Johnson Repr.

--Poems. LC 78-144411. (Bannatyne Club, Edinburgh. Publications: No. 4a). Repr. of 1824 ed. 12.50 (ISBN 0-404-52705-1). AMS Pr.

Bannatyne, Jack. The Mountain Eagles. 192p. 1986. pap. 2.95 (ISBN 0-931773-34-2). Critics Choice Paper.

Bannatyne, Maryl, jt. auth. see Bannatyne, Alexander.

Bannatyne, Richard. Memorials of Transactions in Scotland. Pitcairn, Robert, ed. LC 73-161738. (Bannatyne Club, Edinburgh. Publications: No. 51). Repr. of 1836 ed. 47.50 (ISBN 0-404-52761-2). AMS Pr.

Banner, Arthur S. & Addington, W. W., eds. Management of Common Pulmonary Disorders. 320p. 1980. 49.50 (ISBN 0-8151-0091-4). Year Bk Med.

Banner, Donald W., ed. Intellectual Property Law Review, 1983. LC 79-88703. (Intellectual Property Library). 450p. 1984. 65.00 (ISBN 0-87632-149-X). Boardman.

Banner, F. T. & Collins, M. B. Northwest European Shelf Seas: The Sea-Bed & the Sea in Motion, Vol. 2, Physical & Chemical Oceanography & Physical Resources. (Oceanography Ser.: Vol. 24B). 338p. 1980. 95.75 (ISBN 0-444-41739-7). Elsevier.

Banner, F. T. & Lord, A. R., eds. Aspects of Micropalaeontology. (Illus.). 362p. 1982. text ed. 60.00x (ISBN 0-04-562003-2). Allen Unwin.

Banner, F. T., et al, eds. The North-West European Shelf Seas: The Sea-Bed & the Sea in Motion, Vol. 1, Geology & Sedimentology. LC 78-14524. (Elsevier Oceanography Ser.: Vol. 24b). 300p. 1979. 74.50. Elsevier.

Banner, Hubert S. Calamities of the World. LC 74-159880. (Tower Bks.). (Illus.). 1971. Repr. of 1932 ed. 40.00x (ISBN 0-8103-3918-8). Gale.

Banner, James M. The Anatomy of Teacher Institutes: A Design for Professional Development. 30p. 1985. pap. 4.95 (ISBN 0-931989-25-6). Coun Basic Educ.

Banner, Lois. Elizabeth Cady Stanton: A Radical for Woman's Rights. (Library of American Biography). 1980. 12.95 (ISBN 0-316-08031-4). Little.

Banner, Lois W. American Beauty. LC 82-4738. 352p. 1983. 20.00 (ISBN 0-394-51923-X). Knopf.

--American Beauty. LC 84-2562. (Illus.). x, 372p. 1984. pap. 9.95 (ISBN 0-226-03700-2). U of Chicago Pr.

--Elizabeth Cady Stanton: A Radical for Women's Rights. (Library of American Biography). 189p. 1980. pap. text ed. 6.95 (ISBN 0-316-08030-6). Little.

--Women in Modern America: A Brief History. 2nd ed. 294p. 1984. pap. text ed. 12.95 (ISBN 0-15-596196-9, HC). HarBraceJ.

Banner, Mary. Miss Angelina Adorable. LC 28-17283. (Illus.). 102p. 1981. Repr. of 1928 ed. 25.00 (ISBN 0-940070-11-1). Doll Works.

Banner, William A. Moral Norms & Moral Order: The Philosophy of Human Affairs. LC 80-24206. xiv, 112p. 1981. 10.00 (ISBN 0-8130-0661-9). U Presses Fla.

Bannergee, Sanjoy. Dominant Classes & The State in Development. (Replica Edition Ser.). 140p. 1985. softcover 13.95x (ISBN 0-86531-850-6). Westview.

Bannerjee, Brojendra N. Religious Conversions in India. 384p. 1982. 29.95x (ISBN 0-317-12337-8, Pub. by Harnam Pub India). Asia Bk Corp.

Bannerjee, M. Invitation to Hinduism. (Illus.). 1978. text ed. 10.75x (ISBN 0-391-01082-4). Humanities.

--Invitation to Hinduism. 1979. pap. 5.95 (ISBN 0-89684-081-6, Pub. by Arnold Heinemann India). Orient Bk Dist.

Bannerman, D. A. History of the Birds of the Balearic Islands. 384p. 1982. 100.00x (ISBN 0-686-78891-5, Pub. by Wheldon & Wesley England). State Mutual Bk.

Bannerman, David. Call of Honor. 1985. pap. 2.50 (ISBN 0-8217-1593-3). Zebra.

--The Gamov Factor. (Magic Man Ser.: Vol. 2). 1983. pap. 2.50 (ISBN 0-8217-1252-7). Zebra.

--The Magic Man. 1983. pap. 3.50 (ISBN 0-8217-1158-X). Zebra.

--Pipeline from Hell. (The Magic Man Ser.: No. 3). 1984. pap. 2.50 (ISBN 0-8217-1327-2). Zebra.

Bannerman, David & Bannerman, W. Mary. Birds of the Balearics. (Illus.). 230p. 1983. 45.00 (ISBN 0-88072-022-0, Pub. by Tanager). Longwood Pub Group.

Bannerman, Elizabeth, ed. see Chase, Emily.

Bannerman, Glenn & Fakkema, Robert. Guide for Recreation Leaders. LC 74-28523. 120p. (Orig.). 1975. pap. 6.95 (ISBN 0-8042-2154-5). John Knox.

Bannerman, Helen. Little Black Sambo. (A Pandaback Book). (Illus.). (gr. 1-3). 1978. pap. 1.25 (ISBN 0-448-49608-9, G&D). Putnam Pub Group.

--Little Black Sambo. 114p. 1983. Repr. lib. bdg. 11.95x (ISBN 0-686-47486-4). Buccaneer Bks.

--Story of Little Black Sambo. (Illus.). (gr. k-3). 1923. 6.25 (ISBN 0-397-30006-9). Har-Row.

Bannerman, J. Beatons: A Medical Kindred in the Classical Gaelic Tradition. 150p. 1985. text ed. 34.25x (ISBN 0-85976-139-8, Pub. by Donald Scotland). Humanities.

Bannerman, John W. Studies in the History of Dalriada. 178p. 1974. 15.00x (ISBN 0-87471-522-9). Rowman.

Bannerman, R. M. Thalassemia. LC 61-17667. 144p. 1962. 35.00 (ISBN 0-8089-0795-6, 790415). Grune.

Bannerman, W. Mary, jt. auth. see Bannerman, David.

Bannermann, R. H., jt. auth. see Mace, D. R.

Bannerman-Richter, Gabriel. The Practice of Witchcraft in Ghana. (Ghanaian Witchcraft Ser.: Bk. 1). 149p. (Orig.). 1982. pap. 8.95x (ISBN 0-916073-01-7). Gabari Pub Co.

Bannert, Valerie, tr. see Yano, Shigeko.

Bannet, J., jt. ed. see Belmaker, R. H.

Banning, Evelyn. Helen Hunt Jackson. LC 73-83038. 248p. (gr. 6-10). 1973. 10.95 (ISBN 0-8149-0735-0). Vanguard.

Banning, Lance. The Jeffersonian Persuasion: Evolution of a Party Ideology. LC 77-14666. (Cornell Paperbacks Ser.). 312p. 1980. pap. 8.50x (ISBN 0-8014-9200-9). Cornell U Pr.

--The Jeffersonian Persuasion: Evolution of a Party Ideology. LC 77-14666. 307p. 1978. 29.95x (ISBN 0-8014-1151-3). Cornell U Pr.

Banning, Margaret C. Country Club People. 1976. lib. bdg. 14.85x (ISBN 0-89968-006-2). Lightyear.

--Echo Answers. 2nd ed. 1968. pap. 1.25 (ISBN 0-532-12191-0). Woodhill.

--Spellbinders. 1976. lib. bdg. 14.35x (ISBN 0-89968-008-9). Lightyear.

Banning, Robert. StarPack: A Guide to WordStar Brand Word Processing. (Illus.). 1983. lab manual 24.95 (ISBN 0-934832-34-X). Word Power.

Bannink, B. A., ed. Integration of Ecological Aspects in Coastal Engineering Projects: Proceedings of a Symposium held in Rotterdam, the Netherlands, June 6-10, 1983, 2 vols, Vol. 16:1-4. LC 83-25745. (Illus.). 800p. 1984. Set. pap. 160.00 (ISBN 0-08-031036-2). Pergamon.

Bannister & Halliwell. Free Radicals in Biological Medicine. 277p. 1985. 69.00 (ISBN 3-7186-0285-7). Harwood Academic.

Bannister, A. & Raymond, S. Surveying. 2nd ed. (Illus.). 1977. pap. text ed. 26.95x (ISBN 0-8464-0903-8). Beekman Pubs.

--Surveying. 5th ed. 528p. 1984. pap. 24.95 (ISBN 0-89397-205-3). Nichols Pub.

Bannister, Barbara & Ford, Edna P. State Capitals Quilt Blocks: Fifty Patchwork Patterns from "Hearth & Home Magazine". 13.00 (ISBN 0-8446-5666-6). Peter Smith.

--The United States Patchwork Pattern Book: 50 Quilt Blocks for 50 States from "Hearth & Home" Magazine. 12.00 (ISBN 0-8446-5509-0). Peter Smith.

Bannister, Barbara & Ford, Edna P., eds. State Capitals Quilt Blocks: Fifty Patchwork Patterns from "Hearth & Home Magazine". (Dover Needlework Ser.). (Orig.). 1977. pap. 2.95 (ISBN 0-486-23557-2). Dover.

--The United States Patchwork Pattern Book: Fifty Quilt Blocks for Fifty States from "Hearth & Home" Magazine. LC 75-2821. 128p. (Orig.). 1976. pap. 2.95 (ISBN 0-486-23243-3). Dover.

Bannister, Barbara A. Infectious Diseases. (Illus.). 288p. 1983. pap. 15.95 (ISBN 0-7216-0941-4, Pub. by Bailliere-Tindall). Saunders.

Bannister, D. & Fransella, F. Inquiring Man. LC 82-13016. 218p. 1982. Repr. of 1980 ed. lib. bdg. 12.50 (ISBN 0-89874-541-1). Krieger.

Bannister, D., jt. auth. see Fransella, F.

Bannister, D., ed. Issues & Approaches in Psychological Therapies. LC 74-6996. Repr. of 1975 ed. 75.00 (ISBN 0-8357-9918-2, 2017800). Bks Demand UMI.

--New Perspectives in Personal Construct Theory. 1977. 47.50 (ISBN 0-12-077940-4). Acad Pr.

--Perspectives in Personal Construct Theory. 1971. 44.00 (ISBN 0-12-077960-9). Acad Pr.

Bannister, D., jt. ed. see Stringer, P.

Bannister, Don. The Summer Boy. 240p. 1985. 15.95 (ISBN 0-317-20397-5, Pub. by W Heinemann Ltd). David & Charles.

Bannister, Don, ed. Issues & Approaches in Personal Construct Theory. 1985. 46.50 (ISBN 0-12-077980-3). Acad Pr.

Bannister, Hank & Crane, Tim. The Guide to Computing Around Portland. rev. ed. Berard, Barbara, ed. 1984. pap. 8.95 (ISBN 0-916241-01-7). MicroConsulting NW.

Bannister, Helen H. A Coat of Blue & a Coat of Gray. (Illus.). 64p. 1984. 7.50 (ISBN 0-682-40192-7). Exposition Pr FL.

Bannister, Henry S. Donn Byrne: A Descriptive Bibliography, 1912-1935. LC 80-8485. 350p. 1982. lib. bdg. 61.00 (ISBN 0-8240-9502-2). Garland Pub.

Bannister, Ivy. The Shavian Woman: A Study of Women in the Life & Works of George Bernard Shaw. (Illus.). 368p. 1985. cancelled (ISBN 0-906187-31-1, Pub. by Univ Pr of Ireland). Longwood Pub Group.

Bannister, J. V., ed. The Biology & Chemistry of Active Oxygen. (Developments in Biochemistry Ser.: Vol. 26). 280p. 1984. 55.00 (ISBN 0-444-00924-8). Elsevier.

Bannister, J. V. & Bannister, W. H., eds. Biological & Clinical Aspects of Superoxide & Superoxide Dismutase. (Developments in Biochemistry Ser.: Vol. 11B). 1980. 68.25 (ISBN 0-444-00443-2). Elsevier.

Bannister, J. V. & Hill, H. A., eds. Chemical & Biochemical Aspects of Superoxide & Superoxide Dismutase. (Developments in Biochemistry Ser.: Vol. 11A). 414p. 1980. 68.25 (ISBN 0-444-00442-4). Elsevier.

Bannister, Jim & Bawcutt, Paul. Practical Risk Management. 240p. 1981. 90.00x (ISBN 0-900886-22-6, Pub. by Witherby & Co England). State Mutual Bk.

Bannister, Jo. Striving with Gods. LC 84-1632. (Crime Club Ser.). 192p. 1984. 11.95 (ISBN 0-385-19482-X). Doubleday.

Bannister, John, jt. auth. see Lemmons, Reuel.

Bannister, Mark. Privileged Mortals: The French Heroic Novel, 1630-1660. (Modern Languages & Literature Monographs). 1983. 27.50x (ISBN 0-19-815539-5). Oxford U Pr.

Bannister, Peter. Introduction to Physiological Plant Ecology. LC 76-16743. 273p. 1978. pap. text ed. 24.95x (ISBN 0-470-99389-8). Halsted Pr.

Bannister, Robert C. Social Darwinism: Science & Myth in Anglo-American Social Thought. LC 79-615. (American Civilization Ser.). 292p. 1979. lib. bdg. 34.95 (ISBN 0-87722-155-3). Temple U Pr.

Bannister, Roberta. Math: Grade 1. Hoffman, Joan, ed. (An I Know It! Bk.). 32p. (gr. 1). 1979. pap. text ed. 1.95 (ISBN 0-938256-28-9). Sch Zone Pub Co.

--Math: Grade 2. Hoffman, Joan, ed. (An I Know It! Bk.). (Illus.). 32p. (gr. 2). 1979. pap. text ed. 1.95 (ISBN 0-938256-30-0). Sch Zone Pub Co.

--Math: Grade 3. Hoffman, Joan, ed. (An I Know It! Bk.). (Illus.). 32p. (gr. 3). 1979. pap. text ed. 1.95 (ISBN 0-938256-31-9). Sch Zone Pub Co.

--Math: Grade 4. Hoffman, Joan, ed. (An I Know It! Bk.). (Illus.). 32p. (gr. 4). 1979. pap. text ed. 1.95 (ISBN 0-938256-33-5). Sch Zone Pub Co.

--Math: Grades 5-6. Hoffman, Joan, ed. (An I Know It! Bk.). (Illus.). 32p. (gr. 5-6). 1980. pap. text ed. 1.95 (ISBN 0-938256-35-1). Sch Zone Pub Co.

Bannister, Roger. The Four-Minute Mile. LC 80-28211. 1981. pap. 5.95 (ISBN 0-396-07946-6). Dodd.

Bannister, Roger, ed. Autonomic Failure: A Textbook of Clinical Disorders of the Autonomic Nervous System. (Illus.). 680p. 1983. 98.00x (ISBN 0-19-261339-1). Oxford U Pr.

--Brain's Clinical Neurology. 6th ed. (Illus.). 1985. 35.00x (ISBN 0-19-261455-X); pap. 24.95x (ISBN 0-19-261454-1). Oxford U Pr.

Bannister, Rosella, jt. auth. see Bonnice, Joseph.

Bannister, Saxe. Humane Policy: Justice to the Aborigines. LC 71-75539. Repr. of 1830 ed. cancelled (ISBN 0-8371-0993-0, BAH&, Pub. by Negro U Pr). Greenwood.

Bannister, Saxe, ed. see Paterson, William.

Bannister, Saxe, ed. see Sheridan, Thomas.

Bannister, W. H., jt. ed. see Bannister, J. V.

Bannister, Winifred. James Bridie & His Theatre. 262p. 1980. Repr. lib. bdg. 25.00 (ISBN 0-89984-057-4). Century Bookbindery.

Banno, Masataka. China & the West, Eighteen Fifty-Eight to Eighteen Sixty-One: The Origins of the Tsungli Yamen. LC 64-13419. (Harvard East Asian Ser.: No. 15). pap. 106.80 (ISBN 0-317-08154-3, 2006413). Bks Demand UMI.

Bannock, Graham, jt. auth. see Auld, Douglas.

Bannon, Ann. Beebo Brinker. 2nd ed. (Beebo Brinker Ser.). 208p. 1983. pap. 3.95 (ISBN 0-930044-38-X). Naiad Pr.

--I Am A Woman. 2nd ed. (Beebo Brinker Ser.). 224p. 1983. pap. 3.95 (ISBN 0-930044-35-5). Naiad Pr.

--Journey to a Woman. 2nd ed. (Beebo Brinker Ser.). 224p. 1983. pap. 3.95 (ISBN 0-930044-37-1). Naiad Pr.

--Odd Girl Out. 2nd ed. (Beebo Brinker Ser.). 192p. 1983. pap. 3.95 (ISBN 0-930044-34-7). Naiad Pr.

--Women in the Shadows. 2nd ed. (Beebo Brinker Ser.). 176p. 1983. pap. 3.95 (ISBN 0-930044-36-3). Naiad Pr.

Bannon, J. J. Outreach: Extending Community Service in Urban Areas. (Illus.). 288p. 1973. 16.25x (ISBN 0-398-02887-7). C C Thomas.

Bannon, John F. Herbert Eugene Bolton: The Historian & the Man, 1870-1953. LC 77-20951. 296p. 1978. pap. 12.50x (ISBN 0-8165-0644-2). U of Ariz Pr.

--The Spanish Borderlands Frontier, 1513-1821. LC 74-110887. (Histories of the American Frontier Series). (Illus.). 308p. 1974. pap. 10.95x (ISBN 0-8263-0309-9). U of NM Pr.

Bannon, John F., ed. see Bolton, Herbert E.

Bannon, John Francis. Colonial World of Latin America. LC 81-69334. (World of Latin Amer. Ser.). 1982. pap. text ed. 5.95x (ISBN 0-88273-601-9). Forum Pr IL.

Bannon, Joseph J. Problem Solving in Recreation & Parks. 2nd ed. 400p. 1981. text ed. 25.95 (ISBN 0-13-711770-1). P-H.

Bannon, Liam & Barry, Ursala, eds. Information Technology: Impact on the Way of Life. (Information & Technology Development Ser.: Vol. 1). 381p. 1983. 55.00 (ISBN 0-907567-34-7, TYP114, TYP); pap. 30.00 (ISBN 0-907567-35-5, TYP112). Unipub.

Bannon, Lois & Clark, Taylor. Handbook of Audubon Prints. LC 79-1319. (Illus.). 122p. 1980. 12.50 (ISBN 0-88289-202-9). Pelican.

Bannon, Lois, et al. Magnolia Mound: A Louisiana River Plantation. 96p. 1984. pap. 6.95 (ISBN 0-88289-381-5). Pelican.

Bannon, William J., jt. auth. see Donovan, Suzanne.

Banoczy, J. Oral Leukoplakia. 1982. lib. bdg. 42.00 (ISBN 90-247-2655-7, Pub. by Martinus Nijhoff Netherlands). Kluwer Academic.

Banovetz, James M., ed. Managing the Modern City. LC 58-9090. (Municipal Management Ser.). 1971. text ed. 30.00 (ISBN 0-87326-004-X). Intl City Mgt.

--Small Cities & Counties: A Guide to Managing Services. LC 83-26397. (Municipal Management Ser.). (Illus.). 355p. (Orig.). 1984. pap. text ed. 28.50 (ISBN 0-87326-030-9). Intl City Mgt.

Banowetz, Joseph. The Pianist's Guide to Pedaling. LC 84-47534. (Illus.). 448p. 1985. 27.50x (ISBN 0-253-34494-8). Ind U Pr.

Bansal, V. K. Design of Microprocessor Based Systems. 148p. 1985. 19.95 (ISBN 0-470-20113-4). Halsted Pr.

Banse, Timothy P. Home Applications & Games. (Microcomputer Bookshelf Ser.). 1985. IBM. pap. 14.50 (ISBN 0-316-08049-7); Commodore 64. pap. 14.50 (ISBN 0-316-08048-9); Coleco ADAM 600. pap. 14.50 (ISBN 0-316-08047-0). Little.

--Home Applications & Games for Atari Home Computers. (Microcomputer Bookshelf Ser.). 134p. 1983. pap. text ed. 14.50 (ISBN 0-316-08044-6). Little.

--Home Applications & Games for the Apple II, II Plus & IIe Computers. (Microcomputer Bookshelf Ser.). 170p. (Orig.). 1984. pap. 14.50 (ISBN 0-316-08045-4). Little.

--Home Applications & Games for the Coleco Adam. 132p. 1985. lib. bdg. 15.95 (ISBN 0-934523-00-2); pap. 14.95 (ISBN 0-934523-01-0). Version One Point-Zero.

--Home Applications & Games for the VIC-20 Personal Computer. (Microcomputer Bookshelf Ser.). 170p. (Orig.). 1984. pap. 9.95 (ISBN 0-316-08046-2). Little.

--How to Keep Your Powerboat Shipshape. (Illus.). 198p. 1985. 14.95 (ISBN 0-934523-75-4); pap. 12.95 (ISBN 0-934523-76-2). Version One Point-Zero.

Bansemer, Richard. Chosen & the Changed. 1978. pap. 5.50 (ISBN 0-89536-262-7). CSS of Ohio.

--Grace & the Grave. 1981. 3.25 (ISBN 0-89536-506-5). CSS of Ohio.

--In Plain Sight. 1982. 7.00 (ISBN 0-89536-577-4). CSS of Ohio.

--Risen Indeed. 1982. pap. 3.25 (ISBN 0-89536-521-9). CSS of Ohio.

Bansemer, Richard E. People Prayers. 1976. pap. 5.25 (ISBN 0-89536-194-9). CSS of Ohio.

Bansil, P. C. Agricultural Problems of India. 2nd ed. 1977. 11.00x (ISBN 0-686-26275-1). Intl Bk Dist.

Banskota, N. P. Indo-Nepal Trade & Economic Relations. 299p. 1981. text ed. 19.50x (ISBN 0-391-02337-3, Pub. by Concept India). Humanities.

Bansul, H. C. see Silano, V., et al.

Banta, David, et al. Toward Rational Technology in Medicine: Considerations for Health Policy. (Health Care & Society Ser.: No. 5). 1981. text ed. 28.50 (ISBN 0-8261-3200-6); pap. text ed. cancelled (ISBN 0-8261-3201-4). Springer Pub.

Banta, Gordon R. Asian Cropping System Research: Microeconomic Evaluation Procedures. 56p. 1982. pap. 8.00 (ISBN 0-88936-335-8, IDRC197, IDRC). Unipub.

Banta, H. David. The Management of Health Care Technology in Nine Countries. (Springer Series on Health Care & Society: Vol. 7). 256p. 1982. 35.95 (ISBN 0-8261-3770-9). Springer Pub.

Banta, H. David, ed. Resources for Health: Technology Assessment for Policy Makings. LC 81-21079. 256p. 1982. 35.95 (ISBN 0-03-061341-8). Praeger.

Banta, James E., jt. auth. see Doyle, Patrick J.

Banta, John S., jt. auth. see Babcock, Richard F.

Banta, Martha. Failure & Success in America: A Literary Debate. LC 78-51156. 1978. text ed. 45.00 (ISBN 0-691-06366-4); pap. 21.00 LPE (ISBN 0-691-10070-5). Princeton U Pr.

--Henry James & the Occult: The Great Extension. LC 72-75386. Repr. of 1972 ed. 54.60 (ISBN 0-8357-9215-3, 2013010). Bks Demand UMI.

Banta, Richard E. Hoosier Caravan: A Treasury of Indiana life & Lore, Selected with Comment. LC 73-16521. pap. 160.00 (ISBN 0-317-09634-6, 2055209). Bks Demand UMI.

Bantas, T., jt. auth. see Levitchi, V.

Bantel, Linda, ed. The Alice M. Kaplan Collection. (Illus.). 217p. 1981. 25.00 (ISBN 0-231-05322-3). Columbia U Pr.

--William Rush: American Sculptor. LC 82-80636. (Illus.). 211p. (Orig.). 1982. 21.95x (ISBN 0-943836-00-X, Pub. by Penn Acad Fine Arts). U Pr of Va.

Bantens, Robert J. Eugene Carriere: His Work & His Influence. Foster, Stephen, ed. LC 82-4919. (Studies in the Fine Arts: The Avant-Garde: No. 29). 290p. 1983. 39.95 (ISBN 0-8357-1329-6). UMI Res Pr.

Banthin, Joanna, jt. auth. see Stelzer, Leigh.

Banti, Alberto. Corpus Nummorum Romanorum: Roman Republican Coins, 9 vols. Repr. of 1981 ed. 330.00 (ISBN 0-686-35946-1). Numismatic Fine Arts.

--I Grandi Bronzi Imperiali, 2 Vols. 1984. Vol. I. 45.00 (ISBN 0-318-01499-8); Vol. II. 48.00 (ISBN 0-318-01500-5); Vol. III. 40.00. Numismatic Fine Arts.

Banti, Alberto & Simonetti, L. Corpus Nummorum Romanorum (Roman Imperial, 18 vols. 1978. Set. 650.00 (ISBN 0-686-37929-2). Numismatic Fine Arts.

Banting, Keith & Simeon, Richard, eds. Redesigning the State: The Politics of Constitutional Change. 269p. 1985. 30.00x (ISBN 0-8020-5665-2); pap. 14.50x (ISBN 0-8020-6569-4). U of Toronto Pr.

Banting, Keith G. Poverty, Politics & Policy: Britain in the Nineteen Sixties. (Studies in Policy Making). 1979. text ed. 30.50x (ISBN 0-333-23324-7). Humanities.

--The Welfare State & Canadian Federalism. 216p. 1982. pap. 12.95 (ISBN 0-7735-0384-6). McGill-Queens U Pr.

Bantleman, Lawrence. The Award. 9.00 (ISBN 0-89253-648-9); flexible cloth 4.80 (ISBN 0-89253-649-7). Ind-US Inc.

--Graffiti: Poems. 3rd ed. (Redbird Bk.). 1976. lib. bdg. 8.00 (ISBN 0-89253-095-2); pap. text ed. 4.00 (ISBN 0-89253-132-0). Ind-US Inc.

--Kanchanjanga. 8.00 (ISBN 0-89253-493-1); flexible cloth 4.00 (ISBN 0-89253-494-X). Ind-US Inc.

--New Poems. 8.00 (ISBN 0-89253-491-5); flexible cloth 4.00 (ISBN 0-89253-492-3). Ind-US Inc.

Bantly, Harold A., jt. ed. see Freedman, Janet L.

Bantock, Cuillin. The Story of Life. LC 83-25730. 44p. 1984. 10.95 (ISBN 0-911745-51-3). P Bedrick Bks.

Bantock, G. A. Studies in the History of Educational Theory: Artifice & Nature, 1350-1765, Vol. 1. 1980. text ed. 32.50x (ISBN 0-04-370092-6). Allen Unwin.

Bantock, G. H. Dilemmas of the Curriculum. LC 80-11764. 146p. 1980. 23.95x (ISBN 0-470-26920-0). Halsted Pr.

--Studies in the History of Educational Theory: The Minds & Masses, 1760-1980, Vol. 2. (Illus.). 368p. 1984. text ed. 37.50x (ISBN 0-04-370119-1). Allen Unwin.

Bantock, Gavin. Anhaga. 1972. pap. 1.95 (ISBN 0-685-27670-8, Pub. by Anvil Pr); pap. 5.00 signed ltd. ed. (ISBN 0-685-27671-6). Small Pr Dist.

--Eirenikon. 1972. 5.00 (ISBN 0-685-27672-4, Pub. by Anvil Pr); signed ltd. ed 15.00 (ISBN 0-685-27673-2). Small Pr Dist.

--New Thing Breathing. 6.95 (ISBN 0-685-00944-0, Pub. by Anvil Pr); signed ed. 50 copies 15.00 (ISBN 0-685-00945-9); pap. 3.50 (ISBN 0-685-00946-7). Small Pr Dist.

Bantock, Granville, ed. see Melvill, David.

Banton, Michael. The Idea of Race. 1979. lib. bdg. 28.00x (ISBN 0-89158-719-5). Westview.

--Promoting Racial Harmony. 146p. 1985. 29.95 (ISBN 0-521-30082-7). Cambridge U Pr.

--Racial & Ethnic Competition. LC 82-23558. (Comparative Ethnic & Race Relations Ser.). (Illus.). 500p. 1983. 52.50 (ISBN 0-521-25463-9); pap. 15.95 (ISBN 0-521-27475-3). Cambridge U Pr.

--West African City: A Study of Tribal Life in Freetown. (International African Institute Ser.). 1957. 27.50x (ISBN 0-19-724102-6). Oxford U Pr.

Banton, Michael, ed. Anthropological Approaches to the Study of Religion. 1968. pap. 11.95 (ISBN 0-422-72510-2, NO.2068, Pub. by Tavistock England). Methuen Inc.

--Social Anthropology of Complex Societies. (Orig.). 1968. pap. 14.95x (ISBN 0-422-72520-X, NO. 2069, Pub. by Tavistock England). Methuen Inc.

Banton, Michael P. White & Coloured: The Behavior of the British People Towards Coloured Immigrants. LC 76-43335. 1976. Repr. of 1960 ed. lib. bdg. 18.00x (ISBN 0-8371-9290-0, BAWAC). Greenwood.

Banton, R. Politics of Mental Health. (Critical Texts in Social Work & the Welfare State Ser.). 192p. 1985. text ed. 35.50x (ISBN 0-333-36128-8, Pub. by Macmillan England); pap. text ed. 13.00 (ISBN 0-333-36129-6, Pub. by Macmillan England). Humanities.

Banton, Vera Van see Van Banton, Vera.

Bantuzo, Renee M. Exercise Tests & Sports Medicine: Medical Subject Analysis & Research Index with Bibliography. LC 83-45293. 150p. 1984. 29.95 (ISBN 0-88164-068-9); pap. 21.95 (ISBN 0-88164-069-7). ABBE Pubs Assn.

Banu (Sons of) Musa Bin Shakir. The Book of Ingenious Devices. Hill, Donald R., tr. 1978. lib. bdg. 68.50 (ISBN 90-277-0833-9, Pub. by Reidel Holland). Kluwer Academic.

Banuazizi, Ali & Goodarzi, Prouchestia. Social Stratification in the Middle East & North Africa. 266p. 1984. 36.00x (ISBN 0-7201-1711-9). Mansell.

Banus, B. S., et al. The Developmental Therapist. 2nd ed. LC 79-65452. 405p. 1979. 29.95 (ISBN 0-913590-66-5). Slack Inc.

Banvard, Joseph. The American Statesman: Illustrations of the Life & Character of Daniel Webster. 1863. Repr. 45.00 (ISBN 0-8274-1857-4). R West.

--The American Statesman: Or Illustration of the Life & Character of Daniel Webster. 334p. 1983. Repr. of 1863 ed. lib. bdg. 65.00 (ISBN 0-89984-133-3). Century Bookbindery.

Banville, Aurelian. European Independence & the Approaching Third World Conflagration. (Illus.). 171p. 1980. deluxe ed. 69.95x (ISBN 0-930008-67-7). Inst Econ Pol.

Banville, John. Birchwood. 176p. 1973. 5.95 (ISBN 0-393-08572-4). Norton.

--Docter Copernicus. LC 83-48893. 256p. 1984. pap. 8.95 (ISBN 0-87923-513-6). Godine.

--Kepler. LC 82-3142. 208p. 1983. 14.95 (ISBN 0-87923-438-5); pap. 8.95 (ISBN 0-87923-527-6). Godine.

Banville, Theodore De. Poesies de Theodore De Banville, "Les Cariatides". LC 75-41015. 1976. Repr. of 1877 ed. 22.00 (ISBN 0-404-14504-3). AMS Pr.

--Poesies De Theodore De Banville, "Odes Funambulesques". LC 75-41016. (BCL Ser. II). Repr. of 1880 ed. 26.00 (ISBN 0-404-14505-1). AMS Pr.

Banville, Thomas G. How to Listen-How to Be Heard. LC 77-17961. 236p. 1978. 19.95x (ISBN 0-88229-332-X); pap. 9.95x. Nelson-Hall.

Banwart, Don. Rails, Rivalry, & Romance. (Illus.). 577p. pap. 24.95 (ISBN 0-9601568-7-9); pap. 19.95 (ISBN 0-9601568-8-7). Historic Pres Bourbon.

Banwart, George J. Basic Food Microbiology. abr. ed. (Illus.). 1981. text ed. 27.50 (ISBN 0-87055-384-4). AVI.

Banwart, George J., ed. Basic Food Microbiology. unabridged ed. (Illus.). 1981. lib. bdg. 45.00 (ISBN 0-87055-385-2). AVI.

Banwart, L., jt. ed. see Stucki, J. W.

Banz, Hans. Building Construction Details: Practical Drawings. 272p. pap. 14.95 (ISBN 0-442-21325-5). Van Nos Reinhold.

Banzhaf, Jane C. & Wallas, Charles H., eds. Strategies for Instruction in the Blood Bank. 120p. 1982. 17.10 (ISBN 0-914404-79-2). Am Assn Blood.

Banzhaf, Robert A. Screen Process Printing. 1983. text ed. 10.00 (ISBN 0-87345-206-2). McKnight.

Baouendi, Salah M., et al, eds. Microlocal Analysis. LC 84-2852. (Contemporary Mathematics Ser.: No. 27). 256p. 1984. pap. 26.00 (ISBN 0-8218-5031-8). Am Math.

Bapat. Shanty Town City: The Case of Poona. (Progress in Planning Ser.: Vol. 15, Pt. 3). 85p. 1981. pap. 14.75 (ISBN 0-08-026811-0). Pergamon.

Bapna, Ashok, ed. One World One Future: New International Strategies for Development. 364p. 1985. 42.95 (ISBN 0-03-004963-6). Praeger.

Bappu, M. K., ed. see Symposium No. 49 of the International Astronomical Union, Buenos Aires, Argentina. Aug. 1971.

Baptist, C. Tanker Handbook for Deck Officers. 6th rev. ed. (Illus.). 1980. 50.00 (ISBN 0-85174-386-2). Heinman.

--Tanker Handbook for Desk Officers. 6th ed. 298p. 1980. 48.00x (ISBN 0-85174-386-2). Sheridan.

Baptist, C. N. Salvage Operations. 160p. 1979. 19.50x (ISBN 0-540-07378-4). Sheridan.

Baptista Mantuanus. The Eclogues of Mantuan. Bush, Douglas, ed. Turbervile, George, tr. LC 38-12665. 208p. 1977. Repr. of 1567 ed. 35.00x (ISBN 0-8201-1181-3). Schol Facsimiles.

Baptiste, H. Prentice, Jr. Multicultural Education: A Synopsis. LC 79-89924. 1979. pap. text ed. 8.00 (ISBN 0-8191-0851-0). U Pr of Amer.

Baptiste, H. Prentice, Jr. & Baptiste, Mira L. Developing the Multicultural Process in Classroom Instruction: Competencies for Teachers. LC 79-89993. 1979. pap. text ed. 13.50 (ISBN 0-8191-0855-3). U Pr of Amer.

Baptiste, H. Prentice, Jr., et al, eds. Multicultural Teacher Education: Preparing Educators to Provide Educational Equity, Vol. 1. 218p. (Orig.). 1980. pap. text ed. 6.50 (ISBN 0-89333-017-5). AACTE.

Baptiste, Mira L., jt. auth. see Baptiste, H. Prentice, Jr.

Baptiste De Boyer Argens, Jean. Chinese Letters, Seventeen Forty-One. (The Flowering of the Novel, 1740-1775 Ser: Vol. 4). 1974. lib. bdg. 61.00 (ISBN 0-8240-1103-1). Garland Pub.

Baptist-Metz, Johannes, jt. auth. see Schillebeeckx, Edward.

Baquedano, Sarah. Rombo y Otros Momentos. LC 83-82850. (Coleccion Caniqui Ser.). 309p. (Span.). 1984. pap. 9.95 (ISBN 0-89729-345-2). Ediciones.

Bar, Antonio. Syndicalism & Revolution in Spain. (History of Anarchism Ser.). 1981. lib. bdg. 69.95 (ISBN 0-8490-3208-3). Gordon Pr.

Bar Association Of The District Of Columbia. Federal Administrative Practice Manual. 1966. 8.50 (ISBN 0-685-14183-7). Lerner Law.

Bar, Lois E. Le see Le Bar, Lois E.

Bar, O. Pediatric Sports Medicine for the Practitioner: From Physiologic Principles to Clinical Applications. (Comprehensive Manuals in Pediatrics). (Illus.). 350p. 1983. 37.00 (ISBN 0-387-90873-0). Springer-Verlag.

Bara, B. G. & Guida, G. Computational Models of Natural Language Processing. (Fundamental Studies in Computer Science: Vol. 9). 1984. 50.00 (ISBN 0-444-87598-0). Elsevier.

Bara, Louis. Science de la Paix. LC 78-147448. (Library of War & Peace; Problems of the Organized Peace Movement: Selected Documents). lib. bdg. 46.00 (ISBN 0-8240-0238-5). Garland Pub.

Bara, Nina. Bara-Facts. 1985. write for info. Nin Ra Ent.

Bara, Nina see Linke, Frances, pseud.

Barabas, Andras, jt. auth. see Calnan, James.

Barabash, Y. Aesthetics & Poetics. 292p. 1977. 6.95 (ISBN 0-8285-0189-0, Pub. by Progress Pubs USSR). Imported Pubns.

Barabasz, Arreed F. New Techniques in Behavior Therapy & Hypnosis: Including Advanced Techniques in Sex Therapy. 15.50 (ISBN 0-87505-265-7). Borden.

Baraboshkin, A. N., ed. Electrochemistry of Molten & Solid Electrolytes, 9 vols. Incl. Vol. 1. 106p. 1961. 29.50 (ISBN 0-306-18001-4); Vol. 2. 96p. 1964. 30.00 (ISBN 0-306-18002-2); Vol. 3. 133p. 1966. 29.50x (ISBN 0-306-18003-0); Vol. 4. 165p. 1967. 35.00 (ISBN 0-306-18004-9); Vol. 5. Physiochemical Properties of Electrolyte & Electrode Processes. 158p. 1967. 35.00x (ISBN 0-306-18005-7); Vol. 6. Structure & Properties of Electrolytes & Kinetics of Electrode Properties. 138p. 1968. 29.50x (ISBN 0-306-18006-5); Vol. 7. Physiochemical Properties of Electrolytes. 99p. 1969. 29.50x (ISBN 0-306-18007-3); Vol. 8. Mechanism & Kinetics of Electrode Processes. 84p. 1970. 30.00 (ISBN 0-306-18008-1); Vol. 9. Thermodynamics of Salt & Oxide Systems. 110p. 1972. 30.00 (ISBN 0-306-18009-X). LC 61-15178 (Consultants). Plenum Pub.

Barabtarlo, G., tr. see Nabokov, Vladimir.

Barac, Antun. A History of Yugoslav Literature. (Joint Committee on Eastern Europe Publication Ser.: No. 1). 15.00 (ISBN 0-930042-19-0). Mich Slavic Pubns.

Barach, Alvan L. Treatment Manual for Pulmonary Emphysema. LC 70-75403. (Illus.). 114p. 1969. 24.50 (ISBN 0-8089-0030-7, 790425). Grune.

Barach, Arnold. Famous American Trademarks. 1971. pap. 9.00 (ISBN 0-8183-0165-1). Pub Aff Pr.

Barach, Carol. Help Me Say It. 1984. pap. 7.95 (ISBN 0-452-25623-2, Plume). NAL.

Barack, Boaz. The Application of the Competition Rules (Antitrust Law) of the European Economic Community to Enterprises & Arrangements External to the Common Market. 474p. 1982. cancelled 45.00 (ISBN 90-654-4012-7, Pub. by Kluwer Law Netherlands). Kluwer Academic.

Barack, Nathan A. God Speaks Naturally: An Organic Perspective on the Prophets. LC 83-7836. 242p. 1983. 12.50 (ISBN 0-8246-0299-4). Jonathan David.

Barack, Priscilla, jt. auth. see Costales, Claire.

Barad, Dianne S. All the Games Kids Like. rev. ed. 229p. 1983. pap. text ed. 24.95 (ISBN 0-88450-876-5, 7013-B). Communication Skill.

--Speech News. Rev. ed. (gr. 7-12). 1983. manual 15.95 (ISBN 0-686-69810-X, 3135-B). Communication Skill.

--Talk It Up. 40p. (Orig.). 1984. pap. text ed. 15.95 (ISBN 0-88450-880-3, 7021-B). Communication Skill.

--Unfamiliar Fables. 1979. pap. text ed. 11.95 (ISBN 0-88450-702-5, 3102-B). Communication Skill.

--Words & Sounds Ahoy. 55p. (gr. 1-8). 1983. pap. text ed. 15.95 spiral bdg. (ISBN 0-88450-875-7, 4692-B). Communication Skill.

Baradat, Leon P. Political Ideologies: Their Origins & Impact. 2nd ed. (Illus.). 384p. 1984. pap. 18.95 (ISBN 0-13-684365-4). P-H.

--Soviet Political Society. (Illus.). 416p. 1986. pap. text ed. 18.95 (ISBN 0-13-823592-9). P-H.

Baradei, Mohamed El see El Baradei, Mohamed & Gavin, Chloe.

Baradei, Mohamed El, et al. Model Rules for Disaster Relief Operations. (Policy & Efficacy Studies Series). 68p. 1982. 5.00 (ISBN 0-318-02106-4, E.82.XV.PE/8). Unitar.

Bar-Adon, Aaron. Modern Israeli Hebrew. wrappers 8.00 (ISBN 0-8363-0072-6). Jenkins.

--The Rise & Decline of a Dialect: A Study in the Revival of Modern Hebrew. LC 74-80121. (Janua Linguarum, Ser. Practica: No. 197). 116p. (Orig.). 1975. pap. text ed. 19.20x (ISBN 90-2793-206-9). Mouton.

Baraga, Frederick, ed. Chippewa Indians As Recorded by Rev. Frederick Baraga in Eighteen Forty-Seven. LC 77-375214. 82p. 1976. 5.00 (ISBN 0-686-28384-8). Studia Slovenica.

Baraheni, Reza. The Crowned Cannibals: Writings on Repression in Iran. 1977. pap. 3.95 (ISBN 0-394-72357-0, V-357, Vin). Random.

--God's Shadow: Prison Poems. LC 75-34731. pap. 25.80 (ISBN 0-317-27949-1, 2056023). Bks Demand UMI.

Baraitser, Francis & Winter, Robin. A Colour Atlas of Clinical Genetics. (Illus.). 159p. 1983. text ed. 79.50x (ISBN 0-7234-0800-9, Pub. by Wolfe Medical England). Sheridan.

Baraitser, Michael. The Genetics of Neurological Disorders. 1982. text ed. 69.00x (ISBN 0-19-261155-0). Oxford U Pr.

--The Genetics of Neurological Disorders. (Oxford Monographs on Medical Genetics). (Illus.). 528p. 1985. pap. 24.95 (ISBN 0-19-261540-8). Oxford U Pr.

Barak, Aharon, jt. auth. see Kahan, Yitzhak.

Barak, Gregg. In Defense of Whom? A Critique of Criminal Justice Reform. (Criminal Justice Studies). 148p. (Orig.). 1980. pap. text ed. 7.95 (ISBN 0-87084-080-0). Anderson Pub Co.

Barak, M., ed. Electrochemical Power Sources: Primary & Secondary Batteries. (IEE Energy Ser.: No. 1). (Illus.). 516p. 1980. 86.00 (ISBN 0-906048-26-5). Inst Elect Eng.

Barak, Michael. Double Cross. 1982. pap. 2.95 (ISBN 0-451-11547-3, AE1547, Sig). NAL.

Barak, Ronald S. Foreign Investment in U. S. Real Estate. 561p. 1981. 55.00 (ISBN 0-15-100024-7, H39905). HarBraceJ.

Baraka, Amina, jt. ed. see Baraka, Amiri.

Baraka, Amiri. The Autobiography of Leroi Jones-Amiri Baraka. 329p. 1984. 16.95 (ISBN 0-88191-000-7). Freundlich.

Baraka, Amiri, pseud. Blues People: Negro Music in White America. 1963. pap. 8.70 (ISBN 0-688-18474-X). Morrow.

Baraka, Amiri. Daggers & Javelins: Essays, 1974-1979. LC 84-60089. 335p. 1984. 19.95 (ISBN 0-688-03431-4). Morrow.

--Daggers & Javelins: Essays, 1974-1979. LC 84-60088. 335p. 1984. pap. 9.95 (ISBN 0-688-03432-2, Quill). Morrow.

Baraka, Amiri, pseud. Dutchman & the Slave, 2 Plays. 1964. pap. 4.95 (ISBN 0-688-21084-8). Morrow.

Baraka, Amiri. The Motion of History & Other Plays. LC 77-3291. 1978. 8.95 (ISBN 0-688-03272-9); pap. 3.95 (ISBN 0-688-08272-6). Morrow.

--Reggae or Not! (Contact II Publications Chapbook Ser.). (Illus.). 32p. 1982. pap. 3.00 (ISBN 0-936556-04-8). Contact Two.

--Selected Poetry of Amiri Baraka-Leroi Jones. LC 79-9488. 1979. 12.95 (ISBN 0-688-03496-9); pap. 5.95 (ISBN 0-688-08496-6, Quill). Morrow.

--The Sidney Poet Heroical. LC 78-66005. 1979. pap. 5.95 (ISBN 0-918408-12-1). Reed & Cannon.

Baraka, Amiri & Baraka, Amina, eds. Confirmation: An Anthology of African-American Women. LC 82-21425. 416p. 1983. pap. 10.95 (ISBN 0-688-01582-4, Quill). Morrow.

Baraka, Imamu A. Black Music. LC 80-15439. (Illus.). 221p. 1980. Repr. of 1967 ed. lib. bdg. 22.50x (ISBN 0-313-22518-4, JOBK). Greenwood.

--Blues People: Negro Music in White America. LC 80-15648. xii, 244p. 1980. Repr. of 1963 ed. lib. bdg. 27.50x (ISBN 0-313-22519-2, JOBP). Greenwood.

Baraka, Imamu A., pseud. It's Nation Time. 1970. pap. 0.50 (ISBN 0-88378-008-9). Third World.

--Raise Race Rays Raze: Essays since 1965. 1971. 10.00 (ISBN 0-685-77057-5). Univ Place.

Barakat, Ahmad. Muhammad & the Jews: A Re-Examination. 140p. 1980. text ed. 16.95x (ISBN 0-7069-0804-X, Pub. by Vikas India). Advent NY.

Barakat, Gamal. English-Arabic Dictionary of Diplomacy & Related Terminology. (Eng. & Arabic.). 1982. 25.00x (ISBN 0-86685-290-5). Intl Bk Ctr.

Barakat, Halim. Days of Dust. 2nd ed. Le Gassick, Trevor, tr. from Arabic. (Illus.). 200p. 1983. 18.00 (ISBN 0-89410-359-8); pap. 8.00 (ISBN 0-89410-360-1). Three Continents.

--Lebanon in Strife: Student Preludes to the Civil War. (Modern Middle East Ser.: No. 2). 256p. 1977. text ed. 17.50x (ISBN 0-292-70322-8). U of Tex Pr.

Barakat, Layyah & Kirban, Salem. Lebanon-A Harvest of Love. (Illus.). 1975. pap. 3.95 (ISBN 0-685-52516-3). Kirban.

Barakat, Robert. Cistercian Sign Language. LC 70-152476. (Cistercian Studies: No. 11). 1976. 14.95 (ISBN 0-87907-811-1). Cistercian Pubns.

Barket, Irene, tr. see Fisher, Andrew, et al.

Barak-Glantz, Israel L. & Huff, C. Ronald. The Mad, the Bad & the Different: Essays in Honor of Simon Dinitz. LC 80-8316. 304p. 1981. 24.00 (ISBN 0-669-03997-7). Lexington Bks.

Barak-Glantz, Israel L., et al. Comparative Criminology: Theory & Applications. LC 83-17853. (Sage Research Progress Series in Criminology: Vol. 31). 1983. 16.95 (ISBN 0-8039-2141-1). Sage.

Baraks, Brad. Quad City Sports Greats. (Illus.). 208p. 1982. 9.95 (ISBN 0-940286-50-5). Quest Pub IL.

Baral, David P. Achievement Levels among Foreign-Born & Native-Born Mexican American Students. LC 77-81020. 1977. soft bdg. 10.95 (ISBN 0-88247-472-3). R & E Pubs.

Baral, Jaya K. The Pentagon & the Making of US Foreign Policy: A Case Study of Vietnam 1960-1968. LC 77-13333. 1978. text ed. 18.00x (ISBN 0-391-00549-9). Humanities.

Baral, Lok R. Nepal's Politics of Referendum: A Study of Groups, Personalities & Trends. (Illus.). vi, 243p. 1984. text ed. 30.00x (ISBN 0-7069-2461-4, Pub. by Vikas India). Advent NY.

--Opposition Politics in Nepal. 1977. 12.00x (ISBN 0-8364-0049-6). South Asia Bks.

Baral, Robert. Revue. LC 62-7579. (Illus.). 1970. 16.95 (ISBN 0-8303-0091-0). Fleet.

--Turn West on Twenty-Third. LC 65-24028. (Illus.). 1966. 10.00 (ISBN 0-8303-0055-4). Fleet.

Baralt, Guillermo A. Esclavos Rebeldes. LC 81-70982. (Coleccion Semilla Ser.). 190p. 1982. pap. 4.95 (ISBN 0-940238-07-1). Ediciones Huracan.

Baralt, Luis A., tr. see Marti, Jose.

Baram, Michael, et al. Marine Mining of the Continental Shelf: An Assessment of Legal, Technical & Environmental Factors. LC 77-23831. 424p. 1978. prof ref 35.00 (ISBN 0-88410-616-0). Ballinger Pub.

Baram, Michael S. Alternatives to Regulation: Managing Risks to Health, Safety, & the Environment. LC 81-47560. 256p. 1981. 27.50x (ISBN 0-669-04666-3). Lexington Bks.
Baram, Phillip J. The Department of State in the Middle East, 1919-1945. LC 77-20300. 1978. 40.00x (ISBN 0-8122-7743-0). U of Pa Pr.
Baram, R., et al, eds. see Midwest Autumn Immunology Conference, 7th Meeting, Michigan, Nov. 1978.
Baramki, D. C., jt. auth. see Sellers, O. R.
Baramki, Dimitri. Coins Exhibited in the Archaeological Museum of the American University of Beirut. (Illus.). 1968. pap. 16.95x (ISBN 0-8156-6010-3, Am U Beirut). Syracuse U Pr.
Baramki, Dimitri, jt. auth. see Kelso, James L.
Baramki, Dimtri C., ed. Coin Collection of the American University of Beirut Museum. 1974. 49.95x (ISBN 0-8156-6043-X, Am U Beirut). Syracuse U Pr.
Baran, Elaine V. Modern Spoken Italian: Active Italian Conversation, Part A. 124p. (Orig.). 1981. pap. text ed. 125.00 plus 8 cassettes (ISBN 0-88432-073-1, Z501). J Norton Pubs.
--Modern Spoken Italian: Active Italian Communication, Part B. 136p. (Orig.). 1981. pap. 125.00x (ISBN 0-88432-074-X, Z551); 8 audio cassettes incl. J Norton Pubs.
Baran, Michael. Atlantis Reconsidered: A New Look at the Ancient Deluge Legends & an Analysis of Mysterious Modern Phenomena. 96p. 1981. 6.00 (ISBN 0-682-49761-4). Exposition Pr FL.
--Insights into Prehistory. 128p. 1982. 7.00 (ISBN 0-682-49876-9). Exposition Pr FL.
--Twilight of the Gods. 192p. 9.00 (ISBN 0-682-40131-5). Exposition Pr FL.
Baran, Nicholas, jt. auth. see Erickson, Jonathan.
Baran, Paul. Potential Market Demand for Two-Way Information Services to the Home, 1970-1990. 139p. 1971. 10.50 (ISBN 0-318-14418-2, R26). Inst Future.
Baran, Paul & Lipinski, Andrew J. The Future of the Telephone Industry: 1970-1985. 180p. 1971. 12.00 (ISBN 0-318-14415-8, R 20). Inst Future.
Baran, Paul A. Longer View: Essays Toward a Critique of Political Economy. LC 68-13656. 464p. 1969. pap. 6.95 (ISBN 0-85345-220-2). Monthly Rev.
--Political Economy of Growth. LC 57-7953. 352p. 1957. pap. 9.00 (ISBN 0-85345-076-5). Monthly Rev.
Baran, Paul A. & Sweezy, Paul M. Monopoly Capital: An Essay on the American Economic & Social Order. LC 65-15269. 416p. 1968. pap. 6.50 (ISBN 0-85345-073-0). Monthly Rev.
Baran, Stanley J. The Viewer's Television Book: A Personal Guide to Understanding Television & Its Influence. LC 80-81369. 109p. (Orig.). 1980. pap. 6.95 (ISBN 0-936522-00-3). Penrith.
Baran, Stanley J., jt. auth. see Davis, Dennis K.
Baran, Stanley J., et al. Self, Symbols & Society: An Introduction to Mass Communication. (Illus.). 336p. 1984. pap. text ed. 16.95 (ISBN 0-394-35002-2, RanC). Random.
Baranauskas, et al, trs. see Kreve, Vincas.
Baranczak, Stanislaw. Under My Own Roof. Kujawinski, Frank, tr. (Poetry Chapbook Ser.). 1980. Bilingual edition. 3.00 (ISBN 0-932191-03-7). Mr Cogito Pr.
Baranczak, Stanislaw, jt. auth. see Karasek, Krzysztof.
Baranek, Patricia M., jt. auth. see Ericson, Richard V.
Baranger, Michel & Vogt, Erich, eds. Advances in Nuclear Physics. Incl. Vol. 1. 416p. 1968. 59.50x (ISBN 0-306-39101-5); Vol. 2. 430p. 1969. 59.50x (ISBN 0-306-39102-3); Vol. 3. 480p. 1969. 65.00x (ISBN 0-306-39103-1); Vol. 4. 448p. 1971. 52.50x (ISBN 0-306-39104-X); Vol. 5. 484p. 1972. 65.00x (ISBN 0-306-39105-8); Vol. 6. 462p. 1973. 65.00x (ISBN 0-306-39106-6); Vol. 7. 329p. 1973. 49.50x (ISBN 0-306-39107-4); Vol. 8. 383p. 1975. 55.00x (ISBN 0-306-39108-2); Vol. 9. 264p. 1977. 49.50x (ISBN 0-306-39109-0); Vol. 10. 350p. 1978. 55.00x (ISBN 0-306-39110-4). LC 67-29001 (Plenum Pr). Plenum Pub.
Baranishyn, Barbara, jt. auth. see Wernig, Julie K.
Baranoff, Timy. Kindergarten Minute by Minute. LC 78-72076. 1979. pap. 6.95 (ISBN 0-8224-4100-4). Pitman Learning.
Baranov, A. Basic Latin for Plant Taxonomists. 1971. pap. text ed. 16.00 (ISBN 3-7682-0727-7). Lubrecht & Cramer.
Baranov, Alvin B. Divorces: California Style. (Illus.). 90p. 1984. 8.95 (ISBN 0-910531-05-6). Wolcotts.
--How to Evict a Tenant. 11th ed. (Illus.). 147p. 1983. Repr. of 1978 ed. 9.95 (ISBN 0-910531-04-8). Wolcotts.
Baranov, Alvin B. & Sirkin, Esther. What Every Husband & Wife Should Know Before It's Too Late. 165p. pap. 3.00 (ISBN 0-686-36142-3). Legal Pubns CA.
Baranov, Alvin B., ed. Incorporation Made Easy. (Illus.). 138p. (Orig.). 1984. pap. 19.95 (ISBN 0-910531-02-1). Wolcotts.
Baranov, I. The Ulyanov Family: Lenin's Domestic Environment. pap. 4.00x (ISBN 0-8464-0943-7). Beekman Pubs.
Baranov, Wladimir. Potential Fields & Their Transformations in Applied Geophysics. (Geoexploration Monographs: Series 1, No. 6). (Illus.). 121p. 1975. lib. bdg. 23.10x (ISBN 3-4431-3008-9). Lubrecht & Cramer.
Baranovic, T. M., et al. Eleven Papers on Topology & Algebra. LC 51-5559. (Translations Ser.: No. 2, Vol. 55). 1966. 37.00 (ISBN 0-8218-1755-8, TRANS 2-55). Am Math.
Baranovskii, E. P., jt. auth. see Ryyskov, S. S.
Baranowski, Dave, jt. auth. see Leptich, John.
Baranowski, Henry K. Bibliografia Kopernikowska 1509-1955. 1969. Repr. of 1958 ed. 32.00 (ISBN 0-8337-0161-4). B Franklin.
Baranowski, Richard M., jt. auth. see Slater, James A.
Baranowski, Zdzislaw. The International Horseman's Dictionary. (Illus.). write for info (ISBN 0-85131-262-4, Dist. by Miller). J A Allen.
--Woerterbuch Pferd und Reiter. (Eng., Fr. & Ger., Dictionary of Horses and Horsemanship). 1977. 24.95 (ISBN 0-273-00937-0, M-6910). French & Eur.
Baranski, Johnny. Lonesome Journey. LC 73-85734. (Sunburst Originals Ser.: No. 2). 125p. (Orig.). 1973. pap. 2.00 (ISBN 0-934648-06-9). Sunburst Pr.
--Pencil Flowers. LC 82-12057. (Kestrel Ser.). 24p. 1983. 3.00 (ISBN 0-914974-36-X). Holmgangers.
--Poems from Prison. (Sunburst Originals Ser.: No. 7). 16p. (Orig.). 1979. pap. 2.00 (ISBN 0-934648-02-6). Sunburst Pr.
--Silent Silos: A Counterbomb Haiku Sequence. (Sunburst Matchbooks Ser.: No. 1). (Illus.). 16p. (Orig.). 1985. pap. 3.00x (ISBN 0-934648-10-7). Sunburst Pr.
Baranski, Zygmunt G. & Short, John R., eds. Developing Contemporary Marxism. LC 84-17695. 272p. 1985. 27.50 (ISBN 0-312-19659-8). St Martin.
Baranskii, V. A., et al. Sixteen Papers on Logic & Algebra. LC 51-5559. (Translations Ser.: No. 2, Vol. 94). 1970. 33.00 (ISBN 0-8218-1794-9, TRANS 2-94). Am Math.
Baranson, Jack. Automotive Industries in Developing Countries. LC 77-85339. (World Bank Staff Occasional Papers Ser.: No. 8). pap. 30.00 (ISBN 0-317-29924-7, 2021733). Bks Demand UMI.
--The Japanese Challenge to U. S. Industry. (Illus.). 208p. 1981. 23.50x (ISBN 0-669-04402-4). Lexington Bks.
--North-South Technology Transfer: Financing & Institution Building. LC 81-80543. 160p. 1981. 15.75x (ISBN 0-912338-27-X); microfiche 12.75x (ISBN 0-912338-28-8). Lomond.
--Robots in Manufacturing: Key to International Competitiveness. LC 83-81240. 152p. 1983. 32.50 (ISBN 0-912338-39-3); microfiche 16.50 (ISBN 0-912338-40-7). Lomond.
--Technology & the Multinationals. LC 77-14699. 1978. 25.00x (ISBN 0-669-02021-4). Lexington Bks.
Barante, Amable G. Histoire de la Convention Nationale, 6 vols. LC 77-161739. Repr. of 1853 ed. 27.50 ea.; 165.00 (ISBN 0-404-07780-3). AMS Pr.
--Histoire du directoire de la Republique francaise, 3 vols. LC 71-161740. Repr. of 1855 ed. Set. 125.00 (ISBN 0-404-07770-6). AMS Pr.
Barany, F. R., et al, eds. Gastrointestinal Emergencies Two: Proceedings of the 2nd International Symposium on Gastrointestinal Emergencies, Rome, 7-8 June 1979. (Advances in the Biosciences: Vol. 27). (Illus.). 186p. 1980. 33.00 (ISBN 0-08-024927-2). Pergamon.
Barany, Franz R. & Torsoli, Aldo, eds. Gastrointestinal Emergencies: First International Symposium on Gastrointestinal Emergencies, Stockholm, 1975 - Proceedings. 1977. text ed. 61.00 (ISBN 0-08-020494-5). Pergamon.
Barany Society Meeting, Toronto, Aug. 1971. Current Studies in Otoneurology: Proceedings. Barber, H. O. & Frederickson, J. M., eds. (Advances in Oto-Rhino-Laryngology: Vol. 19). (Illus.). 1973. 65.75 (ISBN 3-8055-1448-4). S Karger.
Baranzini, Mauro. Advances in Economic Theory. LC 82-42613. 330p. 1982. 35.00 (ISBN 0-312-00636-5). St Martin.
Bararee, Charlotte. The Jumbled Gymnast. 1982. pap. 1.95 (ISBN 0-570-08406-7, 39-1081). Concordia.
Baras, Edward M. The Osborne-McGraw-Hill Guide to Using Lotus 1-2-3. 250p. 1984. 16.95 (ISBN 0-88134-123-1, 123-1, Osborne-McGraw). McGraw.
--Symphony Book. 300p. (Orig.). 1985. pap. 19.95 (ISBN 0-07-881160-0, 160-0). Osborne-McGraw.
--Symphony Master: The Expert's Guide. 352p. (Orig.). 1985. pap. 19.95 (ISBN 0-07-881170-8, 170-8). Osborne McGraw.
Baras, F., jt. ed. see Nicolis, G.
Baras, Victor, jt. ed. see Himmelfarb, Milton.
Barasch, Clarence S., jt. ed. see Biskind, Elliott L.
Barasch, Frances. Monarch Notes on Shakespeare's Henry Fourth, Part 2. (Orig.). pap. 2.95 (ISBN 0-671-00634-7). Monarch Pr.
Barasch, Frances K. The Grotesque: A Study in Meanings. (De Proprietatibus Litterarum, Ser. Major: No. 20). 1971. text ed. 19.60x (ISBN 90-2791-788-4). Mouton.
Barasch, Kenneth, jt. auth. see Chase, Cohrane.
Barasch, Marc, ed. Breaking One Hundred: Americans Who Have Lived over a Century. LC 82-23033. (Illus.). 64p. 1983. pap. 5.70 (ISBN 0-688-01926-9, Quill NY). Morrow.
Barasch, Marc & Aguilera-Hellweg, Max, eds. Breaking One Hundred: Americans Who Have Lived Over a Century. LC 82-22899. (Illus.). 64p. (Orig.). 1983. 12.95 (ISBN 0-688-01925-0). Morrow.
Barasch, Marc, jt. ed. see Martin, Russell.
Barasch, Marc I. The Little Black Book of Atomic War. (Illus.). 112p. (Orig.). 1983. pap. 3.95 (ISBN 0-440-54703-2, Dell Trade Pbks). Dell.
Barasch, Moshe. Light & Color in the Italian Renaissance Theory of Art. LC 77-92324. 232p. 1978. 30.00x (ISBN 0-8147-0995-8). NYU Pr.
--Theories of Art: From Plato to Winckelman. 352p. 1985. 30.00 (ISBN 0-8147-1060-3); pap. 15.00 (ISBN 0-8147-1061-1). NYU Pr.
Barasch, Moshe & Friedman, Lucy, eds. Art the Ape of Nature: Studies in Honor of H. W. Janson. (Illus.). 1981. 75.00 (ISBN 0-8109-1153-1). Abrams.
Barasch, Seymour. High School Equivalency Diploma Test. LC 81-1618. (Arco's Preparation for the GED Examination Ser.). 480p. 1983. lib. bdg. 14.00 (ISBN 0-668-05375-5); pap. 7.95 (ISBN 0-668-05382-8). Arco.
Barash, D. P. Sociobiology & Behavior. 2nd ed. 426p. 1982. 41.00 (ISBN 0-444-99091-7); pap. 17.00 (ISBN 0-444-99088-7). Elsevier.
Barash, David. The Whisperings Within. 288p. 1981. pap. 6.95 (ISBN 0-14-005699-8). Penguin.
--The Whisperings Within: Evolution & the Origin of Human Nature. LC 78-20155. 1979. 13.41i (ISBN 0-06-010341-8, HarpT). Har-Row.
Barash, David P. Aging: An Exploration. LC 82-48868. 232p. 1983. 17.50x (ISBN 0-295-95993-2). U of Wash Pr.
Barash, David P. & Lipton, Judith E. The Caveman & the Bomb: Human Nature, Evolution & Nuclear War. 320p. 1985. 16.95 (ISBN 0-07-003654-3). McGraw.
Barash, Meyer, tr. see Caillois, Roger.
Barash, Samuel, ed. Complete Guide to Appraising Condominiums & Cooperatives. LC 81-4441. 288p. 1981. 34.50 (ISBN 0-13-159822-8, Busn). P-H.
Barash, Samuel T. Encyclopedia of Real Estate Appraising Forms & Model Reports. LC 83-3029. 398p. 1983. 64.95 (ISBN 0-13-276212-9). P-H.
Barath, A., jt. auth. see Augusti, G.
Baratta, Alessandro, ed. The Impact of Sociology of Law on Government Action: Proceedings of a Conference on Sociology of Law, Saabrucken, Federal Republic of Germany,September 5-8, 1977. 448p. 1981. 33.55 (ISBN 3-8204-6173-6). P Lang Pubs.
Baratta, Anthony, jt. auth. see Hedley, Carolyn.
Baratta, Ron & Stone, Linda. How to Meet Girls Without Really Trying. 200p. (Orig.). 1985. pap. 11.95 (ISBN 0-9605628-3-4). Mutual Pr IL.
--How to Win With Women. LC 83-19419. Orig. Title: How to Take Advantage of A Woman. 200p. (Orig.). 1982. pap. 11.95 (ISBN 0-9605628-1-8). Mutual Pr IL.
--Sex Power. LC 83-19418. 175p. (Orig.). 1983. pap. 11.95 (ISBN 0-9605628-2-6). Mutual Pr IL.
Baratta, Ron & Stone, Linda I. How to Take Advantage of a Woman. (Orig.). 1981. pap. 10.00 (ISBN 0-9605628-0-X). Mutual Pr IL.
Baratta-Lorton, Robert. Dekodiphukan. LC 85-70308. (Illus.). 116p. 1985. pap. 24.95 (ISBN 0-9614646-0-7). Ctr Innovation.
Baratz, Morton S. Commodity Money Management Yearbook, Vol. 3. 303p. 1982. 59.95x (ISBN 0-471-87628-3, Pub. by Ronald Pr). Wiley.
--The Investor's Guide to Futures Money Management. (Illus.). 160p. (Orig.). 1984. pap. 19.50 (ISBN 0-936624-28-0). Futures Pub.
--The Union & the Coal Industry. LC 82-25141. (Yale Studies in Economics: Vol. 4). xvii, 170p. 1983. Repr. of 1955 ed. lib. bdg. 29.75x (ISBN 0-313-23698-4, BAUC). Greenwood.
Baratz, Morton S., jt. auth. see Bachrach, Peter.
Baratz, Morton S., ed. Nineteen Eighty-Four Futures: Money Management Fact Book. (Illus.). 52p. (Orig.). 1984. pap. 18.50 (ISBN 0-936624-27-2). Futures Pub.
Baravalle, Hermann Von see Von Baravalle, Hermann.
Baraveli, G. G. The Policy of Public Works under the Fascist Regime. 1976. lib. bdg. 59.95 (ISBN 0-8490-2450-1). Gordon Pr.
Baravykas, V., jt. auth. see Piesarskas, B.
Barb, S., ed. see Dyson, Stephen L.
Barba, jt. auth. see Naimark.
Barba, Harry. The Day the World Went Sane: A Fictive Ballet & a Dramatic Opera by Harry Barba. LC 78-70762. 1979. 9.95 (ISBN 0-911906-14-2); pap. 5.95 (ISBN 0-911906-13-4). Harian Creative.
--Love in the Persian Way. 1970. pap. 1.20 (ISBN 0-911906-07-X). Harian Creative.
--One of a Kind (the Many Faces & Voices of America) LC 75-41743. 1976. pap. 5.95 (ISBN 0-911906-12-6). Harian Creative.
--Round Trip to Byzantium. LC 84-80153. 379p. (Orig.). 1985. lib. bdg. 15.95x (ISBN 0-911906-28-2); pap. 7.95x quality (ISBN 0-911906-29-0). Harian Creative.
--Three by Harry Barba. LC 67-27073. (Orig.). 1967. pap. 15.00 (ISBN 0-911906-00-2). Harian Creative.
--Trip a Go-Go. (Mini-Book Ser). (Orig.). 1970. pap. 0.75 (ISBN 0-911906-03-7). Harian Creative.
Barba, Harry & Barba, Marian, eds. What's Cooking in Congress? LC 79-83777. (Orig. Ser.). 1979. pap. 5.95 (ISBN 0-911906-15-0). Harian Creative.
--What's Cooking in Congress, Vol. II. LC 79-83777. (What's Cooking Ser.). (Illus.). 250p. (Orig.). 1982. 12.95 (ISBN 0-911906-20-7, 0278-4947); pap. 7.95 (ISBN 0-911906-21-5). Harian Creative.
Barba, Harry, ed. see Avila, Kay, et al.
Barba, J. The Use of Steel. (Works of J. Barba Ser.). ix, 110p. Date not set. Repr. of 1875 ed. lib. bdg. 29.00 (ISBN 0-932051-61-8). Am Repr Serv.
Barba, Marian, jt. ed. see Barba, Harry.
Barba, Preston A. Cooper in Germany. 59.95 (ISBN 0-87968-944-7). Gordon Pr.
Barba, Preston A., jt. auth. see Treher, Charles H.
Barba, Sharon, jt. ed. see Chester, Laura.
Barbacci, M., jt. ed. see Uehara, T.
Barbacci, Mario, jt. auth. see Siewiorek, Daniel P.
Barbach, L., jt. auth. see Levine, L.
Barbach, Lonnie. For Each Other: Sharing Sexual Intimacy. LC 83-8804. (Illus.). 320p. 1982. pap. 8.95 (ISBN 0-385-17297-4, Anch). Doubleday.
--For Each Other: Sharing Sexual Intimacy. 1984. pap. 3.95 (ISBN 0-451-12802-8, Sig). NAL.
--For Each Other: Sharing Sexual Intimacy. 1984. pap. 4.50 (ISBN 0-451-13989-5, Sig). NAL.
--Pleasures: Women Write Erotica. LC 84-5922. 264p. 1984. 14.95 (ISBN 0-385-18811-0). Doubleday.
--Pleasures: Women Write Erotica. LC 85-42550. 304p. 1985. pap. 6.95 (ISBN 0-06-097002-2, PL 7002, PL). Har-Row.
Barbach, Lonnie & Levine, Linda. Shared Intimacies. 368p. 1981. pap. 4.50 (ISBN 0-553-25449-9). Bantam.
Barbach, Lonnie, jt. auth. see Levine, Linda.
Barbach, Lonnie G. For Yourself: Fulfillment of Female Sexuality-a Guide to Orgasmic Response. 1976. pap. 3.50 (ISBN 0-451-13982-8, Sig). NAL.
--For Yourself: The Fulfillment of Female Sexuality. LC 74-4873. 240p. 1975. pap. 6.95 (ISBN 0-385-11245-9, Anchor Pr). Doubleday.
--Women Discover Orgasm: A Therapist's Guide to a New Treatment Approach. LC 79-7847. (Illus.). 1980. 24.95 (ISBN 0-02-901800-5). Free Pr.
Barback, R. H. The Firm & Its Environment. (Industrial Studies). 288p. 1984. text ed. 25.75x (ISBN 0-86003-526-3, Pub. by Philip Allan England); pap. text ed. 13.00x (ISBN 0-86003-628-6, Pub. by Philip Allan England). Humanities.
Barbacovi, Don R. & Clelland, Richard W. Public Law 94-142: Special Education in Transition. 1978. pap. 4.95 (ISBN 0-686-02453-2, 02100323). Am Assn Sch Admin.
Barbaer, Lynda G. & Warren, Elizabeth V. Personality Decorating. 288p. (Orig.). 1986. pap. 14.95 (ISBN 0-449-90111-4, Columbine). Fawcett.
Barbaernitz, Patricia. R. C. I. A: The Rite of Christian Initiation for Adults. 48p. 1983. pap. 2.95 (ISBN 0-89243-190-3). Liguori Pubns.
Barbagallo-Sangiorgi, G. & Exton-Smith, A. N., eds. Aging & Drug Therapy. (Ettore Majoram International Science Series-Life Sciences: Vol. 15). 534p. 1984. 85.00x (ISBN 0-306-41739-1, Plenum Pr). Plenum Pub.
--The Aging Brain: Neurological & Mental Disturbances. LC 80-24567. (Ettore Majorana International Science Series-Life Sciences: Vol. 5). 406p. 1981. 52.50x (ISBN 0-306-40625-X, Plenum Pr). Plenum Pub.
Barbagli, Marzio. Educating for Unemployment: Origins of Crisis in the Italian University, 1859-1973. Ross, Robert, tr. from italian. 385p. 1982. 37.00x (ISBN 0-231-05284-7). Columbia U Pr.
Barbag-Stoll, Anna. Social & Linguistic History of Nigerian Pidgin English: As Spoken by the Yoruba with Special Reference to the English Derived Lexicon. 128p. (Orig.). 1983. pap. 14.00x (ISBN 3-923721-04-8, Pub by Stauffenberg Verlag W Germany). Benjamins North Am.
Barbalet, J. M. Marx's Construction of Social Theory. 240p. 1983. 26.95x (ISBN 0-7100-9540-6). Routledge & Kegan.
Barban, Arnold, et al. Essentials of Media Planning: A Marketing Viewpoint. LC 75-21743. (Illus.). 96p. (Orig.). 1976. pap. text ed. 9.95x (ISBN 0-87251-019-0). Crain Bks.
Barban, Arnold M., jt. auth. see Dunn, S. Watson.
Barban, Arnold M., et al. Advertising Media Sourcebook & Workbook. 2nd ed. LC 81-1018. (Grid Series in Advertising & Journalism). 176p. 1981. pap. text ed. 16.50 (ISBN 0-471-84148-X, Pub. by Grid). Wiley.
Barbanell, Maurice. Works of Spiritualism & Healing, 6 vols. 800.00 (ISBN 0-8490-1331-3). Gordon Pr.
Barbanis, B., ed. see European Astronomical Meeting, 1st, Athens, 1972.
Barbano, Joseph, et al. Changes among Registered Nurses Between 1972 to 1977-78. Olmstead, Mary, ed. (Series 12: No. 27). 50p. 1982. pap. 1.75 (ISBN 0-8406-0247-2). Natl Ctr Health.
Barbara, Dominick A. Art of Listening. 208p. 1974. 21.50x (ISBN 0-398-00086-7). C C Thomas.
--How to Make People Listen to You. 188p. 1971. 10.75x (ISBN 0-398-02223-2). C C Thomas.

--New Directions in Stuttering: Theory & Practice. (Illus.). 200p. 1965. 17.50x (ISBN 0-398-00087-5). C C Thomas.

--A Practical, Self-Help Guide for Stutterers. 68p. 1983. pap. 8.75x (ISBN 0-398-04794-4). C C Thomas.

--The Psychodynamics of Stuttering. 104p. 1982. 13.75x (ISBN 0-398-04714-6). C C Thomas.

--The Psychotherapy of Stuttering. (Illus.). 308p. 1962. 24.75x (ISBN 0-398-04199-7). C C Thomas.

--Questions & Answers on Stuttering. 112p. 1965. 11.75x (ISBN 0-398-00088-3). C C Thomas.

--Your Speech Reveals Your Personality. 192p. 1970. 10.75x (ISBN 0-398-00089-1). C C Thomas.

Barbara, Dominick A., jt. auth. see Oliver, Robert T.

Barbara, L., et al. New Trends in Pathophysiology & Therapy of the Large Bowel. (Giovanni Lorenzini Foundation Symposia Ser.: Vol. 17). 1984. 73.00 (ISBN 0-444-80534-6). Elsevier.

Barbara, Luigi, et al, eds. Recent Advances in Bile Acid Research. 1985. text ed. price not set (ISBN 0-88167-146-0). Raven.

Barbara, Michael A. Kansas Evidence Objections with Evidentiary Foundations. 1981. 50.00 (ISBN 0-318-04145-6). KS Bar CLE.

Barbarese, J. T. Under the Blue Moon. LC 85-5880. 72p. 1985. 10.95 (ISBN 0-8203-0801-3); pap. 6.95 (ISBN 0-8203-0802-1). U of Ga Pr.

Barbaresi, Nina. A Fox Jumped up One Winter's Night. (Little Golden Book Special Editions). (Illus.). 32p. (ps-2). 1985. 4.95 (ISBN 0-307-11631-X, 11631, Pub. by Golden Bks). Western Pub.

--Frog Went A-Courting. (Illus.). 40p. (Orig.). (gr. k-3). 1985. pap. 4.95 (ISBN 0-590-33301-1, Seesaw Bks). Scholastic Inc.

Barbaresi, Nina, illus. Santa Mouse Pencil, Puzzle & Fun Book. (Illus.). 48p. (ps-3). 1984. pap. 1.50 (ISBN 0-448-07327-7, G&D). Putnam Pub Group.

--The Three Little Pigs. (Golden Storytime Bk.). (Illus.). 24p. (ps-1). 1981. 1.95 (ISBN 0-307-11955-6, Golden Bks). Western Pub.

Barbaresi, Sara M. How to Raise & Train a Boxer. pap. 2.95 (ISBN 0-87666-253-X, DS-1006). TFH Pubns.

--How to Raise & Train a Collie. pap. 2.95 (ISBN 0-87666-272-6, DS-1010). TFH Pubns.

--How to Raise & Train a German Shepherd. pap. 2.95 (ISBN 0-87666-296-3, DS-1017). TFH Pubns.

Barbaresi, Sara M., jt. auth. see Ferguson, Estelle.

Barbaresi, Sara M., jt. auth. see Martin, Leda B.

Barbaresi, Sara M., jt. auth. see Meistrell, Lois.

Barbaresi, Sara M., jt. auth. see Shay, Sunny.

Barbaresi, Sara M., jt. auth. see Stebbins, Natalie.

Barbaresi, Sara M., jt. auth. see Ward, Mary A.

Barbarino, Joseph. The Evolution of the Latin -B-U-Merger: A Quantitative & Comparative Analysis of the B-V Alternation in Latin Inscriptions from Britain, the Balkans, Dalmattia, North Africa, Spain & Italy. LC 78-20445. (Studies in the Romance Languages & Literatures Ser.: No. 203). 184p. 1979. pap. 12.50x (ISBN 0-8078-9203-3). U of NC Pr.

Barbaro, Josafa & Contarini, Amrogio. Travels to Tana & Persia. Thomas, William, tr. (Hakluyt Soc. First Ser.: No. 49). 1963. 23.50 (ISBN 0-8337-0162-2). B Franklin.

Barbaro, Ronald & Cross, Frank L., Jr. Primer on Environmental Impact Statements. LC 73-78925. 140p. 1973. pap. 4.95 (ISBN 0-87762-112-8). Technomic.

Barbarossa, Fred. The Car Care Book. 1983. pap. text ed. 8.35 (ISBN 0-538-33030-9, IE03). SW Pub.

Barbaroux, Charles O. Memoires de Robert Guillemard, Sergent en Retraite, Suivis de Documents Historiques, 2 Vols. Repr. of 1826 ed. Set. 30.00 (ISBN 0-404-07537-1); 15.00 ea. Vol. 1 (ISBN 0-404-07538-X). Vol. 2 (ISBN 0-404-07539-8). AMS Pr.

Barbash, Heather, jt. auth. see Marshall, John.

Barbash, Jack. The Elements of Industrial Relations. LC 83-40258. (Illus.). 170p. 1984. pap. 17.50x (ISBN 0-299-09610-6); pap. text ed. 9.95x (ISBN 0-299-09614-9). U of Wis Pr.

--Job Satisfaction Attitudes Surveys: Industrial Relations Programme, Special Studies. 1976. 2.00x (ISBN 92-64-11537-4). OECD.

--Labor's Grass Roots: A Study of the Local Union. LC 73-11839. 250p. 1974. Repr. of 1961 ed. lib. bdg. 22.25x (ISBN 0-8371-7064-8, BALG). Greenwood.

Barbash, Joseph & Feerick, John D. Unjust Dismissal & at Will Employment. (Litigation & Administrative Practice Course Handbook Ser.). 343p. 1982. pap. 35.00 (H4-4885). PLI.

Barbash, Joseph & Kauff, Jerome. Unjust Dismissal, 1983: Litigating, Settling, & Advocating Claims. Practising Law Institute, ed. LC 84-101023. (Litigation & Administrative Practice Ser.: No. 240). 560p. 1983. 35.00. PLI.

Barbash, Joseph, jt. auth. see Practising Law Institute.

Barbasin, E. A., et al. Twelve Papers on Analysis, Applied Mathematics & Algebraic Topology. LC 51-5559. (Translations Ser.: No. 2, Vol. 25). 1963. 27.00 (ISBN 0-8218-1725-6, TRANS 2-25). Am Math.

Barbata, Jean, jt. auth. see Koch, Marianna.

Barbata, Jean C., jt. auth. see Garnett, Theodosia V.

Barbato & Ayer. Atmospheres. 250p. 1981. pap. text ed. 12.95 (ISBN 0-08-025582-5). Pergamon.

Barbato, Juli. Mom's Night Out. LC 85-3096. (Illus.). 32p. (gr. k-3). 1985. PLB 11.95 (ISBN 0-02-708480-9). Macmillan.

Barbato, Julie. From Bed to Bus. LC 84-20159. 32p. (ps-2). 1985. 10.95 (ISBN 0-02-708380-2). Macmillan.

Barbaud, Pierre. Haydn. (Illustrated Composer Ser.). (Illus.). 192p. 1986. pap. 5.95 (ISBN 0-7145-3582-6). Riverrun NY.

Barbauld, Anna L., ed. see Richardson, Samuel.

Barbe. Strips. 48p. 1983. pap. 4.95 (ISBN 0-918348-05-6). NBM.

Barbe, jt. auth. see St. Barbe, Richard.

Barbe, B. F., ed. Very Large Scale Integration (VLSI) Fundamentals & Applications. 2nd, updated ed. (Springer Series in Electrophysics: Vol. 5). (Illus.). 302p. 1982. 27.00 (ISBN 0-387-11368-1). Springer-Verlag.

Barbe, D. F., ed. Charge-Coupled Devices. (Topics in Applied Physics Ser.: Vol. 38). (Illus.). 1980. 45.00 (ISBN 0-387-09832-1). Springer-Verlag.

Barbe, Louis A. Viscount Dundee. 159p. 1980. Repr. lib. bdg. 20.00 (ISBN 0-89987-053-8). Darby Bks.

Barbe, Waitman. Famous Poems Explained. 1976. lib. bdg. 59.95 (ISBN 0-8490-1803-X). Gordon Pr.

--Famous Poems Explained. LC 78-73480. (Granger Poetry Library). 1979. Repr. of 1909 ed. 18.75x (ISBN 0-89609-106-6). Granger Bk.

--Famous Poems Explained. 237p. 1980. Repr. of 1909 ed. lib. bdg. 35.00 (ISBN 0-8482-0132-9). Norwood Edns.

--Famous Poems Explained: Helps to Reading with the Understanding. LC 79-14267. 1979. lib. bdg. 30.00 (ISBN 0-8414-9826-1). Folcroft.

--Great Poems Interpreted. LC 79-14197. 1914. Repr. 40.00 (ISBN 0-8414-9833-4). Folcroft.

--Great Poems Interpreted, with Biographical Notes of the Authors Represented. 368p. 1980. Repr. of 1914 ed. lib. bdg. 38.50 (ISBN 0-8482-0149-3). Norwood Edns.

Barbe, Walter & Abbott, Jerry. Personalized Reading Instruction: New Techniques That Increase Reading Skill and Comprehension. 1975. 12.95 (ISBN 0-13-658104-8). P-H.

Barbe, Walter, jt. auth. see Allen, Henriette.

Barbe, Walter B. Highlights for Children: Growing up Smarter. (Illus.). 200p. 1985. pap. 8.95 (ISBN 0-87491-790-5). Acropolis.

--Resource Book for the Kindergarten Teacher. (Illus.). 1980. 36.95 (ISBN 0-88309-103-8). Zaner-Bloser.

--Zaner-Bloser Handwriting Workbook: Cursive. (Illus.). 1977. 3.95 (ISBN 0-88309-098-8). Zaner-Bloser.

--Zaner-Bloser Handwriting Workbook: Manuscript. (Illus.). 1977. 3.95 (ISBN 0-88309-097-X). Zaner-Bloser.

Barbe, Walter B. & Francis, Azalia S. Pupil, Bk. 2. (Zaner-Bloser Spelling: Basic Skills & Application Ser.). (gr. k-8). 1984. pap. text ed. 3.94 (ISBN 0-88309-343-X). Zaner-Bloser.

--Pupil, Bk. 3. (Zaner-Bloser Spelling: Basic Skills & Application Ser.). (gr. k-8). 1984. pap. text ed. 3.94 (ISBN 0-88309-344-8). Zaner-Bloser.

--Pupil: Manual-Courses, Bk. 2. (Zaner-Bloser Spelling: Basic Skills & Application Ser.). (gr. k-8). 1984. pap. text ed. 3.94 (ISBN 0-88309-350-2). Zaner-Bloser.

--Zaner-Bloser Spelling: Basic Skills & Application. Incl. Grade 1 soft cover (ISBN 0-88309-268-9). Grade 2 soft cover, Grade 2 Man-Cur softcover, (0-88309-270-0 (ISBN 0-88309-269-7). Grade 3 soft cover (ISBN 0-88309-271-9). Grade 4 soft cover (ISBN 0-88309-272-7). Grade 5 soft cover (ISBN 0-88309-273-5). Grade 6 soft cover (ISBN 0-88309-274-3). Grade 7 soft cover (ISBN 0-88309-275-1). Grade 8 (ISBN 0-88309-276-X). 1983. softcover, Grade 1 3.94 ea. Zaner-Bloser.

--Zaner-Bloser Spelling: Basic Skills & Application, 8 Grades. Incl. Grade 1. pap. 3.94 (ISBN 0-88309-342-1); tchrs' ed. 10.95 (ISBN 0-88309-367-7); Grade 2. 7.68 (ISBN 0-88309-351-0); Man-Cur 7.68 (ISBN 0-88309-358-8); toughcover 5.68 (ISBN 0-88309-359-6); toughcover Man-Cur 5.68 (ISBN 0-88309-366-9); tchrs' ed. 10.95 (ISBN 0-88309-368-5); Grade 3. 7.68 (ISBN 0-88309-352-9); toughcover 5.68 (ISBN 0-88309-360-X); tchrs' ed. 10.95 (ISBN 0-88309-369-3); Grade 4. 7.68 (ISBN 0-88309-353-7); toughcover 5.68 (ISBN 0-88309-361-8); tchrs' ed. 10.95 (ISBN 0-88309-370-7); Grade 5. 7.68 (ISBN 0-88309-354-5); toughcover 5.68 (ISBN 0-88309-362-6); tchrs' ed. 10.95 (ISBN 0-88309-371-5); Grade 6. 7.68 (ISBN 0-88309-355-3); toughcover 5.68 (ISBN 0-88309-363-4); tchrs' ed. 10.95 (ISBN 0-88309-372-3); Grade 7. 7.68 (ISBN 0-88309-356-1); toughcover 5.68 (ISBN 0-88309-364-2); tchrs' ed. 10.95 (ISBN 0-88309-373-1); Grade 8. 7.68 (ISBN 0-88309-357-X); toughcover 5.68 (ISBN 0-88309-365-0); tchrs' ed. 10.95 (ISBN 0-88309-374-X). (gr. 1-8). 1984. Zaner-Bloser.

Barbe, Walter B. & Lucas, Virginia H. Zaner-Bloser Handwriting: Basic Skills & Application. Incl. Readiness (ISBN 0-88309-302-2); Grade 1 (ISBN 0-88309-303-0); Grade 2 (ISBN 0-88309-304-9); Grade 2 Man-Cur (ISBN 0-88309-311-1); Grade 3 (ISBN 0-88309-305-7). Grade 4 (ISBN 0-88309-306-5). Grade 5 (ISBN 0-88309-307-3). Grade 6 (ISBN 0-88309-308-1). Grade 7 (ISBN 0-88309-309-X). Grade 8 (ISBN 0-88309-310-3); Readiness Non-Consumable (ISBN 0-88309-322-7). Grade 1 Non-Consumable (ISBN 0-88309-323-5). Grade 2 Non-Consumable (ISBN 0-88309-324-3). Grade 2 Man-Cur Non-Consumable (ISBN 0-88309-331-6). Grade 3 Non-Consumable (ISBN 0-88309-325-1). Grade 4 Non-Consumable (ISBN 0-88309-326-X); Grade 5 Non-Consumable (ISBN 0-88309-327-8). Grade 6 Non-Consumable (ISBN 0-88309-328-6). Grade 7 Non-Consumable (ISBN 0-88309-329-4). Grade 8 Non-Consumable (ISBN 0-88309-330-8); Readiness Tchr's Ed (ISBN 0-88309-312-X). Grade 1 Tchr's Ed (ISBN 0-88309-313-8). Grade 2 Tchr's Ed (ISBN 0-88309-314-6). Grade 2 Man-Cur Tchr's Ed (ISBN 0-88309-321-9). Grade 3 Tchr's Ed (ISBN 0-88309-315-4); Grade 4 Tchr's Ed (ISBN 0-88309-316-2). Grade 5 Tchr's Ed (ISBN 0-88309-317-0). Grade 6 Tchr's Ed (ISBN 0-88309-318-9). Grade 7 Tchr's Ed (ISBN 0-88309-319-7). Grade 8 Tchr's Ed (ISBN 0-88309-320-0). (Illus.). 1984. pupil bk., consumable 2.87 ea.; non-consumable 3.07 ea.; tchrs.' edition 7.95 ea. Zaner-Bloser.

Barbe, Walter B. & Swassing, Raymond H. Teaching Through Modality Strengths: Concepts & Practices. LC 79-66953. 1979. 10.00 (ISBN 0-88309-100-3). Zaner-Bloser.

Barbe, Walter B., jt. auth. see Lucas, Virginia H.

Barbe, Walter B., ed. Fables & Folktales from Many Lands. (Illus.). 33p. (gr. 2-6). 1972. pap. 2.50 (ISBN 0-87534-147-0). Highlights.

Barbe, Walter B. & Renzulli, Joseph S., eds. Psychology & Education of the Gifted. 3rd ed. LC 80-11174. 544p. 1981. text ed. 19.95x (ISBN 0-8290-0234-0). Irvington.

Barbe, Walter B., ed. see Levin, A. Joyce.

Barbe, Walter B., et al. Barbe Reading Skills Check List & Activities: Readiness to Advanced Level. (Illus.). 1976. pap. 17.60x ea. spiral bdg.; Readiness Level. (ISBN 0-87628-723-2); First Level. (ISBN 0-87628-724-0); Second Level. (ISBN 0-87628-725-9); Third Level. (ISBN 0-87628-726-7); Fourth Level. (ISBN 0-87628-727-5); Fifth Level. (ISBN 0-87628-728-3); Sixth Level. (ISBN 0-87628-729-1); Advanced Level. (ISBN 0-87628-730-5). Ctr Appl Res.

--Competency Tests for Basic Reading Skills, 16 bks. Incl. Readiness Level. 16.90x (ISBN 0-87628-668-6); dupl. master 18.70x (ISBN 0-87628-669-4); First Level. 16.90x (ISBN 0-87628-670-8); dupl. master 18.70x (ISBN 0-87628-671-6); Second Level. 16.90x (ISBN 0-87628-672-4); dupl. master 18.70x (ISBN 0-87628-673-2); Third Level. 16.90x (ISBN 0-87628-674-0); dupl. master 18.70x (ISBN 0-87628-675-9); Fourth Level. 16.90x (ISBN 0-87628-676-7); dupl. master 18.70x (ISBN 0-87628-677-5); Fifth Level. 16.90x (ISBN 0-87628-678-3); dupl. master 18.70x (ISBN 0-87628-679-1); Sixth Level. 16.90x (ISBN 0-87628-680-5); dupl. master 18.70x (ISBN 0-87628-681-3); Advanced Level. 16.90x (ISBN 0-87628-682-1); dupl. master 18.70x (ISBN 0-87628-683-X). 1979. Ctr Appl Res.

--Creative Growth with Handwriting. Incl. Readiness. tchrs.' manual 11.95 (ISBN 0-88309-244-1); consumable; non-consumable (ISBN 0-88309-255-7); Grade One. tchrs.' manual 11.95 (ISBN 0-88309-245-X); consumable (ISBN 0-88309-234-4); non-consumable (ISBN 0-88309-256-5); Grade Two. tchrs.' manual 11.95 (ISBN 0-88309-246-8); consumable (ISBN 0-88309-235-2); non-consumable (ISBN 0-88309-257-3); Book 2T. tchrs.' manual 11.95 (ISBN 0-88309-247-6); consumable (ISBN 0-88309-236-0); non-consumable (ISBN 0-88309-258-1); Grade 3T. tchrs.' manual 11.95 (ISBN 0-88309-248-4); consumable (ISBN 0-88309-237-9); non-consumable (ISBN 0-88309-259-X); Grade 4. tchrs.' manual 11.95 (ISBN 0-88309-250-6); consumable (ISBN 0-88309-239-5); non-consumable (ISBN 0-88309-261-1); Grade 5. tchrs.' manual 11.95 (ISBN 0-88309-251-4); consumable (ISBN 0-88309-240-9); non-consumable (ISBN 0-88309-262-X); Grade 6. tchrs.' manual 11.95 (ISBN 0-88309-252-2); consumable (ISBN 0-88309-241-7); non-consumable (ISBN 0-88309-263-8); Grade 7. tchrs.' manual 7.95 (ISBN 0-88309-253-0); consumable (ISBN 0-88309-242-5); non-consumable (ISBN 0-88309-264-6); Grade 8. tchrs.' manual 7.95 (ISBN 0-88309-254-9); consumable (ISBN 0-88309-243-3); non-consumable (ISBN 0-88309-265-4). (Illus.). 1979. pupil bk., consumable 2.85 ea. (ISBN 0-88309-233-6); non-consumable 3.05 ea. Zaner-Bloser.

--Basic Skills in Kindergarten: Foundations for Formal Learning. 1980. 10.00 (ISBN 0-88309-104-6). Zaner-Bloser.

Barbe, Walter B., et al, eds. Spelling: Basic Skills for Effective Communication. 1982. 10.00 (ISBN 0-88309-118-6). Zaner-Bloser.

Barbe, Wren, ed. Young Japan Views Uncle Sam: A Collection of Opinions on America. LC 65-13413. (gr. 7 up). 1965. 4.15 (ISBN 0-8048-0641-1). C E Tuttle.

Barbeau, A., et al, eds. Huntington's Chorea: Advances in Neurology, Vol. 1. LC 72-93317. 848p. 1973. 96.00 (ISBN 0-911216-40-5). Raven.

Barbeau, Andre & Huxtable, Ryan, eds. Taurine & Neurological Disorders. LC 77-85076. 482p. 1978. 64.50 (ISBN 0-89004-202-0). Raven.

Barbeau, Andre, jt. ed. see Huxtable, Ryan.

Barbeau, Anne T. Intellectual Design of John Dryden's Heroic Plays. LC 71-81412. pap. 58.00 (ISBN 0-8357-9288-9, 2013191). Bks Demand UMI.

Barbeau, Arthur E. & Henri, Florette. Unknown Soldiers: Black American Troops in World War I. LC 72-95880. (Illus.). 303p. 1974. 24.95 (ISBN 0-87722-063-8). Temple U Pr.

Barbeau, Clayton C. Delivering the Male: Out of the Tough-Guy Trap into a Better Marriage. 120p. (Orig.). 1982. pap. 6.95 (ISBN 0-86683-642-X). Winston Pr.

--Joy of Marriage. Orig. Title: Creative Marriage: the Middle Years. 132p. 1980. pap. 5.95 (ISBN 0-86683-759-0). Winston Pr.

Barbeau, Gerard. The Qualified Security Guard. Scotti, Anthony J., tr. (Illus.). 232p. 1981. pap. 27.50x spiral photocopy ed. (ISBN 0-398-04177-6). C C Thomas.

Barbeau, Marius. All Hands Aboard Scrimshawing. (Illus.). 1973. pap. 3.50 (ISBN 0-87577-030-4). Peabody Mus Salem.

--Assomption Sash. (Illus.). 1972. pap. text ed. 3.25x (ISBN 0-660-00130-6, 56268-9, Pub. by Natl Mus Canada). U of Chicago Pr.

--Modern Growth of the Totem Pole on the Northwest Coast. facs. ed. (Shorey Indian Ser.). 16p. pap. 0.95 (ISBN 0-8466-0098-6, S98). Shorey.

Barbeau, Maurice. Art of the Totem. (Illus.). 64p. 1984. 5.95 (ISBN 0-88839-168-4). Hancock House.

Barbedette, Hippolyte. Stephen Heller: His Life & Works. LC 74-75886. (Detroit Reprints in Music). 132p. 1974. Repr. of 1877 ed. 5.00 (ISBN 0-911772-69-3). Info Coord.

Barbee, A. H. Behind the Iron Curtain. 74p. 1985. pap. write for info. (ISBN 0-89084-280-9). Bob Jones Univ Pr.

Barbellion, W. N. Enjoying Life & Other Literary Remains. 75.00 (ISBN 0-87968-257-4). Gordon Pr.

--Journal of a Disappointed Man. lib. bdg. 75.00 (ISBN 0-87968-150-0). Gordon Pr.

--A Last Diary. 75.00 (ISBN 0-87968-382-1). Gordon Pr.

Barbellion, W. N., et al. The Journal of a Disappointed Man & a Last Diary. 464p. (Orig.). 1984. pap. 8.95 (ISBN 0-7012-1906-8). Merrimack Pub Cir.

Barbely, A A. Pharmacological Modifications of Evolked Brain Potentials. 138p. 1973. 60.00 (ISBN 3-456-00356-0, Pub. by Holdan Bk Ltd UK). State Mutual Bk.

Barbe-Marbois, Francois. The History of Louisiana, Particularly of the Cession of That Colony to the United States of America. Lyon, E. Wilson, ed. LC 77-5665. (Louisiana Bicentennial Reprint Ser.). xviii, 460p. 1977. 27.50x (ISBN 0-8071-0186-9). La State U Pr.

--Our Revolutionary Forefathers: The Letters of Francois, Marquis De Barbe-Marbois During His Residence in the United States As Secretary of the French Legation 1779-1785. facsimile ed. LC 71-99659. (Select Bibliographies Reprint Ser). 1929. 23.50 (ISBN 0-8369-5088-7). Ayer Co Pubs.

Barber & Dillman. Package for Emergency Patient Care for the EMT-A. 1981. text ed. 25.00 (ISBN 0-8359-5412-9). Reston.

Barber, Adwin A., jt. auth. see Atlee, Barber A.

Barber, Aldyth A., jt. auth. see Barber, Cyril J.

Barber, Alfred. Digital ICs: How They Work. 240p. 1981. pap. 7.95 (ISBN 0-13-212233-2, Reward). P-H.

Barber, Alfred W. Experimenter's Guide to Solid State Electronics Projects. (Illus.). 1980. 17.95 (ISBN 0-13-295451-6, Parker). P-H.

--Handbook of Hi Fi Audio Systems & Projects. 224p. 1981. 18.95 (ISBN 0-686-92208-5, Parker). P-H.

--Handbook of HiFi-Audio Systems & Projects. (Illus.). 1984. pap. 12.95 (ISBN 0-13-378299-9, Busn); cloth 18.95. P-H.

--Practical Guide to Digital Integrated Circuits. 2nd ed. LC 83-21208. (Illus.). 1984. 21.95 (ISBN 0-13-690751-2, Busn). P-H.

--Practical Guide to Integrated Circuits. 2nd ed. price not set. P-H.

Barber, Allan W., jt. auth. see Green, John L.

Barber, Anthony. Great Britain's Tax Credit Income Supplement. LC 74-32639. (Illus.). 36p. 1975. pap. 3.00 (ISBN 0-915312-00-X). Inst Socioecon.

Barber, Antonia. The Ghosts. (gr. 5-7). 1975. pap. 2.25 (ISBN 0-671-42454-8). Archway.

Barber, B., ed. Medical Informatics, Berlin, 1979: Proceedings. (Lecture Notes in Medical Informatics: Vol. 5). 1979. pap. 44.30 (ISBN 0-387-09549-7). Springer-Verlag.

Barber, Benjamin. Strong Democracy: Participatory Politics for a New Age. LC 83-4842. 320p. 1984. 16.95 (ISBN 0-520-05115-7, CAL 762); pap. 9.95 (ISBN 0-520-05616-7). U of Cal Pr.

Barber, Benjamin & McGrath, Michael J., eds. The Artist & Political Vision. LC 80-80317. 408p. 1981. 39.95 (ISBN 0-87855-380-0). Transaction Bks.

Barber, Benjamin A. Robert Louis Stevenson: An Appreciation. LC 74-17085. Repr. of 1910 ed. lib. bdg. 8.50 (ISBN 0-8414-3114-0). Folcroft.

Barber, Benjamin R. Death of Communal Liberty: A History of Freedom in a Swiss Mountain Canton. 1974. 33.00 (ISBN 0-691-07554-9, 344). Princeton U Pr.

Barber, Bernard. Informed Consent in Medical Therapy & Research. 1980. 20.00x (ISBN 0-8135-0889-4). Rutgers U Pr.

--The Logic & Limits of Trust. 203p. 1983. 27.50 (ISBN 0-8135-0958-0); pap. 9.95 (ISBN 0-8135-1002-3). Rutgers U Pr.

--Mass Apathy & Voluntary Social Participation in the United States. Zuckerman, Harriet & Merton, Robert K., eds. LC 79-8972. (Dissertations on Sociology). 1980. lib. bdg. 22.00x (ISBN 0-405-12949-1). Ayer Co Pubs.

--Science & the Social Order. LC 78-1569. 228p. 1978. Repr. of 1952 ed. lib. bdg. 32.50 (ISBN 0-313-20356-3, BASSO). Greenwood.

Barber, Bernard & Barber, Elinor G. European Social Class: Stability & Change. LC 77-13508. (Main Themes in European History). 1977. Repr. of 1965 ed. lib. bdg. 22.50x (ISBN 0-8371-9860-7, BAEU). Greenwood.

Barber, Bernard & Hirsch, Walter, eds. The Sociology of Science. LC 78-5937. viii, 662p. 1978. Repr. of 1962 ed. lib. bdg. 55.00 (ISBN 0-313-20403-9, BASOS). Greenwood.

Barber, Bernard, ed. see Henderson, L. J.

Barber, Bernard, et al. Research on Human Subjects: Problems of Social Control in Medical Experimentation. LC 70-83831. 264p. 1973. 10.50x (ISBN 0-87154-090-8). Russell Sage.

--Research on Human Subjects: Problems of Social Control in Medical Experimentation. LC 78-55938. 263p. 1979. pap. text ed. 9.95x (ISBN 0-87855-649-4). Transaction Bks.

Barber, Bruce, jt. auth. see Nennsberg, Tatiana O.

Barber, Bruce T. Designer's Dictionary Two. (Illus.). 407p. 1981. 28.00 (ISBN 0-911380-54-X). Signs of Times.

Barber, C. The Theme of Honour's Tongue. 171p. 1985. pap. text ed. 20.00x (ISBN 91-7346-138-5, Pub. by Acta-Universitatis Sweden). Humanities.

Barber, C., et al. Dictionary of Physiological Measurement. 1984. pap. text ed. 11.00 (ISBN 0-85200-737-X, Pub. by MTP Pr England). Kluwer Academic.

Barber, C. L. Shakespeare. Repr. of 1957 ed. lib. bdg. 15.00 (ISBN 0-8414-1625-7). Folcroft.

--Shakespeare's Festive Comedy. 1972. pap. 8.95x (ISBN 0-691-01304-7, 271). Princeton U Pr.

Barber, Charles. Early Modern English. Crystal, David, ed. (Language Library). 360p. 1976. 14.95x (ISBN 0-233-96262-X). Basil Blackwell.

--Poetry in English: An Introduction. LC 82-23099. 220p. 1983. 19.95 (ISBN 0-312-61888-3). St Martin.

Barber, Chris. Mysterious Wales. (Illus.). 256p. 1982. 18.95 (ISBN 0-7153-8366-3). David & Charles.

--Mysterious Wales. (Illus.). 256p. pap. 6.95 (ISBN 0-586-08419-3, Pub. by Granada England). Academy Chi Pubs.

Barber, Cyril J. Dynamic Personal Bible Study: Principles of Inductive Bible Study Based on the Life of Abraham. LC 81-8443. 1981. pap. 4.95 (ISBN 0-87213-023-1). Loizeaux.

--Habakkuk & Zephaniah. (Everyman's Bible Commentary Ser.). 1985. pap. 5.95 (ISBN 0-8024-2069-9). Moody.

--Introduction to Theological Research. 1982. pap. 9.95 (ISBN 0-8024-4134-3). Moody.

--The Minister's Library, Vol. I. 1985. 15.95 (ISBN 0-8024-5296-5). Moody.

--The Minister's Library, Vol. 2. 228p. 1983. 14.95 (ISBN 0-8010-0830-1). Baker Bk.

--Nehemiah & the Dynamics of Effective Leadership: Study Guide. (Illus.). 56p. 1980. pap. text ed. 3.25 (ISBN 0-87213-022-3). Loizeaux.

--Nehemiah & the Dynamics of Effective Leadership. LC 76-22567. 1976. pap. 3.95 (ISBN 0-87213-021-5). Loizeaux.

--Periodic Supplement No. 1 to the Minister's Library. 32p. 1975. pap. 4.95 (ISBN 0-8010-0647-3). Baker Bk.

--Periodic Supplement No. 3 to the Minister's Library. 1980. pap. 4.95 (ISBN 0-8010-0787-9). Baker Bk.

--Periodic Supplement No. 4 to The Minister's Library. 80p. (Orig.). 1982. pap. 5.95 (ISBN 0-8010-0813-1). Baker Bk.

Barber, Cyril J. & Barber, Aldyth A. You Can Have a Happy Marriage. LC 83-25542. 192p. (Orig.). 1984. pap. 6.95 (ISBN 0-8254-2248-5). Kregel.

--Your Marriage Has Real Possibilities. LC 83-25537. 168p. (Orig.). 1984. pap. text ed. 6.95 (ISBN 0-8254-2249-3). Kregel.

Barber, Cyril J. & Carter, John D. Always a Winner. LC 77-72556. 160p. 1977. pap. 3.50 (ISBN 0-8307-0497-3, S321106). Regal.

Barber, Cyril J. & Strauss, Gary H. Leadership: The Dynamics of Success. 126p. 1982. pap. 4.95 (ISBN 0-87921-068-0). Attic Pr.

Barber, D. L., jt. auth. see Davies, D. W.

Barber, Daniel M. Citizen Participation in American Communities: Strategies for Success. LC 80-83336. 144p. 1980. pap. 11.95 (ISBN 0-8403-2299-2). Kendall-Hunt.

Barber, David, jt. auth. see Berwin, Derek.

Barber, David H. Power Think. (Winning in Law School Ser.: Bk. 2). (Illus.). 201p. (Orig.). 1984. pap. 10.95 (ISBN 0-915667-05-3). Spectra Pub Co.

--Practice Exams & Model Answers in Torts. (Winning in Law School Ser.: Bk. 3). (Illus.). 175p. (Orig.). 1984. pap. 10.95 (ISBN 0-915667-04-5). Spectra Pub Co.

--Surviving Your Role As a Lawyer. (Illus.). 379p. (Orig.). 1983. text ed. 17.95 (ISBN 0-915667-02-9). Spectra Pub Co.

--Winning in Law School. (Illus.). 227p. (Orig.). 1983. pap. text ed. 10.95 (ISBN 0-915667-03-7). Spectra Pub Co.

Barber, DeNonie. Their Last Lap at Indy: A Book of Tributes. (Illus.). 1980. 8.95 (ISBN 0-916620-49-2). Portals Pr.

Barber, Derek, ed. Data Networks: Development & Uses. 690p. 1980. pap. text ed. 168.00x (ISBN 0-903796-59-7, Pub. by Online Conferences England). Brookfield Pub Co.

Barber, E. A. Pottery & Porcelain of the U. S. LC 79-96939. 20.00 (ISBN 0-87282-010-6). CHB-ALF.

Barber, E. A., jt. ed. see Powell, J. U.

Barber, E. A., ed. see Propertius.

Barber, E. A., et al, eds. see Liddell, Henry G. & Scott, Robert.

Barber, Edward A. & Lockwood, Luke V. The Ceramic Furniture & Silver Collectors' Glossary. (Architecture & Decorative Art Ser.). 1976. pap. 6.95 (ISBN 0-306-80049-7). Da Capo.

Barber, Edwin A. The Ceramic Collectors' Glossary. LC 76-8172. (Architecture & Decorative Art Ser). 1967. Repr. of 1914 ed. 16.50 (ISBN 0-306-70967-8). Da Capo.

--Marks of American Potters. (Illus.). 1976. Repr. of 1904 ed. 15.00 (ISBN 0-89344-001-9). Ars Ceramica.

--Marks of American Potters--with Facisimles of 1000 Marks & Illustrations of Rare Examples of American Wares. 1976. Repr. of 1904 ed. 29.00x (ISBN 0-403-06291-8, Regency). Scholarly.

Barber, Elinor, et al, eds. Bridges to Knowledge: Foreign Students in Comparative Perspective. LC 84-16374. 264p. 1985. lib. bdg. 25.00x (ISBN 0-226-03708-8); pap. 12.95 (ISBN 0-226-03709-6). U of Chicago Pr.

Barber, Elinor G. Bourgeoisie in Eighteenth Century France. 1955. 21.00x (ISBN 0-691-09309-1); pap. 6.95x (ISBN 0-691-02801-X, 98). Princeton U Pr.

Barber, Elinor G., jt. auth. see Barber, Bernard.

Barber, Ezekiel. The Bene-Israel of India: Images & Reality. LC 81-40006. (Illus.). 176p. 1981. lib. bdg. 21.75 (ISBN 0-8191-1594-0); pap. text ed. 10.50 (ISBN 0-8191-1645-9). U Pr of Amer.

Barber, Florence H. Fellow of Infinite Jest: Recollections & Anecdotes of William Lyon Phelps. 1949. 29.50x (ISBN 0-685-89752-4). Elliots Bks.

Barber, Geoffrey. Country Doctor. (Illus.). 108p. 1975. 11.50 (ISBN 0-85115-037-3, Pub. by Boydell & Brewer); pap. cancelled. Longwood Pub Group.

--The Country Doctor. (Illus.). 200p. 1985. pap. 5.95 (ISBN 0-85115-234-1, Pub. by Boydell England). Academy Chi Pubs.

Barber, George & Reader, Larry. Decoy Carving Techniques: For the Intermediate Carver. LC 83-51212. (Illus.). 56p. 1984. pap. 6.95 (ISBN 0-916838-95-1). Schiffer.

Barber, George E. Guide to Marketing Financial Planning Success. 1983p. 25.00 (ISBN 0-318-04488-9, MFPS). Bank MKTG Assn.

Barber, Godfrey L. The Historian Ephorus. LC 76-29429. (BCL Series II). Repr. of 1935 ed. 18.50 (ISBN 0-404-15343-7). AMS Pr.

Barber, H. Electroheat. (Illus.). 300p. 1983. pap. 26.50x (ISBN 0-246-11739-7, Pub. by Granad England). Sheridan.

Barber, H. O., ed. see Barany Society Meeting, Toronto, Aug. 1971.

Barber, Henrietta D., ed. see Neeb, Karen J.

Barber, Henry. British Family Names. 2nd ed. LC 68-17914. 1968. Repr. of 1903 ed. 34.00x (ISBN 0-8103-3109-8). Gale.

--British Family Names. 59.95 (ISBN 0-87968-791-6). Gordon Pr.

Barber, Hugh R. Manual of Gynecologic Oncology. 356p. 1980. pap. text ed. 23.75 (ISBN 0-397-50474-8, 65-06158, Lippincott Medical). Lippincott.

--Ovarian Carcinoma: Etiology, Diagnosis, & Treatment. 2nd ed. LC 82-7176. (Illus.). 420p. 1982. 59.50x (ISBN 0-89352-168-X). Masson Pub.

Barber, Hugh R. & Graber, Edward A. Septic Shock in Obstetrics & Gynecology. 84p. 1971. spiral 9.50x (ISBN 0-398-00091-3). C C Thomas.

--Surgical Disease in Pregnancy. LC 73-89171. (Illus.). Repr. of 1974 ed. 160.00 (ISBN 0-8357-9559-4, 2016652). Bks Demand UMI.

Barber, Hugh R., jt. ed. see Van Nagell, John R., Jr.

Barber, Hugh R. K. & Sommers, Sheldon C., eds. Carcinoma of the Endometrium: Etiology, Diagnosis & Treatment. LC 81-14264. (Illus.). 248p. 1981. 43.50x (ISBN 0-89352-072-1). Masson Pub.

Barber, J. & Magee, D. The Western Isles. (Illus.). 128p. 1985. text ed. 9.50x (ISBN 0-85976-142-8, Pub. by Donald Scotland). Humanities.

Barber, J., ed. Electron Transport & Photophosphorylation. (Topics in Photosynthesis Ser.: Vol. 4). 288p. 1982. 82.25 (ISBN 0-444-80375-0). Elsevier.

--The Intact Chloroplast. (Topics in Photosynthesis: Vol. 1). 476p. 1976. 95.75 (ISBN 0-444-41451-7, North Holland). Elsevier.

--Photosynthesis in Relation to Model Systems. (Topics in Photosynthesis Ser.: Vol. 3). 534p. 1979. 119.75 (ISBN 0-444-80066-2, North Holland). Elsevier.

Barber, J., jt. ed. see Baker, N. R.

Barber, J. H., ed. General Practice Medicine. 2nd ed. (Illus.). 389p. 1984. pap. text ed. 35.00 (ISBN 0-443-02693-9). Churchill.

Barber, J. H. & Kratz, Charlotte R., eds. Towards Team Care. (Illus.). 176p. 1980. pap. text ed. 10.75 (ISBN 0-443-02031-0). Churchill.

Barber, James. Who Makes British Foreign Policy? 140p. 1976. pap. 9.00x (ISBN 0-335-01962-5, Pub. by Open Univ Pr). Taylor & Francis.

Barber, James, jt. auth. see Hill, Christopher.

Barber, James A., Jr., jt. ed. see Ambrose, Stephen E.

Barber, James D. Erasmus: A Play on Words. LC 81-40002. 80p. (Orig.). 1982. lib. bdg. 21.00 (ISBN 0-8191-1868-0); pap. text ed. 5.75 (ISBN 0-8191-1869-9). U Pr of Amer.

--The Lawmakers: Recruitment & Adaptation to Legislative Life. xii, 314p. 1980. Repr. of 1965 ed. lib. bdg. 32.50x (ISBN 0-313-22200-2, BALA). Greenwood.

--The Presidential Character: Predicting Performance in the White House. 2nd ed. LC 77-4094. 1977. 19.95 (ISBN 0-13-697847-9). P-H.

--The Pulse of Politics: The Rhythm of Presidential Elections in the Twentieth Century. 1980. 14.95 (ISBN 0-393-01341-3). Norton.

Barber, James D. & Kellerman, Barbara. Women in American Poltics. (Illus.). 448p. 1986. pap. text ed. 18.95 (ISBN 0-13-962267-5). P-H.

Barber, James D., jt. auth. see Sherrill, Robert.

Barber, James D., ed. Choosing the President. 1974. 7.95 (ISBN 0-13-133561-8); pap. 3.95 (ISBN 0-13-133553-7). Am Assembly.

Barber, Janet, jt. auth. see Budassi, Susan A.

Barber, Janet M. & Budassi, Susan A. Mosby's Manual of Emergency Care: Practices & Procedures. LC 79-31708. (Illus.). 652p. 1979. pap. text ed. 24.95 (ISBN 0-8016-0447-8). Mosby.

Barber, Janet M., et al. Adult & Child Care: A Client Approach to Nursing. 2nd ed. LC 76-26637. (Illus.). 1036p. 1977. 35.95 (ISBN 0-8016-0444-3). Mosby.

Barber, Joel. Wild Fowl Decoys. (Illus.). pap. 6.95 (ISBN 0-486-20011-6). Dover.

--Wild Fowl Decoys. (Illus.). 15.25 (ISBN 0-8446-1590-0). Peter Smith.

Barber, John. Soviet Historians in Crisis 1928-1932. LC 80-13798. 194p. 1981. text ed. 39.50x (ISBN 0-8419-0614-9). Holmes & Meier.

Barber, John C. Consulting Foresters 1984. 96p. (Orig.). 1984. pap. 7.50 (ISBN 0-939970-22-8, SAF 84-02). Soc Am Foresters.

Barber, John F. Yellowstone Ski Tours. (Illus.). 1979. pap. 3.95 (ISBN 0-89646-079-7). Outbooks.

Barber, John W. History of the Amistad Captives. LC 76-82168. (Anti-Slavery Crusade in America Ser). 1969. Repr. of 1840 ed. 11.00 (ISBN 0-405-00608-X). Ayer Co Pubs.

Barber, John W. & Howe, Henry. Early Woodcut Views of New York & New Jersey: 304 Illustrations from the "Historical Collection". 12.00 (ISBN 0-8446-5156-7). Peter Smith.

--Historical Collections of New Jersey. LC 66-63919. (Illus.). 1966. Repr. of 1868 ed. 25.00 (ISBN 0-87152-029-X). Reprint.

Barber, Joseph & Adrian, Cheri, eds. Psychological Approaches to the Management of Pain. LC 82-45471. 224p. 1982. 25.00 (ISBN 0-87630-303-3). Brunner-Mazel.

Barber, Josephine. German for Musicians. LC 84-48545. (Illus.). 320p. 1985. 25.95 (ISBN 0-253-32571-4); pap. 12.95 (ISBN 0-253-21260-X). Ind U Pr.

Barber, Karin. Yoruba Dun un So: Yoruba Course for Beginners. LC 84-40667. (Yale Language Ser.). 148p. 1985. pap. 16.95x (ISBN 0-300-02958-6). Yale U Pr.

Barber, Lester E., ed. see Rudd, Anthony.

Barber, Lilah. Lilah: A Memoir. Algonquin Bks.

Barber, Linda L. & Lampert, Junko. The Tofu Gourmet. (Illus.). 128p. 1984. 14.95 (ISBN 0-87040-589-6). Japan Pubns USA.

Barber, Lucie, jt. auth. see Union College Character Research Project.

Barber, Lucie W. Celebrating the Second Year of Life: A Parent's Guide for a Happy Child. LC 78-21484. 148p. (Orig.). 1979. pap. 5.95 (ISBN 0-89135-015-2). Religious Educ.

--The Religious Education of Preschool Children. LC 80-27623. 196p. (Orig.). 1981. pap. 8.95 (ISBN 0-89135-026-8). Religious Educ.

--Teaching Christian Values. LC 83-22981. 250p. (Orig.). 1984. pap. 12.95 (ISBN 0-89135-041-1). Religious Educ.

--When a Story Would Help: An Approach to Creative Parenting. LC 80-70550. (When Bk.). (Illus.). 88p. (Orig.). 1981. pap. 2.45 (ISBN 0-87029-173-4, 20267-1). Abbey.

Barber, Lucie W. & Peatling, John H. Manual for the Barber Scales of Self-Regard: Preschool Form. (Illus.). 1977. pap. 6.50 (ISBN 0-915744-09-0). Character Res.

Barber, Lucie W. & Williams, Herman. Your Baby's First Thirty Months. LC 81-80307. (Illus.). 160p. 1981. pap. 7.95 (ISBN 0-89586-062-7). H P Bks.

Barber, Lucie W., jt. auth. see Union College Character Research Project.

Barber, Lucius W. Army Memoirs of Lucius W. Barber. LC 83-24236. (Collector's Library of the Civil War Ser.). (gr. 7 up). 1984. kivar bdg. 26.60 (ISBN 0-8094-4458-5, Pub. by Time-Life). Silver.

Barber, Lylah. Lylah: A Memoir. 176p. 1985. 14.95 (ISBN 0-912697-18-0). Algonquin Bks.

Barber, M. C. The Trial of the Templars. LC 77-85716. 320p. 1978. 54.50 (ISBN 0-521-21896-9); pap. 14.95 (ISBN 0-521-28018-4). Cambridge U Pr.

Barber, M. C., et al. Transactions of the Royal Historical Society, 1984. (RHS Transactions, 5th Ser.). 1985. 12.75 (ISBN 0-86193-104-1, Pub. by Boydell & Brewer). Longwood Pub Group.

Barber, M. N. & Ninham, B. W. Random & Restricted Walks: Theory & Applications. (Mathematics & Its Applications Ser.). 190p. 1970. 46.25 (ISBN 0-677-02620-X). Gordon.

Barber, M. S., jt. ed. see Timmerhaus, K. D.

Barber, Margaret F. Grey Brethren, & Other Fragments in Prose & Verse. facs. ed. LC 75-125202. (Short Story Index Reprint Ser). 1905. 12.00 (ISBN 0-8369-3569-1). Ayer Co Pubs.

Barber, Marie-Claire, tr. see Ferraris, Luigi V.

Barber, Marjorie, jt. auth. see Beall, James L.

Barber, N. F. & Ghey, G. Water Waves. (Wykeham Science Ser.: No. 5). 152p. 1969. 5.75x (ISBN 0-8448-1107-6). Crane Russak Co.

Barber, Natalie. Doctor & Mrs. Fix-It: The Story of Frank & Bessie Beck. LC 79-130776. (Bold Believers Ser). (Orig.). 1969. pap. 0.95 (ISBN 0-377-84181-1). Friend Pr.

Barber, Noel. The Black Hole of Calcutta: A Reconstruction. (Illus.). 256p. 1982. 6.95 (ISBN 0-02-030390-4). Macmillan.

--A Farewell to France. 704p. 1983. 17.95 (ISBN 0-02-506830-X). Macmillan.

--A Farewell to France. 832p. 1984. pap. 3.95 (ISBN 0-380-68064-5, 68064-5). Avon.

--The Natives Were Friendly. 2.95 (ISBN 0-86072-021-7, Pub. by Quartet England). Charles River Bks.

--Sakkara: A Novel of Cairo. 544p. 1985. 17.95 (ISBN 0-02-506820-2). Macmillan.

--Seven Days of Freedom. LC 74-78536. 1975. pap. 2.95 (ISBN 0-8128-1861-X). Stein & Day.

--Week France Fell. LC 75-34398. (Illus.). 266p. 1976. 10.95 (ISBN 0-8128-1921-7); pap. 2.50 (ISBN 0-8128-7018-2). Stein & Day.

--The Week France Fell. 320p. 1984. pap. 3.95 (ISBN 0-8128-8037-4). Stein & Day.

Barber, Olive. Meet Me in Juneau. LC 60-53461. (Illus.). 1960. 8.95 (ISBN 0-8323-0079-9). Binford.

--Meet Me in Juneau. LC 60-53461. 258p. 1975. pap. 5.95 (ISBN 0-8323-0256-2). Binford.

Barber, Otto. H. G. Wells' Verhaltnis Zum Darwinismus. pap. 8.00 (ISBN 0-384-03380-6). Johnson Repr.

Barber, P. & Phillips, C. E. Rothschild Rhododendrons: A Record of the Gardens at Exbury. 1981. 79.00x (ISBN 0-686-78782-X, Pub. by RHS Ent England). State Mutual Bk.

Barber, Paul J. & Legge, David. Information & Human Performance. 194p. 1985. pap. 5.95 (ISBN 0-416-34950-1, NO. 9181). Methuen Inc.

--Perception & Information. (Essential Psychology Ser.). 1976. pap. 4.50x (ISBN 0-416-82040-9, NO. 2615). Methuen Inc.

Barber, Paul J., jt. auth. see Legge, David.

Barber, Peggy, ed. Sixty-Eight Great Ideas: The Library Awareness Handbook. LC 82-11518. 66p. 1982. pap. 7.50x (ISBN 0-8389-0376-2). ALA.

Barber, Peter. Diplomacy: The World of the Honest Spy. 152p. 1981. 30.00x (ISBN 0-904654-29-X, Pub. by Brit Lib England); pap. 20.00x (ISBN 0-904654-30-3). State Mutual Bk.

--Diplomacy: The World of the Honest Spy. (Illus.). 152p. (Orig.). 1979. 11.95 (ISBN 0-904654-29-X, Pub. by British Lib); pap. 7.50 (ISBN 0-904654-30-3). Longwood Pub Group.

Barber, Peter N., jt. aeth. see Phillips, C. E.

Barber, Phyllis. Smiley Snake's Adventure. Jordan, Alton, ed. (Buppet Series). (Illus.). (gr. k-3). 1981. PLB 5.95 (ISBN 0-89868-098-0, Read Res); pap. text ed. 1.95 (ISBN 0-89868-109-X). ARO Pub.

Barber, Randy, jt. auth. see Rifkin, Jeremy.

Barber, Red. Nineteen Forty-Seven: The Year All Hell Broke Loose in Baseball. (Quality Paperbacks Ser.). 380p. 1984. pap. 8.95 (ISBN 0-306-80212-0). Da Capo.

Barber, Richard. The Knight & Chivalry. LC 81-47800. (Illus.). 424p. (Orig.). 1982. pap. 8.17i (ISBN 0-06-090911-0, CN 911, CN). Har-Row.

--The Knight & Chivalry. 2nd ed. (Illus.). 400p. 1975. 22.50x (ISBN 0-87471-653-5). Rowman.

--The Pastons: The Letters of a Family in the Wars of the Roses. (Lives & Letters Ser.). 208p. 1984. pap. 5.95 (ISBN 0-14-057002-0). Penguin.
--The Penguin Guide to Medieval Europe. (Penguin Handbooks). 400p. 1984. pap. 10.95 (ISBN 0-14-046633-9). Penguin.
--Samuel Pepys Esq. LC 70-123622. (Illus.). 1970. 16.95 (ISBN 0-520-01763-3). U of Cal Pr.
Barber, Richard, ed. The Arthurian Legends: An Illustrated Anthology, No. 600. (Illus.). 224p. 1979. 27.95 (ISBN 0-8226-0600-3). Littlefield.
--Arthurian Literature I, 1981. 182p. 1981. 33.50x (ISBN 0-8476-7051-1). Rowman.
--Arthurian Literature II. (Illus.). 176p. 1982. text ed. 42.50x (ISBN 0-8476-7196-8). Rowman.
--Arthurian Literature III. LC 83-640196. 142p. 1984. 39.95x (ISBN 0-389-20431-5, 07317). B&N Imports.
--Arthurian Literature IV. LC 83-640196. 178p. 1985. 39.95x (ISBN 0-389-20432-3, BNB-07318). B&N Imports.
Barber, Richard, ed. see Aubrey, John.
Barber, Richard J. Politics of Research. 9.50 (ISBN 0-8183-0194-5). Pub Aff Pr.
Barber, Rowland. The Night They Raided Minsky's. 16.95 (ISBN 0-88411-097-4, Pub. by Aeonian Pr). Amereon Ltd.
Barber, Rowland, jt. auth. see Marx, Harpo.
Barber, Russell J. The Wheeler's Site: A Specialized Shellfish Processing Station on the Merrimack River. (Peabody Museum Monographs: No. 7). (Illus.). 96p. 1983. pap. 10.00x (ISBN 0-87365-907-4). Peabody Harvard.
Barber, Ruth. Teddy Bears Go Everywhere. (Teddy Bears Are Ser.). (Illus.). 24p. (gr. 1-6). 1984. pap. 1.95 (ISBN 0-89954-279-4). Antioch Pub Co.
Barber, S. A. & Bouldin, D. R., eds. Roots, Nutrient & Water Influx, & Plant Growth. 136p. 1984. 16.00 (ISBN 0-89118-082-6). Am Soc Agron.
Barber, Sandra & Mihankhah, Kianpour. Learning by Doing BASIC. 101p. (Orig.). 1983. pap. text ed. 8.50x (ISBN 0-89917-393-4). Tichenor Pub.
Barber, Sigmund J. Amadis De Gaule & the German Enlightenment. LC 83-49097. (American University Studies I (Germanic Languages & Literature) Vol. 30 & European University Studies I, Vol. 771). 188p. (Orig.). 1985. pap. text ed. 18.80 (ISBN 0-8204-0075-0); (ISBN 3-261-03396-7). P Lang Pubs.
Barber, Sotirios A. The Constitution & the Delegation of Congressional Power. LC 74-16688. x, 154p. 1975. 17.50x (ISBN 0-226-03705-3). U of Chicago Pr.
--On What the Constitution Means. LC 83-48049. 256p. 1983. 20.00x (ISBN 0-8018-3020-6). Johns Hopkins.
Barber, Stanley A. Soil Nutrient Bioavailability: A Mechanistic Approach. LC 83-23331. 398p. 1984. 39.95x (ISBN 0-471-09032-8, Pub. by Wiley-Interscience). Wiley.
Barber, T. Lynwood & Jochim, Michael M. Bluetongue & Related Orbiviruses. LC 85-5170. (Progress in Clinical & Biological Research Ser.: Vol. 178). 772p. 1985. 110.00 (ISBN 0-8451-5028-6). A R Liss.
Barber, Theodore X. LSD, Marihuana, Yoga, & Hypnosis. LC 73-115935. 1970. text ed. 44.95 (ISBN 0-202-25004-0). Aldine Pub.
--Pitfalls in Human Research: Ten Pivotal Points. LC 76-13488. 128p. 1977. 11.25 (ISBN 0-08-020935-1). Pergamon.
Barber, Theodore X., et al. Hypnosis, Imagination & Human Potentialities. LC 73-19539. 1974. pap. 9.95 (ISBN 0-08-017931-2). Pergamon.
Barber, Theodore X., et al, eds. Advances in Altered States of Consciousness & Human Potentialities, Vol. 1. LC 76-42132. 700p. 1980. 69.95x (ISBN 0-88437-002-X). Psych Dimensions.
Barber, Thomas G. Byron & Where He Is Buried. LC 74-8562. 1939. lib. bdg. 20.00 (ISBN 0-8414-3203-1). Folcroft.
Barber, Thomas H. Where We Are At. (Right Wing Individualist Tradition in America Ser). 1972. Repr. of 1950 ed. 19.00 (ISBN 0-405-00412-5, 71-172202). Ayer Co Pubs.
Barber, Thomas K. & Luke, Larry S., eds. Pediatric Dentistry. (Illus.). 448p. 1982. 52.00 (ISBN 0-88416-167-6). PSG Pub Co.
Barber, Triphy & Langfitt, Dot E. Teaching the Medical-Surgical Patient: Diagnostics & Procedures. (Illus.). 160p. 1983. pap. text ed. 21.95 (ISBN 0-89303-881-4). Brady Comm.
Barber, Virginia & Skaggs, Merrill M. The Mother Person. LC 76-48850. 1977. pap. 5.95 (ISBN 0-8052-0565-9). Schocken.
Barber, W. H. Leibniz in France-From Arnauld to Voltaire: A Study in French Reactions to Leibnizianism, 1670-1760. Sleigh, R. C., Jr., ed. LC 84-48416. (The Philosophy of Leibniz Ser.). 276p. 1985. lib. bdg. 40.00 (ISBN 0-8240-6529-8). Garland Pub.
Barber, W. H., et al, eds. see Besterman, Theodore.
Barber, W. T. Exploring Wales. LC 81-67020. (Illus.). 192p. 1982. 19.95 (ISBN 0-7153-8179-2). David & Charles.
Barber, William, ed. Within Doors: Poems Written by Residents of a Nursing Home. 1977. pap. 2.35 (ISBN 0-686-22748-4). Printed Word.
Barber, William J. The Economy of British Cental Africa: A Case Study of Economic Development in a Dualistic Society. LC 84-19119. xii, 271p. 1984. Repr. of 1961 ed. lib. bdg. 45.00x (ISBN 0-313-24619-X, BBCA). Greenwood.
--The History of Economic Thought. 1977. pap. 4.95 (ISBN 0-14-020890-9, Pelican). Penguin.
Barber, William W. From New Era to New Deal: Herbert Hoover, the Economists, & American Economic Policy, 1921-1933. (Historical Perspectives on Modern Economics Ser.). Date not set. price not set (ISBN 0-521-30526-8). Cambridge U Pr.
Barbera, Jack, ed. see Smith, Stevie.
Barbera, John J., jt. auth. see Armandi, Barry R.
Barbereux-Parry, M. Vocal Resonance: Its Source & Command. 1979. Repr. of 1941 ed. 9.50 (ISBN 0-8158-0380-X). Chris Mass.
Barberi, F., jt. ed. see Sheridan, M. F.
Barberis, France. Would You Like a Parrot? LC 67-28671. (Illus.). 32p. (ps-k). 8.95 (ISBN 0-87592-060-8). Scroll Pr.
Barberis, P. Balzac: Une Mythologie Realiste. (Collection Themes et Textes). 288p. (Fr.). 1971. pap. 6.75 (ISBN 2-03-035001-X, 2681). Larousse.
--Pere Goriot de Balzac: Ecriture, structures, significations. new ed. (Collection themes et textes). 296p. (Orig., Fr.). 1972. pap. 6.75 (ISBN 2-03-035010-9, 2681). Larousse.
Barberis, Pierre, ed. see Balpe, Jean-Pierre.
Barberis, Pierre, ed. see Goupil, Armand.
Barberis, Pierre, ed. see Sadeler, Joel.
Barberousse, Michel, ed. Dictionnaire de la Voile. 256p. (Fr.). 1970. pap. 14.95 (ISBN 0-686-56828-1, M-6606). French & Eur.
Barbet, Jean. Architecture of Altars & Chimneys, 2 vols. (Printed Sources of Western Art Ser.). (Illus., Fr.). 1981. pap. 35.00 slipcase (ISBN 0-915346-59-1). A Wofsy Fine Arts.
Barbet, Pierre. Doctor at Calvary. pap. 3.95 (ISBN 0-385-06687-2, Im). Doubleday.
Barbey, Bruno. Portrait of Poland. LC 82-50740. (Illus.). 1982. 37.50 (ISBN 0-500-54083-7). Thames Hudson.
Barbey, K. & Konig, H. Abstract Analytic Function Theory & Hardy Algebras. (Lecture Notes in Mathematics Ser.: Vol. 593). 1977. pap. 18.00 (ISBN 0-387-08252-2). Springer-Verlag.
Barbie, Earl R. Apple LOGO for Teachers. 335p. 1984. pap. write for info. (ISBN 0-534-03392-X). Wadsworth Pub.
Barbier. Dictionnaire Des Ouvrages Anonymes, 4 Vols. (Fr.). Set. 325.00 (ISBN 0-685-11143-1, F-12410). French & Eur.
Barbier, Andre, ed. see Ronsard, Pierre de.
Barbier, E., ed. The Application of Nuclear Techniques in Geothermal Investigations. 192p. 1983. pap. 55.00 (ISBN 0-08-030269-6, 2304, 1506, 1901). Pergamon.
--The Application of Nuclear Techniques to Geothermal Studies: Proceedings. 1978. pap. text ed. 85.00 (ISBN 0-08-021670-6). Pergamon.
--Cerro Prieto Geothermal Field: Proceedings of the First Symposium Held at San Diego, California, Sept. 1978. (Illus.). 300p. 1981. 85.00 (ISBN 0-08-026241-4). Pergamon.
--Cerro Prieto Geothermal Field: Proceedings of the Second Symposium, 17-19 October 1979, Mexicali, Mexico-Selected Papers. 144p. 1982. pap. 42.00 (ISBN 0-08-028746-8). Pergamon.
Barbier, Edmond J. Journal Historique et Anecdotique Du Regne De Louis XV, 4 Vols. Set. 170.00 (ISBN 0-384-03391-1); Set. pap. 148.00 (ISBN 0-384-03390-3). Johnson Repr.
Barbier, George. The Illustrations of George Barbier in Full Color. LC 76-42589. (Illus.). 47p. (Orig.). 1977. pap. 5.95 (ISBN 0-486-23476-2). Dover.
Barbier, J. L., ed. see De Lamartine, A.
Barbier, Jacques A. & Kuethe, Allan J., eds. The North American Role in the Spanish Imperial Economy, 1760-1819. LC 83-25643. 288p. 1984. 35.00 (ISBN 0-7190-0964-2, Pub. by Manchester Univ Pr). Longwood Pub Group.
Barbier, Jean P. Tobaland: The Shreds of Tradition. (Illus.). 237p. 1983. pap. 29.95 (ISBN 2-88104-004-7, Pub. by Barbier Muller Mus Switzerland). Ethnographic Arts Pubns.
Barbier, Jean Philippe & Hugues, Francois Claude. Dictionnaires Des Maladies. 528p. (Fr.). 1973. 42.95 (ISBN 0-686-56744-7, M-6022). French & Eur.
Barbier, Ken. CP-M Assembly Language Programming: A Guide to Integrated Learning of the CP-M Operating & Assembly Language Programming. (Illus.). 226p. 1982. 19.95 (ISBN 0-13-188268-6, Spec); pap. 12.95 (ISBN 0-13-188250-3). P-H.
--CP-M Solutions. (Illus.). 144p. 1985. 22.95 (ISBN 0-13-188186-8); pap. 14.95 (ISBN 0-13-188178-7). P H.
--CP M Techniques. (Illus.). 224p. 1984. 27.95 (ISBN 0-13-187865-4); pap. 19.95 (ISBN 0-13-187857-3). P-H.
Barbier, Maurice. Diccionario Tecnico Ilustrado De Edificacion y Obras Publicas. 177p. (Span.). 1976. pap. 11.50 (ISBN 84-252-0327-9, S-50273). French & Eur.
Barbier, Maurice G. The Mini Sosie Method. LC 82-80775. (Illus.). 96p. 1983. text ed. 28.00 (ISBN 0-934634-41-6). Intl Human Res.
--Pulse Coding. LC 82-80776. (Short Course Handbooks). (Illus.). 89p. (Orig.). 1982. text ed. 26.00 (ISBN 0-934634-52-1); pap. 16.00 (ISBN 0-934634-40-8). Intl Human Res.
Barbieri, Alexander F. Pennsylvania Workmen's Compensation & Occupational Disease, 3 vols. with case finder. 1975. 150.00. Bisel Co.
Barbieri, Elaine. Amber Fire. (Orig.). 1981. pap. 3.50 (ISBN 0-89083-848-8). Zebra.
--Amber Passion. 1985. pap. 3.95 (ISBN 0-8217-1501-1). Zebra.
--Amber Treasure. (Orig.). 1983. pap. 3.50 (ISBN 0-8217-1201-2). Zebra.
--Captive Ecstasy. 1981. pap. 2.75 (ISBN 0-89083-738-4). Zebra.
--Love's Fiery Jewel. 1983. pap. 3.75 (ISBN 0-8217-1128-8). Zebra.
--Passions Dawn. 1985. pap. 3.95 (ISBN 0-8217-1655-7). Zebra.
--Sweet Torment. 496p. 1984. pap. 3.75 (ISBN 0-8217-1385-X). Zebra.
Barbieri, Louis. First & Second Peter. (Everyman's Bible Commentary Ser.). 1977. pap. 5.95 (ISBN 0-8024-2061-3). Moody.
Barbieri, Louis A. Primera y Segunda Pedro, Comentario Biblico Portavoz. Orig. Title: First & Second Peter, Everyman's Bible Commentary. (Span.). 1981. pap. 3.95 (ISBN 0-8254-1051-7). Kregel.
Barbieri, Marcello. The Semantic Theory of Evolution. (Models of Scientific Thought Ser.: Vol. 2). 200p. 1985. text ed. 39.00 (ISBN 3-7186-0243-1). Harwood Academic.
Barbieri, R. H., et al. Process Heat in California: Applications & Potential for Solar Energy in the Industrial, Agricultural & Commercial Sectors. 1978. pap. 14.95x (ISBN 0-930978-72-2, D-004). Solar Energy Info.
Barbieri, Santa U. Anthology of Poetry & Prose. LC 82-70400. 1983. 4.95 (ISBN 0-8358-0441-0). Upper Room.
Barbir, Karl K. Ottoman Rule in Damascus, Seventeen Eight to Seventeen Fifty-Eight. LC 79-3189. (Princeton Studies in the Near East Ser.). 1980. 28.00x (ISBN 0-691-05297-2). Princeton U Pr.
Barbira-Freedman, Francois, jt. auth. see Kroeger, Axel.
Barborka, Geoffrey. Divine Plan: Commentary on the Secret Doctrine. 3rd ed. 1972. 19.95 (ISBN 0-8356-7167-4). Theos Pub Hse.
--Mahatmas & Their Letters. 1973. 8.95 (ISBN 0-8356-7062-7). Theos Pub Hse.
--The Peopling of the Earth. LC 75-4243. (Illus.). 240p. 1975. 10.00 (ISBN 0-8356-0221-4). Theos Pub Hse.
Barborka, Geoffrey A. Glossary of Sanskrit Terms & Key to Their Correct Pronunciation. 76p. (Orig.). 1972. pap. 1.75 (ISBN 0-913004-04-9). Point Loma Pub.
--H. P. Blavatsky: Tibet & Tulku. (Illus.). 1974. 12.95 (ISBN 0-8356-7159-3). Theos Pub Hse.
Barbosa, Duarte. The Book of Duarte Barbosa, 2 vols. Dames, Mansel L., tr. (Hakluyt Society Works Ser.: No. 2, Vol. 49). 1921. 63.00 (ISBN 0-317-16490-2). Kraus Repr.
--Description of the Coasts of East Africa & Malabar in the Beginning of the Sixteenth Century. LC 4-40434. (Landmarks in Anthropology Ser). Repr. of 1866 ed. 24.00 (ISBN 0-384-03405-5, L121). Johnson Repr.
Barbosa, Manuel P. Growth, Migration & the Balance of Payments in a Small Open Economy: Portugal. LC 79-53646. (Outstanding Dissertions in Economics Ser.). 330p. 1984. lib. bdg. 36.00 (ISBN 0-8240-4169-0). Garland Pub.
Barbosa del Rosario, Pilar. Historia Del Pacto Sagastino a Traves De un Epistolario Inedito: El Pacto Produce Desconcierto, 1897-1890. LC 80-22173. 282p. 1981. 12.00 (ISBN 0-8477-0866-7); pap. 10.00 (ISBN 0-8477-0867-5). U of PR Pr.
Barbosa de Rosario, Pilar, ed. De Baldorioty a Barbosa: Historia del Autonomismo puertorriqueno, 1887-1896, Vol. V. (La Obra de Jose Celso Barbosa Ser.). (Illus.). xiii, 367p. (Span.). 1974. pap. 6.25 (ISBN 0-8477-2453-0). U of PR Pr.
Barbou, Alfred. Victor Hugo & His Time. 59.95 (ISBN 0-8490-1259-7). Gordon Pr.
Barbour, Alan G. Cliffhanger. 1978. pap. 9.95 (ISBN 0-8065-0669-5). Citadel Pr.
Barbour, Amy L., ed. Selections from Herodotus. (Illus.). 1977. pap. 9.95x (ISBN 0-8061-1427-4). U of Okla Pr.
Barbour, Arthur J. Painting the Seasons in Watercolor. rev. ed. (Illus.). 160p. 1980. 21.95 (ISBN 0-8230-3859-9). Watson-Guptill.
--Watercolor: The Wet Technique. (Illus.). 1978. 22.50 (ISBN 0-8230-5681-3). Watson-Guptill.
Barbour, Beverly. Easy, Elegant Luncheon Menus. (Illus.). 1980. 14.95 (ISBN 0-8019-6831-3). Chilton.
--Low Salt Diet & Recipe Book. 128p. 1982. pap. 4.95 (ISBN 0-346-12548-0). Cornerstone.
--The Low Salt Diet & Recipe Book. (Illus.). 1985. pap. 5.95 (ISBN 0-671-55745-9, Fireside). S&S.
Barbour, Brian M., ed. American Transcendentalism: An Anthology of Criticism. LC 72-12640. 384p. 1973. pap. 8.95x (ISBN 0-268-00494-3). U of Notre Dame Pr.
--Benjamin Franklin: A Collection of Critical Essays. (Twentieth Century Views Ser.). 1979. text ed. 12.95 (ISBN 0-13-074856-0, Spec). P-H.
Barbour, David M. Theory of Bimetallism & the Effects of the Partial Demonetisation of Silver on England & India. LC 69-18298. Repr. of 1885 ed. lib. bdg. 15.00 (ISBN 0-8371-0295-2, BATB). Greenwood.
Barbour, Erwin H. Windmills & Wells in Nebraska-1899. (Illus.). 102p. 1984. pap. 7.50 (ISBN 0-934646-15-5). TX S & S Pr.
Barbour, Floyd B., ed. Black Power Revolt. LC 67-31432. (Extending Horizons Ser). 1968. 5.95 (ISBN 0-87558-038-6). Porter Sargent.
--Black Seventies. LC 74-133967. (Extending Horizons Ser). 1970. pap. 2.95 (ISBN 0-87558-059-9). Porter Sargent.
Barbour, Frederick K. & Barbour, Margaret R. Frederick K. & Margaret R. Barbour's Furniture Collection. (Illus.). 72p. 1963. 6.00 (ISBN 0-940748-14-2); pap. 5.00x (ISBN 0-940748-15-0); supplement 3.00 (ISBN 0-940748-16-9). Conn Hist Soc.
Barbour, George M. Florida for Tourists, Invalids & Settlers. Peter, Emmett B., Jr., ed. LC 64-19152. (Floridiana Facsimile & Reprint Ser). (Illus.). 1964. Repr. of 1882 ed. 10.75 (ISBN 0-8130-0012-2). U Presses Fla.
Barbour, Harriet & Freeman, Warren S. The Children's Record Book. LC 78-6156. 1978. Repr. of 1947 ed. lib. bdg. 18.75x (ISBN 0-313-20424-1, BACB). Greenwood.
Barbour, Hugh. Margaret Fell Speaking. LC 76-4224. (Orig.). 1976. pap. 5.00x (ISBN 0-87574-206-8). Pendle Hill.
--The Quakers in Puritan England. LC 85-6963. 300p. Date not set. pap. 14.95 (ISBN 0-913408-87-5). Friends United.
Barbour, Ian. Energy & American Values. Brooks, Harvey, et al, eds. LC 82-13174. 256p. 1982. 32.95x (ISBN 0-03-062468-1); pap. 14.95x (ISBN 0-03-062469-X). Praeger.
Barbour, Ian G. Issues in Science & Religion. 1971. pap. 8.95xi (ISBN 0-06-131566-4, TB1566, Torch). Har-Row.
--Myths, Models, & Paradigms. LC 73-18690. 1976. pap. text ed. 8.95x (ISBN 0-06-060388-7, RD 183, HarpR). Har-Row.
--Technology, Environment & Human Values. LC 80-12330. 344p. 1980. 16.95 (ISBN 0-03-055886-7); pap. 16.95 (ISBN 0-03-055881-6). Praeger.
Barbour, J. Murray. Trumpets, Horns & Music. 1964. 10.00 (ISBN 0-87013-079-X). Mich St U Pr.
Barbour, James M. The Church Music of William Billings. LC 72-39000. 167p. 1972. Repr. of 1960 ed. lib. bdg. 22.50 (ISBN 0-306-70434-X). Da Capo.
Barbour, James Murray. Tuning & Temperament: A Historical Survey. LC 74-37288. (Illus.). 228p. 1972. Repr. of 1951 ed. lib. bdg. 27.50 (ISBN 0-306-70422-6). Da Capo.
Barbour, John. Buik of the Most Noble & Vailzeand Conqueror Alexander the Great. Laing, David, ed. LC 70-161748. (Bannatyne Club, Edinburgh. Publications: No. 46). Repr. of 1831 ed. 35.00 (ISBN 0-404-52756-6). AMS Pr.
--The Buik of the Most Noble & Vailzeand Conqueror Alexander the Great. Repr. of 1831 ed. 45.00 (ISBN 0-384-03421-7). Johnson Repr.
--Selections from Barbour's Bruce, Pts. 1 & 4. Skeat, W. W., ed. (EETS, ES: No. 11). Repr. of 1900 ed. Set. 23.00 (ISBN 0-527-00225-9). Kraus Repr.
Barbour, John, ed. The Bruce, 2 Vols. Set. 85.00 (ISBN 0-384-03415-2). Johnson Repr.
Barbour, John D. Tragedy as a Critique of Virtue. LC 83-20028. (Scholars Press Studies in the Humanities). 214p. 1984. text ed. 20.95 (ISBN 0-89130-661-7, 00 01 02); pap. text ed. 13.95 (ISBN 0-89130-662-5). Scholars Pr GA.
Barbour, John G. Unique Traditions Chiefly of the West & South of Scotland. (Folklore Ser). 12.50 (ISBN 0-8482-7419-9). Norwood Edns.
Barbour, Judy. Elegant Elk: Delicious Deer. 3rd ed. (Illus.). 196p. 1983. Repr. of 1978 ed. 13.95 (ISBN 0-686-33178-8). P Peters Studio.
Barbour, K. M., et al, eds. Nigeria in Maps. Oguntoyinbo, J. S. & Onyenelukwe, J. C. 160p. 1982. 35.00x (ISBN 0-8419-0763-3). Holmes & Meier.
Barbour, Kenneth M. & Prothero, R. M., eds. Essays on African Population. LC 75-26210. (Illus.). 336p. 1976. Repr. of 1962 ed. lib. bdg. 22.50 (ISBN 0-8371-8399-5, BAEP). Greenwood.
Barbour, Lucius B. Families of Early Hartford, Connecticut. LC 77-71625. 742p. 1982. Repr. of 1977 ed. 35.00 (ISBN 0-8063-0764-1). Genealog Pub.
Barbour, M. Laboratory Studies in Botany. 6th ed. 263p. 1982. pap. text ed. 17.95 (ISBN 0-471-86185-5). Wiley.
Barbour, Margaret R., jt. auth. see Barbour, Frederick K.
Barbour, Mary, tr. see De Monfort, St. Louis.
Barbour, Mary E. You Can Teach Two's & Three's. 64p. 1981. pap. 2.50 (ISBN 0-88207-149-1). Victor Bks.
Barbour, Michael G. & Major, Jack, eds. Terrestrial Vegetation of California. LC 76-53769. 1002p. 1977. 99.95x (ISBN 0-471-56536-9, Pub. by Wiley-Interscience). Wiley.

Barbour, Michael G., et al. Terrestrial Plant Ecology. 1980. 31.95 (ISBN 0-8053-0540-8). Benjamin-Cummings.

--Coastal Ecology: Bodega Head. LC 70-173902. (Illus.). 1974. 30.00x (ISBN 0-520-02147-9). U of Cal Pr.

Barbour, Nevill. Nisi Dominus: A Survey of the Palestine Controversy. 248p. 1969. Repr. of 1946 ed. 11.95 (ISBN 0-88728-091-9). Inst Palestine.

Barbour, Pamela G. & Spivey, Norma G. The Exchange Cookbook for Diabetic & Weight Control Programs. LC 82-83512. (Illus.). 198p. (Orig.). 1982. pap. 9.95 spiral bdg. (ISBN 0-9610028-0-8). G&G Pub.

Barbour, Philip L., tr. see Pushkin, Alexander.

Barbour, R. Glassblowing for Laboratory Technicians. 2nd ed. 1979. text ed. 53.00 (ISBN 0-08-022155-6); pap. text ed. 14.00 (ISBN 0-08-022156-4). Pergamon.

--Greek Literary Hands A. D. Four Hundred-Sixteen Hundred. (Illus.). 1981. 39.95x (ISBN 0-19-818229-5). Oxford U Pr.

Barbour, Richard T. Pyrotechnics in Industry. LC 80-11152. (Illus.). 190p. 1981. 25.95 (ISBN 0-07-003653-5). McGraw.

Barbour, Roger W. & Davis, Wayne H. Bats of America. LC 73-80086. (Illus.). 312p. 1979. Repr. of 1969 ed. 35.00x (ISBN 0-8131-1186-2). U Pr of Ky.

--Mammals of Kentucky. LC 74-7870. (Illus.). 368p. 1974. 18.00 (ISBN 0-8131-1314-8). U Pr of Ky.

Barbour, Roger W., jt. auth. see Ernst, Carl H.

Barbour, Roger W., jt. auth. see Kuehne, Robert A.

Barbour, Roger W., jt. auth. see Wharton, Mary E.

Barbour, Roger W., et al. Kentucky Birds: A Finding Guide. LC 72-91662. (Illus.). Repr. of 1973 ed. 81.50 (ISBN 0-8357-9787-2, 2016184). Bks Demand UMI.

Barbour, Ruth P. Cruise of the Snap Dragon. LC 76-40443. (YA) 1976. 8.95 (ISBN 0-910244-88-X). Blair.

Barbour, Violet. Capitalism in Amsterdam in the Seventeenth Century. LC 78-64208. (Johns Hopkins University. Studies in the Social Sciences. Sixty-Seventh Ser. 1949: 1). Repr. of 1950 ed. 24.50 (ISBN 0-404-61313-6). AMS Pr.

Barbrook, Alec. Patterns of Political Behaviour. 1975. pap. text ed. 9.95 (ISBN 0-87581-191-4). Peacock Pubs.

Barbrook, Alec & Bolt, Christine. Power & Protest in American Life. 1980. 29.00 (ISBN 0-312-63369-6). St Martin.

Barbrook, Alec T. God Save the Commonwealth: An Electoral History of Massachusetts. LC 72-77572. 234p. 1973. 13.50x (ISBN 0-87023-110-3). U of Mass Pr.

Barbs, S., ed. see Verducci.

Barbu. Optimal Control of Variational Inequalities. (Research Notes in Mathematics: No. 100). 312p. 1984. 23.95 (ISBN 0-273-08629-4). Pitman Pub MA.

Barbu, V. Convexity & Optimisation in Banach Spaces. 328p. 1978. 30.00x (ISBN 90-286-0018-3). Sijthoff & Noordhoff.

--Nonlinear Semigroups & Differential Equations in Banach Spaces. 252p. 1976. 32.50x (ISBN 90-286-0205-4). Sijthoff & Noordhoff.

Barbu, V. & Da Prato, G. Hamilton-Jacobi Equations in Hilbert Space. (Research Notes in Mathematics Ser.: No. 86). 240p. 1983. pap. text ed. 18.95 (ISBN 0-273-08597-2). Pitman Pub MA.

Barbu, V. & Precupanu, T. Convexity & Optimization in Banach Spaces. (Mathematics & its Applications: East European Ser.). 1985. lib. bdg. 64.00 (ISBN 90-277-1761-3, Pub. by Reidel Holland). Kluwer-Academic.

Barbu, Zevedei. Problems of Historical Psychology. LC 75-28659. 1976. Repr. of 1960 ed. lib. bdg. 19.75 (ISBN 0-8371-8476-2, BAHP). Greenwood.

--Society, Personality & Culture. (Blackwell's Sociology Ser.). 183p. 1971. pap. text ed. 6.95 (ISBN 0-8464-1162-8). Beekman Pubs.

Barbusse, Henri. Under Fire. Wray, W. Fitzwater, tr. 362p. 1984. pap. 3.50x (ISBN 0-460-11798-X, DEL-05087, Evman). Biblio Dist.

--Under Fire: The Story of a Squad. Wray, Fitzwater, tr. 1975. Repr. of 1926 ed. 9.95x (ISBN 0-460-00798-X, Evman). Biblio Dist.

Barca, Calderon de la see Bentley, Eric.

Barca, Francis C. de la see Calderon de la Barca, Frances.

Barca, Pedro C. de la see De la Barca, Pedro C.

Barca, Pedro Calderon de la see Calderon de la Barca, Pedro.

Barca Pedro de la, Calderon see Calderon de la Barca, Pedro.

Barcelo, J. R. Spanish-English, English-Spanish Chemical Vocabulary. (Span. & Eng.). pap. 7.50 (ISBN 84-205-0696-6). Heinman.

Barcelo Matutano, Jose R. Diccionario Terminologico de Quimica. 2nd ed. 1100p. (Span., Ger. & Eng.). 1976. pap. 46.00 (ISBN 84-205-0521-8, S-50090). French & Eur.

Barcelona, Biblioteca Central, Seccion De Musica. La Musica De las Cantigas De Santa Maria Del Rey Alfonso el Sabio, 4 pts. in 3 vols. LC 80-2193. Repr. of 1958 ed. Set. 375.00 (ISBN 0-404-19046-4). AMS Pr.

Barcelona, Delia & Bautista, Paulina. Contraception: A Guide to Birth Planning Methods. (Illus.). 147p. (Orig.). 1982. pap. 6.00 (ISBN 0-89836-031-5). Comm & Family.

Barcham, William L. The Imaginary View Scenes of Antonio Canaletto. LC 76-23603. (Outstanding Dissertations in the Fine Arts - 18th Century). (Illus.). 1977. Repr. of 1974 ed. lib. bdg. 76.00 (ISBN 0-8240-2677-2). Garland Pub.

Barchard, David. Turkey & the West. (Chatham House Papers). 128p. 1985. pap. 10.95x (ISBN 0-7102-0618-6). Routledge & Kegan.

Barchas, Jack. Serotonin & Behavior. Usdin, Earl, ed. 1973. 68.00 (ISBN 0-12-078150-6). Acad Pr.

Barchas, Jack D., et al, eds. Psychopharmacology: From Theory to Practice. (Illus.). 1977. pap. text ed. 21.95x (ISBN 0-19-502215-7). Oxford U Pr.

Barchas, Patricia R., ed. Social Hierarchies: Essays Toward a Sociophysiological Perspective. LC 83-22600. (Contributions in Sociology Ser.: No. 47). (Illus.). xvi, 160p. 1984. lib. bdg. 27.95 (ISBN 0-313-23165-6, BSH/). Greenwood.

Barchas, Patricia R. & Mendoza, Sally P., eds. Social Cohesion: Essays Toward a Sociophysiological Perspective. LC 83-22594. (Contributions in Sociology Ser.: No. 49). (Illus.). xvi, 219p. 1984. lib. bdg. 29.95 (ISBN 0-313-24395-6, BCH/). Greenwood.

Barchi, Robert L., jt. auth. see Lisak, Robert P.

Barchilon, Jacques. A Concordance to Charles Perrault's Tales, Volume I: Contes De Ma Mere L'oye. 1978. Repr. of 1977 ed. lib. bdg. 30.00 (ISBN 0-8492-3718-1). R West.

Barchilon, Jacques, et al. A Concordance to Charles Perrault's Tales, Vol.1. 1977. lib. bdg. 35.00 (ISBN 0-8482-0329-1). Norwood Edns.

--A Concordance to Charles Perrault's Tales, Vol. 2. 1979. lib. bdg. 35.00 (ISBN 0-8482-3417-0). Norwood Edns.

Barchilon, John. The Crown Prince: A Novel. 1984. 15.95 (ISBN 0-393-01765-6). Norton.

Barcia, Jose R. Americo Castro & the Meaning of Spanish Civilization. LC 74-27282. 1977. 38.50x (ISBN 0-520-02920-8). U of Cal Pr.

Barcia, Jose R., tr. see Vallejo, Cesar.

Barcia, Jose R., et al. Lengua y Cultura. LC 72-90216. 1973. 27.95 (ISBN 0-03-083624-7, HoltC). HR&W.

Barcia, Roque. Sinonimus Castellanos. 17th ed. 590p. (Span.). 1978. 27.50 (ISBN 0-686-56660-2, S-11889). French & Eur.

Barcia Carballido Y Zuniga, Andres Gonzalez de. Barcia's Chronological History of the Continent of Florida: From the Year 1512, in Which Juan Ponce de Leon Discovered Florida, Until the Year 1722. Kerrigan, Anthony, tr. LC 77-106667. 426p. Repr. of 1951 ed. lib. bdg. 39.50x (ISBN 0-8371-3419-6, BAHF). Greenwood.

Barcikowski, Robert S., ed. Computer Packages & Research Design: Vol. 1-BMDP with Annotations of Input & Output from the BMDP, SAS, SPSS & SPSSX Statistical Packages. (Illus.). 572p. (Orig.). 1983. pap. text ed. 29.50 (ISBN 0-8191-3494-5). U Pr of Amer.

--Computer Packages & Research Design: Vol. 2-SAS with Annotations of Input & Output from the BMDP, SAS, SPSS & SPSSX Statistical Packages. (Illus.). 620p. (Orig.). 1983. pap. text ed. 30.50 (ISBN 0-8191-3495-3). U Pr of Amer.

--Computer Packages & Research Design: Vol. 3-SPSS & SPSSX with Annotations of Input & Output from the BMDP, SAS, SPSS & SPSSX Statistical Packages. (Illus.). 620p. (Orig.). 1983. pap. text ed. 36.00 (ISBN 0-8191-3496-1). U Pr of Amer.

Barck, Oscar T. & Blake, Nelson M. Since Nineteen Hundred: A History of the United States in Our Times. 5th ed. 1974. write for info. (ISBN 0-02-305930-3, 30593). Macmillan.

Barck, Oscar T., Jr. & Lefler, Hugh T. History of the United States-Since 1865. LC 68-12884. (Illus.). Repr. of 1968 ed. 160.00 (ISBN 0-8357-9907-7, 2012466). Bks Demand UMI.

Barckhausen. Montesquieu Ses Idees et Ses Oeuvres d'apres les Papiers de La Brede. 49.90 (ISBN 0-685-34049-X). French & Eur.

Barclay. History of Balmville. 3.98x (ISBN 0-686-14962-9). T E Henderson.

Barclay, Alexander. Certayne Egloges of Alexander Barclay Priest. Siluius, Eneas, compiled by. (Spenser Society Ser.: No. 39). 1966. Repr. of 1570 ed. 41.00 (ISBN 0-8337-0164-9). B Franklin.

--Practical View of the Present State of Slavery in the West Indies. facs. ed. LC 74-83955. (Black Heritage Library Collection Ser). 1828. 22.50 (ISBN 0-8369-8508-7). Ayer Co Pubs.

Barclay, Alexander, tr. see Brant, Sebastian.

Barclay, Alexander, tr. see Mancinus, Domineus.

Barclay, Allan G., jt. ed. see McNamara, Regis.

Barclay, Andrew. Introduction to Human Sexuality. 1973. pap. text ed. 3.75 (ISBN 0-685-48763-6). Collegiate Pub.

Barclay, Barbara, jt. auth. see Cole, Malcolm S.

Barclay, Bob. A Dictionary of Graffiti. 1984. 29.00x (ISBN 0-906549-41-8, Pub. by J Clare Bks UK); pap. 13.00x (ISBN 0-906549-42-6, Pub. by J Clare Bks UK). State Mutual Bk.

--Sex on the Wall. 1984. 25.00x (ISBN 0-906549-33-7, Pub. by J Clare Bks Uk); pap. 10.00x (ISBN 0-906549-34-5, Pub. by J Clare Bks UK). State Mutual Bk.

Barclay, Charles E. The Socratic Method of Educational Stimulation. (Illus.). 1979. 47.75 (ISBN 0-89266-151-8). Am Classical Coll Pr.

Barclay, Cyril N. The New Warfare. LC 82-18375. x, 66p. 1983. Repr. of 1953 ed. lib. bdg. 27.50x (ISBN 0-313-23793-X, BANW). Greenwood.

Barclay, Edwin W. Brand of Mirra Peena: An Outback Story. 1982. 7.95 (ISBN 0-533-04864-8). Vantage.

Barclay, George W. Colonial Development & Population in Taiwan. LC 72-159081. 1971. Repr. of 1954 ed. 25.00x (ISBN 0-8046-1623-X, Pub. by Kennikat). Assoc Faculty Pr.

--Techniques of Population Analysis. LC 58-59899. 31p. 1958. 35.50x (ISBN 0-471-04818-6). Wiley.

Barclay, Glen S. Friends in High Places: The Australian-American Security Relationship since 1945. 300p. 1985. 39.95x (ISBN 0-19-554608-3). Oxford U Pr.

Barclay, H. People Without Government: The Anthropology of Anarchism. 1984. lib. bdg. 79.95 (ISBN 0-87700-636-9). Revisionist Pr.

Barclay, Harold. People Without Government: An Anthropology of Anarchism. 150p. (Orig.). 1982. pap. 8.00 (ISBN 0-904564-47-9). Left Bank.

Barclay, Ian. The Crime Minister. 400p. (Orig.). 1984. pap. 3.50 (ISBN 0-446-30941-9). Warner Bks.

--The Crime Minister: Reprisal. 320p. 1985. pap. 3.50 (ISBN 0-446-32784-0). Warner Bks.

Barclay, James R. Foundations of Counseling Strategies. LC 78-15407. 480p. 1978. Repr. of 1971 ed. lib. bdg. 27.50 (ISBN 0-88275-709-1). Krieger.

Barclay, James T. The City of the Great King: Jerusalem As It Was, As It Is, & As It Is to Be. Davis, Moshe, ed. LC 77-70664. (America & the Holy Land Ser.). 1977. Repr. of 1858 ed. lib. bdg. 49.50x (ISBN 0-405-10225-9). Ayer Co Pubs.

Barclay, Janet M., ed. Emily Bronte Criticism Nineteen Hundred to Nineteen Eighty: An Annotated Check List. LC 83-17433. 1984. 40.00x (ISBN 0-930466-63-2). Meckler Pub.

Barclay, Marion S., et al. Teen Guide to Homemaking. 3rd ed. (gr. 7-9). text ed. 18.28 (ISBN 0-07-003644-6). McGraw.

Barclay, Morgan J. & Strong, Jean W. The Samuel Milton Jones Papers: An Inventory to the Microfilm Edition. 95p. 1978. 5.95 (ISBN 0-318-03217-1). Ohio Hist Soc.

Barclay, Oliver R. The Intellect & Beyond. 144p. (Orig.). 1985. pap. 6.95 (ISBN 0-310-33291-5, Pub. by Academie Bks). Zondervan.

Barclay, R. A., tr. see Auerbach, Elias.

Barclay, R. Mary, tr. see Kraepelin, Emil.

Barclay, Shelley, compiled by. Guide to California Foundations. 5th ed. 480p. 1983. Directory 17.00 (ISBN 0-936434-11-2). Northern Cal.

Barclay, William. All-Sufficient Christ: Studies in Paul's Letter to the Colossians. LC 63-18385. 142p. 1963. pap. 6.95 (ISBN 0-664-24480-7). Westminster.

--Ambassador for Christ. LC 73-9762. 192p. 1974. pap. 4.95 (ISBN 0-8170-0631-1). Judson.

--And He Had Compassion. LC 75-28099. 272p. 1976. pap. 5.95 (ISBN 0-8170-0686-9). Judson.

--And Jesus Said: A Handbook on the Parables of Jesus. LC 77-120410. 224p. 1970. pap. 7.95 (ISBN 0-664-24898-5). Westminster.

--The Beatitudes & the Lord's Prayer for Everyman. LC 75-9309. 256p. 1975. pap. 7.64i (ISBN 0-06-060393-3, RD112, HarpR). Har-Row.

--Christian Ethics for Today. LC 83-48994. 224p. 1984. pap. 7.95 (ISBN 0-06-060412-3, RD 512). Har-Row.

--Communicating the Gospel. 1978. pap. 3.25x (ISBN 0-7152-0401-7). Outlook.

--Everyday Prayers. LC 60-5326. 160p. 1981. pap. 5.72i (ISBN 0-06-060411-5, RD 361, HarpR). Har-Row.

--Fishers of Men. LC 66-22246. 120p. 1979. pap. 4.95 (ISBN 0-664-24224-3). Westminster.

--Flesh & Spirit. 128p. 1976. pap. 3.50 (ISBN 0-8010-0664-3). Baker Bk.

--Great Themes of the New Testament. LC 79-18213. 122p. 1979. pap. 4.95 (ISBN 0-664-24286-3). Westminster.

--Guide to Daily Prayer. LC 62-11473. 1974. pap. 5.72i (ISBN 0-06-060401-8, RD75, HarpR). Har-Row.

--In the Hands of God. LC 80-25261. 1981. pap. 4.95 (ISBN 0-664-24362-2). Westminster.

--Introducing the Bible. (Festival Bks). 1979. pap. 2.75 (ISBN 0-687-19488-1, Festival). Abingdon.

--Introduction to John & the Acts of the Apostles. LC 75-38902. 352p. 1976. softcover 5.95 (ISBN 0-664-24771-7). Westminster.

--Introduction to the First Three Gospels: A Revised Edition of the First Three Gospels. LC 75-37545. 314p. 1976. pap. 9.95 (ISBN 0-664-24798-9). Westminster.

--Jesus as They Saw Him. LC 78-18224. 1978. pap. 7.95 (ISBN 0-8028-1775-0). Eerdmans.

--Jesus of Nazareth. 288p. 1985. pap. 12.95 (ISBN 0-8407-5759-X). Nelson.

--The King & Kingdom. 211p. 1980. pap. 3.95 (ISBN 0-8010-0786-0). Baker Bk.

--Letters to the Seven Churches. LC 82-2760. 128p. 1982. pap. 6.95 (ISBN 0-664-24433-5). Westminster.

--The Life of Jesus for Everyman. LC 75-12282. 96p. 1975. pap. 5.72i (ISBN 0-06-060404-2, RD 319, HarpR). Har-Row.

--The Lord Is My Shepherd: Expositions of Selected Psalms. LC 79-27096. 154p. 1980. pap. 5.95 (ISBN 0-664-24317-7). Westminster.

--The Lord's Supper. LC 82-2774. 128p. 1982. pap. 5.95 (ISBN 0-664-24432-7). Westminster.

--The Master's Men. (Festival Books). 1976. pap. 3.25 (ISBN 0-687-23732-7). Abingdon.

--Meditations on Communicating the Gospel. 1971. pap. 2.25x (ISBN 0-8358-0253-1). Upper Room.

--The Men, the Meaning, the Message of the New Testament Books. LC 77-22184. 156p. 1978. pap. 4.95 (ISBN 0-664-24188-3). Westminster.

--The Mind of Jesus. LC 61-7332. 352p. 1976. pap. 7.95i (ISBN 0-06-060451-4, RD143, HarpR). Har-Row.

--The Mind of St. Paul. LC 75-9310. 256p. 1975. pap. 7.64i (ISBN 0-06-060471-9, RD110, HarpR). Har-Row.

--The New Testament: A New Translation. 576p. 1980. pap. 4.95 (ISBN 0-664-24358-4). Westminster.

--New Testament Words. LC 73-12737. 302p. 1976. softcover 5.95 (ISBN 0-664-24761-X). Westminster.

--The Old Law & the New Law. LC 72-1412. (Illus.). 128p. 1972. Westminster.

--Palabras Griegas Del Nuevo Testamento. Marin, Javier J., tr. 220p. 1985. pap. 4.50 (ISBN 0-311-42052-4). Casa Bautista.

--Prayers for Help & Healing. LC 74-25682. 128p. 1975. pap. 4.95i (ISBN 0-06-060481-6, RD-89, HarpR). Har-Row.

--The Promise of the Spirit. LC 60-11200. 120p. 1978. pap. 5.50 (ISBN 0-664-24205-7). Westminster.

--The Ten Commandments for Today. LC 83-6103. 208p. (Orig.). 1983. pap. 6.68i (ISBN 0-06-060417-4, RD 476, HarpR). Har-Row.

--Turning to God. 1978. pap. 3.25x (ISBN 0-7152-0388-6). Outlook.

--Turning to God: A Study of Conversion in the Book of Acts & Today. pap. 2.95 (ISBN 0-8010-0564-7). Baker Bk.

--William Barclay: A Spiritual Autobiography. LC 73-76528. 1977. pap. 1.50 (ISBN 0-8028-1667-3). Eerdmans.

Barclay, William, ed. Racial Conflict, Discrimination, & Power: Historical & Contemporary Studies. LC 75-11964. (AMS Studies in Modern Society--Political & Social Issues). 1976. lib. bdg. 29.50 (ISBN 0-404-13140-9); pap. 11.95 (ISBN 0-404-13144-1). AMS Pr.

Barclay, William R., ed. Manual for Authors & Editors: Editorial Style & Manuscript Preparation. LC 81-83310. 184p. 1981. 8.50x (ISBN 0-87041-243-4). Lange.

Barcley, Alexander, tr. see Brant, Sebastian.

Barco, Miguel Del see Del Barco, Miguel.

Bar-Cohen, A., jt. auth. see Kraus, A. D.

Barcomb, David. Office Automation: A Survey of Tools & Technology. 241p. 1981. pap. 21.00 (ISBN 0-932376-15-0, EY-00004-DP). Digital Pr.

--Office Automation: A Survey of Tools & Technology. 256p. 1981. 15.00 (ISBN 0-686-98086-7). Telecom Lib.

Barcovitch, Sacvan, ed. Aspects of Puritan Religious Thought: Library, Vol. VI. LC 83-12782. (Library of American Puritan Writings). 728p. 1984. Repr. 57.50 (ISBN 0-404-60806-X). AMS Pr.

Barcroft, J. Features in the Architecture of Physiological Functions. 1972. Repr. of 1938 ed. 21.50x (ISBN 0-02-840820-9). Hafner.

Barcroft, Joseph. The Brain & Its Environment. LC 72-85306. 128p. 1973. Repr. of 1938 ed. 19.50x (ISBN 0-8046-1718-X, Pub. by Kennikat). Assoc Faculty Pr.

Barcroft, Michael. Luckiest of All. 96p. 1984. 25.00x (ISBN 0-906791-35-9, Pub. by Minimax Bks Uk). State Mutual Bk.

Barcus, Earlynne, et al. Echoes of a Dream. 11.95 (ISBN 0-9611922-0-8); pap. 6.95 (ISBN 0-9611922-1-6). E Barcus.

Barcus, F. Earle. Images of Life on Children's Television: Sex Roles, Minorities & Families. 238p. 1983. 25.95 (ISBN 0-03-063883-6). Praeger.

Barcus, James E., ed. Shelley: The Critical Heritage. (The Critical Heritage Ser.). 1975. 36.00x (ISBN 0-7100-8148-0). Routledge & Kegan.

Barcus, Nancy B. The Family Takes A Child. 96p. 1983. pap. 5.95 (ISBN 0-8170-0998-1). Judson.

--Help Me, God, I'm a Working Mother! 64p. 1982. pap. 3.95 (ISBN 0-8170-0954-X). Judson.

Bard. Electroanalytical Chemistry, Vol. 13. 344p. 1983. 75.00 (ISBN 0-8247-7028-5). Dekker.

--Encyclopedia of Electrochemistry of the Elements, Vol. 15. 1984. 129.50 (ISBN 0-8247-2515-8). Dekker.

--Oxidation-Reduction Potentials in Aqueous Solutions: A Selective & Critical Source Book. (Monographs in Electroanalytical Chemistry & Electrochemistry). 544p. 1985. 29.95 (ISBN 0-8247-7291-1). Dekker.

Bard & Lund. Encyclopedia of Electrochemistry of the Elements, Vol. 9A. 486p. 1982. 119.50 (ISBN 0-8247-2509-3). Dekker.
--Encyclopedia of Electrochemistry of the Elements, Vol. 9B. 352p. 1985. write for info. (ISBN 0-8247-2519-0). Dekker.
--Encyclopedia of the Electrochemistry of the Elements. 328p. 1980. write for info. Dekker.
Bard, A. & Lund, Henning, eds. Encyclopedia of Electrochemicals of the Elements, Vol. 13. 1979. 119.50 (ISBN 0-8247-2513-1). Dekker.
--Encyclopedia of Electrochemistry of the Elements, Vol. 12. 1978. 119.50 (ISBN 0-8247-2512-3). Dekker.
Bard, A. J. Electroanalytical Chemistry, Vol. 12: A Series of Advances. 208p. 1982. 75.00 (ISBN 0-8247-1690-6). Dekker.
Bard, Allen, ed. Encyclopedia of Electrochemistry of the Elements, Vol. 7. 1976. 119.50 (ISBN 0-8247-2507-7). Dekker.
--Encyclopedia of Electrochemistry of the Elements, Vol. 8. 1978. 119.50 (ISBN 0-8247-2508-5). Dekker.
Bard, Allen J. Chemical Equilibrium. (Illus.). 1968. pap. text ed. 13.50 scp (ISBN 0-06-040451-5, HarpC). Har-Row.
--Electroanalytical Chemistry: A Series of Advances, Vol. 11. 1979. 75.00 (ISBN 0-8247-6542-7). Dekker.
Bard, Allen J. & Faulkner, Larry R. Electrochemical Methods: Fundamentals & Applications. LC 79-24712. 718p. 1980. text ed. 45.00x (ISBN 0-471-05542-5). Wiley.
Bard, Allen J., ed. Electroanalytical Chemistry, Vol. 4. 1970. 75.00 (ISBN 0-8247-1038-X). Dekker.
--Electroanalytical Chemistry: A Series of Advances, Vol. 1. LC 66-11287. pap. 109.00 (ISBN 0-317-08017-2, 2021504). Bks Demand UMI.
--Electroanalytical Chemistry: A Series of Advances, Vol. 2. LC 66-11287. pap. 72.00 (ISBN 0-317-08518-2, 2055066). Bks Demand UMI.
--Electroanalytical Chemistry: A Series of Advances, Vol. 3. LC 66-11287. (Illus.). pap. 80.50 (ISBN 0-317-07926-3, 2021505). Bks Demand UMI.
--Electroanalytical Chemistry: A Series of Advances, Vol. 5. 1971. 46.40 (ISBN 0-8247-1041-X). Dekker.
--Electroanalytical Chemistry: A Series of Advances, Vol. 7. 304p. 1974. 75.00 (ISBN 0-8247-6101-4). Dekker.
--Encyclopedia of Electrochemistry of the Elements, Vol. 1. 1973. 119.50 (ISBN 0-8247-2501-8). Dekker.
--Encyclopedia of Electrochemistry of the Elements, Vol. 2. 1974. 119.50 (ISBN 0-8247-2502-6). Dekker.
--Encyclopedia of Electrochemistry of the Elements, Vol. 3. 1975. 119.50 (ISBN 0-8247-2503-4). Dekker.
--Encyclopedia of Electrochemistry of the Elements, Vol. 4. 1975. 119.50 (ISBN 0-8247-2504-2). Dekker.
--Encyclopedia of Electrochemistry of the Elements, Vol. 5. 1976. 119.50 (ISBN 0-8247-2505-0). Dekker.
--Encyclopedia of Electrochemistry of the Elements, Vol. 6. 1976. 119.50 (ISBN 0-8247-2556-5). Dekker.
Bard, E. M. The Cat I.Q. Test. LC 79-7854. (Illus.). 1980. pap. 3.95 (ISBN 0-385-15517-4, Dolp). Doubleday.
Bard, Erwin W. Port of New York Authority. LC 68-58547. (Columbia University Studies in the Social Sciences: No. 468). Repr. of 1942 ed. 24.50 (ISBN 0-404-51468-5). AMS Pr.
Bard, Harry E. The City School District, Statutory Provisions for Organizational & Fiscal Affairs. LC 76-176536. (Columbia University. Teachers College. Contributions to Education Ser.: No. 28). Repr. of 1909 ed. 22.50 (ISBN 0-404-55028-2). AMS Pr.
Bard, J. H. Anthelmintic Index. 71p. 1972. 40.00x (ISBN 0-85198-257-3, Pub. by CAB Bks England). State Mutual Bk.
--Nematicide Index. 92p. 1974. cloth 39.00x (ISBN 0-85198-309-X, Pub. by CAB Bks England). State Mutual Bk.
Bard, Lori. Hello! World. LC 71-124681. (Illus.). 129p. 1970. 6.00 (ISBN 0-87787-001-2). Mara.
Bard, Morton & Sangrey, Dawn. The Crime Victim's Book. 2nd ed. (Psychosocial Stress Ser.: No. 6). 240p. 1985. 20.00 (ISBN 0-317-26468-0); pap. 13.50. Brunner-Mazel.
Bard, Rachel. Country Inns of the Far West: Pacific NW. rev. ed. LC 84-3611. (Country Inns Ser.). (Illus.). 228p. 1984. pap. 7.95 (ISBN 0-89286-232-7). One Hund One Prods.
--Navarra: The Durable Kingdom. LC 82-8660. (Basque Bk.). 254p. 1982. 14.00 (ISBN 0-87417-073-7). U of Nev Pr.
--Newswriting Guide: A Handbook for Student Reporters. 83p. (Orig.). 1985. pap. 6.00 (ISBN 0-9603666-0-1). Writers Help.
Bard, Rachel & Kellogg, Caroline. Zucchini & All That Squash. LC 84-52215. 96p. (Orig.). 1985. pap. 7.95 (ISBN 0-9603666-1-X). Writers Help.
Bard, Ray & Davis, Larry. Winning Ways: A Management Performance Game. LC 79-20395. 1979. vinyl binder 99.50 (ISBN 0-89384-043-2). Learning Concepts.
Bard, Ray & Moody, Fran. Breaking In: The Guide to over 500 Top Corporate Training Programs. LC 85-6571. 705p. (Orig.). 1985. pap. 11.95 (ISBN 0-688-05893-0, Quill). Morrow.
Bard, Samuel A., pseud. Waikna, or, Adventures on the Mosquito Shore. Alleger, Daniel E., ed. LC 65-28697. (Latin American Gateway Ser.). (Illus.). 1965. Repr. of 1855 ed. 12.50 (ISBN 0-8130-0217-6). U Presses Fla.
Bard, Yonathan. Nonlinear Parameter Estimation. 1974. 65.00 (ISBN 0-12-078250-2). Acad Pr.
Barda, Clive, illus. The Sculpture of David Wynne, Nineteen Sixty-Eight to Nineteen Seventy-Four. (Illus.). 172p. 1975. 25.00 (ISBN 0-8390-0167-3, Phaidon Press). Abner Schram Ltd.
Bardach, Eugene. The Implementation Game: What Happens After a Bill Becomes Law. 1977. 27.50x (ISBN 0-262-02125-0); pap. 8.95x (ISBN 0-262-52049-4). MIT Pr.
Bardach, Eugene & Angelides, Sotirios. Water Banking: How to Stop Wasting Agricultural Water. LC 78-50766. 56p. 1978. pap. 2.00 (ISBN 0-917616-26-X). ICS Pr.
Bardach, Eugene & Kagan, Robert A. Going by the Book: The Problem of Regulatory Unreasonableness. 375p. 1982. 29.95x (ISBN 0-87722-251-7); pap. 12.95 (ISBN 0-87722-252-5). Temple U Pr.
Bardach, Eugene & Kagan, Robert A., eds. Social Regulation: Strategies for Reform. LC 81-85279. 420p. 1982. text ed. 19.95 (ISBN 0-917616-47-2); pap. text ed. 8.95 (ISBN 0-917616-46-4). ICS Pr.
Bardach, John E., et al. Aquaculture: The Farming & Husbandry of Freshwater & Marine Organisms. LC 72-2516. 868p. 1972. pap. 34.95x (ISBN 0-471-04826-7, Pub. by Wiley-Interscience). Wiley.
Bardack, David. Localities of Fossil Vertebrates Obtained from the Niobrara Formation (Cretaceous) of Kansas. (Museum Ser.: Vol. 17,No. 1). 14p. 1965. 1.25 (ISBN 0-317-04783-3). U of KS Mus Nat Hist.
Bardack, David, jt. auth. see Teller, Susan.
Bardakjian, Kevork B. & Thomson, Robert W. Textbook of Modern Western Armenian. LC 77-1774. 1977. text ed. 15.00x (ISBN 0-88206-012-0). Caravan Bks.
Bardeche. Marcel Proust: Romancier, 2 tomes. Set. deluxe ed. 31.95 (ISBN 0-685-37073-9). French & Eur.
Bardeche, Maurice. Nuremberg, 2 vols. 650p. 1975. lib. bdg. 250.00 (ISBN 0-8490-0742-9). Gordon Pr.
Bardeche, Maurice & Brasillach, Robert. History of Motion Pictures. LC 70-112565. (Literature of Cinema Ser.). Repr. of 1938 ed. 21.00 (ISBN 0-405-01602-6). Ayer Co Pubs.
Bardeen, Charles W., ed. see Comenius, John A.
Bardell, Geoff, jt. auth. see Craft, Alma.
Barden, John A., jt. auth. see Halfacre, Gordon.
Barden, John G. A Suggested Program of Teacher Training for Mission Schools Among the Batetela. LC 75-176517. (Columbia University. Teachers College. Contributions to Education: No. 853). Repr. of 1941 ed. 22.50 (ISBN 0-404-55853-4). AMS Pr.
Barden, Julian A., jt. ed. see Dos Remedios, Cristobal G.
Barden, L. W. The Ruy Lopez: Winning Chess with IP-K4. 12.00 (ISBN 0-08-013006-2). Pergamon.
Barden, Leonard. Book of Chess Puzzles. (Illus.). 190p. 1977. pap. 2.95 (ISBN 0-571-11091-6). Faber & Faber.
--How Good Is Your Chess. LC 75-28848. 128p. 1976. pap. 2.50 (ISBN 0-486-23294-8). Dover.
--Introduction to Chess Moves & Tactics Simply Explained. (Illus., Orig.). 1959. pap. 2.50 (ISBN 0-486-21210-6). Dover.
Barden, Leonard & Harding, Tim. Batsford Guide to Chess Openings. (Illus.). 168p. 1981. pap. 12.95 (ISBN 0-7134-3214-4, Pub. by Batsford England). David & Charles.
Barden, Leonard & Heidenfeld, Wolfgang. Modern Chess Miniatures. LC 77-78590. 1977. pap. 3.95 (ISBN 0-486-23541-6). Dover.
Barden, R. G. Sound Pollution. (Australian Environment Ser.: No.4). (Illus.). 66p. 1976. 19.75 (ISBN 0-7022-1012-9); pap. 9.95x (ISBN 0-7022-1013-7). U of Queensland Pr.
Barden, Renardo. Tamashiwara: The Art of Breaking Bricks & Boards with Your Bare Hands & Feet. (Illus.). 128p. 1985. pap. 7.95 (ISBN 0-8092-5186-8). Contemp Bks.
Barden, William. Microcomputer Math. LC 81-86554. 128p. 1982. pap. 12.95 (ISBN 0-672-21927-1, 21927). Sams.
Barden, William, Jr. Assembly Language Programming for the IBM PC & PCjr. 500p. pap. cancelled (ISBN 0-88134-146-0, 146-0). Osborne-McGraw.
--Guidebook to Small Computers. LC 80-50047. 128p. 1980. pap. 6.95 (ISBN 0-672-21698-1, 21698). Sams.
--How to Do It on the TRS-80. 352p. 1983. 29.95 (ISBN 0-936200-08-1). Blue Cat.
--How to Program Microcomputers. LC 77-77412. 256p. 1978. pap. 11.95 (ISBN 0-672-21459-8, 21459). Sams.
--IBM PC Encyclopedia. 1985. 19.95 (ISBN 0-03-072016-8). CBS Ed.
--IBM PC Programs. 1985. FPT 17.95 (ISBN 0-03-072017-6). CBS Ed.
--Microcomputers for Business Applications. LC 78-64984. 256p. 1979. pap. 9.95 (ISBN 0-672-21583-7, 21583). Sams.
--TRS-80 Assembly Language Subroutines. (Illus.). 282p. 1982. pap. 18.95 (ISBN 0-13-931188-2). P-H.
--TRS-80 Model I, III, & Color Computer Interfacing Projects. LC 82-60876. 276p. 1983. pap. 14.95 (ISBN 0-672-22009-1, 22009). Sams.
--What Do You Do after You Plug It In? LC 82-62199. 200p. 1983. pap. 10.95 (ISBN 0-672-22008-3, 22008). Sams.
--Z80 Microcomputer Design Projects. LC 80-50046. 208p. 1980. pap. 14.95 (ISBN 0-672-21682-5, 21682). Sams.
--Z80 Microcomputer Handbook. LC 77-93166. 304p. 1978. pap. 13.95 (ISBN 0-672-21500-4, 21500). Sams.
Barder, Richard C. English Country Grandfather Clocks. (Illus.). 192p. 1983. 31.50 (ISBN 0-7153-8314-0). David & Charles.
Bardes, B A., jt. auth. see Dubnick, M. J.
Bardham Roy, B K., jt. auth. see Abeles, P W.
Bardhan, K. D., jt. ed. see Porro, G. B.
Bardhan, Pranab. The Political Economy of Development in India. 130p. 1984. 24.95x (ISBN 0-631-13544-8). Basil Blackwell.
Bardhan, Pranab K. Land, Labor, & Rural Poverty: Essays in Development Economics. 288p. 1984. 27.50 (ISBN 0-231-05388-6). Columbia U Pr.
Bardi, Edward, jt. auth. see Coyle, John J.
Bardi, Edward J., jt. auth. see Coyle, John J.
Bardi, Panos D. History of Thanatology: Philosophical, Religious, Psychological, & Sociological Ideas Concerning Death from Primitive Times to the Present. LC 81-43026. 102p. (Orig.). 1981. lib. bdg. 19.00 (ISBN 0-8191-1648-3); pap. text ed. 8.00 (ISBN 0-8191-1649-1). U Pr of Amer.
Bardige, Betty, ed. see Segal, Marilyn.
Bardill, Donald R., jt. auth. see Mueller, Charles S.
Bardill, John E. & Cobbe, James H. Lesotho: Profiles. (Nations of Contemporary Africa Ser.). 130p. 1985. 26.50x (ISBN 0-86531-440-3). Westview.
Bardin, C. Wayne, ed. The Cell Biology of the Testis, Vol. 383. 450p. 1982. 118.00x (ISBN 0-89766-156-7); pap. 118.00. NY Acad Sci.
Bardin, C. Wayne, jt. ed. see Krieger, Dorothy T.
Bardin, C. Wayne, et al, eds. Progesterone & Progestins. (Illus.). 480p. 1983. text ed. 90.00 (ISBN 0-89004-769-3). Raven.
Bardin, John F. The John Franklin Bardin Omnibus. 1976. pap. 7.95 (ISBN 0-14-004130-3). Penguin.
Bardin, Perla. Artesanias Argentinas Tradicionales: (Traditional Argentine Artcrafts) (Illus.). 108p. (Eng. & Span.). 1981. 29.95 (ISBN 0-295-96199-6). U of Wash Pr.
Bardin, Shlomo. Pioneer Youth in Palestine. LC 75-6420. (The Rise of Jewish Nationalism & the Middle East Ser.). 182p. 1976. Repr. of 1932 ed. 17.00 (ISBN 0-88355-308-2). Hyperion Conn.
Bardin, Shlomo, ed. Self-Fulfillment Through Zionism: A Study in Jewish Adjustment. LC 70-142605. (Biography Index Reprint Ser). Repr. of 1943 ed. 17.00 (ISBN 0-8369-8076-X). Ayer Co Pubs.
Barding, LeRoy F. Air-Condition Handbook. 48p. (Orig.). 1981. pap. 3.00 (ISBN 0-9605848-0-3). Barding Pub.
Bardis, Panos. Dictionary of Quotations in Sociology. LC 85-943. 384p. 1985. lib. bdg. 45.00 (ISBN 0-313-23778-6, BDQ/). Greenwood.
Bardis, Panos D. The Future of the Greek Language in the United States. LC 75-36574. 1976. softbound 11.95 (ISBN 0-88247-396-4). R & E Pubs.
Bardis, Panos D., jt. ed. see Das, Man S.
Bardo, John W. & Hartman, John J. Urban Sociology: A Systematic Introduction. LC 81-82886. 401p. 1982. text ed. 19.95 (ISBN 0-87581-277-5). Peacock Pubs.
Bardo, Pamela P. English & Continental Portrait Miniatures: The Latter-Schlesinger Collection. LC 78-59762. (Illus.). 120p. 1978. pap. 7.95 (ISBN 0-89494-006-6). New Orleans Mus Art.
Bardoff, O., jt. auth. see Downing, Frank.
Bardoloi, Nirmalprabha, ed. Assamese Short Stories: An Anthology. (Vikas Library of Modern Indian Writing: No. 23). 180p. 1982. text ed. 20.00x (ISBN 0-7069-1590-9, Pub. by Vikas India). Advent NY.
Bardoloi, Nirmalprbha, ed. Assamese Short Stories: An Anthology. 1982. 40.00x (ISBN 0-7069-1590-9, Pub. by Garlandfold England). State Mutual Bk.
Bardolph, Richard. The Negro Vanguard. LC 77-135592. 388p. 1972. Repr. of 1959 ed. text ed. 33.50x (ISBN 0-8371-5183-X, BNV&, Pub. by Negro U Pr). Greenwood.
Bardon, ed. see Lesage, Alain-Rene.
Bardon, Edward J. The Sexual Arena & Women's Liberation. LC 77-23937. 260p. 1978. 20.95x (ISBN 0-88229-219-6). Nelson-Hall.
Bardon, Franz. Frabato the Magician. Dimai, Peter A., tr. from Ger. (Illus.). 184p. 1982. 9.00 (ISBN 0-914732-13-7). Bro Life Inc.
--Initiation into Hermetics. 4th ed. Radspieler, A., tr. from Ger. (Illus.). 294p. 1981. 17.00 (ISBN 0-914732-10-2). Bro Life Inc.
--The Key to the True Quabbalah. 2nd ed. Dimai, Peter A., tr. from Ger. (Illus.). 270p. 1975. 16.00 (ISBN 0-914732-12-9). Bro Life Inc.
--The Practice of Magical Evocation. 4th ed. Dimai, Peter, tr. from Ger. (Illus.). 435p. 1983. 22.00 (ISBN 0-914732-11-0). Bro Life Inc.
Bardon, Jack I. & Bennett, Virginia C. School Psychology. LC 73-11419. (Foundations of Modern Psychology Ser). (Illus.). 224p. 1973. pap. text ed. 12.95 (ISBN 0-13-794412-8). P-H.
Bardon, Jonathan. Belfast: An Illustrated History. rev. ed. (Illus.). 332p. 1983. 26.95 (Pub. by Blackstaff Pr). Longwood Pub Group.
--Dublin: One Thousand Years of Wood Quay. (Illus.). 36p. 1984. 18.95 (ISBN 0-85640-318-0, Pub. by Blackstaff Pr). Longwood Pub Group.
Bardoni, Avril, tr. see Sciascia, Leonardo.
Bardos, C., ed. Bifurcation & Nonlinear Eigenvalue Problems: Proceedings. (Lecture Notes in Mathematics: Vol. 782). 296p. 1980. pap. 23.00 (ISBN 0-387-09758-9). Springer-Verlag.
Bardos, C. & Damlamian, A., eds. Contributions to Nonlinear Partial Differential Equations. (Research Notes in Mathematics: No. 89). 360p. 1983. pap. text ed. 24.95 (ISBN 0-273-08595-6). Pitman Pub MA.
Bardos, Claude, ed. see NATO Advanced Study Institute, Cargese, Corsica, June 24 - July, 1979.
Bardos, T. J. & Kalman, T. I., eds. New Approaches to the Design of Antineoplastic Agents. 344p. 1983. 78.00 (ISBN 0-444-00724-5, Biomedical Pr). Elsevier.
Bardossy, G. Karst Bauxites: Bauxite Deposits on Carbonate Rocks. (Developments in Economic Geology Ser.: Vol. 14). 442p. 1982. 83.00 (ISBN 0-444-99727-X). Elsevier.
Bardsley, C. W. Curiosities of Puritan Nomenclature. (The International Library of Names). 252p. Repr. of 1880 ed. text ed. cancelled (ISBN 0-8290-1239-7). Irvington.
Bardsley, Charles W. A Dictionary of English & Welsh Surnames with Special American Instances. LC 67-25404. 837p. 1980. Repr. of 1901 ed. 30.00 (ISBN 0-8063-0022-1). Genealog Pub.
--Romance of the London Directory. LC 72-78115. 1971. Repr. of 1879 ed. 40.00x (ISBN 0-8103-3782-7). Gale.
Bardsley, Herbert J. Reconstructions of Early Christian Documents. 1977. lib. bdg. 59.95 (ISBN 0-8490-2504-4). Gordon Pr.
Bardsley, Kathryn, ed. see Esposito, Barbara, et al.
Bardsley, W., et al, eds. Crystal Growth: A Tutorial Approach. (North Holland Series in Crystal Growth: Vol. 2). 408p. 1979. 68.00 (ISBN 0-444-85371-5, North Holland). Elsevier.
Bardwell, Edward C. New Profits: Business Interruption Insurance. 4th ed. 1982. 16.00 (ISBN 0-942326-20-2, 26621). Rough Notes.
Bardwell, George, jt. auth. see Seligson, Harry.
Bardwell, Lorena. Modern Meatless Menus Cookbook. 1963. spiral bdg. 2.50 (ISBN 0-87511-002-9). Claitors.
Bardwick, J. M. Women in Transition. 1981. 35.00x (ISBN 0-686-78802-8, Pub. by Turoe Pr). State Mutual Bk.
Bardwick, Judith. In Transition: How Feminism, Sexual Liberation, & the Search for Self-Fulfillment Have Altered America. LC 78-14168. 17.95 (ISBN 0-03-043061-5, HoltC). HR&W.
Bardwick, Judith M., et al. Feminine Personality & Conflict. LC 80-24191. (Contemporary Psychology Ser.). vii, 102p. 1981. Repr. of 1970 ed. lib. bdg. 19.75x (ISBN 0-313-22504-4, BAFP). Greenwood.
Bare, Charles L. Nebraska Economic Projections II, 1980-2000. Keefe, Jean, ed. (Nebraska Economic & Business Report Ser.: No. 19). 1978. 7.50 (ISBN 0-686-28409-7). Bur Busn Res U Nebr.
--Nebraska Gross State Product Nineteen Sixty to Ninety Seventy-Six. (Nebraska Economic & Business Report Ser.: No. 22). 1978. 5.00 (ISBN 0-686-28411-9). Bur Busn Res U Nebr.
Bare, Colleen S. The Durable Desert Tortoise. LC 79-12806. (A Skylight Bk.). (Illus.). (gr. 2-5). 1979. 7.95 (ISBN 0-396-07706-4). Dodd.
--Ground Squirrels. LC 80-13649. (A Skylight Bk.). (Illus.). 64p. (gr. 2-5). 1980. 7.95 (ISBN 0-396-07852-4). Dodd.
--Guinea Pigs Don't Read Books. (Illus.). 32p. (ps-3). 1985. 10.95 (ISBN 0-396-08538-5). Dodd.
--Mule Deer. (A Skylight Bk.). (Illus.). 64p. (gr. 3-5). 1981. 7.95 (ISBN 0-396-07971-7). Dodd.
--Rabbits & Hares. LC 82-45992. (Illus.). 80p. (gr. 4 up). 1983. pap. 8.95 (ISBN 0-396-08127-4). Dodd.
--Tree Squirrels. (Illus.). (gr. 9 up). 1983. PLB 8.95 (ISBN 0-396-08208-4). Dodd.
Bare, Harold R. One-Room Rural Schools: The Building Blocks for Today's Schools. (Illus.). 64p. 1984. pap. 7.50 (ISBN 0-682-40134-X). Exposition Pr FL.
Bare, Janet E. Wildflowers & Weeds of Kansas. LC 78-16862. (Illus.). 1979. 29.95 (ISBN 0-7006-0176-7). U Pr of KS.
Bare, Richard L. The Film Director: A Practical Guide to Motion Pictures & Television Techniques. LC 76-130944. (Illus.). 243p. 1973. pap. 7.95 (ISBN 0-02-012130-X, Collier). Macmillan.
Bare, William K. Fundamentals of Fire Prevention. LC 76-23221. (Fire Science Ser.). 213p. 1977. text ed. 27.95 (ISBN 0-471-04835-6). Wiley.
--Introduction to Fire Science & Fire Prevention. LC 77-14002. (Fire Science Ser.). 290p. 1978. text ed. 26.95x (ISBN 0-471-01708-6); tchrs. manual (ISBN 0-471-03779-6). Wiley.

Barea, Arturo. Lorca: The Poet & His People. LC 72-92121. xv, 176p. 1973. Repr. of 1949 ed. lib. bdg. 18.50 (ISBN 0-8154-0447-6). Cooper Sq.

Bareau, Paul. The Disorder in World Money. (Institute of Economic Affairs, Occasional Papers Ser.: No. 61). pap. 4.25 technical (ISBN 0-255-36148-3). Transatlantic.

Barefield, James P., et al. Medieval & Other Studies: In Honor of Floyd Seyward Lear. (Rice University Studies: Vol. 60, No. 4). (Illus.). 111p. (Orig.). 1975. pap. 10.00x (ISBN 0-89263-222-4). Rice Univ.

Barefield, Marilyn D. Butler County, Alabama Obituaries. (Illus.). 158p. 1985. pap. 17.50 (ISBN 0-89308-549-9). Southern Hist Pr.

--Historical Records of Randolph County, Alabama, 1832-1900. (Illus.). 230p. 1985. 22.50 (ISBN 0-89308-548-0). Southern Hist Pr.

Barefield, Russell M. The Impact of Audit Frequency on the Quality of Internal Control, Vol. 11. (Studies in Accounting Research). 86p. 1975. 6.00 (ISBN 0-86539-023-1); members 4.00. Am Accounting.

Barefield, Russell M. & Holstrum, Gary L., eds. Disclosure Criteria & Segment Reporting. LC 79-21130. (University of Florida Accounting Ser.: No. 10). (Illus.). ix, 156p. 1979. pap. 8.00 (ISBN 0-8130-0651-1). U Presses Fla.

Barefoot, A. C. & Hankins, Frank W. Identification of Modern Tertiary Woods. (Illus.). 1982. 98.00x (ISBN 0-19-854378-6). Oxford U Pr.

Barefoot, J. Kirk. Employee Theft Investigation. LC 79-9764. 1979. 21.95 (ISBN 0-913708-33-X). Butterworth.

--Undercover Investigation. 2nd ed. 130p. 1983. text ed. 19.95 (ISBN 0-409-95076-9). Butterworth.

Bareh, Hamlet. The Language & Literature of Meghalaya. LC 78-670053. 1977. 7.50x (ISBN 0-89684-427-7). Intl Pubns Serv.

Bareham, T. & Gatrell, S. Bibliography of George Crabbe. 194p. 1978. 22.50 (ISBN 0-208-01723-2, Archon). Shoe String.

Bareham, Terence. George Crabbe. (Critical Studies Ser.). 245p. 1977. 25.00x (ISBN 0-06-490305-2). B&N Imports.

Bareham, Tony, ed. Anthony Trollope. (Barnes & Noble Critical Studies). 207p. 1980. 28.50x (ISBN 0-389-20027-1, 06800). B&N Imports.

Bareis, Charles J. & Porter, James W., eds. American Bottom Archaeology: A Summary of the FAI-270 Project Contribution to the Culture History of the Mississippi River Valley. LC 83-15366. (Illus.). 304p. 1984. 22.50x (ISBN 0-252-01111-2). U of Ill Pr.

Bareis, Charles J., ed. see McElrath, Dale L. & Fortier, Andrew C.

Bareiss, Karl-Heinz. Comoedia. (European University Studies: No. 14, Vol. 100). 525p. (Ger.). 1982. 43.70 (ISBN 3-8204-5986-3). P Lang Pubs.

Bareiss, Philip. Creative West: Taos & Northern New Mexico. Parsons, James, ed. (Illus.). 1983. 1.50 (ISBN 0-9610550-2-2). Gallery West.

Barel, Yves. Le Developpement Economique De la Russie Tsariste. (Economie Du Developpement: No. 4). 1968. pap. 16.40x (ISBN 90-2796-351-7). Mouton.

Barell, John. Playgrounds of Our Minds. LC 79-27084. 1980. pap. text ed. 11.95x (ISBN 0-8077-2580-3). Tchrs Coll.

Barella Campos, Ana G., jt. auth. see Barella Campos, Juana.

Barella Campos, Juana & Barella Campos, Ana G. Diccionario de Refranes. 534p. (Span.). 1975. pap. 44.95 (ISBN 84-600-6609-6, S-50116). French & Eur.

Barelli, Rea. Winds of Love. (YA) (gr. 9-12). 1984. 8.95 (ISBN 0-8034-8457-7, Avalon). Bouregy.

Baren, William S. How to Sell Securities. Seibert, Claude D. & Sweitnickie, Edward, eds. LC 85-90807. 112p. (Orig.). 1985. pap. 8.95 (ISBN 0-9614837-0-9). Dana Co.

Barenblatt, G. I., ed. Similarity, Self-Similarity & Intermediate Asymptotics. LC 79-14621. (Illus.). 236p. 1980. 55.00 (ISBN 0-306-10956-5, Consultants). Plenum Pub.

Barenblatt, G. I. & Iooss, G., eds. Nonlinear Dynamics & Turbulence. 360p. 1983. text ed. 59.95 (ISBN 0-273-08560-3). Pitman Pub MA.

Barenboim, Grigory M., et al. Luminescence of Biopolymers & Cells. LC 68-26768. 229p. 1969. 29.50x (ISBN 0-306-30350-7, Plenum Pr). Plenum Pub.

Barendrecht, Cor. In a Strange Land. 3.50 (ISBN 0-686-15984-5). Being Pubns.

Barendregt, H. P. The Lambda Calculus: Its Syntax & Semantics. (Studies in Logic & the Foundation of Mathematics Ser.: Vol. 103). 616p. 1981. 95.75 (ISBN 0-444-85490-8, North-Holland). Elsevier.

--The Lambda Calculus: Its Syntax & Semantics. 2nd, rev. ed. (Studies in Logic & the Foundations of Mathematics: No. 103). xiv, 616p. 1984. 70.00 (ISBN 0-444-86748-1, 1-127-84, North-Holland); pap. 35.00 (ISBN 0-444-87508-5). Elsevier.

Barendse, Michael A. Social Expectations & Perception: The Case of the Slavic Anthracite Workers. LC 80-8610. (Penn State Studies: No. 47). (Illus.). 72p. (Orig.). 1981. pap. text ed. 4.95x (ISBN 0-271-00277-8). Pa St U Pr.

Barendsen, G. W. & Broerse, J., eds. High Let Radiations in Clinical Radiotherapy. Breur, K. (Illus.). 1980. 170.00 (ISBN 0-08-024383-5). Pergamon.

Barenie, James, jt. ed. see Ripa, Louis.

Barentsen, A., ed. South Slavic & Balkan Linguistics. (Studies in Slavic & General Linguistics: Vol. 2). 340p. 1982. pap. text ed. 32.75x (ISBN 90-6203-634-1, Pub. by Rodopi Holland). Humanities.

--Studies in Slavic & General Linguistics, Vol. 1. 472p. 1980. pap. text ed. 46.50x (ISBN 90-6203-523-X, Pub. by Rodopi Holland). Humanities.

Barer, R., jt. auth. see Cosslett, V. E.

Barer, R., jt. ed. see Cosslett, V. E.

Barer, R. D. & Peters, B. F. Why Metals Fail-Selected Case Histories. 350p. 1970. 70.50x (ISBN 0-677-02630-7). Gordon.

--Why Metals Fall. (Illus.). 345p. 1970. 38.00 (ISBN 0-318-17219-4, 1182). Am Soc Nondestructive.

Bares, R. A., ed. Plastics in Material & Structural Engineering. (Illus.). 962p. 1982. 164.00 (ISBN 0-686-48179-8, 0706). T-C Pubns CA.

--Plastics in Material & Structural Engineering: Proceedings ICP-RILEM-IBK International Symposium, Prague, June 23-25, 1981. (Developments in Civil Engineering Ser.: Vol. 5). 962p. 1982. 164.00 (ISBN 0-444-99710-5). Elsevier.

Baressi, Barry J., ed. Ocular Assessment. 384p. 1983. text ed. 49.95 (ISBN 0-409-95034-3). Butterworth.

Baretti, Guiseppe. Journey from London to Genoa. 1983. 90.00 (ISBN 0-900000-71-6, Pub. by Centaur Pr England). State Mutual Bk.

Barfield, Claude. Science Policy From Ford to Reagan: Change & Continuity. 1983. 13.95 (ISBN 0-8447-3495-0); pap. 5.95 (ISBN 0-8447-3494-2). Am Enterprise.

Barfield, Claude E. Rethinking Federalism. 1981. pap. 4.25 (ISBN 0-8447-3479-9). Am Enterprise.

Barfield, John, jt. auth. see Craven, Henry.

Barfield, Owen. History, Guilt, & Habit. LC 79-65333. 104p. 1981. pap. 8.95 (ISBN 0-8195-6064-2). Wesleyan U Pr.

--Orpheus: A Poetic Drama. LC 82-83247. 144p. (Orig.). 1983. pap. 6.95 (ISBN 0-940262-01-0). Lindisfarne Pr.

--Owen Barfield & the Origin of Language. 1979. pap. 2.50 (ISBN 0-916786-42-0). St George Bk Serv.

--Poetic Diction: A Study in Meaning. 3rd ed. LC 72-10631. 232p. 1973. pap. 9.50 (ISBN 0-8195-6026-X). Wesleyan U Pr.

--Poetic Diction: A Study in Meaning. 230p. 1982. Repr. of 1975 ed. lib. bdg. 45.00 (ISBN 0-8495-0630-1). Arden Lib.

--The Rediscovery of Meaning & Other Essays. LC 76-41479. 1977. 15.00x (ISBN 0-8195-5006-X). Wesleyan U Pr.

--Rediscovery of Meaning & Other Essays. vi, 260p. 1985. pap. 10.95 (ISBN 0-8195-6124-X). Wesleyan U Pr.

--Saving the Appearances: A Study in Idolatry. LC 65-23538. 1965. pap. 4.95 (ISBN 0-15-679490-X, Harv). HarBraceJ.

--The Silver Trumpet. LC 85-71803. 156p. (gr. 1-5). 1985. 16.95 (ISBN 0-917665-05-8); pap. 10.95 (ISBN 0-917665-06-6). Bookmakers Guild.

--Speaker's Meaning. 1984. pap. 9.95 (ISBN 0-8195-6113-4). Wesleyan U Pr.

--What Coleridge Thought. LC 73-153100. 1971. 17.50x (ISBN 0-8195-4040-4). Wesleyan U Pr.

--What Coleridge Thought. 1983. pap. 9.95 (ISBN 0-8195-6084-7). Wesleyan U Pr.

--Worlds Apart. LC 63-17798. 1964. pap. 9.95 (ISBN 0-8195-6017-0). Wesleyan U Pr.

Barfield, Owen, ed. see Harwood, A. Cecil.

Barfield, Owen, tr. see Steiner, Rudolf.

Barfield, Richard E. & Morgan, James N. Early Retirement: The Decision & the Experience & A Second Look. rev. ed. LC 70-626137. 345p. 1970. pap. 12.00x (ISBN 0-87944-067-8). Inst Soc Res.

Barfield, Thomas J. The Central Asian Arabs of Afghanistan: Pastoral Nomadism in Transition. 204p. 1981. text ed. 22.50x (ISBN 0-292-71066-6). U of Tex Pr.

Barfield, Velma. Woman on Death Row. 1985. pap. 6.95 (ISBN 0-8407-9531-9). Nelson.

Barfknecht, Gary W. Mich-Again's Day. (Illus.). 265p. (Orig.). 1984. pap. 7.95 (ISBN 0-9608588-2-2). Friede Pubns.

--Michillaneous. (Illus.). 272p. (Orig.). 1982. pap. 7.95 (ISBN 0-9608588-0-6). Friede Pubns.

--Michillaneous II. (Illus.). 320p. (Orig.). 1985. pap. 9.95 (ISBN 0-9608588-3-0). Friede Pubns.

--Murder, Michigan. 238p. (Orig.). 1983. pap. 6.95 (ISBN 0-9608588-1-4). Friede Pubns.

Barfoot, Audrey. Everyday Costume in Britain. 1972. 13.95 (ISBN 0-7134-1901-6, Pub. by Batsford England). David & Charles.

Barfoot, C. C. Thread of Connection: Aspects of Fate in the Novels of Jane Austen & Others. (Costerus New Ser.: No. XXXII). 215p. 1981. pap. text ed. 21.25x (ISBN 90-6203-903-0, Pub. by Rodopi Holland). Humanities.

Barfoot, Joan. Dancing in the Dark. 192p. 1984. pap. 3.50 (ISBN 0-380-67058-5, 67447-5). Avon.

Barfoot, K. M., jt. auth. see Mitchell, I. V.

Barford, N. C. Experimental Measurements: Precision, Error & Truth. 2nd ed. 1985. write for info. (ISBN 0-471-90701-4). Wiley.

Barford, Philip. Bruckner Symphonies. LC 75-27956. (BBC Music Guides). (Illus.). 64p. (Orig.). pap. 4.95 (ISBN 0-295-95479-5). U of Wash Pr.

--Keyboard Music of C.P.E. Bach. 1966. 15.00 (ISBN 0-8079-0072-9). October.

--Mahler Symphonies & Songs. LC 72-127651. 64p. 1971. pap. 4.95 (ISBN 0-295-95104-4). U of Wash Pr.

Barfuss, Gerald. David Stone in Sunset Valley: The Story of the KSTP Sunset Valley Barn Dance. (Illus.). 1983. 19.95 (ISBN 0-911506-17-9). Thueson.

Barg, Barbara, ed. see Friedman, Ed.

Barg, Joanne. Computers: First Steps in PET BASIC. (Illus.). 112p. (gr. 3-6). 1983. pap. 9.95 (ISBN 0-912526-33-5). Lib Res.

Barg, W. T. de see De Bary, W. T.

Bargad, Warren. Ideas in Fiction: The Works of Hayim Hazaz. LC 81-13621. (Brown Judiac Studies). 1982. pap. 13.50 (ISBN 0-89130-518-1, 14-00-31). Scholars Pr GA.

Bargad, Warren & Chyet, Stanley F., trs. from Hebrew. Israeli Poetry: A Contemporary Anthology. LC 84-48247. (Jewish Literature & Culture Ser.). 224p. 1985. 29.95 (ISBN 0-253-33140-4). Ind U Pr.

Bargainnier, Earl. Ten Women of Mystery. LC 80-85393. 1981. 21.95 (ISBN 0-87972-172-3); pap. 10.95 (ISBN 0-87972-173-1). Bowling Green Univ.

--Twelve Englishmen of Mystery. LC 83-72499. 1984. 22.95 (ISBN 0-87972-249-5); pap. 11.95 (ISBN 0-87972-250-9). Bowling Green Univ.

Bargainnier, Earl F. The Gentle Art of Murder: The Detective Fiction of Agatha Christie. LC 80-83187. 232p. 1981. 16.95 (ISBN 0-87972-158-8); pap. 8.95 (ISBN 0-87972-159-6). Bowling Green Univ.

Bargar, Bradley D. Royal South Carolina, 1719-1763. LC 77-133843. (Tricentennial Booklet: No. 7). viii, 76p. 1970. pap. 3.95 (ISBN 0-87249-206-0). U of SC Pr.

Bargar, Gary W. Life is Not Fair. LC 83-15299. 180p. (gr. 4-7). 1984. PLB 11.95 (ISBN 0-89919-218-1, Clarion). HM.

--What Happened to Mr. Forster? LC 80-28259. 192p. (gr. 3-6). 1981. 8.95 (ISBN 0-395-31021-0, Clarion). HM.

Barge, C. D., jt. auth. see Haynes, J. H.

Bargebuhr, Fredrick P. The Alhambra: A Cycle of Studies on the Eleventh Century in Moorish Spain. 1968. 80.00 (ISBN 3-11-000524-7). De Gruyter.

Bargellini, P. L., ed. Communications Satellite Systems, Vol. 32. LC 73-15613. (Illus.). 480p. 1974. 35.00 (ISBN 0-262-02100-5, PAAS32); members 19.00 (ISBN 0-317-32136-6). AIAA.

--Communications Satellite Technology. LC 73-15612. (Illus.). 540p. 1974. 35.00 (ISBN 0-262-02101-3, PAAS33); members 19.00 (ISBN 0-317-32137-4). AIAA.

Bargen, Doris G. The Fiction of Stanley Elkin. (Studien und Texte zur Amerikanistik: Vol. 8). 338p. 1979. pap. 32.95 (ISBN 3-8204-6430-1). P Lang Pubs.

Bargen, Richard. The Vegetarian's Self-Defense Manual. LC 79-645097. (Illus.). 1979. pap. 4.95 (ISBN 0-8356-0530-2, Quest). Theos Pub Hse.

Barger, et al. The PPO Handbook. 200p. 1984. 32.50 (ISBN 0-89443-569-8). Aspen Systems.

Barger, Adele E. Gardening Success with Lunar Aspects. 112p. 1983. Repr. 6.00 (ISBN 0-86690-249-X, 2115-01). Am Fed Astrologers.

Barger, Geoffrey R., jt. auth. see Farber, Jason E.

Barger, Gerald L., jt. ed. see Jen-Yu Wang.

Barger, Gerald L., jt. ed. see Wang, Jen Y.

Barger, Gwyneth, jt. auth. see Barger, Harold.

Barger, Harold. American Agriculture, 1899-1939: A Study of Output, Employment & Productivity. LC 75-41017. (BCL Ser. II). Repr. of 1942 ed. 22.50 (ISBN 0-404-14640-6). AMS Pr.

--The Transportation Industries, 1889-1946: A Study of Output, Employment & Productivity. LC 75-19692. (National Bureau of Economic Research Ser.). (Illus.). 1975. Repr. of 1951 ed. 23.50x (ISBN 0-405-07573-1). Ayer Co Pubs.

Barger, Harold & Barger, Gwyneth. College on Credit: A History of United Student Aid Funds, 1960-1980. LC 81-6537. 122p. 1981. 8.50 (ISBN 0-915145-20-0). Hackett Pub.

Barger, Harold & Landsberg, Hans H. American Agriculture, 1899-1939: A Study of Output, Employment, & Productivity. LC 75-19693. (National Bureau of Economic Research Ser.). (Illus.). 1975. Repr. of 1942 ed. 33.00x (ISBN 0-405-07574-X). Ayer Co Pubs.

Barger, Harold & Schurr, Sam H. The Mining Industries, 1899-1939: A Study of Output, Employment & Productivity. LC 72-2833. (Use & Abuse of America's Natural Resources Ser). 474p. 1972. Repr. of 1944 ed. 30.00 (ISBN 0-405-04502-6). Ayer Co Pubs.

--The Mining Industries, 1899-1939: A Study of Output, Employment, & Productivity. LC 75-19694. (National Bureau of Economic Research Ser.). (Illus.). 1975. Repr. 32.00x (ISBN 0-405-07575-8). Ayer Co Pubs.

Barger, Harold M. The Impossible Presidency: Illusions & Realities of Executive Power. 1984. pap. text ed. 10.80 (ISBN 0-673-15576-5). Scott F.

Barger, James. Ernest Hemingway: American Literary Giant. new ed. Rahmas, D. Steve, ed. (Outstanding Personalities Ser.). 32p. 1975. lib. bdg. 3.50 incl. catalog cards (ISBN 0-87157-580-9); pap. 1.95 vinyl laminated covers (ISBN 0-87157-080-7). SamHar Pr.

--James Joyce: Modern Irish Writer. Rahmas, D. Steve, ed. LC 74-14701. (Outstanding Personalities Ser.). 32p. 1974. lib. bdg. 3.50 incl. catalog cards (ISBN 0-87157-577-9); pap. 1.95 vinyl laminated covers (ISBN 0-87157-077-7). SamHar Pr.

--William Faulkner: Modern American Novelist & Nobel Prize Winner. Rahmas, D. Steve, ed. (Outstanding Personalities Ser.: No. 63). 32p. (Orig.). (YA) (gr. 7-12). 1973. lib. bdg. 3.50 incl. catalog cards (ISBN 0-87157-563-9); pap. 1.95 vinyl laminated covers (ISBN 0-87157-063-7). SamHar Pr.

Barger, M. Susan. Bibliography of Photographic Processes in Use Before 1880: Their Materials, Processing, & Conservation. LC 80-84390. 160p. 1980. pap. 37.50 (ISBN 0-89938-003-4). Tech & Ed Ctr Graph Arts RIT.

Barger, R. Curtis. Don't You Know? Haven't You Heard? Woolsey, Raymond H., ed. (Banner Ser.). 128p. (Orig.). 1985. pap. 5.95 (ISBN 0-8280-0278-9). Review & Herald.

Barger, Susan M., ed. Selected Bibliography: Photographic Processes in Use Before 1880. LC 84-84390. 149p. 1980. pap. 37.50 (ISBN 0-89938-003-4). Tech & Ed Ctr Graph Arts RIT.

Barger, V., et al, eds. see AIP Conference Proceedings No. 85 Madsion, Wisconsin, 1982.

Barger, Vernon & Cline, David. Neutrino Mass & Gauge Structure of Weak Interactions (Telemark, 1982) AIP Conference Proceedings 99, Particles & Fields Subseries 30. LC 83-71072. 283p. 1983. lib. bdg. 34.50 (ISBN 0-88318-198-3). Am Inst Physics.

Barger, Vernon D. & Olsson, Martin G. Classical Mechanics: A Modern Perspective. LC 72-5697. (Illus.). 352p. 1973. text ed. 34.95 (ISBN 0-07-003723-X). McGraw.

Bargerstock, Charles T. Educational Fund Raising & the Law. 81p. 1984. 14.50 (ISBN 0-89964-226-8). Coun Adv & Supp Ed.

Bargh, David J. De see De Bargh, David J.

Barghahn, Barbara von see Von Barghahn, Barbara.

Barghoorn, E., et al. The Boylston Street Fishweir, Vol. 4. Johnson, F., ed. LC 50-4864. 1949. 6.00 (ISBN 0-939312-05-0). Peabody Found.

Barghoorn, Frederick C. Detente & the Democratic Movement in the U. S. S. R. LC 76-4425. 1976. 15.95 (ISBN 0-02-901850-1). Free Pr.

--Politics in the U. S. S. R. 2nd ed. (Comparative Politics Ser.). 1972. pap. 12.95 (ISBN 0-316-08089-6). Little.

--The Soviet Cultural Offensive: The Role of Cultural Diplomacy in Soviet Foreign Policy. LC 60-12227. pap. 90.30 (ISBN 0-317-09488-2, 2000893). Bks Demand UMI.

--Soviet Foreign Propaganda. 1964. 35.00x (ISBN 0-691-08713-X). Princeton U Pr.

--Soviet Image of the United States. LC 70-85983. 1969. Repr. of 1950 ed. 24.50x (ISBN 0-8046-0599-8, Pub. by Kennikat). Assoc Faculty Pr.

--Soviet Russian Nationalism. LC 76-6861. 1976. Repr. of 1956 ed. lib. bdg. 35.00x (ISBN 0-8371-8429-0, BASRN). Greenwood.

Barghoorn, Frederick G. The Soviet Cultural Offensive. LC 75-18397. 353p. 1976. Repr. of 1960 ed. lib. bdg. 35.00x (ISBN 0-8371-8334-0, BASCO). Greenwood.

Bargmann, Eve. Uranium; the Real Facts: A Medical Response to the Marline Corporation's Uranium Fact Book. 1982. pap. 2.00 (ISBN 0-937188-23-9). Pub Citizen Inc.

Bargmann, Eve & Grove, Cynthia. Surgery in Maryland Hospitals Nineteen Seventy-Nine & Nineteen Eighty Charges & Deaths. 158p. (Orig.). 1982. pap. 5.00 (ISBN 0-937188-13-1). Pub Citizen Inc.

Bargmann, Eve, et al. Stopping Valium, Ativan, Centrax, Dalmane, Librium, Paxipam, Restoril, Serax, Tranxene & Xanax. 108p. 1982. pap. 3.00 (ISBN 0-317-03369-7). Pub Citizen Inc.

--Stopping Valium: And Ativan, Centrax, Dalmane, Librium, Paxipam, Restoril, Serax, Tranxene, Xanax. 1983. pap. 5.95 (ISBN 0-446-37582-9). Warner Bks.

Bargmann, V., ed. Group Representations in Mathematics & Physics: Battelle Seattle 1969 Rencontres. LC 75-146233. (Lecture Notes in Physics: Vol. 6). 1970. pap. 18.30 (ISBN 0-387-05310-7). Springer-Verlag.

Bargmann, W., et al, eds. Neurosecretion & Neuroendocrine Activity: Evolution, Structure & Function. (Illus.). 1978. 63.00 (ISBN 0-387-08637-4). Springer-Verlag.

Bargon, J., ed. Methods & Materials in Microelectronic Technology. (IBM Research Symposia Ser.). 376p. 1984. 59.50x (ISBN 0-306-41803-7, Plenum Pr). Plenum Pub.

Bargon, Joachim, ed. Computational Methods in Chemistry. LC 80-14881. (IBM Research Symposia Ser.). 340p. 1980. 49.50x (ISBN 0-306-40505-9, Plenum Pr). Plenum Pub.

Bargone, Charles. Useless Hands. LC 74-15969. (Science Fiction Ser). 300p. 1975. Repr. of 1926 ed. 25.50x (ISBN 0-405-06289-3). Ayer Co Pubs.

Bargrave, John. Pope Alexander the Seventh & the College of Cardinals. Robertson, James C., ed. LC 78-160001. (Camden Society, London. Publications, First Ser.: No. 92). Repr. of 1867 ed. 19.00 (ISBN 0-404-50192-3). AMS Pr.
--Pope Alexander the Seventh & the College of Cardinals. 19.00 (ISBN 0-384-03435-7). Johnson Repr.
Bargyla, ed. see Corley, Hugh.
Bargyla, ed. see Hainsworth, P. H.
Bargyla, ed. see Leatherbarrow, Margaret.
Bargyla, ed. see Stephenson, W. A.
Bargyla, ed. see Sykes, Friend.
Bargyla, ed. see Turner, F. Newman.
Barham, Jerry N. Mechanical Kinesiology. LC 77-23969. (Illus.). 510p. 1978. 19.95 (ISBN 0-8016-0476-1). Mosby.
Barham, Jerry N. & Thomas, William L. Anatomical Kinesiology: A Programmed Text. (Illus., Prog. Bk.). 1969. pap. text ed. write for info. (ISBN 0-02-306010-7, 30601). Macmillan.
Barham, Jerry N. & Wooten, Edna L. Structural Kinesiology. (Illus.). 448p. 1973. text ed. write for info. (ISBN 0-02-306000-X, 30600). Macmillan.
Barham, Martha. Bridging Two Worlds. Greene, Tom, ed. LC 84-194533. 246p. (Orig.). 1981. pap. 7.95x (ISBN 0-9609680-0-8). MJB Bks.
Barham, Mary L. San Jacinto College: South Campus Library Handbook. 96p. 1981. pap. text ed. 4.95 (ISBN 0-8403-2553-3). Kendall-Hunt.
Barham, Peter. Schizophrenia & Human Value: Chronic Schizophrenia, Science & Society. 232p. 1985. 19.95 (ISBN 0-631-13474-3). Basil Blackwell.
Barhan, P. K., jt. auth. see Rudra, Ashok.
Bar Hebraeus. The Laughable Stories. Budge, Ernest A., tr. from Syriac. LC 73-18852. (Luzac's Semitic Text & Translation Ser.: No. 1). (Eng.). Repr. of 1897 ed. 35.00 (ISBN 0-404-11347-8). AMS Pr.
Bar-Hillel, Y., ed. Pragmatics of Natural Languages. LC 77-159653. (Synthese Library: No. 41). 231p. 1971. lib. bdg. 31.50 (ISBN 90-277-0194-6, Pub. by Reidel Holland); pap. 18.50 (ISBN 90-277-0599-2, Pub. by Reidel Holland). Kluwer Academic.
Barhorp, Michael. British Cavalry Uniform Since 1660. (Illus.). 192p. 1984. 18.95 (ISBN 0-7137-1043-8, Pub. by Blanford Pr England). Sterling.
Bari, N. K., et al. Series & Approximation, Vol. 3. (Translations Ser.: No. 1). 1962. 24.00 (ISBN 0-8218-1603-9, TRANS 1-3). Am Math.
Bari, R. A., ed. see Capital Conference on Graph Theory & Conbinatorics, George Washington University, June 18-22, 1973.
Baric, L. Kinship in Industrial Society. 1971. pap. text ed. 2.45x (ISBN 0-02-972330-2). Macmillan.
Barica, J. & Mur, L., eds. Hypertrophic Ecosystems. (Developments in Hydrobiology Ser.: No. 2). 330p. 1981. PLB 87.00 (ISBN 90-6193-752-3, Pub. by Junk Pubs. Netherlands). Kluwer Academic.
Barice, E. Joan & Jonah, Kathleen. The Palm Beach Long-Life Diet. 224p. 1985. 14.95 (ISBN 0-671-50363-4). S&S.
Barich, Bill. Laughing in the Hills. 240p. 1981. pap. 5.95 (ISBN 0-14-005832-X). Penguin.
--Laughing in the Hills. 228p. 1980. 10.95 (ISBN 0-670-41997-4). Viking.
--Traveling Light. LC 83-47998. 210p. 1984. 15.95 (ISBN 0-670-72477-7). Viking.
--Travelling Light. (Penguin Nonfiction Ser.). 1985. pap. 5.95 (ISBN 0-14-007418-X). Penguin.
Barich, Dewey F. & Smith, Leonard C. Metal Work for Industrial Arts Shops. LC 52-8345. pap. 25.80 (ISBN 0-317-08910-2, 2004570). Bks Demand UMI.
Barich, Madeline C. Confetti. 64p. 1983. 5.50 (ISBN 0-682-49981-1). Exposition Pr FL.
Barickman, Richard, et al. Corrupt Relations: Dickens, Trollope, Thackeray, Collins & the Victorian Sexual System. 304p. 1982. 27.50x (ISBN 0-231-05258-8). Columbia U Pr.
Barigozzi, Claudio, ed. Mechanisms of Speciation. LC 82-13014. (Progress in Clinical & Biological Research Ser.: Vol. 96). 560p. 1982. 88.00 (ISBN 0-8451-0096-3). A R Liss.
--Origin & Natural History of Cell Lines: Proceedings of a Conference Held at Accademia Nazionale Dei Lincei, Rome, Italy, October 1977. LC 78-12805. (Progress in Clinical & Biological Research: Vol. 26). 208p. 1979. 29.00 (ISBN 0-8451-0026-2). A R Liss.
--Vito Volterra Symposium on Mathematical Models in Biology: Proceedings. (LN in Biomathematics Ser.: Vol. 39). (Illus.). 417p. 1980. pap. 32.00 (ISBN 0-387-10279-5). Springer-Verlag.
Baril, Jacques. Dictionnaire de Danse. 288p. (Fr.). 1964. pap. 14.95 (ISBN 0-686-56812-5, M-6590). French & Eur.
Barile, M. F., jt. ed. see Razin, S.
Barile, M. F., et al, eds. The Mycoplasmas Vol. 1: Cell Biology. LC 78-20895. 1979. 69.00 (ISBN 0-12-078401-7). Acad Pr.
--The Mycoplasmas Vol. 2: Human & Animal Mycoplasmas. LC 78-20895. 1979. 67.00 (ISBN 0-12-078402-5). Acad Pr.
--The Mycoplasmas Vol. 3: Plant & Insect Mycoplasmas. 1979. 55.00 (ISBN 0-12-078403-3). Acad Pr.
Barilleaux, Rene P. Holography Redefined Thresholds. LC 84-61634. (Illus.). 32p. (Orig.). 1984. pap. 4.00 (ISBN 0-936210-14-1). Mus Holography.
Barilleaux, Ryan J. The Politics of Southwestern Water. (Southwestern Studies: No. 73). (Illus.). 48p. 1984. pap. 4.00 (ISBN 0-87404-149-X). Tex Western.
--The President & Foreign Affairs: Evaluation, Performance & Power. LC 84-26282. 224p. 1985. 33.95 (ISBN 0-03-002883-3). Praeger.
Barin. Omnipotent. LC 85-61820. (Popular Ser.). 140p. Date not set. 9.95 (ISBN 0-935075-00-3). Sri Aurobindo.
Barincou, Edmond. Machiavelli. Lane, Helen, tr. LC 75-11427. 192p. 1975. Repr. of 1962 ed. lib. bdg. 17.00x (ISBN 0-8371-8185-2, BAMA). Greenwood.
Baring, Frances. Observations on the Establishment of the Bank of England. Bd. with Further Observations. 16p. LC 66-21659. 81p. Repr. of 1797 ed. 22.50x (ISBN 0-678-00281-9). Kelley.
Baring, G. & Fellman, W., eds. Hans Denck Sckriften, Vol. 3: Exegetische Schriften, Gedichte und Briefe. (Tauferakten Kommission Ser.). 1960. pap. 11.95x (ISBN 0-8361-1125-7). Herald Pr.
Baring, Maurice. Cat's Cradle. 1925. 25.00 (ISBN 0-8274-2009-9). R West.
--The Collected Poems of Maurice Baring. LC 75-41018. Repr. of 1911 ed. 16.00 (ISBN 0-404-14756-9). AMS Pr.
--Daphne Adzane. 1926. 25.00 (ISBN 0-8274-2142-7). R West.
--Dead Letters. 1925. 25.00 (ISBN 0-8274-2157-5). R West.
--Diminutive Dramas. 4th ed. LC 77-70343. (One-Act Plays in Reprint Ser.). 1977. Repr. of 1938 ed. 18.50x (ISBN 0-8486-2012-7). Core Collection.
--Diminutive Dramas. 1910. 25.00 (ISBN 0-8274-2187-7). R West.
--Half a Minute's Silence & Other Stories. facsimile ed. LC 71-113647. (Short Story Index Reprint Ser.). 1925. 17.00 (ISBN 0-8369-3376-1). Ayer Co Pubs.
--Have You Anything to Declare? 1936. 25.00 (ISBN 0-8274-2472-8). R West.
--In My End Is My Beginning. 1931. 25.00 (ISBN 0-8274-2562-7). R West.
--Landmarks in Russian Literature. 1910. Repr. 25.00 (ISBN 0-8274-3873-7). R West.
--The Lonely Lady of Dulwich. 1934. 25.00 (ISBN 0-8274-2982-7). R West.
--Lost Diaries. 1913. 25.00 (ISBN 0-8274-2993-2). R West.
--Lost Lectures. LC 76-118411. (Essay & General Literature Index Reprint Ser). 1971. Repr. of 1932 ed. 23.50x (ISBN 0-8046-1399-0, Pub.by Kennikat). Assoc Faculty Pr.
--Lost Lectures or the Fruits of Experience. 1932. 25.00 (ISBN 0-8274-2995-9). R West.
--An Outline of Russian Literature. LC 79-114461. vii, 256p. Repr. of 1915 ed. lib. bdg. 27.50 (ISBN 0-8371-4808-1, BARL). Greenwood.
--An Outline of Russian Literature. 1973. Repr. of 1915 ed. 20.00 (ISBN 0-8274-1489-7). R West.
--Punch & Judy & Other Essays. facs. ed. LC 68-16904. (Essay Index Reprint Ser). 1968. Repr. of 1924 ed. 20.00 (ISBN 0-8369-0172-X). Ayer Co Pubs.
--The Puppet Show of Memory. 1922. 25.00 (ISBN 0-8274-3227-5). R West.
--Sarah Bernhardt. LC 78-91893. 1933. 18.00 (ISBN 0-405-08237-1, Blom Pubns). Ayer Co Pubs.
--Sarah Bernhardt. LC 70-98809. Repr. of 1934 ed. lib. bdg. 18.75 (ISBN 0-8371-3018-2, BASB). Greenwood.
--Tinker's Leave. 1928. 25.00 (ISBN 0-8274-3630-0). R West.
--Unreliable History. 1934. 25.00 (ISBN 0-8274-3662-9). R West.
--When They Love. 1928. 25.00 (ISBN 0-8274-3697-1). R West.
--A Year in Russia. LC 79-2891. 296p. 1981. Repr. of 1917 ed. 23.50 (ISBN 0-8305-0060-X). Hyperion Conn.
Baringer, William. Lincoln's Rise to Power. (Illus.). 1971. Repr. of 1937 ed. 39.00 (ISBN 0-403-00853-0). Scholarly.
Baringer, William E., et al. Politics & the Crisis of Eighteen-Sixty. LC 61-14350. pap. 42.50 (ISBN 0-317-28735-4, 2020243). Bks Demand UMI.
Baring-Gould, Cecil, jt. ed. see Baring-Gould, William S.
Baring-Gould, Ceil, jt. auth. see Baring-Gould, William S.
Baring-Gould, S. A Book of Nursery Songs & Rhymes. 59.95 (ISBN 0-87968-768-1). Gordon Pr.
--Cornish Characters & Strange Events. 1973. Repr. of 1909 ed. 30.00 (ISBN 0-8274-1490-0). R West.
--Curious Myths of the Middle Ages. (Works of S. Baring-Gould Ser.). 254p. Date not set. Repr. of 1867 ed. lib. bdg. 29.00 (ISBN 0-932051-19-7). Am Repr Serv.
--Family Names & Their Story. 59.95 (ISBN 0-8490-0152-8). Gordon Pr.
--Freaks of Fanaticism, & Other Strange Events. 59.95 (ISBN 0-8490-0193-5). Gordon Pr.
--Further Reminiscences, Eighteen Sixty four-Eighteen Ninety Four: 1864-1894. 1925. Repr. 10.00 (ISBN 0-8274-2387-X). R West.
--A Garland of Country Song: English Folk Songs with Their Traditional Melodies. 59.95 (ISBN 0-8490-0211-7). Gordon Pr.
--Legends of the Patriarchs & Prophets & Other Old Testament Characters. LC 74-9741. 1872. lib. bdg. 42.00 (ISBN 0-8414-3205-8). Folcroft.
--Mehalah. 313p. pap. 7.95 (ISBN 0-85115-215-5, Pub. by Boydell & Brewer). Academy Chi Pubs.
--Old Century Life. 59.95 (ISBN 0-8490-0754-2). Gordon Pr.
--An Old English Home & Its Dependencies. 59.95 (ISBN 0-8490-0756-9). Gordon Pr.
--A Study of St. Paul: His Character & Opinions. 1977. lib. bdg. 59.95 (ISBN 0-8490-2712-8). Gordon Pr.
--The Vicar of Morwenstow: A Life of Robert Stephen Hawker. 1973. 20.00 (ISBN 0-8274-1426-9). R West.
Baring-Gould, Sabine. Book of Nursery Songs & Rhymes. LC 68-23135. 1969. Repr. of 1895 ed. 30.00x (ISBN 0-8103-3471-2). Gale.
--Book of Werewolves: Being an Account of Terrible Superstition. Repr. of 1865 ed. 35.00x (ISBN 0-685-32595-4). Gale.
--Cliff Castles & Cave Dwellings of Europe. LC 68-17983. (Illus.). 1968. Repr. of 1911 ed. 35.00x (ISBN 0-8103-3423-2). Gale.
--Curious Myths of the Middle Ages. 69.95 (ISBN 0-87968-261-2). Gordon Pr.
--Curious Myths of the Middle Ages. 1976. Repr. of 1867 ed. 69.00x (ISBN 0-403-06309-4, Regency). Scholarly.
--Early Reminiscences, 1834-1864. LC 67-23868. 1967. Repr. of 1923 ed. 35.00x (ISBN 0-8103-3049-0). Gale.
--Family Names & Their Story. LC 68-23136. 1969. Repr. of 1910 ed. 30.00x (ISBN 0-8103-0151-2). Gale.
--Freaks of Fanaticism & Other Strange Events. LC 68-21754. 1968. Repr. of 1891 ed. 40.00x (ISBN 0-8103-3503-4). Gale.
--Further Reminiscences, Eighteen Sixty-Four to Eighteen Ninety-four. LC 67-23869. 1967. Repr. of 1925 ed. 35.00x (ISBN 0-8103-3050-4). Gale.
--A Garland of Country Song. 112p. 1980. Repr. of 1895 ed. lib. bdg. 15.00 (ISBN 0-8495-0459-7). Arden Lib.
--A Garland of Country Song. LC 76-16147. 1976. Repr. of 1895 ed. lib. bdg. 18.50 (ISBN 0-8414-3311-9). Folcroft.
--Mehalah, a Story of the Salt Marshes, 2 vols. in 1. LC 79-8231. Repr. of 1880 ed. 44.50 (ISBN 0-404-61769-7). AMS Pr.
--Old Country Life. LC 78-77086. 1969. Repr. of 1890 ed. 40.00x (ISBN 0-8103-3848-3). Gale.
--Old English Home & Its Dependencies. LC 74-77085. 1969. Repr. of 1898 ed. 40.00x (ISBN 0-8103-3847-5). Gale.
--Red Spider, 2 vols. in 1. LC 79-8232. Repr. of 1887 ed. 44.50 (ISBN 0-404-61772-7). AMS Pr.
--The Story of Germany. 1886. 40.00 (ISBN 0-8482-7411-3). Norwood Edns.
--Strange Survivals, Some Chapters in the History of Man. LC 67-23909. (Illus.). 1968. Repr. of 1892 ed. 35.00x (ISBN 0-8103-3422-4). Gale.
--Strange Survivals: Some Chapters in the History of Man. 59.95 (ISBN 0-8490-1142-6). Gordon Pr.
--Surnames. (The International Library of Names). 1985. Repr. of 1860 ed. text ed. 39.50x (ISBN 0-8290-1235-4). Irvington.
Baring-Gould, Sabine & Bamfylde, C. A. A History of Sarawak under Its Two White Rajas. LC 77-86981. Repr. of 1909 ed. 41.50 (ISBN 0-404-16696-2). AMS Pr.
Baring-Gould, Sabine & Hitchcock, Gordon, eds. Folk Songs of the West Country. 1974. 5.50 (ISBN 0-7153-6419-7). David & Charles.
Baring-Gould, William S. Lure of the Limerick. (Illus.). 1967. 8.95 (ISBN 0-517-08323-X, C N Potter Bks); pap. 4.95 (ISBN 0-517-53856-3). Crown.
--Nero Wolfe of West Thirty-Fifth Street. (Crime Ser.). 1982. pap. 5.95 (ISBN 0-14-006194-0). Penguin.
Baring-Gould, William S. & Baring-Gould, Ceil. Annotated Mother Goose. (Illus.). 352p. 1982. 25.00 (ISBN 0-517-54629-9, C N Potter Bks). Crown.
Baring-Gould, William S. & Baring-Gould, Cecil, eds. Annotated Mother Goose. (Illus.). 1967. pap. 6.95 (ISBN 0-452-00662-7, Mer). NAL.
Baring-Gould, William S., ed. see Doyle, Arthur Conan.
Bario, Joanne. Fatal Dreams. LC 84-12071. 312p. 1985. 16.95 (ISBN 0-385-27938-8, Dial). Doubleday.
Barish, Frances. Frommer's Guide for the Disabled Traveler: Unites States, Canada & Europe. 362p. 1984. pap. 10.95 (ISBN 0-671-47359-X). S&S.
Barish, Jonas. The Antitheatrical Prejudice. LC 78-59445. 1981. 28.50x (ISBN 0-520-03735-9). U of Cal Pr.
--The Antitheatrical Prejudice. (Cal Ser.: No. 691). (Illus.). 510p. 1984. pap. 12.95 (ISBN 0-520-05216-1, CAL 691). U of Cal Pr.
Barish, Jonas A. Ben Jonson & the Language of Prose Comedy. 1970. pap. 2.45x (ISBN 0-393-00554-2, Norton Lib). Norton.
Barish, Jonas A., ed. see Jonson, Ben.
Barish, Louis & Barish, Rebecca. Varieties of Jewish Belief. 1979. Repr. 9.95 (ISBN 0-8246-0242-0). Jonathan David.
Barish, Norman N. Economic Analysis for Engineering & Managerial Decision Making. 2nd ed. (Industrial Engineering & Management Science). (Illus.). 1978. text ed. 42.00 (ISBN 0-07-003649-7). McGraw.
Barish, Rebecca, jt. auth. see Barish, Louis.
Barish, Wendy, jt. auth. see Dixon, Franklin W.
Barish, Wendy, jt. auth. see Lawson, Don.
Barish, Wendy, jt. auth. see Riedman, Sarah R.
Barish, Wendy, jt. auth. see Rotsler, William.
Barish, Wendy, ed. I Can Draw Horses. (I Can Draw Ser.). 80p. (gr. 3-7). 1983. pap. 3.50 (ISBN 0-671-46447-7). Wanderer Bks.
--The Simon & Schuster Color Illustrated Question & Answer Book: What Is It? (Simon & Schuster Question & Answer Books Ser.). (Illus.). 128p. (gr. 8-12). 1984. Repr. of 1982 ed. text ed. 8.95 (ISBN 0-671-53129-8). Wanderer Bks.
Barish, Wendy, ed. see Alcott, Louisa May.
Barish, Wendy, ed. see Appleton, Victor.
Barish, Wendy, ed. see Beal, George.
Barish, Wendy, ed. see Benton, Michael J.
Barish, Wendy, ed. see Brett, Bernard.
Barish, Wendy, ed. see Brothers Grimm.
Barish, Wendy, ed. see Burgess, Jan.
Barish, Wendy, ed. see Carroll, Lewis.
Barish, Wendy, ed. see Cohen, Daniel.
Barish, Wendy, ed. see Daly, Kathleen N.
Barish, Wendy, ed. see Darden, Ellington.
Barish, Wendy, ed. see Dixon, Franklin W.
Barish, Wendy, ed. see Grisewood, John.
Barish, Wendy, ed. see Heck, Joseph.
Barish, Wendy, ed. see Hope, Laura L.
Barish, Wendy, ed. see Hyman, Jane & Millen-Posner, Barbara.
Barish, Wendy, ed. see Keene, Carolyn.
Barish, Wendy, ed. see Keene, Carolyn & Dixon, Franklin W.
Barish, Wendy, ed. see May, Robin.
Barish, Wendy, ed. see Packard, Mary.
Barish, Wendy, ed. see Rotsler, William.
Barish, Wendy, ed. see Saunders, Rubie.
Barish, Wendy, ed. see Seaver, Tom & Appel, Martin.
Barish, Wendy, ed. see Sewell, Anna.
Barish, Wendy, ed. see Sheldon, Ann.
Barish, Wendy, ed. see Smith, Frank.
Barish, Wendy, ed. see Spyri, Johanna.
Barish, Wendy, ed. see Taylor, L. B., Jr.
Barish, Wendy, ed. see Twain, Mark.
Barish, Wendy, ed. see Wright, Jill & Wright, David.
Barish, Wendy, jt. auth. see Dixon, Franklin W.
Barisic, S., et al, eds. Quasi One-Dimensional Conductors One. (Lecture Notes in Physics: Vol. 95). 1979. pap. 22.00 (ISBN 0-387-09240-4). Springer-Verlag.
Barisse, Rita, tr. see Vercors.
Baritz, Loren. Backfire: A History of How American Culture Led Us into Vietnam & Made Us Fight the Way We Did. LC 84-22625. 416p. (Orig.). 1985. 17.95 (ISBN 0-688-04185-X). Morrow.
--City on a Hill: A History of Ideas & Myths in America. LC 80-11468. xi, 367p. 1980. Repr. of 1964 ed. lib. bdg. 32.50x (ISBN 0-313-22268-1, BACI). Greenwood.
--The Servants of Power. LC 73-17924. 273p. 1974. Repr. of 1960 ed. lib. bdg. 22.75 (ISBN 0-8371-7275-6, BASP). Greenwood.
Baritz, Loren, ed. & intro. by. The Culture of the Twenties. LC 69-14821. (American Heritage Ser). (Illus.). 1970. pap. write for info. (ISBN 0-02-306110-3, AHS83). Macmillan.
Barjon, J. Radio-Diagnosis of Pleuro-Pulmonary Affections. 1918. 59.50x (ISBN 0-685-89775-3). Elliots Bks.
Bark, Dennis, ed. The Red Orchestra: Instruments of Soviet Policy in Latin America & the Caribbean. (Publication Ser.: No. 308). 250p. 1986. pap. 6.95 (ISBN 0-8179-8082-2). Hoover Inst Pr.
Bark, Dennis L. Berlin-Frage 1949-1955: Verhandlungsgrundlagen und Eindaemmungspolitik. (Veroeffentlichungen der Historischen Kommission Zu Berlin Ser.: Vol. 36). xiv, 544p. 1972. 57.60x (ISBN 3-11-003639-8). De Gruyter.
Bark, Dennis L., ed. To Promote Peace: U. S. Foreign Policy in the Mid-1980's. (Publication Ser.: No. 294). 328p. 1984. 19.95t. Hoover Inst Pr.
Bark, L. S. & Allen, N. S. Analysis of Polymer Systems. (Illus.). 311p. 1982. 55.50 (ISBN 0-85334-122-2, Pub. by Elsevier Applied Sci England). Elsevier.
Bark, Voss. West Country Fly Fishing. (Illus.). 192p. 1983. 19.95 (ISBN 0-7134-1882-6, Pub. by Batsford England). David & Charles.
Bark, William C. Origins of the Medieval World. 1958. 15.00x (ISBN 0-8047-0513-5); pap. 5.95x (ISBN 0-8047-0514-3). Stanford U Pr.
Barkachba, Libby & Osrow, Laural. Getting It Done. 164p. (Orig.). 1982. write for info. (ISBN 0-9607540-0-8). Double Lee.
Barkai, Haim. Growth Patterns of the Kibbutz Economy. LC 76-44024. (Contributions to Economic Analysis: Vol. 108). 298p. 1977. 70.25 (ISBN 0-7204-0556-4, North-Holland). Elsevier.
Barkai, Meyer, tr. The Ghetto Fighters. 1977. pap. text ed. 1.75 (ISBN 0-505-51159-2, Pub. by Tower Bks). Dorchester Pub Co.

Barkan, E. R., ed. see Burke, Edmund.

Barkan, Hans, ed. Johannes Brahms & Theodor Billroth: Letters from a Musical Friendship. LC 77-798. 1977. Repr. of 1957 ed. lib. bdg. 22.50x (ISBN 0-8371-9500-4, BRJB). Greenwood.

Barkan, Irving, jt. auth. see Lofbarg, John O.

Barkan, Janice M. Voyager. LC 84-73411. (Illus.). 64p. Date not set. 8.00 (ISBN 0-8233-0406-X). Golden Quill.

Barkan, Joann. Visions of Emancipation: The Italian Workers' Movement since 1945. LC 82-22763. 288p. 1984. 24.95 (ISBN 0-03-059626-2). Praeger.

Barkan, Joel D. & Okumu, John J. Politics & Public Policy in Kenya & Tanzania. 1979. 15.95 (ISBN 0-03-023206-6); pap. 15.95 (ISBN 0-03-052336-2). Praeger.

Barkan, Joel D. & Okumu, John J., eds. Politics & Public Policy in Kenya & Tanzania. rev. ed. 394p. 1984. 34.95 (ISBN 0-03-061358-2); pap. 13.95 (ISBN 0-03-061357-4). Praeger.

Barkan, Leonard. Renaissance Drama New Series. LC 67-29872. 216p. 1981. 24.95 (ISBN 0-8101-0545-4). Northwestern U Pr.

Barkan, Leonard, ed. The Celebratory Mode. LC 67-29872. (Renaissance Drama Ser.: New Ser. VIII). (Illus.). 1978. 23.95 (ISBN 0-8101-0468-7). Northwestern U Pr.

--Renaissance Drama in the Theater. (Renaissance Drama New Ser.: IX). 1979. lib. bdg. 24.95 (ISBN 0-8101-0524-1). Northwestern U Pr.

--Renaissance Drama New Series XV: Modes, Motifs, & Genres. (Renaissance Drama New Ser.). 220p. 1985. 25.95 (ISBN 0-8101-0676-0). Northwestern U Pr.

Barkan, Stanley, jt. ed. see Harding, Gunnar.

Barkan, Stanley H. The Blacklines Scrawl. (Poetry Ser.). 1976. signed ltd. ed. 10.00 (ISBN 0-89304-017-7); pap. 3.00x (ISBN 0-89304-010-X). Cross Cult.

Barkan, Stanley H., compiled by. Five Contemporary Turkish Poets. Sait, Talat, tr. (Cross-Cultural Review Ser.: No. 6). (Illus.). 48p. (Turkish & Eng.). 1980. 10.00 (ISBN 0-89304-610-8); pap. 4.00 (ISBN 0-89304-611-6). Cross Cult.

--Four Postwar Catalan Poets. Rosenthal, David H., tr. LC 78-67773. (Cross Cultural Review Ser.: No. 1). (Illus., Catalan-Eng.). 1978. 10.00x (ISBN 0-89304-600-0, CCC14); pap. 4.00x (ISBN 0-89304-601-9). Cross Cult.

--South Korean Poets of Resistance. Ko Won, tr. LC 79-90037. (Cross-Cultural Review Ser.: No. 4). (Illus., Korean-Eng.). 1980. 10.00x (ISBN 0-89304-606-X, CCC124); pap. 4.00x (ISBN 0-89304-607-8). Cross Cult.

Barkan, Stanley H., ed. To Struga with Love. LC 78-67775. (Illus., Orig.). 1978. in-folio 10.00 (ISBN 0-89304-028-2, CCC115); in-folio boxed 15.00 (ISBN 0-89304-050-9). Cross Cult.

Barkan, Stanley H. & Feiler, Eva, eds. International Festival of Poetry & Art. (International Poetry Festival Ser.: No. 2). (Illus.). 1973. 10.00x (ISBN 0-89304-019-3, CCC101); pap. 4.50x (ISBN 0-89304-002-9). Cross Cult.

Barkan, Stanley H. & Scammacca, Saverio A., eds. Sicilian Antigruppo. (Illus.). 30p. 1976. 5.00 (ISBN 0-89304-008-8). Cross Cult.

Barkan, Stanley H., ed. see Akpalu, Vinoko.

Barkan, Stanley H., ed. see Aspenstrom, Werner.

Barkan, Stanley H., ed. see Axelrod, David B.

Barkan, Stanley H., ed. see Balbin, Julius.

Barkan, Stanley H., ed. see Bruchac, Joseph.

Barkan, Stanley H., ed. see Butscher, Edward.

Barkan, Stanley H., ed. see Cassian, Nina.

Barkan, Stanley H., ed. see Daglarca, Fazil Husnu.

Barkan, Stanley H., ed. see Dame, Enid.

Barkan, Stanley H., jt. ed. see De Wit, Joost.

Barkan, Stanley H., ed. see Dobrin, Arthur.

Barkan, Stanley H., ed. see Hartman, Susan.

Barkan, Stanley H., ed. see Lev, Donald.

Barkan, Stanley H., ed. see Mulisch, Harry.

Barkan, Stanley H., ed. see Scammacca, Nat.

Barkan, Stanley H., jt. ed. see Van De Waarsenburg, Hans.

Barkan, Stanley H., et al, eds. Americana Anthology: Bicentennial Edition 1776-1976, Vol. 1. LC 76-47154. (New York Poetry Forum Ser.). (Illus.). 1976. 14.95x (ISBN 0-89304-011-8, CCC107); pap. 6.95x (ISBN 0-89304-009-6). Cross Cult.

Barkans, V. & Zhdanov, V. Radio Receivers: Operating Principles & Design. 503p. 1975. 19.95x (ISBN 0-8464-1126-1). Beekman Pubs.

Barkas, J. L. Creative Time Management: Become More Productive & Still Have Time for Fun. 240p. 1984. 16.95 (ISBN 0-13-191222-4); pap. 7.95 (ISBN 0-13-191214-3). P-H.

--How to Write Like a Professional. 224p. 1984. 12.95 (ISBN 0-668-05676-2, 5676). Arco.

Barkas, Jan L. Friendship: A Selected Annotated Bibliography. LC 84-48381. (Reference Library of Social Science & Bibliographies in Sociology). 144p. 1985. lib. bdg. 34.00 (ISBN 0-8240-8937-5). Garland Pub.

Barkash, V. A. & Shubin, V. G. Contemporary Problems in Carbonium Ion Chemistry I-II, 2 Vols. (Topics in Current Chemistry Ser.: Vols. 116-117). (Illus.). 320p. 1984. Set. 45.50 (ISBN 0-387-12555-8). Springer Verlag.

Barkdull, Tom. Lonesome Walls: An Odyssey Through Ghost Towns of the Old West. LC 79-159490. 1971. 7.50 (ISBN 0-682-47298-0, Lochinvar). Exposition Pr FL.

Barke, Harvey E., jt. auth. see Pyenson, Louis L.

Barke, James. The Wind That Shakes the Barley: A Novel of the Life & Loves of Robert Burns. 384p. 1982. Repr. of 1945 ed. lib. bdg. 30.00 (ISBN 0-89987-087-2). Darby Bks.

Barke, James, ed. see Burns, Robert, et al.

Barke, Richard P., jt. auth. see Stone, Alan.

Barkely, William D., jt. auth. see Martin, Alexander C.

Barken, Stanley H., ed. see Oliver, Louis.

Barkenbus, Jack N. Deep Seabed Resources: Politics & Technology. LC 78-73024. 1979. 24.95 (ISBN 0-02-901830-7). Free Pr.

Barker. Basic Child Psychiatry. 4th ed. (Illus.). 336p. 1983. pap. text ed. 18.50 (ISBN 0-8391-1820-1, 19844). Univ Park.

--Dictionary of Concrete. LC 82-19825. 1984. text ed. 34.95 (ISBN 0-86095-042-5). Longman.

--Kayode & His Village in Nigeria. 12.95 (ISBN 0-19-279737-9, Pub. by Oxford U Pr Childrens). Merrimack Pub Cir.

--Marketing Research: Text with Cases. 1983. text ed. 26.95 (ISBN 0-8359-4259-7); instr's. manual avail. (ISBN 0-8359-4260-0). Reston.

--Science & Religion: An Annotated Bibliography. 1985. lib. bdg. 40.00 (ISBN 0-8240-8762-3). Garland Pub.

Barker, et al. Principles of Ambulatory Medicine. (Illus.). 1280p. 1986. price not set (ISBN 0-683-00436-0). Williams & Wilkins.

Barker, A. E., ed. see Milton, John.

Barker, A. J. Arab-Israeli Wars. 1982. 19.95 (ISBN 0-88254-587-6). Hippocrene Bks.

--British & American Infantry Weapons of World War Two. LC 69-13594. (Illus.). 1978. pap. 2.95 (ISBN 0-668-04526-4, 4526). Arco.

--Midway. (Illus.). 64p. 1983. pap. 4.95 (ISBN 0-13-582932-1). P-H.

--Stuka-JU-87. (Illus.). 64p. 1983. pap. 4.95 (ISBN 0-13-858837-6). P-H.

--Waffen-SS at War. (Illus.). 128p. 1984. 19.95 (ISBN 0-88254-882-4). Hippocrene Bks.

Barker, A. L. A Heavy Feather. LC 78-26479. 234p. 1979. Repr. of 1978 ed. 8.95 (ISBN 0-8076-0911-0). Braziller.

Barker, A. N. & Gould, G. W., eds. Spore Research 1971. 1972. 66.00 (ISBN 0-12-078750-4). Acad Pr.

Barker, A. N., et al, eds. Spore Research. 1974. 55.00 (ISBN 0-12-078752-0). Acad Pr.

--Spore Research. 1978. Vol. 1. 66.00 (ISBN 0-12-078701-6); Vol. 2. 79.00 (ISBN 0-12-078702-4). Acad Pr.

Barker, A. Trevor, compiled by. The Letters of H. P. Blavatsky to A. P. Sinnett. facsimile of 1925 ed. LC 73-84138. 1973. 12.00 (ISBN 0-911500-23-5). Theos U Pr.

Barker, A. Trevor, ed. Mahatma Letters to A. P. Sinnett. 3rd ed. 1972. 13.25 (ISBN 0-8356-7013-9). Theos Pub Hse.

Barker, A. Trevor, compiled by. The Mahatma Letters to A. P. Sinnett. facsimile of 1926, 2nd ed. LC 75-10574. 1975. 12.00 (ISBN 0-911500-20-0); pap. 7.00 (ISBN 0-911500-21-9). Theos U Pr.

Barker, Alan. Civil War in America. LC 61-11594. pap. 3.50 (ISBN 0-385-09871-5, Anch). Doubleday.

Barker, Albert. Gift from Berlin. 160p. 1980. pap. 1.95 (ISBN 0-441-28828-6, Pub. by Charter Bks). Ace Bks.

Barker, Allen, ed. see Barker, Diana L.

Barker, Andrew. A Report of Captain Ward & Danseker, Pirates. LC 68-54615. (English Experience Ser.: No. 21). 56p. 1968. Repr. of 1609 ed. 8.00 (ISBN 90-221-0021-9). Walter J Johnson.

Barker, Andrew, ed. Greek Musical Writings: Vol. 1-The Musician & His Art. LC 83-20924. (Readings in the Literature of Music Ser.). (Illus.). 350p. 1984. 54.50 (ISBN 0-521-23593-6). Cambridge U Pr.

Barker, Anthony. Public Participation in Britain. 192p. 1979. pap. text ed. 19.50x (ISBN 0-7199-1029-3, Pub. by Bedford England). Brookfield Pub Co.

Barker, Arthur. Milton's Schoolmasters. LC 73-16488. 1937. lib. bdg. 8.50 (ISBN 0-8414-9887-3). Folcroft.

--Milton's Schoolmasters. 1982. lib. bdg. 34.50 (ISBN 0-685-94335-6). Porter.

Barker, Arthur E. Milton & the Puritan Dilemma, 1641-1660. LC 58-3195. 1942. 30.00x (ISBN 0-8020-5025-5); pap. 8.50 o. p. (ISBN 0-8020-6306-3). U of Toronto Pr.

Barker, Arthur E., compiled by. The Seventeenth Century: Bacon Through Marvell. LC 76-4657. (Goldentree Bibliographies in Language & Literature). 1980. text ed. 24.95x (ISBN 0-88295-570-5); pap. text ed. 14.95 (ISBN 0-88295-548-9). Harlan Davidson.

Barker, B. M. Vitamins in Medicine, Vol. 1. 1980. 83.95 (ISBN 0-8151-0422-7). Year Bk Med.

Barker, Ballard M. & Jameson, William C. Platt National Park: Chickasaw National Recreation Area. (Illus.). 1979. pap. 5.95 (ISBN 0-8061-1540-8). U of Okla Pr.

Barker, Barbara. Ballet or Ballyhoo. 280p. 1984. 37.50 (ISBN 0-87127-137-0). Dance Horiz.

Barker, Barbara M., jt. auth. see Barker, Harry R.

Barker, Becky. Answers. 2nd ed. 57p. 1984. 18.95 (ISBN 0-917875-01-X). Answers Period.

Barker, Ben D., jt. ed. see DeFriese, Gordon H.

Barker, Berta L. Dr. Laurie's Conquest. (YA) 1980. 8.95 (ISBN 0-686-73930-2, Avalon). Bouregy.

--A Dream House for Nurse Rhonda. (YA) 1979. 8.95 (ISBN 0-685-65269-6, Avalon). Bouregy.

--Lianne's Island Love. (YA) 1979. 8.95 (ISBN 0-686-52552-3, Avalon). Bouregy.

--Lost in a Mist. (YA) 1981. 8.95 (ISBN 0-686-73954-X, Avalon). Bouregy.

--The Magic of Paris. (YA) 1981. 8.95 (ISBN 0-686-73958-2, Avalon). Bouregy.

Barker, Berta LaVan. Dangerous Waters. (YA) 1978. 8.95 (ISBN 0-685-19056-0, Avalon). Bouregy.

--A Nurse for Dr. Turner. (YA) 1979. 8.95 (ISBN 0-685-93877-8, Avalon). Bouregy.

--A Thousand Happiness. (YA) 1978. 8.95 (ISBN 0-685-87351-X, Avalon). Bouregy.

Barker, Bill. The Whole Famn Damily. (Illus.). 221p. 1981. 9.95 (ISBN 0-937050-03-2). Stonehenge.

Barker, Brian. The Symbols of Sovereignty. (Illus.). 254p. 1979. 19.50x (ISBN 0-8476-6192-X). Rowman.

Barker, C. J. How You Can Achieve Total Success Through Self-Hypnosis. 32p. 1984. pap. 5.95 (ISBN 0-934650-05-5). Sunnyside.

Barker, Carol. A Family in Nigeria. LC 85-6932. (Families the World over Ser.). (Illus.). 32p. (gr. 2-5). 1985. PLB 8.95 (ISBN 0-8225-1659-4). Lerner Pubns.

--Kayode & His Village in Nigeria. (Illus.). 40p. (gr. 1-6). 10.95 (ISBN 0-19-279737-9, Pub. Oxford U PrChildrens). Merrimack Pub Cir.

Barker, Carol, ed. see Savannah Junior Auxiliary.

Barker, Carol M. & Fox, Matthew H. Classified Files: The Yellowing Pages. LC 72-80587. 1974. pap. 10.00 (ISBN 0-527-02850-9). Kraus Repr.

Barker, Charles A. Background of the Revolution in Maryland. x, 414p. 1967. Repr. of 1940 ed. 29.50 (ISBN 0-208-00470-X, Archon). Shoe String.

--Henry George. LC 74-12949. (Illus.). 696p. 1974. Repr. of 1955 ed. lib. bdg. 33.00x (ISBN 0-8371-7775-8, BAHG). Greenwood.

Barker, Charles A., ed. Power & Law: American Dilemma in World Affairs. LC 76-135660. (Illus.). 224p. 1971. 21.00x (ISBN 0-8018-1254-2). Johns Hopkins.

Barker, Chris A. Teakwood Decks. (Illus.). 600p. 15.00x (ISBN 0-9609382-1-4). Susquehanna.

Barker, Christine R. & Last, Rex W. Erich Maria Remarque. LC 79-10837. 174p. 1979. text ed. 28.50x (ISBN 0-685-97225-9, 06339). B&N Imports.

Barker, Cicely M. Flower Fairies Address Book. (Flower Fairies Ser.). (Illus.). 120p. 1984. 5.95 (ISBN 0-911745-46-7, Bedrick Blackie). P Bedrick Bks.

--Flower Fairies Birthday Book. (Flower Fairies Ser.). (Illus.). 154p. 1984. 5.95 (ISBN 0-911745-44-0, Bedrick Blackie). P Bedrick Bks.

--The Flower Fairies Miniature ABC. (Flower Fairies Ser.). (Illus.). 48p. 1984. fold-out 4.95 (ISBN 0-911745-75-0, Bedrick Blackie). P Bedrick Bks.

--The Flower Fairies Miniature Library, 4 vols. (Illus.). 1981. boxed set 6.95 (ISBN 0-399-20823-2, Philomel). Putnam Pub Group.

--Flower Fairies of the Autumn. LC 84-45890. (The Original Flower Fairies Bks.). (Illus.). 40p. 1985. 4.95 (ISBN 0-911745-92-0, Bedrick Blackie). P Bedrick Bks.

--Flower Fairies of the Garden. (The Flower Fairies Ser.). (Illus.). 1984. 6.95 (ISBN 0-911745-37-8, Bedrick Blackie). P Bedrick Bks.

--Flower Fairies of the Garden. LC 85-70559. (The Flower Fairies Ser.). (Illus.). 40p. (gr. k up). 1985. 4.95 (ISBN 0-87226-021-6). P Bedrick Bks.

--Flower Fairies of the Seasons. LC 83-73462. (Flower Fairies Ser.). (Illus.). 96p. 1984. 14.95 (ISBN 0-911745-48-3, Bedrick Blackie). P Bedrick Bks.

--Flower Fairies of the Spring. LC 84-85887. (Original Flower Fairies Bks.). (Illus.). 40p. 1985. 4.95 (ISBN 0-911745-90-4, Bedrick Blackie). P Bedrick Bks.

--Flower Fairies of the Summer. LC 84-45889. (The Original Flower Fairies Bks.). (Illus.). 40p. 1985. 4.95 (ISBN 0-911745-91-2, Bedrick Blackie). P Bedrick Bks.

--Flower Fairies of the Trees. LC 85-70558. (The Flower Fairies Ser.). (Illus.). 40p. (gr. k up). 1985. 4.95 (ISBN 0-87226-022-4). P Bedrick Bks.

--Flower Fairies of the Wayside. LC 85-70560. (The Flower Fairies Ser.). (Illus.). 40p. (gr. k up). 1985. 4.95 (ISBN 0-87226-020-8). P Bedrick Bks.

--Flower Fairies of the Winter. LC 84-45888. (The Original Flower Fairies Bks.). (Illus.). 40p. 1985. 4.95 (ISBN 0-911745-93-9, Bedrick Blackie). P Bedrick Bks.

--Flower Fairies of the Woodland. (Flower Fairies Ser.). (Illus.). 1984. 6.95 (ISBN 0-911745-38-6, Bedrick Blackie). P Bedrick Bks.

--A Flower Fairy Alphabet. LC 85-70557. (The Flower Fairies Ser.). (Illus.). 48p. (gr. k up). 1985. 4.95 (ISBN 0-87226-023-2). P Bedrick Bks.

Barker, Clive. Books of Blood, Vols. I-III. (Illus.). 384p. 1985. Repr. of 1984 ed. 25.00 (ISBN 0-910489-14-9). Scream Pr.

--Clive Barker's Book of Blood, Vol. 1. 224p. 1985. pap. 2.95 (ISBN 0-425-08389-6). Berkley Pub.

--Theatre Games. LC 78-665. (Illus.). 240p. 1978. pap. 10.95x (ISBN 0-910482-93-4). Drama Bk.

Barker, Cornelius L. Democracy in the Classroom. 1984. 5.95 (ISBN 0-8062-2290-5). Carlton.

Barker, Craig. Starting a Marine Aquarium. 1972. 4.95 (ISBN 0-87666-751-5, PS-305). TFH Pubns.

Barker, D. E. & Farrington, B. The Basic Arts of Buying. 249p. 1980. text ed. 24.50x (ISBN 0-220-66295-9, Pub. by Busn Bks England). Brookfield Pub Co.

Barker, D. J. Practical Epidemiology. rev. 2nd ed. (Medicine in the Tropics Ser.). (Illus.). 1976. pap. text ed. 10.75 (ISBN 0-443-01471-X). Churchill.

Barker, D. J., jt. auth. see Rose, Geoffrey.

Barker, Daniel. Igneous Rocks. (Illus.). 448p. 1983. 38.95 (ISBN 0-13-450692-8). P-H.

Barker, Danny, jt. auth. see Buerkle, Jack V.

Barker, Dave. TA & Training: The Theory & Use of Transactional Analysis in Organisations. 232p. 1979. text ed. 40.50x (ISBN 0-566-02118-8). Gower Pub Co.

Barker, David. Inside the Big O. 1975. 2.00 (ISBN 0-917554-03-5). Maelstrom.

--One Thing & Another. 15.00x (ISBN 0-392-13089-0, SpS). Sportshelf.

--Scenes from a Marriage. 40p. 1979. pap. 2.50 (ISBN 0-935390-04-9). Wormwood Rev.

Barker, David, jt. auth. see Robertson, Kirk.

Barker, David T., jt. auth. see Clark, Robert L.

Barker, Dennis. One Man's Estate: The Preservation of an English Inheritance. 227p. 1984. 19.95 (ISBN 0-233-97519-5). Andre Deutsch.

--One Man's Estate: The Preservation of an English Inheritance. (Illus.). 227p. 1984. 19.95 (ISBN 0-233-97519-5, Pub. by A Deutsch England). David & Charles.

--Parian Ware. (Shire Album Ser.: No. 142). (Illus.). 32p. (Orig.). 1985. pap. 3.50 (ISBN 0-85263-737-3, Pub. by Shire Pubns England). Seven Hills Bks.

--Soldiering On: An Unofficial Portrait of the British Army. (Illus.). 272p. 1981. 19.95 (ISBN 0-233-97391-5). Andre Deutsch.

--Soldiering On: An Unofficial Portrait of the British Army. (Illus.). 272p. 1981. 19.95 (ISBN 0-233-97391-5, Pub. by A Deutsch England). David & Charles.

Barker, Diana L. Sexual Divisions & Society. Barker, Allen, ed. 1976. 12.95x (ISBN 0-422-74820-X, NO. 2616, Pub. by Tavistock England); (Pub. by Tavistock England). Methuen Inc.

Barker, Dudley. G. K. Chesterton. LC 72-95988. 1975. 5.95 (ISBN 0-8128-1804-0). Stein & Day.

--Man of Principle: A Biography of John Galsworthy. LC 69-17943. 1970. pap. 4.95 (ISBN 0-8128-1297-2). Stein & Day.

Barker, E. Greek Political Theory. 5th ed. 468p. 1960. 16.95x (ISBN 0-416-67530-1, NO. 2070). Methuen Inc.

Barker, Earnest, ed. see Heath, Thomas L.

Barker, Edmund S. Webb Society Deep-Sky Observer's Handbook: Vol. 4, Galaxies. Glyn-Jones, Kenneth, ed. 250p. 1982. 40.00x (ISBN 0-7188-2527-6, Pub. by Lutterworth Pr England). State Mutual Bk.

Barker, Edward B., ed. Syria & Egypt under the Last Five Sultans of Turkey, 2 vols. in 1. LC 73-6269. (The Middle East Ser.). Repr. of 1876 ed. 51.00 (ISBN 0-405-05324-X). Ayer Co Pubs.

Barker, Eileen. The Making of a Moonie: Choice or Brainwashing. (Illus.). 299p. 1984. 19.95x (ISBN 0-631-13246-5). Basil Blackwell.

Barker, Eileen, ed. New Religious Movements: A Perspective for Understanding Society. LC 82-8263. (Studies in Religion & Society: Vol. 3). 440p. 1982. 69.95x (ISBN 0-88946-864-8). E Mellen.

--Of Gods & Men: New Religious Movements in the West. LC 83-23822. 359p. 1984. 26.50x (ISBN 0-86554-095-0, MUP/H87). Mercer Univ Pr.

Barker, Elisabeth. The British Between the Superpowers, 1945-1950. 282p. 1983. 22.50 (ISBN 0-8020-2512-9). U of Toronto Pr.

--Macedonia: Its Place in Balkan Power Politics. LC 80-16769. (Illus.). 129p. 1980. Repr. of 1950 ed. lib. bdg. 22.50x (ISBN 0-313-22587-7, BAMI). Greenwood.

Barker, Elliott S. Smokey Bear & the Great Wilderness. LC 82-19373. (Illus.). 150p. (Orig.). 1982. pap. 12.95 (ISBN 0-86534-017-X). Sunstone Pr.

--Western Life & Adventures in the Great Southwest. LC 74-15149. Orig. Title: Western Life & Adventure, 1889-1970. (Illus.). 316p. 1974. Repr. of 1970 ed. 9.95 (ISBN 0-913504-19-X). Lowell Pr.

Barker, Ernest. Britain & the British People. LC 75-28660. (Illus.). 1978. Repr. of 1955 ed. lib. bdg. 19.75x (ISBN 0-8371-8483-5, BABB). Greenwood.

--Character of England. LC 76-22422. 1976. Repr. of 1947 ed. lib. bdg. 43.00x (ISBN 0-8371-9020-7, BACOE). Greenwood.

--Church, State & Study: Essays. LC 72-7829. 280p. 1974. Repr. of 1930 ed. lib. bdg. 15.00 (ISBN 0-8371-6534-2, BACS). Greenwood.

--Citizen's Choice. LC 72-300. (Essay Index Reprint Ser.). Repr. of 1937 ed. 17.00 (ISBN 0-8369-2784-2). Ayer Co Pubs.

--The Crusades. facsimile ed. LC 76-160956. (Select Bibliographies Reprint Ser). Repr. of 1923 ed. 12.00 (ISBN 0-8369-5823-3). Ayer Co Pubs.

--Development of Public Services in Western Europe, 1660-1930. viii, 93p. 1966. Repr. of 1944 ed. 13.50 (ISBN 0-208-00043-7, Archon). Shoe String.

--National Character & the Factors in Its Formation. 4th, rev. ed. LC 83-45699. Repr. of 1948 ed. 29.50 (ISBN 0-404-20017-6). AMS Pr.

--Oliver Cromwell & the English People. facsimile ed. LC 72-37329. (Select Bibliographies Reprint Ser). Repr. of 1937 ed. 12.00 (ISBN 0-8369-6674-0). Ayer Co Pubs.

--Political Thought in England, Eighteen Forty-Eight to Nineteen Fourteen. 2nd ed. LC 80-19766. (Home University Library of Modern Knowledge: 104). 256p. 1980. Repr. of 1928 ed. lib. bdg. 24.75x (ISBN 0-313-22216-9, BAPL). Greenwood.

--Political Thought of Plato & Aristotle. 1959. pap. 7.50 (ISBN 0-486-20521-5). Dover.

--Political Thought of Plato & Aristotle. 15.00 (ISBN 0-8446-1594-3). Peter Smith.

--Principles of Social & Political Theory. LC 80-10811. viii, 284p. 1980. Repr. of 1961 ed. lib. bdg. 22.50x (ISBN 0-313-22329-7, BAPRS). Greenwood.

--The Study of Political Science & Its Relation to Cognate Studies. 1979. Repr. of 1928 ed. lib. bdg. 12.50 (ISBN 0-8482-3416-2). Norwood Edns.

--Traditions of Civility: Eight Essays. viii, 370p. 1967. Repr. of 1948 ed. 26.00 (ISBN 0-208-00037-2, Archon). Shoe String.

Barker, Ernest, ed. Library of Greek Thought, 9 Vols. Repr. of 1934 ed. Set. 147.00 (ISBN 0-404-07800-1). AMS Pr.

--Social Contract: Essays by Locke, Hume, & Rousseau. LC 80-22006. xliv, 307p. 1980. Repr. of 1947 ed. lib. bdg. 32.50x (ISBN 0-313-22409-9, BACT). Greenwood.

--Social Contract: Essays by Locke, Hume & Rousseau. (YA) (gr. 9 up). 1962. pap. 7.95x (ISBN 0-19-500309-8, 68). Oxford U Pr.

Barker, Ernest & Clark, George, eds. The European Inheritance, 3 Vols. LC 82-6116. (Illus.). 1340p. 1982. Repr. of 1954 ed. lib. bdg. 150.00x set (ISBN 0-313-23546-5, BARN). Greenwood.

Barker, Ernest, tr. From Alexander to Constantine: Passages & Documents Illustrating the History of Social & Political Ideas, 336 B. C.-A. D. 337. 532p. 1985. pap. text ed. 19.75 (ISBN 0-8191-4757-5). U Pr of Amer.

Barker, Ernest, tr. see Aristotle.

Barker, Sir Ernest. National Character & the Factors in Its Formation. LC 78-59002. 1979. Repr. of 1948 ed. 21.00 (ISBN 0-88355-678-2). Hyperion Conn.

Barker, Esther T. Book of Modern Tongue Twisters. LC 72-108712. 58p. 1970. pap. text ed. 3.40x (ISBN 0-8134-1160-2, 1160). Interstate.

--Tongue Twister Tales for "L", "R", & "S". LC 74-75416. vi, 74p. 1974. pap. text ed. 3.25x (ISBN 0-8134-1640-X, 1640). Interstate.

--Unused Cradle. pap. 1.50x (ISBN 0-8358-0231-0). Upper Room.

Barker, Eugene C. Life of Stephen F. Austin, Founder of Texas, 1793-1836. LC 70-111473. (BCL Ser. I). Repr. of 1925 ed. 24.50 (ISBN 0-404-00653-1). AMS Pr.

--Life of Stephen F. Austin, Founder of Texas, 1793-1836. LC 68-27723. (American Scene Ser). (Illus.). 1968. Repr. of 1925 ed. 65.00 (ISBN 0-306-71153-2). Da Capo.

--The Life of Stephen F. Austin: Founder of Texas, 1793-1836. (Texas History Paperbacks Ser.: Vol. 1). 495p. 1969. pap. 8.95 (ISBN 0-292-78421-X). U of Tex Pr.

--Life of Stephen F. Austin, Founder of Texas, 1793-1836: A Chapter in the Westward Movement of the Anglo-American People. 1949. 19.95 (ISBN 0-87611-002-2). Tex St Hist Assn.

Barker, Eugene C., jt. ed. see Williams, Amelia W.

Barker, Evelyn M. Everyday Reasoning. (Illus.). 304p. 1981. pap. text ed. 17.95 (ISBN 0-13-293407-8). P-H.

Barker, F., ed. Trondhjemites, Dacites, & Related Rocks. LC 78-24338. (Developments in Petrology Ser.: Vol. 6). 660p. 1979. 76.75 (ISBN 0-444-41765-6). Elsevier.

Barker, F. A. The Modern Prison System of India: A Report to the Department - the Progress of Prison Reform in India During the Twenty Years Following the Publication of the Report of the 1919-1920 Indian Jails Committee. (Cambridge Studies in Criminology: Vol. 3). pap. 23.00 (ISBN 0-317-16744-8). Kraus Repr.

Barker, Felix. Laurence Olivier. Smith, John L., ed. (Film & Theatre Stars Ser.). (Illus.). 96p. 1984. 6.95 (ISBN 0-88254-943-X). Hippocrene Bks.

Barker, Felix & Hyde, Ralph. London: As It Might Have Been. 224p. 1982. 40.00x (ISBN 0-7195-3857-2, Pub. by Murray England). State Mutual Bk.

Barker, Forrest. Problems in Technical Mathematics for Electricity-Electronics. LC 76-12728. 1976. pap. 12.95 (ISBN 0-8465-0403-0). Benjamin-Cummings.

Barker, Forrest L. & Wheeler, Gershon J. Mathematics for Electronics. 2nd ed. LC 77-80492. 1978. 31.95 (ISBN 0-8053-0340-5); instr's guide 6.95 (ISBN 0-8053-0341-3). Benjamin-Cummings.

Barker, Francis. Solzhenitsyn: Politics & Form. LC 77-22631. 112p. 1977. text ed. 27.50x (ISBN 0-06-490307-9, 06338). B&N Imports.

--The Tremulous Private Body: Essays on Subjection. 128p. 1985. text ed. 19.95 (ISBN 0-416-37840-4, NO. 9321); pap. 8.50 (ISBN 0-416-37850-1, NO. 9322). Methuen Inc.

Barker, Frank G. The Flying Dutchman. LC 79-65706. (Masterworks of Opera Ser.). 160p. (gr. 6 up). PLB 15.96 (ISBN 0-382-06311-2). Silver.

Barker, G. Russell, ed. see Walpole, Horace.

Barker, George. Anno Domini. LC 82-25160. 56p. 1983. pap. 8.95 (ISBN 0-571-13026-7). Faber & Faber.

--Thurgarton Church. 1969. write for info. (ISBN 0-685-01054-6, Pub. by Trigram Pr); signed ed. 100 copies 12.00 ea.; pap. 2.00 (ISBN 0-685-01056-2). Small Pr Dist.

Barker, George C. Pachuco: An American-Spanish Argot & Its Social Functions in Tucson, Arizona. LC 50-63360. 1970. pap. 1.95x (ISBN 0-8165-0253-6). U of Ariz Pr.

--Social Functions of Language in a Mexican-American Community. LC 70-186238. (Anthropological Papers: No. 22). 56p. 1972. pap. 3.95x (ISBN 0-8165-0317-6). U of Ariz Pr.

Barker, George E. Death & after Death. LC 78-65349. 1978. pap. text ed. 9.00 (ISBN 0-8191-0653-4). U Pr of Amer.

Barker, George F; see Draper, John W.

Barker, Gerard A. Grandison's Heirs: The Paragon's Progress in the Late Eighteenth Century English Novel. LC 83-40616. (Illus.). 192p. 1985. 26.50 (ISBN 0-87413-270-3). U Delaware Pr.

--Twice-Told Tales: An Anthology of Short Fiction. LC 78-69561. 1979. pap. text ed. 17.50 (ISBN 0-395-26635-1). HM.

Barker, Gilbert W. Antoine Watteau. 1978. Repr. of 1939 ed. lib. bdg. 40.00 (ISBN 0-8495-0365-5). Arden Lib.

Barker, Graeme. Landscape & Society: Prehistoric Central Italy. LC 80-41630. (Studies in Archaeology). 288p. 1981. 40.00 (ISBN 0-12-078650-8). Acad Pr.

--Prehistoric Farming in Europe. (New Studies in Archaeology). (Illus.). 352p. 1985. 44.50 (ISBN 0-521-22810-7); pap. 14.95 (ISBN 0-521-26969-5). Cambridge U Pr.

Barker, Graeme & Gamble, Clive, eds. Beyond Domestication: Subsistence Archaeology & Social Complexity in Ancient Europe. (Studies in Archaeology). Date not set. 45.00 (ISBN 0-12-078840-3). Acad Pr.

Barker, Graham H. Chemotherapy of Gynaecological Malignancies. (Illus.). 159p. 1983. 32.00 (ISBN 0-7194-0082-1, Castle House Publications Great Britain). Masson Pub.

--Your Search for Fertility: A Sympathetic Guide to Achieving Pregnancy for Childless Couples. LC 80-81515. (Illus.). 208p. 1981. 9.95 (ISBN 0-688-00184-X). Morrow.

--Your Search for Fertility: A Sympathetic Guide to Achieving Pregnancy for Childless Couples. Bronson, Richard A., frwd. by. LC 82-61676. 208p. 1983. pap. 5.70 (ISBN 0-688-01593-X, Quill). Morrow.

Barker, Gray. Gray Barker at Giant Rock. (Illus.). 100p. (Orig.). 1975. pap. 6.95 (ISBN 0-685-50455-7). G Barker Bks.

--The Secret Terror Among Us. (Illus., Orig.). 1982. pap. 9.95 (ISBN 0-911306-29-3). G Barker Bks.

--The Year of the Saucer, 1983. (UFO Annuals Ser.). (Illus.). 102p. (Orig.). 1983. pap. 12.95 (ISBN 0-911306-34-X). G Barker Bks.

Barker, Gray, ed. The Strange Case of Dr. M. K. Jessup. 4th ed. (Illus.). 82p. pap. 12.95 (ISBN 0-685-51759-4). G Barker Bks.

Barker, H. Granville, jt. ed. see Archer, William.

Barker, Harley G. The Madras House. 160p. 1977. pap. 6.95 (ISBN 0-413-38430-6, NO. 3014). Methuen Inc.

--Prefaces to Shakespeare: Othello. 160p. 1982. pap. 11.95 (ISBN 0-7134-4326-X, Pub. by Batsford England). David & Charles.

Barker, Harold. Secure Forever. LC 73-81552. 192p. 1974. pap. 3.50 (ISBN 0-87213-017-7). Loizeaux.

Barker, Harold R. History of the Forty-Third Division Artillery in World War II, 1941-1945: World War II, 1941-1945. (Illus.). 251p. 1961. 12.95 (ISBN 0-917012-45-3). RI Pubns Soc.

--History of the Rhode Island Combat Units in the Civil War, 1861-1865. (Illus.). 338p. 1964. 12.95 (ISBN 0-917012-44-5). RI Pubns Soc.

Barker, Harriett. Gourmet on Wheels: Two Hundred Fifty Easy & Delicious Recipes for the RV. 208p. (Orig.). 1985. pap. 7.95 (ISBN 0-8092-5402-6). Contemp Bks.

--The One-Burner Gourmet. rev. ed. (Illus.). 1981. pap. 8.95 (ISBN 0-8092-5883-8). Contemp Bks.

--Supermarket Backpacker. (Illus.). 1977. 8.95 (ISBN 0-8092-7307-1). Contemp Bks.

Barker, Harry R. & Barker, Barbara M. Multivariate Analysis of Variance (Manova) A Practical Guide to Its Use in Scientific Decision Making. LC 82-16122. (Illus.). 129p. 1984. text ed. 24.50x o. p. (ISBN 0-8173-0141-0); pap. text ed. 13.95x (ISBN 0-8173-0142-9). U of Ala Pr.

Barker, Howard. Crimes in Hot Countries: Also Contains Fair Slaughter. (Orig.). 1984. pap. 7.95 (ISBN 0-7145-4046-3). Riverrun NY.

--Fair Slaughter. 64p. 1980. pap. 3.95 (ISBN 0-7145-3654-7). Riverrun NY.

--The Hang of the Gaol. 1981. pap. 7.95 (ISBN 0-7145-3769-1). Riverrun NY.

--The Love of a Good Man. 1982. pap. 9.95 (ISBN 0-7145-3767-5). Riverrun NY.

--No End of Blame. 1981. pap. 7.95 (ISBN 0-7145-3912-0). Riverrun NY.

--The Passion in Six Days. 128p. (Orig.). 1985. pap. 4.95 (ISBN 0-7145-3985-6). Riverrun NY.

--Stripwell & Claw. 1980. pap. 4.50 (ISBN 0-7145-3572-9). Riverrun NY.

--That Good Between Us. 1981. pap. 9.95 (ISBN 0-7145-3765-9). Riverrun NY.

--Two Plays for the Right: Birth on a Hard Shoulder & Loud Boy. 150p. 1984. pap. 7.95 (ISBN 0-7145-3896-5). Riverrun NY.

--Victory. 224p. (Orig.). 1984. pap. 4.95 (ISBN 0-7145-3985-6). Riverrun NY.

Barker, J. & Smith, T., eds. The Role of Peptides in Neuronal Function. 1980. 99.75 (ISBN 0-8247-6926-0). Dekker.

Barker, J. Ellis. Foundations of Germany. LC 70-110894. 1970. Repr. of 1916 ed. 22.00x (ISBN 0-8046-0877-6, Pub. by Kennikat). Assoc Faculty Pr.

Barker, J. S., ed. Future Developments in the Genetic Improvement of Animals. 256p. 1983. 29.00 (ISBN 0-12-078830-6). Acad Pr.

Barker, J. S. & Starmer, T., eds. Ecological Genetics & Evolutions: The Cactus-Yeast-Drosophila Model. LC 82-72224. 376p. 1982. 52.50 (ISBN 0-12-078820-9). Acad Pr.

Barker, J. W. Agricultural Marketing. (Illus.). 1981. 35.00x (ISBN 0-19-859468-2). Oxford U Pr.

--Teach Yourself Portuguese. (Teach Yourself Ser.). pap. 4.95 (ISBN 0-679-10193-4). McKay.

Barker, Jack, et al. Arithmetic. 3rd ed. 1983. pap. text ed. 27.95 (ISBN 0-03-062397-9); instr's manual 19.95 (ISBN 0-03-062398-7); test bank 200.00 (ISBN 0-03-062847-4); audio tapes avail. (ISBN 0-03-062844-X). HR&W.

--Basic Algebra. 1983. pap. text ed. 27.95 (ISBN 0-03-058962-2); instr's manual 20.00 (ISBN 0-03-058963-0); prepared tests 20.00. (ISBN 0-03-062788-5); diagnostic tests avail. (ISBN 0-03-062787-7); test bank 200.00 (ISBN 0-03-062789-3); audio tapes avail. (ISBN 0-03-062792-3). HR&W.

--Intermediate Algebra. 1983. pap. text ed. 28.95 (ISBN 0-03-058959-2); instr's manual 20.00 (ISBN 0-03-058961-4); prepared test 200.00 (ISBN 0-03-062842-3); test bank 200.00 (ISBN 0-03-062843-1); audio tapes avail. (ISBN 0-03-062841-5). HR&W.

--Algebra for College Students. 525p. 1984. text ed. 27.95x (ISBN 0-03-069324-1). SCP.

--Elementary Algebra. 420p. 1984. text ed. 27.95x (ISBN 0-03-069326-8). SCP.

Barker, Jacob. Incidents in the Life of Jacob Barker of New Orleans, Louisiana. LC 74-121487. (Select Bibliographies Reprint Ser.). 1972. Repr. of 1855 ed. 20.00 (ISBN 0-8369-5455-6). Ayer Co Pubs.

Barker, James, jt. auth. see Lucas, James S.

Barker, James D. The Presidential Character: Predicting Performance in the White House. 3rd ed. (Illus.). 528p. 1985. pap. text ed. 22.95 (ISBN 0-13-698986-1). P-H.

Barker, Jane V. Historic Homes of Boulder County. (Illus.). 1979. 24.95 (ISBN 0-87108-550-X). Pruett.

Barker, Jane V. & Downing, Sybil. Adventures in the West. (Colorado Heritage Ser.: Bk. 5). (Illus.). 45p. (gr. 3-4). 1979. pap. text ed. 2.50x (ISBN 0-87108-220-9). Pruett.

--Beauty in the Rockies. (Colorado Heritage Ser.: Bk. 10). (Illus.). 50p. (gr. 3-4). 1980. pap. 2.50x (ISBN 0-87108-226-8). Pruett.

--Building up. (Colorado Heritage Ser.: Bk. 7). (Illus.). 44p. (gr. 3-4). 1979. pap. text ed. 2.50x (ISBN 0-87108-228-4). Pruett.

--Happy Harvest. (Colorado Heritage Ser.: Bk. 2). (Illus.). 45p. (gr. 3-4). 1978. pap. text ed. 2.50x (ISBN 0-87108-213-6); tchr's ed. 3.00x (ISBN 0-87108-223-3). Pruett.

--Magic, Mystery & Monsters. (Colorado Heritage Ser.: Bk. 6). (Illus.). 45p. (gr. 3-4). 1979. pap. text ed. 2.50x (ISBN 0-87108-219-5). Pruett.

--Mesas to Mountains. (Colorado Heritage Ser.: Bk. 4). (Illus.). 45p. (gr. 3-4). 1979. pap. text ed. 2.50x (ISBN 0-87108-215-2). Pruett.

--Mountain Treasures. (Colorado Heritage Ser.: Bk. 1). (Illus.). 45p. (gr. 3-4). 1978. pap. text ed. 2.50x (ISBN 0-87108-212-8); tchr's. ed. 3.00x (ISBN 0-87108-222-5). Pruett.

--Settling Down. (Colorado Heritage Ser.: Bk. 8). (Illus.). 59p. (gr. 3-4). 1979. pap. text ed. 2.50x (ISBN 0-87108-227-6). Pruett.

--Trappers & Traders. (Colorado Heritage Ser.: Bk. 3). (Illus.). 45p. (gr. 3-4). 1979. pap. text ed. 2.50x (ISBN 0-87108-214-4). Pruett.

--Wagons & Rails. (Colorado Heritage Ser.: Bk. 9). (Illus.). 44p. (gr. 3-4). 1980. pap. 3.50x (ISBN 0-87108-225-X). Pruett.

Barker, Jane V. & Downings, Sybil. Martha Maxwell: Pioneer Naturalist. LC 81-20988. (Women of the West Ser.). (Illus., Orig.). (gr. 5-6). 1982. pap. 5.50 (ISBN 0-87108-617-4). Pruett.

Barker, Jane V., jt. auth. see Downing, Sybil.

Barker, Jeffery L. & McKelvy, Jeffrey F. Current Methods in Cellular Neurobiology: Vol. I-Anatomical Techniques. LC 83-1282. (Neurobiology Ser.: I-662). 325p. 1983. 59.50 (ISBN 0-471-09328-9, Pub. by Wiley-Interscience). Wiley.

Barker, Jeffrey L. & McKelvy, Jeffery F. Current Methods in Cellular Neurobiology: Vol. 4 Model Systems. LC 83-1282. (Neurobiology Ser.: I-662). 192p. 1983. 49.50 (ISBN 0-471-09327-0, Pub. by Wiley-Interscience). Wiley.

Barker, Jeffrey L. & McKelvy, Jeffrey F., eds. Current Methods in Cellular Neurobiology: Vol. 2: Biochemical Techniques. LC 83-1282. 319p. 1983. 59.50 (ISBN 0-471-09344-0, Pub. by Wiley-Interscience). Wiley.

--Current Methods in Cellular Neurobiology: Vol. 3: Electrophysiological & Optical Techniques. LC 83-1282. 320p. 1983. 59.50 (ISBN 0-471-09343-2, Pub. by Wiley-Interscience). Wiley.

Barker, Jimmie. The Two Worlds of Jimmie Barker: The Life of an Australian Aboriginal 1900-1912 As Told to Janet Matthews. (AIAS Ethnohistory Ser.: No. 4). 1977. pap. text ed. 7.75x (ISBN 0-85575-056-1). Humanities.

Barker, John. British in Boston: Being the Diary of Lieutenant John Barker of the King's Own Regiment from Nov. 15, 1774-May 31, 1776. Decker, Peter, ed. LC 72-76555. (Eyewitness Accounts of the American Revolution Ser., No. 2). (Illus.). 1969. Repr. of 1924 ed. 14.00 (ISBN 0-405-01144-X). Ayer Co Pubs.

--Dictionary of Soil Mechanics & Foundation Engineering. 1981. pap. text ed. 31.00x (ISBN 0-86095-885-X). Longman.

--The Superhistorians: Makers of Our Past. 365p. 1983. pap. text ed. price not set (ISBN 0-02-306070-0, Pub. by Scribner). Macmillan.

Barker, John A. Reinforced Concrete Detailing. 2nd ed. (Illus.). 1981. 98.00x (ISBN 0-19-859523-9). Oxford U Pr.

Barker, John C. Strange Contrarieties: Pascal in England During the Age of Reason. (Illus.). 352p. 1976. 20.00x (ISBN 0-7735-0188-6). McGill-Queens U Pr.

Barker, John M. Saloon Problem & Social Reform. LC 76-112521. (Rise of Urban America Ser.). 1970. Repr. of 1905 ed. 23.50 (ISBN 0-405-02434-7). Ayer Co Pubs.

Barker, John N. & Bray, John. The Indian Princess, 2 vols in 1. LC 77-169587. (Earlier American Music Ser.: No. 11). 1973. Repr. of 1808 ed. 23.50 (ISBN 0-306-77311-2). Da Capo.

Barker, John W. Justinian & the Later Roman Empire. LC 66-11804. (Illus.). 336p. 1966. pap. text ed. 9.95x (ISBN 0-299-03944-7). U of Wis Pr.

Barker, Jonathan. The Politics of Agriculture in Tropical Africa. LC 84-2013. (Sage Series on African Modernization & Development: Vol. 11). 1984. 29.95 (ISBN 0-8039-2295-7). Sage.

Barker, Judith, jt. auth. see Sandbrook, Richard.

Barker, Juliet R., ed. see Bronte, Anne.

Barker, K. R., et al, eds. An Advanced Treatise on Meloidogyne, Vol. II: Methodology. LC 84-61978. (Illus.). 223p. 1985. text ed. 25.00 (ISBN 0-931901-02-2); text ed. 65.00 2 vol. set (ISBN 0-931901-00-6). Intl Melo Proj.

Barker, Kenneth. Religious Education, Catechesis & Freedom. LC 81-13962. 255p. (Orig.). 1981. pap. 12.95 (ISBN 0-89135-028-4). Religious Educ.

Barker, Kenneth & Breland, O. P. Laboratory Manual of Comparative Anatomy. 3rd ed. (Organismal Ser.). (Illus.). 208p. 1980. 21.95 (ISBN 0-07-003656-X). McGraw.

Barker, Larry. Communication in the Classroom. 208p. 1982. 21.95 (ISBN 0-13-153551-X). P-H.

Barker, Larry & Edwards, Renee. Intrapersonal Communication. (Comm Comp Ser.). (Illus.). 52p. 1979. pap. text ed. 2.95x (ISBN 0-89787-301-7). Gorsuch Scarisbrick.

Barker, Larry L. Communication. 3rd ed. (Illus.). 464p. 1984. pap. text ed. 19.95 (ISBN 0-13-153718-0). P-H.

Barker, Larry L. & Wahlers, Kathy J. Groups in Process: An Introduction to Small Group Communication. 2nd ed. (Illus.). 288p. 1983. text ed. 24.95 (ISBN 0-13-365254-8). P-H.

Barker, Larry L., jt. auth. see Malandro, Loretta A.

Barker, Lewellys F., jt. auth. see Dodd, Roger Y.

Barker, Lewis M. Psychobiology of Human Food Selection. (Illus.). 1982. lib. bdg. 29.50 (ISBN 0-87055-409-3). AVI.

Barker, Lewis M., et al, eds. Learning Mechanisms in Food Selection. LC 77-76779. 632p. 1977. 40.00 (ISBN 0-918954-19-3). Baylor Univ Pr.

Barker, Lexington. Propagate Me in Tangiers, Morocco. 187p. 1985. 10.95 (ISBN 0-533-06081-8). Vantage.

Barker, Louisa & Poe, Tina. The Diet Cookbook. 45p. (Orig.). 1983. pap. 6.50 (ISBN 0-943938-00-7). Res Assocs.

Barker, Lucius J. & Barker, Twiley W., Jr. Civil Liberties & the Constitution: Cases & Commentaries. 5th ed. 720p. 1986. pap. text ed. 24.95 (ISBN 0-13-134792-6). P-H.

Barker, Lucius J. & McCorry, Jesse J., Jr. Black Americans & the Political System. 2nd ed. (Orig.). 1980. pap. text ed. 15.95 (ISBN 0-316-08095-0). Little.

Barker, Lucius J., Jr. & Barker, Twiley W. Civil Liberties & the Constitution. 736p. 1982. 24.95 (ISBN 0-13-134882-5). P-H.

Barker, M. A. Flamesong. 1985. pap. 3.50 (ISBN 0-88677-076-9). DAW Bks.

Barker, M. A., et al. Urdu-English Vocabulary: Student's Dictionary. LC 79-92847. 382p. (Urdu & Eng.). 1980. pap. text ed. 10.00x (ISBN 0-87950-438-2). Spoken Lang Serv.

--A Reader of Modern Urdu Poetry. 334p. 1968. pap. 5.00x (ISBN 0-7735-9066-8). McGill-Queens U Pr.

Barker, M. A. R. The Man of Gold. 1985. pap. 3.95 (ISBN 0-88677-082-3). DAW Bks.

Barker, M. L. & Homeyer, H., eds. The Pocket Oxford German Dictionary, 2 vols. in 1. Incl. Pt. 1. German-English. 3rd ed. (Eng. & Ger.). 1975; Pt. 2. English-German. Carr, C. T., compiled by. (Eng. & Ger.). 1975. (Ger.). pap. 6.95x (ISBN 0-19-864138-9). Oxford U Pr.

Barker, Malcolm E. Bummer & Lazarus: San Francisco's Famous Dogs. LC 84-15491. (Illus.). 96p. (Orig.). 1984. 12.95 (ISBN 0-930235-00-2); pap. 6.95 (ISBN 0-930235-01-0). Londonborn Pubns.

Barker, Mark. Th Rag Mag Collection. Larry, ed. (Illus.). 1984. 25.00x (ISBN 0-906549-22-1, Pub. by J Clare Bks UK); pap. 10.00x (ISBN 0-317-07187-4, Pub. by J Clare Bks Uk). State Mutual Bk.

Barker, Martin. A Haunt of Fears: The Strange History of the British Horror Comics Campaign. 227p. (Orig.). 1984. pap. 7.50 (ISBN 0-86104-751-6, Pub. by Pluto Pr). Longwood Pub Group.

--The New Racism: Conservatives & the Ideology of the Tribe. 183p. 1981. lib. bdg. 24.00 (ISBN 0-89093-471-1, Aletheia Bks). U Pubns Amer.

Barker, Martin, ed. The Video Nasties: Freedom & Censorship in the Media. 131p. (Orig.). 1984. pap. 5.25 (ISBN 0-86104-667-6, Pub. by Pluto Pr). Longwood Pub Group.

Barker, Mary, jt. ed. see Hardiker, Pauline.

Barker, Mary L. Natural Resources of British Columbia & the Yukon Territory. (Illus.). 166p. 1977. 14.95x (ISBN 0-295-95561-9). U of Wash Pr.

Barker, Michael. Studies in Renewable Resource Policy, 2 vols. 1981. pap. write for info. (ISBN 0-934842-74-4). Coun State Plan.

Barker, Michael, ed. Financing State & Local Economic Development. LC 83-1561. (Duke Press Policy Studies). 490p. 1983. 37.50 (ISBN 0-8223-0536-4). Duke.

--Rebuilding America's Infrastructure: An Agenda for the 1980's. (Duke Press Policy Studies). 368p. 1983. 27.50x (ISBN 0-8223-0568-2). Duke.

--State Employment Policy in Hard Times. LC 83-5674. (Duke Press Policy Studies). 260p. 1983. 32.50 (ISBN 0-8223-0538-0). Duke.

--State Taxation Policy & Economic Growth, No. 1. (Policy Studies). 290p. 1983. 31.75 (ISBN 0-8223-0535-6). Duke.

--Studies in State Development Policy, 12 vols, Vol. 1. 1979. pap. 66.00x (ISBN 0-934842-24-8). Coun State Plan.

Barker, Michael, ed. see DeVoy, Robert & Wise, Harold.

Barker, Michael, ed. see Gordon, David M.

Barker, Michael, ed. see Hansen, Derek.

Barker, Michael, ed. see Hollister, Robert & Lee, Tunney.

Barker, Michael, ed. see Keischnick, Michael.

Barker, Michael, ed. see Kieschnick, Michael.

Barker, Michael, ed. see Litvak, Larry & Daniels, Belden.

Barker, Michael, ed. see Litvak, Lawrence.

Barker, Michael, ed. see Peirce, Neal, et al.

Barker, Michael, ed. see Vaughan, Roger J.

Barker, Michael B. Building Underground for People. (Illus.). 1978. pap. 3.00 (ISBN 0-913962-27-9); pap. 2.50 members. Am Inst Arch.

Barker, Michael J. Directory for the Environment: Organisations in Britain & Ireland, 1984-85. 296p. (Orig.). 1984. pap. 19.95x (ISBN 0-7102-0227-X). Routledge & Kegan.

Barker, Muhammad. Spoken Urdu. LC 75-15183. (Spoken Language Ser.). 530p. (gr. 9-12). 1975. pap. 10.00x Bk. 1 (ISBN 0-87950-340-8); pap. 10.00x Bk. 2, 576p. (ISBN 0-87950-341-6); pap. 8.00x Bk. 3, 230p. (ISBN 0-87950-342-4); 3 bk. set 25.00x (ISBN 0-87950-343-2); 6 dual track cassettes for bk. 1 90.00x (ISBN 0-87950-344-0); bk. 1 & cassette 95.00x (ISBN 0-87950-347-5); 6 dual track cassettes for bk. 2 75.00x (ISBN 0-87950-345-9); bk. 2 & cassettes 80.00x (ISBN 0-87950-348-3); Bks. 1-2 & cassettes 1 & 2 165.00x (ISBN 0-87950-349-1). Spoken Lang Serv.

Barker, Muhammad & Hamdani. Spoken Urdu, Vol. I. 497p. 1975. with 9 cassettes 135.00x (ISBN 0-88432-106-1, U200). J Norton Pubs.

--Spoken Urdu, Vol. II. 568p. 1976. with 5 cassettes 115.00x (ISBN 0-88432-107-X, U250). J Norton Pubs.

Barker, Muhammad A. A Reader of Classical Urdu Poetry, 3 vols. 1977. 3 vol. set 24.00x (ISBN 0-87950-433-1); vol. 1, 530p. 10.00x (ISBN 0-87950-430-7); vol. 2, 430p. 10.00x (ISBN 0-87950-431-5); vol. 3, 500p. 10.00x (ISBN 0-87950-432-3); Set. 3 vols. & cassettes 95.00x (ISBN 0-87950-435-8); cassettes, 6 dual track 75.00x (ISBN 0-87950-434-X). Spoken Lang Serv.

Barker, Muhammad Abd-al-Rahman, et al. Urdu Newspaper Reader. LC 74-21940. (Spoken Language Ser.). (Illus.). 472p. 1974. Repr. of 1968 ed. 10.00x (ISBN 0-87950-337-8); cassettes 4 dual track 50.00x (ISBN 0-87950-338-6); cassettes with course-bk. 55.00x (ISBN 0-87950-339-4). Spoken Lang Serv.

Barker, Murl G., tr. see Solugub, Fedor.

Barker, Nancy N. French Experience in Mexico, 1821-1861: A History of Constant Misunderstanding. LC 78-12935. xv, 264p. 1979. 22.50 (ISBN 0-8078-1339-7). U of NC Pr.

Barker, Nancy N., ed. French Legation in Texas, 2 vols. (Illus.). 1971-73. 14.95 ea. Vol. 1 (ISBN 0-87611-026-X). Vol. 2 (ISBN 0-87611-030-8). Tex St Hist Assn.

Barker, Nicolas. The Oxford University Press & the Spread of Learning: An Illustrated History, 1478-1978. (Illus.). 1978. 35.00x (ISBN 0-19-951086-5). Oxford U Pr.

Barker, Nicolas & Collins, John. A Sequel to an Enquiry: The Forgeries of Forman & Wise Re-examined. (Illus.). 368p. 1984. 70.00 (ISBN 0-85967-638-2). Scolar.

Barker, Nicolas, jt. auth. see Lambourne, Lionel.

Barker, Nicolas, ed. see Carter, John & Pollard, Graham.

Barker, Nicolas, ed. see Morison, Stanley.

Barker, Nicolas, ed. see Morison, Stanley, et al.

Barker, Nicolas, ed. see Munby, A. N.

Barker, Nicolas J. Stanley Morison. LC 76-189157. (Illus.). 1972. 35.00x (ISBN 0-674-83425-9). Harvard U Pr.

Barker, P. G. Computers in Analytical Chemistry. LC 82-22276. (Pergamon Ser. in Analytical Chemistry: Vol. 6). (Illus.). 472p. 1983. 75.00 (ISBN 0-08-024008-9). Pergamon.

Barker, Pat. Blow Your House Down. 180p. 1984. 13.95 (ISBN 0-399-13011-X, Putnam). Putnam Pub Group.

--Blow Your House Down. 224p. 1985. pap. 3.50 (ISBN 0-345-32361-0). Ballantine.

--Union Street. 256p. 1984. pap. 3.50 (ISBN 0-345-31501-4). Ballantine.

Barker, Paul, ed. Founders of the Welfare State: A Series from "New Society". 160p. (Orig.). 1985. pap. text ed. 28.95x (ISBN 0-435-82060-5). Gower Pub Co.

--The Other Britain: A New Society Collection. 276p. 1983. 24.95x (ISBN 0-7100-9308-X); pap. 11.95x (ISBN 0-7100-9340-3). Routledge & Kegan.

--The Social Sciences Today. (Quality Paperback Ser.: No. 328). 118p. 1977. pap. 1.50 (ISBN 0-8226-0328-4). Littlefield.

Barker, Peggy. What Happened When Grandma Died. 4.95 (ISBN 0-570-04090-6, 56-1458). Concordia.

Barker, Peter. Eastern Europe. LC 79-65841. (Countries Ser.). PLB 13.96 (ISBN 0-382-06326-0). Silver.

Barker, Peter, ed. see Einstein Centennial Celebration, Memphis State University, March 14-16, 1979.

Barker, Philip. Basic Family Therapy. (Illus.). 224p. (Orig.). 1981. pap. 21.00 (ISBN 0-8391-1673-X). Univ Park.

--The Techniques of Archaeological Excavation. LC 77-24786. (Illus.). 1977. text ed. 20.00x (ISBN 0-87663-291-6). Universe.

--Techniques of Archaeological Excavation. 2nd, rev., & extended ed. LC 82-23792. (Illus.). 288p. 1983. text ed. 25.00x (ISBN 0-87663-399-8); pap. text ed. 12.50x (ISBN 0-87663-587-7). Universe.

--Using Metaphors in Psychotherapy. 220p. 1985. 30.00 (ISBN 0-87630-410-2). Brunner-Mazel.

Barker, Philip, ed. The Residential Psychiatric Treatment of Children. Battezzati, M. & Donini, I. LC 74-7208. 354p. 1974. 48.95x (ISBN 0-470-04910-3). Halsted Pr.

Barker, Philip J. Behaviour Therapy Nursing. 276p. 1982. pap. 17.00 (ISBN 0-7099-0637-4, Pub. by Croom Helm Ltd). Longwood Pub Group.

--Patient Assessment in Psychiatric Nursing. 300p. 1985. pap. 14.95 (ISBN 0-7099-3254-5, Pub. by Croom Helm Ltd). Longwood Pub Group.

Barker, Philip J. & Fraser, Douglas, eds. The Nurse As Therapist: A Behavioural Model. LC 85-10935. 320p. (Orig.). 1985. pap. 12.95 (ISBN 0-7099-3253-7, Pub. by Croom Helm Ltd). Longwood Pub Group.

Barker, Rachel. Conscience, Government, & War: Conscientious Objection in Great Britain, 1939-1945. 180p. (Orig.). 1982. pap. 15.95X (ISBN 0-7100-9000-5). Routledge & Kegan.

Barker, Raleigh E. Tales from a Reservation Storekeeper. Hicks, John, ed. 64p. 1979. pap. 3.00 (ISBN 0-934996-01-6). Am Stud Pr.

Barker, Ralph. The Last Blue Mountain. LC 79-83801. (Illus.). 1979. pap. 7.95 (ISBN 0-916890-85-6). Mountaineers.

--The RAF at War. LC 81-5207. (Epic of Flight Ser.). lib. bdg. 21.27 (ISBN 0-8094-3292-7, Pub. by Time-Life). Silver.

--The RAF at War. (Epic of Flight Ser.). (Illus.). 175p. 1982. 14.95 (ISBN 0-8094-3291-9). Time-Life.

Barker, Ralph & Time-Life Book Editors. The RAF at War. (The Epic of Flight Ser.). (Illus.). 176p. 1981. 14.95 (ISBN 0-8094-3291-9). Time-Life.

Barker, Randolph & Sinha, Radha P., eds. The Chinese Agricultural Economy. LC 82-8549. (Special Studies on China & East Asia). 266p. 1982. lib. bdg. 30.00x (ISBN 0-86531-253-2); pap. 13.50x (ISBN 0-86531-342-3). Westview.

Barker, Randolph, et al. The Rice Economy of Asia. LC 84-43086. 328p. 1985. lib. bdg. 30.00 (ISBN 0-915707-14-4); pap. text ed. 12.00 (ISBN 0-915707-15-2). Resources Future.

Barker, Raymond C. The Power of Decision. LC 68-29810. 1968. 8.95 (ISBN 0-396-05806-X). Dodd.

--The Science of Successful Living. LC 57-11392. 145p. 1984. pap. 5.50 (ISBN 0-87516-536-2). De Vorss.

--Treat Yourself to Life. LC 54-9462. 1954. 9.95 (ISBN 0-396-03596-5). Dodd.

Barker, Raymond C., jt. auth. see Holmes, Ernest.

Barker, Raymond J. & McDole, Robert E. Idaho Soils Atlas. LC 82-60201. (Illus.). 148p. 1983. 18.95 (ISBN 0-89301-088-X). U Pr of Idaho.

Barker, Reginald W. Taxonomic Notes on the Species. LC 62-6771. (Society of Economic Paleontologists & Mineralogists, Special Publication: No. 9). pap. 65.50 (ISBN 0-317-27163-6, 2024735). Bks Demand UMI.

Barker, Richard H. Mr. Cibber of Drury Lane. LC 71-160002. Repr. of 1939 ed. 18.00 (ISBN 0-404-00654-X). AMS Pr.

--Thomas Middleton. LC 74-12880. 216p. 1975. Repr. of 1958 ed. lib. bdg. 19.75x (ISBN 0-8371-7767-7, BATM). Greenwood.

Barker, Robert. Social Work in Private Practice: Principles, Issues & Dilemmas. 250p. 1984. 15.95 (ISBN 0-87101-123-9). Natl Assn Soc Wkrs.

Barker, Robert L. The Business of Psychotherapy. LC 82-1307. (Illus.). 376p. 1982. 27.50x (ISBN 0-231-05438-6). Columbia U Pr.

--Treating Couples in Crisis: The Fundamentals & Practice of Marital Therapy. 304p. 1984. 19.95x (ISBN 0-02-901790-4). Free Pr.

Barker, Rodney. The Hiroshima Maidens. 256p. 1985. 16.95 (ISBN 0-670-80609-9). Viking.

--Political Ideas in Modern Britain. 1978. 24.00x (ISBN 0-416-76250-6, NO. 2033); pap. 15.95x (ISBN 0-416-76260-3, NO. 2079). Methuen Inc.

Barker, Rodney, ed. Studies in Opposition. LC 70-167757. 300p. 1972. 25.00 (ISBN 0-312-77105-3). St Martin.

Barker, Roger, et al. Frustration & Regression: An Experiment with Young Children. LC 75-34765. (Studies in Play & Games). (Illus.). 1976. Repr. of 1941 ed. 25.50x (ISBN 0-405-07934-6). Ayer Co Pubs.

Barker, Roger G. Ecological Psychology: Concepts & Methods for Studying the Environment of Human Behavior. LC 68-21287. 1968. 18.50x (ISBN 0-8047-0658-1). Stanford U Pr.

Barker, Roger G. & Gump, Paul V. Big School, Small School: High School Size & Student Behavior. 1964. 20.00x (ISBN 0-8047-0195-4). Stanford U Pr.

Barker, Roger G. & Schoggen, Phil. Qualities of Community Life: Measurement of Environment & Behavior in an American & an English Town. LC 72-13601. (Social & Behavioral Science Ser.). 1973. 50.00x (ISBN 0-87589-172-1). Jossey-Bass.

Barker, Roger G., ed. Stream of Behavior: Explorations of Its Structure & Content. LC 62-18400. (Century Psychology Ser.). (Illus.). 1963. 39.50x (ISBN 0-89197-427-X); pap. text ed. 19.95x (ISBN 0-89197-428-8). Irvington.

Barker, Roger G., et al. Adjustment to Physical Handicap & Illness. rev. ed. LC 53-7245. (Social Science Research Council Bulletin Ser.). 1953. pap. 17.00 (ISBN 0-527-03284-0). Kraus Repr.

--Habitats, Enviroments, & Human Behavior: Studies in Ecological Psychology & Eco-Behavioral Science. LC 77-82912. (Social & Behavioral Science Ser.). 1978. text ed. 27.95x (ISBN 0-87589-356-2). Jossey-Bass.

Barker, Ronald & Escarpit, Robert, eds. The Book Hunger. 155p. (Orig.). 1974. pap. 8.25 (ISBN 92-3-101085-9, U56, UNESCO). Unipub.

Barker, Ronnie. Ooh-La-La! The Ladies of Paris. (Illus.). 192p. 1984. 18.95 (ISBN 0-340-32347-7, Pub. by Hodder & Stoughton UK); pap. 14.94 (ISBN 0-340-32346-9). David & Charles.

Barker, Ruth B. Casey. LC 84-90147. 136p. 1985. 10.95 (ISBN 0-533-06220-9). Vantage.

--He Took Me to Heaven. 96p. 1984. 6.50 (ISBN 0-682-40195-1). Exposition Pr FL.

Barker, Ruth L. Caballeros. Cortes, Carlos E., ed. Van Sweringen, Norma, tr. LC 76-1237. (Chicano Heritage Ser.). (Illus.). 1976. Repr. of 1932 ed. lib. bdg. 30.00x (ISBN 0-405-09484-1). Ayer Co Pubs.

Barker, S. F. Elements of Logic. 4th ed. 416p. 1985. 26.95 (ISBN 0-07-003726-4); Written Cavalier & Dreisbach, 168p. study guide 9.95 (ISBN 0-07-003728-0). McGraw.

Barker, Sandy. It Began with an Island. 192p. 1985. pap. 6.95 (ISBN 0-8407-5971-1). Nelson.

Barker, Sebastian. Who Is Eddie Linden? 1982. 25.00x (ISBN 0-905150-13-9, Pub. by J Landesman England). State Mutual Bk.

Barker, Shirley. Dark Hills Under. LC 76-144739. (Yale Ser. of Younger Poets: No. 32). Repr. of 1933 ed. 18.00 (ISBN 0-404-53832-0). AMS Pr.

Barker, Stanley A. The Signs of the Times: The Neptune Factor & America's Destiny. Weschcke, Carl L., ed. LC 84-20177. (Popular Astrology Ser.). (Illus.). 348p. 1984. pap. 12.95 (ISBN 0-87542-030-3, L-030). Llewellyn Pubns.

Barker, Stephen F. & Beauchamp, Tom L. Thomas Reid: Critical Interpretations. 148p. 1976. pap. 19.95 (ISBN 0-87722-124-3). Temple U Pr.

Barker, Stephen F., jt. ed. see Achinstein, Peter.

Barker, Sue. Playing Tennis. LC 79-66012. (Illus.). 134p. 1982. pap. 5.95 (ISBN 0-8008-6322-4). Taplinger.

--Playing Tennis. LC 79-66012. (Illus.). 128p. 1980. 9.95 (ISBN 0-8008-6323-2). Taplinger.

Barker, T. C. & Harris, J. R. Merseyside Town in the Industrial Revolution: St. Helens 1750-1900. (Illus.). 508p. 1959. Repr. of 1954 ed. 27.50x (ISBN 0-7146-1268-5, F Cass Co). Biblio Dist.

Barker, T. C., jt. auth. see Alford, B. W.

Barker, T. E., et al, eds. Perspectives on Economic Development: Essays in the Honour of W. Arthur Lewis. LC 81-43790. (Illus.). 324p. (Orig.). 1982. PLB 27.50 (ISBN 0-8191-2381-1); pap. text ed. 14.25 (ISBN 0-8191-2382-X). U Pr of Amer.

Barker, T. S. & Brailovsky, Vladimiro, eds. Oil or Industry: Energy, Industrialization & Economic Policy in Canada, Mexico, Norway, the Netherlands & the United Kingdom. LC 81-67884. 1981. 55.00 (ISBN 0-12-078620-6). Acad Pr.

Barker, Theo. The Transport Contractors of Rye: John Jempson & Son, a Chapter in the History of British Road Haulage. (Illus.). 88p. 1982. 18.95 (ISBN 0-485-11234-5, Pub. by Athlone Pr Ltd). Longwood Pub Group.

Barker, Theo & Drake, Michael, eds. Population & Society in Britain, 1850-1980. 240p. 1982. 30.00x (ISBN 0-8147-1043-3). NYU Pr.

Barker, Thomas, ed. Frederick the Great & the Making of Prussia. LC 76-23215. (European Problem Studies). 116p. 1976. pap. 5.95 (ISBN 0-88275-456-4). Krieger.

Barker, Thomas B. Greenberg's American Flyer S Gauge Operating & Repair Manual, 1945-1965. 2nd ed. Greenberg, Linda, ed. (Illus.). 80p. 1983. pap. 10.95 (ISBN 0-89778-017-5, 6434). Greenberg Pub Co.

Barker, Thomas M. Double Eagle & Crescent: Vienna's 2nd Turkish Siege & Its Historical Setting. LC 67-63760. (Illus.). pap. 88.40 (ISBN 0-8357-9592-6, 2010104). Bks Demand UMI.

--The Military Intellectual & Battle: Raimondo Montecuccoli & the Thirty Years War. LC 74-837. (Illus.). 1975. 39.50x (ISBN 0-87395-250-2). State U NY Pr.

Barker, Thomas M. & Moritsch, Andreas. The Slovenes Minority of Carinthia. LC 84-80620. (East European Monographs: No. 169). 415p. 1984. 40.00x (ISBN 0-88033-061-9). East Eur Quarterly.

Barker, Twiley W., jt. auth. see Barker, Lucius J., Jr.

Barker, Twiley W., Jr., jt. auth. see Barker, Lucius J.

Barker, Vernon C. & Aufmann, Richard N. Essential Mathematics with Applications. LC 82-82928. 288p. 1982. pap. text ed. 12.95 (ISBN 0-395-33195-1); answer booklet 1.25 (ISBN 0-395-33196-X). HM.

Barker, Vernon C., jt. auth. see Aufmann, Richard N.

Barker, Virgil. From Realism to Reality in Recent American Painting. facs. ed. LC 68-57301. (Essay Index Reprint Ser). 1959. 11.00 (ISBN 0-8369-0173-8). Ayer Co Pubs.

Barker, W. A. & St. Aubyn, G. R., eds. Documents of English History: 1832-1950. 1954. 29.50x (ISBN 0-317-07647-7). Elliots Bks.

Barker, Wade. Dragon Rising. 288p. (Orig.). 1985. pap. 2.95 (ISBN 0-446-32391-8). Warner Bks.

--Lions Fire. 280p. (Orig.). 1985. pap. 2.95 (ISBN 0-446-32392-6). Warner Bks.

--Phoenix Sword. 256p. (Orig.). 1986. pap. 2.95 (ISBN 0-446-32396-9). Warner Bks.

--Serpent's Eye. 288p. 1985. pap. 2.95 (ISBN 0-446-32394-2). Warner Bks.

Barker, Wayne G. Cryptanalysis of an Enciphered Code Problem: Where an "Additive" Method of Encipherement Has Been Used. (Cryptographic Ser.). (Orig.). 1979. pap. 23.80 (ISBN 0-89412-037-9). Aegean Park Pr.

--Cryptanalysis of Shift-Register Generated Stream Cipher Systems. (Orig.). 1984. pap. text ed. 48.80 (ISBN 0-89412-062-X). Aegean Park Pr.

--Cryptanalysis of the Hagelin Cryptograph. (Cryptographic Ser.). 1977. 24.80 (ISBN 0-89412-022-0). Aegean Park Pr.

--Cryptanalysis of the Simple Substitution Cipher with Word Divisions: Using Non-Pattern Word Lists. LC 75-18083. (Cryptographic Ser.). 1975. pap. 16.00 (ISBN 0-89412-000-X). Aegean Park Pr.

--Cryptograms. 119p. (gr. 9 up). 1980. pap. text ed. 4.95 (ISBN 0-89412-043-3). Aegean Park Pr.

--Medical Schools of the World Where Instruction Is Given in English. rev. ed. LC 76-47072. 1978. pap. 4.95 (ISBN 0-89412-007-7). Aegean Park Pr.

Barker, Wayne G. & Coffman, Rodney. The Anatomy of Two Traitors: Story of the Defection of Two Americans to the Soviet Union. LC 81-69674. 1981. pap. 4.95 (ISBN 0-89412-041-7). Aegean Park Pr.

Barker, Wayne G., jt. auth. see Denney, George.

Barker, Wayne G., ed. The History of Codes & Ciphers in the United States During World War I. (Cryptographic Ser.). (Illus.). 1979. 20.80 (ISBN 0-89412-031-X). Aegean Park Pr.

--History of Codes & Ciphers in the United States Prior to World War I. (Cryptographic Ser.). 1978. 16.80 (ISBN 0-89412-026-3). Aegean Park Pr.

--Manual of Cryptography. 1981. pap. text ed. 14.80 (ISBN 0-89412-042-5). Aegean Park Pr.

Barker, Wayne G., ed. see Friedman, William F.

Barker, Wiley F., jt. auth. see Gaspar, Max R.

Barker, William F. & Doeff, Annick M. Preschool Behavior Rating Scale. LC 80-11444. (Orig.). 1980. pap. text ed. 4.35 instructions & scoring sample (ISBN 0-87868-148-5, J-60A); blank scale 0.60 (ISBN 0-87868-185-X, J-60B); Methodology 2.50 (ISBN 0-87868-187-6, J-60C). Child Welfare.

Barker, William H. West African Folk-Tales. LC 72-99339. (Illus.). 209p. 1972. Repr. of 1917 ed. lib. bdg. 12.50 (ISBN 0-8411-0010-1). Metro Bks.

Barker, William H., ed. Teaching Preventive Medicine in Primary Care. (Springer Series in Medical Education: Vol. 5). 336p. 1983. text ed. 41.50 (ISBN 0-8261-4080-7). Springer Pub.

Barker, William P. Everyone in the Bible. 384p. 1966. 15.95 (ISBN 0-8007-0084-8). Revell.

Barker, William P., ed. Tarbell's Teacher's Guide: 1984-85. 1984. pap. 7.95 (ISBN 0-8007-1420-2). Revell.

Barker-Lunn, Joan C. Streaming in the Primary School. 536p. 1970. 18.00x (ISBN 0-901225-19-3, Pub. by NFER Nelson UK). Taylor & Francis.

Barket, Khuda E., et al. Power Structure in Rural Bangladesh: Some Reflections from a Village in Commilla. (Development Studies Centre-Occasional Paper: No. 28). 37p. (Orig.). 1981. pap. text ed. 2.00 (ISBN 0-909150-55-9, 1004, Pub. by ANUP Australia). Australia N U P.

Barkey, Jim, jt. auth. see Tracy, Jack.

Barkhatov, A. N. Modeling of Sound Propagation in the Sea. LC 74-136985. 91p. 1971. 25.00x (ISBN 0-306-10855-0, Consultants). Plenum Pub.

Barkhaus, Robert S. & Bolyard, Charles W. Threads: A Tapestry of Self & Career Exploration. 2nd ed. (Orig.). 1980. pap. text ed. 7.95 (ISBN 0-8403-2152-X). Kendall-Hunt.

Barkhouse, Bob. Engine Repair: Head Assembly & Valve Gear. LC 74-21562. 500p. (gr. 10-12). 1974. text ed. 19.96 (ISBN 0-87345-101-5). McKnight.

Barkie, Karen E. Fancy, Sweet & Sugarfree. 176p. 1985. pap. 5.95 (ISBN 0-312-28164-1). St Martin.

--Sweet & Sugar Free: Nutritional Sweets Cookbook. 5.95 ea. Hypoglycemia Foun.

--Sweet & Sugarfree: An All Natural Fruit-Sweetened Dessert Cookbook. LC 82-5606. 192p. 1982. 12.95 (ISBN 0-312-78065-6); pap. 5.95 (ISBN 0-312-78066-4). St Martin.

Barkin, Carol & James, Elizabeth. The Complete Babysitter's Handbook. (Illus.). 160p. (Orig.). (gr. 5 up). 1980. pap. 5.95 (ISBN 0-671-33067-5). Wanderer Bks.

--Helpful Hints for Your Pregnancy. Paton, Kathi, ed. 128p. (Orig.). 1984. pap. 7.95 (ISBN 0-671-46779-4, Fireside). S&S.

--The Scary Halloween Costume Book. LC 81-14249. (Illus.). (gr. 3-6). 1983. 10.25 (ISBN 0-688-00956-5); PLB 10.88 (ISBN 0-688-00957-3). Lothrop.

Barkin, Carol, jt. auth. see James, Elizabeth.

Barkin, David & King, Timothy. Regional Economic Development: The River Basin Approach in Mexico. LC 76-111122. (Cambridge Latin American Studies, No. 7). (Illus.). 1970. 44.50 (ISBN 0-521-07837-7). Cambridge U Pr.

Barkin, Florence, et al, eds. Bilingualism & Language Contact: Spanish, English, & Native American Languages. (Bilingual Education Ser.). 1982. pap. text ed. 24.95x (ISBN 0-8077-2671-0). Tchrs Coll.

Barkin, George, ed. see Bierce, Ambrose.

Barkin, Kenneth. Controversy Over German Industrialization, 1890-1902. LC 78-101359. 1970. 25.00x (ISBN 0-226-03712-6). U of Chicago Pr.

Barkin, Roger M. & Rosen, Peter, eds. Emergency Pediatrics. (Illus.). 576p. 1983. text ed. 26.95 (ISBN 0-8016-0487-7). Mosby.

Barkin, Solomon, ed. Worker Militancy & Its Consequences: The Changing Climate of Western Industrial Relations. 2nd ed. 460p. 1983. 43.95 (ISBN 0-03-061793-6); text ed. 16.95 (ISBN 0-03-061792-8). Praeger.

Barklem, Jill. Autumn Story. LC 80-15433. (The Brambly Hedge Bks.). (Illus.). 32p. (gr. 1 up). 1980. 7.95 (ISBN 0-399-20745-7, Philomel). Putnam Pub Group.

--The Secret Staircase. LC 83-6270. (Brambly Hedge Ser.). (Illus.). (ps-3). 1983. 8.95 (ISBN 0-399-20994-8, Philomel). Putnam Pub Group.

--Spring Story. LC 80-15300. (The Brambly Hedge Bks.). (Illus.). 32p. (gr. 1 up). 1980. 7.95 (ISBN 0-399-20746-5, Philomel); PLB 6.99 (ISBN 0-399-61156-8). Putnam Pub Group.

--Summer Story. LC 80-15423. (The Brambly Hedge Bks.). (Illus.). 32p. (gr. 1 up). 1980. 7.95 (ISBN 0-399-20747-3, Philomel); PLB 6.99 (ISBN 0-399-61157-6). Putnam Pub Group.

--Winter Story. LC 80-15422. (The Brambly Hedge Bks.). (Illus.). 32p. (gr. 1 up). 1980. 7.95 (ISBN 0-399-20748-1, Philomel); PLB 6.99 (ISBN 0-399-61158-4). Putnam Pub Group.

Barkley, Alben. Atrocities & Other Conditions in Concentration Camps in Germany. (Witness to the Holocaust Ser.: No. 3). 16p. 1981. pap. 1.00 (ISBN 0-89937-032-2). Ctr Res Soc Chg.

Barkley, Frederick R., jt. auth. see Tucker, Ray T.

Barkley, Katherine T. The Ambulance: The Story of Emergency Transportation of Sick & Wounded Through the Centuries. (Illus.). 1978. 8.50 (ISBN 0-682-48983-2). Exposition Pr FL.

Barkley, Paul W. An Introduction to Macroeconomics. (Illus.). 418p. 1977. pap. text ed. 14.95 (ISBN 0-15-518816-X, HC); instructor's manual avail. (ISBN 0-15-518819-4); study guide by Sam Cordes 6.95 (ISBN 0-15-518818-6); test bklet avail. (ISBN 0-15-518825-9). HarBraceJ.

--An Introduction to Microeconomics. (Illus.). 327p. 1977. pap. text ed. 14.95 (ISBN 0-15-518817-8, HC); instructor's guide avail. (ISBN 0-15-518827-5); test booklet avail. (ISBN 0-15-518828-3). HarBraceJ.

Barkley, Paul W. & Seckler, David. Economic Growth & Environmental Decay: The Solution Becomes the Problem. 193p. 1972. pap. text ed. 11.95 (ISBN 0-15-518795-3, HC). HarBraceJ.

Barkley, Richard A. Oceanographic Atlas of the Pacific Ocean. (Illus.). 1969. text ed. 50.00x (ISBN 0-87022-050-0). UH Pr.

Barkley, Russell. Hyperactive Children: A Handbook for Diagnosis & Treatment. LC 81-1382. 458p. 1981. 25.00 (ISBN 0-89862-609-9, 2609). Guilford Pr.

Barkley, T. M. Field Guide to the Common Weeds of Kansas. LC 82-21914. (Illus.). 160p. 1983. 17.95x (ISBN 0-7006-0233-X); pap. 7.95 (ISBN 0-7006-0224-0). U Pr of KS.

Barklon, L. I., et al. Eighteen Papers on Analysis & Quantum Mechanics. LC 51-5559. (Translations Ser.: No. 2, Vol. 91). 1970. 38.00 (ISBN 0-8218-1791-4, TRANS 2-91). Am Math.

Barkman, Alma. Days Remembered. (Illus.). 96p. 1983. pap. 8.95 (ISBN 0-8024-0188-0). Moody.

--Sunny-Side Up. (Quiet Time Bks.). 1984. pap. 3.25 (ISBN 0-8024-8431-X). Moody.

Barkman, Betty. For Buds in His Bouquet. 135p. 1980. pap. 4.95. Herald Hse.

Barkman, Bruce. Seven Sinners in Grand Opera: Level 6. McConochie, Jean, ed. (Regents Readers Ser.). 1985. pap. text ed. 2.75 (ISBN 0-88345-462-9, 21066). Regents Pub.

Barko, Carol, tr. see Chalon, Jean.

Bar-Kochva, B. The Seleucid Army. (Cambridge Classical Studies Ser.). 1976. 34.50 (ISBN 0-521-20667-7). Cambridge U Pr.

Barkow, Al, jt. auth. see Casper, Billy.

Barkow, Al, jt. auth. see Low, George.

Barkow, Al, jt. auth. see Rodgers, Phil.

Barkow, Al, jt. auth. see Venturi, Ken.

Barks, Carl. Donald Duck. LC 78-14844. (Walt Disney Best Comics Ser.). (Illus.). 196p. 1978. 15.95 (ISBN 0-89659-006-2). Abbeville Pr.

Barks, Coleman, tr. see Rumi.

Barks, Coleman, tr. see Rumi, Jelaluddin.

Barksdale, A. Beverly. The Printed Note: Five Hundred Years of Music Printing & Engraving. (Music Ser.). (Illus.). 145p. 1981. Repr. of 1957 ed. lib. bdg. 25.00 (ISBN 0-306-76087-8). Da Capo.

Barksdale, Byron L. Investment Broker Malpractice. 64p. (Orig.). 1984. pap. text ed. 25.00 (ISBN 0-930631-00-5). Yellow Rose Fin.

Barksdale, E. C. Cosmologies of Consciousness. 148p. 1980. text ed. 18.50x (ISBN 0-87073-969-7); pap. text ed. 11.25x (ISBN 0-87073-970-0). Schenkman Bks Inc.

--The Dacha & the Duchess. LC 74-75086. 203p. 1975. 7.50 (ISBN 0-8022-2143-2). Philos Lib.

--Daggers of the Mind: The Russian Literary Imagination. 212p. 1979. 12.50 (ISBN 0-87291-099-7). Coronado Pr.

Barksdale, Hiram C., jt. ed. see Reynolds, Fred D.

Barksdale, Jo, jt. auth. see Furrh, Mary L.

Barksdale, Julian D., et al. Laboratory Manual for Elementary Geology. 2nd ed. (Illus., Orig.). 1969. pap. text ed. 4.95x (ISBN 0-87015-175-4). Pacific Bks.

Barksdale, Lilburn S. Building Self-Esteem. 1972. softbound 3.95x (ISBN 0-918588-01-4). Barksdale Foun.

--Building Self-Esteem: Study Guide. 1972. 5.60x (ISBN 0-918588-02-2). Barksdale Foun.

--Essays on Self-Esteem. LC 77-73169. 1977. softbound 7.90 (ISBN 0-918588-00-6). Barksdale Foun.

Barksdale, Richard & Kinnamon, Keneth. Black Writers of America: A Comprehensive Anthology. 980p. 1972. text ed. write for info. (ISBN 0-02-306080-8, 30608). Macmillan.

Barksdale, Richard K. Langston Hughes: The Poet & his Critics. LC 77-8599. pap. 41.80 (ISBN 0-317-27976-9, 2025610). Bks Demand UMI.

Barksdale, William C., jt. auth. see Wood, Oliver G., Jr.

Barkuizen, B. The Succulents of Southern Africa. 1980. 60.00x (ISBN 0-686-69985-8, Pub. by Bailey & Swinton South Africa). State Mutual Bk.

Barkun, Michael. Disaster & the Millennium. LC 73-86884. 272p. 1974. 22.50x (ISBN 0-300-01725-1). Yale U Pr.

Barkun, Michael, ed. Law & the Social System. (Controversy Ser). 136p. 1973. 11.95x (ISBN 0-88311-006-7); pap. 5.95x (ISBN 0-88311-007-5). Lieber-Atherton.

Barkus, Philip. How to Prepare for the Postal Clerk Carrier Examination. LC 82-24296. 256p. 1982. pap. 7.95 (ISBN 0-8120-2524-5). Barron.

Barkway, Lunsden & Menzies, Lucy, eds. An Anthology of the Love of God: From the Writings of Evelyn Underhill. 220p. 1981. Repr. of 1953 ed. lib. bdg. 30.00 (ISBN 0-8495-0067-2). Arden Lib.

Barkworth, Peter. About Acting. 176p. 1980. 14.95 (ISBN 0-436-03290-2, Pub. by Secker & Warburg UK); pap. text ed. 12.95 (ISBN 0-436-03291-0, Pub. by Secker & Warburg UK). David & Charles.

--First Houses: On Becoming an Actor. (Illus.). 160p. 1983. 18.95 (ISBN 0-436-03292-9, Pub. by Secker & Warburg UK). David & Charles.

--More About Acting. 224p. 1984. 18.95 (ISBN 0-436-03293-7, Pub. by Secker & Warburg UK); pap. 9.95 (ISBN 0-436-03294-5, Pub. by Secker & Warburg UK). David & Charles.

Barlag, R., jt. auth. see Andersen, R.

Barlas, John see Douglas, Evelyn, pseud.

Barlas, John E. Poems. 34.95 (ISBN 0-8490-0845-X). Gordon Pr.

Barlas, Nefise, jt. ed. see Muftuoglu, Asuman U.

Barlay, Stephen. In the Company of Spies. 1983. pap. 3.50 (ISBN 0-449-20378-6, Crest). Fawcett.

Barlea, Octavian. Romania si Romanii: Romania & the Romanians. Muresan, George C. & Motiu, Enea, trs. from Romanian. (American Romanian Academy Ser.: Vol. I). (Illus.). 1977. 7.00 (ISBN 0-686-23262-3). Am Romanian.

Barlee, N. L. Gold Creeks & Gold Towns. rev. ed. (Illus.). 192p. 1984. 9.95 (ISBN 0-88839-988-X). Hancock House.

--The Guide To Gold Panning. rev. ed. (Illus.). 192p. 1984. 9.95 (ISBN 0-88839-986-3). Hancock House.

--Lost Mines, in British Columbia. rev. ed. 96p. Date not set. 7.95 (ISBN 0-317-04996-8). Hancock House.

--Similkameen Country. Rev. ed. (Illus.). 96p. Date not set. 7.95 (ISBN 0-88839-990-1). Hancock House.

Barlen, M. E. Foundations of Modern Europe, 1789-1871. 17.50 (ISBN 0-8044-1055-0). Ungar.

Barlett. Agricultural Decision Making. 1984. 19.50 (ISBN 0-12-078882-9). Acad Pr.

Barlett, Donald L. & Steele, James B. Empire: The Life, Legend & Madness of Howard Hughes. (Illus.). 1979. pap. 11.95 (ISBN 0-393-00025-7). Norton.

--Forevermore: Nuclear Waste in America. LC 84-22761. (Illus.). 352p. 1985. 17.95 (ISBN 0-393-01920-9). Norton.

Barlett, Kenneth G. The Evening College & Its Relationship to "Community Politics". 1960. 2.50 (ISBN 0-87060-082-6, PUC 16). Syracuse U Cont Ed.

Barlett, Peggy F. Agricultural Choice & Change: Decision Making in a Costa Rican Community. (Illus.). 208p. 1982. 25.00 (ISBN 0-8135-0936-X). Rutgers U Pr.

Barlett, Peggy F., ed. Agricultural Decision Making: Anthropological Contributions to Rural Development. LC 80-513. (Studies in Anthropology Ser.). 1980. 37.50 (ISBN 0-12-078880-2). Acad Pr.

Barlett, Richard A. Exploring the American West, 1803-1879. 128p. 1983. pap. 6.50 (ISBN 0-318-11781-9). Gov Printing Office.

Barletta, Barbara. Ionic Influence in Archaic Sicily: The Monumental Art. (Studies in Mediterranean Archaeology, Pocketbks.: No. 23). (Illus.). 360p. 1983. pap. text ed. 46.50x (ISBN 91-86098-11-X, Pub. by Paul Astroms Sweden). Humanities.

Barletta, Nicloas A., et al. Economic Liberalization & Stabilization Policies in Argentina, Chile, & Uruguay: Applications of the Monetary Approach to the Balance of Payments. 240p. 1984. pap. 17.50 (ISBN 0-318-11919-6, BK 0305). World Bank.

Barlette, Danielle. Hurray for Hollywood. (Mirrors Ser.: No. 3). 144p. 1985. pap. 2.25 (ISBN 0-425-08420-5, Pub. by Berkley-Pace). Berkley Pub.

--I'll Take Manhattan. (Mirrors Ser.: No. 1). 144p. 1985. pap. 2.25 (ISBN 0-425-08410-8). Berkley Pub.

--Perfect for Paris. (Mirrors Ser.: No. 4). 144p. 1985. pap. 2.50 (ISBN 0-425-08435-3, Pub. by Berkley-Pacer). Berkley Pub.

--To London with Love. (Mirrors Ser.: No. 2). 144p. 1985. pap. 2.25 (ISBN 0-425-08411-6). Berkley Pub.

Barley, Elizabeth G. & Bloom, Mark. Young Runner's Handbook. 128p. 1981. pap. 1.95 (ISBN 0-446-90999-8). Warner Bks.

Barley, M. W. A Guide to British Topographical Collections. 159p. 1974. pap. text ed. 18.45x (ISBN 0-686-74108-0, Pub. by Coun Brit Archaeological). Humanities.

Barley, M. W., ed. The Archaeology & History of the European Town. 1978. 86.00 (ISBN 0-12-078850-0). Acad Pr.

Barley, Margaret, jt. auth. see Jeffers, Janet.

Barley, Nigel. Adventures in a Mud Hut: An Innocent Anthropologist Abroad. LC 83-26014. (Illus.). 192p. 1985. 12.95 (ISBN 0-8149-0880-2). Vanguard.

--Symbolic Structures: An Exploration of the Culture of the Dowayos. LC 82-23651. (Illus.). 160p. 1983. 29.95 (ISBN 0-521-24745-4). Cambridge U Pr.

Barlin, G. B. Chemistry of Heterocyclic Compounds: Pyrazines - A Series of Monographs, Vol. 41. 712p. 1982. 193.50 (ISBN 0-471-38119-5, Pub. by Wiley-Interscience). Wiley.

Barling, E. M. Back to G. B. S. 1948. Repr. 12.50 (ISBN 0-8274-1909-0). R West.

Barlingay, et al. A Critical Survey of Western Philosophy. 1980. text ed. 9.00x (ISBN 0-8364-0626-5, Pub. by Macmillan India). South Asia Bks.

Barlingay, S. S. A Modern Introduction to Indian Logic. 2nd, rev. ed. 1976. 7.50 (ISBN 0-89684-541-9). Orient Bk Dist.

--Poverty Power Progress. 227p. 1983. text ed. 15.50x (ISBN 0-391-03174-0, Pub. by Panchsheel Pubs India). Humanities.

Barlotti, A. Combinatorial & Geometric Structures & Their Applications. (Mathematical Studies: Vol. 63). 294p. 1982. 40.50 (ISBN 0-444-86384-2, I-97-82, North Holland). Elsevier.

Barlotti, A. & Ceccerini, P. V. Combinatorics, 1981. (Mathematical Studies: Vol. 78). 826p. 1983. 89.50 (ISBN 0-444-86546-2, I-465-82, North Holland). Elsevier.

Barlow, Alex, jt. ed. see Hill, Marjie.

Barlow, Andrew. Beat On. 192p. 1982. 30.00x (ISBN 0-901482-29-3, Pub. by Golden Eagle England). State Mutual Bk.

Barlow, Anna M; see Corrigan, Robert W.

Barlow, Annette C., jt. auth. see Celorio, Marta.

Barlow, B. V. The Astronomical Telescope. (Wykeham Science Ser.: No. 31). 220p. 1975. pap. cancelled (ISBN 0-85109-440-6). Taylor & Francis.

Barlow, B. V. & Everest, A. S. The Astronomical Telescope. (Wykeham Science Ser.: No. 31). 220p. 1975. 9.95x (ISBN 0-8448-1158-0). Crane Russak Co.

Barlow, Betty. Easy Baroque Duets. 32p. 1984. pap. text ed. 5.95 (ISBN 0-87487-262-6). Birch Tree Gr.

Barlow, Brent. What Husbands Expect of Wives. LC 83-70707. 160p. 1983. 7.95 (ISBN 0-87747-971-2). Deseret Bk.

--What Wives Expect of Husbands. LC 82-70919. 164p. 1982. 7.95 (ISBN 0-87747-911-9). Deseret Bk.

Barlow, Brent A. Understanding Death. LC 79-16414. 1979. 7.95 (ISBN 0-87747-781-7). Deseret Bk.

Barlow, C. W. & Eisen, Glen P. Purchasing Negotiations. 200p. 1983. 18.95 (ISBN 0-8436-0881-1). Van Nos Reinhold.

Barlow, C. Wayne. The Buyer & the Law. 144p. 1982. 19.95 (ISBN 0-686-79743-4). Van Nos Reinhold.

Barlow, Charles F. Headaches & Migraine in Childhood. (Clinics in Development Medicine Ser.: No. 91). (Illus.). 288p. 1985. text ed. 34.95 (ISBN 0-632-01326-5). Lippincott.

--Mental Retardation & Related Disorders. LC 77-14933. (Contemporary Neurology Ser.: No. 17). 1978. text ed. 25.00x (ISBN 0-8036-0615-X). Davis Co.

Barlow, Christopher. Islam. (Today's World Ser.). (Illus.). 72p. (gr. 7-12). 1983. 14.95 (ISBN 0-7134-3659-X, Pub. by Batsford England). David & Charles.

--The Third World. 1979. 14.95 (ISBN 0-7134-1878-8, Pub. by Batsford England). David & Charles.

Barlow, Connie, jt. auth. see Tussing, Arlon R.

Barlow, D. W., et al, eds. Grinding, Vol. 2. (Engineering Craftsmen: No. H.31). 1972. spiral bdg. 49.95x (ISBN 0-85083-380-9). Trans-Atlantic.

Barlow, Daniel L. Educational Psychology: The Teaching-Learning Process. 1985. 15.95 (ISBN 0-8024-8754-8). Moody.

Barlow, David. Sexually Transmitted Diseases: The Facts. (Illus.). 1979. text ed. 14.95x (ISBN 0-19-261157-7). Oxford U Pr.

--Sexually Transmitted Diseases: The Facts. (Illus.). 1979. pap. 6.95 (ISBN 0-19-520276-7, GB 657, GB). Oxford U Pr.

Barlow, David H. & Hayes, Steven C. The Scientist Practitioner: Research & Accountability in Clinical & Educational Settings. (Pergamon General Psychology Ser.: No. 128). 360p. 1983. 43.00 (ISBN 0-08-027217-7); pap. 16.50 (ISBN 0-08-027216-9). Pergamon.

Barlow, David H. & Hersen, Michel. Single Case Experimental Designs: Strategies for Studying Behavior Change. 2nd ed. (Pergamon General Psychology Ser.: No. 56). 432p. 1984. 39.50 (ISBN 0-08-030136-3); pap. 17.50 (ISBN 0-08-030135-5). Pergamon.

Barlow, David H., ed. Behavioral Assessment of Adult Disorders. LC 80-14673. (Behavioral Assessment Ser.). 500p. 1981. 35.00 (ISBN 0-89862-140-2, 2140). Guilford Pr.

--Behavioral Assessment of Adult Disorders. 1983. pap. 15.00 (ISBN 0-89862-901-2, 2901). Guilford Pr.

--Clinical Handbook of Psychological Disorders: A Step by Step Treatment Manual. 660p. 1985. text ed. write for info. (ISBN 0-89862-648-X). Guilford Pr.

Barlow, David H., jt. ed. see Mavissakalian, Matig.

Barlow, E. R. & Wender, Ira T. Foreign Investment & Taxation. LC 55-9771. (Illus.). 508p. 1955. 4.00x (ISBN 0-915506-01-7). Harvard Law Intl Tax.

Barlow, Elizabeth, jt. auth. see Epstein, Jason.

Barnabas. Gospel of Barnabas. 1981. pap. 9.95 (ISBN 0-686-77427-2). Kazi Pubns.

Barnabas, Bentley. Beatitudes for the Balmy. 1985. 6.95 (ISBN 0-682-40211-7). Exposition Pr FL.

Barnabas, Manorama, ed. Challenges of Societies in Transition. 1979. 12.50x (ISBN 0-8364-0274-X). South Asia Bks.

Barnabee, Henry C. Reminiscences of Henry Clay Barnabee. facsimile ed. Varney, George L., ed. LC 73-169779. (Select Bibliographies Reprint Ser). Repr. of 1913 ed. 42.00 (ISBN 0-8369-5999-X). Ayer Co Pubs.

Barnaby, Frank. Prospects for Peace. (Illus.). 105p. 1980. 24.00 (ISBN 0-08-027399-8); pap. 12.75 (ISBN 0-08-027398-X). Pergamon.

Barnaby, Frank, jt. auth. see Jasani, Bhupendra.

Barnaby, Frank & Thomas, Geoffrey, eds. The Nuclear Arms Race: Control or Catastrophe. LC 81-21282. 265p. 1982. 25.00x (ISBN 0-312-57974-8). St Martin.

Barnaby, Frank, et al, eds. Arms Uncontrolled. LC 75-2815. (Stockholm International Peace Research Institute Ser). 256p. 1975. text ed. 14.00x (ISBN 0-674-04655-2). Harvard U Pr.

Barnard, A. V., jt. auth. see Flaschka, H. A.

Barnard, Alan. Visions & Profits: Studies in the Business Career of Thomas Sutcliffe Mort. 1961. 14.00x (ISBN 0-522-83523-6, Pub. by Melbourne U Pr). Intl Spec Bk.

Barnard, Alan & Good, Anthony. Research Practices in the Study of Kinship. (Research Methods in Social Anthropology Ser.). 1984. 32.00 (ISBN 0-12-078980-9). Acad Pr.

Barnard, Anne. Auld Robin Gray. Scott, Walter, ed. LC 79-144414. Repr. of 1825 ed. 15.50 (ISBN 0-404-52709-4). AMS Pr.

--South Africa a Century Ago. Wilkins, W. H., ed. LC 71-116271. x, 316p. 1972. Repr. of 1901 ed. 29.00 (ISBN 0-403-00461-6). Scholarly.

Barnard, Anne L. Auld Robin Gray. Scott, Walter, ed. Repr. of 1825 ed. 20.00 (ISBN 0-384-03440-3). Johnson Repr.

--South Africa a Century Ago: Letters Written from the Cape of Good Hope, 1797-1801. Wilkins, W. H., ed. Repr. of 1901 ed. 22.00 (ISBN 0-527-05300-7). Kraus Repr.

Barnard, C. & Evens, P. Your Healthy Heart: The Family Guide to Staying Healthy & Living Longer. 224p. 1984. 18.95 (ISBN 0-07-003729-9). McGraw.

Barnard, C. J. Animal Behaviour: Ecology & Evolution. 339p. 1983. 21.50 (ISBN 0-471-88929-6, Pub. by Wiley-Interscience). Wiley.

Barnard, C. J. & Thompson, D. B. Gulls & Plovers: The Ecology of Mixed-Species Feeding Groups. 320p. 1985. 30.00x (ISBN 0-231-06262-1). COlumbia U Pr.

Barnard, C. J., ed. Producers & Scroungers Strategics of Exploitation & Parasitism. 267p. 1984. 39.95 (ISBN 0-412-00541-7, NO. 9017, Pub. by Chapman & Hall England). Methuen Inc.

Barnard, C. S. & Nix, J. S. Farm Planning & Control. 2nd ed. LC 79-10572. 1980. pap. 32.50 (ISBN 0-521-29604-8). Cambridge U Pr.

Barnard, Caroline K. Sylvia Plath. (United States Authors Ser.). 1978. lib. bdg. 13.50 (ISBN 0-8057-7219-7, Twayne). G K Hall.

Barnard, Carolyn & Potter, Loren D. New Mexico Grasses: A Vegetative Key. LC 83-21901. (Illus.). 160p. 1984. pap. 8.95 (ISBN 0-8263-0744-2). U of NM Pr.

Barnard, Charles P. Families, Alcoholism & Therapy. 176p. 1981. 16.50x (ISBN 0-398-04157-1). C C Thomas.

Barnard, Charles P. & Corrales, Ramon G. The Theory & Technique of Family Therapy. (Illus.). 352p. 1981. 19.75x (ISBN 0-398-03859-7). C C Thomas.

Barnard, Charles P., ed. Families, Incest & Therapy. (Special Issue IJFT Ser.: Vol. 5, No. 2). 92p. 1983. 9.95 (ISBN 0-686-47619-0). Human Sci Pr.

Barnard, Chester I. Functions of the Executive. 30th anniversary ed. LC 68-28690. 1968. pap. 8.95x (ISBN 0-674-32803-5). Harvard U Pr.

Barnard, Christiaan. Good Life Good Death: A Doctor's Case for Euthanasia & Suicide. LC 80-18839. 120p. 1980. 7.95 (ISBN 0-13-360370-9). P-H.

--South Africa: Sharp Dissection. LC 77-99151. 1977. 9.95 (ISBN 0-916728-02-1). Bks in Focus.

Barnard, Christiaan & Evans, Peter. Christiaan Barnard's Program for Living with Arthritis. (Illus.). 160p. 1984. 9.95 (ISBN 0-671-47052-3, Fireside). S&S.

--Christiaan Barnard's Program for Living with Arthritis. 240p. 1985. pap. 3.95 (ISBN 0-553-24888-X). Bantam.

Barnard, Christian. Christian Barnard's Program for Living with Arthritis. 1984. 9.95 (ISBN 0-317-18536-5, Fireside). S&S.

Barnard, David, jt. ed. see Rogers, William R.

Barnard, David T., et al. Microcomputer Programming with Microsoft BASIC. (Illus.). 1983. text ed. 22.95 (ISBN 0-8359-4357-7); pap. 17.95 (ISBN 0-8359-4356-9). Reston.

Barnard, Edward C. Naked & a Prisoner: Captain Edward C. Bernard's Narrative of Shipwreck in Palau, 1832-33. Martin, Kenneth R., ed. LC 80-83347. (Illus.). 60p. (Orig.). 1980. pap. 8.50 (ISBN 0-937854-01-8). Kendall Whaling.

Barnard, Ellsworth. English for Everybody. LC 79-18238. (Orig.). 1979. pap. 6.00 (ISBN 0-9605458-0-8). Dinosaur.

--A Hill Farm Boyhood. (Illus.). 178p. 1983. 7.50 (ISBN 0-9605458-1-6). Dinosaur.

--Wendell Willkie: Fighter for Freedom. LC 66-19668. 628p. 1971. 20.00x (ISBN 0-87023-088-3); pap. 12.50 (ISBN 0-87023-095-6). U of Mass Pr.

Barnard, Etwell A. New Links with Shakespeare. LC 73-153301. Repr. of 1930 ed. 15.00 (ISBN 0-404-00655-8). AMS Pr.

--New Links with Shakespeare. 1973. Repr. of 1930 ed. 9.95 (ISBN 0-8274-1679-2). R West.

Barnard, F. L. Three Years' Cruize in the Mozambique Channel: For the Suppression of the Slave Trade. facs. ed. LC 79-149863. (Black Heritage Library Collection Ser). 1848. 19.25 (ISBN 0-8369-8745-4). Ayer Co Pubs.

Barnard, F. M., ed. J. G. Herder on Social & Political Culture. LC 69-11022. (Cambridge Studies in the History & Theory of Politics). (Illus.). 1969. 44.50 (ISBN 0-521-07336-7). Cambridge U Pr.

Barnard, Francis P. Edward Fourth's French Expedition of 1475: The Leaders & Their Badges, Being MS. 2.M. 16. College of Arms. (Illus.). 162p. 1975. Repr. of 1925 ed. 18.75x (ISBN 0-87471-745-0). Rowman.

--Edward IV's French Expedition of Fourteen Seventy-Five. (Illus.). 162p. 1982. Repr. of 1925 ed. text ed. 21.50x (ISBN 0-904586-01-4, Pub. by Alan Sutton England). Humanities.

Barnard, Frederick A., ed. see American Unitarian Association.

Barnard, Frederick A., ed. see Campbell, Thomas M.

Barnard, Frederick A., jt. ed. see Cremin, Lawrence A.

Barnard, Geoffrey, jt. auth. see Cage, John.

Barnard, George N. Photographic Views of Sherman's Campaign. LC 76-45964. (Illus.). 1977. pap. 6.00 (ISBN 0-486-23445-2). Dover.

--Photographic Views of Sherman's Campaign. 15.25 (ISBN 0-8446-5553-8). Peter Smith.

Barnard, H. C. Fenelon on Education. (Cambridge Texts & Studies in the History of Education: No. 1). 1966. 29.95 (ISBN 0-521-04107-4). Cambridge U Pr.

--Madame de Maintenon & Saint-Cyr. 1977. Repr. of 1934 ed. 12.50x (ISBN 0-85409-702-3). Charles River Bks.

Barnard, Harry. Chats on Wedgwood Ware. (Illus.). 1977. Repr. of 1924 ed. 17.50x (ISBN 0-85409-799-6). Charles River Bks.

--Eagle Forgotten: Life of John Peter Altgeld. 496p. 1973. 10.95 (ISBN 0-88286-100-X). C H Kerr.

--Forging of an American Jew: The Life & Times of Judge Julian W. Mack. 1974. 7.95 (ISBN 0-685-52984-3). Herzl Pr.

--Wedgwood Chats. 1970. Repr. of 1924 ed. 7.50 (ISBN 0-912014-07-5). Buten Mus.

Barnard, Helen. Advanced English Vocabulary. 1971. tchrs' bk 2.95 (ISBN 0-912066-48-2); wkbk 1 8.95 (ISBN 0-912066-19-9). Newbury Hse.

--Advanced English Vocabulary. 1975. pap. 8.95 wkbk 3B (ISBN 0-912066-44-X). Newbury Hse.

--Advanced English Vocabulary. 1975. pap. 8.95 wkbk 3A (ISBN 0-912066-43-1). Newbury Hse.

--Advanced English Vocabulary. 1972. wkbk 2A 8.95 (ISBN 0-88377-037-7); pap. 8.95 wkbk 2b (ISBN 0-88377-038-5). Newbury Hse.

Barnard, Henry. Education & Employment: Education & Labor... (Works of Henry Barnard Ser.). Date not set. Repr. of 1842 ed. lib. bdg. 29.00 (ISBN 0-932051-82-0). Am Repr Serv.

--German Teachers & Educators. 59.95 (ISBN 0-8490-0230-3). Gordon Pr.

--Henry Barnard on Education. Brubacher, John S., ed. LC 64-66388. (Illus.). 1965. Repr. of 1931 ed. 8.50x (ISBN 0-8462-0553-X). Russell.

--Normal Schools, 2 vols. Date not set. Repr. of 1851 ed. lib. bdg. 69.00 (ISBN 0-932051-87-1). Am Repr Serv.

--Reformatory Education. 361p. 1980. Repr. of 1857 ed. lib. bdg. 32.50 (ISBN 0-8492-3589-8). R West.

--Reformatory Education: Papers on Preventive, Correctional & Reformatory Institutions & Agencies in Different Countries. 1978. Repr. lib. bdg. 20.00 (ISBN 0-8414-9927-6). Folcroft.

Barnard, Henry, ed. Memoirs of Teachers, Educators, & Promoters & Benefactors of Education, Literature, & Science. LC 74-89147. (American Education: Its Men, Institutions & Ideas, Ser. 1). 1969. Repr. of 1861 ed. 32.00 (ISBN 0-405-01384-1). Ayer Co Pubs.

Barnard, Henry, compiled by. Military Schools & Courses of Instruction in the Science & Art of War. LC 68-54786. Repr. of 1872 ed. lib. bdg. 37.50x (ISBN 0-8371-1325-3, BAMS). Greenwood.

Barnard, Henry, ed. Pamphlets in American History, Group I: A Bibliographic Guide to the Microform Collection. 416p. 1979. 35.00 (ISBN 0-667-00566-8). Microfilming Corp.

--Slavery: A Bibliography & Union List of the Microfilm Collection, Part I. 402p. 1980. pap. 50.00 (ISBN 0-667-00613-3). Microfilming Corp.

Barnard, Hollinger F., ed. see Durr, Virginia F.

Barnard, J. A & Bradley, J. N. Flame & Combustion. 2nd ed. 344p. 1985. text ed. 55.00 (ISBN 0-412-23030-5, NO. 9254, Pub. by Chapman & Hall England); pap. text ed. 27.00 (ISBN 0-412-23040-2, NO. 9255, Pub. by Chapman & Hall England). Methuen Inc.

Barnard, J. H., ed. The Odes of Solomon. (Texts & Studies Ser.: No. 1, Vol. 8, Pt. 3). pap. 13.00 (ISBN 0-317-16758-8). Kraus Repr.

Barnard, J. L. Gammaridean Amphipoda in the Collections of Bishop Museum. (BMB). 1955. pap. 8.00 (ISBN 0-527-02323-X). Kraus Repr.

Barnard, Jerry. Something Worse Than Hell & Better Than Heaven. 1979. pap. 3.25 (ISBN 0-917726-31-6). Hunter Bks.

Barnard, John. Ashton's Memorial: A History of the Strange Adventure, & Signal Deliverances of Mr. Philip Ashton, Sun of Marblehead. Knight, Russell W., ed. 1976. 12.50 (ISBN 0-87577-051-7). Peabody Mus Salem.

--From Evangelicalism to Progressivism at Oberlin College, 1866-1917. LC 68-25865. 191p. 1969. 7.50 (ISBN 0-8142-0022-7). Ohio St U Pr.

--Walter Reuther & the Rise of the Autoworkers. 1982. pap. text ed. 6.95 (ISBN 0-316-08142-6). Little.

Barnard, John, ed. Pope: The Critical Heritage. (Critical Heritage Ser.). 550p. 1973. 42.00x (ISBN 0-7100-7390-9); pap. 15.00 (ISBN 0-7102-0516-3). Routledge & Kegan.

--Pope: The Critical Heritage. 560p. 1985. pap. 15.00 (ISBN 0-7102-0516-3). Routledge & Kegan.

Barnard, John, ed. see Etherege, George.

Barnard, John, ed. see Keats, John.

Barnard, John M., ed. Computer Handling of Generic Chemical Structures. LC 84-13725. 242p. 1984. text ed. 53.95x (ISBN 0-566-03515-4). Gower Pub Co.

Barnard, Judith. The Indestructible Crown: The Life of Albert Pick, Jr. LC 80-16389. (Illus.). 246p. 1980. 16.95 (ISBN 0-88229-718-X). Nelson-Hall.

Barnard, Julian. Collecting Victorian Ceramic Tiles. (The Christies International Collectors Ser.). (Illus.). 128p. 1980. 14.95 (ISBN 0-8317-9168-3, Mayflower Bks). Smith Pubs.

Barnard, Julien. Guide to Bach Flower Remedies. 1980. pap. 4.95x (ISBN 0-317-07342-7, Regent House). B of A.

Barnard, Keith & Lee, Kenneth, eds. Conflicts in the National Health Service. LC 76-57740. 1977. 22.50 (ISBN 0-88202-114-1, Prodist). Watson Pub Intl.

Barnard, Kevin F. & Diamond, Joseph. Demutualization: The New Conversion Options for Savings Banks, Savings & Loans, & Insurance Companies. LC 84-170669. (Illus.). Date not set. price not set (Law & Business). HarBraceJ.

Barnard, Laura B. & Hill, Georgia. Touching the Untouchables. 224p. 1985. pap. 6.95 (ISBN 0-317-17143-7). Tyndale.

Barnard, M. U., jt. auth. see Scipien, G. M.

Barnard, Martha, jt. auth. see Hymovich, Debra.

Barnard, Martha U., et al. Handbook of Comprehensive Pediatric Nursing. (Illus.). 592p. 1981. pap. text ed. 19.95 (ISBN 0-07-003740-X). McGraw.

--Human Sexuality for Health Professionals. LC 77-84663. (Illus.). 1978. pap. text ed. 11.95 (ISBN 0-7216-1544-9). Saunders.

Barnard, Mary. Assault on Mount Helicon: A Literary Memoir. LC 83-6887. (Illus.). 331p. 1984. 19.95 (ISBN 0-520-04818-0). U of Cal Pr.

--Collected Poems. LC 79-54693. 1979. deluxe ed. 100.00 (ISBN 0-932576-02-8). Breitenbush Bks.

--Collected Poems: 1979. LC 79-54693. 1981. pap. 8.95 (ISBN 0-932576-09-5). Breitenbush Bks.

--Mythmakers. LC 66-20061. 213p. 1979. 16.95 (ISBN 0-8214-0024-X, 82-80265); pap. 6.50 (ISBN 0-8214-0562-4, 82-80273). Ohio U Pr.

Barnard, Mary, tr. see Sappho.

Barnard, Mary E. Three Fables. LC 83-19719. 56p. 1983. 9.95 (ISBN 0-932576-20-6); pap. 4.95 (ISBN 0-932576-21-4). Breitenbush Bks.

Barnard, Melanie, ed. see Greer, Anne L.

Barnard, Naomi H. The Wonder of Christmas. LC 78-67996. 1979. 5.95 (ISBN 0-8054-5165-X). Broadman.

Barnard, P. M., ed. The Biblical Text of Clement of Alexandria in the Four Gospels & the Acts of the Apostles. (Texts & Studies Ser.: No. 1, Vol. 5, Pt. 5). pap. 13.00 (ISBN 0-317-16754-5). Kraus Repr.

--Clement of Alexandria: Qui Dives Salvetur. (Texts & Studies Ser.: No. 1, Vol. 5, Pt. 2). pap. 19.00 (ISBN 0-317-16752-9). Kraus Repr.

Barnard, Philip. Don't Tickle the Elephant Tree: Sensitive Plants. LC 81-16834. (Illus.). 64p. (gr. 4-6). 1982. PLB 8.97 (ISBN 0-671-41625-1). Messner.

Barnard, Philip, tr. see Sarduy, Severo.

Barnard, Phillip, tr. see Sollers, Philippe.

Barnard, Robert. Blood Brotherhood. 1978. 7.95 (ISBN 0-8027-5387-6). Walker & Co.

--Blood Brotherhood. 196p. 1983. pap. 2.95 (ISBN 0-14-006552-0). Penguin.

--The Case of the Missing Bronte. (Scene of the Crime Ser.: No. 74). 1986. pap. 3.50 (ISBN 0-440-11108-0). Dell.

--The Case of the Missing Bronte. (Nightingale Paperbacks Ser.). 244p. 1984. pap. 8.95 (ISBN 0-8161-3590-8, Large Print Bks). G K Hall.

--The Case of the Missing Bronte: A Perry Trethowan Mystery. 192p. 1983. 11.95 (ISBN 0-684-17910-5, ScribT). Scribner.

--Corpse in a Gilded Cage. 224p. 1984. 12.95 (ISBN 0-684-18192-4, ScribT). Scribner.

--Corpse in a Gilded Cage. (Nightingale Paperbacks (Large Print) Ser.). 1985. pap. 10.95 (ISBN 0-317-19803-3). G K Hall.

--Corpse in a Gilded Cage. 1985. pap. 3.50 (ISBN 0-317-29223-4). Dell.

--Death & the Princess. 192p. 1982. 10.95 (ISBN 0-684-17759-5, ScribT). Scribner.

--Death & the Princess. (Scene of the Crime Ser.: No. 66). 192p. 1985. pap. 3.25 (ISBN 0-440-12153-1). Dell.

--Death by Sheer Torture. 192p. 1982. 10.95 (ISBN 0-684-17437-5, ScribT). Scribner.

--Death by Sheer Torture. (Nightingale Ser.). 1982. pap. 9.95 (ISBN 0-8161-3456-1, Large Print Bks). G K Hall.

--Death by Sheer Torture. 192p. 1985. pap. 3.50 (ISBN 0-440-11976-6). Dell.

--Death in a Cold Climate. (Scene of the Crime Ser.: No. 42). 1986. pap. 3.50 (ISBN 0-440-11829-8). Dell.

--Death in a Cold Climate. (General Ser.). 1981. lib. bdg. 12.95 (ISBN 0-8161-3309-3, Large Print Bks). G K Hall.

--Death of a Literary Widow. 192p. 1985. pap. 2.95 (ISBN 0-440-11821-2). Dell.

--Death of a Literary Widow. (General Ser.). 1981. lib. bdg. 11.95 (ISBN 0-8161-3249-6, Large Print Bks). G K Hall.

--Death of a Literary Widow. 1980. 8.95 (ISBN 0-684-16648-8, ScribT). Scribner.

--Death of a Mystery Writer. 224p. 1985. pap. 2.95 (ISBN 0-440-12168-X). Dell.

--Death of a Mystery Writer. (General Ser.). 1980. lib. bdg. 11.95 (ISBN 0-8161-3081-7, Large Print Bks). G K Hall.

--Death of a Perfect Mother. (Nightingale Ser.). 1982. pap. 9.95 (ISBN 0-8161-3356-5, Large Print Bks). G K Hall.

--Death of a Perfect Mother. 1985. pap. 2.95 (ISBN 0-440-12030-6). Dell.

--Death of an Old Goat. 1983. pap. 3.50 (ISBN 0-14-006537-7). Penguin.

--Death on the High C's. 1985. pap. 3.50 (ISBN 0-440-11900-6). Dell.

--Fete Fatale. 192p. 1985. 13.95 (ISBN 0-684-18469-9, ScribT). Scribner.

--A Little Local Murder. 192p. 1983. 11.95 (ISBN 0-684-17882-6, ScribT). Scribner.

--A Little Local Murder. (Scene of the Crime Ser.: No. 70). 1984. pap. 2.95 (ISBN 0-440-14882-0). Dell.

--Out of the Blackout. 208p. 1985. 12.95 (ISBN 0-684-18282-3, ScribT). Scribner.

--School for Murder. 192p. 1984. 12.95 (ISBN 0-684-18113-4, ScribT). Scribner.

--School for Murder. 1985. pap. 2.95 (ISBN 0-440-17605-0). Dell.

--A Short History of English Literature. 375p. 1984. 24.95x (ISBN 0-631-13761-0); pap. 9.95x (ISBN 0-631-13762-9). Basil Blackwell.

--A Talent to Deceive: An Appreciation of Agatha Christie. LC 79-27435. 208p. 1980. 10.00 (ISBN 0-396-07827-3). Dodd.

Barnard, Robert L. Intrusion Detection Systems. 300p. 1981. text ed. 24.95 (ISBN 0-409-95026-2). Butterworth.

Barnard, Robin O., et al. An Atlas of Tumours Involving the Central Nervous System. (Illus.). 1976. text ed. 45.00 (ISBN 0-02-857250-5). Macmillan.

Barnard, S. A., jt. auth. see Beagley, H. A.

Barnard, T. C. Cromwellian Ireland: English Government & Reform in Ireland 1649-1660. (Oxford Historical Monographs). 1975. text ed. 42.00x (ISBN 0-19-821858-3). Oxford U Pr.

Barnard, Tom. How to Grow an Adult Class. 88p. (Orig.). 1983. pap. 2.95 (ISBN 0-8341-0840-2). Beacon Hill.

Barnard, William D. Dixiecrats & Democrats: Alabama Politics 1942-1950. LC 73-22711. 208p. 1974. 20.00 (ISBN 0-8173-4820-4); pap. 12.50 (ISBN 0-8173-0255-7). U of Ala Pr.

Barnas, Andrew, tr. see Levelt, W. J.

Barndollar, W. W. The Validity of Dispensationalism. LC 67-23370. 1967. pap. 1.50 (ISBN 0-87227-023-8). Reg Baptist.

Barnds, William J., ed. Japan & the United States: Challenges & Opportunities. LC 79-1551. 1979. 27.00x (ISBN 0-8147-1020-4); pap. 15.50x (ISBN 0-8147-1021-2). NYU Pr.

--The Two Koreas in East Asian Affairs. LC 75-27379. 216p. 1976. 25.00x (ISBN 0-8147-0988-5). NYU Pr.

Barnds, William J., et al. Pakistan: The Long View. Ziring, Lawrence, ed. LC 76-4320. (Duke University Center for Commonwealth & Comparatives Studies Publication: No. 43). pap. 125.80 (ISBN 0-317-26810-4, 2023477). Bks Demand UMI.

Barndt, Deborah. Education & Social Change: A Photographic Study of Peru. LC 80-82833. 1980. pap. text ed. 21.95 (ISBN 0-8403-2283-6). Kendall-Hunt.

Barndt, Joseph R., jt. auth. see Smith, Louis A.

Barne, Arpad. Operational Amplifiers. LC 70-150608. (Illus.). pap. 39.80 (ISBN 0-317-09119-0, 2055525). Bks Demand UMI.

Barne, Kitty. Listening to the Orchestra. LC 72-13098. (Essay Index Reprint Ser.). Repr. of 1946 ed. 18.50 (ISBN 0-8369-8146-4). Ayer Co Pubs.

Barnea, Amir, et al. Agency Problems & Financial Contracting. (Illus.). 160p. 1985. text ed. 21.95 (ISBN 0-13-018854-9); pap. text ed. 15.95 (ISBN 0-13-018847-6). P-H.

Barneby, R. C. & Krukoff, B. A. Supplementary Notes on American Menispermaceae Eight: A Generic Survey of the American Triclisiea & Anomospermeae, Vol. 20(2) (Memoirs of the New York Botanical Garden Ser.). 89p. 1971. 12.00 (ISBN 0-317-35530-9). NY Botanical.

Barneby, R. C., jt. auth. see Irwin, H. S.

Barneby, R. C., jt. auth. see Krukoff, B. A.

Barneby, Rupert C. Atlas of North American Astragalus, 2 vols. (Memoirs of the New York Botanical Garden Ser.: Vol. 13). 1964. Set. 40.00x (ISBN 0-89327-225-6); Set. pap. 35.00x (ISBN 0-89327-224-8). Vol. 1 (ISBN 0-89327-226-4). Vol. 2 (ISBN 0-89327-227-2). NY Botanical.

--Daleae Imagines. LC 66-6394. (Memoirs of the New Botanical Garden Ser.: Vol. 27). 1977. pap. 50.00x (ISBN 0-89327-002-4). NY Botanical.

Barneby, Rupert C., jt. auth. see Irwin, Howard S.

Barnefield, George, jt. auth. see Carpenter, Edward.

Barner, R. D., jt. auth. see Merchant, I. A.

Barner, Ralph D., jt. auth. see Merchant, I. A.

Barner, Wilfried & Reh, Albert M., eds. Nation und Gelehrtenrepublik: Lessing im Europaischen Zusammenhang. (Lessing Yearbook Supplement Ser.). 364p. (Orig.). 1985. pap. 30.00 (ISBN 0-8143-1793-6). Wayne St U Pr.

Barner-Barry, Carol & Rosenwein, Robert. Psychological Perspectives: Politics. (Illus.). 352p. 1985. pap. text ed. 18.95 (ISBN 0-13-732298-4). P-H.

Barner-Barry, Carol, jt. auth. see Barry, Donald.

Barnes. Applications of Plasma Emission Spectrochemistry. 160p. 1979. 45.95 (ISBN 0-471-25595-5, Pub. by Wiley Heyden). Wiley.

--Developments in Plasma Emission Spectrochemistry. write for info. (ISBN 0-85501-621-3). Wiley.

--Programming in Ada. 300p. (Orig.). 1983. pap. 21.95 (ISBN 0-201-13799-2). Addison-Wesley.

--Surgical Pathology of the Head & Neck, 2 vols. 1032p. 1985. Vol. 1. 125.00; Vol. 2. 125.00; Set. 250.00. Dekker.

Barnes, jt. auth. see Nivens.

Barnes see Baum, H. & Gergely, J.

Barnes, jt. ed. see Bua.

Barnes, A. C., tr. see Sheng-Tao, Yeh.

Barnes, A. C., tr. see Tsao, Yu.

Barnes, A. C., tr. see Zhou Erfu.

Barnes, A. D., jt. auth. see Clarke, D. B.

Barnes, A. J., et al, eds. Molecular Liquids: Dynamics & Interactions. 1984. lib. bdg. 79.50 (ISBN 90-277-1817-2, Pub. by Reidel Holland). Kluwer Academic.

Barnes, Al. Vinegar Pie & Other Tales of the Grand Traverse Region. LC 58-12684. (Illus.). 184p. 1984. 14.50 (ISBN 0-915937-00-X). Hor Bks MI.

Barnes, Albert. Acts & Romans. 18.95 (ISBN 0-8010-0844-1). Baker Bk.

--The Atonement. LC 80-65582. 1980. pap. 6.95 (ISBN 0-87123-016-X, 210016). Bethany Hse.

--Barnes' Notes on the New Testament. LC 62-8727. 1966. 34.95 (ISBN 0-8254-2200-0). Kregel.

--Barnes' Notes on the Old & New Testaments, 14 vols. 249.50 (ISBN 0-8010-0834-4). Baker Bk.

--Church & Slavery. LC 71-98714. Repr. of 1857 ed. 17.50 (ISBN 0-8371-2771-8, BAC&, Pub. by Negro U Pr). Greenwood.

--Church & Slavery. LC 79-82416. 15.00x (ISBN 0-403-00150-1). Scholarly.

--Daniel. 16.95 (ISBN 0-8010-0841-7). Baker Bk.

--Daniel II. 10.95 (ISBN 0-8010-0504-3). Baker Bk.

--Ephesians-Philemon. 15.95 (ISBN 0-8010-0847-6). Baker Bk.

--Exodus-Esther. 24.95 (ISBN 0-8010-0836-0). Baker Bk.

--First Corinthians, Galatians. 18.95 (ISBN 0-8010-0846-8). Baker Bk.

--Genesis. 13.95 (ISBN 0-8010-0835-2). Baker Bk.

--The Gospels. 19.95 (ISBN 0-8010-0843-3). Baker Bk.

--Hebrews-Jude. 18.95 (ISBN 0-8010-0848-4). Baker Bk.

--Inquiry into Scriptural Views of Slavery. LC 75-92415. 1855. 23.00x (ISBN 0-403-00151-X). Scholarly.

--Inquiry into the Scriptural Views of Slavery. LC 68-58048. Repr. of 1857 ed. 25.00x (ISBN 0-8371-0893-4, BAV&, Pub. by Negro U Pr). Greenwood.

--Isaiah. 23.95 (ISBN 0-8010-0840-9). Baker Bk.

--Job. 18.95 (ISBN 0-8010-0837-9). Baker Bk.

--Minor Prophets. 23.95 (ISBN 0-8010-0842-5). Baker Bk.

--Portland Celebration: Three Hundred Fiftieth. (Illus.). 247p. 1984. pap. 19.95 (ISBN 0-930096-58-4). G gannett.

--Proverbs-Ezekiel. 10.95 (ISBN 0-8010-0839-5). Baker Bk.

--Revelation. 12.95 (ISBN 0-8010-0849-2). Baker Bk.

Barnes, Alfred T., ed. Interactive Cable TV Handbook. 4th ed. (Illus.). 360p. 1984. pap. text ed. 97.00 (ISBN 0-934960-16-X). Phillips Pub Inc.

--The Nineteen Eighty-Five Directory. 7th ed. (Illus.). 948p. 1985. pap. 197.00 (ISBN 0-934960-25-9). Phillips Pub Inc.

Barnes, Allan C. & Seeds, A. Elmore. The Water Metabolism of the Fetus. (Illus.). 184p. 1972. photocopy ed. 18.75x (ISBN 0-398-02224-0). C C Thomas.

Barnes, Allan C., ed. The Social Responsibility of Gynecology & Obstetrics. LC 65-24793. (Illus.). pap. 56.00 (ISBN 0-317-07931-X, 2015431). Bks Demand UMI.

Barnes, Ann, jt. ed. see Berkeley, A. E.

Barnes, Annie S. The Black Middle Class Family: A Study of Black Subsociety, Neighborhood & Home in Interaction. 215p. (Orig.). 1985. pap. 15.95 (ISBN 0-932269-50-8). Wyndham Hall.

Barnes, Arthur S. Christianity at Rome in the Apostolic Age. LC 72-114462. (Illus.). 1971. Repr. of 1938 ed. lib. bdg. 15.00 (ISBN 0-8371-4760-3, BACR). Greenwood.

Barnes, Asa & Nelson, Ilene F., eds. Safe Transfusion. (Illus.). 104p. 1981. 15.20 (ISBN 0-914404-68-7). Am Assn Blood.

Barnes, Asa, Jr., jt. ed. see Judd, W. John.

Barnes, Austin, et al, eds. Matrix Isolation Spectroscopy. x, 606p. 1981. 69.50 (ISBN 90-277-1328-6, Pub. by Reidel Holland). Kluwer Academic.

Barnes, B. A. & Murphy, G. J. Riesz & Fredholm Theory in Banach Algebras. (Research Notes in Mathematics Ser.: No. 67). 300p. 1982. pap. text ed. 19.95 (ISBN 0-273-08563-8). Pitman Pub MA.

Barnes, B. A., jt. auth. see Csaky, T. Z.

Barnes, B. H., jt. ed. see Metzner, John R.

Barnes, B. J., jt. ed. see Hill, Shirley.

Barnes, Barnabe. Devil's Charter. LC 71-133638. (Tudor Facsimile Texts. Old English Plays: No. 121). Repr. of 1913 ed. 49.50 (ISBN 0-404-53421-X). AMS Pr.

--The Devil's Charter (1607) Pogue, Jim C. & Orgel, Stephen, eds. LC 79-54358. (Renaissance Drama Second Ser.). 225p. 1980. lib. bdg. 31.00 (ISBN 0-8240-4474-6). Garland Pub.

--The Devil's Charter, 1607. McKerrow, R. B., ed. (Material for the Study of the Old English Drama Ser.: No. 1, Vol. 6). pap. 16.00 (ISBN 0-317-16733-2). Kraus Repr.

--Foure Bookes of Offices: Enabling Privat Persons for the Service of All Good Princes & Policies. LC 74-28830. (English Experience Ser.: No. 712). 1975. Repr. of 1606 ed. 24.00 (ISBN 9-0221-0712-4). Walter J Johnson.

Barnes, Barry. About Science. 208p. 1985. 24.95x (ISBN 0-631-14157-X); pap. 8.95 (ISBN 0-631-14158-8). Basil Blackwell.

--Interests & the Growth of Knowledge. (Direct Editions Ser.). (Orig.). 1977. pap. 11.95x (ISBN 0-7100-8669-5). Routledge & Kegan.

--Scientific Knowledge & Sociological Theory. (Monographs in Social Theory). 204p. 1974. pap. 9.95X (ISBN 0-7100-7962-1). Routledge & Kegan.

--T. S. Kuhn & Social Science. 192p. 1982. 24.00x (ISBN 0-231-05436-X); pap. 16.50x (ISBN 0-231-05437-8). Columbia U Pr.

Barnes, Barry & Edge, David, eds. Science in Context: Readings in the Sociology of Science. 384p. (Orig.). 1982. pap. text ed. 10.95x (ISBN 0-262-52076-1). MIT Pr.

Barnes, Barry & Shapin, Steven, eds. Natural Order: Historical Studies of Scientific Culture. LC 78-19650. (Sage Focus Editions: Vol. 6). 255p. 1979. 24.00 (ISBN 0-8039-0958-6). Sage.

Barnes, Ben E., jt. auth. see Gay, Kathlyn.

Barnes, Bernard. Man & the Changing Landscape. (Work Notes Ser.: No. 3). (Illus.). 144p. pap. text ed. 14.00x (ISBN 0-906367-12-3, Merseyside County Mus of Liverpool England). Smithsonian.

Barnes, Beverly C. & Coplon, Jennifer. The Single Parent Experience: A Time For Growth. LC 80-5953. 168p. 1980. 14.95 (ISBN 0-86618-002-8). Family Serv.

Barnes, Bill. Building Outdoor Playthings for Kids, with Project Plans. (Illus.). 240p. (Orig.). 1985. 21.95 (ISBN 0-8306-0971-7, 1971); pap. 12.95 (ISBN 0-8306-1971-2). TAB Bks.

Barnes, Bill, et al. The New A to Z on Fuchsias. (Illus.). 1976. 11.95 (ISBN 0-686-19065-3); pap. 9.95. Natl Fuchsia.

Barnes, Bonnie M. & Clarke, Tisha. How to Get a Man to Make a Commitment: Or Know When He Never Will. 160p. 1985. 12.95 (ISBN 0-312-39558-2). St Martin.

Barnes, Brian. Time & Chance. 336p. (Orig.). 1982. pap. 3.25 (ISBN 0-505-51815-5, Pub. by Tower Bks). Dorchester Pub Co.

Barnes, Broda. Hope for Hypoglycemia. 4.00x (ISBN 0-686-29861-6). Cancer Control Soc.

--Hope for Hypoglycemia. 1978. 5.95 (ISBN 0-913730-25-4). Robinson Pr.

--Hope for Hypoglycemia. 57p. 4.00 (ISBN 0-318-15667-9). Natl Health Fed.

--Hypothroidism: Unsuspected Illness. 13.95x (ISBN 0-690-01029-X). Cancer Control Soc.

--Solved: Riddle-Heart Attacks. 4.00x (ISBN 0-686-29860-8). Cancer Control Soc.

--Solved: The Riddle of Heart Attacks. 1976. 5.95 (ISBN 0-913730-27-0). Robinson Pr.

Barnes, Broda & Galton, Lawrence. Hypothyroidism: The Unsuspected Illness. LC 75-29251. 224p. 1976. 14.37 (ISBN 0-690-01029-X). T Y Crowell.

Barnes, Broda O. & Barnes, Charlotte W. Heart Attack Rareness in Thyroid-Treated Patients. 104p. 1972. 12.75x (ISBN 0-398-02519-3). C C Thomas.

Barnes, Bruce. Introduction to Islam. (Illus.). 192p. (Orig.). 1984. pap. text ed. 7.00 (ISBN 0-913811-01-7). Northeast A S.

--Middle East Perspective. (Illus.). 224p. (Orig.). 1983. pap. text ed. 7.00 (ISBN 0-913811-00-9). Northeast A S.

Barnes, Burton V. & Wagner, Warren H., Jr. Michigan Trees: A Guide to the Trees of Michigan & the Great Lakes. (Biological Science). (Illus.). 384p. 1981. text ed. 15.00x (ISBN 0-472-08017-2); pap. text ed. 8.95x (ISBN 0-472-08018-0). U of Mich Pr.

Barnes, Burton V., jt. auth. see Spurr, Stephen H.

Barnes, C. D. & Eltherington, L. G. Drug Dosage in Laboratory Animals: A Handbook. 2nd rev. & enl. ed. LC 64-21066. 1973. 42.50x (ISBN 0-520-02273-4). U of Cal Pr.

Barnes, C. D., jt. ed. see Orem, J.

Barnes, C. G., jt. ed. see Lehner, T.

Barnes, C. L. Dante: His Life & Works. 1973. Repr. of 1922 ed. 8.50 (ISBN 0-8274-1680-6). R West.

--Parallels in Dante & Milton. LC 74-3180. 1917. lib. bdg. 9.50 (ISBN 0-8414-9926-8). Folcroft.

--Parallels in Dante & Milton. 1979. 24.50 (ISBN 0-685-67812-1). Porter.

Barnes, C. W. Earth, Time & Life: An Introduction to Geology. 583p. 1980. 35.50 (ISBN 0-471-05616-2). Wiley.

--Handley Page Aircraft since 1907. (Putnam Aeronautical Books). (Illus.). 666p. 1979. 31.95 (ISBN 0-370-00030-7, Pub. by the Bodley Head). Merrimack Pub Cir.

Barnes, Caren M., jt. auth. see Armstrong, Thomas H.

Barnes, Carl F., Jr. Villard de Honnecourt-The Artist & His Drawings: A Critical Bibliography. 1982. lib. bdg. 30.50 (ISBN 0-8161-8481-X, Hall Reference). G K Hall.

Barnes, Carol P., jt. auth. see Ellner, Carolyn L.

Barnes, Caroline. The Star Wars Book about Flight. LC 82-20423. (Illus.). 32p. (gr. 3-8). 1983. pap. 1.25 (ISBN 0-394-85689-9). Random.

Barnes, Catherine. Men of the Supreme Court: Profiles of the Justices. 236p. 1978. lib. bdg. 22.50x (ISBN 0-87196-459-7). Facts on File.

Barnes, Catherine A. Journey from Jim Crow: The Desegregation of Southern Transit. LC 83-7566. (Contemporary American History Ser.). 320p. 1983. 30.00x (ISBN 0-231-05380-0). Columbia U Pr.

Barnes, Charles & Blake, David. One Hundred Twenty Needlepoint Design Projects. (Arts & Crafts Ser.). (Illus.). (YA) 1974. pap. 2.98 (ISBN 0-517-51473-7). Crown.

Barnes, Charles & Blake, David P. Creative Macrame Projects. LC 76-8115. (Illus.). 256p. 1976. pap. 4.95 (ISBN 0-486-23370-7). Dover.

--Creative Macrame Projects. 1983. 11.75 (ISBN 0-8446-6022-1). Peter Smith.

Barnes, Charles see Crass, Maurice, 3rd.

Barnes, Charles A., et al, eds. Essays in Nuclear Astrophysics. LC 81-9992. 555p. 1982. 85.00 (ISBN 0-521-24410-2); pap. 34.50 (ISBN 0-521-28876-2). Cambridge U Pr.

Barnes, Charles B. The Longshoremen. Stein, Leon, ed. LC 77-70482. (Work Ser.). (Illus.). 1977. Repr. of 1915 ed. lib. bdg. 32.00x (ISBN 0-405-10156-2). Ayer Co Pubs.

Barnes, Charles D., ed. Brain Stem Control of Spinal Cord Function. LC 83-11800. (Research Topics in Physiology Ser.). 1984. 55.00 (ISBN 0-12-079040-8). Acad Pr.

Barnes, Charles D., jt. ed. see Davies, Donald G.

Barnes, Charles D., jt. ed. see Hughes, Maysie J.

Barnes, Charles D., jt. ed. see McGrath, James J.

Barnes, Charlotte W., jt. auth. see Barnes, Broda O.

Barnes, Chester. Table Tennis. 1977. text ed. 5.95 (ISBN 0-8120-5149-1). Barron.

Barnes, Chris. Chris Baines Wildlife Garden Notebook. (Illus.). 64p. 4.95 (ISBN 0-946609-17-9, P117). Haynes Pubns.

Barnes, Christopher J., ed. Studies in Twentieth-Century Russian Literature. LC 75-40543. 91p. 1976. text ed. 23.50x (ISBN 0-06-490316-8, 06340). B&N Imports.

--Studies in Twentieth Century Russian Literature. LC 75-40543. 91p. 1976. 20.00 (ISBN 0-317-07250-1, BNB 06340). B&N Imports.

Barnes, Clive. Inside American Ballet Theatre. (Quality Paperbacks Ser.). (Illus.). 192p. 1983. pap. 11.95 (ISBN 0-306-80192-2). Da Capo.

--Nureyev. (Illus.). 272p. 1982. 35.00 (ISBN 0-9609736-2-1, Dist. by Aux. to Bellevue Hos. Ctr. Inc. NY NY). Helene Obolensky Ent.

Barnes, Clive, ed. Best American Plays. (The John Gossner Best Plays Ser.: Eighth Ser. 1974-1982). 512p. 1983. 19.95 (ISBN 0-517-54480-6). Crown.

--Best American Plays: Seventh Series. LC 57-12830. 640p. 1975. 19.95 (ISBN 0-517-51387-0). Crown.

Barnes, Clive, jt. ed. see Gassner, John.

Barnes, Cyril G. Medical Disorders in Obstetric Practice. 4th ed. (Illus.). 1974. text ed. 42.50 (ISBN 0-8016-0518-0, Blackwell). Mosby.

Barnes, D. & Bliss, P. Biological Control of Nitrogen in Wastewater Treatment. 150p. 1983. 35.00 (ISBN 0-419-12350-4, NO. 6765, E & FN Spon). Methuen Inc.

Barnes, D. & Wilson, F. Chemistry & Unit Operations in Sewage Treatment. (Illus.). 339p. 1978. 48.00 (ISBN 0-85334-783-2, Pub. by Elsevier Applied Sci England). Elsevier.

--Chemistry & Unit Operations in Water Treatment. (Illus.). 325p. 1983. 61.00 (ISBN 0-85334-169-9, I-463-82, Pub. by Elsevier Applied Sci England). Elsevier.

--The Design & Operation of Small Sewage Works. 180p. 1976. 29.95x (ISBN 0-419-10980-3, NO.6024, Pub. by E & FN Spon England). Methuen Inc.

Barnes, D., et al. Water & Wastewater Engineering Systems. (Water Resources Engineering Ser.). 416p. 1981. text ed. 39.95 (ISBN 0-273-01138-3). Pitman Pub MA.

Barnes, D., et al, eds. Surveys in Industrial Wastewater Treatment, 2 vols. (Water Resources Engineering Ser.). 700p. 1984. Vol. 1. 64.95 (ISBN 0-273-08586-7); Vol. 2. 44.95 (ISBN 0-273-08588-3). Pitman Pub MA.

Barnes, D. M. Edgar Allan Poe: Centenary. 1977. 16.50 (ISBN 0-685-81587-0). Porter.

Barnes, D. W. & Mack, J. M. An Algebraic Introduction to Mathematical Logic. LC 74-22241. (Graduate Texts in Mathematics Ser.: Vol. 22). (Illus.). 230p. 1975. 21.00 (ISBN 0-387-90109-4). Springer-Verlag.

Barnes, David, photos by. Seattle. LC 80-60. (Illus.). 80p. 1980. pap. 12.95 (ISBN 0-914718-50-9). Pacific Search.

Barnes, David H., jt. auth. see Morrison, Clinton D.

Barnes, David W. Statistical Evidence in American Courts. write for info. Little.

--Statistics As Proof: Fundamentals of Quantitative Evidence. 464p. 1983. 15.00 (ISBN 0-316-08149-3). Little.

Barnes, David W., et al. Methods for Preparation of Media Supplements, & Substrata for Serum-Free Animal Cell Culture. LC 84-7203. (Cell Culture Methods for Molecular & Cell Biology Ser.: Vol. 1). 378p. 1984. 49.50 (ISBN 0-8451-3800-6). A R Liss.

--Methods for Serum-Free Culture of Cells of the Endocrine System. LC 84-7202. (Cell Culture Methods for Molecular & Cell Biology Ser.: Vol. 2). 272p. 1984. 39.00 (ISBN 0-8451-3801-4). A R Liss.

--Methods for Serum-Free Culture of Neuronal & Lymphoid Cells. LC 84-7204. (Cell Culture Methods for Molecular & Cell Biology Ser.: Vol. 4). 280p. 1984. 39.50 (ISBN 0-8451-3803-0). A R Liss.

Barnes, Demas. From the Atlantic to the Pacific Overland. LC 72-9426. (The Far Western Frontier Ser.). (Illus.). 142p. 1973. Repr. of 1866 ed. 19.00 (ISBN 0-405-04957-9). Ayer Co Pubs.

Barnes, Derek. An Anthology of Animal Poetry of the Last Fifty Years. 1946. 22.50 (ISBN 0-89984-032-9). Century Bookbindery.

Barnes, Derek G. Lords of Life: An Anthology of Animal Poetry of the Last Fifty Years. (Illus.). 1979. Repr. of 1946 ed. write for info (ISBN 0-8495-0528-3). Arden Lib.

--Lords of Life: An Anthology of Animal Poetry of the Last Fifty Years. 1977. Repr. of 1946 ed. 22.50 (ISBN 0-89984-153-8). Century Bookbindery.

Barnes, Derek G., ed. Lords of Life: An Anthology of Animal Poetry of the Last Fifty Years. 1977. Repr. of 1946 ed. lib. bdg. 20.00 (ISBN 0-8495-0321-3). Arden Lib.

Barnes, Djuna. Greenwich Village As It Is. Wilson, Robert A., ed. (Illus.). 1978. 20.00 (ISBN 0-916228-08-8). Phoenix Bk Shop.

--Interviews. Barry, Alyce, ed. (Illus.). 400p. 1985. 16.95 (ISBN 0-940650-36-3); pap. 10.95 (ISBN 0-940650-37-1). Sun & Moon MD.

--Nightwood. LC 49-1384. 1946. pap. 5.25 (ISBN 0-8112-0005-1, NDP98); 14.00 (ISBN 0-8112-0927-X). New Directions.

--Ryder. 352p. 1980. pap. 5.95 (ISBN 0-312-69641-8). St Martin.

--Selected Works of Djuna Barnes. 366p. 1962. 12.95 (ISBN 0-374-25936-4). FS&G.

--Smoke & Other Early Stories. Messerli, Douglas, ed. LC 82-10627. (Illus.). 184p. 1982. 12.95 (ISBN 0-940650-17-7); pap. 8.00 (ISBN 0-940650-12-6). Sun & Moon MD.

Barnes, Djuna, et al see Andre, Michael.

Barnes, Don. Democratic Classrooms: Theory & Behavior. pap. 4.95x (ISBN 0-89741-002-5). Roadrunner Tech.

Barnes, Donald G. George Third & William Pitt, 1783-1806. 1965. lib. bdg. 37.50x (ISBN 0-374-90399-9). Octagon.

--History of the English Corn Laws from 1660-1846. LC 65-24375. 1930. 32.50x (ISBN 0-678-00103-0). Kelley.

Barnes, Donald L. & Burgdorf, Arlene. Study Skills for Information Retrieval, Bk. 1. (gr. 4-8). 1979. pap. text ed. 6.16 (ISBN 0-205-06436-1, 4964365); tchrs'. ed. 7.44 (ISBN 0-205-06440-X, 4964403). Allyn.

--Study Skills for Information Retrieval, Bk. 2. (gr. 4-8). 1979. pap. text ed. 6.16 (ISBN 0-205-06437-X, 4964373); tchrs'. ed. 7.44 (ISBN 0-205-06441-8, 4964411). Allyn.

--Study Skills for Information Retrieval, Bk. 3. (gr. 4-8). 1979. pap. text ed. 6.16 (ISBN 0-205-06438-8, 496438-1); tchrs'. ed. 7.44 (ISBN 0-205-06442-6, 496442-X). Allyn.

Barnes, Donna A. Farmers in Rebellion: The Rise & Fall of the Southern Farmers Alliance & People's Party in Texas. 238p. 1984. text ed. 19.95x (ISBN 0-292-77030-8). U of Tex Pr.

Barnes, Donna M. Songs of the Sand Dunes. 1984. 6.75 (ISBN 0-8062-2168-2). Carlton.

Barnes, Dora M. Edgar Allan Poe. 1978. Repr. of 1949 ed. lib. bdg. 10.00 (ISBN 0-8492-3719-X). R West.

--Edgar Allan Poe: Centenary Commemoration. LC 72-13509. 1974. Repr. of 1949 ed. lib. bdg. 15.00 (ISBN 0-8414-1193-X). Folcroft.

Barnes, Dorothy & Barnes, Douglas. Versions of English. 448p. 1984. text ed. 30.00x (ISBN 0-435-10170-6). Heinemann Ed.

Barnes, Dorothy L. Rape: A Bibliography 1965-1975. LC 77-89641. 1977. 15.00x (ISBN 0-87875-120-3). Whitston Pub.

Barnes, Dorothy L., jt. auth. see Stephens, Irving E.

Barnes, Dorothy L., jt. ed. see Stephens, Irving E.

Barnes, Douglas. From Communication to Curriculum. 208p. (Orig.). 1976. pap. text ed. 6.00x (ISBN 0-14-080382-3). Boynton Cook Pub.

--Practical Curriculum Study. (Rutledge Education Bks.). 160p. 1983. pap. 19.95x (ISBN 0-7100-0979-8). Routledge & Kegan.

Barnes, Douglas & Britton, James. Language, the Learner & the School. 176p. (Orig.). 1969. pap. 7.00x (ISBN 0-14-080094-8). Boynton Cook Pubs.

Barnes, Douglas, jt. auth. see Barnes, Dorothy.

Barnes, Duncan. History of Winchester Firearms, 1866-1980. 5th, rev. ed. LC 85-50225. (Illus.). 256p. 1985. 16.95 (ISBN 0-8329-0397-3, Pub. by Winchester Pr). New Century.

Barnes, Duncan & American Kennel Club Staff. The AKC'S World of the Pure-Bred Dog. LC 83-6117. (Illus.). 352p. 1983. 15.00 (ISBN 0-87605-406-8). Howell Bk.

Barnes, E. B., jt. ed. see Dougherty, David M.

Barnes, E. G. Rise of the Midland Railway 1844-1874. LC 76-83157. (Illus.). 1969. 24.95x (ISBN 0-678-06000-2). Kelley.

Barnes, Ellen, et al. What's the Difference? 1978. 6.00 (ISBN 0-937540-08-0, HPP-11). Human Policy Pr.

Barnes, Emilie. Emilie's Household Hints. LC 83-82317. 160p. 1984. pap. 4.95 (ISBN 0-89081-391-4). Harvest Hse.

--More Hours in My Day. (Orig.). 1982. pap. 4.95 (ISBN 0-89081-355-8). Harvest Hse.

Barnes, Ernest W. Scientific Theory & Religion. LC 77-27198. (Gifford Lectures: 1927-29). Repr. of 1933 ed. 42.50 (ISBN 0-404-60483-8). AMS Pr.

Barnes, Ervin H. Atlas & Manual of Plant Pathology. 2nd ed. LC 79-10575. 343p. 1979. 24.50x (ISBN 0-306-40168-1, Plenum Pr). Plenum Pub.

Barnes, Eugene B., jt. ed. see Dougherty, David M.

Barnes, F. A. Canyon Country. LC 85-80605. (Illus.). 112p. (Orig.). 1985. pap. 14.95 cancelled (ISBN 0-934318-60-3). Falcon Pr MT.

--Canyon Country Camping. new ed. LC 77-95041. (Illus.). 1978. pap. 2.50 (ISBN 0-915272-16-4). Wasatch Pubs.

--Canyon Country Exploring. new ed. (Canyon Country Ser.). (Illus.). 1978. pap. 1.95 (ISBN 0-915272-12-1). Wasatch Pubs.

--Canyon Country Geology for the Layman & Rockhound. new ed. LC 77-95050. (Illus.). 1978. pap. 4.50 (ISBN 0-915272-17-2). Wasatch Pubs.

--Canyon Country Off-Road Vehicle Trails: Arches & la Sals Areas. new ed. LC 77-95043. (Canyon Country Ser.). (Illus.). 1978. pap. 2.50 (ISBN 0-915272-13-X). Wasatch Pubs.

--Canyon Country Off-Road Vehicle Trails: Canyon Rims & Needles Areas. LC 77-95043. (Canyon Country Ser.). (Illus.). 1978. pap. 2.50 (ISBN 0-915272-14-8). Wasatch Pubs.

--Canyon Country Off-Road Vehicle Trails: Island Area. new ed. LC 77-95043. (Canyon Country Ser.). (Illus.). 1978. pap. 2.50 (ISBN 0-915272-15-6). Wasatch Pubs.

--Canyon Country Prehistoric Rock Art. LC 82-60129. (Canyon Country Ser.). (Illus.). 304p. 1982. pap. 7.50 (ISBN 0-915272-25-3). Wasatch Pubs.

Barnes, F. A., jt. auth. see Pendleton, Michalene.

Barnes, F. L. Canyon Country Hiking & Natural History. LC 76-58119. (Canyon Country Ser.). (Illus.). 1977. pap. 4.50 (ISBN 0-915272-07-5). Wasatch Pubs.

Barnes, Florence E., ed. Ambulatory Maternal Health Care & Family Planning Services: Policies, Principles, Practices. LC 78-9724. 276p. 1978. 12.00 (ISBN 0-87553-089-3, 033); pap. 8.00x (ISBN 0-87553-085-0, 029). Am Pub Health.

Barnes, Frank C. Cartridges of the World. 5th ed. (Illus.). 416p. 1985. pap. 15.95 (ISBN 0-910676-95-X). DBI.

Barnes, Fred L. Division of Plymouth Proposed in 1855 & 1856. (Pilgrim Society Notes Ser.: No. 11). 1962. 1.00 (ISBN 0-940628-12-0). Pilgrim Hall.

Barnes, George W. How to Make Bamboo Fly Rods. LC 77-6738. 1977. 14.95 (ISBN 0-8329-2374-5, Pub. by Winchester Pr). New Century.

Barnes, Gilbert H. & Dumond, Dwight L., eds. Letters of Theodore Dwight Weld, Angelina Grimke Weld & Sarah Grimke, 1822-1844, 2 vols. 1934. Set. 32.00 (ISBN 0-8446-1055-0). Peter Smith.

--Letters of Theodore Dwight Weld, Angelina Grimke Weld, & Sarah Grimke. LC 77-121103. (American Public Figures Ser). 1970. Repr. of 1934 ed. lib. bdg. 95.00 (ISBN 0-306-71981-9). Da Capo.

Barnes, Gina, tr. see Miki, Fumio.

Barnes, Grace M., compiled by. Alcohol & Youth: A Comprehensive Bibliography. LC 82-15397. xvi, 432p. 1982. lib. bdg. 45.00 (ISBN 0-313-23136-2, BAY/). Greenwood.

Barnes, Grace M., et al. Alcohol & the Elderly: A Comprehensive Bibliography. LC 80-1786. xvii, 138p. 1980. lib. bdg. 29.95 (ISBN 0-313-22132-4, BAE/). Greenwood.

Barnes, Gregory. Crisscross: Structured Writing in Context. (Illus.). 208p. 1981. pap. text ed. 12.95 (ISBN 0-13-193920-3). P-H.

Barnes, Gregory A. The American University: A World Guide. (Illus.). 196p. 1984. 21.95 (ISBN 0-89495-030-4); pap. 14.95 (ISBN 0-89495-031-2). ISI Pr.

--Communication Skills for the Foreign-Born Professional. (Professional Writing Ser.). (Illus.). 198p. 1982. 18.95 (ISBN 0-89495-013-4); pap. 13.95 (ISBN 0-89495-014-2). ISI Pr.

Barnes, H. Oceanography & Marine Biology. 1959. 10.75 (ISBN 0-08-026258-9). Pergamon.

Barnes, H. L., ed. Geochemistry of Hydrothermal Ore Deposits. 2nd ed. LC 79-354. 798p. 1979. 42.50x (ISBN 0-471-05056-3, Pub. by Wiley-Interscience). Wiley.

Barnes, H. Verdain, jt. auth. see Spivak, Jerry L.

Barnes, Harold, ed. Oceanography & Marine Biology: An Annual Review, Vol. 15. 1977. 75.00 (ISBN 0-900015-39-X). Taylor-Carlisle.

--Oceanography & Marine Biology: An Annual Review, Vol. 16. 1978. 80.00 (ISBN 0-900015-44-6). Taylor-Carlisle.

--Oceanography & Marine Biology: Annual Review, Vol. 14. 1976. 75.00 (ISBN 0-900015-37-3). Taylor-Carlisle.

--Proceedings of the Ninth European Marine Biology Symposium, Oban, 1974. 1976. 65.00x (ISBN 0-900015-34-9). Taylor-Carlisle.

Barnes, Harold, jt. ed. see Barnes, Margaret.

Barnes, Harry E. American Way of Life: An Introduction to the Study of Contemporary Society. 2nd ed. LC 72-138200. (Illus.). 1971. Repr. of 1950 ed. lib. bdg. 43.00x (ISBN 0-8371-5553-3, BAAW). Greenwood.

--The Barnes Trilogy. 140p. 1980. pap. 4.00 (ISBN 0-911038-56-6). Inst Hist Rev.

--The Barnes Trilogy. Brandon, Lewis, ed. 1980. pap. 4.00 (ISBN 0-911038-56-6, 336, Inst Hist Rev). Noontide.

--The Barnes Trilogy: Blasting the Historical Blackout, The Court Historians Versus Revisionism, Revisionism & Brainwashing. Brandon, Lewis, ed. 1981. lib. bdg. 79.95 (ISBN 0-686-73177-8). Revisionist Pr.

--Blasting the Historical Blackout. 59.95 (ISBN 0-87700-027-1). Revisionist Pr.

--Can Man Be Civilized? 69.95 (ISBN 0-87700-028-X). Revisionist Pr.

--The Chickens of the Interventionist Liberals Have Come to Roost. 59.95 (ISBN 0-87700-194-4). Revisionist Pr.

--The Court Historians Versus Revisionism. 59.95 (ISBN 0-87700-193-6). Revisionist Pr.

--Crucifying the Savior of France: Petain. 59.95 (ISBN 0-87700-281-9). Revisionist Pr.

--Economic History of Europe. 75.00 (ISBN 0-87700-243-6). Revisionist Pr.

--An Economic History of the Western World. 125.00 (ISBN 0-87700-026-3). Revisionist Pr.

--An Economic History of the Western World. 790p. Date not set. lib. bdg. 50.00 (ISBN 0-8495-0619-0). Arden Lib.

--Evolution of Penology in Pennsylvania, a Study in American Social History. LC 68-55768. (Criminology, Law Enforcement, & Social Problems Ser.: No. 21). (Illus.). 1968. Repr. of 1927 ed. 20.00x (ISBN 0-87585-021-9). Patterson Smith.

--Genesis of the World War, & Introduction to the Problem of War Guilt. 1968. 79.00 (ISBN 0-403-00140-4). Scholarly.

--Historical Sociology: It's Origin & Developments. Winks, Robin W., ed. (History & Historiography Ser.). 20.00 (ISBN 0-8240-6350-3). Garland Pub.

--History & Prospects of the Social Sciences. 75.00 (ISBN 0-87700-029-8). Revisionist Pr.

--History & Social Intelligence. 75.00 (ISBN 0-87700-030-1). Revisionist Pr.

--History of Historical Writing. 2nd ed. 1962. pap. 7.50 (ISBN 0-486-20104-X). Dover.

--A History of the Penal, Reformatory, & Correctional Institutions of the State of New Jersey: Analytical & Documentary. facsimile ed. LC 74-3817. (Criminal Justice in America Ser.). (Illus.). 1974. Repr. of 1918 ed. 49.50x (ISBN 0-405-06137-4). Ayer Co Pubs.

--In Quest of Truth & Justice: De-Bunking the War Guilt Myth. LC 79-172204. (Right Wing Individualist Tradition in America Ser). 1972. Repr. of 1928 ed. 27.00 (ISBN 0-405-00414-1). Ayer Co Pubs.

--In Quest of Truth & Justice: Debunking the War Guilt Myth. LC 72-78407. 1972. 17.50 (ISBN 0-87926-011-4); pap. 2.95 (ISBN 0-87926-012-2). R Myles.

--The Making of a Nation. 69.95 (ISBN 0-87700-032-8). Revisionist Pr.

--The New History & the Social Studies. (The Harry Elmer Barnes Ser). (Illus.). 624p. 1972. Repr. of 1925 ed. lib. bdg. 79.95 (ISBN 0-87700-033-6). Revisionist Pr.

--Pearl Harbor After a Quarter Century. 134p. 1980. pap. 6.00 (ISBN 0-911038-95-7). Inst Hist Rev.

--Pearl Harbor After a Quarter of a Century. LC 75-172203. (Right Wing Individualist Tradition in America Ser). 1972. Repr. of 1968 ed. 17.00 (ISBN 0-405-00413-3). Ayer Co Pubs.

--Pearl Harbor After a Quarter of a Century. 1981. lib. bdg. 59.95 (ISBN 0-686-73185-9). Revisionist Pr.

--Perpetual War for Perpetual Peace. rev. & enl. ed. 1982. lib. bdg. 79.95 (ISBN 0-87700-454-4). Revisionist Pr.

--Psychology & History. 59.95 (ISBN 0-87700-034-4). Revisionist Pr.

--The Public Stake in Revisionism. 59.95 (ISBN 0-87700-282-7). Revisionist Pr.

--Rauch on Roosevelt. 59.95 (ISBN 0-87700-283-5). Revisionist Pr.

--Repression of Crime, Studies in Historical Penology. LC 69-14911. (Criminology, Law Enforcement, & Social Problems Ser.: No. 56). 1969. Repr. of 1926 ed. 16.00x (ISBN 0-87585-056-1). Patterson Smith.

--Revisionism: A Key to Peace. 59.95 (ISBN 0-87700-192-8). Revisionist Pr.

--Revisionism & Brainwashing. 59.95 (ISBN 0-685-26298-7). Revisionist Pr.

--Revisionism & the Promotion of Peace. 59.95 (ISBN 0-87700-284-3). Revisionist Pr.

--Select Bibliography of Revisionist Books. rev. ed. 59.95 (ISBN 0-685-26300-2). Revisionist Pr.

--Selected Revisionist Pamphlets: An Original Arno Press Compilation. LC 72-172205. (Right Wing Individualist Tradition in America Ser). 1972. Repr. of 1971 ed. 19.00 (ISBN 0-405-00415-X). Ayer Co Pubs.

--Social History of the Western World. 59.95 (ISBN 0-87700-035-2). Revisionist Pr.

--Social Institutions in an Era of World Upheaval. LC 77-6677. 1977. Repr. of 1946 ed. lib. bdg. 39.50x (ISBN 0-8371-9654-X, BASO). Greenwood.

--Society in Transition. 2nd ed. LC 68-23271. 1968. Repr. of 1952 ed. lib. bdg. 39.25x (ISBN 0-8371-0012-7, BAST). Greenwood.

--Sociology & Political Theory. LC 74-185842. 1972. Repr. of 1924 ed. lib. bdg. 69.95 (ISBN 0-87700-036-0). Revisionist Pr.

--Sociology Before Comte. 59.95 (ISBN 0-87700-202-9). Revisionist Pr.

--Story of Punishment: A Record of Man's Inhumanity to Man. 2nd rev. ed. LC 74-108229. (Criminology, Law Enforcement, & Social Problems Ser.: No. 112). (Illus.). 1972. 20.00x (ISBN 0-87585-112-6); pap. 8.50x (ISBN 0-87585-913-5). Patterson Smith.

--The Struggle Against the Historical Blackout. 59.95 (ISBN 0-87700-195-2). Revisionist Pr.

--The Twilight of Christianity. 75.00 (ISBN 0-87700-037-9). Revisionist Pr.

--Was Roosevelt Pushed into War? 59.95 (ISBN 0-87700-285-1). Revisionist Pr.

--Who Started the First World War? 1985. lib. bdg. 79.95 (ISBN 0-87700-651-2). Revisionist Pr.

--World Politics in Modern Civilization, 2 vols. Set. 150.00 (ISBN 0-87700-038-7). Revisionist Pr.

Barnes, Harry E., jt. auth. see Becker, Howard.

Barnes, Harry E., ed. Introduction to the History of Sociology. LC 47-12522. 1948. 30.00x (ISBN 0-226-03723-1). U of Chicago Pr.

--Perpetual War for Perpetual Peace. LC 70-90468. Repr. of 1953 ed. lib. bdg. 26.00 (ISBN 0-8371-2144-2, BAPW). Greenwood.

--Perpetual War for Perpetual Peace. 680p. 1982. pap. 11.00 (ISBN 0-939484-01-3). Inst Hist Rev.

Barnes, Harry E., ed. see Jenks, Leland H.

Barnes, Hazel E. Eixistentialist Ethics. LC 78-55038. xii, 468p. 1985. pap. 16.00 (ISBN 0-226-03729-0). U of Chicago Pr.

--An Existentialist Ethics. LC 78-55038. (Midway Reprint Ser.). 1985. (Phoen); pap. 16.00 (ISBN 0-226-03729-0). U of Chicago Pr.

--Humanistic Existentialism: The Literature of Possibility. LC 59-11732. pap. 107.00 (ISBN 0-317-10295-8, 2022611). Bks Demand UMI.

--The Meddling Gods: Four Essays on Classical Themes. LC 73-92003. x, 141p. 1974. 12.50x (ISBN 0-8032-0838-3). U of Nebr Pr.

--Sartre & Flaubert. LC 80-26872. 416p. 25.00x (ISBN 0-226-03720-7). U of Chicago Pr.

--Sartre & Flaubert. LC 80-26872. x, 450p. 1982. pap. 10.95 (ISBN 0-226-03721-5, PHOEN). U of Chicago Pr.

Barnes, Hazel E., ed. see Schopenhauer, Arthur.

Barnes, Hazel E., tr. see Sartre, Jean-Paul.

Barnes, Henrietta. The Individual & the School. 1975. pap. text ed. 6.95 (ISBN 0-88429-009-3). Collegiate Pub.

Barnes, Homer F. Charles Fenno Hoffman. LC 75-160003. (BCL Ser. I). Repr. of 1930 ed. 26.00 (ISBN 0-404-00656-6). AMS Pr.

Barnes, Howard. Backyard Boatyard. LC 81-81417. (Illus.). 144p. 1982. pap. 10.95 (ISBN 0-87742-144-7). Intl Marine.

Barnes, Howard P. Eel River & Plymouth Beach. (Pilgrim Society Notes Ser.: No. 8). 1958. 1.00 (ISBN 0-940628-13-9). Pilgrim Hall.

Barnes, I. E. Surgical Endodontics. 1984. lib. bdg. 32.00 (ISBN 0-85200-738-8, Pub. by MTP Pr England). Kluwer Academic.

Barnes, Irston R. Public Utility Control in Massachusetts. 1930. 59.50x (ISBN 0-685-89774-5). Elliots Bks.

Barnes, Irston R. & Gude, Gilbert. Landscaping for Birds. Briggs, Shirley A., ed. (Illus.). 54p. 1973. pap. 3.75 (ISBN 0-318-13601-5); pap. 3.00 members (ISBN 0-318-13602-3). Audubon Naturalist.

Barnes, Irwin. Truth Is Immortal: The Story of Baptists in Europe. 127p. 1950. 4.50 (ISBN 0-87921-015-X); pap. 2.50 (ISBN 0-87921-019-2). Attic Pr.

Barnes, J. The Treatyse of Fysshinge with an Angle. (English Dialect Society Publications Ser.: No. 41). pap. 15.00 (ISBN 0-317-15917-8). Kraus Repr.

Barnes, J., tr. see Patzig, G.

Barnes, J. A. Three Styles in the Study of Kinship. LC 74-142057. 1972. 29.50x (ISBN 0-520-01879-6). U of Cal Pr.

--Who Should Know What? LC 79-9656. 232p. 1980. 24.95 (ISBN 0-521-23359-3); pap. 7.95 (ISBN 0-521-29934-9). Cambridge U Pr.

Barnes, J. C. Voluntary Isolation of Control in a Natural Muscle Group. Bd. with Psycho-Motor Norms for Practical Diagnosis. Wallin, J. E. Repr. of 1916 ed; Apparatus & Experiments on Sound Intensity. Weiss, A. P. Repr. of 1916 ed; No. 2. Wellesley College Studies in Psychology. Gamble, E. A., ed. Repr. of 1916 ed; Children's Association Frequency Tables. Woodrow, H. Repr. of 1916 ed. (Psychology Monographs General & Applied: Vol. 22). pap. 29.00 (ISBN 0-317-16768-5). Kraus Repr.

Barnes, J. G. Rtl-2 Design & Philosophy. 176p. 1976. 49.95 (ISBN 0-471-25596-3, Wiley Heyden). Wiley.

Barnes, J. G. & Fisher, G., eds. Ida in Use: Proceedings of the ADA International Conference, Paris. (Ada Companion Ser.). 350p. 1985. 49.50 (ISBN 0-521-30968-9). Cambridge U Pr.

Barnes, J. H., tr. see Abarbanel, Judah.

Barnes, J. S. Fascism. LC 72-7055. (Select Bibliographies Reprint Ser.). 1972. Repr. of 1931 ed. 18.00 (ISBN 0-8369-6922-7). Ayer Co Pubs.

Barnes, J. Wesley, jt. auth. see Jensen, Paul A.

Barnes, Jack. Social Care Research. 163p. 1978. pap. text ed. 12.15x (ISBN 0-7199-0947-3, Pub. by Bedford England). Brookfield Pub Co.

Barnes, Jack & Clark, Steve, eds. Changing Face of U. S. Politics: Building a Party of Socialist Workers. 375p. 1981. lib. bdg. 27.00 (ISBN 0-87348-613-7); pap. 7.95 (ISBN 0-87348-614-5). Path Pr NY.

Barnes, Jack, ed. see Dobbs, Farrell.

Barnes, Jack, et al. Prospects for Socialism in America. LC 76-15820. 1976. 23.00 (ISBN 0-87348-466-5); pap. 5.95 (ISBN 0-87348-467-3). Path Pr NY.

Barnes, James. David G. Farragut. 132p. 1982. Repr. of 1899 ed. lib. bdg. 25.00 (ISBN 0-89987-089-9). Darby Bks.

--Yankee Ships & Yankee Sailors: Tales of 1812. 1977. lib. bdg. 59.95 (ISBN 0-8490-2850-7). Gordon Pr.

Barnes, James, et al. The World of Politics: A Concise Introduction. 2nd ed. LC 83-61601. 220p. 1984. pap. text ed. 13.95 (ISBN 0-312-89228-4). St Martin.

Barnes, James A. John Carlisle: Financial Statesman. 16.00 (ISBN 0-8446-1056-9). Peter Smith.

Barnes, James F. Gabon. (Profiles of Nations of Contemporary Africa Ser.). 135p. 1986. 26.50 (ISBN 0-686-46794-9). Westview.

Barnes, James J. Authors, Publishers, & Politicians: The Quest for an Anglo-American Copyright Agreement, 1815-1854. LC 74-12489. 316p. 1974. 13.00 (ISBN 0-8142-0210-1). Ohio St U Pr.

Barnes, James J. & Barnes, Patience P. Hitler's Mein Kampf in Britain & America: A Publishing History, 1930-39. LC 79-54014. 1980. pap. 24.95 (ISBN 0-521-22691-0). Cambridge U Pr.

Barnes, James N. Let's Save Antarctica! (Illus.). 112p. 1983. pap. 6.95 (ISBN 0-87663-408-0). Universe.

Barnes, James R., et al, eds. Stream Ecology: Application & Testing of General Ecological Theory. 408p. 1983. 55.00x (ISBN 0-306-41460-0, Plenum Pr). Plenum Pub.

Barnes, Jane, ed. see Goldring, Elizabeth O.

Barnes, Jim. The American Book of the Dead. LC 81-11458. 120p. 1982. 10.00 (ISBN 0-252-00937-1); pap. 5.95 (ISBN 0-252-00938-X). U of Ill Pr.

--The Fish on Poteau Mountain. 1980. 6.00 (ISBN 0-935286-00-4); pap. 2.50 (ISBN 0-935286-01-2). Cedar Creek OK.

--A Season of Loss. (Illus.). 84p. (Orig.). 1985. pap. 5.50 (ISBN 0-911198-75-X). Purdue U Pr.

Barnes, Jim, ed. Five Missouri Poets. LC 79-9319. 124p. 1979. pap. 3.00 (ISBN 0-933428-01-4). Chariton Review.

Barnes, Jim, tr. see Nick, Dagmar.

Barnes, Jimmie N. Life with Rev. Ev & Before: The Autobiography of a Methodist Minister's Wife. (Illus.). 1983. 9.95 (ISBN 0-916620-70-0). Portals Pr.

Barnes, Joanna. The Deceivers. LC 74-122642. 1970. 6.95 (ISBN 0-87795-007-5). Arbor Hse.

--Pastora. LC 77-79533. 1980. 12.95 (ISBN 0-87795-170-5). Arbor Hse.

--Pastora. 768p. 1981. pap. 3.50 (ISBN 0-380-56184-0, 56184-0). Avon.

--Silverwood. 432p. 1985. 16.95 (ISBN 0-671-45940-6, Linden Pr). S&S.

--Who Is Carla Hart? LC 72-82170. 1973. 6.95 (ISBN 0-87795-039-3). Arbor Hse.

Barnes, Joe. Man on a Mountain. LC 68-58686. 1969. 4.95 (ISBN 0-87651-200-7); pap. 3.50 (ISBN 0-87651-201-5); cloth 4.95 (ISBN 0-686-86751-3). Southern U Pr.

Barnes, John. The Ashmolean Ostracon of Sinuhe. 40p. 1968. Repr. of 1952 ed. text ed. 37.50x (ISBN 0-900416-16-5, Pub. by Aris England). Humanities.

--Evita--First Lady: A Biography of Eva Peron. LC 78-3185. 1978. 2.95 (ISBN 0-394-17087-3, B425, BC). Grove.

--How to Have More Money. LC 73-21960. 288p. 1974. 8.95 (ISBN 0-688-00255-2). Morrow.

--How to Learn Basic Bookkeeping in Ten Easy Lessons. rev. ed. (Illus.). 156p. 1982. 16.95 (ISBN 0-13-414995-5); pap. 9.95 (ISBN 0-13-414987-4). P-H.

--What Investing Is All about. 1984. pap. 6.75 wkbk. (ISBN 0-538-14570-6, N57). SW Pub.

Barnes, John, ed. Five Ramesseum Papyro. 44p. 1956. text ed. 18.50x (ISBN 0-900416-21-1, Pub. by Aris England). Humanities.

Barnes, John, ed. see Furphy, Joseph.

Barnes, John A. & Von Bodungen, Bodo. The Bermuda Marine Environment, Vol. II. (Bermuda Biological Station Special Pubn Ser.: No. 17). (Illus.). 1978. pap. 6.50 (ISBN 0-917642-17-1). Bermuda Bio.

Barnes, John E. & Waring, Alan J. Pocket Programmable Calculators in Biochemistry. LC 79-2547. 363p. 1980. 47.50x (ISBN 0-471-06434-3, Pub. by Wiley-Interscience); pap. 29.95 (ISBN 0-471-04713-9). Wiley.

Barnes, John G. Titmice of the British Isles. LC 74-33156. (Illus.). 224p. 1975. 15.95 (ISBN 0-7153-6955-5). David & Charles.

Barnes, John S., ed. see Fanning, Nathaniel.

Barnes, John S., ed. see Wolfe, Thomas.

Barnes, John W. Basic Geological Mapping. (Geological Society of London Handbook Ser.). 128p. 1981. 14.95x (ISBN 0-470-27250-3). Halsted Pr.

Barnes, Jonathan. Aristotle. (Past Masters Ser.). 82p. 1982. 13.95x (ISBN 0-19-287582-5); pap. 3.95 (ISBN 0-19-287581-7). Oxford U Pr.

--The Pre-Socratic Philosophers, 2 vols. Incl. Vol. 1. Thales to Zeno. 25.00 (ISBN 0-7100-8860-4); Vol. 2 o.p. Empedocles to Democritus (ISBN 0-7100-8861-2). (The Arguments of the Philosophers). 1979. o.p. 45.00x set (ISBN 0-7100-0180-0); Set. 25.00x ea. Routledge & Kegan.

--The Presocratic Philosophers. Rev. ed. (Arguments of the Philosophers Ser.). 680p. 1982. pap. 19.95 (ISBN 0-7100-9200-8). Routledge & Kegan.

Barnes, Jonathan, jt. auth. see Annas, Julia.

Barnes, Jonathan & Schofield, Malcolm, eds. Articles on Aristotle: Metaphysics. LC 77-20604. (Vol. 3). 223p. 1979. 27.50 (ISBN 0-312-05479-3). St Martin.

Barnes, Jonathan, ed. see Aristotle.

Barnes, Jonathan, et al, eds. Articles on Aristotle: Ethics & Politics, Vol. 2. LC 77-2064. 1978. 27.50 (ISBN 0-312-05478-5). St Martin.

--Science & Speculation. LC 82-4221. (Studies in Hellinistic Theory & Practice). 352p. 1983. 47.50 (ISBN 0-521-24689-X). Cambridge U Pr.

--Articles on Aristotle, Vol. I: Science. LC 77-20604. 1979. 27.50 (ISBN 0-312-05477-7). St Martin.

--Articles on Aristotle, Vol. IV: Psychology & Aesthetics. LC 77-20604. 1979. 27.50 (ISBN 0-312-05480-7). St Martin.

Barnes, Joseph, ed. Empire in the East. facsimile ed. LC 71-128203. (Essay Index Reprint Ser). Repr. of 1934 ed. 21.50 (ISBN 0-8369-1863-0). Ayer Co Pubs.

Barnes, Joseph E. How to Write & Publish the Book You Have Always Dreamed About. LC 76-26435. (Illus.). 176p. 1985. 14.95 (ISBN 0-917732-06-5, 768); pap. 9.95. Barnes Bks.

--SuperPro-crastinators. LC 84-71554. 200p. 1985. 14.95 (ISBN 0-917732-34-0, 767); pap. 10.95 (ISBN 0-917732-35-9). Barnes-Bks.

Barnes, Julia. Why Racism Is Used Against Welfare Programs: Why Workers Should Join Welfare Recipients' Struggles. 1971. pap. 0.10 (ISBN 0-87898-068-7). New Outlook.

Barnes, Julian. Flaubert's Parrot. LC 84-48550. 190p. 1985. 13.95 (ISBN 0-394-54272-X). Knopf.

Barnes, K. K. see Mann, C. K.

Barnes, Kate. Using MultiMate. LC 84-60141. 280p. 1985. 16.95 (ISBN 0-88022-114-3, 116). Que Corp.

Barnes, Kathleen & Pearce, Virginia. You & Yours. (Illus.). 41p. (Orig.). (gr. 3-6). 1980. pap. 3.95 (ISBN 0-87747-823-6). Deseret Bk.

Barnes, Kathleen, jt. auth. see Gregory, Homer E.

Barnes, Keith E. Preschool Screening: The Measurement & Prediction of Children At-Risk. (Illus.). 266p. 1982. 22.50x (ISBN 0-398-04668-9). C C Thomas.

Barnes, L. Introducing dBASE III. 304p. 1985. 18.95 (ISBN 0-07-003777-9, BYTE Bks). McGraw.

Barnes, Lan. The dBASE Demystified: dBASE II-III Applications & Solutions to Real Problems. 320p. (Orig.). 1985. pap. 19.95 (ISBN 0-915391-12-0, Pub. by Microtrend). Slawson Comm.

--Introducing dBASE II. LC 84-26170. (Illus.). 380p. 1985. pap. 18.95 (ISBN 0-07-041807-1). McGraw.

Barnes, Linda. Bitter Finish. 208p. 1985. pap. 2.95 (ISBN 0-449-20690-4, Crest). Fawcett.

--Dead Heat. 224p. 1984. 11.95 (ISBN 0-312-18498-0). St Martin.

--Dead Heat. 256p. 1985. pap. 2.95 (ISBN 0-449-20689-0, Crest). Fawcett.

Barnes, Linda H. The Dialectics of Black Humor: Process & Product. (European University Studies: Series 18, Comparative Literature, Vol. 15). 135p. 1978. pap. 17.05 (ISBN 3-261-03014-3). P Lang Pubs.

Barnes, Linda J. Bitter Finish. 192p. 1983. 11.95 (ISBN 0-312-08236-3). St Martin.

Barnes, Liz. Hand-Me-Downs. 275p. (Orig.). 1985. pap. 7.95 (ISBN 0-933216-18-1). Spinsters Ink.

Barnes, Louis B. Organizational Systems & Engineering Groups: A Comparative Study of Two Technical Groups in Industry. LC 60-13102. pap. 52.50 (ISBN 0-317-10897-2, 2002208). Bks Demand UMI.

Barnes, Louis B., jt. auth. see Lorsch, Jay W.

Barnes, M. Oceanography & Marine Biology: An Annual Review, Vol. 20. (Illus.). 778p. 1983. 82.80 (ISBN 0-08-028460-4). Pergamon.

Barnes, M., ed. Oceanography & Marine Biology: An Annual Review, Vol. 21. (Oceanography & Marine Biology Ser.). (Illus.). 590p. 1983. 82.80 (ISBN 0-08-030360-9). Pergamon.

Barnes, M., et al, eds. see Foote, P.

Barnes, Malcolm, tr. see Descola, Jean.

Barnes, Malcolm, tr. see Levaillant, Maurice.

Barnes, Malcolm, tr. see Troyat, Henri.

Barnes, Margaret, ed. Oceanography & Marine Biology: An Annual Review. LC 64-1930. (Oceanography & Marine Biology Ser.: Vol. 22). (Illus.). 590p. 1984. 76.80 (ISBN 0-08-030392-7). Pergamon.

Barnes, Margaret & Barnes, Harold, eds. Oceanography & Marine Biology: An Annual Review, Vol. 18. (Illus.). 528p. 1980. 63.00 (ISBN 0-08-025732-1). Pergamon.

Barnes, Margaret A. Murder in Coweta County. LC 75-23340. 287p. 1983. Repr. of 1976 ed. 12.95 (ISBN 0-88289-419-6). Pelican.

--Years of Grace. 27.95 (ISBN 0-317-28525-4, Pub. by Am Repr). Amereon Ltd.

Barnes, Margaret C. The King's Bed. 258p. 1981. pap. 2.75 (ISBN 0-441-44518-7). Ace Bks.

--The King's Fool. 300p. 1982. pap. 2.75 (ISBN 0-441-44522-5). Ace Bks.

--Mary of Carisbrooke. 1982. pap. 2.75 (ISBN 0-441-52047-2). Ace Bks.

Barnes, Marilyn G. Love (& Baby Powder) Cover All. 96p. (Orig.). 1985. pap. 5.95 (ISBN 0-86605-156-2). Campus Crusade.

Barnes, Mark & May, Ron. Mexican Majolica in Northern New Spain. 1980. Repr. 4.95 (ISBN 0-686-62076-3). Acoma Bks.

Barnes, Martin. Civil Engineering Standard Method of Measurement: Examples. 106p. 1977. pap. 6.50x (ISBN 0-7277-0035-9). Am Soc Civil Eng.

--Measurement in Contract Control. 304p. 1977. 23.75x (ISBN 0-7277-0040-5). Am Soc Civil Eng.

Barnes, Marvin P. Computer-Assisted Mineral Appraisal & Feasibility. LC 79-52270. (Illus.). 167p. 1980. text ed. 33.00x (ISBN 0-89520-262-X). Soc Mining Eng.

Barnes, Mary. Is There a Chef in the Kitchen. (Illus., Orig.). 1969. pap. 9.50x (ISBN 0-392-06983-0, AUS68-2523, ABC). Sportshelf.

Barnes, Marylou R. & Crutchfield, Carolyn A. The Patient at Home. LC 72-85638. 144p. 1973. 14.95 (ISBN 0-913590-02-9). Slack Inc.

Barnes, Marylou R., et al. The Neurophysiological Basis of Patient Treatment: Reflexes in Motor Development, Vol. II. LC 72-87895. (Illus.). 1973. pap. 13.75x (ISBN 0-936030-01-1). Stokesville Pub.

Barnes, Maude. Renaissance Vistas. facs. ed. LC 68-55838. (Essay Index Reprint Ser). 1930. 17.00 (ISBN 0-8369-0178-9). Ayer Co Pubs.

Barnes, Michael, jt. auth. see Ely, Vivian.

Barnes, Michael F. Measurement & Modelling Methods for Computer Systems Performance Studies. 177p. 1979. pap. 44.50x (ISBN 0-905897-18-8). Gower Pub Co.

Barnes, Michael H. In the Presence of Mystery: An Introduction to the Study of Human Religiousness. 324p. (Orig.). 1984. pap. 9.95 (ISBN 0-89622-205-5). Twenty-Third.

Barnes, Michael J., ed. Politics & Personality Seventeen Sixty-Eighteen Twenty-Seven. LC 68-97214. (Selections from History Today Ser.: No. 6). (Illus.). 1967. 7.95 (ISBN 0-686-85915-4); pap. 5.95 (ISBN 0-05-001535-4). Dufour.

Barnes, Mildred, jt. ed. see Barnes, Virgil.

Barnes, Mildred J. Women's Basketball. 2nd ed. (Illus.). 1980. text ed. 30.54 (ISBN 0-205-06604-6, 6266045). Allyn.

Barnes, Mildred J. & Kentwell, Richard G. Field Hockey: The Coach & the Player. 2nd ed. 1978. text ed. 30.54 (ISBN 0-205-06512-0, 626512). Allyn.

Barnes, Myra J. Linguistics & Languages in Science Fiction-Fantasy. new ed. LC 74-17864. (Science Fiction Ser). 208p. 1975. Repr. of 1974 ed. 13.00x (ISBN 0-405-06319-9). Ayer Co Pubs.

Barnes, N. D. & Robertson, N. R. Paediatrics. 130p. 1982. 59.00x (ISBN 0-906141-15-X, Pub. by MTP Pr). State Mutual Bk.

Barnes, Nathaniel W., jt. auth. see Brown, Rollo W.

Barnes, P. Open Your Mouth for the Dumb. 1984. pap. 1.45 booklet (ISBN 0-85151-390-5). Banner of Truth.

Barnes, P., ed. Structure & Performance of Cements. 576p. 1984. 111.00 (ISBN 0-85334-233-4, Pub. by Elsevier Applied Sci England). Elsevier.

Barnes, P. D., et al, eds. Meson-Nuclear Physics - 1976: Carnegie-Mellon Conference. LC 76-26811. (AIP Conference Proceedings: No. 33). 1976. 24.75 (ISBN 0-88318-132-0). Am Inst Physics.

Barnes, Patience P., jt. auth. see Barnes, James J.

Barnes, Patricia M., ed. The Great Roll of the Pipe for the Fourteenth Year of the Reign of John: Michaelmas 1212. (Pipe Roll Soceity London Ser.: No. 2, Vol. 30). Repr. of 1955 ed. 36.00 (ISBN 0-317-15146-0). Kraus Repr.

--The Great Roll of the Pipe for the Sixteenth Year of the Reign of John, Michaelmas 1214. (Pipe Roll Society, London, Ser.: No. 2, Vol. 35). Repr. of 1962 ed. 48.00 (ISBN 0-317-17876-8). Kraus Intl.

Barnes, Patricia M. & Powell, W. R., eds. Interdict Documents. (Pipe Roll Society London Ser.: No. 2, Vol. 34). Repr. of 1960 ed. 31.00 (ISBN 0-317-16597-6). Kraus Repr.

Barnes, Patricia M. & Slade, C. F., eds. Medieval Miscellany for Doris M. Stenton. (Pipe Roll Society London Ser. 2: No. 2, Vol. 36). Repr. of 1962 ed. 60.00 (ISBN 0-317-15934-8). Kraus Intl.

Barnes, Peter. Barnes People II: Seven Duologues. LC 83-12718. (Orig.). 1984. pap. text ed. 6.00x (ISBN 0-435-23065-4). Heinemann Ed.

--The Bewitched. 1974. pap. text ed. 5.00x (ISBN 0-435-23061-1). Heinemann Ed.

--Collected Plays. (Orig.). 1981. pap. text ed. 12.50x (ISBN 0-435-18281-1). Heinemann Ed.

--The Frontiers of Farce. 1977. pap. text ed. 6.00x (ISBN 0-435-23063-8). Heinemann Ed.

--Laughter. 1978. pap. text ed. 6.00x (ISBN 0-435-23064-6). Heinemann Ed.

--Milk of the World. 80p. (Orig.). 1985. pap. 2.95 (ISBN 0-85151-434-0). Banner of Truth.

--The Ruling Class: A Baroque Comedy. 1969. pap. text ed. 5.00x (ISBN 0-435-20965-5). Heinemann Ed.

Barnes, Peter, ed. Lipids in Cereal Technology. (Food Science & Technology Ser.). 1984. 70.00 (ISBN 0-12-079020-3). Acad Pr.

Barnes, Peter, et al, eds. The Alaskan Beaufort Sea. 1984. 39.00 (ISBN 0-12-079030-0). Acad Pr.

Barnes, R. Get Your Tenses Right. (Cambridge English Language Learning Ser). 1977. 6.95 (ISBN 0-521-21296-0); cassette 13.95 (ISBN 0-521-21297-9). Cambridge U Pr.

Barnes, R. A. Fundamentals of Music: A Program for Self-Instruction. 1964. pap. text ed. 22.95 (ISBN 0-07-003771-X). McGraw.

--PL-One for Programmers. 562p. 1979. 29.50 (ISBN 0-444-00284-7, North Holland). Elsevier.

Barnes, R. H. Two Crows Denies It: A History of Controversy in Omaha Sociology. LC 84-2276. (Illus.). xiv, 272p. 1984. 24.95x (ISBN 0-8032-1182-1). U of Nebr Pr.

Barnes, R. H., ed. see Kohler, Josef.

Barnes, R. J., jt. ed. see Johnson, T. B.

Barnes, R. M. Plasma Spectrochemistry: Proceeding of the 1984 Winter Conference on Plasma Spectrochemistry, San Diego, USA, 2-6 Jan. 1984, No. 2. 412p. 1985. 59.50 (ISBN 0-08-030246-7, Pub. by P P L). Pergamon.

Barnes, R. M., ed. Plasma Spectrochemistry: Proceedings of the Winter Conference, Orlando, Florida, January 4-9, 1982. 436p. 1983. 50.00 (ISBN 0-08-028745-X). Pergamon.

Barnes, R. P., jt. auth. see White, J. M.

Barnes, R. S. Coastal Lagoons. LC 80-40041. (Cambridge Studies in Modern Biology: No. 1). (Illus.). 130p. 1980. 37.50 (ISBN 0-521-23422-0); pap. 13.95 (ISBN 0-521-29945-4). Cambridge U Pr.

--Estuarine Biology. (Studies in Biology: No. 49). 80p. 1974. pap. text ed. 8.95 (ISBN 0-7131-2466-0). E Arnold.

--Estuarine Biology. 2nd ed. (Studies in Biology: No. 49). 80p. 1984. pap. text ed. 8.95 (ISBN 0-7131-2905-0). E Arnold.

--A Synoptic Classification of Living Organisms. LC 84-1237. (Illus.). 276p. (Orig.). 1984. pap. text ed. 14.00x (ISBN 0-87893-048-5). Sinauer Assoc.

Barnes, R. S. & Hughes, R. N. An Introduction to Marine Ecology. (Illus.). 234p. 1982. pap. text ed. 19.95 (ISBN 0-632-00892-X, B0536-9). Mosby.

--An Introduction to Marine Ecology. (Illus.). 348p. 1982. pap. text ed. 23.95x (ISBN 0-632-00892-X). Blackwell Pubns.

Barnes, R. S., ed. The Coastline: A Contribution to Our Understanding of Its Ecology & Physiography in Relation to Land-Use & Management & the Pressures to Which It Is Subject. LC 76-51343. 356p. 1977. 59.95x (ISBN 0-471-99470-7, Pub. by Wiley-Interscience). Wiley.

--Estuarine Environment. Green, J. (Illus.). 133p. 1972. 26.00 (ISBN 0-85334-539-2, Pub. by Elsevier Applied Sci England). Elsevier.

Barnes, R. S. & Mann, K. H., eds. Fundamentals of Aquatic Ecosystems. (Illus.). 240p. 1980. 16.00x (ISBN 0-632-00014-7). Blackwell Pubns.

Barnes, Rachel. The V & A Alphabet Book. (Illus.). 32p. (Orig.). 1985. pap. 3.95 (ISBN 0-948107-10-3, Pub. by Victoria & Albert Mus UK). Faber & Faber.

Barnes, Ralph see White, Denis, et al.

Barnes, Ralph M. Early Days in Clifton Mills. (Illus.). 176p. 1985. 13.95 (ISBN 0-9614933-0-5). McClain.

--Industrial Engineering & Management Problems & Policies. (Management History Ser.: No. 62). (Illus.). 373p. 1973. Repr. of 1931 ed. 20.00 (ISBN 0-87960-066-7). Hive Pub.

--Motion & Time Study: Design & Measurement of Work. 7th ed. LC 80-173. 689p. 1980. text ed. 44.50x (ISBN 0-471-05905-6). Wiley.

Barnes, Ramon M., ed. Development in Atomic Plasma Spectrochemical Analysis. 1981. 84.95 (ISBN 0-471-26138-6). Wiley.

--Emission Spectroscopy. LC 75-30672. 1976. 73.50 (ISBN 0-12-786137-8). Acad Pr.

Barnes, Richard. The Who: Maximum R&B. (Illus.). 168p. 1982. pap. 13.95 (ISBN 0-312-86989-4). St Martin.

Barnes, Richard, jt. auth. see Giffin, Kim.

Barnes, Richard, jt. auth. see Williams, George A.

Barnes, Richard E., jt. auth. see Mabry, Edward A.

Barnes, Richard W., jt. auth. see Wilkinson, Bruce W.

Barnes, Rik. The Complete Guide to American Bed & Breakfast. 416p. 1985. pap. 10.95 (ISBN 0-88289-432-3). Pelican.

Barnes, Robert. Marriages & Deaths from Baltimore Newspapers, 1796-1816. LC 78-61144. 383p. 1978. 20.00 (ISBN 0-8063-0826-5). Genealog Pub.

--Marriages & Deaths from the Maryland Gazette, 1727 to 1839. LC 73-12383. 234p. 1979. Repr. of 1973 ed. 15.00 (ISBN 0-8063-0580-0). Genealog Pub.

--Maryland Marriages: 1778-1800. LC 77-88843. 300p. 1979. 17.50 (ISBN 0-8063-0791-9). Genealog Pub.

--Megaprofit Commodity Methods. 1983. 69.95. Windsor.

--Profitable New Commodity Trading Methods. 1986. cancelled (ISBN 0-442-21273-9). Van Nos Reinhold.

--Silent Thunder. (Orig.). 1980. pap. text ed. 1.75 (ISBN 0-505-51551-2, Pub. by Tower Bks). Dorchester Pub Co.

--A Supplicatyon... Unto Henry the Eighth. LC 73-6098. (English Experience Ser.: No. 567). 1973. Repr. of 1534 ed. 18.50 (ISBN 90-221-0567-9). Walter J Johnson.

Barnes, Robert C. Trails to Glory. (Orig.). 1982. pap. 3.25 (ISBN 0-440-08891-7). Dell.

Barnes, Robert D. Invertebrate Zoology. 4th ed. 1980. text ed. 39.95 (ISBN 0-03-056747-5, CBS C). SCP.

Barnes, Robert D. & Pickering, James D., eds. Nature vs. Nurture: Gettysburg College Senior Scholars' Seminar 1983-1984. 264p. (Orig.). 1985. pap. text ed. 14.75 (ISBN 0-8191-4554-8). U Pr of Amer.

Barnes, Robert G., Jr. Single Parenting: A Wilderness Journey. 176p. 1984. pap. 5.95 (ISBN 0-8423-5892-7). Tyndale.

Barnes, Robert J., jt. ed. see Hagelman, Charles W., Jr.

Barnes, Robert M. Commodity Profits Through Trend Trading: Price Model & Strategies. LC 81-13108. 276p. 1982. 47.50 (ISBN 0-471-08515-4, Pub. by Ronald Pr). Wiley.

--Making High Profits in Uncertain Times: Successful Investing in Inflation & Depression. 208p. 1982. text ed. 35.00 (ISBN 0-442-21299-2). Van Nos Reinhold.

--Taming the Pits: A Technical Approach to Commodity Trading. LC 79-12107. 272p. 1979. 54.95x (ISBN 0-471-05795-9, Pub. by Wiley-Interscience). Wiley.

Barnes, Roger. A Guide to Successful Time Management for the Data Processing Professional. LC 82-74001. (Illus.). 185p. (Orig.). 1983. pap. text ed. 9.95 (ISBN 0-9610220-0-0). Dynabyte Books.

Barnes, Roger W., et al. Urology. 3rd. ed. (Medical Outline Ser.). 1980. pap. 26.50 (ISBN 0-87488-611-2). Med Exam.

Barnes, Rory & Broderick, Damien. Valencies. LC 83-10394. 230p. (Orig.). 1984. pap. 7.95 (ISBN 0-7022-1763-8). U of Queensland Pr.

Barnes, S. Brandi. Blackberries in the China Cabinet. (Illus.). 50p. (Orig.). 1984. pap. 4.95 (ISBN 0-915867-03-6). ENAAQ Pubns.

Barnes, Samuel. Identity. (Illus.). 260p. 1981. 12.95 (ISBN 0-941192-00-8). Best West Pr.

Barnes, Samuel H. & Kasse, Max. Political Action: Mass Participation in Five Western Democracies. LC 78-19649. (Illus.). 607p. 1979. 29.95 (ISBN 0-8039-0957-8). Sage.

Barnes, Samuel Henry. Representation in Italy: Institutionalized Tradition & Electoral Choice. LC 76-51819. (Illus.). 1977. 20.00 (ISBN 0-226-03726-6). U of Chicago Pr.

Barnes, Sandra T. Ogun: An Old God for a New Age. LC 79-26577. (ISHI Occasional Papers in Social Change: No. 3). 72p. 1980. pap. text ed. 5.95x (ISBN 0-89727-011-8). ISHI PA.

Barnes, Simon. China in Focus. (The "In Focus" Ser.). (Illus.). 64p. (Orig.). 1981. pap. 5.95 (ISBN 962-7031-12-7). C E Tuttle.

--Philippines in Focus. (The "In Focus" Ser.). (Illus.). 64p. (Orig.). 1981. pap. 5.95. C E Tuttle.

--Singapore in Focus. (The "In Focus" Ser.). (Illus.). 64p. (Orig.). 1981. pap. 5.95 (ISBN 962-7031-11-9). C E Tuttle.

Barnes, Sondra A. Life Is the Way It Is. LC 78-73124. 85p. 1978. pap. 3.95 (ISBN 0-9602534-0-8). Brason Sargar.

Barnes, Stanley. Two Hundred Million Hungry Children. 1981. 20.00x (ISBN 0-686-78922-9, Pub. by Grosvenor Bks England). State Mutual Bk.

Barnes, Stephen H., ed. A Cross-Section of Research in Music Education. LC 81-43496. 336p. 1982. lib. bdg. 27.25 (ISBN 0-8191-2285-8); pap. text ed. 12.75 (ISBN 0-8191-2286-6). U Pr of Amer.

Barnes, Steve. Ki: How to Generate the Dragon Spirit. Goodman, David, ed. (Sendo Martial Arts: No. 1). (Illus.). 51p. 1976. 2.95 (ISBN 0-686-15598-X); pap. 1.00 (ISBN 0-686-15599-8). Senseis DoJo.

Barnes, Steven. Streetlethal. 1983. pap. 2.95 (ISBN 0-441-79068-2, Ace Science Fiction). Ace Bks.

Barnes, Steven, jt. auth. see Niven, Larry.

Barnes, Sue N., jt. auth. see Curtis, Helena.

Barnes, T. R. English Verse. 1967. 49.50 (ISBN 0-521-04109-0); pap. 11.95x (ISBN 0-521-09433-X, 433). Cambridge U Pr.

Barnes, Thomas. Origin & Destiny of the Earth's Magnetic Field. LC 73-79065. (ICR Technical Monograph: No. 4). (Illus.). 64p. 1973. pap. 7.95 (ISBN 0-89051-013-X). Master Bks.

Barnes, Thomas A. & Israel, Jacob S. Brady's Programmed Introduction to Respiratory Therapy. 2nd ed. LC 79-27753. (Illus.). 365p. 1981. pap. text ed. 16.95 (ISBN 0-87619-624-5). Brady Comm.

Barnes, Thomas C., et al. Northern New Spain: A Research Guide. LC 80-24860. 147p. 1981. pap. text ed. 14.95x (ISBN 0-8165-0709-0). U of Ariz Pr.

Barnes, Thomas G. List & Index to the Proceedings in Star Chamber for the Reign of James I (1603-1625) in the Public Record Office, London: Class STAC8, 3 vols. LC 75-542. 2312p. 1975. 120.00 set (ISBN 0-910058-68-7). Am Bar Foun.

--Somerset, Sixteen Twenty-Five to Sixteen Forty: A County's Government During the "Personal Rule". LC 82-11012. (Midway Reprint Ser.). xviii, 370p. 1982. pap. 21.00x (ISBN 0-226-03719-3). U of Chicago Pr.

Barnes, Thomas G., ed. & intro. by. The Book of the General Lawes & Libertyes Concerning the Inhabitants of the Massachusetts. Fasc. ed. LC 75-12004. 88p. 1975. pap. 5.00 (ISBN 0-87328-066-0). Huntington Lib.

Barnes, Thomas G. & Feldman, Gerald D., eds. Breakdown & Rebirth: 1914 to the Present, a Documentary History of Modern Europe, Vol. IV. LC 82-45164. 288p. 1982. pap. text ed. 10.25 (ISBN 0-8191-2366-8). U Pr of Amer.

--Breakdown & Rebirth: 1914 to the Present. 273p. 1972. pap. 7.95 (ISBN 0-316-08173-6). Little.

--Nationalism, Industrialization, & Democracy, 1815-1914: A Documenatary History of Modern Europe, Vol. III. LC 80-5383. 331p. 1980. pap. text ed. 11.75 (ISBN 0-8191-1079-5). U Pr of Amer.

--Rationalism & Revolution Sixteen Sixty to Eighteen Fifteen, Vol. II. LC 79-66686. 1979. pap. text ed. 10.00 (ISBN 0-8191-0850-2). U Pr of Amer.

--Renaissance, Reformation, & Absolutism Fourteen Hundred to Sixteen Sixty, Vol. I. LC 79-66685. 1979. pap. text ed. 10.50 (ISBN 0-8191-0847-2). U Pr of Amer.

Barnes, Thurlow W., ed. see Weed, Thurlow.

Barnes, Timothy. Constantine & Eusebius. LC 81-4248. (Illus.). 448p. 1981. text ed. 35.00x (ISBN 0-674-16530-6). Harvard U Pr.

Barnes, Timothy D. Constantine & Eusebius. 472p. 1984. pap. text ed. 12.50x (ISBN 0-674-16531-4). Harvard U Pr.

--The New Empire of Diocletian & Constantine. LC 81-4248. 336p. 1982. text ed. 35.00x (ISBN 0-674-61126-8). Harvard U Pr.

--Tertullian: A Historical & Literary Study. 328p. 1985. 34.50 (ISBN 0-19-814362-1). Oxford U Pr.

Barnes, V. E. Geologic Atlas of Texas: Amarillo Sheet, Leroy Thompson Patton Memorial Edition. 1969. Repr. 4.00 (ISBN 0-686-36619-0). Bur Econ Geology.

--Geologic Atlas of Texas: Austin Sheet, Francis Luther Whitney Memorial Edition. rev ed. 1981. 4.00 (ISBN 0-686-36621-2). Bur Econ Geology.

Barnes, V. E. & Bell, W. C. The Moore Hollow Group of Central Texas. (Report of Investigations Ser.: RI 88). (Illus.). 169p. 1977. 5.00 (ISBN 0-318-03228-7). Bur Econ Geology.

Barnes, V. E. & Schofield, D. A. Potential Low-Grade Iron Ore & Hydraulic-Fracturing Sand in Cambrian Sandstones, Northwestern Llano Region, Texas. (Report of Investigations Ser.: RI 53). (Illus.). 58p. 1964. 2.00 (ISBN 0-686-29335-5). Bur Econ Geology.

Barnes, V. E., et al. Stratigraphy of the Pre-Simpson Paleozoic Subsurface Rocks of Texas & Southeast New Mexico, 2 Vols. (Pub. Ser.: 5924). (Illus.). 836p. 1959. 7.75 (ISBN 0-318-03311-9). Bur Econ Geology.

--Geology of the Llano Region & Austin Area. rev. ed. (Guidebook Ser.: GB 13). 154p. 1983. Repr. of 1972 ed. 2.50 (ISBN 0-686-29321-5). Bur Econ Geology.

Barnes, Valerie, jt. auth. see Murray, Thomas C.

Barnes, Vera F. Daybreak Below the Border. 1975. Repr. 2.50 (ISBN 0-87509-078-8). Chr Pubns.

--Miles Beyond in Brazil. 3.50 (ISBN 0-87509-104-0); pap. 2.00 (ISBN 0-87509-105-9). Chr Pubns.

Barnes, Virgil & Barnes, Mildred, eds. Tektites. LC 72-95942. (Benchmark Papers in Geology Ser: Vol. 4). 445p. 1973. 57.95 (ISBN 0-87933-027-9). Van Nos Reinhold.

Barnes, W. E., ed. Basic Physics of Radiotracers. 1983. Vol. I, 216p. 67.00 (ISBN 0-8493-6001-3); Vol. II, 176p. 56.00 (ISBN 0-8493-6002-1). CRC Pr.

Barnes, W. W., jt. auth. see Allison, William H.

Barnes, Walter. The Children's Poets. 59.95 (ISBN 0-87968-851-3). Gordon Pr.

--The Children's Poets: Stevenson, Christina Rossetti, Blake, Lear, Lewis Carroll, Eugene Field, James Whitcomb Riley. 1925. Repr. 20.00 (ISBN 0-8274-2055-2). R West.

--Early England & the Saxon English. 59.95 (ISBN 0-8490-0069-6). Gordon Pr.

--Types of Children's Literature. 59.95 (ISBN 0-8490-1239-2). Gordon Pr.

Barnes, Warner, jt. auth. see Brack, O. M., Jr.

Barnes, Warner, compiled by. The Browning Collection at the University of Texas. LC 66-63479. (Tower Bibliographical Ser.: No. 4). (Illus.). 1966. 10.00 (ISBN 0-87959-036-X). U of Tex H Ransom Ctr.

Barnes, Wesley. Existentialism. LC 67-28536. (Orig.). (gr. 10 up). 1968. pap. text ed. 5.50 (ISBN 0-8120-0275-X). Barron.

Barnes, Will C. Apaches & Longhorns. LC 82-7043. 214p. 1982. 17.50 (ISBN 0-8165-0781-3); pap. 8.50 (ISBN 0-8165-0784-8). U of Ariz Pr.

Barnes, William. Poems of William Barnes, 2 Vols. Jones, Bernard, ed. LC 61-6478. (Centaur Classics Ser.). 993p. 1962. Set. 32.50x (ISBN 0-8093-0069-9). S Ill U Pr.

--A Prose Anthology. Hearl, Trevor, ed. 384p. 1983. text ed. 21.50x (ISBN 0-85635-407-4, Pub. by Carcanet Pr England). Humanities.

--A Selection from Poems of Rural Life in the Dorset Dialect. 1977. Repr. of 1909 ed. 20.00 (ISBN 0-89984-042-6). Century Bookbindery.

Barnes, William & Morgan, John H. The Foreign Service of the U. S. Origins, Developments & Functions. LC 78-13977. (U. S. Dept. of States Publication 7050, Dept. of Foreign Services Ser.: No. 96). (Illus.). 1978. Repr. of 1961 ed. lib. bdg. 42.50x (ISBN 0-313-20675-9, BAFO). Greenwood.

Barnes, William C. Western Grazing Grounds & Forest Ranges. Bruchey, Stuart, ed. LC 78-56685. (Management of Public Lands in the U.S. Ser.). (Illus.). 1979. Repr. of 1913 ed. lib. bdg. 26.50x (ISBN 0-405-11317-X). Ayer Co Pubs.

Barnes, William E., ed. Labor Problem: Plain Questions & Practical Answers. LC 75-156404. (American Labor Ser., No. 2). 1971. Repr. of 1886 ed. 17.00 (ISBN 0-405-02914-4). Ayer Co Pubs.

Barnes, William H. History of the Thirty-Ninth Congress of the United States. LC 77-77189. Repr. of 1868 ed. 31.00x (ISBN 0-8371-1288-5, BAT&, Pub. by Negro U Pr). Greenwood.

Barnes, William N. International Marketing Indicators. 1980. 69.00x (ISBN 0-86176-059-X, Pub. by MCB Pubns). State Mutual Bk.

Barnes-Murphy, Rowan. Dragon Spell. (Mervyn & Magician Pop-Up Magic Spells Ser.). (Illus.). 12p. (gr. 1-3). 1985. pap. 1.95 (ISBN 0-434-95179-X, Pub. by W Heinemann Ltd.). David & Charles.

--Giant Spell. (Mervyn the Magician's Pop-Up Magic Spells Ser.). (Illus.). 12p. (gr. 1-3). 1985. pap. 1.95 (ISBN 0-434-95177-3, Pub. by W Heinemann Ltd.). David & Charles.

--Old Macdonald Had a Farm. 1985. 8.95 (ISBN 0-8120-5693-0); bk. & cassette 12.95 (ISBN 0-8120-7380-0); cassette seperately avail. (ISBN 0-8120-3641-7). Barron.

--Owl Spell. (Mervyn the Magician's Pop-Up Magic Spell Ser.). (Illus.). 12p. (gr. 1-3). 1985. pap. 1.95 (ISBN 0-434-95176-5, Pub. by W Heinemann Ltd.). David & Charles.

--Witch Spell. (Mervyn the Magician's Pop-Up Magic Spells Ser.). (Illus.). 12p. (gr. 1-3). 1985. pap. 1.95 (ISBN 0-434-95178-1, Pub. by W Heinemann Ltd.). David & Charles.

Barness, Lewis. Advances in Pediatrics, Vol. 28. 1981. 55.95 (ISBN 0-8151-0500-2). Year Bk Med.

--Advances in Pediatrics, Vol. 30. 1984. 55.95 (ISBN 0-8151-0503-7). Year Bk Med.

--Advances in Pediatrics, Vol. 31. 1984. 55.95 (ISBN 0-8151-0504-5). Year Bk Med.

Barness, Lewis A. Advances in Pediatrics, Vols. 25-27. (Illus.). 1978-80. Vol. 25. 55.95 (ISBN 0-8151-0497-9); Vol. 26. 55.95 (ISBN 0-8151-0498-7); Vol.27. 55.95 (ISBN 0-8151-0499-5). Year Bk Med.

--Manual of Pediatric Physical Diagnosis. 5th ed. 1980. 19.95 (ISBN 0-8151-0493-6). Year Bk Med.

Barness, Lewis A., ed. Advances in Pediatrics, Vol. 29. 1982. 55.95 (ISBN 0-8151-0501-0). Year Bk Med.

Barness, Lewis A., et al, eds. Nutrition & Medical Practice. (Illus.). 1981. text ed. 29.50 (ISBN 0-87055-365-8). AVI.

Barness, Richard. Graystone College. LC 72-7654. (Adult & Young Adult Bks.). (Illus.). (gr. 9 up). 1973. PLB 5.95 (ISBN 0-8225-0753-6). Lerner Pubns.

--Listen to Me! LC 74-11901. (Books for Adults & Young Adults Ser.). 96p. (gr. 6 up). 1976. PLB 5.95g (ISBN 0-8225-0758-7). Lerner Pubns.

Barnet, Charlie & Dance, Stanley. Those Swinging Years: The Autobiography of Charlie Barnet. LC 83-14923. (Illus.). 288p. 1984. 19.95 (ISBN 0-8071-1128-7). La State U Pr.

Barnet, G., et al, eds. Mechanical Fitting, Vol. 2. 2nd ed. (Engineering Craftsmen: No. H25). (Illus.). 1973. spiral bdg. 39.95x (ISBN 0-85083-186-5). Intl Ideas.

Barnet, Judith M. Culture's Storehouse: Building Humanities Skills Through Folklore. 72p. 5.00 (ISBN 0-318-14207-4, GPH 101). Global Perspectives.

Barnet, Richard. Roots of War. 1973. pap. 6.95 (ISBN 0-14-021698-7, Pelican). Penguin.

Barnet, Richard J. The Alliance: America, Europe, Japan-Makers of the Post-War World. (Illus.). 544p. 1983. 19.95 (ISBN 0-671-42502-1). S&S.

--The Alliance: America, Europe, Japan-Makers of the Postwar World. 528p. 1985. pap. 10.95 (ISBN 0-671-54184-6, Touchstone Bks). S&S.

--The Giants: Russia & America. 1977. (Touchstone Bks); pap. 5.95 (ISBN 0-671-24403-5). S&S.

--Intervention & Revolution: The United States in the Third World. 1969. pap. 7.95 (ISBN 0-452-00770-4, Mer). NAL.

--The Lean Years: Politics in the Age of Scarcity. 1982. pap. 7.95 (ISBN 0-671-43829-8, Touchstone Bks). S&S.

Barnet, Richard J. & Muller, Ronald E. Global Reach: The Power of the Multinational Corporations. LC 74-2794. 1975. (Touchstone Bks); pap. 10.95 (ISBN 0-671-22104-3). S&S.

Barnet, Richard J., jt. ed. see Falk, Richard J.

Barnet, Sylvan. A Short Guide to Shakespeare. LC 73-13359. 206p. 1974. pap. 4.95 (ISBN 0-15-681800-0, Harv). HarBraceJ.

--A Short Guide to Writing about Art. 2nd ed. 1985. pap. 6.95 (ISBN 0-316-08223-6). Little.

Barnet, Sylvan & Burto, William. Zen Ink Paintings. LC 82-80648. (Great Japanese Art Ser.). (Illus.). 96p. 1982. 18.75 (ISBN 0-87011-521-9). Kodansha.

Barnet, Sylvan & Stubbs, Marcia. Barnet & Stubbs' Practical Guide to Writing. 4th ed. 1983. pap. text ed. 10.95 (ISBN 0-316-08215-5); Tchr's. manual avail. (ISBN 0-316-08216-3). Little.

--Barnet & Stubbs's: Practical Guide to Writings with Additional Readings. 4th ed. 1983. pap. text ed. 14.95 (ISBN 0-316-08153-1); Teacher's Manual Avail. (ISBN 0-316-08216-3). Little.

Barnet, Sylvan, jt. auth. see Stubbs, Marcia.

Barnet, Sylvan, ed. The Complete Signet Classic Shakespeare. 1176p. 1972. text ed. 30.95 (ISBN 0-15-512610-5, HC). HarBraceJ.

Barnet, Sylvan, intro. by. Three Plays by George Bernard Shaw. 1985. pap. 4.95 (ISBN 0-451-51903-5, Sig Classics). NAL.

Barnet, Sylvan, ed. see Marlowe, Christopher.

Barnet, Sylvan, ed. see Shakespeare, William.

Barnet, Sylvan, et al. A Dictionary of Literary, Dramatic, & Cinematic Terms. 2nd ed. 124p. 1971. pap. 6.95 (ISBN 0-316-08194-9). Little.

--An Introduction to Literature: Fiction, Poetry, Drama. 8th ed. 1985. pap. text ed. 14.95 (ISBN 0-316-08227-9); tchr's. ed. (ISBN 0-316-08228-7). Little.

--Nine Modern Classics: An Anthology of Short Novels. 681p. 1973. pap. text ed. 14.95 (ISBN 0-316-08169-8). Little.

--Types of Drama: Plays & Essays. 4th ed. 1984. pap. text ed. 17.95 (ISBN 0-316-08222-8). Little.

Barnet, Sylvan, et al, eds. Eight Great Comedies: Clouds, Mandragola, Twelfth Night, Miser, Beggar's Opera, Importance of Being Earnest, Uncle Vanya, Arms & the Man. pap. 4.95 (ISBN 0-451-62364-9, Ment). NAL.

--Eight Great Tragedies: Prometheus Bound, Oedipus the King, Hippolytus, King Lear, Ghosts, Miss Julie, On Bailles Strand, Desire under the Elms. pap. 3.95 (ISBN 0-451-62409-2, ME2258, Ment). NAL.

--Genius of the Early English Theater: Abraham & Isaac, Second Shepherd's Play, Everyman, Doctor Faustus, Macbeth, Volpone, Samson Agonistes. 1962. pap. 3.95 (ISBN 0-451-62221-9, ME2221, Ment). NAL.

--Literature for Composition: Essays, Fiction, Poetry, & Drama. 1984. 15.95 (ISBN 0-316-08151-5); tchr's manual avail. (ISBN 0-316-08152-3). Little.

Barnetson, John. Critter Chronicles: Tales for Here & Now. LC 80-66262. (Illus.). 96p. 1982. 9.95 (ISBN 0-89742-291-0, Dawne-Leigh). Celestial Arts.

Barnett, jt. ed. see Barnett, Vic.

Barnett, A. & Bell, R. M. Rural Energy & the Third World: A Review of Social Science Research & Technology Policy Problems. LC 82-373. (Illus.). 302p. 1982. 40.00 (ISBN 0-08-028953-3); 18.00 (ISBN 0-08-028954-1). Pergamon.

Barnett, A., jt. auth. see Helbling, Robert E.

Barnett, A. Doak. Cadres, Bureaucracy, & Political Power in Communist China. LC 67-15895. (Studies of the East Asian Institute Ser.). 565p. 1967. 31.00x (ISBN 0-231-03035-5). Columbia U Pr.

--China after Mao: With Selected Documents. 1967. 32.00 (ISBN 0-691-03008-1); pap. 10.95 (ISBN 0-691-00000-X). Princeton U Pr.

--China & the Major Powers in East Asia. 1977. 29.95 (ISBN 0-8157-0824-6); pap. 10.95 (ISBN 0-8157-0823-8). Brookings.

--China & the World Food System. LC 79-87912. (Monographs: No. 12). 128p. 1979. 5.00 (ISBN 0-686-28683-9). Overseas Dev Council.

--China on the Eve of Communist Takeover. (A Westview Encore Reprint Ser.). 371p. 1985. Repr. of 1963 ed. softcover 30.00x (ISBN 0-8133-0163-7). Westview.

--China Policy: Old Problems & New Challenges. LC 76-51538. 1977. 22.95 (ISBN 0-8157-0822-X); pap. 8.95 (ISBN 0-8157-0821-1). Brookings.

--China's Economy in Global Perspective. LC 81-1193. 750p. 1981. 32.95 (ISBN 0-8157-0826-2); pap. 16.95 (ISBN 0-8157-0825-4). Brookings.

--Communist Economic Strategy: The Rise of Mainland China. LC 75-28661. (Economics of Competive Coexistence Ser). 106p. 1976. Repr. of 1959 ed. lib. bdg. 15.00x (ISBN 0-8371-8478-9, BACE). Greenwood.

--The FX Decision: Another Crucial Moment in U.S.-China-Taiwan Relations. LC 81-70778. (Studies in Defense Policy). 60p. 1981. pap. 6.95 (ISBN 0-8157-0827-0). Brookings.

--The Making of Foreign Policy in China: Structure & Process. (SAIS Papers in International Affairs). 110p. 1985. 18.50x (ISBN 0-8133-0232-3); pap. 10.95x (ISBN 0-8133-0233-1). Westview.

--Uncertain Passage: China's Transition to the Post-Mao Era. LC 73-22482. pap. 101.30 (ISBN 0-317-30179-9, 2025361). Bks Demand UMI.

--U. S. Arms Sales: The China-Taiwan Tangle. LC 82-72117. (Studies in Defense Policy). 70p. 1982. pap. 6.95 (ISBN 0-8157-0829-7). Brookings.

Barnett, A. Doak, ed. Chinese Communist Politics in Action. LC 69-14203. (Studies in Chinese Government & Politics: No. 1). (Illus.). 648p. 1969. pap. 7.95x (ISBN 0-295-78584-5, WPRA7). U of Wash Pr.

--Communist Strategies in Asia. LC 75-32454. 293p. 1976. Repr. of 1963 ed. lib. bdg. 22.50x (ISBN 0-8371-8547-5, BACSA). Greenwood.

Barnett, Alan W. Community Murals. LC 79-21552. (Illus.). 520p. 1984. 60.00 (ISBN 0-8453-4731-4). Cornwall Bks.

--Murals of Protest. LC 79-21552. (Illus.). 520p. 1984. 60.00 (ISBN 0-87982-030-6). Art Alliance.

Barnett, Alfred J. Scleroderma: Progressive Systemic Sclerosis. (Illus.). 270p. 1974. 31.25x (ISBN 0-398-02955-5). C C Thomas.

Barnett, Annie. A Little Book of English Proses. 335p. 1982. Repr. of 1900 ed. lib. bdg. 25.00 (ISBN 0-8495-0078-8). Arden Lib.

Barnett, Anthony. Fear & Misadventure & Mud Settles. 1977. 15.00 (ISBN 0-686-20794-7, Pub. by Ferry Pr); sewn in wrappers 5.00 (ISBN 0-686-20795-5). Small Pr Dist.

--A Forest Utilization Family. (Burning Deck Poetry Ser.). 28p. (Orig.). 1982. pap. 3.00 (ISBN 0-930901-09-6). Burning Deck.

--Iron Britannia. 160p. (Orig.). Date not set. pap. 5.95 (ISBN 0-8052-8149-5, Pub. by Allison & Busby England). Schocken.

--Poem About Music. (Burning Deck Poetry Ser.). 1974. 15.00 (ISBN 0-930900-00-6); pap. 4.00 (ISBN 0-930900-01-4). Burning Deck.

--Titular. 1975. signed 6.00 (ISBN 0-685-78958-6, Pub. by Grosseteste); sewn in wrappers 0.75 (ISBN 0-685-78959-4). Small Pr Dist.

Barnett, Anthony see Barnett, S. A.

Barnett, B. Aspects of Vocal Multiphonics. Date not set. 7.25 (ISBN 0-939044-19-6). Lingua Pr.

Barnett, Canon. The Ideal City. Meller, Helen, ed. (The Victorian Library). 1979. text ed. 18.75x (ISBN 0-7185-5061-7, Leicester). Humanities.

Barnett, Carne S. & Young, Sharon. Teaching Kids Math: Problem-Solving Activities to Help Young Children Learn & Enjoy Mathematics. (Illus.). 163p. 1982. 14.95 (ISBN 0-13-893537-8); pap. 7.95 (ISBN 0-13-893529-7). P-H.

Barnett, Carolyn, jt. auth. see Casella, Jeanne.

Barnett, Charles. Team Teaching in the Elementary School. Reed, R., ed. LC 81-83631. (Orig.). 1982. 13.95 (ISBN 0-88247-640-8); pap. 8.95 (ISBN 0-88247-606-8). R & E Pubs.

Barnett, Clifford R., jt. auth. see MacGaffey, Wyatt.

Barnett, Clifford R., et al. Poland. LC 58-11469. (Area & Country Surveys Ser.). 479p. 1958. 18.00x (ISBN 0-87536-901-4). HRAFP.

Barnett, Coleman. An Introduction to Structured Programming Using BASIC. 520p. 1984. pap. text ed. 23.95x (ISBN 0-89787-402-1). Gorsuch Scarisbrick.

Barnett, Correlli. Bonaparte. (Illus.). 224p. 1978. 19.95 (ISBN 0-8090-3049-7). Hill & Wang.

--The Desert Generals: New Edition. LC 82-47957. (Illus.). 352p. (Orig.). 1983. 17.95 (ISBN 0-253-11600-7). Ind U Pr.

--The Swordbearers: Supreme Command in the First World War. LC 74-19057. (Midland Bks.: No. 175). (Illus.). 416p. 1975. 22.50x (ISBN 0-253-35584-2); pap. 9.95x (ISBN 0-253-20175-6). Ind U Pr.

Barnett, Cynthia. Ben's Gift. (Sundown Fiction Ser.). 64p. 1981. 2.00 (ISBN 0-88336-705-X). New Readers.

Barnett, David. Stevenson Study, Treasure Island. LC 73-16347. 1924. lib. bdg. 8.50 (ISBN 0-8414-3339-9). Folcroft.

--Treasure Island: A Stevenson Study. 1979. 24.50 (ISBN 0-685-65707-8). Porter.

Barnett, David W. Nondiscriminatory Multifactored Assessment: A Sourcebook. (Illus.). 1982. 29.95x (ISBN 0-89885-080-0); pap. 14.95x (ISBN 0-89885-082-7). Human Sci Pr.

Barnett, Dick. Inside Basketball. (Inside Sports Ser.). (Illus.). 87p. 1971. PLB avail (ISBN 0-685-28676-2); pap. 6.95 (ISBN 0-8092-8860-5). Contemp Bks.

Barnett, Donald F. & Schorsch, Louis. Steel: Upheaval in a Basic Industry. LC 82-10012. 344p. 1983. prof. ref. 29.95x (ISBN 0-88410-397-8). Ballinger Pub.

Barnett, Donald L. & Njama, Karari. Mau Mau from Within: An Analysis of Kenya's Peasant Revolt. LC 65-24519. 512p. 1968. pap. 7.50 (ISBN 0-85345-135-4). Monthly Rev.

Barnett, Edgar. Unlock Your Mind & Be Free! A Practical Approach to Hypnotherapy. 153p. 1984. pap. 8.95 (ISBN 0-930298-49-7). Westwood Pub Co.

Barnett, F. J., et al, eds. History & Structure of French: Essays in Honour of Professor T. B. W. Reid. 268p. 1972. 17.50x (ISBN 0-87471-125-8). Rowman.

Barnett, Franklin. Dictionary of Prehistoric Indian Artifacts of the American Southwest. LC 73-82865. (Illus.). 288p. 1973. pap. 8.95 (ISBN 0-87358-120-2). Northland.

--Excavation of Main Pueblo at Fitzmaurice Ruin. (Illus.). 1974. pap. 7.50 (ISBN 0-89734-017-5). Mus Northern Ariz.

Barnett, G. J., tr. see Moreau, J. J., et al.

Barnett, Gabriel. The Magic Watch. 208p. 1984. 14.95 (ISBN 0-8059-2953-3). Dorrance.

Barnett, Gabrielle, jt. auth. see Barnett, Michael.

Barnett, Gene & Chang, C. Nora, eds. Pharmacokinetics & Pharmacodynamics of Psychoactive Drugs. LC 85-70734. (Illus.). 500p. 1985. text ed. 35.00 (ISBN 0-931890-20-9). Biomed Pubns.

Barnett, George E. Chapters on Machinery & Labor. LC 68-25563. (Arcturus Books Paperbacks Ser.). 191p. 1969. pap. 2.25x (ISBN 0-8093-0398-1). S Ill U Pr.

--Chapters on Machinery & Labor. LC 68-25563. (Masterworks in Industrial Relations Ser.). 191p. 1969. Repr. of 1926 ed. 6.95x (ISBN 0-8093-0397-3). S Ill U Pr.

--The Printers: A Study in American Trade Unionism. 1977. lib. bdg. 59.95 (ISBN 0-8490-2481-1). Gordon Pr.

--State Banking in the United States. 59.95 (ISBN 0-8490-1122-1). Gordon Pr.

--State Banking in the United States Since the Passage of the National Bank Act. LC 78-63887. (Johns Hopkins University. Studies in the Social Sciences. Twentieth Ser. 1902: 2-3). Repr. of 1902 ed. 24.50 (ISBN 0-404-61141-9). AMS Pr.

--State Banks & Trust Companies. LC 68-30516. 1911. 35.00x (ISBN 0-678-00503-6). Kelley.

Barnett, George E. & McCabe, David A. Mediation, Investigation & Arbitration in Industrial Disputes. LC 75-156403. (American Labor Ser., No. 2). Repr. of 1916 ed. 19.00 (ISBN 0-405-02913-6). Ayer Co Pubs.

Barnett, George E., jt. auth. see Hollander, Jacob H.

Barnett, George E., ed. A Trial Bibliography of American Trade-Union Publications. LC 78-63900. (Johns Hopkins Univesity. Studies in the Social Sciences. Twenty-Second Ser. 1904: 1-2). Repr. of 1904 ed. 16.00 (ISBN 0-404-61153-2). AMS Pr.

Barnett, George E., jt. ed. see Hollander, Jacob H.

Barnett, George L. Charles Lamb: The Evolution of Elia. LC 72-6858. (English Literature Ser., No. 33). 1972. Repr. of 1964 ed. lib. bdg. 49.95x (ISBN 0-8383-1652-2). Haskell.

Barnett, George L., ed. Eighteenth Century British Novelists on the Novel. LC 68-19045. (Goldentree Books in English Literature). (Orig.). 1968. pap. text ed. 6.95x (ISBN 0-89197-136-X). Irvington.

--Nineteenth-Century British Novelists on the Novel. LC 75-130791. (Goldentree Books in English Literature). (Orig.). 1971. 32.00x (ISBN 0-89197-317-6); pap. text ed. 10.95x (ISBN 0-89197-318-4). Irvington.

Barnett, Graham K., jt. auth. see Barnett, Michael P.

Barnett, Gregg. Commodore 64 Games Book II. (Illus.). 206p. (Orig.). (gr. 6up). 1984. pap. 12.95 (ISBN 0-86161-178-0). Melbourne Hse.

Barnett, H. G. Qualitative Science. LC 82-90249. 1983. 15.00 (ISBN 0-533-05373-0). Vantage.

Barnett, H. J., et al, eds. Acetylsalicylic Acid: New Uses for an Old Drug. 288p. 1982. text ed. 57.00 (ISBN 0-89004-647-6). Raven.

--Cerebrovascular Diseases: New Trends in Surgical & Medical Aspects. (Symposium of the Giovanni Lorenzini Foundation: Vol. 12). 408p. 1982. 78.50 (ISBN 0-444-80381-5). Elsevier.

Barnett, H. J., jt. ed. see Handa, Hajime.

Barnett, H. Villiers, tr. see Massenet, Jules E.

Barnett, Harold J. Atomic Energy in the United States Economy: A Consideration of Certain Industrial, Regional, & Economic Development Aspects. Bruchey, Stuart, ed. LC 78-22658. (Energy in the American Economy Ser.). (Illus.). 1979. lib. bdg. 25.50x (ISBN 0-405-11962-3). Ayer Co Pubs.

Barnett, Harold J. & Morse, Chandler. Scarcity & Growth: The Economics of Natural Resource Availability. (Resources for the Future Ser). (Illus.). 304p. 1963. 25.00x (ISBN 0-8018-0056-0); pap. 8.00x (ISBN 0-8018-0057-9). Johns Hopkins.

Barnett, Harold J & Morse, Chandler. Scarcity & Growth: The Economics of Natural Resource Availability. 304p. 1963. 25.00 (ISBN 0-8018-0056-0); 8.00 (ISBN 0-8018-0057-9). Resources Future.

Barnett, Henrietta O., jt. auth. see Barnett, Samuel A.

Barnett, Herbert E. & Fraser, Hugh, eds. Who's Who in Canada, 1980-1981. 70th ed. (Illus.). 1496p. 1980. 75.00x (ISBN 0-8002-2744-1). Intl Pubns Serv.

Barnett, Hert E. & Fraser, Hugh, eds. Who's Who in Canada, 1982-83. LC 17-16282. (Illus.). 1608p. 1982. 82.50x (ISBN 0-919339-02-6). Intl Pubns Serv.

Barnett, Homer. Indian Shakers: A Messianic Cult of the Pacific Northwest. LC 72-5482. (Arcturus Books Paperbacks). (Illus.). 383p. 1972. pap. 7.95 (ISBN 0-8093-0595-X). S Ill U Pr.

Barnett, Homer G. Being a Palauan: Fieldwork Edition. 2nd ed. LC 78-16350. 1979. pap. text ed. 9.95 (ISBN 0-03-045366-6, HoltC). HR&W.

--The Coast Salish of British Columbia. LC 75-25251. (Univ. of Oregon Monographs, Studies in Anthropology: No. 4). (Illus.). 320p. 1975. Repr. of 1955 ed. lib. bdg. 25.00x (ISBN 0-8371-8381-2, BACSB). Greenwood.

Barnett, Horace L. & Hunter, Barry B. Illustrated Genera of Imperfect Fungi. 3rd ed. LC 71-163710. 1972. spiral bdg. 13.95x (ISBN 0-8087-0266-1). Burgess.

Barnett, J. A., et al. A Guide to Identifying & Classifying Yeasts. LC 79-11136. (Illus.). 1979. 99.00 (ISBN 0-521-22762-3). Cambridge U Pr.

--Yeasts: Characteristics & Identification. LC 83-8390. 811p. 1984. 150.00 (ISBN 0-521-25296-2). Cambridge U Pr.

Barnett, J. H. The American Divorce Novel. 59.95 (ISBN 0-87968-597-2). Gordon Pr.

Barnett, J. R., ed. Xylem Cell Development. (Illus.). 315p. 1981. text ed. 62.50 (ISBN 0-7194-0050-3, Pub. by Castle Hse England). J K Burgess.

Barnett, James H. The American Christmas: A Study in National Culture. LC 75-22799. (America in Two Centuries Ser.). 1976. Repr. of 1954 ed. 17.00x (ISBN 0-405-07671-1). Ayer Co Pubs.

Barnett, James M. The Diaconate: A Full & Equal Order. 256p. (Orig.). 1981. pap. 9.95 (ISBN 0-8164-2331-8, Pub. by Seabury). Winston Pr.

Barnett, Joe R. Just for Today. (Direction Bks.). pap. 2.95 (ISBN 0-8010-0785-2). Baker Bk.

--Live, with Peace, Power & Purpose. Thomas, J. D., ed. (Twentieth Century Sermons Ser.). 1978. 11.95 (ISBN 0-89112-311-3). Bibl Res Pr.

Barnett, Joe R. & Gipson, John D. Some Quiet Place. (Illus.). 1981. gift ed. 7.95 (ISBN 0-915720-53-1). Brownlow Pub Co.

Barnett, Joel. Inside the Treasury: British. (Illus.). 272p. 1981. 19.95 (ISBN 0-233-97394-X). Andre Deutsch.

--Inside the Treasury: British. (Illus.). 272p. 1981. 21.00 (ISBN 0-233-97394-X, Pub. by A Deutsch England). David & Charles.

Barnett, Jonathan. An Introduction to Urban Design. LC 81-47792. (Icon Editions Ser.). (Illus.). 1982. 20.14i (ISBN 0-06-430376-4, HarpT). Har-Row.

Barnett, L. D. Brahma-Knowledge, Philosophy of Vedanta. 59.95 (ISBN 0-87968-780-0). Gordon Pr.

--Panjabi Printed Books in the British Museum: A Supplementary Catalogue. 132p. 1981. 40.00x (ISBN 0-7141-0624-0, CPub. by Brit Lib England). State Mutual Bk.

Barnett, L. D., ed. Catalogue of Sanskrit, Pali & Prakrit Books in the British Museum: 3rd Supplement, (1906-1928) 856p. 1928. 60.00 (ISBN 0-7141-0633-X, Pub. by British Lib). Longwood Pub Group.

Barnett, L. D., tr. A Jain Scripture: The Anuttarovava-Dasao. 1984. pap. 3.95 (ISBN 0-916411-47-8, Pub. by Oriental Classics). Holmes Pub.

Barnett, L. D., tr. see Joachim, Hermann.

Barnett, L. Margaret. British Food Policy During the First World War. 256p. 1985. text ed. 30.00x (ISBN 0-04-942189-1). Allen Unwin.

Barnett, Larry D. Population Policy & the U. S. Constitution. (Studies in Human Issues). 1982. lib. bdg. 25.00 (ISBN 0-89838-082-0). Kluwer-Nijhoff.

Barnett, Larry D. & Reed, Emily F. Law, Society, & Population: Issues in a New Field. LC 84-71502. 210p. 1985. text ed. 29.95 (ISBN 0-88105-053-9). Cap & Gown.

Barnett, Laurie, jt. ed. see Keylin, Arlene.

Barnett, Leonard. Homosexuality: Time to Tell the Truth. 1975. 14.95 (ISBN 0-575-01935-2, Pub. by Gollancz England). David & Charles.

Barnett, Lincoln. The Universe & Dr. Einstein. 14.95 (ISBN 0-8488-0146-6, Pub. by Amereon Hse). Amereon Ltd.

Barnett, Lionel. Greek Drama. LC 73-9662. 1900. lib. bdg. 16.50 (ISBN 0-8414-3143-4). Folcroft.

Barnett, Lionel D. The Greek Drama. 1979. Repr. of 1900 ed. lib. bdg. 15.00 (ISBN 0-8495-0450-3). Arden Lib.

Barnett, Louise K. Ignoble Savage: American Literary Racism, 1790-1890. LC 75-16964. (Contributions in American Studies: No. 18). 220p. 1975. lib. bdg. 29.95x (ISBN 0-8371-8281-6, BIG/). Greenwood.

--Swift's Poetic Worlds. LC 80-54538. 224p. 1981. 22.50 (ISBN 0-87413-187-1). U Delaware Pr.

Barnett, Louise K., jt. ed. see Jeannet, Angela M.

Barnett, M. E., jt. auth. see Klemperer, Otto.

Barnett, M. R. The Politics of Cultural Nationalism in South India. 1976. 40.00 (ISBN 0-691-07577-8). Princeton U Pr.

Barnett, Margaret E. Introduction to Medical Microbiology. LC 85-4141. 210p. 1985. pap. 25.00 (ISBN 0-933195-00-1). Cal College Pr.

Barnett, Marguerite, tr. see Domalain, Jean-Yves.

Barnett, Marva T. Writing for Technicians. Rev. ed. LC 80-69550. (Technical Communications Ser.). 358p. 1982. pap. text ed. 14.00 (ISBN 0-8273-1867-7); instr's. guide 4.20 (ISBN 0-8273-1868-5). Delmar.

Barnett, Michael & Barnett, Gabrielle. Beginning Graphics for the Commodore 64. 1984. cancelled. Reston.

Barnett, Michael & Barnett, Simon. Your Family & the Timex-Sinclair 1000. 1983. 12.95 (ISBN 0-8359-9502-X). Reston.

Barnett, Michael P. & Barnett, Graham K. Personal Graphics for Profit & Pleasure on the Apple II Plus and IIe Personal Computers. (Microcomputer Bookshelf Ser.). 208p. 1982. pap. text ed. 14.50 (ISBN 0-316-08164-7). Little.

--Personal Graphics for Profit & Pleasure on the IBM Personal Computer. (Little, Brown Microcomputer Bookshelf Ser.). 225p. (Orig.). 1984. pap. 14.50 (ISBN 0-316-08220-1). Little.

Barnett, Nancy B. & Baker, John T. Texas Instruments Compact Computer Forty User's Guide. 336p. (Orig.). 1983. pap. 14.95 (ISBN 0-89512-057-7). Tex Instr Inc.

Barnett, Pankhurst. A New Key to the Yeasts. LC 73-86076. 273p. 1974. 98.75 (ISBN 0-444-10580-8, Biomedical Pr). Elsevier.

Barnett, Paul, tr. see Vassal, Jacques.

Barnett, Peggy, jt. auth. see Spicer, Jerry.

Barnett, Peter. Tools of Thought: The Practical Foundations of Formal Reasoning. 310p. 1981. 18.95x (ISBN 0-87073-655-8); pap. text ed. 9.95x (ISBN 0-87073-656-6). Schenkman Bks Inc.

Barnett, Peter & McKenzie, Joseph. Alternative Mortgage Instruments. 1984. 72.00 (ISBN 0-88712-070-9). Warren.

Barnett, Peter, et al. Parenting Children of Divorce. LC 80-11044. (Workshop Models for Family Life Education Ser.). 111p. 1980. plastic comb 13.95 (ISBN 0-87304-178-X). Family Serv.

Barnett, Peter H. Can You Tell Me How What You Are Doing Now Is to Do Something Philosophical? pap. 5.00 (ISBN 0-686-62107-7). Assembling Pr.

--Time Trap. LC 79-57447. (Illus.). 50p. 1980. pap. 5.00 (ISBN 0-686-65258-4). Assembling Pr.

Barnett, R., jt. auth. see Baruch, G.

Barnett, R. A. College Algebra, Trigonometry & Analytic Geometry. 608p. 1984. 31.95 (ISBN 0-07-003881-3). McGraw.

--Functions & Graphs: A Precalculus Course. LC 84-12519. 800p. 1985. 31.95 (ISBN 0-07-003896-1); 12.95 (ISBN 0-07-003898-8). McGraw.

Barnett, Randy & Hagel, John, eds. Assessing the Criminal: Restitution, Retribution & the Legal Process. LC 77-21388. 432p. 1977. prof ref 29.95 (ISBN 0-88410-785-X). Ballinger Pub.

Barnett, Raymond A. Algebra: An Elementary Course. (Illus.). 560p. 1983. text ed. 26.95 wkbk. (ISBN 0-07-003741-8). McGraw.

--Analytic Trigonometry with Applications. 3rd ed. 320p. write for info. (ISBN 0-534-02858-6). Wadsworth Pub.

--Calculus for Management, Life, & Social Science. 3rd ed. (Illus.). 385p. 1984. text ed. 27.95 (ISBN 0-02-306130-8). Dellen Pub.

--College Algebra. 2nd ed. (Illus.). 1979. text ed. 26.95 (ISBN 0-07-003778-7). McGraw.

--College Algebra. 3rd, rev. ed. (Illus.). 544p. text ed. 29.95 (ISBN 0-07-003861-9). McGraw.

--College Mathematics for Management, Life, & Social Sciences. 3rd ed. LC 83-26147. (Illus.). 689p. 1984. text ed. 29.95 (ISBN 0-02-306220-7). Dellen Pub.

--Elementary Algebra: Structure & Use. 3rd ed. 1980. text ed. 27.95x (ISBN 0-07-003840-6). McGraw.

--Essentials of Algebra for College Students. 1976. text ed. 27.95 (ISBN 0-07-003756-6). McGraw.

--Finite Mathematics for Management, Life & Social Science. 3rd ed. (Illus.). 487p. 1984. text ed. 28.95 (ISBN 0-02-306370-X). Dellen Pub.

--Intermediate Algebra. 2nd ed. (Illus.). 1980. text ed. 27.95 (ISBN 0-07-003750-7). McGraw.

Barnett, Raymond A. & Burke, Charles J. Applied Mathematics for Business & Economics, Life Sciences & Social Sciences. (Illus.). 856p. 1983. text ed. 24.95 (ISBN 0-02-306310-6). Dellen Pub.

Barnett, Raymond A. & Fujii, John N. Vectors. LC 75-12664. 140p. 1975. Repr. of 1963 ed. text ed. 11.50 (ISBN 0-88275-290-1). Krieger.

Barnett, Raymond A. & Ziegler, Michael R. Applied Calculus. (Illus.). 674p. 1982. text ed. 28.95 (ISBN 0-89517-036-1). Dellen Pub.

Barnett, Regina R. Create, Two. 31p. (Orig.). (ps). 1979. pap. text ed. 5.95 student work pad (ISBN 0-697-01705-2); tchrs.' manual 12.95 (ISBN 0-697-01706-0). Wm C Brown.

--Let Out the Sunshine. 144p. (Orig.). (YA) 1981. pap. text ed. 12.00 (ISBN 0-697-01762-1). Wm C Brown.

Barnett, Richard, ed. Scanner Master Connecticut & Rhode Island Guide: Code & Unit Manual. (Scanner Master Frequency Guides Ser.: No. 3). 96p. 1983. 9.95 (ISBN 0-939430-02-9). Scanner Master.

--Scanner Master Connecticut & Rhode Island Guide: Frequency Manual. (Scanner Master Frequency Guides Ser.: No. 2). (Illus.). 96p. 1983. 9.95 (ISBN 0-939430-01-0). Scanner Master.

--Scanner Master Massachusetts Supplement. (Scanner Master Frequency Guides Ser.: No. 7). 50p. (Orig.). 1983. 7.95 (ISBN 0-939430-06-1). Scanner Master.

Barnett, Richard & Soomre, Edward, eds. Scanner Master Massachusetts Guide. 2nd ed. (Frequency Guides Ser.: No. 9). (Illus.). 1985. write for info. (ISBN 0-939430-08-8). Scanner Master.

--Scanner Master New England Guide. (Frequency Guides Ser.: No. 10). (Illus.). 1985. write for info. (ISBN 0-939430-09-6). Scanner Master.

Barnett, Richard B. North India Between Empires: Awadh, the Mughals, & the British, 1720-1801. LC 78-64459. (Center for South & Southeast Asian Studies). 294p. 1980. 35.00x (ISBN 0-520-03787-1). U of Cal Pr.

Barnett, Robert E. Responsibilities & Liabilities of Bank & Bank Holding Company Directors. 120p. 1985. 10.00 (ISBN 0-317-30610-3, 4763). Commerce.

--Responsibilities & Liabilities of Bank Directors. 88p. 1980. pap. 8.50 (ISBN 0-317-04295-5, 5203). Commerce.

--Responsibilities & Liabilities of Savings Institutions Directors. 112p. 1984. pap. 10.50 (ISBN 0-317-19244-2, 4828). Commerce.

Barnett, Robert M. Analysis, Computation, Presentation of Engineering Information. 8.50 (ISBN 0-89741-000-9); pap. 7.95x (ISBN 0-686-96874-3). Roadrunner Tech.

Barnett, Robert W. Beyond War: Japan's Concept of Comprehensive National Security. (Illus.). 176p. 1984. 21.00 (ISBN 0-08-031617-4); pap. 14.00 (ISBN 0-08-031952-1). Pergamon.

--Economic Shanghai: Hostage to Politics, 1937-1941. LC 75-30094. (Institute of Pacific Relations). Repr. of 1941 ed. 20.00 (ISBN 0-404-59504-9). AMS Pr.

Barnett, Rosalind & Baruch, Grace K. The Competent Woman: Perspectives on Development. (Social Relations Ser.). 184p. 1978. 12.95X (ISBN 0-470-26424-1). Halsted Pr.

Barnett, Rosalind, jt. auth. see Rivers, Caryl.

Barnett, Rosalind C. & Baruch, Grace K. Competent Woman: Perspectives on Development. LC 78-8380. (Irvington Social Relations Ser.). 1980. text ed. 17.50x (ISBN 0-8290-0853-5); pap. text ed. 7.95x (ISBN 0-8290-0092-5). Irvington.

Barnett, Roy N. Clinical Laboratory Statistics. 2nd ed. (Series in Laboratory Medicine). 224p. 1979. 28.50 (ISBN 0-316-08196-5). Little.

Barnett, S. & Cronin, T. M. Mathematical Formulae for Engineering & Science Students. 1981. 25.00x (ISBN 0-901945-35-8, Pub. by Bradford U Pr England). State Mutual Bk.

Barnett, S. A. The Human Species: The Biology of Man. (Illus.). 12.75 (ISBN 0-8446-0477-1). Peter Smith.

--Modern Ethology: The Science of Animal Behavior. (Illus.). 1981. text ed. 25.95x (ISBN 0-19-502780-9). Oxford U Pr.

--The Rat: A Study in Behavior. 3rd, rev. ed. LC 74-33509. xiv, 318p. 1976. lib. bdg. 22.00x (ISBN 0-226-03740-1); pap. 11.00x (ISBN 0-226-03742-8). U of Chicago Pr.

Barnett, S. A., ed. Ethology & Development. (Clinics in Developmental Medicine Ser.: Vol. 47). 128p. 1973. text ed. 17.00 (ISBN 0-686-86965-6, Pub. by Spastics Intl England). Lippincott.

--Lessons from Animal Behaviour for the Clinician. (Clinics in Developmental Medicine Ser. No. 7). 50p. 1962. 4.00i (ISBN 0-685-24713-9). Har-Row.

Barnett, Samuel, ed. Century of Darwin. facs. ed. LC 71-76891. (Essay Index Reprint Ser). 1958. 21.25 (ISBN 0-8369-1019-2). Ayer Co Pubs.

Barnett, Samuel A. & Barnett, Henrietta O. Practicable Socialism: Essays on Social Reform. LC 72-3394. (Essay Index Reprint Ser.). Repr. of 1888 ed. 15.00 (ISBN 0-8369-2891-1). Ayer Co Pubs.

Barnett, Simon, jt. auth. see Barnett, Michael.

Barnett, Stanley M., ed. see North Eastern Regional Antipollution Conference, 6th, 1975, et al.

Barnett, Stephen. Introduction to Mathematical Control Theory. (Oxford Applied Mathematics & Engineering Sciences Ser). (Illus.). 1975. pap. 20.95x (ISBN 0-19-859619-7). Oxford U Pr.

--Matrices in Control Theory. rev. ed. LC 82-21321. 206p. 1984. lib. bdg. 14.50 (ISBN 0-89874-590-X). Krieger.

--Matrix Methods for Engineers & Scientists. 185p. 1979. pap. text ed. 23.95 (ISBN 0-07-084084-9). McGraw.

Barnett, Steve. Cross-Country Downhill & Other Nordic Mountain Skiing Techniques. 3rd ed. LC 79-20673. (Illus.). 112p. 1983. pap. text ed. 10.95 (ISBN 0-914718-84-3). Pacific Search.

Barnett, Steve & Silverman, Martin G. Ideology & Everyday Life: Anthropology, Neomarxist Thought, & the Problem of Ideology & the Social Whole. 192p. 1979. pap. 7.95x (ISBN 0-472-02704-2). U of Mich Pr.

Barnett, Suzanne W. & Fairbank, John K., eds. Christianity in China: Early Protestant Missionary Writings. (Harvard Studies in American-East Asian Relations: 9). 280p. 1984. text ed. 20.00x (ISBN 0-674-12881-8). Harvard U Pr.

Barnett, Timothy L. & Flora, Steven R. Exploring God's Web of Life. 80p. 1982. pap. 5.25 (ISBN 0-942684-01-X). Camp Guidepts.

Barnett, Tony. The Gezira Scheme: An Illusion of Development. 192p. 1977. 32.50x (ISBN 0-7146-3060-8, F Cass Co). Biblio Dist.

Barnett, Ursula A. A Vision of Order: A Study of Black South African Literature in English, 1914-1980. LC 83-9296. 336p. 1983. lib. bdg. 21.00x (ISBN 0-87023-406-4). U of Mass Pr.

Barnett, V. Comparative Statistical Inference. LC 73-1833. (Probability & Mathematical Statistics Ser.: Probability Section). 287p. 1973. 49.95x (ISBN 0-471-05401-1, Pub. by Wiley-Interscience). Wiley.

Barnett, Vic. Comparative Statistical Inference. 2nd ed. (Probability & Mathematical Statistics Ser.: Applied Probability & Statistics Section). 325p. 1982. 44.95x (ISBN 0-471-10076-5, Pub. by Wiley Interscience). Wiley.

--Elements of Sampling Theory. 152p. 1975. pap. text ed. 12.50x (ISBN 0-8448-0614-5). Crane-Russak Co.

Barnett, Vic & Lewis, Toby. Outlines in Statistical Data. LC 77-21024. (Probability & Mathematical Statistics Ser.: Applied Section). 365p. 1978. 74.95x (ISBN 0-471-99599-1, Pub. by Wiley-Interscience). Wiley.

Barnett, Vic & Barnett, eds. Interpreting Multivariate Data: Proceedings. (Wiley Ser. in Probability & Mathematical Statistics - Applied Probability & Statistics Section). 374p. 1981. 64.95x (ISBN 0-471-28039-9, Pub. by Wiley-Interscience). Wiley.

Barnett, Vivian E. Handbook: The Guggenheim Museum Collection 1900-1980. 2nd ed. (Illus.). 528p. 1984. pap. 18.00 (ISBN 0-89207-046-3). S R Guggenheim.

--Kandinsky at the Guggenheim. LC 83-3903. (Illus.). 312p. 1983. 45.00 (ISBN 0-89659-398-3). Abbeville Pr.

--One Hundred Works by Modern Masters from the Guggenheim Museum. (Illus.). 212p. 1984. 49.50 (ISBN 0-8109-0370-9). Abrams.

Barnett, Vivian E., jt. auth. see Guggenheim, Solomon R., Foundation.

Barnett, W. A. Consumer Demand & Labor Supply: Goods, Monetary Assets & Time. (Studies in Mathematical & Managerial Economics: Vol. 29). 378p. 1981. 70.25 (ISBN 0-444-86097-5). Elsevier.

Barnett, W. Steven. A Benefit-Cost Analysis of the Perry Preschool Program & its Long-Term Effects. 115p. (Orig.). 1985. pap. 15.00 (ISBN 0-931114-34-9, #54). High-Scope.

Barnett, Walter. Homosexuality & the Bible: An Interpretation. LC 79-84920. 1979. pap. 2.30x (ISBN 0-87574-226-2). Pendle Hill.

--Jesus: the Story of His Life: A Modern Retelling Based on the Gospels. LC 75-28260. 1976. 19.95x (ISBN 0-88229-308-7). Nelson Hall.

Barnett Duster, Alfreda M., ed. see Wells, Ida B.

Barnette, Curtis H., et al. Corporate Law Departments & Outside Counsel II. LC 84-137513. vii, 85p. Date not set. price not set (Law & Business). HarBraceJ.

Barnette, David W. Map Coloring, Polyhedra & the Four-Color Problem. (Dolciani Mathematical Expositions Ser.: Vol. 8). 1984. 30.00 (ISBN 0-88385-309-4, 82062783). Math Assn.

Barnette, Helen P. Your Child's Mind: Making the Most of Public Schools. LC 83-26109. (Potentials: Guides for Productive Living Ser.: Vol. 2). 112p. (Orig.). 1984. pap. 7.95 (ISBN 0-664-24519-6). Westminster.

Barnette, Henlee. Your Freedom to Be Whole. LC 84-2381. (Potentials: Guides to Productive Living Ser.: Vol. 7). 118p. 1984. pap. 7.95 (ISBN 0-664-24526-9). Westminster.

Barnette, Henlee H. Exploring Medical Ethics. LC 82-2116. 183p. 1982. 12.95x (ISBN 0-86554-031-4). Mercer Univ Pr.

--Introducing Christian Ethics. LC 61-5629. 1961. 9.95 (ISBN 0-8054-6102-7). Broadman.

Barnett-Mizrahi, Carol, jt. ed. see Trueba, Henry T.

Barney, Frances. Summer of Awakening. (YA) 1979. 8.95 (ISBN 0-685-93879-4, Avalon). Bouregy.

Barney, G. C. & Dos Santos, S. M. Lift (Elevator) Traffic Analysis, Design & Control. (IEE Control Engineering Ser.: No. 2). (Illus.). 331p. 1977. 62.00 (ISBN 0-901223-86-7, CE002). Inst Elect Eng.

Barney, G. O., et al. Global Two Thousand: Implications for Canada. (Illus.). 196p. 1981. 39.00 (ISBN 0-08-025390-3); pap. 11.00 (ISBN 0-08-025389-X). Pergamon.

Barney, G. Scott, et al, eds. Geochemical Behavior of Disposed Radioactive Waste. LC 83-3106. (ACS Symposium Ser.: No. 246). 413p. 1984. lib. bdg. 79.95x (ISBN 0-8412-0827-1). Am Chemical.

Barney, George C. Intelligent Instrumentation: Microprocessor Applications in Measurement & Control. (Illus.). 528p. 1986. text ed. 39.95 (ISBN 0-13-468943-7). P-H.

Barney, Gerald O. The Global Two Thousand Report to the President of the U. S. Entering the 21st Century, 3 vols. Incl. Vl. I. Summary Report; Vol. II. Technical Supplement; Vol. III. Global Modeling. 35.00 (ISBN 0-08-025990-1). (Pergamon Policy Studies on Policy, Planning & Modeling). 800p. 83.00 (ISBN 0-08-025991-X). Pergamon.

Barney, Gerald O., ed. The Global Two Thousand Report to the President of the U. S.-Entering the 21st Century: The Summary Report--Special Edition with Environment Projections & the Government's Global Model, Vol. 1. (Pergamon Policy Studies Ser.). 200p. 1984. 33.00 (ISBN 0-08-024617-6); pap. 10.95 (ISBN 0-08-024616-8). Pergamon.

--The Unfinished Agenda. LC 76-30486. 1977. pap. 3.95i (ISBN 0-690-01482-1). T Y Crowell.

Barney, Kenneth D. Directions, Please. LC 82-82080. 128p. (Orig.). 1983. pap. 2.50 (ISBN 0-88243-856-5, 02-0856); tchr's. ed. 3.95 (ISBN 0-88243-197-8, 32-0197). Gospel Pub.

--A Faith to Live by. LC 76-27929. (Radiant Life Ser.). 128p. 1977. pap. 2.50 (ISBN 0-88243-899-9, 02-0899); teacher's ed. 3.95 (ISBN 0-88243-171-4, 32-0171). Gospel Pub.

--The Fellowship of the Holy Spirit. LC 77-70475. 96p. 1977. pap. 1.25 (ISBN 0-88243-515-9, 02-0515). Gospel Pub.

--Fourth Watch of the Night. 96p. 1973. 1.50 (ISBN 0-88243-724-0, 02-0724). Gospel Pub.

--Freedom: A Guarantee for Everybody. LC 75-34644. (Radiant Life Ser.). 128p. 1976. pap. 2.50 (ISBN 0-88243-891-3, 02-0891, Radiant Bks); teacher's ed 3.95 (ISBN 0-88243-165-X, 32-0165). Gospel Pub.

--If You Love Me... LC 75-22611. (Radiant Life Ser.). 128p. 1977. pap. 2.50 (ISBN 0-88243-889-1, 02-0889); teacher's ed 2.50 (ISBN 0-88243-163-3, 32-0163). Gospel Pub.

--It Began in an Upper Room. LC 78-67445. 128p. 1978. pap. 1.50 (ISBN 0-88243-528-0, 02-0528, Radiant Bks). Gospel Pub.

--The Longest War. LC 82-83915. 128p. (Orig.). 1984. pap. 2.50 (ISBN 0-88243-536-1, 02-0536). Gospel Pub.

--Preparing for the Storm. LC 74-21021. 96p. 1975. pap. 1.25 (ISBN 0-88243-576-0, 02-0576). Gospel Pub.

--We Interrupt This Crisis. 63p. 1970. pap. 1.25 (ISBN 0-88243-704-6, 02-0704). Gospel Pub.

--You'd Better Believe It! LC 75-22608. (Radiant Bks.). 128p. 1976. pap. 2.50 (ISBN 0-88243-887-5, 02-0887); teacher's ed 3.95 (ISBN 0-88243-161-7, 32-0161). Gospel Pub.

Barney, Laura C., tr. see Abdu'l-Baha.

Barney, Natalie. Traits et Portraits. LC 75-12303. (Homosexuality: Lesbians & Gay Men in Society, History & Literature Ser.). (French.). 1975. Repr. of 1963 ed. 13.00x (ISBN 0-405-07395-X). Ayer Co Pubs.

Barney, Natalie C. Aventures De L'esprit. LC 75-12302. (Homosexuality Ser.). (French.). 1975. Repr. of 1929 ed. 20.00x (ISBN 0-405-07394-1). Ayer Co Pubs.

Barney, Philip L. Pathology of the Nose & Paranasal Sinuses. LC 82-720085. (Atlases of the Pathology of the Head & Neck Ser.). 1982. incl. slides 110.00 (ISBN 0-89189-082-3, 15-1-029-00). Am Soc Clinical.

Barney, Ralph D., jt. ed. see Merril, John C.

Barney, Richard & Loveless, Bob. How to Make Knives. 5th ed. (Illus.). 182p. Repr. of 1977 ed. 16.95 (ISBN 0-911881-00-X). Am Blade Bk Serv.

Barney, Stephen, ed. Chaucer's "Troilus": Essays in Criticism. x, 323p. 1980. 22.50 (ISBN 0-208-01822-0, Archon). Shoe String.

Barney, Stephen A. Allegories of History, Allegories of Love. 323p. 1979. 23.00 (ISBN 0-208-01749-6, Archon). Shoe String.

--Word Hoard Introduction to Old English Vocabulary. 2nd ed. LC 76-47003. (Yale Language Ser.). 96p. 1985. pap. 6.95x (ISBN 0-300-03506-3). Yale U Pr.

Barney, Stephen A., et al. Word-Hoard: An Introduction to Old English Vocabulary. LC 76-47003. 1977. pap. 6.95x (ISBN 0-300-02110-0). Yale U Pr.

Barney, William. The Killdeer Crying: Selected Poems of William Barney. 2nd ed. Oliphant, Dave, ed. (Illus.). 80p. 1983. lib. bdg. 11.95 (ISBN 0-933384-09-2); pap. 7.95 (ISBN 0-933384-07-6). Prickly Pear.

--A Little Kiss of the Nettle. pap. 4.00 (ISBN 0-914476-98-X). Thorp Springs.

Barney, William L. Flawed Victory: A New Perspective on the Civil War. LC 80-68972. 225p. 1980. lib. bdg. 24.25 (ISBN 0-8191-1273-9); pap. text ed. 10.00 (ISBN 0-8191-1274-7). U Pr of Amer.

--The Secessionist Impulse: Alabama & Mississippi in 1860. LC 73-2470. 1974. text ed. 39.00x (ISBN 0-691-04622-0). Princeton U Pr.

Barnfield, George, jt. auth. see Carpenter, Edward.

Barnfield, Richard. The Encomion of Lady Pecunia: Or, the Praise of Money. LC 74-80162. (English Experience Ser.: No. 642). 24p. 1974. Repr. of 1598 ed. 3.50 (ISBN 90-221-0642-X). Walter J Johnson.

Barngrover, Charles L. & Johnson, Timothy E. Personal Finance: Student Workbook. 2nd ed. 67p. 1981. pap. text ed. 12.00 (ISBN 0-471-87781-6). Wiley.

Barngrover, Charles L., et al. Personal Finance. 2nd ed. LC 80-18010. (Finance Ser.). 505p. 1981. text ed. 28.95 (ISBN 0-471-84149-8, Pub. by Grid). Wiley.

Barnham, Henry D., tr. see Nasr Al-Din.

Barnhardt, Marion I., jt. auth. see Lusher, Jeanne M.

Barnhardt, Ray, et al. Anthropology & Educational Administration. 1980. pap. 10.00 (ISBN 0-686-32638-5). Impresora Sahuaro.

Barnhart, Clarence L., jt. auth. see Bloomfield, Leonard.

Barnhart, Clarence L., ed. Scott, Foresman Advanced Dictionary. rev. ed. 1978. 19.95 (ISBN 0-385-14852-6). Doubleday.

--Scott, Foresman Beginning Dictionary. (Illus.). 19.95 (ISBN 0-385-13330-8). Doubleday.

--Scott, Foresman Intermediate Dictionary. (Illus.). 1978. 22.50 (ISBN 0-385-14853-4). Doubleday.

--Thorndike Barnhart Handy Dictionary. 1971. pap. 2.50 (ISBN 0-553-24287-3). Bantam.

Barnhart, Clarence L. & Barnhart, Robert K., eds. The World Book Dictionary, 2 vols. LC 84-45720. (Illus.). 1554p. (gr. 4-12). 1985. Set. lib. bdg. write for info. (ISBN 0-7166-0285-7). World Bk.

Barnhart, Clarence L., et al. Second Barnhart Dictionary of New English. LC 79-6815. 1980. 19.95i (ISBN 0-06-010154-7, HarpT). Har-Row.

Barnhart, Edward N., jt. auth. see Chandler, Albert R.

Barnhart, Edward R., ed. Physician's Desk Reference. (Illus.). 42p. 29.95 (ISBN 0-87489-886-2). Med Economics.

Barnhart, Helene S. How to Write & Sell the Eight Easiest Article Types. LC 85-3227. 256p. 1985. 14.95 (ISBN 0-89879-169-3). Writers Digest.

--Writing Romance Fiction-For Love & Money. LC 83-10585. 272p. 1983. 14.95 (ISBN 0-89879-105-7). Writers Digest.

Barnhart, J. The Study of Religion & Its Meaning. 1977. 19.40x (ISBN 90-279-7762-3). Mouton.

Barnhart, J. D. Valley of Democracy: The Frontier Versus the Plantation in the Ohio Valley, 1775-1818. Repr. of 1953 ed. 22.00 (ISBN 0-527-05350-3). Kraus Repr.

Barnhart, J. E. Religion & the Challenge of Philosophy. (Quality Paperback Ser.: No. 291). 400p. (Orig.). 1975. pap. 5.95 (ISBN 0-8226-0291-1). Littlefield.

Barnhart, Joe, jt. auth. see Warren, Thomas B.

Barnhart, Joe E. & Barnhart, Mary A. The New Birth: A Naturalist View of Religious Conversion. LC 81-9557. xiv, 174p. 1981. 15.50x (ISBN 0-86554-009-8). Mercer Univ Pr.

Barnhart, John D. & Riker, Dorothy L. Indiana to Eighteen Sixteen: The Colonial Period. 536p. 1971. 15.00x (ISBN 0-253-37018-3). Ind U Pr.

Barnhart, Marion I., jt. ed. see Lusher, Jeanne M.

Barnhart, Mary A., jt. auth. see Barnhart, Joe E.

Barnhart, Phil. More Seasonings for Sermons. 1985. 5.95 (ISBN 0-89536-723-8, 5807). CSS of Ohio.

Barnhart, Phillip. Devotions for Insomniacs. (Devotions Ser.). 96p. 1982. pap. 1.95 (ISBN 0-8007-8442-1, Spire Bks). Revell.

--Devotions for Patients. (Devotions Ser.). 96p. 1982. pap. 1.95 (ISBN 0-8007-8455-3, Spire Bks). Revell.

Barnhart, Phillip H. Seasonings for Sermons. 88p. (Orig.). 1980. pap. text ed. 6.25 (ISBN 0-89536-451-4). CSS of Ohio.

Barnhart, Richard M. Along the Border of Heaven: Sung & Yuan Painting from the C. C. Wang Collection. Ohrstrom, Joan, ed. (Illus.). 192p. 1983. 25.00 (ISBN 0-87099-291-0). Metro Mus Art.

--Peach Blossom Spring: Gardens & Flowers in Chinese Paintings. (Illus.). 144p. 1983. 29.50 (ISBN 0-87099-357-7); pap. 19.95 (ISBN 0-87099-358-5). Metro Mus Art.

Barnhart, Robert K., jt. ed. see Barnhart, Clarence L.

Barnhill, Herschel J. From Surplus to Substitution: Energy in Texas. (Texas History Ser.). (Illus.). 45p. (Orig.). 1983. pap. text ed. 1.95x (ISBN 0-89641-118-4). American Pr.

Barnhill, J. B. & McCall, John E. Selections from "The Eagle & the Serpent" & "Nationality". (Men & Movements in the History & Philosophy of Anarchism Ser.). 1979. lib. bdg. 34.50 (ISBN 0-87700-286-X). Revisionist Pr.

Barnhill, Robert E. & Boehm, Wolfgang, eds. Surfaces in Computer Aided Geometric Design: Proceedings of a Conference, Mathematisches Forschungsinstitut, Oberwolfach, F.R.G., April 25-30, 1982. xvi, 216p. 1983. 47.00 (ISBN 0-444-86550-0, I-32-83, North-Holland). Elsevier.

Barnhill, Robert E. & Riesenfeld, Richard F., eds. Computer Aided Geometric Design: Proceedings of a Conference. 1974. 60.00 (ISBN 0-12-079050-5). Acad Pr.

Barnhisel, jt. auth. see Hayes.

Barnhouse, Donald. Is Anybody Up There. LC 76-51734. 1977. 6.95 (ISBN 0-9606562-0-0, BT1102-B26). L Victor Pr.

Barnhouse, Donald C. Expositions of Bible Doctrines, 10 vols. in four. (Bible Study). 1952-64. Set. 49.95 (ISBN 0-8028-3014-5). Eerdmans.

Barnhouse, Donald G. Bible Truth Illustrated. LC 79-64829. (Shepherd Illustrated Ser.). (Illus.). 1980. pap. 5.95 (ISBN 0-87983-208-8). Keats.

--Genesis: A Devotional Commentary in One Volume. 564p. 1973. 11.95 (ISBN 0-310-20471-2). Zondervan.

--The Invisible War. 288p. 1980. pap. 7.95 (ISBN 0-310-20481-X). Zondervan.

--Teaching the Word of Truth. 1958. Repr. 4.95 (ISBN 0-8028-1610-X). Eerdmans.

Barnhouse, Donald G. & Ehrenstein, Herbert H. Acts: An Expositional Commentary. 1979. 7.95 (ISBN 0-310-20511-5). Zondervan.

Barnhouse, Margaret N. That Man Barnhouse. 1983. pap. 9.95 (ISBN 0-8423-7033-1). Tyndale.

Barnhouse, Ruth T. Identity. LC 84-3664. (Choices: Guides for Today's Woman Ser.,: Vol. 7). 120p. (Orig.). 1984. pap. 6.95 (ISBN 0-664-24545-5). Westminster.

Barniak, Carl K. The Food of Angels. 96p. (Orig.). 1984. pap. 4.95 (ISBN 0-9613803-0-6). Barniak Pubns.

Barnicoat, John. Concise History of Posters. (The World of Art Ser.). (Illus.). 288p. 1985. pap. 9.95 (ISBN 0-500-20118-8). Thames Hudson.

Barnidge, Thomas & Grow, Douglas. The Jim Hart Story. (Illus.). 1977. 6.95 (ISBN 0-8272-1705-6); pap. 4.95 (ISBN 0-8272-1704-8). CBP.

Barnitz, Harry W. Existentialism & the New Christianity. LC 69-14353. 1969. 10.00 (ISBN 0-8022-2279-X). Philos Lib.

Barnitz, Jacqueline. Abstract Currents in Ecuadorian Art. annual (Illus.). 48p. 1977. pap. text ed. 3.00 (ISBN 0-89192-235-0, Pub. by Ctr Inter-Am Rel). Interbk Inc.

--Young Mexicans. (Illus.). 1971. pap. 2.00 (ISBN 0-913456-13-6, Pub. by Ctr Inter-Am Rel). Interbk Inc.

Bar-Niv, Ran, jt. auth. see Bickelhaupt, David L.

Bar-Niv, Zvi H., et al. International Labour Law Reports, Vol. 3: 1976 - 1977. 420p. 1981. 40.00 (ISBN 90-286-2711-1). Sijthoff & Noordhoff.

Barnlund, Dean C. Public & Private Self in Japan & the United States. (Illus.). 201p. 1975. pap. 13.50x (ISBN 0-89955-244-7, Pub. by Simul). Intl Spec Bk.

Barnoon, Shlomo & Wolfe, Harvey. Measuring the Effectiveness of Medical Decisions: An Operations Research Approach. (Illus.). 248p. 1972. 36.50x (ISBN 0-398-02225-9). C C Thomas.

Barnoski, Michael, ed. Fundamentals of Optical Fiber Communications. 2nd ed. LC 81-12883. 1981. 26.50 (ISBN 0-12-079151-X). Acad Pr.

Barnoski, Michael K., ed. An Introduction to Integrated Optics. LC 74-5444. 515p. 1974. 59.50x (ISBN 0-306-30784-7, Plenum Pr). Plenum Pub.

Barnothy, Madeline F., ed. Biological Effects of Magnetic Fields. Incl. Vol. 1. 335p. 1964. 39.50x (ISBN 0-306-37601-6); Vol. 2. 327p. 1969. 39.50x (ISBN 0-306-37602-4). LC 64-13146 (Plenum Pr). Plenum Pub.

Barnouw, Adriaan J. Anglo-Saxon Christian Poetry. LC 74-20776. 1974. Repr. of 1914 ed. lib. bdg. 12.50 (ISBN 0-8414-3291-0). Folcroft.

Barnouw, Adriaan J. & Wohlrabe, Raymond A. Land & People of Holland. rev. ed. LC 79-37249. (Ports. of the Nations Ser.). (Illus.). (gr. 6 up). 1972. PLB 9.89 (ISBN 0-397-31254-7). Lipp Jr Bks.

Barnouw, Adrian J. Anglo-Saxon Christian Poetry. 1977. lib. bdg. 59.95 (ISBN 0-8490-1429-8). Gordon Pr.

Barnouw, Elsa & Swan, Arthur. Adventures with Children in the Early School Years. 280p. 1985. 15.00x (ISBN 0-87586-070-2); pap. 7.95x (ISBN 0-87586-069-9). Agathon.

Barnouw, Eric. Documentary: A History of the Non-Fiction Film. rev. ed. (Illus.). 1983. 8.95 (ISBN 0-19-503301-9). Oxford U Pr.

Barnouw, Erik. A History of Broadcasting in the United States, 3 vols. Incl. Vol. 1. A Tower in Babel: To 1933. 1966. 25.00x (ISBN 0-19-500474-4); Vol. 2. The Golden Web: 1933 to 1953. 1968. 25.00x (ISBN 0-19-500475-2); Vol. 3. The Image Empire: From 1950. 1970. 25.00x (ISBN 0-19-501259-3). Oxford U Pr.

--The Magician & the Cinema. (Illus.). 1981. 19.95x (ISBN 0-19-502918-6). Oxford U Pr.

--The Sponsor: Notes on a Modern Potentate. (Illus.). 1978. pap. 7.95 (ISBN 0-19-502614-4, GB 580, GB). Oxford U Pr.

--Tube of Plenty: The Evolution of American Television. (Illus.). 1982. rev. ed. 22.50x (ISBN 0-19-501949-0). Oxford U Pr.

--Tube of Plenty: The Evolution of American Television. rev. ed. (Illus.). 1982. pap. 9.95 (ISBN 0-19-503092-3, GB 481, GB). Oxford U Pr.

Barnouw, Erik & Krishnaswamy, S. Indian Film. 2nd ed. (Illus.). 1980. 22.50x (ISBN 0-19-502682-9); pap. 9.95 (ISBN 0-19-502683-7, GB 592, GB). Oxford U Pr.

Barnouw, Victor. Acculturation & Personality among the Wisconsin Chippewa. LC 76-43646. (AAA Memoir Ser.: No. 72). Repr. of 1950 ed. 19.50 (ISBN 0-404-15481-6). AMS Pr.

--Anthropology: A General Introduction. 1979. 30.00x (ISBN 0-256-02113-9); text ed. 6.00x study guide (ISBN 0-256-02221-6). Dorsey.

--An Introduction to Anthropology, 2 vols. 4th ed. 1982. pap. 20.00x Vol. 1 (ISBN 0-256-02658-0); pap. 20.00x Vol. 2 (ISBN 0-256-02659-9). Dorsey.

--Wisconsin Chippewa Myths & Tales & Their Relation to Chippewa Life. LC 76-53647. 304p. 1977. 25.00x (ISBN 0-299-07310-6). U of Wis Pr.

Barnow, Renee. How to Moderate with Style. pap. 2.00 (ISBN 0-914548-47-6). Soc Tech Comm.

Barnow, Renee, ed. International Technical Communication Conference, 31st: Proceedings. 600p. 1984. pap. text ed. 45.00x (ISBN 0-914548-46-8). Soc Tech Comm.

Barnridge, Mary S. Piano Player at the Dionysia. 76p. (Orig.). 1984. pap. 6.95 (ISBN 0-914739-00-X). T Hill.

Barns, Cass G. The Sod House. LC 73-100812. (Illus.). iv, 301p. 1970. 22.50x (ISBN 0-8032-1153-8); pap. 7.95 (ISBN 0-8032-5700-7, BB 511, Bison). U of Nebr Pr.

Barns, J. W., jt. auth. see Reymond, E. A.

Barns, Marylon R., jt. auth. see Crutchfield, Carolyn A.

Barns, Marylon R., et al. Neurophysiological Basis of Patient Treatment: The Vestibular System, Vol. IV. (Illus.). 1986. pap. 12.75x (ISBN 0-936030-04-6). Stokesville Pub.

Barnsley, John. Jumping off the Donkey. 192p. 1984. 35.00x (ISBN 0-906791-36-7, Pub. by Minimax Bks Uk). State Mutual Bk.

Barnstead, John, tr. see Kuzmin, Mikhail.

Barnstein. As Meeke As Is Mayde. 1985. text ed. 28.00 (ISBN 0-8240-9002-0). Garland Pub.

Barnstone, Aliki & Barnstone, Willis. A Book of Women Poets, Book of Puzzlements: From Antiquity to Now. 640p. (Orig.). 1981. 29.95 (ISBN 0-8052-3693-7); pap. 12.95 (ISBN 0-8052-0680-9). Schocken.

Barnstone, Howard, et al. The Architecture of John F. Staub: Houston & the South. LC 79-105687. (Illus.). 402p. 1979. 35.00 (ISBN 0-292-74012-3); special ed. 100.00 (ISBN 0-292-74013-1). U of Tex Pr.

Barnstone, Willis. China Poems. LC 75-43525. (Breakthrough Bks.). 64p. 1976. 6.95x (ISBN 0-8262-0194-6). U of Mo Pr.

--The Poetics of Ecstasy. 331p. 1983. text ed. 39.50x (ISBN 0-8419-0814-1); pap. text ed. 17.50x (ISBN 0-8419-0849-4). Holmes & Meier.

Barnstone, Willis, jt. auth. see Barnstone, Aliki.

Barnstone, Willis, ed. Borges at Eighty: Conversations. LC 81-47294. (Illus.). 192p. 1982. 17.50x (ISBN 0-253-16626-8). Ind U Pr.

--Eighteen Texts: Writings by Contemporary Greek Authors. LC 74-188347. 1972. 14.50x (ISBN 0-674-24175-4). Harvard U Pr.

--The Other Bible. LC 83-48416. 768p. 1984. cloth 23.99i (ISBN 0-06-250031-7, HarpR); pap. 14.37i (ISBN 0-06-250030-9, CN 4087). Har-Row.

Barnstone, Willis, tr. from Gr. Greek Lyric Poetry. LC 67-25140. (Illus.). 320p. 1972. 11.00x (ISBN 0-8052-3447-0); pap. 7.95 (ISBN 0-8052-0339-7). Schocken.

Barnstone, Willis, tr. see Aleixandre, Vicente.

Barnstone, Willis, tr. see De Leon, Fray L.

Barnstone, Willis, tr. see Machado, Antonio.

Barnstone, Willis, tr. & intro. by see St. John Of The Cross.

Barnstone, Willis, tr. see Salinas, Pedro.

Barnstone, Willis, tr. see Suarez, Nicomedes.

Barnstorff, D. A Key to Shakespeare's Sonnets. LC 70-113549. Repr. of 1862 ed. 21.50 (ISBN 0-404-00657-4). AMS Pr.

Barnstorff, H. German Literature in Translation, 1891-1939. 59.95 (ISBN 0-8490-0228-1). Gordon Pr.

Barnum, H. Gardiner. Market Centers & Hinterlands in Baden-Wuerttemburg. LC 65-28149. (Research Papers: No. 103). 172p. 1966. pap. 10.00 (ISBN 0-89065-013-6). U Chicago Dept Geog.

Barnum, H. L. The Spy Unmasked: Or, the Memoirs of Enoch Crosby, Alias Harvey Birch, the Hero of James Fenimore Cooper's "the Spy". facsimile ed. LC 75-29452. (Illus.). 264p. 1975. Repr. of 1828 ed. 11.50 (ISBN 0-916346-15-3). Harbor Hill Bks.

Barnum, Howard, et al. A Resource Allocation Model for Child Survival. LC 80-17933. 216p. 1980. text ed. 45.00 (ISBN 0-89946-052-6). Oelgeschlager.

Barnum, Howard N. & Squire, Lyn A. A Model of an Agricultural Household: Theory & Evidence. LC 78-21397. (World Bank Ser.). 120p. 1980. pap. 6.95x (ISBN 0-8018-2225-4). Johns Hopkins.

Barnum, Marvin R. Human Form & Function: A Health Science. LC 78-23374. 1979. 25.55x (ISBN 0-673-16247-8); pap. 10.95, study guide (ISBN 0-673-16248-6). Scott F.

Barnum, P. T. Animal Stories. Repr. lib. bdg. 15.95x (ISBN 0-89190-447-6, Pub. by River City Pr). Amereon Ltd.

--Struggles & Triumphs. Bode, Carl, ed. (Penguin American Library). 1981. pap. 5.95 (ISBN 0-14-039004-9). Penguin.

--There's One Born Every Minute: A Blank Book. 60p. 1982. pap. 1.50 (ISBN 0-86541-011-9). Filter.

Barnum, Phineas T. Barnum's Own Story: Autobiography. Browne, Waldo R., ed. (Illus.). 1962. 11.25 (ISBN 0-8446-1597-8). Peter Smith.

--Struggles & Triumphs. LC 77-125677. (American Journalists Ser). 1970. Repr. of 1869 ed. 48.50 (ISBN 0-405-01651-4). Ayer Co Pubs.

Barnum, Priscilla H. Dives & Pauper, Vol. 1, Pt. 1. (Early English Text Society, Original Ser.: No. 275). (Illus.). 1976. text ed. 21.95x (ISBN 0-19-722277-3). Oxford U Pr.

Barnum, Priscilla H., ed. Dives & Pauper, Vol. I, Pt. 2. (Early English Text Society Original Ser.). (Illus.). 1980. 32.50x (ISBN 0-19-722282-X). Oxford U Pr.

Barnwell, F. Aster. The Meaning of Christ for Our Age. Weschcke, Carl L., ed. LC 83-82531. (Spiritual Renaissance Ser.). 280p. 1984. pap. 9.95 (ISBN 0-87542-032-X, L-032). Llewellyn Pubns.

Barnwell, H. T. The Tragic Drama of Corneille & Racine: An Old Parallel Revisited. 1982. 42.00x (ISBN 0-19-815779-7). Oxford U Pr.

Barnwell, H. T., ed. see Racine, Jean.

Barnwell, John. Love of Order: South Carolina's First Secession Crisis. LC 81-11441. xv, 256p. 1982. 25.00x (ISBN 0-8078-1498-9). U of NC Pr.

Barnwell, John, jt. auth. see Montgomery, Robert.

Barnwell, William. The Blessing Papers. 1980. pap. 2.50 (ISBN 0-671-83219-0, Timescape). PB.

--Curve of the Sigmord. (The Blessing Trilogy Ser.: Vol. III). 1981. pap. 2.75 (ISBN 0-671-83451-7, Timescape). PB.

--Writing for a Reason. LC 82-83174. 432p. 1983. pap. text ed. 15.95 (ISBN 0-395-32597-8); instr's. manual 2.00 (ISBN 0-395-32598-6). HM.

Barnwell, William H. Our Story According to St. Mark. 288p. (Orig.). 1982. pap. 9.95 (ISBN 0-86683-634-9). Winston Pr.

Barnwell, William H. & Price, Julie. Reflections: A Thematic Reader. LC 84-81984. 448p. 1984. pap. text ed. 11.95; instr's. manual 2.00. HM.

Baro, Gene. Carol Summers: Woodcuts. (Illus.). 40p. pap. 2.50 (ISBN 0-686-74783-6). Bklyn Mus.

--Graphicstudio U. S. F. An Experiment in Art & Education. LC 78-6796. (Illus.). 1978. pap. 5.45 (ISBN 0-87273-068-9). Bklyn Mus.

--Misch Kohn. (Illus.). 24p. pap. 2.50 (ISBN 0-87273-081-6). Bklyn Mus.

--Nineteen Eighty-Two Carnegie International. (Illus.). 128p. 1982. pap. text ed. 19.95 (ISBN 0-88039-004-2). Mus Art Carnegie.

--Peter Milton: Drawing Toward Etching. (Illus.). 20p. pap. 2.00 (ISBN 0-87273-077-8). Bklyn Mus.

--Robert Gordy: Paintings & Drawings. LC 81-81139. (Illus.). 112p. 1981. pap. 10.95 (ISBN 0-89494-011-2). New Orleans Mus Art.

--Twenty-First National Print Exhibition. LC 78-26421. (Illus.). 1978. pap. 5.95 (ISBN 0-87273-072-7). Bklyn Mus.

--Twenty-Second National Print Exhibition. (Illus.). 100p. 1981. pap. 4.95 (ISBN 0-87273-084-0). Bklyn Mus.

--William Conlon: Paintings 1969-1981. (Illus.). 16p. 1981. pap. text ed. 6.00 (ISBN 0-88039-001-8). Mus Art Carnegie.

Baro, Gene & Weber, Nicholas F. Anni Albers. LC 77-82324. (Illus.). 1977. pap. 2.95 (ISBN 0-87273-062-X). Bklyn Mus.

Baro, Gene, ed. After Appomatox: The Image of the South in Its Fiction, 1865-1900. 1963. 5.75 (ISBN 0-87091-023-X); pap. 1.95 (ISBN 0-87091-022-1). Corinth Bks.

--Famous American Poets. (Pocket Poet Ser.). 1962. pap. 2.00 (ISBN 0-8023-9038-2). Dufour.

Barocas, David N., tr. see Magriso, Yitzchak.

Barocas, Harvey, et al. Personal Adjustment & Growth: A Life-Span Approach. LC 82-60476. 530p. 1983. text ed. 26.95 (ISBN 0-312-60221-9); instr's manual avail.; study guide 7.95 (ISBN 0-312-60222-7). St Martin.

Barocchini, Peter. Holding out for the Moon. 1986. price not set (ISBN 0-87795-773-8). Arbor Hse.

Barocci, Thomas A. Non-Profit Hospitals: Their Structure, Human Resources, & Economic Importance. LC 80-22075. 256p. 1981. 24.95 (ISBN 0-86569-054-5). Auburn Hse.

Barocci, Thomas A., jt. auth. see Jerrett, Robert.

Barocio, Ernesto. Bosquejos de Sermones Selectos. 144p. 1981. pap. 5.95 (ISBN 0-311-43039-2). Casa Bautista.

Barocio, Ernesto, tr. see Broadus, J. A.

Barocio, Teofilo, tr. see Vedder, Enrique C.

Baroff, George S. Mental Retardation: Nature, Cause & Management. 2nd ed. (Illus.). 400p. 1986. 39.95 (ISBN 0-89116-263-1); pap. 24.50 (ISBN 0-89116-457-X). Hemisphere Pub.

Barofsky, I. & Budson, R. D., eds. The Chronic Psychiatric Patient in the Community: Principles of Treatment. LC 82-7338. 570p. 1983. text ed. 49.95 (ISBN 0-89335-164-4). SP Med & Sci Bks.

Barofsky, Semour, tr. see Sendak, Philip.

Baroja. Las Inquietudes de Shanti Andia. (Easy Reader, B). 1973. pap. 4.25 (ISBN 0-88436-062-8, 70267). EMC.

Baroja, Julio C. The World of Witches. Glendinning, O. N., tr. LC 64-15829. (Nature of Human Society Ser.). xiv, 314p. 1973. pap. 12.00x (ISBN 0-226-03763-0, P497, Phoen). U of Chicago Pr.

Baroja, Pio. Arbol de la Ciencia. Flynn, Gerard C., ed. LC 78-106643. (Orig., Span.). 1977. pap. text ed. 9.95x (ISBN 0-89197-028-2). Irvington.

--Caesar or Nothing. How, Louis, tr. from Span. 337p. 1980. Repr. lib. bdg. 17.50 (ISBN 0-8492-3581-2). R West.

--Caesar or Nothing. How, Louis, tr. 336p. 1983. Repr. of 1919 ed. lib. bdg. 25.00 (ISBN 0-89987-952-7). Darby Bks.

Barold, S. Serge, ed. Modern Cardiac Pacing. (Illus.). 1016p. 1985. 98.00 (ISBN 0-87993-256-2). Futura Pub.

Barold, Serge S. & Mugica, Jacques, eds. The Third Decade of Cardiac Pacing: Advances in Technology & Clinical Applications. LC 81-67066. (Illus.). 480p. 1982. 47.50 (ISBN 0-87993-159-0). Futura Pub.

Barolini, Helen, ed. The Dream Book: An Anthology of Writings by Italian American Women. 416p. 1985. 19.95 (ISBN 0-8052-3972-3). Schocken.

Barolini, Helen, tr. see Zizola, Giancarlo.

Barolini, Teodolinda. Dante's Poets: Textuality & Truth in the Comedy. LC 84-42586. 320p. 1984. text ed. 30.00x (ISBN 0-691-06609-4). Princeton U Pr.

Barolsky, Paul. Daniele da Volterra a Catalogue Raisonne. LC 78-68252. (Reference Library of Humanities Ser.). 1984. lib. bdg. 55.00 (ISBN 0-8240-9811-0). Garland Pub.

--Infinite Jest: Wit & Humor in Italian Renaissance Art. LC 77-15843. (Illus.). 272p. 1978. 34.00x (ISBN 0-8262-0241-1). U of Mo Pr.

Baron. Understanding Human Relations: A Practical Guide to People at Work. 1985. 24.29 (ISBN 0-205-08287-4, 798287). Allyn.

Baron, Alan & Schneider, William. The Radical Center. Date not set. price not set. S&S.

Baron, Augustine, Jr. The Utilization of Mental Health Services by Mexican-Americans: A Critical Analysis. LC 78-68460. 1979. perfect bdg. 12.00 (ISBN 0-88247-557-6). R & E Pubs.

Baron, Augustine, Jr., ed. Explorations in Chicano Psychology. 240p. 1981. 33.95 (ISBN 0-03-058016-1). Praeger.

Baron, Bruce, et al. What Did You Learn in School Today? A Comprehensive Guide to Getting the Best Possible Education for Your Child. 304p. 1983. pap. 7.95 (ISBN 0-446-37210-2). Warner Bks.

Baron, C. Technology, Employment & Basic Needs in Food Processing in Developing Countries. 44.00 (ISBN 0-08-025228-1). Pergamon.

Baron, Carl E., ed. A Memoir of D. H. Lawrence: The Betrayal by G. H. Neville. LC 81-7656. (Illus.). 200p. 1982. 39.50 (ISBN 0-521-24097-2). Cambridge U Pr.

Baron, Charles H., jt. ed. see Saks, Michael J.

Baron, Charles Le see Le Baron, Charles.

Baron, Christopher, jt. ed. see Van Ginneken, Wouter.

Baron, D. N. Essentials of Clinical Biochemistry. 292p. 1982. 28.95 (ISBN 0-444-00684-2). Elsevier.

Baron, David. Israel in the Plan of God. LC 82-18678. 320p. 1983. 12.95 (ISBN 0-8254-2241-8). Kregel.

--Types, Psalms & Prophecies. 1981. lib. bdg. 14.00 (ISBN 0-86524-077-9, 9511). Klock & Klock.

--Visions & Prophecies of Zechariah. LC 70-180834. (Kregel Reprint Library). 1972. 14.95 (ISBN 0-8254-2216-7). Kregel.

Baron, David P., ed. The Export-Import Bank: An Economic Analysis. (Mathematical Economics, Econometrics & Economic Theory Monographs). 1983. 41.50 (ISBN 0-12-079080-7). Acad Pr.

Baron, Dennis E. Going Native: The Regeneration of Saxon English. (Publications of the American Dialect Society (PADS): No. 69). 63p. (Orig.). 1982. pap. text ed. 5.25 (ISBN 0-8173-0011-2). U of Ala Pr.

--Grammar & Good Taste: Reforming the American Language. LC 82-1873. (Illus.). 272p. 1982. 24.50x (ISBN 0-300-02799-0). Yale U Pr.

--Grammar & Good Taste: Reforming the American Language. LC 82-1873. 272p. 1984. pap. 7.95 (ISBN 0-300-03080-0, Y-486). Yale U Pr.

Baron, Dona, ed. The National Purpose Reconsidered. LC 78-6103. 139p. 1978. 18.50x (ISBN 0-231-04472-0). Columbia U Pr.

Baron, Frank, ed. see Liebnitz, Jennifer & Holmes, Joan E.

Baron, Frank, et al, eds. Rilke: The Alchemy of Alienation. LC 79-19759. 1980. 25.00x (ISBN 0-7006-0198-8). U Pr of KS.

Baron, Frederick M. Handling Occupational Disease Cases. LC 80-82945. 453p. 1981. 55.00 (ISBN 0-915544-08-3). Lawpress Ca.

Baron, G. Society, Schools & Progress in England. 1966. pap. text ed. 11.75 (ISBN 0-08-011593-4). Pergamon.

Baron, G., ed. The Politics of School Government. LC 80-40913. (International Studies in Education & Social Change). 304p. 1981. 53.00 (ISBN 0-08-025213-3). Pergamon.

Baron, G. E. Neutron Physics. (The Wykeham Science Ser.: No. 2). 256p. 1969. pap. cancelled (ISBN 0-85109-020-6). Taylor & Francis.

Baron, George & Howell, D. A. The Government & Management of Schools. 245p. 38.50 (ISBN 0-485-11142-X, Pub. by Athlone Pr Ltd). Longwood Pub Group.

Baron, Hans. Crisis of the Early Italian Renaissance: Civic Humanism & Republican Liberty in an Age of Classicism & Tyranny. rev. ed. 1966. pap. 13.50 (ISBN 0-691-00752-7). Princeton U Pr.

Baron, Harold, et al. Practical Record Keeping & Bookkeeping. (gr. 9-12). 1983. text ed. 11.50 (ISBN 0-538-02100-4, B10). SW Pub.

Baron, Harry. Card Tricks for Beginners. rev. & enl. ed. (Illus.). 1970. Repr. of 1961 ed. 8.95 (ISBN 0-87523-171-3). Emerson.

Baron, Henry. Touchstones, 4 vols. Incl. Vol. 1. Around Us (ISBN 0-8028-1532-4); Vol. 2. Within Us (ISBN 0-8028-1533-2); Vol. 3. Between Us (ISBN 0-8028-1534-0); Vol. 4. Above Us (ISBN 0-8028-1535-9). 1973. pap. 4.95 ea.; pap. 5.50 tchr's guide (ISBN 0-8028-1645-2). Eerdmans.

Baron, Henry, ed. Soundings, 5 vols. Incl. Vol. 1. Voyage. pap. text ed. 5.95 (ISBN 0-8028-1625-8); Vol. 2. I Am Waiting. pap. text ed. 4.95 (ISBN 0-8028-1626-6); Vol. 3. Nothing Ever Happens. pap. text ed. 4.95 (ISBN 0-8028-1629-0); Vol. 4. A Smiling Hippopotamus. pap. text ed. 4.95 (ISBN 0-8028-1628-2); Vol. 5. The Nest. pap. text ed. 4.95 (ISBN 0-8028-1627-4). 1976. Eerdmans.

Baron, Herman. Author Index to Esquire 1933-1973. LC 76-10625. 299p. 1976. 16.00 (ISBN 0-8108-0935-4). Scarecrow.

Baron, Howard C. & Gorin, Edward. Varicose Veins: A Commonsense Approach to Their Management. LC 78-31727. 160p. 1980. pap. 4.95 (ISBN 0-688-08459-1, Quill NY). Morrow.

Baron, J. H. Clinical Tests of Gastric Secretion. (Illus.). 1979. text ed. 39.50x (ISBN 0-19-520129-9). Oxford U Pr.

Baron, J. H. & Moody, F., eds. BIMR Gastroenterology Vol. 1: Foregut. (Butterworth International Medical Reviews). 1981. text ed. 49.95 (ISBN 0-407-02287-2). Butterworth.

Baron, J. W. Blaze. 192p. (Orig.). 1983. pap. 2.25 (ISBN 0-523-41745-4). Pinnacle Bks.

Baron, Jason D. Kids & Drugs: A Parent's Handbook of Drug Abuse Treatment & Prevention. 224p. (Orig.). 1984. pap. 7.95 (ISBN 0-399-50847-3, G&D). Putnam Pub Group.

Baron, Jennette M., jt. auth. see Salo, Baron W.

Baron, Joan. Cat Couples. LC 82-48798. 160p. (Orig.). 1983. pap. 8.61i (ISBN 0-06-090986-2, CN 986, CN). Har-Row.

--Cats Are Like That. LC 83-48935. 96p. (Orig.). 1984. pap. 9.95i (ISBN 0-06-091148-4, CN 1148, CN). Har-Row.

Baron, John, compiled by. Piano Music from New Orleans Eighteen Fifty-One to Eighteen Ninety-Eight. (Music Reprint Ser.). (Illus.). 194p. 1980. Repr. lib. bdg. 27.50 (ISBN 0-306-76034-7). Da Capo.

Baron, Jonathon. Rationality & Intelligence. 332p. Date not set. price not set. (ISBN 0-521-26717-X). Cambridge U Pr.

Baron, Joseph L., ed. Treasury of Jewish Quotations. 624p. 1985. 25.00 (ISBN 0-87668-894-6). Aronson.

Baron, Judith P. A Study Guide for Radiologic Technologists. (Illus.). 560p. 1978. 8.95x (ISBN 0-398-03726-4). C C Thomas.

Baron, Katheleen, jt. auth. see Thornton, G. H.

Baron, Lawrence. The Eclectic Anarchism of Eric Muhsam. 1975. lib. bdg. 69.95 (ISBN 0-87700-228-2). Revisionist Pr.

Baron, Leora, jt. auth. see Kishon, Ephraim.

Baron, Lindamichelle. The Sun Is On. rev. ed. (Illus.). 48p. (gr. 1-6). 1982. pap. 5.95 (ISBN 0-940938-02-2). Harlin Jacque.

Baron, Mary. Letters for the New England Dead. Schreiber, Jan, ed. LC 73-84885. (Chapbook Series One). 32p. 1974. 5.00 (ISBN 0-87923-083-5). Godine.

--Wheat among Bones. LC 79-90839. 94p. 1980. 9.95 (ISBN 0-935296-04-2); pap. 4.95 (ISBN 0-935296-05-0). Sheep Meadow.

Baron, N. S. Language & Historical Change. (North-Holland Linguistic Ser: Vol. 36). 320p. 1978. 53.25 (ISBN 0-444-85077-5, North-Holland). Elsevier.

Baron, Nancy. Getting Started in Calligraphy. LC 78-66311. (Illus.). (gr. 7 up). 1979. 14.95 (ISBN 0-8069-5392-6); spiral bdg. 8.95 (ISBN 0-8069-8840-1); PLB 17.79 (ISBN 0-8069-5393-4). Sterling.

--Tuesday's Child. LC 84-2944. 120p. (gr. 4-6). 1984. 9.95 (ISBN 0-689-31042-0). Atheneum.

Baron, Naomi S. Speech, Writing, & Sign: A Functional View of Linguistic Representation. LC 79-3626. (Illus.). 320p. 1981. 25.00x (ISBN 0-253-19373-7). Ind U Pr.

Baron, Paul B. When You Buy or Sell a Company. LC 80-66938. 396p. 1980. three ring binder 85.00 (ISBN 0-936936-50-9). Ctr Busn Info.

--When You Buy or Sell a Company. LC 80-66938. 396p. 1980. 3 ring binder 85.00 (ISBN 0-936936-51-7). Ctr Busn Info.

Baron, R. A. Human Aggression. LC 77-24567. (Perspectives in Social Psychology Ser.). (Illus.). 315p. 1977. 23.50x (ISBN 0-306-31050-3, Plenum Pr). Plenum Pub.

Baron, Richard, et al. Raid: The Untold Story of Patton's Secret Mission. 288p. 1981. 12.95 (ISBN 0-399-12597-3, Putnam). Putnam Pub Group.

--Raid: The Untold Story of Patton's Secret Mission. 288p. 1984. pap. 3.95 (ISBN 0-425-05937-5). Berkley Pub.

Baron, Robert, et al. Psychology: Understanding Behavior. 2nd ed. LC 79-22453. 848p. 1980. text ed. 30.95 (ISBN 0-03-054241-3, HoltC); instr's. manual 25.00 (ISBN 0-03-057044-1); study guide 11.95 (ISBN 0-03-055106-4). HR&W.

Baron, Robert A. & Byrne, Donn. Exploring Social Psychology. 2nd ed. 384p. pap. text ed. 21.37 (ISBN 0-205-07606-8, 797606); inst's man (ISBN 0-205-07607-6). Allyn.

--Social Psychology: Understanding Human Interaction. 4th ed. 1983. text ed. 31.83 for info. (ISBN 0-205-08054-5, 798054); write for info. tchr's. manual (ISBN 0-205-08055-3); student guide 9.99 (ISBN 0-205-08056-1, 798056). Allyn.

Baron, Robert A. & Greenberg, Jerald. Behavior in Organizations: Principles, Findings, & Applications. 500p. 1983. scp 32.84 (ISBN 0-205-07851-6, 797851); casebook by Frantzve 16.51 (ISBN 0-205-07853-2, 797853). Allyn.

Baron, Robert E., et al. Chemical Equilibria in Carbon-Hydrogen-Oxygen Systems. LC 75-44374. (Energy Laboratory Ser.). 120p. 1976. 27.50x (ISBN 0-262-02121-8). MIT Pr.

Baron, Robert J. & Shapiro, Linda G. Data Structures & Their Implementation. (University Computer Science Ser.). 416p. 1980. 23.95 (ISBN 0-442-20586-4). Van Nos Reinhold.

--Data Structures & Their Implementation. 469p. pap. text ed. write for info (ISBN 0-87150-429-4, 8070). PWS Pubs.

Baron, Roger. Hugh of St. Victor. (Mediaeval Studies Ser.: No. 20). 1966. 16.95 (ISBN 0-268-00121-9). U of Notre Dame Pr.

Baron, S. Medical Microbiology: Principles & Concepts. 1982. text ed. 45.00 (ISBN 0-201-10175-0, 10175, Med-Nurse). Addison-Wesley.

Baron, Salo W. The Jewish Community, 3 vols. LC 74-97269. 1972. Repr. of 1942 ed. Set. lib. bdg. 53.50x (ISBN 0-8371-3274-6, BAJC). Greenwood.

--Modern Nationalism & Religion. facs. ed. LC 79-134050. (Essay Index Reprint Ser). 1947. 19.50 (ISBN 0-8369-2142-9). Ayer Co Pubs.

--A Social & Religious History of the Jews, 18 vols. 2nd, rev. & enl. ed. Incl. Vol. 1. Ancient Times to the Beginning of the Christian Era. 1952 (ISBN 0-231-08838-8); Vol. 2. Ancient Times: Christian Era: the First Five Centuries. 1952 (ISBN 0-231-08839-6); Vol. 3. High Middle Ages: Heirs of Rome & Persia. 1957 (ISBN 0-231-08840-X); Vol. 4. High Middle Ages: Meeting of the East & West. 1957 (ISBN 0-231-08841-8); Vol. 5. High Middle Ages: Religious Controls & Dissensions. 1957 (ISBN 0-231-08842-6); Vol. 6. High Middle Ages: Laws, Homilies & the Bible. 1958 (ISBN 0-231-08843-4); Vol. 7. High Middle Ages: Hebrew Language & Letters. 1958 (ISBN 0-231-08844-2); Vol. 8. High Middle Ages: Philosophy & Science. 1958 (ISBN 0-231-08845-0); Vol. 9. Late Middle Ages & Era of European Expansion, 1200-1650: Under Church & Empire. 1965 (ISBN 0-231-08846-9); Vol. 10. Late Middle Ages & Era of European Expansion, 1200-1650: On the Empire's Periphery. 1965 (ISBN 0-231-08847-7); Vol. 11. Late Middle Ages & Era of European Expansion, 1200-1650: Citizen or Alien Conjurer. 1967 (ISBN 0-231-08848-5); Vol. 12. Late Middle Ages & Era of European Expansion, 1200-1650: Economic Catalyst. 1967 (ISBN 0-231-08849-3); Vol. 13. Late Middle Ages & Era of European Expansion, 1200-1650: Inquisition, Renaissance & Reformation. 1969 (ISBN 0-231-08850-7); Vol. 14. Late Middle Ages & Era of European Expansion, 1200-1650: Catholic Restoration & Wars of Religion. 1969 (ISBN 0-231-08851-5); Vol. 15. Late Middle Ages & Era of European Expansion, 1200-1650: Resettlement & Exploration. 1973 (ISBN 0-231-08852-3); Index. 42.00x (ISBN 0-231-08877-9). LC 52-404. 40.00x ea. Columbia U Pr.

--Steeled in Adversity. (Texts & Studies). (Hebrew.). 1977. 15.00 (ISBN 0-911934-15-4). Am Jewish Hist Soc.

Baron, Salo W., ed. Essays on Maimonides. LC 79-160004. Repr. of 1941 ed. 24.50 (ISBN 0-404-00658-2). AMS Pr.

Baron, Salo W. & Barzilay, Isaac, eds. Jubilee Volume: The American Academy for Jewish Research, 2 vols. 710p. 1980. text ed. 63.00x (ISBN 0-231-05150-6). Columbia U Pr.

Baron, Salo W., et al. Economic History of the Jews. Gross, Nachum, ed. LC 75-534. (Illus.). 1976. pap. 5.50 (ISBN 0-8052-0538-1). Schocken.

Baron, Samuel & Pletsch, Carl, eds. Psycholgy & the Biographer. (Emotions & Behavior Monograph Ser.: No. 5). 1984. text ed. write for info. (ISBN 0-8236-5575-X). Intl Univs Pr.

Baron, Samuel H. Muscovite Russia. 362p. 1980. 75.00x (ISBN 0-86078-063-5, Pub. by Variorum England). State Mutual Bk.

--Plekhanov, the Father of Russian Marxism. (Illus.). 1963. 39.50x (ISBN 0-8047-0104-0). Stanford U Pr.

Baron, Samuel H., tr. see Olearius, Adam.

Baron, Sandra. The Regional Economic Impacts of Outer Continental Shelf Oil & Gas Development. 95p. 8.00 (ISBN 0-318-16298-9, D-7). Public Int Econ.

Baron, Stanley W. Brewed in America: A History of Beer & Ale in the United States. LC 72-5030. (Technology & Society Ser.). (Illus.). 424p. 1972. Repr. of 1962 ed. 33.00 (ISBN 0-405-04683-9). Ayer Co Pubs.

Baron, Stephen L. Manual of Energy Saving in Existing Buildings & Plants, Vol. I. (Illus.). 1978. 39.95 (ISBN 0-13-553578-6, Busn). P-H.

--Manual of Energy Saving in Existing Buildings & Plants: Vol. 2, Facility Modification. (Illus.). 1978. 49.95 (ISBN 0-13-553586-7, Busn). P-H.

Baron, Sylvia, jt. auth. see Hicks, Bruce.

Baron, V. V., jt. ed. see Savitskii, E. M.

Baron, W. M. Organization in Plants. 3rd ed. LC 78-12085. 264p. 1979. pap. 29.95x (ISBN 0-470-26558-2). Halsted Pr.

Baron, Wendy. The Camden Town Group. 1979. 85.00. Scolar.

Baron, William, jt. auth. see Perloff, William H.

Baron Baltimore, jt. auth. see Calvert, Cecil.

Barondes, Samuel H., ed. Neuronal Recognition. LC 75-45291. (Illus.). 384p. 1976. 39.50x (ISBN 0-306-30885-1, Plenum Pr). Plenum Pub.

Barondes, Samuel H., ed. see International Society for Cell Biology.

Barondess, Jeremiah, et al. The Persisting Osler. 1985. pap. text ed. 46.00 (ISBN 0-8391-2094-X, 22233). Univ Park.

Barone, Antonio & Paterno, Gianfranco. The Physics & Applications of the Josephson Effect. 529p. 1982. 58.95x (ISBN 0-471-01469-9, Pub. by Wiley-Interscience). Wiley.

Barone, Charles A. Marxist Thought on Imperialism: Survey & Critique. LC 84-23556. 225p. 1985. 30.00 (ISBN 0-87332-291-6); pap. 13.95 (ISBN 0-87332-345-9). M E Sharpe.

Barone, Michael. Almanac of American Politics Nineteen Eighty-Six. Ujifusa, Grant, ed. 1400p. 1985. 36.95 (ISBN 0-89234-032-0); pap. 30.95 (ISBN 0-89234-033-9). Natl Journal.

Barone, Michael & Ujifusa, Grant. The Almanac of American Politics, 1982. LC 70-160417. (Illus.). 1258p. 1981. O.P. 29.95 (ISBN 0-686-85694-5); pap. 16.95 (ISBN 0-940702-01-0). Barone & Co.

Barone, Michael, jt. auth. see Peirce, Neal R.

Barongo, Yolamu. Political Science in Africa: A Critical Review. 272p. 1983. 24.75x (ISBN 0-86232-033-X, Pub. by Zed Pr England); pap. 10.25 (ISBN 0-86232-034-8, Pub. by Zed Pr England). Biblio Dist.

Baroni, Daniele. The Furniture of Gerrit Thomas Rietveld. LC 77-17883. 1978. 19.95 (ISBN 0-8120-5201-3). Barron.

Baroni, Daniele & D'Auria, Antonio. Kolo Moser. LC 85-43052. (Illus.). 144p. 1985. pap. 17.50 (ISBN 0-8478-0667-7). Rizzoli Intl.

Baroni, T. J. A Revision of the Genus Rhodocybe Maire (Agaricales) rev. ed. (Nova Hedwigia Beiheft). (Illus.). 300p. 1981. text ed. 42.00x (ISBN 3-7682-5467-4). Lubrecht & Cramer.

--A Revision of the Genus Rhodocybe Maire: Agaricales. (Nova Hedwigia Beiheft: No. 67). (Illus.). 300p. 1981. lib. bdg. 42.00x (ISBN 3-7682-5467-4). Lubrecht & Cramer.

Baronian, Hagop. The Honorable Beggars. Antreassian, Jack, tr. from Armenian. LC 79-24482. (Illus.). 132p. (Orig.). 1980. pap. 4.95 (ISBN 0-935102-03-5). Ashod Pr.

--The Perils of Politeness. Antreassian, Jack, tr. from Armenian. LC 83-2524. (Illus.). 160p. (Orig.). 1983. pap. 7.50 (ISBN 0-935102-10-8). Ashod Pr.

Baronio, Giuseppe. On Grafting in Animals: The Degli Innesti Animali. Sax, Joan B., tr. 112p. 1985. bds. 125.00 decorated leather (ISBN 0-318-04638-5). F A Countway.

Baronio, Joyce. Forty-Second Street Studio. LC 80-80678. (Illus.). 96p. 1980. 50.00 (ISBN 0-936568-00-3). Pyxidium Pr.

Baron Jose de Vinck, jt. auth. see Archbishop Joseph Raya.

Baron Von Mullenheim-Rechberg, Burkhard. Battleship Bismarck: A Survivor's Story. LC 80-81093. 284p. 1980. 17.95 (ISBN 0-87021-096-3). Naval Inst Pr.

Barooah, Nirode Kumar. India & the Official Germany, 1886-1914. (European University Studies: Series 3, History & Allied Studies: Vol. 77). 254p. 1977. 26.10 (ISBN 3-261-02102-0). P Lang Pubs.

Baroody, Leila, ed. The Arabs under Israeli Occupation, 1977. 128p. 1979. 7.50 (ISBN 0-88728-055-2). Inst Palestine.

Baroolshian, Vahab D. Brik & Mayakovsky. (Slavistic Printings & Reprintings Ser.: No. 301). 1978. pap. text ed. 26.75x (ISBN 90-279-7826-3). Mouton.

Barooshian, Vahan D. Russian Cubo-Futurism, 1910-1930: A Study in Avant-Gardism. LC 73-81271. (De Proprietatibus Litterarum, Ser. Major: No. 24). 176p. 1974. text ed. 19.20x (ISBN 90-2792-659-X). Mouton.

Baroux, Louis. An Early Indian Mission. (Illus.). 95p. 1976. Repr. of 1913 ed. 4.50 (ISBN 0-915056-04-6). Hardscrabble Bks.

Barow, Wulf & Kampa, Theo. This Is Photography Afloat. 160p. 35.00x (ISBN 0-333-31811-0, Pub. by Nautical England). State Mutual Bk.

Barozzi, A., tr. see Lambros, P.

Barquero, J. A. Estampas Espanolas. (Span.). 10.50 (ISBN 84-241-5632-3). E Torres & Sons.

Barquin, R. C. & Mead, G. P., eds. Towards the Information Society: Selected Papers from the Hong-Kong Computer Conference, 1983. 164p. 1984. 37.00 (ISBN 0-444-87564-6, North Holland). Elsevier.

Barquin, Ramon C. Cultural Differences & the World of Computers: The Unanswered Questions. 256p. (YA) 1983. 22.95x (ISBN 0-03-059311-5). Praeger.

Barr. Early Methodist under Persecution. pap. 4.95 (ISBN 0-686-23582-7). Schmul Pub Co.

Barr, Alfred, jt. ed. see Cahill, Holger.

Barr, Alfred H. Painting and Sculpture in the Museum of Modern Art, 1929-1967. LC 68-54923. (Illus.). 1977. 40.00 (ISBN 0-87070-540-7). Museum Mod Art.

Barr, Alfred H., et al. Three American Modernist Painters. LC 70-86440. (The Museum of Modern Art Publications in Reprint Ser). (Illus.). 1968-1972. Repr. of 1933 ed. 19.00 (ISBN 0-405-01528-3). Ayer Co Pubs.

Barr, Alfred H., Jr. Art in Our Time: Tenth Anniversary Exhibition. LC 79-169294. (The Museum of Modern Art Publications in Reprint from Arno Press). (Illus.). 384p. 1972. Repr. of 1939 ed. 43.00 (ISBN 0-405-01554-2). Ayer Co Pubs.

--Cezanne, Gauguin, Seurat, Van Gogh: First Loan Exhibition. LC 72-169295. (The Museum of Modern Art Publications in Reprint from Arno Press). (Illus.). 152p. 1972. Repr. of 1929 ed. 24.50 (ISBN 0-405-01555-0). Ayer Co Pubs.

--Cubism & Abstract Art. LC 66-26123. (Museum of Modern Art: Publications in Repr. Ser). Repr. of 1936 ed. 27.50 (ISBN 0-405-01509-7). Ayer Co Pubs.

--Cubism & Abstract Art. LC 66-26123. (Illus.). 248p. 1974. pap. 7.95 (ISBN 0-87070-274-2, Pub. by Museum Mod Art). NYGS.

--Matisse: His Art & His Public. LC 66-26118. (Museum of Modern Art Publications in Reprint Ser). Repr. of 1951 ed. 30.00 (ISBN 0-405-01525-9). Ayer Co Pubs.

--Modern German Painting & Sculpture. LC 76-169296. (The Museum of Modern Art Publications in Reprint from Arno Press). (Illus.). 96p. 1972. Repr. of 1931 ed. 19.00 (ISBN 0-405-01556-9). Ayer Co Pubs.

--The New American Painting As Shown in Eight European Countries, 1958-1959. LC 70-169297. (The Museum of Modern Art Publications in Reprint from Arno Press). (Illus.). 96p. 1972. Repr. of 1959 ed. 17.00 (ISBN 0-405-01557-7). Ayer Co Pubs.

--Picasso Fifty Years of His Art. LC 66-26126. (Museum of Modern Art Publications in Repr. Ser). Repr. of 1955 ed. 14.95 (ISBN 0-405-01519-4). Ayer Co Pubs.

--Picasso: Fifty Years of His Art. rev. & enl. ed. LC 66-26126. (Illus.). 312p. 1974. pap. 14.95 (ISBN 0-87070-539-3, Pub. by Museum Mod Art). NYGS.

--What Is Modern Painting. 5th rev. ed. (Illus., Orig.). 1966. pap. 3.50 (ISBN 0-87070-631-4, Pub. by Museum Mod Art). NYGS.

Barr, Alfred H., Jr. & Brooks, Charles M., Jr. Vincent Van Gogh: A Monograph. LC 66-26121. (Museum of Modern Art Publications in Repr. Ser). Repr. of 1942 ed. 18.00 (ISBN 0-405-01514-3). Ayer Co Pubs.

Barr, Alfred H., Jr., jt. auth. see Soby, James.

Barr, Alfred H., Jr., ed. Fantastic Art, Dada, Surrealism. LC 68-8367. (Museum of Modern Art Publications in Reprint Ser). (Illus.). 1970. Repr. of 1937 ed. 23.00 (ISBN 0-405-01510-0). Ayer Co Pubs.

Barr, Alfred H., Jr., jt. ed. see Miller, Dorothy C.

Barr, Alfred H., Jr., ed. see New York Museum of Modern Art.

Barr, Alfred H., Jr., et al. American Art of the Twenties & Thirties: Paintings by Nineteen Living Americans. LC 76-86439. (The Museum of Modern Art Publications in Reprint Ser.). (Illus.). 218p. Repr. of 1930 ed. 25.50 (ISBN 0-405-01529-1). Ayer Co Pubs.

Barr, Alwyn. Black Texans: A History of Negroes in Texas 1528-1971. LC 72-97935. (Negro Heritage Ser., No. 12). (Illus.). 259p. 1973. 17.50 (ISBN 0-8363-0016-5). Jenkins.

Barr, Amelia. Christopher, & Other Stories. facsimile ed. LC 72-167440. (Short Story Index Reprint Ser.). Repr. of 1888 ed. 20.00 (ISBN 0-8369-3966-2). Ayer Co Pubs.

--Remember the Alamo. 329p. 1980. Repr. of 1880 ed. lib. bdg. 11.95x (ISBN 0-89968-215-4). Lightyear.

--Scottish Sketches. facsimile ed. LC 70-157771. (Short Story Index Reprint Ser.). Repr. of 1883 ed. 19.00 (ISBN 0-8369-3883-6). Ayer Co Pubs.

Barr, Amelia E. All the Days of My Life. Baxter, Annette K., ed. LC 79-8772. (Signal Lives Ser.). (Illus.). 1980. Repr. of 1913 ed. lib. bdg. 57.50x (ISBN 0-405-12822-3). Ayer Co Pubs.

--Remember the Alamo. 1888. 35.00 (ISBN 0-932062-10-5). Sharon Hill.

Barr, Andrew M. Master Guide to High-Income Real Estate Selling. 1974. 11.95 (ISBN 0-13-560011-1). Exec Reports.

Barr, Anita. Piano for Fun, Bk. 1. (Illus.). 64p. (Orig.). (gr. k-7). 1984. pap. 4.95 (ISBN 0-9611130-0-6). Funn Music.

--Piano for Fun, Bk. 2. (Illus.). 48p. (Orig.). (gr. k-7). 1984. pap. 4.95 (ISBN 0-9611130-1-4). Funn Music.

--Piano for Fun, Bk. 3. (Illus.). 48p. (Orig.). (gr. 1-7). 1985. pap. 4.95 (ISBN 0-9611130-2-2). Funn Music.

--Piano for Fun, Bk. 4. (Illus., Orig.). (gr. 1-7). 1985. pap. 4.95 (ISBN 0-9611130-3-0). Funn Music.

Barr, Ann & Levy, Paul. The Official Foodie Handbook. (Illus.). 1985. 17.95 (ISBN 0-87795-770-3); pap. 12.95 (ISBN 0-87795-727-4). Arbor Hse.

Barr, Ann & York, Peter. The Official Sloane Ranger Handbook: How the British Upper Class Prepares Its Offspring for Life. 160p. 1983. 6.95 (ISBN 0-312-58229-3). St Martin.

Barr, Art. You Can Be a Chalk Artist. LC 77-93247. (Illus.). 1978. pap. 4.95 spiral bdg. (ISBN 0-89636-001-6). Accent Bks.

Barr, Avron, et al, eds. The Handbook of Artificial Intelligence, 3 vols. LC 80-28621. 1982. Set. 120.00x (ISBN 0-86576-004-7). Vol. 1. 39.50x (ISBN 0-86576-005-5); Vol. 2. 42.50x (ISBN 0-86576-006-3); Vol. 3. 59.50x (ISBN 0-86576-007-1). W Kaufmann.

--The Handbook of Artificial Intelligence, 3 vols. 1985. Set. pap. 79.95 (ISBN 0-86576-088-8); Vol. 1. pap. 27.95 (ISBN 0-86576-089-6); Vol. 2. pap. 28.95 (ISBN 0-86576-090-X); Vol. 3. pap. 32.95 (ISBN 0-86576-091-8). W Kaufmann.

Barr, Ben, et al. Short Audit Case: The Valley Publishing Company. 5th ed. 1985. 18.95x (ISBN 0-256-03284-X). Irwin.

Barr, Browne. East Bay & Eden. rev., 2nd ed. LC 84-82244. 148p. 1985. pap. 7.00 (ISBN 0-937088-11-0). Illum Pr.

--High Flying Geese: Unexpected Reflections on the Church & Its Ministry. (Illus.). 96p. (Orig.). 1983. pap. 6.95 (ISBN 0-86683-900-3, Pub. by Seabury). Winston Pr.

Barr, Browne, jt. auth. see Jeske, Richard L.

Barr, Charles. Ealing Studios. LC 79-51033. (Illus.). 200p. 1982. pap. 12.95 (ISBN 0-87951-147-8). Overlook Pr.

--Ealing Studios. LC 79-51033. (Illus.). 200p. 1980. 22.95 (ISBN 0-87951-101-X). Overlook Pr.

--Understanding Synthesizers: A Beginner's Guide to Electronic Music. (Illus.). 48p. (Orig.). 1985. pap. 4.95 (ISBN 0-9611130-7-3). Funn Music.

Barr, Claude A. Jewels of the Plains: Wild Flowers of the Great Plains Grasslands & Hills. LC 82-13691. 256p. 1983. 19.95 (ISBN 0-8166-1127-0). U of Minn Pr.

Barr, David. Making Money at the Races. pap. 3.00 (ISBN 0-87980-268-5). Wilshire.

Barr, David & Piediscalzi, Nicholas, eds. The Bible in American Education. LC 81-14436. (SBL The Bible in American Culture Ser.). 1982. 12.95 (ISBN 0-89130-538-6, 061205, Co-pub Fortress Pr). Scholars Pr GA.

Barr, David F. Auditory Perceptual Disorders. 2nd ed. (Illus.). 152p. 1976. 17.75x (ISBN 0-398-03411-7). C C Thomas.

Barr, David F. & Miller, Richard K. Basic Industrial Hearing Conservation. 26.95 (ISBN 0-686-74625-2). Fairmont Pr.

Barr, David L. & Piediscalzi, Nicholas, eds. The Bible in American Education. LC 81-71385. (The Bible in American Culture Ser.). 196p. 1982. text ed. 12.95 (ISBN 0-8006-0612-4, 1-612). Fortress.

Barr, David S. Advertising on Cable: Practical Guide for Advertisers. (Illus.). 160p. 1985. text ed. 24.95 (ISBN 0-13-014531-9). P-H.

Barr, Don, jt. auth. see Zehna, Peter.

Barr, Donald. Primitive Man. (How & Why Wonder Books Ser.). (Illus.). (gr. 4-6). pap. 1.25 (ISBN 0-8431-4255-3). Wonder.

Barr, Donald R. & Zehna, Peter W. Probability: Modeling Uncertainty. (Illus.). 480p. 1983. text ed. 30.95 (ISBN 0-201-10798-8); solution manual 2.00 (ISBN 0-201-10799-6). Addison-Wesley.

Barr, E. Scott. Index to Biographical Fragments in Unspecialized Scientific Journals. LC 73-13434. 300p. 1974. 22.00 (ISBN 0-8173-9603-9). U of Ala Pr.

Barr, Fiona & Walsh, Barbara H. Sisters: Blackstaff Short Stories Ser. 112p. (Orig.). 1980. 2.50 (ISBN 0-85640-165-X, Pub. by Blackstaff Pr). Longwood Pub Group.

Barr, George, jt. auth. see Rees, Ruth.

Barr, Helen W. Thy Word Is True. Date not set. 5.75 (ISBN 0-8062-2355-3). Carlton.

Barr, Howard N. Fifty Best of Baltimore & Ohio Railroad, Bk. 1. (Illus.). 1977. 12.00 (ISBN 0-934118-16-7). Barnard Robert.

Barr, Howard N. & Barringer, W. A. Q-Baltimore & Ohio Railroad Q-Class Mikado Locomotives. LC 78-52708. (Illus.). 1978. 30.00 (ISBN 0-934118-15-9). Barnard Robert.

Barr, J., et al, eds. Instrument Fitting. (Engineering Craftsmen: No. H24). (Illus.). 1969. spiral bdg 39.95x (ISBN 0-85083-069-9). Intl Ideas.

Barr, James. American Humorous Verse. 1977. lib. bdg. 12.50 (ISBN 0-8495-0308-6). Arden Lib.

--Beyond Fundamentalism. LC 84-12029. 206p. 1984. pap. 9.95 (ISBN 0-664-24620-6). Westminster.

--Fundamentalism. LC 77-14512. 396p. 1978. Westminster.

--Holy Scripture: Canon, Authority, Criticism. LC 82-20123. 190p. 1983. 18.95 (ISBN 0-664-21395-2); pap. 9.95 (ISBN 0-664-24477-7). Westminster.

--The Humour of America. 1977. lib. bdg. 25.00 (ISBN 0-8495-0307-8). Arden Lib.

Barr, James, pseud. Quatrefoil. 1982. pap. 6.95 (ISBN 0-932870-16-3). Alyson Pubns.

Barr, James. The Scope & Authority of the Bible. LC 80-21394. 164p. 1981. pap. 7.95 (ISBN 0-664-24361-4). Westminster.

Barr, James R, jt. auth. see Schleicher, Robert.

Barr, Jane J. The Essential You. LC 82-60127. 1982. pap. 7.95 (ISBN 0-87397-211-2). Strode.

Barr, Janet L., tr. see Balbi, Adriano.

Barr, Jean, et al. Standards for Clinical Education in Physical Therapy. 1981. pap. 5.00 (ISBN 0-912452-33-1). Am Phys Therapy Assn.

Barr, Jean S., ed. Planning Curricula in Physical Therapy Education. (Illus.). 158p. (Orig.). 1982. pap. text ed. 19.95 (ISBN 0-912919-00-0, B100). Pathway Al.

Barr, Jene, jt. auth. see Antonacci, Robert J.

Barr, John. The Officina Bodoni. (Illus.). 96p. 1981. pap. 18.50 (ISBN 0-913720-33-X, Sandstone). Beil.

--Stanley Morison: A Portrait. (Illus.). 64p. 15.00 (ISBN 0-913720-47-X). Beil.

Barr, John H. & Stephens, G. Dental Radiology: Pertinent Basic Concepts & Their Applications in Clinical Practice. LC 77-16995. pap. 112.80 (ISBN 0-317-30398-8, 2024964). Bks Demand UMI.

Barr, John H. & Stephens, Russell G. Dental Radiology: Pertinent Basic Concepts & Their Applications in Clinical Practice. LC 77-16995. (Illus.). 439p. 1980. 32.00 (ISBN 0-7216-1542-2). Saunders.

Barr, John L., jt. auth. see Eastman, Peggy.

Barr, John R; see O'Neal, William B.

Barr, Ken, illus. Frankenstein. LC 81-15703. (Step-up Adventures Ser.: No. 2). (Illus.). 96p. (gr. 2-5). 1982. PLB 4.99 (ISBN 0-394-94827-0); pap. 1.95 (ISBN 0-394-84827-6). Random.

Barr, L. D., et al, eds. Advanced Technology Optical Telescopes II, Vol. 444. 332p. 57.00 (ISBN 0-89252-479-0). Photo-Optical.

Barr, Larry, ed. Library Education: 2000 A.D. & After. 38p. 1977. 5.00x (ISBN 0-931510-05-8). Hi Willow.

Barr, Larry, tr. see Balbi, Adriano.

Barr, Larry, jt. auth. see McMullen, Haynes.

Barr, Lily. For a Dream Cometh. LC 77-99161. 1979. 14.95 (ISBN 0-87949-083-7). Ashley Bks.

Barr, Lockwood. Ancient Town of Pelham, Westchester County, N.Y. 1946. 5.00 (ISBN 0-685-09005-1). Dietz.

Barr, Lou & Barr, Nancy. Under Alaskan Seas. (Illus.). 224p. 1983. pap. 14.95 (ISBN 0-88240-235-8). Alaska Northwest.

Barr, M. Autonomous Categories. (Lecture Notes in Mathematics Ser.: Vol. 752). 1979. pap. 13.00 (ISBN 0-387-09563-2). Springer-Verlag.

Barr, M. & Wells, C. Toposes, Triples & Theories. (Grundlehren der Mathematischen Wissenschaften Ser.: Vol. 278). (Illus.). xiii, 345p. 1985. 36.00 (ISBN 0-387-96115-1). Springer-Verlag.

Barr, M. E. Diaporthales in North America with Emphasis on Gnomonia & Its Segregates. (Mycologia Memoirs: No. 7). (Illus.). 1977. lib. bdg. 28.00 (ISBN 3-7682-1189-4). Lubrecht & Cramer.

Barr, Margaret J., ed. Student Affairs & the Law. LC 82-84204. (Student Services Ser.: No. 22). 105p. 1983. 8.95x (ISBN 0-87589-970-6). Jossey-Bass.

Barr, Margaret J., et al. Developing Effective Student Services Programs: Systematic Approaches for Practitioners. LC 84-47978. (Higher Education Ser.). 1985. text ed. 21.95x (ISBN 0-87589-610-3). Jossey-Bass.

Barr, Margaret S. Medardo Rosso. LC 73-169298. (The Museum of Modern Art Publications in Reprint). (Illus.). 94p. 1972. Repr. of 1963 ed. 17.00 (ISBN 0-405-01558-5). Ayer Co Pubs.

Barr, Marleen. Future Females: A Critical Anthology. LC 81-80215. 1981. 16.95 (ISBN 0-87972-174-X); pap. 8.95 (ISBN 0-87972-175-8). Bowling Green.

Barr, Marleen & Smith, Nicholas D. Women & Utopia: Critical Interpretations. LC 83-16920. 171p. (Orig.). 1984. lib. bdg. 22.75 (ISBN 0-8191-3558-5); pap. text ed. 10.25 (ISBN 0-8191-3559-3). U Pr of Amer.

Barr, Marleen S., et al. Suzy McKee Charnas, Octavia Butler, & Joan D. Vinge. (Starmont Reader's Guides Ser.: No. 23). 96p. 1985. Repr. lib. bdg. 15.95x (ISBN 0-89370-950-6). Borgo Pr.

--Reader's Guide to Suzy Mckee Charnas, Octavia Butler & Joan Vinge. Schlobin, Roger C., ed. (Starmont Reader's Guide to Contemporary Science Fiction & Fantasy Authors Ser.: Vol. 23). (Illus., Orig.). 1985. 15.95x (ISBN 0-916732-92-4); pap. text ed. 7.95x (ISBN 0-916732-91-6). Starmont Hse.

Barr, Martin W. Mental Defectives: Their History, Treatment & Training. LC 73-2383. (Mental Illness & Social Policy; the American Experience Ser.). Repr. of 1904 ed. 29.00 (ISBN 0-405-05191-3). Ayer Co Pubs.

Barr, Mary & D'Aroy, Pat, eds. What's Going On? Language Learning Episode in British & American Classroom, Grades 4-13. LC 81-18119. (Illus.). 240p. 1982. pap. text ed. 10.00x (ISBN 0-86709-013-8). Boynton Cook Pubs.

Barr, Mary M. Voltaire in America: 1744-1800. Repr. of 1941 ed. 14.00 (ISBN 0-384-03441-1). Johnson Repr.

Barr, Meyer B. Studies in Social & Legal Theories: An Historical Account of the Social, Ethical, Political & Legal Doctrines of the Foremost Ancient & Medieval Philosophers. 148p. 1982. Repr. of 1932 ed. lib. bdg. 20.00x (ISBN 0-8377-0327-1). Rothman.

Barr, Murray, jt. auth. see Norman, Edward.

Barr, Murray L. El Sistema Nervioso Humano. 2nd ed. 1975. text ed. 16.00 (ISBN 0-06-310057-6, IntlDept). Har-Row.

Barr, Murray L. & Kiernan, John A. The Human Nervous System: An Anatomical Viewpoint. 4th ed. 1983. pap. text ed. 24.75 (ISBN 0-06-140311-3, 14-03112, Harper Medical). Lippincott.

Barr, N. A., jt. auth. see Prest, A. R.

Barr, N. A., et al. Self-Assessment for Income Tax. 1977. text ed. 30.00x (ISBN 0-435-84060-6). Gower Pub Co.

Barr, Nancy, jt. auth. see Barr, Lou.

Barr, Nevada. Bittersweet. 352p. 1984. 15.95 (ISBN 0-312-08244-4). St Martin.

Barr, Pat. Foreign Devils: Westerners in the Far East, the Sixteenth Century to the Present Day. (Illus.). 11.00 (ISBN 0-8446-0024-5). Peter Smith.

--Jade: A Novel of China. 640p. 1982. 14.95 (ISBN 0-312-43943-1). St Martin.

--Jade: A Novel of China. 784p. 1983. pap. 3.95 (ISBN 0-446-30620-7). Warner Bks.

--Japan. (Illus.). 160p. 1980. 22.50 (ISBN 0-7134-0578-3, Pub. by Batsford England). David & Charles.

--Taming the Jungle in British Malaya. 1977. 12.50 (ISBN 0-436-03365-8, Pub. by Secker & Warburg UK). David & Charles.

--To China With Love: The Lives & Times of Protestant Missionaries in China, 1860-1900. 1972. 16.95 (ISBN 0-436-03355-0, Pub. by Secker & Warburg UK). David & Charles.

Barr, Pat & Desmond, Ray. Simla: A Hill Station in British India. 1982. pap. 15.00 (ISBN 0-85967-659-5). Scolar.

Barr, Paul, et al. CAD: Principles & Applications. (Illus.). 208p. 1985. text ed. 21.95 (ISBN 0-13-110198-6). P-H.

Barr, Pauline, et al. Advanced Reading Skills. (English As a Second Language Bk.). 1981. pap. text ed. 7.50x (ISBN 0-582-55904-9). Longman.

Barr, R. & Robson, I. A Census Atlas of Greater Manchester. LC 84-675626. (Orig.). Date not set. 10.50 (ISBN 0-7190-1773-4, Pub. by Manchester Univ Pr). Longwood Pub Group.

Barr, R. S., et al. Enhancements of Spanning Tree Labeling Procedures for Network Optimization. 1977. 2.50 (ISBN 0-686-64192-2). U CO Busn Res Div.

--A New Alternating Basis Algorithm for Semi-Assignment Networks. 1977. 2.50 (ISBN 0-686-64190-6). U CO Busn Res Div.

--The Alternating Basis Algorithm for Assignment Problems. 1977. 2.50 (ISBN 0-686-64191-4). U CO Busn Res Div.

Barr, Rebecca & Dreeben, Robert. How Schools Work. LC 83-6904. 208p. 1983. lib. bdg. 22.50x (ISBN 0-226-03811-4). U of Chicago Pr.

Barr, Robert. In a Steamer Chair, & Other Shipboard Stories. facs. ed. LC 74-116935. (Short Story Index Reprint Ser). 1892. 18.00 (ISBN 0-8369-3437-7). Ayer Co Pubs.

--The Triumphs of Eugene Valmont. 192p. 1985. pap. 3.95 (ISBN 0-486-24894-1). Dover.

Barr, Robert, jt. auth. see Crane, Stephen.

Barr, Robert, jt. auth. see Smith, Vernon.

Barr, Robert, tr. see Bussmann, Claus.

Barr, Robert C. Transportation Bleves: Causes - Effects - Guidelines. Lyons, Paul R., ed. LC 78-720334. 1979. pap. 49.50 incl. slides & tape (ISBN 0-87765-139-6, SL-36). Natl Fire Prot.

Barr, Robert D., et al. Defining the Social Studies. LC 77-85192. (Bulletin Ser.: No. 51). (Illus.). 1977. pap. 7.25 (ISBN 0-87986-012-X, 498-15260). Nat Coun Soc Studies.

--The Nature of the Social Studies. LC 77-2014. 1978. pap. 7.95 (ISBN 0-88280-049-3). ETC Pubns.

Barr, Robert J., ed. American Trade with Asia & the Far East. 1959. 6.95 (ISBN 0-87462-432-0). Marquette.

Barr, Robert R. What Is the Bible? A Nazareth Book. 128p. (gr. 7-12). 1984. pap. 4.95 (ISBN 0-86683-727-2). Winston Pr.

Barr, Robert R., tr. see Boff, Clodovis & Boff, Leonardo.

Barr, Robert R., tr. see Buhlmann, Walbert.

Barr, Robert R., tr. see Cabestrero, Teofilo.

Barr, Robert R., tr. see Carretto, Carlo.

Barr, Robert R., tr. see De Rosny, Eric.

Barr, Robert R., tr. see Eboussi Boulaga, F.

Barr, Robert R., tr. see Galilea, Segundo.

Barr, Robert R., tr. see Gutierrez, Gustavo.

Barr, Robert R., tr. see Maduro, Otto.

Barr, Robert R., tr. see Miguez-Bonino, Jose.

Barr, Robert R., tr. see Miranda, Jose.

Barr, Robert R., tr. see Perez-Esquivel, Adolfo.

Barr, Samuel J. & Abelow, Dan. A Woman's Choice: The Best Modern Guide to Unplanned Pregnancy. pap. 4.95 (ISBN 0-934954-11-9). Public Info Pr.

Barr, Stephen. Experiments in Topology. LC 64-10866. (Illus.). (gr. 7 up). 1964. 11.49i (ISBN 0-690-27862-4). Crowell Jr Bks.

--Mathematical Brain Benders: Second Miscellany of Puzzles. (Illus.). 224p. (gr. 6 up). 1982. pap. 4.50 (ISBN 0-486-24260-9). Dover.

--Puzzlequiz: Wit Twisters, Brain Teasers, Riddles, Puzzles & Tough Questions. LC 77-2647. (Illus.). (gr. 4 up). 1978. Crowell Jr Bks.

Barr, Stringfellow. Mazzini: Portrait of an Exile. 1971. lib. bdg. 26.00 (ISBN 0-374-90415-4). Octagon.

--The Pilgrimage of Western Man. LC 73-21283. 369p. 1974. Repr. of 1962 ed. lib. bdg. 21.00x (ISBN 0-8371-6152-5, BAPI). Greenwood.

--Three Worlds of Man. LC 63-9943. 104p. 1963. 5.00x (ISBN 0-8262-0019-2). U of Mo Pr.

Barr, Susan H., jt. ed. see Huberman, Eliezer.

Barr, Thomas F. & Tockstein, Tara J. Before Your Child Attends Counseling. 1983. text ed. 22.00x (ISBN 0-8290-1069-6). Irvington.

Barr, Thomas P. The Pottawatomie Baptist Manual Labor Training School. LC 84-80938. (Illus.). 58p. 1984. 3.00 (ISBN 0-87726-029-X). Kansas St Hist.

Barr, Tony. Acting for the Camera. LC 81-1157. (Illus.). 319p. 1981. pap. 20.95x (ISBN 0-205-07368-9, 487368, Pub. by Longwood Div). Allyn.

Barr, V. & Broudy, C. Designing to Sell: A Complete Guide to Retail Store Planning & Design. 1985. 40.00 (ISBN 0-07-003838-4). McGraw.

Barr, W. Montfort & Wilkerson, William R. Innovative Financing of Public School Facilities. LC 72-94974. 177p. 1973. pap. text ed. 3.95x (ISBN 0-8134-1543-8, 1543). Interstate.

Barr, William, ed. see Starokadomskiy, Leonid M.

Barr, William D. Counseling with Confidence. LC 80-84569. (Orig.). 1981. pap. 5.95 (ISBN 0-88270-492-3, Pub. by Logos). Bridge Pub.

Barra, Donald. The Dynamic Performance: A Performer's Guide to Musical Expression & Interpretation. (Illus.). 192p. 1983. 21.95 (ISBN 0-13-221556-X). P-H.

Barra, J. R., et al, eds. Recent Developments in Statistics: European Meeting of Statisticians, Sept. 6-11, 1976, Grenoble, France. 808p. 1977. 95.75 (ISBN 0-7204-0751-6, North-Holland). Elsevier.

Barra, Jean-Rene. Mathematical Basis of Statistics. Hernach, L., tr. LC 80-519. (Probability & Mathematical Statistical Ser.). 1981. 49.50 (ISBN 0-12-079240-0). Acad Pr.

Barra, Ralph. Putting Quality Circles to Work: A Practical Strategy for Boosting Productivity & Profits. (Illus.). 224p. 1983. 21.50 (ISBN 0-07-003799-X). McGraw.

Barracato, John & Michelmore, Peter. Arson! 1977. pap. 1.75 (ISBN 0-380-01715-6, 34041). Avon.

--Arson! 1976. 8.95 (ISBN 0-393-08744-1). Norton.

Barrack, Charles & Rabura, Horst. Mosaik. 1982. Deutsche Grammatik, 416p. pap. text ed. 16.00 (ISBN 0-394-32870-1, RanC); Deutsche Kultur, 260p. pap. text ed. 9.95 (ISBN 0-394-32871-X); Deutsche Literatur, 250p. pap. text ed. 9.95 (ISBN 0-394-32974-0); wkbk.-lab manual 8.95 (ISBN 0-394-32944-9). Random.

--Mosaik. 2nd ed. 1986. Deutsche Grammatik. pap. text ed. 15.00 (ISBN 0-394-34254-2, RanC); Deutsche Kultur. pap. text ed. 12.00 (ISBN 0-394-34253-4); Deutsche Literatur. pap. text ed. 12.00 (ISBN 0-394-34252-6); lab manual 9.00 (ISBN 0-394-34251-8); tapes 100.00 (ISBN 0-394-34248-8). Random.

Barrack, Charles Michael. A Diachronic Phonology from Proto-Germanic to Old English Stressing West-Saxon Conditions. LC 72-94519. (Janua Linguarum Ser. Practica: No. 144). (Illus.). 134p. (Orig.). 1975. pap. text ed. 21.60x (ISBN 90-2793-216-6). Mouton.

Barracliffe, Ron. The New Hampshire Insider's Guide. LC 83-60054. (Illus.). 160p. (Orig.). 1983. pap. 2.95 (ISBN 0-9611606-0-8). New Impressions.

Barraclough, Frances H., tr. see Arguedas, Jose M.

Barraclough, Geoffrey. The Crucible of Europe: The Ninth & Tenth Centuries in European History. LC 75-21934. (Illus.). 180p. 1976. 36.50 (ISBN 0-520-03105-9); pap. 6.95 (ISBN 0-520-03118-0, CAL 326). U of Cal Pr.

--Factors in German History. LC 78-21483. (Illus.). 1979. Repr. of 1946 ed. lib. bdg. 24.75x (ISBN 0-313-21066-7, BAFG). Greenwood.

--From Agadir to Armageddon. 208p. 1982. text ed. 22.50x (ISBN 0-8419-0824-9). Holmes & Meier.

--History in a Changing World. LC 84-12976. vii, 246p. 1984. Repr. of 1955 ed. lib. bdg. 37.50x (ISBN 0-313-24369-7, BAHC). Greenwood.

--Introduction to Contemporary History. (YA) (gr. 9 up). 1968. pap. 4.95 (ISBN 0-14-020827-5, Pelican). Penguin.

--Main Trends in History. LC 79-12662. (Main Trends in the Social & Human Sciences Ser.). 259p. 1979. pap. text ed. 12.50x (ISBN 0-8419-0505-3). Holmes & Meier.

--The Medieval Papacy. (Library of World Civilization). (Illus.). 1979. pap. text ed. 7.95x (ISBN 0-393-95100-6). Norton.

--The Origins of Modern Germany. 504p. 1984. pap. 12.95 (ISBN 0-393-30153-2). Norton.

--The Times Concise Atlas of World History. LC 82-50111. (Illus.). 192p. 1982. 40.00 (ISBN 0-7230-0247-9). Hammond Inc.

Barraclough, Geoffrey, ed. The Times Atlas of World History. rev. ed. LC 84-675088. 360p. 75.00 (ISBN 0-7230-0261-4). Hammond Inc.

Barraclough, Geoffrey, ed. see Historical Association, London.

Barraclough, Geoffrey, ed. see Mosse, W. E.

Barraclough, Geoffrey, tr. Mediaeval Germany, Nine Eleven to Twelve Fifty: Essays by German Historians, 2 vols. LC 75-41019. (BCL Ser. II). Repr. of 1938 ed. Set. 40.00 (ISBN 0-404-14800-X). AMS Pr.

Barraclough, June, tr. see Condorcet, Marie J.

Barraclough, Norman. Preology: The Scientific Study of the Planning of Human Development. LC 80-40600. 265p. 1981. pap. 15.75 (ISBN 0-08-026083-7). Pergamon.

Barraclough, Robin I., jt. auth. see Jarman, Lytton P.

Barradas, Efrain & Rodriguez, Rafael. Herejes y Mitificadores. LC 80-69123. 168p. 1980. pap. 4.50 (ISBN 0-940238-18-7). Ediciones Huracan.

Barradas, Efrain, intro. by. Apalabramiento: Diez Cuentistas Puertorriquenos de Hoy. 250p. (Span.). 1983. pap. 9.00 (ISBN 0-910061-09-2, 1109). Ediciones Norte.

Barraga, Natalie. Increased Visual Behavior in Low Vision Children. (Research Ser.: No. 13). 180p. 1964. pap. 5.00 (ISBN 0-89128-041-3, PLR041). Am Foun Blind.

--Visual Handicaps & Learning. rev. ed. (Orig.). 1983. pap. text ed. 10.95 (ISBN 0-935594-06-X). Exceptional Res.

Barraga, Natalie, jt. auth. see Dorward, Barbara.

Barragar, Pam. Spiritual Growth Through Creative Drama. 128p. 1981. pap. 6.95 (ISBN 0-8170-0923-X). Judson.

Barrager, Diane & Perkins, Rodney. The Hearing Book. Orig. Title: Come Again, Please... (Illus.). 128p. 1980. pap. 10.00x (ISBN 0-89106-016-2, 7274). Consulting Psychol.

Barragy, Terrence J. & Huebel, Harry R., eds. From Colony to Republic: Readings in American History to 1877. 279p. 1983. pap. text ed. 10.75 (ISBN 0-9611604-1-1). C Del Grullo.

--From Republic to Empire: Readings in American History Since 1877. 283p. (Orig.). 1982. pap. 10.75 (ISBN 0-918464-51-X). Texas Univ.

--From Republic to Empire: Readings in American History since 1877. 283p. 1982. pap. text ed. 10.75 (ISBN 0-9611604-0-3). C Del Grullo.

Barraine, Raymond. Nouveau Dictionnaire de Droit et de Sciences Economiques. 540p. (Fr.). 1974. 39.95 (ISBN 0-686-56779-X, M-6023). French & Eur.

Barral, Henri. Tiogo: Etude Geographidue D'un Terroir Lela (Haute-Volta) (Atlas Des Structures Agraires Au Sud Sahara: No. 2). 1968. pap. 14.00x (ISBN 90-2796-057-7). Mouton.

Barral, Mary R. The Body in Interpersonal Relations: Merleau-Ponty. 312p. 1984. pap. text ed. 14.25 (ISBN 0-8191-3755-3). U Pr of Amer.

Barral, R. M. Progressive Neutralism: A Philosophical Aspect of American Education. Matczak, Sebastian A., ed. LC 72-80678. (Philosophical Questions Ser.: No. 6). 1970. 18.00x (ISBN 0-912116-03-X). Learned Pubns.

Barrales, H., et al. The Plant Kingdom: A Laboratory Manual. 400p. 1981. pap. text ed. 17.95 (ISBN 0-8403-2372-7). Kendall-Hunt.

Barrall, Bob. The Whole World Knows. (Illus.). 158p. 1981. 7.95 (ISBN 0-682-49773-8). Exposition Pr FL.

Barran, D. H., et al. Rebuilding the Liberal Order. (Institute of Economic Affairs, Occasional Papers Ser.: No. 27). pap. 2.50 technical (ISBN 0-255-69646-9). Transatlantic.

Barran, Fracesca. London. (England in Cameracolour Ser.). (Illus.). 111p. 1985. 14.95 (ISBN 0-86364-007-9, Pub. by Town & Country Bks England). Hippocrene Bks.

Barranco, Clara De see Dinkmeyer, Don & McKay, Gary.

Barranco, Manuel. Mexico: Its Educational Problems. 1976. lib. bdg. 59.95 (ISBN 0-8490-2248-7). Gordon Pr.

--Mexico; Its Educational Problems: Suggestions for the Solution. LC 79-176518. (Columbia University. Teachers College. Contributions to Education: No. 73). Repr. of 1915 ed. 22.50 (ISBN 0-404-55073-8). AMS Pr.

Barranger. Theatre: A Way of Seeing. 2nd ed. 1985. pap. text ed. write for info. (ISBN 0-534-05646-6). Wadsworth Pub.

Barranger, John A. & Brady, Roscoe O., eds. Molecular Basis of Lysosomal Storage Disorders. 1984. 45.00 (ISBN 0-12-079280-X). Acad Pr.

Barranger, Milly S. Barron's Simplified Approach to Ibsen's Ghosts, the Wild Duck, & Hedda Gabler. LC 73-78047. 1969. pap. text ed. 1.95 (ISBN 0-8120-0376-4). Barron.

--Barron's Simplified Approach to Ibsen's Peer Gynt, a Doll's House, & an Enemy of the People. LC 72-75838. 1969. pap. text ed. 1.95 (ISBN 0-8120-0375-6). Barron.

--Theatre Past & Present: An Introduction. 510p. 1984. pap. text ed. write for info. (ISBN 0-534-02842-X). Wadsworth Pub.

Barrante, James R. Applied Mathematics for Physical Chemistry. (Illus.). 160p. 1974. pap. text ed. 23.95 (ISBN 0-13-041384-4). P-H.

Barras, Diane M., jt. auth. see Carbo, Margarete.

Barras, Diane M., jt. auth. see Corbo, Margaret S.

Barras, Diane M., jt. auth. see Corbo, Margarete S.

Barras, Laurence I. Memoirs of an Ex-Jesuit. 1982. 10.00 (ISBN 0-533-05010-3). Vantage.

Barras, Moses. Stage Controversy in France from Corneille to Rousseau. LC 78-159116. 1973. Repr. of 1933 ed. text ed. 12.00x (ISBN 0-87753-051-3). Phaeton.

Barrass, R. Scientists Must Write: A Guide to Better Writing for Scientists, Engineers & Students. 1978. pap. 9.95x (ISBN 0-412-15430-7, NO. 6385, Pub. by Chapman & Hall England). Methuen Inc.

Barrass, Robert. Students Must Write: A Guide to Better Writing in Course Work & Examinations. LC 82-8237. (Illus.). 120p. 1982. pap. 6.95 (ISBN 0-416-33620-5, NO. 3650). Methuen Inc.

--Study: A Guide to Effective Study, Revision & Examination Techniques. 200p. 1984. 26.95 (ISBN 0-412-25680-0, NO. 9158); pap. 8.95 (ISBN 0-412-25690-8, NO. 9186). Methuen Inc.

Barrat, Glynn R. I.I. Kozlov: The Translations from Byron, Slavonic Languages & Literatures. (European University Studies: No. 16, Vol. 1). 128p. 1972. pap. 23.50 (ISBN 3-261-00695-1). P Lang Pubs.

Barrat, John & Louw, Michael, eds. International Aspects of Overpopulation. LC 71-179498. 1972. 26.00 (ISBN 0-312-41965-1). St Martin.

Barratt, Alexandra & Ayto, John, eds. Aelred of Rievaulx's De Instutione Iclusarum. (Early English Text Society Original Ser.: No. 287). (Illus.). 1984. 14.95x (ISBN 0-19-722289-7). Oxford U Pr.

Barratt, Barnaby. Psychic Reality & Psychoanalytic Knowing. 400p. 1984. text ed. 29.95 (ISBN 0-88163-013-6). Analytic Pr.

Barratt, Carol & Sinclair, Jacqueline. The Mother Goose Songbook. (Illus.). 32p. (ps-1). 1985. 11.95 (ISBN 0-434-92841-0, Pub. by W Heinemann Ltd). David & Charles.

Barratt, Glen. The Russians at Port Jackson. 1980. text ed. 16.00x (ISBN 0-391-02165-6); pap. text ed. 11.00x (ISBN 0-391-02166-4). Humanities.

Barratt, Glynn. M. S. Lunin: Catholic Decembrist. (Slavistic Printings & Reprintings Ser.: No. 272). (Illus.). 137p. 1976. pap. text ed. 20.00x (ISBN 90-2793-444-4). Mouton.

--The Rebel on the Bridge: A Life of the Decembrist Baron Andrey Rozen, 1800-84. LC 75-21990. (Illus.). xvii, 310p. 1976. 19.00x (ISBN 0-8214-0217-X, 82-82238). Ohio U Pr.

Barratt, Glynn R. Voices in Exile: The Decembrist Memoirs. LC 75-310670. pap. 100.80 (ISBN 0-317-26443-5, 2023852). Bks Demand UMI.

Barratt, Glynn R., tr. see Ivashintsov, Nikolai A.

Barratt, John, jt. ed. see Hero, Alfred O.

Barratt, John, jt. ed. see Rotberg, Robert I.

Barratt, John, et al, eds. Accelerated Development in Southern Africa. LC 73-82636. 300p. 1974. 29.95 (ISBN 0-312-00210-6). St Martin.

--Strategy for Development. LC 76-1339. 320p. 1976. 26.00 (ISBN 0-312-76475-8). St Martin.

Barratt, Krome. Logic & Design: The Syntax of Art, Art & Mathematics. (Illus.). 328p. 1980. 25.00 (ISBN 0-89860-033-2). Eastview.

Barratt, M. B. & Mahowald, M. E., eds. Geometric Applications of Homotopy Theory I: Proceedings, Evanston, March 21-26, 1977. LC 78-16038. (Lecture Notes in Mathematics: Vol. 657). 1978. pap. 25.00 (ISBN 0-387-08858-X). Springer-Verlag.

--Geometric Applications of Homotopy Theory II: Proceedings, Evanston, March 21-26, 1977. LC 78-16038. (Lecture Notes in Mathematics: Vol. 658). 1978. pap. 25.00 (ISBN 0-387-08859-8). Springer-Verlag.

Barratt, Robert S., jt. auth. see Wilson, Otto.

Barratt, S., jt. auth. see Haszonics, J. J.

Barratt-Boyes, B., jt. auth. see Kirklin, J. W.

Barrau, Jacques. Subsistence Agriculture in Melanesia, 2 vols. (BMB). 1958-1961. Repr. of 1958 ed. Vol. 1. 15.00 (ISBN 0-527-02327-2); Vol. 2. 14.00 (ISBN 0-527-02331-0). Kraus Repr.

Barraud, Cecile. Tanebar-Evav. LC 78-56176. (Atelier D'anthropologie Sociale). (Illus.). 1980. 97.50 (ISBN 0-521-22386-5). Cambridge U Pr.

Barraud, P. J. Diptera: Family Calcidae, Tribe Megarhinini & Cuiicini, Vol. 5. (Fauna of British India Ser.). (Illus.). xxviii, 484p. 1977. Repr. of 1934 ed. 30.00 (Pub. by Messers Today & Tomorrows Printers & Publishers India). Scholarly Pubns.

Barrault, Jean L. Reflections on the Theatre. Wall, Barbara, tr. LC 78-59003. (Illus.). 1979. Repr. of 1951 ed. 21.50 (ISBN 0-88355-679-0). Hyperion Conn.

Barrault, Jean-Louis. Rabelais: A Dramatic Game in Two Parts. Baldick, Robert, tr. from Fr. (Mermaid Dramabook Ser.). 120p. 1971. 4.95 (ISBN 0-8090-8002-8); pap. 1.95 (ISBN 0-8090-1224-3). Hill & Wang.

Barrault, Jean-Louis, jt. auth. see Gide, Andre.

Barrax, Gerald. An Audience of One. LC 79-3050. (Contemporary Poetry Ser.). 94p. 1980. 9.95 (ISBN 0-8203-0500-6); pap. 5.95 (ISBN 0-8203-0502-2). U of Ga Pr.

--The Deaths of Animals & Lesser Gods. Rowell, Charles H., ed. (Callaloo Poetry Ser.: No. 4). (Orig.). 1984. pap. 6.00 (ISBN 0-912759-02-X). Callaloo Journ.

Barre, Andre. Le Symbolisme: bibliographie de la poesie symboliste. (Bibliography & Reference Ser: No. 140). 1968. Repr. of 1911 ed. 23.50 (ISBN 0-8337-0169-X). B Franklin.

--Symbolisme: essai historique sur le mouvement symboliste en France de 1885 a 1900. 1967. Repr. of 1911 ed. 25.50 (ISBN 0-8337-3970-0). B Franklin.

Barre, Michael. The Case Against the Andersons. 320p. 1983. 15.95 (ISBN 0-385-29227-9). Delacorte.

--The Case Against the Andersons. (Orig.). 1984. pap. 3.50 (ISBN 0-440-11008-4). Dell.

--The God-List in the Treaty Between Hannibal & Philip V of Macedonia: A Study in Light of the Ancient Near Eastern Treaty Tradition. LC 82-13961. (Near Eastern Studies). 208p. 1983. text ed. 22.50x (ISBN 0-8018-2787-6). Johns Hopkins.

Barre, Virginia, ed. see Byers, Robert A.

Barre, W. L. Life & Public Services of Millard Fillmore. LC 70-170962. (American Classics in History & Social Science Ser.: No. 203). 1971. Repr. of 1856 ed. 25.50 (ISBN 0-8337-4634-0). B Franklin.

Barre, W. La see La Barre, W.

Barre, Weston La see La Barre, Weston.

Barreca, Christopher A., et al, eds. Labor Arbitrator Development: A Handbook. LC 83-10129. 538p. 1983. pap. 35.00 (ISBN 0-87179-413-6). BNA.

Barreda, Pedro. The Black Protagonist in the Cuban Novel. Bancroft, Page, tr. from Sp. LC 78-19689. 192p. 1979. lib. bdg. 12.50x (ISBN 0-87023-262-2). U of Mass Pr.

Barredo-Carneiro, Paulo E. De & Arnaud, Pierre, eds. Auguste Comte, Correspondance Generale et Confessions: Tome II, Avril 1841-Mars 1845, Textes Establis et Presentes. (Archives Positivistes Ser.: No. 7). 461p. 1975. pap. text ed. 35.60x (ISBN 0-686-22605-4). Mouton.

Barreiro, Alvaro. Basic Ecclesial Communities: The Evangelization of the Poor. Campbell, Barbara, tr. from Portuguese. LC 81-16898. Orig. Title: Comunidades Eclesiais De Base E Evangelizacao Dos Pobres. 96p. (Orig.). 1982. pap. 5.95 (ISBN 0-88344-026-1). Orbis Bks.

Barreiro, Antonio see Carroll, H. Bailey & Haggard, J. Villasana.

Barreiro, Jose & Wright, Robin M., eds. Native Peoples in Struggle: Russell Tribunal & Other International Forums. LC 82-72533. (Illus.). 166p. 1982. pap. 12.00 (ISBN 0-932978-07-X). Anthropology Res.

Barrekette, E. S., ed. Pollution: Engineering & Scientific Solutions. LC 72-91328. (Environmental Science Research Ser.: Vol. 2). 799p. 1973. 79.50 (ISBN 0-306-36302-X, Plenum Pr). Plenum Pub.

Barrekette, E. S., et al, eds. Applications of Holography. LC 76-148415. 396p. 1971. 59.50x (ISBN 0-306-30526-7, Plenum Pr). Plenum Pub.

--Optical Information Processing, Vol. 2. LC 77-17579. 463p. 1978. 69.50x (ISBN 0-306-34472-6, Plenum Pr). Plenum Pub.

Barrel, John. The Dark Side of the Landscape: The Rural Poor in English Painting 1730-1840. LC 78-72334. 180p. 1983. pap. 15.95 (ISBN 0-521-27655-1). Cambridge U pr.

Barrell, J. The Dark Side of the Landscape. LC 78-72334. (Illus.). 1980. 47.50 (ISBN 0-521-22509-4). Cambridge U Pr.

Barrell, James J., jt. auth. see Lyons, Joseph.

Barrell, John. English Literature in History, 1730-1780: An Equal, Wide Survey. LC 83-16104. 228p. 1983. 22.50 (ISBN 0-312-25433-4). St Martin.

Barrell, John & Bull, John, eds. The Penguin Book of English Pastoral Verse. 1982. pap. 6.95 (ISBN 0-14-042178-5). Penguin.

Barrell, John, ed. & intro. by see Coleridge, Samuel T.

Barreman, Gerald. The Politics of Truth: Essays in Critical Anthropology. (Sunderlal Series in Humanistic Social Science: No. 1). 298p. 1982. text ed. 17.75x (ISBN 0-391-02665-8). Humanities.

Barren, T. P. Van see Van Baaren, T. P. & Driljvers, H. J.

Barrer, Harry G., ed. Orthodontics: The State of the Art. LC 79-5043. (Illus.). 448p. 1981. 70.00x (ISBN 0-8122-7767-8). U of Pa Pr.

Barrer, Lester A., ed. Adult & Community Education Organizations & Leaders Directory, 1981. LC 75-7599. (National Professional Directory Ser.). 400p. 1982. 80.00 (ISBN 0-87999-011-2). Today News.

Barrer, Lester A. & Barrer, Myra E., eds. Documentation Index to the Richard M. Nixon Impeachment Proceedings - Including the Watergate & Related Investigations, Hearings, & Prosecutions, 2 vols. Incl. Vol. 1. 1972, 1973, 1974. 500p. 1982. lib. bdg. 60.00 (ISBN 0-87999-008-2); Vol. 2. 1976-1977. 400p. 1982. lib. bdg. 60.00 (ISBN 0-87999-009-0). LC 74-19332. (Illus.). 1982. lib. bdg. 150.00 set (ISBN 0-87999-010-4). Today News.

Barrer, Myra E., jt. ed. see Barrer, Lester A.

Barrer, R. M. Hydrothermal Chemistry of Zeolites: Synthesis, Isomorphous Replacements & Transformations. 1982. 60.00 (ISBN 0-12-079360-1). Acad Pr.

Barrera, Heather. Tax Incidence: A Selected Bibliography. (CPL Bibliographies Ser.: No. 109). 67p. 1983. 13.00 (ISBN 0-86602-109-4). Coun Plan Librarians.

Barrera, Mario. Modernization & Coercion. (Politics of Modernization Ser.: No. 6). 1969. pap. 1.50x (ISBN 0-87725-206-8). U of Cal Intl St.

--Race & Class in the Southwest: A Theory of Racial Inequality. LC 78-62970. 1979. text ed. 22.95 (ISBN 0-268-01600-3). U of Notre Dame Pr.

--Race & Class in the Southwest: A Theory of Racial Inequality. LC 78-62970. 261p. 1980. pap. text ed. 7.95 (ISBN 0-268-01601-1). U of Notre Dame Pr.

Barrera, Mario, ed. Work Family Sex Roles Language. LC 80-53691. 1980. pap. 6.00 (ISBN 0-89229-007-2). Tonatiuh-Quinto Sol Intl.

Barrera-Benitez, Heriberto, jt. ed. see Teranishi, Roy.

Barrere, Dorothy B. Kamehameha in Kona: Two Documentary Studies. Incl. Kamakahonu: Kamehameha's Las Residence; The Morning Star Alone Knows...: A Documentary Search for the Bones of Kamehameha. (Pacific Anthropological Records: No. 23). 108p. 1975. pap. 6.00 (ISBN 0-910240-68-X). Bishop Mus.

--The Kumuhonua Legends: A Study of Late 19th Century Hawaiian Stories of Creation & Origins. (Pacific Anthropological Records: No. 3). 47p. 1969. pap. 2.50 (ISBN 0-910240-59-0). Bishop Mus.

Barrere, Dorothy B. & Pukui, Mary K. Hula: Historical Perspectives. LC 79-56806. (Pacific Anthropological Records: No. 30). 160p. 1980. pap. 10.00 (ISBN 0-910240-49-3). Bishop Mus.

Barrere, Dorothy B., ed. see Kamakau, S. M.

Barrere, Dorothy B., ed. see Papa, John.

Barrere, Jean B., ed. see Hugo, Victor.

Barres, Maurice. Les Traits Eternels de la France. 1918. 24.50x (ISBN 0-685-89791-5). Elliots Bks.

--The Undying Spirit of France. 1917. 24.50x (ISBN 0-686-51322-3). Elliots Bks.

Barrese, Pauline. Home Style Italian Cookery. 1981. pap. 4.50 (ISBN 0-440-13718-7). Dell.

Barrese, Pauline N. Italian Cookery-Home Style. rev. ed. LC 74-82514. 1977. pap. 6.95 (ISBN 0-912656-69-7). H P Bks.

Barresi, Anthony L., jt. auth. see Taylor, Fannie.

Barresi, Josephine G., jt. ed. see Del Polito, Carolyn M.

Barret. Methode de prononciation de francais. 20.50 (ISBN 0-685-36698-7). French & Eur.

Barret, Andre. Florence Observed. 168p. 1973. 24.95 (ISBN 0-19-519750-X). Oxford U Pr.

Barret, Ethel. Muffy & the Mystery of the Stolen Eggs. (Stories to Grow on Ser.). (gr. 2-6). 1980. pap. 6.95 incl. cassette (ISBN 0-8307-0689-5, 5606691). Regal.

Barret, James E., ed. see Hall, Linda B.

Barret, P., ed. see International Meeting of the Societe de Chemie Physique, 25th, July, 1974.

Barret, Richard C. How to Identify Bennington Pottery. LC 64-17558. (Orig.). 1973. pap. 4.95 (ISBN 0-8289-0193-7). Greene.

Barret, Robert. The Theorike & Practike of Moderne Warres. LC 74-26523. (English Experience Ser.: No. 155). (Illus.). 247p. 1969. Repr. of 1598 ed. 42.00 (ISBN 90-221-0155-X). Walter J Johnson.

Barret, Stephen, jt. auth. see Reynolds, Linda.

Barret-Hamilton, Gerald E. & Hinton, Martin A. A History of British Mammals, 2 vols. Sterling, Keir B., ed. LC 77-81081. (Biologists & Their World Ser.). (Illus.). 1978. Repr. of 1921 ed. Set. lib. bdg. 92.00x (ISBN 0-405-10648-3); lib. bdg. 46.00x ea. Vol. 1 (ISBN 0-405-10649-1). Vol. 2 (ISBN 0-405-10650-5). Ayer Co Pubs.

Barreto, Delia. Muscles: A Study Aid for Students of the Allied Health Professions. (Illus.). 48p. 1974. pap. 2.75x (ISBN 0-87936-005-4). Scholium Intl.

Barrett. Coast of Maine. (Illus.). 1984. 15.00 (ISBN 0-19-540610-9). Skyline Press.

Barrett & Gifford. Miwok Material Culture: Indian Life of the Yosemite Region. (Indians). 377p. 6.95 (ISBN 0-939666-12-X). Yosemite Natl Hist.

Barrett & Ovenden. The Sea Coast. pap. 8.95 (ISBN 0-00-219780-4, Collins Pub England). Greene.

Barrett & Yonge. Collins Pocket Guide to the Seashore. 29.95 (ISBN 0-00-219321-3, Collins Pub England). Greene.

Barrett, A. J. Mammalian Proteases: A Glossary & Bibliography: Vol. 2, Exopeptidases. McDonald, J. K., ed. Date not set. write for info. (ISBN 0-12-079502-7). Acad Pr.

Barrett, A. J., ed. Proteinases in Mammalian Cells & Tissues. (Research Monographs in Cell & Tissue Physiology: Vol. 2). 736p. 1977. 110.25 (ISBN 0-7204-0619-6, Biomedical Pr). Elsevier.

Barrett, Alan & McDonald, J. Ken. Mammalian Proteases: a Glossary & Bibliography: Vol. 1: Endopeptidases. 1980. 44.00 (ISBN 0-12-079501-9). Acad Pr.

Barrett, Alan H., ed. see Bekefi, George.

Barrett, Albert M. People under Pressure. 1960. 8.95x (ISBN 0-8084-0405-9). New Coll U Pr.

Barrett, Andrea. The Diabetic's Brand-Name Food Exchange Handbook. LC 84-2105. 176p. 1984. 14.95 (ISBN 0-89471-256-X); lib. bdg. 24.80 (ISBN 0-89471-237-3). Running Pr.

Barrett, Anna P. The Middlebatchers: Throw a Party for the Marriage of Hetty Wish & Lester Leg, Vol. 1. Darst, Shelia S., ed. (Illus.). 118p. (Orig.). (gr. 3-7). 1984. pap. 5.95 (ISBN 0-89896-105-X). Larksdale.

Barrett, Anthony A. & Liscombe, Rhodri W. Francis Rattenbury & British Columbia: Architecture & Challenge in the Imperial Age. (Illus.). 256p. 1983. 29.95 (ISBN 0-7748-0178-6, Pub. by U of BC). Intl Spec Bk.

Barrett, Anthony N., jt. ed. see Geisow, Michael J.

Barrett, Arthur, jt. auth. see Magnani, Duane.

Barrett, B. R., ed. see Tucson International Topical Conference on Nuclear Physics Held at the University of Arizona, Tucson, Jun 2-6, 1975.

Barrett, Benjamin, ed. see Brewer, J. E.

Barrett, Benjamin, ed. see Salinger, John P.

Barrett, Benjamin, ed. see Salinger, John. P.

Barrett, Bernard. The Civic Frontier. LC 79-670360. 1979. 27.50x (ISBN 0-522-84171-6, Pub. by Melbourne U Pr). Intl Spec Bk.

Barrett, Bernard M., ed. Manual of Patient Care in Plastic Surgery. (Spiral Manual Ser.). 1982. spiralbound 18.95 (ISBN 0-316-08217-1). Little.

Barrett, Bob. Pembrook vs the West. LC 77-11773. (Double D Western Ser.). 1978. 6.95 (ISBN 0-385-13526-2). Doubleday.

Barrett, Buckley B. The Barstow Printer: A Personal Name & Subject Index to the Years 1910-1920. LC 84-14550. (San Bernardino County Studies: No. 1). 100p. 1985. lib. bdg. 19.95x (ISBN 0-89370-840-2); pap. 9.95x (ISBN 0-89370-940-9). Borgo Pr.

Barrett, C., et al. The Principles of Engineering Materials. 1973. 34.95 (ISBN 0-13-709394-2). P-H.

Barrett, C. K. Church, Ministry, & Sacraments in the New Testament. 112p. (Orig.). 1985. pap. 6.95 (ISBN 0-8028-1994-X). Eerdmans.

--Essays on John. LC 82-2759. 176p. 1982. 18.95 (ISBN 0-664-21389-8). Westminster.

--Essays on Paul. LC 82-2764. 180p. 1982. 18.95 (ISBN 0-664-21390-1). Westminster.

--The Gospel According to St. John. 2nd ed. LC 78-2587. 654p. 1978. 28.95 (ISBN 0-664-21364-2). Westminster.

--The Gospel of John & Judaism. Smith, D. M., tr. LC 75-15435. 112p. 1975. 5.95 (ISBN 0-8006-0431-8, 1-431). Fortress.

--The Prologue of St. John's Gospel. (Ethel M. Wood Lectures). 28p. 1971. pap. 12.95 (ISBN 0-485-14315-1, Pub. by Athlone Pr Ltd). Longwood Pub Group.

--Reading Through Romans. LC 76-55828. 96p. 1977. pap. 3.95 (ISBN 0-8006-1250-7, 1-1250). Fortress.

Barrett, C. K., jt. ed. see Bammel, E.

Barrett, C. S. & Massalski, T. B. Structure of Metals: Crystallographic Methods, Principles & Data. 3rd rev. ed. LC 80-49878. (International Ser. on Materials Science & Technology: Vol. 14). (Illus.). 675p. 1980. 77.00 (ISBN 0-08-026171-X); pap. 22.00 (ISBN 0-08-026172-8). Pergamon.

Barrett, C. S., et al, eds. Advances in X-Ray Analysis. Incl. Vol. 1. 494p. 1960; Vol. 2. o.p. (ISBN 0-306-38102-8); Vol. 3; Vol. 4. 568p. 1961; Vol. 5. o.p. (ISBN 0-306-38105-2); Vol. 6. 480p. 1963; Vol. 7. 662p. 1964; Vol. 10. 558p. 1967; Vol. 11. 495p. 1968. 65.00x (ISBN 0-306-38111-7); Vol. 12. 652p. 1969. 65.00x (ISBN 0-306-38112-5). LC 58-35928 (Plenum Pr). Plenum Pub.

Barrett, C. Waller & Davidson, Alexander, Jr. Exhibition Celebrating the Seventy-Fifth Anniversary of the Grolier Club. LC 59-15011. 44p. 1959. pap. 4.00x (ISBN 0-8139-0449-8, Dist. by U Prof Va). Grolier Club.

--An Exhibition Celebrating the Seventy-Fifth Anniversary of the Grolier Club. 44p. 1959. pap. 4.00x (ISBN 0-8139-0449-8). U Pr of Va.

Barrett, Charles. Heritage of Stone. (Illus.). 1979. pap. 1.95x (ISBN 0-85091-110-9, Pub. by Lothian). Intl Spec Bk.

Barrett, Charles D. Understanding the Christian Faith. (Illus.). 1980. text ed. 23.95 (ISBN 0-13-935882-X). P-H.

Barrett, Charles K. The Epistle to the Romans. LC 57-12722. 1958. 14.95i (ISBN 0-06-060550-2, HarpR). Har-Row.

--The First Epistle to the Corinthians. LC 68-17594. (New Testament Commentaries Ser., Vol. 9). 1968. 17.95i (ISBN 0-06-060551-0, HarpR). Har-Row.

--The Second Epistle to the Corinthians. LC 73-18682. 366p. 1974. 13.95i (ISBN 0-06-060552-9, HarpR). Har-Row.

Barrett, Charles K., ed. New Testament Background: Selected Documents. pap. 5.95xi (ISBN 0-06-130086-1, TB86, Torch). Har-Row.

Barrett, Charles R. The History of the Society of Apothecaries of London. LC 75-23680. (Illus.). Repr. of 1905 ed. 28.00 (ISBN 0-404-13233-2). AMS Pr.

Barrett, Charles S., et al, eds. Advances in X-Ray Analysis, Vol. 14. LC 58-35928. 500p. 1971. 65.00x (ISBN 0-306-38114-1, Plenum Pr). Plenum Pub.

--Advances in X-Ray Analysis, Vol. 21. LC 58-35928. 341p. 1978. 52.50x (ISBN 0-306-38421-3, Plenum Pr). Plenum Pub.

--Advances in X-Ray Analysis, Vol. 28. 410p. 1985. 52.50x (ISBN 0-306-41939-4, Plenum Pr). Plenum Pub.

Barrett, Charles S., jt. ed. see Russ, John C.

Barrett, Charlotte. Diary & Letters of Madame D'Arblay, 1778-1840, 4 vols. 200.00 (ISBN 0-8274-2173-7). R West.

Barrett, Charls R. Short Story Writing. 257p. 1981. Repr. lib. bdg. 30.00 (ISBN 0-8495-0465-1). Arden Lib.

Barrett, Claire R. Psychological Perspectives in Education. 353p. (Orig.). 1980. pap. text ed. 10.95 (ISBN 0-89669-058-X). Collegium Bk Pubs.

Barrett, Clotilde. Boundweave. 100p. (Orig.). 1982. text ed. 9.95 (ISBN 0-937452-04-1). Colo Fiber.

--Shadow Weave & Corkscrew Weave. 55p. (Orig.). 1980. pap. 5.00 (ISBN 0-937452-02-5). Colo Fiber.

--Summer & Winter & Beyond. Rev. ed. 50p. 1982. pap. 5.00 (ISBN 0-937452-05-X). Colo Fiber.

Barrett, Clotilde & Smith, Eunice. Double Two-Tie Unit Weaves. 88p. 1983. pap. 12.00 (ISBN 0-937452-06-8); 1.50. Colo Fiber.

Barrett, Colin. The Practical Handbook of Private Trucking. LC 83-50039. 208p. 1983. 26.00 (ISBN 0-87408-026-6). Traffic Serv.

--Traffic World's Questions & Answers, Vol. 29. 1985. write for info. Traffic Serv.

Barrett, Cyril, ed. see Wittgenstein, Ludwig.

Barrett, D., ed. see Gordon, Douglas H.

Barrett, David, ed. World Christian Encyclopedia: A Comparative Survey of Churches & Religions in the Modern World, A. D. 1900 to 2000. (Illus.). 1982. text ed. 145.00x (ISBN 0-19-572435-6). Oxford U Pr.

Barrett, David & Sommerstein, Alan H., trs. Aristophanes: The Knights, Peace, the Birds, the Assembly Women, Wealth. (Classics Ser). 1978. pap. 3.95 (ISBN 0-14-044332-0). Penguin.

Barrett, David, tr. see Aristophanes.

Barrett, David D. Dixie Mission: The United States Army Observer Group in Yenan, 1944. (China Research Monographs: No. 6). (Illus.). 92p. 1970. pap. 4.00x (ISBN 0-912966-07-6). IEAS.

Barrett, David M. & Wein, Alan J., eds. Controversies in Neuro-Urology. (Illus.). 549p. 1984. text ed. 75.00 (ISBN 0-443-08106-9). Churchill.

Barrett, Dean, jt. auth. see Armentrout, Fred.

Barrett, Dee. That Saturday Night in Munich. 369p. 1980. pap. 3.95 (ISBN 0-89877-022-X). Jeremy Bks.

Barrett, Diana. Multihospital Systems: The Process of Development. LC 79-26111. 200p. 1980. text ed. 35.00 (ISBN 0-89946-011-9). Oelgeschlager.

Barrett, Don C. The Greenbacks & the Resumption of Specie Payments. 1965. 11.75 (ISBN 0-8446-1057-7). Peter Smith.

Barrett, Donald N., ed. Problem of Population, Vol. 1: Moral & Theological Considerations. (Orig.). 1964. 5.95 (ISBN 0-268-00218-5); pap. 0.95x (ISBN 0-268-00219-3). U of Notre Dame Pr.

--Values in America. 1961. pap. 1.95x (ISBN 0-268-00291-6). U of Notre Dame Pr.

Barrett, Dora & Miller, Rose C. My First Love Wears Two Masks. LC 80-54266. (Illus.). 408p. 1981. 20.00x (ISBN 0-9606048-0-4). Seaview Pr.

Barrett, Douglas & Gray, Basil. Indian Painting. LC 63-8982. (Illus.). 1978. pap. 17.50 (ISBN 0-8478-0158-6). Rizzoli Intl.

Barrett, Douglas B. & Gray, Basil. Indian Painting. (Illus.). 216p. pap. 17.50 (ISBN 0-317-31435-1). Rizzoli Intl.

Barrett, E. C. Climatology from Satellites. (Illus.). 418p. 1974. pap. 17.00x (ISBN 0-416-72150-8, NO.2614). Methuen Inc.

Barrett, E. C. & Curtis, L. R. Introduction to Environmental Remote Sensing. 2nd ed. (Illus.). 300p. 1982. 60.00x (ISBN 0-412-23080-1, NO. 6734, Pub. by Chapman & Hall); pap. 31.00x (ISBN 0-412-23090-9, NO. 6735). Methuen Inc.

Barrett, Eaton S. The Heroine. 1977. Repr. of 1927 ed. lib. bdg. 30.00 (ISBN 0-8482-3374-3). Norwood Edns.

--The Heroine; or, Adventures of a Fair Romance Reader, 3 vols. in 1. LC 79-8233. Repr. of 1813 ed. 44.50 (ISBN 0-404-61775-1). AMS Pr.

Barrett, Edward, Jr. & Cohen, William. Constitutional Law, Cases & Materials, 6th Edition, 1984 Supplement. (University Casebook Ser.). 474p. 1984. pap. text ed. 9.50 (ISBN 0-88277-207-4). Foundation Pr.

Barrett, Edward L., Jr. The Tenney Committee: Legislative Investigation of Subversive Activities in California. Repr. of 1951 ed. 37.00 (ISBN 0-384-03445-4). Johnson Repr.

Barrett, Edward L., Jr. & Cohen, William. Constitutional Law, Cases & Materials. 6th ed. LC 81-2359. (University Casebook Ser.). 1594p. 1981. text ed. 27.50 (ISBN 0-88277-024-1). Foundation Pr.

--Constitutional Law, Cases & Materials. 7th ed. LC 84-29979. (University Casebook Ser.). 1507p. 1985. text ed. write for info. (ISBN 0-88277-224-4). Foundation Pr.

--Constitutional Law: The Structure of Government. LC 81-67412. (University Casebook Ser.). 594p. 1981. pap. text ed. 14.50 (ISBN 0-88277-037-3). Foundation Pr.

Barrett, Elizabeth. Elizabeth Barrett to Miss Mitford. Miller, ed. 1954. 49.50x (ISBN 0-685-69789-4). Elliots Bks.

--Tailor-Made. (Loveswept Ser.: No. 76). 208p. 1985. pap. 2.25 (ISBN 0-553-21683-X). Bantam.

Barrett, Elizabeth B. & Haydon, Benjamin R. Invisible Friends: The Correspondence of Elizabeth Barrett Barrett & Benjamin Robert Haydon, 1842-1845. Pope, Willard B., ed. LC 72-80659. (Illus.). 220p. 1972. 14.50x (ISBN 0-674-46586-5). Harvard U Pr.

Barrett, Elston. Hot Summer Night. 1980. pap. 1.95 (ISBN 0-8439-0711-8, Leisure Bks). Dorchester Pub Co.

Barrett, Eric & Martin, David. The Use of Satellite Data in Rainfall Monitoring. LC 81-66677. 1981. 59.50 (ISBN 0-12-079680-5). Acad Pr.

Barrett, Eric C. & Curtis, Leonard F., eds. Environmental Remote Sensing: Practices & Problems, Vol. 2. LC 73-91531. 309p. 1977. 40.00x (ISBN 0-8448-0967-5). Crane-Russak Co.

Barrett, Eric C. & Fisher, David, eds. Scientists Who Believe: Twenty-One Tell Their Own Stories. 1984. pap. 4.50 (ISBN 0-8024-7634-1). Moody.

Barrett, Ethel. Abraham: God's Faithful Pilgrim. LC 82-12330. (Bible Biography Ser.). 128p. (Orig.). (gr. 3 up). 1982. pap. 2.50 (ISBN 0-8307-0769-7, 5810906). Regal.

--Blister Lamb. 1978. pap. 6.95 (ISBN 0-8307-0420-5, 5602718). Regal.

--Cracker, the Horse Who Lost His Temper: Communicating Christian Values to Children. (Stories to Grow on Ser.). (gr. 2-6). 1979. pap. 6.95 incl. cassette (ISBN 0-8307-0687-9, 5606403). Regal.

--Daniel. LC 79-65230. (Bible Biography Ser.). 128p. (gr. 3-9). 1979. pap. 1.95 (ISBN 0-8307-0761-1, 5810306). Regal.

--David: The Giant-Slayer. LC 82-80009. (Bible Biography Ser.). 128p. (gr. 3). 1982. pap. 2.50 (ISBN 0-8307-0770-0, 5811007). Regal.

--Ethel Barrett Tells Bible Stories to Children, Vol. 2. LC 76-45256. (Bible Biography Ser.). Orig. Title: Stories of Moses & Jesus. 144p. 3.25 (ISBN 0-8307-0475-2, 5603005). Regal.

--Ethel Barrett Tells Favorite Bible Stories. LC 77-93051. (Bible Biography Ser.). 128p. 1978. pap. 3.95 (ISBN 0-8307-0615-1, 5605806). Regal.

--Fanny Crosby. LC 83-23064. 128p. (Orig.). 1984. pap. 4.95 (ISBN 0-8307-0929-0, 5418149). Regal.

--God, Have You Got It All Together? LC 76-29888. (Venture Stories Ser.). 160p. 1977. pap. 1.95 (ISBN 0-8307-0434-5, S064154). Regal.

--Gregory the Grub. (ps-1). 1978. pap. 6.95 (ISBN 0-8307-0421-3, 5602823). Regal.

--Ice, Water & Snow. (Stories to Grow on Ser.: II). (gr. 2-6). 1980. pap. 6.95 (ISBN 0-8307-0690-9, 5606721). Regal.

--Joseph. LC 79-65232. (Bible Biography Bible Ser.). 128p. (gr. 3-9). 1979. pap. 1.95 (ISBN 0-8307-0715-8, 5607701). Regal.

--Joshua. LC 79-65233. (Bible Biography Ser.). 128p. (gr. 3-9). 1979. pap. 2.50 (ISBN 0-8307-0707-7, 5607000). Regal.

--Master of Mystery & Dreams: Daniel. (Bible Biography Ser.). 128p. (gr. 3 up). 1983. pap. text ed. 1.95 (ISBN 0-8307-0717-4, 5810306). Regal.

--Men of Mystery & Miracles. LC 79-65231. (Bible Biography Ser.). 128p. (gr. 3-9). 1979. pap. 1.95 (ISBN 0-8307-0760-3, 5810007). Regal.

--Moses: Mission Impossible! LC 82-16521. (Bible Biographies Ser.). 1982. pap. text ed. 2.50 (ISBN 0-8307-0772-7, 5811201). Regal.

--Paul. LC 81-51740. (Bible Biography Ser.). 128p. (gr. 3 up). 1981. pap. text ed. 1.95 (ISBN 0-8307-0767-0, 5810701). Regal.

--The People Who Couldn't Be Stopped. LC 79-96703. (Orig.). (gr. 4-8). 1970. pap. 1.95 (ISBN 0-8307-0007-2, S063107). Regal.

--Peter. LC 81-52942. (Bible Biography Ser.). 128p. (Orig.). (gr. 3 up). 1982. pap. text ed. 1.95 (ISBN 0-8307-0768-9, 5810809). Regal.

--Quacky & Wacky. (ps-1). 1978. pap. 6.95 book & cassette pac (ISBN 0-8307-0418-3, 5602593). Regal.

--Rules - Who Needs Them? LC 73-90623. (Orig.). (gr. 4-8). 1974. pap. 1.95 (ISBN 0-8307-0282-2, 5407001). Regal.

--Ruth. LC 80-52961. (Bible Biography Ser.). 128p. (gr. 3-9). 1980. pap. 1.95 (ISBN 0-8307-0764-6, 5810418). Regal.

--Steve Paxon: Can't Lose for Winning. LC 84-26238. 1985. pap. 4.95 (ISBN 0-8307-1022-1, 5418424). Regal.

--Storytelling, It's Easy. pap. 5.95 (ISBN 0-310-20561-1, Pub. by Cowman). Zondervan.

--The Strangest Thing Happened. LC 76-84599. 144p. (gr. 4-8). 1971. pap. 1.95 (ISBN 0-8307-0005-6, S061104). Regal.

--Sylvester the Three-Spined Stickleback. (Stories to Grow on Ser.). 24p. (gr. 2-6). 1980. pap. 6.95 incl. cassette (ISBN 0-8307-0688-7, 5606691). Regal.

--Will the Real Phony Please Stand Up? rev. ed. LC 84-17777. 224p. 1984. pap. 4.95 (ISBN 0-8307-1001-9, 5418383); Leader's Guide 3.95 (ISBN 0-8307-1009-4, 6101966). Regal.

Barrett, Francis. The Magus. 374p. pap. 30.00x (ISBN 0-7225-0409-8, Pub. by Aquarian Pr England). State Mutual Bk.

--The Magus: A Complete System of Occult Philosophy. 200p. 1975. pap. 12.00 (ISBN 0-8065-0462-5). Citadel Pr.

Barrett, Francis, ed. The Secret Book of Artephius. pap. 2.95 (ISBN 0-916411-28-1). Alchemical Pr.

Barrett, Francis, ed. see Freher, Dionysius.

Barrett, G. Vincent & Blair, John P. How to Conduct & Analyze Real Estate Market & Feasibility Studies. 352p. 1981. text ed. 28.95 (ISBN 0-442-22568-7). Van Nos Reinhold.

Barrett, G. Vincent & Tandy, Janet K. The International Real Estate & Land Economics Bookshelf, 1975-1985. 420p. (Orig.). 1985. pap. 35.00 (ISBN 0-934471-00-2). NM St U Ctr Real Est.

Barrett, G. W. Ancient China. Reeves, Marjorie, ed. (Then & There Ser.). (Illus.). 96p. (YA) (gr. 7-12). 1969. pap. text ed. 3.40x (ISBN 0-582-20453-4). Longman.

Barrett, Gary W. & Rosenberg, Rutger, eds. Stress Effects on Natural Ecosystems. LC 80-40851. (Environmental Monographs & Symposia, Environmental Science). 305p. 1981. 56.95x (ISBN 0-471-27834-3, Pub. by Wiley-Interscience). Wiley.

Barrett, Gerald, jt. auth. see Bass, Bernard.

Barrett, Gerlad R. & Brabner, Wendy. Stan Brakhage: A Guide to References & Resources. 336p. (gr. 10-12). 1983. lib. bdg. 44.00 (ISBN 0-8161-7890-9, Hall Reference). G K Hall.

Barrett, Glen. Boise State University: Searching for Excellence, 1932-1984. Keiser, John H., epilogue by. 230p. 1984. text ed. 12.95 (ISBN 0-932129-00-5); pap. text ed. 9.95 (ISBN 0-932129-01-3). Boise St Univ.

Barrett, Glenn, ed. see Anderson, John.

Barrett, Graham C., ed. Chemistry & Biochemistry of the Amino Acids. 720p. 1985. 99.00 (ISBN 0-412-23410-6, NO. 6835, Pub. by Chapman & Hall). Methuen Inc.

Barrett, Gregory, tr. see Sato, Tadao.

Barrett, Gwynn W., jt. auth. see Adler, Jacob.

Barrett, H. H. Radiological Imaging, Vol. I: The Theory of Image Formation, Detection, & Processing. Swindell, W., ed. LC 80-69416. 1981. 55.00 (ISBN 0-12-079601-5). Acad Pr.

Barrett, H. H. & Swindell, W. Radiological Imaging: The Theory of Formation & Detection & Processing, Vol. 2. LC 80-69416. (Biophysics & Bioengineering Ser.). 1981. 55.00 (ISBN 0-12-079602-3). Acad Pr.

Barrett, H. J., jt. auth. see Rohl, J. S.

Barrett, Harold. Daring to Be: Love & the Art of Rhetorical Intercourse. LC 82-2237. 152p. 1982. text ed. 18.95x (ISBN 0-88229-609-4). Nelson-Hall.

--Practical Uses of Speech Communication. 5th ed. LC 80-18332. 312p. 1981. pap. text ed. 17.95 (ISBN 0-03-049591-1, HoltC). HR&W.

--Speaking Practically: An Introduction to Speech Communication. LC 80-24041. 212p. 1981. pap. text ed. 16.95 (ISBN 0-03-054091-7, HoltC). HR&W.

Barrett, Helen, ed. see Jenkins, Will D.

Barrett, Helen M. Boethius: Some Aspects of His Times & Works. LC 65-18789. 1965. Repr. of 1940 ed. 7.50x (ISBN 0-8462-0653-6). Russell.

Barrett, Helena M. One Way to Write Anything. 144p. (Orig.). 1982. pap. 4.09i (ISBN 0-06-463551-1, EH 551, EH). B&N NY.

--One Way to Write Anything. 1982. pap. 4.09 (ISBN 0-06-463551-1, EH-551). Har-Row.

Barrett, Henry. The Viola: Complete Guide for Teachers & Students. 2nd ed. LC 70-169498. 232p. 1978. 19.95 (ISBN 0-8173-6402-1). U of Ala Pr.

Barrett, Ian. Tundra & People. LC 82-50395. (Nature's Landscape Ser.). PLB 15.96 (ISBN 0-382-06670-7). Silver.

Barrett, Ivan J. Joseph Smith & the Restoration: A History of the LDS Church to 1846. rev. ed. LC 70-167990. (Illus.). 1973. pap. 9.95 (ISBN 0-8425-0672-1). Brigham.

Barrett, J. Mexico. 1976. lib. bdg. 59.95 (ISBN 0-8490-2241-X). Gordon Pr.

Barrett, J., jt. auth. see Golding, D. N.

Barrett, J. Carl & Tennant, Raymond W., eds. Mammalian Cell Transformation: Mechanisms of Carcinogenesis & Assays for Carcinogens. (Carcinogenesis: A Comprehensive Survey Ser.: Vol. 9). 432p. 1985. text ed. 59.50 (ISBN 0-88167-116-9). Raven.

Barrett, J. Edward. Faith in Focus: A Compact Introduction to Christian Theology. LC 81-40167. 130p. (Orig.). 1982. lib. bdg. 21.75 (ISBN 0-8191-1878-8); pap. text ed. 9.25 (ISBN 0-8191-1879-6). U Pr of Amer.

Barrett, J. O. The Book of Revelation: Missionary Message of the New Testament. 123p. 1947. Repr. 4.50 (ISBN 0-87921-005-2). Attic Pr.

Barrett, James & Williams, Geoffrey. Test Your Own Job Aptitude: Exploring Your Career Potential. 128p. 1981. pap. 2.95 (ISBN 0-14-005809-5). Penguin.

Barrett, James E. The Psalmnary: Gradual Psalms for Cantor & Congregation. 196p. 1982. incl. binder 22.50 (ISBN 0-942466-04-7); 19.50 (ISBN 0-942466-03-9). Hymnary Pr.

Barrett, James E., ed. The Daily Lectionary. 70p. 1982. 2.45 (ISBN 0-942466-02-0). Hymnary Pr.

--The Hymnary: A Table for Service Planning. 95p. 1979. incl. binder 15.00 (ISBN 0-942466-01-2); 12.50 (ISBN 0-942466-00-4). Hymnary Pr.

--Stress & Mental Disorder. LC 79-2202. (American Psychopathological Association Ser.). 310p. 1979. text ed. 41.00 (ISBN 0-89004-384-1). Raven.

Barrett, James E., jt. ed. see Clayton, Paula J.

Barrett, James E., jt. ed. see Cole, Jonathan O.

Barrett, James H. Gerontological Psychology. 184p. 1972. 19.75x (ISBN 0-398-02226-7). C C Thomas.

Barrett, James T. Basic Immunology & Its Medical Application. 2nd ed. LC 80-14328. (Illus.). 304p. 1980. pap. text ed. 22.95 (ISBN 0-8016-0495-8). Mosby.

Barrett, James T., ed. Citation Classics in the Life Sciences. (Citation Classics Ser.). 600p. 1985. 39.95 (ISBN 0-89495-053-3). ISI Pr.

Barrett, James W., ed. End of 'The World' facs. ed. LC 72-117866. (Select Bibliographies Reprint Ser). 1931. 24.50 (ISBN 0-8369-5319-3). Ayer Co Pubs.

Barrett, Janice R. & Schuller, Linda C. Illinois Artisans & Craftsmen: A Guide, Resource, & Reference. (Illinois Artisans & Craftsmen Ser.: No. 1). (Illus.). 352p. 1983. 35.00 (ISBN 0-943902-00-2); pap. 21.90 (ISBN 0-943902-01-0). Insearch Pr.

Barrett, Jay A. Evolution of the Ordinance of Seventeen Eighty-Seven with an Account of the Earlier Plans for the Government of the Northwest Territory. LC 79-146372. (First American Frontier Ser). (Illus.). 1971. Repr. of 1891 ed. 14.00 (ISBN 0-405-02823-7). Ayer Co Pubs.

Barrett, Jean. Archery. 3rd ed. 1980. pap. 8.65x (ISBN 0-673-16181-1). Scott F.

--Fire Bird. (Second Chance at Love Ser.: No. 242). 192p. 1985. pap. 1.95 (ISBN 0-425-07769-1). Jove Pubns.

--The Head Nurse: Her Leadership Role. 3rd ed. 450p. 1975. 23.95 (ISBN 0-8385-3651-4). ACC.

Barrett, Jeffrey W. Impulse to Revolution in Latin America. LC 84-26297. 368p. 1985. 37.95 (ISBN 0-03-001558-8). Praeger.

Barrett, Joan & Goldfarb, Sally. The Insider's Guide to the Prep Schools. 1979. pap. 5.95 (ISBN 0-525-03643-1, Thomas Congdon Book). Dutton.

Barrett, John. The Bear Who Slept Through Christmas. LC 75-37678. (Bear Bks.). (Illus.). 32p. (gr. k-4). 1976. PLB 10.60 (ISBN 0-516-09480-7). Childrens.

--The Bears Find Thanksgiving. (Bear Bks). (Illus.). 32p. (gr. k-4). 1981. PLB 10.60 (ISBN 0-516-09192-1). Childrens.

--The Bears Find Thanksgiving. 32p. (gr. k-6). 1981. 3.95 (ISBN 0-8249-8019-0). Ideals.

--Biochemistry of Parasitic Helminths. (Illus.). 320p. 1981. pap. text ed. 21.00 (ISBN 0-8391-4141-6). Univ Park.

--Christmas Comes to Monster Mountain. (Bear Bks). (Illus.). 32p. (gr. k-4). 1981. PLB 10.60 (ISBN 0-516-09181-6). Childrens.

--Daniel Discovers Daniel. LC 79-17897. 32p. 1980. 10.95 (ISBN 0-87705-423-1). Human Sci Pr.

--The Day the Toys Came to Silver Dollar City. (Silver Dollar City Stories). (Illus.). (gr. k-10). 1978. 1.99 (ISBN 0-686-22891-X). Silver Dollar.

--The Easter Bear. (Illus.). 32p. (gr. k-4). 1981. PLB 10.60 (ISBN 0-516-09190-5). Childrens.

--The Easter Bear. 32p. (gr. k-6). 1981. 3.95 (ISBN 0-8249-8007-7). Ideals.

--The Great Bear Scare. (Bear Bks). (Illus.). 32p. (gr. k-4). 1981. PLB 10.60 (ISBN 0-516-09191-3). Childrens.

--The Great Bear Scare. 32p. (gr. k-6). 1981. 3.95 (ISBN 0-8249-8018-2). Ideals.

--The Littlest Mule. Silver Dollar City, Inc., ed. (Silver Dollar City Stories). (Illus.). (ps-5). 1977. 2.99g (ISBN 0-686-19125-0). Silver Dollar.

--Oscar, the Selfish Octopus. LC 78-18760. (Illus.). 32p. 1978. 10.95 (ISBN 0-87705-335-9). Human Sci Pr.

--The Pan American Union. 1977. lib. bdg. 59.95 (ISBN 0-8490-2401-3). Gordon Pr.

--That Better Country. 1966. 15.50x (ISBN 0-522-83525-2, Pub. by Melbourne U Pr). Intl Spec Bk.

--Zeke Hatfield & a Ghost Named Rocky. (Silver Dollar City Stories). (Illus.). (gr. k-10). 1978. 1.99 (ISBN 0-686-22892-8). Silver Dollar.

Barrett, John, jt. auth. see Iredale, David.

Barrett, John, ed. New York in Twelve Easy Walks. (Easy Walk Ser.: No. 1). (Illus.). 84p. 1986. pap. 5.95 (ISBN 0-915857-00-6). Barrett Pr.

--The World of Tennis 1973. cancelled (ISBN 0-671-21623-6, Fireside). S&S.

Barrett, John, ed. see Kaminski, Lee.

Barrett, John E. & View-Master International, photos by. Big Bird's Mother Goose. LC 83-63404. (Chunky Bks). (Illus.). 28p. (ps). 1984. bds. 2.95 (ISBN 0-394-86745-9, Pub. by BYR). Random.

Barrett, John G. The Civil War in North Carolina. LC 63-22810. xi, 484p. 1963. 17.95 (ISBN 0-8078-0874-1). U of NC Pr.

--North Carolina As a Civil War Battleground, 1861-1865. (Illus.). viii, 99p. 1984. pap. 2.00 (ISBN 0-86526-088-5). NC Archives.

--Sherman's March Through the Carolinas. LC 56-14242. x, 325p. 1956. 17.95 (ISBN 0-8078-0701-X). U of NC Pr.

Barrett, John G., jt. ed. see Yearns, W. Buck.

Barrett, John M. No Time for Me: Learning to Live with Busy Parents. LC 78-21257. 32p. 1979. 10.95 (ISBN 0-87705-385-5). Human Sci Pr.

Barrett, John W., ed. Regional Silviculture of the United States. 2nd ed. 551p. 1980. 42.50 (ISBN 0-471-05645-6). Wiley.

Barrett, Jon H. Individual Goals & Organizational Objectives. LC 77-632403. 119p. 1970. 12.00x (ISBN 0-87944-080-5). Inst Soc Res.

Barrett, Joseph H. Life of Abraham Lincoln. 842p. 1981. Repr. of 1865 ed. lib. bdg. 125.00 (ISBN 0-89987-070-8). Darby Bks.

--Life of Abraham Lincoln. 1865. Repr. 100.00 (ISBN 0-8274-2917-7). R West.

Barrett, Judi. Animals Should Definitely Not Act Like People. LC 80-13364. (Illus.). 32p. (ps-2). 1980. 9.95 (ISBN 0-689-30768-3); pap. 3.95 (ISBN 0-689-30768-3). Atheneum.

--Animals Should Definitely Not Act Like People. LC 80-13364. (Illus.). 32p. (ps-2). 1985. pap. 3.95 (ISBN 0-689-71033-X, A-147, Aladdin). Atheneum.

--I'm Too Small, You're Too Big. LC 80-23883. (Illus.). 32p. (ps-1). 1981. PLB 12.95 (ISBN 0-689-30800-0). Atheneum.

--A Snake Is Totally Tail. LC 83-2657. (Illus.). 32p. (ps-1). 1983. PLB 9.95 (ISBN 0-689-30979-1). Atheneum.

--What's Left? LC 82-12824. (Illus.). 32p. (ps). 1983. 10.95 (ISBN 0-689-30874-4). Atheneum.

Barrett, Judith. Animals Should Definitely Not Wear Clothing. LC 70-115078. (Illus.). 32p. (ps-2). 1970. PLB 12.95 (ISBN 0-689-20592-9). Atheneum.

--Animals Should Definitely Not Wear Clothing. (Illus.). (ps-2). 1980. pap. 3.95 (ISBN 0-689-70412-7, A-36, Aladdin). Atheneum.

--Benjamin's Three Hundred Sixty-Five Birthdays. LC 72-86926. (Illus.). 40p. (gr. k-2). 1974. 7.95 (ISBN 0-689-30130-8); pap. 1.95 (ISBN 0-689-70443-7). Atheneum.

--Benjamin's Three Hundred Sixty Five Birthdays. (Illus.). 1978. pap. 1.95 (ISBN 0-689-70443-7, A-73, Aladdin). Atheneum.

--Cloudy with a Chance of Meatballs. LC 78-2945. (Illus.). (ps-3). 1978. 12.95 (ISBN 0-689-30647-4); pap. 2.95 (ISBN 0-689-70749-5). Atheneum.

--Old McDonald Had a Apartment House. (Illus.). 32p. (ps-3). pap. 2.95 (ISBN 0-689-70401-1, A-35, Aladdin). Atheneum.

Barrett, Judy. Joys of Computer Networking: The Personal Connection Handbook. 219p. 1984. pap. 9.95 (ISBN 0-07-003768-X, BYTE Bks). McGraw.

Barrett, Junelle P., et al. Teaching Global Awareness: An Approach for Grades 1-6. (Illus.). 217p. (Orig.). (gr. 1-6). pap. 19.95 (ISBN 0-943804-13-2). U of Denver Teach.

Barrett, Kate W. Some Practical Suggestions on the Conduct of a Rescue Home: Including Life of Dr. Kate Waller Barrett. facsimile ed. LC 74-3928. (Women in America Ser.). Orig. Title: Fifty Years Work with Girls. 186p. 1974. Repr. of 1903 ed. 20.00x (ISBN 0-405-06075-0). Ayer Co Pubs.

Barrett, Keith E. Dispersion Polymerization in Organic Media. LC 74-5491. 322p. 1975. 79.95x (ISBN 0-471-05418-6, Pub. by Wiley-Interscience). Wiley.

Barrett, Kevin & Amthor, Terry K. Future Law. (Illus.). 80p. (gr. 10-12). 1985. 10.00 (ISBN 0-915795-36-1). Iron Crown Ent Inc.

--Tech Law. (Illus.). 96p. (gr. 10-12). 12.00 (ISBN 0-915795-38-8). Iron Crown Ent Inc.

Barrett, L. L., tr. see Verissimo, Erico.

Barrett, Lady. Personality Survives Death. 59.95 (ISBN 0-8490-0819-0). Gordon Pr.

Barrett, Laurence I. Gambling with History: Ronald Reagan in the White House. 511p. 1984. pap. 8.95 (ISBN 0-14-007275-6). Penguin.

Barrett, Lawrence. Charlotte Cushman, a Lecture. LC 79-130086. (Dunlap Society Publications: No. 9). 1970. Repr. of 1889 ed. lib. bdg. 16.50 (ISBN 0-8337-0171-1). B Franklin.

--Edwin Forrest. LC 71-91894. 1881. 18.00 (ISBN 0-405-08238-X, Pub. by Blom). Ayer Co Pubs.

--Edwin Forrest. 1881. 9.00x (ISBN 0-403-00242-7). Scholarly.

Barrett, Leonard E. The Rastafarians: Sounds of Cultural Dissonance. LC 76-48491. (Illus.). 1977. pap. 9.95 (ISBN 0-8070-1115-0, BP559). Beacon Pr.

--The Sun & the Drum: African Roots in the Jamaican Folk Tradition. 1976. pap. text ed. 10.00x (ISBN 0-435-89454-4). Heinemann Ed.

Barrett, Lindsay. Song for Mumu. LC 73-99065. 1974. 8.95 (ISBN 0-88258-006-X). Howard U Pr.

Barrett, Linton L., ed. Five Centuries of Spanish Literature: From the Cid Through the Golden Age. (Orig., Span.). 1962. pap. text ed. 14.10 scp (ISBN 0-06-040499-X, HarpC). Har-Row.

Barrett, Lois. The Vision & the Reality: The Story of Home Missions in the General Conference Mennonite Church. LC 83-80402. 339p. (Orig.). 1983. pap. 16.95 (ISBN 0-87303-079-6). Faith & Life.

Barrett, Louis C., jt. auth. see Wylie, C. Ray.

Barrett, M., et al. Occasional Papers in Human Biology, Vol. I. 1979. pap. text ed. 11.50x (ISBN 0-391-00999-0). Humanities.

Barrett, M. Edgar & Bruns, William J. Case Problems in Management Accounting. 2nd ed. 1985. 28.50x (ISBN 0-256-03181-9). Irwin.

Barrett, M. Edgar & Cormack, Mary P. Management Strategy in the Oil & Gas Industries: Cases & Readings. LC 82-15524. 594p. 1983. 36.95x (ISBN 0-87201-506-8). Gulf Pub.

Barrett, Marcia, et al. Foundations for Movement. 2nd ed. 124p. 1968. write for info wire coil (ISBN 0-697-07103-0). Wm C Brown.

Barrett, Marsha. Early Christians: Workers for Jesus. (BibLearn Ser.). (Illus.). (gr. 1-6). 1979. 5.95 (ISBN 0-8054-4247-2, 4242-47). Broadman.

--Servant with a Smile. (Illus.). 40p. (Orig.). (gr. 1-3). 1985. pap. 2.00 (ISBN 0-317-18029-0). Home Mission.

--Vena Aguillard: Woman of Faith. LC 82-73664. (Meet the Missionary Ser.). (gr. 4-6). 1983. 5.50 (ISBN 0-8054-4281-2, 4242-81). Broadman.

Barrett, Martyn D. Children's Single-Word Speech. Date not set. 44.95 (ISBN 0-471-90374-4). Wiley.

Barrett, Marvin. Meet Thomas Jefferson. (Step-up Books Ser.). (gr. 2-6). 1967. 4.95 (ISBN 0-394-80067-2, BYR); PLB 5.99 (ISBN 0-394-90067-7). Random.

--Rich News, Poor News: The Sixth Alfred I. duPont - Columbia University Survey of Broadcast Journalism. LC 77-95161. 1978. 14.37i (ISBN 0-690-01740-5); pap. 5.95i (ISBN 0-690-01741-3, TYC-T). T Y Crowell.

Barrett, Marvin, ed. Broadcast Journalism. LC 82-5067. 256p. 1982. 15.95 (ISBN 0-89696-160-5, An Everest House Book). Dodd.

Barrett, Mary E., jt. auth. see Arnaudet, Martin.

Barrett, Mary E., jt. auth. see Arnaudet, Martin L.

Barrett, Maurice. Art Education: A Strategy for Course Design. 1979. pap. text ed. 10.95x (ISBN 0-435-75053-4). Heinemann Ed.

Barrett, Maye. The Lady of Stantonwyck. 1981. pap. 2.50 (ISBN 0-89083-752-X). Zebra.

Barrett, Michael D. Asylum & Circus. 1978. pap. 1.95 (ISBN 0-532-19172-2). Woodhill.

Barrett, Michael J. & Brink, Victor Z. Evaluating Internal-External Audit Services & Relationships. (Research Report Ser.: No. 24). (Illus.). 80p. 1981. pap. 6.00 (ISBN 0-89413-088-9). Inst Inter Aud.

Barrett, Michele. Women's Oppression Today: Problems in Marxist Feminst Analysis. 280p. 1981. 19.50x (ISBN 0-8052-7091-4, Pub. by NLB England); pap. 8.50 (ISBN 0-8052-7090-6). Schocken.

Barrett, Michele & McIntosh, Mary. The Anti-Social Family. 164p. 1983. 18.50 (ISBN 0-8052-7134-1); pap. 7.50 (ISBN 0-8052-7135-X). Schocken.

Barrett, Michele, intro. by see Woolf, Virginia.

Barrett, Michele, et al, eds. Ideology & Cultural Production. LC 78-26901. 1979. 27.50x (ISBN 0-312-40451-4). St Martin.

Barrett, Morris. Health Education Guide: A Design for Teaching. 2nd ed. LC 73-20279. (Illus.). 338p. 1974. pap. 12.00 (ISBN 0-8121-0481-1). Lea & Febiger.

Barrett, N. S. Airliners. (Picture Library). (Illus.). 32p. (gr. k-3). 1985. lib. bdg. 9.40 (ISBN 0-531-03720-7). Watts.

--Computers. (Picture Library). (Illus.). 32p. (gr. k-6). 1985. PLB 9.40 (ISBN 0-531-04945-0). Watts.

--Helicopters. (Picture Library Ser.). (Illus.). 32p. (gr. k-3). 1984. lib. bdg. 8.90 (ISBN 0-531-03721-5). Watts.

--Lasers & Holograms. (Picture Library). (Illus.). 32p. (gr. 1-6). 1985. PLB 9.40 (ISBN 0-531-04946-9). Watts.

--Motorcycles. (Picture Library). (Illus.). (gr. k-3). 1985. lib. bdg. 9.40 (ISBN 0-531-03783-5). Watts.

--Racing Cars. (Picture Library). (Illus.). 32p. (gr. k-3). 1985. lib. bdg. 9.40 (ISBN 0-531-03784-3). Watts.

--Robots. (Picture Library). (Illus.). 32p. (gr. 1-6). 1985. PLB 9.40 (ISBN 0-531-04947-7). Watts.

--Satellites. (Picture Library). (gr. 3 up). 1985. PLB 9.40 (ISBN 0-531-04948-5). Watts.

--Ships. (Illus.). 32p. (gr. k-3). PLB 8.90 (ISBN 0-531-03722-3). Watts.

--Space Shuttle. (Picture Library). (Illus.). 32p. (gr. 1-6). 1985. PLB 9.40 (ISBN 0-531-04949-3). Watts.

--Trucks. (Picture Library). (Illus.). (gr. k-3). 1984. PLB 8.90 (ISBN 0-531-03723-1). Watts.

--TV & Video. (Picture Library). 32p. (gr. 1-3). 1985. PLB 9.40 (ISBN 0-531-04950-7). Watts.

Barrett, Nancy S. The Theory of Microeconomic Policy. 1974. text ed. 13.95x (ISBN 0-669-83170-0). Heath.

Barrett, Nathan N. Bars of Adamant. LC 66-16527. 1966. 5.95 (ISBN 0-8303-0019-8). Fleet.

Barrett, Neal, Jr. Karma Corps. 1984. pap. 2.75 (ISBN 0-87997-976-3). DAW Bks.

Barrett, Nicholas. Fledger. LC 85-5037. 208p. 1985. 13.95 (ISBN 0-02-507410-5). Macmillan.

Barrett, Norman, jt. auth. see Dempsey, Michael.

Barrett, Pat & Dalton, Rosemary. The Kid's Cookbook. LC 74-161817. (Illus., Orig.). 1973. pap. 6.95 (ISBN 0-911954-68-6). Nitty Gritty.

Barrett, Paul. The Automobile & Urban Transit: The Formation of Public Policy in Chicago, 1900-1930. 360p. 1983. 34.95 (ISBN 0-87722-294-0). Temple U Pr.

Barrett, Paul, tr. see Dumery, Henry.

Barrett, Paul, tr. see Le Deaut, Roger.

Barrett, Paul, et al, eds. Concordance to Darwin's "Origin of Species". 864p. 1981. 49.50x (ISBN 0-8014-1319-2). Cornell U Pr.

Barrett, Paul H., ed. see Darwin, Charles.

Barrett, Peter & Barrett, Susan. The Circle Sarah Drew. Incl. The Line Sophie Drew. LC 76-174716 (ISBN 0-87592-029-2); The Square Ben Drew (ISBN 0-87592-049-7). LC 72-89449. (Illus.). 32p. (ps-2). 1973. 7.95 ea. (ISBN 0-87592-012-8). Scroll Pr.

Barrett, R. Developments in Optical Disc Technology & the Implications for Information Storage & Retrieval. 80p. 1981. 129.00x (ISBN 0-905984-71-4, Pub. by Brit Lib England). State Mutual Bk.

--Developments in Optical Disc Technology & the Implications for Information Storage & Retrieval. (R&D Report: No. 5623). (Illus.). 80p. (Orig.). 1981. pap. 71.25 (ISBN 0-905984-71-4, Pub. by British Lib). Longwood Pub Group.

--Further Developments in Optical Disc Technology & Applications. (LIR Report 27). (Illus.). 43p. (Orig.). 1984. pap. 14.25 (ISBN 0-7123-3038-0, Pub. by British Lib). Longwood Pub Group.

Barrett, Ralph Pat. The Administration of Intensive English Language Programs. 109p. 1982. 1.00 (ISBN 0-318-18145-2). Tchrs Eng Spkrs.

Barrett, Ralph Pat, ed. The Administration of Intensive English Language Programs. 109p. 1982. 1.00 (ISBN 0-317-36686-6); bulk rates avail. Natl Assn Foreign Students.

Barrett, Richard. The Commission. LC 82-72373. (Illus.). 438p. 1982. 25.00 (ISBN 0-9609396-0-1). Barrett.

Barrett, Richard A. Culture & Conduct: An Excursion in Anthropology. LC 83-14836. 240p. 1983. pap. write for info. (ISBN 0-534-03034-3). Wadsworth Pub.

Barrett, Richard N. International Dimensions of the Environmental Crisis. (A Westview Replica Ser.). 300p. 1982. softcover 27.50x (ISBN 0-86531-343-1). Westview.

Barrett, Robert S. The Care of the Unmarried Mother. Rothman, David J. & Rothman, Sheila M., eds. (Women & Children First Ser.). 30.00 (ISBN 0-8240-7651-6). Garland Pub.

Barrett, Roger C. & Jackson, Daphne F. Nuclear Sizes & Structure. (International Series of Monographs on Physics). 1977. 69.00x (ISBN 0-19-851272-4). Oxford U Pr.

Barrett, Roger K., jt. auth. see Herbert, David L.

Barrett, Ron. Hi-Yo Fido! LC 83-15110. (Illus.). 32p. (gr. 2-5). 1984. PLB 9.95 (ISBN 0-517-55215-9). Crown.

Barrett, Ron & Manes, Steve. Encyclopedia Placemates. price not set. Workman Pub.

Barrett, Rowland P., jt. ed. see Matson, Johnny L.

Barrett, S. & Rovin, S., eds. Tooth Robbers. 160p. 1980. pap. 8.50 (ISBN 0-89313-024-9). G F Stickley Co.

Barrett, S. A. The Cayapa Indians of Ecuador, 2 vols. 1977. Set. lib. bdg. 250.00 (ISBN 0-8490-1588-X). Gordon Pr.

--The Dream Dance of the Chippewa & Menominee Indians of Northern Wisconsin. (Classics of Anthropology Ser.). 26.00 (ISBN 0-8240-9634-7). Garland PUb.

Barrett, S. A. & Gifford, E. W. Miwok Material Culture. (Illus.). 257p. pap. 6.95 (ISBN 0-939666-12-X). Yosemite Natl Hist.

Barrett, S. L. Parties with a Purpose: A Handbook for Activity Directors. 128p. 1980. spiral 19.50x (ISBN 0-398-03986-0). C C Thomas.

Barrett, S. M. Geronimo's Story of His Life. 1981. Repr. lib. bdg. 29.00 (ISBN 0-686-71919-0). Scholarly.

Barrett, S. M., ed. see Geronimo.

Barrett, Sally. The Sound of the Week. (gr. k-4). 1980. 9.95 (ISBN 0-916456-63-3, GA 184). Good Apple.

Barrett, Samuel A. Ancient Aztalan. LC 70-11394. Repr. of 1933 ed. lib. bdg. 28.25x (ISBN 0-8371-4624-0, BAAA). Greenwood.

--The Dream Dance of the Chippewa & Menominee Indians of Northern Wisconsin. LC 76-43647. (Bulletin of the Public Museum of the City of Milwaukee: Vol. 1). Repr. of 1911 ed. 24.50 (ISBN 0-404-15482-4). AMS Pr.

--Material Aspects of Pomo Culture, 2 pts. in 1 vol. LC 76-43649. (Bulletin of the Public Museum of the City of Milwaukee Ser.: Vol. 20). Repr. of 1952 ed. 57.50 (ISBN 0-404-15483-2). AMS Pr.

--The Washo Indians. LC 76-43651. (Bulletin of the Public Museum of the City of Milwaukee Ser.: Vol. 2, No. 1). Repr. of 1917 ed. 14.00 (ISBN 0-404-15485-9). AMS Pr.

Barrett, Samuel A., et al, eds. Cudahy-Massee-Milwaukee Museum African Expedition 1928-29. LC 71-11397. Repr. of 1930 ed. lib. bdg. 37.50x (ISBN 0-8371-4625-9, BAAE). Greenwood.

Barrett, Stanley R. The Rebirth of Anthropological Theory. 288p. 1984. 25.00 (ISBN 0-8020-5638-5). U of Toronto Pr.

--The Rise & Fall of an African Utopia: A Wealthy Theocracy in Comparative Perspective. Boyd, Rosalind E., ed. (Development Perspectives Ser.: No. 1). 251p. 1977. text ed. 17.75x (ISBN 0-88920-054-8, Pub. by Wilfred Laurier U Pr Canada); pap. text ed. 12.00x (ISBN 0-88920-053-X). Humanities.

Barrett, Stephen, jt. auth. see Cornacchia, Harold J.

Barrett, Stephen, jt. auth. see Herbert, Victor.

Barrett, Stephen, ed. Passport to Successful Alumni Travel Programs. 96p. 1983. 14.50 (ISBN 0-89964-211-X). Coun Adv & Supp Ed.

Barrett, Stephen & Knight, Gilda, eds. Health Robbers: How to Protect Your Money & Your Life. 2nd ed. 408p. 1981. 13.95 (ISBN 0-89313-023-0). G F Stickley Co.

Barrett, Stephen, ed. see Marshall, Charles W.

Barrett, Stephen, ed. see Morelock, Michael & Vap, J. G.

Barrett, Susan, jt. auth. see Barrett, Peter.

Barrett, Susan & Fudge, Colin, eds. Policy & Action: Essays on the Implementation of Public Policy. 1981. 33.00x (ISBN 0-416-30670-5, NO. 3526); pap. 16.95x (ISBN 0-416-30680-2, NO. 3525). Methuen Inc.

Barrett, Susan E. Inbetween Yesterday. 2nd ed. LC 77-74036. (Illus.). 1976. pap. 4.00 (ISBN 0-89430-001-6). Palos Verdes.

--Spill Your Life Open: Poetry. (Illus.). 90p. (Orig.). 1985. pap. 7.00 (ISBN 0-9603916-0-6). Artichoke.

Barrett, Susan L. It's All in Your Head: A Student Guide for Increasing Brain Power. (Challenge Bks.). (Illus.). 120p. (Orig.). (gr. 4-9). 1985. pap. 7.95 (ISBN 0-915793-03-2). Free Spirit Pub Co.

Barrett, Terry & Colwill, Stephen. Winning Games on the Commodore 64. (Recreation Computing Ser.: No. 1-704). 221p. 1984. pap. 12.95 (ISBN 0-471-80725-7, 1-704). Wiley.

Barrett, Terry P. & Jones, Antonia J. Winning Games on the VIC-20. (Recreational Computing Ser.: No. 1-704). 143p. (Orig.). 1983. pap. 12.95 (ISBN 0-471-80601-3, 1-704, Pub. by Wiley Pr). Wiley.

Barrett, Theodosia. Russel County. LC 81-69331. 148p. 1981. 10.95 (ISBN 0-89227-047-0). Commonwealth Pr.

Barrett, Thomas. Great Hanging at Gainesville. 1961. 10.50 (ISBN 0-87611-003-0); pap. 7.50 (ISBN 0-87611-004-9). Tex St Hist Assn.

Barrett, Thomas & Morrissey, Robert, Jr. Marathon Runners. LC 81-11204. (Illus.). 160p. (gr. 7 up). 1981. PLB 9.79 (ISBN 0-671-34019-0). Messner.

Barrett, Thomas & Johnson, Dale, eds. Views on Elementary Reading Instruction. LC 73-78986. (Convention Publications Ser.). 1973. 3.00 (ISBN 0-87207-461-7). Intl Reading.

Barrett, Thomas C., jt. auth. see Clymer, Theodore W.

Barrett, Thomas C., jt. auth. see Smith, Richard J.

Barrett, Thomas J. Harnessing the Earthworm. (Illus.). 192p. 1976. 7.95 (ISBN 0-916302-14-8); pap. 5.95 (ISBN 0-916302-09-1). Bookworm Pub.

--Harnessing the Earthworm. (Illus.). 1947. pap. 5.00 (ISBN 0-914116-08-8). Shields.

Barrett, Thomas S. & Livermore, Putnam. The Conservation Easement in California. 256p. 1983. 44.95 (ISBN 0-933280-20-3); pap. 24.95 (ISBN 0-933280-19-X). Island CA.

Barrett, Thomas Van Braam. Great Morning of the World: The Unforgettable Story of Harry Barrett. LC 75-16416. Repr. of 1975 ed. 47.30 (ISBN 0-8357-9011-8, 2016366). Bks Demand UMI.

Barrett, Timothy. Japanese Papermaking: Traditions, Tools & Techniques. LC 83-5790. (Illus.). 320p. 1984. 32.50 (ISBN 0-8348-0185-X). Weatherhill.

Barrett, W. A., jt. auth. see Stainer, J.

Barrett, W. A., jt. auth. see Stainer, John.

Barrett, W. F. Psychical Research. 1979. Repr. of 1911 ed. lib. bdg. 20.00 (ISBN 0-8492-3738-6). R West.

Barrett, W. S., ed. see Euripides.

Barrett, Wayne. Coast of Massachusetts. (Illus.). 1984. 15.00 (ISBN 0-19-540611-7). Skyline Press.

Barrett, Wayne, photos by. Kings Landing. (Illus.). 1979. 19.95x (ISBN 0-19-540301-0). Oxford U Pr.

Barrett, William. The History & Antiquities of the City of Bristol. 704p. 1982. text ed. 75.50x (ISBN 0-904387-48-8, Pub. by Alan Sutton England). Humanities.

--The Illusion of Technique: A Search for Meaning in a Technological Civilization. LC 77-27765. 1978. pap. 6.95 (ISBN 0-385-11202-5, Anchor Pr). Doubleday.

--Irrational Man. LC 58-8081. 1958. pap. 5.50 (ISBN 0-385-03138-6, Anch). Doubleday.

--Irrational Man: A Study in Existential Philosophy. LC 77-7371. 1977. Repr. of 1958 ed. lib. bdg. 29.75 (ISBN 0-8371-9671-X, BAIM). Greenwood.

--The Lilies of the Field. 128p. 1982. pap. 2.50 (ISBN 0-446-31042-5). Warner Bks.

--Time of Need: Forms of Imagination in the Twentieth Century. write for info.; pap. 10.95 (ISBN 0-8195-6121-5). Wesleyan U Pr.

Barrett, William & Besterman, Theodore. Divining Rod. (Illus.). 1967. 7.50 (ISBN 0-8216-0071-0). Univ Bks.

Barrett, William A. English Church Composers: The Great Musicians. facsimile ed. LC 70-102224. (Select Bibliographies Reprint Ser). 1882. 19.00 (ISBN 0-8369-5109-3). Ayer Co Pubs.

--English Folk-Songs: Collected, Arranged, & Provided with Symphonies & Accompaniments for the Pianoforte. 1978. Repr. of 1891 ed. lib. bdg. 10.00 (ISBN 0-8414-1720-2). Folcroft.

--English Folk Songs Collected, Arranged & Provided with Symphonies & Accompaniments for the Pianoforte. 95p. 1980. Repr. of 1891 ed. lib. bdg. 20.00 (ISBN 0-8492-3758-0). R West.

--English Glee & Madrigal Writers. LC 77-75190. 1977. Repr. of 1877 ed. lib. bdg. 10.00 (ISBN 0-89341-089-6). Longwood Pub Group.

--English Glees & Part Songs. LC 77-75200. 1977. Repr. of 1886 ed. lib. bdg. 40.00 (ISBN 0-89341-104-3). Longwood Pub Group.

Barrett, William A. & Couch, John D. Compiler Construction: Theory & Practice. LC 78-26183. 512p. 1979. text ed. 33.95 (ISBN 0-574-21335-X, 13-4335). SRA.

Barrett, William E. The Left Hand of God. 15.95 (ISBN 0-317-27907-6, Pub. by Aeonian Pr). Amereon Ltd.

--Lilies of the Field. LC 62-8085. (Illus.). (YA) (gr. 7 up). 1962. 8.95 (ISBN 0-385-01785-5, Im); pap. 2.50 (ISBN 0-385-07246-5, Im). Doubleday.

Barrett-Ayres, Reginald. Joseph Haydn & the String Quartet. LC 74-494. (Illus.). 1975. Repr. of 1974 ed. 22.95 (ISBN 0-02-870400-2). Schirmer Bks.

Barrette, Paul. Robert De Blois's: Floris et Lyriope. LC 68-6610. 152p. 1983. Repr. of 1968 ed. lib. bdg. 19.95x (ISBN 0-89370-767-8). Borgo Pr.

Barrette, Paul & Braun, Theodore. Second French. LC 68-12943. 1968. text ed. 14.95 (ISBN 0-394-33391-8, RanC). Random.

Barrette, Pierre. Microcomputers in K-Twelve Education: Second Annual Conference Proceedings. LC 83-2101. 141p. 1983. 30.00 (ISBN 0-914894-87-0). Computer Sci.

Barrette, Pierre, ed. Microcomputers in K-Twelve Education, First Annual Conference Proceedings. LC 82-2522. 123p. 1982. pap. text ed. 30.00 (ISBN 0-914894-32-3). Computer Sci.

Barrette, Roy. Countryman's Journal: Views of Life & Nature from a Maine Coastal Farm. LC 81-7367. 192p. 1985. pap. 8.95 (ISBN 0-87923-558-6). Godine.

Barrett-Keach, Camillia N., ed. The Syntax & Interpretation of the Relative Clause Constructure in Swahili. (Outstanding Dissertations in Linguistics Ser.). 255p. 1985. lib. bdg. 30.00 (ISBN 0-8240-5432-6). Garland Pub.

Barrett-Lennard, C. E. Travels in British Columbia. LC 73-4861. (Illus.). 317p. 1973. Repr. of 1862 ed. lib. bdg. 25.00 (ISBN 0-685-32345-5). Milford Hse.

Barrett-Lennard, Thomas. The Position in Law of Women: A Concise & Comprehensive Treatise on the Position of Women at Common Law as Modified by the Doctrines of Equity & by Recent Legislation, Together with the Married Women's Property Acts, 1870, 1874, 1882: The Rules of the Supreme Court, 1883, Relating to Taking Acknowledgments & the Postal Regulations, 1883, Affecting Married Women. xxviii, 181p. 1983. Repr. of 1883 ed. lib. bdg. 25.00x (ISBN 0-8377-0336-0). Rothman.

Barretto, L. Bright Mexico. 1976. lib. bdg. 59.95 (ISBN 0-8490-1554-5). Gordon Pr.

Barricell, Jean-Pierre, ed. see Barricelli, Jean-Pierre, et al.

Barricelli, Jean P. & Weinstein, Leo. Ernest Chausson: The Composer's Life & Works. LC 73-7192. (Illus.). 241p. 1973. Repr. of 1955 ed. lib. bdg. 15.00 (ISBN 0-8371-6915-1, BAEC). Greenwood.

Barricelli, Jean-Pierre. The Prince: An Analysis of Machiavelli's Treatise on Power Politics. LC 74-1301. 1977. pap. 3.95 (ISBN 0-8120-0524-4). Barron.

Barricelli, Jean-Pierre, ed. Chekhov's Great Plays: A Critical Anthology. (The Gotham Library). 296p. 1981. 29.50x (ISBN 0-8147-1036-0). NYU Pr.

--Chekhov's Great Plays: A Critical Anthology. 268p. 1985. pap. text ed. 12.50x (ISBN 0-8147-1074-3). NYU Pr.

Barricelli, Jean-Pierre, et al. Interrelations of Literature. Barricell, Jean-Pierre & Gibaldi, Joseph, eds. LC 82-7956. vi, 329p. 1982. 25.00x (ISBN 0-87352-090-4, T160C); pap. 11.00 (ISBN 0-87352-091-2, T160P). Modern Lang.

Barrick, Augusta I. The Power of Effective Speech. (Orig.). 1959. pap. 7.95x (ISBN 0-8084-0251-X). New Coll U Pr.

Barrick, Mac E., ed. see Gomez De Toledo, Gaspar.

Barrick, Nolan E. The Unobserved Heritage of Texas Tech. LC 84-51938. (Illus.). 64p. 1985. pap. 5.00 (ISBN 0-89672-125-6). Tex Tech Pr.

Barrick, W. Boyd & Spencer, John S., eds. In the Shelter of Elyon: Essays on Ancient Palestinian Life & Literature in Honor of G. W. Ahlstrom. (JSOT Supplement Ser.: No. 31). 330p. 1984. text ed. 35.00 (ISBN 0-905774-65-5, Pub. by JSOT Pr England). Eisenbrauns.

Barrickman, Ray E. Big Dollar & Small Change. 1985. 16.95 (ISBN 0-87949-259-7). Ashley Bks.

Barrie, D. S. A Regional History of the Railways of Great Britain: South Wales, Vol. 12. LC 80-67609. (Illus.). 1980. 25.00 (ISBN 0-7153-7970-4). David & Charles.

Barrie, Donald S. Directions in Managing Construction: A Critical Look at Present & Future Industry Practices, Problems & Policies. (Construction Management & Engineering Ser.). 468p. 1981. 57.50x (ISBN 0-471-04642-6, Pub. by Wiley-Interscience). Wiley.

Barrie, Donald S. & Paulson, Boyd C. Professional Construction Management. 2nd. ed. Verma, Kiran, ed. (Construction Management Ser.). (Illus.). 512p. 1984. text ed. 45.00 (ISBN 0-07-003847-3). McGraw.

Barrie, Francis. The Commonwealth. (Today's World Ser.). (Illus.). 72p. (gr. 7-12). 1983. 14.95 (ISBN 0-7134-0260-1, Pub. by Batsford England). David & Charles.

Barrie, H. Practical Homecraft Handbook: How to Do It Manual. 22.00 (ISBN 0-87559-108-6). Shalom.

Barrie, J. M. Courage. 8.95 (ISBN 0-89190-519-7, Pub. by Am Repr). Amereon Ltd.

--Farewell Miss Julie Logan. 9.95 (ISBN 0-88411-599-2, Pub. by Aeonian Pr). Amereon Ltd.

--Ibsen's Ghost: A Play in One Act. Griffin, P., ed. 110p. 1975. text ed. 18.50x (ISBN 0-900821-33-7, Pub. by C. Woolf UK). Humanities.

--The Little Minister. 232p. 1981. Repr. PLB 18.95 (ISBN 0-89966-329-X). Buccaneer Bks.

--The Little Minister. 300p. 1980. Repr. PLB 18.95x (ISBN 0-89967-007-5). Harmony Raine.

--Peter Pan. (gr. 4 up). 1979. pap. 1.25 (ISBN 0-448-16069-2, Pub. by Tempo). Ace Bks.

--Peter Pan. Hyman, Trina S., ed. (Illus.). 192p. (gr. 1 up). 1980. 16.95 (ISBN 0-684-16611-9, ScribJ). Scribner.

--Peter Pan. Frank, Josette, adapted by. LC 82-13288. (The Looking Glass Library). (Illus.). 72p. (ps-4). 1983. PLB 7.99 (ISBN 0-394-95717-2); pap. 6.95 (ISBN 0-394-85717-8). Random.

--Peter Pan. (Illus.). 1985. bds. 1.98 (ISBN 0-517-48144-8). Outlet Bk Co.

--Peter Pan. (Great 3-D Fairy Tale Bks.). (Illus.). 2.98 (ISBN 0-517-45984-1). Outlet Bk Co.

--Peter Pan in Kensington Gardens. 175p. 1981. Repr. PLB 16.95x (ISBN 0-89966-328-1). Buccaneer Bks.

--Peter Pan in Kensington Gardens. 150p. 1980. Repr. PLB 16.95x (ISBN 0-89967-006-7). Harmony Raine.

--The Truth about the Russian Dancers. pap. 6.00 (ISBN 0-384-03452-7). Johnson Repr.

Barrie, James. Little Minister. (Classics Ser). (gr. 10 up). 1968. pap. 0.75 (ISBN 0-8049-0187-2, CL-187). Airmont.

Barrie, James M. Auld Licht Idylls & Better Dead. facsimile ed. LC 76-106246. (Short Story Index Reprint Ser.). 1896. 18.00 (ISBN 0-8369-3282-X). Ayer Co Pubs.

--Auld Licht Manse, - Other Sketches. facs. ed. LC 78-116936. (Short Story Index Reprint Ser.). 1893. 17.00 (ISBN 0-8369-3438-5). Ayer Co Pubs.

--George Meredith. 1978. Repr. of 1909 ed. lib. bdg. 8.50 (ISBN 0-8495-0445-7). Arden Lib.

--George Meredith. LC 74-8046. 1909. lib. bdg. 10.00 (ISBN 0-8414-3192-2). Folcroft.

--The Little White Bird or Adventures in Kensington Gardens. LC 77-85624. 1977. Repr. of 1902 ed. lib. bdg. 25.00 (ISBN 0-89341-451-4). Longwood Pub Group.

--M'Connachie & J. M. B. Speeches. facsimile ed. LC 78-156611. (Essay Index Reprint Ser.). Repr. of 1938 ed. 20.00 (ISBN 0-8369-2343-X). Ayer Co Pubs.

--Margaret Ogilvy. 1896. 29.00x (ISBN 0-403-00243-5). Scholarly.

--Peter Pan. 160p. (gr. 3 up). 1985. pap. 2.95 (ISBN 0-553-21178-1). Bantam.

--Peter Pan. Unwin, Noras, ed. (Illus.). (gr. 4-6). 1950. 12.95 (ISBN 0-684-13214-1, ScribJ). Scribner.

--Peter Pan: Or the Boy Who Would Not Grow Up. 208p. 1982. pap. 2.95 (ISBN 0-380-57752-6, Bard). Avon.

--Plays of J. M. Barrie. 1928. 8.95 (ISBN 0-684-10017-7, ScribT). Scribner.

--Selections from the Plays of J. M. Barrie. 1929. 20.00 (ISBN 0-8274-3361-1). R West.

--Selections from the Prose Works of J. M. Barrie. 1929. 20.00 (ISBN 0-8274-3362-X). R West.

--Window in Thrums. 1896. 39.00 (ISBN 0-403-00118-8). Scholarly.

--The Works of J. M. Barrie, 18 vols. Incl. Vol. 1. Auld Licht Idylls, etc. Repr. of 1929 ed (ISBN 0-404-08781-7); Vol. 2. My Lady Nicotine, etc. Repr. of 1929 ed (ISBN 0-404-08782-5); Vol. 3. When a Man's Single. Repr. of 1929 ed (ISBN 0-404-08783-3); Vol. 4. The Little Minister. Repr. of 1929 ed (ISBN 0-404-08784-1); Vol. 5. Sentimental Tommy. Repr. of 1929 ed (ISBN 0-404-08785-X); Vol. 6. Tommy & Grizel. Repr. of 1929 ed (ISBN 0-404-08786-8); Vol. 7. The Little White Bird. Repr. of 1930 ed (ISBN 0-404-08787-6); Vol. 8. Margaret Ogilvy & Others. Repr. of 1930 ed (ISBN 0-404-08788-4); Vol. 9. Courage, etc. Repr. of 1930 ed (ISBN 0-404-08789-2); Vol. 10. Peter Pan & Other Plays. Repr. of 1930 ed (ISBN 0-404-08790-6); Vol. 11. The Admirable Crichton etc. Repr. of 1930 ed (ISBN 0-404-08791-4); Vol. 12. What Every Woman Knows & Other Plays. Repr. of 1930 ed (ISBN 0-404-08792-2); Vol. 13. Dear Brutus & Other Plays. Repr. of 1931 ed (ISBN 0-404-08793-0); Vol. 14. Mary Rose & Other Plays. Repr. of 1931 ed (ISBN 0-404-08794-9); Vol. 15. M'Connachie & J. M. B., etc. Repr. of 1940 ed (ISBN 0-404-08795-7); Vol. 16. The Greenwood Hat, etc. Repr. of 1940 ed (ISBN 0-404-08796-5); Vol. 17. The Boy David, etc. Repr. of 1941 ed (ISBN 0-404-08797-3); Vol. 18. The Professor's Love-Story, etc. Repr. of 1941 ed (ISBN 0-404-08798-1). LC 79-146660. 32.50 ea.; 585.00 set (ISBN 0-404-08780-9). AMS Pr.

Barrie, James M. & Hardy, Thomas. George Meredith: A Tribute. 59.95 (ISBN 0-8490-0223-0). Gordon Pr.

Barrie, Sir James M. Holiday in Bed, & Other Sketches: With a Short Biographical Sketch of the Author. facsimile ed. LC 70-160930. (Short Story Index Reprint Ser.). Repr. of 1892 ed. 14.00 (ISBN 0-8369-3909-3). Ayer Co Pubs.

--The Letters of James Matthew Barrie. Meynell, Viola, ed. LC 72-6723. (BCL Ser. I). 1976. Repr. of 1947 ed. 18.50 (ISBN 0-404-10640-4). AMS Pr.

--Tillyloss Scandal. facsimile ed. LC 77-98560. (Short Story Index Reprint Ser.). 1893. 17.00 (ISBN 0-8369-3134-3). Ayer Co Pubs.

Barrie, Monica. Gentle Fury. (Tapestry Romance Ser.). 320p. (Orig.). 1983. pap. 2.95 (ISBN 0-671-49426-0). PB.

--Silver Moon. (Tapestry Ser.: No. 60). (Orig.). 1985. pap. 2.95 (ISBN 0-671-52843-2). PB.

Barrie, W., jt. auth. see Bell, P. R.

Barrie-Blackey, Sandie, et al. Clinical Oral Language Sampling: Handbook for Students & Clinicians. LC 78-52399. 178p. 1978. pap. text ed. 3.95x (ISBN 0-8134-2007-5, 2007). Interstate.

Barrientos, Alberto. Principios y Alternativas de Trabajo Pastoral. 368p. (Orig.). 1982. pap. 7.25 (ISBN 0-89922-220-X). Edit Caribe.

Barrientos, Lawless J. Maryland Business Kit for Starting & Existing Businesses. LC 85-105171. (Illus.). Date not set. price not set (ISBN 0-671-49214-4). S&S.

--New Jersey Business Kit for Starting & Existing Businesses. LC 84-174276. (Illus.). Date not set. price not set (ISBN 0-671-49212-8). S&S.

--New York Business Kit for Starting & Existing Business. LC 83-113851. (Illus.). 1982. 14.95 (ISBN 0-671-46522-8). S&S.

Barrientos, Lawless J., Jr. Starting Business Kit & Existing Business Aid: Florida. Shelfer, Fred G., ed. 96p. pap. 14.95 (ISBN 0-941058-00-X). Govt Requirement Kits.

Barrientos, Parra O. Revision der Gattung Pediastrum Meyen (Chlorophyta) (Bibliotheca Phycologica: No. 48). (Illus.). 1979. 21.00x (ISBN 3-7682-1254-8). Lubrecht & Cramer.

Barrier, Gerald, jt. ed. see Juergensmeyer, Mark.

Barrier, Gerald N., ed. The Census in British India: New Perspectives. 1982. 18.00x (ISBN 0-8364-0847-0, Pub. By Manohar India). South Asia Bks.

Barrier, Gerard, jt. auth. see Musset, Alfred de.

Barrier, Jean & Kennedy, Alice. English Is Fun. (English Is Fun: Bk. 1). (Illus.). 96p. (gr. k-6). 1981. pap. 4.80 (ISBN 0-911743-01-4). Barrier & Kennedy.

--Expanded Ideas for English Is Fun 1. (English is Fun). 115p. 1982. 12.00 (ISBN 0-911743-02-2). Barrier & Kennedy.

Barrier, Michael. Carl Barks & the Art of the Comic Book. (Illus.). 228p. 1982. 49.95 (ISBN 0-9607652-0-4). M Lilien.

Barrier, Michael & Williams, Martin. A Smithsonian Book of Comic Book Comics. LC 81-607842. (Illus.). 300p. 1982. 25.00 (ISBN 0-8109-0696-1). Abrams.

Barrier, Michael & Williams, Martin, eds. A Smithsonian Book of Comic Book Comics. LC 81-607842. (Illus.). 336p. 1982. 25.00 (ISBN 0-87474-228-5). Smithsonian.

Barrier, N. G., ed. The Roots of Communal Politics: The Cawnpur Riot Commission Report. LC 76-6253. 1976. Repr. of 1933 ed. 16.00x (ISBN 0-88386-609-9); text ed. 9.00 (ISBN 0-8364-0462-9). South Asia Bks.

Barrier, N. G. & Crane, Robert I., eds. British Imperial Policy in India & Sri Lanka, Eighteen Fifty-Eight to Nineteen Twelve: A Reassessment. 1981. 18.50x (ISBN 0-8364-0726-1). South Asia Bks.

Barrier, N. Gerald. Punjab History in Printed British Documents: A Bibliographic Guide to Parliamentary Papers & Select, Nonserial Publications, 1843-1947. LC 69-13332. 109p. 1969. 9.00x (ISBN 0-8262-0077-X). U of Mo Pr.

Barrier, Smith. All Basketball Trivia Trip. (Illus.). 208p. 1984. 2.98 (ISBN 0-943860-03-2). UMI.

--On Tobacco Road: Basketball in North Carolina. LC 83-80743. (Illus.). 208p. (Orig.). 1983. pap. 10.95 (ISBN 0-88011-175-5). Leisure Pr.

Barriere, R. Pallu De La see Pallu De La Barriere, R.

Barriere, Steven L., jt. auth. see Conte, John E., Jr.

Barriga, Omar O. Immunology of Parasitic Infections. (Illus.). 368p. (Orig.). 1981. pap. text ed. 31.50 (ISBN 0-8391-1621-7). Univ Park.

Barriga, Patricio & Ickis, Valerie. Facilitator Model, No. 11. (Technical Notes Ser.). 32p. (Orig.). 1975. pap. 1.00 ea. Eng (ISBN 0-932288-24-3). Span (ISBN 0-932288-25-1). Ctr Intl Ed U of MA.

Barriga, Patricio & Villacis, Rodrigo. Fotonovela, No. 13. (Technical Notes Ser.). 12p. (Orig.). 1975. pap. 1.00 ea. Eng (ISBN 0-932288-28-6). Span (ISBN 0-932288-29-4). Ctr Intl Ed U of MA.

Barrigan, Alice N. Reflections of Lovable Aging. 37p. 1983. 5.95 (ISBN 0-533-05617-9). Vantage.

Barrile, Jackie. Confessions of a Closet Eater. 199p. 1983. 6.95 (ISBN 0-8423-0438-X). Tyndale.

Barrilleaux, Doris. Forever Fit: The First Lady of Bodybuilding Shares Her Secrets on Health & Beauty. (Illus.). 1984. 17.95 (ISBN 0-89651-216-9); pap. 10.95 (ISBN 0-89651-217-7). Icarus.

Barrilleaux, Doris & Murray, Jim. Inside Weight Training for Women. 1978. pap. 5.95 (ISBN 0-8092-7500-7). Contemp Bks.

Barring, G. In Mexican Waters. 1976. lib. bdg. 59.95 (ISBN 0-8490-2044-1). Gordon Pr.

Barringer, Felicity. Flight from Sorrow: The Life & Death of Tamara Wall. LC 83-45063. 288p. 1984. 15.95 (ISBN 0-689-11389-7). Atheneum.

Barringer, H. A Survey of Verification Techniques for Parallel Programs. (Lecture Notes in Computer Science: Vol. 191). vi, 115p. 1985. pap. 11.20 (ISBN 0-387-15239-3). Springer-Verlag.

Barringer, Leslie. Gerfalcon. Reginald, R. & Menville, Douglas, eds. LC 80-19243. (Newcastle Forgotten Fantasy Library: Vol. 7). 310p. 1980. Repr. of 1976 ed. lib. bdg. 14.95x (ISBN 0-89370-506-3). Borgo Pr.

--Gerfalcon: The Neustrian Cycle, Book One. (Forgotten Fantasy Library: Vol. 7). (Illus.). 310p. 1976. pap. 4.95 (ISBN 0-87877-106-9, F-106). Newcastle Pub.

--Joris of the Rock: The Neustrian Cycle, Bk. 2. (Forgotten Fantasy Library: Vol. 9). 318p. 1976. pap. 4.95 (ISBN 0-87877-108-5, F-108). Newcastle Pub.

--Joris of the Rock: The Neustrian Cycle, Bk. 2. Reginald, R. & Menville, Douglas, eds. LC 80-19241. (Newcastle Forgotten Fantasy Library: Vol. 9). 318p. 1980. Repr. of 1976 ed. lib. bdg. 14.95x (ISBN 0-89370-508-X). Borgo Pr.

--Shy Leopardess: The Neustrian Cycle, Bk. 3. Reginald, R. & Menville, Douglas, eds. LC 80-19240. (Newcastle Forgotten Fantasy Library Ser.: Vol. 13). 392p. 1980. Repr. of 1977 ed. lib. bdg. 15.95x (ISBN 0-89370-512-8). Borgo Pr.

--Shy Leopardess: The Neustrian Cycle, Book Three. (Forgotten Fantasy Library: Vol. 13). 1977. pap. 5.95 (ISBN 0-87877-112-3, F-112). Newcastle Pub.

Barringer, Robert, tr. see Staniloae, Dumitru.

Barringer, W. A., jt. auth. see Barr, Howard N.

Barrington, Brian. Industrial Purchase Price Management. 208p. 1980. text ed. 43.25x (ISBN 0-566-02186-2). Gower Pub Co.

Barrington, Carol. Day Trips From Houston. rev. ed. LC 85-71256. (Day Trips America Ser.). 176p. 1985. pap. 7.95 (ISBN 0-88742-055-9). East Woods.

--Shifra Stein's Day Trips from Houston: Getaways Less Than Two Hours. LC 83-49041. (Day Trips Ser.). 192p. 1984. pap. 6.95 (ISBN 0-88742-006-0). East Woods.

Barrington, Daines, tr. see Mourelle, Francisco A.

Barrington, E. J. Environmental Biology. LC 80-12090. (Resource & Environmental Science Ser.). 244p. 1980. pap. 21.95X (ISBN 0-470-26967-7). Halsted Pr.

--Intervertebrate Structure & Function. 2nd ed. 765p. 1979. pap. 24.95x (ISBN 0-470-26503-5). Halsted Pr.

Barrington, E. J., ed. Hormones & Evolution. Vol. 1, 1979. 79.50 (ISBN 0-12-079401-2); Vol. 2, 1980. 79.50 (ISBN 0-12-079402-0). Acad Pr.

Barrington, E. J., jt. ed. see Hamburgh, Max.

Barrington, Emilie I. Life, Letters & Work of Frederic Baron Leighton, 2 Vols. LC 70-140032. (Illus.). Repr. of 1906 ed. Set. 95.00 (ISBN 0-404-00659-0); 47.50 ea. AMS Pr.

Barrington, George. The Life, Times, & Adventures of George Barrington, the Celebrated Thief & Pickpocket. Bd. with The Memoirs of George Barrington, Containing Every Remarkable Circumstance, from His Birth to the Present Time. LC 80-2470. 1981. 29.50 (ISBN 0-404-19102-9). AMS Pr.

--Use Even Me. 1983. pap. 10.00 (ISBN 0-8309-0375-5). Herald Hse.

Barrington, John. Red Sky at Night. (Illus.). 224p. 1985. 14.95 (ISBN 0-7181-1808-1, Pub. by Michael Joseph). Merrimack Pub Cir.

Barrington, Jonah. Ireland of Sir Jonah Barrington: Selections from His Personal Sketches. Staples, Hugh B., ed. LC 67-21201. (Illus.). 352p. 1967. 20.00x (ISBN 0-295-95127-3). U of Wash Pr.

Barrington, Margaret. David's Daughter, Tamar. 176p. 1982. 11.95 (ISBN 0-905473-74-4, Pub. by Wolfhound Pr Ireland); pap. 4.95 (ISBN 0-905473-75-2). Irish Bks Media.

Barrington, Rupert. Making & Managing a Trout Lake. 135p. 1983. pap. text ed. 12.00 (ISBN 0-85238-126-3, FN103, FNB). Unipub.

Barrington, Ruth & Cooney, John. Inside the EEC: An Irish Guide. (Illus.). 200p. 1984. 15.95 (ISBN 0-86278-057-8, Pub. by O'Brien Pr Ireland); pap. 8.50 (ISBN 0-86278-058-6, Pub. by O'Brien Pr Ireland). Irish Bks Media.

Barrington, Thomas, ed. see Carson, William.

Barrio, Raymond. Barrio's Political Forum. (Orig.). 1985. pap. 3.75 (ISBN 0-317-27080-X). Ventura Pr.

--Plum Plum Pickers. (Orig.). 1970. pap. 9.95 (ISBN 0-917438-05-1). Ventura Pr.

--The Plum Plum Pickers. 2nd ed. LC 84-70568. 232p. 1984. pap. 9.95x (ISBN 0-916950-51-4). Biling Rev-Pr.

--A Political Portfolio. 212p. 1985. pap. 3.75 (ISBN 0-917438-12-4). Ventura Pr.

Barrio-Garay, Jose L. Jose Guitierrez Solana: Paintings & Writings. LC 72-3524. (Illus.). 426p. 1976. 60.00 (ISBN 0-8387-1228-2). Bucknell U Pr.

Barrio-Garay, Jose Luis. Antoni Tapies: Thirty-Three Years of His Work. Jones, H. M., ed. LC 77-71151. (Illus.). 95p. 1977. pap. 15.00 (ISBN 0-914782-11-8). Buffalo Acad.

Barrios, Alfred A. Stress Test Biofeedback Card & Booklet. 1985. 3.95 (ISBN 0-9601926-3-8). Self-Prog Control.

--Towards Greater Freedom & Happiness. 3rd ed. LC 78-63152. 1985. 15.95 (ISBN 0-9601926-1-1); pap. 9.95; pap. 10.95 incl. stress control card. Self-Prog Control.

Barrios, Miguel De see De Barrios, Miguel.

Barrios, Virginia B. de see De Barrios, Virginia B.

Barrios-Schley, Vicki. Mexican Cooking. Lammers, Susan, ed. LC 85-70886. (California Culinary Academy Ser.). (Illus.). 128p. (Orig.). 1985. pap. 7.95 (ISBN 0-89721-053-0). Ortho.

Barris, Chuck. Confessions of a Dangerous Mind: An Unauthorized Autobiography. 288p. 1984. 12.95 (ISBN 0-312-16214-6). St Martin.

--You & Me Babe. 1980. pap. 2.50 (ISBN 0-671-81654-3). PB.

Barris, George & Scagnetti, Jack. Cars of the Stars. LC 74-226. (Illus.). 264p. 1974. 16.95 (ISBN 0-8246-0166-1). Jonathan David.

--Famous Custom & Show Cars. (Illus.). 160p. (YA) 1973. 12.95 (ISBN 0-525-29610-7). Dutton.

Barris, R. & Kielhofner, G. Psychosocial Occupational Therapy: Practice in a Pluralistic Arena. (Illus.). 352p. 1983. pap. text ed. 22.50 (ISBN 0-943596-03-3, RAMSCO 00600). Ramsco Pub.

Barrish, Harriet H. & Barrish, I. J. Managing Parental Anger. (The Coping Parent Ser.). 57p. (Orig.). 1985. pap. 4.95 (ISBN 0-930851-02-1). Overland Pr.

Barrish, I. J., jt. auth. see Barrish, Harriet H.

Barrister, Amanda M. A Practical Guide to Trade Marks. 216p. 1982. 39.00x (ISBN 0-686-97894-3, Pub. by ESC Pub England). State Mutual Bk.

Barritt, C. W., jt. auth. see Stockwell, R. P.

Barritt, D. W., jt. ed. see Read, A. E.

Barro, R. J. & Grossman, H. I. Money, Employment & Inflation. LC 75-13449. (Illus.). 304p. 1976. 34.50 (ISBN 0-521-20906-4). Cambridge U Pr.

Barro, Robert. Macroeconomics. LC 83-21692. 580p. 1984. text ed. 34.00 (ISBN 0-471-87407-8); write for info tchrs ed. (ISBN 0-471-88398-0); study guide 13.45 (ISBN 0-471-88397-2) (ISBN 0-471-88139-2). Wiley.

Barro, Robert J. The Impact of Social Security on Private Saving. 1978. pap. 4.25 (ISBN 0-8447-3301-6). Am Enterprise.

--Money, Expectations & Business Cycles: Essays in Macroeconomics. (Economic Theory, Econometrics & Mathematical Economic Ser.). 1981. 33.50 (ISBN 0-12-079550-7). Acad Pr.

Barrodale, Ian, et al. Elementary Computer Applications: In Science, Engineering & Business. LC 74-150609. 254p. 1971. pap. 26.45x (ISBN 0-471-05423-2). Wiley.

Barrois, Georges, jt. auth. see Ware, Kallistos.

Barrois, Georges A. The Face of Christ in the Old Testament. 172p. 1974. pap. 5.95 (ISBN 0-913836-22-2). St Vladimirs.

--Jesus Christ & the Temple. LC 80-19700. 163p. (Orig.). 1980. pap. 5.95 (ISBN 0-913836-73-7, BS680 T4837). St Martin.

--Jesus Christ & the Temple. LC 80-19700. 163p. 1980. pap. 5.95 (ISBN 0-913836-73-7). St Vladimirs.

--Scripture Readings in Orthodox Worship. 197p. 1977. pap. 5.95 (ISBN 0-913836-41-9). St Vladimirs.

Barrois, Maurice. Journal de l'annee: 1977-78. new ed. (Illus.). 400p. (Back issues available). (YA) 29.95x (ISBN 0-685-53376-X). Larousse.

Barrois, Maurice, ed. Journal de l'annee: 1974-1975. new ed. (Illus.). 415p. (Fr.). 1975. 32.95x (ISBN 0-686-67325-5). Larousse.

Barroitt, Denis P. & Carter, Charles F. The Northern Ireland Problem: A Study in Group Relations. LC 82-15568. 163p. 1982. Repr. of 1962 ed. lib. bdg. 22.50x (ISBN 0-313-23262-8, BANI). Greenwood.

Barroll, Clare. The Shadow Man. 192p. (Orig.). 1984. pap. 2.95 (ISBN 0-380-89235-9). Avon.

Barroll, J. Leeds. Artificial Persons: The Formation of Character in the Tragedies of Shakespeare. LC 73-13991. 1974. 19.95x (ISBN 0-87249-294-X); pap. text ed. 7.95x (ISBN 0-87249-377-6). U of SC Pr.

--Shakespeare Studies: An Annual Gathering of Research, Criticism & Reviews, Vol. XI. 1978. lib. bdg. 25.00x (ISBN 0-89102-148-5). B Franklin.

--Shakespearean Tragedy. LC 82-49309. 312p. 1984. 35.00 (ISBN 0-918016-18-5). Folger Bks.

Barroll, J. Leeds, ed. Medieval & Renaissance Drama in England, Vol. 1. LC 83-45280. 304p. 1984. 42.50 (ISBN 0-404-62300-X). AMS Pr.

Barroll, J. Leeds, et al. Revels History of Drama in English, Vol. 3: 1576-1613. LC 74-15177. (Revels History of the Drama in English Ser.). 400p. 1975. 19.95x (ISBN 0-416-13040-2, NO. 2076). Methuen Inc.

Barroll, J. Leeds, 3rd. Shakespeare Studies: An Annual Gathering of Research, Criticism, Reviews. Incl. Vol. 1. 25.00 (ISBN 0-89102-079-9); Vol. 2. 25.00 (ISBN 0-89102-080-2); Vol. 3. 25.00 (ISBN 0-89102-081-0); Vol. 4. 25.00 (ISBN 0-89102-082-9); Vol. 5. 25.00 (ISBN 0-89102-083-7); Vol. 6. 25.00 (ISBN 0-89102-084-5); Vol. 7. 25.00 (ISBN 0-89102-085-3); Vol. 8. 25.00 (ISBN 0-89102-068-3); Vol. 9. 25.00 (ISBN 0-89102-070-5); Vol. 10. 25.00 (ISBN 0-89102-086-1); Vol. 12. 25.00 (ISBN 0-89102-188-4). 1976. Vol. 13. 29.95 (ISBN 0-89102-229-5). B Franklin.

Barromi, Joel see Kaufman, Edy.

Barron, Alfred, ed. see Noyes, John H.

Barron, Almen L., jt. ed. see Rose, Noel R.

Barron, Ann F. Windswept. 464p. 1985. pap. 3.95 (ISBN 0-380-89589-7). Avon.

Barron, Anne D., jt. auth. see Daniels, Diane.

Barron, Bill. The Vaudreuil Papers: 1743-1753. 1975. 25.00 (ISBN 0-686-20900-1). Polyanthos.

Barron, Bill, ed. Census of Pointe Coupee, Louisiana: 1745. LC 77-92116. 1978. pap. 12.50x (ISBN 0-686-09335-6). Polyanthos.

Barron, C. H. Numerical Control for Machine Tools. 1971. 32.00 (ISBN 0-07-003824-4). McGraw.

Barron, Cheryl C. & Scherzer, Cathy C. Great Parties for Young Children. LC 81-50232. (Illus.). 155p. 1981. 10.95 (ISBN 0-8027-0684-3); pap. 5.95 (ISBN 0-8027-7175-0). Walker & Co.

Barron, Clarence W. More They Told Barron. Pound, Arthur & Moore, Samuel T., eds. LC 73-1991. (Big Business; Economic Power in a Free Society Ser.). Repr. of 1931 ed. 21.00 (ISBN 0-405-05075-5). Ayer Co Pubs.

Barron, D. Assemblers & Loaders. 3rd ed. 120p. 1978. 24.75 (ISBN 0-444-19462-2). Elsevier.

Barron, D. W. Computer Operating Systems: For Micros, Minis & Mainframes. 2nd ed. 184p. 1984. 35.00 (ISBN 0-412-15620-2, NO. 6708, Pub. by Chapman & Hall); pap. 15.95 (ISBN 0-412-15630-X, NO. 6588). Methuen Inc.

--An Introduction to the Study of Programming Languages. LC 76-11070. (Cambridge Computer Science Texts Ser.: No. 7). (Illus.). 1977. 27.50 (ISBN 0-521-21317-7); pap. 9.95x (ISBN 0-521-29101-1). Cambridge U Pr.

--Pascal: The Language & Its Implementation. (Computing Ser.). 301p. 1981. 44.95x (ISBN 0-471-27835-1, Pub. by Wiley-Interscience). Wiley.

--Recursive Techniques in Programming. 2nd ed. (Computer Monograph Series: Vol. 3). 1974. text ed. 24.75 (ISBN 0-444-19524-6). Elsevier.

Barron, D. W. & Bishop, J. M. Advanced Programming: A Practical Course. (Wiley Series in Computing: 1-320). 277p. 1984. 24.95x (ISBN 0-471-90319-1). Wiley.

Barron, David W. Anaesthesia & Related Subjects in Orthopaedic Surgery. (Illus.). 216p. 1982. text ed. 24.95 (ISBN 0-632-00675-7, B0512-1). Mosby.

Barron, Don, ed. Creativity, Ten. LC 74-168254. (Illus.). 368p. 1982. 29.50 (ISBN 0-910158-10-X). Art Dir.

--Creativity, Seven. LC 59-14827. (Creativity Ser.: Vol. 7). (Illus.). 1978. 26.50 (ISBN 0-910158-35-5). Art Dir.

--Creativity, Eleven. LC 74-168254. (Creativity Annuals Ser.). (Illus.). 368p. 1982. 31.50 (ISBN 0-910158-93-2). Art Dir.

--Creativity Twelve. LC 74-168254. (Illus.). 1983. 32.50 (ISBN 0-910158-99-1). Art Dir.

Barron, Don & Art Direction Staff, eds. Creativity, Eight. LC 59-14827. (Creativity Ser.: No. 8). (Illus.). 1979. 27.50 (ISBN 0-910158-54-1). Art Dir.

Barron, Emily, jt. auth. see Gidcomb, Johnny.

Barron, Frank see National Art Education Association.

Barron, Frank X. Artists in the Making. LC 72-77220. 256p. 1972. 40.00 (ISBN 0-12-785042-2). Acad Pr.

Barron, George L. Genera of Hyphomycetes from Soil. LC 68-14275. 378p. 1977. Repr. of 1968 ed. 25.50 (ISBN 0-88275-004-6). Krieger.

Barron, Gloria J. Leadership in Crisis: FDR & the Path to Intervention. LC 73-75576. 1973. 14.95x (ISBN 0-8046-9038-3, Pub. by Kennikat). Assoc Faculty Pr.

--Leadership in Crisis: FDR & the Path to Prevention. 158p. 1973. 14.95x (9038). Assoc Faculty Pr.

Barron, Hal S. Those Who Stayed Behind: Rural Society in Nineteenth-Century New England. LC 83-26354. (Illus.). 212p. 1984. 24.95 (ISBN 0-521-25784-0). Cambridge U Pr.

Barron, Howard H. Judah, Past & Future: LDS Teachings Concerning God's Covenant People. LC 79-89350. 1979. 8.95 (ISBN 0-88290-121-4). Horizon Utah.

--Orson Hyde: Missionary, Apostle, Colonizer. LC 77-74490. (Illus.). 1977. 9.95 (ISBN 0-88290-076-5). Horizon Utah.

Barron, Howard H., ed. Of Everlasting Value, Vol. 1. (Orig.). 1978. pap. 5.95 (ISBN 0-89036-129-0). Hawkes Pub Inc.

--Of Everlasting Value, Vol. 2. (Orig.). pap. 5.95 (ISBN 0-89036-130-4). Hawkes Pub Inc.

Barron, Hugh see Hirschfeld, Burt, pseud.

Barron, Iann & Curnow, R. C. The Future with Microelectronics: Forecasting the Effects of Information Technology. 243p. 1979. write for info (ISBN 0-89397-055-7). Nichols Pub.

Barron, Iann & Curnow, Ray. The Future with Microelectronics. 256p. 1979. pap. 13.00x (ISBN 0-335-00268-4, Pub. by Open Univ Pr). Taylor & Francis.

Barron, J. Operative Plastic & Reconstructive Surgery, Vol. 3. Saad, M. N., ed. (Illus.). 352p. 1981. text ed. 72.00 (ISBN 0-443-02212-7). Churchill.

Barron, J. & Saad, M. N. Operative Plastic & Reconstructive Surgery, Vols. 1 & 2. 1981. text ed. 186.00 (ISBN 0-443-02522-3). Churchill.

Barron, J. N. & Saad, M. N. Operative Plastic & Reconstructive Surgery, 3 vols. 1981. text ed. 245.00 (ISBN 0-443-01600-3). Churchill.

Barron, Jerome & Dienes, Thomas. Constitutional Law. LC 83-12554. (Black Letter Ser.). 310p. 1983. pap. text ed. 13.95 (ISBN 0-314-74263-8). West Pub.

Barron, Jerome A. & Dienes, C. Thomas. Constitutional Law: Principles & Policy, Cases & Materials. LC 74-2945. (Contemporary Legal Education Ser.). 1177p. 1982. text ed. 28.50 (ISBN 0-87215-411-4); 1984 Supplement 8.00 (ISBN 0-87215-793-8). Michie Co.

--Handbook of Free Speech & Free Press. 1979. text ed. 60.00 (ISBN 0-316-08230-9). Little.

Barron, Jerome A., jt. auth. see Gillmor, Donald M.

Barron, Jerome A., et al. West's Review Covering Multistate Subjects. LC 79-24976. 448p. 1979. pap. text ed. 23.95 (ISBN 0-8299-2081-1). West Pub.

Barron, John. An Introduction to Greek Sculpture. LC 84-1429. (Illus.). 176p. (Orig.). 1984. pap. 8.95 (ISBN 0-8052-0760-0). Schocken.

--KGB. (Illus.). 640p. 1974. pap. 4.95 (ISBN 0-553-23894-9). Bantam.

--KGB Today: The Hidden Hand. LC 83-4645. 496p. 1983. 19.95 (ISBN 0-88349-164-8). Readers Digest Pr.

--KGB Today: The Hidden Hand. 464p. 1985. pap. 4.95 (ISBN 0-425-07584-2). Berkley Pub.

--Mig Pilot. 1980. 10.95 (ISBN 0-07-003850-3). Readers Digest Pr.

--MIG Pilot: The Final Escape of Lieutenant Belenko. 232p. 1981. pap. 3.50 (ISBN 0-380-53868-7, 67520-X). Avon.

--MIG Pilot: The Story of Viktor Belenko. 1980. 10.95 (ISBN 0-07-003850-3). McGraw.

--The Silver Coins of Samos. 244p. 1966. 95.00 (ISBN 0-485-11080-6, Pub. by Athlone Pr Ltd). Longwood Pub Group.

Barron, Jonathan C. BASIC Programming Using Structured Modules. 1984. text ed. 20.95 (ISBN 0-03-059241-0). HR&W.

Barron, L. D., et al. Structural Chemistry. (Topics in Current Chemistry. Fortschritte der Chemischen Forschung: Vol. 123). (Illus.). 200p. 1984. 36.50 (ISBN 0-387-13099-3). Springer Verlag.

Barron, L. Smythe. The Nazis in Africa. (Lost Documents of the Third Reich Ser.: Vol. 3). 1978. 27.95x (ISBN 0-89712-076-0). Documentary Pubns.

Barron, Lawrence D. Molecular Light Scattering & Optical Activity. 425p. 1983. 72.50 (ISBN 0-521-24602-4). Cambridge U Pr.

Barron, Sr. Mary C. Unveiled Faces: Men & Women of the Bible. LC 80-27728. 95p. 1981. softcover 4.50 (ISBN 0-8146-1212-1). Liturgical Pr.

Barron, Michael & Targett, David. A Manager's Guide to Business Forecasting. 224p. 1985. 39.95x (ISBN 0-631-14034-4). Basil Blackwell.

Barron, Michael M. & Graham, Samuel R. Texas Condemnation Litigation. 1986. pap. price not set (ISBN 0-409-25087-2). Butterworth TX.

Barron, Milton L. The Aging American: An Introduction to Social Gerontology & Geriatrics. LC 74-8874. (Illus.). 269p. 1974. Repr. of 1961 ed. lib. bdg. 20.50 (ISBN 0-8371-7595-X, BAAG). Greenwood.

Barron, Neil. Anatomy of Wonder: A Critical Guide to Science Fiction. 2nd ed. 724p. 1981. 34.95 (ISBN 0-8352-1339-0); pap. 24.95 (ISBN 0-8352-1404-4). Bowker.

Barron, Neil & Reginald, R., eds. Science Fiction & Fantasy Book Review, Nos. 1-13. LC 78-2211. 144p. 1983. lib. bdg. 29.95x (ISBN 0-89370-624-8); pap. text ed. 19.95x (ISBN 0-89370-609-4). Borgo Pr.

Barron, Norman. Dairy Farmer's Veterinary Book. 10th ed. (Illus.). 256p. 1979. 18.95 (ISBN 0-85236-099-1). Diamond Farm Bk.

--Pig Farmer's Vet Book. 10th ed. (Illus.). 180p. 1978. Repr. 18.95 (ISBN 0-85236-086-X, Pub. by Farming Pr UK). Diamond Farm Bk.

Barron, Pamela & Burley, Jennifer. Jump over the Moon: A Reader for Childrens Literature. 1984. pap. text ed. 12.95 (ISBN 0-03-063383-4). HR&W.

Barron, Paul. Federal Regulation of Real Estate: Cumulative Supplementation. 2nd ed. 1983. 64.00 (ISBN 0-88262-086-X). Warren.

Barron, Robert, jt. auth. see Fisk, Jim.

Barron, Robert, jt. auth. see Weist, Dwight.

Barron, S. L., tr. see Cassel, Gustav.

Barron, S. Leonard & Thomson, Angus M., eds. Obstetrical Epidemiology. 1983. 65.00 (ISBN 0-12-079620-1). Acad Pr.

Barron, Samuel B. Lone Star Defenders: A Chronicle of the Third Texas Cavalry Regiment in the Civil War. 1983. Repr. of 1908 ed. 19.95 (ISBN 0-89201-103-3). Zenger Pub.

Barron, Stephanie. German Expressionist Sculpture. (Illus.). 224p. 1985. pap. 22.95 (ISBN 0-226-03821-1). U of Chicago Pr.

--German Expressionist Sculpture. (Illus.). 224p. 1983. 39.95x (ISBN 0-226-03820-3). U of Chicago Pr.

Barron, Stephanie & Tuchman, Maurice, eds. Avant-Garde in Russia, 1910-1930: New Perspectives. (Illus.). 288p. 1980. o. p. 35.00 (ISBN 0-262-20040-6); pap. 15.00 (ISBN 0-262-52077-X). MIT Pr.

Barron, Terry. The Aluminum Industry of Texas. (Mineral Resource Circular Ser.: No. 67). (Illus.). 16p. 1981. 1.50 (ISBN 0-686-36996-3). Bur Econ Geology.

Barron, W. R. Trawthe & Treason: The Sin of Gawain Reconsidered; A Thematic Study of "Sir Gawain & the Green Knight". 150p. 1980. 24.50x (ISBN 0-389-20028-X, 06801). B&N Imports.

Barron, W. R., ed. Robert Henryson: Selected Poems. (The Fyfield Ser.). 126p. pap. 7.50 (ISBN 0-85635-301-9). Carcanet.

--Sir Gawain & the Green Knight. LC 74-21. (Manchester Medieval Classics Ser). 179p. 1976. pap. text ed. 11.95x (ISBN 0-06-490311-7, 06341). B&N Imports.

Barron, William, jt. auth. see Riesenkampff, Alexander.

Barro-Neto & Artino. Hypoellyptic Boundary-Value Problems. (Lecture Notes in Pure & Applied Mathematics: Vol. 53). 104p. 1980. 29.75 (ISBN 0-8247-6886-8). Dekker.

Barron's College Division, et al, eds. Guide to the Best, Most Popular & Most Exciting Colleges. 3rd ed. 1984. pap. 7.95 (ISBN 0-8120-2827-9). Barron.

Barron's Editorial Staff. Shopper's Guide, U.S. Department of Agriculture. LC 74-600137. (Illus.). 368p. 1975. pap. text ed. 0.95 (ISBN 0-8120-0607-0). Barron.

Barron's Educational Series, Inc. College Division, compiled by. Barron's Compact Guide to College Transfer. LC 79-18806. 1979. pap. 3.95 (ISBN 0-8120-2117-7). Barron.

Barron's Educational Series, Inc. College Division. Barron's Profiles of American Colleges: Descriptions of the Colleges, Vol. 1. rev. ed. LC 81-21243. 1088p. 1982. 25.95 (ISBN 0-8120-5449-0); pap. 11.95 (ISBN 0-8120-2459-1). Barron.

--Barrons Profiles of American Colleges: The Northeast. Rev. ed. 336p. (gr. 10-12). 1982. pap. 6.95 (ISBN 0-8120-2467-2). Barron.

Barrons, Keith C. Are Pesticides Really Necessary? LC 80-54684. 245p. 1981. pap. 6.95 (ISBN 0-89526-888-4). Regnery-Gateway.

Barron's Technical Staff, compiled by. Barron's Metric Conversion Tables. LC 76-8425. (Barron's Educational Ser.). 224p. 1976. pap. text ed. 4.50 (ISBN 0-8120-0659-3). Barron.

Barros, James. Betrayal from Within: Joseph Avenol, Secretary-General of the League of Nations, 1933-1940. LC 75-81413. pap. 75.30 (ISBN 0-317-09493-9, 2021978). Bks Demand UMI.

--Britain, Greece & the Politics of Sanctions. (Royal Historical Society, Studies in History: No. 33). 248p. 1982. text ed. 36.00x (ISBN 0-391-02690-9, Pub. by Swiftbks England). Humanities.

--Corfu Incident of Nineteen Twenty-Three: Mussolini & the League of Nations. 1965. 35.00 (ISBN 0-691-05113-5). Princeton U Pr.

--Office Without Power: Secretary-General Sir Eric Drummond 1919-1933. 1979. 64.00x (ISBN 0-19-822551-2). Oxford U Pr.

Barros, Leda Watson de see Sutton, Joan L. & Watson de Barros, Leda.

Barros-Neto, Josbe. An Introduction to the Theory of Distributions. LC 72-90371. (Pure & Applied Mathematics Ser.: No. 14). pap. 57.50 (ISBN 0-317-08375-9, 2055024). Bks Demand UMI.

Barros-Neto, Jose. Algebra & Trigonometry for College Students. (Illus.). 550p. 1985. text ed. 28.95 (ISBN 0-314-85218-2). West Pub.

--College Algebra with Applications. (Illus.). 450p. 1985. text ed. 27.95 (ISBN 0-314-85217-4). West Pub.

--An Introduction to the Theory of Distributions. LC 80-11323. 234p. 1981. Repr. of 1973 ed. lib. bdg. 16.50 (ISBN 0-89874-128-9). Krieger.

Barroso, J. A. Introduction to Holomorphy. (Mathematics Studies: Vol. 106). 302p. 1985. 48.25 (ISBN 0-444-87666-9, North-Holland). Elsevier.

Barroso, J. A., ed. Advances in Holomorphy. (Mathematics Studies: Vol. 34). 766p. 1979. 76.75 (ISBN 0-444-85265-4, North Holland). Elsevier.

--Aspects of Mathematics & Its Applications: In Honour of Professor L. Nachbin. (North-Holland Mathematical Library). 1984. write for info. (North-Holland). Elsevier.

--Functional Analysis, Holomorphy & Approximation Theory: Proceedings of the Seminario de Analise Funcional, Holomorfia e Teoria da Approximacao, Universidade Federal do Rio de Janeiro, Aug. 4-8, 1980. (Mathematics Studies: Vol. 71). 486p. 1983. 64.00 (ISBN 0-444-86527-6, I-421-82, North Holland). Elsevier.

Barroso, Memo. Yucatan: Mexico's Hidden Beaches & Ruins. 1983. pap. 8.95 (ISBN 0-517-54789-9). Crown.

Barrot, Theodore-Adolphe. Unless Haste Is Made: A French Skeptic's Account of the Sandwich Islands in 1836. Pagliaro, Penny, ed. Dole, Daniel, tr. from Fr. LC 77-27597. Orig. Title: Visit of the French Frigate Sloop of War to the Sandwich Islands, 1836. (Illus.). 1978. 10.00 (ISBN 0-916630-05-6); pap. 4.95 (ISBN 0-916630-04-8). Pr Pacifica.

Barroux, Marius. Les Sources de l'ancien etat-civil parisien: repertoire critique. 1968. Repr. of 1908 ed. 20.50 (ISBN 0-8337-0179-7). B Franklin.

Barrow, A. E., jt. auth. see Dayal, Baghubir.

Barrow, A. E., jt. auth. see Dayal, Raghubir.

Barrow, Al. Gettin' to the Dance Floor: An Oral History of American Golf. LC 95-47662. (Illus.). 288p. 1985. 14.95 (ISBN 0-689-11517-2). Atheneum.

Barrow, Alfred. Fifty Years in Western Africa. LC 79-92739. Repr. of 1900 ed. cancelled (ISBN 0-8371-2193-0, BAW&, Pub. by Negro U Pr). Greenwood.

Barrow, Andrew. The Gossip Family Handbook. (Illus.). 128p. 1984. 14.95 (ISBN 0-241-11097-1, Pub. by Hamish Hamilton England). David & Charles.

Barrow, Bennet H. Plantation Life in the Florida Parishes of Louisiana 1836-1846, As Reflected in the Diary of Bennet H. Barrow. Davis, Edwin A., ed. LC 74-163680. Repr. of 1943 ed. 29.50 (ISBN 0-404-01989-7). AMS Pr.

Barrow, Charles G. French Art at the End of the Nineteenth Century: An Illustrated Survey. (Illus.). 123p. 1981. 57.85 (ISBN 0-930582-88-8). Gloucester Art.

Barrow, Christopher J., jt. auth. see Saha, Suranjit K.

Barrow, David, jt. auth. see Tootill, Alan.

Barrow, G. L. The Round Towers of Ireland. (Illus.). 232p. 1979. 19.95 (ISBN 0-906187-64-8); lib. bdg. cancelled (ISBN 0-906187-04-4); pap. cancelled (ISBN 0-906187-44-3). Univ Press.

Barrow, G. W. The Anglo-Norman Era in Scottish History. 1980. 54.00x (ISBN 0-19-822473-7). Oxford U Pr.

--Kingship & Unity: Scotland 1000-1306. 192p. 1981. 40.00x (ISBN 0-7131-6306-2, Pub. by E Arnold England). State Mutual Bk.

--Robert Bruce & the Community of the Realm of Scotland. 502p. 1976. 12.00x (ISBN 0-85224-307-3, Pub. by Edinburgh U Pr Scotland). Columbia U Pr.

Barrow, George. Wild Wales. (Century Travellers Travel Classics Ser.). 640p. 1984. pap. 11.95 (ISBN 0-88254-981-2). Hippocrene Bks.

Barrow, George L. The Round Towers of Ireland. (Illus.). 232p. 1979. 35.00 (ISBN 0-906187-04-4, Pub. by Acad Pr Ireland). Devin.

Barrow, Georgia M. & Smith, Patricia A. Aging: The Individual & Society. 2nd ed. (Illus.). 400p. 1983. pap. text ed. 20.95 (ISBN 0-314-69635-0). West Pub.

Barrow, Gordon. Physical Chemistry. 4th ed. (Illus.). 1979. text ed. 34.95 (ISBN 0-07-003825-2). McGraw.

--Physical Chemistry for the Life Sciences. 2nd ed. (Illus.). 448p. 1981. text ed. 34.95 (ISBN 0-07-003858-9). McGraw.

Barrow, Gordon M. Structure of Molecules: An Introduction to Molecular Spectroscopy. (Orig.). 1963. pap. 18.95 (ISBN 0-8053-0521-1). Benjamin-Cummings.

Barrow, Graeme. Canberra Region Car Tours. LC 80-65767. 85p. (Orig.). 1981. pap. text ed. 3.95 (ISBN 0-7081-1087-8, 1076, Pub. by ANUP Australia). Australia N U P.

Barrow, Graeme T. Canberra's Embassies. LC 78-54412. 1978. pap. 2.75 (ISBN 0-7081-1060-6, Pub by ANUP Australia). Australia N U P.

Barrow, Harold M. Man & Movement: Principles of Physical Education. 3rd ed. LC 82-20398. 381p. 1983. text ed. 22.50 (ISBN 0-8121-0861-2). Lea & Febiger.

Barrow, Harold M. & McGee, Rosemary. A Practical Approach to Measurement in Physical Education. 3rd ed. LC 79-10504. (Illus.). 596p. 1979. text ed. 19.50 (ISBN 0-8121-0673-3). Lea & Febiger.

Barrow, Iris. Know Your Strengths & Be Confident. 91p. 1983. pap. 3.95x (ISBN 0-86863-441-7, Pub. by Heinemann Pub New Zealand). Intl Spec Bk.

--Your Marriage Can Work: A Practical Guide to Marriage Happiness. 96p. 1983. pap. 3.95x (ISBN 0-908592-00-0, Pub. by Heinemann Pub New Zealand). Intl Spec Bk.

Barrow, Isaac. The Geometrical Lectures. Child, J. M., ed. 218p. 14.95 (ISBN 0-912050-54-3). Open Court.

--Mathematical Works. Whewell, W., ed. Repr. of 1860 ed. 128.00x (ISBN 3-4870-4788-8). Adlers Foreign Bks.

--Theological Works of Isaac Barrow, 9 Vols. Napier, Alexander, ed. LC 72-161751. Repr. of 1859 ed. Set. lib. bdg. 215.00 (ISBN 0-404-00670-1); lib. bdg. 25.00 ea. AMS Pr.

--Usefulness of Mathematical Learning. Kirby, J., tr. (Illus.). 458p. 1970. Repr. of 1734 ed. 32.50x (ISBN 0-7146-1591-9, F Cass Co). Biblio Dist.

Barrow, John. Sketches of the Royal Society & Royal Society Club. 216p. 1971. Repr. of 1849 ed. 30.00x (ISBN 0-7146-2405-5, F Cass Co). Biblio Dist.

Barrow, John, ed. see Coats, William S.

Barrow, John, ed. see Cook, James.

Barrow, John D. & Silk, Joseph. The Left Hand of Creation: The Origin & Evolution of the Expanding Universe. LC 83-70766. (Illus.). 256p. 1983. text ed. 17.95 (ISBN 0-465-03895-6). Basic.

Barrow, John D. & Tipler, Frank J. The Anthropic Cosmological Principle. (Illus.). 640p. 1985. 24.95 (ISBN 0-19-851949-4). Oxford U Pr.

Barrow, Sir John. An Account of Travels into the Interior of Southern Africa, in the Years 1797 & 1798, 2 Vols. in 1. (Landmarks in Anthropology Ser). 1968. Repr. of 1801 ed. 68.00 (ISBN 0-384-03455-1). Johnson Repr.

--Mutiny of the Bounty. Kennedy, Gavin, ed. LC 80-66459. (Illus.). 216p. 1980. 17.95 (ISBN 0-87923-343-5). Godine.

Barrow, Kenneth. Helen Hayes: First Lady of the American Theater. LC 85-4540. (Illus.). 1985. 15.95 (ISBN 0-385-23196-2). Doubleday.

Barrow, Leo, jt. auth. see Olstad, Charles.

Barrow, Lu Ann, jt. auth. see Huffman, Carolyn.

Barrow, M. H., jt. auth. see Rase, Howard F.

Barrow, Mark V., et al. Health & Disease of American Indians North of Mexico: A Bibliography, 1800-1969. LC 70-161004. 1972. 8.00 (ISBN 0-8130-0331-8). U Presses Fla.

Barrow, Mary R. The Virginia Beach Harvest Cookbook. Browder, Robyn, ed. LC 83-16330. (Regional Cookbks.). (Illus.). 250p. 1985. pap. 7.95 (ISBN 0-89865-334-7). Donning Co.

Barrow, Mary R. & Browder, Robyn. The Great Taste of Virginia Seafood. (Illus.). 274p. 1984. pap. text ed. 10.95 (ISBN 0-913243-03-5). O'Connor Hse-Pubs.

Barrow, R. Radical Education: A Critique of Preschooling & Deschooling. 207p. 1978. pap. 21.95 (ISBN 0-470-26845-X). Halsted Pr.

Barrow, R. St., jt. auth. see Woods, R. G.

Barrow, R. W., jt. auth. see Gray, J. A.

Barrow, Reginald H. Plutarch & His Times. LC 76-6599. (BCL Ser. II). Repr. of 1967 ed. 19.00 (ISBN 0-404-15276-7). AMS Pr.

--The Romans. (Orig.). (YA) (gr. 9 up). 1975. pap. 4.95 (ISBN 0-14-020196-3, Pelican). Penguin.

Barrow, Robin. Common Sense & the Curriculum. (Unwin Education Books). 1976. pap. text ed. 8.95x (ISBN 0-04-370074-8). Allen Unwin.

--Common Sense & the Curriculum. 169p. 1976. 19.50 (ISBN 0-208-01590-6, Linnet). Shoe String.

--Giving Teaching Back to Teachers: A Critical Introduction to Curriculum Theory. LC 84-14468. 318p. 1984. 27.95x (ISBN 0-389-20524-9, BNB-08086). B&N Imports.

--Happiness & Schooling. 175p. 1980. 25.00x (ISBN 0-312-36177-7). St Martin.

--Injustice, Inequality & Ethics: A Philosophical Introduction to Moral Problems. LC 82-1603. 216p. 1982. text ed. 28.50 (ISBN 0-389-20269-X, 07087). B&N Imports.

--Injustice, Inequality, & Ethics: A Philosophical Introduction to Moral Problems. 216p. 1982. 27.50 (ISBN 0-318-02910-3). Biblio Dist.

--Moral Philosophy for Education. (Unwin Education Books). 1975. pap. text ed. 9.95x (ISBN 0-04-370060-8). Allen Unwin.

--Philosophy of Schooling. 240p. 1981. text ed. 17.50x (ISBN 0-7108-0105-X, Pub. by Harvester England). Humanities.

--Philosphy of Schooling. LC 81-7445. 211p. 1981. 18.95x (ISBN 0-470-27180-9). Halsted Pr.

--Sparta. (Greek & Roman Topics Ser.). 1975. pap. text ed. 3.95x (ISBN 0-04-930002-4). Allen Unwin.

Barrow, S. M., ed. Major Companies of the Far East 1985: Southeast Asia, Vol. 1. 350p. 1982. 135.00x (ISBN 0-86010-324-2, Pub. by Graham & Trotman England); 96.00x (ISBN 0-686-92029-5). State Mutual Bk.

Barrow, S. M., jt. ed. see Graham & Trotman Ltd.

Barrow, Sarah F. Medieval Society Romances. LC 72-195329. 1924. lib. bdg. 17.50 (ISBN 0-8414-1626-5). Folcroft.

--The Medieval Society Romances. LC 73-13967. 141p. 1973. Repr. of 1924 ed. lib. bdg. 17.00x (ISBN 0-374-90416-2). Octagon.

Barrow, Simon M., ed. Arab Business Yearbook, 1985. 175p. 1982. 290.00x (ISBN 0-86010-372-2, Pub. by Graham & Trotman England); pap. 210.00x (ISBN 0-86010-344-7). State Mutual BK.

Barrow, T. Music of the Maori. 50p. 1965. 3.95 (ISBN 0-85467-034-3, Pub. by Viking New Zealand). Intl Spec Bk.

Barrow, Terence. An Illustrated Guide to Maori Art. (Illus.). 104p. 1984. pap. 15.95 (ISBN 0-8248-0979-3). UH Pr.

--Incredible Hawaii. LC 74-77226. (Illus.). 1974. pap. 3.75 (ISBN 0-8048-1137-7). C E Tuttle.

Barrow, Terence, jt. auth. see Nicholson, Bronwen.

Barrow, Thomas C. Trade & Empire: The British Customs Service in Colonial America, 1660-1775. LC 67-11666. 1967. 20.00x (ISBN 0-674-89925-3). Harvard U Pr.

Barrow, Thomas C. see Weaver, Glenn.

Barrow, Thomas F., et al, eds. Reading into Photography: Selected Essays, 1959-1980. 320p. 1982. pap. 12.50x (ISBN 0-8263-0647-0). U of NM Pr.

Barrow, Tony. Bucks Fizz. (Illus.). 32p. 1984. pap. 3.95 (ISBN 0-86276-179-4). Proteus Pub NY.

Barrow, W. J. Manuscripts & Documents: Their Deterioration & Restoration. rev. ed. LC 72-89855. (Illus.). 84p. 1972. Repr. of 1976 ed. 9.95x (ISBN 0-8139-0408-0). U Pr of Va.

Barrowby, William, ed. see Astruc, Jean.

Barrowcliffe, A. J., pseud. Normanton. LC 79-8235. Repr. of 1862 ed. 44.50 (ISBN 0-404-61779-4). AMS Pr.

Barrowclough, Christine & Fleming, Ian. Goal Planning with Elderly People. LC 85-7120. 72p. (Orig.). 1985. pap. 7.00 (ISBN 0-7190-1802-1, Pub. by Manchester Univ Pr). Longwood Pub Group.

Barrowe, John. A Description of Pitcairn's Island & Its Inhabitants. LC 72-302. (World History Ser., No. 48). 1972. Repr. of 1900 ed. lib. bdg. 52.95x (ISBN 0-8383-1409-0). Haskell.

Barrowman, J. A. Physiology of the Gastro-Intestinal Lymphatic System. LC 77-22823. (Physiological Society Monographs: No. 33). (Illus.). 1978. 67.50 (ISBN 0-521-21710-5). Cambridge U Pr.

Barrows & Case. Speech Drills for Children in Form of Play. 1973. text ed. 2.00 (ISBN 0-686-09392-5). Expression.

Barrows & Hall. Jack in the Box. 1973. text ed. 1.25 (ISBN 0-686-09391-7). Expression.

Barrows, A. B. Bakery Specialities. (Illus.). 336p. 1985. 42.00 (ISBN 0-85334-291-1, Pub. by Elsevier Applied Sci England). Elsevier.

--Everyday Production of Baked Goods. 2nd ed. (Illus.). 396p. 1975. 40.75 (ISBN 0-85334-560-0, Pub. by Elsevier Applied Sci England). Elsevier.

Barrows, Anita, tr. see Duras, Marguerite.

Barrows, Anita, tr. see Kristeva, Julia.

Barrows, Anita, tr. see Martini, Plinio.

Barrows, David P. Berbers & Blacks: Impressions of Morocco, Timbuktu & the Western Sudan. LC 70-129938. (Illus.). Repr. of 1927 ed. 22.50x (ISBN 0-8371-1003-3, BBB&, Pub. by Negro U Pr). Greenwood.

--The Ethno-Botany of the Coahuilla Indians of Southern California. LC 76-43653. Repr. of 1900 ed. 14.00 (ISBN 0-404-15487-5). AMS Pr.

--Ethnobotany of the Coahuilla Indians of Southern California. 1977. pap. 5.95 (ISBN 0-939046-16-4). Malki Mus Pr.

--History of the Philippines. 33.00 (ISBN 0-8369-7152-3, 7984). Ayer Co Pubs.

Barrows, Edward M. The Great Commodore: The Exploits of Matthew Calbraith. LC 72-23. (Select Bibliographies Reprint Ser). 1972. Repr. of 1935 ed. 24.00 (ISBN 0-8369-9952-5). Ayer Co Pubs.

Barrows, Elijah P. View of the American Slavery Question. LC 75-107468. Repr. of 1836 ed. 15.00x (ISBN 0-8371-3747-0, BVS&). Greenwood.

Barrows, Gordon H. Worldwide Concession Contracts & Petroleum Legislation. LC 83-2221. 320p. 1983. 59.95 (ISBN 0-87814-226-6, P-4323). Pennwell Bks.

Barrows, Herbert, et al, eds. see Allison, Alexander W.

Barrows, Howard. How to Design a Problem-Based Curriculum for the Preclinical Years. (Springer Series in Medical Education: Vol. 8). 160p. 1985. 25.95 (ISBN 0-8261-4900-6). Springer Pub.

Barrows, Howard S. Guide to Neurological Assessment. (Illus.). 144p. 1980. text ed. 14.50 (ISBN 0-397-52093-X, 65-06141, Lippincott Medical). Lippincott.

--Simulated Patients (Programmed Patients) The Development & Use of a New Technique in Medical Education. (Illus.). 80p. 1971. spiral 16.50 (ISBN 0-398-02227-5). C C Thomas.

Barrows, Howard S. & Tamblyn, Robyn M. Problem Based Learning: An Approach to Medical Education. (Medical Education Ser.: Vol. 1). 1980. text ed. 21.95 (ISBN 0-8261-2840-8). Springer Pub.

Barrows, John A., jt. auth. see Waterman, Thomas T.

Barrows, Marjorie. One Thousand Beautiful Things. (Library of Beautiful Things: Vol. 1). (gr. 7 up). 1955. 9.95 (ISBN 0-8015-5562-0, Hawthorn). Dutton.

Barrows, Susanna. Distorting Mirrors: Visions of the Crowd in Late Nineteenth-Century France. LC 81-3014. (Historical Publications, Miscellany Ser.: No. 127). 224p. 1981. text ed. 23.00x (ISBN 0-300-02588-2). Yale U Pr.

Barrows, Suzanne S., jt. ed. see Goode, John W., Jr.

Barrows, Thomas S., et al. What College Students Know About Their World. LC 80-69768. 56p. (Orig.). 1981. pap. 5.95 (ISBN 0-915390-30-2, Pub. by Change Mag). Transaction Pubs.

--What College Students Know & Believe about Their World. 48p. 1981. pap. 5.95 (ISBN 0-915390-30-2). Transaction Bks.

Barrows, Walter. Grassroots Politics in an African State: Integration & Development in Sierra Leone. LC 74-84655. 250p. 1976. text ed. 35.00x (ISBN 0-8419-0183-X, Africana). Holmes & Meier.

Barrows, William. The Indian's Side of the Indian Question. LC 72-5517. (Select Bibliographies Reprint Ser.). 1972. Repr. of 1887 ed. 13.00 (ISBN 0-8369-6895-6). Ayer Co Pubs.

--Oregon: The Struggle for Possession. LC 72-3766. (American Commonwealths: No. 2). Repr. of 1892 ed. 32.50 (ISBN 0-404-57202-2). AMS Pr.

Barrows, William, ed. The General: Twelve Nights in the Hunters' Camp. facsimile ed. LC 70-179504. (Select Bibliographies Reprint Ser). Repr. of 1869 ed. 20.00 (ISBN 0-8369-6633-3). Ayer Co Pubs.

Barro Y Segura, Antonio. The Truth about Sugar in Cuba. 1976. lib. bdg. 59.95 (ISBN 0-8490-2775-6). Gordon Pr.

Barrs, Jerram. Who Are the Peacemakers? The Christian Case for Nuclear Deterrence. LC 83-62684. 60p. 1983. pap. 2.95 (ISBN 0-89107-307-8, Crossway Bks). Good News.

Barrs, Jerram, jt. auth. see Macaulay, Ranald.

Barr-Sharrar, Beryl, ed. see Borza, Eugene N., et al.

Barrum, James A., et al. Community Based Corrections. 19p. 1983. 2.00 (ISBN 0-318-02514-0). S Houston Employ.

Barrus, Clara. John Burroughs Boy & Man. 385p. 1983. Repr. of 1928 ed. lib. bdg. 45.00 (ISBN 0-8495-0634-4). Arden Lib.

--Our Friend, John Burroughs. LC 76-130262. (American Biography Ser., No. 32). 1970. Repr. of 1914 ed. lib. bdg. 53.95x (ISBN 0-8383-1169-5). Haskell.

--Our Friend, John Burroughs. 1973. Repr. of 1914 ed. 30.00 (ISBN 0-8274-1162-6). R West.

--Whitman & Burroughs: Comrades. LC 67-27575. 1931. Repr. 29.50x (ISBN 0-8046-0017-1, Pub. by Kennikat). Assoc Faculty Pr.

Barrus, Clara, ed. The Heart of Burrough's Journals. 1979. Repr. of 1928 ed. lib. bdg. 30.00 (ISBN 0-8495-0504-6). Arden Lib.

Barrus, David F. The Way to the Sun. 1972. 5.50 (ISBN 0-88290-008-0). Horizon Utah.

Barrus, J. Scott, jt. auth. see Gilder, Jules H.

Barrus, Tim. My Brother, My Lover. 160p. (Orig.). 1985. pap. 7.95 (ISBN 0-917342-08-9). Gay Sunshine.

Barrutia, Richard. Linguistic Theory of Language Learning as Related to Machine Teaching. 119p. (Orig.). 1969. pap. 14.50x (ISBN 0-317-07615-9, Pub. by J Groos W Germany). Benjamins North Am.

Barrutia, Richard & Terrell, Tracy David. Fonetica y Fonologia Espanolas. LC 81-13155. 189p. 1982. text ed. 23.50x (ISBN 0-471-08461-1); avail. tapes. Wiley.

Barry. Applying Ethics: A Text with Readings. 2nd ed. 1984. write for info (ISBN 0-534-03687-2). Wadsworth Pub.

--Dermatological Formation. (Drugs & the Pharmaceutical Science Ser.). 472p. 1983. 69.50 (ISBN 0-8247-1729-5). Dekker.

Barry, Ada L. Yunini's Story of the Trail of Tears. LC 74-7924. (Illus.). Repr. of 1932 ed. 34.50 (ISBN 0-404-11810-0). AMS Pr.

Barry, Alfred. The Life & Works of Sir Charles Barry. LC 72-83088. (Illus.). Repr. of 1867 ed. 29.00 (ISBN 0-405-08239-8, Blom Pubns). Ayer Co Pubs.

Barry, Alyce, ed. see Barnes, Djuna.

Barry, Sr. Anna. Aortic & Tricuspid Valvular Disease. (Continuing Education in Cardiovascular Nursing Ser.). (Illus.). 82p. 1980. pap. 6.95x (ISBN 0-8385-0189-3). ACC.

Barry, Arthur L. The Antimicrobic Susceptibility Test: Principles & Practices. LC 76-18846. pap. 62.00 (ISBN 0-317-26678-0, 2055996). Bks Demand UMI.

Barry, B. Sociologists, Economists & Democracy. 1970. pap. text ed. 2.45x (ISBN 0-02-972350-7). Macmillan.

Barry, B. Austin. Construction Measurements. LC 72-13073. (Practical Construction Guides Ser.). 304p. 1973. 41.50x (ISBN 0-471-05428-3, Pub. by Wiley-Interscience). Wiley.

--Errors in Practical Measurement in Science, Engineering & Technology. LC 78-9751. 183p. 1978. 32.50x (ISBN 0-471-03156-9, Pub. by Wiley-Interscience). Wiley.

Barry, B. T. & Thwaites, C. G. Tin & Its Alloys & Compounds. LC 83-12760. (Industrial Metals Ser.). 268p. 1983. 69.95x (ISBN 0-470-27480-8). Halsted Pr.

Barry, Bernard, jt. auth. see Sadler, Philip J.

Barry, Brett De see Nee, Victor G. & De Barry, Brett.

Barry, Brian. Power & Political Theory: Some European Perspectives. LC 74-20693. 322p. 1976. 48.95x (ISBN 0-471-05424-0, Pub. by Wiley-Interscience). Wiley.

--Sociologists, Economists & Democracy. LC 78-55039. (Illus.). vi, 202p. 1978. pap. 8.00x (ISBN 0-226-03823-8). U of Chicago Pr.

Barry, Brian & Hardin, Russell. Rational Man & Irrational Society? An Introduction & Sourcebook. (Illus.). 432p. 1982. 30.00 (ISBN 0-8039-1850-X); pap. 14.95 (ISBN 0-8039-1851-8). Sage.

Barry, Brian, ed. see Bates, Robert H.

Barry, Brian, jt. ed. see Sikora, R. I.

Barry, Brian M. Political Argument. (International Library of Philosophy & Scientific Method). 1976. text ed. 32.75x (ISBN 0-391-00585-5). Humanities.

Barry, C. H. & Tye, F. Running A School. X ed. 248p. 1982. 25.00x (ISBN 0-85117-190-7, Pub. by M Temple Smith). State Mutual Bk.

Barry, C. J. Home Brewed Beers & Stouts. 5th ed. (Illus.). 172p. Date not set. pap. 4.95 (ISBN 0-900841-58-3, Pub. by Aztex Corp). Argus Bks.

Barry, Catherine, jt. auth. see Mollencott, Virginia.

Barry, Charlie. Keep on Trusting & Trying. (Contemporary Poets of Dorrance Ser.). 88p. 1982. 6.95 (ISBN 0-8059-2822-7). Dorrance.

Barry, Colman J. Worship & Work. LC 80-10753. (Illus.). 526p. 1980. pap. text ed. 12.50 (ISBN 0-8146-1123-0). Liturgical Pr.

Barry, Colman J., ed. Readings in Church History, 3 vols. in 1. 1985. pap. 50.00 (ISBN 0-87061-104-6). Chr Classics.

Barry, Dave. Babies & Other Hazards of Sex. Yepsen, Roger, ed. (Illus.). 96p. 1984. pap. 4.95 (ISBN 0-87857-510-3). Rodale Pr Inc.

--Bad Habits: A One Hundred Percent Fact Free Book. LC 84-18639. 240p. 1985. 14.95 (ISBN 0-385-18954-0). Doubleday.

--Stay Fit & Healthy until You're Dead. Yepsen, Roger, ed. (Illus.). 96p. 1985. pap. 4.95 (ISBN 0-87857-570-7). Rodale Pr Inc.

--Taming of the Screw: Several Million Homeowner's Problems. (Illus.). 96p. (Orig.). 1983. pap. 4.95 (ISBN 0-87857-484-0). Rodale Pr Inc.

Barry, David S. Forty Years in Washington. (American Newspapermen 1790-1933 Ser.). (Illus.). xi, 349p. 1974. Repr. of 1924 ed. 17.50x (ISBN 0-8464-0031-6). Beekman Pubs.

Barry, David W. Ministry of Reconciliation: Modern Lessons from Scripture & Sacrament. LC 75-4630. 129p. (Orig.). 1975. pap. 2.95 (ISBN 0-8189-0317-1). Alba.

Barry, Donald & Barner-Barry, Carol. Contemporary Soviet Politics: An Introduction. 464p. 1982. pap. 19.95 reference (ISBN 0-13-170191-6). P-H.

Barry, Donald D. & Whitcomb, Howard R. The Legal Foundations of Public Administration. LC 80-39909. 890p. 1980. text ed. 17.95 (ISBN 0-8299-2120-6). West Pub.

Barry, Donna. Jan-Louise: A Poetic Narrative. 112p. 1976. 5.00 (ISBN 0-8233-0245-8). Golden Quill.

Barry, Elaine. Robert Frost. LC 72-79942. (Literature and Life Ser.). 1973. 12.95 (ISBN 0-8044-2016-5). Ungar.

Barry, F. V., intro. by. Jane Taylor: Prose & Poetry. 177p. 1981. Repr. of 1925 ed. lib. bdg. 25.00 (ISBN 0-8495-0479-1). Arden Lib.

--Jane Taylor: Prose & Poetry. 177p. 1980. Repr. of 1925 ed. lib. bdg. 30.00 (ISBN 0-89760-075-4). Telegraph Bks.

Barry, Florence V. A Century of Children's Books. 59.95 (ISBN 0-87968-828-9). Gordon Pr.

Barry, Frederick. Scientific Habit of Thought. Repr. of 1927 ed. 26.00 (ISBN 0-404-00666-3). AMS Pr.

Barry, Frederick, ed. see Pascal, Blaise.

Barry, Herbert, III & Schlegel, Alice, eds. Cross-Cultural Samples & Codes. LC 79-3878. 1980. 34.95x (ISBN 0-8229-3417-5); pap. 14.95x (ISBN 0-8229-5317-X). U of Pittsburgh Pr.

Barry, Herbert, III, jt. ed. see Yacobi, Avraham.

Barry, Iris. Let's Go to the Movies. LC 79-169357. (Arno Press Cinema Program). (Illus.). 318p. 1972. Repr. of 1926 ed. 24.50 (ISBN 0-405-03911-5). Ayer Co Pubs.

--Portrait of Lady Mary Montagu. 1928. Repr. 17.50 (ISBN 0-8274-3187-2). R West.

Barry, Iris & Bowser, Ellen. D. W. Griffith, American Film Master: With An Annotated List of Films. LC 82-49224. (Cinema Classics Ser.). 136p. 1985. lib. bdg. 35.00 (ISBN 0-8240-5762-7). Garland Pub.

Barry, J. V., et al. An Introduction to the Criminal Law in Australia. (Cambridge Studies in Criminology: Vol. 6). pap. 16.00. Kraus Repr.

Barry, Jackson G. Dramatic Structure: The Shaping of Experience. LC 78-100607. 1970. 37.50x (ISBN 0-520-01624-6). U of Cal Pr.

Barry, James C., ed. Preaching in Today's World. LC 83-24021. (Orig.). 1984. pap. 5.95 (ISBN 0-8054-2113-0). Broadman.

Barry, James D. Ball Lightning & Bead Lightning: Extreme Forms of Atmospheric Electricity. LC 79-19017. (Illus.). 308p. 1980. 35.00x (ISBN 0-306-40272-6, Plenum Pr). Plenum Pub.

Barry, James D., ed. see McMahon, Thomas F., et al.

Barry, James P. Ships of the Great Lakes: 300 Years of Navigation. LC 73-90191. (Illus.). 1973. 15.00 (ISBN 0-8310-7105-2). Howell-North.

--Wrecks & Rescues of the Great Lakes: A Photographic History. LC 81-6199. (Illus.). 128p. 1981. 15.00 (ISBN 0-8310-7149-4). Howell-North.

Barry, Jan. Veteran's Day. 12p. 1983. pap. 1.00 (ISBN 0-686-46874-0). Samisdat.

--War Baby. 12p. 1984. pap. 1.00 (ISBN 0-317-07608-6). Samisdat.

Barry, Jan & Ehrhart, W. D. Demilitarized Zones: Veterans After Vietnam. LC 76-17200. (Illus.). 1976. pap. 2.95 (ISBN 0-917238-01-X). East River Anthol.

Barry, Jean. Emergency Nursing. LC 77-1436. (Illus.). 1977. pap. text ed. 33.95 (ISBN 0-07-003839-2). McGraw.

Barry, John. American Indian Pottery: Identification & Value Guide. 2nd ed. 232p. 1985. 29.95 (ISBN 0-89689-047-3). Wallace-Homestead.

--The Great Climbing Adventure. (Great Adventure Ser.). (Illus.). 256p. 1985. 12.95 (ISBN 0-946609-07-1, Pub. by Oxford Ill Pr). Interbook.

Barry, John, jt. auth. see Tennant, Rich.

Barry, John M. The Natural Vegetation of South Carolina. LC 79-19678. (Illus.). 214p. 1980. lib. bdg. 19.95 (ISBN 0-87249-384-9); pap. 6.95 (ISBN 0-87249-214-1). U of SC Pr.

Barry, John R. & Wingrove, C. Ray, eds. Let's Learn About Aging: A Book of Readings. 350p. 1977. text ed. 18.50 (ISBN 0-87073-673-6). Schenkman Bks Inc.

Barry, John W. American Indian Pottery: An Identification & Value Guide. 2nd ed. (Illus.). 213p. (Orig.). 1984. pap. 29.95 (ISBN 0-89689-047-3). Bks Americana.

Barry, John W. & Henry, Porter J. Effective Sales Incentive Compensation. (Illus.). 192p. 1980. 21.50 (ISBN 0-07-003860-0). McGraw.

Barry, Kathleen. Female Sexual Slavery. 336p. 1981. pap. 3.95 (ISBN 0-380-54213-7, 54213-7, Discus). Avon.

--Female Sexual Slavery. 336p. 1985. 30.00x (ISBN 0-8147-1070-0); pap. 10.50x (ISBN 0-8147-1069-7). NYU Pr.

Barry, Kenneth H. & Connelly, Patricia A. Research on Law Students: An Annotated Bibliography. 54p. (Reprinted from 1978 ABF Res. J., No. 1). 1978. 2.50 (ISBN 0-317-33356-9). Amer Bar Assn.

Barry, Lord David. Ram Alley. LC 75-133639. (Tudor Facsimile Texts. Old English Plays: No. 129). Repr. of 1913 ed. 49.50 (ISBN 0-404-53429-5). AMS Pr.

Barry, Lording. Ram-Alley or Merrie Trickes: From Quarto of 1611. Jones, Claude E., ed. (Material for the Study of the Old English Drama Ser.: No. 2, Vol. 23). pap. 14.00 (ISBN 0-317-16741-3). Kraus Repr.

Barry, Louise. The Beginning of the West: Annals of the Kansas Gateway to the American West 1540-1854. LC 78-172252. (Illus.). 1296p. 1972. 10.95 (ISBN 0-87726-001-X). Kansas St Hist.

--Comprehensive Index to Publications 1875-1930. 515p. 1959. 5.00 (ISBN 0-87726-011-7). Kansas St Hist.

Barry, Lynda J. Big Ideas. LC 83-61229. (Illus.). 128p. (Orig.). 1983. pap. 5.95 (ISBN 0-941104-07-9). Real Comet.

--Girls & Boys. (Illus.). 96p. (Orig.). 1981. pap. 5.95 (ISBN 0-941104-00-1). Real Comet.

--Naked Ladies, Naked Ladies, Naked Ladies. LC 84-62027. (Illus.). 60p. (Orig.). 1984. pap. 7.95 (ISBN 0-941104-13-3). Real Comet.

Barry, Sr. M. Martin. An Analysis of the Prosodic Structure of Selected Poems of T. S. Eliot. LC 69-19281. 148p. 1969. pap. 5.95x (ISBN 0-8132-0254-X). Cath U Pr.

Barry, Michael P., jt. auth. see Cummings, Frank.

Barry, Mike. Playing Dirty. 128p. 1983. pap. 4.95 (ISBN 0-312-61622-8). St Martin.

Barry, Norman P. Hayek's Social & Economic Philosophy. 1979. text ed. 31.75x (ISBN 0-333-25618-2). Humanities.

--An Introduction to Modern Political Theory. 1981. 26.00 (ISBN 0-312-43098-1). St Martin.

Barry, Patricia D. Mental Health & Mental Illness. 3rd ed. 354p. 1985. pap. text ed. 15.95 (ISBN 0-397-54392-1, Nursing). Lippincott.

--Psychosocial Nursing Assessment & Intervention. 400p. 1984. pap. text ed. 16.95 (ISBN 0-397-54392-1, 64-03331, Lippincott Nursing). Lippincott.

Barry, Patricia S. The King in Tudor Drama. (Salzburg Studies in English Literature: Elizabethan & Renaissance Studies: No. 58). (Orig.). 1977. pap. text ed. 25.50x (ISBN 0-391-01313-0). Humanities.

Barry, Patrick. The Theory & Practice of the International Trade of the United States & England, & of the Trade of the United States & Canada. (The Neglected American Economists Ser.). 1974. lib. bdg. 61.00 (ISBN 0-8240-1014-0). Garland Pub.

Barry, Patrick D., ed. see Boole, George.

Barry, Peter J. see Hopkin, John A., et al.

Barry, Peter J., ed. Risk Management in Agriculture. (Illus.). 1984. text ed. 34.95 (ISBN 0-8138-1523-1). Iowa St U Pr.

Barry, Philip. The Philadelphia Story: A Comedy in Three Acts. LC 83-45700. Repr. of 1939 ed. 24.50 (ISBN 0-404-20018-4). AMS Pr.

Barry, Philip see MacGowan, Kenneth.

Barry, Phillips, et al. British Ballads from Maine. (Music Ser.). (Illus.). 535p. 1982. Repr. of 1929 ed. lib. bdg. 42.50 (ISBN 0-306-76135-1). Da Capo.

Barry, R. Basic Business English. 1981. pap. 19.95 (ISBN 0-13-057208-X). P-H.

--Construction of Buildings, 5 vols. (Illus.). 508p. 1971. Set. spiral bdg. 40.00x (ISBN 0-8464-0276-9). Beekman Pubs.

--The Construction of Buildings: Foundations, Walls, Floors & Roofs. Incl. Vol. I. 3rd ed. 1969. pap. text ed. 12.50x (ISBN 0-258-96765-X); Vol. II. 2nd ed. 140p. 1970. pap. text ed. 13.50x (ISBN 0-258-96798-6); Vol. III. 2nd ed. 101p. 1972. pap. text ed. 13.50x (ISBN 0-258-96844-3); Vol. IV. 2nd ed. 120p. 1971. pap. text ed. 13.50x (ISBN 0-258-96829-X); Vol. V. 108p. 1978. pap. text ed. 13.50x (ISBN 0-258-97077-4). pap. (Pub. by Granada England). Brookfield Pub Co.

Barry, R. D., jt. ed. see Mahy, B. W.

Barry, R. G. & Perry, A. H. Synoptic Climatology: Methods & Applications. 500p. 1973. 56.00x (ISBN 0-416-08500-8, 2078). Methuen Inc.

Barry, Richard. Mr. Rutledge of South Carolina. facsimile ed. LC 71-146851. (Select Bibliographies Reprint Ser). Repr. of 1942 ed. 21.00 (ISBN 0-8369-5618-4). Ayer Co Pubs.

Barry, Richard, tr. see Hoffmann, Peter.

Barry, Robert. Mr. Willoby's Christmas Tree. (Illus.). (gr. k-3). 1963. PLB 10.95 (ISBN 0-07-003877-5). McGraw.

Barry, Robert E. Business English for the Eighties. 2nd ed. (Illus.). 448p. 1985. pap. text ed. 21.95 (ISBN 0-13-095423-3). P-H.

Barry, Robert E., jt. ed. see Webb, Ralph L.

Barry, Robin. Barry: Construction of Building, Vol. 1. 4th ed. 128p. 1980. 9.95x (ISBN 0-246-11261-1, Pub. by Granada England). Sheridan.

--Barry: Construction of Building, Vol. 2. 3rd ed. 136p. 1982. 9.95x (ISBN 0-246-11263-8, Pub. by Granada England). Sheridan.

--Barry: Construction of Building, Vol. 3. 3th ed. 112p. 1972. 9.95x (ISBN 0-246-11950-0, Pub. by Granada England). Sheridan.

--Barry: Construction of Building, Vol. 4. 2nd ed. 128p. 1971. 9.95x (ISBN 0-246-11547-5, Pub. by Granada England). Sheridan.

--Barry: Construction of Building, Vol. 5. 112p. 1978. 9.95x (ISBN 0-246-11275-1, Pub. by Granada England). Sheridan.

Barry, Roger G. Mountain Weather & Climate. LC 80-42348. (Illus.). 313p. 1981. 43.00x (ISBN 0-416-73730-7, NO. 3464). Methuen Inc.

Barry, Roger G. & Chorley, R. J. Atmosphere, Weather & Climate. 4th ed. 425p. 1982. 33.00x (ISBN 0-416-33690-6, NO. 3748); pap. 14.95x (ISBN 0-416-33700-7, 3740). Methuen Inc.

Barry, Roger G., jt. auth. see Ives, Jack D.

Barry, Ruth & Wolf, Beverly. Motives, Values, & Realities: A Framework for Counseling. LC 76-40268. 1976. Repr. of 1965 ed. lib. bdg. 24.75x (ISBN 0-8371-9066-5, WOMV). Greenwood.

Barry, Scott. The Kingdom of Wolves. LC 78-9895. (Illus.). (gr. 6-8). 1979. 9.95 (ISBN 0-399-20657-4, Putnam). Putnam Pub Group.

Barry, Sheila A. Super-Colossal Book of Puzzles, Tricks & Games. LC 77-93325. (Illus.). 640p. (gr. 2-6). 1981. 6.98 (ISBN 0-8069-4720-9); PLB 29.49 (ISBN 0-8069-4581-8); pap. 12.95 (ISBN 0-8069-7524-5). Sterling.

--Tricks & Stunts to Fool Your Friends. LC 84-87. (Illus.). 128p. (gr. 4-6). 1984. PLB 10.99 (ISBN 0-8069-4694-6); 8.95 (ISBN 0-317-02845-6); pap. 3.50 (ISBN 0-8069-7856-2). Sterling.

Barry, Sheila M., jt. ed. see Oxley, T. A.

Barry, Stephen. Royal Service. (General Ser.). 387p. 1983. lib. bdg. 14.95 (ISBN 0-8161-3530-4, Large Print Bks). G K Hall.

--Royal Service: My Twelve Years As Valet to Prince Charles. (Illus.). 320p. 1983. 14.95 (ISBN 0-02-507490-3). Macmillan.

Barry, Stephen P. Royal Secrets: The View from Downstairs. Reverand, Diane, ed. LC 84-40604. 256p. 1985. 16.45 (ISBN 0-394-54403-X, Pub. by Villard Bks). Random.

--Royal Service. 288p. 1984. pap. 3.50 (ISBN 0-380-67397-5, 67397). Avon.

Barry, Susan & Litzky, Harriet. Atlanta Takeout, Vol. 1. 88p. (Orig.). 1985. pap. 2.95 (ISBN 0-9614544-0-7). Atlanta Takeout.

Barry, Susan, jt. auth. see Freeling, Paul.

Barry, Thomas E., et al, eds. Marketing & the Black Consumer: An Annotated Bibliography. LC 76-3722. (American Marketing Association Bibliography Ser.: No. 22). pap. 20.00 (ISBN 0-317-10881-6, 2014622). Bks Demand UMI.

Barry, Tim, jt. auth. see Miller, Merl.

Barry, Tim, ed. see McCabe, C. Kevin.

Barry, Tim, ed. see Townsend, Carl.

Barry, Timothy C., et al. Tones, Tunes & Trills: Sound & Music on the Commodore 64. (Illus.). 224p. 1984. pap. 12.95 (ISBN 0-88056-345-1); incl. disk 29.95 (ISBN 0-88056-230-7). Dilithium Pr.

Barry, Tom & Preusch, Deb. The Central America Fact Book. 288p. (Orig.). 1985. 27.50 (ISBN 0-394-55011-0); pap. 8.95 (ISBN 0-394-62079-8). Grove.

Barry, Tom & Wood, Beth. Dollars & Dictators: A Guide to Central America. 272p. (Orig.). 1982. pap. 5.95 (ISBN 0-911213-00-7). Resource Ctr.

Barry, Tom, et al. Dollars & Dictators: A Guide to Central America. LC 83-81370. 288p. 1983. pap. 6.95 (ISBN 0-394-62485-8, E864, Ever). Grove.

--The Other Side of Paradise: Foreign Control in the Caribbean. LC 83-49370. 416p. 1985. 22.50 (ISBN 0-394-53852-8, GP 890). Grove.

--Other Side of Paradise: Foreign Control in the Caribbean. LC 83-49377. 1985. pap. 9.95 (ISBN 0-394-62056-9, E-904, Ever). Grove.

Barry, Ursala, jt. ed. see Bannon, Liam.

Barry, Vincent. Good Reason for Writing: A Text with Readings. 400p. 1982. pap. text ed. write for info. (ISBN 0-534-01232-9). Wadsworth Pub.

--Moral Aspects of Health Care. 528p. 1982. pap. text ed. write for info. (ISBN 0-534-01090-3). Wadsworth Pub.

--Moral Issues in Business. 3rd ed. 480p. 1985. text ed. 28.50 (ISBN 0-534-05484-6). Wadsworth Pub.

--Philosophy: A Text with Readings. 2nd ed. 544p. 1982. text ed. write for info. (ISBN 0-534-01216-7). Wadsworth Pub.

Barry, Vincent E. Invitation to Critical Thinking. 1984. pap. text ed. 18.95 (ISBN 0-03-059383-2). HR&W.

--Practical Logic. 2nd ed. LC 80-21202. 1981. text ed. 24.95 (ISBN 0-03-056836-6, HoltC). HR&W.

Barry, W. R., ed. Architectural, Construction, Manufacturing & Engineering Glossary of Terms. 519p. 1979. pap. 40.00 (ISBN 0-930284-05-4). Am Assn Cost Engineers.

Barry, Whit. Making Love: A Man's Guide. 1984. pap. 2.95 (ISBN 0-451-12957-1, Sig). NAL.

Barry, William. Cardinal Newman. 1973. Repr. of 1904 ed. 20.00 (ISBN 0-8274-1797-7). R West.

--Ernest Renan. 1905. Repr. 25.00 (ISBN 0-8274-3825-7). R West.

Barry, William, jt. auth. see Dominic, Randolph.

Barry, William A. & Connolly, William J. The Practice of Spiritual Direction. 224p. (Orig.). 1982. pap. 11.95 (ISBN 0-8164-2357-1, AY7870, Pub. by Seabury). Winston Pr.

Barry, William F. Roma Sacra: Essays on Christian Rome. facs. ed. LC 68-14896. (Essay Index Reprint Ser). 1927. 18.00 (ISBN 0-8369-0174-6). Ayer Co Pubs.

--The Two Standards. Wolff, Robert L., ed. LC 75-466. (Victorian Fiction Ser). 1976. Repr. of 1898 ed. lib. bdg. 73.00 (ISBN 0-8240-1544-4). Garland Pub.

Barry, Wm. A History of Framingham, Mass. iv, 456p. 1983. Repr. of 1847 ed. 35.00 (ISBN 0-917890-28-0). Heritage Bk.

Barrymaine, Norman. Time Bomb: A Veteran Journalist Assesses Today's China from the Inside. LC 76-164415. (Illus.). 1971. 6.50 (ISBN 0-8008-7730-6). Taplinger.

Barry-Martin, D. E. Heartfelt Journey. (Illus.). 276p. 1984. 23.95 (ISBN 0-911378-50-2). Sheridan.

Barrymore, D., jt. auth. see Barrymore, Frank.

Barrymore, Ethel. Memories: An Autobiography. LC 55-6565. 1968. Repr. of 1955 ed. 16.00 (ISBN 0-527-05400-3). Kraus Repr.

Barrymore, Frank & Barrymore, D. Too Much, Too Soon. 1981. Repr. lib. bdg. 21.95 (ISBN 0-89966-425-3). Buccaneer Bks.

Barrymore, John. Confessions of an Actor. LC 70-84506. (Illus.). 1926. 18.00 (ISBN 0-405-08240-1, Blom Pubns). Ayer Co Pubs.

Barrymore, Lionel. We Barrymores. LC 74-7602. (Illus.). 311p. 1974. Repr. of 1951 ed. lib. bdg. 24.75x (ISBN 0-8371-7550-X, BAB). Greenwood.

Barrys, Brook, ed. see Croft, William.

Bars, Itzhak, et al, eds. Symmetries in Particle Physics. 320p. 1984. 47.50x (ISBN 0-306-41801-0, Plenum Pr). Plenum Pub.

Barsacq, Andre, ed. see Labiche, Eugene.

Barsan, Uasile C., tr. see Ronnett, Alexander.

Barsby, J. A., ed. see Plautus.

Barsch, Karl-Heinrich. Pushkin & Merimee As Short Story Writers. LC 83-6175. 90p. 1983. pap. 7.00 (ISBN 0-938920-35-9). Hermitage.

Barsch, Ray. Configurations. 1980. Bk. 1. 5.00 ea. (ISBN 0-87879-225-2). Bk. 2 (ISBN 0-87879-226-0). Bk. 3 (ISBN 0-87879-227-9). Acad Therapy.

Barsch, Ray H. Parent of the Handicapped Child: The Study of Child-Rearing Practices. (Illus.). 452p. 1976. pap. 14.75x (ISBN 0-398-03559-8). C C Thomas.

Barschall, Henry H., ed. see Symposium - 3rd - Madison - 1970.

Barselou, P. E. The Genus Agrias. 96p. 1983. 190.00x (ISBN 0-317-07085-1, Pub. by EW Classey UK). State Mutual Bk.

Barsewisch, B. von. Perinatal Retinal Haemorrhages: Morphology, Aetiology & Significanace. (Illus.). 1979. 42.00 (ISBN 0-387-09167-X). Springer-Verlag.

Barsh, Elizabeth T., jt. auth. see Blackard, M. Kay.

Barsh, Laurence I. Dental Treatment Planning: For the Adult Patient. (Illus.). 376p. 1981. text ed. 32.50 (ISBN 0-7216-1533-3). Saunders.

Barsh, Russel L. The Washington Fishing Rights Controversy: An Economic Critique. 1977. pap. text ed. 7.00 (ISBN 0-686-22795-6). U of Wash Grad Sch Busn.

Barsh, Russel L. & Henderson, J. Youngblood. The Road: Indian Tribes & Political Liberty. LC 77-91777. 1980. 22.50x (ISBN 0-520-03629-8, CAL 543); pap. 7.95 (ISBN 0-520-04636-6). U of Cal Pr.

Barshay, Robert H. Philip Wylie: The Man & His Work. LC 79-63682. 1979. pap. text ed. 9.25 (ISBN 0-8191-0733-6). U Pr of Amer.

Barsic, S., ed. Quasi One-Dimensional Conductors Two. (Lecture Notes in Physics: Vol. 96). 1979. pap. 26.00 (ISBN 0-387-09241-2). Springer-Verlag.

Bar-Siman-Tov, Yaacov. Linkage Politics in the Middle East: Syria Between Domestic & External Conflict, 1961-1970. LC 82-21878. (Replica Edition Ser.). 176p. 1983. softcover 20.00x (ISBN 0-86531-945-6). Westview.

Bar-Simon-Tov, Yaacov. The Israeli-Egyptian War of Attrition, Nineteen Sixty-Nine to Nineteen Seventy: A Case-Study of Limited Local War. LC 80-11124. 256p. 1980. 26.00x (ISBN 0-231-04982-X). Columbia U Pr.

Barsis, Max. The Common Man Through the Centuries: A Book of Costume Drawings. LC 68-31447. (Illus.). 380p. 1973. 35.00 (ISBN 0-8044-1075-5). Ungar.

Barskaya, A. French Painting: The Hermitage Museum, Leningrad. (Second Half of the 19th to Early 20th Century). 1975. 80.00x (ISBN 0-317-14232-1, Pub. by Collet's). State Mutual Bk.

--Paul Cezanne. 155p. 1985. 40.00 (ISBN 0-8285-2993-0, Pub. by Aurura Pubs USSR). Imported Pubns.

Barskaya, A. & Georgiyevskaya, E. Paul Cezanne. 200p. 1982. 50.00x (ISBN 0-317-14277-1, Pub. by Collet's). State Mutual Bk.

Barskett, James. History of the Island of Saint Domingo from Its First Discovery by Columbus. 446p. 1972. Repr. of 1818 ed. 30.00x (ISBN 0-7146-2703-8, F Cass Co). Biblio Dist.

--History of the Island of St. Domingo. LC 74-137233. Repr. of 1824 ed. 22.50x (ISBN 0-8371-5800-1, BSD&). Greenwood.

Barsky, Hannah K. Guillaume Dupuytren: A Surgeon in His Place & Time. LC 82-99963. 295p. 1984. 14.95 (ISBN 0-533-05600-4). Vantage.

Barsley, Michael. Left-Handed People. pap. 5.00 (ISBN 0-87980-087-9). Wilshire.

--Modern American Humour: An Anthology. 1977. Repr. of 1943 ed. lib. bdg. 10.00 (ISBN 0-8495-0306-X). Arden Lib.

--The Phoenix Book of Modern American Humour. 1977. Repr. of 1957 ed. lib. bdg. 10.00 (ISBN 0-8495-0305-1). Arden Lib.

Barsley, Michael, ed. The Phoenix Book of Wit & Humour. rev. ed. 255p. 1980. Repr. of 1951 ed. lib. bdg. 20.00 (ISBN 0-8495-0394-9). Arden Lib.

Barsness, John. Hunting the Great Plains. LC 79-22096. (Illus.). 164p. 1979. pap. 6.95 (ISBN 0-87842-117-3). Mountain Pr.

Barsness, Larry. The Bison in Art: A Graphic Chronicle of the American Bison. LC 76-52543. (Illus.). 142p. 1977. pap. 14.50 (ISBN 0-87358-158-X). Amon Carter.

--The Bison in Art: A Graphic Chronicle of the American Bison. pap. 14.50 (ISBN 0-317-31513-7, Dist. by Univ. of Texas Pr.). Amon Carter.

Barsness, Larry, intro. by. see Linderman, Frank B.

Barsness, Larry V. Heads, Hides & Horns: The Compleat Buffalo Book. LC 85-2606. (Illus.). 256p. 1985. 40.00 (ISBN 0-87565-008-2); pap. 19.50 (ISBN 0-87565-017-1). Tex Christian.

Barsocchini, Peter, jt. auth. see Griffin, Merv.

Barsocchini, Peter, ed. see Griffin, Merv.

Barson. Laboratory Investigation of Fetal Disease. 520p. 1981. 56.50. PSG Pub Co.

Barson, Alan. Motivational Games for Mathematics. (Illus.). 40p. (gr. 3-7). 1981. pap. 6.95 (ISBN 0-937138-02-9). Fabmath.

Barson, Alfred T. A Way of Seeing: A Critical Study of James Agee. LC 75-181365. 232p. 1971. 13.50x (ISBN 0-87023-094-8). U of Mass Pr.

Barson, John. La Grammaire a l'Oeuvre. 3rd ed. LC 80-27639. 249p. 1981. pap. text ed. 18.95x (ISBN 0-03-050891-6, HoltC). HR&W.

Barson, John & Bertrand, Vida. Intrigues. 1979. text ed. 15.95 (ISBN 0-03-045161-2). HR&W.

Barson, John, jt. auth. see Rolfe, Stan.

Barson, Kalman A., et al. Investigative Accounting: Techniques & Procedures for Determining the Reality Behind the Financial Statements. (Illus.). 224p. 1985. 34.50 (ISBN 0-442-21163-5). Van Nos Reinhold.

Barsotti, Charles. Kings Don't Carry Money. LC 81-67420. 128p. 1981. 8.95 (ISBN 0-396-08020-0). Dodd.

Barsoum, R. S., ed. Simplified Methods in Pressure Vessel Analysis, PVP-PB-029. (Pressure Vessel & Piping Division Ser.: Bk. No. G00137). 1978. 18.00 (ISBN 0-685-37581-1). ASME.

Barsov, A. S. Que el la Programacion Lineal. 112p. (Span.). 1977. pap. 2.45 (ISBN 0-8285-1458-5, Pub. by Mir Pubs USSR). Imported Pubns.

Barstad, H. The Religious Polemics of Amos. (Vetus Testamentum Supplement Ser.: No. 34). 224p. 1984. text ed. 35.50x (ISBN 90-04-07017-6, Pub. by E. J. Brill). Humanities.

Barstad, Noel, tr. see Gebser, Jean.

Barston, R. P. & Birnie, Patricia, eds. The Maritime Dimension. (Illus.). 272p. 1981. text ed. 27.50x (ISBN 0-04-341015-4); pap. text ed. 12.50x (ISBN 0-04-341016-2). Allen Unwin.

Barstow, Anne L. Married Priests & the Reforming Papacy: The 11th Century Debates. LC 82-7914. (Texts & Studies in Religion: Vol. 12). 288p. 1982. 49.95x (ISBN 0-88946-987-3). E Mellen.

Barstow, Charley. Hard Rider. (Orig.). 1981. pap. 1.95 (ISBN 0-505-51653-5, Pub. by Tower Bks). Dorchester Pub Co.

--Showdown Country. (Orig.). 1980. pap. 1.75 (ISBN 0-505-51491-5, Pub. by Tower Bks). Dorchester Pub Co.

Barstow, Charlie. Showdown Country. 208p. 1985. pap. 2.25 (ISBN 0-8439-2243-5, Leisure Bks). Dorchester Pub Co.

--Vengeance Breed. 224p. (Orig.). 1982. pap. 2.25 (ISBN 0-505-51768-X, Pub. by Tower Bks). Dorchester Pub Co.

Barstow, D. R. Knowledge-Based Program Construction. (Programming Language Ser.: Vol. 6). 262p. 1979. 28.50 (ISBN 0-444-00340-1, North Holland); pap. 17.50 (ISBN 0-444-00341-X). Elsevier.

Barstow, D. R., et al. Interactive Programming Environments. 1983. 37.95 (ISBN 0-07-003885-6). McGraw.

Barstow, David O., ed. The Threat of Nuclear Annihilation: A Psychotherapeutic View-A Special Issue of Pilgrimage. 72p. 1984. pap. 9.95 (ISBN 0-89885-213-7). Human Sci Pr.

Barstow, Frank. Beat the Casino. LC 79-54146. 1979. 13.95 (ISBN 0-935084-00-2); pap. 10.95 (ISBN 0-935084-01-0). Carlyle Assocs.

--Beat the Casino. 224p. 1984. pap. 7.95 (ISBN 0-671-49820-7). S&S.

Barstow, Mrs. Montagu see Orczy, Baroness.

Barstow, Mrs. Montagu see Orczy, Emmuska.

Barstow, Stan. An Enemy of the People. Lbsen, Henrick, ed. 1980. pap. 3.95 (ISBN 0-7145-3651-2). Riverrun NY.

--The Glad Eye & Other Stories. 224p. 1984. 14.95 (ISBN 0-7181-2440-5, Pub. by Michael Joseph). Merrimack Pub Cir.

Barsuhn, Rochelle N. Afraid. LC 82-4559. (What Does it Mean? Ser.). (Illus.). 32p. (gr. 1-2). 1982. PLB 5.95 (ISBN 0-89565-235-8, 4894, Pub. by Childs World). Standard Pub.

--Angry. LC 82-4570. (What Does it Mean? Ser.). (Illus.). 32p. (gr. 1-2). 1982. PLB 5.95 (ISBN 0-89565-234-X, 4895, Pub. by Childs World). Standard Pub.

--Feeling Afraid. LC 82-19946. (What's in a Word Ser.). (Illus.). (gr. 1-2). 1983. PLB 7.45 (ISBN 0-89565-246-3). Childs World.

--Feeling Afraid. (What's In a Word Ser.). (Illus.). 32p. (ps-2). 1983. 9.95 (ISBN 0-516-06322-7). Childrens.

--Feeling Angry. LC 82-19911. (What's in a Word Ser.). (Illus.). 32p. (gr. 1-2). 1983. PLB 7.45 (ISBN 0-89565-244-7). Childs World.

--Feeling Angry. (What's In a Word?). (Illus.). 32p. (ps-2). 1983. 9.95 (ISBN 0-516-06321-9). Childrens.

--The Winds Obey Him! LC 83-7344. (Illus.). 32p. (gr. 3-4). 1983. PLB 4.95 (ISBN 0-89693-216-8). Dandelion Hse.

Barsy, Kalman. Del Nacimiento de la Isla de Boriken. LC 82-83288. (Coleccion Sur Ser.). (Illus.). 76p. (Span.). 1982. pap. 5.95 (ISBN 0-940238-01-2). Ediciones Huracan.

Bart, B. F. & Cook, R. F. The Legendary Sources of Flaubert's Saint Julian. LC 77-7892. 1977. 25.00x (ISBN 0-8020-5373-4). U of Toronto Pr.

Bart, Benjamin F. Flaubert. LC 67-27410. pap. 160.00 (ISBN 0-317-29209-9, 2022230). Bks Demand UMI.

Bart, Benjamin F., jt. auth. see Trapp, Frank.

Bart, H., et al. Minimal Factorization of Matrix & Operator Functions. (Operator Theory: Advances & Applications Ser.: No. 1). 236p. 1979. pap. 20.95x (ISBN 0-8176-1139-8). Birkhauser.

Bart, Joe. The Ten Dollar Book That Can Make You Rich. 1976. 10.00 (ISBN 0-8184-0232-6); lib. bdg. 10.00 (ISBN 0-685-69538-7). Lyle Stuart.

Bart, Kay. Chain to Freedom: A Collection of Links. LC 80-54067. 36p. 1981. 5.95 (ISBN 0-533-04891-5). Vantage.

Bart, Pauline & Frankel, Linda. The Student Sociologist's Handbook. 3rd ed. LC 80-13829. 1980. pap. text ed. 8.00 (ISBN 0-394-33302-0, RanC). Random.

--Student Sociologist's Handbook. 4th ed. 228p. 1986. pap. text ed. 8.00 (ISBN 0-394-35109-6, RanC). Random.

Bart, Pauline B. & O'Brien, Patricia H. Stopping Rape: Successful Survival Strategies. LC 85-6589. (Athene Ser.). 200p. 1985. 24.95 (ISBN 0-08-032814-8, Pub. by Aberdeen Scotland); pap. 10.95 (ISBN 0-08-032813-X, Pub. by Aberdeen Scotland). Pergamon.

Bart, Phil. Working Class Unity: The Role of Communists in the Chicago Federation of Labor, 1919-1923. 1975. pap. 0.40 (ISBN 0-87898-114-4). New Outlook.

Bart, Philip, et al, eds. Highlights of a Fighting History: Sixty Years of the Communist Party, U. S. A. LC 79-14000. (Illus.). 540p. 1979. 15.00 (ISBN 0-7178-0559-X); pap. 5.25 (ISBN 0-7178-0502-6). Intl Pubs Co.

Bart, Polly, et al, eds. Design Through Knowledge. 500p. 1982. 33.00 (ISBN 0-939922-04-5). EDRA.

Bart, Sheldon. Ruby Sweetwater & the Ringo Kid. LC 80-14683. 384p. 1980. 11.95 (ISBN 0-07-003872-4). McGraw.

Bart, William M. & Wong, Martin R., eds. Psychology of School Learning, 2 vols. Incl. Vol. 1. Environmentalism. 249p. pap. text ed. 9.95x (ISBN 0-8422-0447-4); Vol. 2. Nativism & Interactionism. 29.50x (ISBN 0-8422-5210-X); pap. text ed. 9.95x (ISBN 0-8422-0466-0). 1974. pap. Irvington.

Barta, B., et al. Fertility, Female Employment & Policy Measures in Hungary. International Labour Office Staff, ed. (Women, Work & Development Ser.: No. 6). viii, 88p. (Orig.). 1984. pap. 8.55 (ISBN 92-2-103594-8). Intl Labour Office.

Barta, B. Z. & Raab, B. H., eds. The Impact of Informatics on Vocational & Continuing Education: Proceedings of the IFIP WG 3.4 Working Conference, Jerusalem, Israel, 14-18 May, 1984. 240p. 1985. 35.25 (ISBN 0-444-87663-4, North-Holland). Elsevier.

Barta, Barnabas, et al. Fertility, Female Employment & Policy Measures in Hungary. (Wpmen, Work, & Development Ser.: No. 6). 88p. 1984. pap. text ed. 8.55 (ISBN 92-2-103624-3, ILO282, ILO). Unipub.

Barta, E. Market Research Reports & Industry Surveys. 68p. 1982. pap. 39.00x (ISBN 0-902914-63-4, Pub. by Brit Lib England). State Mutual Bk.

Barta, Ernie. Sailing the "Annapolis Way". Senko, Peggy, ed. (Illus.). 160p. 1984. pap. 9.95 (ISBN 0-8117-2262-7). Stackpole.

Barta, Ginevera. Metric Cooking for Beginners. LC 78-6737. (Illus.). 95p. (gr. 5-9). 1978. PLB 10.95 (ISBN 0-89490-009-9). Enslow Pubs.

Barta, Ota. Laboratory Techniques of Veterinary Clinical Immunology. (Illus.). 202p. 1984. spiral binding 22.50x (ISBN 0-398-04980-7). C C Thomas.

Bar-Tal, Daniel & Saxe, Leonard. Social Psychology of Education: Theory & Research. LC 77-28746. 384p. 1978. text ed. 16.95x (ISBN 0-470-26306-7). Halsted Pr.

Bartalini. Opera Psychotherapy. (Illus.). 88p. 1981. 10.00 (ISBN 0-682-49703-7). Exposition Pr FL.

Bartas, Guillaume D. Du see Du Bartas, Guillaume D.

Bartas, Jolanda & Spicer, D. G. Latin American Costumes Illustrated with Plates & Bibliography. (Latin America Ser.). 1979. lib. bdg. 86.95 (ISBN 0-8490-2955-4). Gordon Pr.

Bartas, Sieur Du see Du Saluste, Guillaume & Du Bartas, Sieur.

Bartch, Marian & Mallett, Jerry. Reading Rousers. 1980. pap. 9.95 (ISBN 0-673-16424-1). Scott F.

Bartch, Marian, jt. auth. see Mallett, Jerry J.

Bartch, Marian R. & Mallett, Jerry J. Poor Old Ernie. (Bartch & Mallett's Ernie Ser.: Bk. 2). 1983. 7.95 (ISBN 0-8062-2108-9). Carlton.

Bartch, Marian R., jt. auth. see Mallett, Jerry J.

Bartch, Marion, jt. auth. see Mallett, Jerry J.

Bartch-Mallett. Good Old Ernie. (Bartch & Mallett's Ernie Ser.: Bk. 1). 7.95 (ISBN 0-8062-0932-1). Carlton.

Barteau, F. Les Romans de Tristan et Iseut: Introduction a une lecture plurielle. new ed. (Collection L). 288p. (Orig., Fr.). 1972. pap. 19.95 (ISBN 2-03-036007-4). Larousse.

Bartee, Alice F. Cases Lost, Causes Won: The Supreme Court & the Judicial Process. LC 83-61609. 207p. 1984. pap. text ed. 10.95 (ISBN 0-312-12337-X). St Martin.

Bartee, Thomas. Digital Computer Fundamentals. 5th ed. (Illus.). 576p. 1980. text ed. 33.95 (ISBN 0-07-003894-5). McGraw.

Bartee, Thomas, ed. Data Communication Network & Systems. LC 84-51868. 39.95 (ISBN 0-672-22235-3). Sams.

Bartee, Thomas C. BASIC Computer Programming. 2nd ed. 368p. 1985. pap. text ed. 20.50 scp (ISBN 0-06-040519-8, HarpC). Har-Row.

--Introduction to Computer Science. 1974. 38.95 (ISBN 0-07-003880-5). McGraw.

--Learning BASIC on the IBM PCjr. 372p. 1984. pap. text ed. 18.70 scp (ISBN 0-06-040521-X, HarpC). Har-Row.

Bartee, Tom. Data Communications, Networks & Systems. Date not set. 39.95 (ISBN 0-672-22407-0, 22235). Sams.

Bartek, Edward J. Mind of Future Man. 106p. 1965. pap. 6.95 (ISBN 0-9609866-4-2). Selene Bks.

--The Mind of Future Man. rev. ed. (Illus.). 106p. 1977. pap. text ed. 6.95 (ISBN 0-317-18439-3). Trinity Bks.

--Unifying Principles of the Mind. 178p. (Orig.). 1969. pap. 8.95 (ISBN 0-9609866-5-0). Selene Bks.

Bartel, Bonnie. Night the Animals Talked. 1982. pap. 3.15 (ISBN 0-89536-551-0). CSS of Ohio.

Bartel, C. R. Instructional Analysis & Materials Development. 1977. 18.95 (ISBN 0-8269-4273-3). Am Technical.

Bartel, Constance. A Woman Like That. 432p. (Orig.). 1985. pap. 3.95 (ISBN 0-445-20120-7, Pub. by Popular Lib). Warner Bks.

Bartel, D. Advances in Bioengineering: 1983. 1983. pap. text ed. 34.00 (ISBN 0-317-02540-6, H00276). ASME.

Bartel, Floyd. A New Look at Church Growth. LC 79-53523. 1979. pap. 2.95 (ISBN 0-87303-027-3). Faith & Life.

Bartel, Grace H. David & Eileen. 1985. pap. 3.95 (ISBN 0-8100-0202-7, 17N1620). Northwest Pub.

Bartel, Janice R. & Belt, Sage C. A Guide to Botanical Resources of Southern California. (Illus.). 88p. 1977. 2.00 (ISBN 0-938644-13-0). Nat Hist Mus.

Bartel, Klaus J. German Literary History, Seventeen Seventy-Seven to Eighteen Thirty Five: An Annotated Bibliography. (Germanic Studies in America: Vol. 22). 227p. 1976. 26.75 (ISBN 3-261-01854-2). P Lang Pubs.

Bartel, N., ed. Supernovae As Distance Indicators. (Lecture Notes in Physics: Vol. 224). vi, 226p. 1985. pap. 13.70 (ISBN 0-387-15206-7). Springer-Verlag.

Bartel, Nettie R., jt. auth. see Hammill, Donald D.

Bartel, Ranier. Ideas for Use on Your Commodore. Dykema, Greg, tr. from Ger. 225p. (Orig.). 1984. pap. text ed. 12.95 (ISBN 0-916439-07-0). Abacus Soft.

--Science & Engineering for the Commodore. Dykema, Greg, tr. from Ger. 343p. (Orig.). 1985. pap. text ed. 19.95 (ISBN 0-916439-09-7). Abacus Soft.

Bartel, Richard D., ed. & intro. by. The Challenge of Economics: Readings from "Challenge" the Magazine of Economic Affairs. LC 83-27108. 320p. 1984. pap. 9.95 (ISBN 0-87332-252-5). M E Sharpe.

Bartel, Roland. Metaphors & Symbols: Forays into Language. 83p. 1983. pap. 6.50 (ISBN 0-8141-3147-6). NCTE.

Bartela, Robert. Credit Management. LC 67-11256. (Illus.). pap. 124.00 (ISBN 0-317-10062-9, 2012391). Bks Demand UMI.

Bartelds, G. & Schliekelmann, R. J., eds. Progress in Advanced Materials & Processes Durability, Reliability & Quality Control: Proceedings of the Sixth International European Chapter Conference of the Society for the Advancement of Material & Process Engineering, Scheveningen, The Netherlands May 28-30, 1985. (Materials Science Monographs: No. 29). 310p. 1985. 61.00 (ISBN 0-444-42499-7). Elsevier.

Bartell, D. P., jt. auth. see Neece, K. C.

Bartell, Don G., ed. Paper Coating Additives: Description of Functional Properties & Lists of Available Products. (TAPPI Press Report). 60p. 1978. 24.95 (ISBN 0-317-36028-0, 01-02 R072). TAPPI.

Bartell, Ernest. Costs & Benefits of Catholic Elementary & Secondary Schools. 1969. pap. 14.95 (ISBN 0-268-00336-X). U of Notre Dame Pr.

Bartell, Joyce J., ed. see Center for Study of the American Experience.

Bartell, Steven M., jt. ed. see Fontaine, Thomas D., III.

Bartels, Cornelius P. & Ketellapper, Ronald H. Exploratory & Explanatory Statistical Analysis of Spatial Data. 1979. lib. bdg. 34.50 (ISBN 0-89838-004-9, Pub. by Martinus Nijhoff Netherlands). Kluwer Academic.

Bartels, Francis L. The Roots of Ghana Methodism. LC 64-21525. pap. 95.50 (ISBN 0-317-08427-5, 2050799). Bks Demand UMI.

Bartels, J. see Fluegge, E.

Bartels, M. Bibliography on Transnational Law of Natural Resources, Vol. 3. 227p. 1983. 28.00 (ISBN 90-65-4404-10, Pub. by Kluwer Law Netherlands). Kluwer Academic.

Bartels, Martin. Selbstbewusstsein und Unbewusstes: Studien Zu Freud und Heidegger. (Quellen und Studien Zur Philosophie Ser.: Vol. 10). 1976. 36.40x (ISBN 3-11-005778-6). De Gruyter.

Bartels, R., et al, trs. see Stoer, J. & Bulirsch, R.

Bartels, Robert. Global Development & Marketing. LC 80-11542. (Marketing Ser.). 128p. 1984. pap. text ed. 19.50 (ISBN 0-471-84150-1, Pub. by Grid). Wiley.

--The History of Marketing Thought. 2nd ed. LC 76-6015. (Marketing Ser.). 1976. text ed. 29.95 (ISBN 0-88244-085-3). Pub Horizons.

--Marketing Literature. Assael, Henry, ed. LC 78-228. (Century of Marketing Ser.). 1978. lib. bdg. 43.00x (ISBN 0-405-11165-7). Ayer Co Pubs.

--Marketing Theory & Metatheory. LC 72-105536. Repr. of 1970 ed. 77.50 (ISBN 0-8357-9035-5, 2017789). Bks Demand UMI.

Bartels, Robert, ed. Comparative Marketing: Wholesaling in Fifteen Countries. LC 82-25149. (Illus.). xii, 317p. 1963. lib. bdg. 39.75x (ISBN 0-313-23838-3, BARC). Greenwood.

Bartels, Susan L. Step Carefully in Night Grass. LC 74-75750. 55p. 1974. 5.95 (ISBN 0-910244-76-6). Blair.

Bartels-De Vries, Tineke & Van Zon, Egbert. Your Pony Book. (Illus.). 96p. 1982. pap. text ed. 7.95 (ISBN 0-8065-0794-2). Citadel Pr.

Barten, H. F., jt. tr. see Richtie, J. M.

Barten, Harvey H. & Barten, Sybil S., eds. Children & Their Parents in Brief Therapy. LC 72-10161. 323p. 1973. text ed. 26.95 (ISBN 0-87705-082-1). Human Sci Pr.

Barten, Harvey H. & Bellak, Leopold, eds. Progress in Community Mental Health, Vol. 2. LC 73-6067. 288p. 1972. 41.00 (ISBN 0-8089-0747-6, 790440). Grune.
Barten, Harvey H., jt. ed. see Bellak, Leopold.
Barten, Sybil S. & Franklin, Margery B., eds. Developmental Processes: Heinz Werner's Selected Writings, 2 vols. LC 77-92187. 562p. (Orig.). 1978. Set. text ed. 80.00 (ISBN 0-8236-8405-9). Vol. 1:General Theory & Perceptual Experience (ISBN 0-8236-1250-3). Vol. 2:Cognition, Language & Symbolization (ISBN 0-8236-1251-1). Intl Univs Pr.
Barten, Sybil S., jt. ed. see Barten, Harvey H.
Barten, Sybil S., jt. ed. see Franklin, Margery B.
Bartenev, G. M. & Lavrentev, V. V. Friction & Wear of Polymers. (Tribilogy Ser.: Vol. 6). 320p. 1981. 74.50 (ISBN 0-444-42000-2). Elsevier.
Bartenev, G. M. & Zuyev, Yu. S. Strength & Failure of Visco-Elastic Materials. 1968. 72.00 (ISBN 0-08-012183-7). Pergamon.
Bartenieff, I. & Lewis, D. Body Movement: Coping with the Environment. 304p. 1980. 45.25 (ISBN 0-677-05500-5). Gordon.
Bartenieff, Irmgard, et al. Four Adaptations of Effort Theory in Research & Teaching. LC 73-47570. (Illus.). viii, 72p. 1970. pap. text ed. 8.70x (ISBN 0-932582-06-0). Dance Notation.
Barter, A. Scenes from Eighteenth Century Comedies. 1910. 15.00 (ISBN 0-8482-7405-9). Norwood Edns.
Barter, A. R. Learning Languages. 1970. 7.50 (ISBN 0-8022-2334-6). Philos Lib.
Barter, Amy. Elizabethan Lyrics. 1979. lib. bdg. 15.00 (ISBN 0-8495-0547-X). Arden Lib.
Barter, Judith A., jt. auth. see Trapp, Frank.
Barter, Judith A., et al. Decorative Arts at Amherst College. Trapp, Frank, ed. (Mead Museum Monographs: Vol. 3). 27p. 1982. pap. 3.00 (ISBN 0-914337-03-3). Mead Art Mus.
Barter Publishing. Cookbook Bartering. 20p. 1984. pap. text ed. 1.95 (ISBN 0-911617-49-3, Pub. by Barter Pub). Prosperity & Profits.
--Recipe Bartering. 1984. pap. text ed. 1.95 (ISBN 0-911617-06-X, Pub. by Barter Pub). Prosperity & Profits.
--Telephone Maintenence the Barter Way. 20p. 1984. pap. text ed. 1.75 (ISBN 0-317-06873-3, Pub. by Barter Pub). Prosperity & Profits.
Barter Publishing Research Division Staff. Barter Education, Schools, Workshops, Centers, etc. 30p. 1985. pap. text ed. 5.95 (ISBN 0-911617-40-X, Pub. by Barter Pub). Prosperity & Profits.
Barter Publishing Research Project. Barter Referral Directory: Craftperson's Edition. 300p. 1983. pap. text ed. 29.95 (ISBN 0-911617-60-4, Pub. by Barter Pub). Prosperity & Profits.
--Barter Referral Directory: International Business Edition. 300p. 1983. pap. text ed. 29.95 (ISBN 0-911617-61-2, Pub. by Barter Pub). Prosperity & Profits.
--Barter Referral Directory: Manufacturing Edition. 300p. 1983. pap. text ed. 29.95 (ISBN 0-911617-59-0, Pub. by Barter Pub). Prosperity & Profits.
--Barter Referral Directory: Small Business Edition. 300p. 1983. pap. text ed. 29.95 (ISBN 0-911617-64-7, Pub. by Barter Pub). Prosperity & Profits.
--Barter Referral Directory: Vacation Time Exchanges, Share-A-Transportation Edition. 300p. 1983. pap. text ed. 29.95 (ISBN 0-911617-58-2, Pub. by Barter Pub). Prosperity & Profits.
--Barter Referral Directory: Women's Edition. 300p. 1985. pap. text ed. 29.95 (ISBN 0-911617-63-9, Pub. by Barter Pub). Prosperity & Profits.
Barter Publishing Research Project Staff. Observations of a Barter Community: Report Number One. 10p. 1985. pap. text ed. 3.00 (ISBN 0-911617-38-8, Pub. by Barter Pub). Prosperity & Profits.
--Observations of a Barter Community: Report Number Two. 10p. 1985. pap. text ed. 3.00 (ISBN 0-911617-40-X, Pub. by Barter Pub). Prosperity & Profits.
Barter Publishing Staff. Barter Alert. LC 83-90679. 8p. 1983. pap. text ed. 7.95 (ISBN 0-911617-00-0, Pub. by Barter Pub); wkbk. 20 pgs. 5.95 (ISBN 0-911617-65-5). Prosperity & Profits.
--Barter Alert Workbook. 25p. 1984. pap. 4.50 (ISBN 0-911617-65-5, Pub. by Barter Pub). Prosperity & Profits.
--Barter Referral Directory: Black Business Edition. 300p. 1985. pap. text ed. 29.95 (ISBN 0-911617-62-0, Pub. by Barter Pub). Prosperity & Profits.
--Barter Tax References: A Bibliography. 25p. 1983. pap. text ed. 8.95 (ISBN 0-911617-57-4, Pub. by Barter Pub). Prosperity & Profits.
--Business Bartering: A Bibliography. LC 83-90677. 15p. 1983. pap. text ed. 7.95 (ISBN 0-911617-02-7, Pub. by Barter Pub). Prosperity & Profits.
--The Piggy Back Concept: Reference Pages. LC 83-90676. 10p. 1983. pap. text ed. 3.00 (ISBN 0-911617-03-5, Pub. by Barter Pub). Prosperity & Profits.
Barter Publishing Staff, ed. Barter Associations & Organizations Based in California & the West: A Directory. 25p. 1986. pap. 9.95 (ISBN 0-911617-07-8, Pub. by Barter Pub). Prosperity & Profits.
--Barter Associations & Organizations Based in Colorado & the South Central & Southwest States: A Directory. 50p. 1986. pap. 9.95 (ISBN 0-911617-08-6, Pub. by Barter Pub). Prosperity & Profits.
--Barter Associations & Organizations Based in the Great Lakes Area: A Directory. LC 83-90674. 50p. 1986. pap. 9.95 (ISBN 0-911617-12-4, Pub. by Barter Pub). Prosperity & Profits.
--Barter Associations & Organizations Based in the Middle Atlantic States: A Directory. 35p. 1986. pap. 9.95 (ISBN 0-911617-22-1, Pub. by Barter Pub). Prosperity & Profits.
--Barter Associations & Organizations Based in the Northeastern States: A Directory. 40p. 1986. pap. 9.95 (ISBN 0-911617-36-1, Pub. by Barter Pub). Prosperity & Profits.
--Barter Associations & Organizations Based in the Northwest & Great Plains States: A Directory. 50p. 1986. pap. 9.95 (ISBN 0-911617-05-1, Pub. by Barter Pub). Prosperity & Profits.
--Barter Associations & Organizations Based in the Southeastern States: A Directory. 30p. 1986. pap. 9.95 (ISBN 0-911617-21-3, Pub. by Barter Pub). Prosperity & Profits.
Barter, Tanya & Dunnigan, John. Bentwood. LC 84-60339. (Illus.). 48p. (Orig.). 1984. pap. 10.00 (ISBN 0-911517-02-2). Mus of Art RI.
Bartfai, P. & Tomko, J. Point Process Queuing Problems. (Colloquia Mathematics Ser.: Vol. 24). 426p. 1981. 76.75 (ISBN 0-444-85432-0). Elsevier.
Bartfeld, Fernande, ed. see Vigny, Alfred de.
Barth. The Modern Jew Faces Eternal Problems. 7.50 (ISBN 0-685-48595-1). Feldheim.
Barth & Deal. The Effective Principal: A Research Summary. Lucas, Pat, ed. 48p. 1982. pap. text ed. 5.00 (ISBN 0-88210-141-2). Natl Assn Principals.
Barth, A. Religions of India. 6th ed. Wood, J., tr. from Fr. 309p. 1980. Repr. of 1880 ed. 23.95x (ISBN 0-940500-64-7). Asia Bk Corp.
Barth, Alan. Government by Investigation. LC 71-122068. Repr. of 1955 ed. 25.00x (ISBN 0-678-03150-9). Kelley.
--The Price of Liberty. LC 74-176486. (Civil Liberties in American History Ser.). 1972. Repr. of 1961 ed. lib. bdg. 29.50 (ISBN 0-306-70416-1). Da Capo.
--The Rights of Free Men: An Essential Guide to Civil Liberties. Clayton, James E., ed. LC 83-47886. 352p. 1984. 17.95 (ISBN 0-394-52717-8). Knopf.
Barth, Alan, ed. Presidential Impeachment. 1974. pap. 6.50 (ISBN 0-8183-0134-1). Pub Aff Pr.
Barth, Bruno. Liebe und Ehe Im Altfranzosischen Fabel und in der Mittelhochdeutschen Novelle. 27.00 (ISBN 0-384-03465-9); pap. 22.00 (ISBN 0-685-02215-3). Johnson Repr.
Barth, Carl. Letters, 1961-1968. Fangmeier, Jurgen & Stoevesandt, Hinrich, eds. LC 80-29140. pap. 99.50 (ISBN 0-317-19815-7, 2023208). Bks Demand UMI.
Barth, Christina. Bodywork: Look Good, Keep Fit, Feel Great. (Illus.). 120p. 1985. 12.95 (ISBN 0-668-06397-1). Arco.
Barth, Claire H., ed. see Wingeier, Carol.
Barth, Diana, ed. see International Conference London, Aug. 29-30, 1973.
Barth, E. M. The Logic of the Articles in Traditional Philosophy: A Contribution to the Study of Conceptual Structures. Potts, P., tr. from Dutch. LC 73-94452. (Synthese Historical Library: No. 10). 520p. 1974. lib. bdg. 84.00 (ISBN 90-277-0350-7, Pub. by Reidel Holland). Kluwer Academic.
Barth, E. M. & Krabbe, E. C., eds. From Axiom to Dialogue. (Foundations of Communication Ser.). xi, 337p. 1982. 55.20x (ISBN 3-11-008489-9). De Gruyter.
Barth, E. M., jt. ed. see Marten, J.
Barth, Edna. Balder & the Mistletoe: A Story for the Winter Holidays. LC 78-4523. (Illus.). 64p. (gr. 3). 1979. 10.95 (ISBN 0-395-28956-4, Clarion). HM.
--A Christmas Feast: Poems, Sayings, Greetings, & Wishes. (Illus.). 176p. (gr. 3-6). 1979. 10.60 (ISBN 0-395-28965-3, Clarion). HM.
--Cupid & Psyche: A Love Story. LC 76-8821. (Illus.). 64p. (gr. 3-6). 1976. 10.95 (ISBN 0-395-28840-1, Clarion). HM.
--Hearts, Cupids & Red Roses. LC 73-7128. (Illus.). 64p. (gr. 3-6). 11.95 (ISBN 0-395-28841-X, Clarion). HM.
--Hearts, Cupids, & Red Roses: The Story of the Valentine Symbols. LC 73-7128. (Illus.). 64p. (gr. 3-6). 1982. pap. 4.95 (ISBN 0-89919-036-7, Clarion). HM.
--Holly, Reindeer, & Colored Lights: The Story of the Christmas Symbols. LC 71-157731. (Illus.). 96p. (gr. 3-6). 1981. pap. 4.95 (ISBN 0-89919-037-5, Clarion). HM.
--Holly, Reindeer, & Colored Lights: The Story of the Christmas Symbols. LC 71-157731. (Illus.). 96p. (gr. 3-6). 1971. 8.95 (ISBN 0-395-28842-8, Clarion). HM.
--I'm Nobody, Who Are You: The Story of Emily Dickinson. LC 72-129211. (Illus.). 128p. (gr. 3-6). 1971. 10.95 (ISBN 0-395-28843-6, Clarion). HM.
--Jack O'Lantern. LC 73-20194. (Illus.). 48p. (ps-3). 1974. 8.95 (ISBN 0-395-28763-4, Clarion); pap. 3.95 (ISBN 0-89919-123-1). HM.
--Lilies, Rabbits, & Painted Eggs: The Story of the Easter Symbols. LC 74-79033. (Illus.). (gr. 3-6). 1970. 8.95 (ISBN 0-395-28844-4, Clarion). HM.
--Lilies, Rabbits & Painted Eggs: The Story of the Easter Symbols. (Illus.). 64p. (gr. 3-6). 1981. pap. 4.95 (ISBN 0-395-30550-0, Clarion). HM.
--Shamrocks, Harps, & Shillelaghs: The Story of the St. Patrick's Day Symbols. LC 77-369. (Illus.). 96p. (gr. 3-6). 1982. pap. 4.95 (ISBN 0-89919-038-3, Clarion). HM.
--Shamrocks, Harps, & Shillelaghs: The Story of the St. Patrick's Day Symbols. LC 77-369. (Illus.). 96p. (gr. 3-6). 1977. 9.95 (ISBN 0-395-28845-2, Clarion). HM.
--Turkeys, Pilgrims, & Indian Corn: The Story of the Thanksgiving Symbols. LC 75-4703. (Illus.). 96p. (gr. 3-6). 1981. pap. 4.95 (ISBN 0-89919-039-1, Clarion). HM.
--Turkeys, Pilgrims, & Indian Corn: The Story of the Thanksgiving Symbols. LC 75-4703. (Illus.). 96p. (gr. 3-6). 1975. 12.95 (ISBN 0-395-28846-0, Clarion). HM.
--Witches, Pumpkins, & Grinning Ghosts: The Story of the Halloween Symbols. LC 72-75705. (Illus.). 96p. (gr. 3-6). 1981. pap. 3.95 (ISBN 0-89919-040-5, Clarion). HM.
--Witches, Pumpkins & Grinning Ghosts: The Story of the Halloween Symbols. LC 72-75705. (Illus.). 96p. (gr. 3-6). 1972. 8.95 (ISBN 0-395-28847-9, Clarion). HM.
Barth, Edna, illus. Jack-O-Lantern. 48p. (ps-3). 1982. pap. 3.95 (ISBN 0-89919-123-1, Clarion). HM.
Barth, Edwin J. Asphalt: Science & Technology. (Illus.). 720p. 1962. 160.75 (ISBN 0-677-00040-5). Gordon.
Barth, F. G., ed. Neurobiology of Arachnids. (Illus.). 400p. 1985. 69.50 (ISBN 0-387-15303-9). Springer-Verlag.
Barth, Frederick. The Last Wali of Swat. 225p. 1985. 30.00 (ISBN 0-231-06162-5). Columbia U Pr.
Barth, Fredrik. Features of Person & Society in Swat-Collected Essays on Pathans: Selected Essays of Frederik Barth, Vol. II. (International Library of Anthropology Ser.). 208p. 1981. 33.00x (ISBN 0-7100-0620-9). Routledge & Kegan.
--Human Resources: Social & Cultural Features of the Jebel Marra Project Area. (Bergen Studies in Social Anthropology: No. 1). 97p. (Orig.). 1985. pap. text ed. 7.95x (ISBN 0-936508-50-7, Pub. by Dept Soc Anthropology, Unuversity of Bergen, Norway). Barber Pr.
--Nomads of South Persia: The Basseri Tribe of the Khamseh Confederacy. (Series in Anthropology). 161p. 1968. pap. 7.95 (ISBN 0-316-08245-7). Little.
--Political Leadership among Swat Pathans. (London School of Economics Monographs on Social Anthropology: No. 19). 144p. 1965. pap. 16.50 (ISBN 0-485-19619-0, Pub. by Athlone Pr Ltd). Longwood Pub Group.
--Principles of Social Organization in Southern Kurdistan. LC 77-87641. Repr. of 1953 ed. 16.50 (ISBN 0-404-16423-4). AMS Pr.
--Ritual & Knowledge among the Baktaman of New Guinea. LC 74-19572. (Illus.). pap. 74.00 (ISBN 0-317-11336-4, 2021979). Bks Demand UMI.
--Selected Essays of Fredrik Barth: Process & Form in Social Life. (International Library of Anthropology). 1981. 35.00x (ISBN 0-7100-0720-5). Routledge & Kegan.
--Sohar: Culture & Society in an Omani Town. LC 82-9925. 304p. 1983. 26.00x (ISBN 0-8018-2840-6). Johns Hopkins.
Barth, Fredrik, ed. Ethnic Groups & Boundaries: The Social Organization of Culture Difference. (Series in Anthropology). 153p. 1969. pap. 8.95 (ISBN 0-316-08246-5). Little.
Barth, Friedrich G. Insects & Flowers: The Biology of a Partnership. Biederman-Thorson, M. A., tr. LC 84-9887. (Illus.). 309p. 1985. 35.00x (ISBN 0-691-08368-1). Princeton U Pr.
Barth, Gunter, ed. see Bensell, Royal A.
Barth, Gunther. City People. (Illus.). 1980. 27.50x (ISBN 0-19-502755-8). Oxford U Pr.
--City People: The Rise of Modern City Culture in Nineteenth-Century America. (Illus.). 1980. pap. 8.95 (ISBN 0-19-503194-6, GB 703, GB). Oxford U Pr.
Barth, H. The Idea of Order: Contributions to a Philosophy of Politics. Hankamer, Ernest W. & Newell, William M., trs. from Ger. 209p. 1960. 24.00 (ISBN 90-277-0001-X, Pub. by Reidel Holland). Kluwer Academic.
Barth, Hans. Truth & Ideology. LC 74-81430. Orig. Title: Wahrheit und Ideologie. 1977. 29.50x (ISBN 0-520-02820-1). U of Cal Pr.
--Wahrheit und Ideologie: Truth & Ideology. LC 74-25738. (European Sociology Ser.). 352p. 1975. Repr. 25.50x (ISBN 0-405-06494-2). Ayer Co Pubs.
Barth, Heinrich, ed. Collection of Vocabularies of Central African Languages, 2 vols. 1971. Repr. of 1862 ed. Set. 120.00x (ISBN 0-7146-1914-0, F Cass Co). Biblio Dist.
--Travels & Discoveries in North & Central Africa, 3 vols. 1965. Repr. of 1857 ed. 185.00x set (ISBN 0-7146-1790-3, F Cass Co). Biblio Dist.
Barth, Howard G., et al, eds. Modern Methods of Particle Size Analysis. Elving, P. J. & Winefordner, J. D. LC 84-3630. (Chemical Analysis: A Series of Monographs on Analytical Chemistry & its Applications: 1-075). 309p. 1984. text ed. 55.00x (ISBN 0-471-87571-6, Pub. by Wiley Interscience). Wiley.
Barth, J. R. The Symbolic Imagination: Coleridge & the Romantic Tradition. LC 76-44333. (Princeton Essays in Literature). 1977. 22.00 (ISBN 0-691-06320-6). Princeton U Pr.
Barth, J. Robert. Coleridge & Christian Doctrine. LC 75-75426. 1969. text ed. 16.50x (ISBN 0-674-13691-8). Harvard U Pr.
Barth, J. Robert, ed. Religious Perspectives in Faulkner's Fiction: Yoknapatawpha & Beyond. LC 75-185896. 244p. 1972. pap. 6.95x (ISBN 0-268-00512-5). U of Notre Dame Pr.
Barth, Jack, jt. auth. see Kessler, Stephen.
Barth, James L. Elementary & Junior High-Middle School Social Studies Curriculum, Activities, & Materials. 2nd ed. (Illus.). 320p. 1983. pap. text ed. 14.25 (ISBN 0-8191-3197-0). U Pr of Amer.
--Secondary Social Studies Curriculum, Activities, & Materials. 342p. (Orig.). 1984. pap. text ed. 16.00 (ISBN 0-8191-3797-9). U Pr of Amer.
Barth, James L. & Shermis, S. Samuel. Methods of Instruction in Social Studies Education. 2nd ed. LC 84-7221. 352p. 1984. wkbk. 18.50 (ISBN 0-8191-3980-7). U Pr of Amer.
Barth, James L., et al. Principles of Social Studies: The Why, What & How of Social Studies Instruction. 2nd ed. 194p. 1984. pap. text ed. 13.00 (ISBN 0-8191-3724-3). U Pr of Amer.
Barth, Jeffrey T., jt. auth. see Jarvis, Paul E.
Barth, John. Chimera. 1978. pap. 2.95 (ISBN 0-449-23797-4, Crest). Fawcett.
--Chimera. 1972. 12.95 (ISBN 0-394-48139-9). Random.
--Don't Count on It: A Note on the Number of the 1001 Nights. 40p. 1984. deluxe ed. 75.00 Deluxe Signe (ISBN 0-935716-31-9). Lord John.
--End of the Road. 1969. pap. 3.95 (ISBN 0-553-24276-8). Bantam.
--The Floating Opera. 256p. 1972. pap. 3.95 (ISBN 0-553-24098-6). Bantam.
--The Friday Book: Essays & Other Nonfiction. 304p. 1984. 17.95 (ISBN 0-399-12997-9, Putnam); pap. 8.95 (ISBN 0-399-51209-8). Putnam Pub Group.
--Giles Goat-Boy. 1978. pap. 2.50 (ISBN 0-449-23524-6, Crest). Fawcett.
--Giles Goat-Boy or, the Revised New Syllabus. LC 66-15666. Limited edition 25.00 (ISBN 0-385-07364-X). Doubleday.
--Letters. 1982. pap. write for info. (ISBN 0-449-90090-8, Columbine). Fawcett.
--The Literature of Exhaustion. Bd. with The Literature of Replenishment. 100p. 1982. deluxe ed. 75.00 signed (ISBN 0-935716-16-5). Lord John.
Barth, Joseph. Art of Staying Sane. facs. ed. LC 70-117757. (Essay Index Reprint Ser). 1948. 18.00 (ISBN 0-8369-1783-9). Ayer Co Pubs.
Barth, Jurgen. Porsche Pocket History. (Pocket History Ser.). (Illus.). 66p. (Orig.). 1982. pap. 5.95 (ISBN 88-85058-16-7, Pub. by Automobilia Italy). Motorbooks Intl.
Barth, Jurgen, jt. auth. see Boschen, Lothar.
Barth, Karl. Action in Waiting. Bd. with Joy in the Lord. Blumhardt, Christoph. LC 75-90295. 80p. 1969. pap. 3.50 (ISBN 0-87486-203-5). Plough.
--Anselm: Fides Quaerens Intellectum. Robertson, Ian W., tr. from Ger. LC 76-10795. (Pittsburgh Reprint Ser.: No. 2). 1984. text ed. 12.50 (ISBN 0-915138-09-3). Pickwick.
--The Christian Life. Bromiley, Geoffrey W., ed. LC 80-39942. 328p. 1981. 17.95 (ISBN 0-8028-3523-6). Eerdmans.
--Community, State & Church: Three Essays. 11.00 (ISBN 0-8446-1058-5). Peter Smith.
--Deliverance to the Captives. LC 78-12767. 1979. Repr. of 1978 ed. lib. bdg. 24.75x (ISBN 0-313-21179-5, BADC). Greenwood.
--Deliverance to the Captives. LC 61-7333. (Ministers Paperback Library Ser). 1978. pap. 4.95i (ISBN 0-06-060571-5, RD-267, HarpR). Har-Row.
--Epistle to the Romans. 6th ed. Hoskyns, Edwyn C., tr. 1968. pap. 12.95 (ISBN 0-19-500294-6, GB). Oxford U Pr.
--Ethics. 1981. 34.95 (ISBN 0-8164-0484-4, Pub. by Seabury). Winston Pr.
--Evangelical Theology: An Introduction. Foley, Grover, tr. LC 79-16735. 1979. pap. 5.95 (ISBN 0-8028-1819-6). Eerdmans.
--Great Promise. (Orig.). pap. 0.95 (ISBN 0-685-19404-3, 107, WL). Citadel Pr.
--Great Promise. LC 61-15239. 1963. 5.00 (ISBN 0-8022-0074-5). Philos Lib.
--Humanity of God. Weiser, Thomas & Thomas, John N., trs. LC 60-3479. 1960. pap. 6.95 (ISBN 0-8042-0612-0). John Knox.
--The Knowledge of God & the Service of God According to the Teaching of the Reformation: Recalling the Scottish Confession of 1560. LC 77-27187. (Gifford Lectures: 1937-38). Repr. of 1939 ed. 24.00 (ISBN 0-404-60495-1). AMS Pr.
--Learning Jesus Christ Through the Heidelberg Catechism. 144p. (Orig.). 1982. pap. 4.95 (ISBN 0-8028-1893-5). Eerdmans.

--Prayer. 2nd ed. Saliers, Don E., ed. Terrien, Sara F., tr. from German. LC 84-25782. 96p. 1985. pap. 7.95 (ISBN 0-664-24626-5). Westminster.
--Protestant Thought. facs. ed. LC 73-142606. (Essay Index Reprint Ser). 1959. 23.50 (ISBN 0-8369-2102-X). Ayer Co Pubs.
--The Resurrection of the Dead. Kastenbaum, Robert, ed. LC 76-19559. (Death and Dying Ser.). 1977. Repr. of 1933 ed. lib. bdg. 23.50x (ISBN 0-405-09555-4). Ayer Co Pubs.
--The Theology of Schleiermacher. Bromiley, Geoffrey W., tr. 287p. 1982. 13.95 (ISBN 0-8028-3565-1). Eerdmans.
--Wolfgang Amadeus Mozart. 48p. 1985. pap. 3.95 (ISBN 0-8028-0007-6). Eerdmans.
--The Word of God & the Word of Man. Horton, Douglas, tr. 1958. 12.50 (ISBN 0-8446-1599-4). Peter Smith.
Barth, Karl & Bultmann, Rudolf. Barth-Bultmann Letters, Nineteen Twenty-Two to Nineteen Sixty-Six. Bromiley, Geoffrey W., tr. 224p. 1981. 13.95 (ISBN 0-8028-3560-0). Eerdmans.
Barth, Karl & Zuckmayer, Carl. A Late Friendship: The Letters of Carl Zuckmayer & Karl Barth. Bromiley, Geoffrey W., tr. 80p. 1983. 8.95 (ISBN 0-8028-3574-0). Eerdmans.
Barth, Karl, et al. Christ & Adam: Man & Humanity in Romans Five. Small, T. A., tr. 96p. 1983. Repr. of 1957 ed. lib. bdg. 12.00 (ISBN 0-88254-864-6). Octagon.
Barth, Lewis M. Analysis of Vatican Thirty. 1973. 20.00x (ISBN 0-87820-400-8, Pub. by Hebrew Union). Ktav.
Barth, M. A. Bulletin of Religion, ISPP Vol. 1, No. 4. 60p. 1974. Repr. 2.00 (ISBN 0-88065-050-8, Pub. by Messers Today & Tomorrow Printers & Publishers India). Scholarly Pubns.
Barth, Markus. The People of God. (Journal for the Study of the New Testament, Supplement Ser.: No. 5). 100p. 1983. text ed. 15.95x (ISBN 0-905774-54-X, Pub. by JSOT Pr England); pap. text ed. 7.95x (ISBN 0-905774-55-8, Pub. by JSOT Pr England). Eisenbrauns.
Barth, Michael C. & Titus, James G. Greenhouse Effect & Sea Level Rise. 384p. 1984. 24.50 (ISBN 0-442-20991-6). Van Nos Reinhold.
Barth, Peter S. & Hunt, H. Allan. Workers' Compensation & Work-Related Illnesses & Diseases. 391p. 1980. pap. 12.50x (ISBN 0-262-52080-X). MIT Pr.
Barth, Peter S. & Hunt, H. Allen. Workers' Compensation & Work-Related Illnesses & Diseases. 1980. text ed. 47.50x (ISBN 0-262-02141-2). MIT Pr.
Barth, R. Carl, ed. Journal of the Johannes Schwalm Historical Association, Inc, Vol. 2, No. 5. 92p. (Orig.). 1985. pap. 8.00 (ISBN 0-939016-10-9). Johannes Schwalm Hist.
Barth, R. L. Forced-Marching to the Styx. (Poetry Chapbks.). 20p. 1983. pap. 2.50 (ISBN 0-912288-21-3, PER-17). Perivale Pr.
--Occasions. 1984. pap. 4.00 (ISBN 0-941150-18-6). Barth.
--To Be Brief: X Poems from the Latin. Barth, R. L., tr. from Latin. 8p. (Orig.). 1983. pap. 2.00 (ISBN 0-941150-08-9). Barth.
Barth, Richard. The Condo Kill. (Margaret Binton Mystery Ser.). 192p. 1985. 13.95 (ISBN 0-684-18474-5, ScribT). Scribner.
Barth, Robert H. & Broshears, Robert. The Invertebrate World. 1982. text ed. 37.95 (ISBN 0-03-013276-2, CBS C). SCP.
Barth, Roland S. Open Education & the American School. LC 72-80265. 1972. 8.95x (ISBN 0-87586-036-2). Agathon.
--Run School Run. LC 79-25686. (Illus.). 1980. text ed. 20.00x (ISBN 0-674-78036-1). Harvard U Pr.
--Run School Run. 288p. 1985. pap. text ed. 7.95x (ISBN 0-674-78037-X). Harvard U Pr.
Barth, Volker. Atlas of Diseases of the Breast. (Illus.). 1979. 99.95 (ISBN 0-8151-0418-9). Year Bk Med.
Barth, W. & Peters, C. A. Compact Complex Surfaces. (A Series of Modern Surveys in Mathematics, Band 4: Vol. 4). 320p. 1984. 38.00 (ISBN 0-317-04553-9). Springer-Verlag.
Bartha, Georges De see Duncan, Alastair & De Bartha, Georges.
Bartha, Richard, jt. auth. see Atlas, Ronald M.
Barthe, Joe De see De Barthe, Joe.
Barthel, Bruce, photos by. Skiing the Rockies. LC 80-65133. (Belding Imprint Ser.). (Illus.). 128p. (Text by Charlie Meyers). 1980. 32.50 (ISBN 0-912856-60-2). Graphic Arts Ctr.
Barthel, Diane L. Amana: From Pietist Sect to American Community. LC 83-14624. (Illus.). xvi, 222p. 1984. 19.95 (ISBN 0-8032-1181-3). U of Nebr Pr.
Barthel, Joan. A Death in California. 1982. pap. 4.50 (ISBN 0-440-12038-1). Dell.
Barthel, Manfred. The Jesuits: Legend & Truth of the Society of Jesus - Yesterday, Today, Tomorrow. Howson, Mark, tr. LC 84-60446. (Illus.). 384p. 1984. 17.95 (ISBN 0-688-02861-6). Morrow.
--What the Bible Really Says: Casting New Light on the Book of Books. Howson, Mark, tr. LC 81-18679. Orig. Title: Was Wirklich in der Bibel Steht. (Illus.). 416p. 1982. 15.50 (ISBN 0-688-00821-6). Morrow.
--What the Bible Really Says: Casting New Light on the Book of Books. Howson, Mark, tr. from Ger. LC 83-3001. (Illus.). 416p. 1983. pap. 7.25 (ISBN 0-688-01979-X, Quill). Morrow.
Barthel, Thomas. The Eighth Land: The Polynesian Discovery & Settlement of Easter Island. Martin, Anneliese, tr. from Ger. LC 78-21945. 1978. text ed. 20.00x (ISBN 0-8248-0553-4). UH Pr.
Barthelemy-Madaule. Bergson et Teilhard de Chardin. 23.50 (ISBN 0-685-36604-9). French & Eur.
Barthelemy-Madaule, Madeleine. Lamarck the Mythical Precursor: A Study of the Relations Between Science & Ideology. Shank, Michael, tr. from Fr. 176p. 1982. 22.50x (ISBN 0-262-02179-X). MIT Pr.
Barthell, Edward E., Jr. Gods & Goddesses of Ancient Greece. LC 72-129664. 1981. 49.50 (ISBN 0-87024-165-6). U of Miami Pr.
Barthelme, Donald. Amateurs. 184p. 1976. 7.95 (ISBN 0-374-10379-8). FS&G.
--City Life. 1978. pap. 2.25 (ISBN 0-671-82304-3). PB.
--Come Back, Dr. Caligari. 1971. pap. 6.70 (ISBN 0-316-08254-6). Little.
--The Dead Father. LC 75-25566. 177p. 1975. 7.95 (ISBN 0-374-13535-5). FS&G.
--The Dead Father. 1978. pap. 2.25 (ISBN 0-671-82305-1). PB.
--Great Days. 172p. 1979. 7.95 (ISBN 0-374-16628-5). FS&G.
--Great Days. 1980. pap. 2.50 (ISBN 0-671-83673-0). PB.
--Overnight to Many Distant Cities. LC 83-4594. 144p. 1983. 13.95 (ISBN 0-399-12868-9, Putnam). Putnam Pub Group.
--Overnight to Many Distant Cities. (Contemporary American Fiction Ser.). 176p. 1985. pap. 5.95 (ISBN 0-14-007580-1). Penguin.
--Paradise. 1986. 16.95 (ISBN 0-399-12921-9). Putnam Pub Group.
--Paradise. 256p. 1986. 16.95 (ISBN 0-399-12921-9). Putnam Pub Group.
--Presents. (Limited Edition Ser.). (Illus.). 1981. limited ed. 60.00 (ISBN 0-939722-01-1). Pressworks.
--Sadness. 1980. pap. 2.95 (ISBN 0-671-83204-2). PB.
--Sixty Stories. 464p. 1982. pap. 8.95 (ISBN 0-525-48018-8, 0869-260, Obelisk). Dutton.
--Snow White. LC 67-14324. 1967. pap. 5.95 (ISBN 0-689-70331-7, 191). Atheneum.
--Unspeakable Practices, Unnatural Acts. 1978. pap. 2.25 (ISBN 0-671-82306-X). PB.
Barthelme, Frederick. Moon Deluxe Stories. (Contemporary American Fiction Ser.). 240p. 1984. pap. 5.95 (ISBN 0-14-007130-X). Penguin.
--Second Marriage. 204p. 1984. 15.95 (ISBN 0-671-47441-3). S&S.
--Second Marriage. (Contemporary American Fiction Ser.). 224p. 1985. pap. 5.95 (ISBN 0-14-008274-3). Penguin.
--Tracer. 104p. 1985. 13.95 (ISBN 0-671-54253-2). S&S.
Barthelmeh, Volker. Street Murals. LC 82-80836. 1982. 20.00 (ISBN 0-394-52783-6); pap. 11.95 (ISBN 0-394-71196-3). Knopf.
Barthelmess, Harriet M. The Validity of Intelligence Test Elements. LC 70-176537. (Columbia University. Teachers College. Contributions to Education: No. 505). Repr. of 1931 ed. 22.50 (ISBN 0-404-55505-5). AMS Pr.
Barthels, Katherine, jt. auth. see Kreigbaum, Ellen.
Barthes, et al. Apparatus. Cha, Theresa H., ed. 448p. 1981. 25.95 (ISBN 0-934378-22-3); pap. 12.95 (ISBN 0-934378-21-5). Tanam Pr.
Barthes, R., et al. Structural Analysis & Biblical Exegesis. Johnson, Alfred M., Jr., tr. LC 74-31334. (Pittsburgh Theological Monographs: No. 3). 1974. pap. 10.25 (ISBN 0-915138-02-6). Pickwick.
Barthes, Roland. Arcimboldo (SOM) (Illus.). 188p. 1980. limited, numbered ed. 150.00 (ISBN 0-8478-5309-8). Rizzoli Intl.
--Barthes. 192p. 1975. 6.50 (ISBN 0-686-53928-1). French & Eur.
--A Barthes Reader. Sontag, Susan, ed. LC 80-26762. (Illus.). 495p. 1982. 20.00 (ISBN 0-8090-2815-8); pap. 8.95 (ISBN 0-8090-1394-0). Hill & Wang.
--Camera Lucida: Reflections on Photography. Howard, Richard, tr. (Illus.). 119p. 1981. 10.95 (ISBN 0-8090-3340-2); pap. 6.95 (ISBN 0-8090-1398-3). Hill & Wang.
--Critical Essays. Howard, Richard, tr. xxi, 279p. 1972. 20.95 (ISBN 0-8101-0370-2); pap. 9.95 (ISBN 0-8101-0589-6). Northwestern U Pr.
--Critique et Verite. 1966. 6.95 (ISBN 0-686-53929-X). French & Eur.
--Le Degre Zero de l'Ecriture. 1953. 9.95 (ISBN 0-686-53930-3); pap. 4.95 (ISBN 0-686-53931-1). French & Eur.
--The Eiffel Tower & Other Mythologies. Howard, Richard, tr. from Fr. 152p. 1979. 9.95 (ISBN 0-8090-4115-4); pap. 5.25 (ISBN 0-8090-1391-6). Hill & Wang.
--Elements of Semiology. Lavers, Annette & Smith, Colin, trs. from Fr. 111p. 1977. 8.95 (ISBN 0-8090-4180-4); pap. 3.95 (ISBN 0-8090-1383-5). Hill & Wang.
--L' Empire des Signes. (Illus.). 152p. 1970. 25.00 (ISBN 0-686-53933-8). French & Eur.
--The Empire of Signs. Howard, Richard, tr. (Illus.). 109p. 1982. 12.95 (ISBN 0-8090-4222-3); pap. 5.95 (ISBN 0-8090-1502-1). Hill & Wang.
--Essais Critiques. 1964. 16.95 (ISBN 0-686-53934-6). French & Eur.
--Et la Chine? 16p. 1976. 7.95 (ISBN 0-686-53935-4). French & Eur.
--The Fashion System. Ward, Matthew & Howard, Richard, trs. from Fr. 1983. 20.50 (ISBN 0-8090-4437-4); pap. 7.95 (ISBN 0-8090-1503-X). Hill & Wang.
--Fragments d'un Discours Amoureux. 280p. 1977. 17.50 (ISBN 0-686-53936-2). French & Eur.
--The Grain of the Voice. Coverdale, Linda, tr. (Illus.). 384p. 1985. 24.95 (ISBN 0-8090-5088-9, Pub. by Hill & Wang); pap. 9.95 (ISBN 0-8090-1521-8). FS&G.
--The Grain of the Voice: Interviews, 1962-1980. Coverdale, Linda, tr. from Fr. (Illus.). 320p. 1985. 24.95 (ISBN 0-8090-5088-9). Hill & Wang.
--Image-Music-Text. Heath, Stephen, tr. from Fr. LC 84-16821. 220p. 1978. 8.95 (ISBN 0-8090-5740-9); pap. 7.25 (ISBN 0-8090-1387-8). Hill & Wang.
--A Lover's Discourse: Fragments. Howard, Richard, tr. from Fr. LC 78-7794. 224p. 1978. 10.00 (ISBN 0-8090-6689-0); pap. 7.25 (ISBN 0-8090-1388-6). Hill & Wang.
--Michelet. (Illus.). 192p. 1954. 6.50 (ISBN 0-686-53937-0). French & Eur.
--Mythologies. 1957. 16.95 (ISBN 0-686-53938-9); pap. 5.95 (ISBN 0-686-53939-7). French & Eur.
--Mythologies. Lavers, Annette, tr. from Fr. LC 75-185427. 160p. 1972. pap. 4.25 (ISBN 0-8090-1369-X). Hill & Wang.
--Mythologies. 1983. 13.25 (ISBN 0-8446-5982-7). Peter Smith.
--New Critical Essays. Howard, Richard, tr. from Fr. 121p. 1980. 10.95 (ISBN 0-8090-7257-2); pap. 4.95 (ISBN 0-8090-1396-7). Hill & Wang.
--On Racine. 1983. pap. 7.95 (ISBN 0-933826-56-7). Performing Arts.
--Le Plaisir du Texte. 1973. 7.95 (ISBN 0-686-53940-0). French & Eur.
--The Pleasure of the Text. Miller, Richard, tr. from Fr. 80p. 1975. 5.95 (ISBN 0-8090-7722-1); pap. 5.25 (ISBN 0-8090-1380-0). Hill & Wang.
--The Responsibility of Forms. Howard, Richard, tr. (Illus.). 320p. 1985. 22.95 (ISBN 0-8090-8075-3, Pub by Hill & Wang); pap. 9.95 (ISBN 0-8090-1522-6). FS&G.
--The Responsibility of Forms: Critical Essays on Music, Art, & Representation. Howard, Richard, tr. from Fr. LC 84-12913. 320p. 1985. 22.95 (ISBN 0-8090-8075-3). Hill & Wang.
--Roland Barthes. Howard, Richard, tr. from Fr. (Illus.). 188p. 1977. 8.95 (ISBN 0-8090-8245-4); pap. 7.25 (ISBN 0-8090-1385-1). Hill & Wang.
--The Rustle of Language. Howard, Richard, tr. from Fr. 1985. 20.00 (ISBN 0-8090-8344-2), Hill & Wang.
--The Rustle of Language. Howard, Richard, tr. 320p. 1985. 20.00 (ISBN 0-8090-8344-2, Pub by Hill & Wang). S&G.
--S-Z. 280p. 1970. 16.95 (ISBN 0-686-53944-3); pap. 5.95 (ISBN 0-686-53945-1). French & Eur.
--S-Z. Miller, Richard, tr. from Fr. 271p. 1974. 10.95 (ISBN 0-8090-8375-2); pap. 7.95 (ISBN 0-8090-1377-0). Hill & Wang.
--Sade, Fourier, Loyola. 1971. 14.95 (ISBN 0-686-53941-9). French & Eur.
--Sade-Fourier-Loyola. Miller, Richard, tr. from Fr. 184p. 1976. 8.95 (ISBN 0-8090-8380-9); pap. 8.25 (ISBN 0-8090-1381-9). Hill & Wang.
--Sur Racine. 1963. 13.95 (ISBN 0-686-53942-7). French & Eur.
--Systemes de la Mode. 1967. 17.95 (ISBN 0-686-53943-5). French & Eur.
--La Tour Eiffel. 116p. 1964. 19.95 (ISBN 0-686-53946-X). French & Eur.
--Writing Degree Zero. Laver, Annette & Smith, Colin, trs. from Fr. 94p. 1977. 8.95 (ISBN 0-8090-9865-2); pap. 4.95 (ISBN 0-8090-1384-3). Hill & Wang.
Barthes, Roland, jt. auth. see Lambert, Yvon.
Barthes, Roland, et al. Ecrire Pour Quoi? Pour Qui. 1974. 6.95 (ISBN 0-686-53932-X). French & Eur.
--Analyse Structurale et Exegese Biblique. 128p. 1973. 17.50 (ISBN 0-686-53927-3). French & Eur.
Barthes, Ronald. The Fashion System. Ward, Matthew & Howard, Richard, trs. from Fr. 1983. 20.50 (ISBN 0-8090-4437-4). Hill & Wang.
Barthlet, John. The Pedegrewe of Heretiques. LC 79-76432. (English Experience Ser.: No. 76). 180p. 1969. Repr. of 1566 ed. 21.00 (ISBN 90-221-0076-6). Walter J Johnson.
Barthol, Robert G. Protect Yourself: A Self Defense Guide for Women-from Prevention to Counterattack. (Illus.). 1979. 13.95 (ISBN 0-13-731430-2, Spec); pap. 6.95 (ISBN 0-13-731422-1). P-H.
Barthold, Bonnie J. Black Time: Fiction of Africa, the Caribbean, & the United States. LC 80-24336. (Illus.). 224p. 1981. 22.00x (ISBN 0-300-02573-4). Yale U Pr.
Barthold, W. An Historical Geography of Iran. Bosworth, C. E., ed. LC 83-24548. (Modern Classics in Neareastern Studies). (Illus.). 275p. 1984. text ed. 35.00x (ISBN 0-691-05418-5). Princeton U Pr.
Barthold, Walter. Attorney's Guide to Effective Discovery Techniques. 304p. 1974. 26.50 (ISBN 0-13-050484-X, Busn). P-H.
Bartholdy, Paul, ed. see Mendelssohn, Felix.
Bartholini, G., et al, eds. Epilepsy & Gaba Receptor Agonists: Basic & Therapeutic Research. (L. E. R. S. Monograph: Vol. 3). 496p. 1985. text ed. 29.50 (ISBN 0-88167-106-1). Raven.
--Gaba & Mood Disorders: Animal & Clinical Studies. (L. E. R. S. Monograph: Vol. 4). 1985. text ed. price not set (ISBN 0-88167-129-0). Raven.
Bartholmew, Barbara. Anne & Jay. 1982. pap. 1.75 (ISBN 0-451-11655-0, AE1655, Sig Vista). NAL.
Bartholomaeo, S., jt. auth. see Paulinus, A. S.
Bartholomaeus, Anglicus. Medieval Lore. Steele, R., ed. LC 66-23970. (Medieval Library). Repr. of 1926 ed. 18.50 (ISBN 0-8154-0016-0). Cooper Sq.
Bartholomay, Julia A. The Shield of Perseus: The Vision & Imagination of Howard Nemerov. LC 70-137851. 168p. 1972. 8.00 (ISBN 0-8130-0317-2). U Presses Fla.
Bartholomen, A. T., ed. see Butler, Samuel.
Bartholomeusz, Dennis. Macbeth & the Players. LC 69-10270. (Illus.). 1969. 49.50 (ISBN 0-521-06925-4, 4); pap. 13.95 (ISBN 0-521-29322-7). Cambridge U Pr.
--The Winter's Tale in Performance in England & America, 1611-1976. LC 81-24198. (Illus.). 324p. 1982. 49.50 (ISBN 0-521-24529-X). Cambridge U Pr.
Bartholomeusz, Mark. Boomerang. 1983. 7.50 (ISBN 0-8062-1792-8). Carlton.
Bartholomew. The Bible Tells Me. 1982. pap. 0.75 (ISBN 0-570-04074-4, 56-1377). Concordia.
--God Loves Me. 1982. pap. 0.75 (ISBN 0-570-04073-6, 56-1376). Concordia.
--I Come As A Brother. Moore, Mary-Margaret, ed. 177p. 1985. pap. 9.95 (ISBN 0-9614010-0-1, Dist. by Coleman Pub). High Mesa Pr.
--I Go To Church. 1982. pap. 0.75 (ISBN 0-570-04072-8, 56-1375). Concordia.
--Jesus Teaches Me. 1982. pap. 0.75 (ISBN 0-570-04071-X, 56-1374). Concordia.
--Jimmy & the White Lie. (Illus.). 32p. (gr. k-9). 1976. 3.95 (ISBN 0-570-03460-4, 56-1341). Concordia.
Bartholomew & Orr. Learning to Read & Make Mechanical Drawings. (gr. 7-9). 1982. pap. text ed. 7.08 (ISBN 0-02-664820-2). Bennett IL.
Bartholomew, A. T. Butleriana. 1932. 25.00 (ISBN 0-8274-1988-0). R West.
Bartholomew, A. T., ed. see Butler, Samuel.
Bartholomew, Alexander. Conservatories, Greenhouses & Garden Rooms. 1985. 22.95 (ISBN 0-03-002992-9). HR&W.
Bartholomew, Barbara. Child of Tomorrow. (Time Keeper Fantasy Stories Ser.: Bk. 2). 1985. pap. 2.50 (ISBN 0-451-13674-8, Sig Vista). NAL.
--Flight into the Unknown. (Making Choices Ser.: No. 2). (Orig.). (gr. 3-8). 1982. pap. 2.50 (ISBN 0-89191-561-3, 55616). Cook.
--The Great Gradepoint Mystery. LC 83-61239. (A Microkid Mystery Ser.: Bk. 1). (Illus.). 96p. (gr. 4-7). 1983. 9.95 (ISBN 0-02-708510-4). Macmillan.
--The Great Gradepoint Mystery. (Microkid Mystery Ser.: No. 1). 96p. (ps-5). 1985. pap. 2.50 (ISBN 0-380-69834-X, Camelot). Avon.
--Julie's Magic Moment. 160p. (Orig.). 1983. pap. 2.25 (ISBN 0-451-12628-9, Sig Vista). NAL.
--A Love Like This. (Magic Moments Ser.: No. 5). 1984. pap. 1.95 (ISBN 0-451-13207-6, Sig Vista). NAL.
--Lucky at Love. (Magic Moments Ser.: No. 12). 1985. pap. 2.50 (ISBN 0-451-13579-2, Sig Vista). NAL.
--Mirror Image. 1983. pap. 2.50 (ISBN 0-451-13985-2, Sig Vista). NAL.
--Someone New. (Magic Moments Ser.: No. 2). (gr. 7 up). 1984. pap. 1.95 (ISBN 0-451-12980-6, Sig Vista). NAL.
--Something Special. (Nightingale Paperbacks Ser.). 1984. lib. bdg. 11.95 (ISBN 0-8161-3730-7, Large Print Bks); pap. 9.95 (ISBN 0-8161-3696-3). G K Hall.
--The Time Keeper. 1985. pap. 2.50 (ISBN 0-451-13629-2, Sig). NAL.
--When Dreamers Cease to Dream. (Time Keeper Ser.: Bk. 3). 1985. pap. 2.50 (ISBN 0-451-13869-4, Sig Vista). NAL.
Bartholomew, Bruce, jt. auth. see Hung Ta, Chang.
Bartholomew, D. J. Stochastic Models for Social Processes. 3rd ed. (Wiley Ser. in Probability & Mathematical Statistics: Applied Probability & Statistics Section). 365p. 1982. 57.95x (ISBN 0-471-28040-2, Pub. by Wiley-Interscience). Wiley.
--Stochastic Models for Social Processes. 2nd ed. LC 73-2776. (Probability & Mathematical Statistics Ser.: Applied Probability & Statistic Section). 408p. 1974. 68.95 (ISBN 0-471-05451-8, Pub. by Wiley-Interscience). Wiley.
Bartholomew, David. Mathematical Methods in Social Science. LC 80-41593. (Handbook of Applicable Mathematics Ser.). 153p. 1981. 34.95 (ISBN 0-471-27932-3, Pub. by Wiley-Interscience); pap. 19.95 (ISBN 0-471-27933-1, Pub. by Wiley-Interscience). Wiley.

Bartholomew, David J. & Forbes, Andrew F. Statistical Techniques for Manpower Planning. LC 78-8604. (Probability & Mathematical Statistics: Applied Section Ser.). 288p. 1979. 69.95x (ISBN 0-471-99670-X, Pub. by Wiley-Interscience). Wiley.

Bartholomew, Doris. A Manual for Practical Grammars. 44p. 1976. pap. 2.50 (ISBN 0-88312-839-X); microfiche 1.93 (ISBN 0-88312-330-4). Summer Inst Ling.

Bartholomew, George A., jt. auth. see Peterson, Richard S.

Bartholomew, J. G. A Literary & Historical Atlas of Asia. Rhys, Ernest, ed. 226p. 1984. Repr. of 1984 ed. lib. bdg. 30.00 (ISBN 0-89987-972-1). DArby Books.

--A Literary Historical Atlas of Europe. 253p. 1983. Repr. of 1982 ed. lib. bdg. 30.00 (ISBN 0-89984-092-2). Century Bookbindery.

Bartholomew, James W. Laboratory Textbook & Experiments in Microbiology. rev. ed. 1977. pap. text ed. 10.95 (ISBN 0-8403-1722-0). Kendall-Hunt.

Bartholomew, John. The Random House Concise World Atlas. Date not set. 7.95 (ISBN 0-394-74007-6). Random.

--The Random House Mini World Atlas. Date not set. 4.95 (ISBN 0-394-74008-4). Random.

Bartholomew, Lloyd C. Hum Drum Thrum. (Illus.). 48p. 1981. pap. 5.00 (ISBN 0-933992-14-9). Coffee Break.

--Pursuit of Pinnacles. (Illus.). 44p. (Orig.). 1980. pap. 5.00 (ISBN 0-933992-10-6). Coffee Break.

--Sylvan Shadows. (Illus.). 52p. (Orig.). 1981. pap. 5.00 (ISBN 0-933992-13-0). Coffee Break.

Bartholomew, Mel. Cash from Square Foot Gardening. LC 85-50122. 192p. 1985. 17.95 (ISBN 0-88266-396-8, Pub. by Storey Pub); pap. 9.95 (ISBN 0-88266-395-X, Pub. by Storey Pub). Storey Comm Inc.

--Square Foot Gardening: A New Way to Garden in Less Space with Less Work. Halpin, Anne, ed. (Illus.). 288p. 1981. 14.95 (ISBN 0-87857-340-2); pap. 11.95 (ISBN 0-87857-341-0). Rodale Pr Inc.

Bartholomew, Mervin J., ed. The Grenville Event in the Appalachians & Related Topics. (Special Paper: No. 194). (Illus.). 1984. pap. 31.00 (ISBN 0-8137-2194-6). Geol Soc.

Bartholomew, Paul. American Constitutional Law, Vol. 2. 2nd ed. 398p. 1978. pap. 6.95 (ISBN 0-318-02926-X). Biblio Dist.

--Summaries of Leading Cases on the Constitution. 12th ed. Menez, Joseph, ed. 460p. 1983. pap. 8.95 (ISBN 0-8226-0364-0). Biblio Dist.

Bartholomew, Paul C. American Constitutional Law, Vol. 1. 2nd ed. 350p. 1978. pap. 6.95 (ISBN 0-318-02925-1). Biblio Dist.

--American Constitutional Law Vol. 1: Governmental Organization, Powers, & Procedure. 2nd ed. (Quality Paperback Ser.: No. 240). 350p. 1978. pap. 6.95 (ISBN 0-8226-0240-7). Littlefield.

--American Constitutional Law Vol. 2: Limitations on Government. 2nd ed. (Quality Paperback: No. 241). 398p. 1978. pap. 6.95 (ISBN 0-8226-0241-5). Littlefield.

--Indiana Third Congressional District: A Political History. 1970. 14.95 (ISBN 0-268-00346-7). U of Notre Dame Pr.

--The Irish Judiciary. LC 70-175024. 112p. (Orig.). 1972. pap. 3.95x (ISBN 0-268-00457-9). U of Notre Dame Pr.

--Public Administration. 3rd ed. (Quality Paperback Ser.: No. 29). (Orig.). 1977. Repr. of 1972 ed. 3.95 (ISBN 0-8226-0029-3). Littlefield.

--Summaries of Leading Cases on the Constitution. 12th ed. (Quality Paperback Ser.: No. 50). 460p. (Orig.). 1983. pap. text ed. 8.95 (ISBN 0-8226-0364-0). Littlefield.

--Summaries of Leading Cases on the Constitution. 11th ed. LC 81-5052. 448p. 1981. 15.00x (ISBN 0-8476-7012-0). Rowman.

Bartholomew, Paul C. & Menez, Joseph F. Summaries of Leading Cases on the Constitution. X12 ed. 464p. 1983. pap. 7.95x (ISBN 0-8226-0374-8). Rowman & Allanheld.

Bartholomew, Paul J. Shadows of Turning. LC 84-90202. 81p. 1985. 7.95 (ISBN 0-533-06253-5). Vantage.

Bartholomew, Ralph L. Gopher Hole Treasure Hunt. LC 77-80443. 120p. 1977. pap. 2.95 (ISBN 0-88207-479-2). Victor Bks.

Bartholomew, Ray, ed. see Hill, Richard B.

Bartholomew, Richard. Poems. (Writers Workshop Redbird Ser.). 1975. 8.00 (ISBN 0-88253-610-9); pap. text ed. 4.00 (ISBN 0-88253-609-5). Ind-US Inc.

--The Story of Siddhartha's Release. (Writers Workshop Redbird Ser.). 1975. 8.00 (ISBN 0-88253-648-6); pap. text ed. 4.00 (ISBN 0-88253-647-8). Ind-US Inc.

Bartholomew, Robert, et al. Child Care Centers: Indoor Lighting Outdoor Playspace. LC 72-90516. (Illus.). 1973. pap. 3.45 (ISBN 0-87868-099-3, J-57). Child Welfare.

Bartholomew, Wilmer T. Acoustics of Music. LC 79-17650. (Illus.). 1980. Repr. of 1942 ed. lib. bdg. 22.50x (ISBN 0-313-22087-5, BAAC). Greenwood.

Bartholomew-Biggs, Michael. The Essentials of Numerical Computation. (The Hatfield Poytechnic Computer Science Ser.). 241p. (Orig.). 1982. pap. text ed. 19.50x (ISBN 0-86238-029-4, Pub. by Chartwell-Bratt England). Brookfield Pub Co.

Bartholomew's Cartographic Staff, illus. Bartholomew World Atlas. rev. ed. (Illus.). 168p. 1982. 35.00 (ISBN 0-7028-0404-5). Hammond Inc.

Bartholomy, David. Sometimes You Just Have to Stand Naked: A Guide to Interesting Writing. (Illus.). 224p. 1983. pap. text ed. 12.95 (ISBN 0-13-822593-1). P-H.

Barthorp, Michael. The North-West Frontier: The Ramparts of British India 1839-1947. (Illus.). 192p. 1982. 17.95 (ISBN 0-7137-1133-7, Pub. by Blandford Pr England). Sterling.

--War on the Nile: Britain, Egypt & the Sudan 1882-1898. (Illus.). 190p. 1985. 18.95 (ISBN 0-7137-1310-0, Pub. by Blandford England). Sterling.

Barthou, Louis. Mirabeau. LC 72-7091. (Select Bibliographies Reprint Ser.). 1972. Repr. of 1913 ed. 24.50 (ISBN 0-8369-6923-5). Ayer Co Pubs.

Bartik, M. & Piskac, A., eds. Veterinary Toxicology. (Developments in Animal & Veterinary Science Ser.: Vol. 7). 346p. 1981. 72.50 (ISBN 0-444-99757-1). Elsevier.

Bartilucci, A. & Durgin, J. Giving Medications Correctly & Safely. rev. ed. 1978. pap. 13.95 (ISBN 0-87489-216-3). Med Economics.

Bartimole, Carmella, jt. auth. see Bartimole, John.

Bartimole, John & Bartimole, Carmella. Teenage Alcoholism & Substance Abuse: Causes, Cures & Consequences. (Illus.). 160p. (Orig.). 1985. pap. 6.95 (ISBN 0-936320-18-4, Pub. by Compact Bks). Interbook.

Bartiromo, Sandra. Positively Pasta. Keenan, Mackie, ed. LC 83-51536. (Illus.). 54p. (Orig.). 1983. 4.95 (ISBN 0-916005-00-3). Silver Sea.

Bartiromo, Sandra & Weir, Debbie. Try It! Simple Vegetarian Recipes for the Non-Vegetarian. (Illus., Orig.). 1984. 4.95 (ISBN 0-916005-02-X). Silver Sea.

Bartke, Wolfgang. China's Economic Aid. LC 74-78315. 206p. 1975. 30.00x (ISBN 0-8419-0179-1). Holmes & Meier.

--Who's Who in the People's Republic of China. LC 80-27599. (Illus.). 729p. 1981. 125.00 (ISBN 0-87332-183-9). M E Sharpe.

Bartke, Wolfgang & Schier, Peter. China's New Party Leadership. LC 84-14130. 289p. 1984. 50.00 (ISBN 0-87332-281-9). M E Sharpe.

Bartknecht, W. Explosions: Course, Prevention, Protection. Burg, H. & Almond, T., trs. from Ger. (Illus.). 251p. 1981. 76.50 (ISBN 0-387-10216-7). Springer-Verlag.

Bartkowiak, Robert A. Electric Circuit Analysis. 704p. 1985. text ed. 32.50 scp (ISBN 0-06-040463-9, HarpC); solutions manual avail. (ISBN 0-06-360547-3). Har-Row.

--Electric Circuits. LC 72-14366. 478p. 1973. text ed. 28.95 scp (ISBN 0-7002-2421-1, HarpC); solution manual avail. (ISBN 0-7002-2530-7). Har-Row.

Bartky, Walter. Highlights of Astronomy. (Illus.). 1961. pap. 2.95x (ISBN 0-226-03840-8, P509, Phoen). U of Chicago Pr.

Bartl, R. & Frisch, B. Bone Marrow Biopsies Revisited. (Illus.). x, 94p. 1982. 24.75 (ISBN 3-8055-3572-4). S Karger.

Bartl, R., jt. ed. see Frisch, Bertha.

Bartl, R., et al. Bone Marrow Biopsies Revisited. (Illus.). xiv, 138p. 1984. 24.75 (ISBN 3-8055-3937-1). S Karger.

--Knochenmarkbiopsie. (Illus.). xvi, 140p. 1984. 24.75 (ISBN 3-8055-3875-8). S Karger.

Bartle, Dorothy B., ed. see Wait, George W.

Bartle, Nicole, tr. see Decarpentry.

Bartle, R. G. Studies in Functional Analysis. LC 80-81042. (MAA Studies in Mathematics: No. 21). 229p. 1980. 19.00 (ISBN 0-88385-121-0). Math Assn.

Bartle, Robert G. The Elements of Real Analysis. 2nd ed. LC 75-15979. 480p. 1976. text ed. 41.50x (ISBN 0-471-05464-X); Arabic Translation, 598p. pap. 17.00 (ISBN 0-471-06391-6). Wiley.

Bartle, Wilmot T., ed. see Spencer, Anne M.

Bartle, Wilmot T., jt. ed. see Sweeney, Mary S.

Bartleman, Frank. Another Wave of Revival. rev. ed. Meyers, John, ed. Orig. Title: Another Wave Rolls In. 176p. 1982. pap. text ed. 3.50 (ISBN 0-88368-111-0). Whitaker Hse.

--Azusa Street. LC 80-82806. 1980. pap. 4.95 (ISBN 0-88270-439-7, Pub. by Logos). Bridge Pub.

Bartleson, C. James, jt. auth. see Grum, Fran.

Bartleson, C. James, jt. ed. see Grum, Franc C.

Bartleson, James, jt. ed. see Grum, Fran.

Bartlet, James V. Church Life & Church Order During the First Four Centuries. Cadoux, Cecil J., ed. 1980. lib. bdg. 59.95 (ISBN 0-8490-3147-8). Gordon Pr.

Bartlett. Life Support Systems in Intensive Care. 1984. 49.95 (ISBN 0-8151-0525-8). Year Bk Med.

--Pneumonia. Date not set. write for info. (ISBN 0-444-00843-8). Elsevier.

Bartlett, A., jt. ed. see Voller, A.

Bartlett, Adeline C. Larger Rhetorical Patterns in Anglo-Saxon Poetry. LC 72-159999. Repr. of 1935 ed. 14.50 (ISBN 0-404-00667-1). AMS Pr.

Bartlett, Albert B. Improve Your Health & Save Money at the Same Time. 1977. pap. 3.50 (ISBN 0-89036-077-4). Hawkes Pub Inc.

Bartlett, Alice. The Anthology of Cities. 1977. Repr. of 1927 ed. 30.00 (ISBN 0-89984-043-4). Century Bookbindery.

Bartlett, Amy. Afterwards. (The National Poetry Ser.). 66p. (Orig.). 1985. 13.95 (ISBN 0-89255-090-2); pap. 7.95 (ISBN 0-89255-091-0). Persea Bks.

Bartlett, Barrie E. Beauzee's Grammaire Generale: Theory & Methodology. LC 74-81133. (Janua Linguarum Series Maior: No. 82). 202p. 1975. text ed. 28.80x (ISBN 90-2793-433-9). Mouton.

Bartlett, Bede. Social Theories of the Middle Ages, Twelve Hundred to Twelve-Fifty. 1976. lib. bdg. 59.95 (ISBN 0-8490-2619-9). Gordon Pr.

Bartlett, Bob. Power Pack. 100p. 1985. pap. 4.95 (ISBN 0-89221-124-5). New Leaf.

Bartlett, Bruce & Roth, Timothy P., eds. The Supply-Side Solution. LC 83-7619. 1983. pap. text ed. 14.95x (ISBN 0-934540-18-7). Chatham Hse Pubs.

Bartlett, Bruce R. Reaganomics: Supply Side Economics in Action. 256p. 1981. 3.98 (ISBN 0-517-54817-8, Arlington Hse). Crown.

--Reaganomics: Supply-Side Economics in Action. LC 82-472. 264p. 1982. pap. 7.25 (ISBN 0-688-01182-9, Quill). Morrow.

--Reaganomics: Supply-Side Economics in Action. 1982. pap. 7.50 (ISBN 0-686-94035-0). Morrow.

Bartlett, C. J. Global Conflict: International Rivalry of the Great Powers. 408p. 1984. text ed. 35.00 (ISBN 0-582-49069-3); pap. text ed. 15.95 (ISBN 0-582-49070-7). Longman.

--A History of Postwar Britain, 1945-74. LC 77-3000. 1977. pap. text ed. 13.95x (ISBN 0-582-48320-4). Longman.

--The Rise & Fall of the Pax Americana: U. S. Foreign Policy in the Twentieth Century. LC 74-24742. 300p. 1975. 23.00 (ISBN 0-312-68355-3). St Martin.

Bartlett, C. J., ed. Britain Pre-Eminent: Studies in British World Influence in the Nineteenth Century. LC 75-93447. (Problems in Focus Ser). 1969. 22.50 (ISBN 0-312-09835-9). St Martin.

--The Long Retreat: A Short History of British Defense Policy, 1945-70. LC 79-177925. 1972. 25.00 (ISBN 0-312-49665-6). St Martin.

Bartlett, Carol, jt. auth. see Bartlett, David.

Bartlett, Charles H. Tales of Kankakee Land. 1977. Repr. of 1907 ed. 7.50 (ISBN 0-915056-07-0). Hardscrabble Bks.

Bartlett, David & Bartlett, Carol. Adam's New Friend & Other Stories from the Bible. 96p. 1980. pap. 4.95 (ISBN 0-8170-0882-9). Judson.

Bartlett, David F., ed. The Metric Debate. LC 79-53270. 19.50x (ISBN 0-87081-083-9). Colo Assoc.

Bartlett, David L. Paul's Vision for the Teaching Church. LC 77-1106. 1977. pap. 4.95 (ISBN 0-8170-0738-5). Judson.

--The Shape of Scriptural Authority. LC 83-48009. 176p. 1983. pap. 8.95 (ISBN 0-8006-1713-4, 1-1713). Fortress.

Bartlett, David L., jt. auth. see Orr, Dick.

Bartlett, David M. Modern Agitators. facs. ed. LC 70-133146. (Black Heritage Library Collection Ser). 1854. 19.25 (ISBN 0-8369-8702-0). Ayer Co Pubs.

Bartlett, David W. Life & Public Services of Hon. Abraham Lincoln, with a Portrait on Steel, to Which Is Added a Biographical Sketch of Hon. Hannibal Hamlin. facsimile ed. LC 78-95064. (Select Bibliographies Reprint Ser). 1860. 29.00 (ISBN 0-8369-5066-6). Ayer Co Pubs.

Bartlett, Donald A. Plant Engineering Management. LC 74-144106. (Manufacturing Management Ser.: Vol. 5). pap. write for info. (2055737). Bks Demand UMI.

Bartlett, E. G. Basic Karate. (Illus.). 96p. 1980. 13.95 (ISBN 0-571-11435-0); pap. 6.95 (ISBN 0-571-11436-9). Faber & Faber.

--Weight Training. (Illus.). 96p. 1984. 9.95 (ISBN 0-7153-8512-7). David & Charles.

Bartlett, Edward T., 3rd, jt. auth. see Armour, Leslie.

Bartlett, Elizabeth. Address in Time. LC 78-75102. 1979. 13.95 (ISBN 0-8023-1271-3). Dufour.

--Memory Is No Stranger. LC 81-1484. xii, 68p. 1981. text ed. 13.95x (ISBN 0-8214-0602-7, 82-83863); pap. 7.95 (ISBN 0-8214-0645-0, 82-83871). Ohio U Pr.

Bartlett, Elsa J. & Staton, Jana. Learning to Write: Some Cognitive & Linguistic Components. LC 81-38506. (Linguistics & Literary Ser.: No. 2). 33p. 1981. pap. 5.50 (ISBN 0-15-599004-7, 1530). Ctr Appl Ling.

Bartlett, F. C. Political Propaganda. 158p. 1973. Repr. of 1940 ed. lib. bdg. 18.00x (ISBN 0-374-90425-1). Octagon.

Bartlett, Fred S., frwd. by. Walt Kuhn: An Imaginary History of the West. LC 64-+012. (Illus.). 52p. 1964. pap. 3.50 (ISBN 0-88360-008-0). Amon Carter.

Bartlett, Frederic C. Psychology & Primitive Culture. LC 71-98209. Repr. of 1923 ed. lib. bdg. 18.75 (ISBN 0-8371-3244-4, BPPC). Greenwood.

--Remembering: A Study in Experimental & Social Psychology. 1932. 39.50 (ISBN 0-521-04114-7); pap. 12.95 (ISBN 0-521-09441-0). Cambridge U Pr.

--Thinking: An Experimental & Social Study. LC 82-983. 203p. 1982. Repr. of 1964 ed. lib. bdg. 24.75x (ISBN 0-313-23412-4, BART). Greenwood.

Bartlett, Gene E. The Authentic Pastor. 1978. pap. 3.95 (ISBN 0-8170-0777-6). Judson.

--Postscript to Preaching: After Forty Years, How Will I Preach Today? 88p. 1981. pap. 3.95 (ISBN 0-8170-0909-4). Judson.

Bartlett, Grace. The Wallawa Country, Eighteen Sixty-Seven to Eighteen Seventy-Seven. 110p. 1984. 14.95 (ISBN 0-87770-330-2). Ye Galleon.

Bartlett, Gretchen H. Nourishing Thoughts: For Your Food Fantasies. LC 76-50903. 1976. pap. 3.00x (ISBN 0-9601198-1-7). Nourishing Thoughts.

Bartlett, Gretchen H. & Williams, Luann. My Munch Book. (Illus.). 1981p. pap. 7.95 (ISBN 0-9601198-2-5). Nourishing Thoughts.

Bartlett, Harriett M. Common Base of Social Work Practice. LC 72-116893. 224p. (Orig.). 1970. pap. 6.95x (ISBN 0-87101-054-2). Natl Assn Soc Wkrs.

--Social Work Practice in the Health Field. LC 61-17630. 285p. 1961. 6.95x (ISBN 0-87101-035-6). Natl Assn Soc Wkrs.

Bartlett, Hazel & Gregory, Julia. Catalogue of Early Books on Music (Before 1800) LC 69-12684. (Music Ser). 1969. Repr. of 1913 ed. lib. bdg. 42.50 (ISBN 0-306-71223-7). Da Capo.

Bartlett, Henrietta & Pollard, Alfred. A Census of Shakespeare's Plays in Quarto, 1594-1709. LC 70-135724. Repr. of 1916 ed. 24.50 (ISBN 0-404-00669-8). AMS Pr.

Bartlett, Henrietta C. Mr. William Shakespeare Original & Early Editions of His Quartos & Folios, His Source Books & Those Containing Contemporary Notices. 1922. 75.00x (ISBN 0-685-89767-2). Elliots Bks.

Bartlett, Irving H. The American Mind in the Mid-Nineteenth Century. 2nd ed. (The American History Ser.). 160p. 1982. pap. text ed. 7.95x (ISBN 0-88295-809-7). Harlan Davidson.

--Daniel Webster. (Illus.). 352p. 1981. pap. 6.95 (ISBN 0-393-00996-3). Norton.

--Wendell & Ann Phillips: The Community of Reform, 1840-1880. (Illus.). 256p. 1982. pap. 5.95x (ISBN 0-393-00061-3). Norton.

--Wendell Phillips, Brahmin Radical. LC 73-11849. 438p. 1973. Repr. of 1961 ed. lib. bdg. 22.50x (ISBN 0-8371-7071-0, BAWP). Greenwood.

Bartlett, J. L., jt. auth. see Helmrath, M. O.

Bartlett, J. R., ed. The First & Second Books of the Maccabees: Cambridge Bible Commentary on the New English Bible. LC 72-87436. (Old Testament Ser.). (Orig.). 1973. 42.50 (ISBN 0-521-08658-2); pap. 15.95 (ISBN 0-521-09749-5). Cambridge U Pr.

Bartlett, J. V. Handy Farm & Home Devices & How to Make Them. (Illus.). 320p. (Orig.). 1981. pap. 9.95 (ISBN 0-262-52064-8). MIT Pr.

Bartlett, James H. Classical & Modern Mechanics. LC 74-5588. 489p. 1975. 22.00 (ISBN 0-8173-3100-X); pap. 7.50 (ISBN 0-8173-3101-8). U of Ala Pr.

Bartlett, Jane & Gibbon, David. Animal Draught Technology: An Annotated Bibliography. (Illus.). 90p. (Orig.). 1984. pap. 9.75x (ISBN 0-946688-31-1, Pub. by Intermediate Tech England). Intermediate Tech.

Bartlett, Janet L., jt. auth. see Helmrath, Marilyn O.

Bartlett, Jennifer. History of the Universe. (Illus.). 256p. 1985. 15.95 (ISBN 0-918825-12-1). Moyer Bell Ltd.

--Jennifer Bartlett: Rhapsody. (Contemporary Artists Ser.). (Illus.). 96p. 1985. 35.00 (ISBN 0-8109-1577-4). Abrams.

Bartlett, Jerry F. Getting Started in Alabama Real Estate. (Real Estate Ser.). 1978. pap. text ed. 14.50 (ISBN 0-8403-1879-0). Kendall-Hunt.

Bartlett, Jimmy D. & Jaanus, Siret D., eds. Clinical Ocular Pharmacology. (Illus.). 1008p. 1984. text ed. 69.95 (ISBN 0-409-95041-6). Butterworth.

Bartlett, John. Bartlett's Familiar Quotations: Fifteenth & 125th Anniversary Edition. rev. & enl. ed. LC 68-15664. 1980. 29.45 (ISBN 0-316-08275-9). Little.

--Familiar Quotations. 128p. 1983. pap. 3.95 (ISBN 0-8065-0250-9). Citadel Pr.

--Jericho. 128p. 1982. 35.00x (ISBN 0-7188-2456-3, Pub. by Lutterworth Pr England). State Mutual Bk.

Bartlett, John, jt. auth. see Megaw, T. M.

Bartlett, John, compiled by. Complete Concordance to Shakespeare. 1910p. 1983. Repr. of 1979 ed. 60.00x (ISBN 0-312-15645-6). St Martin.

Bartlett, John A. Jericho. Davies, Graham I., ed. (Cities of the Biblical World Ser.). 128p. (Orig.). 1983. pap. 6.95 (ISBN 0-8028-1033-0). Eerdmans.

Bartlett, John R. Census of the Inhabitants of the Colony of Rhode Island & Providence Plantations: 1774. 246p. 1984. pap. 12.50 (ISBN 0-912606-20-7). Hunterdon Hse.

--Dictionary of Americanism: A Glossary of Words & Phrases, Usually Regarded As Peculiar to the United States. 1976. Repr. of 1848 ed. 69.00x (ISBN 0-403-06365-5, Regency). Scholarly.

--Dictionary of Americanisms: A Glossary of Words & Phrases Usually Regarded As Peculiar to the United States. 2nd ed. Repr. of 1859 ed. 48.00 (ISBN 0-384-03475-6). Johnson Repr.

--The Literature of the Rebellion. 59.95 (ISBN 0-8490-0545-0). Gordon Pr.

--Literature of the Rebellion. LC 77-109311. Repr. of 1866 ed. 27.50x (ISBN 0-8371-3568-0, BLR&, Pub. by Negro U Pr). Greenwood.

--Personal Narrative of Explorations & Incidents in Texas, New Mexico, California, Sonora & Chihuahua in Connection With the U. S. Mexican Boundary Survey, 1851-1853, 2 vols. (Beautiful Rio Grande Classics Ser.). (Illus.). 1413p. 1983. Repr. of 1854 ed. 40.00 (ISBN 0-87380-018-4). Rio Grande.

--Shakespeare Concordance, 4 vols. Set. 600.00 (ISBN 0-87968-266-3). Gordon Pr.

--A Shakespeare Phrase-Book, 2 vols. Set. 250.00 (ISBN 0-87968-260-4). Gordon Pr.

Bartlett, John R., ed. Records of the Colony of Rhode Island & Providence Plantations in New England, 10 Vols. Repr. of 1856 ed. Set. lib. bdg. 550.00 (ISBN 0-404-00680-9); lib. bdg. 55.00 ea. AMS Pr.

Bartlett, Jonathan, ed. Northern Ireland. 163p. 1983. 8.00 (ISBN 0-8242-0670-3). Wilson.

--The Ocean Environment. (Reference Shelf Ser.). 1977. 8.00 (ISBN 0-8242-0600-2). Wilson.

Bartlett, Joseph W. The Law Business: A Tired Monopoly. vii, 198p. 1982. text ed. 17.50x (ISBN 0-8377-0324-7). Rothman.

Bartlett, Josiah. The Papers of Josiah Bartlett. Mevers, Frank C., ed. LC 78-63147. (Illus.). 517p. 1979. 42.50x (ISBN 0-87451-168-2, Pub. for the New Hampshire Hist. Soc.). U Pr of New Eng.

Bartlett, June, tr. see Ekman, Kerstin.

Bartlett, K. Towards Still Greater Professionalism. (Tolley Medal Ser.). 1971. 1.50 (ISBN 0-686-52206-0, WPT 4). Syracuse U Cont Ed.

Bartlett, Kim. Buying Time: An Established Business Fights for Survival. 224p. 1985. 16.95 (ISBN 0-316-08276-7). Little.

Bartlett, Laile. PSI Trek. 300p. 1981. 12.95 (ISBN 0-07-003915-1). McGraw.

Bartlett, Lanier, ed. see Bell, Horace.

Bartlett, Laurence. William Congreve: A Reference Guide. 1979. lib. bdg. 25.00 (ISBN 0-8161-8142-X, Hall Reference). G K Hall.

Bartlett, Lee. The Beats: Essays in Criticism. LC 80-28179. 243p. 1981. lib. bdg. 19.95x (ISBN 0-89950-026-9). McFarland & Co.

--Karl Shapiro: A Descriptive Bibliography. LC 78-68245. (Reference Library of Humanities Ser.). 1979. lib. bdg. 28.00 (ISBN 0-8240-9812-9). Garland Pub.

--William Everson. LC 85-70127. (Western Writers Ser.: No. 67). (Illus.). 50p. (Orig.). 1985. pap. 2.00x (ISBN 0-88430-041-2). Boise St Univ.

Bartlett, Lee & Campo, Allan. William Everson: A Descriptive Bibliography, 1934-1976. LC 77-5397. (Author Bibliographies Ser.: No. 33). 119p. 1977. 16.50 (ISBN 0-8108-1037-9). Scarecrow.

Bartlett, Lee, ed. Benchmark & Blaze: The Emergence of William Everson. LC 78-27137. 292p. 1979. lib. bdg. 18.50 (ISBN 0-8108-1198-7). Scarecrow.

--William Everson - On Writing the Waterbirds & Other Presentations: Collected Forewords & Afterwords 1935-1981. LC 83-3123. 288p. 1983. 17.50 (ISBN 0-8108-1617-2). Scarecrow.

Bartlett, Lee, ed. see Everson, William.

Bartlett, Lee, ed. see Spender, Stephen.

Bartlett, Lester W. State Control of Private Incorporated Institutions of Higher Education As Defined in Decisions of the U. S. Supreme Court: Laws of the States Governing the Incorporation of Institutions of Higher Education, & Charters of Selected Private Colleges & Universities. LC 73-176538. (Columbia University. Teachers College. Contributions to Education: No. 207). Repr. of 1926 ed. 22.50 (ISBN 0-404-55207-2). AMS Pr.

Bartlett, Lu, jt. auth. see Elder, William V., III.

Bartlett, Lynn M. Promise Me Love. 1982. pap. 3.95 (ISBN 0-380-60418-3, 69815-3). Avon.

Bartlett, M. S. Introduction to Stochastic Processes. 3rd ed. LC 76-57094. (Illus.). 404p. 1981. pap. 22.95 (ISBN 0-521-28085-0). Cambridge U Pr.

--An Introduction to Stochastic Processes with Special Reference to Methods & Applications. 3rd ed. LC 76-57094. (Illus.). 1978. 59.50 (ISBN 0-521-21585-4). Cambridge U Pr.

--Probability, Statistics & Time: A Collection of Essays. (Monographs on Applied Probability & Statistics). 1975. 17.95x (ISBN 0-412-14150-7, NO. 6029, Pub. by Chapman & Hall England); pap. 12.95x (ISBN 0-412-22260-4, NO. 2964). Methuen Inc.

--Statistical Analysis of Spatial Pattern. (Monographs in Applied Probability & Statistics). 1976. 17.95x (ISBN 0-412-14290-2, NO.6030, Pub. by Chapman & Hall). Methuen Inc.

--Stochastic Population Models in Ecology & Epidemology. (Monographs in Applied Probability & Statistics). 1960. 10.95x (ISBN 0-416-52330-7, NO.6429). Methuen Inc.

Bartlett, Margaret F. Clean Brook. LC 60-8257. (A Let's-Read-&-Find-Out Science Bk). (Illus.). (gr. k-3). 1960. PLB 11.89 (ISBN 0-690-19556-7). Crowell Jr Bks.

--Where the Brook Begins. LC 60-9773. (A Let's-Read-&-Find-Out Science Bks.). (Illus.). (gr. k-3). 1961. Crowell Jr Bks.

Bartlett, Mary. Gentians. (Illus.). 144p. 1981. text ed. 20.00x (ISBN 0-87663-363-7). Universe.

Bartlett, Merrill L. Assault from the Sea: Essays on the History of Amphibious Warfare. (Illus.). 312p. 1983. 26.95 (ISBN 0-87021-088-2). Naval Inst Pr.

Bartlett, Michael & Best Report Editors. The Book of Bests. (Illus.). 464p. 1984. pap. 8.95 (ISBN 0-8362-7918-2). Andrews Mcmeel Parker.

Bartlett, Michael & Fishman, Joanne A. The Sailing Book. LC 81-71663. 1982. 22.95 (ISBN 0-87795-369-4). Arbor Hse.

Bartlett, Neville. Carpeting the Millions: A History of the British Carpet Industry. 310p. 1982. 50.00x (ISBN 0-85976-025-1, Pub. by Donald Pubs Scotland). State Mutual Bk.

Bartlett, Oso, jt. auth. see Duryea, John S.

Bartlett, Patricia M. An Investigation of Child Abuse: Neglect Instruction Offered in Early Childhood & Elementary Education Preservice Programs. Reed, R., ed. LC 81-84975. (Orig.). 1982. 12.95 (ISBN 0-88247-641-6); pap. 7.95 (ISBN 0-88247-631-9). R & E Pubs.

Bartlett, Phyllis B., ed. see Meredith, George.

Bartlett, R. Rolling Rivers. 1984. 29.95 (ISBN 0-07-003910-0). McGraw.

Bartlett, R., jt. auth. see Clendenning, P. H.

Bartlett, R. B., ed. Wastewater Treatment: Public Health Engineering Design in Metric. 326p. 1971. 39.00 (ISBN 0-85334-504-X, Pub. by Elsevier Applied Sci England). Elsevier.

Bartlett, R. E. Public Health Engineering-Sewarage. 2nd ed. 196p. 1979. 33.50 (ISBN 0-85334-796-4, Pub. by Elsevier Applied Sci England). Elsevier.

--Pumping Stations for Water & Sewage. (Illus.). 150p. 1974. 26.00 (ISBN 0-85334-577-5, Pub. by Elsevier Applied Sci England). Elsevier.

Bartlett, R. E. & Madill, W. Hydraulics for Public Health Engineers. (Illus.). 198p. 1982. 33.50 (ISBN 0-85334-148-6, I-431-82, Pub. by Elsevier Applied Sci England). Elsevier.

Bartlett, R. E., ed. Developments in Sewerage, Vol. 1. (Illus.). 180p. 1979. 33.50 (ISBN 0-85334-831-6, Pub. by Elsevier Applied Sci England). Elsevier.

Bartlett, R. H., et al, eds. see Symposium, Boston, 1970.

Bartlett, Randall. Economic Foundations of Political Power. LC 73-3899. 1973. 14.95 (ISBN 0-02-901870-6). Free Pr.

Bartlett, Raymond C. Medical Microbiology: Quality & Clinical Relevance. LC 73-18482. (Wiley Biomedical Health Publications Ser.). (Illus.). pap. 51.20 (ISBN 0-317-09253-7, 2055168). Bks Demand UMI.

Bartlett, Richard & Keller, Clair. Freedom's Trail. LC 78-53884. (Illus., Gr. 8). 1979. text ed. 22.88 (ISBN 0-395-26197-X); tchr's ed. 23.56 (ISBN 0-395-26198-8). HM.

--Freedom's Trail. 1981. text ed. 22.64 (ISBN 0-395-30250-1); tchr's ed. 23.62 (ISBN 0-395-30251-X). HM.

Bartlett, Richard A. Great Surveys of the American West. LC 62-16475. (The American Exploration & Travel Ser.: Vol. 38). (Illus.). 464p. 1980. pap. 13.95 (ISBN 0-8061-1653-6). U of Okla Pr.

--The New Country: A Social History of the American Frontier 1776-1890. LC 74-79619. (Illus.). 1974. pap. 10.95 (ISBN 0-19-502021-9, 452, GB). Oxford U Pr.

--Yellowstone: A Wilderness Beseiged. LC 85-988. 1985. 24.95 (ISBN 0-8165-0890-9). U of Ariz Pr.

Bartlett, Robert. Gerald of Wales, 1146-1223. (Incl. a Family Tree). 1982. 49.00x (ISBN 0-19-821892-3). Oxford U Pr.

Bartlett, Robert M. The Faith of the Pilgrims: An American Heritage. LC 77-16308. (Illus.). 1978. 8.95 (ISBN 0-8298-0337-8). Pilgrim NY.

--My Corner of New England: Thoughts on Nature & Human Nature from a Pilgrim House on Cape Cod Bay. (Illus.). 182p. 1984. 12.95 (ISBN 0-914339-05-2). P E Randall Pub.

--The Pilgrim Way. LC 70-172790. 384p. 1971. 15.00 (ISBN 0-8298-0222-3). Pilgrim NY.

--Thanksgiving Day. LC 65-16178. (Holiday Ser.). (Illus.). (gr. 1-3). 1965. PLB 10.89 (ISBN 0-690-81045-8). Crowell Jr Bks.

--They Dared to Live. facs. ed. LC 76-90606. (Essay Index Reprint Ser.). 1937. 20.00 (ISBN 0-8369-1273-X). Ayer Co Pubs.

--They Did Something About It. facsimile ed. LC 70-90607. (Essay Index Reprint Ser). 1939. 17.00 (ISBN 0-8369-1243-8). Ayer Co Pubs.

--They Work for Tomorrow. facsimile ed. LC 70-111813. (Essay Index Reprint Ser.). 1943. 17.00 (ISBN 0-8369-1592-5). Ayer Co Pubs.

Bartlett, Robert V. The Reserve Mining Controversy: Science, Technology & Environmental Quality. LC 79-48019. 312p. 1980. 17.50x (ISBN 0-253-14556-2). Ind U Pr.

Bartlett, Roger W. Power Base Attribution & the Perceived Legitimacy of Managerial Accounting. Farmer, Richard N., ed. LC 82-23697. (Research for Business Decisions: No. 57). 145p. 1983. 39.95 (ISBN 0-8357-1393-8). Univ Microfilms.

Bartlett, Roland W. American Foreign Policy in Retrospective. LC 77-99312. 1978. 10.00 (ISBN 0-913228-24-9). Dillon-Liederbach.

--The Fans Vote! One Hundred Baseball Superstars. LC 82-5118. (Illus.). 256p. 1983. 17.95; pap. 9.95 (ISBN 0-88280-089-2). ETC Pubns.

--Modern Private Enterprise: Is It Successful. LC 72-93331. 1973. pap. 3.95 (ISBN 0-8134-1540-3, 1540); text ed. 2.95x. Interstate.

--Success of Modern Private Enterprise. LC 70-106133. 1970. 7.95 (ISBN 0-8134-1148-3, 1148); text ed. 5.95x. Interstate.

Bartlett, Ronald E. Surface Water Sewerage. 2nd ed. LC 80-42202. 147p. 1981. 39.95x (ISBN 0-470-27144-2). Halsted Pr.

Bartlett, Ronald W. & Wolfson, Marty. Galbraiths Garbled Economics. (Illus.). 1974. pap. 1.95 (ISBN 0-916114-03-1). Wolfson.

Bartlett, Ruhl J. John C. Fremont & the Republican Party. LC 73-87663. (American Scene Ser). 1970. Repr. of 1930 ed. lib. bdg. 24.50 (ISBN 0-306-71763-8). Da Capo.

--Policy & Power: Two Centuries of American Foreign Relations. LC 79-25201. (American Century Ser.). (Illus.). 303p. 1980. Repr. of 1963 ed. lib. bdg. 24.75x (ISBN 0-313-22217-7, BAPN). Greenwood.

Bartlett, Samuel C. From Egypt to Palestine: Through Sinai, the Wilderness & the South Country: History of the Israelites. Davis, Moshe, ed. LC 77-70668. (America & the Holy Land Ser.). (Illus.). 1977. Repr. of 1879 ed. lib. bdg. 43.00x (ISBN 0-405-10227-5). Ayer Co Pubs.

--Historical Sketches of the Missions of the American Board. LC 78-38436. (Religion in America, Ser. 2). 210p. 1972. Repr. of 1972 ed. 21.00 (ISBN 0-405-04057-1). Ayer Co Pubs.

Bartlett, Sy, jt. auth. see Lay, Beirne, Jr.

Bartlett, Truman H. The Art Life of William Rimmer: Sculptor, Painter, & Physician. LC 68-27718. (Library of American Art Ser.). (Illus.). 1970. Repr. of 1890 ed. lib. bdg. 32.50 (ISBN 0-306-71166-4). Da Capo.

Bartlett, Vernon. Topsy-Turvy. facsimile ed. LC 77-110179. (Short Story Index Reprint Ser.). 1927. 18.00 (ISBN 0-8369-3330-3). Ayer Co Pubs.

Bartlett, Virginia. Pickles & Pretzels: Pennsylvania's World of Food. LC 79-3996. 1980. pap. 5.95 (ISBN 0-8229-5308-0). U of Pittsburgh Pr.

Bartlett, W. A. & Gallatin, D. B. B & G Cartridge Manual. 2.00 (ISBN 0-913150-12-6). Pioneer Pr.

Bartlett, William I. Jones Very, Emerson's Brave Saint. LC 68-29741. (Illus.). 1968. Repr. of 1942 ed. lib. bdg. 24.75x (ISBN 0-8371-0296-0, BAJV). Greenwood.

Bartlett, William W. To Fathoms in Hell & Back. 208p. 1981. 9.00 (ISBN 0-682-49790-8). Exposition Pr FL.

Bartley, Douglas. Job Evaluation-Wage & Salary Administration. LC 80-21099. 272p. 1981. text ed. 18.95 (ISBN 0-201-00095-4); manual 2.50instr's. (ISBN 0-201-11200-0). Addison-Wesley.

Bartley, Ernest R. The Tidelands Oil Controversy. Bruchey, Stuart, ed. LC 78-53555. (Development of Public Lands Law in the U. S. Ser.). 1979. Repr. of 1953 ed. lib. bdg. 23.00x (ISBN 0-405-11368-4). Ayer Co Pubs.

Bartley, J., et al. Geological Survey of Norway: NGU Bulletin 96. (Illus.). 80p. 1985. pap. 17.00x (ISBN 82-00-31470-7). Universitet.

Bartley, Lynwood, jt. ed. see Cialdella, Gary.

Bartley, Numan V. The Creation of Modern Georgia. LC 82-24791. (Illus.). 256p. 1983. 20.00x (ISBN 0-8203-0668-1); pap. 10.00x (ISBN 0-8203-0680-0). U of Ga Pr.

Bartley, Numan V. & Graham, Hugh D. Southern Elections: County & Precinct Data, 1950-1972. LC 78-5525. 416p. 1977. 35.00x (ISBN 0-8071-0278-4). La State U Pr.

--Southern Politics & the Second Reconstruction. 256p. 1976. 24.50x (ISBN 0-8018-1667-X). Johns Hopkins.

Bartley, Regina. The Joy of Machine Embroidery. LC 76-6259. (Illus.). 160p. 1976. 12.95 (ISBN 0-8092-8346-8); pap. 4.95 (ISBN 0-8092-7966-5). Contemp Bks.

Bartley, Russell H. Imperial Russia & the Struggle for Latin America Independence, 1808-1828. (Latin American Monographs: No. 43). 244p. 1978. 14.95x (ISBN 0-292-73811-0); pap. text ed. 6.95x (ISBN 0-292-73812-9). U of Tex Pr.

Bartley, Russell H. & Wagner, Stuart L. Latin America in Basic Historical Collections: A Working Guide. LC 77-170204. (Bibliographical Ser.: No. 51). 212p. 1972. 12.95x (ISBN 0-8179-2511-2). Hoover Inst Pr.

Bartley, Russell H., ed. Soviet Historians on Latin America: Recent Scholarly Contributions. LC 77-53648. 364p. 1978. 30.00x (ISBN 0-299-07250-9). U of Wis Pr.

Bartley, S. Howard. Fatigue: Mechanism & Management. 112p. 1965. 14.75x (ISBN 0-398-00099-9). C C Thomas.

Bartley, W. W., ed. see Carroll, Lewis.

Bartley, W. W., III. Wittgenstein. 130p. 1985. pap. 9.95 (ISBN 0-87548-441-7). Open Court.

Bartley, W. W., III, ed. see Popper, Karl.

Bartley, W. W., III, ed. see Popper, Karl R.

Bartley, William W., III. The Retreat to Commitment. LC 84-14862. xxviii, 285p. 18.95 (ISBN 0-87548-420-4). Open Court.

Bartman, Joeffrey. Habit Blue. 1980. pap. 3.95 (ISBN 0-918222-13-3). Apple Wood.

Bartmann & Bartmann, W. Biopolymers Complexes. 213p. 1982. 42.95x (ISBN 0-471-26144-0, Pub. by Wiley Heyden). Wiley.

Bartmann, W., jt. auth. see Bartmann.

Bartmann, Wilhelm & Trost, Barry M., eds. Selectivity: A Goal for Synthetic Efficiency. 424p. 1983. text ed. 42.50x (ISBN 0-89573-205-X). VCH Pubs.

Bartnikas, R. & Eichhorn, R. M., eds. Engineering Dielectrics, Volume IIA, Electrical Properties of Solid Insulating Materials: Molecular Structure & Electrical Behavior. LC 82-70637. (Special Technical Publications Ser.: No. 783). 695p. 1983. text ed. 60.00 (ISBN 0-8031-0228-3, 04-783000-21). ASTM.

Barto, A. How Vova Changed His Ways. 12p. 1977. pap. 0.99 (ISBN 0-8285-1165-9, Pub. by Progress Pubs USSR). Imported Pubns.

--Mashenka. 14p. 1976. pap. 0.99 (ISBN 0-8285-1204-3, Pub. by Progress Pubs USSR). Imported Pubns.

--Merry Rhymes. 78p. 1976. 3.95 (ISBN 0-8285-1704-5, Pub. by Progress Pubs USSR). Imported Pubns.

--The Skipping Rope. 52p. 1971. pap. 1.99 (ISBN 0-8285-1228-0, Pub. by Progress Pubs USSR). Imported Pubns.

Barto, P. S. Tannhauser & the Mountain of Venus: A Study in the Legend of the Germanic Paradise. 1977. lib. bdg. 59.95. Gordon Pr.

Barto, Renzo, illus. Pop-Up Book of Cars. LC 75-39338. (Pop-up Ser.: No. 32). (Illus.). (gr. 3 up). 1976. 5.95 (ISBN 0-394-83259-0, BYR). Random.

Bartocci, Barbara. My Angry Son: Sometimes Love Is Not Enough. LC 84-73515. 224p. 1985. 15.95 (ISBN 0-917657-16-0). D I Fine.

Bartocha, Bodo, jt. ed. see Cetron, Marvin J.

Bartoe, Edith. Does the Key to the Future Lie in the Past? (Illus.). 1977. pap. 4.95 (ISBN 0-917200-21-7). ESPress.

Bartoe, Edith F. Now Is the Time. (Orig.). 1979. pap. 3.50 (ISBN 0-917200-26-8). ESPress.

--Tell the World. (Orig.). 1978. pap. 3.95 (ISBN 0-917200-24-1). ESPress.

Bartok. Carols & Christmas Songs: Colinde, Vol. 4. (Rumanian Folk Music Ser). 1975. lib. bdg. 131.50 (ISBN 90-247-1737-X, Pub. by Martinus Nijhoff Netherlands). Kluwer Academic.

--Instrumental Melodies. (Rumanian Folk Music Ser: Vol. 1). lib. bdg. 53.00 (ISBN 90-247-0623-8, Pub. by Martinus Nijhoff Netherlands). Kluwer Academic.

--Maramures County, Vol. 5. (Rumanian Folk Music Ser). 1975. lib. bdg. 79.00 (ISBN 90-247-1738-8, Pub. by Martinus Nijhoff Pubns). Kluwer Academic.

--Romanian Folk Music Texts. (Rumanian Folk Music Ser: Vol. 3). lib. bdg. 53.00 (ISBN 90-247-0625-4, Pub. by Martinus Nijhoff Netherlands). Kluwer Academic.

--Vocal Melodies. (Rumanian Folk Music Ser: Vol. 2). lib. bdg. 53.00 (ISBN 90-247-0624-6, Pub. by Martinus Nijhoff Netherlands). Kluwer Academic.

Bartok, Bela. Hungarian Folk Music. Calvocoressi, M. D., tr. LC 77-87537. 320p. Repr. of 1931 ed. 37.00 (ISBN 0-404-16600-8). AMS Pr.

--Hungarian Folk Music. Calvocoressi, M. D., tr. LC 78-62328. (Encore Music Editions). (Illus.). 1979. Repr. of 1931 ed. 35.00 (ISBN 0-88355-722-3). Hyperion Conn.

--The Hungarian Folk Song. Suchoff, Benjamin, ed. Calvocoressi, M. D., tr. (Bartok Studies in Musicology). 1980. 59.50x (ISBN 0-87395-410-6); pap. 19.50x (ISBN 0-87395-439-4). State U NY Pr.

--Piano Music of Bela Bartok. Suchoff, Benjamin, ed. (Series I-Archive Edition). 18.00 (ISBN 0-8446-5875-8). Peter Smith.

--Piano Music of Bela Bartok. Suchoff, Benjamin, ed. (Series II-Archive Edition). 18.00 (ISBN 0-8446-5876-6). Peter Smith.

--Piano Music of Bela Bartok, Series I. 1982. pap. 6.95 (ISBN 0-486-24108-4). Dover.

--Piano Music of Bela Bartok, Series II. 1982. pap. 6.95 (ISBN 0-486-24109-2). Dover.

--Turkish Folk Music from Asia Minor. Suchoff, Benjamin, ed. LC 75-23186. (Studies in Musicology). 1976. 29.00x (ISBN 0-691-09120-X). Princeton U Pr.

--Yugoslav Folk Music, 4 vols. Suchoff, Benjamin, ed. LC 78-8188. 1979. Set. 395.00x (ISBN 0-87395-383-5). State U NY Pr.

Bartok, John W. Heating with Coal. LC 80-24941. (Illus.). 192p. 1980. pap. 7.95 (ISBN 0-88266-243-0). Garden Way Pub.

Bartok, John W., Jr. Solid Fuel Furnaces & Boilers: Low-Cost Central Heating Systems. LC 82-1003. (Illus.). 224p. (Orig.). 1982. pap. 8.95 (ISBN 0-88266-264-3). Garden Way Pub.

Bartok, M., et al. Stereochemistry of Catalytic Reactions on Metals. LC 84-13085. 1985. 115.00 (ISBN 0-471-90553-4). Wiley.

Bartok, William, ed. Combustion of Synthetic Fuels. LC 83-2822. (ACS Symposium Ser.: No. 217). 246p. 1983. lib. bdg. 34.95x (ISBN 0-8412-0773-9). Am Chemical.

Bartol, Curt R. Criminal Behavior: A Psychosocial Approach. (Criminal Justice Ser.). (Illus.). 1980. text ed. 27.95 (ISBN 0-13-193169-5). P-H.

--Psychology & American Law. 384p. 1982. text ed. write for info. (ISBN 0-534-01217-5). Wadsworth Pub.

Bartol, Cyrus A. Discourses on the Christian Spirit & Life: With an Introduction. 2nd ed. LC 72-4951. (The Romantic Tradition in American Literature Ser.). 418p. 1972. Repr. of 1850 ed. 30.00 (ISBN 0-405-04622-7). Ayer Co Pubs.

Bartol, Kathryn. Male & Female Leaders in Small Work Groups. LC 73-620233. 154p. 1973. pap. 6.00 (ISBN 0-87744-116-2). Mich St U Pr.
Bartol'd, Vasilii V. Histoire des Turcs D'Asie Centrale. Donskis, M., tr. from Turkish. LC 77-10594. (Studies in Islamic History: No. 2). (Illus.). 202p. 1978. Repr. of 1945 ed. lib. bdg. 17.50x (ISBN 0-87991-451-3). Porcupine Pr.
--Mussulman Culture. Suhrawardy, Shahid, tr. from Rus. LC 77-10749. (Studies in Islamic History: No. 3). xxviii, 146p. 1978. Repr. lib. bdg. 19.50x (ISBN 0-87991-452-1). Porcupine Pr.
--Turkestan Down to the Mongol Invasion. 3rd ed. Minorsky, V. M., tr. LC 77-8278. xix, 513p. 1978. Repr. of 1968 ed. lib. bdg. 37.50x (ISBN 0-87991-453-X). Porcupine Pr.
Bartolet, Sam. Eclipses & Lunations in Astrology. 68p. 4.50 (ISBN 0-86690-058-6, 1021-01). Am Fed Astrologers.
Bartoletti, Susan & Lisandrelli, Elaine. Easy Writer: Student Worksheets, Level G. (Illus.). 38p. (Orig.). (gr. 7-9). 1985. pap. text ed. 14.95 (ISBN 0-913935-37-9). ERA-CCR.
--Easy Writer: Student Worksheets, Level H. (Level H Ser.). (Illus.). 38p. (Orig.). (gr. 8-10). 1985. pap. text ed. 14.95 (ISBN 0-913935-38-7). ERA-CCR.
Bartoli, Cecilia & Swenson, Pina. Basic Conversational Italian. 2nd ed. LC 77-15655. (Ital.). 1979. text ed. 26.95 (ISBN 0-03-021681-8); lab manual 11.95 (ISBN 0-03-021686-9). HR&W.
Bartoli, Cosimo. Measurement & Perspective. (Printed Sources of Western Art Ser.). 294p. (Italian.). 1981. pap. 40.00 slipcase (ISBN 0-915346-67-2). A Wofsy Fine Arts.
Bartoli, E., ed. see International Symposium on: HBsAg Containing Immune Complexes: Renal & Other Extra-Hepatic Manifestations: Italy, Sept. 1979, et al.
Bartoli, Jennifer. In a Meadow, Two Hares Hide. Pacini, Kathy, ed. LC 78-15221. (Illus.). (gr. k-2). 1978. PLB 10.75 (ISBN 0-8075-3628-8). A Whitman.
--Snow on Bear's Nose. Rubin, Caroline, ed. LC 76-40261. (Illus.). 24p. (gr. k-7). 1977. PLB 10.75 (ISBN 0-8075-7520-8). A Whitman.
Bartoli, Pietro S. & Bellori, Giovanni P. Ancient Funerary Lamps, 3 vols. (Printed Sources of Western Art Ser.). (Illus.). 324p. (Italian.). pap. 40.00 slipcase (ISBN 0-915346-70-2). A Wofsy Fine Arts.
Bartoli, Renator, ed. see Axelrod, Donald C., et al.
Bartolini, Stefano & Mair, Peter, eds. Party Politics in Contemporary Western Europe. 192p. 1985. 24.00x (ISBN 0-7146-3271-6, F Cass Co). Biblio Dist.
Bartolke-Bergmann. Integrated Cooperatives in the Industrial Society. 1980. text ed. 23.00x (ISBN 90-232-1772-1). Humanities.
Bartollas, et al. Introduction to the American Criminal Justice System. Date not set. price not set (ISBN 0-471-82415-1). Wiley.
Bartollas, C., et al. Juvenile Victimization: The Institutional Paradox. LC 76-3476. 324p. 1976. 18.95x (ISBN 0-470-05490-5). Halsted Pr.
Bartollas, Clemens. Correctional Treatment: Theory & Practice. LC 84-4702. 368p. 1985. text ed. 26.95 (ISBN 0-13-178328-9). P-H.
--Introduction to Corrections. LC 80-25092. (Illus.). 490p. 1981. text ed. 22.85 scp (ISBN 0-06-040516-3, HarpC); instructor's manual avail. (ISBN 0-06-360370-5). Har-Row.
--Juvenile Delinquency. LC 84-14864. 633p. 1985. 25.95 (ISBN 0-471-89364-1). Wiley.
Bartollas, Clemens & Miller, Stuart J. Correctional Administration: Theory & Practice. (Illus.). 1978. text ed. 29.20 (ISBN 0-07-003950-X). McGraw.
Bartollas, Clemens, et al. Juvenile Victimization: The Institutional Paradox. LC 76-3476. 324p. 1976. 19.50 (ISBN 0-470-05490-5, Pub. by Wiley). Krieger.
Bartolo, B. Di see Di Bartolo, B.
Bartolo, Baldassare Di see Di Bartolo, Baldassare & Powell, Richard C.
Bartolo, Baldassare Di see Di Bartolo, Baldassare.
Bartolo, Baldassare di see Di Bartolo, Baldassare.
Bartolo, Dick De see De Bartolo, Dick.
Bartolo, Dick De see De Bartolo, Dick & Clarke, Bob.
Bartolo, Dick De see De Bartolo, Dick & North, Henry.
Bartolomei De La Cruz, Hector G. Protection Against Anti-Union Discrimination. 1976. 11.40 (ISBN 92-2-101348-0). Intl Labour Office.
Bartolomeo, Glen. Insincerity. 1983. 8.95 (ISBN 0-8062-1792-8). Carlton.
Bartoloni, Gilda, jt. auth. see Sprenger, Maja.
Bartolozzi, Bruno. New Sounds for Woodwind. 2nd ed. Brindle, Reginald S., ed. 1981. 29.95x (ISBN 0-19-318611-X). Oxford U Pr.
Bartolus of Sassoferrato. Bartolus on the Conflict of Laws. Beale, Joseph H., tr. LC 78-59004. 1979. Repr. of 1914 ed. 15.00 (ISBN 0-88355-680-4). Hyperion Conn.
Barton, et al, eds. see Paquette, Leo A.
Barton, A. F., ed. see Kertes, A. S.
Barton, Allan F. Handbook of Solubility Parameters & other Cohesion Parameters. 608p. 1983. 99.50 (ISBN 0-8493-3295-8). CRC Pr.
--Resource Recovery & Recycling. LC 78-13601. (Environmental Science & Technology Ser.). 418p. 1979. 72.50x (ISBN 0-471-02773-1, Pub. by Wiley-Interscience). Wiley.
Barton, Allen H. Organizational Measurement & Its Bearing on the Study of College Environments. (Research Monograph: No. 2). 91p. 1961. pap. 5.00 (ISBN 0-87447-067-6, 254730). College Bd.
Barton, Allen H., jt. ed. see Weiss, Carol H.
Barton, Amelia. The Becky Barton Thank You Book. 1983. 5.95 (ISBN 0-8062-2165-8). Carlton.
Barton, Andrew. The Disappointment; or, The Force of Credulity. Mays, David, ed. LC 76-26470. 1976. 7.50 (ISBN 0-8130-0562-0). U Presses Fla.
Barton, Anne. Ben Jonson, Dramatist. LC 83-23196. (Illus.). 380p. 1984. 54.50 (ISBN 0-521-25883-9); pap. 17.95 (ISBN 0-521-27748-5). Cambridge U Pr.
--Shakespeare & the Idea of the Play. LC 76-58419. 1977. Repr. of 1962 ed. lib. bdg. 22.50x (ISBN 0-8371-9446-6, BASI). Greenwood.
Barton, Anthony & Barton, Mary. The Management & Prevention of Pressure Sores. (Illus.). 96p. 1981. pap. 8.50 (ISBN 0-571-11673-6). Faber & Faber.
Barton, Benjamin S. New Views of the Origin of the Tribes & Nations of America. 1976. 22.00 (ISBN 0-527-05480-1). Kraus Repr.
--Notes on the Animals of North America, 1793. Sterling, Keir B., ed. & intro. by. LC 73-17801. (Natural Sciences in America Ser.). 150p. 1974. 12.00 (ISBN 0-405-05719-9). Ayer Co Pubs.
Barton, Brigid S. Otto Dix & "Die Neue Sachlichkeit". 1918-1925. Foster, Stephen, ed. LC 80-39539. (Studies in the Fine Arts. The Avant-Garde: No. 11). 186p. 1981. 39.95 (ISBN 0-8357-1151-X). UMI Res Pr.
Barton, Bruce. Man Nobody Knows. 1925. pap. 6.95 (ISBN 0-672-50743-9). Bobbs.
Barton, Bruce W. The Tree at the Center of the World: The Story of the California Missions. LC 79-26434. (Illus., Orig.). 1980. lib. bdg. 19.95 (ISBN 0-915520-30-3); pap. 12.95 (ISBN 0-915520-29-X). Ross-Erikson.
Barton, Byron. Airport. LC 79-7816. (Illus.). 32p. (ps-k). 1982. 10.53i (ISBN 0-690-04168-3); PLB 10.89g (ISBN 0-690-04169-1). Crowell Jr Bks.
--Building a House. LC 80-22674. (Illus.). 32p. (ps-1). 1981. 10.75 (ISBN 0-688-80291-5); PLB 10.88 (ISBN 0-688-84291-7). Greenwillow.
--Building a House: Picture Puffins. 32p. (gr. k-3). 1984. pap. 3.95 (ISBN 0-14-050470-2, Puffin). Penguin.
--Buzz, Buzz, Buzz. (Picture Puffins Ser.). (Illus.). 1979. pap. 2.95 (ISBN 0-14-050307-2, Puffin). Penguin.
--Elephant. LC 74-154301. (Illus.). (ps-3). 1971. 4.95 (ISBN 0-395-28764-2, Clarion). HM.
--Hester. (Picture Puffins Ser.). (Illus.). (gr. 1-3). 1978. pap. 3.50 (ISBN 0-14-050281-5, Puffin). Penguin.
--Wheels. LC 78-20541. (Illus.). (ps-3). 1979. o. p. 9.57i (ISBN 0-690-03951-4); PLB 10.89 (ISBN 0-690-03952-2). Crowell Jr Bks.
--Where's Al. LC 78-171866. (Illus.). 32p. (ps-3). 1972. 7.95 (ISBN 0-395-28765-0, Clarion). HM.
Barton, Charles. Howard Hughes & His Flying Boat. 274p. 1982. 19.95 (ISBN 0-8168-6457-8); pap. 14.95 (ISBN 0-8168-6456-X). Aero.
Barton, Charles R. & Chappell, William L. Public Administration: The Work of Government. 1985. text ed. 21.95x (ISBN 0-673-15646-X). Scott F.
Barton, Christopher. Cohabitation Contracts. LC 84-6102. 138p. 1984. text ed. 35.50 (ISBN 0-566-00711-8). Gower Pub Co.
Barton, Clara. The Story of My Childhood. Baxter, Annette K., ed. LC 79-8773. (Signal Lives Ser.). (Illus.). 1980. Repr. of 1907 ed. lib. bdg. 16.00x (ISBN 0-405-12823-1). Ayer Co Pubs.
--Story of the Red Cross. (Classics Ser). (gr. 4 up). 1968. pap. 1.50 (ISBN 0-8049-0170-8, CL-170). Airmont.
Barton, Cyril. So Grows the Tree: Life & Memories of Cyril Barton 1921-1971, Vol. 1. (Illus.). 250p. 1984. write for info. (ISBN 0-9613277-0-7); pap. write for info. (ISBN 0-9613277-1-5). C Barton.
Barton, D. E., jt. auth. see David, F. N.
Barton, D. H., ed. see Simonsen, John.
Barton, D. H., et al. Comprehensive Organic Chemistry. Incl. Vol. 1: Stereochemistry, Hydrocarbons, Halo Compounds, & Oxygen Compounds. 230.00x (ISBN 0-08-021313-8); Vol. 2: Nitrogen Compounds, Carboxylic Acids, & Phosphorus Compounds. 230.00x (ISBN 0-08-021314-6); Vol. 3: Sulphur, Selenium, Boron, & Organometallic Compounds. 230.00x (ISBN 0-08-021315-4); Vol. 4: Heterocyclic Compounds. 230.00x (ISBN 0-08-021316-2); Vol. 5: Biological Compounds. 230.00x (ISBN 0-08-021317-0); Vol. 6: Formula, Subject, Author, Reaction & Reagent Indexes. 230.00x (ISBN 0-08-022931-X); Vols. 1-3. half set 687.50; Vols. 4-6. half set 687.50 (ISBN 0-08-023815-7). Vol. 1-3. half set 687.50 (ISBN 0-08-021319-7); Vol. 4-6. half set 687.50 (ISBN 0-08-023815-7). Pergamon.
Barton, D. S., ed. see McCorkle, John.
Barton, David. Notes from the Exile. LC 82-84118. 70p. (Orig.). pap. 3.95 (ISBN 0-941692-05-1). Elysian Pr.
Barton, David K. Monopulse Radar. LC 74-82597. (Radars: Vol. 1). pap. 85.80 (ISBN 0-317-27665-4, 2025059). Bks Demand UMI.
--Pulse Compression. LC 74-82597. (Radars: Vol. 3). pap. 59.30 (ISBN 0-317-27659-X, 2025060). Bks Demand UMI.
--Radar Resolution & Multipath Effects. LC 74-82597. (Radars Ser.: Vol. 4). pap. 94.00 (ISBN 0-317-27647-6, 2025061). Bks Demand UMI.
--Radar Systems Analysis. LC 76-45811. (Artech Radar Library). 1976. Repr. of 1964 ed. 48.00x (ISBN 0-89006-043-6). Artech Hse.
--Radars, Vol. 7: CW & Doppler Radar. LC 78-24055. (Artech Radar Library). 1979. pap. 25.00 (ISBN 0-89006-075-4). Artech Hse.
Barton, David K. & Ward, Harold R. Handbook of Radar Measurement. 425p. 1984. text ed. 55.00 (ISBN 0-89006-155-6). Artech Hse.
Barton, David K., ed. Radars: Radar Clutter, Vol. 5. LC 74-82597. (Artech Radar Library). 1975. pap. 25.00 (ISBN 0-89006-034-7). Artech Hse.
--Radars: The Radar Equation, Vol. 2. 2nd ed. LC 74-82597. (Artech Radar Library). 1975. pap. 25.00 (ISBN 0-89006-031-2). Artech Hse.
Barton, David K., tr. see Basalov, F. A. & Ostrovityanov, R. V.
Barton, Donald F. Their Blood Runneth Orange: Inside Clemson Football. LC 83-80727. (Illus.). 192p. 1983. 7.95 (ISBN 0-88011-174-7). Leisure Pr.
Barton, Donald K., et al. Beginning Spanish Course. 3rd ed. 1976. text ed. 23.95x (ISBN 0-669-96776-9); wkbk. 9.95x (ISBN 0-669-96784-X); tape set 8 reels 50.00 (ISBN 0-669-96792-0); 8 cassettes 30.00 (ISBN 0-669-00082-5); transcript 1.95 (ISBN 0-669-00344-1); demonstration tape 1.95 (ISBN 0-669-00006-X). Heath.
Barton, Donald W. Ministry of Prayer. 165p. 1983. pap. 4.95 (ISBN 0-938736-10-8). LIFE ENRICH.
Barton, Dorothea M., tr. see Andersson, Efraim.
Barton, F. R., ed. R. B. Woodward Remembered: A Collection of Papers in Honour of Robert Burns Woodward 1917-1979. (Illus.). 542p. 1982. 83.00 (ISBN 0-08-029238-0). Pergamon.
Barton, F. R., ed. see Fitzgerald, Edward.
Barton, Florence. Gone to the Cats. LC 84-90350. (Illus.). 160p. (Orig.). 1984. pap. 4.95 (ISBN 0-9613554-0-9). Clin Soc Assn.
--A Trip Through the Magic Valley. (Illus.). 7.95 (ISBN 0-89015-408-2); pap. 5.95 (ISBN 0-89015-421-X). Eakin Pubns.
Barton, Frank. The Press of Africa: Persecution & Perseverence. LC 78-7363. 304p. 1979. text ed. 44.50x (ISBN 0-8419-0393-X, Africana). Holmes & Meier.
Barton, Fredrick. The El Cholo Feeling Passes. 416p. 1985. 14.95 (ISBN 0-931948-78-9). Peachtree Pubs.
Barton, Freeman, ed. Advent Christians & the Bible. 2nd, rev. ed. LC 84-80020. 96p. pap. 4.00 (ISBN 0-913439-03-7). Henceforth.
--Putting the Pieces Together: Advent Christians Interpret Prophecy. 80p. (Orig.). 1983. pap. 3.00 (ISBN 0-913439-02-9). Henceforth.
--Sovereignty & Freedom: A Struggle for Balance. 92p. (Orig.). 1978. pap. 2.50 (ISBN 0-913439-00-2). Henceforth.
Barton, Gail M., jt. auth. see Barton, Walter E.
Barton, George A. Religions of the World. LC 74-90469. Repr. of 1929 ed. lib. bdg. 17.75x (ISBN 0-8371-2216-3, BARW). Greenwood.
Barton, George E. Ordered Pluralism: A Philosophical Plan of Action for Teaching. 2.50 (ISBN 0-8156-7022-2, NES 42). Syracuse U Cont Ed.
--Teaching the Sick: A Manual of Occupational Therapy & Re-Education. Phillips, William R. & Rosenberg, Janet, eds. LC 79-6895. (Physically Handicapped in Society Ser.). (Illus.). 1980. Repr. of 1919 ed. lib. bdg. 17.00x (ISBN 0-405-13106-2). Ayer Co Pubs.
Barton, George S. How to Really Save Money & Energy in Cooling Your Home. rev. ed. LC 78-54385. (Illus.). 1980. pap. 9.95 (ISBN 0-931624-01-0). Chester-Leeds.
Barton, H. Arnold. Letters from the Promised Land: Swedes in America 1840-1914. 344p. 1975. 17.50 (ISBN 0-318-16617-8); pap. 9.95 (ISBN 0-318-16618-6). Swedish-Am.
--Scandinavia in the Revolutionary Era, 1760-1815. Date not set. 39.50 (ISBN 0-8166-1392-3); pap. 16.95 (ISBN 0-8166-1393-1). U of Minn Pr.
--The Search for Ancestors: A Swedish-American Family Saga. LC 78-15537. (Illus.). 189p. 1979. 13.95x (ISBN 0-8093-0893-2). S Ill U Pr.
--The Search for Ancestors: A Swedish-American Family Saga. 178p. 1979. 11.95 (ISBN 0-318-16621-6). Swedish-Am.
Barton, H. Arnold, ed. Letters from the Promised Land: Swedes in America, 1840-1914. LC 74-22843. (Illus.). 350p. 1975. 19.50x (ISBN 0-8166-0740-0); pap. 9.95 (ISBN 0-8166-1009-6). U of Minn Pr.
--Scandinavians & America. 1974. pap. 1.50 (ISBN 0-318-03682-7). Swedish Am.
Barton, Helen B. Nervous Tension, Behavior & Body Function. LC 65-10657. 1965. 6.00 (ISBN 0-8022-0078-8). Philos Lib.
Barton, Hildor A. Clipper Ship & Covered Wagon: Essays from the Swedish Pioneer Historical Quarterly. Scott, Franklyn D., ed. LC 78-14619. (Scandinavians in America Ser.). (Illus.). 1979. 28.50 (ISBN 0-405-11666-7). Ayer Co Pubs.
Barton, J. Amos' Oracles Against the Nations. LC 78-67630. (Society for Old Testament Study Ser.). 1980. 22.95 (ISBN 0-521-22501-9). Cambridge U Pr.
Barton, J. E. Purpose & Admiration: A Law Study of the Visual Arts. 1978. Repr. of 1933 ed. lib. bdg. 30.00 (ISBN 0-8492-3562-6). R West.
Barton, J. J. Domestic Heating & Hot Water Supply. 310p. 1970. 40.75 (ISBN 0-85334-111-7, Pub. by Elsevier Applied Sci England). Elsevier.
Barton, J. L., ed. see Novotny, Frantisek.
Barton, J. W. see Ortmann, Otto.
Barton, Jack S., et al. Future Technical Needs & Trends in the Paper Industry II. (TAPPI PRESS Reports). (Illus.). 82p. 1976. pap. 19.95 (ISBN 0-89852-364-8, 01-01-R064). TAPPI.
Barton, Jerome, ed. Barton's Comic Recitations & Humorous Dialogues... facsimile ed. LC 79-167474. (Granger Index Reprint Ser.). Repr. of 1871 ed. 12.00 (ISBN 0-8369-6279-6). Ayer Co Pubs.
Barton, Jim T. Eighter from Decatur: Growing up in North Texas. LC 79-5279. (Illus.). 172p. 1980. 14.50 (ISBN 0-89096-089-5). Tex A&M Univ Pr.
Barton, Joel R., III & Grice, William A. Tennis. 3rd ed. (Illus.). 118p. 1984. pap. text ed. 4.95x (ISBN 0-89641-147-8). American Pr.
Barton, John. Playing Shakespeare. 208p. 1984. pap. 9.95 (ISBN 0-413-54790-6, NO. 9041); 19.95 (ISBN 0-413-54780-9, NO. 9040). Methuen Inc.
--Reading the Old Testament: Method in Biblical Study. LC 84-3640. 272p. 1984. pap. 12.95 (ISBN 0-664-24555-2). Westminster.
Barton, John & Cavander, Kenneth. The Greeks: Ten Greek Plays Given As a Trilogy. (Orig.). 1981. pap. text ed. 18.50x (ISBN 0-435-23068-9). Heinemann Ed.
Barton, John, jt. auth. see Biokinesiology Institute.
Barton, John & Imai, Ryukichi, eds. Arms Control II: A New Approach to International Security. LC 80-22700. 352p. 1981. text ed. 35.00 (ISBN 0-89946-069-0). Oelgeschlager.
Barton, John, adapted by see Schnitzler, Arthur.
Barton, John H. The Politics of Peace: An Evaluation of Arms Control. LC 79-67776. xii, 257p. 1981. 25.00x (ISBN 0-8047-1081-3). Stanford U Pr.
Barton, John H., et al. Law in Radically Different Cultures. LC 82-24802. (American Casebook Ser.). 960p. 1983. text ed. 27.95 (ISBN 0-314-70396-9). West Pub.
Barton, John P. & Von Der Hardt, Peter. Neutron Radiography. 1983. lib. bdg. 126.00 (ISBN 90-2771-528-9, Pub. by Reidel Holland). Kluwer Academic.
Barton, Josef. Peasants & Strangers: Italians, Rumanians, & Slovaks in an American City, 1890-1950. LC 74-14085. (Studies in Urban History). 240p. 1975. text ed. 15.00x (ISBN 0-674-65930-9). Harvard U Pr.
Barton, Josef J., compiled by. Brief Ethnic Bibliography: An Annotated Guide to the Ethnic Experience in the U. S. LC 76-1282. 56p. pap. 2.75 (ISBN 0-916704-00-9). Langdon Assocs.
Barton, Judith S., ed. Guide to the Bureau of Applied Social Research. LC 81-6133. vi, 222p. 1984. 49.00 (ISBN 0-88354-055-X). Clearwater Pub.
Barton, Keith, jt. auth. see Dielman, Ted.
Barton, Lela V., ed. Bibliography of Seeds. LC 66-20492. 858p. 1967. 85.00x (ISBN 0-231-02937-3). Columbia U Pr.
Barton, Len & Meighan, Roland. Schooling, Ideology & the Curriculum. LC 81-154107. 208p. 1981. text ed. 30.00x (ISBN 0-905273-13-3, Pub. by Falmer Pr); pap. 16.00x (ISBN 0-905273-12-5). Taylor & Francis.
Barton, Len & Walker, Stephen. Schools, Teachers & Teaching. 358p. 1981. text ed. 33.00x (ISBN 0-905273-23-0, Pub. by Falmer Pr); pap. 20.00x (ISBN 0-905273-22-2). Taylor & Francis.
Barton, Len & Meighan, Roland, eds. School Pupils & Deviance. 180p. 1979. pap. 20.00x (ISBN 0-905484-12-6, Pub. by Nafferton England). State Mutual Bk.
--Sociological Interpretations of Schooling & Classrooms: A Reappraisal. 144p. 1979. pap. 20.00x (ISBN 0-905484-04-5, Pub. by Nafferton England). State Mutual Bk.
Barton, Len & Tomlinson, Sally, eds. Special Education & Social Interests. 224p. 1984. 28.50 (ISBN 0-89397-194-4). Nichols Pub.
Barton, Len & Walker, Stephen, eds. Gender, Class & Education. 210p. 1983. 30.00x (ISBN 0-8002-3310-7, Pub. by Falmer Pr); pap. 16.00x (ISBN 0-8002-3300-X). Taylor & Francis.
--Race, Class & Education. 235p. 1983. pap. 11.50 (ISBN 0-7099-0684-6, Pub. by Croom Helm Ltd). Longwood Pub Group.
--Social Crisis & Educational Research. 347p. 1984. 28.00 (ISBN 0-7099-3235-9, Pub. by Croom Helm Ltd); pap. 14.50 (ISBN 0-7099-3248-0). Longwood Pub Group.
Barton, Len, jt. ed. see Lawn, Martin.
Barton, Leonard L. Australians in the Waikato War 1863-1864. 150p. 1981. 15.95 (ISBN 0-908120-27-3, Pub. by Lib Australian Hist). Australia N U P.

Barton, Leslie M. A Study of Eighty-One Principal American Markets. LC 75-22800. (America in Two Centuries Ser). (Illus.). 1976. Repr. of 1925 ed. 34.50x (ISBN 0-405-07672-X). Ayer Co Pubs.

Barton, Lois. Spencer Butte Pioneers: One Hundred Years on the Sunny Side of the Butte 1850-1950. Mills, Charlotte & Northwest Matrix, eds. LC 82-61837. (Illus.). 144p. 1982. pap. 11.95x (ISBN 0-9609420-0-9). S Butte Pr.

Barton, Lucy. Appreciating Costume. 1969. pap. 5.50 (ISBN 0-87440-001-5). Baker's Plays.

--Historic Costume for the Stage. rev. ed. (Illus.). 1961. 20.95 (ISBN 0-87440-002-3). Baker's Plays.

Barton, Lucy & Edson, Doris. Period Patterns. (Illus.). 1942. 7.95 (ISBN 0-87440-003-1). Baker's Plays.

Barton, Lucy, frwd. by see O'Donnol, Shirley M.

Barton, Lyndon O. Mechanism Analysis: Simplified Graphical & Analytical Techniques. (Mechanical Engineering Ser.: Vol. 32). (Illus.). 464p. 1984. 59.75 (ISBN 0-8247-7086-2). Dekker.

Barton, M. Impressions of Mexico with Brush & Pen. 1976. lib. bdg. 59.95 (ISBN 0-8490-3064-1). Gordon Pr.

Barton, Margaret. Garrick. LC 78-612. (Illus.). 312p. 1978. Repr. of 1949 ed. lib. bdg. 27.50x (ISBN 0-313-20270-2, BAGAR). Greenwood.

Barton, Marianne, ed. British Music Yearbook 1982. 8th ed. 512p. 1982. pap. text ed. 24.50x (ISBN 0-8476-4523-1). Rowman.

Barton, Marianne, jt. ed. see Jacobs, Arthur.

Barton, Mary, jt. auth. see Barton, Anthony.

Barton, Mary N., jt. ed. see Kennedy, Virginia W.

Barton, Michael. Goodmen: The Character of Civil War Soldiers. LC 81-139. 144p. 1981. 18.75x (ISBN 0-271-00284-0). Pa St U Pr.

--Life by the Moving Road: An Illustrated History of Greater Harrisburg. (Illus.). 224p. 1983. 24.95 (ISBN 0-89781-064-3). Windsor Pubns Inc.

Barton, P. J., jt. auth. see Darnell, W. H.

Barton, P. K. Building Services Integration. (Illus.). 1983. 27.00 (ISBN 0-419-12030-0, NO. 6830, Pub. by E & FN Spon). Methuen INc.

Barton, Pat. A Week is a Long Time. 28p. write for info (ISBN 0-200-72464-9). Academy Chi Pubs.

Barton, Paul, et al. A New Generation of Leadership: Education for the Gifted in Leadership. 85p. 5.25 (ISBN 0-318-02127-7). NSLTIGT.

Barton, Paul E. Worklife Transitions: Adult Learning. 1982. 19.95 (ISBN 0-07-003974-7). McGraw.

Barton, Paule. The Woe Shirt. Norman, Howard, tr. from Creole. LC 80-81728. (Illus.). 64p. 1980. deluxe ed. 40.00x (ISBN 0-915778-36-X). Penmaen Pr.

--The Woe Shirt. Norman, Howard, tr. from Creole. (Illus.). 64p. (Orig.). 1982. pap. 5.00 (ISBN 0-915308-36-3). Graywolf.

Barton, Phyllis S. Sassone Serigraphs: Catalogue Raisonne. LC 84-71654. 90p. (Orig.). 1984. pap. 25.00 (ISBN 0-935194-01-0). Arti Grafiche.

Barton, R. F. Religion of the Ifugaos. LC 48-3664. (American Anthropological Association Memoirs Ser). Repr. of 1946 ed. 21.00 (ISBN 0-527-00564-9). Kraus Repr.

Barton, R. M. A History of the Cornish China-Clay Industry. 1966. 17.50 (ISBN 0-685-53310-7). ARS Ceramica.

--Life in Cornwall: Early Nineteenth Century. 248p. 1981. 29.00x (ISBN 0-686-97157-4, Pub. by D B Barton England). State Mutual Bk.

--Life in Cornwall: Late 19th Century. 280p. 1981. 29.00x (ISBN 0-686-97163-9, Pub. by D B Barton England). State Mutual Bk.

--Life in Cornwall: Mid Nineteenth Century. 244p. 1981. 29.00x (ISBN 0-686-97164-7, Pub. by D B Barton England). State Mutual Bk.

--Waterfalls of the World. 1981. 30.00x (ISBN 0-686-97153-1, Pub. by D B Barton England). State Mutual Bk.

Barton, Ralph. God's Country. 59.95 (ISBN 0-8490-0242-7). Gordon Pr.

--Science in Rhyme Without Reason. 59.95 (ISBN 0-8490-1000-4). Gordon Pr.

Barton, Rebecca C. Black Voices in American Fiction Nineteen Hundred to Nineteen Thirty. LC 76-10511. 1976. pap. 5.50 (ISBN 0-917428-00-5). Dowling.

--Witnesses for Freedom: Negro Americans in Autobiography. LC 76-29575. 1977. pap. 6.50 (ISBN 0-917428-02-1). Dowling.

Barton, Richard F. The Imaginative Management Game. pap. 12.50 (ISBN 0-914460-00-5). Active Learning.

--The Imaginit Management Game. (Illus.). 320p. 1974. pap. text ed. 9.95x (ISBN 0-685-40092-1). Active Learning.

--The Imaginit Oil Industry Game. 1980. pap. 14.95 (ISBN 0-933836-12-0). Simtek.

Barton, Richard T. Religious Doctrine & Medical Practice. 106p. 1958. 9.75x (ISBN 0-398-00100-6). C C Thomas.

Barton, Robert. Atlas of the Sea. LC 73-18541. (John Day Bk.). (Illus.). 128p. 1974. 10.95i (ISBN 0-381-98267-X). T Y Crowell.

--The Oceans. 336p. 1980. 24.95x (ISBN 0-87196-414-7). Facts on File.

Barton, Robinson J. The Psychological Acumen of Some of the Leading Detectives of All Time in Solving the Most Celebrated Crimes in History. (Illus.). 1982. 67.35 (ISBN 0-89920-039-7). Am Inst Psych.

Barton, Roger E., jt. auth. see Richardson, Richard E.

Barton, Roy F. The Half-Way Sun: Life Among the Headhunters of the Philippines. LC 76-44685. Repr. of 1930 ed. 32.50 (ISBN 0-404-15902-8). AMS Pr.

--Ifugao Law. LC 78-76334. (Illus.). 1969. Repr. of 1919 ed. 26.50x (ISBN 0-520-01427-8). U of Cal Pr.

--Kalingas, Their Institutions & Custom Law. LC 72-161778. Repr. of 1949 ed. 18.00 (ISBN 0-404-09015-X). AMS Pr.

--Philippine Pagans: The Autobiographies of Three Ifugaos. LC 76-44686. Repr. of 1938 ed. 24.50 (ISBN 0-404-15903-6). AMS Pr.

Barton, S. N., ed. Rural Health & Health Communications. (Biosciences Communications: Vol. 4, No. 1). (Illus.). 1977. 11.25 (ISBN 3-8055-2838-8). S Karger.

Barton, S. W., jt. auth. see Kurland, Michael.

Barton, T. C., jt. ed. see Reid, Duncan E.

Barton, Taylor J. The Illustrated JAZZ Book. (Illustrated Ser.). (Illus.). 300p. (Orig.). 1985. pap. 16.98 (ISBN 0-915381-77-X). Wordware Pub.

--The Illustrated Symphony Book. Berliner, Thomas H., ed. LC 84-29181. (Illus.). 240p. Date not set. pap. 17.95 (ISBN 0-915381-69-9). WordWare Pub.

Barton, Thomas, jt. auth. see Moore, James A.

Barton, Thomas J., jt. auth. see Moore, James A.

Barton, Tomlinson. Special Education. 512p. 1982. text ed. 23.50 (ISBN 0-06-318199-1, Pub. by Har-Row Ltd England); pap. text ed. 12.95 (ISBN 0-06-318200-9, Pub. by Har-Row Ltd England). Har-Row.

Barton, W. B., tr. see Heidegger, Martin.

Barton, W. B., Jr., tr. see Heidegger, Martin.

Barton, W. Perry, jt. ed. see Roosevelt, Rita K.

Barton, Walter E. Administration in Psychiatry. (Illus.). 792p. 1962. 64.50x (ISBN 0-398-00101-4). C C Thomas.

Barton, Walter E. & Barton, Gail M. Ethics & Law in Mental Health Administration. LC 84-4610. xxi, 378p. 1984. text ed. 35.00 (ISBN 0-8236-1765-3). Intl Univs Pr.

--Mental Health Administration: Principles & Practice, 2 vols. LC 81-7064. 1008p. 1982. 45.00 ea. Vol. I (ISBN 0-89885-061-4). Vol. II (ISBN 0-89885-062-2). Set. 90.00 (ISBN 0-89885-110-6). Human Sci Pr.

Barton, Walter E. & Sanborn, Charlotte J., eds. Law & the Mental Health Professions: Friction at the Interface. LC 77-90226. 330p. (Orig.). 1978. text ed. 30.00 (ISBN 0-8236-2950-3). Intl Univs Pr.

Barton, Wayne. Chip Carving: Techniques & Patterns. LC 84-8779. (Illus.). 128p. (Orig.). 1985. pap. 8.95 (ISBN 0-8069-7924-0). Sterling.

Barton, Wilfrid C. Shelley & the New Criticism: The Anatomy of a Critical Misvaluation. (Salzburg Studies in English Literature, Romantic Reassessment: No. 5). 228p. 1973. pap. text ed. 25.50x (ISBN 0-391-01314-9). Humanities.

Barton, William A. Outlining As a Study Procedure. LC 77-176539. (Columbia University. Teachers College. Contributions to Education: No. 411). Repr. of 1930 ed. 22.50 (ISBN 0-404-55411-3). AMS Pr.

Barton, William E. Abraham Lincoln & His Books. LC 76-5911. 1976. Repr. lib. bdg. 10.00 (ISBN 0-8414-3346-1). Folcroft.

--Life of Clara Barton, 2 Vols. LC 71-86171. Repr. of 1922 ed. Set. 44.50 (ISBN 0-404-00730-9). AMS Pr.

--Old Plantation Hymns. LC 72-38499. Repr. of 1899 ed. 11.50 (ISBN 0-404-09918-1). AMS Pr.

--Safed the Sage. pap. 3.50 (ISBN 0-8042-3424-8). John Knox.

Barton, William F., tr. see Basalov, F. A. & Ostrovityanov, R. V.

Barton, William H. Fort Bridger: A Brief History. 2nd ed. (Illus.). 80p. 1982. pap. 3.50x (ISBN 0-943398-04-5). Wyoming State Archives.

Barton, Winifred W. John P. Williamson: A Brother to the Sioux. LC 80-53176. (Illus.). 308p. 1980. Repr. of 1919 ed. 16.00 (ISBN 0-9610012-0-8). Sunnycrest Pub.

Bartone, J. C. Computers in Medicine: Current Medical Subject Analysis & Research Directory with Bibliography. LC 81-71809. 162p. 1983. 29.95 (ISBN 0-941864-32-4); pap. 21.95 (ISBN 0-941864-33-2). ABBE Pubs Assn.

Bartone, J. C., ed. see American Health Research Institute.

Bartone, J. C., ed. see American Health Research Institute Ltd.

Bartone, J. C., ed. see Reynolds, Brenda, et al.

Bartone, J. C., et al, eds. see American Health Research Institute.

Bartone, J. C., et al, eds. see American Health Research Institute Ltd.

Bartone, John C. Automatic Data Processing, Artificial Intelligence & Computers: Medical Subject Analysis with Bibliography. LC 83-71669. 144p. 1984. 29.95 (ISBN 0-88164-076-X); pap. 21.95 (ISBN 0-88164-075-1). ABBE Pubs Assn.

--Developing Countries: Status & Progress by Medical Subject Analysis & Research Index with Bibliography. LC 83-71652. 140p. 1984. 29.95 (ISBN 0-941864-93-6); pap. 21.95 (ISBN 0-941864-92-8). ABBE Pubs Assn.

--Diagnosis: General Survey with Medical Research Subject Directory & Bibliography. LC 82-72023. 145p. 1985. 29.95 (ISBN 0-941864-62-6); soft cover 21.95 (ISBN 0-941864-63-4). ABBE Pubs Assn.

--Diagnostic Tests: Medical Subject Analysis with Research Bibliography. LC 84-45646. 150p. 1985. 29.95 (ISBN 0-88164-238-X); pap. 21.95 (ISBN 0-88164-239-8). ABBE Pubs Assn.

--Drug Addiction, Substance Abuse & Narcotic Dependence: A Medical Subject Analysis & Research Index With Bibliography. LC 83-71653. 150p. 1983. 29.95 (ISBN 0-88164-006-9); pap. 21.95 (ISBN 0-88164-007-7). ABBE Pubs Assn.

--Expert Testimony in Medicine, Law & Allied Subjects, I: Subject Analysis with Research Bibliography. LC 84-45867. 150p. 1985. 29.95 (ISBN 0-88164-286-X); pap. 21.95 members (ISBN 0-88164-287-8). ABBE Pubs Assn.

--Family Therapy: Medical Subject Analysis with Research Bibliography. LC 84-45653. 150p. 1985. 29.95 (ISBN 0-88164-224-X); pap. 21.95 (ISBN 0-88164-225-8). ABBE Pubs Assn.

--Hypnosis: Guidebook for Medicine, Reference & Research. LC 83-46102. 150p. 1985. 29.95 (ISBN 0-88164-136-7); pap. 21.95 (ISBN 0-88164-137-5). ABBE Pubs Assn.

--Intelligence Tests: General Survey with Research Subject Index & Bibliography. LC 82-72024. 155p. 1984. 29.95 (ISBN 0-941864-64-2); pap. 21.95 (ISBN 0-941864-65-0). ABBE Pubs Assn.

--Laboratory Diagnosis: Medical Subject Analysis & Research Bibliography. LC 84-45666. 150p. 1985. 29.95 (ISBN 0-88164-196-0); pap. 21.95 (ISBN 0-88164-197-9). ABBE Pubs Assn.

--Marriage & Marital Therapy: Current Medical Subject Analysis & Research Directory with Bibliography. LC 81-71811. 180p. 1984. 29.95 (ISBN 0-941864-78-2); pap. 21.95 members (ISBN 0-941864-79-0). ABBE Pubs Assn.

--Methods in Hypnosis: Guidebook for Medicine, Reference & Research. LC 83-46103. 150p. 1984. 29.95 (ISBN 0-88164-138-3); pap. 21.95 (ISBN 0-88164-139-1). ABBE Pubs Assn.

--Occupational Diseases: International Survey with Medical Research Subject Directory & Bibliography. LC 82-72017. 152p. 1983. 29.95 (ISBN 0-941864-50-2); pap. 21.95 (ISBN 0-941864-51-0). ABBE Pubs Assn.

--Politics & Biomedicine: Subject Analysis & Research Index with Bibliography. LC 83-48714. 155p. 1984. 29.95 (ISBN 0-88164-078-6); pap. 21.95 (ISBN 0-88164-079-4). ABBE Pubs Assn.

--Psychotherapy, Medical & Psychological Research Subject Index with Bibliography. LC 82-72022. 120p. 1983. 29.95 (ISBN 0-941864-60-X); pap. 21.95 (ISBN 0-941864-61-8). ABBE Pubs Assn.

--War: A Medical, Psychological & Scientific Subject Analysis with Research Index & Bibliography. LC 83-71661. 160p. 1984. 29.95 (ISBN 0-941864-91-X); pap. 21.95 (ISBN 0-941864-90-1). ABBE Pubs Assn.

--World Health & the World Health Organization: A Medical Subject Analysis & Research Index with Bibliography. LC 83-71663. 152p. 1985. 29.95 (ISBN 0-88164-020-4); pap. 21.95 (ISBN 0-88164-021-2). ABBE Pubs Assn.

Bartone, John C., ed. see American Health Research Institute.

Bartone, John C., ed. see American Health Research Institute, Ltd.

Bartone, John C., ed. see American Health Research Institute Ltd.

Bartone, John C., ed. see American Health Research Institute, LTD.

Bartone, John C., ed. see American Health Research Institute LTD.

Bartone, John C., ed. see American Health Research Institute Staff.

Bartone, John C., ed. see Holt, Katie L.

Bartone, John C., ed. see Reynolds, Brenda.

Bartone, John C., II. Current Status of Computers in Medicine: Medical Subject Analysis & Bibliography. LC 83-71675. 150p. 1984. 29.95 (ISBN 0-88164-093-X); pap. 21.95 (ISBN 0-88164-092-1). ABBE Pubs Assn.

--Drug Effects on Memory: Medical Subject Analysis with Research Bibliography. LC 84-45656. 150p. 1985. 29.95 (ISBN 0-88164-218-5); pap. 21.95 (ISBN 0-88164-219-3). ABBE Pubs Assn.

--Health & Medical Aspects of Chemical Industries: Subject Analysis & Research Guide. LC 83-45536. 153p. 1984. 29.95 (ISBN 0-88164-104-9); pap. 21.95 (ISBN 0-88164-105-7). ABBE Pubs Assn.

--Medical Electronics & Instrumentation: Research Subject Analysis. LC 83-45291. 166p. 1983. 34.00 (ISBN 0-88164-066-2); pap. 29.95 (ISBN 0-88164-067-0). ABBE Pubs Assn.

--Microwaves & Radiation: Medical Analysis Index with Research Bibliography. LC 85-47580. 150p. 1985. 29.95 (ISBN 0-88164-334-3); pap. 21.95 (ISBN 0-88164-335-1). ABBE Pubs Assn.

--Muscles & Drug Effects: Medical Subject Analysis with Research Bibliography. LC 84-45657. 150p. 1985. 29.95 (ISBN 0-88164-216-9); pap. 21.95 (ISBN 0-88164-217-7). ABBE Pubs Assn.

--Radio & Radio Waves: Medical Research Index with Reference Bibliography. LC 85-47571. 150p. 1985. 29.95 (ISBN 0-88164-316-5); pap. 21.95 (ISBN 0-88164-317-3). ABBE Pubs Assn.

--Science & Medicine of Sports: With Research Subject Analysis & Bibliography. LC 83-71668. 166p. 1984. 29.95 (ISBN 0-88164-065-4); pap. 21.95 (ISBN 0-88164-064-6). ABBE Pubs Assn.

--Ultraviolet Rays, Factors & Adverse Effects: Medical Analysis Index with Research Bibliography. LC 85-47862. 150p. 1985. 29.95 (ISBN 0-88164-398-X); pap. 21.95 (ISBN 0-88164-399-8). ABBE Pubs Assn.

Bartone, Mary R. Communication in Medicine & Psychology: Reference & Research Guide. LC 84-45658. 150p. 1985. 29.95 (ISBN 0-88164-214-2); pap. 21.95 (ISBN 0-88164-215-0). ABBE Pubs Assn.

--Computer-Assisted Instruction & Education: Medical Applications & Subject Analysis with Bibliography. LC 83-71672. 146p. 1984. 29.95 (ISBN 0-88164-056-5); pap. 21.95 (ISBN 0-88164-057-3). ABBE Pubs Assn.

--Health Policy With Plans, Priorities, Problems & Politics: Medical Analysis Index With Bibliography. LC 85-47853. 1985. 29.95 (ISBN 0-88164-380-7); pap. 21.95 (ISBN 0-88164-381-5). ABBE Pubs Assn.

--Hospital Economics & Medical Services: Subject Analysis Index With Reference Bibliography. LC 85-47856. 150p. 1985. 29.95 (ISBN 0-88164-386-6); pap. 21.95 (ISBN 0-88164-387-4). ABBE Pubs Assn.

--Insurance Liability: Medical Subject Analysis & Research Guide with Bibliography. LC 83-45532. 139p. 1984. 29.95 (ISBN 0-88164-116-2); pap. 21.95 (ISBN 0-88164-117-0). ABBE Pubs Assn.

--Life Change Events & Health Sciences: Subject Analysis Index With Research Bibliography. LC 85-47584. 150p. 1985. 29.95 (ISBN 0-88164-342-4); pap. 21.95 (ISBN 0-88164-343-2). ABBE Pubs Assn.

--Medical Economics: International Subject Analysis & Research Index with Bibliography. LC 83-71670. 142p. 1983. 29.95 (ISBN 0-88164-050-6); pap. 21.95 (ISBN 0-88164-051-4). ABBE Pubs Assn.

--Physical Fitness & Sports Medicine: Subject Analysis & Research Index with Bibliography. LC 83-71676. 151p. 1984. 29.95 (ISBN 0-88164-062-X); pap. 21.95 (ISBN 0-88164-063-8). ABBE Pubs Assn.

--Protective Devices for Sports & Work II: Research Subject Analysis with Bibliography. LC 84-45655. 150p. 1985. 29.95 (ISBN 0-88164-220-7); pap. 21.95 (ISBN 0-88164-221-5). ABBE Pubs Assn.

--Research on Health: A Medical Subject Analysis with Bibliography. LC 84-45738. 150p. 1985. 29.95 (ISBN 0-88164-254-1); pap. 21.95 (ISBN 0-88164-255-X). ABBE Pubs Assn.

--Television in Medicine & Science: Subject Analysis & Research Guide with Bibliography. LC 83-45546. 152p. 1984. 29.95 (ISBN 0-88164-088-3); pap. 21.95 (ISBN 0-88164-089-1). ABBE Pubs Assn.

Barton-Jay, David. The Enema as an Erotic Art & Its History. (Illus.). 336p. (Orig.). 1984. pap. 47.50 (ISBN 0-910409-00-5). Barton-Jay Proj.

Bartoo, Glenn. Decisions by Consensus: A Study of the Quaker Method. (Studies in Quakerism: No. 4). 48p. (Orig.). 1978. pap. 2.00 (ISBN 0-89670-003-8). Progresiv Pub.

Bartorillo, Andrew. PCjr BASIC Programs for the Home: Programs That Make the PCjr a Useful Member of the Family. 272p. 1984. pap. 14.95 (ISBN 0-88693-069-3). Banbury Bks.

Bartos, Beth, ed. see Junior Service League of Brooksville Florida.

Bartos, Bob. The Dog for You-- America's Most Popular Breeds. 1980. pap. 1.95 (ISBN 0-451-09130-2, J9130, Sig). NAL.

Bartos, J. & Pesez, M. Colormetric & Fluorimetric Analysis of Steroids. 1977. 55.00 (ISBN 0-12-080150-7). Acad Pr.

Bartos, J., jt. auth. see Pesez, M.

Bartos, Otomar. The Process & Outcome of Negotiations. LC 73-12473. 451p. 1974. 40.00x (ISBN 0-231-03242-0). Columbia U Pr.

Bartos, Otomar J. Simple Models of Group Behavior. LC 67-21498. (Illus.). 345p. 1967. 36.00x (ISBN 0-231-02894-6); pap. 18.00x (ISBN 0-231-02893-8). Columbia U Pr.

Bartos, P., ed. Bond in Concrete. (Applied Science Ser.). (Illus.). 446p. 1982. 77.75 (ISBN 0-85334-156-7, Pub. by Elsevier Applied Sci England). Elsevier.

Bartos, Rena. The Moving Target: What Every Marketer Should Know About Women. LC 81-70148. (Illus.). 320p. 1982. text ed. 17.95 (ISBN 0-02-901700-9). Free Pr.

Bartosek, Ivan, et al, eds. Animals in Toxicological Research. (Monographs of the Mario Negri Institute for Pharmacological Research). 224p. 1982. text ed. 38.50 (ISBN 0-89004-811-8). Raven.

Bartosic, Florian. Labor Relations Law in the Private Sector. 322p. 1977. 30.00 (ISBN 0-317-32231-1, B234). Am Law Inst.

Bartosova, Ludmila, et al. Diseases of the Hair & the Scalp. (Current Problems in Dermatology: Vol. 12). (Illus.). x, 252p. 1984. 35.00 (ISBN 3-8055-3783-2). S Karger.

Bartove, Liisa, tr. see Siikala, Kalervo.

Bartow, Charles L. The Preaching Moment: A Guide to Sermon Delivery. LC 80-12370. (Abingdon Preacher's Library). (Orig.). 1980. pap. 5.95 (ISBN 0-687-33907-3). Abingdon.

Bartow, Donald W. The Adventures of Healing: How to Use New Testament Practices & Receive New Testament Results. rev. ed. 371p. 1981. pap. 5.95 (ISBN 0-938736-02-7). Life Enrich.

Bartow, Gene & Smith, Chuck. Winning Basketball. LC 78-73265. (Illus.). 1978. text ed. 13.95x (ISBN 0-88273-711-2). Forum Pr IL.

Bartram. Radiology in Inflammatory Bowel Disease. (Diagnostic Radiology Ser.). 448p. 1983. 55.00 (ISBN 0-8247-1804-6). Dekker.

Bartram, Alan. Lettering in Architecture. 176p. 1980. 40.00x (ISBN 0-85331-382-2, Pub. by Lund Humphries England). State Mutual Bk.

Bartram, Alan, jt. auth. see Sutton, James.

Bartram, Clive I. & Kumar, Parveen. Clinical Radiology in Gastroenterology. (Illus.). 252p. 1981. text ed. 36.50 (ISBN 0-632-00213-1, B 0533-4). Mosby.

Bartram, E. B. Manual of Hawaiian Mosses. (BMB). Repr. of 1933 ed. 37.00 (ISBN 0-527-02207-1). Kraus Repr.

--Mosses of the Phillipines. (Illus.). 437p. 1972. Repr. of 1939 ed. lib. bdg. 47.25x (ISBN 3-87429-033-6). Lubrecht & Cramer.

Bartram, G. & Waine, A. Brecht in Perspective. LC 81-13755. (Illus.). 288p. (Orig.). 1982. pap. text ed. 12.95x (ISBN 0-582-49205-X). Longman.

Bartram, George. Under the Freeze. 400p. (Orig.). 1984. pap. 3.50 (ISBN 0-523-42055-2). Pinnacle Bks.

Bartram, Gerry, ed. see Zanzucchi, Anne M.

Bartram, Thomas. Nature's Plan for Your Health. (Illus.). 160p. (Orig.). 1984. pap. 7.95 (ISBN 0-7137-1471-9, Pub. by Blandford Pr England). Sterling.

Bartram, W. Travels Through North & South Carolina. 59.95 (ISBN 0-8490-1229-5). Gordon Pr.

Bartram, William. Travels. 1928. pap. 6.00 (ISBN 0-486-20013-2). Dover.

--Travels. Van Doren, Mark, ed. (Illus.). 15.50 (ISBN 0-8446-1600-1). Peter Smith.

--The Travels of William Bartram. Peck, Robert M., ed. & intro. by. (Literature of the American Wilderness). 382p. 1980. pap. 3.95 (ISBN 0-87905-079-9, Peregrine Smith). Gibbs M Smith.

--Travels Through North & South Carolina, Georgia, East & West Florida. LC 73-84685. (Illus.). 534p. 1980. Repr. of 1973 ed. 14.95 (ISBN 0-8139-0871-X). U Pr of Va.

Bartrip, P. W. & Burman, S. B. The Wounded Soldiers of Industry: Industrial Compensation Policy, 1833-1897. LC 83-8229. (Oxford Socio-Legal Studies). (Illus.). 1983. 29.95x (ISBN 0-19-827509-9). Oxford U Pr.

Bartrum, P. C., ed. Early Welsh Genealogical Tracts. 228p. 1966. text ed. 12.50x (ISBN 0-7083-0049-9, Pub. by Univ of Wales Pr England). Humanities.

Bartrum, Royal J., jt. auth. see Young, Stuart W., Jr.

Bartrum, Royal J., Jr. & Crow, Harte C. Case Studies in Ultrasound. (Illus.). 1979. text ed. 28.95 (ISBN 0-7216-1553-8). Saunders.

--Real Time Ultrasound: A Manual for Physician & Technical Personnel. 2nd ed. LC 77-72802. (Illus.). 1983. text ed. 26.00 (ISBN 0-7216-1552-X). Saunders.

Bartsch, Hans-Jochen. Handbook of Mathematical Formulas. 1974. 35.00 (ISBN 0-12-080050-0). Acad Pr.

Bartsch, Karl F. Chrestomathie Provencal. 6th ed. LC 72-38500. (Fr.). Repr. of 1904 ed. 26.00 (ISBN 0-404-08346-3). AMS Pr.

--Untersuchungen Zur Jenaer Leiderhandschrift. 18.00 (ISBN 0-384-03490-X); pap. 13.00 (ISBN 0-685-02216-1). Johnson Repr.

Bartsch, R. Grammar of Adverbials. (Linguistics Ser.: Vol. 16). 390p. 1976. 59.75 (ISBN 0-444-10964-1, North-Holland). Elsevier.

Bartscht, Waltraud. Goethe's "Das Marchen". Translation and Analysis. LC 72-132826. (Studies in Germanic Languages & Literations: No. 3). 112p. 1972. 11.00x (ISBN 0-8131-1237-0). U Pr of Ky.

Bartsocas, Christos S. Progress in Dermatoglyphic Research. LC 82-215. (Progress in Clinical & Biological Research Ser.: Vol. 84). 474p. 1982. 48.00 (ISBN 0-8451-0084-X). A R Liss.

Bartsocas, Christos S. & Papadatos, Constantine J., eds. The Management of Genetic Disorders: Proceedings. LC 79-5298. (Progress in Clinical & Biological Research Ser.: Vol. 34). 430p. 1979. 42.00x (ISBN 0-8451-0034-3). A R Liss.

Bartsocas, Christos S., jt. ed. see Papadatos, Costas J.

Bartson, Lester, ed. see Hammond, Mason.

Bartusch, Nancy, jt. auth. see Geiger, Michael.

Bart-Williams, P. J. Evolution & the Word of God. LC 83-91501. 87p. 1985. 8.95 (ISBN 0-533-06080-X). Vantage.

Barty-King, Hugh. Girdle Round the Earth-Story of Cable & Wireless. 1979. 21.50 (ISBN 0-434-04902-6, Pub. by W Heinemann Ltd). David & Charles.

Barty-King, Hugh & Massel, Anton. Rum: Yesterday & Today. (Illus.). 281p. 1984. 19.95 (ISBN 0-434-45280-7, Pub. by W Heinemann Ltd). David & Charles.

Bartz, Albert E. Basic Statistical Concepts. 2nd ed. LC 80-70169. 1981. text ed. 19.95x (ISBN 0-8087-4041-5). Burgess.

--Descriptive Statistics for Education & the Behavioral Sciences. 5th ed. LC 77-91504. Orig. Title: Basic Descriptive Statistics for Education & the Behavioral Sciences. 1979. pap. text ed. 8.95x (ISBN 0-8087-2853-9). Burgess.

Bartz, Carl. Operating Internationally: A Sourcebook of Assistance for Associations, Businesses, Professionals, & Plain Citizens. 136p. 1981. pap. 30.00 (ISBN 0-88034-001-0). Am Soc Assn Execs.

Bartz, Christine E., ed. see Case, Frederick W., Jr.

Bartz, Fritz. San Francisco-Oakland Metropolitan Area, Strukturwandlungen Eines U. S. Amerikanischen Grossstadtkomplexes. Repr. of 1954 ed. 20.00 (ISBN 0-384-03495-0). Johnson Repr.

Bartz, Patricia M. South Korea. (Illus.). 1972. 42.00x (ISBN 0-19-874008-5). Oxford U Pr.

Bartz, Walter H. Testing Oral Communication in the Foreign Language Classroom. (Language in Education Ser.: No. 17). 25p. 1979. pap. 3.95 (ISBN 0-15-599005-5). Ctr Appl Ling.

Bartz, Wayne & Rasor, Richard. Surviving with Kids. LC 78-13328. (Illus.). 1978. pap. 5.95 (ISBN 0-915166-55-0). Impact Pubs Cal.

Bartz, Wayne R., jt. auth. see Vogler, Roger E.

Baru, A. V. The Brain & Hearing: Hearing Disturbances Associated with Local Brain Lesions. LC 72-82624. 126p. 1972. 25.00x (ISBN 0-306-10876-3, Consultants). Plenum Pub.

Barua, B. P. Politics & Constitution-Making in India & Pakistan. 216p. 1984. text ed. 22.50x (ISBN 0-391-03266-6, Pub. by Deep & Deep India). Humanities.

Barua, Benimadhab. A History of Pre-Buddhistic Indian Philosophy. 1981. Repr. of 1921 ed. 28.50x (ISBN 0-8364-0800-4, Pub. by Motilal Banarsidass). South Asia Bks.

Barua, Tushar Kanti. Political Elite in Bangladesh: A Socio-Anthropological & Historical Analysis of the Processes of Their Formation. (European University Studies: Series 19, Anthropology-Ethnology, Section B, Ethnology: Vol. 4). 354p. 1978. 42.15 (ISBN 3-261-03131-X). P Lang Pubs.

Baruah, Amrit. The Nineteen Fifty's & One Foreign Student. 300p. 1984. text ed. 30.00x (ISBN 0-391-03160-0, Pub. by Radiant Pub India). Humanities.

Baruah, H. K. Textbook of Plant Pathology. 486p. 1979. 50.00 (ISBN 0-686-84470-X, Pub. by Oxford & I B H India). State Mutual Bk.

Baruah, T. C. The English Teacher's Handbook. xvi, 352p. 1984. text ed. 35.00x (ISBN 0-86590-419-7, Pub. by Sterling Pubs India). Apt Bks.

Baruch, et al. Life Prints: New Patterns of Love & Work for Todays Women. 1985. pap. 4.50 (ISBN 0-451-13860-0, Sig). NAL.

Baruch, Dorothy W. New Ways in Discipline. 1949. 12.95 (ISBN 0-07-004040-0). McGraw.

--One Little Boy. 256p. 1983. pap. 3.95 (ISBN 0-440-36631-3, LE). Dell.

Baruch, Elaine H., jt. ed. see Rohrlich, Ruby.

Baruch, G. & Barnett, R. Lifeprints: New Patterns of Love & Work for Today's Women. 368p. 1983. 14.95 (ISBN 0-07-052981-7). McGraw.

Baruch, Grace & Brooks-Gunn, Jeanne, eds. Women in Midlife. (Women in Context Ser.). 400p. 1984. 35.00x (ISBN 0-306-41444-9, Plenum Pr). Plenum Pub.

Baruch, Grace, et al. Lifeprints: New Patterns of Love & Work for Today's Women. LC 83-22045. 304p. 1984. pap. 8.95 (ISBN 0-452-25533-3, Plume). NAL.

Baruch, Grace K., jt. auth. see Barnett, Rosalind.

Baruch, Grace K., jt. auth. see Barnett, Rosalind C.

Baruch, Ismar. Position Classification in the Public Service. 1965. 10.00 (ISBN 0-87373-000-3). Intl Personnel Mgmt.

Baruch, Knei-Paz see Knei-Paz, Baruch.

Baruch, Miriam S. Diary of the "Y". 120p. 1978. write for info. (ISBN 0-8187-0049-1). Harlo Pr.

Baruchello, Gianfranco & Martin, Henry. How to Imagine. Date not set. 3.95 (ISBN 0-317-31354-1). Bantam.

--How to Imagine: A Narrative on Art & Agriculture. LC 83-14954. 160p. 1984. 20.00 (ISBN 0-914232-51-7, Documentext); pap. 10.00 (ISBN 0-914232-52-5); limited ed. 100.00 (ISBN 0-914232-53-3). McPherson & Co.

--Why Duchamp: An Essay on Aesthetic Impact. 160p. 1985. 20.00 (ISBN 0-914232-71-1); pap. 10.00 (ISBN 0-914232-73-8); deluxe ed. 200.00 (ISBN 0-914232-72-X). McPherson & Co.

Barukinamwo, Matthieu. Edith Stein: Pour une Ontologie Dynamique, Ouverte a la Transcendance Totale. (European University Studies: Ser. No. 23, Vol. 169). 184p. (Fr.). 1982. 24.20 (ISBN 3-8204-5974-X). P Lang Pubs.

Barus, Carl. Experiments with the Displacement Interferometer. LC 15-26885. (Carnegie Institution of Washington. Publication: No.229). pap. 29.80 (ISBN 0-317-08462-3, 2003129). Bks Demand UMI.

Barut, A. O. Electrodynamics & Classical Theory of Fields & Particles. (Illus.). 256p. 1980. pap. text ed. 4.50 (ISBN 0-486-64038-8). Dover.

Barut, A. O., ed. Foundations of Radiation Theory & Quantum Electrodynamics. LC 79-25715. (Illus.). 230p. 1980. 35.00x (ISBN 0-306-40277-7, Plenum Pr). Plenum Pub.

--Quantum Electrodynamics & Quantum Optics. (NATO ASI Ser. B, Physics: Vol. 110). 482p. 1984. 75.00x (ISBN 0-306-41730-8, Plenum Pr). Plenum Pub.

--Quantum Theory, Groups, Fields & Particles. 1983. lib. bdg. 45.50 (ISBN 90-277-1552-1, Pub. by Reidel Holland). Kluwer Academic.

Barut, A. O. & Brittin, Wesley E., eds. Lectures in Theoretical Physics, Vol. 14A: Topics in Strong Interactions. (Illus.). 455p. 1972. text ed. 22.50x (ISBN 0-87081-043-X). Colo Assoc.

Barut, A. O., jt. ed. see Brittin, Wesley E.

Barut, A. O., ed. see NATO Advanced Study Institute, Istanbul, Turkey, Aug., 1970.

Barut, A. O., ed. see NATO Advanced Study Institute, Istanbul, Turkey, Aug, 1972.

Barut, Asim O., ed. Scattering Theory: Aspects of Scattering Processes in Atomic, Nuclear, & Particle Physics. 440p. 1969. 119.25 (ISBN 0-677-12730-8). Gordon.

Barut, Asim O. & Brittin, Wesley E., eds. Lectures in Theoretical Physics Vol. 13: Desitter & Conformal Groups & Their Applications. 1971. 22.50x (ISBN 0-87081-014-6); pap. text ed. 10.00x (ISBN 0-87081-039-1). Colo Assoc.

Barut, Asim O., et al, eds. Quantum Space & Time-the Quest Continues: Studies & Essays in Honour of Louis de Broglie, Paul Dirac & Eugene Wigner. (Monographs in Physics). (Illus.). 680p. 1984. pap. 49.50 (ISBN 0-521-31911-0). Cambridge U Pr.

Baruth & Duff, eds. Early Childhood Education. (Special Education Ser.). (Illus., Orig.). 1979. pap. text ed. 16.00 (ISBN 0-89568-100-5). Spec Learn Corp.

Baruth & Lane, eds. Child Psychology. (Special Education Ser.). (Illus., Orig.). 1979. pap. text ed. 16.00 (ISBN 0-89568-101-3). Spec Learn Corp.

Baruth, Leroy & Huber, Charles. Counseling & Psychotherapy: Theoretical Analysis & Skills Applications. 480p. 1984. text ed. 24.95 (ISBN 0-675-20299-X). Additional supplements may be obtained from publisher. Merrill.

Baruth, Leroy G. A Single Parent's Survival Guide: How to Raise the Children. 1979. pap. text ed. 6.95 (ISBN 0-8403-2053-1). Kendall-Hunt.

Baruth, Leroy G. & Eckstein, Daniel G. Life Style: Theory, Practice, & Research. 2nd ed. 224p. 1981. pap. text ed. 13.95 (ISBN 0-8403-2375-1, 40237501). Kendall-Hunt.

Baruth, Leroy G. & Huber, Charles H. An Introduction to Marital Theory & Therapy. LC 83-14275. (Psychology Ser.). 300p. 1983. text ed. 18.75 pub net (ISBN 0-534-02820-9). Brooks-Cole.

Baruth, Leroy G., jt. auth. see Huber, Charles H.

Barutio, William H., jt. auth. see Eizenstat, Stuart E.

Barva, Cecile M. Castle Country. 128p. 1982. 8.95 (ISBN 0-89962-229-1). Todd & Honeywell.

Barvicks, Alex. VHF Antenna Handbook. 94p. 1975-1980. pap. 5.95 (ISBN 0-88006-014-X, BK 7368). Green Pub Inc.

Barwell, Anna, tr. see Stern, William.

Barwell, Anna, tr. see Von Hanstein, Otfrid.

Barwell, Eve. Disguises You Can Make. LC 77-24998. (Lothrop Craft Ser.). (Illus.). (gr. 3-7). 1977. PLB 11.88 (ISBN 0-688-51810-9). Lothrop.

Barwell, F. T. Automation & Control in Transport. 2nd rev. ed. LC 82-18981. 400p. 1983. 66.00 (ISBN 0-08-026712-2). Pergamon.

--Bearing Systems: Principles & Practice. (Illus.). 1979. 78.00x (ISBN 0-19-856319-1). Oxford U Pr.

Barwell, I., et al. Rural Transport in Developing Countries. (Illus.). 145p. 1985. pap. 13.50 (ISBN 0-8133-0271-4). Westview.

Barwick, D., et al, eds. Handbook for Aboriginal & Islander History. 187p. 1980. pap. text ed. 5.00 (ISBN 0-908160-15-1, 0339, Pub. by ANUP Australia). Australia N U P.

Barwick, Dee, compiled by. A Treasury of Days. (Illus.). 1983. 8.00 (ISBN 0-8378-1803-6). Gibson.

Barwick, Diane & Urry, James, eds. Aboriginal History, Vol. 5. 178p. (Orig.). 1982. pap. text ed. 8.50 (ISBN 0-686-37604-8, 1188, Pub. by ANUP Australia). Australia N U P.

--Aboriginal History, Vol. 6. (Illus.). 179p. 1984. pap. text ed. 8.50x (ISBN 0-317-00619-3). Australia N U P.

Barwick, Frances. Pictures from the Douglas M. Duncan Collections. LC 74-75587. pap. 40.00 (ISBN 0-317-26832-5, 2023491). Bks Demand UMI.

Barwick, Humphrey. Concerning the Force & Effect of Manual Weapons of Fire. LC 74-80163. (English Experience Ser.: No. 643). 86p. 1974. Repr. of 1594 ed. 8.00 (ISBN 90-221-0643-8). Walter J Johnson.

Barwick, Humphrey, jt. auth. see Smythe, John.

Barwick, James. The Hangman's Crusade. 1983. pap. 2.95 (ISBN 0-686-80983-1). Ballantine.

--Shadow of the Wolf. 1981. pap. 2.75 (ISBN 0-345-28316-3). Ballantine.

Barwick, Karl. Remmius Palaemon und Die Romische Ars Grammatica. Repr. of 1922 ed. 17.00 (ISBN 0-384-03505-1). Johnson Repr.

Barwick, Sandra. A Century of Style. (Illus.). 192p. 1984. 24.50x (ISBN 0-04-391009-2). Allen Unwin.

Barwick, Steven. The Franco Codex of the Cathedral of Mexico: Transcription & Commentary. LC 64-20256. 190p. 1965. 10.00x (ISBN 0-8093-0165-2). S Ill U Pr.

Barwick, Steven, tr. Two Mexico City Choirbooks of Seventeen Hundred Seventeen: An Anthology of Sacred Polyphony from the Cathedral of Mexico. LC 82-3047. 213p. 1982. 16.95x (ISBN 0-8093-1065-1). S Ill U Pr.

Barwig, Regis N. Waiting for Rain: Meantime Reflections on the Life of Religious Consecration. 1975. pap. 5.00 (ISBN 0-686-18875-6). Benziger Sis.

Barwig, Regis N., ed. More Than a Prophet. 1978. 2.25 (ISBN 0-686-10181-2). Benziger Sis.

Barwig, Regis N., tr. & pref. by see Confalonieri, Cardinal Carlo.

Barwin, B. Norman, et al. Self-Assessment of Current Knowledge in Infertility & Gynecologic Endocrinology. 1979. spiral bdg. 21.00 (ISBN 0-87488-231-1). Med Exam.

Barwin, Norman B. & Belisle, Serge, eds. Adolescent Gynecology & Sexuality. LC 82-6583. (Illus.). 128p. 1982. flexicover 16.50 (ISBN 0-89352-167-1). Masson Pub.

Barwise, J. Handbook of Mathematical Logic. (Studies in Logic & Foundations of Mathematics: Vol. 90). 1166p. 1982. 95.00 (ISBN 0-7204-2285-X, North Holland); pap. 50.00 (ISBN 0-444-86388-5). Elsevier.

Barwise, J., ed. Syntax & Semantics of Infinitary Languages. LC 68-57175. (Lecture Notes in Mathematics: Vol. 72). 1968. pap. 14.70 (ISBN 0-387-04242-3). Springer-Verlag.

Barwise, J. & Feferman, S., eds. Model-Theoretic Logics. (Perspectives in Mathematical Logic). (Illus.). 750p. 1985. 140.00 (ISBN 0-387-90936-2). Springer-Verlag.

Barwise, J., et al, eds. Kleene Symposium. (Studies in Logic: Vol. 101). 426p. 1980. 70.25 (ISBN 0-444-85345-6). Elsevier.

Barwise, Jon & Perry, John. Situations & Attitudes. 256p. 1983. 27.50x (ISBN 0-262-02189-7). MIT Pr.

--Situations & Attitudes. 376p. 1985. pap. text ed. 9.95x (ISBN 0-262-52099-0, Pub. by BradFord). MIT Pr.

Barwise, K. J. Admissible Sets & Structures: An Approach to Definability Theory. (Perspectives in Mathematical Logic Ser.). (Illus.). 400p. 1975. 47.50 (ISBN 0-387-07451-1). Springer-Verlag.

Bary, Anton De see De Bary, Anton.

Bary, Constantine W. Operational Economics of Electric Utilities. LC 63-9807. (Illus.). 221p. 1963. 30.00x (ISBN 0-231-02614-5). Columbia U Pr.

Bary, Valeska, jt. auth. see Cahn, Frances.

Bary, W. Theodore de see Conference on Oriental Classics in General Education (1958: Columbia University) Staff.

Bary, William T. De see Saikaku, Ihara.

Bary, William T. De see De Bary, W. Theodore & Bloom, Irene.

Bary, William T. De see De Bary, William T.

Bar-Yaacov, Nissim. The Israel-Syrian Armistice: Problems of Implementation, 1949-1966. LC 68-988. (Illus.). pap. 95.50 (ISBN 0-317-11312-7, 2051593). Bks Demand UMI.

--The Israel-Syrian Armistice: Problems of Implementation, 1949-1966. LC 68-988. pap. 95.50 (ISBN 0-317-28633-1, 2051593). Bks Demand UMI.

Bar Yohai, Shimon. Hashmotot Zohar: Hebrew Text. 1969. 20.00 (ISBN 0-943688-20-5). Res Ctr Kabbalah.

--Zohar: Hebrew Text, 21 vols. 378.00 set (ISBN 0-686-21743-8); 18.00 ea. Res Ctr Kabbalah.

--Zohar: Hebrew Text, 10 vols. condensed ed. 1981. 15.00 ea.; 150.00 set. Res Ctr Kabbalah.

Baryollas, Clemens & Miller, Staurt. Participants in American Criminal Justice: The Promise & the Performance. (Illus.). 416p. 1983. prof. ref. 27.95 (ISBN 0-13-651349-2). P-H.

Baryshnikov, Mikhail. Baryshnikov. France, Charles E., ed. (Illus.). 64p. 1980. 14.95 (ISBN 0-8109-2225-8, 2225-8). Abrams.

Baryshnikov, Mikhail & Swope, Martha. Baryshnikov at Work. 1976. 35.00 (ISBN 0-394-40345-2). Knopf.

--Baryshnikov at Work. LC 76-13685. 1978. pap. 17.95 (ISBN 0-394-73587-0). Knopf.

Barz, Sandra B., ed. Inuit Artists Print Workbook. (Illus.). 324p. (Orig.). 1981. pap. 58.00 (ISBN 0-9605898-0-5). Arts & Culture.

Barza, Michael, jt. auth. see Proger, Samuel.

Barzakovskii, V. P., jt. auth. see Toropov, N. A.

Barzan, A. Automation in Electrical Power Systems. 430p. 1977. 9.45 (ISBN 0-8285-0670-1, Pub. by Mir Pubs USSR). Imported Pubns.

Barzanti, Sergio. Underdeveloped Areas Within the Common Market. 1965. 41.00x (ISBN 0-691-04188-1); pap. 13.50x (ISBN 0-691-00353-X). Princeton U Pr.

Barzel, Uriel S., ed. Osteoporosis II. 304p. 1979. 44.50 (ISBN 0-8089-1181-3, 790446). Grune.

Barzel, Yoram & Hall, Christopher D. The Political Economy of the Oil Import Quota. LC 76-41087. (Publications Ser.: No. 172). 1977. 9.95x (ISBN 0-8179-6721-4). Hoover Inst Pr.

Barzelay, Michael. The Politicized Market Economy: Alcohol in the Brazilian Energy Strategy. 1986. 28.50x (ISBN 0-520-05382-6). U of Cal Pr.

Barzen, J., ed. see Heberden, M. V.

Barzilay, David. British Army in Ulster. (Illus.). 1976. Repr. of 1973 ed. 29.95x set (ISBN 0-8464-0209-2). Beekman Pubs.

Barzilay, Isaac, jt. ed. see Baron, Salo W.

Barzini, Luigi. The Europeans. 272p. 1984. pap. 6.95 (ISBN 0-14-007150-4). Penguin.

--The Italians. LC 63-17858. 1977. pap. 8.95 (ISBN 0-689-70540-9, 225). Atheneum.

--The Italians. 16.25 (ISBN 0-8446-6146-5). Peter Smith.

--O America: When You & I Were Young. (Penguin Nonfiction Ser.). 1985. pap. 5.95 (ISBN 0-317-19372-4). Penguin.

Barzman, Ben & Barzman, Norma. Rich Dreams. 528p. 1982. pap. 3.50 (ISBN 0-446-90034-6). Warner Bks.

Barzman, Norma, jt. auth. see Barzman, Ben.

Barzman, Sol. The Complete Guide for Credit & Collection Letters. Andover, James J., ed. LC 82-22548. 240p. 1983. 26.95 (ISBN 0-934914-48-6). NACM.

--Credit in Early America. 1975. pap. 4.95 (ISBN 0-934914-11-7). NACM.

--Everyday Credit Checking: A Practical Guide. rev. ed. Andover, James J., ed. LC 80-82080. 289p. 1980. 15.95 (ISBN 0-934914-36-2). NACM.

--Everyday Credit Checking: A Practical Guide. 256p. 1973. 9.95i (ISBN 0-690-27107-7). T Y Crowell.

--The Marginal Account: A Practical Guide. Andover, James J., ed. LC 83-21961. 175p. 1984. 20.95 (ISBN 0-934914-52-4). NACM.

Bar-Zohar, Michael. Arrows of the Almighty. (Illus.). 224p. 1985. 15.95 (ISBN 0-02-507610-8). Macmillan.

Bar-Zohar, Michael & Haber, Eitan. The Quest for the Red Prince. LC 83-60936. (Illus.). 320p. 1983. 15.95 (ISBN 0-688-02043-7). Morrow.

Barzum, Jacques, ed. see Crispin, Edmund.

Barzun, Isabel, tr. see Fabre, Michel.

Barzun, J., ed. see Arthur, Frank.

Barzun, J., ed. see Atkinson, Alex.

Barzun, J., ed. see Bonett, John & Bonett, Emery.

Barzun, J., ed. see Brown, Fredric.

Barzun, J., ed. see Bruce, Leo.

Barzun, J., ed. see Bulik, Robert V.

Barzun, J., ed. see Cannan, Joanna.

Barzun, J., ed. see Carr, A. H.

Barzun, J., ed. see Carr, Glynn.

Barzun, J., ed. see Clark, Philip.

Barzun, J., ed. see Constantine, K. C.

Barzun, J., ed. see Cross, Amanda.

Barzun, J., ed. see Daly, Elizabeth.

Barzun, J., ed. see Dewey, Thomas B.

Barzun, J., ed. see Ellin, Stanley.

Barzun, J., ed. see Fitzgerald, Nigel.

Barzun, J., ed. see Francis, Dick.

Barzun, J., ed. see Grierson, Edward.

Barzun, J., ed. see Hamilton, Bruce.

Barzun, J., ed. see Hillerman, Tony.

Barzun, J., ed. see Hough, Stanley.

Barzun, J., ed. see Hubbard, P. M.

Barzun, J., ed. see Innes, Michael.

Barzun, J., ed. see James, P. D.

Barzun, J., ed. see Keith, Carlton.

Barzun, J., ed. see Kuttner, Henry.

Barzun, J., ed. see Landon, Christopher.

Barzun, J., ed. see Lathen, Emma.

Barzun, J., ed. see Longmate, Norman.

Barzun, J., ed. see MacDonald, John D.

Barzun, J., ed. see Marric, J. J.

Barzun, J., ed. see Miles, John.

Barzun, J., ed. see Mole, William.

Barzun, J., ed. see Moyes, Patricia.

Barzun, J., ed. see Nash, Simon.

Barzun, J., ed. see Peters, Ellis.

Barzun, J., ed. see Priestley, J. B.

Barzun, J., ed. see Procter, Maurice.

Barzun, J., ed. see Rendell, Ruth.

Barzun, J., ed. see Robertson, Helen.

Barzun, J., ed. see Scholey, Jean.

Barzun, J., ed. see Swinnerton, Frank.

Barzun, J., ed. see Symons, Julian.

Barzun, J., ed. see Trey, Josephine.

Barzun, J., ed. see Troy, Simon.

Barzun, J., ed. see Tyrer, Walter.

Barzun, J., ed. see Waugh, Hillary.

Barzun, J., tr. see Carr, J. D., et al.

Barzun, Jacques. Berlioz & His Century: An Introduction to the Age of Romanticism. LC 81-16072. 1982. pap. 9.95 (ISBN 0-226-03861-0). U of Chicago Pr.

--The Bibliophile of the Future: His Complaints About the Twentieth Century. 1976. 3.00 (ISBN 0-89073-048-2). Boston Public Lib.

--Classic, Romantic & Modern. xvi, 256p. 1975. pap. 5.50 (ISBN 0-226-03852-1, P643, Phoen). U of Chicago Pr.

--Clio & the Doctors: History, Psycho-History, Quanto History. LC 74-5723. 1974. pap. 3.45 (ISBN 0-226-03850-5, P687, Phoen). U of Chicago Pr.

--Critical Questions: On Music & Letters, Culture & Biography. Friedland, Bea, ed. LC 81-22023. 1982. lib. bdg. 22.50x (ISBN 0-226-03863-7). U of Chicago Pr.

--Critical Questions: On Music & Letters, Culture & Biography, 1940-1980. Friedland, Bea, ed. LC 81-22023. xviii, 270p. 1984. pap. 8.95 (ISBN 0-226-03864-5). U of Chicago Pr.

--Darwin, Marx, Wagner: Critique of a Heritage. 2nd ed. LC 80-27274. xxii, 374p. 1981. pap. 12.95x (ISBN 0-226-03859-9). U of Chicago Pr.

--The Energies of Art: Studies of Authors Classic & Modern. LC 74-3686. 355p. 1975. Repr. of 1956 ed. lib. bdg. 71.50 (ISBN 0-8371-6856-2, BAEA). Greenwood.

--God's Country & Mine. LC 73-3919. 344p. 1973. Repr. of 1954 ed. lib. bdg. 17.50x (ISBN 0-8371-6860-0, BAGC). Greenwood.

--The House of Intellect. LC 77-28070. 1978. Repr. of 1959 ed. lib. bdg. 24.50 (ISBN 0-313-20071-8, BAHI). Greenwood.

--The House of Intellect. (Midway Reprint Ser.). viii, 274p. 1975. pap. text ed. 12.00x (ISBN 0-226-03855-6). U of Chicago Pr.

--Of Human Freedom. rev., 2nd ed. LC 76-47651. 1977. Repr. of 1964 ed. lib. bdg. 17.75x (ISBN 0-8371-9321-4, BAOH). Greenwood.

--On Writing, Editing, & Publishing: Essays Explicative & Hortatory. LC 71-161602. 1971. pap. 1.50 (ISBN 0-226-03848-3, P430, Phoen). U of Chicago Pr.

--Race: A Study in Superstition. Rev. ed. LC 78-63649. (Studies in Fascism: Ideology & Practice). 288p. Repr. of 1965 ed. 28.50 (ISBN 0-404-16899-X). AMS Pr.

--Simple & Direct: A Rhetoric for Writers. rev. ed. LC 83-48936. 256p. 1985. 14.42 (ISBN 0-06-015283-4, HarpT). Har-Row.

--Simple & Direct: A Rhetoric for Writers. rev. ed. LC 83-48936. 256p. 1984. pap. 6.68i (ISBN 0-06-091122-0, CN 1122, CN). Har-Row.

--A Stroll with William James. LC 82-48108. 288p. 1983. 19.18i (ISBN 0-06-015090-4, HarpT). Har-Row.

--A Stroll with William James. LC 84-2612. viii, 344p. 1984. pap. 10.95 (ISBN 0-226-03866-1); 25.00x (ISBN 0-226-03865-3). U of Chicago Pr.

--Teacher in America. LC 80-82370. 496p. 1981. 9.00 (ISBN 0-913966-78-9, Liberty Clas); pap. 4.00 (ISBN 0-913966-79-7). Liberty Fund.

--The Use & Abuse of Art. LC 73-16780. (The A. W. Mellon Lectures in the Fine Arts No. 22, Bollingen Ser.: Vol. 35). 150p. 1974. 22.00x (ISBN 0-691-09903-0); pap. 6.95x (ISBN 0-691-01804-9). Princeton U Pr.

Barzun, Jacques & Dunbar, Georgia. Simple & Direct: A Rhetoric for Writers. 256p. 1976. pap. text ed. 12.85 scp (ISBN 0-06-040513-9, HarpC). Har-Row.

Barzun, Jacques & Graff, Henry F. The Modern Researcher. 3rd ed. LC 76-27411. 378p. 1977. pap. text ed. 13.95 (ISBN 0-15-562511-X, HC). HarBraceJ.

--The Modern Researcher. 4th ed. LC 76-27411. 450p. 1985. pap. text ed. 13.50 (ISBN 0-15-562512-8, HC). HarBraceJ.

--The Modern Researcher. 4th ed. Boynton, John F., ed. 480p. 1985. 24.95 (ISBN 0-15-161479-2). HarBraceJ.

Barzun, Jacques, ed. Pleasures of Music: An Anthology of Writings About Music & Musicians from Cellini to Bernard Shaw. abr. ed. 1977. 15.00x (ISBN 0-226-03856-4); pap. 10.95x (ISBN 0-226-03854-8, P727, Phoen). U of Chicago Pr.

Barzun, Jacques, ed. & tr. see Berlioz, Hector.

Barzun, Jacques, ed. see Follett, Wilson.

Barzun, Jacques, ed. see Hough, Stanley.

Barzun, Jacques, ed. see MacDonald, Ross.

Barzun, Jacques, tr. & intro. by see Berlioz, Hector.

Barzun, Jacques, tr. see Diderot, Denis.

Bas, Joe, jt. ed. see Carter, E. Dale, Jr.

Bas, M. J. Le see Le Bas, M. J.

Bas, Mauricio O., Sr. Philippine Martial Law. 1984. 13.95 (ISBN 0-533-05827-9). Vantage.

Basa, Eniko M. Sandor Petofi. (World Authors Ser.). 1980. lib. bdg. 16.95 (ISBN 0-8057-6429-1, Twayne). G K Hall.

Basabe, Fernando M. Japanese Youth Confronts Religion: A Sociological Survey. LC 67-28418. 1967. 6.00 (ISBN 0-8048-0324-2). C E Tuttle.

--Religious Attitudes of Japanese Men. LC 68-57415. 1969. bds. 15.00 (ISBN 0-8048-0651-9). C E Tuttle.

Basagni, Fabio. International Monetary Relations After Jamaica. (The Atlantic Papers: No. 76/4). (Orig.). 1977. pap. text ed. 4.75x (ISBN 0-686-83641-3). Allanheld.

Basagni, Fabio & Sauzey, Francois. Employee Participation & Company Reform. (The Atlantic Papers: No. 75/4). (Orig.). 1976. pap. text ed. 4.75x (ISBN 0-686-83643-X). Allanheld.

Basagni, Fabio, ed. International Debt, Financial Stability & Growth. (The Atlantic Papers: No. 51). (Illus.). 60p. 1983. pap. 7.00x (ISBN 0-8476-7348-0). Rowman & Allanheld.

Basagni, Fabio & Uri, Pierre, eds. Monetary Relations & World Development. LC 77-15650. 144p. 1977. 29.95 (ISBN 0-03-041591-8). Praeger.

Basak, Bijan K. Pharmacology for the Anesthesiologist. 209p. 1981. 9.95 (ISBN 0-87762-301-5). Technomic.

Basalov, F. A. & Ostrovityanov, R. V. Statistical Theory of Extended Radar Targets. Barton, William F. & Barton, David K., trs. from Rus. Orig. Title: Statisticheskaya Teoriya Radiolokatsii Protyazhennyz Tselei. 200p. 1984. text ed. 65.00 (ISBN 0-89006-144-0). Artech Hse.

Basar, E. EEG Brain Dynamics: Relation Between EEG & Brain Evoked Potential. 412p. 1980. 96.75 (ISBN 0-444-80249-5). Elsevier.

Basar, E. & Weiss, C. Vasculature & Circulation: The Role of Myogenic Reactivity in the Regulation of Blood Flow. 272p. 1981. 90.00 (ISBN 0-444-80271-1). Elsevier.

Basar, E, et al, eds. Synergetics of the Brain. (Series in Synergetics: Vol. 23). (Illus.). 390p. 1983. 34.00 (ISBN 0-387-12960-X). Springer-Verlag.

Basar, T. Dynamic Modelling & Control of National Economies, 1983: Proceedings of the IFAC-IFORS Symposium, 4th, Washington, DC, June 1983. Pau, F. L., ed. 550p. 116.00 (ISBN 0-08-030557-1). Pergamon.

Basar, Tamer & Olsder, G. J. Dynamic Noncooperative Game Theory. LC 81-67913. (Mathematics in Science Engineering Ser.). 1982. 59.50 (ISBN 0-12-080220-1). Acad Pr.

Basarab, Stephen, et al. The Ukrainians of Maryland. LC 77-85157. (Illus.). 519p. (Orig.). 1977. pap. 8.95 (ISBN 0-9606178-0-9). Ukrainian Ed Assn.

Basaroff, F. The Sacrament of Matrimony According to the Doctrine & Ritual of the Eastern Orthodox Church. Bjerring, N., tr. from Russian. pap. 1.95 (ISBN 0-686-16370-2). Eastern Orthodox.

Basart, Ann. Serial Music: A Classified Bibliography of Writings on 12 Tone & Electronic Music. LC 75-45460. 151p. 1976. Repr. of 1961 ed. lib. bdg. 18.25x (ISBN 0-8371-8753-2, BASM). Greenwood.

Basart, Ann P. Perspectives of New Music: An Index, 1962-1982. (Reference Books in Music: No. 1). ix, 127p. (Orig.). 1984. pap. 13.95 (ISBN 0-914913-00-X, 83-82609). Fallen Leaf.

--The Sound of the Fortepiano: A Discography of Music on Early Pianos. LC 85-1660. (Fallen Leaf Reference Books In Music: No. 2). 300p. (Orig.). 1985. pap. 29.95 (ISBN 0-914913-01-8). Fallen Leaf.

Basawa, I. V. & Scott, D. J. Asymptotic Optimal Inference for Non-Ergodic Models. (Lecture Notes in Statistics Ser.: Vol. 17). 170p. 1983. pap. 16.00 (ISBN 0-387-90810-2). Springer-Verlag.

Basawa, Ishwar & Rao, Prakasa, eds. Statistical Interference for Stochastic Processes. LC 79-50533. (Probability & Mathematical Statistics Ser.). 1980. 75.00 (ISBN 0-12-080250-3). Acad Pr.

Basch, Antonin. Capital Markets of the European Economic Community. (Michigan International Business Studies: No. 3). 1965. pap. 2.00 (ISBN 0-87712-117-6). U Mich Busn Div Res.

Basch, Ernst. The Fascist: His State & His Mind. LC 72-180386. (Studies in Fascism, Ideology & Practice). Repr. of 1937 ed. 29.50 (ISBN 0-404-56101-2). AMS Pr.

Basch, Lester D. & Finkelstein, Milton. Spelling Made Easy. 1974. pap. 3.00 (ISBN 0-87980-288-X). Wilshire.

Basch, Michael, tr. see Rektorys, Karel.

Basch, Michael F. Doing Psychotherapy. LC 79-3084. 1980. text ed. 17.50x (ISBN 0-465-01684-7). Basic.

Basch, Norma. In the Eyes of the Law: Women, Marriage, & Property in Nineteenth Century New York. LC 82-2454. 255p. 1982. 22.50x (ISBN 0-8014-1466-0). Cornell U Pr.

Basch, Paul F. International Health. 1978. text ed. 28.95x (ISBN 0-19-502328-5); pap. text ed. 14.95x (ISBN 0-19-502329-3). Oxford U Pr.

Basch, Peter, jt. auth. see Gwynne, Fred.

Basch, Samuel. Memories of Mexico: History of the Last Ten Months of the Empire. Oechler, Hugh M., tr. LC 78-175806. 253p. 1973. text ed. 9.00 (ISBN 0-911536-41-8). Trinity U Pr.

Basch, Victor. Schumann, a Life of Suffering. facsimile ed. Phillips, Catherine A., tr. LC 76-107791. (Select Bibliographies Reprint Ser). 1931. 22.00 (ISBN 0-8369-5175-1). Ayer Co Pubs.

Basche, James R. U. S. Business Support for International Public Service Activities, Pt. 2. Incl. Support from Foreign Affiliates - Brazil. (No. 616). 25p. 1974. 10.00 (ISBN 0-8237-0058-5); members 2.00 (ISBN 0-317-31506-4); Support from Foreign Affiliates - Argentina. (No. 624). 25p. 1974. 10.00 (ISBN 0-8237-0058-5); Support from Foreign Affiliates - Columbia. (No. 643). 24p. 1974. 20.00 (ISBN 0-8237-0056-9); members 4.00 (ISBN 0-317-31507-2); Support from Foreign Affiliates - Philippines. (No. 657). 1975. 20.00 (ISBN 0-8237-0076-3); members 4.00 (ISBN 0-317-31508-0); Support from Foreign Affiliates - Mexico. (No. 617). 26p. 1974. 10.00 (ISBN 0-8237-0059-3); members 2.00 (ISBN 0-317-31509-9). (Report Ser.). Conference Bd.

Basche, James R., Jr. Evolving Corporate Policy & Organization for East-West Trade. (Report Ser: No. 635). 61p. 1974. pap. 15.00 (ISBN 0-8237-0018-6); pap. 3.00 member. Conference Bd.

--Production Cost Trends & Outlook. (Report Ser.: No. 724). (Illus.). 39p. 1977. pap. 15.00 (ISBN 0-8237-0158-1); pap. 5.00 member. Conference Bd.

Basche, James R., Jr. & Duerr, Michael G. Experience with Foreign Production Work Forces. (Report Ser.: No. 661). 35p. (Orig.). 1975. pap. 15.00 (ISBN 0-8237-0080-1); pap. 3.00 member. Conference Bd.

Baschek, B., et al, eds. Problems in Stellar Atmospheres & Envelopes. LC 74-32493. (Illus.). 390p. 1975. 34.00 (ISBN 0-387-07092-3). Springer-Verlag.

Baschek, R. B., jt. auth. see Unsold, A.

Bascio, Patrick. Building a Just Society. LC 80-27238. 176p. (Orig.). 1981. pap. 5.95 (ISBN 0-88344-205-1). Orbis Bks.

Basco, E., jt. auth. see Hajos, F.

Bascom, Arlene, jt. auth. see Hanks, Darla.

Bascom, John. Aesthetics: Or the Science of Beauty. rev. ed. LC 75-3030. (Philosophy in America Ser.). Repr. of 1872 ed. 19.50 (ISBN 0-404-59029-2). AMS Pr.

--Philosophy of English Literature. xiii, 318p. Date not set. Repr. of 1874 ed. lib. bdg. 39.00 (ISBN 0-932051-94-4). Am Repr Serv.

--A Philosophy of Religion: Or, the Rational Grounds of Religious Belief. LC 75-3037. Repr. of 1876 ed. 40.00 (ISBN 0-404-59035-7). AMS Pr.

--Science, Philosophy & Religion. LC 75-3041. Repr. of 1871 ed. 21.50 (ISBN 0-404-59039-X). AMS Pr.

Bascom, W. R. The Sociological Role of the Yoruba Cult-Group. LC 44-47266. (American Anthro. Association Memoirs). Repr. of 1944 ed. 15.00 (ISBN 0-527-00562-2). Kraus Repr.

Bascom, Willard. Waves & Beaches: The Dynamics of the Ocean Surface. rev. updated ed. LC 79-7038. (Illus.). 1980. pap. 8.95 (ISBN 0-385-14844-5, Anchor Pr). Doubleday.

Bascom, William. African Art in Cultural Perspective: An Introduction. (Illus.). 192p. 1973. pap. 7.95x (ISBN 0-393-09375-1). Norton.

--IFA Divination: Communication Between Gods & Men in West Africa. LC 69-10349. (Illus.). 604p. 1969. 42.50x (ISBN 0-253-32890-X). Ind U Pr.

--Ponape: A Pacific Economy in Transition. LC 65-64597. (University of California, Anthropological Records: Vol. 22). pap. 41.50 (ISBN 0-317-29120-3, 2021322). Bks Demand UMI.

--Sixteen Cowries: Yoruba Divination from Africa to the New World. LC 78-3239. (Illus.). 800p. 1980. 37.50x (ISBN 0-253-35280-0). Ind U Pr.

--The Yoruba of Southwestern Nigeria. (Illus.). 118p. 1984. pap. text ed. 6.95x (ISBN 0-88133-038-8). Waveland Pr.

Bascom, William R. & Herskovits, Melville J., eds. Continuity & Change in African Cultures. LC 58-13135. 1958. pap. 4.25x (ISBN 0-226-03880-7, P85, Phoen). U of Chicago Pr.

Basdekis, Demetrios. Miguel De Unamuno. LC 74-92029. (Columbia Essays on Modern Writers Ser.: No. 44). 48p. (Orig.). 1969. pap. 2.50 (ISBN 0-231-03259-5). Columbia U Pr.

--Unamuno & Spanish Literature. LC 68-63733. 101p. 1983. Repr. of 1967 ed. lib. bdg. 19.95x (ISBN 0-89370-781-3). Borgo Pr.

Basden, G. T. Among the Ibos of Nigeria. new ed. 352p. 1966. 29.50x (ISBN 0-7146-1633-8, F Cass Co). Biblio Dist.

--Niger Ibos. (Illus.). 456p. 1966. Repr. of 1938 ed. 29.50x (ISBN 0-7146-1632-X, F Cass Co). Biblio Dist.

Basdevant, J. L. & Gastmans, R., eds. Fundamental Interactions: Cargese 1981. LC 82-10164. (NATO Advanced Study Institutes Series B, Physics: Vol. 85). 714p. 1982. 95.00x (ISBN 0-306-41116-4, Plenum Pr). Plenum Pub.

Basedow, Herbert. The Australian Aboriginal. LC 76-44687. (Illus.). Repr. of 1925 ed. 34.50 (ISBN 0-404-15904-4). AMS Pr.

Basehore, C. J. & Marantette, Carter H. Securing an Executive Position in the Sunbelt. 57p. (Orig.). 1980. pap. 5.95 (ISBN 0-939148-00-5). Exec West.

Basel, G. I. Pak Six, A Story of the Air-War over North Vietnam. LC 82-72150. (Illus.). 176p. (Orig.). 1982. pap. 7.95 (ISBN 0-933362-07-2). Assoc Creative Writers.

Baseley, Godfrey. A Country Compendium. (Illus.). 1977. text ed. 15.95x (ISBN 0-8464-0296-3). Beekman Pubs.

Baselt, Randall C. Analytical Procedures for Therapeutic Drug Monitoring & Emergency Toxicology. LC 79-50639. 316p. 1980. text ed. 35.00 (ISBN 0-931890-03-9). Biomed Pubns.

--Biological Monitoring Methods for Industrial Chemicals. LC 79-56927. 306p. 1980. text ed. 47.00 (ISBN 0-931890-04-7). Biomed Pubns.

--Disposition of Toxic Drugs & Chemicals in Man. 2nd ed. LC 81-66543. (Illus.). 800p. 1982. text ed. 49.50 (ISBN 0-931890-08-X). Biomed Pubns.

Baselt, Randall C., jt. ed. see Cravey, Robert H.

Basen, Michele Margolin, jt. auth. see Ashery, Rebecca Sager.

Baserga, R., ed. Tissue Growth Factors. (Handbook of Experimental Pharmacology: Vol. 57). (Illus.). 500p. 1981. 176.00 (ISBN 0-387-10623-5). Springer-Verlag.

Baserga, Renato. Biochemistry of Cell Division. (Illus.). 228p. 1969. 17.50x (ISBN 0-398-00103-0). C C Thomas.

--The Biology of Cell Reproduction. (Illus.). 256p. 1985. text ed. 25.00x (ISBN 0-674-07406-8). Harvard U Pr.

Baserga, Renato, ed. Cell Cycle & Cancer. (Biochemistry of Disease Ser: Vol. 1). 1971. 75.00 (ISBN 0-8247-1039-8). Dekker.
--Multiplication & Division in Mammalian Cells. (Biochemistry of Disease Ser.: Vol.6). 256p. 1976. 49.75 (ISBN 0-8247-6353-X). Dekker.
Baserga, Renato, ed. see Conference in Honor of Anna Goldfeder, Feb 17-19, 1982.
Baserga, Renato, et al, eds. Introduction of Macromolecules into Viable Mammalian Cells. LC 79-91743. (Wistar Symposium Ser.: Vol. 1). 354p. 1980. 35.00x (ISBN 0-8451-2000-X). A R Liss.
Basetti-Sami, Giulio. Koran in the Light of Christ. 1977. 8.50 (ISBN 0-8199-0713-8). Franciscan Herald.
Basetti-Sani, Biuolio. Louis Massignon: Christian Ecumenist. 1974. 6.95 (ISBN 0-8199-0496-1). Franciscan Herald.
Basetto, A., et al, eds. see International University Courses on Nuclear Physics, 13th, Schladming, Austria, 1974.
Basevi, Abramo. Studio Sulle Opere Di Giuseppe Verdi. LC 80-2255. Repr. of 1859 ed. 35.50 (ISBN 0-404-18802-8). AMS Pr.
Basevi, Giorgio, jt. auth. see Kohl, Wilfied L.
Basey, Harold E. Discovering Sierra Reptiles & Amphibians. (Discovering Sierra Ser.). (Illus.). 50p. (Orig.). 1976. pap. 2.50 (ISBN 0-939666-03-0). Yosemite Natl Hist.
Basford, Kathleen. The Green Man. (Illus.). 128p. 1978. 30.00x (ISBN 0-8476-1353-4). Rowman.
Basgoz, Ihlan & Tietze, Andreas. Bilmece: A Corpus of Turkish Riddles. (Publications in Folklore Studies: Vol. 22). 1974. pap. 44.00x (ISBN 0-520-09145-0). U of Cal Pr.
Basgoz, Ilhan & Wilson, H. E. Educational Problems in Turkey, 1920-1940. LC 67-65317. (Uralic & Altaic Ser: Vol. 86). 1968. pap. text ed. 8.50x (ISBN 0-87750-077-0). Res Ctr Lang Semiotic.
Basgoz, Ilhan & Halman, Talat S., eds. Yunus Emre: Selected Poems. 1984. record 8.95 (ISBN 0-253-39803-7). Ind U Pr.
Bash, Deborah M. & Gold, Winifred A. The Nurse & the Childbearing Family. LC 80-22945. 718p. 1981. 28.50 (ISBN 0-471-05520-4). Wiley.
Bash, Dick. The Final Exam: General Class. 3rd ed. Bash, Richard M., ed. (Illus.). 128p. 1981. pap. 9.95 (ISBN 0-938408-05-4). Bash Educ Serv.
--Novice Class: Amateur Radio Operator Test Guide. Rev., 3rd ed. Bash, Richard M., ed. (Illus.). 104p. 1984. pap. 9.95 (ISBN 0-938408-13-5). Bash Educ Serv.
Bash, Ewald. Legends from the Future. (Illus., Orig.). 1972. pap. 1.75 (ISBN 0-377-02101-6). Friend Pr.
--Little Us & the Great Big Power Machine. (Orig.). 1973. pap. 1.50 (ISBN 0-377-03401-0). Friend Pr.
Bash, Frank N. Astronomy. (Illus.). 1977. pap. text ed. 22.85 scp (ISBN 0-06-043853-3, HarpC). Har-Row.
Bash, H. H. Sociology, Race & Ethnicity: A Critique of American Ideological Intrusions Upon Sociological Theory. (Monographs in Sociology). 264p. 1979. 33.75 (ISBN 0-677-05390-8). Gordon.
Bash, Lee, jt. auth. see Kuzmich, John, Jr.
Bash, Lee, jt. ed. see Runfola, Maria.
Bash, Mary A., jt. auth. see Camp, Bonnie W.
Bash, Mary Ann & Camp, Bonnie. Think Aloud: Increasing Social & Cognitive Skills-A Problem-Solving Program for Children, Classrom Program, Grades 3 & 4. LC 85-61576. (Illus.). 1985. pap. 35.95 (ISBN 0-87822-241-3). Res Press.
Bash, Mary Ann S. & Camp, Bonnie W. Think Aloud: Increasing Social & Cognitive Skills-A Problem-Solving Program for Children Classroom Programming, Classroom Program, Grades 5 & 6. LC 85-61577. (Illus.). 275p. 1985. pap. 35.95 (ISBN 0-87822-242-1). Res Press.
Bash, Mary Ann S., jt. auth. see Camp, Bonnie W.
Bash, Richard M. The Final Exam: Advanced Class. rev., 4th ed. (Illus.). 120p. 1982. pap. 9.95 (ISBN 0-938408-08-9). Bash Educ Serv.
--Final Exam: Extra Class. 3rd ed. 1981. 9.95 (ISBN 0-938408-07-0). Bash Educ Serv.
--The Final Exam: Novice Class. (Illus.). 104p. (Orig.). 1981. pap. 4.95 (ISBN 0-938408-04-6). Bash Educ Serv.
Bash, Richard M., ed. see Bash, Dick.
Bash, Richard M., ed. see Dersch, James E.
Bash, Richard M., ed. see Gregg, Stuart.
Bash, Robert. Robert's Rhetorics. 96p. 1984. 7.95 (ISBN 0-89962-350-6). Todd & Honeywell.
Basha, Anwar, jt. auth. see Atta-Ur-Rahman.
Bashah. The Day Before: Nuclear War of Nineteen Eighty-Nine & Escape. (Orig.). Date not set. 11.95 (ISBN 0-913429-04-X); pap. 4.95 (ISBN 0-913429-05-8). Cosmos Humanists.
--Your Hidden Companion. (Orig.). pap. 4.95 (ISBN 0-913429-06-6). Cosmos Humanists.
Basham, A. L. The History & Doctrines of the Ajivikas. (Illus.). 326p. 1981. Repr. 22.50 (ISBN 0-89581-377-7). Asian Human Pr.
--The Wonder That Was India. (Illus.). 568p. 1983. 34.95 (ISBN 0-283-35457-7, Pub by Sidgwick & Jackson). Merrimack Pub Cir.
Basham, A. L., ed. A Cultural History of India. (Illus.). 1975. 42.00x (ISBN 0-19-561520-4). Oxford U Pr.
Basham, Carl. Workbook for Modern Business Law. 1983. pap. text ed. 12.95 (ISBN 0-8359-8811-2). Reston.
Basham, Don. Deliver Us from Evil. 224p. 1972. pap. 5.95 (ISBN 0-310-60091-X, Pub by Chosen Bks). Zondervan.
--Face up with a Miracle. 190p. 1971. pap. 3.50 (ISBN 0-88368-002-5). Whitaker Hse.
--A Handbook on Holy Spirit Baptism. (Handbk. Ser: No. 1). 118p. 1969. pap. 3.50 (ISBN 0-88368-003-3). Whitaker Hse.
--Handbook on Tongues, Interpretation & Prophecy. (Handbk. Ser.: No. 2). 1971. pap. 3.50 (ISBN 0-88368-004-1). Whitaker Hse.
--Libranos del Mal. 240p. 1977. 3.25 (ISBN 0-88113-313-2). Edit Betania.
--Spiritual Power. rev ed. 92p. 1976. pap. 3.50 (ISBN 0-88368-075-0). Whitaker Hse.
Basham, Donald J. Traffic Accident Management. (Illus.). 232p. 1979. photocopy ed. 15.25x (ISBN 0-398-03827-9). C C Thomas.
--Traffic Law Enforcement. (Illus.). 176p. 1978. 10.75x (ISBN 0-398-03772-8). C C Thomas.
Bashara, N. M., jt. auth. see Azzam, R. M.
Bashaw, Donald E. & Lohr, Mary K. I Am Me! Primary Action Skills for LD's. 1979. pap. 8.95 (ISBN 0-87804-320-9). Mafex.
Bashaw, Ed. Digestion, Assimilation, Elimination & You. 2.95 (ISBN 0-89557-073-4). Bi World Indus.
Bashaw, W. L. Mathematics for Statistics. LC 84-11228. 344p. 1984. Repr. of 1969 ed. lib. bdg. 23.50 (ISBN 0-89874-762-7). Krieger.
Bashe, Charles, et al. IBM's Early Computers: A Technical History. (History of Computing Ser.). (Illus.). 650p. 1985. text ed. 27.50x (ISBN 0-262-02225-7). MIT Pr.
Bashe, Philip. Heavy Metal Thunder. LC 85-4558. (Illus.). 224p. 1985. pap. 12.95 (ISBN 0-385-19797-7, Dolp). Doubleday.
Bashear, Vokom M. McGrandad an Elephant & Other Stories. Ascher, R. E., tr. from Malaym. 203p. 1981. 15.00x (ISBN 0-85224-386-3, Pub. by Edinburgh U Pr Scotland); pap. 7.50x (ISBN 0-85224-408-8, Pub. by Edinburgh U Pr Scotland). Columbia U Pr.
Basheer, M. Voices-The Walls. 1977. 4.00x (ISBN 0-88386-211-5). South Asia Bks.
Basheer, S. & Ahmed, Alice P., eds. Technology, International Stability, & Growth. LC 83-3696. 180p. 1983. 19.50 (ISBN 0-8046-9314-5, Natl U). Assoc Faculty Pr.
Basheer, Vaikom M. The Love Letter & Other Stories. Abdulla, V., tr. from Malayalam. 192p. 1983. pap. text ed. 4.25 (ISBN 0-86131-447-6, Pub. by Orient Longman Ltd. India). Apt Bks.
Bashevis Singer, Isaac see Singer, Isaac B. & Burgin, Richard.
Bashier, Zakaria. Hijra: Story & Significance. 110p. (Orig.). 1983. pap. 4.95x (ISBN 0-86037-124-7, Pub by Islamic Found UK). New Era Pubns MI.
Bashinski, Marian C. Improving Sentences: A Diagnostic Approach. 200p. 1982. tchrs. ed. 11.95 (ISBN 0-89892-034-5). Contemp Pub Co Raleigh.
Bashinsky, Sloan. Home Buyers: Lambs to the Slaughter? LC 84-6692. (Illus.). 128p. 1984. casebound 12.95 (ISBN 0-89732-027-1). Menasha Ridge.
--Home Buyers: Lambs to the Slaughter? 1985. 12.95 (ISBN 0-671-55729-7). S&S.
--Selling Your Home Sweet Home. 1985. 12.95 (ISBN 0-671-60213-6). S&S.
Bashir, Iskandar. Civil Service Reform in Lebanon. 1977. 17.95x (ISBN 0-8156-6050-2, Am U Beirut). Syracuse U Pr.
Bashiri, Iraj. The Fiction of Sadeq Hedayat. LC 84-61088. 241p. 1984. 17.95 (ISBN 0-939214-22-9); pap. text ed. 12.00 (ISBN 0-939214-24-5). Mazda Pubs.
Bashiriyeh, Hossein. The State & Revolution in Iran: 1962-1982. LC 83-40183. 203p. 1984. 27.50 (ISBN 0-312-75612-7). St Martin.
Bashkin, S. & Stoner, J. O., Jr. Atomic Energy-Level & Grotrian Diagrams: Vol. 3: Vanadium I - Chromium XXIV. 550p. 1981. 115.00 (ISBN 0-444-86006-1). Elsevier.
--Atomic Energy-Level & Grotrian Diagrams, Vol. 4: Manganese I-XXV. 354p. 1983. 78.75 (ISBN 0-444-86463-6, I-517-82, North Holland). Elsevier.
--Atomic Energy Levels & Grotrian Diagrams, Vol. 1: Hydrogen 1 - Phosphorous XV. 1976. 115.00 (ISBN 0-444-10827-0, North-Holland); Addenda. 40.50 (ISBN 0-444-85236-0). Elsevier.
--Atomic Energy Levels & Grotrian Diagrams, Vol. 2: Sulphur I to Titanium XXII. 1978. 115.00 (ISBN 0-444-85149-6, North-Holland). Elsevier.
Bashkin, S., ed. Beam-Foil Spectroscopy. (Topics in Current Physics: Vol. 1). 1976. 42.00 (ISBN 0-387-07914-9). Springer-Verlag.
Bashkin, Stanley, ed. Beam-Foil Spectroscopy, 2 Vols. LC 68-8275. (Illus.). 678p. 1968. Set. 180.50 (ISBN 0-677-12940-8). Gordon.
Bashkina, Nina H. & Trask, David, eds. United States & Russia: The Beginning of Relations, U. S. Department of State. LC 80-607939. 1982. Repr. of 1980 ed. lib. bdg. 44.00 (ISBN 0-89941-229-7). W S Hein.
Bashkirtseff, Marie. Journal of Marie Bashkirtseff. 1977. lib. bdg. 59.95 (ISBN 0-8490-2110-3). Gordon Pr.
Bashline, L. James, ed. The Eastern Trail. (Illus.). 320p. 1972. 8.95 (ISBN 0-88395-014-6). Freshet Pr.
Bashline, L. James, ed. see Hitchcock, John C.
Bashline, Sylvia. Cleaning & Cooking Fish. (Hunting & Fishing Library). 1985. 16.95 (ISBN 0-13-136599-1). P-H.
--Cleaning & Cooking Fish. (Hunting & Fishing Library). (Illus.). 160p. 1982. 16.95 (ISBN 0-86573-011-3). Cy De Cosse.
--Sylvia Bashline's Savory Game Cookbook. 224p. 1983. 13.95 (ISBN 0-8117-0604-4). Stackpole.
Bashline, Sylvia G. The Bounty of the Earth Cookbook. LC 79-13475. 1979. 15.95 (ISBN 0-8329-3010-5, Pub. by Winchester Pr). New Century.
Basho. A Haiku Journey: Basho's "The Narrow Road to the Far North" & Selected Haiku. Britton, Dorothy, tr. from Japanese. LC 74-24903. (Illus.). 111p. 1982. 25.00 (ISBN 0-87011-239-2); pap. 4.25 (ISBN 0-87011-423-9). Kodansha.
--On Love & Barley: Haiku of Basho. Stryk, Lucien, tr. (Illus.). 92p. 1985. 12.00 (ISBN 0-8248-1012-0). UH Pr.
Basho, et al. One Man's Moon: Fifty Haiku by Basho, Buson, Issa, Hakuin, Shiki, Santoka. Corman, Cid, tr. from Japanese. LC 84-80472. 72p. (Orig.). 1984. ltd. ed. 25.00x (ISBN 0-917788-25-7); pap. 5.00 (ISBN 0-917788-26-5). Gnomon Pr.
Basho, Matsuo. The Narrow Road to the Deep North & Other Travel Sketches. Yuasa, Nobuyuki, tr. from Japanese. (Classics Ser.). 167p. (Orig.). 1967. pap. 3.95 (ISBN 0-14-044185-9). Penguin.
Bashour, Dora, jt. auth. see Ernst, Frederic.
Bashshur, Rashid L., et al. Telemedicine: Explorations in the Use of Telecommunications in Health Care. (Illus.). 376p. 1975. write for info.; pap. 47.50x spiral bdg. (ISBN 0-398-03311-0). C C Thomas.
Bashshur, Rashid L., et al, eds. Arabic Essays, 2 pts. (Contemporary Arabic Readers Ser.: Vol. II). 1962. Set. 7.50x (ISBN 0-916798-12-7). Pt. 1, Texts; vi, 78p. Pt. 2, Notes & Glossaries; iv, 208p. U of Mich Pr.
Basic Environmental Problems of Man in Space II, 6th International Symposium, Bonn, Germany, 3-6 November 1980 & Klein, K. E. Proceedings. Hordinsky, J. R., ed. 250p. 1982. pap. 70.00 (ISBN 0-08-028697-6, A140). Pergamon.
Basic Medical Sciences, Annual Symposium & Piper, Priscilla J. SRS-A & Leukotrienes: Proceedings of the Annual Symposium of Basic Medical Sciences, 10th. LC 80-41758. (Prostaglandis Research Studies Press Ser.). 282p. 1981. 74.95x (ISBN 0-471-27959-5, Pub. by Wiley-Interscience). Wiley.
Basichis, Gordon. Beautiful Bad Girl: The Vicki Morgan Story. (Illus.). 400p. 1985. 17.95 (ISBN 0-915643-14-6). Santa Barb Pr.
Basie, Count. Good Morning Blues: The Autobiography of Count Basie. (Illus.). 1985. 19.45 (ISBN 0-394-54864-7). Random.
Basil Blackwell Staff. Blackwell's Guide for Authors. 56p. 1984. pap. 6.95x (ISBN 0-631-13707-6). Basil Blackwell.
Basil, Cynthia. How Ships Play Cards: A Beginning Book of Homonyms. LC 79-18420. (Illus.). 32p. (gr. k-3). 1980. 11.25 (ISBN 0-688-22217-X); PLB 11.88 (ISBN 0-688-32217-4). Morrow.
Basil, Douglas & Cook, Curtis W. The Management of Change. 1974. 37.50 (ISBN 0-07-084440-2). McGraw.
Basil, Douglas C. & Traver, Edna. Women in Management. 140p. 1972. text ed. 14.50x (ISBN 0-8290-1568-X). Irvington.
Basil, Douglas C., et al, eds. Purchasing Information Sources. LC 76-7037. (Management Information Guide Ser.: No. 30). 380p. 1977. 60.00x (ISBN 0-8103-0830-4). Gale.
Basil, John D. The Mensheviks in the Revolution of 1917. 220p. 1984. 18.95 (ISBN 0-89357-109-1). Slavica.
Basil, St. Ascetical Works. LC 50-10735. (Fathers of the Church Ser.: Vol. 9). 525p. 1950. 26.95x (ISBN 0-8132-0009-1). Cath U Pr.
--Exegetic Homilies. LC 63-12483. (Father of the Church Ser.: Vol. 46). 378p. 1963. 19.95x (ISBN 0-8132-0046-6). Cath U Pr.
Basil, Saint Letters, 4 Vols. (Loeb Classical Library: No. 190, 215, 243, 270). 12.50x ea. Vol. 1 (ISBN 0-674-99209-1). Vol. 2 (ISBN 0-674-99237-7). Vol. 3 (ISBN 0-674-99268-7). Vol. 4 (ISBN 0-674-99298-9). Harvard U Pr.
Basil, St. Letters, Nos. 1-185. (Fathers of the Church Ser.: Vol. 13). 345p. 1951. 18.95x (ISBN 0-8132-0013-X). Cath U Pr.
--Letters, Nos. 186-368. LC 65-18318. (Fathers of the Church Ser.: Vol. 28). 369p. 1955. 19.95x (ISBN 0-8132-0028-8). Cath U Pr.
Basil, Saint St. Basil the Great on The Forty Martyrs of Sebaste, Paradise, & the Catholic Faith. 1979. pap. 3.95 (ISBN 0-686-25227-6). Eastern Orthodox.
Basile. The Jackal Helix. (Global Two Thousand Ser.: Bk. 2). 672p. (Orig.). 1984. pap. 3.95 (ISBN 0-523-41961-9). Pinnacle Bks.
Basile, A., jt. auth. see OECD Organization for Economic Co-operation & Development.
Basile, Frank M. Back to Basics with Basile. 6th ed. 305p. (Orig.). 1978. pap. 15.00 (ISBN 0-937008-01-X). Charisma Pubns.
--Beyond the Basics. 3rd ed. (Illus.). 173p. (Orig.). 1980. pap. 12.00 (ISBN 0-937008-02-8). Charisma Pubns.
--Come Fly with Me. 18th ed. Holliday, Carol, ed. 52p. (Orig.). 1978. pap. 5.00 (ISBN 0-937008-00-1). Charisma Pubns.
--Flying to Your Success. Snellenbarger, Jan, ed. LC 83-80682. (Illus.). 235p. (Orig.). 1983. pap. 10.00 (ISBN 0-937008-03-6). Charisma Pubns.
--The Motivated Bible. 72p. (Orig.). 1984. pap. 6.00 (ISBN 0-937008-04-4). Charisma Pubns.
Basile, G., ed. see CISM (International Center for Mechanical Sciences), Dept. of Automation & Information, Univ of Geneva, 1971.
Basile, Giovanni B. The Pentamerone of Giambattista Basile, 2 vols. Penzer, N. M., ed. Croce, Benedetto, tr. from It. LC 75-136519. (Illus.). Repr. of 1932 ed. lib. bdg. 60.50x (ISBN 0-8371-5438-3, BAPE). Greenwood.
Basile, Gloria. The Manipulators, Part 1. 1979. pap. 3.50 (ISBN 0-523-41794-2). Pinnacle Bks.
Basile, Gloria V. Born to Power: Manipulators II. (Orig.). 1982. pap. 3.50 (ISBN 0-523-41822-1). Pinnacle Bks.
--Giants in the Shadows. 512p. 1982. pap. 3.50 (ISBN 0-523-41898-1). Pinnacle Bks.
--Global Two Thousand: Eye of the Eagle. 624p. (Orig.). 1983. pap. 3.95 (ISBN 0-523-41960-0). Pinnacle Bks.
--The Sting of the Scorpion: Global 2000, Bk. III. (Orig.). 1984. pap. 3.95 (ISBN 0-523-41962-7). Pinnacle Bks.
Basile, Leon, ed. The Civil War Diary of Amos E. Stearns, A Prisoner at Andersonville. (Illus.). 144p. 1981. 15.50 (ISBN 0-8386-3017-0). Fairleigh Dickinson.
Basile, Leonard & Cernak, Anne. The Teacher's Idea Catalog: How to Create Learning Materials for Young Children. (Illus.). 161p. 1982. 13.95 (ISBN 0-13-888511-7); pap. 6.95 (ISBN 0-13-888503-6). P-H.
Basile, Louis J., jt. ed. see Ferraro, John R.
Basile, Ralph J., et al. Downtown Development Handbook. LC 80-50928. (Community Builder Handbook Ser.). (Illus.). 264p. 1980. 48.00 (ISBN 0-87420-591-3, D12); members 36.00. Urban Land.
Basilevsky, A. Applied Matrix Algebra in the Statistical Sciences. 390p. 1983. 39.50 (ISBN 0-444-00756-3). Elsevier.
Basilevsky, A. & Hum, Derek. The Estimation of Labor Supply Using Experimental Data: The U. S. Guaranteed Income Experiments (Monograph) (Quantitative Studies in Social Relations). 1984. 40.00 (ISBN 0-12-080280-5). Acad Pr.
Basili, Victor R. Tutorial on Models & Metrics for Software Management & Engineering. 343p. 1980. 25.00 (ISBN 0-8186-0310-0, Q310). IEEE Comp Soc.
Basili, Victor R. & Baker, F. Terry. Tutorial on Structured Programming: Integrated Practices. 290p. 1981. 22.00 (ISBN 0-8186-0362-3, Q362) (ISBN 0-317-12376-9). IEEE Comp Soc.
Basili, Victor R. & Turner, Albert J. SIMPL-T: A Structured Programming Language. 1976. coil bdg. 5.95 (ISBN 0-88252-062-8). Paladin Hse.
Basilius. The Ascetic Works of Saint Basil. Clarke, W. K., tr. & intro. by. LC 80-2352. Repr. of 1925 ed. 47.50 (ISBN 0-404-18902-4). AMS Pr.
Basilius, Harold A., tr. see Bodenheimer, Aron-Ronald.
Basilov, V. N., jt. ed. see Dube, S. C.
Basily, Lascelle De see De Basily, Lascelle.
Basily, Nicolas de. The Abdication of Emperor Nicholas II of Russia. 200p. 1984. 25.00 (ISBN 0-940670-26-7). Kingston Pr.
Basily, Nicolas De see De Basily, Nicolas.
Basin, Thomas. Histoire Des Regnes De Charles VII et De Louis XI, 4 Vols. Set. 154.00 (ISBN 0-384-03510-8); Set. pap. 130.00 (ISBN 0-685-13455-5). Johnson Repr.
Basin, Y. Semantic Philosophy of Art. 240p. 1979. 8.45 (ISBN 0-8285-0210-2, Pub. by Progress Pubs USSR). Imported Pubns.
Basinger, David & Basinger, Randall. Predestination & Free Will. 180p. 1985. pap. 6.95 (ISBN 0-87784-567-0). Inter-Varsity.
Basinger, Jeanine. Anthony Mann. (Filmmakers Ser.). 1979. lib. bdg. 13.50 (ISBN 0-8057-9263-5, Twayne). G K Hall.
Basinger, Louis F. The Techniques of Observation & Learning Retention: A Handbook for the Policeman & the Lawyer. (Illus.). 88p. 1973. pap. 1.75x (ISBN 0-398-02935-0). C C Thomas.
Basinger, Randall, jt. auth. see Basinger, David.
Basini, Richard. The Business Person's Guide to Social Drinking. 128p. pap. cancelled (ISBN 0-312-92070-9). Congdon & Weed.
--How to Cut Down Your Social Drinking. 128p. 1985. 12.95 (ISBN 0-399-13109-4). Putnam Pub Group.
Basinski, Michael. The Women Are Called Girls. 22p. 1983. 3.00 (ISBN 0-938838-10-5). Textile Bridge.
Basisu, Mu'in. Descent into the Water: Palestinian Notes from Arab Exile. Omar, Saleh, tr. LC 79-90810. (Monograph Ser.: No. 13). 102p. 1980. pap. 4.50 (ISBN 0-914456-21-0). Medina Pr.
Basiuk, Victor. Technology, World Politics, & American Policy. LC 76-51841. (Institute of War & Peace Studies). 409p. 1977. 34.00x (ISBN 0-685-74998-3). Columbia U Pr.

Baskauskas, Liucija. An Urban Enclave: Lithuanian Refugees in Los Angeles. LC 84-45348. (Immigrant Communities & Ethnic Minorities in the United States & Canada Ser.). 1985. 35.00 (ISBN 0-404-19402-8). AMS Pr.

Baske, Edwin A., jt. auth. see Heusinkveld, Arthur H.

Baskervill, Charles R. English Elements in Johnson's Early Comedy. LC 67-21711. 1967. Repr. of 1911 ed. 12.50 (ISBN 0-87752-004-6). Gordian.

--English Elements in Johnson's Early Comedy. Repr. of 1911 ed. 20.00 (ISBN 0-384-03520-5). Johnson Repr.

Baskerville, B. C. The Polish Jew. 75.00 (ISBN 0-8490-0870-0). Gordon Pr.

Baskerville, Barnet. The People's Voice: The Orator in American Society. LC 79-4001. 272p. 1979. 17.00x (ISBN 0-8131-1385-7). U Pr of Ky.

Baskerville, C. R. Early Fame of the Shepherds Calendar. 1911. lib. bdg. 8.50 (ISBN 0-8414-1629-X). Folcroft.

Baskerville, David. Music Business Handbook & Career Guide. 3rd ed. LC 81-51753. (Illus.). 1981. 18.95x (ISBN 0-933056-02-8). Sherwood Co.

--Music Business Handbook & Career Guide. 4th ed. LC 85-50766. (Illus.). 1985. 19.95x (ISBN 0-933056-04-4). Sherwood Co.

Baskerville, Edward J. A Chronological Bibliography of Propaganda & Polemic: Published in England Between 1553 & 1558, from the Death of Edward VI to the Death of Mary I. LC 79-51543. (Memoirs Ser.: Vol. 136). 1979. 10.00 (ISBN 0-87169-136-1). Am Philos.

Baskerville, Rosetta G. Flame Tree & Other Folklore Stories from Uganda. LC 75-90106. (Illus.). Repr. of 1925 ed. cancelled (ISBN 0-8371-2013-6, BAF&, Pub. by Negro U Pr). Greenwood.

--The King of the Snakes & Other Folk-Lore Stories from Uganda. LC 78-67685. (The Folktale). Repr. of 1922 ed. 14.50 (ISBN 0-404-16054-9). AMS Pr.

Baskett, Edward. Entrapped. LC 75-41812. 160p. 1976. 6.50 (ISBN 0-88208-064-4). Lawrence Hill.

Baskett, Mary. Footprints of the Buddha. LC 80-80133. (Illus.). 125p. (Orig.). 1980. pap. 8.95 (ISBN 0-87633-034-0). Phila Mus Art.

Baskett, T. F. Essential Management of Obstetric Emergencies. 1985. 35.00 (ISBN 0-471-90333-7). Wiley.

Baskett, William D. Parts of the Body in the Later Germanic Dialects. LC 75-161725. (Chicago. University. Linguistic Studies in Germanic: No. 5). Repr. of 1920 ed. 20.00 (ISBN 0-404-50285-7). AMS Pr.

Baskette, Floyd K., et al. The Art of Editing. 3rd ed. 1982. text ed. 25.95 (ISBN 0-02-306280-0). Macmillan.

Baskin, Alex, ed. The American Civil Liberties Union Papers: A Guide to the Records of the A.C.L.U. Cases 1912-1946. LC 70-28011. 1972. 8.95 (ISBN 0-914924-00-1). Archives Soc Hist.

--Studies in the Social Aspects of the Depression: Social Science Research Council, 13 Vols. 1972. Repr. Set. 219.00 (ISBN 0-405-00840-6). Ayer Co Pubs.

--The Unemployed. LC 74-20094. 1975. 22.95 (ISBN 0-914924-01-X). Archives Soc Hist.

Baskin, Alex, jt. ed. see Sanger, Margaret.

Baskin, Barbara & Harris, Karen. Books for the Gifted Child. (The Serving Special Populations Ser.). 263p. 1981. pap. 14.95 (ISBN 0-8352-1428-1). Bowker.

--Books for the Gifted Child. LC 79-27431. (The Serving Special Populations Ser.). 263p. 1980. 24.95 (ISBN 0-8352-1161-4). Bowker.

Baskin, Barbara, ed. Mainstreamed Library: Issues, Ideas, Innovations. Harris, Karen. LC 82-16463. 293p. 1982. lib. bdg. 35.00x (ISBN 0-8389-0359-2). ALA.

Baskin, Barbara H. & Harris, Karen H. More Notes from a Different Drummer: A Guide to Juvenile Fiction Portraying the Disabled. LC 84-12283. (Serving Special Populations Ser.). 495p. 1984. 27.50 (ISBN 0-8352-1871-6). Bowker.

--Notes from a Different Drummer: A Guide to Juvenile Fiction Portraying the Handicapped. LC 77-15067. (Serving Special Populations Ser.). 375p. 1977. 21.95 (ISBN 0-8352-0978-4). Bowker.

Baskin, Barbara H. & Harris, Karen H., eds. The Special Child in the Library. LC 76-21268. pap. 51.80 (ISBN 0-317-26574-1, 2023955). Bks Demand UMI.

Baskin, Hosie, jt. auth. see Baskin, Leonard.

Baskin, Judith R. Pharaoh's Counsellors: Job, Jethro, & Balaam in Rabbinic & Patristic Tradition. LC 83-11535. (Brown Judaic Studies). 200p. 1983. pap. 18.00 (ISBN 0-89130-637-4, 14 00 47). Scholars Pr GA.

Baskin, Leonard. Baskin: Sculpture, Drawings, Prints. LC 73-132198. 1970. 25.00 (ISBN 0-8076-0577-8). Braziller.

--Figures of Dead Men. LC 68-19668. (Illus.). 80p. 1968. signed woodcut ltd ed 150.00x. U of Mass Pr.

--Imps, Demons, Hobgoblins, Witches, Fairies & Elves. LC 84-2911. (Illus.). 48p. (ps up). 1984. 12.95 (ISBN 0-394-85963-4, Pant Bks Young); PLB 12.99 (ISBN 0-394-95963-9). Pantheon.

--Leonard Baskin's Miniature Natural History, 4 vols. LC 82-12612. (Illus., Each vol. 32 pages). 1983. Set. slipcased 9.95 (ISBN 0-394-85567-1). Pantheon.

Baskin, Leonard & Baskin, Hosie. A Book of Dragons. LC 85-6581. (Illus.). 48p. 1985. PLB 12.99 (ISBN 0-394-96298-2); pap. 12.95 (ISBN 0-394-86298-8). Knopf.

Baskin, Leonard, et al. Hosie's Alphabet. (Illus.). 64p. (gr. k-3). 1972. PLB 10.00 (ISBN 0-670-37958-1). Viking.

Baskin, Otis, jt. auth. see Starling, Grover.

Baskin, Otis W., jt. auth. see Aronoff, Craig.

Baskin, Rosemary M. The Low (Sodium, Sugar, Fat) Cookbook. (Illus.). 224p. 1984. laminated cover 11.95 (ISBN 0-9614289-0-2). JRB Pub.

Baskin, Vlasta, tr. see Kretschmer, Ernst.

Baskin, W., tr. see Sartre, Jean-Paul.

Baskin, Wade, ed. Classics in Chinese Philosophy from Mo Tzu to Mao Tse-Tung. (Quality Paperback: No. 274). 737p. 1974. pap. 7.95 (ISBN 0-8226-0274-1). Littlefield.

Baskin, Wade & Powers, G. Pat, eds. New Outlooks in Psychology. LC 67-20466. 1968. 15.00 (ISBN 0-8022-0080-X). Philos Lib.

Baskin, Wade, jt. ed. see Wedeck, Harry E.

Baskin, Wade, tr. see Alberes, Rene M. & De Boisdeffre, Pierre.

Baskin, Wade see Brehier, Emile.

Baskin, Wade, tr. see De Saussure, Ferdinand.

Baskin, Wade, tr. see Kretschmer, Ernst.

Baskin, Yvonne. The Gene Doctors: Medical Genetics at the Frontier. LC 83-61743. 288p. 1984. 13.95 (ISBN 0-688-02645-1). Morrow.

Baskin, Yvonne, jt. auth. see Keeton, Kathy.

Baskind, Frank R. Defining Generalist Social Work Practice. (Illus.). 142p. (Orig.). 1983. lib. bdg. 20.75 (ISBN 0-8191-3718-9); pap. text ed. 9.25 (ISBN 0-8191-3719-7). U Pr of Amer.

Baskir, Lawrence M. & Straus, William A. Chance & Circumstance: The Draft, the War & the Vietnam Generation. (Giant Ser.). pap. 4.95 (ISBN 0-394-72749-5, V-749, Vin). Random.

Baskiyar, Dharni D. The Inextinguishable Flame: Shelley Poetic & Creative Practice. (Salzburg Studies in English Literature: Romantic Reassessment Ser.: No. 68). 1977. pap. text ed. 25.50x (ISBN 0-391-01315-7). Humanities.

Baskoff, Florence. Guided Composition. 2nd ed. 224p. 1984. pap. text ed. 13.50 (ISBN 0-395-34624-X); instr's manual 14.50 (ISBN 0-395-34625-8). HM.

Baskower, Pat & Williams, Joanne. Women's Winning Doubles. Erikson, George, ed. (Illus.). 176p. (Orig.). 1985. pap. 8.95 (ISBN 0-915643-10-3). Santa Barb Pr.

Basler, Beatrice K. & Basler, Thomas G., eds. Health Sciences Librarianship: A Guide to Information Sources. LC 74-11552. (Books, Publishing, & Libraries Information Guide Ser.: Vol. 1). 180p. 1977. 60.00x (ISBN 0-8103-1284-0). Gale.

Basler, K., jt. auth. see Kollbrunner, C. F.

Basler, Lucile. St. Genevieve, Mother of the West. Palmer, Kathleen, ed. (Illus.). 52p. 1978. pap. 2.50 (ISBN 0-9601726-1-0). Wehmeyer Print.

Basler, Lucille. Church of St. Genevieve. Holland, James, ed. (Illus.). 23p. 1980. pap. 1.00 (ISBN 0-686-32909-0). Wehmeyer Print.

--District of Ste. Genevieve: 1725-1980. Kellogg, Dennis & Palmer, Kathleen, eds. LC 80-70736. (Illus.). 360p. 1980. 22.50 (ISBN 0-686-32932-5). Vedette Print.

--A Tour of Old Ste. Genevieve. Wehmeyer Printing, ed. (Illus.). 30p. pap. 1.00 (ISBN 0-686-32910-4). Wehmeyer Print.

Basler, Roy P. Lincoln. 192p. 1976. Repr. of 1961 ed. lib. bdg. 18.50 (ISBN 0-374-90454-5). Octagon.

--The Lincoln Legend. LC 70-75989. (Illus.). 1969. Repr. of 1935 ed. lib. bdg. 26.00x (ISBN 0-374-90456-1). Octagon.

--The Muse & the Librarian. LC 72-780. (Contributions in American Studies: No. 10). 1974. lib. bdg. 29.95x (ISBN 0-8371-6134-7, BML/). Greenwood.

--A Touchstone for Greatness: Essays, Addresses & Occasional Pieces about Abraham Lincoln. LC 72-781. (Contributions in American Studies: No. 4). 1973. lib. bdg. 29.95x (ISBN 0-8371-6135-5, BTG/). Greenwood.

Basler, Roy P., ed. see Lincoln, Abraham.

Basler, Roy P., ed. see Scripps, John L.

Basler, Roy P., ed. see Whitman, Walt.

Basler, Thomas G., jt. ed. see Basler, Beatrice K.

Basmadejian, Garig. Armenian-American Poets: A Bilingual Anthology. LC 75-38094. 158p. 1978. pap. 5.95 (ISBN 0-8143-1617-4). Wayne St U Pr.

Basmajian, J. V. & Kirby, R. L. Medical Rehabilitation: A Student's Textbook. (RML). (Illus.). 380p. 1984. lib. bdg. 24.95 (ISBN 0-683-00415-8). Williams & Wilkins.

Basmajian, J. V. & MacConaill, M. A. Muscles & Movements: A Basis for Human Kinesiology. rev. ed. LC 76-6883. 412p. 1977. 25.50 (ISBN 0-88275-398-3). Krieger.

Basmajian, John V. Biofeedback: Principles & Practice for Clinicians. 2nd ed. (Illus.). 390p. 1983. lib. bdg. 39.95 (ISBN 0-683-00356-9). Williams & Wilkins.

--Manipulation Traction & Massage. 3rd ed. 300p. 1985. 36.95 (ISBN 0-683-00378-X). Williams & Wilkins.

--Primary Anatomy. 8th ed. (Illus.). 436p. 1982. text ed. 24.00 (ISBN 0-683-00550-2). Williams & Wilkins.

--Therapeutic Exercise. 4th ed. (Illus.). 640p. 1984. lib. bdg. 34.95 (ISBN 0-683-00434-4). Williams & Wilkins.

Basmajian, John V. & DeLuca, Carlo J. Muscles Alive. 5th ed. (Illus.). 561p. 1985. 45.00 (ISBN 0-683-00414-X). Williams & Wilkins.

Basmajian, John V., jt. auth. see Lehmann, Justus F.

Basmajian, John V., ed. Therapeutic Exercise: Student Edition. LC 83-9815. 280p. 1983. Repr. of 1980 ed. text ed. 16.95 (ISBN 0-89874-641-8). Krieger.

Basmann, R. L. & Rhodes, George F. Advances in Econometrics, Vol. 3: Economic Inequality Measurement & Policy. 57.50 (ISBN 0-89232-443-0). Jai Pr.

Basmann, R. L. & Rhodes, George F., eds. Advances in Econometrics, Vol. 1. (Orig.). 1982. lib. bdg. 49.50 (ISBN 0-89232-138-5). Jai Pr.

Basmann, R. L. & Rhodes, George F., Jr., eds. Advances in Econometrics, Vol. 2. 315p. 1983. 49.50 (ISBN 0-89232-183-0). Jai Pr.

Basmanov, M. The Revolutionary Vanguard: Battle of Ideologies. 318p. 1977. 6.45 (ISBN 0-8285-1501-8, Pub. by Progress Pubs USSR). Imported Pubns.

Basnage De Beauval, Henry. Tolerance Des Religions. Repr. 20.00 (ISBN 0-384-03522-1). Johnson Repr.

Basoli, Antonio. Collezione Di Varie Scene Teatrali. LC 68-21205. (Illus., Ital., It). 1968. Repr. of 1821 ed. 24.50 (ISBN 0-405-08241-X, Blom Pubns). Ayer Co Pubs.

Basolo, Fred. Inorganic Syntheses, Vol. 16. LC 79-642684. 270p. 1982. Repr. of 1976 ed. lib. bdg. cancelled (ISBN 0-89874-540-3). Krieger.

Basolo, Fred & Pearson, R. G. Mechanisms of Inorganic Reactions. 2nd ed. LC 66-28755. 701p. 1967. 55.00x (ISBN 0-471-05545-X, Pub. by Wiley-Interscience). Wiley.

Basolo, Fred, ed. Inorganic Syntheses, Vol. 16. LC 79-642684. (Inorgnic Syntheses Ser.). 256p. 1975. Repr. lib. bdg. 25.00 (ISBN 0-07-004015-X). Krieger.

Basolo, Fred & Burwell, Robert L., Jr., eds. Catalysis: Progress in Research. LC 73-81490. 193p. 1973. 35.00x (ISBN 0-306-30753-7, Plenum Pr). Plenum Pub.

Basolo, Fred, et al, eds. Transition Metal Chemistry, Vols. 1-2. LC 72-95642. (ACS Reprint Collection). Vol. 1 1973. 13.95 (ISBN 0-8412-0158-7); pap. 10.95 (ISBN 0-8412-0356-3). Am Chemical.

Bason, Cecilia H. Study of the Homeland & Civilization in the Elementary Schools of Germany. (Columbia University. Teachers College. Contributions to Education: No. 710). Repr. of 1937 ed. 22.50 (ISBN 0-404-55710-4). AMS Pr.

Bason, F. T. A Bibliography of the Writings of William Somerset Maugham. LC 74-6376. (Bibliography Ser., No. 59). 1974. lib. bdg. 49.95x (ISBN 0-8383-1880-0). Haskell.

--Bibliography of William Somerset Maugham. 1977. 22.50 (ISBN 0-685-81152-2). Porter.

Bason, Frederick T. A Bibliography of the Writings of William Somerset Maugham. 1979. Repr. of 1931 ed. lib. bdg. 18.00 (ISBN 0-8495-0508-9). Arden Lib.

--Bibliography of the Writings of William Somerset Maugham. LC 73-16154. 1931. lib. bdg. 15.00 (ISBN 0-8414-9879-2). Folcroft.

Bason, M. L., ed. see Baker, Leighton L.

Bason, M. L., ed. see Boren, Kerry R.

Bason, William A. Now Comes the Tribulation, Vol. I. Wright, Betty & Hughey, Roberta, eds. LC 84-71054. (Illus.). 220p. (Orig.). 1984. pap. write for info. (ISBN 0-9611028-6-1). Salt Warrior Pr.

Basov, N. G. Lasers & Holographic Data Processing. 142p. 1985. pap. 4.95 (ISBN 0-8285-2883-7, Pub by Mir Pubns USSR). Imported Pubns.

Basov, N. G., ed. Coherent Cooperative Phenomena. LC 78-2008. (P. N. Lebedev Physics Institute Ser.: Vol. 87). (Illus.). 161p. 1978. 65.00 (ISBN 0-306-10945-X, Consultants). Plenum Pub.

--Cosmic Rays in the Stratosphere & in Near Space. LC 78-2007. (P. N. Lebedev Physics Institute Ser.: Vol. 88). (Illus.). 186p. 1978. 59.50x (ISBN 0-306-10946-8, Consultants). Plenum Pub.

--The Dissipation of Electromagnetic Waves in Plasmas. McNeill, Donald H., tr. from Russian. (Lebedev Trudy Ser.: Vol. 92). 109p. 1982. 49.50 (ISBN 0-306-10969-7, Consultants). Plenum Pub.

--Electrical & Optical Properties of Type III-V Semiconductors. LC 77-26132. (P. N. Lebedev Physics Institute Ser.: Vol. 89). (Illus.). 126p. 1977. pap. 55.00x (ISBN 0-306-10944-1, Consultants). Plenum Pub.

--Electronic Characteristics & Electron-Phonon Interaction in Superconducting Metals & Alloys. LC 77-16799. (P. N. Lebedev Physics Institute Ser.: Vol. 82). (Illus.). 104p. 1977. 55.00 (ISBN 0-306-10937-9, Consultants). Plenum Pub.

--Exciton & Domain Luminescence of Semiconductors. LC 79-14567. (P. N. Levedev Physics Institute Ser.: Vol. 97). (Illus.). 119p. 1979. 55.00 (ISBN 0-306-10958-1, Consultants). Plenum Pub.

--High-Power Lasers & Laser Plasmas. LC 78-794. (P. N. Lebedev Physics Institute Ser.: Vol. 85). (Illus.). 249p. 1978. 65.00 (ISBN 0-306-10943-3, Consultants). Plenum Pub.

--The Kinetics of Simple Models in the Theory of Oscillations. LC 78-5936. (P.N. Lebedev Physics Institute Ser.: Vol. 90). (Illus.). 216p. 1978. 59.50 (ISBN 0-306-10948-4, Consultants). Plenum Pub.

--Lasers & Their Applications. LC 76-26590. (P. N. Lebedev Physics Institute Ser.: Vol. 76). (Illus.). 223p. 1976. 65.00x (ISBN 0-306-10927-1, Consultants). Plenum Pub.

--Lasers & Their Applications in Physical Research. LC 78-13582. (P. N. Lebedev Physics Institute Ser.: Vol. 91). (Illus.). 234p. 1979. 65.00x (ISBN 0-306-10949-2, Consultants). Plenum Pub.

--Luminescence Centers in Crystals. LC 76-41167. (P. N. Lebedev Physics Institute Ser.: Vol. 79). (Illus.). 174p. 1976. pap. 55.00x (ISBN 0-306-10929-8, Consultants). Plenum Pub.

--Material & Apparatus in Quantum Radiophysics. LC 80-21931. (The Lebedev Physics Institute Ser.: Vol. 98). (Illus.). 171p. 1981. 65.00 (ISBN 0-306-10964-6, Consultants). Plenum Pub.

--Microwave Studies of Exciton Condensation in Germanium. LC 78-10160. (P. N. Lebedev Physics Institute Ser.: Vol. 100). (Illus.). 98p. 1979. 55.00 (ISBN 0-306-10952-2, Consultants). Plenum Pub.

--Neutral Current Sheets in Plasmas. LC 76-17087. (P. N. Lebedev Physics Institute Ser.: Vol. 74). (Illus.). 163p. 1976. 55.00 (ISBN 0-306-10926-3, Consultants). Plenum Pub.

--Optical Properties of Semiconductors. LC 75-37609. (P. N. Lebedev Physics Institute Ser.: Vol. 75). (Illus.). 181p. 1976. 55.00x (ISBN 0-306-10916-6, Consultants). Plenum Pub.

--Problems in the General Theory of Relativity & the Theory of Group Representations. LC 78-12612. (P. N. Lebedev Physics Institutes Ser.: Vol. 96). (Illus.). 193p. 1979. 55.00 (ISBN 0-306-10951-4, Consultants). Plenum Pub.

--Pulse Gas-Discharge Atomic & Molecular Lasers. LC 76-57191. (P. N. Lebedev Physics Institute Ser.: Vol. 81). (Illus.). 186p. 1976. 65.00x (ISBN 0-306-10931-X, Consultants). Plenum Pub.

--Pulsed Neutron Research. LC 78-12997. (P. N. Lebedev Physics Institutes Ser.: Vol. 94). (Illus.). 112p. 1979. 49.50x (ISBN 0-306-10950-6, Consultants). Plenum Pub.

--Radio, Submillimeter, & X-Ray Telescopes. LC 76-48290. (P. N. Lebedev Physics Institute Ser.: Vol. 77). (Illus.). 221p. 1976. 59.50 (ISBN 0-306-10930-1, Consultants). Plenum Pub.

--Research in Molecular Laser Plasmas. LC 76-25553. (P. N. Lebedev Physics Institute Ser.: Vol. 78). (Illus.). 115p. 1976. 59.50x (ISBN 0-306-10928-X, Consultants). Plenum Pub.

--Stimulated Raman Scattering. Adashko, J. George, tr. LC 82-18238. (Proceedings (Trudy) of the Lebedev Physics Institute: Vol. 99). 144p. 1982. 55.00x (ISBN 0-306-10968-9, Consultants Bureau). Plenum Pub.

--Strong & Electromagnetic Interactions of Elementary Particles & Nuclei. LC 80-21933. (The Lebedev Physics Institute Ser.: Vol. 95). (Illus.). 214p. 1980. 65.00 (ISBN 0-306-10965-4, Consultants). Plenum Pub.

--Superconductivity. LC 77-17959. (P. N. Lebedev Physics Institute Ser: Vol. 86). (Illus.). 178p. 1977. 55.00x (ISBN 0-306-10939-5, Consultants). Plenum Pub.

--Synchrotron Radiation. LC 76-54915. (P. N. Lebedev Physics Institute Ser.: Vol. 80). (Illus.). 224p. 1976. 65.00 (ISBN 0-306-10932-8, Consultants). Plenum Pub.

--Techniques & Methods of Radio-Astronomic Reception. LC 78-26720. (P. N. Lebedev Physics Institutes Ser.: Vol. 93). (Illus.). 156p. 1979. 59.50x (ISBN 0-306-10955-7, Consultants). Plenum Pub.

--Temporal Characteristics of Laser Pulses & Interaction of Laser Radiation with Matter. LC 77-13406. (P. N. Lebedev Physics Institute Ser.: Vol. 84). (Illus.). 208p. 1978. 65.00 (ISBN 0-306-10942-5, Consultants). Plenum Pub.

--Theoretical Problems in Spectroscopy & Gas Dynamics of Lasers. LC 79-17616. (P. N. Lebedev Physics Institute Ser.: Vol. 83). (Illus.). 232p. 1978. 65.00 (ISBN 0-306-10938-7, Consultants). Plenum Pub.

Basow, Susan. Sex Role Stereotypes: Traditions & Alternatives. LC 80-19086. 320p. (Orig.). 1980. pap. text ed. 13.75 pub net (ISBN 0-8185-0394-7). Brooks-Cole.

Baspoly, Victor, tr. see Pogosov, V. S.

Basquette, Lina. Your Great Dane. LC 70-187772. (Your Dog Bk.). (Illus.). 128p. 1972. 12.95 (ISBN 0-87714-000-6). Denlingers.

Basrani, Enrique. Fractures of the Teeth: Prevention & Treatment of the Vital & Non-Vital Pulp. LC 84-27783. (Illus.). 156p. 1985. text ed. write for info. (ISBN 0-8121-0954-6). Lea & Febiger.

Bass & Dills. Instructural Development: State of the Art, II. 632p. 1984. pap. text ed. 29.95 (ISBN 0-8403-3270-X). Kendall-Hunt.

Bass, jt. auth. see Smith.

Bass, Alan, tr. see Derrida, Jacques.

Bass, Althea. Grandfather Grey Owl Told Me. (Indian Culture Ser.). 1973. 1.95 (ISBN 0-89992-051-9). Coun India Ed.

--Nightwalker & the Buffalo. (Indian Culture Ser.). (gr. 4-9). 1972. 1.95 (ISBN 0-89992-032-2). Coun India Ed.

Bass, Arnold M. & Broida, H. P., eds. Formation & Trapping of Free Radicals. (Illus.). 1960. 72.00 (ISBN 0-12-080350-X). Acad Pr.

Bass, Barbara, et al, eds. The Afro-American Family: Assessment, Treatment, & Research Issues. LC 81-13267. (Seminars in Psychiatry Ser.). 384p. 1982. 28.00 (ISBN 0-8089-1377-8, 790448). Grune.

Bass, Bernard & Barrett, Gerald. People, Work & Organizations: An Introduction to Industrial & Organizational Psychology. 2nd ed. 1980. text ed. 34.29 (ISBN 0-205-06809-X, 796809). Allyn.

Bass, Bernard, jt. ed. see Klauss, Rudi.

Bass, Bernard M. Leadership & Performance Beyond Expectations. LC 84-24724. 224p. 1985. 26.50x (ISBN 0-02-901810-2). Free Pr.

--Leadership, Psychology, & Organizational Behavior. LC 72-10715. (Illus.). 548p. 1973. Repr. of 1960 ed. lib. bdg. 37.00 (ISBN 0-8371-6631-4, BALP, BAL). Greenwood.

--Organizational Decision Making. 1983. 21.95x (ISBN 0-256-02922-9). Irwin.

--Stogdill's Handbook of Leadership. 2nd rev. ed. (Illus.). 1057p. 1981. text ed. 45.00 (ISBN 0-02-901820-X). Free Pr.

Bass, Bernard M., et al. Assessment of Managers: An International Comparison. LC 78-24670. (Illus.). 1979. 21.95 (ISBN 0-02-901960-5). Free Pr.

Bass, Charlotte C. Applique Quiltmaking. 179p. 1985. pap. 18.95 (ISBN 0-668-05873-0). Wallace-Homestead.

--Applique Quiltmaking: Contemporary Techniques with an Amish Touch. LC 84-346. (Illus.). 208p. 1984. 18.95 (ISBN 0-668-05873-0). Arco.

Bass, Clarence. The Lean Advantage. LC 84-71083. (Illus.). 251p. 1984. pap. 13.95 (ISBN 0-9609714-2-4). Clarence Bass.

--Ripped: The Sensible Way to Achieve Ultimate Muscularity. LC 80-81446. (Illus.). 104p. 1980. pap. 9.95 (ISBN 0-9609714-0-8). Clarence Bass.

--Ripped Two. LC 80-81446. (Illus.). 179p. 1982. pap. 12.95 (ISBN 0-9609714-1-6). Clarence Bass.

Bass, Clifford W., et al. Periodicals & Newspapers Acquired by the State Historical Society of Wisconsin Library July, 1974-December, 1984. Danky, James P., ed. 1000p. 1984. 70.00. State Hist Soc Wis.

Bass, Cyrus. Sex from a Different Position. 320p. (Orig.). 1984. pap. 11.00 (ISBN 0-915911-01-9). Publishers Assocs.

Bass, Cyrus, ed. see Rappaport, Fred.

Bass, David, ed. Biblyografye Fun Yidishe Bikher Vegn Khurbn un Gvure. LC 73-209624. (Joint Documentary Projects Bibliographical Ser.: No. 11). 54p. (Yiddish.). 1970. pap. 5.00 (ISBN 0-914512-10-2). Yivo Inst.

Bass, Donna, et al. The Tale of the Dark Crystal. (Illus.). 48p. (gr. k-3). 1982. 9.95 (ISBN 0-03-062414-2). HR&W.

Bass, Eben, jt. auth. see Bass, Geri.

Bass, Eben E. Aldous Huxley: An Annotated Bibliography. LC 79-7907. (Garland Reference Library of Humanities). 275p. 1981. lib. bdg. 36.00 (ISBN 0-8240-9525-1). Garland Pub.

Bass, Ellen. For Earthly Survival. 40p. 1980. pap. 4.95 (ISBN 0-939952-01-7). Moving Parts.

--I'm Not Your Laughing Daughter. LC 73-79503. 96p. 1973. 8.00x (ISBN 0-87023-128-6); pap. 4.95 (ISBN 0-87023-129-4). U of Mass Pr.

--Our Stunning Harvest & Other Poems. 128p. (Orig.). 1986. lib. bdg. write for info. (ISBN 0-939952-04-1). Moving Parts.

--Our Stunning Harvest: Poems by Ellen Bass. 140p. 1985. lib. bdg. 19.95 (ISBN 0-86571-052-X); pap. 6.95 (ISBN 0-86571-053-8). New Soc Pubs.

Bass, Ellen & Thornton, Louise, eds. I Never Told Anyone: Writing by Women Survivors of Child Sexual Abuse. 1983. 17.26 (ISBN 0-06-015149-8, HarpT); pap. 5.72 (ISBN 0-06-091050-X). Har-Row.

Bass, Ellen, jt. ed. see Howe, Florence.

Bass, F. G. & Fuchs, M. Wave Scattering from Statistically Rough Surfaces. LC 77-23113. 1979. text ed. 125.00 (ISBN 0-08-019896-1). Pergamon.

Bass, George. The Tree, the Tomb, & the Trumpet. 1984. 5.75 (ISBN 0-89536-708-4, 4852). CSS of Ohio.

Bass, George F., et al. Yassi Ada, Volume I: A Seventh-Century Byzantine Shipwreck. LC 81-40401. (Nautical Archaeology Ser.: No. 1). (Illus.). 368p. 1982. 79.50x (ISBN 0-89096-063-1). Tex A&M Univ Pr.

Bass, George M. The Gift, the Glitter & the Glory. 1981. 5.25 (ISBN 0-89536-502-2). CSS of Ohio.

--The Man, the Message, & the Mission. 1982. 5.75 (ISBN 0-89536-565-0). CSS of Ohio.

--Plastic Flowers in the Holy Water. 1981. 4.25 (ISBN 0-89536-480-8). CSS of Ohio.

--The Song & the Story. 1984. 7.00 (ISBN 0-89536-652-5). CSS of Ohio.

--Telling the Whole Story. 1983. 5.75 (ISBN 0-89536-642-8). CSS of Ohio.

Bass, George M., jt. auth. see Kemper, Frederick.

Bass, Geri & Bass, Eben. U. S. Guide to Literary Landmarks. (Illus.). 144p. (Orig.). 1984. pap. 8.95 (ISBN 0-939332-09-4). Pohl Assoc.

Bass, H., ed. Algebraic K-Theory 3: Hermitian K-Theory & Geometric Applications. LC 73-13421. (Lecture Notes in Mathematics: Vol. 343). xv, 572p. 1973. pap. 27.00 (ISBN 0-387-06436-2). Springer-Verlag.

Bass, Helen, jt. auth. see Gulati, Bodh R.

Bass, Herbert J. I Am a Democrat: The Political Career of David Bennett Hill. LC 61-13986. (Illus.). 1961. 12.95x (ISBN 0-8156-0021-6). Syracuse U Pr.

Bass, Howard. Ice Skating for Pleasure. (Illus.). 96p. 8.95 (ISBN 0-902280-59-7, P959). Haynes Pubns.

Bass, Hyman. Introduction to Some Methods of Algebraic K-Theory. LC 73-19925. (CBMS Regional Conference Series in Mathematics: No. 20). 68p. 1982. pap. 16.00 (ISBN 0-8218-1670-5, CBMS-20). Am Math.

Bass, Hyman, jt. auth. see Morgan, John W.

Bass, Hyman, et al, eds. Contributions to Algebra: A Collection of Papers Dedicated to Ellis Kolchin. LC 76-45980. 1977. 75.00 (ISBN 0-12-080550-2). Acad Pr.

Bass, J. & Fischer, K. H. Metals: Electronic Transport Phenomena. (Landolt Boernstein Ser.: Group III, Vol. 15, Subvol. A). (Illus.). 400p. 1982. 263.60 (ISBN 0-387-11082-8). Springer-Verlag.

Bass, Jack & De Vries, Walter. Transformation of Southern Politics: Social Change & Political Consequence Since 1945. 1977. pap. 5.95 (ISBN 0-452-00470-5, F470, Mer). NAL.

Bass, Jack & Nelson, Jack. The Orangeburg Massacre. rev. ed. LC 84-9092. xviii, 248p. 1984. 18.50 (ISBN 0-86554-120-5, MUP-H113). Mercer Univ Pr.

Bass, Jean. Exercises in Mathematics. Scripta Technica, tr. 1966. 76.00 (ISBN 0-12-080750-5). Acad Pr.

Bass, Jeffrey, jt. auth. see Ehrenfeld, John.

Bass, Lawrence W. Management by Task Forces: A Manual on the Operation of Interdisciplinary Teams. LC 74-82702. 1975. 12.50 (ISBN 0-912338-09-1); microfiche 9.50 (ISBN 0-912338-10-5). Lomond.

Bass, Lorena L. Honey & Spice: A Nutritional Guide to Natural Dessert Cookery. LC 83-15221. (Illus.). 352p. (Orig.). 1983. pap. 11.95 (ISBN 0-912837-00-4). Coriander Pr.

Bass, Louis N., ed. see Justice, Oren L.

Bass, M., ed. Laser Materials Processing. (Material Processing Theory & Practice: Vol. 3). 475p. 1983. 97.75 (ISBN 0-686-46005-7, North Holland). Elsevier.

Bass, Michael, ed. Materials Processing Symposium ICALEO '82: Proceedings, Vol. 31. 165p. 1983. pap. 55.00 (ISBN 0-912035-00-5). Laser Inst.

Bass, Michael A. The Story of the Century. (Divisional Ser.: No. 9). (Illus.). 1979. Repr. of 1946 ed. 25.00 (ISBN 0-89839-023-0). Battery Pr.

Bass, Nelly, jt. auth. see Wellek, Susanne.

Bass, R. Nuclear Reactions with Heavy Ions. (Texts & Monographs in Physics). (Illus.). 1980. 57.00 (ISBN 0-387-09611-6). Springer-Verlag.

Bass, R. M. Credit Management: How to Manage Credit Effectively. 352p. 1979. text ed. 36.75x (ISBN 0-220-67026-9, Pub. by Busn Bks England); pap. text ed. 14.75x (ISBN 0-220-67029-3). Brookfield Pub Co.

Bass, Ralph, jt. auth. see Kalt, Bryson.

Bass, Rick. The Deer Pasture. LC 84-40556. (A Wardlaw Bk.). (Illus.). 140p. 1985. 12.50 (ISBN 0-89096-228-6). Tex A&M Univ Pr.

Bass, Robert. Swamp Fox. LC 59-5368. (Illus.). 1982. pap. 7.50 (ISBN 0-87844-051-8). Sandlapper Pub Co.

Bass, Robert D. Ninety-Six: The Struggle for the South Carolina Back Country. LC 77-20551. (Illus.). 1978. 12.50 (ISBN 0-87844-039-9); ltd. signed 15.00 (ISBN 0-87844-017-8). Sandlapper Pub Co.

--Swamp Fox. LC 59-5368. 1976. pap. 7.50 (ISBN 0-87844-007-0). Sandlapper Pub Co.

Bass, Robert E. Some Features of Organization in Nature: A Contribution to Philosophy. 1980. 6.00 (ISBN 0-686-29224-3). Print Mail Serv.

Bass, Ronald. The Emerald Illusion. Golbitz, Pat, ed. LC 83-17277. 320p. 1984. 14.95 (ISBN 0-688-02622-2). Morrow.

--The Emerald Illusion. 1984. pap. 3.95 (ISBN 0-451-13238-6, Sig). NAL.

--Lime's Crisis. LC 81-22470. 352p. 1982. 15.50 (ISBN 0-688-01025-3). Morrow.

--Lime's Crisis. 1985. pap. 3.95 (ISBN 0-451-13850-3, Sig). NAL.

Bass, Ronald K., et al, eds. Instructional Development: The State of the Art. (Illus.). 258p. (Orig.). 1978. pap. 8.95x (ISBN 0-88429-099-9, 095-1). Collegiate Pub.

Bass, Rosaly. The Big Tall Man on Skis. (YA) 1974. 4.50 (ISBN 0-87233-035-4). Bauhan.

Bass, Sharyn P. This Is the Maine Coon Cat. (Illus.). 160p. 1983. 19.95 (ISBN 0-87666-867-8, H-1057). TFH Pubns.

Bass, Sophie F. Pig-Tail Days in Old Seattle. LC 72-77591. (Illus.). 190p. 1973. 12.50 (ISBN 0-8323-0206-6). Binford.

Bass, Thomas A. The Eudaemonic Pie: Or Why Would Anyone Play Roulette Without a Computer in His Shoe? 324p. 1985. 15.95 (ISBN 0-395-35335-1); pap. write for info. HM.

Bass, Virginia. Dimensions of Man's Spirit. (Illus.). 274p. 1975. pap. 12.00 (ISBN 0-911336-60-5). Sci of Mind.

Bass, Virginia, ed. Dreams Can Point the Way. (Illus.). 166p. 1984. pap. write for info. (ISBN 0-911197-05-2). Miracle Pub Co TX.

Bass, Virginia W., ed. Young in Heart. (Illus.). (YA) 1966. 12.95 (ISBN 0-915720-77-9); deluxe ed. 17.95 (ISBN 0-915720-78-7). Brownlow Pub Co.

Bass, William G., jt. auth. see Maurer, Stephen G.

Bass, William M. Human Osteology: A Laboratory & Field Manual of the Human Skeleton. 2nd ed. Evans, David R., ed. LC 77-172091. (Special Publications Ser.: No. 2). (Illus.). 288p. (Orig.). 1971. pap. 9.00 (ISBN 0-943414-07-5). MO Arch Soc.

Bass, William M., III, et al. Fay Tolton & the Initial Middle Missouri Variant. Wood, W. Raymond, ed. LC 76-620007. (Research Ser.: No. 13). (Illus.). 43p. (Orig.). 1976. pap. 5.00 (ISBN 0-943414-14-8). MO Arch Soc.

Bassage, Harold. Time for Choice. (Orig.). 1970. pap. 0.95 (ISBN 0-377-80601-3). Friend Pr.

Bassan, Fernande & Chevalley, Sylvie. Alfred de Vigny et la Comedie-Francaise. (Etudes litteraires francaises: No. 31). (Illus.). xvi, 164p. (Orig., Fr.). 1984. pap. 19.00x (ISBN 3-87808-730-6, Pub. by G N Verlag Germany). Benjamins North Am.

Bassan, Fernande, jt. auth. see Dumas, Alexandre.

Bassan, Fernande, et al. An Annotated Bibliography of French Language & Literature. LC 75-24079. (Reference Library of the Humanities: Vol. 26). 300p. 1975. lib. bdg. 40.00 (ISBN 0-8240-9986-9). Garland Pub.

Bassan, M., ed. Stephen Crane: A Collection of Critical Essays. 1967. 12.95 (ISBN 0-13-188888-9, Spec). P-H.

Bassan, Maurice. Hawthorne's Son: The Life & Literary Career of Julian Hawthorne. LC 70-83142. (Illus.). 304p. 1970. 10.00 (ISBN 0-8142-0003-6). Ohio St U Pr.

Bassanese, Fiore A. Gaspara Stampa. (World Authors Ser.). 1982. lib. bdg. 19.95 (ISBN 0-8057-6501-8, Twayne). G K Hall.

Bassani, F. & Parravicini, Pastori. Electron States & Optical Transitions in Solids. 312p. 1975. text ed. 52.00 (ISBN 0-08-016846-9). Pergamon.

Bassani, F., et al, eds. Highlights of Condensed Matter Theory: Proceedings of the International School of Physics, Enrico Fermi, Course LXXXIX Varenna, Italy, June 28 - July 16, 1983. (Enrico Fermi International Summer School of Physics Ser.). 89p. 1984. write for info. (North-Holland). Elsevier.

Bassani, Giorgio. Behind the Door. Weaver, William, tr. 150p. Date not set. pap. 2.25 (ISBN 0-15-611685-5). HarBraceJ.

--The Garden of the Finzi-Continis. Weaver, William, tr. LC 77-77261. (Helen & Kurt Wolff Bk.). 200p. 1977. pap. 4.95 (ISBN 0-15-634570-6, Harv). HarBraceJ.

Bassano, S., jt. ed. see Christison, M. A.

Bassano, Sharron. Consonants Sound Easy! Phonics. (Illus.). 50p. 1981. pap. text ed. 3.95x (ISBN 0-88084-042-0). Alemany Pr.

--Final Clusters Sound Easy. (Sound Easy Ser.). (Illus.). 90p. 1983. pap. text ed. 3.95 (ISBN 0-88084-200-8). Alemany Pr.

--Initial Clusters Sound Easy. (Sound Easy Ser.). (Illus.). 58p. 1983. pap. text ed. 3.95 (ISBN 0-88084-044-7). Alemany Pr.

--Sounds Easy! (Sounds Easy Ser.). (Illus.). 57p. 1980. pap. text ed. 4.25x (ISBN 0-88084-040-4); cassette 10.95x (ISBN 0-88084-041-2). Alemany Pr.

Bassano, Sharron & Christison, Mary A. Drawing Out: Second Language Acquisition Through Student-Created Images. Olsen, Roger E., ed. 136p. 1982. pap. text ed. 12.95 (ISBN 0-88084-006-4). Alemany Pr.

Bassano, Sharron, jt. auth. see Christison, Mary Ann.

Bassauer, Rochus E., tr. see Putz, Helmut.

Bass de Martinez, Bernice B., jt. auth. see Sims, William E.

Basse, J. H., tr. see Faust, Bernhard C.

Basse, Laura. An Uncertain Memory. LC 81-16798. 256p. 1982. 13.50 (ISBN 0-688-00749-X). Morrow.

Basseches, Bruno. A Bibliography of Brazilian Bibliographies: Bibliografia das Bibliografias Brasileiras. LC 78-2290. 1978. 16.00 (ISBN 0-87917-064-6). Ethridge.

Basseches, Michael. Dialectical Thinking & Adult Development. Broughton, John, et al, eds. LC 84-2935. (Path Ser.). 436p. 1985. inst. ed. 49.50 (ISBN 0-89391-017-1); pers. ed. 36.50. Ablex Pub.

Bassegoda Muste, Buenaventura. Nuevo Glosario, Diccionario Poliglota de la Arquitectura. 366p. (Span., Ger., Catalan, Fr., Eng. & Ital.). 1976. pap. 44.95 (ISBN 84-600-0588-7, S-50134). French & Eur.

Bassein, Beth A. Women & Death: Linkages in Western Thought & Literature. LC 83-8544. (Contributions in Women's Studies: No. 44). xii, 236p. 1984. lib. bdg. 27.95 (ISBN 0-313-23924-X, BWD/). Greenwood.

Bassell, G. M., jt. auth. see Marx, G. F.

Basselman, James A., jt. auth. see Farrall, Arthur W.

Basser, Herbert W. Midrashic Interpretations of the Song of Moses. LC 83-49003. (American University Studies VII: Vol. 2). 312p. 1983. pap. text ed. 28.85 (ISBN 0-8204-0065-3). P Lang Pubs.

Basset, F., ed. see International Symposium on Pulmonary Interstitium, Paris, May 1974.

Basset, R. Contes Arabes. LC 78-20116. (Collection de contes et de chansons populaires: Vol. 7). Repr. of 1883 ed. 21.50 (ISBN 0-404-60357-2). AMS Pr.

--Contes populaires berberes. LC 78-20121. (Collection de contes et de chansons populaires: Vol. 12). Repr. of 1887 ed. 21.50 (ISBN 0-404-60362-9). AMS Pr.

--Nouveaux contes berberes. LC 78-20132. (Collection de contes et de chansons populaires: Vol. 23). Repr. of 1897 ed. 21.50 (ISBN 0-404-60373-4). AMS Pr.

Basset, Rene. Moorish Literature. 1977. Repr. of 1901 ed. 30.00 (ISBN 0-89984-044-2). Century Bookbindery.

Basset, Rene, ed. Moorish Literature. 280p. 1981. Repr. of 1901 ed. lib. bdg. 35.00 (ISBN 0-89984-072-8). Century Bookbindery.

Bassett, ed. Developments in Crystalline Polymers, Vol. 1. 279p. 1982. 64.75 (ISBN 0-85334-116-8, Pub. by Elsevier Applied Sci England). Elsevier.

Bassett, Allen M. & O'Dunn, Shannon. General Geology of the Western United States: A Laboratory Manual. rev. ed. (Illus.). 176p. 1980. pap. text ed. 13.95x (ISBN 0-917962-67-2). Peek Pubns.

Bassett, Arland R., ed. Selected Readings in Crime & Justice. 430p. (Orig.). 1982. pap. 9.95 (ISBN 0-942728-04-1). Custom Pub Co.

Bassett, D. C. Principles of Polymer Morphology. (Cambrige Solid State Science Ser.). (Illus.). 220p. 1981. 64.50 (ISBN 0-521-23270-8); pap. 24.95 (ISBN 0-521-29886-5). Cambridge U Pr.

Bassett, D. R. & Hamielac, Alvin E., eds. Emulsion Polymers & Emulsion Polymerization. LC 81-10823. (ACS Symposium Ser.: No. 165). 1981. 59.95 (ISBN 0-8412-0642-2). Am Chemical.

Bassett, Edward, ed. see Miles International Symposium, 12th.

Bassett, Edward G., jt. ed. see Beers, Roland F.

Bassett, Edward G., jt. ed. see Beers, Roland F., Jr.

Bassett, Edward M. Zoning: The Laws, Administration, & Court Decisions During the First Twenty Five Years. LC 73-11916. (Metropolitan America Ser.). 280p. 1974. Repr. of 1936 ed. 17.00x (ISBN 0-405-05385-1). Ayer Co Pubs.

Bassett, Ernest D. & Goodman, David E. Alphabetic Filing Procedure: Simulation. (gr. 9-12). 1981. 5.90 (ISBN 0-538-11136-4, K136). SW Pub.

Bassett, Ernest D., et al. Business Records Control. (gr. 9-12). 1981. text ed. 8.15 (ISBN 0-538-11130-5, K13). SW Pub.

Bassett, F. S. The Folk-Lorist. 1978. Repr. of 1973 ed. lib. bdg. 25.00 (ISBN 0-8414-0506-9). Folcroft.

--The Folk-Lorist. 260p. 1980. lib. bdg. 30.00 (ISBN 0-8492-3587-1). R West.

Bassett, Fletcher S. The Folk-Lore Manual. LC 76-49139. 1976. Repr. of 1892 ed. lib. bdg. 17.00 (ISBN 0-8414-1755-5). Folcroft.

Bassett, Frank E. & Smith, Richard A. Farwell's Rules of the Nautical Road. 6th ed. LC 77-74417. (Illus.). 640p. 1982. 21.95x (ISBN 0-87021-180-3). Naval Inst Pr.

--Farwell's Rules of the Nautical Road. 6th ed. (Illus.). 500p. 1982. 21.95 (ISBN 0-87021-180-3); bulk rates avail. Naval Inst Pr.

Bassett, Frank E., jt. auth. see Noel, John V., Jr.

Bassett, G. W. & Jacka, Brian. The Modern Primary School in Australia. 280p. 1982. text ed. 28.50x (ISBN 0-86861-172-7). Allen Unwin.

Bassett, Helen W. & Starr, Frederick, eds. International Folk-Lore Congress of the World's Columbian Exposition, July, 1893. LC 80-788. (Folklore of the World Ser.). (Illus.). 1980. Repr. of 1898 ed. lib. bdg. 48.50x (ISBN 0-405-13327-8). Ayer Co Pubs.

Bassett, J. Inorganic Chemistry. 1965. text ed. 28.00 (ISBN 0-08-011207-2). Pergamon.

Bassett, J., et al, eds. see Vogel, A. I.

Bassett, J. S., ed. see Byrd, William.

Bassett, James. Commander Prince, USN. 1977. pap. 1.95 (ISBN 0-532-19148-X). Woodhill.

Bassett, John, ed. William Faulkner: The Critical Heritage. (The Critical Heritage Ser.). 1975. 36.00x (ISBN 0-7100-8124-3). Routledge & Kegan.

Bassett, John E. Faulkner: An Annotated Checklist of Recent Criticism. LC 83-11277. (Serif Ser.: No. 42). 250p. 1983. 30.00x (ISBN 0-87338-291-9). Kent St U Pr.

Bassett, John S. Anti-Slavery Leaders of North Carolina. LC 78-63864. (Johns Hopkins University. Studies in the Social Sciences. Sixteenth Ser. 1898: 6). Repr. of 1898 ed. 11.50 (ISBN 0-404-61120-6). AMS Pr.

--Anti-Slavery Leaders of North Carolina. pap. 9.00 (ISBN 0-384-03526-4). Johnson Repr.

--The Constitutional Beginnings of North Carolina (1653-1729) LC 78-63829. (Johns Hopkins University. Studies in the Social Sciences. Twelfth Ser. 1894: 3). Repr. of 1894 ed. 11.50 (ISBN 0-404-61089-7). AMS Pr.

--The Constitutional Beginnings of North Carolina: 1662-1729. pap. 9.00 (ISBN 0-384-03523-X). Johnson Repr.

--Federalist System: Seventeen Eighty-Nine to Eighteen Hundred & One. LC 68-19308. 1968. Repr. of 1906 ed. 22.50 (ISBN 0-8154-0017-9). Cooper Sq.

--Makers of a New Nation. 1928. 22.50x (ISBN 0-686-83612-X). Elliots Bks.

--Middle Group of American Historians. facs. ed. LC 67-22070. (Essay Index Reprint Ser). 1917. 20.00 (ISBN 0-8369-0175-4). Ayer Co Pubs.
--Slavery & Servitude in the Colonies of North Carolina. LC 78-63849. (Johns Hopkins Univesity. Studies in the Social Sciences. Fourteenth Ser. 1896: 4-5). Repr. of 1896 ed. 11.50 (ISBN 0-404-61106-0). AMS Pr.
--Slavery & Servitude in the Colony of North Carolina. Repr. of 1896 ed. 9.00 (ISBN 0-384-03524-8). Johnson Repr.
--Slavery in the State of North Carolina. LC 79-161726. (John Hopkins University Studies in the Social Sciences Seventeenth Ser.: No. 1899: 7-8). Repr. of 1899 ed. 11.50 (ISBN 0-404-00246-3). AMS Pr.
--Slavery in the State of North Carolina. Repr. of 1899 ed. 13.00 (ISBN 0-384-03527-2). Johnson Repr.
Bassett, John S see Gabriel, Ralph H.
Bassett, John S., ed. Selections from the Federalist. 1979. Repr. of 1921 ed. lib. bdg. 25.00 (ISBN 0-8495-0541-0). Arden Lib.
--Southern Plantation Overseer As Revealed in His Letters. LC 68-55870. (Illus.). 1968. Repr. of 1925 ed. lib. bdg. 22.50x (ISBN 0-8371-0297-9, BAO&). Greenwood.
Bassett, L. & Gold, R. Breast Ultrasonography. LC 85-61595. 150p. 1985. 49.50 (ISBN 0-943432-53-7). Slack Inc.
Bassett, Lawrence W. & Gold, Richard H., eds. Mammography, Thermography & Ultrasound in Breast Cancer Detention. 208p. 1982. 49.50 (ISBN 0-8089-1509-6, 790449). Grune.
Bassett, Lee. Gauguin & Food. 48p. 1982. pap. 8.00 (ISBN 0-937160-06-7). Dooryard.
--The Mapmaker's Lost Daughter. 32p. 1980. pap. 3.50 (ISBN 0-937160-00-8). Dooryard.
--News from the Past-Mistakes Hermitage. (Illus.). 24p. 1983. 5.00 (ISBN 0-911287-01-9). Blue Begonia.
Bassett, Libby, jt. auth. see Baker, Mark.
Bassett, Libby, ed. Conference Proceedings -- Environment & Development: The Future for Consulting Firms. LC 83-16903. (Illus.). 431p. 1983. pap. 85.00 (ISBN 0-317-17555-6). World Enviro.
Bassett, Libby & Quandt, Anna, eds. Conference Proceedings Environment & Development: The Future for Consulting Firms in Asia. LC 84-51748. 345p. (Orig.). 1984. pap. 42.50 (ISBN 0-910499-02-0). World Enviro.
Bassett, Lisa. A Clock for Beany. (Illus.). 32p. (gr. k-3). 1985. 11.95 (ISBN 0-396-08484-2). Dodd.
Bassett, Margaret. Abraham & Mary Todd Lincoln. (Illus.). 64p. 1974. 3.75 (ISBN 0-87027-153-9). Cumberland Pr.
Bassett, Michael G. & Cocks, Leonard R. A Review of Silvrian Brachiopods from Gotland. (Fossils & Strata Ser: No. 3). 1974. 10.50x (ISBN 8-200-09349-2, Dist. by Columbia U Pr). Universitet.
Bassett, Paul M. Keep the Wonder. 61p. 1979. pap. 1.95 (ISBN 0-8341-0608-6). Beacon Hill.
Bassett, Paul M. & Greathouse, William M. Exploring Christian Holiness, Vol. 2. 250p. 1984. 15.95 (ISBN 0-8341-0926-3). Beacon Hill.
Bassett, Preston C. Benefit Accrual Requirements: No. B351. (Requirements for Qualification of Plans Ser.). 10p. 1978. pap. 4.50 (ISBN 0-317-31154-9). Am Law Inst.
Bassett, R. L., et al. Deep Brine Aquifers in the Palo Duro Basin: Regional Flow & Geochemical Constraints. (Report of Investigations Ser.: RI 130). (Illus.). 59p. 1983. 2.50 (ISBN 0-318-03280-5). Bur Econ Geology.
Bassett, Randall K., jt. auth. see Burns, Paul C.
Bassett, Reginald G. Democracy & Foreign Policy: Case History of the Sino-Japanese Dispute 1931-33. 680p. 1968. Repr. of 1952 ed. 35.00x (ISBN 0-7146-2209-5, F Cass Co). Biblio Dist.
--Essentials of Parliamentary Democracy. 2nd ed. 1964. Repr. of 1935 ed. 24.00x (ISBN 0-7146-1547-1, F Cass Co). Biblio Dist.
Bassett, Richard, ed. The Open Eye in Learning: The Role of Art in General Education. 216p. 1969. pap. 4.95x (ISBN 0-262-52032-X). MIT Pr.
Bassett, Ronald E. & Smythe, Mary-Jeanette. Communication & Instruction. LC 78-23390. 1979. text ed. 17.50 scp (ISBN 0-06-040526-0, HarpC); inst. manual avail. (ISBN 0-06-360544-9). Har-Row.
Bassett, S. Denton. Public Religious Services in the Hospital. (Illus.). 80p. 1976. 14.75x (ISBN 0-398-03563-6). C C Thomas.
Bassett, S. R. Saffron Walden: Excavations & Research 1972-1980. (CBA Research Report: No. 45). 134p. 1982. pap. text ed. 32.50x (ISBN 0-906780-15-2, Pub. by Coun Brit Archaelolgy England). Humanities.
Bassett, Scott & Bassett, Tammy. Artemus & the Alphabet. (Illus.). 32p. (ps-k). 1980. 5.95x (ISBN 0-9605548-0-7); PLB 5.95x (ISBN 0-9605548-1-5). Bassett & Brush.
Bassett, Seymour, ed. Outsiders Inside Vermont. LC 67-27301. 1976. pap. 4.95 (ISBN 0-914016-30-X). Phoenix Pub.
Bassett, Steve. The Battered Rich. Ashton, Sylvia, ed. LC 79-15043. 1980. 14.95 (ISBN 0-87949-159-0). Ashley Bks.
Bassett, T. D. Vermont: A Bibliography of Its History. LC 83-19874. (Bibliographies of New England Ser.). 427p. 1984. 40.00x (ISBN 0-87451-285-9). U Pr of New Eng.
Bassett, T. D., jt. ed. see Haskell, John D., Jr.
Bassett, T. D., et al. Bibliographies of New England History. Date not set. price not set. U Pr of New Eng.
Bassett, Tammy, jt. auth. see Bassett, Scott.
Bassett, Wilbur. Wander Ships. 136p. 1980. Repr. of 1917 ed. lib. bdg. 20.00 (ISBN 0-8492-3586-3). R West.
--Wander-Ships: Folk Stories of the Sea with Notes Upon Their Origin. LC 78-23905. 1978. Repr. of 1917 ed. lib. bdg. 20.00 (ISBN 0-8414-9900-4). Folcroft.
Bassett, William & Huizing, Peter, eds. The Financial Administration of the Church. (Concilium Ser.: Vol. 117). (Orig.). 1978. pap. 6.95x (ISBN 0-8245-0278-7). Crossroad NY.
Bassett, William B. Historic American Buildings Survey of New Jersey. (Illus.). 210p. 1977. 13.95 (ISBN 0-686-81818-0); pap. 9.95 (ISBN 0-686-81819-9). NJ Hist Soc.
Bassetti, Fred & Ruchlis, Hy. Math Projects: Polyhedral Shapes. (Science-Math Projects Ser.). (Illus., Orig.). (gr. 4-9). 1968. pap. 3.50 (ISBN 0-87594-016-1). Book-Lab.
Bassey, E. J. Exercise: The Facts. (Illus.). 1981. 19.95x (ISBN 0-19-217716-8). Oxford U Pr.
Bassey, Linus. Africa on Life. 126p. 5.00 (ISBN 0-317-18533-0). Ctr for African.
--African Bedtime Stories, Vol. I & II. each vol. 5.00 (ISBN 0-317-18532-2). Ctr for African.
Bassey, Linus A. African Fables. (Illus.). 53p. pap. text ed. write for info. African Policy.
--Rulers of Africa: Recent Past & Present. 5.00 (ISBN 0-317-18530-6). Ctr for African.
Bassey, Linus A., ed. African Wise Sayings. 1980. pap. write for info. African Policy.
Bassey, Michael. Nine Hundred Primary School Teachers. 128p. 1978. 11.00x (ISBN 0-85633-157-0, Pub. by NFER Nelson UK). Taylor & Francis.
--Practical Classroom Organization in the Primary School. (Ward Lock Educational Ser.). 29.00x (ISBN 0-7062-3665-3, Pub. by Ward Lock Educational England). State Mutual Bk.
Bassey, Shirley. Never, Never, Never. pap. 3.50 (ISBN 0-686-09062-4, Pub. by Peer-Southern). Columbia Pictures.
Bassham, Ben L. The Theatrical Photographs of Napoleon Sarony. LC 78-4933. (Illus.). 150p. 1978. pap. 11.00 (ISBN 0-87338-213-7). Kent St U Pr.
Bassham, Ben L., ed. see Warshawsky, Abel G.
Bassham, Rodger C. Mission Theology, Nineteen Forty Eight to Nineteen Seventy-Five: Years of Worldwide Creative Tension--Ecumenical, Evangelical & Roman Catholic. LC 79-17116. 1980. 10.95 (ISBN 0-87808-330-8). William Carey Lib.
Basshe, Em Jo. The Centuries. facsimile ed. LC 71-168508. (Black Heritage Library Collection). Repr. of 1927 ed. 17.25 (ISBN 0-8369-8878-7, Pub. by Blom). Ayer Co Pubs.
Bassi, C., jt. auth. see Aloi, R.
Bassi, Elena. The Convento della Carita. LC 72-1140. (Corpus Palladianum Ser.: Vol. 6). (Illus.). 252p. 1974. 56.00x (ISBN 0-271-01155-6). Pa St U Pr.
Bassin, Alexander, et al, eds. The Reality Therapy Reader: A Survey of the Work of William Glasser. LC 74-1789. 704p. 1976. 17.26i (ISBN 0-06-010238-1, HarpT). Har-Row.
Bassin, Joan. Architectural Competitions in Nineteenth-Century England. Foster, Stephen, ed. LC 84-2599. (Architecture & Urban Design Ser.: No. 6). 206p. 1984. 39.95 (ISBN 0-8357-1565-5). UMI Res Pr.
Bassin, Milton, et al. Statics & Strength of Materials. 3rd ed. (Illus.). 1979. text ed. 32.45 (ISBN 0-07-004030-3). McGraw.
Bassin, William M. Quantitative Business Analysis. LC 80-21090. 256p. (gr. 11-12). 1981. text ed. 21.17 scp (ISBN 0-672-97696-X); scp tchr's. ed. 3.67 (ISBN 0-672-97697-8). Bobbs.
Bassindale, A., ed. The Third Dimension in Organic Chemistry. 1983. pap. 15.00x (ISBN 0-686-90154-1, Pub. by Open Univ Pr). Taylor & Francis.
Bassindale, Alan. The Third Dimension in Organic Chemistry. 242p. 1984. pap. 17.95x (ISBN 0-471-90189-X, Pub. by Wiley Interscience). Wiley.
Bassingthwaighte, Brian see Bruton, Sheila.
Bassiouni, M. C., ed. International Extradition: U. S. Law & Practice, Releases 1 & 2. LC 82-22373. (Releases 1 & 2). 1983. Set. looseleaf 170.00 (ISBN 0-379-20746-X). Oceana.
--The Islamic Criminal Justice System. LC 81-22370. 288p. 1982. pap. 8.00 (ISBN 0-379-20749-4); 30.00 (ISBN 0-379-20745-1). Oceana.
Bassiouni, M. Cherif. Citizen's Arrest: The Law of Arrest, Search & Seizure for Private Citizens & Private Police. (Illus.). 144p. 1977. spiral 17.75x (ISBN 0-398-03626-8). C C Thomas.
--International Criminal Law: A Draft International Criminal Code. LC 80-50452. 286p. 1980. 50.00x (ISBN 90-286-0130-9). Sijthoff & Noordhoff.
--International Extradition & World Public Order. 630p. 1974. lib. bdg. 32.50 (ISBN 0-379-00203-5). Oceana.
--International Terrorism & Political Crimes. 624p. 1975. pap. 29.75x (ISBN 0-398-03296-3). C C Thomas.
--The Palestinians' Rights of Self-Determination & National Independence. (Information Papers: No. 22). 47p. (Orig.). 1978. pap. 4.00 (ISBN 0-937694-38-X). Assn Arab-Amer U Grads.
--Substantive Criminal Law. 676p. 1978. 55.75x (ISBN 0-398-03628-4). C C Thomas.
Bassiouni, M. Cherif & Savitski, V. M. The Criminal Justice System of the USSR. 296p. 1979. 29.75x (ISBN 0-398-03868-6). C C Thomas.
Bassiouni, M. Cherif, ed. Law of Dissent & Riots. 510p. 1971. 60.00x (ISBN 0-398-00107-3). C C Thomas.
Bassiry, Reza. Power vs. Profit: Multinational Corporation-Nation State Interaction. Bruchey, Stuart, ed. LC 80-566. (Multinational Corporations Ser.). 1980. lib. bdg. 28.50x (ISBN 0-405-13363-4). Ayer Co Pubs.
Bassis, Michael, et al. Sociology: An Introduction. 2nd ed. 608p. 1984. pap. 17.00 (ISBN 0-394-32948-1). Random.
Bassis, Michael S., et al. Sociology: An Introduction. 512p. 1980. text ed. 17.00 (RanC); wkbk. o.p. 8.95 (ISBN 0-394-32510-9). Random.
--Social Problems. Merton, Robert K., ed. 586p. 1982. text ed. 24.95 (ISBN 0-15-581430-3, HC); tests avail. (ISBN 0-15-581431-1); study guide 8.95 (ISBN 0-15-581432-X). HarBraceJ.
Bassler, G. Clayton, jt. auth. see Silverstein, Robert M.
Bassler, Jouette M. Divine Impartiality: Paul & a Theological Axiom. Baird, William, ed. LC 81-1367. (Society of Biblical Literature Dissertation Ser.). 1981. pap. text ed. 13.50 (ISBN 0-89130-475-4, 0-06-01-59). Scholars Pr GA.
Bassler, Richard & Logan, Jimmie. Technology of Data Base Management Systems. 3rd ed. 1976. pap. 9.95 (ISBN 0-916580-03-2). College Readings.
Bassler, Richard, jt. auth. see Enger, Norman.
Bassler, Richard, jt. auth. see Joslin, Edward.
Bassler, Richard A. & Joslin, Edward O. Applications of Computer Systems. 1974. pap. 5.95 (ISBN 0-916580-06-7). College Readings.
--Introduction to Computer Systems. 3rd rev. ed. 1974. pap. 6.95 (ISBN 0-916580-04-0). College Readings.
Bassler, Thomas J. & Burger, Robert E. The Whole Life Diet: An Integrated Program of Nutrition & Exercise for a Lifestyle of Total Health. LC 79-19375. 204p. 1979. 9.95 (ISBN 0-87131-305-7). M Evans.
Bassler, U. Neural Basis of Elementary Behavior in Stick Insects. Strausfeld, C., tr. (Studies in Brain Function: Vol.10). (Illus.). 180p. 1983. 35.00 (ISBN 0-387-11918-3). Springer-Verlag.
Bassliouni, M. Cherif, ed. International Criminal Law, 2 vols. 1200p. Vol. 1: 07/1985. lib. bdg. 60.00 (ISBN 0-941320-28-6); Vol. 2: 09/1985. lib. bdg. 60.00 (ISBN 0-941320-31-6). Transnatl Pubs.
Bassman, Stuart W. & Wester, William C., II. Hypnosis, Headache & Pain Control: An Indirect Approach. (Illus.). 70p. (Orig.). 1984. pap. text ed. 9.00x (ISBN 0-910707-05-7). Ohio Psych Pub.
Bassnett-McGuire, Susan. Luigi Pirandello. LC 83-47990. (Modern Dramatists Ser.). (Illus.). 108p. 1983. 17.50 (ISBN 0-394-53498-0, GP-874); pap. 9.95 (ISBN 0-394-62410-6, E 865). Grove.
--Translation Studies. (New Accents Ser.). 1981. pap. 9.95x (ISBN 0-416-72880-4, NO. 2364). Methuen Inc.
Basso, Aldo P. Coins, Medals & Tokens of the Philippines. (Illus.). 144p. 1968. 7.95 (ISBN 0-912496-10-X). Shirjieh Pubs.
Basso, Daivd T. & Schwartz, Ronald D. Programming with FORTRAN-WATFOR-WATFIV. (Orig.). 1981. pap. text ed. 15.95 (ISBN 0-316-08315-1); tchr's ed. avail. (ISBN 0-316-08317-8). Little.
Basso, Dave, ed. Nevada Historical Marker Guidebook. (Nevada Classics Ser.). (Illus.). 92p. (Orig.). 1982. pap. 5.95 (ISBN 0-936332-01-8). Falcon Hill Pr.
--Nevada Small Press Books in Print: 1984. (Illus.). 48p. (Orig.). 1984. pap. 19.95x (ISBN 0-936332-26-3). Falcon Hill Pr.
--Nevada's Public Museums: A Guide. (Nevada Classics Ser.). (Illus.). 88p. (Orig.). 1983. pap. 5.95 (ISBN 0-936332-08-5). Falcon Hill Pr.
--The Works of C. B. McClellan: Special Collector's Edition. (Illus.). 48p. 1983. 89.00 (ISBN 0-936332-24-7). Falcon Hill Pr.
Basso, Dave, ed. see Martin, Anne H., et al.
Basso, David, jt. auth. see Schwartz, Ron.
Basso, David, jt. auth. see Schwartz, Ronald.
Basso, Ellen B. A Musical View of the Universe: Kalapalo Myth & Ritual Performances. LC 84-5166. (Conduct & Communication Ser.). (Illus.). 464p. 1985. text ed. 35.00 (ISBN 0-8122-7931-X). U of Pa Pr.
Basso, Etolia S., ed. World from Jackson Square. LC 72-8579. (Essay Index Reprint Ser.). 1972. Repr. of 1948 ed. 22.00 (ISBN 0-8369-7306-2). Ayer Co Pubs.
Basso, Hamilton. Mainstream. facs. ed. LC 73-106406. (Essay Index Reprint Ser.). 1943. 19.00 (ISBN 0-8369-1444-9). Ayer Co Pubs.
--The View from Pompey's Head. 1985. 6.95 (ISBN 0-87795-708-8). Arbor Hse.
Basso, Keith & Selby, Henry A., eds. Meaning in Anthropology. LC 75-21189. (School of American Research: Advanced Seminar Ser.). 1977. pap. 9.95x (ISBN 0-8263-0456-7). U of NM Pr.
Basso, Keith H. Portraits of the Whiteman. LC 78-31535. 1979. 21.95 (ISBN 0-521-22640-6); pap. 7.95 (ISBN 0-521-29593-9). Cambridge U Pr.
--Western Apache Witchcraft. LC 69-16329. (University of Arizona, Anthroplological Papers: No. 15). pap. 20.30 (ISBN 0-317-28645-5, 2055359). Bks Demand UMI.
Basso, Keith H. & Opler, Morris, eds. Apachean Culture History & Ethnology. LC 70-140453. (Anthropological Papers: No. 21). (Illus.). 168p. (Orig.). 1971. pap. 6.95x (ISBN 0-8165-0295-1). U of Ariz Pr.
Basso, Keith H., ed. see Goodwin, Grenville.
Bassoff, Bruce. The Secret Sharers: Studies in Contemporary Fictions. LC 82-20766. (Ars Poetica Ser.: No. 1). (Illus.). 152p. 1984. 29.50 (ISBN 0-404-62501-0). AMS Pr.
--Toward Loving: The Poetics of the Novel & the Practice of Henry Green. LC 75-22071. 180p. 1975. lib. bdg. 14.95x (ISBN 0-87249-324-5). U of SC Pr.
Bassoli, F., jt. auth. see Gareff, G.
Bassols, C. & Blanco, L. Ingles, Primer Curso. 1974. text ed. write for info (ISBN 0-07-090582-7). McGraw.
Basson, A. H. David Hume. LC 78-26704. 183p. 1981. Repr. of 1958 ed. lib. bdg. 19.75x (ISBN 0-313-20668-6, BADH). Greenwood.
Basson, Marc D., ed. Ethics, Humanism, & Medicine. LC 79-3650. (Progress in Clinical & Biological Research Ser.: Vol. 38). 346p. 1980. 26.00x (ISBN 0-8451-0038-6). A R Liss.
--Rights & Responsibilities in Modern Medicine: The Second Volume in a Series on Ethics, Humanism, & Medicine. LC 80-29391. (Progress in Clinical & Biological Research: Vol. 50). 272p. 1981. 22.00 (ISBN 0-8451-0050-5). A R Liss.
Basson, Marc D., jt. auth. see Ethics, Humanisms & Medicine Conference, University of Michigan, Ann Arbor, MI. 1981.
Basson, Philip W. Fossil Flora of the Drywood Formation of Southwestern Missouri. LC 67-63045. (Illus.). 184p. 1968. 18.00x (ISBN 0-8262-7516-8). U of Mo Pr.
Basstaire, Jean, jt. auth. see Peguy, Charles.
Bassuk, Daniel, ed. see Zielinski, Stanislaw.
Bassuk, Ellen, ed. Lifelines: Clinical Perspectives on Suicide. LC 82-9105. 249p. 1982. 25.00x (ISBN 0-306-40971-2, Plenum Pr). Plenum Pub.
Bassuk, Ellen L. & Fox, Sandra S. Behavioral Emergencies: A Field Guide for EMT's & Paramedics. 1983. pap. text ed. 14.95 (ISBN 0-316-08330-5); instrs.' manual avail. (ISBN 0-316-08331-3). Little.
Bassuk, Ellen L. & Schoonover, Stephen C. The Practitioner's Guide to Psychoactive Drugs. LC 76-40466. (Topics in General Psychiatry Ser). 331p. 1977. 19.95x (ISBN 0-306-30953-X, Plenum Pr). Plenum Pub.
Bassuk, Ellen L. & Birk, Ann W., eds. Emergency Psychiatry: Concepts, Methods, & Practices. (Critical Issues in Psychiatry Ser.). 468p. 1984. 45.00x (ISBN 0-306-41655-7, Plenum Pr). Plenum Pub.
Bassuk, Ellen L. & Gelenberg, Alan J., eds. The Practitioner's Guide to Psychoactive Drugs. 2nd ed. (Topics in General Psychiatry Ser.). 456p. 1983. 27.50x (ISBN 0-306-41093-1, Plenum Pr). Plenum Pub.
Bast, Henry. The Lord's Prayer. 2.50 (ISBN 0-686-23480-4). Rose Pub MI.
Bast, Rochelle, ed. Handbook for Senior Adult Camping. 68p. 1977. pap. 4.00 (ISBN 0-943272-11-4). Inst Recreation Res.
Bast, Theodore H. & Anson, Barry J. The Temporal Bone & the Ear. (Illus.). 502p. 1949. photocopy ed. 59.50x (ISBN 0-398-04200-4). C C Thomas.
Basta, Daniel J. & Bower, Blair T., eds. Analyzing Natural Systems: Analysis for Regional Residuals--Environmental Quality Management. LC 81-48248. (Research Paper). 564p. 1982. pap. 30.00X (ISBN 0-8018-2820-1). Johns Hopkins.
Basta, Daniel J., et al. Analysis for Residuals-Environmental Quality Management: Case Study of the Ljubljana Area of Yugoslavia. LC 77-17250. (Resources for the Future). pap. 64.50 (ISBN 0-317-26216-5, 2052112). Bks Demand UMI.
Basta, Lofty L. Cardiovascular Diseases: Essentials of Primary Care. 1983. 29.00 (ISBN 0-87488-738-0); pap. 29.00 (ISBN 0-87488-746-1). Med Exam.
Bastard, Thomas. Chrestoleros: Seven Books of Epigrames. (Spencer Society Publications Ser.: No. 47). 1966. Repr. of 1598 ed. 29.50 (ISBN 0-8337-0184-3). B Franklin.
Basten, Fred, jt. auth. see Miller, Robert.
Basten, Fred E. Beverly Hills: Portrait of a Fabled City. LC 75-22571. (Illus.). 384p. 1975. 28.50 (ISBN 0-913264-23-7). Douglas-West.
--Glorious Technicolor: The Movies' Magic Rainbow. LC 78-67469. (Illus.). 1980. 30.00 (ISBN 0-498-02317-6). A S Barnes.
--An Illustrated Guide to the Legendary Trees of Santa Monica Bay. LC 80-83609. (Illus.). 128p. (Orig.). 1980. pap. 6.95 (ISBN 0-937536-01-6). Graphics Calif.

--Main St. to Malibu: Yesterday & Today. LC 80-83608. (Illus.). 128p. (Orig.). 1980. pap. 6.95 (ISBN 0-937536-00-8). Graphics Calif.

--Santa Monica Bay: The First One Hundred Years. LC 74-83618. 1984. limited ed. 24.95 (ISBN 0-318-01901-9). Graphics Pr.

Basten, Fred E., jt. auth. see Sarlot, Raymond R.

Bastenie, P. A. & Bonny, eds. Recent Progress in the Diagnosis & Treatment of Hypothyroid Conditions. (International Congress Ser.: Vol. 529). 158p. 1980. 42.25 (ISBN 0-444-90161-2). Elsevier.

Baster, A. S. The Imperial Banks. Wilkins, Mira, ed. LC 76-29994. (European Business Ser.). 1977. Repr. of 1929 ed. lib. bdg. 23.50x (ISBN 0-405-09752-2). Ayer Co Pubs.

--The International Banks. Wilkins, Mira, ed. LC 76-29995. (European Business Ser.). 1977. Repr. of 1935 ed. lib. bdg. 21.00x (ISBN 0-405-09753-0). Ayer Co Pubs.

Baster, Nancy, ed. Measuring Development: The Role & Adequacy of Development Indicators. 182p. 1972. 29.50x (ISBN 0-7146-2967-7, F Cass Co). Biblio Dist.

Bastgem, Z. Let's Learn Polish. 1982. 7.50 (ISBN 0-89918-329-8, P509). Vanous.

Bastgen, Zofia. Polish, Lets Learn. 4th ed. (Illus.). 1982. pap. text ed. 7.50x (ISBN 0-89918-509-6, P-509). Vanous.

Bastiaenen, J. A. Moral Tone of Jacobean & Caroline Drama. LC 68-951. (Studies in Drama, No. 39). 1969. Repr. of 1930 ed. lib. bdg. 39.95x (ISBN 0-8383-0507-5). Haskell.

Bastian, Adolf. Afrikanische Reisen: Ein Besuch in San Salvador der Hauptstadt Des Konigreichs Congo. (Landmarks in Anthropology Ser). Repr. of 1859 ed. 33.00 (ISBN 0-384-03525-6). Johnson Repr.

--Inselgruppen in Oceanien. LC 75-35174. Repr. of 1833 ed. 24.50 (ISBN 0-404-14203-6). AMS Pr.

Bastian, Donald N. Along the Way. 128p. 1977. pap. 3.95 (ISBN 0-89367-008-1). Light & Life.

--Belonging! Adventures in Church Membership. 1978. pap. 4.95 (ISBN 0-89367-044-8). Light & Life.

Bastian, Dwight R., ed. see Little, Ernest F.

Bastian, F. Defoe's Early Life. (Illus.). 390p. 1981. 32.50x (ISBN 0-389-20094-8, 06867). B&N Imports.

Bastian, Gerd, et al. Generals for Peace & Disarmament. LC 84-4035. 144p. 1984. text ed. 15.00x (ISBN 0-87663-447-1); pap. 6.95 (ISBN 0-87663-862-0). Universe.

Bastian, Hartmut. Ullstein Lexikon der Pflanzenwelt. (Ger.). 1973. 27.50 (ISBN 0-686-56471-5, M-7675, Pub. by Ullstein Verlag VA). French & Eur.

--Ullstein Lexikon der Tierwelt. (Ger.). 1967. 27.50 (ISBN 3-550-06014-9, M-7676, Pub. by Ullstein Verlag/VVA). French & Eur.

Bastian, Heiner. Cy Twombley: The Printed Graphic Work, 1953-84. 1985. 40.00 (ISBN 0-317-28719-2); pap. 19.95 (ISBN 0-317-28720-6). NYU Pr.

--Cy Twombly: The Printed Graphic Work 1953-1984. (Illus.). 80p. 1985. pap. 19.95 (ISBN 0-8147-1077-8); 40.00s (ISBN 0-8147-1076-X). NYU Pr.

Bastian, Henry C. A Treatise on Aphasia & Other Speech Defects. LC 78-72786. (Brainedness, Handedness & Mental Ability Ser.). Repr. of 1898 ed. 37.50 (ISBN 0-404-60851-5). AMS Pr.

Bastian, Katherine. Joyce Carol Oates's Short Stories Between Tradition & Innovation, Vol. 26. (Neue Studien zur Anglistik und Amerikanistik). 173p. 1982. pap. 21.05 (ISBN 3-8204-7215-0). P Lang Pubs.

Bastian, Marlene Y. How to Shop Wisely. 108p. (Orig.). 1982. pap. 5.95x (ISBN 0-9609058-0-4). M Y Bastian.

Bastian, Ralph J., tr. see Portalie, Eugene.

Bastiansen, William. Instrumental Analysis. 1979. pap. text ed. 8.50 (ISBN 0-89669-016-4). Collegium Bk Pubs.

Bastias, John C., jt. ed. see Christopoulos, George A.

Bastiat, Frederic. Economic Harmonies. 596p. 1968. pap. 7.00 (ISBN 0-910614-13-X). Foun Econ Ed.

--Economic Sophisms. 291p. 1968. pap. 5.00 (ISBN 0-910614-14-8). Foun Econ Ed.

--The Law. 76p. 1961. 3.50 (ISBN 0-910614-30-X); pap. 2.00 (ISBN 0-910614-01-6). Foun Econ Ed.

--Paix et Liberte,ou Le Budget Republicain. Bd. with On the Causes of War, & the Means of Reducing Their Number. Laveleye, Emile L. LC 72-147492. (Library of War & Peace; the Political Economy of War). lib. bdg. 46.00 (ISBN 0-8240-0286-5). Garland Pub.

--Selected Essays on Political Economy. 352p. 1968. pap. 6.00 (ISBN 0-910614-15-6). Foun Econ Ed.

Bastiat, Frederick. Incongruities, Inconsistencies, Absurdities & Outright Stupidities in Scientific Economics. (Illus.). 198p. 1984. Repr. of 1920 ed. 137.45 (ISBN 0-89901-191-8). Found Class Reprints.

Bastible, James C., ed. see Ott, Ludwig.

Bastick, Tony. Intuition: How We Think & Act. LC 80-42060. 494p. 1982. 57.95x (ISBN 0-471-27992-7, Pub. by Wiley-Interscience). Wiley.

Bastid, Marianne. Educational Reform in Early Twentieth-Century China. Bailey, Paul J., tr. from Fr. (Michigan Monographs in Chinese Studies: No. 53). 200p. 1985. text ed. 17.50 (ISBN 0-89264-061-8); pap. text ed. 10.00 (ISBN 0-89264-062-6). U of Mich Ctr Chinese.

Bastida, Julio R. Encyclopedia of Mathematics & Its Applications: Field Extensions & Galois Theory, Vol. 22. 1984. 47.50 (ISBN 0-317-14400-6, 30242-0). Cambridge U Pr.

Bastidas, Juanita. Mis Lecciones de Amor. new ed. (Pimienta Collection Ser). 160p. (Span.). 1974. pap. 1.00 (ISBN 0-88473-205-3). Fiesta Pub.

Bastide, Charles. Anglo-French Entente in the Seventeenth Century. LC 78-146136. (Research & Source Works Ser.: No. 825). 1971. Repr. of 1914 ed. lib. bdg. 21.00 (ISBN 0-8337-0185-1). B Franklin.

Bastide, R. see Poirier, J.

Bastide, R., et al. Les Haitiens en France. (Publications de l'Institut d'Etudes et de Recherches Interethniques et Interculturelles Ser.: No. 4). (Illus.). 229p. (Fr.). 1975. pap. text ed. 20.80x (ISBN 90-2797-515-9). Mouton.

Bastide, Roger. The African Religions of Brazil: Toward a Sociology of the Interpenetration of Civilizations. Sebba, Helen, tr. (Johns Hopkins Studies in Atlantic History & Culture Ser.). 1978. text ed. 42.50x (ISBN 0-8018-2056-1); pap. text ed. 14.95x (ISBN 0-8018-2130-4). Johns Hopkins.

Bastide, Roger, ed. Les Sciences De la Folie. (Publications Du Centre De Psychiatrie Sociale: No. 5). 1972. pap. 10.40 (ISBN 90-2796-992-2). Mouton.

--Sens et Usages Du Terme Structure Dans les Sciences Humaines et Sociales. 2nd ed. (Janua Linguarum, Series Minor: No. 16). 165p. (Fr.). 1972. pap. text ed. 15.20x (ISBN 90-2792-312-4). Mouton.

Bastien, Charles. QC Sources. 420p. (Orig.). 1984. 17.95 (ISBN 0-916429-00-8). IAQC Pr.

Bastien, Dorothy. I Want to Be Me. (Orig.). (gr. 7 up). pap. 1.95 (ISBN 0-590-32205-2, Wildfire). Scholastic Inc.

--The Night Skiers. 144p. (Orig.). (gr. 7 up). 1982. pap. 1.95 (ISBN 0-590-32449-7, Wishing Star Bks). Scholastic Inc.

--Remember to Love. (YA) (gr. 7 up). 1979. pap. 1.95 (ISBN 0-590-32398-9, Wishing Star Bks). Scholastic Inc.

Bastien, James W. How to Teach Piano Successfully. 2nd ed. LC 77-75481. (Illus.). 1977. pap. text ed. 19.95 (ISBN 0-8497-6109-3, GP40, Pub. by GWM). Kjos.

--A Parent's Guide to Piano Lessons. LC 76-21927. (Illus.). 1976. pap. 2.50 (ISBN 0-910842-05-1, WP29, Pub by Kjos West). Kjos.

Bastien, James W. & Bastien, Jane S. Beginning Piano for Adults. LC 68-25633. (Illus.). 1968. 12.95 (ISBN 0-910842-02-7, GP23, Pub. by GWM). Kjos.

Bastien, Jane S., jt. auth. see Bastien, James W.

Bastien, Joseph W. Mountain of the Condor: Metaphor & Ritual in an Andean Ayllu. (Illus.). 227p. 1985. pap. text ed. 7.95x (ISBN 0-88133-143-0). Waveland Pr.

Bastien, Joseph W. & Donahue, John N., eds. Health in the Andes. 1981. pap. 15.00 (ISBN 0-686-36592-5). Am Anthro Assn.

Bastien, Remy, jt. auth. see Courlander, Harold.

Bastin, Bruce. Crying for the Carolines. (The Paul Oliver Blues Ser.). pap. 2.95 (ISBN 0-913714-31-3). Legacy Bks.

Bastin, Edson S. Interpretation of Ore Textures. LC 51-3907. (Geological Society of America, Memoir Ser.: No. 45). pap. 32.30 (ISBN 0-317-10251-6, 2007947). Bks Demand UMI.

Bastin, G. Diccionario De Psicologia Sexual. 2nd ed. 412p. (Span.). 1976. 19.95 (ISBN 84-254-0585-8, S-13099). French & Eur.

Bastin, Marcel, et al. God Day by Day, Vol. 2: Ordinary Time: Matthew. 576p. (Orig.). 1984. pap. 16.95t (ISBN 0-8091-2643-5). Paulist Pr.

--God Day by Day, Vol. 1: Lent & the Easter Season. 320p. (Orig.). 1984. pap. 9.95 (ISBN 0-8091-2642-7). Paulist Pr.

--God Day by Day, Vol. 4: Advent & Christmas. 176p. (Orig.). 1985. pap. 8.95 (ISBN 0-8091-2699-0). Paulist Pr.

Bastin, Marjolein. My Name Is Vera. (Illus.). 28p. 1985. 2.50 (ISBN 0-8120-5690-6). Barron.

--Vera & Her Friends. (Illus.). 28p. 1985. 2.50 (ISBN 0-8120-5689-2). Barron.

--Vera's Dressing up. 28p. 1985. 2.50 (ISBN 0-8120-5691-4). Barron.

--Vera's Nature Book. (Illus.). 28p. 1985. 2.50 (ISBN 0-8120-5692-2). Barron.

Basting, Alan. Singing from the Abdomen. 1976. pap. 2.50 (ISBN 0-685-79281-1). Stone-Marrow Pr.

Bastl-Bullock, Elaine. The Marketing of Cooperative Advertising. (Illus.). 110p. 1983. 15.95 (ISBN 0-912875-00-3). Bullock Pub Co.

Bastos, Hugo, jt. auth. see Zarate, Armando.

Bastos, Maria L. Borges Ante la Critica Argentina: 1923-1960. 356p. 1974. 8.00 (ISBN 0-935318-00-3). Edins Hispamerica.

Bastow, Donald. W.O. Bentley: Engineer. 39.95 (ISBN 0-85429-215-2, F215). Haynes Pubns.

Bastress, E. K., ed. Gas Turbine Combustion & Fuels Technology. 84p. 1977. 14.00 (ISBN 0-317-33532-4, H00107); members 7.00 (ISBN 0-317-33533-2). ASME.

Bastress, Frances. Teachers in New Careers: Stories for Successful Transitions. LC 84-12647. 240p. 1984. 10.95 (ISBN 0-910328-40-4). Carroll Pr.

Bastron, R. Dennis & Deutsch, Stanley. Anesthesia & the Kidney. LC 76-41193. (Scientific Basis of Clinical Anesthesia Ser.). (Illus.). 128p. 1976. 37.00 (ISBN 0-8089-0974-6, 790450). Grune.

Bastwick, John. The Letany of J. Bastwick. Bd. with The Answer of J. Bastwick to the Exceptions Against His Letany; The Vanity & Mischief of the Old Letany; A More Full Answer of J. Bastwick Made to the Former Exceptions Newly Propounded. LC 76-57354. (English Experience Ser.: No. 773). 1977. Repr. of 1637 ed. lib. bdg. 9.50 (ISBN 90-221-0773-6). Walter J Johnson.

Bastyai, Lorant de see De Bastyai, Lorant.

Basu, A. K., jt. auth. see Bhattacharjee, P. K.

Basu, Aparna. Essays in the History of Indian Education. 116p. 1982. text ed. 12.50x (ISBN 0-391-02642-9, Pub. by Concept India). Humanities.

Basu, Arindam. Picaro or Me. (Writers Workshop Greenbird Ser.). 90p. 1975. 12.00 (ISBN 0-88253-608-7); pap. text ed. 4.80 (ISBN 0-88253-607-9). Ind-US Inc.

Basu, Asoke, jt. auth. see Segalman, Ralph.

Basu, C. R. Central Banking in a Planned Economy: The Indian Experiment. 1977. 16.00x (ISBN 0-88386-987-X). South Asia Bks.

Basu, Dilip & Murphey, Rhoads, eds. Nineteenth-Century China: Five Imperialist Perspectives. (Michigan Monographs in Chinese Studies: No. 13). 82p. 1972. pap. 1.50 (ISBN 0-89264-013-8). U of Mich Ctr Chinese.

Basu, Dilip K., ed. The Rise & Growth of the Colonial Port Cities in Asia. LC 85-11095. (Monograph Ser.: No. 25). (Illus.). 332p. (Orig.). 1985. lib. bdg. 26.75 (ISBN 0-8191-4761-3, Co-Pub by Center for South & Southeast Asia Studies); pap. text ed. 14.75 (ISBN 0-8191-4762-1). U Pr of Amer.

Basu, Dipak R. Future Energy Policies for the U. K. 164p. 1981. text ed. 40.50x (ISBN 0-333-31277-5, Pub. by Macmillan England). Humanities.

Basu, Duga D. Constitutional Law of India. LC 83-903490. xi, 488p. Date not set. price not set (ISBN 0-87692-024-5). P-H.

Basu, Durga D. Introduction to the Constitution of India. 10th, rev. ed. 1984. pap. 9.00x (ISBN 0-8364-1097-1, Pub. by P-H India). South Asia Bks.

Basu, K. S. Management Similarities & Differences Under Different Culture. 56p. 1970. pap. 38.50 (ISBN 0-677-61505-1). Gordon.

Basu, Kaushik. The Less Developed Economy: A Critique of Contemporary Theory. (Illus.). 224p. 1984. 29.95x (ISBN 0-631-13111-6). Basil Blackwell.

Basu, Keith. Revealed Preference of Government. LC 78-67300. 1980. 32.50 (ISBN 0-521-22489-6). Cambridge U Pr.

Basu, Manoje. The Beauty. Ghosh, Sachindra L., tr. 103p. 1969. pap. 1.80 (ISBN 0-88253-011-9). Ind-US Inc.

--Trappings of Gold. Ghosh, S. L., tr. 176p. 1969. pap. 2.00 (ISBN 0-88253-013-5). Ind-US Inc.

Basu, Nitish K. English Literary Criticism & the Classical Background. 1962. Repr. 25.00 (ISBN 0-8274-2259-8). R West.

--English Literary Criticism & the Classical Background. 544p. 1982. Repr. of 1962 ed. lib. bdg. 50.00 (ISBN 0-89760-016-9). Telegraph Bks.

--A History of English Literature. Incl. Pt. 1. The Old English Period; Pt. 2. From the Norman Conquest to the Dawn of Renaissance & Geoffrey Chaucer. 1978. Repr. of 1969 ed. Set. lib. bdg. 25.00 (ISBN 0-8482-3410-3). Norwood Edns.

--A History of English Literature, 2 vols. 1963. Repr. 12.50 ea. (ISBN 0-8274-2512-0); Part 1: The Old English Period. (ISBN 0-8492-3592-8); Part 2: The Norman Conquest To The Dawn Of Renaissance & Geoffrey Chaucer. (ISBN 0-8492-3593-6). R West.

--Literature & Criticism. LC 76-30433. 1977. Repr. of 1963 ed. lib. bdg. 20.00 (ISBN 0-8414-1767-9). Folcroft.

Basu, P., ed. Fluidized Bed Boilers & Combustors: Design & Operation: Proceedings of the International Workshop on the Design & Operation of Fluidized Bed Boilers, Halifax, Canada, June 23-24, 1984. (Illus.). 198p. 1984. 50.00 (ISBN 0-08-025410-1). Pergamon.

Basu, P. K., ed. The New Managerial Order in Asia. 1981. 20.00x (ISBN 0-8364-0740-7, Pub. by Macmillan India). South Asia Bks.

Basu, Romen. Canvas & the Brush. 116p. 1970. 5.95 (Pub. by Filma K L Mukhopadhyay India). R Basu.

--A Gift of Love. (Greenbird Bk.). 176p. 1975. 12.00 (ISBN 0-88253-823-3); pap. 5.00 (ISBN 0-88253-824-1). Ind-US Inc.

--A Gift of Love. 176p. 1974. 7.95 (ISBN 0-910586-46-2, Pub. by Writers Wksp India). R Basu.

--A House Full of People. 186p. 1968. 6.95 (Pub. by Navana Publishers India). R Basu.

--Portrait on the Roof. 152p. 1980. 11.95 (ISBN 0-86578-193-1). Sterling.

--The Tamarind Tree. 227p. 1976. 7.95 (Pub. by Writers Wksp India). R Basu.

--Your Life to Live. 180p. 1972. 7.95 (Pub. by Filma K L Mukhopadhyay India). R Basu.

Basu, S. N. Jagadis Chandra Bose. (National Biography Ser.). (Orig.). 1979. pap. 3.25 (ISBN 0-89744-205-9). Auromere.

Basu, Sajal. The Politics of Violence: A Case Study of West Bengal. 1982. 11.00x (ISBN 0-685-59390-8). South Asia Bks.

Basu, Sankar. Chekhov & Tagore: A Comparative Study of Their Short Stories. 1985. text ed. 20.00x (ISBN 0-86590-619-X, Pub. by Sterling Pubs India). Apt Bks.

Basu, Shankar. Culture & Civilization of the U. S. S. R. 126p. 1984. text ed. 18.95x (ISBN 0-86590-269-0, Sterling Pubs India). Apt Bks.

Basu, Subhas K. Commercial Banks & Agricultural Credit: A Study in Regional Disparity in India. 1979. 15.00x (ISBN 0-8364-0542-0). South Asia Bks.

Basu, T. K. Clinical Implications of Drug Use, 2 vols. 1980. Vol. 1, 160p. 59.00 (ISBN 0-8493-5391-2); Vol. 2, 144p. 59.00 (ISBN 0-8493-5392-0). CRC Pr.

Basu, T. K. & Schorah, C. J. Vitamin C in Health & Disease. (Illus., Orig.). 1982. lib. bdg. 21.50 (ISBN 0-87055-406-9). AVI.

Basye. Clearing Land Titles: Second Edition. write for info. West Pub.

Bat, Alfred De see De Bat, Alfred.

Bata, L., ed. Advances in Liquid Crystal Research & Applications: Proceedings of the Third Liquid Crystal Conference of the Socialist Countries, Budapest, 27-31 August 1979. 1000p. 1981. 215.00 (ISBN 0-08-026191-4). Pergamon.

Bataille, F. Les Reactions Macrochimiques chez les Champignons Suives d'Indications sur la Morphologie des Spores. 1969. Repr. of 1948 ed. 14.00 (ISBN 3-7682-0654-8). Lubrecht & Cramer.

Bataille, Georges. Blue of Noon. Matthews, Harry, tr. from Fr. 155p. 1985. 13.95 (ISBN 0-7145-2683-5, Dist. by Scribner). M Boyars.

--Blue of Noon. Mathews, Harry, tr. from Fr. 160p. 1985. pap. 8.95 (ISBN 0-7145-2850-1). M Boyars.

--Death & Sensuality: A Study of Eroticism & the Taboo. Kastenbaum, Robert, ed. LC 76-19560. (Death and Dying Ser.). 1977. Repr. of 1962 ed. lib. bdg. 29.00x (ISBN 0-405-09556-2). Ayer Co Pubs.

--L'Abbe C. Facey, Philip A., tr. from Fr. LC 82-17704. 160p. 1983. 13.95 (ISBN 0-7145-2709-2, Dist. by Scribner). M Boyars.

--Literature & Evil. Hamilton, Alastair, tr. from Fr. LC 83-25872. 208p. 1985. 15.00 (ISBN 0-7145-0345-2, Dist. by Scribner). M Boyars.

--Manet. Skira-Rizzoli. LC 83-591. (Illus.). 140p. 1983. pap. 17.50 (ISBN 0-8478-0490-9). Rizzoli Intl.

--Visions of Excess: Selected Writings, 1927-1939. Stoekl, Allan, tr. (Theory & History of Literature Ser.: Vol. 14). 1985. 29.50 (ISBN 0-8166-1280-3); pap. 14.95 (ISBN 0-8166-1283-8). U of Minn Pr.

Bataille, Gretchen M. & Sands, Kathleen M. American Indian Women: Telling Their Lives. LC 83-10234. xii, 209p. 1984. 18.95x (ISBN 0-8032-1159-7). U of Nebr Pr.

Bataille, Gretchen M. & Silet, Charles L. P. Images of American Indians on Film: An Annotated Bibliography. LC 84-48882. 200p. 1985. lib. bdg. 27.00 (ISBN 0-8240-8737-2). Garland Pub.

Bataille, Gretchen M., jt. auth. see Silet, Charles L.

Bataille, Gretchen M., et al, eds. The Worlds Between Two Rivers: Perspectives on American Indians in Iowa. (Illus.). 1978. 8.50 (ISBN 0-8138-1795-1). Iowa St U Pr.

Bataillon, Lionel, jt. auth. see Febvre, Lucien.

Bataire, Jean, jt. auth. see Peguy, Charles.

Batalden, Paul B. & O'Conner, J. Paul. Quality Assurance in Ambulatory Care. LC 79-24700. 1980. text ed. 79.50 loose-leaf 3-ring binder (ISBN 0-89443-165-X). Aspen Systems.

Batalden, Stephen K. Catherine II's Greek Prelate: Eugenios Voulgaris in Russia, 1771-1806. (East European Monographs: No. 115). 197p. 1983. 26.00x (ISBN 0-88033-006-6). East Eur Quarterly.

Batangtaris, Daim. Hand Dynamics. (Illus.). 224p. 1983. pap. 12.95 (ISBN 0-87040-532-2). Japan Pubns USA.

Batarec, Evelyn. Lexique des Termes de Prothese Dentaire. 90p. (Fr.). 1973. pap. 19.95 (ISBN 0-686-56749-8, M-6024). French & Eur.

Batatu, John. The Old Social Classes & the Revolutionary Movements of Iraq: A Study of Iraq's Old Landed & Commercial Classes & of Its Communists, Ba'thists & Free Officers. LC 78-51157. (Princeton Studies on the Near East). (Illus.). 1979. 120.00x (ISBN 0-691-05241-7); pap. 32.50x (ISBN 0-691-02198-8). Princeton U Pr.

Batch, Donald L., jt. auth. see Branson, Branley A.

Batchelder, Alan & Haitani, Kanji. International Economics: Theory & Practice. LC 70-21770. (Economics Ser.). 488p. 1981. text ed. 33.95 (ISBN 0-471-84151-X, Pub. by Grid). Wiley.

Batchelder, Alan B. Economics of Poverty. LC 78-140175. (Illus.). Repr. of 1971 ed. 48.70 (ISBN 0-8357-9876-3, 2011153). Bks Demand UMI.

Batchelder, Charles Foster. An Account of the Nuttall Ornithological Club 1873 to 1919. (Memoirs: Vol. VIII). (Illus.). 109p. 1937. 2.50 (ISBN 0-318-16022-6). Nuttall Ornith.

Batchelder, J. W. Metric Madness. (Illus.). 256p. 1981. 12.95 (ISBN 0-8159-6220-7); pap. 5.95 (ISBN 0-8159-6219-3). Devin.

Batchelder, M. Hooked-Rug Making. rev. ed. (Illus.). pap. 6.95 (ISBN 0-87282-112-9). CHB-ALF.

Batchelder, Martha. The Art of Hooked-Rug Making. (Illus.). 160p. 1983. pap. 7.95 (ISBN 0-89272-138-3). Down East.

Batchelder, Samuel. Introduction & Early Progress of the Cotton Manufacture in the U.S. 59.95 (ISBN 0-8490-0414-4). Gordon Pr.

--Introduction & Early Progress of the Cotton Manufacture in the United States. LC 68-55476. Repr. of 1863 ed. 22.50x (ISBN 0-678-00903-1). Kelley.

Batcheller, John M. & Monsour, Sally. Music in Recreation & Leisure. 2nd ed. 208p. 1982. write for info. wire coil (ISBN 0-697-03561-1). Wm C Brown.

Batchelor. Beginner's BASIC. Lear, Peter. (Getting Ahead Ser.). (Illus.). 48p. (gr. 5-8). 1984. PLB 12.95 (ISBN 0-88110-205-9); pap. 5.95 (ISBN 0-88110-193-1). EDC.

--My Family Myself. 32p. 1983. pap. 3.95 (ISBN 0-88625-043-9). EDC.

Batchelor, et al. Automated Visual Inspection. 1985. 59.00 (ISBN 0-444-87577-8). Elsevier.

Batchelor, Bruce G. Practical Approach to Pattern Classification. LC 74-1614. 240p. 1974. 39.50 (ISBN 0-306-30796-0, Plenum Pr). Plenum Pub.

Batchelor, Bruce G., ed. Pattern Recognition. LC 77-12488. (Illus.). 501p. 1977. 55.00 (ISBN 0-306-31020-1, Plenum Pr). Plenum Pub.

Batchelor, D. Ferrari: The Early Spyders & Competition Roadsters. (Illus.). 128p. (Orig.). 1975. pap. 10.95 (ISBN 0-914792-01-6, Pub. by DB Pubns). Motorbooks Intl.

--Ferrari: The Gran Turismo & Competition Berlinettas. (Illus.). 94p. (Orig.). 1977. pap. 10.95 (ISBN 0-914792-02-4, Pub. by DB Pubns). Motorbooks Intl.

Batchelor, Dean. Illustrated Ferrari Buyer's Guide. (Illus.). 176p. 1981. pap. 13.95 (ISBN 0-87938-118-3). Motorbooks Intl.

--Illustrated Porsche Buyers Guide. (Illus.). 176p. 1983. pap. 13.95 (ISBN 0-87938-159-0). Motorbooks Intl.

Batchelor, Edward, Jr., ed. Abortion: The Moral Issues. LC 82-7505. 256p. 1982. 15.95 (ISBN 0-8298-0611-3); pap. 8.95 (ISBN 0-8298-0612-1). Pilgrim NY.

--Homosexuality & Ethics. rev. ed. LC 80-10533. 1982. 15.95 (ISBN 0-8298-0392-0); pap. 8.95 (ISBN 0-8298-0615-6). Pilgrim NY.

Batchelor, G. K., ed. see Taylor, Geoffrey I.

Batchelor, George K. Introduction to Fluid Dynamics. (Illus.). 634p. 1967. 95.00 (ISBN 0-521-04118-X); pap. 32.50 (ISBN 0-521-09817-3). Cambridge U Pr.

Batchelor, John. The Ainu & Their Folklore. lib. bdg. 79.95 (ISBN 0-87968-478-X). Krishna Pr.

--Ainu Life & Lore: Echoes of a Departing Race. Repr. of 1927 ed. 37.00 (ISBN 0-384-03528-0). Johnson Repr.

--The Ainu of Japan: The Religion, Superstitions, & General History of the Hairy Aborigines of Japan. 26.00 (ISBN 0-8369-7153-1, 7985). Ayer Co Pubs.

--H. G. Wells. 192p. 1985. 34.50 (ISBN 0-521-26026-4); pap. 10.95 (ISBN 0-521-27804-X). Cambridge U Pr.

--Mervyn Peake. 176p. 1974. 34.00x (ISBN 0-7156-0679-4, Pub. by Duckworth England); pap. 13.50x (ISBN 0-7156-1201-8, Pub. by Duckworth England). Biblio Dist.

Batchelor, John & Batchelor, Julie. The Congo. LC 80-50938. (Rivers of the World Ser.). PLB 13.96 (ISBN 0-382-06370-8). Silver.

--The Euphrates. LC 80-53605. (Rivers of the World Ser.). 68p. (gr. 4 up). PLB 13.96 (ISBN 0-382-06518-2). Silver.

Batchelor, John, jt. auth. see Forty, George.

Batchelor, John, ed. see Conrad, Joseph.

Batchelor, John C. American Falls. 1985. 16.95 (ISBN 0-393-02211-0). Norton.

--The Birth of the People's Republic of Antarctica. LC 82-22182. 384p. 1983. 16.95 (ISBN 0-385-27811-X, Dial). Doubleday.

--The Birth of the People's Republic of Antarctica. (Contemporary American Fiction Ser.). 416p. 1984. pap. 6.95 (ISBN 0-14-007151-2). Penguin.

--The Further Adventures of Halley's Comet. 384p. 1980. St Martin.

Batchelor, John H. & Hogg, Ian. Artillery. LC 72-6654. (Illus.). 1972. 9.95 (ISBN 0-684-13092-0, ScribT). Scribner.

Batchelor, Julie, jt. auth. see Batchelor, John.

Batchelor, Mary. Our Family Christmas Book. 96p. 1984. 9.95 (ISBN 0-687-29587-4). Abingdon.

Batchelor, Peter. People in Rural Development. 160p. 1981. pap. text ed. 7.95 (ISBN 0-85364-310-5). Attic Pr.

Batchelor, R. A., et al. Industrialisation & the Basis for Trade. LC 79-41582. (Economic & Social Studies: No. 32). 350p. 1980. 49.50 (ISBN 0-521-23302-X). Cambridge U Pr.

Batchelor, R. E. & Offord, Malcolm. A Guide to Contemporary French Usage. LC 82-4558. (Illus.). 156p. 1983. pap. 11.95 (ISBN 0-521-28037-0). Cambridge U Pr.

Batchelor, Roy. Edwardian Novelists. 1982. 26.00 (ISBN 0-312-23907-6). St Martin.

Batchelor, Roy A. & Wood, Geoffrey E., eds. Exchange Rate Policy. LC 81-23262. 265p. 1982. 27.50x (ISBN 0-312-27389-4). St Martin.

Batchelor, Stephen. Alone with Others. Rosset, Hannelore, ed. LC 82-21054. (Grove Press Eastern Philosophy & Religion Ser.). 144p. 1983. pap. 5.95 (ISBN 0-394-62457-2, E843, Ever). Grove.

Batchelor, Stephen, tr. see Rabten, Geshe.

Batchelor, Walter D. Gateway to Survival Is Storage. 128p. 1974. pap. 3.95 (ISBN 0-89036-127-4). Hawkes Pub Inc.

Batcher, Elaine. Emotion in the Classroom: A Study of Children's Experience. LC 81-10700. 218p. 1981. 32.95x (ISBN 0-03-059386-7). Praeger.

Batcher, Joyce. Microwaving with a Gourmet Flair. Hamernik, Arlene, ed. (Illus.). 67p. 1983. pap. 2.50 (ISBN 0-9602930-1-9). Microwave Helps.

Bate, D. M. see Joint Expedition of the British School of Archaelogy in Jerusalem & the American School of Prehistoric Research, 1929-1934.

Bate, G., et al, eds. Optical & Magnetic Data Storage Materials: Materials Research Society Symposia Proceedings. 500p. 1984. write for info. (ISBN 0-444-00908-6, North-Holland). Elsevier.

Bate, H. Maclear. Report from Formosa. 1952. cancelled (ISBN 0-89984-003-5). Century Bookbindery.

Bate, John. The Mysterys of Nature & Art: In Foure Tretises. LC 77-6850. (English Experience Ser.: No. 845). 1977. Repr. of 1634 ed. lib. bdg. 20.00 (ISBN 90-221-0845-7). Walter J Johnson.

--Second Booke Teaching the Composing of Fireworks. facs. ed. (Shorey Lost Arts Ser.). 45p. pap. 2.95 (ISBN 0-8466-0120-6, S120). Shorey.

Bate, Joseph St. John see St. John Bate, Joseph & Burgess, Ross.

Bate, Lucy. Little Rabbit's Loose Tooth. LC 75-6833. (Illus.). 32p. (gr. k-3). 1975. reinforced lib. bdg. 8.95 (ISBN 0-517-52240-3); pap. 2.95 (ISBN 0-517-55122-5). Crown.

Bate, Margaret, et al. A Review of Tests & Assessments in Early Education (3-5 Years) 124p. 1981. 10.00x (ISBN 0-85633-198-8, Pub. by NFER Nelson UK). Taylor & Francis.

Bate, Marjorie D. & Casey, Mary C. Legal Office Procedures. 2nd ed. (Illus.). 544p. 1980. pap. text ed. 24.25 (ISBN 0-07-004058-3). McGraw.

Bate, Norman. What a Wonderful Machine Is the Submarine. LC 61-13609. (Illus.). (gr. k-3). 1961. reinforced bdg. 4.95 (ISBN 0-684-13447-0, ScribJ). Scribner.

Bate, Paul & Mangham, Ian. Exploring Participation. LC 80-41415. 320p. 1981. 41.95x (ISBN 0-471-27921-8, Pub. by Wiley-Interscience). Wiley.

Bate, Percy. English Pre-Raphaelite Painters. facs. ed. LC 71-140350. (Select Bibliographies Reprint Ser). 1901. 30.00 (ISBN 0-8369-5593-5). Ayer Co Pubs.

Bate, Percy H. The English Pre-Raphaelite Painters: Their Associates & Successors. enl. & rev. ed. LC 79-129383. Repr. of 1901 ed. 24.00 (ISBN 0-404-00691-4). AMS Pr.

Bate, R. H. & Robinson, E., eds. A Stratigraphical Index of British Ostracoda: Geological Journal Special Issue, Vol. 8. (Liverpool Geological Society & the Manchester Geological Association Ser.). 552p. 1978. 159.95x (ISBN 0-471-27755-X, Pub. by Wiley-Interscience). Wiley.

Bate, R. H., et al. Fossil & Recent Ostracods. (British Micropalaeontological Society Ser.). 350p. 1982. 112.95x (ISBN 0-470-27314-3). Halsted Pr.

Bate, R. R., et al. Fundamentals of Astrodynamics. (Illus.). 16.00 (ISBN 0-8446-0025-3). Peter Smith.

Bate, Roger R., et al. Fundamentals of Astrodynamics. 1971. pap. 6.95 (ISBN 0-486-60061-0). Dover.

Bate, Simon, jt. auth. see Kenan, Larry.

Bate, Simon F., jt. auth. see Kenah, Lawrence J.

Bate, W. J., ed. see Johnson, Samuel.

Bate, W. J., et al, eds. see Johnson, Samuel.

Bate, W. Jackson. Burden of the Past & the English Poet. LC 70-102666. (Illus.). 1970. text ed. 10.00x (ISBN 0-674-08586-8, Belknap Pr). Harvard U Pr.

--The Burden of the Past & the English Poet. 1972. 3.95x (ISBN 0-393-00590-9, Norton Lib). Norton.

--John Keats. LC 63-17194. (Harvard Paperback Ser.: No. 142). (Illus.). 1979. 30.00x (ISBN 0-674-47800-2, Belknap Pr); pap. 12.50 (ISBN 0-674-47825-8, Belknap Pr). Harvard U Pr.

--Samuel Johnson. LC 77-73044. (Illus.). 1977. 19.95 (ISBN 0-15-179260-7). HarBraceJ.

--Samuel Johnson. LC 79-10586. (Illus.). 1979. pap. 7.95 (ISBN 0-15-679259-1, Harv). HarBraceJ.

Bate, W. Jackson, ed. see Coleridge, Samuel Taylor.

Bate, W. N. General Sidney Sherman. 1975. 12.95 (ISBN 0-685-51444-7). Texian.

Bate, Walter J. The Achievement of Samuel Johnson. LC 78-56308. 1978. pap. 4.95 (ISBN 0-226-03895-5, P804, Phoen). U of Chicago Pr.

--Criticism: The Major Texts. enl. ed. 719p. 1970. text ed. 26.95 (ISBN 0-15-516148-2, HC). HarBraceJ.

--Negative Capability: The Intuitive Approach in Keats. LC 75-28991. Repr. of 1939 ed. 14.50 (ISBN 0-404-14002-5). AMS Pr.

--The Stylistic Development of Keats. LC 83-48836. Repr. of 1958 ed. 23.00 (ISBN 0-404-20019-2). AMS Pr.

Bate, Walter J., ed. Keats: A Collection of Critical Essays. (Orig.). 1964. pap. 2.95 (ISBN 0-13-514745-X, STC43, Spec). P-H.

Bate, Walter J., ed. see Burke, Edmund.

Bate, Weston. A History of Brighton. 2nd ed. (Illus.). 454p. 1983. Repr. of 1963 ed. 23.00x (ISBN 0-522-84270-4, Pub. by Melbourne U Pr Australia). Intl Spec Bk.

--The Lucky City: The First Generation at Ballarat 1851-1901. 1978. 22.00x (ISBN 0-522-84157-0, Pub. by Melbourne U Pr). Intl Spec Bk.

Bately, Janet, ed. The Anglo-Saxon Chronicle 3, MS. A. (Anglo-Saxon Chronicle Ser.: No. 3). 128p. 1985. 37.50 (ISBN 0-85991-103-9, Pub. by Boydell & Brewer). Longwood Pub Group.

--The Old English Orosius. (Early English Text Society Ser.). (Illus.). 1980. 65.00x (ISBN 0-19-722406-7). Oxford U Pr.

Bateman & Ferris. Methods & Analysis in Organization Research. 1984. text ed. 27.95 (ISBN 0-8359-4339-9). Reston.

Bateman, A. M., jt. auth. see Jensen, M. L.

Bateman, Audray. An Austin Album. (Illus.). 1979. 17.50 (ISBN 0-88426-056-9). Encino Pr.

Bateman, Barbara. So You're Going To Hearing: Preparing for a Public Law 94-142 Due Process Hearing. 36p. (Orig.). 1980. pap. text ed. 3.95 (ISBN 0-8331-1905-2). Hubbard Sci.

Bateman, Barbara, jt. auth. see Haring, Norris.

Bateman, Barry L. & Pitts, Gerald N. JCL in a System-370 Environment. 192p. 1981. 17.95 (ISBN 0-8436-1606-7). Van Nos Reinhold.

Bateman, Barry L., jt. auth. see Pitts, Gerald N.

Bateman, C. A., et al. Preservation & Reproduction of Clay Tablets & the Conservation of Wall Paintings. (Colt Archaeological Institute Monograph: Vol. 3). 36p. 1966. pap. text ed. 14.00x (ISBN 0-85668-065-6, Pub. by Aris & Phillips). Humanities.

Bateman, David N. Business Communication Concepts: Cases, Decisions, & Applications. 1982. pap. text ed. 10.80 (ISBN 0-673-15605-2). Scott F.

Bateman, David N., jt. auth. see Sigband, Norman B.

Bateman, Donald & Zidonis, Frank. Effect of a Study of Transformational Grammar on the Writing of Ninth & Tenth Graders. 1966. pap. 2.60 (ISBN 0-8141-1295-1); pap. 2.00 members. NCTE.

Bateman, Earl. Map of the Ocean Floor. 9.95 (ISBN 0-89087-416-6). Celestial Arts.

Bateman, Edward A. Development of the County-Unit School District in Utah: A Study in Adaptability. LC 75-176541. (Columbia University. Teachers College. Contributions to Education: No. 790). Repr. of 1940 ed. 22.50 (ISBN 0-404-55790-2). AMS Pr.

Bateman, F., jt. auth. see Soal, Samuel G.

Bateman, Fred & Weiss, Thomas. A Deplorable Scarcity: The Failure of Industrialization in the Slave Economy. LC 80-13238. xiii, 237p. 1981. 20.00x (ISBN 0-8078-1447-4). U of NC Pr.

Bateman, Fred, ed. see Audretsch, David B.

Bateman, Fred, ed. see Brunner, Lawrence P.

Bateman, Fred, ed. see Harris, Barry C.

Bateman, Fred, ed. see Kang Rae Cho.

Bateman, Fred, ed. see Kelton, Christina M.

Bateman, Fred, ed. see Maskus, Keith E.

Bateman, Fred, ed. see White, Alice P.

Bateman, Fred, ed. see Williams, Mansfield W.

Bateman, George W. Zanzibar Tales Translated from the Swahili. LC 74-99342. 1970. Repr. of 1901 ed. lib. bdg. 11.50 (ISBN 0-8411-0013-6). Metro Bks.

Bateman, Glenn. MHD Instabilities. 1978. text ed. 34.50x (ISBN 0-262-02131-5). MIT Pr.

Bateman, Harry. Differential Equations. LC 66-23754. 1967. 14.95 (ISBN 0-8284-0190-X). Chelsea Pub.

Bateman, Helen R. Roots & Wings. LC 83-1868. (Illus.). 160p. 1983. 7.95 (ISBN 0-87747-950-X). Deseret Bk.

Bateman, Helen R., et al. With Singleness of Heart: Recipes for Sunday Meals. Knowles, Eleanor, ed. LC 84-71871. 144p. 8.95 (ISBN 0-87747-731-0). Deseret Bk.

Bateman, Hugh E., et al. Applied Anatomy & Physiology of the Speech & Hearing Mechanism. (Illus.). 644p. 1984. 39.75x (ISBN 0-398-04912-2). C C Thomas.

Bateman, J. E. Trapping: A Practical Guide. LC 78-15117. (Illus.). 190p. 1979. 14.95 (ISBN 0-8117-1743-7). Stackpole.

Bateman, James. The Orchidaceae of Mexico & Guatemala. 250.00 (ISBN 0-384-03530-2). Johnson Repr.

Bateman, James & Trott, Arthur. The Foot & Ankle. 1980. 37.50 (ISBN 0-913258-71-7). Thieme Stratton.

Bateman, James A. Animal Traps & Trapping. LC 70-144110. (Illus.). 228p. 1971. 12.95 (ISBN 0-8117-0103-4). Stackpole.

Bateman, James E. The Shoulder & Neck. 2nd ed. LC 77-84658. (Illus.). 1978. text ed. 62.50 (ISBN 0-7216-1571-6). Saunders.

Bateman, Kitty & Charry, Myrna. The New York Times Reading Experience. 40p. 1979. pap. text ed. write for info. (ISBN 0-912853-02-6). NY Times.

Bateman, Michael. Office Development: A Geographical Analysis. LC 84-18172. 192p. 1985. 25.00 (ISBN 0-312-58211-0). St Martin.

Bateman, Nigel T., jt. auth. see Cameron, Ian R.

Bateman, Py. Fear into Anger: A Manual of Self-Defense for Women. LC 77-19122. (Illus.). 144p. 1978. 24.95x (ISBN 0-88229-441-5); pap. 13.95 (ISBN 0-88229-603-5). Nelson-Hall.

Bateman, Richard M. Cased-Hole Log Analysis & Reservoir Performance Monitoring. (Illus.). 336p. 1984. text ed. 52.00 (ISBN 0-934634-92-0). Intl Human Res.

--Log Quality Control. (Illus.). 416p. 1984. 52.00 (ISBN 0-934634-89-0). Intl Human Res.

--Open-Hole Log Analysis & Formation Evalution. (Illus.). 719p. 1985. text ed. write for info. (ISBN 0-88746-060-7). Intl Human Res.

Bateman, Robert. The Art of Robert Bateman. LC 81-43019. (Illus.). 180p. 1981. 50.00 (ISBN 0-670-13497-X, Studio). Viking.

--The Robert Bateman Naturalist's Diary 1986. Date not set. price not set. Random.

Bateman, Robert, illus. The World of Robert Bateman. Derry, Ramsay. (Illus.). 1985. 49.50 (ISBN 0-394-54654-7). Random.

Bateman, Ruth C. The Zucchini & Carrot Cookbook. (Illus.). 192p. 1980. pap. 4.95 (ISBN 0-517-53771-0). Crown.

Bateman, Wayne. Introduction to Computer Music. LC 79-26361. 314p. 1980. 34.95x (ISBN 0-471-05266-3, Pub. by Wiley-Interscience). Wiley.

--Introduction to Computer Music. 314p. 1982. pap. 19.95 (ISBN 0-471-86839-6, Pub. by Wiley-Interscience). Wiley.

Baten, Anderson M. Slang from Shakespeare. LC 72-6402. 1931. lib. bdg. 17.50 (ISBN 0-8414-0154-3). Folcroft.

Bater, James H. Saint Petersburg: Industrialization & Change. (Studies in Urban History: Vol. 4). (Illus.). 469p. 1982. text ed. 49.50x (ISBN 0-8419-5829-7, Pub by E Arnold Ltd UK). Holmes & Meier.

--The Soviet City: Ideal & Reality. LC 80-51193. (Explorations in Urban Analysis: Vol. 2). 196p. 1980. 24.00 (ISBN 0-8039-1466-0); pap. 12.00 (ISBN 0-8039-1467-9). Sage.

Bater, James H. & French, R. Anthony. Studies in Russian Historical Geography. 1983. Vol. 1. 39.00 (ISBN 0-12-081201-0); Vol. 2. 39.00 (ISBN 0-12-081202-9). Acad Pr.

Bates. Commercial Language Systems. (Infotech Computer State of the Art Reports). 555p. 1974. 85.00 (ISBN 0-08-028537-6). Pergamon.

--Input-Output. (Infotech Computer State of the Art Reports). 524p. 1975. 85.00 (ISBN 0-08-028499-X). Pergamon.

--Network Systems & Software. (Infotech Computer State of the Art Reports). 692p. 1975. 85.00 (ISBN 0-08-028507-4). Pergamon.

--Removable Partial Denture Construction. 160p. 1978. 21.00 (ISBN 0-7236-0481-9). PSG Pub Co.

--Software Engineering Techniques, 2 vols. (Infotech Computer State of the Art Reports). 600p. 1972. Set. pap. 105.00 (ISBN 0-08-028521-X). Pergamon.

Bates & Fullerton. How to Think Metric. LC 74-75325. (gr. 5-12). 1974. pap. 4.95 (ISBN 0-8224-3763-5). Pitman Learning.

Bates, A. W., ed. The Role of Technology in Distance Education. LC 84-40035. 231p. 1984. 25.00 (ISBN 0-312-68942-X). St Martin.

Bates, Abert, ed. Shut Down: Nuclear Power on Trial. (Illus.). 1979. pap. 5.00 (ISBN 0-913990-22-1). Book Pub Co.

Bates, Alan, compiled by. Directory of Stage Coach Services, 1836. LC 69-11233. 1969. 19.95x (ISBN 0-678-05579-3). Kelley.

Bates, Alan P. & Julian, Joseph. Sociology: Understanding Social Behavior. (Instructors guide written by Patricia Harvey). 1975. text ed. 29.95 (ISBN 0-395-18652-8); instr's. guide & resource manual 1.90 (ISBN 0-395-18794-X). HM.

Bates, Albert C. The Charter of Connecticut: A Study. 72p. 1932. pap. 2.00 (ISBN 0-940748-03-7). Conn Hist Soc.

--Sketch of the Congregational Society & Church of East Granby, Connecticut. 18p. Repr. of 1930 ed. 2.00 (ISBN 0-940748-53-3). Conn Hist Soc.

--The Work of Hartford's First Printer. 16p. 1925. pap. 1.00 (ISBN 0-940748-47-9). Conn Hist Soc.

Bates, Alfred, et al, eds. The Drama, Its History, Literature & Influence on Civilization, 22 Vols. (Illus.). Repr. of 1904 ed. Set. 990.00 (ISBN 0-404-02190-5); 45.00 ea. AMS Pr.

Bates, Alma S. Speed Phonics. (Illus.). (gr. k-12). 1980. Vol. 1 Tchr's. Resource Guide Bk. 58.00 (ISBN 0-936928-50-6); Vol. 2, Pupils Consonant Wkbk. pkg. of 10 36.00 (ISBN 0-936928-52-2); Vol. 3, Pupils Vowel wkbk. pkg. of 10 36.00 (ISBN 0-936928-53-0); Vol. 4, Consonant wkbk. tchr's ed. 3.60 (ISBN 0-936928-54-9); Vol. 5, Vowel wkbk. tchr's ed. 3.60 (ISBN 0-936928-55-7); Set 3, wall carts wire bound Consonants 40.00 (ISBN 0-936928-56-5); Set 3, wall charts wire bound Vowels 40.00 (ISBN 0-936928-57-3); Consonant Voiced Casette Tape 13.00; Vowel Voiced Casette Tape 13.00. Word-Craft Pub.

Bates, Arlo. In the Bundle of Time. facs. ed. LC 71-116937. (Short Story Index Reprint Ser). 1893. 21.00 (ISBN 0-8369-3439-3). Ayer Co Pubs.

--The Intoxicated Ghost & Other Stories, Vol 1. LC 72-4419. (Short Story Index Reprint Ser). Repr. of 1908 ed. 20.00 (ISBN 0-8369-4170-5). Ayer Co Pubs.

--The Pagans. LC 70-104411. Repr. of 1884 ed. lib. bdg. 15.00 (ISBN 0-8398-0153-X). Irvington.

--The Philistines. LC 74-104412. Repr. of 1889 ed. lib. bdg. 16.00 (ISBN 0-8398-0154-8). Irvington.

--The Puritans. LC 68-20005. (Americans in Fiction Ser.). lib. bdg. 16.00 (ISBN 0-8398-0155-6); pap. text ed. 4.95x (ISBN 0-89197-911-5). Irvington.
--Talks on the Study of Literature. 260p. 1981. Repr. of 1900 ed. lib. bdg. 25.00 (ISBN 0-8495-0482-1). Arden Lib.
--Talks on the Study of Literature. 1973. Repr. of 1897 ed. 20.00 (ISBN 0-8274-1677-6). R West.
--Talks on Writing English. 1897. Repr. 20.00 (ISBN 0-8274-3569-X). R West.
Bates, Arthenia J. Seeds Beneath the Snow: Vignettes from the South. LC 69-18851. 146p. 1975. 8.95 (ISBN 0-88258-046-9). Howard U Pr.
Bates, Barbara. A Guide to Physical Examination. 3rd ed. (Illus.). 580p. 1983. text ed. 35.95 (ISBN 0-397-54399-9, 64-03406, Lippincott Medical). Lippincott.
Bates, Betty. Bugs in Your Ears. (gr. 4-6). 1979. pap. 1.95 (ISBN 0-671-44144-2). Archway.
--Call Me Friday the Thirteenth. LC 83-6146. (Illus.). 112p. (gr. 3-6). 1983. 9.95 (ISBN 0-8234-0498-6). Holiday.
--Call Me Friday the Thirteenth. (Illus.). 112p. (gr. 3-7). 1985. pap. 2.25 (ISBN 0-440-40984-5, LFL). Dell.
--Herbert & Hortense. Tucker, Kathleen, ed. LC 84-2387. (Just for Fun Bks.). (Illus.). 32p. (gr. 1-4). 1984. PLB 10.25 (ISBN 0-8075-3222-3). A Whitman.
--It Must've Been the Fishsticks. 144p. (gr. 5-7). 1983. pap. text ed. 1.95 (ISBN 0-671-46540-6). Archway.
--Love Is Like Peanuts. (gr. 7-9). 1981. pap. 1.75 (ISBN 0-671-56109-X). Archway.
--Love Is Like Peanuts. LC 79-21686. 128p. (gr. 6 up). 1980. 7.95 (ISBN 0-8234-0402-1). Holiday.
--My Mom, the Money Nut. (gr. 4-6). 1981. pap. 1.95 (ISBN 0-671-56065-4). Archway.
--My Mom, the Money Nut. LC 78-24213. 160p. (gr. 4-6). 1979. 9.95 (ISBN 0-8234-0347-5). Holiday.
--Picking up the Pieces. (gr. 7 up). 1982. pap. 1.95 (ISBN 0-671-43939-1). Archway.
--Picking up the Pieces. LC 80-8811. 160p. 1981. 8.95 (ISBN 0-8234-0390-4). Holiday.
--Say Cheese. LC 84-47837. (Illus.). 112p. (gr. 3-6). 1984. 10.95 (ISBN 0-8234-0540-0). Holiday.
--Thatcher Payne-in-the-Neck. LC 85-42879. (Illus.). 144p. (gr. 3-7). 1985. 10.95 (ISBN 0-8234-0584-2). Holiday.
--That's What T. J. Says. LC 82-80815. 160p. (gr. 5-7). 1982. 10.95 (ISBN 0-8234-0465-X). Holiday.
--The Ups & Downs of Jorie Jenkins. (gr. 4-6). 1981. pap. 1.75 (ISBN 0-671-29950-6). Archway.
Bates, Billy P. I. S. Q. D. (Identification System for Questioned Documents) (Illus.). 112p. 1970. 12.25x (ISBN 0-398-00108-1). C C Thomas.
--Typewriting Identification (I.S.Q.T.) Identification System for Questioned Typewriting. (Illus.). 112p. 1971. 10.00x (ISBN 0-398-00110-3). C C Thomas.
Bates, Bob. Expressive Drawing: Mastering the Art of Sketching. (Illus., Orig.). 1985. pap. 9.95 (ISBN 0-917121-02-3, 45-100). M F Weber Co.
Bates, Brian. The Way of Wyrd: The Book of a Sorcerer's Apprentice. LC 83-48417. 224p. 1984. 12.45 (ISBN 0-06-250040-6, HarpR). Har-Row.
Bates, C. C. & Gaskell, T. F. Geophysics in the Affairs of Man: A Personalized History of Exploration Geophysics & Its Allied Sciences of Seismology & Oceanography. (Illus.). 536p. 1982. 66.00 (ISBN 0-08-024026-7); pap. 25.00 (ISBN 0-08-024025-9). Pergamon.
Bates, Charles F. Central Information File: Conversion and Implementation. LC 76-55780. (Bank Study Ser.). (Illus.). 1976. pap. text ed. 25.00 (ISBN 0-87267-025-2). Bankers.
Bates, Charlotte F. Cambridge Book of Poetry. facs. ed. LC 72-80371. (Granger Index Reprint Ser). 1882. 29.00 (ISBN 0-8369-6052-1). Ayer Co Pubs.
Bates, Cornelia F., tr. see Becquer, Gustavo A.
Bates, D. Normandy Before Ten Sixty-Six. LC 81-17154. (Illus.). 320p. 1982. pap. text ed. 14.95x (ISBN 0-582-48492-8). Longman.
Bates, D. & Cartlidge, N. E. Multiple Choice Questions in Neurology. 192p. (Orig.). 1984. pap. text ed. 9.75 (ISBN 0-272-79700-6, Pitman Med UK). Urban & S.
Bates, D. B. Incidents on Land & Water; or Four Years on the Pacific Coast: Being a Narrative of the Burning of the Ships Nonantum, Humayoon, & Fanchon. LC 74-3930. (Women in America Ser). (Illus.). 344p. 1974. Repr. of 1858 ed. 26.50x (ISBN 0-405-06076-9). Ayer Co Pubs.
Bates, D. R. Carpentry & Joinery, Vol. 1. (Illus.). 208p. 1982. pap. text ed. 18.95x (ISBN 0-7121-0394-5). Trans-Atlantic.
Bates, D. R. & Esterman, L., eds. Advances in Atomic & Molecular Physics, Vol. 20. (Serial Publication Ser.). 1985. 95.00 (ISBN 0-12-003820-X). Acad Pr.
Bates, D. R., et al, eds. Advances in Atomic & Molecular Physics, Vols. 1-14. Incl. Vol. 1. 1965. 85.00 (ISBN 0-12-003801-3); Vol. 2. 1966. 85.00 (ISBN 0-12-003802-1); Vol. 3. 1968. 85.00 (ISBN 0-12-003803-X); Vol. 4. 1968. 85.00 (ISBN 0-12-003804-8); Vol. 5. 1969. 85.00 (ISBN 0-12-003805-6); Vol. 6. 1970. 85.00 (ISBN 0-12-003806-4); Vol. 7. 1971. 85.00 (ISBN 0-12-003807-2); Vol. 8. 1972. 85.00 (ISBN 0-12-003808-0); Vol. 9. 1974. 78.00 (ISBN 0-12-003809-9); Vol. 10. 1974. 85.00 (ISBN 0-12-003810-2); Vol. 11. 1976. 95.00 (ISBN 0-12-003811-0); Vol. 12. 1976. 90.00 (ISBN 0-12-003812-9); Vol. 13. 1978. 90.00 (ISBN 0-12-003813-7); Vol. 14. 1979. 80.00 (ISBN 0-12-003814-5). Acad Pr.
Bates, Daniel & Rassam, Amal. Peoples & Cultures of the Middle East. (Illus.). 288p. 1983. pap. 19.95 (ISBN 0-13-656793-2). P-H.
Bates, Daniel, jt. auth. see Plog, Fred.
Bates, Darrel. The Fasheda Incident of 1898: Encounter on the Nile . (Illus.). 1984. 29.95x (ISBN 0-19-211771-8). Oxford U Pr.
Bates, David. A Citizen's Guide to Air Pollution. (Environmental Damage & Control in Canada Ser.: Vol. 2). 250p. 1972. pap. 4.95 (ISBN 0-7735-0145-2). McGill-Queens U Pr.
Bates, David & Bederson, Benjamin. Advances in Atomic & Molecular Physics, Vol. 18. (Serial Publication Ser.). 1982. 70.00 (ISBN 0-12-003818-8). Acad Pr.
--Advances in Atomic & Molecular Physics, Vol. 19. (Serial Publication Ser.). 1983. 65.00 (ISBN 0-12-003819-6). Acad Pr.
Bates, David R. & Bederson, Benjamin, eds. Advances in Atomic & Molecular Physics, Vol. 15. LC 65-18423. (Serial Publication Ser.). 1979. 70.00 (ISBN 0-12-003815-3). Acad Pr.
Bates, Sir David R. & Bederson, Benjamin, eds. Advances in Atomic & Molecular Physics, Vol. 16. LC 65-18423. (Serial Publication Ser.). 1980. 70.00 (ISBN 0-12-003816-1). Acad Pr.
Bates, Donald L. Cases for Strategy & Policy Analysis. 272p. 1981. pap. text ed. write for info. (ISBN 0-697-08066-8). Wm C Brown.
Bates, Donald L. & Eldredge, David L. Strategy & Policy: Analysis, Formulation & Implementation. 2nd ed. 628p. 1984. text ed. write for info (ISBN 0-697-08238-5); instrs.' manual avail. (ISBN 0-697-08195-8); game players' manual avail. (ISBN 0-697-08281-4); admin. manual for game avail. (ISBN 0-697-08316-0); ASCII tape avail.; EBCDIC tape avail.; card deck avail. Wm C Brown.
Bates, Dorothy R. How to Run a Real Estate Office. 1981. 16.95 (ISBN 0-8359-2970-1). Reston.
Bates, E. Language & Context: The Acquisition of Pragmatics. (Language, Thought & Culture Ser.). 1976. 40.00 (ISBN 0-12-081550-8). Acad Pr.
Bates, E. Katharine. Seen & Unseen: A Story of Psychic Experiences. LC 75-32535. 1908. lib. bdg. 20.00 (ISBN 0-8414-3234-1). Folcroft.
Bates, E. Stuart. Inside Out: An Introduction to Autobiography. 1937. Repr. 45.00 (ISBN 0-8274-2576-7). R West.
Bates, Earnest S. The Story of the Supreme Court. 377p. 1982. Repr. of 1936 ed. lib. bdg. 30.00x (ISBN 0-8377-0322-0). Rothman.
Bates, Edward B. Elements of Fire & Arson Investigation. 1975. 8.50 (ISBN 0-89368-313-2). Davis Pub Co.
Bates, Elizabeth. The Emergence of Symbols: Cognition & Communication in Infancy. LC 78-20040. (Language, Thought & Culture Ser.). 1979. 40.00 (ISBN 0-12-081540-0). Acad Pr.
Bates, Elizabeth B., jt. auth. see Fairbanks, Jonathan.
Bates, Erica. Health Systems & Public Scrutiny: Australia, Britain & the United States. LC 83-2861. 224p. 1984. 29.95x (ISBN 0-312-36773-2). St Martin.
--Models of Madness. 1978. 19.95x (ISBN 0-7022-1069-2); pap. 9.95x (ISBN 0-7022-1068-4). U of Queensland Pr.
Bates, Erica M. & Wilson, Paul R. Mental Disorder or Madness: Alternative Theories. 257p. 1980. 24.95x (ISBN 0-7022-1388-8); pap. 15.75x (ISBN 0-7022-1389-6). U of Queensland Pr.
Bates, Ernest. This Land of Liberty. LC 73-19817. (Civil Liberties in American History Ser.). 383p. 1974. Repr. of 1930 ed. lib. bdg. 42.50 (ISBN 0-306-70597-4). Da Capo.
Bates, Ernest S. Study of Shelley's Drama-The Cenci. LC 73-16185. 1908. lib. bdg. 15.00 (ISBN 0-8414-3343-7). Folcroft.
--Touring in 1600: Study in the Development of Travel As a Means of Education. 1964. Repr. of 1911 ed. 23.50 (ISBN 0-8337-0186-X). B Franklin.
Bates, Ernest S., jt. auth. see Carlson, Oliver.
Bates, Esther W. Edwin Arlington Robinson & His Manuscripts. LC 73-16085. 1944. lib. bdg. 10.00 (ISBN 0-8414-9874-1). Folcroft.
Bates, Finis L. The Escape & Suicide of John Wilkes Booth: The First True Account of Lincoln's Assassination, Containing a Complete Confession of Booth Many Years after His Crime. 1979. Repr. of 1907 ed. 49.00x (ISBN 0-403-06413-9, Regency). Scholarly.
Bates, Frank & Douglas, Mary L. Programming Language One: With Structured Programming. 3rd ed. 1975. pap. 18.95 (ISBN 0-13-730473-0). P-H.
Bates, Frank G. Rhode Island & the Formation of the Union. LC 68-1297. (Columbia University Studies in the Social Sciences: No. 27). Repr. of 1898 ed. 16.50 (ISBN 0-404-51027-2). AMS Pr.
Bates, Frederick L. & Harvey, Clyde C. The Structure of Social Systems. LC 85-10009. 432p. 1985. Repr. of 1975 ed. lib. bdg. price not set (ISBN 0-89874-874-7). Krieger.
Bates, George E. Byzantine Coins, Nineteen Fifty-Eight to Nineteen Sixty-Eight. LC 76-95917. (Archaeological Exploration of Sardis Monograph Ser: No. 1). (Illus.). 1971. 17.50x (ISBN 0-674-08965-0). Harvard U Pr.
Bates, Grace E. Probability. (Orig.). (gr. 12). 1965. pap. 6.95 (ISBN 0-201-00405-4). Addison-Wesley.
Bates, H. Central America, the West Indies & South America. 1976. lib. bdg. 59.95 (ISBN 0-8490-1592-8). Gordon Pr.
Bates, H. E. The Best of H. E. Bates. facsimile ed. LC 76-167441. (Short Story Index Reprint Ser.). Repr. of 1963 ed. 24.50 (ISBN 0-8369-3967-0). Ayer Co Pubs.
--In the Heart of the Country. (Illus.). 160p. 1985. pap. 6.95 (ISBN 0-88162-110-2, Pub. by Salem Hse Ltd). Merrimack Pub Cir.
--Love for Lydia. 1979. pap. 3.95 (ISBN 0-14-001165-X). Penguin.
--My Uncle Silas. LC 84-81625. 190p. 1984. o.s.i 16.00 (ISBN 0-915308-62-2); pap. 7.00 (ISBN 0-915308-63-0). Graywolf.
--My Uncle Silas. (Twentieth-Century Classics Ser.). (Illus.). 1984. pap. 5.95 (ISBN 0-19-281854-6). Oxford U Pr.
Bates, Henry & Busenbark, R. Finches & Softbilled Birds. 19.95 (ISBN 0-87666-421-4, H-908). TFH Pubns.
Bates, Henry & Busenbark, Robert. Guide to Mynahs. (Orig.). 4.95 (ISBN 0-87666-769-8, PS-633). TFH Pubns.
--Introduction to Finches & Softbilled Birds. (Orig.). 7.95 (ISBN 0-87666-762-0, PS-648). TFH Pubns.
--Parrots. (Orig.). pap. 2.95 (ISBN 0-87666-427-3, M-506). TFH Pubns.
Bates, Henry J. & Busenbark, Robert I. Parrots & Related Birds. (Illus.). 543p. 19.95 (ISBN 0-87666-967-4, TFH H-912). TFH Pubns.
Bates, Herbert E. Black Boxer: Tales. facsimile ed. LC 73-178437. (Short Story Index Reprint Ser.). Repr. of 1932 ed. 18.00 (ISBN 0-8369-4037-7). Ayer Co Pubs.
--Day's End & Other Stories. 1971. Repr. of 1928 ed. 39.00 (ISBN 0-403-00504-3). Scholarly.
--Edward Garnett. LC 74-8320. 1974. Repr. of 1950 ed. lib. bdg. 12.50 (ISBN 0-8414-4505-2). Folcroft.
--The Fallow Land. LC 79-144867. (Literature Ser). 328p. 1972. Repr. of 1932 ed. 39.00 (ISBN 0-403-00854-9). Scholarly.
--Woman Who Had Imagination & Other Stories. facs. ed. LC 77-103239. (Short Story Index Reprint Ser.). 1934. 18.00 (ISBN 0-8369-3276-5). Ayer Co Pubs.
Bates, I., et al. Schooling for the Dole? The New Vocationalism. (Youth Questions Ser.). 192p. 1984. text ed. 29.25x (ISBN 0-333-36728-6, Pub. by Macmillan England); pap. text ed. 11.25 (ISBN 0-333-36729-4). Humanities.
Bates, Ira J. & Winder, Alvin E. Introduction to Health Education. (Illus.). 262p. 1984. text ed. 18.95 (ISBN 0-87484-586-6, 586). Mayfield Pub.
Bates, J. D., jt. auth. see Jeffries, J. R.
Bates, J. H. U. K. Marine Pollution Law. 1984. 85.00 (ISBN 1-850-44028-X). Lloyds London Pr.
Bates, James D. Minnesota Legal Forms: Probate. 1981. looseleaf 27.50 (ISBN 0-917126-98-X). Butterworth MN.
Bates, James L. The Origins of Teapot Dome: Progressive Parties & Petroleum. LC 78-5265. (Illus.). viii, 278p. 1978. Repr. of 1963 ed. lib. bdg. 25.75 (ISBN 0-313-20383-0, BAOT). Greenwood.
Bates, Jefferson D. Dictating Effectively: A Time Saving Manual. LC 80-23158. (Illus.). 169p. 1980. 12.50 (ISBN 0-87491-411-6); pap. 7.95 (ISBN 0-87491-737-9). Acropolis.
--Writing with Precision: How to Write So That You Cannot Possibly Be Misunderstood. LC 78-1924. (Illus.). 226p. 1978. 12.50 (ISBN 0-87491-184-2); pap. 6.95 (ISBN 0-87491-185-0). Acropolis.
--Writing with Precision: How to Write So That You Cannot Possibly Be Misunderstood. rev. ed. 232p. 1985. 12.50 (ISBN 0-87491-782-4); 12.50 (ISBN 0-87491-783-2). Acropolis.
Bates, Jenny. Dazzled. 192p. 1984. pap. 1.75 (ISBN 0-515-07590-6). Jove Pubns.
--Gilded Spring, No. 5. 192p. 1983. pap. 1.95 (ISBN 0-515-06932-9). Jove Pubns.
Bates, John, et al. The Factors Affecting Household Car Ownership. 184p. 1981. text ed. 46.25x (ISBN 0-566-00475-5). Gower Pub Co.
Bates, John R., jt. auth. see O'Steen, Van.
Bates, Joseph D., Jr. Fishing: An Encyclopedic Guide. (Illus.). 800p. 1985. 29.95 (ISBN 0-525-24322-4, 02908-870). Dutton.
--How to Find Fish & Make Them Strike. LC 73-93268. (An Outdoor Life Bk). (Illus.). 224p. 1975. 11.49i (ISBN 0-06-010241-1, HarpT). Har-Row.
--Outdoor Cook's Bible. LC 63-19269. 1964. pap. 4.50 (ISBN 0-385-02107-0). Doubleday.
--Streamers & Bucktails: The Big Fish Flies. LC 79-2163. (Illus.). 1979. 16.95 (ISBN 0-394-41588-4). Knopf.
Bates, Katharine L. American Literature. 1973. Repr. of 1908 ed. 15.00 (ISBN 0-8274-1678-4). R West.
--The English Religious Drama. 1975. Repr. of 1911 ed. 30.00 (ISBN 0-8274-4103-7). R West.
Bates, Katharine L., ed. Ballad Book. facs. ed. LC 78-103081. (Granger Index Reprint Ser.). 1890. 18.00 (ISBN 0-8369-6096-3). Ayer Co Pubs.
Bates, Katharine L. & Coman, Katharine, eds. English History As Told by English Poets. facsimile ed. LC 71-103082. (Granger Index Reprint Ser). 1902. 23.50 (ISBN 0-8369-6097-1). Ayer Co Pubs.
Bates, Katharine L., tr. see Becquer, Gustavo A.
Bates, Katherine L. The English Religious Drama. (Works of Katherine Lee Bates Ser.). 254p. Date not set. Repr. of 1893 ed. lib. bdg. 34.00 (ISBN 0-932051-81-2). Am Repr Serv.
Bates, Katherine L. & Coman, Katherine, eds. English History Told by English Poets. LC 71-103082. (Granger Index Reprint Ser.). 452p. Repr. of 1902 ed. lib. bdg. 20.00 (ISBN 0-8290-0506-4). Irvington.
Bates, Kenneth F. Enameling: Principles & Practices. (Funk & W Bk.). (Illus.). 272p. 1974. pap. 3.95i (ISBN 0-308-10137-5, F103). T Y Crowell.
--The Enamelist. LC 75-7618. (Funk & W Bk.). (Illus.). 256p. 1975. pap. 3.50i (ISBN 0-308-10196-0, F-127). T Y Crowell.
Bates, L. M. Somerset House. 14.50x (ISBN 0-392-04666-0, SpS). Sportshelf.
--The Spirit of London's River. 200p. 1984. 30.00x (ISBN 0-905418-43-3, Pub. by Gresham England). State Mutual Bk.
Bates, La Donna G., jt. auth. see Bates, William E.
Bates, M., ed. Bronchial Carcinoma: An Integrated Approach to Diagnosis & Management. (Illus.). 240p. Date not set. 52.00 (ISBN 0-387-13234-1). Springer-Verlag.
Bates, M. Searle. Religious Liberty: An Inquiry. LC 77-166096. (Civil Liberties in American History Ser.). 1972. Repr. of 1945 ed. lib. bdg. 59.50 (ISBN 0-306-70235-5). Da Capo.
Bates, Margaret. The Belfast Cookery Book. 222p. 1975. pap. 10.75 (ISBN 0-08-018952-0). Pergamon.
--Lake City. pap. 2.50 (ISBN 0-936564-08-3). Little London.
Bates, Marilyn, jt. auth. see Keirsey, David.
Bates, Marilyn, et al. Group Leadership: A Manual for Group Counseling Leaders. 2nd ed. 281p. 1981. pap. text ed. 14.95 (ISBN 0-89108-105-4). Love Pub Co.
Bates, Marston. Gluttons & Libertines: Human Problems of Being Natural. LC 66-11978. 1971. pap. 2.95 (ISBN 0-394-71267-6, V-267, Vin). Random.
--Jungle in the House: Essays in Natural & Unnatural History. LC 70-103375. 1970. 7.50 (ISBN 0-8027-0159-0). Walker & Co.
--The Natural History of Mosquitos. (Illus.). 11.75 (ISBN 0-8446-0480-1). Peter Smith.
Bates, Martin. High Blood Pressure: How to Live with It, How to Lower It. (Illus.). 132p. 1982. 10.95 (ISBN 0-13-387381-1); pap. 4.95 (ISBN 0-13-387373-0). P-H.
Bates, Martin & Dudley-Evans, Tony, eds. Nucleus: English for Science & Technology. Incl. Agriculture. Denny, Stephen, et al. pap. text ed. write for info. student's bk. (ISBN 0-582-51301-4); write for info. tchr's. notes (ISBN 0-582-55287-7); write for info. cassette (ISBN 0-582-74827-5); Architecture & Building Construction. Cumming, James. 1982. pap. text ed. write for info. student's bk. (ISBN 0-582-74808-9); write for info. tchr's. notes (ISBN 0-582-74807-0); write for info. cassette (ISBN 0-582-74849-6). (English As a Second Language Bk.). 1982. write for info. Longman.
Bates, Milton J. Wallace Stevens: A Mythology of Self. LC 84-8468. 302p. 1985. 24.95 (ISBN 0-520-04909-8). U of Cal Pr.
Bates, Myrtle & Stern, Renee. The Grammar Game. (Illus.). 368p. (Orig.). 1983. pap. text ed. 12.04 scp (ISBN 0-672-61567-3); scp instr's. guide 3.67 (ISBN 0-672-61568-1). Bobbs.
--The Grammar Game. 368p. 1983. pap. text ed. write for info. (ISBN 0-02-305460-3). Macmillan.
Bates, Natica I., jt. ed. see Hooton, Earnest A.
Bates, Natica I., ed. see Murray, G. W.
Bates, Natica I., ed. see Reisner, G. A.
Bates, Oric. Eastern Libyans. (Illus.). 298p. 1970. Repr. of 1914 ed. 45.00x (ISBN 0-7146-1634-6, F Cass Co). Biblio Dist.
Bates, Oric, ed. Varia Africana Two. LC 33-6339. (Harvard African Studies: Vol. 2). 1976. Repr. of 1918 ed. 27.00 (ISBN 0-527-01025-1). Kraus Repr.
Bates, Oric & Sterns, F. H., eds. Varia Africana One. LC 33-6339. (Harvard African Studies: Vol. 1). 1976. Repr. of 1917 ed. 27.00 (ISBN 0-527-01024-3). Kraus Repr.
Bates, Paul A., ed. Faust: Sources, Works, Criticism. (Harbrace Sourcebook Ser.). 240p. (Orig.). 1969. pap. text ed. 8.95 (ISBN 0-15-527102-4, HC). HarBraceJ.
Bates, R. B. & Ogle, C. A. Carbanian Chemistry. (Reactivity & Structure Ser.: Vol. 17). 110p. 1983. 21.50 (ISBN 0-387-12345-8). Springer-Verlag.

Bates, R. W. & Fraser, N. M. Investment Decisions in the Nationalized Fuel Industries. LC 74-76575. (Illus.). 208p. 1974. 32.50 (ISBN 0-521-20455-0). Cambridge U Pr.

Bates, Ralph K. Looking at Christmas from the Inside. LC 82-50304. 80p. (Orig.). 1982. pap. 3.95 (ISBN 0-8358-0432-1). Upper Room.

Bates, Robert B. & Beavers, William A. Carbon-Thirteen NMR Spectral Problems. LC 79-92216. (Organic Chemistry Ser.). 288p. 1981. text ed. 34.50x (ISBN 0-89603-010-5); pap. text ed. 14.95x (ISBN 0-89603-016-4). Humana.

Bates, Robert C., ed. L' Hystore Job. (Yale Romanic Studies: No. 14). Repr. of 1937 ed. 16.50 (ISBN 0-404-53214-4). AMS Pr.

Bates, Robert C., ed. see Chevalier Au Barisel.

Bates, Robert C., ed. see De Blois, Pierre.

Bates, Robert H. Essays on the Political Economy of Rural Africa. LC 82-19757. (African Studies: No. 38). (Illus.). 200p. 1983. 32.50 (ISBN 0-521-24563-X). Cambridge U Pr.

--Ethnicity in Contemporary Africa. LC 73-86994. (Foreign & Comparative Studies Program, Eastern African Ser.: No. 14). 59p. 1973. pap. 4.50x (ISBN 0-915984-11-3). Syracuse U Foreign Comp.

--Markets & States in Tropical Africa: The Political Basis of Agricultural Policies. Barry, Brian & Popkin, Samuel L., eds. LC 80-39732. (Social Choice & Political Economy Ser.). 176p. 1981. 26.50x (ISBN 0-520-04253-0, CAMPUS 320); pap. 6.95 (ISBN 0-520-05229-3). U of Cal Pr.

--Patterns of Uneven Development: Causes & Consequences in Zambia. (Monograph Series in World Affairs: Vol. 11, 1973-74 Ser., Bk. 3). 54p. (Orig.). 1974. 5.95 (ISBN 0-87940-039-0). Monograph Series.

--Rural Responses to Industrialization: A Study of Village Zambia. LC 75-43301. 1976. 36.00x (ISBN 0-300-01920-3). Yale U Pr.

--Unions, Parties, & Political Development: A Study of Mineworkers in Zambia. LC 78-158135. pap. 75.80 (ISBN 0-317-29593-4, 2021980). Bks Demand UMI.

Bates, Robert H. & Lofchie, Michael F. Agricultural Development in Africa: Issues of Public Policy. LC 79-24914. 464p. 1980. 53.95x (ISBN 0-03-056173-6). Praeger.

Bates, Robert L. Geology of the Industrial Rocks & Minerals. LC 69-15364. (Illus.). 1969. pap. 8.50 (ISBN 0-486-62213-4). Dover.

--Geology of the Industrial Rocks & Minerals. (Illus.). 15.25 (ISBN 0-8446-0481-X). Peter Smith.

Bates, Robert L. & Jackson, Julia A. Dictionary of Geologic Terms. 571p. 1984. 7.95 (ISBN 0-385-18101-9). Am Geol.

Bates, Robert L. & Jackson, Julie. Our Modern Stone Age. LC 81-17219. (Illus.). 150p. (Orig.). 1981. 18.95 (ISBN 0-86576-027-6). W Kaufmann.

Bates, Robert L. & Sweet, Walter C. Geology: An Introduction. 2nd ed. 1973. text ed. 27.95 (ISBN 0-669-74328-3). Heath.

Bates, Robert L. & Jackson, Julia A., eds. Glossary of Geology. 2nd ed. LC 79-57360. 749p. 1980. 60.00 (ISBN 0-913312-15-0). Am Geol.

Bates, Robin & Simon, Cheryl. The Dinosaurs & the Dark Star. LC 84-3922. (Illus.). 48p. (gr. 3-7). 1984. 11.95 (ISBN 0-02-708340-3). Macmillan.

Bates, Roger G. Determination of PH: Theory & Practice. 2nd ed. LC 72-8779. (Illus.). pap. 123.80 (ISBN 0-317-09107-7, 2019293). Bks Demand UMI.

Bates, Samuel P. A Biographical History of Greene County, Pennsylvania. LC 75-7875. 337p. 1975. Repr. of 1888 ed. 18.50 (ISBN 0-8063-0676-9). Genealog Pub.

Bates, Sandra, jt. ed. see Sjoden, Per-Olow.

Bates, Sanford. Prisons & Beyond. facsimile ed. LC 72-157324. (Select Bibliographies Reprint Ser.). Repr. of 1936 ed. 24.50 (ISBN 0-8369-5784-9). Ayer Co Pubs.

Bates, Sarah M., jt. ed. see Brenneman, Russell L.

Bates, Scott. The ABC of Radical Ecology. 100p. 5.00 (ISBN 0-9602226-5-0). Highlander.

Bates, Shirley. Popular Pottery. (Illus.). 128p. 1982. 14.95 (ISBN 0-7134-4168-2, Pub. by Batsford England). David & Charles.

--Pottery. (Teaching Today Ser.). (Illus.). 72p. 1981. 14.95 (ISBN 0-7134-3976-9, Pub. by Batsford England). David & Charles.

Bates, Stephen, jt. auth. see Diamond, Edwin.

Bates, Steven L. & Orr, Sidney D. Concordance to the Poems of Ben Jonson. LC 76-25613. xiv, 878p. 1978. 48.00x (ISBN 0-8214-0359-1, 82-82493). Ohio U Pr.

Bates, Steven S. Fundamentals for Assisting in Primary Care Optometry. LC 82-61251. 1983. 50.00 (ISBN 0-87873-031-1). Prof Press.

Bates, Susan, jt. auth. see Edginton, John.

Bates, Susannah. The Pendex: An Index of Pen Names & House Names in Fantastic, Thriller & Series Literature. LC 80-8486. 200p. 1981. lib. bdg. 36.00 (ISBN 0-8240-9501-4). Garland Pub.

Bates, T. D. & Berry, R. J., eds. High Dose-Rate Afterloading in the Treatment of Cancer of the Uterus. 1980. 55.00x (ISBN 0-686-69951-3, Pub. by Brit Inst Radiology). State Mutual Bk.

Bates, Timothy & Bradford, William. Financing Black Economic Development. (Institute for Research on Poverty Policy Analysis Ser.). 1979. 19.50 (ISBN 0-12-081650-4); pap. 10.00 (ISBN 0-12-081652-0). Acad Pr.

Bates, Timothy & Wright, Judith. Evaluating Your Business Computer Needs. 150p. pap. 12.95 (6200). Hayden.

Bates, Timothy, jt. auth. see Fusfeld, Daniel R.

Bates, Tom H. The General's Mess. 1981. 18.00x (ISBN 0-7223-1396-9, Pub. by Stockwell). State Mutual Bk.

Bates, Tony & Robinson, John, eds. Evaluating Educational Television & Radio. 432p. 1977. 53.00x (ISBN 0-335-00045-2, Pub. by Open Univ Pr). Taylor & Francis.

Bates, Virginia H. Geometry Now. (Illus.). 1978. pap. text ed. 9.95 (ISBN 0-89529-049-9). Avery Pub.

Bates, Virginia T. & Chamberlain, Beverly. Antique Bottle Finds in New England. LC 68-9146. pap. 20.00 (ISBN 0-317-28814-8, 2020941). Bks Demand UMI.

Bates, W. H. Better Eyesight Without Glasses. 208p. (Orig.). 1981. pap. 5.95 (ISBN 0-03-058012-9, Owl Bks.). HR&W.

Bates, William. The Computer Cookbook: How to Create Small Computer Systems That Work for You. (Illus.). 380p. 1983. 24.95 (ISBN 0-13-164558-7, Spec); pap. 12.95 (ISBN 0-13-165167-6). P-H.

Bates, William & Crowther, Betty. Toward a Typology of Opiate Users. 160p. 1974. pap. text ed. 7.50 (ISBN 0-87073-960-3). Schenkman Bks Inc.

Bates, William, ed. A Gallery of Illustrious Literary Characters, 1830-1838. 1977. lib. bdg. 59.95 (ISBN 0-8490-1875-7). Gordon Pr.

Bates, William E. & Bates, La Donna G. Ten Roads to the Top. LC 81-82937. 203p. 1981. pap. 8.75 (ISBN 0-87218-019-0). Natl Underwriter.

Bates, Williams S. The Computer Cookbook, 1984: Computers & the Computer Industry from A to Z. LC 83-40142. 416p. 1984. pap. 14.95 (ISBN 0-385-19291-6, Quantum Pr). Doubleday.

Bateson. Problems of Genetics. LC 79-15467. 1979. text ed. 33.00x (ISBN 0-300-02435-5); pap. 9.95x (ISBN 0-300-02436-3, Y-350). Yale U Pr.

Bateson, Beatrice. William Bateson, F. R. S. (Cambridge, England 1928) Rosenberg, Charles, ed. LC 83-48530. (The History of Hereditarian Thought Ser.). 473p. 1985. Repr. of 1928 ed. lib. bdg. 56.00 (ISBN 0-8240-5801-1). Garland Pub.

Bateson, Charles. Gold Fleet for California: Forty-Niners from Australia & New Zealand. (Illus.). 1964. 7.50 (ISBN 0-87013-080-3). Mich St U Pr.

Bateson, F. W. Essays in Critical Dissent. 253p. 1972. 12.00x (ISBN 0-87471-085-5). Rowman.

Bateson, F. W. & Meserole, Harrison T. A Guide to English & American Literature. 3rd ed. LC 76-19083. 352p. 1977. 15.00x (ISBN 0-87752-186-7). Gordian.

Bateson, F. W., ed. The Selected Poems of William Blake. (The Poetry Bookshelf). 1957. pap. text ed. 5.00x (ISBN 0-435-15011-1). Heinemann Ed.

Bateson, F. W., ed. see Sheridan, Richard B.

Bateson, F. W., et al. A Guide to English & American Literature. 3rd ed. 352p. 1976. pap. text ed. 13.95x (ISBN 0-582-48417-0). Longman.

Bateson, Frederick W. English Poetry: A Critical Introduction. LC 78-6657. 1978. Repr. of 1966 ed. lib. bdg. 24.75 (ISBN 0-313-20461-6, BAEN). Greenwood.

--Wordsworth: A Re-Interpretation. LC 83-45410. Repr. of 1954 ed. 27.50 (ISBN 0-404-20020-6). AMS Pr.

Bateson, Gregory. Mind & Nature. (New Age Ser.). 1979. pap. 4.95 (ISBN 0-553-24283-0). Bantam.

--Naven: A Survey of the Problems Suggested by a Composite Picture of the Culture of a New Guinea Tribe Drawn from Three Points of View. 2nd ed. (Illus.). 1958. 25.00x (ISBN 0-8047-0519-4); pap. 8.95x (ISBN 0-8047-0520-8). Stanford U Pr.

--Step to an Ecology of Mind. 1975. pap. 3.50 (ISBN 0-345-29351-7). Ballantine.

Bateson, Gregory, jt. auth. see Ruesch, Jurgen.

Bateson, Gregory, ed. see Perceval, John.

Bateson, Hartley, ed. Patience: A West Midland Poem of the Fourteenth Century. LC 72-187860. 1912. lib. bdg. 20.00 (ISBN 0-8414-1630-3). Folcroft.

Bateson, John T. In-Circuit Testing. (Illus.). 256p. 1985. 32.95 (ISBN 0-442-21284-4). Van Nos Reinhold.

Bateson, M., ed. see Newcastle, Phelman-Holles T.

Bateson, Malcolm C. & Bouchier, Ian A. Clinical Investigation of Gastrointestinal Function. 2nd ed. (Illus.). 296p. 1982. pap. text ed. 19.50 (ISBN 0-632-00742-7, B 0510-5). Mosby.

Bateson, Mary. Mediaeval England, Ten Sixty-Six to Thirteen Fifty. facsimile ed. LC 70-152973. (Select Bibliographies Reprint Ser). Repr. of 1903 ed. 32.00 (ISBN 0-8369-5725-3). Ayer Co Pubs.

--Mediaeval England Ten Sixty-Six to Thirteen Fifty. 1973. Repr. of 1903 ed. 30.00 (ISBN 0-8274-1675-X). R West.

Bateson, Mary C. With a Daughter's Eye. 1985. pap. 4.95 (ISBN 0-671-55424-7). WSP.

--With a Daughter's Eye: A Memoir of Margaret Mead & Gregory Bateson. Golbitz, Pat, ed. LC 84-60564. (Illus.). 256p. 1984. 15.95 (ISBN 0-688-03962-6). Morrow.

Bateson, Nicholas. Data Construction in Social Surveys. Bulmer, Martin, ed. (Contemporary Social Research Ser.: No. 10). 176p. 1984. text ed. 28.50 (ISBN 0-04-312021-0); pap. text ed. 12.50 (ISBN 0-04-312022-9). Allen Unwin.

Bateson, P. P. & Hinde, R. A., eds. Growing Points in Ethology. LC 76-8291. (Illus.). 500p. 1976. 72.50 (ISBN 0-521-21287-1); pap. 21.95x (ISBN 0-521-29086-4). Cambridge U Pr.

Bateson, P. P. & Klopfer, Peter H., eds. Perspectives in Ethology, 3 vols. Incl. Vol. 1. 350p. 1973. 32.50x (ISBN 0-306-36601-0); Vol. 2. 351p. 1976. 32.50x (ISBN 0-306-36602-9); Vol. 3: Social Behavior. 277p. 1978. 29.50x (ISBN 0-306-36603-7). (Illus., Plenum Pr). Plenum Pub.

--Perspectives in Ethology, Vol. 4: Advantages of Diversity. 276p. 1980. 29.50x (ISBN 0-306-40511-3, Plenum Pr). Plenum Pub.

--Perspectives in Ethology, Vol. 5: Ontogeny. 536p. 1982. 39.50x (ISBN 0-306-41063-X, Plenum Pr). Plenum Pub.

--Perspectives in Ethology, Vol. 6: Mechanisms. 324p. 1985. 39.50x (ISBN 0-306-41846-0, Plenum Pr). Plenum Pub.

Bateson, Patrick, ed. Mate Choice. LC 82-14669. (Illus.). 440p. 1983. 62.50 (ISBN 0-521-25112-5); pap. 21.95 (ISBN 0-521-27207-6). Cambridge U Pr.

Bateson, Robert. Introduction to Control Systems Technology. 2nd ed. (Technology Ser.). 560p. 1980. text ed. 29.95 (ISBN 0-675-08255-2). Additional supplements may be obtained from publisher. Merrill.

Bateson, Robert & Raygor, Robin. BASIC Programming for the Apple Computer. (Illus.). 250p. 1985. pap. text ed. 14.95 (ISBN 0-314-85290-5). West Pub.

Bateson, Spencer. The Complete Guide for the Commodore 64. 320p. 1984. pap. 18.95 (ISBN 0-946576-21-1, Pub. by Phoenix Pub). David & Charles.

Bateson, Vaughan. Kipling & the Doctors. LC 73-15769. 1929. lib. bdg. 15.00 (ISBN 0-8414-3294-5). Folcroft.

Bateson, William. Scientific Papers of William Bateson, 2 Vols. Punnett, R. C., ed. Repr. of 1928 ed. Set. 90.00 (ISBN 0-384-03533-7). Johnson Repr.

Bates-Yakobson, Helen, jt. auth. see Von Gronicka, Andre.

Batey. Habeas Corpus. (The Law in Florida Ser.). 24.95 (ISBN 0-686-90245-9). Harrison Co GA.

Batey, Dan. One More for the Hill. (Illus.). 50p. 1984. pap. write for info. (ISBN 0-917459-00-8). Center Hill.

--Return of the Alumni. (Illus.). 64p. (Orig.). 1984. pap. 6.95 (ISBN 0-917459-01-6). Center Hill.

Batey, Mavis. Oxford Gardens: The University's Influence on Garden History. 192p. 1982. text ed. 29.00x (ISBN 0-86127-002-9, Pub. by Avebury England); pap. text ed. 14.75x (ISBN 0-86127-005-3, Pub. by Avebury England). Humanities.

Batey, P. W. Theory & Method in Urban & Regional Analysis. (London Papers in Regional Science). 184p. 1978. pap. 16.00x (ISBN 0-85086-066-0, NO. 2928, Pub. by Pion England). Methuen Inc.

Batey, P. W., jt. ed. see Massey, Doreen B.

Batey, P. W. J. & Madden, M., eds. Integrated Analysis of Regional Systems. (London Papers in Regional Science: No. 15). 190p. 1985. pap. 15.95 (ISBN 0-85086-116-0, 9647, Pub. by Pion England). Methuen Inc.

Bath, C. Richard, jt. ed. see Applegate, Howard G.

Bath, Donald L., et al. Dairy Cattle: Principles, Practices, Problems Profits. 3rd ed. LC 84-20096. (Illus.). 473p. 1985. text ed. 39.50 (ISBN 0-8121-0955-4). Lea & Febiger.

Bath, Geoffrey, ed. The State of the Universe. (Illus.). 1980. 27.50x (ISBN 0-19-857549-1). Oxford U Pr.

Bath, M. Spectral Analysis in Geophysics. (Developments in Solid Earth Geophysics: Vol. 7). 563p. 1974. Repr. of 1974 ed. 106.50 (ISBN 0-444-41222-0). Elsevier.

Bath, Markus. Introduction to Seismology. (Wissenschaft und Kultur Band: No. 27). (Illus.). 428p. 1979. 31.95 (ISBN 0-8176-0956-3). Birkhauser.

Bathe, Dorothy, jt. auth. see Bathe, Greville.

Bathe, Greville & Bathe, Dorothy. Oliver Evans: A Chronicle of Early American Engineering. LC 72-5031. (Technology & Society Ser.). (Illus.). 380p. 1972. Repr. of 1935 ed. 42.00 (ISBN 0-405-04684-7). Ayer Co Pubs.

Bathe, Klaus, et al, eds. Formulations & Computational Algorithms in Finite-Element Analysis: U. S. German Symposium. 1977. 65.00x (ISBN 0-262-02127-7). MIT Pr.

Bathe, Klaus-Jurgen. Finite Element Procedures Engineering Analysis. (Illus.). 736p. 1982. 43.95 (ISBN 0-13-317305-4). P-H.

Bathe, Klaus-Jurgen & Wilson, Edward L. Numerical Methods in Finite Element Analysis. (Illus.). 544p. 1976. ref. ed. 43.95 (ISBN 0-13-627190-1). P-H.

Bathe, P., jt. auth. see Chalmers, L.

Bather, Francis A., tr. see Nordenskiold, Nils A.

Batherman, Muriel. Before Columbus. (Illus.). 32p. (gr. k-3). 1981. PLB 8.95 (ISBN 0-395-30088-6). HM.

Bathersfield, Arnold. In Being: The Name of the Game. Evergreen Productions, ed. (Illus.). 90p. pap. write for info. (ISBN 0-9613919-0-1). Evergreen Prods.

Bathgate, M. A. The Structure of Rural Supply to the Honiara Market in the Solomon Islands. (The Australian National University Development Studies Centre Occasional Paper: No. 11). (Illus.). 1979. pap. text ed. 2.00 (ISBN 0-909150-62-1, Pub. by ANUP Australia). Australia N U P.

Bathhurst, Charles. Remarks on the Differences in Shakespeare's Versification in Different Periods of His Life. LC 75-113550. 1970. Repr. of 1857 ed. 18.00 (ISBN 0-404-00692-2). AMS Pr.

Bathhurst, Effie G. A Teachers College Follow-up Service: Its Factors & Development in an Unsupervised Service Area. LC 79-176542. (Columbia University. Teachers College. Contributions to Education: No. 478). Repr. of 1931 ed. 22.50 (ISBN 0-404-55478-4). AMS Pr.

Bathie, H. Perrier de La see De La Bathie, H. Perrier.

Bathie, William W. Fundamentals of Gas Turbines. LC 83-21609. 358p. 1984. text ed. 37.50 (ISBN 0-471-86285-1). Wiley.

Batho, Margot. Sandcasting. LC 72-13345. (Early Crafts Bks.). (Illus.). 36p. (gr. 1-4). 1973. PLB 4.95 (ISBN 0-8225-0860-5). Lerner Pubns.

Bathorey, Dennis, jt. auth. see McWilliams, Wilson C.

Bathory, Peter D. Political Theory As Public Confession. LC 80-15667. 180p. 1981. 24.95 (ISBN 0-87855-405-X). Transaction Bks.

Bathrick, David D. Agricultural Credit for Small Farm Development: Policies & Practices. (Westview Special Studies in Social, Political, & Economic Development). (Illus.). 1981. hardcover 23.50x (ISBN 0-86531-037-8). Westview.

Bathum, Mike. Four-Step Color Projects. (Portfolio of Illustrated Four-Step Art Projects Ser.). (Illus.). 72p. 1983. tchr's aid 7.95x (ISBN 0-87628-321-0). Ctr Appl Res.

--Four-Step Crafts Projects. (Portfolio of Illustrated Four-Step Art Projects Ser.). (Illus.). 72p. 1984. tchr's aid 7.95x (ISBN 0-87628-322-9). Ctr Appl Res.

--Four-Step Design Projects. (Portfolio of Illustrated Four-Step Art Projects Ser.). (Illus.). 72p. 1983. tchr's aid 7.95x (ISBN 0-87628-323-7). Ctr Appl Res.

--Four-Step Drawing & Composition Projects. (Portfolio of Illustrated Four-Step Art Projects Ser.). (Illus.). 72p. 1983. tchr's aid 7.95X (ISBN 0-87628-324-5). Ctr Appl Res.

--Four-Step Illustration Projects. (Portfolio of Illustrated Four-Step Art Projects Ser.). (Illus.). 72p. 1983. tchr's aid 7.95x (ISBN 0-87628-325-3). Ctr Appl Res.

--Four-Step Painting Projects. (Portfolio of Illustrated Four-Step Art Projects Ser.). (Illus.). 72p. 1983. tchr's aid 7.95x (ISBN 0-87628-326-1). Ctr Appl Res.

--Four-Step Printmaking Projects. (Portfolio of Illustrated Four-Step Art Projects Ser.). (Illus.). 72p. 1983. tchr's aid 7.95x (ISBN 0-87628-327-X). Ctr Appl Res.

--Four-Step Three-Dimensional Art Projects. (Portfolio of Illustrated Four-Step Art Projects Ser.). (Illus.). 72p. 1983. tchr's aid 7.95x (ISBN 0-87628-328-8). Ctr Appl Res.

Bathurst, Bill. How to Continue. LC 72-85134. 1973. pap. 2.95 (ISBN 0-912078-27-8). Volcano Pr.

Bathurst, R. G. Carbonate Sediments & Their Diagenesis. 2nd ed. (Developments in Sedimentology: Vol. 12). 608p. 1975. pap. text ed. 29.75 (ISBN 0-444-41353-7). Elsevier.

Batie, Sandra S. Soil Erosion: Crisis in America's Croplands? LC 83-1942. (Illus.). 136p. (Orig.). 1983. pap. 8.50 (ISBN 0-89164-068-1). Conservation Foun.

Batie, Sandra S. & Healy, Robert G., eds. The Future of American Agriculture As a Strategic Resource. LC 80-70162. 294p. 1980. pap. 11.50 (ISBN 0-89164-064-9). Conservation Foun.

Batiffol, Louis. Century of the Renaissance. (National History of France: No. 3). Repr. of 1935 ed. 30.00 (ISBN 0-404-50793-X). AMS Pr.

--Marie De Medicis & the French Court in the Seventeenth Century. Davis, H. W., ed. King, Mary, tr. from Fr. LC 72-137368. (Select Bibliographies Reprint Ser.). 1972. Repr. of 1908 ed. 17.00 (ISBN 0-8369-5569-2). Ayer Co Pubs.

Batin, Christopher. How to Catch Alaska's Trophy Sportfish. LC 84-70673. (Illus.). 368p. (Orig.). 1984. 60.00 (ISBN 0-916771-01-6); pap. 19.95 (ISBN 0-916771-00-8). Alaska Angler.

Batino. Nitrogen & Air: Gas Solubilities. LC 82-15046. (Solubility Data Ser.: Vol. 10). 1982. 100.00 (ISBN 0-08-023922-6). Pergamon.

Batish, Jonas. All's Well That Ends Well. rev. ed. Harbage, Alfred, ed. (Shakespeare Ser.). 1965. pap. 2.95 (ISBN 0-14-071430-8, Pelican). Penguin.

Batist, Bessie, ed. A Treasure for My Daughter. pap. 5.95 (ISBN 0-8015-7939-2, 0577-180, Hawthorn). Dutton.

Batista, Fulgencio. Growth & Decline of the Cuban Republic. 1964. 7.50 (ISBN 0-8159-5614-2). Devin.

Batista, Jaoa, ed. see Getz, Gene.

Batista, Joao, jt. ed. see Balthazar, Vera.

Batista, O. A. Microcrystal Polymer Science. LC 74-13742. (Illus.). 30.00 (ISBN 0-07-004084-2). RSC Pubs.

Batiuk, Tom. Funky Winkerbean. 96p. 1984. pap. 3.95 (ISBN 0-449-90112-2, Columbine). Fawcett.

Batki, John, tr. see Jozsef, Attila.

Batkin, Maureen. Wedgwood Ceramics, Eighteen Fourty-Six to Nineteen Fifty-Nine: A New Appraisal. (Illus.). 244p. 1982. 95.00 (ISBN 0-903685-11-6, 1250029, Pub. by R Dennis Pubns UK). Seven Hills Bks.

Batley, E. M. A Preface to the Magic Flute. 176p. 1981. 35.00x (ISBN 0-234-77205-0, Pub. by Dobson Bks England). State Mutual Bk.

Batley, Richard. Power Through Bureaucracy: Urban Political Analysis in Brazil. LC 82-16872. 240p. 1983. 27.50x (ISBN 0-312-63437-4). St Martin.

Batley, Richard, jt. auth. see Edwards, John.

Batman, Richard. American Ecclesiastes: The Stories of James Pattie. (Illus.). 328p. 1985. pap. 24.95 (ISBN 0-15-105578-5). HarBraceJ.

--The Outer Coast. LC 85-7613. (Illus.). 400p. 1985. 18.95 (ISBN 0-15-170450-3). HarBraceJ.

Batman, Stephen. Doom Warning All Men to the Judgement. LC 84-1441. 1984. Repr. of 1581 ed. 60.00x (ISBN 0-8201-1393-X). Schol Facsimiles.

--The Golden Booke of the Leaden Gods, Repr. Of 1577 Ed. Bd. with The Third Part of the Countess of Pembroke's Yvychurch. Fraunce, Abraham. Repr. of 1592 ed; The Fountaine of Ancient Fiction. Lynche, Richard. Repr. of 1599 ed. LC 75-27856. (Renaissance & the Gods Ser.: Vol. 13). (Illus.). 1976. lib. bdg. 88.00 (ISBN 0-8240-2062-6). Garland Pub.

Bator, J. W. International Airline Phrase Book. 236p. 1983. pap. 5.95 (ISBN 0-8351-1246-2). China Bks.

Bator, Joseph. International Airline Phrase Book in Six Languages: English, French, German, Italian, Portuguese, Spanish. LC 67-25870. (Orig.). 1968. pap. 4.50 (ISBN 0-486-22017-6). Dover.

Bator, Paul, et al. A Constitutional Convention: How Well Would It Work? 41p. 1979. 3.75 (ISBN 0-8447-2164-6). Am Enterprise.

Bator, Paul M. The International Trade in Art. LC 82-17405. viii, 108p. 1983. lib. bdg. 16.00x (ISBN 0-226-03909-9); pap. 6.95x (ISBN 0-226-03910-2). U of Chicago Pr.

Bator, Robert. Signposts to Criticism of Children's Literature. 360p. 1983. lib. bdg. 30.00x (ISBN 0-8389-0372-X, 82-18498). ALA.

Bator, Robert, ed. Masterworks of Children's Literature, Vol. III & IV: The Middle Period, 1740-1836, 2 vols. 1984. 37.50 ea. Vol. III (ISBN 0-87754-377-1). Vol. 4 (ISBN 0-87754-378-X). Chelsea Hse.

Bator, Victor. Vietnam, a Diplomatic Tragedy: Origins of U. S. Involvement. LC 65-17939. 256p. 1965. 12.50 (ISBN 0-379-00253-1). Oceana.

Batorska, Danuta, frwd. by. Yoruba Sculpture in Los Angeles Collections. (Illus.). 40p. 1969. 1.00 (ISBN 0-915478-17-X). Galleries Coll.

Batoutah, Ibn. Voyages d'ibn Batoutah, 4 vols. Defremery, G. & Sanguinetti, B. R., trs. 2047p. (Fr.). 1985. Repr. of 1879 ed. Set. lib. bdg. 295.00x (ISBN 0-89241-177-5). Caratzas.

Batra, Gretchen, jt. ed. see Markson, Elizabeth.

Batra, Lekh R., ed. Insect Fungus Symbiosis: Nutrition, Mutualism & Commensalism. LC 78-20640. 288p. 1979. text ed. 27.50x (ISBN 0-470-26671-6). Allanheld.

--Insect-Fungus Symbiosis: Nutrition, Mutualism & Commensalism. LC 78-20640. (Illus.). 276p. 1979. text ed. 44.95x (ISBN 0-470-26671-6). Halsted Pr.

Batra, Neelam. Clinical Pathology for Medical Students. 240p. 1983. text ed. 25.00x (ISBN 0-7069-1117-2, Pub. by Vikas India). Advent NY.

--Clinical Pathology for Medical Students. 1982. 39.00x (ISBN 0-7069-1118-0, Pub. by Garlandfold England). State Mutual Bk.

Batra, Raveendra N. The Downfall of Capitalism & Communism: A New Study of History. 1978. text ed. 25.50x (ISBN 0-333-21645-8). Humanities.

Batra, Ravi. The Great Depression of Nineteen Ninety. LC 85-50275. (Illus.). 176p. (Orig.). 1985. 15.00 (ISBN 0-939352-02-8); pap. 10.00 (ISBN 0-939352-03-6). Venus Bks.

--Muslim Civilization & the Crisis in Iran. LC 80-53736. 218p. (Orig.). 1981. 15.00 (ISBN 0-939352-00-1); pap. 8.00 (ISBN 0-686-36905-X). Venus Bks.

--Muslim Civilization & the Crisis in Iran. 218p. 1980. pap. 2.00 (ISBN 0-686-95468-8). Ananda Marga.

--Proust: The Alternative to Capitalism & Marxism. LC 80-67184. 221p. 1980. lib. bdg. 22.25 (ISBN 0-8191-1187-2); pap. text ed. 10.50 (ISBN 0-8191-1188-0). U Pr of Amer.

--Prout: The Alternative to Capitalism & Marxism. 209p. 1980. pap. 5.00 (ISBN 0-686-95463-7). Ananda Marga.

--Regular Cycles of Money, Inflation, Regulation & Depression. LC 85-50598. (Illus.). 192p. 1985. 16.00x (ISBN 0-939352-04-4). Venus Bks.

Batra, Sushma. Social Integration of the Blind. 200p. 1981. text ed. 17.75x (ISBN 0-391-02495-7, Pub. by Concept India). Humanities.

Batran, Aziz A. Islam & Revolution in Africa. LC 84-72246. 51p. 1985. pap. 4.95 (ISBN 0-915597-17-9). Amana bks.

Batsakis, John G. Tumors of the Head & Neck: Clinical & Pathological Considerations. 2nd ed. (Illus.). 584p. 1979. 62.00 (ISBN 0-683-00476-X). Williams & Wilkins.

Batsakis, John G. & Briere, Russell O. Interpretive Enzymology. (Illus.). 312p. 1967. photocopy ed. 29.50x (ISBN 0-398-00111-1). C C Thomas.

Batsakis, John G., jt. auth. see Homburger, Henry A.

Batsakis, John G., jt. ed. see Homburger, Henry A.

Batsakis, John G., et al. Pathology of the Salivary Glands. LC 77-3537. (Atlases of the Pathology of the Head & Neck Ser.). (Illus.). 57p. 1977. slide atlas 100.00 (ISBN 0-89189-031-9, 15-1-0019-00). Am Soc Clinical.

Batschelet, E. Introduction to Mathematics for Life Scientists. 2nd ed. LC 75-11755. (Biomathematics Ser.: Vol. 2). (Illus.). 643p. 1979. 45.00 (ISBN 0-387-09662-0). Springer-Verlag.

--Introduction to Mathematics for Life Scientists. 3rd ed. (Springer Study Edition). (Illus.). 1979. pap. 24.00 (ISBN 0-387-09648-5). Springer-Verlag.

Batschelet, Edward. Circular Statistics in Biology. LC 81-66364. (Mathematics in Biology Ser.). 1981. 69.50 (ISBN 0-12-081050-6). Acad Pr.

Batshaw, Mark L. & Perret, Yvonne M. Children with Handicaps: A Medical Primer. LC 81-9961. (Illus.). 464p. 1981. text ed. 22.95 (ISBN 0-933716-16-8, 168). P H Brookes.

Batson, Benjamin A. The End of the Absolute Monarchy in Siam. (Illus.). 372p. 1985. pap. 22.95x (ISBN 0-19-582612-4). Oxford U Pr.

Batson, C. Daniel, et al. Commitment Without Ideology. LC 72-13000. 1973. 6.95 (ISBN 0-8298-0245-2). Pilgrim NY.

Batson, Daniel C. & Ventis, W. Larry. The Religious Experience: A Social-Psychological Perspective. (Illus.). 1982. text ed. 29.95x (ISBN 0-19-503030-3); pap. text ed. 14.95x (ISBN 0-19-503031-1). Oxford U Pr.

Batson, E. Beatrice. John Bunyan: Allegory & Imagination. 168p. 1984. 27.50x (ISBN 0-389-20442-0, 08004). B&N Imports.

Batson, H. E., tr. see Von Mises, Ludwig.

Batson, Harold E. Select Bibliography of Modern Economic Theory 1870-1929. LC 67-27787. 1930. 27.50x (ISBN 0-678-06509-8). Kelley.

Batson, Larry. An Interview with Alan Page. (Interviews Ser.). (Illus.). (gr. 3-8). 1977. PLB 6.95 (ISBN 0-87191-569-3). Creative Ed.

--An Interview with Jim Plunkett. (Interviews Ser.). (Illus.). (gr. 3-8). 1977. PLB 6.95 (ISBN 0-87191-570-7). Creative Ed.

Batson, Robert G., tr. see Masaryk, Thomas G.

Batson, Sallie, jt. auth. see Pinckney, Callan.

Batson, Trenton W. & Bergman, Eugene, eds. The Deaf Experience: An Anthology of Literature by & about the Deaf. 2nd ed. LC 76-27476. 384p. 1976. pap. 9.00 (ISBN 0-914562-03-7). Merriam-Eddy.

Batson, W. H. see Haines, Thomas H.

Batson, Wade T. Genera of the Eastern Plants. (Illus.). 203p. 1984. pap. 8.95 (ISBN 0-87249-450-0). U of SC Pr.

--Genera of the Western Plants. (Illus.). 210p. 1984. pap. 8.95 (ISBN 0-87249-451-9). U of SC Pr.

--Landscape Plants for the Southeast: Botanical Sketch of Each Plant. LC 84-5267. (Illus.). xxi, 406p. 1984. 14.95 (ISBN 0-87249-433-0). U of SC Pr.

--Wild Flowers in South Carolina. LC 64-23760. (Illus.). 146p. 1980. pap. 6.95 (ISBN 0-87249-257-5). U of SC Pr.

Batstone, Eric. Working Order. 376p. 1985. 39.95x (ISBN 0-631-13751-3). Basil Blackwell.

Batstone, Eric, et al. Consent & Efficiency: Labour Relations & Management Strategy in a State Enterprise. (Warwick Studies in Industrial Relations). 250p. 1984. 24.95x (ISBN 0-631-13517-0). Basil Blackwell.

--Unions on the Board: An Experiment in Industrial Democracy. (Warwick Studies in Industrial Relations). 206p. 1984. 24.95x (ISBN 0-631-13317-8). Basil Blackwell.

--Unions on the Board: An Experiment in Industrial Democracy. 206p. 1985. 24.95x (ISBN 0-631-13317-8); pap. 14.95x (ISBN 0-631-13661-4). Basil Blackwell.

Batt, Alan, ed. see Sadar, Albin.

Batt, Cara M., jt. auth. see Arrigo, Joseph A.

Batt, Elisabeth. The Moncks & Charleville House: A Wicklow Family in the Nineteenth Century. 1981. 40.00x (ISBN 0-686-97834-X, Pub. by Blackwater Pr Ireland). State Mutual Bk.

Batt, John & James, William. The Family Law Decision-Making Process: Annotated Law, Psychology & Policy Science Bibliography. LC 79-63673. 262p. 1979. lib. bdg. 30.00 (ISBN 0-930342-93-3). W S Hein.

Batt, Max. The Treatment of Nature in German Literature from Guenther to Goethe's Werner. 1976. lib. bdg. 59.95 (ISBN 0-8490-2764-0). Gordon Pr.

--Treatment of Nature in German Literature from Gunther to the Appearance of Goethe's Werther. LC 72-91034. 1969. Repr. of 1902 ed. 15.50x (ISBN 0-8046-0644-7, Pub by Kennikat). Assoc Faculty Pr.

Battaglia, Anthony. Toward a Reformulation of Natural Law. 1981. 14.95 (ISBN 0-8164-0490-9, Pub. by Seabury). Winston Pr.

Battaglia, Aurelius, ed. Mother Goose. (ps-1). 1973. pap. 1.95 (ISBN 0-394-82661-2, BYR). Random.

Battaglia, Aurelius, illus. Animal Homemakers. LC 77-10368. (A Pandaback Bks.). (Illus.). (gr. 1-3). 1978. PLB 3.99 (ISBN 0-448-13131-5, G&D). Putnam Pub Group.

--Animal Sounds. (Golden Sturdy Bks.). (Illus.). 14p. (ps). 1981. 2.95 (ISBN 0-307-12122-4, Golden Bks). Western Pub.

--A Farm. LC 77-83860. (A Pandaback Book). (Illus.). (gr. 1-3). 1978. pap. 0.95 (ISBN 0-448-49605-4, G&D). Putnam Pub Group.

--Mother Goose. LC 73-2447. (Pictureback Library Editions). (ps-2). 1978. PLB 4.99 (ISBN 0-394-92661-7, BYR). Random.

--Seasons. LC 76-43128. (Cricket Bk.). (Illus.). (ps-1). 1978. 2.50 (ISBN 0-448-46514-0, G&D). Putnam Pub Group.

--Three Little Pigs. LC 76-24170. (Picturebacks Ser.). (Illus.). 32p. (ps-2). 1982. PLB 4.99 (ISBN 0-394-93459-8); pap. 1.95 saddle stitched (ISBN 0-394-83459-3). Random.

Battaglia, Bruno & Beardmore, John A., eds. Marine Organisms: Genetics, Ecology, & Evolution. LC 78-9715. (NATO Conference Series IV, Marine Science: Vol. 2). 767p. 1978. 85.00x (ISBN 0-306-40020-0, Plenum Pr). Plenum Pub.

Battaglia, Cathy, jt. auth. see Weber, Patricia.

Battaglia, J. & Fisher, M., eds. Yoshi Goes To New York: Authentic Discourse for Listening Comprehension. (Materials for Language Practice Ser.). (Illus.). 64p. 1982. 4.90 (ISBN 0-08-028648-8). Pergamon.

Battaglia, John & Fisher, Marilyn. Yoshi Goes to New York. (Illus.). 142p. 1983. 5.95 (ISBN 0-88084-077-3); cassette 12.95 (ISBN 0-88084-155-9). Alemany Pr.

Battaglia, R. A. & Mayrose, V. Handbook of Livestock Management Techniques. 1981. text ed. 25.95x (ISBN 0-8087-2957-8). Burgess.

Battaini, Andre, jt. auth. see Bordeau, Annette.

Battan, Louis J. Cloud Physics & Cloud Seeding. LC 78-25711. (Illus.). 1979. Repr. of 1962 ed. lib. bdg. 24.75x (ISBN 0-313-20770-4, BACL). Greenwood.

--Fundamentals of Meteorolgy. 2nd ed. (Illus.). 336p. 1984. 31.95 (ISBN 0-13-341123-0). P-H.

--The Nature of Violent Storms. LC 80-24986. (Science Study Ser.: No. S19). (Illus.). 158p. 1981. Repr. of 1961 ed. lib. bdg. 22.50x (ISBN 0-313-22582-6, BANV). Greenwood.

--Radar Observation of the Atmosphere. rev. ed. (Illus.). 1981. pap. 18.00x (ISBN 0-226-03921-8). U of Chicago Pr.

--The Unclean Sky: A Meteorologist Looks at Air Pollution. LC 80-23434. (Selected Topics in the Atmospheric Sciences, Science Study Ser.). (Illus.). xii, 141p. 1980. Repr. of 1966 ed. lib. bdg. 24.75x (ISBN 0-313-22710-1, BAUS). Greenwood.

--Weather. 2nd ed. (Illus.). 160p. 1985. text ed. 18.95 (ISBN 0-13-947698-9); pap. text ed. 15.95 (ISBN 0-13-947680-6). P-H.

--Weather in Your Life. (Illus.). 308p. 1985. pap. 12.95 (ISBN 0-7167-1437-X). W H Freeman.

Battcher, Joyce, jt. auth. see Dlugosch, Sharon.

Battcock, Gregory. Performance Art. 1984. pap. 15.95 (ISBN 0-525-48039-0, 01549-460). Dutton.

Battcock, Gregory, ed. Idea Art: A Critique. 1973. pap. 5.50 (ISBN 0-525-47344-0, 0533-120). Dutton.

--Minimal Art: A Critical Anthology. 1968. pap. 9.95 (ISBN 0-525-47211-8, 0966-290). Dutton.

--The New Art: A Critical Anthology. rev. ed. 1973. pap. 5.75 (ISBN 0-525-47361-0, 0558-170). Dutton.

Battcock, Gregory & Nickas, Robert, eds. The Art of Performance: A Critical Anthology. LC 79-53323. (Illus.). 344p. 1984. pap. 15.95 (ISBN 0-525-48039-0, 01549-460). Dutton.

Batteau, Allen, ed. Appalachia & America: Autonomy & Regional Dependence. LC 82-40462. (Illus.). 296p. 1983. 26.00x (ISBN 0-8131-1480-2). U Pr of Ky.

Batteiger. Business Writing: Process & Forms. 496p. 1985. write for info (ISBN 0-534-04620-7). Wadsworth Pub.

Battell, Andrew see Ravenstein, E. G.

Battelle Columbus Laboratories. Installation of a Modular Photovoltaic Array Field with Low Balance-of-System Costs. Sandia National Labs for U. S. Dept. of Energy, ed. 71p. 1984. pap. 9.95x (P-056). Solar Energy Info.

--Preliminary Environmental Assessment of Biomass Conversion to Synthetic Fuels. 346p. 1980. pap. 49.95x (ISBN 0-89934-049-0, B049-PP). Solar Energy Info.

--Solar Energy Employment & Requirements: 1978-1983. 200p. 1981. pap. 29.50x (ISBN 0-89934-102-0, V.065). Solar Energy Info.

Battelle Columbus Laboratories, jt. auth. see Duffy, A. R.

Battelle Memorial Institute. Agriculture Two-Thousand: A Look at the Future. Bucher, Mary, ed. LC 82-25308. (Illus.). 183p. (Orig.). 1983. pap. 6.95 (ISBN 0-935470-15-8). Battelle.

--Agriculture Two Thousand: A Look at the Future. Bucher, Mary, ed. LC 82-25308. (Illus.). 199p. 1983. 17.00x (ISBN 0-935470-18-2). Battelle.

--Development of Increased Use of Copper as an Alloy in Cast Iron. 61p. 1964. 9.15 (ISBN 0-317-34506-0, 13). Intl Copper.

--Strength & Water Resistance of Adhesive-Bonded Copper Metals. 96p. 1970. 14.40 (ISBN 0-317-34548-6, 108). Intl Copper.

--A Survey of Corrosion Inhibitors & Related Additives to Improve the Corrosion Resistance & Heat Transfer of Copper & Its Alloys. 59p. 1969. 8.85 (ISBN 0-317-34552-4, 148). Intl Copper.

Battelle Memorial Institute Conference - Seattle - 1968. Category Theory, Homology Theory & Their Applications, 1: Proceedings. Hilton, P. J., ed. LC 75-75931. (Lecture Notes in Mathematics: Vol. 86). 1969. pap. 14.70 (ISBN 0-387-04605-4). Springer-Verlag.

--Category Theory, Homology Theory & Their Applications, 2: Proceedings. Hilton, Peter J., ed. LC 75-75931. (Lecture Notes in Mathematics: Vol. 92). (Orig.). 1969. pap. 18.30 (ISBN 0-387-04611-9). Springer-Verlag.

--Category Theory, Homology Theory, & Their Applications, 3: Proceedings. Hilton, Peter J., ed. LC 75-75931. (Lecture Notes in Mathematics: Vol. 99). (Orig.). 1969. pap. 21.90 (ISBN 0-387-04618-6). Springer-Verlag.

Battelle Northwest Laboratory. Analysis of Federal Incentives Used to Stimulate Energy Production. 416p. 1980. Repr. of 1978 ed. 49.50x (ISBN 0-89934-174-8, V052-PP). Solar Energy Info.

Battelle Pacific Northwest Laboratories. Plutonium Utilization in Commercial Power Reactors: Proceedings. 220p. 1972. 15.50 (ISBN 0-317-33073-X, 120004). Am Nuclear Soc.

Battelle Pacific Northwest Labs Staff. Biomass Thermochemical Conversion Program Annual Report, 1983. 51p. Date not set. pap. 9.95 (ISBN 0-914287-34-6, B-052). Solar Energy Info.

Battelle Seattle Research Center Symposium, 1969. Molecular Orbital Studies in Chemical Pharmacology: Proceedings. Kier, Lemont B., ed. LC 77-120374. 1970. 29.50 (ISBN 0-387-04972-X). Springer-Verlag.

Battelli, G., ed. Codex Vindobonesis. (Umbrae Codicum Occidentalium Ser.: Vol. 2). 1960. 10.75 (ISBN 0-7204-6102-2, North Holland). Elsevier.

Battello, Carol. Tell Us a Cormak, & Other Stories. 90p. 1984. 7.95 (ISBN 0-533-06150-4). Vantage.

Battelstein, Sandra L. Celebrity Cookbook. LC 85-70975. (Illus.). 214p. (Orig.). 1985. pap. 12.95 (ISBN 0-933903-00-6). Chefs Pub Co.

Batten, jt. auth. see Baker.

Batten, A. H., jt. auth. see International Astrological Union Symposium, No. 51, Parksville, B. C., Canada Sept. 6-12, 1972.

Batten, Adrian. Four Anthems. Evans, David, ed. LC 68-65217. (Penn State Music Series, No. 17). 232p. pap. 3.25x (ISBN 0-271-09117-7). Pa St U Pr.

Batten, Alan, tr. see Couteau, Paul.

Batten, Charles L., Jr. Pleasurable Instruction: Form & Convention in Eighteenth-Century Travel Literature. LC 76-14316. 1978. 27.50x (ISBN 0-520-03260-8). U of Cal Pr.

Batten, David F. Spatial Analysis of Interacting Economies. 1982. lib. bdg. 26.00 (ISBN 0-89838-109-6). Kluwer-Nijhoff.

Batten, J. R. Golden Foot (Adoniram Judson) (Faith & Fame Ser.). 1956. pap. text ed. 2.50 (ISBN 0-87508-628-4). Chr Lit.

Batten, J. W. & Gibson, J. Sullivan. Soils, Their Nature, Classes, Distribution, Uses, & Care. rev. 2nd ed. LC 76-40302. (Illus.). 314p. 1977. 14.50 (ISBN 0-8173-2876-9). U of Ala Pr.

Batten, Joe D. Beyond Management by Objectives. LC 66-29660. pap. 28.00 (ISBN 0-317-26954-2, 2023580). Bks Demand UMI.

--Tough-Minded Management. 14.95 (ISBN 0-8144-5477-1). AMACOM.

--Tough-Minded Management. 3rd ed. LC 78-15465. 240p. 1984. pap. 10.95 (ISBN 0-8144-7620-1). AMACOM.

Batten, Joseph D. Expectations & Possiblities. LC 80-17102. 368p. 1981. text ed. 10.95 (ISBN 0-201-00093-8). Addison-Wesley.

Batten, Mary. The Tropical Forest: Ants, Ants, Animals & Plants. LC 73-4196. (Illus.). (gr. 5-9). 1973. 12.45i (ISBN 0-690-00138-X). Crowell Jr Bks.

Batten, R. L., tr. see Heim, U. & Pfeiffer, K. M.

Batten, Robert W. Mortality Table Construction. LC 77-12349. (Risk, Insurance & Security Ser.). (Illus.). 1978. 27.95 (ISBN 0-13-601302-3). P-H.

Batten, Robert W. & Hider, George M. Group Life & Health Insurance, Vols. 1 & 2. LC 78-71257. (FLMI Insurance Education Program Ser.). 1979. Set. pap. text ed. 25.00 (ISBN 0-915322-31-5). LOMA.

Batten, Roger L., jt. auth. see Dott, Robert H., Jr.

Batten, Thomas R. Communities & Their Development: An Introductory Study with Special Reference to the Tropics. LC 80-14699. (Illus.). vi, 248p. 1980. Repr. of 1957 ed. lib. bdg. 24.75x (ISBN 0-313-22447-1, BACD). Greenwood.

Battenhouse, H. M. The Philosophy of Friedrich Nietzsche. 59.95 (ISBN 0-8490-0826-3). Gordon Pr.

Battenhouse, Roy W., ed. A Companion to the Study of St. Augustine. (Twin Brooks Ser.). 1979. pap. 7.95 (ISBN 0-8010-0760-7). Baker Bk.

Batterham, T. J. NMR Spectra of Simple Heterocycles. LC 80-11724. 560p. 1982. Repr. of 1973 ed. lib. bdg. 64.50 (ISBN 0-89874-140-8). Krieger.

Batterie, Varta. Sealed Nickel Cadmium Batteries. 1982. pap. 31.00 (ISBN 0-9961074-9-5, Pub. by VDI W Germany). Heyden.

Batterman, Charles A. Techniques of Springboard Diving. LC 68-14457. (Illus.). 1968. 22.00x (ISBN 0-262-02038-6). MIT Pr.

Batterman, Deborah. Manager's Desk Book on Employment Law. 1984. pap. 49.95 (ISBN 0-88057-196-9). Exec Ent Inc.

Battersby, Alan R., jt. ed. see Taylor, William I.

Battersby, Albert. Guide to Stock Control. 2nd ed. 1971. 12.95x (ISBN 0-8464-0463-X). Beekman Pubs.

Battersby, Gregory J., jt. auth. see Grimes, Charles W.

Battersby, H. Prevost. Man Outside Himself: The Methods of Astral Projection. 1979. pap. 2.95 (ISBN 0-8065-0709-8). Citadel Pr.

Battersby, James J. Elder Olson: An Annotated Bibliography. LC 82-48273. 250p. 1982. lib. bdg. 33.00 (ISBN 0-8240-9254-6). Garland Pub.

Battersby, James L. Rational Praise & Natural Lamentation: Johnson, Lycidas, & Principles of Criticism. LC 77-89774. 288p. 1979. 22.50 (ISBN 0-8386-2148-1). Fairleigh Dickinson.

Battersby, Jean. Cultural Policy in Australia. (Studies & Documents on Cultural Policies). (Illus.). 86p. 1980. pap. 6.25 (ISBN 92-3-101778-0, U1031, UNESCO). Unipub.

Battersby, Mark E. & Newhouse, Bertha S. How to Prepare for the CPA Examination: Accounting Practice Section. 1978. pap. text ed. 9.95 (ISBN 0-07-004095-8). McGraw.

Battersby, Martin. Art Deco Fashion: French Designers Nineteen Eight to Nineteen Twenty-Five. (Illus.). 112p. 1984. pap. 10.95 (ISBN 0-312-05181-6). St Martin.

--Decorative Thirties. LC 77-159515. 1971. 20.00 (ISBN 0-8027-0353-4). Walker & Co.

Battersby, W. J. De la Salle: A Pioneer of Modern Education. 236p. 1981. Repr. of 1949 ed. lib. bdg. 40.00 (ISBN 0-89987-065-1). Darby Bks.

Battershaw, Brian, tr. see Gorlitz, Walter.

Battershaw, Brian, tr. see Schucking, Levin L.

Battershill, Norman. Draw Landscapes. LC 78-14063. (Learn to Draw Ser.). (Illus.). 1980. pap. 2.25 (ISBN 0-8008-4583-8, Pentalic). Taplinger.

--Draw Seascapes. LC 79-64255. (Learn to Draw Ser.). (Illus.). 48p. 1981. pap. 2.25 (ISBN 0-8008-2285-4, Pentalic). Taplinger.

--Draw Trees. LC 78-14062. (Learn to Draw Ser.). (Illus.). 1980. pap. 2.25 (ISBN 0-8008-4588-9, Pentalic). Taplinger.

Batterson, Herman G. Sketchbook of the American Episcopate, During One Hundred Years, 1783-1883. 1980. Repr. cancelled (ISBN 0-87921-047-8). Attic Pr.

Battestin, Martin, ed. see Fielding, Henry.

Battestin, Martin C. Moral Basis of Fielding's Art: A Study of Joseph Andrews. LC 59-10177. 1959. 17.50x (ISBN 0-8195-3007-7); pap. 9.50x (ISBN 0-8195-6038-3). Wesleyan U Pr.

Battestin, Martin C., ed. British Novelists, Sixteen Sixty to Eighteen Hundred, 2 pts. (Dictionary of Literary Biography Ser.: Vol.39). 450p. 1985. 176.00x (ISBN 0-8103-1717-6). Gale.

Battestin, Martin C., ed. see Fielding, Henry.

Battestini, M., ed. see Cesaire, Aime.

Battestini, M., ed. see Dadie, Bernard B.

Batteux, Charles. Les Beaux Arts Reduits a un Meme Principe. (Classics in Art & Literary Criticism Ser). Repr. of 1747 ed. 33.00 (ISBN 0-384-03535-3). Johnson Repr.

Battey, George M., Jr. History of Rome & Floyd County, Georgia. LC 74-76719. (Illus.). 728p. 1974. Repr. of 1922 ed. bds. 25.00 (ISBN 0-87797-003-3). Cherokee.

Battey, M. H. Mineralogy for Students. 2nd ed. (Illus.). 356p. 1981. pap. text ed. 21.95x (ISBN 0-582-44005-X). Longman.

Battey, Thomas C. The Life & Adventures of a Quaker Among the Indians. 339p. 1972. Repr. of 1875 ed. 17.50 (ISBN 0-87928-025-5). Corner Hse.

Battezzati, M. & Donini, I. The Lymphatic System. rev. ed. LC 73-9924. 496p. 1974. 85.95x (ISBN 0-470-05706-8). Halsted Pr.

Battezzati, M. see Barker, Philip.

Battie & Turner. Price Guide to Nineteenth & Twentieth Century British Porcelain. (Illus.). 1980. 29.50 (ISBN 0-902028-38-3). Apollo.

--Price Guide to Nineteenth & Twentieth Century British Pottery. (Illus.). 1979. 39.50 (ISBN 0-902028-80-4). Apollo.

Battie, David & Turner, Michael. The Price Guide to Nineteenth & Twentieth Century British Porcelain. (Price Guide Ser.). (Illus.). 486p. 1975. 29.50 (ISBN 0-902028-38-3). Antique Collect.

--The Price Guide to Nineteenth & Twentieth Century British Pottery. (Price Guide Ser.). (Illus.). 244p. 1979. 39.50 (ISBN 0-902028-80-4). Antique Collect.

Battie, William & Monro, John. A Treatise on Madness. (Illus.). 160p. 1962. Repr. of 1758 ed. 18.50x (ISBN 0-8464-0936-4). Beekman Pubs.

Battilega, John A. & Grange, Judith K., eds. Military Appliations of Modeling. LC 84-70088. 568p. 1984. 18.00 (ISBN 0-318-11804-1). Gov Printing Office.

Battin, B. W. Angel of the Night. 256p. (Orig.). 1983. pap. 2.95 (ISBN 0-449-12380-4, GM). Fawcett.

--Programmed for Terror. 256p. 1985. pap. 2.95 (ISBN 0-449-12703-6, GM). Fawcett.

Battin, Buck. Mary, Mary. (Orig.). 1985. pap. 3.50 (ISBN 0-671-47787-0). PB.

Battin, Margaret. Suicide & Ethics. (Special Issue S Ser.: Vol. 13, No. 3). 112p. 1983. 9.95 (ISBN 0-89885-167-X). Human Sci Pr.

Battin, Margaret & Rudick, Michael, eds. John Donne's Biathanatos: A Modern-Spelling Critical Edition. (Garland English Texts Ser.). 1982. lib. bdg. 55.00 (ISBN 0-8240-9481-6). Garland Pub.

Battin, Margaret P. Ethical Issues in Suicide. 250p. 1982. 16.95 (ISBN 0-13-290155-2). P-H.

Battin, R. Ray, ed. Vestibulography. (Illus.). 116p. 1974. photocopy ed. 16.50x (ISBN 0-398-02848-6). C C Thomas.

Battin, R. Ray & Fox, Donna R., eds. Private Practice in Audiology & Speech Pathology. 336p. 1978. 31.00 (ISBN 0-8089-1132-5, 790455). Grune.

Battin, R. Ray, et al. Speech & Language Delay: A Home Training Program. 3rd ed. (Illus.). 120p. 1978. 14.75x (ISBN 0-398-03724-8). C C Thomas.

Battin, Richard H., jt. auth. see Laning, J. Halcombe, Jr.

Battin, Wendy. In the Solar Wind. LC 83-20811. (National Poetry Ser.). 80p. 1984. 10.95 (ISBN 0-385-19384-X); pap. 6.95 (ISBN 0-385-19385-8). Doubleday.

Battino. Oxygen & Ozone: Gas Solubilities. (Solubility Data Ser.). 1981. 100.00 (ISBN 0-08-023915-3). Pergamon.

Battis, Emma, jt. auth. see Evans, Ruth.

Battiscomb, Georgina. Charlotte M. Yonge. 1943. 20.00 (ISBN 0-8274-2046-3). R West.

Battiscombe, Georgina. Christina Rossetti. 240p. 1981. 39.00x (ISBN 0-09-461950-6, Pub. by Constable Pubs). State Mutual Bk.

--Shaftesbury: The Great Reformer 1801-1885. LC 74-32370. 1975. 15.00 (ISBN 0-395-19953-0). HM.

Battison, Robbin, jt. auth. see Baker, Charlotte.

Battison, Robbin, jt. ed. see Baker, Charlotte.

Battison, Robin. Lexical Borrowing in American Sign Language. LC 78-59164. (Illus.). 1978. pap. text ed. 8.00x (ISBN 0-932130-02-X). Linstok Pr.

Battista, H. K., jt. auth. see Battista, O. A.

Battista, O. A. Dictionary of Quotoons. LC 66-12694. 9.95 (ISBN 0-915074-04-4). RSC Pubs.

--Olympiad of Knowledge, 1984: A Novel. LC 75-8352. 1981. 9.95 (ISBN 0-915074-09-5). RSC Pubs.

--People Power. LC 76-58684. Orig. Title: The Power to Influence People. pap. 8.95 (ISBN 0-915074-07-9). RSC Pubs.

--Research for Profit. LC 74-16902. pap. 3.95 (ISBN 0-915074-01-X). RSC Pubs.

--Speaker's Dictionary of Quotoons. LC 77-80327. 12.95 (ISBN 0-915074-08-7). RSC Pubs.

--Work for Profit: Fun, Health, Happiness, Security. LC 75-8351. pap. 3.95 (ISBN 0-915074-02-8). RSC Pubs.

Battista, O. A. & Battista, H. K. Childish Questions? LC 73-85069. (Illus.). 8.95 (ISBN 0-915074-05-2). RSC Pubs.

Battista, Orlando A., ed. Synthetic Fibers in Papermaking. LC 64-13211. 340p. 1964. text ed. 21.00 (ISBN 0-470-05894-3, Pub. by Wiley). Krieger.

Battiste see Jackson, et al.

Battistella, B. Little White Hood. 1980. pap. 1.50 (ISBN 0-8198-4405-5). Dghtrs St Paul.

Battistella, Roger M. & Rundall, Thomas G., eds. Health Care Policy in a Changing Environment. LC 78-57148. 1979. 26.25x (ISBN 0-8211-0131-5); text ed. 24.00x in ten or more copies. McCutchan.

Battisti, Eugenio. Cimabue. LC 66-25463. (Illus.). 1966. 75.00x (ISBN 0-271-73119-2). Pa St U Pr.

--Filippo Brunelleschi: The Complete Work. LC 78-68509. (Illus.). 412p. 1981. 75.00 (ISBN 0-8478-5015-3). Rizzoli Intl.

Battistin, Leontino, et al. Clinical & Biological Aspect of Peripheral Nerve Diseases. LC 83-11295. (Neurology & Neurobiology Ser.: Vol. 4). 402p. 1983. 48.00 (ISBN 0-8451-2703-9). A R Liss.

Battistin, Leontino, et al, eds. Neurochemistry & Clinical Neurology. LC 80-7475. (Progress in Clinical & Biological Research Ser.: Vol. 39). 512p. 1980. 51.00 (ISBN 0-8451-0039-4). A R Liss.

Battistini, Lawrence H. Japan & America from Earliest Times to the Present. LC 76-98210. Repr. of 1954 ed. lib. bdg. 15.00 (ISBN 0-8371-3245-2, BAJA). Greenwood.

--Rise of American Influence in Asia & the Pacific. LC 74-12576. 241p. 1974. Repr. of 1960 ed. lib. bdg. 22.50 (ISBN 0-8371-7728-6, BAAI). Greenwood.

Battistini, Pietro M. The Most Impressive Paintings by Edouard Manet. (The Art Library of the Great Masters of the World). (Illus.). 131p. 1983. 79.95x (ISBN 0-86650-086-3). Gloucester Art.

Battisto, J. R. & Knight, K. L. Immunoglobulin Genes & B Cell Differentiation. (Developments in Immunology Ser.: Vol. 12). 212p. 1980. 61.00 (ISBN 0-444-00580-3). Elsevier.

Battisto, Jack R., ed. see New York Academy of Sciences Annals of, October 19-21, 1981.

Battistone, Joseph. The Great Controversy Theme in E. G. White Writings. xiv, 134p. 1978. pap. 3.95 (ISBN 0-943872-76-6). Andrews Univ Pr.

Battistoni, Richard M. Public Schooling & the Education of Democratic Citizens. 1985. 20.00x (ISBN 0-87805-280-1). U Pr of Miss.

Battle Abbey. Custumals of Battle Abbey, in the Reigns of Edward I & Edward II: 1283-1312. Scargill-Bird, S. R., ed. 27.00 (ISBN 0-384-03545-0). Johnson Repr.

Battle, Brendan P. & Weston, Paul B. Arson Detection & Investigation. LC 78-5308. 1978. lib. bdg. 9.95 (ISBN 0-668-04532-9, 4532). Arco.

Battle, C., ed. see Fulton, Stanley R. & Rawlins, John C.

Battle, C., ed. see Masten, Larry B.

Battle, C., ed. see Schmitt, Neil M. & Farwell, Robert F.

Battle, Charles, ed. see Cannon, Don L.

Battle, Charles W., ed. see Cannon, Don L.

Battle, Charles W., ed. see Walker, Roger S.

Battle, J. H., ed. see Perrin, W. H.

Battle, Jackson B. Environmental Law. LC 84-9341. Date not set. price not set (ISBN 0-87084-084-3). Anderson Pub Co.

Battle, James. Basic Visual-Motor Association Test (BVMAT) 1982. pap. 19.50 for complete battery (ISBN 0-87562-074-4). Spec Child.

--Culture-Free Self-Esteem Inventories for Children & Adults Complete Battery. Preston, J. B., ed. 1981. pap. 51.00 (ISBN 0-87562-067-1). Spec Child.

--Enhancing Self-Esteem & Achievement: A Handbook for Professionals. 160p. (Orig.). 1983. pap. text ed. 16.50 (ISBN 0-87562-076-0). Spec Child.

Battle, Kemp P. History of the University of North Carolina, 2 vols. LC 74-13351. (Illus.). 1974. Repr. of 1907 ed. Set. 50.00 (ISBN 0-87152-308-6); 25.00 ea.; Vol. 1. (ISBN 0-87152-187-3); Vol. 2. (ISBN 0-87152-188-1). Reprint.

Battle, Lois. Season of Change. 280p. 1980. 11.95 (ISBN 0-312-70818-1). St Martin.

--Season of Change. 288p. 1983. pap. 2.95 (ISBN 0-449-20054-X, Crest). Fawcett.

--Southern Women. LC 83-22999. 384p. 1984. 14.95 (ISBN 0-312-74747-0). St Martin.

--Southern Women. 432p. 1985. pap. 3.95 (ISBN 0-312-90328-6). St Martin.

--War Brides. 384p. 1982. 13.95 (ISBN 0-312-85557-5). St Martin.

--War Brides. large print ed. LC 82-7347. 693p. 1982. Repr. of 1982 ed. 15.95 (ISBN 0-89621-374-9). Thorndike Pr.

--War Brides. 384p. 1983. pap. 3.95 (ISBN 0-425-06155-8). Berkley Pub.

Battle, Lynne D. & College Placement Council. Career Planning, Placement, & Recruitment Law: A Sourcebook for Practitioners. LC 83-226670. 1983. 35.00. Coll Placement.

Battles, Ford L. & Miller, Charles. A Concordance to Calvin's Institutio. LC 73-206014. (Bibliographia Tripotamopolitana Ser.: No. 8). 1974. 90.00x (ISBN 0-931222-07-9). C E Barbour.

Battles, Ford L. & Walchenbach, John. An Analysis of "The Institute of the Christian Religion" of John Calvin. LC 79-57385. 1980. pap. 10.95 (ISBN 0-8010-0766-6). Baker Bk.

Battles, Ford L., jt. auth. see Rosenstock-Huessy, Eugen.

Battles, Ford L., ed. see Calvin, John.

Battles, Ford L., jt. ed. see Keiling, Hanns P.

Battocletti, Joseph H. Electromagnetism, Man, & the Environment. LC 76-7905. (Environmental Studies). 1976. 18.50x (ISBN 0-89158-612-1). Westview.

Battrick, B., ed. see Astrophysics & Space Science.

Battro, A. M. Dictionnaire d'Epistemologie Genetique. 188p. (Fr.). 1966. 29.00 (ISBN 90-277-0002-8, Pub. by Reidel Holland). Kluwer Academic.

Batts, H. Lewis & Evans, Monica A., eds. Proceedings: Great Lakes Solar Greenhouse Conference IV. Kalamazoo, Michigan, Nov. 6-7, 1981. 177p. 1982. pap. 10.00 (ISBN 0-939294-05-2, SB-416-G7). Beech Leaf.

Batts, H. Lewis, Jr. & Tenenbaum, Michael, eds. Proceedings: Great Lakes Solar Greenhouse Conference II Kalamazoo, Michigan, June, 8-9, 1979. (Illus.). xiiii, 137p. (Orig.). 1980. pap. 10.00 (ISBN 0-939294-02-8, SB-416-G7). Beech Leaf.

Batts, H. Lewis, ed. & illus. see Bystrom, Robert.

Batts, John S. British Manuscript Diaries of the 19th Century: An Annotated Listing. 345p. 1976. 29.50x (ISBN 0-87471-685-3). Rowman.

--British Manuscript Diaries of the 19th Century. 1983. 75.00 (ISBN 0-900000-84-8, Pub. by Centaur Pr England). State Mutual Bk.

Batts, Michael, et al, eds. Essays on German Literature, in Honour of G. Joyce Hallamore. LC 68-117292. (Illus.). pap. 66.80 (ISBN 0-317-09114-X, 2014126). Bks Demand UMI.

Batts, Michael S. The Bibliography of German Literature: An Historical & Critical Survey. (Canadian Studies in German Language & Literature: Vol. 19). 239p. 1978. pap. 27.15 (ISBN 3-261-03026-7). P Lang Pubs.

Battson, R. K. Modelling Tudor Ships. (Illus.). 76p. 1985. pap. 3.50 (ISBN 0-85242-692-5, Pub. by Argus). Aztex.

Batty, Bob H. Complete Guide to Pressed Glass. LC 77-19211. (Illus.). 261p. 1978. 19.95 (ISBN 0-88289-057-3). Pelican.

Batty, C. D. An Introduction to the 19th Edition of the Dewey Decimal Classification. 168p. 1981. 12.00 (ISBN 0-85157-303-7, Pub. by Bingley England). Shoe String.

Batty, David, ed. Knowledge & Its Organization. LC 76-620022. (Student Contribution Ser.: No. 8). 1976. pap. 8.75 (ISBN 0-911808-12-4). U of Md Lib Serv.

Batty, Eric. Coaching Modern Soccer: Attack. (Illus.). 128p. 1980. 15.95 (ISBN 0-571-09840-1); pap. 6.95 (ISBN 0-571-11605-1). Faber & Faber.

--Coaching Modern Soccer: Defence. (Illus.). 128p. 1981. pap. 8.95 (ISBN 0-571-11773-2). Faber & Faber.

Batty, Eric G., ed. International Football (Soccer) Book, No. 24. 144p. 1983. text ed. 23.50x (ISBN 0-285-62533-0, SpS). Sportshelf.

Batty, J. Accounting for Research & Development. 237p. 1976. text ed. 26.95x (ISBN 0-686-70288-3, Pub. by Busn Bks England). Brookfield Pub Co.

--Advanced Cost Accountancy. 512p. (Orig.). 1978. pap. 21.00x (ISBN 0-7121-0168-3). Trans-Atlantic.

--Domesticated Ducks & Geese. 2nd ed. (Illus.). 1985. 14.75 (ISBN 0-947647-02-3, Pub. by Fanciers Supplies). Longwood Pub Group.

--Lewis Wright's Poultry. (Illus.). 200p. 1984. 32.50 (ISBN 0-946474-10-9). Triplegate.

--Management Accountancy. 5th ed. 896p. 1982. pap. text ed. 37.50x (ISBN 0-7121-1272-3). Intl Ideas.

--Pictorial Poultry Keeping. 2nd ed. 216p. 1980. 15.50 (ISBN 0-904558-50-9). Saiga.

--The Spirit & Influence of Chivalry. 1976. lib. bdg. 59.95 (ISBN 0-8490-2658-X). Gordon Pr.

Batty, J., et al. Industrial Administration & Management. 4th ed. (Illus.). 592p. 1979. pap. 26.95x (ISBN 0-7121-0954-4, Pub. by Macdonald & Evans England). Trans-Atlantic.

Batty, J. Clair & Folkman, Steven L. Food Engineering Fundamentals. 300p. 1983. text ed. 35.45x (ISBN 0-471-05694-4). Wiley.

Batty, M. Urban Modelling. (Urban & Architectural Studies). (Illus.). 384p. 1976. 75.00 (ISBN 0-521-20811-4). Cambridge U Pr.

Batty, Michael & Hutchinson, Bruce, eds. Systems Analysis in Urban Policy-Making & Planning. (NATO Conference Series II, Systems Science: Vol. 12). 605p. 1983. 85.00x (ISBN 0-306-41118-0). Plenum Pub.

Batty, Peter. The House of Krupp. LC 67-14093. 1969. pap. 4.95 (ISBN 0-8128-1232-8). Stein & Day.

Battye, Evelyn. Costumes & Characters of the British Raj. (Illus.). 1982. 12.95 (ISBN 0-03-061461-9). Webb & Bower.

Battye, J. S. Western Australia: A History from Its Discovery to the Inauguration of the Commonwealth. LC 79-670401. 1979. 35.00x (ISBN 0-85564-136-3, Pub. by U of W Austral Pr). Intl Spec Bk.

Baturin, G. N. Phosphorites on the Sea Floor: Origin, Composition & Distribution. (Developments in Sedimentology Ser.: Vol. 33). 344p. 1983. 93.75 (ISBN 0-444-41990-X). Elsevier.

Baty, et al. Bridging Theory & Practice. 96p. 1984. pap. 6.95 (ISBN 0-8403-3421-4). Kendall-Hunt.

Baty, Gordon. Entrepreneurship in the Eighties. 1981. text ed. 19.95 (ISBN 0-8359-1745-2); pap. 16.95 (ISBN 0-8359-1744-4). Reston.

Baty, Jennie S. Twin Rivers. 1980. 12.50 (ISBN 0-682-49459-3, Lochinvar). Exposition Pr FL.

Baty, Roger M. Re-Educating Teachers for Cultural Awareness: Preparation for Educating Mexican-American Children in Northern California. LC 75-173278. (Special Studies in U.S. Economic, Social & Political Issues). 1971. 49.50x (ISBN 0-89197-917-4). Irvington.

--Regional Crafts of Mexico: Book I: Pottery Making. LC 78-104575. (Illus.). 73p. 1983. Repr. of 1978 ed. lib. bdg. 24.95x (ISBN 0-89370-756-2). Borgo Pr.

Baty, Wayne M., jt. auth. see Himstreet, William C.

Batya, Judith, jt. auth. see Penn, Gerald M.

Batygin, K., jt. auth. see Lisitsin, Yu.

Batygin, V. V. & Toptygin, I. N. Problems in Electrodynamics. 2nd ed. 1978. 44.00 (ISBN 0-12-082160-5). Acad Pr.

Batyuk, V. A., jt. auth. see Sergeev, G. B.

Batz, Laila. Banking Language. LC 77-610. (Orig.). 1977. lib. bdg. 12.90 (ISBN 0-914294-67-9); pap. 2.95 (ISBN 0-914294-68-7). Running Pr.

Batzer, Hans & Lohse, Friedrich. Introduction to Macromolecular Chemistry. 2nd ed. LC 78-6175. 297p. 1979. 58.95x (ISBN 0-471-99645-9, Pub. by Wiley-Interscience). Wiley.

Batzler, L. Richard. Journeys on Your Spiritual Path. 1982. 7.95 (ISBN 0-935710-04-3). Hidden Valley.

--Through the Valley of the Shadow: A Guide for the Care of the Dying & Their Loved Ones. 1983. 10.95 (ISBN 0-935710-05-1). Hidden Valley.

Batzler, L. Richard, jt. auth. see Tauraso, Nicola M.

Bau, Iqnatius. This Ground Is Holy: The Provision of Church Sanctuary for Central American Refugees. 288p. (Orig.). 1985. pap. 9.95 (ISBN 0-8091-2720-2). Paulist Pr.

Bau, Mingchien J. Modern Democracy in China: Studies in Chinese Government & Law. 467p. 1977. Repr. of 1923 ed. 25.00 (ISBN 0-89093-060-0). U Pubns Amer.

Bauande, William, tr. see Ferrarius Montanus, Joannes.

Baublitz, E. Raymond. Pop-Pop: An Octogenarian Looks at His Life. 1984. 5.95 (ISBN 0-8062-2232-8). Carlton.

Baublitz, Jacinth I. Relationshift. 216p. (Orig.). 1983. pap. 13.95 (ISBN 0-9610316-0-3). J I Baublitz.

Bauby, Cathrina. Understanding Each Other: Improving Communication Through Effective Dialogue. LC 76-43576. (Illus.). 59p. 1976. pap. text ed. 3.70x (ISBN 0-918970-20-2). Intl Gen Semantics.

Bauch, Kurt. Das Mittelalterliche Grabbild: Figuerliche Grabbilder Des 11.bis 15. Jahrhunderts in Europa. (Illus.). 376p. 1976. 158.00x (ISBN 3-11-004482-X). De Gruyter.

Bauchop, T., jt. ed. see Clarke, R.

Bauchot, M. L., jt. ed. see Whitehead, P. J. P.

Bauchum, Rosalind G. Needs Assessment Methodologies in the Development of Impact Statements. (Public Administration Ser.: Bibliography P 1640). 1985. pap. 2.00 (ISBN 0-89028-330-3). Vance Biblios.

Bauckham, Richard. Tudor Apocalypse. 391p. 1981. 90.00x (ISBN 0-686-79495-8, Pub. by Sutton Courtenay). State Mutual Bk.

Baucom, Marta E. & Causby, Ralph E. Total Communication Used in Experience Based Speech Reading & Auditory Training Lesson Plans: For Hard of Hearing & Deaf Individuals. (Illus.). 160p. 1981. spiral binding 18.50x (ISBN 0-398-04125-3). C C Thomas.

Baud, Charles A. Harmonie der Gesichtszuege. (Illus.). xx, 150p. 1982. pap. 21.00 (ISBN 3-8055-0067-X). S Karger.

Baudelaire. Baudelaire: Selected Poems. rev. ed. Richardson, Joanna, tr. from Fr. (Poets Ser.). 272p. 1975. pap. 3.95 (ISBN 0-14-042188-2). Penguin.

Baudelaire, tr. see Poe, Edgar Allan.

Baudelaire, C. To a Courtesan. (Orig.). pap. 1.95 (ISBN 0-87067-705-5, BA705). Holloway.

Baudelaire, Charles. Art in Paris Eighteen Forty-Five to Eighteen Sixty-Two: Review of Salons & Other Exhibitions. Mayne, Jonathan, ed. LC 81-66146. (Cornell Paperbacks Ser.: Landmarks in Art History). (Illus.). 297p. 1981. pap. 11.95x (ISBN 0-8014-9227-0, Cornell Phaidon Bks.). Cornell U Pr.

--Baudelaire Revisited. Lappin, Kendall E., tr. from French. 1983. Deluxe 25.00 (ISBN 0-87482-120-7); pap. 15.00 (ISBN 0-87482-123-1). Wake Brook.

--Baudelaire's Flowers of Evil & Other Poems. Duke, Francis, tr. 1982. 10.00 (ISBN 0-533-05105-3). Vantage.

--Be Drunk & Athena's Owl. Oshiro, Catherine, tr. from Fr. (Illus.). 1984. pap. 3.00 (ISBN 0-934834-45-8). White Pine.

--Correspondance: Janvier 1832-Fevrier 1860, Vol. 1. 1973. 37.50 (ISBN 0-686-51922-1). French & Eur.

--Correspondance: Mars 1860-Mars 1866, Vol. 2. 1973. 37.50 (ISBN 0-686-51923-X). French & Eur.

--Curiosites Esthetiques, l'art Romantique et Autres Oeuvres Esthetiques. Lemaitre, ed. (Class. Garnier). pap. 16.25 (ISBN 0-685-34098-8). French & Eur.

--Curiosites Esthetiques, l'Art Romantique et Autres Oeuvres Esthetiques. Lemaitre, ed. (Coll. Prestige). 22.65 (ISBN 0-685-34099-6). French & Eur.

--Ecrits sur l'Art, 2 vols. 1971. Set. pap. 7.90 (ISBN 0-686-51926-4). French & Eur.

--Fatal Destinies: The Edgar Allen Poe Essays. Mele, Joan F., tr. from Fr. 1981. pap. 4.95 (ISBN 0-916696-17-0). Cross Country.

--Les Fleurs du Mal, 2 vols. 1857. 32.00x (ISBN 0-685-37409-2). Adlers Foreign Bks.

--Les Fleurs du Mal. Starkie, Enid, ed. (French Texts Ser.). 262p. 1970. pap. text ed. 9.95x (ISBN 0-631-00410-6). Basil Blackwell.

--Fleurs du Mal. (Coll. Prestige). 1961. 29.95 (ISBN 0-685-11190-3). French & Eur.

--Les Fleurs du Mal. (Coll. GF). pap. 4.50 (ISBN 0-685-34101-1). French & Eur.

--Les Fleurs du Mal. Adam, ed. (Class. Garnier). pap. 9.95 (ISBN 0-685-34100-3). French & Eur.

--Les Fleurs du Mal. (Documentation thematique Ser.). (Illus., Fr.). pap. 2.95 (ISBN 0-685-13922-0, 60). Larousse.

--Les Fleurs du Mal. Howard, Richard, tr. from Fr. LC 81-13283. (Illus.). 400p. 1982. 25.00 (ISBN 0-87923-425-3); pap. 13.95 (ISBN 0-87923-462-8). Godine.

--Les Fleurs du Mal. Howard, Richard, tr. from French. LC 81-13283. (Illus.). 416p. 1983. 25.00; pap. 15.95 (ISBN 0-87923-462-8). Godine.

--Flowers of Evil. rev. ed. Mathews, Jackson & Mathews, Marthiel, eds. LC 54-9871. (Fr. & Eng.). 1962. 18.95 (ISBN 0-8112-0249-6). New Directions.

--Intimate Journals. 124p. 1983. pap. 4.95 (ISBN 0-87286-146-5). City Lights.

--Journaux Intimes. pap. 45.00 (ISBN 0-686-50132-2). French & Eur.

--Letters of Charles Baudelaire to His Mother: Eighteen Thirty-Three - Eighteen Sixty-Six. Symons, Arthur, ed. LC 73-153490. (Studies in French Literature, No. 45). 1971. Repr. of 1928 ed. lib. bdg. 52.95x (ISBN 0-8383-1241-1). Haskell.

--Letters of Charles Baudelaire to His Mother, 1833-1866. Symons, Arthur, tr. LC 70-173184. Repr. of 1927 ed. 22.00 (ISBN 0-405-08242-8, Blom Pubns). Ayer Co Pubs.

--Lettres Inedites aux Siens. 1966. 11.00 (ISBN 0-686-51924-8). French & Eur.

--My Heart Laid Bare & Other Essays. Quennell, Peter, ed. LC 75-34313. (Studies in French Literature, No. 45). 1974. lib. bdg. 49.95x (ISBN 0-8383-1870-3). Haskell.

--Oeuvres Completes. 1931-1952. 1 vol. lea. 16.50 (ISBN 0-685-11439-2); pap. 115.00 13 vol. ed (ISBN 0-685-11440-6). French & Eur.

--Oeuvres Completes. Le Dantec, ed. (Bibliotheque de la Pleiade). 45.00 (ISBN 0-685-34097-X). French & Eur.

--Oeuvres critiques: Petits Poemes en Prose. (Nouveaux Classiques Larousse). (Fr). pap. 2.95 (ISBN 0-685-14010-5, 20). Larousse.

--Paradis Artificiels. 1964. pap. 3.95 pocket ed. (ISBN 0-685-11476-7, 1326). French & Eur.

--Paris Spleen. Varese, Louise, tr. LC 48-5012. 1970. pap. 4.95 (ISBN 0-8112-0007-8, NDP294). New Directions.

--Petits Poemes en Prose (Le Spleen de Paris) Lemaitre, ed. (Class. Garnier). pap. 9.95 (ISBN 0-685-34102-X). French & Eur.

--Petits Poemes en Prose (Le Spleen de Paris) Lemaitre, ed. (Coll. Prestige). 29.95 (ISBN 0-685-34103-8). French & Eur.

--Petits Poemes en Prose: Oeuvres Critiques. (Nouveaux Classiques Larousse Ser.). (Fr.). pap. 2.95 (ISBN 0-685-14037-7, 20). Larousse.

--Petits Poemes En Prose: Spleen De Paris. Ruff, ed. (Coll. GF). 1962. pap. 3.95 (ISBN 0-685-11489-9, 1179). French & Eur.

--Selected Flowers of Evil. rev. ed. Mathews, Marthiel & Mathews, Jackson, eds. LC 58-9276. (Eng & Fr). 1946. pap. 4.95 (ISBN 0-8112-0006-X, NDP71). New Directions.

--Selected Poems. Wagner, Geoffrey, tr. from Fr. LC 74-7679. 1974. pap. 2.95 (ISBN 0-394-17831-9, B375, BC). Grove.

--Selected Writings on Art & Artists. Charvet, P. E., tr. 460p. 1981. pap. 19.95 (ISBN 0-521-28287-X). Cambridge U Pr.

--Le Sleende Paris. 1973. pap. 3.95 (ISBN 0-686-51925-6). French & Eur.

Baudelaire, Charles, et al. Baudelaire, Rimbaud & Verlaine: Selected Verse & Prose Poems. Bernstein, Joseph M., ed. 352p. 1983. pap. 6.95 (ISBN 0-8065-0196-0, 67). Citadel Pr.

Baudelaire, Charles P. Baudelaire: A Self-Portrait. Boe, Lois & Hyslop, Francis E., Jr., eds. LC 78-16875. 1979. Repr. of 1957 ed. lib. bdg. 24.75x (ISBN 0-313-20568-X, BASE). Greenwood.

--Baudelaire: A Self-Portrait. Hyslop, Lois B. & Hyslop, Francis E., eds. LC 78-20447. 1981. Repr. of 1957 ed. 24.00 (ISBN 0-88355-827-0). Hyperion Conn.

--Baudelaire As a Literary Critic. Hyslop, Lois B. & Hyslop, Francis E., Jr., trs. LC 64-15067. 1964. 27.50x (ISBN 0-271-73051-X). Pa St U Pr.

--Baudelaire on Poe: Critical Papers. Hyslop, Lois & Hyslop, Francis, trs. (Bald Eagle Ser.). 1952. 19.75x (ISBN 0-271-00317-0, Pub. by Bald Eagle). Pa St U Pr.

--Charles Baudelaire, un poete maudit: Choix de poemes traduits en vers anglais avec une biographie et des notes. LC 77-10245. Repr. of 1942 ed. 18.50 (ISBN 0-404-16301-7). AMS Pr.

--Intimate Journals. Isherwood, Christopher, tr. from Fr. LC 76-48417. (Library of World Literature Ser.). (Illus.). 1978. Repr. of 1930 ed. 14.00 (ISBN 0-88355-532-8). Hyperion Conn.

--The Mirror of Art, Critical Studies. Mayne, Jonathan, ed. LC 77-10247. (Illus.). Repr. of 1955 ed. 32.50 (ISBN 0-404-16303-3). AMS Pr.

--Poemes d'amour de Baudelaire: Avec des documents nouveaux. LC 77-10249. (Illus.). Repr. of 1927 ed. 20.50 (ISBN 0-404-16305-X). AMS Pr.

--The Poems of Charles Baudelaire. Sturm, F. P., tr. LC 77-10250. 192p. Repr. of 1906 ed. 27.50 (ISBN 0-404-16306-8). AMS Pr.

--Selected Critical Studies of Baudelaire. Parmee, D., ed. LC 76-29452. Repr. of 1949 ed. 21.00 (ISBN 0-404-15300-3). AMS Pr.

Baudendistel. Horticulture: A Basic Awareness. 2nd ed. 368p. 1982. pap. text ed. 18.95 (ISBN 0-8359-2895-0); instr's. manual free (ISBN 0-8359-2896-9). Reston.

Baudendistel, Robert. Modern Carpentry. 1984. text ed. 28.95 (ISBN 0-8359-4542-1); instr's. manual avail. (ISBN 0-8359-4543-X). Reston.

Baudendistel, Robert F. Lawn & Garden Construction. 1983. text ed. 22.95 (ISBN 0-8359-3952-9). Reston.

Bauder, Donald C. Captain Money & the Golden Girl: The J. David Affair. (Illus.). 256p. 1985. 15.95 (ISBN 0-15-115501-1). HarBraceJ.

Bauder, Thomas. Write English, Bk. 3. (Speak English Ser.). (Illus.). 64p. (Orig.). 1981. pap. text ed. 4.95 (ISBN 0-88499-686-7). Inst Mod Lang.

--Write English, Bk. 4. (Speak English Ser.). (Illus.). 64p. (Orig.). 1983. pap. text ed. 4.95 (ISBN 0-88499-687-5). Inst Mod Lang.

Baudet, Henri. Paradise on Earth: Some Thoughts on European Images of Non-European Man. Wentholt, Elizabeth, tr. LC 76-21632. 1976. Repr. of 1965 ed. lib. bdg. 23.25 (ISBN 0-8371-8973-X, BAPOE). Greenwood.

Baudet, Henri & Van Der Meulen, Henk, eds. Consumer Behaviour & Economic Growth in the Modern Economy. (Illus.). 283p. 1982. 27.50 (ISBN 0-7099-0646-3, Pub. by Croom Helm Ltd). Longwood Pub Group.

Baudhuin, John. Now about Sex. (Orig.). 1985. pap. 1.15 (ISBN 0-89486-293-6). Hazelden.

Baudhuin, John & Hawks, Linda. Living Longer, Living Better. 120p. 1983. pap. 7.95 (ISBN 0-86683-671-3). Winston Pr.

Baudin. Etudes Historiques et Critiques sur la Philosophie de Pascal, 3 tomes. Incl. Tome I. Pascal et Descartes. 11.95 (ISBN 0-685-34021-X); Tome II. Pascal, les Libertins et les Jansenites. 22.50 (ISBN 0-685-34022-8); Tome III. Pascal et la Casuistique. 11.50 (ISBN 0-685-34023-6). (Coll. Etre et Penser). French & Eur.

Baudin, Maurice. Les Batards Au Theatre En France De la Renaissance a la Fin Du XVIII Siecle. Repr. of 1932 ed. 14.00 (ISBN 0-384-03555-8). Johnson Repr.

Baudis, J. Czech Folk Tales. Repr. of 1917 ed. 17.00 (ISBN 0-527-05600-6). Kraus Repr.

Baudoin, Anne-Marie. Vocabulaire Francais-Anglais De L'automobile: Le Moteur. 174p. (Eng. & Fr.). 1973. pap. 9.95 (ISBN 0-686-56909-1, M-6025). French & Eur.

Baudoin, E. Margaret, et al. Reader's Choice: A Reading Skills Textbook for Students of English As a Second Language. 1977. pap. 8.95x (ISBN 0-472-08100-4). U of Mich Pr.

Baudot, Marcel, et al. Historical Encyclopedia of World War II. Dilson, Jesse, tr. (Cultural Atlas Ser.). 548p. 1980. 24.95 (ISBN 0-87196-401-5). Facts on File.

Baudouin, C. Tolstoi the Teacher. 59.95 (ISBN 0-8490-1218-X). Gordon Pr.

Baudouin, Charles. Contemporary Studies. facs. ed. LC 75-76892. (Essay Index Reprint Ser). 1924. 18.00 (ISBN 0-8369-0002-2). Ayer Co Pubs.

--Power Within Us. facs. ed. LC 68-16905. (Essay Index Reprint Ser). 1923. 15.00 (ISBN 0-8369-0176-2). Ayer Co Pubs.

--Suggestion & Autosuggestion. LC 76-25523. (Educational Ser.). 1920. Repr. 45.00 (ISBN 0-8482-0259-7). Norwood Edns.

--Suggestions & Autosuggestions. 1978. Repr. of 1920 ed. lib. bdg. 45.00 (ISBN 0-8495-0350-7). Arden Lib.

Baudouin, Charles, et al. Studies in Psychoanalysis: An Account of Twenty-Seven Concrete Cases Preceded by a Theoretical Exposition. Comprising Lectures Delivered in Geneva at the Jean Jacques Rousseau Institute and at the Faculty of Letters in the University. Paul, Eden & Paul, Cedar, trs. 1979. Repr. of 1922 ed. lib. bdg. 30.00 (ISBN 0-8495-0532-1). Arden Lib.

Baudouy, Michel-Aime. More Than Courage. Ponsot, Marie, tr. LC 61-13241. (gr. 7 up). 1966. pap. 1.65 (ISBN 0-15-662145-2, VoyB). HarBraceJ.

--Old One-Toe. Ponsot, Marie, tr. LC 59-10944. (Illus.). (gr. 4 up). 1959. 6.50 (ISBN 0-15-257780-7, HJ). HarBraceJ.

Baudrand, D. W., jt. auth. see Muller, G.

Baudrillard, Jean. For a Critique of the Political Economy of the Sign. Levin, Charles, tr. from Fr. lib. bdg. 14.00 (ISBN 0-914386-23-9); pap. 5.50 (ISBN 0-914386-24-7). Telos Pr.

--The Mirror of Production. Poster, Mark, tr. LC 74-82994. 1975. pap. 4.50 (ISBN 0-914386-06-9). Telos Pr.

Baudrillart, Henri. Publicistes Modernes. Mayer, J. P., ed. LC 78-67330. (European Political Thought Ser.). 1979. Repr. of 1863 ed. lib. bdg. 39.00x (ISBN 0-405-11676-4). Ayer Co Pubs.

Baudrillart, Henri J. Jean Bodin et son temps: Tableau des theories politiques et des idees economiques au seizieme siecle. LC 68-58466. (Research & Source Ser.: No. 330). (Fr). 1969. Repr. of 1853 ed. 29.50 (ISBN 0-8337-0188-6). B Franklin.

Baue, Arthur E., jt. auth. see Kreis, David J.

Bauer. Diccionario De Teologia Biblica. 2nd ed. 582p. (Span.). 1976. 38.95 (ISBN 84-254-0360-X, S-50203). French & Eur.

--Products Liability. (The Law in Ohio Ser.). 24.95 (ISBN 0-686-90962-3). Harrison Co GA.

Bauer, jt. auth. see Shea.

Bauer, Armand, tr. see Sallet, Richard.

Bauer, Arnold. Carl Zuckmayer. LC 75-29600. (Literature and Life Ser.). 1976. 12.95 (ISBN 0-8044-2026-2). Ungar.

--Rainer Maria Rilke. Lamm, Ursula, tr. LC 75-163151. (Literature & Life Ser.). 128p. 1972. 12.95 (ISBN 0-8044-2025-4). Ungar.

Bauer, Arnold J. Chilean Rural Society from the Spanish Conquest to 1930. LC 75-2724. (Cambridge Latin American Studies: No. 21). pap. 71.80 (ISBN 0-317-26054-5, 2024421). Bks Demand UMI.

Bauer, Arthur O. Making Mission Happen. 1974. pap. 4.50 (ISBN 0-377-00019-1). Friend Pr.

Bauer, Bertrand, jt. auth. see Chou, Ya-Lun.

Bauer, Betsy. Getting Work Experience: The Student's Directory of Professional Internship Programs. (Orig.). 1985. pap. 7.95 (ISBN 0-440-52815-1, Dell Trade Pbks). Dell.

Bauer, C., et al, eds. Biophysics & Physiology of Carbon Dioxide. (Proceedings in Life Sciences). (Illus.). 480p. 1980. 49.00 (ISBN 0-387-09892-5). Springer-Verlag.

Bauer, C. F. Latin Perfect Endings -ere & -erunt. (LD). 1933. pap. 9.00 (ISBN 0-527-00759-5). Kraus Repr.

Bauer, C. O. Screw Joints in Aluminium Components. 1983. 30.00 (ISBN 0-9911000-3-4, Pub. by Aluminium W Germany). Heyden.

Bauer, C. R. & Peluso, A. P. Basic FORTRAN IV with WATFOR & WATFIV. 1974. 21.95 (ISBN 0-201-00411-9). Addison-Wesley.

Bauer, Camille & Bond, Otto F. Graded French Reader, Deuxieme Etape. 2nd ed. 240p. 1982. pap. text ed. 8.95 (ISBN 0-669-04337-0). Heath.

Bauer, Camille, jt. auth. see Campbell, Hugh D.

Bauer, Camille & Bond, Otto, eds. Graded French Reader: Premiere Etape. 3rd ed. 1978. pap. text ed. 8.95x (ISBN 0-669-00876-1). Heath.

Bauer, Carlos, ed. Cries from a Wounded Madrid: Poetry of the Spanish Civil War. LC 83-18304. xviii, 158p. 1984. text ed. 16.95x (ISBN 0-8040-0421-8, 82-75653, Swallow); pap. 9.95 (ISBN 0-8040-0376-9, 82-75661). Ohio U Pr.

Bauer, Carlos, tr. see Lorca, Federico Garcia.

Bauer, Carol & Ritt, Lawrence, eds. Free & Ennobled: Source Readings in the Development of Victorian Feminism. (Illus.). 1979. 49.00 (ISBN 0-08-022272-2); pap. 20.00 (ISBN 0-08-022271-4). Pergamon.

Bauer, Caroline F. Celebrations: Read-Aloud Holiday & Theme Book Programs. (Illus.). 272p. 1985. 30.00x (ISBN 0-8242-0708-4). Wilson.

--Handbook for Storytellers. (Illus.). 400p. 1977. pap. 15.00x (ISBN 0-8389-0293-6). ALA.

--Handbook for Storytellers. 400p. 1977. 15.00 (ISBN 0-8389-0225-1); pap. 10.00 (ISBN 0-318-13446-2). Assn Library Serv.

--My Mom Travels a Lot. LC 81-2296. (Illus.). 48p. (gr. k-3). 1981. 11.95 (ISBN 0-7232-6203-9); pap. 4.95 (ISBN 0-7232-6249-7). Warne.

--My Mom Travels a Lot. 48p. (ps-3). 1985. pap. 3.95 (ISBN 0-14-050545-8, Puffin). Penguin.

--This Way to Books. 376p. 1983. 30.00 (ISBN 0-8242-0678-9). Wilson.

--Too Many Books! LC 84-7305. (Illus.). (gr. k-4). 1984. 11.95 (ISBN 0-7232-6263-2). Warne.

Bauer, Caroline Feller. My Mom Travels a Lot. (Illus.). (gr. k-3). 1982. incl. cassette 19.95 (ISBN 0-941078-23-X); pap. 12.95 incl. cassette (ISBN 0-941078-21-3); pap. 27.95 4 bks., cassette & guide (ISBN 0-941078-22-1); sound filmstrip 22.95 (ISBN 0-941078-24-8). Live Oak Media.

Bauer, Catherine. Modern Housing. LC 73-11908. (Metropolitan America Ser.). (Illus.). 380p. 1974. Repr. 23.00x (ISBN 0-405-05386-X). Ayer Co Pubs.

Bauer, Catherine K., jt. auth. see Hitchcock, Henry-Russell, Jr.

Bauer, Cathy & Andersen, Juel. The Tofu Cookbook. 1979. 9.95 (ISBN 0-87857-246-5). Rodale Pr Inc.

Bauer, Charles J. To the Moon from Balloon in Two Hundred Years. (Illus.). 305p. 1985. pap. 12.50 (ISBN 0-317-18534-9). Independence House.

Bauer, Charles R., ed. see Weiland, Richard J.

Bauer, Cheryl, jt. auth. see McNutt, Randy.

Bauer, Cornelius. The Battle of Arnhem. (Zebra World at War Ser.: No. 17). 1979. pap. 2.50 (ISBN 0-89083-538-1). Zebra.

Bauer, David. Winning Grants: Leader's Guide. 86p. (Orig.). 1985. pap. text ed. 9.95 (ISBN 0-9614949-4-8). Great Plains.

Bauer, David, jt. auth. see Hein, John.

Bauer, David G., jt. auth. see American Council on Education.

Bauer, Douglas. Prairie City, Iowa: Three Seasons at Home. 330p. 1982. pap. 8.95 (ISBN 0-8138-1329-8). Iowa St U Pr.

Bauer, E. E. Turning Point in China. 248p. 1986. 19.95 (ISBN 0-295-96298-4). U of Wash Pr.

Bauer, E. S. Theoretical Biology. 294p. 1983. text ed. 20.50x (ISBN 963-05-3014-7, Pub. by Kultura Hungary). Humanities.

Bauer, Eddie, Sr., jt. auth. see Satterfield, Archie, Sr.

Bauer, Eddy. The Illustrated World War Two Encyclopedia, 24 vols. 1980. 167.52 (ISBN 0-87475-520-4). Stuttman.

Bauer, Edward E., jt. auth. see Thornburn, Thomas H.

Bauer, Edward L. Statistical Manual for Chemists. 2nd ed. 1971. 39.00 (ISBN 0-12-082756-5). Acad Pr.

Bauer, Erwin. Digest Book of Deer Hunting. LC 79-84930. 96p. pap. 3.95 (ISBN 0-695-81322-6). DBI.

--Saltwater Fisherman's Bible. rev. ed. LC 82-2388. (Outdoor Bible Ser.). (Illus.). 208p. 1983. pap. text ed. 5.95 (ISBN 0-385-17220-6). Doubleday.

Bauer, Erwin & Bauer, Peggy. Camper's Digest. 3rd ed. LC 73-83467. (Illus.). 256p. 1980. pap. 7.95 (ISBN 0-910676-06-2). DBI.

--Digest Book of Camping. LC 79-50064. 96p. pap. 3.95 (ISBN 0-695-81281-5). DBI.

--Digest Book of Cross-Country Skiing. LC 79-84929. 96p. pap. 3.95 (ISBN 0-695-81321-8). DBI.

--Photographing Wild Texas. (Illus.). 144p. 1985. 24.95 (ISBN 0-292-76495-2); pap. 14.95 (ISBN 0-292-76497-9). U of Tex Pr.

--Wildlife Adventures with a Camera. (Illus.). 208p. 1984. 45.00 (ISBN 0-8109-1755-6). Abrams.

Bauer, Erwin A. The Bass Fisherman's Bible. rev. ed. LC 79-7680. (Outdoor Bible Ser.). (Illus.). 1980. pap. 5.95 (ISBN 0-385-14993-X). Doubleday.

--The Cross-Country Skier's Bible. LC 76-52001. (Illus.). 1977. pap. 4.50 (ISBN 0-385-01321-3). Doubleday.

--Duck Hunter's Bible. LC 65-15543. 1965. pap. 4.95 (ISBN 0-385-04373-2). Doubleday.

Bauer, F., et al. Magnetohydrodynamic Equilibrium & Stability of Stellarators. (Illus.). x, 196p. 1984. 40.00 (ISBN 0-387-90966-4). Springer Verlag.

--A Computational Method in Plasma Physics. LC 78-8982. (Springer Ser. in Computational Physics). (Illus.). 1978. 25.00 (ISBN 0-387-08833-4). Springer-Verlag.

Bauer, F. L. & Woessner, H. Algorithmic Language & Program Development. (Texts & Monographs in Computer Science). (Illus.). 520p. 1982. pap. 32.00 (ISBN 0-387-11148-4). Springer-Verlag.

Bauer, F. L., ed. Software Engineering. 1977. pap. 24.00 (ISBN 0-387-08364-2). Springer-Verlag.

Bauer, F. L. & Broy, M., eds. Program Construction: International Summer School. (Lecture Notes in Computer Science Ser.: Vol. 69). 1979. pap. 31.00 (ISBN 0-387-09251-X). Springer-Verlag.

Bauer, F. L. & Samelson, K., eds. Language Hierarchies & Interfaces. (Lectures in Computer Science Ser.: Vol. 46). 1976. pap. 23.00 (ISBN 0-387-07994-7). Springer-Verlag.

Bauer, F. L., et al. Compiler Construction: An Advanced Course. 2nd ed. (Lecture Notes in Computer Science: Vol. 21). 1977. 17.00 (ISBN 0-387-08046-5). Springer-Verlag.

Bauer, F. L., et al, eds. see Grau, A. A., et al.

Bauer, F. L., et al, eds. see Wilkinson, J. H. & Reinsch, C.

Bauer, Frantisek, et al. Isentropic Gas Flow: Tables & Correction Nomograms. LC 62-28534. pap. 160.00 (ISBN 0-317-09432-7, 2019388). Bks Demand UMI.

Bauer, Fred & Reufenacht, Peter. Chilp. LC 72-89351. (Illus.). 24p. (gr. k-4). 1973. 7.95 (ISBN 0-87592-011-X). Scroll Pr.

Bauer, Fred, jt. auth. see Van Buskirk, Robert.

Bauer, Frederick, jt. auth. see Bollinger, Edward T.

Bauer, G., et al. Solid-State Physics. (Tracts in Modern Physics Ser.: Vol. 74). (Illus.). v, 153p. 1974. 46.10 (ISBN 0-387-06946-1). Springer-Verlag.

Bauer, G., et al, eds. Two-Dimensional Systems, Heterostructures & Superlattices: Proceedings of the International Winterschool Mauterndorf, Austria, Feb. 26-Mar. 2, 1984. (Springer Series in Solid-State Sciences: Vol. 53). (Illus.). 290p. 1984. 29.50 (ISBN 0-387-13584-7). Springer-Verlag.

Bauer, G. S. & McDonald, A., eds. Nuclear Technologies in a Sustainable Energy System. (Illus.). 329p. 1983. 29.50 (ISBN 0-387-12154-4). Springer-Verlag.

Bauer, George. Helping Teachers Learn Mathematics: A Competency-Based Content Approach. 288p. 1984. pap. text ed. 14.95 (ISBN 0-8403-3509-1). Kendall-Hunt.

Bauer, George H. Sartre & the Artist. LC 76-88232. pap. 61.50 (ISBN 0-317-26640-3, 2024082). Bks Demand UMI.

Bauer, Gerhard. How to Succeed at Soccer. (Illus.). 128p. 1982. pap. 6.95 (ISBN 0-8069-4148-0). Sterling.

Bauer, Gerhard, jt. auth. see Breitmaier, Eberhard.

Bauer, H. Probability Theory & Elements of Measure Theory. (Probability & Mathematical Statistics Ser.). 1981. 79.50 (ISBN 0-12-082820-0). Acad Pr.

--Wirtschaftsgeschichte. 304p. 1982. 45.95 (ISBN 0-8176-1225-4). Birkhauser.

Bauer, H., ed. see Seminar on Potential Theory, 2nd.

Bauer, H. J., ed. Progress in Multiple Sclerosis Research. (Illus.). 630p. 1980. 52.00 (ISBN 0-387-09867-4). Springer-Verlag.

Bauer, H. W. & Weissbach, L., eds. Forum 1982 Fuer Experimentelle und Klinische Urologie. (Beitraege zur Urologie: Band 3). (Illus.). x, 324p. 1983. pap. 42.75 (ISBN 3-8055-3718-2). S Karger.

Bauer, Hanskurt. Color Atlas of Colposcopy. LC 78-62047. (Illus.). 1979. 45.00 (ISBN 0-89640-031-X). Igaku-Shoin.

Bauer, Harold. Harold Bauer: His Book. LC 76-94577. Repr. of 1948 ed. lib. bdg. 15.00 (ISBN 0-8371-2489-1, BAHB). Greenwood.

Bauer, Heinrich. Vollstaendige Grammatik der neuhochdeutschen Sprache, 5 vols. 1967. Repr. of 1833 ed. Set. 232.00 (ISBN 3-11-000365-1). De Gruyter.

Bauer, Helen. Hawaii: The Aloha State. rev. ed. LC 82-72319. (Illus.). 192p. (gr. 4-7). 1982. 14.45 (ISBN 0-935848-13-4); pap. 11.95 (ISBN 0-935848-15-0). Bess Pr.

Bauer, Henry H. Beyond Velikovsky: The History of a Public Controversy. LC 83-17935. (Illus.). 368p. 1984. 21.95 (ISBN 0-252-01104-X). U of Ill Pr.

Bauer, Henry H., et al. Instrumental Analysis. 1978. text ed. 45.00 (ISBN 0-205-05922-8, 685922). Allyn.

Bauer, J. B. Encyclopedia of Biblical Theology: The Concise Sacramentum Verbi. 1172p. 1981. 39.50 (ISBN 0-8245-0042-3). Crossroad NY.

Bauer, Jeffrey C., jt. auth. see Luke, Roice D.

Bauer, Jeffrey C., jt. auth. see Snyder, Thomas L.

Bauer, Johannes B. Bibeltheologisches Woerterbuch, 2 vols. 3rd ed. (Ger.). 1967. Set. 150.00 (ISBN 3-222-10240-6, M-7308, Pub. by Styria). French & Eur.

Bauer, John. Effective Regulation of Public Utilities. LC 75-39230. (Getting & Spending: the Consumer's Dilemma). 1976. Repr. of 1925 ed. 30.00x (ISBN 0-405-08007-7). Ayer Co Pubs.

Bauer, John, tr. see Lundbergh, Holger.

Bauer, John D. & Ackermann, Philip G. Clinical Laboratory Methods. 9th ed. LC 81-16820. (Illus.). 1235p. 1982. pap. 39.95 (ISBN 0-8016-0508-3). Mosby.

Bauer, Joseph P., jt. auth. see Kintner, Earl W.

Bauer, June B. & Mollah, W. S. Two North Australian Cropping Studies. (North Australia Research Bulletin: No. 7). 191p. 1981. pap. text ed. 8.00 (ISBN 0-909596-67-0, 0100, Pub. by ANUP Australia). Australia N U P.

Bauer, K. & Garbe, D. Common Fragrance & Flavor Substances & Materials. LC 84-26993. 190p. 1985. text ed. 49.75 (ISBN 0-89573-063-4). VCH Pubs.

Bauer, K. & Haller, G. Organometallic Compounds - Models of Synthesis, Physical Constants & Chemical Reactions, Vol. 1: Compounds of Transition Metals. 2nd ed. Dub, M., ed. LC 66-28249. xxvi, 1171p. 1975. 83.00 (ISBN 0-387-07196-2). Springer-Verlag.

Bauer, K. Jack. Zachary Taylor: Soldier, Planter, Statesman of the Old Southwest. Cooper, William J., Jr., ed. (Southern Biography Ser.). (Illus.). 384p. 1985. text ed. 29.95 (ISBN 0-8071-1237-2). La State U Pr.

Bauer, K. Jack, ed. The New American State Papers: Naval Affairs, 1789 to 1860, 10 vols. LC 80-53884. 3000p. 1981. Set. lib. bdg. 600.00 (ISBN 0-8420-2173-6). Scholarly Res Inc.

Bauer, K. Jack, jt. ed. see Coletta, Paolo E.

Bauer, K. Jack, jt. ed. see Gilbert, Benjamin F.

Bauer, K. W. & Ruscheweyh, S. Differential Operators for Partial Differential Equations & Function-Theoretic Applications. (Lecture Notes in Mathematics: Vol. 791). 258p. 1980. pap. 20.00 (ISBN 0-387-09975-1). Springer-Verlag.

Bauer, Karl M. Cystoscopic Diagnosis: Technique & Typical Findings. Mukherjee, K. K., tr. LC 69-15642. (Illus.). pap. 41.80 (ISBN 0-317-07853-4, 2014524). Bks Demand UMI.

Bauer, Laurie. English Word-Formation. LC 82-14693. (Cambridge Textbooks in Linguistics). 330p. 1983. 37.50 (ISBN 0-521-24167-7); pap. 13.95 (ISBN 0-521-28492-9). Cambridge U Pr.

Bauer, Lois M. & Reed, Barbara A. Dance & Play Activities for the Elementary Grades, 2 Vols. (Illus.). 1951-1967. Vol. 1. Gr. 1-3 4.50 (ISBN 0-910354-02-2); Vol. 2. Gr. 4-6 4.98 (ISBN 0-910354-07-3). Chartwell.

Bauer, Maria. Beyond the Chestnut Trees. LC 83-42917. (Illus.). 224p. 1984. 15.95 (ISBN 0-87951-190-7). Overlook Pr.

Bauer, Marion. Sonata for Viola (or Clarinet) & Piano. (Women Composers Ser.: No. 18). 50p. 1985. Repr. of 1951 ed. lib. bdg. 23.50 (ISBN 0-306-76249-8). Da Capo.

--Twentieth Century Music: How It Developed, How to Listen to It. (Music Ser.). 354p. 1978. Repr. of 1933 ed. lib. bdg. 32.50 (ISBN 0-306-79503-5). Da Capo.

Bauer, Marion D. Like Mother, Like Daughter. LC 85-479. 156p. (gr. 5-9). 1985. 11.95 (ISBN 0-89919-356-0, Clarion). HM.

--Rain of Fire. LC 83-2065. 160p. (gr. 4-8). 1983. 10.95 (ISBN 0-89919-190-8, Clarion). HM.

--Shelter from the Wind. LC 75-28184. 112p. (gr. 6 up). 1976. 7.95 (ISBN 0-395-28890-8, Clarion). HM.

--Tangled Butterfly. LC 79-23405. 162p. (gr. 6 up). 1980. 8.95 (ISBN 0-395-29110-0, Clarion). HM.

Bauer, Marion Dane. Foster Child. LC 76-54291. 168p. (gr. 6 up). 1976. 7.95 (ISBN 0-395-28889-4, Clarion). HM.

Bauer, Mary. Simply Entertaining. LC 83-91259. 184p. 1983. pap. 6.95 (ISBN 0-9613619-0-5). M A Bauer.

Bauer, Max. Precious Stones, 2 vols. (Illus.). Set. 32.00 (ISBN 0-8446-1608-7). Peter Smith.

--Precious Stones: A Popular Account of Their Characters, Occurence & Applications. Spencer, L. J., tr. LC 69-12082. (Illus.). 1969. 52.50 (ISBN 0-8048-0489-3). C E Tuttle.

--Precious Stones: A Popular Account of Their Characters, Occurrence & Applications with an Introduction to Their Determination with an Appendix on Pearls & Coral, 2 Vols. Spencer, L. J., tr. (Illus.). 1968. Vol. 1. pap. 6.95 (ISBN 0-486-21910-0); Vol. 2. pap. 7.95 (ISBN 0-486-21911-9). Dover.

Bauer, N. The American Way. 1979. text ed. 22.64 (ISBN 0-03-040741-9, HoltE); tchr's ed. 32.16 (ISBN 0-03-040746-X); wkbk. 6.12 (ISBN 0-03-048426-X); T.E. of wkbk. 10.20 (ISBN 0-03-048421-9); tests (dup. masters) avail. (ISBN 0-03-040751-6). HR&W.

Bauer, N. S., ed. William Wordsworth: A Reference Guide to British Criticism, 1793-1899. 1978. lib. bdg. 42.00 (ISBN 0-8161-7828-3, Hall Reference). G K Hall.

Bauer, Oswald G. Richard Wagner: The Stage Designs & Productions from the Premieres to the Present. LC 82-42889. (Illus.). 288p. 1983. 60.00 (ISBN 0-8478-0478-X). Rizzoli Intl.

Bauer, Otto. Austrian Revolution. Stenning, H. J., tr. LC 70-80243. (Research & Source Works Ser.: No. 424). 1970. Repr. of 1925 ed. text ed. 15.00 (ISBN 0-8337-0189-4). B Franklin.

Bauer, P. T. Dissent on Development: Studies & Debates in Development Economics. LC 70-189158. 1972. 27.50x (ISBN 0-674-21281-9); pap. 8.95x (ISBN 0-674-21282-7). Harvard U Pr.

--Equality, the Third World & Economic Delusion. 304p. 1983. pap. text ed. 7.95x (ISBN 0-674-25986-6). Harvard U Pr.

--Reality & Rhetoric: Studies in the Economics of Development. 192p. 1984. text ed. 15.00x (ISBN 0-674-74946-4). Harvard U Pr.

Bauer, Paul E. & Collicott, Howard E. Entry Vehicle Heating & Thermal Protection Systems: Space Shuttle, Solar Starprobe, Jupiter Galileo Probe. 45.00 (ISBN 0-915928-74-4). AIAA.

Bauer, Paul E., jt. auth. see Collicott, Howard E.

Bauer, Peggy, jt. auth. see Bauer, Erwin.

Bauer, Peter T. Economic Analysis & Policy in Underdeveloped Countries. LC 81-13361. (Duke University Commonwealth-Studies Center Publication: No. 4). xiii, 145p. 1982. Repr. of 1957 ed. lib. bdg. 18.75x (ISBN 0-313-23272-5, BACA). Greenwood.

--West African Trade. LC 67-19585. 1954. 37.50x (ISBN 0-678-06510-1). Kelley.

Bauer, R. & Koslowski, H. J. Chemiefaser-Lexikon. 230p. (Ger.). 1977. 24.95 (ISBN 3-87150-093-3, M-7318, Pub. by Deutscher Fachverlag). French & Eur.

Bauer, R. & Loeschen, R. Chemistry for the Allied Health Sciences. 1980. 28.95 (ISBN 0-13-129205-6); lab manual 16.95 (ISBN 0-13-129213-7); student guide 10.95 (ISBN 0-13-129197-1). P-H.

Bauer, R. A. & Gergen, K. J. Study of Policy Formation. 1971. pap. text ed. 12.95 (ISBN 0-02-901930-3). Free Pr.

Bauer, R. D. & Busse, R., eds. The Arterial System: Dynamics, Control Theory & Regulation. (Illus.). 1978. pap. 30.00 (ISBN 0-387-08897-0). Springer-Verlag.

Bauer, R. F. & Kafka, D. M. United States Federal Election Laws. 1982. loose-leaf 100.00 (ISBN 0-317-30268-X). Oceana.

Bauer, R. S., ed. Surfaces & Interfaces: Physics & Electronics. 650p. 1984. 77.00 (ISBN 0-444-86784-8, I-200-84, North Holland). Elsevier.

Bauer, Raymond A. The New Man in Soviet Psychology. LC 52-5385. (Harvard University, Russian Research Center, Studies: No. 7). 1952. pap. 48.50 (ISBN 0-317-08039-3, 2017683). Bks Demand UMI.

Bauer, Raymond A. & Fenn, Dan H., Jr. The Corporate Social Audit. LC 72-83832. (Social Science Frontiers Ser.). 109p. 1972. pap. 4.95x (ISBN 0-87154-103-3). Russell Sage.

Bauer, Raymond A. & Wasiolek, Edward. Nine Soviet Portraits. LC 79-4609. (Illus.). 1979. Repr. of 1965 ed. lib. bdg. 24.75x (ISBN 0-313-20929-4, BANS). Greenwood.

Bauer, Raymond A., et al. American Business & Public Policy: The Politics of Foreign Trade. 2nd ed. LC 63-8171. (Illus.). 1972. 39.95x (ISBN 0-202-24128-9); pap. 19.95x (ISBN 0-202-24129-7). Aldine Pub.

--How the Soviet System Works: Cultural, Psychological, & Social Themes. LC 56-8549. (Russian Research Center Studies: No. 24). 274p. 1956. 17.50x (ISBN 0-674-41050-5). Harvard U Pr.

Bauer, Raymond B., jt. ed. see Berguer, Ramon.

Bauer, Richard E. The Spirit of the Guard. 122p. 1981. pap. 7.95 (ISBN 0-89279-071-7). R E Bauer.

Bauer, Robert. The New Catalogue of Historical Records: 1898 to 1908-09. 2nd ed. LC 48-1665. 494p. Repr. of 1947 ed. lib. bdg. 19.50x (ISBN 0-8371-9104-1, BAHR). Greenwood.

Bauer, Robert A. The Austrian Solution: International Conflict & Cooperation. LC 81-21916. 217p. 1982. 13.95x (ISBN 0-8139-0903-1). U Pr of Va.

Bauer, Robert A., ed. The Interaction of Economics & Foreign Policy. LC 75-2243. (A Kenyon Public Affairs Forum Publication Ser). 154p. 1975. 10.00x (ISBN 0-8139-0639-3); pap. 2.95x (ISBN 0-8139-0640-7). U Pr of Va.

--The United States in World Affairs Leadership, Partnership, or Disengagement? Essays on Alternatives of United States Foreign Policy. LC 74-14990. (Kenyon Public Affairs Forum Ser.). 136p. 1975. 10.00x (ISBN 0-8139-0593-1); pap. 2.95x (ISBN 0-8139-0637-7). U Pr of Va.

Bauer, Robert F. & Kafka, Doris M. U. S. Federal Election Law: Federal Regulation of Political Campaign Finance & Participation. LC 82-12455. 1982. loose-leaf 100.00 (ISBN 0-379-20743-5). Oceana.

Bauer, Roger. Coping with Stress. 1981. pap. 4.50 (ISBN 0-8309-0313-5). Herald Hse.

Bauer, Ronald S., ed. Epoxy Resin Chemistry. LC 79-21858. (ACS Symposium Ser.: No. 114). 1979. 34.95 (ISBN 0-8412-0525-6). Am Chemical.

--Epoxy Resin Chemistry II. LC 83-6385. (ACS Symposium Ser.: No. 221). 310p. 1983. lib. bdg. 39.95 (ISBN 0-8412-0777-1). Am Chemical.

Bauer, Royal D. & Darby, Paul H. Elementary Accounting. rev. 4th ed. (Orig.). 1973. pap. 4.95 (ISBN 0-06-460150-1, CO 150, COS). B&N NY.

Bauer, S. J. Physics of Planetary Ionospheres. LC 72-15455. (Physics & Chemistry in Space Ser.: Vol. 6). (Illus.). 230p. 1973. 55.00 (ISBN 0-387-06173-8). Springer-Verlag.

Bauer, Stephen, adapted by see Dillon, Robert.

Bauer, Steven. Satyrday. 224p. 1985. pap. 2.75 (ISBN 0-425-07964-3). Berkley Pub.

Bauer, W. German Economic Policy. 1982. lib. bdg. 69.95 (ISBN 0-87700-348-3). Revisionist Pr.

Bauer, W., ed. see Gesellschaft fuer Informatik: 3 Jahrestagung, Hamburg 1973.

Bauer, Walter. Griechisch-Deutsches Woerterbuch zu den Schriften des Neuen Testaments und der uebrigen urchristlichen Literatur. 5th rev. ed. (Gr. & Ger.). 1981. Repr. 43.20x (ISBN 3-11-002073-4). De Gruyter.

--Orthodoxy & Heresy in Earliest Christianity. Kraft, Robert A. & Krodel, Gerhard, eds. LC 71-141252. 360p. 1979. pap. 10.95 (ISBN 0-8006-1363-5, 1-1363). Fortress.

Bauer, Walter, et al, eds. A Greek-English Lexicon of the New Testament & Other Early Christian Literature. Arndt, William F., tr. from Ger. LC 78-14293. (2nd rev. & augmented edition). 1979. lib. bdg. 45.00x (ISBN 0-226-03932-3). U of Chicago Pr.

Bauer, Wolfgang. Change & Other Plays. 237p. 1973. 10.00 (ISBN 0-8090-3403-4); pap. 3.95 (ISBN 0-8090-0750-9). Hill & Wang.

--China & the Search for Happiness: Recurring Themes in Four Thousand Years of Chinese Cultural History. Shaw, Michael, tr. from Ger. LC 76-10679. 1976. 22.50 (ISBN 0-8264-0078-7). Continuum.

--The Golden Caskets: Chinese Novellas of Two Millennia. Levenson, Christopher & Franke, Herbert, trs. from Ger. LC 77-26034. Orig. Title: Die Goldeme Truhe. (Illus.). 1978. Repr. of 1964 ed. lib. bdg. 32.50 (ISBN 0-313-20091-2, BAGO). Greenwood.

Bauer, Yehuda. American Jewry & the Holocaust: The American Jewish Joint Distribution Committee, 1939-1945. LC 80-26035. 522p. 1981. 25.00 (ISBN 0-8143-1672-7). Wayne St U Pr.

--From Diplomacy to Resistance: A History of Jewish Palestine 1939-1945. Winters, Alton M., tr. from Heb. LC 70-105065. (Temple Bks). 1973. pap. 4.65 (ISBN 0-689-70344-9, T24). Atheneum.

--The Holocaust in Historical Perspective. LC 78-2988. (The Samuel & Althea Stroum Lectures in Jewish Studies). (Illus.). 192p. 1982. 18.00x (ISBN 0-295-95606-2); pap. 8.95 (ISBN 0-295-95902-9). U of Wash Pr.

--The Jewish Emergence from Powerlessness. LC 78-25830. pap. 25.80 (ISBN 0-317-26941-0, 2023592). Bks Demand UMI.

--They Chose Life: Jewish Resistance in the Holocaust. LC 73-89085. (Illus.). 64p. (Orig.). 1973. pap. 2.00 (ISBN 0-87495-000-7). Am Jewish Comm.

Bauer, Yehuda & Rotenstreich, Nathan, eds. Holocaust as Historical Experience. 300p. 1981. text ed. 29.50x (ISBN 0-8419-0635-1); pap. text ed. 14.50x (ISBN 0-8419-0636-X). Holmes & Meier.

Bauerfeind, Jack C., ed. Carotenoid As Colorants & Vitamin A Precursors: Technological & Nutritional Applications. LC 80-984. (Food Science & Technology Ser.). 1981. 90.00 (ISBN 0-12-082850-2). Acad Pr.

Bauerie, R., et al, eds. Semantics from Different Points of View. (Springer Series in Language & Communication: Vol. 6). (Illus.). 1979. 31.00 (ISBN 0-387-09676-0). Springer-Verlag.

Bauerle, D; see Hoehler, G.

Bauerle, Rainer, et al, eds. Meaning, Use, & Interpretation of Language. 1983. 66.00 (ISBN 3-11-008901-7). De Gruyter.

Bauerle, Richard E. I, the Prophet. 1981. pap. 6.75 (ISBN 0-570-03835-9, 12YY2800). Concordia.

Bauerle, Richard E. & Kemper, Frederick W. Up to Jerusalem. 1979. pap. 5.95 (ISBN 0-570-03795-6, 12-2777). Concordia.

Bauerle, Ruth. The James Joyce Songbook. LC 81-43329. (Reference Library of the Humanities). 759p. 1984. Repr. lib. bdg. 121.00 (ISBN 0-8240-9345-3). Garland Pub.

--A Word List to James Joyce's "Exiles". LC 80-8487. 240p. 1981. lib. bdg. 48.00 (ISBN 0-8240-9500-6). Garland Pub.

Bauer-Lechner, Natalie. Recollections of Gustav Mahler. Franklin, P., ed. Newlin, D., tr. from Ger. LC 80-834. (Illus.). 241p. 1980. 29.95 (ISBN 0-521-23572-3). Cambridge U Pr.

Bauernfeind, George. Income Taxation: Accounting Methods & Periods. (Tax & Estate Planning Ser.). 1984. 140.00 (ISBN 0-07-004096-6, Shepards-McGraw). McGraw.

Bauers, Mary, ed. see Sverge, Rijk.

Bauersfeld, Karl-Heinz, et al. Track & Field: Text Book for Coaches & Sports Teachers. 2nd ed. Schmolinsky, Gerhardt, ed. Mode, Irene, tr. (Illus.). 400p. 1983. 15.00 (ISBN 0-8285-6039-0, Pub by Sportverlag Berlin GDR). Imported Pubns.

Baues, H. J. Commutator Calculus & Groups of Homotopy Classes. (London Mathematical Society Lecture Note Ser.: No. 50). (Illus.). 220p. 1981. pap. 27.95 (ISBN 0-521-28424-4). Cambridge U Pr.

--Obstruction Theory on the Homotopy Classification of Maps. (Lecture Notes in Mathematics Ser: Vol. 628). 1977. pap. 22.00 (ISBN 0-387-08534-3). Springer-Verlag.

Baues, Hans J. Geometry of Loop Spaces & the Cobar Construction. LC 80-12430. (Memoirs Vol. 230). 171p. 1980. pap. 10.00 (ISBN 0-8218-2230-6, MEMO-230). Am Math.

Baugardner, D., jt. auth. see Elseth, G. D.

Baugh, A., ed. Chaucers Major Poetry. 1963. 28.95 (ISBN 0-13-128223-9). P-H.

Baugh, A., et al, eds. Literary History of England. 2nd student ed. 1967. 55.95 (ISBN 0-13-537605-X). P-H.

--Mechanical Maintenance, Pt. I. (Engineering Craftsmen: No. J1). (Illus.). 1978. spiral bdg. 43.50x (ISBN 0-85083-016-8). Intl Ideas.

Baugh, Albert C. & Cable, Thomas. History of the English Language. 3rd ed. LC 77-26324. (Illus.). 1978. ref. ed. 25.95 (ISBN 0-13-389239-5). P-H.

Baugh, Daniel A. British Naval Administration in the Age of Walpole. (Illus.). 1965. 50.00x (ISBN 0-691-05107-0). Princeton U Pr.

Baugh, G. C., ed. Shropshire, Vol. III. (Victoria History of the Counties of Encland Ser.). (Illus.). 1979. 145.00x (ISBN 0-19-722730-9). Oxford U Pr.

--Victoria History of the Counties of England: Shropshire, Vol. 11. (Illus.). 1984. 98.00x (ISBN 0-19-722763-5). Oxford U Pr.

Baugh, James R. Solution Training: Overcoming Blocks in Problem Solving. LC 79-20717. 256p. 1980. 9.95 (ISBN 0-88289-246-0). Pelican.

Baugh, John. Black Street Speech: Its History, Structure, & Survival. (Texas Linguistics Ser.). 160p. 1983. text ed. 15.95x (ISBN 0-292-70743-6); pap. 7.95 (ISBN 0-292-70745-2). U of Tex Pr.

Baugh, John & Sherzer, Joel. Language in Use: Readings in Sociolinguistics. (Illus.). 350p. 1984. pap. text ed. 20.95 (ISBN 0-13-522996-0). P-H.

Baugh, Ruth E. Geographic Regions of California. (Illus., Orig.). 1955. pap. text ed. 3.95x (ISBN 0-87015-057-X). Pacific Bks.

Baugh, Virgil E. Rendezvous at the Alamo: Highlights in the Lives of Bowie, Crockett, & Travis. LC 85-8570. (Illus.). 262p. 1985. 19.95 (ISBN 0-8032-1190-2); pap. 7.95 (ISBN 0-8032-6074-1, BB 929, Bison). U of Nebr Pr.

Baugh, William H. The Politics of Nuclear Balance: Ambiguity & Continuity in Strategic Policies. LC 82-24995. 320p. 1983. 27.50 (ISBN 0-582-28214-4); pap. 17.95 (ISBN 0-582-28423-6). Longman.

Baughan, E. C; see Dunitz, J. D., et al.

Baughan, Michalina, et al. Social Change in France. 1980. 26.00x (ISBN 0-312-73161-2). St Martin.

Baughan, Peter E. Chester & Holyhead Railway: The Main Line up 1880, Vol. 1. (Railway History Ser.). (Illus.). 17.95 (ISBN 0-7153-5617-8). David & Charles.

--Railways of Wharfedale. LC 76-91236. (Illus.). 1969. 19.95x (ISBN 0-678-05650-1). Kelley.

--A Regional History of the Railways of Great Britain: North & Mid Wales, Vol. 11. LC 79-56255. (Illus.). 208p. 1980. 24.00 (ISBN 0-7153-7850-3). David & Charles.

Baughcum, Allan & Faulhaber, Gerald. Telecommunications Access & Public Policy. Voigt, Melvin J., ed. LC 84-6233. (Telecommunications & Information Science Ser.). 300p. 1984. text ed. 35.00 (ISBN 0-89391-259-X). Ablex Pub.

Baughen, Michael. Breaking the Prayer Barrier: Getting Through to God in Prayer. LC 81-5342. 162p. 1981. pap. 5.95 (ISBN 0-87788-688-1). Shaw Pubs.

--The Moses Principle: Leadership & the Venture of Faith. LC 78-27498. 118p. 1978. pap. 2.95 (ISBN 0-87788-558-3). Shaw Pubs.

--Strengthened by Struggle: The Stress Factor in 2 Corinthians. 128p. 1984. pap. 5.95 (ISBN 0-87788-792-6). Shaw Pubs.

Baugher, Jacob I. Organization & Administration of Practice-Teaching in Privately Endowed Colleges of Liberal Arts. LC 72-176543. (Columbia University. Teachers College. Contributions to Education: No. 487). Repr. of 1931 ed. 22.50 (ISBN 0-404-55487-3). AMS Pr.

Baugher, Joseph F. On Civilized Stars: The Search for Intelligent Life in Outer Space. (Illus.). 288p. 1985. 21.95 (ISBN 0-13-634429-1); pap. 9.95 (ISBN 0-13-634411-9). P-H.

Baughman, Dorothy. Icy Terror. 1984. 8.95 (ISBN 0-8034-8414-3, Avalon). Bouregy.

--Secret of Montoya Mission. (YA) 1981. 8.95 (ISBN 0-686-73950-7, Avalon). Bouregy.

Baughman, Ernest W. Type & Motif-Index of the Folktales of England & North America. 1966. pap. text ed. 44.80x (ISBN 90-2790-046-9). Mouton.

Baughman, Gary L., jt. ed. see Raese, Jon W.

Baughman, James L. Television's Guardians: The FCC & the Politics of Programming, 1958-1967. LC 84-13178. 328p. 1985. text ed. 27.50x (ISBN 0-87049-448-1). U of Tenn Pr.

Baughman, James P. The Mallorys of Mystic: Six Generations in American Maritime Enterprise. LC 70-184363. (The American Maritime Library: Vol. 4). (Illus.). 496p. 1972. 22.50 (ISBN 0-8195-4048-X); limited ed. 40.00 (ISBN 0-8195-4049-8). Mystic Seaport.

Baughman, James P., et al. Environmental Analysis for Management. 1974. 31.95x (ISBN 0-256-01561-9). Irwin.

Baughman, M. Dale. Baughman's Handbook of Humor in Education. 1974. 16.50 (ISBN 0-13-072504-8). P-H.

Baughman, M. Dale, ed. Administration of the Junior High School. LC 66-28866. 74p. 1966. pap. text ed. 2.00x (ISBN 0-8134-6893-0, 6893). Interstate.

--Foreign Language Instruction in the Junior High School Grades. 58p. pap. text ed. 1.50x (ISBN 0-8134-0590-4, 590). Interstate.

--Junior High School Staff Personnel. 114p. 1966. pap. text ed. 1.75x (ISBN 0-8134-6874-4, 6874). Interstate.

Baughman, Martin L., et al. Electric Power in the United States: Models & Policy Analysis. 1979. text ed. 45.00x (ISBN 0-262-02130-7). MIT Pr.

Baughman, Michael. A Full Moon Collage. 1984. 6.95 (ISBN 0-533-05966-6). Vantage.

Baughman, Mike. The Perfect Fishing Trip. 180p. 1985. 14.95 (ISBN 0-13-656984-6); pap. 6.95 (ISBN 0-13-656976-5). P H.

Baughman, Ray. La Vida Abundante. Orig. Title: The Abundant Life. 192p. (Span.). 1959. pap. 3.50 (ISBN 0-8254-1056-8). Kregel.

Baughman, Ray E. Abundant Life. 1959. pap. 2.95 (ISBN 0-8024-0047-7). Moody.

Baughman, Robert W. Kansas in Maps. LC 60-63876. (Illus.). 104p. 1961. 9.95 (ISBN 0-87726-006-0). Kansas St Hist.

--Kansas Post Offices. 2nd ed. LC 62-34174. (Illus.). 256p. 1977. pap. 5.50 (ISBN 0-87726-004-4). Kansas St Hist.

Baughman, Ronald. Understanding James Dickey. (Understanding Contemporary American Literature Ser.). 200p. 1985. 19.95 (ISBN 0-87249-471-3); pap. 9.95 (ISBN 0-87249-472-1). U of SC Pr.

Baughman, SaraL., jt. auth. see Field, Richard.

Baughman, Susan S. & Clagett, Patricia D., eds. Video Games & Human Development: A Research Agenda for the '80s. 72p. 1983. pap. 20.00 (ISBN 0-943484-01-4). Gutman Lib.

Baughn, William H., ed. Advanced Bank Holding Company Management Problems. LC 75-17748. 252p. 1975. pap. 14.95 (ISBN 0-87074-151-9). SMU Press.

Baughn, William H. & Mandich, Donald R., eds. The International Banking Handbook. LC 82-73620. 850p. 1983. 50.00 (ISBN 0-87094-303-0). Dow Jones-Irwin.

Baughn, William H. & Walker, Charls E., eds. The Banker's Handbook. rev. ed. LC 77-89797. 1978. 50.00 (ISBN 0-87094-154-2). Dow Jones-Irwin.

Bauland, Peter. Gerhart Hauptmann's "Before Daybreak". a Translation & an Introduction. (Studies in the Germanic Languages & Literatures: No. 92). xxiv, 87p. 1978. 9.95x (ISBN 0-8078-8092-2). U of NC Pr.

--Hooded Eagle: Modern German Drama on the New York Stage. LC 67-31564. 1968. 19.95x (ISBN 0-8156-2119-1). Syracuse U Pr.

Bauld, Nelson. Mechanics of Materials. 2nd ed. 580p. 1985. text ed. 39.25 (ISBN 0-534-05718-7, Pub. by PWS Enginering). PWS Pubs.

Bauld, Thomas J. Planning, Execution & Evaluation of In-Service Training Programs. (Illus.). 60p. 1983. pap. text ed. 30.00 (ISBN 0-910275-33-5); 20.00. Assn Adv Med Instrn.

Bauldree, John, et al. Biophysical Lab Manual. 1976. spiral bdg. 21.95 (ISBN 0-88252-057-1). Paladin Hse.

Baulieu, E. E. Etude sur le Mode D'Action des Hormones Steroides Sexuelles: Metabolisme Au Niveau des Organes Cibles et Liaison a Des Proteines Specifiques. LC 74-185798. (Cours & Documents de Biologie Ser.). (Illus.). 150p. 1974. 52.00 (ISBN 0-677-50650-3). Gordon.

Baulin, N. Ia. Treasures of the U. S. S. R. Diamond Fund. 1980. 80.00x (ISBN 0-317-14304-2, Pub. by Collet's). State Mutual Bk.

Bauling, Jayne. Valentine's Day. (Harlequin Presents Ser.). 192p. 1984. pap. 1.95 (ISBN 0-373-10663-7). Harlequin Bks.

Bauly, C. B., jt. ed. see Bauly, J. A.

Bauly, J. A. & Bauly, C. B., eds. World Energy Directory. 2nd ed. 600p. 1985. 180.00x (ISBN 0-317-31613-3, Pub. by Longman). Gale.

--World Energy Directory: A Guide to Organizations & Research Activities in Non-Atomic Energy. 600p. 1981. 210.00x (ISBN 0-582-90011-5, Pub. by Longman). Gale.

Baum & Roman, I. Modern Aspects of Medicine, Vol. 3, No. 5. (Illus.). 133p. 1980. 13.25 (ISBN 0-08-027378-5). Pergamon.

Baum, A. & Valins, S. Architecture & Social Behavior: Psychological Studies of Social Density. 128p. 1977. 19.95 (ISBN 0-89859-355-7). L Erlbaum Assocs.

Baum, A. & Epstein, Y. M., eds. Human Response to Crowding. 432p. 1978. 39.95x (ISBN 0-89859-359-X). L Erlbaum Assocs.

Baum, A. & Singer, J. E., eds. Advances in Environmental Psychology: Applications of Personal Control, Vol. 2. 208p. 1980. 29.95x (ISBN 0-89859-018-3). L Erlbaum Assocs.

--Advances in Environmental Psychology: The Urban Environment, Vol. 1. 224p. 1978. 29.95x (ISBN 0-89859-371-9). L Erlbaum Assocs.

--Issues in Child Health & Adolescent Health: Handbook of Psychology & Health. (Vol. 2). (Illus.). 304p. 1982. text ed. 29.95x (ISBN 0-89859-184-8). L Erlbaum Assocs.

Baum, A., jt. ed. see Aiello, J. R.

Baum, Alan. Montesquieu & Social Theory. 1979. 33.00 (ISBN 0-08-024317-7). Pergamon.

Baum, Alan, et al. Applied Calculus. LC 84-19316. 364p. 1985. 25.95 (ISBN 0-471-80306-5). Wiley.

Baum, Andrew, jt. auth. see Gatchel, Robert J.

Baum, Andrew, jt. auth. see Krantz, David S.

Baum, Andrew & Singer, Jerome E., eds. Applications of Personal Control. LC 79-25025. (Advances in Environmental Psychology Ser.: Vol. 2). (Illus.). 208p. 1980. text ed. 29.95x (ISBN 0-89859-018-3). L Erlbaum Assocs.

--Energy Conservation: Psychological Perspectives. LC 81-2820. (Advances in Environmental Psychology Ser.: Vol. 3). 224p. 1981. text ed. 29.95x (ISBN 0-89859-063-9). L Erlbaum Assocs.

--Environment & Health. (Advances in Environmental Psychology Ser.: Vol. 4). (Illus.). 352p. 1982. text ed. 39.95x (ISBN 0-89859-174-0). L Erlbaum Assocs.

Baum, Andrew, et al. Environment & Health. Baum, Andrew & Singer, Jerome E., eds. (Handbook of Psychology & Health Ser.: Vol. 5). 288p. 1985. 29.95 (ISBN 0-89859-680-7). L Erlbaum Assocs.

--Social Psychology. 700p. 1984. text ed. 25.95 (ISBN 0-394-32405-6, RanC). Random.

Baum, Andrew, et al, eds. Handbook of Psychology & Health: Social Psychological Aspects of Health, Vol. 4. Taylor, Shelly E. 1984. text ed. write for info (ISBN 0-89859-186-4). L Erlbaum Assocs.

Baum, B. R. Oats - Wild & Cultivated: A Monograph of the Genus Avena L. (Poaceae) 480p. 1977. 85.00x (ISBN 0-660-00513-1, Pub. by CAB Bks England). State Mutual Bk.

Baum, Mrs. C. L. Studies in Divine Science. 1964. 6.50 (ISBN 0-686-24362-5). Divine Sci Fed.

Baum, Carolyn & Luebben, Aimee. Perspectives in Management: Prospective Payment System. LC 85-61727. (Current Practice Ser.). 150p. 1985. pap. text ed. 14.50 (ISBN 0-943432-52-9). Slack Inc.

Baum, Claude. The System Builders: The Story of SDC. (Illus.). ix, 302p. 1981. 20.00x (ISBN 0-916368-02-5). System Dev CA.

Baum, Dale. The Civil War Party System: The Case of Massachusetts, 1848-1876. LC 83-19687. xviii, 289p. 1984. 29.95 (ISBN 0-8078-1588-8). U of NC Pr.

Baum, Dale D. The Human Side of Exceptionality. LC 81-12956. 296p. (Orig.). 1981. pap. 17.00 (ISBN 0-8391-1693-4). Pro Ed.

Baum, Daniel J. Introduction to Law. (gr. 9-12). 1982. text ed. 4.70 wkbk. (ISBN 0-538-12210-2, L21). SW Pub.

--The Investment Function of Canadian Financial Institutions. LC 72-86435. (Special Studies in International Economics & Development). 1973. 49.50x (ISBN 0-275-28684-3). Irvington.

Baum, Daniel J., jt. auth. see Force, Robert.

Baum, David, jt. ed. see Buckley, Mary.

Baum, David B. & Conason, Robert. Proving & Defending Against Damages in Catastrophic Injury Cases. LC 83-60621. (Litigation & Administrative Practice Ser.). 360p. 1983. 30.00 (ISBN 0-317-12899-X). PLI.

Baum, Doris L. Traditionalism in the Works of Francisco De Quevedo y Villegas. (Studies in the Romance Languages & Literatures: No. 91). 210p. 1970. pap. 11.50x (ISBN 0-8078-9091-X). U of NC Pr.

Baum, E. S., jt. auth. see Pochedly, C.

Baum, Edward & Gagliano, Felix. Chief Executives in Black Africa & Southeast Asia: A Descriptive Analysis of Social Background Characteristics. LC 76-620039. (Papers in International Studies: Africa Ser.: No. 29). (Illus.). 1976. pap. 4.00x (ISBN 0-89680-025-3, 82-91809, Ohio U Ctr Intl). Ohio U Pr.

Baum, Edward, compiled by. A Comprehensive Periodical Bibliography of Nigeria: 1960-1970. LC 75-620025. (Papers in International Studies: Africa Ser.: No. 24). 1975. pap. 13.00x (ISBN 0-89680-057-1, 82-91759, Ohio U Ctr Intl). Ohio U Pr.

Baum, Frank L. Dorothy & the Wizard of Oz. 13.50 (ISBN 0-8446-6141-4). Peter Smith.

--Glinda of Oz. 224p. 1981. pap. 2.25 (ISBN 0-345-28236-1, Del Rey). Ballantine.

--Over the Rainbow. Naden, C. J., ed. LC 79-84151. (Illus.). 32p. (gr. 2-5). 1980. PLB 9.79 (ISBN 0-89375-197-9); pap. text ed. 2.50 (ISBN 0-89375-193-6). Troll Assocs.

--Ozma of Oz. 13.50 (ISBN 0-8446-6180-5). Peter Smith.

--The Wonderful Wizard of Oz. (Children's Illustrated Classics). (Illus.). 159p. 1975. 11.00x (ISBN 0-460-05068-0, BKA 01574, Pub. by J M Dent England). Biblio Dist.

Baum, Frederic S. & Baum, J. Law of Self-Defense. LC 70-127325. (Legal Almanac Ser.: No. 64). 123p. 1970. 5.95 (ISBN 0-379-11070-9). Oceana.

Baum, G. The Earth Shelter Handbook. 15.95 (ISBN 0-937816-13-2). Tech Data.

Baum, G., et al, eds. see Calvin, Jean.

Baum, Gerald L., ed. Textbook of Pulmonary Diseases. 3rd ed. 1983. 95.00 (ISBN 0-316-08386-0). Little.

Baum, Gregory. Journeys: The Impact of Personal Experience on Religious Thought. LC 75-31401. pap. 52.90 (ISBN 0-8357-9486-5, 2013525). Bks Demand UMI.

--The Priority of Labor: A Commentary on "Laborem Exercens", Encyclical Letter of Pope John Paul II. 112p. 1982. pap. 5.95 (ISBN 0-8091-2479-3). Paulist Pr.

--Truth Beyond Relativism: Karl Mannheim's Sociology of Knowledge. LC 77-76605. (Pere Marquette Ser.). 1977. 7.95 (ISBN 0-87462-509-2). Marquette.

Baum, Gregory, ed. Religion & Alienation: A Theological Reading of Sociology. LC 75-28652. 304p. 1976. pap. 7.95 (ISBN 0-8091-1917-X). Paulist Pr.

--Sociology & Human Destiny: Studies in Sociology, Religion & Society. 224p. 1980. 14.50 (ISBN 0-8164-0110-1, Pub. by Seabury). Winston Pr.

--Work & Religion. (Concilium Ser.: Vol. 131). 128p. (Orig.). 1980. pap. 5.95 (ISBN 0-8164-2273-7, Pub. by Seabury). Winston Pr.

Baum, Gregory & Coleman, John, eds. Neo-Conservatism: Social & Religious Phenomenon. (Concilium 1981 Ser.: Vol. 141). 128p. (Orig.). 1981. pap. 6.95 (ISBN 0-8164-2308-3, Pub. by Seabury). Winston Pr.

--New Religious Movements. (Concilium Ser. 1983: Vol. 161). 128p. (Orig.). 1983. pap. 6.95 (ISBN 0-8164-2441-1, Pub. by Seabury); pap. 62.55 10 Volume Subscription (ISBN 0-8164-2453-5). Winston Pr.

--Sexuality, Religion & Society. (Concilium Ser.: Vol.173). 128p. pap. 6.95 (ISBN 0-317-31462-9, 30-30053-1902) (ISBN 0-317-31463-7). Fortress.

Baum, Gregory & Greeley, Andrew, eds. Communication in the Church, Vol. III. (Concilium Ser.). 1978. pap. 6.95x (ISBN 0-8245-0271-X). Crossroad NY.

Baum, Gregory, jt. ed. see Coleman, John.

Baum, Gregory, et al. The Earth Shelter Handbook. (Illus.). 252p. (Orig.). 1980. pap. 12.95 (ISBN 0-937816-05-1). Tech Data.

Baum, Gregory B. & Coleman, John, eds. The Church & Racism. (Concilium Ser.: Vol. 151). 128p. (Orig.). 1982. pap. 6.95 (ISBN 0-8164-2382-2, Pub. by Seabury). Winston Pr.

Baum, Gunter. Basic Values on Single Span Beams: Tables for Calculating Continuous Beams & Frame Constructions, Including Prestressed Beams. (Illus.). 1966. 28.00 (ISBN 0-387-03464-1). Springer-Verlag.

Baum, H. The Biochemist's Songbook. (Illus.). 64p. 1982. pap. 5.50 (ISBN 0-08-027370-X). Pergamon.

Baum, H. & Gergely, J., eds. Molecular Aspects of Medicine, 6 pts, Vol. 1. Incl. Pt. 1. Radioimmunoassay & Reproductive Endocrinology. 1976. pap. text ed. 8.00 (ISBN 0-08-021518-1); Pt. 2. Haemoglobin Structure & Functions: Its Relevance in Biochemistry & Medicine. 1977; Pt. 3. Oedema in the Newborn. Barnes, ed. 1977. pap. text ed. 9.25 (ISBN 0-08-021538-6); Pt. 4. Enzymic Regulation & Its Clinical Significance. 1977. pap. text ed. 9.25 (ISBN 0-08-022642-6). pap. write for info. Pergamon.

--Molecular Aspects of Medicine, Vol. 2. LC 80-40473. (Illus.). 453p. 1980. 77.00 (ISBN 0-08-026355-0). Pergamon.

--Molecular Aspects of Medicine, Vol. 4. (Illus.). 452p. 1982. 165.00 (ISBN 0-08-030007-3). Pergamon.

--Molecular Aspects of Medicine, Vol. 5. (Illus.). 470p. 1983. 162.00 (ISBN 0-08-030429-X). Pergamon.

--Molecular Aspects of Medicine: Vol. 1, Complete. 600p. 1978. 77.00 (ISBN 0-08-020277-2). Pergamon.

Baum, H., et al, eds. Molecular Aspects of Medicine, Vol. 6. (Illus.). 584p. 1984. 162.00 (ISBN 0-08-031724-3). Pergamon.

Baum, Harold. General Biology: Biorhythms, No. 2. Shade, Peter, ed. 67p. 1984. pap. 17.95bk & cassette (ISBN 0-85066-292-3). Taylor & Francis.

--Human Biology: Biorhythms, No. 1. Shade, Peter, ed. 78p. 1984. pap. 17.95 bk & cassette (ISBN 0-85066-291-5). Taylor & Francis.

Baum, Harold & Shade, Peter. Biorhythms 1: Human Biology. 86p. 1984. 17.95 (ISBN 0-85066-291-5). Taylor & Francis.
--Biorhythms 2: General Biology. 86p. 1984. 17.95 (ISBN 0-85066-292-3). Taylor & Francis.
Baum, Herman. House Doctor's Book of Simple Home Repairs. 192p. 1982. pap. 2.95 (ISBN 0-523-41270-3). Pinnacle Bks.
Baum, Hilary, jt. auth. see Baum, Ruth.
Baum, Howell S. Planners & Public Expectations. 306p. 1983. 15.95 (ISBN 0-87073-634-5); pap. 9.95 (ISBN 0-87073-635-3). Schenkman Bks Inc.
Baum, J., jt. auth. see Baum, Frederic S.
Baum, J. D., jt. ed. see Williams, A. F.
Baum, Jay. Umpiring Baseball. (Orig.). 1979. pap. 4.95 (ISBN 0-8092-7476-0). Contemp Bks.
Baum, Joan M. The Theatrical, Composition of the Major English Romantic Poets. (Salzburg Studies in Poetic Drama: No. 57). 1980. pap. text ed. 25.50x (ISBN 0-391-02187-7). Humanities.
Baum, Joanne. One Step Over the Line: A No-Nonsense Guide to Recognizing & Treating Cocaine Dependency. LC 85-42769. 224p. 1985. pap. text ed. 15.95 (ISBN 0-06-250045-7, HarpR). Har-Row.
Baum, Kenneth H & Schertz, Lyle P. Modeling Farm Decisions for Policy Analysis. 500p. 1983. lib. bdg. 21.00x (ISBN 0-86531-589-2). Westview.
Baum, L. F. The Surprising Adventures of the Magical Monarch of Mo & His People. 15.95 (ISBN 0-88411-771-5, Pub. by Aeonian Pr). Amereon Ltd.
--The Wizard of Oz. Scrocco, Jean L., ed. LC 85-8479. (Illus.). 184p. 1985. 14.95 (ISBN 0-88101-018-9). Unicorn Pub.
Baum, L. Frank. Adventures in Oz: Ozma of Oz & Marvelous Land of Oz, The Original Editions Complete & Unabridged. (Juveniles Ser.). 575p. (gr. 2 up). 1985. pap. 9.90 (ISBN 0-486-24880-1). Dover.
--American Fairy Tales. (Illus.). xxi, 224p. 1978. pap. 4.50 (ISBN 0-486-23643-9). Dover.
--American Fairy Tales. (Illus.). 13.25 (ISBN 0-8446-5731-X). Peter Smith.
--By the Candelabra's Glare. LC 80-28443. 1981. Repr. of 1898 ed. 30.00x (ISBN 0-8201-1361-1). Schol Facsimiles.
--Dorothy & the Wicked Witch. Naden, C. J., ed. LC 79-84149. (Illus.). 32p. (gr. 2-5). 1980. PLB 9.79 (ISBN 0-89375-195-2); pap. 2.50 (ISBN 0-89375-191-X). Troll Assocs.
--Dorothy & the Wizard. Naden, C. J., ed. LC 79-84150. (Illus.). 32p. (gr. 2-5). 1980. PLB 9.79 (ISBN 0-89375-196-0); pap. 2.50 (ISBN 0-89375-192-8). Troll Assocs.
--Dorothy & the Wizard in Oz. (Illus.). 256p. (gr. 5-10). 1984. pap. 4.95 (ISBN 0-486-24714-7). Dover.
--The Emerald City of Oz. LC 79-88481. 1985. pap. 2.50 (ISBN 0-345-32028-X, Del Rey). Ballantine.
--Land of Oz. (Classics Ser). (Illus.). (gr. 4 up). 1968. pap. 1.25 (ISBN 0-8049-0181-3, CL-181). Airmont.
--The Land of Oz. LC 79-52645. 1983. 2.25 (ISBN 0-345-31060-8); pap. 2.25 (ISBN 0-345-31060-8). Ballantine.
--The Life & Adventures of Santa Claus. (Illus.). 256p. 1976. pap. 3.95 (ISBN 0-486-23297-2). Dover.
--The Life & Adventures of Santa Claus. (Illus.). 1971. 6.95 (ISBN 0-682-47386-3, Classic). Exposition Pr FL.
--The Life & Adventures of Santa Claus. 11.75 (ISBN 0-8446-5450-7). Peter Smith.
--Little Wizard Stories of Oz. (Illus.). 160p. (ps-4). 1985. Repr. 14.95 (ISBN 0-8052-4005-5). Schocken.
--The Magic of Oz. 256p. 1981. pap. 2.25 (ISBN 0-345-28235-3, Del Rey). Ballantine.
--The Magical Monarch of Mo. (Illus.). 13.00 (ISBN 0-8446-1609-5). Peter Smith.
--The Magical Monarch of Mo. (Illus.). 220p. 1985. pap. 5.95 (ISBN 0-486-21892-9). Dover.
--The Magical World of Oz, 4 vols. (YA) Date not set. Boxed set. pap. 9.00 (ISBN 0-345-29088-7, Del Rey). Ballantine.
--Marvelous Land of Oz. (Illus.). xvii, 287p. (gr. 4-6). 1969. pap. 4.95 (ISBN 0-486-20692-0). Dover.
--Marvelous Land of Oz. (Illus.). 192p. 1985. pap. 2.25 (ISBN 0-14-035041-1, Puffin). Penguin.
--The Marvelous Land of Oz. LC 85-4856. (Illus.). 288p. 1985. 15.00 (ISBN 0-688-05439-0). Morrow.
--The Marvelous Land of Oz. 17.95 (ISBN 0-88411-773-1, Pub. by Aeonian Pr). Amereon Ltd.
--The Marvelous Land of Oz. 13.50 (ISBN 0-8446-6197-X). Peter Smith.
--Master Key: An Electrical Fairy Tale. LC 73-13247. (Classics of Science Fiction Ser.). (Illus.). 256p. 1973. 12.50 (ISBN 0-88355-103-9); pap. 10.00 (ISBN 0-88355-132-2). Hyperion Conn.
--Off to See the Wizard. Naden, C. J., ed. LC 78-84171. 32p. (gr. 2-5). 1980. PLB 9.79 (ISBN 0-89375-194-4); pap. 2.50 (ISBN 0-89375-190-1). Troll Assocs.
--Ozma of Oz. LC 77-89301. (Orig.). 1984. pap. 2.25 (ISBN 0-345-31888-9). Ballantine.
--Ozma of Oz. (Juveniles Ser.). 272p. (gr. 2 up). 1985. pap. 4.95 (ISBN 0-486-24779-1). Dover.
--The Patchwork Girl of Oz. LC 79-88483. 1979. pap. 1.95 (ISBN 0-345-28229-9). Ballantine.
--Policeman Bluejay. LC 81-9044. 1981. Repr. of 1907 ed. 35.00x (ISBN 0-8201-1367-0). Schol Facsimiles.
--The Pop-Up Wizard of Oz. (Windmill Pop-up Bks.). (Illus.). 12p. (ps-2). 1982. bds. 7.95 (ISBN 0-671-44433-6). Windmill Bks.
--The Purple Dragon & Other Fantasies. LC 76-44600. (Illus.). 1976. 8.50 (ISBN 0-934882-01-0). Fictioneer Bks.
--Queen Zixi of Ix: Or, the Story of the Magic Cloak. (Illus.). 231p. (gr. 1-3). 1971. pap. 3.50 (ISBN 0-486-22691-3). Dover.
--Queen Zixi of Ix: The Story of the Magic Cloak. (Illus.). 13.25 (ISBN 0-8446-0026-1). Peter Smith.
--The Road to Oz. LC 79-88480. 1984. 2.25 (ISBN 0-345-31947-8); pap. 1.95 (ISBN 0-345-28227-2). Ballantine.
--Surprising Adventures of the Magical Monarch of Mo & His People. (Illus.). (ps-4). 1968. pap. 5.95 (ISBN 0-486-21892-9). Dover.
--The Tin Woodman of Oz. 272p. 1981. pap. 2.25 (ISBN 0-345-28234-5, Del Rey). Ballantine.
--The Wizard of Oz. (Tempo Classic Ser.). (YA) 1982. pap. 1.95 (ISBN 0-448-16941-X, Pub. by Tempo). Ace Bks.
--The Wizard of Oz. LC 79-52644. 1985. 2.25 (ISBN 0-345-31363-1, Del Rey); pap. 1.95 (ISBN 0-345-28223-X). Ballantine.
--Wizard of Oz. (Illus.). (gr. 4-6). 1956. il. jr. lib. o.p. 5.95 (ISBN 0-448-05826-X, G&D); deluxe ed. 10.95 (ISBN 0-448-06026-4); Companion Lib. Ed. 2.95 (ISBN 0-448-05470-1). Putnam Pub Group.
--The Wizard of Oz. (Illus.). (gr. 2-4). 1984. pap. 1.95 (ISBN 0-590-08604-9). Scholastic Inc.
--The Wizard of Oz. (Bambi Classics Ser.). (Illus.). 224p. (Orig.). 1981. pap. 3.95 (ISBN 0-89531-060-0, 0221-48). Sharon Pubns.
--The Wizard of Oz. (Puffin Classics Ser.). (gr. 3-7). 1983. pap. 2.25 (ISBN 0-14-035001-2, Puffin). Penguin.
--The Wizard of Oz. LC 83-13792. (Looking Glass Library). (Illus.). 64p. (ps-3). 1984. PLB 7.99 (ISBN 0-394-95331-2, BYR); 6.95 (ISBN 0-394-85331-8). Random.
--The Woggle-Bug Book. LC 78-6887. 1978. Repr. of 1905 ed. 30.00x (ISBN 0-8201-1308-5). Schol Facsimiles.
--The Wonderful Wizard of Oz. (Classics Ser.). (gr. 4 up). pap. 1.75 (ISBN 0-8049-0069-8, CL-69). Airmont.
--The Wonderful Wizard of Oz. 139p. 1981. Repr. PLB 15.95x (ISBN 0-89966-347-8). Buccaneer Bks.
--Wonderful Wizard of Oz. (Illus.). vii, 268p. (gr. k-6). 1960. pap. 4.50 (ISBN 0-486-20691-2). Dover.
--The Wonderful Wizard of Oz. 193p. 1981. Repr. PLB 11.95x (ISBN 0-89967-021-0). Harmony Raine.
--Wonderful Wizard of Oz. (Illus.). 13.25 (ISBN 0-8446-1610-9). Peter Smith.
--The Wonderful Wizard of Oz. 15.95 (ISBN 0-88411-772-3, Pub. by Aeonian Pr). Amereon Ltd.
--Wonderful Wizard of Oz Coloring Book. 64p. (ps-2). 1974. pap. 2.50 (ISBN 0-486-20452-9). Dover.
Baum, L. Frank, et al. The Wizard of Oz. LC 82-1109. (Illus.). 232p. (gr. 2-4). 1982. 18.95 (ISBN 0-03-061661-1); signed & numbered, ltd. ed. 100.00 (ISBN 0-03-062426-6). HR&W.
Baum, Lawrence & C Q Press Staff. The Supreme Court. 2nd ed. LC 84-23864. 270p. 1985. pap. 12.95 (ISBN 0-87187-327-3); 17.95 (ISBN 0-87187-343-5). Congr Quarterly.
Baum, Lloyd. Advanced Restorative Dentistry: Modern Materials & Techniques. LC 72-86444. (Illus.). Repr. of 1973 ed. 89.80 (ISBN 0-8357-9531-4, 2012278). Bks Demand UMI.
--Operative Dentistry for the General Practitioner: Some Useful Applications of Pins & Other Materials. (Illus.). 232p. 1974. photocopy ed. 30.50x (ISBN 0-398-03055-3). C C Thomas.
Baum, Lloyd & McCoy, Richard B. Advanced Restorative Dentistry. 2nd ed. (Illus.). 580p. 1984. 39.95 (ISBN 0-7216-1599-6). Saunders.
Baum, Lloyd, ed. Restorative Techniques for Individual Teeth. LC 80-81989. (Masson Monographs in Dentistry: Vol. 2). (Illus.). 224p. 1980. 36.00x (ISBN 0-89352-113-2). Masson Pub.
Baum, Lloyd, et al. Textbook of Operative Dentistry. (Illus.). 450p. 1981. text ed. 35.00 (ISBN 0-7216-1601-1). Saunders.
Baum, Louis. Juju & the Pirate. LC 83-21372. (Illus.). 25p. (gr. k-3). 1984. 9.95 (ISBN 0-911745-14-9). P Bedrick Bks.
Baum, Lyman F. Father Goose: His Book. 1976. Repr. of 1899 ed. 25.00 (ISBN 0-403-06424-4). Scholarly.
Baum, M, jt. auth. see Ray, C.
Baum, M. & Kay, R., eds. Clinical Trails in Early Breast Cancer. (Experientia Supplementum: Vol. 41). 676p. 1983. text ed. 52.95x (ISBN 0-8176-1358-7). Birkhauser.
Baum, Martha, jt. auth. see Rich, Bennett M.
Baum, Maud G. In Other Lands Than Ours. LC 82-10254. 1983. 30.00x (ISBN 0-8201-1385-9). Schol Facsimiles.
Baum, Michael. Breast Cancer: The Facts. (The Facts Ser.). (Illus.). 1981. text ed. 13.95x (ISBN 0-19-261265-4). Oxford U Pr.
Baum, Myra, jt. auth. see Armstrong, Fiona.
Baum, Nathan, jt. auth. see Douglas, Nancy E.
Baum, Paul F. Chaucer: A Critical Appreciation. xi, 229p. Repr. of 1968 ed. 21.50 (ISBN 0-374-90465-0). Octagon.
--Tennyson Sixty Years after. 331p. 1976. Repr. of 1948 ed. lib. bdg. 26.00 (ISBN 0-374-90467-7). Octagon.
Baum, Paull F. see Anderson, Charles R.
Baum, Paull F., ed. see Duke University Library.
Baum, Paull F., ed. see Rossetti, William M.
Baum, R. F. Doctors of Modernity: Darwin, Marx, & Freud. 148p. (Orig.). Date not set. pap. 6.95 (ISBN 0-317-30088-1). Sugden.
Baum, Rainer C. The Holocaust & the German Elite: Genocide & National Suicide in Germany 1871 to 1945. LC 80-25937. 384p. 1981. 29.95x (ISBN 0-8476-6970-X). Rowman.
Baum, Richard. Prelude to Revolution: Mao, the Party, & the Peasant Question, 1962-66. LC 74-23894. 222p. 1975. 24.00x (ISBN 0-231-03900-X). Columbia U Pr.
Baum, Robert J. Ethical Arguments for Analysis. 2nd ed. LC 76-1952. 1976. pap. text ed. 19.95 (ISBN 0-03-089646-0, HoltC). HR&W.
--Ethical Arguments for Analysis: Brief Edition. 2nd ed. LC 78-10770. 1979. pap. text ed. 15.95 (ISBN 0-03-045011-X, HoltC). HR&W.
--Ethics & Engineering Curricula. LC 80-10099. (The Teaching of Ethics Ser.). 79p. 1980. pap. 4.00 (ISBN 0-916558-12-6). Hastings Ctr Inst Soc.
--Logic. 2nd ed. LC 80-11084. 608p. 1980. text ed. 29.95 (ISBN 0-03-046396-3, HoltC); answer key 20.00 (ISBN 0-03-056878-1). HR&W.
Baum, Robert J., ed. Philosophy & Mathematics: From Plato to the Present. LC 73-84704. 320p. 1973. pap. 12.00x (ISBN 0-87735-514-2). Freeman Cooper.
Baum, Ruth & Baum, Hilary. Lifespice Salt-Free Cookbook. (Illus.). 192p. (Orig.). 1985. pap. 9.95 (ISBN 0-399-51093-1, Perigee). Putnam Pub Group.
Baum, S. J. & Young, W. McEwan. Flexible Working Hours: A Practical Guide. LC 73-91148. (Illus.). 190p. 1974. 15.00 (ISBN 0-8155-0521-3). Noyes.
Baum, S. J., ed. Current Methodology in Experimental Hematology. (Bibliotheca Haematologica: No. 48). (Illus.). vi, 418p. 1985. 105.75 (ISBN 3-8055-3722-0). S Karger.
Baum, S. J. & Ledney, G. D., eds. Experimental Hematology Today. (Illus.). 1977. pap. 45.00 (ISBN 0-387-90208-2). Springer-Verlag.
--Experimental Hematology Today 1978. LC 78-8054. (Illus.). 1978. 49.50 (ISBN 0-387-90323-2). Springer-Verlag.
--Experimental Hematology Today 1979. (Illus.). 1979. 79.00 (ISBN 0-387-90380-1). Springer-Verlag.
Baum, S. J., et al, eds. Experimental Hematology Today: 1980. (Illus.). xiv, 342p. 1981. 74.25 (ISBN 3-8055-1705-X). S Karger.
--Experimental Hematology Today 1981. (Illus.). xiv, 250p. 1981. 69.75 (ISBN 3-8055-2255-X). S Karger.
--Experimental Hematology Today, 1982. (Illus.). xx, 270p. 1982. 84.25 (ISBN 3-8055-3486-8). S Karger.
Baum, Sheldon, et al, eds. Atlas of Nuclear Medicine Imaging. (Illus.). 462p. 1981. 81.00 (ISBN 0-8385-0447-7). ACC.
Baum, Stuart, et al. Exercises in Organic & Biological Chemistry. 2nd ed. 1981. write for info. (ISBN 0-02-306540-0). Macmillan.
Baum, Stuart J. Introduction to Organic & Biological Chemistry. 3rd ed. 1981. write for info. (ISBN 0-02-306640-7); pap. write for info. (ISBN 0-02-306580-X). Macmillan.
Baum, Stuart J. & Scaife, Charles W. Chemistry: A Life Science Approach. 2nd ed. (Illus.). 1980. text ed. write for info. (ISBN 0-02-306610-5). Macmillan.
Baum, Susan E. & Cray-Andrews, Martha. Creativity One, Two, Three: Fostering the Creative Potential of Young Children. 7.50 (ISBN 0-89824-076-X). Trillium Pr.
Baum, Thomas. Hugo the Hippo. LC 76-14354. (Illus.). 64p. (ps-3). 1976. 5.95 (ISBN 0-15-237300-4, HJ). HarBraceJ.
Baum, Timothy, jt. auth. see Kaplan, Gilbert E.
Baum, Urban, ed. see Twesten, Gary.
Baum, V. A. Semiconductor Solar Energy Converters. LC 69-17884. 222p. 1969. 35.00x (ISBN 0-306-10830-5, Consultants). Plenum Pub.
Baum, Vicki. Grand Hotel. 1976. Repr. of 1931 ed. lib. bdg. 15.95x (ISBN 0-89190-431-X, Pub. by River City Pr). Amereon Ltd.
--Written on Water. 256p. 1974. pap. 1.50 (ISBN 0-532-15131-3). Woodhill.
Baum, Vicki, jt. auth. see Ogilvie, Elizabeth.
Baum, Vladimir, ed. Energy Planning in Developing Countries. (Illus.). 318p. 1984. 29.95x (ISBN 0-19-828462-4). Oxford U Pr.
Baum, Warren C. The French Economy & the State. LC 82-15539. xvi, 391p. 1982. lib. bdg. 39.95 (ISBN 0-313-23650-X, BAFE). Greenwood.
Baum, Willa K. Oral History for the Local Historical Society. rev. ed. (Illus.). 64p. 1971. pap. 5.00 (ISBN 0-910050-06-6). AASLH Pr.
--Transcribing & Editing Oral History. LC 77-3340. (Illus.). 127p. 1977. pap. 9.00 (ISBN 0-910050-26-0). AASLH Pr.
Baum, Willa K., jt. auth. see Dunaway, David K.
Baumahn, U., jt. ed. see Bobon, D.
Bauman. Alkali- & Alkaline-Earth Metal Oxides & Hydroxides in Water: Solubilities of Solids. (Solubility Data Ser.). 1986. 100.01 (ISBN 0-08-023920-X). Pergamon.
Bauman, Bonnie. Super Reader: How to Teach Your Child to Speed Read. LC 76-56192. 1978. pap. 7.95 (ISBN 0-8128-6044-6). Stein & Day.
Bauman, Chester W. Faith & Works. 1976. pap. 0.95 (ISBN 0-686-15483-5). Rod & Staff.
Bauman, Clarence. The Sermon on the Mount: The Modern Quest for Its Meaning. 420p. 1985. 32.95x (ISBN 0-86554-113-2, MUP/H107). Mercer Univ Pr.
Bauman, David. Test-Taking Skills. (Illus.). 1980. pap. text ed. 135.00 (ISBN 0-89290-185-3, A603-SATC). Soc for Visual.
Bauman, Edward J., ed. Guidance & Control, 1981. LC 57-43769. (Advances in the Astronautical Sciences Ser.: Vol. 45). (Illus.). 506p. 1981. lib. bdg. 60.00x (ISBN 0-87703-150-9, Pub. by Am Astronaut); pap. text ed. 50.00x (ISBN 0-87703-151-7); fiche suppl. 10.00x (ISBN 0-87703-156-8). Univelt Inc.
Bauman, Edward J. & Emsley, Zubin W., eds. Guidance & Control: 1983. LC 57-43769. (Advances in the Astronautical Sciences Ser.: Vol. 51). (Illus.). 494p. 1983. lib. bdg. 60.00x (ISBN 0-87703-182-7, Pub. by Am Astronaut); pap. text ed. 50.00x (ISBN 0-87703-183-5); fiche suppl. 6.00x. Univelt Inc.
Bauman, Edward J., jt. ed. see Culp, Robert D.
Bauman, Edward W. God's Presence in My Life. LC 81-3600. (Journeys in Faith Ser.). 144p. 1981. 7.95 (ISBN 0-687-15444-8). Abingdon.
--An Introduction to the New Testament. 1961. pap. 5.00 (ISBN 0-664-20365-5). Westminster.
--An Introduction to the New Testament. LC 61-10616. 190p. 1979. pap. 5.95 (ISBN 0-664-24279-0). Westminster.
--Life & Teaching of Jesus. LC 60-7038. 240p. 1978. pap. 6.95 (ISBN 0-664-24221-9). Westminster.
Bauman, Elizabeth. Ascuas de Fuego. Patzan, Flora, tr. 128p. (Span.). 1982. pap. 3.95 (ISBN 0-8361-3315-3). Herald Pr.
Bauman, Elizabeth H. Coals of Fire. LC 53-12197. (Christian Peace Shelf Ser.). (Illus.). (gr. 5-9). 1954. 3.95 (ISBN 0-8361-1957-6). Herald Pr.
Bauman, Gustave. Frijoles Canyon Pictographs. (Illus.). 1980. 75.00 (ISBN 0-317-11274-0). Press Pegacycle.
Bauman, Jacqueline A. & Wangler, Hans-Heinrich. Measurements of Sound Durations in the Speech of Apraxic Adults. (Hamburger Phonetische Beitrage Ser.: No. 23). 123p. (Orig.). 1977. pap. text ed. 12.00x (ISBN 3-87118-292-3, Pub. by Helmut Buske Verlag Hamburg). Benjamins North Am.
Bauman, James J. Guide to Issues in Indian Language Retention. 70p. 1980. pap. text ed. 6.95 (ISBN 0-15-599006-3). Ctr Appl Ling.
Bauman, John A., jt. auth. see York, Kenneth H.
Bauman, John F., jt. auth. see Coode, Thomas H.
Bauman, Karl E. Predicting Adolescent Drug Use: Utility Structure & Marijuana. LC 79-22736. 192p. 1980. 35.95x (ISBN 0-03-050636-0). Praeger.
--Research Methods for Community Health & Welfare: An Introduction. 1980. pap. 10.95x (ISBN 0-19-502699-3). Oxford U Pr.
Bauman, Kathleen. On Stage with Johnny Cash. (gr. 6-12). 1975. PLB 6.95 (ISBN 0-87191-486-7). Creative Ed.
Bauman, Louis. The Faith. pap. 2.95 (ISBN 0-88469-026-1). BMH Bks.
Bauman, Mark K. Warren Akin Candler: The Conservative As Idealist. LC 80-22230. 290p. 1981. 18.00 (ISBN 0-8108-1368-8). Scarecrow.
Bauman, Mary K. & Yoder, Norman M. Adjustment to Blindness--Reviewed. (Illus.). 288p. 1966. 26.50x (ISBN 0-398-00116-2). C C Thomas.
Bauman, Mary K., ed. Blindness, Visual Impairment, Deaf-Blindness: Annotated Listing of the Literature, 1953-75. LC 76-14724. 553p. 1976. 39.95 (ISBN 0-87722-067-0). Temple U Pr.
Bauman, Richard. Let Your Words Be Few: Symbolism of Speaking & Silence Among Seventeenth Century Quakers. LC 83-1982. (Cambridge Studies in Oral & Literate Culture Ser.: No. 8). 208p. 1984. 32.50 (ISBN 0-521-25506-6); pap. 9.95 (ISBN 0-521-27514-8). Cambridge U Pr.
--Verbal Art As Performance. 150p. 1984. pap. text ed. 6.95x (ISBN 0-88133-048-5). Waveland Pr.
Bauman, Richard & Abrahams, Roger D., eds. And Other Neighborly Names: Social Process & Cultural Image in Texas Folklore. (Illus.). 332p. 1981. text ed. 25.00x (ISBN 0-292-70352-X). U of Tex Pr.
Bauman, Robert. The Gentleman from Maryland. Date not set. cancelled. Arbor Hse.
Bauman, Robert P. Plants As Pets. (Illus.). 110p. 1982. 9.95 (ISBN 0-396-08021-9); pap. 6.95 (ISBN 0-396-08028-6). Dodd.
Bauman, Thomas. North German Opera in the Age of Goethe. 400p. Date not set. price not set. (ISBN 0-521-26027-2). Cambridge U Pr.
Bauman, Thomas, ed. German Opera Librettos, Seventeen Seventy to Eighteen Hundred, Vol. 18. (German Opera Ser., 1770-1800). 30.00 (ISBN 0-8240-8867-0). Garland Pub.

--German Opera Librettos, Seventeen Seventy to Eighteen Hundred, Vol. 19. (German Opera Ser., 1770-1800). 30.00 (ISBN 0-8240-8868-9). Garland Pub.
--German Opera Librettos, Seventeen Seventy to Eighteen Hundred, Vol. 20. (German Opera Ser., 1770-1800). 40.00 (ISBN 0-8240-8869-7). Garland Pub.
--German Opera, Seventeen Seventy to Eighteen Hundred, Vol. 21. (German Opera Ser., 1770-1800). 40.00 (ISBN 0-8240-8870-0). Garland Pub.
--German Opera, Seventeen Seventy to Eighteen Hundred, Vol. 22. (German Opera Ser., 1770-1800). 40.00 (ISBN 0-8240-8871-9). Garland Pub.
Bauman, Thomas, ed. see Andre, Johann.
Bauman, Thomas, ed. see Benda, Georg A. & Reichardt, Johann F.
Bauman, Thomas, ed. see Dittersdorf, Von & Ditters, Carl.
Bauman, Thomas, ed. see Hiller, Johann A.
Bauman, Thomas, ed. see Salieri, Antonio.
Bauman, Thomas, ed. see Schweitzer, Anton.
Bauman, Thomas, ed. see Sussmayr, Franz X.
Bauman, Thomas, ed. see Umlauf, Ignaz.
Bauman, Thomas, ed. see Vogler, Georg J.
Bauman, Thomas, ed. see Wolf, Ernst W.
Bauman, Thomas, ed. see Zumsteeg, Johann R.
Bauman, Toni & Zinkgraf, June. Spring Surprises. (gr. k-6). 1979. 12.95 (ISBN 0-916456-54-4, GA109). Good Apple.
--Winter Wonders. (gr. k-6). 1978. 12.95 (ISBN 0-916456-29-3, GA89). Good Apple.
Bauman, Toni, jt. auth. see Zinkgraf, June.
Bauman, W. Scott & Klein, Thomas A. Investment Profit Correlation: A Regression Model of Profits from Common Stock Investments. (Michigan Business Reports: No. 55). 1968. pap. 3.00 (ISBN 0-87712-073-0). U Mich Busn Div Res.
Bauman, W. Scott, jt. auth. see Hayes, Douglas A.
Bauman, Wes, et al. Country Kitchen Cookbook. 1981. pap. 9.95 spiral (ISBN 0-8423-0448-7). Tyndale.
Bauman, William. Smart Handicapping Made Easy. pap. 5.00 (ISBN 0-87980-270-7). Wilshire.
Bauman, William A. & Randolph, Therese. Together at Confirmation. LC 72-94177. (Illus.). 96p. (Orig.). 1973. pap. 1.50 (ISBN 0-87793-052-X). Ave Maria.
Bauman, Zygmunt. Memories of Class. (International Library of Sociology). 224p. 1983. 26.95x (ISBN 0-7100-9196-6). Routledge & Kegan.
--Socialism: The Active Utopia. (Controversies in Sociology: No. 3). 1976. pap. text ed. 8.95x (ISBN 0-04-300060-6). Allen Unwin.
--Socialism: The Active Utopia. LC 75-28243. 148p. 1976. text ed. 19.75x (ISBN 0-8419-0240-2). Holmes & Meier.
--Towards a Critical Sociology: An Essay on Commonsense & Emancipation. (Direct Edition Ser.). 1976. pap. 10.95x (ISBN 0-7100-8306-8). Routledge & Kegan.
Baumanis, Vilnis, tr. see Brigadere, Anna.
Baumann. They Travel Outside Their Bodies. (gr. 7 up). 1980. PLB 7.90 (ISBN 0-531-02880-1, B52). Watts.
Baumann, ed. see Lang, Weidmueller.
Baumann, Arthur. The Last Victorians. (Victorian Age Ser). 1927. Repr. 20.00 (ISBN 0-8482-7392-3). Norwood Edns.
Baumann, Arthur A. Last Victorians. facsimile ed. LC 70-104991. (Essay Index Reprint Ser.). 1927. 21.50 (ISBN 0-8369-1445-7). Ayer Co Pubs.
--Personalities. facs. ed. LC 68-54323. (Essay Index Reprint Ser.). 1936. 18.00 (ISBN 0-8369-0177-0). Ayer Co Pubs.
Baumann, Bommi. How It All Began: A Personal Account of a West German Urban Guerilla. Ellenbogen, Hellene & Parker, Wayne, trs. from Ger. Orig. Title: Wie Alles Anfing. 136p. 1977. pap. 5.95 (ISBN 0-88978-045-5). Left Bank.
Baumann, Carl L., tr. see Baegert, Johann J.
Baumann, Cecilia C. Wilhelm Muller: The Poet of the Schubert Song Cycles. LC 80-12806. (Studies in German Literature). (Illus.). 208p. 1981. 24.95x (ISBN 0-271-00266-2). Pa St U Pr.
Baumann, Charles H. The Influence of Angus Snead MacDonald & the Snead Bookstack on Library Architecture. LC 74-171928. (Illus.). 307p. 1972. 16.00 (ISBN 0-8108-0390-9). Scarecrow.
Baumann, Dan. Clearing Life's Hurdles: Workable Solutions to Issues That Affect All of Us. LC 83-21238. 168p. 1984. pap. 3.95 (ISBN 0-8307-0926-6, S381103). Regal.
--Confronted by Love. (Bible Commentary for Laymen Ser.). 144p. 1985. pap. 3.95 (ISBN 0-8307-1050-7, S391101). Regal.
--Which Way to Happiness? LC 81-50302. 144p. 1981. pap. 3.50 (ISBN 0-8307-0773-5, S351100). Regal.
Baumann, Duane. The Recreational Use of Domestic Water Supply Reservoirs: Perception & Choice. LC 69-318025. (Research Papers Ser.: No. 121). 125p. 1969. pap. 10.00 (ISBN 0-89065-028-4). U Chicago Dept Geog.
Baumann, Duane & Dworkin, Daniel. Water Resources for Our Cities. Natoli, Salvatore J., ed. LC 78-59100. (Resource Papers for College Geography Ser.). (Illus.). 1978. pap. text ed. 4.00 (ISBN 0-89291-130-1). Assn Am Geographers.
Baumann, Duane D. & Dworkin, Daniel M., eds. Planning for Water Reuse. 1980. 25.00x (ISBN 0-416-60121-9, NO. 2864). Methuen Inc.
Baumann, Ed, jt. auth. see O'Brien, John.
Baumann, Edward W., jt. auth. see O'Brien, John.
Baumann, Elwood D. An Album of Motorcycles & Motorcycle Racing. (Picture Albums Ser.). (Illus.). 96p. (gr. 5 up). 1982. PLB 9.60 (ISBN 0-531-04469-6). Watts.
--Rip-Roaring Races & Rallies. (Illus.). 128p. (gr. 7 up). 1981. lib. bdg. 8.90 (ISBN 0-531-04344-4). Watts.
Baumann, Friedrich. Sprachpsychologie und Sprachunterricht: Eine Kritische Studie. 142p. 1983. Repr. of 1905 ed. lib. bdg. 45.00 (ISBN 0-89760-055-X). Telegraph Bks.
Baumann, Hans. Chip Has Many Brothers. (Illus.). 26p. (gr. 1-5). 1985. 11.95 (ISBN 0-399-21283-3, Philomel). Putnam Pub Group.
--Mischa & His Brothers. Neumeyer, Peter, tr. from Ger. (Illus.). 32p. (gr. 1 up). 1985. 11.95 (ISBN 0-88138-051-2, Star & Elephant Bks.). Green Tiger Pr.
--What Time Is It Around the World? LC 75-24710. (Illus.). (gr. k-5). 1979. 6.95 (ISBN 0-87592-061-6). Scroll Pr.
Baumann, Hermann. Les Peuples et les civilisations de l'Afrique. LC 74-15010. Repr. of 1948 ed. 42.50 (ISBN 0-404-12005-9). AMS Pr.
Baumann, Horst, ed. see Lang, Weidmueller.
Baumann, J. Daniel. An Introduction to Contemporary Preaching. 1972. 14.95 (ISBN 0-8010-0572-8). Baker Bk.
Baumann, James F. & Johnson, Dale D. Reading Instruction & the Beginning Teacher. (Illus.). 416p. 1984. 21.95x (ISBN 0-8087-4092-X). Burgess.
Baumann, Judy, ed. Community Human Service Centers: Three Successful Experiments. LC 79-18801. (Community & Neighborhood Development Ser.). (Orig.). 1979. pap. 4.95 (ISBN 0-89995-020-5). Social Matrix.
Baumann, Lotte, tr. see Ranke, Kurt.
Baumann, Ludwig. Introduction to Ore Deposits. 1976. 12.50x (ISBN 0-7073-0207-2, Pub. by Scottish Academic Pr Scotland). Columbia U Pr.
Baumann, M. A. & Bahntge, M. A. Legal Keyboarding: Typewriters, Electric Typewriters, Word Processors. 286p. 1985. pap. 14.95 (ISBN 0-471-88590-8). Wiley.
Baumann, Mary A. & Bahntge, Mary A. Legal Terminology & Transcription: Word Processing. 1985. pap. text ed. write for info.; tchrs.' ed. avail. (ISBN 0-471-82042-3). Wiley.
Baumann, N. Neurological Mutants Affecting Myelination. (Inserm Symposia Ser.: Vol. 14). 566p. 1980. 92.00 (ISBN 0-444-80270-3, Biomedical Pr). Elsevier.
Baumann, Oscar. Durch Massailand Zur Nilquelle: Reisen & Forschungen der Massai Expedition Des Deutschen Antisklaverei-Komitee in Den Jahren 1891-1893. (Landmarks in Anthropology Ser). (Illus., Ger). 1968. Repr. of 1894 ed. 37.00 (ISBN 0-384-03560-4). Johnson Repr.
Baumann, P., ed. see International Symposium, Prilly-Lausanne, July 6-7, 1978.
Baumann, Paul. Collecting Antique Marbles. 86p. 1970. pap. 9.95 softbound (ISBN 0-87069-017-5). Wallace-Homestead.
Baumann, Richard G. Retrospective: Lawrence McKinin. (Illus.). 48p. (Orig.). 1983. pap. 5.00x (ISBN 0-910501-01-7). U of Missouri Mus Art Arch.
Baumann, Roland & Wallace, Diane S. Guide to the Microfilm Collections in the Pennsylvania State Archives. 117p. 1980. pap. 5.95 (ISBN 0-89271-013-6). Pa Hist & Mus.
Baumann, Roland, ed. A Manual of Archival Techniques. rev. ed. 150p. 1982. pap. 5.75 (ISBN 0-89271-020-9). Pa Hist & Mus.
Baumann, Roland M., ed. Dissertations on Pennsylvania History, 1886-1976: A Bibliography. LC 79-622900. 80p. 1978. pap. 2.95 (ISBN 0-911124-93-4). Pa Hist & Mus.
--Guide to the Microfilm of the Records of Pennsylvania's Revolutionary Governments, 1775-1790. LC 79-624725. 1978. 11.95 (ISBN 0-911124-96-9); pap. 9.95 (ISBN 0-911124-95-0). Pa Hist & Mus.
Baumann, Winfried. Erinnerung und Erinnertes In Gor'kijs "Kindheit". (European University Studies Ser.: No. 16, Vol. 21). 196p. (Ger.). 1982. 25.80 (ISBN 3-8204-5760-7). P Lang Pubs.
Baumbach, Jonathan. Babble. LC 76-2876. 117p. 1976. 8.95 (ISBN 0-914590-26-X); pap. 3.95 (ISBN 0-914590-27-8). Fiction Coll.
--Chez Charlotte & Emily. LC 79-52033. 1979. 9.95 (ISBN 0-914590-56-1); pap. 4.95 (ISBN 0-914590-57-X). Fiction Coll.
--The Landscape of Nightmare: Studies in the Contemporary American Novel. LC 65-11761. (The Gotham Library). (Orig.). 1965. 22.00x (ISBN 0-8147-0031-4); pap. 13.50x (ISBN 0-8147-0032-2). NYU Pr.
--My Father More or Less. LC 81-71644. 161p. 1982. 11.95 (ISBN 0-914590-66-9); pap. 5.95 (ISBN 0-914590-67-7). Fiction Coll.
--Reruns. LC 74-77780. 1974. 7.95 (ISBN 0-914590-00-6); pap. 3.95 (ISBN 0-914590-01-4). Fiction Coll.
--The Return of Service. LC 79-18102. (Illinois Short Fiction Ser.). 140p. 1979. 11.95x (ISBN 0-252-00784-0); pap. 5.95 (ISBN 0-252-00785-9). U of Ill Pr.
Baumbach, Jonathan & Edelstein, Arthur. Moderns & Contemporaries. 2nd ed. 1977. pap. text ed. 6.95 (ISBN 0-394-31287-2, RanC). Random.
Baumbach, Jonathan & Spielberg, Peter, eds. Statements Two. LC 76-56053. 1977. 8.95 (ISBN 0-914590-36-7); pap. 2.95 (ISBN 0-914590-37-5). Fiction Coll.
Baumbach, Richard O. & Borah, William E. The Second Battle of New Orleans: A History of the Vieux Carre Riverfront-Expressway Controversy. (Illus.). 326p. 27.50 (ISBN 0-8173-4840-9); members 12.95 (ISBN 0-8173-4841-7). Preservation Pr.
Baumbach, Richard O., Jr. & Borah, William E. The Second Battle of New Orleans: A History of the Vieux Carre Riverfront Expressway Controversy. (Illus.). 384p. 1981. 27.50x (ISBN 0-8173-4840-9); pap. 12.95 (ISBN 0-8173-4841-7). U of Ala Pr.
Baumback, C. Baumback's Guide to Entrepreneurship. 1981. 19.95 (ISBN 0-13-066761-7). P-H.
Baumback, Clifford M. Basic Small Business Management. (Illus.). 528p. 1983. 26.95 (ISBN 0-13-066415-4). P-H.
--How to Organize & Operate a Small Business. 7th ed. (Illus.). 608p. 1985. text ed. 27.95 (ISBN 0-13-425646-8); study guide 11.95 (ISBN 0-13-425661-1). P-H.
Baumback, Clifford M. & Mancuso, Joseph R. Entrepreneurship & Venture Management: Text & Readings. (Illus.). 368p. 1975. pap. text ed. 19.95 (ISBN 0-13-283119-8). P-H.
Baume, L. J. The Biology of Pulp & Dentine. (Monographs in Oral Science: Vol. 8). (Illus.). 1979. pap. 41.75 (ISBN 3-8055-3032-3). S Karger.
Baumeister, E. T., ed. Standard Handbook for Mechanical Engineers. 8th ed. 1978. pap. 69.50 (ISBN 0-685-99211-X, E00028); 46.00. ASME.
Baumeister, Theodore. Marks' Standard Handbook for Mechanical Engineers. 8th ed. (Illus.). 1978. 75.00 (ISBN 0-07-004123-7). McGraw.
Baumeister, W. Pflanzenlexikon. 1280p. (Ger.). 1969. pap. 49.95 (ISBN 3-499-16100-1, M-7580). French & Eur.
Baumel, Howard B. Biology: Its Historical Development. LC 77-87937. (Illus.). 1978. 6.00 (ISBN 0-8022-2217-X). Philos Lib.
Baumel, Howard B. & Berger, J. Joel. Biology - Its People & Its Papers. 1973. pap. 5.00 (ISBN 0-87355-002-1). Natl Sci Tchrs.
Baumel, Julian, et al, eds. Nomina Anatomica Avium. LC 78-67890. 1980. 79.00 (ISBN 0-12-083150-3). Acad Pr.
Baumel, Philip, jt. auth. see Semat, Henry.
Baumer, Donald C., et al. The Politics of Unemployment. LC 84-14222. 224p. 1985. pap. 8.95 (ISBN 0-87187-323-0). Congr Quarterly.
Baumer, Franklin L. Main Currents of Western Thought: Readings in Western European Intellectual History from the Middle Ages to the Present. 4th ed. LC 77-90945. 1978. 52.00x (ISBN 0-300-02162-3); pap. 15.95x (ISBN 0-300-02233-6). Yale U Pr.
--Modern European Thought: Continuity & Change in Ideas, 1600-1950. (Illus.). 1978. 15.95 (ISBN 0-02-306450-1). Macmillan.
Baumer, Franz. Franz Kafka. Farbstein, Abraham, tr. from Ger. LC 68-3144. (Literature & Life Ser.). 1971. 12.95 (ISBN 0-8044-2024-6). Ungar.
Baumer, Mary P. Seasonal Kindergarten Units. 1972. pap. 6.95 (ISBN 0-8224-6330-X). Pitman Learning.
Baumer, Rachel & Brandon, James R. Sanskrit Drama in Performance. LC 80-26900. (Illus.). 334p. 1981. text ed. 27.50x (ISBN 0-8248-0688-3). UH Pr.
Baumer, Rachel, ed. Aspects of Bengali History & Society. LC 73-90491. (Asian Studies at Hawaii Ser.: No. 12). 1975. pap. text ed. 10.50x (ISBN 0-8248-0318-3). UH Pr.
Baumer, Terry L. & Rosenbaum, Dennis P. Combatting Retail Theft: Programs & Strategies. 256p. 1984. text ed. 21.95 (ISBN 0-409-95107-2). Butterworth.
Baumer, William. Not All Warriors. facsimile ed. (Essay Index Reprint Ser.). 325p. 1982. Repr. of 1941 ed. lib. bdg. 16.00 (ISBN 0-8290-0790-3). Irvington.
Baumer, William H. Not All Warriors. facs. ed. LC 70-152156. (Essay Index Reprint Ser.). 1941. 19.00 (ISBN 0-8369-2180-1). Ayer Co Pubs.
Baumer, William H., jt. auth. see Darby, William O.
Baumert, Gerhard, et al. German Election Studies, 1961. Hildebrandt, Kai, tr. from Ger. LC 75-40620. 1975. codebk. write for info. (ISBN 0-89138-122-8). ICPSR.
Baumert, J. H., ed. see Alksne, Z. K. & Ikaunieks, Ya Y.
Baumert, John H., jt. auth. see Jackson, Joseph H.
Baumert, L. Cyclic Difference Sets. LC 73-153466. (Lecture Notes in Mathematics: Vol. 182). 1971. pap. 11.00 (ISBN 0-387-05368-9). Springer-Verlag.
Baumgaertner, F., et al, eds. Nukleare Entsorgung: Nuclear Fuel Cycle, Vol. 2. (Illus.). xiii, 352p. 1983. 65.00 (ISBN 3-527-25947-3). VCH Pubs.
Baumgardner, jt. auth. see Perls, Fritz.
Baumgardner, Patricia see Perls, Fritz & Baumgardner.
Baumgardner, Robert W., et al. Formation of the Wink Sink, a Salt Dissolution & Collapse Feature, Winkler County, Texas. (Report of Investigations Ser.: RI 114). (Illus.). 50p. 1982. 1.50 (ISBN 0-686-37544-0). Bur Econ Geology.
Baumgardt, John P. How to Identify Flowering Plant Families. (Illus.). 269p. 1982. pap. 22.95 (ISBN 0-917304-21-7). Timber.
Baumgarner, James, ed. see Levin, Paul.
Baumgart, R. A., jt. ed. see McCuen, Gary E.
Baumgart, W., et al, eds. Process Mineralogy of Ceramic Materials. 229p. 1984. pap. 27.50 (ISBN 0-444-00963-9). Elsevier.
Baumgart, Winfried. Imperialism: The Idea & Reality of British & French Colonial Expansion, 1880-1914. Mast, Ben V., tr. (Illus.). 1982. 29.95x (ISBN 0-19-873040-3); pap. 9.95x (ISBN 0-19-873041-1). Oxford U Pr.
Baumgartel, Elise. Petrie's Naqada Excavation a Supplement. 75p. 1970. text ed. 40.50x (ISBN 0-85388-005-0, Pub. by Aris & Phillips England). Humanities.
Baumgartel, Elise J. The Cultures of Prehistoric Egypt, 2 vols. in 1. LC 80-24186. (Illus.). xxiii, 286p. 1981. Repr. of 1955 ed. lib. bdg. 60.00x (ISBN 0-313-22524-9, BACU). Greenwood.
--The Cultures of Prehistoric Egypt. 189p. 1960. 50.00x (ISBN 0-900416-26-2, Pub. by Griffith Inst). State Mutual Bk.
Baumgartel, Hellmut & Wollenberg, Manfred. Mathematical Scattering Theory. (Operator Theory: Advances & Applications, Vol. 9). 1983. text ed. 44.95 (ISBN 3-7643-1519-9). Birkhauser.
Baumgarten, Alexander & Richards, Frank F. Handbook Series in Clinical Laboratory Science, CRC: Section F, Immunology, 2 pts, Vol. 1. 1978-79. Pt. 1. 63.95 (ISBN 0-8493-7021-3); Pt. 2, 480p. 62.95 (ISBN 0-8493-7022-1). CRC Pr.
Baumgarten, H. E. Organic Syntheses: Collective Volumes, Vol. 5. 1234p. 1973. Vols. 40-49. 59.50 (ISBN 0-471-05707-X). Wiley.
Baumgarten, Henry E., jt. auth. see Linstromberg, Walter W.
Baumgarten, Jon A. & Latman, Alan. Corporate Copyright & Information Practices. LC 83-234204. (Illus.). iv, 200p. Date not set. price not set (Law & Business). HarBraceJ.
Baumgarten, Murray. City Scriptures: Modern Jewish Writing. LC 81-6879. 240p. 1982. text ed. 16.50x (ISBN 0-674-13278-5). Harvard U Pr.
Baumgarten, Murray, tr. see De Ayala, Ramon P.
Baumgarten, Otto, et al. Geistige Und Sittliche Wirkungen des Krieges in Deutschland. (Wirtschafts-Und Sozialgeschichte des Weltkrieges (Deutsche Serie)). (Ger.). 1927. 85.00x (ISBN 0-317-27472-4). Elliots Bks.
Baumgarten, P. M. Henry Charles Lea's Historical Writings. 69.95 (ISBN 0-87968-262-0). Gordon Pr.
Baumgarten, Paul, jt. auth. see Farber, Donald C.
Baumgarten, Sandor. Le Crepuscule Neo-Classique Thomas Hope. 1979. Repr. of 1958 ed. lib. bdg. 40.00 (ISBN 0-8495-0503-8). Arden Lib.
Baumgartmer, Thomas, et al. The Shaping of the Socio-Economic Systems. (Studies In Cybernetics). 369p. 1985. text ed. 56.00 (ISBN 2-88124-003-8); pap. text ed. 24.00 (ISBN 2-88124-027-5). Gordon.
Baumgartner, A. & Reichel, E. World Water Balance. 182p. (Eng. & Ger.). 1975. 95.75 (ISBN 0-444-99858-6). Elsevier.
Baumgartner, Aline & Fisher, Carl, eds. Jesus: Friend, Teacher, Leader. 1986. dupl. masterbook 9.95 (ISBN 0-89837-104-X, Pub. by Pflaum Pr). Peter Li.
Baumgartner, Andreas. William Wordsworth. LC 72-219784. (Ger.). 1897. lib. bdg. 15.00 (ISBN 0-8414-3177-9). Folcroft.
Baumgartner, Anne S. Ye Gods! 192p. 1984. 14.95 (ISBN 0-8184-0349-7). Lyle Stuart.
Baumgartner, Apollinaris W. Catholic Journalism. LC 75-159997. (BCL Ser. I). Repr. of 1931 ed. 11.50 (ISBN 0-404-00693-0). AMS Pr.
Baumgartner, Bernice B. Helping Every Trainable Mentally Retarded Child. LC 75-2494. 1975. pap. 5.00x (ISBN 0-8077-2472-6). Tchrs Coll.
Baumgartner, Dan. The Park Avenue Money Diet: How to Escape from the Middle Class Forever! Moretz, Judith M., ed. LC 83-50234. (Illus.). 240p. 1983. 14.95 (ISBN 0-913221-00-7). Safe Harbor Pr.
--The Park Avenue Money Diet: How to Escape the Middle Class Forever. 1984. 9.95 (ISBN 0-449-90139-4). Fawcett.
Baumgartner, Diane. Melissa. (Orig.). 1980. pap. 4.95 (ISBN 0-89191-233-9). Cook.
Baumgartner, J. S. Systems Management. 522p. 1979. 27.50 (ISBN 0-87179-297-4). BNA.
Baumgartner, James E., et al, eds. Axiomatic Set Theory. LC 84-18457. (Contemporary Mathematics Ser.: Vol. 31). 25.00 (ISBN 0-8218-5026-1). Am Math.
Baumgartner, Keith A. & Schiff, Marty. The Armageddon Color & Game Book. (Orig.). 1984. pap. 2.95 (ISBN 0-939332-14-0). Pohl Assoc.
Baumgartner, M. On Dryden's Relation to Germany. (Studies in Dryden: No. 10). 1979. pap. text ed. 29.95x (ISBN 0-8383-0084-7). Haskell.
Baumgartner, Richard, ed. see Ebelshauser, Gustav.
Baumgartner, Richard A., ed. see Nagel, Fritz.

Baumgartner, Richard A., ed. & intro. by see Rizzi, Joseph N.

Baumgartner, Ted A. & Jackson, Andrew S. Measurement for Evaluation in Physical Education. 2nd ed. 560p. 1982. text ed. write for info. (ISBN 0-697-07194-4); instr's manual avail. (ISBN 0-697-07195-2). Wm C Brown.

Baumgartner, Thomas, ed. Transitions to Alternative Energy Systems. (Replica Edition Ser.). 270p. 1984. softcover 23.50x (ISBN 0-86531-907-3). Westview.

Baumgartner, Victor. Graphic Games: From Pattern to Composition. (Illus.). 160p. 1983. text ed. 16.95 (ISBN 0-13-363333-0). P-H.

Baumgartner, Walter, jt. auth. see Koehler, Ludwig.

Baumgartner, William. Pulse Fundamentals & Small Scale Digital Design. LC 84-6888. 1983. text ed. 32.95 (ISBN 0-8359-5757-8); solutions manual avail. (ISBN 0-8359-5758-6). Reston.

Baumhammers, Andrejs. Temporary & Semipermanent Splinting: An Atlas of Clinical Procedures. (Illus.). 128p. 1971. photocopy ed. 14.75x (ISBN 0-398-00117-0). C C Thomas.

Baumhoff, Martin A., jt. auth. see Heizer, Robert F.

Baumhover, Lorin S. & Jones, Joan D., eds. Handbook of American Aging Programs. LC 76-28641. 1977. lib. bdg. 29.95x (ISBN 0-8371-9287-0, BAA/). Greenwood.

Bauml, Betty J. & Bauml, Franz H. A Dictionary of Gestures. LC 75-3144. 284p. 1975. 18.00 (ISBN 0-8108-0863-3). Scarecrow.

Bauml, Franz H., jt. auth. see Bauml, Betty J.

Bauml, Franz H., ed. Kudrun: Die Handschrift. (Ger). 1969. 55.20x (ISBN 3-11-000376-7). De Gruyter.

Baumler, Ernest. Paul Ehrlich, Scientist for Life: A Biography. Edwards, Grant, tr. from Ger. 304p. 1984. text ed. 39.50x (ISBN 0-8419-0837-0). Holmes & Meier.

Baumol, Hilda & Baumol, William J., eds. Inflation & the Performing Arts. 200p. 1984. 25.00x (ISBN 0-8147-1044-1). NYU Pr.

Baumol, W. Economic Theory & Operations Analysis. 4th ed. 1977. 32.95 (ISBN 0-13-227132-X). P-H.

Baumol, W. J. Performing Arts, the Economic Dilemma. LC 77-16008. Repr. of 1966 ed. 35.00 (ISBN 0-527-02813-4). Kraus Repr.

Baumol, William. Growth, Environment & Public Policy. 57p. 4.00 (ISBN 0-318-16276-8, G-1). Public Int Econ.

Baumol, William G. & Bowen, William G. Performing Arts: The Economic Dilemma. 1968. pap. 14.50x (ISBN 0-262-52011-7). MIT Pr.

Baumol, William J. Economic Dynamics. 3rd ed. (Illus.). 1970. text ed. write for info. (ISBN 0-02-306660-1, 30666). Macmillan.

--Stock Market & Economic Efficiency. LC 65-24469. (Millar Lecture Ser.: No. 6). xiv, 95p. 1965. 8.00 (ISBN 0-8232-0660-2). Fordham.

Baumol, William J. & Blinder, Alan S. Economics: Principles & Policy. 3rd ed. 893p. 1985. text ed. 30.95 (ISBN 0-15-518841-0, HC); study guide 9.95 (ISBN 0-15-518842-9); instr's. manual avail. (ISBN 0-15-518844-5); test bank avail. (ISBN 0-15-518845-3); transparency masters avail. (ISBN 0-15-518846-1). HarBraceJ.

Baumol, William J. & Panzar, John C. Contestable Markets & the Theory of Industry Structure. 510p. 1982. text ed. 34.95 (ISBN 0-15-513910-X, HC). HarBraceJ.

Baumol, William J see Knorr, Klaus E.

Baumol, William J. & McLennan, Kenneth, eds. Productivity, Growth & U. S. Competitiveness. (CED Supplementary Paper). 240p. 1985. lib. bdg. 19.95 (ISBN 0-87186-245-X). Comm Econ Dev.

--Productivity, Growth & U.S. Competitiveness. 1985. 19.95x (ISBN 0-19-503526-7). Oxford U Pr.

Baumol, William J., jt. ed. see Baumol, Hilda.

Baumol, William J., et al. Economics, Environmental Policy & the Quality of Life. 1979. 24.95 (ISBN 0-13-231365-0); pap. 18.95 (ISBN 0-13-231357-X). P-H.

Baumont, Maurice. The Origins of the Second World War. Ferguson, Simone D., tr. LC 77-16652. 1978. 33.00x (ISBN 0-300-02215-8). Yale U Pr.

Baumrin, Bernard & Freedman, Benjamin. Moral Responsibility & the Professions. LC 83-83296. (Professional Ethics Ser.). 400p. (Orig.). 1983. pap. text ed. 20.50 (ISBN 0-930586-10-7). Haven Pubns.

Baums, Roosevelt. A Minority View of How to Campaign for Political Office. Augst, Nancy & Mathews, Michelle, eds. (Illus.). 76p. (Orig.). 1982. pap. 4.95 (ISBN 0-934138-00-1). Rosey-Royce.

--My Children's Struggles. Ellis, Edwin A. & Michels, Joanne, eds. LC 82-60222. 126p. 1983. pap. 2.25 (ISBN 0-934138-02-8). Rosey-Royce.

Baumslag, C. B. & Chandler, B. Group Theory. LC 68-6033. (Schaum's Outline Ser). (Illus.). 1968. pap. 8.95 (ISBN 0-07-004124-5). McGraw.

Baumslag, G., ed. see Magnus, W.

Baumslag, Gilbert. Lecture Notes on Nilpotent Groups. LC 78-145636. (CBMS Regional Conference Series in Mathematics: No. 2). 73p. 1971. 10.00 (ISBN 0-8218-1651-9, CBMS-2). Am Math.

Baumstark, Anton. Festbrevier und Kirchenjahr der Syrischen Jakobiten. Repr. of 1910 ed. 22.00 (ISBN 0-384-03575-2). Johnson Repr.

--Die Modestianischen und Die Konstantinischen Bauten Am Heiligen Grabe Zu Jerusalem. Repr. of 1915 ed. 15.00 (ISBN 0-384-03585-X). Johnson Repr.

Baumstark, Reinhold. Masterpieces from the Collection of the Princes of Liechtenstein. Wolf, Robert E., tr. from Ger. LC 80-18070. (Illus.). 322p. 1981. 100.00 (ISBN 0-933920-09-1). Hudson Hills.

Baumwoll, Dennis & Saitz, Robert L. Advanced Reading & Writing: Exercises in English As a Second Language. 2nd ed. LC 77-16446. 1978. text ed. 13.95 (ISBN 0-03-089946-X, HoltC). HR&W.

Baun, Elizabeth. T. S. Eliot Als Kritiker. (Salzburg Studies in Elizabethan Literature: Poetic Drama Ser.: No. 58). 1980. pap. text ed. 25.50x (ISBN 0-391-01906-6). Humanities.

Baun, L. Frank. The Wonderful Wizard of Oz. 1984. pap. 2.25 (ISBN 0-451-51864-0, Sig Classics). NAL.

Baunach, Phyllis J. Mothers in Prison. 172p. 1985. 19.95 (ISBN 0-88738-027-1). Transaction Bks.

Baunach, Phyllis J., jt. ed. see Price, Barbara R.

Baur, Arthur, tr. see Wodehouse, P. G.

Baur, Benedict. Frequent Confession. 224p. 1980. 7.00 (ISBN 0-906127-20-3). Lumen Christi.

Baur, F. J., ed. Bird Control in Plants: It's a Flying Shame. LC 81-71370. 90p. 1982. pap. text ed. 14.00 (ISBN 0-913250-27-9); pap. text ed. 12.00 members. Am Assn Cereal Chem.

--Insect Management for Food Storage & Processing. 384p. 1984. 65.00 (ISBN 0-913250-38-4). Am Assn Cereal Chem.

Baur, Ferdinand C. The Church History of the First Three Centuries, 2 vols. Menzies, A., ed. 1980. lib. bdg. 199.75 (ISBN 0-8490-3146-X). Gordon Pr.

Baur, Francis. Life in Abundance: A Contemporary Spirituality. 240p. 1983. pap. 7.95 (ISBN 0-8091-2507-2). Paulist Pr.

Baur, George. Helping Children Learn Mathematics: A Competency-Bases Laboratory Approach. 2nd ed. 352p. 1985. pap. text ed. 18.95 (ISBN 0-8403-3462-1). Kendall-Hunt.

Baur, Harry. Flying Mystique. 1982. 10.95 (ISBN 0-02-507920-4). Macmillan.

Baur, John. The Inlander: The Life & Work of Charles Burchfield, 1893-1967. LC 80-51780. (Illus.). 288p. 1981. 50.00 (ISBN 0-8453-4734-9). Cornwall Bks.

--Music Theory Through Literature, Vol. I. (Illus.). 350p. 1985. text ed. 24.95 (ISBN 0-13-607821-4); wkbk. 15.95 (ISBN 0-13-607839-7). P-H.

--Music Theory Through Literature, Vol. II. (Illus.). 400p. 1985. text ed. 24.95 (ISBN 0-13-607847-8); wkbk. 14.95 (ISBN 0-13-607854-0). P-H.

Baur, John E. Dogs on the Frontier. LC 82-12765. (Other Dog Bks.). (Illus.). 1985. pap. 9.95 (ISBN 0-87714-101-0). Denlingers.

Baur, John I. American Painting, 1900-1976. LC 75-27361. (Illus.). 102p. 1976. pap. 6.00 (ISBN 0-89062-022-9, Pub. by Katonah Gallery.). Pub Ctr Cult Res.

--American Painting 1900-1976. LC 75-27361. (Illus.). 96p. 1975. pap. 6.95 (ISBN 0-89062-022-9). Katonah Gal.

--The Inlander: Life & Work of Charles Burchfield, 1893-1967. LC 80-51780. (Illus.). 208p. 1982. 50.00 (ISBN 0-87413-186-3). U Delaware Pr.

Baur, John I., ed. see Whittredge, Worthington.

Baur, John I., et al. Masterpieces of American Painting from the Brooklyn Museum. LC 76-8976. (Illus.). 98p. (Orig.). 1976. pap. 2.50 (ISBN 0-87273-059-X). Bklyn Mus.

Baur, Karla, jt. auth. see Crooks, Robert.

Baur, P. V. Catalogue of the Rebecca Darlington Stoddard Collection of Greek & Roman Vases. LC 78-63552. (Yale Oriental Ser. Researches: 8). Repr. of 1922 ed. 74.50 (ISBN 0-404-60278-9). AMS Pr.

--Preliminary Catalogue of the Rebecca Darlington Stoddard Collection of Greek & Italian Vases. 1914. pap. 29.50x (ISBN 0-686-51289-8). Elliots Bks.

Baur, P. V., jt. auth. see Hopkins, C.

Baur, R. Morphometry of the Placental Exchange Area. LC 77-3148. (Advances in Anatomy, Embryology & Cell Biology: Vol. 53, No. 1). 1977. pap. 22.00 (ISBN 0-387-08159-3). Springer-Verlag.

Baur, Rupprecht S., et al. Resuemierende Auswahlbibliographie Zur Neueren Sowjetischen Sprachlehrforschung (Gesteuerter Fremdsprachenerwerb) (Language & Literary Ser. in Eastern Europe: No. 3). lxviii, 318p. 1980. 43.00x (ISBN 90-272-1504-9). Benjamins North Am.

Baur, W. & Schilling, G. Audiovisuelle Medien im Sport - Schriftenreihe der ETS. (STSM Ser.: No. 27). 424p. (Ger.). 1980. pap. 38.95x (ISBN 0-8176-1157-6). Birkhauser.

Baus, Herb. Best Restaurants Orange County. rev., exp. ed. LC 84-7491. (Best Restaurants Ser.). (Illus.). 240p. 1984. pap. 4.95 (ISBN -089286-235-1). One Hund One Prods.

Baus, Herbert M. The Experts Crossword Puzzle Dictionary. LC 72-84960. pap. 6.95 (ISBN 0-385-04788-6, Dolp). Doubleday.

--The Master Crossword Puzzle Dictionary. LC 79-7681. 1981. 29.95 (ISBN 0-385-15118-7). Doubleday.

Bausch, Michael & Duck, Ruth. Everflowing Streams. LC 81-701. 96p. (Orig.). 1981. pap. 3.95 (ISBN 0-8298-0428-5). Pilgrim NY.

Bausch, Richard. Last Good Time. LC 84-4940. 240p. 1984. 14.95 (ISBN 0-385-27231-6, Dial). Doubleday.

Bausch, Robert. The Lives of Riley Chance. LC 83-16037. 304p. 1984. 14.95 (ISBN 0-312-48889-0). St Martin.

--On the Way Home. LC 81-18227. 260p. 1982. 13.95 (ISBN 0-312-58459-8). St Martin.

--On the Way Home. 240p. 1983. pap. 3.50 (ISBN 0-380-63131-8, 63131-8, Bard). Avon.

Bausch, Thomas. The Spiritual Exercises & Today's CLC: Making the Exercises Come to Life. 24p. 1973. pap. text ed. 1.50x (ISBN 0-913605-01-8). NFCLC.

Bausch, Thomas A. The Spiritual Exercises & CLC: The Role of the Exercises in Today's CLC's. 24p. 1973. pap. text ed. 1.50x (ISBN 0-913605-00-X). NFCLC.

Bausch, William. A New Look at the Sacraments. 2nd ed. 288p. 1983. pap. 5.95 (ISBN 0-89622-174-1). Twenty-Third.

Bausch, William J. Ministry: Traditions, Tensions, Transitions. LC 81-86345. 192p. 1982. pap. 7.95 (ISBN 0-89622-153-9). Twenty-Third.

--Pilgrim Church. LC 73-6608. 560p. 1980. pap. 9.95 (ISBN 0-89622-140-7). Twenty-Third.

--Storytelling, Imagination & Faith. 240p. (Orig.). 1984. pap. 7.95 (ISBN 0-89622-199-7). Twenty-Third.

Bauschatz, Paul C. The Well & the Tree: World & Time in Early Germanic Culture. LC 81-14766. 280p. 1982. lib. bdg. 25.00x (ISBN 0-87023-352-1). U of Mass Pr.

Bauschinger, J. & Peters, J. Logarithmic Trigonometrical Tables to 8 Decimal Places or Numbers 1-200,000 & Trigon: Functions for Sexagesmil Second of the Quadrant, 2vols. 3rd ed. 1971. 45.00 (ISBN 0-934454-57-4). Lubrecht & Cramer.

Bause, Dave. The Best Season of Your Life. (Illus.). 1985. 14.95 (ISBN 0-317-20848-9). Copy Fast.

--How to Promote More Wedding Business Without Headaches. (Illus.). 1985. 11.95. Copy Fast.

Bause, Dave, et al. Create Your Own Newsletter Handbook. LC 83-91092. (Illus.). 80p. 1983. 24.95 (ISBN 0-9612032-0-X). Copy Fast.

Bausell, Barker R., jt. auth. see Waltz, Carolyn.

Bausell, R. Barker, et al. The Bausell Home Learning Guide: Teach Your Child Math. LC 81-50842. 256p. (Orig.). 1981. pap. 12.95 (ISBN 0-03-059652-1, HoltC). HR&W.

Bauske, Robert J. Home Horticulture. LC 76-2733. (Illus.). 200p. 1976. text ed. 18.95 (ISBN 0-8299-0112-4). West Pub.

Bautista, jt. auth. see Enriquez.

Bautista, Paulina, jt. auth. see Barcelona, Delia.

Bautista, Renato G. Hydrometallurgical Process Fundamentals. (NATO Conference Series VI, Materials Science). 635p. 1985. 95.00x (ISBN 0-306-41880-0, Plenum Pr). Plenum Pub.

Bautista, Romeo M. Exhange Rate Adjustment under Generalized Currency Floating: Comparative Analysis among Developing Countries. (Working Paper: No. 436). 99p. 1980. 5.00 (ISBN 0-686-36172-5, WP-0436). World Bank.

Bautista, Romeo M., et al, eds. Capital Utilization in Manufacturing: Colombia, Israel, Malaysia & the Philippines. (World Bank Research Publications Ser.). (Illus.). 1981. 27.50x (ISBN 0-19-520268-6). Oxford U Pr.

Bautista, Sara, tr. see Collingwood, Guillermo.

Bautista, Sara, tr. see Cutting, Jorge.

Bautista, Sara, tr. see Mackintosh, Carlos H.

Bautista, Sara, tr. see Marshall, Alejandro & Bennett, Gordon H.

Bautista, SAra, tr. see Pollock, Algernon J.

Bautista, Sara, tr. see Pollock, Algernon J. & Bennett, Gordon H.

Bautista, Sara, tr. see Rossier, H.

Bautista, Sara, tr. see Thomas, Terry C.

Bautista, Sara, tr. see Voorehoeve, H. C. & Bennett, Gordon H.

Bautista, Veltisezar B. How to Earn Twenty Thousand a Year in the U. S. Postal Service: The Complete System for Scoring 95-100 Percent on Post Office Exams. (Illus.). 94p. 1984. pap. 13.95 (ISBN 0-931613-00-0). Bookhse.

Bautz, E., ed. see Gesellschaft Fuer Biologische Chemie, 24th, Mossbach-Baden, 1973.

Bauw, F. De see De Bauw, F. & Dewit, B.

Bauwens, Eleanor E., jt. auth. see Anderson, Sandra V.

Bauwens, L. Bayesian Full Information Analysis of Simultaneous Equation Models Using Integration by Monte Carlo. (Lecture Notes in Economics & Mathematical Systems Ser.: Vol. 232). vi, 114p. 1984. pap. 11.00 (ISBN 0-387-13384-4). Springer-Verlag.

Bauzen, Peter & Bauzen, Susanne. Flower Pressing. Kuttner, Paul, tr. from Ger. LC 77-167661. (Little Craft Book Ser.). (gr. 7 up). 1982. pap. 4.95 (ISBN 0-8069-7674-8). Sterling.

Bauzen, Susanne, jt. auth. see Bauzen, Peter.

Bava, Domenick. Favorite Stories for Boys & Girls. 160p. (gr. k-6). 1980. PLB 6.95 (ISBN 0-89962-023-X). Todd & Honeywell.

Bavarel, Michel. New Communities, New Ministries: The Church Resurgent in Africa, Asia, & Latin America. Martin, Francis, tr. from Fr. LC 82-22318. Orig. Title: Chretienes Du Bout Du Monde. 128p. (Orig.). 1983. pap. 5.95 (ISBN 0-88344-337-6). Orbis Bks.

Baveja, Malik R. Woman in Islam. Orig. Title: Awrat Awr Islami T'alim. 138p. 1980. pap. text ed. 5.95x (ISBN 0-89891-001-3). Advent NY.

--Women in Islam. 138p. 1982. 40.00x (ISBN 0-7069-1498-8, Pub. by Garlandfold England). State Mutual Bk.

Bavel, Zamir. Introduction to the Theory of Automata & Sequential Machines. 1983. text ed. 31.95 (ISBN 0-8359-3271-0). Reston.

--A Math Companion for Computer Science. 1981. 23.95 (ISBN 0-8359-4300-3); pap. 18.95 (ISBN 0-8359-4299-6); solutions manual avail. (ISBN 0-8359-4301-1). Reston.

Bavendam, Fred. Beneath Cold Waters: The Marine Life of New England. LC 79-67413. (Illus.). 128p. 1980. pap. 14.95 (ISBN 0-89272-184-7). Down East.

Baver, Leonard D., et al. Soil Physics. 4th ed. LC 72-5318. 498p. 1972. 37.50x (ISBN 0-471-05974-9). Wiley.

Baver, Wolfgang. All Change. 1984. pap. 5.95 (ISBN 0-7145-0946-9). Riverrun NY.

Baverle, Ruth H. The James Joyce Songbook. LC 81-43329. 730p. pap. 35.00 (ISBN 0-8240-8925-1). Garland Pub.

Baverstock, Leslie. The Angling Times Book of the Wye. LC 81-68500. (Illus.). 192p. 1982. 22.50 (ISBN 0-7153-8254-3). David & Charles.

Bavetta, Lucien A., jt. ed. see Slavkin, Harold C.

Baviello, Mary A. & Bowie, Alexandra. The Scrubber Strategy: The How & Why of Flue Gas Desulfurization. LC 82-81547. (Orig.). 1982. 37.50 (ISBN 0-918780-19-5). INFORM.

Bavier, Robert N., Jr. Keys to Racing Success. LC 82-2358. (Illus.). 1982. 19.95 (ISBN 0-396-08064-2). Dodd.

--The New Yacht Racing Rules, 1973-1976. (Illus.). 176p. 1974. 7.95 (ISBN 0-393-03177-2). Norton.

--New Yacht, Rules - Racing. 1969. 5.95 (ISBN 0-393-03135-7). Norton.

--Sailing to Win. LC 82-22040. (Illus.). 1983. 17.95 (ISBN 0-396-08050-2). Dodd.

Bavinck, Herman. Doctrine of God. (Twin Brooks Ser.). 1977. pap. 13.95 (ISBN 0-8010-0723-2). Baker Bk.

--The Doctrine of God. Hendricksen, W., tr. (Student's Reformed Theological Library Ser.). 1977. 15.95 (ISBN 0-85151-255-0). Banner of Truth.

--Our Reasonable Faith: A Survey of Christian Doctrine. Zylstra, Henry, tr. (Twin Brooks Ser). 1977. pap. 13.95 (ISBN 0-8010-0513-2). Baker Bk.

--Philosophy of Revelation. (Twin Brooks Ser.). 1980. pap. 7.95 (ISBN 0-8010-0767-4). Baker Bk.

Bavinck, J. H. Introduction to the Science of Missions. 1977. pap. 5.95 (ISBN 0-8010-0600-7). Baker Bk.

Bavinck, Johan H. The Church Between Temple & Mosque: A Study of the Relationship Between the Christian Faith & Other Religions. LC 66-22946. pap. 51.50 (ISBN 0-317-30133-0, 2025316). Bks Demand UMI.

Bavinck, John H. Introduction to Science of Missions. 1960. pap. 5.95 (ISBN 0-87552-124-X). Presby & Reformed.

Bavink, Bernhard. The Natural Sciences. LC 74-26248. (History, Philosophy & Sociology of Science Ser). 1975. Repr. of 1932 ed. 53.00x (ISBN 0-405-06578-7). Ayer Co Pubs.

Bavishi, Vinod B. & Wyman, Harold E. Who Audits the World: Trends in the Worldwide Accounting Profession. 900p. 1983. pap. 75.00 (ISBN 0-913795-01-1). Ctr Trans Acct Fin.

Bavly, Dan & Salpeter, Eliahu. Fire in Beirut: Israel's War in Lebanon with the PLO - Prelude to Aftermath. LC 83-42636. (Illus.). 264p. 1984. 18.95 (ISBN 0-8128-2924-7). Stein & Day.

Bavly, Sarah. Family Food Consumption in Palestine. LC 76-176544. (Columbia University. Teachers College. Contributions to Education: No. 946). Repr. of 1949 ed. 22.50 (ISBN 0-404-55946-8). AMS Pr.

Baw, Cindy & Brownlow, Paul C. Children of the Bible: Twenty-Six Exciting Stories about Children of the Bible. (Illus.). 1984. 10.95 (ISBN 0-915720-19-1). Brownlow Pub Co.

Bawa, V. S., et al. Estimation Risk & Optimal Portfolio Choice. (Studies in Bayesian Econometrics: Vol. 3). 190p. 1979. 46.75 (ISBN 0-444-85344-8, North Holland). Elsevier.

Bawa, Vasant K. Latin American Integration. 225p. 1980. text ed. 13.50x (ISBN 0-391-01899-X). Humanities.

Bawa Muhaiyaddeen, M. R. The Asma'ul-Husna: The 99 Beautiful Names of Allah. LC 79-19619. (Illus.). 211p. 1979. pap. 4.95 (ISBN 0-914390-13-9). Fellowship Pr PA.

--A Book of God's Love. LC 81-4503. (Illus.). 126p. 1981. 7.95 (ISBN 0-914390-19-8). Fellowship Pr PA.

--The Divine Luminous Wisdom That Dispels the Darkness God-Man Man-God. rev. ed. (Illus.). 288p. 1977. pap. 6.95 (ISBN 0-914390-11-2). Fellowship Pr PA.

--Four Steps to Pure Iman. LC 81-1429. (Illus.). 65p. 1979. pap. 3.95 (ISBN 0-914390-17-1). Fellowship Pr PA.

--God, His Prophets & His Children. LC 78-12891. (Illus.). 1978. pap. 5.95 (ISBN 0-914390-09-0). Fellowship Pr PA.

--The Guidebook to the True Secret of the Heart, Vol. 2. LC 75-44557. (Illus.). 232p. 1976. pap. 5.95 (ISBN 0-914390-08-2). Fellowship Pr PA.

--Songs of God's Grace. LC 73-91016. (Illus.). 154p. 1974. pap. 4.95 (ISBN 0-914390-02-3). Fellowship Pr PA.

--Truth & Light: Brief Explanations. LC 74-76219. (Illus.). 144p. 1974. pap. 3.95 (ISBN 0-914390-04-X). Fellowship Pr PA.

--The Truth & Unity of Man: Letters in Response to a Crisis. LC 80-18050. 144p. 1980. pap. 3.95 (ISBN 0-914390-14-7). Fellowship Pr PA.

--Wisdom of Man: Selected Discourses. LC 80-20541. (Illus.). 168p. 1980. 7.95 (ISBN 0-914390-16-3). Fellowship Pr PA.

--Zikr, the Remembrance of God. LC 75-27816. 52p. 1975. pap. 2.95 (ISBN 0-914390-05-8). Fellowship Pr PA.

Bawcutt, N. W., ed. see Ford, John.

Bawcutt, N. W., ed. see Marlowe, Christopher.

Bawcutt, N. W., ed. see Middleton, Thomas & Rowley, Wm.

Bawcutt, N. W., ed. see Shakespeare, William.

Bawcutt, P. A. Captive Insurance Companies. LC 81-69039. 420p. 1982. 40.00 (ISBN 0-87094-293-X). Dow Jones-Irwin.

Bawcutt, Paul, jt. auth. see Bannister, Jim.

Bawcutt, Priscilla, jt. ed. see Riddy, Felicity.

Bawden, C. R. Shamans, Lamas & Evangelicals: The English Missionaries in Siberia. (Illus.). 400p. 1985. 50.00x (ISBN 0-7102-0064-1). Routledge & Kegan.

Bawden, D. Lee, ed. The Social Contract Revisited: Aims & Outcomes of President Reagan's Welfare Policy (Conference Volume) LC 84-7209. (Changing Domestic Priorities Ser.). 250p. 1984. pap. 10.95x (ISBN 0-87766-334-3). Urban Inst.

Bawden, Edward. A Book of Cuts. 1979. 15.00 (ISBN 0-85967-456-8). Scolar.

Bawden, Garth & Conrad, Geoffrey W. The Andean Heritage: Peruvian Art From the Collections of the Peabody Museum. (Peabody Museum Press Ser.). (Illus.). 100p. (Orig.). 1982. pap. 9.00x (ISBN 0-87365-805-1). Peabody Harvard.

Bawden, H. Heath see Breese, B. B.

Bawden, Henry H. The Principles of Pragmatism: A Philosophical Interpretation of Experience. LC 75-3034. (Philosophy in America Ser.). 1976. Repr. of 1910 ed. 25.00 (ISBN 0-404-59042-X). AMS Pr.

Bawden, Nina. Carrie's War. LC 72-13253. (gr. 7 up). 1973. lib. bdg. 11.89 (ISBN 0-397-31450-7). Lipp Jr Bks.

--Carrie's War. 144p. (gr. 4-6). 1975. pap. 1.95 (ISBN 0-14-030689-7, Puffin). Penguin.

--Carrie's War: T.V. Ed. (Illus.). 1980. pap. 2.95 (ISBN 0-14-005581-9). Penguin.

--Devil by the Sea. 1978. pap. 1.95 (ISBN 0-380-01922-1, 57695). Avon.

--Devil by the Sea. LC 76-13177. (gr. 7-12). 1976. 11.49i (ISBN 0-397-31683-6). Lipp Jr Bks.

--The Finding. LC 84-25069. 160p. (gr. 3 up). 1985. 10.25 (ISBN 0-688-04979-6). Lothrop.

--The Grain of Truth. 13.95 (ISBN 0-88411-121-0, Pub. by Aeonian Pr). Amereon Ltd.

--The Ice House. LC 83-9722. 236p. 1983. 11.95 (ISBN 0-312-40386-0). St Martin.

--Kept in the Dark. LC 81-20765. 160p. (gr. 5-8). 1982. 11.75 (ISBN 0-688-00900-X). Lothrop.

--Kept in the Dark. 176p. (gr. 4-6). 1984. pap. 1.95 (ISBN 0-590-32848-4, Apple Paperbacks). Scholastic Inc.

--A Little Love, A Little Learning. 14.95 (ISBN 0-88411-122-9, Pub. by Aeonian Pr). Amereon Ltd.

--Odd Flamingo. 15.95 (ISBN 0-88411-126-1, Pub. by Aeonian Pr). Amereon Ltd.

--The Peppermint Pig. LC 74-26922. (gr. 3-6). 1975. lib. bdg. 11.89i (ISBN 0-397-31618-6). Lipp Jr Bks.

--The Peppermint Pig. (Story Bks.). (gr. 2-7). 1977. pap. 2.95 (ISBN 0-14-030944-6, Puffin). Penguin.

--The Robbers. LC 79-4152. (gr. 5-8). 1979. 11.25 (ISBN 0-688-41902-X); PLB 11.88 (ISBN 0-688-51902-4). Lothrop.

--Runaway Summer. LC 77-82408. (gr. 4-6). 1969. 11.49i (ISBN 0-397-31102-8). Lipp Jr Bks.

--St. Francis of Assisi. LC 82-13105. (Illus.). 32p. (gr. 1-3). 1983. 10.25 (ISBN 0-688-01649-9); PLB 10.88 (ISBN 0-688-01653-7). Lothrop.

--Squib. LC 82-75. (Illus.). 160p. (gr. 5 up). 1982. Repr. 11.75 (ISBN 0-688-01299-X). Lothrop.

--Squib. (gr. 4-6). 1982. 11.75 (ISBN 0-688-01299-X). Morrow.

--Tortoise by Candlelight. 14.95 (ISBN 0-88411-123-7, Pub. by Aeonian Pr). Amereon Ltd.

--Under the Skin. 15.95 (ISBN 0-88411-124-5, Pub. by Aeonian Pr). Amereon Ltd.

--Walking Naked. 224p. 1982. 10.95 (ISBN 0-312-85456-0). St Martin.

--William Tell. LC 80-24786. (Illus.). 32p. (gr. 1-3). 1981. 11.25 (ISBN 0-688-41985-2); PLB 11.88 (ISBN 0-688-51985-7). Lothrop.

--Witch's Daughter. LC 66-10349. (Illus.). (gr. 4-6). 1966. 11.49i (ISBN 0-397-30922-8). Lipp Jr Bks.

--A Woman of My Age. 159p. 1976. Repr. of 1967 ed. lib. bdg. 7.00x (ISBN 0-685-66152-0, Pub. by Queens Hse). Amereon Ltd.

--A Woman of My Age. 11.95 (ISBN 0-88411-125-3, Pub. by Aeonian Pr). Amereon Ltd.

Bawkoff, S. G., jt. ed. see Chew, J. C.

Bawtree, Michael & Bradbeer, Robin. The Student's Calculator's Book. 202p. (Orig.). 1981. pap. text ed. 12.25 (ISBN 0-86238-007-3, Pub. by Chartwell-Bratt England). Brookfield Pub Co.

Bax, Ad. Two-Dimensional Nuclear Magnetic Resonance in Liquids. 1982. 29.50 (ISBN 90-277-1412-6, Pub. by Reidel Holland). Kluwer Academic.

Bax, Arnold E. Farewell My Youth. LC 78-100221. Repr. of 1943 ed. lib. bdg. 22.50 (ISBN 0-8371-3246-0, BAMY). Greenwood.

Bax, Clifford. Bianca Capello. (Women Ser.). 1927. 10.00 (ISBN 0-8482-0142-6). Norwood Edns.

--Highways & Byways in Essex. Repr. of 1939 ed. 10.00 (ISBN 0-8482-3420-0). Norwood Edns.

--Highways & Byways in Essex. 25.00 (ISBN 0-686-17219-1). Scholars Ref Lib.

--Leonardo Da Vinci. 160p. 1980. Repr. of 1932 ed. lib. bdg. 27.50 (ISBN 0-8495-0464-3). Arden Lib.

--Polite Satires. LC 76-40385. (One-Act Plays in Reprint Ser.). 1976. Repr. of 1922 ed. 15.00x (ISBN 0-8486-2001-1). Core Collection.

--Pretty Witty Nell: An Account of Nell Gwyn & Her Environment. LC 76-83871. (Illus.). Repr. of 1932 ed. 22.00 (ISBN 0-405-08243-6, Blom Pubns). Ayer Co Pubs.

Bax, Clifford, ed. Florence Farr, Bernard Shaw & W. B. Yeats. 104p. 1971. Repr. of 1941 ed. 12.50x (ISBN 0-7165-1394-3, BBA 02046, Pub. by Cuala Press Ireland). Biblio Dist.

Bax, Clifford, tr. see Goldoni, Carlo.

Bax, E. Belfort. Jean-Paul Marat: The People's Friend. 59.95 (ISBN 0-8490-0439-X). Gordon Pr.

--Reminiscences & Reflexions of a Mid & Late Victorian. LC 67-27466. 1918. 27.50x (ISBN 0-678-00313-0). Kelley.

--Rise & Fall of the Anabaptists. 59.95 (ISBN 0-8490-0958-8). Gordon Pr.

--The Social Side of the Reformation in Germany, 3 vols. Incl. Vol. 1. German Society at the Close of the Middle Ages. LC 67-25997. 276p. Repr. of 1894 ed. lib. bdg. 25.00x (ISBN 0-678-00312-2); Vol. 2. The Peasants' War in Germany 1525-1526. LC 68-57371. 367p. Repr. of 1899 ed. lib. bdg. 35.00x (ISBN 0-678-00445-5); Vol. 3. The Rise & Fall of the Anapabtists. LC 75-101125. 407p. Repr. of 1903 ed. lib. bdg. 37.50x (ISBN 0-678-00593-1). lib. bdg. 87.50x set (ISBN 0-678-00772-1). Kelley.

Bax, E. Belfort, jt. auth. see Morris, William.

Bax, Ernest B. German Society at the Close of the Middle Ages. 1977. lib. bdg. 59.95 (ISBN 0-8490-1885-4). Gordon Pr.

--German Society at the Close of the Middle Ages. LC 83-45653. Date not set. Repr. of 1894 ed. 32.50 (ISBN 0-404-19803-1). AMS Pr.

--Last Episodes of the French Revolution. LC 74-159489. (World History Ser., No. 48). 1971. lib. bdg. 51.95x (ISBN 0-8383-1282-9). Haskell.

--Outlooks from the New Standpoint. LC 78-39669. (Essay Index Reprint Ser.). Repr. of 1903 ed. 18.00 (ISBN 0-8369-2742-7). Ayer Co Pubs.

--Religion of Socialism: Being Essays in Modern Socialist Criticism. LC 74-39668. (Essay Index Reprint Ser.). Repr. of 1886 ed. 18.00 (ISBN 0-8369-2743-5). Ayer Co Pubs.

Bax, Mart. Harpstrings & Confessions: Machine-Style Politics in the Irish Republic. 1977. pap. text ed. 23.75x (ISBN 90-232-1481-1). Humanities.

Bax, Martin. The Hospital Ship. LC 76-16033. 1976. 7.95 (ISBN 0-8112-0584-3); pap. 3.95 (ISBN 0-8112-0585-1, NDP402). New Directions.

Baxa, Donald E. & Petska, Darrell E. Noise Control in Internal Combustion Engines. 511p. 1982. 68.50 (ISBN 0-471-05870-X). Wiley.

Baxandall, Lee. World Guide to Nude Beaches & Recreations. (Illus.). 216p. 1982. pap. 14.95 (ISBN 0-517-54597-7, Harmony). Crown.

--World Guide to Nude Beaches & Recreation. Rev. ed. 216p. 1986. pap. 15.00 (ISBN 0-517-54983-2). Crown.

Baxandall, Lee, ed. Marxism & Aesthetics: A Selcctive Annotated Bibliography. LC 68-28865. 1978. text ed. 18.00x (ISBN 0-391-00298-8). Humanities.

Baxandall, Lee & Morawski, Stefan, eds. Marx & Engels on Literature & Art: A Selection of Writings. LC 73-93501. 150p. 1973. 12.00 (ISBN 0-914386-01-8); pap. 4.50 (ISBN 0-914386-02-6). Telos Pr.

Baxandall, Lee, ed. see Marx, Karl & Engels, Friedrich.

Baxandall, Michael. The Limewood Sculptors of Renaissance Germany Fourteen Seventy-Five to Fifteen Twenty-Five. LC 79-23258. (Illus.). 1980. 70.00x (ISBN 0-300-02423-1); pap. 17.95x (ISBN 0-300-02829-6, Y-414). Yale U Pr.

--Painting & Experience in Fifteenth Century Italy: A Primer in the Social History of Pictorial Style. 1974. pap. 8.95 (ISBN 0-19-881329-5, GB411, GB). Oxford U Pr.

--Patterns of Intention: On the Historical Explanation of Pictures. LC 85-6049. (Illus.). 196p. 1985. 18.95 (ISBN 0-300-03465-2). Yale U Pr.

Baxardall, Rosalyn, et al. America's Working Women: A Documentary History - 1600 to the Present. 1976. pap. 8.95 (ISBN 0-394-72208-6, V-208, Vin). Random.

Baxby, Derrick. Jenner's Smallpox Vaccine: The Riddle of Vaccinia Virus & Its Origin. (Illus.). 215p. 1981. 25.00x (ISBN 0-435-54057-2). Heinemann Ed.

Baxendale, J. & Busi, F. The Study of Fast Processes & Transient Species by Electron Pulse Radiolysis. 1982. 74.50 (ISBN 90-277-1431-2, Pub. by Reidel Holland). Kluwer Academic.

Baxendale, Jean. Fifty-Two Preschool Activity Patterns. (Illus.). 48p. (Orig.). 1982. pap. 4.50 (ISBN 0-87239-491-3, 2152). Standard Pub.

--First Bible Lessons: A Course for Two and Three-Year-Olds. rev. ed. LC 81-53021. (Illus.). 144p. 1982. pap. 7.95 (ISBN 0-87239-486-7, 3369). Standard Pub.

--Preschool Bible Activities, 4 vols. (Illus.). 24p. (Orig.). 1982. No. 1. pap. 1.25 (ISBN 0-87239-487-5, 2459); No. 2. pap. 1.25 (ISBN 0-87239-488-3, 2460); No. 3. pap. 1.25 (ISBN 0-87239-489-1, 2461); No. 4. pap. 1.25 (ISBN 0-87239-490-5, 2462). Standard Pub.

Baxes, Gary. Digital Image Processing. 1983. 22.95 (ISBN 0-13-214064-0, Spec); pap. 14.95 (ISBN 0-13-214056-X). P-H.

Baxi, Nilesh & Asrani, C. H. Speaking of Alternative Medicine: Accupuncture, the Needle That Heals All Ailments. (Health & Cure Ser.). 1985. text ed. 17.95x (ISBN 0-86590-612-2, Pub. by Sterling Pubs India). Apt Bks.

Baxi, Upendra. Alternatives in Developmental Law: The Crisis of the Indian Legal System. 200p. 1983. text ed. 35.00x (ISBN 0-7069-1369-8, Pub. by Vikas India). Advent NY.

--The Crisis of the Indian Legal System. 200p. 1982. 39.00x (ISBN 0-7069-1369-8, Pub. by Garlandfold England). State Mutual Bk.

Baxt, George. The Dorothy Parker Murder Case. LC 84-13271. 304p. 1984. 14.95 (ISBN 0-312-21791-9). St Martin.

--Process of Elimination. 288p. 1984. 13.95 (ISBN 0-312-64777-8). St Martin.

--A Queer Kind of Death. LC 78-19248. 1979. pap. 4.95 (ISBN 0-312-66022-7). St Martin.

Baxt, William G., ed. Trauma: The First Hour. 336p. 1984. 32.50 (ISBN 0-8385-9005-5). ACC.

Baxter, Angus. In Search of Your British & Irish Roots: A Complete Guide to Tracing Your English, Welsh, & Scottish & Irish Ancestors. LC 82-7895. 320p. 1982. 15.00 (ISBN 0-688-01350-3). Morrow.

--In Search of Your European Roots: A Complete Guide to Tracing Your Ancestors in Every Country in Europe. LC 84-73426. 300p. 1985. pap. 12.95 (ISBN 0-8063-1114-2). Genealog Pub.

Baxter, Anne. Intermission. 1978. pap. 2.50 (ISBN 0-345-29267-7). Ballantine.

Baxter, Annette & Jacobs, Constance. To Be a Woman in America, 1850-1930. LC 78-53299. 1978. pap. 7.95 (ISBN 0-8129-6306-7). Times Bks.

Baxter, Annette K. Women's History - American History. LC 83-61357. (Selected Syllabi from American Colleges & Universities in History Ser.). pap. text ed. 14.50x (ISBN 0-910129-12-6). Wiener Pub Inc.

Baxter, Annette K., ed. Madeleine. LC 79-8767. (Signal Lives Ser.). 1980. Repr. of 1919 ed. lib. bdg. 34.50x (ISBN 0-405-12817-7). Ayer Co Pubs.

--Sex & Equality: An Original Anthology. LC 74-3972. (Women in America Ser). 220p. 1974. Repr. of 1974 ed. 20.00x (ISBN 0-405-06121-8). Ayer Co Pubs.

--Signal Lives Series, 51 bks. 1980. Set. lib. bdg. 1889.50x (ISBN 0-405-12815-0). Ayer Co Pubs.

Baxter, Annette K. & Stein, Leon, eds. American Women: Images & Realities, 44 bks. 17788p. 1972. Repr. Set. 1088.00 (ISBN 0-405-04445-3). Ayer Co Pubs.

Baxter, Annette K., ed. see Antin, Mary.

Baxter, Annette K., ed. see Atherton, Gertrude F.

Baxter, Annette K., ed. see Bacon, Albion F.

Baxter, Annette K., ed. see Bailey, Abigail.

Baxter, Annette K., ed. see Barr, Amelia E.

Baxter, Annette K., ed. see Barton, Clara.

Baxter, Annette K., ed. see Belmont, Eleanor R.

Baxter, Annette K., ed. see Boyle, Sarah P.

Baxter, Annette K., ed. see Brown, Harriet C.

Baxter, Annette K., ed. see Carson, Ann.

Baxter, Annette K., ed. see Churchill, Caroline N.

Baxter, Annette K., ed. see Cleghorn, Sarah N.

Baxter, Annette K., ed. see Dall, Caroline W.

Baxter, Annette K., ed. see Daviess, Maria T.

Baxter, Annette K., ed. see Dorr, Rheta C.

Baxter, Annette K., ed. see Dumond, Annie H.

Baxter, Annette K., ed. see Eaton, Margaret O.

Baxter, Annette K., ed. see Farrar, Elizabeth R.

Baxter, Annette K., ed. see Felton, Rebeca L.

Baxter, Annette K., ed. see Garden, Mary & Biancolli, Louis.

Baxter, Annette K., ed. see Gilson, Mary B.

Baxter, Annette K., ed. see Hurst, Fannie.

Baxter, Annette K., ed. see Jacobs-Bond, Carrie.

Baxter, Annette K., ed. see Jelliffe, Belinda D.

Baxter, Annette K., ed. see Jones, Amanda T.

Baxter, Annette K., ed. see Logan, Kate V.

Baxter, Annette K., ed. see Longworth, Alice R.

Baxter, Annette K., ed. see MacDougall, Alice F.

Baxter, Annette K., ed. see Meyer, Agnes E.

Baxter, Annette K., ed. see Mowatt, Anna C.

Baxter, Annette K., ed. see Odlum, Hortense.

Baxter, Annette K., ed. see Phelps, Elizabeth S.

Baxter, Annette K., ed. see Potter, Eliza.

Baxter, Annette K., ed. see Rinehart, Mary R.

Baxter, Annette K., ed. see Robinson, Josephine D.

Baxter, Annette K., ed. see Roe, Elizabeth A.

Baxter, Annette K., ed. see Sanders, Sue.

Baxter, Annette K., ed. see Sangster, Margaret E.

Baxter, Annette K., ed. see Sherwood, Mary E.

Baxter, Annette K., ed. see Sigourney, Lydia H.

Baxter, Annette K., ed. see Smith, Elizabeth O.

Baxter, Annette K., jt. ed. see Stein, Leon.

Baxter, Annette K., ed. see Terhune, Mary V.

Baxter, Annette K., ed. see Terrell, Mary C.

Baxter, Annette K., ed. see Ueland, Brenda.

Baxter, Annette K., ed. see Van Hoosen, Bertha.

Baxter, Annette K., ed. see Vorse, Mary H.

Baxter, Annette K., ed. see Wilcox, Ella W.

Baxter, Annette K., ed. see Wilson, Edith B.

Baxter, Arlene. Techniques for Dealing with Child Abuse. 146p. 1985. 19.50x (ISBN 0-398-05110-0). C C Thomas.

Baxter, Arthur B. Men, Martyrs & Mountebanks. facsimile ed. LC 73-104992. (Essay Index Reprint Ser.). 1940. 20.00 (ISBN 0-8369-1446-5). Ayer Co Pubs.

Baxter, B. Naval Architecture: Examples & Theory. 240p. 1977. pap. text ed. 29.75x (ISBN 0-85264-179-6). Lubrecht & Cramer.

--Naval Architecture: Examples & Theory. 450p. 1978. 39.95x (ISBN 0-85264-179-6, Pub. by Griffin England). State Mutual Bk.

Baxter, B., jt. auth. see Walton, Thomas.

Baxter, B., ed. see Walton, T.

Baxter, Batsell B. Family of God. 1980. pap. 6.95 (ISBN 0-89225-208-1). Gospel Advocate.

--I Believe Because. 1971. pap. 8.95 (ISBN 0-8010-0548-5). Baker Bk.

--Speaking for the Master. pap. 4.50 (ISBN 0-8010-0588-4). Baker Bk.

--When Life Tumbles in. (Direction Bks.). 136p. 1976. pap. 3.95 (ISBN 0-8010-0630-9). Baker Bk.

Baxter, Batsell B. & Hazelip, Harold. Anchors in Troubled Waters. Abr. ed. LC 82-50267. (Journey Adult Ser.). 124p. pap. text ed. 2.95 (ISBN 0-8344-0120-7). Sweet.

Baxter, Batsell B., et al. Anchors in Troubled Waters: How to Survive the Crises in Your Life. 176p. (Orig.). 1981. pap. 4.95 (ISBN 0-8010-0806-9). Baker Bk.

Baxter, Beverley. First Nights & Noises off. 239p. 1982. Repr. of 1982 ed. lib. bdg. 45.00 (ISBN 0-89987-098-8). Darby Bks.

--First Nights & Noises off. 1949. 15.00 (ISBN 0-8482-7364-8). Norwood Edns.

Baxter, Bob. Baxter's Complete Beginning Folk Guitar Manual. (Illus.). 168p. pap. 8.95 (ISBN 0-8256-2601-3, Amsco Music). Music Sales.

--Baxter's Private Guitar Lessons, 3 bks. (incl. Songbook) LC 76-17437. 1976. pap. 4.95 ea. (Acorn). Bk. 1 (ISBN 0-8256-2371-5). Bk. 2 (ISBN 0-8256-2372-3). Music Sales.

Baxter, Brian. Alienation & Authenticity. 240p. 1982. 32.00 (ISBN 0-422-78280-7, NO. 3708, Pub. by Tavistock). Methuen Inc.

--The Films of Judy Garland. Castell, David, ed. (The Films of...Ser.). (Illus.). (gr. 7-12). 1978. Repr. of 1974 ed. PLB 6.95 (ISBN 0-912616-81-4). Greenhaven.

Baxter, Carol. Business Report Writing. LC 82-21340. 392p. 1983. text ed. write for info. (ISBN 0-534-01392-9). Kent Pub Co.

Baxter, Carolyn. Prison Solitary. LC 79-54299. 1979. 2.00 (ISBN 0-912678-41-0). Greenfld Rev Pr.

Baxter, Charles. Chameleon. (Illus.). 1970. pap. 10.00 signed (ISBN 0-685-02575-6). New Rivers Pr.

--Harmony of the World Stories. LC 83-16799. (Associated Writer's Program Ser.: No. 6). 160p. 1984. pap. 8.95 (ISBN 0-8262-0428-7). U of MO Pr.

--The South Dakota Guidebook. (Illus.). 1974. signed ltd. ed. 10.00 (ISBN 0-685-46812-7); pap. 2.50 (ISBN 0-685-46813-5). New Rivers Pr.

--Through the Safety Net. 208p. 1985. 14.95 (ISBN 0-670-80477-0). Viking.

Baxter, Claude & Melnechuk, Theodore, eds. Perspectives in Schizophrenia Research. 463p. 1980. text ed. 73.00 (ISBN 0-89004-517-8). Raven.

Baxter, Colin, photos by. Scotland: The Light & the Land. (Illus.). 92p. 1985. 19.95 (ISBN 0-88162-086-6, Pub. by Salem Hse Ltd). Merrimack Pub Cir.

Baxter, Colles, jt. auth. see Fisher, Jay M.

Baxter, Craig. Bangladesh. (Profiles on Nations of Contemporary Asia Ser.). 135p. 1984. 16.50x (ISBN 0-86531-630-9). Westview.

--Jana Sangh: A Biography of an Indian Political Party. LC 69-17750. 1969. 15.00x (ISBN 0-8122-7583-7). U of Pa Pr.

Baxter, Craig, ed. Zia's Pakistan: Politics & Stability in a Frontline State. (Westview Special Studies on South & Southeast Asia). 160p. 1985. pap. 16.50 (ISBN 0-8133-7113-9). Westview.

Baxter, D. British Locomotive Catalogue 1825-1923, Vol. 1. 1977. 25.00 (ISBN 0-685-87550-4). State Mutual Bk.

Baxter, D., jt. auth. see Olszewsky, J.

Baxter, David, intro. by. Texas Wildlife: Photographs from Texas Parks & Wildlife Magazine. LC 77-99281. (Louise Lindsey Merrick Texas Environment Ser.: No. 1). (Illus.). 196p. 1978. 24.95 (ISBN 0-89096-047-X). Tex A&M Univ Pr.

Baxter, Derrick S. Ma Rainey & the Classic Blues Singers. LC 72-120110. (Blues Ser). (Illus.). 1970. pap. 2.95 (ISBN 0-8128-1321-9). Stein & Day.

Baxter, Dow V. Disease in Forest Plantations. LC 67-18144. (Bulletin Ser.: No. 51). (Illus.). 251p. 1967. text ed. 4.25x (ISBN 0-87737-028-1). Cranbrook.

Baxter, Ellen & Hopper, Kim. Private Lives-Public Spaces: Homeless Adults on the Streets of New York City. LC 82-234971. 129p. (Orig.). 1981. pap. 6.50 (ISBN 0-88156-002-2). Comm Serv Soc NY.

Baxter, Ellen & Hopper, Kin. The New Mendicancy: Homeless in New York City (with Some Proposals for Service Providers) 1981. pap. 2.00 (ISBN 0-318-00884-X). Comm Serv Soc NY.

Baxter, Elmar, jt. auth. see Miller, Tom.

Baxter, G. W. see Ssu-Ma Kuang.

Baxter, George & McDowell, Bob, eds. Colorado-Wyoming Chapter American Fisheries Society: Proceedings of the Nineteenth Annual Meeting. 168p. 1984. 10.00 (ISBN 0-913235-34-2). Am Fisheries Soc.

Baxter, Glen. Atlas. LC 82-48728. 1983. 7.95 (ISBN 0-394-52994-4). Knopf.

--Glen Baxter His Life: The Years of Struggle. LC 83-47946. (Illus.). 1984. 13.95 (ISBN 0-394-53311-9). Knopf.

--The Impending Gleam. LC 81-48126. 1982. pap. 6.95 bds. (ISBN 0-394-52473-X). Knopf.

Baxter, Gordon. How to Fly. (Illus.). 224p. 1981. 12.95 (ISBN 0-671-44801-3). Summit Bks.

--Jenny 'n Dad. 1985. 15.95 (ISBN 0-671-46954-1). Summit Bks.

--Village Creek. 328p. 1981. pap. 7.95 (ISBN 0-940672-03-0). Shearer Pub.

Baxter, Ian. Essays on Private Law: Foreign Law & Foreign Judgments. LC 66-9312. pap. 54.50 (ISBN 0-317-27651-4, 2014127). Bks Demand UMI.

Baxter, Ian A. A Brief Guide to Biographical Sources. 57p. (Orig.). 1979. pap. 3.00 (ISBN 0-903359-18-9, Pub. by British Lib). Longwood Pub Group.

Baxter, Ian F. Marital Property. LC 72-97627. (American Family Law Library). 640p. 1973. 64.50 (ISBN 0-686-05456-3); Suppl. 1984. 21.00; Suppl. 1983. 19.00. Lawyers Co-Op.

Baxter, J. & Harvey, L. Sonnets for Ethiopians. facsimile ed. LC 74-38009. (Black Heritage Library Collection). Repr. of 1936 ed. 12.50 (ISBN 0-8369-8977-5). Ayer Co Pubs.

--That Which Concerneth Me. facs. ed. LC 79-178468. (Black Heritage Library Collection). Repr. of 1934 ed. 12.00 (ISBN 0-8369-8911-2). Ayer Co Pubs.

Baxter, J. D. & Rousseau, G. G., eds. Glucocorticoid Hormone Action. (Monographs on Endocrinology: Vol. 12). (Illus.). 1979. 75.00 (ISBN 0-387-08973-X). Springer-Verlag.

Baxter, J. Sidlow. Awake My Heart. 12.95 (ISBN 0-310-20590-5). Zondervan.

--Explore the Book. 29.95 (ISBN 0-310-20620-0). Zondervan.

--The Hidden Hand. (Living Bks.). 512p. 1985. pap. 4.95 (ISBN 0-8423-1397-4). Tyndale.

--Majesty! The God You Should Know. LC 84-47805. 228p. 1984. 12.95 (ISBN 0-89840-070-8). Heres Life.

--Master Theme of the Bible. 1978. pap. 5.95 (ISBN 0-8423-4186-2). Tyndale.

Baxter, James H. An Old St. Andrews Music Book. facsimile ed. LC 70-178515. (Medieval Studies Ser.). Repr. of 1931 ed. 34.50 (ISBN 0-404-56525-5). AMS Pr.

--Printing Postage Stamps by Line Engraving. LC 81-50924. Repr. of 1939 ed. lib. bdg. 25.00x (ISBN 0-88000-129-1). Quarterman.

Baxter, James H., tr. see Augustine, St. Aurelius.

Baxter, James K. Collected Poems. Weir, J. E., ed. 1979. 65.00x (ISBN 0-19-558037-0). Oxford U Pr.

Baxter, James K., ed. see Bigwood, Kenneth & Bigwood, Jean.

Baxter, James P. The Greatest of Literary Problems: The Authorship of the Shakespeare Works. LC 79-161734. Repr. of 1915 ed. lib. bdg. 43.50 (ISBN 0-404-00694-9). AMS Pr.

--Introduction of the Ironclad Warship. (Illus.). x, 398p. 1968. Repr. of 1933 ed. 27.50 (ISBN 0-208-00621-4, Archon). Shoe String.

--The Pioneers of New France in New England. 450p. 1980. Repr. of 1894 ed. 25.00 (ISBN 0-917890-20-5). Heritage Bk.

--Sir Ferdinando Gorges (1565-1647) & His Province of Maine, 3 vols. 1966. Set. 62.00 (ISBN 0-8337-0190-8). B Franklin.

Baxter, James P., ed. The British Invasion from the North: The Campaigns of Generals Carleton & Burgoyne from Canada, 1776-1777. LC 74-114756. (Era of the American Revolution Ser). 1970. Repr. of 1887 ed. 49.50 (ISBN 0-306-71926-6). Da Capo.

Baxter, John. The Bidders. LC 79-12325. 1979. 10.95i (ISBN 0-397-01365-5). Har-Row.

--Black Yacht. 336p. 1982. pap. 2.95 (ISBN 0-515-06159-X). Jove Pubns.

--The Hollywood Exiles. LC 75-34734. (Illus.). 232p. 1976. 14.95 (ISBN 0-8008-3918-8). Taplinger.

--Hollywood in the Sixties. LC 70-181065. (Hollywood Ser.). (Illus.). 192p. 1972. pap. 5.95 (ISBN 0-498-01096-1). A S Barnes.

--Hollywood in the Thirties. LC 68-24003. (Hollywood Ser.). 1968. pap. 5.95 (ISBN 0-498-06927-3). A S Barnes.

--Science Fiction in the Cinema. LC 69-14896. pap. 4.95 (ISBN 0-498-07416-1). A S Barnes.

Baxter, John W. William Dunbar: A Biographical Study. LC 71-148872. (Select Bibliographies Reprint Ser). 1972. Repr. of 1952 ed. 20.00 (ISBN 0-8369-5672-9). Ayer Co Pubs.

Baxter, Kathleen M. Come & Get It: A Natural Foods Cookbook for Children. LC 81-70782. (Illus.). 128p. 1981. plastic comb 10.95 (ISBN 0-9603696-1-9); pap. 6.95 spiral bdg (ISBN 0-9603696-2-7). Children First.

Baxter, Lorna. The Eggchild. 160p. 1985. pap. 2.75 (ISBN 0-441-19258-0). Ace Bks.

Baxter, Lucy E. The Cathedral Builders: The Story of a Great Masonic Guild. LC 78-58191. 1978. Repr. of 1899 ed. lib. bdg. 50.00 (ISBN 0-89341-354-2). Longwood Pub Group.

--Sculpture, Renaissance & Modern. LC 79-23263. 1980. Repr. of 1891 ed. lib. bdg. 30.00 (ISBN 0-89341-366-6). Longwood Pub Group.

Baxter, Lucy W. Thackeray's Letters to an American Family. (Illus.). 1904. 25.00 (ISBN 0-8274-3590-8). R West.

Baxter, M. W. Food in Fiji: The Produce & Processed Foods Distribution Systems. (Development Studies Centre-Monographs: No. 22). 282p. 1980. pap. text ed. 9.00 (ISBN 0-909150-03-6, 0064, Pub. by ANUP Australia). Australia N U P.

Baxter, Mary, jt. auth. see Stone, Elizabeth.

Baxter, Maurice G. Daniel Webster & the Supreme Court. LC 66-28116. 280p. 1966. 17.50x (ISBN 0-87023-008-5). U of Mass Pr.

--One & Inseparable: Daniel Webster & the Union. LC 83-26597. (Illus.). 656p. 1984. 25.00 (ISBN 0-674-63821-2, Belknap). Harvard U Pr.

Baxter, Michael, jt. auth. see Benor, Daniel.

Baxter, Neale. Opportunities in Government Service. (VGM Career Bks.). (Illus.). 160p. 1983. 7.95 (ISBN 0-8442-6618-3, 6618-3, Passport Bks.); pap. 5.95 (ISBN 0-8442-6619-1, 6619-1). Natl Textbk.

Baxter, Nevins D. Commercial Paper Market. LC 65-29170. pap. 32.20 (ISBN 0-8357-9038-X, 2051727). Bks Demand UMI.

Baxter, Norman. A Line on Texas. LC 80-15870. (Illus.). 128p. (Orig.). 1980. pap. 9.95x (ISBN 0-88415-429-7, Lone Star Bks). Gulf Pub.

Baxter, P. T. & Almagor, Uri, eds. Age, Generation & Time: Some Features of East African Age Organizations. LC 78-18952. (Illus.). 1978. 30.00 (ISBN 0-312-01172-5). St Martin.

Baxter, Pam M., jt. auth. see Reed, Jeffrey G.

Baxter, Paul R., jt. auth. see Drummond, Lewis A.

Baxter, Peter, ed. Sternberg. (British Film Institute Bks.). (Illus.). 144p. 1980. 13.95x (ISBN 0-85170-098-5); pap. 7.95 (ISBN 0-85170-099-3). U of Ill Pr.

Baxter, R. E. & Phillips, C. Ports, Inland Waterways & Civil Aviation. Maunder, W. F., ed. 1979. text ed. 65.00 (ISBN 0-08-022460-1). Pergamon.

Baxter, R. J. Exactly Solved Models in Statistical Mechanics. LC 81-68965. (Theoretical Chemistry Ser.). 1982. 81.00 (ISBN 0-12-083180-5). Acad Pr.

Baxter, R. R. & Carroll, D. The Panama Canal: Background Papers & Proceedings. LC 65-22162. (Hammarskjold Forum Ser.: No. 6). 118p. 1965. 10.00 (ISBN 0-379-11806-8). Oceana.

Baxter, Ralph. Sexual Harassment in the Workplace. 1980. pap. 5.95 (ISBN 0-917386-63-9). Exec Ent Inc.

Baxter, Richard. Practical Works of Richard Baxter, 23 Vols. Orme, William, ed. LC 72-161735. Repr. of 1830 ed. Set. lib. bdg. 431.25 (ISBN 0-404-00700-7); lib. bdg. 19.50 ea. AMS Pr.

--The Practical Works of Richard Baxter. (Giant Summit Books). 1000p. 1981. pap. 14.95 (ISBN 0-8010-0804-2). Baker Bk.

--The Reformed Pastor. 1979. pap. 4.45 (ISBN 0-85151-191-0). Banner of Truth.

--The Reformed Pastor: A Pattern for Personal Growth & Ministry. rev. ed. Houston, James M., ed. LC 82-18825. (Classics of Faith & Devotion Ser.). 150p. 1983. 10.95 (ISBN 0-88070-003-3). Multnomah.

Baxter, Richard, jt. ed. see Perraton, Jean.

Baxter, Richard, et al, eds. Urban Development Models. LC 79-301020. (Cambridge University Centre for Land Use & Built Form Studies Conference Proceedings: No. 3). pap. 85.80 (ISBN 0-317-27680-8, 2025216). Bks Demand UMI.

Baxter, Richard S. Computer & Statistical Techniques for Planners. 1976. pap. 22.00x (ISBN 0-416-84630-0, NO.2613). Methuen Inc.

Baxter, Robert. Baxter's Alaska. 1985. 9.95 (ISBN 0-913384-47-X). Rail Europe-Baxter.

--Baxter's Britrail Guide. LC 72-83184. 1985. 9.95 (ISBN 0-913384-06-2). Rail-Europe-Baxter.

--Baxter's California: Vol. 1, Southern California. 1985. 9.95 (ISBN 0-913384-51-8). Rail-Europe-Baxter.

--Baxter's California: Vol. 2, Northern California. 1985. 9.95 (ISBN 0-913384-52-6). Rail-Europe-Baxter.

--Baxter's Eurailpass Travel Guide. LC 74-169913. 1985. 9.95 (ISBN 0-913384-65-8). Rail-Europe-Baxter.

--Baxter's Florida. 1985. 9.95 (ISBN 0-913384-34-8). Rail-Europe-Baxter.

--Baxter's Mexico. 1985. 9.95 (ISBN 0-913384-42-9). Rail-Europe-Baxter.

--Baxter's National Parks: Vol. 1, Grand Canyon. 1985. 9.95 (ISBN 0-913384-53-4). Rail-Europe-Baxter.

--Baxter's National Parks: Vol. 2, Yellowstone. 1985. 9.95 (ISBN 0-913384-54-2). Rail-Europe-Baxter.

--Baxter's U. S. A. (the U. S. A. by Car, Bus, Train & Plane) LC 77-92700. 1980-81. perfect bdg. 12.95 (ISBN 0-913384-44-5). Rail-Europe-Baxter.

--Baxter's Western Canada. 1985. 9.95 (ISBN 0-913384-41-0). Rail-Europe-Baxter.

--Bicentennial Images. 1976. perfect bdg. 14.95 (ISBN 0-913384-19-4). Rail-Europe-Baxter.

--Panic of Eighteen Sixty-Six with Its Lessons on the Currency Act. LC 73-101233. (Research & Source Works Ser.: No. 390). 1970. Repr. of 1866 ed. lib. bdg. 20.50 (ISBN 0-8337-0194-0). B Franklin.

Baxter, Ronald E. The Charismatic Gift of Tongues. LC 81-17182. 162p. 1982. pap. 7.95 (ISBN 0-8254-2225-6). Kregel.

--Gifts of the Spirit. LC 83-14963. 280p. (Orig.). 1983. pap. 8.95 (ISBN 0-8254-2243-4). Kregel.

Baxter, Ruth H. A Norwegian Birthday Party. LC 78-63421. (Illus.). 25p. cancelled (ISBN 0-533-03978-9). Vantage.

Baxter, Sandra & Lansing, Marjorie. Women & Politics: The Visible Majority. Rev. ed. (Women & Culture Ser.). 1983. text ed. 19.95 (ISBN 0-472-10043-2); pap. text ed. 10.95 (ISBN 0-472-08043-1). U of Mich Pr.

Baxter, Seaton. Intensive Pig Production: Environmental Management & Design. (Illus.). 599p. 1984. text ed. 42.50x (ISBN 0-246-11234-4). Sheridan.

Baxter, Stephen, ed. England's Rise to Greatness, 1660-1763. LC 82-40095. (Clark Library Professorship). (Illus.). 400p. 1983. text ed. 35.00x (ISBN 0-520-04572-6). U of Cal Pr.

Baxter, Stephen B. William Third & the Defense of European Liberty, 1650-1702. LC 75-8476. (Illus.). 1976. Repr. of 1966 ed. lib. bdg. 31.50 (ISBN 0-8371-8161-5, BAWI). Greenwood.

Baxter, Terry. Hailstone. 1984. pap. 3.50 (ISBN 0-8217-1325-6). Zebra.

Baxter, W. Depreciating Assets. 1981. pap. 13.95 (ISBN 0-85258-204-8). Van Nos Reinhold.

--Inflation Accounting. 296p. 1984. text ed. 42.50x (ISBN 0-86003-524-7, Pub. by PHilip Allan England); pap. text ed. 21.50x (ISBN 0-86003-623-5). Humanities.

Baxter, William D., jt. auth. see Bowen, William R.

Baxter, William F. People or Penguins: The Case for Optimal Pollution. 110p. 1974. 17.00x (ISBN 0-231-03820-8); pap. 8.00x (ISBN 0-231-03821-6). Columbia U Pr.

Baxter, William F., et al. Retail Banking in the Electronic Age: The Law & Economics of Electronic Funds Transfer. LC 76-28594. (Illus.). 200p. 1977. text ed. 22.00x (ISBN 0-916672-06-9). Allanheld.

Baxter, William P. Soviet Airland Battle Tactics. 304p. 1986. 18.95 (ISBN 0-89141-160-7). Presidio Pr.

Baxter, William T. Collected Papers on Accounting: Original Anthology. new ed. Brief, Richard P., ed. LC 77-87311. (Contemporary Accounting Thought Ser.). 1978. lib. bdg. 34.50x (ISBN 0-405-10924-5). Ayer Co Pubs.

Bay, Adela. Method & Techniques for Understanding Music Notation. LC 80-10292. (Illus.). 143p. 1980. pap. text ed. 14.95 (ISBN 0-89116-190-2). Hemisphere Pub.

Bay, Alfred, jt. auth. see Gambrill, Don.

Bay Area Committee for Responsive Philanthropy. Small Change from Big Bucks. 1979. pap. 6.00 (ISBN 0-912078-64-2). Volcano Pr.

Bay, Austin. The Coyote Cried Twice. 167p. 1985. 14.95 (ISBN 0-87795-728-2). Arbor Hse.

--The Coyote Cried Twice. Date not set. 14.95 (ISBN 0-87795-728-2). Arbor Hse.

Bay, Austin, jt. auth. see Dunnigan, James F.

Bay, Bertie C. Some Preachers Do. 150p. 1975. pap. 1.95 (ISBN 0-89114-072-7). Baptist Pub Hse.

Bay, Bill. The Liturgical Guitarist. 360p. 1980. spiral bdg. 9.95 (ISBN 0-89228-055-7). Impact Bks MO.

--Mel Bay's Deluxe Guitar Praise Book. 64p. (Orig.). 1973. pap. 2.95 (ISBN 0-89228-007-7). Impact Bks MO.

--Mel Bay's Guitar Hymnal. 80p. (Orig.). 1972. pap. 2.95 (ISBN 0-89228-009-3). Impact Bks MO.

Bay, Christian. Strategies of Political Emancipation. LC 80-53117. 240p. 1981. text ed. 18.95 (ISBN 0-268-01702-6). U of Notre Dame Pr.

--The Structure of Freedom. rev. ed. LC 58-10475. 1970. 30.00x (ISBN 0-8047-0539-9); pap. 8.95 (ISBN 0-8047-0540-2, SP120). Stanford U Pr.

Bay, Edna, ed. Women & Work in Africa. (Special Studies on Africa). 290p. 1982. pap. 23.00x (ISBN 0-86531-312-1). Westview.

Bay, Edna, jt. ed. see McCall, Daniel.

Bay, Edna G., jt. ed. see Hafkin, Nancy J.

Bay, Kenneth E., ed. The American Fly Tyer's Handbook. LC 78-31584. (Illus.). 1979. 19.95 (ISBN 0-8329-2870-4, Pub. by Winchester Pr). New Century.

Bay, Taco. We & Our Relationship to the Three Worlds Around Us. LC 79-27423. 29p. (Orig.). 1980. pap. 2.95 (ISBN 0-935690-00-X). Schaumburg Pubns.

Bay, Timothy. Fake Giants & Other Great Hoaxes. LC 80-21132. (Monsters & Mysteries Ser.). (gr. 4-10). 1980. pap. 2.25 (ISBN 0-88436-766-5, 35289). EMC.

--How to Turn Problems into Solutions: A Manager's Guide. LC 81-69249. (Hands on Management Guide Ser.). 79p. 1982. 9.95 (ISBN 0-13-435669-1); pap. 4.95 (ISBN 0-13-435651-9). P-H.

Bayan, Richard. Words That Sell. LC 84-71532. (Orig.). Date not set. 19.95 (ISBN 0-87280-150-0). Caddylak Pub.

Bayard, Charles J. The Development of the Public Land Policy, 1783-1820, with Special Reference to Indiana. Bruchey, Stuart, ed. LC 78-53556. (Development of Public Lands Law in the U. S. Ser.). 1979. lib. bdg. 27.50x (ISBN 0-405-11364-1). Ayer Co Pubs.

Bayard, James A. Papers of James A. Bayard. Donnan, Elizabeth, ed. LC 75-75312. (The American Scene: Comments & Commentators Ser.). 1971. Repr. of 1915 ed. lib. bdg. 59.50 (ISBN 0-306-71273-3). Da Capo.

Bayard, Jean. Attachment: Toward the Liberation of the Essential Person. 489p. 1985. 14.95 (ISBN 0-9606078-1-1); pap. 9.95 (ISBN 0-9606078-2-X). Accord Pr.

Bayard, Jean, jt. auth. see Bayard, Robert T.

Bayard, Ralph. Lone-Star Vanguard: The Catholic Re-Occupation of Texas (1838-1848) LC 45-10779. 453p. 1982. lib. bdg. 59.95x (ISBN 0-89370-723-6). Borgo Pr.

Bayard, Robert T. & Bayard, Jean. How to Deal with Your Acting-Up Teenager: Practical Help for Desperate Parents. LC 83-1414. 228p. 1983. 11.95 (ISBN 0-87131-407-X). M Evans.

Bayard, Samuel P. Dance to the Fiddle-March to the Fife: Instrumental Folk Tunes in Pennsylvania. LC 81-83146. 656p. 1982. 32.50x (ISBN 0-271-00299-9). Pa St U Pr.

Bayard, Samuel P., ed. Hill Country Tunes. LC 45-7228. (American Folklore Soc. Memoirs). Repr. of 1944 ed. 15.00 (ISBN 0-527-01091-X). Kraus Repr.

Bayard, Tania. Bourges Cathedral: The West Portals. LC 75-23780. (Outstanding Dissertations in the Fine Arts Ser. - Medieval). (Illus.). 1976. lib. bdg. 55.00 (ISBN 0-8240-1977-6). Garland Pub.

Bayat, Mangol. Mysticism & Dissent: Socioreligious Thought in Qajar Iran. LC 82-5498. 320p. 1982. 25.00x (ISBN 0-8156-2260-0). Syracuse U Pr.

Baybak, Michael. Viewpoints. 32p. 1976. pap. 6.00 (ISBN 0-915598-09-4). Church of Scient Info.

Baybars, Taner, tr. see Hikmet, Nazim.

Bayberry, Austin J. Your Family Herb Guide. 1980. pap. 4.95x (ISBN 0-317-07339-7, Regent House). B of A.

Baybutt, Ron. Codlitz: The Great Escapes. (Illus.). 128p. 1983. 14.45i (ISBN 0-316-08394-1). Little.

Baydo, Gerald. U. S. A. Synoptic History of America's Past, 2 vols. 1981. Set. pap. text ed. 20.50 (ISBN 0-394-34165-1, RanC); pap. text ed. 15.50 ea. (RanC). Vol. 1 (352 pg. (ISBN 0-394-34163-5). Vol. 2 (336 pg. (ISBN 0-394-34164-3). Random.

Baydo, Gerald, ed. The Evolution of Mass Culture in America, 1877 to the Present. LC 81-69861. 1982. pap. text ed. 11.95x (ISBN 0-88273-260-9). Forum Pr IL.

Baydo, Gerald R. A Topical History of the United States. (Illus.). 1978. pap. text ed. 16.95x (ISBN 0-88273-008-8). Forum Pr IL.

Baydun, M., ed. Quran. (Arabic.). medium sized. 20.00x (ISBN 0-86685-134-8). Intl Bk Ctr.

Bayer, Alan E. The Assimilation of American Family Patterns by European Immigrants & Their Children. Cordasco, Francesco, ed. LC 80-839. (American Ethnic Groups Ser.). 1981. lib. bdg. 17.00x (ISBN 0-405-13403-7). Ayer Co Pubs.

Bayer, B., jt. auth. see Adler, Israel.

Bayer, Barry D. & Sobel, Joseph J. Dynamics of VisiCalc. LC 82-73621. 225p. 1983. 19.95 (ISBN 0-87094-391-X). Dow Jones-Irwin.

Bayer, Cary, jt. auth. see Levine, Bob.

Bayer, Edward J. Rape Within Marriage: A Moral Analysis Delayed. LC 85-5289. 160p. (Orig.). 1985. lib. bdg. 22.50 (ISBN 0-8191-4613-7); pap. text ed. 9.75 (ISBN 0-8191-4614-5). U Pr of Amer.

Bayer, Edward J., jt. auth. see McCarthy, Donald G.

Bayer, Edward J., jt. ed. see McCarthy, Donald G.

Bayer, Edward J., ed. see Pope John Center Staff.

Bayer, Erich. Woerterbuch zur Geschichte. 3rd ed. (Ger.). 1974. pap. 19.95 (ISBN 3-520-28903-2, M-6905). French & Eur.

Bayer, Frank J. I Love Credit. (Illus.). 128p. 1982. 7.95 (ISBN 0-89962-249-6). Todd & Honeywell.

Bayer, Frederick M. & Voss, Gilbert L., eds. Studies in Tropical American Mollusks. LC 70-170142. 1971. 12.50x (ISBN 0-87024-230-X). U of Miami Pr.

Bayer, Frederick M. & Weinheimer, Alfred J., eds. Prostaglandins from Plexaura-homomalla: Ecology, Utilization & Conservation of a Major Medical Marine Resource, a Symposium. LC 74-3562. (Studies in Tropical Oceanography Ser: No. 12). 1974. 15.00x (ISBN 0-87024-275-X). U Miami Marine.

Bayer, Herbert, et al, eds. Bauhaus Nineteen Nineteen to Nineteen Twenty-Eight. LC 77-169299. (Illus.). 1976. pap. 9.95 (ISBN 0-87070-240-8, 083763). NYGS.

--Bauhaus: 1919-1928. LC 77-169299. (The Museum of Modern Art Publications in Reprint). (Illus.). 224p. 1972. Repr. of 1938 ed. 33.00 (ISBN 0-405-01559-3). Ayer Co Pubs.

Bayer, Jane. A, My Name Is Alice. (Illus.). (gr. k-3). 1984. 10.95 (ISBN 0-8037-0123-3, 01063320); PLB 10.89 (ISBN 0-8037-0124-1, 01063320). Dial Bks Young.

Bayer, Leona M. & Green, Edith. Kitchen Strategy: The Family Angle on Nutrition. 3rd ed. (Illus.). 112p. 1952. spiral 9.75x (ISBN 0-398-04201-2). C C Thomas.

Bayer, Leona M. & Honzik, Marjorie P. Children with Congenital Intracardiac Defects: A Pictorial Atlas of Individual Somatic & Neuropsychologic Development Before & After Open Heart Surgery. (Illus.). 276p. 1976. photocopy ed. 49.50x (ISBN 0-398-03185-1). C C Thomas.

Bayer, Marc J. Toxicologic Emergencies. LC 83-15758. (Illus.). 352p. 1983. pap. text ed. 19.95 (ISBN 0-89303-188-7). Brady Comm.

Bayer, Marc J. & Rumack, Barry H., eds. Poisoning & Overdose. LC 82-13770. 145p. 1982. 28.00 (ISBN 0-89443-809-3). Aspen Systems.

Bayer, Patricia, ed. see Castle, Wendell & Hunter-Stiebel, Penelope.

Bayer, R., ed. Selection & Use of Wear Tests for Coatings - STP 769. 179p. 1982. 21.00 (ISBN 0-8031-0710-2, 04-769000-29). ASTM.

Bayer, Ronald. Homosexuality & American Psychiatry: The Politics of Diagnosis. LC 80-68182. (Illus.). 224p. 1980. 12.95 (ISBN 0-465-03048-3). Basic.

Bayer, Ronald, et al, eds. In Search of Equity: Health Needs & the Health Care System. (The Hastings Center Series in Ethics). 230p. 1983. 25.00x (ISBN 0-306-41212-8, Plenum Pr). Plenum Pub.

Bayer, Ronald M, et al. Equipment Leasing, 1983. LC 84-119901. (Commercial Law & Practice Course Handbook Ser.: No. 313). 429p. 1983. 35.00 (A4-4072). PLI.

Bayer, S., jt. auth. see Altman, J.

Bayer, S. A., jt. auth. see Altman, J.

Bayer Symposium, 2nd. New Aspects of Storage & Release Mechanisms of Catecholamines. new ed. Schuemann, H. J. & Kroneberg, G., eds. LC 70-123307. (Illus.). 1970. 32.70 (ISBN 0-387-05051-5). Springer-Verlag.

Bayer Symposium, 4th. Psychic Dependence: Definition, Assessment in Animals & Man, Theoretical and Clinical Implications. Hoffmeister, F. & Goldberg, L., eds. LC 73-13497. (Illus.). 244p. 1973. 45.00 (ISBN 0-387-06478-8). Springer-Verlag.

Bayer, U. Pattern Recognition Problems in Geology & Paleontology. (Lecture Notes in Earth Sciences: Vol. 2). vii, 229p. 1985. pap. 19.50 (ISBN 0-387-13983-4). Springer-Verlag.

Bayer, U. & Seilacher, A., eds. Sedimentary & Evolutionary Cycles. (Lecture Notes in Earth Sciences: Vol. 1). vi, 465p. 1985. pap. 29.50 (ISBN 0-387-13982-6). Springer-Verlag.

Bayer, William. Peregrine. 256p. 1983. pap. 2.95 (ISBN 0-345-30618-X). Ballantine.

--Punish Me with Kisses. 1981. pap. 2.95 (ISBN 0-671-41991-9). PB.

--Punish Me with Kisses. 288p. 1982. 20.00x (ISBN 0-7278-0684-X, Pub. by Severn Hse). State Mutual Bk.

--Switch. 1984. 14.95 (ISBN 0-671-49424-4, Linden Pr). S&S.

--Switch. 1984. 13.95 (ISBN 0-317-05158-X, Linden P). S&S.

--Switch. 1985. pap. 3.95 (ISBN 0-451-13603-9, Sig). NAL.

Bayerle, Gustav. Ottoman Diplomacy in Hungary: Letter from the Pashas of Buda, 1590-1593. LC 74-188493. (Uralic & Altaic Ser.: Vol. 101). 196p. (Orig.). 1972. pap. text ed. 7.50x (ISBN 0-87750-169-6). Res Ctr Lang Semiotic.

--Ottoman Tributes in Hungary According to Sixteenth Century Tapu Registers of Novigrad. (Near & Middle East Monographs: No. 8). 1973. text ed. 40.00x (ISBN 90-2792-437-6). Mouton.

Bayerschmidt, Carl F. & Friis, Erik, eds. Scandinavian Studies. LC 65-22388. 1965. 10.95x (ISBN 0-89067-043-9). Am Scandinavian.

Bayerschmidt, Carl F. & Friis, Erik J., eds. Scandinavian Studies: Essays Presented to Dr. Henry Goddard Leach. LC 65-22388. (American-Scandinavian Foundation Scandinavian Studies). (Illus.). 472p. 1965. 20.00x (ISBN 0-295-73924-X). U of Wash Pr.

Bayerschmidt, Carl F. & Hollander, Lee M., eds. Njal's Saga. LC 79-10657. (Illus.). 1979. Repr. of 1956 ed. lib. bdg. 37.50x (ISBN 0-313-20814-X, NJSA). Greenwood.

Bayerschmidt, Carl F. & Hollander, Lee M., trs. from Old Icelandic. Njal's Saga. LC 54-11996. (Library of Scandinavian Literature: Vol. 3). 1955. 7.00x (ISBN 0-89067-011-0). Am Scandinavian.

Bayerschmidt, Carl F., tr. see Reuter, Fritz.

Bayes, Jane H. Ideologies & Interest-Group Politics: The United States As a Special-Interest State in the Global Economy. Jones, Victor, ed. LC 82-14742. (Chandler & Sharp Publications in Political Science Ser.). 288p. (Orig.). 1982. pap. text ed. 9.95x (ISBN 0-88316-547-3). Chandler & Sharp.

--Minority Politics & Ideologies in the United States. Jones, Victor, ed. LC 82-17698. (Chandler & Sharp Publications in Political Science Ser.). 144p. (Orig.). 1982. pap. text ed. 6.95x (ISBN 0-88316-551-1). Chandler & Sharp.

Bayes, Jonathan, jt. auth. see Photographer's Gallery.

Bayes, Marjorie, jt. ed. see Howell, Elizabeth.

Bayes, Ronald. X-Ing Warm. 34p. (Orig.). 1968. pap. 2.00 (ISBN 0-932264-06-9). Trask Hse Bks.

Bayes, Ronald H. A Beast in View. 62p. (Orig.). 1985. pap. 7.00 (ISBN 0-932662-53-6). St Andrews NC.

--The Casketmaker. LC 72-76482. 128p. 1972. 7.95 (ISBN 0-910244-66-9); pap. 4.95 (ISBN 0-910244-67-7). Blair.

--King of August. Ghandour, N., et al, trs. from Japanese & Arabic. (Orig.). 1979. pap. 4.00 (ISBN 0-932662-25-0). St Andrews NC.

Bayes, Ronald H., ed. see Blackburn, Kate & McDonald, Agnes.

Bayes, Ronald H., ed. see Flanagan, Roy K.

Bayes, Ronald H., ed. see Fortner, Ethel.

Bayes, Ronald H., ed. see Gurkin, Kathryn B.

Bayes, Ronald H., ed. see Kimzey, Ardis.

Bayes, Ronald H., ed. see Miller, Rob H.

Bayes, Ronald H., ed. see Oppenheimer, Joel.

Bayes, Ronald H., ed. see Ragan, Sam.

Bayes, Ronald H., ed. see Sibley, Susan K.

Bayes De Luna, A. J., ed. see International Symposium on Diagnosis & Treatment of Cardiac Arrhythmias, Barcelona, Spain, 5-8 October 1977.

Bayet, Albert. Le Suicide et la Morale: Suicide & Morality. LC 74-25739. (European Sociology Ser.). 830p. 1975. Repr. 60.50x (ISBN 0-405-06495-0). Ayer Co Pubs.

Bayfield, M. A. Measures of the Poets. LC 72-195419. 1919. lib. bdg. 15.00 (ISBN 0-8414-1631-1). Folcroft.

--Study of Shakespeare's Versification. LC 74-4224. 1920. lib. bdg. 40.00 (ISBN 0-8414-9920-9). Folcroft.

Bayfield, Matthew A. Study of Shakespeare's Versification, with an Inquiry into the Trustworthiness of the Early Texts. LC 77-130616. Repr. of 1920 ed. 34.50 (ISBN 0-404-00695-7). AMS Pr.

Baygan, Lee. Makeup for Theatre, Film & Television: A Step by Step Photographic Guide. LC 81-1911. (Illus.). 208p. 1982. 29.95x (ISBN 0-89676-023-5). Drama Bk.

--Techniques of Three-Dimensional Make-up: A Step by Step Guide. (Illus.). 184p. 1982. 24.95 (ISBN 0-8230-5260-5). Watson-Guptill.

Baygents, Jeffrey I. Aikido: A Supplement to Dojo Training. LC 81-69692. (Illus.). 150p. 1981. pap. text ed. 14.00 (ISBN 0-9607326-0-8). M E Benefield Pub.

Bayh, Marvella & Kotz, Mary L. Marvella: A Personal Journey. LC 80-25195. 1981. pap. 4.95 (ISBN 0-15-657402-0, Harv). HarbraceJ.

Bayitch, Stojan A. & Siqueiros, Jose L. Conflict of Laws: Mexico & the United States-a Bilateral Study. LC 68-31040. (Studies in Inter-American Law Ser: No. 1). 1968. 15.00x (ISBN 0-87024-090-0). U of Miami Pr.

Bayitch, Stojan A., ed. Latin America & the Caribbean: A Bibliographical Guide to Works in English. LC 67-28900. (Interamerican Legal Studies: Vol. 10). 943p. 1967. 45.00 (ISBN 0-379-00397-X). Oceana.

Bayizian, Elise A. Mesrob Mashtotz: A Fifth Century Life. (Armenian Church Classics Ser.). (Illus.). 39p. (Orig.). 1984. pap. 4.00 (ISBN 0-934728-14-3). D O A C.

Bayizian, Elise A., tr. see Zaroukian, Andranik.

Baykov, Alexander. The Development of the Soviet Economic System: An Essay on the Experience of Planning in the U.S.S.R. LC 83-45411. Repr. of 1946 ed. 49.50 (ISBN 0-404-20021-4). AMS Pr.

Baylac, G., ed. Inelastic Analysis & Life Prediction In Elevated Temperature Design. (PVP Ser.: Vol. 59). 250p. 1982. 44.00 (H00216). ASME.

Bayle, Antoine L. Traite des Maladies Du Cerveau et De Ses Membranes: Maladies Mentales. LC 75-16682. (Classics in Psychiatry Ser.). (Fr.). 1976. Repr. of 1826 ed. 46.50x (ISBN 0-405-07414-X). Ayer Co Pubs.

Bayle, Francis & Rohden, Peter R. Les Idees Politiques de Joseph de Maistre & Joseph de Maistre als Politischer Theoretiker, 2 vols. in one. Mayer, J. P., ed. LC 78-67331. (European Political Thought Ser.). (Fr. & Ger.). 1979. Repr. of 1929 ed. lib. bdg. 32.50x (ISBN 0-405-11677-2). Ayer Co Pubs.

Bayle, Pierre. The Dictionary Historical & Critical of Mr. Peter Bayle, London, 1734-38. Feldman, Burton & Richardson, Robert D., eds. (Myth & Romanticism Ser.). 400.00 (ISBN 0-8240-3551-8). Garland Pub.

--Oeuvres Diverses, 5 Vols. Labrousse, E., ed. Orig. Title: Oeuvres completes. 1969. Repr. of 1727 ed. 780.00x set (ISBN 3-487-05456-6). Adlers Foreign Bks.

Baylen, J. O. & Gossman, N. J. The Biographical Dictionary of Modern British Radicals: Since 1770-1832, Vol. 1. 500p. 1979. text ed. 87.00x (ISBN 0-391-00914-1). Humanities.

Baylen, Joseph O. & Conway, Alan, eds. Soldier-Surgeon: The Crimean War Letters of Dr. Douglas A. Reid, 1855-1856. LC 67-21109. (Illus.). Repr. of 1968 ed. 42.00 (ISBN 0-8357-9765-1, 2016171). Bks Demand UMI.

Baylen, Joseph O. & Gossman, Norbert J., eds. Biographical Dictionary of Modern British Radicals, Vol. 2, 1830-1870. 600p. 1984. 66.00x (ISBN 0-85527-494-8, Pub. by Salem Acad). Merrimack Pub Cir.

Bayles, Jennifer L., jt. auth. see Maurer, Evan E.

Bayles, M. D. Contemporary Utilitarianism. 11.00 (ISBN 0-8446-1612-5). Peter Smith.

Bayles, Mary Ann & Evans, Gail G. Administration of Gymnastics Meets: A Handbook for Teachers & Coaches. 49p. (Orig.). 1983. pap. 6.25x (ISBN 0-88314-241-4). AAHPERD.

Bayles, Michael. Reproductive Ethics. 192p. 1984. pap. text ed. 11.95 (ISBN 0-13-773904-4). P-H.

Bayles, Michael & Henley, Kenneth. Right Conduct: Theories & Applications. 480p. 1982. pap. text ed. 14.00 (ISBN 0-394-32609-1, RanC). Random.

Bayles, Michael D. Morality & Population Policy. LC 79-23965. 208p. 1980. 15.75 (ISBN 0-8173-0032-5); pap. text ed. 7.50 (ISBN 0-8173-0033-3). U of Ala Pr.

--Principles of Legislation: The Uses of Political Authority. LC 78-3220. 280p. 1978. 17.95 (ISBN 0-8143-1599-2). Wayne St U Pr.

--Professional Ethics. 176p. 1981. pap. text ed. write for info. (ISBN 0-534-00998-0). Wadsworth Pub.

Bayles, Michael D. & Chapman, Bruce. Justice, Rights & Tort Law. 1983. lib. bdg. 39.50 (ISBN 90-277-1639-0, Pub. by Reidel Holland). Kluwer Academic.

Bayles, Michael D., ed. Medical Treatment of the Dying: Moral Issues. 180p. 1978. pap. 9.95 (ISBN 0-87073-366-4). Schenkman Bks Inc.

Bayles, W. H. Old Taverns of New York. 1977. lib. bdg. 59.95 (ISBN 0-8490-2373-4). Gordon Pr.

Bayless, jt. auth. see Adams.

Bayless, Allen E. Compact Sight Reduction Tables. LC 80-15129. 32p. 1980. pap. 4.50 (ISBN 0-87033-269-4). Cornell Maritime.

Bayless, B. A., jt. auth. see Kline, M. S.

Bayless, Charles. Charleston Ironwork. (Illus.). Date not set. price not set (ISBN 0-87844-061-5). Sandlapper Pub Co.

Bayless, Hugh. The Best Towns in America: A Where-To-Go Guide for a Better Life. 1983. 15.95 (ISBN 0-395-34391-7); pap. 9.95 (ISBN 0-395-34833-1). HM.

Bayless, Kathleen M. & Ramsey, Marjorie E. Music: A Way of Life for the Young Child. 2nd ed. LC 81-14055. (Illus.). 251p. 1982. pap. text ed. 14.95 (ISBN 0-8016-0521-0). Mosby.

Bayless, Kathleen M., jt. auth. see Ramsey, Marjorie E.

Bayless, Kathy G., jt. auth. see Mull, Richard F.

Bayless, Raymond. Animal Ghosts. 1970. 5.95 (ISBN 0-8216-0054-0). Univ Bks.

Bayless, Raymond, jt. auth. see McAdams, Elizabeth.

Bayless, Theodore M., jt. ed. see Paige, David M.

Bayless, William C. & Pacela, Allan F. Guide to Biomedical Standards. 10th ed. LC 7-640292. 1984. Quest Pub.

Bayless, William C. & Pacela, Allan F., eds. Guide to Biomedical Standards 1984-1985. 11th ed. (Orig.). 1984. pap. 12.00x (ISBN 0-930844-13-0). Quest Pub.

Bayley, Ada E. Donovan, a Novel, 1882. Wolff, Robert L., ed. LC 75-1529. (Victorian Fiction Series). 1975. lib. bdg. 73.00 (ISBN 0-8240-1601-7). Garland Pub.

Bayley, Barrington J. Annihilation Factor. 144p. 1980. 11.95 (ISBN 0-8052-8018-9, Pub. by Allison & Busby England); pap. 4.95 (ISBN 0-8052-8017-0, Pub. by Allison & Busby England). Schocken.

--Empire of Two Worlds. 160p. 1980. 11.95 (ISBN 0-8052-8016-2, Pub. by Allison & Busby England); pap. 4.95 (ISBN 0-8052-8015-4, Pub. by Allison & Busby England). Schocken.

--The Forest of Peldain. 1985. pap. 2.75 (ISBN 0-88677-068-8). DAW Bks.

--The Seed of Evil. 176p. 1980. 11.95 (ISBN 0-8052-8014-6, Pub. by Allison & Busby England); pap. 4.95 (ISBN 0-8052-8013-8, Pub. by Allison & Busby England). Schocken.

--The Zen Gun. 1983. pap. 2.50 (ISBN 0-87997-851-1). DAW Bks.

Bayley, Bruce. Commodore 64 Exposed. (Illus.). 196p. (Orig.). 1983. pap. 14.95 (ISBN 0-86161-133-0). Melbourne Hse.

Bayley, Charles C. Mercenaris for the Crimes: The German, Swiss, & Italian Legions in British Service, 1854-1856. LC 77-357169. pap. 51.30 (ISBN 0-317-26453-2, 2023859). Bks Demand UMI.

Bayley, David H. Forces of Order: Police Behavior in Japan & the United States. LC 75-17304. 1976. 28.50x (ISBN 0-520-03069-9, CAL 388); pap. 7.95 (ISBN 0-520-03641-7). U of Cal Pr.

--Patterns of Policing: A Comparative International Perspective. LC 84-24908. (Crime, Law & Deviance Ser.). 1985. 27.00 (ISBN 0-8135-1094-5). Rutgers U Pr.

Bayley, David H., ed. Police & Society. LC 77-22571. (Sage Focus Editions: Vol. 1). 1977. 28.00 (ISBN 0-8039-0862-8); pap. 14.00 (ISBN 0-8039-0863-6). Sage.

Bayley, Edwin. Joe McCarthy & the Press. LC 81-50824. 288p. 1981. 25.00x (ISBN 0-299-08620-8). U of Wis Pr.

Bayley, Edwin R. Joe McCarthy & the Press. 1982. pap. 6.95 (ISBN 0-394-71246-3). Pantheon.

Bayley, Frank W., et al, eds. see Dunlap, William.

Bayley, Gordon. Local Government: Is It Manageable? 1979. 18.00 (ISBN 0-08-024279-0). Pergamon.

Bayley, H. Photogenerated Reagents in Biochemistry & Molecular Biology. (Laboratory Techniques in Biochemistry & Molecular Biology Ser.: Vol. 12). 208p. 1984. pap. 22.50 (ISBN 0-444-80520-6, I-022-84). Elsevier.

Bayley, Harold. The Lost Language of Symbolism. (Illus.). 763p. 1974. Repr. of 1912 ed. 23.50x (ISBN 0-87471-743-4). Rowman.

--New Light on the Renaissance Displayed in Contemporary Emblems. LC 67-23851. (Illus.). 1967. Repr. of 1909 ed. 22.00 (ISBN 0-405-08244-4, Blom Pubns). Ayer Co Pubs.

--Tragedy of Sir Francis Bacon. LC 70-133281. (English Biography Ser., No. 31). 1970. Repr. of 1902 ed. lib. bdg. 39.95x (ISBN 0-8383-1180-6). Haskell.

Bayley, J. I. & Kessel, L. Shoulder Surgery. (Illus.). 320p. 1982. 67.00 (ISBN 0-387-11040-2). Springer-Verlag.

Bayley, James R. A Brief Sketch of the Early History of the Catholic Church on the Island of New York. LC 77-359171. (Monograph Ser.: No. 29). 1973. Repr. of 1870 ed. 8.50x (ISBN 0-930060-09-1). US Cath Hist.

Bayley, John. An Essay on Hardy. LC 77-80826. 237p. (Orig.). 1981. pap. 14.95 (ISBN 0-521-28462-7). Cambridge U Pr.

--An Essay on Hardy. LC 77-80826. 1978. 29.95 (ISBN 0-521-21814-4). Cambridge U Pr.

--Keats & Reality. LC 73-16442. 1962. lib. bdg. 6.50 (ISBN 0-8414-9877-6). Folcroft.

--Selected Essays. LC 83-15222. 240p. 1984. 39.50 (ISBN 0-521-25828-6); pap. 14.95 (ISBN 0-521-27845-7). Cambridge U Pr.

--Shakespeare & Tragedy. 224p. 1981. pap. 9.95 (ISBN 0-7100-0607-1). Routledge & Kegan.

Bayley, John, ed. The Portable Tolstoy. (Viking Portable Library: No. 91). 1978. 14.95 (ISBN 0-670-71869-6). Viking.

Bayley, John, ed. see Tolstoy, Leo.

Bayley, Linda, et al. Jail Library Service: A Guide for Librarians & Jail Administrators. LC 81-2023. 126p. 1981. pap. 17.50x (ISBN 0-8389-3258-4). ALA.

Bayley, Monica. Wonderful Wizard of Oz Cook Book. LC 81-3708. (Illus.). 128p. (gr. 3 up). 1981. 7.95 (ISBN 0-02-708530-9). Macmillan.

Bayley, Monica & Schulz, Charles M. Snoopy Omnibus. LC 82-71285. (Illus.). 1983. 6.95 (ISBN 0-915696-54-1); pap. 4.95 (ISBN 0-915696-81-9). Determined Prods.

Bayley, Nancy. Development of Motor Abilities During the First Three Years. (SRCD. M). 1935. pap. 14.00 (ISBN 0-527-01486-9). Kraus Repr.

Bayley, Nicola. Crab Cat. LC 84-773. (Copycats Ser.). (Illus.). 24p. (gr. k up). pap. 3.95 (ISBN 0-394-86499-9). Knopf.

--Elephant Cat. LC 84-774. (Copycats Ser.). (Illus.). 24p. (gr. k up). pap. 3.95 (ISBN 0-394-86497-2). Knopf.

--Parrot Cat. LC 83-23749. (Copycats Ser.). (Illus.). 24p. (gr. k up). pap. 3.95 (ISBN 0-394-86496-4). Knopf.

--Polar Bear Cat. LC 83-23744. (Copycats Ser.). (Illus.). 24p. (gr. k up). pap. 3.95 (ISBN 0-394-86501-4). Knopf.

--Spider Cat. LC 84-772. (Copycats Ser.). (Illus.). 24p. (gr. k up). pap. 3.95 (ISBN 0-394-86500-6). Knopf.

Bayley, Nicola, jt. auth. see Adams, Richard.

Bayley, Nicola, jt. auth. see Hoban, Russell.

Bayley, P. French Pulpit Oratory: Fifteen Ninety-Eight to Sixteen Fifty. LC 79-50175. 1980. 57.50 (ISBN 0-521-22765-8). Cambridge U Pr.

Bayley, P. C., ed. see Spenser, Edmund.

Bayley, Peter. Selected Sermons of the French Baroque. LC 82-48767. 326p. 1983. lib. bdg. 85.00 (ISBN 0-8240-9218-X). Garland Pub.

Bayley, Peter & Coleman, Dorothy G., eds. The Equilibrium of Wit: Essays for Odette de Mourgues. LC 81-71433. (French Forum Monographs: No. 36). 286p. (Orig.). 1982. pap. 25.00x (ISBN 0-917058-35-6). French Forum.

Bayley, Rafael, ed. see U. S. Treasury Department.

Bayley, Robert G. The Healing Ministry of the Local Church. 32p. 1983. 2.00x (ISBN 0-318-04132-4). Presby Ref Ren.

Bayley, S. C., jt. auth. see Sheeler, W. D.

Bayley, Stephen. The Albert Memorial: The Monument in its Social & Architectural Context. 1981. 37.00. Scolar.

--Harley Earl & the Dream Machine. LC 83-48024. (Illus.). 128p. 1983. 20.00 (ISBN 0-394-53244-9). Knopf.

Baylie, Simon. The Wizard, From Durham & London MSS. De Vocht, H., ed. (Material for the Study of the Old English Drama Ser.: No. 2, Vol. 4). pap. 24.00 (ISBN 0-317-16739-1). Kraus Repr.

Baylies, Francis. An Historical Memoir of the Colony of New Plymouth... 1608 to 1692, 2 vols. LC 75-31110. Repr. of 1866 ed. 91.00 set (ISBN 0-404-13630-3). AMS Pr.

--A Narrative of Major General Wool's Campaign in Mexico in the Years 1846, 1847, & 1848. (Illus.). Repr. of 1851 ed. 8.95 (ISBN 0-8363-0141-2). Jenkins.

Baylin, Frank & Toner, Amy. Satellites Today: The Complete Guide to Satellite Television. (Illus.). 163p. (Orig.). 1983. pap. 9.95 (ISBN 0-917893-01-8). ConSol.

Baylis & Padfield. The Posterior Pituitary: Hormone Secretion in Health & Disease. (Basic & Clinical Endocrinology Ser.). 528p. 1986. price not set (ISBN 0-8247-7359-4). Dekker.

Baylis, Albert H., Jr. Old Testament Themes. (Living Theology Ser.). 1986. pap. 8.95 (ISBN 0-88070-105-6). Multnomah.

Baylis, H. A. Nematoda: Ascaroidea & Strongyloidea. (Fauna of British India Ser.). xxxvi, 416p. 1978. Repr. of 1936 ed. 30.00 (ISBN 0-88065-051-6, Pub. by Messers Today & Tomorrows Printers & PublishersIndia). Scholarly Pubns.

--Nematoda: Filaricidea, Dictophymoidea & Trichinelloidea, Vol. 2. (Fauna of British India Ser.). xxviii, 280p. 1978. Repr. of 1939 ed. 30.00 (ISBN 0-88065-052-4, Pub. by Messers Today & Tomorrows Printers & Publishers India). Scholarly Pubns.

Baylis, J. A., ed. Safety of Computer Control Systems, 1983: Achieving Safe Real Time Computer Systems, Proceedings of the Third IFAC-IFIP Workshop, SAFECOMP 'Eighty-Three, Cambridge, U. K., September 20-22, 1983. (IFAC Proceedings Ser.). 233p. 1983. 58.00 (ISBN 0-08-030563-6, 11/2). Pergamon.

Baylis, Janice. Sleep on It: The Practical Side of Dreaming. LC 77-74164. 1977. pap. 4.95 (ISBN 0-87516-234-7). De Vorss.

Baylis, Janice F. Dream Dynamics & Decoding: An Interpretation Manual. LC 76-29261. (Illus.). 1977. pap. 10.00 (ISBN 0-917738-00-4). Sun Man Moon.

--Personal Dream Journal. (Illus.). 1977. notebk. 2.50 (ISBN 0-917738-01-2). Sun Man Moon.

Baylis, John. Anglo-American Defense Relations 1939-1979: The Special Relationship. 200p. 1981. 27.50x (ISBN 0-312-03669-8). St Martin.

--Anglo-American Defense Relations, 1939-1984: The Special Relationship. 2nd ed. LC 83-40509. 290p. 1984. 30.00 (ISBN 0-312-03670-1). St Martin.

Baylis, John, ed. Alternative Approaches to British Defence Policy. LC 83-40164. 272p. 1983. 27.95 (ISBN 0-312-02146-1). St Martin.

--British Defence Policy in a Changing World. 295p. 1977. 29.00x (ISBN 0-85664-374-2, Pub. by Croom Helm Ltd). Longwood Pub Group.

Baylis, John & Segal, Gerald, eds. Soviet Strategy. LC 80-28515. 263p. 1981. text ed. 19.95x (ISBN 0-86598-050-0). Allanheld.

Baylis, John, et al. Contemporary Strategy: Theories & Policies. LC 75-19410. 350p. 1975. 24.50x (ISBN 0-8419-0221-6); pap. 14.50x (ISBN 0-8419-0222-4). Holmes & Meier.

Baylis, Maggie. House Plants for the Purple Thumb. Rev. ed. LC 81-11174. (Illus.). 192p. (Orig.). 1981. pap. 6.95 (ISBN 0-89286-194-0). One Hund One Prods.

--Practicing Plant Parenthood. LC 75-22361. (Illus.). 192p. (Orig.). 1975. 4.95 (ISBN 0-912238-62-3); pap. 4.95 (ISBN 0-912238-61-5). One Hund One Prods.

Baylis, Maggie & Castle, Coralie. Real Bread. LC 80-21929. (Illus.). 240p. (Orig.). 1980. pap. 7.95 (ISBN 0-89286-179-7). One Hund One Prods.

Baylis, Robert. Ephesians: Living in God's Household. LC 76-43523. (Fisherman Bible Studyguide). 45p. 1976. saddle stitched 2.95 (ISBN 0-87788-223-1). Shaw Pubs.

Baylis, Robert H. Europe on Purpose: The Christian Traveler's Guide. LC 77-72672. (Illus.). 1977. pap. 3.95 (ISBN 0-918550-01-7). Pilgrimage.

Baylis, Thomas A. The Technical Intelligentsia & the East German Elite: Legitimacy & Social Change in Mature Communism. LC 72-95306. (Illus.). 1974. 37.50x (ISBN 0-520-02395-1). U of Cal Pr.

Bayliss, A. E., ed. Invitation to Verse: An Anthology. facsimile ed. LC 72-167475. (Granger Index Reprint Ser.). Repr. of 1943 ed. 15.00 (ISBN 0-8369-6280-X). Ayer Co Pubs.

Bayliss, B. T. & Philip, A. Butt. Capital Markets & Industrial Investment in Germany & France: Lessons for the U. K. 212p. 1980. text ed. 37.95x (ISBN 0-566-00335-X). Gower Pub Co.

Bayliss, Brian. Planning & Control in the Transport Sector. 216p. 1981. text ed. 47.00x (ISBN 0-566-00407-0). Gower Pub Co.

Bayliss, R. I. Thyroid Disease. (The Facts Ser.). (Illus., Orig.). 1982. 13.95x (ISBN 0-19-261350-2). Oxford U Pr.

Bayliss, William B. An Evaluation of a Plan for Character Education Involving the Use of a Pledge, an Award & a Sponsor. LC 70-176545. (Columbia University. Teachers College. Contributions to Education: No. 695). Repr. of 1936 ed. 22.50 (ISBN 0-404-55695-7). AMS Pr.

Bayliss, Wyke. Five Great Painters of the Victorian Era: Leighton, Millais, Burne-Jones, Watts, Holman Hunt. LC 72-129384. (Illus.). Repr. of 1902 ed. 16.00 (ISBN 0-404-00696-5). AMS Pr.

Bayliss-Smith, T. P. The Ecology of Agricultural Systems. 2nd ed. LC 82-1132. (Cambridge Topics in Geography Ser.: No. 2). (Illus.). 96p. 1982. 14.95 (ISBN 0-521-23125-6); pap. 7.95 (ISBN 0-521-29829-6). Cambridge U Pr.

Bayliss-Smith, Tim, ed. Understanding Green Revolutions: Agrarian Change & Development Planning in South Asia. Wanmali, Sudhir. LC 83-14434. (Illus.). 320p. 1984. 59.50 (ISBN 0-521-24942-2). Cambridge U Pr.

Bayliss-Smith, Timothy & Feachem, Richard, eds. Subsistence & Survival: Rural Ecology in the Pacific. 1978. 68.00 (ISBN 0-12-083250-X). Acad Pr.

Baylon, David, jt. auth. see Eklund, Ken.

Baylor, Ann, jt. auth. see Falls, Harold.

Baylor, Byrd. Before You Came This Way. (Illus.). (gr. 1-5). 1969. 8.95 (ISBN 0-525-26312-8). Dutton.

--The Best Town in the World. LC 83-9033. (Illus.). 32p. (gr. k-3). 1983. 12.95 (ISBN 0-684-18035-9, ScribJ). Scribner.

--Coyote Cry. LC 74-138553. (Illus.). 48p. (gr. 1-5). 1972. PLB 11.88 (ISBN 0-688-51624-6). Lothrop.

--The Desert Is Theirs. (Illus.). 32p. (gr. 1-5). pap. 2.95 (ISBN 0-689-70481-X, A-108, Aladdin). Atheneum.

--The Desert Is Theirs. LC 74-24417. (Illus.). 32p. (gr. 1-5). 1975. reinforced bdg. 13.95 (ISBN 0-684-14266-X, ScribJ); pap. 2.95 (ISBN 0-689-70481-X, ScribJ). Scribner.

--Desert Voices. (Illus.). 32p. (gr. 1-5). 1981. 12.95 (ISBN 0-684-16712-3, ScribJ). Scribner.

--Everybody Needs a Rock. LC 74-9163. (Illus.). 32p. (gr. k-3). 1974. reinforced bdg. 13.95 (ISBN 0-684-13899-9, ScribJ). Scribner.

--Everybody Needs a Rock. LC 74-9163. (Illus.). 32p. (Orig.). (gr. k-3). 1985. pap. 3.95 (ISBN 0-689-71051-8, A-165, Aladdin). Atheneum.

--A God on Every Mountain Top. (Illus.). 64p. (gr. 3-7). 1981. 9.95 (ISBN 0-684-16758-1, ScribJ). Scribner.

--Guess Who My Favorite Person Is. LC 77-7151. (Illus.). (gr. 1-5). 1977. reinforced bdg. 7.95 (ISBN 0-684-15197-9, ScribJ). Scribner.

--Guess Who My Favorite Person Is? LC 77-7151. (Illus.). 32p. (Orig.). (gr. 1-5). 1985. pap. 3.95 (ISBN 0-689-71052-6, A-156, Aladdin). Atheneum.

--Hawk, I'm Your Brother. LC 75-39296. (Illus.). 48p. (gr. 1-5). 1976. reinforced bdg. 11.95 (ISBN 0-684-14571-5, ScribJ); (ScribJ). Scribner.

--If You Are a Hunter of Fossils. LC 79-17926. (Illus.). (gr. 2 up). 1980. 11.95 (ISBN 0-684-16419-1, ScribJ); pap. 3.95 (ISBN 0-689-70773-8). Scribner.

--If You Are a Hunter of Fossils. LC 79-17926. (Illus.). 32p. (gr. 3-6). 1984. pap. 3.95 (ISBN 0-689-70773-8, A-138, Aladdin). Atheneum.

--Moon Song. (Illus.). 24p. (gr. 1-5). 1982. 10.95 (ISBN 0-684-17463-4, ScribJ). Scribner.

--The Other Way to Listen. LC 78-23430. (Illus.). (gr. 1-4). 1978. reinforced bdg 7.95 (ISBN 0-684-16017-X, ScribJ). Scribner.

--The Way to Start a Day. LC 78-113. (Illus.). (gr. 1-4). 1978. reinforced bdg. 12.95 (ISBN 0-684-15651-2, ScribJ). Scribner.

--When Clay Sings. (Illus.). 32p. (gr. 1-5). pap. 2.95 (ISBN 0-689-70482-8, A-109, Aladdin). Atheneum.

--Your Own Best Secret Place. (Illus.). 12.95 (ISBN 0-684-16111-7). Scribner.

Baylor County Historical Society. History of Baylor County: Salt Pork to Sirloin. Vol. 1, 1968. 19.95 (ISBN 0-89015-017-6); Vol. 2, 1977. 25.00 (ISBN 0-89015-167-9). Eakin Pubns.

Baylor, George. Bull Run to Bull Run: Four Years in the Army of Northern Virginia. 1983. Repr. of 1900 ed. 21.95 (ISBN 0-89201-106-8). Zenger Pub.

Baylor, J. & Moore, James. People & Ideas: A Rhetoric Reader. (Illus.). 1980. text ed. 18.95 (ISBN 0-07-004162-8). McGraw.

Baylor, John R., jt. auth. see Miller, Robert W.

Baylor, Robert & Stokes, Brenda. Fine Frenzy: Enduring Themes in Poetry. 2d ed. LC 77-5605. 1978. 19.95 (ISBN 0-07-004160-1). McGraw.

Baylor, Robert & Moore, James, eds. In the Presence of This Continent: American Themes & Ideas. LC 75-130653. 1971. pap. text ed. 12.95x (ISBN 0-03-084397-9). Irvington.

Baylor, Robert A. Detail & Pattern: Essays for Composition. 3rd rev. ed. (Illus.). 224p. 1975. text ed. 19.95 (ISBN 0-07-004145-8). McGraw.

Baylot, R. Beef Basics. 1986. cancelled (ISBN 0-442-21391-3). Van Nos Reinhold.

Bayly, Anselm. An Introduction to Languages: Literary & Philosophical. (Works of Anselm Bayly Ser.). 188p. 1985. Repr. of 1758 ed. lib. bdg. 29.00 (ISBN 0-932051-65-0). Am Repr Serv.

Bayly, Brian. Introduction to Petrology. 1968. text ed. 34.95 (ISBN 0-13-491621-2). P-H.

Bayly, C. A. Rulers, Townsmen & Bazaars: North Indian Society in the Age of British Expansion, 1770-1870. LC 82-4420. (South Asian Studies: No. 28). (Illus.). 488p. 1983. 64.50 (ISBN 0-521-22932-4). Cambridge U Pr.

Bayly, Doreen E. Reflexology Today: The Stimulation of the Body's Healing Forces Through Foot Massage. 64p. (Orig.). 1984. pap. 5.95 (ISBN 0-7225-0705-4). Thorsons Pubs.

Bayly, Joseph. The Gospel Blimp & Other Stories. 1983. pap. 4.95 (ISBN 0-89191-731-4). Cook.

--Heaven. LC 77-71035. (Illus.). 1977. pap. 2.95 (ISBN 0-89191-070-0). Cook.

--The Last Thing We Talk About. rev. & enl. ed. LC 70-87318. Orig. Title: View from a Hearse. 122p. 1973. pap. 2.50 (ISBN 0-912692-07-3). Cook.

--Psalms of My Life. 1969. pap. 0.95 pock. pap. (ISBN 0-8423-5002-0). Tyndale.

Bayly, Lewis. The Practice of Piety: Directing a Christian How to Walk, That He May Please God. LC 75-31081. Repr. of 1718 ed. 34.50 (ISBN 0-404-13500-5). AMS Pr.

Baym. Landav Fermi: Liquid Theory & Low Temperature Properties of Normal Liquid Helium. 1985. price not set (ISBN 0-471-82418-6). Wiley.

Baym, M. I. French Education of Henry Adams. Repr. of 1951 ed. 22.00 (ISBN 0-527-05800-9). Kraus Repr.

Baym, Max I. A History of Literary Aesthetics in America. LC 77-163149. 392p. 1973. 16.00 (ISBN 0-8044-2030-0). Ungar.

Baym, Nina. Novels, Readers, & Reviewers: Responses to Fiction in Antebellum America. LC 84-5033. 288p. 1984. 24.95x (ISBN 0-8014-1709-0). Cornell U Pr.

--The Shape of Hawthorne's Career. LC 75-36994. 288p. 1976. 25.00x (ISBN 0-8014-0996-9). Cornell U Pr.

--Woman's Fiction: A Guide to Novels by & About Women in America, 1820-1870. 336p. 1978. pap. 7.95x (ISBN 0-8014-9184-3). Cornell U Pr.

Baym, Nina, ed. see Chopin, Kate.

Baym, Nina, et al, eds. The Norton Anthology of American Literature, Vols. I & II. 2nd ed. 1984. Vol. I. pap. 18.95 (ISBN 0-393-95377-7). Vol. II. pap. 18.95 (ISBN 0-393-95383-1). Norton.

--Norton Anthology of American Literature. short ed. (Course guide by Marjorie Pryse). 1985. text ed. cancelled; pap. text ed. write for info. (ISBN 0-393-95389-0); write for info. (ISBN 0-393-95452-8). Norton.

Bayman, B. F. & Hamermesh, M. A Review of Undergraduate Physics. 1985. pap. 20.95 (ISBN 0-471-81684-1). Wiley.

Bayn, Nina, ed. see Chopin, Kate.

Bayne, B. L., ed. Cellular Toxicology & Marine Pollution. 44p. 1985. pap. 7.50 (ISBN 0-08-032621-8, Pub by PPL). Pergamon.

--Marine Mussels. LC 75-25426. (International Biological Programme Ser.: No. 10). (Illus.). 400p. 1976. 110.00 (ISBN 0-521-21058-5). Cambridge U Pr.

Bayne, Bradford, ed. see Tinkham, Michael.

Bayne, Brian L., ed. The Effects of Stress & Pollution on Marine Animals. LC 84-18145. 400p. 1984. 45.95x (ISBN 0-03-057019-0). Praeger.

Bayne, Charles J. The Fall of Utopia. LC 76-42718. (Communal Societies in America Ser.). Repr. of 1900 ed. 17.50 (ISBN 0-404-60053-0). AMS Pr.

Bayne, David C. Conscience, Obligation & the Law: The Moral Binding Power of the Civil Law. LC 66-12757. (Jesuit Studies). 1966. 3.45 (ISBN 0-8294-0001-X). Loyola.

Bayne, E. A. Four Ways of Politics: State & Nation in Italy, Somalia, Israel, Iran. LC 65-14723. 316p. 1965. 7.50 (ISBN 0-910116-60-1). U Field Staff Intl.

--Persian Kingship in Transition. LC 68-30502. 1968. 7.50 (ISBN 0-910116-65-2). U Field Staff Intl.

Bayne, James W., jt. auth. see Konzo, Seichi.

Bayne, Neil. Inoculate! 1979. pap. 2.25 (ISBN 0-8439-0664-2, Leisure Bks). Dorchester Pub Co.

Bayne, Neil & Sarginson, Wes. Fast Eddie. 352p. (Orig.). 1983. pap. 3.50 (ISBN 0-8439-1070-4, Leisure Bks). Dorchester Pub Co.

Bayne, Nicholas, jt. auth. see Putnam, Robert D.

Bayne, Peter. Essay in Biography & Criticism: Second Series. LC 73-39681. (Essay Index Reprint Ser.). Repr. of 1858 ed. 25.50 (ISBN 0-8369-2744-3). Ayer Co Pubs.

Bayne, Raymond. Mini Messages on Stewardship. 130p. 1984. pap. 3.95 (ISBN 0-8010-0858-1). Baker Bk.

Bayne, Sheila P. Tears & Weeping: An Aspect of Emotional Climate Reflected in 17th-Century French Literature. (Etudes litteraires francaises: 16). (Orig.). 1981. pap. 19.00x (ISBN 3-87808-895-7). Benjamins North Am.

Bayne, Stephen. Now Is the Accepted Time. Woodhams, Wilbur, ed. 80p. (Orig.). 1983. pap. 2.00 (ISBN 0-88028-022-0). Forward Movement.

Bayne, Stephen F. The Optional God. LC 80-80876. 134p. 1980. pap. 6.95 (ISBN 0-8192-1268-7). Morehouse.

Bayne, William. James Thomson. LC 77-16794. 1898. 20.00 (ISBN 0-8492-0160-8). R West.

Bayne-Jardine, C. C. World War Two. (Modern Times Ser.). (Illus.). 143p. (Orig.). (gr. 9-12). 1968. pap. text ed. 4.75 (ISBN 0-582-20435-6). Longman.

Bayne-Powell, Robert L. Catalogue of Portrait Miniatures in the Fitzwilliam Museum. (Illus.). 256p. 1985. 90.00 (ISBN 0-521-26777-3). Cambridge U Pr.

Bayne-Powell, Rosamond. Travellers in Eighteenth-Century England. LC 74-174875. (Illus.). Repr. of 1951 ed. 20.00 (ISBN 0-405-08245-2, Blom Pubns). Ayer Co Pubs.

Baynes. Eminent Domain & Condemnation. (The Law in Florida Ser.). incl. latest pocket part supplement 24.95 (ISBN 0-686-90239-4); separate pocket part supplement, 1981_(for use in 1982) 10.45 (ISBN 0-686-90240-8). Harrison Co GA.

--Mortgages. (The Law in Florida Ser.). 24.95 (ISBN 0-686-90248-3); separate pocket part supplement, 1984 9.95 (ISBN 0-686-90249-1). Harrison Co GA.

Baynes, C. F. & Wilhelm, R., trs. I Ching or Book of Changes. 3rd ed. LC 67-24740. (Bollingen Ser.: No. 19). 1967. 16.50 (ISBN 0-691-09750-X). Princeton U Pr.

Baynes, C. F., tr. see Wilhelm, Hellmut.

Baynes, Cary F., tr. see Jung, Emma.

Baynes, E. S. Catalogue of Irish Macrolepidoptera. rev. ed. 120p. 1973. Repr. of 1964 ed. 50.00x (ISBN 0-317-07050-9, Pub. by EW Classey UK). State Mutual Bk.

Baynes, Helton G. Germany Possessed. LC 73-180389. (Studies in Fascism Ser.). Repr. of 1941 ed. 28.50 (ISBN 0-404-56106-3). AMS Pr.

Baynes, Kate, jt. auth. see Baynes, Ken.

Baynes, Ken & Baynes, Kate. Gordon Russell. (Design Council Ser.). (Illus.). 72p. 1982. pap. text ed. 12.50x (ISBN 0-87663-572-9). Universe.

Baynes, Ken & Pugh, Francis. The Art of the Engineer. LC 80-29190. (Illus.). 240p. 1981. 85.00 (ISBN 0-87951-128-1); deluxe ed. 175.00 (ISBN 0-87951-140-0). Overlook Pr.

Baynes, Ken, ed. Hospital Research & Briefing Problems: Report on Methods Used in the Department of Health & Social Security's Greenwich Hospital Development Project. 150p. 1971. 30.00x (ISBN 0-900889-52-7, Pub. by Kings Fund). State Mutual Bk.

Baynes, Norman H. The Byzantine Empire. LC 75-41020. Repr. of 1926 ed. 21.50 (ISBN 0-404-14641-4). AMS Pr.

--Byzantine Studies & Other Essays. LC 74-11586. (Illus.). 392p. 1974. Repr. of 1955 ed. lib. bdg. 29.75x (ISBN 0-8371-7673-5, BABYS). Greenwood.

--Constantine the Great & the Christian Church. 1974. lib. bdg. 59.95 (ISBN 0-87968-934-X). Gordon Pr.

--Constantine the Great & the Christian Church. LC 74-34500. (World History Ser., No. 48). 1972. Repr. of 1930 ed. lib. bdg. 50.00x (ISBN 0-8383-0131-2). Haskell.

Baynes, Norman H., jt. tr. see Dawes, Elizabeth.

Baynes, Richard W. God's OK-You're OK? Perspective on Christian Worship. LC 79-67440. 96p. (Orig.). 1981. pap. 2.25 (ISBN 0-87239-382-8, 40088). Standard Pub.

Baynes, Thomas S. Essay on the New Analytic of Logical Forms. LC 73-168274. (Research & Source Works Ser.: No. 897). 170p. (Philosophy Monographs, No. 88). 1972. Repr. of 1850 ed. lib. bdg. 21.00 (ISBN 0-8337-0197-5). B Franklin.

--Shakespeare Studies & an Essay on English Dictionaries. Repr. of 1894 ed. 22.50 (ISBN 0-404-00697-3). AMS Pr.

--Shakespeare Studies & an Essay on English Dictionaries. 1973. Repr. of 1894 ed. 17.45 (ISBN 0-8274-1674-1). R West.

Baynton, Barbara. The Portable Barbara Baynton. Krimmer, Sally & Lawson, Alan, eds. (Portable Australian Authors Ser.). 340p. 1981. text ed. 30.25 (ISBN 0-7022-1377-2); pap. 12.00 (ISBN 0-7022-1469-8). U of Queensland Pr.

Baynton-Power, Henry. How to Compose Music: A Simple Guide for the Amateur to the Composition of Melodies & to Their Effective Harmonization. 2nd ed. LC 79-23654. (Illus.). 1980. Repr. of 1948 ed. lib. bdg. 19.75x (ISBN 0-313-22214-2, BPHC). Greenwood.

Bayo, Alberto. One Hundred Fifty Questions for a Guerrilla. Brown, Robert K., ed. Hartenstein, Hugo & Harber, Dennis, trs. from Span. LC 63-2215. (Illus.). 86p. 1963. pap. 8.00 (ISBN 0-87364-022-5). Paladin Pr.

Bayod Serrat, Ramon. Diccionario Laboral. 546p. (Span.). 1969. pap. 6.95 (ISBN 84-290-0937-X, S-50139). French & Eur.

Bayon, Alejandro & Drucker-Colin, Rene, eds. In Vivo Perfusion & Release of Neuroactive Substances. Date not set. 62.50 (ISBN 0-12-083350-6). Acad Pr.

Bayon, Damian. The Changing Shape of Latin American Architecture: Conversations with Ten Leading Architects. Greaser, Galen D., tr. LC 78-31583. 254p. 1979. 74.95x (ISBN 0-471-27568-9, Pub. by Wiley-Interscience). Wiley.

Bayon, Damian, jt. auth. see Duncan, Barbara.

Bayon, Damian C. Construccion de Lo Visual. LC 76-10371. (Illus., Span.). 1976. pap. 5.00 (ISBN 0-8477-2108-6). U of PR Pr.

Bayon, Mlle., jt. auth. see Lebrun, Francesca.

Bayor, Ronald H. Neighborhoods in Urban America. (Interdisciplinary Urban Ser.). 1982. 27.50x (ISBN 0-8046-9284-X, Pub. by Kennikat). Assoc Faculty Pr.

--Neighbors in Conflict: The Irish, Germans, Jews, & Italians of New York City, 1929-1941. LC 77-14260. (Studies in Historical & Political Science, 96th Ser: No. 2). 1978. pap. 7.95x (ISBN 0-8018-2370-6). Johns Hopkins.

Bayrak, Tosun, tr. see Al-Husayn al-Sulami, Ibn.

Bayraktar, B. A. & Muller-Merbach, H., eds. Education in Systems Science. (NATO Conference Ser.). 384p. 1978. 29.00x (ISBN 0-85066-182-X). Taylor & Francis.

Bayraktar, B. A., et al, eds. Energy Policy Planning. LC 80-26897. (NATO Conference Series II-Systems Science: Vol. 9). 478p. 1981. 69.50x (ISBN 0-306-40631-4, Plenum Pr). Plenum Pub.

Bayrd, Edwin A., jt. auth. see Kyle, Robert A.

Bayrd, Ned & Quilter, Chris. Food for Champions: How to Eat to Win. 224p. 1984. pap. 3.50 (ISBN 0-425-06771-8). Berkley Pub.

Bayros, Franz von. The Amorous Drawings of the Marquis Von Bayros. LC 83-49388. 240p. 1984. 24.95 (ISBN 0-394-53853-6, GP 906); pap. 12.50 (ISBN 0-394-62054-2, E 926). Grove.

Bays, Daniel, jt. auth. see Suleski, Ronald.

Bays, Daniel H. China Enters the Twentieth Century: Chang Chih-Tung & the Issues of a New Age, 1895-1909. LC 77-14261. (Michigan Studies on China). text ed. 19.95x (ISBN 0-472-08105-5). U of Mich Pr.

Bays, Gwendolyn, tr. see Sutra, Buddhist.

Bays, L. R., jt. ed. see Urbistondo, R.

Baysinger, Barry D., et al. Barriers to Corporate Growth. LC 80-8603. 144p. 1981. 21.50 (ISBN 0-669-04323-0). Lexington Bks.

Baysinger, Patricia R. see Dewey, John.

Bayston, Darwin M. CFA, jt. ed. see Fogler, Russell.

Bayt, Phyllis. Medical Assisting: An Introduction to Clinical Practice. 1984. pap. text ed. 19.95 (ISBN 0-8359-4327-5). Reston.

Bayt, Phyllis T. Administering Medications. (Health Occupations Ser.). 1982. pap. 17.55 scp (ISBN 0-672-61522-3); scp answer key 3.67 (ISBN 0-672-61538-X). Bobbs.

Baytop, Turhan, jt. auth. see Mathew, Brian.

Bayvel, L. P. & Jones, A. R. Electromagnetic Scattering & Its Applications. (Illus.). 1981. 63.00 (ISBN 0-85334-955-X, Pub. by Elsevier Applied Sci England). Elsevier.

Baz, Petros D., ed. Dictionary of Proverbs. LC 62-21555. 1963. pap. 5.95. Philos Lib.

Baz, Petros De see De Baz, Petros.

Bazak, Jacob. Jewish Law & Jewish Life, 8 bks. in 4 vols. Passamaneck, Stephen M., ed. Incl. Bk. 1. Selected Rabbinical Response (ISBN 0-8074-0034-3, 180210); Bks. 2-4. Contracts, Real Estate, Sales & Usury (180211); Bks. 5-6. Credit, Law Enforcement & Taxation (180212); Bks. 7-8. Criminal & Domestic Relations (ISBN 0-8074-0037-8, 180213). 1978. pap. 12.50 complete vol. (ISBN 0-8074-0038-6, 180218); pap. 5.00 ea. UAHC.

Bazak Publishing Co. Staff. Bazak Guide to Israel, 1985-86: With City & Touring Maps. (Illus.). 528p. (Orig.). 1985. pap. 11.49i (ISBN 0-06-091206-5, CN 1206, CN). Har-Row.

Bazalgette, Leon. Henry Thoreau Bachelor of Nature. Brooks, Wyck Van, tr. LC 80-2679. (BCL Ser. I). Repr. of 1924 ed. 37.50 (ISBN 0-404-19076-6). AMS Pr.

--Walt Whitman: The Man & His Work. Fitzgerald, Ellen, tr. LC 72-128770. 1971. Repr. of 1920 ed. lib. bdg. 25.00 (ISBN 0-8154-0352-6). Cooper Sq.

Bazan, N. G. & Lolley, R. N., eds. Neurochemistry of the Retina: Proceedings of the International Symposium on the Neurochemistry of the Retina, 28 August - 1 September 1979, Athens, Greece. (Illus.). 584p. 1980. 105.00 (ISBN 0-08-025485-3). Pergamon.

Bazan, N. G., et al, eds. Function & Biosynthesis of Lipids. LC 77-6831. (Advances in Experimental Medicine & Biology Ser.: Vol. 83). 658p. 1977. 79.50x (ISBN 0-306-39083-3, Plenum Pr). Plenum Pub.

Bazan, Nicolas G., et al. New Trends in Nutrition, Lipid Research, & Cardiovascular Diseases. LC 81-15650. (Current Topics in Nutrition & Disease: Vol. 5). 332p. 1981. 30.00 (ISBN 0-8451-1604-5). A R Liss.

Bazant, J. A Concise History of Mexico from Hidalgo to Cardenas 1805-1940. (Illus.). 1977. pap. 11.95 (ISBN 0-521-29173-9). Cambridge U Pr.

Bazant, Vladimir, et al, eds. Handbook of Organosilicon Compounds: Advances Since 1961, Vol. 2. 628p. 1975. 125.00 (ISBN 0-8247-6267-3). Dekker.

--Handbook of Organosilicon Compounds: Advances Since 1961, Vol. 3. 736p. 1975. 125.00 (ISBN 0-8247-6268-1). Dekker.

--Handbook of Organosilicon Compounds: Advances Since 1961, Vol. 4. 1008p. 1975. 125.00 (ISBN 0-8247-6269-X). Dekker.

--Handbook of Organosilicon Compounds: Advances Since 1961, Vol.1. 768p. 1975. 125.00 (ISBN 0-8247-6259-2). Dekker.

Bazant, Z. Methods of Foundation Engineering. LC 78-15933. (Developments in Geotechnical Engineering Ser.: Vol. 24). 616p. 1979. 102.25 (ISBN 0-444-99789-X). Elsevier.

Bazant, Z. P. Mechanics of Geomaterials: Rocks, Concretes & Soils. (Numerical Methods in Engineering Ser.). 1985. 85.00 (ISBN 0-471-90541-0). Wiley.

Bazant, Z. P. & Wittmann, F. H. Creep & Shrinkage in Concrete Structures. LC 82-4766. (Numerical Methods in Engineering Ser.: I-405). 363p. 1983. 58.95x (ISBN 0-471-10409-4, Pub. by Wiley Interscience). Wiley.

Bazaraa, M. S. & Shetty, C. M. Foundations of Optimization. (Lecture Notes in Economics & Mathematical Systems: Vol. 122). 1976. pap. 13.00 (ISBN 0-387-07680-8). Springer-Verlag.

Bazaraa, Mokhtar S. & Jarvis, John J. Linear Programming & Network Flows. LC 76-42241. 565p. 1977. text ed. 46.50x (ISBN 0-471-06015-1). Wiley.

Bazaraa, Mokhtar S. & Shetty, C. M. Nonlinear Programming: Theory & Algorithms. LC 78-986. 560p. 1979. text ed. 47.00 (ISBN 0-471-78610-1). Wiley.

Bazargan, Mehdi. The Inevitable Victory. Yousefi, Mohammad, tr. from Persian. 35p. 1979. pap. 1.25x (ISBN 0-941722-03-1). Book-Dist-Ctr.

--Work & Islam. Yousefi, Mohammack, tr. from Persian. 62p. 1979. 4.00 (ISBN 0-941722-04-X). Book-Dist-Ctr.

Bazarov, Konstantine. Landscape Painting. (Illus.). 224p. (YA) 1981. 25.00 (ISBN 0-7064-1230-3, Mayflower Bks). Smith Pubs.

Bazaz, Nagin. Ahead of His Times: Press Nath Bazaz, His Life & Work. 282p. 1983. text ed. 27.50x (ISBN 0-86590-118-X, Pub by Sterling Pubs India). Apt Bks.

Bazaz, Prem N. Democracy Through Intimidation & Terror: The Untold Story of Kashmiri Politics. 1978. 12.00x (ISBN 0-8364-0270-7). South Asia Bks.

Baze, David, jt. auth. see Scott, Lawrence.

Bazeley, Canon, jt. auth. see Hyett, Francis A.

Bazelon, Bruce S. Defending the Commonwealth: Catalogue of the Militia Exhibit at the Will Penn Memorial Museum in Harrisburg, PA. (Illus.). 28p. 1980. pap. 4.00 (ISBN 0-917218-14-0). Mowbray.

Bazelon, David T. The Paper Economy. LC 78-11587. 1979. Repr. of 1963 ed. lib. bdg. 32.50x (ISBN 0-313-21001-2, BATP). Greenwood.

Bazergui, A. & Marchand, L. PVRC Milestone Gasket Tests: First Results. 1984. bulletin no. 292 14.00 (ISBN 0-318-01897-7). Welding Res Coun.

Bazerman, Charles. The Informed Writer. LC 80-68140. 320p. 1981. pap. text ed. 14.95 (ISBN 0-395-29715-X); instr's manual 1.00 (ISBN 0-395-29716-8). HM.

--The Informed Writer: Using Sources in the Disciplines. 2nd ed. LC 84-82364. 544p. 1984. pap. text ed. write for info. (ISBN 0-395-35499-4); write for info. instr's manual (ISBN 0-395-35500-1). HM.

Bazerman, Charles, jt. auth. see Wiener, Harvey.

Bazerman, Charles, jt. auth. see Wiener, Harvey S.

Bazerman, Max H. & Lewicki, Roy J., eds. Negotiating in Organizations. 392p. 1983. 29.95 (ISBN 0-8039-2035-0); pap. 14.95 (ISBN 0-8039-2036-9). Sage.

Bazett, L. Margery. Beyond the Five Senses. 59.95 (ISBN 0-87968-726-6). Gordon Pr.

Bazhanov, N. Rachmaninov. 343p. 1983. 11.95 (ISBN 0-8285-2624-9, Pub. by Raduga Pubs USSR). Imported Pubns.

Bazhenova, T. V., ed. see CISM (International Center for Mechanical Sciences), Dept. of Hydro & Gas Dynamics, 1970.

Bazigos, G. P. Mathematics for Fishery Statisticians. (Fisheries Technical Papers: No. 169). 193p. (2nd Printing 1978). 1977. pap. 14.00 (ISBN 92-5-100314-9, F1241, FAO). Unipub.

Bazik, Martha. The Life & Works of Luis Carlos Lopez. (Studies in the Romance Languages & Literatures Ser: No. 183). 147p. 1977. 8.00x (ISBN 0-8078-9183-5). U of NC Pr.

Bazilevic, I. E., et al. Thirteen Papers on Algebra, Topology, Complex Variables, & Linear Programming. LC 51-5559. (Translations Ser.: No. 2, Vol. 71). 1968. 32.00 (ISBN 0-8218-1771-X, TRANS 2-71). Am Math.

Bazilevskaya, N. A. On the Races of the Opium Poppy Growing in Semirech'e & the Origin of Their Culture. 1981. 25.00x (ISBN 0-686-76652-0, Pub. by Oxford & IBH India). State Mutual Bk.

Bazin, Andre. The Cinema of Cruelty. Fliss, Tiffany, tr. from Fr. LC 81-13545. Orig. Title: La Cinema De la Cruaute. 224p. 1982. 17.95 (ISBN 0-394-51808-X); pap. 9.95 (ISBN 0-394-17826-2). Seaver Bks.

--French Cinema of the Occupation & Resistance: The Birth of a Critical Esthetic. Hochman, Stanley, tr. from Fr. LC 80-5343. (Ungar Film Library). (Illus.). 256p. 1981. 13.95x (ISBN 0-8044-2022-X). Ungar.

--French Cinema of the Occupation & Resistance: The Birth of a Critical Esthetic. Hochman, Stanley, tr. 174p. 1984. pap. 8.95 (ISBN 0-8044-6024-8). Ungar.

--Orson Welles: A Critical View. Rosenbaum, Jonathan, tr. from Fr. LC 74-15810. (Illus.). 1978. 12.50i (ISBN 0-06-010274-8, HarpT). Har-Row.

--What Is Cinema, Vol. 1. Gray, Hugh, tr. LC 67-18899. 1967. 19.95x (ISBN 0-520-00091-9); pap. 5.95 (ISBN 0-520-00092-7, CAL151). U of Cal Pr.

--What Is Cinema, Vol. 2. Gray, Hugh, tr. & compiled by. 1971. pap. 5.95 (ISBN 0-520-02255-6, CAL250). U of Cal Pr.

Bazin, Germain. Baroque & Rococo. (The World of Art Ser.). (Illus.). 288p. 1985. pap. 9.95 (ISBN 0-500-20018-1). Thames Hudson.

--The Baroque: Principles, Styles, Modes, Themes. (Illus.). 368p. 1978. pap. text ed. 10.95 (ISBN 0-393-09055-8). Norton.

--Mont-Saint-Michel. LC 75-24825. (Fr.). 1978. Repr. of 1933 ed. lib. bdg. 100.00 (ISBN 0-87817-190-8). Hacker.

Bazin, Germain, jt. ed. see Huyghe, Rene.

Bazin, Herve. Madame Ex. Crant, Phillip & Platt, Helen, trs. from Fr. 267p. 1978. 9.95 (ISBN 0-917786-06-8). Summa Pubns.

Bazin, M., ed. Microbial Population Dynamics, Vol. I. 216p. 1982. 69.50 (ISBN 0-8493-5951-1). CRC Pr.

Bazin, M. J. & Smith, O. L. Soil Microbiology: A Model of Nitrification. 272p. 1982. 79.50 (ISBN 0-8493-5952-X). CRC Pr.

Bazin, Michael. Mathematics in Microbiology. 1983. 70.00 (ISBN 0-12-083480-4). Acad Pr.

Bazin, Rene. Marriage of Mademoiselle Gimel, & Other Stories. facs. ed. Hoyt, Edna K., tr. LC 71-128719. (Short Story Index Reprint Ser). 1913. 17.00 (ISBN 0-8369-3610-8). Ayer Co Pubs.

Bazley, John D., jt. auth. see Nikolai, Loren A.

Bazzato, Giorgio & Onesti, Gaddo. Hemodialysis in the Home: Techniques & Clinical Results. (Illus.). 120p. 1975. 13.75x (ISBN 0-398-03156-8). C C Thomas.

Bazzi, Maria. Enciclopedia De las Tecnicas Pictoricas. 342p. (Espn.). 1965. 12.25 (ISBN 84-279-4511-6, S-50549). French & Eur.

BB. Indian Summer. (Illus.). 224p. 1985. 13.95 (ISBN 0-7181-2367-0, Pub. by Michael Joseph). Merrimack Pub Cir.

--Recollections of a Longshore Gunner. 216p. 1979. 11.25 (ISBN 0-85115-067-5, Pub. by Boydell & Brewer). Longwood Pub Group.

BBB Giles Cooper Award Winners. Best Radio Plays of 1983. (Modern Plays Ser.). 212p. 1984. 19.95 (ISBN 0-413-55220-9, NO. 9046). Methuen Inc.

BBC Publications, ed. BBC Music Library, 4 vols. (Orchestral Catalogue Ser.). 1982. 300.00x ea. (Pub. by BBC Pubns); Set. 1200.00x. State Mutual Bk.

--The Computer Book. 208p. 1982. pap. 30.00x (ISBN 0-563-16484-0, Pub. by BBC Pubns). State Mutual Bk.

--Gardeners' World Cottage Garden. 1982. 29.00x (ISBN 0-563-20059-6, Pub. by BBC Pubns). State Mutual Bk.

--Grand Slam. 144p. 1982. 29.00x (ISBN 0-563-20047-2, Pub. by BBC Pubns). State Mutual Bk.

--Muggeridge Ancient & Modern. 268p. 1981. 40.00x (ISBN 0-563-17905-8, Pub. by BBC Pubns). State Mutual Bk.

--Priestland's Progress. 180p. 1981. 30.00x (ISBN 0-563-17968-6, Pub. by BBC Pubns). State Mutual Bk.

--Taking the Strain. 1982. pap. 25.00x (ISBN 0-563-16499-9, Pub. by BBC Pubns). State Mutual Bk.

BCAS. China from Mao to Deng: The Politics & Economics of Socialist Development. (Illus.). 100p. (Orig.). 1983. pap. text ed. 8.95 (ISBN 0-87332-244-4). M E Sharpe.

Bcklemishev, Iurii S. see Krymov, Iurii S., pseud.

B. de Galinanes, Maria T., ed. see Universidad de Puerto Rico, Centro de Investigaciones Sociales.

B. D'Herbelot de Molainville, et al. Bibliotheque Orientale, ou Dictionnaire Universel, Contenant Generalment tout ce qui regarde la Connaissance des Peuples de l'Orient, 4 vols. 2864p. (Fr.). Repr. of 1782 ed. Set. lib. bdg. 525.00x (ISBN 0-89241-342-5). Caratzas.

Bea, Augustin. Church & Mankind. 6.50 (ISBN 0-8199-0012-5, L38112). Franciscan Herald.

--Word of God & Mankind. 1968. 6.50 (ISBN 0-8199-0149-0, L39003). Franciscan Herald.

Bea, Harvey D. The Ambassadors Notes. 1969. pap. text ed. 3.95 (ISBN 0-8220-0161-6). Cliffs.

Bea, Louise de, jt. auth. see Sandahl, Pierre.

Beable, William H. Epitaphs: Graveyard Humour & Eulogy. LC 79-154494. 246p. Repr. of 1925 ed. 35.00x (ISBN 0-8103-3374-0). Gale.

Beach, Amy. Piano Music. (Women Composers Ser.: No. 10). 1982. Repr. lib. bdg. 26.50 (ISBN 0-306-76088-6). Da Capo.

--Quintet for Piano & Strings in F-Sharp Minor, Op. 67. (Women Composers Ser.: No. 1). 1979. Repr. of 1909 ed. lib. bdg. 24.50 (ISBN 0-306-79550-7). Da Capo.

--Sonata for Violin & Piano: Op. 34, No. 19. (Women Composers Ser.: No. 19). 46p. 1985. Repr. of 1899 ed. lib. bdg. 23.50 (ISBN 0-306-76250-1). Da Capo.

Beach, Belle. Riding & Driving for Women. LC 77-3505. (Illus.). 1978. Repr. of 1912 ed. 30.00 (ISBN 0-88427-028-9). North River.

Beach, Charles. The Not-So-Amazing Mormonism. (Truthway Ser.). 39p. 1981. pap. text ed. 1.25 (ISBN 0-87148-629-6). Pathway Pr.

Beach, Charles & Fordyce, Edward, eds. A Solar World: Proceedings of the Annual Meeting of the International Solar Energy Society, 3 vols. 1977. Set. pap. text ed. 115.00x (ISBN 0-89553-004-X). Am Solar Energy.

Beach, Charles M., et al. Distribution of Income & Wealth in Ontario: Theory & Evidence. (Ontario Economic Council Research Studies). 1981. pap. 17.50 (ISBN 0-8020-3369-5). U of Toronto Pr.

Beach, D. N. The Shona & Zimbabwe Nine Hundred to Eighteen Fifty: An Outline of Shona History. LC 80-14116. 424p. 1980. text ed. 45.00x (ISBN 0-8419-0624-6, Africana). Holmes & Meier.

Beach, Dale S. Managing People at Work: Readings in Personnel. 3rd ed. (Illus.). 1980. pap. text ed. write for info. (ISBN 0-02-307030-7). Macmillan.

--Personnel. 5th. ed. 1985. text ed. write for info. (ISBN 0-02-307060-9); text ed. write for info. study guide (ISBN 0-02-307080-3). Macmillan.

--Personnel: The Mangement of People at Work. 4th ed. (Illus.). 1980. text ed. write for info. (ISBN 0-02-307040-4). Macmillan.

Beach, Dan, jt. auth. see Moore, Ralph.

Beach, David. Aspects of Schenkerian Theory. LC 82-13498. 240p. 1983. text ed. 27.50x (ISBN 0-300-02800-8); pap. text ed. 8.95x (ISBN 0-300-02803-2). Yale U Pr.

Beach, David, ed. see Kirnberger, Jonann P.

Beach, Don M. Reaching Teenagers: Learning Centers for the Secondary Classroom. LC 76-40778. (Illus.). 1977. 14.95 (ISBN 0-673-16416-0); pap. 12.95 (ISBN 0-673-16417-9). Scott F.

Beach, Don M., jt. auth. see Reinhartz, Judy.

Beach, Don M., et al. Applications of the Learning Process: A Laboratory Approach. 1979. pap. 10.95 (ISBN 0-8403-2085-X). Kendall-Hunt.

Beach, Donald P. & Lyons, Richard A. Solid State Electronic Amplifiers: An Empirical Approach. 1984. text ed. 28.95 (ISBN 0-8359-6951-7). Reston.

Beach, Dore & Shimberg, Elaine. Two for the Money: A Woman's Guide to a Double Career Marriage. 204p. 1981. 10.95 (ISBN 0-13-935270-8); pap. 5.95 (ISBN 0-13-935262-7). P-H.

Beach, E. F. Economic Models: An Exposition. LC 57-10800. 227p. 1957. text ed. 12.50 (ISBN 0-471-06072-0, Pub. by Wiley). Krieger.

Beach, Edward. Dance of the Dialectic: A Dramatic Dialogue Presenting Hegel's Philosophy of Religion. LC 78-63255. pap. text ed. 6.75 (ISBN 0-8191-0615-1). U Pr of Amer.

Beach, Edward L. Keepers of the Sea: A Profile. LC 82-61291. (Illus.). 256p. 1983. clothbound 45.00 (ISBN 0-87021-727-5); deluxe ed. 75.00 deluxe ed. (ISBN 0-87021-736-4). Naval Inst Pr.

--The United States Navy. (Illus.). 544p. 1985. 25.00 (ISBN 0-03-044711-9). HR&W.

--The Wreck of the Memphis. 17.95 (ISBN 0-88411-774-X, Pub. by Aeonian Pr). Amereon Ltd.

Beach, Edward L., jt. auth. see Noel, John V., Jr.

Beach, Elizabeth. Shakespeare & the Tenth Muse. LC 76-85797. 1969. 6.00 (ISBN 0-686-00965-7). Willoughby.

Beach, Frank A. Human Sexuality in Four Perspectives. Diamond, Milton, et al, eds. LC 76-17235. pap. 84.00 (ISBN 0-317-09724-5, 2019114). Bks Demand UMI.

Beach, Frank A., jt. auth. see Ford, Clellan S.

Beach, Fred F. The Custody of School Funds: An Appraisal of Systems of School Fund Custody with Particular Reference to New York State. LC 73-176546. (Columbia University. Teachers College. Contributions to Education: No. 577). Repr. of 1933 ed. 22.50 (ISBN 0-404-55577-2). AMS Pr.

Beach, Janet L. How to Get a Job in the San Francisco Bay Area. 352p. (Orig.). 1983. pap. 10.95 (ISBN 0-8092-5692-4). Contemp Bks.

Beach, John M. Butterfly: A Journey into Consciousness. 207p. (Orig.). 1984. pap. 7.95 (ISBN 0-913299-00-6). Stillpoint.

Beach, Joseph W. Method of Henry James. rev. ed. 1954. 10.00x (ISBN 0-87556-020-2). Saifer.

--Obsessive Images. O'Connor, William V., ed. LC 73-11620. 396p. 1973. Repr. of 1960 ed. lib. bdg. 22.50 (ISBN 0-8371-7079-6, BEOI). Greenwood.

--Outlook for American Prose. facs. ed. LC 68-22901. (Essay Index Reprint Ser). 1926. 18.00 (ISBN 0-8369-0179-7). Ayer Co Pubs.

--Outlook for American Prose. LC 68-26244. 1934. Repr. 19.50x (ISBN 0-8046-0023-6, Pub. by Kennikat). Assoc Faculty Pr.

--Romantic View of Poetry. Repr. of 1944 ed. 29.00x (ISBN 0-403-03886-3). Somerset Pub.

--A Romantic View of Poetry. 11.25 (ISBN 0-8446-1061-5). Peter Smith.

--Technique of Thomas Hardy. LC 61-14870. 1962. Repr. of 1922 ed. 14.00x (ISBN 0-8462-0120-8). Russell.

Beach, Kenneth M., Jr., jt. auth. see Mager, Robert F.

Beach, Leonard B., jt. auth. see Williams, Stanley T.

Beach, Lynn. Attack of the Insecticons: Find Your Fate Junior-Transformers. (No. 2). 80p. (Orig.). 1985. pap. 1.95 (ISBN 0-345-32671-7). Ballantine.

--The Haunted Castle of Ravencurse. (Wizards, Warriors & You Ser.: Bk. 5). 112p. (gr. 4 up). 1985. pap. 2.25 (ISBN 0-380-89523-4). Avon.

--Secrets of the Lost Island. (Twistaplot Ser.: No. 16). (Illus.). 96p. (Orig.). (gr. 4 up). 1985. pap. 1.95 (ISBN 0-590-33233-3). Scholastic Inc.

Beach, Marie H., ed. Guide to Richmond. rev. ed. pap. write for info. (ISBN 0-9607442-0-7). Guide to Rich.

Beach, Mark. A Bibliographic Guide to American Colleges & Universities: From Colonial Times to the Present. LC 74-11704. 315p. 1975. lib. bdg. 35.00x (ISBN 0-8371-7690-5, BCU/). Greenwood.

--Desegregated Housing & Interracial Neighborhoods: A Bibliographic Guide. 91p. 1975. 1.00 (ISBN 0-318-15821-3, N-5). Natl Neighbors.

--Editing Your Newletter: A Guide to Writing, Design & Production. 122p. 9.95 (ISBN 0-318-17939-3, E06A). NASCO.

--Editing Your Newsletter. 122p. 1983. pap. 14.95 (ISBN 0-88908-553-6). Self Counsel Pr.

--Editing Your Newsletter: A Guide to Writing, Design & Production. 2nd ed. LC 81-70670. 128p. 1982. pap. 9.95 (ISBN 0-9602664-6-1). Coast to Coast.

Beach, Mark, compiled by. A Subject Bibliography of the History of American Higher Education. LC 83-22565. vii, 165p. 1984. lib. bdg. 29.95 (ISBN 0-313-23276-8, BEH/). Greenwood.

Beach, Mark, et al. Getting It Printed: How to Work with Printers & Other Graphic Arts Services to Control Quality, Schedule, & Costs. LC 85-70831. 224p. 1986. 48.50 (ISBN 0-9602664-8-8); pap. 34.50 (ISBN 0-9602664-7-X). Coast to Coast.

Beach, Mary. A Two-Fisted Banana: Electric & Gothic. LC 79-14957. 1980. pap. 4.00x (ISBN 0-916156-35-4). Cherry Valley.

Beach, Mary, tr. see Mansour, Joyce.

Beach, Milo C. The Adventures of Rama. LC 83-1473. (Illus.). 64p. (Orig.). 1983. 15.00 (ISBN 0-934686-51-3). Freer.

--The Imperial Image: Paintings for the Mughal Court. LC 81-8762. (Illus.). 240p. 1982. 45.00x (ISBN 0-934686-37-8); pap. 22.50x (ISBN 0-934686-38-6). Freer.

Beach, Milo C., jt. auth. see Welch, Stuart C.

Beach, Rex. The Barrier. 1975. lib. bdg. 14.85x (ISBN 0-89966-009-6). Buccaneer Bks.

--The Crimson Gardenia. 1975. lib. bdg. 16.70x (ISBN 0-89966-015-0). Buccaneer Bks.

--Heart of the Sunset. 1975. lib. bdg. 16.30x (ISBN 0-89966-016-9). Buccaneer Bks.

--The Iron Trail. 1977. pap. 2.25 (ISBN 0-89174-022-8). Comstock Edns.

--The Net. 1975. lib. bdg. 15.30x (ISBN 0-89966-014-2). Buccaneer Bks.

--The Silver Horde. 1975. lib. bdg. 17.25x (ISBN 0-89966-013-4). Buccaneer Bks.

Beach, Rex E. Pardners. facsimile ed. LC 74-101792. (Short Story Index Reprint Ser). 1905. 18.00 (ISBN 0-8369-3180-7). Ayer Co Pubs.

--The Spoilers. LC 71-96874. 324p. Repr. of 1906 ed. lib. bdg. 10.50 (ISBN 0-8398-0157-2). Irvington.

--The Spoilers. LC 76-144869. (Illus.). 323p. Repr. of 1905 ed. 10.00x (ISBN 0-403-00856-5). Scholarly.

Beach, Richard, jt. auth. see Purves, Alan C.

Beach, Richard & Bridwell, Lillian, eds. New Directions in Composition Research. LC 83-5716. (Perspectives in Writing Research Ser.). 398p. 1984. text ed. 35.00 (ISBN 0-89862-250-6, 2250). Guilford Pr.

Beach, Richard A. Nixon's Inheritance: A Drunken Economy. LC 72-76585. 1972. 5.95 (ISBN 0-87212-024-4). Libra.

Beach, Scott. Musicdotes. LC 76-30883. (Illus.). 1977. 9.00 (ISBN 0-913668-78-8); pap. 4.00 (ISBN 0-913668-64-8). Ten Speed Pr.

Beach, Seth C. Daughters of the Puritans: A Group of Brief Biographies. facs. ed. LC 67-22054. (Essay Index Reprint Ser). 1905. 19.00 (ISBN 0-8369-0180-0). Ayer Co Pubs.

Beach, Stewart. Good Morning-Sun's Up. LC 79-108178. (Illus.). 32p. (ps-3). 8.95 (ISBN 0-87592-021-7). Scroll Pr.

--Lexington & Concord in Color. (Profiles of America Ser.). 1970. 8.95 (ISBN 0-8038-4269-4, 8038-4269-4). Hastings.

--New England in Color. (Profiles of America Ser). 1969. 8.95 (ISBN 0-8038-5013-1). Hastings.

Beach, Sylvia. Shakespeare & Company. LC 81-22361. xvi, 230p. 1982. Repr. of 1959 ed. lib. bdg. 23.00 (ISBN 0-374-90485-5). Octagon.

--Shakespeare & Company. LC 79-26571. (Illus.). xiv, 246p. 1980. pap. 4.95 (ISBN 0-8032-6056-3, BB 733, Bison). U of Nebr Pr.

Beach, Sylvia, tr. see Michaux, Henri.

Beach, T. J., jt. auth. see Alexander, C. H.

Beach, Thomas M. see LeCaron, Henri, pseud.

Beach, Thomas P. Specialty Board Review: Anesthesiology. LC 78-1942. (Illus.). 1984. pap. 19.95 (ISBN 0-8385-8625-2). ACC.

Beach, Waldo. Wheel & the Cross: A Christian Response to the Technological Revolution. pap. 5.95 (ISBN 0-8042-0866-2). John Knox.

Beach, Waldo & Niebuhr, H. Richard, eds. Christian Ethics-Sources of the Living Tradition. 2nd ed. 550p. 1973. text ed. 30.95 (ISBN 0-394-34414-6). Random.

Beach, Walter E. British International Gold Movements & Banking Policy, 1881-1913. LC 76-138201. (Illus.). xiv, 218p. Repr. of 1935 ed. lib. bdg. 17.25x (ISBN 0-8371-5554-1, BEBG). Greenwood.

Beach, Walter G. Oriental Crime in California. LC 75-155608. (Stanford University. Stanford Studies in History, Economics, & Political Science: No. 3). (Illus.). Repr. of 1972 ed. 16.00 (ISBN 0-404-50966-5). AMS Pr.

Beacham, Daniel W. & Beacham, Woodward D. Synopsis of Gynecology. 10th ed. LC 81-18845. (Illus.). 331p. 1982. pap. text ed. 23.95 (ISBN 0-8016-0526-1). Mosby.

Beacham, Deborah, jt. auth. see Beacham, Walton.

Beacham, Ian, ed. Barry Sheene: The Story So Far. 14.95 (ISBN 0-904584-21-6, B1421). Haynes Pubns.

Beacham, Walton & Beacham, Deborah. Using Displaywrite. LC 84-62131. 280p. 1985. 16.95 (ISBN 0-88022-127-5, 158). Que Corp.

--Using WordPerfect. LC 84-62131. 320p. 1985. 16.95 (ISBN 0-88022-132-1, 162). Que Corp.

Beacham, Walton, ed. Research Guide to Biography & Criticism, 2 vols. LC 85-2188. (Literature Ser.). 1350p. 1985. lib. bdg. 129.00 (ISBN 0-933833-00-8). Research Pub.

Beacham, Walton, ed. see Janowitz, Phyllis.

Beacham, Woodward D., jt. auth. see Beacham, Daniel W.

Beachcroft, Thomas O. You Must Break Out Sometimes & Other Stories. facsimile ed. LC 75-113648. (Short Story Index Reprint Ser.). 1937. 18.00 (ISBN 0-8369-3377-X). Ayer Co Pubs.

Beachem, Cedric D., ed. see American Society for Metals.

Beachey, Duane. Faith in a Nuclear Age. LC 82-11785. (Christian Peace Shelf Ser.). 136p. (Orig.). 1983. pap. 6.95 (ISBN 0-8361-3308-0). Herald Pr.

--Faith in a Nuclear Age. LC 82-11785. 136p. 1983. pap. 6.95 (ISBN 0-8361-3308-0). Herald Hse.

Beachey, R. W. The British & West Indies Sugar Industry in the Late 19th Century. LC 77-26800. (Illus.). 1978. Repr. of 1957 ed. lib. bdg. 39.75x (ISBN 0-313-20165-X, BEBW). Greenwood.

--A Collection of Documents on the Slave Trade of Eastern Africa. LC 76-15785. 140p. 1976. text ed. 15.00x (ISBN 0-06-490328-1, 06343). B&N Imports.

Beachley, M. C. Bone Tumors. Ranninger, K., ed. (Encyclopedia of Medical Radiology: Vol. 5, Pt. 6). 1977. 234.00 (ISBN 0-387-08312-X). Springer-Verlag.

Beachley, Michael C., jt. ed. see Hazra, Tapan A.

Beachley, Norman H. & Harrison, Howard L. Introduction to Dynamic System Analysis. (Illus.). 1978. text ed. 31.95 scp (ISBN 0-06-040557-0, HarpC). Har-Row.

Beachy, Alvin J. Worship As Celebration of Covenant & Incarnation. LC 68-57497. 1968. pap. 2.00 (ISBN 0-87303-940-8). Faith & Life.

Beachy, J. Wayne. A Bird of Peace is Born in Petersburg. (Illus., Orig.). (gr. 5). 1981. pap. 2.50 (ISBN 0-9608084-0-X). B Hawkins Studio.

--The Extraordinary Ordinary Christmas Matoaca, 1870. (Illus.). 20p. (Orig.). (gr. 5). 1984. pap. 2.50 (ISBN 0-9608084-2-6). B Hawkins Studio.

--Fire at the Richmond Theater, Richmond, Va., 1911. (Illus.). 25p. (Orig.). (gr. 5 up). 1985. pap. text ed. 2.50 (ISBN 0-9608084-3-4). B Hawkins Studio.

--The Ghost of Rat Castle: A Story of Old Petersburg. (Illus.). 24p. (gr. 5). 1983. pap. 2.50 (ISBN 0-9608084-1-8). B Hawkins Studio.

Beacon Bible Commentary. Genesis-Deuteronomy, Vol. I. 13.95 (ISBN 0-8010-0688-0). Baker Bk.

--Hebrews-Revelation, Vol. X. 13.95 (ISBN 0-8010-0698-8). Baker Bk.

--Hosea-Malachi, Vol. V. 13.95 (ISBN 0-8010-0692-9). Baker Bk.

--Isaiah-Daniel, Vol. IV. 13.95 (ISBN 0-8010-0691-0). Baker Bk.

--Job-Song of Solomon, Vol. III. 13.95 (ISBN 0-8010-0690-2). Baker Bk.

--John: Acts, Vol. VII. 13.95 (ISBN 0-8010-0694-5). Baker Bk.

--Joshua-Esther, Vol. II. 13.95 (ISBN 0-8010-0689-9). Baker Bk.

--Matthew-Luke, Vol. VI. 13.95 (ISBN 0-8010-0693-7). Baker Bk.

--Romans, II-Corinthians, Vol. VIII. 13.95 (ISBN 0-8010-0695-3). Baker Bk.

Beacon Bible Commentary Staff. Galatians-Philemon, Vol. IX. 13.95 (ISBN 0-8010-0696-1). Baker Bk.

Beacon Bible Expositions. Acts, Vol. 5. 6.95 (ISBN 0-8010-0679-1). Baker Bk.

--Corinthians, Vol. 7. 6.95 (ISBN 0-8010-0681-3). Baker Bk.

--Hebrews, James, I-II Peter, Vol. 11. 6.95 (ISBN 0-8010-0677-5). Baker Bk.

--John, Vol. 4. 6.95 (ISBN 0-8010-0777-1). Baker Bk.

--Luke, Vol. 3. 6.95 (ISBN 0-8010-0678-3). Baker Bk.

--Mark, Vol. 2. 6.95 (ISBN 0-8010-0755-0). Baker Bk.

--Matthew, Vol. 1. 6.95 (ISBN 0-8010-0676-7). Baker Bk.

--Romans, Vol. 6. 6.95 (ISBN 0-8010-0680-5). Baker Bk.

--Thessalonians, Vol. 10. 6.95 (ISBN 0-8010-0743-7). Baker Bk.

Beacon Hill Staff. Beacon Small-Group Bible Studies, 1 Corinthians, Living As a Responsible Christian. 60p. 1982. pap. 2.50 (ISBN 0-8341-0755-4). Beacon Hill.

Beacon Presse Staff, ed. Who's Who Among Asian-Americans: Five Thousand Brief Biographies. LC 81-70646. (Ethnic Reference Ser.: No. 4). 224p. 1982. lib. bdg. 979.95 (ISBN 0-935954-58-9). Gormezano Ref.

--Who's Who among Native Americans, 1982: Forty Five Hundred Brief Biographies. LC 81-70648. (Ethnic Reference Ser.: No. 3). 293p. 1982. lib. bdg. 979.95 (ISBN 0-935954-60-0). Gormezano Ref.

--Who's Who in Iowa. LC 80-67912. 64p. (Orig.). 1980. pap. 964.95 (ISBN 0-935954-03-1). Gormezano Ref.

--Who's Who in Montana, 1982: Four Thousand One Hundred Brief Biographies. LC 81-70639. (Who's Who Reference Ser.: No. 6). 204p. 1981. lib. bdg. 959.95 (ISBN 0-935954-16-3). Gormezano Ref.

--Who's Who in Puerto Rico, Virgin Islands & American Samoa, 1982. LC 81-70647. (Who's Who Reference Ser.: No. 48). 211p. 1982. lib. bdg. 959.95 (ISBN 0-935954-59-7). Gormezano Ref.

Beacon Presse Staff & Gormezano, Keith S., eds. Who's Who Among Handicapped Americans: Forty-Seven Hundred Brief Biographies. LC 81-70617. 278p. 1982. lib. bdg. 979.95 (ISBN 0-935954-67-8). Gormezano Ref.

Beacon Publishing, ed. The Fishing Handbook. 448p. 1982. 50.00x (ISBN 0-906358-22-1, Pub. by Beacon Pub Jub Hse England). State Mutual Bk.

--The Jeddah Commercial Directory, 1985. 1985. 175.00 (ISBN 0-686-98474-9, Pub. by Parrish-Rogers England). State Mutual Bk.

--The Oman Business Directory. 1984. 150.00x (ISBN 0-686-92070-8, Pub. by Parrish-Rogers England). State Mutual Bk.

Beacon Publishing Staff, ed. The Arabian Transport Directory, 1984. 1985. 150.00x (ISBN 0-686-98473-0, Pub. by Parrish-Rogers England). State Mutual Bk.

Beaconsfield, B. D. Home Letters. LC 78-137427. Repr. of 1885 ed. 12.00 (ISBN 0-527-06200-6). Kraus Repr.

Beaconsfield, Benjamin D. First Earl of Lothair. 1981. Repr. lib. bdg. 16.00x (ISBN 0-403-00458-6). Scholarly.

--First Earl of Tancred, or the New Crusade. 1981. Repr. lib. bdg. 17.00x (ISBN 0-403-00457-8). Scholarly.

--Popanilla & Other Tales. fasc. ed. LC 79-113649. (Short Story Index Reprint Ser.). 1934. 21.00 (ISBN 0-8369-3378-8). Ayer Co Pubs.

--Sybil; Or, the Two Nations. LC 83-45412. Repr. of 1925 ed. 42.50 (ISBN 0-404-20022-2). AMS Pr.

Beaconsfield, P. Placenta-a Neglected Experimental Animal. 1979. 80.00 (ISBN 0-08-024430-0); pap. 30.00 (ISBN 0-08-024435-1). Pergamon.

Beaconsfield, R. & Birdwood, G., eds. Placenta: The Largest Human Biopsy. (Illus.). 174p. 1982. 44.00 (ISBN 0-08-028028-5). Pergamon.

Beacroft, B. W. The Last Fighting Indians of the American West. Reeves, Marjorie, ed. (Then & There Ser.). (Illus.). 96p. (Orig.). (gr. 7-12). 1976. pap. text ed. 3.75 (ISBN 0-582-20538-7). Longman.

Beacroft, Bernard. The Voyages of Christopher Columbus. Reeves, Marjorie, ed. (Then & There Ser.). (Illus.). 96p. (Orig.). (gr. 7-12). 1978. pap. text ed. 3.75 (ISBN 0-582-21727-X). Longman.

Beadle, B. A. see Royal Geography Society.

Beadle, George W. Genetics & Modern Biology. LC 63-21535. (Memoirs Ser.: Vol. 57). (Illus.). 1963. 5.00 (ISBN 0-87169-057-8). Am Philos.

--Genetics & Modern Biology. LC 63-21535. (American Philosophical Society Ser.: Vol. 57). pap. 20.80 (ISBN 0-317-27906-8, 2025134). Bks Demand UMI.

Beadle, Jeremy, jt. auth. see Winn, Chris.

Beadle, John H. The Undeveloped West; or, Five Years in the Territories. LC 72-9427. (The Far Western Frontier Ser.). (Illus.). 828p. 1973. Repr. of 1873 ed. 51.00 (ISBN 0-405-04958-7). Ayer Co Pubs.

Beadle, Leigh P. The New Brew It Yourself: The Complete Guide to Home Brewing. 99p. 1981. 5.95 (ISBN 0-374-51536-0). FS&G.

Beadle, Muriel. The Cat. 1979. 4.95 (ISBN 0-671-25190-2, Fireside). S&S.

--These Ruins Are Inhabited. LC 77-83865. (Midway Reprint Ser.). 1977. pap. text ed. 10.00x (ISBN 0-226-03967-6). U of Chicago Pr.

--Where Has All the Ivy Gone: A Memoir of University Life with a New Epilogue. LC 77-89292. (Midway Reprint Ser.). 1978. pap. text ed. 10.00x (ISBN 0-226-03966-8). U of Chicago Pr.

Beadle, N. C. The Vegetation of Australia. LC 81-2662. (Illus.). 656p. 1981. 125.00 (ISBN 0-521-24195-2). Cambridge U Pr.

Beadle, Richard & King, Pamela M. York Mystery Plays. 1984. 29.95x (ISBN 0-19-811189-4); pap. 12.95 (ISBN 0-19-811197-5). Oxford U Pr.

Beadle, Richard, ed. The York Plays. 600p. 1982. text ed. 98.50 (ISBN 0-7131-6326-7). E Arnold.

Beadle, Richard & Owen, A. E., eds. The Findern Manuscript. (Medieval Manuscripts Ser.). 1977. 70.00 (ISBN 0-85967-351-0). Scolar.

Beadle, Richard, ed. see Chaucer, Geoffrey.

Beadle, Robert W., jt. ed. see Semonin, Richard W.

Beadle, W. E., et al. Quick Reference Manual for Silicon Integrated Circuit Technology. 736p. 1985. 65.00 (ISBN 0-471-81588-8). Wiley.

Beadles, William T., jt. auth. see Greider, Janice E.

Beadnell, Charles M. Encyclopaedic Dictionary of Science & War. LC 74-164093. 1971. Repr. of 1943 ed. 43.00x (ISBN 0-8103-3753-3). Gale.

Beagle, Ben & Osborne, Ozzie. J. Lindsay Almond: Virginia's Reluctant Rebel. 1984. write for info. (ISBN 0-913767-03-4). Full Court VA.

Beagle, Peter. The Fantasy Worlds of Peter Beagle. (Illus.). 1978. 14.95 (ISBN 0-670-30725-4). Viking.

--Last Unicorn. 1976. pap. 2.25 (ISBN 0-345-28620-0). Ballantine.

Beagle, Peter S. A Fine & Private Place. 256p. 1976. pap. 2.25 (ISBN 0-345-29001-1). Ballantine.

--I See by My Outfit. (Travel Library). 256p. 1985. pap. 5.95 (ISBN 0-14-009553-5). Penguin.

Beaglehole, E. & Beaglehole, P. Ethnology of Pukapuka. (BMB). Repr. of 1938 ed. 51.00 (ISBN 0-527-02258-6). Kraus Repr.

Beaglehole, Ernest. Notes on Hopi Economic Life. LC 76-43655. (Yale University Publications in Anthropology: No. 15). Repr. of 1937 ed. 18.50 (ISBN 0-404-15489-1). AMS Pr.

--Property: A Study in Social Psychology. LC 73-14147. (Perspectives in Social Inquiry Ser.). 332p. 1974. Repr. of 1932 ed. 50.50x (ISBN 0-405-05493-9). Ayer Co Pubs.

Beaglehole, Ernest & Beaglehole, Pearl. Hopi of the Second Mesa. LC 36-5468. (American Anthro. Association Memoirs). 1935. pap. 15.00 (ISBN 0-527-00543-6). Kraus Repr.

Beaglehole, J. C. The Life of Captain James Cook. LC 73-87124. (Illus.). xiv, 804p. 1974. 29.50 (ISBN 0-8047-0848-7). Stanford U Pr.

Beaglehole, John C. The Exploration of the Pacific. 3rd ed. (Illus.). 1966. 27.50x (ISBN 0-8047-0310-8); pap. 8.95x (ISBN 0-8047-0311-6). Stanford U Pr.

Beaglehole, P., jt. auth. see Beaglehole, E.

Beaglehole, Pearl, jt. auth. see Beaglehole, Ernest.

Beaglehole, T. H. Thomas Munro & the Development of Administrative Policy in Madras, 1792-1818: The Origins of the Munro System. LC 65-17209. pap. 48.30 (ISBN 0-317-26048-0, 2024419). Bks Demand UMI.

Beagley, H. A. Deafness: The Facts. (The Facts Ser.). (Illus.). 1984. 13.95x (ISBN 0-19-261411-8). Oxford U Pr.

Beagley, H. A. & Barnard, S. A. Manual of Audiometric Techniques. (Illus.). 1982. pap. 18.95x (ISBN 0-19-261372-3). Oxford U Pr.

Beagley, H. A., ed. Audiology & Audiological Medicine. (Illus.). 1981. text ed. 95.00x (ISBN 0-19-261154-2). Oxford U Pr.

--Auditory Investigation: The Scientific & Technological Basis. (Illus.). 1979. text ed. 95.00x (ISBN 0-19-857526-2). Oxford U Pr.

Beahm, George. Kirk's Works. (Fantasy Artists Ser.: No. 2). (Illus., Orig.). 1980. 25.00x; pap. 10.00x (ISBN 0-9603276-1-4). Heresy Pr.

Beahrs, John O. Unity & Multiplicity: Multilevel Consciousness of Self in Hypnosis, Psychiatric Disorder & Mental Health. LC 81-38538. 256p. 1981. 25.00 (ISBN 0-87630-273-8). Brunner-Mazel.

Beahrs, Oliver H. & Beart, Robert W., eds. General Surgery Therapy. 536p. 1981. 75.00x (ISBN 0-471-09548-6). Wiley.

Beahrs, Oliver H. & Beart, Robert W., Jr., eds. General Surgery-Therapy Update Service. LC 78-62752. 1984. core book w/binder 120.00 (ISBN 0-932036-07-4). Harwal Pub Co.

Beahrs, Oliver H., ed. see American Joint Committee on Cancer.

Beahrs, Oliver H., et al. An Atlas of the Surgical Techniques of Oliver H. Beahrs. (Illus.). 350p. 1984. write for info (ISBN 0-7216-1602-X). Saunders.

Beail, Nigel. Repertory Grid Technique & Personal Constructs: Applications in Clinical & Educational Settings. (Illus.). 400p. 1985. 35.00 (ISBN 0-914797-16-6, Pub. by Croom Helm Ltd.). Brookline Book.

Beaird, Dick. Sweet Revenge. (Orig.). 1982. pap. 2.95 (ISBN 0-89083-911-5). Zebra.

Beaird, Richard F. Death Screen. 1983. pap. 2.95 (ISBN 0-8217-1253-5). Zebra.

Beakley, George C. Careers in Engineering & Technology. 3rd ed. 400p. 1984. pap. text ed. write for info. (ISBN 0-02-307110-9). Macmillan.

--Electronic Drafting. 1982. pap. text ed. write for info. (ISBN 0-02-307600-3). Macmillan.

--Electronic Hand Calculators. 4th ed. 1983. pap. 10.95 cancelled (ISBN 0-686-82939-5). Macmillan.

--Freehand Drawing & Visualization. LC 81-3803. (gr. 12). 1982. pap. text ed. 12.04 scp (ISBN 0-672-97972-1). Bobbs.

--Introduction to Engineering Graphics. (Illus.). 341p. 1975. pap. text ed. write for info. (ISBN 0-02-307210-5, 30721). Macmillan.

Beakley, George C. & Autore, Donald D. Graphics for Design & Visualization: Problem Series B. 1975. pap. 15.95 (ISBN 0-02-307270-9, 30727). Macmillan.

--Introduction to Technical Illustration. (Illus.). 256p. (Orig.). 1983. pap. text ed. write for info. (ISBN 0-02-307610-0). Macmillan.

Beakley, George C. & Leach, H. W. Engineering: An Introduction to a Creative Profession. 4th ed. 1982. text ed. write for info. (ISBN 0-02-307130-3). Macmillan.

Beakley, George C. & Lovell, Robert E. Computation, Calculators & Computers: Tools of Engineering Problem Solving-Including FORTRAN. 368p. 1983. pap. text ed. write for info. (ISBN 0-02-307150-8). Macmillan.

Beakley, George C., et al. Engineering: An Introduction to a Creative Profession. 5th ed. 1066p. 1986. text ed. price not set (ISBN 0-02-307090-0). Macmillan.

Beakley, George C., Jr. Graphics for Design & Visualization: Problem Series A. (Illus.). 120p. 1973. pap. text ed. write for info. (ISBN 0-02-307260-1, 30726). Macmillan.

Beal, David. Travel with a Camera. (Photographer's Library). (Illus.). 144p. pap. text ed. 15.95 (ISBN 0-240-51221-9). Focal Pr.

Beal, Doug. Spike: The Story of the Victorious U. S. Volleyball Team. LC 85-71269. 224p. 1985. pap. 9.95 (ISBN 0-932238-30-0, Pub. by Avant Bks). Slawson Comm.

Beal, Edwin F. & Begin, James P. The Practice of Collective Bargaining. 6th ed. 1982. 26.95 (ISBN 0-256-02489-8). Irwin.

Beal, Fred E. Proletarian Journey. LC 70-146158. (Civil Liberties in American History Ser). 1971. Repr. of 1937 ed. lib. bdg. 45.00 (ISBN 0-306-70096-4). Da Capo.

--Proletarian Journey: New England, Gastonia, Moscow. facsimile ed. LC 73-179505. (Select Bibliographies Reprint Ser). Repr. of 1937 ed. 24.50 (ISBN 0-8369-6634-1). Ayer Co Pubs.

Beal, George. The Julian Messner Young Readers' Thesaurus. Barish, Wendy, ed. (Illus.). 192p. (gr. 3-7). 1984. lib. bdg. 9.79 (ISBN 0-671-50834-2). Messner.

--The Julian Messner Young Reader's Thesaurus. 1984. PLB 9.79 (ISBN 0-671-50834-2). Messner.

--The Julian Messner Young Reader's Thesaurus. 1984. pap. 5.95 (ISBN 0-671-50816-4). Wanderer Bks.

--See Inside a TV Studio. (See Inside Bks.). (Illus.). (gr. 5 up). 1978. PLB 9.40 s&l (ISBN 0-531-09064-7, Warwick Press). Watts.

--The Simon & Schuster Young Readers' Thesaurus. Barish, Wendy, ed. (Illus.). 192p. (gr. 3-7). 1984. pap. 5.95 (ISBN 0-671-50816-4). Wanderer Bks.

Beal, George M., et al. Leadership & Dynamic Group Action. (Illus.). 366p. 1962. pap. text ed. 7.95x (ISBN 0-8138-0981-9). Iowa St U Pr.

Beal, Graham & Dine, Jim. Jim Dine: Five Themes. LC 83-21467. (Illus.). 156p. 1984. 35.00 (ISBN 0-89659-414-9). Abbeville Pr.

Beal, Graham, et al. Robert Hudson: A Survey. LC 85-8239. (Illus.). 80p. 1985. pap. 14.95 (ISBN 0-918471-02-8). San Fran Mod.

Beal, Graham W. The Charles Parsons Collection of Paintings. LC 77-3962. (Illus.). 80p. 1977. pap. 5.00 (ISBN 0-936316-08-X). Wash U Gallery.

Beal, H. E. Indian Ink. 1977. Repr. of 1954 ed. 5.00x (ISBN 0-8364-0112-3). South Asia Bks.

Beal, John M. Critical Care for Surgical Patients. (Illus.). 704p. 1982. text ed. write for info. (ISBN 0-02-307410-8). Macmillan.

Beal, John M. & Raffensperger, John G. Diagnosis of Acute Abdominal Disease. LC 79-811. pap. 44.30 (ISBN 0-317-07819-4, 2055415). Bks Demand UMI.

Beal, John M., jt. auth. see Preston, Frederick W.

Beal, John R. John Foster Dulles: Eighteen Eighty-Eight to Nineteen Fifty-Nine. LC 74-12626. (Illus.). 358p. 1974. Repr. of 1959 ed. lib. bdg. 22.25x (ISBN 0-8371-7730-8, BEJFD). Greenwood.

Beal, Judy. Issues & Advanced Practice in Pediatric Nursing. 1983. text ed. 22.95 (ISBN 0-8359-3306-7). Reston.

Beal, Kathleen. Bob Dylan. LC 74-13936. (Rock'n Pop Stars Ser.). (Illus.). 32p. (gr. 4-12). 1974. PLB 7.95 (ISBN 0-87191-399-2). Creative Ed.

Beal, Mary. A Study of Richard Symonds: His Italian Notebooks & Their Relevance to Seventeenth Century Painting Techniques. LC 83-48688. (Theses from the Courtauld Institute of Art Ser.). 420p. 1984. lib. bdg. 50.00 (ISBN 0-8240-5976-X). Garland Pub.

Beal, Mary R. & Gilbert, Janet P. Music Curriculum Guidelines For Moderately Retarded Adolescents. 122p. 1982. spiral bdg. 14.75x (ISBN 0-398-04757-X). C C Thomas.

Beal, Merrill D. Grand Canyon: The Story Behind the Scenery. rev. ed. LC 75-14775. (Illus.). 1978. 8.95 (ISBN 0-916122-31-X); pap. 3.75 (ISBN 0-916122-06-9). KC Pubns.

--I Will Fight No More Forever. 1985. pap. 3.95 (ISBN 0-345-32131-6). Ballantine.

--I Will Fight No More Forever: Chief Joseph & the Nez Perce War. LC 62-13278. (Illus.). 384p. 1963. pap. 9.95 (ISBN 0-295-74009-4). U of Wash Pr.

Beal, Peter. Index of English Literature Manuscripts, 1450-1625, Vol. I, Pts. 1 & 2. (Illus.). 1258p. 1980. 424.00 (ISBN 0-7201-0807-1). Mansell.

--Roses. (Illus.). 384p. 1985. 45.00 (ISBN 0-03-006022-2). HR&W.

Beal, Peter W; see O'Neal, William B.

Beal, R. W., jt. ed. see Moore, B. P.

Beal, Rebecca J. Jacob Eichholtz, 1776-1842, Portrait Painter of Pennsylvania. 1969. 15.00 (ISBN 0-910732-07-8). Pa Hist Soc.

Beal, Rendy. Never Take Candy from Strangers. 20p. (Orig.). (ps-4). 1984. pap. 3.50 (ISBN 0-9613579-0-8). R B Pubns.

Beal, Richard S. Systems Analysis of International Crises. LC 79-66860. 1979. text ed. 24.00 (ISBN 0-8191-0858-8); pap. text ed. 16.75 (ISBN 0-8191-0859-6). U Pr of Amer.

Beal, Robert C., et al, eds. Spaceborne Synthetic Aperture Radar for Oceanography. LC 81-5966. (The Johns Hopkins Oceanographic Studies: No. 7). 216p. 1981. text ed. 27.00x (ISBN 0-8018-2668-3). Johns Hopkins.

Beal, Ronald L., jt. auth. see Bocchino, Anthony J.

Beal, Samuel. Abstract of Four Lectures on Buddhist Literature in China. LC 78-72376. Repr. of 1882 ed. 26.00 (ISBN 0-404-17226-1). AMS Pr.

--Buddhism in China. lib. bdg. 79.95 (ISBN 0-87968-479-8). Krishna Pr.

--Buddhism in China. 16.75 (ISBN 0-8369-7129-9, 7963). Ayer Co Pubs.

--Buddhist Records of the Western World: Si-Yu-Ki. 428p. 1981. Repr. 30.00 (ISBN 0-89581-131-6). Asian Human Pr.

--The Fo-sho-hing-tsan-king. (Sacred Bks. of the East: Vol. 19). 18.00 (ISBN 0-89581-523-0). Asian Human Pr.

Beal, Samuel, tr. see Dhammapada.

Beal, Samuel, tr. see Fa-Hsien.

Beal, Samuel, tr. from Chines see Hwuy-Le.

Beal, Virginia A. Nutrition in the Life Span. LC 79-24610. 467p. 1980. text ed. 35.00 (ISBN 0-471-03664-1). Wiley.

Beal, Virginia A., jt. auth. see Martin, Ethel A.

Beal, Walter B. The First German War Crimes Trial: Chief Judge Walter B. Beals' Desk Notebook of the Doctors' Trial, held in Nuernberg, Germany, December, 1946 to August, 1947, 2 vols. in 1. 346p. text ed. 44.95x ltd. ed. (ISBN 0-89712-124-4). Documentary Pubns.

Beal, Walter S., et al. Dr. Walter Scott Beal Poetry & Prose: My Favorite Collection. Nichols, Virginia, ed. (Illus.). 100p. 1984. pap. 5.00x (ISBN 0-940178-25-7). Sitare Inc.

Bealby, J. T., tr. see Hedin, Sven A.

Bealby, J. T., tr. see Hoffman, Ernst T.

Beale, jt. auth. see Griffin.

Beale, Arthur, jt. auth. see Wasserman, Jeanne L.

Beale, B. D. The Beale Family of Halifax County Virginia. LC 78-73073. 227p. (Orig.). 1978. pap. 11.00 (ISBN 0-9602132-1-X). B D Beale.

Beale, B. DeRoy. Tucker Trails in Virginia. 1985. pap. write for info. B D Beale.

--Tucker Trails Through Southside Virginia. 250p. (Orig.). 1985. pap. write for info. (ISBN 0-9602132-2-8). B D Beale.

Beale, C. W; see Bleiler, E. F.

Beale, Charles W. The Secret of the Earth. LC 74-15950. (Science Fiction Ser). 256p. 1975. Repr. of 1899 ed. 21.00x (ISBN 0-405-06276-1). Ayer Co Pubs.

Beale, David. A Pictorial History of Our English Bible. (Illus.). 79p. (Orig.). 1982. pap. 2.45 (ISBN 0-89084-149-7). Bob Jones Univ Pr.

Beale, David O. S. B. C.: House on the Sand? 246p. (Orig.). 1985. pap. 4.95 (ISBN 0-89084-281-7). Bob Jones Univ Pr.

Beale, Edgar. Sturt: The Chipped Idol. LC 80-670049. (Illus.). 1980. 33.00x (ISBN 0-424-00069-5, Pub. by Sydney U Pr). Intl Spec Bk.

Beale, Erica, ed. see Kyasht, Lydia.

Beale, Evelyn M. Mathematical Programming in Practice. LC 68-95780. (Illus.). pap. 51.80 (ISBN 0-317-10735-6, 2051898). Bks Demand UMI.

Beale, G. K. The Use of Daniel in Jewish Apocalyptic Literature & in the Relevation of St. John. 364p. (Orig.). 1985. lib. bdg. 23.50 (ISBN 0-8191-4290-5); pap. text ed. 15.00 (ISBN 0-8191-4291-3). U Pr of Amer.

Beale, Griffin. TV & Video. (Electronic World Ser.). 32p. (gr. 4-8). 1983. 7.95 (ISBN 0-86020-640-8); PLB 12.95 (ISBN 0-88110-000-5); pap. 4.95 (ISBN 0-86020-639-4). EDC.

Beale, Helen P., ed. Bibliography of Plant Viruses & Index to Research. LC 73-3200. 1495p. 1976. 130.00x (ISBN 0-231-03763-5). Columbia U Pr.

Beale, Howard. This Inch of Time: Memoirs of Politics & Diplomacy. 1978. 25.00x (ISBN 0-522-84127-9, Pub. by Melbourne U Pr). Intl Spec Bk.

Beale, Howard K. Are American Teachers Free? LC 74-159166. xxiv, 855p. 1971. Repr. of 1936 ed. lib. bdg. 46.00x (ISBN 0-374-90492-8). Octagon.

--Are American Teachers Free? An Analysis of Restraints upon the Freedom of Teaching in American Schools. 855p. 1984. Repr. of 1936 ed. lib. bdg. 50.00 (ISBN 0-8492-3759-9). R West.

--Charles A. Beard: An Appraisal. 1976. lib. bdg. 24.50x (ISBN 0-374-90493-6). Octagon.

--History of Freedom of Teaching in American Schools. 1966. lib. bdg. 24.50x (ISBN 0-374-90494-4). Octagon.

--Theodore Roosevelt & the Rise of America to World Power. LC 83-25584. 624p. 1984. pap. 10.95x (ISBN 0-8018-3249-7). Johns Hopkins.

Beale, Howard K., ed. The Diary of Edward Bates: 1859-1866. LC 75-75304. (American History, Politics & Law Ser). 1971. Repr. of 1933 ed. lib. bdg. 85.00 (ISBN 0-306-71260-1). Da Capo.

Beale, Irene A. Genesee Valley People: 1743-1962. LC 83-71772. 224p. (Orig.). 1983. pap. 9.00 (ISBN 0-9608132-1-7). Chestnut Hill Pr.

--Genesee Valley Women: Seventeen Forty-Three to Nineteen Eighty-Five. LC 84-73387. 223p. (Orig.). 1985. pap. 9.00 (ISBN 0-9608132-2-5). Chestnut Hill Pr.

--William P. Letchworth: A Man for Others. LC 1-90673. 214p. (Orig.). 1982. pap. 9.00 (ISBN 0-9608132-0-9). Chestnut Hill Pr.

Beale, Ivan L., jt. auth. see Corballis, Michael C.

Beale, Jack G. The Manager & the Environment: General Theory & Practice of Environmental Management. LC 79-40712. (Illus.). 192p. 1980. 39.00 (ISBN 0-08-024043-7); pap. 18.00 (ISBN 0-08-024044-5). Pergamon.

Beale, James. A History of the Burgh & Parochial Schools of Fife. (SCRE Publication Ser.: No. 82). 222p. 1983. text ed. 25.75x (Pub. by Scottish Coun Res UK). Humanities.

Beale, Joseph H. A Bibliography of Early English Law Books. LC 26-16217. viii, 304p. 1966. Repr. of 1926 ed. lib. bdg. 38.50 (ISBN 0-89941-351-X). W S Hein.

Beale, Joseph H., tr. see Bartolus of Sassoferrato.

Beale, Kenneth, jt. auth. see Bojarski, Richard.

Beale, Kenneth, jt. auth. see Bojarsky, Richard.

Beale, Lionel S. Our Morality & the Moral Question: From the Medical Side. LC 73-20615. (Sex, Marriage & Society Ser.). 208p. 1974. Repr. of 1887 ed. 19.00x (ISBN 0-405-05793-8). Ayer Co Pubs.

Beale, Morris A. The Drug Story. 6.95 (ISBN 0-89557-011-4). Bi World Indus.

Beale, O. C. Racial Decay: A Compilation of Evidence from World Sources. 1976. lib. bdg. 59.95 (ISBN 0-8490-2498-6). Gordon Pr.

Beale, Robert. Trading in Gold Futures. 180p. 1985. 26.50 (ISBN 0-89397-219-3). Nichols Pub.

Beale, Robert C. The Development of the Short Story in the South. LC 72-13256. 1974. Repr. of 1911 ed. lib. bdg. 20.00 (ISBN 0-8414-1156-5). Folcroft.

Beale, Thomas W. Oriental Biographical Dictionary. rev. & enl. ed. Keene, H. G., ed. 1894. 40.00 (ISBN 0-527-06250-2). Kraus Repr.

Beale, Thomas W., et al. Excavations at Tepe Yaha: The Early Periods. (American School of Prehistoric Research Bulletin: No. 38). (Illus.). 240p. 1986. 25.00x (ISBN 0-87365-541-9). Peabody Harvard.

Beale, Walter H. Old & Middle English Poetry: A Guide to Information Sources. LC 74-11538. (American Literature, English Literature & World Literatures in English Information Guide Ser.: Vol. 7). 1976. 60.00x (ISBN 0-8103-1247-6). Gale.

--Real Writing: Argumentation, Reflection, Information. 2nd ed. 1985. pap. text ed. 13.95x (ISBN 0-673-18153-7). Scott F.

Beale, Walter H., et al. Stylistic Options: The Sentence & the Paragraph. 1982. pap. text ed. 11.90x (ISBN 0-673-15444-0). Scott F.

--Real Writing: Argumentation, Reflection, Information, with Stylistic Options: The Sentence & the Paragraph. 1982. text ed. 18.40 (ISBN 0-673-15585-4); pap. text ed. 14.70x (ISBN 0-673-15446-7). Scott F.

Bealer, Alex. Only the Names Remain: The Cherokees & the Trail of Tears. (gr. 4-6). 1972. 10.45i (ISBN 0-316-08520-0). Little.

Bealer, Alex W. The Art of Blacksmithing. 3rd, rev. ed. McRaven, Charles, ed. LC 83-48320. (Illus.). 480p. 1984. 21.10i (ISBN 0-06-015225-7, HarpT). Har-Row.

--Old Ways of Working Wood. rev. ed. (Illus.). 1980. 12.50 (ISBN 0-517-54047-9, C N Potter Bks). Crown.

Bealer, Alex W. & Ellis, John O. The Log Cabin. (Illus.). 1978. 17.95 (ISBN 0-517-52892-4, Dist. by Crown); pap. 10.95 (ISBN 0-517-53379-0). Barre.

Bealer, George. Quality & Concept. (Clarendon Library of Logic & Philosophy). (Illus.). 1982. 29.95x (ISBN 0-19-824428-2). Oxford U Pr.

--Quality & Concept. 1982. pap. 14.95 (ISBN 0-19-824726-5). Oxford U Pr.

Beales, A. C. Education under Penalty: English Catholic Education from the Reformation to the Fall of James II. 306p. 1963. 42.00 (ISBN 0-485-11062-8, Pub. by Athlone Pr Ltd). Longwood Pub Group.

Beales, A. C., et al. Education, a Framework for Choice. (Institute of Economic Affairs, Readings in Political Economy Ser.: No. 1). pap. 4.25 technical (ISBN 0-255-35987-X). Transatlantic.

Beales, D. The Risorgimento & the Unification of Italy. (Illus.). 176p. 1982. pap. text ed. 8.95x (ISBN 0-582-49217-3). Longman.

Beales, D. & Best, G., eds. History, Society & the Churches: Essays in Honour of Owen Chadwick. 335p. 1985. 49.50 (ISBN 0-521-25486-8). Cambridge U Pr.

Beales, Derek. From Castlereagh to Gladstone, Eighteen Fifteen to Eighteen Eighty-Five. (History of England Ser.). (Illus.). 1969. pap. 8.95 (ISBN 0-393-00367-1, Norton Lib). Norton.

Beales, H. L. Industrial Revolution, 1750-1850. 2nd ed. LC 67-17931. 1958. 15.00x (ISBN 0-678-00216-9). Kelley.

Beales, H. L. & Lambert, R. S. Memoirs of the Unemployed. Leventhal, F. M., ed. (English Wokers & the Coming of the Welfare State Ser., 1918-1945). 287p. 1985. lib. bdg. 35.00 (ISBN 0-8240-7600-1). Garland Pub.

Beales, J. Gerald. Sick Health Centers & How to Make Them Better. 147p. 1978. 14.95x (ISBN 0-8464-1136-9). Beekman Pubs.

Beales, Philip. Otosclerosis. (Illus.). 216p. 1981. text ed. 31.50 (ISBN 0-7236-0598-X). PSG Pub Co.

Bealey, Frank & Pelling, Henry. Labour & Politics, 1900-1906: A History of the Labour Representation Committee. LC 82-15828. xi, 317p. 1982. lib. bdg. 45.00x (ISBN 0-313-23693-3, BELAP). Greenwood.

Bealey, Frank W. & Sewel, John. The Politics of Independence: A Study of a Scottish Town. 280p. 1981. 27.00 (ISBN 0-08-025736-4). Pergamon.

Beall, C. M., ed. Cross-Cultural Studies of Biological Aging. 100p. 1982. 19.50 (ISBN 0-08-028946-0). Pergamon.

Beall, Carl M. The Thunderbird Song. 1970. 5.50 (ISBN 0-682-47055-4). Exposition Pr FL.

Beall, Chandler B. Chateaubriand et le Tasse. (Johns Hopkins University Studies in Romance Literatures & Languages: Vol. 24). 80p. Repr. of 1934 ed. 14.00 (ISBN 0-384-03675-9). Johnson Repr.

--La Fortune du Tasse en France. 1942. pap. 2.00 (ISBN 0-87114-001-2). U of Oreg Bks.

Beall, Christine. Masonry Design & Detailing: For Architects, Engineers & Builders. (Illus.). 448p. 1984. text ed. 46.95 (ISBN 0-13-559153-8). P-H.

Beall, Elizabeth. The Relation of Various Anthropometric Measurements of Selected College Women to Success in Certain Physical Activities. LC 77-176547. (Columbia University. Teachers College. Contributions to Education: No. 774). Repr. of 1939 ed. 22.50 (ISBN 0-404-55774-0). AMS Pr.

Beall, Gildon N. Allergy & Clinical Immunology. LC 82-20183. (UCLA Internal Medicine Today: A Comprehensive Postgraduate Library). 352p. 1983. 35.00 (ISBN 0-471-09568-0, Pub. by Wiley Med). Wiley.

Beall, Gretchen H. Music As Experience: Structure & Sequence for the Elementary School. 416p. 1980. plastic comb write for info (ISBN 0-697-03444-5). Wm C Brown.

Beall, J. H. Hickey, the Days...Are Wider Than the Sky. LC 79-65655. (Orig.). 1980. perfect bdg. 5.95 (ISBN 0-915380-09-9). Word Works.

Beall, James L. How to Achieve Security, Confidence, & Peace. LC 78-50752. 1978. pap. 6.95 (ISBN 0-88270-268-8, Pub. by Logos). Bridge Pub.

--Laying the Foundation. LC 76-42084. 389p. 1976. pap. 5.95 (ISBN 0-88270-198-3, Pub. by Logos). Bridge Pub.

Beall, James L. & Barber, Marjorie. Your Pastor, Your Shepherd. LC 77-77579. 1977. pap. 4.95 (ISBN 0-88270-216-5, Pub. by Logos). Bridge Pub.

Beall, James R. & Downing, Robert E. Helicopter Utilization in Municipal Law Enforcement: Administrative Considerations. (Illus.). 96p. 1973. 14.75x (ISBN 0-398-02780-3). C C Thomas.

Beall, John, et al. Toward a Faculty Self-Appraisal System. LC 70-630596. (Research Monograph: No. 49). 1969. spiral bdg. 5.00 (ISBN 0-88406-062-4). Ga St U Busn Pub.

Beall, Karen F., ed. Cries & Itinerant Trades: A Bibliography. 1975. 235.00x (ISBN 0-8103-4352-5, Pub. by Dr. E. Hauswedell). Gale.

Beall, P. T., et al. NMR Data Handbook for Biomedical Applications. 224p. 1984. 59.95 (ISBN 0-08-030774-4); pap. 29.95 (ISBN 0-08-030775-2). Pergamon.

Beall, Pam & Nipp, Susan. Wee Sing for Christmas. (Illus.). 64p. (Orig.). 1984. pap. 2.25 (ISBN 0-8431-1197-6). Price Stern.

Beall, Pamela. Wee Sing Campfire Songs. (Illus.). 64p. (Orig.). 1982. pap. 2.25 (ISBN 0-8431-0311-6). Price Stern.

Beall, Pamela & Nipp, Susan. Wee Sing. 1982. pap. 2.25 (ISBN 0-8431-0676-X). Price Stern.

--Wee Sing & Play. (Wee Sing Ser.). (Illus.). (ps-6). 1983. pap. 7.95 (ISBN 0-8431-0743-X); cassette incl. Price Stern.

--Wee Sing Around the Campfire. (Wee Sing Ser.). (Illus.). 64p. (ps-6). 1983. pap. 7.95 (ISBN 0-8431-0742-1); cassette incl. Price Stern.

--Wee Sing: Children' Song & Fingerplays. pap. write for info. (ISBN 0-8431-0522-4). Price Stern.

--Wee Sing Silly Songs. (Wee Sing Ser.). (Illus.). 64p. (ps-6). 1983. pap. 7.95 (ISBN 0-8431-0310-8); Cassette incl. Price Stern.

Beall, Pamela C. & Nipp, Susan H. Wee Color: Wee Sing. 48p. 1985. pap. 1.50 (ISBN 0-8431-1423-1). Price Stern.

--Wee Sing Nursery Rhymes & Lullabies. (Wee Sing Ser.). (Illus.). 64p. (Orig.). (ps-2). 1985. pap. 7.95 incl. cassette (ISBN 0-8431-1422-3); pap. 2.25 (ISBN 0-8431-1438-X). Price Stern.

Bealle, Morris. The Drug Story. 239p. 6.95 (ISBN 0-318-15650-4). Natl Health Fed.

Beals. Nomads & Empire Builders: Native Peoples & Cultures of South America. pap. 2.25 (ISBN 0-8065-0087-5). Citadel Pr.

Beals, Alan R. Culture in Progress. 3rd ed. LC 78-27459. 1979. pap. text ed. 16.95 (ISBN 0-03-042806-8, HoltC); inst. manual 25.00 (ISBN 0-03-049271-8). HR&W.

--Golpalpur. LC 79-20364. 125p. 1980. pap. 9.95 fieldwork ed. (ISBN 0-03-045371-2, HoltC). HR&W.

Bean, Michael J. The Evolution of National Wildlife Law. rev. & expanded ed. LC 83-11138. 1983. 42.95 (ISBN 0-03-063503-9); pap. 14.95 (ISBN 0-03-063502-0). HR&W.

--The Evolution of National Wildlife Law. rev. & expanded ed. 464p. 1983. 42.95; pap. 14.95. Praeger.

Bean, Orson. Me & the Orgone: One Man's Sexual Revolution. LC 70-145430. 1978. pap. 3.95 (ISBN 0-312-52372-6). St Martin.

Bean, Philip. Compulsory Admissions to Mental Hospitals. LC 79-41786. 278p. 1980. 62.95x (ISBN 0-471-27758-4, Pub. by Wiley-Interscience). Wiley.

--Punishment: A Philosophical & Criminological Inquiry. 224p. 1981. 40.00x (ISBN 0-85520-391-9, Pub. by Robertson & Co England). State Mutual Bk.

--Punishment: A Philosophical & Criminological Inquiry. 224p. 1982. pap. 12.95x (ISBN 0-85520-478-8). Basil Blackwell.

Bean, Philip, ed. Adoption: Essays in Social Policy, Law, & Sociology. 336p. 1984. 33.00 (ISBN 0-422-78410-9, NO. 9152, Pub. by Tavistock England). Methuen Inc.

--Mental Illness: Changes & Trends. LC 82-8603. 482p. 1983. 69.95 (ISBN 0-471-10240-7, Pub. by Wiley-Interscience). Wiley.

Bean, Philip & MacPherson, Stewart, eds. Approaches to Welfare. 300p. 1983. 28.95x (ISBN 0-7100-9423-X); pap. 15.95x (ISBN 0-7100-9424-8). Routledge & Kegan.

Bean, Phillip, et al, eds. In Defense of Welfare. 250p. 1985. pap. 19.95 (ISBN 0-422-79090-7, 9647, Pub. by Tavistock England). Methuen Inc.

Bean, Reynold & Clemes, Harris. Elementary Principal's Handbook: New Approaches to Administrative Action. 1978. 26.50x (ISBN 0-13-259473-0, Parker). P-H.

--How to Discipline Children Without Feeling Guilty. rev. ed. (The Whole Child Ser.). (Illus.). 80p. 1980. pap. 3.95 (ISBN 0-933358-77-6). Enrich.

--How to Raise Children's Self-Esteem. rev. ed. (The Whole Child Ser.). (Illus.). 80p. 1980. pap. 3.95 (ISBN 0-933358-75-X). Enrich.

--How to Teach Children Responsibility. rev. ed. (The Whole Child Ser.). (Illus.). 80p. 1980. pap. 3.95 (ISBN 0-933358-78-4). Enrich.

Bean, Reynold, jt. auth. see Clemes, Harris.

Bean, Reynold, et al. How to Raise Teenagers' Self-Esteem. rev. ed. (The Whole Child Ser.). (Illus.). 96p. 1980. pap. 3.95 (ISBN 0-933358-76-8). Enrich.

Bean, Richard N. The British Trans-Atlantic Slave Trade, Sixteen Fifty to Seventeen Seventy-Five. LC 75-2575. (Dissertations in American Economic History). (Illus.). 1975. 30.00x (ISBN 0-405-07256-2). Ayer Co Pubs.

Bean, Rita & Wilson, Robert. Effecting Change in School Reading Programs: The Resource Role. 75p. 1981. 5.00 (ISBN 0-87207-945-7). Intl Reading.

Bean, Ron. Comparative Industrial Relations: An Introduction to Cross-National Perspectives. LC 84-22889. 288p. 1985. 32.50 (ISBN 0-312-15335-X). St Martin.

Bean, Roy E. Helping Your Health with Pointed Pressure Therapy. 1975. 15.95 (ISBN 0-13-386466-9); pap. 4.95 (ISBN 0-13-386391-3). P-H.

Bean, S. & Wabun. The Medicine Wheel: Earth Astrology. 1980. pap. 5.95 (ISBN 0-13-572982-3). P-H.

Bean, Susan S. Symbolic & Pragmatic Semantic: A Kannada System of Address. LC 77-18198. (Illus.). 1978. lib. bdg. 17.00x (ISBN 0-226-03989-7). U of Chicago Pr.

Bean, Thomas W., et al. Rapid Reading for Professional Success. 176p. 1983. pap. text ed. 10.95 (ISBN 0-8403-2882-6). Kendall-Hunt.

Bean, Walton. Boss Ruef's San Francisco: The Story of the Union Labor Party, Big Business, & the Graft Prosecution. LC 81-13392. (Illus.). xii, 345p. 1982. Repr. of 1967 ed. lib. bdg. 18.75x (ISBN 0-313-23211-3, BESF). Greenwood.

--Boss Ruef's San Francisco: The Story of the Union Labor Party, Big Business, & the Graft Prosecution. 1952. pap. 4.95 (ISBN 0-520-00094-3, CAL138). U of Cal Pr.

Bean, Walton & Rawls, James J. California: An Interpretive History. 4th ed. (Illus.). 544p. 1982. text ed. 30.95 (ISBN 0-07-004206-3). McGraw.

Bean, William & McClintock, Margery. Introduction to Individualized Reading. 2nd ed. 140p. 1985. pap. text ed. 10.95 (ISBN 0-89892-001-9). Contemp Pub Co Raleigh.

Bean, William B. Rare Diseases & Lesions: Their Contributions to Clinical Medicine. 320p. 1967. 29.50x (ISBN 0-398-04203-9). C C Thomas.

--Vascular Spiders & Related Lesions of the Skin. (Illus.). 338p. 1959. photocopy ed. 37.50x (ISBN 0-398-04204-7). C C Thomas.

--Walter Reed: A Biography. LC 81-16123. (Illus.). 1982. 14.95x (ISBN 0-8139-0913-9). U Pr of Va.

Beanblossom, Ronald, ed. see Reid, Thomas.

Beane. Business Torts. 1987. price not set (ISBN 0-471-82665-0). Wiley.

Beane, jt. auth. see Lipka.

Beane, Leona. Business Law. (Business Review Ser.). 288p. 1985. pap. 8.95 (ISBN 0-8120-3495-3). Barron.

--The Essentials of Corporation Law. 288p. 1984. pap. text ed. 14.95 (ISBN 0-8403-3264-5). Kendall Hunt.

--The Essentials of Partnership Law. 200p. 1982. pap. text ed. 13.95 (ISBN 0-8403-2785-4). Kendall-Hunt.

--Legal Materials in the Study of Commercial Transactions. 320p. 1984. pap. text ed. 17.95 (ISBN 0-8403-3454-0). Kendall-Hunt.

Beane, Leona, jt. auth. see Lakin, Leonard.

Beane, William. The Drama of the Renaissance: Essays for Leicester Bradner. Blistein, Elmer M., ed. LC 72-91635. 213p. 1970. 17.50x (ISBN 0-87057-117-6). U Pr of New Eng.

Beaney, Jan. Embroidery: New Approaches. 96p. 11.95 (ISBN 0-7207-1389-7, Pub. by Michael Joseph). Merrimack Pub Cir.

--Fun with Collage. (Learning with Fun Ser.). (Illus.). 64p. (gr. 5 up). 1980. text ed. 13.50x (ISBN 0-7182-1320-3). Sportshelf.

Beaney, William M. The Right to Counsel in American Courts. LC 72-5275. (University of Michigan Publications History & Political Science Ser.: Vol. 19). 268p. 1972. Repr. of 1955 ed. lib. bdg. 15.00x (ISBN 0-8371-5725-0, BERC). Greenwood.

Beaney, William M., jt. auth. see Mason, Alpheus T.

Beaney-Longi, J., ed. see Sgaravatti, E.

Bear, Alice C. Winter Sunshine. 1983. 8.95 (ISBN 0-8062-2068-6). Carlton.

Bear, C. D. Digby: The Biggest Dog in the World. LC 74-9678. (Illus.). (gr. 5 up). 1974. 10.89 (ISBN 0-200-00145-0, AbS-J). Har-Row.

Bear, D., ed. Telecommunication Traffic Engineering. 244p. 1980. 32.00 (ISBN 0-906048-36-2, TE002). Inst Elect Eng.

Bear, Firman E. Soils in Relation to Crop Growth. LC 65-23863. 304p. 1977. Repr. of 1965 ed. 19.50 (ISBN 0-88275-927-2). Krieger.

Bear, Fred. The Archer's Bible. rev. ed. LC 79-7585. (Outdoor Bible Ser.). (Illus.). 1980. pap. 5.95 (ISBN 0-385-15155-1). Doubleday.

--Fred Bear's Field Notes. LC 76-2752. 1976. 17.95 (ISBN 0-385-11690-X). Doubleday.

Bear, Geoffrey. Craftsmen & Interior Decoration in England, 1660-1820. 320p. 1981. 125.00x (ISBN 0-7028-8430-8, Pub. by Bartholomew & Son England). State Mutual Bk.

Bear, George G. & Callahan, Carolyn M. On the Nose: Fostering Creativity, Problem Solving & Social Reasoning. (Orig.). 1984. pap. 12.95 (ISBN 0-936386-23-1). Creative Learning.

Bear, Greg. Blood Music. 248p. 1985. 14.95 (ISBN 0-87795-720-7). Arbor Hse.

--Corona. (Star Trek Ser.). 192p. (Orig.). 1984. pap. 2.95 (ISBN 0-671-47390-5). PB.

--Corona. (Gregg Fiction Star Trek Ser.). 1985. lib. bdg. 11.95 (ISBN 0-8398-2889-6, Gregg). G K Hall.

--Eon. 16.95 (ISBN 0-312-94144-7, Dist. by St. Martin). Bluejay Bks.

--The Infinity Concert. 352p. 1984. pap. 2.95 (ISBN 0-425-07308-4). Berkley Pub.

--Strength of Stones, Flesh of Brass. 256p. (Orig.). 1981. pap. 2.50 (ISBN 0-441-79069-0). Ace Bks.

--The Wind from a Burning Woman. (Illus.). 270p. 1983. 13.95 (ISBN 0-87054-094-7). Arkham.

--The Wind from a Burning Woman. 256p. 1984. pap. 2.75 (ISBN 0-441-89212-4). Ace Bks.

Bear, H. S. Algebra & Elementary Functions. 2nd ed. LC 76-184869. (Page-Ficklin Math Ser). 1976. pap. text ed. 15.95x (ISBN 0-8087-2855-5). Burgess.

--College Algebra. 2nd ed. LC 79-83675. (Page-Ficklin Math Ser.). 1979. text ed. 14.95x (ISBN 0-8087-2892-X). Burgess.

Bear, Jacob. Hydraulics of Ground Water. (Water Resources & Environmental Engineering Ser.). (Illus.). 1979. text ed. 75.00 (ISBN 0-07-004170-9). McGraw.

Bear, Jacob & Corapcioglu, M. Yavuz, eds. Fundamentals of Transport Phenomena in Porous Media. (NATO Advanced Science Institute Series E: Applied Science: Vol. 82). 1013p. 1984. 132.50 (ISBN 90-247-2982-3, Pub. by Martinus Nijhoff Netherlands). Kluwer Academic.

Bear, James see Mayo, Bernard.

Bear, James A., Jr., jt. auth. see Nichols, Frederick D.

Bear, James A., Jr., ed. Jefferson at Monticello. Incl. Memoirs of a Monticello Slave. Campbell, Isaac; The Private Life of Thomas Jefferson. Pierson, Hamilton W. LC 67-17629. (Illus.). 144p. 1967. pap. 4.95 (ISBN 0-8139-0022-0). U Pr of Va.

Bear, John. Bear's Guide to Money for College. 144p. 1984. pap. 5.95 (ISBN 0-89815-126-0). Ten Speed Pr.

--The Blackmail Diet. LC 84-50971. 144p. 1984. 9.95 (ISBN 0-89815-119-8). Ten Speed Pr.

--Computer Wimp. LC 83-40024. 296p. 1983. 14.95 (ISBN 0-89815-102-3); pap. 9.95 (ISBN 0-89815-101-5). Ten Speed Pr.

--How to Get the Degree You Want: Bear's Guide to Non-Traditional College Degrees. 8th ed. LC 82-905. 273p. (Orig.). 1982. pap. 9.95 (ISBN 0-89815-080-9). Ten Speed Pr.

--United States of America. LC 75-44862. (Countries Ser.). (Illus.). (gr. 6 up). 1976. PLB 13.96 (ISBN 0-382-06109-8). Silver.

Bear, John, jt. auth. see Fox, Margaret S.

Bear, Leroy Little see Little Bear, Leroy, et al.

Bear, Lily A. Safe in His Care. 1984. 8.85 (ISBN 0-318-03659-2). Rod & Staff.

Bear, Philip O'Sullivan see O'Sullivan Bear, Philip.

Bear, Ruedi. Pianta Su: Ski Like the Best. (Sports Illustrated Books). 1976. 10.95 (ISBN 0-316-08550-2). Little.

Bear, Sun, et al. Sun Bear: The Path of Power. LC 83-72949. (Illus.). 272p. 1984. pap. 8.95 (ISBN 0-943404-03-7). Bear Tribe.

Bear, T. The Vascular Systems of the Cerebral Cortex. (Advances in Anatomy, Embryology & Cell Biology: Vol. 59). (Illus.). 1980. pap. 26.00 (ISBN 0-387-09652-3). Springer-Verlag.

Bear, W. Forrest. Electric Motors, Principles, Controls, Service & Maintenance. Hoerner, Harry J. & Hoerner, Thomas A., eds. (Illus.). 202p. 1983. pap. text ed. 10.00x (ISBN 0-913163-15-5, 183); tchr's. ed. 2.50x (ISBN 0-913163-16-3, 283). Hobar Pubns.

Bear, W. Forrest & Hoerner, Thomas A. Planning, Organizing & Teaching Agricultural Mechanics. rev. ed. (Illus.). 224p. 1980. pap. text ed. 13.00x (ISBN 0-913163-14-7, 178). Hobar Pubns.

--Rafter Layout with the Framing Square. rev. ed. (Illus.). 48p. 1982. pap. text ed. 3.00x (ISBN 0-913163-02-3, 166). Hobar Pubns.

--Sawhorse Layout with the Framing Square. rev. ed. (Illus.). 8p. 1971. pap. text ed. 1.10x (ISBN 0-913163-01-5, 165). Hobar Pubns.

--Torque & Torque Wrenches. (Illus.). 24p. 1971. pap. text ed. 2.65x (ISBN 0-913163-05-8, 171). Hobar Pubns.

Bear, W. Forrest, jt. auth. see Hoerner, Thomas A.

Bear, W. Forrest, jt. auth. see Hoerner, Harry.

Bearce, George D. British Attitudes Towards India 1748-1858. LC 81-20244. viii, 315p. 1982. Repr. lib. bdg. 29.75x (ISBN 0-313-23367-5, BEBA). Greenwood.

Beard, A. F. Crusade of Brotherhood, a History of the American Missionary Association. 1909. 18.00 (ISBN 0-527-06300-2). Kraus Repr.

Beard, Adelia, jt. auth. see Beard, Lina.

Beard, Annie E. Our Foreign-Born Citizens. 6th ed. LC 68-17083. (gr. 4 up). 1968. 14.38i (ISBN 0-690-60525-0). Crowell Jr Bks.

Beard, Augustus F. Crusade of Brotherhood, a History of the American Missionary Association. LC 76-161728. Repr. of 1909 ed. 26.50 (ISBN 0-404-00004-5). AMS Pr.

Beard, Belle B. Juvenile Probation: An Analysis of the Case Records of Five Hundred Children Studies at the Judge Baker Guidance Clinic & Placed on Probation in the Juvenile Court of Boston. LC 69-16224. (Criminology, Law Enforcement, & Social Problems Ser.: No. 95). 1969. Repr. of 1934 ed. 12.00x (ISBN 0-87585-095-2). Patterson Smith.

Beard, Betty J. Fashions from the Loom. LC 80-82154. 96p. (Orig.). 1980. 10.00 (ISBN 0-934026-03-3). Interweave.

Beard, Butch, et al. Butch Beards Basic Basketball: The Complete Player. (Illus.). 190p. 1985. 14.95 (ISBN 0-935576-14-2). Kesend Pub Ltd.

Beard, Charles. The Industrial Revolution. 59.95 (ISBN 0-8490-0406-3). Gordon Pr.

--Martin Luther & the Reformation in Germany until the Close of the Diet of Worms. LC 83-45638. Date not set. Repr. of 1889 ed. 49.50 (ISBN 0-404-19822-8). AMS Pr.

--The Reformation of the Sixteenth Century in Its Relations to Modern Thought & Knowledge. new ed. LC 77-27168. (Hibbert Lectures: 1883). Repr. of 1927 ed. 47.50 (ISBN 0-404-60404-8). AMS Pr.

--The Reformation of the Sixteenth Century in Its Relation to Modern Thought & Knowledge. LC 80-12915. xxviii, 450p. 1980. Repr. of 1962 ed. lib. bdg. 37.50x (ISBN 0-313-22410-2, BERF). Greenwood.

Beard, Charles, tr. see Renan, Ernest.

Beard, Charles A. American City Government: A Survey of Newer Tendencies. LC 70-112522. (Rise of Urban America). (Illus.). 1970. Repr. of 1912 ed. 26.50 (ISBN 0-405-02435-5). Ayer Co Pubs.

--Contemporary American History 1877-1913. LC 76-137902. (American History & Culture in the Nineteenth Century Ser). 1971. Repr. of 1914 ed. 29.50x (ISBN 0-8046-1470-9, Pub. by Kennikat). Assoc Faculty Pr.

--Devil Theory of War: An Inquiry into the Nature of History & the Possibility of Keeping Out of War. LC 68-54771. (Illus.). 1968. Repr. of 1936 ed. lib. bdg. 22.50 (ISBN 0-8371-0300-2, BEDT). Greenwood.

--Economic Basis of Politics. 3rd rev. facsimile ed. LC 70-37513. (Essay Index Reprint Ser). Repr. of 1945 ed. 14.00 (ISBN 0-8369-2535-1). Ayer Co Pubs.

--Economic Interpretation of the Constitution of the United States. 1965. pap. 10.95x (ISBN 0-02-902030-1). Free Pr.

--Enduring Federalist. LC 59-9146. (American Classics Ser.). (Illus.). 16.00 (ISBN 0-8044-1094-1); pap. 5.95 (ISBN 0-8044-6025-6). Ungar.

--The Idea of National Interest: An Analytical Study in American Foreign Policy. LC 77-10053. 1977. Repr. of 1934 ed. lib. bdg. 39.25 (ISBN 0-8371-9755-4, BEIN). Greenwood.

--Industrial Revolution. LC 69-13813. Repr. of 1927 ed. lib. bdg. 39.75 (ISBN 0-8371-2168-X, BEIR). Greenwood.

--Introduction to the English Historians. LC 68-56748. (Research & Source Works Ser: No. 231). 1968. Repr. of 1906 ed. 18.50 (ISBN 0-8337-0199-1). B Franklin.

--The Nature of the Social Sciences: In Relation to Objectives of Instruction. LC 73-14148. (Perspectives in Social Inquiry Ser.). 256p. 1974. Repr. of 1934 ed. 15.00x (ISBN 0-405-05494-7). Ayer Co Pubs.

--The Nature of the Social Sciences in Relation to Objectives of Instruction. 236p. Date not set. Repr. of 1934 ed. lib. bdg. 35.00 (ISBN 0-8482-7456-3). Norwood Edns.

--The Nature of the Social Sciences in Relation to Objectives of Instruction. 236p. 1985. Repr. of 1934 ed. lib. bdg. 40.00 (ISBN 0-918377-83-8). Russell Pr.

--Office of Justice of the Peace in England in Its Origin & Development. LC 74-18913. (Columbia University Studies in the Social Sciences: No. 52). Repr. of 1904 ed. 10.00 (ISBN 0-404-51052-3). AMS Pr.

--Office of the Justice of the Peace in England in Its Origin and Development. 1962. Repr. of 1904 ed. 15.00 (ISBN 0-8337-0198-3). B Franklin.

--The Open Door at Home: A Trial Philosophy of National Interest. LC 76-140650. 331p. 1972. Repr. of 1934 ed. lib. bdg. 22.50x (ISBN 0-8371-5811-7, BEOD). Greenwood.

--Presidents in American History. rev. ed. LC 77-908. (Illus.). (gr. 7 up). 1981. PLB 9.79 (ISBN 0-671-44026-8). Messner.

--The Republic: Conversations on Fundamentals. LC 80-12036. xiii, 366p. 1980. Repr. of 1962 ed. lib. bdg. 32.50x (ISBN 0-313-22411-0, BERP). Greenwood.

--Written History As an Act of Faith. 1960. pap. 3.00 (ISBN 0-87404-084-1). Tex Western.

Beard, Charles A. & Beard, Mary R. America in Mid-Passage. (Rise of American Civilization Ser. Vol. 3). 1966. 19.00 (ISBN 0-8446-1062-3). Peter Smith.

Beard, Charles A. & Schultz, Birl E. Documents on the State-Wide Initiative, Referendum & Recall. LC 70-120853. (American Constitutional & Legal History Ser.). 1970. Repr. of 1912 ed. lib. bdg. 49.50 (ISBN 0-306-71958-4). Da Capo.

Beard, Charles A. & Smith, George H. The Future Comes: A Study of the New Deal. LC 73-143307. 178p. 1972. Repr. of 1933 ed. lib. bdg. 15.00 (ISBN 0-8371-5808-7, BEFC). Greenwood.

Beard, Charles A. & Vagts, Detlev. The Presidents in American History: Washington-Reagan. rev. ed. 232p. (gr. 7 up). 1985. 9.79 (ISBN 0-671-60532-1). Messner.

Beard, Charles A., ed. America Faces the Future. facsimile ed. LC 73-90608. (Essay Index Reprint Ser). 1932. 25.50 (ISBN 0-8369-1244-6). Ayer Co Pubs.

--Century of Progress. facs. ed. LC 79-128205. (Essay Index Reprint Ser). 1932. 27.50 (ISBN 0-8369-1903-3). Ayer Co Pubs.

--Whither Mankind. LC 78-109708. 408p. 1973. Repr. of 1934 ed. lib. bdg. 18.50x (ISBN 0-8371-4199-0, BEWM). Greenwood.

--Whither Mankind: A Panorama of Modern Civilization. facs. ed. LC 72-128206. (Essay Index Reprint Ser). Repr. of 1928 ed. 24.50 (ISBN 0-8369-2344-8). Ayer Co Pubs.

Beard, Charles R. Lucks & Talismans: A Chapter of Popular Superstition. LC 72-80494. Repr. of 1934 ed. 22.00 (ISBN 0-405-08246-0, Blom Pubns). Ayer Co Pubs.

--Lucks & Talismans: A Chapter of Popular Superstition. LC 74-174903. xxii, 258p. Repr. of 1934 ed. 40.00x (ISBN 0-8103-3871-8). Gale.

Beard, Crowell. Ptosis. 3rd ed. LC 80-21576. (Illus.). 276p. 1980. text ed. 52.50 (ISBN 0-8016-0532-6). Mosby.

Beard, Daniel C. American Boys Handy Book: What to Do & How to Do It. facs. ed. LC 66-15858. (Illus.). (gr. 4 up). 1966. 11.95 (ISBN 0-8048-0006-5). C E Tuttle.

--The American Boy's Handy Book: What to Do & How to Do It. LC 82-8155. (Illus.). 320p. (gr. 4 up). 1983. pap. 9.95 (ISBN 0-87923-449-0, Nonpareil Bks). Godine.

--Moonblight & Six Feet of Romance. LC 74-22767. (Labor Movement in Fiction & Non-Fiction). (Illus.). 1976. Repr. of 1904 ed. 19.50 (ISBN 0-404-58405-5). AMS Pr.

Beard, Donald. Dakota Love Story. LC 76-2299. 1977. 11.95 (ISBN 0-87949-058-6). Ashley Bks.

Beard, E., et al. Risk Theory: The Stochastic Basis of Insurance. 2nd ed. (Monographs on Applied Probability & Statistics). 1977. 17.50x (ISBN 0-412-15100-6, NO.6031, Pub. by Chapman & Hall). Methuen Inc.

Beard, Edmund. Developing the ICBM: A Study in Bureaucratic Politics. (Institute of War & Peace Studies). 273p. 1976. 30.00x (ISBN 0-231-04012-1). Columbia U Pr.

Beard, Estle, jt. auth. see Carranco, Lynwood.

Beard, Frank A., et al. Maine's Historic Places. (Illus.). 1982. 10.95 (ISBN 0-89272-140-5). Down East.

Beard, G., ed. Historical Records Survey: Checklist of Washington Imprints, 1853-1876. 1942. 12.00 (ISBN 0-527-01930-5). Kraus Repr.

Beard, G. M. Practical Treatise on Nervous Exhaustion (Neurasthenia) Its Symptoms, Nature, Sequences, Treatment. 5th enl. ed. Rockwell, A. D., ed. Repr. of 1905 ed. 22.00 (ISBN 0-527-06340-1). Kraus Repr.

Beard, Geoffery. National Trust Book of English Furniture. 1985. 20.00 (ISBN 0-670-80141-0). Viking.

Beard, Geoffrey. Craftsmen & Interior Decoration in England 1660 - 1820. LC 81-2648. (Illus.). 320p. 1981. 85.00x (ISBN 0-8419-0703-X). Holmes & Meier.

--Stucco & Decorative Plasterwork in Europe. LC 82-49006. (Icon Editions). (Illus.). 165p. 1983. 48.08i (ISBN 0-06-430383-7, HarpT). Har-Row.

Beard, George M. American Nervousness, Its Causes & Consequences: A Supplement to Nervous Exhaustion. LC 72-180552. (Medicine & Society in America Ser.). 382p. 1972. Repr. of 1881 ed. 22.00 (ISBN 0-405-03932-8). Ayer Co Pubs.

--Sexual Neurasthenia, Its Hygiene, Causes, Symptoms & Treatment with a Chapter on Diet for the Nervous. 5th ed. Rockwell, A. D., ed. LC 76-180553. (Medicine & Society in America Ser). 312p. 1972. Repr. of 1898 ed. 18.00 (ISBN 0-405-03933-6). Ayer Co Pubs.

--Stimulants & Narcotics: Medically, Philosophically, & Morally Considered. Grob, Gerald N., ed. LC 80-1213. (Addiction in America Ser.). 1981. Repr. of 1871 ed. lib. bdg. 15.00x (ISBN 0-405-13569-6). Ayer Co Pubs.

Beard, H. Anthrone Test & Your Cancer Problem Today. 1.50 (ISBN 0-553-01293-2). Cancer Control Soc.

--Conquest of Cancer, Rheumatic & Heart Disease. pap. 5.00 (ISBN 0-943080-00-2). Cancer Control Soc.

Beard, H., jt. auth. see Meyerowitz, R.

Beard, Helen. Women in Ministry Today. (Orig.). 1980. (Pub. by Logos). Bridge Pub.

Beard, Henry & McKie, Roy. Cooking: The Art of Using Appliances & Utensils to Convert Ingredients & Seasonings into Excuses & Apologies. (Illus.). 112p. (Orig.). 1985. pap. 5.95 (ISBN 0-89480-843-5, 843). Workman Pub.

--Fishing. LC 82-40498. 96p. 1983. pap. 4.95 (ISBN 0-89480-355-7, 355). Workman Pub.

--Gardening. (Illus.). 1982. pap. 4.95 (ISBN 0-89480-200-3). Workman Pub.

--Sailing. LC 80-54621. (Illus.). 96p. 1981. 8.95 (ISBN 0-89480-158-9, 332); pap. 4.95 (ISBN 0-89480-144-9). Workman Pub.

Beard, Henry, ed. Miss Piggy's Treasury of Art Masterpieces: From the Kermitage Collection. (Illus.). 1984. pap. 12.95 (ISBN 0-03-000743-7). HR&W.

Beard, Howard. New Approach to Etiology Diagnosis, Treatment & Prevention of the Degenerative Diseases. 1965. 10.00x (ISBN 0-943080-14-2). Cancer Control Soc.

Beard, J. Turfgrass: Science & Culture. (Illus.). 1972. ref. ed. 30.95 (ISBN 0-13-933002-X). P-H.

Beard, J. B. & Beard, J. B., eds. International Turgrass Research Conference, 3rd: Proceedings. (Illus.). 1980. 18.00 (ISBN 0-89118-061-3). Am Soc Agron.

Beard, J. S. Vegetation Survey of Western Australia: SWAN - Explanatory Notes to Sheet 7. (Vegetation Survey Ser.). (Illus.). 221p. 1982. pap. 20.50x (ISBN 0-85564-094-4, Pub. by U of W Austral Pr). Intl Spec Bk.

--Vegetation Surveys of Western Australia: Murchison Memoir No. 6. (Vegetation Surveys of W. Australia Ser.). (Illus.). 1977. pap. 12.00x (ISBN 0-85564-093-6, Pub. by U of W Austral Pr). Intl Spec Bk.

--Vegetation Surveys of Western Australia: Swan Memoir No. 7. (Illus.). 1977. pap. 20.50x (ISBN 0-85564-094-4, Pub. by U of W Austral Pr). Intl Spec Bk.

--Vegetation Surveys of Western Australia (1: 1,000,000 Scale Series), Memoir No. 3: Great Victoria Desert. (Illus.). xii, 136p. (Orig.). 1976. pap. 12.00x (ISBN 0-85564-085-5, Pub. by U of W Austral Pr). Intl Spec Bk.

--Vegetation Surveys of Western Australia (1: 1,000,000 Scale Series), Memoir No. 4: Nullarbor. (Illus.). xx, 136p. 1975. pap. 12.00x (ISBN 0-85564-089-8, Pub. by U of W Austral Pr). Intl Spec Bk.

Beard, J. S. & Webb, M. J. Vegetation Surveys of Western Australia: Map & Memoir, No. 5. Incl. Pilbara. (Illus.). 1976. pap. 12.00x (ISBN 0-85564-092-8, Pub. by U of W Austral Pr). Intl Spec Bk.

--Vegetation Surveys of Western Australia (1: 1,000,000 Scale Series), Memoir No. 2: Great Sandy Desert. (Illus.). vii, 64p. 1976. pap. 12.00x (ISBN 0-85564-045-6, Pub. by U of W Austral Pr). Intl Spec Bk.

Beard, J. S., jt. ed. see Pate, J. S.

Beard, James. Barbecue with Beard. 240p. 1976. pap. 2.75 (ISBN 0-446-35062-1). Warner Bks.

--Beard on Bread. (Illus.). 1973. 12.95 (ISBN 0-394-47345-0). Knopf.

--Beard on Pasta. LC 82-48727. 1983. 13.95 (ISBN 0-394-52291-5). Knopf.

--Delights & Prejudices. LC 80-24560. (Illus.). 1964. 6.95 (ISBN 0-689-00007-3); pap. 7.95 (ISBN 0-689-70605-7, 266). Atheneum.

--Fowl & Game Bird Cookery. LC 78-71061. (Illus.). 1979. pap. 5.95 (ISBN 0-15-633340-6, Harv). HarBraceJ.

--Fowl & Game Bird Cookery. 1983. 13.00 (ISBN 0-8446-6079-5). Peter Smith.

--Hors d'Oeuvre & Canapes. LC 84-22339. 228p. 1985. pap. 5.95 (ISBN 0-688-04226-0, Quill). Morrow.

--How to Eat & Drink Your Way Through a French or Italian Menu. LC 70-108820. 1971. pap. 2.95 (ISBN 0-689-70332-5, 190). Atheneum.

--Menus for Entertaining. 1979. pap. 3.95 (ISBN 0-440-15569-X). Dell.

--The New James Beard. LC 80-29305. (Illus.). 640p. 1981. 16.95 (ISBN 0-394-41154-4); pap. 11.95 (ISBN 0-394-72470-4). Knopf.

Beard, James & Jerome, Carl. New Recipes for the Cuisinart Food Processor. 4th ed. 96p. 1978. pap. 5.00 (ISBN 0-936662-00-X, FP-250). Cuisinart Cooking.

Beard, James & Wilson, Jose. Beard on Food. (Illus.). 1974. 17.50 (ISBN 0-394-48505-X). Knopf.

Beard, James, intro. by. Portland Woman's Exchange Cookbook, 1913. new ed. LC 73-89993. (Illus.). 380p. 1973. pap. 5.95 pap. comb binding (ISBN 0-87595-045-0). Oreg Hist Soc.

Beard, James, et al. The Great Cook's Guide to Appetizers. Glaser, Milton & Wolf, Burton, eds. Incl. Appetizers. pap. 2.95 (ISBN 0-394-73607-9); Breads. pap. 2.95 (ISBN 0-394-73421-1); Cakes; Clay Cookery. pap. 2.95 (ISBN 0-394-73420-3); Crepes & Souffles. pap. 2.95 (ISBN 0-394-73422-X); Fish Cookery. pap. 2.95 (ISBN 0-394-73424-6); Ice Cream & Other Frozen Deserts. pap. 2.95 (ISBN 0-394-73606-0); Pasta & Noodle Dishes. pap. 2.95 (ISBN 0-394-73602-8); Pies & Tarts. pap. 2.95 (ISBN 0-394-73604-4); Salads. pap. 2.95 (ISBN 0-394-73423-8); Soups. pap. 2.95 (ISBN 0-394-73608-7); Woks, Steamers & Fire Pots. pap. 2.95 (ISBN 0-394-73425-4). (Illus.). 1977-78. pap. 2.95 ea. Random.

Beard, James, et al, eds. The Cooks' Catalogue. LC 75-6329. (Illus.). 576p. 1975. 21.10i (ISBN 0-06-011563-7, HarpT). Har-Row.

Beard, James A. Beard on Bread. 1981. pap. 2.50 (ISBN 0-345-29550-1). Ballantine.

--The James Beard Cookbook. rev. ed. 1970. 15.95 (ISBN 0-525-13621-5, 01549-460). Dutton.

--James Beard: The Fireside Cookbook. 320p. 1982. pap. 9.95 (ISBN 0-671-44774-2, Fireside). S&S.

--James Beard's American Cookery. 1972. 29.45 (ISBN 0-316-08564-2); pap. 14.95 (ISBN 0-316-08566-9). Little.

--James Beard's Casserole Cookbook. 160p. 1981. pap. 2.50 (ISBN 0-449-13871-2). Fawcett.

--James Beard's Fish Cookery. 1967. pap. 3.95 (ISBN 0-446-32126-5). Warner Bks.

--James Beard's New Fish Cookery. 1976. 15.00 (ISBN 0-316-08565-0). Little.

--James Beard's Theory & Practice of Good Cooking. Bd. with The New James Beard. LC 76-47701. 10.95 (ISBN 0-394-72475-5). LC 76-4770. 1984. boxed set 23.00 (ISBN 0-394-72471-2). Knopf.

--James Beard's Theory & Practice of Good Cooking. (Illus.). 1977. 18.95 (ISBN 0-394-48493-2). Knopf.

Beard, James A. & Callvert, Isabel. James Beard Cookbook. rev. ed. (Orig.). 1959. pap. 4.95 (ISBN 0-440-14174-5, LE). Dell.

Beard, James B. Turf Management for Golf Courses. (Orig.). 1982. 45.00x (ISBN 0-8087-2872-5). Burgess.

Beard, James B., et al, eds. Turfgrass Bibliography from 1672-1972. 730p. 1977. 35.00x (ISBN 0-87013-195-8). Mich St U Pr.

Beard, James F. & Elliott, James P. The Writings of James Fenimore Cooper: A Statement of Editorial Principles & Procedures. LC 77-2995. 1977. pap. 2.00x (ISBN 0-914206-09-5). Clark U Pr.

Beard, James F., ed. Gleanings in Europe: The Rhine by James Fenninore Cooper. (The Writings of James Fennimore Cooper Ser.). (Text established with explanatory notes by Thomas Philbrick & Maurice Geracht). 1985. lib. bdg. 39.50x (ISBN 0-87395-366-5); pap. text ed. 14.95x (ISBN 0-87395-928-0). State U NY Pr.

Beard, James F., ed. see Cooper, James F.

Beard, John R. Life of Toussaint L'Ouverture, the Negro Patriot of Haiti. LC 75-109316. (Illus.). Repr. of 1853 ed. 19.75x (ISBN 0-8371-3572-9, BTL&, Pub. by Negro U Pr). Greenwood.

Beard, Joseph W., jt. auth. see Powell, Marjorie.

Beard, L. R. see Maxwell, H. C.

Beard, Leo R. & Maxwell, W. H., eds. Water Resources Management in Industrial Areas. (Water Resources Ser.: Vol. 1). 463p. 1982. 71.25 (ISBN 0-907567-30-4, TYP129, TYP); pap. 48.75 (ISBN 0-907567-31-2, TYP128). Unipub.

Beard, Lina & Beard, Adelia. American Girls Handy Book. LC 69-11086. (Illus.). (gr. 2-8). 1968. Repr. of 1888 ed. 12.50 (ISBN 0-8048-0008-1). C E Tuttle.

Beard, Marna L. & McGahey, Michael J. Alternative Careers for Teachers. LC 82-20742. 192p. (Orig.). 1983. pap. 9.95 (ISBN 0-668-05571-5). Arco.

--Alternative Careers for Teachers. 2nd ed. 256p. 1985. pap. 9.95 (ISBN 0-668-06373-4). Arco.

Beard, Mary. The American Labor Movement. LC 71-89717. (American Labor Series One). 206p. 1969. Repr. of 1931 ed. 9.50 (ISBN 0-405-02103-8). Ayer Co Pubs.

--Force of Women in Japanese History. 1953. 10.00 (ISBN 0-8183-0167-8). Pub Aff Pr.

Beard, Mary & Crawford, Michael. Rome in the Late Republic. LC 85-480. 128p. 1985. text ed. 22.50x (ISBN 0-8014-1824-0). Cornell U Pr.

Beard, Mary R. On Understanding Women. LC 68-54773. (Illus.). 1968. Repr. of 1931 ed. lib. bdg. 28.50 (ISBN 0-8371-0302-9, BEUW). Greenwood.

--On Understanding Women. 1977. Repr. of 1931 ed. 30.00 (ISBN 0-8274-4311-0). R West.

--Woman As Force in History. 1985. Repr. of 1946 ed. lib. bdg. 27.50x (ISBN 0-374-90503-7). Octagon.

--Woman's Work in Municipalities. LC 72-2588. (American Women Ser). Repr. of 1915 ed. 20.00 (ISBN 0-405-04446-1). Ayer Co Pubs.

Beard, Mary R., jt. auth. see Beard, Charles A.

Beard, Mary R., jt. auth. see Bruere, Martha B.

Beard, Michael & Shyshka, Jeff. Duet. LC 76-58640. (Illus.). 1977. pap. 10.00 (ISBN 0-915346-25-7). A Wofsy Fine Arts.

Beard, Michael, tr. see Hawi, Khalil.

Beard, Miriam, tr. see Francesco, Grete de.

Beard, Oliver T. Bristling with Thorns. LC 68-20006. (Americans in Fiction Ser.). (Illus.). lib. bdg. 14.50 (ISBN 0-8398-0158-0); pap. text ed. 4.95x (ISBN 0-89197-687-6). Irvington.

Beard, Patten. The Pantalette Doll. LC 31-21184. (Illus.). 160p. 1981. Repr. of 1931 ed. lib. bdg. 30.00 (ISBN 0-940070-12-X). Doll Works.

Beard, Paul. Living on: How Consciousness Continues & Evolves after Death. 212p. 1981. 12.95 (ISBN 0-8264-0036-1); pap. 5.95 (ISBN 0-8264-0037-X). Continuum.

Beard, Peter. Longing for Darkness. 35.00 (ISBN 0-686-46612-8). Yankee Peddler.

Beard, R. The Indo-European Lexicon: Synchronic Theory. (North Holland Linguistic Ser.: Vol. 44). 390p. 1981. 47.00 (ISBN 0-444-86214-5, North-Holland). Elsevier.

Beard, R. E. & Pentikainen, T. Risk Theory: The Stochastic Basis of Insurance. 3rd ed. 230p. 1984. 49.95 (ISBN 0-412-24260-5, NO. 6816, Pub. by Chapman & Hall); pap. 24.00 (ISBN 0-412-25980-X, NO. 9013, Pub. by Chapman & Hall). Methuen Inc.

Beard, R. W. & Nathanielsz, P. W. Fetal Physiology & Medicine. LC 76-20126. (Illus.). Repr. of 1976 ed. 138.50 (ISBN 0-8357-9543-8, 2016654). Bks Demand UMI.

Beard, Ray, jt. auth. see Matthews, Velda.

Beard, Richard R. Walt Disney's EPCOT: Creating the New World of Tomorrow. (Illus.). 240p. 1982. 35.00 (ISBN 0-8109-0819-0). Abrams.

Beard, Robert W., jt. auth. see Copi, Irving M.

Beard, Ross E., Jr. Carbine: The Story of David Marshall Williams. LC 76-20847. 1977. ltd ed, signed 15.00 (ISBN 0-87844-047-X). Sandlapper Pub Co.

Beard, Ruth M. An Outline of Piaget's Developmental Psychology. (Student's Library of Education). 144p. 1983. pap. 7.95 (ISBN 0-7100-6344-X). Routledge & Kegan.

--An Outline of Piaget's Developmental Psychology for Students & Teachers. 1972. pap. 3.50 (ISBN 0-451-62438-6, Ment). NAL.

Beard, Ruth M., jt. auth. see Verma, Gajendra K.

Beard, Selma W., jt. auth. see Wight, Rebecca S.

Beard, Thomas R., ed. Louisiana Economy. LC 69-7622. (University Studies, Social Science Ser.: Vol. 15). (Illus.). viii, 232p. 1969. 22.50x (ISBN 0-8071-0307-1). La State U Pr.

Beard, Trudy. Canvas Painting Big & Easy. rev. ed. (Illus.). 72p. 1983. pap. 9.95 (ISBN 0-917119-19-3, 45-1042). Priscillas Pubns.

--Minis Grow Up. (Illus.). 52p. (Orig.). 1978. pap. 8.95 (ISBN 0-917119-13-4, 45-1031). Priscillas Pubns.

Beard, Yolande S. The Wappo: A Report. 1979. pap. 5.25 (ISBN 0-939046-26-1). Malki Mus Pr.

Bearden, Donna. Atari LOGO in the Classroom. 1984. pap. text ed. 14.95 (ISBN 0-8359-0121-1). Reston.

--A Bit of LOGO Magic: Apple. 1984. pap. text ed. 12.95 (ISBN 0-8359-0495-4). Reston.

--Monica the Computer Mouse. (Illus.). 64p. (gr. k-3). 1984. 8.95 (ISBN 0-89588-214-0). SYBEX.

Bearden, Donna & Muller, Jim. One-Two-Three, My Computer & Me. 1983. pap. 12.95 (ISBN 0-8359-5228-2). Reston.

Bearden, H. Joe & Fuquay, John. Applied Animal Reproduction. 2nd. ed. 1984. text ed. 23.95 (ISBN 0-8359-0106-8); instr's manual avail. (ISBN 0-8359-0107-6). Reston.

Bearden, Romare & Holty, Carl. The Painter's Mind: A Study of the Relations of Structure & Space. in Painting. LC 80-8527. 240p. 1981. lib. bdg. 48.00 (ISBN 0-8240-9457-3). Garland Pub.

Bearden, Susan E. A Study of Basketmaker II Settlement on Northern Black Mesa, Arizona: Excavations 1973-1979. LC 84-72847. (Center for Archaeological Investigations Research Paper: No. 44). (Illus.). xv, 198p. 1984. pap. 8.00 (ISBN 0-88104-021-5). Center Archaeo.

Bearden, T E. Solutions to Tesla's Secrets & the Soviet Tesla Weapons with Reference Articles for Solutions to Tesla's Secrets, 2 pts. LC 81-85737. (Illus.). 188p. (Orig.). 1982. Set. pap. 14.00 (ISBN 0-9603536-3-1). Tesla Bk Co.

Bearden, Thomas E. The Excalibur Briefing: Understanding Paranormal Phenomena. 2nd ed. (A Walnut Hill Bk.). (Illus., Orig.). 1986. pap. 11.95 (ISBN 0-89407-060-6). Strawberry Hill.

Beardmore, John A., jt. ed. see Battaglia, Bruno.

Beardon, A. F. Complex Analysis: The Argument Principle in Analysis & Topology. LC 78-8540. 239p. 1979. 69.95x (ISBN 0-471-99671-8, Pub. by Wiley-Interscience). Wiley.

--The Geometry of Discrete Groups. (Graduate Texts in Mathematics: Vol. 91). (Illus.). 337p. 1983. 41.00 (ISBN 0-387-90788-2). Springer-Verlag.

Beardon, Alan. A Primer on Riemann Surfaces. LC 82-4439. (London Mathematical Society Lecture Note Ser.: No. 78). 150p. 1984. pap. 24.95 (ISBN 0-521-27104-5). Cambridge U Pr.

Beards, C. F. Structural Vibration Analysis: Modelling, Analysis & Damping of Vibrating Structures. LC 82-25482. 153p. 1983. 44.95x (ISBN 0-470-27422-0). Halsted Pr.

--Vibration Analysis & Control System Dynamic. LC 81-6646. (Ser. in Engineering Science: Civil Engineering). 169p. 1981. 54.95x (ISBN 0-470-27255-4). Halsted Pr.

Beards, P. H., ed. see Robinson, Joseph F.

Beards, Peter. Electronics: Level II. (Illus.). 192p. 1980. pap. text ed. 17.95x (ISBN 0-7121-0581-6). Trans-Atlantic.

Beardsell, P. R., ed. Ricardo Guiraldes: Don Segundo Sombra. 252p. 1973. pap. text ed. 8.30 (ISBN 0-08-017010-2). Pergamon.

Beardshaw, John. Economics: A Student's Guide. (Illus.). 698p. 1984. pap. text ed. 24.00x (ISBN 0-7121-0598-0). Trans-Atlantic.

Beardshaw, John & Palfreman, David. The Organization in It's Environment. 2nd ed. 625p. 1982. pap. text ed. 27.50x (ISBN 0-7121-1541-2). Trans-Atlantic.

Beardslee, Edward C., jt. auth. see Jerman, Max E.

Beardslee, John W., III, ed. see Turrettin, Thomas.

Beardslee, William A. Human Achievement & Divine Vocation in the Message of Paul. LC 61-4760. (Studies in Biblical Theology: No. 31). 1961. pap. 10.00x (ISBN 0-8401-3031-7). A R Allenson.

--Literary Criticism of the New Testament. Via, Dan O., Jr., ed. LC 77-94817. (Guides to Biblical Scholarship: New Testament Ser.). 96p. (Orig.). 1970. pap. 3.95 (ISBN 0-8006-0185-8, 1-185). Fortress.

Beardslee, William A., ed. see Pregeant, Russell.

Beardslee, William A., ed. see Tannehill, Robert C.

Beardslee, William R. The Way Out Must Lead In. LC 77-77695. 1977. pap. 5.00 (ISBN 0-89937-002-0). Ctr Res Soc Chg.

--The Way Out Must Lead In: Life Histories in the Civil Rights Movement. rev. ed. 208p. 1983. 14.95 (ISBN 0-88208-153-5); pap. 7.95 (ISBN 0-88208-120-9). Lawrence Hill.

Beardsley, Aubrey. Aubrey Beardsley Bookplates. Theodore, Menten, ed. pap. 2.95 (ISBN 0-486-23350-2). Dover.

--Aubrey Beardsley Greeting Card Book. Menten, Theodore, ed. (Illus.). 64p. 1975. pap. 4.00 (ISBN 0-486-23173-9). Dover.

--Beardsley's Illustrations for le Morte d'Arthur. (Facsimile Dent Edition). Repr. of 1893 ed. 13.25 (ISBN 0-8446-4507-9). Peter Smith.

--Collected Drawings of Aubrey Beardsley. Harris, Bruce, ed. (Bounty Bk. Ser). (Illus.). 1969. 4.98 (ISBN 0-517-08326-4, Pub. by Bounty Bks.). Crown.

--Early Work of Aubrey Beardsley. rev. ed. (Illus.). (YA) (gr. 7-12). pap. 6.50 (ISBN 0-486-21816-3). Dover.

--Early Work of Aubrey Beardsley. (Illus.). 14.25 (ISBN 0-8446-1616-8). Peter Smith.

--Illustrations for le Morte Darthur. 250p. 1972. pap. 6.00 (ISBN 0-486-22348-5). Dover.

--Later Work of Aubrey Beardsley. rev. ed. (Illus.). (YA) (gr. 7-12). pap. 5.95 (ISBN 0-486-21817-1). Dover.

--Later Work of Aubrey Beardsley. (Illus.). 14.00 (ISBN 0-8446-1617-6). Peter Smith.

Beardsley, Aubrey & Pope, Alexander. The Rape of the Lock. pap. 3.95 (ISBN 0-486-21963-1). Dover.

Beardsley, Aubrey & Wilde, Oscar. Salome: A Tragedy in One Act. Douglas, Alfred, tr. pap. 4.00 (ISBN 0-486-21830-9). Dover.

Beardsley, Aubrey V. Last Letters of Aubrey Beardsley. 158p. 1980. Repr. of 1904 ed. lib. bdg. 20.00 (ISBN 0-8482-4200-9). Norwood Edns.

--Letters from Aubrey Beardsley to Leonard Smithers. Walker, R. A., ed. LC 79-8049. Repr. of 1937 ed. 27.50 (ISBN 0-404-18360-3). AMS Pr.

Beardsley, Charles. Guam: Past & Present. LC 63-22540. (gr. 9 up). 1964. bds. 12.95 (ISBN 0-8048-0223-8). C E Tuttle.

--Hollywood's Master Showman: The Legendary Sid Grauman. LC 80-69966. (Illus.). 192p. 1981. 25.00 (ISBN 0-8453-4703-9). Cornwall Bks.

Beardsley, Charles, jt. auth. see Seward, Jack.

Beardsley, E. Edwards. Life & Times of William Samuel Johnson. LC 72-4207. (Select Bibliographies Reprint Ser.). 1972. Repr. of 1876 ed. 18.00 (ISBN 0-8369-6872-7). Ayer Co Pubs.

Beardsley, Edward H. Harry L. Russell & Agricultural Science in Wisconsin. (Illus.). 252p. 1969. 25.00x (ISBN 0-299-05470-5). U of Wis Pr.

--Harry L. Russell & Agricultural Science in Wisconsin. LC 77-84950. pap. 67.30 (ISBN 0-317-28985-3, 2023728). Bks Demand UMI.

--The Rise of the American Chemistry Profession, 1850-1900. LC 64-65130. (University of Florida Social Sciences Monographs: No. 23). 1964. 3.50 (ISBN 0-8130-0014-9). U Presses Fla.

Beardsley, John. Art in Public Places. Harney, Andy L., ed. LC 81-85019. (Illus.). 149p. (Orig.). 1981. pap. 9.95 (ISBN 0-941182-05-3). Partners Livable.

--Earthworks & Beyond: Contemporary Art in the Landscape. LC 83-21424. (Illus.). 144p. 1984. 29.95 (ISBN 0-89659-422-X); pap. 19.95 (ISBN 0-89659-465-3). Abbeville Pr.

--A Landscape for Modern Sculpture. 112p. 1985. 35.00 (ISBN 0-89659-587-0). Abbeville Pr.

--Probing the Earth: Contemporary Land Projects. LC 77-12419. (Illus.). 113p. 1978. 19.95 (ISBN 0-87474-232-3). Smithsonian.

Beardsley, Lou. Mothers-in-Law Can Be Fun. LC 80-84763. 1981. pap. 3.95 (ISBN 0-89081-281-0). Harvest Hse.

Beardsley, Lou & Spry, Toni. The Fulfilled Woman. LC 74-29206. 1977. 2.95 (ISBN 0-89081-072-9). Harvest Hse.

Beardsley, M. C. Writing with Reason: Logic for Composition. (Illus.). 176p. 1976. pap. text ed. 10.95 (ISBN 0-13-970301-2). P-H.

Beardsley, Monroe. Practical Logic. 1950. text ed. 22.95 (ISBN 0-13-692111-6). P-H.

Beardsley, Monroe C. The Aesthetic Point of View: Selected Essays. Callen, Donald M., ed. Wreen, Michael. LC 82-71601. 424p. 1982. 37.50x (ISBN 0-8014-1250-1); pap. 19.95x (ISBN 0-8014-9880-5). Cornell U Pr.

--Aesthetics from Classical Greece to the Present: A Short History. LC 75-20138. (Studies in the Humanities: No. 13). 418p. 1975. pap. 8.95 (ISBN 0-8173-6623-7). U of Ala Pr.

--Aesthetics: Problems in the Philosophy of Criticism. 2nd ed. LC 80-28899. (Illus.). 688p. 1981. 30.00 (ISBN 0-915145-09-X); pap. text ed. 15.00 (ISBN 0-915145-08-1). Hackett Pub.

--Thinking Straight: Principles of Reasoning for Readers & Writers. 4th ed. LC 74-16349. (Illus.). 1975. pap. text ed. 14.95 (ISBN 0-13-918227-6). P-H.

Beardsley, Monroe C., ed. The European Philosophers from Descartes to Nietzsche. LC 60-10004. 1960. 8.95 (ISBN 0-394-60412-1). Modern Lib.

Beardsley, Monroe C., et al, eds. Theme & Form: An Introduction to Literature. 4th ed. 704p. 1975. text ed. 24.95 (ISBN 0-13-912972-3). P-H.

Beardsley, Paul, jt. auth. see Jones, Lem.

Beardsley, Philip L. Conflicting Ideologies in Political Economy: A Synthesis. LC 80-39916. (Sage Library of Social Research: Vol. 18). 200p. 1981. 24.00 (ISBN 0-8039-1527-6); pap. 12.00. Sage.

--Redefining Rigor: Ideology & Statistics in Political Inquiry. (Library of Social Research: Vol. 104). (Illus.). 199p. 1980. 24.00 (ISBN 0-8039-1472-5); pap. 12.00 (ISBN 0-8039-1473-3). Sage.

Beardsley, Richard. Trail & Camp Cooking with the Chinese Wok. LC 81-21046. (Illus.). 100p. (Orig.). 1982. pap. 3.50 (ISBN 0-87108-619-0). Pruett.

Beardsley, Richard, ed. The Videolog: General Interest & Education. 1980-81 ed. (Videolog Ser.). 500p. 1981. pap. 39.50x (ISBN 0-88432-071-5). J Norton Pubs.

--The Videolog in Business. 1980-81 ed. (Videolog Ser.). 1981. pap. 39.50x (ISBN 0-88432-070-7). J Norton Pubs.

--The Videolog in the Health Sciences. 1980-81 ed. (Videolog Ser.). 1981. pap. 49.50x (ISBN 0-88432-069-3). J Norton Pubs.

Beardsley, Richard K., ed. see Pacific Science Congress, 10th, Honolulu 1961.

Beardsley, Richard K., et al. Village Japan. LC 58-13802. (Illus.). xvi, 498p. 1969. pap. 3.95 (ISBN 0-226-03998-6, 327, Phoenix). U of Chicago Pr.

Beardsley, Theodore S., Jr. Hispano-Classical Translations. 188p. 1970. 7.95 (ISBN 0-89192-064-1, Pub. by Hispanic Soc). Interbk Inc.

--Hispano-Classical Translations Printed Between 1482 & 1699. (Illus.). 176p. 1970. 9.50 (ISBN 0-87535-113-1). Hispanic Soc.

--Hispano-Classical Translations: Printed Between 1482 & 1699. Koren, J., ed. LC 72-107356. (Duquesne Philological Ser.: No. 12). 1970. text ed. 10.00x (ISBN 0-8207-0115-7). Humanities.

Beardsley, Wilfred A. Infinitive Construction in Old Spanish. LC 77-159992. (Columbia University. Studies in Romance Philology & Literature: No. 28). Repr. of 1921 ed. 22.50 (ISBN 0-404-50628-3). AMS Pr.

Beardwood, Lynette, et al. A First Course in Technical English, Bk. 1. 1978. 6.50x (ISBN 0-435-28755-9); tchrs ed. 9.75x (ISBN 0-435-28756-7); reading tape 28.00x (ISBN 0-435-28757-5); reading cassette 22.00x (ISBN 0-435-28030-9); drills tapes 88.00x (ISBN 0-435-28027-9); drills cassettes 70.00x (ISBN 0-435-28026-0). Heinemann Ed.

--A First Course in Technical English, Bk. 2. (Illus.). 1979. pap. text ed. 6.50x (ISBN 0-435-28758-3); tchr's ed. 9.75x (ISBN 0-435-28759-1); tape 28.00x (ISBN 0-435-28760-5); cassette 22.00x (ISBN 0-435-28031-7). Heinemann Ed.

Beare, A. S., ed. Recent Influenza Research & Progress Towards Epidemiological Control. 288p. 1982. write for info. (ISBN 0-8493-6250-4). CRC Pr.

Beare, F. W. The Gospel According to Matthew: Translation, Commentary, & Notes. LC 81-47837. 575p. 1982. 28.80i (ISBN 0-06-060731-9, HarpR). Har-Row.

Beare, Geraldine, compiled by. Index to the Strand Magazine, 1891-1950. LC 82-11769. xxxviii, 859p. 1982. lib. bdg. 85.00 (ISBN 0-313-23122-2, BIM/). Greenwood.

Beare, J. I., tr. see Aristotle.

Beare, Patricia & Chaney, Harriet S. Nursing Review for NCLEX RN: Content Review & Practice Test. (Illus.). 592p. 1985. pap. text ed. 15.75 (ISBN 0-397-54405-7, Nursing). Lippincott.

Beare, Patricia G. & Rahr, Virginia A. Quick Reference to Nursing Implications of Diagnostic Tests. (Quick References for Nurses Ser.). (Illus.). 438p. 1982. pap. text ed. 13.75 (ISBN 0-397-54366-2, 64-03083, Lippincott Nursing). Lippincott.

Beare, Patricia G., et al. Nursing Implications of Diagnostic Tests. 2nd ed. 480p. 1985. text ed. 15.75 (ISBN 0-317-30587-5, Lippincott Nursing). Lippincott.

Beare, W. The Roman Stage. (Illus.). 416p. 1977. Repr. of 1950 ed. 29.50x (ISBN 0-87471-881-3). Rowman.

Bearman, Graham. The French Revolution. (History Broadsheets Ser.). (Illus.). 1977. pap. text ed. 8.50x (ISBN 0-435-31749-0). Heinemann Ed.

Bearman, Graham, jt. auth. see Lee, Peter.

Bearman, Jane. David. LC 65-21753. (Illus.). (gr. 3 up). 1975. 1.95 (ISBN 0-8246-0085-1). Jonathan David.

--The Eight Nights: A Chanukah Counting Book. Syme, Daniel B., ed. LC 78-60781. (Illus.). 1979. pap. 4.50 (ISBN 0-8074-0025-4, 102562). UAHC.

--Jonathan. LC 65-21754. (Illus.). (gr. 3 up). 1975. 1.95 (ISBN 0-8246-0089-4). Jonathan David.

Bearman, Toni C. & Kunberger, William. A Study of Coverage Overlap Among Major Science & Technology Abstracting & Indexing Services. 1977. 20.00 (ISBN 0-942308-12-3). NFAIS.

Bearn, Alexander G., ed. Antibiotics in the Management of Infections: Outlook for the 1980's: Medac 1982. 270p. 1982. text ed. 36.00 (ISBN 0-89004-880-0). Raven.

Bearn, Alexander G., jt. ed. see Doyle, Austin E.

Bearn, Alexander G., jt. ed. see Steinberg, Arthur G.

Bearne, Colin, tr. see Davydov, Gavriil.

Bear Nicol, W. B. De see Jones, Thora B. & De Bear, Nicol.

Bearns, Robert J. The Awakening Electromagnetic Spectrum. new ed. LC 74-76050. (Illus.). 128p. (Orig.). 1974. pap. 9.98 (ISBN 0-914706-00-4). Awakening Prods.

Bearon, Lucille B., jt. auth. see George, Linda K.

Bears, Edwin C. Hardluck Ironclad: The Sinking & Salvage of the Cairo. rev. ed. LC 79-25985. xiv, 258p. 1980. text ed. 25.00x (ISBN 0-8071-0683-6); pap. 7.95 (ISBN 0-8071-0684-4). La State U Pr.

Bearse, Austin. Reminiscences of Fugitive Slave Law Days in Boston. LC 74-82170. (Anti-Slavery Crusade in America Ser). 1969. Repr. of 1880 ed. 13.00 (ISBN 0-405-00609-8). Ayer Co Pubs.

Bearse, Peter J., ed. Mobilizing Capital: Program Innovation & the Changing Public-Private Interface in Development Finance. LC 82-1447. xvii, 478p. 1982. lib. bdg. 35.00 (ISBN 0-444-00690-7, BMC/, Pub. by Elsevier North Holland, Inc.). Greenwood.

Bearss, Edwin C. The Battle of Brice's Cross Roads. LC 79-84857. (Illus.). 1979. 22.50. Pr of Morningside.

Bearss, Margie, jt. auth. see Kerksis, Sydney C.

Beart, Robert, jt. ed. see Irving, Miles.

Beart, Robert W., jt. ed. see Beahrs, Oliver H.

Beart, Robert W., Jr., jt. ed. see Beahrs, Oliver H.

Bearth, Thomas. L'Enonce Toura (Cote d'Ivoire) (Publications in Linguistics & Related Fields Ser.: No. 30). 481p. (Fr.). 1971. pap. 7.00 (ISBN 0-88312-032-1); microfiche (5) 5.72 (ISBN 0-88312-432-7). Summer Inst Ling.

Beary, Evalena. Sugar Loaf Springs: Heber's Elegant Watering Place. (Illus.). 120p. 1985. write for info. River Road Pr.

Beary, John F., 3rd, et al. Manual of Rheumatology & Outpatient Orthopedic Disorders: Diagnosis & Therapy. (Little, Brown Spiral Manual Ser.). 1981. 16.95 (ISBN 0-316-08575-8). Little.

Beasant, John. The Santo Rebellion: An Imperial Reckoning. (Illus.). 172p. 1984. text ed. 18.95X (ISBN 0-8248-0947-5). UH Pr.

Beasch, Anthony, tr. see Mozart, Wolfgang A.

Bease, W. Lyon. A Short History of English Liberalism. 1976. lib. bdg. 59.95 (ISBN 0-8490-2600-8). Gordon Pr.

Beasley, Audrey, ed. see Junior League of Richardson, Inc.

Beasley, Conger, Jr., ed. Missouri Short Fiction. LC 84-72899. 240p. 1984. pap. 8.50 (ISBN 0-933532-44-X). BkMk.

Beasley, Conger, Jr., jt. ed. see Findlay, Ted.

Beasley, Daniel S., ed. Audition in Childhood: Methods of Study. LC 83-26772. (Illus.). 184p. 1984. pap. text ed. 25.00t (ISBN 0-933014-12-0). College-Hill.

Beasley, Daniel S. & Davis, G. A., eds. Aging: Communication Processes & Disorders. 375p. 1980. 36.50 (ISBN 0-8089-1281-X, 790457). Grune.

Beasley, David. Design Illustration. (Orig.). 1979. pap. text ed. 7.50x (ISBN 0-435-75063-1). Heinemann Ed.

--Through Paphlagonia with a Donkey. (An Adventure in the Turkish Isfendyars). (Illus.). 235p. 1984. 30.00 (ISBN 0-915317-01-X). Davus Pub.

--Through Paphlagonia with a Donkey: An Adventure in the Turkish Isfendyars. (Illus.). 235p. 1983. pap. 9.95 (ISBN 0-915317-00-1). Davus Pub.

Beasley, Delilah L. Negro Trail Blazers of California. LC 73-88400. Repr. 29.75x (ISBN 0-8371-1768-2, BEN&, Pub. by Negro U Pr). Greenwood.

Beasley, Jack O. Microcomputers on the Farm. LC 83-60164. 206p. 1983. pap. text ed. 14.95 (ISBN 0-672-22011-3, 22011). Sams.

Beasley, James, ed. see Bonar, John A.

Beasley, James E. Products Liability & the Unreasonably Dangerous Requirement. 864p. 1981. 65.00 (ISBN 0-686-32426-9, B189). Am Law Inst.

--Products Liability & the Unreasonably Dangerous Requirement. 846p. 1981. 65.00 (ISBN 0-317-32248-6, B189). Am Law Inst.

Beasley, Jerry. Novels of the Seventeen Forties. LC 81-10390. 256p. 1982. 20.00x (ISBN 0-8203-0590-1). U of Ga Pr.

Beasley, Jerry, ed. The Development of American Karate: History & Skills. LC 83-62681. (Illus.). 96p. 1983. pap. 9.95 (ISBN 0-943736-02-1). Ormsby.

--English Fiction, Sixteen Sixty to Eighteen Hundred: A Guide to Information Sources. LC 74-11526. (American Literature, English Literature & World Literatures in English Information Guide Ser.: Vol. 14). 1978. 60.00x (ISBN 0-8103-1226-3). Gale.

Beasley, Jerry C., jt. ed. see Hogan, Robert.

Beasley, Jim. Missions Study: Brazil. (Illus.). 32p. (Orig.). (ps). 1985. pap. 1.00 (ISBN 0-89114-155-3). Baptist Pub Hse.

Beasley, Kenneth L., et al. The Administration of Sponsored Programs: Handbook for Developing & Managing Research Activities & Other Projects. LC 82-48074. (Higher Education & Social & Behavioral Science Ser.). 1982. text ed. 27.95x (ISBN 0-87589-542-5). Jossey Bass.

Beasley, Manley & Robinson, Ras. Laws for Liberated Living. 212p. 1980. pap. 5.00 (ISBN 0-937778-01-X); 3.00 (ISBN 0-937778-02-8). Fulness Hse.

Beasley, Maurine & Gibbons, Sheila. Women in Media: A Documentary Source Book. 198p. 1977. 5.95 (ISBN 0-930470-00-1); pap. 5.00 (tchrs ed. (ISBN 0-318-16870-7). Womens Inst Free Press.

Beasley, Maurine, ed. see Hickok, Lorena.

Beasley, Maurine H. & Harlow, Richard R. Voices of Change: Southern Pulitzer Winners. LC 79-52511. 1979. pap. text ed. 10.00 (ISBN 0-8191-0771-9). U Pr of Amer.

Beasley, N., jt. auth. see Smith, R.

Beasley, Norman, jt. auth. see Smith, Rixey.

Beasley, R. P., et al. Erosion & Sediment Pollution Control. 2nd ed. (Illus.). 304p. 1984. text ed. 27.95x (ISBN 0-8138-1530-4). Iowa St U Pr.

Beasley, Robert W. Injuries to the Hand. (Illus.). 320p. 1981. text ed. 58.00 (ISBN 0-7216-1607-0). Saunders.

Beasley, Sonia. The Spirulina Cookbook: Recipes for Rejuvenating the Body. LC 81-40027. (Illus.). 192p. (Orig.). 1981. pap. 6.95 (ISBN 0-916438-39-2). Univ of Trees.

Beasley, Victor R. Subtle-Body Healing. Hills, Christopher, ed. LC 79-15736. (Illus.). 160p. (Orig.). 1979. pap. 5.95 (ISBN 0-916438-28-7, Dist. by New Era Pr). Univ of Trees.

Beasley, W. Conger, Jr. Over DeSoto's Bones. 2nd ed. Burmaster, O. C., ed. LC 78-74299. (Modern & Contemporary Poets of the West). (Orig.). 1979. pap. 3.00 (ISBN 0-916272-11-7). Ahsahta Pr.

Beasley, W. G. The Meiji Restoration. LC 72-78868. xiv, 514p. 1972. 35.00x (ISBN 0-8047-0815-0). Stanford U Pr.

--The Modern History of Japan. 2nd ed. LC 73-7837. 1974. pap. text ed. 17.95 (ISBN 0-275-84620-2, HoltC). HR&W.

--The Modern History of Japan. 3rd ed. 1981. 27.50 (ISBN 0-312-53999-1). St Martin.

Beasley, W. G., ed. Modern Japan: Aspects of History, Literature & Society. (Campus Ser.: No. 195). 1977. pap. 9.95x (ISBN 0-520-03495-3). U of Cal Pr.

Beasley, W. Wayne, jt. auth. see Henry, Marvin A.

Beasley-Murray, G. R. Baptism in the New Testament. 434p. 1973. pap. 8.95 (ISBN 0-8028-1493-X). Eerdmans.

--The Book of Revelation. (New Century Bible Commentay Ser.). 1981. pap. 7.95 (ISBN 0-8028-1885-4). Eerdmans.

Beasley-Murray, George R. The Coming of God. 64p. 1983. pap. 3.95 (ISBN 0-85364-350-4, Pub. by Paternoster UK). Attic Pr.

--Jesus & the Kingdom of God. 512p. 1985. 29.95 (ISBN 0-8028-3609-7). Eerdmans.

Beasley-Murray, Stephen. Toward a Metaphysics of the Sacred: Development of the Concept of the Holy. LC 82-8288. 118p. 1982. 7.95x (ISBN 0-86554-038-1). Mercer Univ Pr.

--Towards a Metaphysics of the Sacred. LC 82-8288. (Special Studies: No. 8). 1982. pap. 7.95 (ISBN 0-86554-038-1). NABPR.

Beasom, Sam L. & Roberson, Sheila F., eds. Game Harvest Management. (Illus.). 300p. 1985. 20.00 (ISBN 0-912229-08-X); pap. 15.00 (ISBN 0-912229-09-8). CK Wildlife Res.

Beason, Robert G. Hanging On. 1984. 15.95 (ISBN 0-15-138440-1). HarBraceJ.

Beastall, G. H., jt. auth. see Grant, J. K.

Beater, Jack. Pirates & Buried Treasure on Florida Islands. rev. ed. LC 65-1579. (Illus.). pap. 2.95 (ISBN 0-8200-1019-7). Great Outdoors.

Beath, O. A., jt. auth. see Rosenfeld, Irene.

Beath, Paul R., compiled by. Febold Feboldson: Tall Tales from the Great Plains. LC 62-8725. (Illus.). xii, 139p. 1962. pap. 4.25 (ISBN 0-8032-5012-6, BB 161, Bison). U of Nebr Pr.

Beatie, Russel H. Saddles. LC 79-6708. (Illus.). 408p. 1981. 39.50 (ISBN 0-8061-1584-X). U of Okla Pr.

Beatie, S. A Revolution in London Housing. (Illus.). 128p. 1980. pap. text ed. 15.75x (ISBN 0-85139-560-0, Pub. by Architectural Pr England). Humanities.

Beatles. Beatlemania: Nineteen Sixty-Seven to Nineteen Seventy, Vol. II. 127p. 1967. pap. 7.95 (ISBN 0-89524-110-2, 1308). Cherry Lane.

--Beatlemania: Nineteen Sixty-Three to Nineteen Sixty-Six. 128p. 1963. pap. 7.95 (ISBN 0-89524-109-9, 1307). Cherry Lane.

--The Beatles Lyrics Illustrated. (Illus.). 272p. pap. 2.50 (ISBN 0-440-90615-6, LFL). Dell.

Beatley, B. Achievement in the Junior High School. Repr. of 1932 ed. 19.00 (ISBN 0-384-03685-6). Johnson Repr.

Beatley, Janice C. & ERDA Technical Information Center. Vascular Plants of the Nevada Test Site & Central Southern Nevada: Ecologic & Geographic Distributions. LC 76-21839. 316p. 1976. pap. 16.00 (ISBN 0-87079-033-1, TID-26881); microfiche 4.50 (ISBN 0-87079-216-4, TID-26881). DOE.

Beatley, R., jt. auth. see Birkhoff, George D.

Beato, M., ed. Steroid Induced Utherine Proteins: Proceedings Symposium, Marburg, September 27-29, 1979. (Developments in Endocrinology Ser.: Vol. 8). 1980. 68.00 (ISBN 0-444-80203-7). Elsevier.

Beaton, A. E., jt. auth. see Rosenthal, E.

Beaton, A. E., et al. Changes in the Verbal Abilities of High School Seniors, College Entrants, & SAT Candidates Between 1960 & 1972. 1977. 6.00 (ISBN 0-87447-011-0, 251705). College Bd.

Beaton, Albert E., jt. ed. see Juster, Francis T.

Beaton, G. H. & McHenry, E. W., eds. Nutrition: A Comprehensive Treatise, 3 vols. Incl. Vol. 1. Macronutrients & Nutrient Elements. 1964. 85.50 (ISBN 0-12-084101-0); Vol. 2. Vitamins, Nutrient Requirements & Food Selections. 1964. 85.50 (ISBN 0-12-084102-9); Vol. 3. Nutritional Status: Assessment & Application. 1966. 73.00 (ISBN 0-12-084103-7). Acad Pr.

Beaton, J. D., jt. ed. see Walsh, L. M.

Beaton, J. R., et al, eds. Horizontal Boring. 2nd ed. (Engineering Craftsmen: No. H28/2). (Illus.). 1976. spiral bdg. 39.95x (ISBN 0-85083-307-8). Intl Ideas.

Beaton, Jeffrey. Dostoyevsky's Political Revelation: "A Leap of Faith". 1981. 5.95 (ISBN 0-8062-1825-8). Carlton.

Beaton, Leonard & Maddox, John. The Spread of Nuclear Weapons. LC 76-16061. (Studies in International Security: No. 5). 1976. Repr. of 1962 ed. lib. bdg. 24.75x (ISBN 0-8371-8949-7, BENW). Greenwood.

Beaton, M. C. Death of a Gossip. 192p. 1985. 12.95 (ISBN 0-312-18637-1). St Martin.

Beaton, P., tr. see Frankl, Ludwig A.

Beaton, Patrick. Creoles & Coolies. LC 77-118457. 1971. Repr. of 1859 ed. 21.00 (ISBN 0-8046-1207-2, Pub. by Kennikat). Assoc Faculty Pr.

Beaton, Patrick W., ed. Municipal Expenditures, Revenues, & Services. 266p. 1983. pap. 12.95 (ISBN 0-88285-087-3). Transaction Bks.

Beaton, Roderick. Folk Poetry of Modern Greece. LC 79-7644. (Illus.). 272p. 1980. 34.50 (ISBN 0-521-22853-0). Cambridge U Pr.

Beaton, W. Patrick, jt. auth. see Listokin, David.

Beaton, W. Patrick, jt. auth. see Sternlieb, George S.

Beaton, Welford. Know Your Movies. 1976. lib. bdg. 59.95 (ISBN 0-8490-2119-7). Gordon Pr.

Beaton, Welford, ed. Film Spectator Anthology. 1976. lib. bdg. 95.00 (ISBN 0-8490-1836-6). Gordon Pr.

Beaton, William R. Real Estate Finance. 2nd ed. (Illus.). 480p. 1982. text ed. 29.95 (ISBN 0-13-762716-5). P-H.

Beaton, William R., et al. Real Estate. 2nd ed. 1982. text ed. 27.75x (ISBN 0-673-16003-3). Scott F.

Beatrice. It Can Happen to You. (Illus.). 75p. 1983. 12.00 (ISBN 0-682-49960-9). Exposition Pr FL.

Beatson, J. & Matthews, M. H. Administrative Law: Cases & Materials. LC 83-40122. 1983. 47.50x (ISBN 0-19-825340-0); pap. 34.50x (ISBN 0-19-825341-9). Oxford U Pr.

Beatson, Robert. Naval & Military Memoirs of Great Britain, from 1727-1783, 6 vols. LC 72-8675. (American Revolutionary Ser.). Repr. of 1804 ed. Set. lib. bdg. 360.00x (ISBN 0-8398-0189-0). Irvington.

Beatteay, Robert E. Fire Officer's Guide to Waterfront Fires. LC 75-18738. (Fire Officer's Guide Ser.). (Illus.). 150p. 1975. 8.50 (ISBN 0-87765-046-2, FSP-42). Natl Fire Prot.

Beattie, A. D. & Ireland, J. T., eds. Emergencies in Medicine. 256p. 1984. text ed. 45.00 (ISBN 0-272-79746-4, Pub. by Pitman Bks Ltd Uk). Urban & S.

Beattie, Andrew J. The Evolutionary Ecology of Ant-Plant Mutualisms. (Illus.). 176p. Date not set. price not set (ISBN 0-521-25281-4); pap. price not set (ISBN 0-521-27272-6). Cambridge U Pr.

Beattie, Ann. The Burning House. LC 82-5292. 256p. 1982. 12.95 (ISBN 0-394-52494-2). Random.

--The Burning House. 256p. pap. 3.50 (ISBN 0-345-31041-1). Ballantine.

--Chilly Scenes of Winter. 320p. 1983. pap. 3.50 (ISBN 0-446-31108-1). Warner Bks.

--Distortions. 288p. 1983. pap. 3.95 (ISBN 0-446-31338-6). Warner Bks.

--Falling in Place. 1980. 10.95 (ISBN 0-394-50323-6). Random.

--Falling in Place. 320p. 1983. pap. 3.50 (ISBN 0-446-31112-X). Warner Bks.

--Jacklighting. (Metacom Limited Edition Ser.: No. 3). 24p. 1981. ltd. 25.00 (ISBN 0-911381-02-3). Metacom Pr.

--Love Always. LC 84-45749. 1985. 16.95 (ISBN 0-394-53965-6). Random.

--Secrets & Suprises. 320p. 1983. pap. 3.50 (ISBN 0-446-31114-6). Warner Bks.

--Spectacles. (Goblin Tales Ser.). 1985. 10.95 (ISBN 0-317-30492-5). Workman Pub.

Beattie, Arthur H., ed. & tr. see Pascal, Blaise.

Beattie, Arthur H., tr. see Montaigne, Michel De.

Beattie, Arthur H., tr. see Rousseau, Jean-Jacques.

Beattie, Bob. My Ten Secrets of Skiing. (Illus.). 1968. 9.95 (ISBN 0-670-50144-1). Viking.

Beattie, Bruce R. & Taylor, C. Robert. The Economics of Production. LC 84-17432. 258p. 1985. 38.95 (ISBN 0-471-80810-5). Wiley.

Beattie, D. H. & Somerville, W. M. Ship's Gear: A Review of Deck Machinery. (Marine Engineering Practice Ser.: Vol. 2, Pt. 16). 1979. pap. 9.00x (ISBN 0-900976-78-0, Pub. by Inst Marine Eng). Intl Spec Bk.

Beattie, Frank. Jesus on the Cross. (Orig.). 1981. pap. 1.95 (ISBN 0-937172-17-0). JLJ Pubs.

Beattie, Frank A., Jr. Coming Down from the Mountain. (Orig.). 1982. pap. 1.75 (ISBN 0-937172-38-3). JLJ Pubs.

--I Went to School with Jesus. (Orig.). 1982. pap. 1.75 (ISBN 0-937172-37-5). JLJ Pubs.

--The Innkeeper's Son. (Orig.). 1981. pap. 1.75 (ISBN 0-937172-24-3). JLJ Pubs.

Beattie, Frank, Jr. Hey! That's My Donkey. (Orig.). 1981. pap. 1.50 (ISBN 0-937172-16-2). JLJ Pubs.

--In the Dark of Night. (Orig.). 1981. pap. 1.95 (ISBN 0-937172-18-9). JLJ Pubs.

Beattie, Geoffrey. Talk: An Analysis of Speech & Non-Verbal Behaviour in Conversation. 160p. 1983. pap. 19.00x (ISBN 0-335-10414-2, Open Univ Pr). Taylor & Francis.

Beattie, Hilary J. Land & Lineage in China. LC 77-91080. (Cambridge Studies in Chinese History, Literature & Institutions). 1979. 42.50 (ISBN 0-521-21974-4). Cambridge U Pr.

Beattie, Ian. The Complete Book of Automobile Body Design. 12.95 (ISBN 0-85429-217-9, 217). Haynes Pubns.

Beattie, J. Anatomy of the Common Marmoset. LC 78-72711. Repr. of 1927 ed. 27.50 (ISBN 0-404-18281-X). AMS Pr.

Beattie, J. A. & Oppenheim, J. Principles of Thermodynamics. (Studies in Modern Thermodynamics: Vol. 2). 330p. 1980. 41.75 (ISBN 0-444-41806-7). Elsevier.

Beattie, J. M. Crime & the Courts in England, 1660-1800. LC 84-42875. 1986. 72.00 (ISBN 0-691-05437-1); pap. 19.95 (ISBN 0-691-10166-3). Princeton U Pr.

Beattie, James. Elements of Moral Science, 2 vols. Wellek, Rene, ed. LC 75-11195. (British Philosophers & Theologians of the 17th & 18th Centuries: Vol. 2). 1976. Repr. of 1793 ed. Set. lib. bdg. 101.00 (ISBN 0-8240-1751-X); lib. bdg. write for info. Garland Pub.

--Elements of Moral Science. LC 75-45348. 1168p. 1976. Repr. of 1790 ed. lib. bdg. 100.00x (ISBN 0-8201-1167-8). Schol Facsimilies.

--Essay on the Nature & Immutability of Truth. LC 82-48340. (The Philosophy of David Hume Ser.). 511p. 1983. lib. bdg. 55.00 (ISBN 0-8240-5400-8). Garland Pub.

--An Essay on the Nature & Immutability of Truth, in Opposition to Sophistry & Skepticism. LC 78-67645. (Scottish Enlightenment Ser.). Repr. of 1770 ed. 45.00 (ISBN 0-404-17122-2). AMS Pr.

--The Minstrel: The Progress of Genius. LC 78-67646. (Scottish Enlightenment Ser.). Repr. of 1774 ed. 27.50 (ISBN 0-404-17176-1). AMS Pr.

--Poetical Works. LC 72-25. (Select Bibliographies Reprint Ser). 1972. Repr. of 1854 ed. 17.00 (ISBN 0-8369-9953-3). Ayer Co Pubs.

--Poetical Works of Beattie, Blair, & Falconer. Gilfillian, George, ed. LC 73-144580. Repr. of 1854 ed. 13.50 (ISBN 0-404-08552-0). AMS Pr.

--Scoticisms, Arranged in Alphabetical Order, Designed to Correct Improprieties of Speech & Writing. LC 78-67647. (Scottish Enlightenment Ser.). Repr. of 1779 ed. 18.50 (ISBN 0-404-17177-X). AMS Pr.

--Theory of Language, Pts. 1 & 2. LC 78-147953. Repr. of 1788 ed. 36.50 (ISBN 0-404-08201-7). AMS Pr.

Beattie, John. Bunyoro: An African Kingdom. LC 60-7331. 86p. (Orig.). 1960. pap. text ed. 9.95 (ISBN 0-03-004785-4, HoltC). HR&W.

--Lifeboats to the Rescue. LC 80-70704. (Illus.). 160p. 1981. 14.95 (ISBN 0-7153-8103-2). David & Charles.

--Other Cultures: Aims, Methods & Achievements in Social Anthropology. LC 64-16952. 1968. pap. text ed. 14.95x (ISBN 0-02-902050-6). Free Pr.

Beattie, John & Middleton, John. Spirit Mediumship & Society in Africa. LC 70-80849. 310p. 1969. 35.00x (ISBN 0-8419-0009-4, Africana). Holmes & Meier.

Beattie, John M. The English Court in the Reign of George I. LC 67-10776. pap. 79.50 (ISBN 0-317-26057-X, 2024422). Bks Demand UMI.

Beattie, Kotewall, ed. Burns: Selected Poems. 1950. pap. 4.95 (ISBN 0-14-042003-7). Penguin.

Beattie, Melody, jt. auth. see Owens, Carolyn P.

Beattie, Mollie, et al. Working with Your Woodland: A Landowner's Guide. LC 83-40016. (Futures of New England Ser.). (Illus.). 334p. 1983. 27.50x (ISBN 0-87451-265-4); pap. 12.95 (ISBN 0-87451-266-2). U Pr of New Eng.

--Yankee Forestry: A Landowner's Guide. 240p. 25.00X (ISBN 0-87451-265-4); pap. 12.00 (ISBN 0-87451-266-2). U Pr of New Eng.

Beattie, Ronald H., jt. auth. see Morse, Wayne L.

Beattie, Russell. Saddles. (Illus.). 800p. 55.00 (ISBN 0-87556-611-1). Saifer.

Beattie, Susan. Alfred Stevens, 1817-1875. (Illus.). 48p. (Orig.). 1984. pap. 3.95 (ISBN 0-901486-88-4, Pub. by Victoria & Albert Mus UK). Faber & Faber.

--The New Sculpture. LC 83-42876. (Studies in British Art Ser.). (Illus.). 352p. 1983. 50.00x (ISBN 0-300-02860-1). Yale U Pr.

--The New Sculpture. LC 83-42876. (Studies in British Art). (Illus.). 288p. 1985. pap. text ed. 16.95x (ISBN 0-300-03359-1, Y-517). Yale U Pr.

Beattie, William. Life & Letters of Thomas Campbell, 3 Vols. LC 70-161729. Repr. of 1849 ed. Set. 140.00 (ISBN 0-404-07630-0). AMS Pr.

Beatts, Anne & Head, John, eds. Saturday Night Live. (Illus.). 1977. pap. 7.95 (ISBN 0-380-01801-2, 51342). Avon.

Beatts, Anne, et al. Titters One Hundred One: An Introduction to Women's Literature. (Orig.). 1984. pap. 9.95 (ISBN 0-399-51079-6); 44.75 (ISBN 0-399-51106-7). Putnam Pub Group.

Beatty, jt. auth. see Davies.

Beatty, Alice & Sargent, Mary. Basic Rug Hooking. (Illus.). 160p. 1983. pap. 10.95 (ISBN 0-8117-2155-8). Stackpole.

Beatty, Arthur. Browning's Verse-Form: Its Organic Character. LC 74-3133. 1897. lib. bdg. 10.00 (ISBN 0-8414-9924-1). Folcroft.

--William Wordsworth, His Doctrine & Art in Their Historical Relations. 2nd ed. LC 75-28992. Repr. of 1927 ed. 32.50 (ISBN 0-404-14003-3). AMS Pr.

Beatty, Bernard. Byron's "Don Juan". LC 85-13436. 256p. 1985. 28.50x (ISBN 0-389-20589-3). B&N Imports.

Beatty, Betsy & Kirkpatrick, Libby. The Auction Book: A Comprehensive Fundraising Resource for Nonprofit Organizations. rev. ed. LC 85-70258. (Illus.). 159p. 1984. pap. 25.00 (ISBN 0-9613483-1-3). Auction Pr.

Beatty, Charles. Journal of a Two-Months Tour, with a View to Promoting Religion. LC 72-108459. 1768. 25.00x (ISBN 0-403-00456-X). Scholarly.

Beatty, David. He That Wins Souls Is Wise. 1982. pap. 0.75 (ISBN 0-88144-005-1, CPS-005). Christian Pub.

Beatty, Dorothy. New Zealand Cake Decorating Guide. 52p. 1980. pap. 2.50 (ISBN 0-85467-049-1, Pub. by Viking Sevenseas New Zealand). Intl Spec Bk.

Beatty, Edward C. William Penn As Social Philosopher. 1972. lib. bdg. 24.50x (ISBN 0-374-90506-1). Octagon.

Beatty, Eleanor & Schnitger, Carol. Center in on Music: Individualized Learning Centers in the Elementary Classroom. LC 77-76865. (Illus.). 1977. pap. 10.95 (ISBN 0-916656-06-3); material packet 12.95 (ISBN 0-916656-07-1). Mark Foster Mus.

Beatty, Frederika. William Wordsworth of Rydal Mount. LC 74-161730. (Illus.). Repr. of 1939 ed. 24.50 (ISBN 0-404-07927-X). AMS Pr.

Beatty, Grace J., jt. auth. see Gardner, David C.

Beatty, Homer G. & Homewood, A. E. Anatomical Adjustive Technic. rev. ed. 331p. Repr. of 1939 ed. text ed. 25.00x (ISBN 0-317-11382-8). Parker Chiro.

Beatty, J. Kelly, jt. ed. see O'Leary, Brian.

Beatty, J. Kelly, et al, eds. The New Solar System. 2nd ed. LC 81-2661. pap. 62.00 (ISBN 0-317-20616-8, 2024570). Bks Demand UMI.

Beatty, J. Kelly, jt. ed. see O'Leary, Brian.

Beatty, Jackson & Legewie, Heiner, eds. Biofeedback & Behavior. LC 77-830. (NATO Conference Series III, Human Factors: Vol. 2). 541p. 1977. 49.50x (ISBN 0-306-32882-8, Plenum Pr). Plenum Pub.

Beatty, James J., jt. auth. see Beatty, James W.

Beatty, James W. & Beatty, James J. The Elements of Style in Chemistry: A Computer Assisted Instruction Supported Text. LC 81-40530. 116p. (Orig.). 1982. pap. text ed. 8.50 (ISBN 0-8191-1941-5). U Pr of Amer.

Beatty, Jerome, Jr. Maria Looney & the Cosmic Circus. (Illus.). 144p. (Orig.). (gr. 3-7). 1978. pap. 1.95 (ISBN 0-380-40311-0, 77040-7, Camelot). Avon.

--Maria Looney & the Remarkable Robot. (Illus.). 144p. (Orig.). (gr. 3-7). 1979. pap. 1.95 (ISBN 0-380-43232-3, 78626-5, Camelot). Avon.

--Maria Looney on the Red Planet. (Illus.). (gr. 3-7). 1977. pap. 1.50 (ISBN 0-380-01729-6, 75523, Camelot). Avon.

--Matthew Looney & the Space Pirates. (Illus.). 144p. (gr. 4-8). 1974. pap. 1.75 (ISBN 0-380-00848-3, 55905-6, Camelot). Avon.

--Matthew Looney in the Outback. (Illus.). 224p. (gr. 3-7). pap. 1.95 (ISBN 0-380-00847-5, Camelot). Avon.

--Matthew Looney's Invasion of the Earth. (Illus.). 160p. (gr. 3-7). pap. 1.95 (ISBN 0-380-01493-9, Camelot). Avon.

--Matthew Looney's Voyage to Earth. (Illus.). 136p. (gr. 3-7). 1972. pap. 1.95 (ISBN 0-380-01494-7, 53660-9, Camelot). Avon.

--The Tunnel to Yesterday. (Illus.). 160p. (gr. 3-5). 1983. pap. 2.25 (ISBN 0-380-82537-6, 380-82537-6, Camelot). Avon.

Beatty, John. The Citizen-Soldier. LC 82-17004. (Collector's Library of the Civil War). (gr. 7 up). 1983. 26.60 (ISBN 0-8094-4258-2, Pub. by Time-Life). Silver.

Beatty, John C. & Booth, Kellogg S. Computer Graphics. 2nd ed. (Tutorial Texts Ser.). 570p. 1982. 39.00 (ISBN 0-8186-0425-5, Q425). IEEE Comp Soc.

Beatty, John L., jt. auth. see Johnson, Oliver A.

Beatty, Kenneth J. Human Leopards: Account of the Trials of Human Leopards Before the Special Commisson Court. LC 74-15011. (Illus.). Repr. of 1915 ed. 18.50 (ISBN 0-404-12006-7). AMS Pr.

Beatty, LaMond F. Filmstrips. Duane, James E., ed. LC 80-21338. (The Instructional Media Library: Vol. 4). (Illus.). 104p. 1981. 19.95 (ISBN 0-87778-164-8). Educ Tech Pubns.

--Instructional Materials Centers. Duane, James E., ed. LC 80-21451. (The Instructional Media Library: Vol. 5). (Illus.). 104p. 1981. 19.95 (ISBN 0-87778-165-6). Educ Tech Pubns.

--Motion Pictures. Duane, James E., ed. LC 80-21340. (The Instructional Media Library: Vol. 8). (Illus.). 112p. 1981. 19.95 (ISBN 0-87778-168-0). Educ Tech Pubns.

--Still Pictures. Duane, James E., ed. LC 80-21448. (The Instructional Media Library: Vol. 14). (Illus.). 112p. 1981. 19.95 (ISBN 0-87778-174-5). Educ Tech Pubns.

Beatty, M. T., et al, eds. Planning the Uses & Management of Land. (Illus.). 1979. 30.00 (ISBN 0-89118-058-3). Am Soc Agron.

Beatty, Marvin T., jt. ed. see Petersen, Gary W.

Beatty, Mary A. Tales of a Tag-Along. 220p. 12.95 (ISBN 0-87397-257-0). Strode.

--Then Came a Young Man in His Flying Machine. 300p. 1984. 19.95 (ISBN 0-87397-257-0). Strode.

Beatty, Michael & Nulte, James. Guide to Art Museums: Midwest Edition. LC 84-81547. (Illus.). 200p. (Orig.). 1984. pap. 9.95 (ISBN 0-89708-128-5). And Bks.

Beatty, Michael, et al. Studebaker: Less Than They Promised. LC 84-81548. (Illus.). 94p. (Orig.). 1984. pap. 3.95 (ISBN 0-89708-129-3). And Bks.

Beatty, Noelle B. & Pariser, Ursula R. Dumbarton Oaks Gardens: Their History, Design & Ornaments. LC 78-67477. 64p. 1978. pap. 5.95 (ISBN 0-87491-232-6). Acropolis.

Beatty, Patricia. The Bad Bell of San Salvador. (Illus.). 256p. (gr. 5-9). 1973. PLB 11.88 (ISBN 0-688-30081-2). Morrow.

--The Coach That Never Came. 160p. (gr. 5-9). 1985. 10.25 (ISBN 0-688-05477-3, Morrow Junior Bks). Morrow.

--Eight Mules from Monterey. LC 81-22284. 224p. (gr. 4-6). 1982. 11.75 (ISBN 0-688-01047-4). Morrow.

--Jonathan Down under. 224p. 1982. 9.00 (ISBN 0-688-01467-4). Macmillan.

--Jonathan Down under. (gr. 5-9). 1982. 10.25 (ISBN 0-688-01467-4). Morrow.

--Lacy Makes a Match. LC 79-9813. (gr. 7-9). 1979. 11.50 (ISBN 0-688-22200-5); PLB 12.50 (ISBN 0-688-32200-X). Morrow.

--Lupita Manana. (gr. 7-9). 1981. 11.25 (ISBN 0-688-00358-3); PLB 11.88 (ISBN 0-688-00359-1). Morrow.

--Melinda Takes a Hand. LC 83-7971. 160p. (gr. 5-9). 1983. 10.25 (ISBN 0-688-02422-X). Morrow.

--Melinda Takes a Hand. 1983. pap. 10.25 (ISBN 0-688-02422-X). Morrow.

--Red Rock Over the River. LC 72-5883. 256p. (gr. 7-9). 1973. PLB 12.88 (ISBN 0-688-30065-0). Morrow.

--Rufus, Red Rufus. LC 74-26981. (Illus.). 192p. (gr. 7 up). 1975. 11.25 (ISBN 0-688-22021-5); PLB 10.80 (ISBN 0-688-32021-X). Morrow.

--That's One Ornery Orphan. LC 80-10200. 224p. (gr. 7-9). 1980. 11.25 (ISBN 0-688-22227-7); PLB 11.88 (ISBN 0-688-32227-1). Morrow.

--Turn Homeward, Hannalee. LC 84-8960. 208p. (gr. 5-9). 1984. 10.25 (ISBN 0-688-03871-9, Morrow Junior Books). Morrow.

--Wait for Me, Watch for Me, Eula Bee. (gr. 7-9). 1978. 12.50 (ISBN 0-688-22151-3); PLB 12.88 (ISBN 0-688-32151-8). Morrow.

Beatty, R., et al, eds. The Human Resource Information Systems Sourcebook. 200p. 1985. pap. text ed. 25.00 (ISBN 0-914234-97-8). Human Res Dev Pr.

Beatty, Richard H. The Resume Kit. LC 83-23451. 265p. 1984. pap. 9.95 (ISBN 0-471-88148-1). Wiley.

Beatty, Richard W. & Schneier, Craig E. Personnel Administration: An Experiential Skill-Building Approach. 576p. 1981. pap. text ed. 26.95 (ISBN 0-201-00172-1); implementor's manual 25.95 (ISBN 0-201-00176-4). Addison-Wesley.

Beatty, Richard W., jt. auth. see Bernardin, H. John.

Beatty, Richard W., jt. auth. see Schneier, Craig E.

Beatty, Richmond C. James Russell Lowell. (Illus.). xviii, 316p. 1969. Repr. of 1942 ed. 25.00 (ISBN 0-208-00752-0, Archon). Shoe String.

--William Byrd of Westover. 2nd ed. Inge, M. Thomas, pref. by. xxxix, 243p. 1970. Repr. of 1932 ed. 21.00 (ISBN 0-208-00944-2, Archon). Shoe String.

Beatty, Richmond C., ed. see Clemens, Samuel L.

Beatty, Sally R., ed. Continuity of Care: The Hospital & the Community. (Illus.). 272p. 1980. 24.50 (ISBN 0-8089-1304-2, 790458). Grune.

Beatty, Willard W., ed. see Underhill, Ruth M.

Beatty, William K., jt. auth. see Marks, Geoffrey.

Beatty-Kingston, W., tr. see Busch, Moritz.

Beaty, Betty, jt. auth. see Beaty, David.

Beaty, David. Strange Encounters: Mysteries of the Air. LC 83-45497. (Illus.). 160p. 1984. 13.95 (ISBN 0-689-11447-8). Atheneum.

Beaty, David & Beaty, Betty. Wings of the Morning. 1984. pap. 3.95 (ISBN 0-8217-1369-8). Zebra.

Beaty, Frederick L. Byron the Satirist. LC 85-2943. 235p. 1985. 22.50 (ISBN 0-87580-109-9). N Ill U Pr.

--Light from Heaven: Love in British Romantic Literature. LC 70-157649. 288p. 1971. 10.00 (ISBN 0-87580-028-9). N Ill U Pr.

Beaty, H. Wayne, jt. auth. see Fink, Donald G.

Beaty, Janice J. Skills for Preschool Teachers. 2nd ed. 1984. pap. text ed. 13.95 (ISBN 0-675-20086-5). Merrill.

Beaty, Jerome. Middlemarch from Notebook to Novel: A Study of George Eliot's Creative Method. LC 81-6588. ix, 134p. 1981. Repr. of 1960 ed. lib. bdg. 22.50x (ISBN 0-313-22412-9, BEMF). Greenwood.

--Norton Introduction to Fiction. 3rd ed. 1985. pap. text ed. 11.95 (ISBN 0-393-95429-3); classroom guide avail. (ISBN 0-393-95431-5). Norton.

Beaty, Jerome, ed. The Norton Introduction to Fiction. 2nd ed. 640p. 1981. pap. text ed. 11.95 (ISBN 0-393-95156-1); classroom guide 2.95x (ISBN 0-393-95159-6). Norton.

--Norton Introduction to Literature: Fiction. 600p. 1973. pap. text ed. 8.95x (ISBN 0-393-09359-X); tchr's guide 1.25x (ISBN 0-393-09336-0). Norton.

--The Norton Introduction to the Short Novel. (gr. 12). 1981. pap. text ed. 13.95x (ISBN 0-393-95187-1); classroom guide avail. (ISBN 0-393-95190-1). Norton.

Beaty, John. Iron Curtain Over America. pap. 4.00 (ISBN 0-913022-30-6). Angriff Pr.

--Iron Curtain Over America. 1979. lib. bdg. 69.95 (ISBN 0-8490-2950-3). Gordon Pr.

Beaty, John O. John Esten Cooke, Virginian. LC 65-27110. 1922. Repr. 15.00x (ISBN 0-8046-0024-4, Pub. by Kennikat). Assoc Faculty Pr.

Beau, Bryan F. Le see Le Beau, Bryan F.

Beau, Claude Le see Le Beau, Claude.

Beaubelle, Marcy. Coastal Connecticut: Western Region. (Illus., Orig.). 1979. pap. 4.95 (ISBN 0-933614-02-0). Peregrine Pr.

Beaubien, Anne K., et al. Learning the Library: Concepts & Methods for Effective Bibliographic Instruction. 269p. 1982. 39.95 (ISBN 0-8352-1505-9). Bowker.

Beaucamp, Ernest & Hansen, Dorothea. Take Thirty Dictionary. (gr. 12). 1971. pap. 5.25 (ISBN 0-89420-099-2, 219905). Natl Book.

Beaucamp, Ernest & Hansen, Dorthea. Take Thirty Shorthand: Student Syllabus, 2 vols. (gr. 11-12). 1976. Vol. 1. pap. text ed. 5.95 (ISBN 0-89420-097-6, 218999); cassette recordings 244.75 (ISBN 0-89420-211-1, 219105); Vol. 2. pap. text ed. 5.80 (ISBN 0-89420-098-4, 219105). Natl Book.

Beauchamp, Dan E. Beyond Alcoholism: Alcohol & Public Health Policy. 240p. 1980. 29.95 (ISBN 0-87722-189-8). Temple U Pr.

--Beyond Alcoholism: Alcohol & Public Health Policy. 222p. 1982. pap. 9.95 (ISBN 0-87722-286-X). Temple U Pr.

Beauchamp, Deanna, jt. auth. see Beauchamp, Gary.

Beauchamp, Edward. An American Teacher in Early Meiji Japan. (Asian Studies at Hawaii Ser: No. 17). 176p. 1976. pap. text ed. 8.00x (ISBN 0-8248-0404-X). UH Pr.

Beauchamp, Edward R. Billingual Education: An International Perspective Policy. LC 85-61794. (Fastback Ser.: No. 227). 50p. (Orig.). 1985. pap. 0.75 (ISBN 0-87367-227-5). Phi Delta Kappa.

--Dissertations in the History of Education 1970-1980. LC 84-14125. 267p. 1984. 22.50 (ISBN 0-8108-1742-X). Scarecrow.

--Education in Contemporary Japan. LC 81-86313. (Fastback Ser.: No. 171). 50p. (Orig.). 1982. pap. 0.75 (ISBN 0-87367-171-6). Phi Delta Kappa.

--Learning to Be Japanese: Selected Readings on Japanese Society & Education. 408p. 1978. 35.00 (ISBN 0-208-01717-8, Linnet). Shoe String.

Beauchamp, Edward R., ed. see Rust, Val D.

Beauchamp, Elizabeth. The Braes O'Balguhidder. 1981. 20.00x (ISBN 0-905192-29-X, Pub. by Heartherbank England). State Mutual Bk.

Beauchamp, Gary & Beauchamp, Deanna. Religiously Mixed Marriage. 4.95 (ISBN 0-89137-528-7). Quality Pubns.

Beauchamp, Gary R. Sermons for Today. LC 80-70788. 1981. 11.95 (ISBN 0-89112-403-9). Bibl Res Pr.

Beauchamp, George A. Curriculum Theory. 4th ed. LC 80-84104. 221p. 1981. pap. text ed. 11.95 (ISBN 0-87581-270-8). Peacock Pubs.

Beauchamp, Gorman. Jack London. LC 84-28483. (Starmont Reader's Guide Ser.: No. 15). 96p. 1984. Repr. lib. bdg. 13.95x (ISBN 0-89370-046-0). Borgo Pr.

--Reader's Guide to Jack London. Schlobin, Roger C., ed. LC 82-7345. (Starmont Reader's Guides to Contemporary Science Fiction & Fantasy Authors Ser.: Vol. 15). (Illus., Orig.). 1984. 13.95x (ISBN 0-916732-40-1); pap. text ed. 5.95x (ISBN 0-916732-39-8). Starmont Hse.

Beauchamp, James W., jt. ed. see Von Foerster, H.

Beauchamp, Jose J. Imagen Del Puertoriqueno En la Novela: En Alejandro Tapia y Rivera, Manuel Zeno Gandia y Enrique A. Laguerre. LC 76-22555. (Coleccion Mente y Palabra). (Span.). 1977. 6.25 (ISBN 0-8477-0540-4); pap. text ed. 5.00 (ISBN 0-8477-0541-2). U of PR Pr.

Beauchamp, K. G. Walsh Functions & Their Applications. (Techniques of Physics Ser.). 1976. 39.50 (ISBN 0-12-084050-2). Acad Pr.

Beauchamp, K. G. & Yuen, C. K. Data Acquisitions for Signal Analysis. (Illus.). 288p. 1980. text ed. 50.00x (ISBN 0-04-621028-8). Allen Unwin.

--Digital Methods for Signal Analysis. (Illus.). 1979. text ed. 50.00x (ISBN 0-04-621027-X). Allen Unwin.

Beauchamp, K. G., ed. Information Technology & the Computer Network. (NATO ASI Series, Computer & Systems Sciences: Ser. F, No. 6). x, 281p. 1984. 34.50 (ISBN 0-387-12883-2). Springer-Verlag.

Beauchamp, Ken G. Applications of Walsh & Related Functions. (Microelectronics & Signal Processing Ser.). 1984. 55.00 (ISBN 0-12-084180-0). Acad Pr.

Beauchamp, Kenneth G., ed. Interlinking of Computer Networks. (NATO Advanced Study Institutes Ser.). 1979. lib. bdg. 42.00 (ISBN 90-277-0979-3, Pub. by Reider Holland). Kluwer Academic.

Beauchamp, Kenneth G., ed. see NATO Advanced Study Institute, Bonas, France, June 15-26, 1981.

Beauchamp, Kenneth P., jt. auth. see McDorman, Ted L.

Beauchamp, R. Mitchell, ed. see Reid, C. & Dyer, R. Allen.

Beauchamp, Thom & Perlin, Seymour. Ethical Issues in Death & Dying. 1978. pap. 19.95 (ISBN 0-13-290114-5). P-H.

Beauchamp, Tom L. Case Studies in Business, Society & Ethics. 256p. 1983. pap. 16.95 (ISBN 0-13-119263-9). P-H.

--Philosophical Ethics: An Introduction to Moral Philosophy. Pace, Kaye, ed. 416p. 1982. 26.95x (ISBN 0-07-004203-9). McGraw.

Beauchamp, Tom L. & Bowie, Norman E. Ethical Theory & Business. 2nd ed. 640p. 1983. text ed. 28.95 (ISBN 0-13-290452-7). P-H.

Beauchamp, Tom L. & Childress, James F. Prinicples of Biomedical Ethics. 2nd ed. 1983. 24.95x (ISBN 0-19-503285-3); pap. 14.95 (ISBN 0-19-503286-1). Oxford U Pr.

Beauchamp, Tom L. & McCullough, Laurence B. Medical Ethics: The Moral Responsibilities of Physicians. (Illus.). 160p. 1984. pap. 13.95 (ISBN 0-13-572652-2). P-H.

Beauchamp, Tom L. & Rosenberg, Alexander. Hume & the Problem of Causation. 1981. 27.00x (ISBN 0-19-520236-8). Oxford U Pr.

Beauchamp, Tom L. & Walters, LeRoy. Contemporary Issues in Bioethics. 2nd ed. 624p. 1982. text ed. write for info. (ISBN 0-534-01102-0). Wadsworth Pub.

Beauchamp, Tom L., jt. auth. see Barker, Stephen F.

Beauchamp, Tom L. & Faden, Ruth, eds. Ethical Issues in Social Science Research. LC 81-12419. 448p. 1982. text ed. 30.00x (ISBN 0-8018-2655-1); pap. text ed. 12.95x (ISBN 0-8018-2656-X). Johns Hopkins.

Beauchamp, Tom L. & Pinkard, Terry P., eds. Ethics & Public Policy: Introduction to Ethics. (Illus.). 416p. 1983. pap. 20.95 (ISBN 0-13-290957-X). P-H.

Beauchamp, Tom L., et al. Philosophy & the Human Condition. (Illus.). 640p. 1980. text ed. 25.95 (ISBN 0-13-662528-2). P-H.

--A History & Theory of Informed Consent. LC 85-13858. Date not set. price not set (ISBN 0-19-503686-7). Oxford U Pr.

Beauchamp, Virgil. The Life of Christ in the Paintings by Tissot. 1979. deluxe ed. 49.75 (ISBN 0-930582-29-2). Gloucester Art.

Beauchamp, William. The Style of Nerval's Aurelia. (De Proprietatibus Litterarum Series Practica: No. 109). 108p. 1976. pap. text ed. 15.20x (ISBN 90-2793-284-0). Mouton.

Beauchamp, William M. Aboriginal Chipped Stone Implements of New York. LC 76-43659. (New York State Museum Bulletin: Vol. 4, No. 16). Repr. of 1897 ed. 14.50 (ISBN 0-404-15495-6). AMS Pr.

--Aboriginal Occupation of New York. LC 76-43660. (New York State Museum Bulletin: No. 32, Vol. 7). Repr. of 1900 ed. 22.00 (ISBN 0-404-15492-1). AMS Pr.

--Aboriginal Place Names of New York. LC 68-17915. 333p. 1972. Repr. of 1907 ed. 44.00x (ISBN 0-8103-3231-0). Gale.

--Aboriginal Use of Wood in New York. LC 76-43661. (New York State Museum Bulletin: 89). Repr. of 1905 ed. 27.50 (ISBN 0-404-15493-X). AMS Pr.

--A History of the New York Iroquois, Now Commonly Called the Six Nations. LC 74-7925. (Illus.). Repr. of 1905 ed. 27.50 (ISBN 0-404-11811-9). AMS Pr.

--Horn & Bone Implements of the New York Indians. LC 76-43662. (New York State Museum Bulletin: 50). Repr. of 1902 ed. 19.50 (ISBN 0-404-15494-8). AMS Pr.

--Iroquois Folk Lore. LC 74-7926. Repr. of 1922 ed. 21.00 (ISBN 0-404-11812-7). AMS Pr.

--The Iroquois Trail. LC 74-7927. Repr. of 1892 ed. 15.00 (ISBN 0-404-11813-5). AMS Pr.

--Metallic Ornaments of the New York Indians. LC 74-7928. Repr. of 1903 ed. 16.00 (ISBN 0-404-11814-3). AMS Pr.

--Moravian Journals Relating to Central New York. LC 72-8246. (Communal Societies in America Ser). Repr. of 1916 ed. 20.00 (ISBN 0-404-11000-2). AMS Pr.

--Perch Lake Mounds, with Notes on Other New York Mounds & Some Accounts of Indian Trails. LC 74-7929. Repr. of 1905 ed. 14.50 (ISBN 0-404-11815-1). AMS Pr.

--Polished Stone Articles Used by the New York Aborigines Before & During European Occupation. LC 74-7930. Repr. of 1897 ed. 17.50 (ISBN 0-404-11816-X). AMS Pr.

--Wampum & Shell Articles Used by the New York Indians. LC 76-43663. (New York State Museum Bulletin: No. 41, Vol. 8). Repr. of 1901 ed. 21.50 (ISBN 0-404-15496-4). AMS Pr.

Beauchene, Roy E., et al. Enzyme Activities & Aging. LC 74-5496. 208p. 1974. text ed. 34.50x (ISBN 0-8422-7217-8). Irvington.

Beauchesne, Alcide. Louis the Seventeenth, 2 vols. LC 78-161731. (Illus.). Repr. of 1855 ed. 76.50 (ISBN 0-404-07546-0). AMS Pr.

Beau Chesne, John De see De Beau Chesne, John & Baildon, John.

Beauchet, Ludovic. Histoire Du Droit Prive De la Republique Athenienne, 4 vols. facsimile ed. LC 75-13256. (History of Ideas in Ancient Greece Ser.). (Fr.). 1976. Repr. of 1897 ed. Set. 154.00x (ISBN 0-405-07294-5); 38.50x ea. Vol. 1 (ISBN 0-405-07295-3). Vol. 2 (ISBN 0-405-07296-1). Vol. 3. Vol. 4. Ayer Co Pubs.

Beauclair, Inez de see De Beauclair, Inez.

Beauclerk, Helen, tr. see Colette.

Beaucourt, C. Main-d'Oeuvre Potentielle et Emploi Regional en Union Sovietique. Bd. with Mouvements Migratoires de Population Urbaine en Chine. Lieberherr, I. G; Deux Cents Ans de Statistiques Russes et Sovietiques: Deux Cents Ans de Statistiques Russes et Sovietiques. Makhroff, C. (Economies et Societes Series G: No. 24). 1966. pap. 34.00 (ISBN 0-317-16114-8). Kraus Repr.

Beaucourt, C., et al. Tiers Monde Sovietique? Le Kazakhstan. (Economies et Societes Ser. G: No. 17). 1963. pap. 34.00 (ISBN 0-317-16023-0). Kraus Repr.

Beaucourt, Gaston L. Captivite et derniers moments de Louis seize, 2 Vols. LC 71-161732. Repr. of 1892 ed. Set. 35.00 (ISBN 0-404-07622-X); 18.00 ea. Vol, 1 (ISBN 0-404-07623-8). Vol. 2 (ISBN 0-404-07624-6). AMS Pr.

Beaud, Michel. A History of Capitalism, 1500-1980. Dickman, Tom & Lefebvre, Anny, trs. from Fr. LC 83-42522. Orig. Title: Histoire du Capitalism. 288p. 1983. 22.00 (ISBN 0-85345-626-7); pap. 10.00 (ISBN 0-85345-627-5). Monthly Rev.

Beaudelaire, Charles. Mon Coeur mis a nu. 1972. pap. 3.95 (ISBN 0-686-52226-5). French & Eur.

Beaudin, Michael. Willie de Wit: Lord of the Ring. 304p. 1984. pap. 3.25 (ISBN 0-380-89485-8). Avon.

Beaudiquez, Marcelle. Bibliographies Services Throughout the World. Incl. 1950-1959. 1961. pap. 7.50 (U44, UNESCO); 1970-1974. 419p. 1977. 22.50 (ISBN 92-3-101394-7, U817, UNESCO); 1975-1979. 462p. 1985. pap. 33.75 (ISBN 92-3-101982-1, U1406, UNESCO). (Documentation, Libraries, & Archivies: Bibliographies & Reference Works Ser.). Unipub.

Beaudoin, Viola K. Beaudoin Easy Method of Identifying Wildflowers: Over 475 Mountain Flowers. LC 83-72033. (Illus.). 234p. (Orig.). 1983. pap. 8.95 (ISBN 0-9611960-0-9). Evergreen Co.

Beaudouin, John T. & Mattlin, Everett. The Phrase-Droppers Handbook. LC 75-38161. 128p. 1976. 5.95 (ISBN 0-385-05519-6). Doubleday.

Beaudreau, George S., ed. see Biology Colloquium, 34th, Oregon State University, 1973.

Beaudry, Antoinette. Jungle of Desire. 352p. (Orig.). 1982. pap. 2.95 (ISBN 0-523-41401-3). Pinnacle Bks.

--Strands of Desire. 288p. (Orig.). 1981. pap. 2.50 (ISBN 0-523-40925-7). Pinnacle Bks.

Beaudry, Harry R. The English Theatre & John Keats. (Salzburg Studies in English Literature, Poetic Drama & Poetic Theory: No. 13). 240p. 1973. pap. 25.50x (ISBN 0-391-01321-1). Humanities.

Beaudry, Jo & Ketchum, Lynne. Carla Goes to Court. LC 82-2854. (Illus.). 32p. (gr. 1-5). 1982. 11.95 (ISBN 0-89885-088-6). Human Sci Pr.

Beaufort County Open Land Trust. Sea Island Seasons. 1980. 9.95 (ISBN 0-918544-40-8). Wimmer Bks.

Beaufort, John. Five Hundred-Five Theatre Questions Your Friends Can't Answer. (Five Hundred-Five Quiz Ser.). 1982. cancelled (ISBN 0-8027-0711-4); pap. 3.95 (ISBN 0-8027-7194-7). Walker & Co.

Beaufort, Simon de see De Beaufort, Simon.

Beaufort, Simon De see De Beaufort, Simon.

Beaufre, Andre. Strategy for Tomorrow. LC 73-94041. 91p. 1975. pap. 10.50x (ISBN 0-8448-1096-7). Crane-Russak Co.

Beaug, Mark, ed. Planning Education for Reducing Inequalities: An IIEP Seminar. Eide, Kjell. 142p. 1981. pap. 18.75 (ISBN 92-803-1089-5, U1218, UNESCO). Unipub.

Beaugrand. Manuel Pratique de Composition Francaise. 6.50 (ISBN 0-685-36705-3). French & Eur.

Beaugrand, Honore. Jeanne la fileuse. (Novels by Franco-Americans in New England 1850-1940 Ser.). 188p. (Fr.). (gr. 10 up). 1980. pap. 4.50 (ISBN 0-911409-17-3). Natl Mat Dev.

Beaugrande, R. de see De Beaugrande, R. & Dressler, W.

Beaugrande, Robert de. Text Production. Freedle, Roy O., ed. LC 83-25756. (Advances in Discourse Processes Ser.: Vol. 11). 400p. 1983. text ed. 42.50 (ISBN 0-89391-158-5); pap. text ed. 24.95 (ISBN 0-89391-159-3). Ablex Pub.

--Writing Step by Step: Easy Strategies for Writing & Revising. 382p. 1985. pap. text ed. 12.95 (ISBN 0-15-598258-3, HC); instr's manual avail. (ISBN 0-15-598259-1). HarBraceJ.

Beaugrande, Robert De see De Beaugrande, Robert.

Beaugrande, Robert De see Schmidt, Siegfried J.

Beaugue, Jean de. L'Histoire de la guerre d'Ecosse. Bain, Joseph, ed. LC 70-159993. (Maitland Club, Glasgow. Publications: No. 2). Repr. of 1830 ed. 17.50 (ISBN 0-404-52923-2). AMS Pr.

Beaujean, ed. see Littre.

Beaujean, Von Marion Herausgegeben see Von Marion Beaujean, Herausgegeben.

Beaujour, Elizabeth K. The Invisible Land: A Study of the Artistic Imagination of Iurii Olesha. LC 71-130959. 222p. 1970. 27.00x (ISBN 0-231-03428-8). Columbia U Pr.

Beaujour, Michel & Regalado, Nancy. RSVP: Invitation a Ecrire. 253p. (Orig., Fr.). 1965. pap. text ed. 2.50 (ISBN 0-15-577920-6, HC). HarBraceJ.

Beaujour, Michel, et al. Poetiques: Theorie et Critique Litteraires, Vol. 1. Gray, Floyd, ed. LC 81-50963. (Michigan Romance Studies: Vol. I). 207p. (Orig.). 1980. pap. 8.00 (ISBN 0-939730-00-6). Mich Romance.

Beaujoyeulx, Balthazar De see De Beaujoyeulx, Balthazar.

Beaulac, Willard L. Diplomat Looks at Aid to Latin America. LC 70-95591. 157p. 1970. 6.95x (ISBN 0-8093-0429-5). S Ill U Pr.

--The Fractured Continent: Latin America in Close-Up. LC 78-70885. (Publication Ser.: No. 225). (Illus.). 252p. 1980. 11.95x (ISBN 0-8179-7251-X). Hoover Inst Pr.

Beauliaux, Charles, ed. see Paris. Universite. Bibliotheque.

Beaulieu, Harry J. & Buchan, Roy M. Quantitative Industrial Hygiene. 1981. lib. bdg. 19.00 (ISBN 0-8240-7180-8). Garland Pub.

Beaulieu, John E. Stretching for All Sports. LC 80-12695. (Illus.). 214p. 8.95 (ISBN 0-87095-079-7). Athletic.

Beaulieu, Victor A. The Reconstruction of Pythagoras System on the Vibrational Theory of Numbers: The Essential Library of the Great Philosophers. (Illus.). 91p. 1983. Repr. of 1905 ed. 117.45 (ISBN 0-89920-050-8). Am Inst Psych.

Beauman, Nicola. A Very Great Profession: The Woman's Novel Nineteen Fourteen to Nineteen Thirty-Nine. 274p. (Orig.). 1984. pap. 9.95 (ISBN 0-86068-309-5, Pub. by Virago Pr). Merrimack Pub Cir.

Beauman, Sally. The Royal Shakespeare Company: A History of Ten Decades. 1982. 29.95x (ISBN 0-19-212209-6). Oxford U Pr.

Beaumaont, G. P. Introductory Applied Probability. LC 83-10700. (Mathematics & Its Applications, Ellis Horwood Ser.). 235p. 1983. 58.95x (ISBN 0-470-27481-6). Halsted Pr.

Beaumarchais, Pierre. Le Mariage De Figaro. Arnould, E. J., ed. (French Texts Ser.). 1976. pap. text ed. 9.95x (ISBN 0-631-00540-4). Basil Blackwell.

Beaumarchais, Pierre & Bonneville, Georges. Le Barbier de Seville. 64p. 1976. 2.95 (ISBN 0-686-54082-4). French & Eur.

Beaumarchais, Pierre-Augustin. Barber of Seville. Ellis, Brobury P., ed. & tr. LC 65-27803. (Crofts Classics Ser). 1966. pap. 1.25x (ISBN 0-88295-009-6). Harlan Davidson.

--Le Barbier de Seville. Arnould, E. F., ed. (French Texts Ser.). 174p. (Fr.). 1963. pap. 9.95x (ISBN 0-631-00620-6). Basil Blackwell.

Beaumarchais, Pierre de. Lettres Inedites Publiees Par G. Chinard. 130p. 1929. 22.50 (ISBN 0-686-54083-2). French & Eur.

--Le Mariage de Figaro. 192p. 1970. 2.95 (ISBN 0-686-54084-0). French & Eur.

--Theatre Complet: Lettres. 876p. 1934. 31.95 (ISBN 0-686-54088-3). French & Eur.

--Theatre Complet: Paris, Eighteen Sixty-Nine to Eighteen Seventy-One, 4 vols. 1967. 250.00 (ISBN 0-686-54087-5). French & Eur.

Beaumarchais, Pierre de & Morton, Brian N. Correspondance, 3 vols. 250p. 1969. 17.50 ea.; Vol. 1, 1745-1772. Vol. 2, 1773-1776. Vol. 3, 1777. French & Eur.

Beaumarchais, Pierre de & Pomeau, Rene. Theatre: Avec: Le Barbier de Seville, Le Marriage de Figaro, La Mere Coupable. 320p. 1965. 4.50 (ISBN 0-686-54086-7). French & Eur.

Beaumarchais, Pierre de & Rat, Maurice. Theatre: Avec: Le Barbier de Seville, Le Marriage de Figaro, La Mere Coupable. (Illus.). 320p. 10.95 (ISBN 0-686-54085-9). French & Eur.

Beaumarchais, Pierre De see De Beaumarchais, Pierre.

Beaumont & Fletcher. Songs & Lyrics from the Plays of Beaumont & Fletcher. Fellows, E. H., ed. LC 79-180038. Repr. of 1928 ed. 24.50 (ISBN 0-405-08249-5, Blom Pubns). Ayer Co Pubs.

Beaumont, et al. RT-11 Training Set, 4 Vols. 800p. 1984. Set. pap. 100.00 (EY-00036-DP). Digital Pr.

Beaumont, A. P. Intermediate Mathematical Statistics. 225p. 1980. pap. 14.95x (ISBN 0-412-15480-3, 2890, Pub. by Chapmman & Hall England). Methuen Inc.

Beaumont, Anthony. Steam at Work: Road & Farm Engines. LC 81-67002. (Illus.). 96p. 1981. 18.95 (ISBN 0-7153-8121-0). David & Charles.

--Traction Engines & Steam Vehicles in Pictures. LC 79-93192. (Illus.). 1969. lib. bdg. 17.95x (ISBN 0-678-05549-1). Kelley.

Beaumont, Antony. Busoni the Composer. LC 84-47699. 432p. 1985. 32.50x (ISBN 0-253-31270-1). Ind U Pr.

Beaumont, Barbara. Flaubert & Turgenev: A Friendship in Letters: The Complete Correspondence. 1985. 19.95 (ISBN 0-393-02206-4). Norton.

Beaumont, Barbara, tr. see Lange, Monique.

Beaumont, C. W. Vaslav Nijinsky. LC 74-1080. (Studies in Music, No. 42). 1974. lib. bdg. 29.95x (ISBN 0-8383-1752-9). Haskell.

Beaumont, Charles. A Modest Proposal. LC 70-79858. (Literary Casebook Ser.). 1969. pap. text ed. 6.95 (ISBN 0-675-09441-0). Merrill.

Beaumont, Charles, ed. see Thompson, Rose.

Beaumont, Cyril W. The Ballet Called Swan Lake. LC 81-70094. (Illus.). 176p. 1982. 9.95 (ISBN 0-87127-128-1). Dance Horiz.

--Bibliography of Dancing. LC 63-23181. Repr. of 1929 ed. 20.00 (ISBN 0-405-08247-9, Blom Pubns). Ayer Co Pubs.

--History of Harlequin. LC 65-27909. (Illus.). 1967. Repr. of 1926 ed. 18.00 (ISBN 0-405-08248-7, Blom Pubns). Ayer Co Pubs.

--Michel Fokine & His Ballets. LC 80-69956. (Illus.). 170p. 1981. pap. 8.95 (ISBN 0-87127-120-6). Dance Horiz.

--The Mysterious Toyshop. (Illus.). 32p. 1985. 14.00 (ISBN 0-03-005852-X). HR&W.

Beaumont, Cyril W. & Idzikowski, Stanislas. A Manual of the Theory & Practice of Classical Theatrical Dancing (Methode Cecchetti) LC 70-17363. (Illus.). 232p. 1975. pap. 3.95 (ISBN 0-486-23223-9). Dover.

--A Manual of the Theory & Practice of Classical Theatrical Dancing (Methode Cecchetti) (Illus.). 12.75 (ISBN 0-8446-5157-5). Peter Smith.

Beaumont, Cyril W., ed. see Polunin, Vladimir.

Beaumont, Cyril W., tr. see Noverre, Jean G.

Beaumont, David, et al. Working with RT-II. (Illus.). 150p. 1984. pap. 24.00 (ISBN 0-932376-31-2, EY-00021-DP). Digital Pr.

Beaver, Paul C. & Jung, Rodney C. Clinical Parasitology. 9th ed. LC 83-11338. (Illus.). 825p. 1984. text ed. 51.50 (ISBN 0-8121-0876-0). Lea & Febiger.

Beaver, Paul C. & Jung, Rodney C., eds. Animal Agents & Vectors of Human Disease. 5th ed. LC 85-183. (Illus.). 281p. 1985. text ed. write for info. (ISBN 0-8121-0987-2). Lea & Febiger.

Beaver, Philip. African Memoranda: Relative Attempt to Establish a British Settlement on the Island of Bulama, on the Western Coast of Africa in the Year 1792. LC 79-109317. Repr. of 1805 ed. 20.00x (ISBN 0-8371-3573-7, BME&, Pub. by Negro U Pr). Greenwood.

Beaver, R. Pierce. American Protestant Women in World Mission. LC 80-14366. Orig. Title: All Loves Excelling. Repr. of 1960 ed. 45.10 (ISBN 0-8357-9122-X, 2019317). Bks Demand UMI.

Beaver, R. Pierce, ed. American Missions in Bicentennial Perspective. LC 77-7569. 1977. pap. 10.95 (ISBN 0-87808-153-4). William Carey Lib.

--The Native American Christian Community: A Directory of Indian, Aleut, & Eskimo Churches. 395p. 1979. text ed. 6.00 (ISBN 0-912552-25-5). MARC.

Beaver, Rachel, jt. auth. see Beaver, Richard.

Beaver, Richard & Beaver, Rachel. All about the St. Bernard. (All About Ser.). 160p. 1980. 12.95 (ISBN 0-7207-1197-5, Pub. by Michael Joseph). Merrimack Pub Cir.

Beaver, Robert P. Christianity & African Education: The Papers of a Conference at the University of Chicago. LC 65-25184. pap. 58.30 (ISBN 0-317-09800-4, 2012940). Bks Demand UMI.

Beaver, Roy C. Bessemer & Lake Erie Railroad, 1869-1969. LC 73-97230. (Illus.). 200p. 1969. 20.95 (ISBN 0-87095-033-9). Golden West.

Beaver, Wilfred N. Unexplored New Guinea. LC 75-32799. (Illus.). Repr. of 1920 ed. 32.50 (ISBN 0-404-14102-1). AMS Pr.

Beaver, William H. Financial Reporting: An Accounting Revolution. (Contemporary Topics in Accounting Ser.). (Illus.). 240p. 1981. text ed. 20.95. P-H.

Beaver, William H. & Landsman, Wayne R. Incremental Information Content of Statement Thirty-Three Disclosures. LC 83-82489. (Financial Accounting Standards Board Research Report). (Illus., Orig.). 1983. pap. 25.00 (ISBN 0-910065-19-5). Finan Acct.

Beaverbrook, W. M. Men & Power, Nineteen Seventeen to Nineteen Eighteen. (Illus.). xlii, 447p. 1968. Repr. of 1956 ed. 27.50 (ISBN 0-208-00717-2, Archon). Shoe String.

--Politicians & the War, 1914-1916. (Illus.). 556p. 1968. Repr. of 1928 ed. 28.00 (ISBN 0-208-00718-0, Archon). Shoe String.

Beaverbrook, William M. The Decline & Fall of Lloyd George. LC 81-4565. (Illus.). 320p. 1981. Repr. of 1963 ed. lib. bdg. 35.00x (ISBN 0-313-23007-2, BEDF). Greenwood.

Beavers, Dorothy J. Autism: Nightmare Without End. Hammond, Debbie, ed. LC 79-27669. 1982. 17.95 (ISBN 0-87949-167-1). Ashley Bks.

Beavers, Dustin. A Duck Named Bob. 5.95 (ISBN 0-911505-22-9). Lifecraft.

Beavers, Eleanor, jt. ed. see Gerson, Cyrelle K.

Beavers, John P. Ohio Coporations: Ohio Practice Systems Library Selection. LC 79-91157. write for info. Lawyers Co-Op.

--Ohio Forms-Legal & Business, 6 Vols. LC 72-134918. write for info. Lawyers Co-Op.

Beavers, Mary K. Essential Mathematics. 611p. 1983. pap. text ed. 23.50 scp (ISBN 0-06-040591-0, HarpC); instr's. manual & test bank avail. (ISBN 0-06-360553-8). Har-Row.

Beavers, Mary-Kay. Basic Mathematics with Algebra & Geometry. 570p. 1985. pap. text ed. 23.95 scp (ISBN 0-06-040592-9, HarpC). Har-Row.

Beavers, W. Robert. Psychotherapy & Growth: A Family Systems Perspective. LC 77-2639. 1977. 27.50 (ISBN 0-87630-143-X). Brunner-Mazel.

--Successful Marriage: A Family Systems Approach to Couples Therapy. 1985. 19.95 (ISBN 0-393-70006-2). Norton.

Beavers, William A., jt. auth. see Bates, Robert B.

Beavis, Bill. Bows Amidships. (Illus.). 128p. (Orig.). 1984. pap. 4.95 (ISBN 0-229-11717-1). Sheridan.

Beavis, Bill & McCloskey, Richard G. Salty Dog Talk: The Nautical Origins of Everyday Expressions. (Illus.). 96p. 1983. pap. 4.95 (ISBN 0-229-11705-8, Pub. by Adlard Coles). Sheridan.

Beavis, Bill, jt. auth. see Jarman, Colin.

Beavis, F. C. Engineering Geology. (Illus.). 280p. 1985. text ed. 33.00x (ISBN 0-86793-200-7, Pub. by Blackwell Sci Australia); pap. text ed. 18.00x (ISBN 0-86793-128-0). Blackwell Pubns.

Beavis, J. R. S. & Medlik, S. Manual of Hotel Reception. 1981. pap. 13.95 (ISBN 0-434-91243-3, Pub. by W Heinemann Ltd). David & Charles.

Beazer, Cyril H. Random Reflections of a West Country Master Craftsman. 168p. 1981. 35.00x (ISBN 0-9507709-0-6, Pub. by Beazer England). State Mutual Bk.

Beazer, William F. The Commercial Future of Hong Kong. LC 76-24343. 176p. 1978. 37.95x (ISBN 0-275-23670-6). Praeger.

Beazley, C. R. Prince Henry the Navigator. (Illus.). 336p. 1968. Repr. of 1923 ed. 29.50x (ISBN 0-7146-1452-1, F Cass Co). Biblio Dist.

Beazley, C. Raymond. Voyages & Travels, 2 Vols. LC 64-16743. (Arber's an English Garner Ser.). 1964. Repr. of 1890 ed. 35.00x (ISBN 0-8154-0020-9). Cooper Sq.

Beazley, Charles R. Dawn of Modern Geography, 3 vols. (Illus.). 60.00 (ISBN 0-8446-1063-1). Peter Smith.

--John & Sebastian Cabot: The Discovery of North America. (Builders of Great Britain Ser). 1967. Repr. of 1898 ed. 20.50 (ISBN 0-8337-0206-8). B Franklin.

--A Note-Book of Mediaeval History, A. D. 323 - A. D. 1453. facsimile ed. LC 70-160957. (Select Bibliographies Reprint Ser). Repr. of 1917 ed. 18.00 (ISBN 0-8369-5824-1). Ayer Co Pubs.

--Prince Henry the Navigator, the Hero of Portugal & of Modern Discovery 1394-1460. LC 68-57121. (Research & Source Works Ser: No. 316). (Illus.). 1968. Repr. of 1911 ed. 21.50 (ISBN 0-8337-0210-6). B Franklin.

Beazley, E. & Haverson, M. Living with the Desert: Working Buildings of the Iranian Plateau. (Illus.). 140p. 1983. pap. text ed. 48.50x (ISBN 0-85668-192-X, 60245, Pub. by Aris & Phillips England). Humanities.

Beazley, J. D. Attic Black Figure Vase-Painters. LC 75-44909. 1978. Repr. of 1956 ed. lib. bdg. 45.00 (ISBN 0-87817-191-6). Hacker.

--Attic Red-Figure Vase-Painters, 3 Vols. 2036p. 1983. Repr. of 1963 ed. Set. 125.00 (ISBN 0-87817-289-0). Hacker.

Beazley, J. D., tr. see Pfuhl, Ernst.

Beazley, J. M. & Lobb, M. O. Aspects of Care in Labour. LC 83-7357. (Current Reviews in Obstetrics & Gynaecology Ser.: Vol. 6). (Illus.). 142p. (Orig.). 1983. pap. text ed. 17.00 (ISBN 0-443-02927-X). Churchill.

Beazley, Mary, jt. auth. see Scott, Margaret K.

Beazley, Peter C., jt. auth. see Sobeslavsky, Vladimir.

Beazley, Richard M. Library Statistics of Colleges & Universities, 1976 Institutional Data (Libgis II, Hegis XI) (Monograph: No. 16). 184p. 1979. pap. 5.00x (ISBN 0-87845-061-0, NCES 78-234). U of Ill Lib Info Sci.

Bebb, Evelyn D. Nonconformity & Social & Economic Life 1660-1800. LC 80-21180. 1981. Repr. of 1935 ed. lib. bdg. 19.50x (ISBN 0-87991-867-5). Porcupine Pr.

Bebb, Philip N., ed. see Verkamp, Bernard J.

Bebb, Phillip, jt. auth. see Sessions, Kyle.

Bebb, Russ. The Big Orange: A Story of Tennessee Football. LC 73-86998. (College Sports Ser.). 1982. 10.95 (ISBN 0-87397-214-7). Strode.

Bebbington, D. W. The Nonconformist Conscience: Chapel & Politics 1870-1914. 192p. 1982. text ed. 25.00x (ISBN 0-04-942173-5). Allen Unwin.

Bebbington, Jim. The Young Player's Guide to Soccer. LC 78-66970. 1979. 12.95 (ISBN 0-7153-7536-9). David & Charles.

Bebbington, W. G. The Original Manuscript of Thomas Hardy's "the Trumpet Major". LC 73-4599. 1973. lib. bdg. 10.00 (ISBN 0-8414-1753-9). Folcroft.

Bebbington, W. G., compiled by. Introducing Modern Poetry. 146p. 1981. Repr. of 1955 ed. lib. bdg. 20.00 (ISBN 0-8495-0485-6). Arden Lib.

Bebek, Borna. The Third City: Philosophy at War with Positivism. 352p. 1983. 29.95x (ISBN 0-7100-9042-0). Routledge & Kegan.

Bebel, August. My Life, by August Bebel. LC 83-1556. 343p. 1983. Repr. of 1912 ed. lib. bdg. 35.00x (ISBN 0-313-23927-4, BEMY). Greenwood.

--Nicht Stehendes Heer, Sondern Volkswehr. LC 71-147544. (Library of War & Peace; Control & Limitation of Arms). lib. bdg. 46.00 (ISBN 0-8240-0325-X). Garland Pub.

--Woman in the Past, Present, & Future. LC 72-9616. (International Library of Social Sciences Ser.: Vol. 1). Repr. of 1885 ed. 25.00 (ISBN 0-404-57409-2). AMS Pr.

Bebensee, Elisabeth L., jt. auth. see Adams, Anne H.

Beberfall, Lester, tr. see Blasco-Ibanez, Vicente.

Bebermeyer, Ruth. And Master of None. (Illus.). 1976. 5.00 (ISBN 0-686-16393-1). Impermanent Pr.

Bebessay, Araya, jt. auth. see Bloom, Robert.

Bebey, Francis. African Music: A People's Art. Bennett, Josephine, tr. from French. LC 74-9348. (Illus.). 192p. 1975. 12.95 (ISBN 0-88208-051-2); pap. 9.95 (ISBN 0-88208-050-4). Lawrence Hill.

--Agatha Moudio's Son. Hutchinson, Joyce, tr. from Fr. LC 72-96591. 160p. (Orig.). 1973. pap. 3.95 (ISBN 0-88208-038-5). Lawrence Hill.

--The Ashanti Doll. Hutchinson, Joyce, tr. LC 76-52658. 192p. 1977. 7.50 (ISBN 0-88208-075-X). Lawrence Hill.

--King Albert. Hutchinson, Joyce, tr. from Fr. 179p. 1981. 10.00 (ISBN 0-88208-138-1); pap. 5.95 (ISBN 0-88208-139-X). Lawrence Hill.

Bebie, Philip. Proclaim Her Name. 58p. 1982. pap. 1.98 (ISBN 0-911988-46-7). AMI Pr.

Bebis, George S., tr. see Trempelas, Panagiotes N.

Bebko, Claudia & Krestan, Jo A. The Responsibility Trap: A Blueprint for Treating the Alcholic Family. 320p. 1984. 25.00x (ISBN 0-02-902880-9). Free Pr.

Beblawi, Hazem. The Arab Gulf Economy in a Turbulent Age. LC 83-40505. 240p. 1984. 27.50 (ISBN 0-312-04700-2). St Martin.

Bebout, D. G. & Loucks, R. G. Stuart City Trend, Lower Cretaceous, South Texas: A Carbonate Shelf-Margin for Hydrocarbon Exploration. (Report of Investigations Ser.: RI 78). (Illus.). 80p. 1980. Repr. of 1974 ed. 3.00 (ISBN 0-318-03198-1). Bur Econ Geology.

Bebout, D. G. & Loucks, R. G., eds. Cretaceous Carbonates of Texas & Mexico: Applications to Subsurface Exploration. (Report of Investigations Ser.: No. 89). 322p. 1977. Repr. 8.50 (ISBN 0-686-36611-5). Bur Econ Geology.

Bebout, D. G., et al. Depositional & Diagenetic History of the Sligo & Hosston Formations (Lower Cretaceous) in South Texas. (Report of Investigations Ser.: No. 109). (Illus.). 69p. 1981. 4.00 (ISBN 0-686-36993-9). Bur Econ Geology.

--Frio Sandstone Reservoirs in the Deep Subsurface along the Texas Gulf Coast: Their Potential for the Production of Geopressured Geothermal Energy. (Report of Investigations Ser.: RI 91). (Illus.). 92p. 1983. Repr. of 1978 ed. 5.50 (ISBN 0-318-03230-9). Bur Econ Geology.

--Wilcox Sandstone Reservoirs in the Deep Subsurface along the Texas Gulf Coast, Their Potential for Production of Geopressured Geothermal Energy. (Report of Investigations Ser.: RI 117). (Illus.). 125p. 1982. 5.00 (ISBN 0-318-03251-1). Bur Econ Geology.

Bebr, Gerhard. Development of Judicial Control of the European Communities. 840p. 1981. lib. bdg. 150.00 (ISBN 90-247-2541-0, Pub. by Martinus Nijhoff Netherlands). Kluwer Netherlands.

Bec, Christian. Les Marchands Ecrivains: Affaires et Humanisme a Florence, 1375-1434. 1967. pap. 34.80 (ISBN 0-686-22141-9). Mouton.

Bec, Pierre. The Fundus Periphery. Blodi, Frederick, tr. from Fr. 400p. write for info. (ISBN 0-89352-211-2). Masson Pub.

Becan-McBride, K., jt. auth. see Garza, D.

Becan-McBride, Kathleen, ed. Textbook of Clinical Laboratory Supervision. (Illus.). 352p. 1982. 26.50 (ISBN 0-8385-8871-9). ACC.

Beccaria, Cesare. On Crimes & Punishments. Paolucci, Henry, tr. LC 61-18589. 1963. pap. 5.99 scp (ISBN 0-672-60302-0, LLA107). Bobbs.

--On Crimes & Punishments. (International Pocket Library). 1983. pap. 3.00 (ISBN 0-8283-1800-X). Branden Pub Co.

Beccaria, Cesare B. Discourse on Public Economy & Commerce. LC 73-80244. 1970. Repr. of 1769 ed. lib. bdg. 18.50 (ISBN 0-8337-0211-4). B Franklin.

Beccar-Varela, Adele, jt. auth. see Lappe, Frances M.

Bec-Crespin, Jean du see Du Bec-Crespin, Jean.

Becerra, A. T., ed. see International Symposium on Peritoneal Dialysis, 1st, Chapala, Jalisco, Mexico, June 25-28, 1978.

Becerra, Rosina, jt. auth. see Giovannoni, Jeanne M.

Becerra, Rosina M. & Greenblatt, Milton. Hispanics Seek Health Care: A Study of 1,088 Veterans of Three War Eras. LC 83-6718. (Illus.). 164p. 1983. lib. bdg. 24.25 (ISBN 0-8191-3263-2); pap. text ed. 11.25 (ISBN 0-8191-3264-0). U Pr of Amer.

Becerra, Rosina M. & Shaw, David. The Hispanic Elderly: A Research Reference Guide. 152p. (Orig.). 1984. lib. bdg. 24.00 (ISBN 0-8191-3626-3); pap. text ed. 11.25 (ISBN 0-8191-3627-1). U Pr of Amer.

Becerra, Rosina M. & Escobar, Javier I., eds. Mental Health & Hispanic-Americans: Clinical Perspectives. LC 81-22931. (Seminars in Psychiatry Monograph). 256p. 1982. 29.00 (ISBN 0-8089-1452-9, 790463). Grune.

Bechdel, Les & Ray, Slim. River Rescue. (Illus.). 220p. (Orig.). 1985. pap. 9.95 (ISBN 0-910146-55-1). Appalach Mtn.

Bechdolt, Fred R., jt. auth. see Hopper, James M.

Bechdolt, Frederick R. Giants of the Old West. facs. ed. LC 73-80382. (Essay Index Reprint Ser). 1930. 16.50 (ISBN 0-8369-1020-6). Ayer Co Pubs.

Becher. Encyclopedia of Emulsion Technology, Vol. 1. 648p. 1983. 115.00 (ISBN 0-8247-1876-3). Dekker.

--Encyclopedia of Emulsion Technology: Application of Emulsions, Vol. 2. 472p. 1985. 95.00 (ISBN 0-8247-1877-1). Dekker.

Becher & Yudenfreund. Emulsions Latices & Dispersions. 1978. 59.75 (ISBN 0-8247-6797-7). Dekker.

Becher, Belle & Linscott, Robert N., eds. Bedside Book of Famous French Stories. 427p. 1985. Repr. of 1945 ed. lib. bdg. 40.00 (ISBN 0-8414-2297-4). Folcroft.

Becher, H. Woerterbuch der Deutschen und Spanischen Rects und Wirtschaftssprache, Vol. 2. (Ger. & Span.). 1972. 79.95 (ISBN 3-406-00470-9, M-7022). French & Eur.

--Woerterbuch der Spanischen und Deutschen Rechts und Wirtschaftssprache, Vol. 1. (Span. & Ger.). 1971. 85.00 (ISBN 3-406-00469-5, M-6956). French & Eur.

Becher, Paul. Emulsions: Theory & Practice. 2nd ed. LC 77-22344. (ACS Monographs Ser.: No. 162). 452p. 1977. Repr. of 1965 ed. 30.50 (ISBN 0-88275-589-7). Krieger.

Becher, Peter. Der Untergang Kakaniens. (European University Studies: No. 1, Vol. 520). 410p. (Ger.). 1982. 44.20 (ISBN 3-8204-6260-0). P Lang Pubs.

Becher, Peter & Bohm, Manfred. Gauge Theories of Strong & Electroweak Interactions. LC 83-6456. 306p. 1984. 58.95x (ISBN 0-471-10429-9, Pub by Wiley Interscience). Wiley.

Becher, Rolf. Schooling by the Natural Method. (Illus.). 5.95 (ISBN 0-85131-105-9, BL2565, Dist. by Miller). J A Allen.

Becher, Tony & Kogan, Maurice. Process & Structure in Higher Education. (Studies in Social Policy & Welfare). 1980. text ed. 27.00x (ISBN 0-435-82507-0). Gower Pub Co.

Becher, Tony & Maclure, Stuart, eds. Accountability in Education. 256p. 1979. 20.00x (ISBN 0-85633-167-8, Pub. by NFER Nelson UK). Taylor & Francis.

Becher, Tony, et al. Systems of Higher Education: United Kingdom. 1978. pap. 6.00 (ISBN 0-89192-200-8, Pub. by ICED). Interbk Inc.

--Policies for Educational Accountability. (Organization in Schools Ser.). 168p. 1981. text ed. 25.00x (ISBN 0-435-80060-4). Heinemann Ed.

Becher, William D. Logical Design Using Integrated Circuits. 1977. text ed. 21.50x (ISBN 0-8104-5859-4). Hayden.

Becherer, Richard. Science Plus Sentiment: Cesar Daly's Formula for Modern Architecture. Foster, Stephen C., ed. LC 84-2453. (Architecture & Urban Design). 451p. 1984. 54.95 (ISBN 0-8357-1566-3). UMI Res Pr.

Becherer, Richard, jt. auth. see Grum, Franc C.

Becherer, Richard, jt. ed. see Grum, Franc.

Bechert, Heinz & Gombrich, Richard, eds. The World of Buddhism: Buddhist Monks & Nuns in Society & Culture. LC 84-8125. 1984. 49.95 (ISBN 0-87196-982-3). Facts on File.

Bechervaise, John. Science: Men on Ice in Antarctica. (Australian Life Ser.: No. 2). 1979. pap. 6.95x (ISBN 0-85091-054-4, Pub. by Lothian). Intl Spec Bk.

Bechet, Sidney. Treat It Gentle: An Autobiography. LC 74-23412. (Roots of Jazz Ser.). (Illus.). vi, 245p. 1978. lib. bdg. 25.00 (ISBN 0-306-70657-1); pap. 6.95 (ISBN 0-306-80086-1). Da Capo.

Bechett, Wendy M., tr. John of Ford: Sermons on the Song of Songs I. LC 77-3697. (Cistercian Fathers Ser.: No. 29): 1977. 14.95 (ISBN 0-87907-629-1). Cistercian Pubns.

Bechhoefer, Bernhard G. Postwar Negotiations for Arms Control. LC 74-31353. (Illus.). 641p. 1975. Repr. of 1961 ed. lib. bdg. 33.50x (ISBN 0-8371-7892-4, BEPN). Greenwood.

Bechhoefer, Ina S., ed. Guide to Real Estate & Mortgage Banking Software, 2 vols. 1200p. 1985. Set. 115.00 (ISBN 0-917935-02-0). Real Est Sol.

Bechhofer, C. E. In Denikin's Russia & the Caucasus, 1919-1920. LC 76-115507. (Russia Observed Ser). (Illus.). 1971. Repr. of 1921 ed. 17.00 (ISBN 0-405-03077-0). Ayer Co Pubs.

Bechhofer, C. E., tr. Five Russian Plays with One from the Ukrainian. LC 77-89719. (One-Act Plays in Reprint Ser.). 1977. 18.50x (ISBN 0-8486-2016-X). Core Collection.

Bechhofer, Robert E., et al. Sequential Identification & Ranking Procedures: With Special Reference to Koopman-Darmois Populations. LC 67-28463. (Statistical Research Monographs Ser.: Vol. 3). pap. 109.50 (ISBN 0-317-09299-5, 2019954). Bks Demand UMI.

Bechko, Peggy. Dark Side of Love. (Superromances Ser.). 384p. 1983. pap. 2.50 (ISBN 0-373-70047-4, Pub. by Worldwide). Harlequin Bks.

--Harmonie Mexicaine. (Harlequin Seduction Ser.). 332p. 1984. pap. 3.25 (ISBN 0-373-45035-4). Harlequin Bks.

Bechler, Z. Contemporary Newtonian Research. 1982. 39.50 (ISBN 90-277-1303-0, Pub. by Reidel Holland). Kluwer Academic.

Bechman, R. see Hellwege, K. H.

Bechman, R., et al see Hellwege, K. H.

Bechofer, Frank & Elliot, Brian, eds. The Petite Bourgeoise. 1981. 26.00x (ISBN 0-312-60365-7). St Martin.

Becht, J. Edwin & Belzung, L. D. World Resource Management: Key to Civilizations & Social Achievement. (Illus.). 336p. 1975. text ed. 29.95 (ISBN 0-13-968107-8). P-H.

Becht, R. Revision der Sektion Alopecuroideae DC. der Gattung Astragalus L. (Phanerogamarum Monographiae Ser: No. 10). (Illus.). 1979. lib. bdg. 21.00 (ISBN 3-7682-1188-6). Lubrecht & Cramer.

Bechtel. Improving Writing & Learning. 1985. 24.95 (ISBN 0-205-08201-7, 238201). Allyn.

Bechtel, Beverley. Lancelot the Ocelot. LC 78-186859. (Illus.). 32p. (gr. k-3). 1972. PLB 5.95g (ISBN 0-87614-031-2). Carolrhoda Bks.

Bechtel, D. B., ed. New Frontiers in Food Microstructure. LC 83-70795. (Illus.). 392p. 1983. text ed. 48.00 nonmember (ISBN 0-913250-32-5); text ed. 44.00 member. Am Assn Cereal Chem.

Bechtel, Faythelma. The Creative Touch, No. 1. 1973. 5.50x (ISBN 0-87813-909-5). Christian Light.

--Creative Touch, No. 2. 1982. 5.50x (ISBN 0-87813-919-2). Christian Light.

--God's Marvelous Gifts. (Christian Day School Ser.). (gr. 5). 1982. 13.75x (ISBN 0-87813-920-6). Christian Light.

Bechtel, Gordon C. Multidimensional Preference Scaling. (Methods & Models in Social Science: No. 6). 1976. pap. 16.80x (ISBN 90-2797-592-2). Mouton.

Bechtel, John H. Slips of Speech. LC 77-159889. Repr. of 1901 ed. 40.00x (ISBN 0-8103-4041-0). Gale.

Bechtel, John H., ed. Select Speeches for Declamation. facsimile ed. LC 75-103083. (Granger Index Reprint Ser). 1898. 17.00 (ISBN 0-8369-6098-X). Ayer Co Pubs.

--Temperance Selections. facsimile ed. LC 71-116393. (Granger Index Reprint Ser). 1893. 14.00 (ISBN 0-8369-6134-X). Ayer Co Pubs.

Bechtel, Judith. Improving Writing & Learning: A Handbook for Teachers in Every Class. 216p. 1985. 26.95x (ISBN 0-205-08201-7, Pub. by Longwood Div). Allyn.

Bechtel, Judith & Franzblau, Bettie. Reading in the Science Classroom. 64p. 1980. 6.95 (ISBN 0-8106-3201-2). NEA.

Bechtel, Lenore & Curtis, Marcia. The Head First Diet. (Orig.). 1985. write for info. (ISBN 0-9611916-3-5). Write-On Creations.

Bechtel, Marilyn, ed. By & for the People: Building an Advanced Socialist Society in Bulgaria. LC 76-62559. 1977. pap. 1.95 (ISBN 0-916972-01-1). NWR Pubns.

Bechtel, Marilyn & Laibman, David, eds. Peace, Plan & Progress: The Twenty-Sixth Congress of the Communist Party of the Soviet Union. (Illus.). 228p. 1981. pap. 2.95 (ISBN 0-916972-08-9). NWR Pubns.

Bechtel, Marilyn, et al, eds. Six Decades That Changed the World: The USSR After 60 Years. LC 77-93161. (Illus.). 1978. pap. 2.95 (ISBN 0-916972-02-X). NWR Pubns.

Bechtel National, Inc. Photovoltaic Power Systems: Handbook for Battery Energy Storage. 127p. 1982. pap. 29.95x (ISBN 0-89934-164-0, P046). Solar Energy Info.

Bechtel, Paul. Wheaton College: A Heritage Remembered 1860-1985. 384p. 1984. text ed. 17.95 (ISBN 0-87788-347-5). Shaw Pubs.

Bechtel, Paul, ed. The Confessions of St. Augustine. LC 81-11163. 1981. 8.95 (ISBN 0-8024-1618-7). Moody.

Bechtel, Paul M., ed. see Thomas A'Kempis.

Bechtel, R. M., ed. Salus: Low-Cost Rural Health Care & Health Manpower Training: An Annotated Bibliography with Special Emphasis on Developing Countries, Vol. 5. 94p. 1980. pap. 10.00 (ISBN 0-88936-233-5, IDRC144, IDRC). Unipub.

Bechtel, Robert B. Enclosing Behavior. LC 77-2850. (Community Development Ser.: Vol. 31). 1977. 34.95 (ISBN 0-87933-069-4). Van Nos Reinhold.

Bechtel, Rosanna M., ed. Salus: Low-Cost Rural Health Care & Health Manpower Training, Vol. 10. 148p. 1984. pap. text ed. 13.00 (ISBN 0-88936-388-9, IDRC216, IDRC). Unipub.

--Salus: Low-Cost Rural Health Care & Health Manpower Training: A Cumulative Index of Volumes One Through Ten. 150p. 1984. pap. text ed. 13.00 (ISBN 0-88936-389-7, IDRC217, IDRC). Unipub.

--SALUS: Low-Cost Rural Health Care & Health Manpower Training: A Cumulative Index to Volumes 11-15. 97p. 1985. pap. 13.00 (ISBN 0-88936-428-1, IDRC232 5071, IDRC). Unipub.

--Salus: Low-Cost Rural Health Care & Health Manpower Training: An Annotated Bibliography with Special Emphasis on Developing Countries, Vol. 9. 149p. 1983. pap. 13.00 (ISBN 0-88936-322-6, IDRC187, IDRC). Unipub.

--SALUS: Low-Cost Rural Health Care & Health Manpower Training: An Annotated Bibliography with Special Emphasis on Developing Countries, Vols. 12-14. 1984. Vol. 12, 137p. pap. 13.00 (ISBN 0-88936-417-6, IDRC225, IDRC); Vol. 13, 140p. pap. 13.00 (ISBN 0-88936-420-6, IDRC227); Vol. 14, 143p. pap. 13.00 (ISBN 0-88936-421-4, IDRC228). Unipub.

--SALUS: Low-Cost Rural Health Care & Health Manpower Training: An Annotated Bibliography with Special Emphasis on Developing Countries, Vol. 15. 145p. 1985. pap. 13.00 (ISBN 0-88936-425-7, IDRC230, IDRC). Unipub.

Bechterev, Vladimir M. General Principles of Human Reflexology: An Introduction to the Objective Study of Personality. LC 73-2961. (Classics in Psychology Ser.). Repr. of 1932 ed. 21.00 (ISBN 0-405-05134-4). Ayer Co Pubs.

Bechtereva, N. P. Psychophysiology Today & Tomorrow. 66.00 (ISBN 0-08-025930-8). Pergamon.

Bechtle, Thomas C. & Riley, Mary F. Dissertations in Philosophy Accepted in American Universities, 1861-1975. (Reference Library of the Humanities: Vol. 112). (LC 77-083392). 1978. lib. bdg. 73.00 (ISBN 0-8240-9835-8). Garland Pub.

Bechtle-Pierce, Ruth C. The Well Child, Vol. 4. (RN Nursing Assessment Ser.). 190p. 1986. pap. 12.95 (ISBN 0-87489-290-2). Med Economics.

Bechtler, Thomas W., ed. Law in a Social Context. 1978. lib. bdg. 34.00 (ISBN 90-2680-973-5, Pub. by Kluwer Law Netherlands). Kluwer Academic.

Bechtold, Paul F. A Larger Life: From Greed to Greatness. LC 75-2137. 143p. (Orig.). 1975. pap. 2.95 (ISBN 0-87178-514-5). Brethren.

Bechtolsheim, Lulu. Die Kunst des Sehens in der Mathematik. Finetti, Bruno, ed. (Science & Civilization Ser.: No. 28). 92p. (Ger.). 1974. 23.95 (ISBN 0-8176-0677-7). Birkhauser.

Beck. Not for Love Alone: A Critical Analysis. (EPC Ser.). 30p. 1985. pap. 7.95 (ISBN 0-932582-49-4). Dance Notation.

Beck, A. see Keller, Mark.

Beck, A., ed. Probability in Banach Spaces III: Proceedings. (Lecture Notes in Mathematics Ser.: Vol. 860). 329p. 1981. pap. 20.00 (ISBN 0-387-10822-X). Springer-Verlag.

--Probability in Banach Spaces Two. (Lecture Notes in Mathematics Ser.: Vol. 709). 1979. pap. 17.00 (ISBN 0-387-09242-0). Springer-Verlag.

Beck, A. & Jacobs, K., eds. Probability in Banach Spaces IV. (Lecture Notes in Mathematics Ser.: Vol. 990). 234p. 1983. pap. 13.00 (ISBN 0-387-12295-8). Springer-Verlag.

Beck, A., ed. see Conference in Topological Dynamics, Yale University, June 19-23, 1972.

Beck, A., ed. see International Conference on Probability in Banach Spaces, First, Oberwolfach, July 20-26, 1975.

Beck, A., et al. Continuous Flows in the Plane. LC 73-11952. (Grundlehren der Mathematischen Wissenschaften Ser.: Vol. 201). (Illus.). 480p. 1974. 66.00 (ISBN 0-387-06157-6). Springer-Verlag.

Beck, A. E. Physical Principles of Exploration Methods: An Introductory Text for Geology & Geophysics Students. LC 81-80411. 234p. 1981. pap. 17.95 (ISBN 0-470-27128-0). Halsted Pr.

Beck, Aaron T. Cognitive Therapy & Emotional Disorders. LC 75-33518. 365p. (Orig.). 1976. text ed. 30.00 (ISBN 0-8236-0990-1). Intl Univs Pr.

--Cognitive Therapy & the Emotional Disorders. 368p. 1979. pap. 6.95 (ISBN 0-452-00788-7, Mer). NAL.

--Depression: Causes & Treatment. LC 67-23826. 1972. 30.00x (ISBN 0-8122-7652-3); pap. 11.95x (ISBN 0-8122-1032-8, Pa Paperbks). U of Pa Pr.

--Diagnosis & Management of Depression. LC 73-83290. 160p. 1973. 11.95x (ISBN 0-8122-7674-4). U of Pa Pr.

Beck, Aaron T. & Emery, Gary. Anxiety Disorders & Phobias: A Cognitive Perspective. LC 84-42849. 416p. 1985. 26.95x (ISBN 0-465-00384-2). Basic.

Beck, Aaron T., et al. Cognitive Therapy of Depression. LC 79-19967. (Clinical Psychology & Psychotherapy Ser.). 425p. 1979. 25.00 (ISBN 0-89862-000-7, 2000). Guilford Pr.

--Cognitive Therapy of Depression. LC 79-19967. pap. 109.30 (ISBN 0-317-26155-X, 2024273). Bks Demand UMI.

Beck, Adams, jt. auth. see Moresby, Lily.

Beck, Adams L. The Story of Oriental Philosophy. 1931. 20.00 (ISBN 0-8495-6281-3). Arden Lib.

Beck, Alan & Katcher, Aaron. Between Pets & People: The Importance of Animal Companionship. LC 83-4592. 256p. 1983. 14.95 (ISBN 0-399-12775-5, Putnam). Putnam Pub Group.

--Between Pets & People: The Importance of Animal Companionship. (Illus.). 204p. 1984. pap. 8.95 (ISBN 0-399-51069-9, Perigee). Putnam Pub Group.

Beck, Alan & Katcher, Aaron, eds. New Perspectives on Our Lives with Companion Animals. LC 82-40484. (Illus.). 640p. 1983. 26.95x (ISBN 0-8122-7877-1). U of Pa Pr.

Beck, Anatole, et al. Excursions into Mathematics. LC 68-57963. (Illus.). 1969. text ed. 21.95x (ISBN 0-87901-004-5). Worth.

Beck, Ann. History of the British Medical Administration of East Africa, 1900-1950. LC 70-115472. (Commonwealth Fund Publications Ser). 1970. 17.50x (ISBN 0-674-40170-0). Harvard U Pr.

--Medicine & Society in Tanganyika. LC 76-50176. (Transactions Ser.: Vol. 67, Pt. 3). 1977. 7.00 (ISBN 0-87169-673-8). Am Philos.

--Medicine, Tradition, & Development in Kenya & Tanzania, 1920-1970. 125p. 1981. 12.00 (ISBN 0-918456-44-4). African Studies Assn.

Beck, Art. The Discovery of Music. (Chapbook: No. 9). 1977. pap. 1.00 (ISBN 0-912824-18-2). Vagabond Pr.

--Enlightenment: Shorthand for a Scurillious Life (the Re-Discovered Poems of Giacoma Casanova) 1977. pap. 3.00 (ISBN 0-88031-035-9). Invisible-Red Hill.

--Rilke. LC 82-84119. 70p. (Orig.). pap. 3.95 (ISBN 0-941692-06-X). Elysian Pr.

Beck, Arthur C. & Hillmar, Ellis D. Making MBO-R Work. LC 75-18151. 239p. 1975. text ed. 10.95 (ISBN 0-201-00469-0). Addison-Wesley.

Beck, Arthur C., Jr. & Hillmar, Ellis D. A Practical Approach to Organization Development Through MBO: Selected Readings. LC 71-183665. (Illus.). 280p. 1972. pap. text ed. 9.95 (ISBN 0-201-00447-X). Addison-Wesley.

Beck, Barbara L. The Ancient Maya. rev. ed. (First Bks.). (Illus.). 72p. (gr. 4 up). 1983. PLB 8.90 (ISBN 0-531-04529-3). Watts.

--The Aztecs. rev. ed. (First Bks.). (Illus.). 72p. (gr. 4 up). 1983. PLB 8.90 (ISBN 0-531-04522-6). Watts.

--The Incas. rev. ed. (First Bks.). (Illus.). 72p. (gr. 4 up). 1983. PLB 8.90 (ISBN 0-531-04528-5). Watts.

Beck, Benjamin B. & Wemmer, Christen, eds. The Biology & Management of an Extinct Species: Pere David's Deer. LC 83-2364. (Animal Behavior, Ecology, Conservation & Management Ser.). (Illus.). 193p. (Orig.). 1983. 26.00 (ISBN 0-8155-0938-3, Noyes Pubns). Noyes.

Beck, Bertram M. Empowerment: A Future Goal for Social Work. 20p. (Orig.). pap. 2.00 (ISBN 0-88156-015-4). Comm Serv Soc NY.

Beck, Billy De see De Beck, Billy.

Beck, Brenda E. Perspectives on a Regional Culture: Essays About the Coimbatore Area of South India. 1979. text ed. 20.00x (ISBN 0-7069-0723-X, Pub. by Vikas India). Advent NY.

--The Three Twins: The Telling of a South Indian Folk Epic. LC 80-8841. (Illus.). 256p. 1982. 22.50x (ISBN 0-253-36014-5). Ind U Pr.

Beck, Bruce. Produce: A Fruit & Vegetable Lovers' Guide. LC 83-49410. (Illus.). 213p. 1984. 35.00 (ISBN 0-914919-01-6). Friendly Pr NY.

Beck, Bruce, jt. ed. see Young, Bruce.

Beck, C. H. & Matthew Bender. Beck's English-German Dictionary, 2 vols. (Ger. & Eng.). 1979. casebound 200.00 (262). Bender.

Beck, Carl. Contempt of Congress: A Study of the Prosecutions Initiated by the Committee on Un-American Activities, 1945-1957. LC 75-166090. (American Constitutional & Legal History Ser.). 264p. 1974. Repr. of 1959 ed. lib. bdg. 32.50 (ISBN 0-306-70229-0). Da Capo.

--Law & Justice: Essays in Honor of Robert S. Rankin. LC 74-86476. pap. 92.50 (ISBN 0-317-20086-0, 2023376). Bks Demand UMI.

Beck, Carl, jt. ed. see Mesa-Lago, Carmelo.

Beck, Carl, et al. Political Science Thesaurus. LC 75-326011. pap. 117.80 (ISBN 0-317-10235-4, 2017799). Bks Demand UMI.

Beck, Charles A. & Isaacs, I. Beck's Theory & Principles of Pleading in Civil Actions. LC 83-183839. 358p. Date not set. price not set (ISBN 0-409-01235-1). Butterworth.

Beck, Charles B., ed. Origin & Early Evolution of Angiosperms. LC 75-15939. (Illus.). 341p. 1976. 45.00x (ISBN 0-231-03857-7). Columbia U Pr.

Beck, Charlotte H. Worlds & Lives: The Poetry of Randall Jarrell. LC 81-19361. 108p. 1983. 12.00x (ISBN 0-8046-9300-5, Natl U). Assoc Faculty Pr.

Beck, Clark L. & Burks, Ardath W. Aspects of Meiji Modernization: The Japan Helpers & the Helped. 45p. 1983. pap. text ed. 4.95x (ISBN 0-87855-936-1). Transaction Bks.

Beck, Cornelia M. & Rawlins, Ruth Parmelee. Mental Health in Psychiatric Nursing: A Holistic Life-Cycle Approach. (Illus.). 1200p. 1984. write for info. Mosby.

Beck, Curt W., ed. Archeological Chemistry. LC 74-22372. (Advances in Chemistry Ser: No. 138). 1974. 39.95 (ISBN 0-8412-0211-7). Am Chemical.

Beck, D Elden & Braithwaite, Lee F. Invertebrate Zoology: Laboratory Workbook. 3rd ed. (Illus.). 1968. spiral bdg. 16.95x (ISBN 0-8087-0211-4). Burgess.

Beck, David. Ski Touring in California. 2nd ed. LC 79-90502. (Illus.). 1979. pap. 7.95 (ISBN 0-686-59506-8). Pika Pr.

--Ski Touring in California. 2nd ed. LC 83-51473. (Illus.). 224p. 1983. pap. 9.95 (ISBN 0-89997-034-6). Wilderness Pr.

Beck, Dawn. Where to Go Dancing in San Francisco. LC 83-50447. 128p. (Orig.). 1983. pap. 4.95 (ISBN 0-9609740-1-6). Sharain Bks.

--Where To Go Dancing in Silicon Valley. LC 82-61728. 96p. (Orig.). 1982. pap. 4.95 (ISBN 0-9609740-0-8). Sharain Bks.

Beck, Donald. Principles of Reimbursement in Health Care. LC 83-12300. 320p. 1983. 34.50 (ISBN 0-89443-887-5). Aspen Systems.

Beck, Donald R. Basic Hospital Financial Management. LC 80-19598. 300p. 1981. text ed. 31.50 (ISBN 0-89443-329-6). Aspen Systems.

Beck, Donald R., jt. ed. see Nicolaides, Cleanthes A.

Beck, Dorothy. Northern Lights: Writers from the Upper Valley of Vermont & New Hampshire. (Chapbook Ser: No. 1). 170p. 1972. pap. 2.00 (ISBN 0-685-40131-6). Bluefish.

Beck, Dorothy F. Marriage & the Family Under Challenge: An Outline of Issues, Trends, & Alternatives. LC 76-26307. 101p. 1976. 5.00 (ISBN 0-87304-145-3). Family Serv.

--Marriage & the Family Under Challenge. 2nd ed. LC 76-26307. 1976. pap. 5.00 (ISBN 0-87304-145-3). Family Serv.

--New Treatment Modalities: An Outline of Some Options & Source Materials. 85p. 1978. 6.00 (ISBN 0-87304-166-6). Family Serv.

Beck, Dorothy F. & Jones, Mary A. How to Conduct a Client Follow-Up Study. 2nd ed. 126p. 1980. 12.00 (ISBN 0-87304-181-X). Family Serv.

Beck, Dorothy F. & Jones, Mary Ann. How to Conduct a Client Follow-up Study. 2nd ed. LC 73-94027. 1980. pap. 14.00 with 1979 & 1980 supplements (ISBN 0-87304-181-X). Family Serv.

--Ptogress on Family Problems: A Nationwide Study of Clients' & Counselors' Views on Family Agency Services. LC 73-81256. 1973. pap. 17.00 (ISBN 0-87304-107-0). Family Serv.

Beck, E. A. & Furlan, M., eds. Variants of Human Fibrinogen. (Current Problems in Clinical Biochemistry Ser.: No. 14). (Illus.). 328p. (Orig.). 1984. pap. text ed. write for info. (ISBN 3-456-81359-7, Pub. by Hans Huber Switzerland). J K Burgess.

Beck, E. C. They Knew Paul Bunyan. Dorson, Richard M., ed. LC 80-789. (Folklore of the World Ser.). 1980. Repr. of 1956 ed. lib. bdg. 26.50x (ISBN 0-405-13328-6). Ayer Co Pubs.

Beck, Earl C. Lore of the Lumber Camps. enl., rev. ed. LC 49-7123. (University of Michigan Studies & Publications Ser.). (Illus.). pap. 94.50 (ISBN 0-317-09889-6, 2051078). Bks Demand UMI.

--Songs of the Michigan Lumberjacks. (University of Michigan Studies & Publications). pap. 76.80 (ISBN 0-317-29151-3, 2055620). Bks Demand UMI.

Beck, Earl R. Death of the Prussian Republic: A Study of Reich-Prussian Relations, 1932-1934. (Florida State University Studies: No. 31). 283p. 1959. 7.50 (ISBN 0-8130-0473-X). U Presses Fla.

--Germany Rediscovers America. LC 68-54592. 1968. 12.00 (ISBN 0-8130-0424-1). U Presses Fla.

--On Teaching History in Colleges & Universities. LC 66-64094. (Florida State Univ. Studies: No. 50). 1966. 7.50 (ISBN 0-8130-0497-7). U Presses Fla.

--A Time of Triumph & of Sorrow: Spanish Politics During the Reign of Alfonso XII, 1874-1885. LC 78-23282. 320p. 1979. 22.50x (ISBN 0-8093-0902-5). S Ill U Pr.

Beck, Edward N., jt. ed. see Browne, Ellen V.

Beck, Elmer A. & Westburg, John, eds. The Sewer Socialists: A History of the Socialist Party of Wisconsin, 1897-1940, 2 Vols. Incl. Vol. 1. The Socialist Trinity of the Party, the Unions & the Press. 204p; Vol. 2. The Nineteen Twenties & Nineteen Thirties. (Illus.). 168p. LC 82-70072. (Illus.). 1982. Set. pap. 20.00 (ISBN 0-87423-031-4). Westburg.

Beck, Emily M., ed. Sailor Historian: The Best of Samuel Eliot Morison. 1977. 15.00 (ISBN 0-395-25444-2). HM.

Beck, Eric. Climber's Guide to Lake Tahoe & Donner Summit. (Illus.). 48p. 1978. pap. 3.95 (ISBN 0-89646-046-0). Outbooks.

--Tutorials in Differential Diagnosis. 2nd ed. 256p. 1982. 35.00x (ISBN 0-272-79638-7, Pub. by Pitman Bks England). State Mutual Bk.

Beck, Eric R., et al. Differential Diagnosis: Internal Medicine. LC 82-71362. (Illus.). 229p. (Orig.). 1983. pap. 17.95 (ISBN 0-668-05622-3, 5622). ACC.

Beck, Ernest W. & Monsen, Harry. Mosby's Atlas of Functional Human Anatomy. LC 81-14110. (Illus.). 310p. 1982. pap. 16.95 (ISBN 0-8016-0554-7). Mosby.

Beck, Eugen A., tr. see Bizzozero, Julius.

Beck, Evelyn T. Kafka & the Yiddish Theater: Its Impact on His Work. LC 75-143763. 270p. 1971. 27.50x (ISBN 0-299-05881-6). U of Wis Pr.

Beck, Evelyn T., jt. auth. see Hermand, Jost.

Beck, Evelyn T., ed. Nice Jewish Girls: A Lesbian Anthology. (Feminist Ser.). 288p. 1984. 20.95 (ISBN 0-89594-138-4); pap. 9.95 (ISBN 0-89594-137-6). Crossing Pr.

Beck, Evelyn T., jt. ed. see Sherman, Julia A.

Beck, F., jt. ed. see Lierse, W.

Beck, Felix & Lloyd, John B., eds. The Cell in Medical Science, 4 vols. Vol. 1, 1974. 49.50 (ISBN 0-12-084201-7); Vol. 2, 1975. 65.00 (ISBN 0-12-084202-5); Vol. 3, 1976. 57.50 (ISBN 0-12-084203-3); Vol. 4, 1976. 57.50 (ISBN 0-12-084204-1). Acad Pr.

Beck, H. & Gundtherodt, H. J., eds. Classy Metals, Vol. 1. (Topics in Applied Physics Ser.: Vol. 46). (Illus.). 350p. 1981. 43.00 (ISBN 0-387-10440-2). Springer-Verlag.

--Glassy Metals I. (Topics in Applied Physics: Vol. 46). (Illus.). 350p. 1981. 43.00 (ISBN 0-387-10440-2). Springer-Verlag.

Beck, H., jt. ed. see Guntherodt, H. J.

Beck, H. G., et al, eds. Kyklos: Griechisches und Byzantinisches: Rudolf Keydell Zum 90. Geburstag. 1978. 46.40x (ISBN 3-11-007211-4). De Gruyter.

Beck, Hans-Georg. Byzantinistik Heute. 1977. 3.90x (ISBN 3-11-007220-3). De Gruyter.

Beck, Harry. The Scarlet Hills. 160p. 1982. 9.95 (ISBN 0-8027-4005-7). Walker & Co.

Beck, Helen. How Books Get That Way. LC 83-71280. (Illus.). 50p. (gr. 3-6). 1983. PLB 15.95 (ISBN 0-940730-01-4); pap. 9.95 (ISBN 0-940730-02-2). Athena Pr ND.

Beck, Henry C. Forgotten Towns of Southern New Jersey. 1984. pap. 9.95 (ISBN 0-8135-1016-3). Rutgers U Pr.

--Jersey Genesis: The Story of the Mullica River. 338p. 1983. pap. 9.95 (ISBN 0-8135-1015-5). Rutgers U Pr.

--The Jersey Midlands. 1983. pap. 11.95 (ISBN 0-8135-1029-5). Rutgers U Pr.

--More Forgotten Towns of Southern New Jersey. 1984. pap. 9.95 (ISBN 0-8135-0432-5). Rutgers U Pr.

--The Roads of Home: Lanes & Legends of New Jersey. 1962. pap. 9.95 (ISBN 0-8135-0405-8). Rutgers U Pr.

--The Roads of Home: Lanes & Legends of New Jersey. 301p. 1983. pap. 9.95 (ISBN 0-8135-1018-X). Rutgers U Pr.

--Tales & Towns of Northern New Jersey. (Illus., Orig.). 1967. pap. 9.95 (ISBN 0-8135-0534-8). Rutgers U Pr.

--Tales & Towns of Northern New Jersey. 357p. 1983. pap. 9.95 (ISBN 0-8135-1019-8). Rutgers U Pr.

Beck, Hilary. Victorian Engravings. (Illus.). 188p. (Orig.). 1984. pap. 9.95 (ISBN 0-901486-64-7, Pub. by Victoria & Albert Mus UK). Faber & Faber.

Beck, Horace. Classification & Nomenclature of Beads & Pendants. (Illus.). 80p. 1973. pap. 10.00 (ISBN 0-87387-083-2). Shumway.

--Folklore & the Sea. LC 73-6011. (The American Maritime Library: Vol. 6). (Illus.). 480p. 1973. ltd. ed. 40.00 (ISBN 0-8195-4063-3); pap. 16.00 (ISBN 0-913372-36-6). Mystic Seaport.

--Folklore & the Sea. LC 83-1616. (Illus.). 480p. 1983. pap. 10.95 (ISBN 0-8289-0499-5). Greene.

Beck, Horace P., ed. Folklore in Action: Essays for Discussion in Honor of MacEdward Leach. LC 62-12687. (American Folklore Society Bibliographic Special Ser.). Repr. of 1962 ed. 23.00 (ISBN 0-527-01130-4). Kraus Repr.

Beck, Hubert S. Stay in the Son-Shine. (Orig.). 1980. pap. text ed. 4.75 (ISBN 0-89536-460-3). CSS of Ohio.

Beck, I., ed. see North American Symposium on Carbenoxolone, Montreal, 1975.

Beck, Isabel. Comprehension During the Acquisition of Decoding Skills. 55p. 1977. 1.50 (ISBN 0-318-14700-9, E*D 145 385). Learn Res Dev.

Beck, Isabel L. & McCaslin, Ellen S. An Analysis of Dimensions that Affect the Development of Code-Breaking Ability in Eight Beginning Reading Programs. 126p. 1978. 2.00 (ISBN 0-318-14692-4). Learn Res Dev.

Beck, Isabel L. & Mitroff, Donna D. The Rationale & Design of a Primary Grades Reading System for an Individualized Classroom. 89p. 1972. 1.50 (ISBN 0-318-14729-7, ED 063 100). Learn Res Dev.

Beck, Isabel L., et al. The Rationale & Design of a Program to Teach Vocabulary to Fourth-Grade Students. 49p. 1980. 1.00 (ISBN 0-318-14730-0). Learn Res Dev.

--Instructional Dimensions that May Affect Reading Comprehension: Examples from Two Commercial Reading Programs. 142p. 1979. 2.00 (ISBN 0-318-14716-5). Learn Res Dev.

Beck, J. M. Joseph Howe: Conservative Reformer 1804-1848, Vol. 1. 400p. 1983. 37.50x (ISBN 0-7735-0387-0); pap. 17.95 (ISBN 0-7735-0445-1). McGill-Queens U Pr.

--Joseph Howe: Vol. 2, The Briton Becomes Canadian 1848-1873. 448p. 1983. 37.50x (ISBN 0-7735-0388-9); pap. 17.95 (ISBN 0-7735-0447-8). McGill-Queens U Pr.

Beck, J. V. & Yao, L. S., eds. Heat Transfer in Porous Media. (HTD Ser.: Vol. 22). 1982. 24.00 (H00250). ASME.

Beck, J. V., et al. Laboratory Manual for General Microbiology. 3rd ed. 1979. spiral bdg. 9.95x (ISBN 0-8087-2884-9). Burgess.

Beck, J. Walter & Davies, John E. Medical Parasitology. 3rd ed. LC 80-25201. (Illus.). 355p. 1981. text ed. 25.95 (ISBN 0-8016-0552-0). Mosby.

Beck, Jacob. Organizational & Representation in Perception. 400p. 1982. text ed. 39.95x (ISBN 0-89859-175-9). L Erlbaum Assocs.

--Surface Color Perception. LC 76-38118. (Illus.). 224p. 1972. 29.50x (ISBN 0-8014-0704-4). Cornell U Pr.

Beck, Jacob, et al, eds. Human & Machine Vision: Symposium. LC 83-9976. (Notes & Reports in Computer Science & Applied Mathematics Ser.). 1983. 47.00 (ISBN 0-12-084320-X). Acad Pr.

Beck, James. Italian Renaissance Painting. LC 80-8640. (Icon Editions Ser.). (Illus.). 416p. 1981. (HarpT); pap. 15.95xi (ISBN 0-06-430082-X, IN 82). Har-Row.

--Leonardo's Rules of Painting: An Unconventional Approach to Modern Art. (Illus.). 1979. 14.95 (ISBN 0-670-42427-7, Studio). Viking.

--Massacio the Documents With the Collaboration of Gino Corti. LC 78-67679. 1978. 12.00 (ISBN 0-686-92649-8). J J Augustin.

--Raphael. LC 73-12198. (Library of Great Painters). 1976. 40.00 (ISBN 0-8109-0432-2). Abrams.

Beck, James, ed. Raphael Before Rome: A Symposium. (Studies in the History of Art: No. 17). (Illus.). 260p. (Orig.). 1985. pap. 22.50x (ISBN 0-89468-080-3, Dist. by U Pr New Eng). Natl Gallery Art.

Beck, James C. The Potentially Violent Patient & the Tarasoff Decision in Psychiatric Practice. LC 84-28241. (Clinical Insights Monograph Ser.). 160p. 1985. pap. text ed. 12.00x (ISBN 0-88048-075-0, 48-075-0). Am Psychiatric.

Beck, James M. May It Please the Court. 1979. Repr. of 1930 ed. lib. bdg. 30.00 (ISBN 0-8495-0399-X). Arden Lib.

--May It Please the Court. facs. ed. McGuire, O. R., ed. LC 75-121447. (Essay Index Reprint Ser). 1930. 27.50 (ISBN 0-8369-1694-8). Ayer Co Pubs.

Beck, James V. & Arnold, Kenneth J. Parameter Estimation in Engineering & Science. LC 77-40293. (Probability & Statistics: Applied Probability & Statistics Section). 501p. 1976. 51.95x (ISBN 0-471-06118-2, Pub. by Wiley-Interscience). Wiley.

Beck, James V. & St. Clair, C. R. Inverse Heat Conduction. 336p. 1985. 34.50 (ISBN 0-471-08319-4). Wiley.

Beck, Jane. The General Store in Vermont: An Oral History. 44p. 1980. pap. 3.50x (ISBN 0-934720-23-1). VT Hist Soc.

Beck, Jane C. Always in Season: Folk Art & Traditional Culture in Vermont. LC 82-70924. (Vermont Council on Arts Ser.). (Illus.). 144p. 1982. pap. 14.95 (ISBN 0-916718-09-3). U Pr of New Eng.

--To Windward of the Land: The Occult World of Alexander Charles. LC 79-84257. (Illus.). 360p. 1979. 17.50x (ISBN 0-253-16065-0). Ind U Pr.

Beck, Jane C., ed. Always in Season: Folk Art & Traditional Culture in Vermont. LC 82-70924. (Illus.). 144p. (Orig.). 1982. pap. 14.95 (ISBN 0-916718-09-3). VT Council Arts.

Beck, Jean & Beck, Louise, eds. Les Chansonniers des Troubadours et des Trouveres publies par Jean Beck, 4 vols. Incl. Chansonnier Cange, 2 vols. Repr. of 1927 ed (ISBN 0-8450-0002-0); Manuscrit du Roi, 2 vols. Repr. of 1938 ed (ISBN 0-8450-0003-9). (Illus., Fr.). 1964. 370.00x set (ISBN 0-8450-0005-5); 185.00x ea. Broude.

Beck, Jerry, jt. auth. see Friedwald, Will.

Beck, Jo, jt. auth. see Vonde, Dee A.

Beck, Joan. Best Beginnings: Giving Your Child a Head Start in Life. 300p. 1983. 14.95 (ISBN 0-399-12683-X, Putnam). Putnam Pub Group.

--How to Raise a Brighter Child. 336p. 1984. pap. 3.95 (ISBN 0-671-50897-0). PB.

Beck, Johann B. Die Melodien der Troubadours. LC 70-39420. Repr. of 1908 ed. 27.50 (ISBN 0-404-08347-1). AMS Pr.

--La Musique Des Troubadours. (Illus.). Repr. of 1910 ed. 19.00 (ISBN 0-404-56526-3). AMS Pr.

Beck, John & Cox, Charles. Advances in Management Education. LC 80-40117. 360p. 1980. 58.95x (ISBN 0-471-27775-4, Pub. by Wiley-Interscience). Wiley.

Beck, John, jt. ed. see Cox, Charles.

Beck, John, et al, eds. Toward a Sociology of Education. LC 77-80869. Orig. Title: World's Apart: Readings for a Sociology of Education. 570p. 1978. pap. text ed. 8.95x (ISBN 0-87855-643-5). Transaction Bks.

Beck, John A., jt. auth. see Ellis, John T.

Beck, John B., jt. auth. see Beck, Theodoric R.

Beck, John H. Understanding the Automobile. 88p. pap. 6.60 (ISBN 0-8428-2288-7). Cambridge Bk.

Beck, Joseph R., jt. auth. see Trzyna, Thomas N.

Beck, Judy & Matthews, William A. Judy Beck's Gourmet Cookbook for a Slimmer You. (Orig.). 1983. pap. 7.95 (ISBN 0-686-46772-8, Wallaby). S&S.

--Judy Beck's Gourmet Cookbook for a Slimmer You. 1983. 8.95 (ISBN 0-671-47462-6, Wallaby). S&S.

Beck, K. C., jt. auth. see Weaver, C. E.

Beck, K. K. Death in a Deck Chair. 192p. 1984. 12.95 (ISBN 0-8027-5601-8). Walker & Co.

Beck, Ken & Clark, Jim. The Andy Griffith Show Book: From Miracle Slave to Kerosene Cucumbers, the Complete Guide to One of Telvision's Best-Loved Shows. (Illus.). 160p. 1985. pap. 11.95 (ISBN 0-312-03654-X). St Martin.

Beck, Kirsten. Cultivating the Wasteland: Can Cable Put the Vision Back in TV? LC 83-12257. (No. 255). (Illus.). 272p. (Orig.). 1983. pap. 14.95 (ISBN 0-915400-34-0). Am Council Arts.

--Cultivating the Wasteland: Can Cable Put the Vision Back in TV. LC 83-12257. 272p. 1983. 14.95 (ISBN 0-915400-34-0, NO. 255). Am Council Arts.

Beck, Kurt. Color Atlas of Laparoscopy. 2nd ed. (Illus.). 528p. 1984. 120.00 (ISBN 0-7216-1612-7). Saunders.

Beck, L., jt. ed. see Bender, H. G.

Beck, L. W., ed. see International Kant Congress, 3rd, University of Rochester, 1970.

Beck, L. W., ed. see Kant International Congress, 3rd.

Beck, L. W., et al. On History Kant. 1963. pap. text ed. write for info. (ISBN 0-02-307860-X). Macmillan.

Beck, L. W., et al, trs. see Kant, Immanuel.

Beck, Leif C. The Physician's Office. LC 77-87555. (Illus.). 1977. 14.95 (ISBN 90-219-0346-6). Excerpta-Princeton.

Beck, Leland. System Software: An Introduction to Systems Programming. 496p. 1985. text ed. 33.95 (ISBN 0-201-10950-6). Addison-Wesley.

Beck, Leslie J. The Metaphysics of Descartes: A Study of the Meditations. LC 79-14519. 1979. Repr. of 1965 ed. lib. bdg. 25.00x (ISBN 0-313-21480-8, BEMD). Greenwood.

Beck, Lewis C. A Gazetteer of the States of Illinois & Missouri. fascimile ed. LC 75-84. (Mid-American Frontier Ser.). 1975. Repr. of 1823 ed. 34.00x (ISBN 0-405-06853-0). Ayer Co Pubs.

Beck, Lewis W. The Actor & the Spectator. LC 75-2771. (Cassirer Lectures). 160p. 1975. 15.00x (ISBN 0-300-01899-1). Yale U Pr.

--A Commentary of Kant's "Critique of Practical Reason". LC 60-5464. (Midway Reprint Ser.). xiv, 306p. 1984. pap. text ed. 12.00x (ISBN 0-226-04076-3). U of Chicago Pr.

--Critique of Practical Reason: Kant. 1956. pap. text ed. write for info. (ISBN 0-02-307760-3). Macmillan.

--Early German Philosophy: Kant & His Predecessors. LC 79-75427. 1969. 32.50x (ISBN 0-674-22125-7, Belknap Pr). Harvard U Pr.

--Essays on Kant & Hume. LC 77-19999. 1978. 22.50x (ISBN 0-300-02170-4). Yale U Pr.

--Foundations of the Metaphysics of Morals & What Is Enlight? Kant. (LLA Ser.: No. 113). 1959. pap. text ed. write for info. (ISBN 0-02-307720-4). Macmillan.

--Perpetual Peace: Kant. 1957. pap. text ed. write for info. (ISBN 0-02-307750-6). Macmillan.

--Studies in the Philosophy of Kant. LC 81-7247. (Essay & Monograph Series of the Liberal Arts Press). viii, 242p. 1981. Repr. of 1965 ed. lib. bdg. 25.00x (ISBN 0-313-23183-4, BESK). Greenwood.

Beck, Lewis W., jt. auth. see Mahaffy, Carcus.

Beck, Lewis W., ed. Eighteenth Century Philosophy. LC 66-10364. (Orig.). 1966. pap. text ed. 13.95 (ISBN 0-02-902100-6). Free Pr.

--Kant Studies Today. LC 68-57207. ix, 516p. (Orig.). 1969. 29.95x (ISBN 0-87548-028-4). Open Court.

Beck, Lewis W., ed. see Fischer, Kuno.

Beck, Lewis W., ed. see Kant, Immanuel.

Beck, Lewis W., ed. see Macmillan, R. A.

Beck, Lewis W., ed. see Prichard, H. A.

Beck, Lewis W., ed. see Schilpp, Paul A.

Beck, Lewis W., ed. see Seth, Andrew.

Beck, Lewis W., ed. see Vaihinger, Hans.

Beck, Lewis W., ed. see Ward, James.

Beck, Lewis W., ed. see Watson, John.

Beck, Lewis W., tr. see Kant, Immanuel.

Beck, Lewis W., et al. Kant's Latin Writings in English Translation. LC 84-48030. (American University Studies V; Philosophy: Vol. 9). 1986. text ed. 33.00 (ISBN 0-8204-0167-6). P Lang Pubs.

Beck, Lily A. Gallants. facs. ed. LC 76-128207. (Essay Index Reprint Ser.). 1924. 19.00 (ISBN 0-8369-1864-9). Ayer Co Pubs.

--The Ladies' A Shining Constellation of Wit & Beauty. facsimile ed. LC 71-156612. (Essay Index Reprint Ser). Repr. of 1922 ed. 20.00 (ISBN 0-8369-2268-9). Ayer Co Pubs.

Beck, Lois & Keddie, Nikki, eds. Women in the Muslim World. LC 78-3633. 1978. 37.50x (ISBN 0-674-95480-7); pap. 12.50 (ISBN 0-674-95481-5). Harvard U Pr.

Beck, Louise, jt. ed. see Beck, Jean.

Beck, M. B. Water Quality Management: A Review of the Development & Application of Mathematical Models. (Lecture Notes in Engineering Ser.: Vol. 11). viii, 107p. 1985. pap. 10.50 (ISBN 0-387-13986-9). Springer-Verlag.

Beck, M. B. & Van Straten, G., eds. Uncertainty & Forecasting of Water Quality. (Illus.). 386p. 1983. 36.00 (ISBN 0-387-12419-5). Springer-Verlag.

Beck, M. Susan. Kidspeak: How Your Child Develops Language Skills. 144p. 1982. pap. 4.95 (ISBN 0-452-25376-4, Plume). NAL.

Beck, Madeline H. & Williamson, Lamar, Jr. Mastering New Testament Facts, 4 bks. Incl. Bk. 1. Introduction & Synoptic Gospels (ISBN 0-8042-0326-1); Bk. 2. The Fourth Gospel & Acts (ISBN 0-8042-0327-X); Bk. 3. Pauline Letters (ISBN 0-8042-0328-8); Bk. 4. The General Letters & Revelation (ISBN 0-8042-0329-6). (Illus., Orig.). 1973. pap. 4.95 ea.; pap. 14.95 set. John Knox.

--Mastering Old Testament Facts, 4 bks. Incl. Bk. 1. Introduction on-Deut. 1979 (ISBN 0-8042-0134-X); Bk. 2. Joshua-Esther. 1979 (ISBN 0-8042-0135-8). (Illus., Orig.). pap. text ed. 4.95 ea.; pap. text ed. 14.95 set. John Knox.

--Mastering Old Testament Facts, Bk. 4: Isaiah-Malachi. (Mastering Old Testament Facts Ser.). (Illus.). 112p. (Orig.). (gr. 9-12). 1981. pap. 4.95 (ISBN 0-8042-0137-4). John Knox.

Beck, Mary Ann, et al, eds. The Analysis of Hispanic Texts: Current Trends in Methodology. LC 76-5741. (First York College Colloquium). 1976. pap. 14.00x (ISBN 0-916950-00-X). Biling Rev-Pr.

Beck, Mary E. Nutrition & Dietetics for Nurses. 7th ed. (Churchill Livingstone Nursing Texts Ser.). (Illus.). 1984. pap. text ed. 11.50 (ISBN 0-443-03121-5). Churchill.

Beck, Melvin. Secret Contenders: The Myth of Cold War Counterintelligence. (Illus.). 192p. 1984. 14.95 (ISBN 0-940380-05-6); pap. 7.95 (ISBN 0-940380-04-8). Sheridan Square Pubns.

Beck, Morris. Government Spending: Trends & Issues. LC 81-5007. 156p. 1981. 26.95 (ISBN 0-03-058629-1). Praeger.

Beck, Norman A. Mature Christianity: The Recognition & Repudiation of the Anti-Jewish Polemic of the New Testament. LC 83-51047. (Illus.). 328p. 1985. 19.50 (ISBN 0-941664-03-1). Susquehanna U.

--Scripture Notes: Common Consensus Lectionary. (B Ser.). 1984. 7.25 (ISBN 0-89536-687-8, 4863). CSS of Ohio.

Beck, Otto W. Art Principles ub Portrait Photography. LC 72-9181. (The Literature of Photography Ser.). Repr. of 1907 ed. 24.00 (ISBN 0-405-04892-0). Ayer Co Pubs.

Beck, P. Case Exercises in Clinical Reasoning. 1981. 26.50 (ISBN 0-8151-0597-5). Year Bk Med.

Beck, P. G. & Forster, M. C. Six Rural Problem Areas: Relief-Resources-Rehabilitation. LC 71-165679. (Research Monograph: Vol. 1). 1971. Repr. of 1935 ed. lib. bdg. 22.50 (ISBN 0-306-70333-5). Da Capo.

Beck, Pamela & Massman, Patti. Fling. LC 84-4043. 288p. 1984. 13.95 (ISBN 0-87131-432-0). M Evans.

--Fling. 480p. 1985. pap. 3.95 (ISBN 0-440-12615-0). Dell.

Beck, Paul, et al. Individual Energy Conservation Behaviors. LC 80-12699. 240p. 1980. text ed. 35.00 (ISBN 0-89946-018-6). Oelgeschlager.

Beck, Paul A., ed. Electronic Structure & Alloy Chemistry of the Transition Elements. LC 62-18701. pap. 65.30 (ISBN 0-317-08750-9, 2000679). Bks Demand UMI.

Beck, Paul A., jt. ed. see Rowland, T. J.

Beck, Peggy V. & Walters, Anna L. The Sacred: Ways of Knowledge, Sources of Life. (Illus.). 384p. 1977. 14.40x (ISBN 0-912586-24-9). Navajo Coll Pr.

Beck, Phillip. Oradour: Village of the Dead. vii, 88p. 1979. 15.00 (ISBN 0-686-70591-2). Shoe String.

Beck, R. E. & Kolman, B. Computers in Nonassociative Rings & Algebras. 1977. 45.00 (ISBN 0-12-083850-8). Acad Pr.

Beck, R. H., et al. Introductory Soil Science: A Laboratory Manual. (Illus.). 276p. 1984. 10.80x (ISBN 0-87563-222-X). Stipes.

Beck, R. N. & Orr, J. B. Ethical Choice: A Case Study Approach. LC 70-122282. 1970. pap. text ed. 10.95 (ISBN 0-02-902060-3). Free Pr.

Beck, R. Theodore. The Cutting Edge: The Early History of the Surgeons of London. 232p. 1980. 35.00x (ISBN 0-85331-366-0, Pub. by Lund Humphries England). State Mutual Bk.

Beck, Richard. History of Icelandic Poets, Eighteen Hundred to Nineteen-Forty. (Islandica Ser.: Vol. 34). 1950. 24.00 (ISBN 0-527-00364-6). Kraus Repr.

Beck, Richard, ed. Icelandic Poems & Stories. facsimile ed. LC 68-57059. (Short Story Index Reprint Ser.). 1943. 20.00 (ISBN 0-8369-6001-7). Ayer Co Pubs.

Beck, Robert. Airtight Willie & Me. (Orig.). 1979. pap. 2.25 (ISBN 0-87067-031-X, BH031). Holloway.

--Death Wish. (Orig.). 1976. pap. 2.25 (ISBN 0-87067-075-1, BH075). Holloway.

--Experiencing Biography. (gr. 10 up). 1978. pap. text ed. 8.75x (ISBN 0-8104-6034-3); tchr's ed. 1.75 (ISBN --8104-6125-0, 6125). Boynton Cook Pubs.

--Long White Con. (Orig.). 1977. pap. 2.25 (ISBN 0-87067-030-1, BH030). Holloway.

--Mama Black Widow. (Orig.). 1970. pap. 2.95 (ISBN 0-87067-808-6, BH808). Holloway.

--Naked Soul of Iceberg Slim. (Orig.). 1971. pap. 2.75 (ISBN 0-87067-709-8, BH709). Holloway.

--Pimp: The Story of My Life. (Orig.). 1969. pap. 2.95 (ISBN 0-87067-806-X, BH806). Holloway.

--Trick Baby. 1969. pap. 3.25 (ISBN 0-87067-807-8, BH827). Holloway.

Beck, Robert, jt. auth. see Kolman, Bernard.

Beck, Robert, ed. see Brightman, Edgar S.

Beck, Robert A., jt. auth. see Zapsalis, Charles.

Beck, Robert C. Applying Psychology: Understanding People. (Illus.). 480p. 1982. 27.95 (ISBN 0-13-043463-9). P-H.

--Applying Psychology: Understanding People. 2nd ed. (Illus.). 496p. 1986. 26.95 (ISBN 0-13-043480-9). P-H.

--Motivation: Theories & Principles. (Illus.). 480p. 1983. text ed. 28.95 (ISBN 0-13-603910-3). P-H.

Beck, Robert E. & Goplerud, C. Peter, III. Waters & Water Rights, Vol. 3: Water Pollution & Water Quality Legal Controls. 2nd ed. 1984. text ed. 45.00x (ISBN 0-87473-177-1); 1985 suppl. incl. A Smith Co.

--Waters & Water Rights, Vol. 3: Water Pollution & Water Quality: Legal Controls, 1985 Supplement. 1985. pap. text ed. 12.50x (ISBN 0-87473-212-3). A Smith Co.

Beck, Robert H. Change & Harmonization in European Education. LC 75-167299. pap. 55.50 (ISBN 0-317-29401-6, 2055841). Bks Demand UMI.

Beck, Robert H., et al. The Changing Structure of Europe: Economic, Social, & Political Trends. LC 73-110659. pap. 74.00 (ISBN 0-317-29403-2, 2055840). Bks Demand UMI.

Beck, Robert N. Meaning of Americanism. 1957. 5.00 (ISBN 0-8022-0087-7). Philos Lib.

--Perspectives in Philosophy: A Book of Readings. 3rd ed. LC 74-20804. 1975. pap. text ed. 23.95 (ISBN 0-03-089645-2, HoltC). HR&W.

Beck, Roger. Microeconomic Analysis of Issues in Business, Government & Society. (Illus.). 1978. pap. text ed. 26.95 (ISBN 0-07-004253-5). McGraw.

Beck, Roger B. A Bibliography of Africana in the Institute for Sex Research, Indiana University. (African Humanities Ser.). 134p. (Orig.). 1979. pap. text ed. 5.00 (ISBN 0-941934-29-2). Indiana Africa.

Beck, Ron, et al. Market Analysis of the Potential for Wind Systems Use in Remote & Isolated Area Applications. 180p. 1983. pap. 95.00 (ISBN 0-88016-002-0). Windbks.

Beck, Ronald D. Plastic Product Design. 2nd ed. 424p. 1980. 32.95 (ISBN 0-442-20632-1). Van Nos Reinhold.

--Plastic Product Design. 2nd ed. (Illus.). 424p. 1980. 33.00 (ISBN 0-686-48180-1, 0206). T-C Pubns CA.

Beck, Samuel J. Psychological Processes in the Schizophrenic Adaptation. LC 65-12065. (Illus.). 432p. 1965. 62.00 (ISBN 0-8089-0040-4, 790475). Grune.

--Rorschach's Test, 3 vols. Incl. Vol. 1. Basic Processes. 3rd ed. LC 60-15724. (Illus.). 248p. 1961. 30.50 (ISBN 0-8089-0036-6, 790465); Vol. 2. Gradients in Mental Disorder. 3rd ed. Molish, H. B. LC 49-11667. 416p. 1978. 40.50 (ISBN 0-8089-1121-X, 790470); Vol. 3. Advances in Interpretation. LC 44-3779. 320p. 1953. 34.00 (ISBN 0-8089-0038-2, 790467). Grune.

Beck, Sanderson & Holmes, Mark T. Across the Golden Bridge. 1974. 8.00 (ISBN 0-88238-972-6). Baraka Bk.

Beck, Simone. Simca's Cuisine. (Illus.). 1972. 17.95 (ISBN 0-394-47449-X). Knopf.

--Simca's Cuisine. 1976. pap. 6.95 (ISBN 0-394-72105-5, Vin). Random.

Beck, Stanley D. Insect Photoperiodism. 2nd ed. LC 80-10098. 1980. 50.00 (ISBN 0-12-084380-3). Acad Pr.

Beck, Stanley M. & Bernier, Ivan, eds. Canada & the New Constitution: The Unfinished Agenda, 2 Vols. 1983. Vol. 1, 399p. pap. text ed. 16.95x set (ISBN 0-920380-75-1, Pub. by Inst Res Pub Canada); Vol. 2, 289p. pap. text ed. (ISBN 0-920380-77-8). Brookfield Pub Co.

Beck, Stevie, et al. Winnings Ways on the Autoharp, 2 vols, Vol. 1 & 2. Blackley, Becky, ed. (Illus.). 52p. 1985. pap. 8.95 (ISBN 0-912827-05-X); pap. 8.95 (ISBN 0-912827-06-8). I A D Pubns.

Beck, Sue, pseud. How to Buy Your Home... & Do It Right. 252p. 1984. pap. 10.95 (ISBN 0-9614583-0-5). Evans Pub.

Beck, Susan E. see Beck, Sue, pseud.

Beck, Sydney & Roth, Elizabeth. Music in Prints: Fifty-Two Prints Illustrating Musical Instruments from the 15th Century to the Present. LC 65-13045. (Illus.). 1965. 15.00 (ISBN 0-87104-124-3). NY Pub Lib.

Beck, Sydney, ed. see Morley, Thomas.

Beck, Syndey, ed. English Instrumental Music of the Sixteenth & Seventeenth Centuries from Manuscripts in the New York Public Library, 2 vols. Incl. Vol. 1. Nine Fantasies in Four Parts. Byrd, et al.; Vol. 2. Four Suites. Locke, Mathew. write to C.F. Peters Corp. N.Y. for prices (ISBN 0-685-22863-0). NY Pub Lib.

Beck, Mrs. Theodore, tr. see Underhill, Evelyn.

Beck, Theodore R., et al, eds. Electrochemical Contributions to Environmental Protection. LC 72-89668. (Illus.). pap. 45.00 (ISBN 0-317-10703-8, 2052001). Bks Demand UMI.

Beck, Theodric R. & Beck, John B. Elements of Medical Jurisprudence, 2 vols. LC 75-23681. Repr. of 1860 ed. Set. 73.50 (ISBN 0-404-13310-X). AMS Pr.

Beck, Thomas. French Legislators Eighteen Hundred to Eighteen Thirty-Four: A Study in Quantitative History. LC 73-83059. 1975. 38.00x (ISBN 0-520-02535-0). U of Cal Pr.

Beck, Thomasina. Embroidered Gardens. (Illus.). 1979. 19.95 (ISBN 0-670-29260-5, Studio). Viking.

Beck, Trudy, jt. auth. see Green, Laurel.

Beck, Walter G. Beitrage Zur Kulturgeschichte der Afrikanischen Feldarbeit. Repr. of 1943 ed. 19.00 (ISBN 0-384-03705-4). Johnson Repr.

Beck, Warren. Imagination & Four Other One-Act Plays for Boys & Girls. LC 77-89720. (One-Act Plays in Reprint Ser.). (gr. 3-10). Repr. of 1925 ed. 17.00x (ISBN 0-8486-2026-7). Core Collection.

--Rest Is Silence & Other Stories. LC 63-12585. 132p. (Orig.). 1963. pap. 5.95 (ISBN 0-8040-0261-4, 82-71835, Pub. by Swallow). Ohio U Pr.

Beck, Warren A. New Mexico: A History of Four Centuries. LC 62-16470. (Illus.). 1979. Repr. of 1962 ed. 19.95 (ISBN 0-8061-0533-X). U of Okla Pr.

Beck, Warren A. & Clowers, Myles L. Understanding American History Through Fiction, 2 vols. 480p. 1975. Vol. 1: U.S. Colonial to 1877. pap. text ed. 20.95 (ISBN 0-07-004217-9); Vol. 2: 1865 to Present. pap. text ed. 20.95 (ISBN 0-07-004218-7). McGraw.

Beck, Warren A. & Haase, Ynez D. Historical Atlas of California. LC 74-5952. (Illus.). 240p. 1975. pap. 14.95 (ISBN 0-8061-1212-3). U of Okla Pr.

--Historical Atlas of New Mexico. LC 68-31366. (Illus.). 152p. 1969. pap. 11.95 (ISBN 0-8061-0817-7). U of Okla Pr.

Beck, Warren A. & Williams, David A. California: A History of the Golden State. LC 71-186005. (Illus.). 1972. 17.95 (ISBN 0-385-06267-2). Doubleday.

Beck, William. Money & Banking. 1980. lib. bdg. 69.95 (ISBN 0-8490-3095-1). Gordon Pr.

Beck, William C. & Trier, James R. Programmed Course in Basic Algebra. (Mathematics Ser). 1971. pap. 17.95 (ISBN 0-201-00445-3). Addison-Wesley.

Beck, William C. & Meyer, Ralph, eds. Health Care Environment: The User's Viewpoint. 272p. 1982. 84.50 (ISBN 0-8493-6150-8). CRC Pr.

Beck, William F. The Holy Bible in the Language of Today: An American Translation. 1977. 16.95 (ISBN 0-87981-082-3). Holman.

Beck, William F., tr. Christ of the Gospels. rev. ed. LC 59-11068. 1959. pap. 6.95 (ISBN 0-570-03724-7, 12-2626). Concordia.

Beck, William S., jt. auth. see Simpson, George G.

Beck, William S., ed. Hematology. 3rd ed. (Illus.). 448p. 1981. text ed. 40.00x (ISBN 0-262-02216-8); pap. text ed. 17.50x (ISBN 0-262-52097-4). MIT Pr.

Becke, Archibald F. Napoleon & Waterloo: The Emperor's Campaign with the Armee Du Nord 1815, 2 vols. facsimile ed. LC 73-160958. (Select Bibliographies Reprint Ser). Repr. of 1914 ed. Set. 66.00 (ISBN 0-8369-5825-X). Ayer Co Pubs.

Becke, Louis. By Reef & Palm. facs. ed. LC 75-116938. (Short Story Index Reprint Ser). 1895. 17.00 (ISBN 0-8369-3440-7). Ayer Co Pubs.

--Pacific Tales. facsimile ed. LC 70-98561. (Short Story Index Reprint Ser.). 1897. 19.00 (ISBN 0-8369-3135-1). Ayer Co Pubs.

--Rodman the Boat-Steerer, & Other Stories. facs. ed. LC 70-125206. (Short Story Index Reprint Ser). 1924. 19.00 (ISBN 0-8369-3573-X). Ayer Co Pubs.

--South Sea Supercargo. Day, A. Grove, ed. LC 68-18937. (YA) 1967. Repr. 10.00x (ISBN 0-87022-060-8). UH Pr.

--Under Tropic Skies. facsimile ed. LC 73-113650. (Short Story Index Reprint Ser.). 1905. 17.00 (ISBN 0-8369-3379-6). Ayer Co Pubs.

--Yorke the Adventurer, & Other Stories. facsimile ed. LC 71-37535. (Short Story Index Reprint Ser.). Repr. of 1925 ed. 18.00 (ISBN 0-8369-4094-6). Ayer Co Pubs.

Beckelman, Florance & Dreiblatt, Lorraine. Some Things Special for Shabbat. 1977. pap. 6.95 (ISBN 0-933054-03-3). Ricwalt Pub Co.

Beckenbach. College Algebra. 6th ed. write for info. Watts.

Beckenbach, et al. College Algebra. 6th ed. 1984. write for info (ISBN 0-534-03653-8). Wadsworth Pub.

--Modern College Algebra & Trigonometry. 5th ed. 1985. text ed. write for info. Wadsworth Pub.

Beckenbach, E. F. & Bellman, R. Inequalities. LC 62-4593. (Ergebnisse der Mathematik und Ihrer Grenzgebiete: Vol. 30). (Illus.). 1971. 29.50 (ISBN 0-387-03283-5). Springer-Verlag.

--An Introduction to Inequalities. LC 61-6228. (New Mathematical Library: No. 3). 135p. 1975. pap. 8.75 (ISBN 0-88385-603-4). Math Assn.

Beckenbach, Edwin & Grady, Mike. Functions & Graphs. 3rd ed. 592p. 1982. text ed. write for info. (ISBN 0-534-01180-2). Wadsworth Pub.

Beckenbach, Edwin & Walter, Wolfgang. General Inequalities, Pt. 3. (International Numerical Mathematics Ser.: Vol. 64). 592p. 1983. text ed. 54.95 (ISBN 3-7643-1539-3). Birkhauser.

Beckenbach, Edwin, ed. General Inequalities II. (International Ser. of Numerical Mathematics: No. 47). 505p. 1980. pap. 45.95x (ISBN 0-8176-1056-1). Birkhauser.

Beckenbach, Edwin F. & Tompkins, Charles B. Concepts of Communication: Interpersonal, Intrapersonal, & Mathematical. LC 70-161492. 462p. 1971. 29.50 (ISBN 0-471-06120-4). Krieger.

Beckenbach, Edwin F., ed. Applied Combinatorial Mathematics. LC 80-12457. 630p. 1981. Repr. of 1964 ed. lib. bdg. 42.50 (ISBN 0-89874-172-6). Krieger.

Beckenbach, F., ed. General Inequalities I. (International Ser. of Numerical Mathematics: No. 41). 332p. 1978. 44.95x (ISBN 0-8176-0972-5). Birkhauser.

Beckenstein, jt. auth. see Narici.

Beckenstein, Alan, et al. Performance Measurement of the Petroleum Industry: Functional Profitability & Alternatives. LC 79-1951. (Illus.). 1979. 26.50x (ISBN 0-669-03017-1). Lexington Bks.

Beckenstein, E., et al. Topological Algebras. (Mathematical Studies: Vol. 24). 370p. 1977. pap. 59.75 (ISBN 0-7204-0724-9, North-Holland). Elsevier.

Becker. Phosphates & Phosphoric Acid. (Fertilizer Science & Technology Ser.). 592p. 1983. 95.00 (ISBN 0-8247-1712-0). Dekker.

Becker, jt. auth. see Thieme.

Becker, et al. The Garland Dickens Bibliographies: A Concordance to the Poems of John Keats. 1981. lib. bdg. 90.00 (ISBN 0-8240-9807-2). Garland Pub.

Becker, A., tr. see Keller, Conrad.

Becker, A., tr. see Keller, Conrad P.

Becker, A., jt. auth. see Angerhausen, M.

Becker, A. L. & Yengoyan, Aram, eds. The Imagination of Reality: Essays in Southeast Asian Coherence Systems. LC 79-15675. (Language & Being Ser.). (Illus.). 1979. 35.00x (ISBN 0-89391-021-X). Ablex Pub.

Becker, Abraham S. Economic Leverage on the Soviet Union in the 1980's. LC 84-11700. 1984. write for info. (ISBN 0-8330-0577-4). Rand Corp.

--Economic Relations with the U. S. S. R. Issues for the Western Alliance. LC 83-47991. 192p. 1983. 23.00x (ISBN 0-669-06794-6). Lexington Bks.

--Military Expenditure Limitation for Arms Control: Problems & Prospects-With a Documentary History of Recent Proposals. LC 77-8224. 368p. 1977. prof ref 29.95 (ISBN 0-88410-470-2). Ballinger Pub.

--Soviet National Income, Nineteen Fifty-Eight to Nineteen Sixty-Four: National Accounts of the USSR in the Seven Year Plan Period. LC 70-77483. (Illus.). 1969. 53.50x (ISBN 0-520-01437-5). U of Cal Pr.

Becker, Alida, ed. The Tolkien Scrapbook. LC 79-11435. (Illus.). (gr. 5 up). 1979. lib. bdg. 19.80 (ISBN 0-89471-083-4); pap. 7.95 (ISBN 0-89471-082-6). Running Pr.

Becker, Anne, ed. see Yueh, Jean.

Becker, Anton E. & Anderson, Robert H. Cardiac Pathology: An Intergrated Text & Color Atlas. (Illus.). 280p. 1984. text ed. 97.00 (ISBN 0-89004-972-6). Raven.

Becker, Anton E., jt. auth. see Anderson, Robert H.

Becker, Anton E., jt. auth. see Gussenhoven, Elma J.

Becker, Arthur H. The Compassionate Visitor: Resources for Ministering to People Who Are Ill. 128p. (Orig.). 1985. pap. 5.50 (ISBN 0-8066-2094-3, 10-1620). Augsburg.

Becker, Arthur P., ed. see Committee on Taxation Resources & Economic Development Symposium, 4th.

Becker, Benjamin. Legal Checklists: 1982, 2 vols. LC 82-4513. 1968. 150.00; Suppl., 1982. 54.00; Suppl., 1983. 61.00. Callaghan.

Becker, Benjamin & Savin, Bernard. Legal Checklists Specially Selected Forms: 1977, 1 vol. LC 76-56745. Set. 75.00 (ISBN 0-317-12018-2). Callaghan.

Becker, Benjamin M. & Roth, Ben M. A Simplified Approach to Planning Estates: Problems and Solutions. 204p. 1982. 14.95 (ISBN 0-87863-143-7). Farnswth Pub.

Becker, Benjamin M. & Savin, Bernard. Illinois Lawyer's Manual, 2 Vols. LC 60-1143. 1982. 155.00. Callaghan.

Becker, Benjamin M. & Tillman, Fred A. The Family Owned Business. 2nd ed. 400p. 1978. 17.50 (ISBN 0-317-04277-7, 5370). Commerce.

Becker, Bernard H. Scientific London. 340p. 1968. Repr. of 1847 ed. 29.50x (ISBN 0-7146-2328-8, F Cass Co). Biblio Dist.

Becker, Betty G. & Fendler, Dolores T. Vocational & Personal Adjustments in Practical Nursing. 4th ed. LC 81-14041. (Illus.). 180p. 1982. pap. text ed. 12.95 (ISBN 0-8016-0566-0). Mosby.

Becker, Beverly. Someone Special. (Comprehensive Charm Course Ser.). (Illus.). 1978. 14.95 (ISBN 0-9602000-0-2). B Becker.

Becker, Bill. An Immediate Desire to Survive. 32p. 1985. 5.95 (ISBN 0-8059-2989-4). Dorrance.

Becker, Bruce. Backgammon for Blood. 1975. pap. 2.95 (ISBN 0-380-00384-8, 59444-7). Avon.

Becker, C. History of the Catholic Missions in Northeast India. 1980. 32.00x (ISBN 0-8364-0600-1, Pub. by Mukhopadhyay India). South Asia Bks.

Becker, C. D & Fujihara, M. D. The Bacterial Pathogen Flexibacter Columnaris & Its Epizotiology Among Columbia River Fish. (AFS Monographs: No. 2). 94p. 1978. 9.00 (ISBN 0-913235-13-X); members 7.00 (ISBN 0-317-32533-7). Am Fisheries Soc.

Becker, C. H. Christianity & Islam. Chaytor, H. J., tr. LC 74-608. 120p. 1974. Repr. of 1909 ed. lib. bdg. 18.50 (ISBN 0-8337-4816-5). B Franklin.

Becker, C. J. The Joy of Automobile Repair. 1979. pap. 5.95 (ISBN 0-89581-025-5). Asian Human Pr.

Becker, Calvin W. First & Second Timothy & Titus: Letters to Two Young Men. (Teach Yourself the Bible Ser.). 1961. pap. 2.25 (ISBN 0-8024-2646-8). Moody.

Becker, Carl. Declaration of Independence. 14.25 (ISBN 0-8446-1619-2). Peter Smith.

--Eve of the Revolution. 1918. 8.50x (ISBN 0-686-83540-9). Elliots Bks.

Becker, Carl see Johnson, Allen & Nevins, Allan.

Becker, Carl, et al. Spirit of Seventy-Six & Other Essays. (Brookings Institution Reprint Ser). Repr. of 1927 ed. lib. bdg. 20.00x (ISBN 0-697-00150-4). Irvington.

Becker, Carl A., ed. History & Handbook of the American College of Nursing Home Administrators. 148p. 1982. 10.00 (ISBN 0-318-17652-1). Am Coll Health.

Becker, Carl H. Beitrage zur Geschichte Agyptens unter Dem Islam, 2 vols. in 1. LC 77-10579. (Studies in Islamic History: No. 5). 1978. Repr. of 1903 ed. lib. bdg. 19.50x (ISBN 0-87991-454-8). Porcupine Pr.

Becker, Carl L. Declaration of Independence: A Study in the History of Political Ideas. 1958. pap. 4.95 (ISBN 0-394-70060-0, V-60, Vin). Random.

--Detachment & the Writing of History: Essays & Letters of Carl L. Becker. Snyder, Phil L., ed. LC 70-152590. 240p. 1972. Repr. of 1958 ed. lib. bdg. 15.00 (ISBN 0-8371-6023-5, BEWH). Greenwood.

--Freedom & Responsibility in the American Way of Life. LC 80-11156. (University of Michigan, William W. Cook Foundation Lectures: Vol. 1). 1980. Repr. of 1945 ed. lib. bdg. 22.50x (ISBN 0-313-22361-0, BEFA). Greenwood.

--Heavenly City of the Eighteenth-Century Philosophers. (Storrs Lectures Ser.). 1932. pap. 5.95x (ISBN 0-300-00017-0, Y5). Yale U Pr.

--History of Political Parties in the Province of New York, 1760-1776. 324p. 1960. pap. 11.75x (ISBN 0-299-02024-X). U of Wis Pr.

--How New Will the Better World Be? A Discussion of Post-War Reconstruction. facsimile ed. LC 72-134051. (Essay Index Reprint Ser). Repr. of 1944 ed. 20.00 (ISBN 0-8369-2482-7). Ayer Co Pubs.

--Progress & Power. LC 83-45701. Repr. of 1949 ed. 21.50 (ISBN 0-404-20023-0). AMS Pr.

--Safeguarding Civil Liberty Today. 1949. 11.25 (ISBN 0-8446-1064-X). Peter Smith.

Becker, Carl M. The Village: A History of Germantown, Ohio, 1804-1976. LC 80-16683. (Historical Society of Germantown, Ohio Ser.). (Illus.). xvi, 209p. 1980. 15.00 (ISBN 0-8214-0550-0, 82-83434). Ohio U Pr.

Becker, Carol, jt. ed. see Spiegel, Steven L.

Becker, Carol A. Community Information Service: A Directory of Public Library Involvement. LC 74-620019. (Student Contribution Ser.: No. 5). 1974. pap. 5.00 (ISBN 0-911808-09-4). U of Md Lib Serv.

Becker, Charles E. & Row, Robert L. Alcohol as a Drug: A Curriculum on Pharmacology, Neurology & Toxicology. 99p. 1974. 8.00 (ISBN 0-318-15278-9). Natl Coun Alcoholism.

Becker, Charles E., et al. Alcohol As a Drug. LC 78-10584. 114p. 1979. pap. 6.95 (ISBN 0-88275-766-0). Krieger.

Becker, Charles H. Plant Manager's Handbook. 304p. 1974. 42.00. P-H.

Becker, Clarence F. Solar Radiation Availability on Surfaces in the U. S. as Affected by Season, Orientation, Latitude, Altitude, & Cloudiness. Bruchey, Stuart, ed. LC 78-22659. (Energy in the American Economy Ser.). (Illus.). 1979. lib. bdg. 14.00x (ISBN 0-405-11963-1). Ayer Co Pubs.

Becker, Colette, ed. see Zola, Emile.

Becker, Daniel E. Pharmacology for the Health Professional. text ed. 22.95 (ISBN 0-8359-5531-1); instr's. manual avail. (ISBN 0-8359-5532-X). Reston.

Becker, David G. The New Bourgeoisie & the Limits of Dependency: Mining, Class, & Power in "Revolutionary" Peru. LC 82-61352. 368p. 1983. 35.00x (ISBN 0-691-07645-6); pap. 9.95 (ISBN 0-691-02213-5). Princeton U Pr.

Becker, David P. Old Master Drawings at Bowdoin College. LC 84-72390. (Illus.). 260p. (Orig.). 1985. pap. 14.95 (ISBN 0-916606-08-2). Bowdoin Coll.

Becker, Dennis. Study Guide to Hide or Seek. 64p. (Orig.). 1981. pap. 4.95 (ISBN 0-8007-0859-8). Revell.

Becker, Dennis, ed. see Becker, Nancy, et al.

Becker, Dennis, ed. see Becker, Nancy & Braun, Jack.

Becker, Donald. Reverse Dictionary of Urdu. (Urdu.). 1980. 38.00x (ISBN 0-8364-0656-7, Pub. by Manohaar India). South Asia Bks.

Becker, Donald C. Security Administration: A Practical Systems Approach. 224p. 1985. 22.75x (ISBN 0-398-05064-3). C C Thomas.

Becker, Donald P., et al. Head Injury. (Illus.). 700p. Date not set. price not set (ISBN 0-7216-1614-3). Saunders.

Becker, E., ed. see International Congress of Applied Mechanics, 13th, Moscow.

Becker, E. B., jt. auth. see Oden, J. T.

Becker, E. I. & Tsutsui, M., eds. Organometallic Reactions & Syntheses, Vol. 6. LC 74-92108. (Illus.). 314p. 1977. 55.00 (ISBN 0-306-39906-7, Plenum Pr). Plenum Pub.

Becker, Edwin D. High Resolution NMR: Theory & Chemical Applications. 2nd. ed. LC 79-20540. 1980. 36.50 (ISBN 0-12-084660-8). Acad Pr.

Becker, Elle F. Female Sexuality Following Spinal Cord Injury. Cross, Leland L., et al, eds. (Illus.). 1978. pap. 10.95 (ISBN 0-915708-07-8). Cheever Pub.

Becker, Elmer L., et al, eds. Biochemistry of the Acute Allergic Reactions: Fourth International Symposium. LC 81-5975. (Kroc Foundation Ser.: Vol. 14). 370p. 1981. 52.00 (ISBN 0-8451-0304-0). A R Liss.

Becker, Eric B., et al. Finite Elements: An Introduction, Vol. I. (Illus.). 256p. 1981. 37.95 (ISBN 0-13-317057-8). P-H.

Becker, Eric V. de see De Becker, Eric V.

Becker, Ernest. The Birth & Death of Meaning. 2nd ed. LC 62-15359. 228p. 1975. 11.95 (ISBN 0-02-902170-7); pap. 8.95x (ISBN 0-02-902190-1). Free Pr.

--The Denial of Death. LC 73-1860. 1973. 19.95 (ISBN 0-02-902150-2); pap. 8.95x (ISBN 0-02-902310-6). Free Pr.

--Escape from Evil. LC 75-12059. 1975. 11.95 (ISBN 0-02-902300-9). Free Pr.

--Escape from Evil. LC 75-12059. 1976. pap. 8.95 (ISBN 0-02-902340-8). Free Pr.

--The Lost Science of Man. LC 75-142076. 1971. pap. 2.95 (ISBN 0-8076-0599-9). Braziller.

--The Revolution in Psychiatry: The New Understanding of Man. LC 64-11213. 1974. pap. 8.95x (ISBN 0-02-902130-8). Free Pr.

--The Structure of Evil. LC 68-12890. 1976. pap. 8.95x (ISBN 0-02-902290-8). Free Pr.

Becker, Ernest I. & Tsutsui, Minoru, eds. Organometallic Reactions, 2 vols. LC 74-92108. 1971. Vol. 1, 400pp. 29.50 (ISBN 0-471-06135-2); Vol. 2, 462pp. 32.50 (ISBN 0-471-06130-1). Krieger.

Becker, Ernest I., tr. see Lefevre, M. J.

Becker, Ernst. Gas Dynamics. 1969. 70.50 (ISBN 0-12-084450-8). Acad Pr.

Becker, Esther & Anders, Evelyn. The Successful Secretary's Handbook. 480p. 1984. pap. 6.68i (ISBN 0-06-463593-7, EH 593). B&N NY.

Becker, Esther, ed. Dictionary of Personnel & Industrial Relations. 1958. 10.00 (ISBN 0-8022-0088-5). Philos Lib.

Becker, Esther R. & Anders, Evelyn. The Successful Secretary's Handbook. LC 70-83584. (Illus.). 1971. 11.49i (ISBN 0-06-010267-5, HarpT). Har-Row.

Becker, Ethel A. Klondike Ninety Eight: E. A. Hegg's Gold Rush Album. rev. ed. LC 67-27689. 1967. 10.00 (ISBN 0-8323-0000-4). Binford.

Becker, Felix, jt. auth. see Thieme, Ulrich.

Becker, Felix, jt. ed. see Thieme, Ulrich.

Becker, Ferdinand F. Facial Reconstruction with Local & Regional Flaps. (Illus.). 176p. 1985. text ed. 37.00 (ISBN 0-86577-199-5). Thieme-Stratton.

Becker, Franklin. The Successful Office: How to Create a Workspace That's Right for You. LC 82-6680. (Illus.). 256p. 1982. 19.95 (ISBN 0-201-10153-X); pap. 9.95 (ISBN 0-201-10154-8). Addison-Wesley.

Becker, Franklin D. Housing Messages. LC 76-21267. (Community Development Ser: Vol. 30). (Illus.). 1977. 23.95 (ISBN 0-87933-259-X). Van Nos Reinhold.

--Workspace: Creating Environments in Organizations. LC 81-10671. 238p. 1981. 31.95 (ISBN 0-03-059137-6); pap. 15.95 (ISBN 0-03-062184-4). Praeger.

Becker, Frederick F., ed. Cancer: A Comprehensive Treatise. Incl. Vol. 1. Etiology: Chemical & Physical Carcinogenesis. LC 74-31195. 524p. 1975. 52.50x (ISBN 0-306-35201-X); Vol. 2. Etiology: Viral Carcinogenesis. LC 75-11770. 439p. 1975. 57.50x (ISBN 0-306-35202-8); Vol. 3. Biology of Tumors: Cellular Biology & Growth. LC 74-31196. 473p. 1975. 57.50x (ISBN 0-306-35203-6); Vol. 4, Biology of Tumors: Surfaces,Immunology & Comparative Pathology. 440p. 1975. 57.50x (ISBN 0-306-35204-4); Vol. 5, Chemotherapy. LC 77-1142. 666p. 1977. 57.50x (ISBN 0-306-35205-2); Vol. 6. Radiotherapy, Surgery, & Immunotherapy. LC 74-31196. 544p. 57.50x (ISBN 0-306-35206-0). (Illus., Plenum Pr). Plenum Pub.

--The Liver: Normal & Abnormal Functions, 2 pts. (Biochemistry of Disease Ser.: Vol. 5). 592p. 1975. Part A. 85.00 (ISBN 0-8247-6205-3); Part B. 75.00 (ISBN 0-8247-6214-2). Dekker.

Becker, Frederick F., et al, eds. Cancer-A Comprehensive Treatise, Vol. 1: Etiology - Chemical & Physical Carcinogenesis. rev. 2nd ed. LC 81-21050. 736p. 1982. text ed. 85.00x (ISBN 0-306-40701-9, Plenum Pr). Plenum Pub.

Becker, G. & Theden, G., eds. Annual Report on Wood Protection, 1953-1954. vi, 219p. 1955. 28.40 (ISBN 0-387-01928-6). Springer-Verlag.

--Annual Report on Wood Protection, 1955. viii, 170p. 1956. 26.60 (ISBN 0-387-02057-8). Springer-Verlag.

--Annual Report on Wood Protection, 1959-1960. v, 481p. 1969. 67.90 (ISBN 0-387-04576-7). Springer-Verlag.

--Annual Report on Wood Protection, 1961-62. 1972. 57.90 (ISBN 0-387-05827-3). Springer-Verlag.

Becker, Gail. Diet Simply with Soup. (Orig.). 1983. pap. 4.95 (ISBN 0-671-46428-0). PB.

Becker, Gail L. Heart Smart: A Plan for Low-Cholesterol Living. 224p. 1985. pap. 5.95 (ISBN 0-671-55521-9, Fireside). S&S.

--High Points for Healthful Living. LC 81-67072. 1981. write for info. (ISBN 0-87502-091-7). Benjamin Co.

Becker, Gail R. Cooking for the Health of It. LC 81-67070. (Orig.). pap. 5.95 (ISBN 0-87502-090-9). Benjamin Co.

Becker, Gary S. The Economic Approach to Human Behavior. LC 75-43240. 1978. pap. 6.95x (ISBN 0-226-04112-3, P803, Phoen). U of Chicago Pr.

--The Economic Approach to Human Behavior. LC 75-43240. (Illus.). 1977. lib. bdg. 22.00x (ISBN 0-226-04111-5). U of Chicago Pr.

--Economic Theory. 1971. text ed. 25.00 (ISBN 0-394-31492-1, KnopfC). Knopf.

--Economics of Discrimination. rev. 2nd ed. LC 73-157422. (Economics Research Studies Ser.). 1971. pap. 6.00x (ISBN 0-226-04116-6, P393). U of Chicago Pr.

--Human Capital: A Theoretical & Empirical Analysis with Special Reference to Education. 2nd ed. xx, 268p. 1983. pap. text ed. 12.00x (ISBN 0-226-04109-3, Midway Reprint). U of Chicago Pr.

--A Treatise on the Family. LC 81-1306. (Illus.). 320p. 1981. text ed. 20.00x (ISBN 0-674-90696-9). Harvard U Pr.

--A Treatise on the Family. 304p. 1985. pap. text ed. 7.95x (ISBN 0-674-90697-7). Harvard U Pr.

Becker, Gary S., jt. auth. see Ghez, Gilbert R.

Becker, Gary S. & Landes, William M., eds. Essays in the Economics of Crime & Punishment. LC 73-88507. (Human Behavior & Social Institutions Ser.: No. 3). pap. 72.00 (ISBN 0-317-09861-6, 2051703). Bks Demand UMI.

Becker, Gaylene. Growing Old in Silence. LC 79-63548. 160p. 1980. 12.50 (ISBN 0-520-03900-9). U of Cal Pr.

--Growing Old in Silence. 160p. 1983. pap. 6.95 (ISBN 0-520-05058-4, CAL 643). U of Cal Pr.

Becker, George. The Mad Genius Controversy: A Study in the Sociology of Deviance. LC 78-875. (Sociological Observations Ser.: No. 5). pap. 38.00 (ISBN 0-317-08754-1, 2021869). Bks Demand UMI.

Becker, George J. D. H. Lawrence. LC 79-48075. (Literature and Life Ser.). 160p. 1980. 12.95 (ISBN 0-8044-2029-7); pap. 6.95 (ISBN 0-8044-6033-7). Ungar.

--James A. Michener. LC 82-40279. (Literature & Life Ser.). 170p. 1983. 12.95 (ISBN 0-8044-2044-0). Ungar.

--James A. Michener. 7.95 (ISBN 0-8044-6031-0). Ungar.

--John Dos Passos. LC 74-78437. (Literature and Life Ser.). 142p. 1974. 12.95 (ISBN 0-8044-2034-3). Ungar.

--Master European Realists of the Nineteenth Century. LC 81-70124. 225p. 1982. 15.95 (ISBN 0-8044-2046-7). Ungar.

--Realism in Modern Literature. LC 79-4833. 1980. 18.50 (ISBN 0-8044-2031-9). Ungar.

--Shakespeare's Histories. LC 76-15644. (Literature & Life Ser.). (Illus.). 192p. 1977. 13.95 (ISBN 0-8044-2032-7). Ungar.

--Shakespeare's Histories. LC 76-15644. (Literature & Life Ser.). (Illus.). 192p. 1983. pap. 6.95 (ISBN 0-8044-6032-9). Ungar.

Becker, George J., ed. Documents of Modern Literary Realism. 1963. pap. 16.95 (ISBN 0-691-01258-X). Princeton U Pr.

Becker, George J. 1921. Television & the Classroom Reading Program. LC 73-89304. (Reading Aids Ser.). 1973. 2.75 (ISBN 0-87207-214-2). Intl Reading.

Becker, H. A. Dimensionless Parameters: Theory & Methodology. LC 76-1570. 128p. 1976. 37.95x (ISBN 0-470-15048-3). Halsted Pr.

--Dimensionless Parameters: Theory & Methodology. 129p. 1976. 22.25 (ISBN 0-85334-689-5, Pub. by Elsevier Applied Sci England). Elsevier.

Becker, H. A. & Dueuzeide, H. Educational Research in Europe: A New Look at the Relationship Between School Education & Work: Second All-European Conference for Directors of Educational Research Institutions, Madrid, Sept. 11-13, 1979. Carelli, M. Dino, compiled by. (International Studies in Education: No. 37). 164p. 1980. pap. write for info. (U1364, UNESCO). Unipub.

Becker, H. D. & Caspary, W. F. Postgastrectomy & Postvagatomy Syndromes. (Illus.). 500p. 1980. 85.00 (ISBN 0-387-09445-8). Springer-Verlag.

Becker, Hal B. Functional Analysis of Information Networks: A Structured Approach to the Data Communication Environment. LC 80-15347. 294p. 1981. Repr. of 1973 ed. 29.50 (ISBN 0-89874-028-2). Krieger.

--Information Integrity: A Structure for Its Definition & Management. (Illus.). 256p. 1983. 29.95 (ISBN 0-07-004191-1). McGraw.

Becker, Harold K. Police Systems of Europe: A Survey of Selected Police Organizations. 2nd ed. (Illus.). 256p. 1980. pap. 16.75x spiral (ISBN 0-398-04023-0). C C Thomas.

Becker, Harold K. & Hjellemo, Einar O. Justice in Modern Sweden: A Description of the Components of the Swedish Criminal Justice System. (Illus.). 160p. 1976. 18.50x (ISBN 0-398-03486-9). C C Thomas.

Becker, Harold K. & Whitehouse, Jack E. Police of America: A Personal View, Introduction & Commentary. (Illus.). 108p. 1979. 15.50x (ISBN 0-398-03895-3). C C Thomas.

Becker, Harold K., jt. auth. see Felkenes, George T.

Becker, Harriet, jt. auth. see Sommer, Robert.

Becker, Helmut, jt. ed. see Thorelli, Hans.

Becker, Herbert L. Teach Yourself to Type. LC 81-86541. (Illus.). 110p. (Orig.). 1982. text ed. 8.00x (ISBN 0-942418-00-X). Park Ave Bks.

--Typing by Design. 1982. pap. 4.80 (ISBN 0-8224-7191-4). Glencoe.

Becker, Howard. German Youth. LC 76-2674. (Illus.). 286p. 1976. Repr. of 1946 ed. lib. bdg. 20.25 (ISBN 0-8371-8793-1, BEGY). Greenwood.

--Man in Reciprocity. LC 72-12324. 459p. 1973. Repr. of 1956 ed. lib. bdg. 25.00x (ISBN 0-8371-6699-3, BEMR). Greenwood.

Becker, Howard & Barnes, Harry E. Social Thought from Lore to Science, 3 Vols. 3rd ed. 16.50 ea. (ISBN 0-8446-1620-6). Peter Smith.

Becker, Howard P. Through Values to Social Interpretation: Essays on Social Contexts, Actions, Types & Prospects. LC 69-10068. 1968. Repr. of 1950 ed. lib. bdg. 22.50x (ISBN 0-8371-0014-3, BESI). Greenwood.

Becker, Howard S. Art Worlds. LC 81-2694. (Illus.). 408p. 1982. 32.50 (ISBN 0-520-04386-3). U of Cal Pr.

--Art Worlds. (Cal Ser.: No. 692). (Illus.). 406p. 1984. pap. 10.95 (ISBN 0-520-05218-8). U of Cal Pr.

--Outsiders: Studies in the Sociology of Deviance. LC 63-8413. 1966. 14.95 (ISBN 0-02-902200-2); pap. 8.95x (ISBN 0-02-902140-5). Free Pr.

--Role & Career Problems of the Chicago Public School Teacher. Zuckerman, Harriet & Merton, Robert K., eds. LC 79-8974. (Dissertations on Sociology Ser.). 1980. lib. bdg. 28.50x (ISBN 0-405-12951-3). Ayer Co Pubs.

--Sociological Work: Method & Substance. LC 77-115936. 357p. 1976. pap. text ed. 9.95 (ISBN 0-87855-630-3). Transaction Bks.

Becker, Howard S., ed. Campus Power Struggle. 2nd, rev ed. LC 72-91466. 191p. 1970. 9.95 (ISBN 0-87855-059-3); pap. text ed. 3.95x (ISBN 0-87855-556-0). Transaction Bks.

--Culture & Civility in San Francisco. (Illus.). 164p. 1971. pap. text ed. 9.95 (ISBN 0-87855-568-4). Transaction Bks.

--Exploring Society Photographically. 1981. 11.95 (ISBN 0-941680-00-2, 04097-6, Distrib. for Block Gallery, Northwestern University). U of Chicago Pr.

--Other Side: Perspectives on Deviance. LC 64-16953. 1967. pap. 8.95x (ISBN 0-02-902210-X). Free Pr.

Becker, Howard S., et al. Boys in White: Student Culture in Medical School. Repr. of 1961 ed. lib. bdg. 34.50x (ISBN 0-8290-0371-1). Irvington.

Becker, Howard S., et al, eds. Boys in White: Student Culture in Medical School. rev. ed. LC 76-26951. 456p. 1976. pap. text ed. 14.95 (ISBN 0-87855-622-2). Transaction Bks.

Becker, I. Antiviral Drugs. Melnick, J. L., ed. (Monographs in Virology: Vol. 11). (Illus.). 1976. 432.00 (ISBN 3-8055-2248-7). S Karger.

Becker, Irving, jt. auth. see Ellis, Albert.

Becker, J. Formation of the Old Testament. 1.25 (ISBN 0-8199-0513-5). Franciscan Herald.

--Marxian Political Economy. LC 76-9172. (Illus.). 1977. 37.50 (ISBN 0-521-21349-5). Cambridge U Pr.

Becker, J. D. & Eisele, I., eds. WOPPLOT 83 Parallel Processing-Logic, Organization, & Technology: Proceeding of a Workshop Held at the Federal Armed Forces Unversity Munich (HSBwM) Neububerg, Bavaria, Germany, June 27-29, 1983. (Lecture Notes in Physics: Vol. 196). v, 189p. 1984. pap. 13.00 (ISBN 0-387-12917-0). Springer Verlag.

Becker, J. J., et al, eds. Magnetism & Magnetic Materials: Proceedings, 1975. LC 76-10931. (AIP Conference Proceedings: No. 29). 693p. 1976. 30.00 (ISBN 0-88318-128-2). Am Inst Physics.

Becker, Jack D. Introduction to Business Data Processing: Supplement. 216p. 1982. pap. text ed. 13.95 (ISBN 0-8403-2829-X). Kendall-Hunt.

Becker, James M. Teaching about Nuclear Disarmament. LC 85-61792. (Fastback Ser.: No. 229). 50p. 1985. pap. 0.75 (ISBN 0-87367-229-1). Phi Delta Kappa.

Becker, James M. & Hahn, Carole L. Wingspread Workbook for Educational Change. rev. ed. 76p. 1977. pap. 8.95 (ISBN 0-89994-180-X). Soc Sci Ed.

Becker, Jan, et al. Enhance Chance. (Illus., Orig.). (gr. k-9). 1973. pap. 6.50 (ISBN 0-918932-10-6). Activity Resources.

Becker, Jean-Jacques. The Great War & the French People. 304p. 1985. 33.00 (ISBN 0-907582-30-3, Pub. by Berg Pubs); pap. 9.95 (ISBN 0-907582-53-2, Pub. by Berg Pubs). Longwood Pub Group.

Becker, Jillian. The PLO. (Illus.). 336p. 1985. pap. 9.95 (ISBN 0-312-59380-5). St Martin.

--The PLO: The Rise & Fall of the Palestine Liberation Organization. LC 84-40120. 288p. 1984. 19.95 (ISBN 0-312-59379-1). St Martin.

Becker, Jillian, ed. see Goren, Roberta.

Becker, Jim, et al. You Can Be a Doctor in Thirty Minutes. LC 84-3638. 12p. (Orig.). 1984. pap. text ed. 6.95 (ISBN 0-446-38101-2). Warner Bks.

Becker, Joachim. Messianic Expectation in the Old Testament. Green, David E., tr. from Ger. LC 79-8891. 96p. 1980. 8.95 (ISBN 0-8006-0545-4, 1-545). Fortress.

Becker, Joan, tr. see Wolf, Christa.

Becker, Johanna. Karatsu: A Tradition of Diversity. LC 85-45308. (Illus.). 216p. 1986. 45.00 (ISBN 0-87011-749-1). Kodansha.

Becker, John. Jaimie. LC 80-65424. 176p. 1981. 13.95 (ISBN 0-87923-340-0). Godine.

--Seven Little Rabbits. LC 72-86974. (Illus.). PLB 5.85 (ISBN 0-8027-6130-5). Walker & Co.

--Seven Little Rabbits. (Illus.). 32p. (ps-2). 1985. pap. 2.50 (ISBN 0-590-33447-6, Blue Ribbon Bks.). Scholastic Inc.

Becker, John T. & Becker, Stanli K., eds. All Blood is Red: All Shadows Are Dark! xiv, 153p. 1984. pap. 6.50 (ISBN 0-916225-00-3). Seven Shadows.

Becker, Jorg. Information Technology & a New International Order. (Information & Society Ser.). 141p. 1984. pap. text ed. 19.95x (ISBN 0-86238-043-X, Pub. by Chartwell-Bratt England). Brookfield Pub Co.

Becker, Joseph & Hayes, Robert M. Information Storage & Retrieval: Tools, Elements, Theories. LC 63-12279. (Information Sciences Ser.). pap. 115.00 (ISBN 0-317-10285-0, 2019533). Bks Demand UMI.

Becker, Joseph, jt. auth. see Hayes, Robert M.

Becker, Joseph E. de see De Becker, Joseph E.

Becker, Joseph M. Experience Rating in Unemployment Insurance: An Experiment in Competitive Socialism. LC 72-4026. pap. 105.50 (ISBN 0-317-28468-1). Bks Demand UMI.

--Experience Rating in Unemployment Insurance: Virtue or Vice. 94p. 1972. pap. 3.95 (ISBN 0-911558-28-4). W E Upjohn.

--In Aid of the Unemployed. LC 78-17906. (Illus.). 1978. Repr. of 1965 ed. lib. bdg. 31.00x (ISBN 0-313-20534-5, BEIA). Greenwood.

--Shared Government in Employment Security. LC 74-6703. 501p. 1975. Repr. of 1959 ed. lib. bdg. 23.50x (ISBN 0-8371-7547-X, BESG). Greenwood.

--Unemployment Benefits: Should There Be a Compulsory Federal Standard? 1980. pap. 4.25 (ISBN 0-8447-3389-X). Am Enterprise.

--Unemployment Insurance Financing: An Evaluation. 1981. 14.25 (ISBN 0-8447-3462-4); pap. 6.25 (ISBN 0-8447-3463-2). Am Enterprise.

Becker, Joyce. Bible Crafts. LC 82-80820. (Illus.). 128p. (gr. 5 up). 1982. 12.95 (ISBN 0-8234-0467-6); pap. 6.95 (ISBN 0-8234-0469-2). Holiday.

Becker, Judith. Traditional Music in Modern Java. LC 80-19180. (Illus.). 1980. text ed. 30.00x (ISBN 0-8248-0563-1). UH Pr.

Becker, Judith & Feinstein, Alan H., eds. Karawitan: Source Readings in Javanese Gamelan & Vocal Music, Vol. 1. LC 82-72445. (Michigan Papers on South & Southeast Asia: No. 23). xviii, 526p. 1984. 36.50 (ISBN 0-89148-027-7). Ctr S&SE Asian.

Becker, Judith, et al. Fine-Tuning: An NCCB Report on Noncommercial Radio. 1980. pap. 5.00 (ISBN 0-9603466-4-3). T R A C.

Becker, Julie. Animals of the Fields & Meadows. LC 77-8496. (Animals Around Us Ser.). (Illus.). (gr. 2-6). 1977. PLB 7.95 (ISBN 0-88436-394-5, 35451). EMC.

--Animals of the Ponds & Streams. LC 77-8497. (Animals Around Us Ser.). (Illus.). (gr. 2-6). 1977. PLB 7.95 (ISBN 0-88436-398-8, 35453). EMC.

--Animals of the Seashore. LC 77-8106. (Animals Around Us Ser.). (Illus.). (gr. 2-6). 1977. PLB 7.95 (ISBN 0-88436-392-9, 35450). EMC.

--Animals of the Woods & Forests. LC 77-8253. (Animals Around Us Ser.). (Illus.). (gr. 2-6). 1977. PLB 7.95 (ISBN 0-88436-396-1, 35452). EMC.

--Sex Education. 1983. pap. 9.50x (ISBN 0-931460-26-3). Bieler.

Becker, Kenneth L. The Endocrine Lung in Health & Disease. (Illus.). 480p. 1984. 120.00 (ISBN 0-7216-1007-2). Saunders.

Becker, Kenneth M. A Monograph of the Genus Lasianthaea (Asteraceae) (Memoirs Ser.: Vol. 31, No. 2). 1979. pap. 6.50x (ISBN 0-89327-211-6). NY Botanical.

Becker, Laurence A., jt. auth. see Tuttle, Frederick B., Jr.

Becker, Lawrence & Kipnis, Kenneth. Property: Cases, Concepts, Critiques. 352p. 1984. pap. text ed. 16.95 (ISBN 0-13-730912-0). P-H.

Becker, Lawrence C. On Justifying Moral Judgements. (International Library of Philosophy & Scientific Method). 199p. 1973. text ed. 20.45x (ISBN 0-7100-7524-3, Pub. by Routledge Kegan Paul England). Humanities.

--On Justifying Moral Judgments. (International Library of Philosophy & Scientific Method). 1973. text ed. 19.95x (ISBN 0-391-00271-6). Humanities.

--Property Rights: Philosophic Foundations. 148p. 1980. pap. 7.95x (ISBN 0-7100-0606-3). Routledge & Kegan.

--Property Rights: Philosophic Foundations. 1977. 21.95x (ISBN 0-7100-8679-2). Routledge & Kegan.

Becker, Lawrence W., jt. auth. see Stone, George N.

Becker, Lee, jt. auth. see McCombs, Maxwell E.

Becker, Loftus E. & Goldstein, Joseph. Supplement to Criminal Law: Theory & Process. 1982. pap. 9.95x (ISBN 0-02-912320-8). Free Pr.

Becker, Lucille. Henry De Montherlant: A Critical Biography. LC 70-83666. (Crosscurrents-Modern Critiques Ser.). 150p. 1970. 6.95 (ISBN 0-8093-0411-2). S Ill U Pr.

Becker, Lucille F. Louis Aragon. LC 70-110702. (World Authors Ser.). 1971. lib. bdg. 15.95 (ISBN 0-8057-2056-1). Irvington.

Becker, Lucille Frackman see Frackman Becker, Lucille.

Becker, Manning H., jt. auth. see Castle, Emory N.

Becker, Marion R. & Rombauer, Irma. The Joy of Cooking, 2 vols, Vol. 1. Vol. 1. pap. 3.95 (ISBN 0-451-11710-7, AE1710, Sig); Vol. 2. pap. 3.95 (ISBN 0-451-11711-5, AE1711). NAL.

Becker, Marion R., jt. auth. see Rombauer, Irma S.

Becker, Mark, ed. see Elwood, Ann & Raht, John.

Becker, Martin, jt. ed. see Lewins, Jeffery.

Becker, Martin, jt. ed. see Lewins, Jeffrey.

Becker, Martin, et al, eds. Advances in Nuclear Science & Technology, Vol. 12. LC 62-13039. 350p. 1979. 55.00x (ISBN 0-306-40315-3, Plenum Pr). Plenum Pub.

Beckett, Frederick E. College Composition: The Course Where a Student Doesn't Learn to Write. LC 74-78804. 176p. 1974. 16.00x (ISBN 0-9600740-1-5). Calcon Pr.

Beckett, Ian & Gooch, John, eds. Politicians & Defence: Studies in the Formulation of British Defence Policy. 224p. 1982. 20.00 (ISBN 0-7190-0818-2, Pub. by Manchester Univ Pr). Longwood Pub Group.

Beckett, Ian F. & Pimlott, John, eds. Armed Forces & Modern Counter-Insurgency. LC 84-22850. 224p. 1985. 27.50 (ISBN 0-312-04924-2). St Martin.

Beckett, Ian F. & Simpson, Keith R., eds. A Nation in Arms: A Social Study of the British Army in the First World War. LC 84-25048. 1985. 32.50 (ISBN 0-7190-1737-8, Pub. by Manchester Univ Pr). Longwood Pub Group.

Beckett, J. C. The Anglo-Irish Tradition. 160p. pap. 8.95 (ISBN 0-85640-280-X, Pub. by Blackstaff Pr). Longwood Pub Group.

--Belfast: The Making of a City. (Illus.). 194p. 1983. 19.95 (ISBN 0-86281-100-7, Pub. by Salem Hse Ltd). Merrimack Pub Cir.

--Confrontations: Studies in Irish History. 175p. 1972. 13.50x (ISBN 0-87471-147-9). Rowman.

--A Short History of Ireland. 191p. 1982. pap. text ed. 10.75x (ISBN 0-09-139841-X, Hutchinson U Lib). Humanities.

Beckett, J. V. Coal & Tobacco. (Illus.). 280p. 1981. 59.50 (ISBN 0-521-23486-7). Cambridge U Pr.

Beckett, James C. Protestant Dissent in Ireland Sixteen Eighty-Seven to Seventeen Eighty. LC 78-20448. 1980. Repr. of 1948 ed. text ed. 17.60 (ISBN 0-88355-828-9). Hyperion Conn.

--Short History of Ireland. 6th ed. 1975. 17.50x (ISBN 0-391-02079-X, Hutchinson U Lib); pap. text ed. 10.50x (ISBN 0-391-02080-3). Humanities.

Beckett, James G. Making of Modern Ireland, 1603-1923. 1966. 17.95 (ISBN 0-394-43473-0). Knopf.

Beckett, Judith. Silent Recesses. 70p. 1984. 3.65 (ISBN 0-89697-222-4). Intl Univ Pr.

Beckett, Kenneth A. Climbing Plants. (Illus.). 178p. 1983. 17.95 (ISBN 0-917304-76-4). Timber.

--The Complete Book of Evergreens. 168p. 1981. 40.00x (ISBN 0-7063-5989-5, Pub. by Ward Lock Ed England). State Mutual Bk.

--The Concise Encyclopedia of Garden Plants. (Illus.). 440p. 1984. 19.95 (ISBN 0-85613-534-8, Pub. by Salem Hse Ltd). Merrimack Pub Cir.

--The Garden Library: Annuals & Biennials. Dorling Kindersley Ltd., ed. 96p. 1984. pap. 4.95 (ISBN 0-345-30908-1). Ballantine.

--The Garden Library: Flowering Houseplants. Dorling Kindersley Ltd., ed. 96p. 1984. pap. 4.95 (ISBN 0-345-30909-X). Ballantine.

--The Garden Library: Herbs. Dorling Kindersley Ltd., ed. 96p. 1984. pap. 4.95 (ISBN 0-345-30907-3). Ballantine.

--The Garden Library: Roses. Dorling Kindersley Ltd., ed. 96p. 1984. pap. 4.95 (ISBN 0-345-30906-5). Ballantine.

--Growing Hardy Perennials. (Illus.). 182p. 1982. 14.95 (ISBN 0-917304-44-6). Timber.

Beckett, Kenneth A., jt. auth. see Stevens, David.

Beckett, L. C. Movement & Emptiness. 1969. pap. 1.45 (ISBN 0-8356-0414-4, Quest). Theos Pub Hse.

Beckett, Lucy. Richard Wagner: Parsifal. (Cambridge Opera Handbooks Ser.). (Illus.). 220p. 1981. 27.95 (ISBN 0-521-22825-5); pap. 9.95 (ISBN 0-521-29662-5). Cambridge U Pr.

Beckett, Mary. A Belfast Woman. (Poolbeg-Modern Irish Short Story Ser.). 111p. (Orig.). 1980. pap. 3.95 (ISBN 0-905169-25-5, Pub. by Poolbeg Pr Ireland). Irish Bk Ctr.

Beckett, Melvin L. Deep Breathing to Fitness. (Illus.). 17p. 1981. pap. 2.95 (ISBN 0-686-32543-5). MLB Pub.

Beckett, Oliver. J. F. Herring & Sons. 1981. 75.00x (ISBN 0-686-79050-2, Pub. by Allen & Co). State Mutual Bk.

Beckett, Paul, jt. auth. see O'Connell, James.

Beckett, Peter G. Adolescents Out of Step: Their Treatment in a Psychiatric Hospital. LC 65-13538. (Lafayette Clinic Monographs in Psychiatry: No. 2). 191p. 1965. 8.95x (ISBN 0-8143-1269-1). Wayne St U Pr.

Beckett, R. B. Further Documents & Correspondence of John Constable. (Illus.). 371p. 1972. 22.50 (ISBN 0-900716-17-7, Pub. by Boydell & Brewer). Longwood Pub Group.

--John Constable's Correspondence VI: The Fishers. (Suffolk Records Society Ser.: Vol. XII). (Illus.). 299p. 1968. 16.50 (ISBN 0-900716-09-6, Pub. by Boydell & Brewer). Longwood Pub Group.

Beckett, R. B., ed. Constable's Correspondence: VI. The Fishers. (Suffolk Records Society Ser.: Vol. XII). (Illus.). 299p. 1968. 16.50 (ISBN 0-900716-09-6, Pub. by Boydell & Brewer). Longwood Pub Group.

--John Constable's Correspondence I: The Family at East Bergholt 1807-1837. (Suffolk Records Society: Vol. IV). (Illus.). 337p. Repr. of 1962 ed. 16.50 (ISBN 0-85115-064-0, Pub. by Boydell & Brewer). Longwood Pub Group.

--John Constable's Correspondence II: Early Friends & Maria Bicknell (Mrs. Constable) (Suffolk Records Society: Vol. VI). (Illus.). 479p. 1964. 16.50 (ISBN 0-317-19197-7, Pub. by Boydell & Brewer). Longwood Pub Group.

--John Constable's Correspondence III: The Correspondence with C. R. Leslie, R. A. (Suffolk Records Society: Vol. VIII). (Illus.). 163p. 1965. 13.50 (ISBN 0-900716-06-1, Pub. by Boydell & Brewer). Longwood Pub Group.

--John Constable's Correspondence IV: Patrons, Dealers, & Fellow Artists. (Suffolk Records Society: Vol. X). (Illus.). 481p. 1966. 16.50 (ISBN 0-900716-07-X, Pub. by Boydell & Brewer). Longwood Pub Group.

--John Constable's Correspondence V: Various Friends, with Charles Boner & the Artist's Children. (Suffolk Records Society: Vol. XI). (Illus.). 235p. 1967. 13.50 (ISBN 0-900716-08-8, Pub. by Boydell & Brewer). Longwood Pub Group.

--John Constable's Discourses. (Suffolk Records Society: Vol. XIV). (Illus.). 114p. 1970. 13.50 (ISBN 0-900716-01-0, Pub. by Boydell & Brewer). Longwood Pub Group.

Beckett, R. B., ed. see Constable, John.

Beckett, Royce & Hurt, James. Numerical Calculations & Algorithms. LC 81-20894. 1983. 19.50 (ISBN 0-89874-415-6). Krieger.

Beckett, Samuel. Cascando & Other Short Dramatic Pieces. Incl. Words & Music; Eh Joe; Play; Come & Go; Film (Original Version. 1969. 10.00 (ISBN 0-394-47496-1, GP644). Grove.

--Cascando & Other Short Dramatic Pieces. Incl. Words & Music; Eh Joe; Play; Come & Go; Film (Original Version. 1969. pap. 5.95 (ISBN 0-394-17269-8, E471, Ever). Grove.

--Collected Poems in English & French. 1977. pap. 3.95 (ISBN 0-394-17013-X, E700, Ever). Grove.

--The Collected Shorter Plays of Samuel Beckett. LC 83-49371. 320p. (Orig.). 1984. 19.95 (ISBN 0-394-53850-1, GP 892); pap. 6.95 (ISBN 0-394-62098-4, E907). Grove.

--The Collected Works of Samuel Beckett, 29 vols. LC 74-28586. 1981. Set. 175.00 (ISBN 0-394-49789-9, 29V). Grove.

--Comedies et Actes Divers. Incl. Comedie; Va-Et-Vient; Cascando; Paroles et Musique; Dis Joe; Actes sans Paroles II; Film; Souffle. 1966. pap. 5.50 (ISBN 0-685-35878-X). French & Eur.

--Comment C'est. 1961. pap. 9.95 (ISBN 0-685-11097-4). French & Eur.

--Company. LC 80-995. 64p. 1980. 8.95 (ISBN 0-394-51394-0, GP 833). Grove.

--Company. LC 80-995. 64p. 1981. pap. 3.95 (ISBN 0-394-17928-5, E-781, Ever). Grove.

--Le Depeupleur. pap. 3.95 (ISBN 0-685-37197-2). French & Eur.

--Derniere Bande. 1960. pap. 5.25 (ISBN 0-685-11131-8). French & Eur.

--Disjecta. Cohn, Ruby, ed. LC 83-48308. 176p. 1984. 17.50 (ISBN 0-394-53500-6, GP-877); pap. 5.95 (ISBN 0-394-62489-0, E-868). Grove.

--En Attendant Godot. 1952. pap. 5.25 (ISBN 0-685-11159-8). French & Eur.

--En Attendant Godot. Bree, Germaine & Schoenfeld, Eric, eds. (Orig.). 1963. pap. text ed. write for info. (ISBN 0-02-307830-8). Macmillan.

--Endgame. Beckett, Samuel, tr. from Fr. 1958. pap. 3.50 (ISBN 0-394-17208-6, E96, Ever). Grove.

--Endgame & Act Without Words. Beckett, Samuel, tr. from Fr. 1958. 10.00 (ISBN 0-394-47500-3, GP645). Grove.

--Ends & Odds: Dramatic Pieces. LC 76-14510. 1976. 10.00 (ISBN 0-394-40949-3, GP782). Grove.

--Ends & Odds: Dramatic Pieces. 1976. pap. 3.95 (ISBN 0-394-17918-8, E680, Ever). Grove.

--Film, a Film Script. (Illus.). 1969. pap. 6.95 (ISBN 0-394-17276-0, E502, Ever). Grove.

--Fin de Partie. 1957. pap. 4.95 (ISBN 0-685-11186-5). French & Eur.

--First Love & Other Shorts. Beckett, Samuel, tr. from Fr. 180p. 1974. 10.00 (ISBN 0-394-49149-1, GP731). Grove.

--First Love & Other Shorts. Beckett, Samuel, tr. from Fr. (Incl. From An Abandoned Work; Enough; Imagination Dead Imagine; Breath; & Not I). 1974. pap. 4.95 (ISBN 0-394-17850-5, E623, Ever). Grove.

--Fizzles. 1976. 10.00 (ISBN 0-394-40950-7, GP783). Grove.

--Fizzles. 1976. pap. 1.95 (ISBN 0-394-17917-X, E681, Ever). Grove.

--Happy Days. 1961. 10.00 (ISBN 0-394-47507-0, GP647). Grove.

--Happy Days. (Orig.). 1961. pap. 4.95 (ISBN 0-394-17233-7, E318, Ever). Grove.

--How It Is. Beckett, Samuel, tr. from Fr. 1970. 12.50 (ISBN 0-394-47508-9, GP649). Grove.

--How It Is. Beckett, Samuel, tr. from Fr. 1965. pap. 8.95 (ISBN 0-394-17248-5, E388, Ever). Grove.

--Ill Seen Ill Said. LC 81-47695. 64p. 1981. 8.95 (ISBN 0-394-52233-8, GP824). Grove.

--Ill Seen Ill Said. LC 81-47695. 64p. 1982. pap. 4.95 (ISBN 0-394-17953-6, E818, Ever). Grove.

--Ill Seen Ill Said. 50p. 1982. deluxe ed. 100.00 signed (ISBN 0-935716-19-X). Lord John.

--Immobile. 1976. 59.95 (ISBN 0-686-51927-2). French & Eur.

--Innomable. 1953. pap. 12.95 (ISBN 0-685-11252-7). French & Eur.

--Krapp's Last Tape & Other Dramatic Pieces. Incl. All That Fall; Embers (A Play for Radio; Acts Without Words, I & II, Mimes. 1960. 10.00 (ISBN 0-394-47511-9, GP648). Grove.

--Krapp's Last Tape & Other Dramatic Pieces. Incl. All That Fall; Embers (A Play for Radio; Acts Without Words, I & II, (Mimes. 1960. pap. 6.95 (ISBN 0-394-17223-X, E226, Ever). Grove.

--The Lost Ones. LC 72-84341. Orig. Title: Le Depeupleur. 64p. 1972. Repr. of 1972 ed. 10.00 (ISBN 0-394-48276-X, GP708). Grove.

--The Lost Ones. 1972. pap. 6.95 (ISBN 0-394-17786-X, E587, Ever). Grove.

--Malone Dies. Beckett, Samuel, tr. from Fr. LC 56-8440. 1956. 10.00 (ISBN 0-394-47513-5, GP642); pap. 3.95 (ISBN 0-394-17028-8, E39, Ever). Grove.

--Malone Meurt. 1952. pap. 12.95 (ISBN 0-685-11337-X). French & Eur.

--Mercier & Camier. LC 74-21639. 124p. 1975. 10.00 (ISBN 0-394-49722-8, GP764). Grove.

--Mercier & Camier. LC 74-21639. 1975. pap. 6.95 (ISBN 0-394-17835-1, E665, Ever). Grove.

--Mercier et Camier. 9.95 (ISBN 0-685-37198-0). French & Eur.

--Molloy. 14.95 (ISBN 0-685-37199-9). French & Eur.

--Molloy. Beckett, Samuel & Bowles, Patrick, trs. from Fr. 1970. 12.50 (ISBN 0-394-47515-1, GP641). Grove.

--Molloy. Beckett, Samuel & Bowles, Patrick, trs. from Fr. LC 55-5113. 1955. pap. 6.95 (ISBN 0-394-17027-X, E18, Ever). Grove.

--More Pricks Than Kicks. LC 72-119923. 192p. 1970. 12.50 (ISBN 0-394-47516-X, GP655). Grove.

--More Pricks Than Kicks. 1972. pap. 4.95 (ISBN 0-394-17789-4, E588, Ever). Grove.

--Murphy. 1965. pap. 9.95 (ISBN 0-685-11410-4). French & Eur.

--Murphy. 1970. 12.50 (ISBN 0-394-47517-8, GP650). Grove.

--Murphy. 1957. pap. 8.95 (ISBN 0-394-17210-8, E104, Ever). Grove.

--Nouvelles et Textes Pour Rien. 1955. pap. 12.95 (ISBN 0-685-11429-5). French & Eur.

--Oh les Beaux Jours. 1963. pap. 5.25 (ISBN 0-685-11467-8). French & Eur.

--Ohio Impromptu, Catastrophe, & What Where: Three Plays. LC 83-49372. 64p. (Orig.). 1984. 12.95 (ISBN 0-394-53851-X, GP 891); pap. 4.95 (ISBN 0-394-62061-5, E 905). Grove.

--Paroles et Musique. Bd. with Comedie; Dis Joe. (Coll. Bilingue). (Fr. & Eng.). pap. 4.50 (ISBN 0-685-37196-4). French & Eur.

--Poems in English. 1964. pap. 2.95 (ISBN 0-394-17196-9, E379, Ever). Grove.

--Pour Finir Encore. Bd. with Immobile et Autres Foirades. 1976. pap. 4.95 (ISBN 0-686-52220-6). French & Eur.

--Premier Amour. pap. 3.95 (ISBN 0-685-37200-6). French & Eur.

--Proust. 1957. 10.00 (ISBN 0-394-47523-2, GP651). Grove.

--Proust. (Orig.). 1956. pap. 7.95 (ISBN 0-394-17414-3, E50, Ever). Grove.

--Rockaby & Other Works. LC 80-8916. 128p. 1981. 12.50 (ISBN 0-394-51953-1, GP844). Grove.

--Rockaby & Other Works. 128p. 1981. pap. 3.95 (ISBN 0-394-17924-2, E777, Ever). Grove.

--Stories & Texts for Nothing. 1970. 10.00 (ISBN 0-394-47527-5, GP653). Grove.

--Stories & Texts for Nothing. 1967. pap. 4.95 (ISBN 0-394-17268-X, E466, Ever). Grove.

--Tetes Mortes. pap. 3.95 (ISBN 0-685-37201-4). French & Eur.

--Theatre One. Incl. En Attendant Godot; Fin de Partie; Acte sans paroles I et II. 12.95 (ISBN 0-685-37195-6). French & Eur.

--Three Novels. Incl. Molloy; Malone Dies; The Unnamable. 1965. pap. 6.95 (ISBN 0-394-17299-X, B78, BC). Grove.

--Tous Ceux Qui Tombent. 1957. pap. 4.50 (ISBN 0-685-11601-8). French & Eur.

--The Unnamable. Beckett, Samuel, tr. from Fr. 1970. 10.00 (ISBN 0-394-47528-3, GP643). Grove.

--The Unnamable. Beckett, Samuel, tr. from Fr. LC 58-10843. 1958. pap. 3.95 (ISBN 0-394-17030-X, E117, Ever). Grove.

--Waiting for Godot. Beckett, Samuel, tr. from Fr. 1970. 10.00 (ISBN 0-394-47529-1, GP640). Grove.

--Waiting for Godot. Beckett, Samuel, tr. from Fr. 1954. pap. 3.50 (ISBN 0-394-17204-3, E33, Ever). Grove.

--Watt. 14.95 (ISBN 0-685-37202-2). French & Eur.

--Watt. 1970. 12.50 (ISBN 0-394-47530-5, GP652). Grove.

--Watt. (Orig.). 1959. pap. 8.95 (ISBN 0-394-17216-7, E152, Ever). Grove.

--Worstward Ho! LC 83-94626. 64p. (Orig.). 1984. 8.95 (ISBN 0-394-53230-9, GP869). Grove.

Beckett, Samuel see Weiss, Samuel A.

Beckett, Samuel, tr. see Octavio, Paz.

Beckett, Samuel, tr. see Paz, Octavio.

Beckett, Samuel, tr. see Pinget, Robert.

Beckett, Samuel, et al. An Examination of James Joyce. LC 74-1307. (Studies in Joyce, No. 96). 1974. lib. bdg. 44.95 (ISBN 0-8383-2025-2). Haskell.

--James Joyce-Finnegans Wake: a Symposium. LC 44-32829. Orig. Title: Our Exagmination Round His Factification for Incamination of Work in Progress. 202p. 1972. pap. 5.95 (ISBN 0-8112-0446-4, NDP331). New Directions.

--New Writing & Writers, No. 13. 1980. pap. 6.00 (ISBN 0-7145-3541-9); 12.95 (ISBN 0-7145-3552-4). Riverrun NY.

Beckett, Samuel, et al, trs. see Bosquet, Alain.

Beckett, Sarah. Herbs for Cleaning the Skin. 1980. pap. 4.95x (ISBN 0-317-07336-2, Regent House). B of A.

--Herbs for Feminine Ailments. 1980. pap. 4.95x (ISBN 0-317-07337-0, Regent House). B of A.

--Herbs for Prostate & Bladder. 1980. pap. 4.95x (ISBN 0-317-07338-9, Regent House). B of A.

--Herbs for Rheumatism & Arthritis. 1980. pap. 4.95x (ISBN 0-317-07335-4, Regent House). B of A.

--Herbs to Soothe Your Nerves. 1980. pap. 4.95x (ISBN 0-317-07333-8, Regent House). B of A.

Beckett, Sheilah, illus. Jingle Bells. LC 84-60027. (Music Box Bks.). (Illus.). (ps up). 1984. 5.95 (ISBN 0-394-86796-3, Pub. by BYR). Random.

--A Victorian Dollhouse. (Illus.). (gr. k-7). 1982. pap. 6.95 (ISBN 0-394-85280-X). Random.

Beckett, Thomas. The Accountant's Assistant. Brief, Richard P., ed. LC 80-1471. (Dimensions of Accounting Theory & Practice Ser.). 1981. Repr. of 1901 ed. lib. bdg. 16.00x (ISBN 0-405-13501-7). Ayer Co Pubs.

Beckett, W. H. Akokoaso, a Survey of a Gold Coast Village. LC 76-44689. Repr. of 1944 ed. 21.50 (ISBN 0-404-15905-2). AMS Pr.

Beckett, Wendy M., tr. from Latin. John of Ford: Sermons on the Final Verses of the Song of Songs, IV. (Cistercian Fathers Ser.: No. 44). 1983. 24.95 (ISBN 0-87907-644-5). Cistercian Pubns.

--John of Ford: Sermons on the Final Verses of the Song of Songs, V (Sermons 62-82) (Cistercian Fathers Ser.: No. 45). 1983. 24.95 (ISBN 0-87907-645-3). Cistercian Pubns.

Beckett, Wendy M., tr. see John Of Ford.

Beckett, Wendy M., tr. see John of Ford.

Beckey, Fred. Cascade Alpine Guide, Climbing & High Routes: Columbia River to Stevens Pass, Vol. 1. LC 72-83552. (Illus.). 354p. 1974. flexible plastic 14.95 (ISBN 0-916890-32-5). Mountaineers.

--Cascade Alpine Guide: Climbing & High Routes-Rainy Pass to Fraser River, Vol. 3. LC 81-2335. (Illus.). 328p. (Orig.). 1981. pap. 14.95 (ISBN 0-89886-002-4). Mountaineers.

--Cascade Alpine Guide: Climbing & High Routes-Stevens Pass to Rainy Pass, Vol. 2. LC 77-82368. (Illus.). 1978. flexible plastic 14.95 (ISBN 0-916890-51-1). Mountaineers.

--Mountains of North America. LC 82-3315. (Illus.). 288p. 1982. 35.00 (ISBN 0-87156-320-7). Sierra.

Beckey, H. D. Principles of Field Ionization & Field Desorption Mass Spectrometry. LC 77-33014. 1971. 62.00 (ISBN 0-08-017557-0). Pergamon.

Beckford, George & Witter, Michael. Small Garden, Bitter Weed: Struggle & Change in Jamaica. 192p. 1982. 20.00x (ISBN 0-86232-003-8, Pub. by Zed Pr England); pap. 9.50x (ISBN 0-86232-008-9, Pub. by Zed Pr England). Biblio Dist.

Beckford, George L. Persistent Poverty: Underdevelopment in Plantation Economies of the Third World. 270p. Date not set. pap. 9.25 (ISBN 0-86232-207-3, Pub. by Zed Pr England). Biblio Dist.

Beckford, James A. Cult Controversies: The Societal Response to the New Religious Movements. 336p. 1985. 39.95 (ISBN 0-422-79630-1, 9592, Pub. by Tavistock England); pap. 13.95 (ISBN 0-422-79640-9, 9593, Pub. by Tavistock England). Methuen Inc.

--Religious Organization: A Trend Report & Bibliography Prepared for the International Sociological Association Under the Auspices of the International Committee for Social Science Documentation. (Current Sociology La Sociologie Contemporaine: Vol. 21, No. 2). 1973. pap. 11.60x (ISBN 90-2797-851-4). Mouton.

--The Trumpet of Prophecy: A Sociological Study of Jehovah's Witnesses. LC 75-14432. 244p. 1975. 32.95x (ISBN 0-470-06138-3). Halsted Pr.

Beck-Ford, Veda, et al. Leisure Training & Rehabilitation: A Program Manual. 192p. 1984. spiral bdg. 19.75x (ISBN 0-398-05044-9). C C Thomas.

Beckford, W. The Travel-Diaries of William Beckford of Fonthill, 2 vols in 1. Repr. of 1928 ed. 51.00 (ISBN 0-527-06500-5). Kraus Repr.

Beckford, W; see Bleiler.

Beckford, William. Azemia: A Descriptive & Sentimental Novel, Interspersed with Pieces of Poetry, by Jaquetta Agneta Mariana Jenks, 2 vols. Luria, Gina, ed. LC 74-8006. (The Feminist Controversy in England, 1788-1810 Ser.). 1974. Set. lib. bdg. 121.00 (ISBN 0-8240-0850-2). Garland Pub.

--Biographical Memoirs of Extraordinary Painters (1780) Ward, Philip, ed. (Oleander Language & Literature Ser.: Vol. 6). 1977. pap. 18.45 (ISBN 0-900891-13-0). Oleander Pr.

--Biographical Memoirs of Extraordinary Painters. Gemmett, Robert J., ed. LC 69-19434. (Illus.). 112p. 1969. 18.00 (ISBN 0-8386-7367-8). Fairleigh Dickinson.

--Biographical Memoirs of Extraordinary Painters. 1977. 90.00x (ISBN 0-900891-13-0, Pub. by Oleander Pr). State Mutual Bk.

--Dreams, Waking Thoughts & Incidents by William Beckford of Fonthill. Gemmett, Robert J., intro. by. LC 78-139988. (Illus.). 328p. 1972. 28.50 (ISBN 0-8386-7648-0). Fairleigh Dickinson.

--The Episodes of Vathek. Gemmett, Robert J., ed. LC 74-4883. 211p. 1975. 20.00 (ISBN 0-8386-1128-1). Fairleigh Dickinson.

--Modern Novel Writing, 4 vols. in 1. Incl. Azemia. Repr. of 1797 ed. LC 74-81366. 264p. 1970. Repr. of 1796 ed. 45.00x (ISBN 0-8201-1063-9). Schol Facsimiles.

--Modern Novel Writing, or the Elegant Enthusiast: And Interesting Emotions of Arabella Bloomville, a Rhapsodical Romance, Interspersed with Poetry, by the Right Hon. Lady Harriet Marlow, 2 vols. (The Feminist Controversy in England, 1788-1810 Ser.). 1974. Set. lib. bdg. 121.00 (ISBN 0-8240-0851-0). Garland Pub.

--Recollections of an Excursion. 1983. 48.00x (ISBN 0-900000-78-3, Pub. by Centaur Pr England). State Mutual Bk.

--Recollections of an Excursion to the Monasteries of Alcobaca & Baltalha. LC 72-13457. 1974. Repr. of 1835 ed. lib. bdg. 30.00 (ISBN 0-8414-1187-5). Folcroft.

--Recollections of an Excursion to the Monasteries of Alcobaca & Batalha. 1978. lib. bdg. 27.00 (ISBN 0-8482-0126-4). Norwood Edns.

--Recollections of an Excursion to the Monasteries of Alcobaca & Batalha. 27.50 (ISBN 0-87556-541-7). Saifer.

--Vathek. Lonsdale, Roger, ed. (The World's Classics-Paperback Ser.). 1983. pap. 5.95 (ISBN 0-19-281645-4). Oxford U Pr.

--Vathek: An Arabian Tale. 266p. 1984. Repr. of 1924 ed. lib. bdg. 45.00 (ISBN 0-89760-972-7). Telegraph Bks.

--Vathek: The English Translation by Samuel Henley (1786) & the French Editions of Lausanne & Paris -1787, 3 vols. in 1. facsimile ed. LC 72-4324. 768p. (Fr.). 1972. Repr. of 1786 ed. 90.00x (ISBN 0-8201-1102-3). Schol Facsimiles.

Beckford, William see Walpole, Horace.

Beckham, Barry. The Black Student's Guide to Colleges. 508p. 1984. pap. 11.95 (ISBN 0-931761-00-X). Beckham House.

--Runner Mack. LC 83-6140. (Howard University Press Library of Contemporary Literature). 213p. 1984. pap. 6.95 (ISBN 0-88258-116-3). Howard U Pr.

Beckham, Barry, ed. The Black Student's Guide to College. 384p. 1982. 15.95 (ISBN 0-525-93256-9, 01549-460); pap. 8.95 (ISBN 0-525-93257-7, 0869-260). Dutton.

Beckham, E. Ernest & Leber, William R., eds. Handbook for the Diagnosis, Treatment, Assessment, & Research of Depression. (Dursey Profesional Bks.). 1985. 55.00 (ISBN 0-256-03490-7). Dorsey.

Beckham, Eleanor, tr. see Maroger, Jacques.

Beckham, Joseph. Legal Implications of Minimum Competency Testing. LC 79-93114. (Fastback Ser.: No. 138). (Orig.). 1980. pap. 0.75 (ISBN 0-87367-138-4). Phi Delta Kappa.

Beckham, Joseph & Delon, Floyd G. School Officials & the Courts: Update 1982. LC 83-127073. (ERS Monograph). 94p. Date not set. price not set. Ed Research.

Beckham, Joseph & Zirkel, Perry A. Legal Issues in Public School Employment. LC 83-62849. 1983. 7.00 (ISBN 0-87367-789-7). Phi Delta Kappa.

Beckham, Richard. Clinical Simulations in Respiratory Care: Workbook & Study Guide. (Illus.). 271p. 1983. pap. text ed. 25.00 (ISBN 0-397-50625-2, 65-07909, Lippincott Medical). Lippincott.

Beckham, Stephen D. Requiem for a People: The Rogue Indians & the Frontiersmen. LC 79-145497. (Civilization of the American Indian Ser.: Vol. 108). (Illus.). 1971. 14.95 (ISBN 0-8061-0942-4); pap. 7.95 (ISBN 0-8061-1036-8). U of Okla Pr.

Beckhand, Richard, jt. auth. see Schmidt, Warren H.

Beckhard, R. & Harris, R. T. Organizational Transitions: Managing Complex Change. 1977. 10.50 (ISBN 0-201-00335-X). Addison-Wesley.

Beckhard, Richard. Organization Development: Strategies & Models. Schein, Edgar, et al, eds. (Series in Organization Development). 1969. pap. text ed. 10.50 (ISBN 0-201-00448-8). Addison-Wesley.

Beckhardt, Israel. The Small Investor's Guide to Gold. 1979. pap. 2.95 (ISBN 0-532-23232-1). Woodhill.

Beckhardt, Robin, ed. see Hillman, Libby.

Beckhart, Benjamin H., ed. New York Money Market, 4 Vols. LC 79-155152. Repr. of 1932 ed. Set. 150.00 (ISBN 0-404-04550-2). AMS Pr.

Becking, Rudolf W. A Pocket Flora of the Redwood Forest. (Illus.). 262p. (Orig.). 1982. pap. 15.00 (ISBN 0-933280-02-5). Island CA.

Beckingham, C. F. & Huntingford, G. W., eds. Some Records of Ethiopia, Fifteen Ninety-Three to Sixteen Forty-Six. (Hakluyt Society Works Ser.: No. 2, Vol. 107). (Illus.). Repr. of 1954 ed. 42.00 (ISBN 0-317-16516-X). Kraus Repr.

Beckingham, C. F., ed. see Alvares, Francisco.

Beckingham, C. F., et al, eds. The Itinerario of P. Jeronimo Lobo. 1980. 60.00x (ISBN 0-686-79468-0, Pub. by Hakluyt Soc England). State Mutual Bk.

Beckingsale, B. W. Thomas Cromwell: Tudor Minister. (Illus.). 181p. 1978. 18.50x (ISBN 0-8476-6053-2). Rowman.

Beckington, Thomas. Memorials of the Reign of King Henry VI: Official Correspondence of Thomas Bekynton, Secretary to Henry VI & Bishop of Bath & Wells, 2 vols. Williams, George, ed. (Rolls Ser.: No. 56). Repr. of 1872 ed. Set. 88.00 (ISBN 0-317-16779-0). Kraus Repr.

Beckinsale, Monica & Beckinsale, Robert. Southern Europe: A Systematic Geographical Study. LC 74-14940. (Illus.). 352p. 1975. text ed. 55.00x (ISBN 0-8419-0178-3). Holmes & Meier.

Beckinsale, Monica, jt. auth. see Beckinsale, Robert.

Beckinsale, Robert & Beckinsale, Monica. The English Heartland. (Illus.). 446p. 1980. 39.50x (ISBN 0-7156-1389-8, Pub. by Duckworth England). Biblio Dist.

Beckinsale, Robert, jt. auth. see Beckinsale, Monica.

Becklake, John. Man & the Moon. LC 81-51496. (Exploration & Discovery Ser.). PLB 13.80 (ISBN 0-382-06615-4). Silver.

Becklake, Sue. The Mysterious Universe. LC 83-60894. (Exploration & Discovery Ser.). 1983. 13.80 (ISBN 0-382-06699-5). Silver.

Becklake, Susan. The Solar System. LC 81-51498. (Exploration & Discovery Ser.). PLB 13.80 (ISBN 0-382-06614-6). Silver.

Beckler, Alfred W. A Gift of Life: The Powerful True Story of How Family Love & One Man's Indomitable Spirit Brought Him Back from Death to a Joyous Life. 1983. 15.95 (ISBN 0-89256-233-1). Rawson Assocs.

Beckles, Samuel E. Selected Issues in American Education. 1985. 10.00 (ISBN 0-317-28943-8). Vantage.

Beckley, Ed. Government Gold Mines. 368p. 1985. 75.00 (ISBN 0-933623-02-X). Midwest Finan Pubns.

--No Down Payment Formulas. (Illus.). 240p. 1985. 19.95 (ISBN 0-933623-00-3). Midwest Finan Pubns.

--One Hundred Twenty-Five Irresistible Purchase Offers. 1985. 49.95 (ISBN 0-933623-01-1). Midwest Finan Pubns.

--Real Estate Froms & How to Master Them. 103p. 1985. 29.95 (ISBN 0-933623-03-8). Midwest Finan Pubns.

Beckley, Helen, jt. auth. see White, Paul B.

Beckley, John L. The Power of Little Words: Some Ideas to Improve Your Writing. (Illus.). 128p. 1984. 14.95 (ISBN 0-910187-02-9). Economics Pr.

--Why Didn't Somebody Tell Us! Some Curious but Little-Known Facts about the Way We Make Our Living. Flint, Helen, ed. LC 82-12987. (Illus.). 128p. 1982. 12.95 (ISBN 0-910187-00-2). Economic Pr.

--Working with People. 158p. 1985. 14.95 (ISBN 0-910187-03-7). Economics Pr.

Beckley, John L., ed. see Rowland, Daniel.

Beckley, Judi. The Brothers: A Protohistory. 2nd, rev., abr. ed. West, Randall, ed. 85p. (Orig.). 12.95 (ISBN 0-942478-00-2). Photopia Pr.

Beckley, Judi & West, Randy. Rose-A-Down Dilly. (Illus.). 32p. (Orig.). 1981. pap. 2.50x (ISBN 0-942478-01-0). Photopia Pr.

Beckley, Peter. Keeping Bees. (The Garden Farming Ser.). (Illus.). 125p. 1983. pap. 5.95 (ISBN 0-7207-1436-2, Pub. by Michael Joseph). Merrimack Pub Cir.

Beckley, Robert E., jt. auth. see Chalfant, Paul H.

Beckley, Robert M. & Dragos, Stephen F. Downtown Milwaukee. (Illus.). 22p. 1979. pap. 5.00 (ISBN 0-938744-11-9, R79-6). U of Wis Ctr Arch-Urban.

Beckley, Robert M. & Hill, C. The Milwaukee Riverwalk Guidelines. (Illus.). iii, 97p. 1985. write for info. (ISBN 0-938744-28-3). U of Wis Ctr Arch-Urban.

Beckley, Robert M., et al. Theater Facility Impact Study: MRT Facilities: Analysis & Recommendations, Vol. 2. (Illus.). 71p. 1982. 12.50 (ISBN 0-938744-22-4, R82-1). U of Wis Ctr Arch-Urban.

--Theater Facility Impact Study: Theater Facilities: Guidelines & Strategies, Vol. 1. (Illus.). vi, 139p. 1981. 12.50 (ISBN 0-938744-21-6, R81-9). U of Wis Ctr Arch-Urban.

--Historic Third Ward: Urban Design Proposals. (Illus.). 88p. 1985. 10.00 (ISBN 0-938744-29-1). U of Wis Ctr Arch-Urban.

Beckley, Timothy G. Book of Space Contacts. 72p. 1981. pap. 7.95 (ISBN 0-938294-05-9). Global Comm.

--Psychic & UFO Revelations in Last Days. 2nd ed. (Illus.). 72p. 1981. pap. 7.95 (ISBN 0-938294-01-6). Global Comm.

--The Riddle of Hangar Eighteen. (Illus.). 72p. (Orig.). 1981. pap. write for info. (ISBN 0-938294-03-2). Global Comm.

Becklund, Orville A., jt. auth. see Williams, Charles S.

Beckly, Albert. Handbook of Painting & Decorating Products. 240p. 1983. pap. 25.00x (ISBN 0-246-11842-3, Pub. by Granada England). Sheridan.

Beckman, A. L., ed. The Neural Basis of Behavior. (Illus.). 350p. 1982. text ed. 47.50 (ISBN 0-89335-132-6). SP Med & Sci Bks.

Beckman, Barbara J. Underlying Word Order: German as a VSO Language. (German Language & Literature-European University Studies: No. 1, Vol. 322). 155p. 1979. pap. 21.95 (ISBN 3-8204-6633-9). P Lang Pubs.

Beckman, Beatrice. I Can Be a Teacher. (Illus.). 32p. (ps-3). 1985. 2.95 (ISBN 0-516-41843-2). Childrens.

--I Can Be President. LC 84-12653. (I Can Be Bks.). (Illus.). 32p. (gr. k-3). 1984. lib. bdg. 10.60 (ISBN 0-516-01841-8); pap. 2.95 (ISBN 0-516-41841-6). Childrens.

Beckman, Beverly. Shapes in God's World. LC 56-1462. 1984. 5.95 (ISBN 0-570-04094-9). Concordia.

--Sizes in God's World. 1984. 5.95 (ISBN 0-570-04095-7, 56-1463). Concordia.

Beckman, Bob. Building & Flying Giant Scale Radio Control Aircraft. Angle, Burr, ed. (Illus.). 88p. (Orig.). 1983. pap. 9.95 (ISBN 0-89024-049-3). Kalmbach.

Beckman, Carol A., jt. ed. see Crowe, Michael R.

Beckman, Charles R., jt. auth. see Ellis, Jeffery W.

Beckman, Charles R., jt. auth. see Ellis, Jeffrey W.

Beckman, David & Donnelly, Elizabeth Anne. The Overseas List: Opportunities for Living & Working in Developing Countries. 192p. 4.95 (ISBN 0-318-13657-0). Bread for the World.

Beckman, Delores. My Own Private Sky. LC 79-23341. 160p. (gr. 4-6). 1980. 9.95 (ISBN 0-525-35510-3). Dutton.

--Who Loves Sam Grant? LC 82-18211. 160p. (gr. 5-9). 1983. 10.95 (ISBN 0-525-44055-0, 01063-320). Dutton.

--Who Loves Sam Grant? 176p. (gr. 7-12). 1984. pap. 2.25 (ISBN 0-440-99478-0, LFL). Dell.

Beckman, Ed. Love, Praise & Reward: The New Way to Train Your Dog. LC 78-23938. (Illus.). 1979. 9.95 (ISBN 0-698-10886-8, Coward). Putnam Pub Group.

Beckman, Erik. Careers in Criminal Justice: Law Enforcement, Courts, Corrections, Security. 168p. 1981. pap. 16.75x spiral (ISBN 0-398-04497-X). C C Thomas.

--The Criminal Justice Dictionary. 2nd, rev. ed. LC 78-72049. 1983. 24.50 (ISBN 0-87650-153-6); pap. 19.50 (ISBN 0-87650-152-8). Pierian.

--Law Enforcement in a Democratic Society: An Introduction. LC 79-16303. (Justice Administration Ser.). 350p. 1980. 25.95x (ISBN 0-88229-151-3); pap. 15.95x (ISBN 0-88229-753-8). Nelson-Hall.

Beckman, Frank S. Mathematical Foundations of Programming. LC 79-1453. 1980. text ed. 31.95 (ISBN 0-201-14462-X). Addison-Wesley.

Beckman, G. M., jt. ed. see Hoffner, H. A., Jr.

Beckman, Gunnel. Mia Alone. Tate, Joan, tr. 112p. (YA) (gr. 7 up). pap. 1.50 (ISBN 0-440-95586-6). Dell.

Beckman, Gunnell. Admission to the Feast. 144p. (gr. 7 up). 1973. pap. 1.25 (ISBN 0-440-90312-2, LFL). Dell.

Beckman, Harry. Dilemmas in Drug Therapy. LC 67-10428. Repr. of 1967 ed. 104.00 (ISBN 0-8357-9541-1, 2013062). Bks Demand UMI.

Beckman, Henry. How to Sell Your Film Project. (Orig.). 1979. pap. 9.95 (ISBN 0-523-40624-X). Pinnacle Bks.

Beckman, J. E. & Phillips, J. P. Submillimetre Wave Astronomy. LC 82-4487. (Illus.). 370p. 1982. 52.50 (ISBN 0-521-24733-0). Cambridge U Pr.

Beckman, Jean E. Why? There Is More to You Than Meets the Eye. (Illus.). 50p. (Orig.). (gr. 9-12). 1981. pap. 3.95 (ISBN 0-941992-00-4). Los Arboles Pub.

Beckman, John E. & Crivellari, Lucio, eds. Progress in Stellar Spectral Line Formation Theory. 1985. lib. bdg. 59.00 (ISBN 90-277-2007-X, Pub. by Reidel Netherlands). Kluwer Academic.

Beckman, L., ed. see Giannelli, F.

Beckman, L., ed. see International Symposium on Inborn Errors of Metabolism in Man, Tel Aviv, June, 1977.

Beckman, L., ed. see Svejgaard, A.

Beckman, Linda, jt. ed. see Eiduson, Bernice T.

Beckman, Linda J., jt. ed. see Wilsnack, Sharon.

Beckman, Max. Max Beckmann. Selz, Peter, et al, eds. 30.00 (ISBN 0-405-12888-6). Ayer Co Pubs.

Beckman, Neal & Carpenter, Myron. An Approach to Purchasing for Profit. LC 79-50181. 170p. 1979. 24.50 (ISBN 0-87527-199-5). Green.

Beckman, Patti. Spotlight to Fame. (Silhouette Romances Ser.). 1984. lib. bdg. 8.95 (ISBN 0-8398-2804-7, Gregg). G K Hall.

Beckman, Peter R. World Politics in the Twentieth Century. (Illus.). 400p. 1984. pap. 19.95 (ISBN 0-13-968768-8). P-H.

Beckman, Petr. The Health Hazards of Not Going Nuclear. 1980. pap. 2.50 (ISBN 0-686-97299-6). Ace Bks.

Beckman, Ray. Paper Coins. LC 84-71865. (Illus.). 250p. (Orig.). 1985. pap. 9.95 (ISBN 0-9611240-3-2). Basement Pr.

Beckman, Robert C. The Downwave: Survivng the Second Great Depression. (Illus.). 1983. 19.95 (ISBN 0-525-24216-3, 01937-580). Dutton.

Beckman, Robert L. Nuclear Proliferation, Congress, & the Control of Peaceful Nuclear Activities. LC 84-25644. 350p. 1985. pap. 28.00x (ISBN 0-8133-7040-X). Westview.

Beckman, Steven D., tr. see De La Bathie, H. Perrier.

Beckman, Theodore N. & Nolen, Herman C. The Chain Store Problem: A Critical Analysis. LC 75-39231. (Illus.). 1976. Repr. of 1938 ed. 26.50x (ISBN 0-405-08008-5). Ayer Co Pubs.

Beckman, Theodore N., et al. Wholesaling. 3rd ed. LC 59-10138. pap. 160.00 (ISBN 0-317-29068-1, 2017835). Bks Demand UMI.

Beckman, William A., jt. auth. see Duffie, John A.

Beckman, William A., et al. Solar Heating Design: By the F-Chart Method. LC 77-22168. 200p. 1977. 31.95x (ISBN 0-471-03406-1, Pub. by Wiley-Interscience). Wiley.

Beckmann, Beverly. Colors in God's World. 1983. 5.95 (ISBN 0-570-04082-5, 56-1437). Concordia.

--From. (Illus.). 1980. pap. 3.95 (ISBN 0-570-03489-2, 56-1343). Concordia.

--Numbers in God's World. (ps). 1983. 5.95 (ISBN 0-570-04083-3, 56-1438). Concordia.

--Seasons in God's World. (In God's World Ser.). (Illus.). 24p. (gr. 2-5). 1985. 5.95 (ISBN 0-570-04127-9, 56-1538). Concordia.

--Time in God's World. (In God's World Ser.). (Illus.). 24p. (gr. 2-5). 1985. 5.95 (ISBN 0-570-04128-7, 56-1539). Concordia.

Beckmann, Charles R., et al. Williams Obstetrics: Study Guide. 384p. 1985. pap. 29.95 (ISBN 0-8385-9735-1). ACC.

Beckmann, David M. Where Faith & Economics Meet: A Christian Critique. LC 80-67796. 160p. (Orig.). 1981. pap. 7.95 (ISBN 0-8066-1858-2, 10-7068). Augsburg.

Beckmann, David M. & Donnelly, Elizabeth A. The Overseas List: Opportunities for Living & Working in Developing Countries. LC 79-50095. 192p. 1979. pap. 7.50 (ISBN 0-8066-1719-5, 10-4865). Augsburg.

Beckmann, Friedrich & Schmidt, Eckart. N-gons. Garner, Cyril W., tr. LC 70-185699. (Mathematical Expositions Ser.: No. 18). pap. 51.80 (ISBN 0-317-08538-7, 2019448). Bks Demand UMI.

Beckmann, G. & Gilli, P. V. Thermal Energy Storage. (Topics in Energy Ser.). (Illus.). 240p. 1984. 35.50 (ISBN 0-387-81764-6). Springer Verlag.

Beckmann, George M. The Making of the Meiji Constitution: The Oligarchs & the Constitutional Development of Japan, 1868-1891. LC 72-7963. 158p. 1975. Repr. of 1957 ed. lib. bdg. 15.00 (ISBN 0-8371-6553-9, BEMC). Greenwood.

Beckmann, George M. & Genji, Okubo. The Japanese Communist Party, 1922-1945. LC 68-26776. 1969. 32.50x (ISBN 0-8047-0674-3). Stanford U Pr.

Beckmann, H. & Riederer, P., eds. Monoamine Oxidase & Its Selective Inhibitors. (Modern Problems of Pharmacopsychiatry: Vol. 19). (Illus.). x, 354p. 1983. 84.25 (ISBN 3-8055-3595-3). S Karger.

--Pathochemical Markers in Major Psychoses. (Illus.). 175p. 1985. 27.50 (ISBN 0-387-13444-1). Springer-Verlag.

Beckmann, J., jt. ed. see Kuhl, J.

Beckmann, M. & Puu, T. Spatial Economics: Density, Potential & Flow. (Studies in Regional Science & Urban Economics: Vol. 14). 276p. 1985. 46.50 (ISBN 0-444-87771-1, North-Holland). Elsevier.

Beckmann, M. J. Tinbergen Lectures on Organization Theory. (Texts & Monographs in Economics & Mathematical Systems). (Illus.). 176p. 1983. 19.80 (ISBN 0-387-12646-5). Springer-Verlag.

Beckmann, M. J, jt. ed. see Sato, R.

Beckmann, Martin, et al. Studies in the Economics of Transportation. 1956. 59.50x (ISBN 0-685-89787-7). Elliots Bks.

Beckmann, Martin J. Dynamic Programming of Economic Decisions. LC 68-21990. (Econometrics & Operations Research: Vol. 9). 1968. 24.00 (ISBN 0-387-04292-X). Springer-Verlag.

Beckmann, Neal W. Negotiations, Understanding the Bargaining Process. 152p. 1980. 16.50 (ISBN 0-87527-242-8). Green.

Beckmann, Peter. A History of Pi. 1976. pap. 5.95 (ISBN 0-312-38185-9). St Martin.

Beckmann, Petr. Elementary Queue Theory & Telephone Traffic. 1976. 7.75 (ISBN 0-686-98072-7). Telecom Lib.

--The Health Hazards of NOT Going Nuclear. LC 76-12720. (Illus.). 188p. 1976. pap. 7.95x (ISBN 0-911762-17-5). Golem.

--History of Pi. 4th ed. LC 77-24777. (Illus.). 1977. 12.95x (ISBN 0-911762-18-3). Golem.

--Orthogonal Polynomials for Engineers & Physicists. LC 72-87318. 1973. 25.00x (ISBN 0-911762-14-0). Golem.

--The Structure of Language: A New Approach. LC 72-77116. (Illus.). 320p. 1972. 25.00x (ISBN 0-911762-13-2). Golem.

Beckmann, Petr, tr. see Shevchenko, Viktor V.

Beckmann, Petr, tr. see Shifrin, A. S.

Beckmann, Petr, tr. see Zakharyev, L. N., et al.

Beckmann, Till. Studien Zur Bestimmung Des Lebens In Meister Eckharts Deutschen Predigten. (European University Studies: No. 20, Vol. 85). 244p. (Ger.). 1982. 30.00 (ISBN 3-8204-5708-9). P Lang Pubs.

Becknell, Eileen & Smith, Dorothy M. System of Nursing Practice: A Clinical Nursing Assessment Tool. 1975. pap. text ed. 8.50x (ISBN 0-8036-0695-8). Davis Co.

Beckner, Everet. Techniseasonal Commodity Trading. 1984. 65.00 (ISBN 0-318-04207-X). Windsor.

Beckner, Steven K. The Hard Money Book: An Insider's Guide to Successful Investment in Currency, Gold, Silver & Precious Stones. LC 79-84366. (Orig.). 1979. pap. 19.00 (ISBN 0-933722-00-1). Capitalist Reporter.

Beckner, Weldon. The Case for the Smaller School. LC 82-63061. (Fastback Ser.: No. 190). 50p. 1983. pap. 0.75 (ISBN 0-87367-190-2). Phi Delta Kappa.

Beckner, William, et al, eds. Conference on Harmonic Analysis in Honor of Antoni Zygmund. LC 82-11172. (Mathematics Ser.: Vols. I & II). 837p. 1983. write for info. (ISBN 0-534-98043-0). Wadsworth Pub.

Beckoff, Samuel. Monarch Notes on Updike's Rabbit Run & Rabbit Redux. pap. 2.95 (ISBN 0-671-00947-8). Monarch Pr.

Beckson, Karl & Ganz, Arthur. Literary Terms: A Dictionary. rev. ed. 288p. 1975. pap. 6.95 (ISBN 0-374-51225-6). FS&G.

Beckson, Karl, ed. Aesthetes & Decadents of the Eighteen Nineties. (Illus.). 337p. 1981. pap. 6.95 (ISBN 0-89733-044-7). Academy Chi Pubs.

--The Memoirs of Arthur Symons: Life & Art in the 1890s. LC 76-42229. 1977. 24.95x (ISBN 0-271-01244-7). Pa St U Pr.

Beckson, Karl, jt. ed. see Lago, Mary M.

Beckstead, Gayle & Kozub, Mary L. Searching in Illinois: A Reference Guide to Public & Private Records. LC 84-80217. (ISC State Search Bks.: No. 3). 210p. (Orig.). 1984. pap. text ed. 12.95 (ISBN 0-942916-05-0). ISC Pubns.

Beckstrand, O. Garfield. Pray Then, Like This. 39p. 1975. pap. 3.00 (ISBN 0-89536-181-7). CSS of Ohio.

--The Word From the Upper Room. (Orig.). 1977. pap. 3.75 (ISBN 0-89536-265-1). CSS of Ohio.

Beckstrom, Bob. Deck Plans: Includes Complete Plans for 12 Decks. Coolman, Anne, ed. LC 85-60006. (Illus.). 96p. (Orig.). 1985. pap. 5.95 (ISBN 0-89721-043-3). Ortho.

Beckstrom, John H. Sociobiology & the Law: The Biology of Altruism in the Courtroom of the Future. LC 84-16415. 160p. 1985. 19.95x (ISBN 0-252-01171-6). U of Ill Pr.

Beckstrom, Kristen, jt. auth. see Wirt, Sherwood.

Beckstrom, Robert J. Ortho's Home Improvement Encyclopedia. Shakery, Karin, ed. LC 85-70877. (Illus.). 512p. (Orig.). 1985. 24.95 (ISBN 0-89721-066-2). Ortho.

Beckum, William F., Jr. & Langley, Albert M., Jr. Georgia Railroad Album. LC 85-51239. (Illus.). 72p. (Orig.). 1985. pap. 10.95 (ISBN 0-9615257-0-3). Union Sta.

Beckurts, K. H. & Wirtz, K. Neutron Physics. rev. ed. (Illus.). 1964. 55.00 (ISBN 0-387-03096-4). Springer-Verlag.

Beckwith. Lovecrafts Providence & Adjacent Parts. 10.00 (ISBN 0-686-27886-0). D M Grant.

Beckwith, B. P. The Case for Liberal Socialism. 1976. 7.50 (ISBN 0-682-48487-3). Beckwith.

--Liberal Socialism: The Pure Welfare Economics of a Liberal Socialist Economy. 2nd ed. LC 73-92848. 1974. 6.00 (ISBN 0-682-47785-0). Beckwith.

--Radical Essays. 1981. 6.00 (ISBN 0-9603262-2-7). Beckwith.

Beckwith, Burnham P. Contemporary English & American Theories Concerning the Effect of Commercial Banking on the Supply of Physical Capital. LC 35-13250. 45p. 1982. lib. bdg. 19.95x (ISBN 0-89370-707-4). Borgo Pr.

--The Decline of U. S. Religious Faith: Nineteen Twelve to Nineteen Eighty-Four, & the Effect of Education & Intelligence on Such Faith. 1985. 9.00x (ISBN 0-9603262-4-3). Beckwith.

--Government by Experts: The Next Stage in Political Evolution. LC 72-84068. 1972. text ed. 7.50 (ISBN 0-682-47539-4). Beckwith.

--Ideas about the Future: A History of Futurism, 1794-1982. 320p. 1984. 10.00 (ISBN 0-9603262-3-5). Beckwith.

--Liberal Socialism: The Pure Welfare Economics of a Liberal Socialist Economy. 2nd rev. ed. 1974. text ed. 20.00 (ISBN 0-682-47785-0, University). Exposition Pr FL.

--Next Five Hundred Years. 1968. text ed. 10.00 (ISBN 0-682-45791-4, University). Exposition Pr FL.

Beckwith, Carol, jt. auth. see Van Offelen, Marion.

Beckwith, Chant M. The Kumulipo: A Hawaiian Creation. 1957. 6.00 (ISBN 0-910294-10-0). Brown Bk.

Beckwith, Charles E., ed. see Gay, John.

Beckwith, Charlie A. & Knox, Donald. Delta Force. (Illus.). 320p. 1983. 14.95 (ISBN 0-15-124657-2). HarBraceJ.

--Delta Force: The Army's Elite Counterterrorist Unit. (Illus.). 1985. pap. 3.95 (ISBN 0-440-11886-7). Dell.

Beckwith, Francis. Bahai. 64p. 1985. saddle stitched 2.95 (ISBN 0-87123-848-9). Bethany Hse.

Beckwith, George C. The Peace Manual: War & Its Remedies. LC 73-137529. (Peace Movement in America Ser). 1972. Repr. of 1847 ed. lib. bdg. 16.95x (ISBN 0-89198-056-3). Ozer.

Beckwith, George C., ed. The Book of Peace: A Collection of Essays on War & Peace. LC 70-137528. (Peace Movement in America Ser.). iv, 500p. 1972. Repr. of 1845 ed. lib. bdg. 25.95x (ISBN 0-89198-055-5). Ozer.

Beckwith, Glenwood J. How to Make Your Backyard More Interesting Than TV. (McGraw-Hill Paperbacks). (Illus., Orig.). 1980. pap. 6.95 (ISBN 0-07-004266-7). McGraw.

Beckwith, Herbert H., jt. auth. see Williams, Evan W.

Beckwith, Hiram W. The Illinois & Indiana Indians. facsimile ed. LC 75-86. (Mid-American Frontier Ser.). 1975. Repr. of 1884 ed. 13.00 (ISBN 0-405-06854-9). Ayer Co Pubs.

Beckwith, Isbon T. The Apocalypse of John. (Twin Brooks Ser.). 1979. pap. 12.95 (ISBN 0-8010-0761-5). Baker Bk.

Beckwith, John. Early Christian & Byzantine Art. (Pelican History of Art Ser.). 1980. pap. 18.95 (ISBN 0-14-056133-1). Penguin.

--Early Christian & Byzantine Art. rev. ed. (The Pelican History of Art Ser.). 1980. 35.00 (ISBN 0-670-28710-5). Viking.

--Early Medieval Art. LC 84-51844. (World of Art Ser.). (Illus.). 270p. 1985. pap. 9.95 (ISBN 0-500-20019-X). Thames Hudson.

--Ivory Carvings in Early Medieval England. (Illus.). 1972. 49.00x (ISBN 0-19-921007-1). Oxford U Pr.

Beckwith, John A. Gem Minerals of Idaho. LC 70-150817. (Illus., Orig.). 1972. pap. 5.95 enlarged ed. (ISBN 0-87004-228-9). Caxton.

Beckwith, John A. & Coope, Geoffrey G., eds. Contemporary American Biography. facsimile ed. LC 77-142607. (Essay Index Reprint Ser). Repr. of 1941 ed. 22.00 (ISBN 0-8369-2483-5). Ayer Co Pubs.

Beckwith, Jon, et al, eds. Gene Function in Prokaryotes. LC 83-15229. (Cold Spring Harbor Monographs: Vol. 15). 328p. 1984. 52.00x (ISBN 0-87969-164-6). Cold Spring Harbor.

--Gene Function in Prokaryotes. LC 83-15229. (Monograph Ser.: Vol. 15). 328p. 1984. pap. 30.00 (ISBN 0-87969-176-X). Cold Spring Harbor.

Beckwith, Julian R. Basic Electrocardiography & Vectorcardiography. (Illus.). 296p. 1982. pap. text ed. 19.50 (ISBN 0-89004-673-5). Raven.

Beckwith, Lillian. A Shine of Rainbows. 124p. 1984. 9.95 (ISBN 0-312-71738-5). St Martin.

Beckwith, Lynn. Coach Phyllis. 1982. 10.00 (ISBN 0-533-05487-7). Vantage.

Beckwith, Martha W. Black Roadways: A Study of Jamaican Folk Life. LC 69-16597. (Illus.). Repr. of 1929 ed. 25.00x (ISBN 0-8371-1144-7, BEB&, Pub. by Negro U Pr). Greenwood.

--Hawaiian Mythology. LC 70-97998. 1977. pap. 10.95 (ISBN 0-8248-0514-3). UH Pr.

--Jamaica Anansi Stories. LC 26-10368. (American Folklore Soc. Memoirs). Repr. of 1924 ed. 24.00 (ISBN 0-527-01069-3). Kraus Repr.

--Jamaica Folk-Lore. LC 30-18643. (American Folklore Society Memoirs). Repr. of 1928 ed. 29.00 (ISBN 0-527-01073-1). Kraus Repr.

--Jamaica Proverbs. LC 70-100278. Repr. of 1925 ed. 18.75x (ISBN 0-8371-2938-9, BEJ&, Pub. by Negro U Pr). Greenwood.

--Mandan-Hidatsa Myths & Ceremonies. LC 38-19412. (American Folklore Society Memoirs). Repr. of 1938 ed. 29.00 (ISBN 0-527-01084-7). Kraus Repr.

--Myths & Hunting Stories of the Mandan & Hidatsa Sioux. LC 76-43665. (Vassar College Folklore Foundation: Publication No. 10). 1977. Repr. of 1930 ed. 16.00 (ISBN 0-404-15498-0). AMS Pr.

Beckwith, Martha W., ed. The Kumulipo: A Hawaiian Creation Chant. LC 79-118978. 276p. 1981. pap. 5.95 (ISBN 0-8248-0771-5). UH Pr.

Beckwith, Martha W., ed. see Kepelino.

Beckwith, Martha W., et al. Pushkin. facsimile ed. LC 75-168509. (Black Heritage Library Collection). Repr. of 1937 ed. 17.50 (ISBN 0-8369-8862-0). Ayer Co Pubs.

Beckwith, Merle R. A New List of Proverbs. LC 79-92430. cancelled (ISBN 0-8022-2361-3). Philos Lib.

Beckwith, Neil, et al, eds. Nineteen Seventy-Nine AMA Educators Conference. LC 79-14547. (Proceedings Ser.: No. 44). (Illus.). pap. 24.00 (ISBN 0-87757-121-X). Am Mktg.

Beckwith, Osmond. Vernon: An Anecdotal Novel. LC 81-65121. (Illus.). 204p. 1981. 10.00 (ISBN 0-917020-02-2). Breaking Point.

Beckwith, Paul. Notes on the Customs of the Dakotas. (Shorey Indian Ser.). 16p. 1975. pap. 1.95 (ISBN 0-8466-4013-9). Shorey.

Beckwith, Paul, et al, eds. Hymns II. LC 76-47503. 1976. text ed. 10.95 (ISBN 0-87784-898-X); pap. text ed. 6.95 (ISBN 0-87784-783-5); pap. text ed. 10.95 spiral text (ISBN 0-87784-750-9). Inter-Varsity.

Beckwith, Roger. The Old Testament Canon of the New Testament Church. 536p. 1985. 29.95x (ISBN 0-8028-3617-8). Eerdmans.

Beckwith, Roger T. & Scott, Wilfrid. This Is the Day: The Biblical Doctrine of the Christian Sunday in it's Jewish & Early Church Setting. 192p. 1978. 15.00 (ISBN 0-551-05568-5). Attic Pr.

Beckwith, Roger T. & Stott, Wilfred. The Christian Sunday: A Biblical & Historical Study. (Canterbury Ser.). 192p. 1980. pap. 4.95 (ISBN 0-8010-0784-4). Baker Bk.

Beckwith, T. G., et al. Mechanical Measurements. 3rd ed. 1982. 39.95 (ISBN 0-201-00036-9); solutions manual 1.50 (ISBN 0-201-00037-7). Addison-Wesley.

Beckwourth, James P. & Bonner, Thomas D. The Life & Adventures of James P. Beckwourth. LC 73-88092. (Illus.). xiv, 649p. 1972. pap. 10.95 (ISBN 0-8032-6061-X, BB 773, Bison). U of Nebr Pr.

Becnel, Thomas. Labor, Church, & the Sugar Establishment: Louisiana, 1887-1976. LC 80-10572. (Illus.). xx, 276p. 1980. 27.50x (ISBN 0-8071-0660-7). La State U Pr.

Becon, Thomas. The Catechism of Thomas Becon. Repr. of 1884 ed. 55.00 (ISBN 0-384-03715-1). Johnson Repr.

--The Demaundes of Holy Scripture, with Answers to the Same. LC 79-84087. (English Experience Ser.: No.907). 116p. 1979. Repr. of 1577 ed. lib. bdg. 9.00 (ISBN 90-221-0907-0). Walter J Johnson.

--The Early Works of Thomas Becon, Chaplain to Archbishop Cranmer. Repr. of 1843 ed. 41.00 (ISBN 0-384-03725-9). Johnson Repr.

--The Physyke of the Soule. LC 74-28831. (English Experience Ser.: No. 713). 1975. Repr. of 1549 ed. 3.50 (ISBN 90-221-0713-2). Walter J Johnson.

--Prayers & Others Pieces of Thomas Becon, Chaplain to Archbishop Cranmer. Repr. of 1844 ed. 55.00 (ISBN 0-384-03730-5). Johnson Repr.

--The Principles of Christian Religion. LC 76-57355. (English Experience Ser.: No. 774). 1977. Repr. of 1552 ed. lib. bdg. 14.00 (ISBN 90-221-0774-4). Walter J Johnson.

Becque, Hari. La Parisienne. (Livret). pap. 2.95 (ISBN 0-685-34881-4). French & Eur.

Becquer, A., jt. auth. see Armanet, J.

Becquer, Gustavo. The Rimas of Gustavo Becquer. Renard, Jules, tr. 1976. lib. bdg. 59.95 (ISBN 0-8490-2525-7). Gordon Pr.

Becquer, Gustavo A. A Flower on a Volcano. Dubroff, Susanne, tr. from Span. 1980. pap. 2.50 (ISBN 0-915408-21-X); pap. 5.00 signed ed (ISBN 0-915408-22-8, 1-50). Ally Pr.

--Romantic Legends of Spain. facsimile ed. Bates, Cornelia F. & Bates, Katharine L., trs. LC 78-169539. (Short Story Index Reprint Ser.). Repr. of 1909 ed. 19.50 (ISBN 0-8369-4000-8). Ayer Co Pubs.

Becraft, Melvin. Picasso's Guernica: Images Within Images. 1983. 6.95 (ISBN 0-533-05440-0). Vantage.

Becton, Betty G., jt. auth. see Moorhead, Betty B.

Becton, Cleveland M., jt. auth. see Urshan, Nathaniel A.

Becton, Randy. The Beauty of God's Whisper. 1980. pap. 4.75 (ISBN 0-89137-310-1). Quality Pubns.

--The Faithful Father. LC 80-54433. 1981. 6.95 (ISBN 0-89112-055-6). Bibl Res Pr.

--The Gift of Life: A Message of Hope for the Seriously Ill. (Illus.). 1978. pap. 4.75 (ISBN 0-89137-309-8). Quality Pubns.

Becvar, Dorothy S., jt. auth. see Becvar, Raphael J.

Becvar, J., ed. see Symposium, 4th, Marianske Lazne, Sept. 1-5, 1975.

Becvar, Raphael J. Skills for Effective Communication: A Guide to Building Relationships. LC 73-19914. (Wiley Self-Teaching Guides). 218p. 1974. pap. text ed. 7.95 (ISBN 0-471-06143-3). Wiley.

Becvar, Raphael J. & Becvar, Dorothy S. Systems Theory & Family Therapy: A Primer. LC 81-43721. 104p. (Orig.). 1982. PLB 22.25 (ISBN 0-8191-2443-5); pap. text ed. 8.75 (ISBN 0-8191-2444-3). U Pr of Amer.

Bed Post Writers Group. The American Bed & Breakfast Cookbook. LC 84-48886. 192p. 1985. 12.95 (ISBN 0-88742-052-4). East Woods.

Beda. Bedae Opera De Temporibus. Jones, C. W., ed. 1966. Repr. of 1943 ed. 12.50x (ISBN 0-910956-17-0). Medieval Acad.

--The History of the Church of Englande. (English Experience Ser.: No. 234). 382p. Repr. of 1565 ed. 55.00 (ISBN 90-221-0234-3). Walter J Johnson.

Beda Venerabilis. Bedae Venerabilis Expositio Actuum Apostolorum Et Retractatio. Laistner, M. L., ed. (Mediaeval Academy of America Publications). 1939. 18.00 (ISBN 0-527-01702-7). Kraus Repr.

Bedante, Pilar Gomez see Gomez Bedate, Pilar.

Bedard, Brian. Hour of the Beast & Other Stories. 110p. (Orig.). 1984. pap. 5.00 (ISBN 0-933428-04-9). Chariton Review.

Bedard, Hank. Lucky Thirteen. 1980. pap. 1.75 (ISBN 0-686-38385-0). Eldridge Pub.

Bedard, Paul, tr. see Aubry, Joseph.

Bedard, Roger L. Dramatic Literature for Children: A Century in Review. 1983. pap. text ed. 21.00 (ISBN 0-87602-020-1). Anchorage.

Bedarida, Francois. A Social History of England, Eighteen Fifty-One to Nineteen Seventy-Five. 448p. 1979. 14.95x (ISBN 0-416-85910-0, NO. 2833); pap. 14.95x (ISBN 0-416-85920-8, NO. 2834). Methuen Inc.

Bedau, Hugo. Justice & Equality. (Central Issues of Philosophy Ser). (Illus.). 1971. pap. 15.95 ref. ed. (ISBN 0-13-514125-7). P-H.

Bedau, Hugo A. Civil Disobedience: Theory & Practice. 1969. pap. text ed. write for info. (ISBN 0-02-307870-7). Macmillan.

Bedau, Hugo A., jt. auth. see Schur, Edwin M.

Bedau, Hugo A., ed. Civil Disobedience: Theory & Practice. LC 69-27984. (Orig.). 1969. pap. 10.28scp (ISBN 0-672-63514-3). Pegasus.

--The Death Penalty in America. 3rd ed. (Illus.). 1982. 19.95x (ISBN 0-19-502986-0, GB); pap. 10.95 (ISBN 0-19-502987-9). Oxford U Pr.

Bedau, Hugo A. & Pierce, Chester M., eds. Capital Punishment in the United States. LC 76-5828. (AMS Studies in Modern Society. Political & Social Issues: No. 10). lib. bdg. 42.50 (ISBN 0-404-10325-1). AMS Pr.

Bedborough, D. R. & Trott, P. E. The Sensory Measurement of Odours by Dynamic Dilution. 1979. 1981. 69.00x (ISBN 0-686-97168-X, Pub. by W Spring England). State Mutual Bk.

Bedborough, D. R., jt. auth. see Bailey, J. C.

Bedbrook, G., ed. The Care & Management of Spinal Cord Injuries. (Illus.). 351p. 1981. 49.00 (ISBN 0-387-90494-8). Springer-Verlag.

Bedbrook, G. S. Liszt in London. 144p. 1981. 40.00x (ISBN 0-234-72105-7, Pub. by Dobson Bks England). State Mutual Bk.

Bedbrook, Gerald S. Keyboard Music from the Middle Ages to the Beginnings of the Baroque. 2nd ed. LC 69-15605. (Music Ser). (Illus.). 1973. Repr. of 1949 ed. 25.00 (ISBN 0-306-71056-0). Da Capo.

Beddard, G. S. & West, M. A., eds. Flourescent Probes. 1981. 43.00 (ISBN 0-12-084680-2). Acad Pr.

Bedde, Derk, ed. see Fung Yu-Lang.

Beddie, James S., jt. ed. see Sontag, Raymond J.

Beddington. Design for Shopping Centers. 1982. text ed. 59.95. Butterworth.

Beddington, Frances E. All That I Have Met. LC 79-8050. Repr. of 1929 ed. 29.50 (ISBN 0-404-18361-1). AMS Pr.

Beddington, John R. & Rettig, R. Bruce. Approaches to the Regulation of Fishing Effort. (Fisheries Technical Paper Ser.: No. 243). 39p. (Orig.). 1984. pap. 7.50 (ISBN 92-5-101492-2, F2576, FAO). Unipub.

Beddoe, Deirdre. Discovering Women's History: A Practical Handbook. (Illus.). 229p. (Orig.). 1983. pap. 7.95 (ISBN 0-86358-008-4, Pandora Pr). Routledge & Kegan.

Beddoe, John. The Anthropological History Europe. 1982. Repr. 30.00 (ISBN 0-941694-07-0). Cliveden Pr.

--The Races of Britain. 1983. Repr. 40.00 (ISBN 0-941694-13-5). Cliveden Pr.

Beddoes, K., jt. auth. see Smith, W.

Beddoes, Thomas L. The Letters of Thomas Lovell Beddoes. Gosse, Edmund, ed. LC 70-173168. Repr. of 1894 ed. 22.00 (ISBN 0-405-08250-9, Blom Pubns). Ayer Co Pubs.

--The Works of Thomas Lovell Beddoes. Donner, H. W., ed. LC 75-41023. (BCL Ser. II). 1976. Repr. of 1935 ed. 49.50 (ISBN 0-404-14507-8). AMS Pr.

Beddome, R. H. The Ferns of British India, Vols. I & II. 702p. 1978. 99.00x (ISBN 0-686-84451-3, Pub. by Oxford & I B H India). State Mutual Bk.

--Ferns of Southern India. 1969. Repr. of 1873 ed. 45.00 (ISBN 0-934454-31-0). Lubrecht & Cramer.

--Handbook to the Ferns of British India Ceylon & Malay Peninsula. 1969. Repr. of 1883 ed. 16.00 (ISBN 0-934454-47-7). Lubrecht & Cramer.

--Handbook to the Ferns of British India, Ceylon & Malaysia: Peninsula with Supplement. 502p. 1977. 20.00 (ISBN 0-88065-054-0, Pub. by Messers Today & Tomorrows Printers & Publishers India). Scholarly Pubns.

--Icones Plantrum Indiae Orientalis. (Illus.). 70p. 1972. Repr. of 1874 ed. 40.00 (ISBN 0-88065-055-9, Pub. by Messers Today & TomorrowsPrinters & Publishers India). Scholarly Pubns.

Beddow, J. K. Particulate Science & Technology. (Illus.). 1980. 57.50 (ISBN 0-8206-0254-X). Chem Pub.

--The Production of Metal Powders by Atomizaton. (Powder Advisory Centre Publication Ser. (POWTECH)). 106p. 1978. 59.95 (ISBN 0-471-25601-3, Wiley Heyden). Wiley.

Beddow, J. K. & Meloy, T. P., eds. Testing & Characterization of Powders & Fire Particles. (Powder Advisory Centre Publication Ser. (POWTECH)). 176p. 1979. 57.95 (ISBN 0-471-25602-1, Wiley Heyden). Wiley.

Beddow, J. Keith, ed. see International Symposium on Powder Technology, Sept. 27- Oct. 1981, Kyoto, Japan.

Beddow, John K. & Meloy, Thomas P. Advanced Particulate Morphology: Theory & Practice. 208p. 1980. 69.00 (ISBN 0-8493-5781-0). CRC Pr.

Beddow, John K., ed. Particulate Systems: Technology & Fundamentals. LC 82-1099. (Illus.). 362p. 1983. 69.95 (ISBN 0-89116-241-0). Hemisphere Pub.

Beddow, K. Particulate Science & Technology. 1984. text ed. 75.00 (ISBN 0-07-004267-5). McGraw.

Beddow, Michael. The Fiction of Humanity: Studies in the 'Bildungsroman' from Wieland to Thomas Mann. LC 81-18057. (Anglica Germanica Ser.: No. 2). 250p. 1982. 54.50 (ISBN 0-521-24533-8). Cambridge U Pr.

Beddow, Virginia, ed. The Year of the Bible Manual. (Orig.). 1983. pap. 1.95 (ISBN 0-87239-646-0, 3036). Standard Pub.

Bede. Emile Zola. (Columbia Essays on Modern Writers Ser.: No. 69). 1974. pap. 2.50 (ISBN 0-231-02977-2). Columbia U Pr.

--Historical Works, 2 Vols. (Loeb Classical Library: No. 246, 248). 12.50x ea. Vol. 1 (ISBN 0-674-99271-7). Vol. 2 (ISBN 0-674-99273-3). Harvard U Pr.

--History of the English Church & People. Sherley-Price, tr. (Classics Ser.). (Orig.). 1955. pap. 4.95 (ISBN 0-14-044042-9). Penguin.

Bede, Barry, jt. auth. see Piekalkiewicz, Jaroslaw.

Bede, Cuthbert. The Adventures of Mr. Verdant Green. (Oxford Paperback Ser.). (Illus.). 1982. pap. 9.95x (ISBN 0-19-281331-5). Oxford U Pr.

Bede, Elbert. Fabulous Opal Whiteley. (Illus.). 1978. pap. 5.95 (ISBN 0-8323-0360-7). Binford.

--Five Fifteen-Minute Talks. 1981. Repr. of 1972 ed. 4.50 (ISBN 0-686-43321-1). Macoy Pub.

--The Landmarks of Freemasonry. 1980. pap. text ed. 3.00 (ISBN 0-88053-020-0, M-69). Macoy Pub.

--Three-Five-Seven Minute Talks on Freemasonry. 1981. Repr. of 1978 ed. 4.00 (ISBN 0-686-43320-3). Macoy Pub.

Bede, Jean-Albert & Edgerton, William, eds. Columbia Dictionary of Modern European Literature. 2nd ed. 800p. 1980. 65.00x (ISBN 0-231-03717-1). Columbia U Pr.

Bede the Venerable. Ecclesiastical History of England. Giles, John A., ed. LC 78-136367. (Bohn's Antiquarian Lib.). (Illus.). Repr. of 1849 ed. 34.50 (ISBN 0-404-50001-3). AMS Pr.

--Ecclesiastical History of the English People. Colgrave, Bertram & Minors, R. A., eds. (Oxford Medieval Texts Ser). 1969. 85.00x (ISBN 0-19-822202-5). Oxford U Pr.

Bede, Tim. Macroots. 1983. 19.00x (ISBN 0-904265-68-4, Pub. by Macdonald Pub UK). State Mutual Bk.

Bede, Venerable. The Ecclesiastical History of the English People. Hereford, Philip, ed. Stapleton, Thomas, tr. from Latin. 1983. Repr. of 1935 ed. lib. bdg. 45.00 (ISBN 0-89760-062-2). Telegraph Bks.

--History of the English Church & People. Sherley-Price, Leo, tr. 400p. 1985. 16.95 (ISBN 0-88029-042-0, Pub. by Dorset Pr). Hippocrene Bks.

Bedeian, Arthur G. Organizations: Theory & Analysis. 2nd ed. 528p. 1984. text ed. 32.95x (ISBN 0-03-062617-X); instr's. manual 19.95 (ISBN 0-03-062618-8). Dryden Pr.

Bedeian, Arthur G. & Glueck, William F. Management. 3rd ed. 672p. 1983. text ed. 31.95x (ISBN 0-03-061239-X); study guide 12.95 (ISBN 0-03-061242-X). Dryden Pr.

Bedekar, V. M., tr. see Hinze, Oscar M.

Bedeker, V. M., tr. see Frauwallner, Erich.

Bedeler, Harold C., jt. auth. see Schmitt, Bernadotte E.

Bedell, Clyde. How to Write Advertising That Sells. 2nd ed. 1952. 6.95 (ISBN 0-07-004299-3). McGraw.

Bedell, Eugene F. The Computer Solution: Strategies for Success in the Information Age. LC 84-71130. 300p. 1984. 27.50 (ISBN 0-87094-474-6). Dow Jones-Irwin.

Bedell, Gary. Philosophizing with Socrates: An Introduction to the Study of Philosophy. LC 80-5626. 262p. 1980. pap. text ed. 9.25 (ISBN 0-8191-1203-8). U Pr of Amer.

Bedell, George C., et al. Religion in America. 2nd ed. LC 81-8239. 1982. text ed. 21.84 (ISBN 0-02-307810-3). Macmillan.

Bedell, George F., ed. see Bitz, Gregory W.

Bedell, Ginnie. Plain Good Cookin' (Illus.). 7.50 (ISBN 0-918544-79-3). Wimmer Bks.

Bedell, Kenneth. Using Personal Computers in the Church. 112p. 1982. pap. 7.95 (ISBN 0-8170-0948-5). Judson.

Bedell, Kenneth & Rossman, Parker. Computers: New Opportunities for Personalized Ministry. 128p. 1984. pap. 7.95 (ISBN 0-8170-1039-4). Judson.

Bedell, Madelon, ed. see Alcott, Louisa May.

Bedell, Meredith. Stella Benson. (English Authors Ser.). 1983. lib. bdg. 19.95 (ISBN 0-8057-6845-9, Twayne). G K Hall.

Bedell, Sally. Up the Tube: Prime-Time TV in the Silverman Years. LC 80-52002. 336p. 1981. 13.95 (ISBN 0-670-51385-7). Viking.

Bedell, William. True Relation of the Life & Death of the Right Reverend Father in God William Bedell, Lord Bishop of Kilmore in Ireland. Jones, Thomas W., ed. Repr. of 1872 ed. 27.00 (ISBN 0-384-03740-2). Johnson Repr.

Beder, Harold & Smith, Franceska. Developing an Adult Education Program Through Community Linkages. 1977. 5.75 (ISBN 0-88379-009-2). A A A C E.

--Developing an Adult Education Program Through Community Linkages. 79p. 5.75 (ISBN 0-317-32114-5). A A A C E.

Beder, Harold W. & Darkenwald, Gordon G. Development, Demonstration, & Dissemination: Case Studies of Selected Special Projects in Adult Basic Education. LC 74-23656. (Occasional Papers Ser., No. 42). 59p. 1974. pap. 2.75 (ISBN 0-87060-067-2, OCP 42). Syracuse U Cont Ed.

Beder, O. E. Fundamentals for Maxillofacial Prosthetics. (Illus.). 246p. 1974. photocopy ed. 31.50x (ISBN 0-398-02916-4). C C Thomas.

Beder, Oscar E. Surgical & Maxillofacial Prosthesis. rev. ed. LC 49-50002. (Illus.). 94p. 1959. pap. 20.00x spiral bdg. (ISBN 0-295-74090-6). U of Wash Pr.

Bederka, John, jt. ed. see Khan, M. A.

Bederman, Sanford H. Africa: A Bibliography of Geography & Related Disciplines. 3rd ed. LC 74-22175. 1974. pap. 11.00 (ISBN 0-88406-089-6). Ga St U Busn Pub.

Bederson, B. see Marton, L.

Bederson, B., et al, eds. Atomic Physics 1. LC 69-14560. 633p. 1969. 85.00x (ISBN 0-306-30383-3, Plenum Pr). Plenum Pub.

Bederson, Benjamin, jt. auth. see Bates, David.

Bederson, Benjamin, ed. Advances in Atomic & Molecular Physics, Vol. 17. LC 65-18423. (Serial Publication Ser.). 1982. 65.00 (ISBN 0-12-003817-X). Acad Pr.

Bederson, Benjamin, jt. ed. see Bates, David R.

Bederson, Benjamin, jt. ed. see Bates, Sir David R.

Bedeski, Robert E. The Fragile Entente: The Nineteen Seventy-Eight Japan-China Peace Treaty in a Global Context. LC 82-21990. (Replica Edition Ser.). 245p. 1983. softcover 22.00x (ISBN 0-86531-944-8). Westview.

--State Building in Modern China: The Kuomintang in the Prewar Period. (China Research Monographs: No. 18). 181p. 1981. pap. 8.00x (ISBN 0-912966-28-9). IEAS.

Bede the Venerable. Ecclesiastical History of the English Nation & Other Writings. Stevens, John, tr. 1978. Repr. of 1910 ed. 12.95x (ISBN 0-460-00479-4, Evman). Biblio Dist.

Bedford, A. D. Defence of Truth. 1979. 27.00 (ISBN 0-7190-0740-2, Pub. by Manchester Univ Pr). Longwood Pub Group.

Bedford, Annie N. Frosty the Snowman. (Big Golden Christmas Bks.). (Illus.). 24p. (ps-1). 1985. Repr. of 1951 ed. 2.95 (ISBN 0-307-10201-7, 10201, Pub. by Golden Bks). Western Pub.

Bedford, Arthur. The Evil & Danger of Stage Plays. LC 72-170479. (The English Stage Ser.: Vol. 43). lib. bdg. 61.00 (ISBN 0-8240-0626-7). Garland Pub.

--Serious Reflections on the Scandalous Abuse & Effects of the Stage. Bd. with A Second Advertisement Concerning the Profaneness of the Play-House; A Sermon Preached in the Parish-Church of St. Butolph's Algate, in the City of London: Occasioned by the Erecting of a Play-House in the Neighborhood. (The English Stage Ser.: Vol. 41). 1974. lib. bdg. 61.00 (ISBN 0-8240-0624-0). Garland Pub.

Bedford, B. D. & Hoft, R. G. Principles of Inverter Circuits. LC 83-26789. 430p. 1985. Repr. of 1964 ed. lib. bdg. 39.50 (ISBN 0-89874-730-9). Krieger.

Bedford, Burnice D. & Hoft, R. G. Principles of Inverter Circuits. LC 64-20078. 413p. 1964. 42.95x (ISBN 0-471-06134-4, Pub. by Wiley-Interscience). Wiley.

--Principles of Inverter Circuits. LC 64-20078. pap. 107.30 (ISBN 0-317-09138-7, 2020596). Bks Demand UMI.

Bedford, C. Harold. The Seeker: D. S. Merezhkovskiy. LC 74-28496. 222p. 1975. 22.50x (ISBN 0-7006-0131-7). U Pr of KS.

Bedford, Carol. Waiting for the Beatles: An Apple Scruffs Story. (Illus.). 296p. 1984. 15.95 (ISBN 0-7137-1334-8, Pub. by Blandford Pr England); pap. 9.95 (ISBN 0-7137-1414-X, Pub. by Blandford Pr England). Sterling.

Bedford, Clay P., ed. Western North American Indian Baskets from the Collection of Clay P. Bedford. (Illus.). 68p. 1980. pap. 10.00 (ISBN 0-940228-04-1). Calif Acad Sci.

Bedford, Denton R. Tsali. LC 72-91136. (Illus.). 256p. 1972. pap. 6.00 (ISBN 0-913436-24-0). Indian Hist Pr.

Bedford, Frances & Conant, Robert. Twentieth-Century Harpsichord Music: A Classified Catalog. 1974. pap. 9.50 (ISBN 0-913574-08-2). Eur-Am Music.

Bedford, G., ed. see Avens, Roberts.

Bedford, H. The Heroines of George Meredith. 59.95 (ISBN 0-8490-0300-8). Gordon Pr.

Bedford, Henry F. Socialism & the Workers in Massachusetts, Eighteen Eighty-Six to Nineteen Twelve. LC 66-15794. (Illus.). 234p. 1966. 13.50x (ISBN 0-87023-010-7). U of Mass Pr.

--Trouble Downtown: The Local Context of Twentieth Century America. (Harbrace History of the United States Ser.). (Illus.). 213p. 1978. pap. text ed. 10.95 (ISBN 0-15-592369-2, HC). HarBraceJ.

Bedford, Henry F., et al. The Americans: A Brief History, 2 vols. 4th ed. Incl. Pt. 1. A Brief History to 1877. pap. text ed. 9.95x (ISBN 0-15-502618-6); Pt. 2. A Brief History since 1865. pap. text ed. 9.95x (ISBN 0-15-502619-4); test bklt. avail. (ISBN 0-15-502620-8). (Orig.). 1985. Set. pap. text ed. 18.95x (ISBN 0-15-502617-8, HC). HarBraceJ.

Bedford, Herbert. Heroines of George Meredith. LC 78-160742. (Illus.). 1971. Repr. of 1914 ed. 19.50x (ISBN 0-8046-1555-1, Pub. by Kennikat). Assoc Faculty Pr.

--Robert Schumann, His Life & His Work. LC 70-106712. 270p. Repr. of 1933 ed. lib. bdg. 15.00 (ISBN 0-8371-3442-0, BERS). Greenwood.

Bedford, J. R. Metalwork Projects. pap. text ed. 6.50 (ISBN 0-686-89167-8). Transatlantic.

Bedford, Jessie. English Children in the Olden Time. LC 77-1924. 1977. Repr. of 1907 ed. lib. bdg. 30.00 (ISBN 0-8414-4451-X). Folcroft.

--English Children in the Olden Time. 336p. 1980. Repr. of 1907 ed. lib. bdg. 30.00 (ISBN 0-8492-3777-7). R West.

Bedford, John. Discovering English Vineyards. (Discovering Ser.: No. 269). (Illus.). 64p. (Orig.). 1982. pap. 3.95 (ISBN 0-85263-604-0, Pub. by Shire Pubns England). Seven Hills Bks.

Bedford, John, ed. Kibbutz Volunteer. 157p. (Orig.). 1985. pap. 8.95 (ISBN 0-907638-55-4, Pub. by Vacation-Work England). Writers Digest.

Bedford, John R. Basic Course of Practical Metalwork. (gr. 9-12). pap. text ed. 8.95 (ISBN 0-7195-0079-6). Transatlantic.

--Graphic Engineering Geometry. LC 78-67438. 160p. (Orig.). 1979. pap. 9.95x (ISBN 0-87201-325-1). Gulf Pub.

--Metalcraft: Theory & Practice. (Illus.). (gr. 9 up). 1968. text ed. 8.95 (ISBN 0-7195-2251-X). Transatlantic.

Bedford, M. A. Color Atlas of Ocular Tumors. (Illus.). 1979. 55.00 (ISBN 0-8151-0627-0). Year Bk Med.

--Color Atlas of Ophthalmological Diagnosis. (Year Book Color Atlas Ser.). (Illus.). 1971. 39.95 (ISBN 0-8151-0623-8). Year Bk Med.

Bedford, Michael & Dettman, B. The Horror Factory: Universal Pictures & the Horror Film, 1925-1950. 1975. lib. bdg. 69.95 (ISBN 0-87968-443-7). Gordon Pr.

Bedford, Michael J., jt. ed. see Fawcett, Don W.

Bedford, Norton M. The Future of Accounting in a Changing Society. (Author Anderson Lecture Ser.). 101p. 1970. pap. text ed. 1.50x (ISBN 0-686-79307-2). Stipes.

--Introduction to Modern Accounting. LC 68-12885. pap. 160.00 (ISBN 0-317-10060-2, 2012392). Bks Demand UMI.

Bedford, Norton M., et al. Advanced Accounting: An Organizational Approach. 4th ed. LC 78-6961. (Wiley Series Accounting & Information Systems Ser.). 892p. 1979. text ed. 41.95 (ISBN 0-471-02927-0). Wiley.

Bedford, Randolph. Naught to Thirty-Three. 1976. 25.00x (ISBN 0-522-84101-5, Pub. by Melbourne U Pr). Intl Spec Bk.

Bedford, Richard C. English Experienced: Teaching Foreign Students by Staging Communication. LC 70-156068. 260p. 1972. text ed. 9.95x (ISBN 0-8143-1453-8). Wayne St U Pr.

Bedford, Stanley, compiled by. Death: An Interesting Journey; Evidence of Survival. 160p. 15.00x (ISBN 0-85978-030-9, Pub. by Spearman England). State Mutual Bk.

Bedford, Stewart. Instant Replay. (Illus.). 1974. pap. 2.95 (ISBN 0-917476-00-X). Inst Rational-Emotive.

--Prayer Power & Stress Management. pap. 6.95 (ISBN 0-935930-05-1). A & S Pr.

--Stress & Tiger Juice: How to Manage Your Stress & Improve Your Life & Health. LC 79-92277. 128p. 1980. 6.95 (ISBN 0-935930-00-0); pap. 6.95x (ISBN 0-935930-01-9). A & S Pr.

--Tiger Juice: A Book About Stress for Kids (of All Ages) LC 81-9039. 52p. 1981. pap. 2.95 (ISBN 0-935930-02-7). A & S Pr.

Bedford, Sybille. Aldous Huxley. 1974. 17.50 (ISBN 0-394-46587-3, 46587). Knopf.

--Aldous Huxley. 769p. 1985. pap. 14.95 (ISBN 0-88184-145-5). Carroll & Graf.

--A Compass Error: A Novel. (Obelisk Ser.). 288p. 1985. pap. 8.95 (ISBN 0-525-48187-7, 0869-260). Dutton.

--Favourite of the Gods. 256p. 1984. pap. 7.95 (ISBN 0-525-48097-8, 0772-230, Obelisk). Dutton.

--A Legacy. LC 75-34600. (Neglected Books of the Twentieth Century Ser.). 380p. 1976. pap. 8.50 (ISBN 0-912946-26-1). Ecco Pr.

Bedford, William K. The Order or the Hospital of St. John of Jerusalem. LC 76-29831. Repr. of 1902 ed. 25.00 (ISBN 0-404-15412-3). AMS Pr.

Bedfrod, Arthur. A Serious Remonstrance in Behalf of the Christian Religion Against English Play-Houses. LC 79-170478. (The English Stage Ser.: Vol. 42). lib. bdg. 61.00 (ISBN 0-8240-0625-9). Garland Pub.

Bedger, Jean E. Teenage Pregnancy: Research Related to Clients & Services. 224p. 1980. 23.50x (ISBN 0-398-03923-2). C C Thomas.

Bedi, et al. Extradition in International Law & Practice. LC 67-93868. 1968. lib. bdg. 30.00 (ISBN 0-89941-367-6). W S Hein.

Bedi, R. Ladakh: The Trans-Himalayan Kingdom. 192p. 1981. text ed. 64.00x (ISBN 0-391-02908-8, Pub. by Roli Pubns India). Humanities.

Bedi, Rajinder S. I Take This Woman. Singh, Khushwant, tr. 103p. 1967. pap. 2.25 (ISBN 0-88253-014-3). Ind-US Inc.

Bedichek, Roy. Adventures with a Texas Naturalist. (Illus.). 360p. 1961. pap. 8.95 (ISBN 0-292-70311-2). U of Tex Pr.

--Karankaway Country. LC 74-3537. 318p. 1974. 17.95 (ISBN 0-292-74300-9); pap. 8.95 (ISBN 0-292-74304-1). U of Tex Pr.

Bedichek, Wendell, jt. auth. see Tannahill, Neal.

Bedichek, Wendell M. & Tannahill, Neal. Public Policy In Texas. 2nd ed. 1986. pap. text ed. 15.95x (ISBN 0-673-18001-8). Scott F.

Bedichek, Wendell M., jt. auth. see Tannahill, Neal.

Bedient, Calvin. Eight Contemporary Poets: Charles Tomlinson, Donald Davie, R. S. Thomas, Philip Larkin, Ted Hughes, Thomas Kinsella, Stevie Smith, W. S. Graham. 1974. pap. 3.95 (ISBN 0-19-519825-5, 449, GB). Oxford U Pr.

--In the Heart's Last Kingdom: Robert Penn Warren's Major Poetry. 256p. 1984. text ed. 18.50x (ISBN 0-674-44546-5). Harvard U Pr.

Bedient, P. E., jt. auth. see Rainville, E. D.

Bedient, Philip B., ed. see Bosch, Vanden, et al.

Bedier, Joseph. Les Legendes epiques: Recherches sur la formation des chansons de geste, 4 vols. LC 78-63487. Repr. of 1913 ed. Set. 159.00 (ISBN 0-404-17130-3). AMS Pr.

--The Romance of Tristan & Iseult. 1965. pap. 2.95 (ISBN 0-394-70271-9, Vin, V271). Random.

Bedier, Joseph, ed. Bibliographie des travaux de Gaston Paris. Roques, Mario. LC 75-108989. (Bibliography & Reference Ser.: No. 300). (Fr). 1970. Repr. of 1904 ed. text ed. 21.00 (ISBN 0-8337-0212-2). B Franklin.

Bedingfeld, T., tr. see Machiavelli, Niccolo.

Bedingfield, James. Accounting & Federal Regulation. (Illus.). 336p. 1982. pap. text ed. 20.95 (ISBN 0-8359-0051-7). Reston.

Bedingfield, James P. & Rosen, Louis I. Government Contract Accounting. (Government Contract Text Ser.). 500p. 1985. looseleaf 120.00 (ISBN 0-318-04091-3). Fed Pubns Inc.

Bedingfield, Nancy. Oregon's One Hundred Years in Pictures. LC 56-12270. (Illus.). 1958. 3.95 (ISBN 0-8323-0001-2); pap. 2.50 (ISBN 0-8323-0002-0). Binford.

Bedingfield, T., ed. see Cardano, Girolamo.

Bedini, Silvio A. At the Sign of the Compass & Quadrant: The Life & Times of Anthony Lamb. LC 83-73281. (Translations Ser.: Vol. 74, pt. 1). 84p. 1984. 12.00 (ISBN 0-87169-741-6). Am Philos.

--Declaration of Independence Desk: Relic of Revolution. LC 81-607119. (Illus.). 112p. (Orig.). 1982. pap. 5.95 (ISBN 0-87474-241-2). Smithsonian.

--The Life of Benjamin Banneker. LC 78-162755. (Illus.). 1984. Repr. of 1972 ed. 21.00 (ISBN 0-910845-20-4, 904). Landmark Ent.

--Thinkers & Tinkers: Early American Men of Science. (Illus.). 519p. 1983. Repr. of 1975 ed. 21.00 (ISBN 0-910845-19-0, 901). Landmark Ent.

--Thomas Jefferson & His Copying Machines. LC 81-7288. (Monticello Monograph Ser.). (Illus.). 233p. 1984. text ed. 20.00x (ISBN 0-8139-1025-0). U Pr of Va.

Bedjaoui, Mohammed. Towards a New International Economic Order. LC 79-22943. Orig. Title: Pour un Nouvel Ordre Economique International. 287p. 1979. text ed. 35.00x (ISBN 0-8419-0585-1); pap. text ed. 19.85x (ISBN 0-8419-0588-6). Holmes & Meier.

Bedlington, Stanley S. Malaysia & Singapore: The Building of New States. Kahin, G. M., ed. LC 77-3114. (Politics & International Relations of Southeast Asia Ser.). 304p. 1978. 24.50x (ISBN 0-8014-0910-1); pap. 9.95x (ISBN 0-8014-9864-3). Cornell U Pr.

Bednall, John, tr. see Von Heiseler, Brent.

Bednar, Henry H. Pressure Vessel Design Handbook. 336p. 1981. 28.50 (ISBN 0-442-25416-4). Van Nos Reinhold.

--Pressure Vessel Design Handbook. 2nd ed. (Illus.). 448p. 1985. 46.50 (ISBN 0-442-21385-9). Van Nos Reinhold.

Bednar, J. Bee, et al, eds. Conference on Inverse Scattering: Theory & Application. LC 83-51381. x, 290p. 1983. text ed. 26.50 (ISBN 0-89871-190-8). Soc Indus-Appl Math.

Bednar, Jane. Everybody's Dancing: In Socks & on Skates. (Creative's Games, Activities & Projects Ser.). (Illus.). 32p. (gr. 4 up). 1980. PLB 7.95 (ISBN 0-87191-743-2); pap. 3.95 (ISBN 0-89812-211-2). Creative Ed.

Bednar, M. J. The New Atrium. (Illus.). 288p. 1986. price not set (ISBN 0-07-004275-6). McGraw.

Bednar, Michael J, ed. Barrier-Free Environments. LC 76-54798. (Community Development Ser.: Vol. 33). 1977. 38.95 (ISBN 0-87933-277-8). Van Nos Reinhold.

Bednar, Zdenek F. Keep Your Chin up. LC 82-73984. 144p. (Orig.). 1983. pap. 7.95 (ISBN 0-89272-165-0). Down East.

Bednarek, A. R. & Cesari, L., eds. Dynamical Systems. 1977. 55.00 (ISBN 0-12-083750-1). Acad Pr.

--Dynamical Systems: Symposium, II. 1982. 60.00 (ISBN 0-12-084720-5). Acad Pr.

Bednarik, Karl. The Male in Crisis. Sebba, Helen, tr. from Ger. LC 81-7122. xi, 194p. 1981. Repr. of 1970 ed. lib. bdg. 39.75x (ISBN 0-313-22713-6, BEMS). Greenwood.

Bednarowski, Mary F. American Religion: A Cultural Perspective. LC 83-22895. (Illus.). 182p. 1984. pap. text ed. 13.95 (ISBN 0-13-029059-9). P-H.

Bednarski, Betty, tr. see Ferron, Jacques.

Bednarski, Mary W. & Florczyk, Sandra E. Nursing Home Care As a Public Policy Issue. (Learning Packages in Policy Issues Ser.: No. 4). 62p. (Orig.). 1978. pap. text ed. 2.50x (ISBN 0-936826-13-4). Pol Stud Assocs.

Bednarski, Mary W., jt. auth. see Lubliner, Jerry.

Bednarz, Robert S. The Effect of Air Pollution on Property Value in Chicago. LC 75-23057. (Research Papers: No. 166). (Illus.). viii, 114p. 1975. pap. 10.00 (ISBN 0-89065-073-X). U Chicago Dept Geog.

Bednowitz, A. L., ed. World Directory of Crystallographers: & of Other Scientists Employing Crystallographic Methods. 6th ed. 1981. pap. 10.00 (ISBN 90-277-1310-3, Pub. by Reidel Holland). Kluwer Academic.

Bedore, James, jt. auth. see Turner, Louis.

Bedoukian, Kerop. Some of Us Survived: The Story of an Armenian Boy. LC 79-10601. 256p. 1979. 11.95 (ISBN 0-374-37132-6). FS&G.

Bedoukian, Paul Z. Selected Numismatic Studies. bilingual ed. 570p. (Armenian, Eng.). 1981. 35.00 (ISBN 0-9606842-0-4). ANS.

Bedrick, Christina, jt. auth. see Bedrick, Ed.

Bedrick, Ed & Bedrick, Christina. One Hundred & Seventy-Seven Free Oregon Campgrounds. new ed. LC 79-66696. (Illus., Orig.). 1980. pap. 6.95 (ISBN 0-913140-33-3). Signpost Bk Pub.

Bedriomo, Emile. Proust-Wagner et la Coincidence des Arts. (Etudes litteraires francaises: No. 34). 188p. (Orig., Fr.). 1984. pap. 17.00x (ISBN 3-87808-734-9, Pub. by G N Verlag Germany). Benjamins North Am.

Bedrosian, S. D. & Porter, W. A., eds. Recent Trends in Systems Theory. 1976. 36.00 (ISBN 0-08-020590-9). Pergamon.

Bedrossian, Mathias. Armenian-English Dictionary. (Armenian & Eng.). 35.00x (ISBN 0-86685-122-4). Intl Bk Ctr.

Bedson, G. The Notorious Poacher. (Illus.). 160p. 1981. 15.50 (ISBN 0-904558-97-5). Saiga.

BeDunnah, Gary P. A History of the Chinese in Nevada, 1855-1904. LC 73-76004. pap. 9.95 (ISBN 0-88247-206-2). R & E Pubs.

Bedwell. Visual Fields: A Basis for Efficient Investigation. 1982. text ed. 49.95 (ISBN 0-407-00215-4). Butterworth.

Bedwell, A. E. A Catalogue of the Printed Books in the Library of the Honourable Society of the Middle Temple, 4 vols. 1961. Repr. of 1914 ed. Set. lib. bdg. 110.00 (ISBN 0-89941-352-8). W S Hein.

Bedwell, B. L. Sermons for Funeral Occasions. 1960. pap. 2.00 (ISBN 0-88027-029-2). Firm Foun Pub.

Bedwell, C., ed. Developments in Electronics for Offshore Fields, Vol. 1. (Illus.). 230p. 1978. 39.00 (ISBN 0-85334-753-0, Pub. by Elsevier Applied Sci England). Elsevier.

Bedwell, C. H., tr. see Aust, W.

Bedwell, Lance E., et al. Effective Teaching: Preparation & Implementation. 280p. 1984. 26.50x (ISBN 0-398-05004-X). C C Thomas.

Bedwell, Stephen. Fort Rock Basin: Prehistory & Environment. LC 74-169230. 1973. 10.00 (ISBN 0-87114-058-6). U of Oreg Bks.

Bedwell, W., tr. see Salignacus, Bernard.

Bedwell, William. Mesolabium Architectonicum That Is a Most Rare Instrument of Measuring. LC 72-172. (English Experience Ser.: No. 224). 24p. Repr. of 1631 ed. 7.00 (ISBN 90-221-0224-6). Walter J Johnson.

Bedwinek, Anne P. Supplemental Audio Cassettes: For Adults with Neurogenic Communicative Disorders. 1981. 75.00 (ISBN 0-88450-732-7, 3136-B). Communication Skill.

Bedworth. Computer Animation. 1984. write for info. (ISBN 0-07-004269-1). McGraw.

Bedworth, Albert E. & Bedworth, David A. Health for Human Effectiveness: A Holistic Approach. (Illus.). 432p. 1982. 30.95 (ISBN 0-13-385500-7). P-H.

Bedworth, Albert E. & D'Elia, Joseph A. Basics of Drug Education. LC 72-94344. 286p. 1973. text ed. 15.00x (ISBN 0-89503-027-6). Baywood Pub.

Bedworth, David A., jt. auth. see Bedworth, Albert E.

Bedworth, David D. & Bailey, James E. Integrated Production Control Systems: Management, Analysis, Design. LC 81-10506. 433p. 1982. text ed. 37.50x (ISBN 0-471-06223-5); avail solutions. Wiley.

Bee, jt. auth. see Vevers.

Bee, Clifford. Secondary Learning Centers. 1980. pap. 11.95 (ISBN 0-673-16428-4). Scott F.

Bee, Helen. Desarrollo Del Nino. (Span.). 1978. pap. text ed. 12.20 (ISBN 0-06-310061-4, IntlDept). Har-Row.

Bee, Helen L. The Developing Child. 4th ed. 582p. 1984. text ed. 26.50 scp (ISBN 0-06-040577-5, HarpC). Har-Row.

Bee, Helen L. & Mitchell, Sandra K. The Developing Person: A Life-Span Approach. 2nd ed. 653p. 1984. scp 26.95 (ISBN 0-06-040578-3, HarpC); scp instr's. manual 3.00 (ISBN 0-06-360563-5); scp study guide 8.50 (ISBN 0-06-040589-9); test bank 3.25 (ISBN 0-06-360564-3). Har-Row.

Bee, James W. Birds Found on the Arctic Slope of Northern Alaska. (Museum Ser.: Vol. 10, No. 5). 49p. 1958. pap. 2.75 (ISBN 0-317-04585-7). U of KS Mus Nat Hist.

Bee, James W., et al. Mammals in Kansas. Collins, Joseph T., ed. (University of Kansas, Museum of Natural History Public Education Ser.: No. 7). (Illus.). 300p. 17.00 (ISBN 0-89338-015-6); pap. 12.00 (ISBN 0-89338-014-8). U of KS Mus Nat Hist.

Bee, John D. Beyond the Reef: A Story of the Solomon Islands. 1982. 11.95 (ISBN 0-533-05014-6). Vantage.

Bee, Noah. The Impossible Takes Longer. (History of Israel in Cartoons: Vol. II). (Illus.). 207p. 1983. 11.95 (ISBN 0-8197-0491-1). Bloch.

--In Spite of Everything: History of the State of Israel. LC 73-77304. (Illus.). 200p. 1973. 8.95 (ISBN 0-8197-0297-8). Bloch.

Bee, Ooi J. see Ooi Jin Bee.

Bee, Robert L. Crosscurrents Along the Colorado: The Impact of Government Policy on the Quechan Indians. LC 81-7446. 184p. 1981. pap. 7.50x (ISBN 0-8165-0725-2). U of Ariz Pr.

--Patterns & Processes: An Introduction to Anthropological Strategies for the Study of Sociocultural Change. LC 73-10791. 1974. pap. text ed. 12.95 (ISBN 0-02-902090-5). Free Pr.

Bee, Roger & Browne, Gary F. The Chicago Great Western in Minnesota. (Illus.). 115p. 1984. write for info. (ISBN 0-930431-00-6). Blue River Pubns.

Beebe. The Embargo of 1807: A Study in Policy Making. 1972. 5.48 (ISBN 0-201-00465-8, Sch Div). Addison-Wesley.

Beebe, B. W., et al, eds. Natural Gases of North America: A Symposium. LC 68-15769. (American Association of Petroleum Geologists Memoir Ser.: No. 9). Vol. 1. pap. 160.00 (ISBN 0-317-10363-6, 2050025); Vol. 2. pap. 160.00 (ISBN 0-317-10364-4). Bks Demand UMI.

Beebe, Brooke. Best Bets for Babies. (Orig.). 1981. pap. 6.95 (ISBN 0-440-50453-8, Dell Trade Pbks). Dell.

--Tips for Toddlers. (Illus.). 240p. (Orig.). 1983. pap. 6.95 (ISBN 0-440-58658-5, Dell Trade Pbks). Dell.

Beebe, Brooke, et al. Nutrition & Good Health. LC 78-731300. (Illus.). 1978. pap. text ed. 135.00 (ISBN 0-89290-099-7, A576-SATC). Soc for Visual.

Beebe, Brooke M. & Rosenblatt, Ruth Y. The Dictionary. LC 77-730283. (Illus.). (gr. 3-5). 1977. pap. text ed. 125.00 (ISBN 0-89290-121-7, A151-SAR). Soc for Visual.

Beebe, Frank. A Falconry Manual. (Illus.). 200p. 1984. pap. 12.95 (ISBN 0-88839-978-2). Hancock House.

Beebe, Gilbert W. Contraception & Fertility in the Southern Appalachians. LC 79-169373. (Family in America Ser). (Illus.). 396p. 1972. Repr. of 1942 ed. 18.00 (ISBN 0-405-03849-6). Ayer Co Pubs.

Beebe, Gilbert W. & Debakey, Michael E. Battle Casualties: Incidence, Mortality & Logistic Consideration. (Illus.). 296p. 1952. 34.50x (ISBN 0-398-04205-5). C C Thomas.

Beebe, Iola. True Life Story of Swiftwater Bill Gates. facs. ed. (Illus.). 139p. pap. 6.95 (ISBN 0-8466-2163-0, S163). Shorey.

Beebe, John, ed. Money, Food, Drink, Fashion & Analytic Training: Depth Dimensions of Physical Existence. (The Proceedings of the Eighth International Congress for Analytical Psychology). 512p. 40.00 (ISBN 3-87089-304-4, Pub. by Verlag Adolf Germany). Spring Pubns.

Beebe, Joyce. Joy of Canvas Painting, Vol. 2. (Illus.). 80p. (Orig.). 1985. pap. price not set (ISBN 0-917119-43-6, 45-1071). Priscillas Pubns.

--The Joy of Folk Art. (Illus., Orig.). 1983. pap. 9.95 (ISBN 0-917119-29-0, 45-1062). Priscillas Pubns.

Beebe, Lewis. Journal of Dr. Lewis Beebe, a Physician on the Expedition Against Quebec, 1776. Kirkland, Frederic R., ed. LC 77-140854. (Eyewitness Accounts of the American Revolution Ser., No. 3). (Illus.). 1970. Repr. of 1935 ed. 11.50 (ISBN 0-405-01201-2). Ayer Co Pubs.

Beebe, Lucius. The Central Pacific & the Southern Pacific Railroads. LC 63-12942. (Illus.). 1963. 35.00 (ISBN 0-8310-7034-X). Howell-North.

--Mansions on Rails. LC 59-12775. (Illus.). 1959. 16.50 (ISBN 0-8310-7011-0). Howell-North.

--Mixed Train Daily. 4th ed. LC 66-378. (Illus.). 1961. 30.00 (ISBN 0-8310-7026-9). Howell-North.

--Overland Limited. LC 63-22352. (Illus.). 1963. 15.00 (ISBN 0-8310-7038-2). Howell-North.

--Twentieth Century. LC 62-17074. (Illus.). 1962. 17.50 (ISBN 0-8310-7031-5). Howell-North.

--Virginia & Truckee. (Illus.). 68p. 1980. pap. 3.95 (ISBN 0-686-85787-9). Chatham Pub CA.

Beebe, Lucius & Clegg, Charles. The Age of Steam. 2nd ed. LC 72-86410. (Illus.). 304p. 1972. Repr. of 1957 ed. 25.00 (ISBN 0-8310-7095-1). Howell-North.

--Legends of the Comstock Lode. 4th ed. (Illus.). 1956. pap. 3.95 (ISBN 0-8047-0463-5). Stanford U Pr.

--Narrow Gauge in the Rockies. LC 58-5789. (Illus.). 1958. 20.00 (ISBN 0-8310-7003-X). Howell-North.

--Rio Grande. LC 62-13445. (Illus.). 1962. 25.00 (ISBN 0-8310-7028-5). Howell-North.

--Steamcars to the Comstock. 3rd ed. LC 57-2739. (Illus.). 1960. 17.50 (ISBN 0-8310-7004-8). Howell-North.

--The Trains We Rode, 2 Vols. LC 65-25208. 30.00 ea. Vol. 1 (ISBN 0-8310-7054-4). Vol. 2 (ISBN 0-8310-7058-7). Howell-North.

--Virginia & Truckee. LC 63-14279. (Illus.). 64p. 1980. pap. 3.95 (ISBN 0-8310-6007-7). Howell-North.

Beebe, Marjorie H. Claremont Colleges Faculty Exhibition. (Illus.). 1982. 4.00 (ISBN 0-915478-42-0). Galleries Coll.

--Early Twentieth Century German Prints from the Pomona College Collection. (Illus.). 30p. 1983. 4.00 (ISBN 0-915478-49-8). Galleries Coll.

--Printmaking in France Eighteen Fifty to Nineteen Hundred. 1982. 3.00 (ISBN 0-915478-48-X). Galleries Coll.

Beebe, Marjorie H., ed. see Koeninger, Kay, et al.

Beebe, Morton, photos by. San Francisco. (Illus.). 208p. (Text by Herb Caen, Tom Cole, Barnaby Gold, Kevin Starr). 1985. 49.50 (ISBN 0-8109-1608-8). Abrams.

Beebe, Robert P. Voyaging under Power. LC 74-21847. (Illus.). 272p. 1975. 19.95 (ISBN 0-915160-18-8). Seven Seas.

Beebe, Ruth. Sallets, Humbles & Shrewsbery Cakes: An Elizabethan Cookbook with Recipes Adapted for the Modern Kitchen. LC 76-14226. (Illus.). 1977. pap. 7.95 (ISBN 0-87923-238-2). Godine.

Beebe, Steven & Masterson, John. Family Talk. 320p. 1985. pap. text ed. 16.95 (RanC). Random.

Beebe, Steven A. & Masterson, John T. Communicating in Small Groups. 1982. text ed. 17.95x (ISBN 0-673-15389-4). Scott F.

--Communicating in Small Groups: Principles & Practices. 2nd ed. 1985. pap. text ed. 13.95x (ISBN 0-673-18135-9). Scott F.

Beebe, William. The Arcturus Adventure. LC 80-8409. (Nature Library Ser.). 450p. 1981. pap. 5.95i (ISBN 0-06-090846-7, CN 846, CN). Har-Row.

--The Arcturus Adventure: An Account of the New York Zoological Society's First Oceanographic Expedition. 1926. 27.50 (ISBN 0-8482-0138-8). Norwood Edns.

--Edge of the Jungle. 1921. 27.50 (ISBN 0-8482-7358-3). Norwood Edns.

--Edge of the Jungle. 15.95 (ISBN 0-88411-839-8, Pub. by Aeonian Pr). Amereon Ltd.

--Jungle Days. 1923. 27.50 (ISBN 0-8482-7390-7). Norwood Edns.

--The Log of the Sun: A Chronicle of Nature's Year. 321p. 1982. Repr. of 1906 ed. lib. bdg. 25.00 (ISBN 0-89760-087-8). Telegraph Bks.

Beebe, William, intro. by. AUTOFACT West Proceedings, Vol. 1. LC 80-53423. (Illus.). 939p. 1980. pap. 55.00 (ISBN 0-87263-065-X). SME.

Beebee, Trevor J. The Natterjack Toad. (Illus.). 1983. 19.95x (ISBN 0-19-217709-5). Oxford U Pr.

Beeby, C. Planning & the Educational Administrator. (Fundamentals of Educational Planning: No. 4). 36p. (2nd Printing 1980). 1967. pap. 6.00 (ISBN 92-803-1009-7, U1065, UNESCO). Unipub.

Beeby, C. E. Assessment of Indonesian Education: A Guide in Planning. (Illus.). 1979. text ed. 29.95x (ISBN 0-19-580446-5). Oxford U Pr.

Beeby, Clarence E. Quality of Education in Developing Countries. LC 66-14438. 1966. 10.00x (ISBN 0-674-74050-5). Harvard U Pr.

Beech, D., ed. Command Language Directions. 424p. 1980. 57.50 (ISBN 0-444-85450-9, North-Holland). Elsevier.

Beech, D. G. Quality Control of Clay Pipes: Report of the Testing Committee of the Clay Pipe Research Panel. 1969. 25.00x (ISBN 0-686-78818-4, Pub. by Brit Ceramic Soc England). State Mutual Bk.

--Testing Methods for Brick & Tile Manufacture. 1974. 35.00x (ISBN 0-900910-22-4, Pub. by Brit Ceramic Soc England). State Mutual Bk.

Beech, G., ed. Computer Assisted Learning in Science Education. LC 78-40566. 1979. pap. text ed. 50.00 (ISBN 0-08-023010-5). Pergamon.

Beech, George T. A Rural Society in Medieval France: The Gatine of Poitou in the Eleventh & Twelfth Centuries. LC 78-64241. (Johns Hopkins University. Studies in the Social Sciences. Eighty-Second Ser. 1964: 1). Repr. of 1964 ed. 17.00 (ISBN 0-404-61346-2). AMS Pr.

Beech, Graham. FORTRAN IV in Chemistry: An Introduction to Computer-Assisted Methods. LC 75-2488. 303p. 1975. 67.95x (ISBN 0-471-06165-4, Pub. by Wiley-Interscience). Wiley.

--Successful Software for Small Computers: Structured Programming in BASIC. LC 82-10881. 182p. 1982. pap. text ed. 14.95 (ISBN 0-471-87458-2). Wiley.

Beech, H. R., et al. A Behavioural Approach to the Management of Stress: A Practical Guide to Techniques. LC 81-11554. (Studies in Occupational Stress). 132p. 1982. 28.95x (ISBN 0-471-10054-4, Pub. by Wiley Med). Wiley.

Beech, John. Learning to Read: A Cognitive Approach to Reading & Poor Reading. (Illus.). 160p. 1985. 10.00 (ISBN 0-88744-110-6). College-Hill.

--Yancey Railroad. 72p. 1985. pap. 9.95 (ISBN 0-912113-18-9). Railhead Pubns.

Beech, Mervyn W. Suk: Their Language & Folklore. LC 76-75540. (Illus.). Repr. of 1925 ed. cancelled (ISBN 0-8371-0349-5, BTS&, Pub. by Negro U Pr). Greenwood.

Beech, Thomas R., jt. auth. see Chaney, Warren H.

Beecham, John. Ashantee & the Gold Coast, Being a Sketch of the History, Social State & Superstitions of the Inhabitants of Those Countries, with a Notice of the State & Prospects of Christianity Among Them. LC 68-93641. (Landmarks in Anthropology). Repr. of 1841 ed. lib. bdg. 35.00 (ISBN 0-384-03755-0). Johnson Repr.

Beecham, K. J. History of Cirencester. 344p. 1978. Repr. of 1887 ed. text ed. 25.25x (ISBN 0-904387-18-6, Pub. by Alan Sutton England). Humanities.

Beecham, Thomas. Frederick Delius. LC 73-89930. (Studies of Composers). (Illus.). 256p. 1973. pap. 10.00x (ISBN 0-8443-0082-9). Vienna Hse.

--A Mingled Chime: An Autobiography. LC 76-40182. (Music Ser.). 1976. Repr. of 1943 ed. 35.00 (ISBN 0-306-70791-8). Da Capo.

--A Mingled Chime: An Autobiography. LC 76-40238. 1976. Repr. of 1943 ed. lib. bdg. 20.50x (ISBN 0-8371-9274-9, BEMCH). Greenwood.

Beechcroft, William. Image of Evil. 228p. 1985. 14.95 (ISBN 0-396-08558-X). Dodd.

Beechel, Edith E. A Citizenship Program for Elementary Schools. LC 70-176548. (Columbia University. Teachers College. Contributions to Education: No. 335). Repr. of 1929 ed. 22.50 (ISBN 0-404-55335-4). AMS Pr.

Beecher, Addison & Whipple, Colvin. The Racing Yachts. LC 80-20463. (Seafarers Ser.). lib. bdg. 21.27 (ISBN 0-8094-2694-3, Pub. by Time-Life). Silver.

Beecher, Catharine. Letters to the People on Health & Happiness. LC 70-180554. (Medicine & Society in America Ser). (Illus.). 228p. 1972. Repr. of 1855 ed. 15.00 (ISBN 0-405-03934-4). Ayer Co Pubs.

Beecher, Catharine & Stowe, Harriet Beecher. American Woman's Home: Or, Principles of Domestic Science. LC 77-165703. (American Education Ser.: No. 2). 1972. Repr. of 1869 ed. 25.00 (ISBN 0-405-03692-2). Ayer Co Pubs.

Beecher, Catharine E. Essay on Slavery & Abolitionism. facs. ed. LC 74-133147. (Black Heritage Library Collection Ser). 1837. 12.00 (ISBN 0-8369-8703-9). Ayer Co Pubs.

Beecher, Catharine E. & Stowe, Harriet Beecher. American Woman's Home. LC 75-22526. (Library of Victorian Culture). (Illus.). 1975. pap. text ed. 12.50 (ISBN 0-89257-007-5). Am Life Foun.

--The American Woman's Home. LC 75-22526. (Illus.). 1975. pap. 12.95 (ISBN 0-917482-04-2). Stowe-Day.

Beecher, Catherine E. Letters to the People on Health & Happiness. (The Works of Catherine E. Beecher Ser.). vi, 222p. Repr. of 1855 ed. lib. bdg. 29.00 (ISBN 0-932051-03-0, Pub by Am Repr Serv). Am Biog Serv.

Beecher, Charles E. Studies in Evolution. Gould, Stephen J., ed. LC 79-8324. (History of Paleontology Ser.). (Illus.). 1980. Repr. of 1901 ed. lib. bdg. 55.50x (ISBN 0-405-12704-9). Ayer Co Pubs.

Beecher, Donald, tr. see Caro, Annibal.

Beecher, Donald, tr. see De Turnebe, Odet.

Beecher, E. Narrative of Riots at Alton. LC 70-115858. (Studies in Black History & Culture, No. 54). 1970. Repr. of 1838 ed. lib. bdg. 44.95x (ISBN 0-8383-1072-9). Haskell.

Beecher, Edward. Narrative of the Riots at Alton. facs. ed. LC 77-89425. (Black Heritage Library Collection Ser). 1838. 11.00 (ISBN 0-8369-8509-5). Ayer Co Pubs.

--The Papal Conspiracy Exposed & Protestantism Defended. LC 76-46066. (Anti-Movements in America). (Illus.). 1977. Repr. of 1885 ed. lib. bdg. 32.00x (ISBN 0-405-09940-1). Ayer Co Pubs.

Beecher, G. S. B., ed. see Leakey, L. S., et al.

Beecher, Gary R., ed. Human Nutrition Research. LC 79-91006. (Beltsville Symposia in Agricultural Research Ser.: No. 4). (Illus.). 318p. 1981. text ed. 35.00x (ISBN 0-916672-48-4). Allanheld.

Beecher, Henry K. Experimentation in Man. 88p. 1959. spiral 9.75x (ISBN 0-398-00124-3). C C Thomas.

Beecher, Henry W. American Rebellion. facsimile ed. LC 70-168510. (Black Heritage Library Collection). Repr. of 1864 ed. 15.50 (ISBN 0-8369-8863-9). Ayer Co Pubs.

--Freedom & War. facsimile ed. LC 70-157361. (Black Heritage Library Collection Ser.). 1863. 26.00 (ISBN 0-8369-8799-3). Ayer Co Pubs.

--Lectures & Orations. Hillis, Newell D., ed. LC 72-126662. (BCL Ser. II). 1970. Repr. of 1913 ed. 23.00 (ISBN 0-404-00699-X). AMS Pr.

--Patriotic Addresses In. (The Works of Henry Ward Beecher Ser.). 857p. 1985. Repr. of 1891 ed. lib. bdg. 89.00 (ISBN 0-932051-04-9, Pub. by Am Repr Serv). Am Biog Serv.

--Star Papers: Experience of Art & Nature. (The Works of Henry Ward Beecher Ser.). vi, 359p. Repr. of 1855 ed. lib. bdg. 39.00 (ISBN 0-932051-01-4, Pub. by Am Repr Serv). Am Repr Serv.

--Star Papers: Or, Experiences of Art & Nature. LC 75-39679. (Essay Index Reprint Ser.). Repr. of 1855 ed. 24.50 (ISBN 0-8369-2745-1). Ayer Co Pubs.

--Yale Lectures on Preaching. 1976. Repr. of 1872 ed. 39.00x (ISBN 0-403-06546-1, Regency). Scholarly.

--Yale Lectures on Preaching. (The Works of Henry Ward Beecher Ser.). vii, 359p. Repr. of 1873 ed. lib. bdg. 29.00 (ISBN 0-932051-02-2, Pub. by Am Repr Serv). Am Biog Serv.

Beecher, Henry Ward. Norwood: Village Life in New England. 1978. Repr. of 1868 ed. lib. bdg. 45.00 (ISBN 0-8492-3726-2). R West.

Beecher, JoAnn Colbert. Before I Was a Grandparent. (Illus.). 60p. (Orig.). 1984. pap. 5.95 (ISBN 0-9613606-0-7). Beechtree Pr.

Beecher, John. Report to the Stockholders & Other Poems. 3rd ed. LC 62-6046. (Illus.). 1971. 5.00 (ISBN 0-911234-02-0). Red Mtn.

--Report to the Stockholders & Other Poems. 4th ed. (Illus.). 83p. 1980. pap. 1.95 (ISBN 0-917702-08-5). Vanguard Bks.

--To Live & Die in Dixie, & Other Poems. LC 66-28695. (Illus.). 1966. 5.00 (ISBN 0-911234-00-4). Red Mtn.

--Tomorrow Is a Day: A Story of the People in Politics. (Illus.). 386p. (Orig.). 1980. 5.95 (ISBN 0-917702-11-5). Vanguard Bks.

Beecher, Jonathan & Bienvenu, Richard, eds. The Utopian Vision of Charles Fourier: Selected Texts on Work, Love & Passionate Attraction. Beecher, Jonathan & Bienvenu, Richard, trs. LC 83-5897. 448p. 1983. text ed. 28.00 (ISBN 0-8262-0426-0); pap. text ed. 16.00 (ISBN 0-8262-0413-9). U of Mo Pr.

Beecher, Jonathan, tr. see Beecher, Jonathan & Bienvenu, Richard.

Beecher, Lyman. Autobiography of Lyman Beecher, 2 Vols. Cross, Barbara M., ed. LC 61-6348. (The John Harvard Library). (Illus.). 1961. Set. 50.00x (ISBN 0-674-05400-8). Harvard U Pr.

--Lyman Beecher & the Reform of Society: Four Sermons, 1804-1828. LC 71-38437. (Religion in America Series Two). 214p. 1972. Repr. of 1972 ed. 19.00 (ISBN 0-405-04058-X). Ayer Co Pubs.

--A Plea for the West. (The Works of Lyman Beecher Ser.). 190p. 1985. Repr. of 1835 ed. lib. bdg. 29.00 (ISBN 0-932051-00-6, Pub. by Am Repr Serv). Am Biog Serv.

--A Pleas for the West. Grob, Gerald, ed. LC 76-46067. (Anti-Movements in America). 1977. lib. bdg. 17.00x (ISBN 0-405-09941-X). Ayer Co Pubs.

Beecher, Marguerite, jt. auth. see Beecher, Willard.

Beecher, Paul J. Cash Management: Principles & Practices for the 80's. LC 80-22789. (AMA Management Briefing Ser.). (Illus.). pap. cancelled (ISBN 0-317-13002-1, 2051615). Bks Demand UMI.

Beecher, Raymond. Out to Greenville & Beyond, Historical Sketches of Greene County. (Illus.). 1977. pap. 5.50 (ISBN 0-685-88519-4). Hope Farm.

Beecher, Willard & Beecher, Marguerite. Parents on the Run. LC 73-83773. 238p. 1983. pap. 6.95 (ISBN 0-87516-522-2). De Vorss.

--The Sin of Obedience. 88p. (Orig.). 1982. pap. 4.75 (ISBN 0-942350-00-6). Beecher Found.

Beechert, Edward D. Working in Hawaii: A Labor History. 448p. 1985. text ed. 30.00x (ISBN 0-8248-0890-8). UH Pr.

Beechey, Gwilym, ed. see Chilcot, Thomas.

Beechey, Winifred. The Rich Mrs. Robinson. (Illus.). 1984. pap. 12.95 (ISBN 0-19-211783-1). Oxford U pr.

Beechhold, Henry F. The Plain English Maintenance & Repair Guide for the IBM PC & PCjr. 288p. 1985. pap. 14.95 (ISBN 0-671-52864-5, Pub. by Computer Bks). S&S.

--The Plain English Repair & Maintenance Guide for Home Computers. (Illus.). 224p. 1984. pap. 14.95 (ISBN 0-671-49293-4, Pub. by Computer Bks). S&S.

Beechick, Allen. The Pre-Tribulation Rapture. LC 79-53291. 256p. (Orig.). 1980. pap. 4.95 (ISBN 0-89636-040-7). Accent Bks.

Beechick, Ruth. A Biblical Psychology of Learning. LC 81-86503. 160p. (Orig.). 1982. pap. 6.95 (ISBN 0-89636-083-0); 11.95 (ISBN 0-89636-092-X). Accent Bks.

--A Biblical Psychology of Learning. 1982. pap. 5.95 (ISBN 0-89636-083-0). Accent Bks.

--Instant Activities. LC 79-53445. (Orig.). 1981. pap. 5.95 (ISBN 0-89636-032-6). Accent Bks.

--Teaching Juniors. LC 80-68886. (Teacher Training Ser.). 192p. (Orig.). 1981. pap. 4.95 (ISBN 0-89636-062-8). Accent Bks.

--Teaching Kindergarteners. LC 79-53295. (Accent Teacher Training Ser.). 192p. 1980. pap. 4.95 (ISBN 0-89636-038-5). Accent Bks.

--Teaching Preschoolers: It's Not Exactly Easy but Here Is How to Do It. LC 78-73252. (Accent Teacher Training Ser.). 1979. pap. 4.95 (ISBN 0-89636-019-9). Accent Bks.

--Teaching Primaries. LC 80-66723. (Accent Teacher Training Ser.). 128p. (Orig.). 1980. pap. 4.95 (ISBN 0-89636-054-7). Accent Bks.

Beeching, Brian. Interpreting Dental Radiographs. (Illus.). 142p. 1981. PLB 33.50 (ISBN 0-906141-20-6, Pub. by Update Pubns England). Kluwer Academic.

Beeching, Cyril L. A Dictionary of Eponyms. 2nd ed. 160p. 1983. 17.50 (ISBN 0-85157-329-0, Pub. by Bingley England). Shoe String.

Beeching, H. C. Character of Shakespeare. LC 74-13418. 1917. lib. bdg. 8.50 (ISBN 0-8414-3263-5). Folcroft.

Beeching, Henry C. The Character of Shakespeare. 1979. Repr. of 1917 ed. lib. bdg. 10.00 (ISBN 0-8492-3579-0). R West.

--William Shakespeare, Player, Playmaker & Poet. LC 77-168571. (Illus.). Repr. of 1909 ed. 8.50 (ISBN 0-404-00724-4). AMS Pr.

--William Shakespeare: Player, Playmaker & Poet. 1973. Repr. of 1909 ed. 8.45 (ISBN 0-8274-1670-9). R West.

Beeching, Jack. The Chinese Opium Wars. LC 76-40223. (Illus.). 1977. pap. 6.95 (ISBN 0-15-617094-9, Harv). HarBraceJ.

--The Galleys at Lepanto. (Illus.). 272p. 1983. 17.95 (ISBN 0-684-17918-0, ScribT). Scribner.

--Open Path: Christian Missionaries, 1515-1914. LC 80-21270. (Illus.). 350p. 1982. 19.95 (ISBN 0-915520-37-0); pap. 10.95 (ISBN 0-915520-53-2). Ross-Erikson.

Beeching, Jack, ed. see Hakluyt, Richard.

Beechman, Lenore. Song of the Soul: In Celebration of Korea. LC 83-15536. (Illus.). 38p. (Orig.). 1984. pap. 4.95 (ISBN 0-377-00137-6). Friend Pr.

Beechy, T. H. Accountant for Corporate Income Taxes: Conceptual Considerations & Empirical Analysis. 194p. 1983. 26.50 (ISBN 0-88800-102-9). Can Inst Chart Accts.

--La Comptabilisation des impots sur les benefices: Analyse theorique et empirique. 226p. 1983. 26.50 (ISBN 0-88800-103-7). Can Inst Chart Accts.

Beechy, Winifred. The New China. LC 82-11800. 280p. (Orig.). 1982. pap. 6.95 (ISBN 0-8361-3310-2). Herald Pr.

Beeck, Frans J. van see Van Beeck, Frans J.

Beecroft, Glynis. Carving Techniques. LC 82-82918. (Illus.). 144p. 1983. pap. 7.95 (ISBN 0-668-05715-7, 5715). Arco.

Beecroft, John, ed. see Kipling, Rudyard.

Beed, Terence W. & Stimson, Robert J., eds. Survey Interviewing: Theory & Techniques. 224p. 1985. text ed. 27.50x (ISBN 0-86861-436-X). Allen Unwin.

Beede, Benjamin R. Intervention & Counterinsurgency: An Annotated Bibliography of the Small Wars of the United States, 1898-1984. Blanco, Richard L., ed. LC 84-48072. (Reference Library of Social Science- Wars of U.S.). 400p. 1985. lib. bdg. 55.00 (ISBN 0-8240-8944-8). Garland Pub.

Beede, J. W. & Kniker, H. T. Species of the Genus Schwagerina & Their Stratigraphic Significance. (Bull Ser.: 2433). (Illus.). 96p. 1924. 1.00 (ISBN 0-686-29344-4, BULL 2433). Bur Econ Geology.

Beede, Mindy. Dye Transfer Made Easy. 176p. 1981. pap. 16.95 (ISBN 0-8174-3798-3, Pub by Amphoto). Watson-Guptill.

Beedell, Suzanne. Country Living by Sea & Estuary. LC 79-91479. (Illus.). 1980. 22.50 (ISBN 0-7153-7796-5). David & Charles.

--Windmills. (Illus.). 222p. 1982. 21.50 (ISBN 0-7153-6811-7); pap. 9.95 (ISBN 0-7153-7879-1). David & Charles.

Beedham, Christopher. The Passive Aspect in English, German & Russian. (Tubinger Beitrage zur Linguistik (TBL): 186). 186p. (Orig.). 1982. pap. 22.00x (ISBN 3-87808-967-8). Benjamins North Am.

Beeding, Francis. Death Walks in Eastrepps. 272p. 1980. pap. 4.50 (ISBN 0-486-24014-2). Dover.

Beedle, Lynn S. Plastic Design of Steel Frames. LC 58-13454. 406p. 1974. 56.95x (ISBN 0-471-06171-9, Pub. by Wiley-Interscience). Wiley.

Beedome, Thomas. Select Poems Divine & Humane. LC 75-17757. 1973. lib. bdg. 10.00 (ISBN 0-8414-3228-7). Folcroft.

Beedon, Laurel & Heinmiller, Joseph. Writing for Education Journals. LC 79-66532. (Fastback Ser.: No. 136). (Orig.). 1979. pap. 0.75 (ISBN 0-87367-136-8). Phi Delta Kappa.

Beedy, Ted & Granholm, Steve. Discovering Sierra Birds. (Illus.). 175p. 1985. pap. write for info. (ISBN 0-939666-42-1). Yosemite Natl Hist.

Beeftink, Wim G., ed. Vegetation Dynamics. 135p. 1980. pap. 31.50 (ISBN 90-6193-606-3, Pub. by Junk Pubs Netherlands -). Kluwer Academic.

Beeger, Gilda. The Southeast States. (First Book Ser.). 96p. (gr. 4 up). 1984. lib. bdg. 8.90 (ISBN 0-531-04738-5). Watts.

Beeghely, Leonard. Social Stratification in America. LC 78-1551. 1978. text ed. 17.95 (ISBN 0-394-33326-8, RanC). Random.

Beeghley, Leonard. Living Poorly in America. 224p. 1983. 26.95 (ISBN 0-03-063151-3); pap. 13.95 (ISBN 0-03-063152-1). Praeger.

Beeghley, Leonard, jt. auth. see Turner, Jonathan E.

Beegle, Charles W. & Brandt, Richard M., eds. Observational Methods in the Classroom. LC 73-80535. 94p. 1973. 3.50 (ISBN 0-87120-047-3, 611-17948). Assn Supervision.

Beegle, Charles W. & Edelfelt, Roy A., eds. Staff Development: Staff Liberation. 1977. 6.50 (ISBN 0-87120-083-X). Assn Supervision.

Beegle, Dewey M. God's Word into English. LC 79-84556. 1965. pap. 8.95 (ISBN 0-933462-02-6). Pryor Pettengill.

--Moses, the Servant of Yahweh. LC 79-84558. 368p. 1972. pap. text ed. 8.95 (ISBN 0-933462-03-4). Pryor Pettengill.

--Prophecy & Prediction. 274p. 1978. pap. text ed. 8.95 (ISBN 0-933462-01-8). Pryor Pettengill.

--Scripture, Tradition & Infallibility. LC 79-84557. Orig. Title: The Inspiration of Scripture. 332p. pap. text ed. 8.95 (ISBN 0-933462-04-2). Pryor Pettengill.

Beegle, Shirley. Bible Quizzes. 1985. pap. 0.69 pocket size (ISBN 0-87239-823-4, 2813). Standard Pub.

--Easy Bible Quizzes for All Ages. rev. ed. 1983. pap. 1.95 (ISBN 0-87239-657-6, 3137). Standard Pub.

--Jesus Quizzes. 1985. pap. 0.69 (ISBN 0-87239-824-2, 2814). Standard Pub.

--Through the Bible Quizzes for Children. 64p. (Orig.). (gr. 2-7). 1974. pap. 2.50 (ISBN 0-87239-324-0, 3249). Standard Pub.

Beegle, Shirley, ed. Creative Craft Ideas for All Ages. (Illus., Orig.). (gr. k up). 1966. pap. 6.95 (ISBN 0-87239-321-6, 2795). Standard Pub.

Beehler, Bruce, et al. Birds of New Guinea. LC 85-42673. (Illus.). 370p. 1985. 65.00 (ISBN 0-691-08385-1); pap. 37.50 (ISBN 0-691-02394-8). Princeton U Pr.

Beehler, Bruce M. Birdlife of the Adirondack Park. (Illus.). 1978. pap. 5.95 (ISBN 0-935272-05-4). ADK Mtn Club.

Beehler, Paul J. Contemporary Cash Management: Principles, Practices, Perspectives. 2nd ed. LC 82-17358. (Systems & Control for Financial Management Ser.). 447p. 1983. 42.95x (ISBN 0-471-86861-2, Pub by Ronald Pr). Wiley.

Beehler, Rodger. Moral Life. 226p. 1978. 17.50x (ISBN 0-8476-6107-5). Rowman.

Beehler, Roger & Drengson, Alan R., eds. The Philosophy of Society. 1978. pap. 14.50x (ISBN 0-416-83490-6, NO. 2083). Methuen Inc.

Beehr, Terry A. & Bhagat, Rabi S. Human Stress & Cognition in Organizations: An Integrated Perspective. (Organizational Assessment & Change Ser.). 480p. 1985. 39.95 (ISBN 0-471-86954-6). Wiley.

Beek, Gus W. Van see Van Beek, Gus W.

Beek, J. & Frissel, M. J. Simulation of Nitrogen Behaviour in Soils. (Simulation Monographs). 76p. 1974. pap. 10.00 (ISBN 90-220-0440-6, PDC85, PUDOC). Unipub.

Beek, Jan M. van der see Cooke, Philip & Van der Beek, Jan M.

Beek, M. & Foster, D. Wild Flowers of South Australia. (Illus.). 1973. 6.00 (ISBN 0-912728-46-9). Newbury Bks.

Beek, W. J. & Muttzall, K. M. Transport Phenomena. LC 74-4651. 332p. 1975. (Pub. by Wiley-Interscience); pap. text ed. 29.95x (ISBN 0-471-06174-3, Pub. by Wiley-Interscience). Wiley.

Beek, Wil van. Hazrat Inayat Khan: Master of Life-Modern Sufi Mystic. 1983. 12.95 (ISBN 0-533-05453-2). Vantage.

Beekes, R. S. Development of the Proto-Indo-European Laryngeals in Greek. (Janua Linguarum, Ser. Practica: No. 42). 1969. pap. text ed. 46.40x (ISBN 90-2790-693-9). Mouton.

Beek Jan M. van, der see Van der Beek, Jan M. & Bonet, Alieke A.

Beekman, Allan. The Niihau Incident. LC 82-83137. (Illus.). 128p. 1982. 9.95 (ISBN 0-9609132-0-3). Heritage Pac.

Beekman, Betty, jt. auth. see Sutton, Valerie J.

Beekman, Daniel. Forest, Village, Town, City. LC 79-7819. (Illus.). 32p. (gr. 3-6). 1982. 10.10i (ISBN 0-690-04084-9); PLB 9.89g (ISBN 0-690-04085-7). Crowell Jr Bks.

--The Mechanical Baby: A Popular History of Writings on the Theory & Practice of Child Care. LC 76-18055. (Illus.). 320p. 1977. 12.95 (ISBN 0-88208-073-3). Lawrence Hill.

Beekman, E. M. The Verbal Empires of Simon Vestdijk & James Joyce. (Costerus New Ser.). 211p. 1983. text ed. 21.50x (ISBN 90-6203-695-3, Pub. by Rodopi Holland). Humanities.

Beekman, E. M., ed. & tr. from Dutch. The Oyster & the Eagle: Selected Aphorisms of Multatuli. LC 73-93171. 124p. 1974. lib. bdg. 10.00x (ISBN 0-87023-123-5). U of Mass Pr.

Beekman, E. M., ed. Patriotism, Inc & Other Tales by Paul van Ostaijen. LC 79-150314. 192p. 1971. 12.00x (ISBN 0-87023-084-0); pap. 6.00x (ISBN 0-87023-097-2). U of Mass Pr.

Beekman, E. M., ed. see Alberts, A.

Beekman, E. M., ed. see Couperus, L.

Beekman, E. M., ed. see Dermout, Maria.

Beekman, E. M., ed. see Du Perron, E.

Beekman, E. M., ed. see Nieuwenhuys, Rob.

Beekman, E M., ed. see Nijs, E. Breton de.

Beekman, E. M., ed. see Van Schendel, Arthur.

Beekman, E. M., intro. by see Vuyk, Beb & Friedericy, H. J.

Beekman, E. M., tr. see Rumphius.

Beekman, G. K., jt. auth. see Nieger, L.

Beekman, George. Apple II Plus, IIe, IIc Home Companion. (Illus.). 350p. 1985. 19.95 (ISBN 0-8359-0009-6). Reston.

--The Commodore 64 Home Companion. (The Companion Ser.). 360p. (Orig.). 1984. pap. 19.95 (ISBN 0-88190-294-2, BO294). Datamost.

--The Macintosh Home Companion. (Home Companion Ser.). (Illus., Orig.). Date not set. pap. 19.95 (ISBN 0-88190-385-X, BO385). Datamost.

Beekman, George & Corliss, Dennis. Apple Home Companion. (The Companion Ser.). (Illus.). 355p. (Orig.). 1984. pap. 19.95 (ISBN 0-88190-318-3, BO318). Datamost.

Beekman, George & Folts, Jim. The IBM PC Home Companion. (Home Companion Ser.). (Illus.). 360p. (Orig.). Date not set. pap. 19.95 (ISBN 0-88190-314-0, BO314). Datamost.

Beekman, George C. Early Dutch Settlers of Monmouth County. 2nd ed. 1974. 12.00 (ISBN 0-686-11781-6). Neptune His Soc.

Beekman, George C., jt. auth. see Salter, Edwin.

Beekman, J. F., tr. see Broekman, J. M.

Beekman-Love, Gilian & Neiger, L. Materials Management. (Applied Business Logistics Ser.: Vol. 1). 1978. pap. 16.00 (ISBN 90-207-0748-5, Pub. by Martinus Nijhoff Netherlands). Kluwer Academic.

Beelen, Geertruida C., jt. auth. see Sadee, Wolfgang.

Beeler, Duane. Arbitration for the Local Union. 105p. (Orig.). 1977. pap. 3.95 (ISBN 0-317-12246-0). Union Rep.

--Discipline & Discharge. 225p. (Orig.). 1978. pap. 5.95 (ISBN 0-317-12244-4). Union Rep.

--Labor Law for the Union Officer. 103p. 1975. pap. 3.95 (ISBN 0-317-12248-7). Union Rep.

--Negotiating the Contract. 139p. (Orig.). 1981. pap. 4.95 (ISBN 0-317-12243-6). Union Rep.

--Speak Up to Move up: Public Speaking for the Union Representative. 101p. (Orig.). 1979. pap. 3.95 (ISBN 0-317-12254-1). Union Rep.

--Union Professional: The Staff Rep in Action. 109p. 1977. pap. 3.95 (ISBN 0-317-12247-9). Union Rep.

Beeler, Duane & Krushenbaum, Harry. How to Be a More Effective Union Representative. 125p. (Orig.). 1965. pap. 3.95 (ISBN 0-317-12245-2). Union Rep.

--Roles of the Labor Leader. 131p. (Orig.). 1969. pap. 3.95 (ISBN 0-317-12249-5). Union Rep.

Beeler, Duane & McAllister, Frank. Creative Use of Films in Education. (Illus., Orig.). 1968. pap. 1.95 (ISBN 0-317-12255-X). Union Rep.

Beeler, Duane, et al. Why Workers Behave the Way They Do. 240p. (Orig.). 1983. pap. 7.95 (ISBN 0-317-12241-X). Union Rep.

Beeler, J. R. Radiation Effects Computer Experiments. (Defects in Solids Ser.: Vol. 13). 882p. 1983. 168.00 (ISBN 0-444-86315-X, North Holland). Elsevier.

Beeler, Joe. Cowboys & Indians: Characters in Oil & Bronze. LC 67-24616. (Illus.). 80p. 1980. 19.95 (ISBN 0-8061-0761-8); pap. 9.95 (ISBN 0-8061-1634-X). U of Okla Pr.

--Joe Beeler Sketch Book. LC 72-79075. (Illus.). 128p. 1974. 12.50 (ISBN 0-87358-099-0). Northland.

Beeler, John. Warfare in Feudal Europe, 730-1200. LC 74-148018. (Illus.). 288p. 1973. pap. 7.95x (ISBN 0-8014-9120-7, CP120). Cornell U Pr.

Beeler, John H., ed. see Oman, Charles W.

Beeler, M. Fancher, et al. Measuring the Quality of Library Service: A Handbook. LC 74-12107. (Illus.). 220p. 1974. 15.00 (ISBN 0-8108-0732-7). Scarecrow.

Beeler, Myrton F. Interpretations in Clinical Chemistry. 1st. ed. LC 77-95105. (Illus.). 580p. 1978. text ed. 27.50 softbound (ISBN 0-89189-045-9, 45-2-036-00). Am Soc Clinical.

Beeler, Myrton F. & Catrou, Paul G. Interpretations in Clinical Chemistry: A Textbook Approach to Chemical Pathology. 2nd. ed. LC 82-22801. (Illus.). 272p. 1983. text ed. 35.00 (ISBN 0-89189-165-X, 45-2-040-00). Am Soc Clinical.

Beeler, Myrton F., jt. ed. see Freeman, James A.

Beeler, Nelson F. & Branley, Franklyn M. Experiments in Optical Illusion. LC 51-5642. (Illus.). (gr. 5-9). 1951. 10.89 (ISBN 0-690-27507-2). Crowell Jr Bks.

Beeler, Raymond, ed. Princeton Journal: Thematic Studies in Architecture. (Landscape Ser.: Vol. 2). 240p. (Orig.). 1985. pap. text ed. 15.00 (ISBN 0-910413-08-8). Princeton Arch.

Beeley, Arthur L. An Experimental Study in Left-Handedness, with Practical Suggestions for Schoolroom Tests. LC 78-72787. (Brainedness, Handedness, & Mental Ability Ser.). Repr. of 1918 ed. 22.50 (ISBN 0-404-60852-3). AMS Pr.

Beeley, H. Industrial Management Services. (Illus.). 316p. 1981. pap. 14.95x (ISBN 0-7121-0942-0). Trans-Atlantic.

Beeley, P. R. Foundry Technology. 1972. text ed. 89.95 (ISBN 0-408-70348-2). Butterworth.

Beem. The Lorentzian Distance Function & Global Lorentzian Geometry. (Lecture Notes in Pure & Applied Mathematics Ser.: Vol. 67). 1981. 59.75 (ISBN 0-8247-1369-9). Dekker.

Beem, J. K. & Woo, P. Y. Doubly Timelike Surfaces. LC 52-42839. (Memoirs: No. 92). 115p. 1969. pap. 9.00 (ISBN 0-8218-1292-0, MEMO-92). Am Math.

Beeman, D. L., ed. Industrial Power Systems Handbook. 1955. 72.50 (ISBN 0-07-004301-9). McGraw.

Beeman, Don R. & Rump, Richard G. You're Hired! rev. ed. 180p. 1984. pap. text ed. 7.50 (ISBN 0-914399-00-4). DBA Pr.

Beeman, Harris F., et al. Intramural Sports: A Text & Study Guide. 3rd, rev. ed. LC 79-92382. 128p. 1980. pap. text ed. 8.95x (ISBN 0-916622-16-9). Princeton Bk Co.

Beeman, Judith, jt. auth. see Beeman, Martin.

Beeman, Martin & Beeman, Judith. Joys of Hawaiian Cooking. (Illus.). 1981. pap. 5.95 (ISBN 0-912180-41-2). Petroglyph.

Beeman, Richard R. The Evolution of the Southern Backcountry: A Case Study of Lunenburg County, Virginia, 1746-1832. LC 83-27387. (Illus.). 320p. 1984. 25.00 (ISBN 0-8122-7926-3). U of Pa Pr.

--The Old Dominion & the New Nation, 1788-1801. LC 76-190531. 296p. 1972. 25.00x (ISBN 0-8131-1269-9). U Pr of Ky.

Beemer, A. M., et al, eds. see Annual Oholo Biological Conference, 21st, Israel, March 1976.

Beemer, Eleanor. My Luiseno Neighbors. (Illus.). 91p. (Orig.). 1980. pap. 9.95 (ISBN 0-916552-20-9). Acoma Bks.

Beemer, Halsey, jt. ed. see Plucknett, Donald L.

Beemer, Theo., jt. auth. see Bockle, Franz.

Been, Margaret L. Wilderness & Gardens: An American Lady's Prospect. (Illus.). 1974. pap. 5.00 (ISBN 0-87423-011-X). Westburg.

Beene, Gerrie & King, Lourdes. Dining In-Spain: A Guide to Spanish Cooking with Recipes from Its Most Distinguished Restaurants. LC 69-13508. 1969. pap. 2.75 (ISBN 0-8048-0138-X). C E Tuttle.

Beenhakker, Arie. A System for Development Planning & Budgeting. 200p. 1980. text ed. 37.95x (ISBN 0-566-00326-0). Gower Pub Co.

Beenhakker, Henri L. Handbook for the Analysis of Capital Investments. LC 76-5324. (Illus.). 452p. (Orig.). 1976. lib. bdg. 35.00x (ISBN 0-8371-8901-2, BCI). Greenwood.

Beenhakker, Henri L. & Chammari, Abderraouf. Identification & Appraisal of Rural Roads Projects. (Working Paper: No. 362). 74p. 1979. 5.00 (ISBN 0-686-36219-5, WP-0362). World Bank.

Beenstock, et al. Could Do Better. (Institute of Economic Affairs, Occasional Papers Ser.: No. 62). pap. 10.50 technical (ISBN 0-255-36150-5). Transatlantic.

Beenstock, M. A Neoclassical Analysis of Macroeconomic Policy. LC 79-8961. 1981. 42.50 (ISBN 0-521-23077-2). Cambridge U Pr.

Beenstock, Michael. The Foreign Exchanges: Theory, Modelling & Policy. LC 78-1372. 1979. 26.00x (ISBN 0-312-29862-5). St Martin.

--Health, Migration & Development. 192p. 1980. text ed. 37.95x (ISBN 0-566-00369-4). Gower Pub Co.

--The World Economy in Transition. 240p. 1983. text ed. 25.00x (ISBN 0-04-339033-1). Allen Unwin.

--The World Economy in Transition. 2nd ed. 250p. 1984. pap. text ed. 10.95x (ISBN 0-04-339035-8). Allen Unwin.

Beer, jt. ed. see Willardson.

Beer, A., jt. auth. see Beer, P.

Beer, A., jt. ed. see Willardson, R. K.

Beer, A., jt. ed. see Willardson, Robert.

Beer, A., tr. see Roth, G. D.

Beer, A. C., jt. ed. see Willardson, R. K.

Beer, A. C., jt. ed. see Willardson, Robert.

Beer, A. E., jt. ed. see Toder, V.

Beer, Albert C., jt. auth. see Willardson, R. K.

Beer, Albert C., jt. ed. see Willardson, R. K.

Beer, Albert C., jt. ed. see Willardson, Robert K.

Beer, Alice B. Trade Goods: A Study of Indian Chintz. LC 70-125588. (Illus.). 133p. 1970. pap. text ed. 6.95x (ISBN 0-87474-235-8). Smithsonian.

Beer, Alice S. & Graham, Richard. Teaching Music to the Exceptional Child: A Handbook for Mainstreaming. (Illus.). 1980. text ed. 22.95 (ISBN 0-13-893982-9). P-H.

Beer, Barrett L. Northumberland: The Political Career of John Dudley, Earl of Warwick & Duke of Northumberland. LC 73-77386. 235p. 1974. 15.00x (ISBN 0-87338-140-8). Kent St U Pr.

--Rebellion & Riot: Popular Disorder in England During the Reign of Edward VI. LC 81-19341. 260p. 1982. 21.00x (ISBN 0-87338-269-2). Kent St U Pr.

Beer Can Collectors of America. The Beer Can. 1977. pap. 4.95 (ISBN 0-346-12300-3). Cornerstone.

Beer, Chris, et al. Gay Workers: Trade Unions & the Law. 1981. 15.00x (ISBN 0-901108-90-1, Pub. by NCCL England). State Mutual Bk.

Beer, E. S. De see Locke, John.

Beer, E. S. de see Locke, John.

Beer, Edith L. Monarch's Dictionary of Investment Terms. 192p. (Orig.). 1983. pap. 7.95 (ISBN 0-671-45497-8). Monarch Pr.

Beer, Eileene H. Scandinavian Design: Objects of a Life Style. LC 75-25732. (Illus.). 214p. 1975. 35.00 (ISBN 0-89067-055-2). Am Scandinavian.

Beer, F. P. & Johnston, E. R. Mechanics for Engineers, 2 vols. 3rd ed. 1976. Vol. 1: Statics. 39.00 (ISBN 0-07-004271-3); Vol. 2: Dynamics. 39.00 (ISBN 0-07-004273-X); Combined Ed. 46.00 (ISBN 0-07-004270-5). McGraw.

--Vector Mechanics for Engineers: Dynamics, Vol. 2. 4th ed. 1984. 38.95 (ISBN 0-07-004389-2). McGraw.

Beer, F. R., Jr. & Johnston, E. R. Vector Mechanics for Engineers: Combined Volume. 4th ed. 1984. 49.95 (ISBN 0-07-004438-4). McGraw.

Beer, Ferdinand P. & Johnston, E. R., Jr. Vector Mechanics for Engineers Combined. 3rd ed. 1977. text ed. 39.95 (ISBN 0-07-004277-2). McGraw.

--Vector Mechanics for Engineers: Dynamics. 3rd ed. 1977. text ed. 32.95 (ISBN 0-07-004281-0). McGraw.

Beer, Ferdinand P. & Johnston, E. Russell, Jr. Mechanics of Materials. (Illus.). 672p. 1981. text ed. 42.95x (ISBN 0-07-004284-5). McGraw.

Beer, Frances F., tr. see Le Gentil, Pierre.

Beer, Francis A. Integration & Disintegration in NATO: Processes of Alliance Cohesion & Prospects for Atlantic Community. LC 69-12762. 344p. 1969. 10.00 (ISBN 0-8142-0005-2). Ohio St U Pr.

--Peace Against War: The Ecology of International Violence. LC 80-27214. (International Relations Ser.). (Illus.). 447p. 1981. text ed. 24.95 (ISBN 0-7167-1250-4); pap. text ed. 15.95 (ISBN 0-7167-1251-2). W H Freeman.

Beer, G. & Harris, M. The Notebooks of George Meredith. (Salzburg-Romantic Reassessment Ser.: No. 73,2). 216p. 1983. pap. text ed. 25.50x (ISBN 0-391-03142-2, Pub. by Salzburg Austria). Humanities.

Beer, G. R. de see De Beer, G. R.

Beer, Gavin De see De Beer, Gavin.

Beer, Gavin de see De Beer, Gavin.

Beer, Gavin de see DeBeer, Gavin.

Beer, Gavin R. de see De Beer, Gavin R.

Beer, Gavin R. De see Locke, John.

Beer, George A. The Coming of the Italian-Ethiopian War. LC 67-14336. pap. 105.00 (ISBN 0-317-11313-5, 2017258). Bks Demand UMI.

Beer, George L. African Questions at the Paris Peace Conference. LC 73-79813. (Illus.). Repr. of 1923 ed. 28.00x (ISBN 0-8371-1469-1, BEA&, Pub. by Negro U Pr). Greenwood.

--British Colonial Policy, 1754-1765. 13.25 (ISBN 0-8446-1065-8). Peter Smith.

--The Commercial Policy of England Toward the American Colonies. 12.00 (ISBN 0-8446-1068-2). Peter Smith.

--Old Colonial System, 2 vols. 14.50 ea. (ISBN 0-8446-1066-6). Peter Smith.

--Origins of British Colonial System, 1578 to 1660. 13.25 (ISBN 0-8446-1067-4). Peter Smith.

Beer, Gerald A. Applied Calculus for Business & Economics with an Introduction to Matrices. 1978. text ed. 21.95 (ISBN 0-316-08727-0); tchr's ed. avail. (ISBN 0-316-08728-9). Little.

Beer, Gillian. Darwin's Plots: Evolutionary Narrative in Darwin, George Eliot, & Nineteenth-Century Fiction. 384p. 1983. 35.00x (ISBN 0-7100-9505-8); pap. 9.95 (ISBN 0-7448-0021-8). Routledge & Kegan.

--The Romance. (Critical Idiom Ser.: Vol. 10). 1970. pap. 5.50x (ISBN 0-416-17260-1, NO. 2081). Methuen Inc.

Beer, Gretel. Austrian Cooking. 224p. 1984. 9.95 (ISBN 0-233-97653-1). Andre Deutsch.

--Austrian Cooking. 224p. 1984. pap. 9.95 (ISBN 0-233-97653-1, Pub. by A Deutsch England). David & Charles.

--Austrian Cooking & Baking. 224p. 1975. pap. 4.00 (ISBN 0-486-23220-4). Dover.

Beer, J. B. The Achievement of E. M. Forster. 225p. 1983. Repr. of 1962 ed. lib. bdg. 40.00 (ISBN 0-89987-950-0). Darby Bks.

Beer, J. M. & Chigier, N. A. Combustion Aerodynamics. LC 82-13084. 274p. 1982. Repr. of 1972 ed. lib. bdg. 19.50 (ISBN 0-89874-545-4). Krieger.

Beer, J. M., jt. ed. see Palmer, H. B.

Beer, Jeanette, tr. see De Fournival, Richard.

Beer, Jeanette, tr. see De France, Marie.

Beer, Jennifer E., jt. auth. see Friends Suburban Project.

Beer, Johann. Summer Tales. Jordan, Gerda & Hardin, James, trs. from Ger. LC 84-47537. 285p. (Orig.). 1984. pap. 29.50 (ISBN 0-8204-0112-9). P Lang Pubs.

Beer, John. The Emergence of the German Dye Industry. Cohen, I. Bernard, ed. LC 80-2115. (Development of Science Ser.). (Illus.). 1981. lib. bdg. 15.00x (ISBN 0-405-13835-0). Ayer Co Pubs.

--Wordsworth & the Human Heart. LC 78-15767. 277p. 1979. 29.00x (ISBN 0-231-04646-4). Columbia U Pr.

Beer, John, ed. Coleridge's Variety: Bicentenary Studies. LC 74-2051. 1974. 24.95x (ISBN 0-8229-1114-0). U of Pittsburgh Pr.

Beer, John, ed. see Coleridge, Samuel T.

Beer, John, jt. ed. see Das, G. K.

Beer, John B. Coleridge the Visionary. LC 78-2445. 367p. 1978. Repr. of 1970 ed. lib. bdg. 24.75x (ISBN 0-313-20360-1, BECO). Greenwood.

Beer, Lawrence. Freedom of Expression in Japan: A Study in Comparative Law, Politics & Society. LC 83-48288. 416p. 1985. 50.00x (ISBN 0-87011-632-0). Kodansha.

Beer, Lawrence W., jt. auth. see Itoh, Hiroshi.

Beer, Lawrence W., ed. Constitutionalism in Asia: Asian Views of the American Influence. LC 78-57303. 1979. 34.50x (ISBN 0-520-03701-4). U of Cal Pr.

Beer, Lisl. Great Is Kush. (Silver Series of Puppet Plays). 1965. pap. 1.50 (ISBN 0-8283-1258-3). Branden Pub Co.

--Horns of the Moon. (Silver Series of Puppet Plays). pap. 1.50 (ISBN 0-8283-1252-4). Branden Pub Co.

--Jonah & the Whale. (Silver Series of Puppet Plays). pap. 1.50 (ISBN 0-8283-1255-9). Branden Pub Co.

--Mister Vinegar. (Silver Series of Puppet Plays). 1966. pap. 1.50 (ISBN 0-8283-1250-8). Branden Pub Co.

--Prince & the Mermaid. (Silver Series of Puppet Plays). pap. 1.50 (ISBN 0-8283-1247-8). Branden Pub Co.

--Sir Eglamore & the Dragon. (Silver Series of Puppet Plays). pap. 1.50 (ISBN 0-8283-1245-1). Branden Pub Co.

--This My Island. 3.75 (ISBN 0-8283-1103-X). Branden Pub Co.

Beer, Lisl, ed. Punch & Judy. (Silver Series of Puppet Plays). pap. 1.50 (ISBN 0-8283-1244-3). Branden Pub Co.

--Second Shepherd's Play. (Silver Mosque Ser.). pap. 2.00 (ISBN 0-8283-1246-X). Branden Pub Co.

--Somebody-Nothing. (Silver Series of Puppet Plays). pap. 1.50 (ISBN 0-8283-1253-2). Branden Pub Co.

Beer, M. D. Programming Microcomputers with Pascal. 266p. 1982. pap. 13.95 (ISBN 0-442-21368-9). Van Nos Reinhold.

Beer, Martin. Programming with Pascal. 256p. 1982. 17.95 (ISBN 0-442-21368-9). Van Nos Reinhold.

Beer, Martin D. Microcomputer Interfacing & Associated Programming Techniques. (Illus.). 300p. (Orig.). 1985. pap. text ed. 19.95x (ISBN 0-00-383034-9, Pub. by Collins England). Sheridan.

Beer, Maurice, jt. auth. see Covell, Mara B.

Beer, Max. Early British Economics from the Thirteenth to the Middle of the Eighteenth Century. LC 67-17840. 1938. 27.50x (ISBN 0-678-00228-2). Kelley.

--A History of British Socialism, 2 vols. in one. Mayer, J. P., ed. LC 78-67332. (European Political Thought Ser.). 1979. Repr. of 1920 ed. lib. bdg. 55.50x (ISBN 0-405-11678-0). Ayer Co Pubs.

Beer, Michael. Organizational Change & Development: A Systems View. 1980. text ed. 28.20x (ISBN 0-673-16126-9). Scott F.

Beer, Michael & Spector, Bert. Readings in Human Resource Management. LC 84-25977. 752p. 1985. pap. text ed. 17.95 (ISBN 0-02-902370-X). Free Pr.

Beer, Michael, et al. Human Resource Management: A General Manager's Perspective. LC 84-21080. 786p. 1985. text ed. 28.95 (ISBN 0-02-902360-2); P 644. pap. 17.95x (ISBN 0-02-902370-X). Free Pr.

--Managing Human Assets: The Groundbreaking Harvard Business School Program. 288p. 1985. 19.95 (ISBN 0-02-902390-4). Free Pr.

Beer, Myer. Excerpts from Early Italian Opera. (Italian Opera 1810-1840 Ser.). 1985. lib. bdg. 85.00 (ISBN 0-8240-6572-7). Garland Pub.

Beer, P. & Beer, A. Vistas in Astronomy, Vol. 23 Complete. 1980. 125.00 (ISBN 0-08-026046-2). Pergamon.

Beer, P., ed. Vistas in Astronomy, Vol. 26. (Illus.). 426p. 1985. 162.00 (ISBN 0-08-032314-6). Pergamon.

Beer, P. & Pounds, K., eds. Vistas in Astronomy, Vol. 25. (Illus.). 436p. 1983. 144.00 (ISBN 0-08-031042-7). Pergamon.

Beer, Patricia. An Introduction to the Metaphysical Poets. 115p. 1981. Repr. of 1972 ed. text ed. 9.50x (ISBN 0-333-13667-5, Pub. by Macmillan England). Humanities.

--Just Like the Resurrection: Poems. LC 67-11109. 1967. 10.00 (ISBN 0-8023-1131-8). Dufour.

--Mrs. Beer's House. 256p. 1983. pap. 7.50 (ISBN 0-907746-23-3, Pub. by A Mott Ltd). Longwood Pub Group.

--Reader, I Married Him: A Study of the Women Characters of Jane Austen, Charlotte Bronte, Elizabeth Gaskell & George Eliot. LC 74-10054. 1977. Repr. of 1974 ed. 22.50x (ISBN 0-06-490345-1). B&N Imports.

Beer, Peter H. see Leonard, Robert J. & De Beer, Peter H.

Beer, Peter H. de see Leonard, Robert J. & De Beer, Peter H.

Beer, S. A Manager's Guide to Organizational Structure. 19.95 (ISBN 0-471-90675-1). Wiley.

Beer, S., ed. Liquid Metals: Chemistry & Physics. (Monographs & Textbks in Material Science: Vol. 4). 744p. 1972. 125.00 (ISBN 0-8247-1032-0). Dekker.

Beer, Samuel, et al. Patterns of Government: The Major Political Systems of Europe. 3rd ed. 1972. 21.00 (ISBN 0-394-31387-9, RanC). Random.

Beer, Samuel H. Britain Against Itself: The Political Contradictions of Collectivism. 220p. 1982. 18.95 (ISBN 0-393-01564-5); cloth 5.95x (ISBN 0-393-95288-6). Norton.

--British Political System. (Patterns of Government Ser.). 1974. pap. text ed. 8.95 (ISBN 0-394-31817-X, RanC). Random.

--City of Reason. LC 68-23274. (Harvard Political Studies Ser). 1968. Repr. of 1949 ed. lib. bdg. 16.25x (ISBN 0-8371-0016-X, BECR). Greenwood.

--Modern British Politics: Parties & Pressure Groups in the Collectivist Age. Orig. Title: British Politics in the Collectivist Age. 432p. 1982. pap. 7.95x (ISBN 0-393-00952-1). Norton.

--Treasury Control: The Co-ordination of Financial & Economic Policy in Great Britain. LC 82-11843. viii, 138p. 1982. Repr. of 1957 ed. lib. bdg. 25.00x (ISBN 0-313-23626-7, BETRC). Greenwood.

Beer, Samuel H., ed. see Marx, Karl & Engels, Friedrich.

Beer, Stafford. Brain of the Firm. 2nd ed. LC 80-49979. 417p. 1981. 39.95x (ISBN 0-471-27687-1, Pub. by Wiley-Interscience). Wiley.

--Decision & Control: The Meaning of Operational Research & Management Cybernetics. LC 66-25668. 556p. 1966. 52.95x (ISBN 0-471-06210-3, Pub. by Wiley-Interscience). Wiley.

--The Heart of Enterprise. LC 79-40532. 582p. 1980. 39.95 (ISBN 0-471-27599-9, Pub. by Wiley-Interscience). Wiley.

--Platform for Change. LC 73-10741. 457p. 1975. 48.95x (ISBN 0-471-06189-1, Pub. by Wiley-Interscience). Wiley.

Beer, T. The Aerospace Environment. (Wykeham Science Ser.: No. 36). 170p. 1975. pap. cancelled (ISBN 0-85109-021-4). Taylor & Francis.

--Environmental Oceanography: An Introduction to the Behaviour of Coastal Waters. LC 82-18099. (PIL Ser.). (Illus.). 109p. 1983. 30.00 (ISBN 0-08-026291-0); pap. 13.00 (ISBN 0-08-026290-2). Pergamon.

Beer, T. & Kucherawy, M. D. The Aerospace Environment. (Wykeham Science Ser.: No. 36). 170p. 1975. 8.60x (ISBN 0-8448-1163-7). Crane-Russak Co.

Beer, Thomas. Hanna. LC 73-3036. 325p. 1973. Repr. of 1929 ed. lib. bdg. 23.00x (ISBN 0-374-90518-5). Octagon.

--The Mauve Decade: American Life at the End of the Nineteenth Century. 268p. 1980. Repr. of 1926 ed. lib. bdg. 32.50x (ISBN 0-374-90520-7). Octagon.

--Mrs. Egg & Other Americans: Collected Stories. Follett, Wilson, ed. LC 78-23682. 1979. Repr. of 1947 ed. lib. bdg. 37.50x (ISBN 0-313-20648-1, BEMO). Greenwood.

--Stephen Crane. LC 72-4407. 248p. 1972. Repr. of 1923 ed. lib. bdg. 20.50x (ISBN 0-374-90519-3). Octagon.

Beer, William, tr. see Crozier, Michel.

Beer, William R. Househusbands: Men & Housework in American Families. (Illus.). 176p. 1982. 24.95x (ISBN 0-686-78910-5); pap. 12.95 (ISBN 0-89789-046-9). Bergin & Garvey.

--Househusbands: Men & Housework in American Families. 176p. 1982. 24.95 (ISBN 0-03-059978-4). Praeger.

--The Unexpected Rebellion: Ethnic Activism in Contemporary France. LC 79-3515. 1980. 25.00x (ISBN 0-8147-1029-8). NYU Pr.

Beer, William R. & Jacob, James, eds. Language Policy & National Unity. LC 81-67475. 254p. 1985. text ed. 34.50x (ISBN 0-86598-058-6); tables incl. Rowman & Allanheld.

Beerbohm, M. Lytton Strachey. LC 74-7186. (English Literature Ser., No. 33). 1974. lib. bdg. 40.95x (ISBN 0-8383-1936-X). Haskell.

--Rossetti & His Circle. 59.95 (ISBN 0-8490-0974-X). Gordon Pr.

Beerbohm, Max. Around Theatres. LC 69-13814. 1969. Repr. of 1954 ed. lib. bdg. 27.50x (ISBN 0-8371-0303-7, BEAR). Greenwood.

--The Happy Hypocrite. LC 85-70301. (Illus.). 54p. 1985. 13.95 (ISBN 0-88138-038-5, Star & Elephant Bks.). Green Tiger Pr.

--The Illustrated Zuleika Dobson. LC 85-50178. 416p. 1985. 19.95x (ISBN 0-300-03389-3). Yale U Pr.

--Letters to Reggie Turner. Hart-Davis, Rupert, ed. LC 79-8052. Repr. of 1964 ed. 30.00 (ISBN 0-404-18362-X). AMS Pr.

--Lytton Strachey. LC 76-41816. 1976. Repr. of 1943 ed. lib. bdg. 6.00 (ISBN 0-8414-1781-4). Folcroft.

--Lytton Strachey. 1973. Repr. of 1943 ed. 10.00 (ISBN 0-8274-1213-4). R West.

--Mainly on the Air. LC 72-287. (Essay Index Reprint Ser.). Repr. of 1957 ed. 17.00 (ISBN 0-8369-2785-0). Ayer Co Pubs.

--More. facsimile ed. LC 67-28730. (Essay Index Reprint Ser). 1921. 17.00 (ISBN 0-8369-0181-9). Ayer Co Pubs.

--Observations. LC 71-163891. (English Literature Ser., No. 33). 1971. Repr. of 1925 ed. lib. bdg. 56.95x (ISBN 0-8383-1249-7). Haskell.

--The Poet's Corner. 1978. Repr. of 1943 ed. lib. bdg. 12.50 (ISBN 0-8495-0388-4). Arden Lib.

--Seven Men & Two Others. (World's Classics Ser.). (Illus.). 1980. pap. 4.95 (ISBN 0-19-281512-1). Oxford U Pr.

--Works & More. LC 12-30603. 1896. 39.00 (ISBN 0-403-00144-7). Scholarly.

--The Works of Max Beerbohm. 192p. Date not set. Repr. of 1896 ed. lib. bdg. 29.00 (ISBN 0-932051-90-1). Am Repr Serv.

--Zuleika Dobson. 256p. 1983. pap. 4.95 (ISBN 0-14-006713-2). Penguin.

Beerbohm, Max, ed. Herbert Beerbohm Tree. LC 75-91895. (Illus.). 1920. Repr. of 1920 ed. 22.00 (ISBN 0-405-08251-7, Blom Pubns). Ayer Co Pubs.

Beerbower, James R. Search for the Past: An Introduction to Paleontology. 2nd ed. LC 68-18060. (Illus.). 1968. ref. ed. 34.95 (ISBN 0-13-797316-0). P-H.

Beere, Carole A. Women & Women's Issues: A Handbook of Tests & Measures. LC 79-88106. (Social & Behavioral Science Ser.). 1979. text ed. 37.95x (ISBN 0-87589-418-6). Jossey Bass.

Beer-Hofmann, Richard. Jacob's Dream. Wynn, Ida B., tr. from Ger. Orig. Title: Jaakobs Traum. 1946. text ed. 8.50x (ISBN 0-685-52950-9). M S Rosenberg.

Beerits, Henry. The United Nations & Human Survival. 1976. pap. 1.50 (ISBN 0-686-95386-X). Am Fr Serv Comm.

Beermann, W., ed. Biochemical Differentiation in Insect Glands. LC 77-23423. (Results & Problems in Cell Differentiation: Vol. 8). (Illus.). 1977. 51.00 (ISBN 0-387-08286-7). Springer-Verlag.

--Developmental Studies on Giant Chromosomes. LC 74-189387. (Results & Problems in Cell Differentiation Ser.: Vol. 4). (Illus.). 220p. 1972. 28.00 (ISBN 0-387-05748-X). Springer-Verlag.

Beer-Poitevin, F. Enciclopedia Medica para la Familia. Moderma. 1770p. (Span.). 1979. 250.00 (ISBN 0-686-97358-5, S-34968). French & Eur.

Beers. Choosing God's Way to See & Share. 1983. 11.95 (ISBN 0-88207-819-4). Victor Bks.

Beers, A. H., jt. auth. see Coker, W. C.

Beers, Alma, jt. auth. see Coker, William C.

Beers, Alma H., jt. auth. see Coker, William C.

Beers, Burton F. Vain Endeavor: Robert Lansing's Attempts to End the American-Japanese Rivalry. LC 61-16907. Repr. of 1962 ed. 54.80 (ISBN 0-8357-9119-X, 2017884). Bks Demand UMI.

Beers, Burton F., jt. auth. see Clyde, Paul H.

Beers, Clifford W. A Mind That Found Itself. 5th ed. LC 80-5256. (Contemporary Community Health Ser.). 232p. 1981. 14.95 (ISBN 0-8229-3442-6); pap. 5.95 (ISBN 0-8229-5324-2). U of Pittsburgh Pr.

Beers, F. W. Atlas of Windham County, Vermont. 1969. 25.00 (ISBN 0-8289-0107-4). Greene.

Beers, F. W., jt. auth. see Orange County Genealogical Society.

Beers, F. W., et al. Atlas of Bennington County, Vermont. LC 74-653428. (Illus.). 1970. Repr. 35.00 (ISBN 0-8048-0872-4). C E Tuttle.

--Atlas of Chittenden County, Vermont. LC 73-653713. (Illus.). 1970. Repr. 35.00 (ISBN 0-8048-0938-0). C E Tuttle.

--Atlas of the City of Worcester, Worcester County, Massachusetts. LC 74-653716. (Illus.). 1971. Repr. 35.00 (ISBN 0-8048-0939-9). C E Tuttle.

--Atlas of Windsor County, Vermont. LC 72-653430. (Illus.). 1970. Repr. of 1869 ed. 35.00 (ISBN 0-8048-0874-0). C E Tuttle.

--Atlas of Worcester County, Massachusetts. LC 70-653715. (Illus.). 1971. Repr. 35.00 (ISBN 0-8048-0941-0). C E Tuttle.

Beers, Gilbert. Victor Handbook of Bible Knowledge. Popular ed. LC 81-50695. 640p. 1981. 29.95 (ISBN 0-88207-811-9); pap. 19.95 (ISBN 0-88207-808-9). Victor Bks.

--With Sails to the Wind. LC 77-24955. (Muffin Family Ser.). (Illus.). (gr. k-5). 1977. 11.95 (ISBN 0-8024-9570-2). Moody.

Beers, Henry A. Connecticut Wits, & Other Essays. LC 70-153303. Repr. of 1920 ed. 16.00 (ISBN 0-404-04643-6). AMS Pr.

--The Connecticut Wits & Other Essays. 1920. 14.50x (ISBN 0-686-51360-6). Elliots Bks.

--Four Americans. facs. ed. LC 68-54324. (Essay Index Reprint Ser.). 1919. 13.50 (ISBN 0-8369-0182-7). Ayer Co Pubs.

--From Chaucer to Tennyson: English Literature in Eight Chapters. 1973. Repr. of 1890 ed. 15.00 (ISBN 0-8274-1676-8). R West.

--History of English Romanticism in the Eighteenth Century. 1968. pap. 5.50 (ISBN 0-486-21940-2). Dover.

--History of English Romanticism in the Eighteenth Century. LC 66-29374. 1966. Repr. of 1910 ed. 15.00x (ISBN 0-87752-006-2). Gordian.

--History of English Romanticism in the Eighteenth Century. 9.00 (ISBN 0-8446-1623-0). Peter Smith.

--Initial Studies in American Letters. 291p. 1980. Repr. of 1895 ed. lib. bdg. 30.00 (ISBN 0-89987-063-5). Darby Bks.

--Initial Studies in American Letters. 1978. Repr. of 1895 ed. lib. bdg. 20.00 (ISBN 0-8482-3412-X). Norwood Edns.

--Initial Studies in American Letters. 1973. Repr. of 1891 ed. 15.00 (ISBN 0-8274-1671-7). R West.

--Milton's Tercentenary. LC 73-39421. Repr. of 1910 ed. 7.50 (ISBN 0-404-00725-2). AMS Pr.

--Milton's Tercentenary. LC 73-9747. 1910. lib. bdg. 8.50 (ISBN 0-8414-3168-X). Folcroft.

--Nathaniel Parker Willis. LC 70-89458. (BCL Ser. I). Repr. of 1885 ed. 9.50 (ISBN 0-404-00726-0). AMS Pr.

--Nathaniel Parker Willis. 1973. lib. bdg. 9.00 (ISBN 0-8414-1632-X). Folcroft.

--Points at Issue, & Some Other Points. facs. ed. LC 67-22055. (Essay Index Reprint Ser). 1904. 17.00 (ISBN 0-8369-0183-5). Ayer Co Pubs.

Beers, Henry A., ed. see Willis, Nathaniel P.

Beers, Henry P. Bibliographies in American History, Nineteen Forty-Two to Nineteen Seventy-Eight. Research Publications, Inc., ed. LC 81-68886. 978p. 1982. text ed. 260.00 (ISBN 0-89235-038-5). Res Pubns Conn.

--The French & British in the Old Northwest: A Bibliographical Guide to the Archive & Manuscript Sources. LC 64-13305. 302p. 1964. 12.95x (ISBN 0-8143-1235-7). Wayne St U Pr.

--Spanish & Mexican Records of the American Southwest: A Bibliographical Guide to Archive & Manuscript Sources. LC 79-4313. 493p. 1979. 24.95x (ISBN 0-8165-0673-6). U of Ariz Pr.

--The Western Military Frontier 1815-1846. LC 75-25798. (Perspectives in American Hist. Ser.: No. 35). (Illus.). vi, 227p. 1975. Repr. of 1935 ed. lib. bdg. 19.50x (ISBN 0-87991-359-2). Porcupine Pr.

Beers, Henry S., Jr. Computer Leasing. (Data Processing Ser.). (Illus.). 320p. 1983. 31.50 (ISBN 0-534-97929-7). Lifetime Learn.

--Computer Leasing. 320p. 1983. 31.50 (ISBN 0-534-97929-7). Van Nos Reinhold.

Beers, Howard W. An American Experience in Indonesia: The University of Kentucky Affiliation with the Agricultural University at Bogor. LC 75-132824. (Illus.). 288p. 1971. 24.00x (ISBN 0-8131-1235-4). U Pr of Ky.

--Indonesia: Resources & Their Technological Development. LC 78-111503. Repr. of 1970 ed. 72.00 (ISBN 0-8357-9786-4, 2013515). Bks Demand UMI.

Beers, James, jt. ed. see Henderson, Edmund.

Beers, John C., jt. auth. see Gafney, Leo.

Beers, Lorna. The Crystal Cornerstone. LC 53-8533. 218p. (gr. 7 up). 1953. PLB 11.89 (ISBN 0-06-020425-7). HarpJ.

Beers, Paul B. Pennsylvania Politics Today & Yesterday: The Tolerable Accommodation. LC 79-65826. (Keystone Bks.). (Illus.). 416p. 1980. 26.75x (ISBN 0-271-00238-7). Pa St U Pr.

Beers, Portia. Encyclopedie de la Femme, 4: Comment Plaire aux Hommes. 144p. (Fr.-Eng.). 1974. 29.95 (ISBN 0-686-56910-5, M-6026). French & Eur.

Beers, R. & Lash, T. Choosing an Electrical Energy Future for the Pacific Northwest: An Alternative Senario. 177p. 1977. 5.00 (ISBN 0-318-15829-9). Natl Resources Defense Coun.

Beers, R. F., ed. see International Symposium on Molecular Biology, 4th, 1970.

Beers, Richard G. Walk the Distant Hills: The Story of Longri Ao. (Bold Believers Ser.). 1969. pap. 0.95 (ISBN 0-377-84171-4). Friend Pr.

Beers, Robert E. Best Book on BASIC. 448p. 1985. pap. 24.95 (ISBN 0-471-88844-3). Wiley.

Beers, Roland F. & Bassett, Edward G., eds. Mechanisms of Pain & Analgesic Compounds. LC 78-52524. (Miles Symposium Ser.: No. 11). 510p. 1979. text ed. 76.00 (ISBN 0-89004-304-3). Raven.

Beers, Roland F., ed. see Miles International Symposium, 12th.

Beers, Roland F., Jr. & Bassett, Edward G., eds. Cell Fusion: Gene Transfer & Transformation. (Miles International Symposium Ser.: Vol. 14). (Illus.). 438p. 1984. 60.00 (ISBN 0-89004-941-6). Raven.

--Cell Membrane Receptors for Viruses, Antigens & Antibodies, Polypeptide Hormones, & Small Molecules. LC 75-25108. (Miles International Symposium Ser.: No.9). 554p. 1976. 71.00 (ISBN 0-89004-091-5). Raven.

--Recombinant Molecules: Impact on Science & Society. LC 77-5276. (Miles International Symposium Ser.: 10th). 556p. 1977. 70.50 (ISBN 0-89004-131-8). Raven.

--The Role of Immunological Factors in Infectious, Allergic, & Autoimmune Processes. LC 75-25109. (Miles International Symposium Ser: No. 8). 556p. 1976. 64.50 (ISBN 0-89004-073-7). Raven.

Beers, Roland F., Jr., et al, eds. Molecular & Cellular Repair Processes Johns Hopkins Medical Journal Supplement, No. 1. LC 78-184199. (Miles International Symposia on Molecular Biology Ser). Repr. of 1972 ed. 54.60 (ISBN 0-8357-9278-1, 2015685). Bks Demand UMI.

Beers, Ronald, jt. auth. see Beers, V. Gilbert.

Beers, Ronald A., jt. auth. see Beers, V. Gilbert.

Beers, V. Gilbert. Along Thimblelane Trails. LC 81-14197. (Muffin Family Ser.). 96p. 1981. 11.95 (ISBN 0-8024-0298-4). Moody.

--Captain Maxi's Secret Island. (Muffin Family Ser.: No. 11). 96p. 1983. 11.95 (ISBN 0-8024-9573-7). Moody.

--From Castles in the Clouds. (Muffin Family Ser.). (Illus.). 80p. (gr. 1-4). 1980. 11.95 (ISBN 0-8024-2879-7). Moody.

--Muffkins on Parade. LC 82-6338. (Muffin Family Ser.). 96p. 1982. 11.95 (ISBN 0-8024-9572-9). Moody.

--My Picture Bible to See & to Share. (ps-4). 1982. text ed. 11.95 (ISBN 0-88207-818-6, Sonflower Bks). SP Pubns.

--My Picture Bible to See & to Share. (ps-3). 1982. text ed. 11.95 (ISBN 0-88207-818-6). Victor Bks.

--Out of the Treasure Chest. LC 81-1601. (Muffin Family Ser.). (Illus.). 96p. (ps-6). 1981. 11.95 (ISBN 0-8024-6099-2). Moody.

--Over Buttonwood Bridge. LC 78-13103. (Muffin Family Ser.). (ps-4). 1978. 11.95 (ISBN 0-8024-6266-9). Moody.

--Through Golden Windows. LC 75-25535. (Muffin Family Ser.). (Illus.). 144p. 1975. 11.95 (ISBN 0-8024-8753-X). Moody.

--Toyland Tales. (Muffin Family Ser.). (Illus.). (ps). 1984. 11.95 (ISBN 0-8024-9574-5). Moody.

--Treehouse Tales. LC 81-19011. (Muffin Family Ser.). (Illus.). 96p. 1982. 11.95 (ISBN 0-8024-9571-0). Moody.

--Under the Tagalong Tree. LC 76-22173. (Muffin Family Ser.). (Illus.). (gr. k-5). 1976. 11.95 (ISBN 0-8024-9021-2). Moody.

--With Maxi & Mini in Muffkinland. LC 80-39767. (Muffin Family Ser.). 79p. (gr. k-4). 1981. 11.95 (ISBN 0-8024-4063-0). Moody.

Beers, V. Gilbert & Beers, Ronald. The Victor Family Story Bible. 640p. 1985. 19.95 (ISBN 0-88207-822-4). Victor Bks.

Beers, V. Gilbert & Beers, Ronald A. Bible Stories to Live By. LC 82-84616. 192p. (gr. 3-6). 1983. 12.95 (ISBN 0-89840-044-9). Heres Life.

--My Favorite Things to See & Share. (ps-3). 1984. 11.95 (ISBN 0-88207-821-6). Victor Bks.

--Walking with Jesus. 192p. (gr. 1-6). 1984. 14.95 (ISBN 0-89840-069-4). Heres Life.

Beers, Yardley. Theory of Error. 2nd ed. LC 53-8616. (Physics Ser.). (Orig.). 1957. pap. 5.95 (ISBN 0-201-00470-4). Addison-Wesley.

Beery, Angilee. So What Is Peace. (gr. 3-4). 1971. pap. 1.50 (ISBN 0-87178-934-5). Brethren.

Beery, Carrie, ed. Descendants of Solomon Beery. 1965. loose leaf bdg. 4.00x (ISBN 0-87813-126-4). Park View.

Beery, Donald. Call of the Mountains. (Illus.). 1973. 8.00 (ISBN 0-87012-138-3). McClain.

Beery, Galen. Basic Spoken Lao in Sixteen Lessons. 1977. pap. 3.50 (ISBN 0-8048-1207-1). C E Tuttle.

Beery, John R. Current Conceptions of Democracy. LC 70-176686. (Columbia University. Teachers College. Contributions to Education: No. 888). Repr. of 1943 ed. 22.50 (ISBN 0-404-55888-7). AMS Pr.

Beery, Lydia A. Mennonite Maid Cookbook. 1971. pap. 6.50 (ISBN 0-87813-205-8). Park View.

Beery, R. & Todd, R. J. Minnesota Map Studies Program: Activity Manual. 1st ed. Palmer, Princess & Coppock, Darrell, eds. (Illus.). 100p. (gr. 4). 1981. Duplication Masters 49.00 (ISBN 0-943068-43-6); Teacher's guide 5.00 (ISBN 0-943068-42-8). Graphic Learning.

Beery, R. & Todd, Robert J. Doing History. (Illus.). 90p. (gr. 6-8). 1984. pap. text ed. 4.95x (ISBN 0-917009-00-2). Independ Sch.

Beery, R. & Schug, Mark C., eds. Community Study: Applications & Opportunities. LC 84-62025. 128p. (Orig.). 1984. pap. 7.95 (ISBN 0-87986-048-0). Nat Coun Soc Studies.

Beery, W. T., ed. see International Clean Air Congress, 2nd.

Bees, N. A. Chronicon Monembasiae. 50p. 1979. 12.50 (ISBN 0-89005-279-4). Ares.

--Corpus der Griechisch Christlichen Inschriften von Hellas. 1978. 25.00 (ISBN 0-89005-238-7). Ares.

Beesing, Maria, et al. The Enneagram: A Journey of Self Discovery. 1984. pap. 8.95 (ISBN 0-87193-214-8). Dimension Bks.

Beesley, Edward S. Queen Elizabeth. 1978. Repr. of 1908 ed. lib. bdg. 22.50 (ISBN 0-8495-0374-4). Arden Lib.

Beesley, M. J. Lasers & their Applications. 2nd ed. 270p. 1978. cancelled (ISBN 0-85066-045-9). Taylor & Francis.

Beesley, Patrick. Room Forty: British Naval Intelligence 1914-1918. 1983. 15.95 (ISBN 0-15-178634-8). HarBraceJ.

Beesley, Ronald P. The Creative Ethers. 1978. pap. 3.95 (ISBN 0-87516-268-1). De Vorss.

--Yoga of the Inward Path. 1978. pap. 4.95 (ISBN 0-87516-269-X). De Vorss.

Beesly, Edward S. Catiline, Clodius & Tiberius. (Works of Edward Spencer Beesly Ser.). 169p. Date not set. Repr. of 1878 ed. lib. bdg. 29.00 (ISBN 0-932051-84-7). Am Repr Serv.

--Queen Elizabeth. LC 74-39408. (Select Bibliographies Reprint Ser.). 1972. Repr. of 1892 ed. 16.25 (ISBN 0-8369-9901-0). Ayer Co Pubs.

Beesly, Patrick. Very Special Intelligence, No. 9. 304p. 1981. pap. 2.75 (ISBN 0-345-29798-9). Ballantine.

Beeson, Colin R. The Glider Pilot War at Home & Overseas. 263p. (Orig.). 1978. pap. 25.00x (ISBN 0-89126-063-3). MA-AH Pub.

--Target: Death. 1978. pap. 1.50 (ISBN 0-532-15384-7). Woodhill.

Beeson, Irene, jt. auth. see Hirst, David.

Beeson, John. A Plea for the Indians. 148p. 1981. 12.00 (ISBN 0-87770-254-3). Ye Galleon.

Beeson, Kenneth & Matrone, Gennard. The Soil Factor in Nutrition: Animal & Human. (Nutrition & Clinical Nutrition Ser.: Vol. 2). 1976. 39.75 (ISBN 0-8247-6484-6). Dekker.

Beeson, M. Foundations of Constructive Mathematics. (Ergebnisse der Mathematik Ser.: Vol. 6). 480p. 1985. 49.00 (ISBN 0-387-12173-0). Springer-Verlag.

Beeson, Margaret, et al. Hispanic Writers in French Journals: An Annotated Bibliography. LC 77-93922. (SSSAS Bibliographies: No. 102). 1978. pap. 15.00 (ISBN 0-89295-002-1). Society Sp & Sp-Am.

--Memories for Tomorrow: Mexican-American Recollections of Yesteryear. 172p. 1983. pap. 7.95 (ISBN 0-87917-086-7). Ethridge.

Beeson, Marianne S., jt. auth. see Gurel, Lois M.

Beeson, Richard D. & Crutcher, Ernest R. Hardware Cleaning & Sampling for Cleanliness Verification & Contamination Control Microscopy. LC 61-38584. 34p. 1983. pap. text ed. 25.00 (ISBN 0-915414-72-4). Inst Environ Sci.

Beeson, Trevor. Discretion & Valour: Religious Conditions in Russia & Eastern Europe. Rev. ed. LC 81-70664. 416p. 1982. pap. 15.95 (ISBN 0-8006-1621-9, 1-1621). Fortress.

Beeson, Trevor & Pearce, Jenny, eds. A Vision of Hope: The Churches & Change in Latin America. LC 83-48927. 288p. 1984. pap. 6.95 (ISBN 0-8006-1758-4, 1-1758). Fortress.

Beeson, W. Malcolm, et al. Livestock Judging Selection & Evaluation. 2nd ed. LC 76-44040. (gr. 9-12). 1978. 21.65 (ISBN 0-8134-1887-9); text ed. 16.25x. Interstate.

Beeston, A. F. English-French-Arabic Dictionary: Sabaic. 1982. 16.00x (ISBN 0-86685-359-6). Intl Bk Ctr.

Beeston, A. F., ed. The Epistle on Singing-Girls by Jahiz. (Approaches to Arabic Literature: No. 2). 67p. 1980. text ed. 32.50x (ISBN 0-85668-165-2, Pub. by Aris & Phillips England); pap. text ed. 15.00x (ISBN 0-85668-181-4, Pub. by Aris & Phillips England). Humanities.

Beeston, A. F., et al, eds. Arabic Literature to the End of the Umayyad Period. LC 82-23528. (Cambridge History of Arabic Literature Ser.). (Illus.). 570p. 1984. 75.00 (ISBN 0-521-24015-8). Cambridge U Pr.

Beeston, Alfred F. Arabic Historical Phraseology: Supplement to Written Arabic: an Approach to the Basic Structures. LC 68-18342. pap. 37.50 (ISBN 0-317-10958-8, 2022439). Bks Demand UMI.

--Written Arabic: An Approach to the Basic Structures. (Orig.). 1968. 13.95 (ISBN 0-521-09559-X). Cambridge U Pr.

Beeston, B. E., et al, eds. Electron Diffraction & Optical Diffraction Techniques. (Practical Methods in Electron Microscopy Ser.: Vol. 1, Pt. 2). 260p. 1973. 24.00 (ISBN 0-444-10411-9, Biomedical Pr). Elsevier.

Beeston, D. T. Statistical Methods for Building Price Data. 1983. 38.00x (ISBN 0-419-12270-2, NO. 6795, Pub. by E & FN Spon); pap. 19.00 (NO. 6794, Pub. by Chapman & Hall). Methuen Inc.

Beeston, Tom & Tucker, Tom. Hooking In: The Complete Underground Computer Workbook & Guide. Kadison, Ellis, ed. 176p. 1984. pap. 12.75 (ISBN 0-913425-00-1). Coltrane & Beach.

Beetham, David, tr. Marxists in Face of Fascism: Writings by Marxists on Fascism from the Inter-War Period. LC 84-3055. 392p. 1984. 29.95x (ISBN 0-389-20485-4, 08047). B&N Imports.

Beethoben, Livius & Herrick, Gerri L. The Blue Lily. LC 81-86318. (Orig.). 1982. write for info. (ISBN 0-942992-01-6). Peace on Earth.

Beethoven & Forbes, Elliot, eds. Beethoven: Symphony No. Five in C Minor. LC 73-98890. (Critical Score Ser). 1971. pap. 7.95x (ISBN 0-393-09893-1). Norton.

Beethoven Club Staff. Classical Cuisine. 256p. (YA) 1979. pap. 6.50 (ISBN 0-918544-25-4). Wimmer Bks.

Beethoven, Ludwig Van. Beethoven: Letters, Journals & Conversations. Hamburger, Michael, ed. LC 77-13799. 1978. Repr. of 1966 ed. lib. bdg. 24.50 (ISBN 0-8371-9899-2, BELJ). Greenwood.

--Beethoven's Letters. Eaglefield-Hull, A., ed. Shedlock, J. S., tr. from Ger. LC 73-159687. 1972. pap. 6.95 (ISBN 0-486-22769-3). Dover.

--Complete Piano Concertos in Full Score. (Music Ser.). 384p. 1983. pap. 11.95 (ISBN 0-486-24563-2). Dover.

--Complete Piano Sonatas, 2 vols. Schenker, Heinrich, ed. LC 74-83473. 1975. pap. 8.95 ea. Vol. 1 (ISBN 0-486-23134-8). Vol. 2 (ISBN 0-486-23135-6). Dover.

--Complete String Quartets. LC 75-104809. 1970. pap. 11.95 (ISBN 0-486-22361-2). Dover.

--Complete String Quartets Transcribed for Four-Hand Piano, 2 series. unabr. ed. Ser. 1, 320p. pap. 8.95 (ISBN 0-486-23974-8); Ser. 2, 256p. pap. 7.95 (ISBN 0-486-23975-6). Dover.

--Complete String Quartets: Transcribed for Four-Hand Piano. (Series I). 19.00 (ISBN 0-8446-5732-8). Peter Smith.

--Complete String Quartets: Transcribed for Four-Hand Piano. (Series II). 19.00 (ISBN 0-8446-5733-6). Peter Smith.

--Eighth & Ninth Symphonies in Full Orchestral Score. 392p. 1976. pap. 9.95 (ISBN 0-486-23380-4). Dover.

--First, Second & Third Symphonies; in Full Orchestral Score. 368p. 1976. pap. 9.95 (ISBN 0-486-23377-4). Dover.

--Fourth & Fifth Symphonies in Full Orchestral Score. 260p. 1976. pap. 6.95 (ISBN 0-486-23378-2). Dover.

--New Beethoven Letters. MacArdle, Donald W., tr. LC 57-7331. pap. 157.00 (ISBN 0-317-10100-5, 2010097). Bks Demand UMI.

--Six Great Overtures in Full Score. (Music Scores to Play & Study Ser.). 288p. 1985. pap. 9.95 (ISBN 0-486-24789-9). Dover.

--Sixth & Seventh Symphonies; in Full Orchestral Score. 328p. 1976. pap. 8.95 (ISBN 0-486-23379-0). Dover.

--The Symphony of Life: Letters by Ludwig van Beethoven. Steindorff, Ulrich L., tr. LC 74-24037. pap. 17.50 (ISBN 0-404-12860-2). AMS Pr.

Beethoven, Ludwig Van see Van Beethoven, Ludwig.

Beethoven, Ludwig Von see Von Beethoven, Ludwig.

Beethoven, Ludwig Von see Von Beethoven, Ludwig.

Beetles, Chris. S. R. Badmin & the English Landscape. (Illus.). 160p. 1985. 14.95 (ISBN 0-00-412020-5, Pub. by Salem Hse Ltd). Merrimack Pub Cir.

Beetley, David H. Up Old Forge Way. limited ed. Bd. with West Canada Creek. (Illus.). 432p. 1984. 12.95 (ISBN 0-932052-14-2). North Country.

Beeton, I. M. Hot & Cold Sweets. 15.00x (ISBN 0-392-03307-0, LTB). Sportshelf.

Beeton, Isabella. Beeton's Book of Household Management: Illustrated with 500 Engravings. 1112p. 1969. pap. 6.95 (ISBN 0-374-51404-6). FS&G.

Beeton, Mayson M., ed. see Defoe, Daniel.

Beeton, Mrs. Mrs. Beeton's Cookery & Household Management. (Illus.). 59.95x (ISBN 0-8464-0650-0). Beekman Pubs.

--Mrs. Beeton's Cookery in Colour. (Illus.). 256p. 1971. 13.50x (ISBN 0-7063-1425-5). Intl Pubns Serv.

Beets, M. G. Structure-Activity Relationships in Human Chemoreception. (Illus.). 408p. 1978. text ed. 48.25 (ISBN 0-85334-746-8, Pub. by Elsevier Applied Sci England). Elsevier.

Beets, Richard Van Der see Bowen, James K. & Van Der Beets, Richard.

Beets, Willem C. Multiple Cropping & Tropical Farming Systems. 250p. 1982. 33.50x (ISBN 0-86531-518-3). Westview.

Beets Richard Van, Der see Bowen, James K. & Van Der Beets, Richard.

Beetz, Carl P. & Satterthwaite, Linton, Jr. The Monuments & Inscriptions of Caracol, Belize. (University Museum Monographs: No. 45). (Illus.). xiv, 188p. 1982. 30.00x (ISBN 0-934718-41-5). Univ Mus of U PA.

Beetz, Kirk H. Algernon Charles Swinburne: A Bibliography of Secondary Works, 1861-1980. LC 82-3359. (Author Bibliographies Ser.: No. 61). 238p. 1982. 20.00 (ISBN 0-8108-1541-9). Scarecrow.

--John Ruskin: A Bibliography, 1900-1974. LC 76-13611. (Author Bibliographies Ser.: No. 28). 121p. 1976. 16.50 (ISBN 0-8108-0938-9). Scarecrow.

--Tennyson: A Bibliography, 1827-1982. LC 84-1274. (Author Bibliographies Ser.: No. 68). 539p. 1984. 35.00 (ISBN 0-8108-1687-3). Scarecrow.

--Wilkie Collins: An Annotated Bibliography 1889-1976. LC 77-26609. (Author Bibliographies Ser.: No. 35). 175p. 1978. 16.50 (ISBN 0-8108-1103-0). Scarecrow.

Beever, M. & Smith, F. B. Historical Studies: Selected Articles, Second Series. 1967. pap. 10.00x (ISBN 0-522-83826-X, Pub. by Melbourne U Pr Australia). Intl Spec Bk.

Beevers, John. St. Joan of Arc. 1974. pap. 5.00 (ISBN 0-89555-043-1). TAN Bks Pubs.

--Saint Therese, the Little Flower: The Making of a Saint. LC 73-80147. (Orig.). 1976. pap. 3.50 (ISBN 0-89555-035-0). TAN Bks Pubs.

--Storm of Glory. 1977. pap. 3.50 (ISBN 0-385-12617-4, Im). Doubleday.

Beevor, Antony. The Faustian Pact. 208p. 1984. 13.95 (ISBN 0-224-02083-8, Pub. By Jonathan Cape). Merrimack Pub Cir.

--For Reasons of State. 231p. 11.95 (ISBN 0-224-01930-9, Pub. by Jonathan Cape). Merrimack Pub Cir.

--The Spanish Civil War. LC 83-71475. (Illus.). 384p. 1983. 19.95x (ISBN 0-911745-11-4). P Bedrick Bks.

Beezer, A. E., ed. Biological Microcalorimetry. LC 79-41236. 1980. 79.50 (ISBN 0-12-083550-9). Acad Pr.

Beezley, William H. Insurgent Governor: Abraham Gonzalez & the Mexican Revolution in Chihuahua. LC 72-86257. (Illus.). xvi, 195p. 1973. 16.95x (ISBN 0-8032-0821-9). U of Nebr Pr.

Beffel, John N., ed. see Young, Arthur H.

Befu, Ben. Ihara Saikaku: Worldly Mental Calculations. (Publications in Occasional Papers: No. 5). 1976. pap. 20.00x (ISBN 0-520-09406-9). U of Cal Pr.

Befu, Harumi. Japan: An Anthropological Introduction. LC 78-155586. (Culture Area Studies). 1971. pap. text ed. 11.50 scp (ISBN 0-8102-0430-4, HarpC). Har-Row.

Befu, Harumi, jt. auth. see Mannari, Hiroshi.

Befu, Harumi, et al. The Cultural Context: Essays in Honor of Edward Norbeck. Drake, Christine, ed. (Rice University Studies: Vol. 66, No. 1). (Illus.). 224p. (Orig.). 1980. pap. 10.00x (ISBN 0-89263-244-5). Rice Univ.

Beg, Anwer, ed. see Azami, Mustafa.

Beg, Anwer, ed. see Bucaille, Maurice.

Beg, M. A. S. Fine Arts in Islamic Civilisation. 7.95 (ISBN 0-686-83581-6). Kazi Pubns.

Beg, Mahmood A. Universal Humanism & One World Order: Philosociopolinomica. (Illus.). 1983. 8.95 (ISBN 0-533-05236-X). Vantage.

Bega. Last Words of Famous Men (1930) LC 73-405. 1973. lib. bdg. 17.50 (ISBN 0-8414-1378-9). Folcroft.

Begab, Michael J. & Haywood, H. Carl, eds. Psychosocial Influences in Retarded Performance, Vol. 2. LC 80-7106. (Strategies for Improving Competence Ser.). (Illus.). 352p. 1981. 14.00 (ISBN 0-8391-1635-7). Pro-Ed.

Begalla, Patricia. Circles. 65p. 1985. spiral bdg. 3.95 (ISBN 0-932607-00-4). Platen Pub Co.

--Tips for the Serious Beginning Writer. 35p. 1985. spiral 5.00 (ISBN 0-932607-01-2). Platen Pub Co.

Begay, Laura A., tr. see Johnson, Broderick H.

Begay, Shirley M. & Clinton-Tullie, Verna. Kinaalada: A Navajo Puberty Ceremony. rev. ed. LC 83-61661. (Illus.). 171p. 1983. 15.00x (ISBN 0-936008-11-3); pap. 11.00x. Navajo Curr.

Begbie, Eric. Modern Wildfowling. (Illus.). 190p. 1980. 14.95 (ISBN 0-904558-76-2). Saiga.

--Sportsmans Companion. 266p. 1981. 14.95 (ISBN 0-86230-038-X). Saiga.

Begbie, Harold. Mirrors of Downing Street. facs. ed. LC 79-121448. (Essay Index Reprint Ser). 1923. 18.00 (ISBN 0-8369-1695-6). Ayer Co Pubs.

--Mirrors of Downing Street. LC 70-9179. (Essay & General Literature Index Reprint Ser). 1970. Repr. of 1921 ed. 21.00x (ISBN 0-8046-0917-9, Pub. by Kennikat). Assoc Faculty Pr.

--Painted Windows. LC 77-108696. (Essay & General Literature Index Reprint Ser). 1970. Repr. of 1922 ed. 21.00x (ISBN 0-8046-0918-7, Pub. by Kennikat). Assoc Faculty Pr.

--Windows of Westminster. facsimile ed. LC 77-104993. (Essay Index Reprint Ser.). 1924. 19.00 (ISBN 0-8369-1447-3). Ayer Co Pubs.

Begell, William, ed. Glossary of Terms in Heat Transfer, Fluid Flow & Related Topics. LC 82-3153. (A Hemisphere Engineering Paperback Ser.). 112p. (Eng., Rus., Ger., Fr. & Japanese.). 1983. pap. 32.95 (ISBN 0-89116-261-5). Hemisphere Pub.

Begemann, H. & Rastetter, J. Atlas of Clinical Haematology. 3rd ed. Heilmeyer, L., ed. Hirsch, H. J., tr. from Ger. LC 72-86892. (Illus.). xv, 324p. 1979. 195.00 (ISBN 0-387-09404-0). Springer-Verlag.

Begemann, H. & Rastetter, J. W. Atlas of Clinical Haematology. 3rd ed. Hirsch, H. J., tr. from Ger. LC 79-12768. (Illus.). 1979. 195.00 (ISBN 3-540-09404-0). Springer-Verlag.

Begg, A. Charles & Begg, Neil C. The World of John Boultbee. 329p. 1982. 39.00x (ISBN 0-7233-0604-4, Pub. by Whitcoulls New Zealand). State Mutual Bk.

Begg, Alexander. Red River Journal & Other Papers Relative to the Red River Resistance of 1869-1870. Morton, W. L., ed. LC 69-14506. 1969. Repr. of 1956 ed. lib. bdg. 36.75x (ISBN 0-8371-5074-4, BERR). Greenwood.

Begg, David K. The Rational Expectations Revolution in Macroeconomics. 224p. 1982. 50.00x (ISBN 0-86003-044-X, Pub. by Allan Pubs England). State Mutual Bk.

--The Rational Expectations Revolution in Macroeconomics: Theories & Evidence. LC 82-47785. 304p. (Orig.). 1982. 27.50x (ISBN 0-8018-2881-3); pap. 9.95x (ISBN 0-8018-2882-1). Johns Hopkins.

Begg, Ean. The Cult of the Black Virgin. (Illus.). 288p. (Orig.). 1985. pap. 11.95 (ISBN 1-85063-022-4, Ark Paperbacks). Routledge & Kegan.

Begg, Hugh, et al. Expenditure in Scotland, Nineteen Sixty-One to Nineteen Seventy-One. 1974. 10.00x (ISBN 0-7073-0110-6, Pub. by Scottish Academic Pr Scotland). Columbia U Pr.

Begg, Ian, jt. auth. see Paivio, Allan.

Begg, Neil C., jt. auth. see Begg, A. Charles.

Begg, P. R. & Kesling, Peter C. Orthodontic Theory & Technique. 3rd ed. LC 76-14673. (Illus.). 1977. text ed. 52.00 (ISBN 0-7216-1670-4). Saunders.

Begg, R. W., ed. see Canadian Cancer Conference.

Begg, Vivienne. Developing Expert CAD Systems. (High Technology Modular Ser.). 128p. 1984. 19.95 (ISBN 0-89059-042-7, KP101, UPB). Unipub.

Beggerow, G. Heats of Mixing & Solution. (Landolt-Bornstein New Ser.: Group IV, Vol. 2). 1976. 268.80 (ISBN 0-387-07443-0). Springer-Verlag.

Beggerow, O. High-Pressure Properties of Matter. (Landolt-Boernstein Ser.: Group IV, Vol. 4). (Illus.). 1980. 201.60 (ISBN 0-387-09370-2). Springer-Verlag.

Beggiani, Seely J. Early Syriac Theology: With Special Reference to the Maronite Tradition. LC 83-3658. 172p. (Orig.). 1983. lib. bdg. 23.50 (ISBN 0-8191-3152-0); pap. text ed. 10.50 (ISBN 0-8191-3153-9). U Pr of Amer.

Beggs, Dale H. see Brown, Kermit E.

Beggs, David W. America's Schools & Churches. LC 65-12279. pap. 60.30 (ISBN 0-317-28577-7, 2055190). Bks Demand UMI.

Beggs, David W., 3rd, ed. Team Teaching: Bold New Venture. LC 64-17456. (Bold New Venture Ser). (Illus.). Repr. of 1964 ed. 48.00 (ISBN 0-8357-9245-5, 2015810). Bks Demand UMI.

Beggs, H. Dale. Gas Production Operations. 336p. 1984. 46.50 (ISBN 0-930972-06-6). Oil & Gas.

Beggs, Joseph S. Kinematics. LC 82-15835. (Illus.). 223p. 1983. text ed. 24.50 (ISBN 0-89116-355-7). Hemisphere Pub.

Beghi, G. Energy Storage & Transportation: Prospects for New Technologies. 1981. 39.50 (ISBN 90-277-1166-6, Pub. by Reidel Holland). Kluwer Academic.

Beghi, G., ed. Thermal Energy Storage. 1982. 59.50 (ISBN 90-277-1428-2, Pub. by Reidel Holland). Kluwer Academic.

Beghi, Giogio. Performance of Solar Energy Converters: Thermal Collectors & Photovoltaic Cells. 1983. lib. bdg. 69.50 (ISBN 90-277-1545-9, Pub. by Reidel Holland). Kluwer Academic.

Begiebing, Robert J. Acts of Regeneration: Allegory & Archetype in the Works of Norman Mailer. LC 80-50416. 256p. 1980. text ed. 20.00x (ISBN 0-8262-0310-8). U of Mo Pr.

Begin, James P., jt. auth. see Beal, Edwin F.

Begle, E. G. Critical Variables in Mathematics Education: Findings from a Survey of the Empirical Literature. LC 78-78131. 165p. 1979. 9.50 (ISBN 0-88385-430-9). Math Assn.

--Critical Variables in Mathematics Education: Findings from a Survey of the Empirical Literature. LC 78-78131. 165p. 1979. 8.00 (ISBN 0-88385-430-9). NCTM.

Begleiter, Henri, ed. Biological Effects of Alcohol. LC 80-120. (Advances in Experimental Medicine & Biology Ser.: Vol. 126). 845p. 1980. 92.50x (ISBN 0-306-40349-8, Plenum Pr). Plenum Pub.

--Evoked Brain Potentials & Behavior. LC 78-31448. (The Downstate Series of Research in Psychiatry & Psychology: Vol. 2). 579p. 1979. 59.50x (ISBN 0-306-40145-2, Plenum Pr). Plenum Pub.

Begleiter, Henri & Kissin, Benjamin, eds. The Pathogenesis of Alcoholism: Psychosocial Factors. (The Biology of Alcoholism Ser.: Vol. 6). 724p. 1983. 69.50x (ISBN 0-306-41053-2, Plenum Pr). Plenum Pub.

Begleiter, Henri, jt. ed. see Kissin, Benjamin.

Begley, Donal, ed. Handbook on Irish Genealogy. rev. ed. (Illus.). 160p. 1984. pap. 10.95 (ISBN 0-9502455-9-3, Pub. by Heraldic Artists). Irish Bks Media.

Begley, Donal F. The Ancestor Trail in Ireland. (Illus.). 32p. (Orig.). 1982. pap. 3.25 (ISBN 0-9502455-8-5, Pub. by Heraldic Art). Irish Bks Media.

Begley, Donal F., ed. Irish Genealogy: A Record Finder. (Illus.). 256p. (Orig.). 1981. pap. 15.95 (ISBN 0-9502455-7-7, Pub. by Heraldic Artists). Irish Bks Media.

Begley, Eve. Of Scottish Ways. (Illus.). 1978. pap. 5.29 (ISBN 0-06-464020-5, BN4020, BN). B&N NY.

Begley, Kathleen A. Deadline. 160p. (gr. 7 up). 1979. pap. 1.25 (ISBN 0-440-91718-2, LFL). Dell.

Begley, Monie. Rambles in Ireland. LC 77-78830. (Illus.). 1977. 15.00 (ISBN 0-8159-5214-7). Devin.

Begley, W. E. Monumental Islamic Calligraphy from India. LC 84-29717. (Illus.). 144p. 1985. 17.95 (ISBN 0-932815-00-6); pap. 10.95 (ISBN 0-932815-01-4). Islamic Found.

--Monumental Islamic Calligraphy from India. LC 84-29717. 144p. 1985. 17.95 (ISBN 0-295-96259-3); pap. 10.95 (ISBN 0-295-96260-7). U of Wash Pr.

Begnal, Michael. Joseph Sheridan Lefanu. LC 71-126032. (Irish Writers Ser.). 87p. 4.50 (ISBN 0-8387-7766-X); pap. 1.95 (ISBN 0-8387-7735-X). Bucknell U Pr.

Begnal, Michael H. & Eckley, Grace. Narrator & Character in "Finnegans Wake". LC 73-4957. 241p. 1975. 22.50 (ISBN 0-8387-1337-8). Bucknell U Pr.

Begnal, Michael H. & Senn, Fritz, eds. A Conceptual Guide to Finnegans Wake. LC 73-13219. 256p. 1974. 24.95x (ISBN 0-271-01132-7). Pa St U Pr.

Begne, Leopold P. Essentials of Syntactic Design. 232p. 1984. pap. text ed. 15.95x (ISBN 0-89917-412-4). Tichenor Pub.

Begner, Edith. Accident of Birth. 1977. pap. 1.95 (ISBN 0-380-00990-0, 32672). Avon.

--A Dark & Lonely Hiding Place. 1977. pap. 1.95 (ISBN 0-380-01742-3, 34546). Avon.

--Golden Opportunity. 288p. 1980. pap. 2.50 (ISBN 0-380-75085-6, 75085). Avon.

--Just off Fifth. 352p. 1981. pap. 2.95 (ISBN 0-380-77321-X, 77321). Avon.

--Red in the Morning. 1977. pap. 1.75 (ISBN 0-380-01679-6, 33506). Avon.

--Son & Heir. 1977. pap. 1.75 (ISBN 0-380-01787-3, 35311). Avon.

Bego, Mark. Madonna! (Illus.). 192p. (Orig.). 1985. pap. 2.95 (ISBN 0-523-42576-7). Pinnacle Bks.

--Michael! 192p. (Orig.). 1984. pap. 2.95 (ISBN 0-523-42234-2). Pinnacle Bks.

Begon, Michael. Investigating Animal Abundance. (Illus.). 104p. 1979. pap. text ed. 15.00 (ISBN 0-8391-1387-0). Univ Park.

Begon, Michael & Mortimer, Martin. Population Ecology: A Unified Study of Animal & Plants. LC 81-5641. (Illus.). 256p. 1981. pap. text ed. 18.95x (ISBN 0-87893-067-1). Sinauer Assoc.

Begona, Mauricio de see De Begona, Mauricio.

Begue, Claude M., ed. see Duras, Marguerite.

Beguelin, Richard H. The Secrets of Syndication: How to Make Money Using Other People's Money. 1985. 18.45i (ISBN 0-316-08783-1). Little.

Beguin, ed. see Bernanos, Georges.

Beguin, ed. see De Nerval, Gerard.

Beguin, A., et al. Sources of Thermodynamic Data on Mesogens: A Special Issue of the Journal of Molecular Crystals & Liquid Crystals. 340p. 1984. pap. text ed. 94.00 (ISBN 0-677-16575-7). Gordon.

Beguin, Albert. Leon Bloy: A Study in Impatience. Riley, Edith M., tr. from Fr. 247p. 1982. Repr. of 1947 ed. lib. bdg. 45.00 (ISBN 0-89984-081-7). Century Bookbindery.

Beguin, Andre. Dictionnaire Technique et Critique du Dessin. (Fr.). 1978. 99.50 (ISBN 0-686-56911-3, M-6027). French & Eur.

Beguin, J., et al. Vocabulaire Technique des Assurances sur la Vie, Vol. 2. 335p. (Eng. & Fr.). 1979. pap. 9.95 (ISBN 2-551-03302-0, M-9245). French & Eur.

Beguin, L., et al. Vocabulaire Technique des Assurances sur la Vie, Vol. 1. 309p. (Eng. & Fr.). 1979. pap. 9.95 (ISBN 0-7754-2396-3, M-9244). French & Eur.

Beguinus, Jean. Tyrocinium Chymicum. Russell, Richard, tr. from Lat. LC 83-80335. xxiv, 135p. 1983. Repr. of 1669 ed. 15.00 (ISBN 0-935214-05-4). Heptangle.

Begun, James W. Professionalism & the Public Interest: Price & Quality in Optometry. (Health & Public Policy Ser.). 152p. 1981. 25.00x (ISBN 0-262-02156-0). MIT Pr.

Begus, Sarah, et al. An Annotated Bibliography of Recent Research on the Elderly. (Public Administration Ser.: Bibliography P 1083). 63p. 1982. pap. 9.75 (ISBN 0-88066-273-5). Vance Biblios.

Beha ed-Din. The Life of Saladin. lib. bdg. 79.95 (ISBN 0-87968-480-1). Krishna Pr.

Behague, Gerard. The Beginnings of Musical Nationalism in Brazil. LC 79-174730. (Detroit Monographs in Musicology: No. 1). 43p. 1971. pap. 2.00 (ISBN 0-911772-50-2). Info Coord.

--Music in Latin America: An Introduction. (History of Music Ser.). (Illus.). 1979. text ed. 25.95 (ISBN 0-13-608919-4); 18.95 (ISBN 0-13-608901-1). P-H.

Behague, Gerard, ed. Performance Practice: Ethnomusicological Perspectives. LC 83-10842. (Contributions in Intercultural & Comparative Studies: No. 12). (Illus.). vii, 262p. 1984. lib. bdg. 35.00 (ISBN 0-313-24160-0, BPE/). Greenwood.

Behal & Melilli, eds. Stainless Steel Castings - STP 756. 454p. 1982. 45.00 (ISBN 0-8031-0740-4, 04-756000-01). ASTM.

Beham, Hervey. Salvagers. 211p. 1980. 30.00x (ISBN 0-686-78989-X, Pub. by Essex County England). State Mutual Bk.

Behan, Brendan. After the Wake. Fallon, Peter, ed. LC 82-159911. (Classic Irish Fiction Ser.). 156p. 1983. 13.95 (ISBN 0-905140-97-4). Devin.

--Behan: The Complete Plays. Incl. The Hostage; The Quare Fellow; Richard's Cork Leg; Three One Act Plays for Radio. 1978. pap. 8.95 (ISBN 0-394-17052-0, B411, BC). Grove.

--Borstal Boy. LC 81-20115. 384p. 1982. pap. 8.95 (ISBN 0-87923-415-6, Nonpareil Bks). Godine.

--Brendan Behan's Island: An Irish Sketch Book. (Illus.). 192p. 1985. 14.45i (ISBN 0-316-08776-9); pap. 7.70i (ISBN 0-316-08773-4). Little.

--Brendan Behan's New York. (Illus.). 1985. 14.45i (ISBN 0-316-08777-7); pap. 7.70i (ISBN 0-316-08774-2). Little.

--Richard's Cork Leg. 1974. pap. 2.95 (ISBN 0-394-17857-2, E624, Ever). Grove.

--The Scarperer. Repr. lib. bdg. 11.95x (ISBN 0-89190-573-1, Pub. by River City Pr). Amereon Ltd.

Behan, P. O. & Currie, S. Clinical Neuroimmunology. (Major Problems in Neurology: Vol. 8). 1978. text ed. 11.00 (ISBN 0-7216-1672-0). Saunders.

Behan, P. O., et al. Immunology of Nervous System Infections. (Progress in Brain Research Ser.: Vol. 59). 1983. 104.25 (ISBN 0-444-80443-9, I-350-83). Elsevier.

Behan, P. O., et al, eds. Immunology of Nervous System Infections: Proceedings of the Noble Bodman Symposia, London, U.K., November 12-13, 1981. (Progress in Brain Research Ser.). 59p. 1983. 104.25 (ISBN 0-444-80443-9, Biomedical Pr). Elsevier.

Behan, Peter O. & Spreafico, Federico, eds. Neuroimmunology. (Serono Symposia Publications: Vol. 12). 500p. 1984. text ed. 98.50 (ISBN 0-89004-963-7). Raven.

Behar, Moises, jt. ed. see Scrimshaw, Nevin S.

Behar, R. N. Bucket or Murder Near Birmingham Cathedral. LC 83-91490. 67p. 1985. 7.95 (ISBN 0-533-06083-4). Vantage.

Behara, M., et al, eds. Probability & Information Theory 2. LC 75-406171. (Lecture Notes in Mathematics: Vol. 296). v, 223p. 1973. pap. 14.00 (ISBN 0-387-06211-4). Springer-Verlag.

Behara, M., et al, eds. see International Symposium on Probability & Information Theory, McMaster University, Canada, 1968.

Behari, Bepin. Economic Growth & Technological Change in India. 1974. 12.00x (ISBN 0-686-20218-X). Intl Bk Dist.

--Rural Industrialization in India. 1976. 13.50 (ISBN 0-7069-0448-6). Intl Bk Dist.

Behari, Bepin & Behari, Madhuri. Concise Economic Encyclopedia. vii, 340p. 1983. text ed. 35.00x (ISBN 0-86590-106-6). Apt Bks.

--Indian Economy Since Independence Chronology of Events. (Illus.). 328p. 1983. text ed. 37.50x (ISBN 0-86590-136-8). Apt Bks.

Behari, Madhuri, jt. auth. see Behari, Bepin.

Beharrel, Peter, ed. Trade Unions & the Media. Greg, Philo. (Critical Social Studies). 1977. pap. text ed. 7.00x (ISBN 0-333-22055-2). Humanities.

Behasa, Stephanie, jt. auth. see Creekmore, Wayne.

Behavior Modification, Proceedings of the 4th Banff Conference. Behavior Change: Methodology, Concepts, & Practice. Hamerlynck, Leo A., et al, eds. 372p. 1973. pap. text ed. 13.95 (ISBN 0-87822-089-5, 0895). Res Press.

Behavior of Offshore Structures, 2nd International Conference. Boss Seventy-Nine: Proceedings, 3 vols. 1500p. Set. pap. 146.00x (ISBN 0-906085-34-9, Dist. by Air Science Co). BHRA Fluid.

Behbehani, et al, eds. see Symposium on Science & Technology in Kuwait, May 1978.

Behbehani, Abbas M. Human Viral, Bedsonial & Rickettsial Diseases: A Diagnostic Handbook for Physicians. (Illus.). 370p. 1972. 37.50x (ISBN 0-398-02228-3). C C Thomas.

--Laboratory Diagnosis of Viral, Bedsonial & Rickettsial Diseases: A Handbook for Laboratory Workers. (Illus.). 244p. 1972. photocopy ed. 27.50x (ISBN 0-398-02229-1). C C Thomas.

Behbehani, H. S. China's Foreign Policy in the Arab World 1955-75. 400p. 1981. 40.00x (ISBN 0-7103-0008-5). Routledge & Kegan.

Behbehani, Hashim S., ed. China & the People's Democratic Republic of Yemen: A Report. 425p. 1985. 39.95x (ISBN 0-7103-0097-2, Kegan Paul International). Routledge & Kegan.

Behee, John & Saylor, Tom. Wave the Flag for Hudson High. LC 77-89960. (Illus.). 1977. pap. 9.95x (ISBN 0-914464-02-7). J & J Bks.

Behee, John R. Fielding Yost's Legacy. LC 77-173360. (Illus.). 210p. 1971. 7.95 (ISBN 0-914464-00-0). J & J Bks.

--Hail to the Victors. LC 74-75995. 140p. 1974. pap. 6.95 (ISBN 0-914464-01-9). J & J Bks.

Beheler, Laura. The Dragon Thread. LC 80-84202. 164p. 1981. 9.95 (ISBN 0-937884-00-6). Hyst'ry Myst'ry.

Behem, Jacob. Three Principles of the Divine Essence. 1978. Repr. of 1909 ed. 12.00 (ISBN 0-911662-65-0). Yoga.

Beher, W. T. Chemistry & Physiology of Bile Acids & Their Influence on Atherosclerosis. (Monographs on Atherosclerosis: Vol. 6). (Illus.). 1976. 41.75 (ISBN 3-8055-2242-8). S Karger.

Beheshti, H. M., jt. auth. see Eldin, H. K.

Behforooz, Ali & Holoien, Martin O. Problem Solving & Structured Programming with Pascal. 350p. 1984. pap. write for info. Wadsworth Pub.

Behforooz, Ali & Sharma, Onka P. An Introduction to Computer Science: A Structuerd Problem Solving Approach. 1985. text ed. 28.95 (ISBN 0-8359-3212-5); tchr's. manual avail. (ISBN 0-8359-3213-3). Reston.

Behforooz, Ali & Shurma, Onka P. Pascal Syntax. 1985. pap. text ed. 8.95 (ISBN 0-8359-5453-6). Reston.

Behforooz, Ali, jt. auth. see Holoien, Martin O.

Behforooz, ALi, jt. auth. see Holoien, Martin O.

Behishti, Ayatullah. Philosophy of Islam. Ansari, M. A., tr. from Farsi. 580p. 25.00 (ISBN 0-941724-22-0). Islamic Seminary.

Behlen, Charles. Perdition's Keepsake. Oliphant, Dave, ed. (Illus.). 1978. pap. 5.00 (ISBN 0-933384-00-9). Prickly Pear.

Behler, Diana. The Theory of the Novel in Early German Romanticism. (Utah Studies in Literature & Linguistics: Vol. 11). 162p. 1978. pap. 18.95 (ISBN 3-261-03027-5). P Lang Pubs.

Behler, Donna M. & Tippett-Neilson, Terry E. Adult Nurse Practitioner Certification Review. LC 82-16007. 377p. 1983. pap. 19.95 (ISBN 0-471-86410-2, Pub. by Wiley Med.). Wiley.

Behler, Donna M., jt. auth. see Tippett-Neilson, Terry E.

Behler, Ernst, tr. see Schlegel, Friedrich.

Behler, Ernst, et al. Studies in German in Memory of Robert L. Kahn. Eichner, Hans & Kahn, Lisa, eds. (Rice University Studies: Vol. 57, No. 4). 134p. 1971. pap. 10.00x (ISBN 0-89263-210-0). Rice Univ.

Behler, Ernst, et al, eds. Nietzsche-Studien, Vol.9. (Internationales Jahrbuch Fur Die Nietzsche-Forschung). 400p. 1980. text ed. 68.80x (ISBN 3-11-008241-1). De Gruyter.

Behling, John H. Guidelines for Preparing the Research Proposal. rev. ed. LC 83-23362. 88p. 1984. lib. bdg. 18.50 (ISBN 0-8191-3733-2); pap. text ed. 8.75 (ISBN 0-8191-3734-0). U Pr of Amer.

--Research Methods: Statistical Concepts & Research Practicum. 1977. pap. text ed. 7.50 (ISBN 0-8191-0084-6). U Pr of Amer.

Behling, John H. & Merves, Esther S. The Practice of Clinical Research: The Single Case Method. LC 84-13179. (Illus.). 122p. (Orig.). 1984. lib. bdg. 18.75 (ISBN 0-8191-4183-6); pap. text ed. 8.00 (ISBN 0-8191-4184-4). U Pr of Amer.

Behlmer, George K. Child Abuse & Moral Reform in England: 1870-1908. LC 81-51331. (Illus.). 332p. 1982. 32.50x (ISBN 0-8047-1127-5). Stanford U Pr.

Behlmer, Rudy. America's Favorite Movies: Behind the Scenes. LC 81-70117. (Illus.). 344p. 1982. 19.95x (ISBN 0-8044-2036-X); pap. 11.95 (ISBN 0-8044-6034-5). Ungar.

Behlmer, Rudy & Thomas, Tony. Hollywood's Hollywood: The Movies About the Movies. (Illus.). 384p. 1975. 19.95 (ISBN 0-8065-0491-9). Citadel Pr.

Behlmer, Rudy, jt. auth. see Thomas, Tony.

Behlmer, Rudy, ed. Inside Warner Brothers: Nineteen Thirty-Five to Nineteen Fifty-One. 1985. 19.95 (ISBN 0-670-80478-9). Viking.

--Memo from: David O. Selznick. 2nd ed. LC 81-47641. (Illus.). 608p. 1981. pap. 11.95 (ISBN 0-394-17937-4, E783, Ever). Grove.

--The Sea Hawk. LC 81-70418. (Wisconsin-Warner Bros. Screenplay Ser.). (Illus.). 244p. 1982. 17.50x (ISBN 0-299-09010-8); pap. 6.95 (ISBN 0-299-09014-0). U of Wis Pr.

Behlmer, Rudy & Balio, Tino, eds. The Adventures of Robin Hood. LC 79-3971. (Wisconsin-Warner Bros. Screenplay Ser.). (Illus.). 1979. pap. 6.95 (ISBN 0-299-07944-9). U of Wis Pr.

Behm, Carl, III, jt. auth. see Hahn, H. George.

Behm, Douglas R. An Advent Covenant Wreath. 16p. 1981. pap. text ed. 2.50 (ISBN 0-89536-482-4). CSS of Ohio.

--The New Covenant's Power. 1983. 3.00 (ISBN 0-89536-600-2). CSS of Ohio.

Behm, Herbert C., jt. tr. see Place, Edwin B.

Behm, Marc. The Eye of the Beholder. 1981. pap. 2.25 (ISBN 0-345-29260-X). Ballantine.

--The Queen of the Night. 1978. pap. 1.95 (ISBN 0-380-39958-X, 39958). Avon.

Behm, Richard. The Book of Moonlight. LC 78-61837. 1978. pap. 5.00 (ISBN 0-931350-01-8). Moonlight Pubns.

--Simple Explanations. (Juniper Bk: No. 40). 1982. pap. 4.00 (ISBN 0-686-84328-2). Juniper Pr WI.

Behm, Ronald, jt. auth. see Salley, Christopher.

Behme, R., et al. Biology of Nematodes: Current Studies. LC 72-8856. 219p. 1972. text ed. 24.50x (ISBN 0-8422-7043-4). Irvington.

Behn, Aphra. The Lucky Chance. (Royal Court Writers Ser.). 56p. (Orig.). 1984. pap. 4.95 (ISBN 0-413-57120-3, 9238). Methuen Inc.

--Novels of Mrs. Aphra Behn. LC 72-98812. Repr. of 1913 ed. lib. bdg. 19.75x (ISBN 0-8371-2824-2, BENB). Greenwood.

--Oroonoko & Other Prose Narratives. LC 67-25151. 33.00 (ISBN 0-405-08252-5, Blom Pubns). Ayer Co Pubs.

--Oroonoko; or, the Royal Slave. 96p. 1973. pap. 4.95 (ISBN 0-393-00702-2). Norton.

--The Rover. Link, Frederick M., ed. LC 66-20828. (Regents Restoration Drama Ser). xvi, 144p. 1967. 13.95x (ISBN 0-8032-0350-0); pap. 4.25x (ISBN 0-8032-5350-8, BB 260, Bison). U of Nebr Pr.

--Selected Writings of the Ingenious Mrs. Aphra Behn. LC 69-13815. Repr. of 1950 ed. lib. bdg. 18.75 (ISBN 0-8371-1070-X, BESW). Greenwood.

--Works of Aphra Behn, 6 Vols. Summers, Montague, ed. LC 67-22243. 1967. Repr. of 1915 ed. Set. 164.00 (ISBN 0-405-08253-3, Blom Pubns); 27.50 ea. Vol. 1 (ISBN 0-405-08254-1). Vol. 2 (ISBN 0-405-08255-X). Vol. 3 (ISBN 0-405-08256-8). Vol. 4 (ISBN 0-405-08257-6). Vol. 5 (ISBN 0-405-08258-4). Vol. 6 (ISBN 0-405-08259-2). Ayer Co Pubs.

--Works of Aphra Behn, 6 vols. Summers, Montague, ed. LC 67-24964. 1967. Repr. of 1916 ed. Set. 125.00x (ISBN 0-87753-004-1). Phaeton.

Behn, Harry. Crickets & Bullfrogs & Whispers of Thunder: Poems & Pictures by Harry Behn. Hopkins, Lee B., ed. LC 83-18347. (Illus.). 96p. (ps-3). 1984. 11.95 (ISBN 0-15-220885-2, HJ). HarBraceJ.

--The Faraway Lurs. 1981. PLB 9.95 (ISBN 0-8398-2722-9, Gregg). G K Hall.

Behn, Judith, ed. see Public Interest Economics Foundation, et al.

Behn, Noel. Seven Silent Men. 356p. 1984. 16.95 (ISBN 0-87795-499-2). Arbor Hse.

--Seven Silent Men. 1985. pap. 3.95 (ISBN 0-671-54390-3). PB.

Behn, Robert D. & Vaupel, James W. Quick Analysis for Busy Decision Makers. LC 81-68402. 1982. 18.95 (ISBN 0-465-06787-5). Basic.

--Quick Analysis for Busy Decision Makers. LC 81-68402. 415p. 1984. pap. 10.95 (ISBN 0-465-06788-3, CN 5114). Basic.

Behn, Wolfgang, jt. ed. see Pearson, J. D.

Behnke, Daniel J. Fifty Worship Talks for Children. 1982. pap. 4.95 (ISBN 0-570-03850-2, 12-2805). Concordia.

Behnke, Donna A. Religious Issues in Nineteenth Century Feminism. LC 80-52544. 300p. 1982. 22.50x (ISBN 0-87875-203-X). Whitston Pub.

Behnke, H. & Courant, R., eds. Contributions to Functional Analysis. (Eng., Ger. & Fr.). 1965. 28.40 (ISBN 0-387-07768-5). Springer-Verlag.

Behnke, John. Ten Plus One Bible Stories from Creation to Samson, Retold in Everyday Language for Today's Children. LC 83-82022. (Orig.). (gr. k up). 1984. pap. 2.95 (ISBN 0-8091-6552-X). Paulist Pr.

Behnke, John A., et al, eds. The Biology of Aging. LC 78-19012. (Illus.). 400p. 1978. 18.95x (ISBN 0-306-31139-9, Plenum Pr). Plenum Pub.

Behnke, Roy H., Jr. The Herders of Cyrenaica: Ecology, Economy, & Kinship Among the Bedouin of Eastern Libya. LC 79-10605. (Studies in Anthropology: No. 12). (Illus.). 207p. 1980. 14.50x (ISBN 0-252-00729-8). U of Ill Pr.

Behnke, W. B., Jr., et al. Clinch River: The Case for Completion. (Technical & Economic Reports). 1983. 30.00 (ISBN 0-318-02238-9). Atomic Indus Forum.

Behnken, Eloise M. Thomas Carlyle: Calvinist Without the Theology. LC 77-11987. 160p. 1978. 12.50x (ISBN 0-8262-0234-9). U of Mo Pr.

Behr, jt. auth. see Bowen.

Behr, C. A., tr. see Aristides.

Behr, Caroline. T. S. Eliot: A Chronology of His Life & Work. LC 82-16716. 250p. 1983. 25.00x (ISBN 0-312-82185-9). St Martin.

Behr, Edward. The Algerian Problem. LC 75-43947. (Illus.). 256p. 1976. Repr. of 1961 ed. lib. bdg. 22.50x (ISBN 0-8371-8722-2, BEAPR). Greenwood.

Behr, Gustavus E., Jr., jt. auth. see Richards, Theodore W.

Behr, Joyce. Picture Puzzle Riddle Book. LC 83-9160. (Illus.). 128p. (gr. 3 up). 1983. 8.95 (ISBN 0-8069-4676-8); PLB 10.99 (ISBN 0-8069-4677-6). Sterling.

Behr, Marcia W., et al. Drama Integrates Basic Skills: Lesson Plans for the Learning Disabled. (Illus.). 144p. 1979. vinyl spiral 12.75x (ISBN 0-398-03881-3). C C Thomas.

Behr, Marion & Lazar, Wendy. Women Working Home. (Illus.). 256p. 1983. pap. 12.95 (ISBN 0-939240-01-7). Rodale Pr Inc.

--Women Working Home: The Homebased Business Guide & Directory. (Illus.). 176p. (Orig.). 1981. pap. 12.95 (ISBN 0-939240-00-9). WWH Pr.

Behr, Marion & Lazar, Wendy, eds. Women Working Home: The Homebased Business Guide & Directory. 2nd ed. (Illus.). 288p. 1983. pap. 12.95 (ISBN 0-939240-01-7). WWH Pr.

Behr, Merlyn J., jt. auth. see Nichols, Eugene D.

Behrangi, Samad. The Little Black Fish & Other Modern Persian Stories. Hooglund, Mary & Hooglund, Eric, trs. from Persian. LC 75-42512. 1982. pap. 7.00 (ISBN 0-914478-22-2). Three Continents.

Behravesh, Nariman, jt. auth. see Mansfield, Edwin.

Behre, F. Agatha Christie's Writings. 1967. 27.95x (ISBN 0-685-05168-4). Adlers Foreign Bks.

Behrend, Arthur. As from Kemmel Hill: An Adjutant in France & Flanders, 1917 & 1918. LC 75-3861. (Illus.). 176p. 1975. Repr. of 1963 ed. lib. bdg. 15.00 (ISBN 0-8371-8087-2, BEKH). Greenwood.

Behrend, E. Theodor Fontanes Roman "Der Stechlin". pap. 9.00 (ISBN 0-384-03770-4). Johnson Repr.

Behrend, Genevieve. Your Invisible Power. 1921. pap. 2.75 (ISBN 0-87516-004-2). De Vorss.

Behrend, George. Luxury Trains: From the Orient Express to the TGV. LC 81-10366. (Illus.). 216p. 1982. 35.00 (ISBN 0-86565-016-0). Vendome.

Behrend, Hilde. Problems of Labour & Inflation. LC 84-14263. 256p. 1984. 29.00 (ISBN 0-7099-3222-7, Pub. by Croom Helm Ltd). Longwood Pub Group.

Behrend, William. Ludwig Van Beethoven's Pianoforte Sonatas. Lund, Ingeborg, tr. LC 74-24038. (Illus.). Repr. of 1927 ed. 24.50 (ISBN 0-404-12861-0). AMS Pr.

Behrends, E. M-Structured & the Banach-Stone Theorem. (Lecture Notes in Mathematics: Vol. 736). 1979. pap. 17.00 (ISBN 0-387-09533-0). Springer-Verlag.

Behrends, E., et al. L-P Structure in Real Banach Spaces. (Lecture Notes in Mathematics: Vol. 613). 1977. pap. text ed. 14.00 (ISBN 0-387-08441-X). Springer-Verlag.

Behrends, Frederick, ed. see Fulbert.

Behrends, Rainer. Eighteenth Century Moscow. 1975. 150.00x (ISBN 0-686-78983-0, Pub. by Aried Pr). State Mutual Bk.

Behrends, Rainer, et al. Biblia Pauperum: Apocalypsis. (Illus., LC 77-088869). 1978. boxed 500.00 (ISBN 0-87817-239-4). Hacker.

Behrendt, Bill. Pocket Magic: Twenty-Five Intriguing, Animated Games for the TRS-80 PC & the Sharp PC-1211. 96p. 1982. 17.95 (ISBN 0-13-683847-2); pap. 9.95 (ISBN 0-13-683839-1). P-H.

Behrendt, Bill L. Conquering the Commodore 64 Kingdom: 25 Original Games in Dazzling Sight & Sound. 170p. 1984. pap. 14.95 (ISBN 0-13-167917-1); incl. disk 29.95. P-H.

--Conquering the Macintosh Kingdom: Twenty-Five Original Games in Dazzling Sight & Sound. (Illus.). 200p. 1985. pap. 15.95 (ISBN 0-13-167974-0). P-H.

--Conquering the PCjr Kingdom: 25 Original Games in Dazzling Sight & Sound. 180p. 1984. pap. 14.95 (ISBN 0-13-167891-4); incl. disk 29.95 (ISBN 0-13-167909-0). P-H.

--Music & Sound for the Commodore 64. (Illus.). 200p. 1984. pap. text ed. 14.95 (ISBN 0-13-607094-9). P-H.

--Music & Sound for the Macintosh. price not set. P-H.

--Music & Sound for the Macintosh. (Illus.). 200p. 1985. pap. 15.95 (ISBN 0-13-607185-6). P-H.

--Music & Sound for the PCjr. 200p. 1985. pap. 14.95 (ISBN 0-13-607110-4); incl. disk 29.95 (ISBN 0-13-607128-7). P-H.

--Pocket Magic: Graphic Games for the Pocket Computer. LC 82-80271. (Illus.). 96p. (Orig.). 1982. 17.95; pap. 9.95 (ISBN 0-942412-01-X); pre-recorded cassette 8.95 (ISBN 0-686-87025-5). Micro Text Pubns.

--Thirty Games for the Timex-Sinclair Computer. 1983. write for info. P-H.

Behrendt, Bill L. & Librach, Hank. Using the PCjr in the Home. 200p. 1984. pap. 10.95 (ISBN 0-13-939752-3); incl. disk 29.95 (ISBN 0-13-937343-8). P-H.

Behrendt, Douglas M. & Austen, W. Gerald. Patient Care in Cardiac Surgery. 3rd ed. (Little, Brown SPIRAL TM Manual Ser.). 1980. pap. 16.95 (ISBN 0-316-08756-4). Little.

--Patient Care in Cardiac Surgery. 4th ed. 288p. 1985. pap. text ed. 22.50 (ISBN 0-316-08763-7). Little.

Behrendt, H. M. Horsethief Ranch: An Oral History. (Illus.). 130p. (Orig.). 1985. pap. 7.95 (ISBN 0-9613777-0-4). Horsethief Pubns.

Behrendt, Hans. Chemistry of Erythrocytes: Clinical Aspects. (Illus.). 242p. 1957. 24.50x (ISBN 0-398-04206-3). C C Thomas.

Behrendt, Hans & Green, Marvin. Patterns of Skin PH from Birth Through Adolescence: With a Synopsis on Skin Growth. (Illus.). 116p. 1971. 14.75x (ISBN 0-398-00125-1). C C Thomas.

Behrendt, Leo. Ethical Teaching of Hugo of Trimberg. LC 77-140042. (Catholic University of America. Studies in German: No. 1). Repr. of 1926 ed. 18.00 (ISBN 0-404-50221-0). AMS Pr.

Behrendt, Roland, tr. see Arnold, Klaves.

Behrendt, Stephen C. The Moment of Explosion: Blake & the Illustration of Milton. LC 82-13561. (Illus.). xvi, 235p. 1983. 32.50x (ISBN 0-8032-1169-4). U of Nebr Pr.

Behrendt, W., et al. Intensivmedizin und Organversagen. (Beitraege zur Intensiv und Notfallmedizin: Vol. 3). (Illus.). viii, 188p. 1985. 28.50 (ISBN 3-8055-4016-7). S Karger.

Behrendt, W., et al, eds. Organversagen in der Intensivmedizin. (Beitraege zur Intensiv- und Notfallmedizin: Vol. 1). (Illus.). xii, 182p. 1983. pap. 27.00 (ISBN 3-8055-3794-8). S Karger.

Behrendt, Walter C. Modern Building: Its Nature, Problems, & Forms. LC 83-45705. Repr. of 1937 ed. 49.50 (ISBN 0-404-20024-9). AMS Pr.

Behrendt, William. Thirty Games for the Timex-Sinclair 1000. 84p. 1983. 9.95 (ISBN 0-13-918904-1); pap. 4.95 (ISBN 0-13-918896-7). P-H.

Behrendt, William, jt. auth. see Librach, Hank.

Behrens, C., jt. ed. see Rey, L.

Behrens, C. B. The Ancien Regime. (History of European Civilization Library). (Illus.). 215p. 1967. pap. text ed. 11.95 (ISBN 0-15-502750-6, HC). HarBraceJ.

--Merchant Shipping & Demands of War. 1978. 53.00 (ISBN 0-527-35772-3). Kraus Intl.

--Society, Government & the Enlightenment: The Experiences of Eighteenth-Century France & Russia. LC 84-48823. 248p. 1985. 19.23 (ISBN 0-06-430386-1, Icon Edns). Har-Row.

Behrens, D., ed. see Gmehling, J., et al.

Behrens, D., ed. see Gmehling, J. & Onken, U.

Behrens, D., ed. see Sorensen, J. M. & Arlt, W.

Behrens, David W. Pacific Coast Nudibranchs. LC 80-51439. (Illus.). 112p. 1980. pap. 14.95 (ISBN 0-930118-05-7). Western Marine Ent.

Behrens, Dieter, ed. see Gmehling, J., et al.

Behrens, Dieter, ed. see Sorenson, J. M. & Arlt, W.

Behrens, Ernst-August. Ring Theory. (Pure & Applied Mathematics Ser.: Vol. 44). 1972. 66.00 (ISBN 0-12-085250-0). Acad Pr.

Behrens, Frank. Dante's Infernal Guide to Your School. LC 75-154091. 1971. pap. 3.95 (ISBN 0-671-20975-2, Fireside). S&S.

Behrens, H. see Hellwege, K. H.

Behrens, Heinrich. Electron Radial Wave Functions & Nuclear Beta-Decay. (International Series of Monographs in Physics). (Illus.). 1982. 79.00x (ISBN 0-19-851297-X). Oxford U Pr.

Behrens, John C. The Typewriter Guerillas: Closeups of Twenty Top Investigative Reporters. LC 77-3439. 282p. 1977. 21.95x (ISBN 0-88229-266-8). Nelson-Hall.

Behrens, June. Christmas-Magic Wagon. LC 75-14007. (Holiday Play Books). (Illus.). 32p. (gr. k-4). 1975. PLB 9.95 (ISBN 0-516-08880-7, Golden Gate). Childrens.

--Fiesta! (Other Lands, Other Places) LC 78-8468. (Illus.). 32p. (gr. k-4). 1978. PLB 10.60 (ISBN 0-516-08815-7, Golden Gate). Childrens.

--Gung Hay Fat Choy. LC 81-17077. (gr. 1-4). 1982. 10.60 (ISBN 0-516-08842-4). Childrens.

--Hanukkah. LC 82-17890. (Illus.). 32p. (gr. k-4). 1983. PLB 10.60 (ISBN 0-516-02386-1). Childrens.

--I Can Be a Truck Driver. (Illus.). 32p. (ps-3). 1985. 2.95 (ISBN 0-516-41848-3). Childrens.

--I Can Be an Astronaut. LC 84-7601. (I Can Be Bks.). (Illus.). 32p. (gr. k-3). 1984. lib. bdg. 10.60 (ISBN 0-516-01837-X); pap. 2.95 (ISBN 0-516-41837-8). Childrens.

--The Manners Book. LC 79-22377. (Illus.). 32p. (ps-3). 1980. PLB 10.50 (ISBN 0-516-08750-9, Golden Gate). Childrens.

--Martin Luther King, Jr. The Story of a Dream. (Holiday Play Bks). (Illus.). 32p. (gr. k-4). 1979. PLB 9.95 (ISBN 0-516-08879-3, Golden Gate). Childrens.

--A New Flag for a New Country. LC 74-30381. (Holiday Play Books). (Illus.). 32p. (gr. k-3). 1975. PLB 9.95 (ISBN 0-516-08732-0, Golden Gate). Childrens.

--Powwow. LC 83-7274. (Ethnic & Traditional Holidays Ser.). (Illus.). 32p. (gr. k-4). 1983. PLB 10.60 (ISBN 0-516-02387-X). Childrens.

--Ronald Reagan: An All-American. LC 81-9993. (Picture Story Biographies Ser.). (Illus.). 32p. (gr. 2 up). 1981. PLB 10.60 (ISBN 0-516-03565-7). Childrens.
--Sally Ride, Astronaut: An American First. LC 83-23173. (Picture-Story Biographies). (Illus.). 32p. (gr. 2-5). 1984. lib. bdg. 10.60 (ISBN 0-516-03606-8). Childrens.
--Whalewatch! LC 78-7338. (Illus.). (gr. 1-4). 1978. PLB 10.35 (ISBN 0-516-08873-4, Golden Gate); pap. 2.95 (ISBN 0-516-48873-2). Childrens.
Behrens, June & Brower, Pauline. Death Valley. LC 79-23325. (Living Heritage Ser.). (Illus.). 32p. (gr. 1-4). 1980. PLB 10.35 (ISBN 0-516-08714-2, Golden Gate). Childrens.
Behrens, Kathryn L. Paper Money in Maryland. LC 78-64109. (Johns Hopkins University. Studies in the Social Sciences. Forty-First Ser.: 1). Repr. of 1923 ed. 24.50 (ISBN 0-404-61224-5). AMS Pr.
Behrens, Kaye, jt. auth. see Brown, Edgar.
Behrens, Laurence & Rosen, Leonard. Writing & Reading Across the Curriculum. 2nd ed. 1985. pap. text ed. 12.95 (ISBN 0-316-08761-0); tchr's. ed. avail. (ISBN 0-316-08762-9). Little.
Behrens, Richard. Ceramic Glazemaking. 3.95 (ISBN 0-934706-07-7). Prof Pubns Ohio.
--Glaze Projects. 3.95 (ISBN 0-934706-06-9). Prof Pubns Ohio.
Behrens, Robert H. Commercial Loan Officer's Handbook: From Basic Concepts to Advanced Techniques. (Bankers Lending Ser.). 312p. 1984. 45.00 (ISBN 0-87267-049-X). Bankers.
--Commercial Problem Loans: How to Identify, Supervise, & Collect the Problem Loan. 2nd ed. LC 82-16416. (Bankers Lending Ser.). 224p. 1983. text ed. 41.00 (ISBN 0-87267-039-2). Bankers.
Behrens, Robert H., jt. auth. see Frey, Thomas L.
Behrens, Roy R. Design in the Visual Arts. (Illus.). 160p. 1984. pap. text ed. 19.95 (ISBN 0-13-201947-7). P-H.
--Illustration As an Art. (Illus.). 256p. 1986. pap. text ed. 19.95 (ISBN 0-13-451428-9). P-H.
Behrens, Sophia A. Directory of Foreign Language Service Organizations 2. (Language in Education Ser.: No. 33). 58p. 1981. pap. 5.95 (ISBN 0-15-599008-X). Ctr Appl Ling.
Behrens-Abouseif, Doris. The Minarets of Cairo. 1985. 15.00x (ISBN 977-424-035-9, Pub. by Am Univ Cairo Pr). Columbia U Pr.
Behrensmeyer, Anna K. & Hill, Andrew P., eds. Fossils in the Making: Vertebrate Taphonomy & Paleoecology. LC 79-19879. (Prehistoric Archaeology & Ecology Ser.). (Illus.). 1980. lib. bdg. 20.00x (ISBN 0-226-04169-7); pap. text ed. 8.00x (ISBN 0-226-04168-9). U of Chicago Pr.
Behringer, Marjorie P. Techniques & Materials in Biology. LC 80-12458. 608p. 1981. Repr. of 1973 ed. lib. bdg. 30.50 (ISBN 0-89874-175-0). Krieger.
Behrisch, R., ed. Sputtering by Particle Bombardment II. (Topics in Applied Physics: Vol. 52). (Illus.). 385p. 1983. 47.00 (ISBN 0-387-12593-0). Springer Verlag.
--Sputtering by Particle Bombardment I: Physics & Applications. (Topics in Applied Physics Ser.: Vol. 47). (Illus.). 1981. 42.00 (ISBN 0-387-10521-2). Springer-Verlag.
Behrisch, R., et al, eds. Ion Surface Interaction, Sputtering & Related Phenomena. LC 73-85272. 334p. 1973. 80.95 (ISBN 0-677-15850-5). Gordon.
Behrle, Earlamonde. Ruby. 1983. 5.95 (ISBN 0-8062-2125-9). Carlton.
Behrman, Carol H. Miss Dr. Lucy. Wheeler, Gerald, ed. LC 83-23008. (Banner Ser.). 96p. 1984. pap. 5.95 (ISBN 0-8280-0231-2). Review & Herald.
--The Remarkable Writing Machine. LC 80-26648. (Illus.). 64p. (gr. 3-5). 1981. PLB 8.59 (ISBN 0-671-34026-3). Messner.
--There's Only One You. (Better Living Ser.). (Written for girls). (gr. 7-9). 1973. pap. 0.99 (ISBN 0-8127-0071-6). Review & Herald.
Behrman, Cynthia F. Victorian Myths of the Sea. LC 76-51694. 188p. 1977. 15.95 (ISBN 0-8214-0351-6, 82-82428). Ohio U Pr.
Behrman, Daniel. Assault on the Largest Unknown: The International Indian Ocean Expedition, 1959-65. 96p. 1981. pap. 22.50 (ISBN 92-3-101917-1, U1157, UNESCO). Unipub.
--Science & Technology in Development: A UNESCO Approach. (Illus.). 104p. 1979. pap. 5.25 (ISBN 92-3-101726-8, U947, UNESCO). Unipub.
--Solar Energy: The Awakening Science. 1980. pap. 7.95 (ISBN 0-316-08772-6). Little.
Behrman, Debra L. Family and-or Career: Plans of First-Time Mothers. Nathan, Peter, ed. LC 82-17572. (Research in Clinical Psychology: No. 2). 176p. 1982. 34.95 (ISBN 0-8357-1381-4). Univ Microfilms.
--Family & or Career: Plans of First-Time Mothers. Nathan, Peter, ed. LC 82-17572. (Research in Clinical Psychology No.2). 176p. 1982. 34.95 (ISBN 0-8357-1381-4). UMI Res Pr.
Behrman, Harold, jt. ed. see Jaffe, Bernard.
Behrman, Harold R., jt. ed. see Jaffe, Bernard M.
Behrman, Howard T., et al. Common Skin Diseases: Diagnosis & Treatment. 3rd ed. LC 75-152649. (Illus.). 186p. 1978. 49.50 (ISBN 0-8089-1102-3, 790486). Grune.
Behrman, J. R. Macroeconomic Policy in a Developing Country: Chilean Experience. (Contributions to Economic Analysis Ser.: Vol. 109). 340p. 1977. 72.50 (ISBN 0-7204-0548-3, North-Holland). Elsevier.
Behrman, J. R., et al. Socioeconomic Success: A Study of the Effects of Genetic Endowments, Family Environment & Schooling. (Contributions to Economic Analysis Ser.: Vol. 128). 276p. 1980. 66.00 (ISBN 0-444-85410-X, North-Holland). Elsevier.
Behrman, Jack & Mikesell, Raymond. The Impact of U. S. Foreign Direct Investment on U. S. Export Competitiveness in Third World Markets, Vol. II. LC 80-65189. (Significant Issues Ser.: No. 1). 45p. 1980. 5.95 (ISBN 0-89206-014-X). CSI Studies.
Behrman, Jack N. Discourses on Ethics & Business. LC 80-23626. 192p. 1981. text ed. 25.00 (ISBN 0-89946-064-X). Oelgeschlager.
--Industrial Policies: International Restructuring & Transnationals. 272p. 1984. 23.50x (ISBN 0-669-08275-9). Lexington Bks.
--Industry Ties with Science & Technology Policies in Developing Countries. LC 79-25772. 224p. 1980. text ed. 35.00 (ISBN 0-89946-017-8). Oelgeschlager.
--The Role of International Companies in Latin American Integration: Autos & Petrochemicals. LC 79-183711. 185p. 1972. pap. 4.50 (ISBN 0-87186-235-2). Comm Econ Dev.
--Tropical Diseases: Responses of Pharmaceutical Companies. 1980. pap. 4.25 (ISBN 0-8447-3393-8). Am Enterprise.
Behrman, Jack N. & Fischer, William A. Overseas R & D Activities of Transnational Companies. LC 79-25296. 336p. 1980. text ed. 40.00 (ISBN 0-89946-016-X). Oelgeschlager.
--Science & Technology for Development: Corporate & Government Policies & Practices. LC 79-27213. 160p. 1980. text ed. 35.00 (ISBN 0-89946-023-2). Oelgeschlager.
Behrman, Jack N., jt. auth. see Blough, Roy.
Behrman, Jack N. see Driscoll, Robert E.
Behrman, Jere R. Development, the International Economic Order, & Commodity Agreements. LC 78-52500. (Perspectives in Economics). (Illus.). 1978. pap. text ed. 11.95 (ISBN 0-201-08367-1). Addison-Wesley.
--International Commodity Agreements: An Evaluation of the UNCTAD Integrated Commodity Programme. LC 77-90146. (Monographs: No. 9). 112p. 1977. 5.00 (ISBN 0-686-28686-3). Overseas Dev Council.
Behrman, Jere R., jt. auth. see Adams, F. Gerard.
Behrman, Jere R. & Hanson, James A., eds. Short-Term Macroeconomic Policy in Latin America: Conference on Planning & Short-Term Marco-Economic Policy in Latin America. LC 78-24053. (Other Conference Ser.: No.14). 416p. 1979. prof ref 35.00 (ISBN 0-88410-489-3, Pub for the National Bureau of Economic Research). Ballinger Pub.
Behrman, Lucy. Muslim Brotherhoods & Politics in Senegal. LC 70-95918. 1970. 15.00x (ISBN 0-674-59490-8). Harvard U Pr.
Behrman, Marion, ed. see Callen, Anna T.
Behrman, Martin. Martin Behrman of New Orleans: Memoirs of a City Boss. Kemp, John R., ed. LC 77-6781. 1977. 32.50x (ISBN 0-8071-0275-X). La State U Pr.
Behrman, Richard E. & Vaughan, Victor C., III. Nelson Textbook of Pediatrics. 12th ed. (Illus.). 2175p. 1983. 79.00 (ISBN 0-7216-1736-0). Saunders.
Behrman, S. J. & Kistner, Robert W., eds. Progress in Infertility. 2nd ed. 1975. 75.00 (ISBN 0-316-08769-6). Little.
Behrman, S. N. Duveen. (Illus.). 192p. 1982. pap. 6.95 (ISBN 0-517-54628-0, Harmony). Crown.
Behrman, Samuel N; see Clurman, Harold.
Behrmann, Eleanor. General Chemistry. 1975. pap. text ed. 6.95 (ISBN 0-88429-010-7). Collegiate Pub.
Behrmann, Michael. Handbook of Microcomputers in Special Education. (Illus.). 250p. 1984. pap. 25.00 (ISBN 0-933014-35-X). College-Hill.
Behrmann, Michael M., ed. Handbook of Microcomputers in Special Education. 281p. 1984. 22.95 (ISBN 0-933014-35-X). Coun Exc Child.
Behrmann, Michael M. & Lahm, Liz, eds. National Conference on the Use of Microcomputers in Special Education, Proceedings, Hartford, CT, March 10-12, 1983. 217p. 1984. 20.00 (ISBN 0-86586-149-8). Coun Exc Child.
Behrmann, Polly. Activities for Developing Auditory Perception. 1972. pap. 2.50 (ISBN 0-87879-111-6). Acad Therapy.
Behrmann, Polly, jt. auth. see Millman, Joan.
Behrstock, Barry & Trubo, Richard. The Parent's When-Not-to Worry Book: Straight Talk About All Those Myths You've Learned from Your Parents, Friends-- & Even Doctors. LC 80-7894. 256p. 1981. 13.41i (ISBN 0-690-01972-6, HarpT). Har-Row.
Behrstock, Barry & Turbo, Richard. The Parent's When-Not-To-Worry Book. LC 80-7894. 272p. 1983. pap. 4.76i (ISBN 0-686-82652-3, CN 1043, CN). Har-Row.
Behura, N. K. Peasant Potters of Orissa. 1979. text ed. 15.00 (ISBN 0-89684-072-7, Pub. by Sterling New Delhi). Orient Bk Dist.
Behzadnia, A., tr. see Shariati, Ali.
Beichman, Arnold. Herman Wouk: The Novelist As Social Historian. 114p. 1984. 14.95 (ISBN 0-87855-498-X). Transaction Bks.
--Nine Lies About America. LC 76-37468. 345p. 1972. 19.95 (ISBN 0-912050-18-7, Library Pr). Open Court.
Beichman, Arnold & Bernstam, Mikhail S. Andropov: New Challenge to the West. LC 83-42830. 276p. 1983. 16.95 (ISBN 0-8128-2921-2). Stein & Day.
Beichman, Janine. Masaoka Shiki. (World Authors Ser.). 1982. lib. bdg. 19.95 (ISBN 0-8057-6504-2, Twayne). G K Hall.
Beichner, Paul E. Petri Riage Biblia Versificato: Petri Rigue Biblia Versificata, a Verse Commentary on the Bible, 2 vols. (Mediaeval Studies Ser.: No. 19). 1965. 50.00 set (ISBN 0-268-00016-6). U of Notre Dame Pr.
Beidel, Hyun S. see Beidel, Susie L., pseud.
Beidel, Susie L., pseud. The Story of Susie Lee. 1984. 9.95 (ISBN 0-8062-2350-2). Carlton.
Beidelman. The Kaguru: A Matrilineal People of East Africa. (Illus.). 134p. 1983. pap. text ed. 6.95x (ISBN 0-88133-060-4). Waveland Pr.
Beidelman, T. O. Colonial Evangelism: A Socio-Historical Study of an East African Mission at the Grassroots. LC 81-47771. (Midland Bks. Ser.: No. 278). (Illus.). 296p. 1982. 29.95x (ISBN 0-253-31386-4); pap. 12.50x (ISBN 0-253-20278-7). Ind U Pr.
--W. Robertson Smith & the Sociological Study of Religion. LC 73-87311. 1974. pap. 1.95x (ISBN 0-226-04160-3, P618, Phoen). U of Chicago Pr.
Beidelman, Thomas O. A Comparative Analysis of the Jajmani System. 2.50 (ISBN 0-685-71736-4). J J Augustin.
Beidelman, William. Story of the Pennsylvania Germans: Embracing an Account of Their Origin, Their History, Their Dialect. LC 70-81759. 1969. Repr. of 1898 ed. 43.00x (ISBN 0-8103-3571-9). Gale.
Beiderman, Charles & Johnston, William. The Beginner's Handbook of Woodcarving: Tools, Tips, & Techniques for a Successful Start. (Illus.). 173p. 1983. 19.95 (ISBN 0-13-072116-6); pap. 10.95 (ISBN 0-13-072108-5). P-H.
Beiderwieden, George. Heaven. 1957. 1.50 (ISBN 0-570-03680-1, 74-1008). Concordia.
Beidleman, Carl. Valuation of Used Capital Assets. (Studies in Accounting Research: Vol. 7). 84p. 1973. 6.00 (ISBN 0-318-12352-5); members 4.00 (ISBN 0-318-12353-3). Am Accounting.
--Valuation of Used Capital Assets, Vol. 7. (Studies in Accounting Research). 84p. 1973. 6.00 (ISBN 0-86539-019-3); members 4.00. Am Accounting.
Beidleman, Carl R. Financial Swaps: New Strategies in Currency & Coupon Risk Management. LC 84-72997. 1985. 35.00 (ISBN 0-87094-577-7). Dow Jones-Irwin.
Beidler, John. An Introduction to Data Structures. 200p. 1982. scp 33.73 (ISBN 0-205-07711-0, EDP 207711). Allyn.
Beidler, John & Jackowitz, Paul. Modula-Two. LC 85-6298. 300p. 1985. pap. 20.25 (ISBN 0-87150-912-1, 37L8900). PWS Pubs.
Beidler, L. M. see Autrum, H., et al.
Beidler, Peter G. Fig Tree John: An Indian in Fact & Fiction. LC 76-26345. 152p. 1977. pap. 4.95x (ISBN 0-8165-0522-5). U of Ariz Pr.
--John Gower's Literary Transformations in the Confessio Amantis: Original Articles & Translations. 150p. (Orig.). 1982. lib. bdg. 22.50 (ISBN 0-8191-2596-2); pap. text ed. 9.25 (ISBN 0-8191-2597-0). U Pr of Amer.
Beidler, Peter G. & Egge, Marion F. The American Indian in Short Fiction: An Annotated Bibliography. LC 79-20158. 215p. 1979. 16.50 (ISBN 0-8108-1256-8). Scarecrow.
Beidler, Philip D. American Literature & the Experience of Vietnam. LC 81-19845. 240p. 1982. 17.00x (ISBN 0-8203-0612-6). U of Ga Pr.
Beidler, Philip D., jt. ed. see Davis, Sara D.
Beidler, W. Vision of Self in Early Vedanta. 1975. 12.50 (ISBN 0-8426-0990-3). Orient Bk Dist.
Beier, A. L. Masterless Men: The Vagrancy Problem in England, 1560-1640. 250p. 1985. 33.00 (ISBN 0-416-39010-2, 9603). Methuen Inc.
--The Problems of the Poor in Tudor & Early Stuart England. (Lancaster Pamphlet Ser.). 60p. 1983. pap. 3.95 (ISBN 0-416-35060-7, NO. 3895). Methuen Inc.
Beier, Ernst G. & Valens, E. G., Jr. People-Reading: How We Control Others, How They Control Us. LC 74-26977. 256p. 1975. 8.95 (ISBN 0-8128-1781-8). Stein & Day.
Beier, Ernst G. & Young, David M. The Silent Language of Psychotherapy: Social Reinforcement of Unconscious Processes. 2nd ed. LC 84-6287. 318p. 1984. lib. bdg. 29.95x (ISBN 0-202-26097-6); pap. text ed. 14.95x (ISBN 0-202-26098-4). Aldine Pub.
Beier, Freidrich, ed. see Bochnovic, John.
Beier, H. M. & Karlson, P., eds. Proteins & Steroids in Early Pregnancy. (Illus.). 346p. 1981. pap. 42.00 (ISBN 0-387-10457-7). Springer Verlag.
Beier, H. M. & Linder, H. R., eds. Fertilization of the Human Egg in Vitro: Biological Basis & Clinical Applications, Munich, FRG 1982, Proceedings. (Illus.). 424p. 1983. 43.50 (ISBN 0-387-11896-9). Springer-Verlag.
Beier, Karl F. & Schricker, Gerhard. German Industrial Property: Copyright & Antitrust Laws. Ulmer, Eugen, tr. (Vol. 6 I I C Studies). 222p. 1983. pap. 38.00x (ISBN 0-89573-060-X). VCH Pubs.
Beier, Ulli. African Poetry. (Illus., Orig.). 1966. o. p. 10.95 (ISBN 0-521-04140-6); pap. 6.95 (ISBN 0-521-04141-4). Cambridge U Pr.
--Art in Nigeria, 1960. LC 61-16002. pap. 20.00 (ISBN 0-317-10214-1, 2051428). Bks Demand UMI.
--Introduction to African Literature: An Anthology of Critical Writing from Black Orpheus. LC 66-30612. pap. 70.50 (ISBN 0-317-10051-3, 2006935). Bks Demand UMI.
--The Origin of Life & Death. (African Writers Ser.). 1966. pap. text ed. 3.50x (ISBN 0-435-90023-4). Heinemann Ed.
--The Stolen Images. 64p. 1976. pap. 3.95x (ISBN 0-521-20901-3). Cambridge U Pr.
--Yoruba Myths. LC 79-7645. (Illus.). 88p. 1980. 14.95 (ISBN 0-521-22995-2); pap. 5.95 (ISBN 0-521-22865-4). Cambridge U Pr.
--Yoruba Poetry: An Anthology of Traditional Poems. LC 77-92244. pap. 31.50 (ISBN 0-317-26051-0, 2024420). Bks Demand UMI.
Beier, Ulli, jt. auth. see Gbadamosi, Bakare.
Beier, Ulli, ed. Political Spider: An Anthology of Stories from Black Orpheus. LC 79-90296. 118p. (Orig.). 1969. pap. 5.45x (ISBN 0-8419-0017-5, Africana). Holmes & Meier.
--Voices of Independence: New Black Writing from Papua New Guinea. 1980. 20.00 (ISBN 0-312-85084-0). St Martin.
--Words of Paradise: Poetry of Papua New Guinea. Laycock, Don & Natachee, Allan, trs. from New Guinean. LC 72-77912. (Illus.). 1973. 10.00 (ISBN 0-87775-031-9); pap. 3.00 (ISBN 0-87775-081-5). Unicorn Pr.
Beier, Ulli & Moore, Gerald, eds. The Penguin Book of Modern African Poetry. 320p. 1984. pap. 6.95 (ISBN 0-14-042311-7). Penguin.
Beierle, Herbert L. Alles Beginnt im Positiven Denken. 1981. 10.00 (ISBN 0-940480-14-X). U of Healing.
--Art & Science of Wholeness. 1975. 20.00 (ISBN 0-940480-00-X). U of Healing.
--Autobiography of God. 1979. 10.00 (ISBN 0-940480-05-0). U of Healing.
--Dualism. 1979. 10.00 (ISBN 0-940480-06-9). U of Healing.
--Erfolgs-und Gesundheitsbewusstes Denken und Handeln Fur Geschaftslete. 1982. 10.00 (ISBN 0-940480-18-2). U of Healing.
--A Gift from Self to Self. 1981. 10.00 (ISBN 0-940480-12-3). U of Healing.
--How Much of God I Express Is How Much I Profess. 1982. 1.00 (ISBN 0-686-35834-1). U of Healing.
--How to Give a Healing Treatment. 1979. 1.00 (ISBN 0-940480-07-7). U of Healing.
--Illumination: Handbook of Ascended Masters. 1978. 20.00 (ISBN 0-940480-02-6). U of Healing.
--Die Kunst und Wissenschaft der Guettlichen Ganzheit. 20.00 (ISBN 0-940480-13-1). U of Healing.
--Making Energy Work. 1980. 5.00 (ISBN 0-940480-08-5). U of Healing.
--Proclaim Your God. 1.00 (ISBN 0-940480-09-3). U of Healing.
--Quiet Healing Zone. 1980. 10.00 (ISBN 0-940480-10-7). U of Healing.
--School for Masters. 1979. 1.00 (ISBN 0-940480-11-5). U of Healing.
--Song of the Spirit. 1978. 20.00 (ISBN 0-940480-01-8). U of Healing.
--Success & Health Conscious Thoughts & Actions for Business People. 1982. 10.00 (ISBN 0-940480-17-4). U of Healing.
--Syllabus: 1982. 1982. 1.00 (ISBN 0-940480-16-6). U of Healing.
--Warum Ich Sagen Kann: Ich Bin Gott. 1981. 1.00 (ISBN 0-940480-15-8). U of Healing.
--Why I Can Say I Am God. 1978. 1.00 (ISBN 0-940480-04-2). U of Healing.
Beierle, Herbert L., ed. Ministers Manual. 1978. 10.00 (ISBN 0-940480-03-4). U of Healing.
--Minister's Manual. 2nd ed. 1985. 10.00 (ISBN 0-940480-20-4). U of Healing.
Beifuss, Joan T. At the River I Stand: Memphis, the 1968 Strike & Martin Luther King. LC 85-71065. 320p. 1985. pap. 13.95 (ISBN 0-9614996-0-5). B & W Bks.
Beigbeder, Olivier. Lexique des Symboles. 436p. (Fr.). 1969. 45.00 (ISBN 0-686-56912-1, M-6028). French & Eur.
Beigel, Allan, jt. auth. see Russell, Harold E.
Beigel, Allan, jt. ed. see Sharfstein, Steven S.
Beigel, Hugo G. Art Appreciation. 1978. Repr. of 1947 ed. lib. bdg. 30.00 (ISBN 0-8495-0373-6). Arden Lib.
--Dictionary of Psychology & Related Fields. LC 74-115063. (Ger. & Eng.). 15.00 (ISBN 0-8044-0042-3). Ungar.

Beigel, Hugo G. & Johnson, Warren R. Application of Hypnosis in Sex Therapy. 352p. 1980. 29.75x (ISBN 0-398-03965-8). C C Thomas.

Beighey, Clyde & Borchardt, Gordon C. Mathematics for Business, College Course. 5th ed. (Illus.). 256p. 1974. pap. text ed. 18.50 (ISBN 0-07-004370-1). McGraw.

Beightler, Charles S., et al. Foundations of Optimization. 2nd ed. (International Ser. in Industrial & Systems Engineering). (Illus.). 1979. text ed. 35.95 (ISBN 0-13-330332-2). P-H.

Beighton, P. & Cremin, B. J. Sclerosing Bone Dysplasias. (Illus.). 210p. 1980. 69.00 (ISBN 0-387-09471-7). Springer-Verlag.

Beighton, P., jt. auth. see Cremin, B. J.

Beighton, P., jt. auth. see Horan, F. T.

Beighton, P., et al. Hypermobility of Joints. (Illus.). 105p. 1983. 46.00 (ISBN 0-387-12113-7). Springer-Verlag.

Beighton, Peter & Sellars, Sean. Genetics & Otology. LC 82-1273. (Genetics in Medicine & Surgery Ser.). (Illus.). 108p. 1982. text ed. 32.50 (ISBN 0-443-02284-4). Churchill.

Beigie, Carl E. Inflation Is a Social Malady. LC 78-70536. (British-North American Committee Ser.). 92p. 1979. 4.00 (ISBN 0-902594-34-6). Natl Planning.

Beigie, Carl E. & Hero, Alfred O., Jr., eds. Natural Resources in U. S.-Canadian Relations: Volume II: Patterns & Trends in Resource Supplies & Policies. 626p. 1980. 27.50 (ISBN 0-89158-555-9); pap. 12.00 (ISBN 0-89158-878-7). Inst C D Howe.

--Natural Resources in U. S.-Canadian Relations: Volume I: The Evolution of Policies & Issues. 371p. 1980. 25.00 (ISBN 0-89158-554-0); pap. 10.00 (ISBN 0-89158-877-9). Inst C D Howe.

Beigie, Carl E., et al. Seeking a New Accomodation in World Commodity Markets. 1976. 15.00 (ISBN 0-318-02784-4); pap. 4.95 (ISBN 0-318-02785-2). Trilateral Comm.

Beiglbeeck, W., et al, eds. Feynman Path Integrals: Proceedings, International Colloquium, Marseilles May 1978. (Lecture Notes in Physics: Vol. 106). 1979. pap. 24.00 (ISBN 0-387-09532-2). Springer-Verlag.

Beiglboeck, W., et al, eds. Group Theoretical Methods in Physics, Vol. 94. (Lecture Notes in Physics Ser.). 1979. pap. 28.00 (ISBN 0-387-09238-2). Springer-Verlag.

Beihl, Bessie. Blessed Are Your Eyes. pap. 1.00 (ISBN 0-87516-131-6). De Vorss.

--The Lord Is Your Shepherd. 1972. pap. 2.25 (ISBN 0-87516-132-4). De Vorss.

--Peace My Heart. pap. 1.00 (ISBN 0-87516-133-2). De Vorss.

Beijer, Agne. Court Theatres of Drottningholm & Gripsholm. LC 77-180032. (Illus.). Repr. of 1933 ed. 35.00 (ISBN 0-405-08260-6). Ayer Co Pubs.

Beijing Bureau of Parks & Gardens, Staff. Chinese Chrysanthemums. (Illus.). 74p. (Orig.). 1981. pap. 13.95 (ISBN 0-8351-0965-8). China Bks.

Beijing Foreign Language Institute. The Pinyin Chinese-English Dictionary. Wu Jingrong, ed. LC 79-2477. 976p. (Chinese & Eng.). 1979. 85.95x (ISBN 0-471-27557-3, Pub. by Wiley-Interscience); pap. 24.95 (ISBN 0-471-86796-9). Wiley.

Beijing Institute of Foreign Trade Staff, jt. ed. see Beijing Language Institute.

Beijing Institute of Traditional Chinese Medicine Staff. Fundamentals of Chinese Medicine. East Asia Medical Studies Center & Zmiewski, Paul, eds. 486p. 1985. 29.95 (ISBN 0-912111-07-0). Paradigm Pubns.

Beijing Language Institute. Elementary Chinese Reader, Vol. 1. 294p. 1980. pap. 6.95 (ISBN 0-917056-44-2, Pub. by Foreign Lang Pr China); teach ed 4.95 (ISBN 0-917056-17-5); wkbk. 3.95 (ISBN 0-917056-21-3). Cheng & Tsui.

--Elementary Chinese Reader, Vol. 2. 266p. 1980. pap. 6.95 (ISBN 0-917056-45-0, Pub. by Foreign Lang Pr China); teach ed 4.95 (ISBN 0-917056-18-3); wkbk. 3.95 (ISBN 0-917056-29-9). Cheng & Tsui.

--Elementary Chinese Reader, Vol. 3. 295p. pap. 6.95 (ISBN 0-917056-46-9, Pub. by Foreign Lang Pr China); tchr's. ed. 4.95 (ISBN 0-917056-19-1). Cheng & Tsui.

--Elementary Chinese-Readers Supplement. (Elementary Chinese Readers). 277p. 1982. pap. 6.95 (ISBN 0-8351-1038-9). China Bks.

--Elementary Chinese Readers Supplement. 277p. (Orig.). 1982. pap. 6.95 (ISBN 0-917056-07-8, Pub. by Foreign Lang Pr China). Cheng & Tsui.

--Practical Chinese Reader: Elementary, Vol. 1, Pt. 1. 551p. 1981. pap. 8.95 (ISBN 0-917056-48-5, Pub. by Commercial Pr China). Cheng & Tsui.

--Practical Chinese Reader: Elementary, Vol. 2, Pt. 2. 506p. 1981. pap. 8.95 (ISBN 0-917056-49-3, Pub. by Commercial Pr China). Cheng & Tsui.

--Readings from Chinese Writers: Nineteen Nineteen to Nineteen Forty-Nine, Vol. 1. 335p. (Chinese.). 1982. pap. text ed. 7.95x (ISBN 0-88727-038-7). Cheng & Tsui.

--Readings from Chinese Writers: Nineteen Nineteen to Nineteen Forty-Nine, Vol. 2. 363p. (Chinese.). 1982. pap. text ed. 7.95x (ISBN 0-88727-039-5). Cheng & Tsui.

--Vocabulary List-Key to Exercise for Practical Chinese Reader. (Practical Chinese Reader Ser.: No. 1 & 2). 75p. (Orig.). 1982. pap. 1.95 (ISBN 0-8351-1148-2). China Bks.

Beijing Language Institute, ed. Elementary Chinese Reader, Vol. 4. 311p. 1980. pap. 6.95 (ISBN 0-917056-47-7, Pub. by Foreign Lang Pr China); tchrs ed. 4.95 (ISBN 0-917056-20-5). Cheng & Tsui.

--Readings From Chinese Writers Series: Nineteen Nineteen to Nineteen Forty-Nine, Bk. 1. (Readings From Chinese Writers). 333p. (Orig.). 1982. pap. 7.95 (ISBN 0-8351-1117-2). China Bks.

--Readings From Chinese Writers: 1919-1949, Bk. 2. (Readings From Chinese Writers Ser.). 360p. (Orig.). 1982. pap. 7.95 (ISBN 0-8351-1122-9). China Bks.

Beijing Language Institute & Beijing Institute of Foreign Trade Staff, eds. Business Chinese 500. 309p. (Orig.). 1982. pap. 5.95 (ISBN 0-8351-1039-7). China Bks.

Beijing Language Institute Staff. Annotated Chinese Proverbs: Supplementary Readings for Elementary Chinese Readers. 178p. (Orig.). 1982. pap. 6.95 (ISBN 0-917056-13-2, Pub. by Foreign Lang Pr China). Cheng & Tsui.

Beijing Language Institute Staff, ed. Annotated Chinese Proverbs. (Elementary Chinese Readers). (Illus.). 178p. (Orig.). 1982. pap. 6.95 (ISBN 0-8351-1100-8). China Bks.

Beijing Languages Institute. Chinese Character Exercise Book for Practical Chinese Reader. (Practical Chinese Reader Ser.: No. 2). 108p. 1982. pap. 2.95 (ISBN 0-8351-1147-4). China Bks.

Beijing Languages Institute, ed. Chinese Character Exercise Book for Practical Chinese Reader. (Practical Chinese Reader Ser.: No. 1). 208p. (Orig.). 1982. pap. 3.95 (ISBN 0-8351-1146-6). China Bks.

--Chinese Three Hundred. (Chinese Language Library). 193p. (Orig.). 1984. pap. 5.95 (ISBN 0-8351-1162-8). China Bks.

Beijing Symposium on Cardiothoracic Surgery & Brewer, Lyman A. Proceedings on Beijing Symposium on Cardiothoracic Surgery. 382p. 1982. 60.00x (ISBN 0-471-87327-6, Pub. by Wiley Med). Wiley.

Beik, Paul H. Judgment of the Old Regime. LC 44-2365. (Columbia University Studies in the Social Sciences: No. 509). Repr. of 1944 ed. 18.50 (ISBN 0-404-51509-6). AMS Pr.

Beik, William. Absolutism & Society in Seventeenth-Century France: State Power & Provincial Aristocracy in Languedoc. (Cambridge Studies in Early Modern History). (Illus.). 375p. 1985. 44.50 (ISBN 0-521-26309-3). Cambridge U Pr.

Beikman, Helen M., et al. Coal Reserves of Washington. (Bulletin Ser.: No. 47). (Illus.). 115p. 1961. 3.50 (ISBN 0-686-34700-5). Geologic Pubns.

Beil, D. The Bank Street Writer Book: The Rosetta Stone of Word Processing. 256p. 1984. 19.95 (ISBN 0-8359-0361-3). Reston.

Beil, Don. The DIF File: For Users of VisiCalc & Other Software. 1983. 16.95 (ISBN 0-8359-1305-8). Reston.

--Symphony: First Introduction to Business Software. 1984. cancelled (ISBN 0-8359-7440-5). Reston.

Beil, Donald. File Processing with COBOL. (Illus.). 1981. pap. text ed. 20.95 (ISBN 0-8359-1984-6). Reston.

--SuperCalc! The Book. 16.95 (ISBN 0-8359-7305-0). Reston.

Beil, Ivanka. Das Konjugationssystem der Tschechischen Hochsprache der Gegenwart: Versuch einer Generativen Morphologie, Vol. 7. (Slavistische Linguistic). 234p. (Ger.). 1983. 28.95 (ISBN 3-8204-7673-3). P Lang Pubs.

Beil, Norman. The Writer's Legal & Business Guide to Motion Pictures, Television & Book Publishing. LC 83-15832. 224p. 1984. lib. bdg. 14.95 (ISBN 0-668-05579-0); pap. 9.95 (ISBN 0-668-05582-0). Arco.

Beil, Preston J. & Brown, Florence, eds. What to Do in New Jersey. rev. ed. (What to Do Ser.). (Illus.). 160p. 1980. pap. 2.50x (ISBN 0-686-28502-6). What to Do.

Beilan, Michael H. Your Offshore Doctor: A Manual of Medical Self-Sufficiency at Sea. (Illus.). 184p. 1985. pap. 14.95 (ISBN 0-396-08680-2). Dodd.

Beilby, Alvin L., ed. Modern Classics in Analytical Chemistry, Vols. 1-2. LC 75-125864. (ACS Reprint Collection). Vol. 1 1970. pap. 8.95 (ISBN 0-8412-0315-6); Vol. 2 1976. pap. 10.95 (ISBN 0-8412-0332-6). Am Chemical.

Beilby, M. H. Economics & Operational Research. 1976. 37.50 (ISBN 0-12-085750-2). Acad Pr.

Beilen, Aileen V. Hunger Awareness Dinners. 40p. 1978. pap. 0.95. Herald Hse.

Beilen, Aileen Van see Van Beilen, Aileen.

Beilen, Harry. Studies in the Cognitive Basis of Language Development. (Child Psychology Ser.). 1975. 55.00 (ISBN 0-12-085650-6). Acad Pr.

Beilenson, Edna. Festive Cookies. LC 85-61306. (Illus.). 64p. 1985. 4.95 (ISBN 0-88088-176-3, 881763). Peter Pauper.

Beilenson, Edna, ed. A Lover's Almanac. (Illus.). 64p. 1983. 4.95 (ISBN 0-88088-032-5). Peter Pauper.

Beilenson, Evelyn, jt. ed. see Beilenson, Peter.

Beilenson, Evelyn L., ed. Early American Cooking: Recipes from America's Historic Sites. LC 84-62478. (Illus.). 96p. 1985. 9.95 (ISBN 0-88088-913-6, 889136). Peter Pauper.

Beilenson, John & Beilenson, Nick, eds. The Olympics: A Book of Lists. (Illus.). 96p. (Orig.). 1984. pap. 4.95 (ISBN 0-88088-778-8). Peter Pauper.

Beilenson, Lawrence W. Power Through Subversion. 1972. 12.00 (ISBN 0-8183-0195-3). Pub Aff Pr.

Beilenson, Nick, jt. ed. see Beilenson, John.

Beilenson, Peter & Beilenson, Evelyn, eds. The Merrie Christmas Drink Book. rev. ed. LC 84-60959. 64p. 1984. Repr. of 1955 ed. 4.95 (ISBN 0-88088-430-4, 884304). Peter Pauper.

Beiler, Albert H. Recreations in the Theory of Numbers. (Orig.). 1964. pap. 5.95 (ISBN 0-486-21096-0). Dover.

Beiler, Edna. Mattie Mae. LC 67-24800. (Illus.). 128p. (gr. 3-7). 1967. pap. 3.95 (ISBN 0-8361-1789-1). Herald Pr.

Beiler, Henry. Food Is Your Best Medicine. pap. 2.95x (ISBN 0-394-71837-2). Cancer Control Soc.

Beilharz, Edwin A. Felipe De Neve, First Gov. of California. 194p. 1971. 12.95 (ISBN 0-910312-09-5). Calif Hist.

--Filipe De Neve: First Govenor of California. 1971. 12.95 (ISBN 0-317-12125-1). Calif Hist.

--Institutions in Conflict. 548p. 1981. text ed. 25.00 (ISBN 0-686-91827-4, Pub by Pioneer Pub Co). Panorama West.

Beilke, Marlan. Family, Friends, & Poetry. 12p. 1980. pap. 5.00 (ISBN 0-918466-09-1). Quintessence.

--Shining Clarity: God & Man in the Works of Robinson Jeffers. LC 77-70786. 1978. separate ed. 100.00x (ISBN 0-918466-01-6). Quintessence.

Beilke, Patricia F., jt. auth. see Carroll, Frances Laverne.

Beilke, S. & Elshout, A. J., eds. Acid Deposition. 1983. lib. bdg. 32.50 (ISBN 90-2771-588-2, Pub. by Reidel Holland). Kluwer Academic.

Beilner, H. & Gelenbe, E., eds. Measuring, Modelling & Evaluating Computer Systems: Proceedings of the Third International Workshop on Modelling & Performance Evaluation of Computer Systems, Bonn, October, 1977. 470p. 1978. 76.75 (ISBN 0-444-85058-9, North-Holland). Elsevier.

--Modelling & Performance Evaluation of Computer Systems: Proceedings of the International Workshop Organized by the Commission of the European Communities, Italy, 1976. LC 77-1179. 516p. 1977. 72.50 (ISBN 0-7204-0554-8, North-Holland). Elsevier.

Beilock, Richard P., ed. see Boulding, Kenneth E.

Beilstein Institute for Literature of Organic Chemistry. Acyclische Kohlenwasserstoffe, Hydroxy-Verbindungen und Oxo-Verbindungen. (Beilsteins Handbuch der Organischen Chemie, 4th Ed., 4th Suppl.: Vol. 1, Pt. 6). 569p. 1975. 348.60 (ISBN 0-387-07221-7). Springer-Verlag.

--Acyclische Verbindungen. Boit, H. G., ed. LC 72-95756. (Beilsteins Handbuch der Organischen Chemie, Ser., 4th Ed., 4th Suppl.: Vol. 2, Pt. 1). 692p. 1975. 404.90 (ISBN 0-387-07311-6). Springer-Verlag.

--Beilstein-Leitfaden: Eine Anleitung Zur Benutzung Von Beilsteins Handbuch der Organischen Chemie. 56p. 1975. pap. 257.10 (ISBN 0-387-07431-7). Springer-Verlag.

--Heterocyclische Verbindungen. Boit, H. G., ed (Beilsteins Handbuch der Organischen Chemie, 4th Ed., 3rd & 4th Suppl.: Vol. 17, Pt. 6). 868p. 1975. 495.60 (ISBN 0-387-07359-0). Springer-Verlag.

--Heterocyclische Verbindungen. (Beilsteins Handbuch der Orgnaischen Chemie, 4th Ed.,: Vol. 17, Pts. 3-5). 1975. Pt. 3. 505.70 (ISBN 0-387-07084-2); Pt. 4. 701.40 (ISBN 0-387-07220-9); Pt. 5. 446.90 (ISBN 0-387-07310-8). Springer-Verlag.

--Isocyclische Oxoamine, Aminocarbonsauren, Aminossulfinsauren, Aminosulfonsauren. (Beilsteins Handbuch der Organischen Chemie, 4th Ed., 3rd Suppl.: Vol. 14, Pt. 5). 878p. 1975. 215.10 (ISBN 0-387-07099-0). Springer-Verlag.

Beim, Jerrold. The Smallest Boy in the Class. (Illus.). (gr. k-3). 1949. PLB 11.88 (ISBN 0-688-31442-2). Morrow.

Beim, Jerrold, jt. auth. see Beim, Lorraine.

Beim, Lorraine. Triumph Clear. LC 46-3638. (gr. 7 up). 1966. pap. 0.65 (ISBN 0-15-691161-2, VoyB). HarBraceJ.

Beim, Lorraine & Beim, Jerrold. Two Is a Team. LC 73-12939. (Illus.). 58p. (gr. k-3). 1974. pap. 1.25 (ISBN 0-15-692050-6, VoyB). HarBraceJ.

Beimer, Dorothy S. Hovels, Haciendas & House Calls: The Life of Carl H. Gellenthien, M.D. (Illus.). 320p. (Orig.). 1985. pap. 16.95 (ISBN 0-86534-074-9). Sunstone Pr.

Bein, Alex. Theodore Herzl: A Biography of the Founder of Modern Zionism. Samuel, Maurice, tr. from Ger. LC 62-20753. (Temple Bk). 1970. pap. 4.75 (ISBN 0-689-70244-2, T18). Atheneum.

Bein, G. German-English Dictionary of International Transport. 232p. (Ger. & Eng.). 1980. 15.00x (ISBN 0-569-05117-7, Pub. by Collet's). State Mutual Bk.

Bein, Vic. Mountain Skiing. (Illus.). 192p. (Orig.). 1982. pap. 9.95 (ISBN 0-89886-034-2). Mountaineers.

--Mountain Skiing. 1983. 15.25 (ISBN 0-8446-6044-2). Peter Smith.

Beinart, William. The Political Economy of Pondoland, Eighteen Sixty to Nineteen Thirty: Production, Labour, Migrancy & Chiefs in Rural South Africa. LC 81-21619. (Afican Studies: No. 33). (Illus.). 232p. 1982. 44.50 (ISBN 0-521-24393-9). Cambridge U Pr.

Beinecke, Mary A. Basic Needlery Stitches on Mesh Fabrics. LC 73-77444. 64p. (Orig.). 1973. pap. 3.95 (ISBN 0-486-21713-2). Dover.

Beineke, Lowell & Wilson, Robin, eds. Selected Topics in Graphs Theory. 1979. 75.00 (ISBN 0-12-086250-6). Acad Pr.

Beineke, Lowell, jt. ed. see Wilson, Robin.

Beineke, Lowell W. & Wilson, Robin J. Selected Topics in Graph Theory, Vol. 2. 1983. 60.00 (ISBN 0-12-086202-6). Acad Pr.

Beiner, Ronald. Political Judgement. LC 83-50829. 1984. lib. bdg. 20.00x (ISBN 0-226-04164-6); pap. 9.50x (ISBN 0-226-04165-4). U of Chicago Pr.

Beiner, Ronald, ed. see Arendt, Hannah.

Beiner, Stan J. Sedra Scenes: Skits for Every Torah Portion. LC 82-71282. 225p. (Orig.). (gr. 6-12). 1982. pap. text ed. 8.75 (ISBN 0-86705-007-1). AIRE.

Beinhart, Haim. Trujillo: A Jewish Community in Extremadura on the Eve of Expulsion from Spain. (Hispania Judaica Ser.: No. 2). 372p. 1980. text ed. 25.50x (ISBN 965-223-349-8, Pub. by Magnes Israel). Humanities.

Beinhauer, Werner. Spanischer Sprachhumor. pap. 10.00 (ISBN 0-384-03785-2). Johnson Repr.

Beinhorn, George, ed. Food for Fitness. LC 74-16792. (Illus.). 144p. 1975. pap. 3.95 (ISBN 0-89037-084-2). Anderson World.

Beinhorn, George, tr. see Steffny, Manfred.

Beinhorn, George, tr. see Van Aaken, Ernst.

Beinin, L. Medical Consequences of Natural Disasters. (Illus.). 195p. 1985. pap. 39.00 (ISBN 0-387-15506-6). Springer-Verlag.

Beining, Guy. Backroads & Artism. LC 79-84873. 1979. pap. 5.00 (ISBN 0-931350-05-0). Moonlight Pubns.

--Waiting for the Soothsayer. 1981. pap. 1.50 (ISBN 0-686-47954-8). Ghost Dance.

Beining, Guy R. The Raw-Robed Few & Other Poems. 1979. pap. 4.95 (ISBN 0-930090-11-X). Applezaba.

Beintema, David, jt. auth. see Prechtl, Heinz.

Beinum, Hans van see Kolodny, Harvey F. & Van Beinum, Hans.

Beirlein, et al. Principles of Agribusiness Management. 1985. text ed. 23.95 (ISBN 0-8359-5599-0); instrs' manual avail. (ISBN 0-8359-5600-8). Reston.

Beirne, Charles J. The Problem of Americanization in the Catholic Schools of Puerto Rico. 144p. (Orig.). 1976. pap. 5.00 (ISBN 0-8477-2725-4). U of PR Pr.

--El Problema de la "Americanizacion" en las Escuelas Catolicas de Puerto Rico. Estades De Camara, Maria E., tr. LC 76-10347. 228p. (Span.). 1976. pap. 5.00 (ISBN 0-8477-2726-2). U of PR Pr.

Beirne, Francis F. The Amiable Baltimoreans. LC 84-47953. (Maryland Paperback Bookshelf Ser.). 1984. pap. 9.95 (ISBN 0-8018-2513-X). Johns Hopkins.

Beirne, Gerald. The New England Sports Trivia Book. LC 82-50959. (Illus.). 176p. (Orig.). 1983. pap. 10.95 (ISBN 0-911658-47-5). Yankee Bks.

Beirne, Piers & Quinney, Richard, eds. Marxism & Law. LC 81-15927. 381p. 1982. text ed. 24.50x (ISBN 0-471-08758-0). Wiley.

Beirne, Piers & Sharlet, Robert, eds. Pashukanis: Selected Writings on Marxism & Law. LC 79-40895. (Law, State & Society Ser.). 1980. 55.00 (ISBN 0-12-086350-2). Acad Pr.

Beis, Edward B. Mental Health & the Law. LC 83-15825. 390p. 1983. 37.50 (ISBN 0-89443-893-X). Aspen Systems.

Beischer, Norman A. & MacKay, Eric V. Color Atlas of Gynecology. (Illus.). 201p. 1981. 60.00 (ISBN 0-7216-1649-6). Saunders.

--Obstetrics & the Newborn. (Illus.). 532p. 1977. 27.50 (ISBN 0-7216-1673-9). Saunders.

Beiser. Physics. 3rd ed. 1982. 35.95 (ISBN 0-8053-0381-2); study guide 11.95 (ISBN 0-8053-0383-9); instr's. manual with tests 6.95 (ISBN 0-8053-0382-0). Benjamin-Cummings.

Beiser, A. Applied Physics. (Schaum's Outline Ser.). 1976. pap. 8.95 (ISBN 0-07-004377-9). McGraw.

Beiser, A., jt. auth. see Krauskopf, K. B.

Beiser, Arthur. Basic Concepts of Physics. 2nd ed. LC 70-168762. 1972. text ed. 27.95 (ISBN 0-201-00491-7). Addison-Wesley.

--Concepts of Modern Physics. 3rd ed. (Illus.). 544p. 1981. text ed. 34.95 (ISBN 0-07-004382-5). McGraw.

--Earth Sciences. (Schaum's Outline Ser.). 160p. (Orig.). 1975. pap. 5.95 (ISBN 0-07-004375-2). McGraw.

--Modern Technical Physics. 4th ed. 1983. text ed. 31.95 (ISBN 0-8053-0682-X); pap. text ed. 6.95 solution manual (ISBN 0-8053-0683-8). Benjamin-Cummings.

--Physical Science. (Schaum's Outline Ser.). 320p. 1974. pap. text ed. 6.95 (ISBN 0-07-004376-0). McGraw.

--Schaum's Outline of Basic Mathematics for Electricity & Electronics. (Schaum's Outline Ser.). (Illus.). 208p. 1980. pap. 7.95 (ISBN 0-07-004378-7). McGraw.

Beiser, Arthur & Krauskopf, Konrad B. Introduction to Earth Science. (Illus.). 320p. 1975. text ed. 34.95 (ISBN 0-07-004368-X). McGraw.

Beiser, Arthur, jt. auth. see Krauskopf, Konrad B.

Beiser, Karl. Twenty-Five Ski Tours in Maine: From Kittery to Caribou, A Cross-Country Skiers Guide. LC 79-64992. (Twenty-Five Ski Tours Ser.). (Illus.). 128p. 1979. pap. 5.95 (ISBN 0-89725-006-0). Backcountry Pubns.

Beiser, L., ed. Advances in Laser Scanning & Recording, Vol. 396. 224p. 42.00 (ISBN 0-89252-431-6). Photo-Optical.

Beishenvliyev, S. The Horned Lamb. 22p. 1973. pap. 1.49 (ISBN 0-8285-1160-8, Pub. by Progress Pubs USSR). Imported Pubns.

Beishir, Lois. Microbiology in Practice: Individualized Instruction for the Allied Health Sciences. 3rd ed. 320p. 1982. pap. text ed. 16.50 scp (ISBN 0-06-040587-2, HarpC); instrs'. manual avail. (ISBN 0-06-360636-4). Har-Row.

Beishon. Systems Behavior. 3rd ed. 320p. 1982. text ed. 31.50 (ISBN 0-06-318211-4, Pub. by Har-Row Ltd England); pap. text ed. 15.50 (ISBN 0-06-318212-2, Pub. by Har-Row Ltd England). Har-Row.

Beisly, Sidney. Shakespere's Garden. LC 79-113551. Repr. of 1864 ed. 17.00 (ISBN 0-404-00727-9). AMS Pr.

Beisner, E. Calvin. God in Three Persons. 180p. 1984. pap. 4.95 (ISBN 0-8423-1073-8); 2.95 (ISBN 0-8423-1074-6). Tyndale.

Beisner, Monika. An Address Book: With Riddles, Rhymes, Tales, & Tongue Twisters. (Illus.). 182p. 1979. 6.95 (ISBN 0-374-30053-4). FS&G.

--Book of Riddles. LC 83-81529. (Illus.). 32p. (ps-3). 1983. 11.95 (ISBN 0-374-30866-7). FS&G.

--A Folding Alphabet Book. (Illus.). 1981. 5.95 (ISBN 0-374-32420-4). FS&G.

--Secret Spells & Curious Charms. (Illus.). 32p. (ps up). 1985. 12.95 (ISBN 0-374-36692-6). FS&G.

Beisner, Robert L. From the Old Diplomacy to the New: 1865-1900. LC 74-7001. (American History Ser.). 1975. pap. 8.95x (ISBN 0-88295-702-3). Harlan Davidson.

--Twelve Against Empire: The Anti-Imperialist, 1898-1900. LC 84-24116. 310p. 1985. pap. 9.95 (ISBN 0-226-04171-9). U of Chicago Pr.

Beisser, Arnold R. Mental Health Consultation & Education. 1972. pap. 10.95x (ISBN 0-87484-255-7). Inst Pr.

Beiswinger, George L. One to One: The Story of the Big Brothers-Big Sisters Movement in America. LC 84-20399. (Illus.). 290p. 1985. 15.95 (ISBN 0-9613820-0-7). Big Brothers-Big Sisters.

Beite, A. M. Basic Swedish Grammar. 3rd ed. 1976. 20.00 (ISBN 91-21-01551-1). Heinman.

Beith, Alan. The Case for the Liberal Party & the Alliance. LC 82-17168. pap. 45.50 (ISBN 0-317-08593-X, 2022522). Bks Demand UMI.

Beith, G. A. Edward Carpenter. LC 72-3568. (English Literature Ser., No. 33). 1972. Repr. of 1931 ed. lib. bdg. 43.95x (ISBN 0-8383-1558-5). Haskell.

Beith, Gilbert, ed. Edward Carpenter: An Appreciation. 1979. Repr. of 1931 ed. lib. bdg. 25.00 (ISBN 0-8492-3737-8). R West.

Beit-Hallahmi, B., jt. auth. see Rabin, A. I.

Beit-Hallahmi, Benjamin. Psychoanalysis & Religion. 1978. lib. bdg. 27.50 (ISBN 0-8482-7374-5). Norwood Edns.

Beit-Hallahmi, Benjamin, jt. auth. see Argyle, Michael.

Beith-Halahmi, Esther Y. Angell Fayre or Strumpet Lewd: Jane Shaw as an Example of Erring Beauty in 16th Century Literature, 2 vols. (Salzburg Studies in English Literature, Elizabethan & Renaissance Studies: Nos. 26-27). 361p. 1974. Set. pap. text ed. 50.75x (ISBN 0-391-01322-X). Humanities.

Beitinger, jt. auth. see Zimmerman.

Beitler, Ethel J. & Lockhart, Bill. Design for You. 2nd ed. LC 83-14862. 270p. 1985. Repr. of 1969 ed. lib. bdg. 27.95 (ISBN 0-89874-652-3). Krieger.

Beitler, James F. Moments in Time. (Dorrance Contemporary Poets Ser.). 32p. 1984. pap. 3.95 (ISBN 0-8059-2881-2). Dorrance.

Beitler, L. & McDonald, B. English for the Medical Professions. 1982. 7.24 (ISBN 0-07-004521-6). McGraw.

Beitman, Bernard D. & Klerman, Gerald L., eds. Combining Psychotherapy & Drug Therapy in Clinical Practice. LC 84-14144. 288p. 1984. text ed. 35.00 (ISBN 0-89335-214-4). SP Med & Sci Bks.

Beitman, Hartford. Advertising & Direct Mail for Financial Services Salespeople. Beitman, Kristina, ed. (Illus.). 150p. (Orig.). Date not set. pap. 19.95 (ISBN 0-938630-26-1). ARS Enterprises.

--Recorded Sound. (Illus., Orig.). 1981. pap. text ed. 2.00 (ISBN 0-938630-13-X). ARS Enterprises.

Beitman, Hartford & Beitman, Kristina. Seattle Seating. (Illus.). 110p. (Orig.). 1984. pap. 7.95 (ISBN 0-938630-25-3). ARS Enterprises.

Beitman, Kristina, jt. auth. see Beitman, Hartford.

Beitman, Kristina, ed. see Beitman, Hartford.

Beitman, Morris N. Most-Often-Needed Nineteen Twenty-Six-Nineteen Thirty-Eight Radio Diagrams. pap. 9.95 (ISBN 0-914126-12-1). Vintage Radio.

Beitner, R., ed. Regulation of Carbohydrate Metabolism, 2 vols. 240p. 1985. Set. 65.00 (ISBN 0-8493-5262-2); Set. 73.00 (ISBN 0-8493-5263-0). CRC Pr.

Beitz, Charles, jt. ed. see Kuperberg, Mark.

Beitz, Charles, ed. see Kuperberg, Mark.

Beitz, Charles R. Political Theory & International Relations. LC 79-83976. 212p. 1979. 23.50 (ISBN 0-691-07614-6); pap. 8.50 (ISBN 0-691-02192-9). Princeton U Pr.

Beitz, Charles R., et al, eds. International Ethics. LC 84-42938. (A Philosophy & Public Affairs Reader Ser.). 352p. 1985. text ed. 24.50 (ISBN 0-691-07683-9); pap. 8.95 (ISBN 0-691-02234-8). Princeton U Pr.

Beitz, Donald & Hansen, R. G. Animal Products in Human Nutrition. (Nutrition Foundation Monograph). 1982. 69.50 (ISBN 0-12-086380-4). Acad Pr.

Beitz, Ursula, jt. ed. see LeRoy, Gaylord C.

Beitz, W., jt. auth. see Pahl, G.

Beitzel, Barry J. The Moody Atlas of Bible Lands. 1985. text ed. 29.95 (ISBN 0-8024-0438-3). Moody.

Beitzel, Wallace, jt. auth. see Harter, James.

Beitzell, Robert, ed. Tehran-Yalta-Potsdam: The Soviet Protocols. (Russian Ser.: Vol. 17). 25.00 (ISBN 0-87569-013-0). Academic Intl.

Beitzinger, Alfons J. Edward G. Ryan: Lion of the Law. LC 59-6307. (Illus.). 214p. 1960. pap. 7.50 (ISBN 0-87020-002-X). State Hist Soc Wis.

Beizer, Boris. The Architecture & Engineering of Digital Computer Computers, Vols. 1 & 2. LC 71-141244. 1971. Vol. 1, 394p. 59.50x (ISBN 0-306-37151-0, Plenum Pr); Vol. 2, 453 P. 65.00x (ISBN 0-306-37152-9). Plenum Pub.

--Micro-Analysis of Computer System Performance. (Illus.). 340p. 1978. 24.50 (ISBN 0-442-20663-1). Van Nos Reinhold.

--Software Systems Testing & Quality Assurance. (Electrical, Computer Science & Engineering Ser.). (Illus.). 384p. 1984. 34.50 (ISBN 0-442-21306-9). Van Nos Reinhold.

--Software Testing Techniques. (Electrical-Computer Science & Engineering Ser.). 300p. 1982. 29.95 (ISBN 0-442-24592-0). Van Nos Reinhold.

Beja, Morris. Critical Essays on Virginia Woolf. (Critical Essays Ser.). 1985. lib. bdg. 35.00 (ISBN 0-8161-8753-3). G K Hall.

Beja, Morris & Gontarski, S. E., eds. Samuel Beckett: Humanistic Perspectives. LC 82-12468. (Illus.). 227p. 1983. 20.00 (ISBN 0-8142-0334-5). Ohio St U Pr.

Bejan, Adrian. Convection Heat Transfer. LC 84-3583. 477p. 1984. text ed. 39.95x (ISBN 0-471-89612-8, Pub. by Wiley-Interscience). Wiley.

--Entropy Generation Through Heat & Fluid Flow. LC 82-8414. 248p. 1982. 44.95x (ISBN 0-471-09438-2, Pub. by Wiley-Interscience). Wiley.

Bejar, Isaac I. Achievement Testing. LC 83-50514. 88p. 1983. pap. text ed. 5.00 (ISBN 0-8039-2047-4). Sage.

Bejarano & Sanchez. Obligaciones Civiles. 2nd ed. 608p. (Span.). 1983. pap. text ed. write for info (ISBN 0-06-310066-5, Pub. by HarLA Mexico). Har-Row.

Bejarano, Manuel. Obligaciones Civiles. (Span.). 1980. pap. text ed. 16.20 (ISBN 0-06-310063-0, Pub. by HarLA Mexico). Har-Row.

Bejel, Emilio & Panico, Marie J. Huellas-Footprints. LC 82-71933. 122p. (Span. & Eng.). 1982. pap. 6.50 (ISBN 0-935318-07-0). Edins Hispamerica.

Bejerot, Nils. Addiction: An Artificially Induced Drive. (Illus.). 96p. 1972. 13.50x (ISBN 0-398-02527-4). C C Thomas.

--Addiction & Society. (Illus.). 272p. 1970. 27.50x (ISBN 0-398-00126-X). C C Thomas.

Bejin, Andre, jt. auth. see Aries, Philippe.

Bejing Language Institute. New Chinese Three Hundred. (C & T Asian Language Ser.). 351p. Boxed Set. incl. 3 cassettes 35.00x (ISBN 0-88727-002-6). Cheng & Tsui.

Beju, I. Spinor & Non-Euclidean Tensor Calculus with Applications. 267p. 1983. 44.00 (ISBN 0-9961006-8-7, Pub. by Abacus England). Heyden.

Bek, Lilla, jt. auth. see Wilson, Annie.

Beke, B. The Process of Fine Grinding. 1981. 29.50 (ISBN 90-247-2462-7, Pub. by Martinus Nijhoff Netherlands). Kluwer Academic.

Beke, C. T; see Royal Geography Society.

Beke, D. L., jt. ed. see Kedves, F. J.

Bekefi, George. Electromagnetic Vibrations, Waves, & Radiation. Barrett, Alan H., ed. LC 77-10421. 1978. pap. text ed. 27.50x (ISBN 0-262-52047-8). MIT Pr.

--Principles of Laser Plasmas. LC 76-28311. 736p. 1976. 76.95x (ISBN 0-471-06345-2, Pub. by Wiley-Interscience). Wiley.

Bekemeier, H., ed. Trends in Inflammation Research Two. Hirschelmann, R. (Agents & Actions Supplements: Vol. 10). 315p. 1982. text ed. 39.95 (ISBN 0-8176-1344-7). Birkhauser.

Beken, Frank & Beken, Keith. The Beauty of Sail, with One Hundred Full Page Photos of Yachts. text ed. 139.95 (ISBN 0-8490-1483-2). Gordon Pr.

Beken, Keith, jt. auth. see Beken, Frank.

Beken Of Cowes. A Hundred Years of Sail. LC 81-82531. (Illus.). 208p. 1981. 50.00 (ISBN 0-394-52326-1). Knopf.

Beker, Avi. Disarmament Without Order: The Politics of Disarmament at the United Nations. LC 84-6722. (Contributions in Political Science Ser.: No.118). (Illus.). xii, 212p. 1985. lib. bdg. 35.00 (ISBN 0-313-24362-X, BDW/). Greenwood.

Beker, Gisela & Rosenwald, Carol. The Personals. 144p. 1985. pap. 2.95 (ISBN 0-8217-1512-7). Zebra.

Beker, H. J. & Piper, F. C. Secure Speech Communications: A Monograph. (Microelectronics & Signal Processing Ser.). Date not set. 39.50 (ISBN 0-12-084780-9). Acad Pr.

Beker, Henry & Piper, Fred. Cipher Systems: The Protection of Communications. 427p. 1984. 40.50 (ISBN 0-471-89192-4, Pub. by Wiley-Interscience). Wiley.

Beker, J. Christiaan. Paul's Apocalyptic Gospel. LC 82-8670. 128p. (Orig.). 1982. pap. 7.95 (ISBN 0-8006-1649-9, 1-1649). Fortress.

Beker, J. Christian. Paul the Apostle: The Triumph of God in Life & Thought. LC 79-8904. 468p. 1980. pap. 14.95 (ISBN 0-8006-1811-4). Fortress.

Beker, Jerome, jt. auth. see Willie, Charles V.

Beker, Jerome, jt. ed. see Eisikovits, Zvi.

Beker, Jerome, et al. Critical Incidents in Child Care: A Case Book for Child Care Workers. LC 74-174272. (Clinical Applications Ser). 375p. 1972. text ed. 29.95 (ISBN 0-87705-061-9); pap. 12.95 (ISBN 0-87705-074-0). Human Sci Pr.

Beker, Simon, ed. Diagnostic Procedures in the Evaluation of Hepatic Diseases. LC 82-20324. (Laboratory & Research Methods in Biology & Medicine Ser.: Vol. 7). 646p. 1983. 96.00 (ISBN 0-8451-1656-8). A R Liss.

Beker G., Simon, jt. auth. see Grases, Pedro J.

Bekerman, Gerard. Marx & Engels: A Conceptual Concordance. Carver, Terrell, tr. LC 83-11931. 238p. 1983. 33.50x (ISBN 0-389-20427-7, BNB 07313). B&N Imports.

Bekessy, Emery. Barabbas. Repr. lib. bdg. 17.95x (ISBN 0-89190-574-X, Pub. by River City Pr). Amereon Ltd.

Bekesy, G. Von see Von Bekesy, George.

Bekey, G. A., jt. auth. see IFAC Symposium, 6th, Washington, DC, June 1982.

Bekey, Ivan, ed. Permanent Presence - Making It Work. (Science & Technology Ser.: Vol. 60). (Illus.). 190p. (Orig.). 1985. lib. bdg. 40.00 (ISBN 0-87703-207-6, Pub by Am Astro Soc); pap. text ed. 30.00 (ISBN 0-87703-208-4). Univelt Inc.

--Permanent Presence-Making It Work: Twenty-Second Goddard Memorial Symposium, Mar. 15-16, 1984 Greenbelt, MD. (Science & Technology Ser.: Vol. 60). 190p. 1985. 40.00 (ISBN 0-317-27277-2); pap. 30.00 (ISBN 0-317-27278-0). Univelt Inc.

Bekhtereva, Natal'ia P. Biopotentials of Cerebral Hemispheres in Brain Tumors. Haigh, Basil, tr. LC 61-17724. (International Behavioral Sciences Ser.). pap. 47.80 (ISBN 0-317-09877-2, 2020644). Bks Demand UMI.

Bekiroglu, Haluk, ed. Computer Models for Production & Inventory Control, Vol. 12 No. 2. 1984. 30.00 (ISBN 0-318-01063-1). Soc Computer Sim.

--Simulation in Inventory & Production Control. 63p. 1983. softbound 20.00 (ISBN 0-686-42972-9). Soc Computer Sim.

Bekis, A. see Halpern, M., et al.

Bekkari, Muhammad, tr. see Badawi, Gamal.

Bekken, O. B., et al, eds. Spaces of Analytic Functions. (Lecture Notes in Mathematics Ser.: Vol. 512). 1976. pap. 16.00 (ISBN 0-387-07682-4). Springer-Verlag.

Bekker, Balthasar. The World Bewitch'd; or, an Examination of the Common Opinions Concerning Spirits. LC 79-8093. Repr. of 1695 ed. 30.00 (ISBN 0-404-18404-9). AMS Pr.

Bekker, Cajus. Hitler's Naval War. (YA) 1981. pap. 2.75 (ISBN 0-89083-759-7). Zebra.

--The Luftwaffe War Diaries. Ziegler, Frank, tr. 608p. 1975. pap. 3.95 (ISBN 0-345-28799-1). Ballantine.

Bekker, Hugo. Andreas Gryphius: Poet Between Epochs. (Canadian Studies in German Language & Literature: Vol. 10). 83p. 1973. pap. 11.75 (ISBN 3-261-00770-2). P Lang Pubs.

--Friedrich Von Hausen: Inquiries into His Poetry. (Studies in Germanic Languages & Literatures: No. 87). x, 159p. 1977. 12.95x (ISBN 0-8078-8087-6). U of NC Pr.

Bekker, L. J. De see De Bekker, L. J.

Bekker, Paul. Beethoven. Bozman, M. M., tr. LC 75-175938. (BCL Ser. I). (Illus.). 391p. 1972. Repr. of 1925 ed. 34.50 (ISBN 0-404-00728-7). AMS Pr.

--The Changing Opera. Mendel, Arthur, tr. LC 80-2256. Repr. of 1935 ed. 35.50 (ISBN 0-404-18803-6). AMS Pr.

--Jacques Offenbach. LC 74-24039. Repr. of 1909 ed. 14.50 (ISBN 0-404-12862-9). AMS Pr.

--Orchestra. (Illus.). 1963. pap. 4.95 (ISBN 0-393-00219-5, Norton Lib). Norton.

--Richard Wagner: His Life in His Work. facsimile ed. Bozman, M. M., tr. LC 70-107792. (Select Bibliographies Reprint Ser). 1931. 32.00 (ISBN 0-8369-5176-X). Ayer Co Pubs.

--Richard Wagner: His Life in His Work. Bozman, M. M., tr. LC 74-106713. Repr. of 1931 ed. lib. bdg. 20.50x (ISBN 0-8371-3443-9, BERW). Greenwood.

--Story of Music: An Historical Sketch of the Changes in Musical Form. LC 74-124592. (BCL Ser. I). (Illus.). 1970. Repr. of 1927 ed. 22.50 (ISBN 0-404-00729-5). AMS Pr.

Bekker, W. G. Historical & Critical Review of Samuel Butlers' Literary Works. LC 67-8773. (Studies in Fiction, No. 34). 1969. Repr. of 1925 ed. lib. bdg. 47.95x (ISBN 0-8383-0509-1). Haskell.

Bekker-Nielsen, Hans. Old Norse-Icelandic Studies: A Select Bibliography. pap. 23.80 (ISBN 0-317-10304-0, 2019157). Bks Demand UMI.

Bekkum, O. Van see Van Bekkum, O. & De Vries, H.

Beklemishev, V. N. Principles of Comparative Anatomy of Invertebrates, 2 Vols. Kabata, Z., ed. McLennan, J. M., tr. LC 70-97749. 1970. Set. 60.00x (ISBN 0-226-04175-1). U of Chicago Pr.

Bekleshov, D. A. The U. S. S. R. A Guide for Businessmen. 400p. 1978. 7.95 (ISBN 0-8285-0543-8, Pub. by Progress Pubs USSR). Imported Pubns.

Bekoff, Marc, ed. Cayotes: Biology, Behavior & Management. 1978. 55.00 (ISBN 0-12-086050-3). Acad Pr.

Beks, J. W., ed. The Management of Pain. (The Jonxis Lectures Ser.: Vol. 3). 416p. 1980. 47.75 (ISBN 0-444-90109-4, Excerpta Medica). Elsevier.

Beks, J. W., et al, eds. see International Symposium on Intercranial Pressure, U. of Groningen, June 1-3, 1976.

Bektemirov, T. A., jt. auth. see Solov'ev, V. D.

Belack, Allan S., jt. ed. see Hersen, Micheal.

Belady, L. A., jt. ed. see Maekawa, M.

Belafonte, Dennis & Marill, Alvin H. The Films of Tyrone Power. (Illus.). 1979. 14.95 (ISBN 0-8065-0477-3); pap. 7.95 (ISBN 0-686-85804-2). Citadel Pr.

Belaief, Gail. Spinoza's Philosophy of Law. LC 78-118275. (Studies in Philosophy: No. 24). (Illus.). 151p. (Orig.). 1971. pap. text ed. 12.00x (ISBN 90-2791-851-1). Mouton.

Belaief, Lynne. Toward a Whiteheadian Ethics. LC 84-15248. 208p. (Orig.). 1985. lib. bdg. 23.50 (ISBN 0-8191-4229-8); pap. text ed. 12.50 (ISBN 0-8191-4230-1). U Pr of Amer.

Belair, Richard L. Double Take. 192p. (gr. 8 up). pap. 1.95 (ISBN 0-440-92130-9, LFL). Dell.

Belan, F. Water Treatment: Calculations, Examples, Problems. 293p. 1984. pap. 6.95 (ISBN 0-317-07272-2, Pub. by Mir Pubs USSR). Imported Pubns.

Beland, Bernard. Electricity As a Cause of Fires. 5.35 (ISBN 0-318-03822-6). Society Fire Protect.

Beland, Irene & Passos, Joyce. Clinical Nursing: Pathophysiological & Psychosocial Approaches. 4th ed. 1981. text ed. write for info. (ISBN 0-02-307890-1). Macmillan.

Belanger, Jerome. The Homesteader's Handbook to Raising Small Livestock. Stoner, Carol, ed. LC 73-88254. (Illus.). 256p. 1974. 12.95 (ISBN 0-87857-075-6). Rodale Pr Inc.

Belanger, Jerome D. The Homesteader's Handbook to Raising Small Livestock. LC 73-88254. 1976. pap. 9.95 (ISBN 0-87857-122-1). Rodale Pr Inc.

Belanger, Jerry. Raising Milk Goats the Modern Way. LC 75-3493. (Illus.). 160p. 1975. pap. 5.95 (ISBN 0-88266-062-4). Garden Way Pub.

Belanger, Mel. Ah, Sweet Mystery. (Illus.). 150p. (Orig.). 1983. pap. text ed. 5.00 (ISBN 0-9608146-8-X). Western Sun Pubns.

Belanger, Merlyn. On Religious Maturity. LC 61-15238. 1962. 5.00 (ISBN 0-8022-0090-7). Philos Lib.

Belanger, Terry. Lunacy & the Arrangement of Books. ii, 28p. 1982. pap. 10.00 (ISBN 0-938768-08-5). Oak Knoll.

Belasco, Bernard. The Entrepreneur As Culture Hero: Preadaptations for Nigerian Economic Development. LC 79-10475. (Illus.). 256p. 1980. 27.95. Praeger.

Belasco, Carol W. Motivational Bulletin Boards for Speech & Language. 80p. (Orig.). 1985. pap. text ed. 16.95 (ISBN 0-88450-907-9, 7083-B). Communication Skill.

Belasco, David. Theatre Through Its Stage Door. Defoe, Louis V., ed. LC 69-56534. (Illus.). 1968. Repr. of 1919 ed. 22.00 (ISBN 0-405-08261-4, Blom Pubns). Ayer Co Pubs.

Belasco, James A. & Hampton, David R. Management Today: Wiley Series in Management. 2nd ed. LC 80-28981. 460p. 1981. text ed. 32.45 (ISBN 0-471-08579-0); avail. tchrs. manual. Wiley.

Belasco, Leonard, ed. Northwords. LC 80-85225. 66p. (Orig.). 1981. pap. 12.95 (ISBN 0-915032-23-6). Natl Poet Foun.

Belasco, Simon see Bottiglia, William F.

Belasco, Warren J. Americans on the Road: From Autocamp to Motel, Nineteen Ten to Nineteen Forty-Five. (Illus.). 1979. 27.50x (ISBN 0-262-02123-4); pap. 8.95x (ISBN 0-262-52071-0). MIT Pr.

Belash, C. A. Braiding & Knotting: Techniques & Projects. LC 74-75266. 1974. pap. 2.75 (ISBN 0-486-23059-7). Dover.

Belash, Constantine A. Braiding & Knotting: Techniques & Projects. (Illus.). 13.50 (ISBN 0-8446-5002-1). Peter Smith.

Belash, Rachel P., tr. see Almendros, Nestor.

Belaunde, Victor A. Bolivar & the Political Thought of the Spanish-American Revolution. 1967. lib. bdg. 31.50x (ISBN 0-374-90532-0). Octagon.

Belaval, Domitila, jt. ed. see Nash, Rose.

Belaval, Yvon. Histoire de la Philosophie: De la Renaissance a la Revolution, Vol. 2. (Historique Ser.). 1168p. 48.95 (ISBN 0-686-56455-3). French & Eur.

--Histoire de la Philosophie: Du XIX Siecle a nos Jours, Vol. 3. (Historique Ser.). 1408p. 52.50 (ISBN 0-686-56456-1). French & Eur.

--Philosophers & Their Language. Guterman, Norbert, tr. LC 66-18481. pap. 39.30 (ISBN 0-317-08951-X, 2005230). Bks Demand UMI.

Belbase, Lekh, et al. A Selected Annotated Bibliography of Vocational Education: Planning & Implementaion in Developing Countries, with Special Reference to Nepal. 1982. 8.00 (ISBN 0-318-04180-4). Am-Nepal Ed.

--A Selected Annotated Bibliography of Vocational Education (Planning & Implementation) in Developing Countries, with Special Reference to Nepal. 49p. 1982. 8.00 (ISBN 0-318-17076-0, 48). Am-Nepal Ed.

Belbase, Lekh N. Planning & Implementing Vocational Education in Nepal. 326p. 1981. 30.00 (ISBN 0-318-12884-5, 41). Am-Nepal Ed.

Belben, Howard. The Mission of Jesus. 96p. 1985. pap. 4.95 (ISBN 0-89109-529-2). NavPress.

Belbin, R. M. Management Teams: Why They Succeed or Fail. 179p. 1981. 26.95x (ISBN 0-470-27172-8). Halsted Pr.

Belch, Jean, ed. Contemporary Games: A Directory & Bibliography Describing Play Situations or Simulations, Vol. 1: Directory. LC 72-6353. 1973. 100.00x (ISBN 0-8103-0968-8). Gale.

--Contemporary Games: A Directory & Bibliography Describing Play Situations or Simulations, Vol. 2. LC 72-6353. 1974. 90.00x (ISBN 0-8103-0969-6). Gale.

Belchem, David. Victory in Normandy. (Illus.). 192p. 1981. 26.00 (ISBN 0-7011-2546-2, Pub. by Chatto & Windus). Merrimack Pub Cir.

Belcher, et al. Humanities: Life Styles & Human Values, Vol. 3. 376p. 1983. pap. text ed. 25.95 (ISBN 0-8403-2924-5). Kendall-Hunt.

Belcher, Bill. Wind-Vane Self-Steering. LC 81-85260. (Illus.). 128p. 1982. 16.95 (ISBN 0-87742-158-7). Intl Marine.

Belcher, C. David, III, et al. Photocoagulation for Glaucoma & Anterior Segment Disease. 254p. 1984. lib. bdg. 46.50 (ISBN 0-683-00611-8). Williams & Wilkins.

Belcher, Carol, jt. auth. see Belcher, Lee.

Belcher, David W. Compensation Administration. (Industrial Relations & Personnel Ser). (Illus.). 576p. 1974. ref. ed. 28.95 (ISBN 0-13-154161-7). P-H.

Belcher, Diana. The Mutineers of the Bounty & Their Descendants in Pitcairn & Norfolk Islands. LC 75-3439. Repr. of 1870 ed. 34.50 (ISBN 0-404-14443-8). AMS Pr.

Belcher, E. A. see Gunn, Hugh.

Belcher, Edward & Simpkinson, F. G. H. M. S. Sulphur on the Northwest & California Coasts: 1837 & 1839. Pierce, Richard A., ed. (Alaska History Ser.: No. 12). (Illus.). 1979. 15.50x (ISBN 0-919642-65-9). Limestone Pr.

Belcher, Edward R. Notes on Cole's Hill. (Pilgrim Society Notes Ser.: No. 1). 1954. 1.00 (ISBN 0-940628-25-2). Pilgrim Hall.

Belcher, Finley E. & Stickney, Clyde P. Business Combinations & Consolidated Financial Statements. 1983. pap. 18.95x (ISBN 0-256-02788-9). Irwin.

Belcher, George F., jt. auth. see Aumonier, Stacy.

Belcher, J. A., ed. Sign Language Dot-to-Dot. new ed. 32p. (ps-3). 1979. 2.95 (ISBN 0-917002-40-7). Joyce Media.

Belcher, J. R. & Sturridge, M. F. Thoracic Surgical Management. 4th ed. (Illus.). 1982. pap. text ed. 14.50 (ISBN 0-7216-0703-9, Pub. by Bailliere-Tindall). Saunders.

Belcher, James O., jt. auth. see Norton, Robert E.

Belcher, John G., Jr. The Productivity Management Process. (Research Ser.). 65p. 1983. pap. 8.00 (ISBN 0-912841-01-X, 06). Planning Forum.

Belcher, Lady The Mutineers of the Bounty & Their Descendants in Pitcairn. 75.00 (ISBN 0-87968-342-2). Gordon Pr.

Belcher, Lee & Belcher, Carol. Reaching Our Jewish Friends. (Truthway Ser.). 79p. (Orig.). 1981. pap. text ed. 1.50 (ISBN 0-87148-735-7). Pathway Pr.

Belcher, R., ed. Instrumental Organic Elemental Analysis. 1978. 59.50 (ISBN 0-12-085950-5). Acad Pr.

Belcher, Richard P. Layman's Guide to the Inerrancy Debate. LC 79-27015. 1980. pap. 2.95 (ISBN 0-8024-2379-5). Moody.

Belcher, Supply. The Harmony of Maine. Hitchcock, H. Wiley, ed. LC 77-169607. (Earlier American Music Ser: Vol. 6). 104p. 1972. Repr. of 1794 ed. lib. bdg. 22.50 (ISBN 0-306-77306-6). Da Capo.

Belcher, Wyatt W. Economic Rivalry Between St. Louis & Chicago, 1850-1880. LC 68-58548. (Columbia University Studies in the Social Sciences: No. 529). Repr. of 1947 ed. 19.50 (ISBN 0-404-51529-0). AMS Pr.

Belchetz, P. Management of Pituitary Disease. 537p. 1984. 59.95 (ISBN 0-471-81896-8). Wiley.

Beld, Scott G., et al. The Tablets of Ebla: Concordance & Bibliography. 70p. (Orig.). 1984. text ed. 6.50x (ISBN 0-931464-21-8). Eisenbrauns.

Belden. Snake Blossoms. 64p. (Orig.). 1976. pap. 3.00 (ISBN 0-917658-06-X). BPW & P.

Belden, Bauman L. Indian Peace Medals Issued in the United States, 1789-1889. LC 66-20865. (Illus.). 1966. 9.50 (ISBN 0-910598-04-5). Flayderman.

Belden, Donald L. The Role of the Buyer in Mass Merchandising. LC 70-181779. (Chain Store Age Bks). (Illus.). 256p. 1971. 15.95 (ISBN 0-86730-510-X). Lebhar Friedman.

Belden, Henry M., ed. Ballads & Songs Collected by the Missouri Folk-Lore Society. 2nd ed. LC 55-7519. 554p. 1955. 22.00x (ISBN 0-8262-0142-3). U of Mo Pr.

Belden, Jack. China Shakes the World. LC 77-105312. 1970. pap. 10.50 (ISBN 0-85345-159-1). Monthly Rev.

--Retreat with Stillwell. (China in the 20th Century Ser). (Illus.). 368p. 1975. Repr. of 1943 ed. lib. bdg. 32.50 (ISBN 0-306-70734-9). Da Capo.

--Still Time to Die. (China in the 20th Century Ser). xi, 322p. 1975. Repr. of 1944 ed. lib. bdg. 32.50 (ISBN 0-306-70735-7). Da Capo.

Belden, L. Burr. Goodbye, Death Valley. (Illus.). 64p. 1975. wrappers 3.95 (ISBN 0-936932-01-5). Death Valley Fortyniners.

--Mines of Death Valley. (Illus.). 1985. wrappers 3.50 (ISBN 0-910856-16-8). La Siesta.

Belden, Louise C. The Festive Tradition: Table Decoration & Desserts in America, 1650-1900. (Winterthur Museum Bk.). (Illus.). 1983. 35.00 (ISBN 0-393-01618-8). Norton.

--Marks of American Silversmiths in the Ineson-Bissell Collection. LC 78-31816. 505p. 1980. 50.00x (ISBN 0-8139-0798-5). U Pr of Va.

Belden, Mary M. Dramatic Work of Samuel Foote. LC 69-15678. (Yale Studies in English Ser.: No. 80). viii, 218p. 1969. Repr. of 1929 ed. 19.50 (ISBN 0-208-00768-7, Archon). Shoe String.

Belden, Wilanne S. Mind-Call. LC 80-18488. 252p. (gr. 5-9). 1981. PLB 9.95 (ISBN 0-689-30796-9, Argo). Atheneum.

--The Rescue of Ranor. LC 82-13806. 192p. (gr. 5-8). 1983. 10.95 (ISBN 0-689-30951-1, Argo). Atheneum.

Belderson, R. H., et al. Sonographs of the Sea Floor: A Picture Atlas. 185p. 1972. 87.25 (ISBN 0-444-40984-X). Elsevier.

Beldiceanu, Nicoara. Les Actes Des Premiers Sultans Conserves Dans le Manuscrits Turcs De la Bibliotheque Nationale a Paris, 2 tomes. Incl. Tome I. Actes De Mehmed II et De Bayezid II Du Ms. Fonds Turc Ancien 39. (No. 3). 1960. pap. 22.00x (ISBN 90-2796-098-4); Tome II. Reglements Miniers, 1390-1512. (No. 8). 1964. pap. 44.00x (ISBN 90-2796-102-6). (Documents et Recherches Sur L'economie Des Pays Byzantins, Islamiques et Slaves et Leurs Relations Commerciales Au Moyen-Age). pap. Mouton.

Beldieeanu, Nicoara. Le Monde Ottoman Des Balkans (1402-1566) Institutions, Societe, Economie. 340p. 1976. 16.00x (ISBN 0-902089-95-1, Pub. by Variorum). State Mutual Bk.

Belding, D. V. Racing Pigeons. 1982. 14.95 (ISBN 0-86230-014-2). Triplegate.

Belding, John A. Cogeneration. Gyftopoulos, Elias P. & Cohen, Karen C., eds. (Industrial Energy-Conservation Manuals: No. 15). (Illus.). 72p. 1982. loose-leaf 20.00x (ISBN 0-262-02170-6). MIT Pr.

Belding, Lyman. Land Birds of the Pacific District. Repr. of 1890 ed. 37.00 (ISBN 0-384-03792-5). Johnson Repr.

Belding, W. G., ed. ASM Handbook of Engineering Mathematics. 1983. 83.00 (ISBN 0-87170-157-X). ASM.

Beldomandi, Prosdocimo de see Prosdocimo de' Beldomandi.

Belendiuk, Arthur & Robb, Scott. Broadcasting Via Satellite: Legal & Business Considerations. 175p. 1979. pap. 40.00 (ISBN 0-941888-01-0). Comm Media.

Belenkii, B. G. & Vilenchik, I. K. Modern Liquid Chromatography of Macromolecules. (Journal of Chromatography Library: Vol. 25). 400p. 1984. 100.00 (ISBN 0-444-42075-4, I-477-83). Elsevier.

Belenson, Aleksandr, ed. Strelets: Sbornik Pervyi. (Illus., Rus.). 1978. 14.00 (ISBN 0-88233-366-6); pap. 6.00 (ISBN 0-88233-374-7). Ardis Pubs.

Beletskii, A. I. Russkii romantizm, Sbornik statei. 152p. Repr. of 1927 ed. cancelled (ISBN 0-88233-963-X). Ardis Pubs.

Belevitskaya, V. S., et al. Exercises in Russian Syntax, 2 Vols. 2nd ed. 588p. (Rus. & Eng.). 1969. Set. 163.25 (ISBN 0-677-21050-7). Gordon.

Beley, Jim, ed. see Galle, Fred & Fell, Derek.

Beley, Jim, ed. see Williams, T. Jeff.

Beleznay, F., et al, eds. New Developments in Semiconductor Physics: Proceedings. (Lecture Notes in Physics: Vol. 122). (Illus.). 276p. 1980. pap. 23.00 (ISBN 0-387-09988-3). Springer-Verlag.

Belf, Miriam, jt. ed. see Corbin, Richard.

Belfast Free Library, ed. see Williamson, Joseph.

Belfer, Nancy. Designing in Batik & Tie Die. LC 72-185461. (Illus.). 128p. 1972. 14.95 (ISBN 0-87192-047-6). Davis Mass.

Belfield, Eversley. The Boer War. (Concise Campaign Ser.). (Illus.). xxvi, 181p. (Orig.). 1975. 18.00 (ISBN 0-208-01568-X, Archon). Shoe String.

Belfield, Robert, jt. auth. see Sagafi-nejad, Tagi.

Belfield, W. O. & Zucker, M. The Very Healthy Cat Book. 264p. 1983. 14.95 (ISBN 0-07-004367-1); pap. 6.95 (ISBN 0-07-004354-X). McGraw.

Belfield, Wendel & Zucker, Martin. How to Have a Healthier Dog. 1982. pap. 3.50 (ISBN 0-451-12585-1, Sig). NAL.

Belfield, Wendel & Zulker, Martin. How to Have a Healthier Dog: The Benefits of Vitamins & Minerals for Your Dog's Life Cycles. LC 80-1081. 288p. 1981. 13.50 (ISBN 0-385-15992-7). Doubleday.

Belfiglio, Cav V. Best of Italian Cooking, Texas Style: Cav Valentine. 104p. 1985. 11.95 (ISBN 0-89015-459-7). Eakin Pubns.

Belfiglio, Cavaliere V. The Italian Experience in Texas. (Illus.). 264p. 1983. 12.95 (ISBN 0-89015-380-9). Eakin Pubns.

Belfiglio, Jeff, et al. Hazardous Waste Disposal Sites: A Handbook for Public Input & Review. LC 82-121857. x, 168p. 1981. 10.00. Stanford Enviro.

Belfiglio, Valentine J. American Foreign Policy. 2nd ed. (Illus.). 152p. 1983. pap. text ed. 11.25 (ISBN 0-8191-2677-2). U Pr of Amer.

Belfiore, F. Enzyme Regulation & Metabolic Diseases. (Illus.). xxiv, 880p. 1981. 106.00 (ISBN 3-8055-0005-X). S Karger.

--New Events & Facts in Diabetes. (Frontiers in Diabetes: Vol. 2). (Illus.). x, 190p. 1982. 48.70 (ISBN 3-8055-3541-4). S Karger.

--Reviewed Contents of Major Diabetes Congresses. (Frontiers in Diabetes: Vol. 1). xii, 162p. 1981. 38.00 (ISBN 3-8055-3414-0). S Karger.

Belfiore, F. & Iannello, Silvia. Advances in World Diabetes Research. (Frontiers in Diabetes Ser.: Vol. 5). x, 258p. 1984. 70.25 (ISBN 3-8055-3810-3). S Karger.

Belfiore, F. & Galton, D. J., eds. Diabetes Mellitus: Etiopathogenesis & Metabolic Aspects. (Frontiers in Diabetes: Vol. 4). (Illus.). x, 282p. 1984. 90.25 (ISBN 3-8055-3771-9). S Karger.

Belfiore, F. Catania. Current Diabetology. (Frontiers in Diabetes: Vol. 6). x, 190p. 1985. 55.50 (ISBN 3-8055-4029-9). S Karger.

Belford & Dunlap. Mauser Self Loading Pistol. 18.50 (ISBN 0-87505-108-1). Borden.

Belford, G. & Liu, C. L. Pascal. (Illus.). 384p. 1984. pap. 23.95 (ISBN 0-07-038138-0). McGraw.

Belford, Lee A., ed. Religious Dimensions in Literature. 160p. (Orig.). 1982. pap. 6.95 (ISBN 0-8164-2360-1, Pub. by Seabury). Winston Pr.

Belford, William J. Special Ministers of the Eucharist. 1979. pap. 1.95 (ISBN 0-916134-39-3). Pueblo Pub Co.

Belfort, Anne Marie, jt. auth. see Camard, Jean Pierre.

Belfort, Georges. Synthetic Membrane Process: Fundamentals & Water Applications. LC 83-2654. (Water Pollution Ser.). 1984. 72.50 (ISBN 0-12-085480-5). Acad Pr.

Belfort, Georges, jt. ed. see Myers, Alan L.

Belforte, David. International Laser Processing Conference: Proceedings, Vol.30. 448p. 1981. 30.00 (ISBN 0-912035-05-6). Laser Inst.

Belforte, David A., ed. Industrial Laser Materials Processing Bibliography, 5 vols. 4th ed. 500p. 1985. pap. text ed. 145.00 (ISBN 0-916389-05-7). Belforte Assoc.

Belforte, G., ed. see CISM (International Center for Mechanical Sciences).

Belfour, A. O., ed. Twelfth-Century Homilies in Ms. Bodley 343, Pt. I: Text. (EETS OS Ser.: Vol. 131). pap. 15.00 (ISBN 0-317-16542-9). Kraus Repr.

Belfrage, Cedric. Promised Land. Kupelnick, Bruce S., ed. LC 76-52089. (Classics of Film Literature Ser.). 1978. lib. bdg. 24.00 (ISBN 0-8240-2865-1). Garland Pub.

Belfrage, Cedric & Aronson, James. Something to Guard: The Stormy Life of the National Guardian. LC 78-3530. 362p. 1978. 40.00x (ISBN 0-231-04510-7). Columbia U Pr.

Belfrage, Cedric, tr. see Fraginals, Manuel M.

Belfrage, Cedric, tr. see Fraginals, Manuel Moreno.

Belfrage, Cedric, tr. see Galeano, Eduardo.

Belfrage, Cedric, tr. see Quintero-Rivera, Angel.

Belfrage, Cedric, tr. see Selser, Gregorio.

Belfrage, Cedric, tr. see Silen, Juan A.

Belgardt, Raimund. Romantische Poesie. (Ger). 1970. text ed. 37.20x (ISBN 90-2791-248-3). Mouton.

Belgatom. Nuclear Fuel Supply Industry in the European Community. 141p. 85.00x (ISBN 0-686-97540-5, Pub. by Graham & Trotman England). State Mutual Bk.

Belgatom, ed. Nuclear Fuel Supply Industry in the European Community. 194p. 1983. pap. 35.00x (ISBN 0-8448-1424-5). Crane-Russak Co.

Bel Geddes, Norman. Horizons. LC 72-92. (Select Bibliographies Reprint Ser). 1972. Repr. of 1932 ed. 53.25 (ISBN 0-8369-9954-1). Ayer Co Pubs.

--Horizons. (Illus.). 16.50 (ISBN 0-8446-5554-6). Peter Smith.

Belgic Confession Translation Committee. Service Book, Part Six: Belgic Confession. 45p. (Orig.). 1984. pap. 0.60 (ISBN 0-933140-92-4). Bd of Pubns CRC.

Belgion, Montgomery. Human Parrot, & Other Essays. facs. ed. LC 67-22056. (Essay Index Reprint Ser). 1931. 17.00 (ISBN 0-8369-0184-3). Ayer Co Pubs.

Belgion, Montgomery, tr. see De Rougement, Denis.

Belgion, Montgomery, tr. see De Rougemont, Denis.

Belgium. Parliament. Library. Catalogue Systematique de la Bibliotheque de la Chambre des Representants, 2 vols. in 1. LC 68-57256. (Bibliography & Reference Ser.: No. 223). (Fr). 1968. Repr. of 1847 ed. 43.00 (ISBN 0-8337-0218-1). B Franklin.

Belgrado, Fernando D., ed. Songs of the Synagogue of Florence, 2 vols. Incl. Vol. 1. The Three Festivals (ISBN 0-87203-108-X); Vol. 2. The High Holy Days. 0p (ISBN 0-87203-109-8). (Illus.). 60p. 1982. 32.95 ea. Hermon.

Belgrano, Giovanni. Let's Make a Movie. LC 72-90235. (Illus.). 48p. (gr. 4-9). 1973. 7.95 (ISBN 0-87592-028-4). Scroll Pr.

Belgrave, Charles. The Pirate Coast. (Arab Background Ser.). 14.00x (ISBN 0-86685-003-1). Intl Bk Ctr.

Belgrave, Dorothy M. & Hart, Hilda. Tales & Legends from India. 1977. lib. bdg. 25.00 (ISBN 0-8495-0314-0). Arden Lib.

Belgrave, Robert. Energy: Two Decades of Crisis. 400p. 1983. text ed. 42.00x (ISBN 0-566-00612-X). Gower Pub Co.

--Oil Supply & Price: Future Crisis Management. (Atlantic Papers: No. 48). 32p. (Orig.). 1982. pap. text ed. 6.50x (ISBN 0-86598-115-9, ARO 03914). Allanheld.

Belgrave, Robert & Cornell, Margaret. Energy Self-Sufficiency for the U. K. 200p. 1985. text ed. write for info. (ISBN 0-566-00992-7). Gower Pub Co.

Belgum, David. Religion & Personality in the Spiral of Life. LC 79-66478. 1979. pap. text ed. 14.00 (ISBN 0-8191-0832-4). U Pr of Amer.

Belhayes, Iris. Spirit Guides: We Are not Alone. (Inner Visions Ser.). 180p. (Orig.). 1985. pap. 9.95 (ISBN 0-917086-80-5). A C S Pubns Inc.

Beliaev, V. M. Central Asian Music: Essays in the History of the Music of the Peoples of the USSR. Slobin, Mark, ed. Slobin, Greta N., tr. from Rus. LC 74-5913. 340p. 1975. 36.00x (ISBN 0-8195-4083-8). Wesleyan U Pr.

Belic, Z. The Endless Search. 1984. 22.00x (ISBN 0-317-14513-4, Pub. by Selecteditions). State Mutual Bk.

Belin, David. Why Choose Judaism: New Dimensions of Jewish Outreach. 32p. 1985. pap. text ed. 4.00 (ISBN 0-8074-0302-4, 381900). UAHC.

Belin, Jean P. Commerce des Livres Prohibes a Paris de 1750 a 1789. (Illus.). 1962. Repr. of 1913 ed. 19.00 (ISBN 0-8337-0219-X). B Franklin.

--Mouvement philosophique de 1748 a 1789. 1962. Repr. of 1913 ed. 23.50 (ISBN 0-8337-0220-3). B Franklin.

Belin, M. A. Histoire de la Latinite de Constantinople. 2nd ed. R. P. Arsene de Chatel, ed. 547p. (Fr.). Repr. of 1895 ed. lib. bdg. 95.00x (ISBN 0-89241-166-X). Caratzas.

Belin, Peter. Horology on the Half-Shell. LC 78-55929. (Illus.). 77p. 1978. 12.50 (ISBN 0-8048-1482-1). C E Tuttle.

Belina, Tom, et al. Electing the President. (Electing the President Ser.). (Illus.). 64p. (gr. 9 up). 1983. pap. text ed. 3.50 (ISBN 0-88102-013-3). Janus Bks.

Belina, Virginia S. Planning for Your Own Apartment. (gr. 7-12). 1975. pap. 5.00 (ISBN 0-8224-5420-3); tchrs manual free (ISBN 0-8224-5421-1). Pitman Learning.

Belinfante, F. J. Measurements of Time Reversal in Objective Quantum Theory. 1975. text ed. 22.00 (ISBN 0-08-018152-X). Pergamon.

--Survey of Hidden Variables Theories. 376p. 1973. Pergamon.

Belinfante, J. G. F. & Kolman, B. A Survey of Lie Groups & Lie Algebras. LC 72-77081. ix, 164p. 1972. 19.50 (ISBN 0-89871-044-8). Soc Indus-Appl Math.

Beling, Willard A., ed. King Faisal & the Modernisation of Saudi Arabia. LC 79-5134. 1979. 36.00x (ISBN 0-89158-693-8). Westview.

--Role of Labor in African Nation-Building. 15.00 (ISBN 0-685-37307-X). Univ Place.

Belinskii, Vissarion G. Selected Philosophical Works. LC 79-2893. li, 552p. 1981. Repr. of 1948 ed. 48.00 (ISBN 0-8305-0061-8). Hyperion Conn.

Belisle, Bertrand. The Myths of Satan. 64p. 1982. 6.95 (ISBN 0-89962-284-4). Todd & Honeywell.

Belisle, Monique. Cooking Yankee with a French Accent. 1985. pap. write for info. (ISBN 0-89272-207-X). Down East.

Belisle, Serge, jt. ed. see Barwin, Norman B.

Belitt, Ben. The Double Witness: Poems, 1970-1976. LC 77-2534. (Princeton Series of Contemporary Poets). 1977. 13.00 (ISBN 0-691-06346-X); pap. 5.95 (ISBN 0-691-01341-1). Princeton U Pr.

--The Enemy Joy: New & Selected Poems. LC 64-15805. 1964. pap. 1.95 (ISBN 0-226-04192-1, PP2, Phoen). U of Chicago Pr.

--Nowhere but Light. LC 70-108879. 1970. pap. 1.95 (ISBN 0-226-04195-6, PP14, Phoen). U of Chicago Pr.

Belitt, Ben, ed. & tr. see Neruda, Pablo.

Belitt, Ben, ed. & intro. by see Neruda, Pablo.

Belitt, Ben, ed. & tr. see Neruda, Pablo.

Belitt, Ben, tr. see Garcia Lorca, Federico.

Belitt, Ben, tr. see Machado, Antonio.

Belitt, Ben, tr. see Neruda, Pablo.

Belitt, Ben, tr. see Rimbaud, Jean N.

Belitzky, B., tr. see Pavlov, Boris & Terentyev, A.

Beliveau, Andre, jt. auth. see French, Richard.

Beljame, Alexandre. Men of Letters & the English Public in the 18th Century: 1660-1744, Dryden, Addison, Pope. Dobree, Bonamy, ed. Lormier, E. O., tr. LC 71-159815. 1971. Repr. of 1948 ed. 59.00 (ISBN 0-403-03645-3). Scholarly.

Beljanski, M. The Regulation of DNA Replication & Transcription. (Experimental Biology & Medicine Series: Vol. 8). (Illus.). x, 190p. 1983. pap. 53.25 (ISBN 3-8055-3631-3). S Karger.

Belk, Fred R. The Great Trek of the Russian Mennonites to Central Asia. LC 75-28340. (Studies in Anabaptist & Mennonite History: No. 18). pap. 63.00 (ISBN 0-317-26601-2, 2025418). Bks Demand UMI.

Belk, J. A., jt. auth. see Peapell, P. N.

Belk, J. A., ed. Electron Microscopy & Microanalysis of Crystalline Materials. (Illus.). 240p. 1979. 40.75 (ISBN 0-85334-816-2, Pub. by Elsevier Applied Sci England). Elsevier.

Belk, Russell W., ed. Advances in Nonprofit Marketing, Vol. 1. 1985. 47.50 (ISBN 0-89232-254-3). Jai Pr.

Belk, Russell W., jt. ed. see Gardner, David M.

Belk, Russell W., et al. AMA Educators' Proceedings, 1984. LC 84-9240. (Illus.). 431p. (Orig.). 1984. pap. 30.00 (ISBN 0-87757-169-4). Am Mktg.

Belkaoui, Ahmed. Accounting Theory. 2nd ed. 484p. 1985. text ed. 28.95x (ISBN 0-15-500472-7, HC); solutions manual avail. (ISBN 0-15-500473-5). HarBraceJ.

--Conceptual Foundations of Management Accounting. LC 80-16086. (A-W Paperback Series in Accounting). 125p. 1980. pap. 10.50 (ISBN 0-201-00097-0). Addison-Wesley.

--Cost Accounting: A Multidimensional Emphasis. 656p. 1983. text ed. 37.95x (ISBN 0-03-061121-0); solutions manual 21.95 (ISBN 0-03-061122-9). Dryden Pr.

--Industrial Bonds & the Rating Process. LC 83-4600. (Illus.). xii, 198p. 1983. lib. bdg. 35.00 (ISBN 0-89930-046-4, BEB/, Quorum). Greenwood.

--International Accounting: Issues & Solutions. LC 84-11514. (Illus.). xiv, 364p. 1985. lib. bdg. 39.95 (ISBN 0-89930-089-8, BLN/, Quorum). Greenwood.

--Public Policy & the Practice & the Problems of Accounting. LC 85-3568. (Illus.). 224p. 1985. lib. bdg. 35.00 (ISBN 0-89930-105-3, BIF/, Quorum Bks.). Greenwood.

--Socio-Economic Accounting. LC 83-17682. (Illus.). xii, 324p. 1984. lib. bdg. 39.95 (ISBN 0-89930-065-0, BSE, Quorum). Greenwood.

Belker, L. The First Time Manager. 1983. pap. 6.95 (ISBN 0-8144-7588-4). AMACOM.

Belker, Loren B. The First-Time Manager. LC 78-12993. 1979. 14.95 (ISBN 0-8144-5492-5). AMACOM.

--Organizing for Political Victory. LC 82-7855. 208p. 1982. 18.95x (ISBN 0-88229-727-9); pap. 10.95x (ISBN 0-88229-817-8). Nelson-Hall.

--The Successful Secretary: You, Your Boss, & the Job. LC 81-66239. pap. 56.00 (ISBN 0-317-26943-7, 2023590). Bks Demand UMI.

Belkin, G. S. Twelve-Hour Basic for the IBM PC Compatibles. 240p. 1985. price not set (ISBN 0-07-004374-4). McGraw.

Belkin, Gary S. Contemporary Psychotherapies. 1981. pap. 20.95 (ISBN 0-395-30781-3). HM.

--Counseling: Directions in Theory & Practice. LC 73-92087. 1976. perfect bdg. 8.95 (ISBN 0-8403-1446-9). Kendall-Hunt.

--Getting Published: A Guide for Business People & Other Professionals. LC 83-6924. (Wiley Self-Teaching Guides Ser.). 210p. 1983. (Pub. by Wiley Pr); pap. 8.95 (ISBN 0-471-89338-2). Wiley.

--How to Start & Run Your Own Word Processing Business. LC 83-21691. (Small Business Ser.: 1-382). 206p. 1984. pap. 9.95 (ISBN 0-471-88396-4, Pub. by Wiley Pr). Wiley.

--Introduction to Counseling. 2nd ed. 624p. 1984. pap. text ed. write for info (ISBN 0-697-06070-5). Wm C Brown.

--Perspectives in Educational Psychology. 700p. 1979. pap. text ed. write for info. (ISBN 0-697-06009-8). Wm C Brown.

--Practical Counseling in the Schools. 2nd ed. 544p. 1981. pap. text ed. write for info. (ISBN 0-697-06055-1); intrs.' manual avail. (ISBN 0-697-06039-X). Wm C Brown.

--Twelve-Hour BASIC for the IBM PC Compatibles: How to Get the Most from Your Compaq, Corona, Eagle, Columbia, or Other PC Clone. 1985. price not set (ISBN 0-07-004374-4). McGraw.

Belkin, Gary S. & Goodman, N. Marriage, Family & Intimate Relationships. 1980. pap. text ed. 24.95 (ISBN 0-395-30560-8); Instr's. manual 1.00 (ISBN 0-395-30561-6). HM.

Belkin, Gary S. & Nass, Stanley. Psychology of Adjustment. 1983. pap. text ed. 27.86 (ISBN 0-205-08087-1, 798087); write for info. tchr's. manual (798088). Allyn.

Belkin, Gary S. & Skydell, Ruth H. Foundations of Psychology. LC 78-69566. (Illus.). 1979. text ed. 25.95 (ISBN 0-395-25363-2); instr's. annotated ed. 26.95 (ISBN 0-395-25364-0); study guide 11.50 (ISBN 0-395-25365-9); test items 1.00 (ISBN 0-395-25366-7); test items manual II 1.50 (ISBN 0-395-28483-X). HM.

Belkin, John N. Fundamentals of Entomology. 220p. 1976. pap. 12.95x (ISBN 0-916846-10-5). Flora & Fauna.

--Fundamentals of Entomology. 1976. pap. 11.95 (ISBN 0-916846-10-5). World Natural Hist.

Belkin, John N. & Heinemann, Sandra J. The Mosquitoes of the West Indies, 2 vols. 1979. Set. lib. bdg. write for info. (ISBN 0-916846-10-5). World Natural Hist.

Belkin, Mary, tr. see Maklakov, Vasilii A.

Belkin, Samuel. In His Image: The Jewish Philosophy of Man As Expressed in Rabbinic Tradition. LC 78-10192. 1979. Repr. of 1960 ed. lib. bdg. 27.50x (ISBN 0-313-21234-1, BEIH). Greenwood.

--Philo & the Oral Law: The Philonic Interpretation of Biblical Law. (Harvard Semitic Ser.: Vol. 11). Repr. of 1940 ed. 25.00 (ISBN 0-384-03795-X). Johnson Repr.

Belkind, Allen J. Jean-Paul Sartre, Sartre Existentialism in English: A Bibliographical Guide. LC 76-95708. (Serif Ser.: No. 10). Repr. of 1970 ed. 63.50 (ISBN 0-8357-9367-2, 2016107). Bks Demand UMI.

Belknap, Bill & Belknap, Buzz. Canyonlands River Guide: Westwater, Lake Powell, Canyonlands National Park. LC 74-80876. (Illus.). 64p. 1974. waterproof 10.95 (ISBN 0-916370-08-9); pap. 6.95 (ISBN 0-916370-07-0). Westwater.

Belknap, Bill, jt. auth. see Kabotie, Fred.

Belknap, Buzz. Grand Canyon River Guide: Powell Centennial. LC 70-92769. (Illus.). 52p. 1969. waterproof 10.95 (ISBN 0-916370-01-1); pap. 6.95 (ISBN 0-916370-00-3). Westwater.

Belknap, Buzz, jt. auth. see Belknap, Bill.

Belknap, Buzz, jt. auth. see Evans, Laura.

Belknap, Buzz, jt. auth. see Huser, Verne.

Belknap, Dorothy C., jt. auth. see Terenzio, Stephanie.

Belknap, George N. The Blue Ribbon University. 1976. pap. 1.25 (ISBN 0-87114-082-9). U of Oreg Bks.

--Early Oregon Imprints in the Oregon State Archives. 17p. 1981. pap. 6.50 (ISBN 0-912296-52-6). Am Antiquarian.

--Henry Villard & the University of Oregon. 1976. pap. 2.00 (ISBN 0-87114-083-7). U of Oreg Bks.

--Oregon Imprints 1845-1870. LC 78-1013. (Illus.). 1968. 10.00 (ISBN 0-87114-019-5). U of Oreg Bks.

--The University of Oregon Charter. 1976. pap. 1.25 (ISBN 0-87114-081-0). U of Oreg Bks.

Belknap, George N., ed. see Adams, William L.

Belknap, Ivan. Human Problems of a State Mental Hospital. Grob, Gerald N., ed. LC 78-22548. (Historical Issues in Mental Health Ser.). (Illus.). 1979. Repr. of 1956 ed. lib. bdg. 21.00x (ISBN 0-405-11902-X). Ayer Co Pubs.

Belknap, Jeremy. The Foresters: An American Tale. LC 78-104413. Repr. of 1792 ed. lib. bdg. 19.00 (ISBN 0-8398-0159-9). Irvington.

--The Foresters: An American Tale. 216p. Date not set. Repr. of 1792 ed. lib. bdg. 29.00 (ISBN 0-932051-47-2). Am Repr Serv.

--Foresters, an American Tale, 1792. LC 71-100127. 1969. Repr. of 1792 ed. 40.00x (ISBN 0-8201-1071-X). Schol Facsimiles.

--History of New Hampshire, 3 vols. LC 73-141081. (Research Library of Colonial Americana). (Illus.). 1971. Repr. of 1792 ed. 120.00 (ISBN 0-405-03272-2); 40.00 ea. Vol. 1 (ISBN 0-405-03273-0). Vol. 2 (ISBN 0-405-03274-9). Vol. 3 (ISBN 0-405-03275-7). Ayer Co Pubs.

--The History of New Hampshire, 2 Vols. (Sources of Science Ser: No. 88). Repr. of 1812 ed. Set. 75.00 (ISBN 0-384-03803-4). Johnson Repr.

Belknap, Jodi P. Felisa & the Magic Tikling Bird. LC 73-79571. (gr. 1-7). 1973. 5.95 (ISBN 0-89610-014-6). Island Herit.

--Majesty: The Exceptional Trees of Hawaii. Cazimero, Momi, ed. LC 82-60598. 72p. 1982. 12.95 (ISBN 0-686-38728-7). Outdoor Circle.

Belknap, Joel R. The Story of Free Enterprise. 1963. 9.95 (ISBN 0-8159-6825-6). Devin.

Belknap, Michael R. Cold War Political Justice: The Smith Act, the Communist Party, & American Civil Liberties. LC 77-4566. (Contributions in American History: No. 66). xiv, 322p. 1977. lib. bdg. 29.95x (ISBN 0-8371-9692-2, BCW/). Greenwood.

Belknap, Michal R., ed. American Political Trials. LC 80-24911. (Contributions in American History Ser.: No. 94). x, 316p. 1981. lib. bdg. 35.00 (ISBN 0-313-21471-9, BAP/). Greenwood.

Belknap, Robert L. & Kuhns, Richard. Tradition & Innovation: General Education & the Reintegration of the University, a Columbia Report. LC 77-3315. 130p. 1977. 21.00x (ISBN 0-231-04322-8); pap. 10.00x (ISBN 0-231-04323-6). Columbia U Pr.

Belknap, Waldron P., Jr. American Colonial Painting: Materials for a History. Sellers, Charles C., ed. LC 59-10313. (Illus.). 1960. boxed 25.00x (ISBN 0-674-02250-5, Belknap Pr). Harvard U Pr.

--De Peyster Genealogy. LC 56-34875. (Illus.). 1956. 10.00x (ISBN 0-674-19801-8, Belknap Pr). Harvard U Pr.

Bell. Eastern Star. 6.95x (ISBN 0-685-21937-2). Wehman.

--Employment in the Age of Drastic Change: The Future with Reports. 1984. 10.00 (ISBN 0-9901004-0-5, Pub. by Abacus England). Heyden.

--Fundamentals of Engineering Geology. 1983. text ed. 89.95 (ISBN 0-408-01169-6). Butterworth.

--Industrial Noise Control. (Mechanical Engineering Ser.). 536p. 1982. 49.50 (ISBN 0-8247-1787-2). Dekker.

--Multiple Choice Questions in Medicine. 176p. 13.00 (ISBN 0-7236-0646-3). PSG Pub Co.

--One Thousand & One Questions about Radiologic Technology, Vol. 2. (Illus.). 192p. 1982. pap. text ed. 10.50 (ISBN 0-8391-1774-4). Univ Park.

--Orofacial Pains. 3rd ed. 1985. 44.95 (ISBN 0-317-19081-4). Year Bk Med.

--Purdue Thirty-Sixth Industrial Waste Conference Proceedings. LC 77-84415. 997p. 1982. 75.00 (ISBN 0-250-40493-1). Butterworth.

Bell, jt. auth. see Malick.

Bell, ed. Database Performance. (Computer State of the Art Report: Series 12, No. 4). (Illus.). 250p. 1984. 460.00 (ISBN 0-08-028589-9). Pergamon.

Bell, A. Beautiful Rio De Janeiro. 1976. lib. bdg. 69.95 (ISBN 0-8490-1482-4). Gordon Pr.

Bell, A. A., jt. ed. see Mace, M. E.

Bell, A. Craig. Alecandre Dumas: A Biography & Study. 420p. 1980. Repr. of 1950 ed. lib. bdg. 47.50 (ISBN 0-8495-0470-8). Arden Lib.

--Alexandre Dumas. 1973. Repr. of 1950 ed. 47.50 (ISBN 0-8274-1214-2). R West.

--Alexandre Dumas: A Biography & Study. LC 79-1153. 1979. lib. bdg. 45.00 (ISBN 0-8414-9832-6). Folcroft.

--The Last Man & Other Stories. 1985. 22.00x (ISBN 0-317-14520-7, Pub. by Selecteditions). State Mutual Bk.

Bell, A. Craig, ed. & tr. see Dumas, Alexandre.

Bell, A. E., et al, eds. Optical Storage Media, Vol. 420. 357p. 55.00 (ISBN 0-89252-455-3). Photo-Optical.

Bell, A. F. Portugal of the Portuguese. 1976. lib. bdg. 69.95 (ISBN 0-8490-2458-7). Gordon Pr.

--Studies in Portuguese Literature. 69.95 (ISBN 0-87968-243-4). Gordon Pr.

Bell, A. F., tr. & notes by see Vicente, G.

Bell, A. F. G. Portugese Bibliography. 388p. 1976. Repr. of 1922 ed. 8.50 (ISBN 0-317-34220-7). Hispanic Soc.

Bell, A. Fleming, jt. ed. see Burby, Raymond.

Bell, A. G. The Machine Plays Chess. 1978. text ed. 17.00 (ISBN 0-08-021221-2); pap. text ed. 8.95 (ISBN 0-08-021222-0). Pergamon.

Bell, A. Graham. Performance Tuning in Theory & Practice-- Four Strokes. (Illus.). 15.95 (ISBN 0-85429-275-6, F275). Haynes Pubns.

--Performance Tuning in Theory & Practice-- Two STrokes. (Illus.). 229p. pap. 15.95 (ISBN 0-85429-329-9, F329). Haynes Pubns.

Bell, A. J. & Bell, E. Q. Adam User's Guide. 336p. 1984. 7.95 (ISBN 0-89303-300-6). Brady Comm.

Bell, A. T. & Bonet, C., eds. Plasma Chemistry: Font Romeu & Rome, 1975. 1977. text ed. 35.00 (ISBN 0-08-020999-8). Pergamon.

Bell, A. W., et al. Research on Learning & Teaching. 335p. 1983. 20.00x (ISBN 0-7005-0612-8, Pub. by NFER Nelson UK). Taylor & Francis.

Bell, Aaron, tr. see Hiden, Mikael.

Bell, Adrian. The Green Bond. 124p. 1976. 10.00x (ISBN 0-8476-1421-2). Rowman.

Bell, Adrian, et al. The Legacy of England: An Illustrated Survey of the Works of Man in the English County. 30.00 (ISBN 0-89984-232-1). Century Bookbindery.

Bell, Aili R. & Koski, Augustus A. FSI Finnish Graded Reader. 1968. pap. text ed. 17.50X (ISBN 0-686-10710-1); 14 cassettes 84.00x (ISBN 0-686-10711-X). Intl Learn Syst.

Bell, Alan. The Scottish Antiquarian Tradition. (Illus.). 290p. 1982. text ed. 32.00x (ISBN 0-85976-080-4, Pub. by Alan Sutton England). Humanities.

--Sydney Smith. (Illus.). 1980. 32.50x (ISBN 0-19-812050-8). Oxford U Pr.

Bell, Alan, ed. Cockburn: Bicentenary Essays. 1980. 12.50x (ISBN 0-7073-0245-5, Pub. by Scottish Academic Pr). Columbia U Pr.

Bell, Alan P., et al. Sexual Preference: Its Development in Men & Women. LC 81-47006. (Illus.). 256p. 1981. 4.95 (ISBN 0-253-16673-X); statistical appendix 20.00 (ISBN 0-253-16674-8); Set. 24.95x (ISBN 0-253-16672-1). Ind U Pr.

Bell, Albert A. & Decato, Clifford M. A Primer for Administration in Mental Health & Professional Education. (Illus.). 164p. 1982. 19.75x (ISBN 0-398-04662-X). C C Thomas.

Bell, Alexander, ed. see Gaimar, Geoffroy.

Bell, Alexander G. The Bell Telephone: The Deposition of Alexander Graham Bell in the Suit Brought by the United States to Annul the Bell Patents. LC 74-4665. (Telecommunications Ser.). (Illus.). 480p. 1974. Repr. of 1905 ed. 33.00 (ISBN 0-405-06032-7). Ayer Co Pubs.

Bell, Alexander M. The Principles of Elocution. (Works of Alexander Melville Bell Ser.). xvi, 240p. Date not set. Repr. lib. bdg. 29.00 (ISBN 0-932051-80-4). Am Repr Serv.

--Visible Speech the Science of Universal Alphabetics. 1976. Repr. of 1867 ed. 49.00x (ISBN 0-403-06591-7, Regency). Scholarly.

Bell, Alexis T. & Hair, Michael L., eds. Vibrational Spectroscopies for Absorbed Species. LC 80-21181. (ACS Symposium Ser.: No. 137). 1980. 33.95 (ISBN 0-8412-0585-X). Am Chemical.

Bell, Alexis T. & Hegedus, L. Louis, eds. Catalysis under Transient Conditions. LC 82-20639. (ACS Symposium Ser.: No. 178). 1982. 34.95 (ISBN 0-8412-0688-0). Am Chemical.

Bell, Alexis T., jt. ed. see Hollahan, John R.

Bell, Alexis T., jt. ed. see Shen, Mitchel.

Bell, Andrew. A History of Feudalism: British & Continental. 360p. 1982. Repr. of 1863 ed. lib. bdg. 75.00 (ISBN 0-89987-086-4). Darby Bks.

Bell, Anne, jt. auth. see Habenicht, Donna.

Bell, Anne O., ed. Diary of Virginia Woolf: Vol. 1, 1915-1919. LC 78-23882. 1979. pap. 3.95 (ISBN 0-15-626036-0, Harv). HarBraceJ.

--The Diary of Virginia Woolf: Vol. 2, 1920-1924. LC 78-23882. 1980. pap. 5.95 (ISBN 0-15-626037-9, Harv). HarBraceJ.

--Diary of Virginia Woolf: Vol. 3, 1925-1930. LC 77-73111. 400p. 1981. pap. 8.95 (ISBN 0-15-626038-7, Harv). HarBraceJ.

--The Diary of Virginia Woolf: Vol. 4, 1931-1935. 402p. 1983. pap. 7.95 (ISBN 0-15-626039-5, Harv). HarBraceJ.

Bell, Anne O., ed. see Woolf, Virginia.

Bell, Anthea. The Great Menagerie: An Adaptation of the Antique Pop-up Book. LC 79-67762. (Illus.). (gr. k-3). 1980. 10.95 (ISBN 0-670-34979-8, Co-Pub. by Kestrel Books). Viking.

--A London Season. 224p. 1984. 12.95 (ISBN 0-312-49547-1). St Martin.

Bell, Anthea, tr. Stories of the Arabian Nights. LC 83-71485. (Illus.). 92p. 1983. 12.95 (ISBN 0-911745-02-5). P Bedrick Bks.

--Tom Thumb. (Illus.). 32p. (ps-3). 1985. 8.95 (ISBN 0-7207-0914-8, Pub. by Salem Hse Ltd). Merrimack Pub Cir.

Bell, Anthea, tr. see Andersen, Hans Christian.

Bell, Anthea, tr. see Brentano, Clemens.

Bell, Anthea, tr. see Donnelley, Elfie.

Bell, Anthea, tr. see Donnelly, Elfie.

Bell, Anthea, tr. see Dubelaar, Thea.

Bell, Anthea, tr. see Fahrmann, Willi.

Bell, Anthea, tr. see Goscinny & Uderzo.

Bell, Anthea, tr. see Hoffmann, E. T.

Bell, Anthea, tr. see Koenig, Alma J.

Bell, Anthea, tr. see Nostlinger, Christine.

Bell, Anthea, tr. see Peyo.

Bell, Anthea, tr. see Sonnleitner, A. T.

Bell, Anthea, tr. see Tolstoy, Leo.

Bell, Anthea, tr. see Voltaire.

Bell, Anthea, et al. More Favourite Tales From Grimm. (Illus.). 112p. (gr. k-3). 1984. laminated bds 12.95 (ISBN 0-7207-1486-9). Merrimack Pub Cir.

Bell, Arthur & Klammer, Thomas. The Practicing Writer. LC 82-83411. 224p. 1983. 15.95 (ISBN 0-395-32564-1); instr's. manual 2.00 (ISBN 0-395-32565-X). HM.

Bell, Arthur H., jt. auth. see Sigband, Norman B.

Bell, Arthur S., Jr. Peter Charlie: The Cruise of the PC 477. LC 82-71794. (Illus.). 384p. 1982. 14.95 (ISBN 0-910355-00-2). Courtroom Comp.

Bell, Aubrey F. Benito Arias Montano. 1922. pap. 2.50 (ISBN 0-87535-009-7). Hispanic Soc.

--Diogo do Cuoto. (Illus.). 1924. 2.00 (ISBN 0-87535-015-1). Hispanic Soc.

--Fernam Lopez. (Illus.). 1921. 2.00 (ISBN 0-87535-006-2). Hispanic Soc.

--Francisco Sanchez el Brocense. (Illus.). 1925. 4.00 (ISBN 0-87535-017-8). Hispanic Soc.

--Gaspar Correa. (Illus.). 1924. 2.50 (ISBN 0-87535-016-X). Hispanic Soc.

--Juan Gines de Sepulveda. (Illus.). 1925. 3.00 (ISBN 0-87535-018-6). Hispanic Soc.

Bell, Aubrey F., tr. see De Eon, Luis P.

Bell, Aubrey F., tr. see De Oliveira Martins, J. P.

Bell, Aubrey F., tr. see Hollanda, Francisco De.

Bell, B., jt. auth. see Nutini, H. G.

Bell, B. M. Integrated Basic Theory & Practice of Nursing. 852p. 1979. 100.00x (ISBN 0-85896-625-5, Pub. by Pitman Bks England). State Mutual Bk.

Bell, Barbara C. Tools in the Learning Trade. LC 83-15105. 192p. 1984. pap. 7.50 (ISBN 0-8108-1743-8). Scarecrow.

--Tools in the Learning Trade: A Guide to Eight Indispensable Tools for College Students. LC 83-15105. 192p. 1984. text ed. 15.00 (ISBN 0-8108-1655-5). Scarecrow.

Bell, Belden, ed. Nicaragua: An Ally Under Seige. 1978. pap. 15.00 (ISBN 0-685-59450-5). Coun Soc Econ.

Bell, Bernard. Folk Roots of Afro-American Poetry. 1974. 5.00 (ISBN 0-910296-93-6); pap. 2.75 (ISBN 0-910296-98-7). Broadside.

Bell, Bernard I. Crowd Culture. facs. ed. LC 74-117758. (Essay Index Reprint Ser). 1952. 17.00 (ISBN 0-8369-1742-1). Ayer Co Pubs.

Bell, Bernard I., ed. Affirmations, by a Group of American Anglo-Catholics, Clerical & Lay. facs. ed. LC 68-16906. (Essay Index Reprint Ser). 1938. 15.00 (ISBN 0-8369-0185-1). Ayer Co Pubs.

Bell, Beryl, et al. Paper Crafts. (Illus.). 160p. 1984. pap. 6.68i (ISBN 0-06-464084-1, BN 4084). B&N NY.

Bell, Beryle, et al. Papercrafts. 1984. pap. 6.95 (ISBN 0-317-02915-0). Har-Row.

Bell, Betsy. Movietown Nurse. 1984. 8.95 (ISBN 0-8034-8436-4, Avalon). Bouregy.

--Nurse Carrie's Island. 1982. 8.95 (ISBN 0-686-84162-X, Avalon). Bouregy.

--Nurse in the Wilderness. 1983. 8.95 (ISBN 0-8034-8321-X, Avalon). Bouregy.

Bell, Bill. Saxophone Boy. LC 80-53747. (Illus.). 24p. (gr. 4 up). 1980. 4.95 (ISBN 0-912766-98-0). Tundra Bks.

Bell, Bill D. Contemporary Social Gerontology: Significant Developments in the Field of Aging. (Illus.). 480p. 1976. 49.50x (ISBN 0-398-03464-8). C C Thomas.

Bell, Bob. Digest Book of Upland Game Hunting. LC 79-84931. 96p. pap. 3.95 (ISBN 0-695-81319-6). DBI.

--Hunting the Long Tailed Bird. (Illus.). 224p. 1975. 14.95 (ISBN 0-88395-027-8). Freshet Pr.

--Scopes & Mounts: Gun Digest Bk. LC 83-72345. 224p. 1983. pap. 11.95 (ISBN 0-910676-61-5). DBI.

Bell, Brenda. Spuds: Fifty Great Stuffed Potato Recipes. (Illus.). 80p. (Orig.). 1985. pap. 5.95 (ISBN 0-8092-5161-2). Contemp Bks.

Bell, Brian. Farm Machinery. 2nd ed. (Illus.). 256p. 1983. pap. 15.95 (ISBN 0-85236-131-9, Pub. by Farming Pr UK). Diamond Farm Bk.

--Farm Workshop. (Illus.). 224p. pap. 15.95 (ISBN 0-85236-112-2, Pub. by Farming Pr UK). Diamond Farm Bk.

Bell, Bruce & Grainger, David A. Basic Operative Dentistry Procedures. LC 72-123419. pap. 104.80 (ISBN 0-317-26679-9, 2155997). Bks Demand UMI.

Bell, Bruce A., jt. auth. see Mandt, Mikkel G.

Bell, Bruce M., jt. ed. see Edwards, Stephen R.

Bell, Bruce M., jt. ed. see Lee, Welton L.

Bell, Bryan, ed. World Directory of Pharmaceutical Manufacturers. 4th ed. 316p. (Orig.). 1982. pap. 325.00x (ISBN 0-906184-03-7). Intl Pubns Serv.

Bell, Buddy. Ministry of Helps Study Course. 40p. (Orig.). 1983. pap. 1.95 (ISBN 0-89274-292-5). Harrison Hse.

Bell, Buster. Bell-E-Laffs. 1983. 4.95 (ISBN 0-8062-2027-9). Carlton.

Bell, C. Proust. 59.95 (ISBN 0-8490-0907-3). Gordon Pr.

Bell, C. G. & Newall, A. Computer Structures Readings & Examples. 1971. 51.95 (ISBN 0-07-004357-4). McGraw.

Bell, C. Gordon & Mudge, J. Craig. Computer Engineering: A DEC View of Hardware Systems Design. (Illus.). 585p. 1978. 28.00 (ISBN 0-932376-00-2, EY-BX007-DP). Digital Pr.

Bell, C. L., et al. Project Evaluation in Regional Perspective: A Study of an Irrigation Project in Northwest Malaysia. LC 81-48173. (World Bank Ser.). 336p. 1982. text ed. 30.00x (ISBN 0-8018-2802-3). Johns Hopkins.

Bell, C. Ritchie & Taylor, Bryan J. Florida Wild Flowers & Roadside Plants. (Illus.). 1982. 18.50 (ISBN 0-9608688-0-1). Laurel Hill Pr.

Bell, C. Ritchie, jt. auth. see Justice, William S.

Bell, C. William & Blodgett, Diane. Home Care & Rehabilitation in Respiratory Medicine. (Illus.). 320p. 1984. pap. text ed. 25.00 (ISBN 0-397-50585-X, 65-07479, Lippincott Medical). Lippincott.

Bell, Camille G. & Fallon, Berlie J. Consumer & Homemaking Education. LC 70-147277. xviii, 210p. 1971. pap. text ed. 3.50x (ISBN 0-8134-1234-X, 1234). Interstate.

Bell, Carl I. They Knew Franklin Pierce. 1980. 8.95 (ISBN 0-917780-01-9). April Hill.

Bell, Carla H. Olivier Messiaen. (Twayne Music Ser.). 158p. 1984. lib. bdg. 24.95 (ISBN 0-8057-9457-3, Twayne). G K Hall.

Bell, Carol, ed. Seminar on Antigen: Antigen-Antibody Reactions Revisited. 247p. 1982. 24.30 (ISBN 0-914404-80-6). Am Assn Blood.

--A Seminar on Immune Mediated Cell Destruction. (Illus.). 208p. 1981. 20.00 (ISBN 0-914404-70-9). Am Assn Blood.

Bell, Carol W. Columbiana County, Ohio, 1850 Census: Surname Index. 14.00 (ISBN 0-318-04641-5). OH Genealogical.

Bell, Carol W., ed. First Families of Ohio: Official Roster, Vol. 1. 6.00 (ISBN 0-318-04648-2). OH Genealogical.

Bell, Cary B. Speaking in Business: A Basic Survival Guide. 192p. 1984. pap. text ed. 12.95 (ISBN 0-8403-3305-6). Kendall-Hunt.

Bell, Catherine & Peters, Roy. Passing Shots. (Illus.). 112p. 1983. pap. 9.95 (ISBN 0-8253-0142-4). Beaufort Bks NY.

Bell, Cecil H., Jr., jt. auth. see French, Wendell L.

Bell, Charles. The Anatomy & Philosophy of Expression as Connected with the Fine Arts. 265p. 1982. Repr. of 1846 ed. lib. bdg. 100.00 (ISBN 0-89760-096-7). Telegraph Bks.

--The Hand: Its Mechanism & Vital Endowments. LC 78-72789. (Brainedness, Handedness, & Mental Ability Ser.). Repr. of 1885 ed. 27.50 (ISBN 0-404-60853-1). AMS Pr.

Bell, Charles A. The People of Tibet. lib. bdg. 79.95 (ISBN 0-87968-481-X). Krishna Pr.

--The Religion of Tibet. lib. bdg. 79.95 (ISBN 0-87968-482-8). Krishna Pr.

--Tibet: Past & Present. lib. bdg. 79.95 (ISBN 0-87968-483-6). Krishna Pr.

Bell, Charles B. & Miller, Harriett P. A Mysterious Spirit: The Bell Witch of Tennessee. 1972. 20.00 (ISBN 0-918450-06-3); pap. 6.00 (ISBN 0-918450-13-6). C Elder.

Bell, Charles Frederic M. Khedives & Pashas: Sketches of Contemporary Egyptian Rulers & Statesmen, by One Who Knows Them Well. LC 80-2196. Repr. of 1884 ed. 30.00 (ISBN 0-404-18954-7). AMS Pr.

Bell, Charles G. Five Chambered Heart. 84p. 14.95 (ISBN 0-89255-097-X); pap. 8.95 (ISBN 0-89255-098-8). Persea Bks.

--The Half Gods. LC 68-23028. 1968. 20.00 (ISBN 0-89366-085-X). Ultramarine Pub.

Bell, Charles G. & Price, Charles M. California Government Today: Politics of Reform. 2nd ed. 1984. pap. 18.00x (ISBN 0-256-03102-9). Dorsey.

Bell, Charles H. The History of Exeter, N.H. 2nd, rev. ed. LC 79-1226. (Illus.). 1979. Repr. of 1888 ed. 42.50 (ISBN 0-917890-14-0). Heritage Bk.

Bell, Charles N. Henry's Journal. 20p. 1982. pap. 2.00 (ISBN 0-87770-270-5). Ye Galleon.

Bell, Chip R. Influencing: Marketing the Ideas That Matter. LC 82-7772. 185p. 1982. text ed. 19.95 (ISBN 0-89384-051-3). Learning Concepts.

Bell, Chip R. & Nadler, Leonard. Clients & Consultants. 2nd ed. LC 84-10917. 368p. 1985. 19.95x (ISBN 0-87201-119-4). Gulf Pub.

Bell, Christine. Saint. LC 85-12256. 320p. 1985. 14.95 (ISBN 0-910923-21-3). Pineapple Pr.

Bell, Clair H., jt. auth. see Hager, Georg.

Bell, Clair H., ed. see Fabrizius, Peter.

Bell, Clara, tr. see Huysmans, Joris K.

Bell, Clare. Clan Ground. LC 84-6289. 276p. (gr. 7 up). 1984. 12.95 (ISBN 0-689-50304-0, Argo). Atheneum.

--Ratha's Creature. LC 82-13875. 264p. (gr. 7 up). 1983. 12.95 (ISBN 0-689-50262-1, Argo). Atheneum.

Bell, Clint C. Maintenance Mechanics Qualification Program. (Illus.). 49p. 1981. pap. 44.95 (ISBN 0-89852-389-3, 01-01-R089). TAPPI.

--Preventive Maintenance in a Corrugated Container Plant. (Reports Ser.). (Illus.). 50p. 1981. pap. 43.95 (ISBN 0-89852-388-5, 01-01-R088). TAPPI.

Bell, Clive. Aesthetics & Post-Impressionism: A New Theory of Art, 2 vols. (Illus.). 328p. 1985. Repr. Set. 178.75 (ISBN 0-89901-226-4). Found Class Reprints.

--Landmarks in Nineteenth Century Painting. facs. ed. LC 67-30197. (Essay Index Reprint Ser). 1927. 18.00 (ISBN 0-8369-0186-X). Ayer Co Pubs.

--Old Friends: Personal Recollections. LC 83-45703. Repr. of 1956 ed. 22.50 (ISBN 0-404-20025-7). AMS Pr.

--Proust. 1978. Repr. of 1928 ed. lib. bdg. 17.50 (ISBN 0-8495-0429-5). Arden Lib.

--Proust. LC 74-13466. 1928. lib. bdg. 15.00 (ISBN 0-8414-3265-1). Folcroft.

--Since Cezanne. facs. ed. (Essay Index Reprint Ser). 1922. 16.00 (ISBN 0-8369-0034-0). Ayer Co Pubs.

Bell, Colin & Newby, Howard. Community Studies: An Introduction to the Sociology of the Local Community. 3rd ed. (Studies in Sociology). (Illus.). 1979. pap. text ed. 9.95x (ISBN 0-04-300032-0). Allen Unwin.

Bell, Colin & Roberts, Helen. Social Researching: Politics, Problems, Practice. 272p. (Orig.). 1984. pap. 13.95x (ISBN 0-7100-9884-7). Routledge & Kegan.

Bell, Colin & Encel, Sol, eds. Inside the Whale: Ten Personal Accounts of Social Research. 1978. text ed. 20.00 (ISBN 0-08-022244-7); pap. text ed. 15.25 (ISBN 0-08-022243-9). Pergamon.

Bell, Colin & Newby, Howard, eds. Sociology of Community: A Collection of Readings. 424p. 1974. 32.50x (ISBN 0-7146-2970-7, F Cass Co). Biblio Dist.

Bell, Colin F. Principles & Applications of Metal Chelation. (Oxford Chemistry Ser.). (Illus.). 1977. 29.95x (ISBN 0-19-855485-0). Oxford U Pr.

Bell, Coral. The Diplomacy of Detente: The Kissinger Era. LC 77-82634. 1977. 25.00x (ISBN 0-312-21122-8). St Martin.

--Negotiation from Strength: A Study in the Politics of Power. LC 77-1054. 1977. Repr. of 1963 ed. lib. bdg. 20.00x (ISBN 0-8371-9508-X, BENS). Greenwood.

Bell, Coral, ed. Agenda for the Eighties. LC 80-65340. 256p. 1980. pap. text ed. 13.50 (ISBN 0-7081-1086-X, 0469, Pub. by ANUP Australia). Australia N U P.

Bell, D. H., et al. Parallel Programming: A Bibliography. Willis, N., ed. (Mongraphs in Informatics (British Computer Society)). 64p. 1983. 19.95x (ISBN 0-471-26277-3, 1601). Wiley.

Bell, D. J. Planning Corporate Manpower. LC 73-86105. (Manpower Studies Ser.). pap. 47.80 (ISBN 0-317-08448-8, 2010055). Bks Demand UMI.

Bell, D. J. & Jacobson, D. H. Singular Optimal Control Problems. (Mathematics in Science & Engineering Ser.). 1975. 39.50 (ISBN 0-12-085060-5). Acad Pr.

Bell, D. J. & Freemon, B. M., eds. Physiology & Biochemistry of the Domestic Fowl, 3 vols. 1972. Vol. 1. 90.00 (ISBN 0-12-085001-X); Vol. 2. 90.00 (ISBN 0-12-085002-8); Vol. 3. 80.00 (ISBN 0-12-085003-6). Acad Pr.

Bell, D. J., et al, eds. Design of Modern Control Methods. (IEE Control Engineering Ser.: No. 20). 344p. 1982. pap. 64.00 (ISBN 0-906048-74-5, CE020). Inst Elect Eng.

Bell, D. Rayford. Marriages Are Not Made in Heaven. LC 83-72340. 120p. 1983. pap. 3.95 (ISBN 0-9604820-7-5). D R Bell.

--The Philosophy of Christ. LC 80-67408. 104p. 1980. 6.95 (ISBN 0-9604820-0-8); pap. 4.95 (ISBN 0-9604820-1-6). D R Bell.

--Song Book of Israel. LC 80-67409. 303p. 1983. 6.95 (ISBN 0-9604820-3-2); pap. 4.95 (ISBN 0-9604820-2-4). D R Bell.

Bell, D. S., jt. ed. see Kolinsky, Martin.

Bell, Dana. A-10 Thunderbolt II in Detail & Scale. Gentle, Ernest J., ed. (Detail & Scale Ser.: Vol. 19). (Illus.). 72p. (Orig.). pap. 7.95 (ISBN 0-8168-5030-5). Aero.

--Air War over Vietnam, Vol. III. (Warbirds Illustrated Ser.: No. 21). (Illus.). 68p. 1984. pap. 7.95 (ISBN 0-85368-607-6, Pub. by Arms & Armour Pr). Sterling.

--Air War over Vietnam, Vol. IV. (Warbirds Illustrated Ser.: No. 26). 1984. pap. 7.95 (ISBN 0-85368-635-1, Pub. by Arms & Armour Pr). Sterling.

--U. S. A. F. in Color Today. (Warbirds Illustrated Ser.: No.29). (Illus.). 1984. pap. 9.95 (ISBN 0-85368-679-3, Arms & Armour Pr). Sterling.

--Warbirds Illustrated: Air War over Vietnam, No. 10. (Illus.). 68p. 1983. pap. 7.95 (ISBN 0-85368-548-7, Arms & Armour Pr). Sterling.

Bell, Daniel. Coming of Post-Industrial Society: A Venture in Social Forecasting. LC 72-89178. 1976. pap. 9.95x (ISBN 0-465-09713-8, TB-5077). Basic.

--The Cultural Contradictions of Capitalism. LC 75-7271. 384p. 1976. o.s.i 17.95x (ISBN 0-465-01526-3, TB-5040); pap. 8.95x (ISBN 0-465-09727-8, CN-5027). Basic.

--Marxian Socialism in the United States. (Princeton Studies in American Civilization). 1952. pap. 9.95x (ISBN 0-691-02155-4). Princeton U Pr.

--The Social Sciences since the Second World War. LC 80-27957. 104p. 1981. 16.95; pap. text ed. 5.95 (ISBN 0-87855-872-1). Transaction Bks.

--The Winding Passage: Essays & Sociological Journeys, 1960-1980. LC 79-57350. (Illus.). 394p. 1980. 25.00 (ISBN 0-89011-545-1). Abt Bks.

--The Winding Passage: Essays & Sociological Journeys, 1960-1980. LC 81-66858. 372p. 1981. pap. 8.00 (ISBN 0-465-09193-8, CN-5075). Basic.

--The Winding Passage: Essays & Sociological Journeys, 1960-1980. 394p. 1984. Repr. of 1980 ed. lib. bdg. 32.50 (ISBN 0-8191-4142-9). U Pr of Amer.

Bell, Daniel & Thurow, Lester. The Deficits: How Big? How Long? How Dangerous? 100p. 1985. text ed. 15.00x (ISBN 0-8147-1083-2). NYU Pr.

Bell, Daniel, ed. The Radical Right: The New American Right. rev. & enl. facsimile ed. LC 78-167309. (Essay Index Reprint Ser). Repr. of 1963 ed. 23.50 (ISBN 0-8369-2447-9). Ayer Co Pubs.

Bell, Daniel & Kristol, Irving, eds. The Crisis in Economic Theory. LC 80-70392. 242p. 1981. 15.50 (ISBN 0-465-01476-3, CN-5070); pap. 6.95 (ISBN 0-465-01477-1). Basic.

Bell, Darlene. Olive. pap. 4.95 (ISBN 0-318-00389-9). Rod & Staff.

Bell, Darlene, jt. auth. see Bell, Foster.

Bell, David. Electronic Instrumentation & Measurement. 1982. pap. text ed. 29.95 (ISBN 0-8359-1669-3); instrs'. manual avail. (ISBN 0-8359-1670-7). Reston.

--Frege's Theory of Judgement. 1979. text ed. 32.50x (ISBN 0-19-827423-8). Oxford U Pr.

--Fundamentals of Electric Circuits. 3rd ed. 1984. text ed. 32.95 (ISBN 0-8359-2125-5); guide 10.95study (ISBN 0-8359-2126-3). Reston.

--Linear Integrated Circuits: Design & Applications. 1982. text ed. 21.95 (ISBN 0-8359-4074-8); solutions manual avail. (ISBN 0-8359-4075-6). Reston.

--Marxist Local Governments in Western Europe & Japan. LC 84-62670. (Marxist Regimes Ser.). (Illus.). 160p. 1985. lib. bdg. cancelled (ISBN 0-931477-25-5); pap. text ed. cancelled (ISBN 0-931477-26-3). Lynne Rienner.

--Marxist Local Governments in Western Europe & Japan: Politics, Economics & Society. Szajkowski, Bogdan, ed. LC 84-62670. (Marxist Regimes Ser.). (Illus.). 160p. 1986. lib. bdg. 22.50x (ISBN 0-931477-25-5); pap. text ed. 10.95x (ISBN 0-931477-26-3). Lynne Rienner.

--Spinoza in Germany from Sixteen Seventy the Age of Goethe. (Bithell Series of Dissertations: Vol. 7). 192p. 1984. pap. text ed. 19.50x (ISBN 0-85457-117-5, Pub. by Inst Germanic UK). Humanities.

Bell, David & Deeds, Daphne A. William Penhallow Henderson: Master Colorist of Santa Fe. LC 84-61888. (Illus.). 108p. (Orig.). 1984. pap. 13.00x (ISBN 0-910407-12-6). Phoenix Art.

Bell, David, jt. auth. see Deeds, Daphne.

Bell, David, jt. ed. see Manor, Oded.

Bell, David A. Electronic Devices & Circuits. 2nd ed. (Illus.). 480p. 1979. 28.95 (ISBN 0-8359-1634-0); students manual avail. (ISBN 0-8359-1635-9). Reston.

--Solid State Pulse Circuits. 2nd ed. (Illus.). 432p. 1981. 30.95 (ISBN 0-8359-7057-4). Reston.

Bell, David E. Conflicting Objectives in Decisions. LC 77-5064. (Wiley International Ser. on Applied Systems Analysis). 442p. 1977. 54.95x (ISBN 0-471-99506-1, Pub. by Wiley-Interscience). Wiley.

Bell, David F., ed. see Serres, Michel.

Bell, David N. The Image of Likeness: The Augustinian Spirituality of William of St. Thierry. 19.95 (ISBN 0-87907-878-2). Cistercian Pubns.

Bell, David N., ed. see St. Symeon.

Bell, David N., tr. & intro. by. Besa: The Life of Shenoute. (Cistercian Studies: No. 73). 1983. pap. 11.95 (ISBN 0-87907-873-1). Cistercian Pubns.

Bell, David S. Contemporary French Political Parties. LC 81-21301. 1982. 27.50 (ISBN 0-312-16662-1). St Martin.

--Democratic Politics in Spain. LC 82-42708. 210p. 1983. 25.00x (ISBN 0-312-19371-8). St Martin.

Bell, David S. & Criddle, Byron. The French Socialist Party: Resurgence & Victory. LC 83-23707. 311p. 1984. 29.95x (ISBN 0-19-822597-0). Oxford U Pr.

Bell, David S., ed. The Conservative Government: Nineteen Seventy-Nine to Nineteen Eighty-Four: An Interim Report. 224p. 1985. 21.50 (ISBN 0-7099-3258-8, Pub. by Croom Helm Ltd). Longwood Pub Group.

--Labour into the Eighties. 168p. 1980. bds. 25.00x (ISBN 0-7099-0443-6, Pub. by Croom Helm Ltd England). Biblio Dist.

--Labour into the Eighties. 168p. 1980. 25.00 (ISBN 0-7099-0443-6, Pub. by Croom Helm Ltd). Longwood Pub Group.

Bell, Derrick. Civil Rights: Leading Cases. 1980p. 13.50 (ISBN 0-316-08819-6). Little.

--Race, Racism, & American Law. 2nd ed. 1980. text ed. 27.00 (ISBN 0-316-08821-8). Little.

--Race, Racism & American Law, 1984 Supplement. LC 79-90940. 250p. 1984. pap. text ed. 8.95 (ISBN 0-316-08815-3). Little.

Bell, Derrick, ed. Shades of Brown: New Perspectives on School Desegregation. LC 80-21877. 1980. text ed. 12.95x (ISBN 0-8077-2595-1). Tchrs Coll.

Bell, Diane. Daughters of the Dreaming. (Illus.). 297p. 1984. pap. text ed. 14.50x (ISBN 0-86861-472-6). Allen Unwin.

Bell, Diane & Ditton, Pam. Law: The Old Man & the New. (Illus.). 147p. 1980. pap. text ed. 5.95 (ISBN 0-908160-77-1). Australia N U P.

Bell, Dion R. Lecture Notes on Tropical Medicine. (Illus.). 240p. 1981. pap. text ed. 21.00 (ISBN 0-632-00546-7, B 0584-9). Mosby.

Bell, Donald. Being a Man: The Paradox of Masculinity. LC 82-7196. 1982. 12.95 (ISBN 0-86616-013-2). Greene.

--Being a Man: The Paradox of Masculinity. 168p. 1984. pap. 5.95 (ISBN 0-15-611686-3, Harv). HarBraceJ.

Bell, Donald A. Food & Beverage Cost Control. LC 83-62769. 354p. 1984. 25.50x (ISBN 0-8211-0135-8); text ed. 23.00 in copies of ten or more. McCutchan.

--Spirits of Hospitality: An Overview of the Origin, History & Service of Alcoholic Beverages. (Illus.). 166p. 1976. 8.95 (ISBN 0-86612-005-X). Educ Inst Am Hotel.

Bell, Doris. Stranger's Fever: Poems. 1975. 5.00 (ISBN 0-916620-44-1). Portals Pr.

Bell, Doris L. Contemporary Art Trends, Nineteen Sixty to Nineteen Eighty: A Guide to Sources. LC 81-5668. 183p. 1981. 16.00 (ISBN 0-8108-1445-5). Scarecrow.

Bell, Doug. Early Chevrolet History: 1912-1945. Clymer Publications, ed. (Illus.). pap. 5.00 (ISBN 0-89287-269-1, H544). Clymer Pubns.

Bell, Doug, jt. auth. see Pugh, John.

Bell, E. C. & Whitehead, R. W. Basic Electrical Engineering & Instrumentation for Engineers. (Illus.). 1977. pap. 17.95x (ISBN 0-8464-0175-4). Beekman Pubs.

--Basic Electrical Engineering & Instrumentation for Engineers. 2nd ed. 487p. 1981. pap. text ed. 22.00x (ISBN 0-258-97051-0, Pub. by Granada England); pap. 14.75. Brookfield Pub Co.

--Basic Electrical Engineering & Instrumentation for Engineers. 2nd ed. 560p. 1981. pap. 18.00x (ISBN 0-246-11477-0, Pub. by Granada England). Sheridan.

Bell, E. Q., jt. auth. see Bell, A. J.

Bell, E. T. Algebraic Arithmetic. LC 28-28412. (Colloquium Publications). 180p. 1927. 29.00 (ISBN 0-317-32948-0, OP-13793); pap. 24.00 (ISBN 0-317-32949-9). Am Math.

Bell, E. T., pseud. Before the Dawn. LC 74-16522. (Science Fiction Ser). 247p. 1975. Repr. of 1934 ed. 19.00x (ISBN 0-405-06314-8). Ayer Co Pubs.

Bell, E. T. Man & His Lifebelts. 1938. 35.00 (ISBN 0-8482-7395-8). Norwood Edns.

Bell, Edward. Hellenic Architecture. LC 73-39657. (Select Bibliographies Reprint Ser). 1972. Repr. of 1920 ed. 18.75 (ISBN 0-8369-9928-2). Ayer Co Pubs.

Bell, Edward J., Jr., jt. auth. see Burlingame, Merrill G.

Bell, Edward P., ed. World Chancelleries: Sentiments, Ideas Expressed by Famous Statesmen of the World. 1977. lib. bdg. 59.95 (ISBN 0-8490-2845-0). Gordon Pr.

Bell, Elaine, jt. ed. see Benolt, Dick.

Bell, Enid H. Storming the Citadel: The Rise of the Woman Doctor. LC 79-2931. 200p. 1981. Repr. of 1953 ed. 20.00 (ISBN 0-8305-0098-7). Hyperion Conn.

Bell, Eric T. Men of Mathematics. (Illus.). 1937. pap. 10.75 (ISBN 0-671-46401-9, Fireside). S&S.

--Numerology. LC 78-13855. (Illus.). 1979. Repr. of 1933 ed. 18.00 (ISBN 0-88355-774-6). Hyperion Conn.

Bell, Eric T. see Taine, John, pseud.

Bell, Ernest A. Fighting the Traffic in Young Girls: Or, War on the White Slave Traffic. 75.00 (ISBN 0-87968-252-3). Gordon Pr.

Bell, F. Engineering Properties of Soils & Rocks. 2nd ed. 144p. 1983. pap. text ed. 19.95 (ISBN 0-408-01457-1). Butterworth.

Bell, F. A. Eastern Star Ritual. 5.50 (ISBN 0-685-19473-6). Powner.

Bell, F. Howard. Pacific Halibut: The Resource & the Fishery. LC 80-29218. (Illus.). 288p. 1981. 24.95 (ISBN 0-88240-158-0); pap. 19.95 (ISBN 0-88240-141-6). Alaska Northwest.

Bell, F. T. & Smith, F. Seymour. Library Bookselling: A History & Handbook of Current Practice. 128p. 1966. 11.00x (ISBN 0-686-94104-7, 05771-1, Pub. by Gower Pub Co England). Lexington Bks.

Bell, F. W., jt. auth. see Hazleton, J. E.

Bell, Florence. At the Works. 256p. 1985. pap. 7.95 (ISBN 0-86068-415-6, Pub. by Virago Pr). Merrimack Pub Cir.

Bell, Foster & Bell, Darlene. Queener: The Man Behind the Preaching. 1976. pap. 2.95 (ISBN 0-934942-13-7). White Wing Pub.

Bell, Frank. Patient Lifting Devices in Hospitals. 236p. 1984. 25.00 (ISBN 0-7099-3229-4, Pub. by Croom Helm Ltd). Longwood Pub Group.

Bell, Frank C. & Stenstrom, William J. An Atlas of the Peripheral Retina. (Illus.). 244p. 1983. 75.00 (ISBN 0-7216-1669-0). Saunders.

Bell, Frank F. Gladiators of the Glittering Gulches. (Illus.). 176p. (Orig.). 1985. pap. 7.95 (ISBN 0-318-04407-2). Western Horizons Bks.

Bell, Frederic. Jenny's Corner. LC 73-18741. (Illus.). 72p. 1974. 3.95 (ISBN 0-394-82741-4); PLB 5.99 (ISBN 0-394-92741-9). Random.

Bell, Frederick. Apple Programming for Learning & Teaching. (Illus.). 1984. text ed. 21.95 (ISBN 0-8359-0098-3); pap. 16.95 (ISBN 0-8359-0097-5). Reston.

--Teaching Elementary School Mathematics, Methods & Content for Grades K-8. 550p. 1980. pap. text ed. write for info. (ISBN 0-697-06018-7). Wm C Brown.

--TRS-80 Programming for Learning & Teaching. 1984. text ed. 21.95 (ISBN 0-8359-7863-X); pap. text ed. 16.95 (ISBN 0-8359-7862-1). Reston.

Bell, Frederick & Canterbery, Ray. Aquaculture for Developing Countries: A Feasibility Study. LC 76-28400. 288p. 1976. 30.00x (ISBN 0-88410-296-3). Ballinger Pub.

Bell, Frederick H. Teaching & Learning Math in Secondary Schools. 576p. 1978. pap. text ed. write for info. (ISBN 0-697-06017-9). Wm C Brown.

Bell, Frederick W. Food from the Sea: The Economics & Politics of Ocean Fisheries. LC 77-28756. (Special Studies in Natural Resources & Energy Management Ser.). (Illus.). 1978. pap. 14.00x (ISBN 0-89158-403-X). Westview.

Bell, G. & Bowen, P. The Business of Transport. (Illus.). 344p. 1984. pap. text ed. 24.00x (ISBN 0-7121-2406-3). Trans-Atlantic.

Bell, G. & Finlay, D. Basic Radiographic Positioning & Anatomy. (Illus.). 270p. Date not set. price not set (Pub. by Bailliere-Tindall). Saunders.

Bell, G., et al. The Economics & Planning of Transport. 272p. 1984. pap. 19.95 (ISBN 0-434-90133-4, Pub. by W Heinemann Ltd). David & Charles.

Bell, G. K. The English Church. 10.00 (ISBN 0-8414-1634-6). Folcroft.

Bell, Gawain. Shadows on the Sand: The Memoirs of Sir Gawain Bell. LC 83-40286. (Illus.). 253p. 1984. 25.00 (ISBN 0-312-71418-1). St Martin.

Bell, Geoffrey. The British in Ireland: A Suitable Case for Withdrawal. 120p. (Orig.). 1983. pap. 4.50 (ISBN 0-86104-510-6). Pluto Pr.

--The Golden Gate & the Silver Screen. LC 81-71875. (Illus.). 192p. 1984. 24.50 (ISBN 0-8386-3231-9). Fairleigh Dickinson.

--The Golden Gate & the Silver Screen. LC 81-71875. (Illus.). 192p. 1984. 24.50 (ISBN 0-8453-4750-0). Cornwall Bks.

--Protestants of Ulster. 159p. (Orig.). 1976. pap. 5.95 (ISBN 0-904383-08-3). Pluto Pr.

--Troublesome Business: The Labour Party & the Irish Question. 168p. 1982. pap. 8.95 (ISBN 0-86104-373-1). Pluto Pr.

Bell, George, et al, eds. Theoretical Immunology. (Immunology Ser.: Vol. 8). 1978. 79.75 (ISBN 0-8247-6618-0). Dekker.

Bell, George H., et al, eds. Textbook of Physiology. 10th ed. (Illus.). 600p. 1980. pap. 35.00 (ISBN 0-443-02152-X). Churchill.

Bell, George I. & Glasstone, Samuel. Nuclear Reactor Theory. LC 78-22102. 638p. 1979. Repr. of 1970 ed. lib. bdg. 42.50 (ISBN 0-88275-790-3). Krieger.

Bell, George K. The Kingship of Christ: The Story of the World Council of Churches. LC 78-10482. 1979. Repr. of 1954 ed. lib. bdg. 18.75x (ISBN 0-313-21121-3, BEKC). Greenwood.

Bell, George L. Making It Together: Dates Before & After Marriage. (Orig.). 1974. pap. 8.75 (ISBN 0-89536-150-7). CSS of Ohio.

Bell, Georgianna. Passionate Jade. 1981. pap. 2.95 (ISBN 0-671-83657-9). PB.

Bell, Gerald D. Achievers. LC 73-79581. 200p. 1973. pap. 10.95 (ISBN 0-914616-00-5). Preston-Hill.

Bell, Gerald W., ed. Professional Preparation in Athletic Training. LC 82-81094. 184p. 1982. text ed. 15.00x (ISBN 0-931250-32-3, BBEL0032). Human Kinetics.

Bell, Gerard. Le Project de Pole Electro-Metallurgique de Fria: L'Energie Hydro-Electrique et le Developpement. (Economies et Societes Series F: No. 18). 1963. pap. 26.00 (ISBN 0-317-16842-8). Kraus Repr.

Bell, Gertrude. Persian Pictures. Repr. of 1928 ed. 20.00 (ISBN 0-8482-3424-3). Norwood Edns.

Bell, Gertrude L. Syria: The Desert & the Sown. LC 73-6270. (The Middle East Ser.). Repr. of 1908 ed. 32.00 (ISBN 0-405-05325-8). Ayer Co Pubs.

Bell, Gertrude L., jt. auth. see Ramsay, W. M.

Bell, Gordon. The Golden Troubador. 1980. 10.95 (ISBN 0-07-004393-0). McGraw.

Bell, Gordon M., ed. Light Metals 1981: Proceedings. AIME Annual Meeting, Chicago, 1981. (Illus.). 1060p. 55.00 (ISBN 0-89520-359-6); members 32.00 (ISBN 0-317-36292-5); student members 16.00 (ISBN 0-317-36293-3). ASM.

Bell, Gordon M., ed. see Metallurgical Society of AIME.

Bell, Graham. The Masterpiece of Nature: The Evolution & Genetics of Sexuality. LC 81-16045. (Illus.). 600p. 1982. 50.00x (ISBN 0-520-04583-1). U of Cal Pr.

Bell, Griffin, et al. Whom Do Judges Represent? 31p. 1981. 3.75 (ISBN 0-8447-2224-3). Am Enterprise.

Bell, Griffin B. & Ostrow, Ronald J. Taking Care of the Law. LC 82-2245. 290p. 1982. 13.50 (ISBN 0-688-01136-5). Morrow.

Bell, Gwen, ed. Strategies for Human Settlements: Habitat & Environment. LC 76-5416. (Illus.). 195p. (Orig.). 1976. (Eastwest Ctr); pap. 3.95x (ISBN 0-8248-0469-4). UH Pr.

Bell, H. C. Lord Palmerston, 2 Vols. (Illus.). 999p. 1966. Repr. of 1936 ed. Set. 42.50 (ISBN 0-208-00438-6, Archon). Shoe String.

--Woodrow Wilson & the People. iv, 392p. 1968. Repr. of 1945 ed. 25.00 (ISBN 0-208-00601-X, Archon). Shoe String.

Bell, H. C., et al. Guide to British West Indian Archive Materials, in London & in the Islands, for the History of the United States. 1926. 32.00 (ISBN 0-527-00688-2). Kraus Repr.

Bell, H. I. Cults & Creeds in Graeco-Roman Egypt. 1975. pap. 10.00 (ISBN 0-89005-088-0). Ares.

--Egypt from Alexander the Great to the Arab Conquest. 1985. Repr. of 1948 ed. 12.50 (ISBN 0-89005-354-5). Ares.

Bell, H. Idris. Fragments of an Unknown Gospel & Other Early Christian Papyri. 59.95 (ISBN 0-8490-0188-9). Gordon Pr.

--Literature & Life: Addresses to the English Association, 2 vols. 1973. Repr. of 1948 ed. 30.00 (ISBN 0-8274-1288-6). R West.

--Nature of Poetry As Conceived by the Welsh Bards. LC 73-9748. 1955. lib. bdg. 8.50 (ISBN 0-8414-3170-1). Folcroft.

Bell, H. Idris & Skeat, T. C., eds. Fragments of an Unknown Gospel & Other Early Christian Papyri. 76p. 1981. 25.00x (ISBN 0-7141-0438-8, Pub. by Brit Lib England). State Mutual Bk.

Bell, H. Idris, et al. Literature & Life: Addresses to the English Association, 2 Vols. LC 70-105802. 1970. Repr. of 1948 ed. Set. 35.00x (ISBN 0-8046-0959-4, Pub. by Kennikat). Assoc Faculty Pr.

Bell, Harold I. Egypt, from Alexander the Great to the Arab Conquest. LC 77-8057. (Gregynog Lectures for 1946). 1977. Repr. of 1948 ed. lib. bdg. 19.75x (ISBN 0-8371-9093-2, BEEA). Greenwood.

--The Nature of Poetry As Conceived by the Welsh Bards. 1978. Repr. of 1955 ed. lib. bdg. 10.00 (ISBN 0-8495-0410-4). Arden Lib.

Bell, Harold I., ed. Jews & Christians in Egypt. LC 79-97270. (Judaica Ser). (Illus.). 140p. 1972. Repr. of 1924 ed. lib. bdg. 15.50x (ISBN 0-8371-2587-1, BEJA). Greenwood.

Bell, Harriet, jt. auth. see Austen, Jane.

Bell, Harriet, ed. see Haubrick, Judd.

Bell, Harrison B., ed. see Crosby, Lamar H., Jr.

Bell, Henrietta. The Secret of Chapultepec Castle. 1980. pap. 4.95x (ISBN 0-89741-013-0). Roadrunner Tech.

Bell, Henry H. Obeah: Witchcraft in the West Indies. LC 78-106879. Repr. of 1889 ed. 18.75x (ISBN 0-8371-3275-4, BEO&, Pub. by Negro U Pr). Greenwood.

Bell, Herbert W. How to Get Your Book Published. 252p. 1985. 15.95 (ISBN 0-89879-193-6, 1386). Writers Digest.

Bell, Hermon F. & MacFarland, Charles S., eds. Religion Through the Ages: An Anthology. LC 68-23275. 1968. Repr. of 1948 ed. lib. bdg. 22.25x (ISBN 0-8371-0017-8, BERA). Greenwood.

Bell, Horace. On the Old West Coast: Being Further Reminiscences of a Ranger. Bartlett, Lanier, ed. LC 76-1242. (Chicano Heritage Ser.). (Illus.). 1976. Repr. of 1930 ed. lib. bdg. 31.00x (ISBN 0-405-09485-X). Ayer Co Pubs.

Bell, Howard H. Survey of the Negro Convention Movement. LC 74-94129. (American Negro: His History & Literature, Ser. No. 3). 1970. Repr. of 1953 ed. 19.00 (ISBN 0-405-01915-7). Ayer Co Pubs.

Bell, Howard H., ed. Minutes of the Proceedings of the National Negro Conventions 1830-1864. LC 72-105552. (American Negro: His History & Literature, Ser. No. 3). 1970. Repr. of 1969 ed. 26.50 (ISBN 0-405-01916-5). Ayer Co Pubs.

Bell, Howard M. Youth Tell Their Story: A Study of the Conditions & Attitudes of Young People in Maryland Between the Ages of 16 & 24. facsimile ed. LC 74-1665. (Children & Youth Ser.: Social Problems & Social Policy). 290p. 1974. Repr. of 1938 ed. 24.50x (ISBN 0-405-05946-9). Ayer Co Pubs.

Bell, Hugh M. The Adjustment Inventory. prices on request (ISBN 0-8047-1061-9). Stanford U Pr.

Bell, Hugh S. How to Succeed in Life Insurance Selling. 4.50 (ISBN 0-686-31052-7, 29705). Rough Notes.

Bell, I. E. & Chambers, J. D. Story of Lincoln. (Illus.). 1971. 14.95x (ISBN 0-8464-0887-2). Beekman Pubs.

Bell, Ian. The Dominican Republic. LC 80-13968. (Nations of the Modern World Ser.). (Illus.). 360p. 1981. lib. bdg. 36.50x (ISBN 0-89158-780-2). Westview.

Bell, Ian A. Defoe's Fiction. LC 84-28296. 208p. 1985. 28.00x (ISBN 0-389-20559-1). B&N Imports.

Bell, Ian F. Critic as Scientist: The Modernist Poetics of Ezra Pound. LC 80-41826. 302p. 1981. 34.00 (ISBN 0-416-31350-7, NO. 3451). Methuen Inc.

Bell, Ian F., ed. Henry James: Fiction As History. LC 84-18607. 188p. 1985. 27.50x (ISBN 0-389-20515-X, BNB-08071). B&N Imports.

Bell, Ian F. A., ed. Ezra Pound: Tactics for Reading. LC 82-11542. (Critical Studies Ser.). 248p. 1982. text ed. 28.50x (ISBN 0-389-20283-5, 07101). B&N Imports.

Bell, Irene W. Literature Cross-A-Word Book I: Crossword Learning Experiences with Animal Stories, Modern Fantasy, & Space & Time. (Illus.). 96p. 1982. pap. 9.95x (ISBN 0-89774-062-9). Oryx Pr.

--Literature Cross-A-Word Book II: Crossword Learning Experiences with Historical Fiction Mystery & Detective Stories, & Newbery Award Winners. (Illus.). 98p. 1982. pap. 9.95x (ISBN 0-89774-070-X). Oryx Pr.

Bell, Irene W. & Brown, Robert B. Gaming in the Media Center Made Easy. (Illus.). 200p. 1982. lib. bdg. 22.50 (ISBN 0-87287-336-6). Libs Unl.

Bell, Irene W. & Wieckert, Jeanne E. Basic Classroom Skills Through Games. LC 80-351. 1980. 18.50 (ISBN 0-87287-207-6). Libs Unl.

--Basic Media Skills Through Games. LC 79-941. 1979. 18.50 (ISBN 0-87287-194-0). Libs Unl.

--Basic Media Skills Through Games, 2 Vols. 2nd ed. 1985. Vol. 1. lib. bdg. 28.50 415pp (ISBN 0-87287-438-9); Vol. 2. lib. bdg. 23.50 350pp (ISBN 0-87287-470-2). Libs Unl.

Bell, Irene W., jt. auth. see Wieckert, Jeanne E.

Bell, Iris R. Clinical Ecology: A New Medical Approach to Environmental Illness. LC 82-7304. 80p. 1982. pap. 4.95x (ISBN 0-943004-01-2). Common Knowledge.

Bell, Irving. Christmas in Old New England. LC 80-69858. 54p. (gr. 3-8). 1981. 8.95 (ISBN 0-917780-02-7). April Hill.

Bell, J. & Machover, M. A Course in Mathematical Logic. 600p. 1977. text ed. 42.75 (ISBN 0-7204-2844-0, North-Holland). Elsevier.

Bell, J., et al, eds. General Welding & Cutting. (Engineering Craftsmen: No. F10). (Illus.). 1976. spiral bdg. 49.95x (ISBN 0-85083-330-2). Trans-Atlantic.

--Welding Practices, 6 vols. Incl. Vol. 1. General Welding & Cutting; Vol. 2. Advanced Pipe & Tube Welding; Vol. 3. Tungsten Arc Gas Shielded Welding; Vol. 4. Metal Arc Gas Shielded Welding; Vol. 5. Manual Metal Arc Welding; Vol. 6. Oxy-Acetlene Welding. 1977. Set. 200.00x (ISBN 0-89563-037-0). Intl Ideas.

Bell, J. Bowyer. On Revolt: Strategies of National Liberation. 368p. 1976. 17.50x (ISBN 0-674-63655-4). Harvard U Pr.

--The Secret Army: The IRA, 1916-1979. 496p. 1980. pap. 12.50 (ISBN 0-262-52090-7) MIT Pr.

--Terror out of Zion: The Fight for Israeli Independence 1929-1949. Rev. ed. (Illus.). 400p. 1984. Repr. of 1979 ed. cancelled (ISBN 0-906187-11-7). Univ Press.

--Transnational Terror. LC 75-27369. 1975. pap. 4.25 (ISBN 0-8447-3187-0). Am Enterprise.

Bell, J. Bowyer, Jr. The Horn of Africa. LC 73-89523. 64p. 1974. 6.50x (ISBN 0-8448-0255-7); pap. 2.45x (ISBN 0-8448-0256-5). Crane-Russak Co.

Bell, J. D. Peasants in Power: Alexander Stamboliski & the Bulgarian National Union, 1899-1923. 1977. 32.00x (ISBN 0-691-07584-0). Princeton U Pr.

Bell, J. Ellis, ed. Spectroscopy in Biochemistry, 2 vols. 336p. Vol. 1, May 1981. 82.00 (ISBN 0-8493-5551-6); Vol. 2, April, 1981. 82.00 (ISBN 0-8493-5552-4). CRC Pr.

Bell, J. F. Mechanics of Solids, Vol. 1: The Experimental Foundations of Solid Mechanics. (Illus.). 830p. 1984. pap. 36.00 (ISBN 0-387-13160-4). Springer-Verlag.

Bell, J. G., jt. auth. see Stone, Wilfred.

Bell, J. L. Boolean-Valued Models & Independence Proofs in Set Theory. 2nd ed. (Logic Guides Ser.). 1985. 19.95x (ISBN 0-19-853241-5). Oxford U Pr.

Bell, James. George Eliot As a Novelist. LC 74-8912. 1973. Repr. of 1888 ed. lib. bdg. 8.50 (ISBN 0-8414-0404-6). Folcroft.

Bell, James B. Family History Record Book. 1980. pap. 7.95 (ISBN 0-8166-0972-1). U of Minn Pr.

--Roots of Jesus. LC 81-43738. (Illus.). 216p. 1983. 13.95 (ISBN 0-385-18062-4). Doubleday.

Bell, James B. & Abrams, Richard I. In Search of Liberty: The Story of the Statue of Liberty & Ellis Island. LC 83-45554. (Illus.). 128p. 1984. 24.95 (ISBN 0-385-19624-5); pap. 10.95 (ISBN 0-385-19276-2). Doubleday.

Bell, James B., jt. auth. see Doane, Gilbert H.

Bell, James C., Jr. Opening a Highway to the Pacific, 1838-1846. LC 68-56648. (Columbia University Studies in the Social Sciences: No. 217). Repr. of 1921 ed. 18.50 (ISBN 0-404-51217-8). AMS Pr.

Bell, James E., Jr. Selection of New Suppliers by the Mobile Family. LC 69-63016. 1969. 6.50 (ISBN 0-87744-063-8). Mich St U Pr.

Bell, James F. Physics of Large Deformation of Crystalline Solids. (Springer Tracts in Natural Philosophy: Vol. 14). (Illus.). 1968. 35.00 (ISBN 0-387-04343-8). Springer-Verlag.

Bell, James K. & Cohn, Adrian. Rhetoric in a Modern Mode, with Selected Readings. 3rd ed. 1976. pap. text ed. write for info. (ISBN 0-02-470600-0). Macmillan.

--Rhetoric Three: The Rhetoric Section from Rhetoric in a Modern Mode. 3rd ed. 1976. pap. text ed. write for info. (ISBN 0-02-470620-5). Macmillan.

Bell, James K. & Cohn, Adrian A. Handbook of Grammar, Style & Usage. 3rd ed. 1981. pap. text ed. write for info. (ISBN 0-02-470640-X). Macmillan.

Bell, James M. Poetical Works. Arnett, Bishop, ed. LC 70-39423. Repr. of 1901 ed. 11.00 (ISBN 0-404-00005-3). AMS Pr.

--Poetical Works of James Madison Bell. facs. ed. LC 78-133148. (Black Heritage Library Collection). 1901. 14.75 (ISBN 0-8369-8704-7). Ayer Co Pubs.

Bell, James P. Our Quaker Friends of Ye Olden Time. LC 76-22486. (Illus.). 287p. 1976. Repr. of 1905 ed. 17.50 (ISBN 0-8063-0732-3). Genealog Pub.

Bell, James W. Little Rock Handbook. (Illus.). iv, 88p. (Orig.). 1980. pap. 8.95 (ISBN 0-939130-00-9). J W Bell.

Bell, Jan, ed. Accounting Control Systems: A Behavioral & Technical Integration. LC 83-61102. (Managerial Accounting Ser.). 378p. 1983. pap. text ed. 18.00x (ISBN 0-910129-02-9). Wiener Pub Inc.

Bell, Jeanenne. Old Jewelry, Eighteen Forty to Nineteen Fifty. 2nd ed. (Illus.). 307p. (Orig.). 1984. pap. 10.95 (ISBN 0-89689-053-8). Bks Americana.

Bell, Jerry. Howard Hughes. 1977. pap. 2.95 (ISBN 0-89036-069-3). Hawkes Pub Inc.

Bell, Jerry K. The Rapple. (Illus.). 50p. 1985. write for info. (ISBN 0-932784-02-X). Rapple Prod.

--The Rip Off. (Satan's Set: Vol. 11). 539p. 1985. 17.95 (ISBN 0-932784-03-8). Rapple Prod.

--Satan's Set, Vol. 1 666 Divided by 12. (Illus.). 285p. 1985. write for info. (ISBN 0-932784-00-3); pap. 8.95 (ISBN 0-932784-01-1). Rapple Prod.

Bell, Jimmy. The Gulf Coast Guide: Insight & Information on the Mississippi Coast. Woolfolk, Doug, ed. (Illus.). 232p. 1984. pap. 5.95 (ISBN 0-913567-02-7). Guilde Living.

Bell, Joan K., jt. auth. see Bell, Richard O.

Bell, John. Bell's New Pantheon, 2 vols. Feldman, Burton & Richardson, Robert D., eds. LC 78-60919. (Myth & Romanticism Ser.: Vol. 4). 809p. 1979. Set. lib. bdg. 160.00 (ISBN 0-8240-3553-4). Garland Pub.

--The Best of Bell's British Theatre, Consisting of the Most Esteemed English Plays, 41 vols. 1776-1802. Set. 1742.50 (ISBN 0-404-00800-3); 42.50 ea.; write for info. listing. AMS Pr.

--Policy Arguments in Judicial Decisions. LC 83-4207. 1983. 39.95x (ISBN 0-19-825397-4); pap. 14.95 (ISBN 0-19-825522-5). Oxford U Pr.

Bell, John, ed. Bell's British Theatre, 1776-1781, 21 vols. LC 76-44551. (Illus.). 1977. Repr. of 1781 ed. 892.50 set (ISBN 0-404-00800-3); 42.50 ea. AMS Pr.

--Selected Plays from Bell's British Theatre, 16 vols. LC 76-44553. (Illus.). Repr. of 1802 ed. Set. 680.00 (ISBN 0-404-00840-2); 42.50 ea. Ams Pr.

--Supplement to Bell's British Theatre, Farces-1784, 4 vols. LC 76-44552. (Illus.). 1977. Repr. of 1784 ed. 42.50 ea.; 170.00 set (ISBN 0-404-00830-5). AMS Pr.

Bell, John B. Purdue Thirty-Ninth Industrial Waste Conference. 1008p. 1985. text ed. 79.95 (ISBN 0-250-40640-3). Butterworth.

Bell, John D. The Bulgarian Communist Party from Blagoev to Zhivkov. (Publication History of Ruling Communist Parties Ser.: No. 320). (Illus.). 300p. (Orig.). 1985. pap. price not set (ISBN 0-8179-8202-7). Hoover Inst Pr.

Bell, John F. A History of Economic Thought: A Structured Approach to the Data Communications Environment. 2nd ed. LC 79-22893. 754p. 1980. Repr. of 1967 ed. lib. bdg. 38.50 (ISBN 0-89874-065-7). Krieger.

Bell, John L., Jr. Hard Times: Beginnings of the Great Depression in North Carolina, 1929-1933. (Illus.). xi, 87p. 1982. pap. 4.00 (ISBN 0-86526-196-2). NC Archives.

Bell, John M., ed. Purdue Thirty-Eighth Industrial Waste Conference: Proceedings. 1000p. 1984. text ed. 75.00 (ISBN 0-250-40639-X). Butterworth.

--Purdue Thirty-Seventh University Industrial Waste Conference, 1982. LC 77-84415. (Illus.). 952p. 1983. 75.00 (ISBN 0-250-40592-X). Butterworth.

Bell, John P. Crisis in Costa Rica: The 1948 Revolution. LC 77-165920. (Latin American Monographs Ser.: No. 24). 206p. 1971. 13.95x (ISBN 0-292-70147-0). U of Tex Pr.

Bell, Johnny F., jt. auth. see Thompson, Charles L.

Bell, Jonathan W., ed. The Kansas Art Reader. LC 80-621211. (Kansas Studies). 437p. (Orig.). 1976. pap. text ed. 6.75 (ISBN 0-936352-02-7, B926). U of KS Cont Ed.

Bell, Joseph D. Industrial Unionism. LC 74-22732. (Labor Movement in Fiction & Non-Fiction). Repr. of 1949 ed. 11.50 (ISBN 0-404-58485-3). AMS Pr.

Bell, Joseph N. Love Theory in Later Hanbalite Islam. LC 78-5904. 1979. PLB 49.50x (ISBN 0-87395-244-8). State U NY Pr.

Bell, Josephine. A Deadly Place to Stay. 224p. 1983. 12.95 (ISBN 0-8027-5496-1). Walker & Co.

--Death of a Poison Tongue. LC 77-21252. (Jubilee Mystery Ser.). 192p. pap. 2.75 (ISBN 0-8128-7067-0). Stein & Day.

--The Fennister Affair. LC 77-21305. (Jubilee Mystery Ser.). 188p. pap. 2.50 (ISBN 0-8128-7056-5). Stein & Day.

--A Question of Inheritance. 1981. 9.95 (ISBN 0-8027-5438-4). Walker & Co.

--A Question of Inheritance. (British Mysteries Ser.). 1983. pap. 2.95 (ISBN 0-8027-3033-7). Walker & Co.

--Stroke of Death. LC 77-79963. (British Mystery Ser.). 175p. 1984. pap. 2.95 (ISBN 0-8027-3073-6). Walker & Co.

--Treachery in Type. (Walker Mystery Ser.). 1980. 8.95 (ISBN 0-8027-5402-3). Walker & Co.

--Treachery in Type. (British Mysteries Ser.). 1983. pap. 2.95 (ISBN 0-8027-3039-6). Walker & Co.

--The Trouble in Hunter Ward. 1984. pap. 2.95 (ISBN 0-8027-3051-5). Walker & Co.

--Victim. 192p. 1983. pap. 2.95 (ISBN 0-8027-3021-3). Walker & Co.

--The Wilberforce Legacy. 1984. pap. 2.95 (ISBN 0-8027-3096-5). Walker & Co.

--Wolf! Wolf! 190p. 1980. 9.95 (ISBN 0-8027-5425-2). Walker & Co.

--Wolf! Wolf! LC 80-51993. (British Mystery Ser.). 175p. 1984. pap. 2.95 (ISBN 0-8027-3077-9). Walker & Co.

Bell, Julius, jt. auth. see Fomon, Samuel.

Bell, K. & Morgan, G. The Great Historians: An Anthology of British History Arranged in Chronological Order. 1924. 20.00 (ISBN 0-8482-7379-6). Norwood Edns.

Bell, K. W. & Parrish, R. G. Computational Skills with Applications. 448p. 1975. pap. text ed. 19.95 (ISBN 0-669-91082-1); instructor's manual 1.95 (ISBN 0-669-93237-X). Heath.

Bell, Keith. Championship Thinking: The Athletes Guide to Winning Performances in All Sports. 188p. 1983. 17.95 (ISBN 0-13-127597-6); pap. 8.95 (ISBN 0-13-127589-5). P-H.

Bell, L. F., jt. auth. see Grant, Eugene L.

Bell, L. N. Energetics of the Photosynthezing Plant Cell. (Soviet Scientific Reviews Supplement Series Physicochemical Biology: Vol. 5). 420p. 1985. text ed. 175.00 (ISBN 3-7186-0195-8). Harwood Academic.

Bell Laboratories. Human Factors in Telecommunications International Symposium, 9th. 1980. 75.00 (ISBN 0-686-37981-0). Info Gatekeepers.

Bell Labs Staff. UNIX, 2 vols. 1983. Vol. 1, 208 p. pap. 37.45 (ISBN 0-03-061742-1); Vol. II, 320 p. pap. 37.45 (ISBN 0-03-061743-X). HR&W.

Bell, Lady. Landmarks. 1929. 22.50 (ISBN 0-932062-13-X). Sharon Hill.

Bell, Landon C. Charles Parish, York County, Virginia: History & Registers -- Births, 1648-1789; Deaths 1665-1787. LC 33-27865. vi, 285p. 1984. Repr. of 1932 ed. 12.50 (ISBN 0-88490-114-9). VA State Lib.

--Cumberland Parish, Lunenburg County, Virginia 1746-1816 and Vestry Book 1746-1816. LC 74-14283. 633p. 1974. Repr. of 1930 ed. 25.00 (ISBN 0-8063-0632-7). Genealog Pub.

--Lunenburg County, Virginia: Wills 1746-1825. LC 72-83657. 136p. 1972. 15.00 (ISBN 0-685-65057-X). Va Bk.

--The Old Free State: A Contribution to the History of Lunenburg County & Southside Virginia, 2 vols in 1. LC 74-5469. (Illus.). 1267p. 1974. Repr. of 1927 ed. 40.00 (ISBN 0-8063-0623-8). Genealog Pub.

--Poe & Chivers. LC 73-9500. Repr. of 1931 ed. lib. bdg. 10.00 (ISBN 0-8414-3133-7). Folcroft.

Bell, Laurel & Garthwaite, Elloyse M. Accelerated Grammar. 1982. pap. text ed. 17.95 (ISBN 0-8403-2778-1). Kendall-Hunt.

Bell, Leland V. In Hitler's Shadow: The Anatomy of American Nazism. LC 72-89991. 1973. 13.50x (ISBN 0-8046-9029-4, Pub. by Kennikat). Assoc Faculty Pr.

--Treating the Mentally Ill: From Colonial Times to the Present. LC 80-168. 262p. 1980. 36.95. Praeger.

Bell, Leland V., jt. auth. see Tyor, Peter L.

Bell, Lesley, jt. auth. see Klemz, Astrid.

Bell, Linda, ed. Visions of Women. LC 82-4866. (Contemporary Issues in Biomedicine Ethics & Society Ser.). 512p. 1985. 39.50 (ISBN 0-89603-044-X); pap. 7.50 (ISBN 0-89603-054-7). Humana.

Bell, Linda R. The Red Butterfly: Lupus Patients Can Survive. (Orig.). 1983. pap. 4.95 (ISBN 0-8283-1880-8). Branden Pub Co.

Bell, Lorna & Seyfer, Eudora. Gentle Yoga for People with Arthritis, Stroke Damage, Multiple Sclerosis & in Wheelchairs. (Illus.). 140p. 1982. pap. 6.50 (ISBN 0-911119-01-9). Igram Pr.

Bell, Louis. The Telescope. 287p. 1981. pap. 6.95 (ISBN 0-486-24151-3). Dover.

--The Telescope. (Illus.). 13.25 (ISBN 0-8446-5877-4). Peter Smith.

Bell, M. Christina Rossetti. LC 74-156294. (English Literature Ser., No. 33). 1971. Repr. of 1898 ed. lib. bdg. 56.95x (ISBN 0-8383-1292-6). Haskell.

Bell, M. Bannon. Fire! How to Save Your Pet's Life. (Illus.). 30p. 1984. pap. 3.00 (ISBN 0-931573-01-7). Pet Pro Co.

--Lamp in the Labyrinth. (Illus.). 65p. 1984. pap. 3.50 (ISBN 0-931573-00-9). Pet Pro Co.

Bell, M. Robert, jt. auth. see Steinaker, Norman.

Bell, Mackenzie. Christina Rossetti. 1973. Repr. of 1898 ed. 14.95 (ISBN 0-8274-1672-5). R West.

--Christina Rossetti: A Biographical & Critical Study. LC 70-148747. Repr. of 1898 ed. 12.50 (ISBN 0-404-08724-8). AMS Pr.

Bell, Madison S. Waiting for the End of the World. LC 85-2743. 1985. 16.95 (ISBN 0-89919-377-3). Ticknor & Fields.

--The Washington Square Ensemble. 336p. 1983. 15.75 (ISBN 0-670-75005-0). Viking.

--The Washington Square Ensemble. 352p. 1984. pap. 5.95 (ISBN 0-14-007025-7). Penguin.

Bell, Malcolm. Morgantina Studies: Vol. 1, the Terracottas. LC 80-8537. (Illus.). 416p. 1981. 60.00x (ISBN 0-691-03946-1). Princeton U Pr.

--Sir Edward Burne-Jones: A Record & Review. Repr. of 1898 ed. 16.00 (ISBN 0-404-00733-3). AMS Pr.

--The Turkey Shoot: Tracking the Attica Cover-Up. 384p. 1985. 17.50 (ISBN 0-394-55020-X). Grove.

Bell, Margaret. Margaret Fuller. 1930. 11.50 (ISBN 0-8274-2672-0). R West.

--Margaret Fuller: A Biography. facsimile ed. LC 72-164587. (Select Bibliographies Reprint Ser). Repr. of 1930 ed. 20.00 (ISBN 0-8369-5871-3). Ayer Co Pubs.

Bell, Margaret E. Learning & Instruction: Theory into Practice. 546p. 1986. text ed. price not set (ISBN 0-02-307930-4). Macmillan.

Bell, Maria A. Guess Who's Cooking Dinner: One Hundred & Fifty Recipes from the Famous, the Near Famous & the Super Famous. (Illus.). 1979. 12.95 (ISBN 0-8027-0614-2); pap. 6.95 (ISBN 0-8027-7141-6). Walker & Co.

Bell, Marion L. Crusade in the City: Revivalism in Nineteenth-Century Philadelphia. 1978. 22.50 (ISBN 0-8387-1929-5). Bucknell U Pr.

Bell, Marion V. & Swidan, Eleanor A. Reference Books: A Brief Guide. 8th ed. 1978. pap. 5.00 (ISBN 0-910556-11-3). Enoch Pratt.

Bell, Martin. A Deadly Place to Stay. rev. ed. (Walker British Mystery Paperbacks Ser.). 192p. 1985. pap. 2.95 (ISBN 0-8027-3134-1). Walker & Co.

--Nenshu & the Tiger: Parables of Life & Death. 112p. 1982. pap. 5.95 (ISBN 0-8164-2356-3, Pub. by Seabury). Winston Pr.

--Return of the Wolf. 128p. 1983. 12.50 (ISBN 0-8164-0545-X, Pub. by Seabury); pap. 7.95 (ISBN 0-8164-2470-5). Winston Pr.

--Way of the Wolf. (Epiphany Ser.). 144p. 1983. pap. 2.95 (ISBN 0-345-30522-1). Ballantine.

--The Way of the Wolf. 254p. 1985. pap. 7.95 large print ed. (ISBN 0-8027-2483-3). Walker & Co.

--Way of the Wolf: The Gospel in New Images. LC 77-120366. (Illus.). 128p. 1970. pap. 8.95 (ISBN 0-8164-0202-7, AY6445, Pub. by Seabury); 2 records 8.95 ea. Winston Pr.

Bell, Marty. The Legend of Dr. J. The Story of Julius Erving. (RL 8). 1976. pap. 2.95 (ISBN 0-451-12179-1, AE2179, Sig). NAL.

Bell, Marvin. Drawn by Stones, by Earth, by Things That Have Been in the Fire. LC 84-72998. 53p. 1984. 11.95 (ISBN 0-689-11466-4); pap. 6.95 (ISBN 0-689-11467-2). Atheneum.

--Escape into You. LC 79-162967. 1971. pap. 5.95 (ISBN 0-689-10472-3). Atheneum.

--Old Snow Just Melting: Essays & Interviews. (Poets on Poetry Ser.). 200p. 1983. pap. 7.95 (ISBN 0-472-06342-1). U of Mich Pr.

--Probable Volume of Dreams. LC 77-84942. (Orig.). 1969. pap. 3.95 (ISBN 0-689-10030-2). Atheneum.

--Residue of Song. LC 74-80325. (Orig.). 1974. pap. 3.95 (ISBN 0-689-10637-8). Atheneum.

--Stars Which See: Stars Which Do Not See. LC 76-39922. 1977. pap. 4.95 (ISBN 0-689-10779-X). Atheneum.

--These Green-Going-to-Yellow. LC 81-66013. 1981. 10.95 (ISBN 0-689-11228-9); pap. 5.95 (ISBN 0-689-11227-0). Atheneum.

Bell, Marvin, jt. auth. see Stafford, William.

Bell, Mary A. Pearls. 1984. pap. 6.95 (ISBN 0-86666-203-0). Natl Lit Guild.

Bell, Mary B. Colonial Bertie Co., N.C., Deed Books A-H 1720-1757. 328p. 1980. Repr. of 1963 ed. 30.00 (ISBN 0-89308-048-9). Southern Hist Pr.

Bell, Mary W. Terra & the Tornado. (Orig.). 1984. pap. 2.95 (ISBN 0-8024-8589-8). Moody.

Bell, Mervyn, ed. Britain's National Parks. LC 74-20450. (Illus.). 160p. 1975. 17.95 (ISBN 0-7153-6792-7). David & Charles.

Bell, Michael. The Salesman in the Field: viii, 108p. 1980. pap. 8.75 (ISBN 92-2-102308-7, ILO149, ILO). Unipub.

--The Salesman in the Field: Conditions of Work & Employment of Commercial Travellers & Representatives. International Labour Office, Geneva, ed. viii, 108p. (Orig.). 1980. pap. 8.55 (ISBN 92-2-102308-7). Intl Labour Office.

--The Sentiment of Reality. 224p. 1983. text ed. 22.50x (ISBN 0-04-801023-5). Allen Unwin.

Bell, Michael, ed. Context of English Literature 1900-1930. LC 80-7792. (Context of English Literature Ser.). 250p. 1980. 34.50x (ISBN 0-8419-0423-5); pap. 19.75x (ISBN 0-8419-0424-3). Holmes & Meier.

Bell, Michael C., et al. Investigating Living Systems, Pt. I. 2nd ed. 203p. 1982. pap. 11.95x lab manual (ISBN 0-88725-021-1). Hunter Textbks.

--Investigating Living Systems, Pt. II. 2nd ed. 200p. 1982. pap. 11.95x lab manual (ISBN 0-89459-195-9). Hunter Textbks.

Bell, Michael D. Development of American Romance: The Sacrifice of Relation. LC 80-12241. 272p. 1981. lib. bdg. 25.00x (ISBN 0-226-04211-1). U of Chicago Pr.

--The Development of American Romance: The Sacrifice of Relation. LC 80-12241. xiv, 292p. 1984. pap. 10.95x (ISBN 0-226-04213-8). U of Chicago Pr.

Bell, Michael D., ed. see Brackenridge, Hugh H. & Freneau, Philip.

Bell, Michael E. & Lande, Paul S., eds. Regional Dimensions of Industrial Policy. LC 80-8994. 224p. 1981. 26.50x (ISBN 0-669-04491-1). Lexington Bks.

Bell, Michael J. The World from Brown's Lounge: An Ethnography of Black Middle-Class Play. LC 82-4732. 208p. 1983. 14.95x (ISBN 0-252-00956-8). U of Ill Pr.

Bell, Millicent. Hawthorne's View of the Artist. LC 62-13566. 1962. 36.50x (ISBN 0-87395-008-9). State U NY Pr.

--Marquand: An American Life. LC 79-12818. (Illus.). 1979. 17.95 (ISBN 0-316-08828-5, Pub. by Atlantic-Little Brown). Little.

Bell, Millicent, ed. see Hawthorne, Nathaniel.

Bell, Mimi. Offbeat Oregon. LC 83-5229. (Orig.). 1983. pap. 6.95 (ISBN 0-87701-274-1). Chronicle Bks.

Bell, Muriel, tr. see Bianco, Lucien.

Bell, N., tr. see Hohnel, L. Von.

Bell, Neal. Two Small Bodies. pap. 3.35x (ISBN 0-686-63171-4). Dramatists Play.

Bell, Neil. Cover His Face. 1943. 20.00 (ISBN 0-8274-2108-7). R West.

Bell, Neill. The Book of Where: Or How to Be Naturally Geographic. 140p. (gr. 7 up). 1982. 13.45i (ISBN 0-316-08830-7); pap. 7.70 (ISBN 0-316-08831-5). Little.

--Only Human: Why We Are the Way We Are. LC 83-9826. (Illus.). 128p. (gr. 4 up). 1983. 13.45i (ISBN 0-316-08816-1); pap. 7.70 (ISBN 0-316-08818-8). Little.

Bell, Nora K., ed. Who Decides? Conflicts of Rights in Health Care. LC 81-83908. (Contemporary Issues in Biomedicine, Ethics & Society Ser.). 240p. 1982. 29.50 (ISBN 0-89603-034-2). Humana.

Bell, Norman T. & Abedor, Allan J. Developing Audio-Visual Instructional Modules for Vocational & Technical Training. LC 76-50019. (Illus.). 192p. 1977. pap. 26.95 (ISBN 0-87778-094-3). Educ Tech Pubns.

Bell, Norman T., et al. Proposal Writing Guide. 1984. 9.95. Radio Shack.

Bell, Norman W. & Vogel, Ezra F., eds. Modern Introduction to the Family. rev. ed. LC 68-12830. 1968. text ed. 17.95 (ISBN 0-02-902330-0). Free Pr.

Bell, Oliver, ed. America's Changing Population. (Reference Shelf Ser.). 1974. 7.00 (ISBN 0-8242-0522-7). Wilson.

Bell, P. Hightech Writing. 240p. 1985. pap. 19.95 (ISBN 0-471-81864-X). Wiley.

Bell, P. B. & Staines, P. J. Reasoning & Argument in Psychology. 228p. (Orig.). 1983. pap. 11.95x (ISBN 0-7100-0712-4). Routledge & Kegan.

Bell, P. G. Essentials of New Testament: Greek. 1983. pap. 9.95 Wkbk. (ISBN 0-89957-569-2); answer bk. for wkbk. 4.95 (ISBN 0-89957-570-6); answers for essentials 2.95. AMG Pubs.

Bell, P. R. & Barrie, W. Operative Arterial Surgery. 200p. 1981. text ed. 39.50 (ISBN 0-7236-0610-2). PSG Pub Co.

Bell, P. R. & Woodcock, C. L. The Diversity of Green Plants. 3rd ed. 1983. 19.95 (ISBN 0-7131-2866-6). E Arnold.

Bell, Patty & Myrland, Doug. The Official Silicon Valley Guy Handbook. 128p. 1983. pap. 3.95 (ISBN 0-380-84392-7, 84392-7). Avon.

Bell, Paul B., Jr., ed. Scanning Electron Microscopy of Cells in Culture. (Illus.). vi, 314p. 1984. pap. 29.00 (ISBN 0-931288-31-2). Scanning Electron.

Bell, Peter. Timber & Iron: Houses in North Queensland Mining Settlements 1861-1920. (Illus.). 1985. 30.00x (ISBN 0-7022-1714-X). U of Queensland Pr.

Bell, Peter & Evans, Jimmy. Counseling the Black Client: Alcohol Use & Abuse in Black America. 52p. 1981. 3.95 (ISBN 0-89486-124-7). Hazelden.

Bell, Peter & Tilney, N., eds. BIMR Surgery Vol. 4: Vascular Surgery. 320p. 1984. text ed. 39.95 (ISBN 0-407-02320-8). Butterworth.

Bell, Peter D. Peasants in Socialist Transition: Life in a Collectivized Hungarian Village. LC 80-25126. (Illus.). 320p. 1984. lib. bdg. 27.50x (ISBN 0-520-04157-7). U of Cal Pr.

Bell, Peter M. Programming in Decision Tables. (Illus.). 176p. (Orig.). 1984. pap. 24.50 (ISBN 0-930953-01-0). Albion PA.

Bell, Philip. Disestablishment in Ireland & Wales. LC 73-488607. (Church Historical Society Ser.: No. 90). 1969. pap. 21.50x (ISBN 0-8401-5090-3). A R Allenson.

Bell, Philip A., ed. Pacific Appeal, Vol. 1. 1969-1970. 10.95 (ISBN 0-685-40335-1). R & E Pubs.

Bell, Philip W., jt. auth. see Edwards, Edgar O.

Bell, Quentin. The Art Critic & the Art Historian. LC 75-314718. (Leslie Stephen Lecture Ser.: 1973). pap. 20.00 (ISBN 0-317-10217-6, 2051369). Bks Demand UMI.

--The Brandon Papers. Evans, Maurice, ed. 224p. 1985. 15.95 (ISBN 0-317-20393-2). HarBraceJ.

--On Human Finery. 2nd rev. & en. ed. LC 76-9129. (Illus.). 1978. pap. 6.95 (ISBN 0-8052-0606-X). Schocken.

--Ruskin. LC 77-6123. 1978. Repr. of 1963 ed. 8.95 (ISBN 0-8076-0876-9). Braziller.

--Techniques of Terra Cotta. (Illus.). 128p. 1984. 19.95 (ISBN 0-7011-2664-7, Pub. by Chatto & Windus); pap. 8.95 (ISBN 0-7011-2701-5). Merrimack Pub Cir.

--Virginia Woolf: A Biography. LC 73-12870. (Illus.). 530p. 1974. pap. 9.95 (ISBN 0-15-693580-5, Harv). HarBraceJ.

Bell, R. Unequal Allies. 1977. 20.00x (ISBN 0-522-84115-5, Pub. by Melbourne U Pr). Intl Spec Bk.

Bell, R. A., tr. see Gaxotte, Pierre.

Bell, R. C. Board & Table Games from Many Civilizations. LC 79-51819. (Illus.). 1980. pap. 6.50 (ISBN 0-486-23855-5). Dover.

--Board & Table Games from Many Civilizations, 2 vols. in one. rev. ed. 15.75 (ISBN 0-8446-5734-4). Peter Smith.

--Discovering Backgammon. 2nd ed. (Shire Discovering Ser.). (Illus.). 48p. 1983. pap. 2.95 (ISBN 0-85263-474-9, Pub. by Shire Pubns England). Hippocrene Bks.

--Discovering Chess. (Shire Discovering Ser.). (Illus.). 48p. 1983. pap. 2.95 (ISBN 0-85263-478-1, Pub. by Shire Pubns England). Hippocrene Bks.

--Discovering Dice & Dominoes. (Discovering Ser.: No. 255). (Illus.). 63p. (Orig.). 1983. pap. 3.50 (ISBN 0-85263-532-X, Pub. by Shire Pubns England). Seven Hills Bks.

--Discovering Mah-Jong. (Shire Discovering Ser.). (Illus.). 48p. 1984. pap. 2.95 (ISBN 0-686-88517-1, Pub. by Shire Pubns England). Hippocrene Bks.

--Discovering Old Board Games. (Illus.). 80p. 1983. pap. 2.95 (ISBN 0-85263-533-8, Pub. by Shire Pubns England). Hippocrene Bks.

--Discovering Old Board Games. (Discovering Ser.: No. 182). (Illus.). 64p. 1980. pap. 3.50 (ISBN 0-85263-533-8, Pub. by Shire Pubns England). Seven Hills Bks.

--Studies in Ephesians. 1971. pap. 2.75 (ISBN 0-88027-041-1). Firm Foun Pub.

--Studies in Galatians. 1954. pap. 2.75 (ISBN 0-88027-042-X). Firm Foun Pub.

--Studies in Philippians. 1956. pap. 2.75 (ISBN 0-88027-043-8). Firm Foun Pub.

--Studies in Romans. 1957. pap. 2.75 (ISBN 0-88027-025-X). Firm Foun Pub.

Bell, R. D. & Scott, F. B. Moths Lepidoptera: Sphingidae, Vol. 5. (Fauna of British India Ser.). (Illus.). xviii, 537p. 1976. Repr. 40.00 (ISBN 0-88065-056-7, Pub. by Messers Today & Tomorrows Printers & Publishers India). Scholarly Pubns.

Bell, R. Dermont, jt. auth. see Christensen, Edward L.

Bell, R. H., jt. auth. see Prusaczyk, J. E.

Bell, R. J. Introductory Fourier Transform Spectroscopy. 1972. 59.50 (ISBN 0-12-085150-4). Acad Pr.

Bell, R. M., jt. auth. see Barnett, A.

Bell, R. Q. & Harper, L. V. Child Effects on Adults. 272p. 1977. 29.95x (ISBN 0-89859-430-8). L Erlbaum Assocs.

Bell, R. T., jt. auth. see Bhatnagar, R. P.

Bell, R. W., et al, eds. Developmental Psychobiology & Clinical Neuropsychology. (Interfaces in Psychology Ser.: No. 1). 133p. 1984. 24.95 (ISBN 0-89672-120-5); pap. 14.95 (ISBN 0-89672-119-1). Tex Tech Pr.

Bell, Rebecca S. & Severin, C. S. Profiles Cut from the Wave: CSS Sixth Collection of Poetry. (Collection of National Poetry Ser.). (Illus.). 200p. 1984. pap. 9.95 (ISBN 0-942170-06-7). CSS Pubns.

Bell, Rebecca S. & Severin, C. S., eds. The Whisper of Dreams: A Collection of Poetry. (CSS Collection of National Poetry Ser.). (Illus.). 232p. 1982. pap. 9.95 (ISBN 0-942170-04-0). CSS Pubns.

Bell, Rebecca S. & Severin, C. Sherman, eds. I Have Need of the Poets. (Collection of National Poetry Ser.: No. 7). (Illus.). 168p. (Orig.). 1984. pap. 9.95 (ISBN 0-942170-07-5). CSS Pubns.

Bell, Reginald. Public School Education of Second-Generation Japanese in California. Daniels, Roger, ed. LC 78-54808. (Asian Experience in North America Ser.). 1979. Repr. of 1935 ed. lib. bdg. 12.00x (ISBN 0-405-11264-5). Ayer Co Pubs.

Bell, Richard. Origin of Islam in Its Christian Environment. 224p. 1968. Repr. of 1926 ed. 30.00x (ISBN 0-7146-1977-9, F Cass Co). Biblio Dist.

Bell, Richard H. Sensing the Spirit. LC 84-5158. (Spirituality & the Christian Life Ser.: Vol. 6). 120p. 1984. pap. 7.95 (ISBN 0-664-24632-X). Westminster.

Bell, Richard O. & Bell, Joan K. Auditions & Scenes: American & British Theatre. LC 80-80119. 200p. pap. 9.95 postponed (ISBN 0-9603626-1-4). Armado & Moth.

--Auditions & Scenes from Shakespeare. LC 79-54914. 161p. (Orig.). 1979. pap. 7.95 (ISBN 0-9603626-0-6). Armado & Moth.

Bell, Richard Q. & Harper, Lawrence V. Child Effects on Adults. LC 77-24115. 253p. 1977. 16.50x (ISBN 0-470-99267-0). Halsted Pr.

--Child Effects on Adults. LC 80-16565. xiv, 253p. 1980. pap. 5.95x (ISBN 0-8032-6058-X, BB 758, Bison). U of Nebr Pr.

Bell, Rivian & Koenig, Teresa. Careers at a Movie Studio. LC 82-20865. (Early Career Bks.). (Illus.). 36p. (gr. 2-5). 1983. PLB 5.95 (ISBN 0-8225-0347-6). Lerner Pubns.

--Careers in an Airplane Factory. LC 82-17136. (Early Career Bks.). (Illus.). 36p. (gr. 2-5). 1983. PLB 5.95 (ISBN 0-8225-0349-2). Lerner Pubns.

--Careers with a Record Company. LC 82-20840. (Early Career Bks.). (Illus.). 36p. (gr. 2-5). 1983. PLB 5.95 (ISBN 0-8225-0348-4). Lerner Pubns.

Bell, Rivian, jt. auth. see Koenig, Teresa.

Bell, Robert. The Culture of Policy Deliberations. LC 84-23799. 1985. 30.00 (ISBN 0-8135-1093-7). Rutgers U Pr.

--Early Ballads. 59.95 (ISBN 0-8490-0067-X). Gordon Pr.

--Early Ballads. Repr. 11.25 (ISBN 0-8274-2212-1). R West.

--Fairy Tale Plays & How to Act Them. 1896. 20.00 (ISBN 0-8482-7362-1). Norwood Edns.

--How to Win at Office Politics: Techniques, Tips, & Step-by-Step Plans for Coming Out Ahead. LC 84-40095. 258p. 1984. 15.95 (ISBN 0-8129-1118-0). Times Bks.

--Roadwork. 1979. pap. 2.25 (ISBN 0-8439-0697-9, Leisure Bks). Dorchester Pub Co.

--Songs from the Dramatists. 1927. 20.00 (ISBN 0-8482-7408-3). Norwood Edns.

--Stranger in Dodge. Large Print ed. LC 83-17998. 256p. 1983. 12.95 (ISBN 0-89621-498-2). Thorndike Pr.

--To the Death. 192p. (Orig.). 1984. pap. 2.50 (ISBN 0-345-31937-0). Ballantine.

--Valley Called Disappointment. 128p. 1982. pap. 1.95 (ISBN 0-345-30076-9). Ballantine.

--You Can Win at Office Politics: Techniques, Tips, & Step-by-Step Plans for Coming Out Ahead. 272p. 1985. pap. 7.95 (ISBN 0-03-005863-5). HR&W.

Bell, Robert, jt. auth. see Bell, Rosanna.

Bell, Robert, jt. auth. see Hansen, Rosanna.

Bell, Robert, ed. Early Ballads, Illustrative of History, Traditions, & Customs. LC 67-23928. 1968. Repr. of 1877 ed. 43.00x (ISBN 0-8103-3408-9). Gale.

--Siege of the Castle of Edinburgh. LC 78-39425. (Bannatyne Club, Edinburgh. Publications: No. 23). Repr. of 1828 ed. 18.50 (ISBN 0-404-52729-9). AMS Pr.

--Songs from the Dramatists. 268p. 1981. Repr. lib. bdg. 45.00 (ISBN 0-8495-0484-8). Arden Lib.

Bell, Robert, ed. see Courcelles, M.

Bell, Robert, ed. see Howard, Henry.

Bell, Robert, jt. ed. see Spalek, John M.

Bell, Robert E. Dictionary of Classical Mythology: Symbols, Attributes, & Associations. LC 81-19141. 390p. 1982. 30.00 (ISBN 0-87436-305-5). ABC Clio.

Bell, Robert E., ed. Prehistory of Oklahoma. LC 83-12321. (New World Archaeological Record Ser.). 1983. 48.50 (ISBN 0-12-085180-6). Acad Pr.

Bell, Robert P. & Hanks, Joanna. Typewriting Office Practice for Colleges: Simulation. 1983. 7.60 (ISBN 0-538-11770-2, K77). SW Pub.

Bell, Robert R. Contemporary Social Problems. 542p. 1981. 27.00x (ISBN 0-256-02412-X). Dorsey.

--Marriage & Family Interaction. 6th ed. 1983. 25.00x (ISBN 0-256-02868-0). Dorsey.

--Worlds of Friendship. (Sociological Observations Ser.: Vol. 12). 200p. 1981. 25.00 (ISBN 0-8039-1723-6); pap. 12.50 (ISBN 0-8039-1724-4). Sage.

Bell, Robert S. Paul's Letter to the Romans. 1970. pap. 2.75 (ISBN 0-88027-036-5). Firm Foun Pub.

Bell, Robert V. Never Say Die. 160p. (Orig.). 1985. pap. 2.50 (ISBN 0-345-32502-8). Ballantine.

--Platte River Crossing. 144p. (Orig.). 1983. pap. 2.25 (ISBN 0-345-31208-2). Ballantine.

--Stranger in Dodge. 192p. (Orig.). 1983. pap. 2.25 (ISBN 0-345-30875-1). Ballantine.

Bell, Robert W. & Lockerbie, D. Bruce. In Peril on the Sea. LC 84-4153. (Illus.). 288p. 1984. 14.95 (ISBN 0-385-18378-X). Doubleday.

Bell, Robert W. & Smotherman, William F., eds. Maternal Influences & Early Behavior. LC 78-17074. (Illus.). 465p. 1980. text ed. 60.00 (ISBN 0-89335-059-1). SP Med & Sci Bks.

Bell, Robin. Strathinver. 1983. 30.00x (ISBN 0-86334-035-0, Pub. by Macdonald Pub UK); pap. 20.00x (ISBN 0-86334-036-9). State Mutual Bk.

Bell, Roger, et al, eds. Assessing Health & Human Service Needs: Concepts, Methods & Applications. LC 81-20249. (Community Psychology Ser.: Vol. VIII). (Illus.). 352p. 1983. 34.95 (ISBN 0-89885-057-6). Human Sci Pr.

Bell, Roger J. Last among Equals: Hawaiian Statehood & American Politics. LC 83-24330. 387p. 1984. text ed. 24.95x (ISBN 0-8248-0847-9). UH Pr.

Bell, Roger T. Sociolinguistics: Goals, Methods & Problems. LC 76-9423. 1976. 25.00x (ISBN 0-312-73955-9). St Martin.

Bell, Rosanna & Bell, Robert. My First Book about Space: Developed in Conjunction with NASA. (Illus.). 48p. (gr. k-3). 1985. 6.95 (ISBN 0-671-60262-4). Messner.

Bell, Roy. One Thousand & One Questions About Radiologic Technology, Vol. 1. 192p. (Orig.). 1980. pap. text ed. 10.50 (ISBN 0-8391-1607-1). Univ Park.

--One Thousand & One Questions about Radiologic Technology, Vol. 3. LC 80-137150. (Illus.). 192p. 1983. pap. text ed. 10.50 (ISBN 0-8391-1957-7, 20559). Univ Park.

--One Thousand & One Questions about Radiologic Technology, Vol. 4. 1985. pap. text ed. 12.00 (ISBN 0-8391-2086-9, 22144). Univ Park.

--One Thousand & One Questions about Radiation Therapy Technology. 160p. 1981. pap. 10.50 (ISBN 0-8391-1694-2). Univ Park.

--One Thousand One Questions about Diagnostic Medical Sonography. 168p. 1982. pap. text ed. 10.50 (ISBN 0-8391-1749-3). Univ Park.

--One Thousand One Questions about Nuclear Medicine Technology. LC 82-8364. 168p. 1982. pap. text ed. 10.50 (ISBN 0-8391-1756-6). Univ Park.

--Self-Assessment Tests for the Practicing Radiographer. 208p. 1984. pap. text ed. 12.00 (ISBN 0-8391-2079-6, 22055). Univ Park.

Bell, Rudolf. Party & Faction in American Politics: The House of Representatives, 1789-1801. new ed. LC 72-782. (Contributions in American History Ser.: No. 32). 1974. lib. bdg. 29.95x (ISBN 0-8371-6356-0, BPF/). Greenwood.

Bell, Rudolph M. Fate & Honor, Family & Village: Demographic & Cultural Change in Rural Italy Since Eighteen Hundred. LC 79-11011. (Illus.). 1979. 25.00x (ISBN 0-226-04208-1). U of Chicago Pr.

--Holy Anorexia. LC 85-8460. (Illus.). 280p. 1985. 22.50 (ISBN 0-226-04204-9). U of Chicago Pr.

Bell, Rudolph M., jt. auth. see Weinstein, Donald.

Bell, Ruth & Wildflower, Leni. Talking with Your Teenager: A Book for Parents. 150p. 1984. 15.95 (ISBN 0-394-52773-9); pap. 8.95 (ISBN 0-394-71605-1). Random.

Bell, Ruth, jt. auth. see Eisenhart, Connie.

Bell, Ruth, et al. Changing Bodies, Changing Lives: A Book for Teens on Sex & Relationships. (Illus.). 1981. 17.95 (ISBN 0-394-50304-X); pap. 9.95 (ISBN 0-394-73632-X). Random.

Bell, S. Peter. Biographical Index of British Engineers in the 19th Century. LC 75-5114. (Reference Library of the Social Sciences: Vol. 5). 206p. 1975. lib. bdg. 37.00 (ISBN 0-8240-1078-7). Garland Pub.

Bell, S. W., et al. Mathematics for Higher National Certificate: Volume II. 3rd ed. (Illus.). pap. 126.00 (ISBN 0-317-09177-8, 2050773). Bks Demand UMI.

Bell, Sadie. Church, the State, & Education in Virginia. LC 78-89148. (American Education: Its Men, Institutions & Ideas Ser.). 1969. Repr. of 1930 ed. 43.00 (ISBN 0-405-01385-X). Ayer Co Pubs.

Bell, Sally C. & Langdon, Dolly. Romper Room's Miss Sally Presents Two Hundred Fun Things to Do with Little Kids. LC 80-1807. (Illus.). (ps-3). 1983. 7.95 (ISBN 0-385-15735-5). Doubleday.

Bell, Sam, jt. auth. see Steben, Ralph.

Bell, Sam, jt. auth. see Steben, Ralph E.

Bell, Sam, et al. Arts in Ulster: A Symposium. (Illus.). 173p. 1951. 10.00x (ISBN 0-87556-446-1). Saifer.

Bell, Sam H. December Bride. 304p. 1982. pap. 8.95 (ISBN 0-317-02596-1, Pub. by Blackstaff Pr). Longwood Pub Group.

Bell, Samuel E. & Smallwood, James M. Zona Libre. (Southwestern Studies: No. 69). 100p. 1982. pap. 4.00 (ISBN 0-87404-129-5). Tex Western.

Bell, Sarah F. Charles Nodier: His Life & Works: A Critical Bibliography. (Studies in the Romance Languages & Literatures: No. 95). 150p. 1971. pap. 8.50x (ISBN 0-8078-9095-2). U of NC Pr.

Bell, Skip. These Are Gifts: A Study Guide for Understanding Spiritual Gifts. 72p. 1985. pap. write for info. Chatham Comm Inc.

Bell, Stephen. Rebel, Priest & Prophet. 303p. 1968. 3.00 (ISBN 0-911312-28-5). Schalkenbach.

--Rebel, Priest & Prophet: A Biography of Dr. Edward McGlynn. LC 75-301. (The Radical Tradition in America Ser). 303p. 1975. Repr. of 1937 ed. 24.75 (ISBN 0-88355-206-X). Hyperion Conn.

Bell, Steven, jt. auth. see Kettell, Brian.

Bell, Steven, ed. Foreign Exchange Market Handbook. 250p. 1982. 90.00x (ISBN 0-86010-385-4, Pub. by Graham & Trotman England); pap. 50.00x (ISBN 0-86010-384-6). State Mutual Bk.

Bell, Susan, et al. Women & Children First: Home Link- A Neighborhood Education Project. LC 84-6561. (Bernard van Leer Foundation International Series on Education). (Illus.). 213p. (Orig.). 1984. pap. text ed. 10.00 (ISBN 0-931114-26-8). High-Scope.

Bell, Susan G., ed. Women: From the Greeks to the French Revolution. LC 80-51750. xiv, 313p. 1973. 20.00x (ISBN 0-8047-1094-5); pap. 7.95x (ISBN 0-8047-1082-1). Stanford U Pr.

--Women, the Family, & Freedom: The Debate in Documents, Vol.1, 1880-1950. Offen, Karen M. LC 82-61081. xvi, 474p. 1983. 30.00x (ISBN 0-8047-1172-0); pap. 13.95x (ISBN 0-8047-1173-9). Stanford U Pr.

Bell, Susan G. & Offen, Karen M., eds. Women, the Family, & Freedom. The Debate in Documents Vol.1,1750-1880. LC 82-61081. xvi, 561p. 1983. 32.50x (ISBN 0-8047-1170-4); pap. 14.95x (ISBN 0-8047-1171-2). Stanford U Pr.

Bell, Sydney S. Colonial Administration of Great Britain. LC 74-114023. Repr. of 1859 ed. lib. bdg. 45.00x (ISBN 0-678-00639-3). Kelley.

Bell, T. The Fossil Crustacea: London Clay, Pt. 1. pap. 8.00 (ISBN 0-384-03830-1). Johnson Repr.

--The Fossil Malacostracous Crustacea. pap. 6.00 (ISBN 0-384-03838-7). Johnson Repr.

--Surface Heat Treatment of Steel. (Pergamon Materials Engineering Practice Ser.). 250p. 1986. 30.01 (ISBN 0-08-026700-9); pap. 12.51 (ISBN 0-08-026699-1). Pergamon.

Bell, T., jt. auth. see Owen, R.

Bell, T., ed. Ambulatory Facilities Planning. 114p. 1979. pap. text ed. 10.00 (ISBN 0-936164-17-4). Group Health Assoc of Amer.

--Availability & Accessibility: What Do They Mean & How Are They Measured? 114p. 1979. pap. text ed. 10.00 (ISBN 0-936164-20-4). Group Health Assoc of Amer.

--Finance & Marketing in the Nation's Group Practice HMOs. 251p. 1981. pap. text ed. 16.95 (ISBN 0-936164-02-6). Group Health Assoc of Amer.

--Health Assessment & Preventive Care. 115p. 1978. pap. text ed. 10.00 (ISBN 0-936164-16-6). Group Health Assoc of Amer.

--Health Promotion: Who Needs It? 110p. 1980. pap. text ed. 10.00 (ISBN 0-936164-22-0). Group Health Assoc of Amer.

--Heat Treatment Shanghai 83. 552p. 1984. text ed. 96.00x (ISBN 0-904357-65-1, Pub. by Metals Soc). Brookfield Pub Co.

--HMO Quality Assurance Compliance. 103p. 1979. pap. text ed. 10.00 (ISBN 0-936164-18-2). Group Health Assoc of Amer.

--Management & Policy Issues in HMO Development, 1979. 285p. 1979. pap. text ed. 15.95 (ISBN 0-936164-10-7). Group Health Assoc of Amer.

--Medical & Executive Directors on Planning & Managing HMO Growth. 99p. 1980. pap. text ed. 10.00 (ISBN 0-936164-23-9). Group Health Assoc of Amer.

--Medical & Executive Directors on Physician Organization & Health Plan Relationships. 100p. 1979. pap. text ed. 10.00 (ISBN 0-936164-19-0). Group Health Assoc of Amer.

--The Medical Director in Prepaid Group Practice HMOs. 137p. 1973. pap. text ed. 10.00 (ISBN 0-936164-11-5). Group Health Assoc of Amer.

--Medical Information Systems for Prepaid Group Practice. 109p. 1978. pap. text ed. 10.00 (ISBN 0-936164-15-8). Group Health Assoc of Amer.

--Mental Health Services. 126p. 1979. pap. text ed. 10.00 (ISBN 0-936164-21-2). Group Health Assoc of Amer.

--Organizational Considerations in Developing Group Practice: Quality Assurance. 159p. 1977. pap. text ed. 10.00 (ISBN 0-936164-14-X). Group Health Assoc of Amer.

--Physician & Clinical Staffing in Prepaid Group Practice. 143p. 1977. pap. text ed. 10.00 (ISBN 0-936164-13-1). Group Health Assoc of Amer.

--Physician Recruitment, Performance Evaluation, & the Role of the Medical Director. 79p. 1976. pap. text ed. 10.00 (ISBN 0-936164-12-3). Group Health Assoc of Amer.

--Proceedings of 1976 Group Health Institute. 182p. 1976. pap. text ed. 6.00 (ISBN 0-936164-08-5). Group Health Assoc of Amer.

--Proceedings of 1977 Group Health Institute. 420p. 1977. pap. text ed. 15.95 (ISBN 0-936164-09-3). Group Health Assoc of Amer.

--Skills Development for the HMO Managers of the 1980s. 326p. 1980. pap. text ed. 16.95 (ISBN 0-936164-01-8). Group Health Assoc of Amer.

Bell, T., ed. see MacColl, William A.

Bell, T., ed. see Saward, Ernest.

Bell, T. H. Edward Carpenter, the English Tolstoi. 59.95 (ISBN 0-8490-0094-7). Gordon Pr.

Bell, Thomas. The Anatomie of Popish Tyrannie. LC 74-28833. (English Experience Ser.: No. 714). 1975. Repr. of 1603 ed. 16.00 (ISBN 90-221-0714-0). Walter J Johnson.

--Out of This Furnace. LC 76-6657. 1976. pap. 8.95 (ISBN 0-8229-5273-4). U of Pittsburgh Pr.

Bell, Valdemar D., tr. see Mariengof, Anatol.

Bell, Vereen. Swamp Water. LC 80-24570. (Brown Thrasher Ser.). 282p. 1981. 16.00x (ISBN 0-8203-0553-7); pap. 7.95 (ISBN 0-8203-0546-4). U of Ga Pr.

Bell, Vereen M. Robert Lowell: Nihilist as Hero. 272p. 1983. text ed. 17.50x (ISBN 0-674-77585-6). Harvard U Pr.

Bell, W. C., jt. auth. see Barnes, V. E.

Bell, W. E. Clinical Management of Temporomandibular Disorders. (Illus.). 256p. 1982. 42.95 (ISBN 0-8151-0652-1). Year Bk Med.

Bell, W. J. The Laboratory Cockroach. LC 81-16931. (Illus.). 1982. pap. 15.95x (ISBN 0-412-23990-6, NO. 6630, Pub. by Chapman & Hall). Methuen Inc.

Bell, W. J. & Adiyodi, K. G. American Cockroach. 1981. 85.00 (ISBN 0-412-16140-0, NO. 6557, Pub. by Chapman & Hall). Methuen Inc.

Bell, W. S. Old Fort Benton. facs. ed. (Shorey Historical Ser.). 32p. pap. 2.95 (ISBN 0-8466-0084-6, S84). Shorey.

Bell, Wallace. An Elementary Chronicle. 104p. 1984. 4.72 (ISBN 0-89697-199-6). Intl Univ Pr.

--God's Transient House. 124p. 1984. 5.37 (ISBN 0-89697-197-X). Intl Univ Pr.

--The Jamesville Saga. 116p. 1984. 5.11 (ISBN 0-89697-194-5). Intl Univ Pr.

--One Farmers Family. 154p. 1984. 6.34 (ISBN 0-89697-195-3). Intl Univ Pr.

--A Wayward Warrior. 135p. 1984. 5.72 (ISBN 0-89697-198-8). Intl Univ Pr.

Bell, Walter G. Great Fire of London in 1666. LC 70-114464. (Illus.). 1971. Repr. of 1920 ed. lib. bdg. 20.00x (ISBN 0-8371-4774-3, BEGF). Greenwood.

--The Great Plague in London in 1665. LC 75-23682. (Illus.). Repr. of 1924 ed. 37.50 (ISBN 0-404-13235-9). AMS Pr.

Bell, Wendell. Jamaican Leaders: Political Attitudes in a New Nation. LC 64-19447. 1964. 34.50x (ISBN 0-520-00103-6). U of Cal Pr.

Bell, Wendell & Oxaal, Ivan. Decisions of Nationhood: Political & Social Development in the British Caribbean. (Monograph Series in World Affairs: Vol. 1, 1963-64, Bks. 3 & 4). 99p. (Orig.). 1964. 3.95 (ISBN 0-87940-002-1). Monograph Series.

Bell, Wendell, jt. auth. see Shevky, Eshref.

Bell, Wendell & Mau, James, eds. Sociology of the Future. LC 72-158565. 464p. 1971. 13.95x (ISBN 0-87154-106-8). Russell Sage.

Bell, Whitfield, ed. see Franklin, Benjamin.

Bell, Whitfield J., Jr. The Colonial Physician & Other Essays. new ed. LC 75-6652. (Illus.). 236p. 1975. text ed. 16.00 (ISBN 0-88202-024-2, Sci Hist). Watson Pub Intl.

--John Morgan: Continental Doctor. 1965. 12.00 (ISBN 0-686-65682-2). Watson Pub Intl.

--Towards a National Spirit. 1979. pap. 3.00 (ISBN 0-89073-057-1). Boston Public Lib.

Bell, Whitfield J., Jr. & Smith, Murphy D. Guide to the Archives & Manuscript Collections of the American Philosophical Society. LC 66-30208. (Memoirs Ser.: Vol. 66). 1966. 8.00 (ISBN 0-87169-066-7). Am Philos.

Bell, William. Shakespeare's Puck & His Folkslore, 3 Vols. Repr. of 1864 ed. Set. 92.50 (ISBN 0-404-00740-6). AMS Pr.

Bell, William, ed. Papers Relative to the Regalia of Scotland. LC 71-39426. Repr. of 1829 ed. 20.00 (ISBN 0-404-52736-1). AMS Pr.

Bell, William E. & McCormick, William F. Increased Intracranial Pressure in Children. 2nd ed. (Major Problems in Clinical Pediatrics Ser.: Vol. 8). (Illus.). 485p. 1978. 26.00 (ISBN 0-7216-1708-5). Saunders.

--Neurologic Infections in Children. 2nd ed. (Major Problems in Clinical Pediatrics Ser.: Vol. 12). (Illus.). 600p. 1981. text ed. 63.00 (ISBN 0-7216-1676-3). Saunders.

Bell, William G., et al. Will James: The Spirit of the Cowboy. Neil, J. M., pref. by. (Illus.). 96p. (Orig.). 1985. pap. 12.95 (ISBN 0-9614971-1-4); ltd. ed. 50.00 (ISBN 0-9614971-0-6). Nicolaysen Art Mus.

Bell, William G., jt. ed. see Osterbind, Carter C.

Bell, William H. New Concepts in Surgical Correction of Dentofacial Deformities. (Illus.). 850p. Date not set. price not set (ISBN 0-7216-1739-5). Saunders.

Bell, William H., et al. Surgical Correction of Dentofacial Deformities, 2 vols. LC 76-27050. 1980. Set. text ed. 195.00 (ISBN 0-7216-1671-2); Vol. 1. 100.00 (ISBN 0-7216-1675-5); Vol. 2. 100.00 (ISBN 0-7216-1707-7). Saunders.

Bell, William R., jt. auth. see Seifter, Eric J.

Bell, William T. & Carde, Ring T., eds. Chemical Ecology of Insects. LC 83-20212. (Illus.). 550p. 1984. text ed. 45.00x o.p (ISBN 0-87893-069-8); pap. text ed. 29.95x (ISBN 0-87893-070-1). Sinauer Assoc.

Bell, William W. Secrets of a Professional Home Buyer. LC 82-21980. 160p. 1983. softcover 12.95 (ISBN 0-930294-00-9). World Wide OR.

Bell, Willis, jt. auth. see Castetter, Edward F.

Bellace, Janice, jt. auth. see Dunfee, Thomas W.

Bellace, Janice R. The Landrum-Griffin Act: Twenty Years of Federal Protection of Union Members' Rights. LC 79-2465. (Labor Relations & Public Policy Ser.: No. 19). 363p. 1979. pap. 15.00 (ISBN 0-89546-014-9). Indus Res Unit-Wharton.

Bellack, A. S. & Hersen, M., eds. Research & Practice in Social Skills Training. LC 79-12118. (Illus.). 370p. 1979. 32.50x (ISBN 0-306-40233-5, Plenum Pr). Plenum Pub.

--Research Methods in Clinical Psychology. (Pergamon General Psychology Ser.: No. 130). (Illus.). 416p. 1984. 49.00 (ISBN 0-08-029410-3); pap. 19.50 (ISBN 0-08-029409-X). Pergamon.

Bellack, Alan, jt. ed. see Hersen, Michel.

Bellack, Alan S. & Hersen, Michel. Behavior Modification: An Introductory Textbook. 1977. 22.95x (ISBN 0-19-502302-1). Oxford U Pr.

--Introduction to Clinical Psychology. 1980. text ed. 22.95x (ISBN 0-19-502641-1). Oxford U Pr.

Bellack, Alan S., ed. Schizophrenia: Treatment, Management, & Rehabilitation. 432p. 1984. 37.50 (ISBN 0-8089-1640-8, 790497). Grune.

Bellack, Alan S. & Hersen, Michel, eds. Dictionary of Behavior Therapy Techniques. (Pergamon General Psychology Ser.: No. 132). 304p. 1985. 35.00 (ISBN 0-08-030168-1); pap. 14.50 (ISBN 0-08-030167-3). Pergamon.

Bellack, Alan S., jt. ed. see Hersen, Michel.

Bellack, Alan S., et al, eds. International Handbook of Behavior Modification & Therapy: Student Edition. abr. ed. 484p. 1985. pap. text ed. 24.95x (ISBN 0-306-41876-2, Plenum Pr). Plenum Pub.

--International Handbook of Behavior Modification & Therapy. 1052p. 1982. 95.00 (ISBN 0-306-40777-9, Plenum Pr). Plenum Pub.

Bellack, Alison, jt. auth. see Oliphant, David.

Bellack, Arno A., ed. Theory & Research in Teaching. LC 63-18839. (Orig.). 1963. pap. text ed. 5.25x (ISBN 0-8077-1065-2). Tchrs Coll.

Bellack, Arno A. & Kliebard, Herbert E., eds. Curriculum & Evaluation. LC 76-18040. (Readings in Educational Research Ser.). 1977. 32.50x (ISBN 0-8211-0129-3); text ed. 29.50x 10 or more copies. McCutchan.

Bellack, Jan & Bamford, Penny. Nursing Assessment: A Multidimensional Approach. LC 83-23480. (Nursing Ser.). 600p. 1984. text ed. 24.50x pub net (ISBN 0-534-03193-5). Wadsworth Health.

Belladonna, Giorgio, jt. auth. see Wei, C. C.

Belladonna, R., tr. see Piccolomini, A.

Bellafiore, Joseph. Adventures with Words, 2 bks. (gr. 9-12). 1971. Bk. 1. wkbk. 7.08 (ISBN 0-87720-353-9); Bk. 2. wkbk 7.08 (ISBN 0-87720-355-5). AMSCO Sch.

--College English Workshop. 1976. 9.58 (ISBN 0-87720-951-0). AMSCO Sch.

--English Language Arts. rev. ed. (gr. 10-12). 1982. text ed. 14.58 (ISBN 0-87720-439-X); pap. text ed. 8.75 (ISBN 0-87720-438-1). AMSCO Sch.

--English Language Arts Workbook. 2nd ed. (Orig.). (gr. 9-12). pap. 10.25 (ISBN 0-87720-392-X). AMSCO Sch.

--English Made Easier. (Orig.). (gr. 7-12). 1974. wkbk. 9.25 (ISBN 0-87720-344-X); pap. text ed. 7.67 (ISBN 0-87720-342-3). AMSCO Sch.

--Essentials of English. (Orig.). (gr. 9-12). 1970. pap. text ed. 6.17 (ISBN 0-87720-341-5). AMSCO Sch.

--Essentials of English. 3rd ed. (gr. 6-8). 1983. text ed. 9.17 (ISBN 0-87720-678-3, 259H); Key 1.15 (ISBN 0-317-03324-7). Amsco Sch.

--Essentials of English Workbook. 3rd ed. (gr. 10-12). 1982. 7.58 (ISBN 0-87720-441-1). AMSCO Sch.

--Reviewing English Preliminary. (gr. 7-12). 1958. pap. text ed. 5.92 (ISBN 0-87720-305-9). AMSCO Sch.

--Words at Work. 2nd ed. (gr. 10-12). 1968. pap. text ed. 6.00 (ISBN 0-87720-320-2). AMSCO Sch.

Bellah, James. Imperial Express. 320p. (Orig.). 1982. pap. 2.95 (ISBN 0-515-05449-6). Jove Pubns.

Bellah, Robert, jt. ed. see Haan, Norma.

Bellah, Robert N. Beyond Belief. LC 77-109058. 1976. pap. text ed. 7.95x (ISBN 0-06-060775-0, RD129, HarpR). Har-Row.

--Beyond Belief: Essays on Religion in a Post-Traditional World. LC 77-109058. 1970. 7.95x (ISBN 0-06-060774-2, RD-129, HarpR). Har-Row.

--The Broken Covenant: American Civil Religion in Time of Trail. 1976. pap. 5.95 (ISBN 0-8164-2123-4, Pub. by Seabury). Winston Pr.

--Tokugawa Religion. 272p. pap. 9.95 (ISBN 0-02-902460-9). Free Pr.

--Tokugawa Religion: The Cultural Roots of Modern Japan. 272p. 1985. pap. 9.95x (ISBN 0-02-902460-9). Free Pr.

--Tokugawa Religion: The Cultural Roots of Modern Japan. 272p. 1985. pap. 9.95 (ISBN 0-02-902460-9). Free Pr.

Bellah, Robert N. & Hammond, Phillip E. Varieties of Civil Religion. LC 80-7742. 224p. 1982. pap. 7.64i (ISBN 0-06-060769-6, RD-385, HarpR). Har-Row.

Bellah, Robert N., ed. see Durkheim, Emile.

Bellah, Robert N., jt. ed. see Glock, Charles.

Bellah, Robert N., jt. ed. see Glock, Charles Y.

Bellah, Robert N., et al. Habits of the Heart: Individualism & Commitment in American Life. LC 84-16370. 360p. 1985. 16.95 (ISBN 0-520-05388-5). U of Cal Pr.

Bellaigue, Camille. Portraits & Silhouettes of Musicians. Orr, Ellen, tr. LC 77-90807. 1978. Repr. of 1898 ed. lib. bdg. 35.00 (ISBN 0-89341-424-7). Longwood Pub Group.

Bellaigue, G. De see De Bellaigue, Geoffrey.

Bellaigue, Geoffrey de see De Bellaigue, Geoffrey.

Bellaire, Arthur. Bellaire Guide to Controlling Your TV Commercial Cost. 2nd ed. LC 82-72510. 160p. 1982. 15.95 (ISBN 0-87251-075-1). Crain Bks.

Bellaire, Marc. Brush Decoration for Ceramics. 3.95 (ISBN 0-934706-02-6). Prof Pubns Ohio.

--Underglaze Decoration. 3.95 (ISBN 0-934706-01-8). Prof Pubns Ohio.

Bellairs, Charles. Conservatism: Conservative Social & Industrial Reform. 128p. 1977. 20.00x (ISBN 0-686-78987-3, Pub. by Conserv Political Ctr England). State Mutual Bk.

Bellairs, D. A. & Cox, C. B., eds. Morphology & Biology of Reptiles. (Linnean Society Symposium Ser.). 1977. 59.00 (ISBN 0-12-085850-9). Acad Pr.

Bellairs, George. All Roads to Sospel. 176p. 1981. 9.95 (ISBN 0-8027-5454-6). Walker & Co.

--Devious Murder. LC 80-51995. 175p. 1980. 9.95 (ISBN 0-8027-5427-9). Walker & Co.

--Fear Round About. LC 80-54821. 1981. 9.95 (ISBN 0-8027-5441-4). Walker & Co.

--Gone to Her Death. 206p. 1981. 9.95 (ISBN 0-8027-5455-4). Walker & Co.

--Murder Masquerade. (Orig.). 1981. pap. 1.95 (ISBN 0-505-51698-5, Pub. by Tower Bks). Dorchester Pub Co.

Bellairs, Herbert J. & Helsel, James L. Modern Real Estate Practice in Pennsylvania. 3rd ed. Caldwell, Thomas D., ed. (Illus.). 441p. (Orig.). 1982. pap. text ed. 30.95 (ISBN 0-88462-298-3, 1510-17, Real Estate Ed). Longman USA.

Bellairs, John. The Curse of the Blue Figurine. LC 82-73217. (Illus.). 224p. (gr. 5 up). 1983. 11.95 (ISBN 0-8037-1119-0, 01160-350); PLB 11.89 (ISBN 0-8037-1265-0). Dial Bks Young.

--The Curse of the Blue Figurine. (Skylark Ser.). 208p. (gr. 4-6). 1984. pap. 2.50 (ISBN 0-553-15282-3, RL6IL4, Skylark). Bantam.

--The Dark Secret of Weatherend. (Illus.). 208p. (gr. 5 up). 1984. 11.95 (ISBN 0-8037-0072-5, 01160-350); PLB 11.89 (ISBN 0-8037-0074-1). Dial Bks Young.

--The Face in the Frost. 192p. 1984. pap. 2.50 (ISBN 0-441-22530-6, Pub. by Ace Science Fiction). Ace Bks.

--The Figure in the Shadows. 192p. (gr. 4-7). 1977. pap. 2.50 (ISBN 0-440-42551-4, YB). Dell.

--The Figure in the Shadows. LC 74-2885. (Illus.). 168p. (gr. 4-7). 1975. PLB 9.89 (ISBN 0-8037-4917-1). Dial Bks Young.

--The House with a Clock in Its Walls. 192p. (gr. 3 up). 1974. pap. 2.75 (ISBN 0-440-43742-3, YB). Dell.

--The House with a Clock in Its Walls. LC 72-7600. (Illus.). 192p. (gr. 4-7). 1973. 10.95 (ISBN 0-8037-3821-8, 01063-320); PLB 10.89 (ISBN 0-8037-3823-4). Dial Bks Young.

--The Letter, the Witch & the Ring. 192p. (gr. 3-6). 1977. pap. 2.50 (ISBN 0-440-44722-4, YB). Dell.

--The Letter, the Witch, & the Ring. LC 75-28968. (Illus.). (gr. 4-7). 1976. 12.95 (ISBN 0-8037-4740-3, 01258-370). Dial Bks Young.

--The Mummy, the Will, & the Crypt. (Illus.). 192p. (gr. 5 up). 1983. 11.95 (ISBN 0-8037-0029-6, 01160-350); PLB 11.89 (ISBN 0-8037-0030-X). Dial Bks Young.

--The Revenge of the Wizard's Ghost. LC 85-4550. (Illus.). 160p. (gr. 5 up). 1985. 11.95 (ISBN 0-8037-0170-5); PLB 11.89 (ISBN 0-8037-0177-2). Dial Bks Young.

--The Spell of the Sorcerer's Skull. (gr. 5 up). 1984. 11.95 (ISBN 0-8037-0120-9, 01160-350); PLB 11.89 (ISBN 0-8037-0122-5). Dial Bks Young.

Bellairs, Ruth. Developmental Processes in Higher Vertebrates. LC 70-80928. (Illus.). 1971. 19.95x (ISBN 0-87024-204-0). U of Miami Pr.

Bellairs, Ruth, et al, eds. Cell Behaviour: A Tribute to Michael Abercrombie. Ruth & Curtis, Dunn. LC 81-6119. (Illus.). 500p. 1982. 110.00 (ISBN 0-521-24107-3). Cambridge U Pr.

Bellak, George. Come Jericho. LC 81-4858. 356p. 1981. 12.95 (ISBN 0-688-00125-4). Morrow.

Bellak, Leopold. Overload: The New Human Condition. LC 74-19052. 223p. 1975. 24.95 (ISBN 0-87705-245-X). Human Sci Pr.

--Porcupine Dilemma. 1970. 5.95 (ISBN 0-8065-0223-1). Citadel Pr.

--Psychology of Physical Illness. LC 52-14496. 256p. 1953. 48.50 (ISBN 0-8089-0045-5, 790500). Grune.

--The T.A.T., C.A.T., & S.A.T., in Clinical Use. 3rd ed. 352p. 1975. 29.50 (ISBN 0-8089-0865-0, 790515). Grune.

Bellak, Leopold & Baker, Samm S. Reading Faces. LC 80-19235. (Illus.). 163p. 1981. 10.95 (ISBN 0-03-057869-8). HR&W.

Bellak, Leopold & Faithorn, Peri E. Crises & Special Problems in Psychoanalysis & Psychotherapy. LC 80-25670. 264p. 1981. 27.50 (ISBN 0-87630-257-6). Brunner-Mazel.

Bellak, Leopold & Small, Leonard. Emergency Psychotherapy & Brief Psychology. 2nd ed. 288p. 1977. 42.00 (ISBN 0-8089-1057-4, 790507). Grune.

Bellak, Leopold, ed. A Concise Handbook of Community Psychiatry & Community Mental Health. (Illus.). 256p. 1974. 43.50 (ISBN 0-8089-0833-2, 790511). Grune.

--Disorders of the Schizophrenic Syndrome. LC 78-19814. 1980. 28.95x (ISBN 0-465-01675-8). Basic.

--Psychiatric Aspects of Minimal Brain Dysfunction in Adults. 224p. 1979. 31.00 (ISBN 0-8089-1192-9, 790513). Grune.

Bellak, Leopold & Barten, Harvey H., eds. Progress in Community Mental Health, Vol. 1. LC 69-15739. 280p. 1969. 49.50 (ISBN 0-8089-0047-1, 790501). Grune.

Bellak, Leopold & Goldsmith, Lisa A., eds. The Broad Scope of Ego Function Assessment. LC 84-3726. (General & Clinical Psychiatry Ser.: 1-708). 577p. 1984. text ed. 52.00 (ISBN 0-471-89198-3, 1-708, Pub. by Wiley Interscience). Wiley.

Bellak, Leopold & Karasu, T., eds. Geriatric Psychiatry: A Handbook for Psychiatrists & Primary Care Physicians. LC 76-26287. (Illus.). 320p. 1976. 46.50 (ISBN 0-8089-0967-3, 790509). Grune.

Bellak, Leopold, jt. ed. see Barten, Harvey H.

Bellak, Leopold, jt. ed. see Karasu, Toksoz B.

Bellak, Leopold, et al. Ego Functions in Schizophrenics, Neurotics, & Normals: A Systematic Study of Conceptual, Diagnostic, & Therapeutic Aspects. LC 73-3199. (Personality Processes Ser.). 688p. 1973. 63.00x (ISBN 0-471-06413-0, Pub. by Wiley-Interscience). Wiley.

Bellama, J. M., jt. ed. see Brinckman, F. E.

Bellama, J. M., jt. ed. see Chvalovsky, Vaclav.

Bellamak, Lu. Non-Judgemental Sacred Dance: Simple Ways to Pray Through Dance. 1984. 3.00 (ISBN 0-941500-14-4). Sharing Co.

Bellaman, Henry. Cups of Illusion. 59.95 (ISBN 0-87968-976-5). Gordon Pr.

--A Music Teacher's Notebook. 59.95 (ISBN 0-8490-0683-X). Gordon Pr.

Bellamann, Henry. Kings Row. 672p. 1983. pap. 8.95 (ISBN 0-88184-059-9, Publishers Group West). Carroll & Graf.

--Kings Row. Karr, Jay M., ed. (Illus.). 1982. 18.50 (ISBN 0-9609926-1-8); pap. 9.95 (ISBN 0-9609926-2-6); leather, limited, signed, numbered 50.00 (ISBN 0-9609926-0-X). Kingdom Hse.

Bellamann, Katherine J. Two Sides of a Poem. LC 70-179811. (New Poetry Ser.). Repr. of 1955 ed. 16.00 (ISBN 0-404-56011-3). AMS Pr.

Bellamy & Child. Common Market Law of Competition. 1973. 32.50 (ISBN 0-685-40616-4). Bender.

Bellamy, Blanche W. & Goodwin, Maud. Open Sesame Poetry & Prose for School-Days, 3 vols. text ed. 112.00 (ISBN 0-8369-9360-8). Ayer Co Pubs.

Bellamy, Blanche W. & Goodwin, Maud W. Open Sesame! Poetry & Prose for School-Days. rev. & enl. ed. Incl. Arranged for Children from 4 to 12 Yrs. Repr. of 1889 ed. Vol. 1. 18.00 (ISBN 0-8369-6355-5); Arranged for Children from 10 to 14 Yrs. Repr. of 1890 ed. Vol. 2. 20.00 (ISBN 0-8369-6356-3); Arranged for Children Over 14 Yrs. Repr. of 1890 ed. Vol. 3. 19.00 (ISBN 0-8369-6357-1). LC 72-451. (Granger Index Reprint Ser). Ayer Co Pubs.

Bellamy, Charles. Experiment in Marriage. LC 77-16040. 320p. 1977. Repr. of 1889 ed. 45.00x (ISBN 0-8201-1304-2). Schol Facsimiles.

Bellamy, David. Bellamy's New World. (Illus.). 192p. 1985. 24.95 (ISBN 0-88186-025-5). Parkwest Pubns.

--The Mouse Book: The Story of Apodemus, a Longtailed Field Mouse. (Illus.). 96p. 1984. 11.95 (ISBN 0-85362-200-0, Oriel). Routledge & Kegan.

--The Queen's Hidden Garden: Buckingham Palace's Treasury of Wild Plants. (Illus.). 1985. 19.95 (ISBN 0-318-04507-9, Pub. by Salem Hse Ltd). Merrimack Pub Cir.

Bellamy, Edward. The Blindman's World & Other Stories. 1972. Repr. of 1898 ed. 20.75 (ISBN 0-8422-8006-5). Irvington.

--The Blindmans World & Other Stories. (The Works of Edward Bellamy Ser.). 415p. Repr. of 1898 ed. lib. bdg. 49.00 (ISBN 0-932051-08-1, Pub. by Am Repr Serv). Am Biog Serv.

--Doctor Heidenhoff's Process. LC 72-84878. (BCL Ser. I). 1969. Repr. of 1880 ed. 19.50 (ISBN 0-404-00734-1). AMS Pr.

--Dr. Heidenhoff's Process. (The Works of Edward Bellamy Ser.). 140p. 1985. Repr. of 1880 ed. lib. bdg. 29.00 (ISBN 0-932051-09-X, Pub. by Am Repr Serv). Am Biog Serv.

--Edward Bellamy Speaks Again! LC 75-302. (The Radical Tradition in America Ser). (Illus.). 249p. 1975. Repr. of 1937 ed. 20.35 (ISBN 0-88355-207-8). Hyperion Conn.

--Equality. (BCL Ser. II). (Illus.). 1970. Repr. of 1897 ed. 10.00 (ISBN 0-404-00735-X). AMS Pr.

--Equality. 2 ed. 1897. 7.00x (ISBN 0-403-00145-5). Scholarly.

--Equality. (The Works of Edward Bellamy Ser.). 412p. 1985. Repr. of 1899 ed. lib. bdg. 49.00 (ISBN 0-932051-14-6, Pub by Am Repr Serv). Am Biog Serv.

--Looking Backward. 318p. Repr. of 1888 ed. lib. bdg. 17.95 (ISBN 0-89190-238-4, Pub. by River City Pr). Amereon Ltd.

--Looking Backward. (Literature Ser). (gr. 9-12). 1970. pap. text ed. 4.92 (ISBN 0-87720-733-X). AMSCO Sch.

--Looking Backward. White, Frederic R., ed. 272p. 1979. pap. 4.45 (ISBN 0-87532-107-0). Hendricks House.

--Looking Backward. pap. 1.95 (ISBN 0-451-51886-1, Sig Classics). NAL.

--Looking Backward. Tichi, Cecelia, ed. (American Library). 1982. pap. 3.95 (ISBN 0-14-039018-9). Penguin.

--Looking Backward Two Thousand to Eighteen Eighty-Seven. Thomas, John L., ed. LC 67-14337. (The John Harvard Library). 1967. 17.50x (ISBN 0-674-53900-1). Harvard U Pr.

--Looking Backward: Two Thousand to Eighteen Eighty-Seven. Elliott, Robert C., ed. LC 67-2787. (YA) (gr. 9 up). 1966. pap. 5.50 (ISBN 0-395-05194-0, RivEd). HM.

--Looking Backward Two Thousand to Eighteen Eighty-Seven. (Modern Library College Editions Ser.). 275p. 1982. pap. text ed. 3.95 (ISBN 0-394-32980-5, MLCE). Random.

--Miss Ludington's Sister. LC 71-104414. Repr. of 1884 ed. lib. bdg. 24.50 (ISBN 0-8398-0161-0). Irvington.

--Religion of Solidarity. LC 73-9680. 1940. lib. bdg. 10.00 (ISBN 0-8414-3139-6). Folcroft.

--The Religion of Solidarity. (Institute of World Culture Ser.). 132p. 1984. pap. 6.50 (ISBN 0-88695-029-5). Concord Grove.

--Selected Writings on Religion & Society. Schiffman, Joseph, ed. LC 74-40. (The American Heritage Ser.: No. 11). 139p. 1974. Repr. of 1955 ed. lib. bdg. 15.00 (ISBN 0-8371-7359-0, BEWR). Greenwood.

--Talks on Nationalism. facsimile ed. LC 78-102226. (Select Bibliographies Reprint Ser). 1938. 19.00 (ISBN 0-8369-5111-5). Ayer Co Pubs.

Bellamy, Frank. Caribbean Island Hopping. rev. ed. (Handbooks for the Independent traveller Ser.). (Illus.). 288p. 1982. pap. 12.95 (ISBN 0-686-46710-8, Pub. by Regnery-Gateway). Hippocrene Bks.

Bellamy, G. Thomas. Vocational Habilitation of Severely Retarded Adults. LC 78-10161. (Illus.). 256p. 1979. pap. text ed. 15.00 (ISBN 0-936104-81-3). Pro Ed.

Bellamy, G. Thomas, jt. auth. see Wilcox, Barbara.

Bellamy, J. G. Law of Treason in England in the Later Middle Ages. LC 70-111123. (Cambridge Studies in English Legal History). 1970. 47.50 (ISBN 0-521-07830-X). Cambridge U Pr.

--Robin Hood: An Historical Enquiry. LC 84-48552. 160p. 1985. 19.50x (ISBN 0-253-35015-8). Ind U Pr.

Bellamy, James A., et al, eds. Modern Arabic Poetry, 2 pts. (Contemporary Arabic Readers Ser.: Vol. V). 1968. Set. 9.00x (ISBN 0-916798-15-1). Pt. 1, Texts; Xiii, 108p. Pt. 2, Notes & Glossaries; Iv, 308p. U of Mich Pr.

--Short Stories, 2 pts. (Contemporary Arabic Readers Ser.: Vol. IV). 1963. Set. 8.50x (ISBN 0-916798-14-3). Pt. 1, Texts; Xiii, 93p. Pt. 2, Notes & Glossaries; Iv, 274p. U of Mich Pr.

Bellamy, Joe D. The New Fiction: Interviews with Innovative American Writers. LC 74-14841. 225p. 1974. 15.95x (ISBN 0-252-00430-2); pap. 5.95x (ISBN 0-252-00555-4). U of Ill Pr.

--Olympic Gold Medalist. 64p. 1979. pap. 6.95 (ISBN 0-915996-03-0). North Am Rev.

Bellamy, Joe D., ed. American Poetry Observed: Poets on Their Work. LC 83-6961. (Illus.). 328p. 1984. 19.95 (ISBN 0-252-01042-6). U of Ill Pr.

--Moral Fiction. LC 80-67335. 298p. 1980. pap. 6.95 (ISBN 0-931362-02-4). Fiction Intl.

--New Writers for the Eighties. LC 81-71004. 392p. (Orig.). 1981. pap. 14.95 (ISBN 0-931362-06-7). Fiction Intl.

--Superfiction, or the American Story Transformed: An Anthology. (Orig.). 1975. pap. 6.95 (ISBN 0-394-71523-3, Vin). Random.

Bellamy, Joe D. & Weingarten, Roger, eds. Love Stories-Love Poems. LC 82-84443. 300p. (Orig.). 1982. pap. 12.95 (ISBN 0-931362-07-5). Fiction Intl.

Bellamy, John. Digital Telephony. LC 81-11633. 526p. 1982. 54.95x (ISBN 0-471-08089-6, Pub. by Wiley-Interscience). Wiley.

Bellamy, John C. Digital Telephony. 526p. 1982. 37.50 (ISBN 0-686-98112-X). Telecom Lib.

Bellamy, John G. Crime & Public Order in England in the Later Middle Ages. LC 73-163803. (Studies in Social History). pap. 59.30 (ISBN 0-317-26940-2, 2023593). Bks Demand UMI.
--Criminal Law & Society in Late Medieval & Tudor England. LC 83-40623. 180p. 1985. 25.00 (ISBN 0-312-17215-X). St Martin.
Bellamy, Joyce M. & Saville, John, eds. Dictionary of Labour Biography, 6 vols. LC 78-185417. 1972. lib. bdg. 37.50x ea. Vol. 1 (ISBN 0-678-07008-3). Vol. 2 (ISBN 0-678-07018-0). Vol. 3 (ISBN 0-333-14415-5). Vol. 4 (ISBN 0-333-19704-6). Vol. 5 (ISBN 0-333-22015-3). Vol. 6 (ISBN 0-333-24095-2). Vol. 7 (ISBN 0-333-33181-8). Kelley.
Bellamy, L. J. The Infrared Spectra of Complex Molecules, Vol. 1. 3rd ed. 1975. 39.95x (ISBN 0-412-13850-6, NO. 6033, Pub. by Chapman & Hall). Methuen Inc.
--Infrared Spectra of Complex Molecules, Vol. 2. 2nd ed. 299p. 1980. 39.95 (ISBN 0-412-22350-3, NO. 6333, Pub. by Chapman & Hall England). Methuen Inc.
Bellamy, Lin, jt. auth. see Williamson, Tom.
Bellamy, Margot A. & Greenshields, Bruce L., eds. The Rural Challenge: Proceedings of the 17th International Conference of Agricultural Economists, Vol. II. 346p. 1981. text ed. 26.95x (ISBN 0-566-00472-0). Gower Pub Co.
Bellamy, Margot A., jt. ed. see Greenshields, Bruce L.
Bellamy, Nicholas. Colour Atlas of Clinical Rheumatology. 1985. lib. bdg. 68.50 (ISBN 0-85200-761-2, Pub. by MTP Pr England). Kluwer-Academic.
Bellamy, Rex. The Peak District Companion: A Walker's Guide. LC 80-70294. (Illus.). 208p. 1981. 19.95 (ISBN 0-7153-8140-7). David & Charles.
--Walking the Tops: Dartmoor to Scotland. (Illus.). 208p. 1984. 19.95 (ISBN 0-7153-8419-8). David & Charles.
Bellamy, Robert L. Byron, the Man. 245p. 1980. Repr. of 1924 ed. lib. bdg. 35.00 (ISBN 0-8495-0455-4). Arden Lib.
--Byron the Man. LC 75-29104. 1975. Repr. of 1924 ed. lib. bdg. 25.00 (ISBN 0-8414-3326-7). Folcroft.
--Byron the Man. 59.95 (ISBN 0-87968-808-4). Gordon Pr.
Bellamy, T. Vocational Rehabilitation of Severely Handicapped Persons. LC 79-12015. (Illus.). 296p. 1979. 14.00 (ISBN 0-8391-1343-9). Pro Ed.
Bellamy, Virginia W. And the Evening & the Morning. LC 76-41608. 1976. French style bdg. 4.50 (ISBN 0-87027-172-5). Cumberland Pr.
Bellamy, Walter S. The Art of the Ancient World Conquerors. (Illus.). 139p. 1984. 78.85x (ISBN 0-86650-099-5). Gloucester Art.
Bellamy, William. A Second Century of Charades. 1979. Repr. of 1896 ed. lib. bdg. 20.00 (ISBN 0-8495-0527-5). Arden Lib.
--A Second Century of Charades. 1977. Repr. of 1896 ed. 15.00 (ISBN 0-89984-045-0). Century Bookbindery.
Bellan, R. C. Excerpts from Principles of Economics & the Canadian Economy. 6th ed. (FLMI Insurance Education Program Ser.). 1981. pap. text ed. 5.00 (ISBN 0-915322-46-3). LOMA.
Bellanato, J. & Hidalgo, A. Infrared Analysis Ofessential Oils. 1971. 97.00 (ISBN 0-85501-022-3). Wiley.
Bellanca, James A. Quality Circles in Education: The Facilitator's Guidebook. (Illus.). 231p. Date not set. 40.00 (ISBN 0-932935-00-1). Ill Renewal Inst.
--Values & the Search for Self. new ed. LC 75-12724. 112p. 1975. pap. text ed. 7.95 (ISBN 0-8106-1356-5). NEA.
Bellanca, James A., jt. ed. see Simon, Sidney B.
Belland, F. W. Fleshwound. 224p. (Orig.). 1981. pap. 2.25 (ISBN 0-515-05652-9). Jove Pubns.
--The True Sea: A Novel of the Florida Keys. LC 83-18440. 1984. 15.95 (ISBN 0-03-064014-8, William Abrahams Bk). HR&W.
Belland, Kathleen H. & Wells, Mary A., eds. Clinical Nursing Procedures. LC 83-25982. 500p. 1984. pap. text ed. 17.00x pub net (ISBN 0-534-03154-4). Wadsworth Health.
Bellanger, Maurice G. Digital Processing of Signals: Theory & Practice. McMullan, Jean, tr. 336p. 1984. text ed. 49.95x (ISBN 0-471-90318-3, Pub. by Wiley-Interscience). Wiley.
Bellante, Donald M. & Jackson, J. Mark, Jr. Labor Economics: Choice in Labor Markets. 2nd ed. (Illus.). 368p. 1983. text ed. 33.95 (ISBN 0-07-004399-X). McGraw.
Bellanti, Joseph A. Immunology: Basic Process. new ed. LC 79-3947. (Illus.). 1979. pap. text ed. 14.95 (ISBN 0-7216-1677-1). Saunders.
--Immunology II. 2nd ed. LC 77-72808. (Illus.). 1978. text ed. 32.50 (ISBN 0-7216-1681-X). Saunders.
--Immunology in Medicine. 3rd ed. 450p. 1984. pap. write for info. (ISBN 0-7216-1668-2). Saunders.
Bellanti, Joseph A., ed. Acute Diarrhea: Its Nutritional Consequences in Children. (Nestle Nutrition Workshop Ser.: Vol. 2). 240p. 1983. text ed. 30.50 (ISBN 0-89004-991-2). Raven.
Bellanti, Joseph A. & Herscowitz, Herbert B., eds. The Reticuloendothelial System: A Comprehensive Treatise: Vol. 6: Immunology. (Immunology Ser.). 337p. 1984. 55.00x (ISBN 0-306-41421-X, Plenum Pr). Plenum Pub.
Bellanti, Joseph A., et al. Herpesvirus: Recent Studies, 3 vols, Vol. 1. LC 73-13558. 156p. 1974. text ed. 22.50x (ISBN 0-8422-7164-3). Irvington.
Bellanti, Joseph H. Basic Immunology. 2nd ed. 200p. 1984. pap. write for info. (ISBN 0-7216-1244-X). Saunders.
Bellanti, Robert, jt. ed. see Georgi, Charlotte.
Bellany, Ian & Blacker, Coit D., eds. Antiballistic Missile Defense in the 1980s. 100p. 1983. text ed. 27.50x (ISBN 0-7146-3207-4, F Cass Co). Biblio Dist.
--The Verification of Arms Control Agreements. 104p. 1983. 27.50x (ISBN 0-7146-3228-7, F Cass Co). Biblio Dist.
Bellardi, Werner. Die Geschichte der "Christlichen Gemeinschaft" in Strassburg: 1546-1550. 34.00 (ISBN 0-384-03849-2); pap. 28.00 (ISBN 0-384-03850-6). Johnson Repr.
Bellarmino, Saint Roberto F. De Laicis: Or, the Treatise on Civil Government. Murphy, Kathleen E., tr. from Lat. LC 78-20450. 1980. Repr. of 1928 ed. 15.00 (ISBN 0-88355-927-7). Hyperion Conn.
Bellars, John. The Mummy, the Will & the Crypt. 176p. (gr. 6). 1985. pap. 2.50 (ISBN 0-553-15323-4). Bantam.
Bellas, jt. auth. see Kirk.
Bellas, Henry H., jt. auth. see Anderson, Enoch.
Bellaschi, Jules. To Lead & Manage. LC 80-83869. 70p. (Orig.). 1980. pap. 4.95 (ISBN 0-9605144-0-6). MJ Pubns.
Bellasis, Edward. Cherubini: Memorials Illustrative of His Life. (Works of Edward Bellasis Ser.). xv, 429p. Date not set. Repr. of 1874 ed. lib. bdg. 49.00 (ISBN 0-932051-60-X). Am Repr Serv.
--Cherubini: Memorials Illustrative of His Life & Work. LC 70-138497. (Music Ser). 1971. Repr. of 1912 ed. lib. bdg. 37.50 (ISBN 0-306-70071-9). Da Capo.
Bellavance, Diane. Advertising & Public Relations for a Small Business. (Illus.). 88p. 1985. pap. 8.95x (ISBN 0-9605276-0-5). DBA Bks.
--Typing Made Easy. (Illus.). 20p. 1984. pap. 2.00x (ISBN 0-9605276-1-3). DBA Bks.
Bellavance, Russell C., ed. see Institute for Paralegal Training.
Bellavita, Christopher see Wholey, Joseph S., et al.
Bellavita, Christopher, jt. ed. see Meltsner, Aronold J.
Bellay, Joachim Du. Poems. Lawton, H. W., ed. (French Texts Ser.). 206p. 1972. pap. text ed. 9.95x (ISBN 0-631-00600-1). Basil Blackwell.
Bellay, Joachim Du see Du Bellay, Joachim.
Belle, Bella La see La Belle, Bella.
Belle, Deborah, ed. Lives in Stress: Women & Depression. (Sage Focus Editions). (Illus.). 280p. 1982. 24.00 (ISBN 0-8039-1768-6); pap. 12.00 (ISBN 0-8039-1769-4). Sage.
Belle, O. C. Van see Bottcher, C. J., et al.
Belle, Pamela. Alethea. 544p. 1985. pap. 6.95 (ISBN 0-425-08397-7). Berkley Pub.
--The Chains of Fate. 544p. 1984. pap. 5.50 (ISBN 0-425-07367-X). Berkley Pub.
--The Moon in the Water. 544p. 1984. pap. 6.95 (ISBN 0-425-07200-2). Berkley Pub.
--The Moon in the Water. 528p. 1985. pap. 3.95 (ISBN 0-425-08268-7). Berkley Pub.
Belle, Rene & Haas, A. F. Promenades en France. 3rd ed. LC 56-11937. 1972. text ed. 14.95 (ISBN 0-03-080294-6, HoltC). HR&W.
Belle, Thomas J. la see Hawkins, John N. & La Belle, Thomas J.
Bellefonds, Y. Linant De see Linant De Bellefonds, Y.
Bellegarde. Black Heroes & Heroines, Bk 5: Benjamin Banneker's Great Achievements. 64p. 1985. write for info. (ISBN 0-918340-14-4). Bell Ent.
Bellegarde, Dantes. Haiti & Her Problems. 1976. lib. bdg. 59.95 (ISBN 0-8490-1925-7). Gordon Pr.
Bellegarde, Ida. Easy Steps to a Large Vocabulary. LC 77-79111. 1977. 4.45x (ISBN 0-918340-04-7). Bell Ent.
--Pasaderitas Hacia el Ingles Correcto. Lopez, Peter, tr. LC 77-73283. 1977. 4.45x (ISBN 0-918340-05-5). Bell Ent.
Bellegarde, Ida R. Black Heroes & Heroines, Bk. 1. LC 79-51798. 1979. 5.45x (ISBN 0-918340-08-X). Bell Ent.
--Black Heroes & Heroines, Bk. 2. LC 79-51798. 1981. 5.45x (ISBN 0-918340-10-1). Bell Ent.
--Black Heroes & Heroines, Bk. 3. LC 79-51798. 61p. (gr. 5 up). 1983. 5.45x (ISBN 0-918340-11-X). Bell Ent.
--Black Heroes & Heroines, Bk. 4. 64p. (gr. 5 up). 1984. 5.45x (ISBN 0-918340-13-6). Bell Ent.
--Easy Steps to Correct Speech. 3rd ed. LC 77-73289. 1974. 4.45x (ISBN 0-918340-00-4). Bell Ent.
--Easy Steps to Good Grammar. 3rd ed. LC 77-89896. 1974. 4.45x (ISBN 0-918340-01-2). Bell Ent.
--Haiku Reflections. LC 78-72586. 1978. 4.45x (ISBN 0-918340-07-1). Bell Ent.
--Idylls of the Seasons. LC 78-72585. 1978. 4.45x (ISBN 0-918340-06-3). Bell Ent.
--Lisping Leaves. (gr. 9 up). 1976. 4.45 (ISBN 0-918340-03-9). Bell Ent.
--Little Stepping Stones to Correct Speech. 2nd ed. 1974. 4.45x (ISBN 0-918340-02-0). Bell Ent.
--Sunshine & Shadows: Poetry. 62p. 1984. 4.45x (ISBN 0-918340-12-8). Bell Ent.
--Understanding Cultural Values. LC 79-51620. 1979. 4.45x (ISBN 0-918340-09-8). Bell Ent.
Belleggia, Sr. Concetta. God & the Problem of Evil. 1980. 3.75 (ISBN 0-8198-3007-0); pap. 2.50 (ISBN 0-8198-3008-9). Dghtrs St Paul.
Belle Isle, J. Gerald. Dictionnaire Technique General: Anglais-Français. 2nd ed. 555p. (Eng. & Fr.). 1977. 79.95 (ISBN 0-686-56913-X, M-6158). French & Eur.
Bellenden, Jean, jt. auth. see Makgill, Jacques.
Bellenger, Danny, jt. auth. see Greenberg, Barnett.
Bellenger, Danny M. & Ingram, Thomas N. Professional Selling: Text & Cases. 448p. 1984. text ed. write for info. (ISBN 0-02-308060-4). Macmillan.
Bellenger, Danny N. & Berl, Robert L. Sales Management: A Review of the Current Literature. LC 81-6559. (Research Monograph: No. 89). 1981. spiral bdg. 15.00 (ISBN 0-88406-147-7). GA St U Busn Pub.
Bellenger, Danny N. & Goldstucker, Jac L. Retailing Basics. 1983. 27.50x (ISBN 0-256-02529-0). Irwin.
Bellenger, Danny N., jt. auth. see Robertson, Dan H.
Bellenger, Danny N., et al. Qualitative Research in Marketing. LC 76-3765. (American Marketing Association Monographs Ser.). pap. 21.50 (ISBN 0-317-28132-1, 2022482). Bks Demand UMI.
Bellenger, Joseph M., ed. see Maillard, Antoine S.
Bellenger, W. A. A Dictionary of Idioms, French & English. 331p. (Fr. & Eng.). 1983. Repr. of 1830 ed. lib. bdg. 125.00 (ISBN 0-89760-052-5). Telegraph Bks.
Bellenger, Yvonne. Le Jour dans la Poesie Francaise au Temps de la Renaissance. (Etudes Litteraires Francaise Ser.: No. 2). 1979p. (Fr.). pap. 31.00x (ISBN 3-87808-881-7). Benjamins North Am.
Belleni-Morante, A. Applied Semigroups & Evolution Equations. (Oxford Mathematical Monographs). 1980. 36.00x (ISBN 0-19-853529-5). Oxford U Pr.
Beller, A., et al. Coding the Universe. LC 81-2663. (London Mathematical Society Lecture Notes: No. 47). 300p. 1982. 39.50 (ISBN 0-521-28040-0). Cambridge U Pr.
Beller, Dan. Progress Through Pioneer Evangelism. pap. 2.00 (ISBN 0-911866-80-9). Advocate.
Beller, F. K. & Schumacher, G. F. B., eds. The Biology of the Fluids of the Female Genital Tract. 464p. 1979. 72.00 (ISBN 0-444-00362-2, North Holland). Elsevier.
Beller, Janet. A-B-C-ing: An Action Alphabet. LC 83-23925. (Illus.). 32p. 1984. pap. text ed. 8.95 (ISBN 0-517-55208-6). Crown.
Beller, Joel. So You Want to Do a Science Project! LC 81-7943. (Illus.). 160p. (gr. 5 up). 1982. PLB 9.95 (ISBN 0-668-04987-1, 4987). Arco.
Beller, William S., ed. Puerto Rico & the Sea. Balzac, Irma, tr. 1974. pap. 6.25 (ISBN 0-8477-2301-1). U of PR Pr.
Bellerby, Frances. The First-Known & Other Poems. 1974. 5.00 (ISBN 0-685-46795-3, Pub. by Enitharmon Pr); signed, limited to 30 12.50 (ISBN 0-685-46796-1); wrappers 4.00 (ISBN 0-685-46797-X). Small Pr Dist.
Belleroche, J. de see De Belleroche, J. & Dockray, G. J.
Bellerophn Books Editors, jt. auth. see Chesterfield, Fourth Earl of.
Bellers, John. Essays about the Poor, Manufacturers, Trade Plantations, & Immorality, 3 vols. in 1. Bd. with A Discourse Touching Provision. Hale, Sir Matthew. Repr. of 1683 ed; A Discourse of the Poor. North, Roger. Repr. of 1753 ed. (History of English Economic Thought). Repr. of 1699 ed. 17.00 (ISBN 0-384-03860-3). Johnson Repr.
Belles, Donald W. Fire Hazard Analysis from Plastic Insulation in Exterior Walls of Buildings. 1982. 5.35 (ISBN 0-686-37665-X, TR 82-1). Society Fire Protect.
Bellessort, Andre. Balzac et Son Oeuvre. 1924. 30.00 (ISBN 0-8274-1911-2). R West.
Bellestri, Joseph. Sins of the Fathers. 1981. 7.75 (ISBN 0-8062-1612-3). Carlton.
Bellet, Louise Pecquet du see Du Bellet, Louise Pecquet.
Bellet, Samuel. Clinical Disorders of the Heart Beat. 3rd Rev. ed. pap. 160.00 (ISBN 0-317-27965-3, 2056015). Bks Demand UMI.
Bellett, J. G. Short Meditations, 3 vols. pap. 13.95 set (ISBN 0-88172-003-8); pap. 4.95 ea. Believers Bkshelf.
Bellevue Art Museum, ed. see Alps, Glen.
Bellew, Bernard. Desert Yucca: For Health & Arthritis. 1980. pap. 4.95x (ISBN 0-317-07332-X, Regent House). B of A.
Bellew, Frank. The Art of Amusing. LC 74-15725. (Popular Culture in America Ser.). (Illus.). 328p. 1975. Repr. of 1866 ed. 25.50x (ISBN 0-405-06362-8). Ayer Co Pubs.
Bellew, J. C. Poet's Corner: A Manual for Students in English Poetry. 1979. Repr. of 1884 ed. lib. bdg. 50.00 (ISBN 0-8495-0506-2). Arden Lib.
Bellew, John C. Shakespeare's Home at New Place. LC 76-113553. Repr. of 1863 ed. 25.00 (ISBN 0-404-00736-8). AMS Pr.
Bellezza, Fransis S. Improve Your Memory Skills. (Illus.). 145p. 1982. pap. 6.95 (ISBN 0-13-453308-9). P-H.
Belli, G. G. The Roman Sonnets. Norse, Harold, tr. LC 60-9955. 1960. pap. 4.00 (ISBN 0-317-02755-7, Dist. by Inland Bk). Jargon Soc.
Belli, Giuseppe. Sonnets of Giuseppe Belli. Williams, Miller, tr. from Ital. LC 80-24331. xx, 164p. 1981. 17.50x (ISBN 0-8071-0762-X). La State U Pr.
Belli, Giuseppe G. The Roman Sonnets of Giuseppe Gioacchino Belli. Norse, Harold, tr. from It. & intro. by. LC 73-79284. (Perivale Translation Ser.: No. 1). 54p. 1974. pap. 4.75 (ISBN 0-912288-06-X). Perivale Pr.
Belli, Humberto. Breaking Faith. LC 85-70475. 176p. 1985. pap. 6.95 (ISBN 0-89107-359-0, Crossway Bks). Good News.
Belli, M. M. The Law Revolt, 2 vols. 1126p. 1968. Set. 30.00 (ISBN 0-913338-03-6). Condyne-Oceana.
Belli, Melvin. The Belli Files. 275p. 1982. 14.95 (ISBN 0-13-077974-1, Busn). P-H.
--Modern Trials: Second Edition. LC 82-11159. write for info. (ISBN 0-314-68804-8). West Pub.
Belli, Melvin M., Sr. & Carlova, John. Belli for Your Malpractice Defense. Date not set. write for info. (ISBN 0-87489-380-1). Med Economics.
Bellier, Marcel, jt. auth. see Gros-Louis, Max.
Bellimin-Noel, J. Le Texte & l'Avant-Texte: Les Brouillons d'un Poeme de Milosz. new ed. (Collection L). 144p. (Orig., Fr.). 1972. pap. 8.95 (ISBN 2-03-036003-1). Larousse.
Bellin. Classical Dutch. 21.00 (ISBN 0-7134-3211-X, Pub. by Batsford England). David & Charles.
Bellin & Ruhl. Blake & Swedenborg: Opposition is True Friendship. LC 85-50060. 168p. pap. 8.95 (ISBN 0-87785-127-1). Swedenborg.
Bellin, Barbara & Haxby, James. Standard Catalog of Broken Bank Notes of the United States. LC 85-5043. (Illus.). 1986. write for info. (ISBN 0-87341-043-2). Krause Pubns.
Bellin, David. The Children's War. LC 79-54050. 1980. 10.95 (ISBN 0-935210-00-8); pap. 4.95 (ISBN 0-935210-01-6). Dundee Pub.
Bellin, H. & Steinberg, Peter. Dr. Bellin's Beautiful You Book. LC 81-10664. (Illus.). 192p. 1981. 16.95 (ISBN 0-13-216812-X); pap. 7.95 (ISBN 0-13-216804-9). P-H.
Bellin, Mildred G. The Original Jewish Cookbook. 470p. 1984. Repr. of 1958 ed. 14.95 (ISBN 0-8197-0058-4). Bloch.
Bellin, Robert. Queen's Pawn: Veresov System. (Illus.). 96p. 1983. pap. 13.95 (ISBN 0-7134-1877-X, Pub. by Batsford England). David & Charles.
--Trompowski Opening & Torre Attack. (Illus.). 96p. 1983. 14.95 (ISBN 0-7134-2399-4, Pub. by Batsford England). David & Charles.
Bellin, Robert & Ponzetto, Pietro. Test Your Positional Play. (Illus.). 192p. 1985. pap. 8.95 (ISBN 0-02-028090-4). MacMillan.
Bellina, J. H., ed. Gynecologic Laser Surgery. LC 81-7323. 492p. 1981. 55.00x (ISBN 0-306-40741-8, Plenum Pr). Plenum Pub.
Bellina, Joseph H. & Bandieramonte, Gaetano. Principles & Practice of Gynecologic Laser Surgery. 308p. 1984. 39.50x (ISBN 0-306-41543-7, Plenum Pr). Plenum Pub.
Bellina, Joseph H. & Wilson, Josleen. You Can Have a Baby: Everything You Need to Know about Fertility. (Illus.). 1985. 18.95 (ISBN 0-517-55619-7). Crown.
Bellincioni, Gemma, jt. auth. see Stagno Bellincioni, Bianca.
Bellinger, A. R. Essays on the Coinage of Alexander the Great. (Alexander the Great Ser.). (Illus.). 132p. 1981. 30.00 (ISBN 0-916710-93-9). Obol Intl.
Bellinger, Alfred R. Spires & Poplars. LC 72-144711. (Yale Ser. of Younger Poets: No. 4). Repr. of 1920 ed. 18.00 (ISBN 0-404-53804-5). AMS Pr.
--Troy the Coins. LC 81-50603. (Illus.). 1979. Repr. of 1961 ed. lib. bdg. 30.00 (ISBN 0-915262-32-0). S J Durst.
Bellinger, Alfred R. & Bellinger, Charlotte B. Catalogue of the Coins Found at Corinth, Nineteen Twenty-Five, with a Note on the Cleaning of the Coins. (Illus.). 1930. 75.00x (ISBN 0-686-51349-5). Elliots Bks.
Bellinger, Charlotte B., jt. auth. see Bellinger, Alfred R.
Bellinger, Gladys I. Mugsie Magpie's Surprise. LC 80-50318. (Illus.). 24p. (Orig.). (gr. 1-6). 1980. pap. 2.50 (ISBN 0-89301-067-7). U Pr of Idaho.
Bellinger, Louisa, jt. auth. see Kuhnel, Ernst.
Bellinger, Martha F. A Short History of the Drama. 469p. 1980. Repr. lib. bdg. 40.00 (ISBN 0-89984-052-3). Century Bookbindery.
Bellinger, Peter, jt. auth. see Christiansen, Kenneth.
Bellinger, W. H. Psalmody & Prophecy. (JSOT Supplement Ser.: No. 27). 146p. 1984. text ed. 28.50x (ISBN 0-905774-60-4, Pub. by JSOT Pr England); pap. text ed. 11.95x (ISBN 0-905774-61-2, Pub. by JSOT England). Eisenbrauns.
Bellingham, A. J., ed. Advanced Medicine, Vol. 16. 352p. pap. text ed. cancelled (ISBN 0-272-79600-X). Pitman Pub MA.
Bellingham, W., tr. see Simonde De Sismondi, Jean C.
Bellingrath, George C. Qualities Associated with Leadership in the Extra-Curricular Activities of the High School. LC 74-176549. (Columbia University. Teachers College. Contributions: No. 399). Repr. of 1930 ed. 22.50 (ISBN 0-404-55399-0). AMS Pr.

--Robespierre: A Study. LC 72-8441. (Select Bibliographies Reprint Ser.). 1972. Repr. of 1931 ed. 25.50 (ISBN 0-8369-6964-2). Ayer Co Pubs.

--The Servile State. LC 77-2914. 1977. 8.00 (ISBN 0-913966-31-2, Liberty Clas); pap. 3.00 (ISBN 0-913966-32-0). Liberty Fund.

--Short Talks with the Dead, & Others. facs. ed. LC 67-23175. (Essay Index Reprint Ser). 1926. 18.00 (ISBN 0-8369-0192-4). Ayer Co Pubs.

--Silence of the Sea. facs. ed. LC 74-107682. (Essay Index Reprint Ser). 1940. 16.00 (ISBN 0-8369-2038-4). Ayer Co Pubs.

--This & That & the Other. facs. ed. LC 68-22903. (Essay Index Reprint Ser.). 1968. Repr. of 1912 ed. 21.50 (ISBN 0-8369-0193-2). Ayer Co Pubs.

--Towns of Destiny. LC 72-101273. (BCL Ser. I). (Illus.). Repr. of 1927 ed. 20.00 (ISBN 0-404-00745-7). AMS Pr.

--Warfare in England. 254p. 1983. Repr. of 1912 ed. lib. bdg. 35.00 (ISBN 0-89987-094-5). Darby Bks.

--William the Conqueror. 153p. 1983. Repr. of 1938 ed. lib. bdg. 35.00 (ISBN 0-89987-093-7). Darby Bks.

--Wolsey. 1978. Repr. of 1933 ed. lib. bdg. 20.00 (ISBN 0-8495-0382-5). Arden Lib.

Belloc, Hilarie. Richelieu. 1935. Repr. 17.50 (ISBN 0-8274-3281-X). R West.

Belloc, Hillaire. Cruise of the Nona. (Century Travellers). 360p. 1984. pap. 11.95 (ISBN 0-7126-0280-1). Hippocrene Bks.

Belloli, Andrea P., ed. see Ackerman, Evelyn.

Belloli, Andrea P., ed. see Nodal, Al & De Bretteville, Sheila L.

Belloli, G. P., ed. Pediatric Cardiology & Cardiosurgery. (Modern Problems in Paediatrics: Vol. 22). (Illus.). viii, 216p. 1983. pap. 70.25 (ISBN 3-8055-3593-7). S Karger.

Belloli, Jay. Innovations: Contemporary Home Environments. (Illus.). 38p. 1973. 6.00x (ISBN 0-686-99821-9). La Jolla Mus Contemp Art.

--Jim Dine: The Summers Collection. (Illus.). 28p. 1974. 5.00x (ISBN 0-686-99817-0). La Jolla Mus Contemp Art.

--Ron Cooper. (Illus.). 38p. 1973. 6.00x (ISBN 0-686-99822-7). La Jolla Mus Contemp Art.

Belloli, Jay, ed. Myron Hunt, Eighteen Sixty-Eight to Nineteen Fifty-Two: The Search for a Regional Architecture. LC 84-81891. (California Architecture & Architects: No. 4). (Illus.). 120p. (Orig.). 1984. pap. 24.50 (ISBN 0-912158-90-5). Hennessey.

Belloli, Robert C. Contemporary Physical Science: Our Impact on Our World. (Illus.). 1978. write for info. (ISBN 0-02-308070-1). Macmillan.

Bellomo, Chas & Lynch, John. Crash, Fire & Rescue Handbook. (Pilot Training Ser.). 94p. (Orig.). 1984. pap. text ed. 8.95 (ISBN 0-89100-250-2, EA-250-2). Aviation Maintenance.

Bellon, Errol M. Radiologic Interpretation of ERCP: A Clinical Atlas. 1983. pap. text ed. 40.00 (ISBN 0-87488-707-0). Med Exam.

Bellon, Eugen. Scattered to All the Winds (Sixteen Eighty-Five to Seventeen Twenty): Migrations of the Dauphine French Huguenots into Italy, Switzerland, & Germany. rev. ed. Schalliol, Willis, ed. Gautschi, Erika, tr. from Ger. LC 83-70252. Orig. Title: Zerstreut in alle Winde. (Illus.). 284p. (Orig.). 1983. pap. 8.00x (ISBN 0-9605732-1-6). Belle Pubns.

Bellon, Jerry & Handler, Janet R. Curriculum Development & Evaluation: A Design for Improvement. 96p. 1982. pap. text ed. 7.95 (ISBN 0-8403-2720-X). Kendall-Hunt.

Bellon, Jerry J., et al. Classroom Supervision & Instructional Improvement. LC 76-4225. 1978. pap. text ed. 8.95 (ISBN 0-8403-2692-0, 40269202). Kendall-Hunt.

--Instructional Improvement: Principles & Processes. 1978. pap. text ed. 9.95 (ISBN 0-8403-1838-3). Kendall-Hunt.

Bellone, Enrico. A World on Paper: Studies in the Second Scientific Revolution. 220p. 1980. pap. 8.95x (ISBN 0-262-52081-8). MIT Pr.

--The World on Paper: Studies on the Second Scientific Revolution. Giaconni, Mirella & Giaconni, Ricardo, trs. from Italian. Orig. Title: Il Mondo di Carta. 1980. text ed. 27.50x (ISBN 0-262-02147-1). MIT Pr.

Belloni, Lanfranoo, jt. auth. see Brush, Stephen G.

Bellony-Rewald, Alice & Peppiatt, Michael. Imagination's Chamber: Artists & Their Studios. 232p. 1982. 45.00 (ISBN 0-8212-1520-5, 417866). NYGS.

Bellori, Giovanni P. The Lives of Annibale & Agostino Carracci. LC 67-16194. 1967. 12.50x (ISBN 0-271-73128-1). Pa St U Pr.

--Le Vite de' pittori, scultori et architetti moderni. (Documents of Art & Architectural History, Ser. 1: Vol. 4). (Ital.). 1980. Repr. of 1672 ed. 42.50x (ISBN 0-89371-104-7). Broude Intl Edns.

Bellori, Giovanni P., jt. auth. see Bartoli, Pietro S.

Bellos, David, ed. Leo Spitzer: Essays on 17th Century French Literature. LC 82-14581. (Cambridge Studies in French). 400p. 1983. 49.50 (ISBN 0-521-24356-4). Cambridge U Pr.

Bellosi, Luciano. Giotto. (Illus.). 96p. (Orig.). 1981. pap. 12.50 (ISBN 0-935748-03-2). Scala Books.

Bellot, Hugh H. American History & American Historians. LC 73-19305. (Illus.). 336p. 1974. Repr. of 1952 ed. lib. bdg. 22.50x (ISBN 0-8371-7325-6, BEAH). Greenwood.

Bellot, Leland J. William Knox: The Life & Thought of an Eighteenth-Century Imperialist. LC 76-44006. 276p. 1977. text ed. 17.50x (ISBN 0-292-79007-4). U of Tex Pr.

Bellow, A. & Kolzow, D., eds. Measure Theory: Proceedings of the Conference Held at Oberwolfach, 15-21 June, 1975. LC 76-26664. (Lecture Notes in Mathematics Ser.: Vol. 541). 1976. pap. 23.00 (ISBN 0-387-07861-4). Springer-Verlag.

Bellow, Gary & Moulton, Bea. The Lawyering Process: Ethics & Professional Responsibility. LC 81-67777. (University Casebook Ser.). 460p. 1981. pap. text ed. 10.00 (ISBN 0-88277-038-1). Foundation Pr.

--The Lawyering Process: Negotiation. LC 81-67776. (University Casebook Ser.). 297p. 1981. pap. text ed. 7.50 (ISBN 0-88277-039-X). Foundation Pr.

--The Lawyering Process: Preparing & Presenting the Case. LC 81-67655. (University Casebook Ser.). 516p. 1981. pap. text ed. 11.00 (ISBN 0-88277-040-3). Foundation Pr.

Bellow, Saul. The Adventures of Augie March. 1977. pap. 3.95 (ISBN 0-380-00961-7, 64600-5). Avon.

--The Adventures of Augie March. 1953. 12.95 (ISBN 0-670-10602-X). Viking.

Bellow, Sual. The Adventures of Augie March. 544p. 1984. pap. 5.95 (ISBN 0-14-007272-1). Penguin.

--Dangling Man. 1975. pap. 2.25 (ISBN 0-380-00332-5, 50849-4). Avon.

--Dangling Man. 192p. 12.95 (ISBN 0-8149-0024-0). Vanguard.

--The Dean's December. LC 80-8705. 320p. 1982. 14.37i (ISBN 0-06-014849-7, HarpT). Har-Row.

--The Dean's December. (General Ser.). 1982. lib. bdg. 16.95 (ISBN 0-8161-3404-9, Large Print Bks). G K Hall.

--Henderson: The Rain King. 1976. pap. 2.95 (ISBN 0-380-00832-7, 58313-5). Avon.

--Henderson the Rain King. 1959. 12.95 (ISBN 0-670-36655-2). Viking.

--Henderson the Rain King. 352p. 1984. pap. 4.95 (ISBN 0-14-007269-1). Penguin.

--Herzog. 1964. 12.95 (ISBN 0-670-36912-8). Viking.

--Herzog. 1984. pap. 4.95 (ISBN 0-14-007270-5). Penguin.

--Herzog: Text & Criticism. Howe, Irving, ed. LC 75-42290. (Viking Critical Library: No. 10). 1976. 14.95 (ISBN 0-670-36913-6). Viking.

--Herzog: Text & Ctiticism. (Viking Critical Library). 1976. pap. 7.95x (ISBN 0-670-01810-4). Penguin.

--Him with His Foot in His Mouth & Other Stories. LC 82-48322. 304p. 1984. 15.34i (ISBN 0-06-015179-X, HarpT). Har-Row.

--Him with His Foot in His Mouth & Other Stories. 1985. pap. 4.50 (ISBN 0-317-19328-7). PB.

--Humbolbt's Gift. 1984. 5.95 (ISBN 0-14-007271-3). Penguin.

--Humboldt's Gift. LC 75-12595. 416p. 1975. 12.95 (ISBN 0-670-38655-3). Viking.

--Mr. Sammler's Planet. 1984. pap. 5.95 (ISBN 0-14-007317-5). Penguin.

--Mr. Sammler's Planet. 1970. 12.95 (ISBN 0-670-49322-8). Viking.

--Mosby's Memoirs & Other Stories. 1968. 10.95 (ISBN 0-670-48965-4). Viking.

--Mosby's Memoirs & Other Stories. 192p. 1984. pap. 4.95 (ISBN 0-14-007318-3). Penguin.

--The Portable Saul Bellow. (Viking Portable Library: No. 79). 672p. 1977. pap. 9.95 (ISBN 0-14-015079-X, P79). Penguin.

--The Portable Saul Bellow. (Portable Library: No. 79). 1974. 14.95 (ISBN 0-670-15616-7). Viking.

--Seize the Day. 1984. pap. 4.95 (ISBN 0-14-007285-3). Penguin.

--Seize the Day. 1956. 7.95 (ISBN 0-670-63176-0). Viking.

--To Jerusalem & Back. 1977. pap. 1.95 (ISBN 0-380-01676-1, 33472-0). Avon.

--To Jerusalem & Back: A Personal Account. LC 76-42198. 192p. 1976. 11.95 (ISBN 0-670-71729-0). Viking.

--To Jerusalem & Back: A Personal Account. (Nonfiction Ser.). 192p. 1985. pap. 3.95 (ISBN 0-14-007273-X). Penguin.

--The Victim. 1975. pap. 1.95 (ISBN 0-380-00334-1, 36780-7). Avon.

--Victim. LC 47-12088. 302p. 15.95 (ISBN 0-8149-0050-X). Vanguard.

Bellow, Saul, ed. Great Jewish Short Stories. 414p. (Orig.). 1985. pap. 2.50 (ISBN 0-440-33122-6, LE). Dell.

Bellow, Saul, et al. Frontiers of Knowledge: The Frank Nelson Doubleday Lectures at the National Museum of History & Technology at the Smithsonian Institution, Washington, D. C. 416p. 1975. Limited Edition. 20.00 (ISBN 0-385-04826-2). Doubleday.

Bellow, Saul, et al, trs. see Singer, Isaac B.

Bellows, Barbara, jt. auth. see Connelly, Thomas L.

Bellows, Emma L. Memoirs of a Town & Country Doctor. LC 81-51489. 198p. 1982. 10.00 (ISBN 0-533-05079-0). Vantage.

Bellows, George. Drawings of George Bellows. Morgan, Charles, ed. (Master Draughtsman Ser). (Illus.). 48p. treasure trove bdg. 9.95x (ISBN 0-87505-000-X); pap. 4.95 (ISBN 0-87505-153-7). Borden.

Bellows, George K., jt. auth. see Howard, John T.

Bellows, Guy. Chemical Machining. 2nd ed. (Machining Process Ser.MDC 82-102). (Illus.). 96p. 1982. pap. 12.50 (ISBN 0-936974-08-7). Metcut Res Assocs.

--Low Stress Grinding. (Machining Process Ser.: MDC 83-103). (Illus.). 136p. 1983. pap. 17.50 (ISBN 0-936974-09-5). Metcut Res Assocs.

--Machining: A Process Checklist. 3rd ed. (Machining Process Ser.MDC 82-100). (Illus.). 32p. 1982. pap. 5.00 (ISBN 0-936974-07-9). Metcut Res Assocs.

Bellows, John G., ed. Cataract & Abnormalities of the Lens. LC 74-17438. (Illus.). 656p. 1975. text ed. 99.50 (ISBN 0-8089-0842-1, 790525). Grune.

--Glaucoma: Contemporary International Concepts. LC 79-88728. (Illus.). 448p. 1980. 66.00x (ISBN 0-89352-058-6). Masson Pub.

Bellows, Thomas J. The People's Action Party of Singapore: Emergence of a Dominant Party System. LC 73-114788. (Monograph Ser.: No. 14). xii, 195p. 1970. 8.25x (ISBN 0-938692-15-1). Yale U SE Asia.

Bellows, Thomas J., jt. auth. see Winter, Herbert R.

Bellquist, Eric C. Some Aspects of the Recent Foreign Policy of Sweden. 1929. 18.00 (ISBN 0-384-03885-9); pap. 12.00 (ISBN 0-685-13595-0). Johnson Repr.

Bellringer, A. W. & Jones, C. B., eds. The Romantic Age in Prose. (Costerus Ser.: Vol. XXIX). 159p. 1981. pap. text ed. 29.00x (ISBN 90-6203-981-2, Pub. by Rodopi Holland). Humanities.

Bellringer, Alan W. The Ambassadors. Rawson, Claude, ed. (Unwin Critical Library). (Illus.). 208p. 1984. text ed. 24.50x (ISBN 0-04-800026-4). Allen Unwin.

Bellringer, Alan W. & Jones, C. B., eds. The Victorian Sages: An Anthology of Prose. (Rowman & Littlefield University Library). 241p. 1975. 11.50x (ISBN 0-87471-553-9); pap. 6.00x (ISBN 0-87471-554-7). Rowman.

Bellrose, Frank C., rev. by see Kortright, E. H.

Bell-Taylor. Florida Wild Flowers & Roadside Plants. 1984. 18.50 (ISBN 0-9608688-0-1). Horticult FL.

Belluardo, Connie, et al. BASIC Programming 1. LC 84-71291. (Illus.). 103p. (Orig.). 1985. pap. text ed. 9.95 (ISBN 0-917531-04-3); pap. text ed. 16.95 tchr's. guide (ISBN 0-917531-14-0). Compu Tech Pub.

--BASIC Programming 2. LC 84-71291. (Illus.). 112p. (Orig.). 1985. pap. text ed. 9.95 (ISBN 0-917531-05-1); pap. text ed. 16.95 tchr's. guide (ISBN 0-917531-15-9). Compu Tech Pub.

--BASIC Programming 3. LC 84-71291. (Illus.). 120p. (Orig.). 1985. pap. text ed. 9.95 (ISBN 0-917531-06-X); pap. text ed. 16.95 tchr's. guide (ISBN 0-917531-16-7). Compu Tech Pub.

--BASIC Programming 4. LC 84-71291. (Illus., Orig.). 1985. pap. text ed. 9.95 (ISBN 0-917531-07-8); pap. text ed. 16.95 tchr's. guide (ISBN 0-917531-17-5). Compu Tech Pub.

--Discovering BASIC 1. LC 84-71290. (Illus.). 90p. (Orig.). 1985. pap. text ed. 8.95 (ISBN 0-917531-00-0); pap. text ed. 16.95 tchr's guide (ISBN 0-917531-10-8). Compu Tech Pub.

--Discovering BASIC 2. LC 84-71290. (Illus., Orig.). 1985. pap. text ed. 8.95 (ISBN 0-917531-01-9); pap. text ed. 16.95 tchr's guide (ISBN 0-917531-11-6). Compu Tech Pub.

--Discovering BASIC 3. LC 84-71290. (Illus.). 90p. (Orig.). 1985. pap. text ed. 8.95 (ISBN 0-917531-02-7); pap. text ed. 16.95 tchr's guide (ISBN 0-917531-12-4). Compu Tech Pub.

--Discovering BASIC 4. LC 84-71290. (Illus.). 96p. (Orig.). 1985. pap. text ed. 8.95 (ISBN 0-917531-03-5); pap. text ed. 16.95 tchr's guide (ISBN 0-917531-13-2). Compu Tech Pub.

Belluco, Umberto. Organometallic & Coordination Chemistry of Platinum. 1974. 98.00 (ISBN 0-12-085350-7). Acad Pr.

Bellugi, U. & Studdert-Kennedy, M., eds. Signed & Spoken Language: Biological Constraints on Linguistic Form. (Dahlem Workshop Reports, Life Science Research Report Ser.: No. 19). (Illus.). 379p. (Orig.). 1980. pap. 40.00x (ISBN 0-89573-034-0). VCH Pubs.

Bellugi, Ursula & Brown, Roger. Acquisition of Language. LC 70-172101. (Monograph from Cognitive Development in Children - Society for the Research in Child Development Ser). 1972. pap. 3.95x (ISBN 0-226-76757-4, P445, Phoen). U of Chicago Pr.

Bellugi, Ursula, jt. auth. see Klima, Edward.

Bellush, Bernard. The Failure of the NRA. (Norton Essays in American History Ser.). 197p. 1976. pap. 4.95x (ISBN 0-393-09223-2). Norton.

--Franklin D. Roosevelt As Governor of New York. LC 68-54257. (Columbia University Studies in the Social Sciences: No. 585). Repr. of 1955 ed. 17.50 (ISBN 0-404-51585-1). AMS Pr.

Bellush, Bernard, jt. auth. see Bellush, Jewel.

Bellush, Jewel & Bellush, Bernard. Union Power & New York: Victor Gotbaum & District Council 37. LC 84-15926. 496p. 1984. 33.95 (ISBN 0-03-000122-6). Praeger.

--Union Power & New York: Victor Gotbaum & District Council 37. (Illus.). 368p. 1985. pap. 14.95 (ISBN 0-03-001322-4). Praeger.

Bell-Villada, Gene H. Borges & His Fiction: A Guide to His Mind & Art. LC 80-17426. xx, 292p. 1981. 21.00x (ISBN 0-8078-1458-X); pap. 10.00x (ISBN 0-8078-4075-0). U of NC Pr.

Bellville, Cheryl W. All Things Bright & Beautiful. 64p. (Orig.). 1983. pap. 7.95 (ISBN 0-86683-722-1, AY8363). Winston Pr.

--Farming Today-Yesterday's Way. LC 84-3215. (Carolrhoda Photo Bks.). (Illus.). 32p. (gr. 1-5). 1984. PLB 9.95 (ISBN 0-87614-220-X). Carolrhoda Bks.

--Rodeo. LC 84-14981. (Carolrhoda Photo Bks.). (Illus.). 32p. (gr. 1-5). 1985. PLB 11.95 (ISBN 0-87614-272-2). Carolrhoda Bks.

--Round-up. (Illus.). 32p. (gr. k-4). 1982. PLB 9.95g (ISBN 0-87614-187-4). Carolrhoda Bks.

--Theater Magic: Behind the Scenes at a Children's Theater. (Photo Bks.). (Illus.). 48p. (gr. 1-6). 1985. lib. bdg. 12.95 (ISBN 0-87614-278-1). Carolrhoda Bks.

Bellville, Cheryl W., jt. auth. see Bellville, Rod.

Bellville, J. Weldon & Weaver, Charles S. Techniques in Clinical Physiology: A Survey of Methods in Anesthesiology. LC 1-30791. (Illus.). 1969. write for info. (ISBN 0-02-307910-X, 30791). Macmillan.

Bellville, Rod & Bellville, Cheryl W. Large Animal Veterinarians. LC 82-19750. (Illus.). 32p. (gr. 1-4). 1983. PLB 8.95g (ISBN 0-87614-211-0). Carolrhoda Bks.

--Stockyards. LC 83-18839. (Carolrhoda Photo Bks.). (Illus.). 32p. (gr. 1-5). 1984. PLB 9.95 (ISBN 0-87614-224-2). Carolrhoda Bks.

Bellwood, Peter S. Archaeological Research in the Cook Islands. LC 78-65064. (Pacific Anthropological Records: No. 27). 214p. 1978. pap. 10.00 (ISBN 0-910240-50-7). Bishop Mus.

Bellwood, Peter S., jt. auth. see Skjolsvold, Arne.

Belly, J. M., et al, eds. Measure Theory & Its Applications. (Lecture Notes in Mathematics Ser.: Vol. 1033). 317p. 1983. pap. 17.00 (ISBN 0-387-12703-8). Springer-Verlag.

Belmaker, R. H. & Bannet, J., eds. New Directions in Tardive Dyskinesia Research. (Modern Problems of Pharmacopsychiatry: Vol. 21). (Illus.). vi, 222p. 1983. 53.75 (ISBN 3-8055-3735-2). S Karger.

Belmaker, R. H. & Van Praag, H., eds. Mania: An Evolving Concept. (Illus.). 437p. 1980. text ed. 40.00 (ISBN 0-89335-115-6). SP Med & Sci Bks.

Belmaker, R. H., jt. ed. see Zohar, Joseph.

Belmaker, Robert, jt. auth. see Gershon, Samuel.

Belman, A. Barry & Kaplan, George W. Genitourinary Problems in Pediatrics. (Major Problems in Clinical Pediatrics Ser.: Vol. 23). (Illus.). 200p. 1981. text ed. 41.00 (ISBN 0-7216-1678-X). Saunders.

Belmar, John J. Success - It's Yours to Have. 1984. 5.75 (ISBN 0-8062-2305-7). Carlton.

Belmar, Terri. Brezhia. 128p. 1981. 7.00 (ISBN 0-682-49721-5). Exposition Pr FL.

Belmont, Eleanor R. The Fabric of Memory. Baxter, Annette K., ed. LC 79-8775. (Signal Lives Ser.). (Illus.). 1980. Repr. of 1957 ed. lib. bdg. 34.50x (ISBN 0-405-12824-X). Ayer Co Pubs.

Belmont Historic District Commission Project Staff. Belmont, Massachusetts: The Architecture & Development of the Town of Homes. (Illus.). 120p. 1984. write for info. Belmont Hist Dist Comm.

Belmont, Nicole. Arnold van Gennep: The Creator of French Ethnography. Coltman, Derek, tr. LC 78-8680. 1979. lib. bdg. 17.00x (ISBN 0-226-04216-2). U of Chicago Pr.

Belmont, Perry. American Democrat: The Recollections of Perry Belmont. 2nd ed. LC 42-3269. Repr. of 1941 ed. 28.50 (ISBN 0-404-00746-5). AMS Pr.

--Return to Secret Party Funds. LC 73-19127. (Politics & People Ser.). 258p. 1974. Repr. of 1927 ed. 18.00x (ISBN 0-405-05852-7). Ayer Co Pubs.

Belmonte, C., et al, eds. see International Meetings on Arterial Chemoreceptors, 6th, Valladoli, Spain, Sept., 1979.

Belmonte, Mimi. The Diabetic Child & Young Adult. 150p. 1983. pap. 8.95 (ISBN 0-920792-17-0). Eden Pr.

Belmonte, Thomas. The Broken Fountain. LC 78-32167. 160p. 1979. 21.00x (ISBN 0-231-04542-5); pap. 10.00x (ISBN 0-231-04543-3). Columbia U Pr.

Belnap, Nuel D. & Steel, Thomas B., Jr. The Logic of Questions & Answers. LC 75-27761. 1976. 22.50x (ISBN 0-300-01962-9). Yale U Pr.

Belnap, Nuel D., Jr., jt. auth. see Anderson, Alan R.

Belnap, Parley L. Hymn Studies for Organists. pap. 4.95 (ISBN 0-87747-418-4). Deseret Bk.

Belo, Fernando. A Materialist Reading of the Gospel of Mark. O'Connell, Matthew, tr. from Fr. LC 80-24756. 384p. (Orig.). 1981. pap. 12.95 (ISBN 0-88344-323-6). Orbis Bks.

Belo, Jane. Traditional Balinese Culture: Essays. LC 68-54454. pap. 123.80 (ISBN 0-317-08157-8, 2006119). Bks Demand UMI.

--Trance in Bali. LC 77-6361. 1977. Repr. of 1960 ed. lib. bdg. 35.75 (ISBN 0-8371-9652-3, BETR). Greenwood.

Beloch, Julius. Die Bevolkerung der Griechisch-Romischen Welt. Finley, Moses, ed. LC 79-4962. (Ancient Economic History Ser.). (Ger.). 1980. Repr. of 1886 ed. lib. bdg. 44.00x (ISBN 0-405-12349-3). Ayer Co Pubs.

Beloff, Halla. Camera Culture. 304p. 1985. 24.95 (ISBN 0-631-13989-3). Basil Blackwell.

Beloff, John. Psychological Sciences, a Review of Modern Psychology. 361p. 1973. 17.95x (ISBN 0-8464-1125-3). Beekman Pubs.

Beloff, M., ed. see Wiener Library.

Beloff, Max. The Balance of Power. (Beatty Memorial Lectures Ser.). 1967. 4.00 (ISBN 0-7735-0050-2). McGill-Queens U Pr.

--Foreign Policy & the Democratic Process. LC 76-57665. (The Albert Shaw Lectures on Diplomatic History, 1954). 1977. Repr. of 1955 ed. lib. bdg. 15.00 (ISBN 0-8371-9463-6, BEFO). Greenwood.

--Foreign Policy & the Democratic Process. LC 55-9743. (Albert Shaw Lectures on Diplomatic History Ser). pap. 37.80 (ISBN 0-8357-9272-2, 2015876). Bks Demand UMI.

--The Great Powers: Essays in Twentieth Century Politics. LC 78-14402. 1979. Repr. of 1959 ed. lib. bdg. 24.75x (ISBN 0-8371-9297-8, BEGP). Greenwood.

--The Intellectual in Politics & Other Essays. LC 78-141854. 361p. 1971. 19.95 (ISBN 0-912050-02-0, Library Pr). Open Court.

--Public Order & Popular Disturbances: 1660-1714. 168p. 1963. 26.00x (ISBN 0-7146-1270-7, F Cass Co). Biblio Dist.

--Soviet Policy in the Far East, 1944-1951. facsimile ed. LC 75-146852. (Select Bibliographies Reprint Ser). Repr. of 1953 ed. 20.00 (ISBN 0-8369-5619-2). Ayer Co Pubs.

--The United States & the Unity of Europe. LC 75-31355. 124p. 1976. Repr. of 1963 ed. lib. bdg. 45.00 (ISBN 0-8371-8507-6, BEUS). Greenwood.

--Wars & Welfare: Britain 1914-1945. 320p. 1984. text ed. 37.50 (ISBN 0-7131-6163-9). E Arnold.

Beloff, Max & Peele, Gillian. The Government of the United Kingdom: Political Authority in a Changing Society. (Comparative Modern Goverment Ser.). (Orig.). 1980. 17.95 (ISBN 0-393-01344-8); pap. text ed. 8.95x (ISBN 0-393-95135-9). Norton.

Beloff, Max & Vale, Vivian, eds. American Political Institutions in the 1970's. 194p. 1975. 21.50x (ISBN 0-87471-587-3). Rowman.

Beloff, Michael. The Plateglass Universities. LC 70-88559. 208p. 1970. 18.50 (ISBN 0-8386-7550-6). Fairleigh Dickinson.

Belohlav, James. The Art of Disciplining Your Employees: A Manager's Guide. (Illus.). 168p. 1985. pap. 7.95 (ISBN 0-13-046715-4). P-H.

Belohlavek, John M. George Mifflin Dallas: Jacksonian Patrician. LC 77-1415. 1977. 24.95x (ISBN 0-271-00510-6). Pa St U Pr.

--Let the Eagle Soar: The Foreign Policy of Andrew Jackson. LC 85-1007. (Illus.). 336p. 1985. 27.95xt (ISBN 0-8032-1187-2). U of Nebr Pr.

Belok, Michael V. Forming the American Minds: Early School Books & Their Compilers (1783-1837) 1973. 12.50 (ISBN 0-685-81370-3). Heinman.

Belok, Michael V., jt. auth. see Roucek, Joseph S.

Belokhovstikova, V. I., jt. auth. see Kornilovich, Yu. E.

Beloserkovskii, O. M., et al, eds. Rarefied Gas Dynamics. 1418p. 1985. 195.00x (ISBN 0-306-41932-7, Plenum Pr). Plenum Pub.

Belot, Raymond de see De Belot, Raymond.

Belote, James H. & Belote, William M. Corregidor. LC 80-80981. (Blockbusting War Bks.). (Illus.). 288p. 1984. pap. 2.95 (ISBN 0-515-07738-0). Jove Pubns.

--Typhoon of Steel: The Battle for Okinawa. 416p. (Orig.). 1984. pap. text ed. 3.95 (ISBN 0-553-24372-1). Bantam.

Belote, Theodore T. Scioto Speculation & the French Settlement at Gallipolis. LC 75-146138. (Research & Source Works Ser.: No. 717) 1971. Repr. of 1907 ed. lib. bdg. 18.50 (ISBN 0-8337-0221-1). B Franklin.

Belote, William M., jt. auth. see Belote, James H.

Belotserkovskii, Sergei M. Theory of Thin Wings in Subsonic Flow. LC 67-17189. 250p. 1967. 30.00x (ISBN 0-306-30291-8, Plenum Pr). Plenum Pub.

Belotserkovsky, O. M., jt. auth. see Napolitano, L. G.

Belouino, P. Dictionnaire General et Complet des Persecutions, 2 vols. Migne, J. P., ed. (Nouvelle Encyclopedie Theologique Ser.: Vols. 4-5). 1468p. (Fr.). Repr. of 1851 ed. lib. bdg. 186.50x (ISBN 0-89241-255-0). Caratzas.

Belous, Richard, jt. auth. see Levitan, Sar.

Belous, Richard S., jt. auth. see Levitan, Sar A.

Belous, Richard S., jt. auth. see Levitan, Sara.

Belousov, R. What Real Socialism Means to the People. 261p. 1982. pap. 2.95 (ISBN 0-8285-2300-2, Pub. by Progress Pubs USSR). Imported Pubns.

Belousov, V. V. Geotectonics. (Illus.). 330p. 1980. 34.00 (ISBN 0-387-09173-4). Springer-Verlag.

Beloussov, V. V. Continental Endogenous Regimes. 295p. 1981. 10.00 (ISBN 0-8285-2281-2, Pub. by Mir Pubs USSR). Imported Pubns.

Belov, A. F., jt. ed. see Williams, J. C.

Belov, Nikolai V. Crystal Chemistry of Large-Cation Silicates. LC 63-17642. pap. 42.00 (ISBN 0-317-08935-8, 2003357). Bks Demand UMI.

Belov, P. Fundamentals of Petroleum Chemicals Technology. Sobolev, David, tr. from Russian. (Illus.). 430p. 1970. 16.00x (ISBN 0-8464-0438-9). Beekman Pubs.

Belov, V. Morning Rendezous. 383p. 1985. pap. 4.00 (ISBN 0-8285-3006-8, Pub. by Raduga Puds USSR). Imported Pubns.

Belova, E. V., jt. auth. see Sokolov, E. I.

Belove, Charles. A First Circuits Course for Engineering Technology. 1982. text ed. 32.95 (ISBN 0-03-057851-5). HR&W.

--Handbook of Modern Electrical & Electronic Engineering. 2200p. 1985. text ed. 53.45 (ISBN 0-471-09754-3). Wiley.

Belove, Charles & Drossman, Melvyn. Systems & Circuits for Electrical Engineering Technology. new ed. (Illus.). 1976. text ed. 45.00 (ISBN 0-07-004430-9). McGraw.

Belove, Charles, jt. auth. see Schilling, Donald.

Belove, Charles, et al. Digital Analog System Circulation Development. Wade, Charles R., ed. (Illus.). 448p. 1973. text ed. 47.00 (ISBN 0-07-004420-1). McGraw.

Belozerskaya-Bulgakova, L. E. My Life with Mikhail Bulgakov. Thompson, M., tr. from Rus. 136p. 1983. 18.95 (ISBN 0-88233-433-6). Ardis Pubs.

Belpre, P., tr. see Hoff, Syd.

Belpre, Pura. The Dance of the Animals. LC 72-83126. (Illus.). 32p. (gr. 1-3). 1972. PLB 4.95 (ISBN 0-7232-6039-7). Warne.

--The Rainbow-Colored Horse. LC 77-84600. (Illus.). (ps-2). 1978. PLB 8.95 (ISBN 0-7232-6151-2). Warne.

Belpre, Pura, tr. see Bonsall, Crosby N.

Belpre, Pura, tr. see De Paola, Tomie.

Belpre, Pura, tr. see Kessler, Leonard.

Bels, A. Voice of the Herald. 368p. 1980. 8.45 (ISBN 0-8285-1879-3, Pub. by Progress Pubs USSR). Imported Pubns.

Bels, Albert. The Inspector. Cedrins, Inara, tr. from Latvian. 125p. cancelled (ISBN 0-931556-08-2). Translation Pr.

Belschner, H. G. Horse Diseases. 1975. pap. 6.00 (ISBN 0-87980-302-9). Wilshire.

--Horse Diseases. Rose, R. J., rev. by. 264p. 1982. 59.00x (ISBN 0-207-14319-6, Pub. by Angus & Robertson). State Mutual Bk.

Belsey, Catherine. Critical Practice. 176p. 1980. pap. 9.95x (ISBN 0-416-72950-9, NO.2021). Methuen Inc.

--The Subject of Tragedy. 288p. (Orig.). 1985. 25.00 (ISBN 0-416-32700-1, 9446); pap. text ed. 11.95 (ISBN 0-416-32710-9, 9447). Methuen Inc.

Belshaw, Cyril S. Changing Melanesia: Social Economics of Culture Contact. LC 76-44881. (Illus.). 1976. lib. bdg. 17.00x (ISBN 0-8371-9039-8, BELM). Greenwood.

Belshaw, Michael. Economics of Underdeveloped Countries. LC 74-84420. (Real World of Economics Ser). Orig. Title: Economic Development. (Illus.). (gr. 5-11). 1970. PLB 4.95 (ISBN 0-8225-0617-3). Lerner Pubns.

Belshaw, Michael H. A Village Economy: Land & People of Huecorio. LC 66-28489. (Institute of Latin American Studies). (Illus.). 421p. 1967. 36.00x (ISBN 0-231-02928-4). Columbia U Pr.

Belshaw, R. H. Guinea Fowl of the World. (Illus.). 224p. 37.50 (ISBN 0-947647-20-1, Pub. by Fanciers Supplies). Longwood Pub Group.

Belshin, Leon & Mason, Dean T. Love Your Heart. LC 82-80481. (Dialogue Bks.). 176p. (Orig.). 1982. pap. 9.75 (ISBN 0-89881-011-6). Intl Dialogue Pr.

Belsinger, Susan & Dille, Carolyn. Cooking With Herbs. (Illus.). 240p. 1984. 19.95 (ISBN 0-8436-2225-3); pap. 14.95 (ISBN 0-8436-2226-1). Van Nos Reinhold.

Belskaya, Natalia, tr. see Alexeyev, S.

Bels-Koning, H. C. & Van Kuijk, W. M. Mushroom Terms: Polyglot on Research & Cultivation of Edible Fungi. 336p. (Eng., Fr., Ger., Ital., Span., Dutch, Danish & Lat.). 1980. pap. 83.00 (ISBN 90-220-0673-5, PDC211, Pudoc). Unipub.

Belsky, Dick. One for the Money. 200p. 1985. 14.95 (ISBN 0-89733-148-6). Academy Chi Pubs.

Belsky, Janet K. The Psychology of Aging: Theory, Research & Practice. LC 83-20923. (Psychology Ser.). 550p. 1984. text ed. 19.50 pub net (ISBN 0-534-02868-3). Brooks-Cole.

Belsky, Jay. In the Beginning: Readings in Infancy. LC 81-10008. (Illus.). 328p. 1982. 36.00x (ISBN 0-231-05114-X); pap. 14.50x (ISBN 0-231-05115-8). Columbia U Pr.

Belsky, Jay, et al. The Child in the Family. LC 83-12255. (Illus.). 288p. 1984. pap. text ed. 14.95 (ISBN 0-394-34787-0, RanC). Random.

Belsley, David A., et al. Regression Diagnostics: Identifying Influential Data & Sources of Collinearity. LC 79-19876. (Ser. in Probability & Mathematical Statistics: Applied Probability & Statistics). 292p. 1980. 36.95x (ISBN 0-471-05856-4, Pub. by Wiley-Interscience). Wiley.

Belsley, David A., et al, eds. Inflation, Trade, & Taxes. LC 75-19099. (Illus.). 262p. 1976. 15.95 (ISBN 0-8142-0194-6). Ohio St U Pr.

Belson, David. What to Say & How to Say It: For All Occasions. 1961. pap. 4.95 (ISBN 0-8065-0891-4, 98). Citadel Pr.

Belson, David & Belson, Ruth. Chairman & Speaker's Role Made Easy. 1968. pap. 1.95 (ISBN 0-8065-0187-1, C269). Citadel Pr.

Belson, Ruth, jt. auth. see Belson, David.

Belson, William A. The Design & Understanding of Survey Questions. 408p. 1981. 29.00x (ISBN 0-566-00420-8, 04703-1, Pub. by Gower Pub Co England). Lexington Bks.

--Juvenile Theft: The Causal Factors. 1975. 28.80 (ISBN 0-06-318026-X, IntlDept). Har-Row.

--Television Violence & the Adolescent Boy. (Illus.). 1978. 24.50x (ISBN 0-566-00211-6, 02081-8, Pub. by Saxon Hse England). Lexington Bks.

Belstead, John S., jt. auth. see Thomas, Meirion.

Belstock, Alan & Smith, Gerald. Consumer Mathematics with Calculator Applications. Gafney, Leo, ed. (gr. 10-12). 1980. text ed. 17.52x (ISBN 0-07-004436-8). McGraw.

Belt, Elmer. Leonardo the Anatomist. LC 69-13818. (Illus.). 76p. Repr. of 1955 ed. lib. bdg. 18.75 (ISBN 0-8371-0304-5, BELA). Greenwood.

Belt, Elmer, ed. see Da Vinci, Leonardo.

Belt, Sage C., jt. auth. see Bartel, Janice R.

Belt, T. Edwin. Winemaking with Elderberries. (Illus.). 106p. Date not set. pap. 3.95 (ISBN 0-900841-62-1, Pub. by Aztex Corp). Argus Bks.

Belt, Thomas. The Naturalist in Nicaragua. (Illus.). xxxiv, 406p. 1985. lib. bdg. 30.00x (ISBN 0-226-04219-7); pap. 12.95 (ISBN 0-226-04220-0). U of Chicago Pr.

Beltaine, ed. see Yeats, W. B.

Belth, Joseph M. Life Insurance: A Consumer's Handbook. LC 72-76943. 272p. 1973. 12.50x (ISBN 0-253-14800-6). Ind U Pr.

--Life Insurance: A Consumer's Handbook. 2nd ed. LC 84-47705. (Illus.). 240p. 1985. 25.00x (ISBN 0-317-14909-1); pap. 12.50x (ISBN 0-253-20346-5). Ind U Pr.

--Participating Life Insurance Sold by Stock Companies. 1965. 10.00x (ISBN 0-256-00639-3). Irwin.

Belth, Nathan C. A Promise to Keep: A Narrative of the American Encounter with Anti-Semitism. LC 81-40403. (Illus.). 1981. pap. 7.95 (ISBN 0-8052-0682-5). Schocken.

--A Promise to Keep: The American Encounter with Anti-Semitism. 305p. Repr. 6.95 (ISBN 0-686-95111-5). ADL.

Belting, Elizabeth, jt. auth. see Belting, George.

Belting, George & Belting, Elizabeth. Sweet Dreams: Fourteen Ways to Sleep at Will. 1982. pap. 11.95x (ISBN 0-317-06947-0, Regent House). B of A.

Belting, Hans. Images & Its Public. 1985. write for info. (ISBN 0-89241-403-0). Caratzas.

--Studies in the History of Art 1982, Vol. 12. (Illus.). 1983. pap. 9.95 (ISBN 0-89468-063-3, Dist. by U Pr of New Eng). Natl Gallery Art.

Belting, Hans, jt. auth. see Buchthal, Hugo.

Belting, Hans, et al. The Mosaics & Frescoes of St. Mary Pammakaristos (Fethiye Camii) at Istanbul. LC 77-99268. (Dumbarton Oaks Studies: Vol. 15). (Illus.). 118p. 1978. 30.00x (ISBN 0-88402-075-4). Dumbarton Oaks.

Belting, Natalia M. Kaskaskia under the French Regime. 1975. Repr. 15.00 (ISBN 0-686-20878-1). Polyanthos.

Belting, Natalia M. & Hine, James R. Your Wedding Workbook. 5th ed. (Illus.). 1985. pap. 6.95 (ISBN 0-8134-2481-X, 2481). Interstate.

Belting, Paul E. Development of the Free Public High School in Illinois to 1860. LC 71-89149. (American Education: Its Men, Institutions & Ideas, Ser. 1). 1969. Repr. of 1919 ed. 16.00 (ISBN 0-405-01386-8). Ayer Co Pubs.

Beltman, H. A. Vegetative Strukturen der Parmeliaceae und Ihre Entwicklung. (Bibliotheca Lichenologica Ser.: No. 11). (Illus.). 1978. lib. bdg. 21.00x (ISBN 3-7682-1199-1). Lubrecht & Cramer.

Belton, Beth. American Class Society in Numbers. rev. & enl. ed. Howard, Bob & Logue, John, eds. (Illus.). 112p. 1981. pap. 2.95 (ISBN 0-933522-07-X). Kent Popular.

Belton, G. R. & Worrell, W. L., eds. Heterogeneous Kinetics at Elevated Temperatures. LC 70-128401. 532p. 1970. 75.00x (ISBN 0-306-30500-3, Plenum Pr). Plenum Pub.

Belton, John. Cinema Stylists. LC 82-10793. (Filmmakers Ser.: No. 2). (Illus.). 384p. 1983. 21.00 (ISBN 0-8108-1585-0). Scarecrow.

--The Hollywood Professionals, Vol. 3: Hawks, Borzage, & Ulmer. LC 73-13190. (International Film Guide Ser). (Illus.). 192p. 1974. pap. 4.95 (ISBN 0-498-01448-7). A S Barnes.

Belton, John & Cramblit, Joella. Card Games. LC 75-42319. (Games & Activities). (Illus.). 48p. (gr. 3 up). 1976. PLB 13.31 (ISBN 0-8172-0021-5). Raintree Pubs.

--Dice Games. LC 75-43625. (Games & Activities). (Illus.). 48p. (gr. k-3). 1976. 13.31 (ISBN 0-8172-0023-1). Raintree Pubs.

--Domino Games. LC 76-8864. (Games & Activities). (Illus.). 48p. (gr. 4-9). 1976. PLB 13.31 (ISBN 0-8172-0625-6). Raintree Pubs.

--Let's Play Cards. LC 75-9606. (Games & Activities). (Illus.). 48p. (gr. k-3). 1975. PLB 13.31 (ISBN 0-8172-0025-8). Raintree Pubs.

--Solitaire Games. LC 75-25956. (Games & Activities). (Illus.). 48p. (gr. 3 up). 1975. PLB 13.31 (ISBN 0-8172-0027-4). Raintree Pubs.

Belton, John, jt. ed. see Weis, Elisabeth.

Belton, N. R. & Toothill, C., eds. Transport & Inherited Disease. 1982. lib. bdg. 59.00 (ISBN 0-85200-391-9, Pub. by MTP Pr England). Kluwer Academic.

Belton, N. R., et al, eds. Brain: Biochemistry & Inherited Metabolic Disease. 128p. 1983. text ed. 36.00 (ISBN 0-85200-484-2, Pub. by MTP Pr England). Kluwer Academic.

Belton, Sandra & Terbough, Christine. Sparks: Activities to Help Children Learn at Home. LC 74-11878. 120p. 1972. pap. text ed. 9.95 (ISBN 0-87705-710-9). Human Sci Pr.

Beltowski, Gary, jt. auth. see Zavisca, Ernest.

Beltrametti, E. & Van Fraassen, Bas C., eds. Current Issues in Quantum Logic. LC 80-29505. (Ettore Majorana International Science Series Physical Sciences: Vol. 8). 502p. 1981. 79.50x (ISBN 0-306-40652-7, Plenum Pr). Plenum Pub.

Beltrametti, Franco. Another Earthquake. Vangelisti, Paul, tr. 1976. pap. 2.50 (ISBN 0-88031-023-5). Invisible-Red Hill.

--Face to Face. 1973. signed 4.00 (ISBN 0-685-78949-7, Pub. by Grosseteste); sewn in wrappers 2.00 (ISBN 0-685-78950-0). Small Pr Dist.

Beltrametti, Franco, et al. Andiamo. 3.00 (ISBN 0-686-15302-2). Great Raven Pr.

Beltrami, E. Models for Public Systems Analysis. (Operations Research & Industrial Engineering Ser.). 1977. 39.50 (ISBN 0-12-085565-8). Acad Pr.

Beltrami, E. J. Algorithmic Approach to Nonlinear Analysis & Optimization. (Mathematics in Science & Engineering Ser.: Vol. 63). 1970. 55.00 (ISBN 0-12-085560-7). Acad Pr.

Beltrami, E. J. & Wohlers, M. R. Distributions & the Boundary Values of Analytic Functions. 1966. 29.00 (ISBN 0-12-085550-X). Acad Pr.

Beltrami, Edward. The High Cost of Clean Water: Models for Water Quality Management Ser. (The UMAP Expository Monograph). 53p. 1982. pap. text ed. 8.95 (ISBN 0-8176-3098-8). Birkhauser.

Beltramo, Mario & Longo, Giovanni E. The Italian Civil Code, Supplement, 1969-1978. LC 69-15387. 220p. 1978. lib. bdg. 25.00 (ISBN 0-379-20292-1). Oceana.

Beltran, Antonio. Rock Art of the Spanish Levant. LC 81-21694. (The Imprint of Man Ser.). 144p. 1982. 22.95 (ISBN 0-521-24568-0). Cambridge U Pr.

Beltran, George, ed. see Freemesser, Bernard.

Beltrone, Art, ed. Old Bethpage Village Restoration. (Illus.). 48p. pap. 2.00 (ISBN 0-911357-03-3). Friends Long Island.

Beltroy, Manuel, tr. see Hume, Roberto E.

Beltsville Symposia in Agricultural Research, ed. Animal Reproduction, No. 3. LC 78-65535. (Beltsville Symposia in Agricultural Research). (Illus.). 434p. 1979. 42.95 (ISBN 0-470-26672-4). Halsted Pr.

Beltz, George F. Memorials of the Most Noble Order of the Garter from Its Foundation to the Present Time. LC 72-178572. Repr. of 1841 ed. 49.50 (ISBN 0-404-56527-1). AMS Pr.

Beltz, Oliver S., ed. Te Decet Laus: To Thee Belongeth Praise. Revised ed..(Illus.). viii, 223p. 1982. 9.95 (ISBN 0-943872-84-7). Andrews Univ Pr.

Beltz, Walter. God & the Gods: Myths of the Bible. Heinegg, Peter, tr. 272p. 1983. pap. 5.95 (ISBN 0-14-022192-1, Pelican). Penguin.

Belveal, L. Dee. Charting Commodity Market Price Behavior. 2nd ed. LC 85-70189. 250p. 1985. 30.00 (ISBN 0-87094-651-X). Dow Jones-Irwin.

--Speculation in Commodity Contracts & Options. 2nd ed. 250p. 1985. 30.00 (ISBN 0-87094-672-2). Dow Jones-Irwin.

Belvedere Editions. Graphic Editions. 1986. cancelled (ISBN 0-442-21079-5). Van Nos Reinhold.

Belves, Pierre & Mathey, Francois. Enjoying the World of Art. (Illus.). (gr. 6 up). 1966. PLB 14.95 (ISBN 0-87460-100-2). Lion Bks.

--How Artists Work. Bach, Alice, tr. (gr. 6 up). 1968. PLB 14.95 (ISBN 0-87460-101-0). Lion Bks.

Belvianes, Marcel. The Madonna in the Paintings of the Great Masters. (Illus.). 1980. Repr. 77.50 (ISBN 0-89901-010-5). Found Class Reprints.

Belvins, James L., tr. see Herrmann, Siegfried.

Belvins, T. F., ed. see Richardson, Robert M.

Bely, Andrei. Petersburg. Maguire, Robert A. & Malmstad, John E., trs. from Rus. LC 77-74442. (Midland Bks.: No. 219). 384p. 1978. 27.50x (ISBN 0-253-34410-7); pap. 8.95x (ISBN 0-253-20219-1). Ind U Pr.

Bely, Andrey. The First Encounter. Janecek, Gerald, tr. from Rus. LC 78-70276. 1979. 15.00 (ISBN 0-691-06381-8). Princeton U Pr.

Bely, V. A., et al. Friction & Wear in Polymer-Based Materials. LC 80-41825. (Illus.). 400p. 1982. 110.00 (ISBN 0-08-025444-6). Pergamon.

Belyaev, A. I., ed. Surface Phenomena in Metallurgical Processes. LC 65-11335. 288p. 1965. 37.50x (ISBN 0-306-10704-X, Consultants). Plenum Pub.

Belyaev, S. T. Collective Excitations in Nuclei. (Documents on Modern Physics Ser.). 84p. 1968. 38.50 (ISBN 0-677-01870-3). Gordon.

Belyaeva, Natasha. Hunger. HIrschman, Jack, tr. from Rus. 1977. pap. 2.50 (ISBN 0-317-17250-6). DAurora Pr.

Belyavaky, Dmitry, tr. see Tarasov, K., et al.

Belyi, Andre I. Anthroposophy & Russia. 1983. pap. 5.00 (ISBN 0-916786-69-2). St George Bk Serv.

Belyi, Andrei. Masterstvo Gogolia. 328p. (Rus.). 1982. 25.00 (ISBN 0-88233-842-0); pap. 12.50 (ISBN 0-88233-843-9). Ardis Pubs.
--Pochemu Ia Stal Simvolistom. 120p. 1982. 20.00 (ISBN 0-88233-664-9); pap. 6.50 (ISBN 0-88233-665-7). Ardis Pubs.
Belykh, L. N., jt. ed. see Marchuk, G. I.
Belytschko, T. & Geers, T. L., eds. Computational Methods for Fluid-Structure Interaction Problems: Presented at the Winter Annual Meeting of the American Society of Mechanical Engineers, Atlanta, Georgia, Nov. 27-Dec. 2, 1977. LC 77-88000. (American Society of Mechanical Engineers Ser. - Applied Mechanics Division: Vol. 26). (Illus.). pap. 43.50 (ISBN 0-317-09990-6, 2011589). Bks Demand UMI.
Belytschko, T. & Hughes, T. J., eds. Computational Methods for Transient Analysis. (Mechanics & Mathematical Methods: Vol. 1). 540p. 1984. 69.00 (ISBN 0-444-86479-2, I-94-83, North-Holland). Elsevier.
Belytschko, Ted & Marcal, P. V., eds. Finite Element Analysis of Transient Nonlinear Structural Behavior: AMD, Vol. 14. 200p. 1975. pap. text ed. 20.00 (ISBN 0-685-62566-4, 100094). ASME.
Belz, Carl. The Story of Rock. 2nd ed. pap. 6.68i (ISBN 0-06-090344-9, CN344, CN). Har-Row.
--The Story of Rock. 2nd ed. (Illus.). 1972. 19.95x (ISBN 0-19-501554-1). Oxford U Pr.
Belz, Herman. Emancipation & Equal Rights: Politics & Constitutionalism in the Civil War Era. 1978. 10.95x (ISBN 0-393-05692-9); pap. 4.95x (ISBN 0-393-09016-7). Norton.
--A New Birth of Freedom: The Republican Party & Freedmen's Rights, 1861 - 1866. LC 76-5257. (Contributions in American History Ser.: No. 52). xv, 199p. 1976. lib. bdg. 27.50x (ISBN 0-8371-8902-0, BEO/). Greenwood.
--Reconstructing the Union: Theory & Policy During the Civil War. LC 78-21311. 1979. Repr. of 1969 ed. lib. bdg. 27.50x (ISBN 0-313-20862-X, BERU). Greenwood.
Belz, R., jt. auth. see Maarse, H.
Belza, Igor F. Handbook of Soviet Musicians. Bush, Alan, ed. LC 74-114468. (Illus.). 1971. Repr. of 1943 ed. lib. bdg. 22.50 (ISBN 0-8371-4764-6, BOSM). Greenwood.
--Handbook of Soviet Musicians. Bush, Alan, ed. LC 74-166221. (Illus.). 101p. 1972. Repr. of 1943 ed. 29.00 (ISBN 0-403-01348-8). Scholarly.
Belzer. Encyclopedia of Computer Science & Technology, Vol. 13. 1979. 115.00 (ISBN 0-8247-2263-9). Dekker.
--Index to Encyclopedia of Computer Science & Technology, Vol. 16. 464p. 1981. 115.00 (ISBN 0-8247-2266-3). Dekker.
Belzer, Edwin G., jt. auth. see Johnson, Warren R.
Belzer, J., ed. Encyclopedia of Computer Science & Technology, Vol. 15. 1980. 115.00 (ISBN 0-8247-2265-5). Dekker.
Belzer, Jack. Encyclopedia of Computer Science & Technology, Vol. 9. 1978. 115.00 (ISBN 0-8247-2259-0). Dekker.
Belzer, Jack, ed. Encyclopedia of Computer Science & Technology, Vol. 1. 1975. 115.00 (ISBN 0-8247-2251-5). Dekker.
--Encyclopedia of Computer Science & Technology, Vol. 2. 1975. 115.00 (ISBN 0-8247-2252-3). Dekker.
--Encyclopedia of Computer Science & Technology, Vol. 3. 1976. 115.00 (ISBN 0-8247-2253-1). Dekker.
--Encyclopedia of Computer Science & Technology, Vol. 5. 1976. 115.00 (ISBN 0-8247-2255-8). Dekker.
--Encyclopedia of Computer Science & Technology, Vol. 10. 1978. 115.00 (ISBN 0-8247-2260-4). Dekker.
--Encyclopedia of Computer Science & Technology, Vol. 11. 1978. 115.00 (ISBN 0-8247-2261-2). Dekker.
--Encyclopedia of Computer Science & Technology, Vol. 12. 1979. 115.00 (ISBN 0-8247-2262-0). Dekker.
--Encyclopedia of Computer Science & Technology, Vol. 14. 1980. 115.00 (ISBN 0-8247-2264-7). Dekker.
Belzer, Jack & Holzman, Albert G., eds. Encyclopedia of Computer Science & Technology, Vol. 4. 1976. 115.00 (ISBN 0-8247-2254-X). Dekker.
Belzer, Jack, et al, eds. Encyclopedia of Computer Science, Vol. 7. 1977. 115.00 (ISBN 0-8247-2257-4). Dekker.
--Encyclopedia of Computer Science & Technology, Vol. 8. 1977. 115.00 (ISBN 0-8247-2258-2). Dekker.
--Encyclopedia of Computer Science & Technology, Vol. 6. 1977. 115.00 (ISBN 0-8247-2256-6). Dekker.
Belzer, Thomas J. Roadside Plants of Southern California. (Illus.). 172p. 1984. pap. 8.95 (ISBN 0-87842-158-0). Mountain Pr.
Belzoni, Giovanni. Adventures, in Egypt & Nubia. 1843. 29.00 (ISBN 0-403-00454-3). Scholarly.
Belzung, L. D., jt. auth. see Becht, J. Edwin.
Bem, A. L. Dostoevskii: Psikhoanaliticheskie Etiudy. 190p. (Rus.). 1983. Repr. of 1933 ed. 22.50 (ISBN 0-88233-854-4). Ardis Pubs.
Bem, Daryl J. Beliefs, Attitudes, & Human Affairs. LC 71-95057. (Basic Concepts in Psychology Ser). (Orig.). 1970. pap. text ed. 7.25 pub net (ISBN 0-8185-0295-9). Brooks-Cole.
Bem, Jean. Clefs pour "L'Education Sentimentale". (Etudes Litteraires Francaise Ser.: 15). 104p. (Orig., Fr.). 1981. pap. 14.00x (ISBN 3-87808-894-9). Benjamins North Am.
Beman, Lamar T. Selected Articles on Capital Punishment. LC 82-45654. 1983. Repr. of 1925 ed. 42.50 (ISBN 0-404-62401-4). AMS Pr.
Beman, Lamar T., ed. Selected Articles on Censorship of Speech & the Press. LC 77-95404. (BCL Ser. I). 1969. Repr. of 1930 ed. 14.00 (ISBN 0-404-00747-3). AMS Pr.
Beman, Lamar T., compiled by. Selected Articles on Censorship of Speech & the Press. LC 76-98813. 1971. Repr. of 1930 ed. lib. bdg. 19.75x (ISBN 0-8371-3073-5, BECE). Greenwood.
Beman, Lamar T., ed. Selected Articles on Censorship of the Theater & Moving Pictures. LC 78-160229. (Moving Pictures Ser). 385p. 1971. Repr. of 1931 ed. lib. bdg. 20.95x (ISBN 0-89198-030-X). Ozer.
Beman, Wooster W., ed. see Row, Sundara T., et al.
Beman, Wooster W., tr. see Dedekind, Richard.
Bembe, John P., jt. auth. see Darey-Bembe, Francoise.
Bembo, Pietro. Gli Asolani. facsimile ed. Gottfried, Rudolf B., tr. LC 76-168501. (Select Bibliographies Reprint Ser). Repr. of 1954 ed. 18.00 (ISBN 0-8369-5941-8). Ayer Co Pubs.
Bemelmans, Ludwig. Hotel Splendide. 13.95 (ISBN 0-88411-846-0, Pub. by Aeonian Pr). Amereon Ltd.
--Madeline. LC 39-21791. (gr. k-3). 1977. pap. 3.95 (ISBN 0-14-050198-3, Puffin). Penguin.
--Madeline & the Bad Hat. LC 57-62. (Illus.). (gr. k-3). 1977. pap. 3.95 (ISBN 0-14-050206-8, Puffin). Penguin.
--Madeline & the Gypsies. (Illus.). 56p. (ps-3). 1977. pap. 3.95 (ISBN 0-14-050261-0, Puffin). Penguin.
--Madeline in London. (Illus.). 56p. (ps-3). 1977. pap. 3.95 (ISBN 0-14-050199-1, Puffin). Penguin.
--Madeline's Christmas. (Illus.). 32p. (ps-3). 1985. 12.95 (ISBN 0-670-80666-8, Viking Kestrel). Viking.
--Madeline's Rescue. (Illus.). 64p. (gr. k-3). 1977. pap. 3.95 (ISBN 0-14-050207-6, Puffin). Penguin.
--Madeline's Rescue. (Illus.). (gr. k-3). 1953. PLB 13.95 (ISBN 0-670-44716-1). Viking.
--Parsley. LC 55-7682. (Illus.). 48p. (ps-3). 1980. 10.53i (ISBN 0-06-020455-9); PLB 12.89 (ISBN 0-06-020456-7). HarpJ.
--Tell Them It Was Wonderful. 1985. 19.95 (ISBN 0-670-80391-X). Viking.
Bemelmans, T. A. Beyond Productivity: Information Systems Development for Organizational Effectiveness. 1984. 56.00 (ISBN 0-444-86832-1, I-024-84). Elsevier.
Bement, A. L., Jr., ed. Biomaterials: Bioengineering Applied to Materials for Hard & Soft Tissue Replacement. LC 71-152333. (Illus.). 361p. 1971. text ed. 25.00x (ISBN 0-295-95160-5). U of Wash Pr.
Bement, Peter. George Chapman: Action & Contemplation in His Novels. (Salzburg Studies in English Literature, Jacobean Drama Studies: No. 8). 292p. 1974. pap. text ed. 25.50x (ISBN 0-391-01323-8). Humanities.
Bemer, G., ed. see International Workshop on Appropriate Tech., Delft Univ. of Technology, Sept. 4-7, 1979.
Bemert, Gunnar & Ormond, Rupert. Red Sea Coral Reefs. (Illus.). 192p. 1981. 45.00 (ISBN 0-7103-0007-7). Routledge & Kegan.
BeMiller, J. N., jt. ed. see Whistler, R. L.
Bemis, E. W; see Haynes, J.
Bemis, Edward W. Cooperation in New England. LC 78-63779. (Johns Hopkins University. Studies in the Social Sciences. Sixth Ser. 1888: 1). Repr. of 1888 ed. 11.50 (ISBN 0-404-61045-5). AMS Pr.
--Cooperation in New England. facs. ed. LC 73-119926. (Select Bibliographies Reprint Ser.). 1886. 14.50 (ISBN 0-8369-5369-X). Ayer Co Pubs.
--Cooperation in New England. Repr. of 1888 ed. 14.00 (ISBN 0-384-03888-3). Johnson Repr.
--Cooperation in the Middle States. LC 78-63781. (Johns Hopkins University. Studies in the Social Sciences. Sixth Ser. 1888: 2-3). Repr. of 1888 ed. 11.50 (ISBN 0-404-61046-3). AMS Pr.
--Cooperation in the Middle States. 1973. pap. 9.00 (ISBN 0-384-03889-1). Johnson Repr.
--Local Government in Michigan & the Northwest. LC 78-63735. (Johns Hopkins University. Studies in the Social Sciences. First Ser. 1882-1883: 5). Repr. of 1883 ed. 11.50 (ISBN 0-404-61005-6). AMS Pr.
--Local Government in Michigan & the Northwest. pap. 9.00 (ISBN 0-384-03887-5). Johnson Repr.
--Local Government in the South & Southwest. Bd. with Popular Election of United States Senators. Haynes, J. Repr. of 1893 ed. 1973. Repr. of 1893 ed. 13.00 (ISBN 0-384-03886-7). Johnson Repr.
Bemis, Edward W., et al. Local Government in the South & Southwest. LC 78-63824. (Johns Hopkins University. Studies in the Social Sciences. Eleventh Ser. 1893: 11). Repr. of 1893 ed. 11.50 (ISBN 0-404-61085-4). AMS Pr.
Bemis, Pat. Pluto. 1978. pap. 3.50 (ISBN 0-88053-752-3). Macoy Pub.
Bemis, Samuel F. American Foreign Policy & the Blessings of Liberty, & Other Essays. LC 75-11972. 423p. 1975. Repr. of 1962 ed. lib. bdg. 24.50 (ISBN 0-8371-8132-1, BEAF). Greenwood.
--The Diplomacy of the American Revolution. LC 83-12977. xii, 293p. 1983. Repr. of 1957 ed. lib. bdg. 37.50x (ISBN 0-313-24173-2, BEDI). Greenwood.
--Diplomacy of the American Revolution. LC 57-7878. (Midland Bks.: No. 6). pap. cancelled (ISBN 0-8357-9204-8, 2015463). Bks Demand UMI.
--The Hussey-Cumberland Mission & American Independence: An Essay in the Diplomacy of the American Revolution. 15.25 (ISBN 0-8446-1069-0). Peter Smith.
--Jay's Treaty: A Study in Commerce & Diplomacy. LC 75-11844. (Illus.). 1975. Repr. of 1962 ed. lib. bdg. 29.50 (ISBN 0-8371-8133-X, BEJT). Greenwood.
--John Quincy Adams & the Foundations of American Foreign Policy. LC 80-23039. (Illus.). xix, 588p. 1981. Repr. of 1949 ed. lib. bdg. 49.75x (ISBN 0-313-22636-9, BEAD). Greenwood.
--John Quincy Adams & the Union. LC 80-20402. (Illus.). xv, 546p. 1980. Repr. of 1965 ed. lib. bdg. 55.00x (ISBN 0-313-22637-7, BEJQ). Greenwood.
--Pinckney's Treaty: America's Advantage from Europe's Distress, 1783-1800. LC 73-8148. (Illus.). xvi, 372p. 1973. Repr. of 1960 ed. lib. bdg. 65.00x (ISBN 0-8371-6954-2, BEPT). Greenwood.
Bemis, Samuel F., ed. American Secretaries of State & Their Diplomacy, from 1776-1925, 10 Vols. in 5. LC 62-20139. Repr. of 1928 ed. 175.00 (ISBN 0-8154-0021-7). Cooper Sq.
Bemis, Stephen E., et al. Job Analysis: An Effective Management Tool. 240p. 1983. 27.00 (ISBN 0-87179-412-8). BNA.
Bemis, Virginia. Energy Guide: A Directory of Information Resources. LC 77-10470. (Reference Library of Social Science: Vol. 43). 1977. lib. bdg. 33.00 (ISBN 0-8240-9870-6). Garland Pub.
Bemish, Paul. Build Your Own Home for Less Than 15,000 Dollars. LC 84-60483. (Illus.). 128p. (Orig.). 1984. pap. 8.70 (ISBN 0-688-02640-0, Quill). Morrow.
Bemiss, Elijah. The Dyer's Companion. LC 73-77377. 307p. 1973. pap. 4.50 (ISBN 0-486-20601-7). Dover.
--The Dyer's Companion. 3rd enl ed. 11.25 (ISBN 0-8446-5003-X). Peter Smith.
Bemister, Margaret. Thirty Indian Legends of Canada. (Illus.). 154p. (Orig.). 1983. pap. 8.95 (ISBN 0-88894-025-4, Pub. by Salem Hse Ltd). Merrimack Pub Cir.
Bemko, Jane. Substance Abuse Book Review Index. 67p. 1983. 6.95 (ISBN 0-88868-098-8). Addict Res Ont.
Bemmel, J. H. Van see Van Bemmel, J. H., et al.
Bemmel, John V. A Get Well Prayer Book. (Greeting Book Line Ser.). 48p. (Orig.). 1985. pap. 1.50 (ISBN 0-89622-231-4). Twenty Third.
Bemmelen, D. J. Van see Van Bemmelen, D. J.
Bemmelmans, Ludwig. Madeline. (Illus.). (gr. k-3). 1939. PLB 13.95 (ISBN 0-670-44580-0). Viking.
--Madeline & the Bad Hat. (Illus.). (gr. k-3). 1957. PLB 13.95 (ISBN 0-670-44614-9). Viking.
--Madeline & the Gypsies. (Illus.). (gr. k-3). 1959. PLB 9.95 (ISBN 0-670-44682-3). Viking.
--Madeline in London. (Illus.). (gr. k-3). 1961. PLB 13.95 (ISBN 0-670-44648-3). Viking.
Bemont, Charles. Simon De Montfort, Earl of Leicester, 1208-1265. Jacob, E. F., tr. LC 74-9223. (Illus.). 303p. 1974. Repr. of 1930 ed. lib. bdg. 20.50x (ISBN 0-8371-7625-5, BESM). Greenwood.
Bemporad, J., ed. A Rational Faith: Essays in Honor of Levi A. Olan. 15.00x (ISBN 0-87068-448-5). Ktav.
Bemporad, Jules, jt. auth. see Arieti, Silvano.
Bemporad, Jules R. Child Development in Normality & Psychopathology. LC 79-24086. 544p. 1980. 32.50 (ISBN 0-87630-210-X). Brunner-Mazel.
Bemporad, M. & Ferreira, E. Selected Topics in Solid State & Theoretical Physics. 482p. 1968. 132.95 (ISBN 0-677-11900-3). Gordon.
Bemstock, Bernard, ed. Art in Crime Writing: Essays on Detective Fiction. 240p. 1983. pap. 8.95 (ISBN 0-312-05397-5). St Martin.
Benabou, J., et al, eds. see Midwest Category Seminar, 1st.
Benac, ed. see Diderot, Denis.
Benac, Henri. Dictionnaire Des Synonymes. 1026p. (Fr.). 1975. pap. 25.95 (ISBN 0-686-56880-X, M-4558). French & Eur.
Benacerraf, Baruj, jt. auth. see Unanue, Emil R.
Benacerraf, Baruj, ed. Immunogenetics & Immune Regulation. (Illus.). 148p. 1982. 31.00 (ISBN 88-214-1655-0); 29.50. Masson Pub.
Benacerraf, Baruj, jt. ed. see Katz, David.
Benacerraf, Hilary, ed. see Putnam, Hilary.
Benack, Raymond T. What Is Allergy? A Guide for the Allergic Person. (Illus.). 172p. 1967. 17.50x (ISBN 0-398-00128-6). C C Thomas.
Benacka, S. English-Slovak Technical Dictionary. 1358p. (Eng. & Slovak.). 1980. 79.00x (ISBN 0-569-08529-2, Pub. by Collet's). State Mutual Bk.
Benade, A. H. Fundamentals of Musical Acoustics. (Illus.). 1976. text ed. 19.95x (ISBN 0-19-502030-8). Oxford U Pr.
Benade, Arthur H. Horns, Strings, & Harmony. LC 78-25707. (Illus.). 1979. Repr. of 1960 ed. lib. bdg. 22.50x (ISBN 0-313-20771-2, BEHO). Greenwood.
Benagh, Christine L. Meditations on the Book of Job. LC 64-25262. 1964. 3.95 (ISBN 0-686-05041-X). St Thomas.
Benagh, Jim. Picture Story of Wayne Gretzky. LC 82-60640. (Illus.). 64p. (gr. 4 up). 1982. PLB 9.29g (ISBN 0-671-45949-X). Messner.
Benagh, Jim, et al. Monday Morning Quarterback. 1983. pap. 8.95 (ISBN 0-03-063776-7). HR&W.
Benagiano, Giuseppe & Diczfalusy, Egon, eds. Endocrine Mechanisms in Fertility Regulation. (Comprehensive Endocrinology Ser.). 368p. 1983. text ed. 65.50 (ISBN 0-89004-464-3). Raven.
Benagiano, Giuseppe, et al, eds. Progestogens in Therapy. (Serono Symposia Publications Ser.: Vol. 3). (Illus.). 280p. 1983. text ed. 67.00 (ISBN 0-89004-856-8). Raven.
Ben-Ami, Aharon. Social Change in a Hostile Environment: The Crusaders' Kingdom of Jerusalem. (Princeton Studies on the Near East Ser.). (Illus.). 1969. 24.00 (ISBN 0-691-09344-X). Princeton U Pr.
Ben-Ami, Shlomo. Fascism from Above: The Dictatorship of Primo de Rivera in Spain, 1923-1930. 1983. 45.00x (ISBN 0-19-822596-2). Oxford U Pr.
--The Origins of the Second Republic in Spain. (Historical Monographs). 1978. 45.00x (ISBN 0-19-821871-0). Oxford U Pr.
Ben-Ami, Yitshaq. Years of Wrath, Days of Glory. 2nd ed. LC 83-60834. (Illus.). 620p. 1983. Repr. of 1982 ed. 17.50 (ISBN 0-88400-096-6). Shengold.
Ben-Amittay, Jacob. The History of Political Thought. LC 72-181332. 425p. 1973. 20.00 (ISBN 0-8022-2077-0). Philos Lib.
Ben-Amos, Dan. Sweet Words: Storytelling Events in Benin. LC 75-26677. (Illus.). 96p. 1975. text ed. 7.95 (ISBN 0-915980-00-2). ISHI PA.
Ben-Amos, Dan, ed. Folklore Genres. 1975 ed ed. (American Folklore Society Bibliographical & Special Ser.: No. 26). (Illus.). 360p. 1981. pap. 12.95x (ISBN 0-292-72437-3). U of Tex Pr.
Ben-Amos, Dan & Mintz, Jerome R., eds. In Praise of the Baal Shem Tov: The Earliest Collection of Legends About the Founder of Hasidism. Ben-Amos, Dan & Mintz, Jerome R., trs. from Hebrew. LC 83-40455. 384p. 1984. pap. 9.95 (ISBN 0-8052-0758-9). Schocken.
Ben-Amos, Dan, tr. see Ben-Amos, Dan & Mintz, Jerome R.
Benamou, Michael & Ionesco, Eugene. Mise En Train: Premiere Annee De Francais. (gr. 11-12). 1969. text ed. 22.95x (ISBN 0-02-307970-3); write for info. (ISBN 0-02-307980-0). Macmillan.
Benamou, Michel. Wallace Stevens & the Symbolist Imagination. LC 66-11962. (Princeton Essays in Literature Ser.). 156p. 1972. 21.00x (ISBN 0-691-06225-0). Princeton U Pr.
Benamou, Michel & Carduner, Jean. Le Moulin a Paroles. 2nd ed. LC 71-126958. (Illus.). 336p. (Fr.). 1975. pap. text ed. 17.00x (ISBN 0-471-06450-5). Wiley.
Benamy, Arnon, tr. see Chimenti, Elisa.
Benaquist, Lawrence M. Tripartite Structure of Christopher Marlowe's Tamburlaine Plays & Edward II. (Salzburg Studies in English Literature; Elizabethan & Renaissance Studies: No. 43). 223p. (Orig.). 1975. pap. text ed. 25.50x (ISBN 0-391-01324-6). Humanities.
Benard, Cheryl & Khalilzad, Zalmay. The Government of God: Iran's Islamic Republic. 232p. 1984. 26.00x (ISBN 0-231-05376-2). Columbia U Pr.
Benard, Edmond, jt. ed. see Ryan, John K.
Benard, J., et al, eds. Adsorption on Metal Surfaces: An Integrated Approach. (Studies in Surface Science & Catalysis: No. 13). x, 338p. 1983. 83.00 (ISBN 0-444-42163-7). Elsevier.
Benarde, Anita. Games from Many Lands. LC 71-86975. (Illus.). 64p. (gr. 3-7). 1971. PLB 8.95 (ISBN 0-87460-147-9). Lion Bks.
--Mediterranean Mosaic Designs. (International Design Library). (Illus.). 48p. (Orig.). 1984. pap. 3.50 (ISBN 0-88045-049-5). Stemmer Hse.
--Spanish Ceramic Designs. (International Design Library). (Illus.). 48p. (Orig.). 1984. pap. 3.50 (ISBN 0-88045-059-2). Stemmer Hse.
Benarde, Melvin. Our Precarious Habitat. rev. ed. (Illus.). 384p. 1973. 8.25 (ISBN 0-393-06360-7); pap. 6.95x (ISBN 0-393-09372-7). Norton.
Benarde, Melvin A. The Food Additives Dictionary. 96p. 1981. pap. 4.95 (ISBN 0-671-42837-3, Wallaby). S&S.
Benarde, Melvin A., ed. Disinfection. 1970. 85.00 (ISBN 0-8247-1040-1). Dekker.
Benardete, Jane & Moe, Phyllis, eds. Companions of Our Youth: Stories by Women for Young People's Magazines, 1865-1900. LC 80-5339. (Illus.). 1980. 16.95 (ISBN 0-8044-2043-2); pap. 5.95 (ISBN 0-8044-6047-7). Ungar.
Benardete, M. J., jt. auth. see Flores, Angel.
Benardete, Mair Jose. Hispanic Culture & Character of the Sephardic Jews. 2nd rev. ed. 226p. 1981. 15.00 (ISBN 0-87203-100-4). Hermon.
--Hispanic Culture & Character of the Sephardic Jews. 186p. 3.50 (ISBN 0-318-14274-0). Hispanic Inst.
Benardete, Seth, tr. see Plato.

Benardete, Seth G., tr. see Aeschylus.

Benares, Camden. Zen Without Zen Masters. 2nd ed. (Illus.). 128p. 1985. pap. 6.95 (ISBN 0-941404-34-X). Falcon Pr AZ.

Ben-Ari. Amygdaloid Complex. (INSERM Symposia Ser.: Vol. 20). 516p. 1982. 90.00 (ISBN 0-444-80397-1, Biomedical Pr). Elsevier.

Benarie, M. M. Atmospheric Pollution, 1982. (Studies in Environmental Science: Vol. 20). 404p. 1982. 85.00 (ISBN 0-444-42083-5). Elsevier.

Benarie, M. M., ed. Atmospheric Pollution, 1980: Proceedings of the 14th International Colloqium, Paris, May 1980. (Studies in Environmental Science: Vol. 8). 440p. 1980. 85.00 (ISBN 0-444-41889-X). Elsevier.

Benarie, Michael M. Urban Air Pollution Modeling. (Illus.). 1980. text ed. 65.00x (ISBN 0-262-02140-4). MIT Pr.

Ben-Arieh, Y. The Rediscovery of the Holy Land in the Nineteenth Century. 2nd ed. 265p. 1983. Repr. of 1979 ed. text ed. 29.25x (ISBN 965-223-326-9, Pub. by Magnes Israel). Humanities.

Ben-Arieh, Yehoshua. Jerusalem in the Nineteenth Century: The Old City. 417p. 1985. 29.95 (ISBN 0-312-44187-8). St Martin.

--The Rediscovery of the Holy Land in the Nineteenth Century. LC 79-67619. (Illus.). 266p. 1980. 18.95 (ISBN 0-8143-1654-9, Co-Pub by Magnes Press, Hebrew University, & Israel Exploration Society). Wayne St U Pr.

Benario, Herbert W. The Classical World Special Series: Tacitus Annals 11 & 12, Vol. 3. (The Classical World Special Ser.). (Illus.). 248p. (Orig.). 1983. lib. bdg. 24.25 (ISBN 0-8191-3480-5); pap. text ed. 12.25 (ISBN 0-8191-3481-3). U Pr of Amer.

--A Commentary on the Vita Hadriana in the Historia Augusta. LC 80-11953. (American Classical Studies: No. 7). 1980. pap. 10.50x (ISBN 0-89130-392-8, 400407). Scholars Pr GA.

--An Introduction to Tacitus. LC 73-85025. 188p. 1975. pap. text ed. 8.00x (ISBN 0-8203-0361-5). U of Ga Pr.

Benaroya, Alfred. Fundamentals & Application of Centrifugal Pumps for the Practicing Engineer. 222p. 1978. 34.95x (ISBN 0-87814-040-9). Pennwell Bks.

Ben'Ary, Ruth. Touch Typing in Ten Lessons. rev. ed. (Illus., Orig.). 1982. pap. 4.95 (ISBN 0-399-50809-0, G&D). Putnam Pub Group.

Benary-Isbert, Margot. Blue Mystery. LC 57-6558. (Illus.). (gr. 4-7). 1965. pap. 3.95 (ISBN 0-15-613225-7, VoyB). HarBraceJ.

Ben-Asher, David. Fighting Fit: The Official Israel Defense Force Guide to Physical Fitness & Self-Defense. Schlesinger, Miriam, tr. LC 82-402. (Illus.). 320p. 1983. pap. 7.95 (ISBN 0-399-50624-1, Perigee). Putnam Pub Group.

Ben-Asher, Naomi & Leaf, Hayim, eds. Junior Jewish Encyclopedia. 10th, rev. ed. LC 84-51583. (Illus.). (gr. 9-12). 1984. 19.95 (ISBN 0-88400-110-5). Shengold.

Benassy, Jean-Pascal. Economics of Market Disequilibrium. (Mathematical Economics, Economic Theory & Econometric Ser.). 1983. 27.50 (ISBN 0-12-086420-7). Acad Pr.

Benatar, Stephen. When I Was Otherwise. 272p. 1984. 13.95 (ISBN 0-312-86664-X, Pub. by Marek). St Martin.

--Wish Her Safe at Home. LC 82-5815. 192p. 1982. 11.95 (ISBN 0-312-88419-2, Pub. by Marek). St Martin.

Benavente, Jacinto. Malquerida. Manchester, Paul T., ed. (Orig., Span.,). 1961. pap. text ed. 7.95x (ISBN 0-89197-287-0). Irvington.

Benavides, Magdalena, tr. see Davis, Edward M. & Newcomb, William W.

Benavidez, Max, ed. see Schneider, Jerome.

Benaya, Margaret, tr. see Shamir, Moshe.

Benayon, Robert. The Look of the Buster Keaton. Conrad, Randall, tr. from Fr. 208p. 1983. 24.95 (ISBN 0-312-49695-8). St Martin.

Ben-Bassat, Avraham. Reserve-Currency Diversification & the Substitution Account. LC 84-581. (Princeton Studies in International Finance Ser.: No. 53). 1984. pap. text ed. 4.50x (ISBN 0-88165-225-3). Princeton U Int Finan Econ.

Benbow, Camilla P. & Stanley, Julian C., eds. Academic Precocity: Aspects of Its Development. LC 83-48063. (The Hyman Blumberg Symposia on Research in Early Childhood Education Ser.: No. 10). 232p. 1983. text ed. 22.50x (ISBN 0-8018-2990-9); pap. text ed. 7.50x (ISBN 0-8018-2991-7). Johns Hopkins.

Benbow, Doras R. Beyond the Farthest Star. (Illus.). 1977. lib. bdg. 2.00 (ISBN 0-686-19227-3). D R Benbow.

--Lantern in the Moonlight. (Illus.). 1974. lib. bdg. 2.00 (ISBN 0-686-09539-1). D R Benbow.

Benbow, R. Mark see Peele, George.

Benbow, R. Mark, ed. see Wager, W.

Benbow, Terence. Report & Recommendations of the In-Rem Housing Task Force: Committee on Housing & Urban Development. 1981. pap. 2.50 (ISBN 0-318-00895-5). Comm Serv Soc NY.

Bencar, Gary R. Computers for Small Business: A Step by Step Guide on How to Buy. LC 82-21710. (Illus.). 148p. 1983. pap. 9.95 (ISBN 0-935222-05-7). La Cumbre.

Bence, Evelyn. Leaving Home: The Making of an Independent Woman. LC 82-15910. 168p. 1982. A Bridgebooks Publication. 9.95 (ISBN 0-664-27005-0). Westminster.

--Mary Had a Baby: The Story of Christmas. (Illus.). 36p. (Orig.). (gr. k up). 1981. 5.95 (ISBN 0-86702-026-2). Genesis Project.

--The Rainy Day Bible. Janney, Anne, ed. (Illus.). 64p. (Orig.). (gr. k-5). 1981. pap. 1.95 (ISBN 0-86702-011-3). Genesis Project.

--Spread the Word: A Woman's Workshop on Luke. (Woman's Workshop Ser.). 112p. 1984. pap. 2.95 (ISBN 0-310-44781-X, 11314P, Pub. by Lamplighter). Zondervan.

Bence, Evelyn, jt. auth. see Strasheim, Linda.

Bence, Richard. Handbook of Clinical Endodontics. 2nd ed. LC 80-15722. (Illus.). 262p. 1980. pap. text ed. 19.95 (ISBN 0-8016-0587-3). Mosby.

Bence-Jones, Mark. The Viceroys of India. 1982. 40.00x (ISBN 0-09-463810-1, Pub. by Constable & Co England). State Mutual Bk.

--The Viceroys of India. (Illus.). 362p. 1984. 19.95 (ISBN 0-312-83910-3). St Martin.

Bench, Carson E. Chaos. 140p. (Orig.). 1985. pap. 5.00 (ISBN 0-930669-01-0). Western Sun Pubns.

--Of Angels & Dreamers. Galchutt, Kathy, ed. (Illus.). 36p. (Orig.). 1982. pap. 3.95 (ISBN 0-9608146-4-7). Western Sun Pubns.

Bench, Carson E. & Carpenter, Maryann. Common Feelings. Galchutt, Kathy, ed. (Illus.). 56p. 1982. pap. 3.95 (ISBN 0-9608146-0-4). Western Sun Pubns.

Bench, Carson E., ed. see Kolbaska, John.

Bench, Carson E., ed. see Moravec, Lissetta L.

Bench, Carson E., ed. see Stach, Alex G.

Bench, John & Bamford, John, eds. Speech-Hearing Tests & Spoken Language of Hearing-Impaired Children. 1979. 67.00 (ISBN 0-12-088450-X). Acad Pr.

Ben Chaim, Daphna. Distance in the Theatre: The Aesthetics of Audience Response. Beckerman, Bernard, ed. LC 83-24231. (Theatre & Dramatic Studies: No. 17). 124p. 1984. 34.95 (ISBN 0-8357-1531-0). UMI Res Pr.

Benchimol, Alberto. Non-Invasive Diagnostic Techniques in Cardiology. LC 76-4843. 462p. 1977. 32.50 (ISBN 0-683-00525-1). Krieger.

--Noninvasive Techniques in Cardiology for the Nurse & Technician. LC 78-9047. (Illus.). pap. 83.00 (ISBN 0-317-07800-3, 2015847). Bks Demand UMI.

--Vectorcardiography. LC 78-9932. 236p. 1979. Repr. of 1973 ed. lib. bdg. 21.50 (ISBN 0-88275-762-8). Krieger.

Benchley, Nathaniel. Beyond the Mists. LC 75-9389. 160p. (gr. 7 up). 1975. 12.45i (ISBN 0-06-020459-1). HarpJ.

--Bright Candles. LC 73-5477. 264p. (gr. 7 up). 1974. 12.95 (ISBN 0-06-020461-3). HarpJ.

--Demo & the Dolphin. LC 80-8434. (Illus.). 96p. (gr. 4-7). 1981. PLB 10.89g (ISBN 0-06-020510-5). HarpJ.

--Feldman Fieldmouse. LC 72-135773. (Illus.). 96p. (gr. 4-7). 1971. PLB 10.89 (ISBN 0-06-020484-2). HarpJ.

--George the Drummer Boy. LC 76-18398. (History I Can Read Bks.). (Illus.). 64p. (gr. k-3). 1977. 8.61i (ISBN 0-06-020500-8); PLB 9.89 (ISBN 0-06-020501-6). HarpJ.

--Ghost Named Fred. LC 68-24322. (I Can Read Mystery Bk.). (Illus.). 64p. (gr. k-3). 1968. PLB 9.89 (ISBN 0-06-020474-5). HarpJ.

--A Ghost Named Fred. LC 68-24322. (I Can Read Bks). (Illus.). 64p. (gr. k-3). 1979. pap. 2.95 (ISBN 0-06-444022-2, Trophy). HarpJ.

--Gone & Back. LC 73-145998. (gr. 7 up). 1971. pap. 1.95 (ISBN 0-06-440016-6, Trophy). HarpJ.

--Kilroy & the Gull. LC 76-24309. (Illus.). 1978. pap. 2.95 (ISBN 0-06-440090-5, Trophy). HarpJ.

--The Magic Sled. LC 74-183166. (Illus.). 64p. (gr. 2-6). 1972. PLB 10.89 (ISBN 0-06-020490-7). HarpJ.

--A Necessary End. LC 75-37105. 208p. (gr. 7 up). 1976. PLB 12.95 (ISBN 0-06-020499-0). HarpJ.

--Only Earth & Sky Last Forever. LC 72-82891. (gr. 7 up). 1972. pap. 2.95 (ISBN 0-06-440049-2, Trophy). HarpJ.

--Oscar Otter. LC 66-11499. (I Can Read Bk.). (Illus.). 64p. (gr. k-3). 1966. PLB 9.89 (ISBN 0-06-020472-9). HarpJ.

--Oscar Otter. LC 66-11499. (I Can Read Bk.). (Illus.). 64p. (gr. k-3). 1980. pap. 2.95 (ISBN 0-06-444025-7, Trophy). HarpJ.

--Portrait of a Scoundrel. (General Ser.). 1980. pap. 9.95 (ISBN 0-8161-3104-X, Large Print Bks). G K Hall.

--Red Fox & His Canoe. LC 64-16650. (I Can Read Bk.). (Illus.). 64p. (gr. k-3). 1964. PLB 9.89 (ISBN 0-06-020476-1). HarpJ.

--Red Fox & His Canoe. LC 64-16650. (Trophy I Can Read Bk.). (Illus.). 64p. (gr. k-3). 1985. pap. 2.84i (ISBN 0-06-444075-3, Trophy). HarpJ.

--Running Owl the Hunter. LC 78-22156. (I Can Read Bk.). (Illus.). 64p. (gr. k-3). 1979. 8.6100272321x (ISBN 0-06-020453-2); PLB 9.89 (ISBN 0-06-020454-0). HarpJ.

--Sam the Minuteman. LC 68-10211. (I Can Read History Bk.). (Illus.). 64p. (gr. k-3). 1969. 8.61i (ISBN 0-06-020479-6); PLB 9.89 (ISBN 0-06-020480-X). HarpJ.

--Several Tricks of Edgar Dolphin. LC 79-85038. (I Can Read Bk.). (Illus.). 64p. (gr. k-3). 1970. PLB 9.89 (ISBN 0-06-020468-0). HarpJ.

--Small Wolf. LC 70-183170. (I Can Read History Bk.). (Illus.). 64p. (gr. k-3). 1972. PLB 8.89 (ISBN 0-06-020492-3). HarpJ.

--Snorri & the Strangers. LC 76-3290. (History I Can Read Bk.). (Illus.). (gr. k-3). 1976. 8.61i (ISBN 0-06-020457-5). HarpJ.

--Strange Disappearance of Arthur Cluck. LC 67-4151. (I Can Read Mystery Bk.). (Illus.). 64p. (gr. k-3). 1967. PLB 9.89 (ISBN 0-06-020478-8). HarpJ.

--The Strange Disappearance of Arthur Cluck. LC 67-4151. (I Can Read Bks). (Illus.). 64p. (gr. k-3). 1979. pap. 2.95 (ISBN 0-06-444024-9, Trophy). HarpJ.

--Sweet Anarchy. 304p. 1981. pap. 2.50 (ISBN 0-380-53777-X, 53777-X). Avon.

--Walter, the Homing Pigeon. LC 79-2696. (Illus.). 32p. (gr. 1-4). 1981. PLB 10.89g (ISBN 0-06-020508-3). HarpJ.

Benchley, P. J. Fossils & Climate. 352p. 1984. text ed. 49.95 (ISBN 0-471-90418-X, Pub. by Wiley-Interscience). Wiley.

Benchley, Peter. The Deep. LC 75-44521. 312p. 1976. 9.95 (ISBN 0-385-04742-8). Doubleday.

--The Girl of the Sea of Cortez. (General Ser.). 1983. lib. bdg. 14.95 (ISBN 0-8161-3487-1, Large Print Bks). G K Hall.

--The Girl of the Sea of Cortez. 240p. 1983. pap. 3.50 (ISBN 0-425-06005-5). Berkley Pub.

--Jaws. LC 73-80799. 288p. 1974. 9.95 (ISBN 0-385-04771-1). Doubleday.

Benchley, Robert. Benchley at the Theatre. 244p. 1985. 14.95 (ISBN 0-938864-05-X). Ipswich Pr.

--Benchley Beside Himself. 1976. Repr. of 1943 ed. lib. bdg. 16.95 (ISBN 0-88411-307-8, Pub. by Aeonian Pr). Amereon Ltd.

--Benchley Lost & Found. LC 78-88786. 183p. 1970. pap. 3.50 (ISBN 0-486-22410-4). Dover.

--Benchley or Else. 1976. Repr. of 1947 ed. lib. bdg. 16.95 (ISBN 0-88411-306-X, Pub. by Aeonian Pr). Amereon Ltd.

--The Benchley Roundup: A Selection by Nathaniel Benchley of His Favorites. LC 83-5111. (Illus.). xii, 334p. 1983. pap. 9.95 (ISBN 0-226-04218-9). U of Chicago Pr.

--The Best of Robert Benchley: Seventy-Two Timeless Stories of Wit, Wisdom, & Whimsy. (Illus.). 368p. 1983. 5.98 (ISBN 0-517-41139-3, Avenel). Outlet Bk Co.

--Chips off the Old Benchley. 1976. Repr. of 1949 ed. lib. bdg. 16.95 (ISBN 0-88411-301-9, Pub. by Aeonian Pr). Amereon Ltd.

--A Good Old-Fashioned Christmas. (Illus.). 96p. (Orig.). 1981. pap. 5.95 (ISBN 0-938864-02-5). Ipswich Pr.

--Inside Benchley. 1976. Repr. of 1942 ed. lib. bdg. 17.95 (ISBN 0-88411-302-7, Pub. by Aeonian Pr). Amereon Ltd.

--My Ten Years in a Quandry. (Illus.). 1976. Repr. lib. bdg. 19.95x (ISBN 0-88411-303-5, 303, Pub. by Aeonian Pr). Amereon Ltd.

--Penguin Psychology: or, The Mystery of Bridge Building. 12.95 (ISBN 0-88411-299-3, Pub. by Aeonian Pr). Amereon Ltd.

--Pluck & Luck. 296p. Repr. of 1925 ed. lib. bdg. 16.95x (ISBN 0-88411-308-6, Pub. by Aeonian Pr). Amereon Ltd.

--The Robert Benchley Omnibus. 19.95 (ISBN 0-8488-0069-9, Pub. by Amereon Hse). Amereon Ltd.

--The Treasurer's Report; And Other Aspects of Community Singing. (Illus. by Guyas Williams). 1976. Repr. of 1938 ed. lib. bdg. 15.95x (ISBN 0-88411-304-3, Pub. by Aeonian Pr). Amereon Ltd.

--Twenty Thousand Leagues Under the Sea or David Copperfield. 1976. Repr. of 1928 ed. lib. bdg. 16.95x (ISBN 0-88411-305-1, Pub. by Aeonian Pr). Amereon Ltd.

Benchly, Alexandra J. Kiss the Dove Gently. 1983. pap. 3.22 (ISBN 0-914657-00-3). Perci Bks.

Benchly, Robert. Benchley Lost & Found. 13.95 (ISBN 0-89190-498-0, Pub. by Am Repr). Amereon Ltd.

Bencin, Richard L. The Marketing Revolution: Understanding Major Changes in How Businesses Market. 220p. 1984. 29.95x (ISBN 0-915601-01-X). Cresheim Pubns.

Bend, J. R., jt. ed. see Hodgson, E.

Benda, ed. see De La Bruyere, Jean.

Benda, Clemens E. Down's Syndrome: The Scientific Facts on Mongolism. 3rd ed. LC 68-55434. (Illus.). 1969. 73.50 (ISBN 0-8089-0050-1, 790533). Grune.

Benda, Ernst, et al, eds. Handbuch des Verfassungsrechts der Bundesrepublik Deutschland, 2 vols. 1448p. 1983. 107.20 (ISBN 3-11-009512-2); pap. 23.20 (ISBN 3-11-010103-3). De Gruyter.

Benda, Georg A. Romeo und Julie: German Opera, 1770-1800. 280p. 1985. lib. bdg. 60.00 (ISBN 0-317-28812-1). Garland Pub.

Benda, Georg A. & Reichardt, Johann F. Ariadne Auf Naxos (Gotha, 1775); Ino (Leipzig, 1779) Bauman, Thomas, ed. (German Opera 1770-1800 Ser.: Vol. 4). 315p. 1985. lib. bdg. 65.00 (ISBN 0-8240-8853-0). Garland Pub.

Benda, Hansjochen. Introduction to the Basic Principles of Semiconductors. (Siemens Programmed Instruction Ser.: 1). pap. 20.00 (ISBN 0-317-26185-1, 2052078). Bks Demand UMI.

Benda, Harry J. Continuity & Change in Southeast Asia: Collected Journal Articles of Harry J.Benda. LC 72-84083. (Yale University Southeast Asia Studies: Monographs: No. 18). pap. 79.80 (ISBN 0-317-09326-6, 2007479). Bks Demand UMI.

Benda, Harry J. & McVey, Ruth T., eds. Communist Uprisings of Nineteen Twenty-Six to Nineteen Twenty-Seven in Indonesia: Key Documents. (Translation Ser.). 1960. pap. 5.50 (ISBN 0-87763-024-0). Cornell Mod Indo.

Benda, Julien. Treason of the Intellectuals. Aldington, Richard, tr. 1969. pap. 7.95 (ISBN 0-393-00470-8, Norton Lib). Norton.

Benda-Beckmann, Franz von see Thomas, Lynn L. & Von Benda-Beckmann, Franz.

Bendah, David. How to Use Your Hidden Potential to Get Rich. (Illus.). 200p. (Orig.). 1986. pap. price not set (ISBN 0-933301-00-6). Lion Pub.

--Making Five Hundred Thousand Dollars a Year in Mail Order. (Illus.). 200p. 1985. 11.95 (ISBN 0-933301-05-7). Lion Pub.

Ben-Dak, Joseph, jt. auth. see Azar, Edward E.

Bendall, C., jt. tr. see Rouse, W. H.

Bendall, Cecil & Rouse, W. H. Siksha Samuccaya: A Compendium of Buddhist Doctrine. 336p. 1981. Repr. 18.00 (ISBN 0-89581-160-X). Asian Human Pr.

Bendall, Cecil & Rouse, W. H., eds. Siksa Samuccaya: A Compendium of Buddhist Doctrine. 1981. 18.50x (ISBN 0-8364-0793-8, Pub. by Motilal Banarsidass). South Asia Bks.

Bendall, Cecil, tr. see Santideva.

Bendall, D. S., ed. Evolution from Molecules to Men. LC 82-22020. (Illus.). 500p. 1983. 32.50 (ISBN 0-521-24753-5). Cambridge U Pr.

Bendann, Effie. Death Customs: An Analytical Study of Burial Rites. 1971. 37.00x (ISBN 0-8103-3733-9). Gale.

--Death Customs: An Analytical Study of Burial Rites. 59.95 (ISBN 0-8490-0010-6). Gordon Pr.

Ben-Dasan, Isaiah. The Japanese & the Jews. Gage, Richard L., tr. from Japanese. LC 79-28518. 193p. 1981. pap. 4.95 (ISBN 0-8348-0158-2). Weatherhill.

Bendat, Julius S. Principles & Applications of Random Noise Theory. rev. ed. LC 77-7225. 456p. 1977. Repr. of 1958 ed. lib. bdg. 26.00 (ISBN 0-88275-556-0). Krieger.

Bendat, Julius S. & Piersol, Allan G. Engineering Applications of Correction & Spectral Analysis. LC 79-25926. 302p. 1980. 41.95x (ISBN 0-471-05887-4, Pub. by Wiley-Interscience). Wiley.

--Random Data: Analysis & Measurement Procedures. LC 71-160211. (Illus.). 407p. 1971. 45.50x (ISBN 0-471-06470-X, Pub. by Wiley-Interscience). Wiley.

Bendau, Clifford P. Colin Wilson: The Outsider & Beyond. LC 79-288. (The Milford Ser: Popular Writers of Today: Vol. 21). 1979. lib. bdg. 12.95x (ISBN 0-89370-129-7); pap. 4.95x (ISBN 0-89370-229-3). Borgo Pr.

--The Man Behind the Mouse: An Interview with & Remembrance of Leonard Wibberley. LC 84-14642. (Borgo Bioviews Ser.: No. 11). 128p. (Orig.). 1986. lib. bdg. 14.95x (ISBN 0-89370-346-X); pap. text ed. 6.95x (ISBN 0-89370-446-6). Borgo Pr.

--Still Worlds Collide: Philip Wylie & the End of the American Dream. LC 80-10756. (The Milford Ser.: Popular Writers of Today: Vol. 30). 1980. lib. bdg. 12.95x (ISBN 0-89370-144-0); pap. 4.95x (ISBN 0-89370-244-7). Borgo Pr.

Ben-David, Joseph. The Scientist's Role in Society: A Comparative Study with a New Introduction. LC 84-2758. 236p. 1984. 20.00x (ISBN 0-226-04227-8); pap. text ed. 8.95x (ISBN 0-226-04221-9). U of Chicago Pr.

--Trends in American Higher Education. LC 78-177370. (Midway Reprints Ser.). xii, 138p. 1981. 6.00x (ISBN 0-226-04225-1). U of Chicago Pr.

Ben-David, Joseph & Clark, Terry N. Culture & Its Creators. LC 76-610. 1977. 30.00x (ISBN 0-226-04222-7). U of Chicago Pr.

Bendavid-Val, Avron. Regional & Local Economic Analysis for Practitioners. new ed. LC 82-16695. (Illus.). 208p. 1983. 33.95 (ISBN 0-03-062912-8); pap. 14.95 (ISBN 0-03-062913-6). Praeger.

Bendel, Stephanie B. Making Crime Pay: A Practical Guide to Mystery Writing. (Illus.). 234p. 1983. 13.95 (ISBN 0-13-545939-7); pap. 5.95 (ISBN 0-13-545921-4). P-H.

Bender. Dictionary of Nutrition & Food Techonology. 5th ed. 1983. text ed. 34.95. Butterworth.

Bender & Gaston. A Concordance to Conrad's the Arrow of Gold. 1981. lib. bdg. 73.00 (ISBN 0-8240-9370-4). Garland Pub.

Bender, jt. auth. see McCabe.

Bender, A. E. & Bender, D. A. Nutrition for Medical Students. LC 82-133881. 380p. 1982. 48.95x (ISBN 0-471-28041-0, Pub. by Wiley-Interscience). Wiley.

Bender, A. E., jt. auth. see Fisher, Patty.

Bender, Albrecht. Die Natuerliche Gotteserkenntnis bei Laktanz und Seinen Apologetischen Vorgaengern. (European University Studies: No. 15, Vol. 26). 235p. (Ger.). 1983. 27.90 (ISBN 3-8204-7819-1). P Lang Pubs.
Bender, Arnold. Food Processing & Nutrition. (Food Science & Technology Ser.). 1978. 41.50 (ISBN 0-12-086450-9). Acad Pr.
Bender, Arnold & Nash, Tony. Pocket Encyclopedia of Calories & Nutrition. 1979. pap. 4.95 (ISBN 0-671-24839-1). S&S.
Bender, Averam B. Apache Indians, Vol. IX. Horr, David A., ed. (American Indian Ethnohistory Ser.). 1978. lib. bdg. 51.00 (ISBN 0-8240-0711-5). Garland Pub.
--The March of Empire: Frontier Defense in the Southwest, 1848-1860. LC 69-13819. (Illus.). Repr. of 1952 ed. lib. bdg. 20.00 (ISBN 0-8371-0306-1, BEMA). Greenwood.
Bender, Barbara & Caillaud, Robert. The Archaeology of Brittany, Normandy & the Channel Islands: An Introduction & Guide. (Illus.). 192p. 1985. write for info. (ISBN 0-571-09957-2, Dist. by Harper & Row Pubs., Inc). Faber & Faber.
Bender, Barbara L. Growing Up with Lake Forest Park. (Illus.). 488p. 1983. pap. 19.95 (ISBN 0-939116-09-X). Creative Comm.
Bender, Byron W. Spoken Marshallese. (PALI Language Texts: Micronesian). 463p. (Orig., Marshallese & Eng.). 1969. pap. text ed. 13.00x (ISBN 0-87022-070-5). UH Pr.
Bender, Carl M. & Orszag, Steven A. Advanced Mathematical Methods for Scientists & Engineers. (International Series in Pure & Applied Mathematics). (Illus.). 1978. text ed. 49.95 (ISBN 0-07-004452-X). McGraw.
Bender, Coleman C., jt. auth. see Zacharias, John C.
Bender, D. A., jt. auth. see Bender, A. E.
Bender, David, jt. auth. see Glock, Marvin.
Bender, David, jt. auth. see Glock, Marvin D.
Bender, David A. Amino Acid Metabolism. LC 74-20863. 234p. 1975. 64.95x (ISBN 0-471-06498-X, Pub. by Wiley-Interscience). Wiley.
Bender, David L. American Values. 2nd ed. LC 84-5925. (Opposing Viewpoints Ser.). (Illus.). 240p. (gr. 10up). 1984. 11.95 (ISBN 0-89908-345-5); pap. 6.95 (ISBN 0-89908-320-X). Greenhaven.
--The Political Spectrum: Opposing Viewpoints. LC 85-8007. (Opposing Viewpoints Ser.). (gr. 12). 1981. lib. bdg. 11.95 (ISBN 0-89908-325-0); pap. text ed. 6.95 (ISBN 0-89908-300-5). Greenhaven.
--The Welfare State: Opposing Viewpoints. 3rd ed. LC 85-8000. (Opposing Viewpoints Ser.). (gr. 12). 1982. 11.95 (ISBN 0-89908-338-2); pap. 5.95 (ISBN 0-89908-313-7). Greenhaven.
Bender, David L. & Leone, Bruno. The Ecology Controversy: Opposing Viewpoints. 3rd ed. LC 85-7645. (Opposing Viewpoints Ser.). 160p. (gr. 12). 1981. 11.95 (ISBN 0-89908-327-7); pap. 6.95 (ISBN 0-89908-302-1). Greenhaven.
Bender, David L., ed. American Foreign Policy: Opposing Viewpoints. 2nd ed. LC 85-7668. (Opposing Viewpoints Ser.). 156p. (gr. 12). 1981. 11.95 (ISBN 0-89908-336-6); pap. 6.95 (ISBN 0-89908-311-0). Greenhaven.
--The American Military: Opposing Viewpoints. LC 85-8050. (Opposing Viewpoints Ser.). (Illus.). 160p. (Orig.). 1983. lib. bdg. 11.95 (ISBN 0-89908-342-0); pap. text ed. 6.95 (ISBN 0-89908-317-X). Greenhaven.
--The Arms Race: Opposing Viewpoints. LC 85-7685. (Opposing Viewpoints Ser.). 1982. lib. bdg. 11.95 (ISBN 0-89908-339-0); pap. 6.95 (ISBN 0-89908-314-5). Greenhaven.
--Constructing Life Philosophy. 5 th, rev. ed. (Opposing Viewpoints Bks.). (Illus.). 150p. 1985. lib. bdg. 11.95 (ISBN 0-89908-379-X); pap. 6.95 (ISBN 0-89908-354-4). Greenhaven.
--Criminal Justice: Opposing Viewpoints. LC 85-7675. (Opposing Viewpoints Ser.). (gr. 12). 1981. lib. bdg. 11.95 (ISBN 0-89908-332-3); pap. text ed. 6.95 (ISBN 0-89908-307-2). Greenhaven.
--Death & Dying: Opposing Viewpoints. LC 85-8066. (Opposing Viewpoints Ser.). (gr. 12). 1980. lib. bdg. 11.95 (ISBN 0-89908-331-5); pap. text ed. 6.95 (ISBN 0-89908-306-4). Greenhaven.
--Problems of Death: Opposing Viewpoints. 2nd ed. LC 85-8070. (Opposing Viewpoints Ser.). 176p. (gr. 12). 1981. 11.95 (ISBN 0-89908-335-8); pap. 6.95 (ISBN 0-89908-310-2). Greenhaven.
Bender, David L. & Leone, Bruno, eds. Abortion. (Opposing Viewpoints Bks.). (Illus.). 150p. (Orig.). 1986. lib. bdg. 11.95 (ISBN 0-89908-380-3); pap. text ed. 5.95 (ISBN 0-89908-355-2). Greenhaven.
--The Death Penalty. (Opposing Viewpoints Bks.). (Illus.). 150p. (Orig.). 1986. lib. bdg. 11.95 (ISBN 0-89908-381-1); pap. text ed. 5.95 (ISBN 0-89908-356-0). Greenhaven.
--Religion & Human Experience: Opposing Viewpoints. LC 85-7660. 1981. 11.95 (ISBN 0-89908-333-1); pap. text ed. 6.95 (ISBN 0-89908-308-0). Greenhaven.
--Science & Religion: Opposing Viewpoints. LC 85-7641. 1981. 11.95 (ISBN 0-89908-334-X); pap. 6.95 (ISBN 0-89908-309-9). Greenhaven.
--War & Human Nature: Opposing Viewpoints. LC 85-8008. (Opposing Viewpoints Ser.). (Illus.). 160p. 1983. lib. bdg. 11.95 (ISBN 0-89908-341-2); pap. text ed. 6.95 (ISBN 0-89908-316-1). Greenhaven.
Bender, David L., ed. see Church, Carol B.
Bender, David L., ed. see Leone, Bruno.
Bender, David L., et al, eds. Crime & Criminals: Opposing Viewpoints. 2nd, rev. ed. LC 84-13624. (Opposing Viewpoints Ser.). (Illus.). 200p. 1984. lib. bdg. 11.95 (ISBN 0-89908-346-3); pap. text ed. 6.95 (ISBN 0-89908-321-8). Greenhaven.
--The Vietnam War: Opposing Viewpoints. LC 84-13628. (Opposing Viewpoints Ser.). (Illus.). 200p. (Orig.). 1984. lib. bdg. 11.95 (ISBN 0-89908-349-8); pap. text ed. 6.95 (ISBN 0-89908-324-2). Greenhaven.
Bender, David R. Learning Resources & the Instructional Program in Community Colleges. 296p. 1980. text ed. 19.50 (ISBN 0-208-01754-2, Lib Prof Pubns); pap. text ed. 14.50x (ISBN 0-208-01851-4, Lib Prof Pubns). Shoe String.
Bender, David R., jt. auth. see Baker, D. Phillip.
Bender, David S., jt. auth. see Glock, Marvin D.
Bender, Deborah, jt. auth. see Allen, James E.
Bender, Deborah E. & Bean, Cydne. Counseling Skills in Family Planning: Participants Handbook. 1982. pap. 4.00 (ISBN 0-686-47616-6). Carolina Pop Ctr.
--Counseling Skills in Family Planning: Trainer's Handbook. 1982. pap. 10.00 (ISBN 0-686-47615-8). Carolina Pop Ctr.
Bender Editorial Staff. California Forms of Pleading & Practice Annotated, 52 vols. LC 62-52786. (Illus.). 1962. Updates avail. 1525.00 (181); looseleaf 1983 695.00; looseleaf 1984 769.50. Bender.
Bender Editorial Staff, ed. Gilbert Criminal Law & Procedure of New York. 63rd ed. 1980-81. Annual subscription. 74.50 (ISBN 0-317-09855-1, 312); looseleaf 1983 69.50; looseleaf 1984 74.50. Bender.
--Standard California Codes: Uniform Commercial Code. 1963. Updates avail. 30.00 (ISBN 0-317-09840-3, 686). Bender.
--Valuation & Distribution of Marital Property, 2 vols. 1984. Updates avail. looseleaf 160.00 (ISBN 0-317-09744-X, 133). Bender.
Bender Editorial Staff, ed. see Magana, Raoul.
Bender Editorial Staff, ed. see Sparber, Byron L., et al.
Bender Editorial Staff, ed. see Spires, Jeremiah J.
Bender, Edmund J., ed. Bibliographie: Charles Nodier. LC 69-11276. 90p. (Fr). 1969. 4.50 (ISBN 0-911198-21-0). Purdue U Pr.
Bender, Edward A. An Introduction to Mathematical Modeling. LC 77-23840. 256p. 1978. 36.50x (ISBN 0-471-02951-3, Pub. by Wiley-Interscience); solutions manual 9.00 (ISBN 0-471-03407-X). Wiley.
Bender, Eleanor M., et al, eds. All of Us Are Present: The Stephens College Symposium Women's Education the Future. 1984. pap. 15.00 (ISBN 0-916767-01-9). J M Wood Res.
Bender, Ernest. Urdu: Grammar & Reader. LC 66-20832. (Illus.). pap. 122.80 (ISBN 0-317-10103-X, 2051185). Bks Demand UMI.
Bender, Ernest & Riccardi, Theodore, Jr. Introductory Hindi Readings. LC 75-133202. 1971. text ed. 19.50x (ISBN 0-8122-7626-4). U of Pa Pr.
Bender, Ernest, ed. Indological Studies in Honor of W. Norman Brown. (American Oriental Ser.: Vol. 47). 1962. 10.00x (ISBN 0-940490-47-1). Am Orient Soc.
Bender, F. Underground Siting of Nuclear Power Plants: Internationales Symposium, 1981. (Illus.). 409p. (Ger. & Eng.). 1982. 63.25 (ISBN 3-510-65108-1). Lubrecht & Cramer.
Bender, F., ed. The Mineral Resources Potential of the Earth: Proceedings of the International Symposium, 2nd, Hannover, West Germany, 1979. (Illus.). 156p. 1979. pap. text ed. 21.10x (ISBN 3-510-65093-X). Lubrecht & Cramer.
Bender, Filmore E., et al. Statistical Methods for Food & Agriculture. (Illus.). 1982. text ed. 27.50 (ISBN 0-87055-391-7). AVI.
Bender, Fred, jt. auth. see Howorth, Beckett.
Bender, Frederick L., ed. The Betrayal of Marx. 16.50 (ISBN 0-8446-5158-3). Peter Smith.
Bender, Friedrich. Geology of Burma. (Beitraege zur Regionalen Geologie der Erde: Vol. 16). (Illus.). 293p. 1983. lib. bdg. 74.50x (ISBN 3-443-11016-9). Lubrecht & Cramer.
Bender, George & Parascandola, John, eds. American Pharmacy in the Colonial & Revolutionary Periods. 48p. 1977. pap. 3.00 (ISBN 0-686-39601-4). Am Inst Hist Pharm.
--Historical Hobbies for the Pharmacist. 57p. 1980. Repr. of 1974 ed. 4.00 (ISBN 0-317-32898-0). Am Inst Hist Pharm.
Bender, George A. & Parascandola, John, eds. Historical Hobbies for the Pharmacist. 2nd ed. (Publications Ser.: No. 2). (Illus.). iv, 57p. 1980. pap. 4.00 (ISBN 0-931292-10-7). Am Inst Hist Pharm.
Bender, Gerald J. African Crisis Areas & Foreign Policy. 400p. 1985. 40.00x (ISBN 0-520-05548-9); pap. 9.95 (ISBN 0-520-05609-4, CAL 776). U of Cal Pr.
--Angola under the Portuguese: The Myth & the Reality. LC 76-7751. (Perspectives on Southern Africa Ser.: No. 23). 1978. 30.00x (ISBN 0-520-03221-7); pap. 8.50x (ISBN 0-520-04274-3). U of Cal Pr.
Bender, Gordon L., ed. Reference Handbook on the Deserts of North America. LC 80-24791. (Illus.). xiii, 594p. 1982. lib. bdg. 75.00 (ISBN 0-313-21307-0, BRD/). Greenwood.
Bender, H. G. & Beck, L., eds. Cancer of the Uterine Cervix. (Cancer Campaign Ser.: Vol. 8). (Illus.). 231p. 1985. pap. 49.00 (ISBN 0-89574-184-9, Pub. by Gustav Fisher Verlag). VCH Pubs.
Bender, Harold S. Anabaptist Vision. 1944. pap. 1.45 (ISBN 0-8361-1305-5). Herald Pr.
--Conrad Grebel, c. 1498-1526: The Founder of the Swiss Brethren Sometimes Called Anabaptists. (Studies in Anabaptist & Mennonite History Ser.: No. 6). pap. 85.80 (ISBN 0-317-28810-5, 2020335). Bks Demand UMI.
--These Are My People. LC 62-12947. 136p. 1962. pap. 3.95 (ISBN 0-8361-1479-5). Herald Hse.
--These Are My People: The New Testament Church. LC 62-12947. (Conrad Grebel Lecture Ser.). 1962. pap. 3.95 (ISBN 0-8361-1479-5). Herald Pr.
Bender, Harold S. & Horsch, John. Menno Simons su Vida y Escritos. Palomeque, Carmen, tr. 160p. 1979. 4.95x (ISBN 0-8361-1218-0). Herald Pr.
Bender, Harold S. & Smith, C. Henry, eds. Mennonite Encyclopedia, 4vols. 1956-1969. Set. 160.00x (ISBN 0-8361-1018-8); 45.00x ea. Vol. 1 (ISBN 0-8361-1118-4). Vol. 2 (ISBN 0-8361-1119-2). Vol. 3 (ISBN 0-8361-1120-6). Vol. 4 (ISBN 0-8361-1121-4). Herald Pr.
Bender, Henry E. Uintah Railway: The Gilsonite Route. LC 75-135999. (Railroadiana). (Illus.). 1970. 17.50 (ISBN 0-8310-7080-3). Howell-North.
Bender, Jack. A Layman's Guide to Installing A Small Business Computer. (Illus.). 128p. 1979. 15.00 (ISBN 0-89433-097-7). Petrocelli.
Bender, James F. How to Sell Well: The Art & Science of Professional Salesmanship. 1971. pap. 5.95 (ISBN 0-07-004441-4). McGraw.
--How to Talk Well. 1963. pap. 4.95 (ISBN 0-07-004446-5). McGraw.
Bender, James F., jt. auth. see Stark, Judy T.
Bender, Jan. Organ Improvisation for Beginners. LC 75-2934. (Illus.). 71p. 1975. bds. 8.25 (ISBN 0-570-01312-7, 99-1229). Concordia.
Bender, Jay, jt. auth. see Ferguson, A. B.
Bender, John B. Spenser & Literary Pictorialism. LC 71-166361. 224p. 1972. 23.50x (ISBN 0-691-06211-0). Princeton U Pr.
Bender, John F. The Functions of Courts in Enforcing School Attendance. LC 79-176550. (Columbia University. Teachers College. Contributions to Education: No. 262). Repr. of 1927 ed. 22.50 (ISBN 0-404-55262-5). AMS Pr.
Bender, Judith, et al. Half a Childhood: Time for School-Age Child Care. (Illus.). 112p. (Orig.). 1984. pap. 7.95 (ISBN 0-917505-01-8). School Age.
Bender, Kirsten A., jt. auth. see Bender, Todd K.
Bender, Lauretta. Aggression, Hostility & Anxiety in Children. (Illus.). 200p. 1953. photocopy ed. 19.75x (ISBN 0-398-04631-X). C C Thomas.
--Child Psychiatric Techniques. (Illus.). 360p. 1952. photocopy ed. 35.50x (ISBN 0-398-04632-8). C C Thomas.
--A Dynamic Psychopathology of Childhood. (Illus.). 296p. 1954. photocopy ed. 29.75x (ISBN 0-398-04633-6). C C Thomas.
--Psychopathology of Children with Organic Brain Disorders. (Illus.). 168p. 1956. photocopy ed. 16.75x (ISBN 0-398-04634-4). C C Thomas.
Bender, Lauretta, ed. see Schilder, Paul.
Bender, Leonard F. Prostheses & Rehabilitation After Arm Amputation. (Illus.). 196p. 1974. photocopy ed. 27.50x0 (ISBN 0-398-03094-4). C C Thomas.
Bender, Lionel. Lasers in Action. (Tomorrow's World Ser.). (Illus.). 48p. (gr. 7-9). 1985. price not set (Pub. by Bookwright Pr). Watts.
--Understanding Communcaution & Control. LC 85-40218. (Understanding Science Ser.). (Illus.). 64p. (gr. 5 up). PLB 12.95 (ISBN 0-382-09082-9). Silver.
Bender, Lynn D. Perspectivas Politicas. rev. ed. LC 83-82307. 167p. 1983. pap. text ed. 6.95 (ISBN 0-913480-59-2). Inter Am U Pr.
Bender, Lynn-Darrell. Cuba vs. United States: The Politics of Hostility. rev. ed. LC 74-78314. 108p. 1981. 12.50 (ISBN 0-913480-51-7); pap. 5.75 (ISBN 0-913480-52-5). Inter Am U Pr.
Bender, M. L. & Domiyama, M. Cyclodextrin Chemistry. (Relativity & Structure Ser.: Vol. 6). (Illus.). 1978. 30.00 (ISBN 0-387-08577-7). Springer-Verlag.
Bender, M. P. Community Psychology. (Essential Psychology Ser.). 1976. pap. 4.50x (ISBN 0-416-82330-0, NO.2611). Methuen Inc.
Bender, Margaret O. Le Torneiment Anticrist by Huon De Meri: A Critical Edition. LC 75-33765. (Romance Monographs: No. 17). 1976. 17.00x (ISBN 84-399-4702-X). Romance.
Bender, Marilyn & Webb, Paul. Archaeological Investigations at the Roos Site, St. Clair County Illinois. new ed. Jeffries, Richard W., ed. (Research Paper Ser.: No. 43). (Illus.). 59p. 1984. pap. 1.25 (ISBN 0-88104-015-0). Center Archaeo.
Bender, Marjie. Beverly Hills Princess. (The Laughter Library). 48p. (Orig.). 1983. pap. 1.75 (ISBN 0-8431-0547-X). Price Stern.
Bender, Mark. EFTS: Electronic Funds Transfer Systems - Elements & Impact. 112p. 1975. 19.50x (ISBN 0-8046-9119-3, Pub. by Kennikat). Assoc Faculty Pr.
Bender, Mark & Huana, Su, trs. from Chinese. Daur Folktales. (Illus.). 191p. 1984. pap. 4.95 (ISBN 0-8351-1538-0). China Bks.
Bender, Mark A., tr. see Yi Qiong & Xu Junhui.
Bender, Marvin. Language in Ethiopia. (Illus.). 1976. text ed. 26.00x (ISBN 0-19-436102-0). Oxford U Pr.
Bender, Marylin & Marc, Monsieur. Nouveau is Better than No Riche at All. (Illus.). 256p. 1983. 15.95 (ISBN 0-399-12867-0, Putnam). Putnam Pub Group.
Bender, Michael & Bender, Rosemary K. Disadvantaged Preschool Children: A Source Book for Teachers. LC 79-12001. (Illus.). 308p. (Orig.). 1979. pap. text ed. 15.95 (ISBN 0-933716-00-1, 001). P H Brookes.
Bender, Michael & Valletutti, Peter J. Teaching Functional Academics: A Curriculum Guide for Adolescents & Adults with Learning Problems. (Illus.). 296p. 1981. pap. 18.00 (ISBN 0-8391-1662-4). Pro-Ed.
Bender, Michael, jt. auth. see Valletutti, J.
Bender, Michael, et al. Teaching the Moderately & Severely Handicapped, Vol. 3. LC 79-46596. 272p. 1976. pap. text ed. 18.00 (ISBN 0-936104-54-6). Pro Ed.
--Leisure Education For The Handicapped: Curriculum Goals, Activities & Resources. LC 83-23908. (Illus.). 246p. 1984. pap. text ed. 18.50 (ISBN 0-933014-10-4). College Hill.
--Careers, Computers, & the Handicapped. LC 84-3682. 171p. 1985. pap. 17.00 (ISBN 0-936104-45-7). Pro Ed.
--Teaching the Moderately & Severely Handicapped, Vol. I. 2nd ed. LC 84-22861. (Illus.). 280p. 1985. pap. 19.00 (ISBN 0-936104-52-X). Pro Ed.
--Teaching the Moderately & Severely Handicapped, Vol. II. 2nd ed. LC 84-22861. (Illus.). 352p. 1985. pap. 19.00 (ISBN 0-936104-53-8). Pro Ed.
Bender, Miriam. Bender-Purdue Reflex Test & Training Manual. 1974. pap. 16.00x includes manual & recording forms (ISBN 0-87879-137-X). Acad Therapy.
Bender, Morris B., ed. Approach to Diagnosis in Modern Neurology. LC 66-29189. (Illus.). 192p. 1967. 48.50 (ISBN 0-8089-0051-X, 790537). Grune.
Bender, Myron L. Mechanisms of Homogeneous Catalysis from Protons to Proteins. LC 73-153080. pap. 160.00 (ISBN 0-317-08936-6, 2006490). Bks Demand UMI.
Bender, Myron L. & Brubacher, Lewis J. Catalysis. (Illus.). 256p. 1973. text ed. 25.95 (ISBN 0-07-004450-3); pap. text ed. 21.95 (ISBN 0-07-004451-1). McGraw.
Bender, Myron L., et al. The Bioorganic Chemistry of Enzymatic Catalysis. LC 83-19857. 312p. 1984. 39.50x (ISBN 0-471-05991-9, Pub. by Wiley Interscience). Wiley.
Bender, Norman J., ed. Missionaries, Outlaws & Indians: Taylor F. Ealy at Lincoln & Zuni, 1878-1881. LC 84-5075. (New Mexico Historical Society Ser.). (Illus.). 256p. 1984. pap. 9.95 (ISBN 0-8263-0758-2). U of NM Pr.
Bender, P. Phyiscal Resources Management. 32.50 (ISBN 0-471-80026-0). Wiley.
Bender, P. L., ed. see I.A.U. Symposium No. 78, Kiev, USSR, May 23-28, 1977, et al.
Bender, Paul S. Resource Management: An Alternative View of the Management Process. LC 82-13471. (Systems Engineering & Analysis Ser.). 227p. 1983. 42.25x (ISBN 0-471-08179-5, Pub. by Wiley-Interscience); 41.95. Assn Inform & Image Mgmt.
Bender Publishers. California Real Estate Law & Practice. 1983. write for info. (#271). Bender.
Bender, Ralph E., et al. The FFA & You. LC 77-91585. (Illus.). 646p. (gr. 9-12). 1979. text ed. 17.25x (ISBN 0-8134-2009-1, 2009). Interstate.
Bender, Robert M. Five Courtier Poets of the English Renaissance. 1969. pap. 0.50 (ISBN 0-671-48480-X). WSP.
Bender, Robert M., ed. Shaping of Fiction. (Orig.). 1970. pap. text ed. 0.95 (ISBN 0-671-47802-8). WSP.
Bender, Roger J. & Odegard, Warren W. Uniforms, Organization & History of the Panzertruppe. (Illus.). 336p. 1980. 24.95 (ISBN 0-912138-18-1). Bender Pub CA.
Bender, Roger J., jt. auth. see Chalif, Don.
Bender, Roger J., ed. see Thayer, Lucien H.
Bender, Rosemary K., jt. auth. see Bender, Michael.
Bender, Ross T. Christians in Families. LC 82-6058. (Conrad Grebel Lecture Ser.). 184p. (Orig.). pap. 7.95 (ISBN 0-8361-3301-3). Herald Pr.
Bender, Ruth. Be Young & Flexible after Thirty, Forty, Fifty, Sixty.... 1976. spiral bdg. 3.95 (ISBN 0-917434-01-3). Ruben Pub.
--Gentle Relaxing & Strengthening Movements for People with Backproblems, Arthritis & MS. 1983. 1.95 (ISBN 0-917434-03-X). Ruben Pub.
--Yoga Exercises for Every Body. 1975. spiral bdg. 7.95 (ISBN 0-917434-00-5). Ruben Pub.
--Yoga Exercises for More Flexible Bodies. 1977. spiral bdg. 7.95 (ISBN 0-917434-02-1). Ruben Pub.
Bender, Ruth E. & Silverman, S. Richard. The Conquest of Deafness. 3rd ed. 216p. 1981. text ed. 10.95x (ISBN 0-8134-2227-2). Interstate.

Bender, Sheila. Near the Light. 30p. (Orig.). 1983. pap. write for info (ISBN 0-9609476-1-2). J Doe Pr.

Bender, Stephen J., jt. auth. see Sorochan, Walter D.

Bender, Stephen O., et al. Issues in Income Distribution. Soligo, Ronald & Von der Mehden, Fred R., eds. (Rice University Studies: Vol. 61, No. 4). (Illus.). 176p. (Orig.). 1976. pap. 10.00x (ISBN 0-89263-226-7). Rice Univ.

Bender, Tamara L., tr. see Viera, J. L.

Bender, Terry C. & Stiles, Lawrence W. Major College Football; A Record of Scores: Eighteen Sixty-Nine to Nineteen Eighty Two. LC 83-90064. 320p. 1983. pap. 19.95 (ISBN 0-8059-2869-3). Dorrance.

Bender, Thomas. Community & Social Change in America. LC 82-47981. 176p. (Orig.). 1982. pap. text ed. 6.95x (ISBN 0-8018-2924-0). Johns Hopkins.

--Toward an Urban Vision: Ideas & Institutions in Nineteenth-Century America. LC 82-47980. 296p. (Orig.). 1982. pap. text ed. 8.50x (ISBN 0-8018-2925-9). Johns Hopkins.

Bender, Thomas, et al, eds. see DeTocqueville, Alexis.

Bender, Todd K. A Concordance to Conrad's A Set of Six. 1981. lib. bdg. 55.00 (ISBN 0-8240-9340-2). Garland Pub.

--A Concordance to Conrad's "An Outcast of the Islands". LC 83-49320. (Reference Library of the Humanities). 200p. 1984. lib. bdg. 66.00 (ISBN 0-8240-8991-X). Garland Pub.

--A Concordance to Conrad's Heart of Darkness. LC 78-68269. (Garland Reference Library of the Humanities: No. 135). 1980. lib. bdg. 121.00 (ISBN 0-8240-9809-9). Garland Pub.

--Concordance to Conrad's Secret Agent. LC 78-68258. (Reference Library of Humanities Ser.). 1979. lib. bdg. 73.00 (ISBN 0-8240-9810-2). Garland Pub.

--A Concordance to Conrad's the Mirror of the Sea & the Inheritors. LC 83-47608. 330p. 1985. lib. bdg. 50.00 (ISBN 0-8240-9110-8). Garland Pub.

--Concordances to Conrad's Tales of Unrest, Tales of Hearsay. LC 81-43332. 242p. 1982. lib. bdg. 73.00 (ISBN 0-8240-9297-X). Garland Pub.

--Concordances to Conrad's the Shadow Line & Youth. LC 79-8416. 150p. 1980. lib. bdg. 48.00 (ISBN 0-8240-9520-0). Garland Pub.

--Gerard Manley Hopkins: The Classical Background and Critical Reception of His Work. 180p. 1966. 16.00x (ISBN 0-8018-0066-8). Johns Hopkins.

Bender, Todd K. & Bender, Kirsten A. A Concordance to Conrad's: Within the Tide & Typhoon. (British Literature Ser.). 372p. 1982. lib. bdg. 91.00 (ISBN 0-8240-9379-8). Garland Pub.

Bender, Todd K. & Parins, James W. A Concordance to Conrad's Nigger of the Narcissus. LC 79-8417. 150p. 1981. lib. bdg. 48.00 (ISBN 0-8240-9519-7). Garland Pub.

Bender, Todd K., jt. auth. see Briggum, Sue M.

Bender, Todd K., jt. auth. see Higdon, David.

Bender, Todd K., jt. auth. see Higdon, David L.

Bender, Todd K., jt. auth. see Sabol, C. Ruth.

Bender, Todd K., et al. A Concordance to Conrad's Lord Jim. LC 75-34972. (Reference Library in the Humanities: Vol. 10). 1975. lib. bdg. 73.00 (ISBN 0-8240-9995-8). Garland Pub.

--Concordance to Conrad's Victory. LC 78-68275. (Reference Library of Humanities Ser.). 1979. lib. bdg. 121.00 (ISBN 0-8240-9808-0). Garland Pub.

Bender, Urie. Four Earthen Vessels. 320p. 1982. 10.95; pap. 7.95. Herald Pr.

Bender, Urie A. To Walk in the Way. LC 79-83511. 208p. 1979. pap. 5.95 (ISBN 0-8361-1884-7). Herald Pr.

Benderly, Beryl L. Dancing Without Music: Deafness in America. LC 79-6092. 312p. 1980. 15.95 (ISBN 0-385-14703-1, Anchor Pr). Doubleday.

--Thinking about Abortion. LC 83-45243. (Illus.). 216p. 1984. 13.95 (ISBN 0-385-27757-1, Dial). Doubleday.

Bender's Editorial Staff. Appeals & Writs: Unit 5. (California Civil Litigation Forms System). 1985. incl. disks 625.00 (796). Bender.

--Attorney's Guide to Government Studies & Reports. 1984. pamphlet 50.00 (064). Bender.

--California Civil Litigation Forms System, 5 vols. 1985. Complete set. incl. disks 1995.00. Bender.

--California Criminal Defense Practice Reporter. 1981. Updates avail. looseleaf incl. one year's subs. 130.00 (173); looseleaf annual renewal 130.00; looseleaf 1983 90.00; looseleaf 1984 120.00. Bender.

--California Durable Power of Attorney System. 1985. incl. disks 200.00 (644). Bender.

--California Family Law Monthly. 1984. looseleaf incl. one year's subs. 125.00 (110); annual renewal 150.00. Bender.

--California Incorporation System. 1985. incl. disks 500.00 (638). Bender.

--California Partnerships System. 1985. incl. disks 600.00 (639). Bender.

--California Simple Will System. 1985. incl. disks 200.00 (643). Bender.

--Contracts Interrogatories. (Bender's Interrogatories System). 1985. incl. disks 300.00 (653). Bender.

--Defendant's Personal Injury & Products Liability Interrogatories. (Bender's Interrogatories System). 1985. incl. disks 300.00 (649). Bender.

--Delaware Incorporation System. 1985. incl. disks 500.00 (646). Bender.

--Dictionary of Ten Forty Deductions. 1985. Updates avail. pap. 32.00 (306); pap. 25.00, 1983; pap. 32.00, 1984. Bender.

--Discovery: Unit 3. (California Civil Litigation Forms System). 1985. incl. disks 650.00 (794). Bender.

--Divorce Interrogatories. (Bender's Interrogatories System). 1985. incl. disks 300.00 (651). Bender.

--Illinois Simple Will System. 1985. looseleaf incl. disks 200.00 (669). Bender.

--Plaintiff's Personal Injury & Products Liability Interrogatories. (Bender's Interrogatories System). 1985. incl. disks 300.00 (647). Bender.

--Pleadings: Unit 1. (California Civil Litigation Forms System). 1985. incl. disks 625.00 (792). Bender.

--Pretrial Proceedings; Trial & Post-Trial Motions: Unit 4. (California Civil Litigation Forms System). 1985. incl. disks 475.00 (795). Bender.

--Pretrial Proceedings: Unit 2. (California Civil Litigation Forms System). 1985. incl. disks 525.00 (793). Bender.

--Real Property Interrogatories. (Bender's Interrogatories System). 1985. incl. disks 300.00 (652). Bender.

--Standard California Codes: Uniform Commercial Code. 1963. Updates avail. 32.00 (686); 1983 18.50,; 1984 18.50,. Bender.

--Texas Durable Power of Attorney System. 1985. looseleaf incl. disks 200.00 (791). Bender.

--Texas Incorporation System. 1985. looseleaf incl. disks 500.00 (776). Bender.

--Texas Simple Will System. 1985. looseleaf incl. disks 200.00. Bender.

Bender's Editorial Staff, jt. auth. see Reiss, Peter.

Bendersky, David, et al. Resource Recovery Processing Equipment. LC 82-7882. (Pollution Technology Rev. 93). (Illus.). 417p. 1983. 42.00 (ISBN 0-8155-0911-1). Noyes.

Bendersky, Joseph W. Carl Schmitt, Theorist for the Reich. LC 82-61353. 336p. 1983. 30.00x (ISBN 0-691-05380-4). Princeton U Pr.

--A History of Nazi Germany. LC 84-11503. 278p. 1984. text ed. 22.95x (ISBN 0-88229-684-1); pap. text ed. 11.95x (ISBN 0-88229-829-1). Nelson-Hall.

Benderson, Albert E. Critical Approaches to Federico Fellini's Eight & a Half, Vol. 4. LC 74-2078. (Dissertations on Film Ser.). 239p. 1974. 15.00 (ISBN 0-405-04877-7). Ayer Co Pubs.

Bendick, Jeanne. Airplanes. rev. ed. (First Bk.). (Illus.). 72p. (gr. 4-6). 1982. PLB 8.90 (ISBN 0-531-00455-4). Watts.

--Artificial Satellites. (First Bks.). (Illus.). 72p. (gr. 4 up). 1982. PLB 8.90 (ISBN 0-531-04381-9). Watts.

--Automobiles. rev. ed. (First Bks.). (Illus.). 72p. lib. bdg. 8.90 (ISBN 0-531-04821-7). Watts.

--The Big Strawberry Book of Astronomy. LC 78-78321. (Illus.). (gr. 3-7). 1979. 5.95 (ISBN 0-88470-058-5, Pub by One Strawberry); PLB 6.99 (ISBN 0-88470-059-3). Larousse.

--Exploring an Ocean Tide Pool. LC 75-34469. (Good Earth Ser.). (Illus.). 64p. (gr. 2-6). 1976. PLB 8.19 (ISBN 0-8116-6105-9). Garrard.

--Putting the Sun to Work. LC 78-6178. (Good Earth Ser.). (Illus.). (gr. 3). PLB 8.19 (ISBN 0-8116-6111-3). Garrard.

--Scare a Ghost, Tame a Monster. LC 82-23696. (Illus.). 120p. (gr. 3-6). 1983. 11.95 (ISBN 0-664-32701-X). Westminster.

--Space Travel. (First Bks). (Illus.). 72p. (gr. 4 up). 1982. PLB 8.90 (ISBN 0-531-04388-6). Watts.

Bendick, Jeanne & Bendick, Robert. The Consumer's Catalog of Economy & Ecology. LC 74-8081. 160p. (gr. 9-12). 1974. pap. 5.95 (ISBN 0-07-004511-9). McGraw.

Bendick, Jeanne & Levin, Marcia. Mathematics Illustrated Dictionary: Facts, Figures & People, Including the New Math. (Illus.). (gr. 7 up). 1965. 10.95 (ISBN 0-07-004460-0). McGraw.

Bendick, Marc, Jr., jt. auth. see Campbell, Toby H.

Bendick, Marc, Jr., jt. ed. see Struyk, Raymond J.

Bendick, Robert, jt. auth. see Bendick, Jeanne.

Bendict, Benjamin. Duet. 1981. 5.00 (ISBN 0-686-31630-4). Falcon Pub Venice.

Bendinelli, Cesare. The Entire Art of Trumpet Playing. Tarr, Edward H., tr. from It. & commentary by. LC 75-31807. Orig. Title: Volume di Tutta L'Arte della Trombetta. (Illus.). 20p. (Eng.). 1975. pap. text ed. 5.00 (ISBN 0-914282-16-6). Brass Pr.

Bendiner, Alfred. Bendiner's Philadelphia. 8.95 (ISBN 0-8453-6214-3). Cornwall Bks.

Bendiner, Elmer. The Rise & Fall of Paradise: When Arabs & Jews Built a Kingdom in Spring. LC 83-3351. 272p. 1983. 17.95 (ISBN 0-399-12857-3, Putnam). Putnam Pub Group.

Bendiner, Kenneth. An Introduction to Victorian Painting. LC 84-27038. (Illus.). 208p. 1985. 35.00x (ISBN 0-300-03309-5). Yale U Pr.

Bendiner, Winifred, jt. auth. see Schoenfeld, Susan.

Bending, Richard & Eden, Richard. U. K. Energy: Structure, Prospects & Policies. (Illus.). 320p. 1985. 49.50 (ISBN 0-521-26708-0). Cambridge U Pr.

Bendire, Charles E. Life Histories of North American Birds: Their Breeding Habits & Eggs, 2 vols. in one. LC 73-17802. (Natural Sciences in America Ser.). (Illus.). 1042p. 1974. Repr. 68.50x (ISBN 0-405-05720-2). Ayer Co Pubs.

Bendis, Kieth. Lemmings & Other New Yorkers. (Illus.). 32p. 1983. pap. 4.95 (ISBN 0-396-08179-7). Dodd.

Bendisz, K. Pipe Loops & Bends: Design for Flexibility Tables. Bendisz-Siekierski, Anna, ed. LC 84-90195. (Illus.). 288p. (Orig.). 1984. 27.00 (ISBN 0-9613395-0-0). Siren.

Bendisz-Siekierski, Anna, ed. see Bendisz, K.

Bendit, Laurence & Bendit, Phoebe. The Transforming Mind. 2nd ed. LC 74-103415. 161p. 1983. pap. 5.75 (ISBN 0-8356-0012-2, Quest). Theos Pub Hse.

Bendit, Laurence J. Mirror of Life & Death. 1965. pap. 1.35 (ISBN 0-8356-0411-X, Quest). Theos Pub Hse.

--Self Knowledge: A Yoga for the West. LC 67-7871. (Orig.). 1967. pap. 1.25 (ISBN 0-8356-0032-7, Quest). Theos Pub Hse.

Bendit, Laurence J., jt. auth. see Bendit, Phoebe D.

Bendit, Laurence J., jt. auth. see Payne, Phoebe D.

Bendit, Phoebe, jt. auth. see Bendit, Laurence.

Bendit, Phoebe D. & Bendit, Laurence J. The Etheric Body of Man. LC 76-46930. 1977. pap. 3.50 (ISBN 0-8356-0489-6, Quest). Theos Pub Hse.

Benditt, Theodore. Rights. 158p. 1982. 27.50 (ISBN 0-318-02976-6). Biblio Dist.

Benditt, Theodore M. Law As Rule & Principle: Problems of Legal Philosophy. LC 77-89180. 1978. 17.50x (ISBN 0-8047-0963-7). Stanford U Pr.

--Rights. LC 81-23448. (Philosophy & Society Ser.). 158p. 1982. text ed. 27.50 (ISBN 0-8476-6754-5). Rowman.

Bendix, G. Press Point Therapy. 1978. pap. 3.50 (ISBN 0-380-39867-2, 64782-6). Avon.

Bendix, Regina. Progress & Nostalgia. LC 84-28128. (Publications in Folklore & Mythology: Vol. 33). 1985. 28.00x (ISBN 0-520-09959-1). U of Cal Pr.

Bendix, Reinhard. Force, Fate, & Freedom: On Historical Sociology. LC 83-3565. 180p. 1984. 11.95 (ISBN 0-520-04931-4). U of Cal Pr.

--From Berlin to Berkeley: German-Jewish Identities. 320p. 1985. 29.95 (ISBN 0-88738-067-0). Transaction Bks.

--Higher Civil Servants in American Society. LC 73-17856. 129p. 1974. Repr. of 1949 ed. lib. bdg. 15.00 (ISBN 0-8371-7265-9, BEHC). Greenwood.

--Kings or People: Power & the Mandate to Rule. 1978. pap. 9.95 (ISBN 0-520-04090-2). U of Cal Pr.

--Max Weber: An Intellectual Portrait. 1978. 40.00x (ISBN 0-520-03503-8); pap. 9.95x (ISBN 0-520-03194-6). U of Cal Pr.

--Nation-Building & Citizenship: Studies of Our Changing Social Order. 2nd rev. ed. LC 73-91670. 400p. 1977. 45.00x (ISBN 0-520-02676-4); pap. 9.50x (ISBN 0-520-02761-2, CAMPUS 138). U of Cal Pr.

--Scholarship & Partisanship: Essays on Max Weber. (California Reprint Ser.: No. 110). 1980. 29.50x (ISBN 0-520-04171-2). U of Cal Pr.

--Work & Authority in Industry: Ideologies of Management in the Course of Industrialization. LC 73-78553. 1974. pap. 8.95x (ISBN 0-520-02628-4, CAMPUS 115). U of Cal Pr.

Bendix, Reinhard, jt. auth. see Lipset, Seymour M.

Bendix, Reinhard, ed. State & Society: A Reader in Comparative Political Sociology. LC 73-76270. 1974. 10.95x (ISBN 0-520-02490-7, CAMPUS 100). U of Cal Pr.

Bendix, Reinhard & Lipset, Seymour M., eds. Class, Status & Power: A Reader in Social Stratification. rev. ed. LC 65-23025. 1966. text ed. 24.95 (ISBN 0-02-902630-X). Free Pr.

Bendix, Torben. The Anxious Patient. Wright, H. J., ed. Schou, Mogens, tr. LC 81-70694. 70p. 1982. pap. text ed. 4.95 (ISBN 0-443-02295-X). Churchill.

Bendixen, Alfred, ed. Haunted Women: The Best Supernatural Tales by American Women Writers. 260p. 1985. 14.95 (ISBN 0-8044-2052-1). Ungar.

Ben-Dor, Gabriel. The Druzes in Israel: A Political Study. 287p. 1979. text ed. 25.50x (ISBN 965-223-333-1, Pub. by Magnes Israel). Humanities.

--The Druzes in Israel: A Political Study: Political Innovation & Integration in a Middle Eastern Minority. 287p. 1981. lib. bdg. 36.00x (ISBN 0-686-64555-3, Pub. by Magnes Pr). Westview.

--State & Conflict in the Middle East: Emergence of the Post-Colonial State. LC 82-24616. 288p. 1983. 32.95 (ISBN 0-03-063559-4). Praeger.

--State & Conflict in the Middle East. 200p. 1985. text ed. 32.50x (ISBN 0-7146-3224-4, F Cass Co). Biblio Dist.

Bendor, Jonathan B. Parallel Systems: Redundancy in Government. LC 84-2594. 350p. 1985. 27.50x (ISBN 0-520-05149-1). U of Cal Pr.

Ben-Dor, L., jt. ed. see Marcus, Y.

Bendor-Samuel, David. Hierarchical Structures in Guajajara. (Publications in Linguistics & Related Fields, No. 37). 214p. 1972. pap. 4.50x (ISBN 0-88312-039-9); microfiche (3) 3.80x (ISBN 0-88312-439-4). Summer Inst Ling.

--Tupi Studies I. (Publications in Linguistics & Related Fields Ser.: No. 29). 129p. 1971. pap. 1.80 (ISBN 0-88312-031-3); microfiche 2.25x (ISBN 0-88312-431-9). Summer Inst Ling.

Bendor-Samuel, David & Bendor-Samuel, Margaret. Community Literacy Programmes in Northern Ghana. LC 83-61218. 81p. (Orig.). 1983. pap. 8.50 (ISBN 0-88312-927-2); microfiche 1.93 (ISBN 0-88312-539-0). Summer Inst Ling.

Bendor-Samuel, John. Ten Nigerian Tone Languages. (Language Data, African Ser.: No. 4). 129p. 1974. pap. 7.00x (ISBN 0-88312-604-4); microfiche 2.25x (ISBN 0-88312-704-0). Summer Inst Ling.

Bendor-Samuel, John, et al. Duka Sentence, Clause & Phrase. (Language Data, African Ser.: No. 3). 160p. 1973. pap. 5.50 (ISBN 0-88312-603-6); microfiche (3) 3.80x (ISBN 0-88312-703-2). Summer Inst Ling.

Bendor-Samuel, Margaret, jt. auth. see Bendor-Samuel, David.

Ben-Dov, Meir. In the Shadow of the Temple. LC 84-48639. (Illus.). 384p. 1985. 23.99i (ISBN 0-06-015362-8, HarpT). Har-Row.

Bendow, B. & Langeler, B. Polariton - Mediated Light Scattering & Electronic Structure of Noble Metals. (Springer Tracts in Modern Physics Ser.: Vol. 82). (Illus.). 1978. 33.00 (ISBN 0-387-08814-8). Springer-Verlag.

Bendow, B. see Mitra, S. S.

Bendow, B. & Mitra, S. S., eds. Fiber Optics: Advances in Research & Development. 703p. 1979. 95.00x (ISBN 0-306-40167-3, Plenum Pr). Plenum Pub.

Bendow, Bernard & Mitra, Shashanka S., eds. Advances in Ceramics: Physics of Fiber Optics, Vol. 2. (Illus.). 1981. text ed. 50.00 (ISBN 0-916094-42-1); text ed. 30.00 student members. Am Ceramic.

Bendow, Bernard, et al, eds. Theory of Light Scattering in Condensed Matter. LC 76-47492. 540p. 1976. 79.50x (ISBN 0-306-30993-9, Plenum Pr). Plenum Pub.

Bendt, Ingela & Downing, Jim. We Shall Return: Women of Palestine. (Illus.). 144p. (Orig.). 1982. 16.95 (ISBN 0-88208-154-3); pap. 8.50 (ISBN 0-88208-155-1). Lawrence Hill.

Bendure, Zelma & Pfeiffer, Gladys. America's Fabrics: Origin & History, Manufacture, Characteristics & Uses. LC 72-5260. (Technology & Society Ser.). (Illus.). 703p. 1972. Repr. of 1946 ed. 46.00 (ISBN 0-405-04685-5). Ayer Co Pubs.

Bendz, E. P. Joseph Conrad. LC 77-92934. (Studies in Conrad, No. 8). 1970. Repr. of 1923 ed. lib. bdg. 39.95x (ISBN 0-8383-0960-7). Haskell.

Bendz, Ernst. Influence of Pater & Matthew Arnold in the Prose Writings of Oscar Wilde. LC 73-9753. 1914. lib. bdg. 12.50 (ISBN 0-8414-3172-8). Folcroft.

--Oscar Wilde. LC 74-13380. 1921. lib. bdg. 12.50 (ISBN 0-8414-3267-8). Folcroft.

Bendz, Ernst P. Joseph Conrad: An Appreciation. LC 73-9671. 1923. lib. bdg. 9.75 (ISBN 0-8414-3141-8). Folcroft.

Bendz, G. & Lindqvist, I., eds. Biochemistry of Silicon & Related Problems. LC 77-29160. 603p. 1978. 75.00x (ISBN 0-306-33710-X, Plenum Pr). Plenum Pub.

Bendz, Gerd & Santesson, Johann, eds. Chemistry in Botanical Classification. 1974. 66.00 (ISBN 0-12-086650-1). Acad Pr.

Bene. Erasmi Opera Omnia, Vol. 2. Date not set. price not set (ISBN 0-444-86878-X). Elsevier.

Benecerraf, Paul, tr. see Mehlberg, Henry.

Beneck, John. And Why Did You Come to the Emergency Room? LC 80-20360. 1983. pap. 9.95 (ISBN 0-87949-192-2). Ashley Bks.

Benecke, Else C. & Busch, Marie, trs. from Polish. Selected Polish Tales. 1978. Repr. of 1921 ed. lib. bdg. 12.50 (ISBN 0-8495-0417-1). Arden Lib.

Benecke, G. F., et al, eds. see Hartman, Von Aue.

Benecke, G. F., et al, eds. see Von Aue, Hartmann.

Benecke, Gerhard. Germany in the Thirty Years War. LC 78-21443. (Illus.). 1979. 22.50x (ISBN 0-312-32626-2). St Martin.

--Maximillian I, Fourteen Fifty-Nine to Fifteen Nineteen. (Illus.). 224p. 1982. 26.95x (ISBN 0-7100-9023-4). Routledge & Kegan.

Benecke, Gerhard, jt. auth. see Scribner, Bob.

Benecke, Gerhardt, jt. ed. see Bak, Janos M.

Benecke, Roberta, jt. auth. see Knox, Douglas R.

Benedeck, Elissa. The Secret Worry. 32p. (ps-3). 1984. 10.95 (ISBN 0-89885-133-5). Human Sci Pr.

Benedeit. The Anglo-Norman Voyage of St. Brendan. Short, I. & Merrilees, B., eds. (Medieval French Text Ser.). 1979. pap. text ed. 6.00 (ISBN 0-7190-0735-6, Pub. by Manchester Univ Pr). Longwood Pub Group.

Benedek, Elissa, jt. ed. see Schetky, Diane H.

Benedek, Elissa P. & Schetky, Diane H. Merging Issues in Child Psychiatry & the Law. LC 85-9920. 1985. price not set (ISBN 0-87630-393-9). Brunner-Mazel.

Benedek, Elissa P. see Schetky, Diane.

Benedek, G. & Valbusa, U., eds. Dynamics of Gas-Surface Interaction, Sicily, Italy 1981: Proceedings. (Springer Series in Chemical Physics: Vol. 21). (Illus.). 282p. 1982. 36.00 (ISBN 0-387-11693-1). Springer-Verlag.

Benedek, G., jt. ed. see Obal, F.

Benedek, G., et al, eds. Statics & Dynamics of Nonlinear Systems. (Springer Series in Solid-State Sciences: Vol. 47). (Illus.). 311p. 1983. 30.00 (ISBN 0-387-12841-7). Springer Verlag.

Benedek, G. B. Magnetic Resonance at High Pressure. LC 63-18561. (Interscience Tracts on Physics & Astronomy: Vol. 24). pap. 27.30 (ISBN 0-317-08895-5, 2055130). Bks Demand UMI.
Benedek, G. B. & Villars, F. M. Physics with Illustrative Examples from Medicine & Biology, 2 vols. 1974. 25.95 ea.; Vol. 1. 23.95 (ISBN 0-201-00551-4). Vol. 2 (ISBN 0-201-00558-1). Addison-Wesley.
--Physics with Illustrative Examples from Medicine & Biology, Vol. 3. 1979. pap. text ed. 25.95 (ISBN 0-201-00559-X). Addison-Wesley.
Benedek, George, jt. auth. see Miller, David.
Benedek, P., ed. Steady-State Flow-Sheeting of Chemical Plants. (Chemical Engineering Monographs: Vol. 12). 410p. 1981. 72.50 (ISBN 0-444-99765-2). Elsevier.
Benedek, Paul & Otti, Ferenc. Computer Aided Chemical Thermodynamics of Gases & Liquids: Theory, Models & Programs. 832p. 1985. write for info. (ISBN 0-471-87825-1). Wiley.
Benedek, Therese, jt. auth. see Fleming, Joan.
Benedek, Therese, jt. ed. see Anthony, E. James.
Benedek, W., jt. ed. see Ginther, K.
Benedetta, Mary, jt. auth. see Moholy-Nagy, L.
Benedetti & Brunenghi. The Knee: Chronic Capsular Ligament Injuries (Surgical Techniques) 1985. 35.00 (ISBN 88-299-0084-2). Ishiyaku Euro.
Benedetti, Alessandro. Diaria De Bello Carolino (Diary of the Caroline War) new ed. Schullian, Dorothy M., ed. LC 66-21028. (Renaissance Text Ser.: No. 1). x, 276p. 1967. 8.50 (ISBN 0-9602696-0-6). Renaissance Soc Am.
Benedetti, Costantino, et al, eds. Recent Advances in the Management of Pain. LC 84-15111. (Advances in Pain Research & Therapy Ser.: Vol. 7). 712p. 1984. text ed. 98.00 (ISBN 0-88167-021-9). Raven.
Benedetti, David. Nictitating Membrane. (Illus.). 64p. 1976. signed ed. 10.00 (ISBN 0-685-78912-8); perfect bound in wrappers 3.00 (ISBN 0-685-78913-6). Figures.
Benedetti, Edoardo De see De Benedetti, Edoardo.
Benedetti, Eugene, jt. auth. see Garber, Lee O.
Benedetti, Jean. Stanislavski: An Introduction. 1982. pap. 5.95 (ISBN 0-87830-578-5). Theatre Arts.
Benedetti, Robert. The Actor at Work. 3rd ed. (Illus.). 1981. text ed. 25.95 (ISBN 0-13-003673-0). P-H.
--The Director at Work. (Illus.). 256p. 1985. text ed. 19.95 (ISBN 0-13-214909-5). P-H.
--Seeming, Being, & Becoming. LC 76-26668. 136p. 1976. pap. text ed. 6.95x (ISBN 0-89676-011-1); text ed. 6.95 (ISBN 0-910482-77-2). Drama Bk.
Benedetti, Robert L. The Actor at Work. 4th ed. (Illus.). 304p. 1986. text ed. 24.95 (ISBN 0-13-003732-X). P-H.
Benedetti-Pichler, A. A. Identification of Materials Via Physical Properties, Chemical Testing & Microscopy. (Illus.). 1964. 42.00 (ISBN 0-387-80670-9). Springer-Verlag.
Benedetto. Matrix Management: Theory in Practice. 96p. 1985. pap. text ed. 10.95 (ISBN 0-8403-3598-9). Kendall Hunt.
Benedetto, Anthony R., ed. Nuclear Medicine Science Syllabus. 2nd rev. ed. LC 82-19434. 280p. 1983. text ed. 33.00 (ISBN 0-932004-15-6). Soc Nuclear Med.
Benedetto, Don, jt. auth. see Valdes, Juan de.
Benedetto, Gravagnuolo. Adolf Loos: Theory & Works. LC 81-51716. (Illus.). 224p. 1982. 50.00 (ISBN 0-8478-0414-3). Rizzoli Intl.
Benedetto, J. Harmonic Analysis on Totally Disconnected Sets. LC 77-163741. (Lecture Notes in Mathematics: Vol. 202). 1971. pap. 14.00 (ISBN 0-387-05488-X). Springer-Verlag.
Benedetto, J. J., ed. Euclidean Harmonic Analysis: Proceedings. (Lecture Notes in Mathematics: Vol. 779). 177p. 1980. pap. 15.00 (ISBN 0-387-09748-1). Springer-Verlag.
Benedetto, John J. Real Variable & Integration. (Illus.). 1976. pap. 32.50x (ISBN 3-5190-2209-5). Adlers Foreign Bks.
Benèdetto, U. Spanish-English, English-Spanish Dictionary, 2 Vols. (Span. & Eng.). Set. 120.00 (ISBN 8-4716-6211-6). Heinman.
Benedickson, J., et al. Canadian North: Source of Wealth or Vanishing Heritage. 1977. pap. 4.65 (ISBN 0-13-112912-0). P-H.
Benedict, A. A., ed. Avian Immunology. LC 77-2732. (Advances in Experimental Medicine & Biology Ser.: Vol. 88). 423p. 1977. 55.00x (ISBN 0-306-32688-4, Plenum Pr). Plenum Pub.
Benedict, A. A., jt. ed. see Hildemann, W. H.
Benedict, Barbara. Golden Tomorrows. 384p. 1984. pap. 3.75 (ISBN 0-8439-2122-6, Leisure Bks). Dorchester Pub Co.
--Lovestorm. 496p. 1984. pap. 3.75 (ISBN 0-8439-2062-9). Dorchester Pub Co.
--Lovestorm. 496p. 1985. pap. 3.95 (ISBN 0-8439-2328-8, Leisure Bks). Dorchester Pub Co.
Benedict, Benjamin. Duet, 3 bks, No. 2. (Eggs Benedict Ser.). (Illus., Orig.). 1982. pap. 2.95 (ISBN 0-942764-02-1). Falcon Pub Venice.
--Glue. 1981. 4.00 (ISBN 0-686-24853-8). Falcon Pub Venice.
--Glue. Rev. ed. (Eggs Benedict Ser.). (Illus.). 144p. 1982. pap. 2.95 (ISBN 0-942764-01-3). Falcon Pub Venice.
Benedict, Brad. Cool Cats: A Catalog of Portraits. 1982. 1.00 (ISBN 0-517-54760-0, Harmony Bks). Crown.
--Fame. (Illus.). 120p. 1980. 7.98 (ISBN 0-517-54161-0, Harmony); pap. 3.98 (ISBN 0-517-54162-9, Harmony). Crown.
--Fame II. LC 84-80884. (Illus.). 112p. (Orig.). 1984. pap. 12.95 (ISBN 0-394-62303-7, E960, Ever). Grove.
--Love: Art of Romance. (Illus.). 48p. 1982. pap. 1.00 Outlet (ISBN 0-517-54355-9, Harmony). Crown.
Benedict, Brad, ed. The Blue Book. LC 82-84633. (Illus.). 96p. 1983. pap. 13.95 (ISBN 0-394-62439-4, E857, Ever). Grove.
Benedict, Burton. The Anthropology of World's Fairs: San Francisco's Panama Pacific International Exposition of 1915. 175p. 1983. 45.00 (ISBN 0-85967-676-5); pap. 15.00 (ISBN 0-85967-677-3). Scolar.
Benedict, Burton, jt. auth. see Benedict, Marion.
Benedict, Clare M. St. Sharbel, Mystic of the East. 1977. 6.95 (ISBN 0-911218-11-4); pap. 3.45 (ISBN 0-911218-12-2). Ravengate Pr.
Benedict, Clifford J. Old King Penn. 1983. 7.75 (ISBN 0-8062-2213-1). Carlton.
Benedict, David. A General History of the Baptist Denomination in America, 2 vols. 1985. Repr. of 1813 ed. 64.00 (ISBN 0-317-31642-7). Church History.
--General History of the Baptist Denomination in America & Other Parts of the World, 2 vols. facsimile ed. LC 73-152974. (Select Bibliographies Reprint Ser). Repr. of 1813 ed. Set. 60.00 (ISBN 0-8369-5726-1). Ayer Co Pubs.
--History of the Donatists. 1985. Repr. of 1875 ed. 15.00 (ISBN 0-317-31641-9). Church History.
Benedict, Dianne. Shiny Objects. LC 82-10853. (Iowa School of Letters Award for Short Fiction Ser.: No. 13). 170p. 1982. 12.95 (ISBN 0-87745-116-8); pap. 8.95 (ISBN 0-87745-117-6). U of Iowa Pr.
Benedict, Don. Born Again Radical. LC 82-9100. 240p. (Orig.). 1982. pap. 7.95 (ISBN 0-8298-0371-8). Pilgrim NY.
Benedict, Elizabeth. Slow Dancing. LC 84-48499. 288p. 1985. 15.95 (ISBN 0-394-54148-0). Knopf.
Benedict, F. C. The Physiology of Large Reptiles: With Special Reference to the Heat Production of Snakes, Tortoises, Lizards & Alligators. (Illus.). 1973. Repr. of 1932 ed. 48.25 (ISBN 90-6123-263-5). Lubrecht & Cramer.
Benedict, George G. Visions & Verities. LC 57-14845. 1957. 6.95 (ISBN 0-87015-077-4). Pacific Bks.
Benedict, Glen E., jt. auth. see Schulz, Wallace W.
Benedict, Helen. Recovery: How to Survive Sexual Assault for Women, Men, Teenagers, Their Friends & Families. LC 84-13821. 312p. 1985. 15.95 (ISBN 0-385-19206-1). Doubleday.
Benedict, Helen, et al. Women Making History: Conversations with Fifteen New Yorkers. Gold, Maxine, ed. LC 85-2976. 160p. (Orig.). 1985. pap. 4.95 (ISBN 0-9610688-1-7). NYC Comm Women.
Benedict, Howard M., et al. Calculator Techniques for Real Estate. LC 77-11252. 1977. 14.95 (ISBN 0-913652-10-5). Realtors Natl.
Benedict, John T. Metrication for the Manager. Boselovic, Len, ed. LC 77-84932. (Illus.). 1977. pap. text ed. 10.00 (ISBN 0-916148-12-2); subscribers 8.00. Am Natl.
Benedict, Julius. Carl Maria Von Weber. LC 74-24040. Repr. of 1899 ed. 18.00 (ISBN 0-404-12863-7). AMS Pr.
Benedict, Karen M., ed. A Select Bibliography on Business Archives & Records Management. 134p. (Orig.). 1981. pap. 9.00 (ISBN 0-931828-30-9). Soc Am Archivists.
Benedict, Lynn. The Fatal Flower. 1973. pap. 0.75 (ISBN 0-380-01177-8, 15909). Avon.
Benedict, M., jt. ed. see Merriman, J. R.
Benedict, M. R. The Agricultural Commodity Programs, Two Decades of Experience. (Twentieth Century Fund Ser.). Repr. of 1956 ed. 10.00 (ISBN 0-527-02815-0). Kraus Repr.
--Can We Solve the Farm Problem? An Analysis of Federal Aid to Agriculture. (Twentieth Century Fund Ser.). Repr. of 1955 ed. 20.00 (ISBN 0-527-02814-2). Kraus Repr.
Benedict, Madeline. That Bridge Again. LC 73-80457. 78p. 1973. 4.00 (ISBN 0-8233-0188-5). Golden Quill.
Benedict, Manson, et al. Nuclear Chemical Engineering. 2nd ed. (Illus.). 1008p. 1981. text ed. 49.00 (ISBN 0-07-004531-3). McGraw.
Benedict, Marion & Benedict, Burton. Men, Women & Money in Seychelles. LC 81-19853. (Illus.). 250p. 1982. 27.50x (ISBN 0-520-04592-0). U of Cal Pr.
Benedict, Michael L. The Impeachment & Trial of Andrew Johnson. (Norton Essays in American History Ser). 224p. 1973. 6.95x (ISBN 0-393-05473-X); pap. text ed. 3.95x (ISBN 0-393-09418-9). Norton.
Benedict, Paul K. Austro-Thai: Language & Culture, with a Glossary of Roots. LC 67-30152. (Monographs). 510p. 1975. 25.00x (ISBN 0-87536-323-7). HRAFP.
--Sino-Tibetan: A Conspectus. LC 78-154511. (Princeton-Cambridge Studies in Chinese Linguistics: No. 2). 1972. 85.00 (ISBN 0-521-08175-0). Cambridge U Pr.
Benedict, Philip. Rouen During the Wars of Religion. LC 79-50883. (Cambridge Studies in Early Modern History). (Illus.). 324p. 1981. 52.50 (ISBN 0-521-22818-2). Cambridge U Pr.
Benedict, R. Ralph. Electronics for Scientists & Engineers. 2nd ed. (Illus.). 1975. 39.95 (ISBN 0-13-252353-1). P-H.
Benedict, Robert P. Fundamentals of Gas Dynamics. LC 83-1273. 272p. 1983. text ed. 37.45 (ISBN 0-471-09193-6); solutions avail. (ISBN 0-471-87340-3). Wiley.
--Fundamentals of Pipe Flow. LC 79-23924. 531p. 1980. cloth 64.50x (ISBN 0-471-03375-8, Pub. by Wiley-Interscience). Wiley.
--Fundamentals of Temperature, Pressure & Flow Measurements. 3rd ed. LC 83-23558. 532p. 1984. 54.50x (ISBN 0-471-89383-8, Pub. by Wiley-Interscience). Wiley.
Benedict, Robert P. & Carlucci, Nicola A. Handbook of Specific Losses in Flow Systems. LC 65-25129. 193p. 1966. 32.50x (ISBN 0-306-65122-X, IFI Plenum). Plenum Pub.
Benedict, Robert P. & Steltz, W. G. Handbook of Generalized Gas Dynamics. LC 65-25128. 243p. 1966. 52.50x (ISBN 0-306-65118-1, IFI Plenum). Plenum Pub.
Benedict, Ruth. An Anthropologist at Work: Writings of Ruth Benedict. Mead, Margaret, ed. LC 77-3017. (Illus.). 1977. Repr. of 1966 ed. lib. bdg. 31.50x (ISBN 0-8371-9576-4, BEAW). Greenwood.
--Chrysanthemum & the Sword: Patterns of Japanese Culture. 1967. pap. 7.95 (ISBN 0-452-00729-1, Mer). NAL.
--Patterns of Culture. 1961. 10.95 (ISBN 0-395-07405-3). HM.
--Race: Science & Politics. 206p. 1982. Repr. of 1950 ed. lib. bdg. 27.50 (ISBN 0-313-23597-X, BENR). Greenwood.
--Tales of the Cochiti Indians. 1976. lib. bdg. 59.95 (ISBN 0-8490-2729-2). Gordon Pr.
--Tales of the Cochiti Indians. Repr. of 1931 ed. 29.00 (ISBN 0-403-03705-0). Scholarly.
--Tales of the Cochiti Indians. LC 80-54563. 256p. 1981. pap. 12.95 (ISBN 0-8263-0569-5). U of NM Pr.
--Zuni Mythology, 2 Vols. LC 75-82366. (Columbia Univ. Contributions to Anthropology Ser.: No. 21). 1969. Repr. of 1935 ed. Set. 70.00 (ISBN 0-404-50571-6); 35.00 ea. AMS Pr.
Benedict, Ruth, ed. Country People. LC 79-63698. (Illus.). 1979. pap. 9.95 (ISBN 0-89821-029-1). Reiman Assocs.
--Grandma, Book II. 64p. 1984. pap. 5.95 (ISBN 0-89821-061-5). Reiman Assocs.
--Grandma, Book 1. 64p. 1982. pap. 5.95 (ISBN 0-89821-045-3). Reiman Assocs.
--Showers. LC 79-65360. (Orig.). 1980. pap. 7.95 (ISBN 0-89821-030-5). Reiman Assocs.
Benedict, Ruth, ed. see Farmer, Val.
Benedict, Ruth F. Concept of the Guardian Spirit in North America. LC 24-872. (American Anthropology Association Memoirs). 1923. 12.00 (ISBN 0-527-00528-2). Kraus Repr.
Benedict, Saint Rule of Saint Benedict. Gasquet, Cardinal, tr. LC 66-30730. (Medieval Library). (Illus.). 130p. 1966. Repr. of 1926 ed. 18.50 (ISBN 0-8154-0022-5). Cooper Sq.
Benedict, Stephen. Cultural Institutions Across America: Functions & Funding. 28p. 1982. pap. 3.00 (ISBN 0-943006-15-5). Seven Springs.
Benedict, Stephen, compiled by. Arts Management: An Annotated Bibliography. rev. ed. LC 80-25918. 48p. 1980. pap. 5.75 (ISBN 0-89062-049-0, Pub. by Ctr for Arts Info). Pub Ctr Cult Res.
Benedict, Steward, ed. The Literary Guide to the U. S. (Illus.). 256p. 1981. 15.95 (ISBN 0-87196-304-3). Facts on File.
Benedict, Stewart. Street Beat. 288p. (Orig.). 1982. pap. 2.75 (ISBN 0-523-41188-X). Pinnacle Bks.
Benedict, William. To Love. 1984. 5.95 (ISBN 0-533-05905-4). Vantage.
Benedictine Sisters of Clyde Missouri. St. Gertrude the Great: Herald of Divine Love. 1977. pap. 0.75 (ISBN 0-89555-026-1). TAN Bks Pubs.
Benedictine Sisters Of Peking Editors. Art of Chinese Cooking. LC 56-11125. (Illus., Orig.). 1956. pap. 5.95 (ISBN 0-8048-0035-9). C E Tuttle.
Benedictines de la Congregation de Saint-Maur. Dictionnaire de l'art de Verifier les Dates. Migne, J. P., ed. (Nouvelle Encyclopedie Theologique Ser.: Vol. 49). 680p. (Fr.). Date not set. Repr. of 1854 ed. lib. bdg. 86.50x (ISBN 0-89241-287-9). Caratzas.
Benedictis, Daniel J. De see De Benedictis, Daniel J.
Benedictus, David. Local Hero. movie tie-in ed. 224p. 1983. pap. 3.50 (ISBN 0-14-006660-8). Penguin.
Benedictus, Edouard. Benedictus' Art Deco Designs in Color. (Illus.). 1980. pap. 6.00 (ISBN 0-486-23971-3). Dover.
Benedictus, Saint Middle High German Translations of the Regula Sancti Benedicti. Selmer, Carl, ed. & intro. by. (Mediaeval Academy of America Publications). 1933. 28.00 (ISBN 0-527-01689-6). Kraus Repr.
Benedikt, E. T., ed. Weightlessness: Physical Phenomena & Biological Effects. special vol ed. 1960. 20.00x (ISBN 0-87703-000-6, Pub. by Am Astronaut). Univelt Inc.
Benedikt, Michael. The Badminton at Great Barrington; Or, Gustave Mahler & the Chattanooga Choo-Choo. LC 80-5258. (Pitt Poetry Ser.). xii, 81p. 1980. 12.95x (ISBN 0-8229-3423-X); pap. 6.95 (ISBN 0-8229-5322-6). U of Pittsburgh Pr.
--The Body. LC 68-27539. (Wesleyan Poetry Program: Vol. 40). 1968. 15.00x (ISBN 0-8195-2040-3); pap. 6.95 (ISBN 0-8195-1040-8). Wesleyan U Pr.
--Mole Notes. LC 78-161695. (Illus.). 1971. 15.00x (ISBN 0-8195-4038-2). Wesleyan U Pr.
--Night Cries. LC 75-32526. (Wesleyan Poetry Program: Vol. 80). 1976. 15.00x (ISBN 0-8195-2080-2); pap. 6.95 (ISBN 0-8195-1080-7). Wesleyan U Pr.
--Sky. LC 75-120257. (Wesleyan Poetry Program: Vol. 52). 1970. 15.00x (ISBN 0-8195-2052-7); pap. 6.95 (ISBN 0-8195-1052-1). Wesleyan U Pr.
Benedikt, Michael, ed. The Poetry of Surrealism: An Anthology. LC 74-8014. 1975. pap. 10.45 (ISBN 0-316-08898-6). Little.
Benedikt, Michael & Wellwarth, George E., eds. Modern French Theatre: The Avant-Garde, Dada & Surrealism. Benedikt, Michael & Wellwarth, George E., trs. 1966. pap. 7.95 (ISBN 0-525-47176-6, 0772-230). Dutton.
Benedikt, Michael, tr. see Benedikt, Michael & Wellwarth, George E.
Benedikt, Moriz. Anatomical Studies upon Brains of Criminals. Fowler, E. P., tr. from Ger. (Historical Foundations of Forensic Psychiatry & Psychology Ser.). (Illus.). 185p. 1980. Repr. of 1881 ed. lib. bdg. 25.00 (ISBN 0-306-76071-1). Da Capo.
Benediktsson, Thomas E. George Sterling. (United States Authors Ser.). 1980. lib. bdg. 14.50 (ISBN 0-8057-7313-4, Twayne). G K Hall.
Benedikz, B. S., ed. On the Novel: A Present for Walter Allen on His 60th Birthday from His Friends & Colleagues. 239p. 1971. 12.50x (ISBN 0-87471-410-9). Rowman.
Benedikz, Benedickt S. Early Printing in Iceland. Clair, Colin, ed. (Spread of Printing Ser.: No. 1). (Illus.). 1969. pap. 9.75 (ISBN 0-8390-0018-9). Abner Schram Ltd.
Benedikz, S., tr. see Blondal, S.
Beneditttis, Suzanne M. De see De Benedittis, Suzanne M.
Benefield, Larry, et al. Treatment Plant Hydraulics for Environmental Engineers. (Illus.). 240p. 1984. 45.00 (ISBN 0-13-930248-4). P-H.
Benefield, Larry D., jt. auth. see Judkins, Joseph F.
Benefield, Larry D., jt. auth. see Randall, Clifford W.
Benegal, Shyam. The Churning (Mantham) cancelled (ISBN 0-8364-1142-0, Pub. by Seagull Bks India). South Asia Bks.
Benegar, John. Teaching Writing Skills: A Global Approach. rev. ed. (Illus.). 189p. (Orig.). (gr. 6-12). 1985. pap. 16.95 (ISBN 0-943804-31-0). U of Denver Teach.
Benegar, John, jt. auth. see Johnson, Jacquelyn.
Benegar, John, et al. Changing Images of China. (Illus.). 271p. (Orig.). 1983. pap. 16.95 (ISBN 0-317-17329-4). U of Denver Teach.
Beneich, Denis, jt. auth. see Breton, Thierry.
Beneke, E. S. & Rogers, A. L. Medical Mycology Manual. 4th ed. 242p. 1980. pap. 19.95x (ISBN 0-8087-4042-3). Burgess.
Beneke, Lynda, ed. A Grand Heritage: A Culinary Legacy of Columbus, Mississippi. (Illus.). 370p. 1983. pap. text ed. 14.95 (ISBN 0-9612048-0-X). Heritage Acad.
Beneke, Raymond R. & Winterboer, Ronald D. Linear Programming Applications to Agriculture. LC 72-2298. (Illus.). 244p. 1973. text ed. 13.95x (ISBN 0-8138-1035-3). Iowa St U Pr.
Beneke, Timothy. Men on Rape: What They Have to Say about Sexual Violence. LC 82-5628. 192p. 1982. 12.95 (ISBN 0-312-52950-3). St Martin.
--Men on Rape: What They Have to Say about Sexual Violence. 192p. 1983. 5.95 (ISBN 0-312-52951-1). St Martin.
Beneken, J. E. & Lavelle, S. M., eds. Objective Medical Decision Making: Systems Approach in Acute Disease. (Lecture Notes in Medical Informatics: Vol. 22). 243p. 1983. pap. 20.00 (ISBN 0-387-12671-6). Springer-Verlag.
Benemann, John R. Biofuels: A Survey. 106p. 1980. pap. 19.95x (ISBN 0-89934-006-7, B045). Solar Energy Info.
Ben, ed. see Washington Group Staff.
Benenfeld, Alan R., ed. see ASIS Annual Meeting, 43rd, 1980.
Benenson, Abram S., ed. Control of Communicable Diseases in Man. 14th ed. 485p. 1985. 9.00x (ISBN 0-87553-130-X). Am Pub Health.
Benenson, F. C. Probability, Objectivity & Evidence. (International Library of Philosophy). 224p. 1984. 35.00x (ISBN 0-7100-9598-8). Routledge & Kegan.
Benenson, Walter, jt. ed. see Nolen, Jerry A.
Benenzon, Rolando O. Music Therapy in Child Psychosis. (Illus.). 112p. 1982. 15.50x (ISBN 0-398-04646-8). C C Thomas.
--Music Therapy Manual. (Illus.). 178p. 1981. 18.75x (ISBN 0-398-04502-X). C C Thomas.
Ben-Ephraim, Gavriel. The Moon's Dominion: Narrative Dichotomy & Female Dominance in the First Five Novels of D. H. Lawrence. LC 78-75172. 256p. 1981. 24.50 (ISBN 0-8386-2266-6). Fairleigh Dickinson.

Bengtson, Hermann. Introduction to Ancient History. Frank, R. I. & Gilliard, Frank D., trs. LC 78-118685. (California Library Reprint Ser.: No. 63). 1976. 32.50x (ISBN 0-520-03150-4). U of Cal Pr.

Bengtson, Melodie N., ed. see Newhouse, Flower A.

Bengtson, Phil & Hunt, Todd. Packer Dynasty. LC 75-78716. 1969. 8.95 (ISBN 0-385-07164-7). Doubleday.

Bengtsson, A. B. Does Education Have a Future? (Plan Europe 2000 Ser: No. 10). 1975. pap. 21.00 (ISBN 90-247-1760-4). Kluwer Academic.

Bengtsson, Bengt A. The Scythrididae (Lepidoptera) of Northern Europe. (Fauna Entomologica Scandinavica Ser.: Vol. 13). (Illus.). 137p. 1984. write for info. (ISBN 90-04-07312-4). E J Brill.

Bengtsson, Gerda. Danish Floral Charted Designs. 1980. pap. 1.75 (ISBN 0-486-23957-8). Dover.

Bengtsson, Hans, jt. auth. see Atkinson, George.

Bengtsson, Ingmar & Van Boer, Bertil H., Jr., eds. The Symphony in Sweden, Pt. 1. (The Symphony 1720-1840 Series F: Vol. II). 1982. lib. bdg. 90.00 (ISBN 0-8240-3811-8). Garland Pub.

Bengtsson, L. & Lighthill, J., eds. Intense Atmospheric Vortices, Reading UK 1981 Proceedings. (Topics in Atmospheric & Oceanographic Sciences Ser.). (Illus.). 360p. 1982. pap. 29.00 (ISBN 0-387-11657-5). Springer-Verlag.

Ben-Gurion, David. Ben-Gurion Looks at the Bible. Kolatch, Jonathan, tr. LC 70-167600. 320p. 1972. 12.50 (ISBN 0-8246-0127-0). Jonathan David.

--My Talks with Arab Leaders. LC 72-94298. 342p. 1973. 11.95 (ISBN 0-89388-076-0). Okpaku Communications.

Ben-Gurion, David, ed. The Jews in Their Land. LC 66-11274. 405p. 1974. 9.95 (ISBN 0-385-06152-8). Doubleday.

Benhabib, Seyla. Critique, Norm, & Utopia: A Study of the Foundations of Critical Theory. 424p. 1985. 35.00x (ISBN 0-231-06164-1). Columbia U Pr.

Ben-Haim, Yakov. The Assay of Spacially Random Materials. 1985. lib. bdg. 44.00 (ISBN 90-277-2066-5, Pub. by Reidel Holland). Kluwer Academic.

Benham, Allen R. English Literature from Widsith to Death of Chaucer. LC 68-15693. 1967. Repr. of 1916 ed. 17.50x (ISBN 0-87753-005-X). Phaeton.

--English Literature from Widsith to the Death of Chaucer: A Source Book. facsimile ed. LC 73-114903. (Select Bibliographies Reprint Ser). 1916. 32.00 (ISBN 0-8369-5307-X). Ayer Co Pubs.

Benham, Arliss R. The Long Way Back: How One Woman Learned to Live with Divorce. (Direction Bks.). 1982. pap. 2.45 (ISBN 0-8010-0815-8). Baker Bk.

Benham, Benjamin A. Clio & Mr. Croce. LC 74-9707. 1928. lib. bdg. 10.00 (ISBN 0-8414-3117-5). Folcroft.

Benham, George C. A Year of Wreck. facsimile ed. LC 75-38639. (Black Heritage Library Collection). Repr. of 1880 ed. 26.00 (ISBN 0-8369-8997-X). Ayer Co Pubs.

Benham, Harvey. Man's Struggle for Food. LC 80-67188. (Illus.). 506p. 1981. lib. bdg. 33.25 (ISBN 0-8191-1518-5); pap. text ed. 19.75 (ISBN 0-8191-1519-3). U Pr of Amer.

--The Salvagers. (Illus.). 212p. 1980. 10.50 (ISBN 0-9505944-2-3, Pub. by Boydell & Brewer). Longwood Pub Group.

Benham, Hervey. The Codbangers. 35.00x (ISBN 0-9505944-1-5, Pub. by Essex County England). State Mutual Bk.

--The Codbangers. (Illus.). 207p. 1979. 10.50 (ISBN 0-9505944-1-5, Pub. by Boydell & Brewer). Longwood Pub Group.

--The Stowboaters. 1981. 25.00x (ISBN 0-686-79166-5, Pub. by Essex County England). State Mutual Bk.

--The Stowboaters. (Illus.). 49p. 1977. 7.50 (ISBN 0-9505944-0-7, Pub. by Boydell & Brewer). Longwood Pub Group.

Benham, Hugh. Latin Church Music in England, Fourteen Sixty to Fifteen Seventy-Five. (Music Reprint Ser.: 1980). (Illus.). 1980. Repr. of 1977 ed. lib. bdg. 29.50 (ISBN 0-306-76025-8). Da Capo.

Benham, Jack & Benham, Sarah, eds. Rocky Mountains Receipts Remedies. Rev. ed. (Illus.). 60p. (Orig.). 1966. pap. text ed. 2.50 (ISBN 0-941026-08-6). Bear Creek Pub.

Benham, Jack L. Camp Bird & the Revenue. (Illus.). 68p. (Orig.). 1979. pap. 3.50 (ISBN 0-941026-04-3). Bear Creek Pub.

--Ouray. (Illus.). 64p. (Orig.). 1976. pap. 3.50 (ISBN 0-941026-01-9). Bear Creek Pub.

--Silverton. rev. ed. (Illus.). 64p. (Orig.). 1981. pap. 3.50 (ISBN 0-941026-02-7). Bear Creek Pub.

Benham, Jack L., ed. see Jackson, William H. & Holmes, William H.

Benham, Jack L., ed. see McLean, Evalyn W. & Sparkes, Boyden.

Benham, Jack L., ed. see Rice, Frank A.

Benham, Jack L., ed. see Rickard, T. A.

Benham, Phyllis S. Woodstove Cookery. (Soups, Stews & Chowders & Homemade Breads Ser.: Vol. 2). 52p. (Orig.). 1982. pap. 3.95 (ISBN 0-940750-01-5). Country Cooking.

--Woodstove Cookery Cookbook: Soups, Stews, Chowders & Home-Made Breads, Vol. 2. 54p. 1981. pap. 3.95 (ISBN 0-686-81745-1). Country Cooking.

--Woodstove Cookery Cookbook: Volume L, Main Dishes. 44p. 1981. pap. 3.95 (ISBN 0-940750-00-7). Country Cooking.

Benham, Sarah, jt. ed. see Benham, Jack.

Benharbit, Abdelali, jt. auth. see Al-Moajil, Abdullah H.

Benhart, John. The Encyclopedia of Pennsylvania. LC 82-19306. (The Encyclopedia of the U. S. Ser.). (Illus.). 764p. 1984. Repr. 79.00x (ISBN 0-403-09977-3). Somerset Pub.

Benhart-Scull. Regions of the World Today. 256p. 1985. pap. text ed. 23.95 (ISBN 0-8403-3599-7). Kendall Hunt.

Benhazera, Maurice. Six mois chez les Touareg du Ahaggar. LC 77-87619. (Illus.). Repr. of 1908 ed. 22.50 (ISBN 0-404-16446-3). AMS Pr.

Ben-Horim, Moshe & Levy, Haim. Statistics: Decisions & Applications in Business & Economics. 2nd ed. Donnelly, Paul, ed. (Random House Business Division Ser.). 700p. 1984. text ed. 28.95 (ISBN 0-394-33587-2, RanC); write for info. tchr's. ed. Random.

Ben-Horin, Moshe & Levy, Haim. Business Statistics: Fundamentals & Applications. Donnelly, Paul, ed. LC 82-15060. (Random House Business Division Ser.). 564p. 1983. text ed. 28.00 (ISBN 0-394-33022-6, RanC). Random.

Ben Hurin, Meir, jt. auth. see Duker, Abraham G.

Beni, G., jt. auth. see Hackwood, S.

Beni, Ruth. Sir Baldergog the Great. (Illus.). 32p. (gr. 1-3). 1985. 10.95 (ISBN 0-233-97628-0). Andre Deutsch.

Benians, Sylvia. From Renaissance to Revolution. LC 74-110895. 1970. Repr. of 1923 ed. 16.50x (ISBN 0-8046-0878-4, Pub. by Kennikat). Assoc Faculty Pr.

Benice, Daniel. Arithmetic & Algebra. 3rd ed. (Illus.). 464p. 1985. pap. text ed. 26.95 (ISBN 0-13-046111-3). P-H.

Benice, Daniel D. Finite Mathematics with Algebra. (Illus.). 1982. Repr. of 1975 ed. text ed. 19.50x (ISBN 0-8290-0632-X). Irvington.

--Introduction to Computers & Data Processing. (Applied Mathematics Ser). 1970. ref. ed. 21.95 (ISBN 0-13-479543-1). P-H.

--Mathematics: Ideas & Applications. 1978. 19.25i (ISBN 0-12-088250-7); instrs'. ed. 2.50i (ISBN 0-12-088252-3). Acad Pr.

--Precalculus Mathematics. 2nd ed. (Illus.). 512p. 1982. text ed. 29.95 (ISBN 0-13-694976-2). P-H.

--Precalculus Mathematics. 3rd ed. (Illus.). 544p. 1986. pap. text ed. 29.95 (ISBN 0-13-695503-7). P-H.

Benichou, Paul, ed. see Hugo, Victor.

Benidt, Bruce W. The Library Book: Centennial History of the Minneapolis Public Library. (Illus.). 256p. 1984. 19.95 (ISBN 0-9613716-0-9). MPLS Publ Lib.

Beniger, James R. Trafficking in Drug Users: Professional Exchange Networks in the Control of Deviance. LC 83-5251. (ASA Rose Monograph). 224p. 1984. 34.50 (ISBN 0-521-25753-0); pap. 12.95 (ISBN 0-521-27680-2). Cambridge U Pr.

Beningfield, Gordon, illus. Hardy Country. Zeman, Anthea. (Illus.). 25.00 (ISBN 0-7139-1451-3). Allen Lane.

Benington, George, ed. An Abridged Field Guide to the Maine Writer. 36p. (Orig.). 1984. pap. 2.95 (ISBN 0-913341-04-5). Coyote Love.

Benirschke, K., jt. auth. see Hsu, T. C.

Benirschke, K, jt. auth. see Hsu, T. C.

Benirschke, K., jt. auth. see Hsu, T. C.

Benirschke, K. & Hsu, T. C., eds. Chromosome Atlas: Fish, Amphibians, Reptiles & Birds, Vol. 1. LC 73-166079. (Illus.). 225p. 1972. loose leaf 25.00 (ISBN 0-387-05507-X). Springer-Verlag.

Benirschke, K., ed. see International Conference on Comparative Aspects of Reproductive Failure - Dartmouth - 1966.

Benirschke, K., ed. see International Conference on Comparative Mammalian Cytogenetics, Dartmouth Medical School, 1968.

Benirschke, K., et al, eds. Pathology of Laboratory Animals, 2 vols. (Illus.). 1978. Set. 360.00 (ISBN 0-387-90292-9). Springer-Verlag.

Benirshke, Max. Color Source Book of Authentic Art Nouveau Designs: 146 Motifs. (Illus.). 32p. 1984. pap. 4.00 (ISBN 0-486-24547-0). Dover.

Benis, A. M. Toward Self & Sanity: On the Genetic Origins of the Human Character. LC 84-26313. 528p. 1985. 39.95 (ISBN 0-88437-074-7). Psych Dimensions.

Benis, Martin, jt. auth. see Carmichael, D. R.

Benisch, Liselotte. Frag mich - ich antworte dreitausend dreihundertmal. 176p. (Ger.). pap. 2.95 (ISBN 3-581-66023-7). Langenscheidt.

Ben-Israel, Adi, et al. Optimality in Nonlinear Programming: A Feasible Directions Approach. LC 80-36746. (Pure & Applied Mathematics Ser.). 144p. 1981. cloth 37.50 (ISBN 0-471-08057-8, Pub. by Wiley-Interscience). Wiley.

Ben-Israel, Manasseh. The Conciliator: A Reconcilement of the Apparent Contradictions in Holy Scripture. Lindo, E. H., tr. from Span. LC 72-83942. (The Library of Judaic Studies: No. SHP 10). 688p. 1985. pap. 15.95 (ISBN 0-87203-115-2). Hermon.

Benisten, Ellen. Medical & Health Annual, 1984. 448p. 1983. write for info. Ency Brit Inc.

Benites, Frank G., jt. auth. see Young, Carlota B.

Benitez, Ana M. De see De Benitez, Ana M.

Benitez, Fernando. The Poisoned Water. Ellsworth, Mary E., tr. from Span. LC 74-184549. (Contemporary Latin American Classics Ser.). 160p. 1973. 8.95x (ISBN 0-8093-0634-4). S Ill U Pr.

Benitez, Jaime. Junto a la Torre. 5.00 (ISBN 0-8477-2404-2); pap. 2.50 (ISBN 0-8477-2405-0). U of PR Pr.

Benitez, Jesus, tr. see Farr, Kenneth R.

Benitez, Jesus, tr. see Senior, Clarence.

Benitez, Jose G. Anthology of the Poetry of Jose Gautier Benitez. (Puerto Rico Ser.). 1979. lib. bdg. 75.00 (ISBN 0-8490-2865-5). Gordon Pr.

Benitez, William. Housing Rehabilitation: A Guidebook for Municipal Programs. 165p. 1976. 9.00 (ISBN 0-318-14949-4, N580); members 7.00 (ISBN 0-318-14950-8). NAHRO.

Benitez, Zuleyka. Trouble in Paradise. LC 78-17909. (Lost Roads Ser.: No. 19). (Illus.). 56p. (Orig.). 1980. pap. 9.00 (ISBN 0-918786-20-7). Lost Roads.

Benitez de Avila, Crucita, jt. auth. see Diaz Zayas, Carmen E.

Benito Bacho, Jose. Diccionario de la Construccion y Obras Publicas Ingles-Espanol, 2 vols. 268p. (Span. & Eng.). 1975. Set. 38.95 (ISBN 84-85198-10-7, S-50117). French & Eur.

--Diccionario de la Construccion y Obras Publicas, Tomo 2: Span. 110p. (Span.). 1975. 18.95 (ISBN 84-85198-09-3, S-50119). French & Eur.

--Diccionario de la Construcion y de Obras Publicas, Tomo I: Ingles. 168p. (Span.). 1975. 18.95 (ISBN 84-85198-00-X, S-50118). French & Eur.

Benitz, W. G. & Tatro. The Pediatric Drug Handbook. 1981. 16.95 (ISBN 0-8151-0663-7). Year Bk Med.

Benivieni, Antonio. The Hidden Causes of Disease. Singer, Charles, tr. Orig. Title: De Abditis Nunnulis Ac Mirandis Morborum et Sanationum Causis. (Illus.). 272p. 1954. 26.50x (ISBN 0-398-01767-0). C C Thomas.

Benjamin. The Father Who Dwelleth Within. 1979. pap. 2.50 (ISBN 0-87516-293-2). De Vorss.

Benjamin, A. & Hackstaff, L. H. On Free Choice of the Will: Augustine. 1964. pap. text ed. write for info. (ISBN 0-02-308030-2). Macmillan.

Benjamin, A. Corne. Science, Technology & Human Values. LC 65-10698. 306p. 1965. 22.00x (ISBN 0-8262-0035-4). U of Mo Pr.

Benjamin, A. S., tr. see Augustine, Saint.

Benjamin, Alan. A Treasury of Baby Names. 1983. pap. 2.95 (ISBN 0-451-13356-0, Sig). NAL.

Benjamin, Alfred. Behavior in Small Groups. LC 77-73213. 1978. pap. text ed. 11.50 (ISBN 0-395-25447-7). HM.

Benjamin, Alfred D. The Helping Interview. 3rd ed. LC 80-81650. 208p. 1981. pap. text ed. 12.95 (ISBN 0-395-29648-X). HM.

Benjamin, Alice & Corrigan, Harriett. Cooking with Conscience: A Book for People Concerned about World Hungar. 1977. pap. 4.95 (ISBN 0-8164-0902-1, Pub. by Seabury). Winston Pr.

Benjamin, Anna, tr. see Xenophon.

Benjamin, Anne. Kidney Failure: Our Success Story. 150p. 1984. 7.50x (ISBN 0-86516-050-3). Bolchazy-Carducci.

Benjamin, Anne, ed. see Mandela, Winnie.

Benjamin, Arnold. Lost Johannesburg. (Illus.). 102p. 1982. 17.50 (ISBN 0-86954-080-7, Pub. by Macmillan S Africa). Intl Spec Bk.

Benjamin, Asher. The American Builder's Companion. 6th ed. (Illus., New intro. by William Morgan). Repr. of 1827 ed. 15.25 (ISBN 0-8446-1626-5). Peter Smith.

--American Builder's Companion: Or, a System of Architecture, Particularly Adapted to the Present Style of Building. (Illus.). 1969. pap. 6.95 (ISBN 0-486-22236-5). Dover.

--The Practical House Carpenter. 119p. Repr. of 1830 ed. 39.00 (ISBN 0-318-04471-4). Am Repr Serv.

--The Practical House Carpenter: Being a Complete Development of the Grecian Orders of Architecture. 1976. Repr. of 1830 ed. 49.00x (ISBN 0-403-06633-6, Regency). Scholarly.

--The Works of Asher Benjamin: Boston, 1806-1843, 7 vols. Incl. The Country Builder's Assistant: 1797. 84p. 42.50 (ISBN 0-306-71027-7); The American Builder's Companion: 1806. 158p. 42.50 (ISBN 0-306-71026-9); The Rudiments of Architecture: 1814. 162p. 42.50 (ISBN 0-306-71031-5); The Practical House Carpenter: 1830. 248p. 42.50 (ISBN 0-306-71029-3); The Practice of Architecture: 1833. 236p. 42.50 (ISBN 0-306-71030-7); The Builder's Guide: 1839. 174p. 45.00 (ISBN 0-306-70971-6); Elements of Architecture: 1843. 290p. 45.00 (ISBN 0-306-71028-5). (Architecture & Decorative Art Ser.). 1974. Set. 265.00 (ISBN 0-306-71032-3). Da Capo.

Benjamin, B. & Pollard, J. H. Analysis of Mortality & Other Actuarial Statistics. 212p. 1980. 31.50 (ISBN 0-434-90137-7, Pub. by W. Heinemann Ltd). David & Charles.

Benjamin, B. S. Structural Design with Plastics. 2nd ed. 416p. 1981. 34.50 (ISBN 0-442-20167-2). Van Nos Reinhold.

--Structures for Architects. 2nd ed. 1984. 37.50 (ISBN 0-442-21190-2). Van Nos Reinhold.

Benjamin, Ben & Borden, Gale. Listen to Your Pain. LC 82-20066. (Illus.). 288p. 1983. 17.95 (ISBN 0-670-43017-X, Dist. by Penguin). Viking.

--Listen to Your Pain: The Active Person's Guide to Understanding. LC 82-20066. (Illus.). 1984. pap. 9.95 (ISBN 0-14-006687-X). Penguin.

Benjamin, Ben A. Let's Talk Hebrew. 1961. 4.00 (ISBN 0-914080-01-6). Shulsinger Sales.

Benjamin, Ben E. Are You Tense? The Benjamin System of Muscular Therapy. LC 77-88778. 1978. pap. 8.95 (ISBN 0-394-73499-8). Pantheon.

Benjamin, Bernard. General Insurance. 1977. 18.95 (ISBN 0-434-90136-9, Pub. by W Heinemann Ltd). David & Charles.

--Social & Economic Factors Affecting Mortality Confluence. 1965. text ed. 5.20x (ISBN 0-686-22460-4). Mouton.

Benjamin, Bruce. Atlas of Paediatric Endoscopy: Upper Respiratory Tract & Oesophagus. (Illus.). 1981. text ed. 47.50x (ISBN 0-19-261179-8). Oxford U Pr.

Benjamin, Carol. Cartooning for Kids. LC 81-43876. (Illus.). 80p. (gr. 3-7). 1982. pap. 3.80i (ISBN 0-690-04207-8); PLB 10.89 (ISBN 0-690-04208-6). Crowell Jr Bks.

--The Rib Section. LC 81-80615. (Orig.). 1981. pap. 4.95 (ISBN 0-88270-498-2, Pub. by Logos). Bridge Pub.

--So You're Getting Married! 1982. pap. 3.95 (ISBN 0-911739-15-7). Abbott Loop.

Benjamin, Carol L. Dog Problems. LC 80-1082. 192p. 1981. 11.95 (ISBN 0-385-15710-X). Doubleday.

--Dog Training for Kids. LC 76-14019. (Illus.). 96p. (gr. 8-12). 1985. 9.95 (ISBN 0-87605-516-1). Howell Bk.

--Mother Knows Best: The Natural Way to Train Your Dog. LC 84-27871. (Illus.). 256p. 1985. 14.95 (ISBN 0-87605-666-4). Howell Bk.

--Nobody's Baby Now. LC 83-18714. 168p. (gr. 7 up). 1984. 10.95 (ISBN 0-02-708850-2). Macmillan.

--Nobody's Baby Now. 160p. 1985. pap. 2.25 (ISBN 0-425-08415-9, Pub. by Berkley-Pacer). Berkley Pub.

--Writing for Kids. LC 85-47542. (Illus.). 80p. (gr. 3-7). 1985. PLB 10.89g (ISBN 0-690-04490-9). Crowell Jr Bks.

--Writing for Kids. LC 85-42831. (Trophy Nonfiction Bk.). (Illus.). 96p. (gr. 3-7). 1985. pap. 3.80i (ISBN 0-06-446012-6, Trophy). HarpJ.

Benjamin, Carol L., jt. auth. see Haggerty, Arthur J.

Benjamin, Carole L. The Wicked Stepdog. LC 81-43322. (Illus.). 128p. (gr. 3-7). 1982. 10.53i (ISBN 0-690-04170-5); PLB 10.89 (ISBN 0-690-04171-3). Crowell Jr Bks.

Benjamin-Clarke Associates, Inc. Fire Deaths - Causes & Strategies for Control. LC 84-51634. 77p. 1984. pap. 20.00 (ISBN 0-87762-370-8). Technomic.

Benjamin, Claude. Medical Itch. (Illus.). 1964. 9.95 (ISBN 0-8392-1067-1). Astor-Honor.

Benjamin, Curtis G. A Candid Critique of Book Publishing. 187p. 1977. 16.50 (ISBN 0-8352-1033-2). Bowker.

Benjamin, David A. Competitive Tennis: A Parent's & Young Players Guide. 1979. 12.45i (ISBN 0-397-01326-4). Har-Row.

Benjamin, Deborah V. A Road Map to Effective Planning & Time Management. rev. ed. 215p. 1982. pap. write for info. (ISBN 0-911347-00-3). Debron.

Benjamin, Dick. Abortion Is Murder. 1980. pap. 1.75 (ISBN 0-911739-04-1). Abbott Loop.

--Finding Your Place in the Body of Christ. 1980. pap. text ed. 3.95 (ISBN 0-911739-07-6). Abbott Loop.

--Pleading the Case of the Fatherless. 1982. pap. 0.95 (ISBN 0-911739-09-2). Abbott Loop.

--Should I Tithe? 1977. pap. 1.75 (ISBN 0-911739-11-4). Abbott Loop.

--Women's Ministries in the New Testament Church. 1983. pap. 1.75 (ISBN 0-911739-16-5). Abbott Loop.

Benjamin, Dick & Richardson, Jim. Remember the Poor. 1982. pap. 1.75 (ISBN 0-911739-26-2). Abbott Loop.

Benjamin, Don C. Deuteronomy & City Life: A Form Criticism of Texts with the Word City ('ir) in Deuteronomy 4: 41 -26: 19. LC 83-3609. (Illus.). 366p. (Orig.). 1983. lib. bdg. 28.25 (ISBN 0-8191-3138-5); pap. text ed. 15.50 (ISBN 0-8191-3139-3). U Pr of Amer.

Benjamin, Don-Paul. Downhill. (Illus.). 1979. pap. 5.00 (ISBN 0-932624-01-4). Elevation Pr.

--When You Live Alone: More Things Dedicated Singles Do. (Illus., Orig.). 1983. pap. 3.75 (ISBN 0-932624-06-5). Elevation Pr.

--When You Live Alone: Things Dedicated Singles Do. (Illus.). 1979. pap. 3.75 (ISBN 0-932624-00-6). Elevation Pr.

Benjamin, Elsie. Man at Home in the Universe: A Study of the Great Evolutionary Cycle: the "Globes", the "Rounds", "Races", "Root-Races" & "Sub-Races". (Study Ser.: No. 8). 36p. 1981. pap. 3.00 (ISBN 0-913004-43-X). Point Loma Pub.

--Search & Find: Theosophical Reference Index. Small, W. Emmett & Todd, Helen, eds. (Study Ser.: No. 1). 1978. pap. 5.95 (ISBN 0-913004-32-4). Point Loma Pub.

--The Stanzas of Dzyan: Notes for Study on Cosmogenesis & Anthropogenesis. (Study Ser.: No. 5). 45p. 1981. pap. 3.00 (ISBN 0-913004-40-5). Point Loma Pub.

--A Study of the Whole of Man: The Significance of the Seven Principles of Man & The Significance of the Monad. (Study Ser.: No. 6). 41p. 1981. pap. 3.00 (ISBN 0-913004-41-3). Point Loma Pub.

Benjamin, Francis S., Jr. & Toomer, G. J., eds. Campanus of Novara & Medieval Planetary Theory: "Theorica planetarum". (Medieval Science Ser: No. 16). (Illus.). 508p. 1971. 40.00 (ISBN 0-299-05960-X). U of Wis Pr.

Benjamin, Franklin. The Autobiography & Other Writings. Shaw, Peter, ed. (Bantam Classics Ser.). 304p. (gr. 9-12). 1982. pap. 2.50 (ISBN 0-553-21075-0). Bantam.

Benjamin, Fred & Kaplan, Dorothea. Settle Yourself. LC 85-71295. (Illus.). 104p. 1985. pap. 9.95 (ISBN 0-933893-01-9). Bonus Books.

Benjamin, Fred B. Alcohol, Drugs, & Traffic Safety: Where Do We Go from Here? (Illus.). 96p. 1980. 14.75x (ISBN 0-398-04046-X). C C Thomas.

Benjamin, Gerald, jt. auth. see Connery, Robert H.

Benjamin, Gerald, ed. The Communications Revolution in Politics, No. 4. LC 82-72550. (Proceedings of the Academy of Political Science: Vol. 34). 1982. 6.95 (ISBN 0-318-01789-X). Acad Poli Sci.

Benjamin, Guy. More Tales for Me & My Beloved Virgin. 1983. 6.50 (ISBN 0-8062-2115-1). Carlton.

Benjamin, H. Basic Self Knowledge. 1972. pap. 5.95 (ISBN 0-87728-162-9). Weiser.

Benjamin, Harry. Better Sight Without Glasses. 1980. pap. 6.95x (ISBN 0-317-07331-1, Regent House). B of A.

--Common Sense Vegetarianism. 1980. pap. 4.95x (ISBN 0-317-07330-3, Regent House). B of A.

--Everybody's Guide to Nature Cure. 1982. pap. 11.95 (ISBN 0-7225-0703-8). Newcastle Pub.

--Everyone's Guide to Theosophy. 1969. 8.50 (ISBN 0-8356-5079-0). Theos Pub Hse.

Benjamin, Henri, jt. auth. see De Rebecque, Constant.

Benjamin, Israel. Three Years in America: 1859-1862, 2 vols. in 1. facsimile ed. Reznikoff, Charles, tr. from Ger. LC 74-27962. (Modern Jewish Experience Ser.). (Eng.). 1975. Repr. of 1956 ed. 52.00x (ISBN 0-405-06693-7). Ayer Co Pubs.

Benjamin, Jacob. Sing Me a Love Song. (Orig.). 1980. pap. 1.75 (ISBN 0-532-23173-2). Woodhill.

--Thunder in the Earth. (Orig.). 1979. pap. 2.25 (ISBN 0-532-23169-4). Woodhill.

Benjamin, James J. & Kratchman, Stanley H. Practice Problem Two, for Use with Intermediate Accounting. (Illus.). 60p. (Orig.). 1981. pap. text ed. 5.95 (ISBN 0-931920-17-5). Dame Pubns.

Benjamin, James J., et al. Financial Accounting. 5th ed. LC 83-70548. (Illus.). 737p. 1980. pap. text ed. 24.95 (ISBN 0-931920-89-2); practice problems 5.95x (ISBN 0-931920-51-5); study guide 8.95x (ISBN 0-686-70442-8); work papers 8.95x (ISBN 0-931920-52-3). Dame Pubns.

--Principles of Accounting. 3rd ed. LC 80-67313. 1100p. 1985. text ed. 27.95x (ISBN 0-931920-24-8); study guide 8.95 (ISBN 0-931920-56-6); working papers o.p. 7.95 (ISBN 0-686-68563-6); practice problem o.p. 4.95 (ISBN 0-686-68564-4). Dame Pubns.

Benjamin, James M. Successful School Board Service. LC 85-60672. 103p. 1985. write for info. (ISBN 0-914607-05-7). Master Tchr.

--Successful School Board Services. LC 85-60672. 103p. 1985. pap. write for info. (ISBN 0-914607-22-7). Master Tchr.

Benjamin, James M., jt. auth. see DeBruyn, Robert L.

Benjamin, Janice Y., jt. auth. see Vinitsky, Barbara B.

Benjamin, Jean K., jt. auth. see Roethel, Hans K.

Benjamin, Jules R. A Student's Guide to History. 3rd ed. LC 82-60464. 175p. 1983. pap. text ed. 7.95 (ISBN 0-312-77003-0). St Martin.

--The United States & Cuba: Hegemony & Dependent Development, 1880-1934. LC 77-74550. (Pitt Latin American Ser.). 1977. 23.95x (ISBN 0-8229-3347-0). U of Pittsburgh Pr.

Benjamin, Laura. Le Chemin de L'Inca. (Collection Colombine). 192p. 1983. pap. 1.95 (ISBN 0-373-48060-1). Harlequin Bks.

Benjamin, Lewis S. More Stage Favorites of the Eighteenth Century. facs. ed. (Essay Index Reprint Ser). 1929. 17.00 (ISBN 0-8369-0194-0). Ayer Co Pubs.

--South Sea Bubble. (Illus.). 1967. Repr. of 1921 ed. 21.00 (ISBN 0-8337-0225-4). B Franklin.

--Stage Favorites of the Eighteenth Century. facs. ed. LC 68-57303. (Essay Index Reprint Ser). 1928. 18.00 (ISBN 0-8369-0060-X). Ayer Co Pubs.

--William Makepeace Thackeray: A Biography Including Hitherto Uncollected Letters & Speeches & a Bibliography of 1300 Items, 2 Vols. LC 15-5841. 1968. Repr. of 1910 ed. Set. 59.00x (ISBN 0-403-00112-9). Scholarly.

Benjamin, Lewis S. & Hargreaves, Reginald, eds. Great German Short Stories. facsimile ed. LC 72-169540. (Short Story Index Reprint Ser.). Repr. of 1929 ed. 46.50 (ISBN 0-8369-4001-6). Ayer Co Pubs.

Benjamin, Libby, jt. auth. see Walz, Garry R.

Benjamin, Libby, ed. see Arends, Richard I. & Arends, Jane H.

Benjamin, Libby, ed. see Bennett, Lawrence A.

Benjamin, Libby, ed. see Jones, Brian, et al.

Benjamin, Libby, ed. see Lamb, Jackie & Lamb, Wesley.

Benjamin, Libby, ed. see Meerbach, John C.

Benjamin, Libby, ed. see Mehrabian, Albert.

Benjamin, Libby, ed. see Sinick, Daniel.

Benjamin, Linda. Ecstasy's Fury. 1983. pap. 3.50 (ISBN 0-8217-1126-1). Zebra.

--Midnight Desire. 1985. pap. 3.50 (ISBN 0-8217-1573-9). Zebra.

Benjamin, Ludy T. & Lowman, Kathleen D., eds. Activities Handbook for the Teaching of Psychology. LC 81-1648. 244p. (Orig.). 1981. pap. 13.00 (ISBN 0-912704-34-9). Am Psychol.

Benjamin, Ludy T., et al, eds. Handbook for Teaching Introductory Psychology. 272p. 1985. pap. 14.95 (ISBN 0-89859-561-4). L Erlbaum Assocs.

Benjamin, Ludy T., Jr. & Warwick, Robert J. Introduction to Psychology: Selected Readings. 93p. 1971. pap. text ed. 5.95x (ISBN 0-8422-0152-1). Irvington.

Benjamin, Martin & Curtis, Joy. Ethics in Nursing. 1981. text ed. 17.95x (ISBN 0-19-502836-8); pap. text ed. 10.95x (ISBN 0-19-502837-6). Oxford U Pr.

Benjamin, Maxine. Outline of Veterinary Clinical Pathology. 3rd ed. (Illus.). 352p. 1978. 18.50x (ISBN 0-8138-1230-5). Iowa St U Pr.

Benjamin, Medea, et al. No Free Lunch: Food & Revolution in Cuba Today. (Orig.). 1984. pap. 7.95 (ISBN 0-935028-18-8). Inst Food & Develop.

Benjamin, Park. A History of Electricity. LC 74-26249. (History, Philosophy & Sociology of Science Ser). 1975. Repr. 42.00x (ISBN 0-405-06579-5). Ayer Co Pubs.

--Poems of Park Benjamin. LC 70-160914. (Biography Index Reprint Ser). Repr. of 1948 ed. 21.00 (ISBN 0-8369-8077-8). Ayer Co Pubs.

Benjamin, Paul. Squeeze Play. 200p. (Orig.). 1982. 10.95 (ISBN 0-938764-03-9); pap. 5.95 (ISBN 0-938764-04-7). Alpha-Omega Bks.

--Squeeze Play. 208p. 1984. pap. 2.50 (ISBN 0-380-67686-9, 67686). Avon.

Benjamin, Philip S. The Philadelphia Quakers in the Industrial Age, 1865-1920. LC 75-22967. 309p. 1976. 19.95 (ISBN 0-87722-086-7). Temple U Pr.

Benjamin, Phyllis, jt. ed. see Lockwood, Lewis.

Benjamin, Ranana. Origami for Everyone. 120p. 1983. soft cover 10.00 (ISBN 0-89345-950-X, Biograf Pubns). Garber Comm.

Benjamin, Rene. Balzac. 1973. Repr. of 1927 ed. 17.50 (ISBN 0-8274-0709-2). R West.

--Balzac: La Prodigieuse Vie D'Honore De Balzac. 1929. 30.00 (ISBN 0-932062-14-8). Sharon Hill.

Benjamin, Richard K. Introduction & Supplement to Thaxter's Contribution Towards a Monograph of the Laboulbeniacea. 1971. 11.20 (ISBN 3-7682-0708-0). Lubrecht & Cramer.

--The Merosporangiferous Mucorales. (Bibl. Myco.). (Illus.). 1967. Repr. of 1965 ed. 21.00 (ISBN 3-7682-0514-2). Lubrecht & Cramer.

Benjamin, Rick & Richardson, Jim. God Is Greater. 1983. pap. 1.75 (ISBN 0-911739-00-9). Abbott Loop.

Benjamin, Robert. Administrative Adjudication in the State of New York, 6 Vols. LC 42-36978. 1966. Repr. of 1942 ed. lib. bdg. 150.00 (ISBN 0-930342-87-9). W S Hein.

--Making Schools Work: A Reporter's Journey Through Some of America's Most Remarkable Classrooms. 208p. 1981. 12.95 (ISBN 0-8264-0040-X). Continuum.

Benjamin, Robert C. & Kemppainen, Rudolph C. Hospital Administrator's Desk Book. 270p. 1983. 49.95x (ISBN 0-13-394890-0, Busn). P-H.

Benjamin, Robert L. Semantics & Language Analysis. 128p. 1970. pap. text ed. 7.95x (ISBN 0-8290-0330-4). Irvington.

Benjamin, Robert S., ed I Am an American, by Famous Naturalized Americans. facsimile ed. LC 74-104995. (Essay Index Reprint Ser.). 1941. 17.00 (ISBN 0-8369-1449-X). Ayer Co Pubs.

Benjamin, Roger. The Limits of Politics: Collective Goods & Political Change in Post-Industrial Societies. LC 79-19473. (Illus.). 1980. lib. bdg. 15.00x (ISBN 0-226-04233-2). U of Chicago Pr.

--The Limits of Politics: Collective Goods & Political Change in Post-Industrial Societies. LC 79-19473. 148p. 1982. pap. text ed. 5.00x (ISBN 0-226-04234-0). U of Chicago Pr.

Benjamin, Roger & Ori, Kan. Tradition & Change in Postindustrial Japan: The Roles of the Political Parties. LC 80-28559. 192p. 1981. 36.95 (ISBN 0-03-059138-4). Praeger.

Benjamin, Roger & Elkin, Stephen L., eds. The Democratic State. LC 84-21963. (Studies in Government & Public Policy). (Illus.). 356p. 1985. 29.95x (ISBN 0-7006-0262-3). U Pr of KS.

Benjamin, Roger & Kudrle, Robert T., eds. The Industrial Future of the Pacific Basin. (Pacific Basin Project: No. 2). 336p. 1984. lib. bdg. 29.50x (ISBN 0-86531-685-6). Westview.

Benjamin, Ruth. Naked at Forty. 106p. 1984. 10.95 (ISBN 0-8180-0640-4). Horizon.

Benjamin, S. G. Art in America: A Critical & Historical Sketch. Weinberg, H. Barbara, ed. LC 75-28872. (Art Experience in Late 19th Century America Ser.: Vol. 8). (Illus.). 1976. Repr. of 1880 ed. lib. bdg. 70.00 (ISBN 0-8240-2232-7). Garland Pub.

--Contemporary Art in Europe. Weinberg, H. Barbara, ed. LC 75-28868. (Art Experiences in Late 19th Century America Ser.: Vol. 4). (Illus.). 1976. Repr. of 1877 ed. lib. bdg. 73.00 (ISBN 0-8240-2228-9). Garland Pub.

--Our American Artists: With Portraits, Studios & Engravings of Paintings, Repr. Of 1879 Ed. Bd. with Second Series. Painters, Sculptors, Illustrators, Engravers & Architects. Repr. of 1881 ed. LC 75-28870. (Art Experience in Late 19th Century America Ser.: Vol. 6). (Illus.). 1976. lib. bdg. 70.00 (ISBN 0-8240-2230-0). Garland Pub.

--The Story of Persia. 1977. lib. bdg. 59.95 (ISBN 0-8490-2685-7). Gordon Pr.

Benjamin, Samuel G. Persia. LC 70-39191. (Select Bibliographies Reprint Ser.). 1887. 22.00 (ISBN 0-8369-6793-3). Ayer Co Pubs.

Benjamin, Sophia L. Mosaic Trilogy: Poetry. 177p. 1983. 15.00 (ISBN 0-87482-122-3). Wake Brook.

Benjamin, Susan. Enamels. Akre, Nancy, ed. LC 82-72761. (Smithsonian Illustrated Library of Antiques). (Illus.). 128p. (Orig.). 1983. 9.95 (ISBN 0-910503-39-7). Cooper-Hewitt Museum.

--English Enamel Boxes: From the Eighteenth to the Twentieth Centuries. (Illus.). 128p. 1983. 18.95 (ISBN 0-85613-038-9, Pub. by Salem Hse Ltd). Merrimack Pub Cir.

Benjamin, Thomas. The Craft of Modal Counterpoint: A Practice Approach. LC 77-90012. 1979. pap. text ed. 12.95 (ISBN 0-02-870480-0). Schirmer Bks.

Benjamin, Thomas E., et al. Music for Analysis: Examples from the Common Practice Period & the Twentieth Century. 2nd ed. LC 83-82356. 432p. 1984. pap. text ed. 21.95 (ISBN 0-395-34225-2). HM.

--Music for Sight Singing. LC 83-82355. 336p. 1984. pap. text ed. 16.95 (ISBN 0-395-34226-0). HM.

--Techniques & Materials of Tonal Music: With an Introduction to Twentieth-Century Techniques. 2nd ed. LC 78-69578. (Illus.). 1979. text ed. 24.95 (ISBN 0-395-27066-9). HM.

Benjamin, Tritobia H. African Artists in America. (Illus.). 1977. pap. 2.00 (Pub. by African Am Inst). Interbk Inc.

Benjamin, Walter. Illuminations. LC 68-24382. 1969. pap. 7.50 (ISBN 0-8052-0241-2). Schocken.

--The Origin of German Tragic Drama. 1978. 19.00 (ISBN 0-8052-7000-0, Pub by NLB). Schocken.

--Reflections: Essays, Aphorisms, Autobiography Writings. Jephcott, Edmond, tr. 348p. Date not set. pap. 6.95 (ISBN 0-15-676245-5). HarBraceJ.

Benjamin, William A. & Kingston, Irene, eds. Directory of European Business Information. 608p. 1980. prof ref 125.00 (ISBN 2-85993-001-9). Ballinger Pub.

Benjamin, William P. Plastic Tooling: Techniques & Applications. LC 75-39845. (Illus.). 256p. 1972. 57.00 (ISBN 0-07-004554-2). McGraw.

Benjamine, Elbert. How to Use Modern Ephemerides: Computed for Midnight & Noon & Eclipse Dates 1880-1990. rev. ed. 1983. pap. 1.50 (ISBN 0-933646-15-1). Aries Pr.

--The Influence of the Planet Pluto, Including an Ephemeris of Pluto, 1840-1990. 1981. pap. 1.50 (ISBN 0-933646-16-X). Aries Pr.

Benjamini, E., jt. ed. see Atassi, M. Z.

Benjamins, Herman D. Encyclopaedie Van Nederlandsch West Indie. 1976. lib. bdg. 150.00 (ISBN 0-8490-1763-7). Gordon Pr.

Benjaminson, Peter. Death in the Afternoon: America's Newspaper Giants Struggle for Survival. LC 84-14499. 200p. 1984. 14.95 (ISBN 0-8362-7955-7). Andrews McMeel Parker.

--The Story of Motown. LC 79-2332. (Illus.). 1979. pap. 8.95 (ISBN 0-394-17554-9, E745, Ever). Grove.

Benjaminson, Peter, jt. auth. see Anderson, David.

Benjiuja, Nisim, jt. auth. see Coltharp, Joe.

Ben-Jonathan, Nira, et al, eds. Catecholamines As Hormone Regulators. (Serono Symposia Publications from Raven Press Ser.: Vol. 18). 396p. 1985. text ed. 39.50 (ISBN 0-89004-607-7). Raven.

Ben-Joseph, Reuben, tr. see Tene, Benjamin.

Ben-Joseph, Reuben, tr. see Tene, Enjamin.

Benke, Ralph L., Jr. & Edwards, James Don. Transfer Pricing: Techniques & Uses. 154p. pap. 16.95 (ISBN 0-86641-012-0, 80118). Natl Assn Accts.

Benkin, Richard. Sociology: A Way of Seeing. 432p. 1981. pap. text ed. write for info. (ISBN 0-534-00929-8). Wadsworth Pub.

Benko, Edna T., jt. auth. see Benko, James S.

Benko, F. Geological & Cosmogonie Cycles as Reflected by the New Law of Universal Cyclicity. 400p. 1984. text ed. 45.00 (991000382). Heyden.

Benko, James S. Hyec Do: Vital Points for Self-Defense. (Illus.). 60p. (Orig.). 1985. pap. 8.00 (ISBN 0-937314-09-9). Midwest Taekwon-Do.

--Taekwon-Do Hyungs for Blue & Red Belt Levels. LC 81-82100. (Illus.). 118p. (Orig.). 1981. 20.00 (ISBN 0-937314-05-6); pap. 10.00 (ISBN 0-937314-04-8). Midwest Taekwon-Do.

--Taekwon-Do Hyungs for White, Yellow & Green Belt Levels. LC 81-81353. (Illus.). 118p. (Orig.). 1981. 20.00 (ISBN 0-937314-01-3); pap. 10.00 (ISBN 0-937314-02-1). Midwest Taekwon-Do.

--Taekwon-Do, Self-Defense Against Weapons. LC 80-82015. (Illus.). 108p. 1981. 20.00 (ISBN 0-937314-03-X). Midwest Taekwon-Do.

--Taekwon-Do: Self Defense Against Weapons. LC 80-82015. (Illus.). 108p. (Orig.). 1980. pap. 10.00 (ISBN 0-937314-00-5). Midwest Taekwon-Do.

Benko, James S. & Benko, Edna T. Kwan Jyel Sul: Joint Locks, Holds & Throws for Self Defense. (Illus.). 120p. (Orig.). 1983. pap. 10.00 (ISBN 0-937314-07-2). Midwest Taekwon-Do.

Benko, Lorand & Imre, Samu, eds. The Hungarian Language. (Janua Linguarum, Ser. Practica: No. 134). (Illus.). 377p. (Orig.). 1972. pap. text ed. 44.00x (ISBN 90-2792-075-3). Mouton.

Benko, Marietta, et al. Space Law in the United Nations. 1985. lib. bdg. 38.00 (ISBN 90-247-3157-7, Pub. by Martinus Nijhoff Netherlands). Kluwer Academic.

Benko, Stephen. Los Evangelicos, los Catolicos y la Virgen Maria, Los. Olmedo, Alfonso, tr. from Eng. Orig. Title: Protestants, Catholics & Mary. 1981. pap. 6.95 (ISBN 0-311-05041-7). Casa Bautista.

--Meaning of Sanctorum Communio. LC 64-55292. (Studies in Historical Theology: No. 3). 1964. pap. 10.00x (ISBN 0-8401-0178-3). A R Allenson.

--Pagan Rome & the Early Christians. LC 83-48898. 192p. 1984. 20.00x (ISBN 0-253-34286-4). Ind U Pr.

Benkovic, Stephen J., jt. ed. see Blakely, Raymond L.

Benkovic, Stephen J., jt. ed. see Blakley, Raymond L.

Benkovitz, Miriam J., ed. A Bibliography of Ronald Firbank. 2nd ed. 1982. text ed. 45.00x (ISBN 0-19-818188-4). Oxford U Pr.

Benkovitz, Miriam J., ed. see Aldington, Richard.

Benkowitz, Joan B., ed. see International Symposium on Solar Energy.

Benlliure, F., tr. see Vardaman, Jerry.

Benlliure, Felix, tr. see Hester, H. I.

Benlliure, Felix, tr. see Mehl, Roger.

Ben-Meir, Alon. The Middle East Imperatives & Choices. LC 75-26110. (Illus.). 1975. 12.95x (ISBN 0-915474-01-8, Decalogue). Effective Learn.

Ben-Menachem, Yoram. Angiography in Trauma: A Work Atlas. (Illus.). 350p. 1981. text ed. 85.00 (ISBN 0-7216-1733-6). Saunders.

Ben-Menahem, A. & Singh, S. Seismic Waves & Sources. (Illus.). 1000p. 1981. 99.00 (ISBN 0-387-90506-5). Springer-Verlag.

Benn. Carpet Annual, 1984. 1984. 65.00x (ISBN 0-86382-005-0). Intl Pubns Serv.

Benn, A. The Twenty-Seven Most Common Mistakes in Advertising. 1981. pap. 8.95 (ISBN 0-317-31402-5). AMACOM.

Benn, Alec. The Twenty-Seven Most Common Mistakes in Advertising. 1978. 12.95 (ISBN 0-8144-5478-X). AMACOM.

--The Twenty-Three Most Common Mistakes in Public Relations. 256p. 1982. 17.95 (ISBN 0-8144-5715-0). AMACOM.

Benn, Alfred W. Early Greek Philosophy. LC 77-101033. 1969. Repr. of 1908 ed. 14.00x (ISBN 0-8046-0700-1, Pub. by Kennikat). Assoc Faculty Pr.

Benn, Barry, jt. auth. see Mace, Roger.

Benn, Douglas R. Love-God's Greatest Gift. (Illus.). 1981. pap. 4.00 (ISBN 0-682-49736-3). Exposition Pr FL.

Benn, Ernest. Happier Days, Recollections & Reflections. 222p. 1981. Repr. of 1949 ed. lib. bdg. 20.00 (ISBN 0-89987-068-6). Darby Bks.

Benn, Frederick C. Mozart on the Stage. LC 74-24041. Repr. of 1946 ed. 18.00 (ISBN 0-404-12864-5). AMS Pr.

Benn, Gottfried. Primal Vision. Ashton, E. B., ed. LC 58-13434. 1971. pap. 8.95 (ISBN 0-8112-0008-6, NDP322). New Directions.

--Primal Vision: Selected Writings. Ashton, E. B., ed. Hamburger, Michael, et al, trs. from Ger. 292p. 1985. Repr. 18.00 (ISBN 0-7145-2500-6, Dist. by Scribner). M Boyars.

Benn, J. Solomon, III. Preaching from the Bible. (Resources for Black Ministries Ser.). 80p. (Orig.). 1981. pap. 2.45 (ISBN 0-8010-0801-8). Baker Bk.

Benn, M. B. The Drama of Revolt: A Critical Study of Georg Buchner. LC 75-3974. (Anglica Germanica Ser.: No. 2). (Illus.). 300p. 1976. 54.50 (ISBN 0-521-20828-9); pap. 15.95x (ISBN 0-521-29415-0). Cambridge U Pr.

Benn Publications Ltd. Benn's Press Directory: The World Media Guide 1986, 2 vols. (Benn Directories Ser.). 1986. Set. 160.00 (ISBN 0-86382-013-1); Vol. 1-United Kingdom. lib. bdg. 95.00 (ISBN 0-86382-015-8); Vol. 2-International. lib. bdg. 95.00 (ISBN 0-86382-016-6). Nichols Pub.

--Chemical Industry Directory & Who's Who 1986. (Benn Directories). 1986. 98.50 (ISBN 0-86382-018-2). Nichols Pub.

--Chemist & Druggist Directory 1986. (Benn Directories). 1986. 82.50 (ISBN 0-86382-017-4). Nichols Pub.

--Phillips Paper Trade Directory 1986. (Benn Directories Ser.). 1986. 104.00 (ISBN 0-86382-022-0). Nichols Pub.

--Printing Trades Directory, 1986. 1986. 93.50 (ISBN 0-86382-023-9). Nichols Pub.

Benn, S. I. & Peters, R. S. Social Principles & the Democratic State. 1959. pap. text ed. 15.95x (ISBN 0-04-300028-2). Allen Unwin.

Benn, S. I. & Gaus, G. F., eds. Public & Private in Social Life. LC 83-9539. 430p. 1983. 35.00 (ISBN 0-312-65357-3). St Martin.

Benn, S. I. & Mortimore, G. W., eds. Rationality & the Social Sciences: Contributions to the Philosophy & Methodology of the Social Sciences. 400p. 1976. 36.95x (ISBN 0-7100-8170-7). Routledge & Kegan.

Benn, Tony. Arguments for Democracy. 257p. 1982. 14.95 (ISBN 0-224-01878-7, Pub. by Jonathan Cape). Merrimack Pub Cir.

--Arguments for Socialism. 206p. 1982. 14.95 (ISBN 0-224-01770-5, Pub. by Jonathan Cape). Merrimack Pub Cir.

--Parliament, People & Power: Agenda for a Free Society. 160p. 1983. 17.50 (ISBN 0-8052-7139-2, Pub. by NLB England); pap. 6.50 (ISBN 0-8052-7140-6). Schocken.

--Parliament, People & Power Agenda for a Free Society. 152p. 1982. 59.00x (ISBN 0-86091-057-1, Pub. by Verso-NLB England). State Mutual Bk.

Benn, Tony, ed. Writings on the Wall: A Radical & Socialist Anthology, Twelve Fifteen to Nineteen Eighty-Four. 300p. 1984. 22.95 (ISBN 0-571-13334-7); pap. 11.95 (ISBN 0-571-13335-5). Faber & Faber.

Ben-Naim, Arieh. Hydrophobic Interactions. LC 79-510. (Illus.). 319p. 1980. 45.00x (ISBN 0-306-40222-X, Plenum Pr). Plenum Pub.

--Water & Aqueous Solutions: Introduction to a Molecular Theory. LC 74-7325. (Illus.). 474p. 1974. 65.00x (ISBN 0-306-30774-X, Plenum Pr). Plenum Pub.

Bennani, B. M. A Bowl of Sorrow. 1977. perfect bdg. 3.00 (ISBN 0-912678-36-4). Greenfld Rev Pr.

Bennani, B. M., tr. Splinters of Bone. LC 74-25797. Orig. Title: Darweesh. 1974. 2.95 (ISBN 0-912678-17-8). Greenfld Rev Pr.

Bennassar, Bartolome. The Spanish Character: Attitudes & Mentalities from the Sixteenth to the Nineteenth Century. Keen, Benjamin, tr. LC 76-55563. 1979. 30.00x (ISBN 0-520-03401-5). U of Cal Pr.

Bennathan, Esra & Walters, Alan A. Port Pricing & Investment Policy for Developing Countries. 1979. 27.50x (ISBN 0-19-520092-6); pap. 12.50x (ISBN 0-19-520093-4). Oxford U Pr.

Bennaton, Gwendolyn K., jt. auth. see Honduras Information Service.

Benndorf, Cornelie. Die Englische Padagogik Im 16. Jahrhundert. Repr. of 1905 ed. 12.00 (ISBN 0-384-03895-6). Johnson Repr.

Benne, Bart. The Illustrated PC-FOCUS Book. LC 85-3352. (Illustrated Ser.). (Illus.). 160p. 1985. pap. 19.95 (ISBN 0-915381-73-7). Wordware Pub.

Benne, Kenneth D. Conception of Authority: An Introductory Study. LC 75-151538. 1971. Repr. of 1943 ed. 13.00x (ISBN 0-8462-1474-1). Russell.

--Education for Tragedy: Essays in Disenchanted Hope for Modern Man. LC 67-17847. 216p. 1967. pap. 6.00x (ISBN 0-8131-0124-7). U Pr of Ky.

Benne, Kenneth D. & Birnbaum, Max. Teaching & Learning About Science & Social Policy. 132p. 1978. 9.95 (ISBN 0-89994-233-4). Soc Sci Ed.

Benne, Kenneth D., et al, eds. Laboratory Method of Changing & Learning: Theory & Application. LC 74-32598. 1975. 15.95 (ISBN 0-685-59371-1). Sci & Behavior.

Benne, Robert. The Ethic of Democratic Capitalism: A Moral Reassessment. LC 80-2385. 288p. 1981. pap. 11.95 (ISBN 0-8006-1445-3, 1-1445). Fortress.

Bennehoff, Paul W., ed. see Osbeck, Kenneth W.

Benneman, K. H. & Ketterson, J. B., eds. The Physics of Solid and Liquid Helium, Pt. 2. LC 75-20235. 760p. Repr. of 1978 ed. text ed. 80.95 (ISBN 0-471-06601-X). Krieger.

Benner, Allen R., ed. see Homer.

Benner, Bob. Carolina Whitewater. 4th ed. LC 84-115920. (Illus.). 264p. 1977. pap. 11.95 (ISBN 0-89732-008-5). Menasha Ridge.

Benner, David G. Baker Encyclopedia of Psychology. 1376p. 1985. text ed. 39.95 (ISBN 0-8010-0865-4). Baker Bk.

Benner, George. Footprints: A Humanistic View of Science Education. LC 75-41832. (Illus.). 66p. 1976. pap. text ed. 2.95x (ISBN 0-8134-1788-0, 1788). Interstate.

Benner, J. Structure of Decision. 134p. 1983. text ed. 15.25x (ISBN 0-391-03028-0, Pub. by S Asian India). Humanities.

Benner, Jeffrey. The Indian Foreign Policy Bureaucracy. (Replica Edition-Softcover Ser.). 220p. 1985. softcover 19.50x (ISBN 0-86531-875-1). Westview.

Benner, Judith A. Sul Ross: Soldier, Statesman, Educator. LC 82-45891. (Centennial Series of the Association of Former Students: No. 13). (Illus.). 286p. 1983. 19.50 (ISBN 0-89096-142-5). Tex A&M Univ Pr.

Benner, Judith A., jt. auth. see Paschal, George H., Jr.

Benner, Patricia. From Novice to Expert: Excellence & Power in Clinical Nursing Practice. 1984. 17.95 (ISBN 0-201-00299-X, Med-Nurse). Addison-Wesley.

Benner, Patricia & Benner, Richard V. The New Nurse's Work Entry: A Troubled Sponsorship. LC 78-68494. (Illus.). 160p. 1979. flexible 7.95 (ISBN 0-913292-09-5). Tiresias Pr.

Benner, Patricia E. Stress & Satisfaction on the Job: Work Meanings & Coping of Mid-Career Men. LC 84-3252. 176p. 1984. 23.95 (ISBN 0-03-063839-9). Praeger.

Benner, Ralph. Songbird. 192p. 1975. pap. 1.25 (ISBN 0-532-12294-1). Woodhill.

Benner, Reuven. Betting on Ideas: Wars, Invention, Inflation. LC 85-8750. (Illus.). 227p. 1986. lib. bdg. price not set (ISBN 0-226-07400-5). U of Chicago Pr.

Benner, Richard V., jt. auth. see Benner, Patricia.

Benner, Samuel. Benner's Prophecies on the Future of Ups & Downs Commodity Prices with Predictions on Corn, Hogs, Cotton & Other Commodities. 1977. Repr. of 1879 ed. 77.85 (ISBN 0-89266-053-8). Am Classical Coll Pr.

--Benner's Prophecies on the Future of Ups & Downs Commodity Prices with Predictions on Corn, Hogs, Cotton & Other Commodities, 2 vols. (Illus.). 1985. Set. 187.50 (ISBN 0-86654-158-6). Inst Econ Finan.

--Commodity Prophecy & the Mastery of Commodity Futures Trading. (Illus.). 132p. 1983. Repr. of 1879 ed. 99.85x (ISBN 0-86654-080-6). Inst Econ Finan.

Bennet, Arthur. Valley of Vision. 240p. 1983. pap. 7.95 (ISBN 0-85151-228-3). Banner of Truth.

Bennet, Boyce M., Jr., ed. see Miller, Madeleine S. & Miller, J. Lane.

Bennet, C. L. Defining the Manager's Job: The AMA Manual of Position Descriptions. LC 58-14306. (American Management Association Research Study Ser.: No. 33). pap. 111.80 (ISBN 0-317-09571-4, 2051306). Bks Demand UMI.

Bennet, D. & Thomas, J. F. On Rational Grounds: Systems Analysis in Catchment & Land Use Planning. (Development in Landscape Planning & Urban Planning Ser.: Vol. 4). 362p. 1982. 81.00 (ISBN 0-444-42056-8). Elsevier.

Bennet, E. A. What Jung Really Said. LC 67-13153. (What They Really Said Ser). 1971. pap. 4.95 (ISBN 0-8052-0265-X). Schocken.

--What Jung Really Said. 192p. 1983. pap. 6.95 (ISBN 0-8052-0753-8). Schocken.

Bennet, Edward G. Patients & Their Doctors. (Illus.). 1979. pap. text ed. 10.95 (ISBN 0-7216-0704-7, Pub. by Bailliere-Tindall). Saunders.

Bennet, G. A. Electricity & Modern Physics. 2nd ed. 1974. pap. text ed. 28.50x (ISBN 0-7131-2459-8). Intl Ideas.

Bennet, Georgette. A Safe Place to Live: A Management Manual to Help Communities Plan Crime Prevention Programs. 136p. (Orig.). 1982. pap. 4.95 (ISBN 0-932387-07-1). Insur Info.

Bennet, Glin. Beyond Endurance. 272p. 1983. 13.95 (ISBN 0-312-07783-1, Pub. by Marek). St Martin.

Bennet, Gordon C. From Nineveh to Now: Three Dramatic Fantasies Based on the Old Testament. LC 73-3145. (Orig.). 1973. pap. 2.50 (ISBN 0-8272-1004-3). CBP.

Bennet, Harold L. Glimpse at Wall Street & Its Markets: Descriptions of Important Railroad & Industrial Properties. LC 68-28616. 1968. Repr. of 1904 ed. lib. bdg. 16.00x (ISBN 0-8371-0307-X, BEGW). Greenwood.

Bennet, J. V., jt. auth. see Pacsy, V. A.

Bennet, John. Master Skylark. 13.95 (ISBN 0-88411-823-1, Pub. by Aeonian Pr). Amereon Ltd.

Bennet, John & Masia, Seth. Walks in the Catskills. LC 74-81304. (Illus.). 204p. 1974. pap. 7.95 (ISBN 0-914788-00-0). East Woods.

Bennet, John M., jt. auth. see Rosenthal, Susan N.

Bennet, John W. Of Time & Enterprise: North American Family Farm Management in a Context of Resource Marginality. (Illus.). 384p. 1982. 39.50x (ISBN 0-8166-1051-7). U of Minn Pr.

Bennet, Lowitz Barry B., jt. auth. see Casciato, Dennis A.

Bennet, Mark. Public Policy & Industrial Development: The Case of Mexican Auto Parts Industry. LC 83-23456. (Replica Edition Ser.). 115p. 1984. pap. 15.00x (ISBN 0-86531-821-2). Westview.

Bennet, Mel. Stockton's Theatre of Yesterday. LC 78-66214. (Illus.). 1979. 20.00 (ISBN 0-912450-16-9). Willow Hse.

Bennet, Michael. IBM Personal Computer Handbook, Vol. I. 1986. 19.95 (ISBN 0-89303-544-0). Brady Comm.

Bennet, Olivia. A Family in Egypt. LC 84-19468. (Families the World Over Ser.). (Illus.). 32p. (gr. 2-5). 1985. PLB 8.95 (ISBN 0-8225-1652-7). Lerner Pubns.

Bennet, Robert A. The Bowl of Baal. 7.50 (ISBN 0-937986-06-2). D M Grant.

--Thyra: A Romance of the Polar Pit. Reginald, R. & Melville, Douglas, eds. LC 77-84199. (Lost Race & Adult Fantasy Ser.). (Illus.). 1978. Repr. of 1901 ed. lib. bdg. 26.50x (ISBN 0-405-10957-1). Ayer Co Pubs.

Bennet, Roger. Management Research: Guide for the Institutions & Professionals. (Management Development Ser.: No. 20). viii, 245p. 1983. pap. 12.85 (ISBN 92-2-103303-1). Intl Labour Office.

Bennet, S. & Bowers, D. An Introduction to Multivariate Techniques for Social & Behavioral Sciences. LC 74-20108. 156p. 1978. pap. 24.95x (ISBN 0-470-26428-4). Halsted Pr.

Bennet, William S. & Evert, Carl F., Jr. What Every Engineer Should Know about Microcomputers: Hardware-Software Design: a Step by Step Example. (What Every Engineer Should Know Ser.: Vol. 3). (Illus.). 192p. 1980. 19.75 (ISBN 0-8247-6909-0). Dekker.

Bennet-Ruete, Jackie, tr. see Schmidt, Gustav.

Bennett. Cardiac Arrhythmias. 2nd ed. 1985. price not set (ISBN 0-7236-0845-8). PSG Pub Co.

--Georgia Medical Torts: Physicians. 42.95 (ISBN 0-686-90361-7). Harrison Co GA.

--Hamlet in the Nineteen Sixties. 1985. lib. bdg. 39.00 (ISBN 0-8240-8990-1). Garland Pub.

--Spaces for People: Human Factors in Design. LC 76-30847. 1977. pap. 4.95 (ISBN 0-13-823955-X, Spec). P-H.

Bennett & Ciegler. Secondary Metabolism & Differentiation in Fungi. (Mycology Ser.). 472p. 1983. 75.00 (ISBN 0-8247-1819-4). Dekker.

Bennett & Nelson. Mathematics: An Activity Approach. 1985. 21.81 (ISBN 0-205-06518-X, 566518). Allyn.

--Mathematics: An Informal Approach. 2nd ed. 1985. 31.43 (ISBN 0-205-08305-6, 568305). Allyn.

Bennett & Siy. Blueprint Reading for Welders. LC 76-29579. (Illus.). 180p. 1978. instructor's guide o.p. 5.00 (ISBN 0-8273-1060-9); charts 11.40wall (ISBN 0-8273-1063-3); transparencies 160.00 (ISBN 0-8273-1889-8). Delmar.

Bennett & Upton. Zesty Pizzas. (Easy Cooking Ser.). 1983. 4.95 (ISBN 0-8120-5536-5). Barron.

Bennett, jt. auth. see Upton.

Bennett, A. & Velo, G., eds. Mechanisms of Gastrointestinal Motility & Secretion. (NATO ASI Ser.: Series A, Life Sciences). 368p. 1984. 52.50x (ISBN 0-306-41813-4, Plenum Pr). Plenum Pub.

Bennett, A., et al. Workshops in Cognitive Processes. 2nd. ed. 136p. 1982. pap. 9.95x (ISBN 0-7100-0932-1). Routledge & Kegan.

Bennett, A., et al, eds. Selected Medical Terminology. Orig. Title: Medical Terminology for Hospital Employees. (Orig.). 1968. text ed. 18.00 (ISBN 0-686-00455-8). Preston.

Bennett, A. E. & Siy, L. Blueprint Reading for Welders. 4th ed. LC 82-46005. 304p. 1983. text ed. 14.40 (ISBN 0-8273-2144-9); instructors guide 5.10 (ISBN 0-8273-2145-7). Delmar.

Bennett, A. E. & Sly, Louis J. Blueprint Reading for Welders. 3rd ed. 1983. 22.95 (ISBN 0-442-21358-1). Van Nos Reinhold.

Bennett, A. G. Optics of Contact Lenses. 1981. 30.00x (ISBN 0-686-45409-X, Pub. by Assn Disp Opt England). State Mutual Bk.

Bennett, A. L., ed. see Sappington, Joe.

Bennett, A. LeRoy. International Organizations: Principles & Issues. 3rd ed. (Illus.). 544p. 1984. 27.95 (ISBN 0-13-473496-3). P-H.

Bennett, A. R. The Telephone Systems of the Continent of Europe, 1895, 2 vols. in 1. LC 74-4666. (Telecommunications Ser). 395p. 1974. Repr. of 1895 ed. 36.50x (ISBN 0-405-06033-5). Ayer Co Pubs.

Bennett, A. Wayne. Introduction to Computer Simulation. LC 74-4509. 480p. 1974. text ed. 30.95 (ISBN 0-8299-0017-9); solutions manual avail. (ISBN 0-8299-0459-X). West Pub.

Bennett, Addison C. Improving Management Performance in Health Care Institutions: A Total Systems Approach. LC 78-8010. (Illus.). 256p. (Orig.). 1978. casebound 26.00 (ISBN 0-87258-246-9, 001106); pap. 25.00 (ISBN 0-87258-229-9, 001104). AHPI.

--Managing Hospital Costs Effectively As a System: A Primer for Hospital Administration. (Illus.). 72p. (Orig.). 1980. pap. 18.75 (ISBN 0-87258-327-9, 001108). AHPI.

--Managing Hospital Costs Effectively As a System: A Primer for Hospital Administration. 72p. 1980. 18.75 (ISBN 0-87258-327-9, 001108); members 15.00 (ISBN 0-317-32795-X). Am Hospital.

--Productivity & the Quality of Work Life in Hospitals. (Illus.). 100p. 1983. 30.00 (ISBN 0-939450-01-1, 088220). AHPI.

Bennett, Adrian A. John Fryer: The Introduction of Western Science & Technology into Nineteenth-Century China. LC 68-4092. (East Asian Monograph Ser.: No. 24). 1967. pap. 11.00x (ISBN 0-674-47650-6). Harvard U Pr.

--Missionary Journalist in China: Young J. Allen & His Magazines, 1860-1883. LC 81-19761. (Illus.). 336p. 28.00x (ISBN 0-8203-0615-0). U of Ga Pr.

Bennett, Alan. Horsewoman: Louie Dingwall. 200p. 40.00 (ISBN 0-686-75651-7, Pub by Dorset). State Mutual Bk.

--The Old Country. 64p. 1978. pap. 5.95 (ISBN 0-571-11242-0). Faber & Faber.

--A Private Function. LC 84-28734. 110p. (Orig.). 1985. pap. 8.95 (ISBN 0-571-13571-4). Faber & Faber.

--Prostaglandins & the Gut, Vol. 1. 1977. 14.40 (ISBN 0-904406-49-0). Eden Pr.

Bennett, Alberto A. Silas Brown: Pioneer. LC 77-95293. 1978. text ed. 7.95 (ISBN 0-912760-65-6); pap. 5.95 (ISBN 0-685-65243-2). Valkyrie Pub Hse.

Bennett, Allan. A Note on Genesis. (Equinox Reprints: Vol. 1, No. 2). 1976. pap. 1.50 (ISBN 0-87728-338-9). Weiser.

Bennett, Allison P. The People's Choice: A History of Albany County in Art & Architecture. LC 80-66320. (Illus.). 145p. (Orig.). 1980. pap. 10.95 (ISBN 0-89062-124-1). Albany County.

--Times Remembered: Chronicles of the Towns of Bethlehem & New Scotland, N.Y. (Illus.). 110p. 1984. pap. 10.95 (ISBN 0-318-03966-4). Newsgraphics Delmar Inc.

Bennett, Alvin. God the Stonebreaker. (Caribbean Writers Ser.). 1973. pap. text ed. 5.50x (ISBN 0-435-98100-5). Heinemann Ed.

Bennett, Alwina, jt. auth. see Gollay, Elinor.

Bennett, Angeline. Or Even Poetry. 36p. 1976. pap. 3.00 (ISBN 0-911826-43-2). Am Atheist.

Bennett, Anna, ed. Acts of the Tapestry Symposium. LC 77-91645. (Illus.). 1979. pap. 15.00 (ISBN 0-88401-031-7). Fine Arts Mus.

Bennett, Anna E. Little Witch. LC 52-1374. (Illus.). (gr. 4-6). 1953. lib. bdg. 10.89 (ISBN 0-397-30261-4). Lipp Jr Bks.

--Little Witch. (Illus.). 128p. (gr. 2-5). 1981. pap. 2.95 (ISBN 0-06-440119-7, Trophy). HarpJ.

Bennett, Anna G. & Berson, Ruth. Fans in Fashion. LC 81-65612. (Illus.). 128p. (Orig.). 1981. pap. 15.00 (ISBN 0-88401-037-6, Pub by Fine Arts Mus). C E Tuttle.

--Fans in Fashion. LC 81-65612. (Illus.). 128p. 1981. pap. 15.00 (ISBN 0-88401-037-6). Fine Arts Mus.

Bennett, Annette. A Comparative Study of Subnormal Children in Elementary Grades. LC 76-176552. (Columbia University. Teachers College. Contributions to Education: No. 510). Repr. of 1932 ed. 22.50 (ISBN 0-404-55510-1). AMS Pr.

Bennett, Archie. The New Color Picture Dictionary for Children. LC 76-42144. (Illus.). 256p. (gr. 1-4). 1978. 8.95 (ISBN 0-8326-2214-1, 6391). Delair.

--New Color-Picture Dictionary for Children. (Illus.). 252p. (gr. k-4). 1981. PLB 19.95 (ISBN 0-516-00820-X). Childrens.

Bennett, Archie & Gutierrez, Marta. The Beginner's English-Spanish Dictionary: Diccionario Espanol-Ingles para Principiantes. (Illus.). 512p. (Eng. & Span.). 12.95 (ISBN 0-8326-0063-6, 6392); pap. 10.95 (ISBN 0-8326-0064-4, 6392). Delair.

Bennett, Archie, ed. New Illustrated Grosset Dictionary. LC 76-42144. (Illus.). (gr. k-5). 1977. pap. 6.95 (ISBN 0-448-14384-4, G&D). Putnam Pub Group.

Bennett, Arnold. Anna of the Five Towns. LC 74-5320. (Collected Works of Arnold Bennett: Vol. 1). 1976. Repr. of 1902 ed. 20.75 (ISBN 0-518-19082-X). Ayer Co Pubs.

--Anna of the Five Towns. 281p. 1977. Repr. lib. bdg. 13.25x (ISBN 0-89966-282-X). Buccaneer Bks.

--Anna of the Five Towns. 1978. pap. 3.95 (ISBN 0-14-000033-X). Penguin.

--Arnold Bennett. LC 74-5388. (Collected Works of Arnold Bennett: Vol. 2). 1976. Repr. of 1935 ed. 29.00 (ISBN 0-518-19083-8). Ayer Co Pubs.

--The Arnold Bennett Omnibus Book. LC 74-5396. (Collected Works of Arnold Bennett: Vol. 4). 1976. Repr. of 1931 ed. 33.00 (ISBN 0-518-19085-4). Ayer Co Pubs.

--The Author's Craft. LC 74-5396. (Collected Works of Arnold Bennett: Vol. 5). 1976. Repr. of 1914 ed. 18.75 (ISBN 0-518-19086-2). Ayer Co Pubs.

--Author's Craft & Other Critical Writings of Arnold Bennett. Hynes, Samuel, ed. LC 68-12706. (Regents Critics Ser). xx, 281p. 1968. 21.50x (ISBN 0-8032-0451-5); pap. 5.25x (ISBN 0-8032-5451-2, BB 410, Bison). U of Nebr Pr.

--Body & Soul. LC 74-5293. (Collected Works of Arnold Bennett: Vol. 6). 1976. Repr. of 1921 ed. 16.75 (ISBN 0-518-19087-0). Ayer Co Pubs.

--The Book of Carlotta. LC 74-6017. (Collected Works of Arnold Bennett: Vol. 7). 1976. Repr. of 1911 ed. 21.75 (ISBN 0-518-19088-9). Ayer Co Pubs.

--Books & Persons. LC 74-546. (Collected Works of Arnold Bennett: Vol. 8). 1976. Repr. of 1917 ed. 24.25 (ISBN 0-518-19089-7). Ayer Co Pubs.

--Books & Persons. 1917. 15.00 (ISBN 0-8274-1967-8). R West.

--Books & Persons: Being Comments on a Past Epoch, 1908-1911. LC 69-10069. 1969. Repr. of 1917 ed. lib. bdg. 22.50x (ISBN 0-8371-0018-6, BEBP). Greenwood.

--The Bright Island. LC 74-5327. (Collected Works of Arnold Bennett: Vol. 9). 1976. Repr. of 1925 ed. 15.75 (ISBN 0-518-19090-0). Ayer Co Pubs.

--Buried Alive. LC 74-5327. (Collected Works of Arnold Bennett: Vol. 10). 1976. Repr. of 1923 ed. 19.25 (ISBN 0-518-19091-9). Ayer Co Pubs.

--The Card. LC 460011416000006. 224p. 1985. pap. 2.95x (ISBN 0-318-04542-7, Pub. by Evman England). Biblio Dist.

--The City of Pleasure. LC 74-5394. (Collected Works of Arnold Bennett: Vol. 11). 1976. Repr. of 1907 ed. 22.75 (ISBN 0-518-19092-7). Ayer Co Pubs.

--Clayhanger. LC 74-5390. (Collected Works of Arnold Bennett: Vol. 12). 1976. Repr. of 1910 ed. 43.25 (ISBN 0-518-19093-5). Ayer Co Pubs.

--The Collected Works of Arnold Bennett, 90 vols. 1976. Repr. 1897.50set (ISBN 0-8369-7057-8). Ayer Co Pubs.

--Cupid & Commonsense. LC 74-6015. (Collected Works of Arnold Bennett: Vol. 13). 1976. Repr. of 1910 ed. 18.25 (ISBN 0-518-19094-3). Ayer Co Pubs.

--Denry the Audacious. LC 72-6208. (Collected Works of Arnold Bennett: Vol. 14). 1976. Repr. of 1911 ed. 20.75 (ISBN 0-518-19095-1). Ayer Co Pubs.

--Don Juan De Marana. (Collected Works of Arnold Bennett: Vol. 15). 1976. Repr. of 1923 ed. 19.25 (ISBN 0-518-19096-X). Ayer Co Pubs.

--The Evening Standard Years 'Books & Persons' 1926-1931. Mylett, Andrew, ed. xxviii, 481p. (Orig.). 1974. 27.50 (ISBN 0-208-01444-6, Archon). Shoe String.

--Fame & Fiction. LC 74-6011. (Collected Works of Arnold Bennett: Vol. 16). 1976. Repr. of 1901 ed. 22.75 (ISBN 0-518-19097-8). Ayer Co Pubs.

--Fame & Fiction. 59.95 (ISBN 0-8490-0150-1). Gordon Pr.

--Flora. LC 74-5325. (Collected Works of Arnold Bennett: Vol. 17). 1976. Repr. of 1933 ed. 16.75 (ISBN 0-518-19098-6). Ayer Co Pubs.

--Frank Swinnerton: Personal Sketches: Together with Notes and Comments on the Novels of Frank Swinnerton. LC 76-52446. 1977. lib. bdg. 10.00 (ISBN 0-8414-1752-0). Folcroft.

--Friendship & Happiness. LC 74-5432. (Collected Works of Arnold Bennett Ser.: Vol. 19). 1976. Repr. of 1911 ed. 18.75 (ISBN 0-518-19100-1). Ayer Co Pubs.

--From the Log of the Velsa. LC 74-5317. (Collected Works of Arnold Bennett: Vol. 20). 1976. Repr. of 1914 ed. 31.50 (ISBN 0-518-19101-X). Ayer Co Pubs.

--The Gates of Wrath. LC 74-5322. (Collected Works of Arnold Bennett: Vol. 21). 1976. Repr. of 1903 ed. 21.75 (ISBN 0-518-19102-8). Ayer Co Pubs.

--The Ghost. LC 74-5392. (Collected Works of Arnold Bennett: Vol. 22). 1976. Repr. of 1907 ed. 19.75 (ISBN 0-518-19103-6). Ayer Co Pubs.

--The Glimpse. LC 74-5399. (Collected Works of Arnold Bennett: Vol. 23). 1976. Repr. of 1909 ed. 29.00 (ISBN 0-518-19104-4). Ayer Co Pubs.

--The Grand Babylon Hotel. LC 74-5400. (Collected Works of Arnold Bennett: Vol. 24). 1976. Repr. of 1902 ed. 29.00 (ISBN 0-518-19105-2). Ayer Co Pubs.

--The Grand Babylon Hotel: A Fantasia on Modern Themes. 224p. 1976. pap. 4.95 (ISBN 0-14-000176-X). Penguin.

--Grand Babylon Hotel, a Fantasia on Modern Themes. 1904. 27.00x (ISBN 0-403-00004-1). Scholarly.

--The Great Adventure. LC 74-5329. (Collected Works of Arnold Bennett: Vol. 25). 1976. Repr. of 1913 ed. 18.75 (ISBN 0-518-19106-0). Ayer Co Pubs.

--Great Adventure: A Play of Fancy in Four Sets. LC 70-131622. 1970. Repr. of 1913 ed. 16.00x (ISBN 0-403-00509-4). Scholarly.

--A Great Man. LC 74-5321. (Collected Works of Arnold Bennett: Vol. 26). 1976. Repr. of 1911 ed. 20.75 (ISBN 0-518-19107-9). Ayer Co Pubs.

--The Grim Smile of the Five Towns. LC 74-5401. (Collected Works of Arnold Bennett: Vol. 27). 1976. Repr. of 1907 ed. 24.25 (ISBN 0-518-19108-7). Ayer Co Pubs.

--The Grim Smile of the Five Towns. (Fiction Ser.). 192p. 1985. pap. 4.95 (ISBN 0-14-046728-9). Penguin.

--Helen with the High Hand. LC 74-5402. (Collected Works of Arnold Bennett: Vol. 28). 1976. Repr. of 1911 ed. 21.75 (ISBN 0-518-19109-5). Ayer Co Pubs.

--Hilda Lessways. LC 74-5331. (Collected Works of Arnold Bennett Ser.: Vol. 29). 1976. Repr. of 1911 ed. 24.25 (ISBN 0-518-19110-9). Ayer Co Pubs.

--The Honeymoon. LC 74-5328. (Collected Works of Arnold Bennett: Vol. 30). 1976. Repr. of 1910 ed. 18.75 (ISBN 0-518-19111-7). Ayer Co Pubs.

--Honeymoon: A Comedy in Three Acts. LC 74-131623. 1970. Repr. of 1911 ed. 17.00x (ISBN 0-403-00510-8). Scholarly.

--How to Become an Author. 2nd ed. LC 74-5431. (Collected Works of Arnold Bennett: Vol. 31). 1976. Repr. of 1903 ed. 22.75 (ISBN 0-518-19112-5). Ayer Co Pubs.

--How to Live on Twenty-four Hours a Day. LC 74-5288. (Collected Works of Arnold Bennett: Vol. 32). 1976. Repr. of 1910 ed. 18.75 (ISBN 0-518-19113-3). Ayer Co Pubs.

--How to Live on Twenty-Four Hours a Day. 1962. pap. 1.95 (ISBN 0-346-12208-2). Cornerstone.

--How to Make the Best of Life. LC 74-5332. (Collected Works of Arnold Bennett: Vol. 33). 1976. Repr. of 1923 ed. 21.75 (ISBN 0-518-19114-1). Ayer Co Pubs.

--Hugo. LC 74-5403. (Collected Works of Arnold Bennett: Vol. 34). 1976. Repr. of 1906 ed. 22.75 (ISBN 0-518-19115-X). Ayer Co Pubs.

--The Human Machine. LC 74-5290. (Collected Works of Arnold Bennett: Vol. 35). 1976. Repr. of 1908 ed. 16.75 (ISBN 0-518-19116-8). Ayer Co Pubs.

--Imperial Palace. LC 74-5409. (Collected Works of Arnold Bennett: Vol. 36). 1976. Repr. of 1930 ed. 43.00 (ISBN 0-518-19117-6). Ayer Co Pubs.

--Journal of Arnold Bennett. (Collected Works of Arnold Bennett: Vol. 38). 1976. 22.75 (ISBN 0-518-19119-2). Ayer Co Pubs.

--Journal of Arnold Bennett: Pt. 1, 1896-1910. LC 74-5371. (Collected Works of Arnold Bennett: Vol. 37). 1976. Repr. of 1932 ed. 33.00 (ISBN 0-518-19118-4). Ayer Co Pubs.

--Journal of Arnold Bennett: Pt. 2, 1911-1920. LC 74-5371. (Collected Works of Arnold Bennett: Vol. 39). 1976. Repr. of 1932 ed. 29.00 (ISBN 0-518-19120-6). Ayer Co Pubs.

--Journal of Arnold Bennett: Pt. 3, 1921-1928. LC 74-5371. (Collected Works of Arnold Bennett: Vol. 40). 1976. Repr. of 1933 ed. 30.00 (ISBN 0-518-19121-4). Ayer Co Pubs.

--Journal of Things New & Old. LC 74-6178. (Collected Works of Arnold Bennett: Vol. 41). 1976. Repr. of 1930 ed. 24.50 (ISBN 0-518-19122-2). Ayer Co Pubs.

--Judith. LC 74-5397. (Collected Works of Arnold Bennett: Vol. 42). 1976. Repr. of 1919 ed. 16.75 (ISBN 0-518-19123-0). Ayer Co Pubs.

--Leonora. LC 74-5379. (Collected Works of Arnold Bennett: Vol. 43). 1976. Repr. of 1903 ed. 20.75 (ISBN 0-518-19124-9). Ayer Co Pubs.

--Liberty! LC 74-5300. (Collected Works of Arnold Bennett: Vol. 44). 1976. Repr. of 1914 ed. 16.75 (ISBN 0-518-19125-7). Ayer Co Pubs.

--Lilian. LC 74-5330. (Collected Works of Arnold Bennett: Vol. 45). 1976. Repr. of 1922 ed. 21.75 (ISBN 0-518-19126-5). Ayer Co Pubs.

--The Lion's Share. LC 74-17027. (Collected Works of Arnold Bennett: Vol. 46). 1976. Repr. of 1916 ed. 31.50 (ISBN 0-518-19127-3). Ayer Co Pubs.

--Literary Taste: How to Form It. LC 74-16487. (Collected Works of Arnold Bennett: Vol. 47). 1976. Repr. of 1909 ed. 20.25 (ISBN 0-518-19128-1). Ayer Co Pubs.

--London Life. LC 74-16480. (Collected Works of Arnold Bennet: Vol. 48). 1976. Repr. of 1924 ed. 20.75 (ISBN 0-518-19129-X). Ayer Co Pubs.

--The Loot of Cities. LC 74-17025. (Collected Works of Arnold Bennett: Vol. 49). 1976. Repr. of 1911 ed. 22.75 (ISBN 0-518-19130-3). Ayer Co Pubs.

--The Love Match. LC 74-16481. (Collected Works of Arnold Bennett: Vol. 50). 1976. Repr. of 1922 ed. 16.75 (ISBN 0-518-19131-1). Ayer Co Pubs.

--A Man from the North. LC 74-17023. (Collected Works of Arnold Bennett Ser.: Vol. 51). 1976. Repr. of 1911 ed. 22.75 (ISBN 0-518-19132-X). Ayer Co Pubs.

--Married Life. LC 74-17077. (Collected Works of Arnold Bennett: Vol. 52). 1976. Repr. of 1913 ed. 16.75 (ISBN 0-518-19133-8). Ayer Co Pubs.

--The Matador of the Five Towns & Other Stories. LC 74-17074. (Collected Works of Arnold Bennett Ser.: Vol. 53). 1976. Repr. of 1912 ed. 31.50 (ISBN 0-518-19134-6). Ayer Co Pubs.

--Matador of the Five Towns & Other Stories. LC 79-144875. 1971. Repr. of 1905 ed. 25.00 (ISBN 0-403-00862-X). Scholarly.

--Mediterranean Scenes. LC 74-1702. (Collected Works of Arnold Bennett: Vol. 54). 1976. Repr. of 1928 ed. 16.75 (ISBN 0-518-19135-4). Ayer Co Pubs.

--Mental Efficiency & Other Hints to Men & Women. LC 74-17123. (Collected Works of Arnold Bennett: Vol. 55). 1976. Repr. of 1911 ed. 16.75 (ISBN 0-518-19136-2). Ayer Co Pubs.

--Milestones. LC 74-17129. (Collected Works of Arnold Bennett: Vol. 56). 1976. Repr. of 1912 ed. 16.75 (ISBN 0-518-19137-0). Ayer Co Pubs.

--Mr. Prohack: A Comedy in Three Acts. LC 74-17128. (Collected Works of Arnold Bennett: Vol. 58). 1976. Repr. of 1927 ed. 22.75 (ISBN 0-518-19138-9). Ayer Co Pubs.

--The Night Visitor & Other Stories. LC 74-17062. (Collected Works of Arnold Bennett: Vol. 59). 1976. Repr. of 1931 ed. 29.00 (ISBN 0-518-19140-0). Ayer Co Pubs.

--The Old Adam. LC 74-17296. (Collected Works of Arnold Bennett: Vol. 60). 1976. Repr. of 1913 ed. 30.00 (ISBN 0-518-19141-9). Ayer Co Pubs.

--Old Wives' Tale. 632p. 1980. pap. 8.95 (ISBN 0-915864-77-0). Academy Chi Pubs.

--The Old Wives' Tale. LC 74-17060. (Collected Works of Arnold Bennett: Vol. 61). 1976. Repr. of 1911 ed. 43.25 (ISBN 0-518-19142-7). Ayer Co Pubs.

--The Old Wives' Tale. 529p. 1982. pap. text ed. 3.95x (ISBN 0-460-01919-8, Pub. by Evman England). Biblio Dist.

--The Old Wives Tales. Wain, John, ed. (Penguin English Library). 400p. 1983. pap. 5.95 (ISBN 0-14-043163-2). Penguin.

--Our Women. LC 74-17107. (Collected Works of Arnold Bennett: Vol. 62). 1976. Repr. of 1920 ed. 22.75 (ISBN 0-518-19143-5). Ayer Co Pubs.

--Our Women. 250p. 1980. Repr. of 1920 ed. lib. bdg. 25.00 (ISBN 0-8492-3756-4). R West.

--Paris Nights & Other Impressions of Places & People. (Collected Works of Arnold Bennett: Vol. 64). (Illus.). 1976. Repr. of 1913 ed. 33.00 (ISBN 0-518-19145-1, 19145). Ayer Co Pubs.

--Piccadilly. LC 74-17299. (Collected Works of Arnold Bennett: Vol. 65). 1976. Repr. of 1930 ed. 19.75 (ISBN 0-518-19146-X). Ayer Co Pubs.

--The Pretty Lady. LC 74-17298. (Collected Works of Arnold Bennett: Vol. 67). 1976. Repr. of 1918 ed. 22.75 (ISBN 0-518-19148-6). Ayer Co Pubs.

--Pretty Lady. LC 72-144876. 1971. Repr. of 1918 ed. 18.00x (ISBN 0-403-00863-8). Scholarly.

--The Price of Love. LC 74-17050. (Collected Works of Arnold Bennett: Vol. 68). 1976. Repr. of 1914 ed. 35.50 (ISBN 0-518-19149-4). Ayer Co Pubs.

--The Reasonable Life. LC 74-16364. (Collected Works of Arnold Bennett: Vol. 69). 1976. Repr. of 1907 ed. 16.75 (ISBN 0-518-19150-8). Ayer Co Pubs.

--The Regent. LC 74-17073. (Collected Works of Arnold Bennett: Vol. 70). 1976. Repr. of 1913 ed. 23.50 (ISBN 0-518-19151-6). Ayer Co Pubs.

--Riceyman Steps. 393p. pap. 8.95 (ISBN 0-89733-093-5). Academy Chi Pubs.

--The Roll-Call. LC 74-17047. (Collected Works of Arnold Bennett: Vol. 71). 1976. Repr. of 1918 ed. 24.25 (ISBN 0-518-19152-4). Ayer Co Pubs.

--The Savour of Life. LC 74-17048. (Collected Works of Arnold Bennett: Vol. 72). 1976. Repr. of 1928 ed. 24.25 (ISBN 0-518-19153-2). Ayer Co Pubs.

--Self & Self-Management. LC 74-16345. (Collected Works of Arnold Bennett: Vol. 73). 1976. Repr. of 1918 ed. 16.75 (ISBN 0-518-19154-0). Ayer Co Pubs.

--The Sinews of War. LC 74-17139. (Collected Works of Arnold Bennett: Vol. 74). 1976. Repr. 24.25 (ISBN 0-518-19155-9). Ayer Co Pubs.

--Sketches for Autobiography. Hepburn, James, ed. 192p. 1979. text ed. 17.95x (ISBN 0-04-928041-4). Allen Unwin.

--The Statue. LC 74-17141. (Collected Works of Arnold Bennett: Vol. 75). 1976. Repr. of 1911 ed. 19.25 (ISBN 0-518-19156-7). Ayer Co Pubs.

--Stroke of Luck & Dream of Destiny. LC 74-17075. (Collected Works of Arnold Bennett: Vol. 76). 1976. Repr. of 1932 ed. 22.00 (ISBN 0-518-19157-5). Ayer Co Pubs.

--Tales of the Five Towns. LC 74-17131. (Collected Works of Arnold Bennett: Vol. 77). 1976. Repr. of 1910 ed. 21.75 (ISBN 0-518-19158-3). Ayer Co Pubs.

--Teresa of Watling Street. LC 74-17051. (Collected Works of Arnold Bennett: Vol. 78). 1976. Repr. of 1904 ed. 18.75 (ISBN 0-518-19159-1). Ayer Co Pubs.

--These Twain. LC 74-17052. (Collected Works of Arnold Bennett: Vol. 79). 1976. Repr. of 1915 ed. 41.25 (ISBN 0-518-19160-5). Ayer Co Pubs.

--Things That Have Interested Me: First Series. LC 74-17049. (Collected Works of Arnold Bennett: Vol. 80). 1976. Repr. of 1921 ed. 27.50 (ISBN 0-518-19161-3, 19161). Ayer Co Pubs.

--Things That Have Interested Me: Second Series. LC 74-17091. (Collected Works of Arnold Bennett: Vol. 81). 1976. Repr. of 1923 ed. 24.25 (ISBN 0-518-19162-1). Ayer Co Pubs.

--Things That Have Interested Me: Third Series. LC 74-17074. (Collected Works of Arnold Bennett: Vol. 82). 1976. Repr. of 1926 ed. 22.75 (ISBN 0-518-19163-X). Ayer Co Pubs.

--The Title. LC 74-17056. (Collected Works of Arnold Bennett: Vol. 83). 1976. Repr. of 1918 ed. 16.75 (ISBN 0-518-19164-8). Ayer Co Pubs.

--The Truth about an Author. LC 74-17055. (Collected Works of Arnold Bennett: Vol. 84). 1976. Repr. of 1911 ed. 20.25 (ISBN 0-518-19165-6). Ayer Co Pubs.

--The Vanguard. LC 74-17054. (Collected Works of Arnold Bennett: Vol. 85). 1976. Repr. of 1927 ed. 22.75 (ISBN 0-518-19166-4). Ayer Co Pubs.

--What the Public Wants. LC 74-16478. (Collected Works of Arnold Bennett: Vol. 86). 1976. Repr. of 1909 ed. 18.75 (ISBN 0-518-19167-2). Ayer Co Pubs.

--Where Are the Dead? LC 74-17034. (Collected Works of Arnold Bennett: Vol. 87). 1976. Repr. of 1928 ed. 18.75 (ISBN 0-518-19168-0). Ayer Co Pubs.

--Whom God Hath Joined. Date not set. lib. bdg. 11.95 (ISBN 0-915864-82-7); pap. 5.25 (ISBN 0-915864-81-9). Academy Chi Pubs.

--Whom God Hath Joined. LC 74-17007. (Collected Works of Arnold Bennett: Vol. 88). 1976. Repr. of 1906 ed. 31.00 (ISBN 0-518-19169-9). Ayer Co Pubs.

--The Woman Who Stole Everything & Other Stories. LC 74-17057. (Collected Works of Arnold Bennett: Vol. 89). 1976. Repr. of 1927 ed. 28.00 (ISBN 0-518-19170-2). Ayer Co Pubs.

--Your United States. LC 74-16408. (Collected Works of Arnold Bennett: Vol. 90). 1976. Repr. of 1912 ed. 20.75 (ISBN 0-518-19171-0). Ayer Co Pubs.

Bennett, Arnold & Knoblauch, Edward. Milestones, A Play in Three Acts. LC 78-131624. 1971. Repr. of 1912 ed. 15.00x (ISBN 0-403-00511-6). Scholarly.

Bennett, Arnold, et al. Frank Swinnerton. LC 74-5433. (Collected Works of Arnold Bennett: Vol. 18). 1976. Repr. of 1920 ed. 16.75 (ISBN 0-518-19099-4). Ayer Co Pubs.

Bennett, Mrs. Arnold. Arnold Bennett. 1973. Repr. of 1925 ed. 20.00 (ISBN 0-8274-0716-5). R West.

Bennett, Arthur G. & Rabbetts, Ronald B. Clinical Visual Optics. (Illus.). 424p. 1985. text ed. 79.95 (ISBN 0-407-00068-2). Butterworth.

Bennett, B., jt. auth. see Bennett, S.

Bennett, B. A. & Wilkins, D. G., eds. Donatello. (Illus.). 1985. 65.00 (ISBN 0-89835-261-4). Abaris Bks.

Bennett, Barbara. Words Take Wing: A Teaching Guide to Creative Writing for Children. 178p. 1983. text ed. 15.95x (ISBN 0-8138-1932-6). Iowa St U Pr.

Bennett, Barbara, jt. auth. see Prigal, Ken.

Bennett, Barbara, ed. see Glubetich, Dave.

Bennett, Barbara, ed. see Harris, James.

Bennett, Barbara C. Berryhill. (Orig.). 1979. pap. 1.95 (ISBN 0-686-68907-0). Woodhill.

Bennett, Barbara R. see Jacobs, Lenworth M.

Bennett, Ben. Death, Too, for The-Heavy-Runner. (Illus.). 192p. 1982. O.P. 14.95 (ISBN 0-87842-131-9); pap. 7.95 (ISBN 0-87842-132-7). Mountain Pr.

Bennett, Benjamin. Modern Drama & German Classicism: Renaissance from Lessing to Brecht. LC 79-14644. (Illus.). 1979. 29.95x (ISBN 0-8014-1189-0). Cornell U Pr.

Bennett, Betty T., ed. British War Poetry in the Age of Romanticism: 1793-1815. LC 75-31144. (Romantic Context: Poetry 1789-1830 Ser.: Vol. 1). 1977. lib. bdg. 57.00 (ISBN 0-8240-2100-2). Garland Pub.

--The Letters of Mary Wollstonecraft Shelley: Vol. II: "Treading in Unknown Paths". LC 79-24190. 416p. 1983. text ed. 32.00x (ISBN 0-8018-2645-4). Johns Hopkins.

--The Letters of Mary Wollstonecraft Shelley, Vol. 1: A Part of the Elect. LC 79-24190. 1980. 35.00x (ISBN 0-8018-2275-0). Johns Hopkins.

Bennett, Bev. Easy Cooking Step-by-Step. 432p. 1985. 21.95 (ISBN 0-8120-5637-X). Barron.

--Two's Company. (Illus.). 224p. 1985. 14.95 (ISBN 0-8120-5596-9). Barron.

Bennett, Beverly & Upton, Kim. The Joy of Cocktails & Hors D'oeuvre. (Illus.). 208p. 1984. 14.95 (ISBN 0-8120-5592-6). Barron.

Bennett, Bill & Tatchell, Judy. Understanding the Micro. (Usborne Electronics Ser.). (Illus.). 48p. (gr. 7-9). 1982. 8.95 (ISBN 0-86020-638-6, Usborne-Hayes); PLB 12.95 (ISBN 0-88110-008-0); pap. 5.95 (ISBN 0-86020-637-8). EDC.

Bennett, Bill, jt. auth. see Martin, Ken.

Bennett, Blake, ed. see Milkovich, J.

Bennett, Blossom. Blossoms for Gladness. (Contemporary Poets of Dorrance Ser.). 96p. 1982. 8.95 (ISBN 0-8059-2853-7). Dorrance.

Bennett, Bob. Raising Rabbits Successfully. (Illus.). 192p. (Orig.). 1984. pap. 8.95 (ISBN 0-913589-03-9). Williamson Pub Co.

--The T.F.H. Book of Pet Rabbits. (Illus.). 80p. 1982. 6.95 (ISBN 0-87666-815-5, HP-014). TFH Pubns.

Bennett, Bonnie & Wilkins, David. Donatello. (Illus.). 248p. 1985. 49.95 (ISBN 0-918825-03-2). Moyer Bell Ltd.

Bennett, Boyce M. Bennett's Guide to the Bible: Graphic Aids & Outlines. (Illus.). 128p. (Orig.). 1982. pap. 9.95 (ISBN 0-8164-2397-0, Pub. by Seabury). Winston Pr.

Bennett, Brian C. Sutivan: A Dalmatian Village in Social & Economic Transition. LC 73-80724. (Illus.). 1974. 10.00 (ISBN 0-88247-226-7). Ragusan Pr.

Bennett Brother's Printing, ed. see Wagner, Clarence M.

Bennett, Bruce. Straw into Gold. (CSU Poetry Ser.: No. xvi). 52p. (Orig.). 1984. pap. 4.50 (ISBN 0-914946-45-5). Cleveland St Univ Poetry Ctr.

Bennett, Bruce, jt. auth. see Van Dalen, Deobold B.

Bennett, Bruce, ed. History of Physical Education & Sport. LC 72-77548. 1972. soft bdg. 5.00 (ISBN 0-87670-854-8). Athletic Inst.

--The Literature of Western Australia. 1980. 30.00x (ISBN 0-85564-152-5, Pub by U of W Austral Pr). Intl Spec Bk.

Bennett, Bruce L., et al. Comparative Physical Education & Sport. 2nd ed. LC 82-14957. 283p. 1983. pap. 19.00 (ISBN 0-8121-0864-7). Lea & Febiger.

Bennett, C. Practical Time Travel. (Paths to Inner Power Ser.). 1971. pap. 2.50 (ISBN 0-85030-203-X). Weiser.

Bennett, C., et al, eds. Comparative Studies in Adult Education: An Anthology. LC 75-20016. (Occasional Papers Ser.: No. 44). 250p. 1975. pap. 9.00 (ISBN 0-87060-069-9, OCP 44). Syracuse U Cont Ed.

Bennett, C. Mehrl & Bennett, John M. Some Blood: Joint Poems. 16p. 1982. signed & lettered ed. 8.00 (ISBN 0-935350-08-X); pap. 3.00 (ISBN 0-935350-07-1). Luna Bisonte.

Bennett, C. Mehrl, jt. auth. see Bennett, John M.

Bennett, C. O. & Myers, J. E. Momentum, Heat & Mass Transfer. 3rd ed. (Chemical Engineering Ser.). 1981. 46.00 (ISBN 0-07-004671-9). McGraw.

Bennett, C. Richard. Monheim's Local Anesthesia & Pain Control in Dental Practice. 7th ed. (Illus.). 384p. 1984. text ed. 31.95 (ISBN 0-8016-0614-4). Mosby.

Bennett, Carl A. & Lumsdaine, Arthur A., eds. Evaluation & Experiment: Some Critical Issues in Assessing Social Programs (Based upon a Symposium) (Quantitative Studies in Social Relations Ser.). 1975. 49.50 (ISBN 0-12-088850-5). Acad Pr.

Bennett, Carl A., et al. Statistical Analysis in Chemistry & the Chemical Industry. LC 54-11428. (Wiley Publications in Statistics Ser.). pap. 160.00 (ISBN 0-317-09349-5, 2055153). Bks Demand UMI.

Bennett, Cathereen L. Will Rogers: The Cowboy Who Walked with Kings. 9.95 (ISBN 0-88411-848-7, Pub. by Aeonian Pr). Amereon Ltd.

Bennett, Charles & Rogers, W. H., illus. Quarles' Emblems. 321p. 1980. Repr. lib. bdg. 50.00 (ISBN 0-8495-4576-5). Arden Lib.

Bennett, Charles, et al. The Year-Round, All-Occasion Make Your Own Greeting Card Book. LC 84-8459. (Illus.). 1984. pap. 7.95 (ISBN 0-87477-321-0). J P Tarcher.

Bennett, Charles A. Dilemma of Religious Knowledge. LC 71-85986. (Essay & General Literature Index Reprint Ser). 1969. Repr. of 1931 ed. 14.00x (ISBN 0-8046-0538-6, Pub. by Kennikat). Assoc Faculty Pr.

--History of Manual & Industrial Education, 2 vols, Vol. 1. to 1870, Vol. 2. 1870-1917. Vol. 1 to 1870. text ed. 25.32 (ISBN 0-02-664360-X); Vol. 2, 1870-1917. text ed. 25.32 (ISBN 0-02-664370-7). Bennett IL.

Bennett, Charles E. Critique of Some Recent Subjunctive Theories. Repr. of 1898 ed. 10.00 (ISBN 0-384-03901-4). Johnson Repr.

--Florida's French Revolution, Seventeen Ninety-Three to Seventeen Ninety-Five. LC 81-7431. x, 218p. 1981. 16.00 (ISBN 0-8130-0641-4). U Presses Fla.

--Syntax of Early Latin, 2 Vols. Repr. of 1910 ed. Set. 107.50x (ISBN 3-487-01345-2). Adlers Foreign Bks.

Bennett, Charles E., ed. Dialogus de Oratoribus. 1983. lib. bdg. 20.00; pap. 10.00 (ISBN 0-89241-380-8). Caratzas.

--On Old Age-De Senectute: Cicero. (Bolchazy-Carducci Textbook). (Illus.). 446p. 1980. pap. text ed. 8.00x (ISBN 0-86516-001-5). Bolchazy-Carducci.

Bennett, Charles E., ed. see Horace.

Bennett, Charles F. Conservation & Management of Natural Sources in the United States. LC 82-21941. 436p. 1983. text ed. 28.00 (ISBN 0-471-04652-3). Wiley.

Bennett, Charles F., Jr. Man & Earth's Ecosystems: An Introduction to the Geography of Human Modification of the Earth. LC 75-22330. 331p. 1976. text ed. 33.95x (ISBN 0-471-06638-9). Wiley.

Bennett, Charles H., ed. see Walpole, Horace.

Bennett, Chester C. An Inquiry into the Genesis of Poor Reading. LC 70-176553. (Columbia University. Teachers College. Contributions to Education: No. 755). Repr. of 1938 ed. 22.50 (ISBN 0-404-55755-4). AMS Pr.

Bennett, Christine. The Girl of Black Island. (Contemporary Teens Ser.). 224p. (Orig.). 1981. pap. 2.25 (ISBN 0-89531-141-0, 0146-96). Sharon Pubns.

--Gloria's Ghost. (Contemporary Teens Ser.). 224p. (Orig.). 1981. pap. 2.25 (ISBN 0-89531-140-2, 0146-96). Sharon Pubns.

--Wind in the Sage. (Contemporary Teens Ser.). 224p. (Orig.). 1981. pap. 2.25 (ISBN 0-89531-144-5, 0146-96). Sharon Pubns.

Bennett, Clarence. Advance & Retreat to Saratoga, 2 vols. in 1. LC 72-8741. (American Revolutionary Ser.). 1979. Repr. of 1927 ed. lib. bdg. 59.00 (ISBN 0-8398-0186-6). Irvington.

--Physics Problems & How to Solve Them. 3rd ed. (Orig.). 1973. pap. 7.95 (ISBN 0-06-460203-6, CO 203, COS). B&N NY.

Bennett, Clarence E. College Physics. 6th ed. LC 67-16622. (Illus.). 1967. pap. 5.95 (ISBN 0-06-460021-1, CO 21, COS). B&N NY.

--Physics Without Mathematics. rev. ed. LC 76-124362. 1970. pap. 5.95 (ISBN 0-06-460067-X, CO 67, COS). B&N NY.

Bennett, Clifford. Nursing Home Life: What It Is & What It Could Be. LC 80-52650. (Illus.). 192p. 1980. pap. text ed. 7.95 (ISBN 0-913292-19-2). Tiresias Pr.

Bennett, Clinton W., et al, eds. Contemporary Readings in Articulation Disorders. 400p. 1982. pap. text ed. 20.95 (ISBN 0-8403-2656-4). Kendall-Hunt.

Bennett, Clois W. Clinical Serology. (Illus.). 304p. 1980. 19.75x (ISBN 0-398-00130-8). C C Thomas.

Bennett, Colin. What Is Astrology? 124p. 1981. 6.50 (ISBN 0-89540-113-4, SB-113). Sun Pub.

Bennett, Constance. The Pirate's Vixen. 1985. pap. 3.95 (ISBN 0-8217-1636-0). Zebra.

Bennett, Cora N. One Two Three Four Five Six Seven All Dead Children Go to Heaven. 32p. 1986. 5.95 (ISBN 0-89962-509-6). Todd & Honeywell.

Bennett, Curtis. God As Form: Essays in Greek Mythology. LC 75-43851. 1976. 36.50x (ISBN 0-87395-325-8). State U NY Pr.

Bennett, D. Machine Embroidery with Style. LC 80-13914. (Connecting Threads Ser.). (Illus.). 100p. 1980. pap. 9.95 (ISBN 0-914842-45-5). Madrona Pubs.

Bennett, D. Gordon. World Population Problems: An Introduction to Population Geography. LC 83-62691. 250p. 1984. pap. text ed. 9.95 (ISBN 0-941226-04-2). Park Pr Co.

Bennett, D. Gordon, ed. Tension Areas of the World: A Problem Oriented World Regional Geography. LC 81-82632. (Illus.). 342p. 1982. text ed. 19.95 (ISBN 0-941226-01-8). Park Pr Co.

Bennett, D. M., et al, eds. Chromosomes Today: Vol. VII. (Illus.). 336p. 1981. text ed. 38.50x (ISBN 0-04-575021-1). Allen Unwin.

Bennett, D. R., et al. Atlas of Electroencephalography in Coma & Cerebral Death: EEG at the Bedside or in the Intensive Care Unit. LC 74-14470. 254p. 1976. 108.00 (ISBN 0-911216-91-X). Raven.

Bennett, Daphne. Margot: A Life of the Countess of Oxford & Asquith. 452p. 1985. 18.95 (ISBN 0-531-09794-3). Watts.

Bennett, David H. Cardiac Arrhythmias: Practical Notes on Interpretation & Treatment. (Illus.). 176p. 1981. pap. text ed. 20.50 (ISBN 0-7236-0590-4). PSG Pub Co.

Bennett, De Robigne M. Anthony Comstock: His Career of Cruelty & Crime. LC 73-121102. (Civil Liberties in American History Ser). 1971. Repr. of 1878 ed. lib. bdg. 22.50 (ISBN 0-306-71968-1). Da Capo.

Bennett, Dean B. & Young, Barbara E., eds. Maine Dirigo: I Lead. LC 80-68242. (Maine Studies Curriculum Project). (Illus.). 300p. 1980. text ed. 13.50 (ISBN 0-89272-103-0). Down East.

Bennett, Dean B., ed. see Maine Studies Curriculum Project.

Bennett, Debra K. The Fossil Fauna from Lost & Found Quarries (Hemphilliam: Latest Miocene), Wallace County, Kansas. (Occasional Papers: No. 79). 24p. 1979. pap. 1.50 (ISBN 0-686-79812-0). U of KS Mus Nat Hist.

Bennett, Dennis. How to Pray for the Release of the Holy Spirit. 1985. pap. 3.95 (ISBN 0-88270-586-5). Bridge Pub.

--Moving Right Along in the Spirit. 160p. 1982. 5.95 (ISBN 0-8007-5184-1, Power Bks). Revell.

Bennett, Dennis & Bennett, Rita. Holy Spirit & You Supplement. LC 73-75963. (To be used with The Holy Spirit & You). 1973. pap. 3.95 (ISBN 0-88270-031-6, Pub. by Logos). Bridge Pub.

--The Holy Spirit & You: The Text Book of the Charismatic Renewal. LC 71-140673. 224p. 1971. pap. 4.95 (ISBN 0-912106-14-X, Pub. by Logos). Bridge Pub.

--Trinidad Del Hombre. Carrodeguas, Andy, ed. Lievano, Franscisco, tr. from Span. Orig. Title: Trinity of Man. 224p. 1982. pap. 2.50 (ISBN 0-8297-1298-4). Life Pubs Intl.

--Trinity of Man. LC 79-67378. (Illus.). 1979. pap. text ed. 6.95 (ISBN 0-88270-287-4, Pub. by Logos). Bridge Pub.

Bennett, Dennis J. Nine O'clock in the Morning: An Episcopal Priest Discovers the Holy Spirit. LC 72-85205. 1970. pap. 4.95 (ISBN 0-912106-41-7, Pub. by Logos). Bridge Pub.

Bennett, Diane T. & Tarleton, Linda. William Cullen Bryant in Roslyn. LC 87-67782. 163p. 1978. pap. 5.95 (ISBN 0-9602242-1-1). Bryant Library.

Bennett, Dominique, et al. Horizons: An Introduction to French Language & Culture. 1984. text ed. 27.95 (ISBN 0-03-062496-7). HR&W.

Bennett, Donald J. The Elements of Nuclear Power. 2nd ed. LC 80-41121. 1981. pap. text ed. 21.95x (ISBN 0-582-30504-7). Longman.

Bennett, Donald P. & Humphries, David A. Introduction to Field Biology. 2nd ed. 1974. pap. text ed. 18.95x (ISBN 0-7131-2458-X). Intl Ideas.

Bennett, Dorothy C. Arnold Bennett. 1973. Repr. of 1935 ed. 20.00 (ISBN 0-8274-0695-9). R West.

Bennett, Douglas. Collecting Irish Silver. (Illus.). 228p. 1985. 28.95 (ISBN 0-285-62622-1, Pub. by Souvenir Pr Ltd UK). Seven Hills Bks.

Bennett, Douglas C. & Sharpe, Kenneth E. Transnational Corporations versus the State: The Political Economy of the Mexican Auto Industry. LC 85-42674. 329p. 1985. text ed. 42.00x (ISBN 0-691-07689-8); pap. 9.95 (ISBN 0-691-02237-2). Princeton U Pr.

Bennett, Douglas H., jt. ed. see Watts, Fraser N.

Bennett, Dudley. Successful Team Building Through TA. 1980. 14.95 (ISBN 0-8144-5607-3). AMACOM.

--TA & the Manager. (AMACOM Executive Bks). 1978. pap. 5.95 (ISBN 0-8144-7511-6). AMACOM.

--TA & the Manager. (Illus.). 1976. 13.95 (ISBN 0-8144-5422-4). AMACOM.

--TA & the Manager. LC 76-20559. pap. cancelled (ISBN 0-317-10213-3, 2022624). Bks Demand UMI.

Bennett, E. K. History of the German Novelle. rev. ed. Waidson, H. M., rev. by. (Orig.). 1961. 52.50 (ISBN 0-521-04152-X). Cambridge U Pr.

Bennett, E. M. & Trute, B., eds. Mental Health Information Systems: Problems & Prospects. LC 83-23683. (Studies in Health & Human Services: Vol. 1). 318p. 1983. 49.95x (ISBN 0-88946-125-2). E Mellen.

Bennett, E. N. Problems of Village Life. 10.00 (ISBN 0-8482-3447-2). Norwood Edns.

Bennett, E. W. Structural Concrete Elements. (Illus.). 1973. 21.95x (ISBN 0-412-09020-1, 6034, Pub. by Chapman & Hall). Methuen Inc.

Bennett, Edna M. & Bennett, John F. Turquoise Jewelry of the Indians of the Southwest. (Illus.). 1973. 15.00 (ISBN 0-917834-01-1). Turquoise Bks.

Bennett, Edward. Rigid Gas Permeable Contact Lenses. 1985. 49.00 (ISBN 0-87873-057-5). Prof Press.

--A Treatise Touching the Inconveniences, That the Importation of Tobacco Out of Spaine, Hath Brought into This Land. LC 77-6856. (English Experience Ser.: No. 846). 1977. Repr. of 1620 ed. lib. bdg. 3.50 (ISBN 90-221-0846-5). Walter J Johnson.

Bennett, Edward D. Blue's Isle. 610p. 1981. 22.00x (ISBN 0-9605962-0-8). Aozora Pub.

Bennett, Edward H., jt. auth. see Burnham, Daniel H.

Bennett, Edward J. & Bowyer, Denis E. Principles of Pediatric Anesthesia. (Illus.). 392p. 1982. 34.75x (ISBN 0-398-04653-0). C C Thomas.

Bennett, Edward L., jt. ed. see Rosenzweig, Mark R.

Bennett, Edward M. Franklin D. Roosevelt & the Search for Security: American-Soviet Relations, 1933-1939. 224p. 1985. 30.00 (ISBN 0-8420-2246-5); pap. text ed. 9.95 (ISBN 0-8420-2247-3). Scholarly Res Inc.

Bennett, Edward M., jt. ed. see Burns, Richard D.

Bennett, Edward W. German Rearmament & the West, 1932-1933. LC 78-70277. 1979. 57.00 (ISBN 0-691-05269-7). Princeton U Pr.

--Germany & the Diplomacy of the Financial Crisis, 1931. LC 62-13261. (Historical Monographs Ser: No. 50). 1962. 22.50x (ISBN 0-674-35250-5). Harvard U Pr.

Bennett, Elizabeth, jt. auth. see Bennett, John G.

Bennett, Emerson. Forest Rose: A Tale of the Frontier. Facs. of 1885 Ed. LC 72-96394. li, 118p. 1973. 4.95 (ISBN 0-8214-0128-9, 82-81313). Ohio U Pr.

--Mike Fink. LC 75-104415. Repr. of 1848 ed. lib. bdg. 9.50 (ISBN 0-8398-0162-9). Irvington.

--The Prairie Flower. LC 79-104416. Repr. of 1849 ed. lib. bdg. 14.50 (ISBN 0-8398-0163-7). Irvington.

Bennett, Emma. Beneath the Willow Tree. (Candlelight Ecstasy Ser.: No. 167). 192p. (Orig.). 1983. pap. 1.95 (ISBN 0-440-10443-2). Dell.

--By Passion Bound. (Candlelight Ecstasy Ser.: No. 135). (Orig.). 1983. pap. 1.95 (ISBN 0-440-10918-3). Dell.

--Loving Brand. (Candlelight Ecstasy Ser.: No. 228). (Orig.). 1984. pap. 1.95 (ISBN 0-440-15106-6). Dell.

--Loving Persuasion. (Candlelight Ecstasy Romance Ser.: No. 329). 192p. pap. 1.95 (ISBN 0-440-15113-9). Dell.

--River Enchantment. (Candlelight Ecstasy Ser.: No. 139). (Orig.). 1983. pap. 1.95 (ISBN 0-440-17470-8). Dell.

--That Certain Summer. (Candlelight Ecstasy Ser.: No. 120). (Orig.). 1983. pap. 1.95 (ISBN 0-440-18579-3). Dell.

--With Each Passing Hour. (Candlelight Ecstasy Ser.: No. 257). (Orig.). 1984. pap. 1.95 (ISBN 0-440-19741-4). Dell.

Bennett, Emmett L., Jr., ed. see International Colloquium For Mycenaean Studies - 3rd - Wingspread - 1961.

Bennett, Ernest N. Downfall of the Dervishes. LC 71-79818. (Illus.). Repr. of 1899 ed. 19.75x (ISBN 0-8371-1545-0, BEB&). Greenwood.

Bennett, Estelline. Old Deadwood Days. LC 81-14737. (Illus.). xiv, 314p. 1982. 23.95x (ISBN 0-8032-1173-2); pap. 6.50 (ISBN 0-8032-6065-2, BB 794, Bison). U of Nebr Pr.

Bennett, Evan. The Maya Epic. 135p. 1974. 12.95 (ISBN 0-686-27297-8). U Pr Wisc River Falls.

Bennett, F. Lawrence. Critical Path Precedence Networks: A Handbook on Activity-on-Node Networking for the Construction Industry. LC 77-9069. 110p. 1977. 27.50 (ISBN 0-442-12190-3). Krieger.

Bennett, F. M. Religious Cults Associated with the Amazons. v, 79p. 1985. Repr. of 1912 ed. lib. bdg. 20.00x (ISBN 0-89241-204-6). Caratzas.

Bennett, F. V. & Symmons, P. M. A Review of Estimates of the Effectiveness of Certain Control Techniques & Insecticides Against the Desert Locust. 1972. 35.00x (ISBN 0-85135-060-7, Pub. by Centre Overseas Research). State Mutual Bk.

Bennett, Frances & Chang, Sunny. Page a Day Study Guide for Competency Tests. 224p. (Orig.). 1981. pap. 4.95 (ISBN 0-668-05284-8, 5284). Arco.

Bennett, Frances C. & Chang, Sunny. Page a Day SAT Study Guide. 320p. (Orig.). 1981. pap. 4.95 (ISBN 0-668-05196-5, 5196). Arco.

Bennett, Frank M. Steam Navy of the United States. LC 70-98814. Repr. of 1896 ed. lib. bdg. 56.25 (ISBN 0-8371-2949-4, BESN). Greenwood.

Bennett, G. F. When They Ask for Bread: Pastoral Care & Counseling. LC 77-15743. 1978. 8.95 (ISBN 0-8042-1159-0). John Knox.

Bennett, G. W., jt. ed. see Griffiths, E. C.

Bennett, G. Willis. Effective Urban Church Ministry. LC 83-70370. 1983. pap. 5.95 (ISBN 0-8054-5526-4). Broadman.

Bennett, Garry & Perkins, Roberta. Being a Prostitute. 340p. (Orig.). 1985. text ed. 28.00x (ISBN 0-86861-678-8); pap. text ed. 12.50x (ISBN 0-86861-637-0). Allen Unwin.

Bennett, Gary. The Star Sailors. 384p. 1980. 12.95 (ISBN 0-312-75582-1). St Martin.

Bennett, Gary F., ed. Water: Nineteen Eighty. LC 81-93783. (AIChE Symposium Ser.: Vol. 77). 344p. 1981. pap. 38.00 (ISBN 0-8169-0217-8, S-209); pap. 20.00 members. Am Inst Chem Eng.

Bennett, Gary F., et al. Handbook of Hazardous Materials Spills. LC 82-123. (Illus.). 704p. 1982. 57.50 (ISBN 0-07-004680-8). McGraw.

Bennett, Gay. A Family in Sri Lanka. LC 85-6891. (Families the World over Ser.). (Illus.). 32p. (gr. 2-5). 1985. PLB 8.95 (ISBN 0-8225-1661-6). Lerner Pubns.

Bennett, Geoffrey W. & Whitehead, Saffron A. Mammalian Neuroendocrinology. (Illus.). 1983. pap. 19.95x (ISBN 0-19-520416-6). Oxford U Pr.

Bennett, Georgaan. What the Bible Says About Goodness. LC 80-69626. (What the Bible Says Ser.). 405p. 1981. 13.50 (ISBN 0-89900-080-0). College Pr Pub.

Bennett, Georgann. Soulshine. 1978. pap. 2.95 (ISBN 0-89900-133-5). College Pr Pub.

Bennett, George. When the Mental Patient Comes Home, Vol.2. LC 79-23809. (Christian Care Books). 118p. 1980. pap. 6.95 (ISBN 0-664-24295-2). Westminster.

Bennett, George, ed. Great Tales of Action & Adventure. 256p. (YA) (gr. 7 up). 1959. pap. 2.75 (ISBN 0-440-93202-5, LFL). Dell.

Bennett, George, et al. The Historiography of the British Empire- Commonwealth: Trends, Interpretations & Resources. LC 65-15555. pap. 152.50 (ISBN 0-317-26799-X, 2023472). Bks Demand UMI.

Bennett, George N. The Realism of William Dean Howells, 1889-1920. LC 72-1345. 256p. 1973. 14.95x (ISBN 0-8265-1180-5). Vanderbilt U Pr.

Bennett, George W. Management of Lakes & Ponds. 2nd ed. LC 83-6091. 398p. 1983. Repr. of 1970 ed. text ed. 23.95 (ISBN 0-89874-626-4). Krieger.

Bennett, Gerald & Vourakis, Christine. Substance Abuse: Pharmacologic, Developmental & Clinical Perspectives. LC 82-13583. 453p. 1983. cloth 30.00 (ISBN 0-471-08537-5, Pub. by Wiley Med). Wiley.

Bennett, Gerald T., jt. auth. see Chance, Chester B.

Bennett, Gertrude B. The Heads of Cerberus. Reginald, R. & Melville, Douglas, eds. LC 77-84269. (Lost Race & Adult Fantasy Ser.). (Illus.). 1978. Repr. of 1952 ed. lib. bdg. 20.00x (ISBN 0-405-11009-X). Ayer Co Pubs.

Bennett, Gertrude R. Ballads of Colonial Days, with Historical Background. LC 72-91230. 160p. 1972. 5.00 (ISBN 0-8233-0186-9). Golden Quill.

--Fugitive. 1975. 5.00 (ISBN 0-8233-0217-2). Golden Quill.

--Living in a Landmark. (Illus.). 1980. 7.00 (ISBN 0-686-86304-6). M Jones.

--Turning Back the Clock. 1982. 7.00 (ISBN 0-317-07543-8). M Jones.

Bennett, Gordon. Aboriginal Rights in International Law. (RAI Occasional Papers: No. 37). 1978. pap. text ed. 10.00x (ISBN 0-391-01109-X). Humanities.

--Aboriginal Rights in International Law. 1978. 29.00 (ISBN 0-686-98249-5, Pub. by Royal Anthro Ireland). State Mutual bk.

--Yundong: Mass Campaigns in Chinese Communist Leadership. LC 75-620060. (China Research Monographs: No. 12). 1976. pap. text ed. 4.50x (ISBN 0-912966-15-7). IEAS.

Bennett, Gordon, ed. China's Finance & Trade: A Policy Reader. LC 77-99080. 256p. 1978. pap. 11.95 (ISBN 0-87332-115-4). M E Sharpe.

Bennett, Gordon, jt. ed. see Peers, John.

Bennett, Gordon A. & Montaperto, Ronald N. Red Guard: The Political Biography of Dai Hsiao-Ai. 12.00 (ISBN 0-8446-4710-1). Peter Smith.

Bennett, Gordon C. God Is My Fuehrer. (Orig.). 1970. pap. 1.50 (ISBN 0-377-80611-0). Friend Pr.

--Happy Tales, Fables & Plays. LC 75-13464. (Illus.). 120p. 1976. pap. 6.95 (ISBN 0-8042-1947-8). John Knox.

--Reader's Theatre Comes to Church. 2nd ed. LC 85-61999. 128p. 1985. pap. 6.95 (ISBN 0-317-31575-7). Meriwether Pub.

Bennett, Gordon D., jt. ed. see Rosenshein, Joseph.

Bennett, Gordon H., jt. auth. see Marshall, Alejandro.

Bennett, Gordon H., jt. auth. see Pollock, Algernon J.

Bennett, Gordon H., jt. auth. see Voorehoeve, H. C.

Bennett, Gordon H., ed. see Collingwood, Guillermo.

Bennett, Gordon H., ed. see Cutting, Jorge.

Bennett, Gordon H., ed. see Mackintosh, Carlos H.

Bennett, Gordon H., ed. see Rossier, H.

Bennett, Gregory R. Successful Convention Management. 160p. Repr. lib. bdg. cancelled (ISBN 0-89370-079-7). Borgo Pr.

Bennett, Gwen P. A Bibliography of Illinois Archaeology. (Scientific Papers: Vol. XXI). xii, 356p. (Orig.). 1985. pap. text ed. 10.00 (ISBN 0-89792-105-4). Ill St Museum.

Bennett, H. Chemical Specialties. 1978. 28.50 (ISBN 0-8206-0210-8). Chem Pub.

--Concise Chemical & Technical Dictionary. 4th ed. 1986. 95.00 (ISBN 0-8206-0310-4). Chem Pub.
--Cumulative Index of Chemical Formulary, Vols. 1-15. 1972. 33.00 (ISBN 0-8206-0209-4). Chem Pub.
--Encyclopedia of Chemical Trademarks & Synonyms, Vol. 1 A-E. 1981. 65.00 (ISBN 0-8206-0286-8). Chem Pub.
--Encyclopedia of Chemical Trademarks & Synonyms Vol. 2, F-O. 1982. 65.00 (ISBN 0-8206-0293-0). Chem Pub.
--Encyclopedia of Chemical Trademarks & Synonyms Vol. 3, P-Z. 1983. 65.00 (ISBN 0-8206-0302-3). Chem Pub.
--Industrial Waxes, 2 vols. Incl. Vol. 1. Natural Waxes; Synthetic Waxes (ISBN 0-8206-0224-8); Vol. 2. Compounded Waxes; Technology (ISBN 0-8206-0225-6). 1975. 30.00 ea. Chem Pub.
Bennett, H. & Reed, R. A. Chemical Methods of Silicate Analysis. 1981. 55.00x (Pub. by Brit Ceramic Soc England). State Mutual Bk.
--Chemical Methods of Silicate Analysis: A Handbook. 1972. 47.50 (ISBN 0-12-088740-1). Acad Pr.
Bennett, H., ed. Chemical Formulary, 26 vols. Incl. Vol. 1, 1933 (ISBN 0-8206-0259-0). Vol. 2, 1935 (ISBN 0-8206-0260-4). Vol. 3, 1936 (ISBN 0-8206-0261-2). Vol. 4, 1939 (ISBN 0-8206-0262-0). Vol. 5, 1941 (ISBN 0-8206-0263-9). Vol. 6, 1943 (ISBN 0-8206-0264-7). Vol. 7, 1945 (ISBN 0-8206-0265-5); Vol. 8, 1948 (ISBN 0-8206-0266-3). Vol. 9, 1950 (ISBN 0-8206-0267-1). Vol. 10, 1957 (ISBN 0-8206-0268-X). Vol. 11, 1961 (ISBN 0-8206-0269-8). Vol. 12, 1965 (ISBN 0-8206-0270-1). Vol. 13, 1967 (ISBN 0-8206-0271-X). Vol. 14, 1968 (ISBN 0-8206-0272-8); Vol. 15, 1970 (ISBN 0-8206-0273-6). Vol. 16, 1971 (ISBN 0-8206-0274-4). Vol. 17, 1973 (ISBN 0-8206-0275-2). Vol. 18, 1975 (ISBN 0-8206-0276-0). Vol. 19, 1976 (ISBN 0-8206-0277-9). Vol. 20, 1977 (ISBN 0-8206-0278-7). Vol. 21, 1979 (ISBN 0-8206-0279-5). Vol. 22, 1979 (ISBN 0-8206-0280-9). 35.00 ea. Chem Pub.
--Chemical Formulary, Vol. 23. 1981. 35.00 (ISBN 0-8206-0282-5). Chem Pub.
--Chemical Formulary, Vol. 24. 1982. 35.00 (ISBN 0-8206-0291-4). Chem Pub.
--Chemical Formulary, Vol. 25. 1983. 35.00 (ISBN 0-8206-0304-X). Chem Pub.
Bennett, H. S. England from Chaucer to Caxton. LC 73-16144. Repr. of 1928 ed. lib. bdg. 25.00 (ISBN 0-8414-3337-2). Folcroft.
Bennett, H. S., ed. see Marlowe, Christopher.
Bennett, H. Stith. On Becoming a Rock Musician. LC 80-5378. 272p. 1980. lib. bdg. 19.00x (ISBN 0-87023-311-4). U of Mass Pr.
Bennett, Hal. Doctor Within-Natural Healing. 1980. 18.95x (ISBN 0-317-07328-1, Regent House). B of A.
--A Wilderness of Vines. (Library of Contemporary Literature). 350p. 1986. pap. 7.95 (ISBN 0-88258-153-8). Howard U Pr.
Bennett, Hal & Samuels, Michael. The Well-Body Book. (YA) 1973. pap. 9.95 (ISBN 0-394-70969-1). Random.
Bennett, Hal Z. The Complete Bicycle Commuter: The Sierra Club Guide to Wheeling to Work. LC 82-719. (Sierra Club Outdoors Activities Guides Ser.). (Illus.). 256p. (Orig.). 1982. pap. 8.95 (ISBN 0-87156-308-8). Sierra.
--Remembering the Yellow Journal. (Orig.). 1978. pap. 3.95 (ISBN 0-686-24532-6). Hal Z Bennett.
Bennett, Hal Z., jt. auth. see Garfield, Charles A.
Bennett, Hal Z., jt. auth. see Samuels, Mike.
Bennett, Hank & Helms, Harry L. The Complete Shortwave Listener's Handbook. 2nd ed. LC 80-14325. (Illus.). 308p. 1980. pap. 13.95 (ISBN 0-8306-1255-6, 1255). TAB Bks.
Bennett, Harold. Farming with Steam. (History in Camera Ser.). 1984. pap. 6.95 (ISBN 0-85263-285-1, Pub. by Shire Pubns England). Seven Hills Bks.
--Saga of the Steam Plough. 20.50 (ISBN 0-392-15490-0, SpS). Sportshelf.
Bennett, Harold C. God's Awesome Challenge. LC 79-56692. 1980. 7.95 (ISBN 0-8054-6322-4). Broadman.
Bennett, Harold G. Reflections of Faith. LC 81-67326. 1983. pap. 5.95 (ISBN 0-8054-6565-0). Broadman.
Bennett, Heather, ed. see Davis, Joyce E.
Bennett, Henry S. Chaucer & the Fifteenth Century. (Oxford History of English Literature Ser.). 1947. 42.50x (ISBN 0-19-812201-2). Oxford U Pr.
--England from Chaucer to Caxton. 1980. Repr. of 1928 ed. lib. bdg. 27.50 (ISBN 0-8492-3883-8). R West.
--Life on the English Manor. (Cambridge Studies in Medieval Life & Thought). 1960. 44.50 (ISBN 0-521-04154-6); pap. 13.95 (ISBN 0-521-09105-5). Cambridge U Pr.
Bennett, Henry S., ed. England from Chaucer to Caxton. facsimile ed. LC 77-114904. (Select Bibliographies Reprint Ser). 1928. 19.00 (ISBN 0-8369-5308-8). Ayer Co Pubs.
Bennett, Howard F. Precision Power: The First Half Century of Bodine Electric Company. LC 75-41747. (Companies & Men: Business Enterprises in America). (Illus.). 1976. Repr. of 1959 ed. 34.50x (ISBN 0-405-08064-6). Ayer Co Pubs.
Bennett, Hugh H. Soil Conservation. LC 74-125731. (American Environmental Studies). 1970. Repr. of 1939 ed. 51.00 (ISBN 0-405-02656-0). Ayer Co Pubs.
Bennett, I. History of the Panama Canal. 1976. lib. bdg. 59.95 (ISBN 0-8490-2005-0). Gordon Pr.
Bennett, Ian. Oriental Rugs, Vol. 1: Caucasian. (Illus.). 400p. 1981. 69.50 (ISBN 0-902028-58-8). Antique Collect.
Bennett, J. A Packet of Poems. (Illus.). 112p. 1983. bds. 10.95 (ISBN 0-19-276049-1, Pub by Oxford U Pr Childrens). Merrimack Pub Cir.
Bennett, J. A. Chaucer at Oxford & Cambridge. LC 74-81706. (Illus.). 1974. 16.50x (ISBN 0-8020-2155-7). U of Toronto Pr.
--Poetry of the Passion: Studies in Twelve Centuries of English Verse. 1982. 37.50 (ISBN 0-19-812804-5); pap. 14.95x (ISBN 0-19-812832-0). Oxford U Pr.
Bennett, J. A. & Smithers, G. V. Early Middle English Verse & Prose. 2nd ed. 1968. pap. text ed. 23.95x (ISBN 0-19-871101-8); text ed. 27.50x (ISBN 0-19-811493-1). Oxford U Pr.
Bennett, J. A., ed. Langland Piers Plowman. xiv, 259p. 1985. Repr. of 1972 ed. 29.00 (ISBN 0-932051-50-2). Am Repr Serv.
Bennett, J. Claude. Vistas in Connective Tissue Diseases. (Illus.). 328p. 1968. photycopy ed. 32.75x (ISBN 0-398-00131-6). C C Thomas.
Bennett, J. D. Discovering Statues in Central & Northern England. (Discovering Ser.: No. 49). (Illus., Orig.). 1983. pap. 2.95 (ISBN 0-85263-016-6, Pub. by Shire Pubns England). Seven Hills Bks.
Bennett, J. G. Enneagram Studies. LC 82-60166. 160p. 1983. 5.95 (ISBN 0-87728-544-6). Weiser.
--Gurdjieff: A Very Great Enigma 1973. LC 72-91951. 100p. (Orig.). 1984. pap. 4.50 (ISBN 0-87728-581-0). Weiser.
--Intimations. 1976. pap. 4.95 (ISBN 0-87728-327-3). Weiser.
--The Masters of Wisdom. 1980. pap. 7.95 (ISBN 0-85500-069-4). Weiser.
--Sex. 128p. 1981. pap. 4.95 (ISBN 0-87728-533-0). Weiser.
--The Way to Be Free. 1980. pap. 6.95 (ISBN 0-87728-491-1). Weiser.
--Works on Subud, 3 vols. 300.00 (ISBN 0-8490-1332-1). Gordon Pr.
Bennett, J. G. & Montessori, Mario. The Spiritual Hunger of the Modern Child. Addison, Wendy, ed. LC 87-71204. 220p. Date not set. pap. price not set (ISBN 0-934254-06-0). Claymont Comm.
Bennett, J. H. Natural Selection, Heredity & Eugenics. 1983. 47.50x (ISBN 0-19-858177-7). Oxford U Pr.
Bennett, J. M. A Local Matter. 1985. 13.95 (ISBN 0-8027-5603-4). Walker & Co.
Bennett, J. M., ed. Lymphomas, Vol. I. 1981. lib. bdg. 69.50 (ISBN 90-247-2479-1, Pub. by Martinus Nijhoff Netherlands). Kluwer Academic.
Bennett, J. M. & Kalman, R. E., eds. Computers in Developing Nations. 272p. 1981. 47.00 (ISBN 0-444-86270-6, North-Holland). Elsevier.
Bennett, J. M. & Pearcey, T., eds. The New World of the Information Society: Proceedings of the 7th International Conference on Computer Communication Sydney, Australia, 30 Oct. - 2 Nov., 1984. 886p. 1985. 60.00 (ISBN 0-444-87649-9, North Holland). Elsevier.
Bennett, J. V. Heat Engines: Questions & Answers. (Marine Engineering Ser.). 116p. 1975. pap. 9.95x (ISBN 0-540-07340-7). Sheridan.
Bennett, J. V., jt. auth. see Pacsy, V. A.
Bennett, J. W. & Lasure, Linda L., eds. Gene Manipulation in Fungi. Edited Treatise ed. Date not set. price not set (ISBN 0-12-088640-5). Acad Pr.
Bennett, Jack. The Voyage of the Lucky Dragon. 156p. (gr. 7 up). 1982. 9.95 (ISBN 0-13-944165-4). P-H.
--The Voyage of the Lucky Dragons. 156p. (gr. 5 up). 1985. pap. 5.95 (ISBN 0-13-944158-1). P-H.
Bennett, Jack A., ed. see Langland, William.
Bennett, Jack W., jt. auth. see Strange, Marliss G.
Bennett, Jackie P. Chinese Cooking for Everyone. (Illus.). 95p. 5.98 (ISBN 0-8317-1247-3). Smith Pubs.
Bennett, James. Oral History & Delinquency: The Rhetoric of Criminology. LC 81-7514. 1981. 32.00x (ISBN 0-226-04245-6). U of Chicago Pr.
Bennett, James & Pravitz, James. The Miracle of Sports Psychology: How to Win with Mental Dynamics. (Illus.). 169p. 1982. 16.95 (ISBN 0-13-585257-9); pap. 7.95 (ISBN 0-13-585240-4). P-H.
Bennett, James A. The Mathematical Science of Christopher Wren. LC 81-18045. (Illus.). 250p. 1983. 32.50 (ISBN 0-521-24608-3). Cambridge U Pr.
Bennett, James A. & Foster, Benjamin. The American System of Practical Bookkeeping: Adopted to the Commerce of the United States, 2 vols. in 1. LC 75-18457. (History of Accounting Ser.). (Illus.). 1976. Repr. 17.00x (ISBN 0-405-07541-3). Ayer Co Pubs.
Bennett, James C. & Demos, George D. Drug Abuse & What We Can Do About It. 148p. 1972. 14.75x (ISBN 0-398-00132-4). C C Thomas.
Bennett, James C., jt. auth. see Stengel, Anna M.
Bennett, James C., jt. auth. see Wanous, S. J.
Bennett, James D. & Harrison, Lowell H. Writing History Papers. LC 78-66987. (Orig.). 1979. pap. text ed. 3.95x (ISBN 0-88273-105-X). Forum Pr IL.
Bennett, James G. Command-Train Your Dog: Foolproof Obedience Techniques for Home & Show. (Illus.). 1979. (Spec); pap. 5.95 (ISBN 0-13-152611-1). P-H.
Bennett, James T. & DiLorenzo, Thomas J. The Nation's Largest Municipal Bankruptcy: The Tip of the Off-Budget Iceberg. 1983. 7.00 (ISBN 0-943802-07-5). Natl Ctr Pol.
--Off-Budget Spending: The Growth of Underground Government. 1983. 7.00 (ISBN 0-943802-02-4). Natl Ctr Pol.
--Underground Government: The Off-Budget Public Sector. 184p. 1983. pap. 8.95 (ISBN 0-932790-37-2). Cato Inst.
Bennett, James T. & Johnson, Manuel H. Better Government at Half the Price. 1981. pap. 5.95 (ISBN 0-89803-048-X, Dist. by Kampmann). Green Hill.
--The Political Economy of Federal Government Growth. 148p. 1980. 12.95 (ISBN 0-86599-001-8); pap. 4.95 (ISBN 0-86599-002-6). Ctr Educ Res.
Bennett, Jana, jt. auth. see Simpson, John.
Bennett, Jane G. The New Complete German Shepherd Dog. rev. ed. LC 82-1031. (Illus.). 256p. 1984. 14.95 (ISBN 0-87605-151-4). Howell Bk.
Bennett, Janet, jt. auth. see Gordon, Joan.
Bennett, Janice N. The Pioneers. (Orig.). 1979. pap. 1.95 (ISBN 0-532-19237-0). Woodhill.
Bennett, Jay. The Birthday Murderer. 160p. (YA) (gr. 7 up). 1980. pap. 2.25 (ISBN 0-440-90576-1, LFL). Dell.
--The Dangling Witness. 144p. (gr. 7 up). pap. 1.95 (ISBN 0-440-91669-0, LFL). Dell.
--The Executioner. 176p. 1982. pap. 2.50 (ISBN 0-380-79160-9, 89507-2, Flare). Avon.
--I Never Said I Loved You. 128p. 1984. pap. 2.25 (ISBN 0-380-86900-4, 86900-4, Flare). Avon.
--The Killing Tree. (gr. 7 up). 1979. pap. 1.95 (ISBN 0-380-44289-2, 56259, Flare). Avon.
--The Long Black Coat. 128p. (gr. 7 up). 1974. pap. 2.25 (ISBN 0-440-94944-0, LFL). Dell.
--The Pigeon. 144p. (YA) 1981. pap. 2.50 (ISBN 0-380-55848-3, 60163-X, Flare). Avon.
--The Pigeon. LC 79-26270. 1980. 8.95 (ISBN 0-416-30631-4, NO. 0151). Methuen Inc.
--Say Hello to the Hit Man. 144p. (gr. 7 up). 1977. pap. 1.95 (ISBN 0-440-97618-9, LFL). Dell.
--Slowly, Slowly I Raise the Gun. 128p. 1983. pap. 2.25 (ISBN 0-380-84426-5, 84426-5, Flare). Avon.
--To Be a Killer. 128p. (Orig.). (gr. 7 up). 1985. pap. 2.25 (ISBN 0-590-33208-2, Point). Scholastic Inc.
Bennett, Jeanine, jt. auth. see Bellisimo, Louis A.
Bennett, Jeanne C. Martin-Chase Family Album. (Illus.). 174p. 1983. 12.50x (ISBN 0-939684-03-9). Calliope Pr.
Bennett, Jerome V. Administering the Company Accounting Function. 2nd ed. LC 80-25947. 375p. 1981. 39.95 (ISBN 0-13-004804-6). P-H.
Bennett, Jesse Lee. The Diffusion of Science. LC 74-26250. (History, Philosophy & Sociology of Science Ser). 1975. Repr. 17.00x (ISBN 0-405-06580-9). Ayer Co Pubs.
Bennett, Jesse Lee, ed. see Jerrold, Douglas, et al.
Bennett, Jill. Days Are Where We Live & other Poems. LC 81-8353. 48p. (ps-3). 1982. 10.25 (ISBN 0-688-00852-6). Lothrop.
Bennett, Jill & Goodwin, Susanne. Godfrey: A Special Time Remembered. 186p. 1984. 16.95 (ISBN 0-340-33160-7, Pub. by Hodder & Stoughton UK). David & Charles.
Bennett, Jill, retold by. Jack & the Robbers. (An Umbrella Bk.). (Illus.). 32p. (gr. k-3). 1984. bds. 7.95 laminated boards (ISBN 0-19-278204-5, Pub. by Oxford U Pr Childrens). Merrimack Pub Cir.
Bennett, Jill, compiled by. Roger Was a Razor Fish & Other Poems. LC 80-17166. (Illus.). 48p. (gr. 2-6). 1981. 11.25 (ISBN 0-688-41986-0). Lothrop.
Bennett, Joan. Five Metaphysical Poets: Donne, Herbert, Vaughan, Crashaw, Marvell. 1964. 32.50 (ISBN 0-521-04156-2); pap. 9.95 (ISBN 0-521-09238-8). Cambridge U Pr.
--George Eliot: Her Mind & Her Art. (Orig.). 1948. 29.95 (ISBN 0-521-04158-9); pap. 12.95 (ISBN 0-521-09174-8, 174). Cambridge U Pr.
--Virginia Woolf. 2nd ed. 1945. pap. 11.95 (ISBN 0-521-09951-X). Cambridge U Pr.
--Virginia Woolf: Her Art as a Novelist. 131p. Date not set. 25.00 (ISBN 0-8495-0618-2). Arden Lib.
Bennett, Joel P. Winning Attorneys' Fees from the U. S. Government. LC 84-4363. 1984. looseleaf 60.00. NY Law Pub.
Bennett, John. Construction Project Management. (Illus.). 224p. 1985. text ed. 39.95 (ISBN 0-408-01544-6). Butterworth.
--Crazy Girl on the Bus. 1979. pap. 2.00 (ISBN 0-686-65399-8). Vagabond Pr.
--Crime of the Century. (White Paper). 1982. 2.50 (ISBN 0-912824-28-X). Vagabond Pr.
--Hijack. (White Paper). 1982. 2.50 (ISBN 0-912824-29-8). Vagabond Pr.
--In the Course of Human Events. (White Paper). 1982. 2.50 (ISBN 0-912824-27-1). Vagabond Pr.
--Madame Margot: A Legend of Old Charleston. LC 51-13406. 110p. 1951. 8.95 (ISBN 0-87249-027-0). U of SC Pr.
--Managing the Academic Department. 208p. 1983. 12.95 (ISBN 0-02-902650-4). ACE.
--Master Skylark. (Classics Ser). (gr. 5 up). 1.95 (ISBN 0-8049-0092-2, CL-92). Airmont.
--Survival Song, Pt. 1. 111p. 1985. pap. 4.00 (ISBN 0-912824-34-4). Vagabond Pr.
--Survival Song, Pt. 2. 120p. 1985. pap. 4.00 (ISBN 0-912824-35-2). Vagabond Pr.
--Survival Song, Pt. 3. 120p. 1985. pap. 4.00 (ISBN 0-912824-36-0). Vagabond Pr.
--Tripping in America. 160p. 1984. pap. 5.95 (ISBN 0-912824-33-6). Vagabond Pr.
--Whiplash on the Couch. Robertson, Kirk, ed. LC 77-73210. (Orig.). 1979. pap. 3.00 (ISBN 0-916918-06-8). Duck Down.
--The Zoo Manuscript. 1968. 3.00 (ISBN 0-686-20739-4). Sydon.
Bennett, John & Brachman, Philip S. Hospital Infections. 1979. text ed. 37.50 (ISBN 0-316-08989-3). Little.
Bennett, John & Cooley, Peter. The Struck Leviathan & The Company of Strangers: Poetry Readings by John Bennett & Peter Cooley. LC 76-741319. 1977. 7.95 (ISBN 0-8262-0220-9). U of Mo Pr.
Bennett, John, jt. auth. see Bain, George S.
Bennett, John, jt. auth. see Penfold, Gerda.
Bennett, John, jt. auth. see Stone, Phil.
Bennett, John, jt. ed. see Dahlberg, Kenneth.
Bennett, John, et al. A Good Day to Die. 120p. 1985. pap. 4.00 (ISBN 0-912824-37-9). Vagabond Pr.
--The Vagabond Anthology. LC 77-90626. 1978. pap. 4.95 (ISBN 0-912824-45-X). Vagabond Pr.
Bennett, John, et al, eds. Visual Display Terminal: Usability Issues & Health Concerns. 1984. 28.00 (ISBN 0-13-942482-2). P-H.
Bennett, John B. Rational Thinking: A Study in Basic Logic. 1980. 22.95x (ISBN 0-88229-285-4); pap. 10.95x (ISBN 0-88229-739-2). Nelson-Hall.
Bennett, John B. & Doelling, Norman. Investing in Japanese Securities: Profit & Protection for the Intelligent Investor. LC 72-83672. 112p. 1972. pap. 3.00 (ISBN 0-8048-1063-X). C E Tuttle.
Bennett, John C. The Radical Imperative: From Theology to Social Ethics. LC 75-15538. 208p. 1975. 8.50 (ISBN 0-664-20824-X); pap. 7.95 (ISBN 0-664-24769-5). Westminster.
Bennett, John C. & Seifert, Harvey. U. S. Foreign Policy & Christian Ethics. LC 77-5062. 234p. 1977. soft cover 7.95 (ISBN 0-664-24756-3). Westminster.
Bennett, John C., et al. Christian Values & Economic Life. facs. ed. LC 71-99624. (Essay Index Reprint Ser.). 1954. 21.50 (ISBN 0-8369-1559-3). Ayer Co Pubs.
Bennett, John E., ed. Building Voluntary Support for the Two-Year College. 142p. 1981. looseleaf binder 16.50 (ISBN 0-89964-017-6). Coun Adv & Supp Ed.
--Building Voluntary Support for the Two-Year College. rev. 1981 ed. 142p. 1981. 16.50 (ISBN 0-89964-017-6). Coun Adv & Supp Ed.
Bennett, John F., jt. auth. see Bennett, Edna M.
Bennett, John G. Creation. 1978. 5.95 (ISBN 0-900306-41-6, Pub. by Coombe Springs Pr). Claymont Comm.
--Creative Thinking. 3rd ed. 1982. 5.95 (ISBN 0-900306-10-6, Pub. by Coombe Springs Pr). Claymont Comm.
--Existence. 1977. 3.95 (ISBN 0-900306-40-8, Pub. by Coombe Springs Pr). Claymont Comm.
--The First Liberation. 1976. 2.50 (ISBN 0-900306-32-7, Pub. by Coombe Springs Pr). Claymont Comm.
--Food. 1978. 2.95 (ISBN 0-900306-45-9, Pub. by Coombe Springs Pr). Claymont Comm.
--The Foundations of Moral Philosophy, Vol. 2. (Dramatic Universe Ser.). 12.95 (ISBN 0-900306-42-4, Pub. by Coombe Springs Pr). Claymont Comm.
--The Foundations of Natural Philosophy, Vol. 1. (The Dramatic Universe Ser.). 14.95 (ISBN 0-900306-39-4, Pub. by Coombe Springs Pr). Claymont Comm.
--Gurdjieff Today. (Transformation of Man Ser.). 1978. 3.95 (ISBN 0-900306-13-0, Pub. by Coombe Springs Pr). Claymont Comm.
--Hazard. 1976. 3.95 (ISBN 0-900306-33-5, Pub. by Coombe Springs Pr). Claymont Comm.
--History, Vol. 4. (The Dramatic Universe Ser.). 12.95 (ISBN 0-900306-44-0, Pub. by Coombe Springs Pr). Claymont Comm.
--The Image of God in Work. 1976. 2.95 (ISBN 0-900306-27-0, Pub. by Coombe Springs Pr). Claymont Comm.
--The Long Pilgrimage: The Life & Teaching of Shivapuri Baba. LC 81-66139. 191p. pap. 7.95 (ISBN 0-913922-54-4). Dawn Horse Pr.
--Man & His Nature, Vol. 3. (The Dramatic Universe Ser.). 12.95 (ISBN 0-900306-42-4, Pub. by Coombe Springs Pr). Claymont Comm.
--Material Objects. 1977. 2.95 (ISBN 0-900306-35-1, Pub. by Coombe Springs Pr). Claymont Comm.
--Needs of a New Age Community. 1976. 3.95 (ISBN 0-900306-47-5, Pub. by Coombe Springs Pr). Claymont Comm.
--Noticing. 1976. 2.95 (ISBN 0-900306-31-9, Pub. by Coombe Springs Pr). Claymont Comm.
--The Sevenfold Work. LC 79-52758. 1980. 4.95 (ISBN 0-934254-01-X). Claymont Comm.

--A Spiritual Psychology. LC 73-81620. 4.95 (ISBN 0-934254-03-6). Claymont Comm.

--Talks on Beelzebub's Tales. 1977. 6.95 (ISBN 0-900306-36-X, Pub. by Coombe Springs Pr). Claymont Comm.

--Transformation. LC 78-60760. 5.95 (ISBN 0-900306-07-6). Claymont Comm.

--What Are We Living for. 4.95 (ISBN 0-900306-07-6, Pub. by Coombe Springs Pr.). Claymont Comm.

--Witness. 1983. 8.95 (ISBN 0-934254-05-2). Claymont Comm.

Bennett, John G. & Bennett, Elizabeth. Idiots in Paris. 6.95 (ISBN 0-900306-47-5, Pub. by Coombe Springs Pr). Claymont Comm.

Bennett, John L. Building Decision Support Systems. LC 82-1632. (Computer Science Ser.). 1982. text ed. 25.95 (ISBN 0-201-00563-8). Addison-Wesley.

Bennett, John M. Blender. 1983. pap. 1.50 (ISBN 0-686-47952-1). Ghost Dance.

--Burning Dog. 24p. 1983. signed & lettered ed. 9.00 (ISBN 0-935350-10-1); pap. 4.00 (ISBN 0-935350-09-8). Luna Bisonte.

--Contents. 1978. 1.50 (ISBN 0-686-73437-8); signed & lettered 5.00 (ISBN 0-686-73438-6). Luna Bisonte.

--Found Objects. 1973. boxed, signed, numbered 10.00 (ISBN 0-685-37296-0). New Rivers Pr.

--Image Standards. 1975. 2.50 (ISBN 0-686-73433-5). Luna Bisonte.

--Jerks. 1980. 3.00 (ISBN 0-686-86297-X); signed & lettered 7.00 (ISBN 0-686-73428-9). Luna Bisonte.

--Meat Dip: Fifteen Labels. 1976. 2.00 (ISBN 0-686-75948-6); signed & lettered 5.00 (ISBN 0-686-75949-4). Luna Bisonte.

--Meat Watch. 1977. 3.00 (ISBN 0-686-75950-8); signed & lettered 5.00 (ISBN 0-686-75951-6). Luna Bisonte.

--Motel Moods. 1980. 2.50 (ISBN 0-935350-03-9); signed & lettered 6.00 (ISBN 0-686-86299-6). Luna Bisonte.

--Nips Poems. (Illus.). 40p. (Orig.). 1980. pap. 3.00 (ISBN 0-935350-00-4); signed & lettered 6.00 (ISBN 0-686-86300-3). Luna Bisonte.

--Nose Death. 10p. 1984. pap. 2.50 (ISBN 0-935350-12-8); signed & lettered 7.50 (ISBN 0-935350-13-6). Luna Bisonte.

--Puking Horse. 1980. 5.00 (ISBN 0-935350-04-7); signed & lettered 10.00 (ISBN 0-686-73424-6). Luna Bisonte.

--Six Portraits. 1975. 2.00 (ISBN 0-686-73434-3). Luna Bisonte.

--Time Release. 1978. 2.00 (ISBN 0-686-73439-4); signed & lettered 5.00 (ISBN 0-686-73440-8). Luna Bisonte.

--Time's Dipstick. 1976. 2.00 (ISBN 0-686-73435-1). Luna Bisonte.

--White Screen. 1975. signed ed. 7.50 (ISBN 0-685-79003-7); perfect bound in wrappers 2.50 (ISBN 0-685-79004-5). New Rivers Pr.

--White Screen, Poetry & Graphics. 1976. 6.00 (ISBN 0-686-73442-4). Luna Bisonte.

Bennett, John M. & Bennett, C. Mehrl. Applied Appliances. (Orig.). 1981. pap. 2.00 (ISBN 0-686-73840-3); signed & lettered ed. 5.00 (ISBN 0-935350-05-5). Luna Bisonte.

Bennett, John M., jt. auth. see Andrews, Bruce.

Bennett, John M., jt. auth. see Bennett, C. Mehrl.

Bennett, John M., jt. auth. see Crozier, Robin.

Bennett, John M., jt. auth. see Mehrl, C.

Bennett, John M., ed. Controversies in the Management of Lymphomas. (Cancer Treatment & Research Ser.). 1983. lib. bdg. 59.50 (ISBN 0-89838-586-5, Pub. by Martinus Nijhoff Netherlands). Kluwer Academic.

Bennett, John R. A Catalogue of Vocal Recordings from the English Catalogues of the Gramophone Company, 1898-1899; The Gramophone Company Limited, 1899-1900; The Gramophone & Typewriter Company Limited, 1901-1907;; the Gramophone Company Limited, 1907-1925. LC 77-28267. (Series: Voices of the Past: Vol. 1). 1978. Repr. of 1955 ed. lib. bdg. 22.00x (ISBN 0-313-20237-0, BECVE). Greenwood.

--Therapeutic Endoscopy & Radiology of the Gut. 1981. 72.50 (ISBN 0-8151-0674-2). Year Bk Med.

Bennett, John R. & Wimmer, Wilhelm. A Catalogue of Vocal Recordings from the 1898-1926 German Catalogues of the Gramophone Company Limited, Duetsche Grammophon. LC 77-28980. (Voices of the Past: Vol. 7). 1978. Repr. of 1967 ed. lib. bdg. 32.25 (ISBN 0-313-20236-2, BECVG). Greenwood.

Bennett, John R., compiled by. Melodiya: A Soviet Russian L. P. Discography. LC 81-4247. (Discographies Ser.: No. 6). (Illus.). xxii, 832p. 1981. lib. bdg. 85.00 (ISBN 0-313-22596-6, BME/). Greenwood.

Bennett, John W. The Ecological Transition. 1976. pap. text ed. 17.50 (ISBN 0-08-017868-5). Pergamon.

--Hutterian Brethren: The Agricultural Economy & Social Organization of a Communal People. (Illus.). 1967. 25.00x (ISBN 0-8047-0329-9). Stanford U Pr.

--Northern Plainsmen: Adaptive Strategy & Agrarian Life. LC 76-75043. (Worlds of Man Ser.). (Illus.). 1970. text ed. 23.95x (ISBN 0-88295-602-7); pap. text ed. 13.95x (ISBN 0-88295-603-5). Harlan Davidson.

Bennett, John W. & Ishino, Iwao. Paternalism in the Japanese Economy. LC 72-3538. 307p. 1972. Repr. of 1963 ed. lib. bdg. 17.75x (ISBN 0-8371-6424-9, BEJE). Greenwood.

Bennett, John W., jt. auth. see American Ethnological Society.

Bennett, Jonathan. Kant's Analytic. (Orig.). 1966. 44.50 (ISBN 0-521-04157-0); pap. 13.95 (ISBN 0-521-09389-9, 389). Cambridge U Pr.

--Kant's Dialectic. LC 73-89762. 290p. 1974. o. p. 38.50 (ISBN 0-521-20420-8); pap. 13.95 (ISBN 0-521-09849-1). Cambridge U Pr.

--Linguistic Behavior. LC 75-44575. 260p. 1976. 42.50 (ISBN 0-521-21168-9). Cambridge U Pr.

--Linguistic Behavior. LC 75-44575. 1979. pap. 14.95 (ISBN 0-521-29751-6). Cambridge U Pr.

--Locke, Berkeley, Hume: Central Themes. 1971. pap. 12.95x (ISBN 0-19-875016-1). Oxford U Pr.

--Rationality: An Essay Towards an Analysis. (Studies in Philosophical Psychology). 1971. text ed. 13.50x (ISBN 0-7100-3841-0); pap. text ed. 7.45x (ISBN 0-391-00198-1). Humanities.

--A Study of Spinoza's Ethics. LC 83-18568. 416p. 1984. lib. bdg. 25.00 (ISBN 0-915145-82-0); pap. text ed. 13.75 (ISBN 0-915145-83-9). Hackett Pub.

Bennett, Jonathan, ed. see Leibniz, G. W.

Bennett, Joseph A. Problems in Descriptive Geometry, Bk. 2. pap. 20.00 (ISBN 0-317-08629-4, 2007319). Bks Demand UMI.

Bennett, Joseph D. Baudelaire. LC 78-85985. 1969. Repr. of 1946 ed. 15.00x (ISBN 0-8046-0601-3, Pub. by Kennikat). Assoc Faculty Pr.

Bennett, Joseph T., jt. ed. see Dolan, Paul J.

Bennett, Josephine, tr. see Bebey, Francis.

Bennett, Josephine W. Evolution of the Faerie Queene. 1962. Repr. of 1942 ed. lib. bdg. 21.00 (ISBN 0-8337-0231-9). B Franklin.

--Measure for Measure As Royal Entertainment. LC 66-15764. 208p. 1966. 29.00x (ISBN 0-231-02921-7). Columbia U Pr.

--Rediscovery of Sir John Mandeville. (MLA Mono Ser.: 19). 1954. 29.00 (ISBN 0-527-06700-8). Kraus Repr.

Bennett, Josephine W., ed. see Shakespeare, William.

Bennett, Judith. Sex Signs. 384p. 1981. pap. 6.95 (ISBN 0-312-71339-8). St Martin.

Bennett, Judith K. The Ahae Gang Meets Melvin. 112p. 1984. 7.95 (ISBN 0-533-05677-2). Vantage.

Bennett, Julian. Towns in Roman Britain. (Shire Archaeology Ser.: No. 13). (Illus.). 70p. 1984. pap. 5.95 (ISBN 0-85263-672-5, Pub. by Shire Pubns England). Seven Hills Bks.

Bennett, Julius C. Of Men & Gods. LC 81-82234. 1982. 7.95 (ISBN 0-686-80562-3). Libra.

Bennett, June H. Inside the Poet's Mind. LC 83-61190. 64p. (Orig.). 1983. pap. 5.50 (ISBN 0-935834-18-4). Rainbow Books.

Bennett, Keith S. The Tropical Asiatic Slipper Orchids: Genus Paphiopedilum. (Illus.). 91p. 1985. 15.95 (ISBN 0-207-14887-2, Pub. by Salem Hse Ltd). Merrimack Pub Cir.

Bennett, Kenneth A. Fundamentals of Biological Anthropology. 550p. 1979. text ed. write for info. (ISBN 0-697-07553-2). Wm C Brown.

--The Indians of Point of Pines, Arizona: A Comparative Study of their Physical Characteristics. LC 72-76616. (Anthropological Papers of the University of Arizona: No. 23). pap. 20.80 (ISBN 0-317-26807-4, 2024316). Bks Demand UMI.

Bennett, Kenneth A., jt. auth. see Osborne, Richard H.

Bennett, L. Claire & Searl, Sarah S. Communicable Disease Handbook. LC 82-11062. 270p. 1982. pap. 18.50 (ISBN 0-471-09271-1, Pub. by Wiley Med). Wiley.

Bennett, L. H. & Waber, J. T., eds. Energy Bands in Metals & Alloys. LC 67-29668. (Metallurgical Society Conferences Ser.: Vol. 45). pap. 50.80 (ISBN 0-317-10608-2, 2001533). Bks Demand UMI.

Bennett, L. H., ed. see AIME Annual Meeting, New Orleans, 1979.

Bennett, L. H., jt. ed. see Massalski, T. B.

Bennett, L. H., ed. see Metallurgical Society of AIME Staff.

Bennett, L. H., et al, eds. Alloy Phase Diagrams: Proceedings of a Symposium Held in Boston, Nov. 1982. (Materials Research Society Symposia Proceedings Ser.: Vol. 19). 436p. 1983. 77.00 (ISBN 0-444-00809-8, North Holland). Elsevier.

Bennett, L. J. Secretarial Assistance in Teachers Colleges & Normal Schools. LC 73-176554. (Columbia University. Teachers College. Contributions to Education: No. 724). Repr. of 1937 ed. 22.50 (ISBN 0-404-55724-4). AMS Pr.

Bennett, Lawrence, ed. The Western Wind American Tune-Book. 1977. pap. 12.50x (ISBN 0-8450-0076-4). Broude.

Bennett, Lawrence A. Counseling in Correctional Environments. Walz, Garry R. & Benjamin, Libby, eds. LC 77-21269. (New Vistas in Counseling Ser.: Vol. VI). 94p. 1978. text ed. 12.95 (ISBN 0-87705-319-7). Human Sci Pr.

Bennett, Leonard S. Review Workbook for High School Entrance Plus Scholarship Examination. pap. 3.95 (ISBN 0-87738-000-7). Youth Ed.

Bennett, Leonard S., et al. Preparation for Civil Service. pap. 4.95 (ISBN 0-87738-019-8). Youth Ed.

--Review Workbook for Adult Education in Mathematics & English. pap. 5.50 (ISBN 0-87738-001-5). Youth Ed.

Bennett, Lerone, Jr. Before the Mayflower: A History of Black America. 1982. 19.95 (ISBN 0-87485-029-0). Johnson Chi.

--Before the Mayflower: A History of Black America. Rev. ed. 688p. 1984. pap. 6.95 (ISBN 0-14-007214-4). Penguin.

--Black Power U. S. A. The Human Side of Reconstruction, 1867-1877. 1967. 6.95 (ISBN 0-87485-023-1). Johnson Chi.

--Pioneers in Protest. 1968. 5.95 (ISBN 0-87485-026-6). Johnson Chi.

--Shaping of Black America. LC 74-20659. 1975. 15.95 (ISBN 0-87485-071-1). Johnson Chi.

--Wade in the Water: Great Moments in Black American History. (Illus.). 328p. 1979. 14.95 (ISBN 0-87485-078-9). Johnson Chi.

--What Manner of Man: A Biography of Martin Luther King Jr, 1929-1968. 1968. 12.95 (ISBN 0-87485-027-4). Johnson Chi.

Bennett, Lerone, Jr., ed. see Ebony Editors.

Bennett, Linda A. Personal Choice in Ethnic Identity Maintenance: Serbs, Croats & Slovenes in Washington, D. C. LC 77-93261. 230p. 1978. soft cover 10.00 (ISBN 0-918660-06-8). Ragusan Pr.

Bennett, Linda L. Symbolic State Politics: Education Funding in Ohio, 1970-1980. LC 83-48760. (American University Studies X, Political Science: Vol. 1). 160p. 1983. pap. text ed. 17.35 (ISBN 0-8204-0052-1). P Lang Pubs.

--Volunteers in the School Media Center. 250p. 1984. lib. bdg. 23.50 (ISBN 0-87287-351-X). Libs Unl.

Bennett, Luella. Searie Dearie. 28p. 1973. pap. 1.50 (ISBN 0-89036-005-7). Hawkes Pub Inc.

Bennett, Lynn. Dangerous Wives & Sacred Sisters: Social & Symbolic Roles of Women in Nepal. 352p. 1983. 31.50x (ISBN 0-231-04664-2). Columbia U Pr.

Bennett, M. Chemical Formulary, Vol. 26. 1985. 35.00 (ISBN 0-8206-0313-9). Chem Pub.

--Handbook of Chemical Substitutes. 1985. 40.00 (ISBN 0-8206-0307-4). Chem Pub.

Bennett, M. A. The Instant Expert's Guide to the Kaypro II. Dvorak, John C., ed. (Dvorak's Instant Expert Ser.). (Illus.). 192p. (Orig.). 1984. 7.95 (ISBN 0-440-54462-9, Dell Trade Paperback). Dell.

Bennett, M. D., jt. ed. see Brandham, P. E.

Bennett, M. D., et al, eds. Chromosomes Today. (Chromosomes Today Ser.: Vol. VIII). (Illus.). 400p. 1984. text ed. 50.00x (ISBN 0-04-575023-8). Allen Unwin.

Bennett, M. J. Ultrasound in Perinatal Care. (Wiley Perinatal Practice Ser.). 187p. 1984. 37.00 (ISBN 0-471-90384-1). Wiley.

Bennett, M. K. The World's Food: A Study of the Interrelations of World Populations, National Diets & Food Potentials. LC 75-26295. (World Food Supply Ser). (Illus.). 1976. Repr. of 1954 ed. 23.50x (ISBN 0-405-07768-8). Ayer Co Pubs.

Bennett, M. R. Automatic Neuromuscular Transmission. LC 76-182026. (Physiological Society Monographs: No. 30). (Illus.). 400p. 1973. 59.50 (ISBN 0-521-08463-6). Cambridge U Pr.

Bennett, M. V., ed. Synaptic Transmission & Neuronal Interaction. LC 73-83886. (Society of General Physiologists Ser: Vol. 28). 401p. 1974. 50.50 (ISBN 0-911216-56-1). Raven.

Bennett, Marcia J. Shadow Singer. 256p. (Orig.). 1986. pap. 2.75 (ISBN 0-345-31776-9, Del Rey). Ballantine.

--Where the Ni-Lach. 256p. 1986. pap. 2.95 (ISBN 0-345-33123-0, Del Rey). Ballantine.

Bennett, Margaret. Biking for Grown Ups. 249p. Repr. of 1976 ed. 6.95 (ISBN 0-686-35966-6). Sugarfree.

--Cross-Country Skiing for the Fun of It. 206p. Repr. of 1973 ed. 6.95 (ISBN 0-686-35965-8). Sugarfree.

--Peripatetic Diabetic. LC 69-16019. (Illus.). 1969. pap. 5.95 (ISBN 0-8015-5840-9, Hawthorn). Dutton.

Bennett, Margie, jt. auth. see Wigginton, Eliot.

Bennett, Margo L., jt. auth. see Desatnick, Robert L.

Bennett, Marguerite. My Arnold Bennett. 1973. Repr. of 1931 ed. 12.50 (ISBN 0-8274-0717-3). R West.

Bennett, Marian. Baby Jesus ABC's. (Little Happy Day Bks.). (Illus.). 24p. (Orig.). (gr. k-3). 1983. pap. 0.45 (ISBN 0-87239-651-7, 2121). Standard Pub.

--Bible Numbers. (Little Happy Day Bks.). (Illus.). 24p. (Orig.). (gr. k-3). 1983. pap. 0.45 (ISBN 0-87239-653-3, 2123). Standard Pub.

--David, the Shepherd. (Happy Day Bible Stories Bks.). (Illus.). 24p. (ps-2). 1984. 1.39 (ISBN 0-87239-763-7, 3723). Standard Pub.

--God Made Chickens. (Happy Day Bks.). (Illus.). 24p. (ps-2). 1985. 1.39 (ISBN 0-87239-874-9, 3674). Standard Pub.

--God Made Kittens. (A Happy Day Book). (Illus.). 24p. (ps). 1980. 1.39 (ISBN 0-87239-404-2, 3636). Standard Pub.

--God Made Puppies. (A Happy Day Book). (Illus.). 24p. (ps). 1980. 1.39 (ISBN 0-87239-403-4, 3635). Standard Pub.

--God Made the Whole World. LC 84-50288. (Little Happy Day Ser.). (Illus.). 24p. (Orig.). (ps-1). 1984. pap. 0.45 (ISBN 0-87239-801-3, 2161). Standard Pub.

--God's Animals. (My Shape Book Ser.). (Illus.). 10p. (ps). 1985. 2.95 (ISBN 0-87239-909-5, 2749). Standard Pub.

--God's Gifts. (My Shape Book Ser.). (Illus.). 10p. (ps). 1985. 2.95 (ISBN 0-87239-910-9, 2750). Standard Pub.

--Helping. (Wipe-Clean Bks.). (Illus.). 12p. (ps). 1985. pap. 1.29 (ISBN 0-87239-952-4, 3512). Standard Pub.

--House Full of Prayers. (Surprise Bks.). (Illus.). 14p. (Orig.). (ps-3). 1982. pap. 4.95 (ISBN 0-87239-563-4, 2709). Standard Pub.

--I Can. (My Surprise Book Ser.). (Illus.). 10p. (ps). 1985. 4.95 (ISBN 0-87239-905-2, 2729). Standard Pub.

--I Go to Church. (My Shape Book Ser.). (Illus.). 10p. (ps). 1985. 2.95 (ISBN 0-87239-911-7, 2751). Standard Pub.

--I Learn to Pray. (Wipe-Clean Bks.). (Illus.). 12p. (ps). 1985. pap. 1.29 (ISBN 0-87239-953-2). Standard Pub.

--Jesus, God's Son. (Surprise Bks.). (Illus.). 14p. (Orig.). (ps-3). 1982. pap. 4.95 (ISBN 0-87239-564-2, 2705). Standard Pub.

--Loving. (Wipe-Clean Bks.). (Illus.). 12p. (ps). 1985. pap. 1.29 (ISBN 0-87239-955-9, 3515). Standard Pub.

--My Bible Book. (Wipe-Clean Bks.). (Illus.). 12p. (ps). 1985. pap. 1.29 (ISBN 0-87239-956-7, 3516). Standard Pub.

--My Friend Jesus. (Wipe-Clean Bks.). (Illus.). 12p. (ps). 1985. pap. 1.29 (ISBN 0-87239-957-5, 3517). Standard Pub.

--Obeying. (Wipe-Clean Bks.). (Illus.). 12p. (ps). 1985. pap. 1.29 (ISBN 0-87239-958-3, 3518). Standard Pub.

--Preschool Pattern Book. (Illus.). 48p. (Orig.). (gr. k). 1973. pap. 4.50 (ISBN 0-87239-339-9, 2145). Standard Pub.

--Sharing. (Wipe-Clean Bks.). (Illus.). 12p. (ps). 1985. pap. 1.29 (ISBN 0-87239-959-1, 3519). Standard Pub.

--The Story of Baby Jesus. (Illus.). 24p. (Orig.). (ps-k). 1983. pap. 0.45 (ISBN 0-87239-654-1, 2124). Standard Pub.

--Thank You, God. (My Surprise Book Ser.). (Illus.). 10p. (ps). 1985. 4.95 (ISBN 0-87239-906-0, 2780). Standard Pub.

Bennett, Marian & Peltier, Pam. My First Valentine's Day Book. LC 84-21511. (My First Bks.). (Illus.). 32p. (ps-2). 1985. lib. bdg. 10.35 (ISBN 0-516-02906-1); pap. 2.95 (ISBN 0-516-42906-X). Childrens.

Bennett, Marian, ed. Baby Jesus. (My Shape Book Ser.). (Illus.). 10p. (ps). 1985. 2.95 (ISBN 0-87239-907-9, 2747). Standard Pub.

Bennett, Marian, compiled by. Bible Memory Verses. (Little Happy Day Bks.). (Illus.). 24p. (Orig.). (gr. k-3). 1983. pap. 0.45 (ISBN 0-87239-652-5, 2122). Standard Pub.

Bennett, Marian, ed. God Made Me. (My Shape Book Ser.). (Illus.). 10p. (ps). 1985. 2.95 (ISBN 0-87239-908-7, 2748). Standard Pub.

--My Family & Friends. (My Shape Book Ser.). (Illus.). 10p. (ps). 1985. 2.95 (ISBN 0-87239-912-5, 2752). Standard Pub.

--Songs for Preschool Children. LC 80-25091. 96p. (Orig.). 1981. pap. 7.95 (ISBN 0-87239-429-8, 5754). Standard Pub.

Bennett, Martin. Rolls-Royce: The History of the Car. (Illus.). 184p. 19.95 (ISBN 0-946609-00-4, P919). Haynes Pubns.

Bennett, Mary E., jt. ed. see Laustsen, Jean B.

Bennett, Melba. First Nibbles of the Apple Computer. (Illus.). 288p. 1984. pap. 17.95 (ISBN 0-89303-456-8). Brady Comm.

Bennett, Melba B. Robinson Jeffers & the Sea. LC 73-9. 1971. Repr. of 1936 ed. lib. bdg. 20.00 (ISBN 0-8414-3154-X). Folcroft.

Bennett, Merrill K. International Commodity Stockpiling As an Economic Stabilizer. LC 69-10070. 1969. Repr. of 1949 ed. lib. bdg. 15.00 (ISBN 0-8371-0308-8, BECS). Greenwood.

Bennett, Michael. The Battle of Bosworth. 189p. 1985. 29.95 (ISBN 0-312-06972-3). St Martin.

--Refinishing Antique Furniture. (Illus.). 72p. 1980. 8.95 (ISBN 0-7134-4971-3, Pub. by Batsford England). David & Charles.

--Refinishing Antique Furniture. (Illus.). 72p. 1984. 8.95 (ISBN 0-85219-139-1, Pub. by Batsford England). David & Charles.

Bennett, Michael, et al. Papers in Cognitive-Stratificational Linguistics. Copeland, James E. & Davis, Philip W., eds. (Rice University Studies: Vol. 66, No. 2). (Illus.). 208p. (Orig.). 1980. pap. 10.00x (ISBN 0-89263-245-3). Rice Univ.

--Elementary Algebra. (Illus.). 400p. 1985. pap. text ed. 23.00 (ISBN 0-912675-12-8); manual avail. (ISBN 0-912675-13-6). Ardsley.

Bennett, Michael E., et al. Elementary Algebra. LC 80-21563. 400p. 1981. text ed. write for info. (ISBN 0-87150-303-4, 2391, Prindle). PWS Pubs.

Bennett, Wendell C. & D'Harnoncourt, Rene. Ancient Art of the Andes. LC 54-6135. (Museum of Modern Art - Publications in Reprint). (Illus.). Repr. of 1954 ed. 18.00 (ISBN 0-405-01521-6). Ayer Co Pubs.

Bennett, Will. Zero. Owen, Maureen, ed. 1984. pap. 4.00 (ISBN 0-916382-31-1). Telephone Bks.

Bennett, William & Gurin, Joel. The Dieter's Dilemma. LC 81-68403. 329p. 1983. pap. 6.95 (ISBN 0-465-01653-7, CN-5098). Basic.

--The Dieter's Dilemma: Eating Less & Weighing More. LC 81-68403. 1982. 14.95 (ISBN 0-465-01652-9). Basic.

Bennett, William, jt. auth. see Kuehnel, Edward.

Bennett, William H. Catholic Footsteps in Old New York: A Chronicle of Catholicity in the City of New York from 1524 to 1808. LC 77-359169. (Monograph Ser.: No. 28). 1973. Repr. of 1909 ed. 10.00x (ISBN 0-930060-08-3). US Cath Hist.

--An Exposition of the Books of Chronicles. 467p. 1983. lib. bdg. 17.50 (ISBN 0-86524-169-4, 1401). Klock & Klock.

--An Introduction to the Gothic Language. 4th, rev. ed. Lehmann, Winfred P., ed. LC 79-87574. (Introductions to Older Languages Ser.: No. 2). xvii, 190p. 1981. 22.00x (ISBN 0-87352-290-7, Z101). Modern Lang.

Bennett, William P. First Baby in Camp. (Shorey Historical Ser.). 68p. pap. 4.95 (ISBN 0-8466-0161-3, S161). Shorey.

Bennett, William S. Complete Works for Piano Solo, Vol. 17. (The London Pianoforte School 1770-1860 Ser.). 190p. 1984. lib. bdg. 50.00 (ISBN 0-8240-6166-7). Garland Pub.

--Complete Works for Piano Solo, Vol. 18. (The London Pianoforte School 1770-1860 Ser.). 240p. 1984. lib. bdg. 60.00 (ISBN 0-8240-6167-5). Garland Pub.

Bennett, Wilma. Occupations Filing Plan & Bibliography. LC 68-56288. 138p. 1968. pap. text ed. 3.95x book only (ISBN 0-8134-1055-X, 1055). Interstate.

Bennett, Wilma E. Checklist-Guide to Selecting a Small Computer. LC 80-13996. 32p. 1980. pap. 5.00 (ISBN 0-87576-091-0). Pilot Bks.

Bennett-Ashcraft, Sue. The Upper Crust Cookbook. LC 84-91700. 538p. (Orig.). 1984. pap. 14.95 spiral bdg. (ISBN 0-9613757-0-1). Upper Crust.

Bennett-England, Rodney. Dress Optional, the Revolution in Menswear. LC 68-29951. (Illus.). 1968. 15.00 (ISBN 0-7206-0110-X). Dufour.

Bennetton, Norman A. Social Significance of the Duel in Seventh-Century French Drama. 1973. Repr. of 1938 ed. 14.00 (ISBN 0-384-03903-0). Johnson Repr.

Bennett-Ruete, Jackie, tr. see Link, Werner.

Bennetts, John R. Far Away in Australia. 1981. 12.00x (ISBN 0-7223-1411-6, Pub. by Stockwell). State Mutual Bk.

Bennetts, R. G. Introduction to Digital Board Testing. LC 81-3258. (Computer Systems Engineering Ser.). 320p. 1982. text ed. 32.50x (ISBN 0-8448-1385-0). Crane-Russak Co.

Bennett-Sandler, Georgette, et al. Law Enforcement & Criminal Justice: An Introduction. LC 78-69537. (Illus.). 1979. text ed. 25.50 (ISBN 0-395-27467-2); instr's. manual 0.50 (ISBN 0-395-27466-4). HM.

Benneward, Patrice. Banquets for Birds: Suggestions for Supplementary Feeding. Stallings, Constance, ed. (Illus.). 28p. (Orig.). 1983. pap. 1.60 (ISBN 0-930698-11-8). Natl Audubon.

Benneward, Patrice, ed. From Outrage to Action: The Story of the National Audubon Society. (Illus., Orig.). 1982. pap. avail. (ISBN 0-930698-15-0). Natl Audubon.

Bennewith, Walter. Encounter. 1984. 22.00x (ISBN 0-317-14512-6, Pub. by Selecteditions). State Mutual Bk.

Benney, Mark. Low Company: Describing the Evolution of a Burglar. 350p. 1981. 19.75 (ISBN 0-904573-18-4); pap. 9.75 (ISBN 0-904573-75-3). Caliban Bks.

Benni, C. A. & Bolza, Eleanor. South American Timbers. 1982. 60.00x (ISBN 0-686-97897-8, Pub. by CSIRO Australia). State Mutual Bk.

Benni, Stefano. Terra! Cancogni, Annapaoloa, tr. from Italian. LC 84-22600. 342p. 1985. pap. 6.95 (ISBN 0-394-54353-X). Pantheon.

Bennie, Frances. Learning Centers: Development & Operation. LC 76-58528. 340p. 1977. 27.95 (ISBN 0-87778-097-8). Educ Tech Pubns.

Bennie, W. G., ed. see McLaren, J.

Bennigsen, Alexandre & Broxup, Marie. The Islamic Threat to the Soviet State. LC 82-16826. 224p. 1983. 27.50x (ISBN 0-312-43739-0). St Martin.

Bennigsen, Alexandre & Lemercier-Quelquejay, Chantal. Les Mouvements Nationaux Chez les Musulmans De Russie, 2 tomes. Incl. Tome I. Le "Sultangalievisme" Au Tatarstan. (No. 3). 1960. pap. 18.40x (ISBN 0-686-22176-1); Tome II. La Presse et le Mouvement National Chez les Musulmans De Russie Avant 1920. (No. 4). (Illus.). 1964. pap. 31.60x (ISBN 90-2796-244-8). (Mouvements Sociaux et Ideologies, Documents et Temoignages). pap. Mouton.

Bennigsen, Alexandre A. & Wimbush, S. Enders. Muslim National Communism in the Soviet Union: A Revolutionary Strategy for the Colonial World. LC 78-8608. (Publications of the Center for Middle Eastern Studies Ser.: No. 11). 1979. lib. bdg. 20.00x (ISBN 0-226-04235-9). U of Chicago Pr.

Bennike, S. Boisen. Contributions to the Ecology & Biology of the Danish Fresh-Water Leeches. Repr. of 1943 ed. 21.00 (ISBN 0-384-03905-7). Johnson Repr.

Benning, A. H. see Emerich, A. D.

Benning, Calvin J. Plastic Films for Packaging: Technology Applications & Process Economics. 192p. 1983. 35.00 (ISBN 0-87762-320-1). Technomic.

Benningfield, L. M., jt. auth. see Lago, G. V.

Benninghoff, H. Index of Chemicals. (Eng., Ger., & Fr.). 1974. 128.00 (ISBN 0-444-41075-9). Elsevier.

Benninghoven, A., ed. Ion Formation from Organic Solids: Proceedings, Muenster, FRG, 1982. (Springer Series in Chemical Physics: Vol. 25). (Illus.). 269p. 1983. 33.00 (ISBN 0-387-12244-3). Springer-Verlag.

Benninghoven, A., et al, eds. Secondary Ion Mass Spectrometry SIMS III: Proceedings. (Springer Series in Chemical Physics: Vol. 19). (Illus.). 444p. 1982. 42.00 (ISBN 0-387-11372-X). Springer-Verlag.

--Secondary Ion Mass Spectrometry SIMS-II: Proceedings of the International Conference on Secondary Ion Mass Spectrometry. LC 79-23997. (Springer Ser. in Chemical Physics: Vol. 9). (Illus.). 298p. 1979. 42.00 (ISBN 3-540-09843-7). Springer-Verlag.

Benninghoven, A., et al, eds. see International Conference on Secondary Ion Mass Spectrometry, 4th, Minoo-Kanko Hotel, Osaka, Japan, November 13-19, 1984.

Benningsen, Alexandre A. & Wimbush, S. Enders. Muslim National Communism in the Soviet Union: A Revolutionary Strategy for the Colonial World. LC 78-8608. xxii, 268p. 1980. pap. 7.95x (ISBN 0-226-04236-7, P915, Phoen). U of Chicago Pr.

Bennington, Allen, jt. auth. see Kennedy, Lona B.

Bennington, Christian. The Next Horizon. 1981. 29.00x (ISBN 0-575-01639-6, Pub. by Gollancz England). State Mutual Bk.

Bennington, Ed, Jr. Surplus Dollars. 3rd ed. LC 75-23177. (Illus.). 80p. 1982. pap. 4.95 (ISBN 0-686-34360-3). E Bennington.

Bennington, Geoff, tr. see Lyotard, Jean-Francois.

Bennington, James L. Saunders Encyclopedia & Dictionary of Laboratory Medicine & Technology. (Illus.). 1700p. 1984. 45.00 (ISBN 0-7216-1714-X). Saunders.

Bennington, James L. & Kradjian, Robert M. Renal Carcinoma. LC 67-10430. pap. 92.30 (ISBN 0-317-07919-0, 2001766). Bks Demand UMI.

Bennington, Richard R. Furniture Marketing: From Product Development to Distribution. (Illus.). 280p. 1984. text ed. 17.50 (ISBN 0-87005-491-0); instr's guide 2.50 (ISBN 0-87005-499-6). Fairchild.

Bennion, Elizabeth. Antique Medical Instruments. LC 78-55189. 1979. 50.00 (ISBN 0-520-03832-0). U of Cal Pr.

Bennion, Francis A. The Constitutional Law of Ghana. LC 63-3133. (Butterworth's African Law Ser.: No. 5). pap. 140.80 (ISBN 0-317-28446-0, 20512259). Bks Demand UMI.

Bennion, Junius L., jt. auth. see Schneider, Edward W.

Bennion, Lowell. Jesus, the Master Teacher. 63p. 1980. 5.95 (ISBN 0-87747-833-3). Deseret Bk.

Bennion, Lowell L. I Believe. LC 83-70024. 87p. 1983. 5.95 (ISBN 0-87747-954-2). Deseret Bk.

--Understanding the Scriptures. LC 81-66422. 88p. 1981. 6.95 (ISBN 0-87747-863-5). Deseret Bk.

Bennion, Lynn J. Hypoglycemia: Fact or Fad? LC 83-10060. 192p. 1983. 12.95 (ISBN 0-517-55074-1). Crown.

Bennion, Marion. Clinical Nutrition. 1978. text ed. 36.50 scp (ISBN 0-06-453526-6, HarpC). Har-Row.

--Introductory Foods. 592p. 1985. text ed. write for info. (ISBN 0-02-308180-5). Macmillan.

--The Science of Food. 1980. text ed. 24.50 scp (ISBN 0-06-453532-0, HarpC). Har-Row.

Bennis, Warren. The Leaning Ivory Tower. LC 72-7734. (Higher Education Ser.). 1974. 18.95x (ISBN 0-87589-157-8). Jossey-Bass.

Bennis, Warren & Nanus, Burt. Leaders: The Strategies of Taking Charge. LC 83-48323. 200p. 1985. 19.18 (ISBN 0-06-015246-X, HarpT). Har-Row.

Bennis, Warren, et al. Essays in Interpersonal Dynamics. 1979. pap. 15.00x (ISBN 0-256-02231-3). Dorsey.

Bennis, Warren G. Beyond Bureaucracy: Essays on the Development & Evolution of Human Organization. 204p. 1973. pap. 3.50 (ISBN 0-07-004760-X). McGraw.

--Organization Development: Its Nature, Origins & Prospects. Schein, Edgar, et al, eds. (Ser. in Organization Development). 1969. pap. text ed. 10.50 (ISBN 0-201-00523-9). Addison-Wesley.

Bennis, Warren G., ed. American Bureaucracy. (Society Bks). 187p. 1970. 14.95 (ISBN 0-87855-053-4); pap. text ed. 6.95x (ISBN 0-87855-546-3). Transaction Bks.

Bennis, Warren G., et al. Personnel Dialogue for the Seventies. 1971. 3.00 (ISBN 0-87373-284-7, PR 712). Intl Personnel Mgmt.

Bennis, Warren G., et al, eds. Leadership & Motivation: Essays of Douglas McGregor. 1966. pap. 7.95x (ISBN 0-262-63015-X). MIT Pr.

--Planning of Change. 3rd ed. LC 75-41359. 1976. text ed. 28.95 (ISBN 0-03-089518-9, HoltC). HR&W.

Bennish, Lee J. Continuity & Change Xavier University 1831-1981. (Illus.). 252p. 1981. 8.95 (ISBN 0-8294-0388-4). Loyola.

Bennison, G. M. Introduction to Geological Structures & Maps: Metric. 3rd ed. (Illus.). 1975. pap. text ed. 15.95x (ISBN 0-7131-2513-6). Intl Ideas.

Bennison, M. & Casson, J. Manpower Planning Handbook. 320p. 1985. price not set (ISBN 0-07-084727-4). McGraw.

Bennison, R. L. The Impact of Town Centre Shopping Schemes in Britain: Their Impact on Traditional Retail Environments. (Progress in Planning Ser.: Vol. 14, Part 1). (Illus.). 104p. 1980. pap. 14.75 (ISBN 0-08-026789-0). Pergamon.

Bennitt, Mark, ed. History of the Louisiana Purchase Exposition. LC 75-22801. (America in Two Centuries Ser). (Illus.). 1976. Repr. of 1905 ed. 87.00x (ISBN 0-405-07673-8). Ayer Co Pubs.

Benns, F. Lee. American Struggle for the British West India Carrying-Trade 1815-1830. LC 68-55479. Repr. of 1923 ed. lib. bdg. 22.50x (ISBN 0-678-00793-4). Kelley.

Benois, Alexandre. Reminiscences of the Russian Ballet. Britnieva, Mary, tr. LC 77-7791. (Da Capo Series in Dance). (Illus.). 1977. Repr. of 1941 ed. lib. bdg. 35.00 (ISBN 0-306-77426-7). Da Capo.

--The Russian School of Painting. LC 77-94543. 1979. Repr. of 1916 ed. lib. bdg. 30.00 (ISBN 0-89341-224-4). Longwood Pub Group.

Benois, George, jt. auth. see Cox, Beverly.

Benoist, Jean-Marie. The Structural Revolution. LC 78-5298. 1978. 25.00x (ISBN 0-312-76698-X). St Martin.

Benoist De Matougues, L. Dictionnaire de Geographie Sacree et Ecclesiastique, 3 vols. Migne, J. P., ed. (Encyclopedie Theologique Ser.: Vols. 28-30). 1886p. (Fr.). Repr. of 1854 ed. lib. bdg. 240.50x (ISBN 0-89241-241-0). Caratzas.

Benoist Matougues, L. De see Benoist De Matougues, L.

Benoit. Le Dejeuner De Sousceyrac. (Easy Readers Ser. B). 1978. pap. text ed. 4.25 (ISBN 0-88436-293-0, 40268). EMC.

Benoit, Clement F., ed. Children's Poems That Never Grow Old. LC 22-13224. (Granger Poetry Library). (gr. k-6). 1976. Repr. of 1922 ed. 24.50x (ISBN 0-89609-004-3). Granger Bk.

Benoit de Sainte - More. Roman de Troie, 6 Vols. Set. 215.00 (ISBN 0-384-03915-4); Set. pap. 167.00 (ISBN 0-384-03916-2). Johnson Repr.

Benoit, Emile. Europe at Sixes & Sevens. LC 82-2975. (Illus.). xxiv, 276p. 1982. Repr. of 1961 ed. lib. bdg. 35.00x (ISBN 0-313-23500-7, BENE). Greenwood.

--Progress & Survival: An Essay on the the Future of Mankind. Gohn, Jack B., ed. 144p. 1980. 29.95 (ISBN 0-03-056911-7). Praeger.

Benoit, Emile, jt. auth. see McCracken, Paul W.

Benoit, Emile & Boulding, Kenneth E., eds. Disarmament & the Economy. LC 77-25966. 1978. Repr. of 1963 ed. lib. bdg. 22.00x (ISBN 0-313-20076-9, BEDE). Greenwood.

Benoit, H., ed. see International Symposium on Macromolecules, Strasbourg, France.

Benoit, Hendra. Hendra's Book. (Psi Patrol Ser.). 160p. (Orig.). (gr. 7 up). 1985. pap. 2.25 (ISBN 0-590-33202-3, Point). Scholastic Inc.

Benoit, Hubert. The Many Faces of Love: The Psychology of the Emotional & Sexual Life. Mairet, Philip, tr. from Fr. Orig. Title: De l'Amour. 308p. 1980. lib. bdg. 26.00x (ISBN 0-374-90577-0). Octagon.

--The Supreme Doctrine: Psychological Studies in Zen Thought. 248p. 1984. pap. 8.95 (ISBN 0-89281-058-0). Inner Tradit.

Benoit, J. C., et al, eds. see International Congress of Psychotherapy, 10th, Paris, July 1976.

Benoit, Pere, tr. see Lagrange, Maria J.

Benoit, Philip & Hausman, Carl. Do Your Own Public Relations. (Illus.). 256p. 1983. pap. 13.50 (ISBN 0-8306-1595-4, 1595). TAB Bks.

Benoit, Pierre, ed. How Does the Christian Confront the Old Testament. (Concilium Ser.: Vol. 30). 1967. 6.95 (ISBN 0-8091-0074-6). Paulist Pr.

Benoit, Pierre, et al, eds. Dynamism of Biblical Tradition. LC 67-15983. (Concilium Ser.: Vol. 20). 226p. 1967. 6.95 (ISBN 0-8091-0035-5). Paulist Pr.

--Human Reality of Sacred Scripture. LC 65-28869. (Concilium Ser.: Vol. 10). 220p. 6.95 (ISBN 0-8091-0075-4). Paulist Pr.

Benoit, Raymond. Single Nature's Double Name: The Collectedness of the Conflicting in British & American Romanticism. (De Proprietatibus Litterarum Ser.: No. 26). 1973. text ed. 16.00x (ISBN 90-2792-599-2). Mouton.

Benoit-Levy, Jean. Art of the Motion Picture. LC 70-112568. (Literature of Cinema Ser). Repr. of 1946 ed. 16.00 (ISBN 0-405-01603-4). Ayer Co Pubs.

Benoliel, Doug. Northwest Foraging: Wild Edibles of the Pacific Northwest. (Illus., With recipes). 1974. pap. 5.95 (ISBN 0-913140-13-9). Signpost Bk Pubns.

Benoliel, J. O. Death Education for the Health Professional. 1982. 39.95 (ISBN 0-07-004761-8). McGraw.

Benoliel, Jeanne Q., ed. Death Education for the Health Professional. LC 81-20153. (Death Education, Aging & Health Care Ser.). (Illus.). 118p. 1982. text ed. 25.50 (ISBN 0-89116-248-8). Hemisphere Pub.

Benolt, Dick & Bell, Elaine, eds. Geothermal Energy: Bet on It! (Transaction Ser.: Vol. 8). (Illus.). 537p. 1984. 33.00 (ISBN 0-934412-58-8). Geothermal.

Benor, Daniel & Baxter, Michael. Training & Visit Extension. 214p. 15.00 (ISBN 0-318-02826-3, BK0121). World Bank.

Benor, Daniel & Harrison, James Q. Agricultural Extension: The Training & Visit System. 55p. 1977. pap. 5.00 (ISBN 0-686-36060-5, PM-7701). World Bank.

Benor, Daniel, et al. Agricultural Extension: The Training & Visit System. 95p. 5.00 (ISBN 0-318-02827-1, WP0140). World Bank.

Benouis, Mustapha K. Le Dialoque Philosophique Dans la Litterature Francaise Du Seizieme Siecle. (De Proprietatibus Litterarum, Series Maior: No. 31). 1976. text ed. 32.80x (ISBN 90-2793-201-8). Mouton.

--Le Francais Economique et Commercial. 246p. 1982. pap. text ed. 10.95 (ISBN 0-15-528300-6, HC). HarbraceJ.

Benowicz, Robert J. Drugs, Diet & You. 640p. 1984. 9.95 (ISBN 0-671-46174-5, Fireside). S&S.

--Non-Prescription Drugs & Their Side Effects. 1983. pap. 3.50 (ISBN 0-425-06547-2). Berkley Pub.

--Non-Prescription Drugs & Their Side Effects. 2nd, rev. ed. 352p. 1983. pap. 6.95 (ISBN 0-399-50855-4, G&D). Putnam Pub Group.

--Vitamins & You. 352p. 1984. pap. 3.95 (ISBN 0-425-07482-X). Berkley Pub.

Benoyendranath, Banerjea. The Practice of Freedom. 1983. 9.00x (ISBN 0-8364-0918-3, Pub. by Minerva India). South Asia Bks.

Ben-Porat, Josef. My Odyssey in Mother's Womb. 1979. 6.95 (ISBN 0-9603256-0-3). Brighton House.

Ben-Porath, Yoram. Income Distribution & the Family. LC 82-61326. 248p. (Orig.). 1982. pap. 6.95 (ISBN 0-686-43273-8). Population Coun.

Benque, J. P., et al. Engineering Applications of Computational Hydraulics, Vol. 2. Abbott, M. & Cunge, J. A., eds. (Water Resources Engineering Ser.). 224p. 1982. text ed. 48.95 (ISBN 0-273-08543-3). Pitman Pub MA.

Ben-Rafael, Eliezer. The Emergence of Ethnicity: Cultural Groups & Social Conflict in Israel. LC 81-17131. (Contributions in Ethnic Studies: No. 7.). (Illus.). xviii, 258p. 1982. lib. bdg. 29.95x (ISBN 0-313-23088-9, BRE/). Greenwood.

Benrey, Ronald M. Fifty IC Projects You Can Build. (Illus.). 1970. pap. 7.85 (ISBN 0-8104-0723-X). Hayden.

Bens, A. Active English: Pronunciation & Speech. 1977. pap. text ed. 14.95 (ISBN 0-13-003392-8). P-H.

Ben-Sasson, H. H., ed. A History of the Jewish People. 1232p. 1985. pap. 18.95 (ISBN 0-674-39731-2). Harvard U Pr.

Ben-Sasson, Haim, et al. History of the Jewish People. (Illus.). 1040p. 1976. 60.00 (ISBN 0-674-39730-4). Harvard U Pr.

Bensasson, R. V. & Truscott, T. G. Flash Photolysis & Pulse Radiolysis: Contributions to the Chemistry of Biology & Medicine. (Illus.). 272p. 1983. 50.00 (ISBN 0-08-024949-3). Pergamon.

Bensasson, R. V., et al, eds. Primary Photo-Processes in Biology & Medicine. (NATO ASI Series A, Life Sciences: Vol. 8). 528p. 1985. 85.00x (ISBN 0-306-41930-0). Plenum Pub.

Bensch, D. E., jt. auth. see Burke, J. L.

Bensch, E., et al. Schiffbau-Schiffahrt Fischereittechnik: Russisch-English-Deutsch. 784p. (Rus., Eng. & Ger.). 1981. 95.00 (ISBN 0-686-92464-9, M-12665). French & Eur.

Bensch, Erhard, jt. auth. see Dipl-Ling, V.

Benschoten, A. Q. Van see Van Benschoten, A. Q., Jr.

Bense, Walter F, ed. see Holl, Karl.

Bensel, Richard. Sectionalism & American Political Development, 1880-1980. LC 84-40145. (Illus.). 576p. 1984. text ed. 35.00x (ISBN 0-299-09830-3). U of Wis Pr.

Benseler, David P. & Schultz, Renate A. Intensive Foreign Language Courses. (Language in Education Ser.: No. 18). 55p. 1979. pap. 6.95 (ISBN 0-15-599009-8). Ctr Appl Ling.

Benseler, G., ed. see Isocrates.

Bensell, Royal A. All Quiet on the Yamhill: The Civil War in Oregon. Barth, Gunter, ed. (Illus.). 1958. 12.00 (ISBN 0-87071-332-9). Oreg St U Pr.

--All Quiet on the Yamhill: The Civil War in Oregon. Barth, Gunter, ed. LC 60-63172. 1959. 5.00 (ISBN 0-87114-005-5). U of Oreg Bks.

Bensen, D. R., jt. auth. see Woodehouse, P. G.

Bensen, D. R., ed. see Wodehouse, P. G.

Benson, E. S. & Strandjord, P. E., eds. Multiple Laboratory Screening. 1969. 55.00 (ISBN 0-12-089050-X). Acad Pr.

Benson, Edward F. The Blotting Book. LC 75-32734. (Literature of Mystery & Detection). 1976. Repr. of 1908 ed. 20.00x (ISBN 0-405-07864-1). Ayer Co Pubs.

--Freaks of Mayfair. facsimile ed. LC 77-150536. (Short Story Index Reprint Ser.). Repr. of 1917 ed. 17.00 (ISBN 0-8369-3833-X). Ayer Co Pubs.

--Spook Stories. Reginald, R. & Menville, Douglas, eds. LC 75-46252. (Supernatural & Occult Fiction Ser.). 1976. Repr. of 1928 ed. lib. bdg. 21.00x (ISBN 0-405-08112-X). Ayer Co Pubs.

Benson, Egbert. Vindication of the Captors of Major Andre. (American Revolutionary Ser.). Repr. of 1865 ed. lib. bdg. 26.50x (ISBN 0-8398-0187-4). Irvington.

Benson, Eileen, ed. see Taetzsch, Lyn.

Benson, Elizabeth P. A Man & a Feline in Mochica Art. LC 74-18650. (Studies in Pre-Columbian Art & Archaeology: No. 14). (Illus.). 31p. 1974. pap. 3.00x (ISBN 0-88402-058-4). Dumbarton Oaks.

--An Olmec Figure at Dumbarton Oaks. LC 70-184640. (Studies in Pre-Columbian Art & Archaeology: No. 8). (Illus.). 95p. 1971. pap. 4.00x (ISBN 0-88402-035-5). Dumbarton Oaks.

Benson, Elizabeth P., jt. auth. see Coe, Michael D.

Benson, Elizabeth P; see Grove, David C.

Benson, Elizabeth P; see Wilbert, Johannes.

Benson, Elizabeth P., ed. The Cult of the Feline: A Conference in Pre-Columbian Iconography, October 31 & November 1, 1970. LC 72-90080. (Illus.). 166p. 1972. 15.00x (ISBN 0-88402-043-6). Dumbarton Oaks.

--Death & the Afterlife in Pre-Columbian America: A Conference at Dumbarton Oaks, October 27, 1973. LC 74-22694. (Illus.). 196p. 1975. 15.00x (ISBN 0-88402-062-2). Dumbarton Oaks.

--Dumbarton Oaks Conference on Chavin, October 26 and 27, 1968. LC 73-153502. (Illus.). 124p. 1971. 12.00x (ISBN 0-88402-037-1). Dumbarton Oaks.

--Mesoamerican Sites & World-Views: Conference at Dumbarton Oaks, October 16 & 17, 1976. LC 79-92647. (Illus.). 256p. 1981. 24.00x (ISBN 0-88402-097-5). Dumbarton Oaks.

--Mesoamerican Writing Systems: A Conference at Dumbarton Oaks, October 30 & 31, 1971. LC 73-93086. (Illus.). 226p. 1973. 20.00x (ISBN 0-88402-048-7). Dumbarton Oaks.

--The Olmec & Their Neighbors: Essays in Memory of Matthew W. Stirling. LC 79-49262. (Illus.). 346p. 1981. 30.00x (ISBN 0-88402-098-3). Dumbarton Oaks.

--Pre-Columbian Metallurgy of South-America, Proceedings: A Conference at Dumbarton Oaks, October 18 & 19, 1975. LC 79-49261. (Illus.). 107p. 1979. 20.00x (ISBN 0-88402-094-0). Dumbarton Oaks.

Benson, Elizabeth P., ed. see Dumbarton Oaks Collection.

Benson, Ellen. Philip's Little Sister. LC 78-12627. (Social Values Ser.). (Illus.). (gr. 3). 1979. PLB 10.35 (ISBN 0-516-02023-4); pap. 3.95 (ISBN 0-516-42023-2). Childrens.

Benson, Ellis, jt. ed. see Stefanini, Mario.

Benson, Ethel M. Ferocious Sarah. (Illus., Orig.). (gr. k-4). 1979. pap. 1.50 (ISBN 0-934926-01-8). Talespinner.

Benson, Eugene. J. M. Synge. (Grove Press Modern Dramatists Ser.). (Illus.). 224p. (Orig.). 1983. pap. 9.95 (ISBN 0-394-62432-7, E833, Ever). Grove.

Benson, Evelyn P. & DeVitt, Joan Q. Community Health & Nursing Practices. 2nd ed. (Illus.). 1980. text ed. 24.95 (ISBN 0-13-153171-9). P-H.

Benson, Ezra T. Come unto Christ. 136p. 1984. 6.95 (ISBN 0-87747-997-6). Deseret Bk.

--Cross Fire: The Eight Years with Eisenhower. LC 75-25484. 1976. Repr. of 1962 ed. lib. bdg. 38.50x (ISBN 0-8371-8422-3, BECRF). Greenwood.

--Farmers at the Crossroads. 1956. 8.95 (ISBN 0-8159-5501-4). Devin.

--Farmers at the Crossroads. LC 82-997. (Illus.). xvi, 107p. 1982. Repr. of 1956 ed. lib. bdg. 22.50x (ISBN 0-313-23484-1, BENF). Greenwood.

--The Proper Role of Government. 32p. 1975. pap. 1.95 (ISBN 0-89036-122-3). Hawkes Pub Inc.

--This Nation Shall Endure. LC 77-21466. 1977. 8.95 (ISBN 0-87747-658-6). Deseret Bk.

Benson, F. A. Electric Circuit Problems with Solutions: SI-Version. 2nd ed. 1975. pap. 12.95x (ISBN 0-412-21260-9, NO.6035, Pub. by Chapman & Hall). Methuen Inc.

--Problems in Electronics with Solutions. 5th ed. 1976. pap. 14.95x (ISBN 0-412-14770-X, NO. 6036, Pub. by Chapman & Hall). Methuen Inc.

Benson, Francis R. My Memoirs. LC 79-8053. Repr. of 1930 ed. 31.50 (ISBN 0-404-18364-6). AMS Pr.

Benson, Frank & Blumer, Diedrich, eds. Psychiatric Aspects of Neurologic Disease, Vol. 2. (Seminars in Psychiatry Ser.). 352p. 1982. 31.00 (ISBN 0-8089-1430-8, 790543). Grune.

Benson, Frederic R. High Nitrogen Compounds. LC 83-10476. 679p. 1983. 133.95 (ISBN 0-471-02652-2, Pub. by Wiley-Interscience). Wiley.

Benson, G. C. The New Centralization: A Study of Intergovernmental Relationships in the U.S. LC 77-74928. (American Federalism-the Urban Dimension). 1978. Repr. of 1941 ed. lib. bdg. 17.00x (ISBN 0-405-10477-4). Ayer Co Pubs.

Benson, G. R., ed. see Nettleship, Richard L.

Benson, George, jt. auth. see McClave, James T.

Benson, George, jt. auth. see Sachs, William S.

Benson, George A. What to Do When You're Depressed: A Christian Psychoanalyst Helps You Understand & Overcome Your Depression. LC 75-22712. 144p. 1975. pap. 5.95 (ISBN 0-8066-1519-2, 10-7052). Augsburg.

Benson, George C. Business Ethics in America. LC 81-48392. 320p. 1982. 32.50x (ISBN 0-669-05353-8). Lexington Bks.

Benson, George C. & Engeman, Thomas S. Amoral America: Sources of Morality in a Liberal Society. rev. ed. LC 81-70432. 294p. 1982. lib. bdg. 22.75 (ISBN 0-89089-208-3); pap. 9.95 (ISBN 0-89089-209-1). Carolina Acad Pr.

Benson, George C. & McClelland, Harold F. Consolidated Grants: A Means of Maintaining Fiscal Responsibility. 41p. 1961. pap. 3.75 (ISBN 0-8447-3030-0). Am Enterprise.

Benson, George W. The Cross: Its History & Symbolism. LC 73-88643. 1976. Repr. of 1934 ed. lib. bdg. 25.00 (ISBN 0-87817-149-5). Hacker.

Benson, Gordon, Jr., ed. Poul Anderson Myth-Maker & Wonder-Weaver. 2nd ed. (Orig.). 1982. pap. 3.50 (ISBN 0-912613-01-7). Galactic Central.

Benson, H. W. Democratic Rights for Union Members: A Guide to Internal Union Democracy. 245p. 1979. 4.75 (ISBN 0-9602244-1-6). Assn Union Demo.

Benson, Harold J. Human Anatomy Laboratory Textbook. 288p. 1979. write for info. wire coil (ISBN 0-697-04656-7). Wm C Brown.

--Microbiological Applications: A Laboratory Manual in General Microbiology, Complete Version. 4th ed. 472p. 1985. write for info. wire coil (ISBN 0-697-00307-8); instr's. manual avail. (ISBN 0-697-00557-7). Wm C Brown.

--Microbiological Applications: A Laboratory Manual in General Microbiology. Short Versions. 4th ed. 368p. 1985. write for info. wire coil bdg. (ISBN 0-697-00306-X); instr's. manual avail. (ISBN 0-697-00557-7). Wm C Brown.

Benson, Harold J. & Talaro, Arthur. Physiological Applications. 318p. 1982. write for info. wire coil (ISBN 0-697-04717-2); instr's. handbook avail. (ISBN 0-697-04723-7). Wm C Brown.

Benson, Harold J. & Talaro, Kathleen P. Human Anatomy Laboratory Textbook. 2nd ed. 352p. 1984. write for info. wire coil (ISBN 0-697-04924-8); instr's handbk. avail. (ISBN 0-697-04925-6). Wm C Brown.

Benson, Harold J., et al. Anatomy & Physiology Laboratory Textbook. 3rd ed. 448p. 1983. write for info. wire coil short version (ISBN 0-697-04739-3); instr's. manual avail. (ISBN 0-697-04740-7); complete version, 592p. 1983 (ISBN 0-697-04737-7); instr's. manual avail. (ISBN 0-697-04738-5). Wm C Brown.

Benson, Hazel B. Behavior Modification & the Child: An Annotated Bibliography. LC 79-7358. (Contemporary Problems of Childhood Ser.: No. 3). 1979. lib. bdg. 39.95 (ISBN 0-313-21489-1, BBM/). Greenwood.

Benson, Henry C. Life among the Choctaw Indians & Sketches of the Southwest. (American Studies). Repr. of 1860 ed. 19.00 (ISBN 0-384-03928-6). Johnson Repr.

Benson, Herbert & Klipper, Miriam Z. The Relaxation Response. 1976. pap. 3.50 (ISBN 0-380-00676-6, 60110-9). Avon.

Benson, Herbert & Proctor, William. Beyond the Relaxation Response. 192p. 1985. pap. 3.50 (ISBN 0-425-08183-4). Berkley Pub.

--Beyond the Relaxation Response: How to Harness the Healing Power of Your Personal Beliefs. LC 83-45920. (Illus.). 180p. 1984. 12.50 (ISBN 0-8129-1107-5). Times Bks.

Benson, Ian & Lloyd, John. New Technology & Industrial Change. 220p. 1983. 27.50 (ISBN 0-89397-128-6). Nichols Pub.

Benson, Ian, ed. Intelligent Machinery: Theory & Practice. 250p. Date not set. price not set (ISBN 0-521-30836-4). Cambridge U Pr.

Benson, J. & Greaves, W. You & Your Language-The Kinds of English You Use: Styles & Dialects, Vol. 1. LC 83-2359. (Pergamon Institute of English Courses Ser.). (Illus.). 96p. 1984. pap. 4.50 (ISBN 0-08-031092-3); cassette 10.60 (ISBN 0-08-029424-3). Pergamon.

Benson, J. L. Bamboula at Kourion: The Necropolis & the Finds, Excavated by J. F. Daniel. LC 72-133204. (Haney Foundation Ser.). (Illus.). 264p. 1973. 65.00x (ISBN 0-8122-7635-3). U of Pa Pr.

Benson, J. L., jt. auth. see Stillwell, Agnes N.

Benson, J. L., tr. see Buschor, Ernst.

Benson, Jack L. Horse, Bird & Man: The Origins of Greek Painting. LC 70-95787. (Illus.). pap. 63.30 (ISBN 0-317-10543-4, 2022133). Bks Demand UMI.

Benson, Jackson J. Hemingway: The Writer's Art of Self-Defense. LC 70-77139. pap. 53.50 (ISBN 0-317-29400-8, 2055842). Bks Demand UMI.

--The True Adventures of John Steinbeck, Writer: A Biography. (Illus.). 1038p. 1984. 35.00 (ISBN 0-670-16685-5). Viking.

Benson, Jackson J., ed. The Short Stories of Ernest Hemingway: Critical Essays. LC 74-75815. xv, 375p. 1975. 21.00 (ISBN 0-8223-0320-5). Duke.

Benson, Jackson J., jt. ed. see Astro, Richard.

Benson, Jacqueline M. Weeds in Tropical Crops: Review of Abstracts on Constraints in Production Caused by Weeds in Maize, Rice, Sorghum-Millet, Groundnuts, and Cassava, 1952-1980. (Plant Production & Protection Papers: No. 32, Suppl. 1). 68p. 1982. pap. 7.50 (ISBN 92-5-101206-7, F2333, FAO). Unipub.

Benson, James & Greaves, William. Systemic Perspectives on Discourse Selected Applied Papers. Freedle, Roy O., ed. (Advances in Discourse Processes Ser.). 400p. 1985. inst. ed. 42.50 (ISBN 0-89391-202-6); pers. ed. 24.95. Ablex Pub.

--Systemic Perspectives on Discourse: Selected Theoretical Papers. Freedle, Roy, ed. (Advances in Discourse Processes Ser.). 288p. 1984. text ed. 34.50 (ISBN 0-89391-193-3). Ablex Pub.

Benson, Jean. Soft Toys to Stitch & Stuff. LC 82-45099. (Illus.). 144p. 1983. 14.95 (ISBN 0-385-18136-1). Doubleday.

Benson, Jean & Anderson, Joanna. Respond: Teaching Children Self-Protection. 1985. pap. 14.50 (ISBN 0-87562-085-X). Spec Child.

Benson, Jean & Anderson, Joanne. Respond: Teach Your Child Self-Protection. 1984. 7.95 (ISBN 0-917634-13-6). Creative Infomatics.

Benson, Jeanette & Hilyard, Jack. Becoming Family. LC 78-62677. 1978. 9.95 (ISBN 0-88489-107-0). St Mary's.

Benson, Jeffrey & MacKenzie, Alastair. Sauternes: A Study of the Great Sweet Wines of Bordeaux. (Illus.). 172p. 1979. 26.00 (ISBN 0-85667-062-6, Pub. by Sotheby Pubns England). Biblio Dist.

--Sauternes: A Study of the Great Sweet Wines of Bordeaux. (Illus.). 184p. 26.00 (ISBN 0-85667-062-6). Sotheby Pubns.

--The Wines of Saint-Emilion & Pomerol. (Illus.). 300p. 39.95 (ISBN 0-85667-169-X, Pub. by Sotheby Pubns England). Biblio Dist.

Benson, Jim, jt. auth. see Okagaki, Alan.

Benson, Joe, ed. Illustrated Alfa Romeo Buyer's Guide. (Buyer's Guide Ser.). (Illus.). 176p. 1983. pap. 13.95 (ISBN 0-87938-163-9). Motorbooks Intl.

Benson, John. Bibliography of the British Coal Industry. Neville, Robert & Thompson, Charles, eds. 1981. 105.00x (ISBN 0-19-920120-X). Oxford U Pr.

--British Coalminers in the Nineteenth Century: A Social History. 250p. 1980. text ed. 47.50x (ISBN 0-8419-0592-4). Holmes & Meier.

Benson, John, ed. The Working Class in England, 1875-1914. LC 84-17672. 214p. 1984. 27.50 (ISBN 0-7099-0692-7, Pub. by Croom Helm Ltd). Longwood Pub Group.

Benson, John & Neville, Robert G., eds. Studies in the Yorkshire Coal Industry. LC 76-11778. 1976. lib. bdg. 27.50x (ISBN 0-678-06793-7). Kelley.

Benson, John H. & Carey, A. G. Elements of Lettering. 2nd ed. 1962. text ed. 23.10 (ISBN 0-07-004775-8). McGraw.

Benson, John H., tr. First Writing Book: An English Translation & Facsimile Text of Arrighi's Operina. (Illus.). 1966. pap. 4.95x (ISBN 0-300-00020-0, Y178). Yale U Pr.

Benson, John L. Who Is the Antichrist? LC 78-2426. 1978. pap. 2.50 (ISBN 0-87227-058-0). Reg Baptist.

Benson, John W. Social Studies Starters: Games Students Like to Play. 1974. pap. 4.95 (ISBN 0-8224-3270-6). Pitman Learning.

Benson, Kathleen. A Man Called Martin Luther. 1980. 7.50 (ISBN 0-570-03625-9, 39-1067). Concordia.

Benson, Kathleen, jt. auth. see Haskins, James.

Benson, Larry D. Malory's Morte d'Arthur: A 15th Century Chivalric Romance. 256p. 1976. 17.50x (ISBN 0-674-54393-9). Harvard U Pr.

Benson, Larry D., ed. The Learned & the Lewed: Studies in Chaucer & Medieval Literature. LC 74-78719. (English Studies: No. 5). 448p. 1974. pap. 7.95x (ISBN 0-674-51888-8). Harvard U Pr.

Benson, Larry D & Leyerle, John, eds. Chivalric Literature: Essays on Relations Between Literature & Life in the Later Middle Ages. LC 80-17514. (Studies in Medieval Culture: XIV). (Illus.). 176p. (Orig.). 1980. pap. 10.80x (ISBN 0-918720-09-5). Medieval Inst.

Benson, Larry D. & Wenzel, Siegfried, eds. The Wisdom of Poetry: Essays in Early English Literature in Honor of Morton W. Bloomfield. viii, 315p. 1982. 22.95x (ISBN 0-918720-15-X); pap. 13.95x (ISBN 0-918720-16-8). Medieval Inst.

Benson, Lee. Concept of Jacksonian Democracy: New York As a Test Case. 1961. 35.00x (ISBN 0-691-04513-5); pap. 10.95 (ISBN 0-691-00572-9). Princeton U Pr.

--Merchants, Farmers, & Railroads: Railroad Regulation & New York Politics, 1850-1887. LC 68-27048. (Illus.). 310p. 1969. Repr. of 1955 ed. 12.00x (ISBN 0-8462-1271-4). Russell.

--Merchants, Farmers, & Railroads: Railroad Regulation & New York Politics, 1850-1887. 1955. 10.00x (ISBN 0-317-27520-8). Elliots Bks.

--Turner & Beard: American Historical Writing Reconsidered. LC 79-28641. xiii, 241p. 1980. Repr. of 1960 ed. lib. bdg. 22.50x (ISBN 0-313-22281-9, BETU). Greenwood.

Benson, Leslie. Proletarians & Parties: Five Essays in Social Class. 1978. pap. 10.50x (ISBN 0-422-76580-5, NO. 2829, Pub. by Tavistock England). Methuen Inc.

Benson, Lewis. Catholic Quakerism: A Vision for All Men. 108p. 1968. pap. text ed. 2.50 (ISBN 0-941308-03-0). Religious Soc Friends.

Benson, Louis. The English Hymn. (Music Reprint Ser.). 624p. 1985. Repr. of 1915 ed. 65.00 (ISBN 0-306-76261-7). Da Capo.

Benson, Lyman. The Cacti of Arizona. 3rd ed. LC 70-77802. (Illus.). 218p. 1969. pap. 12.50 (ISBN 0-8165-0509-8). U of Ariz Pr.

--The Cacti of the United States & Canada. LC 73-80617. (Illus.). 1104p. 1982. 95.00x (ISBN 0-8047-0863-0). Stanford U Pr.

--The Native Cacti of California. LC 69-13176. (Illus.). 1969. 12.95 (ISBN 0-8047-0696-4). Stanford U Pr.

--Plant Classification. 2nd ed. 1979. text ed. 31.95 (ISBN 0-669-01489-3). Heath.

Benson, Lyman & Darrow, Robert A. Trees & Shrubs of the Southwestern Deserts. rev. ed. LC 81-7617. 416p. 1981. text ed. 49.50 (ISBN 0-8165-0591-8). U of Ariz Pr.

Benson, M. English-Serbocroatian Dictionary. 669p. (Eng. & Serbocroatian.). 1981. 75.00 (ISBN 0-686-97376-3, M-9635). French & Eur.

--Serbocroatian-English Dictionary. 770p. (Serbocroatian & Eng.). 1980. 75.00 (ISBN 0-686-97438-7, M-9630). French & Eur.

--Yugoslavic Dictionary, 2 Vols. 1980p. (Serbocroation & Eng.). 29.50x ea. Vol. 1, Serbocroation-English (ISBN 0-89918-786-2). Vol. 2, English-Serbocroation (ISBN 0-89918-787-0). Vanous.

Benson, M. A. Measurement of Peak Discharge by Indirect Methods. (Technical Note Ser.). 1968. pap. 10.00 (ISBN 0-685-22318-3, W60, WMO). Unipub.

Benson, Marilyn & Benson, Dennis. The Hard Times Catalog for Youth Ministry. LC 82-81332. (Illus.). 288p. (Orig.). 1982. pap. 14.95 (ISBN 0-936664-06-1). Group Bks.

Benson, Marilyn J., jt. auth. see Benson, Dennis C.

Benson, Mary. The Sun Will Rise. X ed. 80p. 1981. 3.00 (ISBN 0-904759-43-1). Intl Defense & Aid.

Benson, Mary S. Women in Eighteenth-Century America: A Study of Opinion & Social Usage. LC 75-41025. (BCL Ser. II). 1976. Repr. of 1935 ed. 31.50 (ISBN 0-404-51405-7). AMS Pr.

Benson, Michael. Vintage Science Fiction Films, 1896-1949. LC 83-42889. (Illus.). 232p. 1985. lib. bdg. 18.95x (ISBN 0-89950-085-4). McFarland & Co.

Benson, Michael, jt. auth. see Benson, Bob.

Benson, Morton. English-Serbocroatian Dictionary. LC 78-64520. (Eng. & Serbocroatian.). 1979. 40.00 (ISBN 0-8122-7764-3). U of Pa Pr.

Benson, Morton, ed. Dictionary of Russian Personal Names. LC 64-19386. 1964. 17.50x (ISBN 0-8122-7452-0). U of Pa Pr.

--Serbocroatian-English Dictionary. LC 79-146959. (Eng. & Serbocroatian.). 1971. text ed. 40.00x (ISBN 0-8122-7636-1). U of Pa Pr.

Benson, N. G., ed. A Century of Fisheries in North America. (AFS Special Publications: No. 7). 330p. 1970. 12.00 (ISBN 0-913235-05-9); members 10.00 (ISBN 0-317-32534-5). Am Fisheries Soc.

Benson, Nella. Amaranth. 176p. (Orig.). 1984. pap. 2.50 (ISBN 0-380-88765-7). Avon.

Benson, Nettie L., ed. Catalogue of "Martin Fierro" Materials in the University of Texas Library. LC 72-97224. (Ilas Guides & Bibliographies Ser.: No. 6). 147p. 1973. pap. 4.50x (ISBN 0-292-71009-7). U of Tex Pr.

--Mexico & the Spanish Cortes, 1810-1822: Eight Essays. (Latin American Monograph Ser.: No. 5). 251p. 1966. 14.50x (ISBN 0-292-73606-1). U of Tex Pr.

Benson, Nettie L., tr. & intro. by see Ramos Arizpe, Miguel.

Benson, Norma, jt. auth. see Zauner, Christian.

Benson, O. G. Cain's Wife. LC 85-42551. 160p. 1985. pap. 3.50 (ISBN 0-06-080773-3, P 773, PL). Har-Row.

Benson, Oscar H., jt. auth. see Tod, Osma G.

Benson, P. F., ed. Screening & Management of Potentially Treatable Genetic Metabolic Disorders. 176p. 1984. lib. bdg. 45.00 (ISBN 0-85200-784-1, Pub. by MTP Pr England). Kluwer Academic.

Benson, P. George, jt. auth. see McClave, James T.

Benson, Pagnar & Christensen, Devon. Live off the Land in the City & Country. 262p. 1983. pap. 9.95 (ISBN 0-8065-0892-2). Citadel Pr.

Benson, Philip F. & Fensom, Anthony H. Genetic Biochemical Disorders. (Oxford Monographs on Medical Genetics). (Illus.). 600p. 1985. 55.00 (ISBN 0-19-261193-3). Oxford U Pr.

Benson, Ragnar. Bull's-Eye: Crossbows by Ragnar Benson. (Illus.). 94p. (Orig.). 1985. pap. 8.00 (ISBN 0-87364-326-7). Paladin Pr.

--Eating Cheap. 120p. 1982. pap. 8.00 (ISBN 0-87364-252-X). Paladin Pr.
--Live off the Land in the City & Country. (Illus.). 263p. 1981. 16.95 (ISBN 0-87364-200-7). Paladin Pr.
--Mantrappping. (Illus.). 88p. 1981. pap. 10.00 (ISBN 0-87364-215-5). Paladin Pr.
--Ragnar's Tall Tales. 90p. 1983. pap. 6.00 (ISBN 0-87364-263-5). Paladin Pr.
--Survival Poaching. (Illus.). 250p. 1980. 14.95 (ISBN 0-87364-183-3). Paladin Pr.
--The Survival Retreat: A Total Plan for Retreat Defense. (Illus.). 136p. 1983. pap. 8.00 (ISBN 0-87364-275-9). Paladin Pr.
--Survivalist's Medicine Chest. (Illus.). 80p. 1982. pap. 5.95 (ISBN 0-87364-256-2). Paladin Pr.
Benson, Ralph C. Handbook of Obstetrics & Gynecology. 8th ed. LC 83-82070. (Illus.). 804p. 1983. lexotone cover 13.00 (ISBN 0-87041-145-4). Lange.
Benson, Ralph C., ed. Current Obstetric & Gynecologic Diagnosis & Treatment. 5th ed. LC 84-81907. (Illus.). 1082p. 1984. lexotone cover 26.50 (ISBN 0-87041-214-0). Lange.
Benson, Ramsey J. & Rochester, Jack B. The Adam's Companion. 400p. 1984. pap. 9.95 (ISBN 0-380-87650-7, 87650-7). Avon.
Benson, Randolph. Thomas Jefferson As Social Scientist. LC 70-118124. 333p. 1971. 27.50 (ISBN 0-8386-7705-3). Fairleigh Dickinson.
Benson, Raymond. The James Bond Bedside Companion. (Illus.). 385p. 1984. 19.95 (ISBN 0-396-08383-8); pap. 12.95 (ISBN 0-396-08384-6). Dodd.
Benson, Renate. German Expressionist Drama: Ernst Toller & Georg Kaiser. (Modern Dramatists Ser.). 192p. 1984. 19.50 (ISBN 0-394-54135-9, GP-936); pap. 7.95 (ISBN 0-394-62268-5, EVER). Grove.
Benson, Richard. Lay This Laurel. LC 73-84997. (Illus.). 96p. 1973. 15.00x (ISBN 0-87130-036-2). Eakins.
Benson, Richard E., jt. ed. see Brossi, Arnold.
Benson, Rita, ed. see Debussy, Claude.
Benson, Robert, ed. see Johnston, William L.
Benson, Robert E. Natural Trigonometric Functions. 6.00 (ISBN 0-685-19493-0). Powner.
Benson, Robert H. Book of Essays. facs. ed. LC 68-54325. (Essay Index Reprint Ser). 1968. Repr. of 1916 ed. 17.00 (ISBN 0-8369-0195-9). Ayer Co Pubs.
--Lord of the World. LC 74-15951. (Science Fiction Ser). 352p. 1975. Repr. of 1908 ed. 25.50x (ISBN 0-405-06277-X). Ayer Co Pubs.
--The Necromancers. LC 75-36826. (Occult Ser.). 1976. Repr. of 1909 ed. 24.50x (ISBN 0-405-07939-7). Ayer Co Pubs.
--Papers of a Pariah. facs. ed. LC 67-23176. (Essay Index Reprint Ser). 1907. 17.00 (ISBN 0-8369-0196-7). Ayer Co Pubs.
Benson, Robert H. & More, Thomas. The Friendship of Christ. (Books to Live Ser.). 156p. 1984. 8.95 (ISBN 0-88347-171-X). Thomas More.
Benson, Robert L. The Bishop-Elect: A Study in Medieval Ecclesiastical Office. LC 65-17130. pap. 115.00 (ISBN 0-317-07842-9, 2010535). Bks Demand UMI.
Benson, Robert L. & Constable, Giles, eds. Renaissance & Renewal in the Twelfth Century. (Illus.). 832p. 1983. text ed. 55.00x (ISBN 0-674-76085-9). Harvard U Pr.
--Renaissance & Renewal in the Twelfth Century. 816p. 1985. pap. text ed. 15.95x (ISBN 0-674-76086-7). Harvard U Pr.
Benson, Rolf. Skydiving. LC 78-26246. (Superwheels & Thrill Sports Bks.). (Illus.). (gr. 4 up). 1979. PLB 8.95 (ISBN 0-8225-0425-1). Lerner Pubns.
Benson, Rowland S. Advanced Engineering Thermodynamics. 2nd ed. 1967. text ed. 45.00 (ISBN 0-08-020719-7); pap. 14.00 (ISBN 0-08-020718-9). Pergamon.
--Thermodynamics & Gas Dynamics of Internal Combustion Engines, Vol. 1. Horlock, J. H. & Winterbone, D., eds. (Illus.). 1982. text ed. 125.00x (ISBN 0-19-856210-1). Oxford U Pr.
Benson, Rowland S. & Whitehouse, N. D. Internal Combustion Engines, 2 vols. LC 79-40359. (Thermodynamics & Fluid Mechanics for Mechanical Engineers). (Illus.). 1979. Set. 28.00 set (ISBN 0-08-031630-1); Vol. 1. pap. 15.75 (ISBN 0-08-022718-X); Vol. 2. pap. 15.75 (ISBN 0-08-022720-1). Pergamon.
Benson, Ruth C. Women in Tolstoy: The Ideal & the Erotic. LC 72-92631. pap. 38.30 (ISBN 0-317-09648-6, 2020225). Bks Demand UMI.
--Women in Tolstoy: The Ideal & the Erotic. LC 72-92631. pap. 38.30 (ISBN 0-317-28788-5, 2020225). Bks Demand UMI.
Benson, Sally. Junior Miss. (gr. 7-9). 1969. pap. 1.75 (ISBN 0-671-42066-6). Archway.
--Stories of the Gods & Heroes. (gr. 4-6). 1940. 12.95 (ISBN 0-8037-8291-8, 01258-370). Dial Bks Young.
--Women & Children First. 1976. Repr. of 1943 ed. lib. bdg. 6.95 (ISBN 0-89190-872-2, Pub. by River City Pr). Amereon Ltd.
Benson, Sidney W. Chemical Calculations: An Introduction to the Use of Mathematics in Chemistry. 3rd ed. LC 76-146670. 279p. 1971. pap. text ed. 16.00 (ISBN 0-471-06769-5). Wiley.
--Foundations of Chemical Kinetics. LC 80-16099. 742p. 1982. Repr. of 1960 ed. lib. bdg. 46.50 (ISBN 0-89874-194-7). Krieger.
--Thermochemical Kinetics: Methods for the Estimation of Thermochemical Data & Rate Parameters. 2nd ed. LC 76-6840. 320p. 1976. 48.95 (ISBN 0-471-06781-4). Wiley.
Benson, Stella. The Far-Away Bride. LC 77-138606. 354p. 1972. Repr. of 1941 ed. lib. bdg. 24.75x (ISBN 0-8371-5714-5, BEFB). Greenwood.
Benson, Steve. As Is. 1978. 10.00 (ISBN 0-685-99352-3); pap. 3.50 (ISBN 0-685-99353-1). Figures.
Benson, Susan. Ambiguous Ethnicity: Interracial Families in London. LC 81-6172. (Changing Cultures Ser.). (Illus.). 192p. 1982. 34.50 (ISBN 0-521-23017-9); pap. 11.95 (ISBN 0-521-29769-9). Cambridge U Pr.
Benson, Susan, ed. see El Shazly, Saad.
Benson, Ted, jt. auth. see MacGregor, Bruce.
Benson, Ted, jt. auth. see Steinheimer, Richard.
Benson, Ted, jt. auth. see Styffe, Dave.
Benson, Tedd & Gruber, James. Building the Timber Frame House. (Illus.). 224p. 1981. pap. 14.95 (ISBN 0-684-17286-0, ScribT). Scribner.
Benson, Theodora. The First Time I... Repr. of 1935 ed. 25.00 (ISBN 0-89987-150-X). Darby Bks.
--In the East My Pleasure Lies. 20.00 (ISBN 0-686-17220-5). Scholars Ref Lib.
Benson, Thomas W. & Prosser, Michael H., eds. Readings in Classical Rhetoric. LC 76-80478. Repr. of 1969 ed. 87.50 (ISBN 0-8357-9237-4, 2017610). Bks Demand UMI.
Benson, Vladimir. The Failure of the American Dream & the Moral Responsibility of the United States for the Crisis in the Middle East & for the Collapse of the World Order. (The Great Currents of History Library Bk.). (Illus.). 141p. 1983. 97.85x (ISBN 0-86722-025-2). Inst Econ Pol.
--The Failure of the American Dream & the Moral Responsibility of the United States for the Crisis in the Middle East & for the Collapse of the World Order, 2 vols. (Illus.). 311p. 1985. Set. 189.75 (ISBN 0-86722-114-3). Inst Econ Finan.
Benson, Warren E., Jr., ed. Car Buyer's Illustrated Fact & Figure Book 1981. (Illus.). 1981. pap. 5.00 (ISBN 0-394-17881-5, E761, Ever). Grove.
Benson, Warren S., jt. auth. see Gangel, Kenneth O.
Benson, Warren S., jt. ed. see Zuck, Roy B.
Benson, Wilbur M. & Schiele, Burtrum C. Tranquilizing & Antidepressive Drugs. (Illus.). 108p. 1962. 9.75x (ISBN 0-398-00134-0). C C Thomas.
Benson, William H. & Jacoby, Oswald. New Recreations with Magic Squares. LC 74-28909. 192p. (Orig.). 1976. pap. 4.95 (ISBN 0-486-23236-0). Dover.
--New Recreations with Magic Squares. (Illus.). 11.25 (ISBN 0-8446-5159-1). Peter Smith.
Benson, William H. & Oswald, Jacoby. Magic Cubes: New Recreations, 2 pts. (Illus.). 96p. (Orig.). 1982. Set. pap. 4.00 (ISBN 0-486-24140-8). Dover.
Benson-von-der-Ohe, Elizabeth E. First & Second Marriages. 200p. Date not set. 29.95 (ISBN 0-03-059239-9). Praeger.
Bensor, N. R. North Atlantic Seaway, Vol. 1. (Illus.). 1975. 19.95 (ISBN 0-668-03679-6). Arco.
Bensoussan, A. Stochastic Control by Functional Analysis Methods. (Studies in Mathematics & Its Applications: Vol. 11). 410p. 1982. 53.25 (ISBN 0-444-86329-X, North-Holland). Elsevier.
Bensoussan, A. & Lions, J. L. Applications of Variational Inequalities in Stochastic Control. (Studies in Mathematics & Its Applications: Vol. 12). Orig. Title: Applications des Inequations Variationnelles en Controle Stochastique. 564p. 1982. 74.50 (ISBN 0-444-86358-3, North-Holland). Elsevier.
Bensoussan, A. & Lions, J. L., eds. Analysis & Optimization of Systems: Proceedings. (Lecture Notes in Control & Information Sciences Ser.: Vol. 28). 999p. 1980. pap. 66.00 (ISBN 0-387-10472-0). Springer-Verlag.
--Analysis & Optimization of Systems: Proceedings of the Sixth International Conference on Analysis & Optimization of Systems, Nice, June 19-22, 1983. (Lecture Notes in Control & Information Sciences,: Vol. 62, Pt. 1). (Illus.). xix, 591p. 1984. pap. 34.50 (ISBN 0-387-13551-0). Springer-Verlag.
--Analysis & Optimization of Systems, Versailles, France, 1982: Proceedings. (Lecture Notes in Control & Information Sciences Ser.: Vol. 44). (Illus.). 987p. 1983. pap. 51.00 (ISBN 0-387-12089-0). Springer-Verlag.
--International Symposium on Systems Optimization & Analysis. (Lecture Notes in Control & Information Sciences: Vol. 14). (Illus.). 1979. pap. 20.00 (ISBN 0-387-09447-4). Springer-Verlag.
Bensoussan, A., et al. Mathematical Theory of Production Planning. (Advanced Series in Management: Vol. 3). 506p. 1983. 76.75 (ISBN 0-444-86740-6, I-403-83, North Holland). Elsevier.
--Advances in Hamiltonian Systems. (Annals of the Ceremade: Vol. 2). 196p. 1983. text ed. 19.95 (ISBN 0-8176-3130-5). Birkhauser.
--Management Applications of Modern Control Theory. (Studies in Mathematical & Managerial Economics: Vol. 18). 346p. 1975. 63.50 (ISBN 0-444-10620-0, North-Holland). Elsevier.
--Asymptotic Analysis for Periodic Structures. (Studies in Mathematics & Its Applications Ser.: Vol. 5). 700p. 1978. 70.25 (ISBN 0-444-85172-0, North-Holland). Elsevier.
Bensoussan, A., et al, eds. Applied Optimal Control. (TIMS Studies in the Management Science: Vol. 9). 204p. 1978. pap. 32.50 (ISBN 0-444-85175-5, North Holland). Elsevier.
--Applied Stochastic Control in Econometrics & Management. (Contributions to Economic Analysis Ser.: Vol. 130). 304p. 1981. 64.00 (ISBN 0-444-85408-8, North-Holland). Elsevier.
Bensoussan, Alain & Lions, Jacques-Louis. Impulse Control & Quasi-Variational Inequalities. 640p. 1984. 76.00 (ISBN 0-9912000-1-2, Pub. by Gauthier-Villars FR). Heyden.
Bensoussan, E. & Lions, J. L., eds. Analysis & Optimization of Systems: Proceedings of the Sixth International Conference on Analysis & Optimization of Systems. Nice, June 19-22, 1983. (Lecture Notes in Control & Information Sciences: Vol. 63, Pt. 2). (Illus.). xix, 700p. 1984. pap. 34.50 (ISBN 0-387-13552-9). Springer-Verlag.
Benstock, B., ed. Pomes for James Joyce. 47p. 1981. pap. text ed. 4.75x (ISBN 0-905261-04-6, 51407, Pub. by Malton Pr Ireland). Humanities.
Benstock, Bernard. Critical Essays on James Joyce. (Critical Essays in American Literature Ser.). 1985. lib. bdg. 29.95 (ISBN 0-8161-8751-7). G K Hall.
--James Joyce. LC 84-28048. (Literature & Life Ser.). 210p. 1985. 13.95 (ISBN 0-8044-2047-5); pap. 7.95 (ISBN 0-8044-6037-X). Ungar.
--Joyce-Again's Wake: An Analysis of Finnegans Wake. LC 75-3981. (Illus.). 312p. 1975. Repr. of 1966 ed. lib. bdg. 24.75 (ISBN 0-8371-7418-X, BEJW). Greenwood.
--Sean O'Casey. LC 72-124101. (Irish Writers Ser). 123p. 1971. 4.50 (ISBN 0-8387-7748-1); pap. 1.95 (ISBN 0-8387-7618-3). Bucknell U Pr.
Benstock, Bernard, jt. auth. see Benstock, Shari.
Benstock, Bernard, ed. Essays on Detective Fiction. LC 83-25025. 200p. 1984. 22.50 (ISBN 0-312-26152-7). St Martin.
--The Seventh of Joyce. LC 81-47775. (Midland Bks: No. 282). 288p. (Orig.). 1982. 25.00X (ISBN 0-253-35184-7); pap. 12.50X (ISBN 0-253-20282-5). Ind U Pr.
Benstock, Bernard, jt. ed. see Bushrui, Suheil B.
Benstock, Bernard, jt. ed. see Staley, Thomas F.
Benstock, Shari & Benstock, Bernard. Who's He When He's at Home: A James Joyce Directory. LC 79-17947. 252p. 1980. 19.95 (ISBN 0-252-00756-5); pap. 8.95 (ISBN 0-252-00757-3). U of Ill Pr.
Benston, George. Financial Services: Changing Institutions & Government Policy. 290p. 1983. 14.95 (ISBN 0-13-316513-2); pap. 7.95 (ISBN 0-13-316505-1). P-H.
--Government Credit Allocation: Where Do We Go from Here? LC 75-32951. 208p. 1975. pap. text ed. 4.95 (ISBN 0-917616-02-2). ICS Pr.
Benston, George J. The Anti-Redlining Rules: An Analysis of the Federal Home Loan Bank Board's Proposed Nondiscrimination Requirements. (LEC Occasional Paper). 1978. pap. text ed. 2.50 (ISBN 0-916770-06-0). Law & Econ U Miami.
--Conglomerate Mergers. 1980. pap. 4.25 (ISBN 0-8447-3373-3). Am Enterprise.
--Investors' Use of Financial Accounting Statement Numbers. 56p. 1981. 25.00x (ISBN 0-85261-166-8, Pub. by U of Glasgow Pr Scotland). State Mutual Bk.
Bensusan, S. L. Charles Lamb: His Homes & Haunts. LC 79-14593. 1979. Repr. lib. bdg. 10.00 (ISBN 0-8414-9834-2). Folcroft.
--Coleridge. 1979. Repr. lib. bdg. 15.00 (ISBN 0-8414-9835-0). Folcroft.
--Morocco. 1977. lib. bdg. 59.95 (ISBN 0-8490-2281-9). Gordon Pr.
--William Shakespeare: His Homes & Haunts. 87p. 1981. lib. bdg. 30.00 (ISBN 0-8495-0478-3). Arden Lib.
Bensusan, Samuel L. Charles Lamb: His Homes & Haunts. 81p. 1980. Repr. of 1910 ed. lib. bdg. 10.00 (ISBN 0-8495-0606-9). Arden Lib.
--William Wordsworth: His Homes & Haunts. LC 77-10639. 1977. Repr. lib. bdg. 12.50 (ISBN 0-8414-0502-6). Folcroft.
Bensusan-Butt, D. M. On Economic Knowledge: A Sceptical Miscellany. 124p. 1980. pap. text ed. 6.50 (ISBN 0-909596-41-7, 0011, Pub. by ANUP Australia). Australia N U P.
Bensussen, Rusty. Making Patterns from Finished Clothes. LC 84-26763. (Illus.). 160p. 1985. 16.95 (ISBN 0-8069-5704-2); pap. 8.95 (ISBN 0-8069-7978-X). Sterling.
Bent. Applied Cost & Schedule Control. (Cost Engineering Series: Vol. 3). 416p. 1982. 39.50 (ISBN 0-8247-1654-X). Dekker.
Bent, A. J. Van Der see Van Der Bent, A. J.
Bent, Alan E. The Politics of Law Enforcement. 1977. pap. text ed. 8.95x (ISBN 0-669-01058-8). Heath.
Bent, Alan E. & Rossum, Ralph A. Police, Criminal Justice, & the Community. 384p. 1976. text ed. 22.85 scp (ISBN 0-06-040637-2, HarpC). Har-Row.
Bent, Alan E. & Rossum, Ralph A., eds. Urban Administration: Management, Politics & Change. 1976. 25.00x (ISBN 0-8046-7106-0, Pub by Kennikat); pap. 12.50x (ISBN 0-8046-7109-5). Assoc Faculty Pr.
Bent, Allen H. Bibliography of the White Mountains. rev. ed. Hanrahan, Jack, ed. LC 79-179457. (Bibliographies of New Hampshire History). (Illus.). 1972. pap. 10.00 (ISBN 0-912274-11-5). NH Pub Co.
Bent, Arthur C. Life Histories of North American Birds of Prey, 2 Vols. (Illus.). 1958. Vol. 1. pap. 8.50 (ISBN 0-486-20931-8); Vol. 2. pap. 8.50 (ISBN 0-486-20932-6). Dover.
--Life Histories of North American Birds of Prey, 2 vols. (Illus.). Set. 32.50 (ISBN 0-8446-1630-3). Peter Smith.
--Life Histories of North American Blackbirds, Orioles, Tanagers & Allies. (Illus.). 1958. 16.75 (ISBN 0-8446-1631-1). Peter Smith.
--Life Histories of North American Blackbirds, Orioles, Tanagers & Their Allies. (Illus.). 1958. pap. 7.95 (ISBN 0-486-21093-6). Dover.
--Life Histories of North American Gallinaceous Birds. (Illus.). 1932. pap. 8.00 (ISBN 0-486-21028-6). Dover.
--Life Histories of North American Gallinaceous Birds. (Illus.). 15.25 (ISBN 0-8446-1635-4). Peter Smith.
--Life Histories of North American Marsh Birds. (Illus.). 1927. pap. 7.50 (ISBN 0-486-21082-0). Dover.
--Life Histories of North American Marsh Birds. (Illus.). 15.00 (ISBN 0-8446-1639-7). Peter Smith.
--Life Histories of North American Nuthatches, Wrens, Thrashers & Their Allies. (Illus.). 1948. pap. 9.95 (ISBN 0-486-21088-X). Dover.
--Life Histories of North American Nuthatches, Wrens, Thrashers & Their Allies. (Illus.). 14.75 (ISBN 0-8446-1640-0). Peter Smith.
--Life Histories of North American Shore Birds, 2 Vols. (Illus.). 1927-29. pap. 7.00 ea.; Vol. 1. pap. (ISBN 0-486-20933-4); Vol. 2. pap. (ISBN 0-486-20934-2). Dover.
--Life Histories of North American Shore Birds, 2 Vols. (Illus.). 13.00 ea. (ISBN 0-8446-1642-7). Peter Smith.
--Life Histories of North American Thrushes, Kinglets & Their Allies. (Illus.). 1949. pap. 7.95 (ISBN 0-486-21086-3). Dover.
--Life Histories of North American Thrushes, Kinglets & Their Allies. (Illus.). 14.50 (ISBN 0-8446-1643-5). Peter Smith.
--Life Histories of North American Wagtails, Shrikes, Vireos & Their Allies. (Illus.). 1950. pap. 8.95 (ISBN 0-486-21085-5). Dover.
--Life Histories of North American Wagtails, Shrikes, Vireos & Their Allies. (Illus.). 14.00 (ISBN 0-8446-1644-3). Peter Smith.
--Life Histories of North American Wood Warblers, 2 Vols. (Illus.). Vol. 1. pap. 6.95 (ISBN 0-486-21153-3); Vol. 2. pap. 6.95 (ISBN 0-486-21154-1). Dover.
--Life Histories of North American Wood Warblers, 2 Vols. (Illus.). 12.00 ea. (ISBN 0-8446-1646-X). Peter Smith.
--Life Histories of North American Woodpeckers. (Illus.). 1939. pap. 7.95 (ISBN 0-486-21083-9). Dover.
--Life Histories of North American Woodpeckers. (Illus.). 15.25 (ISBN 0-8446-1647-8). Peter Smith.
Bent, Bob. How to Cut Your Own or Anybody Else's Hair. (Illus.). 128p. 1983. spiral bound 8.95 (ISBN 0-671-46776-X, Fireside). S&S.
Bent, Bob & Bozzi. How to Cut Your Own or Anybody Else's Hair. LC 75-2295. 1975. 8.95 (ISBN 0-671-22012-8, Fireside). S&S.
Bent, Christine. The New York Times Book of World War I. 14.98 (ISBN 0-405-13465-7). Ayer Co Pubs.
Bent, Christine, jt. auth. see Keylin, Arleen.
Bent, Henry A. Second Law: An Introduction to Classical & Statistical Thermodynamics. 1965. 18.95x (ISBN 0-19-500829-4). Oxford U Pr.
Bent, Ian, ed. Source Materials & the Interpretation of Music: A Memorial Volume to Thurston Dart. (Illus.). 474p. 1981. text ed. 70.00x (ISBN 0-8476-4785-4). Rowman.
Bent, J. Theodore. Early Voyages & Travels in the Levant. 1917. 30.00 (ISBN 0-8482-7357-5). Norwood Edns.
--Early Voyages in The Levant: With Some Account of The Levant Company of Turkey Merchants. 1979. Repr. of 1893 ed. lib. bdg. 45.00 (ISBN 0-8495-0516-X). Arden Lib.
Bent, James T. The Ruined Cities of Mashonaland. facsimile ed. LC 70-161256. (Black Heritage Library Collection). Repr. of 1892 ed. 30.50 (ISBN 0-8369-8528-1). Ayer Co Pubs.
Bent, James T., ed. Early Voyages & Travels in the Levant: The Diary of Thomas Dallam, 1599-1600 & Extracts from the Diaries of Dr. John Covel 1670-1679. 1670-79. 29.50 (ISBN 0-8337-0233-5). B Franklin.
Bent, Jorj. Sometime after the Equinox. (Orig.). 1981. pap. 2.25 (ISBN 0-505-51695-0, Pub. by Tower Bks). Dorchester Pub Co.
Bent, Margarert, tr. see Kirkendale, Warren.

Bent, Margaret. Dunstaple. (Studies of Composers: No. 17). 1981. pap. 21.50x (ISBN 0-19-315225-8). Oxford U Pr.
Bent, R. & McKinley, J. Aircraft Powerplants. 5th ed. 608p. 1985. 28.95 (ISBN 0-07-004797-9). McGraw.
Bent, R. D. & McKinley, J. L. Aircraft Basic Science. 5th ed. 1980. 30.20 (ISBN 0-07-004791-X). McGraw.
Bent, R. D., jt. auth. see Casamassa, J. V.
Bent, Ralph D. & McKinley, James L. Aircraft Electricity & Electronics. 3rd, rev. ed. (Aviation Technology Ser.). (Illus.). 432p. 1981. pap. text ed. 30.20 (ISBN 0-07-004793-6). McGraw.
--Aircraft Maintenance & Repair. 4th ed. (Aviation Technology Ser.). 1979. pap. text ed. 30.20 (ISBN 0-07-004794-4). McGraw.
--Aircraft Powerplants. 4th ed. Orig. Title: Powerplants for Aerospace Vehicles. (Illus.). 1978. 30.20 (ISBN 0-07-004792-8). McGraw.
Bent, Robert & Sethares, George. FORTRAN with Problem Solving: A Structured Approach. 374p. 1981. pap. write for info. Wadsworth Pub.
--Microsoft BASIC: Programming the IBM PC. LC 84-23765. (Computer Science Ser.). 350p. 1985. pap. text ed. 20.00 pub net (ISBN 0-534-04770-X). Brooks-Cole.
Bent, Robert D., ed. Pion Production & Absorption in Nuclei, 1981: Indiana University Cyclatron Facility. LC 82-70678. (AIP Conference Proceedings: No. 79). 432p. 1982. lib. bdg. 36.00 (ISBN 0-88318-178-9). Am Inst Physics.
Bent, Robert J. & Sethares, George C. BASIC: An Introduction to Computer Programming. 2nd ed. LC 81-17033. (Computer Science Ser.). 408p. 1982. pap. text ed. 19.00 pub net (ISBN 0-534-01101-2). Brooks-Cole.
--BASIC: An Introduction to Computer Programming. 2nd ed. 349p. 1982. pap. write for info. Wadsworth Pub.
--BASIC: An Introduction to Computer Programming with the Apple. 1983. pub net 19.00 (ISBN 0-534-01370-8, 82-20572). Brooks-Cole.
--BASIC: An Introduction to Computer Programming with the Apple. 250p. 1983. pap. write for info. Wadsworth Pub.
--Business BASIC. 2nd ed. LC 83-19024. (Computer Science Ser.). 240p. 1984. pap. text ed. 18.25 pub net (ISBN 0-534-03179-X). Brooks-Cole.
--Business BASIC. 2nd ed. 200p. 1984. write for info. Wadsworth Pub.
--FORTRAN with Problem Solving. LC 80-28581. 448p. (Orig.). 1981. pap. text ed. 19.00 pub net (ISBN 0-8185-0436-6). Brooks-Cole.
Bent, Samuel A., ed. Familiar Short Sayings of Great Men. LC 68-30643. 1968. Repr. of 1887 ed. 46.00x (ISBN 0-8103-3182-9). Gale.
Bent, Silas. Justice Oliver Wendell Holmes: A Biography. LC 75-98636. (BCL Ser. I). (Illus.). 1969. Repr. of 1932 ed. 28.00 (ISBN 0-404-00751-1). AMS Pr.
--Newspaper Crusaders. facsimile ed. LC 77-90609. (Essay Index Reprint Ser). 1939. 19.00 (ISBN 0-8369-1245-4). Ayer Co Pubs.
--Newspaper Crusaders: A Neglected Story. LC 73-98815. Repr. of 1939 ed. lib. bdg. 18.75 (ISBN 0-8371-2951-6, BENC). Greenwood.
Bent, Susan, ed. Back in Town. LC 80-23860. (Illus.). 1980. pap. text ed. 7.95 (ISBN 0-918606-02-0). Heidelberg Graph.
Bent, Theodore J. Freak of Freedom: Or the Republic of San Marino. LC 78-110896. 1970. Repr. of 1879 ed. 21.00x (ISBN 0-8046-0879-2, Pub. by Kennikat). Assoc Faculty Pr.
Bente, Elizabeth H. The Farm Plan. 114p. 1981. 6.00 (ISBN 0-682-49671-5). Exposition Pr FL.
Bente, F. Historical Introduction to the Book of Concord. 1965. 11.95 (ISBN 0-570-03287-3, 15-1926). Concordia.
Bente, Paul F., Jr., jt. auth. see Borlaug, Norman E.
Bente, Paul F., Jr., ed. Bio-Energy Directory, April 1980. (Illus.). 768p. (Orig.). 1980. pap. 70.00 (ISBN 0-940222-02-7). Bio Energy.
--Bio-Energy Directory, May 1979. (Illus.). 533p. (Orig.). 1979. pap. 30.00 (ISBN 0-940222-01-9). Bio Energy.
--Bio-Energy 1980: Proceedings. (Illus.). 586p. 1980. pap. 60.00 (ISBN 0-940222-03-5). Bio Energy.
--The Increasing Use of Biomass for Energy & Chemicals: Proceedings. 21p. (Orig.). 1983. pap. 15.00 (ISBN 0-940222-05-1). Bio Energy.
--International Bio-Energy Directory & Handbook - 1984. (Illus.). 628p. (Orig.). 1984. pap. 95.00 (ISBN 0-940222-06-X). Bio Energy.
--International Bio-Energy Directory, 1981. rev. ed. 770p. (Orig.). 1981. pap. 90.00 (ISBN 0-940222-04-3). Bio Energy.
Bentea, Cassandra, tr. see Camon, Ferdinando.
Benteen, John. Apache Raiders. (Fargo Ser.: No. 6). 1980. pap. 1.75 (ISBN 0-505-51562-8, Pub. by Tower Bks). Dorchester Pub Co.
--Bandolero. new ed. De Villa, Alvaro, tr. from Eng. (Compadre Collection: Fargo Ser., No. 1). 160p. (Span.). 1974. pap. 0.75 (ISBN 0-88473-511-7). Fiesta Pub.
--Blood on the Prairie. (Sundance Ser: No. 18). 1978. pap. 1.50 (ISBN 0-8439-0577-8, Leisure Bks). Dorchester Pub Co.
--Bounty Killer. (Sundance Ser.: No. 15). 144p. 1981. pap. 1.75 (ISBN 0-8439-1050-X, Leisure Bks). Dorchester Pub Co.
--Bring Me His Scalp. (Sundance Ser.: No. 8). 160p. 1981. pap. 1.75 (ISBN 0-8439-1047-X, Leisure Bks). Dorchester Pub Co.
--The Bronco Trail. (Sundance Ser.: No. 6). 160p. 1981. pap. 1.75 (ISBN 0-8439-1045-3, Leisure Bks). Dorchester Pub Co.
--Campeon De Violencia. new ed. De Torres, Jacinto, tr. from Eng. (Compadre Collection Ser.: Fargo: No. 5). Orig. Title: Fargo Is His Name, Violence Is His Game. 160p. (Span.). 1975. pap. 0.85 (ISBN 0-88473-515-X). Fiesta Pub.
--Dakota Badlands. (Fargo Ser.). 1977. pap. 1.50 (ISBN 0-505-51173-8, Pub. by Tower Bks). Dorchester Pub Co.
--Dakota Territory. (Sundance: No. 3). 1979. pap. 1.75 (ISBN 0-8439-0708-8, Leisure Bks). Dorchester Pub Co.
--La Danza Mitica. Caballero, E., tr. (Compadre Collection, Sundnace Ser: No. 6). 1976. pap. 0.95 (ISBN 0-88473-536-2). Fiesta Pub.
--Dead Man's Canyon. (Sundance: No. 2). 1979. pap. 1.75 (ISBN 0-8439-0709-6, Leisure Bks). Dorchester Pub Co.
--Death in the Lava. (Sundance Ser.: No. 4). 1979. pap. 1.75 (ISBN 0-8439-0707-X, Leisure Bks). Dorchester Pub Co.
--Fargo, No. 1. 1980. pap. 1.75 (ISBN 0-505-51481-8, Pub. by Tower Bks). Dorchester Pub Co.
--Fargo: Alaska Steel, No. 3. (Orig.). 1980. pap. 1.75 (ISBN 0-505-51502-4, Pub. by Tower Bks). Dorchester Pub Co.
--Fargo & the Texas Rangers. 1977. pap. 1.25 (ISBN 0-505-51126-6, BT51126, Pub. by Tower Bks). Dorchester Pub Co.
--Fargo Bandolero. (Fargo Ser.). 1977. pap. 1.25 (ISBN 0-505-51144-4, Pub. by Tower Bks). Dorchester Pub Co.
--Fargo No. 4: Massacre River. (Orig.). 1980. pap. 1.50 (ISBN 0-505-51521-0, Pub. by Tower Bks). Dorchester Pub Co.
--Fargo: Panama Gold, No. 2. 1980. pap. 1.75 (ISBN 0-505-51482-6, Pub. by Tower Bks). Dorchester Pub Co.
--Los Invasores Apaches. De Villa, Alvaro, tr. from Eng. (Fargo Ser: No. 4). Orig. Title: Apache Raiders. 160p. (Span.). 1974. pap. 0.85 (ISBN 0-88473-514-1). Fiesta Pub.
--Manhunt. (Sundance Ser.: No. 17). 192p. 1982. pap. 2.25 (ISBN 0-8439-1133-6, Leisure Bks). Dorchester Pub Co.
--Orgia de Sangre. new ed. De Torre, Jacinto, tr. from Eng. (Compadre Collection, Fargo: No. 7). (Illus.). 160p. (Span.). 1975. pap. 0.95 (ISBN 0-88473-517-6). Fiesta Pub.
--Oro de Panama. new ed. De Villa, Alvaro, tr. from Eng. (Compadre Collection: Fargo Ser., No. 2). Orig. Title: Panama Gold. 160p. (Span.). 1974. pap. 0.75 (ISBN 0-88473-512-5). Fiesta Pub.
--Overkill. (Sundance Ser.: No. 1). 224p. 1976. pap. 2.25 (ISBN 0-8439-1033-X, Leisure Bks). Dorchester Pub Co.
--Pistolero Fantasma. new ed. De Villa, Alvaro, tr. from Eng. (Compadre Collection, Fargo Ser.: No. 3). Orig. Title: Phantom Gunman. 160p. 1974. pap. 0.85 (ISBN 0-88473-513-3). Fiesta Pub.
--The Pistoleros. (Sundance: No. 5). 1979. pap. 0.95 (ISBN 0-8439-0706-1, Leisure Bks). Dorchester Pub Co.
--Ride the Man Down. (Sundance Ser.: No. 22). 160p. 1981. pap. 1.75 (ISBN 0-8439-1053-4, Leisure Bks). Dorchester Pub Co.
--Riding Shotgun. (Sundance Ser.: No. 20). 160p. 1981. pap. 1.75 (ISBN 0-8439-1051-8, Leisure Bks). Dorchester Pub Co.
--Run for Cover. (Sundance Ser.: No. 16). 176p. 1983. pap. 2.25 (ISBN 0-8439-1172-7, Leisure Bks). Dorchester Pub Co.
--Sharpshooters. (Fargo Ser.: No.9). 160p. 1982. pap. 1.75 (ISBN 0-505-51790-6, Pub. by Tower Bks). Dorchester Pub Co.
--Shotgun Man. (Fargo Ser). (Orig.). 1977. pap. 1.25 (ISBN 0-505-51155-X, Pub. by Tower Bks). Dorchester Pub Co.
--Silent Enemy. (Sundance Ser.: No. 21). 1981. pap. 1.75 (ISBN 0-8439-1052-6, Leisure Bks). Dorchester Pub Co.
--Taps at Little Big Horn. (Sundance Ser.: No. 9). 144p. 1981. pap. 1.75 (ISBN 0-8439-1048-8, Leisure Bks). Dorchester Pub Co.
--El Tesoro de los Modocs. new ed. Diaz, John T., tr. from Eng. (Compadre Collection, Sundance Ser: No. 5). (Illus.). 160p. (Span.). 1975. pap. 0.95 (ISBN 0-88473-535-4). Fiesta Pub.
--Los Toros Negros. new ed. De Torres, Jacinto, tr. from Eng. (Compadre Collection Ser., Fargo Ser: No. 6). Orig. Title: The Black Bulls. (Illus.). 160p. (Span.). 1975. pap. 0.95 (ISBN 0-88473-516-8). Fiesta Pub.
--Traiganme Su Cabellera. new ed. Rios, Juan A., tr. from Eng. (Sundance Ser: No. 3). Orig. Title: Bring Me His Scalp. 160p. (Span.). 1974. pap. 0.85 (ISBN 0-88473-533-8). Fiesta Pub.
--Valley of Skulls. (Fargo Ser.: No. 8). 160p. 1982. pap. 1.95 (ISBN 0-505-51803-1, Pub. by Tower Bks). Dorchester pub Co.
--War Party. (Sundance Ser.: No. 14). 1974. pap. 1.50 (ISBN 0-8439-1009-7, Pub. by Leisure Bks). Dorchester Pub Co.
--War Party, No. 14. (Sundance Ser.). 1981. pap. 1.50 (ISBN 0-317-12912-0). Dorchester Pub Co.
--The Wild Stallions. (Sundance Ser.: No. 7). 160p. 1981. pap. 1.75 (ISBN 0-8439-1046-1, Leisure Bks). Dorchester Pub Co.
--The Wildcatters. (Fargo Ser.: No. 5). (Orig.). 1980. pap. 1.50 (ISBN 0-505-51542-3, Pub. by Tower Bks). Dorchester Pub Co.
Bentel, Gunilla C., et al. Treatment Planning & Dose Calculation & Treatment Planning in Radiation Oncology. (Illus.). 265p. 1982. 39.00 (ISBN 0-08-027176-6, H230); pap. 12.95 (ISBN 0-08-027175-8). Pergamon.
Benthall, Joseph L. Archeological Investigation of the Shannon Site, Montgomery County, Virgini. (Virginia State Library Publications: No. 32). xi, 152p. 1969. pap. 5.00 (ISBN 0-88490-063-0). VA State Lib.
Bentham see Bentham, Jeremy & Mill, John S.
Bentham, C. G., jt. auth. see Haynes, R. M.
Bentham, Frederick. Art of Stage Lighting. 3rd. ed. (Illus.). 1976. 22.00 (ISBN 0-87830-009-0). Theatre Arts.
Bentham, G. The Botany of the Voyage of H. M. S. Sulphur, Under the Command of Captain Sir Edward Belcher 1832-42. (Illus.). 1968. 70.00 (ISBN 3-7682-0542-8). Lubrecht & Cramer.
--Plantae Hartwegianae: Plantas Hartwegianas Imprimis Mexicanas Adjectis Nonullis Grahamianis Enumerat Novasque Describit. 1971. Repr. of 1857 ed. 35.00 (ISBN 3-7682-0673-4). Lubrecht & Cramer.
Bentham, G. & Hooker, J. D. Genera Plantarum, 3 vols. 1966. 231.00 (ISBN 3-7682-0277-1). Lubrecht & Cramer.
--Supplemental Papers to Bentham & Hooker's Genera Plantarum. 1971. Repr. of 1881 ed. 77.00 (ISBN 3-7682-0706-4). Lubrecht & Cramer.
Bentham, G. & Mueller, F. von. Flora Austaliensis: Description of the Plants of the Australian Territory. 4289p. 1966. Repr. of 1863 ed. lib. bdg. 124.00 (ISBN 90-6123-010-1). Lubrecht & Cramer.
Bentham, J. An Introduction to the Principles of Morals & Legislation. 1970. pap. 10.95x (ISBN 0-317-30528-X). Free Pr.
Bentham, Jeremy. Bentham's Theory of Fictions. LC 75-41026. Repr. of 1932 ed. 22.50 (ISBN 0-404-14508-6). AMS Pr.
--Constitutional Code, Vol. 1. Rosen, F. & Burns, J. H., eds. (The Collected Works of Jeremy Bentham Ser.). 1983. 115.00x (ISBN 0-19-822608-X). Oxford U Pr.
--Deontology. Goldworth, Amnon, ed. Incl. A Table of the Springs of Action & the Article on Utilitarianism. (The Collected Works of Jeremy Bentham). (Illus.). 1983. 79.00x (ISBN 0-19-822609-8). Oxford U Pr.
--A Fragment on Government. Montague, F. C., ed. LC 80-10507. xii, 241p. 1980. Repr. of 1931 ed. lib. bdg. 24.75x (ISBN 0-313-22323-8, BEFG). Greenwood.
--Introduction to the Principles of Morals & Legislation. Lafleur, J., ed. (Library of Classics Ser.: No. 6). 1948. pap. text ed. 10.05x (ISBN 0-02-841200-1). Hafner.
--An Introduction to the Principles of Morals & Legislation. Burns, J. H. & Hart, H. L. A, eds. 343p. 1970. text ed. 75.00 (ISBN 0-485-13211-7, Pub. by Athlone Pr Ltd). Longwood Pub Group.
--Limits of Jurisprudence Defined. LC 71-100143. (Illus.). xxii, 358p. Repr. of 1945 ed. lib. bdg. 20.75x (ISBN 0-8371-3249-5, BEJU). Greenwood.
--Plan of Parliamentary Reform, in the Form of a Catechism, with Reasons for Each Article. LC 75-41027. (BCL Ser. II). Repr. of 1818 ed. 16.50 (ISBN 0-404-14777-1). AMS Pr.
Bentham, Jeremy & Hart, H. L. Introduction to the Principles of Morals & Legislation. 385p. 1982. 14.95x (ISBN 0-416-31910-6, NO. 3710). Methuen Inc.
Bentham, Jeremy & Mill, John S. The Utilitarians. Incl. Principles of Morals & Legislation. Bentham; Utilitarianism & on Liberty. Mill, John S. LC 62-1269. pap. 3.50 (ISBN 0-385-08256-8, Anch). Doubleday.
Bentham, Jeremy see McReynolds, Paul.
Bentham, Jeremy, et al. Chrestomathia. (The Collected Works of Jeremy Bentham Ser.). (Illus.). 1983. 76.00x (ISBN 0-19-822610-1). Oxford U Pr.
Bentham-Edwards, M. The Lord of the Harvest. 135p. pap. 5.95 (ISBN 0-85115-218-X, Pub. by Boydell & Brewer). Academy Chi Pubs.
Benthe, Arnold. As I Remember. Sobieszk, Robert A. & Bunnell, Peter C., eds. LC 76-24684. (Sources of Modern Photography Ser.). (Illus.). 1979. Repr. of 1936 ed. lib. bdg. 32.50x (ISBN 0-405-09660-7). Ayer Co Pubs.
Benthem, J. V. The Logic of Time. 1982. 49.50 (ISBN 90-277-1421-5, Pub. by Reidel Holland). Kluwer Academic.
Benthic, Arch E. The Id of the Squid. LC 79-129864. 120p. 4.95 (ISBN 0-685-42028-0). Compass Va.
Benthul, Herman F. Wording Your Way Through Texas. (Illus.). 241p. (Orig.). 1981. 14.95 (ISBN 0-89015-335-3). Eakin Pubns.
Bentinck, William A. The Correspondence of Lord William Bentinck, Governor General of India 1828-1835, 2 vols. Philips, Cyril H., ed. 1977. 149.00x set (ISBN 0-19-713571-4). Oxford U Pr.
Bentinck-Smith, William. Building a Great Library: The Coolidge Years at Harvard. (Illus.). 288p. 1976. 18.50x (ISBN 0-674-08578-7). Harvard U Pr.
Bentinck-Smith, William, ed. The Harvard Book. rev., enl. ed. LC 81-20078. 544p. 1982. text ed. 25.00x (ISBN 0-674-37301-4). Harvard U Pr.
Bentley. National Health Care Controversy. (Impact Bks.). (gr. 7 up). 1979. PLB 9.90 (ISBN 0-531-04262-6). Watts.
Bentley, jt. auth. see Bryson.
Bentley, A. F. Condition of the Western Farmer As Illustrated by the Economic History of a Nebraska Township. pap. 10.00 (ISBN 0-384-03938-3). Johnson Repr.
Bentley, Arnold. Music in Education: A Point of View. 13.00x (ISBN 0-85633-066-3, Pub. by NFER Nelson UK). Taylor & Francis.
Bentley, Arthur F. The Condition of the Western Farmer As Illustrated by the Economic History of a Nebraska Township. LC 78-63821. (Johns Hopkins University. Studies in the Social Sciences. Eleventh Ser. 1893: 7-8). Repr. of 1893 ed. 11.50 (ISBN 0-404-61083-8). AMS Pr.
--Inquiry into Inquiries: Essays in Social Theory. Ratner, Sidney, ed. LC 75-31655. 365p. 1976. Repr. of 1954 ed. lib. bdg. 22.50x (ISBN 0-8371-8463-0, BEII). Greenwood.
--Process of Government. LC 82-19509. (Social Science Classics Ser.). 551p. 1983. pap. 19.95 (ISBN 0-87855-934-5). Transaction Bks.
--Relativity in Man & Society. 1967. lib. bdg. 26.00 (ISBN 0-374-90589-4). Octagon.
Bentley, Arthur F., jt. auth. see Dewey, John.
Bentley, Barbara. Mistress Nancy. LC 80-14264. 384p. 1980. 12.95 (ISBN 0-07-016722-2). McGraw.
--Mistress Nancy. 368p. 1982. pap. 3.50 (ISBN 0-380-56895-0, 56895-0). Avon.
Bentley, Barbara & Elias, Thomas, eds. Biology of Nectaries. (Illus.). 336p. 1983. 37.00x (ISBN 0-231-04446-1). Columbia U Pr.
Bentley, Beth. Country of Resemblances. LC 75-14549. 78p. 1976. 8.95 (ISBN 0-8214-0196-3, 82-82006); pap. 5.95 (ISBN 0-8214-0210-2, 82-82014). Ohio U Pr.
--Phone Calls from the Dead. LC 76-122096. 78p. 1970. 8.95 (ISBN 0-8214-0076-2, 82-80802). Ohio U Pr.
Bentley, Beth, ed. see Hall, Hazel.
Bentley, Christopher, ed. The Tragedy of Othello: The Moor of Venice. 166p. 1983. pap. 9.00x (ISBN 0-424-00093-8, Pub. by Sydney U Pr). Intl Spec Bk.
Bentley, Clerihew. The First Clerihews. (Illus.). 1982. 14.95x (ISBN 0-19-212980-5). Oxford U Pr.
Bentley, Colin. Computer Project Management. (Computing Science Ser.). 107p. 1983. 34.95 (ISBN 0-471-26208-0, Pub. by Wiley Heyden). Wiley.
Bentley, Coulson E. Psychological Approach to Competition Ballroom Dancing. (Ballroom Dance Ser.). 1985. lib. bdg. 79.95 (ISBN 0-87700-655-5). Revisionist Pr.
Bentley, D. J., ed. see Keir, David L. & Lawson, Frederick H.
Bentley, E. C. The Complete Clerihews of E. Clerihew Bentley. (Illus.). 1981. 14.95x (ISBN 0-19-212978-3). Oxford U Pr.
--Trent Intervenes. 259p. 1981. pap. 4.50 (ISBN 0-486-24098-3). Dover.
--Trent's Last Case. LC 75-44955. (Crime Fiction Ser). 1976. Repr. of 1912 ed. lib. bdg. 21.00 (ISBN 0-8240-2353-6). Garland Pub.
--Trent's Last Case. 1978. pap. 3.37i (ISBN 0-06-080440-8, P 440, PL). Har-Row.
--Trent's Last Case. 1976. lib. bdg. 13.95x (ISBN 0-89968-165-4). Lightyear.
--Trent's Own Case. LC 80-7836. 1980. pap. 2.84i (ISBN 0-06-080516-1, P 516, PL). Har-Row.
--Woman in Black. 1976. lib. bdg. 13.95x (ISBN 0-89968-166-2). Lightyear.
Bentley, Elizabeth P. Index to the 1800 Census of Massachusetts. LC 78-58855. 305p. 1978. 20.00 (ISBN 0-8063-0817-6). Genealog Pub.
--Index to the 1800 Census of North Carolina. LC 76-53969. 270p. 1982. Repr. of 1977 ed. 18.50 (ISBN 0-8063-0104-X). Genealog Pub.
--Index to the 1810 Census of North Carolina. LC 77-88140. 282p. 1978. 20.00 (ISBN 0-8063-0788-9). Genealog Pub.
--Index to the 1810 Census of Virginia. LC 79-91510. 366p. 1980. 22.50 (ISBN 0-8063-0875-3). Genealog Pub.
--Index to the 1820 Census of Tennessee. LC 81-81537. 287p. 1981. 21.50 (ISBN 0-8063-0946-6). Genealog Pub.
--Index to the 1850 Census of Pennsylvania: Bucks County. LC 76-17830. 88p. 1976. pap. 7.50 (ISBN 0-8063-0724-2). Genealog Pub.
--Index to the 1850 Census of Pennsylvania: Berks County. LC 75-34362. 106p. 1976. pap. 7.50 (ISBN 0-8063-0695-5). Genealog Pub.
--Index to the 1850 Census of Pennsylvania: Lancaster County. LC 75-20049. 156p. 1975. pap. 10.00 (ISBN 0-8063-0683-1). Genealog Pub.

Benton, Arthur L., et al. Contributions to Neuropsychological Assessment: A Clinical Manual. (Illus.). 1983. text ed. 28.95x (ISBN 0-19-503192-X); pap. text ed. 19.95x (ISBN 0-19-503193-8). Oxford U Pr.

Benton, Barbara. The Babysitter's Handbook. LC 81-3996. (Illus.). 192p. 1981. 12.95 (ISBN 0-688-00641-8); pap. 4.50 (ISBN 0-688-00687-6, Quill). Morrow.

Benton, Bill, et al. Social Services: Federal Legislation vs. State Implemention. 157p. 1978. pap. 7.95x (ISBN 0-87766-237-1, 23700). Urban Inst.

Benton, Charles J. The Data Base Guide: How to Select, Organize & Implement Database Systems for Microcomputers. LC 83-19689. (Illus.). 150p. 1984. pap. 12.95 (ISBN 0-89303-238-7). Brady Comm.

Benton, Charlotte, jt. ed. see Benton, Tim.

Benton, Curtis D., Jr. & Welsh, Robert C. Spectacles for Aphakia. (Illus.). 176p. 1977. photocopy ed. 20.75x (ISBN 0-398-00135-9). C C Thomas.

Benton, E. J. International Law & the Diplomacy of the Spanish-American War. 1977. lib. bdg. 59.95 (ISBN 0-8490-2062-X). Gordon Pr.

Benton, E. V., et al, eds. Nuclear Track Registration: Proceedings of the Fifth Pacific Northwest Conference, Hanford Engineering Development Laboratory, Westinghouse Hanford Company, Richland, Wash. USA, July 28-29 1982. 96p. pap. 55.00 (ISBN 0-08-030274-2). Pergamon.

Benton, Elbert J. International Law & Diplomacy of the Spanish-American War. 300p. 1968. Repr. of 1908 ed. 13.25 (ISBN 0-8446-1072-0). Peter Smith.

--The Movement for Peace Without a Victory During the Civil War. LC 70-176339. (The American Scene Ser.). 1972. Repr. of 1918 ed. lib. bdg. 17.50 (ISBN 0-306-70420-X). Da Capo.

--The Movement for Peace Without Victory During the Civil War. 1976. lib. bdg. 59.95 (ISBN 0-8490-2302-5). Gordon Pr.

--The Wabash Trade Route in the Development of the Old Northwest. LC 78-63893. (Johns Hopkins University. Studies in the Social Sciences. Twenty-First Ser. 1903: 1-2). Repr. of 1903 ed. 24.50 (ISBN 0-404-61147-8). AMS Pr.

Benton, F. Warren. Execucomp: Maximum Management with the New Computers. LC 83-17028. 261p. 1983. cloth 19.95x (ISBN 0-471-89828-7). Wiley.

Benton, Floria. The Hollow Earth at the End Time. 128p. (Orig.). 1983. pap. 9.95 (ISBN 0-911306-36-6). G Barker Bks.

--Hollow Earth Mysteries & the Polar Shift. 100p. (Orig.). pap. 9.95 (ISBN 0-911306-25-0). G Barker Bks.

Benton, Gregor, tr. see Marx, Karl.

Benton, Gregor, tr. see Wang Fan-Hsi.

Benton, Joanna. Keeping Close. (Orig.). 1983. pap. 10.00 (ISBN 0-8065-0839-6). Citadel Pr.

Benton, Joel. Emerson, As a Poet. 1978. Repr. of 1883 ed. lib. bdg. 20.00 (ISBN 0-8495-0371-X). Arden Lib.

--Emerson As a Poet. LC 75-12974. Repr. of 1883 ed. lib. bdg. 20.00 (ISBN 0-8414-3332-1). Folcroft.

--In the Poe Circle. 1978. Repr. of 1899 ed. lib. bdg. 17.25 (ISBN 0-8495-0370-1). Arden Lib.

--In the Poe Circle. LC 72-190703. 1899. lib. bdg. 16.50 (ISBN 0-8414-1640-0). Folcroft.

Benton, John. Candi. (A New Hope Bk). 1983. pap. 2.95 (ISBN 0-8007-8473-1, Spire Bks). Revell.

--Connie. 192p. (Orig.). (gr. 7-12). 1982. pap. 2.95 (ISBN 0-8007-8429-4, New Hope Bks). Revell.

--Debbie. 192p. (Orig.). (gr. 7-12). 1980. pap. 3.50 (ISBN 0-8007-8398-0, New Hope Bks). Revell.

--Denise. 192p. (gr. 7-12). 1982. pap. 2.95 (ISBN 0-8007-8451-0, New Hope Bks.). Revell.

--Do You Know Where Your Children Are? 160p. 1983. pap. 2.95 (ISBN 0-8007-8480-4). Revell.

--Jackie. 192p. (Orig.). (gr. 7-12). 1981. pap. 2.95 (ISBN 0-8007-8406-5, New Hope Bks). Revell.

--Julie. 192p. (Orig.). (gr. 7-12). 1981. pap. 2.95 (ISBN 0-8007-8399-9, New Hope Bks). Revell.

--Kari. 192p. (gr. 7-12). 1984. pap. 2.95 (ISBN 0-8007-8491-X, New Hope). Revell.

--Lefty. 192p. (Orig.). (gr. 7-12). 1981. pap. 2.95 (ISBN 0-8007-8401-4, New Hope Bks). Revell.

--Nikki. 192p. (gr. 7-12). 1982. pap. 2.95 (ISBN 0-8007-8409-X, New Hope Bks). Revell.

--Sheila. 192p. (gr. 7-12). 1982. pap. 2.95 (ISBN 0-8007-8419-7, New Hope Bks.). Revell.

--Stephanie. 1983. pap. 2.95 (ISBN 0-8007-8472-3, Spire Bks). Revell.

--Terri. 192p. (gr. 7-12). 1981. pap. 2.95 (ISBN 0-8007-8408-1, New Hope Bks). Revell.

--Tracy. 192p. (Orig.). (gr. 7-12). 1984. pap. 2.95 (ISBN 0-8007-8495-2, New Hope). Revell.

--Valarie. 192p. (Orig.). (gr. 7-12). 1982. pap. 2.95 (ISBN 0-8007-8430-8, New Hope Bks.). Revell.

Benton, John F., ed. Self & Society in Medieval France: The Memories of Abbot Guibert of Nogent. (Medieval Academy Reprints for Teaching Ser.). 260p. 1984. pap. text ed. 8.95c (ISBN 0-8020-6550-3). U of Toronto Pr.

Benton, Josephine M. A Door Ajar: Facing Death Without Fear. LC 65-16442. 1979. pap. 4.45 (ISBN 0-8298-0366-1). Pilgrim NY.

--Martha & Mary: A Woman's Relationship to Her Home. 1983. pap. 5.00x (ISBN 0-87574-036-7, 036). Pendle Hill.

--The Pace of a Hen. 103p. 1961. 2.95 (ISBN 0-8298-0100-6). Pilgrim NY.

Benton, Josiah H. John Baskerville: Typefounder & Printer, 1706-1775. LC 68-56593. (Bibliography & Reference Ser.: No. 230). (Illus.). 1969. Repr. of 1914 ed. 18.50 (ISBN 0-8337-0238-6). B Franklin.

--Warning Out in New England. facs. ed. LC 70-137370. (Select Bibliographies Reprint Ser). 1911. 13.00 (ISBN 0-8369-5571-4). Ayer Co Pubs.

Benton, Kitty. Classic Designs for Today's Active Children. (Illus.). 192p. 1985. 19.95 (ISBN 0-688-05684-9, Hearst Bks). Morrow.

--Sewing Classic Clothes for Children. 160p. 1981. 19.95 (ISBN 0-87851-204-7). Hearst Bks.

Benton, Lewis, ed. Private Management & Public Policy: Reciprocal Impacts. LC 79-2040. 256p. 1980. 22.50x (ISBN 0-669-03063-5). Lexington Bks.

Benton, Michael. How Dinosaurs Lived. (Do You Know Ser.). (Illus.). 32p. (gr. 1-6). 1985. PLB 9.40 (ISBN 0-531-19002-1, Warwick). Watts.

Benton, Michael J. The Dinosaur Encyclopedia. (Illus.). 192p. (gr. 3-7). 1984. lib. bdg. 9.29 (ISBN 0-671-53131-X). Messner.

--The Dinosaur Encyclopedia. Barish, Wendy, ed. (Illus.). 192p. (gr. 3-7). 1984. pap. 5.95 (ISBN 0-671-51046-0). Wanderer Bks.

Benton, Mike. Comic Book Collecting for Fun & Profit. 1985. pap. 8.95 (ISBN 0-517-55702-9). Crown.

--The Complete Guide to Computer Camps & Workshops. LC 83-15578. 208p. 1984. pap. 10.95 (ISBN 0-672-52796-0). Bobbs.

Benton, Minnie M. Boomtown: A Portrait of Burkburnett. 1980. 9.95 (ISBN 0-89015-013-3). Eakin Pubns.

Benton, P. A. Languages & Peoples of Bornu, Vol. 1. 2nd ed. 304p. 1968. 37.50x (ISBN 0-7146-1635-4, F Cass Co). Biblio Dist.

--Languages & Peoples of Bornu, Vol. 2. new ed. 373p. 1968. 37.50x (ISBN 0-7146-1636-2, F Cass Co). Biblio Dist.

--Sultanate of Bornu. Shultze, A., tr. 401p. 1968. Repr. of 1913 ed. 35.00x (ISBN 0-7146-1717-2, F Cass Co). Biblio Dist.

Benton, Peggie, tr. see Lyon, Ninette.

Benton, Richard. Bedlam Patterns: Love & the Idea of Madness in Poe's Fiction. 1979. pap. 2.75 (ISBN 0-910556-13-X). Enoch Pratt.

Benton, Richard A. Pangasinan Dictionary. LC 75-152456. (Hawaii University Honolulu, Pacific & Asian Linguistics Ser.). pap. 82.30 (ISBN 0-317-10106-4, 2007975). Bks Demand UMI.

--Pangasinan Reference Grammar. McKaughan, Howard P., ed. LC 72-152458. (PALI Language Texts: Philippines). Repr. of 1971 ed. 71.50 (ISBN 0-8357-9826-7, 2017213). Bks Demand UMI.

--Spoken Pangasinan. LC 79-152457. (University of Hawaii, Honolulu. Pacific & Asian Linguistics Institute). pap. 160.00 (ISBN 0-317-10118-8, 2017214). Bks Demand UMI.

Benton, Richard G. Death & Dying. (Illus.). 1978. 16.95 (ISBN 0-442-20708-5). Van Nos Reinhold.

Benton, Rita. The Elf of Discontent & Other Plays. LC 79-50017. (One-Act of Plays in Reprint Ser.). 1980. Repr. of 1927 ed. 23.50x (ISBN 0-8486-2041-0). Core Collection.

--Ignace Pleyel: A Thematic Catalogue of His Compositions. (Thematic Catalogue Ser.: No. 2). 1977. lib. bdg. 72.00 (ISBN 0-918728-04-5). Pendragon NY.

Benton, Robert J. Kant's "Second Critique" & the Problem of Transcendental Arguments. 1978. pap. 24.00 (ISBN 90-247-2055-9, Pub. by Martinus Nijhoff Netherlands). Kluwer Academic.

Benton, Stan & Weekes, Len. Program It Right: Structured Methods in BASIC. (Orig.). 1985. pap. text ed. write for info. Yourdon.

Benton, Stanley H., ed. The Hamilton-Jacobi Equation: A Global Approach. 1977. 37.50 (ISBN 0-12-089350-9). Acad Pr.

Benton, T. H. Historical & Legal Examination of That Part of the Decision of the Supreme Court of the United States in the Dred Scott Case, Which Declares the Unconstitutionality of the Missouri Compromise Act & the Self-Extension of the Constitution to Territories, Carrying Slavery Along with It. Repr. of 1857 ed. 24.00 (ISBN 0-527-06800-4). Kraus Repr.

Benton, Ted. Philosophical Foundations of the Three Sociologies. (International Library of Sociology Ser). 1977. 23.95x (ISBN 0-7100-8593-1). Routledge & Kegan.

Benton, Ten. The Rise & Fall of Structural Marxism: Louis Althusser & His Influence. LC 84-4812. (Theoretical Traditions Ser.). 251p. 1984. 27.95 (ISBN 0-312-68375-8); pap. 12.95 (ISBN 0-312-68376-6). St Martin.

Benton, Thomas. Bank of the United States. 59.95 (ISBN 0-87968-701-0). Gordon Pr.

Benton, Thomas H. An Artist in America. 4th rev. ed. LC 68-20096. (Illus.). 1983. Repr. of 1968 ed. 15.00 (ISBN 0-8262-0071-0). U of Mo Pr.

--An Artist in America. 4th ed. LC 82-20279. (Illus.). 480p. 1983. text ed. 25.00 (ISBN 0-8262-0394-9); pap. 12.95 (ISBN 0-8262-0399-X). U of Mo Pr.

--Historical & Legal Examination of That Part of the Decision of the Supreme Court of the U.S. in the Dred Scott Case Which Declares the Unconstitutionality of the Missouri Compromise Act & the Self-Extension of the Constitution to Territories. Repr. of 1857 ed. 14.00 (ISBN 0-384-03946-4). Johnson Repr.

--Thirty Years' View, or, a History of the Working of the American Government for Thirty Years, from 1820-1850, 2 Vols. LC 68-28617. 1968. Repr. of 1856 ed. Set. lib. bdg. 75.00x (ISBN 0-8371-0309-6, BETY). Greenwood.

Benton, Thomas H., ed. Abridgement of the Debates of Congress, 16 Vols. Repr. of 1857 ed. Set. lib. bdg. 1040.00 (ISBN 0-404-00770-8); lib. bdg. 65.00 ea. AMS Pr.

Benton, Tim. Le Corbusier: The Parisian Villas 1920-1930. 1984. cancelled (ISBN 0-8478-0564-6). Rizzoli Intl.

Benton, Tim & Benton, Charlotte, eds. Form & Function: A Source Book for the History of Architecture & Design 1890-1939. 276p. 1975. pap. 17.50x (ISBN 0-246-11278-6, Pub by Granada England). Sheridan.

Benton, Walter. This Is My Beloved. 1943. 8.50 (ISBN 0-394-40458-0); pocket ed. o.p. 5.00 (ISBN 0-394-40459-9). Knopf.

Benton, Warren F., jt. auth. see Silberstein, Judith.

Benton, Wilbourn E. Drafting the U. S. Constitution. LC 84-40563. 1986. 85.00 (ISBN 0-89096-217-0). Tex A&M Univ Pr.

--Texas Politics: Constraints & Opportunities. 5th ed. LC 83-26458. (Illus.). 416p. 1984. text ed. 26.95x (ISBN 0-8304-1092-9); pap. text ed. 13.95x (ISBN 0-8304-1108-9); instr's. resource manual & test bank avail. (ISBN 0-8304-1114-3). Nelson-Hall.

Benton, Wilbourn E., ed. Seventeen Eighty-Seven: Drafting the U. S. Constitution. LC 84-40563. (Illus.). 1600p. 1985. lib. bdg. 85.00x (ISBN 0-89096-217-0). Tex A&M Univ Pr.

Benton, Wilbourn E. & Grimm, Georg, eds. Nuremberg: German Views of the War Trials. LC 55-5739. 1955. 12.95 (ISBN 0-87074-006-7). SMU Press.

Benton, William. Normal Meanings. 1979. pap. 3.95 (ISBN 0-932792-00-6). Deer Crossing.

--The Voice of Latin America. LC 74-1553. (Illus.). 204p. 1974. Repr. of 1961 ed. lib. bdg. 22.50 (ISBN 0-8371-7393-0, BEVL). Greenwood.

Benton, William A. Whig Loyalism: An Aspect of Political Ideology in the American Revolutionary Era. LC 69-19433. 231p. 1968. 22.50 (ISBN 0-8386-7338-4). Fairleigh Dickinson.

Bentov, Itzhak. Stalking the Wild Pendulum. 1979. pap. 3.95 (ISBN 0-553-20768-7). Bantam.

--Stalking the Wild Pendulum: On the Mechanics of Consciousness. LC 76-46349. 1977. pap. 6.95 (ISBN 0-525-47458-7). Dutton.

Ben-tov, S. During Ceasefire. LC 84-48138. 96p. 1985. 15.34i (ISBN 0-06-015384-9, HarpT); pap. 7.64 (ISBN 0-06-091219-7, CN). Har-Row.

Bentovim, A. Family Therapy: Complementary Frameworks of Theory & Practice, Vol. 2. 1982. 31.00 (ISBN 0-8089-1480-4, 790546). Grune.

Bentovim, A., ed. Family Therapy: Complementary Frameworks of Theory & Practice, Vol. 1. 1982. 31.00 (ISBN 0-8089-1479-0, 790545). Grune.

Bents, jt. ed. see Howey.

Bentsi-Enchill, Kwamina, jt. auth. see Smock, David R.

Bentvelsen, C. L. & Branscheid, V. Yield Response to Water. (Irrigation & Drainage Papers: No. 33). (Illus.). 201p. (Eng., Fr. & Span.). 1979. pap. 14.50 (ISBN 92-5-100744-6, F1843, FAO). Unipub.

Bentwich, N. D. & Martin, A. Commentary on the Charter of the United Nations. 1951. 16.00 (ISBN 0-527-06850-0). Kraus Repr.

Bentwich, Norman. A New Way of Life: The Collective Settlements of Israel. 1949. 15.00 (ISBN 0-686-17691-X). Quality Lib.

--Solomon Schechter. 1964. 6.00 (ISBN 0-8381-3105-0). United Syn Bk.

Bentwich, Norman D. Fulfillment in the Promised Land, 1917-1937. LC 75-6423. (The Rise of Jewish Nationalism & the Middle East Ser). 246p. 1976. Repr. of 1938 ed. 21.50 (ISBN 0-88355-310-4). Hyperion Conn.

--Jewish Youth Comes Home. LC 75-6422. (The Rise of Jewish Nationalism & the Middle East Ser). 159p. 1976. Repr. of 1944 ed. 19.25 (ISBN 0-88355-309-0). Hyperion Conn.

Bentz, John D. Descendants of Martin Benz-Dorothea Schmeller. (Illus.). 310p. 1983. pap. 30.00 (ISBN 0-9612438-0-5). J D Bentz.

Bentz, Stephan. Kennzahlensysteme zur Erfolgskontrolle des Verkaufs und der Marketing-Logistik: Entwicklung und Anwendung in der Konsumguterindustrie, Vol. 8. (Schriften zum Marketing). 395p. (Ger.). 1983. 40.55 (ISBN 3-8204-7551-6). P Lang Pubs.

Bentz, Thomas. New Immigrants: Portraits in Passage. LC 81-5160. (Illus.). 208p. (Orig.). 1981. pap. 7.95 (ISBN 0-8298-0457-9). Pilgrim NY.

Bentz, William F., jt. ed. see Sterling, Robert R.

Bentzen, Warren R. Seeing Young Children: A Guide for Observation & Recording of Behavior. LC 85-1564. 272p. 1985. pap. text ed. 11.80 (ISBN 0-8273-2329-8); write for info. instr's guide (ISBN 0-8273-2330-1). Delmar.

Benua, N. N., jt. auth. see Naumenko, A. I.

Benumof, A. & Jonathan, L. Clinical Frontiers in Anesthesiology: Anesthesia Update. 1983. 32.00 (ISBN 0-8089-1580-0, 790548). Grune.

Benun, Nancy & Berry, Carmen. Kid Power: A Journey to Safety. (Illus.). Date not set. pap. 5.25 (ISBN 0-318-04148-0); instr's. materials 3.75. Priory Bks.

Benveniste & Benson. From Mass to Universal Education. (Plan Europe 2000 Ser: No. 12). 1976. pap. 21.00 (ISBN 90-247-0305-0, Pub. by Martinus Nijhoff Netherlands). Kluwer Academic.

Benveniste, Albert & Hoetis, Themistocles, eds. Zero: A Review of Literature & Art, Nos. 1-7. (Avant Garde Magazine Ser.). Repr. of 1949 ed. 25.50 (ISBN 0-405-01753-7). Ayer Co Pubs.

Benveniste, Asa. Atoz Formula. 1969. 5.00 (ISBN 0-685-01067-8, Pub. by Trigram Pr); signed ed. fifty copies 12.00 ea.; pap. 2.50 (ISBN 0-685-01069-4). Small Pr Dist.

Benveniste, Asa & Marley, Brian. Dense Lens. 1975. 2.50 (ISBN 0-685-78362-6, Pub. by Trigram Pr); signed ltd eds 7.50 (ISBN 0-685-78363-4). Small Pr Dist.

Benveniste, Asa & Vaux, Marc. Colour Theory. (Illus.). 1977. 1.75 (ISBN 0-685-04162-X, Pub. by Trigram Pr). Small Pr Dist.

Benveniste, Emile. Indo-European Language & Society. Palmer, Elizabeth, tr. from Fr. LC 73-77119. (Miami Linguistics Ser: No. 12). (Illus.). 579p. 1973. 29.50x (ISBN 0-87024-250-4). U of Miami Pr.

--Problems in General Linguistics. (Miami Linguistic Ser.: No. 8). 317p. 1973. 15.00 (ISBN 0-87024-310-1). U of Miami Pr.

Benveniste, Guy. Bureaucracy. 2nd ed. 240p. 1983. pap. text ed. 12.50x (ISBN 0-87835-134-5). Boyd & Fraser.

--Politics of Expertise. 2nd ed. LC 77-9200. 1977. text ed. 18.75x (ISBN 0-87835-067-5); pap. text ed. 9.95x (ISBN 0-87835-060-8). Boyd & Fraser.

--Regulation & Planning: The Case of Environmental Politics. LC 80-70765. 250p. 1980. pap. text ed. 12.50x (ISBN 0-87835-075-6). Boyd & Fraser.

Benveniste, J. & Arnou, X. B. Platelet-Activating Factor & Structurally Related Ether-Lipids. (Inserm Symposium Ser.: Vol. 23). 1984. 73.00 (ISBN 0-444-80552-4, I-193-84). Elsevier.

Benvenisti, Meron. Jerusalem: The Torn City. (Illus.). 1977. 22.50x (ISBN 0-8166-0795-8). U of Minn Pr.

--The West Bank Data Project: A Survey of Israel's Policies. LC 84-2984. (AEI Studies: No. 398). 1984. 25.00 (ISBN 0-8447-3545-0); pap. 15.00 (ISBN 0-8447-3544-2). Am Enterprise.

Benvenisty, David. Melakhim Aleph. (Illus.). 70p. pap. 1.80 (ISBN 0-318-13626-0, 14-525). Board Jewish Educ.

--Melakhim Bet. (Illus.). 70p. pap. 1.80 (ISBN 0-318-13627-9, 14-526). Board Jewish Educ.

--Shmuel Aleph. (Illus.). 84p. pap. 1.80 (ISBN 0-318-13635-X, 14-523). Board Jewish Educ.

--Shmuel Bet. (Illus.). 63p. pap. 1.80 (ISBN 0-318-13636-8, 14-524). Board Jewish Educ.

Benvenuti, Stefano & Rizzoni, Gianni. The Whodunit: An Informal History of Detective Fiction. Eyre, Anthony, tr. (Illus.). 224p. 1982. 17.95 (ISBN 0-02-509260-X); pap. 8.95 (ISBN 0-02-048620-0). Macmillan.

Benvenuto, Richard. Amy Lowell (Tusas 483) (Twayne U. S. Authors Ser.). 189p. 1985. lib. bdg. 16.95 (ISBN 0-8057-7436-X, Twayne). G K Hall.

--Emily Bronte. (English Authors Ser.). 1982. lib. bdg. 13.50 (ISBN 0-8057-6813-0, Twayne). G K Hall.

Benward, Bruce. Advanced Ear Training. 144p. 1985. price not set wire coil (ISBN 0-697-00409-0); price not set instr's. manual (ISBN 0-697-00410-4). Wm C Brown.

--Ear Training: A Technique for Listening. 2nd ed. 208p. 1983. write for info. wire coil (ISBN 0-697-03547-6); instr's dictation manual avail. (ISBN 0-697-03548-4); write for info. 14 cassette tapes avail. (ISBN 0-697-03716-9). Wm C Brown.

--Music in Theory & Practice, 2 Vols. 2nd ed. 400p. 1981. Vol. 1. write for info. plastic comb bdg. (ISBN 0-697-03423-2); Vol. 1. instrs.' manual avail. (ISBN 0-697-03447-X); Vol. 1. wkbk. avail. (ISBN 0-697-03445-3); Vol. 1. solns. manual avail. (ISBN 0-697-03535-2); Vol. 2. write for info. (ISBN 0-697-03424-0); Vol. 2. wkbk. avail. (ISBN 0-697-03446-1); Vol. 2. instr's. manual avail. (ISBN 0-697-03519-0); Vol. 2. solns. manual avail. (ISBN 0-697-03569-7). Wm C Brown.

--Music in Theory & Practice, Vol. 1. 3rd ed. 432p. 1984. text ed. write for info. plastic comb. bdgs. (ISBN 0-697-03621-9); instr's. manual avail. (ISBN 0-697-03641-3); solutions manual avail. (ISBN 0-697-03681-2); wkbk. avail. (ISBN 0-697-03660-X). Wm C Brown.

--Sightsinging Complete. 3rd ed. 288p. 1980. plastic comb write for info. (ISBN 0-697-03599-9). Wm C Brown.

--Workbook in Advanced Ear Training. 190p. 1974. write for info. (ISBN 0-697-03589-1); instr's manual avail. Wm C Brown.

--Workbook in Ear Training. 2nd ed. 256p. 1969. (ISBN 0-697-03577-8); tchr's. dictation manual wire coil avail. (ISBN 0-697-03578-6). Wm C Brown.

Benward, Bruce & Jackson, Barbara G. Practical Beginning Theory. 5th ed. 464p. 1982. write for info. plastic comb (ISBN 0-697-03545-X); instr's. manual avail. (ISBN 0-697-03546-8); cassette recordings avail. (ISBN 0-697-03553-0). Wm C Brown.

Benward, Bruce & Wildman, Joan. Jazz Improvisation in Theory & Practice. 256p. 1984. pap. text ed. write for info (ISBN 0-697-03615-4); instr's. manual avail. (ISBN 0-697-00179-2). Wm C Brown.

Benware, Paul. Luke: Gospel of the Son of Man. (Everyman's Bible Commentary Ser.). 1985. pap. 5.95 (ISBN 0-8024-2074-5). Moody.

Benware, Paul N. Ambassadors of Armstrongism. 182p. (Orig.). 1984. pap. 5.95 (ISBN 0-87508-046-4). Chr Lit.

Benwell, Deirdre A., jt. ed. see Repacholi, Michael H.

Beny, Roloff. Odyssey: Mirror of the Mediterranean. LC 81-47220. (Illus.). 371p. 1981. 67.31i (ISBN 0-06-014879-9, HarpT). Har-Row.

Beny, Roloff & Saunders, Pamela. Iceland. (Illus.). 1985. 40.00 (ISBN 0-88162-108-0, Pub. by Salem Hse Ltd). Merrimack Pub Cir.

Beny, Roloff, jt. auth. see Stassinopoulos, Arianna.

Beny, Roloff, photos by. The Romance of Architecture. (Illus.). 312p. 1985. 49.50 (ISBN 0-8109-1589-8). Abrams.

Benyahia, Hadj. Education & Technological Innovations: Academic Performance & Economical Advantages. 163p. (Orig.). 1983. pap. text ed. 12.95x (ISBN 0-317-02590-2). Brookfield Pub Co.

Ben-Yami, M. Fishing with Light. 1978. 16.00 (ISBN 0-685-63423-X). State Mutual Bk.

--Fishing with Light: An FAO Fishing Manual. (Illus.). 132p. (Orig.). 1976. pap. 14.25 (ISBN 0-85238-078-X, FN46, FNB). Unipub.

--Tuna Fishing with Pole & Line. 1980. 21.50x (ISBN 0-686-64740-8, Pub. by Fishing News England); pap. 19.50x (ISBN 0-686-77604-6). State Mutual Bk.

Ben-Yami, M., ed. Tuna Fishing with Pole & Line: An FAO Fishing Manual. (Illus.). 168p. 1981. pap. 24.50 (ISBN 0-85238-111-5, FN88, FNB). Unipub.

Ben-Yehuda, Eliezer, ed. Dictionary & Thesaurus of the Hebrew Language, 8 Vols. Set. 150.00 (ISBN 0-498-07038-7, Yoseloff); lea. bd. set o.p. 250.00 (ISBN 0-498-08915-0). A S Barnes.

Ben-Yehuda, Nachman. Deviance & Moral Boundaries: Witchcraft, the Occult, Science Fiction, Deviant Sciences & Scientists. 248p. 1985. 25.00x (ISBN 0-226-04335-5). U of Chicago Pr.

Benyei, Candace. A Cape Cod Journal. 45p. (Orig.). 1985. pap. 6.95 (ISBN 0-932269-43-5). Wyndham Hall.

Benyei, Candace R. Called to Be Lonely: A Company of Clowns. xvii, 50p. 1984. pap. 5.95 (ISBN 0-932269-10-9). Wyndham Hall.

Benyo, Rich & Provost, Rhoda. Runner's World Advanced Indoor Exercise Book. 1981. spiral bdg. 11.95 (ISBN 0-89037-167-9). Anderson World.

Benyo, Rich & Provost, Rhonda. Runner's World Indoor Exercise Book. 200p. spiral bdg. 11.95 (ISBN 0-89037-190-3). Anderson World.

Benyo, Richard. The Masters of the Marathon. LC 82-73028. 256p. 1983. 14.95 (ISBN 0-689-11340-4). Atheneum.

--Return to Running. LC 78-55787. (Illus.). 235p. 1978. pap. 3.95 (ISBN 0-89037-128-8). Anderson World.

Benyo, Richard, jt. auth. see Herrin, Kym.

Benyon, J., ed. Scarman & After: Essays Reflecting on Lord Scarman's Report, the Riots & Their Aftermath. 270p. 1983. 29.95 (ISBN 0-08-030217-3); pap. 13.50 (ISBN 0-08-030218-1). Pergamon.

Benyus, Janine M. Christmas Tree Pests Manual. 107p. 1983. pap. 14.00 (ISBN 0-318-11762-2). Gov Printing Office.

Benz, C. William. Passion: Program for Algebraic Sequences Specifically of Input-Output Nature. LC 72-126524. (Illus.). 92p. 1971. pap. text ed. 10.95 (ISBN 0-7167-0441-2). W H Freeman.

Benz, Carolyn, jt. auth. see Newman, Isadore.

Benz, Ernst. Dreams, Hallucinations, Visions. pap. 0.50 (ISBN 0-87785-099-2). Swedenborg.

--The Mystical Sources of German Romantic Philosophy. Reynolds, Blair, et al, trs. from Fr. LC 83-21154. (Pittsburgh Theological Monographs: New Ser.: No. 6). vi, 133p. 1983. pap. 12.50 (ISBN 0-915138-50-6). Pickwick.

Benz, G., ed. see European Chemoreception Research Organisation, 2nd Interdisciplinary Symposium, Switzerland, 1975.

Benz, Hamilton. Heroine. (The Lost Play Ser.). Date not set. pap. 1.25x (ISBN 0-912262-18-4). Proscenium.

Benz, Larry L. Standards for Living. LC 77-70791. 1977. pap. 1.99 (ISBN 0-87148-779-9). Pathway Pr.

Benz, M. Flowers: Abstract Form II. LC 78-65678. (Illus.). 288p. 1979. 47.50x (ISBN 0-911982-11-6). San Jacinto.

Benz, Margaret G. Family Counseling Service in a University Community. LC 70-176556. (Columbia University. Teachers College. Contributions to Education: No. 800). Repr. of 1940 ed. 22.50 (ISBN 0-404-55800-3). AMS Pr.

Benz, Morris. Flowers: Free Form-Interpretive Design. LC 59-15356. (Illus.). 250p. 1960. 15.00x (ISBN 0-89096-103-4). San Jacinto.

--Flowers: Geometric Form. rev., 5th ed. LC 80-50568. (Illus.). 336p. 1980. 42.50x (ISBN 0-911982-12-4). San Jacinto.

Benzaquin, Paul. Fire at Boston's Coconut Grove. 1967. 12.00 (ISBN 0-8283-1160-9). Branden Pub Co.

Benzel, Kathryn N., et al. The Little English Workbook. 2nd ed. 1984. pap. text ed. 9.25x (ISBN 0-673-15898-5). Scott F.

Benzie, William. Dr. F. J. Furnivall: A Victorian Scholar Adventurer. 320p. 1983. 32.95 (ISBN 0-937664-57-X). Pilgrim Bks OK.

Benziger, Barbara F. The Prison of My Mind. LC 80-54811. 184p. 1981. pap. 5.95 (ISBN 0-8027-7172-6). Walker & Co.

--Speaking Out: Therapists & Patients; How They Cure & Cope with Mental Illness Today. LC 74-31912. 320p. 1976. pap. 5.95 (ISBN 0-8027-7146-7). Walker & Co.

Benziger, James. Images of Eternity: Studies in the Poetry of Religious Vision, from Wordsworth to T. S. Eliot. LC 62-15007. (Arcturus Books Paperbacks). 333p. 1962. pap. 2.25 (ISBN 0-8093-0136-9). S Ill U Pr.

Benziger, Marieli. Darling Driver. (Illus.). 1978. pap. 9.00x (ISBN 0-686-10179-0). Benziger Sis.

--St. Francis Xavier: A Sixteenth-Century Nobleman. pap. 2.25 (ISBN 0-686-18871-3). Benziger Sis.

Benziger, Marieli & Benziger, Rita. August Benziger: Portrait Painter. 16.00 (ISBN 0-686-18874-8). Benziger Sis.

--Mamma Margherita: St. John Bosco's Mother. 2nd ed. LC 73-84375. 1973. pap. 2.25 (ISBN 0-686-18870-5). Benziger Sis.

--Martin De Porres: Many Sided Martin...The First Negro Saint of the Western Hemisphere. LC 73-86681. 1973. pap. 2.25 (ISBN 0-686-18869-1). Benziger Sis.

--Try It Cook Book: Fun with Unusual Cooking. LC 78-121019. 1970. 5.00 (ISBN 0-686-18876-4). Benziger Sis.

Benziger, Rita, jt. auth. see Benziger, Marieli.

Benziger, Theodore H., ed. Temperature, 2 pts. Incl. Pt. 1. Arts & Concept. 66.00 (ISBN 0-12-786141-6); Pt. 2. Thermal Homeostasis. 73.00 (ISBN 0-12-786142-4). (Benchmark Papers in Human Physiology: Vols. 9 & 10). 1977. Acad Pr.

Benziman, Uzi. Sharon: An Israeli Caesar. LC 85-13461. 256p. 1985. 17.95 (ISBN 0-915361-23-X). Adama Pubs Inc.

Benzing, David H. Biology of the Bromeliads. 305p. (Orig.). 1980. pap. 14.95x (ISBN 0-916422-21-6). Mad River.

Ben Zion, Raphael, tr. from Hebrew. Anthology of Jewish Mysticism. 5.00 (ISBN 0-686-13334-X). Yesod Pubs.

Ben Zion, Raphael see Zion, Raphael Ben.

Benzley, Steven E., jt. ed. see Rybicki, Edmund F.

Benzoni, Girolamo. History of the New World. Smyth, William H., ed. & tr. (Hakluyt Soc., First Ser.: No. 21). 1964. 31.50 (ISBN 0-8337-0239-4). B Franklin.

Benzoni, Juliette. Belle Catherine. 1973. pap. 1.95 (ISBN 0-380-36525-1, 36525). Avon.

--Catherine, Royal Mistress. 1978. pap. 1.95 (ISBN 0-380-37069-7, 37069). Avon.

--Catherine's Quest. 1981. pap. 1.95 (ISBN 0-380-37895-7, 37895). Avon.

--Catherine's Time for Love. 1981. pap. 1.95 (ISBN 0-380-40949-6, 40949). Avon.

Ben-Zvi, Abraham. Alliance Politics & the Limits of Influence: The Case of the U. S. & Israel, 1975-1983. 75p. 1984. pap. 8.00x (ISBN 0-8133-0130-0). Westview.

Beonio-Brocchieri Fumagalli, M. T. The Logic of Abelard. Pleasance, Simon, tr. from It. (Synthese Library: No. 1). 101p. 1969. lib. bdg. 18.50 (ISBN 90-277-0068-0, Pub. by Reidel Holland). Kluwer Academic.

Beougher, Lois. Now Lord, How Did You Manage That? 143p. 1984. 7.95 (ISBN 0-533-05912-7). Vantage.

Beowulf. Beowulf. Collins, Rowland L., ed. LC 64-10837. (A Midland Book: MB-73). pap. 31.80 (ISBN 0-317-28749-4, 2055493). Bks Demand UMI.

--Beowulf, the Oldest English Epic. Kennedy, Charles W., tr. 1940. 15.00x (ISBN 0-19-500929-0). Oxford U Pr.

Bequaert, Joseph C. & Miller, Walter B. The Mollusks of the Arid Southwest. LC 72-187825. 271p. 1973. pap. 8.00x (ISBN 0-8165-0318-4). U of Ariz Pr.

Bequai, August. The Cashless Society: EFTS at the Crossroads. LC 80-21517. 298p. 1981. cloth 34.50x (ISBN 0-471-05654-5). Wiley.

--Computer Crime. LC 77-3857. 1978. pap. 12.00x (ISBN 0-669-05654-5). Lexington Bks.

--How to Prevent Computer Crime: A Guide for Managers. LC 83-6952. 308p. 1983. 29.95x (ISBN 0-471-09367-X, Pub. by Wiley-Interscience). Wiley.

--Making Washington Work for You. LC 82-48602. 304p. 1983. 24.00x (ISBN 0-669-06347-9); pap. 11.95x (ISBN 0-669-06348-7). Lexington Bks.

--Organized Crime. LC 77-18574. 1979. 12.00x (ISBN 0-669-07405-5). Lexington Bks.

--White-Collar Crime. LC 77-11242. (Illus.). 1978. 18.95 (ISBN 0-669-01900-3); pap. 12.00x (ISBN 0-669-05907-2). Lexington Bks.

Berachya. The Ethical Treatises of Berachya, Son of Rabbi Natronai Ha-Nakdan. LC 73-2187. (The Jewish People; History, Religion, Literature Ser.). Repr. of 1902 ed. 37.50 (ISBN 0-405-05253-7). Ayer Co Pubs.

Beraha, Laura, tr. see Davydov, Yu.

Beraha, Laura, et al, trs. see Platonov, Andrei.

Beraldi, Henri, jt. auth. see Portalis, Roger.

Beran. Epilepsy & Its Variants. 150p. 1986. 30.00 (ISBN 0-683-12109-X). Williams & Wilkins.

Beran, jt. auth. see Street-Perrot.

Beran, E. Stoics & Sceptics. 1985. Repr. of 1913 ed. 12.50 (ISBN 0-89005-364-2). Ares.

Beran, George. Viral Zoonoses. (CRC Handbook in Zoonoses Sect B: Vol. 1). 544p. 1981. 76.00 (ISBN 0-8493-2911-6). CRC Pr.

Beran, George, ed. Viral Zoonoses. (Handbook Series in Zoonoses Sect. B: Vol. 2). 528p. 1981. 81.00 (ISBN 0-8493-2912-4). CRC Pr.

Beran, Ladislav. Orthomodular Lattices. 1985. lib. bdg. 69.00 (ISBN 90-277-1715-X, Pub. by Reidel Holland). Kluwer Academic.

Beran, Mark J. & Parrent, George B. Theory of Partial Coherence. pap. 51.80 (ISBN 0-317-08514-X, 2010137). Bks Demand UMI.

Beran, Nancy J. & Toomey, Beverly G., eds. Mentally Ill Offenders & the Criminal Justice System: Issues in Forensic Services. LC 78-19782. 208p. 1979. 37.95 (ISBN 0-03-046426-9). Praeger.

Beranbaum, Rose L. Romantic & Classic Cakes. Sparks, Jennifer, ed. LC 81-68841. (Great American Cooking Schools Ser.). (Illus.). 84p. 1981. pap. 5.95 (ISBN 0-941034-06-2). I Chalmers.

Beranek, B., ed. Annuale Mediaevale, Vol. 22. 126p. 1985. pap. text ed. 13.50x (ISBN 0-317-26979-8). Humanities.

Beranek, Bernard. Annuale Mediaevale, Vol. 21. 138p. 1982. 14.00x (ISBN 0-686-82238-2). Humanities.

Beranek, Leo L. Noise Reduction. LC 79-26956. 762p. 1980. Repr. of 1960 ed. lib. bdg. 45.50 (ISBN 0-89874-108-4). Krieger.

Beranek, Susan K., jt. auth. see Rapp, William F.

Berar-Awad, Azita, ed. see Internatioanl Labour Office Staff & United Nations High Commission for Refugees.

Berard, ed. see De Balzac, Honore.

Berard, Barbara, ed. see Bannister, Hank & Crane, Tim.

Berard, M. F., jt. auth. see Jones, J. T.

Berard, Samuel J. Principles of Machine Design. LC 55-6078. pap. 136.50 (ISBN 0-317-11123-X, 2012447). Bks Demand UMI.

Berardi, Gigi M. & Geisler, Charles C., eds. The Social Consequences & Challenges of New Agricultural Technologies. (Rural Studies). 450p. 1985. pap. 29.50x softcover (ISBN 0-86531-666-X). Westview.

Berardi, Lucy K. MISSION WRITE. (Illus., Orig.). (gr. 7-8). 1978. MISSION WRITE 7. pap. 1.80 (ISBN 0-915441-00-4); MISSION WRITE 8. pap. 1.80 student bk. (ISBN 0-915441-01-2); Teaching Takeoffs 7. 15.00_worksheets (ISBN 0-915441-02-0); Teaching Takeoffs 8. 15.00 (ISBN 0-915441-03-9); Touchstone WRITE Units Overview 7. 1.00 (ISBN 0-915441-05-5); Touchstone WRITE Units Overview 8. 1.00 (ISBN 0-915441-06-3); TOUCHSTONE Analytical Scoring Scale with Guide, 1982. 15.00 (ISBN 0-915441-07-1); MANUEVERING with MISSION WRITE. manual 1.00 (ISBN 0-915441-04-7). W R I T E.

Berardi, Mary. Saint Agnes. (Orig.). (gr. 4-8). 2.00 (ISBN 0-8198-0134-8); pap. 1.25 (ISBN 0-8198-0135-6). Dghtrs St Paul.

--St. Tarcisius. (gr. 4-8). plastic bdg. 2.00 (ISBN 0-8198-0222-0); pap. 1.25 (ISBN 0-8198-0223-9). Dghtrs St Paul.

Berardis, Vincenzo. Italy & Ireland in the Middle Ages. 1977. lib. bdg. 59.95 (ISBN 0-8490-2089-1). Gordon Pr.

Berardo, Felix F., ed. Middle & Late Life Transitions. LC 82-61685. (The Annals of the American Academy of Political & Social Science: Vol. 464). 1982. 15.00 (ISBN 0-8039-1932-8); pap. 7.95 (ISBN 0-8039-1933-6). Sage.

Berardo, Felix M., jt. auth. see Nye, F. Ivan.

Berardo, Felix M., jt. ed. see Nye, F. Ivan.

Beraud, Henri. Twelve Portraits of the French Revolution. facs. ed. Boyd, M., tr. LC 68-16909. (Essay Index Reprint Ser). 1928. 18.00 (ISBN 0-8369-0197-5). Ayer Co Pubs.

Berberi, Dilaver & Berberi, Edel A., eds. Cortina-Grosset Basic Dictionary: Italian. (Ital.). 1977. pap. 2.95 (ISBN 0-448-14030-6, G&D). Putnam Pub Group.

--Cortina-Grosset Basic Italian Dictionary. LC 73-18524. 384p. (Ital.). 1975. 3.95 (ISBN 0-448-14030-6, G&D). Putnam Pub Group.

Berberi, Dilaver, ed. see Laita, Luis M.

Berberi, Dilaver, ed. see Marcy, Teresa & Marcy, Michel.

Berberi, Edel A., jt. ed. see Berberi, Dilaver.

Berberi, Edel A., ed. see Laita, Luis M.

Berberi, Edel A., ed. see Marcy, Teresa & Marcy, Michel.

Berberian, Mimi, jt. ed. see Kasperson, Roger E.

Berberian, S. K. Baer-Rings. LC 72-189105. (Die Grundlehren der Mathematischen Wissenschaften Ser.: Vol. 195). 315p. 1972. 37.00 (ISBN 0-387-05751-X). Springer-Verlag.

--Lectures in Functional Analysis & Operator Theory. (Graduate Texts in Mathematics: Vol. 15). 370p. 1974. 39.0000569725x (ISBN 0-387-90080-2). Springer-Verlag.

Berberian, S. K., tr. see Dixmier, J.

Berberian, Schahan. Fifty Songs. 250p. (Orig.). 1983. pap. 15.00 (ISBN 0-934728-08-9). D O A C.

Berberian, Sterling K. An Introduction to Hilbert Space. 2nd ed. LC 75-29231. 206p. 1976. text ed. 9.95 (ISBN 0-8284-0287-6). Chelsea Pub.

--Measure & Integration. LC 74-128871. 1970. Repr. of 1965 ed. text ed. 14.95 (ISBN 0-8284-0241-8). Chelsea Pub.

Berberoglu, B. Turkey in Crisis: From State Capitalism to Neocolonialism. 150p. 1982. 21.95x (ISBN 0-905762-56-8, Pub. by Zed Pr England); pap. 9.95x (ISBN 0-905762-61-4). Biblio Dist.

Berberoglu, H. Restauranteurs' & Hoteliers' Purchasing Book. 240p. 1981. pap. text ed. 16.95 (ISBN 0-8403-2348-4). Kendall-Hunt.

--The World of Wines, Spirits & Beers. 336p. 1983. pap. text ed. 19.95 (ISBN 0-8403-3170-3, 40317001). Kendall-Hunt.

Berberova, ed. see Tolstoy, Leo.

Berberova, N., ed. see Tolstoy, Leo.

Berberova, Nina. Kursiv Moi, 2 vols. LC 82-61509. (Illus.). 720p. (Orig., Rus.). 1983. Set. 48.00 (ISBN 0-89830-078-9). Vol. 1 (ISBN 0-89830-079-7). Vol.2 (ISBN 0-89830-080-0). Set. pap. 28.50 (ISBN 0-89830-065-7). Vol. 1 (ISBN 0-89830-066-5). Vol. 2 (ISBN 0-89830-067-3). Russica Pubs.

--Liudi i Lozhi: Russkie Masony XX Stoletiia. 450p. (Orig., Russian.). 1985. write for info. (ISBN 0-89830-098-3); pap. write for info. (ISBN 0-89830-099-1). Russica Pubs.

--Stikhi: Nineteen Twenty-One to Nineteen Eighty-Three. LC 84-60081. (Russica Poetry Ser.: No. 4). 120p. (Orig., Rus.). 1984. pap. 7.95 (ISBN 0-89830-072-X). Russica Pubs.

--Zheleznaia Zhenshchina. LC 80-54020. 400p. (Orig., Rus.). 1981. pap. 18.50 (ISBN 0-89830-039-8). Russica Pubs.

Berbrich, Joan D. One Hundred One Ways to Learn Vocabulary. (Orig.). (gr. 10-12). 1971. wkbk. 8.08 (ISBN 0-87720-343-1). AMSCO Sch.

--Reading Today. (Orig.). (gr. 10-12). 1983. pap. 7.00 (ISBN 0-87720-449-7). AMSCO Sch.

--Wide World of Words. (Orig.). (gr. 7-10). 1975. 9.08 (ISBN 0-87720-340-7). AMSCO Sch.

--Writing about Amusing Things. (Orig.). (gr. 10-12). 1981. pap. 5.17 (ISBN 0-87720-427-6). AMSCO Sch.

--Writing about Curious Things. (Orig.). (gr. 8). 1981. pap. text ed. 7.50 (ISBN 0-87720-394-6). AMSCO Sch.

--Writing about Fascinating Things. (Orig.). (gr. 8-10). 1980. wkbk. 7.67 (ISBN 0-87720-391-1). AMSCO Sch.

--Writing about People. (gr. 10-12). 1979. wkbk. 9.25 (ISBN 0-87720-382-2). AMSCO Sch.

--Writing Creatively. (gr. 10-12). 1977. wkbk 11.08 (ISBN 0-87720-375-X). AMSCO Sch.

--Writing Logically. (gr. 11-12). 1978. wkbk. 10.00 (ISBN 0-87720-332-6). AMSCO Sch.

--Writing Practically. (Orig.). (gr. 10-12). 1976. wkbk. 9.17 (ISBN 0-87720-338-5). AMSCO Sch.

Berbrich, Joan D., ed. Stories of Crime & Detection. LC 73-8832. (Patterns in Literary Art Ser). (Illus.). 312p. (gr. 9-12). 1972. pap. text ed. 11.04 (ISBN 0-07-004826-6). McGraw.

Berc. Tess of the D'Urbervilles (Hardy) (Book Notes Ser.). 1984. pap. 2.50 (ISBN 0-8120-3445-7). Barron.

--Tom Jones. (Book Note Ser.). 1985. pap. 2.50 (ISBN 0-8120-3546-1). Barron.

Berceo, Gonzalo De see De Berceo, Gonzalo.

Berch, Bettina. The Endless Day: The Political Economy of Women & Work. 212p. 1982. pap. text ed. 11.95 (ISBN 0-15-517950-0, HC). HarBraceJ.

Berch, Michael A. & Berch, Rebecca W. Introduction to Legal Method & Process Cases & Materials: Teacher's Manual. (American Casebook Ser.). 149p. 1985. write for info. tchr's manual (ISBN 0-314-94997-6). West Pub.

--Legal Method & Process, Introduction. (American Casebook Ser.). 456p. 1985. text ed. 22.95 (ISBN 0-314-89167-6). West Pub.

Berch, Rebecca W., jt. auth. see Berch, Michael A.

Berchan, Richard. Inner Stage: An Essay on the Conflict of Vocations in the Early Works of Paul Claudel. 1966. 3.50 (ISBN 0-87013-097-8). Mich St U Pr.

Berchem, Denis Van see Van Berchem, Denis.

Berchman, Robert M. From Philo to Origen: Middle Platonism in Transition. (Brown Judaic Studies: No. 69). 370p. 1985. 29.95 (ISBN 0-89130-750-8, 14 00 69); pap. 25.95 (ISBN 0-89130-815-6). Scholars Pr GA.

Berchowitz, David, jt. auth. see Urieli, Israel.

Berchtold, Inge M., jt. auth. see Meyer, Mary C.

Berchtold, R., ed. see Paquet, K. J., et al.

Berchtold, W., tr. see Hopper, A. G.

Bercik, Elaine V. Thorns among the Sagebrush. 189p. 1984. 7.95 (ISBN 0-89697-161-9). Intl Univ Pr.

Berckelaer-Onnes, I. A. Early Childhood Autism: A Child Rearing Problem. (Modern Approaches to the Diagnosis & Instruction of Multi-Handicapped Children Ser.: Vol. 17). 169p. 1983. text ed. 10.50 (ISBN 90-265-0451-9, Pub. by Swets). Hogrefe Intl.

Berckhemer, H. & Hsu, K., eds. Alpine-Mediterranean Geodynamics. (Geodynamics Ser.: Vol. 7). 216p. 1982. 22.00 (ISBN 0-87590-503-X). Am Geophysical.

Berckman, Evelyn. The Beckoning Dream. Large Print ed. LC 83-17862. 308p. 1983. Repr. of 1955 ed. 11.95 (ISBN 0-89621-483-4). Thorndike Pr.

--The Beckoning Dream. 13.95 (ISBN 0-88411-269-1, Pub. by Aeonian Pr). Amereon Ltd.

--The Crown Estate. 1978. pap. 1.75 (ISBN 0-380-01960-4, 38422). Avon.

--Do You Know This Voice? LC 60-11930. (Red Badge Mysteries Ser.). 1983. pap. 3.50 (ISBN 0-396-08161-4). Dodd.

--The Evil of Time. 13.95 (ISBN 0-88411-270-5, Pub. by Aeonian Pr). Amereon Ltd.

--The Heir of Starvelings. 14.95 (ISBN 0-88411-271-3, Pub. by Aeonian Pr). Amereon Ltd.

--The Hovering Darkness. 13.95 (ISBN 0-88411-272-1, Pub. by Aeonian Pr). Amereon Ltd.

--Journey's End. 1978. pap. 1.50 (ISBN 0-380-37655-5, 37655). Avon.

--Lament for Four Brides. 13.95 (ISBN 0-88411-273-X, Pub. by Aeonian Pr). Amereon Ltd.

--Strange Bedfellows. 13.95 (ISBN 0-88411-274-8, Pub. by Aeonian Pr). Amereon Ltd.

Bercoon, Norman, jt. auth. see Ullman, James M.

Bercovici, Konrad. Alexander, a Romantic Biography. 335p. 1982. Repr. of 1928 ed. lib. bdg. 30.00 (ISBN 0-89984-085-X). Century Bookbindery.

--Best Short Stories of the World. 25.00 (ISBN 0-89987-135-6). Darby Bks.

--The Crusades. 1979. Repr. of 1929 ed. lib. bdg. 25.00 (ISBN 0-8482-3439-1). Norwood Edns.

--Singing Winds: Stories of Gypsy Life. LC 79-133814. (BCL Ser. I). 1970. Repr. of 1926 ed. 22.00 (ISBN 0-404-00787-2). AMS Pr.

--The Story of the Gypsies. LC 78-164051. (Illus.). xii, 294p. 1975. Repr. of 1928 ed. 37.00x (ISBN 0-8103-4042-9). Gale.

--Volga Boatman. LC 72-131628. 1970. Repr. of 1926 ed. 15.00x (ISBN 0-403-00515-9). Scholarly.

Bercovici, Sylvia M. Barriers to Normalization: The Restrictive Management of Retarded Persons. LC 82-13644. 224p. 1982. pap. text ed. 16.00 (ISBN 0-8391-1766-3). Pro Ed.

Bercovitch, Jacob. Social Conflicts & Third Parties: Strategies of Conflict Resolution. (Replica Edition). 160p. 1983. softcover 20.00x (ISBN 0-86531-961-8). Westview.

Bercovitch, S. The American Puritan Imagination. LC 73-94136. 256p. 1974. 39.50 (ISBN 0-521-20392-9); pap. 13.95 (ISBN 0-521-09841-6). Cambridge U Pr.

Bercovitch, Sacvan. The American Jeremiad. LC 78-53283. 254p. 1979. 29.50x (ISBN 0-299-07350-5); pap. 11.75x (ISBN 0-299-07354-8). U of Wis Pr.

--The Puritan Origins of the American Self. LC 74-29713. 272p. 1975. pap. 8.95x (ISBN 0-300-02117-8). Yale U Pr.

Bercovitch, Sacvan, ed. A Library of American Puritan Writings: The Seventeenth Century, 27 vols. Incl. Vol. 1. Election Day Sermons: Massachusetts. LC 78-253 (ISBN 0-404-60801-9); Vol. 2. Election Day Sermons: Plymouth & Connecticut. LC 78-254 (ISBN 0-404-60802-7); Vol. 3. Fast Day Sermons. LC 78-258 (ISBN 0-404-60803-5); Vol. 4. Sermons on Conduct & Manners. LC 78-259 (ISBN 0-404-60804-3); Vol. 5. Execution Sermons. LC 78-263 (ISBN 0-404-60805-1); Vol. 6. Aspects of Puritan Religious Thought. LC 78-264 (ISBN 0-404-60806-X); Vol. 7. Puritan Personal Writings: Diaries. LC 78-269 (ISBN 0-404-60807-8); Vol. 8. Puritan Personal Writings: Autobiographies & Other Writings. LC 78-270. 240p (ISBN 0-404-60808-6); Vol. 9. Histories & Narratives. LC 78-274 (ISBN 0-404-60809-4); Vol. 10. Tracts Against New England. LC 78-275 (ISBN 0-404-60810-8); Vol. 11. The Orthodox Evangelist. LC 78-280 (ISBN 0-404-60811-6); Vol. 12. John Cotton: The New England Way. LC 78-281 (ISBN 0-404-60812-4); Vol. 13. John Cotton: The Way of Faith. LC 78-286 (ISBN 0-404-60813-2); Vol. 14. John Cotton: The End of the World. LC 78-287 (ISBN 0-404-60814-0); Vol. 15. Thomas Hooker: The Soules Preparation for Christ. LC 78-291 (ISBN 0-404-60815-9); Vol. 16. Thomas Hooker: The Soules Humiliation. LC 78-293 (ISBN 0-404-60816-7); Vol. 17. Thomas Hooker: The Soules Implantation. LC 78-297 (ISBN 0-404-60817-5); Vol. 18. Thomas Hooker: The Soules Exaltation. LC 78-298 (ISBN 0-404-60818-3); Richard Mather: Life, Journal & Selected Writings. LC 78-302 (ISBN 0-404-60819-1); Vol. 20. Increase Mather: Jeremiads. LC 78-303 (ISBN 0-404-60820-5); Vol. 21. Increase Mather: Doctrine. LC 78-308 (ISBN 0-404-60821-3); Vol. 22. Increase Mather: Two Tracts. LC 78-309 (ISBN 0-404-60822-1); Vol. 23. Cotton Mather: Historical Writings. LC 78-314 (ISBN 0-404-60823-X); Vol. 24. Cotton Mather: Apocalyptic Writings. LC 78-319 (ISBN 0-404-60824-8); Vol. 25. Cotton Mather: Sermons on Church & State. LC 78-325 (ISBN 0-404-60825-6); Vol. 26. Samuel Willard: Selected Sermons. LC 78-315 (ISBN 0-404-60826-4); Vol. 27. The Vision of New England: Selected Writings. LC 78-321 (ISBN 0-404-60827-2). LC 84-45975. 360p. 1985. Set. 1552.50 (ISBN 0-404-60800-0); 57.50 ea. AMS Pr.

--Typology & Early American Literature. LC 74-181362. (New England Writers Ser.). 352p. 1971. 17.50x (ISBN 0-87023-096-4). U of Mass Pr.

Bercovitz, Alan. The Financial Freedom Course. 200p. 1985. 3 ring binder 29.50 (ISBN 0-916735-00-1). New Venture.

Bercuson, David J. Confrontation at Winnipeg: Labour, Industrial Relations & the General Strike. 224p. 1974. pap. 10.95 (ISBN 0-7735-0226-2). McGill-Queens U Pr.

--The Secret Army. LC 84-40238. (Illus.). 306p. 1984. 19.95 (ISBN 0-8128-2984-0). Stein & Day.

Bercuson, David J. & Buckner, Phillip A., eds. Eastern & Western Perspectives: Papers from the Joint Atlantic Canada-Western Canadian Studies Conference. 256p. 1981. o. p. 25.00x (ISBN 0-8020-2390-8); pap. 10.00 (ISBN 0-8020-6415-9). U of Toronto Pr.

Bercusson, Brian. Fair Wages Resolutions. (Studies in Labour & Social Law: Vol. 2). 566p. 1978. lib. bdg. 35.00x (ISBN 0-7201-0709-1). Mansell.

Bercy, Drovin De see De Bercy, Drouin.

Berczeller. Medical Treatment of Quadriplegia. 1985. 39.50 (ISBN 0-8151-0700-5). Year Bk Med.

Berczynski, Thomas, tr. see Olesha, Yury.

Berd, Malcolm, jt. ed. see Boehm, Erika.

Berd, Malcolm D. & Boehm, Erika C., eds. Passage III. LC 74-1564. 1977. 3.95 (ISBN 0-931672-02-3). Triton Coll.

Berdahl, Clarence A. War Powers of the Executive in the United States. LC 21-12280. Repr. of 1921 ed. lib. bdg. 22.00 (ISBN 0-384-03970-7). Johnson Repr.

Berdahl, Robert O. British Universities & the State. Metzger, Walter P., ed. LC 76-55198. (The Academic Profession Ser.). 1977. Repr. of 1959 ed. lib. bdg. 19.00x (ISBN 0-405-10029-9). Ayer Co Pubs.

Berdahl, Robert O., jt. ed. see Altbach, Philip.

Berdan, Frances. The Aztecs of Central Mexico: An Imperial Society. 1982. pap. text ed. 9.95 (ISBN 0-03-055736-4). HR&W.

Berdan, John M. Fourteen Stories from One Plot, Based on Mr. Fothergill's Plot. LC 76-131629. 1971. Repr. of 1932 ed. 21.00 (ISBN 0-403-00516-7). Scholarly.

Berde, E. & Eichler, O., eds. Neurohypophysial Hormones & Similar Polypeptides. (Handbook of Experimental Pharmacology: Vol. 23). (Illus.). 1968. 135.70 (ISBN 0-387-04149-4). Springer-Verlag.

Berdecio, Robert, ed. see Posada, Jose G.

Berdell, Dorothy K., ed. see Olivares, Dennis A.

Berden, John M. & Forthergill, John. Fourteen Stories from One Plot, Based on "Mr Fothergill's Plot. 21.00 (ISBN 0-8369-4262-0, 6064). Ayer Co Pubs.

Berdiaer, Nicolaii. The Realm of Spirit & the Realm of Caesar. Luurie, Donald A., tr. from Rus. LC 74-1554. 182p. 1975. Repr. of 1953 ed. lib. bdg. 22.50x (ISBN 0-8371-7395-7, BESC). Greenwood.

Berdiaev, Nicolas. Leontiev. (Russian Ser.: Vol. 15). 1968. pap. 15.00x (ISBN 0-87569-004-1). Academic Intl.

Berdiaev, Nikolai. The Destiny of Man. Duddington, Natalie, tr. LC 78-14100. 1979. Repr. of 1954 ed. 25.85 (ISBN 0-88355-775-4). Hyperion Conn.

--Solitude & Society. Reavey, George, tr. from Rus. LC 70-98211. 207p. 1976. Repr. of 1938 ed. lib. bdg. 25.00x (ISBN 0-8371-3250-9, BESS). Greenwood.

Berdiaev, Nikolai A. The Beginning & the End. French, R. M., tr. from Russian. LC 76-6083. 1976. Repr. of 1952 ed. lib. bdg. 35.00x (ISBN 0-8371-8837-7, BEBE). Greenwood.

--Leontiev. 1978. Repr. of 1940 ed. lib. bdg. 25.00 (ISBN 0-8495-0405-8). Arden Lib.

--The Russian Idea. French, R. M., tr. LC 78-32021. 1979. Repr. of 1948 ed. lib. bdg. 37.50x (ISBN 0-313-20968-5, BERN). Greenwood.

Berdicea, Fernando S. Antonio S. Pedreira. (Puerto Rico Ser.). 1979. lib. bdg. 59.95 (ISBN 0-8490-2867-1). Gordon Pr.

Berdichevsky, M. N. & Zhdanov, M. S. Advanced Theory of Deep Geomagnetic Sounding. (Methods in Geochemistry & Geophysics Ser.: Vol. 19). 400p. 1984. 94.50 (ISBN 0-444-42189-0). Elsevier.

Berdichewsky, Bernardo, ed. Anthropology & Change in Rural Areas. (World Anthropology Ser.). (Illus.). 564p. text ed. 39.20x (ISBN 90-279-7810-7). Mouton.

Berdicio, Marion D., tr. see Frank, Andre G.

Berdie, Douglas R. & Anderson, John F. Questionnaires: Design & Use. LC 74-4174. 225p. 1974. 15.00 (ISBN 0-8108-0719-X). Scarecrow.

Berdie, Mitchell, jt. auth. see Muldoon, Joseph A.

Berdine, William H. & Cegelka, Patricia T. Teaching the Trainable Retarded. (Special Education Ser.). 312p. 1980. text ed. 23.95 (ISBN 0-675-08200-5). Merrill.

Berdine, William H., jt. auth. see Blackhurst, A. Edward.

Berding, Andrew. The Making of Foreign Policy. LC 66-14226. (The U.S.A Survey Ser.). 102p. 1966. 4.95 (ISBN 0-87107-002-2). Potomac.

Berdjis, Charles C. Pathology of Irradiation. LC 71-110278. 722p. 1970. 52.50 (ISBN 0-683-00601-0, Pub. by Williams & Wilkins). Krieger.

Berdnyk, Oles. Svyata Ukrayina. LC 80-51598. 208p. (Ukrainian.). 1980. pap. 8.75 (ISBN 0-914834-29-0). Smoloskyp.

Berdoe, E. Browning & the Christian Faith. LC 79-130244. (Studies in Browning, No. 4). 1970. Repr. of 1896 ed. lib. bdg. 39.95x (ISBN 0-8383-1134-2). Haskell.

--Browning & the Christian Faith. 1973. Repr. of 1896 ed. 22.50 (ISBN 0-8274-1720-9). R West.

--Browning's Message to His Time. LC 73-16003. (Studies in Browning, No. 4). 1974. Repr. of 1893 ed. lib. bdg. 48.95x (ISBN 0-8383-1724-3). Haskell.

Berdoe, Edward. The Browning Cyclopedia: A Guide to the Study of the Works of Robert Browning. 1980. Repr. of 1916 ed. lib. bdg. 55.00 (ISBN 0-89341-479-4). Longwood Pub Group.

--The Browning Cyclopedia: A Guide to the Study of the Works of Robert Browning. 1977. Repr. of 1912 ed. lib. bdg. 65.00 (ISBN 0-8492-0396-1). R West.

--Browning's Message to His Time: His Religion, Philosophy & Science. 1973. Repr. of 1890 ed. 15.00 (ISBN 0-8274-1478-1). R West.

Berdoukas, Vasili, jt. auth. see Modell, B.

Berdt, Dennys De see De Berdt, Dennys.

Berdy, Janos. Antibiotics from Higher Forms of Life: Higher Plants, Vol. VIII, Pt. II. (CRC Handbook of Antibiotic Compounds Ser.). 448p. 1982. 67.00 (ISBN 0-8493-3460-8). CRC Pr.

--Heterocyclic Antibiotics. (CRC Handbook of Antibiotic Compounds: Vol. 5). 576p. 1982. 82.00 (ISBN 0-8493-3456-X). CRC Pr.

Berdy, Janos, ed. Alicyclic, Aromatic & Aliphatic Antibiotics, Vol. 6. (CRC Handbook of Antibiotic Compounds Ser.). 384p. 1981. 75.00 (ISBN 0-8493-3457-8). CRC Pr.

--Antibiotics from Higher Forms of Life: Higher Plants, Vol. VIII, Pt. VI. (CRC Handbook of Antibiotic Compounds Ser.). 424p. 1982. 67.00 (ISBN 0-8493-3459-4). CRC Pr.

--Antibiotics from Higher Forms of Life: Lichens, Algae, & Animal Organisms, Vol. IX. (CRC Handbook of Antibiotic Compounds Ser.). 248p. 1982. 46.00 (ISBN 0-8493-3461-6). CRC Pr.

--CRC Handbook of Antibiotic Compounds, Vol. XII. 704p. 1984. 120.00 (ISBN 0-8493-3465-9). CRC Pr.

--Handbook of Antibiotic Compounds, 4 vols. Incl. Vol. 1. Carbohydrate Antibiotics. 472p. 72.00 (ISBN 0-8493-3451-9); Vol. 2. Macrocyclic Lactone (Lactam) Antibiotics. 552p. 82.00 (ISBN 0-8493-3452-7); Vol. 3. Quinone & Similar Antibiotics. 440p. 66.00 (ISBN 0-8493-3453-5); Vol. 4, 2 pts. Amino Acids & Peptide Antibiotics, Pt. 1, 576 Pgs. 82.00 (ISBN 0-8493-3454-3); Peptolide Macromolecular Antibiotics, Pt. 2, 376 Pgs. 66.00 (ISBN 0-8493-3455-1). 1980. CRC Pr.

--Handbook of Antibiotic Compounds, Vol. X. 560p. 1982. 84.50 (ISBN 0-8493-3462-4). CRC Pr.

--HB Antiobiotic Compounds, Vol. XI: Pts. I & II. 1984. Pt. I, 704p. 110.00 (ISBN 0-8493-3463-2); Pt. II, 408p. 72.50 (ISBN 0-8493-3464-0). CRC Pr.

--Miscellaneous Antibiotics with Unknown Chemical Structure, Vol. 7. (CRC Handbook of Antibiotic Compounds Ser.). 272p. 1980. 56.00 (ISBN 0-8493-3458-6). CRC Pr.

Berdyaev, Nicholas. Freedom & the Spirit. Clarke, Oliver F., tr. 380p. 1982. Repr. of 1935 ed. lib. bdg. 21.00 (ISBN 0-8290-0815-2). Irvington.

--Leontiev. LC 73-9622. 1914. lib. bdg. 20.00 (ISBN 0-8414-3152-3). Folcroft.

Berdyaev, Nicolas. Bourgeois Mind, & Other Essays. facs. ed. LC 67-22072. (Essay Index Reprint Ser). 1934. 10.00 (ISBN 0-8369-0198-3). Ayer Co Pubs.

--Freedom & the Spirit. LC 72-2567. (Select Bibliographies Reprint Ser.). 1972. Repr. of 1935 ed. 24.50 (ISBN 0-8369-6848-4). Ayer Co Pubs.

--The Origin of Russian Communism. 239p. 1980. Repr. of 1937 ed. lib. bdg. 30.00 (ISBN 0-89760-047-9). Telegraph Bks.

--Origin of Russian Communism. 1960. pap. 8.95 (ISBN 0-472-06034-1, 34, AA). U of Mich Pr.

--Toward a New Epoch. 1978. Repr. of 1949 ed. lib. bdg. 12.50 (ISBN 0-8495-0368-X). Arden Lib.

--Towards a New Epoch. LC 73-6799. Repr. of 1949 ed. lib. bdg. 15.00 (ISBN 0-8414-3115-9). Folcroft.

Bere, May. A Comparative Study of the Mental Capacity of Children of Foreign Parentage. (Columbia University. Teachers College. Contributions to Education: No. 154). Repr. of 1924 ed. 22.50 (ISBN 0-404-55154-8). AMS Pr.

Bere, R. De La see De La Bere, R.

Bere, Rennie. Crocodile's Eggs for Supper & Other Animal Tales from Northern Uganda. LC 79-64235. (Illus.). (gr. 2-6). 1979. 5.95 (ISBN 0-233-96424-X). Andre Deutsch.

--The Nature of Cornwall: The County's Wildlife & Its Habitats. 196p. 1982. 39.00x (ISBN 0-86023-163-1, Pub. by Barracuda England). State Mutual Bk.

Bereano, Philip L. Technology As a Social & Political Phenomenon. LC 76-18723. 544p. 1976. text ed. 46.50x cloth (ISBN 0-471-06875-6). Wiley.

Berecz, E. & Balla-Ach, S. M. Gas Hydrates. (Studies in Inorganic Chemistry: Vol. 4). 330p. 1984. 75.00 (ISBN 0-444-99657-5, I-318-83). Elsevier.

Bereday, George Z. Universities for All: International Perspectives on Mass Higher Education. LC 72-11624. (Higher Education Ser.). 1973. 17.95x (ISBN 0-87589-164-0). Jossey-Bass.

Bereday, George Z. & Lauwerys, Joseph A., eds. Yearbook of Education, Nineteen Fifty-Eight: The Secondary School Curriculum. facsimile ed. LC 73-38704. (Essay Index Reprint Ser). Repr. of 1958 ed. 32.00 (ISBN 0-8369-2680-3). Ayer Co Pubs.

--Yearbook of Education, Nineteen Fifty-Nine: Higher Education. facsimile ed. LC 73-38704. (Essay Index Reprint Ser). Repr. of 1959 ed. 29.00 (ISBN 0-8369-2681-1). Ayer Co Pubs.

--Yearbook of Education, Nineteen Fifty-Seven: Education & Philosophy. facsimile ed. LC 73-38704. (Essay Index Reprint Ser). Repr. of 1957 ed. 22.00 (ISBN 0-8369-2679-X). Ayer Co Pubs.

Bereday, George Z. & Masui, Shigeo, eds. American Education Through Japanese Eyes. LC 72-91619. 1973. 15.00x (ISBN 0-8248-0249-7, Eastwest Ctr). UH Pr.

Bereday, George Z. & Pennar, Jaan, eds. The Politics of Soviet Education. LC 75-28662. 217p. 1976. Repr. of 1960 ed. lib. bdg. 22.50x (ISBN 0-8371-8477-0, BEPS). Greenwood.

Bereday, George Z. & Volpicelli, Luigi, eds. Public Education in America: A New Interpretation of Purpose & Practice. LC 77-23510. 1977. Repr. of 1958 ed. lib. bdg. 18.50x (ISBN 0-8371-9702-3, BEPU). Greenwood.

Beredene, Jocelyn. What Difference Did the Deed of Christ Make? 1979. pap. 1.50 (ISBN 0-88010-103-2). Anthroposophic.

Beregi, E. & Varga, I. Renal Biopsy in Glomerular Diseases. 1978. 34.50 (ISBN 0-9960012-1-2, Pub. by Akademiai Kaido Hungary). Heyden.

Beregi, E., et al, eds. Pulmonary Pathology & Aging, Vol. 1. LC 74-6167. 202p. 1974. text ed. 24.50x (ISBN 0-8422-7224-0). Irvington.

Beregovaia, N. A., et al. Contributions to the Archaeology of the Soviet Union: With Special Emphasis on Central Asia, the Caucasus & Armenia. Field, Henry, ed. Klein, Richard G., et al, trs. LC 67-79842. (Harvard University. Peabody Museum of Archaeology & Ethnology. Russian Translation Ser.: No. 1). lib. bdg. 32.50 (ISBN 0-404-52644-6). AMS Pr.

Bereitner, jt. auth. see Anderson.

Berelson, Bernard. Content Analysis in Communications Research. 1971. 22.95x (ISBN 0-02-841210-9). Hafner.

--The Great Debate on Population Policy: An Instructive Entertainment. LC 75-22229. 32p. (Orig.). 1975. pap. text ed. 2.95 (ISBN 0-87834-050-5). Population Coun.

Berelson, Bernard & Ansheim, Lester. The Library's Public: A Report of the Public Library Inquiry. LC 75-31430. 174p. 1976. Repr. of 1949 ed. lib. bdg. 24.75x (ISBN 0-8371-8499-1, BELP). Greenwood.

Berelson, Bernard, ed. Population Policy in Developed Countries. LC 73-18368. 793p. 1974. write for info. Population Coun.

Berelson, Bernard R., et al. Voting: A Study of Opinion Formation in a Presidential Campaign. LC 54-11205. (Illus.). 1954. pap. 10.00x (ISBN 0-226-04349-5). U of Chicago Pr.

Beren, Peter, jt. auth. see Bunnin, Brad.

Berenbaum, Esai. Municipal Public Safety: A Guide for the Implementation of Consolidated Police-Fire Services. (Illus.). 104p. 1977. 20.75x (ISBN 0-398-03612-8). C C Thomas.

Berenbaum, Linda B. The Gothic Imagination: Expansion in Gothic Literature & Art. LC 80-67035. (Illus.). 140p. 1981. 19.50 (ISBN 0-8386-3068-5). Fairleigh Dickinson.

Berenbaum, Michael. The Vision of the Void: Theological Reflections on the Works of Elie Wiesel. LC 78-27321. 1978. 17.50x (ISBN 0-8195-5030-2). Wesleyan U Pr.

Berenbeim, Ronald. Nonunion Complaint Systems: A Corporate Appraisal. LC 79-92986. (Report Ser.: No. 770). (Illus.). v, 50p. (Orig.). 1980. pap. 30.00 (ISBN 0-8237-0206-5); pap. 10.00 member. Conference Bd.

Berenbeim, Ronald E., jt. auth. see Janger, Allen R.

Berenbein, Boris A. Pseudocarcinoma of the Skin. Tatarchenko, V. E., tr. from Russ. 257p. 1985. 49.50x (ISBN 0-306-10981-6, Plenum Pr). Plenum Pub.

Berenberg, Ben R. Clock Book. (Golden Play & Learn Bks.). (Illus.). (gr. 1-3). 1967. 2.95 (ISBN 0-307-10730-2, Golden Bks). Western Pub.

Berenberg, S. R. Puberty. 1975. lib. bdg. 45.00 (ISBN 90-207-0539-3, Pub. by Martinuus Nijhoff Netherlands). Kluwer Academic.

Berenberg, S. R., ed. see International Children's Center Conference, 1972.

Berenberg, Samuel R. Brain: Fetal & Infant. 1977. lib. bdg. 53.00 (ISBN 90-247-2022-2, Pub. by Martinus Nijhoff Netherlands). Kluwer Academic.

Berenblum, I. Cancer Research Today. 1967. pap. 10.25 (ISBN 0-08-012452-6). Pergamon.

--Carcinogenesis As a Biological Problem. 1975. 108.50 (ISBN 0-444-10628-6). Elsevier.

Berenblum, Isaac. Man Against Cancer: The Story of Cancer Research. LC 52-13023. pap. 49.00 (ISBN 0-317-07917-4, 2003830). Bks Demand UMI.

Berenbon, Howard. Mostly BASIC: Application for the Commodore 64. LC 84-50183. Bk. 1. 12.95 (ISBN 0-672-22355-4); Bk. 2. 14.95 (ISBN 0-672-22356-2). Sams.

--Mostly BASIC: Applications for Your Apple II, Bk. 1. LC 80-53273. 160p. 1980. pap. 13.95 (ISBN 0-672-21789-9, 21864). Sams.

--Mostly BASIC: Applications for Your Apple II, Bk. 2. LC 80-53273. 224p. 1982. pap. 12.95 (ISBN 0-672-21864-X). Sams.

--Mostly BASIC: Applications for Your Atari, 2 vols. LC 83-61071. 184p. 1983. Bk. 1, 184 pp. 12.95 (ISBN 0-672-22075-X, 22075); Bk. 2, 224 pp. 15.95 (ISBN 0-672-22092-X, 22092). Sams.

--Mostly BASIC: Applications for Your IBM-PC, 2 Vols. 1983. Bk. 1. 12.95 (ISBN 0-672-22076-8, 22093); Bk. 2. 14.95 (ISBN 0-672-22093-8). Bobbs.

--Mostly BASIC: Applications for Your IBM-PC, 2 vols. LC 83-61072. 1983. Bk. 1, 192 pp. 12.95 (ISBN 0-672-22076-8, 22076); Bk. 2, 248 pp. 14.95 (ISBN 0-672-22093-8, 22093). Sams.

--Mostly BASIC: Applications for Your PET. LC 80-53274. 160p. 1980. Book 1. pap. 13.95 (ISBN 0-672-21790-2, 21790). Sams.

--Mostly BASIC: Applications for Your PET, Bk. 2. LC 80-53274. 224p. 1983. pap. 13.95 (ISBN 0-672-22001-6, 22001). Sams.

--Mostly BASIC: Applications for Your TRS-80, Bk. 1. LC 80-53269. 168p. 1980. pap. 12.95 (ISBN 0-672-21788-0, 21788). Sams.

--Mostly BASIC Applications for Your TRS-80, Bk.2. 224p. 1981. pap. 12.95 (ISBN 0-672-21865-8, 21865). Sams.

--TRS-80 Sharp Pocket Computer Programs. LC 83-50938. 224p. 1984. pap. 15.95 (ISBN 0-672-22078-4, 22078). Sams.

Berend, Ivan & Ranki, Gyorgy. The European Periphery & Industrialisation 1780-1914. LC 81-3893. (Studies in Modern Capitalism). (Illus.). 200p. 1982. 32.50 (ISBN 0-521-24210-X). Cambridge U Pr.

Berend, Ivan R. & Ranki, Gyorgy. The Hungarian Economy in the Twentieth Century. 272p. 1985. 32.50 (ISBN 0-312-40118-3). St Martin.

Berend, Ivan T. & Ranki, Gyorgy, trs. Economic Development in East Central Europe in the Nineteenth & Twentieth Centuries. LC 73-6542. (Institute on East Central Europe Ser.). 402p. 1976. 37.00x (ISBN 0-231-03013-4); pap. 18.00x (ISBN 0-231-08349-1). Columbia U Pr.

Berendes, H. W., jt. ed. see Garattini, S.

Berends, Polly. Ozma & the Wayward Wand. LC 84-17972. (Brand-New Oz Adventure Ser.). (Illus.). 80p. (gr. 2-6). 1985. PLB 4.99 (ISBN 0-394-97068-3, BYR); pap. 1.95 (ISBN 0-394-87068-9). Random.

--Whole Child-Whole Parent. LC 81-480294. (Illus.). 384p. (Orig.). 1983. pap. 10.53i (ISBN 0-06-090949-8, CN 949, CN). Har-Row.

Berends, Polly B. The Case of the Elevator Duck. (Illus.). (gr. 3-6). 1973. PLB 6.99 (ISBN 0-394-92115-1, BYR). Random.

--Ladybug & Dog & the Night Walk. LC 79-20692. (Illus.). 32p. (ps). 1980. (BYR); PLB 4.99 (ISBN 0-394-93398-2). Random.

--Whole Child-Whole Parent: A Spiritual & Practical Guide to Parenthood. rev. ed. LC 81-48029. (Illus.). 1983. 16.30 (ISBN 0-06-014971-X, HarpT). Har-Row.

Berendsen, A. M. Ship Painting Manual. (Illus.). 1975. 45.00 (ISBN 90-228-1951-5). Heinman.

Berendsen, B. S. M. Regional Models of Trade & Development. (Studies in Developing & Planning: Vol. 7). 1978. lib. bdg. 20.50 (ISBN 90-207-0753-1, Pub. by Martinus Nijhoff Netherlands). Kluwer Academic.

Berendsohn, Walter A. August Strindberg: Der Mensh und Seine Umwelt - das Werk - der Schopferische Kunstler. (Amsterdamer Publikationen Zur Sprache und Literatur: No. 4). (Illus.). 473p. (Ger.). 1976. pap. text ed. 29.25x (ISBN 90-6203-061-0). Humanities.

--Selma Lagerlof. 136p. 1979. Repr. of 1931 ed. lib. bdg. 25.00 (ISBN 0-89984-050-7). Century Bookbindery.

--Selma Lagerlof, Her Life & Work. LC 67-27576. (Illus.). 1931. Repr. 14.00x (ISBN 0-8046-0027-9, Pub. by Kennikat). Assoc Faculty Pr.

Berendt, Gerald E. Collective Bargaining. (Contemporary Litigation Ser.). 356p. 1984. 40.00 (ISBN 0-87215-693-1). Michie Co.

Berendt, Joachim. The Jazz Book: From Ragtime to Fusion & Beyond with a New American Discography. rev. ed. Morgenstern, Dan & Bredigkeit, H. B., trs. from German. 436p. 1982. 18.95 (ISBN 0-88208-140-3); pap. 9.95 (ISBN 0-88208-141-1). Lawrence Hill.

Berendt, Joachim-Ernst. Jazz: A Photo History. LC 79-7629. (Illus.). 1979. 35.00 (ISBN 0-02-870290-5). Schirmer Bks.

Berendt, Robert J. & Taft, J. Richard. How to Rate Your Development Office: A Fund-raising Primer for the Chief Executive. LC 83-50709. 88p. 1983. 19.95 (ISBN 0-914756-54-0). Taft Group.

Berendzen. Man Discovers the Galaxies. 1976. 15.95 (ISBN 0-07-004845-2). McGraw.

Berendzen, Richard. Is My Armor Straight? A Year in the Life of a University President. 1986. 16.95 (ISBN 0-917561-01-5). Adler & Adler.

--Man Discovers the Galaxies. 1984. 30.00x; pap. 12.00. Columbia U Pr.

Berenger-Feraud, L. J. Contes populaires de Provencaux de l'Antiquite et du Moyen Age. LC 78-20120. (Collection de contes et de chansons populaires: Vol. 11). Repr. of 1887 ed. 21.50 (ISBN 0-404-60361-0). AMS Pr.

--Recueil de contes populaires de la Senegambie. LC 78-20118. (Collection de contes et de chansons populaires: Vol. 9). Repr. of 1885 ed. 21.50 (ISBN 0-404-60359-9). AMS Pr.

Berens, E. M. The Myths & Legends of Ancient Greece & Rome. LC 77-91528. 1977. Repr. of 1880 ed. lib. bdg. 30.00 (ISBN 0-89341-029-2). Longwood Pub Group.

Berens, H., jt. auth. see Butzer, P. L.

Berens, John F. Providence & Patriotism in Early America, 1640-1815. LC 78-5889. 1978. 15.00x (ISBN 0-8139-0779-9). U Pr of Va.

Berens, John S. Contemporary Retailing: Cases from Today's Market Place. 2nd ed. 237p. 1985. pap. 14.95x (ISBN 0-8134-2356-2, 2356); pap. text ed. 14.95x instr's. aid (ISBN 0-8134-2357-0, 2357). Interstate.

Berenson, Bernard. Aesthetics & History. LC 52-1732. pap. 60.50 (ISBN 0-317-10437-3, 2012984). Bks Demand UMI.

--Contemporary Jewish Fiction. 1976. lib. bdg. 59.95 (ISBN 0-87968-939-0). Gordon Pr.

--Italian Painters of the Renaissance. (Landmarks in Art History Ser.). 438p. 1980. pap. 14.95x (ISBN 0-8014-9195-9). Cornell U Pr.

--Studies in Medieval Painting. LC 73-153884. (Graphic Art Ser.). (Illus.). 148p. 1971. Repr. of 1930 ed. lib. bdg. 37.50 (ISBN 0-306-70292-4). Da Capo.

--Studies in Medieval Painting. LC 74-22036. (Graphic Art Ser.). (Illus.). xxii, 148p. 1975. pap. 5.95 (ISBN 0-306-80010-1). Da Capo.

Berenson, Bernard, ed. see Mariano, Nicky.

Berenson, Bernard G. & Mitchel, Kevin M. Confrontation for Better or Worse. LC 74-75370. (Perspectives Ser.). (Illus.). 106p. 1974. pap. text ed. 15.00 (ISBN 0-914234-81-1). Human Res Dev Pr.

Berenson, Bernard G., jt. auth. see Carkhuff, Robert R.

Berenson, Bernhard. Aesthetics & History. LC 52-1732. 242p. 1955. Repr. 49.00 (ISBN 0-403-03882-0). Somerset Pub.

--Alberto Sani: An Artist Out of His Time. LC 70-138202. (Illus.). 115p. 1972. Repr. of 1950 ed. lib. bdg. 22.50x (ISBN 0-8371-5555-X, BEAS). Greenwood.

--Drawings of the Florentine Painters, 3 Vols. enl. ed. LC 69-13822. (Illus.). 1969. Repr. of 1938 ed. Set. lib. bdg. 42.75x (ISBN 0-8371-0915-9, BEFP). Greenwood.

--The Italian Painters of the Renaissance, 2 vols. (Illus.). 139p. 1982. Repr. of 1897 ed. 145.50 (ISBN 0-89901-070-9). Found Class Reprints.

--The Study & Criticism of Italian Art - First Series. LC 75-41028. (BCL Ser. II). Repr. of 1920 ed. 17.50 (ISBN 0-404-14758-5). AMS Pr.

Berenson, David, et al. The Skills of Teaching: Content Development Skills. (The Skills of Teaching Ser.: Vol. 2). (Illus., Orig.). 1978. pap. text ed. 9.95x (ISBN 0-914234-21-8). Human Res Dev Pr.

Berenson, Edward. Populist Religion & Left-Wing Politics in France, 1830-1852. LC 83-42548. 345p. 1984. 35.00x (ISBN 0-691-05396-0). Princeton U Pr.

Berenson, F. M. Understanding Persons: Personal & Impersonal Relations. 25.00 (ISBN 0-312-83154-4). St Martin.

Berenson, Gerald & White, Harvey M., eds. Annual Review of Family Therapy, Vol. 1. LC 81-4131. 494p. 1980. 34.95 (ISBN 0-87705-508-4). Human Sci Pr.

Berenson, Gerald S. Cardiovascular Risk Factors in Children. 1980. text ed. 45.00x (ISBN 0-19-502589-X). Oxford U Pr.

Berenson, Gerald S., ed. Causation of Cardiovascular Risk Factors in Children: Perspectives on Cardiovascular Risk in Early Life. 1985. text ed. price not set (ISBN 0-88167-138-X). Raven.

Berenson, Marisa. Dressing Up: How to Look & Feel Absolutely Perfect for Any Social Occasion. (Illus.). 144p. 1984. 17.95 (ISBN 0-399-13003-9, Putnam). Putnam Pub Group.

Berenson, Mark & Levine, David. Basic Business Statistics: Concepts & Applications. 3rd ed. (Illus.). 816p. 1986. text ed. 31.95 (ISBN 0-13-057746-4). P-H.

Berenson, Mark L. & Levine, David M. Basic Business Statistics: Concepts & Applications. 2nd ed. (Illus.). 752p. 1983. text ed. 30.95 (ISBN 0-13-057620-4); study guide & wkbk. 10.95. P-H.

Berenson, Mark. L & Levine, David M. Intermediate Statistical Methods & Applications: A Computer Package Approach. (Illus.). 624p. 1983. text ed. 33.95 (ISBN 0-13-470781-8). P-H.

Berenstain, Jan, jt. auth. see Berenstain, Stan.

Berenstain, Jan, jt. auth. see Berestain, Stan.

Berenstain, Janice & Berenstain, Stan. The Berenstain Bears Get in a Fight. LC 81-15866. (Berenstain Bears First Time Bks.). (Illus.). 32p. (ps-1). 1982. pap. 1.95 (ISBN 0-394-85132-3). Random.

--The Berenstain Bears Go to Camp. LC 81-15864. (Berenstain Bears First Time Bks.). (Illus.). 32p. (ps-1). 1982. PLB 4.99 (ISBN 0-394-95131-X); pap. 1.95 (ISBN 0-394-85131-5). Random.

Berenstain, Janice, jt. auth. see Berenstain, Stan.

Berenstain, Janice, jt. auth. see Berenstain, Stanley.

Berenstain, Michael. The Creature Catalog: A Monster Watcher's Guide. LC 82-5365. (Illus.). 64p. (gr. 3-7). 1982. pap. 3.95 perfect bound (ISBN 0-394-85277-X). Random.

--The Dwark Meets the Trash Monster. 48p. (Orig.). (gr. 1-4). 1984. pap. 1.95 (ISBN 0-553-15288-2, Skylark). Bantam.

--The Great Monster Party. (Texas Instruments Magic Wand Speaking Library). (Illus.). 49p. (ps-3). 1983. text ed. 7.30 (ISBN 0-89512-074-7). Tex Instr Inc.

--The Sorcerer's Scrapbook. LC 80-5754. (Illus.). 64p. (gr. 3-7). 1981. PLB 7.99 (ISBN 0-394-94731-2). Random.

--The Troll Book. LC 79-5268. (Illus.). 72p. (gr. 1-7). 1980. bds. o.p. 5.95 (ISBN 0-394-84295-2); PLB 6.99 (ISBN 0-394-94295-7). Random.

Berenstain, Stan & Berenstain, Jan. The Berenstain Bears & the Big Election. LC 83-62399. (Berenstain Bears Mini-Storybooks). (Illus.). 32p. (ps-3). 1984. pap. 1.25 (ISBN 0-394-86542-1, BYR). Random.

--The Berenstain Bears & the Dinosaurs. LC 84-60384. (Berenstain Bears Mini-Storybooks). (Illus.). 32p. (ps-3). 1984. pap. 1.25 . Random.

--The Berenstain Bears & the Neighborly Skunk. LC 84-60383. (Berenstain Bears Mini-Storybooks). (Illus.). 32p. (ps-3). 1984. pap. 1.25. Random.

--The Berenstain Bears & Too Much Junk Food. LC 84-40393. (First Time Bks.). (Illus.). 32p. (ps-1). 1985. PLB 4.99 (ISBN 0-394-97217-1, BYR); pap. 1.95 (ISBN 0-394-87217-7). Random.

--Berenstain Bears Forget Their Manners. LC 84-43156. (Berenstain Bears First Time Books Ser.). (Illus.). 32p. (ps-1). 1985. PLB 4.99 (ISBN 0-394-97333-X); pap. 1.95. Random.

--Berenstain Bears: How to Get Along at School with Your Fellow Bear. (Illus.). 32p. (Orig.). 1984. 8.98 (ISBN 0-87660-014-3). I J E Bk Pub.

--The Berenstain Bears' Make & Do Book. (Illus.). 64p. (ps-3). 1984. pap. 2.95. Random.

--The Berenstain Bears on the Job. (Texas Instruments Magic Wand Speaking Library). (Illus.). 49p. (ps-3). 1983. text ed. 7.30 (ISBN 0-89512-069-0). Tex Instr Inc.

--How to Teach Your Children about God. 1984. pap. 3.95 (ISBN 0-345-29457-2). Ballantine.

--Stan & Jan Berenstains's It's All in the Family. (Orig.). 1985. pap. 5.95. Ballantine.

Berenstain, Stan & Berenstain, Janice. The Bear Detectives. LC 75-1603. (Illus.). 48p. (gr. k-3). 1975. 4.95 (ISBN 0-394-83127-6); PLB 5.99 (ISBN 0-394-93127-0). Beginner.

--The Bears' Nature Guide. LC 75-8070. (Now I Know! Ser). (Illus.). 72p. (ps-3). 1975. 6.95 (ISBN 0-394-83125-X, BYR); PLB 6.99 (ISBN 0-394-93125-4). Random.

--The Berenstain Bears' Almanac. LC 73-2298. (Bear Facts Library). (Illus.). 72p. (ps-4). 1984. pap. 3.95 (ISBN 0-394-86601-0, BYR). Random.

--The Berenstain Bears & Mama's New Job. LC 84-4787. (First Time Bks.). (Illus.). 32p. (ps-1). 1984. pap. 1.95 (ISBN 0-394-86881-1, BYR); PLB 4.99 (ISBN 0-394-96881-6). Random.

--The Berenstain Bears & the Messy Room. (Berenstain Bears First Time Bks.). (Illus.). 32p. (gr. k-2). 1983. PLB 4.99 (ISBN 0-394-95639-7); pap. 1.95 (ISBN 0-394-85639-2). Random.

--The Berenstain Bears & the Missing Dinosaur Bone. LC 79-3458. (Beginner Bks.). (Illus.). 48p. (ps-3). 1980. 4.95; PLB 5.99 (ISBN 0-394-94447-X). Beginner.

--The Berenstain Bears & the Sitter. LC 81-50046. (Berenstain Bears First Time Bks.). (Illus.). 32p. (ps-1). 1981. PLB 4.99 (ISBN 0-394-94837-8); pap. 1.95 (ISBN 0-394-84837-3). Random.

--The Berenstain Bears & the Spooky Old Tree. LC 77-93771. (Bright & Early Bk). (Illus.). (ps-2). 1978. 4.95 (ISBN 0-394-83910-2, BYR); PLB 5.99 (ISBN 0-394-93910-7). Random.

--The Berenstain Bears & the Truth. LC 83-3304. (First Time Bks.). (Illus.). 32p. (ps-k). 1983. PLB 4.99 (ISBN 0-394-95640-0); pap. 1.95 (ISBN 0-394-85640-6). Random.

--The Berenstain Bears & the Wild, Wild Honey. LC 83-60057. (Berenstain Bears Mini-Storybooks). (Illus.). 32p. (ps). 1983. pap. 1.25 (ISBN 0-394-85924-3). Random.

--The Berenstain Bears & Too Much TV. LC 83-22887. (First Time Bks.). (gr. 3-6). 1984. pap. 1.50 (ISBN 0-394-86570-7, BYR); PLB 4.99 (ISBN 0-394-96570-1). Random.

--The Berenstain Bears' Bath Book. (Bathtime Bks.). (Illus.). 10p. (ps). 1985. pap. 2.95 (ISBN 0-394-87116-2, BYR). Random.

--The Berenstain Bears' Christmas Tree. LC 80-5087. (Illus.). 72p. (ps-3). 1980. 7.95 (ISBN 0-394-84566-8); PLB 7.99 (ISBN 0-394-94566-2). Random.

--The Berenstain Bears Go Fly a Kite. LC 83-60056. (Berenstain Bears Mini-Storybooks). (Illus.). 32p. (ps-2). 1983. pap. 1.25 (ISBN 0-394-85921-9). Random.

--The Berenstain Bears Go to School. LC 77-79853. (Picturebacks Ser.). (Illus.). (ps-2). 1978. (BYR); pap. 1.95 (ISBN 0-394-83736-3). Random.

--The Berenstain Bears Go to the Doctor. LC 81-50043. (Berenstain Bears First Time Bks.). (Illus.). 32p. (ps-1). 1981. PLB 4.99 (ISBN 0-394-94835-1); pap. 1.95 (ISBN 0-394-84835-7). Random.

--The Berenstain Bears in the Dark. LC 82-5395. (Berenstain Bears First Time Bks.). 32p. 1982. PLB 4.99 (ISBN 0-394-95443-2); pap. 1.95 saddle-stitched (ISBN 0-394-85443-8). Random.

--Berenstain Bears Learn about Strangers. LC 84-43157. (Berenstain Bears First Time Books Ser.). (Illus.). 32p. (ps-1). 1985. PLB 4.99 (ISBN 0-394-97334-8); pap. 1.95 (ISBN 0-394-87334-3). Random.

--The Berenstain Bears Meet Santa Bear. LC 84-4829. (First Time Bks.). (Illus.). 32p. (ps-1). 1984. pap. 1.95 (ISBN 0-394-86880-3, BYR); PLB 4.99 (ISBN 0-394-96880-8). Random.

--The Berenstain Bears' Moving Day. LC 81-50044. (Berenstain Bears First Time Bks.). (Illus.). 32p. (ps-1). 1981. pap. 1.95 (ISBN 0-394-84838-1). Random.

--The Berenstain Bears' Nature Guide. LC 75-8070. (Bear Facts Library). (Illus.). 72p. (ps-4). 1984. pap. 3.95 (ISBN 0-394-86602-9, BYR). Random.

--The Berenstain Bears' New Baby. (Illus.). 32p. 1985. pap. 4.95 (ISBN 0-394-87661-X, BYR). Random.

--The Berenstain Bears Olympics. (Texas Instruments Magic Wand Speaking Library). (Illus.). 50p. 1983. text ed. 7.30 (ISBN 0-89512-070-4). Tex Instr Inc.

--The Berenstain Bears on the Moon. LC 84-20428. (Bright & Early Bks.). (Illus.). 48p. (ps-3). 1985. PLB 5.99 (ISBN 0-394-97180-9, BYR); pap. 4.95 (ISBN 0-394-87180-4). Random.

--The Berenstain Bears' Science Fair. LC 76-8121. (Bear Facts Library: No. 2). (Illus.). (gr. 1-4). 1977. 5.95 (ISBN 0-394-93294-3, BYR); PLB 7.99. Random.

--The Berenstain Bears' Science Fair. LC 76-8121. (Bear Facts Library). (Illus.). 72p. (ps-4). 1984. pap. 3.95 (ISBN 0-394-86603-7, BYR). Random.

--The Berenstain Bears Shoot the Rapids. LC 83-62400. (Berenstain Bears Mini-Storybooks). (Illus.). 32p. (ps-3). 1984. pap. 1.25 (ISBN 0-394-86543-X, BYR). Random.

--The Berenstain Bears' Soccer Star. LC 83-60055. (Berenstain Bears Mini-Storybooks). (Illus.). 32p. (ps-2). 1983. pap. 1.25 (ISBN 0-394-85922-7). Random.

--The Berenstain Bears' Take-Along Library. Incl. The Berenstain Bears Visit the Dentist. 32p; The Berenstain Bears & Too Much TV. 32p; The Berenstain Bears & the Sitter. 32p; The Berenstain Bears in the Dark. 32p; The Berenstain Bears & the Messy Room. 32p. (Illus.). (ps-3). 1985. bds. 9.75 (ISBN 0-394-87615-6, BYR). Random.

--The Berenstain Bears to the Rescue. LC 83-60058. (Berenstain Bears Mini-Storybooks). (Illus.). 32p. (ps-2). 1983. pap. 1.25 (ISBN 0-394-85923-5). Random.

--The Berenstain Bears' Toy Time. (Cuddle Cloth Books). (Illus.). 12p. 1985. 2.95 (ISBN 0-394-87449-8, BYR). Random.

--The Berenstain Bears' Trouble with Money. LC 83-3305. (First Time Bks.). (Illus.). 32p. (ps-k). 1983. PLB 4.99 (ISBN 0-394-95917-5); pap. 1.95 (ISBN 0-394-85917-0). Random.

--The Berenstain Bears Visit the Dentist. LC 81-50045. (Berenstain Bears First Time Bks.). (Illus.). 32p. (ps-1). 1981. PLB 4.99 (ISBN 0-394-94836-X); pap. 1.95 (ISBN 0-394-84836-5). Random.

--The Berenstains' Baby Book. (Illus.). 192p. 1983. 12.95 (ISBN 0-87795-509-3). Arbor Hse.

--The Berenstains' Baby Book. 208p. 1984. pap. 4.95 (ISBN 0-671-49629-8). PB.

--How to Teach Your Children about Sex. 1984. pap. 3.95 (ISBN 0-345-31971-0). Ballantine.

--Papa's Pizza: A Berenstain Bear Sniffy Book. LC 78-55907. (Illus.). (ps-2). 1978. 3.95 (ISBN 0-394-83922-6, BYR). Random.

Berenstain, Stan, jt. auth. see Berenstain, Janice.

Berenstain, Stanley & Berenstain, Janice. Bear Scouts. LC 67-21919. (gr. k-3). 1967. 4.95 (ISBN 0-394-80046-X); PLB 5.99 (ISBN 0-394-90046-4). Beginner.

--The Bears Almanac. (gr. 1-4). 1973. (BYR); PLB 7.99 (ISBN 0-394-92693-5). Random.

--Bears' Christmas. LC 79-117542. (Illus.). (gr. k-3). 1970. 4.95 (ISBN 0-394-80090-7); PLB 5.99 (ISBN 0-394-90090-1). Beginner.

--Bears in the Night. (Bright & Early Bk). (Illus.). (ps-1). 1971. 4.95 (ISBN 0-394-82286-2, BYR); PLB 5.99 (ISBN 0-394-92286-7). Random.

--Bears on Wheels. LC 72-77840. (Bright & Early Bk). (Illus.). (ps-1). 1969. 4.95 (ISBN 0-394-80967-X, BYR); PLB 5.99 (ISBN 0-394-90967-4). Random.

--Bears' Picnic. LC 66-10156. (Illus.). (gr. k-3). 1966. 4.95 (ISBN 0-394-80041-9); PLB 5.99 (ISBN 0-394-90041-3). Beginner.

--Bears' Vacation. LC 68-28460. (Illus.). (gr. k-3). 1968. 4.95 (ISBN 0-394-80052-4); PLB 5.99 (ISBN 0-394-90052-9). Beginner.

--The Berenstain Bears & the Missing Dinosaur Bone. (Illus.). (ps-1). 1980. 5.99 (ISBN 0-394-94447-X); PLB 4.95 (ISBN 0-394-84447-5). Random.

--The Berenstains' B Book. (Bright & Early Bk.). (Illus.). (ps-1). 1971. lib. bdg. 3.95 (ISBN 0-394-92324-3, BYR); PLB 5.99. Random.

--The Berenstains' Bears' Nursery Tales. (Illus.). (ps-1). 1973. pap. 1.95 (ISBN 0-394-82665-5, BYR). Random.

--Big Honey Hunt. LC 62-15115. (Illus.). (gr. 1-2). 1962. 4.95 (ISBN 0-394-80028-1); PLB 5.99 (ISBN 0-394-90028-6). Beginner.

--Bike Lesson. LC 64-11460. (Illus.). (gr. k-3). 1964. 4.95 (ISBN 0-394-80036-2); PLB 5.99 (ISBN 0-394-90036-7). Beginner.

--C Is for Clown. (Bright & Early Book Ser.: No. 14). (Illus.). (ps-1). 1972. o.s.i 3.95 (ISBN 0-394-82492-X, BYR); PLB 6.99 (ISBN 0-394-92492-4). Random.

--He Bear, She Bear. LC 74-5518. (Bright & Early Bk). (Illus.). 48p. (ps-1). 1974. 4.95 (ISBN 0-394-82997-2, BYR); PLB 5.99 (ISBN 0-394-92997-7). Random.

--Inside, Outside, Upside Down. LC 68-28465. (Bright & Early Bk). (Illus.). (ps-1). 1968. 4.95 (ISBN 0-394-81142-9, BYR); PLB 5.99 (ISBN 0-394-91142-3). Random.

--The New Baby. LC 74-2535. (Picturebacks Ser). (Illus.). 32p. (Orig.). (ps-1). 1974. pap. 1.95 (ISBN 0-394-82908-5, BYR). Random.

--Old Hat, New Hat. (Bright & Early Book Ser.: No. 9). (Illus.). (ps-1). 1970. 4.95 (ISBN 0-394-80669-7, BYR); PLB 5.99 (ISBN 0-394-90669-1). Random.

Berenstein, C. A. & Dostal, M. A. Analytically Uniform Spaces & Their Applications to Convolution Equations. LC 70-189386. (Lecture Notes in Mathematics: Vol. 256). 137p. 1972. pap. 9.00 (ISBN 0-387-05746-3). Springer-Verlag.

Berent, Irving. The Algebra of Suicide. LC 81-4131. 205p. 1981. 25.95 (ISBN 0-89885-006-1). Human Sci Pr.

Berent, Irwin M. & Zubatsky, David S. Jewish Genealogy: A Sourcebook of Family Histories & Genealogies. (Reference Library of Social Science). 335p. 1983. lib. bdg. 33.00 (ISBN 0-8240-9028-4). Garland Pub.

Berentes, Drew. Apple LOGO: A Complete, Illustrated Handbook. (Illus.). 406p. (Orig.). 1984. pap. 13.95 (ISBN 0-8306-1751-5, 1751). TAB Bks.

--MacPascal Programming. 1985. 22.95 (ISBN 0-8306-0891-5, 1891); pap. 16.95 (ISBN 0-8306-1891-0). TAB Bks.

Bereny, J. A., ed. see Central Intelligence Agency.

Bereny, J. A., ed. see Energy Information Administration.

Bereny, J. A., ed. see Federal Energy Administration.

Bereny, Justin A. Survey of the Emerging Solar Energy Industry. De Winter, Francis, ed. LC 77-71664. (Illus.). 405p. 1977. 60.00x (ISBN 0-930978-00-5, V-901); pap. 34.50x (ISBN 0-930978-01-3). Solar Energy Info.

--Technology Transfer: Survey of an Emerging Service Industry, 1970. 130p. pap. 49.50x (ISBN 0-89934-231-0). Business Technology Bks.

Bereny, Justin A. & De Winter, Francis. San Francisco Bay Area Solar Heating Guide & Directory: 1977 Edition. LC 77-86469. 1977. pap. 7.95x (ISBN 0-930978-03-X, H-002). Solar Energy Info.

Bereny, Justin A., jt. auth. see Howell, Yvonne.

Bereny, Justin A., ed. Alcohol Fuels Information Series: Vol. 1, U. S. Government Overviews. LC 80-51918. 1980. 54.95x (ISBN 0-89934-031-8, B941-SS); pap. 39.95x (ISBN 0-89934-032-6, B041-SS). Solar Energy Info.

--Industrial Robots: A Survey of Domestic & Foreign Patents (1969-1983) LC 85-71672. (Robotics & Artificial Intelligence Applications Ser.: Vol. 6). 250p. (Orig.). 1985. pap. 89.50x (ISBN 0-89934-230-2, BT021). Business Technology Bks.

Berenyi, D. & Hock, G., eds. High-Energy Ion-Atom Collisions: Proceedings of the International Seminar on High-Energy Ion-Atom Collision Processes, Debrecen, Hungary, Mar. 17-19, 1982. (Nuclear Methods Monographs: Vol. 2). 276p. 1982. 68.00 (ISBN 0-444-99703-2). Elsevier.

Berenyi, John. The Modern American Business Dictionary: Including Reaganomics & an Appendix of Business Slang. LC 81-22342. 288p. 1982. 22.50 (ISBN 0-688-00986-7). Morrow.

--The Modern American Business Dictionary: Including Reagonomics & an Appendix of Business Slang. LC 81-21185. 288p. 1982. pap. 7.25 (ISBN 0-688-00987-5, Quill). Morrow.

Berer, Margaret & Rinvolucri, Mario. Mazes: A Problem-Solving Reader. (Orig.). 1981. pap. text ed. 4.50x (ISBN 0-435-28719-2). Heinemann Ed.

Bererdi, Gigi M. World Food, Population & Development. 448p. 1985. 29.95x (ISBN 0-8476-7455-X). Rowman.

Bereron, Clifton G. & Risbud, Subhas H., eds. Introduction to Phase Equilibria in Ceramic Systems. 1984. 30.00 (ISBN 0-916094-58-8). Am Ceramic.

Beres, Louis R. Apocalypse: Nuclear Catastrophe in World Politics. LC 80-13541. (Illus.). xvi, 316p. 1982. pap. 8.95 (ISBN 0-226-04361-4). U of Chicago Pr.

--Apocalypse: Nuclear Catastrophe in World Politics. LC 80-13541. (Illus.). 1980. 20.00x (ISBN 0-226-04360-6). U of Chicago Pr.

--The Management of World Power: A Theoretical Analysis. (Monograph Series in World Affairs: Vol. 10, 1972-73, Bk. 3). 93p. (Orig.). 1973. 4.95 (ISBN 0-87940-035-8). Monograph Series.

--Mimicking Sisyphus: America's Countervailing Nuclear Strategy. LC 82-48437. 160p. 1982. 20.00x (ISBN 0-669-06137-9); pap. 12.00x (ISBN 0-669-06419-X). Lexington Bks.

--Nuclear Strategy & World Order: The U. S. Imperative. (Working Papers: No.23). 52p. 1982. pap. 2.00 (ISBN 0-911646-12-4, Dist. by Transaction Bks). World Policy.

--People, States, & World Order. LC 80-83099. 237p. 1981. pap. text ed. 11.95 (ISBN 0-87581-267-8). Peacock Pubs.

--Reasons & Realpolitik: U.S. Foreign Policy & World Order. LC 83-49102. 160p. 1984. 20.00x (ISBN 0-669-07756-9); pap. 9.95 (ISBN 0-669-07758-5). Lexington Bks.

--Terrorism & Global Security: The Nuclear Threat. LC 79-16291. (Westview Special Studies in National & International Terrorism). 161p. 1979. 24.50x (ISBN 0-89158-557-5). Westview.

--Transforming World Politics: The National Roots of World Peace. (Monograph Series in World Affairs: Vol. 12, 1974-75 Ser., Bk. 4). 51p. (Orig.). 1975. 5.95 (ISBN 0-87940-044-7). Monograph Series.

Beres, Louis R., ed. Security or Armageddon: Israel's Nuclear Strategy. LC 84-48505. 1985. pap. 12.95x (ISBN 0-669-11131-7). Lexington Bks.

Beresford, Anne. Songs a Thracian Taught Me. 64p. 1981. 8.95 (ISBN 0-7145-2724-6, Dist by Scribner); pap. 4.50 (ISBN 0-7145-2725-4). M Boyars.

Beresford, Brian, ed. & tr. see Geshe, Rabten & Geshe, Dhargyey.

Beresford, D. R., et al. Accounting for Income Taxes: A Review of Alternatives. LC 83-81594. (Research Reports Ser.). (Illus.). 156p. (Orig.). 1983. pap. 6.00 (ISBN 0-910065-18-7). Finan Acct.

Beresford, Dennis R. & Neary, Robert D. SEC Financial Reporting: Annual Reports to Shareholders, Form 10-K, Quarterly Financial Reporting. 2nd ed. 1977. Updates avail. looseleaf 80.00 (625); looseleaf 1984 35.00. Bender.

Beresford, Dennis R., et al. SEC Financial Reporting: Annual Reports to Shareholders, Form 10-K, Quarterly Financial Reporting, 1 vol. 2nd ed. LC 83-195088. (A Business Reports Publication). (Illus.). 1983. 75.00 (ISBN 0-317-01761-6). Bender.

Beresford, Elisabeth. Awkward Magic. (Illus.). 1978. 8.95x (ISBN 0-8464-0164-9). Beekman Pubs.

--Dangerous Magic. (Illus.). 1978. 8.95x (ISBN 0-8464-0312-9). Beekman Pubs.

--Escape to Happiness. (Orig.). 1980. pap. 1.75 (ISBN 0-8439-8007-9, Tiara Bks). Dorchester Pub Co.

--Veronica. (Orig.). 1980. pap. 1.75 (ISBN 0-8439-8004-4, Tiara Bks). Dorchester Pub Co.

Beresford, G. C. Schooldays of Kipling. 1936. Repr. 35.00 (ISBN 0-8274-3335-2). R West.

Beresford, H. Richard. Legal Aspects of Neurologic Practice. LC 75-16362. (Contemporary Neurology Ser.: No. 13). 150p. 1975. text ed. 25.00x (ISBN 0-8036-0730-X). Davis Co.

Beresford, J. D. H. G. Wells. LC 72-2072. (English Literature Ser., No. 33). 1972. Repr. of 1915 ed. lib. bdg. 29.95x (ISBN 0-8383-1467-8). Haskell.

--The Hampdenshire Wonder. LC 74-15952. (Science Fiction Ser). 304p. 1975. Repr. of 1911 ed. 23.50x (ISBN 0-405-06278-8). Ayer Co Pubs.

Beresford, John. Gossip of the Seventeenth & Eighteenth Centuries. facs. ed. LC 68-29191. (Essays Index Reprint Ser). 1968. Repr. of 1924 ed. 17.00 (ISBN 0-8369-0199-1). Ayer Co Pubs.

--Mister Du Quesne, & Other Essays. facs. ed. LC 68-24845. (Essay Index Reprint Ser). 1932. 17.00 (ISBN 0-8369-0200-9). Ayer Co Pubs.

--Mr. Du Quesne & Other Essays. 1932. Repr. 10.00 (ISBN 0-8274-2767-0). R West.

--Storm & Peace. facs. ed. LC 67-28744. (Essay Index Reprint Ser). 1936. 17.00 (ISBN 0-8369-0201-7). Ayer Co Pubs.

Beresford, John, ed. see Woodforde, James.

Beresford, John D. Nineteen Impressions. facsimile ed. LC 71-103492. (Short Story Index Reprint Ser.). 1918. 17.00 (ISBN 0-8369-3234-X). Ayer Co Pubs.

Beresford, M, ed. see Tolstoi, L. N.

Beresford, M. W. Time & Place. (History Ser.: No. 32). 420p. 1985. 40.00 (ISBN 0-907628-39-7). Hambledon Press.

Beresford, M. W. & St. Joseph, J. K. Medieval England: An Aerial Survey. 2nd ed. LC 77-90200. (Cambridge Air Surveys). 1979. 39.50 (ISBN 0-521-21961-2). Cambridge U Pr.

Beresford, Michael. Complete Russian Course for Beginners. 1965. 14.50x (ISBN 0-19-815642-1). Oxford U Pr.

Beresford, Thomas P. A Father's Handbook. (First Pamphlet Ser.). 16p. (Orig.). 1983. pap. 4.00 (ISBN 0-941150-06-2). Barth.

--Front Range. 20p. 1984. pap. 4.00 (ISBN 0-941150-24-0). Barth.

Beresford, Thomas P., jt. auth. see Hall, Richard C.

Beresford, Thomas P., jt. ed. see Hall, Richard C.

Beresford, W. A. Chondroid Bone, Secondary Cartilage & Metaplasia. LC 80-13411. (Illus.). 471p. (Orig.). 1980. text ed. 45.00 (ISBN 0-8067-0261-3). Urban & S.

Beresford-Jones, R. D. A Manual of Anglo-Gallic Gold Coins. 1964. 12.00 (ISBN 0-685-51544-3, Pub by Spink & Son England). S J Durst.

Beresford-Peirse, H. Forests, Food & People. (Freedom from Hunger Campaign Basic Studies: No. 20). 72p. (Orig.). 1968. pap. 4.50 (ISBN 0-685-09384-0, F199, FAO). Unipub.

Bereshnoi, A. S. Silicon & Its Binary Systems. 283p. 1960. 25.00x (ISBN 0-306-10602-7, Consultants). Plenum Pub.

Beresin, Victor E. & Schiesser, Frank J. The Neutral Zone in Complete & Partial Dentures. 2nd ed. LC 78-59658. (Illus.). 1978. text ed. 44.50 (ISBN 0-8016-0617-9). Mosby.

Beresiner, Yasha. British County Maps: A Reference & Price Guide. (Illus.). 295p. 1983. 62.50 (ISBN 0-902028-97-9). Antique Collect.

Berestov, V. My Basket. 18p. (ps-3). 1981. pap. 2.00 (ISBN 0-8285-2014-3, Pub. by Malysh Pubs USSR). Imported Pubns.

Berestyci, H. & Brezis, H. Recent Contributions to Nonlinear Partial Differential Equations. LC 81-700. (Research Notes in Mathematics Ser.: No. 50). 288p. 1981. pap. text ed. 28.95 (ISBN 0-273-08492-5). Pitman Pub MA.

Beretka, J. Survey of Industrial Wastes & By-Products in Australia. 58p. 1978. pap. 6.00 (ISBN 0-643-02260-0, C041, CSIRO). Unipub.

Bereton, C., tr. see Tarde, Gabriel.

Berey, David, ed. Barron's Regents Exams & Answers Earth Science. rev. ed. LC 57-58736. 300p. (gr. 10-12). 1982. pap. text ed. 4.50 (ISBN 0-8120-3165-2). Barron.

Berez, Natalie R. One World under God. 1985. 6.75 (ISBN 0-533-05900-3). Vantage.

Berezanskii, Ju. M. Expansions in Eigenfunctions of Selfadjoint Operators. LC 67-22347. (Translations of Mathematical Monographs: Vol. 17). 1968. 67.00 (ISBN 0-8218-1567-9, MMONO-17). Am Math.

Berezanskii, Ju. M., et al. Nine Papers on Functional Analysis. (Translations Ser.: No. 2, Vol. 93). 1970. 32.00 (ISBN 0-8218-1793-0, TRANS 2-93). Am Math.

--Twelve Papers on Analysis & Applied Mathematics. LC 51-5559. (Translations Ser.: No. 2, Vol. 35). 1964. 30.00 (ISBN 0-8218-1735-3, TRANS 2-35). Am Math.

Berezhkov, Valentin. History in the Making: Memoirs of World War II Diplomacy. Hagen, Dudely & Jones, Barry, trs. 544p. 1984. 11.95 (ISBN 0-8285-9106-7, Pub. by Progress Pubs USSR). Imported Pubns.

Berezhnoi, A. I. Glass-Ceramics & Photo-Sitalls. LC 69-12509. 444p. 1970. 45.00x (ISBN 0-306-30400-7, Plenum Pr). Plenum Pub.

Berezin, B. D. Coordination Compounds of Porphyrins & Phthalocyanine. LC 80-40958. 286p. 1981. 69.95 (ISBN 0-471-27857-2, Pub. by Wiley-Interscience). Wiley.

Berezin, F. A. Method of Second Quantization. (Pure and Applied Physics Ser.: Vol. 24). 1966. 47.50 (ISBN 0-12-089450-5). Acad Pr.

Berezin, F. A., et al. Eight Papers on Differential Equations & Functional Analysis. LC 51-5559. (Translations, Ser.: No. 2, Vol. 56). 1966. 37.00 (ISBN 0-8218-1756-6, TRANS 2-56). Am Math.

Berezin, Martin A. & Cath, Stanley H., eds. Geriatric Psychiatry: Grief, Loss, & Emotional Disorders in the Aging Process. LC 65-25512. 380p. (Orig.). 1967. text ed. 32.50 (ISBN 0-8236-2120-0). Intl Univs Pr.

Berezin, Nancy. After a Loss in Pregnancy: Help for Families Affected by a Miscarriage, a Still Birth, or a Newborn's Death. (Illus.). 224p. (Orig.). 1982. pap. 9.95 (ISBN 0-671-25525-8, Fireside). S&S.

--The Gentle Birth Book: A Practical Guide to LeBoyer Family-Centered Delivery. 1983. pap. 3.95 (ISBN 0-671-49703-0). PB.

Berezina. The Hermitage: Catalogue of Western European Paintings-French Painting, Early & Mid 19th Century, Vol. 11. LC 83-70709. 1983. 200.00 (ISBN 0-384-03971-5); Subscription Price 160.00. Johnson Repr.

Berezkin, V. G. Chemical Methods in Gas Chromatography. (Journal of Chromatography Library: No. 24). 314p. 1983. 81.00 (ISBN 0-444-41951-9, I-383-83). Elsevier.

Berezkin, V. G. & Tatarinskii, V. S. Gas-Chromatographic Analysis of Trace Impurities. LC 78-16035. 288p. 1973. 45.00 (ISBN 0-306-10879-8, Consultants). Plenum Pub.

Berezkin, Viktor G. Analytical Reaction Gas Chromatography. LC 68-21473. (Illus.). 193p. 1968. 29.50x (ISBN 0-306-30338-8, Plenum Pr). Plenum Pub.

Berfenstam, Ragnar & William-Olsson, Inger. Early Child Care in Sweden. (International Monographs on Early Child Care). 166p. 1973. 31.50x (ISBN 0-677-04890-4). Gordon.

Berg. Oblong Sources. (Carl Bach Ser., 1714-1788). 75.00 (ISBN 0-8240-6455-0). Garland Pub.

Berg, Adriane G. Moneythink: Financial Planning Finally Made Easy. LC 82-12384. 256p. 1982. 13.95 (ISBN 0-8298-0497-8). Pilgrim NY.

--Your Kids, Your Money. 180p. 1985. 16.95 (ISBN 0-13-979949-4, Busn); pap. 7.95 (ISBN 0-13-979931-1, Busn). P-H.

Berg, Alan. Malnourished People: A Policy View. 108p. 1981. 5.00 (ISBN 0-686-36129-6, BN-8104). World Bank.

--The Nutrition Factor: Its Role in National Development. 1973. 22.95 (ISBN 0-8157-0914-5); pap. 8.95 (ISBN 0-8157-0913-7). Brookings.

Berg, Albert Van Den see Van Den Berg, Albert.

Berg, Alter G. Buildings & Structures of American Railroads. 1976. lib. bdg. 134.95 (ISBN 0-8490-1561-8). Gordon Pr.

Berg, Annemarie. Great State Seals of the United States. LC 79-52035. (Illus.). (gr. 5 up). 1979. 8.95 (ISBN 0-396-07705-6). Dodd.

Berg, Barbara J. The Remembered Gate: Origins of American Feminism - the Woman & the City, 1800-1860. (Urban Life in America Ser.). (Illus.). 1978. pap. 8.95 (ISBN 0-19-502704-3, GB 595, GB). Oxford U Pr.

Berg, Bob. Fishing Minnesota. LC 85-70955. 272p. (Orig.). 1985. pap. 13.95 (ISBN 0-932861-00-8). Berg Pub Co.

Berg, Bruce O. Child Neurology: A Clinical Manual. LC 84-80920. (Illus.). 316p. 1984. pap. text ed. 16.95 (ISBN 0-930010-05-1). Jones Med.

Berg, C. Circumpolar Problems: Habitat, Economy & Social Relations in the Arctic. 1973. text ed. 54.00 (ISBN 0-08-017038-2). Pergamon.

Berg, C. & Christensen, J. P. Harmonic Analysis on Semigroups: Theory of Positive Definite & Related Functions. (Graduate Texts in Mathematics Ser.: Vol. 100). (Illus.). 335p. 1984. 39.00 (ISBN 0-387-90925-7). Springer-Verlag.

Berg, C. & Forst, G. Potential Theory on Locally Compact Abelian Groups. (Ergebnisse der Mathematik und Ihrer Grenzgebiete Ser.: Vol. 87). 240p. 1975. 37.00 (ISBN 0-387-07249-7). Springer-Verlag.

Berg, C., et al, eds. Potential Theory Copenhagen Nineteen Seventy-Nine: Proceedings. (Lecture Notes in Mathematics: Vol. 787). 319p. 1980. pap. text ed. 23.00 (ISBN 0-387-09967-0). Springer-Verlag.

--Buildings & Structures of American Railroads, Pt. 3. 9th ed. (Train Shed Cyclopedia Ser., No. 19). (Illus.). 1974. pap. 4.50 (ISBN 0-912318-48-1). N K Gregg.

--Buildings & Structures of American Railroads, Pt. 5. (Train Shed Cyclopedia Ser: No. 33). (Illus.). 72p. 1975. pap. 4.95 (ISBN 0-912318-64-3). N K Gregg.

--Buildings & Structures of American Railroads, Pt. 6. (Train Shed Cyclopedia Ser: No. 38). (Illus.). 72p. 1975. pap. 4.95 (ISBN 0-912318-69-4). N K Gregg.

Berg, Walter G., ed. Building & Structures of American Railroads, Pt. 4. (Train Shed Cyclopedia Ser., No. 24). (Illus.). 1974. pap. 4.95 (ISBN 0-912318-54-6). N K Gregg.

Berg, William. Early Virgil. 222p. 1974. 60.00 (ISBN 0-485-11145-4, Pub. by Athlone Pr Ltd). Longwood Pub Group.

Berg, William, tr. see Bertin, Jacques.

Berg, William J., tr. see Bertin, Jacques.

Berg, William J., et al. Saint Oedipus: Psychocritical Approaches to Flaubert's Art. LC 81-17441. 1982. 25.00x (ISBN 0-8014-1383-4). Cornell U Pr.

Berg, William M & Boguslaw, Robert. Communication & Community: An Approach to Social Psychology. (Illus.). 400p. 1985. text ed. 27.95 (ISBN 0-13-153818-7). P-H.

Berg, William M., jt. auth. see Ross, J. Michael.

Bergad, Laird W. Coffee & the Growth of Agrarian Capitalism in Nineteenth-Century Puerto Rico. LC 82-61354. (Illus.). 264p. 1983. 27.50x (ISBN 0-691-07646-4); pap. 14.50 LPE (ISBN 0-691-10139-6). Princeton U Pr.

Bergama, Daniel, ed. Medical Genetics Today: Papers Presented at the Johns Hopkins Hospital, Baltimore, Maryland, June 15 & 16, 1972, Vol. 10. LC 78-78434. (Birth Defects, Original Article Ser.: no. 10). pap. 78.50 (ISBN 0-317-28476-2, 2020736). Bks Demand UMI.

Bergamasco, Bruno, jt. auth. see Bergamini, Ludovico.

Bergamin, Jose. Beltenebros: De la Naturaleza y Figuracion Fronteriza De la Poesia. 4.65 (ISBN 0-8477-3112-X); pap. 3.75 (ISBN 0-8477-3113-8). U of PR Pr.

Bergamini, Ludovico & Bergamasco, Bruno. Cortical Evoked Potentials in Man. Sprague, James M., tr. (Illus.). 128p. 1967. photocopy ed. 17.50x (ISBN 0-398-00138-3). C C Thomas.

Bergan, Bill, ed. Championship Drills for Basketball, Vol. 1: Offensive Drills, 4 bks. 64p. (Orig.). 1980. pap. 19.95 (ISBN 0-317-14603-3). Championship Bks.

--Championship Drills for Football, Vol. 1: Offensive Drills, 4 bks. 64p. 1982. pap. 18.95 (ISBN 0-317-14607-6). Championship Bks.

Bergan, Francis. The History of the New York Court of Appeals, 1847-1932. 368p. 1985. 35.00X (ISBN 0-231-05950-7). Columbia U Pr.

Bergan, Hans R. The Lingore Paper Airplane Folding Manual: Introduction to Functional Origami. (Illus.). 160p. 1981. pap. 9.95 (ISBN 0-9607146-0-X). Lingore Pr.

Bergan, Helen J. Where the Money is: A Fund Raiser's Guide to the Rich. (Illus.). 104p. (Orig.). 1985. pap. price not set (ISBN 0-9615277-0-6). BioGuide Pr.

Bergan, Jacqueline & Schwan, S. Marie. Forgiveness: A Guide for Prayer. (Take & Receive Ser.). 200p. (Orig.). 1985. pap. 6.95 (ISBN 0-88489-169-0). St Mary's.

--Love: A Guide for Prayer. (Take & Receive Ser.). 96p. (Orig.). 1984. pap. 4.95 (ISBN 0-88489-168-2). St Mary's.

Bergan, John J. & Yao, J. S., eds. Venous Problems. (Illus.). 1978. 59.95 (ISBN 0-8151-0686-6). Year Bk Med.

Bergan, John J. & Yao, James, eds. Aneurysms: Diagnosis & Treatment. LC 81-2006. 704p. 1981. 75.00 (ISBN 0-8089-1440-5, 790557). Grune.

Bergan, John J. & Yao, James S., eds. Cerebrovascular Insufficiency. 640p. 1982. 79.00 (ISBN 0-8089-1540-1, 790555). Grune.

--Operative Techniques in Vascular Surgery. 310p. 1980. 73.00 (ISBN 0-8089-1334-4, 790559). Grune.

--Surgery of the Veins. 576p. 1984. 84.00 (ISBN 0-8089-1699-8, 790553). Grune.

Bergan, John R. School Psychology in Contemporary Society: An Introduction. 544p. 1985. 29.95 (ISBN 0-675-20316-3). Merrill.

Bergan, John R., jt. auth. see Henderson, Ronald W.

Bergan, Ronald. Sports in the Movies. (Illus.). 160p. 1982. pap. 10.95 (ISBN 0-86276-017-8). Proteus Pub NY.

Bergan, Ronald & Karney, Robyn. Movie Mastermind: One Thousand Questions to Addle an Addict & Baffle a Buff. (Illus.). 192p. 1984. 18.95 (ISBN 0-07-004866-5); pap. 8.95 (ISBN 0-07-004865-7). McGraw.

Bergan, T., jt. auth. see Norris, J. R.

Bergant, Dianne. Introduction to the Bible. (Bible Commentary Ser.). 72p. 1985. pap. 2.50 (ISBN 0-8146-1369-1). Liturgical Pr.

--Job, Ecclesiastes. (Old Testament Message Ser.: Vol. 18). 1982. 12.95 (ISBN 0-89453-418-1); pap. 9.95 (ISBN 0-89453-252-9). M Glazier.

--What Are They Saying about Wisdom Literature? LC 83-82027. (WATSA Ser.). (Orig.). 1984. pap. 3.95 (ISBN 0-8091-2605-2). Paulist Pr.

Berganza, Carlos E., jt. ed. see Mezzich, Juan E.

Bergau, Nancy, jt. auth. see Soedharno, R.

Bergaud, Jacques. Close-up. (Illus.). 104p. 1985. 29.95 (ISBN 0-932733-00-X). Collectors Editions.

Berge. Graphs. rev. ed. (Mathematical Library: Vol. 6). 1985. 50.00 (ISBN 0-444-87603-0). Elsevier.

Berge, Andre, et al, eds. Entretiens Sur L'art et la Psychanalyse: Decades Du Centre International De Cerisy-la-Salle. (Nouvelle Serie: No. 6). 1968. pap. 18.40x (ISBN 90-2796-017-8). Mouton.

Berge, C. Graphs & Hypergraphs. 2nd rev. ed. LC 72-88288. (Mathematical Library: Vol. 6). (Illus.). 555p. 1976. 74.50 (ISBN 0-7204-0479-7, North-Holland). Elsevier.

Berge, C. & Bresson, D., eds. Combinatorial Mathematics: Proceedings of the International Colloquium on Graph Theory & Combinatorics, Marseille-Luminy, June, 1981. (Mathematics Studies: Vol. 75). 660p. 1983. 96.00 (ISBN 0-444-86512-8, I-419-83, North Holland). Elsevier.

Berge, C. & Chvatal, V., eds. Topics on Perfect Graphics: Annals of Discreet Mathematics, Vol. 21. (Mathematics Studies: No. 88). 350p. 1984. 92.75 (ISBN 0-444-86587-X, North-Holland). Elsevier.

Berge, C., ed. see Hypergraph Seminar, Ohio State University, 1972.

Berge, Carol. Fierce Metronome: The One-Page Novels & Other Short Fiction. 44p. (Orig.). 1981. signed ed. 25.00 (ISBN 0-939290-05-7); pap. 3.00 (ISBN 0-939290-04-9). Window Edns.

--Secrets, Gossip & Slander. 234p. (Orig.). 1984. pap. 9.95 (ISBN 0-918408-20-2). Reed & Cannon.

Berge, Carol, ed. see Crews, Judson.

Berge, Claude. Principles of Combinatorics. (Mathematics in Science & Engineering Ser.: Vol. 72). 1971. 45.00 (ISBN 0-12-089750-4). Acad Pr.

Berge, Dennis E. The Mexican Republic Eighteen Forty-Seven. (Southwestern Studies Ser.: No. 45). 1975. 3.00 (ISBN 0-87404-103-1). Tex Western.

Berge, George W. The Free Pass Bribery System: Showing How the Railroads, Through the Free Pass Bribery System, Procure the Government Away from the People. LC 73-19128. (Politics & People Ser.). (Illus.). 338p. 1974. Repr. of 1905 ed. 23.50x (ISBN 0-405-05853-5). Ayer Co Pubs.

Bergel, D. H., ed. Cardiovascular Fluid Dynamics, Vol. 2. 1973. 67.00 (ISBN 0-12-089902-7). Acad Pr.

Bergelson, David. When All Is Said & Done. Martin, Bernard, tr. from Yiddish. LC 76-25614. xxi, 310p. 1971. 18.95x (ISBN 0-8214-0360-5, 82-82501); pap. 10.00 (ISBN 0-8214-0392-3, 82-82519). Ohio U Pr.

Bergelson, L. D. Lipid Biochemical Preparations. 306p. 1980. 82.75 (ISBN 0-444-80146-4, Biomedical Pr); pap. 39.25 (ISBN 0-444-80261-4). Elsevier.

Bergen, Arthur R. Power Systems Analysis. (Illus.). 480p. 1986. text ed. 42.95 (ISBN 0-13-687864-4). P-H.

Bergen, Berger Von see Von Bergen, Werner.

Bergen, Bernard J., jt. auth. see Arney, William R.

Bergen, C. M. Some Sources of Children's Science Information: An Investigation of Sources of Information & Attitudes Toward Such Sources As Used or Expressed by Children. LC 71-176689. (Columbia University. Teachers College. Contributions to Education: No. 881). Repr. of 1943 ed. 22.50 (ISBN 0-404-55881-X). AMS Pr.

Bergen, Candice. Knock Wood. (Illus.). 304p. 1984. 17.95 (ISBN 0-671-25294-1, Linden Pr). S&S.

--Knock Wood. (General Ser.). 1984. lib. bdg. 17.95 (ISBN 0-8161-3764-1, Large Print Bks); pap. 9.95 (ISBN 0-8161-3776-5). G K Hall.

--Knock Wood. 384p. 1985. pap. 3.95 (ISBN 0-345-32137-5). Ballantine.

Bergen, Edgar. How to Become a Ventriloquist. (Illus.). 125p. (gr. 4 up). 1983. 14.95x (ISBN 0-943224-21-7). Presto Bks.

Bergen, Fanny D., ed. Animal & Plant Lore, Collected from the Oral Tradition of English Speaking Folk. LC 99-4363. (AFS.M.). Repr. of 1899 ed. 19.00 (ISBN 0-527-01059-6). Kraus Repr.

--Current Superstitions, Collected from the Oral Tradition of English Speaking Folk. LC 4-4052. (AFS.M.). Repr. of 1896 ed. 15.00 (ISBN 0-527-01056-1). Kraus Repr.

Bergen, Frank & Papanikolas, Zeese. Looking Far West: The Search of the American West in History, Myth & Literature. (Illus., Orig.). 1978. pap. 5.95 (ISBN 0-452-00758-5, Mer). NAL.

Bergen, George A. Word Paintings from Life. LC 81-50810. 54p. 1982. 5.95 (ISBN 0-533-05014-6). Vantage.

Bergen, H., ed. Lydgate's Fall of Princes, Pt. I. (EETS ES Ser.: Vol. 121). Repr. of 1918 ed. 25.00 (ISBN 0-317-16545-3). Kraus Repr.

--Lydgate's Fall of Princes, Pt. II. (EETS ES Ser.: Vol. 122). Repr. of 1918 ed. 25.00 (ISBN 0-317-16546-1). Kraus Repr.

--Lydgate's Fall of Princes, Pt. III. (EETS ES Ser.: Vol. 123). Repr. of 1919 ed. 25.00 (ISBN 0-317-16547-X). Kraus Repr.

--Lydgate's Fall of Princes, Pt. IV. (EETS ES Ser.: Vol. 124). Repr. of 1919 ed. 36.00 (ISBN 0-317-16548-8). Kraus Repr.

Bergen, Henry, ed. see Lydgate, John.

Bergen, John. All about Upholstering. LC 77-85359. (Illus.). 1978. pap. 10.95 (ISBN 0-8015-0169-5, 01063-320, Hawthorn). Dutton.

Bergen, John J. & Bills, Garland D., eds. Spanish & Portuguese in Social Context. LC 83-9076. 124p. (Orig.). 1983. pap. 9.95 (ISBN 0-87840-087-7). Georgetown U Pr.

Bergen, Ronald. A-Z of Movie Directors. (Illus.). 160p. 1983. 18.95 (ISBN 0-86276-067-4); pap. 12.95 (ISBN 0-86276-066-6). Proteus Pub NY.

Bergen, S. A. Productivity & the R & D Production Interface. 122p. 1983. text ed. 29.90x (ISBN 0-566-00648-0). Gower Pub Co.

Bergen, Stephen F., jt. auth. see Preston, Jack D.

Bergen, T., jt. ed. see Norris, J. R.

Bergen, Werner Von see Von Bergen, Werner.

Bergendahl, G., jt. ed. see Albach, H.

Bergendahl, Goran & Forlag, P. A., eds. International Financial Management. 175p. 1982. pap. 34.00 (ISBN 0-686-41016-5). Kluwer Academic.

Bergendoff, Conrad. Augustana - A Profession of Faith: A History of Augustana College, 1860-1935. LC 76-92170. (Augustana College Library Ser.: No. 33). (Illus.). 220p. 1969. 5.95x (ISBN 0-910182-33-7). Augustana Coll.

--The Augustana Ministerium: A Study of the Careers of the 2504 Pastors of the Augustana Evangelical Lutheran Synod-Church 1850-1962. LC 80-66400. (Augustana Historical Society Ser.: No. 28). 246p. 1980. 15.00 (ISBN 0-910184-28-3). Augustana.

--One Hundred Years of Oratorio at Augustana: A History of the Handel Oratorio Society, 1881-1980. LC 81-52434. (Augustana Historical Society Publication Ser.: No. 29). 54p. 1981. 7.50 (ISBN 0-910184-00-3); pap. 5.00 (ISBN 0-910184-29-1). Augustana.

Bergendoff, Conrad & Van Doren, Mark. Perspective in American Education, & Doctors & Masters. (Augustana College Library Occasional Papers: No. 7). 20p. 1961. pap. 0.50 (ISBN 0-910182-28-0). Augustana Coll.

Bergendoff, Conrad & Lehman, Helmut H., eds. Luther's Works: Church & Ministry II, Vol. 40. LC 55-9893. 1958. 18.95 (ISBN 0-8006-0340-0, 1-340). Fortress.

Bergendoff, Conrad, tr. see Norelius, Eric.

Bergendoff, Conrad J. Olavus Petri & the Ecclesiastical Transformation in Sweden (1521-1552) A Study in the Swedish Reformation. LC 83-45600. Date not set. Repr. of 1928 ed. 32.50 (ISBN 0-404-19868-6). AMS Pr.

Bergendoff, Conrad L. Pastoral Care for Alcoholism: An Introduction. 36p. 1981. pap. 1.95 (ISBN 0-89486-123-9). Hazelden.

Bergendorff, Fred & Smith, Charles H. Broadcast Advertising & Promotion: A Handbook for TV, Radio & Cable. (Communication Arts Bks.). (Illus.). 480p. (Orig.). 1983. pap. 21.95 (ISBN 0-8038-0801-1). Hastings.

Bergener. Thresholds in Aging. 1985. 25.00 (ISBN 0-317-26971-2). Acad Pr.

Bergener, Manfred. Geropsychiatric Diagnostics & Treatment: Multidimensional Approaches. (Psychiatry Ser.: No. 3). 240p. 1983. text ed. 36.00 (ISBN 0-8261-4420-9). Springer Pub.

Bergener, Manfred, et al. Aging in the Eighties & Beyond. 416p. 1983. text ed. 43.00 (ISBN 0-8261-3690-7). Springer Pub.

Bergenfeld, Nathan. The Adult Beginner. (Acorn Basic Lessons for Piano Ser.). 1977. pap. 2.95 (ISBN 0-8256-2686-2). Music Sales.

--The Older Beginner. (Acorn Basic Lessons for Piano Ser.). 1977. pap. 2.95 (ISBN 0-8256-2685-4). Music Sales.

--The Very Young Beginner. (Acorn Basic Lessons for Piano Ser.). 1977. pap. 2.95 (ISBN 0-8256-2683-8). Music Sales.

--The Young Beginner. (Acorn Basic Lessons for Piano Ser.). 1977. pap. 2.95 (ISBN 0-8256-2684-6). Music Sales.

Bergengren, Ralph W. Perfect Gentleman. facs. ed. LC 67-23177. (Essay Index Reprint Ser). 1919. 10.00 (ISBN 0-8369-0202-5). Ayer Co Pubs.

Bergens. Prevert. (Classiques du XXe Siecle). pap. 4.50 (ISBN 0-685-37054-2). French & Eur.

--Raymond Queneau. 24.50 (ISBN 0-685-37074-7). French & Eur.

Bergens, A. & Noakes, D., eds. Prevert Vous Parle. (Fr.). 1968. pap. 16.95 (ISBN 0-13-699231-5). P-H.

Bergentino, Len. Psychotherapy Insight & Style. 289p. 1985. 25.00 (ISBN 0-87668-906-3). Aronson.

Berger. Taming of the Shrew. 1985. lib. bdg. 54.00 (ISBN 0-8240-8892-1). Garland Pub.

Berger & Hollerweger, eds. Celebrating the Easter Vigil. O'Connell, Matthew J., tr. 160p. (Ger.). 1983. pap. 9.95 (ISBN 0-916134-56-3). Pueblo Pub Co.

Berger & Wint, eds. New Concepts for Coating Protection of Steel Structures - STP 841. 135p. 1984. 28.00 (ISBN 0-8031-0236-4, 04-841000-14). ASTM.

Berger, et al. Management for Nurses: A Multidisciplinary Approach. 2nd ed. LC 79-19965. 1980. pap. 15.95 (ISBN 0-8016-4815-7). Mosby.

--A Visit to the Doctor. (Illus.). pap. 2.95 (ISBN 0-448-14001-2, G&D). Putnam Pub Group.

Berger, A., ed. The Big Bang & George Lemaitre. 1984. lib. bdg. 59.00 (ISBN 90-277-1848-2, Pub. by Reidel Holland). Kluwer Academic.

--The Evangelical Hamburger: Essays on Commonplace Aspects of American Culture & Society. 1970. pap. text ed. 11.95x (ISBN 0-686-79906-2). Irvington.

Berger, A. J., jt. auth. see Kear, Janet.

Berger, A. L. & Nicolis, C. New Perspectives in Climate Modelling, Vol. 16. (Developments in Atmospheric Sciences Ser.). 404p. 1984. 57.75 (ISBN 0-444-42295-1, I-093-84). Elsevier.

Berger, A. L., et al, eds. Milankovitch & Climate: Understanding the Response to Astronomical Forcing, 2 vol. set. 1984. lib. bdg. 117.00 2 volume set, not sold separately (Pub. by Reidel Holland). Kluwer Academic.

--Milankovitch & Climate: Understanding the Response to Astronomical Forcing. 1984. lib. bdg. 64.00 (ISBN 90-277-1791-5, Pub. by Reidel Holland). Kluwer Academic.

Berger, Adrienne F. & Colangelo, Cheryl. Positioning the Client with Central Nervous System Deficits: The Wheelchair & Other Adapted Equipment. 2nd, rev ed. (Illus.). 1985. pap. text ed. 29.95 (ISBN 0-911681-02-7). Valhalla Rehab.

Berger, Alain Y. & Burr, Norman. Berger-Burr's Ultralight & Microlight AirCraft of the World. 2nd ed. (Illus.). 320p. 1986. 17.95 (ISBN 0-85429-481-3, Pub. by G T Foulis Ltd). Interbook.

Berger, Alan A. Witness to the Sacred: Mystical Tales of Primitive Hasidism. (Illus.). 1977. pap. text ed. 4.00x (ISBN 0-914914-10-3). New Horizons.

Berger, Alan S. Longitudinal Studies on the Class of 1961: The Graduate Science Students. (Report Ser: No. 107). 1967. 3.00x (ISBN 0-932132-07-3). NORC.

Berger, Alan Y. & Burr, Norman. Berger-Burr's Ultalight & Microlight Aircraft of the World. (Illus.). 285p. 16.95 (ISBN 0-85429-390-6, F390). Haynes Pubns.

Berger, Albert I. The Magic That Works: John W. Campbell & the American Response to Technology. LC 84-373. (Milford Series: Popular Writers of Today: Vol. 46). 96p. (Orig.). 1985. lib. bdg. 13.95x (ISBN 0-89370-175-0); pap. text ed. 5.95x (ISBN 0-89370-275-7). Borgo Pr.

Berger, Alexander & Coopers & Lybrand International Tax Network, eds. International Tax Summaries 1984: A Guide for Planning & Decisions 1-560. LC 84-5237. (Wiley-Ronald Series in Professional Accounting & Business). 992p. 1984. 65.00x (ISBN 0-471-80728-1, Pub. by Ronald Pr.). Wiley.

Berger, Alfred H., ed. Dictionary of Psychology: English-German. LC 76-15645. (Eng. & Ger.). 1977. 14.50 (ISBN 0-8044-0043-1). Ungar.

Berger, Allen & Hartig, Hugo. Reading Materials Handbook: A Guide to Materials & Sources for Secondary & College Reading Improvement. 1969. pap. 3.00 (ISBN 0-911880-01-1). Academia.

Berger, Allen & Peebles, James D., eds. Rates of Comprehension. rev. ed. (Annotated Bibliographies Ser.). 48p. 1976. pap. text ed. 2.50 (ISBN 0-87207-329-7). Intl Reading.

Berger, Allen & Robinson, H. Alan, eds. Secondary School Reading: What Research Reveals for Classroom Practices. 206p. (Orig.). 1982. pap. 10.75 (ISBN 0-8141-4295-8). NCTE.

Berger, Allen, jt. ed. see Lee, Grace.

Berger & Associates Cost Consultants, Inc. Berger Building & Design Cost File, 1982: General Construction Trades, Vol. 1. LC 82-70008. (Illus.). 477p. 1982. pap. 34.50 perfect (ISBN 0-942564-00-6). Building Cost File.

--The Berger Building & Design Cost File, 1983: General Construction Trades, Vol. 1. LC 83-70008. 477p. 1983. pap. 36.75 (ISBN 0-942564-02-2). Building Cost File.

--Berger Building & Design Cost File, 1982: Mechanical-Electrical Trades, Vol. 2. LC 82-70008. (Illus.). 207p. 1982. pap. 24.50 perfect (ISBN 0-942564-01-4). Building Cost File.

--The Berger Building & Design Cost File, 1983: Mechanical, Electrical Trades, Vol. 2. LC 83-70008. 207p. 1983. pap. 26.45 (ISBN 0-942564-04-9). Building Cost File.

--Berger Building & Design Cost File, 1984: Mechanical, Electrical Trades, Vol. 2. 300 ed. LC 84-70008. (Illus.). 1984. pap. 32.50 (ISBN 0-942564-05-7). Building Cost File.

Berger, Andre L., ed. Climatic Variations & Variability: Facts & Theories. xxvi, 771p. 1981. 87.50 (ISBN 90-277-1300-6, Pub. by Reidel Holland). Kluwer Academic.

Berger, Andrew J. Bird Study. LC 72-143678. (Illus.). 1971. pap. 7.95 (ISBN 0-486-22699-9). Dover.

--Hawaiian Birdlife. 2nd & rev. ed. LC 80-26332. (Illus.). 275p. 1981. 29.95 (ISBN 0-8248-0742-1). UH Pr.

Berger, Andrew J., jt. auth. see George, J. C.

Berger, Andrew J., jt. auth. see Van Tyne, Josselyn.

Berger, Arnold E., ed. Orendel: Ein Deutsches Spielmannsgedicht. cxxxiv, 191p. (Ger.). 1974. Repr. of 1888 ed. 33.60x (ISBN 3-11-003399-2). De Gruyter.

Berger, Arthur. Aaron Copland. LC 79-136055. (Illus.). 1971. Repr. of 1953 ed. lib. bdg. 18.25x (ISBN 0-8371-5205-4, BEAC). Greenwood.

--Aaron Copland. (Music Reprint Ser.). 120p. 1985. Repr. of 1953 ed. lib. bdg. 22.50 (ISBN 0-306-76266-8). Da Capo.

--Liberation of the Person. LC 64-13321. 1964. 6.00 (ISBN 0-8022-0103-2). Philos Lib.

Berger, Arthur A. Media Analysis Techniques. (ComTexts: Vol. 10). (Illus.). 160p. 1982. 17.50 (ISBN 0-8039-0613-7); pap. 8.95 (ISBN 0-8039-0614-5). Sage.

--Signs in Contemporary Culture. (Annenberg Communication Ser.). (Illus.). 224p. 1984. text ed. 29.95 (ISBN 0-582-28487-2). Longman.

--Television As an Instrument of Terror. LC 78-55942. 214p. 1979. 6.95 (ISBN 0-87855-708-3). Transaction Bks.

Berger, Arthur A., ed. Film in Society. LC 78-55943. 151p. 1980. 10.95 (ISBN 0-87855-245-6). Transaction Bks.

Berger, Arthur L., jt. auth. see Volz, Marlin M.

Berger, Barbara. Animalia. 1982. 12.95 (ISBN 0-89087-342-9). Celestial Arts.

--Grandfather Twilight. (Illus.). 32p. (ps-3). 1984. 11.95 (ISBN 0-399-20996-4, Philomel). Putnam Pub Group.

Berger, Barbara H. The Donkey's Dream. (Illus.). 32p. (ps up). 1985. 12.95 (ISBN 0-399-21233-7, Philomel). Putnam Pub Group.

Berger, Bennett M. The Survival of a Counterculture: Ideological Work & Everyday Life Among Rural Communards. LC 72-93531. 251p. 1981. 17.95 (ISBN 0-520-02388-9). U of Cal Pr.

--The Survival of a Counterculture: Ideological Work & Everyday Life among Rural Communards. 278p. 1983. pap. 7.95 (ISBN 0-520-04950-0, CAL 579). U of Cal Pr.

Berger, Bill & Anderson, Ken. Modern Petroleum. 2nd ed. 255p. 1981. 39.95x (ISBN 0-87814-172-3). Pennwell Bks.

--Petroleo Moderno. Pena, Gus, tr. from Eng. 284p. (Span.). 1980. 15.95 (ISBN 0-87814-136-7). Pennwell Bks.

Berger, Bill D. & Anderson, Ken E. Plant Operations Training, Vol. 1. 157p. 1979. 39.95x (ISBN 0-87814-109-X). Pennwell Bks.

--Plant Operations Training, Vol. 2. 165p. 1979. 34.95x (ISBN 0-87814-110-3). Pennwell Bks.

--Plant Operations Training, Vol. 3. 162p. 1980. 34.95x (ISBN 0-87814-111-1). Pennwell Bks.

Berger, Bill D. & Anderson, Kenneth E. Modern Petroleum: A Basic Primer of the Industry. 255p. 1981. 33.95 (ISBN 0-318-17611-4, O-3); members 30.50 (ISBN 0-318-17612-2). Petro Mktg Ed Found.

Berger, Bonnie G. Free Weights for Women. pap. 8.95 (ISBN 0-671-49710-3). S&S.

Berger, Brian. Beautiful Iowa. LC 79-28596. (Illus.). 72p. 1980. 12.95 (ISBN 0-89802-107-3); pap. 7.95 (ISBN 0-89802-106-5). Beautiful Am.

--Beautiful Monterey Peninsula & Big Sur. 2nd ed. LC 80-20374. (Illus.). 72p. 1984. 14.95 (ISBN 0-317-07729-5); pap. 7.95 (ISBN 0-317-07730-9). Beautiful Am.

--Beautiful Oklahoma. LC 80-10968. (Illus.). 72p. 1980. 12.95 (ISBN 0-89802-008-5); pap. 6.95 (ISBN 0-89802-007-7). Beautiful Am.

--Beautiful Wyoming. LC 79-25372. (Illus.). 72p. 1985. 12.95 (ISBN 0-89802-094-8); pap. 7.95 (ISBN 0-89802-093-X). Beautiful Am.

Berger, Brian F. Thomas Wolfe: The Final Journey. (Illus.). 1984. 10.00x (ISBN 0-915443-00-7). Willamette River.

Berger, Brigette, ed. Readings in Sociology: A Biographical Approach. LC 73-82233. 1974. pap. text ed. 9.95x (ISBN 0-465-06853-7). Basic.

Berger, Brigitte. Societies in Change. LC 77-126946. 1971. text ed. 12.50x (ISBN 0-465-07941-5). Basic.

Berger, Brigitte & Berger, Peter L. Sociology: a Biographical Approach. 2nd ed. LC 74-26580. 1975. 14.95x (ISBN 0-465-07985-7). Basic.

--War over the Family: Capturing the Middle Ground. LC 82-45237. 264p. 1984. (Anchor Pr); pap. 7.95 (ISBN 0-385-18006-3, Anchor Pr). Doubleday.

Berger, Brigitte & Callahan, Sidney, eds. Child Care & Mediating Structures. 1979. 11.25 (ISBN 0-8447-2162-X); pap. 4.25. Am Enterprise.

Berger, Bruce. Gordon Snidow Portrays the Cowboy Heritage Hangin'on. LC 80-83021. (Illus.). 128p. 1980. 40.00 (ISBN 0-87358-266-7); pap. 18.50 O.P. (ISBN 0-87358-265-9); ltd. ed. O.P. 3500.00 (ISBN 0-87358-267-5). Northland.

Berger, Bruce, jt. auth. see Qoyawayma, Al.

Berger, C., ed. Photon-Photon Collisions. (Lecture Notes in Physics Ser.: Vol. 191). 417p. 1983. pap. 22.00 (ISBN 0-387-12691-0). Springer-Verlag.

Berger, Carl. B-29: The Superfortress. 1976. pap. 2.50 (ISBN 0-345-24994-1). Ballantine.

--Science, God, & Nature in Victorian Canada. 107p. 1983. 15.00x (ISBN 0-8020-2501-3); pap. 6.50 (ISBN 0-8020-6523-6). U of Toronto Pr.

--Sense of Power: Studies in the Ideas of Canadian Imperialism, 1867-1914. LC 79-470040. 1970. pap. 10.95 (ISBN 0-8020-6113-3). U of Toronto Pr.

Berger, Carl, ed. Approaches to Canadian History. LC 23-16213. (Canadian Historical Readings Ser.: No. 1). 1967. pap. 4.50x (ISBN 0-8020-1459-3). U of Toronto Pr.

--Imperial Relations in the Age of Laurier. LC 23-16213. (Canadian Historical Readings Ser.: No. 6). 1969. pap. 4.00x (ISBN 0-8020-1616-2). U of Toronto Pr.

Berger, Charles. Forms of Farewell: The Late Poetry of Wallace Stevens. LC 84-40489. 224p. 1985. text ed. 22.50x (ISBN 0-299-09920-2). U of Wis Pr.

--Image Tibet. LC 73-80938. 25.00 (ISBN 0-686-22380-2). Artisan Pr.

Berger, Charles, jt. ed. see Lehman, David.

Berger, Charles J. How to Raise & Train an Alaskan Malamute. (Orig.). pap. 2.95 (ISBN 0-87666-235-1, DS-1042). TFH Pubns.

Berger, Charles R. & Bradac, James J. Language & Social Knowledge Uncertainty in Interpersonal Relations. 208p. 1982. pap. text ed. 14.95 (ISBN 0-7131-6196-5). E Arnold.

Berger, Charles R., jt. auth. see Roloff, Michael E.

Berger, Curtis J. Land Ownership & Use. 3rd ed. LC 81-86687. (Illus.). xxxiv, 1199p. 1983. 32.00 (ISBN 0-316-09154-5). Little.

Berger, Curtis J., jt. auth. see Axelrod, Allan.

Berger, D., tr. see Mechnikov, et al.

Berger, David. The Legacy of Jewish Migration: Eighteen Eighty-One & Its Impact. (Social Science Monographs, Brooklyn College Studies on Society in Change). 189p. 1983. 26.00x (ISBN 0-88033-026-0). East Eur Quarterly.

--Security for Small Businesses. 193p. 1981. text ed. 22.95 (ISBN 0-409-95037-8). Butterworth.

Berger, David & Wyschogrod, Michael. Jews & Jewish Christianity. 3.95x (ISBN 0-87068-675-5). Ktav.

Berger, David, tr. see Moll, Albert.

Berger, David, tr. see Stern, Bernhard J.

Berger, David L. Industrial Security. LC 79-628. 1979. 21.95 (ISBN 0-913708-32-1); instr's manual avail. Butterworth.

Berger, Dorothea, jt. auth. see Berger, Erich W.

Berger, Dorothy. An Alternative to Gum Surgery: The Keyes Method. 104p. (Orig.). 1985 (ISBN 0-941568-16-4). pap. 5.95 (ISBN 0-941568-05-9). Stratford Pubns.

Berger, E., jt. auth. see Aebi, H.

Berger, Elena L. Labour, Race & Colonial Rule: The Copperbelt from 1924 to Independence. (Oxford Studies in African Affairs). 1974. 35.00x (ISBN 0-19-821690-4). Oxford U Pr.

Berger, Elmer. Memoirs of an Anti-Zionist Jew. 159p. (Orig.). 1978. pap. 5.00x (ISBN 0-911038-87-6, Inst Hist Rev). Noontide.

--Memoirs of an Anti-Zionist Jew. 1981. lib. bdg. 59.95 (ISBN 0-686-73184-0). Revisionist Pr.

--Memoirs of an Anti-Zionist Jew. 159p. 1978. 4.00 (ISBN 0-88728-127-3). Inst Palestine.

--Who Knows Better Must Say So! 113p. 1970. Repr. of 1955 ed. 6.50 (ISBN 0-88728-094-3). Inst Palestine.

Berger, Erich W. & Berger, Dorothea. New German Self-Taught. 396p. (Ger.). 1982. pap. text ed. 4.76i (ISBN 0-06-463615-1, EH 615, EH). B&N NY.

--New German Self-Taught. 1982. pap. 4.76 (ISBN 0-06-463615-1, EH-615). Har-Row.

Berger, Eugenia H. Parents As Partners in Education: The School & Home Working Together. LC 80-39691. (Illus.). 424p. 1981. pap. text ed. 16.95 (ISBN 0-8016-0637-3). Mosby.

Berger, Evelyn & Winters, Bonnie. Social Studies in the Open Classroom: A Practical Guide. LC 72-97667. 108p. 1973. pap. text ed. 5.00x (ISBN 0-8077-2398-3). Tchrs Coll.

Berger, Evelyn M. This One Thing I Do. 1984. 7.50 (ISBN 0-89536-957-5). CSS of Ohio.

--Triangle: The Betrayed Wife. LC 70-170883. 224p. 1971. 18.95 (ISBN 0-911012-13-3). Nelson-Hall.

Berger, Fred R. Freedom of Expression. 224p. 1979. pap. text ed. write for info. (ISBN 0-534-00749-X). Wadsworth Pub.

--Happiness, Justice & Freedom: The Moral & Political Philosophy of John Stuart Mill. LC 83-6502. 1984. lib. bdg. 24.95x (ISBN 0-520-04867-9). U of Cal Pr.

Berger, Fredericka. Nuisance. LC 82-20848. 272p. (gr. 4 up). 1983. 10.50 (ISBN 0-688-01738-X). Morrow.

Berger, G. & Brenner, W., eds. Second Trimester Abortion. 1981. lib. bdg. 50.00 (ISBN 90-247-2487-2, Pub. by Martinus Nijhoff Netherlands). Kluwer Academic.

Berger, Gary S., et al, eds. Second Trimester Abortion: Perspectives After a Decade of Experience. 364p. 1981. text ed. 39.50 (ISBN 0-88416-256-7). PSG Pub Co.

Berger, Gaston. Recherches Sur les Conditions De la Connaissance Essai D'une Theoretique Pure. Natanson, Maurice, ed. LC 78-66755. (Phenomenology Ser.: Vol. 1). 194p. 1979. lib. bdg. 26.00 (ISBN 0-8240-9569-3). Garland Pub.

Berger, Gilda. Addiction: Its Causes, Problems, & Treatment. 144p. (gr. 9-12). 1982. lib. bdg. 9.90 (ISBN 0-531-04427-0). Watts.

--All in the Family: Animal Species Around the World. (Science Is What & Why Bk.). (Illus.). 48p. (gr. 7-10). 1981. PLB 6.99 (ISBN 0-698-30730-5, Coward). Putnam Pub Group.

--Apes in Fact & Fiction. LC 80-14061. (gr. 5 up). 1980. PLB 8.90 (ISBN 0-531-04152-2). Watts.

--Aviation. (First Bks). (Illus.). 96p. (gr. 4up). PLB 8.90 (ISBN 0-531-04645-1). Watts.

--Easter & Other Spring Holidays. (First Bks.). (Illus.). 72p. (gr. 4 up). 1983. PLB 8.90 (ISBN 0-531-04547-1). Watts.

--Kuwait & the Rim of Arabia: Kuwait, Bahrain, Quatar, United Arab Emirates, Yemen, Oman, People's Democratic Republic of Yemen. (First Bks). (Illus.). (gr. 4-6). 1978. PLB 8.90 s&l (ISBN 0-531-02235-8). Watts.

--Mental Illness. (Illus.). 144p. (gr. 9 up). 1981. lib. bdg. 9.90 (ISBN 0-531-04343-6). Watts.

--PMS: An INFOBOOK for Teenage Women, Their Friends & Families. (Illus.). 96p. 1985. pap. 6.95 (ISBN 0-89793-035-5). Hunter Hse.

--PMS: Premenstrual Syndrome. (Impact Bks.). 128p. (gr. 7-12). 1984. lib. bdg. 10.90 (ISBN 0-531-04857-8). Watts.

--PMS: Premenstrual Syndrome. 96p. 1985. Repr. lib. bdg. 19.95x (ISBN 0-89370-574-8). Borgo Pr.

--Religion. (A Reference First Bk.). 96p. (gr. 4 up). 1983. PLB 8.90 (ISBN 0-531-04538-2). Watts.

--Speech & Language Disorders. LC 80-85052. (Impact Bks.). (YA) (gr. 7 up). 1981. PLB 9.90 (ISBN 0-531-04263-4). Watts.

--Women, Work & Wages. (Illus.). 128p. (gr. 7 up). 1985. PLB 10.90 (ISBN 0-531-10074-X). Watts.

Berger, Gilda & Berger, Melvin. Bizarre Crimes. (Illus.). 96p. (gr. 7 up). 1985. 8.79 (ISBN 0-671-49371-X). Messner.

--Bizarre Murders. LC 82-42880. (Illus.). 128p. (gr. 9-12). 1983. PLB 9.79 (ISBN 0-671-45583-4). Messner.

--The Whole World of Hands. (Illus.). (gr. 2-5). 1982. 8.95 (ISBN 0-395-32862-4). HM.

Berger, Gordon M. Parties Out of Power in Japan, 1931-1941. LC 76-3243. (Illus.). 1976. text ed. 45.00x (ISBN 0-691-03106-1). Princeton U Pr.

Berger, Gordon M., ed. & tr. see Munemitsu, Mutsu.

Berger, Gotthard. Monkeys & Apes. LC 84-2846. (Illus.). 240p. 1984. 24.95 (ISBN 0-668-06204-5, 6204). Arco.

Berger, Harold L. Science Fiction & the New Dark Age. LC 76-1054. 1976. pap. 7.95 (ISBN 0-87972-122-7). Bowling Green Univ.

Berger, Helen, jt. auth. see Sefkow, Paula.

Berger, Hilbert J. Time to Negotiate. 1973. pap. 2.95 (ISBN 0-377-43001-3). Friend Pr.

Berger, Iris. Religion & Resistance: East African Kingdoms in the Precolonial Period. (Annales Serie, in-8, Sciences Humaines: No. 105). 177p. 1981. pap. text ed. 15.50x (Pub. by Musee Royal De L'Afrique Centrale Belgium). Humanities.

Berger, J., et al. Status Characteristics & Social Interaction: An Expectation-States Approach. new ed. 1976. 27.50 (ISBN 0-444-99032-1, BST, Pub. by Elsevier). Greenwood.

Berger, J., et al, eds. Mathematical Models in Medicine. (Lecture Notes in Biomathematics: Vol. 11). 1976. pap. 19.00 (ISBN 0-387-07802-9). Springer-Verlag.

Berger, J. Joel, jt. auth. see Baumel, Howard B.

Berger, J L., ed. Directory of College Seminars & Short Courses in Engineering & Management, Vol. 5, No. 1. rev. ed. 104p. 1985. pap. 24.95 (ISBN 0-941568-14-8). Stratford Pubns.

Berger, J. Louis. How Electronic Gadgets Work. (Illus.). 104p. (gr. 8 up). 1985. pap. 7.95 (ISBN 0-941568-15-6). Stratford Pubns.

Berger, James O. & Wolpert, Robert L. The Likelihood Principle. Gupta, Shanti S., ed. LC 84-48467. (IMS Lecture Notes-Monograph: Vol. 6). 206p. 1984. pap. 25.00 (ISBN 0-940600-06-4). Inst Math.

Berger, James O., jt. ed. see Gupta, Shanti S.

Berger, Jason. A New Deal for the World: Eleanor Roosevelt & American Foreign Policy, 1920-1962. 240p. 1981. 20.00x (ISBN 0-930888-07-3). Brooklyn Coll Pr.

Berger, Jason, ed. The Military Draft. (The Reference Shelf Ser.: Vol. 53, No. 4). 175p. 1981. pap. 8.00 (ISBN 0-8242-0656-8). Wilson.

--Saving Social Security. (Reference Shelf Ser.: Vol. 54, No. 4). 158p. pap. text ed. 8.00 (ISBN 0-8242-0668-1). Wilson.

Berger, Jean, ed. see Perti, Giacomo Antonio.

Berger, Joel. Wild Horses of the Great Basin: Social Competiton & Population Size. LC 85-8604. (Wildlife Behavior & Ecology Ser.). (Illus.). 1986. lib. bdg. price not set (ISBN 0-226-04367-3). U of Chicago Pr.

Berger, Joel S., ed. Making Your News Service More Effective. 3rd ed. 227p. 1981. loose leaf bdg. 19.50 (ISBN 0-89964-177-6). Coun Adv & Supp Ed.

--Making Your News Service More Effective. 227p. 1981. 19.50 (ISBN 0-89964-177-6). Coun Adv & Supp Ed.

Berger, Joerg. The Dialect of Holy Island: Anglo-Saxon Language & Literature. (European University Studies: Ser. 14, Vol. 83). 172p. 1980. pap. 18.85 (ISBN 3-261-04784-4). P Lang Pubs.

Berger, John. About Looking. (Illus.). 1980. 10.95 (ISBN 0-394-51124-7); pap. 5.95 (ISBN 0-394-73907-8). Pantheon.

--And Our Faces, My Heart, Brief as Photos. 92p. 1984. 12.45 (ISBN 0-394-53738-6); pap. 5.95 (ISBN 0-394-72427-5). Pantheon.

--Art in Revolution. LC 68-26045. 1969. pap. 5.95 (ISBN 0-394-41562-0). Pantheon.

--Corker's Freedom. 288p. 1981. 12.95 (ISBN 0-906495-08-3); pap. 5.95 (ISBN 0-904613-40-2). Writers & Readers.

--The Foot of Clive. 160p. 1981. 9.95 (ISBN 0-906495-09-1); pap. 4.95 (ISBN 0-904613-88-7). Writers & Readers.

--A Fortunate Man: The Story of a Country Doctor. (Illus.). 176p. (Orig.). 1981. pap. 3.95 (ISBN 0-904613-11-9). Writers & Readers.

--G. 1980. pap. 6.95 (ISBN 0-394-73967-1). Pantheon.

--Nuclear Power-the Unviable Option: A Critical Look at Our Energy Alternatives. LC 76-2181. (Illus.). 1976. pap. 4.95 (ISBN 0-87867-063-7). Ramparts.

--A Painter of Our Time. 192p. 1981. 11.95 (ISBN 0-904613-12-7); pap. 4.95 (ISBN 0-904613-13-5). Writers & Readers.

--Permanent Red: Essays in Seeing. 223p. 1981. 12.95 (ISBN 0-906495-07-5); pap. 5.95 (ISBN 0-904613-92-5). Writers & Readers.

--Pig Earth. 1982. pap. 6.95 (ISBN 0-394-73989-2). Pantheon.

--A Seventh Man. 1981. pap. 6.95 (ISBN 0-906495-90-3). Writers & Readers.

--The Success & Failure of Picasso. (Illus.). 1980. pap. 5.95 (ISBN 0-394-73900-0). Pantheon.

--Ways of Seeing. 1977. pap. 4.95 (ISBN 0-14-021631-6, Pelican). Penguin.

--Ways of Seeing. 13.25 (ISBN 0-317-28760-5). Peter Smith.

Berger, John & Mohr, Jean. Another Way of Telling. LC 81-47186. 300p. 1982. 17.00 (ISBN 0-394-51294-4); pap. 9.95 (ISBN 0-394-73998-1). Pantheon.

--A Fortunate Man. 1982. pap. 6.95 (ISBN 0-394-73999-X). Pantheon.

Berger, John & Tanner, Alain. Jonah Who Will Be Twenty-Five in the Year Two-Thousand. Palmer, Michael, tr. from Fr. (Illus.). 150p. (Orig.). 1983. 20.00 (ISBN 0-913028-97-5); pap. 9.95 (ISBN 0-913028-98-3). North Atlantic.

Berger, John, tr. see Bielski, Nella.

Berger, John J. Nuclear Power: The Unviable Option. 1977. pap. 2.50 (ISBN 0-440-35994-5, LE). Dell.

--Restoring the Earth: How Americans Are Working to Repair Our Damaged Environment. Goerner, Lee, ed. LC 85-40341. 256p. 1985. 16.95 (ISBN 0-394-52372-5). Knopf.

Berger, Jonathan & Sinton, John W. Water, Earth, & Fire: Land Use & Environmental Planning in the New Jersey Pine Barrens. LC 84-47963. (Illus.). 248p. 1985. text ed. 25.00x (ISBN 0-8018-2398-6). Johns Hopkins.

Berger, Josef, pseud. Cape Cod Pilot. (Illus.). 432p. 1985. pap. 9.95 (ISBN 0-930350-72-3). NE U Pr.

Berger, Joseph & Zelditch, Morris, Jr., eds. Status, Rewards & Influence: How Expectations Organize Behavior. LC 84-47979. (Social & Behavioral Science Ser.). 1985. text ed. 42.95x (ISBN 0-87589-611-1). Jossey-Bass.

Berger, Joseph, ed. see Milinaire, Catherine.

Berger, Joseph, et al. Types of Formalization in Small-Group Research. LC 79-27703. (Illus.). x, 159p. 1980. Repr. of 1962 ed. lib. bdg. 22.50x (ISBN 0-313-22328-9, BETF). Greenwood.

Berger, Joseph, et al, eds. Expectation States Theory: A Theoretical Research Program. Conner, Thomas L. & Fisek, M. Hamit. LC 81-40887. 256p. 1982. lib. bdg. 25.00 (ISBN 0-8191-1998-9); pap. text ed. 12.50 (ISBN 0-8191-1999-7). U Pr of Amer.

Berger, Joseph R., jt. auth. see Caprio, Frank S.

Berger, Judith & Landau, Terry. Butterflies & Rainbows. LC 82-71932. (Illus.). 48p. (ps-2). 1982. 9.95 (ISBN 0-943760-00-3). Bande Hse Pub.

Berger, Judith D., jt. auth. see Koehler, Cortus T.

Berger, Juergen, jt. ed. see Bock, Hans-Michael.

Berger, K. Mykologisches Worterbuch. 432p. (Ger. & Eng. & Fr. & Span. & Lat. & Czech. & Pol. & Rus.). 1980. write for info. (M-9435). French & Eur.

--Rainer Maria Rilkes Fruehe Lyrik. pap. 9.00 (ISBN 0-384-03980-4). Johnson Repr.

Berger, Karen & Bostwick, John, III. A Woman's Decision: Breast Care, Treatment & Reconstruction. 352p. 1984. 15.95 (ISBN 0-317-05521-6). Mosby.

--A Woman's Decision: Breast Care, Treatment & Reconstruction. 1985. pap. 9.95 (ISBN 0-345-32485-4). Ballantine.

Berger, Karen & Fields, Willa. Pocket Guide to Health Assessment. (Illus.). 1980. pap. text ed. 16.95 (ISBN 0-8359-5582-6). Reston.

Berger, Karl. Mycological Dictionary. 432p. 1980. 99.00x (ISBN 0-686-44735-2, Pub. by Collets). State Mutual Bk.

--Schiller, Sein Leben, und Seine Werke, Vols. 1 & 2. rev. ed. LC 70-178909. (BCL Ser. I). (Illus.). Repr. of 1911 ed. Set. 125.00 (ISBN 0-404-00790-2). AMS Pr.

Berger, Karol. Theories of Chromatic & Enharmonic Music in Late Sixteenth-Century Italy. Buelow, George, ed. LC 79-24734. (Studies in Musicology: No. 10). 182p. 1980. 39.95 (ISBN 0-8357-1065-3). UMI Res Pr.

Berger, Kathleen S. The Developing Person. (Illus.). 1980. 27.95x (ISBN 0-87901-117-3); study guide 8.95x (ISBN 0-87901-118-1). Worth.

--The Developing Person Through the Life Span. rev. ed. 686p. 1983. text ed. 28.95 (ISBN 0-87901-194-7); study guide 8.95 (ISBN 0-87901-195-5). Worth.

Berger, Kermit C. Sun, Soil, & Survival: An Introduction to Soils. LC 72-3608. (Illus.). 371p. pap. 12.95x (ISBN 0-8061-1388-X). U of Okla Pr.

Berger, Klaus. Die Amen-Worte Jesu: Eine Untersuchung zum Problem der Legitimation in Apokalyptischer Rede. (Beiheft 39 Zur Zeitschrift fuer Die neutestamentliche Wissenschaft Ser.). (Ger). 1970. 20.80x (ISBN 3-11-006445-6). De Gruyter.

Berger, Klaus, ed. see Gericault, Jean L.

Berger, L., ed. Israel Year Book 1980. 35th ed. LC 51-36641. 1977. 20.00x (ISBN 0-8002-3633-5). Intl Pubns Serv.

Berger, L. I. & Prochukhan, V. D. Ternary Diamond-Like Semiconductors. LC 69-17903. 114p. 1969. 30.00x (ISBN 0-306-10833-X, Consultants). Plenum Pub.

Berger, Lawrence, jt. ed. see Ts'ai-Fan Yu.

Berger, Lesly. The Gourmet's Guide to Chocolate. LC 84-42597. (Gourmet's Guide Ser.). (Illus.). 128p. (Orig.). 1984. pap. 6.95 (ISBN 0-688-02501-3, Quill). Morrow.

Berger, Linda. Guide to Dining on the Outer Banks of North Carolina: 1985-86 Edition. (Guide to Dining Ser.). (Illus.). 42p. 1985. pap. 2.95 (ISBN 0-912367-08-3). Storie McOwen.

Berger, Louis S. Introductory Statistics: A New Approach for Behavioral Science Students. LC 79-2484. 407p. 1981. text ed. 37.50 (ISBN 0-8236-2775-6). Intl Univs Pr.

--Psychoanalytic Theory & Clinical Relevance: What Makes a Theory Consequential for Practice. 150p. 1985. text ed. cancelled (ISBN 0-88163-007-1). L Erlbaum Assocs.

Berger, M., et al. Problems in Geometry. (Problem Books in Mathematics). (Illus.). 184p. 1984. 29.80 (ISBN 0-387-90971-0). Springer-Verlag.

Berger, M. S., ed. J. C. Maxwell, the Sesquicentennial Symposium: Nonlinear Extensions of Maxwell's Electromagnetic Theory. 350p. 1984. 55.00 (ISBN 0-444-86707-4, I-549-83, North-Holland). Elsevier.

Berger, Manfred, et al. German Election Panel Study, 1982. 1974. codebk. write for info. (ISBN 0-89138-108-2). ICPSR.

Berger, Marc A. & Sloan, Alan D. A Method of Generalized Characteristics. LC 82-8741. (Memoirs of the American Mathematical Society Ser.: No. 266). 9.00 (ISBN 0-8218-2266-7, MEMO/266). Am Math.

Berger, Margaret, jt. auth. see Weinstein, Jack B.

Berger, Margaret A., jt. auth. see Weinstein, Jack B.

Berger, Margaret A., ed. see Ford Foundation.

Berger, Margaret L. Aline Meyer Liebman: Pioneer Collector & Artist. (Illus.). 148p. 1982. 30.00 (ISBN 0-9605914-0-0). M L Berger.

Berger, Marjorie S., ed. see O'Harrow, Dennis.

Berger, Mark L. The Revolution in the New York Party System: 1840-1860. LC 72-89990. 184p. 1973. 15.50x (ISBN 0-8046-9030-8, Pub. by kennikat). Assoc Faculty Pr.

Berger, Marshall D. Vest Pocket Russian. LC 60-9758. (Illus.). 182p. (Rus.). 1961. pap. 3.45 (ISBN 0-06-464905-9, BN4905, BN). B&N NY.

Berger, Martin. Engels, Armies & Revolution: The Revolutionary Tactics of Classical Marxism. 239p. 1977. 19.50 (ISBN 0-208-01650-3, Archon). Shoe String.

Berger, Max. British Traveller in America, 1836-1860. LC 78-39433. (Columbia University Studies in the Social Sciences: No. 502). Repr. of 1943 ed. 11.50 (ISBN 0-404-51502-9). AMS Pr.

Berger, Melvin. Animal Hospital. LC 72-2418. (Scientists at Work Ser.). (Illus.). 128p. (gr. 2-4). 1973. lib. bdg. 11.89 (ISBN 0-381-99941-6, A04400, JD-J). Har-Row.

--Bright Stars, Red Giants & White Dwarfs. LC 82-23052. (Illus.). 64p. (gr. 5-9). 1983. PLB 6.99 (ISBN 0-399-61209-2, Putnam). Putnam Pub Group.

--Censorship. LC 82-4754. (Impact Ser.). (Illus.). 96p. (gr. 7 up). 1982. PLB 9.90 (ISBN 0-531-04483-1). Watts.

--Comets, Meteors & Asteroids. (Illus.). 64p. (gr. 10 up). 1981. PLB 6.99 (ISBN 0-399-61148-7, Putnam). Putnam Pub Group.

--Computer Talk. LC 83-22120. (Illus.). 96p. (gr. 4 up). 1984. lib. bdg. 9.29 (ISBN 0-671-47342-5). Messner.

--Computers: A Question & Answer Book. LC 85-47530. 160p. (gr. 5 up). 1985. 11.06i (ISBN 0-690-04479-8); PLB 10.89g (ISBN 0-690-04480-1). Crowell Jr Bks.

--Computers in Your Life. LC 80-2452. (Illus.). 128p. (gr. 5 up). 10.53 (ISBN 0-690-04100-4); PLB 10.89 (ISBN 0-690-04101-2). Crowell Jr Bks.

--Computers in Your Life. LC 80-2452. (A Trophy Nonfiction Bk.). (Illus.). 128p. (gr. 5-8). 1984. pap. 3.80i (ISBN 0-06-446001-0, Trophy). HarpJ.

--Computers in Your Life. (Harper Trophy Ser.). (gr. 5 up). pap. 4.95 (ISBN 0-06-446001-0). Har-Row.

--Consumer Protection Labs. LC 75-6686. (Scientists at Work Ser.). (Illus.). (gr. 2-4). 1950. PLB 11.89 (ISBN 0-381-99622-0, JD-J). Har-Row.

--Data Processing. LC 83-6879. (A Computer Awareness First Bk.). (Illus.). 96p. (gr. 5 up). PLB 8.90 (ISBN 0-531-04640-0). Watts.

--Disastrous Floods & Tidal Waves. LC 81-2959. (First Bks.). (Illus.). 72p. (gr. 4 up). 1981. lib. bdg. 8.90 (ISBN 0-531-04326-6). Watts.

--Disastrous Volcanoes. LC 81-2995. (First Bks.). (Illus.). 72p. (gr. 4 up). 1981. lib. bdg. 8.90 (ISBN 0-531-04329-0). Watts.

--Disease Detectives. LC 77-26589. (Scientists at Work Ser.). (Illus.). (gr. 4 up). 1978. o. p. 9.57i (ISBN 0-690-03907-7); PLB 11.89 (ISBN 0-690-03908-5). Crowell Jr Bks.

--Energy. (A Reference First Bk.). (Illus.). 96p. (gr. 4 up). 1983. PLB 8.90 (ISBN 0-531-04536-6). Watts.

--Energy from the Sun. LC 75-33310. (A Let's Read & Find Out Science Bk.). (Illus.). 40p. (gr. k-3). 1976. PLB 11.89 (ISBN 0-690-01056-7). Crowell Jr Bks.

--Enzymes in Action. LC 76-132291. (gr. 7-9). 1971. 11.06i (ISBN 0-690-26735-5). Crowell Jr Bks.

--Exploring the Mind & Brain. LC 82-45582. (Scientists at Work Ser.). (Illus.). 128p. (gr. 5 up). 1983. 11.49i (ISBN 0-690-04251-5); PLB 11.89g (ISBN 0-690-04252-3). Crowell Jr Bks.

--Germs Make Me Sick! LC 84-45334. (A Let's-Read-&-Find-Out Science Bk.). (Illus.). 32p. (ps-3). 1985. 11.06i (ISBN 0-690-04428-3); PLB 11.89g (ISBN 0-690-04429-1). Crowell Jr Bks.

--Guide to Chamber Music. 608p. 1985. 29.95 (ISBN 0-396-08385-4). Dodd.

--Mad Scientists in Fact & Fiction. (gr. 5 up). 1980. PLB 8.90 (ISBN 0-531-04153-0). Watts.

--Medical Center Lab. LC 76-12964. (Scientists at Work Ser.). (Illus.). (gr. 3 up). 1936. PLB 10.89 (ISBN 0-381-99602-6, JD-J). Har-Row.

--Mind Control. LC 82-46004. 128p. (gr. 5 up). 1985. 11.06i (ISBN 0-690-04348-1); PLB 10.89g (ISBN 0-690-04349-X). Crowell Jr Bks.

--The New Earth Book: Our Changing Planet. LC 79-7828. (Illus.). 128p. (gr. 5 up). 1980. 9.57i (ISBN 0-690-00735-3); PLB 10.89 (ISBN 0-690-04074-1). Crowell Jr Bks.

--The Photo Dictionary of Football. (Illus.). 60p. (gr. 3-7). 1980. 9.95 (ISBN 0-416-30131-2, NO. 0148). Methuen Inc.

--The Photo Dictionary of the Orchestra. 64p. (gr. 3-7). 1980. 9.95 (ISBN 0-416-30681-0, NO. 0193). Methuen Inc.

--Planets, Stars & Galaxies. LC 78-16688. (Illus.). (gr. 6-8). 1978. PLB 7.99 (ISBN 0-399-61104-5, Putnam). Putnam Pub Group.

--Police Lab. LC 75-33198. (Illus.). 1976. PLB 11.89 (ISBN 0-381-99620-4, JD-J). Har-Row.

--Quasars, Pulsars & Black Holes in Space. new ed. LC 76-50057. (Illus.). (gr. 3-6). 1977. PLB 6.99 (ISBN 0-399-61051-0). Putnam Pub Group.

--Space Shots, Shuttles & Satellites. LC 83-19279. (Illus.). 80p. (gr. 4-6). 1984. 7.99 (ISBN 0-399-61210-6, Putnam). Putnam Pub Group.

--Space Talk. (Illus.). 96p. (gr. 4-7). PLB 9.29 (ISBN 0-671-54290-7). Messner.

--Sports. (A Reference First Bk.). (Illus.). 96p. (gr. 4 up). 1983. PLB 8.90 (ISBN 0-531-04540-4). Watts.

--Sports Medicine. LC 81-43891. (Scientists at Work Ser.). (Illus.). 128p. (gr. 5 up). 1982. 11.06 (ISBN 0-690-04209-4); PLB 11.89g (ISBN 0-690-04210-8). Crowell Jr Bks.

--Star Gazing, Comet Tracking & Sky Mapping. (Illus.). 64p. (gr. 5 up). 1985. PLB 7.99 (ISBN 0-399-61211-4). Putnam Pub Group.

--The Story of Folk Music. LC 76-18159. (Illus.). (gr. 6 up). 1976. PLB 11.95 (ISBN 0-87599-215-3). S G Phillips.

--The Supernatural: From ESP to UFO's. LC 77-2829. (gr. 6 up). 1977. 10.53i (ISBN 0-354-17625-0, JD-J). Har-Row.

--The Trumpet Book. LC 78-836. (Illus.). (gr. 3-7). 1978. o. p. 11.25 (ISBN 0-688-41832-5); PLB 11.88 (ISBN 0-688-51832-X). Lothrop.

--Why I Cough, Sneeze, Shiver, Hiccup, & Yawn. LC 82-45587. (A Let's-Read-&-Find-Out Science Bk.). (Illus.). 40p. (gr. k-3). 1983. 11.49 (ISBN 0-690-04253-1); PLB 11.89 (ISBN 0-690-04254-X). Crowell Jr Bks.

--Word Processing. (Computer-Awareness First Bks.). (Illus.). 96p. (gr. 5 up). 1984. lib. bdg. 8.90 (ISBN 0-531-04729-6). Watts.

--The World of Dance. LC 78-14498. (Illus.). (gr. 5 up). 1978. 11.95 (ISBN 0-87599-221-8). S G Phillips.

Berger, Melvin & Handelsman, J. B. The Funny Side of Science. LC 71-187944. (Illus.). (gr. 5 up). 1973. 9.57i (ISBN 0-690-32088-4). Crowell Jr Bks.

Berger, Melvin, jt. auth. see Berger, Gilda.

Berger, Meyer. The Eight Million: Journal of a New York Correspondent. (A Morningside Book). (Illus.). 1983. 34.00 (ISBN 0-231-05710-5); pap. 10.00x (ISBN 0-231-05711-3). Columbia U Pr.

--Story of the New York Times: The First Hundred Years, 1851-1951. LC 75-122933. (American Journalists Ser). 1970. Repr. of 1951 ed. 19.00 (ISBN 0-405-01652-2). Ayer Co Pubs.

Berger, Meyer, jt. auth. see Keller, James G.

Berger, Michael. Violence in the Schools: Causes & Remedies. LC 74-19932. (Fastback Ser.: No. 46). (Orig.). 1974. pap. 0.75 (ISBN 0-87367-046-9). Phi Delta Kappa.

Berger, Michael, jt. auth. see Klemperer, Katharina.

Berger, Michael, ed. see Diabetes & Exercise Symposium, Sept., 1980, Olympia, Greece.

Berger, Michael, et al. Practicing Family Therapy in Diverse Settings: New Approches to the Connections Among Families, Therapists, & Treatment Settings. LC 83-49256. (Social & Behavioral Science Ser.). 1984. text ed. 19.95x (ISBN 0-87589-591-3). Jossey-Bass.

--University of California Union Catalog System Design Overview. (Working Paper: No. 5). 1979. 5.00 (ISBN 0-686-87245-2). UCDLA.

Berger, Michael L. The Devil Wagon in God's Country: The Automobile & Social Change in Rural America Eighteen Ninety-three to Nineteen Twenty-nine. (Illus.). 269p. 1979. 19.50 (ISBN 0-208-01704-6, Archon). Shoe String.

Berger, Michail L. An Album of Modern Aircraft Testing. LC 81-7412. (Picture Album Ser.). (Illus.). 96p. (gr. 5 up). 1981. PLB 9.60 (ISBN 0-531-04341-X). Watts.

Berger, Mike. Bittersweet: True Stories of Decisions That Shaped Eternal Paths. LC 80-81505. 124p. 1980. 6.95 (ISBN 0-88290-144-3). Horizon Utah.

--Testimony: Fragile Thread, Eternal Fabric. LC 78-70364. 1978. 6.95 (ISBN 0-88290-100-1). Horizon Utah.

Berger, Mike, jt. auth. see Radke, Barbara.

Berger, Milton M. Working with People Called Patients. LC 76-46483. 1977. pap. 12.50 (ISBN 0-87630-126-X). Brunner-Mazel.

Berger, Milton M., ed. Videotape Techniques in Psychiatric Training & Treatment. 2nd ed. LC 78-1782. 1978. 35.00 (ISBN 0-87630-163-4). Brunner-Mazel.

Berger, Milton M., jt. ed. see Rosenbaum, Max.

Berger, Morris I. The Settlement, the Immigrant & the Public School: A Study of the Influence of the Settlement Movement & the New Migration Upon Public Education, 1890-1924. Cordasco, Francesco, ed. LC 80-841. (American Ethnic Groups Ser.). 1981. lib. bdg. 22.00x (ISBN 0-405-13405-3). Ayer Co Pubs.

Berger, Morroe. Equality by Statute. 1978. Repr. of 1967 ed. lib. bdg. 20.00x (ISBN 0-374-90606-8). Octagon.

--Islam in Egypt Today: Social & Political Aspects of Popular Religion. LC 70-113597. 1970. 34.50 (ISBN 0-521-07834-2). Cambridge U Pr.

--Military Elite & Social Change: Egypt since Napoleon. (Research Monograph: Center for International Studies, Woodrow Wilson School of Public & International Affairs: No. 6). pap. 20.00 (ISBN 0-317-29730-9, 2015725). Bks Demand UMI.

--Real & Imagined Worlds: The Novel & Social Science. 1977. 20.00x (ISBN 0-674-74941-3). Harvard U Pr.

Berger, Morroe, ed. Madam de Stael on Politics, Literature & National Character. 292p. 1983. Repr. of 1964 ed. lib. bdg. 40.00 (ISBN 0-89760-057-6). Telegraph Bks.

Berger, Morroe, ed. & tr. Madame De Stael on Politics, Literature & National Character. 292p. 1981. Repr. of 1964 ed. lib. bdg. 30.00 (ISBN 0-8495-0483-X). Arden Lib.

Berger, Morroe, ed. The New Metropolis in the Arab World. 1973. lib. bdg. 20.00x (ISBN 0-374-90609-2). Octagon.

Berger, Morroe, et al. Freedom & Control in Modern Society. 1964. lib. bdg. 26.00x (ISBN 0-374-90608-4). Octagon.

--Benny Carter: A Life in American Music, 2 vols. LC 82-10634. (Studies in Jazz: No. 1). 877p. 1982. Set. 47.50 (ISBN 0-8108-1580-X). Vol. I, Biography, 456p. Vol. II, Discography, Filmography, & Bibliography, iv, 417p. Scarecrow.

Berger, Nomi. The Best of Friends. 336p. 1984. pap. 3.50 (ISBN 0-441-05488-9, Pub. by Charter Bks). Ace Bks.

--Devotions. 428p. 1983. pap. 3.25 (ISBN 0-441-14517-5). Ace Bks.

--Echoes of Yesterday. LC 80-82848. 384p. 1984. pap. 3.50 (ISBN 0-441-18625-4). Ace Bks.

--Emerald Enchantment. (Interlude Romance Ser.). 208p. (Orig.). 1982. pap. 1.95 (ISBN 0-441-20479-1). Ace Bks.

Berger, P. William Blake: Poet & Mystic. LC 67-31287. (Studies in Blake, No. 3). 1969. Repr. of 1914 ed. lib. bdg. 49.95x (ISBN 0-8383-0778-7). Haskell.

Berger, Pam, jt. ed. see Dyer, Esther.

Berger, Pamela. The Goddess Obscured: Transformation of the Grain Protectress from Goddess to Saint. LC 85-47524. (Illus.). 250p. 1985. 19.95 (ISBN 0-8070-6722-9). Beacon Pr.

Berger, Pamela C. The Insignia of the Notitia Dignitatum: A Contribution to the Study of Late Antique Illustrated Manuscripts. LC 79-57511. (Outstanding Dissertations in Fine Arts Ser.: No. 5). 375p. 1982. lib. bdg. 53.00 (ISBN 0-8240-3927-0). Garland Pub.

Berger, Paul. Seattle Subtext. (Artist Bk.). 52p. 1984. 15.00 (ISBN 0-89822-037-8). Visual Studies.

--Seattle Subtext. LC 83-26047. (Illus.). 52p. (Orig.). 1984. pap. 15.00 (ISBN 0-941104-09-5). Real Comet.

Berger, Paul & Searle, Leroy. Radical Rational-Space Time: Idea Networks in Photography. LC 83-80314. (Illus.). 72p. (Orig.). 1983. pap. 22.50 (ISBN 0-935558-10-1). Henry Art.

Berger, Paul S. & Hester, Stephen L. Special Problems of Multiemployer Plans: No. B333. (Kinds of Qualified Plans). 45p. 1978. pap. 6.00 (ISBN 0-317-31072-0). Am Law Inst.

Berger, Paul S. & Siegel, Mayer. Pensions & Employee Benefits Under the 1982 Tax Act: Coping with the Greatest Changes Since ERISA. LC 82-234929. (Illus.). 1982. write for info. (Law & Business). HarBraceJ.

Berger, Peter & Kellner, Hansfried. Sociology Reinterpreted: An Essay on Method & Vocation. LC 80-2845. 192p. 1981. pap. 3.95 (ISBN 0-385-17420-9, Anchor Pr). Doubleday.

Berger, Peter L. The Heretical Imperative: Contemporary Possibilities of Religious Affirmation. LC 78-20106. 1979. pap. 4.50 (ISBN 0-385-15967-6, Anch). Doubleday.

--Invitation to Sociology: A Humanistic Perspective. LC 63-8758. 1963. pap. 3.95 (ISBN 0-385-06529-9, Anch). Doubleday.

--The Precarious Vision. LC 76-1981. 238p. 1976. Repr. of 1961 ed. lib. bdg. 22.50x (ISBN 0-8371-8657-9, BEPV). Greenwood.

--Pyramids of Sacrifice: Political Ethics & Social Change. 240p. 1976. pap. 4.95 (ISBN 0-385-07101-9, Anch). Doubleday.

--Religion in a Revolutionary Society. (Bicentennial Lecture Ser.). 16p. 1974. pap. 1.00 (ISBN 0-8447-1306-6). Am Enterprise.

--Rumor of Angels. LC 68-27103. pap. 3.95 (ISBN 0-385-06630-9, Anch). Doubleday.

--Sacred Canopy: Elements of a Sociological Theory of Religion. LC 67-19805. 1969. pap. 4.50 (ISBN 0-385-07305-4, Anch). Doubleday.

Berger, Peter L. & Luckmann, Thomas. Social Construction of Reality: A Treatise in the Sociology of Knowledge. LC 66-14925. 1966. pap. 4.95 (ISBN 0-385-05898-5, Anch). Doubleday.

--Social Construction of Reality: A Treatise in the Sociology of Knowledge. LC 66-14925. 1980. Repr. of 1966 ed. 29.50x (ISBN 0-89197-578-0). Irvington.

Berger, Peter L & Neuhaus, Richard. To Empower People: The Role of Mediating Structures in Public Policy. LC 76-58262. 1977. pap. 3.25 (ISBN 0-8447-3236-2). Am Enterprise.

Berger, Peter L., jt. auth. see Berger, Brigitte.

Berger, Peter L., et al. Homeless Mind: Modernization & Consciousness. 1974. pap. 3.95 (ISBN 0-394-71994-8, V-994, Vin). Random.

Berger, Peter W. & Dunahoo, Kermit L. Iowa Legal Forms-Criminal Law. 1983. looseleaf 34.50 (ISBN 0-86678-192-7). Butterworth MN.

Berger, Phil. Deadly Kisses. 208p. 1984. pap. 2.95 (ISBN 0-441-14216-8). Ace Bks.

--The Last Laugh. rev. ed. (Illus.). 416p. 1985. pap. 10.95 (ISBN 0-87910-053-2). Limelight Edns.

--More Championship Teams of the NFL. LC 74-4199. (NFL Punt, Pass & Kick Library). (Illus.). 160p. (gr. 5 up). 1974. PLB 3.69 (ISBN 0-394-92767-2, BYR). Random.

--The State-of-the-Art Robot Catalog: Robots for Fun, Show, Personal & Home Use & Industry. LC 83-20838. (Illus.). 148p. 1984. pap. 12.95 (ISBN 0-396-08361-7). Dodd.

Berger, Philip. Highland Park: American Suburb at Its Best. (Illus.). 96p. 1983. pap. 4.95 (ISBN 0-9604316-1-6, Highland Pk Landmark Pres Comm). Chicago Review.

Berger, Philip A., jt. ed. see Davis, Kenneth L.

Berger, Rainer, jt. auth. see Nicholson, H. B.

Berger, Rainer, ed. Scientific Methods in Medieval Archaeology. LC 75-99771. (UCLA Center for Medieval & Renaissance Studies: No. 4). (Illus.). 1971. 58.50x (ISBN 0-520-01626-2). U of Cal Pr.

Berger, Ralph. Psyclosis: The Circularity of Experience. LC 77-24398. (Biology Ser.). (Illus.). 221p. 1977. text ed. 23.95 (ISBN 0-7167-0018-2). W H Freeman.

Berger, Raoul. Congress vs. the Supreme Court. LC 75-75426. 1969. text ed. 22.50x (ISBN 0-674-16210-2). Harvard U Pr.

--Death Penalties: The Supreme Court's Obstacle Course. 256p. 1982. 18.50 (ISBN 0-674-19426-8). Harvard U Pr.

--Executive Privilege: A Constitutional Myth. LC 73-93837. (Studies in Legal History). 1974. 22.50x (ISBN 0-674-27425-3). Harvard U Pr.

--Government by Judiciary: The Transformation of the Fourteenth Amendment. 1977. 22.50x (ISBN 0-674-35795-7); pap. 9.95 (ISBN 0-674-35796-5). Harvard U Pr.

--Impeachment: The Constitutional Problems. LC 72-75428. (Studies in Legal History). 360p. 1973. 18.50x (ISBN 0-674-44475-2); pap. 7.95x (ISBN 0-674-44476-0). Harvard U Pr.

Berger, Raymond M. Gay & Gray: The Older Homosexual Man. LC 81-24079. 232p. 1982. 14.95 (ISBN 0-252-00950-9). U of Ill Pr.

--Gay & Gray: The Older Homosexual Man. (Illus.). 233p. 1984. pap. 7.95 (ISBN 0-932870-60-0). Alyson Pubns.

Berger, Regina, jt. auth. see Karlin, Muriel.

Berger, Renee A., jt. auth. see Fosler, Scott.

Berger, Renee A., ed. see Committee for Economic Development.

Berger, Richard A. Applied Exercise Physiology. LC 81-2322. (Illus.). 291p. 1982. text ed. 19.75 (ISBN 0-8121-0773-X). Lea & Febiger.

--Introduction to Weight Training. (Illus.). 160p. 1984. pap. text ed. 11.95 (ISBN 0-13-500745-3). P-H.

Berger, Robert. All about Antiquing & Restoring Furniture. 1974. pap. 5.95 (ISBN 0-8015-0138-5, Hawthorn). Dutton.
--Undecidability of the Domino Problem. LC 52-42839. (Memoirs: No. 66). 72p. 1966. pap. 9.00 (ISBN 0-8218-1266-1, MEMO-66). Am Math.
Berger, Robert & Federico, Ronald. Human Behavior: A Social Work Perspective. LC 81-11763. (Illus., Orig.). 1982. pap. text ed. 14.95x (ISBN 0-582-28180-6). Longman.
Berger, Robert, jt. auth. see Hauser, Priscilla.
Berger, Robert A. Songwriting: A Structured Approach. LC 83-70101. (Illus.). 108p. (Orig.). 1983. pap. 8.95 (ISBN 0-911999-00-0). Beer Flat.
Berger, Robert J. Know Your Broomhandle Mausers. (Know Your Gun Ser.). (Illus.). 96p. (Orig.). 1985. pap. 6.95 (ISBN 0-941540-09-X). Blacksmith Corp.
Berger, Robert J., et al. Experiment in a Juvenile Court: A Study of a Program of Volunteers Working with Juvenile Probationers. LC 75-620133. 490p. 1976. pap. 10.50x (ISBN 0-87944-202-6). Inst Soc Res.
Berger, Robert O. Practical Accounting for Lawyers. LC 81-3319. (Modern Accounting Perspectives & Practice Ser.). 357p. 1981. cloth 55.00 (ISBN 0-471-08486-7). Wiley.
Berger, Robert W. In the Garden of the Sun King: Studies on the Park of Versailles under Louis XIV. LC 85-1603. (Illus.). 220p. 1985. 40.00x (ISBN 0-88402-141-6). Dumbarton Oaks.
Berger, Ronald, jt. auth. see Balkan, Sheila.
Berger, S. A. Clinical Manual of Infectious Diseases. 1982. text ed. 19.95 (ISBN 0-201-10093-2, Med-Nurse). Addison-Wesley.
Berger, Sidney E., ed. see Clemens, Samuel L.
Berger, Stu, ed. Photography Magazine Index, 1978-1983. LC 83-63009. 160p. (Orig.). 1984. pap. 7.95x (ISBN 0-914809-00-8). Paragon Pub CA.
--Photography Magazine Index 1984. 112p. 1985. 11.95 (ISBN 0-914809-01-6). Paragon Pub CA.
Berger, Stuart. Divorce Without Victims: Helping Children Through Divorce with a Minimum of Pain & Trauma. 200p. 1983. 12.95 (ISBN 0-395-33115-3). HM.
--The Southampton Diet. 1983. pap. 3.95 (ISBN 0-671-46483-3). PB.
Berger, Stuart M. Dr. Berger's Immune Power Diet. LC 84-25420. 288p. 1985. 14.95 (ISBN 0-453-00483-0). NAL.
Berger, Suzanne. French Political System. (Patterns of Government Ser.). 1974. pap. text ed. 8.00 (ISBN 0-394-31818-8, RanC). Random.
--Peasants Against Politics: Rural Organization in Britanny, 1911-1967. LC 73-174541. (Center for International Affairs Ser). (Illus.). 508p. 1972. 20.00x (ISBN 0-674-65925-2). Harvard U Pr.
Berger, Suzanne & Piore, Michael. Dualism & Discontinuity in Industrial Societies. LC 79-25172. (Illus.). 176p. 1980. 24.95 (ISBN 0-521-23134-5). Cambridge U Pr.
Berger, Suzanne, ed. Organizing Interests in Western Europe: Pluralism, Corporatism & the Transformation of Politics. LC 80-16378. (Cambridge Studies in Modern Political Economies). (Illus.). 464p. 1981. 44.50 (ISBN 0-521-23174-4). Cambridge U Pr.
--Organizing Interests in Western Europe: Pluralism, Corporatism & the Transformation of Politics. LC 80-16378. (Cambridge Studies in Modern Political Economies). (Illus.). 464p. 1983. pap. 15.95 (ISBN 0-521-27062-6). Cambridge U Pr.
--Religion in West European Politics. (Illus.). 200p. 1982. text ed. 29.50x (ISBN 0-7146-3218-X, F Cass Co). Biblio Dist.
Berger, Suzanne E. Legacies. LC 84-70353. 72p. 1984. 12.95 (ISBN 0-914086-48-0); pap. 6.95 (ISBN 0-914086-49-9). Alicejamesbooks.
--These Rooms. Norris, Joan & Peich, Michael, eds. LC 79-83711. 1979. 12.00 (ISBN 0-915778-38-6); pap. 4.25x (ISBN 0-915778-39-4). Penmaen Pr.
Berger, Terry. Being Alone, Being Together. LC 75-20302. (Moods & Emotions Ser.). (Illus.). 32p. (gr. k-3). 1976. Repr. of 1974 ed. PLB 13.31 (ISBN 0-8172-0047-9). Raintree Pubs.
--Ben's ABC Day. LC 81-13754. (Illus.). 32p. (gr. k-3). 1982. o. p. 11.25 (ISBN 0-688-00881-X); PLB 11.88 (ISBN 0-688-00882-8). Lothrop.
--Black Fairy Tales. (Illus.). (gr. 3-7). pap. 3.95 (ISBN 0-689-70402-X, A-37, Aladdin). Atheneum.
--Country Inns: The Rocky Mountains. 96p. 1983. pap. 10.95 (ISBN 0-03-062211-5). HR&W.
--A Friend Can Help. LC 75-19325. (Moods & Emotions). (Illus.). 32p. (gr. k-3). 1975. Repr. of 1974 ed. PLB 13.30 (ISBN 0-8172-0051-7). Raintree Pubs.
--Friends. LC 80-25940. (Illus.). 64p. (gr. 3 up). 1981. 9.29 (ISBN 0-671-42165-4, 158). Messner.
--I Have Feelings. LC 70-147123. (Illus.). 32p. (ps-3). 1971. 10.95 (ISBN 0-87705-021-X). Human Sci Pr.
--I Have Feelings Too. LC 79-15863. 32p. (ps-3). 1979. 10.95 (ISBN 0-87705-441-X). Human Sci Pr.
--Lucky. LC 73-16817. (Lead-off Bks.). 48p. (ps-3). 1976. 6.95 (ISBN 0-87955-110-0) (ISBN 0-87955-710-9). O'Hara.
Berger, Terry & Reid, Robert. Great American Scenic Railroads. (Illus.). 112p. 1985. pap. 12.95 (ISBN 0-525-48174-5). Dutton.
Berger, Terry, ed. Black Fairy Tales. LC 70-75517. (Illus.). (gr. 3-7). 1969. PLB 5.95 (ISBN 0-689-20622-4); pap. 3.50 (ISBN 0-689-70402-X). Atheneum.
Berger, Terry, et al. The Haunted Dollhouse. LC 82-50640. (Illus.). 96p. 1982. 5.95 (ISBN 0-89480-206-2, 476). Workman Pub.
Berger, Thomas. Arthur Rex. 1978. 11.95 (ISBN 0-385-28039-4, Sey Lawr). Delacorte.
--Arthur Rex. 512p. 1979. pap. 5.95 (ISBN 0-385-28005-X, Delta). Dell.
--Arthur Rex. 1985. pap. 4.95 (ISBN 0-440-30362-1, LE). Dell.
--Crazy in Berlin. 448p. 1982. pap. 8.95 (ISBN 0-385-28117-X, Delta). Dell.
--Crazy in Berlin. 448p. 1982. 16.95 (ISBN 0-385-28123-4, Sey Lawr). Delacorte.
--The Feud. 263p. 1983. 14.95 (ISBN 0-385-29221-X, Sey Lawr). Delacorte.
--The Feud. 288p. 1984. pap. 7.95 (ISBN 0-385-29335-6, Delta). Dell.
--Granted Wishes. 30p. 1984. deluxe ed. 50.00 signed (ISBN 0-935716-33-5). Lord John.
--Killing Time. 1981. pap. 7.95 (ISBN 0-385-28531-0, Delta). Dell.
--Little Big Man. 1979. 10.95 (ISBN 0-385-28606-6, Sey Lawr). Delacorte.
--Little Big Man. 448p. 1978. pap. 3.50 (ISBN 0-449-23854-7, Crest). Fawcett.
--Little Big Man. 448p. pap. 4.95 (ISBN 0-440-34976-1, LE). Dell.
--Neighbors. 1980. 9.95 (ISBN 0-385-28745-3, Sey Lawr). Delacorte.
--Neighbors. 288p. (gr. 11 up). 1981. pap. 5.95 (ISBN 0-385-28682-1, Delta). Dell.
--Nowhere. 192p. 1984. 14.95 (ISBN 0-385-29401-8, Sey Lawr). Delacorte.
--Regiment of Women. (Orig.). 1982. pap. 7.95 (ISBN 0-385-28833-6, Delta). Dell.
--Reinhart in Love. 304p. 1982. pap. 7.95 (ISBN 0-385-28830-1, Delta). Dell.
--Reinhart in Love. 304p. 1982. 16.95 (ISBN 0-385-28841-7, Sey Lawr). Delacorte.
--Reinhart's Women. 1981. 13.95 (ISBN 0-385-28857-3, Sey Lawr). Delacorte.
--Reinhart's Women. 1982. pap. 7.95 (ISBN 0-385-28856-5, Delta). Dell.
--Sneaky People. 1983. pap. 7.95 (ISBN 0-385-29205-8, Delta). Dell.
--Village Journey: The Report of the Alaska Native Review Commission. 1985. 16.95 (ISBN 0-8090-9624-2). Hill & Wang.
--Vital Parts. 448p. 1982. pap. 8.95 (ISBN 0-385-29117-5, Delta). Dell.
--Vital Parts. 448p. 1982. 16.95 (ISBN 0-385-29115-9, Sey Lawr). Delacorte.
--Who Is Teddy Villanova? 1978. pap. 3.95 (ISBN 0-385-29149-3, Delta). Dell.
Berger, Thomas L. A Critical Old-Spelling Edition of Thomas Dekker's Blurt Master Constable. (Salzburg Institute for English Literature Jacobean Drama Studies: 83). (Orig.). 1979. pap. text ed. 25.50x (ISBN 0-391-01735-7). Humanities.
Berger, Thomas R. Village Journey: The Report of the Alaska Native Review Commission. (Illus.). 288p. 1985. 16.95 (ISBN 0-8090-9624-2, Pub. by Hill & Wang). FS&G.
Berger, W., jt. auth. see Seibold, E.
Bergere, R., et al, eds. Intermediate Energy Nuclear Physics: Proceedings of the 3rd COurse of the International School of Imtermediate Energy Nuclear Physics, Verona, Italy, July 1981. viii, 440p. 1982. 42.00x (ISBN 9971-950-08-1, Pub. by World Sci Singapore). Taylor & Francis.
Bergeret, et al. Nourrir En Harmonie Avec L'environnement. 1977. 14.40x (ISBN 90-279-7684-8). Mouton.
Bergeret, Annie & Tenaille, Mabel. Tales from China. LC 80-52513. (The World Folktale Library). 96p. PLB 12.68 (ISBN 0-382-06596-4). Silver.
Bergeret, L. F. The Preventive Obstacle, or Conjugal Onanism. De Marmon, P., tr. from Fr. LC 73-20616. (Sex, Marriage & Society Ser.). 192p. 1974. Repr. of 1870 ed. 18.00x (ISBN 0-405-05794-6). Ayer Co Pubs.
Bergerhoff, Siegfried. Studien Zum Englischen Wortschatz der Gegenwart. pap. 10.00 (ISBN 0-384-03985-5). Johnson Repr.
Bergerhoff, Walther. Atlas of Normal Radiographs of the Skull. (Eng, Ger, Fr, Span.). 1961. 99.20 (ISBN 0-387-02637-1). Springer-Verlag.
Berger Hzn, D. Seedlings of Some Tropical Trees & Shrubs Mainly of South East Asia. (Illus.). 416p. 1972. 35.00 (ISBN 90-220-0416-3, PDC 81, PUDOC). Unipub.
Bergerie, Maurine. They Tasted Bayou Water: A Brief History of Iberia Parish. LC 80-66373. (Illus.). 1980. 10.00 (ISBN 0-686-27535-7). M Bergerie.
Bergerol, Jane, jt. auth. see Wolfers, Michael.
Bergeron, Dave. First Responder: Self-Instructional Workbook. (Illus.). 166p. 1982. 8.50 (ISBN 0-89303-227-1). Brady Comm.
Bergeron, David. Pageants & Entertainments of Anthony Munday: A Critical Edition. (The Renaissance Imagination Ser.). 162p. 1985. lib. bdg. 33.00 (ISBN 0-8240-5453-9). Garland Pub.
Bergeron, David & Wilson, Holly. Coaches Guide to Sport Injuries. 1985. pap. text ed. 12.00x (ISBN 0-931250-37-4, BBER0037). Human Kinetics.
Bergeron, David M. English Civic Pageantry, 1558-1642. LC 70-163908. 338p. 1971. lib. bdg. 17.95x (ISBN 0-87249-238-9). U of SC Pr.
--Shakespeare's Romances & the Royal Family. LC 85-689. xiv, 256p. 1985. 25.00x (ISBN 0-7006-0271-2). U Pr of KS.
--Twentieth-Century Criticism of English Masques, Pageants, & Entertainments: 1558-1642. LC 71-90310. (Checklists in the Humanities & Education Ser.). 67p. 1972. 6.00 (ISBN 0-911536-46-9). Trinity U Pr.
Bergeron, David M., ed. Pageantry in the Shakespearean Theater. LC 83-24221. (Illus.). 251p. 1985. 26.00x (ISBN 0-8203-0716-5). U of Ga Pr.
Bergeron, Eugene. How to Clean Sea Shells. rev. ed. LC 72-12754. (Illus.). 1973. pap. 1.00 (ISBN 0-8200-0206-2). Great Outdoors.
Bergeron, G. La Gouverne Politique. 1977. 15.60x (ISBN 90-279-7873-5). Mouton.
Bergeron, J. David. First Responder. 336p. 1981. pap. text ed. 15.95 (ISBN 0-87619-998-8). Brady Comm.
--First Responder. 2nd ed. (Illus.). 416p. 1986. pap. text ed. 16.95 (ISBN 0-89303-610-2). Brady Comm.
Bergeron, Karen. Swifter Far than Summer's Flight. 1984. 6.50 (ISBN 0-8062-2041-4). Carlton.
Bergeron, L. Dictionnaire de la Langue Quebecoise. 574p. (Fr.). 1980. pap. 75.00 (ISBN 0-686-92606-4, M-9360). French & Eur.
Bergeron, Louis. France under Napoleon. Palmer, R. R., tr. from Fr. LC 81-47115. (Illus.). 240p. 1981. 25.00 (ISBN 0-691-05333-2); pap. 8.95 (ISBN 0-691-00789-6). Princeton U Pr.
Bergeron, Louis J. Water Hammer in Hydraulics & Wave Surges in Electricity. pap. 84.30 (ISBN 0-317-10793-3, 2011588). Bks Demand UMI.
Bergeron, Paul H. Antebellum Politics in Tennessee. LC 82-40170. 224p. 1982. 20.00x (ISBN 0-8131-1469-1). U Pr of Ky.
--Paths of the Past: Tennessee, 1770-1970. LC 79-14896. (Tennessee Three Star Books). (Illus.). 1979. lib. bdg. 8.50x (ISBN 0-87049-283-7); pap. 3.50 (ISBN 0-87049-274-8). U of Tenn Pr.
Bergeron, Paul H., jt. ed. see Weaver, Herbert.
Bergeron, Thomas R., et al. Head & Neck Imaging: Excluding the Brain. (Illus.). 1983. 125.00 (ISBN 0-8016-0622-5). Mosby.
Bergeron, Victor J. Trader Vic's Bartender's Guide. rev. ed. LC 72-76212. (Illus.). 360p. 1972. 15.95 (ISBN 0-385-06805-0). Doubleday.
--Trader Vic's Pacific Island Cookbook: With Side Trips to Hong Kong, Southeast Asia, Mexico & Texas. LC 68-10564. (Illus.). 1968. 14.95 (ISBN 0-385-02502-5). Doubleday.
Bergersen, F. J. Root Nodules of Legumes: Structure & Functions. LC 83-185046. (Botanical Research Studies Press). 164p. 1982. 37.95x (ISBN 0-471-10456-6, Pub. by Res Stud Pr). Wiley.
Bergersen, F. J., ed. Methods for Evaluating Biological Nitrogen Fixation. LC 79-41785. 702p. 1980. cloth 139.95x (ISBN 0-471-27759-2, Pub. by Wiley-Interscience). Wiley.
Bergerson, Frederic A. The Army Gets an Air Force: The Tactics of Insurgent Bureaucratic Politics. LC 79-18191. 1980. 21.00x (ISBN 0-8018-2205-X). Johns Hopkins.
Bergerson, Howard W. Palindromes & Anagrams. 192p. (Orig.). 1973. pap. 3.50 (ISBN 0-486-20664-5). Dover.
Bergerson, Michael, ed. see International Congress of Nephrology, 7th, Montreal, June 18-23, 1978.
Bergert, Fritz. Die Von Den Trobadors Genannten Oder Gefeierten Damen. LC 80-2164. Repr. of 1913 ed. 26.50 (ISBN 0-404-19028-6). AMS Pr.
Bergerud, Marly & Gonzalez, Jean. Understanding Word & Information Processing: A Study Guide & Projects Manual. 125p. 1984. pap. 9.95 (ISBN 0-471-80173-9, Pub. by Wiley-Interscience). Wiley.
--Word Information Processing: Concepts of Office Automation. 2nd ed. LC 83-19815. (Word Processing Ser.: 1-388). 528p. 1984. text ed. 26.95. Wiley.
--Word Processing: Concepts & Careers. 3rd ed. LC 83-10242. (Word Processing Ser.: 1-388). 313p. (YA) 1984. 20.95 (ISBN 0-471-87057-9). Wiley.
Bergerud, Mary & Gonzalez, Jean. Word Information Processing Concepts. 387p. 1981. 16.95 (ISBN 0-686-98088-3). Telecom Lib.
Berges, Emily T. The Flying Circus. LC 84-1112. 256p. 1985. 12.95 (ISBN 0-688-02989-2). Morrow.
Berges, Marshall. The Life & Times of Los Angeles: A Newspaper, a Family & a City. LC 83-9243. (Illus.). 304p. 1984. 17.95 (ISBN 0-689-11427-3). Atheneum.
Berges, Ruth. The Collector's Cabinet. LC 77-84560. (Illus.). 1980. 20.00 (ISBN 0-498-02117-3). A S Barnes.
Bergesen, Albert, ed. Crises in the World-System. (Political Economy of the World-System Annuals Ser.: Vol. 6). (Illus.). 311p. 1983. 28.00 (ISBN 0-8039-1936-0); pap. 14.00 (ISBN 0-8039-1937-9). Sage.
--Studies of the Modern World System. LC 80-10871. (Studies in Social Discontinuity). 1980. 32.00 (ISBN 0-12-090550-7). Acad Pr.
Bergeson, Sandra. I Hate to Diet Dictionary. (A Turnbull & Willoughby Bk.). 96p. 4.95. Contemp Bks.
Bergeson, Sandy. I Hate to Diet Dictionary. (Illus., Orig.). 1984. pap. 4.95 (ISBN 0-943084-09-1). Turnbull & Willoughby.
Bergessen, Albert. The Sacred & the Subversive: Political Witch-Hunts as National Rituals. LC 84-61370. (Society for Scientific Study of Religion: Monograph No. 3). 1984. pap. 5.50 (ISBN 0-932566-03-0). Soc Sci Stud Rel.
Bergessen, Helge O., et al, eds. The Recalcitrant Rich: A Comparative Analysis of the Northern Responses to the Demands for a New International Economic Order. 1982. 25.00x (ISBN 0-312-66573-3). St Martin.
Bergethon, Bjornar & Boardman, Eunice. Musical Growth in the Elementary School. 4th ed. LC 78-16311. 1979. pap. text ed. 23.95 (ISBN 0-03-020856-4, HoltC). HR&W.
Bergethon, Bjorner, jt. auth. see Nye, Robert E.
Bergethon, K. Roald & Finger, Ellis. Grammar for Reading German, Form C. rev. ed. 1979. pap. text ed. 15.95 (ISBN 0-395-26085-X); instr's. ans. key 7.50 (ISBN 0-395-26084-1). HM.
Bergevin, Paul & McKinley, John. Participation Training for Adult Education. (Orig.). 1965. pap. 3.95 (ISBN 0-8272-2900-3). CBP.
Bergey, Alice & Obata. World God Made. LC 65-15145. (Arch Bks: Set 2). 1965. pap. 0.99 (ISBN 0-570-06011-7, 59-1114). Concordia.
Bergey, Alyce. Beggar's Greatest Wish. (Arch Bks: No. 6). (gr. 4-6). 1969. pap. 0.99 (ISBN 0-570-06040-0, 59-1155). Concordia.
--Fishermen's Surprise. (Arch Bks: Set 4). 1967. laminated cover 0.99 (ISBN 0-570-06028-1, 59-1139). Concordia.
Bergey, Alyce & Wind, Betty. Boy Who Saved His Family. (Arch Bks: Set 3). 1966. laminated cover 0.99 (ISBN 0-570-06017-6, 59-1126). Concordia.
Bergfeld, J., ed. see Wagner, Richard.
Bergfeld, R. Herder-Lexikon Biologie. 238p. (Ger.). 1975. pap. 24.95 (ISBN 3-451-16453-1, M-7453, Pub. by Herder). French & Eur.
Bergfeld, Rainer. Diccionario Rioduero: Biologia. 2nd ed. 244p. (Span.). 1977. 9.95 (ISBN 84-220-0683-9, S-50169). French & Eur.
Bergfield, Philip B. California Real Estate Law. (Illus.). 480p. 1983. 33.95 (ISBN 0-07-004896-7). McGraw.
--Principles of Real Estate Law. (Illus.). 1979. text ed. 33.95 (ISBN 0-07-004890-8). McGraw.
Bergflexner, Stuart, ed. Oxford American Dictionary. 1982. pap. 4.95 (ISBN 0-380-60772-7, 60772-7). Avon.
Bergflexner, Stuart, et al, eds. The Oxford American Dictionary. 832p. 1982. pap. 6.95 (ISBN 0-380-51052-9, 10071-4). Avon.
Berggren, Don. The Magnificent Metric System: A Magical Guide to the Marvels of Metrics. LC 76-40527. (Illus., Orig.). 1976. pap. 2.95 (ISBN 0-912800-34-8). Woodbridge Pr.
Berggren, Paula S., jt. ed. see Solomon, Barbara H.
Berggren, R. Economic Benefits of Climatological Services. (Technical Note Ser.: No. 145). 43p. 1975. pap. 15.00 (ISBN 92-63-10424-7, W189, WMO). Unipub.
Berggren, Sture. Etudes Sur la Meningite Otogene Purulente Generalisse. Repr. of 1920 ed. 23.00 (ISBN 0-384-03990-1). Johnson Repr.
Berggren, W. A. & Van Couvering, John, eds. Catastrophes & Earth History: The New Uniformitarianism. LC 83-11026. (Series in Paleontology). (Illus.). 456p. 1983. 65.00x (ISBN 0-691-08328-2); pap. 19.50x (ISBN 0-691-08329-0). Princeton U Pr.
Berggren, W. F. & Van Couvering, J. Late Neogene. 1975. 29.50 (ISBN 0-444-41246-8). Elsevier.
Bergh, Albert A. Plays by Greek, Spanish, French, German & English Dramatists, 2 vols. limited ed. 1900. Set. 100.00 (ISBN 0-685-84519-2). Norwood Edns.
Bergh, Albert E., ed. Plays, 2 vols. Date not set. Repr. of 1900 ed. Set. lib. bdg. 85.00 (ISBN 0-89760-424-5). Vol. 1: 449p, Vol. 2: 512p. Telegraph Bks.
Bergh, Arpad A. & Dean, Paul J. Light-Emitting Diodes. (Monographs in Electrical & Electronic Engineering). (Illus.). 1976. text ed. 79.00x (ISBN 0-19-859317-1). Oxford U Pr.
Bergh, Haakon, jt. auth. see Grenzeback, Joe.
Bergh, J. & Lofstrom, J. Interpolation Spaces: An Introduction. 1976. 38.00 (ISBN 0-387-07875-4). Springer-Verlag.
Bergh, Leonard J. Vanden see Vanden Bergh, Leonard J.
Bergh, Peter. Art of Ogden Pleissner. LC 84-47649. 120p. 1984. 45.00 (ISBN 0-87923-530-6); deluxe ed. 150.00 ltd. ed. (ISBN 0-87923-545-4); 500.00x (ISBN 0-87923-546-2). Godine.
Bergh, Ulf. Physiology of Cross-Country Ski Racing. Brady, Michael & Hadler, Marianne, trs. from Swedish. LC 81-84643. (Illus.). 89p. 1981. pap. 9.95x (ISBN 0-931250-28-5, BBER0028). Human Kinetics.
Berghage, Thomas E., jt. auth. see Adolfson, John A.
Berghahn, Marion. German-Jewish Refugees in England: The Ambiguities of Assimilation. LC 83-9802. 270p. 1984. 30.00 (ISBN 0-312-32571-1). St Martin.
Berghahn, V. R. Germany & the Approach of War in 1914. LC 73-86664. (Making of the Twentieth Century Ser). 256p. 1974. pap. text ed. 11.95 (ISBN 0-312-32480-4). St Martin.

--Militarism: The History of an International Debate, 1860-1979. LC 81-48630. 1982. 19.95 (ISBN 0-312-53232-6). St Martin.

--Modern Germany: Society, Economy & Politics in the Twentieth Century. LC 82-4214. (Illus.). 352p. 1983. 34.50 (ISBN 0-521-23185-X); pap. 9.95 (ISBN 0-521-29859-8). Cambridge U Pr.

Berghahn, Volker R. The Americanisation of West German Industry, 1945-1973. 360p. 1986. 29.50 (ISBN 0-907582-55-9, Pub. by Berg Pubs). Longwood Pub Group.

--Militarism: The History of an International Debate, 1861-1979. LC 83-24072. 1984. 8.95 (ISBN 0-521-26905-9). Cambridge U Pr.

Berghahn, Volker R. & Kitchen, Martin, eds. Germany in the Age of Total War. 266p. 1981. 28.50x (ISBN 0-389-20186-3, 06962). B&N Imports.

Berghahn, Volker R., tr. see Born, Karl B.

Berghe, Christian L. Van den see Van den Berghe, Christian L.

Berghe, Christian van den. Dictionnaire des Idees dans L'oeuvre de Simone de Beauvoir. (Collection Dictionnaires Des Idees, Litterature Francaise: No. 1). (Fr.). 1966. 12.80x (ISBN 0-686-20917-6). Mouton.

Berghe, Guido V. Political Rights for European Citizens. 256p. (Orig.). 1982. text ed. 38.00 (ISBN 0-566-00524-7). Gower Pub Co.

Berghe, Guido van den see Berghe, Guido V.

Berghe, Pierre L. Van Den. Caneville: The Social Structure of a South African Town. LC 63-17796. (Illus.). 1964. 18.00x (ISBN 0-8195-3042-5). Wesleyan U Pr.

--Human Family Systems: An Evolutionary View. LC 83-13694. viii, 254p. 1983. Repr. of 1979 ed. lib. bdg. 35.00x (ISBN 0-313-24202-X, VDHU). Greenwood.

Berghe, Pierre L. Van Den see Van Den Berghe, Pierre L.

Berghe, Pierre van Den see Van den Berghe, Pierre.

Berghe, Pierre Van Den see Van Den Berghe, Pierre L.

Berghoef, Gerard & DeKoster, Lester. The Believers Handbook. LC 82-72686. 295p. 1982. 14.95 (ISBN 0-934874-03-4); pap. 8.95 (ISBN 0-934874-05-0). Chr Lib Pr.

--The Deacon's Handbook. 269p. 14.95 (ISBN 0-934874-01-8). Chr Lib Pr.

--The Elders Handbook. LC 79-54143. 303p. 1979. 14.95 (ISBN 0-934874-00-X). Chr Lib Pr.

--God's Yardstick: For the Abundant Life. 180p. 5.95 (ISBN 0-934874-02-6). Chr Lib Pr.

--Liberation Theology: The Church's Future Shock. 197p. 1984. 14.95 (ISBN 0-934874-07-7). Chr Lib Pr.

Bergholtz, Richard C. Los Angeles Times Drawn & Quartered: The Best Political Cartoons of Paul Conrad. (Illus.). 176p. 1985. 24.95 (ISBN 0-8109-1291-0). Abrams.

Bergholtz, Richard C., ed. Drawn & Quartered: The Best Political Cartoons of Paul Conrad. (Illus.). 176p. 1985. 24.95 (ISBN 0-8109-1291-0). Abrams.

Berghorn, Forrest J., et al. Dynamics of Aging: Original Essays on the Process & Experience of Growing Old. 542p. 1980. pap. 14.50x (ISBN 0-89158-782-9). Westview.

--The Urban Elderly: A Study of Life Satisfaction. LC 77-84407. 256p. 1978. text ed. 18.50x (ISBN 0-916672-98-0). Allanheld.

Bergiel, Blaise J., jt. auth. see Walters, C. Glenn.

Bergier, Francois, ed. see Third International Conference of Economic History, Munich, 1965.

Bergier, Jacques, jt. auth. see Pauwels, Louis.

Bergier, N. S. Dictionnaire de Theologique Dogmatique, Liturgique, Canonique et Disciplinaire, 3 vols. in 4. Migne, J. P., ed. (Encyclopedie Theologique Ser.: Vols. 33-35). 2681p. (Fr.). Repr. of 1851 ed. lib. bdg. 341.00x (ISBN 0-89241-243-7). Caratzas.

Bergin, Allen E., jt. auth. see Garfield, Sol L.

Bergin, Edward J. A Star to Steer Her By: A Self-Teaching Guide to Offshore Navigation. LC 83-71313. 216p. 1983. pap. 16.50 (ISBN 0-87033-309-7). Cornell Maritime.

Bergin, Edward J. & Grandon, Ronald E. The American Survival Guide: How to Survive in Your Toxic Environment. (Illus.). 512p. 1984. pap. 11.95 (ISBN 0-380-87460-1, 87460-1). Avon.

Bergin, James J. & Holmes, Geraldine C. Continuing Medical Education in the Community Hospital. LC 79-55326. (Illus.). 112p. 1979. text ed. 22.00x (ISBN 0-935466-00-2); pap. text ed. 16.00x (ISBN 0-935466-01-0). Pierson Pubs.

Bergin, Joseph. Cardinal Richelieu: Power & the Pursuit of Wealth. 352p. 1985. 30.00x (ISBN 0-300-03495-4). Yale U Pr.

Bergin, Thomas F. & Haskell, Paul G. Preface to Estates in Land & Future Interests. 2nd ed. LC 84-13695. (University Textbook Ser.). 259p. 1984. text ed. 13.50 (ISBN 0-88277-184-1). Foundation Pr.

Bergin, Thomas G. Anthology of the Provencal Troubadours, 2 vols. LC 72-91287. (Yale Romanic Studies, Second Ser.: No. 23). (Illus.). Vol. 1. pap. 75.00 (ISBN 0-8357-9077-0, 2016802); Vol. 2. pap. 62.80. Bks Demand UMI.

--Dante. LC 76-10974. (Illus.). 326p. 1976. Repr. of 1965 ed. lib. bdg. 35.00x (ISBN 0-8371-7973-4, BEDA). Greenwood.

--The Game: The Harvard-Yale Football Rivalry, 1875-1983. Cloney, Will, frwd. by. LC 84-40189. (Illus.). 336p. 1984. 19.95x (ISBN 0-300-03267-6). Yale U Pr.

--Giovanni Verga. 1931. 13.50x (ISBN 0-686-83557-3). Elliots Bks.

--Under Scorpio. LC 82-19377. 56p. 1983. pap. 4.95 (ISBN 0-933760-02-7). Solaris Pr.

Bergin, Thomas G., jt. auth. see Smith, Nathaniel E.

Bergin, Thomas G., ed. & tr. see Dante Alighieri.

Bergin, Thomas G., ed. & tr. see Machiavelli, Niccolo.

Bergin, Thomas G., ed. see Petrarch.

Bergin, Thomas G., rev. by see Wilkins, Ernest H.

Bergin, Thomas G., tr. see Vico, Giambattista.

Bergin, Victoria. Special Education Needs in Bilingual Programs. 52p. (Orig.). 1980. pap. 4.50 (ISBN 0-89763-026-2). Natl Clearinghse Bilingual Ed.

Bergk, Theodorus, ed. see Aristophanes.

Bergland, Glen D. & Gordon, Ronald D. Software Design Strategies. 2nd ed. (Tutorial Texts Ser.). 479p. 1981. 30.00 (ISBN 0-8186-0389-5, Q389). IEEE Comp Soc.

Berglas, Charlotte. Midlife Crisis. LC 82-74317. 109p. 1983. 15.00 (ISBN 0-87762-322-8). Technomic.

Bergle, Rainer, jt. ed. see Libby, Leona M.

Bergler, Edmund. The Basic Neurosis: Oral Regression & Psychic Masochism. rev ed. 371p. 1978. 20.50 (ISBN 0-8089-0054-4, 790564). Grune.

--Counterfeit Sex. 2nd rev. ed. LC 57-10688. 398p. 1958. 54.00 (ISBN 0-8089-0055-2, 790560). Grune.

--Curable & Incurable Neurotics. LC 61-10464. cloth 1961 o.p. 8.95x (ISBN 0-87140-978-X, 1961); pap. 3.95 paper 1972 (ISBN 0-87140-266-1, 1972). Liveright.

--Divorce Won't Help. 1979. 12.95 (ISBN 0-87140-635-7); pap. 5.95 (ISBN 0-87140-124-X). Liveright.

--Money & Emotional Conflicts. LC 84-22390. xiii, 269p. 1985. text ed. 27.50 (ISBN 0-317-17977-2, 03445). Intl Univs Pr.

--Psychology of Gambling. 254p. 1970. text ed. 25.00 (ISBN 0-8236-5570-9); pap. text ed. 9.95 (ISBN 0-8236-8255-2, 025570). Intl Univs Pr.

--The Revolt of the Middle-Aged Man. LC 84-22396. xxi, 312p. 1985. text ed. 28.50 (ISBN 0-8236-5830-9, 05830). Intl Univs Pr.

--Tensions Can Be Reduced to Nuisances. 1979. 12.95 (ISBN 0-87140-976-3); pap. 3.95 (ISBN 0-87140-123-1). Liveright.

Bergler, Reinhold. Advertising & Cigarette Smoking: A Psychological Study. (Illus.). 188p. (Orig.). 1981. pap. text ed. 14.00 (ISBN 3-456-81018-0, Pub. by Hans Huber Switzerland). J K Burgess.

Bergles, A. E. & Ishigai, S. Two Phase Flow Dynamics & Reactor Safety. 1981. 110.00 (ISBN 0-07-004904-1). McGraw.

Bergles, A. E., jt. auth. see Veziroglu, T. N.

Bergles, A. E. & Webb, R. L., eds. Augmentation of Convective Heat & Mass Transfer. LC 75-143215. pap. 42.00 (ISBN 0-317-10889-1, 2015856). Bks Demand UMI.

Bergles, A. E., et al. Two-Phase Flow & Heat Transfer in the Power & Process Industries. (Illus.). 695p. 1981. 69.50 (ISBN 0-07-004902-5). McGraw.

Bergles, Arthur E. & Ishigai, Seiken, eds. Two-Phase Flow Dynamics & Reactor Safety: The Japan-U. S. Seminar 1979. LC 81-4295. (Illus.). 554p. 1981. text ed. 87.50 (ISBN 0-89116-198-8). Hemisphere Pub.

Bergles, Arthur E., et al. Two-Phase Flow & Heat Transfer in the Power & Process Industries. LC 80-22025. (Illus.). 707p. 1980. text ed. 69.50 (ISBN 0-89116-197-X). Hemisphere Pub.

Bergling, J. M. Art Alphabets & Lettering. 9th ed. Bergling, V. C., ed. LC 67-29582. 1967. 19.95 (ISBN 0-910222-01-0). Gem City Coll.

--Art Monograms & Lettering. 20th ed. Bergling, V. C., ed. LC 63-22577. 1964. 19.95 (ISBN 0-910222-02-9). Gem City Coll.

Bergling, John M. Heraldic Designs & Engravings Manual. rev. ed. Bergling, V. C., ed. LC 66-25383. (Illus.). 1966. 19.95 (ISBN 0-910222-04-5). Gem City Coll.

--Ornamental Designs & Illustrations. 4th ed. Bergling, V. C., ed. LC 63-22578. 1964. 19.95 (ISBN 0-910222-05-3). Gem City Coll.

Bergling, V. C., ed. see Bergling, J. M.

Bergling, V. C., ed. see Bergling, John M.

Berglund, Abraham. United States Steel Corporation: A Study of the Growth & Influence of Combination in the Iron & Steel Industry. LC 72-76677. (Columbia University Studies in the Social Sciences Ser.: No. 73). 1968. Repr. of 1907 ed. 16.50 (ISBN 0-404-51073-6). AMS Pr.

Berglund, Abraham & Wright, Phillip G. Tariff on Iron & Steel. (Brookings Institution Reprint Ser). Repr. of 1929 ed. lib. bdg. 34.50x (ISBN 0-697-00151-2). Irvington.

Berglund, Anders R. & Zakharov, Vasilii V. The Novgorod Mint During the Swedish Occupation 1611-1617. (Illus.). v, 56p. (Orig.). 1983. pap. 13.00 (ISBN 0-912671-03-3). Russian Numis.

Berglund, Axel-Ivar. Zulu Thought-Patterns & Symbolism. (Illus.). 402p. 1976. pap. text ed. 30.50x (ISBN 0-8419-5751-7). Holmes & Meier.

Berglund, B. Handbook of Holocene Palaeoecology & Palaeohydrology. 1985. 90.00 (ISBN 0-471-90691-3). Wiley.

Berglund, Berndt & Bolsby, Clare E. The Complete Outdoorsman's Guide to Edible Wild Plants. LC 77-82243. (Illus.). 1978. pap. 4.95 (ISBN 0-684-15481-1). Scribner.

Berglund, Gosta W. Mental Growth: A Study of Changes in Test Ability Between the Ages of Nine & Sixteen Years. (Studia Scientiae Paedagogicae Upsaliensia: No. 6). 1965. pap. 39.50x (ISBN 0-317-27518-6). Elliots Bks.

Berglund, J. F. & Hoffmann, K. H. Compact Semitopological Semigroups & Weakly Almost Periodic Functions. (Lecture Notes in Mathematics: Vol. 42). (Orig.). 1967. pap. 10.70 (ISBN 0-387-03913-9). Springer-Verlag.

Berglund, J. F., et al. A Compact Right Topological Semigroups & Generalizations of Almost Periodicity. (Lecture Notes in Mathematics: Vol. 663). (Illus.). 1978. pap. 17.00 (ISBN 0-387-08919-5). Springer-Verlag.

Berglund, Robert. A Philosophy of Church Music. (Orig.). 1985. pap. 7.95 (ISBN 0-8024-0279-8). Moody.

Berglund, S., et al, eds. Utilisation of Sewage Sludge on Land: Rates of Application & Long-Term Effects of Metals. 1984. lib. bdg. 39.00 (ISBN 90-277-1701-X, Pub. by Reidel Holland). Kluwer Academic.

Bergman & Gittins. Statistical Methods for Planning Pharmaceutical Research. (Statistics-Textbook & Monographs Ser.). 280p. 1985. write for info. (ISBN 0-8247-7146-X). Dekker.

Bergman, Abby, jt. auth. see Jacobson, Willard.

Bergman, Abraham & Choate, Judith. Why Did My Baby Die: The Phenomenon of Sudden Infant Death Syndrome & How to Cope with It. LC 73-92794. 1975. 9.95 (ISBN 0-89388-146-5). Okpaku Communications.

Bergman, Amdrew. The Big Kiss-Off of Nineteen Eighty-Four. LC 83-47579. 224p. 1983. pap. 2.84i (ISBN 0-06-080673-7, P673, PL). Har-Row.

Bergman, Andrew. Hollywood & Levine. LC 83-47580. 224p. 1983. pap. 2.84i (ISBN 0-06-080674-5, P674, PL). Har-Row.

--We're in the Money. 1975. pap. 4.95xi (ISBN 0-06-131948-1, TB1948, Torch). Har-Row.

--We're in the Money: Depression America & Its Films. LC 74-159533. (Illus.). 1971. cusa 20.00x (ISBN 0-8147-0964-8). NYU Pr.

Bergman, Bella. Hebrew Level Two. Band, Ora, ed. (Illus.). 243p. 1983. pap. text ed. 7.95x (ISBN 0-87441-360-5). Behrman.

Bergman, Billy. Goodtime Kings: Emerging African Pop. (Illus.). 144p. (Orig.). 1985. pap. 7.95 (ISBN 0-688-02192-1, Quill). Morrow.

Bergman, Billy & Horn, Richard. Recombinant Do Re Mi: Frontiers of the Rock Era. LC 84-61406. 1985. pap. 7.95 (ISBN 0-688-02395-9, Quill). Morrow.

Bergman, Billy, et al. Hot Sauces: Latin & Caribbean Pop. LC 84-61407. (Illus.). 144p. 1985. pap. 7.70 (ISBN 0-688-02193-X, Quill). Morrow.

Bergman, David & Epstein, Daniel M. The Heath Guide to Literature. 1539p. text ed. 17.95 (ISBN 0-669-04637-X); cassette tapes gratis upon adoption avail. Heath.

Bergman, David, jt. auth. see Pantell, Robert.

Bergman, David, jt. auth. see Plante, Patricia.

Bergman, David F., et al. Retrograde Condensation in Natural Gas Pipelines. 512p. 1975. 12.00 (ISBN 0-318-12698-2, L22277). Am Gas Assn.

Bergman, Denise, jt. auth. see Williams, Lorna.

Bergman, E., jt. ed. see Pullman, B.

Bergman, E. D. & Pullman, Bernard, eds. Conformation of Biological Molecules & Polymers. 1973. 90.00 (ISBN 0-12-091065-9). Acad Pr.

Bergman, Edward F. & Pohl, Thomas W. A Geography of the New York Metropolitan Region. LC 75-20816. (Illus.). 1975. perfect bdg. 7.95 (ISBN 0-8403-1263-6). Kendall Hunt.

Bergman, Elihu, jt. ed. see Silber, Bettina.

Bergman, Elsie O., jt. auth. see Thorndike, Eard L.

Bergman, Eugene, jt. auth. see Bragg, Bernard.

Bergman, Eugene, jt. ed. see Batson, Trenton W.

Bergman, Floyd. Manuscript Diagnosis: The Text Ray. pap. 3.90 (ISBN 0-87506-053-6). Campus.

--Occupation: English Teacher. 1969. looseleaf 6.45 (ISBN 0-87506-040-4). Campus.

--Occupation: English Teacher. 138p. 1969. looseleaf 6.45 (ISBN 0-87506-040-4). Campus.

--Reading: Who? What? When? Where? Why? How? 314p. 1969. looseleaf 7.90 (ISBN 0-87506-041-2). Campus.

--Text Ray. pap. 3.90 (ISBN 0-317-20153-0). Campus.

Bergman, Floyd L. The English Teacher's Activities Handbook: An Ideabook for Middle & Secondary Schools. 2nd ed. 350p. 1982. pap. 26.95x (ISBN 0-205-07383-2, 237383, Pub. by Longwood Div). Allyn.

Bergman, Floyd L. & Bergman, Virginia. A Guidebook for Teaching Grammar. 368p. 1985. pap. 32.50 (ISBN 0-205-08360-9, 23860). Allyn.

Bergman, Goran. Why Does Your Dog Do That. LC 73-165560. (Illus.). 160p. 1985. 11.95 (ISBN 0-87605-808-X). Howell Bk.

Bergman, H., ed. Ureter. (Illus.). 780p. 1981. 88.00 (ISBN 0-387-90561-8). Springer-Verlag.

Bergman, Harold L., et al, eds. Environmental Hazard Assessment of Effluents. (SETAC Special Publications Ser.). (Illus.). 390p. 1985. 40.00 (ISBN 0-08-030165-7). Pergamon.

Bergman, Hjalmar. Four Plays. Johnson, Walter, ed. Pearson, Henry, tr. from Swed. LC 68-11037. 1968. 8.95x (ISBN 0-89067-047-1). Am Scandinavian.

--Four Plays: Markurells of Wadkoping, the Baron's Will, Swedenhielms, Mr. Sleeman Is Coming. Johnson, Walter, ed. LC 68-11037. (American-Scandinavian Foundation Scandinavian Studies). (Illus.). 310p. 1968. 20.00x (ISBN 0-295-97884-8). U of Wash Pr.

Bergman, Ingmar. Four Screenplays of Ingmar Bergman. LC 82-49277. (Cinema Classics Ser.). 381p. 1985. lib. bdg. 50.00 (ISBN 0-8240-5752-X). Garland Pub.

--Persona & Shame: Two Screenplays. Blair, Alan, tr. from Swedish. (Cinema Ser.). (Illus.). 192p. 1984. pap. 6.95 (ISBN 0-7145-0757-1, Dist. by Scribner). M Boyars.

--A Project for the Theatre. Marker, Frederick J. & Marker, Lise-Lone, eds. LC 82-40258. (Ungar Film Library). (Illus.). 224p. 1983. 15.95 (ISBN 0-8044-2050-5). Ungar.

--The Seventh Seal. (Lorrimer Classic Screenplay Ser.). (Illus.). pap. 6.95 (ISBN 0-8044-6038-8). Ungar.

--Wild Strawberries. (Lorrimer Classic Screenplay Ser.). (Illus.). o. s. i. 10.95 (ISBN 0-8044-2049-1); pap. 6.95 (ISBN 0-8044-6039-6). Ungar.

Bergman, Ingrid & Burgess, Alan. Ingrid Bergman: My Story. 1981. pap. 3.95 (ISBN 0-440-14086-2). Dell.

Bergman, Jay. Vera Zasulich: A Biography. LC 82-80927. 280p. 1983. 28.50x (ISBN 0-8047-1156-9). Stanford U Pr.

Bergman, Jerry. Jehovah's Witness & Kindred Groups: An Historical Compendium & Bibliography. LC 83-47603. (Social Science Ser.). 414p. 1985. lib. bdg. 53.00 (ISBN 0-8240-9109-4). Garland Pub.

--Teaching About the Creation-Evolution Controversy. LC 79-66529. (Fastback Ser.: No. 134). (Orig.). 1979. pap. 0.75 (ISBN 0-87367-134-1). Phi Delta Kappa.

--Understanding Educational Measurement & Evaluation. 1981. 26.50 (ISBN 0-395-30782-1). HM.

Bergman, Joel S. Fishing for Barracuda: Pragmatics of Brief Systemic Therapy. 1985. 18.50 (ISBN 0-393-70005-4). Norton.

Bergman, Jules. Anyone Can Fly. rev. ed. LC 73-9141. 1977. 19.95 (ISBN 0-385-02830-X). Doubleday.

Bergman, M., ed. Subsurface Space--Environment Protection, Low Cost Storage, Energy Savings: Proceedings of the International Symposium, Stockholm, Sweden, June 23-27, 1980, 3 vols. (Illus.). 1500p. 1981. 275.00 (ISBN 0-08-026136-1). Pergamon.

Bergman, Mary. Survival Family. new ed. (Illus.). 1977. pap. 3.95 (ISBN 0-89036-091-X). Hawkes Pub Inc.

Bergman, Nina M. Marah: The Woman at the Well. 1983. pap. 3.50 (ISBN 0-8423-4032-7). Tyndale.

Bergman, P. M. Concise Dictionary of Twenty-Six Languages in Simultaneous Translation. pap. 3.95 (ISBN 0-451-12987-3, AE2987, Sig). NAL.

Bergman, Paul, jt. auth. see Binder, David A.

Bergman, Paul B. Trial Advocacy in a Nutshell. LC 78-27734. (Nutshell Ser.). 402p. 1979. pap. text ed. 8.95 (ISBN 0-8299-2030-7). West Pub.

Bergman, Peter, ed. The Basic English-Chinese, Chinese-English Dictionary with PINYIN Transliteration. (Eng. & Chinese.). 1979. text ed. 12.50x (ISBN 0-391-01287-8). Humanities.

Bergman, Peter M., compiled by. The Basic English-Chinese, Chinese-English Dictionary. (Chinese & Eng.). (YA) 1980. pap. 3.95 (ISBN 0-451-12926-1, AE2926, Sig). NAL.

Bergman, R. K., jt. auth. see Munoz, J. J.

Bergman, R. N., jt. ed. see Cobelli, C.

Bergman, Ray & Janes, Edward C. Trout. 1976. 25.00 (ISBN 0-394-49957-3); pap. 15.95 (ISBN 0-394-73144-1). Knopf.

Bergman, Robert P. The Salerno Ivories: Ars Sacra from Medieval Amalfi. LC 79-22616. (Illus.). 268p. 1981. 37.50x (ISBN 0-674-78528-2). Harvard U Pr.

Bergman, Robert P. & Canby, Jeanny V. Three Thousand Years in Glass: Treasures from The Walters Art Gallery. Strohecker, Carol, ed. (Illus.). 16p. (Orig.). 1982. pap. 3.95 (ISBN 0-911886-24-9). Walters Art.

Bergman, Roland W. Amazon Economics: The Simplicity of Shipibo Indian Wealth. LC 80-20198. (Dellplain Latin American Studies Ser.: No. 6). pap. 67.80 (ISBN 0-317-28150-X, 2022595). Bks Demand UMI.

Bergman, Ronald A. & Afifi, Adel K. Atlas of Microscopic Anatomy: A Companion to Histology & Neuroanatomy. LC 72-88844. (Illus.). 426p. 1974. text ed. 32.00 (ISBN 0-7216-1687-9). Saunders.

Bergman, Ronald A., jt. auth. see Afifi, Adel K.

Bergman, Ronald A., et al. A Catalog of Human Variation. (Illus.). 246p. (Orig.). 1984. pap. text ed. 14.50 spiral (ISBN 0-8067-2501-X). Urban & S.

Bergman, Samuel & Bruckner, Steven. Introduction to Computers & Computer Programming. LC 72-140834. 1972. text ed. 28.95 (ISBN 0-201-00552-2). Addison-Wesley.

Bergman, Samuel H. Faith & Reason: An Introduction to Modern Jewish Thought. LC 61-10414. 1963. pap. 3.95 (ISBN 0-8052-0056-8). Schocken.

Bergman, Stefan. Kernel Function & Conformal Mapping. rev. ed. LC 68-58995. (Mathematical Surveys Ser.: No. 5). 257p. 1980. pap. 33.00 (ISBN 0-8218-1505-9, SURV-5). Am Math.

Bergman, T. Dissertation on Elective Attractions. 400p. 1970. Repr. of 1785 ed. 37.50x (ISBN 0-7146-1592-7, F Cass Co). Biblio Dist.

Bergman, Torbern. Dissertation on Elective Attractions. Schufle, J. A., tr. (Sources of Science Ser: No. 43). (Illus.). Repr. of 1968 ed. 22.00 (ISBN 0-384-03995-2). Johnson Repr.

Bergman, Torbern O. Physical & Chemical Essays, 3 vols. 1979. lib. bdg. 350.00 (ISBN 0-8490-2438-2). Gordon Pr.

Bergman, Virginia, jt. auth. see Bergman, Floyd L.

Bergman, Werner & Heller, Wilfried. Angular Light Scattering Maxima & Minima in Monodisperse & Heterodisperse Systems of Spheres. LC 77-6931. (Illus.). pap. 68.80 (ISBN 0-8357-9828-3, 2013660). Bks Demand UMI.

Bergman, Werner, jt. auth. see Heller, Wilfried.

Bergmann, Barbara R., jt. auth. see Bennett, Robert L.

Bergmann, E. D. & Pullman, B., eds. Aromaticity, Pseudoaromaticity, Antiaromaticity. LC 79-134838. 1971. 76.00 (ISBN 0-12-091040-3). Acad Pr.

Bergmann, E. D. & Pullmann, B., eds. Chemical & Biochemical Reactivity, April, 1973. (The Jerusalem Symposia on Quantum Chemistry & Biochemistry: No. 6). 1975. 53.00 (ISBN 90-277-0554-2, Pub. by Reidel Holland). Kluwer Academic.

Bergmann, E. D., ed. see Jerusalem Symposia on Quantum Chemistry & Biochemistry, Vol. 4.

Bergmann, Emilie L. Art Inscribed: Essays on Ekphrasis in Spanish Golden Age Poetry. LC 79-966. (Harvard Studies in Romance Languages: 35). (Illus.). 1980. 20.00x (ISBN 0-674-04805-9). Harvard U Pr.

Bergmann, Ernst & Pullman, Bernard, eds. Molecular & Quantum Pharmacology. new ed. LC 74-83002. (Jerusalem Symposia on Quantum Chemistry & Biochemistry: No. 7). 522p. 1974. lib. bdg. 87.00 (ISBN 90-277-0525-9, Pub. by Reidel Holland). Kluwer Academic.

Bergmann, Frank. Robert Grant. (United States Authors Ser.). 1982. lib. bdg. 16.50 (ISBN 0-8057-7360-6, Twayne). G K Hall.

Bergmann, Frank, ed. Upstate Literature: Essays in Memory of Thomas F. O'Donnell. LC 84-26853. (New York State Studies). 256p. 1985. text ed. 24.00x (ISBN 0-8156-2333-X); pap. text ed. 11.95x (ISBN 0-8156-2331-3). Syracuse U Pr.

Bergmann, Fredrick L., jt. ed. see Pedicord, Harry W.

Bergmann, Frithjof. On Being Free. LC 77-89760. 1979. pap. text ed. 7.95x (ISBN 0-268-01493-0). U of Notre Dame Pr.

--On Being Free. LC 77-89760. 1977. text ed. 19.95 (ISBN 0-268-01492-2). U of Notre Dame Pr.

Bergmann, Gustav. Logic & Reality. LC 64-10261. pap. 91.30 (ISBN 0-317-08977-3, 2004234). Bks Demand UMI.

--Meaning & Existence. 286p. (Orig.). 1960. pap. 8.95x (ISBN 0-299-01984-5). U of Wis Pr.

--The Metaphysics of Logical Positivism. LC 78-28139. 1978. Repr. of 1967 ed. lib. bdg. 26.75x (ISBN 0-313-20235-4, BEML). Greenwood.

--Realism: A Critique of Brentano & Meinong. 468p. (Orig.). 1967. 25.00x (ISBN 0-299-04330-4); pap. 9.95x (ISBN 0-299-04334-7). U of Wis Pr.

Bergmann, Helena. Between Obedience & Freedom: Woman's Role in the Mid-Nineteenth Century Industrial Novel. (Goteborg Studies in English: No. 45). (Orig.). 1979. pap. text ed. 19.50x (ISBN 91-7346-065-6). Humanities.

Bergmann, Hellmuth. Guide to the Economic Evaluation of Irrigation Projects. 134p. 1976. 18.00x (ISBN 9-2641-1021-6). OECD.

Bergmann, Josef. The Peafowl of the World. (Illus.). 192p. 1980. 21.75 (ISBN 0-904558-51-7). Saiga.

Bergmann, Leola N. Americans from Norway. LC 72-12625. 324p. 1973. Repr. of 1950 ed. lib. bdg. 15.00x (ISBN 0-8371-6677-2, BEAN). Greenwood.

--Music Master of the Middle West: The Story of F. Melius Christiansen & the St. Olaf Choir. 2nd ed. LC 68-16222. (Music Ser). 1968. Repr. of 1944 ed. 27.50 (ISBN 0-306-71057-9). Da Capo.

Bergmann, Mark, jt. auth. see Otte, Elmer.

Bergmann, Martin & Jucovy, Milton E., eds. Generations of the Holocaust. 1982. 18.95 (ISBN 0-465-02666-4). Basic.

Bergmann, Merrie, et al. The Logic Book. 608p. 1980. text ed. 27.00 (ISBN 0-394-32679-2, KnopfC). Knopf.

Bergmann, P. G., et al. Physics of Sound in the Sea, 4 pts. Incl. Pt. 1. Transmission. Bergmann, P. G. & Yaspan, A. 266p. 48.75 (ISBN 0-677-01890-8); Pts. 2 & 3. Reverbreration Bd with Reflection of Sound from Submarines & Surface Vessels. Gerjuoy, E., et al, eds. 218p. 32.50 (ISBN 0-677-01900-9); Pt. 4. Acoustic Properties of Wakes. Wildt, R., ed. 128p. 19.75 (ISBN 0-677-01910-6). (Documents on Modern Physics Ser.). 612p. 1968. Set. 145.75 (ISBN 0-677-01920-3). Gordon.

Bergmann, Peter G. Introduction to the Theory of Relativity. 1976. pap. 5.00 (ISBN 0-486-63282-2). Dover.

--Riddle of Gravitation. LC 68-11537. 1968. lib. bdg. 25.00 (ISBN 0-684-15378-5, ScribT). Scribner.

Bergmann, Peter G. & De Sabbath, Venzo, eds. Cosmology & Gravitation: Spin, Torsion, Rotation, & Supergravity. LC 80-23742. (NATO ASI Series B, Physics: Vol. 58). 519p. 1980. 75.00x (ISBN 0-306-40478-8, Plenum Pr). Plenum Pub.

Bergmann, Rolf. Verzeichnis der althochdeutschen und altsaechsischen Glossenhandschriften: Mit Bibliographie der Glosseneditionen, der Handschriftenbeschreibungen und der Dialektbestimmungen. LC 72-76056. (Arbeiten Zur Fruehmittelalterforschung Ser: Vol. 6). (Ger.). 1973. 31.60x (ISBN 3-11-003713-0). De Gruyter.

Bergmann, Theodore. The Development Models of India, the Soviet Union & China. (Publications of European Society for Rural Sociology Ser.: No. 1). (Illus.). 1977. pap. text ed. 31.75x (ISBN 90-232-1497-8). Humanities.

Bergmann, Thesi & Freud, Anna. Children in the Hospital. LC 65-28803. 162p. 1966. text ed. 17.50 (ISBN 0-8236-0800-X); pap. 9.95 (ISBN 0-8236-8017-7, 020800). Intl Univs Pr.

Bergmeister, Karl. The Jewish World Conspiracy. 1982. lib. bdg. 59.95 (ISBN 0-87700-427-7). Revisionist pr.

Bergmeyer, H. U. Lipids, Amino Acids & Related Compounds, Vol. 8. 3rd ed. LC 84-105641. (Methods of Enzymatic Analysis). (Illus.). 600p. 1985. lib. bdg. 135.00 (ISBN 0-89573-238-6). VCH Pubs.

--Principles of Enzymatic Analysis. (Illus.). 264p. 1978. pap. 30.70x (ISBN 0-89573-006-5). VCH Pubs.

Bergmeyer, H. U., ed. Metabolites One, Vol. 6. 3rd ed. (Methods of Enzymatic Analysis). 701p. 1984. 155.60 (ISBN 0-89573-236-X). VCH Pubs.

--Metabolites Two, Vol. 7. 3rd ed. (Methods of Enzymatic Analysis). 637p. 1985. 135.00 (ISBN 0-89573-237-8). VCH Pubs.

--Methods of Enzymatic Analysis: Enzymes 3-Peptides, Protinases & Their Inhibitors, Vol. 5. 3rd ed. 558p. 1984. 120.00x (ISBN 0-89573-235-1). VCH Pubs.

Bergmeyer, Hannelore. Brutus Brown & the Green Forest State. 64p. 1982. 6.95 (ISBN 0-89962-276-3). Todd & Honeywell.

Bergmeyer, Hans U., ed. Methods of Enzymatic Analysis: Enzymes I, Vol. 3. 3rd, English ed. 603p. 1983. 129.00 (ISBN 0-89573-233-5). VCH Pubs.

--Methods of Enzymatic Analysis: Esterases, Glycosidases, Lyases, Ligases, Enzymes 2, Vol. 4. 3rd ed. 426p. 1984. text ed. 102.00 (ISBN 0-89573-234-3). VCH Pubs.

--Methods of Enzymatic Analysis: Fundamentals, Vol. 1. 3rd, English ed. 574p. 1983. 116.00x (ISBN 0-89573-231-9). VCH Pubs.

--Methods of Enzymatic Analysis, Vol. 2: Samples, Reagents, Assessment of Results. 3rd, English ed. 539p. 1983. 122.50x (ISBN 0-89573-232-7). VCH Pubs.

Bergner, Erik E., et al, eds. Compartments, Pools & Spaces in Medical Physiology: Proceedings. LC 67-61865. (AEC Symposium Ser.). 521p. 1967. pap. 21.00 (ISBN 0-87079-167-2, CONF-661010); microfiche 4.50 (ISBN 0-87079-168-0, CONF-661010). DOE.

Bergner, Jeffrey T. The Origin of Formalism in Social Science. LC 80-17484. 160p. 1981. lib. bdg. 16.00x (ISBN 0-226-04362-2). U of Chicago Pr.

Bergner, Lawrence, jt. ed. see Eisenberg, Mickey.

Bergold, Lynn, jt. auth. see Edwards, James D.

Bergon, Frank. Stephen Crane's Artistry. LC 75-19159. 174p. 1975. 22.00x (ISBN 0-231-03905-0). Columbia U Pr.

--The Wilderness Reader. (Orig.). 1980. pap. 3.95 (ISBN 0-451-62284-7, ME2284, Ment). NAL.

Bergonzi, Bernard. Heroes Twilight. 241p. 1980. text ed. 25.50x (ISBN 0-333-28126-8, Pub. by Macmillan England). Humanities.

--Reading the Thirties: Texts & Contexts. LC 78-4262. (Critical Essays in Modern Literature Ser.). 1978. 14.95 (ISBN 0-8229-1135-3). U of Pittsburgh Pr.

--The Turn of a Century: Essays on Victorian & Modern English Literature. 1973. text ed. 10.50x (ISBN 0-333-14636-0). Humanities.

Bergonzi, Bernard, ed. see Gissing, George.

Bergonzo, Jean-Louis. Spanish Inn. 1984. 9.95 (ISBN 0-7145-0535-8). Riverrun NY.

Bergot, Erwan. The French Foreign Legion. 2nd ed. LC 84-50777. (Illus.). 1985. pap. 12.95 (ISBN 0-500-27382-0, Dist. by Norton). Thames Hudson.

--The French Foreign Legion: The Inside Story of the World Famous Fighting Force. LC 84-50777. (Illus.). 212p. 1984. 24.95f (ISBN 0-500-01342-X). Thames Hudson.

Bergot, Francois, jt. auth. see Rosenberg, Pierre.

Berg-Pan, Renata. Bertolt Brecht & China. 1982. 36.00x (ISBN 3-416-01516-9, Pub. by Bouvier Verlag Ger). State Mutual Bk.

--Bertolt Brecht & China. (Studien zur Germanistik, Anglistik und Komparatistik: Vol. 88). 394p. (Orig.). 1979. pap. 33.00x (ISBN 3-416-01516-9, Pub. by Bouvier Verlag W Germany). Benjamins North Am.

--Leni Riefenstahl. (Filmmakers Ser.). 1980. lib. bdg. 14.50 (ISBN 0-8057-9275-9, Twayne). G K Hall.

Bergquist, Barbara J., jt. auth. see DiGiacomo, Kathy.

Bergquist, Charles W. Alternative Approaches to the Problem of Development: A Selected & Annotated Bibliography. LC 77-88665. 264p. 1979. lib. bdg. 19.95 (ISBN 0-89089-081-1); pap. 9.95 (ISBN 0-89089-083-8). Carolina Acad Pr.

--Coffee & Conflict in Columbia, 1886-1910. 1978. 21.00 (ISBN 0-8223-0418-X). Duke.

Bergquist, Craig. Finish Carpentry Techniques. Shakery, Karin, ed. LC 82-63127. (Illus.). 96p. (Orig.). 1983. pap. 5.95 (ISBN 0-89721-013-1). Ortho.

Bergquist, G. William, ed. Three Centuries of English & American Plays: A Check List - England 1500-1800 & United States 1714-1830. 1963. 37.50x (ISBN 0-02-841230-3). Hafner.

Bergquist, Gordon N. The Pen & the Sword: War & Peace in the Prose & Plays of Bernard Shaw. (Salzburg Studies in English Literature, Poetic Drama & Poetic Theory: No. 28). 1977. pap. text ed. 25.50x (ISBN 0-391-01325-4). Humanities.

Bergquist, Lois M. Changing Patterns of Infectious Disease. LC 84-3957. (Illus.). 285p. 1984. pap. 28.50 (ISBN 0-8121-0940-6). Lea & Febiger.

--Microbiology for the Hospital Environment. (Illus.). 719p. 1981. text ed. 29.95 scp (ISBN 0-06-040646-1, HarpC); scp lab manual 17.95 (ISBN 0-06-040644-5); inst's manual avail. (ISBN 0-06-360635-6). Har-Row.

Bergquist, M. Francille. Ibero-Romance: Comparative Phonology & Morphology. LC 81-40657. (Illus.). 186p. (Orig.). 1982. lib. bdg. 24.00 (ISBN 0-8191-2029-4); pap. text ed. 11.25 (ISBN 0-8191-2030-8). U Pr of Amer.

Bergquist, Patricia R. Sponges. LC 77-93644. 1978. 44.50x (ISBN 0-520-03658-1). U of Cal Pr.

Bergquist, Sidney, ed. New Webster's Dictionary: Modern Reference Dictionary. (Illus.). 656p. pap. 3.95 (ISBN 0-8326-0065-2, 6500). Delair.

Bergquist, Sidney R., ed. New Webster's Dictionary of the English Language (Handy School & Office Edition) LC 75-15424. 1975. 5.95 (ISBN 0-8326-0033-4, 6501). Delair.

--New Webster's Dictionary of the English Language (Modern Desk Edition) LC 76-3282. (Illus.). 720p. 1976. 8.95 (ISBN 0-8326-0040-7, 6603). Delair.

Bergquist, William & Shoemaker, William A., eds. Comprehensive Approach to Institutional Development. LC 76-11882. (New Directions for Higher Education Ser.: No. 15). pap. 30.00 (ISBN 0-317-26056-1, 2023779). Bks Demand UMI.

Bergquist, William H. & Phillips, Steven R. A Handbook for Faculty Development, Vol. 2 & 3. LC 80-69254. 1977. Set. pap. 19.00; pap. 13.00 (ISBN 0-937012-09-2); pap. 15.00 (ISBN 0-937012-11-4). Coun Indep Colleges.

Bergquist, William H., jt. auth. see Pilon, Daniel H.

Bergquist, William H., jt. auth. see Sprunger, Benjamin E.

Bergquist, William H., et al. Designing Undergraduate Education: A Systematic Guide. LC 81-47768. (Higher Education Ser.). 1981. text ed. 19.95x (ISBN 0-87589-508-5). Jossey-Bass.

Bergqvist, D. Postoperative Thromboembolism: Frequency, Etiology, Prophylaxis. (Illus.). 248p. 1983. 41.00 (ISBN 0-387-12062-9). Springer-Verlag.

Bergreen, Laurence. James Agee: A Biography. LC 83-25496. 352p. 1984. 20.00 (ISBN 0-525-24253-8, 01942-580). Dutton.

--James Agee: A Life. 480p. 1985. pap. 8.95 (ISBN 0-14-008064-3). Penguin.

Bergren, Ann L. The Etymology & Usage of Peirar in Early Greek Poetry. (American Philological Association, American Classical Studies). 1975. pap. 7.50 (ISBN 0-89130-242-5, 400402). Scholars Pr GA.

Bergren, Victor. The Prophets & the Law. 15.00x (ISBN 0-87820-403-2, Pub. by Hebrew Union College Press). Ktav.

Bergsma, D., ed. Winnipeg Conference, 4th International Workshop on Human Gene Mapping, Winnipeg, August 1977. (Human Gene Mapping: No. 4). (Illus.). 1979. pap. 35.00 (ISBN 3-8055-3052-8). S Karger.

Bergsma, D., ed. see Baltimore Conference, 1975.

Bergsma, D., ed. see Rotterdam Conference, 1974.

Bergsma, D., et al, eds. Bilirubin Metabolism in the Newborn. (International Congress Ser.: No. 380). 1976. 66.00 (ISBN 0-444-15216-4, Excerpta Medica). Elsevier.

--An International System for Human Cytogenetic Nomenclature 1978: Report of the Standing Committee on Human Cytogenetic Nomenclature. (Cytogenetics & Cell Genetics: Vol. 21, No. 6). (Illus.). 1979. pap. 9.00 (ISBN 3-8055-3011-0). S Karger.

Bergsma, Daniel. Cancer & Genetics. (Alan R. Liss, Inc. Ser.: Vol 12, No. 1). 1976. 28.00 (ISBN 0-686-18077-1). March of Dimes.

Bergsma, Daniel, ed. Birth Defects Compendium. 2nd ed. LC 78-20651. 1222p. 1979. 72.00x (ISBN 0-8451-0203-6). A R Liss.

--Congenital Malformations in Singletons: Epidemiologic Survey. LC 74-79906. (March of Dimes Ser.: Vol. 10, No. 11). 1976. 12.50 (ISBN 0-686-14567-4). March of Dimes.

--Cytogenetics, Environmental Malformation Syndromes. LC 76-20510. (Alan R. Liss., Inc. Ser.: Vol 12, No. 5). 1976. 42.00 (ISBN 0-686-18079-8). March of Dimes.

--Developmental Disabilities: Psychologic & Social Implications. LC 76-44446. (Alan R. Liss, Inc. Ser.: Vol. 12, No. 4). 1976. 25.00 (ISBN 0-686-18080-1). March of Dimes.

--Disorders of Connective Tissue. LC 75-17345. (March of Dimes Ser.: Vol. 11, No. 6). 1976. 16.95 (ISBN 0-686-14574-7). March of Dimes.

--Embryology & Pathogenesis & Prenatal Diagnosis. (Alan R. Liss Ser.: Vol 13, No.3d). 1977. 42.00 (ISBN 0-686-23120-1). March of Dimes.

--Ethical Issues Arising in the Genetic Counseling Relationship. LC 78-70429. (National Foundation Ser.: Vol. 14, No. 9). 1978. write for info (ISBN 0-686-23952-0). March of Dimes.

--Ethical, Social & Legal Dimensions of Screening for Human Genetic Disease. (March of Dimes Ser.: Vol. 10, No. 6). 13.95 (ISBN 0-686-10018-2). March of Dimes.

--The Eye & Inborn Error of Metabolism. LC 76-12112. (Alan R. Liss, Inc. Ser.: Vol. 12, No. 3). 1976. 83.00 (ISBN 0-686-18081-X). March of Dimes.

--Genetic Effects on Aging. (Alan R. Liss Ser.: Vol. 14, No. 1). 1978. 70.00 (ISBN 0-686-10130-8). March of Dimes.

--Genetics & Cytogenetics. (March of Dimes Ser.: Vol. 10, No. 9). 12.95 (ISBN 0-686-10016-6). March of Dimes.

--Growth Problems & Clinical Advances. LC 76-21714. (Alan R. Liss, Inc. Ser.: Vol. 12, No. 6). 1976. 42.00 (ISBN 0-686-18083-6). March of Dimes.

--Infant at Risk. (March of Dimes Ser.: Vol. 10, No. 2). 11.50 (ISBN 0-686-10021-2). March of Dimes.

--International Workshop on Human Gene Mapping: Proceedings, New Haven Conference. (March of Dimes Ser.: Vol. 10, No. 3). 13.50 (ISBN 0-686-10020-4). March of Dimes.

--Iron Metabolism & Thalassemia. LC 76-25835. (Alan R. Liss, Inc. Ser: Vol 12, No. 8). 1976. 31.00 (ISBN 0-686-18085-2). March of Dimes.

--Limb Malformations. (Symposia Ser.: Vol. 10, No. 5). 15.00 (ISBN 0-686-10019-0). March of Dimes.

--Malformation Syndromes. (March of Dimes Ser.: Vol. 10 No. 7). 12.95 (ISBN 0-686-10017-4). March of Dimes.

--The Molecular Basis of Cell-Cell Interaction. (Alan R. Liss Ser.: Vol. 14, No. 2). 1978. 80.00 (ISBN 0-686-10131-6). March of Dimes.

--Morphogenesis & Malformation of Face & Brain. LC 75-24570. (Alan R. Liss, Inc. Ser.: Vol. 11, No. 7). 1976. 43.00 (ISBN 0-686-14575-5). March of Dimes.

--Morphogenesis & Malformation of the Limb, Vol. 13, No. 1. LC 76-55004. (Alan R. Liss, Inc. Ser.). 1977. 49.00 (ISBN 0-686-20484-0). March of Dimes.

--Morphogenesis & Malformation of the Genital System, Vol. 13, No. 2. LC 77-535. (Alan R. Liss, Inc. Ser.). 1977. 25.00 (ISBN 0-686-20483-2). March of Dimes.

--Natural History of Specific Birth Defects. (Alan R. Liss Ser.: Vol. 13, No. 3c). 1977. 42.00 (ISBN 0-686-23122-8). March of Dimes.

--New Chromosomal & Malformation Syndromes. LC 75-16885. (March of Dimes Ser.: Vol. 11, No.5). 1976. 16.95 (ISBN 0-686-14573-9). March of Dimes.

--New Syndromes. (Alan R. Liss Ser.: Vol. 13, No.3b). 1977. 42.00 (ISBN 0-686-23123-6). March of Dimes.

--Normal Values for Selected Physical Parameters: An Aid to Syndrome Delineation. LC 75-25485. (National Foundation Ser.: Vol 10, No. 13). 1974. write for info. (ISBN 0-686-18086-0). March of Dimes.

--Numerical Taxonomy of Birth Defects & Polygenic Disorders. (Alan R. Liss Ser.: Vol. 13, No. 3a). 1977. 28.00 (ISBN 0-686-23124-4). March of Dimes.

--Skeletal Dysplasias. (March of Dimes Ser.: Vol. 10, No. 8). 12.95 (ISBN 0-686-10015-8). March of Dimes.

--Trends in Teaching Genetics. (Alan R. Liss Ser.: Vol. 13, No. 6). 1977. 23.00 (ISBN 0-686-23125-2). March of Dimes.

--Urinary System & Others, Pt. 16. (Alan R. Liss Ser.: Vol. 10, No. 4). 1974. 48.00 (ISBN 0-686-23126-0). March of Dimes.

--Urinary System Malformations in Children. (Alan R. Liss Ser.: Vol. 13, No. 5). 1977. 70.00 (ISBN 0-686-23127-9). March of Dimes.

--X-Linked Mental Retardation & Verbal Disability. (March of Dimes Ser.: Vol. 10, No. 1). 11.50 (ISBN 0-686-10022-0). March of Dimes.

Bergsma, Daniel & Goldstein, Allan, eds. Neurochemical & Immunologic Components in Schizophrenia. (Allan R. Liss, Inc. Ser.: Vol. 14, No. 5). 1978. 64.00 (ISBN 0-8451-1019-5). March of Dimes.

Bergsma, Daniel & Goldstein, Allan L., eds. Neurochemical & Immunologic Components in Schizophrenia: Proceedings of a Conference Held at the University of Texas Medical Branch, Oct. 1976. LC 78-8534. (Birth Defects Original Article Ser.: Vol. 14, No. 5). 448p. 1978. 70.00 (ISBN 0-8451-1019-5). A R Liss.

Bergsma, Daniel & Kargar, S., eds. Human Gene Mapping III. LC 76-2955. (Vol. 12, No. 7). 1976. avail. (ISBN 0-686-18084-4). March of Dimes.

Bergsma, Daniel & Lenz, Widukind, eds. Morphogenesis & Malformation of the Limb: Proceedings. LC 76-55004. (Birth Defects Original Article Ser.: Vol. 13, No. 1). 376p. 1977. 54.00x (ISBN 0-8451-1008-X). A R Liss.

Bergsma, Daniel & Lowry, R. Brian, eds. Embryology & Pathogenesis & Prenatal Diagnosis: Part D of Annual Review of Birth Defects, 1976. LC 77-2785. (Birth Defects Original Article Ser.: Vol. 13, No. 3D). 312p. 1977. 46.00x (ISBN 0-8451-1013-6). A R Liss.

--Natural History of Specific Birth Defects: Part C of Annual Review of Birth Defects, 1976. LC 77-23452. (Birth Defects Original Article Ser.: Vol. 13, No. 3C). 270p. 1977. 46.00x (ISBN 0-8451-1012-8). A R Liss.

--New Syndromes: Part B of Annual Review of Birth Defects, 1976. LC 77-23451. (Birth Defects Original Article Ser.: Vol. 13, No. 3B). 284p. 1977. 48.00x (ISBN 0-8451-1011-X). A R Liss.

--Numerical Taxonomy of Birth Defects & Polygenic Disorders: Part A of Annual Review of Birth Defects, 1976. LC 77-23450. (Birth Defects Original Article Ser.: Vol. 13, No. 3A). 178p. 1977. 31.00x (ISBN 0-8451-1010-1). A R Liss.

Bergsma, Daniel & Pulver, Ann E., eds. Developmental Disabilities: Psychologic & Social Implications; Proceedings of a Symposium Sponsored by the National Foundation March of Dimes & the Johns Hopkins University School of Hygiene & Public Health, Baltimore, Md., LC 76-44446. (Birth Defects - Original Article Ser.: Vol. 12, No. 4.). 204p. 1976. 28.00 (ISBN 0-8451-1007-1). A R Liss.

Bergsma, Daniel, ed. see Birth Defects Annual Conference, 10th Memphis, Tenn., June, 1977.

Bergsma, Daniel, ed. see Birth Defects Conference, Kansas City, Mo., May 1975.

Bergsma, Daniel, ed. see Birth Defects Conference-1975, Kansas City, Missouri.

Bergsma, Daniel, ed. see Birth Defects Conference, 1975, Kansas City, Missouri.

Bergsma, Daniel, ed. see Conference Held at Jackson Laboratory, Bar Harbor, Maine, Sept. 1976.

Bergsma, Daniel, ed. see International Conference, la Jolla, Calif., Feb. 1977.

Bergsma, Daniel, ed. see International Conference on Morphogenesis & Malformation, 1st, Airlie House, Va., June 1974, et al.

Bergsma, Daniel, ed. see International Conference on Morphogenesis & Malformation, Lake Wilderness, Washington, 3rd, July 1976.

Bergsma, Daniel, ed. see International Pediatric Urological Seminar, Phila., Pa., Apr. 1976.

Bergsma, Daniel, ed. see International Workshop on Morphogenesis & Malformation, 4th, Grand Canyon, Ariz., 1977.

Bergsma, Daniel, jt. ed. see Myrianthopoulos, Ntinos C.

Bergsma, Daniel, jt. ed. see Rosenquist, Glenn C.

Bergsma, Daniel, ed. see Rotterdam Conference, 2nd 1974.

Bergsma, Daniel, jt. ed. see Summit, Robert.

Bergsma, Daniel, jt. ed. see Summitt, Robert.

Bergsma, Daniel, ed. see Symposium in Conjunction with the 11th World Congress on Neurology, September, 1977, Amsterdam.

Bergsma, Daniel, et al, eds. Trends & Teaching in Clinical Genetics. LC 77-24643. (Birth Defects Original Article Ser.: Vol. 13, No. 6). 200p. 1977. 25.00 (ISBN 0-8451-1015-2). A R Liss.

Bergsma, Daniel, et al, eds. see Conference Sponsored by National Foundation-March of Dimes, Key Biscayne, Florida, Nov. 1975.

Bergsma, Daniel, et al, eds. see Symposium Held at the Radcliffe Infirmary, Oxford, England, April, 1975 Sponsored by the National Foundation - March of Dimes.

Bergsma, Jurrit & Thomasma, David. Health Care: Its Psychosocial Dimensions. Orig. Title: The Other Side of Medicine. (Illus.). 225p. 1981. text ed. 16.00x (ISBN 0-391-01630-X). Duquesne.

Bergsma, Lily C. A Cross-Cultural Study of Conformity in Americans & Chinese. LC 76-55970. 1977. soft bdg. 10.95 (ISBN 0-88247-432-4). R & E Pubs.

Bergsman, Joel. Growth & Equity in Semi-Industrialized Countries. (Working Paper: No. 351). ii, 113p. 1979. 5.00 (ISBN 0-686-36050-8, WP-0351). World Bank.

--Income Distribution & Poverty in Mexico. (Working Paper: No. 395). 1980. pap. 3.00 (ISBN 0-686-39731-2, WP-0395). World Bank.

Bergson, Abram. The Economics of Soviet Planning. LC 80-13737. (Studies in Comparative Economics: No. 5). (Illus.). xxii, 394p. 1980. Repr. of 1964 ed. lib. bdg. 37.50x (ISBN 0-313-22413-7, BEES). Greenwood.

--Essays in Normative Economics. LC 66-13177. (Illus.). 1966. 17.50x (ISBN 0-674-26500-9, Belknap Pr). Harvard U Pr.

--Planning & Productivity Under Soviet Socialism. LC 68-24703. (Benjamin Fairless Memorial Lectures Ser.). 95p. 1968. 17.00x (ISBN 0-231-03116-5). Columbia U Pr.

--Productivity & the Social System-The U. S. S. R. & the West. LC 77-15493. 1978. 18.50x (ISBN 0-674-71165-3). Harvard U Pr.

--Soviet National Income & Product in 1937. LC 75-104222. Repr. of 1953 ed. lib. bdg. 22.50x (ISBN 0-8371-3332-7, BESO). Greenwood.

--Structure of Soviet Wages: A Study in Socialist Economics. LC 44-1242. (Economic Studies: No. 76). 1944. 17.50x (ISBN 0-674-84480-7). Harvard U Pr.

--Welfare, Planning, & Employment: Selected Essays in Economic Theory. 288p. 1982. 35.75x (ISBN 0-262-02175-7). MIT Pr.

Bergson, Abram & Levine, Herbert S., eds. The Soviet Economy: Toward the Year 2000. 496p. (Orig.). 1985. pap. text ed. 18.50x (ISBN 0-04-335053-4). Allen Unwin.

--The Soviet Economy Towards the Year 2000. 496p. 1983. text ed. 37.50x (ISBN 0-04-335045-3). Allen Unwin.

Bergson, Anika & Tuchack, Vladimir. Shiatzu. 1983. pap. 2.50 (ISBN 0-523-42526-0). Pinnacle Bks.

Bergson, Anika, ed. Zone Therapy. Tuchak, Vladimir. (Illus.). 160p. 1982. pap. 2.25 (ISBN 0-523-41860-4). Pinnacle Bks.

Bergson, Henri. Creative Evolution. Mitchell, Arthur, tr. 407p. 1981. Repr. of 1911 ed. lib. bdg. 50.00 (ISBN 0-89760-079-7). Telegraph Bks.

--Creative Evolution. Mitxhell, Arthur, tr. LC 83-19859. 460p. 1984. pap. text ed. 13.50 (ISBN 0-8191-3553-4). U Pr of Amer.

--The Creative Mind: An Introduction to Metaphysics. 256p. 1974. pap. 3.95 (ISBN 0-8065-0421-8). Citadel Pr.

--Les Deux Sources de la Morale et de la Religion. 1976. pap. 18.95 (ISBN 0-686-51928-0). French & Eur.

--Dreams. Slosson, Edwin E., tr. 62p. 1982. Repr. of 1914 ed. lib. bdg. 35.00 (ISBN 0-89987-092-9). Darby Bks.

--Duree et Simultaneite. 1968. pap. 15.95 (ISBN 0-686-51929-9). French & Eur.

--Ecrits et Paroles. 1959. pap. 14.95 (ISBN 0-686-51930-2). French & Eur.

--L' Energie Spirituelle. pap. 15.95 (ISBN 0-685-37205-7). French & Eur.

--Essai sur les Donnees Immediates de la Conscience. pap. 16.50 (ISBN 0-685-37206-5). French & Eur.

--L' Evolution Creatrice. 21.50 (ISBN 0-685-37207-3). French & Eur.

--An Introduction to Metaphysics. 2nd ed. Hulme, T. E., tr. LC 49-3135. 1955. pap. 3.03 scp (ISBN 0-672-60171-0, LLA10). Bobbs.

--An Introduction to Metaphysics: The Creative Mind. (Quality Paperback: No. 164). 1975. pap. 5.95 (ISBN 0-8226-0164-8). Littlefield.

--Laughter: An Essay on the Meaning of the Comic. Brereton, Cloudesley & Rothwell, Fred, trs. 1977. Repr. of 1921 ed. lib. bdg. 35.00 (ISBN 0-8492-0272-8). R West.

--Matiere et Memoire. pap. 16.50 (ISBN 0-685-37208-1). French & Eur.

--Matter & Memory. (Muirhead Library of Philosophy). 1978. text ed. 20.00x (ISBN 0-391-00924-9). Humanities.

--Melanges. Robinet, ed. Incl. L' Idee de Lieu chez Aristote; Duree et Simultaneite; Correspondance; Pieces Diverses; Documents. 59.95 (ISBN 0-685-37209-X). French & Eur.

--Memoire et Vie. 1975. pap. 11.95 (ISBN 0-686-51931-0). French & Eur.

--Mind-Energy, Lectures & Essays. Carr, H. Wildon, tr. from Fr. LC 74-28922. 262p. 1975. Repr. of 1920 ed. lib. bdg. 21.25x (ISBN 0-8371-7931-9, BEEN). Greenwood.

--Oeuvres. 52.50 (ISBN 0-685-37204-9). French & Eur.

--La Pensee et le Mouvement. 21.50 (ISBN 0-685-37210-3). French & Eur.

--Le Rire. pap. 8.95 (ISBN 0-685-37211-1). French & Eur.

--Risa. pap. 2.95 (ISBN 0-685-11531-3). French & Eur.

--Time & Free Will. (Muirhead Library of Philosophy). 1971. text ed. 31.75x (ISBN 0-04-194002-4). Humanities.

--The Two Sources of Morality & Religion. LC 74-10373. 308p. 1974. Repr. of 1935 ed. lib. bdg. 25.00x (ISBN 0-8371-7679-4, BETS). Greenwood.

--The Two Sources of Morality & Religion. Audra, R. Ashley, tr. from Fr. LC 77-89762. 1977. pap. text ed. 8.95 (ISBN 0-268-01835-9). U of Notre Dame Pr.

Bergson, Henri L. Creative Evolution. Mitchell, Arthur, tr. LC 74-28524. 453p. 1975. Repr. of 1944 ed. lib. bdg. 35.00x (ISBN 0-8371-7917-3, BECEV). Greenwood.

--Creative Evolution. 1911. 35.00 (ISBN 0-8274-2111-7). R West.

--Creative Mind. Andison, Mabelle L., tr. LC 68-19264. Repr. of 1946 ed. lib. bdg. 23.75x (ISBN 0-8371-0310-X, BECM). Greenwood.

Bergson, Henry. Laughter. Bd. with Essay on Comedy. Meredith, George. 13.75 (ISBN 0-8446-1666-4). Peter Smith.

Bergson, Peter A. Spaces for Children: Learning-Play Structures for Home & School. (Illus.). 55p. (Orig.). 1984. pap. 5.00 (ISBN 0-9606434-1-9). Open Connections.

Bergson, Peter A., jt. auth. see Shilcock, Susan D.

Bergsten, Bebe. The Great Dane & the Great Northern Film Company. LC 72-97021. (Illus.). 1973. 8.95 (ISBN 0-913986-05-4). Renovare Co.

Bergsten, C. F. The International Economic Policy of the United States: Selected Papers of C. Fred Bergsten, 1977-1979. LC 79-3040. 416p. 1980. 34.00x (ISBN 0-669-03314-6). Lexington Bks.

Bergsten, C. F., et al. Approaches to Greater Flexibility of Exchange Rates: The Burgenstock Papers. LC 78-11633. 1970. 41.00x (ISBN 0-691-04196-2). Princeton U Pr.

Bergsten, C. Fred The Dilemmas of the Dollar: The Economics & Politics of the United States International Monetary Policy. LC 75-10904. 584p. 1975. pap. 18.50x (ISBN 0-8147-1022-0). NYU Pr.

Bergsten, C. Fred. The United States in the World Economy: Selected Papers of C. Fred Bergsten, 1981 to 1982. LC 82-49336. 256p. 1983. 24.00x (ISBN 0-669-06617-6). Lexington Bks.

Bergsten, C. Fred & Cline, William P. U. S. - Japan Economic Problem. (Policy Analyses in International Economics Ser.). (Orig.). 1985. pap. text ed. 10.00 (ISBN 0-88132-039-0). Inst Intl Eco.

Bergsten, C. Fred & Cline, William R. Trade Policy of the Nineteen Eighties. (Policy Analyses in International Economics: No. 3). pap. 21.00 (ISBN 0-317-20818-7, 2024793). Bks Demand UMI.

Bergsten, C. Fred & Schott, Jeffrey J. New International Arrangements for Foreign Direct Investment. (Policy Analyses in International Economics Ser.). 80p. (Orig.). 1986. pap. 10.00x (ISBN 0-88132-024-2). MIT (ISBN 0-262-52092-3, BERAP). Inst Intl Eco.

--New International Arrangements for Foreign Direct Investment. 1984. 25.00x (ISBN 0-262-52092-3). MIT Pr.

Bergsten, C. Fred & Williamson, John. The Multiple Reserve Currency System. (Policy Analyses in International Economics Ser.). 80p. (Orig.). 1986. pap. 10.00x (ISBN 0-88132-003-X). MIT (ISBN 0-262-52089-3, BERMP). Inst Intl Eco.

Bergsten, C. Fred, ed. Global Economic Imbalances. LC 85-8279. (Special Reports Ser.). 150p. (Orig.). 1985. 10.00x (ISBN 0-88132-038-2); MIT. 25.00 (ISBN 0-262-02235-4, BERWP). Inst Intl Eco.

Bergsten, C. Fred & Krause, Lawrence B., eds. World Politics & International Economics. LC 75-15684. pap. 93.30 (ISBN 0-317-20637-0, 2024128). Bks Demand UMI.

Bergsten, C. Fred, et al. American Multinationals & American Interests. LC 77-91786. 1978. 32.95 (ISBN 0-8157-0920-X); pap. 16.95 (ISBN 0-8157-0919-6). Brookings.

--From Rambouillet to Versailles: A Symposium. LC 82-23424. (Essays in International Finance Ser.: No. 149). 1982. pap. text ed. 2.50x (ISBN 0-88165-056-0). Princeton U Int Finan Econ.

--The Reform of International Institutions. 1978. 15.00 (ISBN 0-318-02786-0); pap. 4.95 (ISBN 0-318-02787-9). Trilateral Comm.

--Bank Lending to Developing Countries: The Policy Alternatives. LC 85-60898. (Policy Analyses in International Economics Ser.: No. 10). 221p. (Orig.). 1985. pap. 12.00x (ISBN 0-88132-032-3). MIT (ISBN 0-262-52098-2, BERLP). Inst Intl Eco.

Bergsten, Gunilla. Thomas Mann's Doctor Faustus: The Sources & Structure of the Novel. Winston, Krishna, tr. LC 69-14483. 1969. 14.00x (ISBN 0-226-04365-7). U of Chicago Pr.

Bergsten, Gunilla U. Thomas Mann's Doctor Faustus: The Sources & Structure of the Novel. LC 69-14483. pap. 63.50 (ISBN 0-317-29848-8, 2020031). Bks Demand UMI.

Bergsten, L. Fred. Completing the GATT: Toward New International Rules to Govern Export Controls. (Illus.). 62p. 1974. 2.00 (ISBN 0-902594-26-5, BN16). Inst C D Howe.

Bergsten, Staffan. Mary Poppins & Myth. (Illus.). 1978. text ed. 14.75x (ISBN 91-22-00127-1). Humanities.

Bergsten, T., jt. ed. see Westin, G.

Bergstrasser, Gotthelf. Introduction to the Semitic Languages. rev. ed. Daniels, Peter T., tr. pap. text ed. 24.50x (ISBN 0-931464-10-2); 34.50x (ISBN 0-931464-17-X). Eisenbrauns.

Bergstrom, A. R. Statistical Inference in Continuous Time Economic Models. (Contributions to Economic Analysis Ser.: Vol. 99). 334p. 1976. 74.50 (ISBN 0-444-10991-9, North-Holland). Elsevier.

Bergstrom, A. R., et al, eds. Stability & Inflation: Essays in Memory of A. W. Phillips. LC 77-4420. 323p. 1978. cloth 84.95x (ISBN 0-471-99522-3, Pub. by Wiley-Interscience). Wiley.

Bergstrom, Corinne. Losing Your Best Friend. LC 79-20622. 32p. (ps-3). 1980. 10.95 (ISBN 0-87705-471-1). Human Sci Pr.

Bergstrom, Evelyn J., ed. see Perle, Ruth L.

Bergstrom, Harald. Weak Convergence of Measures. (Probability & Mathematical Statistics Ser.). 1982. 49.50 (ISBN 0-12-091080-2). Acad Pr.

Bergstrom, Ingvar. Dutch Still-Life Painting in the Seventeenth Century. LC 81-81718. (Illus.). xxxii, 330p. 1982. Repr. of 1956 ed. lib. bdg. 60.00 (ISBN 0-87817-279-3). Hacker.

Bergstrom, Jan. Organization, Life & Systematics of Trilobites. (Fossils & Strata Ser: No. 2). 1973. 12.00x (ISBN 8-200-09330-1, Dist. by Columbia U Pr). Universitet.

Bergstrom, Joan M. School's Out: Now What? LC 84-51171. (Illus.). 224p. (Orig.). 1984. pap. 10.95 (ISBN 0-89815-131-7). Ten Speed Pr.

Bergstrom, K., jt. auth. see Muhr, C.

Bergstrom, Kim, jt. auth. see Bergstrom, Leslie.

Bergstrom, Len V., jt. ed. see Rosenberg, Marie B.

Bergstrom, Leslie & Bergstrom, Kim. Trips on Twos. rev. ed. (Illus.). 72p. pap. 2.95 (ISBN 0-9612668-0-5). Talk Town.

Bergstrom, Louise. Magic Island. 1984. 8.95 (ISBN 0-8034-8408-9, Avalon). Bouregy.

--The Moonshell. (Orig.). 1981. pap. 1.75 (ISBN 0-8439-8016-8, Tiara Bks). Dorchester Pub Co.

Bergstrom, Peter V. Markets & Merchants: Economic Diversification in Colonial Virginia, 1700-1775. Bruchey, Stuart, ed. LC 84-45426. (American Economic History Ser.). 270p. 1985. lib. bdg. 35.00 (ISBN 0-8240-6670-7). Garland Pub.

Bergstrom, Staffan, jt. auth. see Bondestam, Lars.

Bergstrom, Stig M., ed. see Symposium on Conodont Biostratigraphy 1969:(Ohio State University).

Bergstrom, Sune, jt. ed. see Vane, John R.

Bergstrom, Villy, jt. ed. see Ruden, Bengt.

Bergtsson, L., et al, eds. Dynamic Meterology: Data Assimilation Methods (Proceedings) (Applied Mathematical Sciences Ser.: Vol. 36). (Illus.). 330p. 1981. pap. 22.00 (ISBN 0-387-90632-0). Springer-Verlag.

Berguer, Ramon & Bauer, Raymond B., eds. Vertebrobasilar Arterial Occlusive Disease: Medical & Surgical Management. (Illus.). 352p. 1984. text ed. 54.50 (ISBN 0-89004-984-X). Raven.

Bergveld, P. Electromedical Instrumentation: A Guide for Medical Personnel. LC 77-85711. (Techniques of Measurement in Medicine Ser.: No. 2). (Illus.). 1980. 34.50 (ISBN 0-521-21892-6); pap. 12.95 (ISBN 0-521-29305-7). Cambridge U Pr.

Berhens, D., ed. see Knapp, H. & Doring, R.

Beria, L. On the History of the Bolshevik Organization in Transcaucasia. 206p. 1975. pap. text ed. 2.95 (ISBN 0-89380-000-7). Proletarian Pubs.

Bericht ueber die Jahresversammlung, 19-21 Juni 1975 in Nyon, Schweizerische Gesellschaft. Gynaekologie. Erb, H., ed. (Gynaekologische Rundschau: Vol. 15, Suppl. 1). (Illus.). 128p. 1976. 17.25 (ISBN 3-8055-2313-0). S Karger.

Bericoff, Steven. The Trial & Metamorphosis. 1984. pap. 6.95 (ISBN 0-87910-214-4). LImelight Edns.

Beriedale. The Little Pepper Book. (Illus.). 64p. 1983. 5.95 (ISBN 0-312-48865-3). St Martin.

Beringause, Arthur, jt. auth. see Lieberman, Leo.

Beringer, Johann B. The Lying Stones of Johann Bartholomew Adam Beringer Being His Lithographiae Wirceburgensis. Jahn, Melvin E. & Woolf, Daniel J., trs. LC 63-8585. 1963. 39.50x (ISBN 0-520-00110-9). U of Cal Pr.

Beringer, Richard E. Historical Analysis: Contemporary Approaches to Clio's Craft. LC 77-10589. pap. 83.30 (ISBN 0-317-09268-5, 2020344). Bks Demand UMI.

--Historical Analysis: Contemporary Approaches to Clio's Craft. LC 84-23368. 334p. 1985. Repr. of 1978 ed. lib. bdg. price not set (ISBN 0-89874-751-1). Krieger.

Beringer, Robert. The Easter People. 1984. 4.75 (ISBN 0-89536-682-7, 4858). CSS of Ohio.

Beringer, Theodore, jt. auth. see Borysenko, Myrin.

Berington, Joseph. The Literary History of the Middle Ages: Comprehending an Account of the State of Learning, from the Close of the Reign of Augustus, to Its Revival in the 15th Century. 1977. Repr. of 1846 ed. lib. bdg. 45.00 (ISBN 0-8495-0326-4). Arden Lib.

Berington, Simon. The Memoirs of Signior Guadentio Di Lucca. LC 74-170596. (Novel in England, 1700-1775 Ser.). lib. bdg. 61.00 (ISBN 0-8240-0578-3). Garland Pub.

Berins, Jane & Samuels, Madilyn. New Orleans Q & A: Trivial Questions, Terrific Answers. (Illus.). 96p. (Orig.). 1985. pap. 5.95 (ISBN 0-9614929-0-2). Royale LA.

Berinstein, Ava. Evidence for Multiattachment in K'Ekchi, Mayan. (Outstanding Publications in Linguistics Ser.). 330p. 1985. lib. bdg. 40.00 (ISBN 0-8240-5421-0). Garland Pub.

Berio, Luciano, et al. Luciano Berio: Two Interviews. Osmond-Smith, David, ed. LC 84-12346. (Illus.). 192p. 1985. 19.95 (ISBN 0-7145-2829-3, Dist. by Scribner). M Boyars.

Berio, Paquita. Ahora Brillan las Estrellas. 134p. (Orig., Span.). 1981. pap. 3.75 (ISBN 0-89922-201-3). Edit Caribe.

Beriozkin, V. Artists of the Bolshoi Theatre. 176p. 1976. 40.00x (ISBN 0-569-08360-5, Pub. by Collet's). State Mutual Bk.

Beriozkina, Patricia, tr. see Rozanov, Herman.

Beris, Sandra. The Pink Panther & the Fancy Party. (Golden Look-Look Bk.). 24p. (ps-3). 1983. pap. 1.50 (ISBN 0-307-11887-8, 11890, Golden Bks). Western Pub.

Beris, Sandra, jt. auth. see Seguin-Fontes, Marthe.

Beris, Sandra, ed. see Seguin-Fontes, Marthe.

Beris, Sandra, tr. see Seguin-Fontes, Martha.

Beritashvili, I. S. Vertebrate Memory. LC 74-157930. 143p. 1971. 25.00x (ISBN 0-306-30524-0, Plenum Pr). Plenum Pub.

Berk, A., et al. Water Shortage: Lessons in Conservation from the Great California Drought, 1976-77. 220p. 1984. Repr. of 1981 ed. lib. bdg. 22.50 (ISBN 0-8191-4092-9). U Pr of Amer.

Berk, A. A. Practical Robotics & Interfacing for the Spectrum. (Illus.). 160p. (Orig.). 1984. pap. 13.95 (ISBN 0-246-12576-4, Pub. by Granada England). Sheridan.

Berk, Emanuel. Downtown Improvement Manual. (APA Planners Press Ser.). 780p. 1976. pap. 28.95. Planners Pr.

--Downtown Improvement Manual. 780p. 1976. pap. 19.00 (ISBN 0-318-12962-0); pap. 16.00 members (ISBN 0-318-12963-9). Am Plan Assn.

Berk, Fred. Chasidic Dance. (YA) (gr. 9 up). 1975. pap. 5.00 (ISBN 0-8074-0083-1, 582050). UAHC.

--Holiday in Israel. Rainer, Beatrice & Venable, Lucy, eds. LC 78-111026. (Illus.). xvii, 70p. (Orig.). 1977. pap. 11.95 (ISBN 0-932582-08-7). Dance Notation.

Berk, Fred & Venable, Lucy. Dances from Israel. rev. ed. ii, 16p. 1967. pap. text ed. 5.00 (ISBN 0-932582-07-9). Dance Notation.

--Ten Folk Dances in Labanotation. i, 32p. 1959. pap. text ed. 5.00 (ISBN 0-932582-09-5). Dance Notation.

Berk, J. Edward, ed. Developments in Digestive Diseases, Vol. 3. (Illus.). 258p. 1980. text ed. 24.00 (ISBN 0-8121-0754-3). Lea & Febiger.

Berk, J. Edward, et al. Bockus Gastroenterology, 7 vols. 4th ed. (Illus.). 4500p. Date not set. Set. price not set (ISBN 0-7216-1777-8). Saunders.

Berk, J. L. & Sampliner, J. E., eds. Handbuch der Intensivmedizin. 3rd, rev. & enl. ed. (Illus.). xvi, 560p. 1985. pap. 41.75 soft cover (ISBN 3-8055-3766-2). S Karger.

Berk, J. L., et al, eds. Handbuch der Intensivmedizin. 1979. pap. 35.00 (ISBN 3-8055-2941-4). S Karger.

Berk, James I. & Sampliner, James F. Handboook of Critical Care. 2nd ed. 1982. 29.95 (ISBN 0-316-09171-5). Little.

Berk, Joseph & Berk, Susan. Financial Analysis on the IBM PC. LC 84-12130. 222p. (Orig.). 1984. pap. 12.95 (ISBN 0-8019-7546-8). Chilton.

--Financial Analysis on TI Computers. LC 84-45158. 220p. (Orig.). 1984. pap. 12.95 (ISBN 0-8019-7518-2). Chilton.

Berk, Juliene. The Down Comforter: How to Beat Depression & Pull Yourself Out of the Blues. 1981. pap. 2.95 (ISBN 0-380-55814-9, 55814). Avon.

Berk, Lynn M., jt. auth. see Ohlgren, Thomas H.

Berk, Paul D. & Chalmers, Thomas C., eds. Frontiers in Liver Disease. (Illus.). 300p. 1981. text ed. 21.00 (ISBN 0-86577-017-4). Thieme-Stratton.

Berk, Paul D., et al. Myelofibrosis & the Biology of Connective Tissue. LC 84-5668. (Progress in Clinical & Biological Research Ser.: Vol. 154). 518p. 1984. 68.00 (ISBN 0-8451-5004-9). A R Liss.

Berk, Phyllis L. Duke's Command. (Illus.). (gr. 2-5). PLB 6.19 (ISBN 0-685-13772-4). Lantern.

Berk, Richard A. & Rossi, Peter H. Prison Reform & State Elites. LC 76-21240. 224p. 1977. prof ref 25.00 (ISBN 0-88410-214-9). Ballinger Pub.

Berk, Richard A., et al. Water Shortage: Lessons in Conservation from the Great California Drought, 1976-77. (Illus.). 232p. 1981. text ed. 20.00 (ISBN 0-89011-560-5). Abt Bks.

Berk, Richard A., et al, eds. A Measure of Justice: An Empirical Study of Changes in the California Penal Code, 1955-1971. (Quantitative Studies in Social Relations). 1977. 39.50 (ISBN 0-12-091550-2). Acad Pr.

Berk, Robert N. & Lasser, Elliott C. Radiology of the Ileocecal Area. LC 74-11684. (Saunders Monographs in Clinical Radiology: Vol. 5). pap. 85.50 (ISBN 0-317-08646-4, 2012284). Bks Demand UMI.

Berk, Robert N., et al. Radiology of the Gallbladder & Bile Ducts: Diagnosis & Intervention. (Illus.). 608p. 1983. 69.50 (ISBN 0-7216-1728-X). Saunders.

Berk, Ronald A. Criterion-Referenced Measurement: The State of the Art. LC 79-18194. 1980. 22.50x (ISBN 0-8018-2264-5). Johns Hopkins.

--Handbook of Methods for Detecting Test Bias. LC 81-48190. (Illus.). 336p. 1982. text ed. 30.00x (ISBN 0-8018-2662-4). Johns Hopkins.

--Screening & Diagnosis of Children with Learning Disabilities. 296p. 1984. 29.75x (ISBN 0-398-04925-4). C C Thomas.

Berk, Ronald A., ed. Educational Evaluation Methodology: The State of the Art. LC 80-8859. 184p. 1981. text ed. 17.50x (ISBN 0-8018-2518-0). Johns Hopkins.

--A Guide to Criterion-Referenced Test Construction. LC 84-47955. 1984. text ed. 32.50x (ISBN 0-8018-2417-6). Johns Hopkins.

Berk, Ruth, jt. auth. see Kramer, Anne.

Berk, Sarah F. The Gender Factory: The Apportionment of Work in American Households. 264p. 1985. 29.50x (ISBN 0-306-41795-2, Plenum Pr). Plenum Pub.

Berk, Sarah F., ed. Women & Household Labor. LC 79-23003. (Sage Yearbooks in Women's Policy Studies: Vol. 5). (Illus.). 295p. 1980. 28.00 (ISBN 0-8039-1211-0); pap. 14.00 (ISBN 0-8039-1212-9). Sage.

Berk, Stephen E. Calvinism vs. Democracy: Timothy Dwight & the Origins of American Evangelical Orthodoxy. xiv, 252p. 1974. 21.50 (ISBN 0-208-01419-5, Archon). Shoe String.

Berk, Stephen M. Year of Crisis, Year of Hope: Russian Jewry & the Pogroms of 1881-1882. LC 84-25216. (Contributions in Ethnic Studies Ser.: No. 11). 1985. lib. bdg. 39.95 (ISBN 0-313-24609-2, BPG/). Greenwood.

Berk, Susan. California: A Programmed History. (gr. 10-12). 1976. pap. text ed. 7.67 (ISBN 0-87720-617-1). AMSCO Sch.

Berk, Susan, jt. auth. see Berk, Joseph.

Berk, Z. Braverman's Introduction to the Biochemistry of Foods. 2nd, rev. ed. 316p. 1976. 41.50 (ISBN 0-444-41450-9, Biomedical Pr). Elsevier.

Berka, Karel. Measurement: Its Concepts, Theories & Problems. 1983. 49.50 (ISBN 90-277-1416-9, Pub. by Reidel Holland). Kluwer Academic.

Berka, Paula M., jt. auth. see Minard, Susan.

Berke, jt. auth. see Gioello.

Berke & Sorass, eds. English-Norwegian Dictionary: Includes New Words since Word War II. 562p. 1963. 30.00 (ISBN 0-317-18988-3, N434). Vanous.

Berke, Art. Unsung Heroes of the Major Leagues. LC 75-34909. (Illus.). 160p. (gr. 5 up). 1976. PLB 3.69 (ISBN 0-394-93096-7, BYR). Random.

Berke, Art & Schmitt, Paul. This Date in Chicago White Sox History. LC 81-40804. (This Date Ser.). (Illus.). 304p. 1982. pap. 10.95 (ISBN 0-8128-6132-9). Stein & Day.

Berke, Beverly, jt. auth. see Gioello, Debbie A.

Berke, Bradley. Tragic Thought & the Grammar of Tragic Myth. LC 81-48675. 128p. 1982. 15.00X (ISBN 0-253-36027-7). Ind U Pr.

Berke, Jacqueline. Twenty Questions for the Writer: A Rhetoric with Readings. 4th ed. 630p. 1985. pap. text ed. 14.95 (ISBN 0-15-592403-6, HC); instr's. manual avail. (ISBN 0-15-592404-4). HarBraceJ.

Berke, Joel S. Answers to Educational Inequity. LC 73-7237. 1974. 24.25x; text ed. 22.25x 10 or more copies. McCutchan.

Berke, Joel S., et al. Financing Equal Educational Opportunity: Alternatives for State Finance. LC 79-190059. 300p. 1972. 22.75x (ISBN 0-8211-0120-X); text ed. 20.50x 10 or more copies. McCutchan.

--Politicians, Judges & City Schools: Reforming School Finance in New York. LC 84-60265. 228p. 1985. 25.00x (ISBN 0-87154-108-4). Russell Sage.

Berke, Joseph & Hernton, Calvin C. The Cannabis Experience: An Interpretative Study of the Effects of Marijuana & Hashish. 288p. 1974. text ed. 17.50x (ISBN 0-7206-0073-1). Humanities.

Berke, Melvyn & Grant, Joanne. Games Divorced People Play. (Illus.). 264p. 1980. 12.95 (ISBN 0-13-346205-6, Busn); pap. 5.95 (ISBN 0-13-346197-1). P-H.

Berke, Roberta. Bounds out of Bounds: A Compass for Recent American & British Poetry. 1981. 19.95x (ISBN 0-19-502872-4). Oxford U Pr.

Berke, Roberta E. Sphere of Light. (Illus.). 1972. 10.00 (ISBN 0-685-29890-6, Pub. by Trigram Pr); signed ed. 18.00 (ISBN 0-685-29891-4). Small Pr Dist.

Berke, Sally. Monster at Loch Ness. LC 77-24715. (Great Unsolved Mysteries). (Illus.). (gr. 4-5). 1977. PLB 14.25 (ISBN 0-8172-1054-7). Raintree Pubs.

--Monster at Loch Ness. LC 77-24715. (Great Unsolved Mysteries Ser.). (Illus.). 48p. (gr. 4up). 1983. pap. 9.27 (ISBN 0-8172-2160-3). Raintree Pubs.

Berkebile, Don H. Carriage Terminology: An Historical Dictionary. LC 77-118. (Illus.). 487p. 1979. 37.50x (ISBN 0-87474-166-1). Smithsonian.

Berkebile, Don H., ed. American Carriages, Sleighs, Sulkies & Carts: 168 Illustrations from Victorian Sources. (Illus.). 14.75 (ISBN 0-8446-5556-2). Peter Smith.

--American Carriages, Sleighs, Sulkies & Carts. LC 76-17222. (Pictorial Archive Ser.). (Illus.). 1977. pap. 6.50 (ISBN 0-486-23328-6). Dover.

Berkebile, Donna. Come Lord Jesus. 1979. pap. 2.25 (ISBN 0-89536-406-9). CSS of Ohio.

--Game of Life. 1975. 2.50 (ISBN 0-317-04048-0, 0702). CSS of Ohio.

--This Is Your Life. 1975. 2.25 (ISBN 0-317-04082-0). CSS of Ohio.

Berkel, Boyce N. How to Prevent Home Accidents & Handle Emergencies Effectively. LC 79-55195. (Illus.). 1979. pap. 7.50 (ISBN 0-9603184-0-2). B Berkel.

Berkeley, A. E. & Barnes, Ann, eds. Labor Relations in Hospitals & Health Care Facilities: Proceedings of a Conference Presented by the American Arbitration Association & the Federal Mediation & Conciliation Service, 1975. LC 75-45236. pap. 27.50 (ISBN 0-317-26526-1, 2023972). Bks Demand UMI.

Berkeley, Anthony. The Piccadilly Murder. (Detective Stories Ser.). 352p. 1983. pap. 5.95 (ISBN 0-486-24518-7). Dover.

--The Poisoned Chocolates Case. 1980. pap. 2.95 (ISBN 0-440-16844-9). Dell.

Berkeley, Anthony, ed. see Christie, Agatha, et al.

Berkeley, Bernard. Floors: Selection & Maintenance. LC 68-23014. (American Library Association Ser.: No. 13). pap. 81.50 (ISBN 0-317-27860-6, 2024196). Bks Demand UMI.

Berkeley, David S. Blood Will Tell in Shakespeare's Plays. (Graduate Studies: No. 28). 107p. 1984. 35.00 (ISBN 0-89672-118-3); pap. text ed. 20.00 (ISBN 0-89672-108-6). Tex Tech Pr.

Berkeley, Dorothy S., jt. auth. see Berkeley, Edmund.

Berkeley, Dorothy S., ed. see Clayton, John.

Berkeley, Edmund & Berkeley, Dorothy S. Dr. John Mitchell: The Man Who Made the Map of North America. LC 73-16162. (Illus.). xix, 283p. 1974. 25.00 (ISBN 0-8078-1221-8). U of NC Pr.

--John Beckley, Zealous Partisan in a Nation Divided. LC 73-86616. (Memoirs Ser.: Vol. 100). (Illus.). 1973. 10.00 (ISBN 0-87169-100-0). Am Philos.

--The Life & Travels of John Bartram: From Lake Ontario to the River St. John. LC 81-4083. (Illus.). xv, 376p. 1982. 25.00 (ISBN 0-8130-0700-3). U Presses Fla.

Berkeley, Edmund, ed. see Clayton, John.

Berkeley, Edmund C. The Computer Book of Lists & the First Computer Almanac. (Illus.). 176p. 1984. pap. 14.95 (ISBN 0-8359-0864-X). Reston.

Berkeley, Edmund, Jr., ed. Autographs & Manuscripts: A Collector's Manual. (Illus.). 1978. 24.95 (ISBN 0-684-15622-9, ScribR). Scribner.

Berkeley, Ellen P. Maverick Cats: Encounters with Feral Cats. (Illus.). 192p. 1982. 12.95 (ISBN 0-8027-0714-9). Walker & Co.

Berkeley, George. Berkeley's Philosophical Writings. Armstrong, David M., ed. (Orig.). 1965. pap. 3.95 (ISBN 0-02-064170-2, Collier). Macmillan.

--Philosophical Works: Including the Works on Vision. (Rowman & Littlefield University Library). 1980. 18.50x (ISBN 0-87471-699-3); pap. 8.75x (ISBN 0-8476-6231-4). Rowman.

--Philosophical Works Including the Works of Vision. 358p. 1975. 20.00 (ISBN 0-460-10483-7, DEL-05137, Evman). Biblio Dist.

--Philosophical Writings. Jessop, T. E., ed. LC 69-13823. Repr. of 1953 ed. lib. bdg. 19.75x (ISBN 0-8371-1056-4, BEPW). Greenwood.

--Principles, Dialogues & Philosophical Correspondence. Turbayne, Colin M., tr. LC 64-66065. 1965. pap. write for info. (ISBN 0-02-421600-3, LLA208). Macmillan.

--The Principles of Human Knowledge & Three Dialogues Between Hylas & Philonous. 12.00 (ISBN 0-8446-5833-2). Peter Smith.

--The Querist: Seventeen Twenty-Six Edition. 1981. write for info. (ISBN 0-08-027641-5, HE 014); microfiche 10.00 (ISBN 0-686-79356-0). Pergamon.

--Selections from Berkeley. LC 72-4216. (Select Bibliographies Reprint Ser.). 1972. Repr. of 1899 ed. 22.00 (ISBN 0-8369-6873-5). Ayer Co Pubs.

--Three Dialogues Between Hylas & Philonous. Turbayne, Colin M., ed. 1954. pap. 5.99 scp (ISBN 0-672-60206-7, LLA39). Bobbs.

--Three Dialogues Between Hylas & Philonous. Adams, Robert M., ed. LC 79-65276. 138p. 1979. lib. bdg. 15.00 (ISBN 0-915144-62-X); pap. text ed. 2.95 (ISBN 0-915144-61-1). Hackett Pub.

--Three Dialogues Between Hylas & Philonous. McCormack, Thomas J., ed. vi, 144p. 1969. pap. 4.95 (ISBN 0-87548-069-1). Open Court.

--Treatise Concerning the Principles of Human Knowledge. Turbayne, Colin M., ed. LC 57-1290. 1957. pap. 4.79 scp (ISBN 0-672-60225-3, LLA53). Bobbs.

--A Treatise Concerning the Principles of Human Knowledge. McCormack, Thomas J., ed. & pref. by. xv, 143p. 1963. 12.00 (ISBN 0-87548-071-3); pap. 4.95 (ISBN 0-87548-072-1). Open Court.

--A Treatise Concerning the Principles of Human Knowledge. Winkler, Kenneth, ed. & intro. by. LC 82-2876. (HPC Philosophical Classics Ser.). 156p. 1982. lib. bdg. 15.00 (ISBN 0-915145-40-5); pap. text ed. 3.45 (ISBN 0-915145-39-1). Hackett Pub.

--A Treatise Concerning the Principles of Human Knowledge: Three Dialogues Between Hylas & Philonous. 288p. 1985. pap. 6.95 (ISBN 0-87548-446-8). Open Court.

--Works on Vision. Turbayne, Colin M., ed. LC 81-7160. (The Library of Liberal Arts: No. 83). iii, 158p. 1981. Repr. of 1963 ed. lib. bdg. 19.75x (ISBN 0-313-23186-9, BEWV). Greenwood.

Berkeley, George, et al. The Empiricists. Incl. Essay Concerning Human Understanding. abr ed. Locke, John; Principles of Human Knowledge. Berkeley, George; Three Dialogues. Berkeley, George; Enquiry Concerning Human Understanding. Hume, David. pap. 7.95 (ISBN 0-385-09622-4, Anch). Doubleday.

Berkeley, George F. Campaign of Adowa & the Rise of Menelik. LC 76-76477. (Illus.). Repr. of 1902 ed. cancelled (ISBN 0-8371-1132-3, BEC&, Pub. by Negro U Pr). Greenwood.

Berkeley Holistic Health Center, compiled by. Holistic Health Lifebook. LC 81-2846. (Illus.). 430p. 1981. pap. 12.95 (ISBN 0-915904-53-5). And-Or Pr.

Berkeley Holistic Health Center Staff, compiled by. The Holistic Health Handbook: A Tool for Attaining Wholeness of Body, Mind & Spirit. (Illus.). 488p. 1984. pap. 12.95 (ISBN 0-8289-0542-8). Greene.

Berkeley Holistic Health Center Staff, tr. The Holistic Health Lifebook: A Guide to Personal & Planetary Well Being. 448p. 1984. pap. 12.95 (ISBN 0-8289-0543-6). Greene.

Berkeley, Humphry. The Life & Death of Rochester Sneath. (Illus.). 96p. 1981. 11.95 (ISBN 0-241-10416-5, Pub. by Hamish Hamilton England). David & Charles.

--The Odyssey of Enoch: A Political Memoir. (Illus.). 1978. 17.95 (ISBN 0-241-89623-1, Pub. by Hamish Hamilton England). David & Charles.

Berkeley, James P. Knowing the Old Testament. (Illus.). (YA) (gr. 9 up). 1954. pap. text ed. 5.95 (ISBN 0-8170-0088-7). Judson.

Berkeley, M. J. & Broome, C. E. Notices of British Fungi: 1841-45, 35 papers bd. in 1 vol. (Bibl. Myco.: Vol. 1). 1967. 49.00 (ISBN 3-7682-0456-1). Lubrecht & Cramer.

Berkeley, Peter E. Computer Training Operations: A Strategy for Change. 336p. 1984. 29.95 (ISBN 0-442-20993-2). Van Nos Reinhold.

Berkeley Planning Associates Inc. & Energyworks Inc. Energy Cost Control Guide for Multifamily Properties. Kirk, Nancye J., ed. (Illus.). 100p. (Orig.). 1981. pap. 26.80 (ISBN 0-912104-67-8, 863). Inst Real Estate.

Berkeley Poets Cooperative, ed. Berkeley Poets Cooperative Anthology, 1970-1980. 256p. 1980. pap. 6.95 (ISBN 0-917658-12-4). BPW & P.

Berkeley, R. C. & Ellwood, D. C., eds. Microbial Polysaccharides & Polysaccharases. (Society for General Microbiology Ser.). 1979. 59.50 (ISBN 0-12-091450-6). Acad Pr.

Berkeley, R. C., et al. Microbial Adhesion to Surfaces. LC 80-41358. 559p. 1981. 125.00x (ISBN 0-470-27083-7). Halsted Pr.

Berkeley, Roger & Goodfellow, Michael, eds. The Aerobic Endosphere-Forming Bacteria: Classification & Identification. (Society for General Microbiology Special Publication: No. 4). 1981. 45.00 (ISBN 0-12-091250-3). Acad Pr.

Berkeley, Selma G. & Jackson, Barbara E. Your Career As a Medical Secretary Transcriber. LC 74-34233. (Wiley Biomedical-Health Publication Ser.). pap. 39.60 (ISBN 0-317-28655-2, 2055088). Bks Demand UMI.

Berkeley, William D. & Foster, Jerry. Long-Range Planning for Independent Schools. 1979. pap. 13.50 (ISBN 0-934338-36-1). NAIS.

Berkery, Michael J. & Bolek, Raymond W. Touche Ross Guide to Selecting a Small Business Computer. LC 84-26528. 337p. 1985. pap. 19.95 (ISBN 0-13-925744-6). P-H.

Berkes, Niyazi, ed. & tr. see Gokalp, Ziya.

Berkey, Arthur L., ed. Teacher Education in Agriculture. 2nd ed. (Illus.). 350p. 1982. text ed. 14.75x (ISBN 0-8134-2217-5). Interstate.

Berkey, Barry R. Halfway Through the Tunnel. LC 72-82790. 180p. 1972. 7.50 (ISBN 0-8022-2099-1). Philos Lib.

--Save Your Marriage. LC 75-45338. 313p. 1976. 20.95x (ISBN 0-88229-235-8). Nelson-Hall.

Berkey, Barry R., et al. Pioneer Decoy Carvers: A Biography of Lemuel & Stephen Ward. LC 77-13075. (Illus.). 172p. 1977. 17.50 (ISBN 0-87033-243-0). Tidewater.

Berkey, Dennis D. Calculus. LC 83-20046. 1194p. 1984. text ed. 42.95x (ISBN 0-03-059522-3). SCP.

Berkey, Gordon, jt. auth. see Holloway, Gordon F.

Berkey, Jim, jt. auth. see Tracy, Jack.

Berkey, Martha L., jt. auth. see Wooden, Wayne S.

Berkey, Rachel L. New Career Opportunities in the Paralegal Profession. LC 82-13929. (Illus.). 160p. 1983. lib. bdg. 11.95 (ISBN 0-668-05478-6). Arco.

--Resumes for Paralegals & Other People with Legal Training: A Complete Resume Preparation & Job-Getting Guide. LC 83-9931. 1983. 11.95 (ISBN 0-668-05754-8); pap. 6.95 (ISBN 0-668-05760-2). Arco.

Berkey, Robert F. & Edwards, Sarah A., eds. Christological Perspectives. 320p. 18.95 (ISBN 0-8298-0491-9); pap. 10.95 (ISBN 0-8298-0606-7). Pilgrim NY.

Berkey, Velma, et al. Chincoteague for Children. LC 75-20185. (Illus.). 61p. 1975. pap. 5.95 (ISBN 0-87033-208-2). Tidewater.

Berkheiser, Samuel W., Jr. Fetid Barite Occurrences, Western Berks County, Pennsylvania. (Mineral Resource Report: No. 84). (Illus.). 43p. 1984. pap. 5.55 (ISBN 0-8182-0053-7). Commonweal PA.

--Reconnaissance Survey of Potential Carbonate Whiting Sources in Pennsylvania. (Mineral Resource Report Ser.: No. 83). (Illus.). 53p. (Orig.). 1983. pap. 3.75 (ISBN 0-8182-0024-3). Commonweal PA.

Berkhof, Hendrik. Christ & the Powers. LC 62-13713. 80p. 1962. pap. 3.95 (ISBN 0-8361-1820-0). Herald Pr.

Berkhof, Hendrikus. Christ, the Meaning of History. (Twin Brooks Ser.). 1979. pap. 4.95 (ISBN 0-8010-0762-3). Baker Bk.

--Doctrine of the Holy Spirit. LC 64-16279. 1976. pap. 6.95 (ISBN 0-8042-0551-5). John Knox.

--Introduction to the Study of Dogmatics. Vriend, John, tr. from Dutch. 120p. (Orig.). 1985. pap. 7.95 (ISBN 0-8028-0045-9). Eerdmans.

Berkhof, Hendrikus, ed. Christian Faith. Woudstra, Sierd, tr. from Dutch. LC 79-12673. 22.95 (ISBN 0-8028-3521-X). Eerdmans.

Berkhof, Louis. The History of Christian Doctrine. 1978. 12.95 (ISBN 0-85151-005-1). Banner of Truth.

--History of Christian Doctrines. (Twin Brooks Ser). 288p. 1975. pap. 7.95 (ISBN 0-8010-0636-8). Baker Bk.

--Introduction to Systematic Theology. (Twin Brooks Ser.). 1979. pap. 5.95 (ISBN 0-8010-0768-2). Baker Bk.

--Manual of Christian Doctrine. 1933. pap. 7.95 (ISBN 0-8028-1647-9). Eerdmans.

--Principles of Biblical Interpretation. 1950. 8.95 (ISBN 0-8010-0549-3). Baker Bk.

--Summary of Christian Doctrine. 1939. pap. 4.95 (ISBN 0-8028-1513-8). Eerdmans.

--Systematic Theology. 1978. 19.95x (ISBN 0-8028-3020-X). Eerdmans.

Berkhofer, Edward, ed. see Dittberner, Job L.

Berkhofer, Edward, ed. see Fine, William F.

Berkhofer, Robert, ed. see Baker, M. Joyce.

Berkhofer, Robert, ed. see Biemer, Linda B.

Berkhofer, Robert, ed. see Blouin, Francis X., Jr.

Berkhofer, Robert, ed. see Conk, Margo A.

Berkhofer, Robert, ed. see De Marco, William M.

Berkhofer, Robert, ed. see Friedman, Jean E.

Berkhofer, Robert, ed. see Geddes, Gordon E.

Berkhofer, Robert, ed. see Goodwin, Everett C.

Berkhofer, Robert, ed. see Gragg, Larry D.

Berkhofer, Robert, ed. see Grigg, Susan.

Berkhofer, Robert, ed. see Hampel, Robert L.

Berkhofer, Robert, ed. see Hanlan, James P.

Berkhofer, Robert, ed. see Hansen, Stephen L.

Berkhofer, Robert, ed. see Harlan, David.

Berkhofer, Robert, ed. see Hast, Adele.

Berkhofer, Robert, ed. see Holmes, Richard.

Berkhofer, Robert, ed. see Hummer, Patricia M.

Berkhofer, Robert, ed. see Kanawada, Leo V., Jr.

Berkhofer, Robert, ed. see Lauderbaugh, Richard A.

Berkhofer, Robert, ed. see Mencke, John G.

Berkhofer, Robert, ed. see Mottus, Jane E.

Berkhofer, Robert, ed. see Nawyn, William.

Berkhofer, Robert, ed. see Nord, David P.

Berkhofer, Robert, ed. see Primer, Ben.

Berkhofer, Robert, ed. see Roeder, George H., Jr.

Berkhofer, Robert, ed. see Rosenberg, Ann E.

Berkhofer, Robert, ed. see Rotella, Elyce J.

Berkhofer, Robert, ed. see Schlereth, Wendy C.

Berkhofer, Robert, ed. see Selcraig, James T.

Berkhofer, Robert, ed. see Singleton, Gregory H.

Berkhofer, Robert, ed. see Stuart, Paul.

Berkhofer, Robert, ed. see Weinbaum, Paul O.

Berkhofer, Robert, ed. see Wharton, Leslie.

Berkhofer, Robert, ed. see Woods, Patricia D.

Berkhofer, Robert, ed. see Young, Christine A.

Berkhofer, Robert, ed. see Zelman, Patricia G.

Berkhofer, Robert F. Salvation & the Savage: An Analysis of Protestant Missions & American Indian Response, 1787-1862. LC 77-22857. 1977. Repr. of 1965 ed. lib. bdg. 22.50x (ISBN 0-8371-9745-7, BESSA). Greenwood.

--The White Man's Indian: Images of the American Indian from Columbus to the Present. LC 77-15568. (Illus.). 1978. 15.00 (ISBN 0-394-48485-1). Knopf.

Berkhofer, Robert F., Jr. Salvation & the Savage: An Analysis of Protestant Missions & American Indian Response, 1787-1862. LC 65-11826. 1972. pap. text ed. 4.95x (ISBN 0-689-70290-6, 184). Atheneum.

--The White Man's Indian: Images of the American Indian from Columbus to the Present. LC 78-11047. (Illus.). 1979. pap. 5.95 (ISBN 0-394-72794-0, V-794, Vin). Random.

Berkhout, A. J. Seismic Migration: Imaging of Acoustic Energy by Wave Field Extrapolation; A Theoretical Aspect. 2nd rev. & enl. ed. (Developments in Solid Earth Geophysics Ser.: Vol. 14A). 352p. 1983. 59.50 (ISBN 0-444-42130-0). Elsevier.

--Seismic Migration: Imaging of Acoustic Energy by Wave Field Extrapolation B, Practical Aspects. (Developments in Solid Earth Geophysics Ser.: No. 14B). 1985. 46.50 (ISBN 0-444-42431-8). Elsevier.

Berkhout, Carl T., jt. ed. see Gatch, Milton McC.

Berkhuijsen, Elly M., ed. see Symposium of the International Astronomical Union, No. 77.

Berki, R. N. The History of Political Thought: A Short Introduction. (Rowman & Littlefield University Library). 216p. 1977. 17.50x (ISBN 0-87471-996-8). Rowman.

--Insight & Vision: The Problem of Communism in Marx's Thought. 218p. 1984. 19.95x (ISBN 0-460-10172-2, Pub. by Evman England); pap. 9.95X (ISBN 0-460-11172-8, Pub. by Evman England). Biblio Dist.

--On Political Realism. 288p. 1981. 27.50x (ISBN 0-460-04367-6, Pub by J M Dent England). Biblio Dist.

Berki, R. N., jt. ed. see Hayward, Jack.

Berki, S. E. & Heston, Alan W., eds. Nation's Health: Some Issues. LC 77-186411. (Annals of the American Academy of Political & Social Science Ser.: No. 399). 1972. pap. 7.95 (ISBN 0-87761-146-7). Am Acad Pol Soc Sci.

Berki, Sylvester & Lepkowski, James. High-Volume & Low-Volume Users of Health Services: United States, 1980. Olmstead, Mary, ed. (Series C: No. 4). 180p. pap. 2.00 (ISBN 0-8406-0324-X). Natl Ctr Health Stats.

Berkin, Carol. Jonathan Sewall: Odyssey of an American Loyalist. 200p. 1974. 21.00x (ISBN 0-231-03851-8). Columbia U Pr.

Berkin, Carol & Norton, Mary B. Women of America: A History. LC 78-69589. (Illus.). 1979. pap. text ed. 17.50 (ISBN 0-395-27067-7). HM.

Berkin, Carol R. & Lovett, Clara M., eds. Women, War & Revolution. LC 79-26450. 310p. 1980. text ed. 34.50x (ISBN 0-8419-0502-9); pap. text ed. 13.50x (ISBN 0-8419-0545-2). Holmes & Meier.

Berklekamp, E. R., ed. Key Papers in the Development of Coding Theory. LC 73-87652. (Illus.). 1974. 27.00 (ISBN 0-87942-031-6, PC00323). Inst Electrical.

Berkley & Saundra, Gould. The Short Story Reader. 2nd ed. 1973. pap. 8.40 scp (ISBN 0-672-73292-0). Bobbs.

Berkley, Carl, ed. Automated Multiphasic Health Testing. LC 79-175127. 432p. 1971. pap. 20.00x (ISBN 0-939204-08-8, 70-21). Eng Found.

Berkley, George. Arthritis Without Aspirin: Effective New Ways to Control Arthritic Pain. 152p. 1982. 10.95 (ISBN 0-13-049114-4); pap. 5.95 (ISBN 0-13-049106-3). P-H.

--Cancer How to Prevent It & How to Help Your Doctor Fight It. 5.95x. Cancer Control Soc.

--Cancer: How to Prevent It, & How to Help Your Doctor Fight It. LC 77-26954. 1978. (Spec); pap. 5.95 (ISBN 0-13-113381-0, Spec). P-H.

--The Craft of Public Administration. 4th ed. 1984. text ed. 30.00 (ISBN 0-205-08127-4, 768127); test items avail. (ISBN 0-205-08128-2). Allyn.

--The Democratic Policeman. LC 73-84791. 256p. 1969. pap. 6.95x (ISBN 0-8070-0887-7, BP470). Beacon Pr.

--How to Manage Your Boss. 160p. 1985. 15.95 (ISBN 0-13-423641-6); pap. 7.95 (ISBN 0-13-423633-5). P H.

--The No-Drug Approach to Lowering Your Blood Pressure. 208p. (Orig.). 1981. pap. 3.50 (ISBN 0-915962-32-2). Larchmont Bks.

--The No-Drug Approach to Lowering Your Blood Pressure. 1981. 2.25x (ISBN 0-915962-32-2). Cancer Control Soc.

--On Being Black & Healthy: How Black Americans Can Live Longer & Healthier Lives. 206p. 1982. 11.95 (ISBN 0-13-634394-5); pap. 5.95 (ISBN 0-13-634386-4). P-H.

--The Querist, Containing Several Queries Proposed to the Consideration of the Public. Repr. of 1737 ed. 16.00 (ISBN 0-384-04010-1). Johnson Repr.

Berkley, Harold B., et al. Reference Card for the Dragon 32 Microcomputer. (Dragon 32 Ser.). (Illus.). 18p. (Orig.). 1983. pap. 5.95 (ISBN 0-915069-17-2). Nanos Sys.

Berkley, Henry J. A Treatise on Mental Diseases. Grob, Gerald N., ed. LC 78-22549. (Historical Issues in Mental Health Ser.). (Illus.). 1979. Repr. of 1900 ed. lib. bdg. 46.00x (ISBN 0-405-11903-8). Ayer Co Pubs.

Berkley, Sandra. Delta's Oral Placement Test Teacher's Manual. 16p. (Orig.). 1982. pap. text ed. 7.95 (ISBN 0-937354-04-X). Delta Systems.

Berkley, Sandra & Moore, Gary W. Delta's Oral Placement Test. 62p. (Orig.). 1982. pap. text ed. 20.95 (ISBN 0-937354-05-8). Delta Systems.

Berkley, Susan, tr. see Keppe, Norberto R., et al.

Berkman, Al. The Actor Sings, Vol. 1. 220p. (Orig.). 1985. pap. text ed. 12.95 (ISBN 0-317-02284-9). Melrose Bk Co.

--It's How You Say It. 1977. 12.50 (ISBN 0-934972-04-4). Melrose Bk Co.

--The Psychology of Singing. 1977. 12.50 (ISBN 0-934972-08-7). Melrose Bk Co.

--The Science of Popular Voice: Voice Production for the Pop Singer. 1979. 12.95 (ISBN 0-934972-09-5). Melrose Bk Co.

--Sex & the Singing Girl. 1975. 12.50 (ISBN 0-934972-03-6). Melrose Bk Co.

--Singers Glossary of Show Business Jargon. 1961. 3.95 (ISBN 0-934972-06-0). Melrose Bk Co.

--Singing Takes More Than a Voice. 1961. 3.95 (ISBN 0-934972-00-1). Melrose Bk Co.

--Song Presentation for Popular Singers: Book II. 1984. 12.50 (ISBN 0-934972-02-8). Melrose Bk Co.

--Song Presentation for Popular Singers: Book I. 1979. 10.00 (ISBN 0-934972-01-X). Melrose Bk Co.

--Vocal Gymnastics for the Pop Singer. 1979. 10.00 (ISBN 0-934972-07-9). Melrose Bk Co.

Berkman, Alexander. ABC of Anarchism. 86p. (Orig.). pap. 3.00 (ISBN 0-686-46369-2). Freedom Pr.

--ABC of Anarchism. 3rd ed. 86p. (Orig.). 1980. pap. 3.00 (ISBN 0-317-00634-7). Left Bank.

--ABC of Anarchism. 1984. lib. bdg. 79.95 (ISBN 0-87700-649-0). Revisionist Pr.

--The Anti-Climax. 59.95 (ISBN 0-87968-647-2). Gordon Pr.

--Prison Memoirs of an Anarchist. (Illus.). 540p. 1970. 8.50 (ISBN 0-686-05057-6); pap. 3.50 (ISBN 0-686-05058-4). Frontier Press Calif.

--The Russian Tragedy. Nowlin, William G., Jr., ed. 1979. 11.25 (ISBN 0-932366-03-1); pap. 4.50 (ISBN 0-932366-02-3). Black Thorn Bks.

--The Russian Tragedy. Nowlin, William G., Jr., ed. (Illus.). 1977. pap. 7.95 (ISBN 0-904564-11-8, Pub by Cienfuegos Pr). Carrier Pigeon.

Berkman, Alexander, jt. auth. see Goldman, Emma.

Berkman, Alexander, ed. see De Cleyre, Voltairine.

Berkman, Fral. Sure You Can Sing. 1983. 10.00 (ISBN 0-317-03727-7). Melrose Bk Co.

Berkman, Frank W., et al. Convention Management & Service. (Illus.). 230p. 1979. Repr. of 1978 ed. 19.95 (ISBN 0-86612-002-5). Educ Inst Am Hotel.

Berkman, Harold W. & Gilson, Christopher. Consumer Behavior: Concepts & Strategies. 2nd ed. LC 80-29645. 483p. 1981. text ed. write for info. (ISBN 0-534-00957-3). Kent Pub Co.

Berkman, Harold W. & Vernan, Ivan R. Contemporary Perspectives in International Business. 1979. 20.95 (ISBN 0-395-30562-4). HM.

Berkman, Harold W., jt. auth. see Gilson, Christopher.

Berkman, James L. The Ballads. (Illus.). 40p. (Orig.). 1984. pap. 10.00 (ISBN 0-943662-04-4, 164-356). Runaway Pubns.

--Concerto for Knife & Axe. (Illus.). 28p. (Orig.). 1977. pap. 2.00 (ISBN 0-943662-00-1, 25-336). Runaway Pubns.

--Last of the Northside Cowboys. (Illus.). 40p. (Orig.). 1980. pap. 3.00 (ISBN 0-943662-01-X, 579-010). Runaway Pubns.

--The Patriot, Vol. 1, No. 1. LC 1-464941. (Illus., Orig.). 1984. pap. 10.00 (ISBN 0-943662-05-2). Runaway Pubns.

--The Patriot: The Scripturion, Vol. 2, No. 1. (Orig.). 1985. pap. text ed. 10.00 (ISBN 0-943662-06-0). Runaway Pubns.

--Shoot Out. 32p. (Orig.). 1983. pap. 4.00 (ISBN 0-943662-02-8, 1-166-723). Runaway Pubns.

Berkman, Joyce. Olive Schreiner: Feminism on the Frontier. LC 78-74842. 1979. 11.95 (ISBN 0-88831-031-5). Eden Pr.

Berkman, Lisa A. & Breslow, Lester. Health & Ways of Living: The Alameda County Studies. (Illus.). 237p. 1983. 24.95x (ISBN 0-19-503216-0). Oxford U Pr.

Berkman, Richard L. & Viscusi, W. Kip. Damming the West: The Report on the Bureau of Reclamation. LC 72-77707. (Ralph Nader Study Group Reports). 286p. 1973. 12.95 (ISBN 0-670-25460-6, Grossman). Viking.

Berkman, Ronald. Opening the Gates: The Rise of the Prisoners Movement. 224p. 1979. 27.00x (ISBN 0-669-02828-2). Lexington Bks.

Berkman, Sylvia. Blackberry Wilderness. facs. ed. LC 79-116939. (Short Story Index Reprint Ser). 1959. 18.00 (ISBN 0-8369-3441-5). Ayer Co Pubs.

Berkmen, Yahya M. Radiology of the Trachea. 1985. 27.50 (ISBN 0-87527-259-2). Green.

Berkner, Dimity S. & Sellen, Betty-Carol, eds. New Options for Librarians: Finding a Job in a Related Field. 300p. 1984. 19.95 (ISBN 0-918212-73-1). Neal-Schuman.

Berkner, L. V. The Scientific Age. LC 75-16841. 137p. 1975. Repr. of 1964 ed. lib. bdg. 22.50x (ISBN 0-8371-8263-8, BESAG). Greenwood.

Berko, Frances G., et al. Management of Brain Damaged Children: A Parents' & Teachers' Guide. 84p. 1970. 12.75x (ISBN 0-398-00141-3). C C Thomas.

Berko, Roy M. & Bostwick, Fran. Basic-ly Communicating: An Activity Approach. 264p. 1982. pap. text ed. write for info. (ISBN 0-697-04208-1); instr's. manual write for info. (ISBN 0-697-04222-7). Wm C Brown.

Berko, Roy M. & Wolvin, Andrew D. Communicating: A Social & Career Focus. 2nd ed. (Illus.). 432p. 1981. pap. text ed. 16.50 (ISBN 0-395-29170-4); handbook with test items 1.00 (ISBN 0-395-29171-2). HM.

--This Business of Communicating. 2nd ed. 336p. 1983. pap. text ed. write for info. (ISBN 0-697-04227-8); instrs' manual avail. (ISBN 0-697-00279-9). Wm C Brown.

Berko, Roy M., et al. Communicating: A Social & Career Focus. 3rd ed. LC 84-81855. 416p. 1984. pap. text ed. write for info. (ISBN 0-395-35919-8); write for info. handbook (ISBN 0-395-36445-0). HM.

Berkoben, L. D. Coleridge's Decline As a Poet. (Studies in English Literature: No. 98). 171p. (Orig.). 1975. pap. text ed. 19.20x (ISBN 90-2793-226-3). Mouton.

Berkoff, Steven. Decadence & the Greeks. 64p. 1983. pap. 5.95 (ISBN 0-7145-3954-6). Riverrun NY.

--East & Other Plays. 1980. 9.95 (ISBN 0-7145-0206-5); pap. 7.95 (ISBN 0-7145-3637-7). Riverrun NY.

--Gross Intrusion & Other Stories. 1980. 9.95 (ISBN 0-7145-3685-7); pap. 4.95 (ISBN 0-7145-3825-6). Riverrun NY.

--West & Other Plays. 96p. (Orig.). 1985. 22.50 (ISBN 0-394-55017-X); pap. 7.95 (ISBN 0-394-62084-4). Grove.

Berkofsky, Louis, et al, eds. Settling the Desert. 290p. 1981. 50.95 (ISBN 0-677-16280-4). Gordon.

Berkom, Bev Ulsrud van. Ancient Scandinavian Designs. (The InternationalDesign Library). (Illus.). 48p. 1985. pap. 3.50 (ISBN 0-88045-073-8). Stemmer Hse.

Berkooz, M. Nuzi Dialect of Akkadian: Orthography & Phonology. (LD). 1937. pap. 9.00 (ISBN 0-527-00769-2). Kraus Repr.

Berkouwer, Gerrit C. Studies in Dogmatics: Theology, 14 vols. Incl. Vol. 1. Faith & Sanctification. 8.95 (ISBN 0-8028-3028-5); Vol. 2. The Providence of God. 10.95 (ISBN 0-8028-3029-3); Vol. 3. Faith & Justification. 8.95 (ISBN 0-8028-3030-7); Vol. 4. The Person of Christ. 9.95 (ISBN 0-8028-3031-5); Vol. 5. General Revelation. 10.95 (ISBN 0-8028-3032-3); Vol. 6. Faith & Perseverance. 8.95 (ISBN 0-8028-3033-1); Vol. 7. Divine Election. 9.95 (ISBN 0-8028-3034-X); Vol. 8. Man-The Image of God. 12.95 (ISBN 0-8028-3035-8); Vol. 9. The Work of Christ. 9.95 (ISBN 0-8028-3036-6); Vol. 10. The Sacraments. 12.95 (ISBN 0-8028-3037-4); Vol. 11. Sin. 17.95 (ISBN 0-8028-3027-7); Vol. 12. The Return of Christ. 13.95 (ISBN 0-8028-3393-4); The Church. 9.95 (ISBN 0-8028-3433-7); Holy Scripture. 11.95 (ISBN 0-8028-3394-2). 1952. Eerdmans.

Berkov, P. N. Literary Contacts Between Russia & the West Since the Fourteenth Century. 488p. 1973. 60.00x (ISBN 0-902089-46-3, Pub. by Variorum). State Mutual Bk.

Berkov, Robert. Strong Man of China. facs. ed. LC 70-124225. (Select Bibliographies Reprint Ser). (Illus.). 1938. 19.00 (ISBN 0-8369-5413-0). Ayer Co Pubs.

Berkove, Laurence I. Ambrose Bierce: A Braver Man Than Anybody Knew. (Illus.). Date not set. 22.00 (ISBN 0-88233-349-6). Ardis Pubs.

Berkovitch, J. Coal-Energy & Chemical Storehouse. 140p. 1981. 60.00x (ISBN 0-86108-023-8, Pub. by Portcullio Pr). State Mutual Bk.

Berkovits, Eliezer. Crisis & Faith. 224p. 1975. 8.95 (ISBN 0-88482-903-0, Sanhedrin Pr). Hebrew Pub.

--Faith After the Holocaust. 1973. 10.00x (ISBN 0-87068-193-1). Ktav.

--God, Man & History. 1979. Repr. of 1959 ed. 9.95 (ISBN 0-8246-0239-0). Jonathan David.

--Major Themes in Modern Philosophies of Judaism. 1974. 20.00x (ISBN 0-87068-264-4). Ktav.

--Not in Heaven: The Nature & Function of Halakha. LC 82-23255. 131p. 1983. 15.00x (ISBN 0-88125-003-1). Ktav.

--With God in Hell: Judaism in the Ghettos & Deathcamps. 1979. 9.95 (ISBN 0-88482-937-5, Sanhedrin Pr). Hebrew Pub.

Berkovitz, et al. Multiple Choice Questions in the Anatomical Sciences for Students of Dentistry. 112p. 1977. 10.00 (ISBN 0-7236-0451-7). PSG Pub Co.

Berkovitz, B. K., et al. A Color Atlas & Textbook of Oral Anatomy. (Illus.). 1978. 65.00 (ISBN 0-8151-0696-3). Year Bk Med.

Berkovitz, B. K. B., et al, eds. The Periodontal Ligament in Health & Disease. (Illus.). 472p. 1982. 110.00 (ISBN 0-08-024412-2); pap. 54.00 (ISBN 0-08-024411-4). Pergamon.

Berkovitz, L. D. Optimal Control Theory. LC 74-20837. (Applied Mathematical Sciences Ser.: Vol. 12). (Illus.). 1974. pap. 19.50 (ISBN 0-387-90106-X). Springer-Verlag.

Berkovitz, Seliger. Expanding Mental Health Interventions in Schools. 320p. 1985. pap. 15.95 (ISBN 0-8403-3545-8). Kendall Hunt.

Berkovsky, Boris, ed. see International Advanced Course & Workshop on Thermomechanics of Magnetic Fluids, Udine, Italy, Oct. 3-7, 1977.

Berkow, Robert. The Merck Manual. 14th ed. LC 1-31760. 1982. 19.75 (ISBN 0-911910-03-4). Merck.

Berkow, Robert, ed. The Merck Manual: General Medicine, Vol. I. 14th ed. 1600p. 1982. pap. 11.95 (ISBN 0-911910-04-2). Merck.

--The Merck Manual: Obstetrics, Gynecology, Pediatrics, Genetics, Vol. II. 14th ed. 600p. 1982. pap. 6.95 (ISBN 0-911910-05-0). Merck.

Berkowitz, A. E. & Kneller, E., eds. Magnetism & Metallurgy, 2 Vols. Vol. 2, 1969. 72.00 (ISBN 0-12-091702-5). Acad Pr.

Berkowitz, Alan. A Guide to the Bright Angel Trail. 1979. pap. 1.25 (ISBN 0-938216-09-0). GCNHA.

--A Guide to the North Kaibab Trail. 1980. pap. 1.25 (ISBN 0-938216-10-4). GCNHA.

Berkowitz, Alan D., jt. auth. see Dereshinsky, Ralph M.

Berkowitz, B., jt. auth. see Newman, M.

Berkowitz, B. J. & Scattergood, R. O., eds. Chemistry & Physics of Rapidly Solidified Materials: Proceedings, TMS Fall Meeting, St. Louis, Missouri, 1982. LC 83-61484. (Illus.). 315p. 1983. 45.00 (ISBN 0-89520-460-6). Metal Soc.

Berkowitz, B. J., jt. ed. see Fiore, N. F.

Berkowitz, Bernard, jt. auth. see Newman, Mildred.

Berkowitz, Bernard, jt. ed. see Newman, Mildred.

Berkowitz, David S. In Remembrance of Creation: Evolution of Art & Scholarship in the Medieval & Renaissance Bible. LC 68-28658. (Illus.). 160p. 1968. 25.00x (ISBN 0-87451-059-7). U Pr of New Eng.

Berkowitz, David S. & Thorne, Samuel E., eds. George Meriton. Sir Henry Spelman. Anon. Charles Fearne. (English Legal History Ser.: Vol. 137). 370p. 1979. lib. bdg. 61.00 (ISBN 0-8240-3174-1). Garland Pub.

--Sir Henry Finch. Edmund Wingate. William Phillips. (English Legal History Ser.: Vol. 68). 462p. 1979. lib. bdg. 61.00 (ISBN 0-8240-3055-9). Garland Pub.

Berkowitz, David S., ed. see De Lolme, Jean L.

Berkowitz, David S., ed. see Hammond, Henry.

Berkowitz, David S., ed. see Littlton, Thomas.

Berkowitz, David S., ed. see Morison, Richard.

Berkowitz, David S., ed. see Prynne, Wiliam, et al.

Berkowitz, David S., ed. see Staunford, William & Romilly, Samuel.

Berkowitz, Edward & McQuaid, Kim. Creating the Welfare State: The Political Economy of Twentieth Century Reform. LC 79-22524. 204p. 1980. 32.95x (ISBN 0-03-056243-0). Praeger.

Berkowitz, Edward D. Rehabilitation: The Federal Government's Response to Disability, 1935 to 1954. Phillips, William R. & Rosenberg, Janet, eds. LC 79-6896. (Physically Handicapped in Society Ser.). 1980. lib. bdg. 33.50x (ISBN 0-405-13107-0). Ayer Co Pubs.

Berkowitz, Edward D., et al, eds. Disability Policies & Government Programs. 206p. 1979. 33.95x (ISBN 0-03-051431-2). Praeger.

Berkowitz, Eric W., jt. auth. see Hillestad, Steven G.

Berkowitz, Freda P. Popular Titles & Subtitles of Musical Compositions. 2nd ed. LC 75-4751. 217p. 1975. 16.00 (ISBN 0-8108-0806-4). Scarecrow.

Berkowitz, Gerald, jt. auth. see Neimark, Paul.

Berkowitz, Gerald, ed. see Garrick, David.

Berkowitz, Gerald M. David Garrick: A Reference Guide. 1980. lib. bdg. 38.50 (ISBN 0-8161-8136-5). G K Hall.

--New Broadways: Theatre Across America 1950-1980. LC 81-21162. (Illus.). 208p. 1982. 26.50 (ISBN 0-8476-7031-7). Rowman.

--Sir John Vanbrugh & the End of Restoration Comedy. (Costerus New Ser.: No. 31). 222p. 1981. pap. text ed. 29.00x (ISBN 90-6203-503-5, Pub. by Rodopi Holland). Humanities.

Berkowitz, Gerald M. & Neimark, Paul. The Berkowitz Diet Switch. 288p. 1981. 2.98 (ISBN 0-517-37008-5, Arlington Hse). Outlet Bk Co.

Berkowitz, Henry. Fish Facts & Fancies. (Illus.). 32p. 1.95 (ISBN 0-916224-66-X). Banyan Bks.

Berkowitz, Herb B., jt. auth. see Feulner, Edwin J.

Berkowitz, Joan B., ed. see Symposium on Energy Storage (1975: Dallas), et al.

Berkowitz, Joan B., et al, eds. Marine Electrochemistry. LC 73-75170. (Illus.). pap. 103.50 (ISBN 0-317-10052-1, 2050445). Bks Demand UMI.

--Unit Operations for Treatment of Hazardous Industrial Wastes. LC 78-62520. (Pollution Technology Review: No. 47). (Illus.). 920p. 1979. 42.00 (ISBN 0-8155-0717-8). Noyes.

Berkowitz, Joseph. Photoabsorption, Photoionization & Photoelectron Spectroscopy. (Pure & Applied Physics Ser.). 1979. 59.50 (ISBN 0-12-091650-9). Acad Pr.

Berkowitz, Joseph & Groeneveld, Karl-Ontjes, eds. Molecular Ions: Geometric & Electronic Structures. (NATO ASI Series B, Physics: Vol. 90). 606p. 1983. 89.50x (ISBN 0-306-41264-0, Plenum Pr). Plenum Pub.

Berkowitz, Julie S. College of Physicians of Philadelphia Portrait Catalogue. LC 84-3206. (Illus.). 244p. text ed. 65.00 (ISBN 0-943060-03-6); pap. text ed. 35.00 (ISBN 0-943060-04-4). Wood Inst.

Berkowitz, L., jt. ed. see Macaulay, J.

Berkowitz, Leonard. Advances in Experimental Social Psychology, Vol. 16. (Serial Publication Ser.). 1984. 29.50 (ISBN 0-12-015216-9). Acad Pr.

--Social Psychology. 1972. pap. 11.90x (ISBN 0-673-07533-8). Scott F.

--A Survey of Social Psychology. 2nd ed. LC 79-23961. 594p. 1980. text ed. 29.95 (ISBN 0-03-042731-2, HoltC); instructor's manual 25.00 (ISBN 0-03-055386-5); study guide 10.95 (ISBN 0-03-056234-1). HR&W.

Berkowitz, Leonard, ed. Advances in Experimental Social Psychology: Equity Theory- Toward a General Theory of Social Interaction, Vol. 9. 1976. 55.00 (ISBN 0-12-015209-6). Acad Pr.

--Advances in Experimental Social Psychology. Incl. Vol. 2. 1966. 60.00 (ISBN 0-12-015202-9); Vol. 3. 1967. 60.00 (ISBN 0-12-015203-7); Vol. 4. 1969. 60.00 (ISBN 0-12-015204-5); Vol. 5. 1971. 60.00 (ISBN 0-12-015205-3); Vol. 6. 1972. 60.00 (ISBN 0-12-015206-1); Vol. 7. 1974. 60.00 (ISBN 0-12-015207-X); Vol. 8. 1975. 60.00 (ISBN 0-12-015208-8); Vol. 10. 1977. 60.00 (ISBN 0-12-015210-X); Vol. 11. 1978. 55.00 (ISBN 0-12-015211-8). LC 64-23452. Acad Pr.

--Advances in Experimental Social Psychology, Vol. 12. (Serial Publication Ser.). 1979. 50.00 (ISBN 0-12-015212-6). Acad Pr.

--Advances in Experimental Social Psychology, Vol. 13. (Serial Publication Ser.). 1980. 40.00 (ISBN 0-12-015213-4). Acad Pr.

--Advances in Experimental Social Psychology, Vol. 14. (Serial Publication Ser.). 1981. 45.00 (ISBN 0-12-015214-2). Acad Pr.

--Advances in Experimental Social Psychology, Vol. 15. 270p. 1982. 35.00 (ISBN 0-12-015215-0). Acad Pr.

--Advances in Experimental Social Psychology, Vol. 17. (Serial Publication Ser.). 1984. 47.50 (ISBN 0-12-015217-7). Acad Pr.

--Advances in Experimental Social Psychology, Vol. 18. LC 64-23452. 1984. 42.50 (ISBN 0-12-015218-5). Acad Pr.

--Cognitive Theories in Social Psychology: Papers from Advances in Experimental Social Psychology. 1978. 24.00 (ISBN 0-12-091850-1). Acad Pr.

--Group Processes. 1978. 23.50 (ISBN 0-12-091840-4). Acad Pr.

Berkowitz, Luci, jt. auth. see Brunner, Theodore F.

Berkowitz, M., et al. The Politics of American Foreign Policy: The Social Contexts of Decisions. (Illus.). 1977. pap. text ed. 18.95 (ISBN 0-13-685073-1). P-H.

Berkowitz, Marc. Gravadores Brasileros. (Illus.). 1969. pap. 1.00 (ISBN 0-913456-07-1, Pub. by Ctr Inter-Am Rel). Interbk Inc.

Berkowitz, Marvin. The Social Costs of Human Underdevelopment: Case Study of Seven New York City Neighborhoods. LC 73-19440. (Special Studies in U.S. Economic, Social & Political Issues). 1974. 49.50x (ISBN 0-275-28821-8). Irvington.

Berkowitz, Mona. How to Raise & Train an Old English Sheepdog. pap. 2.95 (ISBN 0-87666-344-7, DS-1103). TFH Pubns.

Berkowitz, Morton I. A Primer on School Mental Health Consultation. 132p. 1975. 14.75x (ISBN 0-398-03342-0). C C Thomas.

Berkowitz, N. An Introduction to Coal Technology. LC 78-19663. (Energy Science & Engineering Ser.). 1979. 37.00 (ISBN 0-12-091950-8). Acad Pr.

Berkowitz, Pearl H. & Rothman, Esther P. Public Education for Disturbed Children in New York City: Application & Theory. 388p. 1967. 38.75x (ISBN 0-398-00142-1). C C Thomas.

Berkowitz, Raymond S. Modern Radar: Analysis, Evaluation & System Design. LC 65-21446. pap. 160.00 (ISBN 0-317-09180-8, 2017411). Bks Demand UMI.

Berkowitz, Richard L., et al. Handbook for Prescribing Medications During Pregnancy. 1981. pap. text ed. 13.95 (ISBN 0-316-09173-1). Little.

Berkowitz, Robert L., jt. auth. see Shaver, Deborah K.

Berkowitz, Sarah B. In Search of Ashes. LC 83-50495. 128p. 1984. 7.95 (ISBN 0-88400-099-0). Shengold.

Berkowitz, Sol, et al. A New Approach to Sight Singing. rev ed. (Illus.). 346p. 1976. pap. text ed. 17.95x (ISBN 0-393-09194-5). Norton.

Berkowitz, Stan, jt. auth. see Lees, David.

Berkowitz, William R. Community Dreams: Ideas for Enhancing Neighborhood & Community Life. LC 83-22853. 256p. (Orig.). 1984. pap. 8.95 (ISBN 0-915166-29-1). Impact Pubs Cal.

--Community Impact: Creating Grass Roots Change. 304p. 1982. 18.95 (ISBN 0-87073-447-4); pap. 9.95 (ISBN 0-87073-448-2). Schenkman Bks Inc.

Berkowtiz, Marvin W. & Oser, Fritz, eds. Moral Education: International Perspectives. 456p. 1985. text ed. 45.00 (ISBN 0-89859-557-6). L Erlbaum Assocs.

Berkshire Traveller. Treasured Recipes of Country Inns. LC 73-91008. (Illus.). 134p. 1973. pap. 4.95 (ISBN 0-912944-08-0). Berkshire Traveller.

Berkshire Traveller, ed. Country Inn Cookbook. rev. ed. LC 75-2520. (Illus.). 1975. pap. 4.95 (ISBN 0-912944-18-8). Berkshire Traveller.

Berkson, Bill. Blue Is the Hero. 1976. 7.50 (ISBN 0-685-79245-5); signed ed. 15.00 (ISBN 0-685-79246-3); pap. 4.00 (ISBN 0-685-79247-1). L Pubns.

--Lush Life. Elmslie, Kenward, ed. LC 84-51752. 52p. (Orig.). 1985. pap. 6.00 (ISBN 0-915990-26-1). Z Pr.

--Start Over. (Desert Island Chapbook Ser.). 32p. 1983. pap. 3.50 (ISBN 0-939180-24-3). Tombouctou.

Berkson, Bill & LeSeuer, Joe, eds. Homage to Frank O'Hara. (Illus.). 224p. 1980. pap. 8.95 (ISBN 0-916870-29-4). Creative Arts Bk.

Berkson, Carmel, jt. auth. see Del Bonta, Robert J.

Berkson, Carmel, et al. Elephanta: The Cave of Shiva. (Illus.). 144p. 1983. 35.00x (ISBN 0-691-04009-5); pap. 18.50x (ISBN 0-691-00371-8). Princeton U Pr.

Berkson, Devaki. Foot Book. (Everyday Handbook). pap. 5.29 (ISBN 0-06-463474-4, EH 474, EH). B&N NY.

--The Foot Book: Healing with the Integrated Treatment of Foot Reflexology. LC 76-56733. (Funk & W Bk.). (Illus.). 1977. 11.49i (ISBN 0-308-10295-9). T Y Crowell.

Berkson, Isaac B. Ethics, Politics, & Education. LC 68-64524. 1968. 7.50 (ISBN 0-87114-020-9). U of Oreg Bks.

--The Ideal & the Community: A Philosophy of Education. LC 70-115977. Repr. of 1958 ed. lib. bdg. 15.00x (ISBN 0-8371-3056-5, BEIC). Greenwood.

--Theories of Americanization: A Critical Study. LC 77-87743. (American Education: Its Men, Institutions & Ideas, Ser. 1). 1969. Repr. of 1920 ed. 15.00 (ISBN 0-405-01387-6). Ayer Co Pubs.

--Theories of Americanization: A Critical Study, with Special Reference to the Jewish Group. LC 78-176558. (Columbia University. Teachers College. Contributions to Education: No. 109). Repr. of 1920 ed. 22.50 (ISBN 0-404-55109-2). AMS Pr.

Berkson, Larry & Baller, Scott. Judicial Selection in the United States: A Compendium of Provisions. LC 80-70531. 182p. (Orig.). 1981. pap. 7.50 (ISBN 0-938870-02-5, 8565). Am Judicature.

Berkson, Larry C. & Carbon, Susan B. The United States Circuit Judge Nominating Commission: Its Members, Procedures & Candidates. 260p. 1980. 7.50 (ISBN 0-938870-09-2, 8561). Am Judicature.

Berkson, Larry C., jt. auth. see Carbon, Susan B.

Berkson, Larry C. & Vandenberg, Donna, eds. National Roster of Women Judges, 1980. 120p. (Orig.). 1980. pap. 2.95 (ISBN 0-938870-07-6, 8563). Am Judicature.

Berkson, William & Wettersten, John. Learning from Error: Karl Popper's Psychology of Learning. 155p. 1984. cloth 14.95 (ISBN 0-912050-74-8). Open Court.

Berkstresser, Gordon A., III. Textile Marketing Management. LC 83-22096. (Illus.). 135p. 1984. 32.00 (ISBN 0-8155-0975-8). Noyes.

Berkus, Rusty. Appearances: Clearings Through Masks of Our Existence. (Illus.). 34p. (Orig.). 1984. pap. 13.95 (ISBN 0-9609888-1-5). Red Rose Pr.

--Life Is a Gift. (Illus.). 64p. (Orig.). 1982. pap. 13.95 (ISBN 0-9609888-0-7). Red Rose Pr.

Berky, Andrew S., ed. Challenge to American Life. facs. ed. LC 76-134052. (Essay Index Reprint Ser). 1956. 14.00 (ISBN 0-8369-2143-7). Ayer Co Pubs.

Berky, Andrew S., tr. see Sommer, Fedor.

Berl, Robert L., jt. auth. see Bellenger, Danny N.

Berl, Soll, et al, eds. Metabolic Compartmentation & Neurotransmission: Relation to Brain Structure & Function. LC 75-33685. (Illus.). 744p. 1975. 75.00x (ISBN 0-306-35606-6, Plenum Pr). Plenum Pub.

Berlak, Ann & Berlak, Harold. Dilemmas of Schooling. 309p. 1981. pap. 10.95 (ISBN 0-416-74110-X, NO.3565). Methuen Inc.

Berlak, Harold, jt. auth. see Berlak, Ann.

Berland, Alwyn. Culture & Conduct in the Novels of Henry James. 225p. 1981. 44.50 (ISBN 0-521-23343-7). Cambridge U Pr.

Berland, Joseph C. No Five Fingers Are Alike: Cognitive Amplifiers in Social Context. LC 81-7154. (Illus.). 272p. 1982. text ed. 30.00x (ISBN 0-674-62540-4). Harvard U Pr.

Berland, Theodore. The Dieter's Almanac. (A World Almanac Publications Bk.). 224p. 1984. pap. 7.95 (ISBN 0-345-31628-2). Ballantine.

--Rating the Diets. Consumer Guide Editors, ed. 1980. pap. 3.95 (ISBN 0-451-12269-0, AE2269, Sig). NAL.

Berland, Theodore & Addison, Robert. Living with Your Bad Back. 160p. 1983. 5.95 (ISBN 0-312-49036-4). St Martin.

Berland, Theodore & Fischer-Pap, Lucia. Living with Your Allergies & Asthma. 160p. 1983. 5.95 (ISBN 0-312-49249-9). St Martin.

Berland, Theodore & Snider, Gordon. Living with Your Bronchitis & Emphysema. LC 72-89418. (Griffin Paperback Ser.). (Illus.). 197p. 1972. pap. 3.95 (ISBN 0-312-49140-9). St Martin.

Berland, Theodore & Spellberg, Mitchell A. Living with Your Ulcer. LC 77-145432. (Griffin Paperback Ser.). (Illus.). 1974. 5.95 (ISBN 0-312-49210-3, L63000); pap. 3.95 (ISBN 0-312-49245-6). St Martin.

Berland, Theodore, jt. auth. see Warren, Frank Z.

Berland, Thomas. The Dieter's Almanac. (Illus.). 224p. (Orig.). 1984. pap. 7.95. World Almanac.

Berlandier, Jean L., et al. Journey to Mexico During the Years Eighteen Twenty-Six to Eighteen Thirty-Four, 2 vols. Ohlendorf, Sheila M. & Bigelow, Josette, eds. LC 80-52705. (Illus.). 1980. boxed 75.00 (ISBN 0-87611-044-8); special limited ed. 150.00 (ISBN 0-87611-051-0). Tex St Hist Assn.

Berlanstein, Lenard R. The Barristers of Toulouse in the Eighteenth Century, 1740-1793. LC 75-9784. (J. H. Studies in Historical & Political Science Ser: Ninety-Third Series (1975)). (Illus.). 224p. 1975. 21.00x (ISBN 0-8018-1582-7). Johns Hopkins.

--The Working People of Paris, 1871-1914. LC 84-47951. 1985. text ed. 25.95x (ISBN 0-8018-3241-1). Johns Hopkins.

Berlant, Anthony & Kahlenberg, Mary H. Walk in Beauty: The Navajo & Their Blankets. LC 75-37203. (Illus.). 1977. 37.50 (ISBN 0-8212-0691-5, 917966). NYGS.

Berlant, Jeffrey L. Profession & Monopoly: A Study of Medicine in the United States & Great Britain. LC 74-76381. 1975. 36.50x (ISBN 0-520-02734-5). U of Cal Pr.

Berlau, A. Joseph. German Social Democratic Party, 1914-1921. LC 77-120228. 1970. Repr. lib. bdg. 26.00x (ISBN 0-374-90612-2). Octagon.

Berle, A. A., Jr., et al. America's Recovery Program. facs. ed. Wilcox, C., et al, eds. LC 76-104990. (Essay Index Reprint Ser.). 1934. 20.00 (ISBN 0-8369-1591-7). Ayer Co Pubs.

Berle, Adolf A. Latin America: Diplomacy & Reality. LC 81-3818. (Council on Foreign Relations Ser.). xii, 144p. 1981. Repr. of 1962 ed. lib. bdg. 19.75x (ISBN 0-313-22970-8, BELAM). Greenwood.

Berle, Adolf A., Jr. & Means, Gardiner C. The Modern Corporation & Private Property. (Business Enterprises Reprint Ser.). xiii, 396p. 1982. Repr. of 1933 ed. lib. bdg. 30.00 (ISBN 0-89941-183-5). W S Hein.

Berle, Arnie. Arnie Berle's Complete Handbook for Jazz Improvisation. 1972. pap. 6.95 (ISBN 0-8256-2805-9). Music Sales.

--How to Play Bass Guitar. 1980. pap. 4.95 (ISBN 0-8256-2397-9, Amsco Music). Music Sales.

--Solo Book for Bass Guitar. 1983. pap. 3.95 (ISBN 0-8256-2398-7, Amsco Music). Music Sales.

Berle, Beatrice, jt. ed. see Wolf, Stewart.

Berle, Beatrice B. Eighty Puerto Rican Families in New York City: Health & Disease Studied in Context. LC 74-14221. (The Puerto Rican Experience Ser). (Illus.). 356p. 1975. Repr. 26.50x (ISBN 0-405-06211-7). Ayer Co Pubs.

--A Life in Two Worlds: The Autobiography of Beatrice Bishop Berle. LC 83-7033. 288p. 1983. 17.95 (ISBN 0-8027-0743-2). Walker & Co.

Berle, Beatrice B., jt. ed. see Wolf, Stewart.

Berle, Lina W. George Eliot & Thomas Hardy. 1968. 6.50 (ISBN 0-685-26778-4). Bookfinger.

--George Eliot & Thomas Hardy: A Contrast. 174p. 1981. lib. bdg. 30.00 (ISBN 0-8495-0468-6). Arden Lib.

Berle, Peter A. Does the Citizen Stand a Chance? Politics of a State Legislature - New York. Dillon, Mary E., ed. LC 73-13013. (Politics of Government Ser). (gr. 11 up). 1974. pap. 3.95 (ISBN 0-8120-0480-9). Barron.

Berleant-Schiller, Riva & Shanklin, Eugenia, eds. The Keeping of Animals: Adaptation & Social Relations in Livestock Producing Communities. LC 81-65015. (Illus.). 208p. 1982. text ed. 25.95x (ISBN 0-86598-033-0). Allanheld.

Berleant-Schiller, Riva, jt. ed. see Grant, Mary M.

Berlekamp, E. R., ed. see CISM (International Center for Mechanical Sciences).

Berlekamp, Elwyn R. Algebraic Coding Theory. rev. ed. 1984. pap. text ed. 38.80 (ISBN 0-89412-063-8). Aegean Park Pr.

Berlekamp, Elwyn R., et al. Winning Ways. LC 81-66678. 1982. Vol. 1: For Your Mathematical Plays: Games In General. 58.50 (ISBN 0-12-091150-7); Vol. 2: For Your Mathematical Plays: Games In Particular. pap. 28.00 (ISBN 0-12-091102-7). Acad Pr.

Berler, Alexander. New Towns in Israel. 384p. 1970. casebound 14.95x (ISBN 0-87855-174-3). Transaction Bks.

Berler, Beatrice, tr. see Azuela, Mariano.

Berler, Beatrice, tr. see Latorre Cabal, Hugo.

Berler, Beatrice, tr. see Urbanski, Edmund S.

Berler, Beatrice, tr. see Zea, Leopoldo.

Berler, Joan & Young, Sandra. A Teacher's Guide to Using Books with Gifted Children. 1982. pap. 1.00 (ISBN 0-317-00774-2). Dell.

Berlese, A. N. Icones Fungorum Omnium Hucusque Cognitorum: Ad usum sylloges Saccardianae accomodatae, 4 vols. 1968. 126.00 (ISBN 3-7682-0575-4). Lubrecht & Cramer.

Berlev, O., jt. auth. see Hodjash, S.

Berley, Lawrence F. Holographic Mind, Holographic Vision: A New Theory of Vision in Art & Physics. LC 79-92384. (Illus.). 1980. 16.95 (ISBN 0-9603706-0-9); pap. 11.95 (ISBN 0-9603706-1-7). Lakstun Pr.

Berliant, Howard M. & Arbit, Bruce, eds. Jewish Literary Marketplace: A Directory of the Press, Periodicals, Publishers, & Booksellers. LC 79-18114. 1979. pap. 9.95 (ISBN 0-930038-16-9). Arbit.

Berlin, A. Enmerkar & Ensuhkesdanna: A Sumerian Narrative Poem. (Occasional Publications of the Babylonian Fund Ser.: No. 2). (Illus.). xi, 102p. 1979. 15.00 (ISBN 0-934718-29-6). Univ Mus of U Pa.

Berlin, A., ed. Assessment of Toxic Agents at the Workplace. 660p. 1984. text ed. 98.50 (ISBN 0-89838-613-6, Pub. by Martinus Nijhoff Netherlands). Kluwer Academic.

Berlin, A., et al. Monitoring Human Exposure to Carcinogenic & Mutagenic Agents. (International Agency for Research on Cancer Scientific Publications Ser.: No. 59). 1985. 35.00 (ISBN 0-317-17825-3). Oxford U Pr.

--The Use of Biological Specimens for the Assessment of Human Exposure to Environmental Pollutants. 1979. lib. bdg. 50.00 (ISBN 90-247-2168-7, Pub. by Martinus Nijhoff Netherlands). Kluwer Academic.

Berlin, A. A., et al. Foam Based on Reactive Oligomers. 301p. 1982. 49.00 (ISBN 0-87762-307-4). Technomic.

Berlin, Adele. The Dynamics of Biblical Parallelism. LC 84-48250. 176p. 1985. 22.50x (ISBN 0-253-31850-5). Ind U Pr.

--Poetics & Interpretation of Biblical Narrative. (Bible & Literature Ser.: No. 9). 180p. 1983. text ed. 22.95x (ISBN 0-907459-23-4, Pub. by Almond Pr England); pap. text ed. 10.95x (ISBN 0-907459-24-2). Eisenbrauns.
Berlin, Berlin M. Five Hundred Fifty-Five Timer Applications Sourcebook. LC 78-56584. 160p. 1976. pap. 7.50 (ISBN 0-672-21538-1). Sams.
Berlin, Brent. Tzeltal Numerical Classifiers: A Study in Ethnographic Semantics. (Janua Linguarum, Ser. Practica: No. 70). (Orig.). 1968. pap. text ed. 38.40x (ISBN 0-686-22422-1). Mouton.
Berlin, Brent, et al. Principles of Tzeltal Plant Classification: An Introduction to the Botanical Ethnography of a Mayan Speaking People of Highland Chiapas. (Language, Thought & Culture: Advances in the Study of Cognition Ser.). 1974. 80.00 (ISBN 0-12-785047-3). Acad Pr.
Berlin, Charles. Index to Festschriften in Jewish Studies. 1971. 50.00x (ISBN 0-87068-133-8). Ktav.
--Studies in Jewish Bibliography, History & Literature: In Honor of I. Edward Kiev. 1971. 50.00x (ISBN 0-87068-143-5). Ktav.
Berlin, Charles, ed. see Bloch, Joshua, et al.
Berlin, Charles I., ed. Hearing Science: Recent Advances. LC 84-11424. (Illus.). 380p. 1984. 49.50 (ISBN 0-933014-96-1). College-Hill.
Berlin, Edward A. Ragtime: A Musical & Cultural History. LC 78-51759. 1980. 18.95 (ISBN 0-520-03671-9). U of Cal Pr.
--Ragtime: A Musical & Cultural History. (Cal Ser.: No. 693). (Illus.). 267p. 1984. pap. 7.95 (ISBN 0-520-05219-6). U of Cal Pr.
Berlin, Evelyn, jt. auth. see Hubbard, Kate.
Berlin, G. Lennis. Earthquakes & the Urban Environment, 3 Vols. 1980. Vol. 1, 224 Pgs. 74.00 (ISBN 0-8493-5173-1); Vol. 2, 192 Pgs. 66.00 (ISBN 0-8493-5174-X); Vol. 3, 288 Pgs. 88.00 (ISBN 0-8493-5175-8). CRC Pr.
Berlin, Graydon L., jt. auth. see Avery, Thomas E.
Berlin, Helene, ed. see Anderson, Jerry D.
Berlin, Helene, ed. see Brown, Donald R. & Mathews, Wendell G.
Berlin, Helene, ed. see Klock, P.
Berlin, Howard M. Circuit Design Programs for the Apple II. LC 81-85516. 132p. 1982. pap. 15.95 (ISBN 0-672-21863-1, 21863). Sams.
--Circuit Design Programs for the TRS-80. LC 80-52227. 144p. 1980. pap. 14.50 (ISBN 0-672-21741-4, 21741). Sams.
--Design of Op-Amp Circuits, with Experiments. LC 78-56606. 224p. 1978. pap. 11.95 (ISBN 0-672-21537-3). Sams.
--Design of Phase-Locked Loop Circuits, with Experiments. LC 78-57203. 256p. 1978. pap. 11.95 (ISBN 0-672-21545-4). Sams.
--Digital Electronics: Fundamentals, Applications & Experiment. LC 84-2121. 1984. text ed. 28.95 (ISBN 0-8359-1311-2). Reston.
--The Dow Jones-Irwin Guide to Buying & Selling Treasury Securities. LC 83-72199. 210p. 1984. 25.00 (ISBN 0-87094-464-9). Dow Jones-Irwin.
--Experiments in Electronic Devices. 1984. lab manual 16.95 (ISBN 0-675-20234-5). Merrill.
--Guide to CMOS Basics, Circuits, & Experiments. LC 79-67128. 224p. 1979. pap. 9.95 (ISBN 0-672-21654-X). Sams.
Berlin, I. N., jt. ed. see Szurek, S. A.
Berlin, Ira. Slaves Without Masters: The Free Negro in the Antebellum South. 1981. pap. 9.95 (ISBN 0-19-502905-4, GB 629). Oxford U Pr.
--Slaves Without Masters: The Free Negro in the Antebellum South. LC 74-4761. 448p. 1975. 15.00 (ISBN 0-394-49041-X). Pantheon.
Berlin, Ira & Hoffman, Ronald, eds. Slavery & Freedom in the Age of the American Revolution. LC 82-8387. 368p. 1983. 15.95x (ISBN 0-8139-0969-4). U Pr of Va.
Berlin, Ira, et al, eds. Freedom, a Documentary History of Emancipation 1861-1867: The Black Military Experience, No. 2. LC 82-4446. 784p. 1983. 39.50 (ISBN 0-521-22984-7). Cambridge U Pr.
Berlin, Irving, jt. auth. see French, Alfred.
Berlin, Irving N., ed. Bibliography of Child Psychiatry & Child Mental Health: With a Selected List of Films. LC 74-11813. 508p. 1976. 34.95 (ISBN 0-87705-244-1). Human Sci Pr.
Berlin, Irving N. see Noshpitz, Joseph D.
Berlin, Isaiah. Against the Current: Essays in the History of Ideas. Hardy, Henry, ed. 1980. 16.95 (ISBN 0-670-10944-4). Viking.
--Concepts & Categories. Hardy, Henry, ed. 1979. 14.95 (ISBN 0-670-23552-0). Viking.
--Concepts & Categories: Philosophical Essays. Hardy, Henry, ed. 1981. pap. 6.95 (ISBN 0-14-005805-2). Penguin.
--Four Essays on Liberty. 1969. pap. 5.95 (ISBN 0-19-500272-5, GB). Oxford U Pr.
--Personal Impressions. Hardy, Henry, ed. 1982. pap. 6.95 (ISBN 0-14-006313-7). Penguin.
--Russian Thinkers. (Pelican Ser.). 1979. pap. 5.95 (ISBN 0-14-022260-X, Pelican). Penguin.
--Russian Thinkers. 1978. 14.95 (ISBN 0-670-61371-1). Viking.
--Vico & Herder: Two Studies in the History of Ideas. new ed. LC 75-33299. 216p. 1976. 14.95 (ISBN 0-670-74585-5). Viking.
Berlin, Isaiah, ed. Age of Enlightenment. facs. ed. LC 72-117760. (Essay Index Reprint Ser). 1956. 17.00 (ISBN 0-8369-1822-3). Ayer Co Pubs.
--Age of Enlightenment: The Eighteenth Century Philosophers. (Orig.). 1984. pap. 3.50 (ISBN 0-452-00700-3, Mer). NAL.
Berlin, Isaiah, tr. see Turgenev, Ivan.
Berlin, Isaiah see Turgenev, Ivan.
Berlin, Isaiah, tr. see Turgenev, Ivan.
Berlin, Isiah. Karl Marx: His Life & Environment. 4th ed. 1978. 19.95x (ISBN 0-19-219122-5); pap. 7.95 (ISBN 0-19-520052-7, GB 25, GB). Oxford U Pr.
Berlin, James A. Writing Instruction in Nineteenth-Century American Colleges. LC 83-20116. (Studies in Writing & Rhetoric Ser.). 128p. (Orig.). 1984. pap. 8.50x (ISBN 0-8093-1166-6). S Ill U Pr.
Berlin, Johan D. Anledning til Tonometrien - Anleitung zur Tonometrie. Kortsen, Bjarne, ed. LC 79-388385. (Alter Norwegischen Musik Ser.). (Illus.). 52p. (Orig., Eng. & Ger. & Norwegian.). 1976. pap. 16.25 (ISBN 0-934082-12-X, Pub. by Edition Norvegica Norway). Theodore Front.
Berlin, Joyce E., jt. auth. see Erhardt, Carl L.
Berlin, K. D., jt. ed. see McEwen, W. E.
Berlin, K Darrell, jt. auth. see Butler, George B.
Berlin, Laura, ed. see Blank, Marion, et al.
Berlin, Louis, jt. auth. see Smith, Alexander B.
Berlin, Lucia. Phantom Pain. 120p. 1984. pap. 7.00 (ISBN 0-939180-28-6). Tombouctou.
Berlin, Lucia, ed. Angel's Laundromat. (New World Writing Ser). (Illus.). 96p. (Orig.). 1981. pap. 4.95 (ISBN 0-686-69426-0). Turtle Isl Foun.
Berlin, Nathaniel, et al, eds. Polycythemia: A "Seminars in Hematology" Reprint. LC 76-3396. 208p. 1976. 49.50 (ISBN 0-8089-0944-4, 790570). Grune.
Berlin, Normand. Eugene O'Neill. LC 82-47992. (Illus.). 184p. (Orig.). 1982. pap. 9.95 (ISBN 0-394-62418-1, E819, Ever). Grove.
--The Secret Cause: A Discussion of Tragedy. LC 81-4089. 208p. 1981. lib. bdg. 17.50x (ISBN 0-87023-336-X). U of Mass Pr.
--The Secret Cause: A Discussion of Tragedy. LC 81-4089. 208p. 1983. pap. text ed. 11.50x (ISBN 0-87023-398-X). U of Mass Pr.
Berlin, Pamela S., et al. A Missouri Playwrights' Anthology of Prize-Winning Plays. Knittel, Robert E., ed. LC 81-82168. 383p. (Orig.). 1981. pap. 8.95 (ISBN 0-933038-01-1). Grass Hooper Pr.
Berlin, Peggy H., jt. auth. see Robertson, Patricia.
Berlin, Richard, et al, eds. Molecular Basis of Biological Degradative Processes. 1978. 47.50 (ISBN 0-12-092150-2). Acad Pr.
Berlin, Saretta, jt. auth. see Haft, Jacob I.
Berlin, Susan T., jt. ed. see Paulin, Mary Ann.
Berlin, Sven. Jonah's Dream: A Meditation on Fishing. LC 74-14908. (Illus.). 140p. 1975. pap. 4.95 (ISBN 0-913232-78-5). W Kaufmann.
Berlin, William S. On the Edge of Politics: The Roots of Jewish Political Thought in America. (Contributions in Political Science Ser.: No. 14). 1978. lib. bdg. 27.50x (ISBN 0-313-20422-5, BEP/). Greenwood.
Berliner, Abraham. Aus dem Leben der Deuschen Juden im Mittelalter. Katz, Steven, ed. LC 79-7127. (Jewish Philosophy, Mysticism & History of Ideas Ser.). 1980. Repr. of 1900 ed. lib. bdg. 14.00x (ISBN 0-405-12241-1). Ayer Co Pubs.
Berliner, Arthur K. Psychoanalysis & Society: The Social Thought of Sigmund Freud. LC 82-21932. 216p. (Orig.) 1983. lib. bdg. 23.50 (ISBN 0-8191-2893-7); pap. text ed. 12.00 (ISBN 0-8191-2894-5). U Pr of Amer.
Berliner, Baruch. Limits of Insurability of Risks. (Illus.). 128p. 1982. text ed. 20.95 (ISBN 0-13-536789-1). P-H.
Berliner, David, jt. auth. see Gage, Nathaniel.
Berliner, David C., jt. auth. see Fisher, Charles W.
Berliner, Don. Aerobatics. LC 80-10914. (Superwheels & Thrill Sports Bks.). (Illus.). 48p. (gr. 4 up). 1980. PLB 8.95 (ISBN 0-8225-0436-7). Lerner Pubns.
--Airplane Racing. LC 79-4491. (Superwheels & Thrill Sports Bks.). (Illus.). (gr. 4 up). 1979. PLB 8.95 (ISBN 0-8225-0432-4). Lerner Pubns.
--Flying-Model Airplanes. LC 81-20720. (Superwheels & Thrills Sports Bks.). (Illus.). 48p. (gr. 4 up). 1982. PLB 8.95 (ISBN 0-8225-0449-9). Lerner Pubns.
--Helicopters. LC 83-9819. (Superwheels & Thrills Sports Bks.). (Illus.). 48p. (gr. 4 up). 1983. PLB 8.95 (ISBN 0-8225-0448-0). Lerner Pubns.
--Home-Built Airplanes. LC 79-1460. (Superwheels & Thrill Sports Bks.). (Illus.). (gr. 4 up). 1979. PLB 8.95 (ISBN 0-8225-0433-2). Lerner Pubns.
--Personal Airplanes. LC 81-15658. (Superwheels & Thrill Sports Bks.). (Illus.). (gr. 4 up). 1982. PLB 8.95 (ISBN 0-8225-0447-2). Lerner Pubns.
--Record Breaking Airplanes. (Superwheels & Thrill Sports Bks.). (Illus.). 48p. (gr. 4 up) 1985. PLB 8.95 (ISBN 0-8225-0429-4). Lerner Pubns.
--Scale-Model Airplanes. LC 81-17120. (Superwheels & Thrill Sports Bks.). (Illus.). (gr. 4 up). 1982. PLB 8.95 (ISBN 0-8225-0446-4). Lerner Pubns.
--Unusual Airplanes. 1985. 8.95 (ISBN 0-8225-0431-6). Lerner Pubns.
--Want a Job? Get Some Experience. Want Experience? Get a Job. LC 78-18304. pap. 48.00 (ISBN 0-317-26944-5, 2023589). Bks Demand UMI.
--World War Two Jet Fighters. Angle, Burr, ed. (Illus.). 72p. (Orig.). 1982. pap. 8.50 (ISBN 0-89024-041-8). Kalmbach.
--Yesterday's Airplanes. LC 80-10915. (Superwheels & Thrill Sports Books). (Illus.). (gr. 4 up). 1980. PLB 8.95 (ISBN 0-8225-0444-8). Lerner Pubns.
Berliner, Howard. The Flexner Report. 180p. 1985. 29.95 (ISBN 0-422-79520-8, 9619, Pub. by Tavistock England); pap. 13.95 (ISBN 0-422-79530-5, 9620, Pub. by Tavistock England). Methuen Inc.
Berliner, Joseph S. Innovation Decision in Soviet Industry. LC 76-2390. 632p. 1976. pap. 17.50x (ISBN 0-262-52052-4). MIT Pr.
Berliner, L. J., ed. Spin Labeling Two: Theory & Applications. LC 75-3587. (Molecular Biology Ser.). 1979. 65.00 (ISBN 0-12-092352-1). Acad Pr.
Berliner, L. J. & Reuben, J., eds. Biological Magnetic Resonance, Vol. 2. LC 78-16035. (Illus.). 352p. 1980. 52.50x (ISBN 0-306-40264-5, Plenum Pr). Plenum Pub.
Berliner, Larry & Berliner, Susan. ReWriter, Bk. I. (Illus.). 38p. (Orig.). (gr. 5 up). 1985. pap. text ed. 17.95 ea. Bk. I, gr. 5-8 & high school sp. needs (ISBN 0-913935-28-X). Bk. II, gr. 6-9 & high school sp. needs (ISBN 0-913935-29-8). ERA-CCR.
Berliner, Lawrence J., ed. Spin Labeling: Theory & Applications. (Molecular Biology Ser.: Vol. 1). 1976. 93.00 (ISBN 0-12-092350-5). Acad Pr.
Berliner, Lawrence J. & Reuben, Jacques, eds. Biological Magnetic Resonance, Vol. 3. LC 78-16035. 288p. 1981. 45.00x (ISBN 0-306-40612-8, Plenum Pr). Plenum Pub.
--Biological Magnetic Resonance, Vol. 4. LC 78-16035. 360p. 1982. 52.50x (ISBN 0-306-40968-2, Plenum Pr). Plenum Pub.
--Biological Magnetic Resonance, Vol. 6. 318p. 1984. 47.50x (ISBN 0-306-41683-2, Plenum Pr). Plenum Pub.
Berliner, Paul F. The Soul of Mbira: Music & Traditions of the Shona People of Zimbabwe. LC 76-24578. (Perspectives on Southern Africa Ser.: No. 26). 1978. 36.50x (ISBN 0-520-03315-9, CAL 466); pap. 6.95 (ISBN 0-520-04268-9). U of Cal Pr.
Berliner, Robert W., jt. auth. see Cronkite, Eugene D.
Berliner, Susan, jt. auth. see Berliner, Larry.
Berliner, Thomas H. WorkShape: A Working Person's Guide to Staying Fit. 240p. 1985. pap. 9.95 (ISBN 0-697-00768-5). Wm C Brown.
Berliner, Thomas H. & Kathman, Clemens A. The Illustrated TK! Solver Book. LC 84-25692. (Illus.). 240p. 1984. pap. 17.95 (ISBN 0-915381-63-X). WordWare Pub.
Berliner, Thomas H. & Reeves, David T. The Illustrated Lotus 1-2-3 Book. LC 84-29180. (Illus.). 240p. 1985. pap. 17.95 (ISBN 0-915381-52-4). WordWare Pub.
Berliner, Thomas H., jt. auth. see Stone, Paula S.
Berliner, Thomas H., jt. auth. see Templeton, Harley.
Berliner, Thomas H., ed. see Barton, Taylor J.
Berliner, Thomas H., ed. see Beam, Emmett.
Berliner, Thomas H., ed. see Lukers, Tom.
Berliner, Thomas H., ed. see McMahan, Mike.
Berliner, Thomas H., ed. see Mishkoff, Hank.
Berliner, Thomas H., ed. see Pegues, Guy.
Berliner, Thomas H., ed. see Stone, Deborah L.
Berliner, Thomas H., ed. see Stultz, Russell A.
Berliner, Thomas H., ed. see Weyandt, Palmer.
Berliner, William M. Managerial & Supervisory Practice. 7th ed. 1979. 26.95x (ISBN 0-256-02040-X). Irwin.
Berling, Judith A. The Syncretic Religion of Lin Chao-En. LC 79-25606. (Institute for Advanced Studies of World Religions; Neo-Confucian Studies). 1980. 29.00x (ISBN 0-231-04870-X). Columbia U Pr.
Berling, K., ed. Meissen China: An Illustrated History. (Illus.). 300p. 1972. Dover.
--Meissen China: An Illustrated History. 15.75 (ISBN 0-8446-4621-0). Peter Smith.
Berlinger, Josef. Das Zeitgenoessische Deutsche Dialektgedicht. (European University Studies: No. 1, Vol. 688). 392p. (Ger.). 1983. 28.40 (ISBN 3-8204-7813-2); 28.40 (ISBN 3-8204-7553-2). P Lang Pubs.
Berlinger, L. J. & Reuben, J., eds. Biological Magnetic Resonance, Vol. 1. LC 78-16035. (Illus.). 359p. 1978. 52.50x (ISBN 0-306-38981-9, Plenum Pr). Plenum Pub.
Berlinghoff, William P., et al. A Mathematical Panorama: Topics for the Liberal Arts. 1980. text ed. 21.95 (ISBN 0-669-02423-6). Heath.
Berlinski, Allen. Purvis: The Newcastle Conjuror. (Illus.). 39p. (Orig.). 1981. pap. 10.00x (ISBN 0-916638-25-1). Meyerbooks.
Berlinsky, Ellen B. & Biller, Henry B. Parental Death & Psychological Development. LC 82-48015. 176p. 1982. 22.00x (ISBN 0-669-05875-0). Lexington Bks.
Berlioux, Etienne Felix. Slave Trade in Africa in 1872. 78p. 1971. 29.50x (ISBN 0-7146-2307-5, F Cass Co). Biblio Dist.
Berlioz, Hector. Berlioz Symphonie Fantastique. Cone, Edward T., ed. (Critical Scores Ser). 1971. pap. 8.95x (ISBN 0-393-09926-1). Norton.
--Conductor, the Theory of His Art. 1902. 25.00x (ISBN 0-403-00247-8). Scholarly.
--A Critical Study of Beethoven's Nine Symphonies with a Few Words on His Trios & Sonatas, a Criticism of His Fidelio, & an Introductory Essay on Music. LC 70-181109. 165p. 1958. Repr. 39.00x (ISBN 0-403-01508-1). Scholarly.
--Evenings with the Orchestra. Barzun, Jacques, ed. & tr. from Fr. LC 72-95224. 1973. pap. 5.95 (ISBN 0-226-04375-4, P499, Phoen). U of Chicago Pr.
--Gluck & His Operas. Evans, Edwin, tr. LC 73-7695. (Illus.). 167p. 1973. Repr. of 1915 ed. lib. bdg. 22.50 (ISBN 0-8371-6938-0, BEGO). Greenwood.
--Life, As Written by Himself in His Letters & Memoirs. Boult, Katharine F., tr. from Fr. LC 74-24042. Repr. of 1903 ed. 18.00 (ISBN 0-404-12865-3). AMS Pr.
--Memoirs. (Illus.). 1960. pap. 9.95 (ISBN 0-486-21563-6). Dover.
--Memoirs of Hector Berlioz. new ed. Cairns, David, tr. from Fr. (Illus.). 672p. 1975. pap. 8.95 (ISBN 0-393-00698-0, Norton Lib). Norton.
--Mozart, Weber & Wagner. 1976. Repr. of 1918 ed. lib. bdg. 39.00x (ISBN 0-403-08963-8). Scholarly.
--New Letters of Berlioz, 1830-1868. Barzun, Jacques, tr. & intro. by. LC 75-100144. xxix, 322p. Repr. of 1954 ed. lib. bdg. 18.50x (ISBN 0-8371-3251-7, BENL). Greenwood.
--Symphony Fantastique & Harold in Italy in Full Score. (Music Scores & Music to Play Ser.). 320p. 1984. pap. 10.95 (ISBN 0-486-24657-4). Dover.
--A Treatise on Modern Instrumentation & Orchestration. 1976. 69.00x (ISBN 0-403-06679-4, Regency). Scholarly.
--Trojans. Dent, E. J., tr. 1957. 3.00 (ISBN 0-19-313303-2). Oxford U Pr.
Berlioz, Hector & Apthorp, William F. Hector Berlioz: Selections from His Letters, & Aesthetic, Humorous & Satirical Writings. Apthorp, William F., tr. from French. LC 76-22325. 1976. Repr. of 1879 ed. lib. bdg. 40.00 (ISBN 0-89341-018-7). Longwood Pub Group.
Berlitz. Basic French. 1984. cassette course 59.95 (ISBN 0-02-961150-4, Berlitz). Macmillan.
--Basic German. 1984. cassette course 59.95 (ISBN 0-02-961160-1, Berlitz). Macmillan.
--Basic Italian. 1984. cassette course 59.95 (ISBN 0-02-961170-9, Berlitz). Macmillan.
--China Country Guide. 256p. 1984. 7.95 (ISBN 0-317-02970-3, Berlitz). Macmillan.
--Tyrol Travel Guide. 128p. 1984. 4.95 (ISBN 0-02-969920-7, Berlitz). Macmillan.
--U. S. A. Country Guide. 256p. 1984. 7.95 (ISBN 0-02-969900-2, Berlitz). Macmillan.
Berlitz, Charles. Atlantis: The Eighth Continent. (Illus.). 1984. 16.95 (ISBN 0-399-12892-1, Putnam). Putnam Pub Group.
--Atlantis: The Eighth Continent. 256p. 1985. pap. 3.50 (ISBN 0-449-20742-0, Crest). Fawcett.
--Bermuda Triangle. 1975. pap. 2.25 (ISBN 0-380-00465-8, 38315-2). Avon.
--The Bermuda Triangle. LC 74-3691. (Illus.). 216p. 1974. 8.95 (ISBN 0-385-04114-4). Doubleday.
--Doomsday Nineteen Ninety-Nine A.D. 1983. pap. 2.95 (ISBN 0-671-44163-9). PB.
--English Step-By-Step for Spanish Speaking People: Ingles Paso-a-Paso. 336p. 1985. 15.95 (ISBN 0-396-08548-2). Dodd.
--French Step by Step. LC 78-73614. 1979. 15.95 (ISBN 0-89696-026-9, Everest Hse). Dodd.
--French Step-By-Step. 1985. pap. 8.95 (ISBN 0-396-08592-X). Dodd.
--German Step-by-Step. LC 78-73611. 1979. 15.95 (ISBN 0-89696-027-7, An Everest House Book). Dodd.
--German Step-by-Step. 1985. pap. 8.95 (ISBN 0-396-08593-8). Dodd.
--Italian Step by Step. LC 78-73613. 1979. 15.95 (ISBN 0-89696-028-5, An Everest House Book). Dodd.
--Italian Step by Step. 1985. pap. 8.95 (ISBN 0-396-08594-6). Dodd.
--The Mystery of Atlantis. (Illus.). 1976. pap. 2.75 (ISBN 0-380-00546-8, 56747-4). Avon.
--Native Tongues. LC 83-24986. (Illus.). 352p. 1984. pap. 7.95 (ISBN 0-399-50999-2, Wideview). Putnam Pub Group.
--Native Tongues: The Book of Language Facts. (Illus.). 352p. 1982. 14.95 (ISBN 0-448-12336-3, G&D); pap. 7.95 (ISBN 0-399-50999-2). Putnam Pub Group.
--Passport to French. 1974. pap. 2.75 (ISBN 0-451-13094-4, AE3094, Sig). NAL.
--Passport to German. 1974. pap. 2.95 (ISBN 0-451-12735-8, AE2735, Sig). NAL.
--Passport to Italian. 1974. pap. 3.50 (ISBN 0-451-13743-4, AE2946, Sig). NAL.
--Passport to Japanese. 192p. 1985. pap. 3.95 (ISBN 0-451-13824-4, Sig). NAL.
--Passport to Spanish. 224p. 1974. pap. 3.50 (ISBN 0-451-13745-0, AE3095, Sig). NAL.
--Spanish Step-by-Step. LC 78-73610. 1979. 15.95 (ISBN 0-89696-029-3, An Everest House Bk.). Dodd.
--Spanish Step-by-Step. 1985. pap. 8.95 (ISBN 0-396-08595-4). Dodd.
--Without a Trace. 1985. pap. 3.50 (ISBN 0-345-32517-6). Ballantine.
Berlitz, Charles, jt. auth. see Moore, William.

Berlitz Editors. Algrave Travel. (Travel Guides Ser.). 1980. pap. 4.95 (ISBN 0-317-12095-6, Berlitz). Macmillan.
--Amsterdam Travel Guide. (Travel Guides for English Speakers Ser.). 1977. pap. 4.95 (ISBN 0-02-969010-2, Berlitz). Macmillan.
--Arabic for Travel Cassettepack. 1983. 14.95 (ISBN 0-02-962780-X, Berlitz); cassette incl. Macmillan.
--Barcelona Travel Guide. (Travel Guides Ser.). 1976. pap. 4.95 (ISBN 0-317-12101-4, Berlitz). Macmillan.
--Berlin Travel Guide. (Travel Guides for English Speakers Ser.). 1983. pap. 4.95 (ISBN 0-02-969040-4, Berlitz). Macmillan.
--Berlitz Arabic for Travellers. 192p. (Arabic.). 1975. 4.95 (ISBN 0-02-964180-2, Berlitz). Macmillan.
--Berlitz Chinese for Travellers. 192p. 1982. pap. 4.95 (ISBN 0-686-93010-X, Berlitz); pap. 4.95 (ISBN 0-02-964210-8). Macmillan.
--Berlitz European Menu for Travellers. 192p. 1982. pap. 4.95 (ISBN 0-686-93020-7, Berlitz); pap. 4.95 (ISBN 0-02-964200-0). Macmillan.
--Berlitz French for Travellers. 192p. (Fr.). 1982. pap. 4.95 (ISBN 0-02-963920-4, Berlitz). Macmillan.
--Berlitz German for Travellers. 192p. (Ger.). 1982. pap. 4.95 (ISBN 0-686-92970-5, Berlitz); pap. 4.95 (ISBN 0-02-963930-1). Macmillan.
--Berlitz Greek for Travellers. 192p. (Gr.). 1982. pap. 4.95 (ISBN 0-686-92956-X, Berlitz); pap. 4.95 (ISBN 0-02-964040-7). Macmillan.
--Berlitz Hebrew for Travellers. 192p. (Hebrew.). 1975. pap. 4.95 (ISBN 0-02-964050-4, Berlitz). Macmillan.
--Berlitz Italian for Travellers. 192p. (Ital.). 1980. 8.95 (ISBN 0-02-965180-8, Berlitz); pap. 4.95 (ISBN 0-02-963940-9). Macmillan.
--Berlitz Japanese for Travellers. 192p. (Japanese.). 1975. pap. 4.95 (ISBN 0-02-964070-9, Berlitz). Macmillan.
--Berlitz Latin-American Spanish for Travellers. 192p. (Span.). 1982. 8.95 (ISBN 0-02-965510-2, Berlitz); pap. 4.95 (ISBN 0-02-963880-1). Macmillan.
--Berlitz Pocket Dictionaries: Danish-English. 300p. (Danish & Eng.). 1982. pap. 4.95 (ISBN 0-02-964550-6, Berlitz). Macmillan.
--Berlitz Pocket Dictionaries: Dutch-English. 300p. (Eng. & Dutch.). 1982. pap. 4.95 (Berlitz). Macmillan.
--Berlitz Pocket Dictionaries: Finnish-English. 300p. (Eng. & Finnish.). 1982. pap. 4.95 (ISBN 0-02-964580-8, Berlitz). Macmillan.
--Berlitz Pocket Dictionaries: French-English. 300p. (Eng. & Fr.). 1982. pap. 4.95 (ISBN 0-02-964500-X, Berlitz). Macmillan.
--Berlitz Pocket Dictionaries: German-English. 300p. (Eng. & Ger.). 1982. pap. 4.95 (ISBN 0-02-964530-1, Berlitz). Macmillan.
--Berlitz Pocket Dictionaries: Italian-English. 300p. (Eng. & Ital.). 1982. pap. 4.95 (ISBN 0-02-964520-4, Berlitz). Macmillan.
--Berlitz Pocket Dictionaries: Norwegian-English. 300p. (Eng. & Norwegian.). 1982. pap. 4.95 (ISBN 0-02-964560-3, Berlitz). Macmillan.
--Berlitz Pocket Dictionaries: Spanish-English. 300p. (Eng. & Span.). 1982. pap. 4.95 (ISBN 0-02-964510-7, Berlitz). Macmillan.
--Berlitz Pocket Dictionaries: Swedish-English. 300p. (Eng. & Swedish.). 1982. pap. 4.95 (ISBN 0-02-964570-0, Berlitz). Macmillan.
--Berlitz Portuguese for Travellers. 192p. (Port.). 1977. pap. 4.95 (ISBN 0-02-963960-3, Berlitz). Macmillan.
--Berlitz Spanish for Travellers. 192p. (Span.). 1980. 8.95 (ISBN 0-02-965190-5, Berlitz); pap. 4.95 (ISBN 0-02-963970-0). Macmillan.
--Berlitz Swedish for Travellers. 192p. 1977. pap. 4.95 (ISBN 0-02-963990-5, Berlitz). Macmillan.
--Berlitz Travel Guide: Egypt. (Illus.). 128p. 1980. pap. 4.95 (ISBN 0-02-969710-7, Berlitz). Macmillan.
--Berlitz Travel Guide: Hawaii. (Illus.). 128p. 1979. pap. 4.95 (ISBN 0-02-969770-0, Berlitz). Macmillan.
--Berlitz Travel Guide: Ireland. (Illus.). 128p. 1981. pap. 4.95 (ISBN 0-02-969190-7, Berlitz). Macmillan.
--Berlitz Travel Guide: Jerusalem. (Illus.). 128p. 1979. pap. 4.95 (ISBN 0-02-969250-4, Berlitz). Macmillan.
--Berlitz Travel Guide: London. (Illus.). 128p. 1978. pap. 4.95 (ISBN 0-02-969320-9, Berlitz). Macmillan.
--Berlitz Travel Guide: Mexico City. (Illus.). 128p. 1978. pap. 4.95 (ISBN 0-02-969660-7, Berlitz). Macmillan.
--Berlitz Travel Guide: New York. (Illus.). 128p. 1981. pap. 4.95 (ISBN 0-02-969400-0, Berlitz). Macmillan.
--Berlitz Travel Guide: Paris. (Illus.). 128p. 1978. pap. 4.95 (ISBN 0-02-969430-2, Berlitz). Macmillan.
--Berlitz Travel Guide: Rome. (Illus.). 128p. 1976. pap. 4.95 (ISBN 0-02-969470-1, Berlitz). Macmillan.
--Berlitz Travel Guide: Scotland. (Illus.). 128p. 1982. pap. 4.95 (ISBN 0-02-969490-6, Berlitz). Macmillan.
--Berlitz Travel Guide: Southern Caribbean. (Illus.). 128p. 1982. pap. 4.95 (ISBN 0-686-92930-6, Berlitz). Macmillan.
--Berlitz Travel Guide: Vienna. (Illus.). 128p. 1982. pap. 4.95 (ISBN 0-02-969570-8, Berlitz). Macmillan.
--Berlitz Travel Guide: Virgin Islands. (Illus.). 128p. 1982. pap. 4.95 (ISBN 0-686-92912-8, Berlitz). Macmillan.
--Brussels Travel Guide. (Travel Guides Ser.). 1981. pap. 4.95 (ISBN 0-317-12099-9, Berlitz). Macmillan.
--Canary Islands Travel Guide. (Travel Guides Ser.). 1976. pap. 4.95 (ISBN 0-317-12100-6, Berlitz). Macmillan.
--China Country Guide. (Country Guides for English Speakers). 1984. pap. 7.95 (ISBN 0-02-969960-6, Berlitz). Macmillan.
--Chinese for Travellers. 1984. cassettepack 14.95 (ISBN 0-02-962210-7, Berlitz). Macmillan.
--Danish for Travel Cassettepack. 1983. 14.95 (ISBN 0-02-962970-5, Berlitz); cassette incl. Macmillan.
--Danish for Travellers. (Travel Guides Ser.). 1977. pap. 4.95 (ISBN 0-317-12089-1, Berlitz). Macmillan.
--Dutch-English Dictionary. 1979. pap. 4.95 (ISBN 0-02-964540-9, Berlitz). Macmillan.
--Dutch for Travel Cassettepack. 1983. 14.95 (ISBN 0-02-962950-0, Berlitz); cassette incl. Macmillan.
--Dutch for Travellers. 1977. pap. 4.95 (ISBN 0-02-963900-X, Berlitz). Macmillan.
--English (British) for Spanish Travellers. (Travellers Ser. for Non-English Speakers). 1971. pap. 4.95 (ISBN 0-02-966600-7, Berlitz). Macmillan.
--English for Arabic Phrasebook. 1982. pap. 4.95 (ISBN 0-02-965540-4, Berlitz). Macmillan.
--English for Japanese Travellers. 1977. 4.95 (ISBN 0-02-966850-6, Berlitz). Macmillan.
--English for Norwegian Travellers. (Travellers Ser. for Non-English Speakers). 1971. pap. 4.95 (ISBN 0-02-965800-4, Berlitz). Macmillan.
--English (North American) for German Travellers. 1974. pap. 4.95 (ISBN 0-02-965280-4, Berlitz, 96895). Macmillan.
--English (North American) for Spanish Travellers. 1974. pap. 2.95 (ISBN 0-02-966650-3, Berlitz). Macmillan.
--European Menu Reader. (Travel Guides Ser.). 1975. pap. 4.95 (ISBN 0-317-12094-8, Berlitz). Macmillan.
--European Phrase Book. 1974. pap. 4.95 (ISBN 0-02-964290-6, Berlitz). Macmillan.
--Finnish for Travel Cassettepack. 1983. 14.95 (ISBN 0-02-962960-8, Berlitz); cassette incl. Macmillan.
--Finnish for Travelers. 1977. pap. 4.95 (ISBN 0-02-963910-7, Berlitz). Macmillan.
--Florence Travel Guide. (Travel Guides for English Speakers Ser.). 1978. pap. 4.95 (ISBN 0-02-969210-5, Berlitz). Macmillan.
--French for Spanish Travellers. 1977. pap. 4.95 (ISBN 0-02-966610-4, Berlitz). Macmillan.
--French for Travel Cassettepack. 1983. 14.95 (ISBN 0-02-962190-9, Berlitz); cassette incl. Macmillan.
--German for Travel Cassettepack. 1983. 14.95 (ISBN 0-02-962200-X, Berlitz); cassette incl. Macmillan.
--German for Travellers. (Travel Guide Ser.). 1975. pap. 4.95 (ISBN 0-317-12090-5, Berlitz). Macmillan.
--Greek for Travel Cassettepack. 1983. 14.95 (ISBN 0-02-962940-3, Berlitz); cassette incl. Macmillan.
--Greek for Travellers. (Travel Guides Ser.). 1975. pap. 4.95 (ISBN 0-317-12091-3, Berlitz). Macmillan.
--Greek Islands Travel Guide. (Travel Guides Ser.). 1979. pap. 4.95 (ISBN 0-317-12277-0, Berlitz). Macmillan.
--Hungarian for Travellers. 1981. 4.95 (ISBN 0-02-964270-1, Berlitz). Macmillan.
--Hungary Country Guides. (Travel Guides for English Speakers Ser.). 1983. pap. 7.95 (ISBN 0-02-969890-1, Berlitz). Macmillan.
--Ibiza & Formentera Travel Guide. (Travel Guides Ser.). 1978. pap. 4.95 (ISBN 0-317-12106-5, Berlitz). Macmillan.
--Istria Croatian Coast Travel Guide. (Travel Guides Ser.). 1977. pap. 4.95 (ISBN 0-317-12104-9, Berlitz). Macmillan.
--Italian for Travellers. (Travel Guides Ser.). 1983. pap. 14.95 (ISBN 0-317-12084-0, Berlitz). Macmillan.
--Italian Travel Guide. (Travel Guides Ser.). 1978. pap. 4.95 (ISBN 0-317-12109-X, Berlitz). Macmillan.
--Jamaica Travel Guide. (Travel Guides Ser.). 1981. pap. 4.95 (ISBN 0-317-12276-2, Berlitz). Macmillan.
--Japanese for Travel Cassettepack. 1983. 14.95 (ISBN 0-02-962850-4, Berlitz); cassette incl. Macmillan.
--Latin American Spanish for Travel Cassettepack. 1983. 14.95 (ISBN 0-02-962590-4, Berlitz); cassette incl. Macmillan.
--Latin American Spanish for Travellers. (Travel Guides Ser.). 1980. pap. 4.95 (ISBN 0-317-12087-5, Berlitz). Macmillan.
--Madeira Travel Guide. (Travel Guides Ser.). 1977. pap. 4.95 (ISBN 0-317-12110-3, Berlitz). Macmillan.
--Madrid Travel Guide. (Travel Guides Ser.). 1977. pap. 4.95 (ISBN 0-317-12111-1, Berlitz). Macmillan.
--Majorca Travel Guide. (Travel Guides Ser.). 1976. pap. 4.95 (ISBN 0-317-12112-X, Berlitz). Macmillan.
--New Zealand Travel Guide. 1984. pap. 4.95 (ISBN 0-02-969940-1, Berlitz). Macmillan.
--Norwegian for Travel Cassettepack. 1983. 14.95 (ISBN 0-02-962870-9, Berlitz); cassette incl. Macmillan.
--Norwegian for Travellers. 1977. pap. 4.95 (ISBN 0-02-963950-6, Berlitz). Macmillan.
--Oslo Travel Guide. (Travel Guides Ser.). 1980. pap. 4.95 (ISBN 0-317-12113-8, Berlitz). Macmillan.
--Oxford & Stratford Travel Guide. (Travel Guides Ser.). 1981. pap. 4.94 (ISBN 0-317-12116-2, Berlitz). Macmillan.
--Polish for Travellers. LC 73-2273. (Travellers Series for English Speakers). 1973. pap. 4.95 (ISBN 0-02-964160-8, Berlitz). Macmillan.
--Portuguese-English Dictionary. (Port. & Eng.). 1982. 4.95 (ISBN 0-02-964440-2, Berlitz). Macmillan.
--Portuguese for Travel Cassettepack. 1983. 14.95 (ISBN 0-02-962790-7, Berlitz); cassette incl. Macmillan.
--Rhodes Travel Guide. (Travel Guides for English Speakers Ser.). 1976. pap. 4.95 (ISBN 0-02-969460-4, Berlitz). Macmillan.
--Russian for Travel Cassettepack. 1983. 14.95 (ISBN 0-02-962880-6, Berlitz); cassette incl. Macmillan.
--Russian for Travellers. 1973. pap. 4.95 (ISBN 0-02-964090-3, Berlitz). Macmillan.
--Salonica Travel Guide. (Travel Guides Ser.). 1980. pap. 4.95 (ISBN 0-317-12280-0, Berlitz). Macmillan.
--Serbo-Croatian. (Travel Guides Ser.). 1983. pap. 14.95 (ISBN 0-317-12086-7, Berlitz). Macmillan.
--Serbo-Croatian for Travellers. LC 73-2272. (Travellers Ser. for English Speakers). (Illus.). 1974. pap. 4.95 (ISBN 0-02-964150-0, Berlitz); cassettepak, 1976 14.95 (ISBN 0-02-962150-X). Macmillan.
--South Caribbean Travel Guide. (Travel Guides for English Speakers Ser.). 1981. pap. 4.95 (ISBN 0-02-969810-3, Berlitz). Macmillan.
--Spanish for Travel Cassette Pack. 1983. 14.95 (ISBN 0-02-962220-4, Berlitz); cassette incl. Macmillan.
--Split & Dalmatia. (Travel Guides Ser.). 1977. pap. 4.95 (ISBN 0-317-12275-4, Berlitz). Macmillan.
--Sri Lanka Travel Guide. (Travel Guides Ser.). 1982. pap. 4.95 (ISBN 0-317-12282-7, Berlitz). Macmillan.
--Swahili for Travellers. 1974. pap. 4.95 (ISBN 0-02-964220-5, Berlitz). Macmillan.
--Swedish for Travel Cassettepack. 1983. 14.95 (ISBN 0-02-962860-1, Berlitz); cassette incl. Macmillan.
--Switzerland Country Travel Guide. (Travel Guides Ser.). 1985. pap. 7.95 (ISBN 0-317-12283-5, Berlitz). Macmillan.
--Switzerland French Speaking Travel Guide. (Travel Guides Ser.). 1979. pap. 4.95 (ISBN 0-317-12281-9, Berlitz). Macmillan.
--Switzerland Travel Guide. (Travel Guides for German Speakers Ser.). 1978. pap. 4.95 (ISBN 0-02-969540-6, Berlitz). Macmillan.
--Turkish for Travellers. 1975. pap. 4.95 (ISBN 0-02-964230-2, Berlitz). Macmillan.
--Virgin Islands. (Travel Guides for English Speakers Ser.). 1977. pap. 4.95 (ISBN 0-02-969700-X, Berlitz). Macmillan.

Berlitz Schools of Language. Berlitz Self-Teachers: French, Vol. 2. (Illus.). 300p. 1958. 8.95 (ISBN 0-448-01421-1, G&D). Putnam Pub Group.
--Berlitz Self-Teachers: German, Vol. 3. (Illus.). 300p. 1950. 8.95 (ISBN 0-448-01422-X, G&D). Putnam Pub Group.
--Berlitz Self-Teachers: Spanish, Vol. 1. (Illus.). 300p. 1950. 8.95 (ISBN 0-448-01427-0, G&D). Putnam Pub Group.

Berlitz Schools of Languages. Berlitz Sin Maestro Ingles or, English for the Spanish-Speaking People, Vol. 5. (Span). 1960. 8.95 (ISBN 0-448-01428-9, G&D). Putnam Pub Group.

Berlman, I. Energy Transfer Parameters of Aromatic Compounds. 1973. 66.00 (ISBN 0-12-092640-7). Acad Pr.

Berlman, Isadore B. Handbook of Fluorescence Spectra of Aromatic Molecules. 2nd ed. 1971. 76.00 (ISBN 0-12-092656-3). Acad Pr.

Berlmer, Ross. Hiding Places. 1985. pap. 3.95 (ISBN 0-451-13798-1, Sig). NAL.

Berlo, David K. The Process of Communication: An Introduction to Theory & Practice. 1960. pap. text ed. 15.95 (ISBN 0-03-055686-4). HR&W.

Berlo, R., jt. auth. see Clements, W.

Berloquin, Pierre. The Garden of the Sphinx: One Hundred Fifty Challenging & Instructive Puzzles. (Illus.). 224p. (YA) 1985. 11.95 (ISBN 0-684-18342-0). Scribner.
--One Hundred Games of Logic. LC 76-49947. (Illus.). 1977. encore ed. 2.98 (ISBN 0-684-14860-9, ScribT). Scribner.

Berlow, Lawrence H. Mexico in the Nineteen Eighties. (Library Research). (Illus.). 160p. 1983. 12.95 (ISBN 0-912526-23-8). Lib Res.

Berlow, Peter. Introduction to Chemistry of Life. 1982. text ed. 32.95 (ISBN 0-03-058516-3, CBS C); instr's manual 4.95 (ISBN 0-03-058517-1); lab manual 18.95 (ISBN 0-03-058519-8); overheads 400.00 (ISBN 0-03-060583-0). SCP.

Berlowitz, Marvin J. & Chapman, Frank E., Jr., eds. The United States Educational System: Marxist Approaches: Papers from Fourth Midwest Marxist Scholars Conference. LC 80-12394. (Studies in Marxism: Vol. 6). 240p. 1980. 18.95x (ISBN 0-930656-12-1); pap. 7.50 (ISBN 0-930656-11-3). MEP Pubns.

Berlowitz, Marvin J. & Edari, Ronald S., eds. Racism & the Denial of Human Rights: Beyond Ethnicity. LC 83-26796. (Studies in Marxism: Vol. 13). 136p. 1984. 17.95x (ISBN 0-930656-33-4); pap. 6.95 (ISBN 0-930656-34-2). MEP Pubns.

Berlucchi, Jim. Person to Person: How to Be Effective in Evangelism. 144p. (Orig.). 1984. pap. 3.50 (ISBN 0-89283-164-2). Servant.

Berlyand, M. E., ed. Air Pollution & Athmospheric Diffusion. LC 73-1982. 221p. 1973. Vol. 1. cloth 42.95x (ISBN 0-470-07034-X). Halsted Pr.

Berlye, Milton. Your Career in the World of Work. LC 75-12236. 1975. pap. 19.96 scp (ISBN 0-672-97534-3). Bobbs.

Berlye, Milton, jt. auth. see Conover, Hobart.

Berlye, Milton K. Encyclopedia of Working with Glass. 1983. 29.95 (ISBN 0-89696-193-1, An Everest House Book). Dodd.

Berlyn, David. Exploring Careers in Cable-TV. (Careers in Depth Ser.). (Illus.). 128p. 1985. lib. bdg. 8.97 (ISBN 0-8239-0667-1). Rosen Group.

Berlyn, Graeme P. & Miksche, Jerome P. Botanical Microtechnique & Cytochemistry. new ed. (Illus.). 326p. 1976. text ed. 16.50x (ISBN 0-8138-0220-2). Iowa St U Pr.

Berlyne, D. E. & Madsen, K. B. Pleasure, Reward, Preference: Their Nature, Determinants, & Role in Behavior (Based Upon a Symposium Held at the Klarskovgaard Training Institute, Near Korsor, Denmark, June, 1972) 1973. 60.00 (ISBN 0-12-092550-8). Acad Pr.

Berlyne, D. E., ed. Studies in the New Experimental Aesthetics. LC 74-13600. Repr. of 1974 ed. 66.20 (ISBN 0-8357-9148-3, 2050704). Bks Demand UMI.

Berlyne, G. H., ed. Reprinted Selected Top Articles Published 1976 - 1977. (Karger Highlights, Nephrology One). (Illus.). 1978. pap. 6.50 (ISBN 3-8055-2938-4). S Karger.

Berlyne, G. M., ed. see International Symposium on Parathyroid in Uremia, 1st, N.Y., May, 1979.

Berlyne, G. M., et al, eds. see Congress on Toxic Nephropathies, 6th, Parma, June 1977.

Berman. The Glands Regulating Personality: A Study of the Glands of Internal Secretion in Relation to the Types of Human Nature. 341p. 1983. Repr. of 1933 ed. lib. bdg. 40.00 (ISBN 0-89760-051-7). Telegraph Bks.

Berman, A. Total Pressure Measurements in Vacuum Technology. Date not set. 59.50 (ISBN 0-12-092440-4). Acad Pr.

Berman, Abraham & Plemmons, Robert J. Non-Negative Matrices in the Mathematical Sciences. (Computer Sciences & Applied Mathematics Ser.). 1979. 49.50 (ISBN 0-12-092250-9). Acad Pr.

Berman, Alan. A Critical Edition of Greene's Tu Quoque, Or The City Gallant by John Cooke. Orgel, Stephen, ed. (The Renaissance Imagination Ser.). 33.00 (ISBN 0-8240-5456-3). Garland Pub.

Berman, Alex, ed. see Design Engineering Technical Conference Staff.

Berman, Alvin & Jones, Edward G. The Thalamus & Basal Telencephalon of the Cat. (Illus.). 180p. 1982. text ed. 250.00x (ISBN 0-299-08440-X). U of Wis Pr.

Berman, Alvin L. Brain Stem of the Cat: A Cytoarchitectonic Atlas with Stereotaxic Coordinates. (Illus.). 192p. 1968. 250.00x (ISBN 0-299-04860-8). U of Wis Pr.

Berman, Barry & Evans, Joel. Readings in Marketing Management: A Strategic Perspective. 478p. 1984. pap. text ed. 22.45 (ISBN 0-471-86966-X). Wiley.

Berman, Barry & Evans, Joel R. Retail Management. 3rd ed. 866p. 1985. text ed. price not set (ISBN 0-02-308620-3). Macmillan.
--Retailing Management: A Strategic Approach. 2nd ed. 656p. 1983. text ed. write for info. (ISBN 0-02-308520-7); student study guide avail.; instrs'. manual avail. Macmillan.

Berman, Barry, jt. auth. see Evans, Joel R.

Berman, Ben. The Dictionary of Business & Credit Terms. Andover, James J., ed. LC 82-14231. 208p. 1983. 19.95 (ISBN 0-934914-45-1). NACM.

Berman, Bernard A. & MacDonnell, Kenneth F. Differential Diagnosis & Treatment of Pediatric Allergy. 1981. text ed. 37.50 (ISBN 0-316-09182-0). Little.

Berman, Bruce D. Encyclopedia of American Shipwrecks. LC 71-181861. 320p. 1972. 30.00x (ISBN 0-913352-01-2); pap. 25.00x (ISBN 0-913352-00-4). Mariners Boston.

Berman, Claire G. What Am I Doing in a Step-Family? 48p. 1982. 12.00 (ISBN 0-8184-0325-X). Lyle Stuart.

Berman, Connie, et al, eds. The City Magazine. (Illus.). 64p. 1984. pap. 5.95 (ISBN 0-452-25580-5, Plume). NAL.

Berman, D. H. The Role of Law in Population Planning: Working Paper & Proceedings of the Sixteenth Hammarskjold Forum. LC 72-2061. (Hammarskjold Forum Ser.: No. 16). 90p. 1972. 10.00 (ISBN 0-379-11816-5). Oceana.

Berman, D. L., et al. Nineteen Papers on Statistics & Probability. LC 61-9803. (Selected Translations on Mathematical Statistics & Probability Ser: Vol. 5). 1965. 30.00 (ISBN 0-8218-1455-9, STAPRO-5). Am Math.

Berman, Daniel. Death on the Job. LC 78-13914. 260p. 1979. pap. 8.00 (ISBN 0-85345-527-9). Monthly Rev.

--It Is So Ordered. (Orig.). 1966. pap. text ed. 5.95x (ISBN 0-393-09679-3, NortonC). Norton.

Berman, Daniel, jt. ed. see Navarro, Vicente.

Berman, Daniel S. How To Put Together A R.E. Syndicate Or Joint Venture. LC 84-3324. 288p. 1984. 37.50 (ISBN 0-13-430653-8, Busn). P-H.

--How to Put Together a Real Estate Syndicate or Joint Venture, 2 Vols. 1973. Set. 95.00 (ISBN 0-911474-01-3); Vol. 1. 50.00 (ISBN 0-911474-02-1); Vol. 2. 50.00 (ISBN 0-911474-03-X). Syndicate.

Berman, Daniel S. & Mason, Dean T. Clinical Nuclear Cardiology. (Clinical Cardiology Monographs Ser.). (Illus.). 512p. 1981. 59.50 (ISBN 0-8089-1356-5, 790571). Grune.

Berman, David. State & Local Politics. 4th ed. 1984. text ed. 31.36 (ISBN 0-205-08089-8, 768089); write for info. (ISBN 0-205-08090-1). Allyn.

Berman, David R. American Government, Politics & Policymaking. 2nd ed. LC 82-61096. (Illus.). 1983. text ed. 13.95x (ISBN 0-913530-31-X). Palisades Pub.

Berman, David R. & Bollens, John C. American Government: Ideas & Issues. LC 80-83670. 1981. pap. 6.95x (ISBN 0-913530-22-0). Palisades Pub.

Berman, E. Homosexual Acts: Five 'Almost Free' 1981. 20.00x (ISBN 0-686-78800-1, Pub. by Turoe Pr). State Mutual Bk.

--Toxic Metals & Their Analysis. 304p. 1980. cloth 49.95 (ISBN 0-471-25651-X, Pub. by Wiley Heyden). Wiley.

Berman, E., ed. Analysis of the Drugs of Abuse by Chromatographic Methods. new ed. 1976. 25.00 (ISBN 0-912474-09-2). Preston Pubns.

Berman, Edgar. The Solid Gold Stethoscope. 1978. pap. 2.25 (ISBN 0-345-28623-5). Ballantine.

Berman, Edward. Labor Disputes & the President of the United States. LC 75-76691. (Columbia University Studies in the Social Sciences: No. 249). Repr. of 1924 ed. 20.00 (ISBN 0-404-51249-6). AMS Pr.

Berman, Edward B., ed. Contingency Planning for Materials Resources. 234p. 1978. pap. 15.00x (ISBN 0-939204-12-6, 78-06). Eng Found.

Berman, Edward H. African Reactions to Missionary Education. LC 74-22497. (Orig.). 1975. pap. text ed. 10.50x (ISBN 0-8077-2445-9). Tchrs Coll.

--The Influence of the Carnegie, Ford, & Rockefeller Foundations on American Foreign Policy: The Ideology of Philanthropy. LC 82-19494. 227p. 1983. 36.50x (ISBN 0-87395-725-3); pap. 11.95x (ISBN 0-87395-726-1). State U NY Pr.

Berman, Elaine R., jt. ed. see Michaelson, I. C.

Berman, Eleanor. Away for the Weekend: A Guide to Great Getaways Less Than 200 Miles from New York City for Every Season of the Year. (Illus.). 256p. 1984. pap. 9.95 (ISBN 0-517-54647-7, C N Potter Bks). Crown.

--Away for the Weekend: Great Getaways for Every Season of the Year Throughout the Six New England States. 1985. pap. 9.95 (ISBN 0-517-55257-4, Pub. by C. N. Potter). Crown.

Berman, Esme. Art & Artists of South Africa. Enl. ed. (Illus.). 545p. 1984. 65.00 (ISBN 0-8390-0335-8). Abner Schram Ltd.

Berman, Eugene. Eugene Berman. Levy, Julien, ed. LC 73-160915. (Biography Index Reprint Ser). Repr. of 1947 ed. 30.50 (ISBN 0-8369-8078-6). Ayer Co Pubs.

Berman, Filipp. Registrator. 140p. (Rus.). 1984. pap. 8.00 (ISBN 0-88233-730-0). Ardis Pubs.

Berman, Filipp, ed. Katalog, Literaturnyi Almanakh. 300p. (Rus.). 1982. pap. 13.50 (ISBN 0-88233-732-7). Ardis Pubs.

Berman, Gerald & Fryer, K. D. Introduction to Combinatorics. 1972. text ed. 22.50i (ISBN 0-12-092750-0). Acad Pr.

Berman, Greta. The Lost Years: Mural Painting in New York City Under the Works Progress Administration's Federal Art Project 1935-1943. LC 77-94687. (Outstanding Dissertations in the Fine Arts Ser.). 436p. 1978. lib. bdg. 55.00 (ISBN 0-8240-3216-0). Garland Pub.

Berman, H., jt. auth. see Ginzberg, Eli.

Berman, Hannah. Melutovna: A Novel. facsimile ed. LC 74-27963. (Modern Jewish Experience Ser.). 1975. Repr. of 1913 ed. 30.00x (ISBN 0-405-06694-5). Ayer Co Pubs.

Berman, Harold. Encyclopedia of Bronzes, Sculptors & Founders: 1800-1930. LC 74-78612. (Abage Encyclopedia Ser.: Vols. 1-4). 1974-80. Set. lib. bdg. 210.00x (ISBN 0-917350-05-7); Vol. 1. lib. bdg. 45.00x (ISBN 0-917350-01-4); Vol. 2. lib. bdg. 50.00x (ISBN 0-917350-02-2); Vol. 3. lib. bdg. 55.00x (ISBN 0-917350-03-0); Vol. 4. lib. bdg. 60.00x (ISBN 0-917350-04-9). Abage.

--The Law of International Commercial Transactions. 65p. 1982. pap. 12.00 (ISBN 0-686-40802-0, B405). Am Law Inst.

Berman, Harold, tr. see Sachs, Abraham S.

Berman, Harold J. Justice in the U. S. S. R: An Interpretation of the Soviet Law. rev. ed. LC 63-15045. (Russian Research Center Studies: No. 3). 1963. pap. text ed. 14.50x (ISBN 0-674-49151-3). Harvard U Pr.

--Law & Revolution: The Formation of the Western Legal Tradition. 672p. 1983. text ed. 32.50x (ISBN 0-674-51774-1). Harvard U Pr.

--Law & Revolution: The Formation of the Western Legal Tradition. 672p. 1985. pap. text ed. 12.95x (ISBN 0-674-51776-8). Harvard U Pr.

--Russians in Focus. facsimile ed. LC 71-90610. (Essay Index Reprint Ser.). 1953. 20.00 (ISBN 0-8369-1391-4). Ayer Co Pubs.

Berman, Harold J. & Maggs, Peter B. Disarmament Inspection Under Soviet Law. LC 66-13368. 162p. 1967. 10.00 (ISBN 0-379-00293-0). Oceana.

Berman, Harold J., tr. see Russel, Ralph.

Berman, Henry S. & Burhenne, Diane P. The Complete Health Care Advisor: How to Get the Best & Pay the Least. 320p. 1983. 16.95 (ISBN 0-312-15765-7, Pub. by Marek). St Martin.

Berman, Henry S., et al. The Complete Health Care Advisor: How to Get the Best & Pay the Least. 352p. 1984. pap. 8.95 (ISBN 0-312-15766-5, Pub. by Marek). St Martin.

Berman, Herbert J. & Hebert, Normand C., eds. Ion-Selective Microelectrodes. LC 74-14914. (Advances in Experimental Medicine & Biology Ser.: Vol. 50). 210p. 1974. 39.50x (ISBN 0-306-39050-7, Plenum Pr). Plenum Pub.

Berman, Howard J. & Weeks, Lewis E. The Financial Management of Hospitals. 5th ed. LC 81-7169. (Illus.). 904p. 1982. text ed. 35.00x (ISBN 0-914904-74-4). Health Admin Pr.

Berman, Howard J. & Weeks, Lewis E., eds. Economics in Health Care. LC 77-10860. 402p. 1978. text ed. 44.50 (ISBN 0-89443-026-2). Aspen Systems.

Berman, Howard J., jt. ed. see Weeks, Lewis E.

Berman, I. & Schroeder, J. W., eds. Explosive Welding, Forming, Plugging, & Compaction. (PVP: No. 44). 119p. 1980. 20.00 (ISBN 0-686-69850-9, H00171). ASME.

Berman, Irwin, ed. see Syposium on Engineering Computer Software (1971: San Francisco, CA).

Berman, James, ed. see MacDonald & Mack Partnership & Miller-Dunwiddie Architects Inc.

Berman, Jan. Birdseye Writing Skills: Mastery Masters, 3 bks. Incl. Fiction (ISBN 0-8224-0708-6); Non-Fiction (ISBN 0-8224-0709-4); Paragraphs (ISBN 0-8224-0710-8). (gr. 4-6). 1981. pap. 5.95 ea.; pap. 14.85 comp. set (ISBN 0-8224-0713-2). Pitman Learning.

--Fiction Writing. (Learning Workbooks Language Arts). (gr. 4-6). pap. 1.95 (ISBN 0-8224-4182-9). Pitman Learning.

--Nonfiction Writing. (Learning Workbooks Language Arts). (gr. 4-6). pap. 1.95 (ISBN 0-8224-4181-0). Pitman Learning.

--Paragraph Writing. (Learning Workbooks Language Arts). (gr. 4-6). pap. 1.95 (ISBN 0-8224-4180-2). Pitman Learning.

Berman, Jeffery B., jt. auth. see Crump, David.

Berman, Jeffrey. The Talking Cure: Literary Representations of Psychoanalysis. 1985. 42.50x (ISBN 0-8147-1075-1). NYU Pr.

Berman, Jerry J., et al. Comparision of Proposals for Reforming the Intelligence Agencies: A Report. 2nd ed. (Center for National Security Studies Reports: No. 101-102). 79p. 1980. 2.50 (ISBN 0-86566-017-4). Ctr Natl Security.

Berman, Joel, jt. auth. see Seagrave, Barbara G.

Berman, Jonathan. Rachel's Walk. LC 84-90285. 83p. 1985. 8.95 (ISBN 0-533-06325-6). Vantage.

Berman, Judith, jt. auth. see Polit, Denise F.

Berman, Kathleen, jt. auth. see Landesman, Bill.

Berman, L. I. & Sacco, W. J. Glyphs. (Cyometrics Math Enrichement Ser.). 26p. (Orig.). 1981. pap. text ed. 3.00 (ISBN 0-686-36282-9). Cyometrics.

Berman, Larry. The Office of Management & Budget & the Presidency: 1921-1979. LC 79-83977. 1979. 23.50x (ISBN 0-691-07619-7); pap. 9.95 (ISBN 0-691-02197-X). Princeton U Pr.

--Planning a Tragedy: The Americanization of the War in Vietnam. 224p. 1983. pap. 7.95 (ISBN 0-393-95326-2). Norton.

Berman, Lawrence V., et al, eds. The Study of Judaism: Vol. 2. 25.00x (ISBN 0-87068-486-8). Ktav.

Berman, Lee & Leonard, Ken. The BASIC Explorer for the Commodore 64. (Illus.). 200p. 1984. pap. 11.95 (ISBN 0-07-881139-2, 139-2). Osborne-McGraw.

Berman, Leslie & Wood, Heather, eds. Grass Roots International Folk Resource Directory 1985. (Illus.). 200p. 1985. pap. text ed. 12.95x (ISBN 0-9614589-0-9). Grass Roots Productions.

Berman, Linda. The Goodbye Painting. LC 81-20217. 32p. (ps-3). 1982. 11.95 (ISBN 0-89885-074-6). Human Sci Pr.

Berman, Linda, et al. Tenth Year Mathematics. (Arco's Regents Review Ser.). 288p. (Orig.). 1982. pap. 3.95 (ISBN 0-668-05702-5, 5702). Arco.

Berman, Louis & Evans, John C. Exploring the Cosmos. 4th. ed. 1983. 28.95 (ISBN 0-316-09184-7); teacher's manual avail. (ISBN 0-316-09187-1). Little.

Berman, Louis & Kirstein, Laurette. Idiom Workbook. 1979. 6.95 (ISBN 0-88499-530-5). Inst Mod Lang.

Berman, Louis A. Vegetarianism & the Jewish Tradition. LC 81-11729. 120p. 1982. 10.00x (ISBN 0-87068-756-5); pap. 7.95. Ktav.

Berman, Louise M. & Roderick, Jessie A., eds. Feeling, Valuing & the Art of Growing: Insights into the Affective. LC 76-54454. (ASCD Yearbook, 1977). 1977. 9.75 (ISBN 0-87120-082-1, 610-77104). Assn Supervision.

Berman, Mark L., ed. Motivation & Learning: Applying Contingency Management Techniques. LC 70-160894. 222p. 1972. pap. 16.95 (ISBN 0-87778-023-4). Educ Tech Pubns.

Berman, Marshall. All That Is Solid Melts into Air. 1983. pap. 6.95 (ISBN 0-671-45700-4, Touchstone Bks). S&S.

--All That Is Solid Melts into Air: The Experience of Modernity. LC 81-16640. 1982. 17.95 (ISBN 0-671-24602-X). S&S.

--Politics of Authenticity: Radical Individualism & the Emergence of Modern Society. LC 77-124968. 1970. pap. 5.95x (ISBN 0-689-70288-4, 170). Atheneum.

Berman, Maureen, jt. auth. see Zartman, I. William.

Berman, Maureen R. & Johnson, Joseph E., eds. Unofficial Diplomats. LC 77-9376. 1977. 19.50x (ISBN 0-231-04396-1); pap. 9.00x (ISBN 0-231-04397-X). Columbia U Pr.

Berman, Michael. Playing & Working with Words. LC 80-41911. (Materials for Language Practice Ser.). 96p. 1981. pap. 3.95 (ISBN 0-08-025352-0). Pergamon.

--Take Note: Materials for Listening Comprehension & Note Taking in English. 1980. pap. 2.95 (ISBN 0-08-025316-4). Pergamon.

Berman, Michelle & Shevitz, Linda. I Can Make It on My Own: Functional Reading Ideas & Activities for Daily Survival. LC 78-9639. 1978. 12.95 (ISBN 0-673-16375-X); pap. 12.95 (ISBN 0-673-16374-1). Scott F.

Berman, Michelle, jt. auth. see Shevitz, Linda.

Berman, Milton. John Fiske: The Evolution of a Popularizer. LC 62-7334. (Historical Monographs Ser: No. 48). (Illus.). 1961. 18.50x (ISBN 0-674-47551-8). Harvard U Pr.

Berman, Mones. Lipoprotein Kinetics & Modeling. LC 82-6749. 480p. 1982. 70.00 (ISBN 0-12-092480-3). Acad Pr.

Berman, Morris. The Reenchantment of the World. LC 81-67178. (Illus.). 368p. 1981. 39.95x (ISBN 0-8014-1347-8); pap. 10.95x (ISBN 0-8014-9225-4). Cornell U Pr.

--The Reenchantment of the World. (New Age Bks.). 416p. 1984. pap. 4.95 (ISBN 0-553-24171-0). Bantam.

--Social Change & Scientific Organization: The Royal Instutution, Seventeen Ninety-Nine to Eighteen Forty-Four. LC 77-79702. (Illus.). 249p. 1978. 34.95x (ISBN 0-8014-1093-2). Cornell U Pr.

Berman, Myron. The Attitude of American Jewry Towards East European Jewish Immigration, 1881-1914. Cordasco, Francesco, ed. LC 80-842. (American Ethnic Groups Ser.). 1981. lib. bdg. 55.00x (ISBN 0-405-13406-1). Ayer Co Pubs.

--Richmond's Jewry, Seventeen Sixty-Nine to Nineteen Seventy-Six. LC 78-6377. 438p. 1979. 14.95x (ISBN 0-8139-0743-8). U Pr of Va.

Berman, Neil D. Geriatric Cardiology. LC 81-70163. 244p. 1982. 25.95 (ISBN 0-669-04505-5, Collamore). Heath.

--Playful Fictions & Fictional Players: Game, Sport & Survival in Contemporary American Fiction. (National University Publications, Literary Criticism Ser.). 125p. 1981. 13.50x (ISBN 0-8046-9265-3, Pub. by Kennikat). Assoc Faculty Pr.

Berman, Norman, jt. auth. see Pinto, Andrew.

Berman, Paul. The Make-Believe Empire. LC 81-10847. (Illus.). 96p. (gr. 3 up). 1982. PLB 8.95 (ISBN 0-689-30909-0). Atheneum.

Berman, Phil. Catamaran Sailing: From Start to Finish. (Illus.). 1982. pap. 12.95 (ISBN 0-393-00084-2). Norton.

Berman, Phil, jt. auth. see Waltze, Mike.

Berman, Phillip L., ed. & intro. by. Courage of Conviction: Prominent Contemporaries Discuss their Beliefs & how they put them in Action. (Illus.). 256p. 1985. 17.95 (ISBN 0-396-08622-5). Dodd.

Berman, R. Thermal Conductions in Solids. (Oxford Studies in Physics). (Illus.). 1976. 39.95x (ISBN 0-19-851429-8); pap. 19.95x (ISBN 0-19-851430-1). Oxford U Pr.

Berman, R., tr. see Ivanovski, M. N., et al.

Berman, R. J. Browning's Duke. LC 72-167641. (gr. 7 up). 1972. PLB 15.00 (ISBN 0-8239-0247-1). Rosen Group.

--Shepherd's Trade. 1984. limited autographed ed. 100.00 (ISBN 0-317-02338-1); 25.00 (ISBN 0-317-02339-X). Rosen Group.

Berman, Rita. The A-Z of Writing & Selling. LC 81-80002. 1981. 10.00 (ISBN 0-87716-117-8, Pub. by Moore Pub Co). Castle Dist.

Berman, Robert P. Soviet Air Power in Transition. (Studies in Defense Policy). 1978. pap. 6.95 (ISBN 0-8157-0923-4). Brookings.

Berman, Robert P. & Baker, John C. Soviet Strategic Forces: Requirements & Responses. LC 82-70889. (Studies in Defense Policy). 171p. 1982. 22.95 (ISBN 0-8157-0926-9); pap. 8.95 (ISBN 0-8157-0925-0). Brookings.

Berman, Ronald. Advertising & Social Change. (Sage CommTexts Ser.: Vol. 8). 160p. 1981. 17.50 (ISBN 0-8039-1737-6); pap. 8.95 (ISBN 0-8039-1738-4). Sage.

--Culture & Politics. 182p. 1984. lib. bdg. 10.95 (ISBN 0-8191-3706-5). U Pr of Amer.

--Reader's Guide to Shakespeare's Plays: A Discursive Bibliography. 2nd ed. 1973. pap. 8.65x (ISBN 0-673-07878-7). Scott F.

--The Signet Classic Book of Restoration Drama. 1980. pap. 3.95 (ISBN 0-451-51402-5, CE1402, Sig Cl). NAL.

Berman, Ronald, ed. Solzhenitsyn at Harvard: The Address, Twelve Early Responses, & Six Later Reflections. LC 79-26033. 160p. 1980. 11.00 (ISBN 0-89633-034-6); pap. 7.00 (ISBN 0-89633-023-0). Ethics & Public Policy.

Berman, Russell, tr. see Leonhard, Karl.

Berman, Russell A. Between Fontane & Tucholsky: Literary Criticism & the Public Sphere in Imperial Germany. LC 83-9371. (New York University Ottendorfer Ser.: Vol. 17). 176p. (Orig.). 1983. pap. text ed. 18.40 (ISBN 0-8204-0012-2). P Lang Pubs.

Berman, S. D., et al. Nine Papers on Logic & Group Theory. LC 51-5559. (Translations Ser.: No. 2, Vol. 64). 1967. 34.00 (ISBN 0-8218-1764-7, TRANS 2-64). Am Math.

Berman, Sanford. How to Lessen Misunderstandings. LC 72-75525. 29p. 1972. pap. text ed. 3.00x (ISBN 0-918970-12-1). Intl Gen Semantics.

--Joy of Cataloging: Essays, Letters, Reviews & Other Explosions. 264p. 1981. lib. bdg. 35.00x (ISBN 0-912700-51-3); pap. 27.50x (ISBN 0-912700-94-7). Oryx Pr.

--Understanding & Being Understood. LC 72-75526. 77p. 1972. pap. text ed. 4.00x (ISBN 0-918970-13-X). Intl Gen Semantics.

--Words, Meaning & People. LC 82-84221. 102p. 1982. pap. text ed. 5.95x (ISBN 0-918970-31-8). Intl Gen Semantics.

Berman, Sanford, ed. Subject Cataloging: Critiques & Innovations. LC 84-10554. (Technical Services Quarterly Ser.: Vol. 2, No. 1/2). 264p. 1985. text ed. 22.95 (ISBN 0-86656-265-6, B265). Haworth Pr.

Berman, Sanford & Danky, James P., eds. Alternative Library Literature, 1982-1983: A Biennial Anthology. (Illus.). 344p. 1984. pap. 37.50 (ISBN 0-89774-132-3). Oryx Pr.

Berman, Sharon L. With a Face Like Mine. 160p. 1981. 8.95 (ISBN 0-87777-062-X, Pub. by R W Baron). Dutton.

Berman, Shelley. A Hotel is a Funny Place. (Illus.). 120p. 1985. pap. 3.95 (ISBN 0-8431-1418-5). Price Stern.

--A Hotel Is a Place. (Gift Bks. Ser.). (Illus.). 112p. 1972. 4.95 (ISBN 0-8431-0211-X). Price Stern.

Berman, Sol. Horseshoe Film, Facts & Fun. LC 82-46092. (Illus.). 80p. 1984. 4.95 (ISBN 0-8453-4770-5). Cornwall Bks.

Berman, Stephen. Pediatric Decision Making. (Decision Making Ser.). 300p. 1984. text ed. 36.00 (ISBN 0-941158-17-9, D0640-3). Mosby.

Berman, Steve. The Six Demons of Love: A Book About Men & Love. 144p. 6.95 (ISBN 0-07-004915-7). McGraw.

Berman, Steve & Weiss, Vivian. What to Be. (Illus.). (gr. 5-7). 1981. 8.95 (ISBN 0-13-955278-2). P-H.

Berman, Susan. Easy Street. LC 81-7841. 224p. 1981. 13.95 (ISBN 0-385-27185-9, Dial). Doubleday.

Berman, Susan, ed. see Fay, Clifford T., Jr., et al.

Berman, Susan, ed. see Ninemeier, Jack D.

Berman, Susan J., ed. see Jefferies, Jack P.

Berman, W. W., ed. see Row, T. S.

Berman, Wayne L., jt. ed. see Hunter, Robert E.

Berman, William. Beginning Biochemistry. LC 74-29784. (A Sentinel Science Bk.). (Illus., Orig.). (YA) 1968. pap. 3.95 (ISBN 0-668-03235-9). Arco.

--How to Dissect. 4th ed. LC 83-27510. (Illus.). 224p. (Orig.). (gr. 8 up). 1984. lib. bdg. 9.95 (ISBN 0-668-05939-7); pap. 5.95 (ISBN 0-668-05941-9). Arco.

Berman, William C. The Politics of Civil Rights in the Truman Administration. LC 70-114736. 273p. 1970. 8.00 (ISBN 0-8142-0142-3). Ohio St U Pr.

Berman, William, Jr. Pulsed Doppler Ultrasound in Clinical Pediatrics. 248p. 1983. 32.00 (ISBN 0-87993-201-5). Futura Pub.

Bermann, Eric. Scapegoat: The Impact of Death-Fear on an American Family. LC 73-80573. (Illus.). 370p. 1973. 10.00 (ISBN 0-472-14300-X). U of Mich Pr.

Bermann, Richard A. The Mahdi of Allah: The Story of the Dervish, Mohammed Ahmed. John, Robin, tr. LC 80-1935. Repr. of 1932 ed. 36.00 (ISBN 0-404-18955-5). AMS Pr.

Bermann, Sandra, tr. see Manzoni, Alessandro.

Bermant, Chaim. Belshazzar: A Cat's Story for Humans. 64p. 1982. pap. 2.50 (ISBN 0-380-58560-X, 58560-X, Bard). Avon.

--Dancing Bear. 256p. 1985. 13.95 (ISBN 0-312-18211-2). St Martin.

--The House of Women. 304p. 1983. 12.95 (ISBN 0-312-39306-7). St Martin.

--The House of Women. 272p. 1984. pap. 3.50 (ISBN 0-441-34468-2). Ace Bks.
--The Patriarch. 448p. 1981. 14.95 (ISBN 0-312-59804-1). St Martin.
Bermant, Chaine. The Patriarch. 432p. 1982. pap. 3.25 (ISBN 0-441-65366-9). Ace Bks.
Bermanzohn, Paul & Bermanzohn, Sally. The True Story of the Greensboro Massacre. (Illus.). 256p. 1981. pap. text ed. 3.95 (ISBN 0-86686-000-2). Cauce Pubs.
Bermanzohn, Sally, jt. auth. see Bermanzohn, Paul.
Berme, Necip, et al, eds. Biomechanics of Normal & Pathological Human Articulating Joints. (NATO Advanced Science Ser.: E, Applied Sciences). 1985. lib. bdg. 52.50 (ISBN 90-247-3164-X, Pub. by Martinus Nijhoff Netherlands). Kluwer Academic.
Bermek, E., ed. Mechanisms of Protein Synthesis: Structure-Function Relations, Control Mechanisms, & Evolutionary Aspects. (Proceedings in Life Sciences Ser.). (Illus.). 250p. 1984. 25.00 (ISBN 0-387-13653-3). Springer-Verlag.
Bermel, Albert. Contradictory Characters: An Interpretation of the Modern Theatre. LC 84-15246. 308p. 1984. pap. text ed. 13.50 (ISBN 0-8191-4237-9). U Pr of Amer.
--Farce. 1983. pap. 9.95 (ISBN 0-671-25149-X, Touchstone Bks). S&S.
--Six One-Act Farces. LC 82-81872. 75p. (Orig.). 1982. pap. 8.50 (ISBN 0-88127-005-9). Oracle Pr LA.
Bermel, Albert, ed. Three Popular French Comedies. LC 75-1959. x, 187p. 1975. 11.50 (ISBN 0-8044-2041-6); pap. 5.95 (ISBN 0-8044-6044-2). Ungar.
Bermel, Albert, tr. see Moliere.
Bermeo, Nancy. The Revolution Within the Revolution: Workers' Control in Rural Portugal. LC 85-42675. (Illus.). 264p. 1986. 28.50 (ISBN 0-691-07688-X). Princeton U Pr.
Bermingham, Alan. The Small TV Studio: Equipment & Facilities. (Media Manual Ser.). (Illus.). 160p. 1975. pap. 14.95 (ISBN 0-240-50869-6). Focal Pr.
Bermingham, Cedric O. Stars of the Screen 1931. 1976. lib. bdg. 75.00 (ISBN 0-8490-3065-X). Gordon Pr.
Bermingham, E. H. Staunton's Chess Player's Handbook. Repr. of 1929 ed. lib. bdg. 30.00 (ISBN 0-8495-0359-0). Arden Lib.
Bermingham, Jack, jt. auth. see Clausen, Edwin.
Bermingham, Peter. American Art in the Barbizon Mood. LC 74-26664. (Illus.). pap. 48.00 (ISBN 0-317-10477-2, 2011372). Bks Demand UMI.
Bermingham, Peter, jt. auth. see National Museum of American Art.
Bermon, Sonya T. Holistic Assertion Handbook. 1980. pap. text ed. 7.00 (ISBN 0-9603958-0-6). Assert Train Inst.
Bermont, Hubert. The Complete Consultant: A Roadmap to Success. (The Consultant's Library). 125p. 1982. 23.00 (ISBN 0-930686-16-0, Pub. by Consultants Library). Bermont Bks.
--The Consultant's Malpractice Avoidance Manual. (The Consultant's Library). 70p. (Orig.). 1981. pap. 19.00 (ISBN 0-930686-15-2). Bermont Bks.
--How to Become a Successful Consultant in Your Own Field. rev. ed. 150p. 1985. pap. 29.00 (ISBN 0-930686-22-5). Bermont Bks.
--How to Compete Successfully in Your Own Field. 1979. 14.00 (ISBN 0-930686-05-5). Bermont Bks.
--How to Mass Market Your Advice. (The Consultant's Library). 60p. (Orig.). 1981. pap. 18.00 (ISBN 0-930686-13-6). Bermont Bks.
--The Successful Consultant's Guide to Authoring, Publishing & Lecturing. 1979. text ed. 19.00 (ISBN 0-930686-03-9). Bermont Bks.
Bermont, Hubert, jt. auth. see Langston, Shelley.
Bermont, Hubert, jt. auth. see Thomas, David S.
Bermont, Hubert, ed. see Garvin, Andrew P.
Bermont, John. How to Europe: The Complete Travelers Handbook. 2nd ed. LC 85-124822. (Illus.). 502p. 1985. pap. 9.95 (ISBN 0-940792-41-9). Murphy & Broad.
Bermudes, Robert W. Conquering Cancer. 1983. 5.50 (ISBN 0-89536-619-3). CSS of Ohio.
Bermudez, Andrea B. Influence of the Institution of Free Learning on Spanish Education. LC 76-51193. (Coleccion De Estudios Hispanicos (Hispanic Studies Collection)). 1978. pap. 10.00 (ISBN 0-89729-190-5). Ediciones.
Bermudez, Maria T. Mexican Family Favorites Cook Book. 144p. 1983. pap. 5.00 (ISBN 0-914846-17-5). Golden West Pub.
Bermudez, Paul. Timmy Learns to Draw. 1985. 5.95 (ISBN 0-317-18726-0). Todd & Honeywell.
Bern, H. von Dach see Von Dach Bern, H.
Bern, Murray, ed. Urinary Tract Bleeding. (Illus.). 554p. 1985. 69.50 (ISBN 0-87993-236-8, Plenum Pr). Futura Pub.
Berna, Henri. Dictionnaire Technique et Administratif De la Navigation Interieure. 393p. (Fr.). 1977. 82.50 (ISBN 0-686-56914-8, M-6030). French & Eur.
Berna, Kurt. Christ Did Not Perish on the Cross: Christ's Body Buried Alive. 1975. 14.50 (ISBN 0-682-48139-4). Exposition Pr FL.
Bernabe, Emma, et al. Ilokano Lessons. McKaughan, Howard P., ed. LC 76-152459. (PALI Language Texts: Philippines). Repr. of 1971 ed. 89.50 (ISBN 0-8357-9823-2, 2017215). Bks Demand UMI.
Bernabo, M. & Picchi, F. Grande Dizionario di Marina: Inglese-Italiano, Italiano-Inglese. 963p. (Eng. & Ital.). 1970. 95.00 (ISBN 0-686-92551-3, M-9298). French & Eur.
Bernac, Pierre. The Interpretation of French Song. (Illus.). 1978. pap. 8.95x (ISBN 0-393-00878-9, N878, Norton Lib). Norton.
Bernacca, Pier L., ed. Astrophysics from Spacelab. Ruffini, Remo. (Astrophysics & Space Science Library: No. 81). 720p. 1980. lib. bdg. 47.50 (ISBN 90-277-1064-3, Pub. by Reidel Holland). Kluwer Academic.
Bernacchi, Richard L. & Larsen, Gerald H. Data Processing Contracts & the Law. 1974. 50.00 (ISBN 0-316-09183-9). Little.
Bernadete, M. J., jt. auth. see Del Rio, Angel.
Bernadette. French Vegetarian Cooking. (Illus.). 192p. (Orig.). 1983. pap. 6.95 (ISBN 0-399-50841-4, Perigee). Putnam Pub Group.
Bernadette, Ann. Echoes of the Heart. (Orig.). 1981. pap. 2.50 (ISBN 0-8439-8042-7, Tiara Bks). Dorchester Pub Co.
Bernadette, Michael, ed. Creating a Career Choice for Nurses: Long-Term Care. 64p. 1983. 7.95 (ISBN 0-88737-285-6, 20-1917). Natl League Nurse.
Bernadotte Af Wisborg, Folke G. To Jerusalem. LC 75-6424. (The Rise of Jewish Nationalism & the Middle East Ser.). 280p. 1975. Repr. of 1951 ed. 21.50 (ISBN 0-88355-311-2). Hyperion Conn.
Bernal, jt. auth. see Ludwig.
Bernal, Ignacio. A History of Mexican Archaeology: The Vanished Civilizations of Middle America. (Illus.). 1983. pap. 9.95f (ISBN 0-500-79008-6). Thames Hudson.
--The Olmec World. Heyden, Doris & Horcasitas, Fernando, trs. (Illus.). 1969. pap. 7.95 (ISBN 0-520-02891-0, CAL 303). U of Cal Pr.
Bernal, Ignacio see Wauchope, Robert.
Bernal, Ivan, et al. Symmetry: A Stereoscopic Guide for Chemists. LC 75-178258. (Illus.). 180p. 1972. text ed. 35.95 (ISBN 0-7167-0168-5). W H Freeman.
Bernal, J. D. The Analytic Theory of Point Systems, 1923. 1981. pap. 5.00 (ISBN 0-686-45041-8). Polycrystal Bk Serv.
--Science in History, 4 vols. Incl. Vol. 1. The Emergence of Science. pap. 8.95x (ISBN 0-262-52020-6); Vol. 2. The Scientific & Industrial Revolution. pap. 8.95x (ISBN 0-262-52021-4); Vol. 3. The Natural Sciences in Our Time. pap. 8.95x (ISBN 0-262-52022-2); Vol. 4. The Social Sciences: a Conclusion. pap. 8.95x (ISBN 0-262-52023-0). 1971. Set. pap. 30.00x (ISBN 0-262-02142-0). MIT Pr.
--The Social Function of Science. 482p. 1980. Repr. lib. bdg. 40.00 (ISBN 0-8492-3754-8). R West.
Bernal, John D. The Freedom of Necessity. LC 83-45414. Repr. of 1949 ed. 44.50 (ISBN 0-404-20028-1). AMS Pr.
Bernal, Louis C., jt. auth. see Martin, Patricia P.
Bernal, Martin. Chinese Socialism in Nineteen Hundred-Seven. LC 75-16809. (Illus.). 259p. 1976. 29.95x (ISBN 0-8014-0915-2). Cornell U Pr.
Bernanos, Georges. Le Chemin de la Croix des Ames. 1948. pap. 7.95 (ISBN 0-686-51932-9). French & Eur.
--Correspondance, 2 tomes. Beguin & Murray, eds. Set. 35.00 (ISBN 0-685-37213-8). French & Eur.
--Courrier. 5.95 (ISBN 0-685-37214-6). French & Eur.
--Le Crepuscule des Vieux: Essai. 5.95 (ISBN 0-685-37215-4). French & Eur.
--Un Crime. 3.95 (ISBN 0-685-37224-3). French & Eur.
--Dialogue Des Carmelites. 1960. 13.50 (ISBN 0-685-11136-9). French & Eur.
--Dialogue Des Carmelites. (Coll. Le Livre de Vie). pap. 3.95 (ISBN 0-685-37216-2). French & Eur.
--Dialogue d'Ombres. pap. 2.95 (ISBN 0-685-23914-4). French & Eur.
--The Diary of a Country Priest. 304p. 1984. pap. 7.95 (ISBN 0-88184-013-0, Publishers Group West). Carroll & Graf.
--The Diary of a Country Priest: Thomas More Books to Live Ser. Morris, Pamela, tr. (Fr.). 1983. 14.95 (ISBN 0-88347-155-8). Thomas More.
--Les Enfants Humilies Journal (1939-1940) pap. 3.95 (ISBN 0-685-23911-X). French & Eur.
--Essais et Ecrits de Combat. Bridel & Chabot, eds. Incl. Saint-Dominique; Jeanne, Relapse et Sainte; La Grande Peur Des Bien-Pensants; Les Grands Cimetieres Sous la Lune; Scandale de la Verite; Nous Autres Francais; Les Enfants Humilies; Articles (1909-1939. (Bibliotheque de la Pleiade). 35.50 (ISBN 0-685-37212-X). French & Eur.
--Francais, Si Vous Saviez (1945-1948) 4.95 (ISBN 0-685-37217-0). French & Eur.
--La France contre les Robots. 3.95 (ISBN 0-685-37218-9). French & Eur.
--La Grande Peur des Bien-Pensants. pap. 3.95 (ISBN 0-685-23915-2, 2240). French & Eur.
--Grands Cimetieres Sous La Lune. 1962. 3.95 (ISBN 0-685-11223-3). French & Eur.
--Imposture. 1958. 13.95 (ISBN 0-685-11248-9); pap. 3.95 (ISBN 0-686-66426-4). French & Eur.
--Jeanne, Relapse et Sainte. 6.50 (ISBN 0-685-37219-7). French & Eur.
--Joie. 1956. 13.95 (ISBN 0-685-11278-0); pap. 3.95 (ISBN 0-686-66427-2). French & Eur.
--Journal D'un Cure De Campagne. 1955. 13.95 (ISBN 0-685-11280-2). French & Eur.
--Last Essays. LC 68-23409. 1968. Repr. of 1955 ed. lib. bdg. 18.75x (ISBN 0-8371-0019-4, BELE). Greenwood.
--Le Lendemain, C'est Vous. 14.50 (ISBN 0-685-37220-0). French & Eur.
--Lettre aux Anglais: Essai. pap. 6.95 (ISBN 0-685-37221-9). French & Eur.
--La Liberte, Pourquoi Faire? Essai. pap. 13.95 (ISBN 0-685-37222-7). French & Eur.
--Un Mauvais Reve. 13.50 (ISBN 0-685-37225-1). French & Eur.
--Monsieur Ouine. 1960. 12.95 (ISBN 0-685-11404-X). French & Eur.
--Nous Autres Francais: Essai. pap. 4.95 (ISBN 0-685-37223-5). French & Eur.
--Nouvelle Histoire De Mouchette. 1960. 13.50 (ISBN 0-685-11428-7). French & Eur.
--Sous le Soleil De Satan. 1957. 11.95 (ISBN 0-685-11569-0). French and Eur.
--Sous le Soleil de Satan. (Documentation thematique). (Illus., Fr.). pap. 2.95 (ISBN 0-685-14079-2, 79). Larousse.
Bernanos, Georges, et al. Oeuvres Romanesques Completes. Picon, et al, eds. 1962. 45.95 (ISBN 0-685-11464-3). French & Eur.
Bernanos, Michel. The Other Side of the Mountain. LC 68-29550. 107p. 1973. Repr. of 1968 ed. 8.95 (ISBN 0-910220-47-6). Berg.
Bernar, Christine E. Sans Rhyme or Reason. 1984. 6.95 (ISBN 0-533-05879-1). Vantage.
Bernard, A., et al, eds. Leucocyte Typing. (Illus.). 820p. 1984. 48.50 (ISBN 0-387-12056-4). Springer Verlag.
Bernard, A. J., jt. ed. see Amstutz, G. C.
Bernard, Art. Dog Days. LC 69-12374. 1969. 5.95 (ISBN 0-87004-126-6). Caxton.
Bernard, Bruce. The Bible & Its Painters. (Illus.). 300p. 1984. 24.95 (ISBN 0-02-510130-7). Macmillan.
Bernard, C. H. & Epp, C. D. Laboratory Experiments in College Physics. 5th ed. 437p. 1980. 19.45 (ISBN 0-471-05441-0). Wiley.
Bernard, Carl & Norquay, Karen. Practical Effects in Photography. LC 80-40794. (Practical Photography Ser.). (Illus.). 168p. 1982. 19.95 (ISBN 0-240-51082-8). Focal Pr.
Bernard, Christiaan. Junior Body Machine. LC 83-7771. (gr. 3-6). 1984. pap. 8.95 (ISBN 0-517-55091-1). Crown.
Bernard, Christine, ed. see Elder, Gladys.
Bernard, Claude. Introduction to the Study of Experimental Medicine. Greene, Henry C., tr. 1957. pap. 3.95 (ISBN 0-486-20400-6). Dover.
--Lectures on the Phenomena of Life Common to Animals & Plants, Vol. 1. Hoff, Hebbel E., et al, trs. (Illus.). 336p. 1974. 34.75x (ISBN 0-398-02857-5). C C Thomas.
--Memoir on the Pancreas: And the Role of Pancreatic Juice in Digestive Processes Particularly in the Digestion of Neutral Fat. (Monographs of the Physiological Society: No. 42). 1985. 48.00 (ISBN 0-12-092880-9). Acad Pr.
Bernard, Dan, et al, eds. Charging for Computer Services: Principles & Guidelines. Emery, James C. & Nolan, Richard. LC 77-23811. (Computer & Data Processing Professionals Ser). 1977. text ed. 17.50 (ISBN 0-89433-055-1); pap. text ed. 12.00 (ISBN 0-89433-051-9). Petrocelli.
Bernard, David. Essentials of Oneness Theology. (Illus.). 40p. (Orig.). 1985. pap. 2.00 (ISBN 0-912315-89-X). Word Aflame.
Bernard, David K. The New Birth. Wallace, Mary H., ed. 346p. (Orig.). 1984. pap. 6.95 (ISBN 0-912315-77-6). Word Aflame.
--The Oneness of God. Wallace, Mary K., ed. 326p. (Orig.). 1983. pap. 6.95 (ISBN 0-912315-12-1). Word Aflame.
Bernard, David K., jt. auth. see Bernard, Loretta A.
Bernard De Menthon. Le Mystère De S. Bernard De Menthon. 28.00 (ISBN 0-384-04015-2); pap. 22.00 (ISBN 0-384-04016-0). Johnson Repr.
Bernard, Dorothy. So Dear to My Heart. (Candlelight Romance Ecstacy Ser.: No. 351). (Orig.). 1985. pap. 2.25 (ISBN 0-440-18166-6). Dell.
Bernard, Dorothy A. Delicate Dimensions. (Candlelight Ecstasy Ser.: No. 309). (Orig.). 1985. pap. 1.95 (ISBN 0-440-11775-5). Dell.
--Destiny's Touch. (Candlelight Ecstacy Romance Ser.: No. 190). (Orig.). 1983. pap. 1.95 (ISBN 0-440-11889-1). Dell.
--Just Call My Name. (Candlelight Ecstasy Ser.: No. 275). 192p. (Orig.). 1984. pap. 1.95 (ISBN 0-440-14410-8, Dell Trade Pbks). Dell.
--A Question of Trust. (Candlelight Ecstasy Ser.: No. 53). (Orig.). 1982. pap. 1.75 (ISBN 0-440-17315-9). Dell.
--Speak Softly To My Soul. (Candlelight Ecstasy Ser.: No. 104). (Orig.). 1982. pap. 1.95 (ISBN 0-440-18827-X). Dell.
Bernard, E. E. & Kare, M. R. Biological Prototypes & Synthetic Systems. LC 62-9964. 397p. 1962. 39.50x (ISBN 0-306-30114-8, Plenum Pr). Plenum Pub.
Bernard, Edward, pseud. The Name Changers. (Illus.). 528p. (Orig.). 1982. pap. 5.95 (ISBN 0-910797-00-5). Marketing Effect.
Bernard, Eileen. Lies That Came True. Hobe, David, ed. LC 83-70300. (Illus.). 244p. 1983. pap. 9.95 (ISBN 0-89305-050-4). Anna Pub.
Bernard, Elaine. Long Distance Feeling. (Illus.). 280p. 1982. 14.95 (ISBN 0-919573-02-9, Pub. by New Star Bks BC); pap. 7.95 (ISBN 0-919573-03-7). Flatiron Book Dist.
Bernard, Ellsworth. An Academic Apprenticeship. (Illus.). viii, 268p. 1985. 10.00 (ISBN 0-9605458-2-4). Dinosaur.
Bernard, Etienne A. Compendium of Lecture Notes for Training Personnel in the Applications of Meteorology to Economic & Social Development. (Illus.). 186p. (Eng., Fr. & Span.). 1976. pap. 25.00 (ISBN 92-63-10382-8, W152, WMO). Unipub.
Bernard, Felix. Elements de Paleontologie. Gould, Stephen J., ed. LC 79-8325. (The History of Paleontology Ser.). (Illus., Fr.). 1980. Repr. of 1895 ed. lib. bdg. 97.50x (ISBN 0-405-12705-7). Ayer Co Pubs.
Bernard, G. S. War Talks of Confederate Veterans. 335p. 1981. 20.00 (ISBN 0-89029-063-6). Pr of Morningside.
Bernard, G. W. The Power of the Early Tudor Nobility: A Study of the Fourth & Fifth Earls of Shrewsbury. LC 84-16757. 240p. 1985. 27.50x (ISBN 0-389-20525-7, 08087). B&N Imports.
Bernard, Gary D. & Ishimaru, Akira. Tables of the Anger & Lommel-Weber Functions. LC 62-17144. (Illus.). 74p. 1962. pap. 15.00x (ISBN 0-295-73956-8). U of Wash Pr.
Bernard, George. Inside the National Enquirer: Confessions of an Undercover Reporter. Hammond, Debbie, ed. LC 76-44613. 1977. 13.95 (ISBN 0-87949-089-6). Ashley Bks.
--Moment of the Predator. 1980. pap. 2.50 (ISBN 0-8439-0807-6, Pub. by Nordon Pubns). Dorchester Pub Co.
Bernard, George & Paling, John. Grey Squirrel, Vol. 23. LC 82-410. (Illus.). 32p. 1982. 8.95 (ISBN 0-399-20906-9, Putnam). Putnam Pub Group.
Bernard, Graham. Why You Are Who You Are: A Psychic Conversation. 208p. (Orig.). 1985. pap. 8.95 (ISBN 0-89281-100-5). Destiny Bks.
Bernard, H. A. & LeBlanc, R. J., Sr. Recent Sediments of Southeast Texas - a Field Guide to the Brazos Alluvial & Deltaic Plains & the Galveston Barrier Island Complex: Resume of the Quaternary Geology of the Northwestern Gulf of Mexico Province. (Guidebook Ser.: GB 11). 132p. 1970. Repr. 7.00 (ISBN 0-686-29319-3). Bur Econ Geology.
Bernard, H. Russell. Human Way: Readings in Anthropology. 1975. pap. write for info. (ISBN 0-02-308920-2, 30892). Macmillan.
Bernard, H. Russell & Pelto, Pertti J. Technology & Social Change. (Illus.). 352p. 1972. text ed. 24.95x (ISBN 0-02-309010-3, 30901). Macmillan.
Bernard, H. Y. Law of Death & Disposal of the Dead. 2nd ed. LC 79-19160. (Legal Almanac Ser.: No. 57). 114p. 1979. 5.95 (ISBN 0-379-11120-9). Oceana.
--Public Officials, Elected & Appointed. LC 68-54014. (Legal Almanac Ser.: No. 26). 119p. 1969. 5.95 (ISBN 0-379-11026-1). Oceana.
Bernard, Harold. The Greenhouse Effect. LC 80-8710. 256p. 1981. pap. 4.95i (ISBN 0-06-090855-6, CN 855, CN). Har-Row.
Bernard, Harold W., jt. auth. see Strom, Robert D.
Bernard, Helene. Great Women Initiates or the Feminine Mystic. Ziebel, Michelle, tr. from Fr. LC 84-50133. (Illus.). 151p. (Orig.). 1984. pap. 8.00 (ISBN 0-912057-36-X, G-650). AMORC.
Bernard, Henri. Matteo Ricci's Scientific Contribution to China. Werner, Edward C., tr. LC 73-863. (China Studies Ser). (Illus.). 108p. 1973. Repr. of 1935 ed. 13.75 (ISBN 0-88355-059-8). Hyperion Conn.
Bernard, Henry. The Shade of the Balkans. 1978. Repr. of 1904 ed. lib. bdg. 40.00 (ISBN 0-8495-0425-2). Arden Lib.
Bernard, Henry, intro. by. The Shade of the Balkans: Being a Collection of Bulgarian Folksongs & Proverbs. LC 73-15747. Repr. of 1904 ed. lib. bdg. 38.00 (ISBN 0-8414-3331-3). Folcroft.
Bernard, J., et al, eds. Rubidomycin: A New Agent Against Cancer. (Recent Results in Cancer Research: Vol. 20). (Illus.). xiv, 181p. 1969. 36.00 (ISBN 0-387-04682-8). Springer-Verlag.
Bernard, J. H. The Pastoral Epistles: Timothy & Titus. (Thornapple Commentaries Ser.). 272p. 1980. pap. 6.95 (ISBN 0-8010-0797-6). Baker Bk.
Bernard, J. H., tr. see Kant, Immanuel.
Bernard, J. R. A Short Guide to Traditional Grammar. 88p. 1975. pap. 9.00x (ISBN 0-424-06950-4, Pub. by Sydney U Pr). Intl Spec Bk.
Bernard, Jack, ed. see Hartmann, Sven & Hartner, Thoman.
Bernard, Jack, tr. see Diole, Philippe.
Bernard, Jack, tr. see Tazieff, Haroun.
Bernard, Jacqueline. The Children You Gave Us. LC 72-87122. (Illus.). 1972. 6.95 (ISBN 0-8197-0356-7). Bloch.
Bernard, James E. An Overview of Simulation in Highway Transportation, Vol. 7. 1977. two book set 30.00 (ISBN 0-318-01053-4). Soc Computer Sim.

Bernard, James E., ed. An Overview of Simulation in Highway Transportation, 2 vols, Pts. 1 & 2. (SCS Simulation Ser.: Vol. 7, Nos. 1 & 2). Set. 30.00 (ISBN 0-686-36672-7). Soc Computer Sim.
Bernard, Janine & Hackney, Harold. Untying the Knot: A Guide to Civilized Divorce. 204p. (Orig.). 1983. pap. 7.95 (ISBN 0-86683-800-7). Winston Pr.
Bernard, Jean-Jacques. Nationale Six. Kroff, Alexander Y. & Bottke, Karl G., eds. (Illus., Orig., Fr.,). 1961. pap. text ed. 4.95x (ISBN 0-89197-312-5). Irvington.
Bernard, Jean-Louis. Dictionnaire de l'Insolite et du Fantastique. 356p. (Fr.). 1974. 17.95 (ISBN 0-686-56830-3, M-6608). French & Eur.
Bernard, Jeffrey & Taki. High Life, Low Life. 192p. 1981. 35.00 (ISBN 0-905150-27-9, Pub. by J Landesman England). State Mutual Bk.
Bernard, Jessie. The Female World. LC 80-69880. (Illus.). 1981. 27.50 (ISBN 0-02-903000-5). Free Pr.
--The Female World. LC 80-69880. 1982. pap. 11.95 (ISBN 0-02-903060-9). Free Pr.
--The Future of Marriage. LC 82-6991. 384p. 1982. text ed. 31.00x (ISBN 0-300-02912-8); pap. 9.95x (ISBN 0-300-02853-9, Y-441). Yale U Pr.
--Sex Game: Communication Between the Sexes. LC 68-13219. 1972. pap. 4.95 (ISBN 0-689-70293-0, 187). Atheneum.
--Women, Wives, Mothers: Values & Options. LC 74-18210. 294p. 1975. pap. text ed. 13.95x (ISBN 0-202-30281-4). Aldine Pub.
Bernard, Jessie, commentary by. Self-Portrait of a Family: Letters by Jessie, Dorothy Lee, Claude, & David Bernard. LC 77-88361. (Illus.). 1978. pap. 8.95 (ISBN 0-8070-3799-0, BP597). Beacon Pr.
Bernard, Joel. Authority, Autonomy & Radical Commitment: Stephen & Abby Kelley Foster. 39p. 1981. pap. 6.00 (ISBN 0-912296-50-X, Dist. by U Pr of Va). Am Antiquarian.
Bernard, John. Every Man His Own Mechanic. 14.50x (ISBN 0-392-05395-0, LTB). Sportshelf.
--Retrospection of America, Seventeen Ninety-Seven to Eighteen Eleven. Matthews, Brander & Hutton, Laurence, eds. LC 73-83401. 1887. 24.50 (ISBN 0-405-08263-0, Blom Pubns). Ayer Co Pubs.
--This Prayer Called Life. (Infinity Ser.: No. 1). 1972. text ed. 2.50 (ISBN 0-03-004001-9, 227); tchr's. guide by Dennis Pearson 1.15 (ISBN 0-03-004006-X, 228). Winston Pr.
--The Tranquillitie of the Minde. LC 73-6099. (English Experience Ser.: No. 568). 1973. Repr. of 1570 ed. 15.00 (ISBN 90-221-0568-7). Walter J Johnson.
Bernard, Jules E., Jr. Prosody of the Tudor Interlude. LC 69-15677. (Yale Studies in English Ser.: No. 90). ix, 225p. 1969. Repr. of 1939 ed. 18.50 (ISBN 0-208-00782-2, Archon). Shoe String.
Bernard, L. L. Instinct: A Study in Social Psychology. 550p. 1980. Repr. of 1924 ed. lib. bdg. 40.00 (ISBN 0-89760-046-0). Telegraph Bks.
--An Introduction to Social Psychology. 652p. 1980. Repr. lib. bdg. 65.00 (ISBN 0-89984-060-4). Century Bookbindery.
--An Introduction to Social Psychology. 1979. Repr. of 1926 ed. lib. bdg. 35.00 (ISBN 0-8492-3747-5). R West.
--An Introduction to Sociology. 1041p. 1980. Repr. of 1942 ed. lib. bdg. 35.00 (ISBN 0-8492-3755-6). R West.
Bernard, L. L., ed. The Fields & Methods of Sociology. 1934. 25.00 (ISBN 0-8482-7363-X). Norwood Edns.
--An Introduction to Sociology. 1942. 25.00 (ISBN 0-8482-7388-5). Norwood Edns.
Bernard, Leon. Emerging City: Paris in the Age of Louis Fourteenth. LC 71-86478. 326p. 1970. 21.00 (ISBN 0-8223-0214-4). Duke.
Bernard, Loretta A. & Bernard, David K. In Search of Holiness. 288p. (Orig.). 1981. pap. 5.95 (ISBN 0-912315-40-7). Word Aflame.
Bernard, Luther L. Instinct: A Study in Social Psychology. Coser, Lewis A. & Powell, Walter W., eds. LC 79-6984. (Perennial Works in Sociology Ser.). (Illus.). 1979. Repr. of 1924 ed. lib. bdg. 42.00x (ISBN 0-405-12084-2). Ayer Co Pubs.
Bernard, Marc, ed. see Zola, Emile.
Bernard, Marie. The ABC of Graphology. (Illus.). 400p. 1985. 30.00 (ISBN 0-87875-304-4). Whitston Pub.
Bernard, Mary. Agony! Can the Church Survive Without Jesus? LC 79-84343. 1979. pap. 2.95 (ISBN 0-89221-059-1). New Leaf.
--Who Can We Trust? LC 80-80531. 128p. 1980. 2.50 (ISBN 0-89221-075-3). New Leaf.
Bernard, Matt. Mario Lanza. 1971. pap. 1.25 (ISBN 0-532-12113-9). Woodhill.
Bernard, Michael & Schneider, Mark, eds. Symposium on Land Policy. (Orig.). 1984. pap. 8.00 (ISBN 0-918592-70-4). Policy Studies.
Bernard, Michael E. & Joyce, Marie R. Rational-Emotive Therapy with Children & Adolescents: Theory, Treatment Strategies, Preventative Methods. LC 83-23442. (Personality Processes Ser.: 1-341). 489p. 1984. 40.00x (ISBN 0-471-87543-0, Pub. by Wiley-Interscience). Wiley.
Bernard, Michael E., jt. ed. see Ellis, Albert.
Bernard, Michael M., ed. Annotated Bibliography on Taxation As an Instrument of Land Planning Policy. (Lincoln Institute Monograph: No. 80-8). 90p. 1980. pap. text ed. 4.00 (ISBN 0-686-29504-8). Lincoln Inst Land.
Bernard, Miguel A. The Lights of Broadway & Other Essays: Reflections of a Filipino Traveler. 103p. 1981. pap. 4.50x (ISBN 0-686-30671-6, Pub. by New Day Philippines); pap. text ed. 4.75x (ISBN 0-686-30672-4). Cellar.
Bernard, Mitchell, et al. The Rights of Single People. (American Civil Liberties Union Ser.). 144p. (Orig.). 1985. pap. 4.95 (ISBN 0-553-24816-2). Bantam.
Bernard, Mountague. Historical Account of the Neutrality of Great Britain During the American Civil War. LC 70-146237. 1971. Repr. of 1870 ed. lib. bdg. 32.00 (ISBN 0-8337-0246-7). B Franklin.
Bernard, Nelson T. Wildflowers Along Forest & Mesa Trails. LC 83-23344. (A Coyote Bk.). (Illus.). 192p. 1984. pap. 9.95 (ISBN 0-8263-0730-2). U of NM Pr.
Bernard, Nora. Hollywood's Irish Rose. 1978. pap. 1.95 (ISBN 0-380-41061-3, 41061). Avon.
Bernard, Otis. Life With Yankee Wife. 120p. 1982. pap. 4.95 (ISBN 0-89221-093-1, Pub. by SonLife). New Leaf.
--Put a Little Starch in Your Faith. 150p. 1980. pap. 4.95 (ISBN 0-89221-095-8). New Leaf.
Bernard, P. & Dubeif, H. The Decline of the Third Republic 1914-1938. (Cambridge History of Modern France Ser.: No. 5). 358p. 1985. 49.50 (ISBN 0-521-25240-7). Cambridge U Pr.
Bernard, Paul P. Jesuits & Jacobins: Enlightenment & Enlightened Despotism in Austria. LC 78-151997. 207p. 1971. 14.95x (ISBN 0-252-00180-X). U of Ill Pr.
--The Limits of Enlightenment: Joseph II & the Law. LC 79-12030. 160p. 1979. 13.50x (ISBN 0-252-00735-2). U of Ill Pr.
--Rush to the Alps. (Eastern European Monographs: No. 37). 228p. 1978. 22.50x (ISBN 0-914710-30-3). East Eur Quarterly.
Bernard, Philippe J. Le Travailleurs Estrangers en Europe Occidentale: Actes Du Collcque Organise Par la Commission Nationale Pour les Etudes et les Recherches Inter-Ethniques, Paris-Sorbonne, Du 5 Au 7 Juin 1974. (Publications de l'Institut d'Etudes et de Recherches Interethniques et Inter Culturelles: No. 6). (Fr.). 1976. pap. text ed. 26.80x (ISBN 0-686-22611-9). Mouton.
Bernard, Raymond. The Danger We All Face: Suppressed Truth about Radiation. 62p. pap. 4.95 (ISBN 0-88697-045-8). Life Science.
--Eat Your Way to Better Health, Vol. 1. 1974. pap. 4.95 (ISBN 0-685-47352-X). G Barker Bks.
--Eat Your Way to Better Health, Vol. 2. 1974. pap. 4.95 (ISBN 0-685-47353-8). G Barker Bks.
--Escape to the Inner Earth. 1974. pap. 4.95 (ISBN 0-685-47351-1). G Barker Bks.
--The Hollow Earth. (Illus.). 1976. pap. 3.95 (ISBN 0-8065-0546-X). Citadel Pr.
--Hollow Earth. (Illus.). 1969. pap. 9.95 (ISBN 0-685-20197-X). G Barker Bks.
--Meat Eating: A Cause of Disease. 1981. pap. 14.95x (ISBN 0-317-06950-0, Regent House). B of A.
--Mensajes del Sanctum Celestial. 4th ed. AMORC Staff, tr. from Fr. 296p. (Orig., Span.). 1981. pap. 8.00 (ISBN 0-912057-75-0, GS-523). AMORC.
--Messages from the Celestial Sanctum. AMORC, tr. from Fr. LC 79-92677. 354p. (Orig.). 1980. pap. 10.00 (ISBN 0-912057-30-0, G-523). AMORC.
--Nutritional Methods of Blood Regeneration, Pt. 1. 53p. 1960. pap. 8.95 (ISBN 0-88697-037-7). Life Science.
--Nutritional Sex Control & Rejuvenation. 51p. 1960. pap. 5.95 (ISBN 0-88697-038-5). Life Science.
--Secret of Rejuvenation: Professor Brown Squad's Great Discovery of the Fountain of Youth. 39p. 1956. pap. 4.95 (ISBN 0-88697-036-9). Life Science.
Bernard, Reams D., Jr., ed. see Taylor, John N.
Bernard, Richard. Isle of Man, or, the Legal Proceeding in Man-Shire Against Sinne. LC 76-57356. (English Experience Ser.: No. 775). 1977. Repr. of 1630 ed. lib. bdg. 21.00 (ISBN 90-221-0775-2). Walter J Johnson.
Bernard, Richard M. The Melting Pot & the Altar: Marital Assimilation in Early Twentieth-Century Wisconsin. LC 80-16287. (Illus.). 192p. 1981. 17.50x (ISBN 0-8166-0988-8). U of Minn Pr.
--The Poles in Oklahoma. LC 79-6714. (Newcomers to a New Land Ser.: Vol. 1). (Illus.). 90p. (Orig.). 1980. pap. 3.95 (ISBN 0-8061-1630-7). U of Okla Pr.
Bernard, Richard M. & Rice, Bradley R., eds. Sunbelt Cities: Politics & Growth since World War II. LC 83-10222. 358p. 1983. text ed. 25.00x O.P. (ISBN 0-292-77576-8); pap. 9.95 (ISBN 0-292-77580-6). U of Tex Pr.
Bernard, Robert. A Catholic Education. 1982. 15.50 (ISBN 0-03-061123-7). HR&W.
--Death & the Princess. (Nightingale Ser.). 1983. pap. 9.95 (ISBN 0-8161-3520-7, Large Print Bks). G K Hall.
Bernard, Russell H., ed. see Hewitt, John D., et al.
Bernard, Sidney. Metamorphosis of Peace: Essays & Poems. 25p. 1984. pap. 3.00 (ISBN 0-933292-13-9). Arts End.
--This Way to the Apocalypse: The Politics of the 1960's. LC 77-94632. 256p. 1969. 5.95 (ISBN 0-912292-09-1). The Smith.
--Witnessing: The Seventies. LC 77-74623. 1977. 12.95 (ISBN 0-8180-1172-6). Horizon.
Bernard, Susan & Thompson, Grechen. Job Search Strategies for College Grads: The 10 Step Plan for Career Success. 186p. (Orig.). 1984. 3.95 (ISBN 0-937860-34-4). Adams Inc Ma.
Bernard, T. B. Secondary Education under Different Types of District Organization. LC 71-176559. (Columbia University. Teachers College. Contributions to Education: No. 642). Repr. of 1935 ed. 22.50 (ISBN 0-404-55642-6). AMS Pr.
Bernard, Thelma R. La Mansion Tenebrosa. new ed. Reed, John A., tr. from Eng. (Compadre Collection Ser.). 160p. (Span.). 1974. pap. 0.75 (ISBN 0-88473-606-7). Fiesta Pub.
Bernard, Theos. Hindu Philosophy. LC 68-21323. 1968. Repr. of 1947 ed. lib. bdg. 15.00x (ISBN 0-8371-0311-8, BEHP). Greenwood.
--Hindu Philosophy. 1981. Repr. of 1947 ed. 14.00x (ISBN 0-8364-0765-2, Pub. by Motilal Banarsidass). South Asia Bks.
Bernard, Thomas. The Consensus-Conflict Debate: Form & Content in Social Theories. 264p. 1983. 30.00x (ISBN 0-231-05670-2); pap. 15.00x (ISBN 0-231-05671-0). Columbia U Pr.
--Hindu Philosophy. 220p. 1981. 15.00 (ISBN 0-89581-220-7); pap. 9.00 (ISBN 0-89581-541-9). Asian Human Pr.
--Of the Education of the Poor. (Social History of Education Ser.: Second Series, No. 1). 380p. 1983. Repr. of 1809 ed. 24.00x (ISBN 0-7130-0010-4, Woburn Pr England). Biblio Dist.
Bernard, Thomas D. The Central Teaching of Christ: A Study of John 13-17. 426p. 1985. Repr. lib. bdg. 16.25 (ISBN 0-86524-176-7, 9519). Klock & Klock.
Bernard, Thomas J., jt. auth. see Vold, George B.
Bernard, Trevor. Brightlight. 1977. pap. 1.50 (ISBN 0-532-15278-6). Woodhill.
Bernard, W. B., jt. auth. see Johnson, T. W.
Bernard, William S., ed. Americanization Studies: The Acculturation of Immigrant Groups into American Society, 10 vols. Incl. New Homes for Old. Breckinridge, S. P; Immigrant's Day in Court. Claghorn, K. H; America Via the Neighborhood. Daniels, J; Immigrant Health & the Community. Davis, M. M; Americans by Choice. Gavit, J. P; Adjusting Immigrant & Industry. Leiserson, W. M; Immigrant Press & Its Control. Park, R. E; Stake in the Land. Speek, P. A; Old World Traits Transplanted. Thomas, W. I., et al.; Schooling of the Immigrant. Thompson, F. V. LC 73-108242. (Criminology, Law Enforcement, & Social Problems Ser.: No. 125). (Illus., Repr. 1920-24 with intros. to all vols. & indexes added. Available in set only). 1971. Set. 200.00x (ISBN 0-87585-125-8). Patterson Smith.
Bernard, Yves & Colli, Jean-Claude. Vocabulaire Economique et Financier: Coll. Points Economie. 384p. (Fr.). 1976. pap. 10.95 (ISBN 0-686-56915-6, M-6031). French & Eur.
Bernard, Yves, et al. Dictionnaire Economique et Financier. Lewandowski, Dominique, ed. 1200p. (Fr.). 1975. 119.95 (ISBN 0-686-57297-1, M-4643). French & Eur.
Bernard de Clairvaux, Saint Letters. James, Bruno S., tr. LC 78-63344. (The Crusades & Military Orders: Second Ser.). Repr. of 1953 ed. 47.50 (ISBN 0-404-17004-8). AMS Pr.
Bernard de Clairvaux, St. On Loving God: Selections from Sermons by St. Bernard of Clairvaux. Martin, Hugh, ed. LC 79-8706. (A Treasury of Christian Bks.). 125p. 1981. Repr. of 1959 ed. lib. bdg. 29.75x (ISBN 0-313-20787-9, BEOL). Greenwood.
Bernardi, Bernardo. Age Class Systems: Social Institutions & Polities Based on Age. (CAmbridge Studies in Social Anthropology: No. 57). (Illus.). 192p. Date not set. price not set (ISBN 0-521-30747-3); pap. price not set (ISBN 0-521-31482-8). Cambridge U Pr.
--The Mugwe, a Failing Prophet: A Study of a Religious & Public Dignitary of the Meru of Kenya. LC 59-3468. pap. 56.80 (ISBN 0-317-28187-9, 2022785). Bks Demand UMI.
Bernardi, F. & Mangini, A. Organic Sulfur Chemistry: Theoretical & Experimental Advances. (Studies in Organic Chemistry: Vol. 19). 1985. 146.50 (ISBN 0-444-42453-9). Elsevier.
Bernardi, J. Mario De see De Bernardi, J. Mario.
Bernardi, Mario. Conductor's Saga. (Illus.). 240p. 1984. 19.95 (ISBN 0-88962-205-1, Pub by Mosaic Pr Canada). Flatiron Book Dist.
Bernardi, S. D. Bibliography of Schlicht Functions. LC 83-7958. 363p. 1983. 32.50 (ISBN 0-936166-09-6). Mariner Pub.
Bernardin, H. J., ed. Personality Assessment in Organizations. LC 84-26355. 336p. 1985. 47.95 (ISBN 0-03-072023-0). Praeger.
Bernardin, H. John & Beatty, Richard W. Performance Appraisal: Assessing Human Behavior at Work. LC 83-9906. (Human Resource Management Ser.). 416p. 1983. pap. text ed. write for info. (ISBN 0-534-01398-8). Kent Pub Co.
Bernardin, John H. Women in the Work Force. LC 82-13170. 256p. 1982. 29.95 (ISBN 0-03-062471-1). Praeger.
Bernardin, Joseph B. Burial Services: Revised & Updated. 1980. casebound 14.95 (ISBN 0-8192-1267-9). Morehouse.
--Introduction to the Episcopal Church. rev ed. (Orig.). 1978. pap. 4.95 (ISBN 0-8192-1231-8). Morehouse.
Bernardin, Joseph C. Prayer in Our Time. (Illus.). pap. 0.35 (ISBN 0-8198-0269-7). Dghtrs St Paul.
Bernardin, Joseph L. Christ Lives in Me: A Pastoral Reflection on Jesus & His Meaning for Christian Life. 69p. (Orig.). 1985. pap. 3.95 (ISBN 0-86716-044-6). St Anthony Mess Pr.
Bernardin De Saint-Pierre. Paul et Virginie. 1964. 18.50 (ISBN 0-685-11480-5). French & Eur.
--Paul et Virginie. (Coll GF). pap. 3.95 (ISBN 0-685-34034-1). French & Eur.
--Paul et Virginie. Trahard, ed. (Class Garnier). pap. 9.95 (ISBN 0-685-34033-3). French & Eur.
Bernardin De Saint-Pierre, Jacques H. Paul et Virginie. (Documentation thematique). (Illus., Fr.). pap. 2.95 (ISBN 0-685-14023-7, 29). Larousse.
Bernardini, Joe. Singapore: A Novel of the Bronx. (Illus.). 224p. 1983. 1.98 (ISBN 0-517-55062-8, Harmony). Crown.
Bernardino, Bonasea M. God & Atheism: A Philosophical Approach to the Problem of God. LC 78-12064. 378p. 1979. 19.95x (ISBN 0-8132-0549-2). Cath U Pr.
Bernardis, Frank De see De Bernardis, Frank & O'Connor, Fank.
Bernard Le, Bovier De Fontenelle see Le Bovier De Fontenelle, Bernard.
Bernard-Marie, Brother. Praying the Rosary with the Bible. 1983. 6.00 (ISBN 0-8199-0872-X). Franciscan Herald.
Bernard-Munos, Carmen. Les Ayore du Chaco Septentrional: Etude Critique a Partir des Notes de Lucien Sebag. 1977. pap. 17.60x (ISBN 90-279-7525-6). Mouton.
Bernardo, Aldo S. Petrarch, Laura & the "Triumphs". LC 74-22084. 1974. 34.50x (ISBN 0-87395-289-8); pap. 10.00. State U NY Pr.
--Petrarch, Scipio & the "Africa". The Birth of Humanism's Dream. LC 78-19065. 1978. Repr. of 1962 ed. lib. bdg. 24.75x (ISBN 0-313-20535-3, BEPA). Greenwood.
Bernardo, Aldo S. & Mignani, Rigo. Ritratto Dell'Italia. 2nd ed. 1978. pap. text ed. 17.95x (ISBN 0-669-01157-6). Heath.
Bernardo, Aldo S. & Pellegrini, Anthony L., eds. Dante, Petrarch, Boccaccio: Studies in the Italian Trecento In Honour of Charles S. Singleton. LC 83-717. (Medieval & Renaissance Texts & Studies: Vol. 22). 400p. 1983. 25.00 (ISBN 0-86698-061-X). Medieval & Renaissance NY.
Bernardo, Aldo S., ed. see Fallani, Giovanni, et al.
Bernardo, Aldo S., tr. see Petrarca, Francesco.
Bernardo, C. Joseph & Bacon, Eugene H. American Military Policy. LC 74-9697. 548p. 1974. Repr. of 1961 ed. lib. bdg. 32.50x (ISBN 0-8371-7615-8, BEMP). Greenwood.
Bernardo, F. P., Jr. Design & Implementation of Low Cost Automation. LC 72-86487. 116p. 1972. 7.75 (ISBN 92-833-1020-9, APO17, APO). Unipub.
Bernardo, J. M., et al, eds. Bayesian Statistics Two: Proceedings of the Second Valencia International Meeting on Bayesian Statistics, 6-10 Sept., 1983. 770p. 1985. 75.00 (ISBN 0-444-87746-0, North Holland). Elsevier.
Bernardo, Robert M. Theory of Moral Incentives in Cuba. LC 76-148691. 184p. 1971. 12.50 (ISBN 0-8173-4720-8). U of Ala Pr.
Bernardo, Sorj, jt. ed. see Henfrey, Colin.
Bernard Of Clairvaux. Bernard of Clairvaux on the Song of Songs, Vol. II. Walsh, Kilian, tr. (Cistercian Fathers Ser.: No. 7). pap. 5.00 (ISBN 0-87907-707-7). Cistercian Pubns.
--Bernard of Clairvaux: Sermons I on Conversion; Lenten Sermons on the Psalm "He Who Dwells". Said, Marie-Bernard, tr. (Cistercian Fathers Ser.: No. 25). (Lat.). 1982. 25.95 (ISBN 0-87907-125-7); pap. 7.00 (ISBN 0-87907-925-8). Cistercian Pubns.
--Bernard of Clairvaux: Sermons on the Song of Songs, Vol. IV. Edmonds, Irene, tr. (Cistercian Fathers Ser.: No. 40). 1980. 15.95 (ISBN 0-87907-140-0). Cistercian Pubns.
--Song of Solomon. 560p. 1984. smythe sewn 21.00 (ISBN 0-86524-177-5, 2202). Klock & Klock.
Bernard Of Clairvaux & Amadeus Of Lausanne. Magnificat: Homilies in Praise of the Blessed Virgin Mary. LC 78-6249. (Cistercian Fathers Ser.: No. 18). 1979. 15.95 (ISBN 0-87907-118-4). Cistercian Pubns.
Bernard of Clairvaux & William of St. Thierry. The Love of God. Houston, James M., ed. LC 83-10533. (Classics of Faith & Devotion). Orig. Title: Life & Works of St. Bernard. 1983. 11.95 (ISBN 0-88070-017-3). Multnomah.
Bernardoni, Gus. Golf God's Way. LC 77-80414. 1978. 9.95 (ISBN 0-88419-144-3). Creation Hse.
Bernardoni, James. George Cukor: A Critical Study & Filmography. LC 84-43198. 200p. 1985. 18.95 (ISBN 0-89950-176-1). McFarland & Co.
Bernards, Solomon S., jt. auth. see Greenberg, David.
Bernards, Solomon S., ed. The Living Heritage of the High Holy Days. 31p. 1973. pap. 0.50 (ISBN 0-686-74964-2). ADL.

Bernardus Guidonis. Manuel de l'Inquisiteur, 2 vols. in 1. Mollat, G., ed. LC 78-63183. (Heresies of the Early Christian & Medieval Era: Second Ser.). Repr. of 1927 ed. 44.50 set (ISBN 0-404-16199-5). AMS Pr.

Bernardus Silvestris. Commentary on the First Six Books of Virgil's "Aeneid". Schreiber, E. G. & Maresca, Thomas E., trs. LC 79-9138. xxxvi, 129p. 1980. 14.50x (ISBN 0-8032-4108-9). U of Nebr Pr.

Bernart De Ventadorn. Bernart Von Ventadorn. LC 80-2176. Repr. of 1915 ed. 62.50 (ISBN 0-404-19004-9). AMS Pr.

Bernas, Joaquin G. A Historical & Juridical Study of the Philippine Bill of Rights. 1971. wrps. 11.00x (ISBN 0-686-09488-3). Cellar.

Bernasconi, Andrea. La Clemenza Di Tito. LC 80-831. (Italian Opera II Ser.). 822p. 1982. lib. bdg. 83.00 (ISBN 0-8240-4827-X). Garland Pub.

Bernasconi, C. F. Relaxation Kinetics. 1976. 59.00 (ISBN 0-12-092950-3). Acad Pr.

Bernasconi, G. Creep of Engineering Materials & Structures. 420p. 1980. 64.75 (ISBN 0-85334-878-2, Pub. by Elsevier Applied Sci England). Elsevier.

Bernasconi, J. & Schneider, Toni, eds. Physics in One Dimension: Proceedings. (Springer Ser. in Solid-State Sciences: Vol. 23). (Illus.). 368p. 1981. 37.00 (ISBN 0-387-10586-7). Springer-Verlag.

Bernasconi, Robert. The Question of Language in Heidegger's History of Being. (Contempory Studies in Philosophy & the Human Sciences). 110p. 1984. text ed. 16.45x (ISBN 0-391-03093-0, Pub. by Macmillan England). Humanities.

Bernat, Ivan, ed. Iron Metabolism. Gosztonyi, Eva, tr. from Hungarian. 415p. 1983. 39.50 (ISBN 0-306-30829-0, Plenum Pr). Plenum Pub.

Bernat de So. La Vesio de Bernat de So et le Debat entre Honor e Delit de Jacme March, Poemes Provenco-Catalans du 14ieme Siecle, Suivis du Sirventes de Joan de Castelnou. (Bibliotheque Meridionale: 1 Ser., Tome 25). (Fr.). Repr. of 1945 ed. 17.00 (ISBN 0-384-04030-6). Johnson Repr.

Bernath, Clifford. Making the Most of It: A Manual for the Army Family. 224p. 1983. pap. 11.95 (ISBN 0-8117-2159-0). Stackpole.

Bernath, Frances A., ed. Catalogue of Thai Language Holdings, in the Cornell University Libraries Through Nineteen-Sixty Four. 236p. 1964. pap. 3.00 (ISBN 0-87727-054-6, DP 54). Cornell SE Asia.

Bernath, Maja. Parents Book for Your Baby's First Year. 144p. (Orig.). 1983. pap. 3.50 (ISBN 0-345-30442-X). Ballantine.

Bernath, Stefan. The Cactus Coloring Book. (Illus.). 48p. (Orig.). 1981. pap. 2.75 (ISBN 0-486-24097-5). Dover.

--House Plants Coloring Book. (Illus.). 1976. pap. 2.00 (ISBN 0-486-23266-2). Dover.

--Trees of the Northeast Coloring Book. (Illus.). pap. 2.25 (ISBN 0-486-23734-6). Dover.

Bernath, Stefen. Common Weeds Coloring Book. (Illus.). pap. 2.50 (ISBN 0-486-23308-1). Dover.

--Herbs Coloring Book. (Illus.). pap. 1.95 (ISBN 0-486-23499-1). Dover.

--Tropical Fish Coloring Book. (Illus.). pap. 2.00 (ISBN 0-486-23620-X). Dover.

Bernath, Stuart L. Squall Across the Atlantic: American Civil War Prize Cases & Diplomacy. LC 76-79042. 1970. 33.00x (ISBN 0-520-01562-2). U of Cal Pr.

Bernatowicz, Albert J., jt. auth. see Taylor, William R.

Bernatzik, Hugo A. Akha & Miao: Problems of Applied Ethnography in Farther India. LC 73-114702. (Monographs). 780p. 1970. 28.00x (ISBN 0-87536-027-0). HRAFP.

Bernatzky, A. Tree Ecology & Preservation. (Developments in Agricultural & Managed-Forest Ecology Ser.: Vol. 2). 358p. 1978. 72.50 (ISBN 0-444-41606-4). Elsevier.

Bernau, Andreas. Orthopaedic Positioning in Diagnostic Radiology. Berquist, Thomas H., ed. LC 83-12406. (Ger.). 1983. 49.50 (ISBN 0-8067-0281-8). Urban & S.

Bernau, Deborah, ed. Energy Conservation Source Book. 81p. 1981. 5.00 (ISBN 0-317-36330-1). Natl Conf State Legis.

Bernauer, Carol. Modern Day Beasties. (Illus.). 12p. 1983. pap. 1.00 (ISBN 0-686-46875-9). Samisdat.

Bernaver, Carol. Modern Days II. 12p. 1984. pap. 1.00 (ISBN 0-317-13317-9). Samisdat.

Bernays, Anne. The Address Book. 352p. 1983. 14.45i (ISBN 0-316-09195-2). Little.

--The School Book. LC 79-2643. 1980. 12.45i (ISBN 0-06-010332-9, HarpT). Har-Row.

Bernays, Edward L. Public Relations. 1977. pap. 10.95x (ISBN 0-8061-1457-6). U of Okla Pr.

--Your Future in a Public Relations Career. (Careers in Depth Ser.). PLB 8.97 (ISBN 0-8239-0443-1). Rosen Group.

Bernays, Hella, tr. see Argelander, Hermann.

Bernays, Hella F., ed. see Brunn, Fritz.

Bernays, Jakob. Joseph Justus Scaliger. 1965. Repr. of 1885 ed. 23.50 (ISBN 0-8337-0247-5). B Franklin.

Bernays, P., ed. see Symposium, Brussels.

Bernazzani, William P. Defer Payment - Let the Next Generation Pay. LC 80-13862. 1981. 14.95 (ISBN 0-87949-145-0). Ashley Bks.

Bernbach, Linda. Food Service Supervisor-School Lunch Manager. LC 79-15860. 1980. pap. 8.00 (ISBN 0-668-04819-0, 4819-0). Arco.

Bernbaum, Edwin. The Way to Shambhala. LC 78-1234. (Illus.). 336p. (Orig.). 1980. pap. 8.95 (ISBN 0-385-12794-4, Anch). Doubleday.

Bernbaum, Ernest. The Drama of Sensibility: A Sketch of the History of English Comedy and Domestic Tragedy. 11.50 (ISBN 0-8446-1074-7). Peter Smith.

--English Poets of the Eighteenth Century. 1979. Repr. of 1918 ed. lib. bdg. 22.50 (ISBN 0-8495-0526-7). Arden Lib.

--The Mary Carleton Narratives, 1663-73. facsimile ed. LC 76-164588. (Select Bibliographies Reprint Ser). Repr. of 1914 ed. 14.00 (ISBN 0-8369-5872-1). Ayer Co Pubs.

Bernbaum, Gerald. Knowledge & Ideology in the Sociology of Education. (Studies in Sociology Ser.). 1977. pap. text ed. 6.75x (ISBN 0-333-15762-1). Humanities.

Bernbaum, Israel. My Brother's Keeper: The Holocaust Through the Eyes of an Artist. (Illus.). 64p. (gr. 4-8). 1985. 16.95 (ISBN 0-399-21242-6, Putnam). Putnam Pub Group.

Bernbaum, John A., ed. Perspectives on Peacemaking. LC 84-3331. 1984. pap. 6.95 (ISBN 0-8307-0951-7, 5418206). Regal.

Bernbeck, Rupprecht & Sinios, Alexander. Neuro-Orthopedic Screening in Infancy: Schedules, Examination & Findings. LC 78-2505. (Illus.). 120p. 1978. text ed. 16.50 (ISBN 0-8067-0231-1). Urban & S.

Bernd, Clifford A. Theodor Storm's Craft of Fiction: The Torment of a Narrator. LC 67-64644. (North Carolina University. Studies in the Germanic Languages & Literature: No. 43). Repr. of 1963 ed. 27.00 (ISBN 0-404-50943-6). AMS Pr.

Bernd, Ed, Jr. Relax, It's Good for You. write for info. (ISBN 0-913343-35-8). Inst Psych Inc.

Bernd, Edward I. Business Opportunities Brokerage: Strategies & Techniques for Real Estate Professionals. LC 82-25077. 169p. 1983. 29.95 (ISBN 0-13-106724-9). P-H.

Bernd, Joseph L., ed. Mathematical Applications in Political Science, Vol. 4. LC 67-28023. (Illus.). 83p. 1969. 10.00x (ISBN 0-8139-0262-2). U Pr of Va.

Bernd, Joseph L., jt. ed. see Havard, William C.

Bernd, Joseph L., jt. ed. see Herndon, James F.

Berndt, A. Magnetic Properties of Free Radicals: Part D 1: Organic Anion Radicals. (Landolt-Boernstein Ser.: Group II Vol. 9). (Illus.). 920p. 1980. 411.60 (ISBN 0-387-08884-9). Springer-Verlag.

Berndt, A., et al. Organic C-Centered Radicals. LC 62-53136. (Landolt-Boernstein,Group II: Vol. 9, Pt. 8). (Illus.). 1977. 327.60 (ISBN 0-387-08152-6). Springer-Verlag.

Berndt, Alan F. & Stearns, Robert I. Dental Fluoride Chemistry. (Illus.). 144p. 1978. 14.75x (ISBN 0-398-03753-1). C C Thomas.

Berndt, B. C. Ramanujan's Notebooks, Pt. 1. (Illus.). 430p. 1985. 54.00 (ISBN 0-387-96110-0). Springer-Verlag.

Berndt, Bruce C., et al. Chapter Nine of Ramanujan's Second Notebook: Infinite Series Identities, Transformations, & Evaluations, Vol. 23. LC 83-11803. (Contemporary Mathematics Ser.: No. 23). 84p. 1983. pap. 17.00 (ISBN 0-8218-5024-5). Am Math.

Berndt, Catherine H., jt. auth. see Berndt, Ronald M.

Berndt, Catherine H., jt. ed. see Berndt, Ronald M.

Berndt, Elsa. Dame Nature in der Englishen Literatur. (Ger). 18.00 (ISBN 0-384-04033-0); pap. 13.00 (ISBN 0-685-02221-8). Johnson Repr.

Berndt, Ernst R. & Field, Barry C., eds. Modeling & Measuring Natural Resource Substitution. 384p. 1982. text ed. 50.00x (ISBN 0-262-02174-9). MIT Pr.

Berndt, Harry E. New Rulers in the Ghetto: The Community Development Corporation & Urban Poverty. LC 76-47888. (Contributions in Afro-American & African Studies: No. 28). (Illus.). 1977. lib. bdg. 27.50 (ISBN 0-8371-9399-0, BNL/). Greenwood.

Berndt, R. M. The Sacred Site: The Western Arnehem Land Example. (Aias Social Anthropology Ser.: No. 29). 1970. pap. text ed. 8.75x (ISBN 0-85575-097-9). Humanities.

Berndt, R. M. & Stanton, J. E. Australian Aboriginal Art: In the Anthropology Museum of the University of Western Australia. (Illus.). 24p. (Orig.). pap. 7.00x (ISBN 0-85564-188-6, Pub. by U of W Austral Pr). Intl Spec Bk.

Berndt, R. M., ed. Aborigines & Change: Australia in the 70's. (AIAS Social Anthropology Ser.: No. 11). 1977. text ed. 28.50x o.p (ISBN 0-391-00726-2); pap. text ed. 16.75x (ISBN 0-391-00727-0). Humanities.

Berndt, Robert J. Your Beagle. LC 75-41979. (Your Dog Book Ser.). (Illus.). 1976. 12.95 (ISBN 0-87714-034-0). Denlingers.

--Your Bulldog. LC 75-41980. (Your Dog Book Ser.). (Illus.). 1976. 12.95 (ISBN 0-87714-036-7). Denlingers.

--Your Lhasa Aspo. LC 74-77246. (Your Dog Book Ser.). (Illus.). 1982. rev. 12.95 (ISBN 0-87714-078-2). Denlingers.

--Your Maltese. LC 75-20787. (Your Dog Book Ser.). (Illus.). 1975. 12.95 (ISBN 0-87714-033-2). Denlingers.

--Your Pekingese. LC 77-87761. (Your Dog Bk). (Illus.). 1978. 12.95 (ISBN 0-87714-049-9). Denlingers.

--Your Welsh Corgi, Cardigan-Pembroke. LC 77-87762. (Your Dog Bk.). (Illus.). 1978. 12.95 (ISBN 0-87714-052-9). Denlingers.

Berndt, Robert J. & Myers, Richard L. The Labrador Retriever. LC 83-7402. (Illus.). 128p. 1983. 24.95 (ISBN 0-87714-087-1). Denlingers.

Berndt, Robert J., jt. auth. see Hogg, Peggy A.

Berndt, Ronald M. Love Songs of Arnhem Land. LC 77-83828. (Illus.). 1978. lib. bdg. 22.50x (ISBN 0-226-04389-4). U of Chicago Pr.

Berndt, Ronald M. & Berndt, Catherine H. Man, Land & Myth in North Australia: The Gunwinggu People. (Illus.). 262p. 1970. text ed. 10.00x (ISBN 0-87013-165-6). Mich St U Pr.

Berndt, Ronald M., ed. Aboriginal Sites, Rights & Resource Development. 253p. (Orig.). 1983. pap. 12.95x (ISBN 0-85564-221-1, Pub. by U of W Austral Pr). Intl Spec Bk.

--Question of Choice: An Australian Aboriginal Dilemma. LC 72-188167. 123p. 1971. pap. 8.00x (ISBN 0-85564-054-5, Pub. by U of W Austral Pr). Intl Spec Bk.

Berndt, Ronald M. & Berndt, Catherine H., eds. Aborigines of the West. 516p. 1980. 30.00x (ISBN 0-85564-145-2, Pub. by U of W Austral Pr); pap. 36.00x. Intl Spec Bk.

Berndt, Ronald M. & Lawrence, Peter, eds. Politics in New Guinea: Traditional & in the Context of Change, Some Anthropological Perspectives. LC 73-172827. (Illus.). 448p. 1973. text ed. 30.00x (ISBN 0-295-95235-0). U of Wash Pr.

Berndtson, Arthur. Power, Form & Mind. LC 80-65658. 296p. 1981. 27.50 (ISBN 0-8387-5010-9). Bucknell U Pr.

Berne, Barbara. Buzzard Barbara. 1978. pap. 1.75 (ISBN 0-532-17185-3). Woodhill.

Berne, Bruce J. & Pecora, Robert. Dynamic Light Scattering: With Applications to Chemistry, Biology & Physics. LC 75-19140. 376p. 1976. 54.95 (ISBN 0-471-07100-5, Pub. by Wiley-Interscience). Wiley.

Berne, Bruce J., ed. Statistical Mechanics, 2 pts. Incl. Pt. 1: Equilibrium Techniques. 242p. 49.50x (ISBN 0-306-33505-0); Pt. 2: Time-Dependent Processes. 362p. 55.00x (ISBN 0-306-33506-9). LC 76-46977. (Modern Theoretical Chemistry Ser.: Vols. 5 & 6). (Illus.). 1977 (Plenum Pr). Plenum Pub.

Berne, Eric. Games People Play. 1978. pap. 2.75 (ISBN 0-345-29477-7). Ballantine.

--Layman's Guide to Psychiatry & Psychoanalysis. 1982. pap. 3.50 (ISBN 0-345-30922-7). Ballantine.

--What Do You Say after You Say Hello? 480p. 1975. pap. 4.50 (ISBN 0-553-25023-X). Bantam.

Berne, Eric & Steiner, C. Beyond Games & Scripts. 1978. pap. 2.50 (ISBN 0-345-28471-2). Ballantine.

Berne, Eric, et al. Transactional Analysis Bulletin: Selected Articles from Volumes 1 Thru 9. McCormick, Paul, ed. (Illus.). 1976. pap. 3.00x (ISBN 0-89489-000-X). TA Press.

Berne, Frankfurt M., ed. see Ponomareff, Constantin.

Berne, Karin. Bare Acquaintances. 288p. 1985. pap. 2.95 (ISBN 0-445-20008-1, Pub. by Popular Lib). Warner Bks.

--Shock Value. 320p. (Orig.). 1985. pap. 2.95 (ISBN 0-445-20136-3, Pub. by Popular Lib). Warner Bks.

Berne, Pat & Savary, Lou. Building Self-Esteem in Children. 192p. 1985. pap. 8.95 (ISBN 0-8264-0353-0). Crossroad NY.

Berne, Patricia H. & Savary, Louis M. Building Self-Esteem in Children. 220p. 1981. 12.95 (ISBN 0-8264-0050-7). Continuum.

--What Will the Neighbors Say? Facing the Fear of Disapproval. LC 82-14076. 176p. 1982. 10.95 (ISBN 0-8264-0196-1). Continuum.

Berne, Patricia H., jt. auth. see Savary, Louis M.

Berne, R. M., et al, eds. Annual Review of Physiology, Vol. 45. LC 39-15404. (Illus.). 1983. text ed. 27.00 (ISBN 0-8243-0345-8). Annual Reviews.

--Annual Review of Physiology, Vol. 46. LC 39-15404. (Illus.). 1984. text ed. 27.00 (ISBN 0-8243-0346-6). Annual Reviews.

Berne, Robert & Stiefel, Leanna. The Measurement of Equity in School Finance: Conceptual, Methodological & Empirical Dimensions. LC 83-24394. 1984. text ed. 35.00x (ISBN 0-8018-3148-2). Johns Hopkins.

Berne, Robert, ed. see American Physiologial Society.

Berne, Robert M. & Levy, Matthew N. Cardiovascular Physiology. 4th ed. LC 81-2039. (Illus.). 286p. 1981. pap. text ed. 18.95 (ISBN 0-8016-0655-1). Mosby.

Berne, Robert M., ed. Brief Reviews from Circulation Research 1976. LC 77-7123. (AHA Monograph: No. 51). 1977. pap. 6.00 cancelled (ISBN 0-87493-052-9, 3-037A). Am Heart.

Berne, Robert M. & Hoffman, Brian F., eds. Brief Reviews from Circulation Research 1977. (AHA Monograph: No.54). 1977. pap. 6.00 cancelled (ISBN 0-87493-055-3, 73-040A). Am Heart.

Berne, Robert M. & Hoffman, Joseph F., eds. Annual Review of Physiology, Vol. 47. LC 39-15404. (Illus.). 859p. 1985. text ed. 27.00 (ISBN 0-8243-0347-4). Annual Reviews.

Berne, Robert M. & Levy, Matthew N., eds. Physiology. LC 82-22943. (Illus.). 1165p. 1983. text ed. 41.95 (ISBN 0-8016-0644-6). Mosby.

Berne, Robert M., et al, eds. The Regulatory Function of Adenosine. 1983. lib. bdg. 93.50 (ISBN 90-247-2779-0, Pub. by Martinus Nijhoff Netherlands). Kluwer Academic.

Berne, Stanley. The Dialogues. LC 62-7479. (Illus.). 108p. 1962. pap. 100.00 (ISBN 0-913844-15-2). Am Canadian.

--Future Language. LC 75-36891. (Archives of Post-Modern Literature). 1976. pap. 10.95 (ISBN 0-913844-02-0). Am Canadian.

--Future Language. LC 76-21885. 1976. pap. 10.95 (ISBN 0-8180-1167-X). Horizon.

--The Great American Empire. LC 81-85003. (Illus.). 232p. 1982. 18.95 (ISBN 0-686-82851-8); pap. 8.95 (ISBN 0-686-82850-X). Am Canadian.

--The Great American Empire. LC 82-3114. (Illus.). 226p. (Orig.). 1982. pap. 8.95 (ISBN 0-8180-0633-1). Horizon.

--The Multiple Modern Gods & Other Stories. LC 64-21952. (Illus.). 1964. pap. 17.95 (ISBN 0-913844-30-6). Am Canadian.

--The New Rubaiyat of Stanley Berne, Vol. 1. LC 73-77094. (Archives of Post-Modern Literature). 111p. 1973. pap. 17.95 (ISBN 0-913844-00-4). Am Canadian.

--The Unconscious Victorious & Other Stories. LC 69-20442. (Archives of Post-Modern Literature). (Illus.). 1969. pap. 9.95 (ISBN 0-913844-04-7). Am Canadian.

--The Unconscious Victorious & Other Stories. 304p. 1973. pap. 9.95 (ISBN 0-8180-0616-1). Horizon.

Berne, Stanley & Zekowski, Arlene. A First Book of the Neo-Narrative. (Illus.). 1954. 110.00 (ISBN 0-913844-18-7); pap. 85.00 (ISBN 0-913844-09-8). Am Canadian.

Berne, Stanley, jt. auth. see Zekowski, Arlene.

Bernel, Ignacio, et al. National Museum of Anthropology, Mexico: Art, Architecture, Archaeology, Ethnography. (Illus.). 1968. 50.00 (ISBN 0-8109-0342-3). Abrams.

Bernen, Robert. The Hills: More Tales from the Blue Stacks; Stories of Ireland. 160p. 1984. 12.95 (ISBN 0-684-18005-7, ScribT). Scribner.

--Tales from the Blue Stacks. LC 78-3742. 1978. 8.95 (ISBN 0-684-15540-0, ScribT). Scribner.

--Tales from the Blue Stacks. 146p. 1980. pap. 4.95 (ISBN 0-905169-27-1, Pub. by Poolbeg Pr Ireland). Irish Bk Ctr.

Bernen, Robert, jt. auth. see Bernen, Satia.

Bernen, Satia & Bernen, Robert. A Guide to Myth & Religion in European Painting 1270-1700. LC 72-96070. 288p. 1973. 8.95 (ISBN 0-8076-0683-9). Braziller.

Berner, Carl W. Teardrops to Diamonds: How God's Love Turns Sorrow into Joy. LC 83-70505. 96p. (Orig.). 1983. pap. 5.50 (ISBN 0-8066-2011-0, 10-6228). Augsburg.

--Why Me, Lord? Meaning & Comfort in Times of Trouble. LC 73-78267. 112p. (Orig.). 1973. pap. 4.95 (ISBN 0-8066-1331-9, 10-7172). Augsburg.

Berner, Elsa R. Integrating Library Instruction with Classroom Teaching at Plainview Junior High School. LC 58-6978. 1958. pap. 5.00x (ISBN 0-8389-0040-2). ALA.

Berner, Jeff. At Your Fingertips: Making the Most of the Micro. 202p. 1984. pap. 12.95 (ISBN 0-673-18049-2). Scott F.

--The Foolproof Guide to Scripsit Word Processing. LC 83-60044. (Illus.). 179p. pap. cancelled (ISBN 0-89588-098-9). SYBEX.

--Overcoming Computer Fear. LC 83-50714. (Illus.). 92p. 1984. pap. 3.95 (ISBN 0-89588-145-4). SYBEX.

Berner, Jeffrey. The Executive's Guide to Portable Computers. 224p. (Orig.). 1984. pap. 9.95 (ISBN 0-345-31700-9). Ballantine.

Berner, Jerome J. Effects of Diseases on Laboratory Tests. (Illus.). 363p. 1983. pap. text ed. 19.75 (ISBN 0-397-50580-9, 65-07438). Lippincott.

Berner, Loretta. Rancho los Cerritos. (Illus.). 1975. pap. 2.00 (ISBN 0-916552-01-2). Acoma Bks.

Berner, Loretta & Brown, Albert. The Pike on the Sulver Strand. LC 82-83974. (Illus.). 72p. (Orig.). 1982. pap. 10.00 (ISBN 0-9610250-3-4). Hist Soc Long Beach.

Berner, P. & Diehl, L. W., eds. The Treatment of Complicated Epilepsies in Adults. (Bibliotheca Psychiatrica: No. 158). (Illus.). 1978. 24.75 (ISBN 3-8055-2814-0). S Karger.

Berner, P. & Kehrer, H., eds. Kindlicher Autismus. (Bibliotheca Psychiatrica: No. 157). (Illus., Ger.). 1978. 21.00 (ISBN 3-8055-2822-1). S Karger.

Berner, P., ed. see Zapotoczky, H. G.

Berner, P., et al. Diagnosekriterien fuer Schizophrene und Affektive Psychosen. 191p. (Ger.). 1983. pap. 15.00x (ISBN 3-900-48801-0). Am Psychiatric.

--Diagnostic Criteria for Schizophrenic & Affective Psychoses. 183p. 1983. pap. 15.00x (ISBN 0-317-00591-X). Am Psychiatric.

Berner, P., et al, eds. Current Perspectives in Lithium Prophylaxis. (Bibliotheca Psychiatrica: Vol. 161). (Illus.). viii, 248p. 1981. pap. 37.50 (ISBN 3-8055-1753-X). S Karger.

Berner, R. Thomas. Editing. 1982. text ed. 25.95 (ISBN 0-03-057469-2). HR&W.

--Language Skills for Journalists. 2nd ed. LC 83-82323. 320p. 1983. pap. text ed. 12.50 (ISBN 0-395-34098-5); instr's manual 1.50 (ISBN 0-395-34099-3). HM.

Berner, Richard C. Archival Theory & Practice in the United States: A Historical Analysis. LC 82-48869. 240p. 1983. 35.00x (ISBN 0-295-95992-4). U of Wash Pr.

Berner, Robert A. Early Diagenesis: A Theoretical Approach. LC 80-7510. (Princeton Series in Geochemistry: No. 1). (Illus.). 256p. 1980. 35.00 (ISBN 0-691-08258-8); pap. 15.50 (ISBN 0-691-08260-X). Princeton U Pr.

Berner, Samuel, jt. ed. see Cantor, Norman F.

Berner, Wolfgang. The Soviet Union: 1978-1979: Domestic Policy, the Economy, & Foreign Policy, Vol. 5. 340p. 1981. text ed. 39.50x (ISBN 0-8419-0632-7). Holmes & Meier.

--The Soviet Union: 1980-1981, Vol. 6. 348p. 1983. text ed. 30.00x (ISBN 0-8419-0866-4). Holmes & Meier.

Berner, Wolfgang, et al. The Soviet Union: 1973: Domestic Policy, the Economy & Foreign Policy, Vol. 1. LC 74-22285. 200p. 1975. text ed. 39.50x (ISBN 0-8419-0188-0). Holmes & Meier.

--The Soviet Union: 1974-1975: Domestic Policy, the Economics, & Foreign Policy, Vol. 2. LC 74-22285. 288p. 1976. 39.50x (ISBN 0-8419-0216-X). Holmes & Meier.

--The Soviet Union: 1975-1976: Domestic Policy, the Economy, & Foreign Policy, Vol. 3. LC 74-22285. 308p. 1978. text ed. 39.50x (ISBN 0-8419-0316-6). Holmes & Meier.

--The Soviet Union: 1976-1977: Domestic Policy, the Economic & Foreign Policy, Vol. 4. Adomeit, Hannes, tr. from Ger. LC 74-22285. (Illus.). 270p. 1979. text ed. 39.50x (ISBN 0-8419-0450-2). Holmes & Meier.

Berneri, Marie L. Journey Through Utopia. facs. ed. LC 71-93316. (Essay Index Reprint Ser). 1950. 29.00 (ISBN 0-8369-1392-2). Ayer Co Pubs.

Berners, tr. see Steele, Robert.

Berners, Juliana. The Book of Hawking, Hunting & Blasing of Arms. LC 74-25849. (English Experience Ser.: No. 151). 180p. 1969. Repr. of 1486 ed. 42.00 (ISBN 90-221-0151-7). Walter J Johnson.

--A Treatise on Fishing with a Hook. LC 79-20603. 1979. Repr. 15.00 (ISBN 0-88427-038-6). North River.

Berners, Lord. First Childhood & Far from the Madding War. 1983. pap. 5.95x (ISBN 0-19-281417-6). Oxford U Pr.

Berners-Lee, C. M., ed. Models for Decision. 160p. 1965. 44.25 (ISBN 0-677-61100-5). Gordon.

Berney, Arthur L., et al. Legal Problems of the Poor: Cases & Materials. 1440p. 1975. 25.50 (ISBN 0-316-09189-8). Little.

Berney, Donald W. American Government for Law Enforcement Training. LC 75-8915. (Justice Administration Ser.). 336p. 1976. 25.95x (ISBN 0-88229-152-1). Nelson-Hall.

Berney, O., jt. auth. see Jones, K.

Berney, Paul R. & Gartska, Stanley J. Accounting: Concepts & Applications. 1984p. 30.95x (ISBN 0-256-02964-4). Irwin.

Berney, Paul R., et al. Financial Accounting & Reporting. 1980. text ed. 28.95x (ISBN 0-256-02418-9). Business Pubns.

Berney, Saffold. Handbook of Alabama: A Complete Index to the State, with Map. rev. 2nd ed. LC 74-34573. (Illus.). 568p. 1975. Repr. of 1892 ed. 27.50 (ISBN 0-87152-201-2). Reprint.

Berney, William, jt. auth. see Richardson, Howard.

Bernfeld, Marvin, jt. auth. see Cook, Charles E.

Bernfeld, Siegfried. Sisyphus; or, the Limits of Education. Lilge, Frederic, tr. from Ger. LC 77-84784. (Quandum Ser.). 1973. 24.00x (ISBN 0-520-01407-3). U of Cal Pr.

Bernfeld, Stephen R. & Lakshmikantham, V. An Introduction to Nonlinear Boundary Value Problems. (Mathematics in Science & Engineering: A Series of Monographs & Textbooks, Vol. 109). 1974. 60.00 (ISBN 0-12-093150-8). Acad Pr.

Bernhard, Berenson. The Guidebook of the Works of the Great Italian Painters of the Renaissance with Specific Information As to Their Location at the Present Time, 2 vols. (Illus.). 227p. 1984. 175.85x (ISBN 0-89266-450-9). Am Classical Coll Pr.

Bernhard, C. G. & Crawford, E., eds. Science, Technology & Society in the Time of Alfred Nobel: Proceedings of a Nobel Symposium held at Bjorkborn, Karlskoga, Sweden, August 17-22, 1981. LC 82-11254. (Illus.). 440p. 1982. 65.00 (ISBN 0-08-027939-2). Pergamon.

Bernhard, Linda A. & Walsh, Michelle. Leadership: The Key to Professionalization of Nursing. (Illus.). 256p. 1981. pap. text ed. 22.95 (ISBN 0-07-004936-X). McGraw.

Bernhard, S., ed. Patterns of Change in Earth Evolution: Report of the Dahlem Workshop on Patterns of Change in Earth Evolution, Berlin, 1983, May 1-6. (Dahlem Workshop Reports, Physical, Chemical, & Earth Sciences Research Report: Vol. 5). (Illus.). 450p. 1984. 26.00 (ISBN 0-387-12749-6). Springer-Verlag.

Bernhard, Sarah. Ima Hogg: The Governor's Daughter. Lubeck, Scott, ed. (Illus.). 144p. 1984. 18.95 (ISBN 0-932012-68-X). Texas Month Pr.

Bernhard, Thomas. Concrete. McLintock, David, tr. from Ger. LC 83-49356. 154p. 1984. 12.95 (ISBN 0-394-53781-5). Knopf.

--Correction. LC 83-48034. (The Library of Contemporary World Literature). 288p. 1983. pap. 7.95 (ISBN 0-394-72210-8, Vin). Random.

--Gathering Evidence. Janeway, Carol B., ed. McLintock, David, tr. LC 85-40393. 352p. 1985. 22.95 (ISBN 0-394-54707-1). Knopf.

--The President & Eve of Retirement: Two Plays. Honegger, Gitta, tr. LC 82-80615. 1982. 16.95 (ISBN 0-933826-24-9); pap. 6.95 (ISBN 0-933826-25-7). Performing Arts.

Bernhard, Victor M. & Towne, Jonathon B., eds. Complications in Vascular Surgery. 624p. 1980. 83.50 (ISBN 0-8089-1283-6, 790573). Grune.

--Complications in Vascular Surgery. 2nd ed. LC 79-574. 832p. 1985. 89.50 (ISBN 0-8089-1747-1). Grune.

Bernhard, Virginia, ed. Elites, Masses, & Modernization in Latin America, 1850-1930. (Texas Pan American Ser.). 165p. 1979. text ed. 14.95x (ISBN 0-292-76457-X). U of Tex Pr.

Bernhard, Winfred E. Fisher Ames: Federalist & Statesman, 1758-1808. (Institute of Early American History & Culture Ser.). (Illus.). xiii, 372p. 1965. 30.00 (ISBN 0-8078-0967-5). U of NC Pr.

Bernhard, Winfred E. see Wood, William.

Bernhard, Winfred E., jt. ed. see Emerson, Everett.

Bernhardi, Charlotte, ed. see Von Krusenstern, Adam J.

Bernhardi, Robert. The Buildings of Berkeley. (Illus.). 116p. 1984. Repr. of 1971 ed. 10.95 (ISBN 0-317-17550-5, Berkeley Architectural Heritage). Forest Hill.

--Buildings of Oakland with a Section on Piedmont. 116p. 1979. 14.95 (ISBN 0-9605472-0-7). Forest Hill.

Bernhardi, Robert C. Great Buildings of San Francisco. LC 79-51660. (Illus.). 1980. pap. 6.95 (ISBN 0-486-23839-3). Dover.

--Great Buildings of San Francisco: A Photographic Guide. 11.00 (ISBN 0-8446-5736-0). Peter Smith.

Bernhardt, Arthur D. Building Tomorrow: The Mobile-Manufactured Housing Industry. (Illus.). 1980. text ed. 60.00 (ISBN 0-262-02134-X). MIT Pr.

Bernhardt, Bill. Just Writing. (Orig.). 1977. pap. 7.95 (ISBN 0-915924-06-4). Tchrs & Writers Coll.

--Just Writing: Exercises to Improve Your Writing. 104p. 1977. 7.00 (ISBN 0-8141-2537-9); members 5.50 (ISBN 0-317-35278-4). NCTE.

Bernhardt, David K., ed. Being a Parent: Unchanging Values in a Changing World. LC 74-484635. pap. 50.50 (ISBN 0-317-26939-9, 2023594). Bks Demand UMI.

Bernhardt, Debra & Mikusko, M. Brady. Working Womenroots: An Oral History Primer. 2nd ed. 33p. 1980. pap. 3.50 (ISBN 0-87736-342-0). U of Mich Inst Labor.

Bernhardt, Donna B., ed. Recreation for the Disabled Child. LC 84-19330. (Physical & Occupational Therapy in Pediatrics Ser.: Vol. 4, No. 3). 120p. 1985. text ed. 19.95 (ISBN 0-86656-263-X, B263). Haworth Pr.

Bernhardt, Ernest C., ed. Computer Aided Engineering for Injection Molding. 500p. 1984. text ed. 39.50 (ISBN 0-02-948590-8). Macmillan.

Bernhardt, Frances S. Introduction to Library Technical Services. 322p. 1979. 20.00 (ISBN 0-8242-0637-1). Wilson.

Bernhardt, Joshua. The Alaskan Engineering Commission: Its History, Activities & Organization. LC 72-3017. (Brookings Institution. Institute for Government Research. Service Monographs of the U.S. Government: No. 4). Repr. of 1922 ed. 24.50 (ISBN 0-404-57104-2). AMS Pr.

--The Division of Conciliation: Its History, Activities & Organization. LC 73-14847. (Brookings Institution. Institute for Government Research. Service Monographs of the U.S. Government: No. 20). Repr. of 1923 ed. 21.50 (ISBN 0-404-57120-4). AMS Pr.

--The Interstate Commerce Commission: Its History, Activities & Organization. LC 72-3036. (Brookings Institution. Institute for Government Research. Service Monographs of the U.S. Government: No. 18). Repr. of 1923 ed. 25.00 (ISBN 0-404-57118-2). AMS Pr.

--The Railroad Labor Board: Its History, Activities & Organization. LC 72-3037. (Brookings Institution. Institute for Government Research. Service Monographs of the U.S. Government: No. 19). Repr. of 1923 ed. 21.50 (ISBN 0-404-57119-0). AMS Pr.

--The Tariff Commission: Its History, Activities & Organization. LC 72-3018. (Brookings Institution. Institute for Government Research. Service Monographs of the U.S. Government: No. 5). Repr. of 1922 ed. 21.50 (ISBN 0-404-57105-0). AMS Pr.

Bernhardt, Kenneth, et al, eds. The Changing Marketing Environment: New Theories & Applications. LC 81-3552. (Proceedings Ser.: No. 47). (Illus.). 471p. (Orig.). 1981. pap. text ed. 30.00 (ISBN 0-87757-151-1). Am Mktg.

Bernhardt, Kenneth L. & Kinnear, Thomas C. Cases in Marketing Management. 3rd ed. 1985. 29.95x (ISBN 0-256-03055-3). Business Pubns.

Bernhardt, Kenneth L., jt. auth. see Kinnear, Thomas C.

Bernhardt, Lysiane S. Sarah Bernhardt, My Grandmother. Holland, Vyvyan, tr. LC 79-8054. Repr. of 1949 ed. 26.50 (ISBN 0-404-18365-4). AMS Pr.

Bernhardt, Melvin. The Pied Piper of Hamelin. (Children's Theatre Playscript Ser.). 1963. pap. 2.50x (ISBN 0-88020-043-X). Coach Hse.

Bernhardt, Peter, jt. auth. see Calder, Malcolm D.

Bernhardt, R., ed. see International Symposium on the Judicial Settlement of International Disputes.

Bernhardt, R., et al, eds. Digest of the Decisions of the International Court of Justice, 1959-1975. (Fontes Iuris Gentium, A-I-6). 1978. 200.60 (ISBN 0-387-08550-5). Springer-Verlag.

Bernhardt, Roger. California Mortgage & Deed of Trust Practice. LC 78-64976. 457p. 1979. 70.00 (ISBN 0-88124-065-6). Cal Cont Ed Bar.

--Property. LC 83-10320. (Black Letter Ser.). 318p. 1983. pap. text ed. 13.95 (ISBN 0-314-73213-6). West Pub.

Bernhardt, Roger & Martin, David. Self-Mastery Through Self-Hypnosis. 1978. pap. 2.50 (ISBN 0-451-12696-3, AE2696, Sig). NAL.

Bernhardt, Roger H. Real Property in a Nutshell. 2nd ed. LC 81-11662. (Nutshell Ser.). 448p. 1981. pap. text ed. 9.95 (ISBN 0-314-60008-6). West Pub.

Bernhardt, Sarah. Art of the Theatre. LC 70-82819. 1924. 18.00 (ISBN 0-405-08264-9, Blom Pubns). Ayer Co Pubs.

--Art of the Theatre. Stenning, H. J., tr. LC 70-131630. 1971. Repr. of 1924 ed. 11.00 (ISBN 0-403-00517-5). Scholarly.

--Memories of My Life. LC 68-56475. (Illus.). 1968. Repr. of 1908 ed. 27.50 (ISBN 0-405-08265-7, Blom Pubns). Ayer Co Pubs.

--Memories of My Life, Being My Personal Professional, Social Recollections As a Woman & Artist. 1968. Repr. of 1907 ed. 69.00 (ISBN 0-403-00111-0). Scholarly.

Bernhardt, Sarah & Lesberg, Sandy. The Memoirs of Sarah Bernhardt: Early Childhood Through the First American Tour. (Illus.). 256p. 1977. 18.75x (ISBN 0-8464-1197-0). Beekman Pubs.

Bernheim, Alfred L. Business of the Theatre. LC 64-14693. 1932. 22.00 (ISBN 0-405-08266-5, Blom Pubns). Ayer Co Pubs.

Bernheim, Alfred L., ed. see Twentieth Century Fund.

Bernheim, Ernst. Lehrbuch der Historischen Methode und der Geschichtsphilosophie, 2 vols. in 1. 6th ed. 1960. Repr. of 1914 ed. 44.50 (ISBN 0-8337-0250-5). B Franklin.

Bernheim, Evelyne, jt. auth. see Bernheim, Marc.

Bernheim, Gotthardt D. History of the German Settlements & of the Lutheran Church in North & South Carolina. LC 75-969. xvi, 557p. 1975. Repr. of 1872 ed. 20.00 (ISBN 0-8063-8001-2). Regional.

--History of the German Settlements & of the Lutheran Church in North & South Carolina. LC 76-187361. 573p. 1972. Repr. of 1872 ed. 25.00 (ISBN 0-87152-089-3). Reprint.

Bernheim, Hippolyte. Bernheim's New Studies in Hypnotism. Sandor, Richard S., ed. (Illus.). xix, 407p. 1980. text ed. 35.00x (ISBN 0-8236-0496-9). Intl Univs Pr.

--Suggestive Therapeutics. 1957. 8.95 (ISBN 0-87497-135-7). Assoc Bk.

Bernheim, Kayla F. & Lewine, Richard R. J. Schizophrenia: Symptoms, Causes, Treatments. (Illus.). 1979. pap. 8.95x (ISBN 0-393-09017-5). Norton.

Bernheim, Kayla F., et al. The Caring Family: Living with Chronic Mental Illness. LC 80-40248. 1982. 13.50 (ISBN 0-394-51028-3). Random.

Bernheim, Marc & Bernheim, Evelyne. African Success Story: The Ivory Coast. LC 72-84772. (Illus.). (gr. 7 up). 1970. 6.95 (ISBN 0-15-201650-3, HJ). HarBraceJ.

--The Drums Speak: The Story of Kofi, a Boy of West Africa. LC 70-137761. (Illus.). 48p. (gr. 3 up). 1972. 6.50 (ISBN 0-15-224233-3, HJ). HarBraceJ.

Bernheimer, Charles. Flaubert & Kafka: Studies in Psychopoetic Structure. LC 82-1842. 280p. 1982. 25.00x (ISBN 0-300-02633-1). Yale U Pr.

Bernheimer, Charles & Kahane, Claire, eds. In Dora's Case. 320p. 1985. 32.50x (ISBN 0-231-05910-8); pap. 9.50x (ISBN 0-231-05911-6). Columbia U Pr.

Bernheimer, Richard. The Nature of Representation: A Phenomenological Inquiry. Janson, H. W., ed. LC 61-8057. pap. 65.80 (ISBN 0-317-13004-8, 2050263). Bks Demand UMI.

Bernholz, Peter. Flexible Exchange Rates in Historical Perspective. LC 82-6167. (Princeton Studies in International Finance Ser.: No. 49). 1982. pap. text ed. 4.50x (ISBN 0-88165-220-2). Princeton U Int Finan Econ.

--The International Game of Power: Past, Present, & Future. LC 85-4820. (New Babylon, Studies in the Social Sciences: No. 42). write for info. Amer Bar Assn.

Bernice P. Bishop Museum - Honolulu. Dictionary Catalog of the Library of the Bernice P. Bishop Museum, 9 Vols. 1964. Set. lib. bdg. 890.00 (ISBN 0-8161-0679-7, Hall Library); lib. bdg. 120.00 1st suppl. 1967 (ISBN 0-8161-0722-X); lib. bdg. 110.00 2nd suppl. 1969 (ISBN 0-8161-0834-X). G K Hall.

Bernice Pauahi Bishop Museum, Honolulu. Museum of Polynesian Ethnology & Natural History: Honolulu Bulletins, Nos. 1-223. 1922-1961. 4020.00 set (ISBN 0-527-02103-2). Kraus Repr.

Bernick, Deborah & Bershad, Carol. The Doofus Stories. (The Doofus Stories). (Illus.). 88p. (Orig.). (gr. 1-3). 1978. pap. text ed. 6.95 (ISBN 0-913723-00-2); 14.95 (ISBN 0-913723-01-0). Mgmt Sci Health.

Bernick, Deborah, jt. auth. see Bershad, Carol.

Bernick, E. Lee. Legislative Decision-Making & the Politics of Tax Reform: The Oklahoma Senate. (Legislative Research Ser: No. 9). 35p. 1973. pap. 2.50 (ISBN 0-686-20786-6). Univ OK Gov Res.

--Legislative Voting Patterns & Partisan Cohesion in a One-Party Dominant Legislature. (Legislative Research Ser: No. 3). 26p. 1973. pap. 1.00 (ISBN 0-686-20788-2). Univ OK Gov Res.

Bernick, Michael. The Dream of Jobs. LC 84-2287. 202p. 1984. pap. text ed. 10.95 (ISBN 0-913420-48-4). Olympus Pub Co.

Bernier, C. L., jt. auth. see Borko, Harold.

Bernier, Charles L. & Yerkey, A. Neil. Cogent Communication: Overcoming Reading Overload. LC 78-73794. (Contributions in Librarianship & Information Science Ser.: No. 26). (Illus.). xii, 280p. 1979. lib. bdg. 29.95x (ISBN 0-313-20893-X, BEC/). Greenwood.

Bernier, Charles L., jt. auth. see Borko, Harold.

Bernier, Donald R., jt. auth. see Wells, L. David.

Bernier, Donald R., et al. Nuclear Medicine Technology & Techniques. LC 80-17455. (Illus.). 538p. 1981. pap. text ed. 43.95 (ISBN 0-8016-0662-4). Mosby.

Bernier, Georges, ed. The Physiology of Flowers, 2 vols. 1981. Vol. I, 168p. 56.00 (ISBN 0-8493-5709-8); Vol. II 248p. 81.50 (ISBN 0-8493-5710-1). CRC Pr.

Bernier, Ivan. International Legal Aspects of Federalism. viii, 308p. (Orig.). 1973. 22.50 (ISBN 0-208-01384-9, Archon). Shoe String.

Bernier, Ivan, jt. ed. see Beck, Stanley M.

Bernier, J. J., et al. Traite de Gastro-Enterologie, 2 vols. (Illus.). 1600p. (Fr.). 1984. Set. 295.00 (ISBN 2-257-10431-5). S M P F Inc.

Bernier, John M. CIA: Mission to Burundi. (Orig.). 1979. pap. 1.95 (ISBN 0-686-62758-X). Woodhill.

Bernier, Olivier. The Eighteenth Century Woman. LC 81-43302. (Illus.). 168p. 1982. 35.00 (ISBN 0-385-17875-1). Doubleday.

--Lafayette: Hero of Two Worlds. (Illus.). 856p. 1983. 19.95 (ISBN 0-525-24181-7, 01937-580). Dutton.

--Louis the Beloved: The Life of Louis XV. LC 82-46027. (Illus.). 288p. 1984. 18.95 (ISBN 0-385-18402-6). Doubleday.

--Secrets of Marie Antoinette. LC 85-1683. 336p. 1985. 19.95 (ISBN 0-385-19156-1). Doubleday.

Bernier, Paul. Bread Broken & Shared. LC 81-67539. 144p. 1981. pap. 3.95 (ISBN 0-87793-232-8). Ave Maria.

Bernier, Paul, ed. Bread from Heaven: Essays on the Eucharist. LC 77-74581. 182p. 1977. pap. 2.95 (ISBN 0-8091-2029-1). Paulist Pr.

Bernier, Robert. The Pro Golf Teaching Manual. pap. 2.95x (ISBN 0-89741-008-4). Roadrunner Tech.

Bernier, Ronald, et al. Splendours of Kerala. LC 80-901927. (Illus.). 148p. 1979. 32.50x (ISBN 0-89684-457-9). Orient Bk Dist.

Bernier, Ronald M. The Nepalese Pagoda: Origins & Style. 1984. 21.00 (ISBN 0-8364-1231-1, Pub. by S Chand). South Asia Bks.

--Temple Arts of Kerala. (Illus.). 258p. 1982. 99.00x (ISBN 0-940500-79-5, Pub by S Chand India). Asia Bk Corp.

Berniker, Bernard. Great Rabbis. Gorr, Samuel, ed. (Illus.). 1978. 10.00 (ISBN 0-87306-144-6); portfolio ed. 10.00 (ISBN 0-87306-195-0). Feldheim.

Bernikow, Louise. Abel, No. 13. 1982. pap. 2.75 (ISBN 0-345-30212-5). Ballantine.

--Among Women. LC 81-47083. 304p. 1981. pap. 4.95i (ISBN 0-06-090878-5, CN 878, CN). Har-Row.

Bernikow, Louise, ed. The World Split Open: Four Centuries of Women Poets in England & America, 1552-1950. LC 74-8582. 1974. pap. 4.95 (ISBN 0-394-71072-X, Vin). Random.

Berning, Alice, et al. Keyboard Experiences for Classroom Teachers. 3rd ed. 208p. 1983. write for info. wire coil (ISBN 0-697-03617-0). Wm C Brown.

Berning, Randall K. & Snyder, Thomas L. Personalized Guide to Legal Issues. LC 84-8259. (Mosby's Dental Practice Management Ser.: Vol. 7). 1984. 15.95 (ISBN 0-8016-4751-7). Mosby.

Berninger, Louis M. Profitable Garden Center Management. 2nd ed. (Illus.). 1981. 20.95 (ISBN 0-8359-5633-4); instrs's manual avail. (ISBN 0-8359-5634-2). Reston.

Berninghausen, David K. The Flight from Reason: Essays on Intellectual Freedom in the Academy, the Press, & the Library. LC 74-23236. 189p. 1975. pap. text ed. 9.00x (ISBN 0-8389-0192-1). ALA.

Berninghausen, John & Huters, Ted. Revolutionary Literature in China: An Anthology. LC 76-51581. Repr. of 1976 ed. text ed. 27.30 (ISBN 0-317-30479-8, 2024814). Bks Demand UMI.

Bernini, Gian L. Selected Drawings of Bernini. Harris, A. S., ed. (Illus.). 13.25 (ISBN 0-8446-5557-0). Peter Smith.

--Selected Drawings of Gian Lorenzo Bernini. LC 77-70028. (Illus.). 1977. pap. 6.50 (ISBN 0-486-23525-4). Dover.

Bernitsas, M. M., jt. auth. see Imron, A.

Bernitsas, M. M., jt. auth. see Kokarakis, J. E.

Bernitsas, M. M., jt. auth. see Kokkinis, Theodore.

Bernitsas, Michael M. & Guha-Thakurta, S. Program HYDCYL: A Database for Calculation of Hydrodynamic Loading of Circular Cylinders. (University of Michigan, Dept. of Naval Architecture & Marine Engineering, Report: No. 267). pap. 20.00 (ISBN 0-317-27134-2, 2024682). Bks Demand UMI.

Bernitsas, Michael M. & Kekridis, Nikos S. Nonlinear Simulation of Time Dependent Towing of Ocean Vehicles. (University of Michigan Dept. of Naval Architecture & Marine Engineering Ser.: No. 283). pap. 20.00 (ISBN 0-317-30470-4, 2024824). Bks Demand UMI.

Bernitsas, Michael M., et al. Parametric Analysis of Static 2-Dimensional Riser Behavior. (University of Michigan Dept. of Naval Achitecture & Marine Engineering, Report: No. 287). pap. 38.50 (ISBN 0-317-27122-9, 2024686). Bks Demand UMI.

Bernkopf, Michael. Science of Galileo, Level 3. McConochie, Jean, ed. (Regents Readers Ser.). (Illus.). 80p. 1983. pap. text ed. 2.50 (ISBN 0-88345-457-2, 21092). Regents Pub.

Bernold, T. & Albers, G., eds. Artificial Intelligence: Towards Practical Application. (Proceedings of the Joint Technology Assessment Conference of the Gottlieb Duttweiler Institute & the European Coordinating Committee for Artificial Intelligence). 334p. 1985. 44.50 (ISBN 0-444-87719-3, North-Holland). Elsevier.

Bernot, Lucien. Les Paysans Arakanais Du Pakistan Oriental: L'histoire le Monde Vegetal et L'organisation Sociale Des Refugies Marma (Mog, 2 vols. (Le Monde D'outre-Mer Passe et Present, Etudes: No. 16). (Illus.). 1967. pap. text ed. 64.80x (ISBN 90-2796-172-7). Mouton.

Bernoth, E., et al. Gynaekologie. (Illus.). 656p. 1984. 88.25 (ISBN 3-8055-3861-8). S Karger.

Bernoulli, J., ed. Der Briefwechsel von Johann Bernoulli, Vol. I. 531p. (Ger.). 1955. 73.95x (ISBN 0-8176-0027-2). Birkhauser.

Bernoulli, Jakob. Die Gesammelten Werke Vol. 3: Wahrscheinlichkeitsrechnung. (Illus.). 594p. (Ger.). 1975. 85.80x (ISBN 3-7643-0713-7). Birkhauser.

Bernreuter, Robert G. The Personality Inventory. prices on request (ISBN 0-8047-1065-1). Stanford U Pr.

Berns, Gabriel, ed. & tr. see Alberti, Rafael.

Berns, Gabriel, tr. see De Ayala, Ramon P.

Berns, Joel M. The Story of Impacted Wisdom Teeth Kit. 1980. pap. 26.00 (ISBN 0-931386-14-4). Quint Pub Co.

--What Is Periodontal Disease? (Illus.). 64p. (Orig.). 1982. pap. text ed. 18.00 (ISBN 0-86715-109-9). Quint Pub Co.

--Why Replace a Missing Back Tooth? (Illus.). 24p. 1984. pap. text ed. 12.00x (ISBN 0-86715-135-8). Quint Pub Co.

Berns, Kenneth I., ed. The Parvoviruses. (Viruses Ser.). 424p. 1984. 59.50x (ISBN 0-306-41412-0, Plenum Pr). Plenum Pub.

Berns, Laurence, et al. Abraham Lincoln: The Gettysburg Address & American Constitutionalism. DeAlvarez, Leo P., ed. 1976. pap. 7.95x (ISBN 0-918306-03-5). U of Dallas Pr.

Berns, Michael W. Cells. 2nd ed. 1983. pap. text ed. 17.95 (ISBN 0-03-061578-X, CBS C). SCP.

--Hematoporphyrin Derivative Photoradiation Therapy of Cancer. 134p. 1984. 29.50 (ISBN 0-8451-0237-0). A R Liss.

Berns, Michael W. & Mirhoseini, Mahmood. Laser Application to Occlusive Vascular Disease. LC 85-4608. 154p. 1985. 28.00 (ISBN 0-8451-0246-X). A R Liss.

Berns, Robert G., et al. Marketing & Distributive Education: Review & Synthesis of the Research. 140p. 1980. 8.25 (ISBN 0-318-15509-5, IN213). Natl Ctr Res Voc Ed.

Berns, Walter. The First Amendment & the Future of American Democracy. 1985. pap. 8.95 (ISBN 0-89526-820-5). Regnery-Gateway.

--For Capital Punishment: Crime & the Morality of the Death Penalty. 1981. 7.95x (ISBN 0-465-02474-2, TB-5099). Basic.

--Freedom, Virtue & the First Amendment. LC 79-90470. Repr. of 1957 ed. lib. bdg. 15.00x (ISBN 0-8371-2143-4, BEFV). Greenwood.

--In Defense of Liberal Democracy. 376p. 1984. pap. 9.95 (ISBN 0-89526-831-0). Regnery-Gateway.

Berns, Walter, ed. After the People Vote: Steps in Choosing the President. LC 83-15535. (AEI Studies: No. 395). 1983. pap. 2.95 (ISBN 0-8447-3540-X). Am Enterprise.

Bernsheim, Hermit & Sobieszk, Robert A., eds. The Man Behind the Camera. LC 76-24683. (Sources of Modern Photography Ser.). (Illus.). 1979. Repr. of 1948 ed. lib. bdg. 17.00x (ISBN 0-405-09655-0). Ayer Co Pubs.

Bernsohn, Joseph & Grossman, Herbert J., eds. Lipid Storage Diseases: Enzymatic Defects & Clinical Implications. LC 70-137623. 1971. 60.00 (ISBN 0-12-092850-7). Acad Pr.

Bernson, Bernard G., jt. auth. see Carkhuff, Robert R.

Bernstam, Mikhail S., jt. auth. see Beichman, Arnold.

Bernstein. Dermatopharmacology. 1985. 35.00 (ISBN 0-8151-0716-1). Year Bk Med.

Bernstein, jt. auth. see Wong.

Bernstein, jt. auth. see Wong, H.

Bernstein, jt. auth. see Woodward.

Bernstein, A. & Wells. Trouble-Shooting Mathematics Skills. 1979. text ed. 18.48 (ISBN 0-03-041686-8, HoltE); tchr's guide 8.12 (ISBN 0-03-041691-4); tests (dup. masters) 31.40 (ISBN 0-03-041696-5); drill sheets (dup. masters) 42.00 (ISBN 0-03-043581-1). HR&W.

--Troubleshooting Mathematics Skills: Grades 7-12. 1975. text ed. 18.64 (ISBN 0-03-088441-1, HoltE); pap. 8.12 tchr's guide (ISBN 0-03-088442-X); tests (dup. masters) 31.40 (ISBN 0-03-089823-4); 266.60 (ISBN 0-03-016786-8). HR&W.

Bernstein, Aaron. Beating the Harness Races. LC 75-18956. (Illus.). 224p. 1976. pap. 6.95 (ISBN 0-668-03872-1). Arco.

Bernstein, Al. Boxing for Beginners. LC 77-23690. 1978. pap. 5.95 (ISBN 0-8092-7757-3). Contemp Bks.

Bernstein, Alan B. The Emergency Public Relations Manual. LC 82-80824. 94p. Repr. of 1982 ed. 75.00 (ISBN 0-686-38793-7). PASE.

Bernstein, Alison R., jt. auth. see Smith, Virginia B.

Bernstein, Allen. Tax Guide for College Teachers, 1985. 400p. 1984. pap. 18.95 (ISBN 0-916018-27-X). Acad Info Serv.

Bernstein, Alvin H. Tiberius Sempronius Gracchus: Tradition & Apostasy. 272p. 1978. 27.50x (ISBN 0-8014-1078-9). Cornell U Pr.

Bernstein, Alvin H., ed. see Polybius.

Bernstein, Anne E. & Warner, Gloria. An Introduction to Contemporary Psychoanalysis. LC 80-70246. 300p. 1981. 25.00 (ISBN 0-87668-442-8). Aronson.

Bernstein, Anne E. & Warner, Gloria M. Women Treating Women: Case Material from Women Treated by Female Psychoanalysists. LC 84-8996. xv, 310p. 1985. text ed. 32.50x (ISBN 0-8236-6863-0, 06863). Intl Univs Pr.

Bernstein, Arthur. Intern's Manual. 4th ed. (Illus.). 1971. pap. 18.50 (ISBN 0-8151-0712-9). Year Bk Med.

Bernstein, Arthur H. A Trustee's Guide to Hospital Law. LC 81-53758. 300p. 1981. 24.95 (ISBN 0-931028-14-0); pap. 19.95 (ISBN 0-931028-13-2). Teach'em.

Bernstein, B. J., tr. see Garcia-Marquez, Gabriel.

Bernstein, Barton J., ed. The Atomic Bomb: The Critical Issues. (Critical Issues in American History Ser.). 1976. pap. 8.95 (ISBN 0-316-09192-8). Little.

Bernstein, Barton J. & Matusow, Allen J., eds. Twentieth-Century America: Recent Interpretations. 2nd ed. 582p. (Orig.). 1972. pap. text ed. 14.95 (ISBN 0-15-592391-9, HC). HarBraceJ.

Bernstein, Basil. Class, Codes & Control, Vol. 3: Towards a Theory of Educational Transmissions. (Primary Socialization, Language & Education Ser.). 1977. pap. 8.95x (ISBN 0-7100-8666-0). Routledge & Kegan.

Bernstein, Bernard, jt. auth. see Nassi, Robert.

Bernstein, Bernard, jt. auth. see Nassi, Robert J.

Bernstein, Blanche. The Politics of Welfare: The New York City Experience. LC 82-6863. 1982. 22.00 (ISBN 0-89011-570-2). Abt Bks.

--The Politics of Welfare: The New York City Experience. 230p. 1984. Repr. of 1982 ed. lib. bdg. 22.50 (ISBN 0-8191-4070-8). U Pr of Amer.

Bernstein, Bob. Monday Morning Magic. 64p. (gr. k-6). 1982. 5.95 (ISBN 0-86653-080-0, GA 425). Good Apple.

Bernstein, Bonnie. Writing Crafts Workshop. LC 81-85351. (Crafts Workshop Ser.). (gr. 3-8). 1982. pap. 7.95 (ISBN 0-8224-9785-9). Pitman Learning.

Bernstein, Bonnie & Blair, Leigh. Native American Crafts Workshop. LC 81-82041. (Crafts Workshop Ser.). (gr. 3-8). 1982. pap. 7.95 (ISBN 0-8224-9784-0). Pitman Learning.

Bernstein, Bonnie, ed. Day by Day: Three Hundred Calendar-Related Activities, Crafts, & Bulletin Board Ideas for the Elementary Grades. LC 80-81680. (Learning Ideabooks Ser.). 1980. pap. 14.95 (ISBN 0-8224-4252-3). Pitman Learning.

Bernstein, Bruce, jt. auth. see Udell, James.

Bernstein, Burton. Plane Crazy: A Celebration of Flying. (Illus.). 192p. 1985. 16.95 (ISBN 0-89919-390-0). HM.

--Plane Crazy: A Reporter Aloft. (Illus.). 256p. 1985. 16.95 (ISBN 0-89919-390-0). Ticknor & Fields.

--Sinai: The Great & Terrible Wilderness. (Illus.). 1979. 16.95 (ISBN 0-670-34837-6). Viking.

--Thurber: A Biography. 1985. 10.95 (ISBN 0-87795-690-1). Arbor Hse.

Bernstein, Carl & Woodward, Bob. All the President's Men. (Illus.). 1976. pap. 4.50 (ISBN 0-446-32264-4). Warner Bks.

Bernstein, Carl, jt. auth. see Woodward, Bob.

Bernstein, Carol, jt. auth. see Bertherat, Therese.

Bernstein, Carol L. Precarious Enchantment: A Reading of Meredith's Poetry. LC 79-744. 202p. 1979. 17.50x (ISBN 0-8132-0543-3). Cath U Pr.

Bernstein, Charles. Great Restaurant Innovatos. 1981. 19.95 (ISBN 0-86730-239-9). Lebhar Friedman.

--Sambo's. LC 83-81546. 208p. 1984. pap. 9.95 (ISBN 0-86666-202-2). Natl Lit Guild.

--Stigma. 1981. pap. 3.00 (ISBN 0-930794-49-4). Station Hill Pr.

Bernstein, Charles, jt. auth. see Andrews, Bruce.

Bernstein, Charles, ed. Connecticut Time Limitations. 311p. looseleaf 40.00 (ISBN 0-88063-002-7). Butterworth Legal Pubs.

Bernstein, Charles, et al. Perception. Wellman, Don, ed. Guss, David, tr. (Toward a New Poetics Ser: Vol. 2). (Illus.). 224p. 1982. pap. 6.95 (ISBN 0-942030-02-8). O ARS.

Bernstein, Charles S., ed. Connecticut Real Property Statutes. LC 82-73439. 383p. 1982. looseleaf binder 45.00 (ISBN 0-88063-007-8). Butterworth Legal Pubs.

Bernstein, Chuck. The Joy of Birding: A Guide to Better Bird Watching. LC 84-7778. (Illus.). 201p. (Orig.). 1984. pap. 8.95 (ISBN 0-88496-220-2). Capra Pr.

Bernstein, D. L. Existence Theorems in Partial Differential Equations. (Annals of Mathematic Studies: No. 23). 1950. 18.00 (ISBN 0-527-02739-1). Kraus Repr.

Bernstein, Daniel J., ed. Nebraska Symposium on Motivation, 1981: Response Structure & Organization. LC 53-11655. (Nebraska Symposia on Motivation Ser.: Vol. 29). xii, 267p. 1982. 19.95x (ISBN 0-8032-1171-6); pap. 9.95x (ISBN 0-8032-6064-4). U of Nebr Pr.

Bernstein, Deena E. & Tiegerman, Ellen Morris. Language & Communications Disorders in Children. 416p. 1985. 25.95 (ISBN 0-675-20267-1). Merrill.

Bernstein, Dennis, jt. auth. see Lehrer, Warren.

Bernstein, Douglas A. & Borkovec, Thomas D. Progressive Relaxation Training: A Manual for the Helping Professions. 76p. (Orig.). 1973. pap. text ed. 10.95 record incl. (ISBN 0-87822-104-2, 1042). Res Press.

Bernstein, Douglas A. & Nietzel, Michael T. Introduction to Clinical Psychology. (Psychology Ser.). (Illus.). 1980. text ed. 32.95 (ISBN 0-07-005016-3). McGraw.

Bernstein, Eckhard. German Humanism. (World Authors Ser.). 1983. lib. bdg. 19.95 (ISBN 0-8057-6537-9, Twayne). G K Hall.

Bernstein, Eduard. Cromwell & Communism: Socialism & Democracy in the Great English Revolution. new ed. 287p. 1963. 28.50x (ISBN 0-7146-1454-8, F Cass Co). Biblio Dist.

--Evolutionary Socialism: A Criticism & Affirmation. 2nd ed. LC 61-16649. 1961. pap. 5.50 (ISBN 0-8052-0011-8). Schocken.

Bernstein, Edward. Ferdinand Lassalle As a Social Reformer. Aveling, Eleanor Marx, tr. from Ger. LC 74-131631. 1970. Repr. of 1893 ed. 12.00x (ISBN 0-403-00518-3). Scholarly.

Bernstein, Ellen, ed. Medical & Health Annual, 1983. 448p. (YA) 1982. write for info. Ency Brit Inc.

Bernstein, Eugene F. Noninvasive Diagnostic Techniques in Vascular Disease. 2nd ed. LC 81-14049. (Illus.). 626p. 1982. text ed. 79.50 (ISBN 0-8016-0807-4). Mosby.

Bernstein, Gail L. Haruko's World: A Japanese Farm Woman & Her Community. LC 82-61783. (Illus.). xviii, 199p. 1983. 25.00x (ISBN 0-8047-1174-7). Stanford U Pr.

--Japanese Marxist. (East Asia Ser: No. 86). 1976. text ed. 15.00x (ISBN 0-674-47193-8). Harvard U Pr.

Bernstein, Gail S., et al. Behavioral Habilitation Through Proactive Programming. LC 81-10134. (Illus.). 336p. (Orig.). 1981. pap. text ed. 18.95 (ISBN 0-933716-19-2, 192). P H Brookes.

Bernstein, Gary. Pro Techniques of Beauty & Glamour Photography. 160p. 1985. 12.95 (ISBN 0-89586-364-2). H P Bks.

--Pro Techniques of People Photography. (Illus.). 160p. 1984. pap. 12.95 (ISBN 0-89586-269-7). H P Bks.

Bernstein, George see Cordasco, Francesco.

Bernstein, George B. A Fifteen-Year Forecast of Information-Processing Technology. LC 77-128581. 187p. 1969. 19.00 (ISBN 0-403-04486-3). Scholarly.

Bernstein, Gerry. Freezer Cookery. LC 80-11170. (Illus.). 250p. 1980. pap. 6.95 (ISBN 0-914090-84-4). Chicago Review.

Bernstein, H., jt. auth. see Kaufman, L.

Bernstein, Harry. Dom Pedro II. (World Authors Ser.). 267p. Repr. of 1973 ed. text ed. cancelled (ISBN 0-8290-0729-6). Irvington.

--Origins of Inter-American Interest, 1700-1812. LC 66-13164. 1965. Repr. of 1945 ed. 7.00x (ISBN 0-8462-0711-7). Russell.

Bernstein, Henrietta. Cabalah Primer: Introduction to English-Hebrew Cabalah. 192p. 1984. pap. 9.95 (ISBN 0-87516-526-5). De Vorss.

Bernstein, Henry & Campbell, Bonnie. Contradictions of Accumulation in Africa. 1985. 29.95 (ISBN 0-8039-2366-X). Sage.

Bernstein, Henry, jt. ed. see Johnson, Hazel.

Bernstein, Herman. Celebrities of Our Time. facs. ed. LC 68-8438. (Essay Index Reprint Ser). 1924. 18.00 (ISBN 0-8369-0204-1). Ayer Co Pubs.

Bernstein, Hilda. For Their Triumphs & for Their Tears: Women in Apartheid South Africa. rev. ed. (Illus.). 72p. 1978. 2.35 (ISBN 0-317-20231-6). IDAFSA.

--For Their Triumphs & for Their Tears: Women in Apartheid South Africa. 71p. 1978. 2.00 (ISBN 0-317-36677-7). Africa Fund.

--Steve Biko. 149p. 1978. 3.50 (ISBN 0-317-36653-X, 46). Africa Fund.

Bernstein, I. A. Biochemical Responses to Environmental Stress. LC 79-151618. 166p. 1971. 29.50x (ISBN 0-306-30531-3, Plenum Pr). Plenum Pub.

Bernstein, I. A. & Seiji, M., eds. Biochemistry of Normal & Abnormal Epidermal Differentiation. (Current Problems in Dermatology: Vol. 10). (Illus.). x, 442p. 1981. pap. 58.00 (ISBN 3-8055-1915-X). S Karger.

Bernstein, I. A., jt. ed. see Seigi, M. S.

Bernstein, I. M., jt. auth. see Peckner, Donald.

Bernstein, I. M. & Thompson, Anthony W., eds. Hydrogen Effects in Metals: Proceedings of a Meeting held at Moran, Wyoming, 1980. (Illus.). 1059p. 55.00 (ISBN 0-89520-378-2); member 32.00 (ISBN 0-317-36230-5); student members 20.00 (ISBN 0-317-36231-3). ASM.

Bernstein, Ilene N. & Freeman, Howard E. Academic & Entreprenurial Research: The Consequences of Diversity in Federal Evaluation Studies. LC 74-83208. 108p. 1975. text ed. 9.95x (ISBN 0-87154-109-2). Russell Sage.

Bernstein, Ilene N., ed. Validity Issues in Evaluative Research. LC 75-32373. (Sage Contemporary Social Science Issues Ser.: No. 23). pap. 33.50 (ISBN 0-317-29607-8, 2021870). Bks Demand UMI.

Bernstein, Irving. A Caring Society: The New Deal, the Worker & the Great Depression. LC 84-25129. (History of the American Worker Ser.). 336p. 1985. 22.95 (ISBN 0-395-33116-1). HM.

--The Lean Years: A History of the American Worker 1920-1933. (Quality Paperbacks Ser.). 577p. 1983. pap. 11.95 (ISBN 0-306-80202-3). Da Capo.

--The New Deal Collective Bargaining Policy. LC 75-8997. (FDR & the Era of the New Deal Ser.). xi, 178p. 1975. Repr. of 1950 ed. lib. bdg. 27.50 (ISBN 0-306-70703-9). Da Capo.

Bernstein, Irving, ed. Unemployment: Problems & Policies. 73p. 1976. 3.50 (ISBN 0-89215-062-9). U Cal LA Indus Rel.

Bernstein, J. How to Profit from Seasonal Commodity Spreads: A Complete Guide. LC 82-13543. 537p. 1982. cloth 69.95 (ISBN 0-471-86432-3, Pub. by Ronald Pr). Wiley.

Bernstein, J., ed. see Symposium Based on Papers Presented at the Cajal Club Meeting in Conjunction with the American Association of Anatomists, Dallas, Tex., April 1972.

Bernstein, J. J. Neural Prostheses: Materials, Physiology & Histopathology of Electrical Stimulation of the Nervous System. (Journal: Brain, Behav ior & Evolution: Vol. 14, No. 1-2). (Illus.). 1977. 31.50 (ISBN 3-8055-2640-7). S Karger.

Bernstein, J. M. The Philosophy of the Novel: Lukacs, Marxism & the Dialectics of Form. 320p. 1984. 35.00x (ISBN 0-8166-1304-4); pap. 14.95 (ISBN 0-8166-1307-9). U of Minn Pr.

Bernstein, J. S. Benjamin Jarnes. LC 78-110707. (World Authors Ser.). 1985. lib. bdg. 15.95 (ISBN 0-8057-2464-8). Irvington.

Bernstein, J. S., tr. see Garcia-Marquez, Gabriel.

Bernstein, Jacob. Beyond the Investor's Quotient. 1985. 19.95 (ISBN 0-471-82062-8). Wiley.

--Handbook of Commodity Cycles: A Window on Time. 383p. 1982. cloth 49.95x (ISBN 0-471-08197-3, Pub. by Ronald Pr). Wiley.

--An Investor's Guide to Using Cycles in the Precious Metals & Copper. LC 84-19561. 224p. 1985. 34.95x (ISBN 0-471-88746-3, Pub. by Wiley-Interscience). Wiley.

--The Investor's Quotient: The Psychology of Successful Investing in Commodities & Stock. LC 80-17127. 275p. 1980. cloth 19.95 (ISBN 0-471-07849-2). Wiley.

Bernstein, James D., et al. Rural Health Centers in the United States. LC 79-903. (Rural Health Center Ser.: Vol. I). (Illus.). 1979. prof ref 18.50x (ISBN 0-88410-535-0); pap. 10.00x (ISBN 0-88410-541-5). Ballinger Pub.

Bernstein, Jane. Departures. 304p. 1981. pap. 2.50 (ISBN 0-380-53736-2, 53736). Avon.

--Seven Minutes in Heaven. 256p. (Orig.). 1986. pap. 2.50 (ISBN 0-449-70139-5, Juniper). Fawcett.

Bernstein, Jane A., ed. French Chansons of the Sixteenth Century. LC 84-43062. (Illus.). 224p. 1985. 22.50x (ISBN 0-271-00397-9). Pa St U Pr.

Bernstein, Jay, jt. ed. see Rosenberg, Harvey S.

Bernstein, Jay B. The Professional Syndicator: A Guide for Creating Limited Partnerships. 112p. 1981. text ed. 29.95 (ISBN 0-8403-2503-7). Kendall-Hunt.

Bernstein, Jeremy. The Analytical Engine: Computers - Past, Present, & Future. rev. ed. LC 80-29413. 128p. 1981. pap. 8.95 (ISBN 0-688-00488-1). Morrow.

--Ascent: Of the Invention of Mountain Climbing & Its Practice. LC 78-26722. (Illus.). 124p. 1979. 10.95x (ISBN 0-8032-1154-6); pap. 3.25 (ISBN 0-8032-6052-0, BB 689, Bison). U of Nebr Pr.

--Einstein. (Modern Masters Ser.). 1976. pap. 4.95 (ISBN 0-14-004317-9). Penguin.

--Elementary Particles & Their Currents. LC 68-21404. (Physics Ser.). (Illus.). 322p. 1968. text ed. 32.95 (ISBN 0-7167-0324-6). W H Freeman.
--Experiencing Science. LC 77-20415. 1978. 12.50 (ISBN 0-465-02185-9). Basic.
--Hans Bethe: Prophet of Energy. LC 80-50555. (Illus.). 224p. 1980. pap. 12.95 (ISBN 0-465-02903-5). Basic.
--Hans Bethe: Prophet of Energy. 224p. 1985. pap. 7.95 (ISBN 0-87548-313-5). Open Court.
--Mountain Passages. LC 78-15996. (Illus.). x, 278p. 1978. 12.50 (ISBN 0-8032-0983-5). U of Nebr Pr.
--Science Observed: Essays Out of My Mind. 1982. 16.95 (ISBN 0-465-07340-9). Basic.
--Three Degrees Above Zero: Bell Labs in the Information Age. (Illus.). 320p. 1984. 17.95 (ISBN 0-684-18170-3). Scribner.
Bernstein, Jeremy, et al. Science & the Human Imagination: Albert Einstein. Incl. New Jersey's Contributions to the Chemical Industry & Chemical Education. Hass, Henry B. & Bose, A K.. LC 77-92565. (The Leverton Lecture Ser: No. 5). 1978. 9.50 (ISBN 0-8386-2223-2). Fairleigh Dickinson.
Bernstein, Jerome, tr. see De Ventos, Xavier R.
Bernstein, Jerrold G. Handbook of Drug Therapy in Psychiatry. (Illus.). 1983. 29.00 (ISBN 0-7236-7028-5). PSG Pub Co.
Bernstein, Jerrold G., ed. Clinical Psychopharmacology. 2nd ed. LC 76-15733. (Illus.). 286p. 1984. text ed. 23.00 (ISBN 0-7236-7030-7). PSG Pub Co.
Bernstein, Joanne. Fiddle with a Riddle: Write Your Own Riddles. LC 76-11391. (Illus.). (gr. 3-7). 1979. 9.25 (ISBN 0-525-29678-6, 0898-270). Dutton.
--Loss & How to Cope with It. LC 76-50027. (gr. 6 up). 8.95 (ISBN 0-395-28891-6, Clarion). HM.
--Loss & How to Cope with It. 160p. (gr. 6 up). 1981. pap. 3.95 (ISBN 0-395-30012-6, Clarion). HM.
Bernstein, Joanne & Cohen, Paul. Unidentified Flying Riddles. Fay, Ann, ed. LC 83-17097. (Illus.). 32p. (gr. 1-5). 1983. PLB 7.75 (ISBN 0-8075-8329-4). A Whitman.
Bernstein, Joanne, et al. Un-Frog-Getable Riddles. Fay, Ann, ed. LC 81-11548. 32p. (gr. 1-5). 1981. PLB 7.75 (ISBN 0-8075-8322-7). A Whitman.
Bernstein, Joanne E. Books to Help Children Cope with Separation & Loss. 2nd ed. 439p. 1983. 34.95 (ISBN 0-8352-1484-2). Bowker.
--Dmitry: A Young Soviet Immigrant. (Illus.). 80p. (gr. 4-7). 1981. 10.95 (ISBN 0-89919-034-0, Clarion). HM.
Bernstein, Joanne E. & Cohen, Paul. Happy Holiday Riddles to You. Fay, Ann, ed. (Illus.). 32p. (gr. 1-5). 1985. PLB 7.75 (ISBN 0-8075-3154-5). A Whitman.
--More Unidentified Flying Riddles. (Illus.). 32p. (gr. 1-5). 1985. 7.75 (ISBN 0-8075-5279-8). A Whitman.
Bernstein, Joel H. Families that Take in Friends. LC 83-60359. 164p. 1983. 13.95 (ISBN 0-912299-00-2); pap. 8.95 (ISBN 0-912299-01-0). Stoneydale Pr Pub.
Bernstein, John. Pacificism-Rebellion in Herman Melville. 1985. 52.50 (ISBN 0-317-19971-4). Porter.
Bernstein, John A. Shaftsbury, Rousseau & Kant: An Introduction to the Conflict Between Aesthetic & Moral Values in Modern Thought. LC 78-75190. 192p. 1980. 19.50 (ISBN 0-8386-2351-4). Fairleigh Dickinson.
Bernstein, Joseph, tr. see Parturier, Francoise.
Bernstein, Joseph M., ed. see Baudelaire, Charles, et al.
Bernstein, Joseph M., tr. see Escarpit, Robert.
Bernstein, Joseph M., tr. see Par, Isabelle.
Bernstein, Julian L. Audio Systems. LC 78-2563. 424p. 1978. Repr. of 1966 ed. lib. bdg. 24.50 (ISBN 0-88275-668-0). Krieger.
Bernstein, Kenneth. Music Lover's Europe: A Guidebook & Companion. (Illus.). 192p. 1983. 12.95 (ISBN 0-684-17770-6, ScribT). Scribner.
Bernstein, L. Jacobi-Perron Algorithm: Its Theory & Application. LC 70-169956. (Lecture Notes in Mathematics: Vol. 207). 1971. pap. text ed. 11.00 (ISBN 0-387-05497-9). Springer-Verlag.
Bernstein, L. B. Deutsch-Russisches Worterbuch fur Wasserbau. 579p. (Rus. & Ger.). 1961. leatherette 19.95 (ISBN 0-686-92359-6, M-9100). French & Eur.
Bernstein, Lawrence F., ed. see Gero, Ihan.
Bernstein, Leonard. Bernstein on Broadway. Gottlieb, Jack & Wittke, Paul, eds. (Illus.). 352p. (Orig.). 1981. 29.95 (ISBN 0-911320-01-6); pap. 19.95 (ISBN 0-911320-00-8). Schirmer Bks.
--The Joy of Music. 1963. pap. 9.95 (ISBN 0-671-39721-4, Fireside). S&S.
--The Unanswered Question: Six Talks at Harvard. (The Charles Eliot Norton Lectures). 1976. slipcased with 3 records 25.00 (ISBN 0-674-81065-1); pap. 12.50 (ISBN 0-674-92001-5). Harvard U Pr.
Bernstein, Leonard, et al. West Side Story. 1958. 12.95 (ISBN 0-394-40788-1). Random.
--Candide: The Complete Words & Music of the Drama Critics Award Winning Broadway Musical. LC 75-43171. (Illus.). 1976. 35.00 (ISBN 0-02-870450-9); pap. 25.00 (ISBN 0-02-870460-6). Schirmer Bks.
Bernstein, Leonard S. The Official Guide to Wine Snobbery. LC 81-18707. 180p. 1982. 10.95 (ISBN 0-688-00807-0). Morrow.
--The Official Guide to Wine Snobbery. 1984. pap. 5.95 (ISBN 0-688-01605-7, Quill). Morrow.
Bernstein, Leopold A. Analysis of Financial Statements. rev. ed. LC 84-71131. 350p. 1984. 25.00 (ISBN 0-87094-494-0). Dow Jones-Irwin.
--Financial Statement Analysis: Theory, Application & Interpretation. 3rd ed. 1983. 32.95x (ISBN 0-256-02586-X). Irwin.
Bernstein, Leopold A. & Engler, Calvin. Advanced Accounting. 1982. 33.95x (ISBN 0-256-02456-1). Irwin.
Bernstein, Leslie, ed. Plastic & Reconstructive Surgery of the Head & Neck: Aesthetic Surgery, Vol. 1. 272p. 1981. 60.00 (ISBN 0-8089-1372-7, 790576). Grune.
--Plastic & Reconstructive Surgery of the Head & Neck: Rehabilitative Surgery, Vol. 2. 576p. 1981. 82.00 (ISBN 0-8089-1373-5, 790577). Grune.
Bernstein, Levitt & Richardson, Anthony. Specification Clauses for Rehabilitation & Conversion Work. (Illus.). 128p. 1982. 27.50 (ISBN 0-85139-582-1). Nichols Pub.
Bernstein, Lewis. Making an Inter-American Mind. LC 61-11110. 1961. 7.00 (ISBN 0-8130-0019-X). U Presses Fla.
Bernstein, Lewis & Bernstein, Rosalyn S. Interviewing: A Guide for Health Professionals. 3rd ed. (Illus.). 224p. 1980. pap. 13.95x (ISBN 0-8385-4307-3). ACC.
--Interviewing: A Guide for Health Professionals. 4th ed. 240p. 1985. pap. 15.95 (ISBN 0-8385-4317-0). ACC.
Bernstein, Louis. Challenge & Mission. LC 82-60203. 272p. 1982. 13.95 (ISBN 0-88400-081-8). Shengold.
Bernstein, M. D., jt. ed. see Iotti, R. C.
Bernstein, M. D., jt. ed. see Singh, A.
Bernstein, Malcome E., et al. Strategic Sales Development: A Consultative Selling Process, 2 vols. 1985. write for info. Human Equat.
Bernstein, Margery & Kobrin, Janet. The First Morning: An African Myth. LC 75-27705. (Myths You Can Read by Yourself, Encore Edition). (Illus.). 48p. (gr. 1-3). 1976. reinforced bdg. 3.19 (ISBN 0-684-17712-9, ScribJ). Scribner.
Bernstein, Martin D., ed. see National Congress on Pressure Vessel & Piping (3rd: 1979: San Francisco).
Bernstein, Marver H. Politics of Israel: The First Decade of Statehood. LC 69-13825. Repr. of 1957 ed. lib. bdg. 19.25x (ISBN 0-8371-2036-5, BEPI). Greenwood.
--Regulating Business by Independent Commission. LC 77-2985. 1977. Repr. of 1955 ed. lib. bdg. 20.25 (ISBN 0-8371-9563-2, BERB). Greenwood.
Bernstein, Marvin. Mexican Mining Industry, 1890-1950. LC 64-18628. 1965. 39.50 (ISBN 0-87395-016-X). State U NY Pr.
Bernstein, Matt. This Messiah Fellow. 1985. 6.75 (ISBN 0-8062-2344-8). Carlton.
Bernstein, Melvin H. John Jay Chapman. (Twayne's United States Authors Ser). 1964. pap. 5.95x (ISBN 0-8084-0185-8, T70, Twayne). New Coll U Pr.
Bernstein, Melvin H., ed. see Chapman, John Jay.
Bernstein, Melvin H., jt. ed. see Hoy, John C.
Bernstein, Melvin H., ed. see Rush, James.
Bernstein, Meredith, jt. auth. see Fast, Julius.
Bernstein, Michael A. Prima Della Rivoluzione. LC 83-83108. (Poet's Ser.). 65p. 1984. 12.95 (ISBN 0-915032-41-4); pap. 4.95 (ISBN 0-915032-16-3). Natl Poet Foun.
--The Tale of the Tribe: Ezra Pound & the Modern Verse Epic. LC 80-129. 1980. 35.00x (ISBN 0-691-06434-2); pap. 13.50x LPE (ISBN 0-691-10105-1). Princeton U Pr.
Bernstein, Mordecai W., ed. see Kruk, Herman.
Bernstein, Norman. Emotional Care of the Facially Burned & Disfigured. 1976. pap. 15.95 (ISBN 0-316-09193-6). Little.
Bernstein, Norman & Robson, Martin C., eds. Comprehensive Approaches to the Burned Person. 1983. pap. text ed. 23.50 (ISBN 0-87488-741-0). Med Exam.
Bernstein, Norman & Sussex, James, eds. Handbook of Psychiatric Consultation with Children & Youth. LC 84-3376. 416p. 1984. text ed. 40.00 (ISBN 0-89335-188-1). SP Med & Sci Bks.
Bernstein, Norman R. Emotional Care of the Facially Burned & Disfigured Patients. pap. 15.95 (ISBN 0-318-03570-7). Phoenix Soc.
Bernstein, Paul. Workplace Democratization. LC 79-66569. 127p. 1980. pap. text ed. 6.95x (ISBN 0-87855-711-3). Transaction Bks.
Bernstein, Paul & Green, Robert W. History of Civilization, since Sixteen Forty-Eight. (Quality Paperback Ser.: No. 65). 515p. (Orig.). 1976. pap. 5.95 (ISBN 0-8226-0065-X). Littlefield.
--History of Civilization to Sixteen Forty-Eight. (Quality Paperback: No. 64). 355p. (Orig.). 1976. pap. 4.95 (ISBN 0-8226-0064-1). Littlefield.
Bernstein, Paula. Family Ties, Corporate Bonds. LC 82-48695. 192p. 1985. 14.95 (ISBN 0-385-19015-8). Doubleday.
Bernstein, Penny L. Eight Theoretical Approaches in Dance-Movement Therapy. 1979. pap. text ed. 13.95 (ISBN 0-8403-2026-4). Kendall-Hunt.
--Theoretical Approaches in Dance-Movement Therapy, Vol. II. 224p. 1984. pap. text ed. 15.95 (ISBN 0-8403-3463-X). Kendall Hunt.
--Theory & Methods in Dance Movement Therapy: A Manual for Therapists, Students & Educators. 2nd ed. 1981. perfect bdg. 13.95 (ISBN 0-8403-2378-6). Kendall-Hunt.
Bernstein, Peter, ed. see Young, Arthur.
Bernstein, Peter W., ed. see Arthur Young & Company Staff.
Bernstein, Philip. To Dwell in Unity: The Jewish Federation Movement in America, 1960-1980. LC 83-9867. 394p. 1983. 19.95 (ISBN 0-8276-0228-6, 608). Jewish Pubns.
Bernstein, Philip, jt. auth. see Tsichritzis, Dionysios C.
Bernstein, Philip A., et al. Distributed Data Base Management. (Tutorial Texts Ser.). 195p. 1978. 20.00 (ISBN 0-8186-0212-0, Q212). IEEE Comp Soc.
Bernstein, Philip S. What the Jews Believe. LC 77-28446. (Illus.). 1978. Repr. of 1951 ed. lib. bdg. 15.00x (ISBN 0-313-20228-1, BEWJ). Greenwood.
Bernstein, R., ed. Digital Image Processing for Remote Sensing. LC 77-94520. 1978. 49.85 (ISBN 0-87942-105-3, PC01024). Inst Electrical.
Bernstein, R. B. Chemical Dynamics Via Molecular & Laser Techniques. (Illus.). 1982. 59.00x (ISBN 0-19-855154-1); pap. 24.95x (ISBN 0-19-855169-X). Oxford U Pr.
Bernstein, R. B., jt. auth. see Levine, R. D.
Bernstein, R. B., ed. Atom-Molecule Collision Theory: Guide for the Experimentalist. LC 78-27380. (Physics of Atoms & Molecules Ser.). (Illus.). 1979. 95.00x (ISBN 0-306-40121-5, Plenum Pr). Plenum Pub.
Bernstein, Richard. Beyond Objectivism & Relativism: Science, Hermeneutics, & Praxis. 320p. (Orig.). 1983. 27.50x (ISBN 0-8122-7906-9); pap. 9.95 (ISBN 0-8122-1165-0). U of Pa Pr.
--From the Center of the Earth: The Search for the Truth about China. 1982. 15.95 (ISBN 0-316-09194-4). Little.
--Megastar. LC 84-80883. (Illus.). 96p. (Orig.). 1984. pap. 14.95 (ISBN 0-394-62305-3, E961, Ever). Grove.
Bernstein, Richard J. John Dewey. x, 214p. 1981. lib. bdg. 24.00x (ISBN 0-917930-35-5); pap. text ed. 8.50x (ISBN 0-917930-15-0). Ridgeview.
--Philosophical Profiles: Essays in a Pragmatic Mode. 250p. 1985. 25.00 (ISBN 0-8122-7995-6); pap. 10.95 (ISBN 0-8122-1216-9). U of Pa Pr.
--Praxis & Action: Contemporary Philosophies of Human Activity. LC 77-157048. 1971. 30.00x (ISBN 0-8122-7640-X); pap. 10.95x (ISBN 0-8122-1016-6, Pa Paperbks). U of Pa Pr.
--The Restructuring of Social & Political Theory. LC 76-12544. 1978. pap. 9.95x (ISBN 0-8122-7742-2). U of Pa Pr.
Bernstein, Richard J., ed. Perspectives on Peirce: Critical Essays on Charles Sanders Peirce. LC 80-13703. ix, 148p. 1980. Repr. of 1965 ed. lib. bdg. 19.75x (ISBN 0-313-22414-5, BEPP). Greenwood.
Bernstein, Richard W. Habermas & Modernity. 240p. 1985. 20.00x (ISBN 0-262-02227-3); pap. 8.95x (ISBN 0-262-52102-4). MIT Pr.
Bernstein, Robert, et al. Book Publishing in the U.S.S.R. Reports of the Delegations of U.S. Book Publishers Visiting the U.S.S.R., 1962 & 1970. 2nd enl. ed. LC 76-37283. 1972. pap. text ed. 5.95x (ISBN 0-674-07874-8). Harvard U Pr.
Bernstein, Robert A. & Dyer, James A. An Introduction to Political Science Methods. (Illus.). 1979. P-H.
--An Introduction to Political Science Methods. 2nd ed. (Illus.). 304p. 1984. pap. text ed. 16.95 (ISBN 0-13-493313-3). P-H.
Bernstein, Roberta. Jasper Johns' Paintings & Sculptures 1954-1974: "The Changing Focus of the Eye". Foster, Stephen, ed. LC 85-998. (Studies in the Fine Arts: The Avant-Garde: No. 46). 272p. 1985. 39.95 (ISBN 0-8357-1601-5). UMI Res Pr.
Bernstein, Ron. Straight Down: Memoirs by the King of the Beach. 218p. 1977. pap. 4.95 (ISBN 0-915520-08-7). Ross-Erikson.
Bernstein, Ronald A. Successful Direct Selling: How to Plan, Launch, Promote, & Maintain a Profitable Direct Selling Company. (Illus.). 240p. 1984. 21.95 (ISBN 0-13-860726-5). P-H.
Bernstein, Rosalyn S., jt. auth. see Bernstein, Lewis.
Bernstein, Ruth A. & Bernstein, Stephen. Biology: The Study of Life. 654p. 1982. text ed. 27.95 (ISBN 0-15-505440-6, HC); instr's. manual avail. (ISBN 0-15-505441-4); study guide 8.95 (ISBN 0-15-505442-2). HarBraceJ.
Bernstein, S. Technological Assessment of Waste & Water Management Options for Garfield Park Community Area in Chicago, Illinois. 59p. 1978. 5.00 (ISBN 0-318-14680-0). Lake Mich Fed.
Bernstein, S. J., tr. see Garcia-Marquez, Gabriel.
Bernstein, S. P., ed. Labor & Social Welfare in Latin America: A Bibliography. 1976. lib. bdg. 59.95 (ISBN 0-8490-2121-9). Gordon Pr.
Bernstein, Samuel. Connecticut Yankee in an Age of Revolution. 1985. 15.95 (ISBN 0-87469-045-5). Sammis Pub.
--Essays in Political & Intellectual History. facs. ed. LC 73-86729. (Essay Index Reprint Ser). 1955. 18.00 (ISBN 0-8369-1171-7). Ayer Co Pubs.
--First International in America. LC 62-52478. 1962. 27.50x (ISBN 0-678-00102-2). Kelley.
--French Political & Intellectual History. 224p. 1983. pap. text ed. 24.95 (ISBN 0-87855-938-8). Transaction Bks.
Bernstein, Samuel J. The Strands Entwined: A New Direction in American Drama. LC 80-12740. 171p. 1980. 20.95x (ISBN 0-930350-07-3). NE U Pr.
Bernstein, Samuel J. & Mellon, W. Giles. Selected Readings in Quantitative Urban Analysis. LC 77-30458. 1978. pap. text ed. 22.00 (ISBN 0-08-019592-X). Pergamon.
Bernstein, Samuel J., ed. Computers in Public Administration: An International Perspective. 450p. 1976. text ed. 54.00 (ISBN 0-08-017869-3). Pergamon.
Bernstein, Saul. The Renaissance of the Torah Jew. 1985. text ed. 20.00x (ISBN 0-88125-090-2). Ktav.
Bernstein, Saul, ed. Explorations in Group Work: Essays in Theory & Practice. LC 76-50518. 1976. text ed. 12.00x (ISBN 0-89182-000-0); pap. text ed. 6.75x (ISBN 0-89182-001-9). Charles River Bks.
--Further Explorations in Group Work. 1976. text ed. 12.00 (ISBN 0-89182-002-7); pap. 6.75 (ISBN 0-89182-003-5). Charles River Bks.
Bernstein, Serge & Poussin, Charles D. Approximation, 2 Vols. in 1. LC 69-16996. (Fr). 15.95 (ISBN 0-8284-0198-5). Chelsea Pub.
Bernstein, Seymour. New York Tax Handbook: 1984 Edition. 436p. 1984. 11.00x (ISBN 0-686-89040-X, 62061-7). P-H.
--With Your Own Two Hands: Self-Discovery Through Music. (Illus.). 320p. 1981. 18.95 (ISBN 0-02-870310-3). Schirmer Bks.
Bernstein, Seymour, et al. Physical Properties of Steroid Conjugates. LC 68-9218. 1968. 42.00 (ISBN 0-387-04060-9). Springer-Verlag.
Bernstein, Seymour F. New York Tax Handbook 1985. price not set. P-H.
Bernstein, Sidney, ed. see Mason, James.
Bernstein, Stephen, jt. auth. see Bernstein, Ruth A.
Bernstein, Steven. Technique of Film Production. (Illus.). 394p. 1985. text ed. 26.95 (ISBN 0-240-51248-0); pap. text ed. 18.95 (ISBN 0-240-51249-9). Focal Pr.
Bernstein, Susan. Digest Book of Dog Care. LC 79-50063. 96p. pap. 3.95 (ISBN 0-695-81289-0). DBI.
Bernstein, Theodore M. Bernstein's Reverse Dictionary. LC 75-8283. 384p. 1975. 16.95 (ISBN 0-8129-0566-0). Times Bks.
--Careful Writer: A Modern Guide to English Usage. LC 65-12404. 1965. pap. 10.95 (ISBN 0-689-70555-7, 233). Atheneum.
--Do's, Don'ts, & Maybes of English Usage. LC 77-4293. 1977. 15.95 (ISBN 0-8129-0695-0); pap. 8.95 (ISBN 0-8129-6321-0). Times Bks.
--Miss Thistlebottom's Hobgoblins. 1984. pap. 6.95 (ISBN 0-671-50404-5). S&S.
--Watch Your Language. LC 58-12309. 1965. pap. 7.95 (ISBN 0-689-70531-X, 220). Atheneum.
Bernstein, Theodore M., jt. auth. see Garst, Robert E.
Bernstein, Thomas P. Up to the Mountains & Down to the Villages: The Transfer of Youth from Urban to Rural China. LC 77-76291. (Illus.). 1977. 31.00x (ISBN 0-300-02135-6). Yale U Pr.
Bernstein, William & Cawker, Ruth. Contemporary Canadian Architecture. (Illus.). 192p. 1983. 25.00 (ISBN 0-8038-1281-7). Architectural.
Bernstein-Tarrow, Norma, jt. auth. see Lundsteen, Sara.
Bernstine, Richard L. & Molloy, Catherine. Obstetrics-Gynecology: A Problem-Oriented Approach. 1985. pap. text ed. price not set (ISBN 0-87488-801-8). Med Exam.
Bernthal, John E. & Bankson, Nicholas W. Articulation Disorders. (Illus.). 352p. 1981. text ed. 27.95 (ISBN 0-13-049072-5). P-H.
Bernthal, Patricia J. & Spiller, James D. Understanding the Language of Medicine: A Programmed Learning Text. (Illus.). 1981. pap. text ed. 17.95x (ISBN 0-19-502879-1). Oxford U Pr.
Bernthal, Wilmar F., jt. auth. see Schmidt, Martin F.
Bernton, Hal, et al. The Forbidden Fuel: Power Alcohol in the Twentieth Century. LC 81-85112. (Illus.). 312p. 1982. 19.95 (ISBN 0-941726-00-2). Boyd Griffin.
Berntzen, Allen K., jt. auth. see Macy, Ralph W.
Bernus, Edmond. Les Illabakan (Niger) Une Tribu Touaregue Sahelienne et Son Aire De Nomadisation. (Atlas Des Structures Agraires Au Sud Du Sahara: No. 10). 1974. 30.00x (ISBN 90-2797-535-3). Mouton.
Bernussou, J. & Titli, A. Interconnected Dynamical Systems: Stability, Decomposition & Decentralisation. (North-Holland Systems & Control Ser.: Vol. 5). 330p. 1982. 59.75 (ISBN 0-444-86504-7, North Holland). Elsevier.
Bernz, Charles E. The Little Lion. LC 66-28050. (Illus.). 1966. text ed. 7.50 (ISBN 0-8236-3040-4). Intl Univs Pr.

Bernzweig, Eli. The Nurse's Liability for Malpractice: A Programmed Course. 3rd ed. 368p. 1981. pap. text ed. 22.95 (ISBN 0-07-005058-9). McGraw.

Bernzweig, Eli P. By Accident, Not Design: The Case for Comprehensive Injury Reparations. LC 80-20815. 238p. 1980. 38.95x (ISBN 0-03-056961-3). Praeger.

Ber Of Bolechow. The Memoirs of Ber of Bolechow (1723-1805) LC 73-2186. (The Jewish People; History, Religion, Literature Ser.). Repr. of 1922 ed. 19.00 (ISBN 0-405-05252-9). Ayer Co Pubs.

Berofsky, Bernard. Determinism. LC 70-112994. 1971. 36.00 (ISBN 0-691-07169-1). Princeton U Pr.

Berofsky, Bernard, ed. Free Will & Determinism. (Orig.). 1966. pap. text ed. 16.95 scp (ISBN 0-06-040648-8, HarpC). Har-Row.

Berolzheimer, Ruth, ed. The American Woman's Cookbook. 1974. pap. 1.95 (ISBN 0-380-00124-1, 20610). Avon.

--Culinary Arts Institute Encyclopedic Cookbook. 1980. 11.95 (ISBN 0-671-41408-9, Fireside). S&S.

--Encyclopedic Cookbook. 1962. 16.95 (ISBN 0-399-12836-0, G&D). Putnam Pub Group.

Beron, Alberto, et al. Guia de Studios Essential Arithmetic: Spanish Study Guide for Essential Arithmetic. 174p. write for info. Watts.

Beroul. Roman de Tristan & un Anonyme Poeme du 12th Siecle. Muret, E., ed. 38.00 (ISBN 0-384-04045-4); pap. 32.00 (ISBN 0-685-13586-1). Johnson Repr.

--Romance of Tristan. Fredrik, Alan S., tr. (Classics Ser.). 1978. pap. 3.95 (ISBN 0-14-044230-8). Penguin.

Beroza, Morton, ed. Pest Management with Insect Sex Attractants. LC 76-1873. (ACS Symposium Ser: No. 23). 1976. 24.95 (ISBN 0-8412-0308-3). Am Chemical.

Beroza, Morton, ed. see Symposium on the Chemistry & Action of Insect Juvenile Hormones, Washington, D. C., 1971.

Berquam, Hazel H. Miniatures of Nature. LC 80-68645. (Illus.). 1980. pap. 4.95 (ISBN 0-8323-0383-6). Binford.

Berque, Jacques. Arab Rebirth: Pain & Ecstasy. Hoare, Quintin, tr. from Fr. Orig. Title: Les Arabes. 138p. (Orig.). 1984. pap. 6.95 (ISBN 0-86356-015-6, Pub. by Al Saqi UK). Evergreen Dist.

--Cultural Expression in Arab Society Today. Stookey, Robert W., tr. from Fr. LC 76-16845. (Modern Middle East Ser.: No. 3). Orig. Title: Languages arabes du present. 382p. 1978. 27.50x (ISBN 0-292-70330-9). U of Tex Pr.

Berquin, Arnaud. Looking-Glass for the Mind, Or, Intellectual Mirror. (Early Children's Bks). (Illus.). 1969. Repr. of 1794 ed. lib. bdg. 28.00 (ISBN 0-384-04055-1). Johnson Repr.

Berquist, Charles. Labor in the Capitalist World Economy. LC 83-27015. 312p. 1984. 28.00 (ISBN 0-8039-2266-3); pap. 14.00 (ISBN 0-317-18519-5). Sage.

Berquist, Goodwin F. & Bowers, Paul C., Jr. The New Eden: James Kilbourne & the Development of Ohio. (Illus.). 306p. (Orig.). 1983. lib. bdg. 27.75 (ISBN 0-8191-3385-X); pap. text ed. 14.50 (ISBN 0-8191-3386-8). U Pr of Amer.

Berquist, Maurice. The Doctor Is In. (Illus.). 1981. 8.95 (ISBN 0-87162-253-X, D3490). Warner Pr.

--Miracle & Power of Blessing. 1984. pap. 2.95 (ISBN 0-87162-408-7, D8556). Warner Pr.

Berquist, Thomas H. Diagnostic Imaging of the Acutely Injured Patient. (Illus.). 192p. 1985. pap. 47.50 (ISBN 0-8067-2511-7). Urban & S.

Berquist, Thomas H., ed. see Bernau, Andreas.

Berr, Samuel. An Etymological Glossary to the Old Saxon Heliand: German Language & Literature, V l. 33. (European University Studies: Ser. 1). 480p. 1971. pap. 63.10 (ISBN 3-261-00032-5). P Lang Pubs.

Berra, Kathy, jt. auth. see Fry, Gary.

Berra, Tim M. An Atlas of Distribution of the Freshwater Fish Families of the World. LC 80-24666. (Illus.). xxx, 197p. 1981. 26.50x (ISBN 0-8032-1411-1); pap. 12.50x (ISBN 0-8032-6059-8, BB 768, Bison). U of Nebr Pr.

--William Beebe (1877-1962) An Annotated Bibliography. (Illus.). 157p. 1977. 22.50 (ISBN 0-208-01608-2, Archon). Shoe String.

Berrara, William M. & Hommon, Robert. Salvage Archaeology at Wailau, Ka'u, Island of Hawaii. (Departmental Report: No. 72-1). 60p. 1972. pap. 2.75 (ISBN 0-910240-79-5). Bishop Mus.

Berrebi, E., jt. auth. see Abraham-Frois, Gilbert.

Berredo Carneiro, Paulo E. & Arnaud, Pierre, eds. Auguste Comte: Correspondance Generale et Confessions, Tome 1, 1814-1840. (Archives Positivistes Ser.). 1973. pap. 27.20x (ISBN 90-2797-192-7). Mouton.

--Auguste Comte: Ecrits de Jeunesse 1816-1828. (Archives Positivistes Ser.). 1971. pap. 34.40x (ISBN 90-2796-767-9). Mouton.

Berreman, Gerald D. Social Inequality: Comparative & Developmental Approaches. LC 80-68550. (Studies in Anthropology). 1981. 39.50 (ISBN 0-12-093160-5). Acad Pr.

Berreman, Gerard. Caste & Other Inequalities. 1981. 20.00x (ISBN 0-8364-0775-X, Pub. by Folklore Inst). South Asia Bks.

Berreman, J. V. Tribal Distribution in Oregon. LC 37-20181. (American Anthropological Association Memoirs). pap. 15.00 (ISBN 0-527-00546-0). Kraus Repr.

Berrens, L. The Chemistry of Atopic Allergens. (Monographs in Allergy: Vol. 7). 1971. 39.75 (ISBN 3-8055-1150-7). S Karger.

Berreth, David, ed. American Paintings: 1830-1915. LC 82-61415. (Illus.). 40p. (Orig.). 1982. pap. 3.00 (ISBN 0-940784-03-3). Miami Univ Art.

Berrett, A. M., tr. see Gresh, A.

Berrett, A. M., tr. see Lefort, Rene.

Berrett, LaMar C. Discovering the World of the Bible. LC 79-18338. 1979. text ed. 14.95 (ISBN 0-8407-5182-6). Nelson.

Berrett, Tony, tr. see Chaliand, Gerald & Rageau, Jean-Pierre.

Berrett, William E. The Latter-day Saints: A Contemporary History to the Church of Jesus Christ. Knowles, Eleanor, tr. (Illus.). 525p. 1984. 10.95 (ISBN 0-87747-728-0). Deseret Bk.

Berrey, Henry, ed. see Osborne, Michael.

Berri, L. Y., ed. Planning a Socialist Economy, 2 vols. 572p. 9.45 (ISBN 0-8285-0371-0, Pub. by Progress Pubs USSR). Imported Pubns.

Berrian, Brenda. Bibliography of African Women Writers & Journalists. LC 84-52276. (Illus.). 1985. 24.00 (ISBN 0-89410-226-5); pap. 14.00 (ISBN 0-89410-227-3). Three Continents.

Berriault, Gina. The Infinite Passion of Expectation: Twenty-Five Stories. LC 82-81480. 260p. 1982. pap. 12.50 (ISBN 0-86547-082-0). N Point Pr.

--The Lights of Earth: A Novel. 176p. (Orig.). 1984. 12.50 (ISBN 0-86547-141-X). N Point Pr.

--The Son. Bd. with Conference of Victims. Repr. of 1962 ed. 352p. 1985. pap. 13.50 (ISBN 0-86547-198-3). N Point Pr.

Berrichon, Paterne. La Vie De Jean-Arthur Rimbaud. LC 77-10252. (Symbolists Ser.). (Fr.). Repr. of 1897 ed. 27.50 (ISBN 0-404-16307-6). AMS Pr.

Berrichon, Paterne, ed. see Rimbaud, Jean N.

Berrick, A. J. An Approach to Algebraic K-Theory. (Research Notes in Mathematics Ser.: No. 56). 120p. 1982. text ed. 17.95 (ISBN 0-273-08529-8). Pitman Pub MA.

Berrick, Ronald P. & Berrick, Stephen W. How Much is that Computer in the Window? (Illus.). 67p. (Orig.). 1982. spiral bdg. 9.95 (ISBN 0-910045-00-3). R Berrick.

Berrick, Stephen W., jt. auth. see Berrick, Ronald P.

Berridge. A Farewell to Arms (Hemingway) (Book Notes). 1984. pap. 2.50 (ISBN 0-8120-3412-0). Barron.

Berridge, A. E. Product Innovation & Development. 236p. 1977. text ed. 29.50x (ISBN 0-220-66325-4, Pub. by Busn Bks England). Brookfield Pub Co.

Berridge, Celia. Grandmother's Tales. Berridge, Celia, ed. (Illus.). 32p. (ps-2). 1982. 9.95 (ISBN 0-233-97357-5). Andre Deutsch.

Berridge, David. Children's Homes. 176p. 1985. 39.95x (ISBN 0-631-14136-7); pap. 14.95x (ISBN 0-631-14137-5). Basil Blackwell.

Berridge, G. R. & Jennings, A., eds. Diplomacy at the U. N. LC 84-11733. 256p. 1985. 27.50 (ISBN 0-312-21117-1). St Martin.

Berridge, Geoff. Economic Power in Anglo-South African Diplomacy. 225p. 1981. text ed. 40.50x (ISBN 0-333-26592-0, Pub. by Macmillan England). Humanities.

Berridge, M., ed. Advances in Insect Physiology, Vol. 18. Date not set. price not set (ISBN 0-12-024218-4). Acad Pr.

Berridge, M., et al, eds. Advances in Insect Physiology, Vol. 15. LC 63-14039. (Serial Publication). 1981. 96.00 (ISBN 0-12-024215-X). Acad Pr.

Berridge, M. J. see Beament, J. W., et al.

Berridge, M. J., et al. Advances in Insect Physiology, Vol. 17. (Serial Publication Ser.). 1984. 55.00 (ISBN 0-12-024217-6). Acad Pr.

Berridge, Michael J. & Oschman, James L. Transporting Epithelia. (Monographs in the Ultrastructure of Cells & Organisms Ser.). 1972. 27.50 (ISBN 0-12-454135-6). Acad Pr.

Berridge, P. S. Couplings to the Khyber. LC 69-10857. (Illus.). 1969. 24.95x (ISBN 0-678-05580-7). Kelley.

Berridge, Robert I., et al. Training the Community Educator. 150p. 1977. 13.20 (ISBN 0-87812-145-5). Pendell Pub.

Berridge, Virginia & Edwards, Griffith. Opium & the People: Opiate Use in Nineteenth Century England. 1982. 26.00 (ISBN 0-312-58684-1). St Martin.

Berridge, William A., et al. Purchasing Power of the Consumer: A Statistical Index. LC 75-39232. (Getting & Spending: the Consumer's Dilemma). (Illus.). 1976. Repr. of 1925 ed. 26.50x (ISBN 0-405-08009-3). Ayer Co Pubs.

Berrie, T. W. Power System Economics. (IEE Power Engineering Ser.: No. 5). 288p. 1983. pap. 69.00 (ISBN 0-906048-88-5, P0005, Pub. by Peregrinus England). Inst Elect Eng.

Berrie, W. W. Badger. A Theology of Generosity: Principles & Practice of Giving Based on Bible Teaching. 32p. 1982. pap. 2.50 (ISBN 0-8192-1293-8). Morehouse.

Berriedale-Johnson, Michelle. The Food Repair Handbook, or, How to Rescue a Disastrous Dish. (Illus.). 136p. 1985. 10.95 (ISBN 0-356-10518-0, Pub. by Salem Hse Ltd). Merrimack Pub Cir.

--Olde Englishe Recipes. (Illus.). 1984. 13.95 (ISBN 0-86188-091-9, Pub. by Salem Hse Ltd). Merrimack Pub Cir.

Berriedale-Johnson, Michelle, jt. ed. see Driver, Christopher.

Berrien, F. Kenneth. General & Social Systems. LC 68-29552. (Illus.). 1968. 25.00x (ISBN 0-8135-0585-2). Rutgers U Pr.

Berrien, William, jt. auth. see De Moraes, Borba.

Berrier, Harry H. Animal Sanitation & Disease Prevention. 2nd ed. LC 77-73472. 1977. pap. text ed. 11.50 (ISBN 0-8403-1726-3). Kendall-Hunt.

Berrigan, Daniel. Beside the Sea of Glass: The Song of the Lamb. (Classic Prayer Ser.). (Illus.). 112p. 1978. pap. 2.50 (ISBN 0-8164-2174-9, Pub. by Seabury). Winston Pr.

--Block Island. 100p. (Orig.). 1984. 20.00 (ISBN 0-87775-175-7); pap. 7.50 (ISBN 0-87775-176-5). Unicorn Pr.

--A Book of Parables. 160p. 1977. 3.00 (ISBN 0-8164-0328-7, Pub. by Seabury). Winston Pr.

--The Nightmare of God. LC 81-51877. (Sunburst Originals Ser.: No. 9). (Illus.). 144p. (Orig.). 1983. pap. 6.00 (ISBN 0-934648-08-5). Sunburst Pr.

--Portraits. (Crossroad Paperback Ser.). 160p. 1982. pap. 6.95 (ISBN 0-8245-0416-X). Crossroad NY.

--Portraits: Of Those I Love. 1982. pap. 6.95 (ISBN 0-8245-0416-X). Crossroad NY.

--Prison Poems. LC 73-76683. 124p. (Orig.). 1982. pap. 6.00 (ISBN 0-87775-149-8). Unicorn Pr.

--Steadfastness of the Saints: A Journal of Peace & War in Central & North America. LC 85-5120. 160p. 1985. pap. 7.95 (ISBN 0-88344-447-X). Orbis Bks.

--We Die Before We Live: Talking with the Very Ill. 160p. 1980. 9.95 (ISBN 0-8164-0462-3, Pub. by Seabury). Winston Pr.

--The Words Our Saviour Gave Us. 1978. pap. 4.95 (ISBN 0-87243-081-2). Templegate.

Berrigan, Daniel & Hanh, Thich N. The Raft Is Not the Shore: Conversations Toward a Buddhist-Christian Awareness. LC 75-5287. (Illus.). 128p. 1975. 12.95x (ISBN 0-8070-1124-X). Beacon Pr.

Berrigan, Frances J. Community Communications: The Role of Community Media in Development. (Reports & Papers on Mass Communication: No. 90). 50p. 1981. pap. 5.00 (ISBN 92-3-101771-3, U1093, UNESCO). Unipub.

Berrigan, Joseph R., ed. & tr. see Patavino, Rolandino.

Berrigan, Joseph R., tr. from Lat. & Eng. Fabulae Aesopicae: Renaissance Period. 1977. 8.50x (ISBN 0-87291-092-X). Coronado Pr.

Berrigan, Joseph R., Jr., jt. auth. see White, D. S.

Berrigan, Sandy. Summer Sleeper. 43p. 1981. pap. 2.00 (ISBN 0-916382-24-9). Telephone Bks.

Berrigan, Ted. Clear the Range. 1977. perfect bound in wrappers 3.50 (ISBN 0-685-80036-9, Pub. by Adventures Poet). Small Pr Dist.

--Many Happy Returns. 47p. (Orig.). 1968. pap. 2.00 (ISBN 0-87091-039-6). Corinth Bks.

--Red Wagon. LC 76-26054. 1976. 7.95 (ISBN 0-916328-05-8); signed ed. 15.00 (ISBN 0-685-93040-8); pap. 3.00 (ISBN 0-916328-01-5). Yellow Pr.

--So Going Around Cities: New & Selected Poems, 1958-1979. LC 80-10185. (Selected Works Ser.: No. 4). (Illus.). 1980. 24.95 (ISBN 0-912652-62-4); signed, numbered & boxed 75.00x (ISBN 0-912652-63-2); pap. 14.95 (ISBN 0-912652-61-6). Blue Wind.

--Train Ride. 48p. 1978. o. p. 25.00 (ISBN 0-931428-22-X); pap. 6.00 (ISBN 0-931428-21-1). Vehicle Edns.

Berrill, Deborah, jt. auth. see Berrill, Michael.

Berrill, J. N. Tunicata. 1950. 28.00 (ISBN 0-384-04065-9). Johnson Repr.

Berrill, Jacquelyn, jt. auth. see Berrill, N. J.

Berrill, K. Economic Development with Special Reference to East Asia. (International Economic Association Ser.). 1969. 35.00 (ISBN 0-312-23100-8). St Martin.

Berrill, Michael & Berrill, Deborah. A Sierra Club Naturalist's Guide to the North Atlantic Coast: Cape Cod to Newfoundland. LC 80-23086. (Naturalist's Guides Ser.). (Illus.). 512p. 1981. 24.95 (ISBN 0-87156-242-1); pap. 10.95 (ISBN 0-87156-243-X). Sierra.

Berrill, N. J. & Berrill, Jacquelyn. One Thousand & One Questions Answered About the Seashore. LC 76-12889. (The One Thousand & One Questions Ser.). (Illus.). 305p. 1976. pap. 4.95 (ISBN 0-486-23366-9). Dover.

--One Thousand & One Questions Answered About the Seashore. 14.75 (ISBN 0-8446-5558-9). Peter Smith.

Berrill, N. J., jt. auth. see Karp, Gerald.

Berriman, A. E., et al. Industrial Administration: A Series of Lectures. Chandler, Alfred D., ed. LC 79-7546. (History of Management Thought & Practice Ser.). 1980. Repr. of 1920 ed. lib. bdg. 21.00x (ISBN 0-405-12330-2). Ayer Co Pubs.

Berriman, Algernon E. Historical Metrology. LC 70-91753. Repr. of 1953 ed. lib. bdg. 19.75x (ISBN 0-8371-2424-7, BEHM). Greenwood.

Berriman, W. Thomas, et al. Capital Projects for Health Care Facilities. LC 76-15771. 224p. 1976. 37.50 (ISBN 0-912862-24-6). Aspen Systems.

Berrin, Elliott R. Investigative Photography. 1983. 4.65 (ISBN 0-686-40876-4, TR-83-1). Society Fire Protect.

Berrin, Kathleen & Seligman, Thomas K. The Bay Area Collects: Art from Africa, Oceania, & the Americas. LC 82-71433. (Illus.). 112p. 1982. pap. 5.95 (ISBN 0-88401-040-6). Fine Arts Mus.

Berrin, Kathleen & Seligman, Thomas K.intro. by. Art of the Huichol Indians. (Illus.). 1978. o. p. 22.50; pap. 9.95 (ISBN 0-8109-2160-X). Abrams.

Berring, Robert C, jt. auth. see Cohen, Morris L.

Berrington, Hugh, ed. Change in British Politics. (Illus.). 248p. 1984. 29.50x (ISBN 0-7146-3243-0, BHA-03243, F Cass Co). Biblio Dist.

Berrini, James, jt. auth. see Amendola, Joseph.

Berrios, D., tr. see Lopez Pinero, Jose M.

Berrios, G. E. & Dowson, H. Treatment & Management in Adult Psychiatry. (Illus.). 432p. 1983. 45.00 (ISBN 0-7216-0808-6, Pub. by Bailliere-Tindall). Saunders.

Berrios, Jose, jt. auth. see Sahai, Hardeo.

Berrios Burgos, Luis A., et al. Principios de Contabilidad (I) (Span.). 1983. text ed. 15.00 (ISBN 0-538-22500-9, V50). SW Pub.

--Principios de Contabilidad (II) (Span.). 1983. text ed. 15.00 (ISBN 0-538-22800-8, V80). SW Pub.

Berrios-Ortiz, A. & Selandev, R. B. Skeletal Musculature in Larval Phases of the Beetle Epicauta Segmenta, (Coleoptera, Meloidae) (Entomologica Ser.: Vol. 16). (Illus.). 1979. lib. bdg. 26.00 (ISBN 90-6193-126-6, Pub. by Junk Pubs Netherlands). Kluwer Academic.

Berrios-Ortiz, Luis. Abastos de Alimentos Para el Hogar. LC 82-2773. (Illus.). ix, 119p. (Orig.). 1982. pap. 6.25 (ISBN 0-8477-2778-5). U of PR Pr.

Berrisford, Judith. Backyards & Tiny Gardens. 160p. 1977. pap. 5.95 (ISBN 0-571-10837-7). Faber & Faber.

Berrol, Selma C. Immigrants at School: New York City, Eighteen Ninety Eight to Nineteen Fourteen. Cordasco, Francesco, ed. LC 77-90872. (Bilingual-Bicultural Education in the U. S. Ser.). 1978. lib. bdg. 40.00x (ISBN 0-405-11077-4). Ayer Co Pubs.

Berrondo, Marie. Mathematical Games. Dax, Peter & Fitzpatrick, Mariana, trs. (Illus.). 192p. 1983. 15.95 (ISBN 0-13-561399-X); pap. 6.95 (ISBN 0-13-561381-7). P-H.

Berrong, Richard M. Every Man for Himself: Rabelais's Study of Social Order & It's Dissolution. (Stanford French & Italian Studies: Vol. 38). 160p. 1985. pap. 25.00 (ISBN 0-915838-56-7). Anma Libri.

Berrurier, Diane O. le see Le Berrurier, Diane O.

Berruti, A. & Sinclair, J. C. Where to Watch Birds in Southern Africa. (Illus.). 302p. 1985. 24.95 (ISBN 0-88072-066-2). Tanager Bks.

Berry, et al. APL & Insight. (Orig.). 1978. pap. 5.25 (ISBN 0-917326-08-3). APL Pr.

Berry, A. J., ed. see European Symposium on Marine Biology, 12th.

Berry, Adrian. The Iron Sun: Crossing the Universe Through Blackholes. 1977. 7.95 (ISBN 0-525-13490-5). Dutton.

--Koyama's Diamond: A Novel of the Far Future. 1982. 11.95 (ISBN 0-533-04992-X). Vantage.

--Labyrinth of Lies. 1984. 10.95 (ISBN 0-533-05763-9). Vantage.

--The Next Ten Thousand Years: A Vision of Man's Future in the Universe. 1975. pap. 2.25 (ISBN 0-451-61601-4, ME1601, Ment). NAL.

--The Super-Intelligent Machine: An Electronic Odyssey. 192p. 1985. 14.95 (ISBN 0-224-01967-8, Pub. by Jonathan Cape). Merrimack Pub Cir.

Berry, Albert. Essays on Industrialization in Columbia. LC 83-5175. 330p. 1983. 37.95 (ISBN 0-87918-053-6). ASU Lat Am St.

Berry, Albert & Urrutia, Miguel. Income Distribution in Colombia. LC 75-18164. (Illus.). 288p. 1976. 33.00x (ISBN 0-300-01874-6). Yale U Pr.

Berry, Albert R. & Cline, William R. Agrarian Structure & Productivity in Developing Countries. LC 78-20524. 1979. text ed. 25.00x (ISBN 0-8018-2190-8). Johns Hopkins.

Berry, Alice F. Rabelais: Homo Logos. (Studies in the Romance Languages & Literature: No. 208). 130p. 1979. 13.50x (ISBN 0-8078-9208-4). U of NC Pr.

Berry, Ana M. Animals in Art. LC 79-162506. (Tower Bks.). (Illus.). 1971. Repr. of 1929 ed. 40.00x (ISBN 0-8103-3900-5). Gale.

Berry, Arthur. Short History of Astronomy: From Earliest Times Through the 19th Century. (Illus.). 1961. pap. 8.95 (ISBN 0-486-20210-0). Dover.

Berry, B. S., jt. auth. see Nowick, A. S.

Berry, Brian. Geography of Market Centers & Retail Distribution. 1967. pap. 17.95 ref. ed. (ISBN 0-13-351304-1). P-H.

Berry, Brian J. Comparative Urbanization: Divergent Paths in the Twentieth Century. 2nd ed. 235p. 1983. text ed. 15.95 (ISBN 0-312-15475-5); pap. text ed. 11.95 (ISBN 0-312-15476-3). St Martin.

Berry, Brian J. & Hankins, Thomas D. A Bibliographic Guide to the Economic Regions of the United States. LC 75-3862. 101p. 1975. Repr. of 1963 ed. lib. bdg. 18.75x (ISBN 0-8371-8086-4, BEBGU). Greenwood.

Berry, Brian J. & Horton, Frank E. Urban Environmental Management: Planning for Pollution Control. (Illus.). 448p. 1974. 34.95 (ISBN 0-13-939611-X). P-H.

Berry, Brian J., jt. auth. see Cohen, Yehoshua S.

Berry, Brian J., jt. auth. see Teicholz, Eric.

Berry, Brian J., ed. City Classification Handbook: Methods & Application. LC 71-171911. (Wiley Series in Urban Research). pap. 101.50 (ISBN 0-317-09217-0, 2022500). Bks Demand UMI.

--The Nature of Change in Geographical Ideas. LC 75-39294. (Perspectives in Geography Ser.: Vol. 3). (Illus.). 167p. 1978. 17.50 (ISBN 0-87580-063-7); pap. 7.50 (ISBN 0-87580-525-6). N Ill U Pr.

Berry, Brian J., et al. Land Use, Urban Form & Environmental Quality. LC 73-87830. (Research Papers Ser.: No. 155). (Illus.). 440p. 1974. pap. 10.00 (ISBN 0-89065-062-4). U Chicago Dept Geog.

Berry, Brian J. L. & Conkling, Edgar C. Geography of Economic Systems. ref. ed. 544p. 1976. 36.95 (ISBN 0-13-351296-7). P-H.

Berry, Brian J. L., ed. Urbanization & Counterurbanization. LC 76-15864. (Urban Affairs Annual Reviews: Vol. 11). (Illus.). 334p. 1976. 28.00 (ISBN 0-8039-0499-1); pap. 14.00 (ISBN 0-8039-0682-X). Sage.

Berry, C. & Ferguson, J. G. Chapter Six - Discharge, Resist & Special Styles. 75.00x (ISBN 0-686-98198-7, Pub. by Soc Dyers & Colour); pap. 50.00x (ISBN 0-686-98199-5). State Mutual Bk.

Berry, C. J. Amateur Winemaker Recipes. 2nd. ed. (Illus.). 172p. Date not set. pap. 4.95 (ISBN 0-900841-65-6, Pub. by Aztex Corp). Argus Bks.

--First Steps in Winemaking. rev. ed. (Illus.). 222p. Date not set. pap. 7.95 (ISBN 0-900841-66-4, Pub. by Aztex Corp). Argus Bks.

--Hints on Home Brewing. (Illus.). Date not set. pap. 1.95 (ISBN 0-900841-20-6, Pub. by Aztex Corp). Argus Bks.

--One Hundred Thirty New Winemaking Recipes. (Illus.). 135p. Date not set. pap. 5.95 (ISBN 0-900841-63-X, Pub. by Aztex Corp). Argus Bks.

--Winemaking with Canned & Dried Fruit. (Illus.). 92p. Date not set. pap. 4.95 (ISBN 0-900841-00-1, Pub. by Aztex Corp). Argus Bks.

Berry, C. L. The Effects of Estrogen Administration on the Male Breast. (Lectures in Toxicology Ser.: No. 15). (Illus.). 1982. 60.00 (ISBN 0-08-029791-9). Pergamon.

Berry, C. L., ed. Bone & Joint Disease. (Current Topics in Pathology Ser.: Vol. 71). (Illus.). 300p. 1982. 66.00 (ISBN 0-387-11235-9). Springer-Verlag.

--Dermatopathology. (Current Topics in Pathology: Vol. 74). (Illus.). 320p. 1985. 58.00 (ISBN 0-387-13174-4). Springer-Verlag.

--Paediatric Pathology. (Illus.). 710p. 1981. 82.50 (ISBN 0-387-10507-7). Springer-Verlag.

Berry, C. L. & Poswillo, D., eds. Teratology: Trends & Applications. (Illus.). 260p. 1975. 48.00 (ISBN 0-387-07333-7). Springer-Verlag.

Berry, Carmen, jt. auth. see Benun, Nancy.

Berry, Caroline F., jt. auth. see Shaw, Diana.

Berry, Cecilia R. Folk Songs of Old Vincennes. 96p. 1945. pap. 5.00 (ISBN 0-912222-08-5, R557851). FitzSimons.

Berry, Charles A. Introduction to Economics, Economics 101. rev. ed. 1972. text ed. 4.50 (ISBN 0-685-48764-4). Collegiate Pub.

--Introduction to Economics, Economics 103. rev. ed. 1973. text ed. 4.95 (ISBN 0-685-48765-2). Collegiate Pub.

Berry, Charles N. & Hovde, Christian A. Human Anatomy Atlas. (Illus.). 36p. (Orig.). 1960. pap. 2.95x (ISBN 0-8437-9083-0). Hammond Inc.

Berry, Charles R. The Reform in Oaxaca, 1856-76: A Microhistory of the Liberal Revolution. LC 80-15378. (Illus.). xx, 282p. 1981. 22.50x (ISBN 0-8032-1158-9). U of Nebr Pr.

Berry, Christopher J. Hume, Hegel & Human Nature. 1983. lib. bdg. 41.50 (ISBN 90-247-2682-4, Pub. by Martinus Nijhoff Netherlands). Kluwer Academic.

Berry, Cicely. Voice & the Actor. (Illus.). 149p. 1974. 14.95 (ISBN 0-02-510370-9). Macmillan.

Berry, D., et al. The Preservation of Open Space in the New Jersey Pinelands. (Discussion Paper Ser.: No. 73). 1974. pap. 4.50 (ISBN 0-686-32239-8). Regional Sci Res Inst.

Berry, D. B., jt. auth. see Smith, J. E.

Berry, D. R., jt. auth. see Smith, J. E.

Berry, D. R., ed. see Smith, J. E.

Berry, Dave, et al. Where is the Other News? The News Trade & the Radical Press. 30.00x (ISBN 0-906890-01-2, Pub. by Comedia England); pap. 25.00x (ISBN 0-906890-02-0). State Mutual Bk.

Berry, David. The Creative Vision of Guillaume Apollinaire: A Study in Imagination. (Stanford French & Italian Studies: Vol. 25). vi, 165p. 1982. pap. 25.00 (ISBN 0-915838-14-1). Anma Libri.

--Environmental Protection & Collective Action: The Case of Urban Open Space. (Discussion Paper Ser.: No. 61). 1973. pap. 4.50 (ISBN 0-686-32228-2). Regional Sci Res Inst.

--Idling of Farmland in the Philadelphia Region, 1930 to 1970. (Discussion Paper Ser.: No. 88). 1976. pap. 3.25 (ISBN 0-686-32254-1). Regional Sci Res Inst.

--Landscape Aesthetics & Environment Planning: A Critique of Underlying Premises. (Discussion Paper Ser.: No. 85). 1975. pap. 3.25 (ISBN 0-686-32251-7). Regional Sci Res Inst.

--Open Space Values: A Household Survey of Two Philadelphia Parks. (Discussion Paper Ser.: No. 76). 1974. pap. 4.50 (ISBN 0-686-32242-8). Regional Sci Res Inst.

Berry, David & Coughlin, Robert E. Land & Landscape in the Philadelphia Region: Two Thousand Twenty-Five. (Discussion Paper Ser.: No. 95). 1977. pap. 3.25 (ISBN 0-686-32261-4). Regional Sci Res Inst.

Berry, David & Steiker, Gene. The Concept of Justice in Regional Planning: Some Policy Implications. (Discussion Paper Ser.: No. 69). 1973. pap. 4.50 (ISBN 0-686-32235-5). Regional Sci Res Inst.

--An Economic Analysis of Transfer of Development Rights. (Discussion Paper Ser.: No. 81). 1975. pap. 3.25 (ISBN 0-686-32247-9). Regional Sci Res Inst.

--Landscape, Image & Design: A Survey of Open Space Planners. (Discussion Paper Ser.: No. 77). 1974. pap. 4.50 (ISBN 0-686-32243-6). Regional Sci Res Inst.

Berry, David, et al. The Farmer's Response to Urbanization: A Study of the Middle Atlantic States. (Discussion Paper Ser.: No. 92). 1976. pap. 3.25 (ISBN 0-686-32258-4). Regional Sci Res Inst.

Berry, David R. Biology of Yeast. (Studies in Biology: No. 140). 64p. 1982. pap. text ed. 8.95 (ISBN 0-7131-2838-0). E Arnold.

Berry, Dick. Managing Service for Results. LC 83-12821. 288p. 1983. text ed. 26.95x (ISBN 0-87664-775-1). Instru Soc.

--Understanding & Motivating the Manufacturers' Agent. 138p. 1981. 19.95 (ISBN 0-8436-0773-4). Van Nos Reinhold.

Berry, Don. A Majority of Scoundrels. new ed. LC 61-10198. 1977. pap. 3.95 (ISBN 0-89174-028-7). Comstock Edns.

--Moontrap. 1976. pap. 2.50 (ISBN 0-89174-000-7). Comstock Edns.

--To Build a Ship. new ed. LC 60-5835. 1977. pap. 2.50 (ISBN 0-89174-029-5). Comstock Edns.

--Trask. LC 60-5835. 376p. 1976. pap. 3.95 (ISBN 0-89174-001-5). Comstock Edns.

Berry, Don, jt. auth. see Sigler, Cam.

Berry, Donald, jt. auth. see Lindgren, Bernard.

Berry, Donald A. & Fristedt, Bert. Bandit Problems. 200p. 1985. text ed. 25.00 (ISBN 0-412-24810-7, 9637, Pub. by Chapman & Hall England). Methuen Inc.

Berry, Donald L. Mutuality: The Vision of Martin Buber. (SUNY Series in Philosophy). 132p. 1985. lib. bdg. 29.50x (ISBN 0-87395-929-9); pap. text ed. 9.95x (ISBN 0-87395-930-2). State U NY Pr.

Berry, Dorothea M. A Bibliographic Guide to Educational Research. 2nd ed. LC 80-20191. 224p. 1980. 16.50 (ISBN 0-8108-1351-3). Scarecrow.

Berry, Dorothea M. & Martin, Gordon P. A Guide to Writing Research Papers. LC 70-139549. (Illus.). 176p. 1972. pap. text ed. 5.95 (ISBN 0-07-005029-5). McGraw.

Berry, Duane. Psychic Manual. 1978. pap. 1.95 (ISBN 0-686-01317-4). Cathedral of Knowledge.

Berry, Edmund G. Emerson's Plutarch. LC 80-2525. Repr. of 1961 ed. 37.00 (ISBN 0-404-19250-5). AMS Pr.

Berry, Edward. Shakespeare's Comic Rites. 230p. 1984. 34.50 (ISBN 0-521-26303-4). Cambridge U Pr.

Berry, Eliot. A Poetry of Force & Darkness: The Fiction of John Hawkes. LC 79-282. (The Milford Ser.: Popular Writers of Today: Vol. 22). 1979. lib. bdg. 12.95x (ISBN 0-89370-132-7); pap. 4.95x (ISBN 0-89370-232-3). Borgo Pr.

Berry, Elizabeth, jt. auth. see Berry, William D.

Berry, Eric. Horses for the General. (gr. 7 up). 1963. pap. write for info. (ISBN 0-02-041550-8, Acorn). Macmillan.

Berry, Erick. The Land & People of Finland. rev. ed. LC 78-37246. (Portraits of the Nations Ser.). (Illus.). (gr. 6 up). 1972. PLB 10.89 (ISBN 0-397-31255-5). Lipp Jr Bks.

--The Land & People of Iceland. new rev. ed. LC 72-1569. (Portraits of the Nations Ser.). (Illus.). (gr. 6 up). 1972. lib. bdg. 10.89 (ISBN 0-397-31401-9). Lipp Jr Bks.

--When Wagon Trains Rolled to Santa Fe. LC 66-12813. (How They Lived Ser.). (Illus.). (gr. 3-6). 1966. PLB 7.98 (ISBN 0-8116-6902-5). Garrard.

Berry, Evalena. Time & the River: A History of Cleburne County. LC 82-62560. 1983. 21.50 (ISBN 0-914546-42-2). Rose Pub.

Berry, F. J. & Vaughan, D. J. Chemical Bonding: Spectroscopy in Mineral Chemistry. (Illus.). 300p. 1985. 73.00x (ISBN 0-412-25270-8, 9275, Pub. by Chapman & Hall). Methuen Inc.

Berry, Faith. Langston Hughes: Before & Beyond Harlem. 1983. 19.95 (ISBN 0-88208-156-X); pap. 12.95 (ISBN 0-88208-157-8). Lawrence Hill.

Berry, Faith, ed. see Hughes, Langston.

Berry, Francis. Poets' Grammar: Person, Time, & Mood in Poetry. LC 73-14192. 190p. 1974. Repr. of 1958 ed. lib. bdg. 18.75x (ISBN 0-8371-7147-4, BEPG). Greenwood.

Berry, Fred, tr. see Andreyev, Vladimir.

Berry, G. Medieval English Jetons. 1974. 10.00 (ISBN 0-685-51549-4, Pub by Spink & Son England). S J Durst.

Berry, G. G., tr. see Langlois, Charles V. & Seignobos, Charles.

Berry, Geoffrey. Across Northern Hills. 1981. 25.00x (ISBN 0-686-75520-0, Pub. by Westmorland Gazette). State Mutual Bk.

Berry, George R. Berry's Greek-English New Testament Lexicon with Synonyms: Numerically Coded to Strong's Exhaustive Concordance. 208p. (Orig., Gr. & Eng.). 1980. pap. 5.95 (ISBN 0-8010-0791-7). Baker Bk.

--A Dictionary of New Testament Greek Synonyms. (Gr.). 1979. 4.95 (ISBN 0-310-21161-1). Zondervan.

--Interlinear Greek-English New Testament. LC 78-54242. 1978. pap. 13.95 (ISBN 0-8054-1372-3). Broadman.

--Interlinear Greek-English New Testament. 17.95 (ISBN 0-310-21170-0). Zondervan.

Berry, George R. & Strong, James. Interlinear Greek-English New Testament. (Reference Set). 1187p. 24.95 (ISBN 0-915134-74-8). Mott Media.

Berry, George W., et al. The New Improved Good Book of Hot Springs; or, Thermal Springs List for the Western United States. LC 85-10987. 97p. 1985. Repr. lib. bdg. 19.95x (ISBN 0-89370-873-9). Borgo Pr.

Berry, Gordon & Mitchell-Kernan, C., eds. Television & the Socialization of the Minority Child. LC 81-22795. 1982. 33.00 (ISBN 0-12-093220-2). Acad Pr.

Berry, Gordon L. Strategies for Successful Teaching in Urban Schools: Ideas & Techniques from Central City Teachers. Reed, R., ed. LC 81-84973. (Orig.). 1981. 14.95 (ISBN 0-88247-642-4); pap. 9.95 (ISBN 0-88247-632-7). R & E Pubs.

Berry, Graham, jt. auth. see Kennerly, Byron.

Berry, H., jt. auth. see Maini, R. N.

Berry, Harrison M., ed. Emergency Physician's Guide to Dental Care. LC 83-3455. (Illus.). 136p. 1983. 27.50x (ISBN 0-8122-1149-9). U of Pa Pr.

Berry, Harrison M., Jr. Radiologic Anatomy of the Jaws. LC 82-60263. (Illus.). 144p. (Orig.). 1982. 37.50x (ISBN 0-8122-7870-4); pap. 14.95x (ISBN 0-8122-1130-8). U of Pa Pr.

Berry, Hedley, ed. Contemporary Topics in Pain Management: An Update on Zomepirac, No. 52. (Royal Society of Medicine International Congress & Symposium Ser.). 1983. 10.00 (ISBN 0-8089-1536-3, 790579). Grune.

Berry, Hedley, et al, eds. Rheumatology & Rehabilitation: Diagnosis & Management. (Illus.). 266p. 1983. text ed. 35.00x (ISBN 0-7099-0678-1, Pub. by Croom Helm England); pap. text ed. 18.50x (ISBN 0-7099-3204-9). Sheridan.

Berry, Henry. Pathways to Restoration: The Revitalization of the American Spirit. LC 83-90221. 144p. (Orig.). 1983. pap. 8.95 (ISBN 0-9611846-0-4). Greenfield Pr.

--Semper Fi, Mac. 448p. 1983. pap. 3.95 (ISBN 0-425-06253-8). Berkley Pub.

--Semper Fi Mac: Living Memories of the U. S. Marines in World War II. LC 81-71664. (Illus.). 370p. 1982. 16.95 (ISBN 0-87795-370-8). Arbor Hse.

Berry, Herbert. Assembly Language for IBM Compatible Processors: A Systematic Approach. 354p. 1984. pap. text ed. write for info (ISBN 0-87150-695-5, 8200). PWS Pubs.

Berry, Herbert, ed. The First Public Playhouse: The Theatre in Shoreditch, 1576-1598. 1979. pap. 10.95x (ISBN 0-7735-0340-4). McGill-Queens U Pr.

Berry, I. William. Kids on Skis. rev. ed. (Illus.). 240p. 1982. pap. 6.95 (ISBN 0-684-17782-X, ScribT). Scribner.

Berry, J. S., et al, eds. Teaching & Applying Mathematical Modelling. (Mathematics & Its Applications Ser.: 1-176). 491p. 1984. text ed. 75.00x (ISBN 0-470-20079-0). Halsted Pr.

Berry, J. T., jt. ed. see Dantzig, J. A.

Berry, J. W. Human Ecology & Cognitive Style: Comparative Studies in Cultural & Psychological Adaptation. LC 76-9803. (Cross Cultural Research & Methodology Ser.). 242p. 1976. cloth 18.95x (ISBN 0-470-15103-X). Halsted Pr.

Berry, J. W. & Dasen, P. R. Culture & Cognition: Readings in Cross-Cultural Psychology. (Illus.). 525p. 1974. pap. 12.95x (ISBN 0-416-75180-6, NO.2086). Methuen Inc.

Berry, J. W., ed. see International Conference of Selected Papers, 2nd, Kingston. Ont. August, 6-10, 1974.

Berry, James. Chain of Days. 96p. 1985. pap. 7.95 (ISBN 0-19-211964-8). Oxford U Pr.

--Tales of Old Ireland. 224p. 1985. pap. 6.95 (ISBN 0-88162-060-2, Pub. by Salem Hse Ltd). Merrimack Pub Cir.

Berry, James, ed. News for Babylon. (Chatto Poetry Ser.). 224p. 1985. pap. 8.95 (ISBN 0-7011-2797-X, Pub. by Chatto & Windus-Hogarth Pr). Merrimack Pub Cir.

Berry, Jan, jt. auth. see Roberts, Joseph.

Berry, Jason. Amazing Grace: With Charles Evers in Mississippi. 2nd ed. 370p. 1978. pap. 10.00 (ISBN 0-918784-20-4, Pub. by Legacy Pub). Three Continents.

Berry, Jason, et al. Up from the Cradle of Jazz: New Orleans Rhythm & Blues, & Beyond. (Illus.). 392p. 1984. write for info. (ISBN 0-8071-1164-3). La State U Pr.

Berry, Jean S. & Berry, John R. Race Drivers' Wives: Twenty-Four Women Talk about Their Lives. LC 82-70755. (Illus.). 181p. (Orig.). 1982. pap. 4.95 (ISBN 0-942556-00-3). Berry Pub.

Berry, Jeffrey M. Feeding Hungry People: Rulemaking in the Food-Stamp Program. LC 83-8712. 185p. 1984. text ed. 24.00 (ISBN 0-8135-1013-9). Rutgers U Pr.

--The Interest Group Society. 1984. pap. text ed. 8.95 (ISBN 0-316-09212-6). Little.

--Lobbying for the People: The Political Behavior of Public Interest Groups. LC 77-71973. 1977. 38.50x (ISBN 0-691-07588-3); pap. 10.95 (ISBN 0-691-02178-3). Princeton U Pr.

Berry, Jo. Beloved Unbeliever. 176p. (Orig.). 1985. pap. 5.95 (ISBN 0-310-42691-X, Pub. by Lamplight). Zondervan.

--Beloved Unbeliever: Loving Your Husband into the Faith. 176p. (Orig.). 1981. pap. 5.95 (ISBN 0-310-42621-9). Zondervan.

--Can You Love Yourself? LC 77-89395. 160p. 1978. pap. 4.95 (ISBN 0-8307-0579-1, 5407206). Regal.

--Growing, Sharing, Serving. LC 78-73461. 1979. pap. 3.95 (ISBN 0-89191-073-5). Cook.

--The Priscilla Principle: Making Your Life a Ministry. 256p. 1984. pap. 5.95 (ISBN 0-310-42631-6, 11218P). Zondervan.

Berry, Jo, jt. auth. see Costales, Claire.

Berry, Joan P. Reflections in a Shop Window. 1983. 3.60 (ISBN 0-89536-605-3). CSS of Ohio.

--What If...? 1985. 2.75 (ISBN 0-89536-729-7, 5813). CSS of Ohio.

Berry, John, jt. auth. see Waite Group.

Berry, John F., jt. auth. see Green, Mark.

Berry, John R., jt. auth. see Berry, Jean S.

Berry, John S. Darkness of Snow. 1974. 4.25 (ISBN 0-941490-02-5). Solo Pr.

--Those Gallant Men: On Trial in Vietnam. (Illus.). 192p. 1984. 14.95 (ISBN 0-89141-186-0). Presidio Pr.

Berry, John W., jt. ed. see Irvine, Sid H.

Berry, Jon, ed. see Herbert, Jean.

Berry, Joy. Teach Me about Bathtime. Kelly, Orly, ed. (Teach Me about Ser.). (Illus.). 34p. (ps). 1984. 3.98 (ISBN 0-88149-701-0). Peter Pan.

--Teach Me about Bedtime. Kelly, Orly, ed. (Teach Me about Ser.). (Illus.). 34p. (ps). 1984. 3.98 (ISBN 0-88149-703-7). Peter Pan.

--Teach Me about Boredom. Kelly, Orly, ed. (Teach Me about Ser.). (Illus.). 34p. (ps). 1984. 3.98 (ISBN 0-88149-707-X). Peter Pan.

--Teach Me about Crying. Kelly, Orly, ed. (Teach Me about Ser.). (Illus.). 34p. (ps). 1984. 3.98 (ISBN 0-88149-706-1). Peter Pan.

--Teach Me about Danger. Kelly, Orly, ed. (Teach Me about Ser.). (Illus.). 34p. (ps). 1984. 3.98 (ISBN 0-88149-704-5). Peter Pan.

--Teach Me about Getting Dressed. Kelly, Orly, ed. (Teach Me about Ser.). (Illus.). 34p. (ps). 1984. 3.98 (ISBN 0-88149-702-9). Peter Pan.

--Teach Me about Illness. Kelly, Orly, ed. (Teach Me about Ser.). (Illus.). 34p. (ps). 1984. 3.98 (ISBN 0-88149-705-3). Peter Pan.

--Teach Me about Mealtime. Kelly, Orly, ed. (Teach Me about Ser.). (Illus.). 34p. (ps). 1984. 3.98 (ISBN 0-88149-700-2). Peter Pan.

--Teach Me about Potty Training. Kelly, Orly, ed. (Teach Me about Ser.). (Illus.). 34p. (ps). 1984. 3.98 (ISBN 0-88149-711-8). Peter Pan.

--Teach Me about Security Objects. Kelly, Orly, ed. (Teach Me about Ser.). (Illus.). 34p. (ps). 1984. 3.98 (ISBN 0-88149-709-6). Peter Pan.

--Teach Me about Separation. Kelly, Orly, ed. (Teach Me about Ser.). (Illus.). 34p. (ps). 1984. 3.98 (ISBN 0-88149-710-X). Peter Pan.

--Teach Me about Series. Incl. Potty Training; Crying; Travel; Separation; Danger; Illness; Boredom; Mealtime; Bathtime; Getting Dressed; Bedtime; Security Objects. (Illus.). (gr. k up). 1984. pap. 2.98 ea. Peter Pan.

--Teach Me about Travelling. Kelly, Orly, ed. (Teach Me about Ser.). (Illus.). 34p. (ps). 1984. 3.98 (ISBN 0-88149-708-8). Peter Pan.

--You Can Be a Winner! Dickey, Kate, ed. LC 84-52434. (You Can Ser.). (Illus.). 48p. (gr. 1-7). 1984. 4.98 (ISBN 0-941510-27-1). Living Skills.

--You Can Get along with Difficult People! Cochran, Nancy & Motycka, Susan, eds. LC 84-52436. (You Can! Ser.). (Illus.). 48p. (gr. 1-7). 1985. 4.98 (ISBN 0-941510-45-X). Living Skills.

--You Can Get Rid of Bad Habits! Cochran, Nancy, et al, eds. LC 84-52425. (You Can Ser.). (Illus.). 48p. (gr. 1-7). 1985. 4.98 (ISBN 0-941510-32-8). Living Skills.

--You Can Handle Stress! Cochran, Nancy & Motycka, Susan, eds. LC 84-52427. (You Can Ser.). (Illus.). 48p. (gr. 1-7). 1985. 4.98 (ISBN 0-941510-31-X). Living Skills.

--You Can Make Money! Dickey, Kate, ed. LC 84-52433. (You Can Ser.). (Illus.). 48p. (gr. 1-7). 1985. write for info. (ISBN 0-941510-28-X). Living Skills.

--You Can Overcome Fear! Kelly, Orly, et al, eds. LC 84-52423. (You Can Ser.). (Illus.). 48p. (gr. 1-7). 1985. 4.98 (ISBN 0-941510-34-4). Living Skills.

--You Can Survive Trauma! Cochran, Nancy & Motycka, Susan, eds. LC 84-52426. (You Can Ser.). (Illus.). 48p. (gr. 1-7). 1985. 4.98 (ISBN 0-941510-33-6). Living Skills.

Berry, Marilyn. Help Is on the Way for Book Reports. (Skills on Studying Ser.). (Illus.). 48p. (gr. 4-6). 1984. lib. bdg. 10.00 (ISBN 0-516-03231-3). Childrens.
--Help Is on the Way for Reading Skills. (Skills on Studying Ser.). (Illus.). 48p. (gr. 4-6). 1984. lib. bdg. 10.00 (ISBN 0-516-03232-1). Childrens.
--Help Is on the Way for Schoolwork. (Skills on Studying Ser.). (Illus.). 48p. (gr. 4-6). 1984. lib. bdg. 10.00 (ISBN 0-516-03233-X). Childrens.
--Help Is on the Way for Written Reports. (Skills on Studying Ser.). (Illus.). 48p. (gr. 4-6). 1984. lib. bdg. 10.00 (ISBN 0-516-03234-8). Childrens.
--Helping Your Child Through School. 160p. 1986. price not set (ISBN 0-8499-0473-0, 0473-0). Word Bks.
Berry, Mary. Cooking with Cheese. (Illus.). 144p. 1980. 19.95 (ISBN 0-7134-1925-3, Pub. by Batsford England). David & Charles.
--Extracts of Journals & Correspondence, Seventeen Eighty-Three to Eighteen Fifty-Two, 3 vols. Lewis, Theresa, ed. LC 71-148750. Repr. of 1865 ed. Set. 115.00 (ISBN 0-404-00860-7). Vol. 1 (ISBN 0-404-00861-5). Vol. 2 (ISBN 0-404-00862-3). Vol. 3 (ISBN 0-404-00863-1). AMS Pr.
--Gifts of Food. LC 84-8519. (Illus.). 96p. 1984. Repr. of 1983 ed. 6.95 (ISBN 0-943392-55-1). Tribeca Comm.
--Mary Berry's Main Course. (Illus.). 120p. 1981. 22.50 (ISBN 0-7134-0920-7, Pub. by Batsford England); pap. 12.50 (ISBN 0-7134-0921-5). David & Charles.
Berry, Mary, ed. Cantors. LC 78-56178. (Resources of Music Ser.). 1979. pap. 5.95 (ISBN 0-521-22149-8). Cambridge U Pr.
Berry, Mary E. Hideyoshi. (Harvard East Asian Ser.: No. 97). (Illus.). 320p. 1982. text ed. 30.00x (ISBN 0-674-39025-3). Harvard U Pr.
Berry, Mary F. Military Necessity & Civil Rights Policy: Black Citizenship & the Constitution, 1861-1868. LC 76-53822. (National University Publications Ser. in American Studies). 1977. 13.95x (ISBN 0-8046-9166-5, Pub. by Kennikat). Assoc Faculty Pr.
--Stability. Security & Continuity: Mr. Justice Burton & Decision-Making in the Supreme Court, 1945-1958. LC 77-84772. (Contributions in Legal Studies Ser.: No. 1). (Illus.). viii, 296p. 1978. lib. bdg. 29.95x (ISBN 0-8371-9798-8, BSS/). Greenwood.
Berry, Mary F. & Blassingame, John W. Long Memory: The Black Experience in America. LC 80-24748. (Illus.). 512p. 1982. 29.95x (ISBN 0-19-502909-7); pap. 12.95x (ISBN 0-19-502910-0). Oxford U Pr.
Berry, MaryAnn. Answered Prayer. 40p. (Orig.). 1985. 4.95 (ISBN 0-9614947-0-0); pap. 2.50 (ISBN 0-9614947-1-9). First Love Min.
Berry, Michael S. Time: Space & Transition in Anasazi Prehistory. 112p. 1982. 20.00x (ISBN 0-87480-212-1). U of Utah Pr.
Berry, Mildred F. Language Disorders of Children: The Bases & Diagnoses. (Illus.). 1969. O.P. 27.95 (ISBN 0-13-522854-9). P-H.
--Teaching Linguistically Handicapped Children. 1980. text ed. 28.95 (ISBN 0-13-893545-9). P-H.
Berry, N. Injection Mold Handbook. 1986. cancelled (ISBN 0-442-24420-7). Van Nos Reinhold.
Berry, Nancee. At Home with Jesus. (Come Unto Me Library). 1979. pap. 1.65 (ISBN 0-8127-0236-0). Review & Herald.
--Jesus Cares for Me. (Come Unto Me Ser.). 16p. (ps-1). 1979. pap. 1.65 (ISBN 0-8127-0252-2). Review & Herald.
--When Jesus Comes. (Come Unto Me Library). 1979. pap. 1.65 (ISBN 0-8127-0210-7). Review & Herald.
Berry, Newton & Drew, Christopher. The Best of Dial-an-Atheist. 154p. (Orig.). 1982. pap. 3.95 (ISBN 0-910309-06-X). Am Atheist.
Berry, Patricia. Echo's Subtle Body: Contributions to an Archetypal Psychology. LC 82-19506. 198p. (Orig.). 1982. pap. 9.00 (ISBN 0-88214-313-1). Spring Pubns.
Berry, Paul. The Essential Self: An Introduction to Literature. (Illus.). 480p. 1975. pap. text ed. 20.95 (ISBN 0-07-005048-1). McGraw.
Berry, Paulette, jt. auth. see Warner, Laverne.
Berry, Pearlleen D. & Repass, Mary E., eds. Grandpa Says: Superstitions & Sayings of Eastern Kentucky. (Illus.). 24p. (Orig.). (gr. 7-12). pap. text ed. 2.00 (ISBN 0-940502-01-1). Foxhound Ent.
Berry, Peggy. The Corporate Couple: Living the Corporate Game. 320p. 1985. 16.95 (ISBN 0-531-09592-4). Watts.
Berry, Peter E. And the Hits Just Keep on Comin' LC 76-48921. 12.95 (ISBN 0-8156-0134-4); pap. 5.95 (ISBN 0-8156-0135-2). Syracuse U Pr.
Berry, Peter S., ed. Sourcebook for Environmental Studies. 1975. pap. text ed. 11.00x (ISBN 0-8464-0865-1). Beekman Pubs.
Berry, Philip A. A Review of the Mexican War on Christian Principles: And an Essay on the Means of Preventing War. LC 76-143427. (Peace Movement in America Ser.). ix, 87p. 1972. Repr. of 1849 ed. lib. bdg. 9.95x (ISBN 0-89198-057-1). Ozer.
Berry, R. Albert, et al, eds. Politics of Compromise: Coalition Government in Colombia. LC 78-64478. 488p. 1980. 29.95 (ISBN 0-87855-301-0); pap. text ed. 7.95x (ISBN 0-87855-723-7). Transaction Bks.
Berry, R. E. Insects & Mites of Economic Importance in the Northwest. (Illus.). 1978. spiral comb bdg. 11.95 (ISBN 0-88246-002-1). Oreg St U Bkstrs.
--Programming Language Translation. (Computers & Their Applications Ser.). 175p. 1983. pap. 28.95x (ISBN 0-470-27468-9). Halsted Pr.
Berry, R. E. & Meekings, B. A. A Book on C. (Computer Science Ser.). (Illus.). 210p. (Orig.). 1984. pap. text ed. 22.50x (ISBN 0-333-36821-5). Scholium Intl.
Berry, R. G., jt. auth. see Covington, M. V.
Berry, R. J. Charles Darwin: A Commemoration 1882-1982. 140p. 1982. 19.00 (ISBN 0-12-093180-X). Acad Pr.
--Inheritance & Natural History. (The New Natural Ser.). (Illus.). 1978. 14.95 (ISBN 0-8008-4195-6). Taplinger.
--Neo-Darwinism. (Studies in Biology: No. 144). 72p. 1982. pap. text ed. 8.95 (ISBN 0-7131-2849-6). E Arnold.
--The People of Orkney. 250p. 59.00x (ISBN 0-907618-08-1, Pub. by Orkney Pr Uk). State Mutual Bk.
Berry, R. J., ed. Computerized Tomographic Scanners on Radiotheraopy in Europe. 1980. 80.00x (ISBN 0-686-69944-0, Pub. by Brit Inst Radiology England). State Mutual Bk.
Berry, R. J., jt. ed. see Bates, T. D.
Berry, R. J., jt. ed. see Bonner, W. N.
Berry, R. J., ed. see Zoological Society of London - 26th Symposium.
Berry, R. L. Adventures in the Land of Canaan. 128p. pap. 1.00 (ISBN 0-686-29096-8). Faith Pub Hse.
--Around Old Bethany. 83p. pap. 0.75 (ISBN 0-686-29097-6). Faith Pub Hse.
--Steps Heavenward. 123p. pap. 1.00 (ISBN 0-686-29142-5). Faith Pub Hse.
Berry, R. M. Plane Geometry & Other Affairs of the Heart: Stories. LC 84-8172. 189p. 1985. 12.95 (ISBN 0-914590-88-X); pap. 6.95 (ISBN 0-914590-89-8). Fiction Coll.
Berry, R. Stephen, et al. Physical Chemistry. LC 79-790. 1281p. 1980. text ed. 51.50 comb. cloth (ISBN 0-471-04829-1); pap. 17.95 solutions manual (ISBN 0-471-04844-5). Wiley.
--Physical Chemistry, 3 pts. Incl. Pt. 1. The Structure of Matter. 521p. 1980. pap. text ed. 29.50 (ISBN 0-471-05824-6); Pt. 2. Matter in Equilibrium Statistical Mechanics & Thermodynamics. 585p. 1980. pap. text ed. 30.00 (ISBN 0-471-05825-4); Pt. 3. Physical & Chemical Kinetics. 281p. 1980. pap. text ed. 24.95 (ISBN 0-471-05823-8). 1980. Wiley.
Berry, Ralph. Changing Styles in Shakespeare. 128p. 1981. text ed. 12.95x (ISBN 0-04-822042-6). Allen Unwin.
--Shakespeare & the Awareness of Audience. LC 84-9772. 176p. 1985. 21.00 (ISBN 0-312-71423-8). St Martin.
--The Shakespearean Metaphor: Studies in Language & Form. 128p. 1978. 17.50x (ISBN 0-8476-6047-8). Rowman.
--Shakespearean Structures. 164p. 1981. 28.50x (ISBN 0-389-20173-1, 06949). B&N Imports.
Berry, Ralph E. & Boland, James P. The Economic Cost of Alcohol Abuse. LC 76-19642. (Illus.). 1977. 13.95 (ISBN 0-02-903080-3). Free Pr.
Berry, Raymond & Gilbert, C. H., Jr. Raymond Berry's Complete Guide to Coaching Pass Receivers. LC 82-2140. 180p. 1982. 15.95 (ISBN 0-13-753210-5, Parker). P-H.
Berry, Reginald, et al. Smith-Seventeen. LC 64-9367. 1975. pap. 3.00 (ISBN 0-912292-36-9). The Smith.
Berry, Richard. Build Your Own Telescope: Complete Plans for Five High-Quality Telescopes That Anyone Can Build. (Illus.). 240p. 1985. 25.00 (ISBN 0-317-19458-5). Scribner.
Berry, Richard C. Industrial Marketing for Results. LC 80-18222. (Illus.). 144p. 1981. text ed. 25.00 (ISBN 0-201-00075-X). Addison-Wesley.
Berry, Richard L. A Revision of the North American Genus Argoporis: Coleoptera Tenebrionidae Cevenopini. 1980. 10.00 (ISBN 0-86727-089-6). Ohio Bio Survey.
Berry, Richard M. Plastics Additives Marketing Guide & Company Directory. LC 77-150351. 125p. 1972. pap. 7.95 (ISBN 0-87762-058-X). Technomic.
Berry, Richard W., jt. auth. see Tver, David F.
Berry, Robert C. & Wong, Glenn M. Law & Business of the Sports Industries, 2 vols. LC 82-22833. 1280p. 1985. Vol. I. 45.00 ea. Vol. II (ISBN 0-86569-081-2) (ISBN 0-86569-102-9). Auburn Hse.
Berry, Robert C., et al. Labor Relations in Professional Sports. 376p. 1985. professional reference 39.95 (ISBN 0-88410-950-X). Ballinger Pub.
Berry, Roger J., jt. ed. see Holm, Niels W.
Berry, Roger L. God's World-His Story. (Christian Day School Ser.). 1976. 18.80x (ISBN 0-87813-911-7); tchr's guide 19.65x (ISBN 0-87813-914-1). Christian Light.
Berry, Roger W. Creative Writing: A Review of the Study at the College Level. 1984. 12.95 (ISBN 0-533-06025-7). Vantage.
Berry, Roland. Mechanical Giants. (Illus.). 40p. (gr. 3-6). 1982. 9.95 (ISBN 0-241-10765-2, Pub. by Hamish Hamilton England). David & Charles.
Berry, Romeyn. Stoneposts in the Sunset. 1950. 5.00 (ISBN 0-87282-011-4). CHB-ALF.
Berry, S. G., jt. auth. see Ferguson, J. T.
Berry, Sara S. Fathers Work for Their Sons: Accumulation, Mobility, & Class Formation in an Extended Yoruba Community. LC 84-122. 250p. 1985. 32.50x (ISBN 0-520-05164-5). U of Cal Pr.
Berry, Stephen A. The Battle for Terra Two. 256p. (Orig.). 1986. pap. 2.95 (ISBN 0-8125-3191-4, Dist. by Warner Pub Services & St. Martin). Tor Bks.
--The Biofab War. 192p. 1984. pap. 2.75 (ISBN 0-441-06226-1, Pub. by Ace Science Fiction). Ace Bks.
Berry, T. Jazz: The Inside Track. 256p. 1985. pap. 18.95 (ISBN 0-07-005064-3). McGraw.
Berry, Thomas. Buddhism. LC 75-10518. 1967. pap. 5.95 (ISBN 0-89012-017-X). Anima Pubns.
--Management: The Managerial Ethos & the Future of Planet Earth. (Teilhard Studies). 1980. pap. 2.00 (ISBN 0-89012-016-1). Anima Pubns.
--The New Story. (Teilhard Studies). 1978. 2.00 (ISBN 0-89012-012-9). Anima Pubns.
--Teilhard in the Ecological Age. (Teilhard Studies). 1982. 2.00 (ISBN 0-89012-032-3). Anima Pubns.
--Western Prices Before Eighteen Sixty-One: A Study of the Cincinnati Market. (Harvard Economie Studies: Vol. 74). Repr. of 1943 ed. 38.00 (ISBN 0-384-04075-6). Johnson Repr.
Berry, Thomas E. The Craft of Writing. 1974. pap. text ed. 4.95 (ISBN 0-07-005051-1). McGraw.
--Journalism in America: An Introduction to the News Media. (Communication Arts Bks.). 1976. 14.50 (ISBN 0-8038-3712-7); pap. text ed. 8.50x (ISBN 0-8038-3713-5). Hastings.
--Most Common Mistakes in English Usage. 1971. pap. 4.95 (ISBN 0-07-005053-8). McGraw.
--Plots & Characters in Major Russian Fiction, Vol. 1: Pushkin, Lermontov, Turgenev, & Tolstoy. (Plots & Characters Ser.). xiv, 226p. 1977. 20.00 (ISBN 0-208-01584-1, Archon). Shoe String.
Berry, Thomas, Sr. Western Prices Before Eighteen Sixty-One: A Study of the Cincinnati Market. 1943. 35.00x (ISBN 0-317-27656-5). Elliots Bks.
Berry, Timothy. Working Smart with Electronic Spreadsheets. 1985. pap. 18.95 (ISBN 0-8104-6203-6). Hayden.
Berry, Turner W. & Johnson, A. F. Catalogue of Specimens of Printing Types by English & Scottish Printers & Founders 1665-1830. LC 78-74404. (Nineteenth-Century Book Arts & Printing History Ser.: Vol. 12). 1980. lib. bdg. 46.00 (ISBN 0-8240-3886-X). Garland Pub.
Berry, Virginia G., ed. & tr. see Odo of Deuil.
Berry, W. & Roberts, J., eds. International Symposium on Materials in Nuclear Power Systems - Water Reactors: Proceedings. LC 83-63121. (Illus.). 978p. 75.00 (ISBN 0-915567-00-8); members 60.00 (ISBN 0-317-18667-1). Natl Corrosion Eng.
Berry, W., et al, illus. Sierra Wildlife Coloring Book. 16p. 1971. pap. 1.00 (ISBN 0-939666-15-4). Yosemite Natl Hist.
Berry, W. B. Graptolite Faunas of the Marathon Region, West Texas. (Pub Ser.: 6005). (Illus.). 179p. 1960. 3.00 (ISBN 0-318-03312-7). Bur Econ Geology.
Berry, W. B., ed. see En-Zhi, Mu, et al.
Berry, W. Dennis. A Guide to Training the Swimming Pool Lifeguard. (Illus.). 75p. (Orig.). 1984. pap. text ed. 3.95x (ISBN 0-89641-140-0). American Pr.
Berry, W. Grinton. John Milton. LC 73-10007. 1909. lib. bdg. 17.50 (ISBN 0-8414-3150-7). Folcroft.
Berry, W. Grinton, ed. see Foxe, John.
Berry, W. T., Jr., et al. Basic Animal Science. 6th ed. (Illus.). 187p. 1980. Repr. wire coil lab. manual 6.95x (ISBN 0-89641-052-8). American Pr.
Berry, Wallace. Form in Music. 2nd ed. (Illus.). 464p. 1986. text ed. 27.95 (ISBN 0-13-329285-1). P-H.
--Form in Music: An Examination of Traditional Techniques of Musical Structure & Their Application in Historical & Contemporary Styles. 1966. text ed. 29.95 (ISBN 0-13-329201-0). P-H.
Berry, Wallace & Chudacoff, Edward. Eighteenth Century Imitative Counterpoint: Music for Analysis. (Orig.). 1969. pap. 29.95 (ISBN 0-13-246843-3). P-H.
Berry, Wendell. Clearing. LC 76-27422. 1977. pap. 3.95 (ISBN 0-15-618051-0, Harv). HarBraceJ.
--The Collected Poems of Wendell Berry 1957-1982. 288p. 1985. 16.50 (ISBN 0-86547-189-4). N Point Pr.
--A Continuous Harmony: Essays Cultural & Agricultural. LC 74-17016. 182p. 1975. pap. 4.95 (ISBN 0-15-622575-1, Harv). HarBraceJ.
--The Country of Marriage. LC 75-5941. 53p. 1975. pap. 6.95 (ISBN 0-15-622697-9, Harv). HarBraceJ.
--Farming: A Hand Book. LC 71-118828. 1971. pap. 2.95 (ISBN 0-15-630171-7, Harv). HarBraceJ.
--The Gift of Good Land: Further Essays Cultural & Agricultural. LC 81-81507. 304p. 1981. 18.00 (ISBN 0-86547-051-0); pap. 9.50 (ISBN 0-86547-052-9). N Point Pr.
--The Memory of Old Jack. LC 75-6530. 223p. 1975. pap. 4.95 (ISBN 0-15-658670-3, Harv). HarBraceJ.
--Nathan Coulter. 192p. 1985. 8.50 (ISBN 0-86547-184-3). N Point Pr.
--A Part. LC 80-18268. 104p. 1980. pap. 6.00 (ISBN 0-86547-008-1). N Point Pr.
--A Place on Earth. Rev. ed. LC 82-81478. 352p. 1983. pap. 15.00 (ISBN 0-86547-083-9). N Point Pr.
--Recollected Essays, Nineteen Sixty-Five to Nineteen Eighty. LC 80-28812. 352p. 1981. 18.00 (ISBN 0-86547-025-1); pap. 9.50 (ISBN 0-86547-026-X). N Point Pr.
--Sayings & Doings. LC 75-39229. 1975. 5.00 (ISBN 0-917788-03-6). Gnomon Pr.
--Standing by Words: Essays. 224p. (Orig.). 1983. 20.00 (ISBN 0-86547-121-5); pap. 10.50 (ISBN 0-86547-122-3). N Point Pr.
--The Unsettling of America. 1978. pap. 6.95 (ISBN 0-380-40147-9, 64972-1). Avon.
--The Unsettling of America: Culture & Agriculture. LC 77-3729. 238p. 1977. 14.95 (ISBN 0-87156-194-8). Sierra.
--The Wheel: Poems. LC 82-81482. 72p. 1982. 10.00 (ISBN 0-86547-078-2); pap. 5.00 (ISBN 0-86547-079-0). N Point Pr.
Berry, William. The Great North American Ski Book. (Illus.). 480p. 1984. pap. 14.95 (ISBN 0-684-18207-6). Scribner.
Berry, William & Feldman, Stanley. Multiple Regression in Practice. 1985. 5.00 (ISBN 0-8039-2054-7). Sage.
Berry, William, jt. auth. see Gray, Jane.
Berry, William, et al. Master Production Scheduling: Principle & Practice. 184p. 1979. 29.00 (ISBN 0-935406-21-2). Am Prod & Inventory.
Berry, William D. & Berry, Elizabeth. Mammals of the San Francisco Bay Region. (California Natural History Guides: No. 2). 1959. 14.95x (ISBN 0-520-03088-5); pap. 3.95 (ISBN 0-520-00116-8). U of Cal Pr.
Berry, William G. John Milton. 1978. Repr. of 1909 ed. lib. bdg. 20.00 (ISBN 0-8495-0407-4). Arden Lib.
Berry, William L., jt. ed. see Montgomery, Douglas C.
Berry, William L., et al. Management Decision Sciences: Cases & Readings. 1980. 27.95x (ISBN 0-256-02219-4). Irwin.
Berry, William R., ed. Clinical Dysarthria. LC 82-19867. (Illus.). 330p. 1983. pap. 27.50 (ISBN 0-933014-76-7). College-Hill.
Berryhill, Clint. Rifles & Romance. 200p. 1983. pap. 5.00 (ISBN 0-942698-09-6). Trends & Events.
--Take a Chance on Me. 268p. 1983. pap. 5.00 (ISBN 0-942698-09-6). Trends & Events.
Berryhill, Ken. Funny Business: A Professional Guide to Becoming a Comic. (Illus.). 144p. 1985. pap. 9.95 (ISBN 0-13-345406-1). P-H.
Berryman, Alan A. Population Systems: A General Introduction. LC 80-26167. 237p. 1981. 18.95x (ISBN 0-306-40589-X, Plenum Pr). Plenum Pub.
Berryman, Brantley Jo. Circe's Craft: Ezra Pound's "Hugh Selwyn Mauberley". Litz, Walton, ed. LC 83-5936. (Studies in Modern Literature: No. 19). 258p. 1983. 39.95 (ISBN 0-8357-1431-4). UMI Res Pr.
Berryman, Charles. From Wilderness to Wasteland: The Trial of the Puritan God in the American Imagination. (National University Publications, Literary Criticism Ser.). 1979. 19.50x (ISBN 0-8046-9235-1, Pub. by Kennikat). Assoc Faculty Pr.
Berryman, Gregg. Designing Creative Resumes & Portfolios. (Illus.). 175p. 1985. pap. 14.95 (ISBN 0-86576-047-0). W Kaufmann.
--Notes on Graphic Design & Visual Communication. rev. ed. (Illus.). 48p. 1983. pap. 4.95 (ISBN 0-86576-072-1). W Kaufmann.
Berryman, Gwen. Doris Archer's Farm Cookery. 14.50 (ISBN 0-392-05381-0, LTB). Sportshelf.
Berryman, Jack H. & Markley, Merle, eds. International Associaiton of Fish & Wildlife Agencies 73rd Convention, 1983: Proceedings. 300p. lib. bdg. 15.00 (ISBN 0-932108-10-5). Iafwa.
Berryman, John. Berryman's Sonnets. 121p. 1967. 5.50 (ISBN 0-374-11204-5); pap. 4.95 (ISBN 0-374-50800-3). FS&G.
--The Dream Songs. 427p. 1969. 17.50 (ISBN 0-374-14397-8); pap. 8.95 (ISBN 0-374-51670-7). FS&G.
--The Freedom of the Poet. 400p. 1976. 12.50 (ISBN 0-374-15848-7); pap. 6.95 (ISBN 0-374-51392-9). FS&G.
--Henry's Fate & Other Poems. Haffenden, John, selected by. 112p. 1977. 7.95 (ISBN 0-374-16950-0). FS&G.
--His Toy, His Dream, His Rest. 317p. 1968. 6.50 (ISBN 0-374-17028-2). FS&G.
--A Homage to Mistress Bradstreet & Other Poems. LC 68-24596. 1968. pap. 3.50 (ISBN 0-374-50660-4). FS&G.
--Homage to Mistress Bradstreet: Drawings by Ben Shahn. 52p. 1956. 8.95 (ISBN 0-374-17252-8). FS&G.
--Love & Fame. 96p. 1970. 12.95 (ISBN 0-374-19233-2). FS&G.
--Recovery. LC 72-84779. 1973. 12.95 (ISBN 0-374-24817-6); pap. 6.95 (ISBN 0-374-51606-5). FS&G.
--Short Poems. 120p. 1967. 4.95 (ISBN 0-374-26328-0). FS&G.
--Stephen Crane: A Critical Biography. 365p. 1982. pap. 9.25 (ISBN 0-374-51732-0). FS&G.

Berryman, Philip. The Religious Roots of Rebellion: Christians in Central American Revolutions. LC 83-19343. (Orig.). 1984. pap. 19.95 (ISBN 0-88344-105-5). Orbis Bks.

Berryman, Phillip. Inside Central America: The Essential Facts Past & Present on El Salvador, Nicaragua, Honduras, Guatemala, & Costa Rica. LC 84-43002. 166p. 1985. pap. 5.95 (ISBN 0-394-72943-9). Pantheon.

--What's Wrong in Central America, 1983. 75p. pap. write for info. (ISBN 0-910082-10-3). Am Fr Serv Comm.

Berryman, Phillip, tr. see Sobrino, Jon & Pico, Juan H.

Berryman-Fink, Cynthia, ed. see Conference on Communication, Language & Sex, 1st Annual.

Berrywell, Clint. Survivors. 196p. 1983. pap. 5.00 (ISBN 0-942698-13-4). Trends & Events.

Bers, L., ed. see American Mathematical Society Special Session, San Francisco, Jan, 1974.

Bers, L., et al. Contributions to the Theory of Partial Differential Equations. (Annals of Math Studies). Repr. of 1954 ed. 21.00 (ISBN 0-527-02749-9). Kraus Repr.

Bers, Lipman see Knopp, Konrad.

Bers, Lipman, et al. Partial Differential Equations. LC 63-19664. (Lectures in Applied Mathematics Ser.: Vol. 3a). 343p. 1981. pap. 33.00 (ISBN 0-8218-0049-3, LAM-3-1). Am Math.

Bers, Melvin K. Union Policy & the Older Worker. LC 76-14986. 1976. Repr. of 1957 ed. lib. bdg. 35.00x (ISBN 0-8371-8655-2, BEUP). Greenwood.

Bers, Victor. Greek Poetic Syntax in the Classical Age. LC 82-20309. (Yale Classical Monographs: No. 5). 240p. 1984. 21.00x (ISBN 0-300-02812-1). Yale U Pr.

Bersani, Carl A. Crime & Delinquency: A Reader in Selected Areas. (Illus.). 1970. pap. 14.95 (ISBN 0-02-309100-2, 30910). Macmillan.

Bersani, Leo. Baudelaire & Freud. LC 76-55562. (Quantum Ser.). 1978. 18.50x (ISBN 0-520-03402-3). U of Cal Pr.

--The Death of Stephane Mallarme. LC 81-3907. (Cambridge Studies in French). 140p. 1982. 22.95 (ISBN 0-521-23863-3). Cambridge U Pr.

--A Future for Astyanax: Character & Desire in Literature. (A Morningside Book). 350p. 1984. 30.00x (ISBN 0-231-05938-8); pap. 10.00x (ISBN 0-231-05939-6). Columbia U Pr.

--A Future for Astynax. 1984. 30.00x (ISBN 0-317-18767-8); pap. 9.95 (ISBN 0-317-18768-6). Columbia U Pr.

Bersani, Leo & Dutoit, Ulysse. The Forms of Violence: Narrative in Assyrian Art & Modern Culture. (Illus.). 160p. 1985. 19.95 (ISBN 0-8052-3973-1). Schocken.

Bersani, Leo, ed. see Flaubert, Gustave.

Berscheid, Ellen & Walster, Elaine H. Interpersonal Attraction. 2nd ed. LC 77-77726. (Illus.). 231p. 1978. pap. text ed. 12.95 (ISBN 0-394-34805-2, RanC). Random.

Berschin, Walter. Bonizo von Sutri: Leben und Werk. (Beitraege Zur Geschichte und Quellenkunde des Mittelalters Ser. Bd 2). 200p. 1972. 38.80x (ISBN 3-11-001758-X). De Gruyter.

Berse, P. A., ed. see Fraser, G. M. & Blockley, J.

Berselli, Costante & Gharib, Georges, eds. Sing the Joys of Mary. Jenkins, Phil, tr. from Italian. 136p. (Orig., Eng.). 1983. pap. 7.95 (ISBN 0-8192-1329-2). Morehouse.

Bersentes, Harry. Velanidia-The Acorn Tree: The History of a Greek Peasant Family. 1985. 14.95 (ISBN 0-533-06536-4). Vantage.

Bershad, Carol & Bernick, Deborah. Bodyworks: The Kids' Guide to Food & Physical Fitness. (Illus.). 240p. (gr. 5-9). 1981. PLB 8.99 (ISBN 0-394-94752-5). Random.

--From the Inside Out: A Kid's Guide to Food & Physical Fitness. LC 80-26741. (From the Inside Out Ser.). (Illus.). 220p. (Orig.). 1979. pap. text ed. 7.50 (ISBN 0-913723-02-9); 14.95 (ISBN 0-913723-03-7). Mgmt Sci Health.

Bershad, Carol & DiMella, Nancy. The Changer & the Changed: A Working Guide to Personal Change. LC 83-207297. (Illus.). 142p. (Orig.). (gr. 9-12). 1983. pap. 11.95 (ISBN 0-913723-04-5); tchr's. guide 13.95 (ISBN 0-913723-05-3). Mgmt Sci Health.

Bershad, Carol, jt. auth. see Bernick, Deborah.

Bershader, Daniel, ed. see International Shock Tube Symposium, 9th, Stanford Univ., 1973.

Bershadsky, Luba & Millington, Ada. I Know His Touch. LC 83-72042. 192p. (Orig.). 1984. pap. 6.95 (ISBN 0-89107-299-3, Crossway Bks). Good News.

--I Know His Touch. 240p. 1985. pap. 2.95 (ISBN 0-345-32164-2). Ballantine.

Bershas, Henry N., jt. ed. see Sullivan, Howard A.

Bersoff, Edward, et al. Software Configuration Management: An Investment in Product Integrity. 1980. 36.95 (ISBN 0-13-821769-6). P-H.

Berson, Dvera & Roy, Sander. Pain-Free Arthritis. (Illus.). 130p. 1982. 15.95x (ISBN 0-9609608-0-5). S&J Books.

Berson, Ginny. Making a Show of It: A Guide to Concert Production. Worley, Jo-Lynne, et al, eds. 100p. (Orig.). 1980. pap. text ed. 4.95 (ISBN 0-686-97699-1). Redwood Records.

Berson, Harold. Charles & Claudine. LC 79-23693. (Illus.). (gr. 1-4). 1980. 9.95 (ISBN 0-02-709230-5). Macmillan.

--Why the Jackal Won't Speak to the Hedgehog. LC 69-13439. (Illus.). 32p. (ps-3). 1969. 6.95 (ISBN 0-395-28768-5, Clarion). HM.

Berson, Misha, ed. Theatre Directory of the San Francisco Bay Area, 1983-1984. 138p. 1983. pap. 9.00 (ISBN 0-9605896-2-7). Theatre Ctr Bay.

Berson, Misha & Hey, Betty, eds. Theatre Directory of the San Francisco Bay Area 1985-1986. 138p. 1985. pap. 10.00 (ISBN 0-9605896-3-5). Theatre Ctr Bay.

Berson, Misha, jt. ed. see Crane, Debra J.

Berson, Ruth, jt. auth. see Bennett, Anna G.

Berson, S. A. & Yalow, R. S., eds. Peptide Hormones, 2 Vols. LC 72-93088. (Methods in Investigative & Diagnostic Endocrinology: Vol. 2). 1200p. 1973. Set. 285.00 (ISBN 0-444-10453-4, North-Holland). Elsevier.

Berssen, William. Pacific Boating Almanac 1984: Northern California & Nevada Edition. annual ed. 448p. 1983. pap. 9.95 (ISBN 0-930030-21-4). Western Marine Ent.

--Pacific Boating Almanac 1984: Oregon, Washington, British Columbia & Alaska Edition. annual ed. 448p. 1983. pap. 9.95 (ISBN 0-930030-22-2). Western Marine Ent.

--Pacific Boating Almanac 1984: Southern California, Arizona, Baja. LC 76-646468. (Illus.). 448p. 1984. pap. 9.95 (ISBN 0-930030-33-8). Western Marine Ent.

--Pacific Boating Almanac, 1986: Northern California & Nevada. LC 76-646468. (Illus.). 448p. 1986. pap. 9.95 (ISBN 0-930030-41-9). Western Marine Ent.

--Pacific Boating Almanac, 1986: Pacific Northwest & Alaska. LC 76-646468. (Illus.). 448p. 1986. pap. 9.95 (ISBN 0-930030-42-7). Western Marine Ent.

--Pacific Boating Almanac 1986: Southern California, Arizona & Baja California. LC 76-646468. (Illus.). 448p. 1986. pap. 9.95 (ISBN 0-930030-40-0). Western Marine Ent.

Berssenbrugge, Mei-Mei. The Heat Bird. (Burning Deck Poetry Ser.). 74p. 1983. pap. 4.00 (ISBN 0-930901-03-7). Burning Deck.

--Rat Pack Steve. (Contact II Chapbook Ser.). 24p. (Orig.). 1983. pap. 3.00 (ISBN 0-936556-09-9, Pub by Inland Book Co). Contact Two.

Berssenbrugge, Mei Mei. Summits Move with the Tide. 2nd ed. 70p. (Orig.). 1983. pap. 4.00 (ISBN 0-912678-56-9). Greenfld Rev Pr.

Berst, Barbara J. I Love Softball. LC 84-62470. (Illus.). 72p. (Orig.). (gr. 3-6). 1985. 8.95 (ISBN 0-9614126-1-5); pap. 4.25 (ISBN 0-9614126-0-7). Natl Lilac Pub.

Berst, Charles A. Bernard Shaw & the Art of Drama. LC 72-93625. 363p. 1973. 24.95 (ISBN 0-252-00258-X). U of Ill Pr.

Berst, Charles A., ed. Shaw & Religion. LC 81-956. (Shaw: the Annual of Bernard Shaw Studies: Vol 1). 264p. 1981. 20.50x (ISBN 0-271-00280-8). Pa St U Pr.

Berst, Jesse, jt. auth. see Segal, Hillel.

Berst, Jessie. Computhink Guide to Spreadsheet. LC 83-82557. 168p. 1983. pap. 11.95 (ISBN 0-672-22164-0, 22164). Sams.

--The Computhink Guide to Word Processing. LC 83-50169. 192p. 1983. pap. 12.95 (ISBN 0-672-22069-5, 22069). Sams.

Berstein, Gail L. Haruko's World: A Japanese Farm Woman & Her Community. LC 82-61783. (Illus.). xviii, 199p. 1985. pap. 6.95 (ISBN 0-8047-1287-5, SP 117). Stanford U Pr.

Berstein, Joan Z. & Harris, Lucy R. Health Maintenance Organizations: Opportunities & Problems. (Health Care Economics & Technology Ser.). 190p. 1983. 32.95x (ISBN 0-86621-004-0). F&S Pr.

Berstein, M. D. & Iotti, R. C., eds. Advances In Containment Design & Analysis. 127p. 1982. 30.00 (G00214). ASME.

Berstein, Richard K. Diabetes: The Glucograf Method for Normalizing Blood Sugar. (Illus.). 320p. 1981. 15.95 (ISBN 0-517-54155-6). Crown.

--Diabetes: The Glucograf Method for Normalizing Blood Sugar. LC 83-24257. 320p. 1984. pap. 8.95 (ISBN 0-87477-314-8). J P Tarcher.

Berstein, Samuel. French Political & Intellectual History. LC 83-4731. 224p. 1983. pap. text ed. 24.95 (ISBN 0-87855-938-8). Transaction Bks.

Berstel, Jean & Perrin, Dominiqbe. Theory of Codes. (Pure & Applied Mathematics Ser.). Date not set. 60.00 (ISBN 0-12-093420-5). Acad Pr.

Berston, Hyman M. California Real Estate Practice. 4th ed. 1981. 25.95x (ISBN 0-256-02539-8). Irwin.

--California Real Estate Principles. 4th ed. 1983. 25.95x (ISBN 0-256-02725-0). Irwin.

Berston, Hyman M. & Fisher, Paul. Collegiate Business Mathematics. 3rd ed. 1982. 18.95x (ISBN 0-256-02762-5). Irwin.

Bersuker, I. B. The Jahn-Teller Effect: A Bibliographic Review. 600p. 1983. 85.00x (ISBN 0-306-65206-4, IFI-Plenum). Plenum Pub.

--The Jahn-Teller Effect & Vibronic Interactions in Modern Chemistry. (Modern Inorganic Chemistry Ser.). 334p. 1984. 45.00x (ISBN 0-306-41319-1, Plenum Pr). Plenum Pub.

Bert, C. W., ed. Developments in Mechanics: Proceedings of the 14th Midwestern Mechanics Conference, Vol. 8. LC 61-17719. (Illus.). 626p. 39.50 (ISBN 0-8061-1291-3). U of Okla Pr.

--Mechanics of Bimodulus Materials, Bk. No. G00150. LC 90-75422. (Applied Mechanics Division Ser.: Vol. 33). 96p. 1979. 18.00 (ISBN 0-686-62957-4). ASME.

Bert, Diana, et al. Having a Baby. (Illus.). 384p. (Orig.). 1984. pap. 19.95 (ISBN 0-385-29334-8). Delacorte.

Bert, Edmund. An Approved Treatise of Hawkes & Hawking Divided into Three Bookes. LC 68-54618. (English Experience Ser.: No. 23). 110p. 1968. Repr. of 1619 ed. 16.00 (ISBN 90-221-0023-5). Walter J Johnson.

Berta, I., ed. see Horvath, T.

Berta, Michel. De l'androgynie dans les Rougon-Macquart et deux autres etudes sur Zola. (American University Studies II(Romances Languages & Literature): Vol. 22). 158p. 1985. text ed. 21.00 (ISBN 0-8204-0198-6). P Lang Pubs.

Bertaccini, G., ed. Mediators & Drugs in Gastrointestinal Motility II: Endogenous & Exogenous Agents. (Handbook of Experimental Pharmacology: Vol. 59, II). (Illus.). 460p. 1982. 141.00 (ISBN 0-387-11333-9). Springer-Verlag.

--Meditators & Drugs in Gastrointestinal Motility I: Morphological Basis & Neurophysiological Control. (Handbook of Experimental Pharmacology Ser.: Vol. 59, I). (Illus.). 468p. 1982. 160.00 (ISBN 0-387-11296-0). Springer-Verlag.

Bertagnolli, Leslie. Family Photographs. Bensen, Robert, ed. (Chapbook Ser.: No. 1). 24p. 1978. pap. 2.00 (ISBN 0-932884-00-8). Red Herring.

Bertagnolli, Olivia & Rackham, Jeff, eds. Creativity & the Writing Process. 211p. 1982. pap. text ed. 9.75x (ISBN 0-673-15732-6). Scott F.

Bertalanffy, Ludwig Van see Von Bertalanffy, Ludwig.

Bertalanffy, Ludwig von see Von Bertalanffy, Ludwig.

Bertalanffy, Ludwig von see Von Bertalanffy, Ludwig.

Bertalanffy, Ludwig Von see Von Bertalanffy, Ludwig.

Bertalanffy, Maria von see Von Bertalanffy, Ludwig.

Bertaut, J. Paris, Eighteen Seventy to Nineteen Thiry-Five. Repr. of 1936 ed. 28.00 (ISBN 0-527-07200-1). Kraus Repr.

Bertaux, Daniel, ed. Biography & Society: The Life History Approach in the Social Sciences. (Sage Studies in International Sociology: Vol. 23). 308p. 1981. 28.00 (ISBN 0-8039-9800-7). Sage.

Bertaux, Felix. A Panorama of German Literature from 1871-1931. Traunstine, John J., tr. from Fr. LC 73-132940. 1971. Repr. of 1935 ed. lib. bdg. 25.00 (ISBN 0-8154-0354-2). Cooper Sq.

Bertaux, Pierre. Franzosisch-Deutsches, Deutsch-Franzosisches Woerterbuch, Vol. 1. (Ger. & Fr.). 1966. 69.95 (ISBN 3-87097-000-6, M-7411, Pub. by Brandstetter). French & Eur.

--Franzosisch-Deutsches, Deutsch-Franzosisches Woerterbuch, Vol. 2. (Ger. & Fr.). 1966. 69.95 (ISBN 3-87097-001-4, M-7412, Pub. by Brandstetter). French & Eur.

Bertazzoni, U., et al, eds. Contributions of Modern Biology to Medicine: New Approaches in Pathogenesis, Diagnosis, & Therapy in Immunological & Hematological Disorders. (Serono Symposia Publications from Raven Press Ser.: Vol. 17). 262p. 1985. text ed. 34.00 (ISBN 0-88167-092-8). Raven.

Bertazzoni, Umberto & Bollum, Fred J., eds. Terminal Transferase in Immunobiology & Leukemia. LC 82-3691. (Advances in Experimental Medicine & Biology: Vol. 145). 405p. 1982. 55.00x (ISBN 0-306-40989-5, Plenum Pr). Plenum Pub.

Bertcher & Milnes. Verbal Emphatic Responding. Date not set. 3.75 (ISBN 0-317-20155-7). Campus.

Bertcher, Harvey J. Group Participation: Techniques for Leaders & Members. LC 79-175. (Sage Human Services Guides: Vol. 10). 1979. pap. 9.95 (ISBN 0-8039-1204-8). Sage.

Bertcher, Harvey J. & Maple, Frank F. Creating Groups. LC 77-22401. (Sage Human Services Guides: Vol. 2). 96p. 1977. pap. 7.95 (ISBN 0-8039-0881-4). Sage.

--Group Composition: An Instructional Program. Date not set. 3.90 (ISBN 0-317-20154-9). Campus.

Bertcher, Harvey J., jt. auth. see Milnes, John.

Bertcher, Harvey J., et al. Group Composition, an Instructional Program. 88p. 1972. pap. 3.90 (ISBN 0-87506-046-3). Campus.

Berte, John B. Pulmonary Emergencies. LC 77-21473. (Illus.). 1977. flexible bdg. 22.50 (ISBN 0-397-50383-0, 65-00391, Lippincott Medical). Lippincott.

Berte, Neal R., ed. Individualizing Education Through Contract Learning. LC 75-9707. Repr. of 1975 ed. 39.20 (ISBN 0-8357-9618-3, 2051291). Bks Demand UMI.

Berte, Raymond. To Speak Again: My Victory over Throat Cancer. 192p. 1985. 14.95 (ISBN 0-8159-6923-6). Devin.

Berteaux, H. O. Buoy Engineering. LC 75-20046. (Ocean Engineering, a Wiley Ser.). pap. 83.00 (ISBN 0-317-10892-1, 2055605). Bks Demand UMI.

Bertele, Rene, jt. auth. see Prevert, Jacques.

Bertele, Umberto & Brioschi, Francesco. Nonserial Dynamic Programming. (Mathematics in Science & Engineering Ser.: Vol. 91). 1972. 60.00 (ISBN 0-12-093450-7). Acad Pr.

Bertelli, A., ed. Chemotherapy Future Trends. Vol. 1, 1974. 45.00 (ISBN 0-686-51192-1); Vol. 2, 1977. 50.00 (ISBN 0-686-67756-0); Vol. 3, 1978-1980. 115.00 (ISBN 0-686-67757-9); Vol. 4, 1980-1982. 85.00 (ISBN 2-88079-001-8); Vol. 5, 1982-1984. 90.00 (ISBN 2-88079-004-2). Heinman.

Bertelli, A., ed. see International Symposium on Tirrenia, June 1974.

Bertelli, A., ed. see International Symposium, 6-7 May, 1974, Tirrenia.

Bertelli, A., et al, eds. New Anti-Inflammatory & Antirheumatic Drugs: Proceedings. (Illus.). 1977. 55.00 (ISBN 0-685-87097-9). Heinman.

Bertelli, Aldo & Back, Nathan, eds. Shock: Biochemical, Pharmacological & Clinical Aspects. LC 77-122624. (Advances in Experimental Medicine & Biology Ser.: Vol. 9). 366p. 1970. 45.00x (ISBN 0-306-39009-4, Plenum Pr). Plenum Pub.

Bertels, Frank. The First Book on Male Liberation & Sex Equality. LC 81-164329. (Illus.). 415p. (One $10 male-lib study tape free with either book purchased see noticeinside book). 1981. lib. bdg. 25.00 (ISBN 0-932574-05-X); text ed. 15.00 (ISBN 0-932574-06-8). Brun Pr.

--Frank Bertel's Lively Talking Book: Study Tapes of 100 Recent Coast to Coast Appearances on Male Liberation Seminars. 1982. one, one hour tape cassette 10.00 (ISBN 0-932574-07-6). Brun Pr.

Bertelsen, Judy S., ed. Non-State Nations in International Politics: Comparative System Analyses. LC 75-36404. 272p. 1976. 39.95 (ISBN 0-275-56320-0). Praeger.

Bertelsmann, Elizabeth, jt. auth. see Bertelsmann, Heinz.

Bertelsmann, Heinz & Bertelsmann, Elizabeth. The Eye of the Beholder. LC 81-6396. (Illus.). 128p. 1981. 30.00 (ISBN 0-933920-20-2). Hudson Hills.

Bertelson, David. The Lazy South. LC 80-24033. ix, 284p. 1980. Repr. of 1967 ed. lib. bdg. 27.50x (ISBN 0-313-22696-2, BELS). Greenwood.

Bertens, Hans. The Fiction of Paul Bowles: The Soul Is the Weariest Part of the Body. (Costerus Ser.: No. XXI). (Orig.). 1979. pap. text ed. 29.00x (ISBN 90-6203-992-8). Humanities.

Bertensson, Sergei, jt. ed. see Leyda, Jay.

Berteville, John. Recit de l'expedition en Ecosse l'an 1546. LC 79-39436. (Bannatyne Club, Edinburgh. Publications: No. 10). Repr. of 1825 ed. 17.50 (ISBN 0-404-52710-8). AMS Pr.

Berthelot, Joseph A. Michael Drayton. LC 67-19341. (English Authors Ser.). 1967. lib. bdg. 15.95 (ISBN 0-8057-1172-4). Irvington.

Berthelot, Pierre & Ogus, Arthur. Notes on Crystalline Coholomology. LC 78-57039. (Mathematical Notes Ser.: No. 21). 1979. 16.50x (ISBN 0-691-08218-9). Princeton U Pr.

Berthelot, R. M. Socio-Economic Aspects of Urban Hydrology: Prepared at a Workshop in Lund, Sweden. (Studies & Reports in Hydrology: No. 27). (Illus.). 88p. 1979. pap. 10.00 (ISBN 92-3-101702-0, U965, UNESCO). Unipub.

Berthene, Sandra A. Hennepin County Family Law Bench Book. 1983. looseleaf 35.00 (ISBN 0-86678-128-5). Butterworth MN.

Bertherat, Therese & Bernstein, Carol. The Body Has Its Reasons. 1979. pap. 3.50 (ISBN 0-380-44321-X, 61788-9). Avon.

Berthier, A. M. Spectral Theory & Wave Operators for the Schrodinger Equation. (Research Notes in Mathematics Ser.: No. 71). 256p. 1982. pap. text ed. 28.95 (ISBN 0-273-08562-X). Pitman Pub MA.

Berthier, J. Les Physalacriaceae du Globe: Hymenomacetales, Clavariodes. (Bibliotheca Mycologica Ser.: No. 98). (Illus.). 128p. 1985. pap. text ed. 17.50x (ISBN 3-7682-1424-9). Lubrecht & Cramer.

Berthier, Marc P. G. The Art of Knots. 1977. 6.95 (ISBN 0-385-11464-8). Doubleday.

Berthoff, Ann E. Forming-Thinking-Writing: The Composing Imagination. LC 78-3485. 224p. 1978. pap. text ed. 9.50x (ISBN 0-86709-027-8). Boynton Cook Pub.

--The Making of Meaning: Metaphors, Models, & Maxims for Writing Teachers. LC 81-9948. 224p. (Orig.). 1981. pap. text ed. 9.75x (ISBN 0-86709-003-0). Boynton Cook Pubs.

--Reclaiming the Imagination: Philosophical Perspectives for Writers & Teachers of Writing. 320p. (Orig.). 1984. pap. text ed. 11.50x (ISBN 0-86709-059-6). Boynton Cook Pubs.

Berthoff, Warner. Edmund Wilson. LC 68-64750. (Pamphlets on American Writers Ser: No. 67). (Orig.). 1968. pap. 1.25 (ISBN 0-8166-0481-9, MPAW67). U of Minn Pr.

--The Ferment of Realism: American Literature 1884-1919. LC 80-42335. 352p. 1981. 54.50 (ISBN 0-521-24092-1); pap. 15.95 (ISBN 0-521-28435-X). Cambridge U Pr.

Berthoff, Warner, ed. see Melville, Herman.

Berthoff, Werner. A Literature Without Qualities: American Writing Since 1945. LC 78-57305. (Quantum Bks.). 1979. 16.75x (ISBN 0-520-03696-4). U of Cal Pr.

Berthold & Schwarz. UFO-Dynamics: Psychiatric & Psychic Aspects of the UFO Syndrome, Bk. 2. (Illus.). 260p. 1983. pap. 14.95 (ISBN 0-935834-13-3). Rainbow Books.

Berthold, Arthur B. American Colonial Printing As Determined by Contemporary Cultural Forces. 1967. Repr. of 1934 ed. 15.00 (ISBN 0-8337-0261-0). B Franklin.

Berthold, Dennis & Price, Kenneth M., eds. Dear Brother Walt: The Letters of Thomas Jefferson Whitman. LC 83-26775. (Illus.). 225p. 1984. 27.50x (ISBN 0-87338-297-8). Kent St U Pr.

Berthold, George C., ed. Maximus the Confessor. (Classics of Western Spirituality Ser.: Vol. 45). 1985. 14.95 (ISBN 0-8091-0353-2); pap. 11.95 (ISBN 0-8091-2659-1). Paulist Pr.

Berthold, Mary P. Big Hole Journal: Notes & Excerpts. 1973. 5.25 (ISBN 0-8187-0022-X). Harlo Pr.

--Including Two Captains: A Later Look. LC 75-13400. 1975. 6.00 (ISBN 0-8187-0023-8). Harlo Pr.

--Turn Here for the Big Hole. 1970. 3.95 (ISBN 0-8187-0025-4). Harlo Pr.

Berthold, Richard M. Rhodes in the Hellenistic Age. LC 83-23127. (Illus.). 243p. 1984. 25.00x (ISBN 0-8014-1640-X). Cornell U Pr.

Bertholdi, Franz W. Von see Von Bertholdi, Franz W.

Bertholf, Diana. Diana's Star. 145p. 1983. pap. 2.95 (ISBN 0-8423-0545-9). Tyndale.

Bertholf, Judy. Tiger Beetles of the Genus Cicindela in Arizona: Coleoptera: Cicindelidae. (Special Publications of the Museum Ser.: No. 19). (Illus.). 44p. 1983. pap. 7.00 (ISBN 0-89672-110-8). Tex Tech Pr.

Bertholf, Robert. Robert Duncan: A Descriptive Bibliography. (Illus.). 500p. 1985. 65.00 (ISBN 0-87685-620-2); signed ed. 90.00 (ISBN 0-87685-621-0). Black Sparrow.

Bertholf, Robert J. & Levitt, Annette S., eds. William Blake & the Moderns. 352p. 1982. 44.50x (ISBN 0-87395-615-X); pap. 16.95x (ISBN 0-87395-616-8). State U NY Pr.

Bertholf, Robert J. & Reid, Ian W., eds. Robert Duncan: Scales of the Marvelous. LC 79-19861. (New Directions Insights III). 1979. pap. 5.95 (ISBN 0-8112-0735-8, NDP487). New Directions.

Bertholle, Louisette. French Cuisine for All. Manheim, Mary, tr. LC 78-1235. (Illus.). 512p. 1981. 19.95 (ISBN 0-385-13087-2). Doubleday.

Berthollet, Claude L. Essai De Statique Chimique, 2 Vols. Repr. of 1803 ed. Set. 70.00 (ISBN 0-384-04079-9). Johnson Repr.

Berthollet, Claude-Louis. Researches into the Laws of Chemical Affinity. 2nd ed. LC 65-23404. 1966. Repr. of 1809 ed. 27.50 (ISBN 0-306-70914-7). Da Capo.

Berthoud, Jacques. Joseph Conrad: The Major Phase. LC 77-8242. (British Authors Ser.). 1978. 32.50 (ISBN 0-521-21742-3); pap. 11.95 (ISBN 0-521-29273-5). Cambridge U Pr.

Berthoud, Jacques, ed. see Conrad, Joseph.

Berthoud, Jacques, ed. see Trollope, Anthony.

Berthoud, Richard. Challenges to Social Policy. 230p. 1985. text ed. write for info. (ISBN 0-566-05011-0). Gower Pub Co.

--Disadvantages of Inequality: A Study of Social Deprivation. (Illus.). 1976. text ed. 19.95x (ISBN 0-8464-0338-2). Beekman Pubs.

--Unemployed Professionals & Executives. 121p. 1979. 29.00x (ISBN 0-686-87349-1, Pub. by Policy Studies). State Mutual Bk.

Berthoud, Richard & Brown, Joan C. Poverty & the Development of Anti-Poverty Policy in the U. K. (Policy Studies Institute Ser.). 288p. 1981. text ed. 27.00x (ISBN 0-435-83102-X). Gower Pub Co.

Berthoud, Roger. Graham Sutherland: A Biography. (Illus.). 352p. 1982. 26.95 (ISBN 0-571-11882-8). Faber & Faber.

Berthouex, P. Mac & Rudd, Dale F. Strategy of Pollution Control. LC 76-29008. 579p. 1977. text ed. 48.45 (ISBN 0-471-74449-2). Wiley.

Berthoz, A. & Jones, G. M., eds. Adaptive Mechanisms in Gaze Control. (Reviews of Oculomotor Research: No. 1). 1984. 109.25 (ISBN 0-444-80483-8, Biomedical Pr). Elsevier.

Berthrong, Donald J. The Cheyenne & Arapaho Ordeal: Reservations & Agency Life in the Indian Territory 1875-1907. LC 75-17795. (The Civilization of the American Indian Ser: No.136). 418p. 1976. 19.95 (ISBN 0-8061-1277-8). U of Okla Pr.

--The Southern Cheyennes. LC 63-8990. (Civilization of the American Indian Ser.: No. 66). (Illus.). 456p. 1975. pap. 12.95 (ISBN 0-8061-1199-2). U of Okla Pr.

Berti, F. & Folco, G., eds. Leukotrienes & Prostacyclin. (NATO ASI Series A, Life Sciences: Vol. 154). 290p. 42.50x (ISBN 0-306-41173-3, Plenum Press). Plenum Pub.

Berti, F. & Velo, G. P., eds. The Prostaglandin System: Endoperoxides, Prostacyclin & Thromboxanes. LC 80-28197. (NATO ASI Series A, Life Sciences: Vol. 36). 437p. 1981. 49.50x (ISBN 0-306-40645-4, Plenum Pr). Plenum Pub.

Berti, F., et al, eds. Cyclooxygenase & Lipoxygenase Modulators in Lung Reactivity. (Progress in Biochemical Pharmacology: Vol. 20). (Illus.). x, 146p. 1985. 56.75 (ISBN 3-8055-3974-6). S Karger.

--Prostaglandins & Thromboxanes. LC 77-5364. (NATO ASI Series A, Life Sciences: Vol. 13). 458p. 1977. 59.50x (ISBN 0-306-35613-9, Plenum Pr). Plenum Pub.

Berti, Luciano. Florence: The City & It's Art. (Illus.). 160p. (Orig.). 1981. pap. 13.95 (ISBN 0-935748-36-9). Scala Books.

--Michelangelo: All the Works. Glasspool, Susan, tr. from Ital. (Bonechi Guides Ser.). (Illus.). 1984. pap. 8.95 (ISBN 0-88332-333-8, 8260). Larousse.

--Uffizzi. (Illus.). 140p. (Orig.). 1981. pap. 13.95 (ISBN 0-935748-40-7). Scala Books.

Berti, Luciano, intro. by. The Official Catalogue of the Uffizi. (Illus.). 1980. 540.00x (ISBN 88-7038-017-3, Centro Di). Gale.

Bertier de Sauvigny, G. de see De Bertier de Sauvigny, G. & Pinkney, David H.

Bertillon, Alphonse. Alphonse Bertillon's Instructions for Taking Descriptions for the Identification of Criminals, & Others by Means of Anthropometric Indications. LC 72-156004. (Foundations of Criminal Justice Ser.). Repr. of 1889 ed. 19.00 (ISBN 0-404-09104-0). AMS Pr.

Bertim, Jack. The Pyramids from Space. LC 76-9700. 1977. pap. 1.25 (ISBN 0-532-12502-9). Woodhill.

Bertin, Celia. Marie Bonaparte: A Life. (A Helen & Kurt Wolff Bk.). (Illus.). 304p. 1982. 17.95 (ISBN 0-15-157252-6). HarBraceJ.

Bertin, Charles. Two Plays: Christopher Columbus & Don Juan. Smith, William J., tr. LC 78-109941. (Minnesota Drama Edition Ser.: No. 6). pap. 37.00 (ISBN 0-317-29397-4, 2055843). Bks Demand UMI.

Bertin, Emanuel A. Pennsylvania Child Custody: Law, Practice & Procedure - Including Using Expert Witnesses in Custody Cases. LC 82-74396. xxiv, 475p. 1983. 40.00. Bisel Co.

Bertin, Eugene P. Introduction to X-Ray Spectrometric Analysis. LC 77-27244. (Illus.). 499p. 1978. 42.50x (ISBN 0-306-31091-0, Plenum Pr). Plenum Pub.

--Principles & Practice of X-Ray Spectrometric Analysis. 2nd ed. LC 74-28043. (Illus.). 1079p. 1975. 95.00x (ISBN 0-306-30809-6, Plenum Pr). Plenum Pub.

Bertin, J. & Loeb, J. Experimental & Theoretical Aspects of Induced Polarization. Incl. Vol. 1. Presentation & Application of the IP Method. 43.30 (ISBN 3-443-13009-7); Vol. 2. Macroscopic & Microscopic Theories. 22.40 (ISBN 3-443-13010-0). 1976. 76.30 set. Lubrecht & Cramer.

Bertin, Jacques. Graphics & Graphic Information Processing. Berg, William J. & Scott, Paul, trs. from Fr. (Illus.). 273p. 1981. 23.20x (ISBN 3-11-008868-1); pap. 15.20x (ISBN 3-11-006901-6). De Gruyter.

--Semiology of Graphics. Berg, William, tr. from French. LC 83-47755. Orig. Title: Semiologie du Graphiques. (Illus.). 432p. 1983. text ed. 75.00x (ISBN 0-299-09060-4). U of Wis Pr.

Bertin, Jacques, et al. Atlas of Food Crops. (Ecoles Practiques Des Hautes Etudes: Section 6). (Illus.). 41p. 1971. text ed. 40.80x (ISBN 90-2791-798-1). Mouton.

Bertin, John J. Engineering Fluid Mechanics. (Illus.). 576p. 1984. 38.95 (ISBN 0-13-278812-8). P-H.

Bertin, John J. & Smith, Michael L. Aerodynamics for Engineers. (Illus.). 1979. text ed. 38.95 (ISBN 0-13-018234-6). P-H.

Bertin, M. J., ed. Seminaire De Theorie Des Nombres, Paris 1979-1980. (Progress in Mathematics Ser.: Vol. 12). 404p. (Fr. & Eng.). 1981. 27.50x (ISBN 0-8176-3035-X). Birkhauser.

--Seminaire de Theorie des Nombres: Paris 1980-1981. (Progress in Mathematics Ser.: Vol. 22). 360p. 1982. text ed. 22.50 (ISBN 0-8176-3066-X). Birkhauser.

Bertin, Marie-Jose. Seminaire de Theorie des Nombres, Paris 1981-1982. (Progress in Mathematics Ser.: Vol. 38). 359p. 1983. text ed. 27.50 (ISBN 0-8176-3155-0). Birkhauser.

Bertin, Marie-Jose & Goldstein, Catherine, eds. Seminaire de Theorie des Nombres: Nineteen Eighty-Two to Nineteen Eighty-Three. (Progress in Mathematics Ser.: No. 51). 312p. 1984. text ed. 27.95 (ISBN 0-8176-3261-1). Birkhauser.

Bertinchamps, A. J., et al, eds. Effects of Ionizing Radiation on DNA: Physical, Chemical & Biological Aspects. LC 77-25857. (Molecular, Biology, Biochemistry & Biophysics: Vol 27). (Illus.). 1978. 56.00 (ISBN 0-387-08542-4). Springer-Verlag.

Berting, Jan, et al. Problems in International Comparative Research in the Social Sciences. 186p. 1979. 33.00 (ISBN 0-08-025247-8). Pergamon.

Berting, Jan, et al, eds. The Socio-Economic Impact of Microelectronics: International Conference on Socio-Economic Problems & Potentialities of Microelectronics, Sept. 1979, Zandvoort, Netherlands. LC 80-49810. (Vienna Centre Ser.). (Illus.). 263p. 1980. 64.00 (ISBN 0-08-026776-9). Pergamon.

Bertini & Drago. The Coordination Chemistry of Metalloenzymes: The Role of Metals in Reaction Involving Water, Dioxygen & Related Species. 1983. lib. bdg. 56.00 (ISBN 90-277-1530-0, Pub. by Reidel Holland). Kluwer Academic.

Bertini, I., et al, eds. Advances in Solution Chemistry. LC 80-28783. 398p. 1981. 65.00x (ISBN 0-306-40638-1, Plenum Pr). Plenum Pub.

Bertini, Ivano & Drago, Russell, eds. E S R & N M R of Paramagnetic Species in Biological & Related Systems. (Nato Advanced Studies Institute Ser.: No. C-52). 422p. 1980. lib. bdg. 50.00 (ISBN 90-277-1063-5, Pub. by Reidel Holland). Kluwer Academic.

Bertini, M., et al, eds. Field Dependence in Psychological Theory Research & Application: Two Symposia in Memory of H. A. Witkin. 175p. 1985. text ed. 19.95 (ISBN 0-89859-668-8). L Erlbaum Assocs.

Bertleson, Amy D., jt. ed. see Walsh, James K.

Bertling, Ed, jt. auth. see Leen, Edie.

Bertling, Paul. MASH: The Official 4077 Quiz Manual. LC 83-23840. 220p. 1984. pap. 6.95 (ISBN 0-452-25505-8, Plume). NAL.

Bertman, Martin A. Thomas Hobbes: The Natural & the Artifacted Good. (European University Studies: Ser. 20, Philosophy: Vol. 48). 158p. 1981. 16.20 (ISBN 3-261-04770-4). P Lang Pubs.

Bertman, Stephen. Art & the Romans. (Illus.). 83p. 1975. 10.00x (ISBN 0-87291-070-9). Coronado Pr.

Bertman, Stephen, ed. The Conflict of Generations in Ancient Greece & Rome. 1976. text ed. 26.25x (ISBN 90-6032-033-6). Humanities.

Berto, Giuseppe. Sky Is Red. Davidson, Angus, tr. from It. LC 76-138575. 1971. Repr. of 1948 ed. lib. bdg. 22.50x (ISBN 0-8371-5774-9, BESR). Greenwood.

Berto, Hazel. Cooking with Honey. (Illus.). 192p. 1972. 3.98 (ISBN 0-517-24212-5). Outlet Bk Co.

--Cooking with Honey. 1981. 18.95x (ISBN 0-317-06966-7, Regent House); lib. bdg. 18.95x. B of A.

Bertocci, P. A. Empirical Argument for God in Late British Thought. Repr. of 1938 ed. 27.00 (ISBN 0-527-07300-8). Kraus Repr.

Bertocci, Peter. Person God Is. (Muirhead Library of Philosophy). 1970. text ed. 18.00x (ISBN 0-391-00095-0). Humanities.

Bertocci, Peter A. Religion As Creative Insecurity. LC 73-1836. 128p. 1973. Repr. of 1958 ed. lib. bdg. 15.00x (ISBN 0-8371-6803-1, BECI). Greenwood.

Bertocci, Peter A., ed. Mid-Twentieth Century American Philosophy: Personal Statements. LC 73-18467. 251p. 1974. text ed. 13.00x (ISBN 0-391-00340-2). Humanities.

Bertocci, Philip A. Jules Simon: Republican Anticlericalism & Cultural Politics in France, 1848-1886. LC 77-14668. 255p. 1978. 20.00x (ISBN 0-8262-0239-X). U of Mo Pr.

Bertoglio, Jan, jt. auth. see Hudson, Jole.

Bertolazzi, P. & Luccio, F., eds. VLSI: Algorithms & Architectures. (Proceedings of the International Workshop on Parallel Computing & VLSI, Amalfi, Italy, May 23-25, 1984). 388p. 1985. 70.50 (ISBN 0-444-87662-6, North-Holland). Elsevier.

Bertolet, Mary M. & Goldsmith, Lee S., eds. Hospital Liability: Law & Tactics. 4th ed. LC 79-92666. 789p. 1980. text ed. 35.00 (ISBN 0-686-65589-3). PLI.

Bertoli, John. Winter Warriors. (Orig.). 1979. pap. 1.95 (ISBN 0-532-23213-5). Woodhill.

Bertoline, Gary R. Fundamentals of CAD. LC 84-17563. 352p. 1985. pap. text ed. 19.80 (ISBN 0-8273-2332-8); instr's. guide 5.60 (ISBN 0-8273-2333-6). Delmar.

Bertolini, Alberto M. Gerontologic Metabolism. De Sabata, Victor, tr. (Illus.). 716p. 1969. photocopy ed. 64.50x (ISBN 0-398-00147-2). C C Thomas.

Bertolini Guerrieri-Gonzaga, jt. auth. see Rolland, Romain.

Bertolino, James. The Alleged Conception. LC 75-46211. 64p. 1976. pap. 3.00 (ISBN 0-914102-05-2). Bluefish.

--Making Space for Our Living. LC 75-14276. 64p. (Orig.). 1975. pap. 5.00 (ISBN 0-914742-08-6). Copper Canyon.

--New & Selected Poems. LC 77-81274. (Poetry Ser). 1978. pap. 3.95 (ISBN 0-915604-14-0). Carnegie-Mellon.

--Precint Kali & the Gertruce Spicer Story. LC 81-80548. (Illus.). 108p. 1981. pap. 4.00 (ISBN 0-89823-034-9). New Rivers Pr.

--Soft Rock. 1973. perfect bound in wrappers 2.00 (ISBN 0-685-79033-9). Stone-Marrow Pr.

--Terminal Placebos. (Illus.). 1975. saddlestitched in wrappers 1.25 (ISBN 0-685-79002-9). New Rivers Pr.

Bertolotti, Antonino. Artisti Bolognesi, Ferraresi Alcuni Altri del Gia Stato Pontificio in Roma nei Secoli Quindici, Seidici, Dicitasette. LC 79-136047. 1968. Repr. of 1885 ed. 25.50 (ISBN 0-8337-0263-7). B Franklin.

--Artisti Lombardi a Roma nei Secoli XV, XVI & XVII: Studi e Ricerche Archivi Romani, 2 vols. LC 77-146239. 1972. Repr. of 1881 ed. Set. lib. bdg. 50.50 (ISBN 0-8337-0266-1). B Franklin.

Bertolotti, David S., Jr. Culture & Technology. LC 84-71555. 154p. 1984. 18.95 (ISBN 0-87972-307-6); pap. 7.95 (ISBN 0-87972-308-4). Bowling Green Univ.

Bertolotti, M. Masers & Lasers: An Historical Approach. 1983. 29.00 (ISBN 0-9960024-3-X, Pub. by A Hilger England). Heyden.

Bertolotti, M., ed. Physical Processes in Laser-Materials Interactions. (NATO ASI Series B, Physics: Vol. 84). 534p. 1983. 75.00 (ISBN 0-306-41107-5, Plenum Pr). Plenum Pub.

Bertolucci, John. The Disciplines of a Disciple. 136p. (Orig.). 1985. pap. 4.95 (ISBN 0-89283-240-1). Servant.

Bertolucci, John & Lilly, Fred. On Fire with the Spirit. 140p. (Orig.). 1984. pap. 4.95 (ISBN 0-89283-193-6). Servant.

Bertolucci, Michael D., jt. auth. see Harris, Daniel C.

Berton, Alberta D., compiled by. Asbestosis: A Comprehensive Bibliography. (Biomedical Information Guides Ser.: Vol. 1). 395p. 1980. 85.00x (ISBN 0-306-65176-9, IFI Plenum). Plenum Pub.

--Nuclear Medicine: A Comprehensive Bibliography. (Biomedical Information Guides Ser.: Vol. 2). 355p. 1980. 85.00x (ISBN 0-306-65178-5, IFI Plenum). Plenum Pub.

--Smoking & Health: A Comprehensive Bibliography. (Biomedical Information Guides Ser.: Vol. 3). 535p. 1980. 95.00x (ISBN 0-306-65184-X, IFI Plenum). Plenum Pub.

Berton, C. Dictionnaire des Cardinaux. Migne, J. P., ed. (Troisieme et Derniere Encyclopedie Theologique Ser.: Vol. 31). 912p. (Fr.). Repr. of 1857 ed. lib. bdg. 115.00x (ISBN 0-89241-310-7). Caratzas.

--Dictionnaire du Parallele entre Diverses Doctrines Philosophiques et Religieuses. Migne, J. P., ed. (Troisieme et Derniere Encycolpedie Theologique Ser.: Vol. 38). 698p. (Fr.). Repr. of 1858 ed. lib. bdg. 90.00x (ISBN 0-89241-317-4). Caratzas.

Berton, Peter. Soviet Works on China: A Bibliography of Non-Periodical Literature, 1946-1955. LC 58-13210. 158p. 1959. pap. 2.50 (ISBN 0-88474-011-0). U of S Cal Pr.

Berton, Peter & Rubinstein, Alvin Z. Soviet Works on Southeast Asia: A Bibliography of Non-Periodical Literature 1946-1965. 202p. 1967. pap. text ed. 4.50 (ISBN 0-88474-012-9). U of S Cal Pr.

Berton, Peter & Wu, Eugene. Contemporary China: A Research Guide. LC 67-14235. (Bibliographical Ser.: No. 31). 695p. 1967. 25.00x (ISBN 0-8179-2311-X). Hoover Inst Pr.

Berton, Peter, ed. see Symposium on the Comparative Study of Communist Foreign Policy.

Berton, Peter, et al. Japanese Training & Research in the Russian Field. 264p. 1956. pap. text ed. 4.00 (ISBN 0-88474-010-2). U of S Cal Pr.

Berton, Peter A., jt. auth. see Nahm, Andrew C.

Berton, Pierre. Flames Across the Border: The Canadian-American Tragedy. 1982. 19.95 (ISBN 0-316-09217-7, Pub. by Atlantic Monthly Pr). Little.

--The Impossible Railway: The Building of the Canadian Pacific. 1984. 21.75 (ISBN 0-8446-6174-0). Peter Smith.

--The Invasion of Canada: 1812-1813. (Illus.). 320p. 1980. 17.50 (ISBN 0-316-09216-9, An Atlantic Monthly Press Book). Little.

--Klondike Fever. 457p. 1985. pap. 10.95 (ISBN 0-88184-139-0). Carroll & Graf.

--Klondike Fever: The Life & Death of the Last Great Stampede. (Illus.). 1958. 17.95 (ISBN 0-394-43206-1). Knopf.

--The Secret World of Og. (Orig.). (gr. 3-6). 1984. pap. 1.95 (ISBN 0-671-50352-9). Archway.

Berton, Pierre, ed. The Klondike Quest: A Photographic Essay, 1897-1899. LC 83-71421. (Illus.). 240p. 1983. 49.00 (ISBN 0-316-09218-5, An Atlantic-Little, Brown Book). Little.

Bertonasco, Marc F., jt. auth. see Miles, Robert.

Bertone, Michael. Romeo & Juliet of Another Century. LC 78-50635. 1979. 12.95 (ISBN 0-87949-118-3). Ashley Bks.

Bertone, Pamela S., jt. auth. see Dickens, E. Larry.

Bertoni, Phil. Strangers in Computerland. LC 84-40078. 256p. 1984. pap. 7.95 (ISBN 0-394-72613-8, Vin). Random.

--Strangers in Computerland: Getting Comfortable with the New Magick. LC 83-18737. 224p. 1983. 16.95 (ISBN 0-86616-034-5); pap. 9.95 (ISBN 0-86616-035-3). Greene.

Bertot, Cathey. The New Financial Planner: A Guide to Client Service. (Plaid Ser.). Date not set. 25.00 (ISBN 0-87094-587-4). Dow Jones-Irwin.

Bertot, Lillian. Separados Por la Espuma. LC 80-65223. (Coleccion Espejo De Paciencia). 46p. 1980. pap. 5.95 (ISBN 0-89729-250-2). Ediciones.

Bertotti, B., ed. Experimental Gravitation. (Italian Physical Society: Course 56). 1974. 92.50 (ISBN 0-12-368856-6). Acad Pr.

Bertotti-Scamozzi, O. The Buildings & the Designs of Andrea Palladio. pap. 31.50 (ISBN 0-317-29912-3, 2021770). Bks Demand UMI.

Bertotti-Scamozzi, Ottavio. The Buildings & Designs of Andrea Palladio, 2 vols. 1976. boxed o.p. 400.00x (ISBN 0-685-73875-2); Plates. boxed 200.00x (ISBN 0-8139-0932-5); 30 plates o.p. 30.00x (ISBN 0-686-67584-3); 10 plates o.p. 20.00x (ISBN 0-8139-0933-3); eng. trans. only 50.00x (ISBN 0-8139-0934-1). U Pr of Va.

Bertouille, S., jt. ed. see Aalders, Carel A. V.

Bertozzi, W., et al, eds. Electron & Pion Interactions with Nuclei at Intermediate Energies. (Studies in High Energy Physics: Vol. 2). 718p. 1980. 77.50 (ISBN 3-7186-0015-3). Harwood Academic.

Bertram, Burt & Moon, Jeanne. Everything Makes a Difference. LC 83-82061. (Illus.). 116p. (Orig.). 1983. pap. 7.95 (ISBN 0-914419-00-5). High-Touch.

Bertram, Christoph. New Conventional Weapons & East-West Security. LC 78-78216. (Praeger Special Studies). 102p. 1979. 37.95 (ISBN 0-03-052091-6). Praeger.

Bertram, Christoph, jt. auth. see Kincade, William H.

Bertram, Christoph, ed. Arms Control & Military Force. LC 80-67836. (Adelphi Library: Vol. 3). 272p. 1981. text ed. 33.50x (ISBN 0-916672-70-0). Allanheld.

--Defense & Consensus: The Domestic Aspects of Western Security. LC 83-40182. 144p. 1984. 25.00 (ISBN 0-312-19098-0). St Martin.

--The Future of Strategic Deterrence. 108p. 1981. 19.50 (ISBN 0-208-01943-X, Archon). Shoe String.

--Prospects of Soviet Power in the Nineteen Eighties. 126p. 1980. 19.50 (ISBN 0-208-01885-9, Archon). Shoe String.

--Strategic Deterrence in a Changing Environment. LC 80-67841. (Adelphi Library: Vol. 6). 208p. 1981. pap. text ed. 33.50x (ISBN 0-916672-75-1). Allanheld.

--Third-World Conflict & International Security. 120p. 1982. 19.50 (ISBN 0-208-01957-X, Archon). Shoe String.

Bertram, Christoph, jt. ed. see Kincade, William H.

Bertram, Christopher. America's Security in the Nineteen Eighties. LC 82-16814. 200p. 1983. 25.00x (ISBN 0-312-02199-2). St Martin.

Bertram, E. G. & Moore, Keith L. A Concise Atlas of the Human Brain & Spinal Cord. (Illus.). 276p. 1982. text ed. 16.50 (ISBN 0-683-00610-X). Williams & Wilkins.

Bertram, G. L. Conservation of Sirenia: Current Status & Perspectives for Action. 1974. pap. 7.50 (ISBN 2-88032-023-2, IUCN35, IUCN). Unipub.

Bertram, Geoffrey, jt. auth. see Thorp, Rosemary.

Bertram, Gordon W. Consolidated Bargaining in California Construction: An Appraisal of Twenty-Five Years' Experience. (Monograph Ser.: No. 12). 259p. 1966. 6.00 (ISBN 0-89215-013-0). U Cal LA Indus Rel.

Bertram, Hans. The Abbey Cookbook: Inspired Recipes from the Great Atlanta Restaurant. LC 81-20225. (Illus.). 224p. 1982. 15.95 (ISBN 0-916782-23-9); pap. 9.95 spiral (ISBN 0-916782-26-3). Harvard Common Pr.

Bertram, James. Dan Davin. (New Zealand Writers & Their Work Ser.). 1983. pap. 9.95x (ISBN 0-19-558095-8). Oxford U Pr.

Bertram, James M. First Act in China: The Story of the Sian Mutiny. LC 74-31223. (China in the 20th Century Ser). Orig. Title: Crisis in China. (Illus.). xxii, 284p. 1975. Repr. of 1938 ed. lib. bdg. 35.00 (ISBN 0-306-70687-3). Da Capo.

--First Act in China: The Story of the Sian Mutiny. LC 73-864. (China Studies: from Confucius to Mao Ser.). (Illus.). viii, 284p. 1973. Repr. of 1938 ed. 23.50 (ISBN 0-88355-060-1). Hyperion Conn.

--Unconquered: Journal of a Year's Adventure Among the Fighting Peasants of North China. (China in the 20th Century Ser). (Illus.). ix, 340p. 1975. Repr. of 1939 ed. lib. bdg. 39.50 (ISBN 0-306-70688-1). Da Capo.

Bertram, Martin, tr. see Pelikan, Jaroslav.

Bertram, Martin H., tr. Luther's Works, Vol. 23. LC 55-9893. 1958. 16.95 (ISBN 0-570-06423-6, 15-1765). Concordia.

Bertram, Martin H., tr. see Pelikan, Jaroslav.

Bertram, Paul. White Spaces in Shakespeare. 112p. 1981. 12.50x (ISBN 0-934958-01-7); pap. 8.50x (ISBN 0-934958-02-5). Bellflower.

Bertram, Ross. Magic & Methods of Ross Bertram. (Illus.). xiii, 163p. 1978. Repr. 37.50 (ISBN 0-915926-24-5). Magic Ltd.

Bertram, Theodor, jt. auth. see Martin, Genevieve A.

Bertrand, A. R., jt. auth. see Kohnke, Helmut.

Bertrand, Alvin L. & Corty, Floyd L., eds. Rural Land Tenure in the United States: A Socioeconomic Approach to Problems, Programs, & Trends. LC 62-16212. (Illus.). xii, 314p. 1962. 32.50x (ISBN 0-8071-0325-X). La State U Pr.

Bertrand, Armand L., Jr. How to Start Understanding the Computer. (Illus.). 250p. (Orig.). 1984. pap. 12.95 suppl. avail. (ISBN 0-912447-02-8). Eclectical.

Bertrand, Arthur & Cebula, Joseph P. Tests, Measurement & Evaluation: A Developmental Approach. LC 79-21032. (Education Ser.). (Illus.). 1980. 23.05 (ISBN 0-201-00778-9, Sch Div). Addison-Wesley.

Bertrand, D. & Waldschmidt, M., eds. Approximations Diophantiennes et Nombres Transcendants: Proceedings. (Progress in Mathematics Ser.: Vol. 31). 336p. 1983. write for info (ISBN 0-8176-3120-8). Birkhauser.

Bertrand, F. E., ed. Giant Multipole Resonances. Oak Ridge, Tennessee, October 15-17, 1979. (Nuclear Science Research Conference Ser.: Vol. 1). 498p. 1980. 60.25 (ISBN 3-7186-0029-3). Harwood Academic.

Bertrand, F. M. Dictionnaire Universel, Historique et Comparatif des Toutes les Religions du Monde, 4 vols. Migne, J. P., ed. (Encyclopedie Theologique Ser.: Vols. 24-27). 2588p. (Fr.). Repr. of 1851 ed. lib. bdg. 329.50x (ISBN 0-89241-240-2). Caratzas.

Bertrand, J. W. & Wortmann, J. C. Production Control & Information Systems for Component Manufacturing Shops. (Studies in Production & Engineering Economics: Vol. 1). 104p. 1981. 74.50 (ISBN 0-444-41964-0). Elsevier.

Bertrand, Jane T. Audience Research for Improving Family Planning Communication Programs. LC 80-66649. 85p. (Orig.). 1981. pap. 3.50 (ISBN 0-89836-015-3). Comm & Family.

--Communications Pretesting. LC 78-74908. (Orig.). 1979. pap. text ed. 3.50 (ISBN 0-89836-006-4). Comm & Family.

Bertrand, Jane T., et al. Communicating Family Planning to Rural Guatemala. LC 78-72937. Orig. Title: Perspectivas Para la Planificacion Familiar En Areas Rurales de Guatemala. (Orig.). 1978. pap. 3.00 (ISBN 0-89836-010-2). Comm & Family.

Bertrand, John. Born to Win: A Life-Long Struggle to Capture the America's Cup. (Illus.). 1985. 19.95 (ISBN 0-688-04349-6). Morrow.

Bertrand, Joseph. Calcul Des Probabilites. 2nd ed. LC 78-113114. 389p. (Fr.). 1972. text ed. 13.95 (ISBN 0-8284-0262-0). Chelsea Pub.

Bertrand, Louis M. Fin du classicisme et le retour a l'antique dans la seconde moitie du dix-huitieme siecle et les premieres annees du dix-neuvieme. LC 78-170956. (Essays in Literature & Criticism: No. 153). (Fr.). 1897. 26.50 (ISBN 0-8337-3983-2). B Franklin.

Bertrand, M. see Halpern, M., et al.

Bertrand, Marc. L' Oeuvre de Jean Prevost. LC 68-64308. 127p. 1983. Repr. of 1968 ed. lib. bdg. 19.95x (ISBN 0-89370-793-7). Borgo Pr.

--L' Oeuvre de Jean Prevost. LC 68-64308. (U. C. Publ. in Modern Philology: Vol. 90). Repr. of 1968 ed. 25.30 (ISBN 0-8357-9634-5, 2013805). Bks Demand UMI.

Bertrand, Marc, ed. Popular Traditions & Learned Culture in France, 17th-20th Centuries. (Stanford French & Italian Studies: Vol. 35). 160p. 1985. pap. 25.00 (ISBN 0-915838-02-8). Anma Libri.

Bertrand, P., jt. auth. see Jourbel, H.

Bertrand, R. Analyse du Tarif Douanier Francais par Industries. (Economies et Societes Series R.: No. 1). 1957. pap. 11.00 (ISBN 0-317-16400-7). Kraus Repr.

--Comparaison du Niveau des Tarifs Douaniers des Pays Du Marche Commun. (Economies et Societes Series R: No. 2). 1958. pap. 11.00 (ISBN 0-317-16413-9). Kraus Repr.

Bertrand, Trent. Thailand: Case Study of Agricultural Input & Output Pricing. (Working Paper: No. 385). ix, 134p. 1980. 5.00 (ISBN 0-686-36080-X, WP-0385). World Bank.

Bertrand, Vida, jt. auth. see Barson, John.

Bertrand, Yolande. Borrowed Moments. (Orig.). 1984. pap. 1.95 (ISBN 0-87067-232-0). Holloway.

--Come September. 1984. pap. 1.95 (ISBN 0-87067-238-X, BH238). Holloway.

--Dark Road Home. (Orig.). 1984. pap. 1.95 (ISBN 0-87067-247-9, BH247). Holloway.

--A Play for Love. (Orig.). 1983. pap. 1.95 (ISBN 0-87067-229-0, BH229). Holloway.

Bertrin, G. Lourdes: A History of Its Apparitions & Cures. 59.95 (ISBN 0-8490-0560-4). Gordon Pr.

Bertsch, G. F., ed. Nuclear Spectroscopy: Proceedings. (Lecture Notes in Physics: Vol. 119). 250p. 1980. pap. 23.00 (ISBN 0-387-09970-0). Springer-Verlag.

Bertsch, Gary & McIntyre, John R., eds. National Security & Technology Transfer: The Strategic Dimensions of East-West Trade. LC 83-50026. (Illus.). 258p. 1983. pap. 17.95x (ISBN 0-86531-614-7). Westview.

Bertsch, Gary, et al. Comparing Political Systems: Power & Policy in Three Worlds. 2nd ed. LC 81-21863. 548p. 1982. text ed. 28.50 (ISBN 0-471-08446-8); avail. tchrs.' manual (ISBN 0-471-86600-8). Wiley.

Bertsch, Gary K. East-West Strategic Trade, COCOM & the Atlantic Alliance. (The Atlantic Papers: No. 49). (Illus.). 52p. 1983. pap. 7.00x (ISBN 0-86598-143-4). Rowman & Allanheld.

--Policy Making in Communist Party States. (CISE Learning Package Ser.: No. 10). (Illus.). 114p. (Orig.). 1975. pap. text ed. 4.00x (ISBN 0-936876-25-5). Learn Res Intl Stud.

--Power & Policy in Communist Systems. 2nd ed. LC 81-19715. 192p. 1982. pap. text ed. 15.95 (ISBN 0-471-09005-0). Wiley.

--Values & Community in Multinational Yugoslavia. (East European Monographs: No. 17). 160p. 1976. 20.00x (ISBN 0-914710-10-9). East Eur Quarterly.

Bertsch, Gary K. & Rosenbluth, James M. Summit Diplomacy: A Learning Package. (CISE Learning Packages in International Studies). 49p. (Orig.). 1980. pap. text ed. 4.00x (ISBN 0-936876-37-9). Learn Res Intl Stud.

Bertsch, Gary K., ed. Global Policy Studies. LC 82-5693. (Sage Focus Editions). (Illus.). 1982. 24.00 (ISBN 0-8039-0781-8); pap. 12.00 (ISBN 0-8039-0782-6). Sage.

Bertsch, Judith, jt. ed. see Treacy, Margaret.

Bertsch, Kenneth A. & Shaw, Linda S. The Nuclear Weapons Industry. 405p. 1984. pap. text ed. 45.00. Investor Ctr.

Bertsch, Lory. Willie Visits Tulip Time. (Illus.). 40p. 1983. 4.50 (ISBN 0-682-49980-3). Exposition Pr FL.

Bertsche, G. Practitioners Shell Model. 1972. 24.50 (ISBN 0-444-10348-1). Elsevier.

Bertsekas, Dimitri P. Constrained Optimization & Lagrange Multipler Methods. (Computer Science & Applied Mathematics Ser.). 1982. 65.00 (ISBN 0-12-093480-9). Acad Pr.

--Dynamic Programming & Stochastic Control. (Math in Science & Engineering Ser.). 1976. 45.00 (ISBN 0-12-093250-4). Acad Pr.

Bertsekas, Dimitri P. & Shreve, Steven E. Stochastic Optimal Control: The Discrete Time Case. (Mathematics in Science & Engineering Ser.). 1978. 70.00 (ISBN 0-12-093260-1). Acad Pr.

Berttell, Richard R. Paper & Light: The Calotype in France & Great Britain, 1839-1870. LC 83-47983. (Illus.). 192p. 1984. 35.00 (ISBN 0-87923-485-7). Godine.

Bertucci, Bob, jt. auth. see Crawford, Terry.

Bertucci, Bob, jt. auth. see Fields, Bud.

Bertucci, Bob, jt. auth. see Siroky, Mike.

Bertucci, Bob, jt. auth. see Peterson, James A.

Bertucci, Robert, ed. Championship Volleyball by the Experts. 2nd ed. LC 82-81451. (Illus.). 1982. pap. text ed. 7.95 (ISBN 0-88011-076-7). Leisure Pr.

Berube, John-Paul, jt. auth. see Darcy-Berube, Francoise.

Berube, Maurice R. Education & Poverty: Effective Schooling in the United States & Cuba. LC 83-26428. (Contributions to the Study of Education Ser.: No. 13). xi, 163p. 1984. lib. bdg. 27.95 (ISBN 0-313-23468-X, BPV/). Greenwood.

--The Urban University in America. LC 77-87917. 1978. lib. bdg. 27.50x (ISBN 0-313-20031-9, BUU/). Greenwood.

Beruete y Moret, Aureliano De. Velazquez. facsimile ed. LC 77-37330. (Select Bibliographies Reprint Ser). (Illus.). Repr. of 1906 ed. 37.50 (ISBN 0-8369-6677-5). Ayer Co Pubs.

Berulfsen. Norwegian Grammar. pap. 12.00 (ISBN 0-317-19061-X, N436). Vanous.

Berulfsen, B. Engelsk-Norsk Ordbok. 430p. 1978. 24.95 (ISBN 82-573-0007-1, M-9455). French & Eur.

--English-Norwegian Dictionary, Vol. I. 427p. (Eng. & Norwegian.). 1981. 22.00x (ISBN 8-2573-0161-2, N481). Vanous.

--Norwegian Grammar. 4th ed. 82p. 1977. pap. text ed. 12.00x (ISBN 8-2030-4312-7, N436). Vanous.

Berulfsen, B. & Berulfsen, T. Norwegian Dictionary: Engelsk-Norwegina. rev. ed. 433p. 1981. 22.00x (ISBN 82-573-0161-2, N481). Vanous.

Berulfsen, B. & Svenkerud, A. Norwegian Deluxe Dictionary: English-Norse. (Norwegian & Eng.). 1968. 100.00x (ISBN 82-02-09060-1, N461). Vanous.

Berulfsen, B., jt. auth. see Kirkeby, W.

Berulfsen, B. & Scavenius, H., eds. McKay's Modern Norwegian-English & English-Norwegian Dictionary. (Modern Dictionaries Ser.). (Norwegian & Eng.). 1953. 15.95 (ISBN 0-679-10076-8). McKay.

Berulfsen, T., jt. auth. see Berulfsen, B.

Berutti, John. Dreams Don't Make Noise When They Die. (Illus.). 1978. 10.00 (ISBN 0-912950-39-0); pap. 4.50 (ISBN 0-912950-40-4). Blue Oak.

Berve, Helmut. Das Alexanderreich: Auf Prosopographischer Grundlage Esterband; Darstellung; Zweiterband; Prosopographie, 2 vols in 1. LC 72-7885. (Greek History Ser). (Ger.). Repr. of 1926 ed. 52.00 (ISBN 0-405-04779-7). Ayer Co Pubs.

Berwanger, Eugene H. As They Saw Slavery. LC 77-14984. (Illus.). 174p. 1978. pap. text ed. 9.50 (ISBN 0-88275-624-9). Krieger.

--The Frontier Against Slavery: Western Anti-Negro Prejudice & the Slavery Extension Controversy. LC 67-21850. pap. 35.40 (ISBN 0-317-28433-9, 2019006). Bks Demand UMI.

--The West & Reconstruction. LC 80-26357. (Illus.). 280p. 1981. 18.95x (ISBN 0-252-00868-5). U of Ill Pr.

Berwanger, Eugene H., jt. auth. see Nichols, Roy F.

Berwick, Donald M. Reputation of Jonathan Swift 1781-1882. LC 65-21096. (Studies in Irish Literature, No. 16). 1969. Repr. of 1941 ed. lib. bdg. 39.95x (ISBN 0-8383-0508-3). Haskell.

Berwick, Donald M., et al. Cholesterol, Children, & Heart Disease: An Analysis of Alternatives. (Illus.). 1980. 39.50x (ISBN 0-19-502669-1). Oxford U Pr.

Berwick, Ray. How to Train Your Pet Like a Television Star. LC 77-83372. 1977. pap. 3.95 (ISBN 0-915936-02-2). Armstrong Pub.

Berwick, Robert. The Acquisition of Syntactic Knowledge. (Series in Artificial Intelligence). (Illus.). 350p. 1985. text ed. 27.50x (ISBN 0-262-02226-5). MIT Pr.

Berwick, Robert C. & Weinberg, Amy S. The Grammatical Basis of Linguistic Performance: Language Use & Acquisition. (Current Studies in Linguistics). 288p. 1983. text ed. 30.00x (ISBN 0-262-02192-7). MIT Pr.

Berwick, Robert C., jt. ed. see Brady, Michael.

Berwick, Sandy. The Healthy Gourmet Primer. (The Healthy Gourmet Ser.). 74p. (Orig.). 1983. pap. text ed. 7.50 (ISBN 0-912727-00-4). P S Publishing.

Berwin, Derek & Barber, David. Creative Techniques in Underwater Photography. (Illus.). 144p. 1983. 19.95 (ISBN 0-7134-4035-X, Pub. by Batsford England). David & Charles.

Berwitz, Clement J. The Job Analysis Approach to Affirmative Action. LC 75-11660. (Illus.). pap. 64.80 (ISBN 0-317-09927-2, 2016461). Bks Demand UMI.

Beryl, Ruth. Teaching Home Economics in the Integrated Curriculum. 1977. pap. text ed. 4.00x (ISBN 0-435-42268-5). Heinemann Ed.

Berzelius, Jons J. Essai sur la Theorie Des Proportions Chimiques et Sur L'influence Chimique De L'electricite. (Fr.). Repr. of 1819 ed. 36.00 (ISBN 0-384-04082-9). Johnson Repr.

Berzin, Alexander, ed. see Yeshe, Lama & Rinpoche, Zopa.

Berzing, Bud. Sex Songs of the Ancient Letts. LC 69-10779. 320p. 1969. 5.95 (ISBN 0-8216-0151-2). Univ Bks.

Berzins, Alfreds. Two Faces of Co-Existence. 1967. 10.95 (ISBN 0-8315-0018-2). Speller.

Berzins, Gunars. Born in Sorrow: An Essay Concerning Human Nature. 1984. 8.50 (ISBN 0-533-05830-9). Vantage.

Berzoa, Morton, jt. ed. see Leonhardt, Barbara A.

Berzon, Betty. Positively Gay. rev. ed. 232p. 1984. pap. 7.95 (ISBN 0-915893-00-2). Mediamix.

Berzon, Betty, jt. ed. see Solomon, Lawrence N.

Berzon, Judith R. Neither White nor Black: The Mulatto Character in American Fiction. LC 77-94392. 1978. 35.00x (ISBN 0-8147-0996-6); pap. 16.00x (ISBN 0-8147-0997-4). NYU Pr.

Berzon, S., ed. Seismic Wave Propagation in Real Media. LC 74-80752. (Illus.). 208p. 1969. 35.00x (ISBN 0-306-10825-9, Consultants). Plenum Pub.

Berzonsky. Adolescent Development. 1981. write for info. (ISBN 0-02-471360-0). Macmillan.

Berztiss, A. T. Data Structures: Theory & Practice. 2nd ed. (Computer Science & Applied Mathematics Ser.). 586p. 1975. 24.00i (ISBN 0-12-093552-X). Acad Pr.

Bes, A. & Geraud, G., eds. Cerebral Circulation & Neurotransmitters: Proceedings. (International Congress Ser.: No. 507). 268p. 1980. 51.50 (ISBN 0-444-90129-9, Excerpta Medica). Elsevier.

Bes, A., et al. Cerebral Ischemia. (International Congress Ser.: Vol. 654). 1984. 76.00 (ISBN 0-444-80586-9). Elsevier.

Bes, Andre, et al, eds. Proceedings of the Eleventh International Symposium on Cerebral Blood Flow & Metabolism. 704p. 1983. text ed. 79.00 (ISBN 0-89004-748-0). Raven.

Bes, J. Bulk Carriers. 2nd ed. 1972. 30.00 (ISBN 0-685-11996-3). Heinman.

--Chartering & Shipping Terms, Vol. 1. 10th ed. 1978. 50.00 (ISBN 0-900133-08-2). Heinman.

--Chartering & Shipping Terms: Time-Sheet Supplements, Vols. 2 & 3. Set. 70.00 (ISBN 0-685-11999-8). Heinman.

Besag, Frank P. & Besag, Peter L. Statistics for the Helping Professions. 1985. 24.95 (ISBN 0-8039-2340-6). Sage.

Besag, Frank P. & Levine, Leonard P. BASIC for Teachers. 1984. pap. 14.95 (ISBN 0-8039-2329-5). Sage.

--Computer Literacy for Teachers. LC 84-6954. 112p. (Orig.). 1984. pap. 9.95 (ISBN 0-8039-2330-9). Sage.

Besag, Frank P. & Nelson, Jack. Stasis & Change: The Cultural Foundations of Education. 480p. 1984. pap. text ed. 22.00 (ISBN 0-394-32817-5, RanC). Random.

Besag, Peter L., jt. auth. see Besag, Frank P.

Besalel, V. A., jt. auth. see Azrin, Nathan H.

Besalel, Victoria A., jt. auth. see Azrin, Nathan H.

Besalel, Victoria B., jt. auth. see Azrin, Nathan.

Besanceney, Paul H. Interfaith Marriages: Who & Why. 1970. 10.95x (ISBN 0-8084-0164-5); pap. 7.95x (ISBN 0-8084-0165-3). New Coll U Pr.

Besancon, Alain. Education et Societe en Russie dans le Second Tiers du XIXe Siecle. (Civilisations et Societes: No. 40). 1974. pap. 12.80x (ISBN 90-2797-545-0). Mouton.

Besancon, Alain, ed. L' Histoire Psychanalytique: Une Anthologie. (Le Savoir Historique Ser.: No. 7). 1974. pap. 15.60x (ISBN 90-2797-326-1). Mouton.

Besancon, Its'hak, adapted by see Nachman of Breslov.

Besancon, Robert M., ed. The Encyclopedia of Physics. 3rd ed. 1985. 149.50 (ISBN 0-442-25778-3). Van Nos Reinhold.

Besant, Annie. Ancient Wisdom. 9th ed. 1972. 6.25 (ISBN 0-8356-7038-4). Theos Pub Hse.

--Autobiographical Sketches. 59.95 (ISBN 0-87968-683-9). Gordon Pr.

--Avataras. 124p. 1983. pap. 5.95 (ISBN 0-912181-06-0). East School Pr.

--Death & After. 1972. 2.95 (ISBN 0-8356-7039-2). Theos Pub Hse.

--Esoteric Christianity. 59.95 (ISBN 0-8490-0124-2). Gordon Pr.

--Esoteric Christianity. 8th ed. 1966. 7.00 (ISBN 0-8356-7052-X). Theos Pub Hse.

--Esoteric Christianity. abr ed. LC 71-113470. 1971. pap. 4.95 (ISBN 0-8356-0028-9, Quest). Theos Pub Hse.

--The Free Thinker's Textbook. 59.95 (ISBN 0-8490-0194-3). Gordon Pr.

--The Freethinker's Textbook: Christianity, Its Evidences, Its Origin, Its Morality, Its History, Pt. 2. 3rd ed. LC 77-169205. (Atheist Viewpoint Ser). 288p. 1972. Repr. 21.00 (ISBN 0-405-03803-8). Ayer Co Pubs.

--From the Outer Court to the Inner Sanctum. Nicholson, Shirley, ed. LC 82-42703. 130p. 1983. pap. 4.50 (ISBN 0-8356-0574-4, Quest). Theos Pub Hse.

--How India Wrought for Freedom: The Story of the National Congress Told from Official Records. 770p. 1974. Repr. 40.00 (ISBN 0-88065-057-5, Pub. by Messers Todays & Tomorrows Printers & Publishers India). Scholarly Pubns.

--The Inner Government of the World. 81p. 1981. pap. 4.50 (ISBN 0-89540-092-8, SB-092). Sun Pub.

--Introduction to Yoga. 1972. 3.50 (ISBN 0-8356-7120-8). Theos Pub Hse.

--Karma. 10th ed. 1975. 3.50 (ISBN 0-8356-7035-X). Theos Pub Hse.

--Man & His Bodies. 12th ed. 1967. 2.75 (ISBN 0-8356-7083-X). Theos Pub Hse.

--Reincarnation. 11th ed. 1975. 2.50 (ISBN 0-8356-7019-8). Theos Pub Hse.

--Selection of the Social & Political Pamphlets of Annie Besant 1874-1890. LC 78-114024. 1970. 45.00x (ISBN 0-678-00638-5). Kelley.

--Study in Consciousness. 6th ed. 1972. 7.50 (ISBN 0-8356-7287-5). Theos Pub Hse.

--Thought Power: Its Control & Culture. LC 73-7644. 1967. pap. 3.50 (ISBN 0-8356-0312-1, Quest). Theos Pub Hse.

--Yoga: The Hatha Yoga & Raja Yoga of India. 73p. 1974. pap. 4.95 (ISBN 0-88697-035-0). Life Science.

Besant, Annie & Leadbeater, Charles W. Thought Forms. abr. ed. (Illus.). 1969. pap. 4.95 (ISBN 0-8356-0008-4, Quest). Theos Pub Hse.

Besant, Annie, tr. Bhagavad Gita, 8 pts. 1974. 1.95 (ISBN 0-8356-7001-5). Theos Pub Hse.

Besant, Annie Wood. Annie Besant, an Autobiography. 1976. Repr. of 1893 ed. 29.00 (ISBN 0-403-06689-1, Regency). Scholarly.

Besant, C. B. Computer-Aided Design & Manufacture. 2nd ed. LC 79-40971. (Engineering Science Ser.). (Illus.). 232p. 1982. 54.95x (ISBN 0-470-27372-0); pap. 26.95x (ISBN 0-470-27373-9). Halsted Pr.

Besant, Lloyd, et al, eds. Commodity Trading Manual. 1977. 17.50 (ISBN 0-685-73601-6). Chicago Bd Trade.

Besant, Walter. All Sorts & Conditions of Men: An Impossible Story. LC 78-131632. 1971. Repr. of 1899 ed. 39.00x (ISBN 0-403-00519-1). Scholarly.

--Autobiography of Sir Walter Besant. LC 76-144877. 1971. Repr. of 1902 ed. 39.00 (ISBN 0-403-00864-6). Scholarly.

--East London. LC 79-56945. (The English Working Class Ser.). 373p. 1980. lib. bdg. 43.00 (ISBN 0-8240-0100-1). Garland Pub.

--Essays & Historiettes. LC 70-105763. 1970. Repr. of 1903 ed. 24.00x (ISBN 0-8046-0938-1, Pub. by Kennikat). Assoc Faculty Pr.

--The Eulogy of Richard Jefferies. 384p. 1980. Repr. of 1893 ed. lib. bdg. 45.00 (ISBN 0-8495-0453-8). Arden Lib.

--The Eulogy of Richard Jeffries. 1889. Repr. 20.00 (ISBN 0-8274-2319-5). R West.

--The French Humorists: From the Twelfth to the Ninteenth Century. Repr. of 1873 ed. lib. bdg. 40.00 (ISBN 0-8495-0378-7). Arden Lib.

--French Humorists: From the Twelfth to the Nineteenth Century. facsimile ed. LC 74-38774. (Essay Index Reprint Ser). Repr. of 1874 ed. 23.00 (ISBN 0-8369-2635-8). Ayer Co Pubs.

--In Deacon's Orders, & Other Stories. facs. ed. LC 76-128720. (Short Story Index Reprint Ser). 1895. 17.00 (ISBN 0-8369-3611-6). Ayer Co Pubs.

--In Deacon's Orders, 1895. Wolff, Robert L., ed. Bd. with Red Pottage, 1899. Cholmondely, Mary. LC 75-1541. (Victorian Fiction Ser). 1976. lib. bdg. 73.00 (ISBN 0-8240-1612-2). Garland Pub.

--London. 1892. lib. bdg. 50.00 (ISBN 0-8492-3723-8). R West.

--Rabelais. LC 73-12353. Repr. of 1898 ed. lib. bdg. 15.00 (ISBN 0-8414-3220-1). Folcroft.

--Readings in Rabelais. 1973. Repr. of 1883 ed. 25.00 (ISBN 0-8274-1436-6). R West.

--The Rebel Queen. facsimile ed. LC 74-27964. (Modern Jewish Experience Ser.). 1975. Repr. of 1893 ed. 36.50x (ISBN 0-405-06695-3). Ayer Co Pubs.

--Studies in Early French Poetry. LC 72-13206. (Essay Index Reprint Ser.). Repr. of 1868 ed. 20.00 (ISBN 0-8369-8147-2). Ayer Co Pubs.

--Studies in Early French Poetry. LC 72-13206. (Essay Index Reprint Ser.). 319p. Repr. of 1868 ed. lib. bdg. 17.00 (ISBN 0-8290-0522-6). Irvington.

Besant, Walter & Rice, James. Sir Richard Whittington, Lord Maylor of London. 222p. 1982. Repr. of 1881 ed. lib. bdg. 30.00 (ISBN 0-8495-0608-5). Arden Lib.

Besant, Walter, ed. see Conder, Claude R.

Besas, Peter. Behind the Spanish Lens: Spanish Cinema under Fascism & Democracy. (Illus.). 300p. (Orig.). 1985. 26.00 (ISBN 0-912869-06-2). Arden Pr.

Besaw, Victor. The Sword of Shandar. 1978. pap. 1.75 (ISBN 0-532-17195-0). Woodhill.

Besch, Paige. Clinical Radioassay Procedures: A Compendium. LC 74-28803. 338p. 1985. 20.00 (ISBN 0-915274-01-9); members 15.00. Am Assn Clinical Chem.

Besch, Werner & Knoop, Ulrich, eds. Dialektologie: Ein Handbuch Zur Deutschen Und Allgemeinen Dialektforschung, 2 Pts. (Illus.). 1344p. 1982. Pt. 1. 192.00x (ISBN 3-11-005977-0); Pt. 2. 220.00 (ISBN 3-11-009571-8). De Gruyter.

Besch, Werner & Reichmann, Eskar, eds. Sprachgeschichte: Ein Handbuch zur Geschichte der Deutschen Sprache und Ihrer Erforschung, 2 pts. (Handbuecher zur Sprach und Kommunikations Wissenschaft). (Illus.). xxxiiii, 948p. (Ger.). 1984. 216.00x (ISBN 3-11-007396-X). De Gruyter.

Bescherelle. Art de Conjuguer: Douze Mille Verbes. (Fr). 6.95 (ISBN 0-685-20225-9). Schoenhof.

Bescherelle, Louis. Le Nouveau Bescherelle: L'Art De Conjuguer. 7.50 (ISBN 0-685-11014-1). French & Eur.

Beschner & Friedman, eds. Youth Drug Abuse: Problems, Issues, & Treatment. LC 78-21197. 1979. 30.00 (ISBN 0-669-02804-5). Lexington Bks.

Besdine, Richard W., jt. auth. see Rowe, John W.

Besdo, D., ed. see CISM (International Center for Mechanical Sciences).

Besedovskii, Grigorii Z. Revelations of a Soviet Diplomat. Norgate, M., tr. LC 75-39046. (Russian Studies: Perspectives on the Revolution Ser). 276p. 1977. Repr. of 1931 ed. 23.65 (ISBN 0-88355-424-0). Hyperion-Conn.

Beseliev, Veselin. Bulgarisch-Byzantinische Aufsatze. 370p. 1978. 60.00x (ISBN 0-86078-024-4, Pub. by Variorum). State Mutual Bk.

Besemer, Susan P. & Crosman, Christopher, eds. From Museums, Galleries, & Studios: A Guide to Artists on Film & Tape. LC 83-22710. (Art Reference Collection: No. 6). xvi, 199p. 1984. lib. bdg. 35.00 (ISBN 0-313-23881-2, BFM/). Greenwood.

Besemeres, John. Socialist Population Politics: The Political Implications of Demographic Trends in the USSR & Eastern Europe. LC 80-65260. 320p. 1980. 30.00 (ISBN 0-87332-154-5). M E Sharpe.

Besen, Stanley M., et al. Regulation of Media Ownership by the Federal Communications Commission. LC 84-26387. 77p. 1984. 7.50 (ISBN 0-8330-0627-4, R-3206-MF). Rand Corp.

--Misregulating Television: Network Dominance & the F.C.C. LC 84-8738. 160p. 1985. lib. bdg. 24.00x (ISBN 0-226-04415-7). U of Chicago Pr.

Beserra, Sarah S. & Franklin, Sterling C. The Sex Code of California: A Compendium. 2nd ed. Clevenger, Norma K., ed. 191p. Set. pap. 6.95x (ISBN 0-86576-001-2); pap. 5.95x (ISBN 0-686-74351-2). W Kaufmann.

Besford, John. Good Mouthkeeping; or How to Save Your Children's Teeth & Your Own While You're about It. (Illus.). 200p. 1984. 10.95x (ISBN 0-19-261461-4). Oxford U Pr.

Besharon, Douglas J. The Vulnerable Social Worker: Liability for Serving Children & Families. 1985. 12.95 (ISBN 0-87101-136-0). Natl Assn Soc Wkrs.

Besharov, Douglas J. Juvenile Justice Advocacy: Practice in a Unique Court. 1974. 20.00 (ISBN 0-685-85396-9, C1-1144). PLI.

--Protecting Abused & Neglected Children: Identification & Action. 1983. pap. text ed. cancelled (ISBN 0-8391-1797-3, 17949). Univ Park.

Besharov, Douglas J., jt. auth. see Fontana, Vincent J.

Beshenkovsky, Eugene, jt. ed. see Kulik, Eugene J.

Beshers, James M. Urban Social Structure. LC 80-27972. vii, 207p. 1981. Repr. of 1962 ed. lib. bdg. 27.50x (ISBN 0-313-22714-4, BEUR). Greenwood.

Beshlie. Romany Wood. (Illus.). 1977. 7.95x (ISBN 0-8464-0800-7). Beekman Pubs.

--Snailsleap Lane. (Illus.). 7.95x (ISBN 0-8464-0854-6). Beekman Pubs.

Beshlyage, V., et al. Do You Know How the Sun Laughs? 262p. 1976. 3.95 (ISBN 0-8285-0948-4, Pub. by Progress Pubs USSR). Imported Pubns.

Beshoar, Daniel. Violet Soup: Common Edible Plants of the Rockies. (Illus.). 70p. 1982. 8.00 (ISBN 0-86541-009-7); pap. 4.00 (ISBN 0-86541-010-0). Filter.

Besier, Rudolf. The Barretts of Wimpole Street. (Illus.). 1930. 9.95 (ISBN 0-316-09223-1). Little.

Beskin, Wade, tr. see Brehier, Emile.

Beskow, Arne. Look at Norway. (Illus.). xiv, 144p. 1981. 40.00 (ISBN 82-05-13081-7, Pub. by Gyldendal Norsk Forlag Norway). Heinman.

Beskow, Bo. Two by Two. 128p. 1981. pap. 2.95 (ISBN 0-380-55210-8, 55210-8, Bard). Avon.

Beskow, Elsa. Children of the Forest. (Illus.). 1984. laminated bds 11.95 (ISBN 0-510-00128-9, Pub. by Salem Hse Ltd). Merrimack Pub Cir.

--Pelle's New Suit. (Illus.). 16p. (ps-1). 1929. PLB 12.89 (ISBN 0-06-020496-6). HarpJ.

--Peter in Blueberry Land. (Illus.). 34p. 1984. laminated bds 11.95 (ISBN 0-510-00129-7, Pub. By Salem Hse Ltd). Merrimack Pub Cir.

Beskow, Per. Strange Tales About Jesus: A Survey of Unfamiliar Gospels. LC 82-16001. 144p. 1983. pap. 6.95 (ISBN 0-8006-1686-3, 1-1686). Fortress.

Besmer, Fremont E. Horses, Musicians & Gods: The Hausa Cult of Spirit Possession. (Illus.). 304p. 1983. 39.95x (ISBN 0-89789-020-5). Bergin & Garvey.

--Kidan Daran Salla: Music for the Eve of the Muslim Festivals of Id Al-Fitr & Id Al-Kabir in Kano, Nigeria. (African Humanities Ser.). (Illus.). 84p. (Orig.). 1974. pap. text ed. 4.00 (ISBN 0-941934-10-1). Indiana Africa.

Besnard, M. & Coursodon, J. P. Ecritures: Techniques de Composition. 1972. write for info. (ISBN 0-02-309150-9). Macmillan.

Besnard, Philippe, ed. The Sociological Domain: The Durkheimians & the Founding of French Sociology. LC 82-9485. (Illus.). 336p. 1983. 47.50 (ISBN 0-521-23876-5). Cambridge U Pr.

Besnehard, Daniel. Passengers. Vogel, Stephen J., tr. (Ubu Repertory Theater Publications Ser.: No. 11). 100p. (Orig.). 1985. pap. text ed. 6.25 (ISBN 0-913745-12-X, Dist. by Publishing Center for Cultural Resources). Ubu Repertory.

Besner, Edward & Ferrigno, Peter. Practical Endodontics: A Clinical Guide. (Illus.). 184p. 1981. text ed. 23.95 (ISBN 0-683-00607-X). Williams & Wilkins.

Besner, Hilda F. & Robinson, Sandra J. Understanding & Solving your Police Marriage Problems. (Illus.). 174p. 1982. pap. 18.50x (ISBN 0-398-04707-3). C C Thomas.

Besov, O. V., et al. Nine Papers on Functional Analysis & Numerical Analysis. (Translations Ser.: No. 2, Vol. 40). 1964. 25.00 (ISBN 0-8218-1740-X, TRANS 2-40). Am Math.

Besov, Oleg V., et al. Integral Representations of Functions & Imbedding Theorems, 2 vols. (Scripta Series in Mathematics). 1979. Vol. 1, 345p. 19.95x ea. (ISBN 0-470-26540-X). Vol. 2, 311p (ISBN 0-470-26593-0). Halsted Pr.

Besoyan, Rick. Babes in the Wood. 64p. 1983. pap. 4.00 (ISBN 0-88145-011-1). Broadway Play.

Besozzi, Cerbonio. Chronik Des Cerbonio Besozzi: 1548-1563. 185p. pap. 23.00 (ISBN 0-384-15678-9). Johnson Repr.

Bespaloff, Alexis. The New Signet Book of Wine. 1980. pap. 3.50 (ISBN 0-451-12948-2, AE2948, Sig). NAL.

Bespaloff, Alexis, ed. The Fireside Book of Wine. (Illus.). 446p. (Orig.). 1984. pap. 9.95 (ISBN 0-671-53069-0, Fireside). S&S.

Bess, C. W. Object-Centered Children's Sermons. (Object Lesson Ser.). 1978. pap. 3.95 (ISBN 0-8010-0734-8). Baker Bk.

--Sermons for the Seasons. 1985. pap. 4.95 (ISBN 0-8054-2256-0). Broadman.

--Sparkling Object Sermons for Children. (Object Lesson Ser.). 120p. (Orig.). 1982. pap. 4.50 (ISBN 0-8010-0824-7). Baker Bk.

Bess, C. W. & DeBand, Roy E. Bible-Centered Object Sermons for Children. (Object Lesson Ser.). 128p. 1985. pap. 4.95 (ISBN 0-8010-0886-7). Baker Bk.

Bess, Clayton. Big Man & the Burn-Out. 208p. (gr. 5 up). 1985. 12.95 (ISBN 0-395-36173-7). HM.

--Big Man & the Burn Out. 1985. 12.95 (ISBN 0-317-31616-8). HM.

--Story for a Black Night. LC 81-13396. (gr. 7 up). 1982. 7.95 (ISBN 0-395-31857-2). HM.

--The Truth about the Moon. (Illus.). 48p. (gr. k-3). 1983. PLB 8.95 (ISBN 0-395-34551-0). HM.

Bess, Demaree, jt. auth. see Littlepage, John D.

Bess, Fred H. & McConnell, Freeman E. Audiology, Education & the Hearing Impaired Child. LC 80-39517. (Illus.). 321p. 1981. pap. text ed. 23.95 (ISBN 0-8016-0671-3). Mosby.

Bess, Fred H., ed. Childhood Deafness: Causation, Assessment & Management. 368p. 1977. 51.50 (ISBN 0-8089-1043-4, 790575). Grune.

Bess, Fred H., et al, eds. Amplification in Education. LC 81-68721. (Illus.). 400p. (Orig.). pap. 16.95 (ISBN 0-88200-146-9, F3002). Alexander Graham.

Bess, H. David. Marine Transportation. LC 75-28532. 1976. 5.95x (ISBN 0-8134-1772-4, 1772). Interstate.

Bess, H. David & Farris, Martin T. U. S. Maritime Policy: History & Prospects. LC 81-1503. 238p. 1981. 39.95 (ISBN 0-03-059419-7). Praeger.

Bess, James L. College & University Organization. 1984. 30.00 (ISBN 0-317-18433-4); pap. 12.50 (ISBN 0-317-18434-2). NYU pr.

--University Organization: A Matrix Analysis of the Academic Professions. LC 81-8127. 334p. 1982. 29.95x (ISBN 0-89885-036-3). Human Sci Pr.

Bess, James L., ed. College & University Organization: Insights from the Behavioral Sciences. 144p. 1983. 32.50 (ISBN 0-8147-1056-5); pap. 13.50. NYU Pr.

--Motivating Professors to Teach Effectively. LC 81-48583. (Teching & Learning Ser.: No. 10). 1982. 8.95x (ISBN 0-87589-924-2). Jossey-Bass.

Bessant, B., jt. auth. see Spaull, A. D.

Bessant, J. & Dickson, K. Computers & Employment: An Annotated Bibliography. (British Computer Society Ser.). 1981. 21.95 (ISBN 0-471-26205-6). Wiley.

Bessant, J. R. & Dickson, K. E. Issues in the Adoption of Microelectronics. 148p. 1982. 27.00 (ISBN 0-903804-73-5). F Pinter Pubs.

Bessant, J. R., et al. The Impact of Microelectronics: A Review of the Literature. LC 80-54414. (Illus.). 174p. 1981. text ed. 25.00x (ISBN 0-87663-729-2, Pica Special Studies). Universe.

Bessant, John & Cole, Sam. Stacking the Chips. 310p. 1985. 26.95x (ISBN 0-8476-7461-4). Rowman.

Bessant, John & Grunt, Manfred. Management & Manufacturing Innovation in the United Kingdom & West Germany. LC 84-21728. 331p. 1985. text ed. 37.95 (ISBN 0-566-00727-4). Gower Pub Co.

Bessant, John & Cole, Sam, eds. Stacking the Chips. 260p. cancelled (ISBN 0-86187-359-9). F Pinter Pubs.

Bessason, Haraldur, tr. see Johannesson, Jon.

Bessborough, ed. see Schreiber, Charlotte E.

Besse, A. L. Manifolds All of Whose Geodesics Are Closed. (Ergebnisse der Mathmatik und Ihrer Grenzbebiete: Vol. 93). (Illus.). 1978. 51.00 (ISBN 0-387-08158-5). Springer-Verlag.

Besse, B., et al. Lexique Anglais-Francais de L'Aciere Electrique. 135p. (Eng. & Fr.). 1975. pap. 8.95 (ISBN 0-686-92555-6, M-9239). French & Eur.

Bessel, Richard. Political Violence & the Rise of Nazism: The Storm Troopers in Eastern Germany 1925-1934. LC 83-40477. 256p. 1984. 21.00x (ISBN 0-300-03171-8). Yale U Pr.

Bessel, Richard & Feuchtwanger, E. J., eds. Social Change & Political Development in Weimar Germany. LC 80-41179. 298p. 1981. 28.50x (ISBN 0-389-20176-6, 06952). B&N Imports.

Bessel, Richard, jt. ed. see Ehlers, Robert.

Besselaar, A. van den see Van Den Besselaar, A., et al.

Besseling, J. F. & Van Der Heijden, A. M., eds. Trends in Solid Mechanics. 256p. 1980. 45.00x (ISBN 90-286-0699-8). Sijthoff & Noordhoff.

Bessell, Harold. Human Development Program: Activity Guide, Level Pk. rev. ed. 1972. 10.95 (ISBN 0-86584-000-8). Palomares & Assoc.

--Human Development Program: Activity Guide, Level I. rev. ed. 1972. 10.95 (ISBN 0-86584-001-6). Palomares & Assoc.

--Human Development Program: Activity Guide, Level II. rev. ed. 1972. 10.95 (ISBN 0-86584-002-4). Palomares & Assoc.

--Human Development Program: Activity Guide, Level III. rev. ed. 1972. 10.95 (ISBN 0-86584-003-2). Palomares & Assoc.

--Human Development Program: Activity Guide, Level IV. rev. ed. 1972. 10.95 (ISBN 0-86584-004-0). Palomares & Assoc.

--Human Development Program: Activity Guide, Level V. rev. ed. 1972. 10.95 (ISBN 0-86584-005-9). Palomares & Assoc.

--Human Development Program: Activity Guide, Level VI. rev. ed. 1972. 10.95 (ISBN 0-86584-006-7). Palomares & Assoc.

--The Love Test. Golbitz, Pat, ed. LC 83-13312. (Illus.). 316p. 1984. 14.95 (ISBN 0-688-01383-X). Morrow.

--The Love Test. 256p. 1985. pap. 3.50 (ISBN 0-446-32582-1). Warner Bks.

Bessell, Harold & Kelly, Thomas. The Parent Book. new ed. LC 77-71461. 1977. pap. 9.95 (ISBN 0-915190-15-X). Jalmar Pr.

Bessell, Peter. Cover-up: The Jeremy Thorpe Affair. LC 80-52089. (Illus.). 574p. 1981. pap. 10.00 ltd. ed. (ISBN 0-937812-01-3). Simons Bks.

Bessell, Robert. Interviewing & Counselling. 1976. 14.95 (ISBN 0-7134-0965-7, Pub. by Batsford England). David & Charles.

Besser, Daniel. Timesharing: The Dollars & Sense. (Condominium Guideline Ser.). 200p. 1985. 32.95 (ISBN 0-317-26994-1). Wyndham Hse.

Besser, G. M., ed. Advanced Medicine: Proceedings of the 13th Annual Symposium of Advanced Medicine, 1977. (Illus.). 1977. 34.95x (ISBN 0-8464-0111-8). Beekman Pubs.

Besser, G. M. & Martini, Luciano, eds. Clinical Neuroendocrinology, Vol. 2. 450p. 1982. 60.00 (ISBN 0-12-093602-X). Acad Pr.

Besser, G. M., jt. ed. see Martini, Luciano.

Besser, Gretchen R. Nathalie Sarraute. (World Authors Ser.). 1979. lib. bdg. 14.50 (ISBN 0-8057-6376-7, Twayne). G K Hall.

Besser, Joe, et al. Not Just a Stooge: The Autobiography of Hollywood's Most Prolific Third Stooge. (Illus.). 276p. (Orig.). pap. 10.95 (ISBN 0-918283-00-0). Excelsior Bks.

Besserman, G., tr. see Huxley, Aldous.

Besserman, Lawrence L. The Legend of Job in the Middle Ages. LC 78-14936. (Illus.). 1979. 15.00x (ISBN 0-674-52385-7, Belknap Pr). Harvard U Pr.

Besset, Maurice. Art of the Twentieth Century. LC 72-91630. (History of Art Ser.). (Illus.). 200p. 1976. 10.00x (ISBN 0-87663-186-3). Universe.

Bessette, Gerard. The Brawl. Lebel, Marc & Sutherland, Ronald, trs. LC 77-473823. (French Writers of Canada Ser.). pap. 57.50 (ISBN 0-317-30429-1, 2024931). Bks Demand UMI.

Bessette, Joseph M. & Tulis, Jeffrey, eds. The Presidency in the Constitutional Order. LC 80-14250. xvi, 349p. 1981. text ed. 32.50x (ISBN 0-8071-0774-3); pap. text ed. 8.95x (ISBN 0-8071-0781-6). La State U Pr.

Bessey, Ernest A. Morphology & Taxonomy of Fungi. (Illus.). 1973. Repr. of 1950 ed. 21.95x (ISBN 0-02-841320-2). Hafner.

Bessey, M. A., ed. see Bradford, Gamaliel.

Bessie, Alvah. Alvah Bessie's Short Fictions. LC 82-9739. 312p. (Orig.). 1982. pap. 7.95 (ISBN 0-88316-546-5). Chandler & Sharp.

--Bread & a Stone. LC 83-7488. 352p. 1983. pap. 7.95 (ISBN 0-88316-553-8). Chandler & Sharp.

--Men in Battle. new ed. LC 74-28743. 408p. 1975. pap. 6.95 (ISBN 0-88316-513-9). Chandler & Sharp.

--Spain Again. LC 74-28742. (Illus.). 242p. 1975. pap. 5.95 (ISBN 0-88316-516-3). Chandler & Sharp.

Bessiere, Irene. Recit fantastique: La Poetique de l'incertain. new ed. (Collection Themes et Textes). 256p. (Orig., Fr.). 1974. pap. 6.75 (ISBN 2-03-035023-0, 2674). Larousse.

Bessiere, J. Fitzgerald: La Vocation de l'echec. (Collection themes et textes). 256p. (Orig., Fr.). 1972. pap. 6.75 (ISBN 2-03-035002-8, 2682). Larousse.

Bessieres, Albert. Wife, Mother & Mystic: Blessed Anna Maria Taigi. Newton, Douglas, ed. Rigby, Stephen, tr. from Fr. (Eng.). 1977. pap. 5.50 (ISBN 0-89555-058-X). TAN Bks Pubs.

Bessinger, J. B., Jr., ed. A Concordance to Beowulf. (Concordances Series). 407p. (Prog. Bk.). 1969. 39.50x (ISBN 0-8014-0480-0). Cornell U Pr.

--A Concordance to the "Anglo-Saxon Poetic Records". LC 77-6186. (Concordances Ser.). 1503p. 1978. 75.00x (ISBN 0-8014-1146-7). Cornell U Pr.

Bessinger, Jess B. A Short Dictionary of Anglo-Saxon Poetry: In a Normalized Early West-Saxon Orthography. LC 61-2144. pap. 26.30 (ISBN 0-317-09527-7, 2020454). Bks Demand UMI.

Bessinger, Jess B., Jr. & Yeager, Robert F., eds. Approaches to Teaching Beowulf. (Approaches to Teaching Masterpieces of World Literature Ser.: No. 4). 212p. 1984. 25.00x (ISBN 0-87352-481-0); pap. 14.50x (ISBN 0-87352-482-9). Modern Lang.

Bessinger, R. Carlton & Suojanen, Waino, eds. Management & the Brain: An Integrative Approach to Organization Behavior. 285p. 1983. pap. 19.95 (ISBN 0-88406-161-2). Ga St U Busn Pub.

Bessis, D., jt. ed. see Levy, M.

Bessis, Daniel, ed. see NATO Advanced Study Institute, Cargese, Corsica, June 24 - July, 1979.

Bessis, M. Blood Smears Reinterpreted. (Illus.). 1977. 57.00 (ISBN 0-387-07206-3). Springer-Verlag.

--Corpuscles: Atlas of Red Blood Cell Shapes. LC 73-77351. (Illus.). xvi, 140p. 1976. 56.00 (ISBN 0-387-06375-7). Springer-Verlag.

--Living Blood Cells & Their Ultrastructure. Weed, R. I., tr. from Fr. LC 72-88924. (Illus.). 800p. 1973. 91.00 (ISBN 0-387-05981-4). Springer-Verlag.

Bessis, M., ed. Unclassifiable Leukemias. (Illus.). 270p. 1975. pap. 29.00 (ISBN 0-387-07242-X). Springer-Verlag.

Bessis, M. & Brecher, G., eds. Hemopoietic Dysplasias: Proceedings of a Symposium, Held on Oct.11-12, 1974 at the Institute of Cell Pathology, Hopital De Bicetre, Paris, France. (Illus.). 1977. pap. 33.00 (ISBN 0-387-07597-6). Springer-Verlag.

Bessis, M., et al, eds. Red Cell Rheology. (Illus.). 1978. pap. 68.00 (ISBN 0-387-09001-0). Springer-Verlag.

--Red Cell Shape: Physiology, Pathology, Ultrastructure. LC 73-77351. (Illus.). 180p. 1973. 29.00 (ISBN 0-387-06257-2). Springer-Verlag.

Bessmer, Sue. The Laws of Rape. LC 84-18202. (Landmark Dissertations in Women's Studies). 400p. 1984. 29.95 (ISBN 0-03-069524-4). Praeger.

Besso, Henry V. Dramatic Literature of the Sephardic Jews of Amsterdam in the XVII & XVIII Centuries. 118p. 1.00 (ISBN 0-318-14257-0). Hispanic Inst.

Bessom, Malcolm E., et al. Teaching Music in Today's Secondary Schools: A Creative Approach to Contemporary Music Education. 2nd ed. 1980. text ed. 21.95 (ISBN 0-03-021556-0). HR&W.

Besson, Augustin & Saegesser, Frederic. Color Atlas of Chest Trauma & Associated Injuries, 2 vols. 1983. Set. 179.00 (ISBN 0-87489-362-3). Med Economics.

--Color Atlas of Chest Trauma & Associated Injuries, Vol. 1. (Illus.). 384p. (Orig.). 1983. 98.50 (ISBN 0-87489-353-4). Med Economics.

--Color Atlas of Chest Trauma & Associated Injuries, Vol. 2. (Illus.). 360p. 1983. 98.50 (ISBN 0-87489-354-2). Med Economics.

Besson, Clyde C. Growing Together: Growth Coaching for Couples. Goss, Leonard G., ed. 184p. 1985. pap. write for info. (ISBN 0-88062-066-8). Mott Media.

--Picking up the Pieces. 209p. 1982. pap. 5.95 (ISBN 0-317-01575-3). Mott Media.

Besson, J., ed. Advanced Infared Sensor Technology, Vol. 395. 279p. 42.00 (ISBN 0-89252-430-8). Photo-Optical.

Besson, J. A. History of Eufaula, Alabama: The Bluff City of the Chattahoochee. LC 76-50. 72p. 1976. Repr. of 1875 ed. 7.500 (ISBN 0-87152-229-2). Reprint.

Besson, Maurice. Scourge of the Indies: Buccaneers, Corsairs & Filibusters. 1977. lib. bdg. 69.95 (ISBN 0-8490-2574-5). Gordon Pr.

Besson, Pablo, tr. from Greek. Nuevo Testamento de Nuestro Senor Jesucristo. 576p. (Span.). 1981. pap. 6.50 (ISBN 0-311-48710-6, Edit Mundo). Casa Bautista.

Bessonette, Colin. Back Roads & City Streets: Weekend Getaways in & Around Georgia. LC 83-63500. (Illus.). 150p. (Orig.). 1984. pap. 6.95 (ISBN 0-931948-54-1). Peachtree Pubs.

Bessonova, E. N., et al. Investigation of the Mechanism of Earthquakes. LC 60-9255. (Soviet Research in Geophysics Ser.: Trudy No. 40). 1960. 34.50x (ISBN 0-306-10625-6, Consultants). Plenum Pub.

Bessrebrennikov, N., jt. auth. see Chernov, A.

Besst, Nancy. Milton & Matilda. (Illus.). 48p. (Orig.). (gr. 4-9). 1982. pap. 3.95 (ISBN 0-8351-0998-4). China Bks.

Bessy, Maurice. Charlie Chaplin. LC 84-43184. (Illus.). 440p. 1985. 48.08 (ISBN 0-06-015423-3, HarpT). Har-Row.

Best. Small Business Computer Systems. pap. 20.95 (ISBN 0-13-814129-0). P-H.

Best & Ross. River Pollution Studies. 102p. 1982. 30.00x (ISBN 0-85323-363-2, Pub. by Liverpool Univ England). State Mutual Bk.

Best, et al. Planting by the Moon, Including Growers Guide, 1983 -1984. 140p. (Orig.). 1982. pap. 3.95 (ISBN 0-917086-48-1). A C S Pubns Inc.

Best, Alan. Frank Wedekind. Last, R. W., ed. (Modern German Authors Ser: No. 4). 125p. 1975. text ed. 7.50x (ISBN 0-85496-054-6). Humanities.

Best, Alan C. & Blij, Harm J. De. An African Survey. LC 76-44520. 626p. 1977. text ed. 43.00 (ISBN 0-471-20063-8). Wiley.

Best, Alan D. & Wolfshutz, Hans, eds. Modern Austrian Writing: Literature & Society After 1945. 307p. 1980. 28.50x (ISBN 0-389-20038-7, 06810). B&N Imports.

Best, Arthur. When Consumers Complain. 256p. 1981. 25.00x (ISBN 0-231-05124-7). Columbia U Pr.

Best, Bob, jt. auth. see Pagna, Tom.

Best, Catherine T., ed. Hemispheric Function & Collaboration in the Child. (Educational Psychology Ser.). Date not set. 46.50 (ISBN 0-12-093720-4). Acad Pr.

Best, Charles L., jt. auth. see Schwar, James P.

Best, David. Expression in Movement & the Arts. 203p. 1980. 12.00x (ISBN 0-86019-003-X, Pub. by Kimpton). State Mutual Bk.

--Expression in Movement & the Arts: A Philosophical Enquiry. 12.00 (ISBN 0-8238-0200-0). Plays.

--Feeling & Reason in the Arts. 220p. 1985. text ed. 28.50x (ISBN 0-04-370156-6); pap. text ed. 9.95x (ISBN 0-04-370157-4). Allen Unwin.

--Philosophy & Human Movement. (Unwin Education Bks.). 1979. text ed. 21.95x (ISBN 0-04-370088-8); pap. text ed. 7.95x (ISBN 0-04-370089-6). Allen Unwin.

Best, Deborah L., jt. auth. see Williams, John E.

Best, Don & Freeman, Jim. Crystal Clarinets: A Coffee Table Book of Nice. LC 80-83629. (Illus.). 96p. (Orig.). pap. 6.66 (ISBN 0-938104-00-4). Cosmotic Concerns.

Best, E. A. Following Jesus: Discipleship in the Gospel of Mark. (Journal for the Study of the New Testament, Supplement Ser.: No. 4). 283p. 1981. text ed. 27.50x (ISBN 0-905774-28-0, Pub. by JSOT Pr England); pap. text ed. 12.50x (ISBN 0-905774-29-9, Pub. by JSOT Pr England). Eisenbrauns.

Best, E. P. & Haeck, J., eds. Ecological Indicators for the Assessment of the Quality of Air, Water, Soil, & Ecosystems. 1984. lib. bdg. 31.50 (ISBN 0-318-00438-0, Pub. by Reidel Holland). Kluwer Academic.

Best, Elsdon. The Astronomical Knowledge of the Maori, Genuine & Empirical. Bd. with The Maori Division of Time. LC 75-35226. Repr. of 1922 ed. 12.50 (ISBN 0-404-14405-5). AMS Pr.

--Fishing Methods & Devices of the Maori. LC 75-35228. Repr. of 1929 ed. 27.50 (ISBN 0-404-14406-3). AMS Pr.

--Forest Lore of the Maori. LC 75-35229. Repr. of 1942 ed. 42.50 (ISBN 0-404-14407-1). AMS Pr.

--The Maori, 2 vols. LC 75-35231. Repr. of 1924 ed. Set. 95.00 (ISBN 0-404-14310-5). AMS Pr.

--Maori Agriculture. LC 75-35232. Repr. of 1925 ed. 68.00 (ISBN 0-404-14409-8). AMS Pr.

--The Maori Canoe. Bd. with Polynesian Voyagers. LC 75-35234. Repr. of 1925 ed. 57.50 (ISBN 0-404-14411-X). AMS Pr.

--Maori Religion & Mythology. LC 75-35236. Repr. of 1924 ed. 37.50 (ISBN 0-404-14412-8). AMS Pr.

Best, Ernest. From Text to Sermon: Responsible Use of the New Testament in Preaching. LC 77-79584. 1978. 8.95 (ISBN 0-8042-0245-1). John Knox.

--I Peter. Black, Matthew, ed. (The New Century Bible Commentary Ser.). 188p. 1982. pap. 6.95 (ISBN 0-8028-1909-5). Eerdmans.

Best, Ernest, ed. Letter of Paul to the Romans: Cambridge Bible Commentary on the New English Bible. (New Testament Ser.). (Orig.). 1967. 21.95 (ISBN 0-521-04213-5); pap. 8.95x (ISBN 0-521-09401-1, 401). Cambridge U Pr.

Best, Ernest & Wilson, R. McL., eds. Text & Interpretation: Studies in the New Testament. LC 78-2962. pap. 71.50 (ISBN 0-317-26088-X, 2024416). Bks Demand UMI.

Best, Ernest E. Religion & Society in Transition: The Church & Social Change in England, 1560-1850. LC 82-21699. (Texts & Studies in Religion: Vol. 15). 353p. 1983. 59.95x (ISBN 0-88946-804-4). E Mellen.

Best, Fred. Flexible Life Scheduling: Breaking the Education-Work-Retirement Lockstep. LC 80-160. 286p. 1980. 39.95 (ISBN 0-03-050586-0); pap. 15.95 (ISBN 0-03-050591-7). Praeger.

--Work Sharing: Issues, Policy Options & Prospects. 204p. 1981. text ed. 17.95 (ISBN 0-911558-79-9); pap. text ed. 11.95 (ISBN 0-911558-80-2). W E Upjohn.

Best, G., jt. ed. see Beales, D.

Best, G. M. Mexican Narrow Gauge. LC 68-57487. (Illus.). 14.95 (ISBN 0-8310-7073-0). Howell-North.

--Nevada County Narrow Gauge. LC 65-18740. (Illus.). 1965. 17.50 (ISBN 0-8310-7049-8). Howell-North.

Best, Gary D. Herbert Hoover: The Postpresidential Years, 1933-1964, 2 Vols. 538p. 1983. Set. 75.00 (ISBN 0-8179-7761-9). Hoover Inst Pr.

--The Politics of American Individualism: Herbert Hoover in Transition, 1918-1921. LC 75-16960. 202p. 1975. lib. bdg. 29.95x (ISBN 0-8371-8160-7, BPA/). Greenwood.

--To Free a People: American Jewish Leaders & the Jewish Problem in Eastern Europe, 1890 to 1914. LC 81-4265. (Contributions in American History Ser.: No. 98). xi, 240p. 1982. lib. bdg. 29.95 (ISBN 0-313-22532-X, BTO/). Greenwood.

Best, Geoffrey. Honour Among Men & Nations: Transformations of an Idea. 112p. 1982. 13.50x (ISBN 0-8020-2459-9); pap. 7.50 (ISBN 0-8020-6472-8). U of Toronto Pr.

--Humanity in Warfare. 400p. 1980. 34.00x (ISBN 0-231-05158-1); pap. 12.00 (ISBN 0-231-05159-X). Columbia U Pr.

--War & Society in Revolutionary Europe, 1770-1870. LC 82-3261. 336p. 1982. 27.50x (ISBN 0-312-85551-6). St Martin.

Best, Geoffrey & Wheatcroft, Andrew, eds. War, Economy & the Military Mind. 136p. 1976. 12.50x (ISBN 0-87471-757-4). Rowman.

Best, George. The Three Voyages of Martin Frobisher: In Search of a Passage to Cathaia & India by the Northwest, A.D. 1576-78. Collinson, Richard, ed. (Hakluyt Society, First Ser.: No. 38). (Illus.). 1964. 32.00 (ISBN 0-8337-0271-8). B Franklin.

Best, Gerald M. Iron Horses to Promontory Railroad: Central Pacific-Union Pacific. LC 69-20447. (Illus.). 1969. 26.95 (ISBN 0-87095-001-0). Golden West.

--Promontory's Locomotives. (Illus.). 48p. pap. 2.95 (ISBN 0-87095-082-7). Golden West.

--Railroads of Hawaii. LC 78-23666. 194p. 1978. 22.95 (ISBN 0-87095-049-5). Golden West.

--Ships & Narrow Gauge Rails: The Story of the Pacific Coast Company. LC 64-19122. (Illus.). 155p. 1981. Repr. of 1964 ed. 15.00 (ISBN 0-8310-7042-0). Howell-North.

--The Ulster & Delaware: Railroad Through the Catskills. LC 70-190176. (Illus.). 208p. 1972. 21.95 (ISBN 0-87095-041-X). Golden West.

Best, Heidi. How to Book of Riding & Horse Care. (How to Bks.). (Illus.). 96p. (Orig.). 1981. pap. 3.95 (ISBN 0-8069-9694-3, Pub. by Blandford Pr England). Sterling.

Best, Hugh. Debrett's Southern Peerage. 416p. 1985. 25.00 (ISBN 0-399-13026-8). Putnam Pub Group.

--Debrett's Texas Peerage. (Illus.). 352p. 1983. 25.00 (ISBN 0-698-11244-X, Coward). Putnam Pub Group.

Best, James. Another Way to Live: Experiencing Intentional Community. LC 78-51384. 32p. (Orig.). 1978. pap. 2.30x (ISBN 0-87574-218-1). Pendle Hill.

Best, James J. American Popular Illustration: A Reference Guide. LC 83-14150. (American Popular Culture Ser.). x, 121p. 1984. lib. bdg. 29.95 (ISBN 0-313-23389-6, BEI/). Greenwood.

Best, James M. Wind Dance Lane. 1977. pap. 3.95 (ISBN 0-930612-00-0). Cinnamon Pr.

Best, Joan & Erikson, Kate. Recipe Index, 1982. 250p. 1983. pap. text ed. 9.95 (ISBN 0-912023-00-7). Home Index Pubns.

Best, Joel, jt. auth. see Luckenbill, David F.

Best, John. Research in Education. 4th ed. (Illus.). 400p. 1981. text ed. 29.95 (ISBN 0-13-774026-3). P-H.

Best, John H., ed. Benjamin Franklin on Education. LC 62-20697. (Classics in Education Ser.). (Orig.). 1962. pap. text ed. 10.00x (ISBN 0-8077-1080-6). Tchrs Coll.

--Historical Inquiry in Education: A Research Agenda. 1983. members 8.00 (ISBN 0-935302-03-4); non-members 11.00. Am Educ Res.

Best, John W. & Kahn, James V. Research in Education. 5th ed. (Illus.). 416p. 1986. text ed. 28.95 (ISBN 0-13-774035-2). P-H.

Best, Judith. The Case Against Direct Election of the President: A Defense of the Electoral College. LC 74-25366. 256p. 1975. 29.95x (ISBN 0-8014-0916-0). Cornell U Pr.

--National Representation for the District of Columbia. 1983. 20.00 (ISBN 0-89093-562-9). U Pubns Amer.

Best, Judith A. The Mainstream of Western Political Thought. LC 80-11042. 149p. 1980. text ed. 24.95 (ISBN 0-87705-271-9); pap. text ed. 12.95 (ISBN 0-87705-243-3). Human Sci Pr.

Best, Mary A. Rebel Saints. facs. ed. LC 68-55839. (Essay Index Reprint Ser). 1925. 18.00 (ISBN 0-8369-0205-X). Ayer Co Pubs.

--Thomas Paine, Prophet & Martyr of Democracy. 59.95 (ISBN 0-8490-1203-1). Gordon Pr.

Best, Michael H. & Connolly, William E. The Politicized Economy. 2nd ed. 224p. 1982. pap. 9.95 (ISBN 0-669-04005-3). Heath.

Best, Michael J. & Ritter, Klaus. Linear Programming: Active Set Analysis. (Illus.). 336p. 1985. text ed. 33.95 (ISBN 0-13-536996-7). P-H.

Best, Michael R., ed. see Albertus Magnus.

Best, Myron G. Igneous & Metamorphic Petrology. LC 81-17530. (Illus.). 630p. 1982. text ed. 37.95 (ISBN 0-7167-1335-7). W H Freeman.

Best of Bridge. Winners: More Recipes from the Best of Bridge. Date not set. price not set. NAL.

Best, Otto F. Peter Weiss. Molinaro, Ursule, tr. from Ger. LC 75-10104. (Literature and Life Ser.). 170p. 1976. 12.95 (ISBN 0-8044-2038-6). Ungar.

Best, Paul, jt. ed. see Jacobs, Mary.

Best, Peter. Beatle! The Pete Best Story. Doncaster, Patrick, as told to. 192p. (Orig.). 1985. pap. 7.95 (ISBN 0-440-50561-5, Dell Trade Pbks). Dell.

Best, R. I. Bibliography of Irish Philology & of Printed Irish Literature. LC 14-3208. (Library of Literature, Drama & Criticism). 1970. Repr. of 1913 ed. 24.00 (ISBN 0-384-13160-3). Johnson Repr.

Best, R. T., intro. by. Milan Codex: The Commentary on the Psalms With Glosses in Old Irish. 1982. 125.00x (ISBN 0-686-96569-8, Pub by Royal Irish Ireland). State Mutual Bk.

Best, Raphaela. We've All Got Scars: What Boys & Girls Learn in Elementary School. LC 82-49198. 192p. 1983. 15.00x (ISBN 0-253-36420-5). Ind U Pr.

Best, Reba A. & Picquet, Cheryn. Computer Crime, Abuse Liability & Security: A Comprehensive Bibliography, 1970-1985. LC 84-43210. 176p. 1985. pap. 33.00 (ISBN 0-89950-148-6). McFarland & Co.

Best, Reba A., jt. auth. see Picquet, D. Cheryn.

Best, Rebecca, jt. ed. see Fromberg, Robert.

Best Report Editors, jt. auth. see Bartlett, Michael.

Best Report Editors, ed. The Book of Bests. LC 83-1966. 1983. 15.95 (ISBN 0-89696-196-6, An Everest House Book). Dodd.

Best, Richard L. Reconstruction of a Tragedy: The Beverly Hills Supper Club Fire. Dean, Amy E., ed. LC 77-93009. 1978. pap. 5.75 (ISBN 0-87765-113-2, LS-2). Natl Fire Prot.

Best, Robert S. Faith, & Other Poems. 1983. 5.95 (ISBN 0-533-05536-9). Vantage.

Best, Robin H. Land Use & Living Space. 240p. 1981. 25.00x (ISBN 0-416-73760-9, NO. 3535); pap. 12.95x (ISBN 0-416-73770-6, NO. 3536). Methuen Inc.

Best, Ron, et al. Perspectives on Pastoral Care. (Heinemann Organization in Schools Ser.). 1980. text ed. 27.50x (ISBN 0-435-80066-3). Heinemann Ed.

Best, Thomas F., ed. Hearing & Speaking the Word: An Anthology of the Works of James Muilenburg. (Scholars Press Homage Ser.: No. 7). 464p. 1985. 26.95 (ISBN 0-89130-665-X, 00 16 07). Scholars Pr GA.

Best, Thomas W. Eccius Dedolatus: A Reformation Satire. LC 71-111504. (Studies in Germanic Languages & Literatures: No. 1). 88p. 1971. 8.00x (ISBN 0-8131-1232-X). U Pr of Ky.

--Reynard the Fox. (World Authors Ser.). 1983. lib. bdg. 19.95 (ISBN 0-8057-6520-4, Twayne). G K Hall.

Best, W. E. Studies in the Person & Work of Jesus Christ. pap. 2.95 (ISBN 0-8010-0644-9). Baker Bk.

Best, W. M. A Treatise on Presumptions of Law & Fact, with the Theory & Rules of Presumptive or Circumstantial Proof in Criminal Cases. 222p. 1981. Repr. of 1845 ed. lib. bdg. 25.00x (ISBN 0-8377-0319-0). Rothman.

Best, William. The Churches Plea for Her Right. LC 76-57357. (English Experience Ser.: No. 776). 1977. Repr. of 1635 ed. lib. bdg. 10.50 (ISBN 90-221-0776-0). Walter J Johnson.

Bestall, Alfred. Rupert Annual. (Rupert Daily Express Annual Ser.). (Illus.). (gr. 4-6). 1975. 5.95 (ISBN 0-685-56545-9). Scholium Intl.

Beste, C. E. & Humburg, N. E. Herbicide Handbook of the Weed Science Society of America. rev., 5th ed. 664p. pap. 10.00 (ISBN 0-686-39882-3). Weed Sci Soc.

Beste, J. Richard. Wabash, or Adventures of an English Gentleman's Family in the Interior of America, 2 Vols. facs. ed. LC 75-121498. (Select Bibliographies Reprint Ser). 1855. 40.00 (ISBN 0-8369-5456-4). Ayer Co Pubs.

Bester. Deceivers. 2.50 (ISBN 0-317-31841-1). Tor Bks.

Bester, Alfred. The Deceivers. 304p. 1982. pap. 2.50 (ISBN 0-523-48524-7). Pinnacle Bks.

--The Deceivers. 256p. 1981. pap. 6.95 (ISBN 0-671-43432-2, Wallaby). S&S.

--The Demolished Man. Del Rey, Lester, ed. LC 75-396. (Library of Science Fiction). 1975. lib. bdg. 19.00 (ISBN 0-8240-1402-2). Garland Pub.

--The Demolished Man. 1982. pap. 2.95 (ISBN 0-671-47626-2, Timescape). PB.

--Golem Hundred. 432p. 1981. pap. 2.95 (ISBN 0-671-82047-8, Timescape). PB.

Bester, John, tr. see Agawa, Hiroyuki.

Bester, John, tr. see Awakawa, Yasuichi.

Bester, John, tr. see Doi, Takeo.

Bester, John, tr. see Enchi, Fumiko.

Bester, John, tr. see Hasegawa, Nyozekan.

Bester, John, tr. see Ibuse, Masuji.

Bester, John, tr. see Kato, Shuichi.

Bester, John, tr. see Mishima, Yukio.

Bester, John, tr. see Miyazawa, Kenji.

Bester, John, tr. see Nakagawa, Sensaka.

Bester, John, tr. see Narazaki, M.

Bester, John, tr. see Oe, Kenzaburo.

Bester, John, tr. see Shiroyama, Saburo.

Bester, John, tr. see Suzuki, Juzo.

Bester, John, tr. see Suzuki, Juzo & Oka, Isaburo.

Bester, John, tr. see Yoshiyuki, Junnosuke.

Bester, John, et al, trs. see Oe, Kenzaburo, et al.

Bester, Roger. Fireman Jim. LC 81-9694. (Illus.). 32p. (gr. k-3). 1981. 9.95 (ISBN 0-517-54290-0). Crown.

--Guess What? LC 79-24945. (Illus.). 32p. (ps-1). 1980. PLB 1.49 (ISBN 0-517-54104-1). Outlet Bk Co.

Besterfield & O'Hagan. Technical Sketching for Engineers, Technologists & Technicians. 1983. text ed. 22.95 (ISBN 0-8359-7540-1). Reston.

Besterfield, Dale H. Quality Control: A Practical Approach. (Illus.). 1979. ref. 29.95 (ISBN 0-13-745232-2). P-H.

Besterman, ed. see De Voltaire, Francois M.

Besterman, Theodore. The Age of the Enlightenment: Studies Presented to Theodore Besterman. Barber, W. H., et al, eds. (Illus.). 468p. 1967. 15.00x (ISBN 0-87471-217-3). Rowman.

--The Beginning of Systematic Bibliography. 2nd ed. LC 72-79199. 81p. 1936-40. Repr. 25.00 (ISBN 0-403-03317-9). Somerset Pub.

--Beginnings of Systematic Bibliography. 2nd ed. (Illus.). 1966. Repr. of 1936 ed. 20.50 (ISBN 0-8337-0272-6). B Franklin.

--A Bibliography of Sir James George Frazer. 1977. Repr. of 1934 ed. lib. bdg. 27.50 (ISBN 0-8482-0317-8). Norwood Edns.

--Voltaire. 3rd ed. (Illus.). 1977. lib. bdg. 33.00x (ISBN 0-226-04430-0). U of Chicago Pr.

--Voltaire Essays, & Another. LC 80-17075. (Illus.). 181p. 1980. Repr. of 1962 ed. lib. bdg. 27.50x (ISBN 0-313-22527-3, BEVO). Greenwood.

--A World Bibliography of African Bibliographies. Pearson, J. D., rev. by. 105p. 1975. 27.50x (ISBN 0-87471-749-3). Rowman.

--World Bibliography of Bibliographies, 5 Vols. 4th ed. 1963. Set. 275.00x (ISBN 0-87471-294-7). Rowman.

--A World Bibliography of Oriental Bibliographies. Pearson, J. D., rev. by. 339p. 1975. 75.00x (ISBN 0-87471-750-7). Rowman.

Besterman, Theodore, jt. auth. see Barrett, William.

Besterman, Theodore, ed. see Crawley, Alfred E.

Besterman, Theodore, ed. see Crawley, Ernest.

Besterman, Theodore, tr. see Driesch, Hans.

Besterman, Theodore, tr. see Voltaire.

Bestgen, Barbara J. & Reys, Robert E. Films in the Mathematics Classroom. LC 82-3442. 90p. 1982. pap. 5.80 (ISBN 0-87353-195-7). NCTM.

Bestmann, H. & Zimmermann, R. Chemistry of Organophosphorous Compounds, 2. (Topics in Current Chemistry: Vol. 20). 1971. 48.40 (ISBN 0-387-05459-6). Springer-Verlag.

Beston, Elizabeth B. Chimney Farm Bedtime Stories. 1977. pap. 3.50 (ISBN 0-89272-040-9). Down East.

Beston, Henry. The Book of Gallant Vagabonds: Trelawny, Rimbaud. LC 78-27411. 1978. lib. bdg. 30.00 (ISBN 0-8414-9898-9). Folcroft.

--Especially Maine: The Natural World of Henry Beston, from Cape Cod to the St. Lawrence. Coatsworth, Elizabeth, ed. LC 75-118226. 1976. pap. 6.95 (ISBN 0-8289-0267-4). Greene.

--Outermost House. 1976. pap. 2.25 (ISBN 0-345-28978-1). Ballantine.

--The Outermost House. 1976. pap. 4.95 (ISBN 0-14-004315-2). Penguin.

Beston, William C., jt. auth. see Biegen, Joseph R.

Bestor, Arthur. Backwoods Utopias: The Sectarian Origins & the Owenite Phase of Communitarian Socialism in America: 1663-1829. 2nd ed. LC 76-92852. 1970. 30.00 (ISBN 0-8122-7193-9); pap. 11.95x (ISBN 0-8122-1004-2, Pa Paperbks). U of Pa Pr.

--Educational Wastelands: The Retreat from Learning in Our Public Schools. 2nd ed. LC 85-1014. 288p. 1985. 19.95x (ISBN 0-252-01226-7). U of Ill Pr.

Bestor, Arthur E., et al. Three Presidents & Their Books: The Readings of Jefferson, Lincoln, & F. D. Roosevelt. LC 54-12305. (Fifth Annual Windsor Lectures Ser.). pap. 35.30 (ISBN 0-317-28792-3, 2020219). Bks Demand UMI.

Bestor, Arthur E., Jr., ed. see Maclure, William & Fretageot, Marie D.

Bestor, Dorothy K. Aside from Teaching, What in the World Can You Do? Career Strategies for Liberal Arts Graduates. LC 82-2009. 352p. (Orig.). 1982. 25.00x (ISBN 0-295-95960-6); pap. 10.95 (ISBN 0-295-95903-7). U of Wash Pr.

Bestor, William S., jt. ed. see Leakey, L. S.

Bestul, Thomas H. Satire & Allegory in "Wynnere & Wastoure". LC 73-77750. xiv, 121p. 1974. 11.50x (ISBN 0-8032-0829-4). U of Nebr Pr.

Beswick, Barbara A. Every Child an Artist: New Methods & Materials for Elementary Art. LC 82-24626. 257p. 1983. 17.50 (ISBN 0-13-293324-1, Parker). P H.

Beswick, Bill. Beginners Basketball: International Rules. (Illus.). 96p. 1983. 9.95 (ISBN 0-7182-1740-3, Pub. by Kaye & Kaye). David & Charles.

Beswick, David E. & Hill, Toni. Bald Men Always Come Out on Top. (Illus.). 96p. 1984. pap. 5.95 (ISBN 0-9613176-0-4). Beacon Hill Pr Seattle.

Beswick, Norman. Resource-Based Learning. (Organization in Schools Ser.). 1977. text ed. 25.50x (ISBN 0-435-80077-9). Heinemann Ed.

Beswick, Norman J. Organizing Resources: Six Case Studies. (Organization in Schools Ser.). 1975. text ed. 26.50x (ISBN 0-435-80067-1). Heinemann Ed.

Beswick, Raymond & Williams, Alfred, eds. Information Systems & Business Communication. 116p. (Orig.). 1983. pap. text ed. 6.60 (ISBN 0-931874-15-7). Assn Busn Comm.

Beswick, S. L., jt. auth. see Stewart, F. S.

Besznyak, I. & Szende, B. Diagnosis & Surgical Treatment of Mediastinal Tumors & Pseudotumors. (Illus.). 336p. 1984. 55.00 (ISBN 3-8055-3582-1). S Karger.

Beta. Enchanted Closet. (Illus.). (gr. k-2). 1967. PLB 7.21 PLB (ISBN 0-87460-117-7). Lion Bks.

Betances, Ramon. Writings of Ramon Betances, 9 vols. (Puerto Rico Ser.). 1979. Set. lib. bdg. 1500.00 (ISBN 0-8490-3017-X). Gordon Pr.

Betancourt, Esdras, ed. Manual Comprensivo de Sicologia Pastoral. 168p. (Span.). 1980. pap. 4.95 (ISBN 0-87148-580-X). Pathway Pr.

Betancourt, Ethel Rios De see De Betancourt, Ethel Rios.

Betancourt, Hal. The Advertising Answerbook: A Guide for Business & Professional People. (Illus.). 214p. 1982. 16.95 (ISBN 0-13-014514-9); pap. 7.95 (ISBN 0-13-014506-8). P-H.

Betancourt, Jeane. Am I Normal? 96p. (YA) 1983. pap. 1.95 (ISBN 0-380-82040-4, Flare). Avon.

--Dear Diary. (Illus.). 100p. (gr. 6-8). 1983. pap. 2.25 (ISBN 0-380-82057-9, 89501-3, Flare). Avon.

Betancourt, Jeanne. The Edge. 144p. (Orig.). (gr. 7 up). 1985. pap. 2.25 (ISBN 0-590-33259-7, Point). Scholastic Inc.

--The Rainbow Kid. 112p. (Orig.). (gr. 3-7). 1985. pap. 2.25 (ISBN 0-380-84665-9, 84665, Camelot). Avon.

--Smile: How to Cope with Braces. LC 81-11800. (Illus.). 96p. (gr. 5 up). 1982. PLB 8.99 (ISBN 0-394-94732-0); pap. 5.95 (ISBN 0-394-84732-6). Knopf.

--Turtle Time. 112p. 1985. pap. 2.50 (ISBN 0-380-89675-3, Camelot). Avon.

Betancourt, Juan, ed. From the Palm Tree: The Cuban Revolution in Retrospect. 224p. 1983. 12.00 (ISBN 0-8184-0344-6). Lyle Stuart.

Betancourt, Philip. Cooking Vessels from Minoan Kommos: A Preliminary Report. (Occasional Papers: No. 7). (Illus.). 13p. 1980. 3.00 (ISBN 0-917956-16-8). UCLA Arch.

Betancourt, Philip P. The Aeolic Style in Architecture: A Survey of Its Development in Palestine, the Halikarnassos Peninsula, & Greece, 1000-500 B.C. LC 76-45890. (Illus.). 1977. 49.00x (ISBN 0-691-03922-4). Princeton U Pr.

--The History of Minoan Pottery. (Illus.). 264p. 1985. text ed. 57.00 (ISBN 0-691-03579-2); pap. 19.95 (ISBN 0-691-10168-X). Princeton U Pr.

--Minoan Objects Excavated from Vasilike, Pseira, Sphoungaras, Priniatikos Pyrgos, & Other Sites: The Cretan Collection in The University Museum, University of Pennsylvania, Vol. I. (University Museum Monographs: No. 47). (Illus.). 160p. 1983. 45.00 (ISBN 0-934718-46-6). Univ Mus of U Pa.

--Vasilike Ware, One Hundred, Vol. LVI. (Studies in Mediterranean Archaeology). 1979. text ed. 28.50x (ISBN 91-85058-88-2). Humanities.

Betancourt, Philip P., et al. East Cretan White-on-Dark Ware. (University Museum Monographs: No. 51). (Illus.). xx, 200p. 1984. 56.00 (ISBN 0-934718-57-1). Univ Mus of U Pa.

Betancourt, Roger & Clague, Christopher. Capacity Utilization: A Theoretical & Empirical Analysis. LC 80-22410. (Illus.). 320p. 1981. 49.50 (ISBN 0-521-23583-9). Cambridge U Pr.

Betancourt, Romulo. Venezuela's Oil. 1978. pap. 22.50x (ISBN 0-04-338082-4). Allen Unwin.

Betanzos-Palacios, Odon. Conciencia y Reforma. (Span.). 1962. pap. 5.00 (ISBN 0-317-02312-8). Edit Mensaje.

--Diosdado de lo Alto. (Illus., Span.). 1980. pap. 8.80 (ISBN 0-86515-000-1). Edit Mensaje.

--Hombre de Luz. (Illus., Span.). 1972. 12.00 (ISBN 0-317-02311-X). Edit Mensaje.

Betchaku, Teiichi, et al. Biology of Turbellaria: Experimental Advances, II. LC 72-13502. 1973. 29.50x (ISBN 0-8422-7112-0). Irvington.

Betchaku, Yasuko, tr. see Burn, Barbara.

Betchaku, Yasuko, tr. see Utamaro, Kitagawa.

Betchov, Robert & Criminale, William O., Jr. Stability of Parallel Flows. (Applied Mathematics & Mechanics Ser.: Vol. 10). 1967. 75.00 (ISBN 0-12-093750-6). Acad Pr.

Beteille, Andre. Caste, Class & Power: Changing Patterns of Stratification in a Tanjore Village. LC 65-25628. 1965. pap. 9.75x (ISBN 0-520-02053-7). U of Cal Pr.

Beteille, Andre, ed. Equality & Inequality: Theory & Practice. 300p. 1985. pap. 10.95x (ISBN 0-19-561661-8). Oxford U Pr.

Beteille, Andrea. The Idea Of Natural Inequality & Other Essays. (Orig.). 1983. pap. 13.95 (ISBN 0-19-878004-4). Oxford U Pr.

Betelli, Vincent. A Simple Method for Deciphering Any Writing in Italian, French, English & Latin. (Illus.). 117p. 1985. 89.75 (ISBN 0-89920-097-4). Am Inst Psych.

Betenson, Lula P. & Flack, Dora. Butch Cassidy, My Brother. LC 75-2332. (Illus.). Repr. of 1975 ed. 70.30 (ISBN 0-8357-9044-4, 2015648). Bks Demand UMI.

Beter, Peter D. Conspiracy Against the Dollar: The Politics of the New Imperialism. LC 73-79850. 96p. 1973. 5.95 (ISBN 0-8076-0709-6); pap. 2.95 (ISBN 0-8076-0710-X). Braziller.

Beteta, Ramon. Jarano. Upton, John, tr. from Span. (Texas Pan American Ser). (Illus.). 175p. 1970. 11.95x (ISBN 0-292-70036-9). U of Tex Pr.

Beth, E., jt. auth. see Giraldo, G.

Beth, E., jt. ed. see Giraldo, G.

Beth, E. W. Aspects of Modern Logic. De Jongh, D. M. & De Jongh-Kearl, Susan, trs. from Dutch. LC 79-135102. (Synthese Library: No. 32). 176p. 1971. 26.00 (ISBN 90-277-0173-3, Pub. by Reidel Holland). Kluwer Academic.

--Formal Methods: An Introduction to Symbolic Logic & to the Study of Effective Operations in Arithmetic & Logic. (Synthese Library: No.4). 170p. 1962. lib. bdg. 26.00 (ISBN 90-277-0069-9, Pub. by Reidel Holland). Kluwer Academic.

--Formal Methods: An Introduction to Symbolic Logic. 170p. 1962. 37.25 (ISBN 0-677-00050-2). Gordon.

--Mathematical Thought. 220p. 1965. 50.95 (ISBN 0-677-00600-4). Gordon.

--Mathematical Thought: An Introduction to the Philosophy of Mathematics. (Synthese Library Ser.: No. 11). 208p. 1965. lib. bdg. 22.00 (ISBN 90-277-0070-2, Pub. by Reidel Holland). Kluwer Academic.

--Science a Road to Wisdom: Collected Philosophical Studies. Wesly, Peter, tr. from Dutch. 123p. 1968. lib. bdg. 21.00 (ISBN 90-277-0003-6, Pub. by Reidel Holland). Kluwer Academic.

Beth, E. W. & Piaget, J. Mathematical Epistemology & Psychology. 348p. 1966. 73.00 (ISBN 0-677-01290-X). Gordon.

--Mathematical Epistomology & Psychology. Mays, W., tr. from Fr. (Synthese Library: No. 12). 326p. 1966. lib. bdg. 39.50 (ISBN 90-277-0071-0, Pub. by Reidel Holland). Kluwer Academic.

Beth, Elke, jt. ed. see Giraldo, G.

Beth Israel Hospital, Boston. Respiratory Intensive Care Nursing. 2nd ed. 1979. spiral bdg. 14.95 (ISBN 0-316-09237-1). Little.

Beth Israel Hospital Nutrition Services Department. Beth Israel Hospital Diet Manual. LC 81-71959. 208p. 1982. text ed. 9.95 (ISBN 0-669-05523-9, Collamore). Heath.

Beth Israel Hospital Staff & Friedman, Emanuel A. Gynecologic Decision Making. 256p. 1983. text ed. 36.00 (ISBN 0-941158-08-X, D1681-6). Mosby.

Beth Israel Staff, jt. auth. see Friedman, Emanuel A.

Beth Jacob Hebrew Teachers College. Deeds of the Righteous. (Illus.). 160p. 6.95 (ISBN 0-934390-00-2). B J Hebrew Tchrs.

--The Rebbe's Treasure. write for info. (ISBN 0-934390-01-0); pap. write for info. (ISBN 0-934390-02-9). B J Hebrew Tchrs.

Beth, Laurie. Horizons. (Illus.). 48p. 1983. pap. 4.95 (ISBN 0-9610430-0-8). J Jones Prods.

Beth, Loren P. Development of the American Constitution, 1877-1917. LC 79-138707. (New American Nation Ser). (Illus.). 1971. 17.26xi (ISBN 0-06-010314-0, HarpT). Har-Row.

Beth, T., ed. Cryptography: Burg Feuerstein, FRG 1982. (Lecture Notes in Computer Science: Vol. 149). 402p. 1983. pap. 20.50 (ISBN 0-387-11993-0). Springer-Verlag.

Bethall, Brian. The Defense Diaries of W. Morgan Petty. LC 84-22767. (Orig.). 1985. pap. 5.95 (ISBN 0-394-73263-4). Pantheon.

Betham, Ernest. A House of Letters: Coleridge, Lamb. Repr. 30.00 (ISBN 0-8274-2539-2). R West.

Betham Edwards. French Men Women & Books. 1973. Repr. of 1911 ed. 15.00 (ISBN 0-8274-1802-7). R West.

Betham-Edwards, M. French Fireside Poetry: With Metrical Translations. Miall, Bernard, ed. 1979. Repr. of 1921 ed. lib. bdg. 20.00 (ISBN 0-8492-3741-6). R West.

Betham-Edwards, M., ed. see Young, Arthur.

Bethancourt, T. Ernesto. The Dog Days of Arthur Cane. LC 76-15033. 160p. (gr. 7 up). 1976. 10.95 (ISBN 0-8234-0286-X). Holiday.

--Doris Fein: Dead Heat at Long Beach. LC 82-48754. (Doris Fein Ser.). 160p. (YA) (gr. 9 up). 1983. 10.95 (ISBN 0-8234-0485-4). Holiday.

--Doris Fein: Deadly Aphrodite. LC 81-85093. 160p. 1982. 9.95 (ISBN 0-8234-0445-5). Holiday.

--Doris Fein: Murder is No Joke. LC 82-80817. 144p. (YA) 1982. 10.95 (ISBN 0-8234-0468-4). Holiday.

--Doris Fein: Phantom of the Casino. LC 80-8814. 160p. (YA) 1981. 10.95 (ISBN 0-8234-0391-2). Holiday.

--Doris Fein: Quartz Boyar. LC 80-15920. 160p. (YA) (gr. 9 up). 1980. 10.95 (ISBN 0-8234-0378-5). Holiday.

--Doris Fein: Quartz Boyar. (Doris Fein Mystery Ser.). 176p. (gr. 7 up). 1982. pap. 1.95 (ISBN 0-590-32383-0). Scholastic Inc.

--Doris Fein: Superspy. LC 79-23339. 160p. (YA) (gr. 9 up). 1980. 10.95 (ISBN 0-8234-0407-2). Holiday.

--Doris Fein: The Mad Samurai. LC 81-4041. 128p. (YA) 1981. 8.95 (ISBN 0-8234-0431-5). Holiday.

--Doris Felin: Legacy of Terror. LC 83-18497. 144p. (YA) 1984. 10.95 (ISBN 0-8234-0506-0). Holiday.

--The Great Computer Dating Caper. LC 83-20971. 160p. (gr. 7 up). 1984. 10.95 (ISBN 0-517-55213-2). Crown.

--Instruments of Darkness. LC 78-11133. 160p. (YA) 1979. 7.95 (ISBN 0-8234-0346-7). Holiday.

--The Mad Samurai. (Doris Fein Mystery Ser.). 128p. (gr. 7 up). 1983. pap. 1.95 (ISBN 0-590-32385-7). Scholastic Inc.

--The Me Inside of Me. LC 85-10292. 156p. (gr. 5 up). 1985. 10.95 (ISBN 0-8225-0728-5). Lerner Pubns.

--New York City Too Far from Tampa Blues. LC 74-24692. 192p. (gr. 6 up). 1975. 6.95 (ISBN 0-8234-0256-8). Holiday.

--Phantom of the Casino. (Doris Fein Mystery Ser.). 160p. (gr. 7 up). 1983. pap. 1.95 (ISBN 0-590-32384-9, Vagabond). Scholastic Inc.

--T.H.U.M.B.B. LC 83-6119. 160p. (YA) 1983. 10.95 (ISBN 0-8234-0494-3). Holiday.

--The Tomorrow Connection. LC 84-47836. 144p. (YA) 1984. 10.95 (ISBN 0-8234-0543-5). Holiday.

--Where the Deer & the Cantaloupe Play. LC 80-27110. 144p. 1981. 7.95 (ISBN 0-916392-69-4). Oak Tree Pubns.

Bethards, H. Gordon. Salesman Calling. 78p. (Orig.). 1984. pap. 4.95 (ISBN 0-930264-54-1). Century Comm.

--Selling Is a Personal Affair. 190p. (Orig.). 1984. pap. 9.95 (ISBN 0-930264-53-3). Century Comm.

Bethe, Hans A. Splitting of Terms in Crystals. 73p. 1962. 20.00x (ISBN 0-306-10639-6, Consultants). Plenum Pub.

--Splitting of Terms in Crystals. LC 58-2296. (Translated from Annals of Physics Ser.: Vol. 3). (Illus.). pap. 20.00 (ISBN 0-317-09920-5, 2003370). Bks Demand UMI.

Bethe, Hans A. & Jackiw, Roman W. Intermediate Quantum Mechanics. 2nd ed. LC 68-24363. (Lecture Notes & Supplements in Physics Ser.: No. 9). 1968. pap. 34.95 (ISBN 0-8053-0755-9, Adv Bk Prog). Benjamin-Cummings.

Bethe, Hans A. & Salpeter, Edwin E. Quantum Mechanics of One-& Two-Electron Atoms. LC 76-30829. 382p. 1977. pap. 10.95x (ISBN 0-306-20022-8, Plenum Pr). Plenum Pub.

--Quantum Mechanics of One-& Two-Electron Atoms. LC 76-30829. 382p. 1977. pap. 10.95x (ISBN 0-306-20022-8). Plenum Pub.

Bethe, Monica & Brazell, Karen. Dance in the No Theatre, 3 vols. Incl. Vol. 1. Dance Analysis. 193p; Vol. 2. Plays & Scores. 289p; Vol. 3. Dance Patterns. 250p. (East Asia Papers: No. 29). 1982. 9.00 ea.; Set. 24.00 (ISBN 0-318-02254-0). Cornell China-Japan Pgm.

--Dance in the No Theatre, 3 vols. (East Asia Papers: 29). Set. 24.00 (ISBN 0-318-17860-5); Vol. 1, 193p. 9.00 (ISBN 0-318-17861-3); Vol. 2, 289p. 9.00 (ISBN 0-318-17862-1); Vol. 3, 250p. 9.00 (ISBN 0-318-17863-X). Cornell China-Japan Pgm.

--No as Performance: An Analysis of the Kuse Scene of Yamamba. (East Asia Papers: No. 16). 206p. 1978. 9.00 (ISBN 0-318-04622-9). Cornell China-Japan Pgm.

--No as Performance: An Analysis of the Kuse Scene of Yamamba. (East Asia Papers: 16). 206p. 1978. 6.00 (ISBN 0-318-13818-2). Cornell China-Japan Pgm.

Bethe, Monica, tr. see Ito, Toshiko.

Bethe, Monica, tr. see Nishikawa, Kyotaro.

Bethea, David M. Khodasevich: His Life & Art. LC 82-61355. (Illus.). 378p. 1983. 27.50x (ISBN 0-691-06559-4). Princeton U Pr.

Bethea, Doris C. Introductory Maternity Nursing. 4th ed. (Illus.). 464p. 1984. pap. text ed. 14.50 (ISBN 0-397-54466-9, 64-04073, Lippincott Nursing); wkbk. 9.50 (ISBN 0-397-54467-7, 64-04081). Lippincott.

Bethea, Robert M. Air Pollution Control Technology. (Environmental Engineering Ser). 1978. 39.95 (ISBN 0-442-20715-8). Van Nos Reinhold.

Bethel, A. C. Traditional Logic. 332p. (Orig.). 1982. pap. text ed. 13.00 (ISBN 0-8191-2616-0). U Pr of Amer.

Bethel, Dell. Coaching Winning Baseball. 1979. pap. 9.95 (ISBN 0-8092-7459-0). Contemp Bks.

--The Complete Book of Baseball Instruction. LC 77-91148. 1978. pap. 12.95 (ISBN 0-8092-7740-9). Contemp Bks.

--Inside Baseball: Tips & Techniques for Coaches & Players. LC 69-17434. (Illus.). 96p. 1969. 7.95 (ISBN 0-8092-8871-0). Contemp Bks.

Bethel, Elizabeth R. Promiseland: A Century of Life in a Negro Community. 318p. 1981. 29.95 (ISBN 0-87722-211-8). Temple U Pr.

--Promiseland: A Century of Life in a Negro Community. 329p. 1982. pap. 9.95 (ISBN 0-87722-275-4). Temple U Pr.

Bethel, James S., ed. World Trade in Forest Products. LC 83-17012. (Geo. S. Long Publication Series). 551p. 40.00x (ISBN 0-295-96078-7). U of Wash Pr.

Bethel, Lorraine & Smith, Barbara, eds. Conditions: Five-the Black Women's Issue. 4.50 (ISBN 0-686-31642-8). Conditions.

Bethel, May. Healing Power of Herbs. pap. 4.00 (ISBN 0-87980-047-X). Wilshire.

--Healing Power of Natural Foods. 1978. pap. 5.00 (ISBN 0-87980-363-0). Wilshire.

Bethel, Rodman J., et al. A Slumbering Giant of the Past. (Illus.). 91p. (Orig.). 1984. pap. 11.95 (ISBN 0-9614702-0-8). Slumbering.

Bethell, D., jt. ed. see Gold, V.

Bethell, E., et al, eds. Electrical Assembly & Wiring. (Engineering Craftsmen: No. G4). (Illus.). 1969. spiral bdg. 39.95x (ISBN 0-85083-031-1). Trans-Atlantic.

Bethell, Jane. Raggedy Ann & Andy & the Absent-Minded Magician. LC 81-25675. 1982. 4.95 (ISBN 0-672-52721-9). Bobbs.

Bethell, Jean. Playmates. LC 80-20542. 32p. (gr. k-2). 1981. 7.95 (ISBN 0-03-053821-1). HR&W.

Bethell, Jean & Axtell, Susan. A Colonial Williamsburg Activities Book: Fun Things to Do for Children 4 & Up. (Illus.). 40p. (ps). 1984. pap. 2.95 (ISBN 0-87935-068-7). Williamsburg.

Bethell, Leslie. Abolition of the Brazilian Slave Trade. (Latin American Studies). (Illus.). 1970. 49.50 (ISBN 0-521-07583-1). Cambridge U Pr.

Bethell, Leslie, ed. The Cambridge History of Latin America: Colonial Latin America, Vols. I & II. (Illus.). 1985. Vol. I, 600p. 65.00 (ISBN 0-521-23223-6); Vol. II, 850p. 75.00 (ISBN 0-521-24516-8). Cambridge U Pr.

--The Cambridge History of Latin America, Vol. III: From Independence to 1870. (Illus.). 961p. Date not set. 80.00 (ISBN 0-521-23224-4). Cambridge U Pr.

Bethell, Nicholas. Betrayed. LC 85-40277. (Illus.). 224p. 1985. 15.95 (ISBN 0-8129-1188-1). Times Bks.

--Russia Besieged. Time-Life Books, ed. (World War II Ser.). 1977. 14.95 (ISBN 0-8094-2470-3). Time-Life.

Bethell, Nicholas, tr. see Solzhenitsyn, Alexander.

Bethell, Richard S., ed. Pear Pest Management. LC 78-67293. 1978. 3-ring polymer bndr. 20.00x (ISBN 0-931876-26-5, 4086). Ag & Nat Res.

Bethell, Ruth M., tr. see Zeeden, Ernest W.

Bethell, S. L. The Literary Outlook. 1978. Repr. of 1942 ed. lib. bdg. 17.50 (ISBN 0-8495-0376-0). Arden Lib.

Bethell, Samuel L. Essays on Literary Criticism & the Tradition. LC 72-191667. 1948. lib. bdg. 15.00 (ISBN 0-8414-1641-9). Folcroft.

--Literary Outlook. LC 73-9787. 1943. lib. bdg. 15.00 (ISBN 0-8414-3145-0). Folcroft.

Bethell, Thomas N. & Tuck, Deborah E., eds. The Native Home of Hope: People & the Northern Rockies. 275p. 1984. pap. 12.50 (ISBN 0-935704-26-4). Howe Brothers.

Bethell, Tom. George Lewis: A Jazzman from New Orleans. LC 76-3872. 1977. 17.95 (ISBN 0-520-03212-8). U of Cal Pr.

--Television Evening News Covers Inflation: 1978-79. Media Institute, ed. (Illus.). 52p. (Orig.). 1980. pap. 5.00 (ISBN 0-937790-00-1). Media Inst.

Bethemont, Jacques & Pelletier, Jean. Italy: A Geographical Introduction. King, Russel, ed. (Illus.). 224p. 1982. text ed. pap. 16.95 (ISBN 0-582-49149-5). Longman.

Bethge, Eberhard. Costly Grace: An Illustrated Introduction to Dietrich Bonhoeffer in His Own Words. LC 78-19492. (Illus.). 1979. pap. 4.95i (ISBN 0-06-060773-4, RD 294, HarpR). Har-Row.

Bethge, Eberhard, ed. see Bonhoeffer, Dietrich.

Bethge, Ederhard. Dietrich Bonhoeffer. LC 70-10975. 1977. pap. 11.49i (ISBN 0-06-060771-8, RD 165, HarpR). Har-Row.

Bethge, K., et al, eds. Nuclear Physics Methods in Materials Research: Proceedings of the 7th Divisional Conference. 1980. 46.00 (ISBN 0-9940013-9-8, Pub. by Vieweg & Sohn Germany). Heyden.

Bethke, Emil G. Basic Drawing for Biology Students. (Illus.). 100p. 1969. photocopy ed. 16.50x (ISBN 0-398-00148-0). C C Thomas.

Bethke, Frederick J. Three Victorian Travel Writers: An Annotated Bibliography of Criticism on Mrs. Frances Milton Trollope, Samuel Butler, & Robert Louis Stevenson. 1977. lib. bdg. 26.00 (ISBN 0-8161-7852-6, Hall Reference). G K Hall.

Bethke, Robert D. Adirondack Voices: Woodsmen & Woods Lore. LC 80-24054. (Illus.). 160p. 1981. 12.50 (ISBN 0-252-00829-4). U of Ill Pr.

Bethlehem, Douglas. A Social Psychology of Prejudice. 256p. 1985. 27.50 (ISBN 0-312-73478-6). St Martin.

Bethlem, J. Myopathies. 2nd ed. 320p. 1980. 73.75 (ISBN 0-444-80198-7, Biomedical Pr). Elsevier.

Bethlen, Stephen. Treaty of Trianon & European Peace: Four Lectures Delivered in London in November 1933. LC 73-135795. (Eastern European Collection Ser). 1970. Repr. of 1934 ed. 13.00 (ISBN 0-405-02737-0). Ayer Co Pubs.

Bethlen, Steven & Volgyles, Ivan. Europe & the Superpowers: Economic, Political, & Military Policies in the 1980's. (Replica edition-Softcover Ser.). 230p. 1985. pap. 20.00x (ISBN 0-86531-887-5). Westview.

Bethmann, Johannes. Untersuchungen Uber Die Mhd. 18.00 (ISBN 0-384-04083-7); pap. 13.00 (ISBN 0-685-02222-6). Johnson Repr.

Bethune, C. Drinkwater, ed. see Galvao, Antonio.

Bethune, George. The Fruit of the Spirit. pap. 4.95 (ISBN 0-685-88375-2). Reiner.

Bethune, George W. British Female Poets: With Biographical & Critical Notices. facsimile ed. LC 75-38734. (Essay Index Reprint Ser). Repr. of 1848 ed. 28.00 (ISBN 0-8369-2636-6). Ayer Co Pubs.

Bethune, J. Essentials of Drafting. 416p. 1977. text ed. 28.95 (ISBN 0-13-284430-3). P-H.

Bethune, James. Basic Electronic & Electrical Drafting. 2nd ed. (Illus.). 304p. 1985. text ed. 27.95 (ISBN 0-13-060336-8); 21.95 (ISBN 0-13-060351-1). P-H.

Bethune, James D. Basic Electronic & Electrical Drafting. (Illus.). 1980. text ed. 24.95 (ISBN 0-13-060301-5). P-H.

--Technical Illustration. LC 82-8529. 237p. 1983. 29.95 (ISBN 0-471-05308-2). Wiley.

Bethune-Baker, J. F. The Meaning of Homoousios in the "Constantinopolitan" Creed. (Texts & Studies Ser.: No. 1, Vol. 7, Pt. 1). pap. 13.00 (ISBN 0-317-16757-X). Kraus Repr.

--Nestorius & His Teaching. 1908. 15.00 (ISBN 0-527-07500-0). Kraus Repr.

Bethurum, Dorothy, ed. Critical Approaches to Medieval Literature. LC 60-13104. (Essays of the English Institute Ser.). 1960. 20.00x (ISBN 0-231-02417-7). Columbia U Pr.

Bethurum, Dorothy see Columbia University. English Institute.

Beti, Mongo. King Lazarus. Green, Peter, tr. from Fr. (African Writers Ser.: No. 77). (Orig.). 1970. pap. text ed. 5.00x (ISBN 0-435-90077-3). Heinemann Ed.

--Lament for an African Pol. Bjornson, Richard, tr. from French. & intro. by. LC 84-51443. 366p. 1985. 18.00 (ISBN 0-89410-304-0); pap. 10.00 (ISBN 0-89410-305-9). Three Continents.

--Mission to Kala. (African Writers Ser.). 1964. pap. text ed. 4.00x (ISBN 0-435-90013-7). Gower Pub Co.

--Perpetua & the Habit of Unhappiness. (African Writers Ser.). 1978. pap. text ed. 7.00x (ISBN 0-435-90181-8). Heinemann Ed.

--The Poor Christ of Bomba. (African Writers Ser.). 1971. pap. text ed. 5.50x (ISBN 0-435-90088-9). Heinemann Ed.

Beti, Mongo, pseud. Remember Ruben. 350p. (Orig.). 1981. 14.00x (ISBN 0-89410-240-0); pap. 7.00x (ISBN 0-89410-241-9). Three Continents.

Beti, Mongo, ed. Peuples Noirs Peuples Africains, Nos. 1-26. 150p. (Fr.). 1983. pap. 8.00 per issue (ISBN 0-686-88947-9, Pub. by Edit Peuples Noirs France); pap. 185.00 for set. Three Continents.

Betiero, J. T. & Clymer, R. Swinburne. Nedoure: Priestess of the Magi. 248p. 1958. 7.95 (ISBN 0-932785-34-4). Philos Pub.

Betina, V. The Chemistry & Biology of Antibiotics. (Pharmacochemistry Library: No. 5). 590p. 1983. 125.75 (ISBN 0-444-99678-8). Elsevier.

Betina, V., ed. Mycotoxins: Production, Isolation, Separation & Purification, Vol. 8. (Developments in Food Science Ser.). 500p. 1984. 113.50 (ISBN 0-444-42289-7, I-051-84). Elsevier.

Betjeman, John. American's Guide to English Parish Churches. (Illus.). 1959. 15.00 (ISBN 0-8392-1004-3). Astor-Honor.

--John Betjeman. (Pocket Poet Ser.). 1958. pap. 2.00 (ISBN 0-8023-9040-4). Dufour.

--John Betjeman's Collected Poems. 431p. 1985. pap. 9.95 (ISBN 0-88162-070-X, Pub. by Salem Hse Ltd). Merrimack Pub Cir.

--A Life in Pictures. Hiller, Bevis, compiled by. (Illus.). 160p. 1985. text ed. 19.95 (ISBN 0-8052-6003-X, Pub. by J Murray Bk-D Herbert UK). Schocken.

--London's Historic Railway Stations. (Illus.). 1978. pap. 12.95 (ISBN 0-7195-3426-7); 20.00. Transatlantic.

--A Nip in the Air. 1976. pap. 2.50 (ISBN 0-393-04423-8). Norton.

--An Oxford University Chest. (Illus.). 1980. pap. 15.00 (ISBN 0-19-281273-4). Oxford U Pr.

--Victorian & Edwardian London. 1969. pap. 10.50 (ISBN 0-7134-2185-1, Pub. by Batsford England). David & Charles.

Betjeman, John & Rowse, A. L. Victorian & Edwardian Cornwall. 1977. pap. 10.50 (ISBN 0-7134-3167-9, Pub. by Batsford England). David & Charles.

Betjeman, John, ed. Altar & Pew. (Pocket Poet Ser.). 1960. pap. 2.00 (ISBN 0-8023-9041-2). Dufour.

Betjeman, John & Taylor, Geoffrey, eds. English Love Poems. 220p. 1964. pap. 6.95 (ISBN 0-571-07065-5). Faber & Faber.

--English, Scottish & Welsh Landscape, 1700-C. 1860. LC 77-94807. (Granger Poetry Library). (Illus.). 1978. Repr. of 1944 ed. 19.75x (ISBN 0-89609-080-9). Granger Bk.

Betken, William T. The Other Shakespeare: Macbeth. unexpurgated ed. 612p. (Orig.). 1985. 29.95 (ISBN 0-941672-08-5); pap. 12.95 (ISBN 0-941672-09-3). Valentine Pub.

--The Other Shakespeare: Romeo & Juliet. 531p. (Orig.). 1984. 29.95. (ISBN 0-941672-04-2); pap. 12.95 (ISBN 0-941672-05-0). Valentine Pub.

--The Other Shakespeare: The Two Gentlemen of Verona. Unexpurgated Edition ed. LC 81-52512. 284p. (Orig.). 1982. 13.95 (ISBN 0-941672-00-X); pap. 7.95 (ISBN 0-941672-01-8). Valentine Pub.

--The Other Shakespeare: The Two Gentlemen of Verona. 215p. (Orig., Young People (Expurgated) Edition). 13.95 (ISBN 0-941672-02-6); pap. 7.95 (ISBN 0-941672-03-4). Valentine Pub.

Betlyon, John. The Coinage & Mints of Phoenicia: The Pre-Alexandrine Period. (Harvard Semitic Monographs). 184p. 1982. 18.75 (ISBN 0-89130-588-2, 04-00-26). Scholars Pr GA.

Beton. Precast Concrete Connection Details: Part 1-Structural Design manual. 1981. 87.00 (ISBN 0-9960095-3-1, Pub. by Beton Bks W Germany). Heyden.

--Precast Concrete Connection Details: Part 2-Floor Connections. 1978. 71.00 (ISBN 0-9960095-4-X, Pub. by Beton Bks W Germany). Heyden.

Betourne, Henriette D., et al. Direct French Conversation, 2 Bks. (Orig., Fr.). (gr. 9 up). 1966. Bk. 1. pap. text ed. 3.25 (ISBN 0-88345-040-2, 17470); Bk. 2. pap. text ed. 3.25 (ISBN 0-88345-041-0, 17471). Regents Pub.

Betram, James G. see Paterson, Peter, pseud.

Betrock, Alan. Girl Groups: The Story of Sound. LC 81-71010. (Illus.). 176p. (Orig.). 1982. pap. 8.95 (ISBN 0-933328-25-7). Delilah Bks.

Betsky, Sarah Z, ed. Onions & Cucumbers & Plums: Forty-Six Yi ddish Poems in English. Betsky, Sarah Z., tr. from Yiddish. LC 80-20914. 280p. 1981. 12.50 (ISBN 0-8143-1080-X); pap. 6.95 (ISBN 0-8143-1674-3). Wayne St U Pr.

Betsky, Sarah Z., tr. see Betsky, Sarah Z.

Betson, Martin. Here Begynneth a Treatyse to Dyspose Men to Be Vertously Occupyed in Theyr Myndes & Prayers. LC 77-6854. (English Experience Ser.: No. 848). 1977. Repr. of 1500 ed. lib. bdg. 5.00 (ISBN 90-221-0848-1). Walter J Johnson.

Betsworth, Roger G. The Radical Movement of the Nineteen Sixties. LC 80-12534. (ATLA Monograph Ser.: No. 14). viii, 363p. 1980. 20.00 (ISBN 0-8108-1307-6). Scarecrow.

Bett, H. Nursery Rhymes & Tales: Their Origin & History. 59.95 (ISBN 0-8490-0743-7). Gordon Pr.

Bett, Henry. English Myths & Traditions. (Illus.). 144p. 1980. Repr. of 1952 ed. lib. bdg. 17.50 (ISBN 0-8414-2921-9). Folcroft.

--Joachim of Flora. (Great Medieval Churchmen Ser). vii, 184p. 1976. Repr. of 1931 ed. lib. bdg. 16.50x (ISBN 0-915172-24-0). Richwood Pub.

--Johannes Scotus Erigena: A Study in Medieval Philosophy. LC 78-14101. 1980. Repr. of 1925 ed. 18.50 (ISBN 0-88355-830-0). Hyperion Conn.

--Nicholas of Cusa. LC 76-1131. (Great Medieval Churchmen Ser). x, 210p. 1976. Repr. of 1932 ed. lib. bdg. 17.50x (ISBN 0-915172-05-4). Richwood Pub.

--Nursery Rhymes & Tales: Their Origin & History. LC 73-14839. 1924. lib. bdg. 17.50 (ISBN 0-8414-3274-0). Folcroft.

--Some Secrets of Style. LC 73-105764. 1970. Repr. of 1932 ed. 19.50x00351164x (ISBN 0-8046-0939-X, Pub. by Kennikat). Assoc Faculty Pr.

--Studies in Literature. LC 68-8220. 1929. Repr. of 1929 ed. 19.50x (ISBN 0-8046-0028-7, Pub. by Kennikat). Assoc Faculty Pr.

Bett, K. E., et al. Thermodynamics for Chemical Engineers. LC 75-24573. 504p. 1975. text ed. 30.00x (ISBN 0-262-02119-6). MIT Pr.

Bettany, G. T. The Conquerors of the World: Peoples & Races of Europe. 1977. lib. bdg. 59.95 (ISBN 0-8490-1664-9). Gordon Pr.

--Dark Peoples of the Land of Sunshine. facs. ed. LC 73-89424. (Black Heritage Library Collection). 1890. 14.25 (ISBN 0-8369-8510-9). Ayer Co Pubs.

--Life of Charles Darwin. 1977. Repr. of 1887 ed. lib. bdg. 20.00 (ISBN 0-8495-0327-2). Arden Lib.

--Life of Charles Darwin. 1973. Repr. of 1887 ed. 15.00 (ISBN 0-8274-1801-9). R West.

Bettany, George T. Eminent Doctors, 2 vols. facsimile ed. LC 76-39663. (Essay Index Reprint Ser.). Set. 40.00 (ISBN 0-8369-2747-8). Ayer Co Pubs.

--World's Inhabitants. LC 72-5744. (Black Heritage Library Collection). 1972. Repr. of 1888 ed. 82.50 (ISBN 0-8369-9134-6). Ayer Co Pubs.

Bettany, W. A., ed. see Byron, George G.

Bettarel, Robert L. & Smith, Hale G. The Moccasin Bluff Site & the Woodland Cultures of Southwestern Michigan. (Anthropological Papers: No. 49). 1973. pap. 6.00 (ISBN 0-932206-47-6). U Mich Mus Anthro.

Bettelheim, Bruno. Children of the Dream. (YA) 1970. pap. 2.50 (ISBN 0-380-01097-6, 49130-3, Discus). Avon.

--Dialogues with Mothers. 1971. pap. 2.50 (ISBN 0-380-01138-7, 49874-X, Discus). Avon.

--Dialogues with Mothers. LC 62-10583. 1962. text ed. 16.95 (ISBN 0-02-903120-6). Free Pr.

--The Empty Fortress: Infantile Autism & the Birth of the Self. LC 67-10886. 484p. 1972. 10.95 (ISBN 0-02-903130-3); pap. text ed. 10.95 (ISBN 0-02-903140-0). Free Pr.

--Freud & Man's Soul. LC 82-47809. 112p. 1983. 11.95 (ISBN 0-394-52481-0). Knopf.

--Freud & Man's Soul. LC 83-47809. 128p. 1984. 3.95 (ISBN 0-394-71036-3, Vin). Random.

--A Home for the Heart. LC 85-8752. (Illus.). xxii, 470p. 1974. pap. 14.95 (ISBN 0-226-04439-4). U of Chicago Pr.

--Informed Heart. 1971. pap. 4.50 (ISBN 0-380-01302-9, 60049-8, Discus). Avon.

--Informed Heart: Autonomy in a Mass Age. 1960. 17.95 (ISBN 0-02-903200-8). Free Pr.

--Love Is Not Enough. 1971. pap. 3.50 (ISBN 0-380-01405-X, 56846-2, Discus). Avon.

--Love Is Not Enough. 1950. 20.95 (ISBN 0-02-903280-6). Free Pr.

--Surviving & Other Essays. LC 78-20388. 1979. 15.00 (ISBN 0-394-50402-X). Knopf.

--Surviving & Other Essays. LC 79-22029. 1980. pap. 6.95 (ISBN 0-394-74264-8, Vin). Random.

--Truants from Life: The Rehabilitation of Emotionally Disturbed Children. LC 55-7331. 516p. 1955. 18.95 (ISBN 0-02-903440-X); pap. 10.95 (ISBN 0-02-903450-7). Free Pr.

--The Uses of Enchantment: The Meaning & Importance of Fairy Tales. 1976. 16.95 (ISBN 0-394-49771-6). Knopf.

--The Uses of Enchantment: The Meaning & Importance of Fairy Tales. 1977. pap. 5.95 (ISBN 0-394-72265-5, Vin). Random.

Bettelheim, Bruno & Janowitz, Morris B. Social Change & Prejudice. LC 64-11214. 1964. 18.95 (ISBN 0-02-903480-9). Free Pr.

Bettelheim, Bruno & Zelan, Karen. On Learning to Read: The Child's Fascination with Meaning. LC 81-47492. 1982. 13.95 (ISBN 0-394-51592-7). Knopf.

--On Learning to Read: The Child's Fascination with Meaning. 320p. 1983. pap. 5.95 (ISBN 0-394-71194-7, Vin). Random.

Bettelheim, Bruno, commentary by see Carotenuto, Aldo.

Bettelheim, Charles. Class Struggles in the U. S. S. R. First Period, 1917-1923. Pearce, Brian, tr. LC 76-28986. 567p. 1978. pap. 10.00 (ISBN 0-85345-434-5). Monthly Rev.

--Class Struggles in the U. S. S. R. Second Period: 1923-1930, Vol. 11. Pearce, Brian, tr. from Fr. LC 76-28976. 640p. 1978. pap. 8.95 (ISBN 0-85345-514-7). Monthly Rev.

--Class Struggles in the U. S. S. R. Third Period, 1930-1941. Westwood, J., tr. 288p. 1985. 27.00 (ISBN 0-85345-671-2); pap. 11.00 (ISBN 0-85345-672-0). Monthly Rev.

--Cultural Revolution & Industrial Organization in China: Changes in Management & the Division of Labor. Ehrenfeld, Alfred, tr. from Fr. LC 73-90078. 128p. 1975. pap. 2.95 (ISBN 0-85345-351-9). Monthly Rev.

--Economic Calculation & Forms of Property. Taylor, John, tr. from Fr. LC 74-21473. 168p. 1976. 11.50 (ISBN 0-85345-360-8); pap. 3.95 (ISBN 0-85345-427-2). Monthly Rev.

--The Transition to Socialist Economy. Mepham, John, ed. Pearce, Brian, tr. from Fr. (Marxist Theory & Contemporary Capitalism Ser.). 248p. 1975. text ed. 19.00x (ISBN 0-391-00396-8); pap. text ed. 11.00x (ISBN 0-391-00884-6). Humanities.

Bettelheim, Charles & Burton, Neil. China since Mao. LC 78-15623. 130p. 1978. 7.50 (ISBN 0-85345-474-4); pap. 3.95 (ISBN 0-85345-475-2). Monthly Rev.

Bettelheim, Charles, jt. auth. see Sweezy, Paul M.

Bettelheim, Frederick A. & March, Jerry. Introduction to General, Organic & Biochemistry. LC 83-20124. 708p. 1984. text ed. 33.95x (ISBN 0-03-061548-8); study guide 12.95 (ISBN 0-03-064122-5). SCP.

Bettelheim, Frederick A., jt. auth. see Lee, Jessie C.

Bettell, Richard R. & McCullagh, Suzanne F. Degas in the Art Institute of Chicago. Rossen, Susan F., ed. LC 84-6409. (Illus.). 200p. 1984. pap. 18.50 (ISBN 0-86559-058-3). Art Inst Chi.

Bettembourg, Georges & Brame, Michael. The White Death. (Illus.). 300p. 1981. 13.95 (ISBN 0-932998-05-4, Reynard Hse). Noit Amrofer.

--The White Death. 13.95 (ISBN 0-932998-05-4). Reynard Hse.

Betten, Neil. Catholic Activism & the Industrial Worker. LC 76-17280. 1976. 10.00 (ISBN 0-8130-0503-5). U Presses Fla.

Bettencourt, Vladimir. New Discoveries in the Psychology of Management. (Research Center for Economic Psychology Library). (Illus.). 148p. 1983. 79.75x (ISBN 0-86654-061-X). Inst Econ Finan.

Bettendorf, G., jt. ed. see Insler, V.

Bettenson, Henry, ed. Documents of the Christian Church. 2nd ed. 1970. pap. 7.95 (ISBN 0-19-501293-3, GB). Oxford U Pr.

Bettenson, Henry, ed. & tr. The Later Christian Fathers: A Selection from the Writings of the Fathers from St. Cyril of Jerusalem to St. Leo the Great. (OPB No. 293). 1972. pap. 7.95x (ISBN 0-19-283012-0). Oxford U Pr.

Bettenson, Henry, tr. Early Christian Fathers: A Selection from the Writings of the Fathers from St. Clement of Rome to St. Athanasius. (Oxford Paperbacks Ser). 1969. pap. 8.95x (ISBN 0-19-283009-0, 174). Oxford U Pr.
Bettenson, Henry, tr. see Livy.
Better Homes & Gardens. Woodworking Projects You Can Build. (You Can Build Ser.). 1980. pap. 6.95 (ISBN 0-696-01385-1). BH&G.
Better Homes & Gardens, ed. After-Forty Health & Medical Guide. 1980. 24.95 (ISBN 0-696-00810-6). BH&G.
Better Homes & Gardens Books, ed. Classic International Recipes. (Illus.). 192p. 1982. 9.95 (ISBN 0-696-00715-0). BH&G.
Better Homes & Gardens Books Editors. New Cook Book. rev. ed. LC 79-55162. (Illus.). 466p. (YA) 1981. 16.95 (ISBN 0-696-00011-3). BH&G.
--New Decorating Book. LC 80-68456. (Illus.). 432p. (YA) 1981. 29.95 (ISBN 0-696-00092-X). BH&G.
Better Homes & Gardens Books Editor, ed. New Family Medical Guide. rev. ed. (Illus.). 896p. 1982. 29.95 (ISBN 0-696-00344-9). BH&G.
--Step-by-Step Household Repairs. (Step-by-Step Home Repair Ser.). (Illus.). 96p. 1982. pap. 6.95 (ISBN 0-696-00775-4). BH&G.
--Step-by-Step Masonry & Concrete. (Step-by-Step Home Repair Ser.). (Illus.). 96p. 1982. pap. 6.95 (ISBN 0-696-00685-5). BH&G.
Better Homes & Gardens Editors. All Time Favorite Cake & Cookie Recipes. 96p. 1983. 6.95 (ISBN 0-696-01215-4). BH&G.
--All Time Favorite Hamburger Recipes. 96p. 1983. 6.95 (ISBN 0-696-01225-1). BH&G.
--Better Homes & Gardens: Adding On. (All about Your House Ser.). (Illus.). 160p. 1984. 9.95 (ISBN 0-696-02169-2). BH&G.
--Better Homes & Gardens All About Your House: Stretching Your Living Space. LC 81-70035. (All About Your House Ser.). (Illus.). 160p. 1983. 9.95 (ISBN 0-696-02162-5). BH&G.
--Better Homes & Gardens All About Your House: Your Kitchen. (All About your House Ser.). 160p. 1983. 9.95 (ISBN 0-696-02161-7). BH&G.
--Better Homes & Gardens All About Your House: Your Walls & Ceilings. LC 81-70036. (All About Your House Ser.). (Illus.). 160p. 1983. 9.95 (ISBN 0-696-02163-3). BH&G.
--Better Homes & Gardens All-Time Favorite Bread Recipes. LC 78-74937. (All-Time Favorite Ser.). (Illus.). 1979. 6.95 (ISBN 0-696-01210-3). BH&G.
--Better Homes & Gardens All-Time Favorite Fish & Seafood Recipes. LC 80-66392. (All-Time Favorite Recipes Ser.). (Illus.). 96p. 1983. 6.95 (ISBN 0-696-01220-0). BH&G.
--Better Homes & Gardens All-Time Favorite Vegetable Recipes. LC 76-42690. (Illus.). 1977. 6.95 (ISBN 0-696-01340-1). BH&G.
--Better Homes & Gardens American Christmas Crafts & Foods. (Illus.). 320p. 1984. 24.95 (ISBN 0-696-00585-9). BH&G.
--Better Homes & Gardens American Patchwork & Quilting. (Illus.). 320p. 1985. 24.95 (ISBN 0-696-01015-1). BH&G.
--Better Homes & Gardens Anytime Appetizers. Henry, Linda, ed. (Illus.). 96p. 1985. pap. 5.95 (ISBN 0-696-01545-5). BH&G.
--Better Homes & Gardens Bath & Bedroom Projects You Can Build. (You Can Build Ser.). (Illus.). 1979. 6.95 (ISBN 0-696-00335-X). BH&G.
--Better Homes & Gardens Beginner's Cook Books. (Illus.). 96p. 1984. pap. 5.95 (ISBN 0-696-01310-X). BH&G.
--Better Homes & Gardens Best Recipes Yearbook 1986. 192p. 1985. 14.95 (ISBN 0-696-02114-5). BH&G.
--Better Homes & Gardens Brown Bagger's Cook Book. (Illus.). 80p. 1985. pap. 5.95 (ISBN 0-696-01470-X). BH&G.
--Better Homes & Gardens Calorie-Counter's Cook Book. rev. ed. (Illus.). 96p. 1983. 6.95 (ISBN 0-696-00835-1). BH&G.
--Better Homes & Gardens Candy. (Illus.). 96p. 1984. 6.95 (ISBN 0-696-01415-7). BH&G.
--Better Homes & Gardens Chocolate. (Illus.). 96p. 1984. 6.95 (ISBN 0-696-01305-3). BH&G.
--Better Homes & Gardens Christmas Crafts to Make Ahead. (Illus.). 80p. 1983. pap. 6.95 (ISBN -696-00885-8). BH&G.
--Better Homes & Gardens Christmas Joys to Craft & Stitch. (Illus.). 80p. 1985. pap. 6.95 (ISBN 0-696-01432-7). BH&G.
--Better Homes & Gardens Christmas: 1985. (Illus.). 80p. 1985. pap. 3.95 (ISBN 0-696-01505-6). BH&G.
--Better Homes & Gardens Complete Guide to Gardening. (Illus.). 1979. 22.95 (ISBN 0-696-00041-5). BH&G.
--Better Homes & Gardens Complete Guide to Home Repair, Maintenance & Improvement. (Illus.). 1980. 22.95 (ISBN 0-696-00545-X). BH&G.
--Better Homes & Gardens Complete Step-by-Step Cook Book. LC 77-74601. (Illus.). 1978. 19.95 (ISBN 0-696-00125-X). BH&G.
--Better Homes & Gardens Cookies for Christmas. (Illus.). 96p. 1985. 6.95 (ISBN 0-696-01290-1). BH&G.
--Better Homes & Gardens Cookies for Kids. (Illus.). 96p. 1983. pap. 5.95 (ISBN 0-696-00865-3). BH&G.
--Better Homes & Gardens Cooking for Two. rev. ed. (Illus.). 96p. 1982. 6.95 (ISBN 0-696-00452-6). BH&G.
--Better Homes & Gardens: Cooking with Whole Grains. (Illus.). 96p. 1984. pap. 5.95 (ISBN 0-696-01315-0). BH&G.
--Better Homes & Gardens Creative Machine Stitchery. (Illus.). 80p. 1985. pap. 6.95 (ISBN 0-696-01437-8). BH&G.
--Better Homes & Gardens Crocheting & Knitting. (Illus.). 1977. 6.95 (ISBN 0-696-01400-9). BH&G.
--Better Homes & Gardens Crockery Cooker Cook Book. LC 75-40624. (Illus.). 96p. 1976. 6.95 (ISBN 0-696-01020-8). BH&G.
--Better Homes & Gardens Deck & Patio Projects You Can Build. (You Can Build Ser.). (Illus.). 1977. pap. 6.95 (ISBN 0-696-01365-7). BH&G.
--Better Homes & Gardens Decorating Your Home. (All about Your House Ser.). (Illus.). 160p. 1985. 9.95 (ISBN 0-696-02178-1). BH&G.
--Better Homes & Gardens Dieting for One. (Illus.). 96p. (Orig.). 1984. pap. 5.95 (ISBN 0-696-01410-6). BH&G.
--Better Homes & Gardens Do-It-Yourself Home Repairs. (Illus.). 320p. 1985. 14.95 (ISBN 0-696-01520-X). BH&G.
--Better Homes & Gardens Eat & Stay Slim. LC 78-74939. (Illus.). 1979. 6.95 (ISBN 0-696-01115-8). BH&G.
--Better Homes & Gardens Eating Light. (Illus.). 96p. 1985. 6.95 (ISBN 0-696-01475-0). BH&G.
--Better Homes & Gardens Fix It Fast Cook Book. LC 78-73180. (Illus.). 1979. 6.95 (ISBN 0-696-01230-8). BH&G.
--Better Homes & Gardens Food Processor Cook Book. LC 78-73181. (Illus.). 1979. 6.95 (ISBN 0-696-01025-9). BH&G.
--Better Homes & Gardens Furniture Projects You Can Build. (Illus.). 1977. pap. 6.95 (ISBN 0-696-01370-3). BH&G.
--Better Homes & Gardens Garages, Basements & Attics. (All about Your House Ser.). (Illus.). 160p. 1985. lib. bdg. 9.95 (ISBN 0-696-02179-X). BH&G.
--Better Homes & Gardens: Hearts to Stitch & Craft. (Illus.). 80p. 1984. pap. 6.95 (ISBN 0-696-01087-9). BH&G.
--Better Homes & Gardens His Turn to Cook. (Illus.). 96p. 1983. pap. 5.95 (ISBN 0-696-00875-0). BH&G.
--Better Homes & Gardens Homemade Cookies Cook Book. LC 74-75786. (Illus.). 96p. 1975. 6.95 (ISBN 0-696-01140-9). BH&G.
--Better Homes & Gardens Hot & Spicy. (Illus.). 96p. 1984. pap. 5.95 (ISBN 0-696-01420-3). BH&G.
--Better Homes & Gardens Hot off the Grill. (Illus.). 96p. 1985. pap. 5.95 (ISBN 0-696-01465-3). BH&G.
--Better Homes & Gardens Italian Cook Book. LC 78-74935. (Ethnic Ser.). (Illus.). 1979. 6.95 (ISBN 0-696-01235-9). BH&G.
--Better Homes & Gardens Kid's Party Cook Book. (Illus.). 80p. 1985. pap. 5.95 (ISBN 0-696-01555-2). BH&G.
--Better Homes & Gardens Kids' Snacks. (Illus.). 80p. 1985. pap. 5.95 (ISBN 0-696-01480-7). BH&G.
--Better Homes & Gardens Living the Country Life. (Illus.). 320p. 1985. 24.95 (ISBN 0-696-01180-8). BH&G.
--Better Homes & Gardens Lovable Gifts for Babies. (Illus.). 80p. 1985. pap. 6.95 (ISBN 0-696-01442-4). BH&G.
--Better Homes & Gardens Low Calorie Microwave Cooking. (Illus.). 96p. 1984. 6.95 (ISBN 0-696-01450-5). BH&G.
--Better Homes & Gardens Low-Fat Cooking. (Illus.). 96p. 1985. 6.95 (ISBN 0-696-01515-3). BH&G.
--Better Homes & Gardens Low-Salt Cooking. (Illus.). 96p. 1984. 6.95 (ISBN 0-696-01320-7). BH&G.
--Better Homes & Gardens Maintaining Your Home. (All about Your House Ser.). (Illus.). 160p. 1985. 9.95 (ISBN 0-696-02181-1). BH&G.
--Better Homes & Gardens Meals for One or Two. LC 77-8563. (Illus.). 1978. 6.95 (ISBN 0-696-01240-5). BH&G.
--Better Homes & Gardens Mexican Cook Book. LC 77-74591. (Illus.). 1977. 6.95 (ISBN 0-696-01030-5). BH&G.
--Better Homes & Gardens Microwave Cooking for Kids. (Illus.). 96p. 1984. pap. 5.95 (ISBN 0-696-01425-4). BH&G.
--Better Homes & Gardens Microwave Plus Cook Book. (Illus.). 96p. 1983. 6.95 (ISBN 0-696-00850-5). BH&G.
--Better Homes & Gardens My Recipe Collection. (Illus.). 142p. 1983. 14.95 (ISBN 0-696-01070-4). BH&G.
--Better Homes & Gardens New Baby Book. 416p. 1980. pap. 3.95 (ISBN 0-553-23821-3). Bantam.
--Better Homes & Gardens New Baby Book. (Illus.). 1979. 9.95 (ISBN 0-696-00021-0). BH&G.
--Better Homes & Gardens New Baby Book. rev. ed. (Illus.). 264p. 1985. 14.95 (ISBN 0-696-00022-9). BH&G.
--Better Homes & Gardens New Cook Book. 960p. 1982. pap. 4.50 (ISBN 0-553-22528-6). Bantam.
--Better Homes & Gardens New Junior Cook Book. LC 78-73183. (Illus.). 1979. 6.95 (ISBN 0-696-01145-X). BH&G.
--Better Homes & Gardens New Junior Cookbook. (Reading Rainbow Ser.). 1984. pap. 5.95 (ISBN 0-317-05642-5). BH & GB.
--Better Homes & Gardens One-Dish Microwave Meals. Hoppe, Lynn, ed. (Illus.). 80p. 1985. pap. 5.95 (ISBN 0-696-01540-4). BH&G.
--Better Homes & Gardens Oriental Cook Book. LC 77-74592. (Illus.). 1977. 6.95 (ISBN 0-696-01045-3). BH&G.
--Better Homes & Gardens: Outside Your Home. (All About Your House Ser.). (Illus.). 160p. 1985. 10.95 (ISBN 0-696-02177-3). BH&G.
--Better Homes & Gardens Pasta. (Illus.). 96p. 1983. 6.95 (ISBN 0-696-00855-6). BH&G.
--Better Homes & Gardens Patchwork & Quilting. (Illus.). 1977. 6.95 (ISBN 0-696-01395-9). BH&G.
--Better Homes & Gardens: Renewing an Old House. (All About Your House Ser.). 160p. 1984. 9.95 (ISBN 0-696-02174-9). BH&G.
--Better Homes & Gardens Step-by-Step Cabinets & Shelves. (Illus.). 1983. pap. 6.95 (ISBN 0-696-01065-8). BH&G.
--Better Homes & Gardens Step-by-Step Kids' Cookbook. (Illus.). 96p. 1984. pap. 5.95 (ISBN 0-696-01327-4). BH&G.
--Better Homes & Gardens Stir Fry Recipes. (Illus.). 80p. 1985. 6.95 (ISBN 0-696-01485-8). BH&G.
--Better Homes & Gardens: Storage. (All About Your House Ser.). 160p. 1984. 9.95 (ISBN 0-696-02175-7). BH&G.
--Better Homes & Gardens Storage Projects You Can Build. (Illus.). 1977. pap. 6.95 (ISBN 0-696-01380-0). BH&G.
--Better Homes & Gardens: The Pleasures of Cross-Stitch. (Illus.). 80p. 1984. pap. 6.95 (ISBN 0-696-01082-8). BH&G.
--Better Homes & Gardens: Using Color & Light. (All about Your House Ser.). (Illus.). 160p. 1985. 9.95 (ISBN 0-696-02180-3). BH&G.
--Better Homes & Gardens: Working at Home. (All About Your House Ser.). (Illus.). 160p. 1985. 9.95 (ISBN 0-696-02173-0). BH&G.
--Better Homes & Gardens: Your Bedrooms. (All About Your House Ser.). 160p. 1984. 9.95 (ISBN 0-696-02172-2). BH&G.
--Better Homes & Gardens: Your Floors & Stairs. (All About Your House Ser.). (Illus.). 160p. 1985. 9.95 (ISBN 0-696-02176-5). BH&G.
--Better Homes & Gardens: Your Furniture. (All about Your House Ser.). (Illus.). 160p. 1984. 9.95 (ISBN 0-696-02170-6). BH&G.
--Better Homes & Gardens: Your Yard. (All about Your House Ser.). (Illus.). 160p. 1984. 9.95 (ISBN 0-696-02168-4). BH&G.
--Cherished Dolls You Can Make for Fun. (Better Homes & Gardens Bks.). (Illus.). 80p. pap. 6.95 (ISBN 0-696-01077-1). BH&G.
--Cooking Chinese. (Better Homes & Gardens Bks.). (Illus.). 96p. 1983. pap. 5.95 (ISBN 0-696-01095-X). BH&G.
--Country Cooking. (Better Homes & Gardens Bks.). (Illus.). 96p. 1983. 6.95 (ISBN 0-696-01155-7). BH&G.
--Creative Cake Decorating. (Illus.). 96p. 1983. pap. 5.95 (ISBN 0-696-01150-6). BH&G.
--The Dieter's Cook Book. 384p. 1982. 24.95 (ISBN 0-696-00745-2). BH&G.
--Easy Bazaar Crafts. (Illus.). 96p. 1981. 6.95 (ISBN 0-696-00665-0). BH&G.
--Entertaining with Ease Cook Book. Granseth, Sandra, ed. 320p. 1984. 24.95 (ISBN 0-696-00895-5). BH&G.
--Microwave Cooking for One or Two. (Better Homes & Gardens Bks.). (Illus.). 96p. 1983. 6.95 (ISBN 0-696-01160-3). BH&G.
--Microwave Recipes Made Easy. 210p. 1982. 6.95 (ISBN 0-696-00845-9). BH&G.
--More from Your Wok. (Illus.). 96p. 1982. 6.95 (ISBN 0-696-01125-5). BH&G.
--New Cook Book. 14p. 1982. casebound 24.95 (ISBN 0-696-00890-4). BH&G.
--The New Cookbook. (Illus.). 464p. 1984. pap. 9.95 (ISBN 0-696-00825-4). BH&G.
--Solar Living. (All about Your House Ser.). (Illus.). 160p. 1983. 9.95 (ISBN 0-696-02166-8). BH&G.
--Step-by-Step Basic Carpentry. (Step-by-Step Home Repair Ser.). (Illus.). 96p. 1981. pap. 6.95 (ISBN 0-696-01185-9). BH&G.
--Toaster Oven Cook Book. (Illus.). 96p. 1982. 6.95 (ISBN 0-696-01175-1). BH&G.
--Your Baths. (All about Your House Ser.). (Illus.). 160p. 1983. 9.95 (ISBN 0-696-02165-X). BH&G.
--Your Family Centers. (All about Your House Ser.). (Illus.). 160p. 1983. 9.95 (ISBN 0-696-02164-1). BH&G.
Better Homes & Gardens Editors, ed. Better Homes & Gardens Microwave Cook Book. LC 75-38241. (Illus.). 96p. 1976. 6.95 (ISBN 0-696-01035-6). BH&G.
--Better Homes & Gardens Soups & Stews Cook Book. LC 78-56642. (Illus.). 1978. 6.95 (ISBN 0-696-01285-5). BH&G.
--Better Homes & Gardens Story Book. rev. ed. LC 50-9504. (Illus.). (gr. k-3). 1970. 9.95 (ISBN 0-696-00030-X). BH&G.
Betteridge, Barbara, tr. see Steiner, Rudolf.
Betteridge, Harold T. Cassell's German Dictionary: German-English, English-German. rev. ed. LC 77-18452. (Ger. & Eng.). 1978. thumb indexed 21.95 (ISBN 0-02-522930-3); indexed 19.95 (ISBN 0-02-522920-6); concise 9.95 (ISBN 0-02-522650-9). Macmillan.
Betteridge, Terry. An Algebraic Analysis of Storage Fragmentation. Stone, Harold, ed. LC 82-11194. (Computer Science: Systems Programming Ser.: No. 15). 232p. 1983. 44.95 (ISBN 0-8357-1364-4). UMI Res Pr.
Betteridge, W. Cobalt & Its Alloys. (Industrial Metals Ser.). 159p. 1982. 53.95x (ISBN 0-470-27342-9). Halsted Pr.
--Nickel & Its Alloys. (Illus.). 160p. 1977. pap. 18.50x (ISBN 0-7121-0947-1, Pub. by Macdonald & Evans England). Trans-Atlantic.
--Nickel & Its Alloys. (Monographs in Toxicology). 211p. 1984. 49.95 (ISBN 0-470-20117-7). Halsted Pr.
Betteridge, W. & Heslop, J., eds. The Nimonic Alloys. 2nd ed. LC 74-79862. (Illus.). 498p. 1974. 59.00x (ISBN 0-8448-0370-7). Crane-Russak Co.
Betteridge, W., et al, eds. Alloy Eight Hundred: Proceedings of the Petten International Conference, the Netherlands, 14-16 March, 1978. 1979. 83.00 (ISBN 0-444-85228-X, North Holland). Elsevier.
Betterley, Melvin. Sheet Metal Drafting. 2nd ed. (Illus.). 1977. pap. text ed. 26.40 (ISBN 0-07-005126-7). McGraw.
Betters, Francis. Fishing the Adirondacks. LC 82-81857. (Illus.). 114p. pap. cancelled (ISBN 0-918517-06-0). Chauncy Pr.
Betters, P. V. & Williams, J. Kerwin. Cities & the 1936 Congress & Recent Federal-City Relations. LC 77-74929. (American Federalism-the Urban Dimension). 1978. Repr. of 1936 ed. lib. bdg. 17.00x (ISBN 0-405-10478-2). Ayer Co Pubs.
Betters, Paul V. The Bureau of Home Economics: Its History, Activities & Organization. LC 72-3079. (Brookings Institution. Institute for Government Research. Service Monographs of the U.S. Government: No. 62). Repr. of 1930 ed. 24.00 (ISBN 0-404-57162-X). AMS Pr.
--Federal Services to Municipal Governments. LC 77-749330. (American Federalism-the Urban Dimension). 1977. Repr. of 1931 ed. lib. bdg. 17.00x (ISBN 0-405-10479-0). Ayer Co Pubs.
--The Personnel Classification Board: Its History, Activities & Organization. LC 72-3081. (Brookings Institution. Institute for Government Research. Service Monographs of the U.S. Government: No. 64). Repr. of 1931 ed. 24.00 (ISBN 0-404-57164-6). AMS Pr.
Betters, Paul V., jt. auth. see Smith, Darrell H.
Bettersworth, John K. People's University: A History of Mississippi State University. LC 79-13648. 1980. text ed. 25.00x (ISBN 0-87805-104-X). U Pr of Miss.
Betterton, Alec, jt. auth. see Dymond, David.
Bettetini, Gianfranco. The Language & Technique of the Film. (Approaches to Semiotics Ser: No. 28). 1973. text ed. 22.40x (ISBN 90-2792-412-0). Mouton.
Bettex, Albert W. German Novel of Today: A Guide to Contemporary Fiction in Germany, to the Novels of the Emigrants & to Those of German-Speaking Swiss Writers. facsimile ed. LC 77-99655. (Select Bibliographies Reprint Ser). 1939. 13.00 (ISBN 0-8369-5084-4). Ayer Co Pubs.
Bettex, M. & Koch, A., eds. Kinderchirurgische Probleme in der paediatrische Praxis. (Paediatrische Fortbildungskurse fuer die Praxis: Vol. 49). (Illus.). 1980. pap. 17.50 (ISBN 3-8055-0232-X). S Karger.
Bettey, J. H. Church & Community: The Parish Church in English Life. LC 79-14739. (Illus.). 142p. 1979. text ed. 26.50x (ISBN 0-06-490381-8, 06346). B&N Imports.
--Dorset. (City & County Historics Ser). 1974. 4.50 (ISBN 0-7153-6371-9). David & Charles.
Bettey, J. H. & Taylor, C. W. Sacred & Satiric: Medieval Stone Carving in the West Country. (Illus.). 40.00x (ISBN 0-317-20312-6, Pub. by Redcliffe Pr Ltd). State Mutual Bk.
Bettger, Frank. How I Multiplied My Income & Happiness in Selling. 315p. 1982. 12.95 (ISBN 0-13-423962-8); pap. 4.95 (ISBN 0-13-423954-7). P-H.
--How I Raised Myself from Failure to Success in Selling. 1975. pap. 2.95 (ISBN 0-346-12295-3). Cornerstone.
--How I Raised Myself from Failure to Success in Selling. 1958. 8.95 (ISBN 0-13-399402-3). P-H.
--How I Raised Myself from Failure to Success in Selling. 192p. 1983. pap. 4.95 (ISBN 0-13-423970-9). P-H.
Betti, Claudia W. & Sale, Teel. Drawing: A Contemporary Approach. LC 79-26976. 276p. (Orig.). 1980. pap. text ed. 25.95 (ISBN 0-03-045976-1, HoltC). HR&W.
Betti, Franco. Vittorio Alfieri. (World Authors Ser.). 1984. lib. bdg. 18.95 (ISBN 0-8057-6579-4, Twayne). G K Hall.
Betti, Ugo. Two Plays: Frana allo Scalo Nord & L'aiuola bruciata. McWilliam, G. H., ed. (Italian Texts Ser.). 208p. (Ital.). 1965. pap. text ed. 5.95 (ISBN 0-7190-0197-8, Pub. by Manchester Univ Pr). Longwood Pub Group.

Bettina. Pantaloni. LC 57-9103. (Illus.). 32p. (gr. k-3). 1957. PLB 10.89 (ISBN 0-06-020506-7). HarpJ.

Bettinghaus, Erwin P. Persuasive Communication. 3rd ed. 272p. 1980. text ed. 25.95 (ISBN 0-03-089959-1, HoltC). HR&W.

Bettini, S., ed. Arthropod Venoms. (Handbook of Experimental Pharmacology: Vol. 48). (Illus.). 1977. 265.00 (ISBN 0-387-08228-X). Springer-Verlag.

Bettinson, Christopher. Gide: A Study. 104p. 1977. 10.00x (ISBN 0-87471-936-4). Rowman.

Bettis, D. G., ed. see Conference on Numerical Solution of Ordinary Differential Equations.

Bettis, Joseph & Johannesen, S. K., eds. The Return of the Millennium. LC 83-82671. 247p. 1984. pap. 11.95 (ISBN 0-913757-02-0). Rose Sharon Pr.

Bettis, Joseph & Johannesen, Stanley, eds. The Return of the Millenium. LC 83-82671. 232p. (Orig.). pap. 11.95 (ISBN 0-913757-02-0, Pub. by New Era Bks.). Paragon Hse.

Bettis, Mervin, jt. auth. see Hoerner, Thomas.

Bettis, Stan & Doornink, Jon. Place Called Oregon. (Illus.). Date not set. price not set (ISBN 0-685-52885-5). Pacific Bks.

Bettison, Sue. Toilet Training to Independence for the Handicapped: A Manual for Trainers. (Illus.). 144p. 1982. pap. 15.95x spiral (ISBN 0-398-04678-6). C C Thomas.

Bettiza, Enzo. Inspector. Frenaye, F., tr. 1966. 4.00 (ISBN 0-8184-0108-7). Lyle Stuart.

--Italian Communism. Keene, Frances, tr. from Ital. Orig. Title: Il Comunismo Europeo. 1979. text ed. write for info. (ISBN 0-918294-07-X). Karz Pub.

Bettman, James R. Information Processing Theory of Consumer Choice. LC 78-52496. (Advances in Marketing Ser.). 1979. text ed. 35.95 (ISBN 0-201-00834-3). Addison-Wesley.

Bettman, Lynn. Profiles of American Artists. Rev. ed. 1984. pap. 25.00 (ISBN 0-317-26926-7). Kennedy Gall.

Bettmann, Otto L. Good Old Days - They Were Terrible! LC 74-6050. (Illus.). 1974. pap. 6.95 (ISBN 0-394-70941-1). Random.

--Pictorial History of Medicine. (Illus.). 336p. 1979. pap. 16.00x (ISBN 0-398-00149-9). C C Thomas.

Bettmann, Otto L., jt. auth. see Lang, Paul H.

Bettoja, Jo & Cornetto, Anna Maria. Italian Cooking in the Grand Tradition. LC 82-4979. (Illus.). 320p. 1982. 24.95 (ISBN 0-385-27424-6, Dial). Doubleday.

Bettoney, Fred, ed. see Weissenborn, Julius.

Bettoni, Efrem. Duns Scotus: The Basic Principles of His Philosophy. Bonansea, Berbardine, ed. LC 78-14031. 1979. Repr. of 1961 ed. lib. bdg. 35.00x (ISBN 0-313-21142-6, BEDS). Greenwood.

--Saint Bonaventure. Scuola, Editrice, Brescia, Italy, tr. from Ital. LC 81-13371. (The Notre Dame Pocket Library). 127p. 1982. Repr. of 1964 ed. lib. bdg. 17.50x (ISBN 0-313-23271-7, BESB). Greenwood.

Bettotti, B., et al, eds. General Relativity & Gravitation. 1984. lib. bdg. 69.00 (ISBN 90-277-1819-9, Pub. by Reidel Holland). Kluwer Academic.

Betts. Appeals & Certiorari in Lower & Appellate Courts. (The Law in Georgia Ser.). incl. latest pocket part supplement 24.95 (ISBN 0-686-90379-X); separate pocket part supplement, 1979 8.95 (ISBN 0-686-90380-3). Harrison Co GA.

--Elements of Applied Physics. 1983. text ed. 28.95 (ISBN 0-8359-1688-X); solutions manual free (ISBN 0-8359-1689-8). Reston.

--Patient with a Cardiovascular Disorder, Vol. 2. 96p. 1982. pap. text ed. 6.00 (ISBN 0-06-318232-7, Pub. by Har-Row Ltd England). Har-Row.

--Patient with a Respiratory Disorder, Vol. 1. 96p. 1982. pap. text ed. 6.00 (ISBN 0-06-318231-9, Pub. by Har-Row Ltd England). Har-Row.

Betts, jt. auth. see Sexton.

Betts, Ann. Patient with a Genitourinary Disorder. 1983. pap. text ed. 4.50 (ISBN 0-06-318253-X). Har-Row.

--Patient with Gastrointestinal Disorder. 1984. pap. text ed. 4.50 (ISBN 0-06-318254-8). Har-Row.

Betts, Benjamin. Mexican Imperial Coinage: The Medals & Coinage. (Illus.). 1982. Repr. of 1899 ed. softcover 8.00 (ISBN 0-915262-75-4). S J Durst.

Betts, C. J. Early Deism in France. 1984. lib. bdg. 53.50 (ISBN 90-247-2923-8, Pub. by Martinus Nijhoff Netherlands). Kluwer Academic.

Betts, C. J., tr. see Montesquieu, Charles D.

Betts, Carolyn. A Special Kind of Normal. 160p. 10.95 (ISBN 0-684-17778-1, ScribT). Scribner.

Betts, D. S. Refrigeration & Thermometry Below One Kelvin. LC 75-34695. (Illus.). 304p. 1976. 29.50x (ISBN 0-8448-0853-9). Crane-Russak Co.

--Refrigeration & Thermometry Below One Kelvin. 40.00x (ISBN 0-686-97021-7, Pub. by Scottish Academic Pr Scotland). State Mutual Bk.

Betts, D. S., jt. auth. see Turner, R. D.

Betts, Doris, et al. Three by Three: Masterworks of the Southern Gothic. Simpson, Lewis, ed. 768p. (Orig.). 1985. 22.95 (ISBN 0-931948-80-0); pap. 14.95 (ISBN 0-931948-84-3). Peachtree Pubs.

Betts, E. Outbreaks of the African Migratory Locust (Locusta Migratoria Migratoriodes R & F) Since 1871. 1961. 35.00x (ISBN 0-85135-005-4, Pub. by Centre Overseas Research). State Mutual Bk.

Betts, Edward. Creative Seascrape Painting. 160p. 1981. 22.50 (ISBN 0-8230-1113-5). Watson-Guptill.

Betts, Edward C. Historic Huntsville: Eighteen Four to Eighteen Seventy. (Illus.). 1966. pap. 7.95 (ISBN 0-87651-011-X). Southern U Pr.

Betts, Edwin M., ed. Thomas Jefferson's Farm Book: With Commentary & Relevant Extracts from Other Writings. LC 52-13160. (Illus.). 552p. 1976. Repr. of 1953 ed. 25.00x (ISBN 0-8139-0705-5). U Pr of Va.

--Thomas Jefferson's Garden Book. (Memoirs Ser.: Vol. 22). (Illus.). 1944. Repr. of 1981 ed. 20.00 (ISBN 0-87169-022-5). Am Philos.

Betts, Emmett A. The Prevention & Correction of Reading Difficulties. 402p. 1984. Repr. of 1936 ed. lib. bdg. 40.00 (ISBN 0-89987-973-X). Darby Books.

Betts, Frank, ed. Songs & Sayings of Walther Von der Vogelweide. 69.95 (ISBN 0-8490-2631-8). Gordon Pr.

Betts, Frank, tr. see Walther von der Vogelweide.

Betts, G. G. & Plenard, F. J. Future Changes in the Chemical Industry. 34p. 1981. 32.00x (ISBN 0-85295-145-0, Pub. by IChemE). State Mutual Bk.

Betts, George H. The Curriculum of Religious Education. (Educational Ser.). 1924. Repr. 30.00 (ISBN 0-8482-7352-4). Norwood Edns.

--The Distribution & Functions of Mental Imagery. LC 76-176560. (Columbia University. Teachers College. Contributions to Education: No. 26). Repr. of 1909 ed. 22.50 (ISBN 0-404-55026-6). AMS Pr.

--Foundations of Character & Personality. (Educational Ser.). 1937. Repr. 10.00 (ISBN 0-8482-7375-3). Norwood Edns.

--Mind & Its Education. LC 77-164694. Repr. of 1906 ed. 8.50 (ISBN 0-404-00789-9). AMS Pr.

--The Mind & Its Education. (Educational Ser.). 1910. Repr. 10.00 (ISBN 0-8482-7400-8). Norwood Edns.

Betts, Glynne R. Writers in Residence: American Authors at Home. 1981. 16.95 (ISBN 0-670-79108-3, Studio). Viking.

Betts, Grawin N. Sponge Gray. LC 79-93426. 1980. 6.95 (ISBN 0-87212-133-X). Libra.

Betts, Irene D. & Howell, Carol C. Writing Plan. 288p. 1984. pap. text ed. 14.95 (ISBN 0-13-971770-6). P-H.

Betts, Jim. The Million Dollar Idea. 100p. (Orig.). 1985. pap. 6.95 (ISBN 0-911909-01-X). New Prod Develop.

Betts, Jim, jt. auth. see Brewer, Edward S.

Betts, Jim, jt. auth. see Heimbold, Noreen C.

Betts, John E. Physics for Technology. 2nd ed. (Illus.). 675p. 1981. text ed. 29.95 (ISBN 0-8359-5544-3); solutions manual free (ISBN 0-8359-5545-1). Reston.

Betts, John R. America's Sporting Heritage: 1850-1950. LC 73-10590. 1974. text ed. 23.95 (ISBN 0-201-00557-3). Addison-Wesley.

Betts, Leonard C. Garden Pools. (Illus.). 1952. pap. 2.95 (ISBN 0-87666-077-4, M-513). TFH Pubns.

Betts, Otsie V., jt. ed. see Srygley, Ola P.

Betts, P. W. Office Management. (Teach Yourself Ser.). 1975. pap. 4.95 (ISBN 0-679-10383-X). McKay.

--Supervisory Studies. 4th ed. (Illus.). 498p. 1983. pap. text ed. 24.95x (ISBN 0-7121-1992-2). Trans-Atlantic.

Betts, Peter W. The Board & Administrative Management: Management for the Board. 192p. 1977. text ed. 29.50x (ISBN 0-220-66338-6, Pub. by Busn Bks England). Brookfield Pub Co.

Betts, Raymond F. Assimilation & Association in French Colonial Theory 1890-1914. LC 70-130622. (Columbia University Social Science Studies Ser.: No. 604). Repr. of 1961 ed. 17.50 (ISBN 0-404-51604-1). AMS Pr.

--Europe in Retrospect: A Brief History of the Past Hundred Years. (Orig.). 1979. pap. 9.95 (ISBN 0-669-01366-8). Heath.

--The False Dawn: European Imperialism in the Nineteenth Century. Shafer, Boyd C., ed. LC 75-14683. (Europe & the World in the Age of Expansion: Vol. VI). (Illus.). 1975. 15.00x (ISBN 0-8166-0762-1). U of Minn Pr.

--The False Dawn: European Imperialism in the 19th Century. LC 75-14683. (Europe & the World in the Age of Expansion Ser). 1978. pap. 5.95x (ISBN 0-8166-0852-0). U of Minn Pr.

--Uncertain Dimensions: Western Overseas Empires in the Twentieth Century. (Europe & the World in the Age of Expansion Ser.: Vol. 13). (Illus.). Date not set. 22.50 (ISBN 0-8166-1308-7); pap. 11.95 (ISBN 0-8166-1309-5). U of Minn Pr.

Betts, Richard. Cruise Missiles & U.S. Policy. LC 82-72704. 61p. 1982. pap. 6.95 (ISBN 0-8157-0933-1). Brookings.

Betts, Richard K. Soldiers, Statesmen, & Cold War Crises. 1977. 17.50x (ISBN 0-674-81741-9). Harvard U Pr.

--Surprise Attack: Lessons for Defense Planning. LC 82-70887. 318p. 1982. 26.95 (ISBN 0-8157-0930-7); pap. 9.95 (ISBN 0-8157-0929-3). Brookings.

Betts, Richard K., jt. auth. see Gelb, Leslie H.

Betts, Richard K., ed. Cruise Missiles: Technology, Strategy, Politics. LC 81-18149. 612p. 1981. 32.95 (ISBN 0-8157-0932-3); pap. 15.95 (ISBN 0-8157-0931-5). Brookings.

Betts, Richard M. & Ely, Silas J. Basic Real Estate Appraisal. 367p. 1982. text ed. 26.95x (ISBN 0-471-03120-8); test 7.50x (ISBN 0-471-87300-4). Wiley.

Betts, Richard M., jt. auth. see McKenzie, Dennis J.

Betts, Robert B. Along the Ramparts of the Tetons: The Saga of Jackson Hole, Wyoming. LC 77-94083. 1978. 22.50 (ISBN 0-87081-113-4); pap. 10.00 (ISBN 0-87081-117-7). Colo Assoc.

--Christians in the Arab East. LC 78-8674. 1981. 12.50 (ISBN 0-8042-0796-8). John Knox.

--The Search for York: The Black Member of the Lewis & Clark Expedition. 1985. 19.50 (ISBN 0-87081-144-4). Colo Assoc.

Betts, Wilbur, jt. auth. see Schultz, James W.

Bettsworth, Michael. Drownproofing: A Technique for Water Survival. LC 76-48762. 1977. pap. 2.95 (ISBN 0-8052-0558-6). Schocken.

Betty, L. Stafford. Vadiraja's Refutation of Sankara's Non-Dualism: Clearing the Way for Theism. 1978. 9.95 (ISBN 0-89684-001-8). Orient Bk Dist.

Betty, Stafford. The Rich Man: A Galilean Chronicle. LC 83-26882. 209p. 1984. 14.95 (ISBN 0-312-68105-4). St Martin.

Betz. Ecuaciones Diferenciales. (Span.). 1977. pap. text ed. 11.40 (ISBN 0-06-310058-4, IntlDept). Har-Row.

Betz, Albrecht. Hanns Eisler: Political Musician. Hopkins, Bill, tr. from Ger. LC 81-12260. (Illus.). 190p. 1982. 49.50 (ISBN 0-521-24022-0). Cambridge U Pr.

Betz, C. E. Principle of Penetrants. 2nd ed. Catlin, F. S., ed. LC 76-95933. (Illus.). 31.50x (ISBN 0-686-21416-1). Magnaflux.

Betz, Carl E. Principles of Magnetic Particle Testing. 528p. 1966. 37.00 (ISBN 0-318-17207-0, 436); members 31.50 (ISBN 0-318-17208-9). Am Soc Nondestructive.

Betz, Don. Cultivating Leadership: An Approach. LC 80-69039. 120p. (Orig.). 1981. pap. text ed. 6.75 (ISBN 0-8191-1441-3). U Pr of Amer.

Betz, E., ed. Ionic Actions on Vascular Smooth Muscle. (Illus.). 1976. pap. 19.00 (ISBN 0-387-07836-3). Springer-Verlag.

Betz, Eleanor P., et al. Holiday Eating for a Healthy Heart. 1981. pap. write for info. Rush-Presby-St Lukes.

--Summertime Eating for a Healthy Heart: Cook Out-Camp Out-Eat Out the Low Cholesterol Way. 60p. 1981. pap. 3.95 (ISBN 0-686-31628-2). Rush-Presby-St Lukes.

Betz, H. D., ed. see Ebeling, Gerhard, et al.

Betz, Hans D. Essays on the Sermon on the Mount. LC 84-47910. 192p. 1984. 24.95 (ISBN 0-8006-0726-0). Fortress.

--Galatians. LC 77-78625. (Hermenia: A Critical & Historical Commentary on the Bible). 1979. 28.95 (ISBN 0-8006-6009-9, 20-6009). Fortress.

--Second Corinthians Eight & Nine: A Commentary on Two Administrative Letters of the Apostle Paul. LC 84-48904. (Hermeneia Ser.). 288p. 1985. 27.95 (ISBN 0-8006-6014-5, 20-6014). Fortress.

--Second Corithians 8 & 9: A Commentary on Two Administrative Letters of the Apostle Paul. LC 84-48904. 288p. 27.95 (ISBN 0-8006-6014-5); Canada 36.35 (ISBN 0-317-31441-6). Fortress.

Betz, Hans D., ed. Christology & a Modern Pilgrimage: A Discussion with Norman Perrin. rev. ed. LC 79-31605. pap. 27.30 (ISBN 0-317-28877-6, 2020268). Bks Demand UMI.

--The Greek Magical Papyri in Translation, Including the Demonic Spells, Vol. 1: Text. LC 85-1137. (Illus.). 448p. 1986. lib. bdg. 39.95x (ISBN 0-226-04444-0). U of Chicago Pr.

Betz, L. P. Litterature Comparee. LC 68-25307. (Studies in Comparative Literature, No. 35). 1969. Repr. of 1904 ed. lib. bdg. 44.95x (ISBN 0-8383-0911-9). Haskell.

Betz, Louis P. Litterature Comparee. LC 77-101092. (BCL Ser. I). (Fr). 1969. Repr. of 1904 ed. 10.00 (ISBN 0-404-00793-7). AMS Pr.

Betz, Margaret. Faith & Justice. LC 80-50259. 176p. (gr. 11-12). 1980. pap. text ed. 5.00x (ISBN 0-88489-114-3); tchr's guide 9.00x (ISBN 0-88489-121-6). St Mary's.

Betz, Mathew J. & McGowan, Patrick J., eds. Appropiate Technology: Choice & Development. (DPPS Econonmics Ser.). 330p. 1984. PLB 32.50x (ISBN 0-8223-0573-9). Duke.

Betz, Nancy E., jt. auth. see Walsh, W. Burke.

Betz, Paul, ed. see Wordsworth, William.

Betzer, Dan. Beast: A Novel of the Future Dictator. 224p. 1985. 5.95 (ISBN 0-933451-01-6). Prescott Pr.

--Countdown. LC 79-53943. 112p. 1979. pap. 1.95 (ISBN 0-88243-481-0, 02-0481). Gospel Pub.

--Daily in the Word. LC 83-17464. 372p. 1983. pap. 7.95 (ISBN 0-8407-5864-2). Nelson.

Betzig, Laura L. Despotism & Differential Reproduction: A Darwinian View of History. (Biological Foundations of Human Behavior Ser.). (Illus.). 300p. 1986. lib. bdg. price not set (ISBN 0-202-01171-2). Aldine Pub.

Betzler, H., tr. see Von Mellenthin, F. W.

Betzler, M., jt. ed. see Herfarth, C.

Betzner, Jean. Content & Form of Original Compositions Dictated by Children from Five to Eight Years of Age. LC 70-176561. (Columbia University. Teachers College. Contributions to Education: No. 442). Repr. of 1930 ed. 22.50 (ISBN 0-404-55442-3). AMS Pr.

Betzold, Michael J. Sexual Scarcity: The Marital Mistake & the Communal Alternative. 1978. pap. 2.50 (ISBN 0-686-10620-2). Betzold.

Beuaverts, Ana, jt. auth. see Mels, Alberto.

Beube, Douglas S. Manhattan Street Romance. (Artist Bk.). (Illus.). 40p. (Orig.). 1982. pap. text ed. 6.00 (ISBN 0-89822-027-0). Visual Studies.

Beuchame, L., tr. see Melanchthon, Philip.

Beuchat, Henri, jt. auth. see Mauss, Marcel.

Beuchat, L. R. Food & Beverage Mycology. (Illus.). 1978. pap. text ed. 28.50 (ISBN 0-87055-293-7). AVI.

Beucler, Andre. Last of the Bohemians: Twenty Years with Leon-Paul Fargue. Sainsbury, Geoffrey, tr. LC 79-108841. Repr. of 1954 ed. lib. bdg. 18.75x (ISBN 0-8371-3729-2, BEBO). Greenwood.

Beudette. Central Vermont. (Carstens Hobby Bks.: No. C-44). (Illus.). 112p. 1982. pap. 13.95 (ISBN 0-911868-44-5). Carstens Pubns.

Beuf, Ann H. Biting off the Bracelet: A Study of Children in Hospitals. LC 79-5047. 1979. 16.00x (ISBN 0-8122-7766-X). U of Pa Pr.

--Red Children in White America. LC 76-49737. 168p. 1977. 16.00x (ISBN 0-8122-7719-8). U of Pa Pr.

Beukelman, David, et al. Communication Augmentation: A Casebook of Clinical Management. 1985. 34.00 (ISBN 0-85066-502-7). Taylor & Francis.

Beukelman, David R., et al. Communication Augmentation: A Casebook of Clinical Management. (Illus.). 235p. 1985. pap. 25.00 (ISBN 0-88744-102-5). College-Hill.

Beukema, H. J., jt. auth. see Giachino, J. W.

Beukema, Henry J., jt. auth. see Giachino, Joseph W.

Beukenkamp, Cornelius. Fortunate Strangers. 1971. pap. 4.95 (ISBN 0-87877-000-3, S-0). Newcastle Pub.

Beukenkamp, Cornelius, Jr. Fortunate Strangers. LC 80-19260. 269p. 1980. Repr. of 1971 ed. lib. bdg. 12.95x (ISBN 0-89370-600-0). Borgo Pr.

Beukenkamp, Erik J., et al. Exercises in Listening. 144p. 1984. pap. text ed. write for info. (ISBN 0-02-309200-9). Macmillan.

Beum, R., jt. auth. see Shapiro, Karl J.

Beum, Robert, ed. Classic European Short Stories. 276p. (Orig.). 1984. pap. 7.95 (ISBN 0-89385-025-X). Sugden.

Beumont, P. J. & Burrows, G. D., eds. Handbook of Psychiatry & Endocrinology. 448p. 1982. 109.00 (ISBN 0-444-80355-6, Biomedical Pr). Elsevier.

Beumont, P. J., jt. ed. see Touyz, S. W.

Beunat, Joseph. Empire Style Designs & Ornaments. LC 73-91877. (Illus.). 95p. 1974. pap. 5.95 (ISBN 0-486-22984-X). Dover.

--Empire Style Designs & Ornaments. (Illus.). Repr. of 1813 ed. 11.50 (ISBN 0-8446-5004-8). Peter Smith.

Beurdeley, Jean-Michel & Hinz, Hans. Thai Forms. (Illus.). 140p. 1980. 47.50 (ISBN 0-8348-0150-7, 28518). Weatherhill.

Beurdeley, Michel. Chinese Furniture. Watson, Katherine, tr. LC 79-84654. (Illus.). 1983. 69.95 (ISBN 0-87011-387-9). Kodansha.

--Giuseppe Castiglione: A Jesuit Painter at the Court of the Chinese Emperors. LC 77-157257. (Illus.). 1972. 25.00 (ISBN 0-8048-0987-9). C E Tuttle.

Beus, A. A. Geochemistry of the Lithosphere. 1976. 10.00 (ISBN 0-8285-1817-3, Pub. by Mir Pubs USSR). Imported Pubns.

Beus, A. A. & Grigorian, S. V. Geochemical Exploration Methods for Mineral Deposits. Levinson, A. A., ed. Teteruk-Schneider, Rita, tr. LC 77-75045. (Illus.). 1977. 32.00x (ISBN 0-915834-03-0). Applied Pub.

Beus, Carma. One Patch, Two Patch, Three Patch-Four! LC 83-81177. 52p. 1983. pap. 6.95 (ISBN 0-88290-224-5). Horizon-Utah.

Beus, H. L., tr. see Rodin, S. N.

Beus, Stanley S. & Rawson, Richard R., eds. Carboniferous Stratigraphy in the Grand Canyon Country, Northern Arizona & Southern Nevada. LC 78-74894. (AGI Selected Guidebook Ser.: No. 2). 1979. pap. 20.00 (ISBN 0-913312-09-6). Am Geol.

Beusedom, Mark Van see Brooke, Michael Z. & Van Beusedom, Mark.

Beust, Friedrich F. Von see Von Beust, Friedrich F.

Beust Friedrich F., Graf Von see Graf Von Beust, Friedrich F.

Beutel, Frederick K. Democracy of the Scientific Method in Law & Policy Making. 6.25 (ISBN 0-8477-3000-X). U of PR Pr.

--The Operation of the Bad Check Laws of Puerto Rico. 3.75 (ISBN 0-8477-2200-7); pap. 3.10 (ISBN 0-8477-2201-5). U of PR Pr.

Beutel, Frederick K. & Schroeder, Milton R. Bank Officer's Handbook of Commercial Banking Law. 5th ed. 1983. 58.00 (ISBN 0-88262-670-1). Warren.

Beutel, Frederick K., jt. auth. see Brannan, Joseph D.

Beutelspacher, H. & Van Der Marel, H. Atlas of Electron Microscopy of Clay Minerals & Their Admixtures. 333p. 1968. 132.00 (ISBN 0-444-40041-9). Elsevier.

Beutelspacher, H., jt. auth. see Van der Marel, R.

Beutler, Ernest. Hemolytic Anemia in Disorders of Red Cell Metabolism. LC 78-2391. (Topics in Hematology Ser.). (Illus.). 280p. 1978. 34.50x (ISBN 0-306-31112-7, Plenum Med Bk). Plenum Pub.

--Red Cell Metabolism: A Manual of Biochemical Methods. 3rd ed. 208p. 1984. 24.50 (ISBN 0-8089-1672-6, 790582). Grune.

Beutler, Larry E. Eclectic Psychotherapy: A Systematic Approach. (General Psychology Ser.: No. 118). 270p. 1983. 25.00 (ISBN 0-08-028842-1). Pergamon.

Beutler, Larry E. & Greene, Richard, eds. Special Problems in Child & Adolescent Behavior: A Social & Behavioral Approach. LC 78-56115. 1978. 14.95 (ISBN 0-87762-243-4). Technomic.

Beutlich, Tadek. The Technique of Woven Tapestry. 192p. 1980. pap. 9.95 (ISBN 0-7134-2529-6, Pub by Batsford England). David & Charles.

Beutner, Ed. Biblical Ballads. (Illus.). 1985. 4.95 (ISBN 0-911346-09-0). Christianica.

Beutner, Ernst H., ed. Autoimmunity in Psoriasis. 328p. 1982. 82.50 (ISBN 0-8493-5473-0). CRC Pr.

Beutner, Ernst H., et al, eds. Immunopathology of the Skin. 2nd ed. LC 78-24139. (Wiley Medical Publication). (Illus.). pap. 98.80 (ISBN 0-317-09236-7, 2017830). Bks Demand UMI.

--Seventh International Conference on Defined Immunofluorescence, Immunoenzyme Studies, & Related Labeling Techniques, Vol. 420. 84.00 (ISBN 0-89766-238-5); pap. 84.00 (ISBN 0-89766-239-3). NY Acad Sci.

Beuzamy, Bernard. Introduction to Banach Spaces & Their Geometry. (North Holland Mathematical Studies: Vol. 68). 308p. 1982. 38.50 (ISBN 0-444-86416-4, North-Hooand). Elsevier.

Bevacqua, Robert F. & Dye, Thomas S. Archaeological Reconnaissance of Proposed Kapoho-Kalapana Highway, District of Puna, Island of Hawaii. (Departmental Report: No. 72-3). 46p. 1972. pap. 2.00 (ISBN 0-686-47629-8). Bishop Mus.

Bevacqua, Robert F., jt. auth. see Hommon, Robert J.

Bevacqua, Robert F., ed. Archaeological Survey of Portions of Waikoloa, South Kohala District, Island of Hawaii. (Departmental Report: No. 72-4). 24p. 1972. pap. 2.00 (ISBN 0-910240-81-7). Bishop Mus.

Bevan. House of Ptolemy. (Illus.). 434p. 1985. 20.00 (ISBN 0-89005-536-X). Ares.

--House of Seleucus, 2 Vols. 681p. 1985. 25.00 (ISBN 0-89005-537-8). Ares.

Bevan, A. A., ed. The Hymn of the Soul: Contained in the Syriac Acts of St. Thomas. (Texts & Studies Ser.: No. 1, Vol. 5, Pt. 3). Repr. of 1897 ed. 19.00 (ISBN 0-317-16753-7). Kraus Repr.

Bevan, Bernard, tr. see Gomez-Moreno, Manuel.

Bevan, Brian. The Real Francis Bacon. 1983. 48.00x (ISBN 0-900000-67-8, Pub. by Centaur Pr England). State Mutual Bk.

Bevan, Clifford. The Tuba Family. (Illus.). 1978. 27.50 (ISBN 0-684-15477-3, ScribT). Scribner.

Bevan, David. The Art & Poetry of Charles-Ferdinand Ramuz. (Oleander Language & Literature Ser.). 1977. 8.95 (ISBN 0-902675-47-8). Oleander Pr.

--Renal Function in Anaesthesia & Surgery. 240p. 1979. 52.00 (ISBN 0-8089-1160-0, 790581). Grune.

Bevan, Edwyn. Stoics & Sceptics. Vlastos, Gregory, ed. LC 78-15852. (Morals & Law in Ancient Greece Ser.). 1979. Repr. of 1913 ed. lib. bdg. 14.00x (ISBN 0-405-11530-X). Ayer Co Pubs.

Bevan, Edwyn R. Christianity. LC 80-24452. (The Home University Library of Modern Knowledge Ser.: No. 157). 255p. 1981. Repr. of 1948 ed. lib. bdg. 25.00x (ISBN 0-313-22681-4, BECY). Greenwood.

--Hellenism & Christianity. facs. ed. LC 67-26714. (Essay Index Reprint Ser). 1921. 18.00 (ISBN 0-8369-0207-6). Ayer Co Pubs.

--Holy Images: An Inquiry into Idolatry & Image-Worship in Ancient Paganism & in Christianity. LC 77-27191. (Gifford Lectures: 1933). Repr. of 1940 ed. 18.00 (ISBN 0-404-60489-7). AMS Pr.

--Sibyls & Seers. 1979. Repr. of 1928 ed. lib. bdg. 30.00 (ISBN 0-8495-0510-0). Arden Lib.

Bevan, Edwyn R., ed. Later Greek Religion. LC 76-179282. (Library of Greek Thought: No. 9). Repr. of 1927 ed. 12.50 (ISBN 0-404-07807-9). AMS Pr.

Bevan, G. A., ed. see University of Wales Press.

Bevan, Gloria. Beyond the Ranges, Vineyard in a Valley, The Frost & the Fire. (Harlequin Romances Ser.). 576p. 1982. pap. 3.50 (ISBN 0-373-20061-7). Harlequin Bks.

--Emerald Cave. 192p. 1982. pap. 1.50 (ISBN 0-373-02455-X). Harlequin Bks.

--The Rouseabout Girl. (Harlequin Romances Ser.). 192p. 1983. pap. 1.75 (ISBN 0-373-02563-7). Harlequin Bks.

Bevan, Gwyn, et al. Health Care Priorities & Management: Priorities & Management. (Illus.). 294p. 1980. 30.00 (ISBN 0-7099-0093-7, Pub. by Croom Helm Ltd). Longwood Pub Group.

Bevan, J. A., et al, eds. Vascular Neuroeffector Mechanisms: Proceedings of the 5th International Congress on Vascular Neuroeffector Mechanisms held in Paris, France, 6-8 August; 1984. 368p. 1985. 70.50 (ISBN 0-444-80667-9). Elsevier.

Bevan, J. A., et al, eds. see Symposium on the Physiology & the Pharmacology of Vascular Neuroeffector Systems, Interlaken, 1969.

Bevan, Jack, tr. from see Quasimodo, Salvadore.

Bevan, Jack, tr. see Quasimodo, Salvatore.

Bevan, James. The Family First Aid & Medical Guide. 192p. 1984. pap. 7.95 (ISBN 0-671-50891-1). S&S.

--The Simon & Schuster Handbook of Anatomy & Physiology. 8.50 (ISBN 0-671-24998-3); 8.95 (ISBN 0-317-00952-4). S&S.

Bevan, John A. Fundamentos de Farmacologia. 2nd ed. (Span.). 1982. pap. text ed. 21.00 (ISBN 0-06-310065-7, Pub. by HarLA Mexico). Har-Row.

Bevan, John A. & Thompson, Jeremy H. Essentials of Pharmacology: Introduction to the Principles of Drug Action. 3rd ed. (Illus.). 916p. 1983. text ed. 37.50 (ISBN 0-06-140462-4, 14-04623, Lippincott Medical). Lippincott.

Bevan, John A., et al, eds. Vascular Neuroeffector Mechanisms: 4th International Symposium. 456p. 1983. text ed. 91.00 (ISBN 0-89004-738-3). Raven.

Bevan, Jonquil, ed. see Walton, Isaak.

Bevan, N., jt. ed. see Murray, D.

Bevan, P. Gilroy. Reconstructive Procedures in Surgery. (Illus.). 454p. 1982. text ed. 64.95 (ISBN 0-632-00602-1, B 0664-0). Mosby.

Bevan, Ruth A. Marx & Burke: A Revisionist View. LC 73-79625. 208p. 1973. 19.95 (ISBN 0-87548-144-2). Open Court.

Bevan, S. C., ed. see Conference on Vacuum Microbalance Techniques (10th: 1972: Uxbridge, England.

Bevan, Stanley C., et al. A Concise Etymological Dictionary of Chemistry. ix, 140p. 1976. 20.50 (ISBN 0-85334-653-4, Pub. by Elsevier Applied Sci England). Elsevier.

Bevan, W., jt. ed. see Kennedy, H. E.

Bevans, Jerry T., ed. Thermal Design Principles. LC 64-103. (Illus.). 855p. 1969. 43.00 (ISBN 0-317-36814-1); members 21.50 (ISBN 0-317-36815-X). AIAA.

--Thermophysics: Applications to Thermal Design of Spacecraft. LC 64-103. (Illus.). 580p. 1970. 48.00 (ISBN 0-317-36810-9); members 24.00 (ISBN 0-317-36811-7). AIAA.

Bevelander, Gerrit & Ramaley, Judith A. Essentials of Histology. 8th ed. LC 78-4847. 400p. 1979. text ed. 25.95 (ISBN 0-8016-0669-1). Mosby.

Bevell, Ruth Adams. Sheaves of Friendship. 1982. 7.95 (ISBN 0-88053-325-0). Macoy Pub.

Beven, Annette. The Spade Sage. (Jataka Tales for Children Ser.). (Illus.). 24p. (gr. 1-8). 1984. pap. 4.95 (ISBN 0-913546-71-2). Dharma Pub.

Bevenot, Maurice. The Tradition of Manuscripts: A Study in the Transmission of St. Cyprian's Treatises. LC 78-14421. 1979. Repr. of 1961 ed. lib. bdg. 22.50x (ISBN 0-313-20622-8, BETM). Greenwood.

Bevensee, Robert M. Handbook of Conical Antennas & Scatterers. LC 71-172793. (Illus.). 182p. 1973. 67.25 (ISBN 0-677-00480-X). Gordon.

Bever, Bernie. Hojo Supreme. 1978. 1.00 (ISBN 0-916866-03-3); signed ed. 3.00 (ISBN 0-916866-04-1). Cats Pajamas.

Bever, Dale N. Northwest Conifers: A Photographic Key. LC 81-65509. (Illus.). 1981. pap. 18.95 (ISBN 0-8323-0390-9). Binford.

Bever, David L. A Personal Focus. (Illus.). 448p. 1984. pap. text ed. 21.95 (ISBN 0-8016-0681-0). Mosby.

Bever, James A. Coming of Age in America: VERCAP, a Guide for High School Students. 1977. pap. 4.00 (ISBN 0-88210-080-7). Natl Assn Principals.

Bever, M. B., jt. ed. see Henstock, M.

Bever, Thomas & Carroll, John M., eds. Talking Minds: The Study of Language in Cognitive Sciences. 1982. 19.95x (ISBN 0-262-02181-1). MIT Pr.

Bever, Thomas G., ed. Regressions in Mental Development: Basic Phenomena & Theories. 336p. 1982. text ed. 29.95x (ISBN 0-89859-096-5). L Erlbaum Assocs.

Bever, Thomas G. & Terrace, Herbert S., eds. Human Behavior: Prediction & Control in Modern Society. LC 73-7253. 163p. 1974. pap. text ed. 6.95x (ISBN 0-8422-9104-0). Irvington.

Bever, William Van see Van Bever, William & Lal, Harbans.

Beverage, Richard E. The Angels: Los Angeles in the Pacific Coast League, 1919-1957. LC 81-68247. (Illus.). 286p. (Orig.). 1981. 9.95 (ISBN 0-940684-00-4). Deacon Pr.

--The Hollywood Stars: Baseball in Movieland 1926-57. LC 84-70556. (Illus.). 310p. (Orig.). 1984. pap. 11.95 (ISBN 0-940684-01-2). Deacon Pr.

Beveridge, Albert J. The Life of John Marshall. 550.00 (ISBN 0-384-04088-8). Johnson Repr.

--Life of John Marshall: Unabridged, 4 vols. in 2. new ed. LC 34-7756. (Illus.). 2496p. 1974. lib. bdg. 99.95 set (ISBN 0-910220-65-4). Berg.

--Meaning of the Times & Other Speeches. facs. ed. LC 68-54327. (Essay Index Reprint Ser.). 1908. 20.00 (ISBN 0-8369-0208-4). Ayer Co Pubs.

--The Russian Advance. LC 76-27543. (Illus.). 1976. Repr. of 1904 ed. lib. bdg. 45.00 (ISBN 0-89341-040-3). Longwood Pub Group.

Beveridge, Andrew A. & Oberschall, Anthony R. African Businessmen & Social Change in Zambia. LC 79-83978. 1979. 42.00x (ISBN 0-691-03121-5). Princeton U Pr.

Beveridge, Annette S., tr. see Babar, Emperor of Hindustan.

Beveridge, Charles E. & Schuyler, David. The Papers of Frederick Law Olmsted, Vol.III: Creating Central Park, 1857-1861. LC 82-4701. (Olsted Papers). (Illus.). 464p. 1983. text ed. 28.50x (ISBN 0-8018-2751-5). Johns Hopkins.

Beveridge, Charles E. & McLaughlin, Charles C., eds. The Papers of Frederick Law Olmsted: Vol. II: Slavery & the South, 1852-1857. LC 80-8881. (The Papers of Frederick Law Olmsted). (Illus.). 528p. 1981. text ed. 30.00x (ISBN 0-8018-2242-4). Johns Hopkins.

Beveridge, D. L., jt. auth. see Pople, J. A.

Beveridge, Elizabeth. Choosing & Using Home Equipment. 7th ed. (Illus.). 1976. pap. text ed. 6.50x (ISBN 0-8138-0780-8). Iowa St U Pr.

Beveridge, Henry. Comprehensive History of India, 2 vols. 1973. 144.00 (ISBN 0-686-20205-8). Intl Bk Dist.

Beveridge, Henry, ed. see Calvin, John.

Beveridge, Henry, tr. see Abu-L-Fazl.

Beveridge, J. M. & Velton, E. J. Positioning to Win: Planning & Executing the Superior Proposal. (Illus.). 256p. 1982. 27.50 (ISBN 0-8019-7112-8). Chilton.

Beveridge, June, ed. Authentic Algerian Carpet Designs & Motifs. Appelbaum, Stanley, tr. from French. (Illus.). 1978. pap. 3.50 (ISBN 0-486-23650-1). Dover.

Beveridge, Lord. Prices & Wages in England. (Illus.). 756p. 1965. Repr. of 1939 ed. 47.50x (ISBN 0-7146-1271-5, F Cass Co). Biblio Dist.

Beveridge, M., jt. auth. see Lloyd, P.

Beveridge, Malcolm. Cage & Pen Fish Farming: Carrying Capacity Models & Environmental Impact. (Fisheries Technical Papers: No. 255). 131p. 1985. pap. 10.00 (ISBN 92-5-102163-5, F2725, FAO). Unipub.

Beveridge, Michael, ed. Children Thinking Through Language. 280p. 1982. pap. text ed. 19.95 (ISBN 0-7131-6352-6). E Arnold.

Beveridge, N., tr. see Fyodorov, Vadim.

Beveridge, Phyllis, jt. auth. see Corbett, Nancy A.

Beveridge, Phyllis, jt. auth. see Corbett, Nancy Ann.

Beveridge, W. H. Unemployment: A Problem of Industry. LC 79-59646. (The English Working Class Ser.). 421p. 1980. lib. bdg. 46.00 (ISBN 0-8240-0101-X). Garland Pub.

Beveridge, W. I. Influenza: The Last Great Plague: An Unfinished Story of Discovery. 2nd ed. LC 77-2971. 1977. 12.50 (ISBN 0-88202-125-7). Watson Pub Intl.

--Seeds of Discovery. (Illus.). 144p. 1981. 12.95 (ISBN 0-393-01444-4). Norton.

Beveridge, W. I., ed. see International Symposium on Breeding Non-Human Primates for Laboratory Use, Berne, 1971.

Beveridge, William. Complete Works, 12 vols. LC 72-39437. (Library of Anglo-Catholic Theology: No. 2). Repr. of 1848 ed. Set. 360.00 (ISBN 0-404-52040-5). AMS Pr.

--Social Insurance & Allied Services: The Beveridge Report. LC 70-76848. 1969. Repr. 10.00x (ISBN 0-87586-014-1). Agathon.

Beveridge, William H. British Food Control. (Economic & Social History of the World War, British Ser.). 1928. 75.00x (ISBN 0-317-27420-1). Elliots Bks.

--Causes & Cures of Unemployment. LC 75-41030. (BCL Ser. II). 1976. Repr. of 1931 ed. 9.00 (ISBN 0-685-70886-1). AMS Pr.

--Unemployment: A Problem of Industry. LC 79-95398. (BCL Ser. II). Repr. of 1930 ed. 25.00 (ISBN 0-404-00794-5). AMS Pr.

Beveridge, William H. & Wells, Alan F., eds. The Evidence for Voluntary Action, Being Memoranda by Organisations & Individuals & Other Materials Relevant to Voluntary Action. LC 78-5650. (Illus.). 1978. Repr. of 1949 ed. lib. bdg. 24.00x (ISBN 0-313-20485-3, BEEV). Greenwood.

Beveridge, William I. Art of Scientific Investigation. 1960. pap. 3.95 (ISBN 0-394-70129-1, V129, Vin). Random.

Beveridge-Wavering, Agnes. Expressive Language Remediation for the Older Elementary Child. 2nd ed. 1984. pap. 3.50x (ISBN 0-8134-2312-0). Interstate.

--Written Language Remediation for the Older Elementary Child. 226p. 1982. text ed. 17.75 (ISBN 0-8134-2233-7). Interstate.

Beveridge-Wavering, Agnes & Seibert-Shook, Mavis. Reinforcing Home Activities: Program for Articulation Improvement. 2nd ed. 1981. pap. 9.75x (ISBN 0-8134-2158-6, 2158). Interstate.

Beveridgr, James A. Scriptwriting for Short Films. (Reports & Papers on Mass Communication: No. 57). 45p. (2nd Printing 1972). 1969. pap. 5.00 (ISBN 92-3-100744-0, U593, UNESCO). Unipub.

Beverley, George H. Pioneer in the U. S. Air Corps. (Illus.). 70p. 1982. pap. text ed. 9.95x (ISBN 0-89745-029-9). Sunflower U Pr.

Beverley, John. Aspects of Gongora's "Soledades". (Purdue University Monographs in Romance Languages: No. 1). iv, 139p. 1980. 21.00x (ISBN 90-272-1711-4). Benjamins North Am.

Beverley, M. C., tr. see Aksakov, S. T.

Beverley, Mary F. Great Hometown Restaurants of Texas. LC 84-10007. (Illus.). 112p. (Orig.). 1984. pap. 9.95x (ISBN 0-88415-390-8, Lone Star Bks). Gulf Pub.

Beverley, Robert. History & Present State of Virginia. Wright, Louis B., ed. LC 68-58999. (Illus.). pap. 76.40 (ISBN 0-8357-9803-8, 2015745). Bks Demand UMI.

Beverlin, Jack C. Football's Multiple-Motion I Offense. 227p. 1982. 16.95 (ISBN 0-13-324145-9, Parker). P-H.

Beverloo, W. A., jt. auth. see Leniger, H. A.

Beverly, David. The Tale of the Wise Little Sea Turtle. 1982. 4.95 (ISBN 0-533-05506-7). Vantage.

Beverly Hills Bar Association Barristers Committee for the Arts. The Musician's Manual: A Practical Career Guide. Halloran, Mark, ed. 288p. 1981. pap. 9.95 (ISBN 0-8015-5204-4, Hawthorn). Dutton.

--The Visual Artist's Manual: A Practical Guide to Your Career. Grode, Susan A., ed. LC 82-45347. 320p. 1984. pap. 15.95 (ISBN 0-385-18251-1, Dolp). Doubleday.

Beverly, Peter see Prouty, Charles T.

Beversluis, John. C. S. Lewis & the Search for Rational Religion. 200p. (Orig.). 1985. pap. 9.95 (ISBN 0-8028-0046-7). Eerdmans.

Beverton, R. J. H., et al, eds. Marine Mammals & Fisheries. (Illus.). 350p. 1985. text ed. 55.00x (ISBN 0-04-639003-0). Allen Unwin.

Bevier, Abraham G. Indians: Or Narratives of Massacres & Depredations. LC 75-16122. 90p. 1975. pap. 3.95 (ISBN 0-912526-17-3). Lib Res.

Bevier, L. Brief Greek Syntax. (College Classical Ser.). (gr. 11-12). 20.00x (ISBN 0-89241-127-9); pap. 11.00x (ISBN 0-89241-343-3). Caratzas.

Bevier, Michael J. Politics Backstage: Inside the California Legislature. LC 79-1021. 293p. 1979. 29.95 (ISBN 0-87722-150-2). Temple U Pr.

Bevil, C., jt. auth. see Gioiella, E.

Bevilacqua, Joseph J., ed. Changing Government Policies for the Mentally Disabled: Proceedings of the First Annual Fogarty Memorial Conference. LC 81-10968. 320p. 1982. prof ref 32.50 (ISBN 0-88410-384-6). Ballinger Pub.

Bevilacqua, Winifred F. Josephine Herbst. (United States Authors Ser.). 1985. lib. bdg. 15.95 (ISBN 0-8057-7409-2, Twayne). G K Hall.

Bevilacqua, Winifred F. Fiction by American Women: Recent Views. LC 83-2816. 168p. 1983. 17.50x (ISBN 0-8046-9315-3, Natl U). Assoc Faculty Pr.

Bevill, Evangeline. Communicating, Here & Beyond. LC 83-90846. 85p. 1984. 7.95 (ISBN 0-533-05852-X). Vantage.

Beville, Hugh M., Jr. Audience Ratings: Radio, Television, & Cable. 488p. 1985. text ed. 39.95 (ISBN 0-89859-535-5); 24.95. L Erlbaum Assocs.

Beville, Mitchel J. Municipal Structural Reform in Sioux City: The Perennial Question. 1980. write for info. U of SD Gov Res Bur.

--Survey of Attitudes Towards Third Planning & Development District's Programs & Activities: Analysis & Action Recommedations. 1984. write for info. U of SD Gov Res Bur.

Beville, Mitchel J. & Meyer, Kenneth. The Search for Effectiveness & Efficiency in Government: Policy Analysis, Program Evaluation, Social Indicator, & Quality of Life Research. 1983. write for info. U of SD Gov Res Bur.

Beville, Mitchel J., et al. Planning Districts in South Dakota: An Assessment of Economic Change & Development. 1984. write for info. U of SD Gov Res Bur.

Bevin, A. Griswold, jt. auth. see Salisbury, Roger E.

Beving, James, jt. auth. see Bondhus, Willard.

Bevington, D., et al, eds. see Shakespeare, William.

Bevington, David. Action Is Eloquence: Shakespeare's Language of Gesture. 248p. 1984. text ed. 16.50x (ISBN 0-674-00355-1). Harvard U Pr.

--Medieval Drama. 1975. text ed. 31.95 (ISBN 0-395-13915-5). HM.

Bevington, David, jt. auth. see Craig, Hardin.

Bevington, David, ed. The Complete Works of Shakespeare. 3rd ed. 1980. text ed. 32.60x (ISBN 0-673-15193-X). Scott F.

--Macro Plays. Incl. The Castle of Perserverance; Wisdom & Mankind. (Facsimiles Ser). 42.00 (ISBN 0-686-16149-1). Folger Bks.

Bevington, David, compiled by. Shakespeare. LC 76-5220. (Goldentree Bibliographies in Language & Literature). 1978. pap. text ed. 14.95x (ISBN 0-88295-555-1). Harlan Davidson.

Bevington, David & Halio, Jay L., eds. Shakespeare, Pattern of Excelling Nature: Shakespearean Criticism in Honor of America's Bicentennial. LC 77-82878. 304p. 27.50 (ISBN 0-87413-129-4). U Delaware Pr.

Bevington, David M. Tudor Drama & Politics: A Critical Approach to Topical Meaning. LC 68-17637. 1968. 22.50x (ISBN 0-674-91230-6). Harvard U Pr.

Bevington, David M., ed. The Macro Plays. LC 72-3905. 1972. 50.00 (ISBN 0-384-34920-X). Johnson Repr.

--What Does Santa Bring? (Cuddle Doll Books). (Illus.). 12p. (gr. 1-4). 1985. 3.95 (ISBN 0-394-87510-9, BYR). Random.

Beylsmit, J. & Rijlaarsdam, J. C., eds. Linguistic Bibliography for the Year 1976. xlviii, 736p. 1980. lib. bdg. 103.00 (ISBN 90-247-2242-X, Martinus Nijhoff Pubs). Kluwer Academic.

Beylsmit, J. J. Linguistic Bibliography for the Year Nineteen Seventy-Nine. 1982. 135.00 (ISBN 0-686-37163-1, Pub. by Martinus Nijhoff Netherlands). Kluwer Academic.

Beylsmit, J. J., ed. Linguistic Bibliography for the Year 1978. 760p. 1981. 160.00 (ISBN 90-247-2509-7, Pub. by Martinus Nijhoff Netherlands). Kluwer Academic.

--Linguistic Bibliography for the Year 1981. 911p. 1984. 140.00 (ISBN 90-247-2953-X, Pub. by Martinus Nijhoff Netherlands). Kluwer Academic.

Beyme, Klaus Von see Von Beyme, Klaus.

Beyme, Klaus von see Von Beyme, Klaus.

Beyme, Klaus Von see Von Beyme, Klaus.

Beyme, Klaus von see Von Beyme, Klaus.

Beyme, Klaus von see Von Beyme, Klaus & Schmidt, Manfred G.

Beymer, Robert. The Boundary Waters Canoe Area: The Western Region, Vol. I. 3nd ed. Winnett, Thomas, ed. LC 85-40197. (Illus.). 176p. 1985. pap. 9.95 (ISBN 0-89997-053-2). Wilderness Pr.

--The Boundary Waters Canoe Area: The Western Region, Vol 1. Winnett, Thomas, ed. LC 77-88643. (Illus., Orig.). 1985. pap. 8.95 (ISBN 0-911824-68-5). Wilderness Pr.

--Boundary Waters Canoe Area: Vol. 2 the Eastern Region. Winnett, Thomas, ed. LC 77-88643. (Illus.). 160p. (Orig.). 1979. pap. 9.95 (ISBN 0-911824-79-0). Wilderness Pr.

Beyn, Edgar J. The Twelve Volt Doctor's Practical Handbook: For the Boat's Electric System. rev. ed. (Illus.). 1983. write for info. (ISBN 0-911551-07-7). SPA Creek.

Beynen, K., ed. see De Veer, Gerrit.

Beynon, Granville, ed. Solar-Terrestrial Physics: Proceedings of an International Symposium, Innsbruck, Austria, 1978. (Illus.). 240p. 1979. pap. 47.00 (ISBN 0-08-025054-8). Pergamon.

Beynon, Huw, jt. auth. see Nichols, Theo.

Beynon, Huw, ed. Digging Deeper: Issues in the Miners' Strike. 252p. 1985. pap. 4.95 (ISBN 0-8052-7268-2, Pub. by Verso England). Schocken.

Beynon, J. H. & Gilbert, J. R. Application of Transition State Theory to Unimolecular Reactions: An Introduction. LC 83-17016. 85p. 1984. 26.95x (ISBN 0-471-90316-7, Pub. by Wiley-Interscience). Wiley.

Beynon, J. H. & Williams, A. E. Mass & Abundance Tables for Use in Mass Spectrometry. 570p. 1963. 117.00 (ISBN 0-444-40044-3). Elsevier.

Beynon, J. H. & McGlashan, M. L., eds. Current Topics in Mass Spectrometry & Chemical Kinetics: Proceedings of the Symposium in Honour of Professor Allan Maccoll, University College, London, 1981. pap. 41.30 (ISBN 0-317-26147-9, 2025194). Bks Demand UMI.

Beynon, J. H., et al. The Mass Spectra of Organic Molecules. (Illus.). 510p. 1968. 81.00 (ISBN 0-444-40046-X). Elsevier.

Beynon, John. Initial Encounters in the Secondary School. (Issues in Education & Training Ser.: No. 4). 250p. 1985. 27.00x (ISBN 1-85000-031-X, Falmer Pr); pap. 15.00x (ISBN 1-85000-032-8, Falmer Pr). Taylor & Francis.

Beynon, L. R. & Conell, E. B., eds. Ecological Aspects of the Toxicity: Testing of Oils & Dispersants. (Illus.). 149p. 1974. 31.50 (ISBN 0-85334-458-2, Pub. by Elsevier Applied Sci England). Elsevier.

Beyrer, Mary K. Positive Health: Designs for Action. LC 76-22769. (Health Education, Physical Education, & Recreation Ser.). pap. 48.80 (ISBN 0-317-28172-0, 2014525). Bks Demand UMI.

Beys, C. De & Protzman, M. I. Les Illustres Fous of Charles Beys: A Critical Ed. pap. 19.00 (ISBN 0-384-04089-6). Johnson Repr.

Beyshenaliev, S. Un Corderito con Cuernos. 22p. (Span.). 1980. pap. 2.45 (ISBN 0-8285-1814-9, Pub. by Progress Pubs USSR). Imported Pubns.

Beytagh, Francis, jt. auth. see Kauper, Paul.

Beyth-Marom, Ruth. An Elementary Approach to Thinking under Uncertainty. rev. ed. 160p. 1984. text ed. write for info (ISBN 0-89859-379-4). L Erlbaum Assocs.

Bez, H. E., jt. auth. see Cooke, D. J.

Beza, Marcu. Paganism in Roumanian Folklore. LC 74-173102. (Illus.). 1972. Repr. of 1928 ed. lib. bdg. 14.00 (ISBN 0-405-08267-3, Blom Pubns). Ayer Co Pubs.

--Paganism in Roumanian Folklore. 1976. lib. bdg. 59.95 (ISBN 0-8490-2397-1). Gordon Pr.

Beza, Theodore. Bezae Codex Cantabrigiensis: Being an Exact Copy, in Ordinary Type of the Celebrated Uncial Graeco-Latin Manuscript of the Four Gospels & Acts of the Apostles. Scrivener, Frederick H., ed. LC 78-4144. (Pittsburgh Reprint Ser.: No. 5). 1978. pap. 15.75 (ISBN 0-915138-39-5). Pickwick.

Bezanson, Walter E., ed. Clarel. (Complete Works of Herman Melville Ser.). 772p. 1959. 14.00 (ISBN 0-87532-011-2). Hendricks House.

Bezboruah, D. N., tr. see Bhattacharyya, Birendra K.

Bezdechi, Adrian. Manual & Digital Gymnastics. (Illus., Orig.). 1957. pap. 5.00 (ISBN 0-9604092-1-1). Interstate Piano.

--Pianos & Player Pianos: An Informative Guide for Owners & Prospective Buyers. LC 79-318082. (Illus.). 63p. (Orig.). 1979. pap. 7.50 (ISBN 0-9604092-0-3). Interstate Piano.

Bezdek, James C. Pattern Recognition with Fuzzy Objective Function Algorithms. LC 81-4354. (Advanced Applications in Pattern Recognition Ser.). 272p. 1981. 39.50 (ISBN 0-306-40671-3, Plenum Pr). Plenum Pub.

Bezdicek, D. F., et al, eds. Organic Farming: Current Technology & Its Role in a Sustainable Agriculture. (Casa Special Publication Ser.). 192p. 1984. 12.00 (ISBN 0-89118-076-1). Am Soc Agron.

Beze, Theodore de. Abraham Sacrifiant: Tragedie Francoise (Geneve, 1550) (Classiques De la Renaissance En France: No. 2). 1970. 10.40 (ISBN 90-2796-344-4). Mouton.

Beze, Theodore De see De Beze, Theodore.

Beze, Theodore de see De Beze, Theodore.

Bezella, Winfred A., jt. auth. see Ott, Karl O.

Bezier, P. Numerical Control: Mathematics & Applications. LC 70-39230. (Wiley Series in Computing). Repr. of 1972 ed. 48.70 (ISBN 0-8357-9944-1, 2014900). Bks Demand UMI.

Bezilla, Michael. Electric Traction on the Pennsylvania Railroad, 1895-1968. LC 79-65858. (Illus.). 1980. 24.90x (ISBN 0-271-00241-7). Pa St U Pr.

--Engineering Education at Penn State: A Century in the Land-Grant Tradition. LC 81-47170. (Illus.). 180p. 1981. 24.95x (ISBN 0-271-00287-5). Pa St U Pr.

--Penn State: An Illustrated History. LC 84-43057. (Illus.). 580p. 1985. 39.50 (ISBN 0-271-00392-8). Pa St U Pr.

Bezirgan, Basima Q., jt. ed. see Fernea, Elizabeth W.

Bezkorovainy, Anatoly. Basic Protein Chemistry. (Illus.). 248p. 1971. photocopy ed. 24.50x (ISBN 0-398-00151-0). C C Thomas.

--Biochemistry of Nonheme Iron. LC 80-16477. (Biochemistry of the Elments Ser.: Vol. 1). 455p. 1981. 52.50x (ISBN 0-306-40501-6, Plenum Pr). Plenum Pub.

--Science & Medicine in Imperial Russia. (Illus.). 271p. 1980. soft cover, spiral bdg. 12.00 (ISBN 0-9607600-0-8). Bezkorovainy.

Bezner, ed. Dictionary of Electrical Machines. 558p. 1978. 39.00 (ISBN 0-318-01455-6, Pub. by O Brandstetter WG). Heyden.

Beznoska, Dennis, et al. HDE Manual of Fine Restaurant Service. 1985. 20.00 (ISBN 0-682-40223-0). Exposition Pr FL.

Bezodis, P. A. Spitalfields & Mile End New Town. LC 74-6547. (London County Council. Survey of London: No. 27). Repr. of 1957 ed. 74.50 (ISBN 0-404-51677-7). AMS Pr.

Bezold, Clement, jt. auth. see Dator, James.

Bezold, Friedrich. Geschichte der Deutschen Reformation. LC 79-149654. (BCL Ser. I). (Ger.). Repr. of 1890 ed. 37.50 (ISBN 0-404-00797-X). AMS Pr.

Bezou, Henry C. Metairie: A Tongue of Land to Pasture. new ed. LC 73-17038. (Illus.). 183p. 1973. 25.00 (ISBN 0-88289-012-3). Pelican.

Bezou, James F., tr. see Goffin, Robert.

Bezruchka, Stephen. A Guide to Trekking in Nepal. 5th ed. (Illus.). 352p. 1985. pap. 10.95 (ISBN 0-89886-094-6). Mountaineers.

Bezrukov, V. V., jt. auth. see Frolkis, V. V.

Bezucha, Robert J. The Lyon Uprising of 1834: Social & Political Conflict in the Early July Monarchy. LC 74-75780. (Studies in Urban History). 288p. 1974. text ed. 17.50x (ISBN 0-674-53965-6). Harvard U Pr.

Bezuidenhout, L. F. Alone, & Other Poems. LC 82-90618. (Illus.). 39p. 1983. 6.95 (ISBN 0-533-05564-4). Vantage.

Bezuidenhout, S. H. Approaching Realities. 32p. 1983. 5.95 (ISBN 0-533-05686-1). Vantage.

Bezuszka, Stanley & Kenney, Margaret. Wonder-Full World of Numbers. (Contemporary Motivated Mathematics Ser.). 97p. (Orig.). (gr. 3-6). 1971. pap. text ed. 1.50 (ISBN 0-917916-05-0). Boston Coll Math.

Bezuszka, Stanley, et al. Word Problems for Maxima & Minima. (Motivated Math Project Activity Booklets). 96p. (Orig.). 1984. pap. text ed. 4.00 (ISBN 0-917916-20-4). Boston Coll Math.

--Applications of Geometric Series. (Motivated Math Project Activity Bks.). 46p. (Orig.). (gr. 10-12). 1976. pap. text ed. 2.00 (ISBN 0-917916-14-X). Boston Coll Math.

--Finite Differences. (Motivated Math Project Activity Booklets). 108p. (Orig.). (gr. 10-12). 1976. pap. text ed. 2.50 (ISBN 0-917916-11-5). Boston Coll Math.

--Fraction Action 1. (Motivated Math Project Activity Booklets). 47p. (Orig.). (gr. 5-8). 1976. pap. text ed. 2.00 (ISBN 0-917916-12-3). Boston Coll Math.

--Fraction Action 2. (Motivated Math Project Activity Booklets). 68p. (Orig.). (gr. 7-12). 1976. pap. text ed. 2.00 (ISBN 0-917916-13-1). Boston Coll Math.

--Perfect Numbers. (Motivated Math Project Activity Booklets). 169p. (Orig.). (gr. 7-12). 1980. pap. text ed. 3.50 (ISBN 0-917916-19-0). Boston Coll Math.

--Wonder Square. (Motivated Math Project Activity Booklets). 30p. (Orig.). (gr. 6-12). 1976. pap. text ed. 1.25 (ISBN 0-917916-15-8). Boston Coll Math.

--Comtemporary Motivated Mathematics, Bk,. 3. (Comtemporary Motivated Mathematics Ser.). 97p. (Orig.). (gr. 7-10). 1972. pap. text ed. 1.50 (ISBN 0-917916-04-2). Boston Coll Math.

--Contemporary Motivated Mathematics, Bk. 1. (Contemporary Motivated Mathematics Ser.). 97p. (Orig.). (gr. 5-8). 1972. pap. text ed. 1.50 (ISBN 0-917916-02-6). Boston Coll Math.

--Contemporary Motivated Mathematics, Bk. 2. (Comtemporary Motivated Mathematics Ser.). 97p. (Orig.). (gr. 6-9). 1973. pap. text ed. 1.50 (ISBN 0-917916-03-4). Boston Coll Math.

Bezy, John. Bryce Canyon: The Story Behind the Scenery. LC 79-93079. (Illus.). 1980. 8.95 (ISBN 0-916122-70-0); pap. 3.75 (ISBN 0-916122-69-7). KC Pubns.

Bezy, John V. A Guide to the Desert Geology of the Lake Mead National Recreation Area. new ed. Jackson, Earl, ed. LC 78-56673. (Popular Ser.: No. 24). (Illus., Orig.). 1979. pap. 1.75x (ISBN 0-911408-51-7). SW Pks Mnmts.

Bezzant, Norman, jt. auth. see Burroughs, David.

Bezzerides, A. I. William Faulkner: A Life on Paper. LC 79-15371. (Illus.). 1980. 10.00x (ISBN 0-87805-098-1); pap. text ed. 5.00 (ISBN 0-87805-085-X). U Pr of Miss.

Bezzi, Mario. Syrphidae of the Ethiopian Region. Repr. of 1915 ed. 16.00 (ISBN 0-384-04095-0). Johnson Repr.

Bhabha, J., ed. Homi Bhabha as Artist. 1968. 22.50 (ISBN 0-89684-411-0). Orient Bk Dist.

Bhabha, Jacqueline, et al, eds. Worlds Apart: Women under Immigration Law. 176p. (Orig.). 1985. pap. 7.50 (ISBN 0-7453-0021-9, Pub. by Pluto Pr). Longwood Pub Group.

Bhacca, Norman S. & William, Dudley H. Applications of NMR Spectroscopy in Organic Chemistry: Illustrations from the Steroid Field. LC 64-25659. (Holden-Day Series in Physical Techniques in Chemistry). pap. 52.00 (ISBN 0-317-09053-4, 2016285). Bks Demand UMI.

Bhacca, Rosaria D. All'Italiana. Stevens, Cheryl J., ed. LC 81-84607. (Illus.). 133p. (Orig.). 1981. pap. 6.95 (ISBN 0-88127-001-6). Oracle Pr LA.

Bhaduri, Amit. The Economic Structure of Backward Agriculture. (Studies in Political Economy Ser.: Vol. 3). 1984. 33.00 (ISBN 0-12-095420-6). Acad Pr.

Bhaduri, T. C. Chambal, the Valley of Terror. 1972. 9.00 (ISBN 0-89684-375-0). Orient Bk Dist.

Bhaerman, Robert D. Career & Vocational Development of Handicapped Learners: An Annotated Bibliography. 85p. 1978. 5.10 (ISBN 0-318-15403-X, IN134). Natl Ctr Res Voc Ed.

--Community Resources & Community Involvement in Career Education: An Annotated Bibliography. 69p. 1978. 5.10 (ISBN 0-318-15424-2, IN 140). Natl Ctr Res Voc Ed.

--Planning for Adult Career Counseling. 64p. 1985. 6.25 (ISBN 0-318-17845-1, IN 290). Natl Ctr Res Voc Ed.

--Techniques & Strategies for Infusing Career Education into the Educational Program for Exceptional Children: Some Sample Resources. 53p. 1979. 3.80 (ISBN 0-318-15579-6, IN 181). Natl Ctr Res Voc Ed.

Bhaerman, Steve & Denker, Joel. No Particular Place to Go: The Making of a Free High School. LC 81-18248. 263p. (Orig.). pap. 10.95x (ISBN 0-8093-1056-2). S Ill U Pr.

Bhaerman, Steve, jt. auth. see Cole, Raymond.

Bhagat, Budh D. Mode of Action of Autonomic Drugs. LC 78-58696. (Illus.). 170p. 1979. text ed. 21.50x (ISBN 0-932126-00-6); pap. text ed. 17.50x (ISBN 0-932126-01-4). Graceway.

Bhagat, Budh D., et al. Fundamentals of Visceral Innervation. (Illus.). 216p. 1977. photocopy ed. spiral 29.75x (ISBN 0-398-03390-0). C C Thomas.

Bhagat, M. G. Ancient Indian Asceticism. LC 76-104001. 1976. 20.00 (ISBN 0-89684-476-5). Orient Bk Dist.

Bhagat, P. S. Shield & the Sword. 1974. 6.00 (ISBN 0-686-20304-6). Intl Bk Dist.

Bhagat, Rabi S., jt. auth. see Beehr, Terry A.

Bhagat, Shantilal P. The Family Farm: Can It Be Saved? Keylock, Leslie R., ed. 74p. (Orig.). 1985. pap. 2.95 (ISBN 0-87178-227-8). Brethren.

Bhagat, Shantilal P. & Rieman, T. Wayne. What Does It Profit...? Christian Dialogue on the U. S. Economy. LC 83-3687. 144p. (Orig.). 1983. pap. 6.95 (ISBN 0-87178-927-2). Brethren.

Bhagavad-Gita. The Song of God. Prabhavananda, Swami & Isherwood, C., trs. pap. 2.50 (ISBN 0-451-62281-2, ME2281, Ment). NAL.

Bhagavan. Biochemistry. 2nd ed. (Illus.). 1363p. 1978. text ed. 35.00 flexible bdg. (ISBN 0-397-52086-7, 65-00417, Lippincott Medical). Lippincott.

Bhagavan, M. R. Poems. 2nd ed. (Redbird Bk.). 1976. lib. bdg. 8.00 (ISBN 0-89253-125-8); flexible bdg. 4.80 (ISBN 0-89253-139-8). Ind-US Inc.

Bhagavan, M. R., jt. ed. see Arthurs, A. M.

Bhagavantam, S. & Venkatarayudu, T. Theory of Groups & Its Application to Physical Problems. 1969. 32.00 (ISBN 0-12-095460-5). Acad Pr.

Bhagavat Simhaji. A Short History of Aryan Medical Science. LC 75-23683. Repr. of 1896 ed. 23.00 (ISBN 0-404-13236-7). AMS Pr.

Bhagowalia, Urmila. Vaisnavism & Society in Northern India. 1980. 22.00x (ISBN 0-8364-0664-8, Pub. by Intellectual India). South Asia Bks.

Bhagvan, Vishnoo & Bhushan, Vidya. The Constitution of Great Britain. 1984. text ed. 18.95x (ISBN 0-86590-336-0, Pub. by Sterling Pubs India). Apt Bks.

Bhagwan Shree. A Cup of Tea. 2nd ed ed. Somendra, Swami Anand, ed. LC 83-43215. (Early Discourses & Writings Ser.). 272p. 1983. pap. 4.95 (ISBN 0-88050-538-9). Rajneesh Found Intl.

Bhagwan, Vishnoo. Municipal Government & Politics in Haryana: A Case Study of Rohtak City. (Illus.). 356p. 1975. text ed. 12.00x (ISBN 0-8426-0767-6). Verry.

Bhagwan, Vishnoo & Bhushan, Vidya. The Constitution of the United States of America. vii, 164p. 1984. text ed. 18.95x (ISBN 0-86590-490-1, Pub. by Sterling Pubs India). Apt Bks.

--The Constitutions of Switzerland, Canada, Japan & Australia. 228p. 1985. text ed. 27.50x (ISBN 0-86590-693-9, Pub. by Sterling Pubs India). Apt Bks.

--The Constitutions of U. S. S. R. & China. 220p. 1985. text ed. 25.00x (ISBN 0-86590-588-6, Pub. by Sterling Pubs India). Apt Bks.

--World Constitutions. 727p. 1984. text ed. 15.95x (ISBN 0-86590-314-X, Sterling Pubs India). Apt Bks.

Bhagwan Shree Rajneesh. From Sex to Super Consciousness. Vora, V., tr. 157p. (Marathi.). 1975. pap. 2.95 (ISBN 0-89253-060-X). Ind-US Inc.

--The Perfect Way. Mahasattva Swami Krishna Prem, ed. LC 84-42808. (Early Writings & Discourses Ser.). 208p. 1984. pap. 3.95 (ISBN 0-88050-707-1). Rajneesh Found Intl.

--The Rainbow Bridge. Prabhu, Swami Krishna, ed. LC 85-42535. (Initiation Talks Ser.). 368p. (Orig.). 1985. pap. 3.95 (ISBN 0-88050-618-0). Rajneesh Found Intl.

--The Rajneesh Bible, Vol. 1. Academy of Rajneeshism, ed. LC 85-42539. (Academy of Rajneeshism Ser.). 800p. (Orig.). 1985. pap. 6.95 (ISBN 0-88050-200-2). Rajneesh Found Intl.

--Tao: The Golden Gate, Vol. 2. Prabhu, Swami Krishna, ed. LC 84-42615. (Tao Ser.). 304p. (Orig.). 1985. pap. 4.95 (ISBN 0-88050-647-4). Rajneesh Found Intl.

Bhagwat, Ramachandra K., tr. see Jnanadev.

Bhagwati, J. N. The Brain Drain & Taxation: Theory & Empirical Analysis. 1976. (North-Holland); pap. 29.50 (ISBN 0-444-11090-9). Elsevier.

--Illegal Transactions in International Trade: Theory & Measurement. LC 73-88164. (Studies in International Economics Ser.: Vol. 1). 208p. 1974. 51.00 (ISBN 0-444-10581-6, North-Holland); pap. 17.00 (ISBN 0-444-10883-1). Elsevier.

Bhagwati, Jagdish. Dependence & Independence: Essays in Development Economics, Vol. 2. Grossman, Gene, ed. 416p. 1985. text ed. 37.50x (ISBN 0-262-02230-3). MIT Pr.

--Essays in International Economic Theory: Vol. I - The Theory of Commercial Policy. Feenstra, Robert, ed. 605p. 1983. text ed. 45.00x (ISBN 0-262-02196-X). MIT Pr.

--Essays in International Economic Theory: Vol. 2 - International Factor Mobility. Feenstra, Robert, ed. 558p. 1983. text ed. 45.00x (ISBN 0-262-02197-8). MIT Pr.

--Foreign Trade Regimes & Economic Development: Anatomy & Consequences of Exchange Control Regimes, Vol. II. LC 78-18799. (Foreign Trade Regimes & Economic Development Ser.: Vol. XI). 256p. 1978. prof ref 30.00 (ISBN 0-88410-487-7). Ballinger Pub.

--Wealth & Poverty: Essays in Development Economics, Vol. 1. Grossman, Gene, ed. 400p. 1985. text ed. 37.50x (ISBN 0-262-02229-X). MIT Pr.

Bhagwati, Jagdish & Srinivasan, T. N. Lectures on the Theory of International Trade. (Illus.). 464p. 1983. text ed. 24.95x (ISBN 0-262-02185-4); pap. 16.50x (ISBN 0-262-52084-2). MIT Pr.

Bhagwati, Jagdish, ed. The Brain Drain & Income Taxation. 1977. pap. text ed. 14.75 (ISBN 0-08-020600-X). Pergamon.

--Import Competition & Response. LC 81-21831. (National Bureau of Economic Research-Conference Ser.). (Illus.). 352p. 1982. lib. bdg. 32.50x (ISBN 0-226-04538-2); pap. 15.00x (ISBN 0-226-04539-0). U of Chicago Pr.

--International Trade: Selected Readings. 456p. 1981. text ed. 37.50x (ISBN 0-262-02160-9); pap. text ed. 12.50x (ISBN 0-262-52060-5). MIT Pr.

Bhagwati, Jagdish M. Essays in Developmental Economics, 2 Vols. Grossmen, Gene M., ed. Incl. Vol 1. Wealth and Poverty (ISBN 0-262-02229-X); Vol. 2. Dependence & Interdependence (ISBN 0-262-02230-3). 1985. 37.50x (ISBN 0-317-28554-8). MIT Pr.

Bhagwati, Jagdish N. Amount & Sharing of Aid. LC 73-123777. (Monographs: No. 2). 208p. 1970. 1.50 (ISBN 0-686-28693-6). Overseas Dev Council.

Bhat, G. K. Theatric Aspects of Sanskrit Drama. 1985. 12.50x (ISBN 0-8364-1365-2, Pub. by Bhanarkar Oriental Inst). South Asia Bks.

Bhat, G. K., ed. see International Vacuum Metallurgy Conference on Special Melting, 6th.

Bhat, M. R. Brihat Samhit: The Great Composition on Astrology, 2 vols. 1009p. 1982. Vol. 1. 25.00 (ISBN 0-89581-115-4); Vol. 2. 20.00 (ISBN 0-89581-116-2). Asian Human Pr.

--Fundamentals of Astrology. 2nd, rev. ed. 1979. 16.95 (ISBN 0-89684-065-4, Pub. by Motilal Banarsidass India). Orient Bk Dist.

Bhat, M. Ramakrishna. Fundamentals of Astrology. 1974. lib. bdg. 75.00 (ISBN 0-87968-484-4). Krishna Pr.

Bhat, Rajendra R. Managing the Demand for Fashion Items. Farmer, Richard, ed. LC 85-1039. (Research for Business Decisions Ser.: No. 73). 138p. 1985. 34.95 (ISBN 0-8357-1618-X). UMI Res Pr.

Bhat, Shama & Gupta, V. K. Ichneumonologia Orientalis, Pt. VI: The Subfamily Agathidinae (Hym: Braconidae) (Oriental Insects Monograph: No. 6). 1977. 45.00x (ISBN 0-318-01584-6). Oriental Insects.

Bhat, U. Narayan. Elements of Applied Stochastic Processes. LC 70-178140. (Probability & Mathematical Statistics Ser.). 414p. 1972. 45.95x (ISBN 0-471-07199-4, Pub. by Wiley-Interscience). Wiley.

--Elements of Applied Stochastic Processes. 2nd ed. LC 84-7338. (Probability & Mathematical Statistics-Applied Probability & Statistics Section Ser.: 1-346). 685p. 1984. text ed. 44.95x (ISBN 0-471-87826-X, Pub. by Wiley-Interscience). Wiley.

Bhateja, Chander & Lindsay, Richard, eds. Grinding: Theory, Techniques & Trouble Shooting. LC 81-84502. (Manufacturing Update Ser.). (Illus.). 230p. 1982. 32.00 (ISBN 0-87263-077-3). SME.

Bhati, A., jt. ed. see Hamilton, R. J.

Bhatia, A. B. Ultrasonic Absorption: An Introduction to the Theory of Sound Absorption & Dispersion in Gases, Liquids & Solids. 440p. 1985. pap. 8.95 (ISBN 0-486-64917-2). Dover.

Bhatia, A. K. Tourism Development: Principles & Practices. 3rd, rev. ed. (Illus.). 354p. 1985. text ed. 40.00x (ISBN 0-86590-543-6, Pub. by Sterling Pubs India). Apt Bks.

--Tourism in India, History & Development. 1st ed. 1978. 15.00 (ISBN 0-89684-458-7). Orient Bk Dist.

Bhatia, B., jt. ed. see Tajuddin, M.

Bhatia, B. D. & Craig, M. Elements of Psychology & Mental Hygiene for Nurses in India. 376p. 1979. 30.00x (ISBN 0-86125-051-6, Pub. by Orient Longman India). State Mutual Bk.

Bhatia, B. L. Protozoa: Ciliophora. (Fauna of British India Ser.). (Illus.). xxii, 522p. 1979. Repr. 30.00 (ISBN 0-88065-058-3, Pub. by Messers Today & Tomorrows Printers & Publishers India). Scholarly Pubns.

--Protozoa: Sporozoa. (Fauna of British India Ser.). (Illus.). xx, 508p. 1979. Repr. 30.00 (ISBN 0-88065-103-2, Pub. by Messers Today & Tomorrows Printers & Publishers India). Scholarly Pubns.

Bhatia, B. L. & Suri, P. N. Elementary Hygiene. 134p. 1981. 30.00x (ISBN 0-86125-781-2, Pub. by Orient Longman India). State Mutual Bk.

--Elementary Physiology. 180p. 1981. 30.00x (ISBN 0-86125-693-X, Pub. by Orient Longman India). State Mutual Bk.

Bhatia, B. M. History & Social Development, 2 vols. Incl. Vol. 1. Elites in Modern India. text ed. 18.00x (ISBN 0-7069-0309-9); Elites, Democracy & Socialism: Vol. 2. text ed. 20.00x (ISBN 0-7069-0485-0). 1977. Verry.

--Pakistan's Economic Development, Nineteen Forty-Eight to Nineteen Seventy-Eight: The Failure of a Strategy. (Illus.). 1979. text ed. 25.00x (ISBN 0-7069-0766-3, Pub. by Vikas India). Advent NY.

--Poverty, Agriculture & Economic Growth. 1977. 15.00x (ISBN 0-7069-0524-5). Intl Bk Dist.

Bhatia, H. L. Centre-State Financial Relations in India. 1979. 11.00x (ISBN 0-8364-0323-1). South Asia Bks.

--History of Economic Thought. 3rd. ed. 517p. 1982. text ed. 35.00 (ISBN 0-7069-0585-7, Pub. by Vikas India). Advent NY.

--History of Economic Thought. 496p. 1982. 50.00x (ISBN 0-7069-1470-8, Pub. by Garlandfold England). State Mutual Bk.

--Public Finance. 8th ed. 400p. 1982. text ed. 40.00x (ISBN 0-7069-2055-4, Pub. by Vikas India). Advent NY.

Bhatia, H. L., ed. Does Foreign Aid Help? 120p. 1981. 14.95x (ISBN 0-940500-84-1, Pub by Allied Pubs India). Asia Bk Corp.

Bhatia, H. S. Martial Law: Theory & Practice. 1979. text ed. 12.00x (ISBN 0-391-01039-5). Humanities.

--Military History of British India(1607-1947) 1977. pap. text ed. 15.75x (ISBN 0-391-02010-2). Humanities.

Bhatia, H. S., ed. International Law & Practice in Ancient India. 1977. text ed. 14.00x (ISBN 0-391-01081-6). Humanities.

--Political, Legal & Military History of India, 5 vols. 1912p. 1984. Set. text ed. 250.50x (ISBN 0-391-03269-0, Pub by Deep & Deep India). Vol. 1 (ISBN 0-391-03270-4). Vol. 2 (ISBN 0-391-03271-2). Vol. 3 (ISBN 0-391-03272-0). Vol. 4 (ISBN 0-391-03273-9). Vol.5 (ISBN 0-391-03274-7). Humanities.

Bhatia, K. S., jt. auth. see Varute, A. T.

Bhatia, M. V. & Cheremisinoff, Paul N., eds. Solids & Liquids Conveying Systems. (Process Equiptment Ser.: Vol. 4). 254p. 1982. 35.00 (ISBN 0-87762-311-2). Technomic.

Bhatia, Mahesh V. & Cheremisinoff, Paul N. Solids Separation & Mixing. LC 79-63114. (Process Equipment Ser.: Vol. 1). 303p. 1979. 35.00 (ISBN 0-87762-272-8). Technomic.

Bhatia, Mahesh V. & Cheremisinoff, Paul N., eds. Air Movement & Vacuum Devices. LC 79-63114. (Process Equipment Ser.: Vol. 3). 323p. 1981. 35.00 (ISBN 0-87762-291-4). Technomic.

Bhatia, N. P. & Szegoe, G. P. Dynamical Systems: Stability Theory & Applications. (Lecture Notes in Mathematics: Vol. 35). (Illus., Orig.). 1967. pap. 21.90 (ISBN 0-387-03906-6). Springer-Verlag.

Bhatia, Prem. Indian Ordeal in Africa. (Illus.). 1974. 6.00 (ISBN 0-686-20258-9). Intl Bk Dist.

Bhatia, Rattan J. The West African Monetary Union: An Analytical Review. (Occasional Papers: No. 35). 1985. pap. 7.50 (ISBN 0-317-19912-9). Intl Monetary.

Bhatia, Sham L. Technology, Economics of Scale & Gains from Trade & Factor Mobility: An Empirical Study of Indo-U. S. Comparative Advantage in Trade. 1981. 9.75 (ISBN 0-8062-1805-3). Carlton.

Bhatia, V. Indo Soviet Relations: Problems & Prospects. 193p. 1984. text ed. 17.50x (ISBN 0-391-03173-2, Pub. by Panchsheel Pubs India). Humanities.

Bhatkhande, V. N. Music System in India: A Comparative Study of Some Leading Music Systems, 15-18th Centuries. 1985. 8.50x (ISBN 0-8364-1361-X, Pub. by S Lal). South Asia Bks.

Bhatnagar, Ajay S., ed. The Anterior Pituitary Gland. 472p. 1983. text ed. 59.50 (ISBN 0-89004-759-6). Raven.

Bhatnagar, Joti, ed. Educating Immigrants. 250p. 1981. 27.50 (ISBN 0-312-23711-1). St Martin.

Bhatnagar, K. C. The Symbolic Tendency in Irish Renaissance. 1973. Repr. of 1962 ed. 15.00 (ISBN 0-8274-1798-5). R West.

Bhatnagar, Prabhu L. Non-Linear Waves in One-Dimensional Dispersive Systems. (OXMM Ser.). (Illus.). 1981. text ed. 27.50x (ISBN 0-19-853531-7). Oxford U Pr.

Bhatnagar, R. P. & Bell, R. T. Communication in English. 266p. 1979. pap. text ed. 8.95 (ISBN 0-86131-097-7, Pub. by Orient Longman India). Apt Bks.

Bhatnagar, S. K. Network Analysis Techniques. LC 82-23257. 520p. 1985. 24.95x (ISBN 0-470-27395-X). Halsted Pr.

Bhatnagar, S. N., et al. Essentials of Human Embryology. 2nd ed. (Illus.). 244p. 1983. pap. text ed. 14.95x (ISBN 0-86131-381-X, Pub. by Orient Longman India). Apt Bks.

Bhatnagar, S. P., jt. auth. see Bhojwani, S. S.

Bhatnagar, Vijay M. Flammability of Apparel. LC 72-91704. (Progress in Fire Retardancy Ser.: Vol. 7). (Illus.). 230p. 1975. pap. 14.95 (ISBN 0-87762-165-9). Technomic.

--Nonwovens & Disposables: New Technical-Marketing Developments. 86p. 1978. pap. 15.00 (ISBN 0-87762-256-6). Technomic.

Bhatnagar, Vijay M., ed. Advances in Fire Retardant Textiles. LC 72-91704. (Progress in Fire Retardancy Ser.: Vol. 5). 500p. 1974. pap. 14.95 (ISBN 0-87762-143-8). Technomic.

--Advances in Fire Retardants, Pt. Two. LC 72-91704. (Progress in Fire Retardancy Ser.: Vol. 3). 200p. 1974. pap. 9.95 (ISBN 0-87762-111-X). Technomic.

--Fire Retardant Polyurethanes: Formulations Handbook, Vol. 8. LC 72-91704. (Progress in Fire Retardancy Ser.). (Illus.). 1977. pap. 9.95x (ISBN 0-87762-217-5). Technomic.

--Fire Retardants: Proceedings of the First European Conference on Flammability & Fire Retardants. LC 78-66105. 1979. pap. 19.00 (ISBN 0-87762-264-7). Technomic.

--Nonwovens & Disposables: Proceedings of the First Canadian Symposium of Nonwovens & Disposables. LC 78-68591. (Illus.). 1978. pap. 9.95 (ISBN 0-87762-268-X). Technomic.

Bhatnagar, Vijay M., ed. see International Symposium on Flammability & Fire Retardants, 1974.

Bhatnagar, Vijay M., ed. see International Symposium on Flammability & Fire Retardants.

Bhatnagar, Vijay M., ed. see International Symposium on Flammability & Fire Retardants, 1977.

Bhatnager, D. Labour Welfare & Social Security Legislation in India. 302p. 1984. text ed. 25.50x (ISBN 0-391-03231-3, Pub. by Deep & Deep India). Humanities.

Bhatnager, K. C. The Symbolic Tendency in the Irish Renaissance. LC 74-7226. lib. bdg. 17.50 (ISBN 0-8414-3182-5). Folcroft.

Bhatnager, Vijay M., ed. Proceedings: 1976 International Symposium on Flammability & Fire Retardants. LC 75-25478. (Illus.). 1977. pap. 14.95x (ISBN 0-87762-215-9). Technomic.

Bhatt, Anil, jt. auth. see Rao, T. V.

Bhatt, Dibya D. Natural History & Economic Botany of Nepal. 248p. 1981. 20.00x (ISBN 0-86125-412-0, Pub. by Orient Longman India). State Mutual Bk.

Bhatt, H. D. Kalidas. (Illus.). (gr. 3-8). 1979. pap. 3.95 (ISBN 0-89744-144-3). Auromere.

Bhatt, H. G., et al. Management of Toxic & Hazardous Wastes. (Illus.). 548p. 1985. 49.95 (ISBN 0-87371-023-1). Lewis Pubs Inc.

Bhatt, Harasiddhiprasad D., jt. ed. see Sweeney, Thomas L.

Bhatt, Jagdish J. Ocean Enterprise: Domain of Resources, Policies & Conflicts. (Illus.). 242p. (Orig.). Date not set. pap. text ed. price not set (ISBN 0-9600900-5-3). Cambridge Intl.

Bhatt, P. Problems in Structural Analysis by Matrix Methods. (Illus.). 465p. 1981. pap. 22.50x (ISBN 0-86095-881-7). Longman.

Bhatt, Purnima M. Scholars' Guide to Washington, D. C. for African Studies. LC 79-607774. (Scholars' Guide to Washington D.C. Ser.: No. 4). 348p. (Orig.). 1980. text ed. 25.00x (ISBN 0-87474-238-2); pap. text ed. 8.95x (ISBN 0-87474-239-0). Smithsonian.

Bhatt, S. Aviation, Environment & World Order. 196p. 1980. text ed. 16.25x (ISBN 0-391-01809-4). Humanities.

--Legal Controls of Outer Space. 372p. 45.00x (ISBN 0-686-78834-6, Pub. by Bks India England). State Mutual Bk.

Bhatt, S. R. Philosophy of Pancharatra: An Advaitic Approach. 137p. pap. 4.25 (ISBN 0-89744-122-2, Pub. by Ganesh & Co. India). Auromere.

Bhatt, S. R., jt. ed. see Pandey, R. C.

Bhatt, Sudha A. see Johari, Om, et al.

Bhatt, V. V. Development Perspectives: Problems, Strategies & Policies. (Illus.). 352p. 1980. 59.00 (ISBN 0-08-025774-7). Pergamon.

Bhatt, Vinayak V. & Roe, Alan R. Capital Market Imperfections & Economic Development. (Working Paper: No. 338). 87p. 1979. 5.00 (ISBN 0-686-36170-9, WP-0338). World Bank.

Bhattacarya, Jagadishvara. Hasyarnava-the Ocean of Laughter. Nelson, David & Munda, Ramdayal, trs. (Translated from Sanskrit). 1976. 8.00 (ISBN 0-89253-805-8); flexible cloth 4.80 (ISBN 0-89253-806-6). Ind-US Inc.

Bhattacharajee. History of Ancient India. (Illus.). 1980. text ed. 20.50x (ISBN 0-391-01756-X). Humanities.

Bhattacharjee, Arun. Dateline Mujibnagar. 1973. 9.00 (ISBN 0-686-20210-4). Intl Bk Dist.

Bhattacharjee, G. P. Southeast Asia Politics: Malayasia & Indonesia. 1977. 11.00x (ISBN 0-88386-841-5). South Asia Bks.

Bhattacharjee, J. B. Cachar under British Rule in North East India. 1977. 12.00x (ISBN 0-8364-0388-6). South Asia Bks.

Bhattacharjee, J. B., ed. Social Tensions in North-East India. 1983. 14.00x (ISBN 0-8364-0926-4, Pub. by Research India). South Asia Bks.

Bhattacharjee, J. P., ed. Studies in Indian Agricultural Economics. LC 75-26296. (World Food Supply Ser). (Illus.). 1976. Repr. of 1958 ed. 27.50x (ISBN 0-405-07769-6). Ayer Co Pubs.

Bhattacharjee, K. North-East India: A Study. 276p. 1983. text ed. 28.00x (ISBN 0-391-03320-4, Pub. by Cosmo India). Humanities.

Bhattacharjee, P. J. & Shastri, G. N. Population in India: A Study of Inter-State Variations. 1976. 9.00 (ISBN 0-7069-0426-5). Intl Bk Dist.

Bhattacharjee, P. K. & Basu, A. K. A Textbook of Railway Engineering. 188p. 1981. 20.00x (ISBN 0-86125-285-3, Pub. by Orient Longman India). State Mutual Bk.

--A Textbook of Road Engineering. 172p. 1981. 29.00x (Pub. by Orient Longman India). State Mutual Bk.

Bhattacharjee, S. K., jt. auth. see Bosel, T. K.

Bhattacharji, S., jt. ed. see Saxena, S. K.

Bhattacharrya, K. C. Search for the Absolute in Neo-Vedanta. Burch, George B., ed. LC 75-17740. 202p. 1976. text ed. 14.00x (ISBN 0-8248-0296-9). UH Pr.

Bhattacharvya, Amitabha & Ham, Inyong. Design of Cutting Tools: Use of Metal Cutting Theory. LC 68-59237. (American Society of Tool & Manufacturing Engineers Manufacturing Data Ser.). pap. 49.80 (ISBN 0-317-10901-4, 2016001). Bks Demand UMI.

Bhattacharya, A. K., jt. auth. see Lozoya, Jorge A.

Bhattacharya, A. N. & Vyas, R. N. Habitat, Economy & Society: A Study of the Dangis. 1979. text ed. 15.50x (ISBN 0-391-01818-3). Humanities.

Bhattacharya, Aparna. Religious Movements of Bengal, 1800-1850. 1984. pap. 9.00x (ISBN 0-8364-1118-8, Pub. by New Times). South Asia Bks.

Bhattacharya, Arun. A Treatise on Ancient Indian Music. 1978. 12.00x (ISBN 0-8364-0051-8). South Asia Bks.

Bhattacharya, B. B. Public Expenditure, Inflation & Growth: A Macro-Econometric Analysis for India. 228p. 1985. 18.95 (ISBN 0-19-561713-4). Oxford U Pr.

Bhattacharya, B. B., tr. see Nalivkin, D. V.

Bhattacharya, B. C. Indian Images: The Brahmanic Iconography. (Illus.). 79p. 1978. Repr. of 1921 ed. 14.50 (ISBN 0-89684-154-5, Pub. by Cosmo Pubns India). Orient Bk Dist.

--Jaina Iconography. 2nd, rev. ed. (Illus.). 1974. 19.50 (ISBN 0-89684-482-X). Orient Bk Dist.

Bhattacharya, Bhabani. Mahatma Gandhi. (Indian Writers Ser.: Vol. 14). 236p. 1977. 10.00 (ISBN 0-86578-003-X). Ind-US Inc.

--Music for Mohini. 2nd ed. 1976. pap. 2.75 (ISBN 0-89253-071-5). Ind-US Inc.

--Shadow from Ladakh. 359p. 1969. pap. 3.00 (ISBN 0-88253-018-6). Ind-US Inc.

--Socio-Political Currents in Bengal: Nineteenth Century Perspective. 160p. 1980. text ed. 16.50 (ISBN 0-7069-0988-7, Pub. by Vikas India). Advent NY.

--Steel Hawk & Other Stories. 143p. 1968. pap. 2.95 (ISBN 0-88253-020-8). Ind-US Inc.

Bhattacharya, Bhabani, ed. Contemporary Indian Short Stories, 2 vols. 1967. Vol. 1. 3.50 (ISBN 0-88253-409-2); Vol. 2. 3.50 (ISBN 0-88253-327-4). Ind-US Inc.

Bhattacharya, Bhabani, tr. see Tagore, Rabindranath.

Bhattacharya, D. K. Demand for Financial Assets. 208p. 1978. text ed. 44.50x (ISBN 0-566-00228-0). Gower Pub Co.

Bhattacharya, D. S. & Bagchi, T. S. Elements of Geological Map-Reading & Interpretation. 78p. 1981. 30.00x (ISBN 0-86125-433-3, Pub. by Orient Longman India). State Mutual Bk.

Bhattacharya, Deben, ed. Song of Krsna. (Illus.). 1978. cloth 12.50 (ISBN 0-87728-421-0); pap. 5.95 (ISBN 0-87728-422-9). Weiser.

Bhattacharya, Deben, tr. & intro. by. Songs of the Bards of Bengal. 1970. pap. 4.95 (ISBN 0-394-17385-6, E543, Ever). Grove.

Bhattacharya, Dipak C. Studies in Buddhist Iconography. 1978. 22.50x (ISBN 0-8364-0016-X). South Asia Bks.

Bhattacharya, Jatin. Ustad Allauddin Khan & His Music. 1983. 18.50x (ISBN 0-8364-1088-2, Pub. by BS Shah Delhi). South Asia Bks.

Bhattacharya, Kamaleswar, tr. see Johnston, E. H. & Kunst, Arnold.

Bhattacharya, Krishna. An Intensive Course in Bengali. 1984. 12.50x (ISBN 0-8364-1229-X, Pub. by Ctrl Inst). South Asia Bks.

Bhattacharya, Lokenath. Fifteen Prose Poems. Guha, Nikhiles, tr. from Bengali. (Saffronbird Book Ser). 25p. 1975. flexible cloth 4.80 (ISBN 0-88253-709-1). Ind-US Inc.

--The Virgin Fish of Babughat. Mukherjee, Meenakshi, tr. from Bengali. (Indian Novels Ser.). 160p. 1975. 5.95 (ISBN 0-89253-016-2). Ind-US Inc.

Bhattacharya, Mohinimohana. Platonic Ideas in Spenser. LC 72-187921. 1935. lib. bdg. 17.50 (ISBN 0-8414-1643-5). Folcroft.

--Platonic Ideas in Spenser. LC 73-98858. Repr. of 1935 ed. lib. bdg. 18.75x (ISBN 0-8371-3129-4, MOPI). Greenwood.

Bhattacharya, P. B. & Jain, S. K. First Course in Rings, Fields & Vector Spaces. 238p. 1977. cloth 14.95x (ISBN 0-470-99047-3, 76-55303). Halsted Pr.

Bhattacharya, P. B., et al. First Course in Linear Algebra. 190p. 1983. pap. 21.95x cloth (ISBN 0-470-27442-5). Halsted Pr.

Bhattacharya, P. K. Historical Geography of Madhya Pradesh. 1977. 13.95 (ISBN 0-8426-0910-5). Orient Bk Dist.

Bhattacharya, R. N. & Rao, R. R. Normal Approximation & Asymptotic Expansions. LC 83-19559. 288p. 1985. Repr. of 1976 ed. lib. bdg. write for info (ISBN 0-89874-690-6). Krieger.

Bhattacharya, Rameswar. Dynamics of Marine Vehicles. LC 78-950. (Ocean Engineering Ser.). 498p. 1978. text ed. 70.95x cloth (ISBN 0-471-07206-0, Pub. by Wiley-Interscience). Wiley.

Bhattacharya, S. K. & Venkataraman, N. Managing Business Enterprises: Strategies, Structure & Systems. xii, 227p. 1983. text ed. 27.50 o. p. (ISBN 0-7069-2197-6, Pub. by Vikas India); pap. text ed. 10.95x (ISBN 0-7069-2198-4, Pub. by Vikas India). Advent NY.

Bhattacharya, S. N. Indian Rural Economics. 443p. 1984. text ed. 30.50x (ISBN 0-391-03197-X, Pub. by Himalayan Bks India). Humanities.

--Rural Industrialisation in India. 387p. 1981. text ed. 26.50x (ISBN 0-391-02084-6, Pub. by Concept India). Humanities.

Bhattacharya, S. S. Zoology Practicals. 160p. 1981. 30.00x (ISBN 0-86125-643-3, Pub. by Orient Longman India). State Mutual Bk.

Bhattacharya, S. S. & Antia, K. K. Biology Practicals for the Higher Secondary Std.XI. 138p. 1981. 29.00x (ISBN 0-86125-108-3, Pub. by Orient Longman India). State Mutual Bk.

Bhattacharya, S. S., jt. auth. see Antia, K. K.

Bhattacharya, Sachchidananda. A Dictionary of Indian History. LC 77-1105. 1977. Repr. of 1972 ed. lib. bdg. 58.50x (ISBN 0-8371-9515-2, BHDI). Greenwood.

Bhattacharya, Sauripad. Pursuit of National Interest Through Neutralism: India's Foreign Policy in the Nehru Era. 1978. 15.00x (ISBN 0-8364-0139-5). South Asia Bks.

Bhattacharya, Vidhusekhara. The Basic Conception of Buddhism. LC 78-70135. (Adharchandra Mookerjee Lectures. 1932). Repr. of 1934 ed. 20.50 (ISBN 0-404-17405-1). AMS Pr.

Bhattacharya, Vivek. The Spirit of Indian Culture: Saints of India. 622p. 1980. 29.95 (ISBN 0-940500-40-X). Asia Bk Corp.

Bhattacharyya, et al, eds. The Cultural Heritage of India, 5 vols. Incl. Vol. 1. Early Phases. Radhakrishnan, S., intro. by. (ISBN 0-87481-560-6); Vol. 2. Itihasas, Puranas, Dharma & Other Shastras (ISBN 0-87481-561-4); Vol. 3. The Philosophies (ISBN 0-87481-562-2); Vol. 4. The Religions (ISBN 0-87481-563-0); Vol. 5: Languages & Literatures (ISBN 0-87481-564-9). (Illus.). 35.00x ea.; Set. 175.00x (ISBN 0-87481-558-4). Vedanta Pr.

Bhattacharyya, Ajit & Friedman, Gerald M., eds. Modern Carbonate Environments. LC 82-11816. (Benchmark Papers in Geology: Vol. 74). 381p. 1983. 50.00 (ISBN 0-87933-436-3). Van Nos Reinhold.

Bhattacharyya, Amitabha, jt. auth. see Ham, Inyong.

Bhattacharyya, B. K. Humour & Satire in Assamese Literature. 263p. 1982. 45.00x (ISBN 0-940500-46-9, Pub. by Sterling India). Asia Bk Corp.

Bhattacharyya, Benoytosh. An Introduction to Buddhist Esoterism. 1980. Repr. of 1931 ed. 19.00x (ISBN 0-686-69019-2, Pub. by Motilal Banarsidas). South Asia Bks.

Bhattacharyya, Birendra K. Mrityunjay: A Novel in Assamese. Bezboruah, D. N., tr. from Assamese. (Orig.). 1983. 19.95 (ISBN 0-86578-135-4); pap. 8.00 (ISBN 0-86578-176-1). Ind-US Inc.

Bhattacharyya, Buddhadeva. Satyagrahas in Bengal, 1921-1939. 1977. 15.00x (ISBN 0-88386-901-2). South Asia Bks.

Bhattacharyya, Deborah P. Paglami: Ethnopsychiatric Knowledge in Bengal. (Foreign & Comparative Studies-South Asian Ser.: No. 11). (Orig.). 1985. pap. price not set (ISBN 0-915984-89-X). Syracuse U Foreign Comp.

Bhattacharyya, Gouri K. & Johnson, Richard A. Statistical Concepts & Methods. LC 76-53783. (Probability & Mathematical Statistics). 639p. 1977. text ed. 39.45 (ISBN 0-471-07204-4). Wiley.

Bhattacharyya, Gouri K., jt. auth. see Johnson, Richard A.

Bhattacharyya, J. V., tr. Jayantabhatta's Nyaya-Manjari: The Compendium of Indian Speculative Logic, Vol. 1. 1978. 42.00 (ISBN 0-89684-000-X, Pub. by Motilal Banarsidass India). Orient Bk Dist.

Bhattacharyya, M. N. Comparison of Box-Jenkins & Bonn Monetary Prediction Performance. (Lecture Notes in Economics & Mathematical Systems: Vol. 178). (Illus.). 146p. 1980. pap. 18.00 (ISBN 0-387-10011-3). Springer-Verlag.

--Differential Diagnosis in Medicine. 2nd, rev. ed. xii, 360p. 1984. text ed. 35.00x (ISBN 0-86590-236-4, Pub. by Sterling Pubs India). Apt Bks.

Bhattacharyya, N. N. History of the Tantric Religion. 1983. 34.00x (ISBN 0-8364-0942-6, Pub. by Manohar India); pap. 17.50x (ISBN 0-8364-0943-4). South Asia Bks.

--Indian Mother Goddess. 2nd ed. 1977. 16.50x (ISBN 0-88386-736-2). South Asia Bks.

Bhattacharyya, Narendra N. Ancient Indian Rituals & Their Social Contents. 184p. 1975. 14.50x (ISBN 0-87471-735-3). Rowman.

Bhattacharyya, S. & Torok, J., eds. A Critical Study of Materials for Synthetic Gas Quench Systems: Proceedings of the International Gas Research Conference, June 13-16, 1983, London, United Kingdom. LC 81-86225. write for info. Metal Prop Coun.

Bhattacharyya, S. K., et al. Accounting for Management: Text & Cases. 2nd ed. 696p. (Orig.). 1984. pap. text ed. 25.00x (ISBN 0-7069-2479-7, Pub. by Vikas India). Advent NY.

Bhattacharyya, Sailendra N. Mahatma Gandhi the Journalist. LC 84-595. (Illus.). x, 195p. 1984. Repr. of 1965 ed. lib. bdg. 25.00x (ISBN 0-313-24461-8, BHMG). Greenwood.

Bhattacharyya, Swapan K. Farmers Rituals, & Modernization in India: A Sociological Study. 1976. 12.50x (ISBN 0-88386-800-8). South Asia Bks.

Bhattacherje, M. M. Courtesy in Shakespeare. 1978. Repr. of 1940 ed. lib. bdg. 25.00 (ISBN 0-8495-0367-1). Arden Lib.

--Courtesy in Shakespeare. LC 74-13490. 1940. lib. bdg. 17.50 (ISBN 0-8414-3217-1). Folcroft.

--Keats & Spenser. LC 73-9720. 1944. lib. bdg. 17.50 (ISBN 0-8414-3123-X). Folcroft.

--Pictorial Poetry. 1977. Repr. of 1953 ed. lib. bdg. 30.00 (ISBN 0-8495-0320-5). Arden Lib.

--Pictorial Poetry. 184p. Repr. of 1954 ed. lib. bdg. 35.00 (ISBN 0-89760-090-8). Telegraph Bks.

--Pictorial Poetry. 182p. 1983. Repr. of 1982 ed. lib. bdg. 40.00 (ISBN 0-89984-093-0). Century Bookbindery.

--Studies in Spenser. LC 74-13422. 1929. lib. bdg. 17.00 (ISBN 0-8414-3253-8). Folcroft.

Bhattacherje, Mohinimohan. Pictorial Poetry: Chaucer, Keats, Spencer, Tennyson, Rossetti, Morris, Swinburne, Hopkins. Repr. 25.00 (ISBN 0-8274-3136-8). R West.

Bhattasali, B. N. Transfer of Technology Among the Developing Countries. LC 70-186286. 94p. 1972. 10.50 (ISBN 92-833-1013-6, APO4, APO). Unipub.

Bhattasali, B. N. & Bhattasali, Gouri. Productivity & Economic Development. LC 76-186285. 121p. 1972. 11.75 (ISBN 92-833-1015-2, APO60, APO). Unipub.

Bhattasali, Gouri, jt. auth. see Bhattasali, B. N.

Bhatti, A. N. Modern Muslim Cooking of Indo-Pakistan. 1970. 3.50x (ISBN 0-87902-156-X). Orientalia.

Bhave, Vinoba. Democratic Values. Sykes, Marjorie, ed. & tr. from Hindi. 251p. 1980. pap. 5.00 (ISBN 0-934676-24-0). Greenlf Bks.

--Revolutionary Sarvodaya. Nargolkar, Vasant, ed. & tr. from Hindi. 64p. (Orig.). 1980. pap. 1.25 (ISBN 0-934676-23-2). Greenlf Bks.

--Talks on the Gita. 241p. 1983. 10.00 (ISBN 0-934676-37-2). Greenlf Bks.

--Thoughts on Education. Sykes, Marjorie, ed. 288p. (Orig.). 1983. pap. 6.00 (ISBN 0-934676-47-X). Greenlf Bks.

--Vinoba on Gandhi. Shah, K., ed. 199p. 1983. 9.50 (ISBN 0-934676-38-0). Greenlf Bks.

Bhave, W. N. & King, W. R. New Secondary Chemistry. 292p. 1981. 30.00x (ISBN 0-86131-015-2, Pub. by Orient Longman India). State Mutual Bk.

Bhavnani, E. Decorative Designs on Stone & Wood in India. 1978. 27.50x (ISBN 0-89684-560-5). Orient Bk Dist.

Bhavnani, Enakshi. The Dance of India: The Origin & History, Foundation, & Art & Science of the Dance in India - Classical, Folk & Tribal. 3rd ed. (Illus.). xxvi, 260p. 1984. text ed. 60.00x (ISBN 0-86590-056-6, Pub. by Taraporevala India). Apt Bks.

--Decorative Designs & Craftsmanship of India. (Illus.). xv, 109p. 1981. 45.00x (ISBN 0-86590-060-4, Pub. by Taraporevala India). Apt Bks.

--Decorative Designs on Stone & Wood in India. (Illus.). xi, 68p. 1981. text ed. 35.00x (ISBN 0-86590-058-2, Pub. by Taraporevala India). Apt Bks.

--Folk & Tribal Designs of India. xii, 75p. 1981. text ed. 35.00x (ISBN 0-86590-059-0, Pub. by Taraporevala India). Apt Bks.

Bhavvat, H. H., jt. auth. see Jee, Sinh.

Bhavyananda, Swami, ed. see Monks of the Ramakrishna Order.

Bhaya, Hiten. Methods & Techniques of Training Public Enterprise Managers. (ICPE Monograph). 109p. 1983. pap. 10.00x (ISBN 92-9038-905-2, Pub. by Intl Ctr Pub Yugoslavia). Kumarian Pr.

Bhebe, A. H. Lobengula of Zimbabwe. (Illus.). 48p. 1977. pap. text ed. 2.75x (ISBN 0-435-94476-2). Heinemann Ed.

Bhebe, Ngwabi & Ngcongco, L. Junior Certificate History of Southern Africa, Bks 1 & 2. (Orig.). 1981. pap. text ed. 7.50x (ISBN 0-435-94161-5); pap. text ed. 7.50x (ISBN 0-686-98148-0). Heinemann Ed.

Bhiday, M. R. & Joshi, V. A. Introduction to Nuclear Physics. 388p. 1981. 30.00x (ISBN 0-86125-503-8, Pub. by Orient Longman India). State Mutual Bk.

Bhide, Amar. Of Politics & Economic Reality: The Art of Winning Elections with Sound Economic Policies. LC 83-46094. 246p. 1984. 15.95 (ISBN 0-465-05184-7). Basic.

Bhide, Shashanka, jt. ed. see Heady, Earl O.

Bhikshu, Yogi. Bhakti Yoga. 6.00 (ISBN 0-911662-21-9). Yoga.

--Karma Yoga. 1928. 6.00 (ISBN 0-911662-20-0). Yoga.

Bhikshu Heng Shun, et al, trs. see Tripitaka Master Hua.

Bhikshu Hung Ju & Bhikshu Hung Yo. Three Steps, One Bow. (Illus.). 160p. (Orig.). 1976. pap. 5.00 (ISBN 0-917512-18-9). Buddhist Text.

Bhikshu Hung Yo, jt. auth. see Bhikshu Hung Ju.

Bhikshun Heng Tao, et al, trs. see Tripitaka Master Hua.

Bhikshuni Heng Bin, et al, trs. see Tripitaka Master Hua.

Bhikshuni Heng Ch'ih, tr. see Buddhist Text Translation Society.

Bhikshuni Heng Ch'ih, et al, trs. see Hua, Tripitaka Master.

Bhikshuni Heng Ch'ih, et al, trs. see Master Hua, Tripitaka.

Bhikshuni Heng Ch'ih, et al, trs. see Tripitaka Master Hua.

Bhikshuni Heng Hsien, tr. see National Master Ch'ing Liang.

Bhikshuni Heng Hsien, et al, trs. see National Master Ch'ing Liang.

Bhikshuni Heng Hsien, et al, trs. see Tripitaka Master Hua.

Bhikshuni Heng Tao, tr. see Buddhist Text Translation Society.

Bhikshuni Heng Tao, tr. see Hui Seng.

Bhikshuni Heng Tao, et al, trs. from Chinese. Flower Adornment Sutra: Chapter 39, Entering the Dharma Realm, Part VII. 160p. (Orig.). 1983. pap. 9.00 (ISBN 0-88139-050-X). Buddhist Text.

Bhikshuni Heng Tao, et al, trs. see Master Hua, Tripitaka.

Bhikshuni Heng Tao, et al, trs. see Tripitaka Master Hua.

Bhiksuni Heng Hsien, et al, trs. see Master Hua, Tripitaka.

Bhila, H. H. Trade & Politics in a Shona Kingdom: The Manyika & Their African & Portuguese Neighbors, 1575-1902. (Studies in Zimbabwean History). pap. 76.80 (ISBN 0-317-27757-X, 2025233). Bks Demand UMI.

Bhim Sen Savara, ed. see Boyd, Edith.

Bhiwandiwala, Pouru, jt. auth. see Potts, Malcolm.

Bhojwani, S. S. & Bhatnagar, S. P. The Embryology of Angiosperms. 1978. 17.50x (ISBN 0-7069-0335-8, Pub. by Vikas India). Advent NY.

--Embryology of Angiosperms. (Illus.). 1976. 10.50 (ISBN 0-7069-0335-8). Intl Bk Dist.

Bhojwani, S. S. & Razdan, M. N. Plant Tissue Culture: Theory & Practice. (Developments in Crop Science Ser.: Vol. 5). 1984. 113.50 (ISBN 0-444-42164-5, I-075-84). Elsevier.

Bhola, H. S. Campaigning for Literacy: Eight National Experiences of the Twentieth Century, with a Memorandum to Decision-Makers. 203p. 1985. pap. 18.00 (ISBN 92-3-102167-2, U1442, UNESCO). Unipub.

Bhola, Nath T., jt. auth. see Chaturvedi, Mahendra.

Bhooshan, B. S. The Development Experience of Nepal. 1980. text ed. 16.25x (ISBN 0-391-01819-1). Humanities.

Bhooshan, B. S., jt. auth. see Misra, R. P.

Bhooshan, B. S., ed. Towards Alternative Settlement Strategies: The Role of Small & Intermediate Centers in Development Process. x, 404p. 1980. text ed. 30.00x (ISBN 0-86590-005-1). Apt Bks.

Bhoothalingam, Mathuram. Movement in Stone: A Study of Some Chola Temples. LC 70-910892. 1969. 5.00x (ISBN 0-89684-435-8). Orient Bk Dist.

Bhoyrub, J. P. & Morton, H. G. Psychiatric Problems in Childhood: A Guide for Nurses. 180p. 1983. pap. text ed. 11.50 (ISBN 0-272-79711-1, Pub. by Pitman Bks Ltd UK). Urban & S.

Bhruksasri, Wanat, jt. ed. see McKinnon, J. McLachlan.

Bhuinya, Niranjan. Direct Democracy in Switzerland. 1975. 12.00 (ISBN 0-686-20212-0). Intl Bk Dist.

--Parliamentary Democracy in Japan. 1971. 9.00 (ISBN 0-686-20282-1). Intl Bk Dist.

Bhuiyan, Abdul W. Emergence of Bangladesh & the Role of the Awami League. 275p. 1982. text ed. 32.50x (ISBN 0-7069-1773-1, Pub. by Vikas India). Advent NY.

--The Emergence of Bangladesh & the Role the Awami League. 1982. 45.00x (ISBN 0-686-94082-2, Pub. by Garlandfold England). State Mutual Bk.

Bhukaswan, Thirophan. Management of Asian Reservoir Fisheries. (Fisheries Technical Papers: No. 207). 78p. 1980. pap. 7.50 (ISBN 92-5-101023-4, F2156, FAO). Unipub.

Bhumralker, Chandrakant & Teasley, John I., eds. Meteorological Aspects of Acid Rain. (Acid Precipitation Ser.: Vol. 1). 256p. 1984. text ed. 32.50 (ISBN 0-250-40566-0). Butterworth.

Bhumralker, Williams. Atmospheric Effects of Waste Heat Discharges: Energy, Power & Environment, Vol. 13. 203p. 1982. pap. 35.00 (ISBN 0-8247-1653-1). Dekker.

Bhushan, Vidya. Prison Administration in India. 296p. 25.00x (ISBN 0-686-78849-4, Pub. by Bks India England). State Mutual Bk.

Bhushan, Vidya, jt. auth. see Bhagvan, Vishnoo.

Bhushan, Vidya, jt. auth. see Bhagwan, Vishnoo.

Bhutani, Surendra, ed. Contemporary Gulf. 1980. 12.00x (ISBN 0-8364-0667-2, Pub. by Academic India). South Asia Bks.

Bhutto, Zulfikar A. Myth of Independence. 1969. 15.00x (ISBN 0-19-215167-3). Oxford U Pr.

Bhuyan, Suryya K. Anglo-Assamese Relations: Seventeen Seventy-One to Eighteen Twenty-Six. LC 77-87072. Repr. of 1949 ed. 46.00 (ISBN 0-404-16795-0). AMS Pr.

Bia, Fred & Lynch, R. Nihi Hahoodzoodoo-Diijjidi doo Adaadaa: Our Community-Today & Yesterday, Bk. 1. LC 82-83573. (Illus.). 98p. 1982. 12.00x (ISBN 0-936008-04-0). Navajo Curr.

Bia, Fred & McCarthy, T. L. Of Mother Earth & Father Sky. (Illus.). 69p. 1983. 17.00x (ISBN 0-87358-339-6); pap. 12.00. Navajo Curr.

Biaggi, Virgilio, jt. auth. see Aguayo, Carlos A.

Biagi, Adele, jt. ed. see Ragazzini, Giuseppe.

Biagi, Bob. Working Together: A Manual to Help Groups Work More Effectively. 124p. (Citizen Involvement Training Project). 1978. pap. 6.85 (ISBN 0-318-17175-9, C27). Natl Ctr Cit Involv.

Biagi, Gabriella. Francesco Gasparini. Gianturco, Carolyn, ed. (The Italian Cantata in the Seventeenth Century Ser.). 60.00 (ISBN 0-8240-8881-6). Garland Pub.

Biagi, Guido. The Last Days of Percy Bysshe Shelley. LC 76-17878. 1976. Repr. of 1898 ed. lib. bdg. 25.00 (ISBN 0-8414-3344-5). Folcroft.

Biagi, Robert C. Working Together: A Manual to Help Groups Work More Effectively. LC 79-934736. (Illus., Orig.). 1978. pap. 8.00x (ISBN 0-934210-05-5). Citizen Involve.

Biagi, Shirley. How to Write & Sell Magazine Articles. 156p. 1981. 12.95 (ISBN 0-13-441618-X); pap. 4.95 (ISBN 0-13-441600-7). P-H.

--Interviews That Work: A Practical Guide for Journalists. 200p. 1985. pap. text ed. write for info. (ISBN 0-534-05664-4). Wadsworth Pub.

--A Writer's Guide to Word Processors. (Illus.). 160p. 1984. 13.95 (ISBN 0-13-971721-8); pap. 6.95 (ISBN 0-13-971713-7). P-H.

Bial, Morrison D. Liberal Judaism at Home: The Practices of Modern Reform Judaism. rev. ed. 1971. pap. 5.00 (ISBN 0-8074-0075-0, 383110); tchrs'. guide 1.50 (ISBN 0-8074-0225-7, 203110). UAHC.

--Your Jewish Child. Syme, Daniel B., ed. 1978. pap. 5.00 (ISBN 0-8074-0012-2, 101200). UAHC.

Bial, Morrison D., ed. see Stadtler, Bea.

Bial, Raymond. Ivesdale: A Photographic Essay. LC 82-73325. (Champaign County Historical Archives Historical Publications Ser.: No. 5). (Illus.). 126p. 1982. 12.00 (ISBN 0-9609646-0-6). Champaign County.

Bial, Raymond & Schlipf, Frederick A. Upon a Quiet Landscape: The Photographs of Frank Sadorus. LC 83-72993. (Champaign Country Historical Archives Historical Publications Ser.: No. 6). (Illus.). 168p. 1983. 18.00 (ISBN 0-9609646-1-4). Champaign County.

Biale, David. Childhood, Marriage & the Family in the Eastern European Jewish Enlightement. 24p. 1983. pap. 1.50 (ISBN 0-87495-049-X). Am Jewish Comm.

--Gershom Scholem: Kabbalah & Counter-History. LC 78-23620. 1979. text ed. 17.50x (ISBN 0-674-36330-2). Harvard U Pr.

--Gershom Scholem: Kabbalah & Counter-History. 2nd ed. 240p. 1982. pap. text ed. 7.95x (ISBN 0-674-36332-9). Harvard U Pr.

Biale, Rachel. Women & Jewish Law: An Exploration of Women's Issues in Halakhic Sources. LC 83-40457. 256p. 1984. 18.95 (ISBN 0-8052-3887-5). Schocken.

Bialer, Irv., jt. ed. see Gadow, Kenneth D.

Bialer, Seweryn. The Soviet Paradox: External Expansion & Internal Decline. 1984. 18.95 (ISBN 0-394-54095-6). Knopf.

--Stalin's Successors: Leadership, Stability & Change in the Soviet Union. LC 80-12037. 416p. 1980. 32.50 (ISBN 0-521-23518-9); pap. 10.95 (ISBN 0-521-28906-8). Cambridge U Pr.

--The U. S. S. R. after Brezhnev. LC 83-83061. (Headline Ser.: No. 265). (Illus.). 64p. (Orig.). (gr. 11-12). 1983. pap. 3.00 (ISBN 0-87124-086-6). Foreign Policy.

Bialer, Seweryn, ed. The Domestic Context of Soviet Foreign Policy. LC 80-11877. 442p. 1981. lib. bdg. 38.50x (ISBN 0-89158-783-7); pap. 15.95x (ISBN 0-89158-891-4). Westview.

--Stalin & His Generals: Soviet Military Memoirs of World War II. (Encore Edition Ser.). 650p. 1984. softcover 42.50x (ISBN 0-86531-610-4). Westview.

Bialer, Seweryn & Gustafson, Thane, eds. Russia at the Crossroads: The Twenty-Sixth Congress of the CPSU. 256p. 1982. text ed. 28.50x (ISBN 0-04-329039-6). Allen Unwin.

Bialer, Seweryn, et al. Trilateral-Soviet Relations in Transition. write for info. Trilateral Comm.

Bialers, Seweryn & Sluzar, S., eds. Sources of Contemporary Radicalism, Vol. 1. LC 76-39890. (Studies of the Research Institute of International Change, Columbia University). 396p. 1977. lib. bdg. 28.50 (ISBN 0-89158-130-8); lib. bdg. 60.00 3 vol. set (ISBN 0-686-77225-3). Westview.

Bialik, Hayyim N. And It Came to Pass. 281p. 1938. 6.95 (ISBN 0-88482-887-5). Hebrew Pub.

--Knight of Onions & Knight of Garlic. 55p. 1934. 4.95 (ISBN 0-88482-734-8). Hebrew Pub.

Bialkin, Kenneth J., et al. New Techniques in Acquisitions & Takeovers. LC 84-149770. vi, 528p. Date not set. price not set (Law & Business). HarBraceJ.

Bialosiewicz, Frank & Burns, Julie. Game of Childhood Diseases. (Technical Notes Ser.: No. 23). (Illus.). 30p. (Orig.). 1983. pap. text ed. 1.50 (ISBN 0-932288-70-7). Ctr Intl Ed U of Ma.

Bialosiewicz, Frank, jt. auth. see Burns, Julie.

Bialosky, Alan, jt. auth. see Bialosky, Peggy.

Bialosky, Peggy & Bialosky, Alan. Making Your Own Teddy Bear. LC 82-60061. (Illus.). 124p. 1983. pap. 8.95 (ISBN 0-89480-211-9, 484). Workman Pub.

--The Teddy Bear Catalog. LC 83-40040. (Illus.). 224p. 1983. pap. 6.95 (ISBN 0-89480-607-6, 607). Workman Pub.

Bialostocki, Jan. The Art of the Renaissance in Eastern Europe. LC 75-38429. 340p. 1976. 45.00x (ISBN 0-8014-1008-8). Cornell U Pr.

Bialostosky, Don H. Making Tales: The Poetics of Wordsworth's Narrative Experiments. LC 83-5069. 208p. 1984. lib. bdg. 25.00x (ISBN 0-226-04575-7); pap. 12.50x (ISBN 0-226-04576-5). U of Chicago Pr.

Bialoszewski, Miron. The Revolution of Things. Czaykowski, Bogdan & Busza, Andrzej, trs. LC 74-81212. 1974. 7.50 (ISBN 0-910350-01-9). Charioteer.

Bialy, Harvey, ed. Biopoesis. 350p. 1974. pap. 5.00 (ISBN 0-913028-25-8). North Atlantic.

Bialynicey-Birula, J. Quantum Electrodynamics. LC 74-4473. 541p. 1975. text ed. 52.00 (ISBN 0-08-017188-5). Pergamon.

Bialystok, Ellen, jt. auth. see Olson, David R.

Biamonte, Edgar. Window of Eternity. LC 83-9944. 145p. 1984. 13.95 (ISBN 0-87949-230-9). Ashley Bks.

Biancani, Laurent. Nude Photography: The French Way. Orig. Title: Te-Nu. (Illus.). 1980. (Amphoto); pap. 12.95 (ISBN 0-8174-5096-3). Watson-Guptill.

Bianchi, A. L. & Denavit-Saubie, M., eds. Neurogenesis of Central Respiratory Rhythm: Electrophysiological, Pharmacological & Pathological Aspects. 1985. lib. bdg. 89.00 (ISBN 0-85200-903-8, Pub. by MTP Pr England). Kluwer-Academic.

Bianchi, C., ed. Kidney, Small Proteins & Drugs. (Contributions to Nephrology: Vol. 42). (Illus.). x, 262p. 1984. 53.25 (ISBN 3-8055-3913-4). S Karger.

Bianchi, C. Paul, jt. ed. see Narahashi, Toshio.

Bianchi, Claudio, jt. ed. see Blaufox, M. Donald.

Bianchi, Daniel B., jt. auth. see Smith, Julian P.

Bianchi, Donald E., jt. auth. see Sheeler, Phillip.

Bianchi, Doris B., et al. Easily Understood: A Basic Speech Text. 160p. (Orig.). 1981. pap. text ed. 9.95 (ISBN 0-89529-138-X). Avery Pub.

Bianchi, Eugene A. Aging as a Spiritual Journey. 304p. 1984. pap. 9.95 (ISBN 0-8245-0622-7). Crossroad NY.

Bianchi, G., jt. ed. see Sawczuk, A.

Bianchi, G., et al, eds. Man under Vibration: Suffering & Protection. (Studies in Environmental Science: Vol. 13). 438p. 1982. 83.00 (ISBN 0-444-99743-1). Elsevier.

Bianchi, G., jt. ed. see Morecki, A.

Bianchi, L. & Gerok, W., eds. Liver in Metabolic Diseases. 300p. 1983. text ed. write for info. (ISBN 0-85200-730-2, Pub. by MTP Pr England). Kluwer Academic.

--Virus & the Liver. Sickinger, K. 1981. lib. bdg. 55.00 (ISBN 0-85200-350-1, Pub. by MTP Pr England). Kluwer Academic.

Bianchi, L., et al, eds. Trends in Hepatology. 1985. lib. bdg. 48.00 (ISBN 0-85200-868-6, Pub. by MTP Pr Netherlands). Kluwer Academic.

Bianchi, Luciana. Easy Italian Cooking. LC 83-82234. (Illus.). 80p. 1984. 9.95 (ISBN 0-88332-328-1, 8253). Larousse.

Bianchi, Martha D. The Life & Letters of Emily Dickinson. LC 70-162296. 386p. 1972. Repr. of 1924 ed. 15.00x (ISBN 0-8196-0276-0). Biblo.

Bianchi, Martha D., ed. see Dickinson, Emily.

Bianchi, Raymond, jt. auth. see Lyle, Carl.

Bianchi, Robert. Interest Groups & Political Development in Turkey. LC 83-10999. 432p. 1984. 45.00x (ISBN 0-691-07653-7); pap. 17.50x (ISBN 0-691-10149-3). Princeton U Pr.

Bianchi, Susan & Butler, Jan. Warm Ups for Meeting Leaders. Parcher, Jean & Lewis, Cathy, eds. LC 84-61535. (Illus.). 138p. (Orig.). 1984. 14.95x (ISBN 0-930733-00-2). Quality Groups Pub.

Bianchi, Suzanne M. Household Composition & Racial Inequality. 215p. 1981. 22.00x (ISBN 0-8135-0913-0). Rutgers U Pr.

Bianchi, Tony. Richard Vaughan. (Writers of Wales Ser.). 96p. 1984. pap. text ed. 6.75x (ISBN 0-7083-0848-1, Pub. by Univ of Wales Pr England). Humanities.

Bianchin, Helen. Wildfire Encountered. (Harlequin Presents Ser.). 192p. 1982. pap. 1.75 (ISBN 0-373-10527-4). Harlequin Bks.

Bianchina, Paul, ed. see Bianchina, Rose.

Bianchina, Rose. Pet Names. Bianchina, Paul, ed. (Illus.). 45p. (Orig.). 1984. pap. 3.95 (ISBN 0-918783-00-3). Golden Pubns.

Bianchine, Joseph, jt. ed. see Yetiv, Jack.

Bianchine, Joseph R., jt. auth. see Yetiv, Jack.

Bianchini, Thomas. The Overlord. 92p. (Orig.). 1983. pap. 5.00 (ISBN 0-9612286-0-1). Whitewater.

Bianco. Fabulous Cookies. (Easy Cooking Ser.). 1983. 4.95 (ISBN 0-8120-5528-4). Barron.

--Thirty-Two Seafood Dishes. 1983. 4.95 (ISBN 0-8120-5530-6). Barron.

--Wild about Potatoes. (Wild about Ser.). 1985. pap. 5.95 (ISBN 0-8120-2914-3). Barron.

Bianco, Carla. The Two Rosetos. LC 73-16523. (Illus.). Repr. of 1974 ed. 62.30 (ISBN 0-8357-9249-8, 2055234). Bks Demand UMI.

Bianco, David, ed. Who's New Wave in Music: An Illustrated Encyclopedia, 1976-1982. LC 84-61228. (Rock & Roll Reference Ser.: No. 14). 1985. (individuals) 29.50 (ISBN 0-87650-173-0); (institutions) 39.50. Pierian.

Bianco, E. Informatique Fondamental. (Interdisciplinary Systems Research: No. 70). 158p. (Fr.). 1979. pap. 20.95x (ISBN 0-8176-1090-1). Birkhauser.

Bianco, Enzo. Don Bosco's Lay Religious: Essays on the Salesian, Pt. 1. Swain, Peter, tr. 75p. pap. 3.00 (ISBN 0-89944-078-9). Don Bosco Multimedia.

--Don Bosco's Lay Religious: Profiles in Courage, Pt. 2. Swain, Peter, tr. 101p. pap. 3.00 (ISBN 0-89944-079-7). Don Bosco Multimedia.

--Salesian Cooperators: A Practical Way of Life. Swain, Peter, tr. (Salesian Family Ser.). 40p. 1983. pap. 3.25 (ISBN 0-89944-073-8). Don Bosco Multimedia.

Bianco, Jose. The Rats Shadow Play. Miller, Yvette E., ed. Balderston, Daniel, tr. LC 83-775. 88p. 1983. pap. 9.50 (ISBN 0-935480-11-0). Lat Am Lit Rev Pr.

Bianco, Joseph R. My Dear Italian Mother's Peasant Recipes. 1977. pap. 3.95 (ISBN 0-918688-00-0). Touchstone Pr Ore.

Bianco, Lucien. Origins of the Chinese Revolution, 1915-1949. Bell, Muriel, tr. from Fr. LC 75-150321. Orig. Title: Les Origines de la Revolution Chinoise, 1915-1949. xvii, 220p. 1971. 18.50x (ISBN 0-8047-0746-4); pap. 6.95 (ISBN 0-8047-0827-4, SP131). Stanford U Pr.

Bianco, Margery. The Skin Horse. LC 84-145310. (Illus.). 54p. 1982. pap. 6.95 (ISBN 0-914676-25-3). Green Tiger Pr.

Bianco, Margery, tr. see Cendrars, Blaise.

Bianco, Margery W. The Skin Horse. LC 84-145310. (Illus.). 1978. (Star & Elephant Bks.); pap. 6.95 (ISBN 0-914676-25-3). Green Tiger Pr.

Bianco, Pamela. Valentine Party. LC 54-7303. (Illus.). (gr. k-3). 1955. 9.57i (ISBN 0-397-30314-9). Lipp Jr Bks.

Biancolli, Louis & Farkas, Andrew. The Flagstad Manuscript. LC 76-29935. (Opera Biographies). (Illus.). 1977. Repr. of 1952 ed. lib. bdg. 26.50x (ISBN 0-405-09677-1). Ayer Co Pubs.

Biancolli, Louis, jt. auth. see Garden, Mary.

Biancolli, Louis, ed. The Mozart Handbook: A Guide to the Man & His Music. LC 75-32504. (Illus.). 629p. 1976. Repr. of 1954 ed. lib. bdg. 45.00x (ISBN 0-8371-8496-7, BIMH). Greenwood.

--The Opera Reader. 1977. Repr. of 1953 ed. lib. bdg. 43.00x (ISBN 0-8371-9722-8, BIOR). Greenwood.

Biancolli, Louis L. & Peyser, Herbert F. Masters of the Orchestra from Bach to Prokofieff. LC 70-94578. Repr. of 1954 ed. lib. bdg. 19.75x (ISBN 0-8371-2545-6, BIMO). Greenwood.

Biancolli, Louis L., ed. Analytical Concert Guide. LC 77-92295. lib. bdg. 33.75x (ISBN 0-8371-3074-3, BICG). Greenwood.

Bianconi, A., et al, eds. EXAFS & Near Edge Structures: Proceedings, Frascati, Italy, 1982. (Springer Series in Chemical Physics: Vol. 27). (Illus.). 420p. 1983. 39.00 (ISBN 0-387-12411-X). Springer-Verlag.

Bianki, V. The First Hunt. 12p. 1978. pap. 1.49 (ISBN 0-8285-1139-X, Pub. by Progress Pubs USSR). Imported Pubns.

--Forest Homes. 48p. 1978. 5.45 (ISBN 0-8285-1598-0, Pub. by Progress Pubs USSR). Imported Pubns.

--The Fox & the Mouse. 12p. 1975. pap. 1.49 (ISBN 0-8285-1144-6, Pub. by Progress Pubs USSR). Imported Pubns.

Biannual. Long Care News. 6.00 (ISBN 0-317-06761-3). Am Foun Blind.

Biard, Roland. Dictionnaire de l'Extreme-Gauche: De 1945 a Nos Jours. 384p. (Fr.). 1978. pap. 22.50 (ISBN 0-686-56917-2, M-6033). French & Eur.

Biardeau, Madeleine. Theorie De la Connaissance et Philosophie De la Parole Dans le Brahmanisme Classique. (Le Monde D'outre-Mer Passe et Present, Etudes: No. 23). 1963. pap. 34.80x (ISBN 90-2796-178-6). Mouton.

Biardo, John C. Willy's Story. LC 85-80436. (Illus.). 32p. (gr. 3-6). 1985. price not set (ISBN 0-933181-01-9). Elmwood Park Pub.

--The World's Greatest Telvision Trivia Quiz Book. LC 85-70386. 518p. (Orig.). 1985. pap. 12.95 (ISBN 0-933181-00-0). Elmwood Park Pub.

Biart, Lucien. The Aztecs: Their History, Manners, & Customs. 1977. lib. bdg. 59.95 (ISBN 0-8490-1466-2). Gordon Pr.

--The Aztecs: Their History, Manners & Customs. 1976. Repr. of 1887 ed. 39.00x (ISBN 0-685-71094-7, Regency). Scholarly.

Bias, Clifford. The Way Back. LC 84-52289. (Illus.). 224p. (Orig.). 1985. pap. 7.95 (ISBN 0-87728-607-8). Weiser.

Bias, Clifford, compiled by. Ritual Book of Magic. 160p. 1981. pap. 5.95 (ISBN 0-87728-532-2). Weiser.

Biasin, Gian-Paolo. Italian Literary Icons. LC 84-42876. (Illus.). 220p. 1985. text ed. 27.50x (ISBN 0-691-06632-9). Princeton U Pr.

--Literary Diseases: Theme & Metaphor in the Italian Novel. LC 74-30345. 188p. 1975. 12.50x (ISBN 0-292-74614-8). U of Tex Pr.

Biasini, Gian-Paolo. The Smile of the Gods: A Thematic Study of Cesare Pavese's Works. LC 68-9748. 337p. 1968. 20.00x (ISBN 0-915042-19-3). Lib Soc Sci.

Biasiotto, Judd. Hypnotize Me & Make Me Great. Trunzo, Jim, ed. 100p. (Orig.). 1985. pap. 7.00 (ISBN 0-933079-00-1). World Class Enterprises.

--Two Thousand One: A Sports Odyssey Hypnosis Cybernetics Conditioning Biofeedback. 160p. (Orig.). 1984. pap. 8.00 (ISBN 0-933079-04-4). World Class Enterprises.

Biasiotto, Peter R. History of the Development of the Devotion to the Holy Name. 1943. 3.50 (ISBN 0-686-11579-1). Franciscan Inst.

Biass-Ducroux, Francoise. Glossary of Genetics. (Glossaria Inetrpretum: Vol. 16). 436p. (Eng., Fr., Span., Ital., Ger. & Rus.). 1970. 76.75 (ISBN 0-444-40712-X). Elsevier.

Biava, A. Dizionario Italiano-Portoghese, Portoghese-Italiano. 318p. (Ital. & Port.). 1980. leatherette 5.95 (ISBN 0-686-97345-3, M-9172). French & Eur.

Bibago, Abraham. Derek Emunah: The Path of Faith. 204p. 1521. text ed. 49.68x (ISBN 0-576-80102-X, Pub. by Gregg Intl Pubs England). Gregg Intl.

Bibar, Geronimo De see De Bibar, Geronimo.

Bibaud, M. Histoire Du Canada et Des Canadiens Sous la Domination Anglaise. (Canadiana Avant 1867: No. 2). 1968. 26.00x (ISBN 90-2796-323-1). Mouton.

Bibaud, Michel. Histoire Du Canada et Des Canadiens Sous la Domination Anglaise. (Bibliography of Canadiana: No. 2040). (Fr). Repr. of 1844 ed. 26.00 (ISBN 0-384-04190-6). Johnson Repr.

--Histoire Du Canada, Sous La Domination Francaise. Repr. of 1837 ed. 27.00 (ISBN 0-384-04195-7). Johnson Repr.

Bibb, Benjamin O. Other Times, Other Planets: Vardigan Speaks. De Geus, Leonard F., ed. (Orig.). 1985. Vol. 1, July 1979-December 1981, 38p. pap. text ed. 8.95 (ISBN 0-916541-04-5); Vol. 2, January 1982-December 1983, 35p. pap. text ed. 8.95 (ISBN 0-916541-05-3); Vol. 3, January-December 1984, 14p. pap. text ed. 4.95 (ISBN 0-916541-06-1); Set. pap. text ed. 20.50 (ISBN 0-916541-03-7). Woods Creek Pr.

Bibb, Benjamin O. & Weed, Joseph J. Amazing Secrets of Psychic Healing. 1976. pap. 4.95 (ISBN 0-13-023762-0). P-H.

Bibb, Eloise. Poems. facsimile ed. LC 71-173601. (Black Heritage Library Collection). Repr. of 1895 ed. 12.50 (ISBN 0-8369-8897-3). Ayer Co Pubs.

Bibb, Henry. Narrative of the Life & Adventures of Henry Bibb, an American Slave. facs. ed. LC 70-89423. (Black Heritage Library Collection Ser). 1849. 14.25 (ISBN 0-8369-8511-7). Ayer Co Pubs.

--Narrative of the Life & Adventures of Henry Bibb, an American Slave. LC 76-84686. (Illus.). Repr. of 1850 ed. 17.50x (ISBN 0-8371-1267-2, BIH&, Pub. by Negro U Pr). Greenwood.

Bibb, John, jt. auth. see Graham, Lou.

Bibb, Mary. Autumn Leaves Poetry Anthology. LC 83-91091. (Illus.). 160p. (Orig.). 1984. pap. 5.00x (ISBN 0-9608778-2-7). M Bibb.

--Footprints in the Sands of Time. LC 82-90338. (Illus.). 215p. (Orig.). pap. 5.00 (ISBN 0-9608778-0-0). M Bibb.

--Spring Symphony Poetry Anthology. LC 85-70796. 120p. (Orig.). 1985. pap. 5.00x (ISBN 0-9608778-1-9). M Bibb.

Bibb, Porter, et al. The CB Bible. (Illus.). 1976. pap. 4.95 (ISBN 0-385-12323-X, Dolp). Doubleday.

Bibbero, R. J. Portfolio Stock Selection. (Professional Software Ser.). 1984. incl. disk 125.00 (ISBN 0-471-80232-8). Wiley.

Bibbero, Robert J. Microprocessors in Industrial Control: An Independent Learning Module of the Instrument Society of America. LC 82-48556. 256p. 1983. text ed. 39.95x (ISBN 0-87664-624-0, 1624-0). Instru Soc.

--Microprocessors in Instruments & Control. LC 77-9929. 301p. 1977. 32.50x (ISBN 0-471-01595-4, Pub. by Wiley-Interscience). Wiley.

Bibbero, Robert J. & Stern, David. Microprocessor Systems: Interfacing & Applications. 195p. 1982. 25.50x (ISBN 0-471-05306-6, Pub. by Wiley-Interscience). Wiley.

Bibbero, Robert J. & Young, Irving G. Systems Approach to Air Pollution Control. LC 74-8905. pap. 135.50 (ISBN 0-317-11255-4, 2055157). Bks Demand UMI.

Bibbero, Robert J., ed. see Instrument Society of America.

Bibby, Basil G & Shern, Roald J, eds. Methods of Caries Prediction: Proceedings. LC 78-50300. 336p. 1978. 30.00 (ISBN 0-917000-04-8). IRL Pr.

Bibby, Cyril. The Art of the Limerick. (Illus.). 276p. 1978. 19.50 (ISBN 0-208-01761-5, Archon). Shoe String.

Bibby, Geoffrey. Four Thousand Years Ago: A World Panorama of Life in the Second Millennium B. C. LC 83-12743. (Illus.). xix, 398p. 1983. Repr. of 1961 ed. lib. bdg. 49.50x (ISBN 0-313-23411-6, BIFT). Greenwood.

Bibby, John & Toutenburg, Helge. Prediction & Improved Estimation in Linear Models. (Probability & Mathematical Statistics Tracts on Probability & Statistic Section). 188p. 1977. 42.95x (ISBN 0-471-01656-X, Pub. by Wiley-Interscience). Wiley.

Bibby, John, jt. auth. see Johnson, Paul.

Bibby, John, ed. Congress Off the Record: Candid Analyses of Seven Members. 1983. pap. 4.95 (ISBN 0-8447-3526-4). Am Enterprise.

Bibby, John F., et al. Vital Statistics on Congress, 1980. 1980. pap. 5.25 (ISBN 0-8447-3401-2). Am Enterprise.

Bibeau, Simone. Cash in on Today's Educational Market: Teachers-Make Real Money Outside the Classroom! (Illus.). 256p. (Orig.). pap. 14.95x (ISBN 0-940406-11-X). Perception Pubns.

--Developing the Early Learner: Level 1. rev. ed. (Pre-Reading Experience Ser.). (Illus.). 64p. (ps-2). 1983. pap. text ed. 4.95 (ISBN 0-940406-01-2). Perception Pubns.

--Developing the Early Learner: Level 2. rev. ed. (Pre-Reading Experience Ser.). (Illus.). 64p. (ps-2). 1983. pap. text ed. 4.95 (ISBN 0-940406-02-0). Perception Pubns.

--Developing the Early Learner: Level 3. rev. ed. (Pre-Reading Experience Ser.). (Illus.). 64p. (ps-2). 1983. pap. text ed. 4.95 (ISBN 0-940406-03-9). Perception Pubns.

--Developing the Early Learner: Level 4. (Pre-Reading Experience Ser.). (Illus.). 64p. (ps-2). 1983. pap. text ed. 4.95 (ISBN 0-940406-04-7). Perception Pubns.

--IQ Booster Kit: Developing the Early Learner Levels 1-4. (Pre-Reading Experience Ser.). (Illus.). 64p. (ps-2). 1983. pap. text ed. 75.00 (bks. & cassettes) (ISBN 0-940406-05-5). Perception Pubns.

--Writing the Advanced Short Story. 32p. (gr. 1-12). 1983. pap. text ed. 1.95 (ISBN 0-940406-07-1). Perception Pubns.

--Writing the Beginning Short Story. (Illus.). 32p. (Orig.). (gr. 1-9). 1983. pap. text ed. 1.95 (ISBN 0-940406-06-3). Perception Pubns.

--Writing the Fantasy Story. 32p. (Orig.). (gr. 1-9). 1983. pap. text ed. 1.95 (ISBN 0-940406-08-X). Perception Pubns.

Bibeault, Donald. Corporate Turnaround: How Managers Turn Losers into Winners. 416p. 1982. 31.95 (ISBN 0-07-005190-9). McGraw.

Bibee, John. The Magic Bicycle. LC 83-240. (Illus.). 220p. (Orig.). (gr. 4-9). 1983. pap. 5.95 (ISBN 0-87784-348-1). Inter-Varsity.

Bibel, W. & Kowalski, R., eds. Fifth Conference on Automated Deduction: Les Arcs Proceedings. (Lecture Notes in Computer Science: Vol. 87). (Illus.). 385p. 1980. pap. 26.00 (ISBN 0-387-10009-1). Springer-Verlag.

Biber, Barbara. Early Education & Psychological Development. Zigler, Edward, frwd. by. LC 84-40190. (Illus.). 392p. 1984. 30.00x (ISBN 0-300-02802-4). Yale U Pr.

Biber, Barbara, ed. see Johnson, Harriet M.

Biber, Barbara, et al. Promoting Cognitive Growth: A Developmental-Interaction Point of View. 2nd ed. LC 72-154558. (Illus.). 64p. 1977. pap. text ed. 3.00 (NAEYC126). Natl Assn Child Ed.

Biber, Jacob. Survivors: A Personal Story of the Holocaust. (Studies in Judaica & the Holocaust: No. 2). 208p. 1985. lib. bdg. 16.95x (ISBN 0-89370-370-2); pap. text ed. 8.95x (ISBN 0-89370-470-9). Borgo Pr.

--Survivors: A Personal Story of the Holocaust. 208p. 1985. pap. 8.95 (ISBN 0-87877-470-X). Newcastle Pub.

Biber, Yehoash. Adventures in the Galilee. Bacon, Josephine, tr. from Heb. LC 72-87912. (Covenant Ser.). 140p. (gr. 6-10). 1973. 3.95 (ISBN 0-8276-0002-X, 163). Jewish Pubns.

Biberfeld, Henry. David: King of Israel. 1978. pap. 3.95 (ISBN 0-87306-178-0). Feldheim.

Biberfeld, Henry, tr. see Munk, Elie.

Biberfeld, Philip. Universal Jewish History, 3 vols. Vol. 1. 5.95 (ISBN 0-87306-052-0, Spero Foundation); Vol. 2. 7.95 (ISBN 0-87306-053-9); Vol. 3. 9.95 (ISBN 0-87306-054-7); Set. 22.00 (ISBN 0-87306-051-2). Feldheim.

Biberman, Herbert. Salt of the Earth: The Story of a Film. Cortes, Carlos E., ed. LC 76-1248. (Chicano Heritage Ser.). (Illus.). 1976. Repr. of 1965 ed. 14.00x (ISBN 0-405-09486-8). Ayer Co Pubs.

Biberman, L. M., ed. Perception of Displayed Information. LC 72-97695. (Optical Physics & Engineering Ser.). (Illus.). 345p. 1973. 55.00 (ISBN 0-306-30724-3, Plenum Pr). Plenum Pub.

Biberman, L. M. & Nudelman, S., eds. Photoelectronic Imaging Devices, 2 vols. Incl. Vol. 1, Physical Processes & Methods of Analysis. 430p. 59.50x (ISBN 0-306-37081-6); Vol. 2, Devices & Their Evaluation. 584p. 75.00x (ISBN 0-306-37082-4). LC 74-120029. (Optical Physics & Engineering Ser.). 1971 (Plenum Pr). Plenum Pub.

Bibesco, Elizabeth. Whole Story. facsimile ed. LC 75-403493. (Short Story Index Reprint Ser.). 1926. 19.00 (ISBN 0-8369-3235-8). Ayer Co Pubs.

Bibiena, Ferdinando G. Da. Architettura Civile. LC 68-57184. (Illus., It). 1969. 50.00 (ISBN 0-405-08268-1, Blom Pubns). Ayer Co Pubs.

Bibiena, Giuseppe. Architectural & Perspective Designs. (Illus.). 1740. pap. 8.50 (ISBN 0-486-21263-7). Dover.

Bibiena, Giuseppe G. Architectural & Perspective Designs. (Illus.). 16.50 (ISBN 0-8446-1676-1). Peter Smith.

Bibikov, Y. N. Local Theory of Nonlinear Analytic Ordinary Differential Equations. (Lecture Notes in Mathematics: Vol. 702). 1979. pap. 14.00 (ISBN 0-387-09114-9). Springer-Verlag.

Bibin, T., jt. auth. see Fries, Yvonne.

Bible, Douglas S. Real Estate Principles & Practices: Study Questions & Problems. 10th ed. 192p. Date not set. 10.95 (ISBN 0-13-766007-3). P-H.

Bible, Ken. Beacon Small-Group Bible Studies, Genesis, Pt. II: God's Hand in History. Wolf, Earl C., ed. 96p. (Orig.). 1986. pap. 2.50 (ISBN 0-8341-0958-1). Beacon Hill.

Bible, Roy H., Jr. Guide to the NMR Empirical Method: A Workbook. LC 66-11695. 305p. 1967. 32.50 (ISBN 0-306-30233-0, Plenum Pr). Plenum Pub.

--Interpretation of NMR Spectra: An Empirical Approach. LC 64-20741. 150p. 1965. 29.50x (ISBN 0-306-30187-3, Plenum Pr). Plenum Pub.

Bible Temple. The Home Fellowship Meetings. rev. ed. 1975. 4.25 (ISBN 0-914936-14-X). Bible Temple.

Bible, W. & Petkoff, B., eds. Artifical Intelligence: Methodology, Systems, Applications: Proceedings of the International Conference on Artificial Intelligence Varna, Bulgaria, 17-20 Sept., 1984. 248p. 1985. 44.50 (ISBN 0-444-87743-6, North Holland). Elsevier.

Biblio Press. Telegram & Other Gram Rhymes for All Occasions: Any Occasion, That Occasion & Most Occasions. 15p. 1984. pap. text ed. 2.75 (ISBN 0-939476-19-3, Pub. by Biblio Pr GA). Prosperity & Profits.

Bibliographic Research Library Staff. Terrace & Row Houses in Architectural Design: A Selected Bibliography. (Architecture Ser.: Bibliography A-1311). 6p. 1985. pap. 2.00 (ISBN 0-89028-241-2). Vance Biblios.

Bibliographic Society of Northern Illinois. Index to Reviews of Bibliographical Publications, 1978, Vol. 3. Oggel, Terry, ed. 1979. lib. bdg. 27.50 (ISBN 0-8161-8477-1, Hall Reference). G K Hall.

Bibliographical Society of the University of Virginia. William Faulkner: "Man Working", 1919-1962. 1983. 27.50 (ISBN 0-686-89625-4). U Pr of Va.

Bibliotheca Press. Farmer's Markets in the U. S. & Some Other Countries: A Directory. 60p. 1986. pap. text ed. 4.95 (ISBN 0-939476-78-9, Pub. by Biblio Pr GA). Prosperity & Profits.

--Groomed for Doom. (Situational Series for Plays, Skits, etc.: Bk. 2). 14p. 1984. pap. text ed. 2.95 (ISBN 0-317-11742-4, Pub. by Biblio Pr GA). Prosperity & Profits.

--Groomed for Doom. (Situational Series for Plays, Skits, etc.: Bk. 1). 16p. 1984. pap. text ed. 2.95 (ISBN 0-317-11744-0, Pub. by Biblio Pr GA). Prosperity & Profits.

--Nosie the Research Hound. 50p. 1986. pap. 2.75 (ISBN 0-939476-22-3, Pub. by Biblio Pr GA). Prosperity & Profits.

--Recycling Suggestions for Home, Business, Associations, Government etc. 60p. 1986. pap. text ed. 9.95 (ISBN 0-939476-83-5, Pub. by Bibio Pr GA). Prosperity & Profits.

Bibliotheca Press, compiled by. Bibliotheca Press Subject Notebook with Bibliographic Information. 300p. 1983. notebook 35.00 (ISBN 0-939476-64-9, Pub. by Biblio Pr GA). Biblio Pr GA.

Bibliotheca Press, ed. Prescriptions for Survival Index. LC 82-70345. 102p. 1982. pap. text ed. 14.95 (ISBN 0-939476-43-6, Pub. by Biblio Pr GA). Prosperity & Profits.

--Single Source: A Bibliography for Singles. 75p. 1982. pap. 5.95 (ISBN 0-939476-71-1, Pub. by Biblio Pr GA). Prosperity & Profits.

Bibliotheca Press Consulting Services. Suggestions for Using the Piggyback Concept. 6p. pap. 3.95 (ISBN 0-317-01535-4, Pub. by Biblio Pr GA). Prosperity & Profits.

Bibliotheca Press Educational Division. Fundraiser's Workbook: Based on Guide for Fundraisers. 8.95 (ISBN 0-939476-76-2, Pub. by Biblio Pr GA). Prosperity & Profits.

--Recycling Workbook: Based on Recycling for Living, Fun & Profit. 50p. 1983. 5.95 (ISBN 0-939476-50-9, Pub. by Biblio Pr GA). Prosperity & Profits.

--Small Press Publishers Workbook. 50p. 1983. wkbk. 19.95 (ISBN 0-939476-77-0, Pub. by Biblio Pr GA). Prosperity & Profits.

Bibliotheca Press Research. How to Be Your Own Publisher, Advertiser, Promoter, Etc. Date not set. pap. 12.95 (ISBN 0-939476-18-5, Pub. by Biblio Pr GA). Prosperity & Profits.

Bibliotheca Press Research Division. Almost Meat: Nutritional Foods that Can Be Prepared to Taste Like Meat. 50p. 1983. pap. 1.95 (ISBN 0-939476-60-6, Pub. by Biblio Pr GA). Prosperity & Profits.

Bibliotheca Press Research Division, compiled by. The Baby Index. 300p. 1983. pap. 3.95 (ISBN 0-939476-66-5, Pub. by Biblio Pr GA). Prosperity & Profits.

Bibliotheca Press Research Division. Barter Update Directory. 100p. 1983. pap. text ed. 5.95 (ISBN 0-939476-53-3, Pub. by Biblio Pr GA). Prosperity & Profits.

--Guide for Fundraisers. 52p. 1981. pap. text ed. 3.75 (ISBN 0-939476-30-4, Pub. by Biblio Pr GA). Prosperity & Profits.

--Recycling for Living, Fun & Profit. 52p. 1981. pap. text ed. 5.00 (ISBN 0-939476-29-0, Pub. by Biblio Pr GA). Prosperity & Profits.

--Self-Sufficiency & Back to Basics Workbook. 60p. Date not set. 4.95 (ISBN 0-939476-81-9, Pub. by Biblio GA). Prosperity & Profits.

--An Unescorted Women. 1986. pap. 3.00 (ISBN 0-939476-26-6, Pub. by Biblio Pr GA). Prosperity & Profits.

Bibliotheca Press Research Project. The Directory of Special Black Libraries, Museums, Halls of Fames, Colleges, Art Galleries, Etc. 62p. 1983. text ed. 6.00 (ISBN 0-939476-90-8, Pub. by Biblio Pr GA). Prosperity & Profits.

--Selected Topics on Creative Ways to Recycle. (A Recycling Ser.). 1983. text ed. 29.95 (ISBN 0-939476-88-6, Pub. by Biblio Pr GA); pap. text ed. 15.95 (ISBN 0-939476-89-4). Prosperity & Profits.

Bibliotheca Press Research Staff. A Bibliography on Consulting. 25p. 1982. pap. text ed. 2.75 (ISBN 0-939476-70-3, Pub. by Biblio Pr GA). Prosperity & Profits.

--A Bibliography on Fundraising. 50p. 1982. pap. text ed. 2.75 (ISBN 0-939476-73-8, Pub. by Bibio Pr GA). Prosperity & Profits.

--A Bibliography on Travel. 50p. 1982. pap. text ed. 2.75 (ISBN 0-939476-72-X, Pub. by Biblio Pr GA). Prosperity & Profits.

--A Series of Suggestions. 300p. 1983. text ed. 75.00 (ISBN 0-939476-92-4, Pub. by Biblio Pr GA). Prosperity & Profits.

Bibliotheca Press Research Staff, ed. The Children's Index. LC 81-71747. 200p. (Orig.). 1982. pap. text ed. 4.75 (ISBN 0-939476-44-4, Pub. by Biblio Pr GA). Prosperity & Profits.

Bibliotheca Press Research Staff, compiled by. Prosperity References. 35p. 1983. pap. 1.25 (ISBN 0-939476-62-2, Pub. by Biblio Pr GA). Prosperity & Profits.

Bibliotheca Press Research Staff, ed. The Self Sufficiency & Back to Basics Index. LC 82-70238. 55p. (Orig.). 1982. pap. text ed. 6.95 (ISBN 0-939476-46-0, Pub. by Biblio Pr GA). Prosperity & Profits.

Bibliotheca Press Staff. Cookbooks & Recipes for Almost Nothing & More. 75p. 1983. pap. text ed. 6.95 (ISBN 0-939476-67-3, Pub. by Biblio Pr GA). Prosperity & Profits.

--How to Make Simple Potpourri to Give As Gifts. (Creativity Workbook Ser.). 20p. 1984. pap. 3.95 (ISBN 0-317-11741-6, Pub. by Biblio Pr GA). Prosperity & Profits.

--On This Day We Will Pray: Prayers for Sunday Through Saturday. 7p. 1986. pap. 1.75 (ISBN 0-939476-19-3, Pub. by Biblio Pr GA). Prosperity & Profits.

--Vegetarian Cookbooks: A Directory. 70p. 1983. pap. text ed. 3.95 (ISBN 0-939476-68-1, Pub. by Biblio Pr GA). Prosperity & Profits.

Bibliotheca Press Staff, ed. The Cultural & Ethnic Cookbook Index. 60p. 1983. pap. 4.95 (ISBN 0-939476-69-X, Pub. by Biblio Pr GA). Prosperity & Profits.

--Why Not an Answering Service? Telephone Answering Service Ideas. LC 83-90692. 50p. 1983. pap. text ed. 1.95 (ISBN 0-939476-65-7, Pub. by Biblio Pr GA). Prosperity & Profits.

Bibliotheek der Rijksuniversiteit Utrecht, Department of Classification, ed. Dutch Theses Nineteen Seventy-Seven. 132p. 1980. text ed. 30.95 (ISBN 90-265-0330-X, Pub. by Swets Pub Serv Holland). Swets North Am.

Bibliotheek der Rijksunviersiteit Utrecht, Department of Classification, ed. Dutch Theses Nineteen Seventy-Nine. viii, 140p. 1983. text ed. 30.95 (ISBN 90-265-0483-7, Pub. by Swets Pub Serv Holland). Swets North Am.

Bibliotheek der Rijsuniversiteit Utrecht, Department of Classification, ed. Dutch Theses Nineteen Seventy-Eight. x, 136p. 1982. text ed. 30.95 (ISBN 90-265-0388-1, Pub. by Swets Pub Serv Holland). Swets North Am.

Bibliotheque du Musee de l'Homme, Paris. Catalogue Systematique de la Section Afrique (Classified Catalog of the Africa Section, 2 Vols. 1970. Set. lib. bdg. 150.00 (ISBN 0-8161-0827-7, Hall Library). G K Hall.

Bibliotheque Forney. Davis Catalog of Periodical Articles-Decorative & Fine Arts, 4 vols. 1972. Set. lib. bdg. 395.00 (ISBN 0-8161-0965-6, Hall Library). G K Hall.

--Davis Catalog of the Catalogs of Sales of Art, 2 vols. 1972. Set. lib. bdg. 198.00 (ISBN 0-8161-0962-1, Hall Library). G K Hall.

Bibliotheque Imperiale Publique de St. Petersbourg. Catalogue de la Section des Russica: Ecrits Sur la Russie en Langues Etrangere, 2 Vols. LC 72-115679. 1970. Repr. of 1873 ed. Set. lib. bdg. 125.00 (ISBN 0-306-71933-9). Da Capo.

Bibliotheque Nationale. Catalogue General des Livres Imprimes: Auteurs, Collectivites, Auteurs Anonymes (1960-1969, 15 tomes. Set. 1350.00 (ISBN 0-685-35975-1). French & Eur.

--Catalogue Generale des Livres Imprimes: Auteurs, Collectivites-Auteurs, Anonymes, 1960-1969, 15 vols. (Serie I). 1350.00 (ISBN 0-685-11067-2). French & Eur.

Bibliotheque Nationale. Departement des Imprimes, Paris. Catalogue de l'histoire de l'Afrique. LC 77-126406. Repr. of 1895 ed. lib. bdg. 25.50 (ISBN 0-8337-3986-7). B Franklin.

--Catalogue des Ouvrages de Chateaubriand. LC 78-132534. (Bibliography & Reference Ser.: No. 394). 1971. Repr. of 1906 ed. lib. bdg. 15.00 (ISBN 0-8337-0754-X). B Franklin.

Bibliotheque Nationale, Paris. Catalogue de l'histoire de l'Amerique, 6 vols. 1971. Repr. of 1903 ed. Set. lib. bdg. 264.00 (ISBN 0-8337-0177-0). B Franklin.

--Inventaire de la Collection Anisson sur l'histoire de l'imprimerie et la librarie, 2 Vols. Coyecque, Ernest, compiled by. 1964. Repr. of 1900 ed. Set. 59.00 (ISBN 0-8337-0711-6). B Franklin.

Bibliowicz, Meryl, jt. auth. see Goldstein, Paula.

Bibo, Istvan. The Paralysis of International Institutions & the Remedies: A Study of Self-Determination, Concord Among the Major Powers & Political Arbitration. LC 75-17182. 152p. 1976. cloth 37.95x (ISBN 0-470-07208-3). Halsted Pr.

Bibring, Grete L. & Kahana, Ralph J. Lectures in Medical Psychology: An Introduction to the Care of Patients. LC 68-57279. 289p. 1969. text ed. 27.50 (ISBN 0-8236-2970-8). Intl Univs Pr.

Bibring, Grete L., ed. The Teaching of Dynamic Psychiatry: A Reappraisal of the Goals & Techniques in the Teaching of Psychoanalytic Psychiatry. LC 67-27426. 277p. 1968. text ed. 27.50 (ISBN 0-8236-6380-9). Intl Univs Pr.

Bic, Lubomir. MICOS: A Microprogrammable Computer Simulator. LC 82-23627. 123p. 1983. pap. 15.95 (ISBN 0-914894-76-5); IBM diskette 17.50 (ISBN 0-88175-018-2); Apple diskette 17.50 (ISBN 0-88175-029-8). Computer Sci.

Bican, et al. Rings, Modules, & Preradicals. 264p. 1982. 45.00 (ISBN 0-8247-1568-3). Dekker.

Bicanic, R. Economic Policy in Socialist Yugoslavia. LC 72-80588. (Soviet & East European Studies). (Illus.). 270p. 1973. 52.50 (ISBN 0-521-08631-0). Cambridge U Pr.

Bicanic, Rudolf. Problems of Planning, East & West. (Publications of the Institute of Social Studies: No. 15). 1967. text ed. 11.60x (ISBN 90-2790-112-0). Mouton.

Bice, Christopher. Cornish Phrase Book: Lyver Lavarow Kernewek. pap. 4.95 (ISBN 0-686-25500-3). British Am Bks.

Bice, David A. The Legend of John Henry - the Steel Drivin' Man. (The Pringle Tree Ser.). (Illus.). 32p. (gr. 3-6). 1980. PLB 5.95 (ISBN 0-934750-05-X). Jalamap.

--Mad Anne Bailey. (The Pringle Tree Ser.). (Illus.). 36p. (gr. 3-6). 1980. 6.95 (ISBN 0-934750-06-8). Jalamap.

--A Panorama of Tennessee. LC 83-80152. (Illus.). 285p. 1984. 14.99 (ISBN 0-934750-38-6); 4.00 (ISBN 0-934750-39-4); 3.25 (ISBN 0-934750-40-8). Jalamap.

--A Panorama of West Virginia. LC 79-89608. 319p. (gr. 8). 1979. text ed. 12.95 (ISBN 0-934750-00-9); tchr's guide 4.00 (ISBN 0-934750-01-7); wkbk. 3.50 (ISBN 0-934750-03-3). Jalamap.

--A Panorama of West Virginia. (Illus.). 319p. 1981. 15.95 (ISBN 0-934750-08-4); pap. 13.95 (ISBN 0-934750-15-7). Jalamap.

--The Pringle Tree. rev. ed. (Illus.). 54p. (gr. 3). 1981. PLB 5.95 (ISBN 0-934750-12-2); pap. 4.95 (ISBN 0-934750-11-4). Jalamap.

Bice, David A. & Jones, Helen. West Virginia & the Appalachians. 100p. 1983. 8.95 (ISBN 0-934750-47-5); pap. 5.00 (ISBN 0-934750-46-7); wkbk. 2.99 (ISBN 0-934750-49-1); tchr's. ed. 4.00 (ISBN 0-934750-48-3). Jalamap.

Bice, David A., et al. A Panorama of Florida. Armstrong, Alfredlene, ed. (Illus.). 320p. 1982. 15.95 (ISBN 0-934750-13-0); text ed. 14.99 (ISBN 0-934750-21-1). tchrs. ed. 14.99 (ISBN 0-934750-27-0); wkbk. 3.99 (ISBN 0-934750-22-X); tchrs. wkbk. 4.25 (ISBN 0-934750-23-8). Jalamap.

Bice, Thomas, jt. auth. see Salkever, David.

Bicentennial Space Symposium. New Themes for Space - Mankind's Future Needs & Aspirations: Proceedings. Schneider, William C., ed. & intro. by. LC 57-43769. (Advances in the Astronautical Sciences Ser.: Vol. 35). (Illus.). 1977. lib. bdg. 25.00x (ISBN 0-87703-090-1, Pub. by Am Astronaut). Univelt Inc.

Bice-Stephens, Nona. The Arts of Nursing. (Contemporary Poets of Dorrance Ser.). 1983. 5.95 (ISBN 0-8059-2899-5). Dorrance.

Bicha, Karel D. The Czechs in Oklahoma. LC 79-19734. (Newcomers to a New Land Ser.: Vol. 2). (Illus.). 81p. (Orig.). 1980. pap. 4.95 (ISBN 0-8061-1618-8). U of Okla Pr.

--Western Populism: Studies in an Ambivalent Conservatism. (Illus.). 1976. 8.50 (ISBN 0-87291-085-7). Coronado Pr.

Bichakjian, Bernhard H., ed. From Linguistics to Literature: Romance Studies Offered to Francis M. Rogers. 292p. 1981. 35.00x (ISBN 90-272-2007-7). Benjamins North Am.

Bichat, Marie F. Physiological Researches on Life & Death. Kastenbaum, Robert, ed. Gold, F. & Magendie, F., trs. LC 76-19561. (Death & Dying Ser.). 1977. Repr. lib. bdg. 30.00x (ISBN 0-405-09557-0). Ayer Co Pubs.

Bichat, Xavier. Physiological Researches on Life & Death. Gold, F., tr. from Fr. Bd. with Outlines of Phrenology; Phrenology Examined. (Contributions to the History of Psychology, Vol. II, Pt. E: Physiological Psychology). 1978. Repr. of 1827 ed. 30.00 (ISBN 0-89093-175-5). U Pubns Amer.

Bicher, Haim I. & Bruley, Duane F., eds. Hyperthermia. LC 82-18047. (Advances in Experimental Medicine & Biology Ser.: Vol. 157). 202p. 1982. 39.50x (ISBN 0-306-41172-5, Plenum Pr). Plenum Pub.

--Oxygen Transport to Tissue IV. (Advances in Experimental Medicine & Biology: Vol. 159). 650p. 1983. 85.00x (ISBN 0-306-41192-X, Plenum Pr). Plenum Pub.

--Oxygen Transport to Tissue, Vol. 1, 2 pts, Vol. I. Incl. Pt. A, Instrumentation, Methods, & Physiology. 702p. 1973. 75.00x (ISBN 0-306-39093-0); Pt. B: Pharmacology, Mathematical Studies & Neonatology. 552p. 1973. 69.50x (ISBN 0-306-39094-9). LC 73-13821. (Advances in Experimental Medicine & Biology Ser.: Vols. 37A & 37B, Plenum Pr). Plenum Pub.

Bichowsky, F. Russell. Industrial Research. LC 72-5033. (Technology & Society Ser.). (Illus.). 132p. 1972. Repr. of 1942 ed. 14.00 (ISBN 0-405-04686-3). Ayer Co Pubs.

Bichsel, Peter. Stories for Children. Hamberger, Michael, tr. from Ger. 60p. 1984. pap. 5.95 (ISBN 0-7145-0689-3). M Boyars.

Bichteler, K. Stochastic Integration & Stochastic Differential Equations. (North-Holland Mathematics Studies). 1984. write for info. (North-Holland). Elsevier.

Bick, Edgard M., ed. Classics of Orthopaedics. (Illus.). 1976. 36.00 (ISBN 0-397-58194-7, 65-70196, Lippincott Medical). Lippincott.

Bick, H. Ciliated Protozoa: An Illustrated Guide to the Species Used As Biological Indicators in Fresh Water Biology. 198p. 1972. pap. 9.60 (ISBN 92-4-154028-1, 1308). World Health.

Bick, Rodger L., jt. ed. see Murano, Genesio.

Bick, Roger L., ed. Disseminated Intravascular Coagulation & Related Syndromes. 144p. 1983. 57.00 (ISBN 0-8493-6636-4). CRC Pr.

Bickart, Theodore, jt. auth. see Balabanian, Norman.

Bickel, Alexander M. The Caseload of the Supreme Court: And What If Anything to Do About It? 37p. 1973. pap. 3.25 (ISBN 0-8447-3121-8). Am Enterprise.

--The Least Dangerous Branch: The Supreme Court at the Bar of Politics. LC 62-20685. pap. 78.80 (ISBN 0-317-28616-1, 2055404). Bks Demand UMI.

--The Morality of Consent. LC 75-10988. 176p. 1975. 21.00x (ISBN 0-300-01911-4); pap. 6.95x (ISBN 0-300-02119-4). Yale U Pr.

--Politics & the Warren Court. LC 73-398. (American Constitutional & Legal History Ser.). 314p. 1973. Repr. of 1955 ed. lib. bdg. 35.00 (ISBN 0-306-70573-7). Da Capo.

--The Supreme Court & the Idea of Progress. LC 77-18365. 1978. 20.00x (ISBN 0-300-02238-7); pap. 8.95x (ISBN 0-300-02239-5). Yale U Pr.

Bickel, Alexander M. & Schmidt, Benno C., Jr. History of the Supreme Court of the United States: The Judiciary & Responsible Government 1910-1921, Vol. IV. (Illus.). 1984. 75.00 (ISBN 0-02-541420-8). Macmillan.

Bickel, Bruce, ed. see Jantz, Stan & Jantz, Karin.

Bickel, H. & Schutz, Y., eds. Digestion & Absorption of Nutrients. (International Journal for Vitamin & Nutrition Research, Supplement: No. 25). (Illus.). 94p. (Orig.). 1983. pap. 15.00 (ISBN 3-456-81335-X, Pub. by Hans Huber). J K Burgess.

Bickel, H., et al, eds. Neonatal Screening for Inborn Errors of Metabolism. (Illus.). 300p. 1980. 56.00 (ISBN 0-387-09779-1). Springer-Verlag.

Bickel, Hans, ed. Palatability & Flavor Use in Animal Feeds. (Advances in Animal Physiology & Animal Nutrition: Vol. 11). (Illus.). 148p. (Orig.). 1980. pap. text ed. 34.10 (ISBN 3-490-41115-3). Parey Sci Pubs.

Bickel, John O. & Kuesel, T. R., eds. Tunnel Engineering Handbook. 640p. 1982. 57.50 (ISBN 0-442-28127-7). Van Nos Reinhold.

Bickel, Lennard. The Deadly Element: The Story of Uranium. LC 78-66243. (Illus.). 320p. 1980. pap. 7.95 (ISBN 0-8128-6089-6). Stein & Day.

Bickel, Margot & Steigert, Hermann. Harvest the Day. Frost, Gerhard E., ed. (Illus.). 64p. (Orig.). pap. 7.95 (ISBN 0-86683-730-2). Winston Pr.

Bickel, P. J. & Doksum, K. A. Mathematical Statistics: Basic Ideas & Selected Topics. LC 76-8724. 1977. 40.00x (ISBN 0-8162-0784-4). Holden-Day.

Bickel, Peter J. & Doksum, Kjell, eds. A Festschrift for Erich L. Lehmann. (Wadsworth Statistics-Probability Ser.). 461p. 1982. write for info. (ISBN 0-534-98044-9). Wadsworth Pub.

Bickel, Peter J., ed. see Becker, Richard A., et al.

Bickel, Robert D., ed. The College Administrator & the Courts. 1978. write for info. Coll Admin Pubns.

Bickel, Walter, ed. Hering's Dictionary of Classical & Modern Cookery. 5th ed. 1974. 39.95 (ISBN 0-8436-2189-3, Pub. by Virtuea Col Ltd. England). Van Nos Reinhold.

Bickel, Walter, tr. see Hering, Richard.

Bickelhaupt, David L. General Insurance. 11th ed. 1983. text ed. 28.95x (ISBN 0-256-02821-4). Irwin.

Bickelhaupt, David L. & Bar-Niv, Ran. International Insurance: Managing Risk in the World. 176p. 1983. text ed. 15.95 (ISBN 0-932387-03-9); pap. 9.95 (ISBN 0-932387-04-7). Insur Info.

Bickerdyke, John. The Curiosities of Ale & Beer. LC 78-174387. (Illus.). Repr. of 1889 ed. 22.00 (ISBN 0-405-08269-X, Blom Pubns). Ayer Co Pubs.

Bickerman, E. J. Chronology of the Ancient World. 2nd ed. (Aspects of Greek & Roman Life Ser.). (Illus.). 260p. 1980. 27.50x (ISBN 0-8014-1282-X). Cornell U Pr.

Bickerman, Elias. Four Strange Books of the Bible: Jonah, Daniel, Koheleth, Esther. (Illus.). 252p. 1984. pap. 8.95 (ISBN 0-8052-0774-0). Schocken.

--From Ezra to the Last of the Maccabees: Foundations of Post-Biblical Judaism. 1962. pap. 4.95 (ISBN 0-8052-0036-3). Schocken.

Bickerman, Elias & Smith, Morton. The Ancient History of Western Civilization. (Illus.). 288p. 1976. scp 15.95 (ISBN 0-06-040668-2, HarpC). Har-Row.

Bickerman, Elias J., ed. see Rostovtzeff, Mikhail I.

Bickers, Bernard W., jt. auth. see Holmes, Derek J.

Bickers, David R., jt. auth. see Harber, Leonard C.

Bickers, David R., et al, eds. Clinical Pharmacology of Skin Disease. (Monographs in Clinical Pharmacology: Vol. 7). (Illus.). 321p. 1984. text ed. 39.50 (ISBN 0-443-08057-7). Churchill.

Bickerstaff, Issac. The Plays of Isaac Bickerstaff, 3 vols. Tasch, Peter A., ed. (Eighteenth Century English Drama Ser.). 1981. lib. bdg. 218.00 (ISBN 0-8240-3578-X). Garland Pub.

Bickerstaff, Laura. Pioneer Artists of Taos. rev. ed. 1984. 25.00 (ISBN 0-912094-21-4). Old West.

Bickerstaffe-Drew, Francis B. Discourses & Essays. facsimile ed. LC 78-107683. (Essay Index Reprint Ser.). Repr. of 1922 ed. 18.00 (ISBN 0-8369-1489-9). Ayer Co Pubs.

--Levia-Pondera. facs. ed. LC 67-26715. (Essay Index Reprint Ser). 1913. 20.00 (ISBN 0-8369-0210-6). Ayer Co Pubs.

Bickerstaffe-Drew, Frank. John Ayscough's Letters to His Mother, During 1914, 1915, & 1916. 1919. 15.00 (ISBN 0-932062-07-5). Sharon Hill.

Bickersteth, Edward H. Holy Spirit. LC 59-13640. 1976. pap. 4.95 (ISBN 0-8254-2227-2). Kregel.

--The Trinity. LC 59-13770. 1976. pap. 5.95 (ISBN 0-8254-2226-4). Kregel.

Bickersteth, Geoffrey, tr. see Dante Alighieri.

Bickersteth, Geoffrey L. The Golden World of "King Lear". 1978. Repr. of 1946 ed. lib. bdg. 12.50 (ISBN 0-8482-0332-1). Norwood Edns.

--Golden World of" King Lear". 1979. 28.50 (ISBN 0-685-94332-1). Porter.

--The Golden World of "King Lear". A Lecture. LC 73-9789. lib. bdg. 10.00 (ISBN 0-8414-3174-4). Folcroft.

--Leopardi & Wordsworth: A Lecture. LC 73-9786. lib. bdg. 10.00 (ISBN 0-8414-3175-2). Folcroft.

Bickersteth, J. Burgon. The Land of Open Doors: Being Letters from Western Canada, 1911-1913. LC 76-41611. 1976. pap. 7.50 (ISBN 0-8020-6266-0). U of Toronto Pr.

Bickerton. Neurology for Nurses. (Illus.). 216p. 1982. pap. text ed. 18.00 (ISBN 0-8391-1742-6). Univ Park.

Bickerton, D. Dynamics of a Creole System. LC 74-12971. (Illus.). 288p. 1975. 39.50 (ISBN 0-521-20514-X). Cambridge U Pr.

Bickerton, Derek. Roots of Language. (Illus.). xiii, 351p. 1981. 24.95x (ISBN 0-89720-044-6). Karoma.

Bickerton, Derek, et al. The Genesis of Language: The First Michigan Colloquium, 1979. Hill, Kenneth C., ed. 159p. 1979. 15.50 (ISBN 0-89720-024-1); pap. 12.50 (ISBN 0-89720-025-X). Karoma.

Bickerton, L. M. English Drinking Glasses, 1675-1825. (Shire Album Ser.: No. 116). (Illus.). 32p. (Orig.). 1984. pap. 2.95 (ISBN 0-85263-661-X, Pub. by Shire Pubns England). Seven Hills Bks.

Bicket, Zenas J. The Effective Pastor. LC 74-80729. 185p. 1973. 3.95 (ISBN 0-88243-512-4, 02-0512). Gospel Pub.

--Walking in the Spirit. LC 76-51000. 96p. 1977. pap. 1.25 (ISBN 0-88243-611-2, 02-0611, Radiant Bks). Gospel Pub.

--We Hold These Truths. LC 78-56133. (Workers Training Book of the Year). (Illus.). 128p. 1978. pap. 1.50 (ISBN 0-88243-631-7, 02-0631). Gospel Pub.

Bickford. An Introduction to the Design & Behavior of Bolted Joints. (Mechanical Engineering Ser.). 632p. 1981. 59.75 (ISBN 0-8247-1508-X). Dekker.

Bickford, Charlene B. & Veit, Helen E. Documentary History of the First Federal Congress of the United States of America, March 4, 1789-March 3, 1791: Legislative Histories: Funding Act (HR-63) Through Militia Bill (HR-112, Vol. 5. LC 84-15465. 864p. 1985. text ed. 42.50x (ISBN 0-8018-3167-9). Johns Hopkins.

Bickford, Charlene B. & Veit, Helen E., eds. Documentary History of the First Federal Congress of the United States of America, March 4, 1789-March 3, 1791: Legislative Histories: Amendments to the Constitution Through Foreign Officers Bill (HR-116, Vol. 4. LC 84-15465. 736p. 1985. text ed. 37.50 (ISBN 0-8018-3163-6). Johns Hopkins.

--Documentary History of the First Federal Congress of the United States of America, March 4, 1789-March 3, 1791: Legislative Histories: Mitigation of Fines Bill (HR-38) Through Resolution on Unclaimed Western Lands, Vol. 6. LC 84-15465. 720p. 1985. text ed. 37.50x (ISBN 0-8018-3169-5). Johns Hopkins.

Bickford, Christopher P. Farmington in Connecticut. LC 82-18575. (Illus.). 496p. 1982. 19.95 (ISBN 0-914016-92-X). Phoenix Pub.

Bickford, J. P. & Mullineux, N. Computation of Power-System Transients. (IEE Monograph Ser.: No. 18). 186p. 1980. pap. 32.00 (ISBN 0-906048-35-4). Inst Elect Eng.

Bickford, John H. Mechanisms for Intermittent Motion. LC 75-184639. 272p. 1972. 28.50 (ISBN 0-8311-1091-0). Krieger.

Bickford, Maggie, et al. Bones of Jade, Soul of Ice: The Flowering Plum in Chinese Art. Schwartz, Sheila & Hofmaier, Barbara, eds. (Illus.). 256p. (Orig.). 1985. pap. 18.95x (ISBN 0-89467-032-8). Yale Art Gallery.

Bickford, Marion E. & Mose, D. G. Geochronology of Precambrian Rocks in the St. Francois Mountains, Southeastern Missouri. LC 75-25345. (Geological Society of America Special Paper Ser.: No. 165). pap. 20.00 (ISBN 0-317-30059-8, 2025033). Bks Demand UMI.

Bickford, Paul. Poems & Other Stuff. (Illus.). 37p. 1982. pap. 4.95x (ISBN 0-910303-00-2). Writers Pub Serv.

Bickford, Sam. Pilippino-English: English-Pilippino Concise Dictionary. (Hippocrene Concise Dictionaries Ser.). 550p. 1985. pap. 5.95 (ISBN 0-87052-028-8). Hippocrene Bks.

Bickford, Ted, jt. auth. see Arnell, Peter.

Bickford, Ted, ed. see Andrews, Mason.

Bickford, Ted, jt. ed. see Arnell, Peter.

Bickford, Ted, ed. see Stern, Robert A.

Bickford, Vahadah O. Method for Classic Guitar. pap. 10.00 (ISBN 0-686-09073-X). Peer-Southern.

Bickford, Zarh M. Twentieth Century Tenor Banjo Method, Bk. I. 1941. 1.25 (ISBN 0-913650-25-0). Columbia Pictures.

Bickham, George. The Universal Penman. (Illus.). 1941. pap. 10.95 (ISBN 0-486-20616-5). Dover.

--The Universal Penman. (Illus.). 18.50 (ISBN 0-8446-4712-8). Peter Smith.

Bickham, Jack. All the Days Were Summer. 224p. 1982. pap. 2.25 (ISBN 0-448-16926-6, Pub. by Tempo). Ace Bks.

--Baker's Hawk. 240p. 1984. pap. 2.50 (ISBN 0-441-04690-8). Ace Bks.

--Gunman's Gamble. 184p. 1981. pap. 1.95 (ISBN 0-441-30810-4). Ace Bks.

--Halls of Dishonor. (Orig.). 1980. pap. 2.50 (ISBN 0-671-82508-9). PB.

--Hangmen's Territory. 1981. pap. 1.95 (ISBN 0-441-31632-8). Ace Bks.

Bickham, Jack M. The Apple Dumpling Gang. 192p. 1983. pap. 1.95 (ISBN 0-441-02587-0). Ace Bks.

--Ariel. LC 84-11740. 416p. 1984. 15.95 (ISBN 0-312-04917-X). St Martin.

--Ariel. 384p. 1985. pap. 3.95 (ISBN 0-8125-8086-9, Dist. by Pinnacle Bks, Warner Pub Services & St. Martin). Tor Bks.

--The Regensburg Legacy. 320p. 1985. pap. 3.50 (ISBN 0-8125-8088-5, Dist. by Warner Pub Services & St. Martin). Tor Bks.

Bickhard, Mark H. Cognition, Convention, & Communication. LC 80-20799. 288p. 1980. 37.95x (ISBN 0-03-056098-5). Praeger.

--On the Nature of Representation: A Case Study of James Gibson's Theory of Perception. 122p. 1983. text ed. 26.95 (ISBN 0-03-069526-0). Praeger.

Bickimer, David Arthur. Christ the Placenta. LC 82-24097. 239p. (Orig.). 1983. pap. 12.95 (ISBN 0-89135-034-9). Religious Educ.

Bicklecombe, Peter. Goodwill, the Wasted Asset. 175p. 1971. 19.95x (ISBN 0-8464-1103-2). Beekman Pubs.

Bickley, A. C. see Gomme, George L., et al.

Bickley, F. L. J. M. Synge & the Irish Dramatic Movement. 59.95 (ISBN 0-8490-0430-6). Gordon Pr.

Bickley, Francis. Life of Matthew Prior. LC 74-2441. 1914. lib. bdg. 25.00 (ISBN 0-8414-9934-9). Folcroft.

Bickley, Francis L. Matthew Arnold & His Poetry. LC 77-120977. Repr. of 1912 ed. 7.25 (ISBN 0-404-52501-6). AMS Pr.

--Matthew Arnold & His Poetry. 1912. 10.00 (ISBN 0-8274-2690-9). R West.

Bickley, George W. L. History of the Settlement & Indian Wars of Tazewell County, Virginia. 1974. 25.00 (ISBN 0-87012-147-2). McClain.

Bickley, Harmon. Modular Concepts in Human Disease. 319p. wkbk. & study guide 7.00 (ISBN 0-318-16768-9). U IA Audiovisual.

Bickley, John S. Impact of a State Disability Act on Insurance Companies. 1954. pap. 1.00x (ISBN 0-87776-071-3, R71). Ohio St U Admin Sci.

--Trends & Problems in the Distribution of Property Liability Insurance. 1956. pap. text ed. 2.00x (ISBN 0-87776-091-8, R91). Ohio St U Admin Sci.

Bickley, N. M. Manual of Etiquette. 18.50 (ISBN 0-87559-116-7). Shalom.

Bickley, Nora, ed. Letters from & to Joseph Joachim. LC 70-183496. 470p. 1972. Repr. of 1914 ed. 45.00x (ISBN 0-8443-0043-8). Vienna Hse.

Bickley, R. Bruce. The Method of Melville's Short Fiction. LC 74-28904. 1975. 14.00 (ISBN 0-8223-0334-5). Duke.

Bickley, R. Bruce, Jr. Critical Essays on Joel Chandler Harris. (Critical Essays on American Literature Ser.). 1981. 26.00 (ISBN 0-8161-8381-3, Twayne). G K Hall.

Bickley, Verner C. & Puthenparampil, J. Philip, eds. Cultural Relations in the Global Community: Problems & Prospects. 1981. 17.50x (ISBN 0-8364-0728-8, Pub. by Abhinav India). South Asia Bks.

Bickman, Jack. Dinah, Blow Your Horn. 224p. 1982. pap. 2.25 (ISBN 0-448-15689-X). Ace Bks.

Bickman, Jack M. I Still Dream about Columbus. LC 82-5742. 240p. 1982. 13.95 (ISBN 0-312-40276-7). St Martin.

Bickman, Leonard, ed. Applied Social Psychology Annual, Vol. 1. (Illus.). 296p. 1981. 28.00 (ISBN 0-8039-1400-8); pap. 14.00 (ISBN 0-8039-1401-6). Sage.

--Applied Social Psychology Annual, Vol. 2. (Illus.). 296p. 1981. 28.00 (ISBN 0-8039-1642-6); pap. 14.00 (ISBN 0-8039-1643-4). Sage.

--Applied Social Psychology Annual, Vol. 3. (Illus.). 312p. 1982. 28.00 (ISBN 0-8039-0796-6); pap. 14.00 (ISBN 0-8039-0797-4). Sage.

--Applied Social Psychology Annual, Vol. 4. 280p. 1983. 28.00 (ISBN 0-8039-2106-3); pap. text ed. 14.00 (ISBN 0-8039-2107-1). Sage.

Bickman, Martin. Approaches to Teaching Melville's "Moby Dick". (Approaches to Teaching Masterpieces of World Literature. Ser.: No. 8). 158p. 1985. 25.00 (ISBN 0-87352-489-6); 14.50 (ISBN 0-87352-490-X). Modern Lang.

--The Unsounded Centre: Jungian Studies in American Romanticism. LC 79-26042. ix, 182p. 1980. 17.50 (ISBN 0-8078-1428-8). U of NC Pr.

Bickmore, Kathy, jt. auth. see Northeast Ohio Alternatives to Violence Committee.

Bicknell & Sines. Community Mental Handicap Care. 1984. pap. text ed. 16.50 (ISBN 0-06-318246-7, Pub. by Har-Row Ltd England). Har-Row.

Bicknell, A. J. Bicknell's Victorian Buildings: Floor Plans & Elevations for 45 Houses & Other Structures. 16.00 (ISBN 0-8446-5737-9). Peter Smith.

--Wooden & Brick Buildings with Details. (Architecture & Decorative Art Ser.). 1977. Repr. of 1875 ed. 85.00 (ISBN 0-306-70832-9). Da Capo.

Bicknell, A. J. & Comstock, William T. Victorian Architecture: Two Pattern Books. LC 75-22530. (Athenaeum Library of Nineteenth Century America). (Illus.). 1975. Repr. 18.00 (ISBN 0-89257-001-6). Am Life Foun.

Bicknell, Arthur. Masterpieces. 1979. pap. 3.35x (ISBN 0-685-95392-0). Dramatists Play.

Bicknell, David L. & Brengle, Richard L., eds. Image & Event: America Now. LC 75-146363. (Illus., Orig.). 1971. pap. text ed. 9.95x (ISBN 0-89197-225-0). Irvington.

Bicknell, F. & Prescott, F. Vitamins in Medicine. 47.50 (ISBN 0-911238-63-8). B Of A.

Bicknell, Franklin. Chemicals in Your Food. LC 61-11031. 1970. 9.95 (ISBN 0-87523-130-6). Emerson.

Bicknell, Peter, ed. see Wordsworth, William.

Bickner, Mei L. & Shaughnessey, Marlene. Women at Work: Annotated Bibliography. 420p. 1977. Vol. II. 12.00 (ISBN 0-89215-064-5). U Cal LA Indus Rel.

Bickner, Robert J., et al, eds. Papers from a Conference on Thai Studies in Honor of William J. Gedney. LC 84-45446. (Michigan Papers on South & Southeast Asia: No. 25). (Illus.). 300p. 1985. 24.95 (ISBN 0-89148-030-7); pap. 11.95 (ISBN 0-89148-031-5). Ctr S&SE Asian.

Bicknese, Gunther. Hier und Heute: Lessen Leicht Gemacht. LC 82-84304. 96p. 1983. pap. text ed. 8.95 (ISBN 0-395-33249-4). HM.

Bicks, Alexander. Contracts for the Sale of Realty. 6th ed. 149p. 1973. 15.00 (ISBN 0-686-79995-X, N1-0333). PLI.

Bicksler, J. L., ed. Handbook of Financial Economics. 470p. 1980. 102.25 (ISBN 0-444-85224-7, North Holland). Elsevier.

Bicksler, James L., ed. Capital Market Equilibrium & Efficiency: Implications for Accounting, Finance, & Portfolio Decision Making. 1977. 41.00x (ISBN 0-669-86660-1). Lexington Bks.

Bicksler, James L. & Samuelson, Paul A., eds. Investment Portfolio Decision-Making. LC 73-1561. 1974. 24.00x (ISBN 0-669-86215-0). Lexington Bks.

Bickston, Diana. Street Birth. (Prison Writing Ser.). 36p. 1982. pap. 2.00 (ISBN 0-912678-52-6). Greenfld Rev Pr.

Bicudo, C. & Sormus, L. Desmidioflorula Paulista II: Genero Micrasterias C. Agardh ex Ralfs. (Bibliotheca Phycologica Ser.: No. 57). (Illus.). 230p. (Span.). 1982. pap. text ed. 31.50x (ISBN 3-7682-1225-4). Lubrecht & Cramer.

Bicudo, C., jt. ed. see Acleto, O.

Bicudo, C. E. & Azevedo, M. T. Desmidioflorula Paulista I: Genero Arthordesmus Ehr. ex Ralfs Emend. Arch. (Bibliotheca Phycologica Ser.: No. 36). (Illus., Port.). 1978. text ed. 14.00 (ISBN 3-7682-1156-8). Lubrecht & Cramer.

Bicudo, C. E. & Samanez, I. M. Desmidioflorula Paulista III: Generos Bambu ina, Desmidium, Groenbladia, Nyalotheca, Onychonema, Phymatodos, Spondylosium, Teilingia. (Bibliotheca Phycologica Ser.: No. 68). (Illus.). 138p. (Port.). 1984. pap. text ed. 17.50x (ISBN 3-7682-1388-9). Lubrecht & Cramer.

Bicudo, Carlos E., jt. auth. see Croasdale, Hannah.

Bicudo, Carlos E., jt. auth. see Prescott, G. W.

Bicudo, Carlos M. Contribution to the Knowledge of the Desmids of the State of Sao Paulo. (Illus.). 1969. 10.00 (ISBN 3-7682-0653-X). Lubrecht & Cramer.

Bicycle Magazine Staff. Bicycle Repair. (Illus., Orig.). 1985. pap. 4.50 (ISBN 0-87857-543-X). Rodale Pr Inc.

Bicycling Magazine Staff. All-Terrain Bikes. Wolf, Ray, ed. 1985. pap. 4.50 (ISBN 0-87857-546-4). Rodale Pr Inc.

--Bicycle Touring. Wolf, Ray, ed. 96p. 1985. pap. 4.50 (ISBN 0-87857-547-2). Rodale Pr Inc.

--Easy Bicycle Maintenance. Wolf, Ray, ed. 1985. 4.50 (ISBN 0-87857-544-8). Rodale Pr Inc.

--Fitness Through Cycling. Wolf, Ray, ed. (Illus., Orig.). 1985. pap. 4.50 (ISBN 0-87857-548-0). Rodale Pr Inc.

--Riding & Racing Techniques. Wolf, Ray, ed. (Illus.). 1985. pap. 4.50 (ISBN 0-87857-545-6). Rodale Pr Inc.

Biczok, I. Concrete Corrosion & Concrete Protection. 3rd ed. 1972. 38.50x (ISBN 0-685-27529-9). Adlers Foreign Bks.

Bidart, Frank. The Book of the Body. 56p. 1977. pap. 4.95 (ISBN 0-374-51438-0). FS&G.

--Golden State. LC 72-94953. 96p. 1973. 5.95 (ISBN 0-8076-0676-6); pap. 2.95 (ISBN 0-8076-0677-4). Braziller.

--The Sacrifice. LC 83-47794. 96p. 1983. 10.00 (ISBN 0-394-53297-X, Vin); pap. 5.95 (ISBN 0-394-71638-8). Random.

Bidault, M. L'Abbe, jt. auth. see Tardy.

Bidder, Hans & Bidder, Irmgard. Filztteppiche. (Illus.). 172p. (Ger.). 1984. pap. 45.00 (ISBN 0-911403-09-4, Pub. by Klinkhardt & Biermann WG). Seven Hills Bks.

Bidder, Irmgard, jt. auth. see Bidder, Hans.

Biddick, Kathleen, ed. Archaeological Approaches to Medical Europe. LC 84-14759. (Studies in Medieval Culture: No. XVIII). (Illus.). 301p. 1985. 27.95x (ISBN 0-918720-53-2); pap. 16.95x (ISBN 0-918720-52-4). Medieval Inst.

Biddiss, Michael D. The Age of the Masses: Ideas & Society in Europe Since 1870. LC 77-7542. 1977. text ed. 25.25x (ISBN 0-391-00736-X). Humanities.

Biddiss, Michael D., ed. Images of Race. LC 78-31825. 259p. 1979. text ed. 32.50x (ISBN 0-8419-0482-0); pap. text ed. 18.00x (ISBN 0-8419-0483-9). Holmes & Meier.

Biddle, A. J. Drexel, Jr. Poland & the Coming of the Second World War: Diplomatic Papers of A. J. Drexel Biddle, Jr., the United States Ambassador to Poland, 1937-1939. Cannistraro, Philip V., et al, eds. LC 75-45433. (Illus.). 374p. 1976. 17.50 (ISBN 0-8142-0237-3). Ohio St U Pr.

Biddle, A. W. Writer to Writer. 256p. 1984. 11.95 (ISBN 0-07-005213-1). McGraw.

Biddle, Arthur. A Treatise on the Law of Warranties in the Sale of Chattels. xx, 308p. 1981. Repr. of 1884 ed. lib. bdg. 30.00x (ISBN 0-8377-0316-6). Rothman.

Biddle, B. J. & Thomas, E. J. Role Theory: Concepts & Research. LC 78-25644. 484p. 1979. Repr. of 1966 ed. lib. bdg. 27.50 (ISBN 0-88275-817-9). Krieger.

Biddle, Bruce J. Role Theory: Expectations, Identities & Behaviors. 1979. 25.00 (ISBN 0-12-095950-X). Acad Pr.

Biddle, Bruce J., jt. auth. see Dunkin, Michael J.

Biddle, Bruce J., jt. ed. see Rossi, Peter H.

Biddle, Bruce J., jt. auth. see Good, Thomas L.

Biddle, Edward & Fielding, Mantle. Life & Works of Thomas Sully. LC 74-77716. (Library of American Art Ser). 1970. Repr. of 1921 ed. lib. bdg. 42.50 (ISBN 0-306-71354-3). Da Capo.

Biddle, Francis. Fear of Freedom. LC 76-138496. (Civil Liberties in American History Ser). 1971. Repr. of 1951 ed. lib. bdg. 39.50 (ISBN 0-306-70073-5). Da Capo.

--In Brief Authority. LC 76-5432. (Illus.). 494p. 1976. Repr. of 1962 ed. lib. bdg. 19.75x (ISBN 0-8371-8807-5, BIIB). Greenwood.

--The World's Best Hope. (Midway Reprint Ser). xiv, 176p. 1974. pap. 8.50x (ISBN 0-226-04621-4). U of Chicago Pr.

Biddle, Gordon & Nock, O. S. The Railway Heritage of Britain: One Hundred Fifty Years of Railway Architecture & Engineering. (Illus.). 256p. 1984. 21.95 (ISBN 0-7181-2355-7, Pub. by Michael Joseph). Merrimack Pub Cir.

Biddle, Gordon & Spence, Geoffrey. British Railway Station. LC 77-89382. 1977. 13.50 (ISBN 0-7153-7467-2). David & Charles.

Biddle, Gordon, jt. auth. see Hadfield, Charles.

Biddle, J., jt. auth. see Dunkin, M.

Biddle, K. H. & Rivinus, M. W. Lights Along the Delaware. 1965. 4.95 (ISBN 0-8059-0245-7). Dorrance.

Biddle, Marcia M. Contributions of Women: Labor. LC 78-23303. (Contributions of Women Ser.). (Illus.). (gr. 6 up). 1979. PLB 8.95 (ISBN 0-87518-167-8). Dillon.

Biddle, Maureen. Fifty Craft Projects with Bible Verses & Patterns. LC 80-53862. (Illus.). 64p. (Orig.). 1981. pap. 4.50 (ISBN 0-87239-428-X, 2148). Standard Pub.

Biddle, Msartin, contrib. by see Clarke, Giles.

Biddle, Nicholas. Correspondence of Nicholas Biddle Dealing with National Affairs, 1807-1844. McGrane, Reginald C., ed. 1966. Repr. of 1919 ed. 15.00x (ISBN 0-910324-02-6). Canner.

Biddle, Perry H., Jr. Abingdon Funeral Manual. 176p. 1984. pap. 9.95 (ISBN 0-687-00470-5). Abingdon.

--Abingdon Marriage Manual. LC 73-21799. 256p. 1974. 10.95 (ISBN 0-687-00484-5). Abingdon.

--The Goodness of Marriage: A Devotional Book for Newlyweds. LC 84-50840. 144p. 1984. 6.95 (ISBN 0-8358-0490-9). Upper Room.

Biddle, Richard. Memoir of Sebastian Cabot, with a Review of the History of Maritime Discovery, Illustrated by Documents from the Rolls. facsimile ed. LC 73-107793. (Select Bibliographies Reprint Ser). 1831. 24.50 (ISBN 0-8369-5211-1). Ayer Co Pubs.

Biddle, Richard E. Discrimination: What Does It Mean? 1973. 4.50 (ISBN 0-685-47832-7). Intl Personnel Mgmt.

Biddle, Sara J. Lost & Found. (Illus.). 32p. 1984. 5.95 (ISBN 0-89962-394-8). Todd & Honeywell.

Biddle, W. Earl. Hypnosis in the Psychoses. 152p. 1967. 12.75x (ISBN 0-398-00152-9). C C Thomas.

Biddle, Wayne. Coming to Terms: From Alpha to X-Ray, a Lexicon for the Science-Watcher. 128p. 1982. pap. 4.95 (ISBN 0-380-61093-0, 61093-0). Avon.

--Coming to Terms: Lexicon for the Science Watcher. LC 80-54198. (Illus.). 128p. 1981. 8.95 (ISBN 0-670-33092-2). Viking.

Biddle, William W. Propaganda & Education. LC 73-176562. (Columbia University. Teachers College. Contributions to Education: No. 531). Repr. of 1932 ed. 22.50 (ISBN 0-404-55531-4). AMS Pr.

Biddlecomb, George. The Art of Rigging. LC 76-57844. 1977. lib. bdg. 75.00 (ISBN 0-8490-1453-0). Gordon Pr.

Biddulph, C. E., ed. & tr. see Khush-Hal Khan, Khattack.

Biddulph, M. W., jt. ed. see Henstock, M. E.

Biddulph, Peter, jt. auth. see Biddulph, William.

Biddulph, William & Biddulph, Peter. Travels of Certaine Englishmen into Africa, Asia & to the Blacke Sea, Finished 1608. LC 72-6344. (English Experience Ser.: No. 22). 144p. 1968. Repr. of 1609 ed. 25.00 (ISBN 90-221-0022-7). Walter J Johnson.

Bideleux, Robert. Communism & Development. 320p. 1985. 39.95 (ISBN 0-416-73410-3, 4028). Methuen Inc.

Bidelman, Patrick K. Pariahs Stand Up! The Founding of the Liberal Feminist Movement in France, 1858-1889. LC 81-4222. (Contributions in Women's Studies: No. 31). xi, 240p. 1982. lib. bdg. 29.95 (ISBN 0-313-23006-4, BPU/). Greenwood.

Bider, Djemma. The Buried Treasure. LC 81-43216. (Illus.). 32p. (gr. k-3). 1982. 10.95 (ISBN 0-396-07991-1). Dodd.

Bider, Djemma, tr. see Zhitkov, Boris.

Biderberg Conference, Arnhem, Holland, April 17-21, 1967. The Structure of the Quiet Photospher & the Low Chromosphere: Proceedings. De Jager, C., ed. 240p. 1968. lib. bdg. 47.50 (ISBN 90-277-0120-2, Pub. by Reidel Holland). Kluwer Academic.

Biderman, A. E. Cry the Unborn: A Modern Myth. 72p. (Orig.). 1985. pap. 6.95 (ISBN 0-934435-00-6). Old Man Pr.

Biderman, Albert D. March to Calumny. Kohn, Richard H., ed. LC 78-22376. (American Military Experience Ser.). 1979. Repr. of 1963 ed. lib. bdg. 23.00x (ISBN 0-405-11853-8). Ayer Co Pubs.

Biderman, Bob. Letters to Nanette. LC 82-5180. (Contemporary Lit. Ser.). 256p. 1982. 11.95 (ISBN 0-915786-07-9); pap. 5.95 (ISBN 0-915786-08-7). Early Stages.

Biderman, Jaime, jt. auth. see Carnemark, Curt.

Bidermann, Jacob. Cenodoxus. Dyer, D. G. & Longrigg, Cecily, trs. from Latin. LC 74-15527. (Edinburgh Bilingual Library: No. 9). 211p. 1975. pap. 6.95x (ISBN 0-292-71028-3). U of Tex Pr.

Bidez, J. & Parmentier, L., eds. The Ecclesiastical History of Evagrius. LC 76-24994. (Byzantine Texts: No. 4). Repr. of 1898 ed. 32.00 (ISBN 0-404-60004-2). AMS Pr.

Bidez, Joseph. Eos: Ou, Platon et l'Orient. LC 77-27185. (Gifford Lectures: 1939). Repr. of 1945 ed. 27.00 (ISBN 0-404-60496-X). AMS Pr.

Bidez, Joseph & Cumont, Franz. Les Mages Hellenises: Zoroastre, Ostanes & Hystaspe d'Apres la Tradition Grecque, 2 vols. in 1. facsimile ed. LC 75-10629. (Ancient Religion & Mythology Ser.). (Fr. & Gr.). 1976. Repr. of 1938 ed. 53.00x (ISBN 0-405-07005-5). Ayer Co Pubs.

Bidgood, R. J. The Holy Trinity. 1983. 8.95 (ISBN 0-533-05696-9). Vantage.

Bidgood, Reginald. Future Markets for Consultancy. 160p. 1981. 30.00x (ISBN 0-7198-2830-9, Pub. by Northwood Bks). State Mutual Bk.

Bidgood, Ruth. Lighting Candles: New & Selected Poems. 75p. 1982. pap. 8.95 (ISBN 0-907476-13-9). Dufour.

Bidlack, Gerald H. Unlikely Beginnings. LC 82-90984. 1984. 10.95 (ISBN 0-87212-164-X). Libra.

Bidlingmaier, F. & Knorr, D. Oestrogens: Physiological & Clinical Aspects. (Pediatric & Adolescent Endocrinology: Vol. 4). (Illus.). 1978. 29.00 (ISBN 3-8055-2845-0). S Karger.

Bidney, David. Theoretical Anthropology. LC 53-12098. 506p. 1953. 40.00x (ISBN 0-231-01910-6). Columbia U Pr.

Bidney, David, ed. Concept of Freedom in Anthropology. (Studies in General Anthropology). 1963. text ed. 23.60x (ISBN 90-2790-316-6). Mouton.

Bidol, Patricia. Improving Local Union Women's Committees. Kleiner, Lydia & Kornbluh, Joyce L., eds. (Program on Women & Work Ser.). 38p. 1981. pap. 3.50 (ISBN 0-87736-345-5). U of Mich Inst Labor.

Bidstrup, Sondra. Cooking with Wood. 1980. pap. 3.00 (ISBN 0-89166-012-7). Cobblesmith.

Bidwell, Alice T. & Rosenstiel, Isabelle D. Places of English Literature. LC 77-105765. 1970. Repr. of 1924 ed. 19.50x (ISBN 0-8046-0940-3, Pub. by Kennikat). Assoc Faculty Pr.

Bidwell, Bruce & Heffer, Linda. The Joycean Way: A Topographic Guide to Joyce's Dubliners & A Portait. 144p. 1982. 49.00x (ISBN 0-905473-39-6, Pub. by Wolfhound Pr Ireland). State Mutual Bk.

--The Joycean Way: A Topographical Guide to "Dubliners" & "A Portrait of the Artist As a Young Man". LC 82-80660. 144p. 1982. 25.00x (ISBN 0-8018-2879-1). Johns Hopkins.

Bidwell, Charles, jt. ed. see Windham, Douglas.

Bidwell, Charles E. & Kasarda, John. The Organization & Its Ecosystem. (Monographs in Organizational Behavior & Industrial Relations: Vol. 2). 1985. 49.50 (ISBN 0-89232-500-3). Jai Pr.

Bidwell, Charles E. & Wise, Sheldon. English for Jugo-Slavs (Kurs Govornog Engleskog Jezika) (English for Foreigners Ser.). 374p. (Eng. & Serbo-Croation., Prog. Bk.). 1980. pap. 90.00x incl. 9 dual cassettes (ISBN 0-87950-609-1). Spoken Lang Serv.

Bidwell, James K. & Clason, Robert G., eds. Readings in the History of Mathematics Education. LC 74-113172. (Illus.). 706p. 1970. 16.90 (ISBN 0-87353-087-X). NCTM.

Bidwell, John. Echoes of the Past: An Account of the First Emigrant Train to California, Fremont in the Conquest of California, the Discovery of Gold & Early Reminiscences. LC 72-9428. (The Far Western Frontier Ser.). (Illus.). 824p. 1973. Repr. of 1914 ed. 11.00 (ISBN 0-405-04959-5). Ayer Co Pubs.

--The Size of the Sheet in America: Paper-Moulds Manufactured by N & D Sellers of Philadelphia. (Illus.). 1978. pap. 4.00x (ISBN 0-912296-31-3, Dist. by U Pr of Va). Am Antiquarian.

Bidwell, John, ed. see American Type Founders Co.

Bidwell, John, ed. see Arnett, John A.

Bidwell, John, ed. see Balston, Thomas.

Bidwell, John, ed. see Brightly, Charles.

Bidwell, John, ed. see De Vinne, Theodore L.

Bidwell, John, ed. see Legros, Lucien & Grant, John C.

Bidwell, John, ed. see Munsell, Joel.

Bidwell, John, ed. see Nicholson, James B.

Bidwell, John, ed. see R. Hoe & Co.

Bidwell, John, jt. ed. see Ringwalt, J. Luther.

Bidwell, John, ed. see Thompson, John S.

Bidwell, Joseph P. & Spotte, Stephen. Artificial Seawaters: Formulas & Methods. 360p. 1985. write for info. (ISBN 0-86720-057-X). Jones & Bartlett.

Bidwell, Percy & Falconer, John I. History of Agriculture in the Northern United States 1620-1860. LC 72-11914. Repr. of 1925 ed. 45.00x (ISBN 0-678-00956-2). Kelley.

Bidwell, Percy W. History of Agriculture in the Northern United States: 1620-1860. 19.00 (ISBN 0-8446-1075-5). Peter Smith.

--Raw Materials: A Study of American Policy. LC 74-9649. (Council on Foreign Relations Ser). (Illus.). 403p. 1974. Repr. of 1958 ed. lib. bdg. 22.50x (ISBN 0-8371-7616-6, BIRM). Greenwood.

--Rural Economy in New England at the Beginning of the 19th Century. LC 68-55480. (Illus.). 1972. Repr. of 1916 ed. 25.00x (ISBN 0-678-00815-9). Kelley.

--What the Tariff Means to American Industries. LC 82-6133. xvi, 304p. 1982. Repr. of 1956 ed. lib. bdg. 35.00x (ISBN 0-313-23574-0, BIWT). Greenwood.

Bidwell, R. G. Plant Physiology. 2nd ed. 1979. text ed. write for info. (ISBN 0-02-309430-3). Macmillan.

Bidwell, R. G., jt. ed. see Steward, F. C.

Bidwell, R. L., jt. auth. see Serjeant, R. B.

Bidwell, R. L. see Serjeant, R. B.

Bidwell, R. L. & Smith, Rex, eds. Arabian & Islamic Studies: Articles. LC 83-12027. (Illus.). 320p. 1984. text ed. 44.00 (ISBN 0-582-78308-9). Longman.

Bidwell, Robin. Morocco Under Colonial Rule: French Administration of Tribal Areas, 1912-1956. 349p. 1973. 35.00x (ISBN 0-7146-2877-8, F Cass Co). Biblio Dist.

--The Two Yemens. LC 82-15352. 350p. 1983. lib. bdg. 27.50X (ISBN 0-86531-295-8). Westview.

Bidwell, Robin, ed. Affairs of Arabia: 1905-1906, 2 vols. new ed. 1971. Set. 125.00x (ISBN 0-7146-2694-5, F Cass Co). Biblio Dist.

--Affairs of Kuwait: 1896-1905, 2 vols. new ed. 1971. Set. 125.00x (ISBN 0-7146-2692-9, F Cass Co). Biblio Dist.

--British Documents on Foreign Affairs: Reports & Papers from the Foreign Office Confidential Print, 35 vols. (Turkey, Iran, & the Middle East Ser.). 1985. Set. 2450.00x (ISBN 0-89093-603-X). U Pubns Amer.

--Guide to Government Ministers: Arab World 1900-1972, Vol. 2. 124p. 1973. 35.00x (ISBN 0-7146-3001-2, F Cass Co). Biblio Dist.

--Guide to Government Ministers: Major Powers & Western Europe 1900-1971, Vol. 1. 298p. 1973. 35.00x (ISBN 0-7146-2977-4, F Cass Co). Biblio Dist.

--Guide to Government Ministers: The British Empire & Successor States 1900-1972, Vol. 3. 168p. 1974. 35.00x (ISBN 0-7146-3017-9, F Cass Co). Biblio Dist.

Bidwell, Robin L. Guide to African Ministers. 79p. 1978. 22.50x (ISBN 0-8476-6126-1). Rowman.

Bidwell, Shelford. Brassey's Artillery of the World. 2nd rev. ed. 270p. 1981. 49.50 (ISBN 0-08-027035-2). Pergamon.

Bidwell, Shelford & Graham, Dominick. Fire Power: British Army Weapons & Theories of War, 1904-1945. (Illus.). 1982. 27.50 (ISBN 0-04-942176-X). Allen Unwin.

--Fire Power: British Army Weapons & Theories (1904-1945) (Illus.). 366p. 1985. pap. text ed. 14.95x (ISBN 0-04-942190-5). Allen Unwin.

Bidwell, Wilma W., jt. auth. see Curtis, Thomas E.

Bie, Oscar. History of the Pianoforte & Pianoforte Players. 2nd ed. LC 66-28445. 1966. Repr. of 1899 ed. lib. bdg. 29.50 (ISBN 0-306-70938-4). Da Capo.

--Schubert, the Man. facsimile ed. LC 77-107794. (Select Bibliographies Reprint Ser). 1928. 24.50 (ISBN 0-8369-5177-8). Ayer Co Pubs.

Bie, Oskar. Schubert, the Man. LC 76-109710. (Illus.). xvii, 215p. Repr. of 1928 ed. lib. bdg. 15.00x (ISBN 0-8371-4201-6, BISM). Greenwood.

Bie, S. W., jt. ed. see Burrough, P. A.

Bie, S. W., ed. see ISSS Working Group on Soil Information Systems.

Biebel, David B. Jonathan: You Left Too Soon. LC 80-28276. 192p. 1982. pap. 4.95 (ISBN 0-8407-5809-X). Nelson.

--Jonathan, You Left Too Soon. 1982. pap. 2.25 (ISBN 0-451-11775-1, AE1775, Sig). NAL.

Bieber, Albert A. American Plays, Poetry & Songsters. LC 63-20133. (Illus.). 1923. 18.50 (ISBN 0-8154-0024-1). Cooper Sq.

Bieber, Doris M. Current American Legal Citations with 2100 Examples. LC 82-84586. iii, 342p. 1983. pap. text ed. 9.25 (ISBN 0-89941-188-6). W S Hein.

--Dictionary of Legal Abbreviations Used in American Law Books. LC 78-60173. 337p. 1979. pap. text ed. 7.95 (ISBN 0-930342-96-8). W S Hein.

--Dictionary of Legal Abbreviations Used in American Law Books. 2nd ed. LC 84-81483. 490p. 1985. lib. bdg. 35.00 (ISBN 0-89941-347-1). W S Hein.

Bieber, Doris M., jt. auth. see Kavass, Igor I.

Bieber, Doris M., jt. ed. see Kavass, Igor I.

Bieber, Hugo. Johann Adolf Schlegels Poetische Theorie. 18.00 (ISBN 0-384-04236-8); pap. 13.00 (ISBN 0-384-04235-X). Johnson Repr.

Bieber, Irving. Cognitive Psychoanalysis. LC 80-66921. 300p. 1980. 30.00 (ISBN 0-87668-423-1). Aronson.

Bieber, Konrad. Simone de Beauvoir. (World Authors Ser.). 1979. lib. bdg. 14.50 (ISBN 0-8057-6374-0, Twayne). G K Hall.

Bieber, Margaret. History of the Greek & Roman Theater. rev. ed. (Illus.). 360p. 1980. 60.00 (ISBN 0-691-03521-0); pap. 17.95 (ISBN 0-691-00212-6). Princeton U Pr.

Bieber, Margarete. Alexander the Great in Greek & Roman Art. (Illus.). 98p. 1979. 20.00 (ISBN 0-916710-69-6). Obol Intl.

--Ancient Copies: Contributions to the History of Greek & Roman Art. LC 72-95529. (Illus.). 600p. 1977. 150.00x (ISBN 0-8147-0970-2). NYU Pr.

--Griechische Kleidung. (Illus.). vi, 100p. 1977. Repr. of 1928 ed. 164.00x (ISBN 3-11-004835-3). De Gruyter.

--The Sculpture of the Hellenistic Age. rev. ed. LC 79-91814. (Illus.). 256p. 1980. Repr. of 1961 ed. lib. bdg. 60.00 (ISBN 0-87817-257-2). Hacker.

Bieber, Richard. Rebirth of the Congregation. 1973. pap. 1.25 (ISBN 0-87508-012-X). Chr Lit.

Bieberach, Ludwig, tr. Lehrbuch der Funktionentheorie, 2 Vols. (Bibliotheca Mathematica Teubneriana Ser: Nos. 21, 22). Repr. of 1921 ed. Set. 50.00 (ISBN 0-384-04244-9). Johnson Repr.

Bieberbach, Ludwig. Conformal Mapping. LC 53-7209. 6.95 (ISBN 0-8284-0090-3); pap. 2.95 o. p. (ISBN 0-8284-0176-4). Chelsea Pub.

--Differentialgeometrie. (Bibliothecha Mathematica Teubneriana Ser: No. 35). (Ger). 1969. 20.00 (ISBN 0-384-04240-6). Johnson Repr.

Bieber-Moses, Jeanette J. SuperSCRIPSIT Word Processing for the TRS-80 Models III, 4, & 4P. 1985. pap. 17.95 (ISBN 0-673-18086-7). Scott F.

Bieberstein, F. Marschall Von see Von Bieberstein, F. Marschall.

Biebuych, Tony, jt. auth. see Drake, Madeline.

Biebuyck, Brunhilde, tr. see Rossen, Gilbert.

Biebuyck, Daniel. Hero & Chief: Epic Literature from the Banyanga(Zaire Republic) LC 76-50242. 1978. 36.50x (ISBN 0-520-03386-8). U of Cal Pr.

--Tradition & Creativity in Tribal Art. LC 69-12457. 1969. 47.50x (ISBN 0-520-01509-6, CAL 220); pap. 4.95 (ISBN 0-520-02487-7). U of Cal Pr.

Biebuyck, Daniel P., et al. Symbolism of the Lega Stool & An Ethnoscientific Approach to Akan Arts & Aesthetics. LC 77-14571. (Working Papers in the Traditional Arts: Nos. 2 & 3). (Illus.). 72p. 1978. pap. text ed. 5.95 (ISBN 0-915980-81-9). ISHI PA.

Biechler, James E. The Religious Language of Nicholas of Cusa. LC 75-23096. (American Academy of Religion, Dissertation Ser.). 240p. 1975. pap. 10.25 (ISBN 0-89130-021-X, 01 01 08). Scholars Pr GA.

Biedenbach, J. M. & Grayson, L. P, eds. Teaching Aids in the College Classroom: A Pragmatic Approach. 137p. 1975. 5.00 (ISBN 0-317-33264-3). Am Soc Ag Eng.

Biedenbach, J. M., jt. ed. see Curtis, J. A.

Biedenbach, J. M., jt. ed. see Eliott, C. S.

Biedenbach, J. M., jt. ed. see Grayson, L. P.

Biedenharn, C., ed. Quantum Theory of Angular Momentum: A Collection of Reprints & Original Papers. (Perspectives in Physics Ser.). (Illus., Orig.). 1965. pap. 44.00 (ISBN 0-12-096056-7). Acad Pr.

Biedenharn, L. C. & Louck, J. D. Encyclopedia of Mathematics & Its Applications: The Racah-Wigner Algebra in Quantum Theory, Vol. 9. 1984. 59.50 (ISBN 0-521-30229-3). Cambridge U Pr.

Biedenharn, L. C., et al. Algebra of Representations of Some Finite Groups. (Rice University Studies: Vol. 54, No. 2). 68p. 1968. pap. 10.00x (ISBN 0-89263-196-1). Rice Univ.

Biedenhern, L. C. & Louck, J. D. Encyclopedia of Mathematics & Its Applications: Angular Momentum in Quantum Physics, Vol. 8. 1984. 69.50 (ISBN 0-521-30228-5). Cambridge U Pr.

Bieder, L., et al. Handbook of Alcoholism for Health Professionals. 128p. 1984. 11.00 (ISBN 0-433-24721-5, 991430069, Pub. by Heinemann Medical). Heyden.

Bieder, Ludwig, et al. Handbook on Alcoholism for Health Professionals. Paton, Alex, ed. x, 102p. (Orig.). 1985. pap. 12.50 (ISBN 0-433-24721-5, Pub. by Heinemann-Med England). Heinman.

Bieder, Maryellen. Narrative Perspective in the Post-Civil War Novels of Francisco Ayala: Muertes de Perro & El Fondo del Vaso. (Studies in the Romance Languages & Literatures: No. 207). 133p. 1979. 10.00x (ISBN 0-8078-9207-6). U of NC Pr.

Biederman, Charles. New Cezanne. LC 58-10644. 1958. 7.50 (ISBN 0-9600002-2-4). Art History.

--Search for New Arts. LC 79-90835. 1979. 20.00 (ISBN 0-9605614-0-4); pap. 15.00 (ISBN 0-9605614-1-2). Art History.

Biederman, Danny. The Book of Kisses. LC 84-7667. (Illus., Orig.). 1984. pap. 6.95 (ISBN 0-934878-42-0). Dembner Bks.

Biederman, Jerry. He's a Girl. 96p. 1984. pap. 2.95 (ISBN 0-8431-0616-6). Price Stern.

Biederman, Jerry & Silberkleit, Tom. Your First Romance: Twenty Do-It-Yourself Novels You Can Complete & Sell. 176p. 1984. pap. 8.95 (ISBN 0-312-89790-1). St Martin.

Biederman, Jerry & Silberkleit, Tom, eds. My First Real Romance: Twenty Bestselling Romance Novelists Reveal the Stories of Their Own First Real Romances. LC 84-40618. 296p. 1985. 15.95 (ISBN 0-8128-3015-6). Stein & Day.

--My First Real Romance: Twenty Bestselling Romance Novelists Reveal the Stories of Their Own First Real Romances. LC 84-40618. 296p. 1985. pap. 8.95 (ISBN 0-8128-6248-1). Stein & Day.

Biederman, Marcia. The Makeover. 240p. 1984. 13.95 (ISBN 0-89733-107-9). Academy Chi Pubs.

Biederman, Paul. The U. S. Airline Industry: End of an Era. LC 81-17845. 222p. 1982. 29.95 (ISBN 0-03-060324-2). Praeger.

Biederman, Robert, ed. see Schmitt.

Biedermann, Gertrude & Anderson, Martha. Traditional Bobbin Lace: Patterns in Torchin, Guipure & Indria. Kliot, Jules & Kliot, Kaethe, eds. 1983. pap. 21.00 (ISBN 0-916896-07-2). Lacis Pubns.

Biederman-Thorson, M. A., tr. see Barth, Friedrich G.

Biederman-Thorson, M. A., tr. see Larcher, W.

Biederman-Thorson, M. A., tr. see Nachtigall, W.

Biederman-Thorson, M. A., tr. see Schmidt, R. F. & Thews, G.

Biederman-Thorson, M. A., tr. see Schmidt, Robert F.

Biederman-Thorson, M. A., tr. see Thews, G. & Vaupel, P.

Biederwolf, William E. Study of the Holy Spirit. LC 84-25099. 128p. 1985. pap. 5.95 (ISBN 0-8254-2244-2). Kregel.

Biefang, S., et al. Manual for the Planning & Implementation of Therapeutic Studies. (Lecture Notes in Medical Informatics Ser.: Vol. 20). 100p. 1983. pap. 14.00 (ISBN 0-387-11979-5). Springer-Verlag.

Biefus, Doreen. How to Start Your Own Mail Order Business Without Capital. (Illus.). 48p. 1985. 6.95 (ISBN 0-89962-421-9). Todd & Honeywell.

Bieg, Bernard J., jt. auth. see Keeling, B. Lewis.

Biegel, David & Naparstek, Arthur J. Community Support Systems & Mental Health: Research, Practice & Policy. 384p. 1982. text ed. 25.95 (ISBN 0-8261-3420-3). Springer Pub.

Biegel, David E., et al. Social Networks & Mental Health. 1985. 25.00 (ISBN 0-8039-2420-8). Sage.

--Building Support Networks for the Elderly. LC 84-8337. 158p. 1984. pap. 9.95 (ISBN 0-8039-2350-3). Sage.

Biegel, Harvey M. Battleship Country: The Battle Fleet at Long Beach-San Pedro, California, 1919-1940. LC 82-63060. (Illus.). 76p. 1983. 6.95 (ISBN 0-933126-30-1). Pictorial Hist.

Biegel, Len, ed. Physical Fitness & the Older Person: A Guide to Exercise for Health Care Professionals. LC 84-6328. 165p. 1984. 25.00 (ISBN 0-89443-894-8). Aspen Systems.

Biegel, Paul. The King of the Copper Mountains. (Illus.). 182p. 1977. Repr. of 1969 ed. 11.00x (ISBN 0-460-05746-4, BKA 01640, Pub. by J M Dent England). Biblio Dist.

Biegel, Peter. Peter Biegel's Racing Pictures. (Illus.). 160p. 1984. 75.00 (ISBN 0-7181-2358-1, Pub. by Michael Joseph). Merrimack Pub Cir.

Biegeleisen, H. I. Varicose Veins, Related Diseases & Sclerotherapy: A Guide for Practitioners. 255p. 1984. text ed. 35.00 (ISBN 0-920792-18-9). Eden Pr.

Biegeleisen, J. I. The ABC of Lettering. 5th ed. 272p. 1984. pap. 7.95i (ISBN 0-06-464079-5, BN 4079). Har-Row.

--Antique Alphabets. (Illus.). 1969. 11.95 (ISBN 0-911380-01-9). Signs of Times.

--The Book of Sixty Hand-Lettered Alphabets. 1976. 8.00 (ISBN 0-911380-40-X). Signs of Times.

--Complete Book of Silk Screen Printing Production. (Illus., Orig.). 1963. pap. 4.50 (ISBN 0-486-21100-2). Dover.

--Design & Print Your Own Posters. (Illus.). 168p. 1976. 16.95 (ISBN 0-8230-1309-X). Watson-Guptill.

--Design & Print Your Own Posters. (Illus.). 168p. 1984. pap. 12.95 (ISBN 0-8230-1310-3). Watson-Guptill.

--Handbook of Type Faces & Lettering. 4th ed. LC 81-19111. (Illus.). 272p. 1982. pap. 14.95 (ISBN 0-668-05420-4, 5420). Arco.

--Make Your Job Interview a Success: A Guide for the Career-Minded Jobseeker. LC 83-22448. 176p. 1984. lib. bdg. 11.95 (ISBN 0-668-06016-6); pap. 6.95 (ISBN 0-668-05487-5). Arco.

--Screen Printing. (Illus.). 160p. 1971. 19.50 (ISBN 0-8230-4665-6). Watson-Guptill.

Biegeleisen, J. I. & Cohn, J. A. Silk Screen Techniques. (Illus.). 1958. pap. 3.95 (ISBN 0-486-20433-2). Dover.

Biegeleisen, J. I. & Cohn, M. A. Silk Screen Techniques. (Illus.). 14.75 (ISBN 0-8446-0491-7). Peter Smith.

Biegeleisen, Jacob I. Book of One Hundred Type Face Alphabets. 1974. 10.00 (ISBN 0-911380-03-5). Signs of Times.

--Complete Book of Silk Screen Printing Production. (Illus.). 14.75 (ISBN 0-8446-1677-X). Peter Smith.

--Job Resumes. 112p. 1976. pap. 4.95 (ISBN 0-399-50822-8, G&D). Putnam Pub Group.

--Job Resumes. rev. ed. 112p. pap. cancelled (ISBN 0-448-00947-1, G&D). Putnam Pub Group.

Biegeleison, J. I. The ABC of Lettering. 5th, rev., enl. ed. LC 76-5165. (Illus.). 296p. 1976. 19.18xi (ISBN 0-06-010329-9, HarpT). Har-Row.

Biegelsen, D. K., et al, eds. Energy Beam-Solid Interactions & Transient Thermal Processing, 1985, Vol. 35. LC 85-5113. 1985. text ed. 50.00 (ISBN 0-931837-00-6). Materials Res.

Biegen, Joseph R. & Beston, William C. Introduction to Computer Graphics: CADDS-3. (Illus.). 210p. 1984. 16.50 (ISBN 0-911597-00-X). Redcomp Servs.

Biegert. Looking Up...While Lying Down. (Looking Up Ser.). 1979. pap. 1.25 booklet (ISBN 0-8298-0364-5). Pilgrim NY.

--So We're Growing Older. (Looking Up Ser.). 1982. pap. 1.25 booklet (ISBN 0-8298-0436-6). Pilgrim NY.

--When Death has Touched Your Life. 1981. pap. 1.25 (ISBN 0-8298-0455-2). Pilgrim NY.

Biegert, E., ed. A Topical Guide to "Folia Primatologica", Volumes 1-30 (1963-1978) 160p. 1980. pap. 16.75 (ISBN 3-8055-0781-X). S Karger.

Biegert, J. see International Congress of Primatology, 3rd, Zurich, 1970.

Biegert, John E. Mirando Hacia Arriba en Medio de la Enfermedad: Looking Up...While Lying Down. (Looking Up Ser.). 24p. (Orig., Span.). 1983. pap. 1.25 booklet (ISBN 0-8298-0663-6). Pilgrim NY.

--Staying In. (Looking Up Ser.). 1985. pap. 1.25 (ISBN 0-8298-0567-2). Pilgrim NY.

Biegun, Dov. David's Castle. 156p. pap. 15.00 (ISBN 0-317-36699-8). Kosciuszko.

Biehl, Dieter, et al, eds. Public Finance & Economic Growth: Proceedings of the 37th Congress of the International Institute of Public Finance, Tokyo 1981. LC 83-12477. 358p. 1983. 40.00 (ISBN 0-8143-1750-2). Wayne St U Pr.

Biehler, Fred. Aviation Maintenance Law. 172p. 1976. text ed. 18.95x (ISBN 0-89100-067-4, EA-AML-2). pap. 16.95x (ISBN 0-89100-061-5, EA-AML-1). Aviation Maintenance.

Biehler, Robert F. Child Development: An Introduction. 2nd ed. LC 80-82347. (Illus.). 704p. 1981. text ed. 26.95 (ISBN 0-395-29833-4); study guide 9.95 (ISBN 0-395-29835-0); instr's manual 1.00 (ISBN 0-395-29834-2). HM.

Biehler, Robert F. & Snowran, Jack. Psychology Applied to Teaching. 4th ed. LC 81-82572. 1982. 25.95 (ISBN 0-395-31681-2); instr's man. & test 2.00 (ISBN 0-395-31682-0); study guide 10.50 (ISBN 0-395-31683-9). HM.

Biehler, Susan, jt. auth. see Bogue, Donald J.

Biek, David. The Mushrooms of Northern California. LC 84-90157. (Illus.). 304p. (Orig.). 1984. pap. 12.95 (ISBN 0-9612020-0-9). Spore Prints.

Bieker, Beverly, jt. auth. see Roth, Sandra.

Bielasiak, Jack, ed. Polish Politics: Edge of the Abyss. LC 83-24759. 384p. 1984. 37.95 (ISBN 0-03-069633-X). Praeger.

Bielawski, Maxwell M. How to Heal & Cure Anything: My Favorite Remedies. 300p. (Orig.). 1984. 125.00 (ISBN 0-317-14873-7). Bielawski.

Bielchowsky, Albert. Goethe, Sein Leben und Seine Werke, 2 vols. 1973. Repr. of 1910 ed. 75.00 set (ISBN 0-8274-1215-0). R West.

Biele, Pam, jt. auth. see Walter, Susan.

Bielefeld, Carole, jt. auth. see Young, Lorelle.

Bielen, Peggy & McDaniel, Sandy. Project Self-Esteem. 250p. (Orig.). 1985. pap. text ed. write for info. (ISBN 0-935266-16-X). B L Winch.

Bielenberg, Christabel. The Past Is Myself. 285p. 1982. pap. 9.95 (Pub. by Ward River Pr Ireland). Irish Bks Media.

--Ride Out the Dark: The Experiences of an Englishwoman in Wartime Germany. LC 84-10717. 1984. pap. 6.95 (ISBN 0-8398-2853-5). G K Hall.

Bielenstein, Hans. The Bureaucracy of Han Times. LC 78-72080. (Cambridge Studies in Chinese History, Literature & Institutions). (Illus.). 1980. 47.50 (ISBN 0-521-22510-8). Cambridge U Pr.

Bieler, Arthur, et al. Perspectives de France. 3rd ed. (Illus.). 576p. 1982. text ed. 28.95 (ISBN 0-13-660563-X). P-H.

Bieler, E. F. Three Great Gothic Novels. 18.95 (ISBN 0-8488-0060-5, Pub. by Amereon Hse). Amereon Ltd.

Bieler, H. G. Food Is Your Best Medicine. 256p. 1982. pap. 2.95 (ISBN 0-345-30190-0). Ballantine.

Bieler, Henry G. Food Is Your Best Medicine. 256p. 1973. pap. 2.95 (ISBN 0-345-30190-0, V-837, Vin). Random.

--Natural Way to Sexual Health. Fried, Jerome, ed. LC 72-83312. 300p. 1972. 6.95 (ISBN 0-912880-03-1). Charles Pub.

Bieler, L., ed. see O'Meara, John J.

Bieler, Ludwig. The Grammarian's Craft. 1.50 (ISBN 0-686-23372-7). Classical Folia.

Bieleski, R. L., jt. ed. see Lauchli, A.

Bielfeld. Guinea Pigs. (Pet Care Ser.). 1983. pap. 3.95 (ISBN 0-8120-2629-2). Barron.

Bielfeld, Horst & Heidenreich, Manfred. Handbook of Lovebirds: With Special Section on Diseases of Parrots. Arrens, Christa, tr. (Illus.). 111p. 1982. 16.95 (ISBN 0-87666-820-1, H-1040). TFH Pubns.

Bieliauskas, Linas A. The Influence of Individual Differences in Health & Illness. (Behavioral Sciences for Health Care Professionals Ser.). 128p. (Orig.). 1982. lib. bdg. 21.00x (ISBN 0-86531-004-1); pap. text ed. 8.95x (ISBN 0-86531-005-X). Westview.

--Stress & Its Relationship to Health & Illness. (Behavioral Sciences for Health Care Professionals Ser.). 128p. (Orig.). 1982. pap. text ed. 7.95x (ISBN 0-86531-003-3). Westview.

Bielier, E. F. The Big Bow Mystery. 12.95 (ISBN 0-8488-0063-X, Pub. by Amereon Hse). Amereon Ltd.

--Five Victorian Ghost Novels. 22.95 (ISBN 0-89190-683-5, Pub. by Am Repr). Amereon Ltd.

--My Lady's Money. 10.95 (ISBN 0-8488-0062-1, Pub. by Amereon Hse). Amereon Ltd.

--Three Supernatural Novels of the Victorian Period. 18.95 (ISBN 0-89190-697-5, Pub. by Am Repr). Amereon Ltd.

Bielig, Hans J. Fruit Juice Processing. (Agricultural Services Bulletins: No. 13). (Illus.). 108p. (Eng. & Span., 3rd Printing 1977). 1973. pap. 8.00 (ISBN 92-5-100174-X, F708, FAO). Unipub.

Bielka, Heinz, ed. The Eukaryotic Ribosome. (Illus.). 320p. 1982. 35.00 (ISBN 0-387-11059-3). Springer-Verlag.

Biella, Joan C. Dictionary of Old South Arabic: Sabaen Dialect. LC 81-8946. (Harvard Semitic Studies). (Arabic.). 1982. 33.00 (ISBN 0-89130-455-X, 04-04-25). Scholars Pr GA.

Bielschowsky, A. Life of Goethe, 3 Vols. LC 70-92935. (Studies in German Literature, No. 13). 1969. Repr. of 1905 ed. lib. bdg. 99.95x (ISBN 0-8383-1000-1). Haskell.

Bielschowsky, Albert. Life of Goethe, 3 Vols. Cooper, William A., tr. LC 73-113555. (BCL Ser. I). (Illus.). Repr. of 1908 ed. Set. 80.00 (ISBN 0-404-00870-4). Vol. 1 (ISBN 0-404-00871-2). Vol. 2 (ISBN 0-404-00872-0). Vol. 3 (ISBN 0-404-00873-9). AMS Pr.

Bielski, Benon H. & Gebicki, Janusz M. Atlas of Electron Spin Resonance Spectra. 1967. 95.00 (ISBN 0-12-096650-6). Acad Pr.

Bielski, Benon H., jt. auth. see Capellos, Christos.

Bielski, Nella. Oranges for the Son of Alexander Levy. 1981. 7.95 (ISBN 0-686-32050-6). Writers & Readers.

--Oranges for the Son of Alexander Levy. Berger, John & Appignanesi, Lisa, trs. 140p. 1984. pap. 3.95 (ISBN 0-906495-71-7). Writers & Readers.

--Oranges for the Son of Asher Levy. Berger, John & Appignanesi, Lisa, trs. (Fr.). 1982. 11.95 (ISBN 0-906495-70-9). Writers & Readers.

Bielstein, R. M. The Practical Approach to Industrial Relations for Line Supervisors. 109p. 1965. 6.95x (ISBN 0-87201-381-2). Gulf Pub.

Biely, Andrey. St. Petersburg. Cournos, John, tr. from Rus. & intro. by. (Illus., Orig.). (YA) (gr. 9 up). 1959. pap. 7.95 (ISBN 0-394-17237-X, E331, Ever). Grove.

--Silver Dove. Reavey, George, tr. from Rus. LC 73-21039. 1974. pap. 7.95 (ISBN 0-394-17859-9, E637, Ever). Grove.

Biemel. Phanomelogie Heute. (Phaenomenologica Ser: No. 51). 1972. lib. bdg. 22.50 (ISBN 90-247-1336-6, Pub. by Martinus Nijhoff Netherlands). Kluwer Academic.

--Philosophischen Analysen Zur Kunst der Gegenwart. (Phaenomenologica Ser: No. 28). 1968. lib. bdg. 34.00 (ISBN 90-247-0263-1, Pub. by Martinus Nijhoff Netherlands); pap. 18.50 (ISBN 90-247-0262-3, Pub. by Martinus Nijhoff Netherlands). Kluwer Academic.

Biemel, W. Die Welt Des Menschen-Die Welt der Philosophie: Festschrift Fur Jan Patocka. (Phaenomenologica Ser: No. 72). 1976. lib. bdg. 71.00 (ISBN 90-247-1899-6, Pub. by Martinus Nijhoff Netherlands). Kluwer Academic.

Biemer, E. & Duspiva, W. Reconstructive Microvascular Surgery. (Illus.). 151p. 1982. 97.00 (ISBN 0-387-11320-7). Springer-Verlag.

Biemer, Linda. New York: Our Communities. (Illus.). 328p. (gr. 4). 1983. text ed. 17.25x (ISBN 0-87905-111-6, Peregrine Smith). Gibbs M Smith.

Biemer, Linda B. Women & Property in Colonial New York: The Transition from Dutch to English Law, 1643-1727. Berkhofer, Robert, ed. LC 82-23701. (Studies in American History & Culture: No. 38). 170p. 1983. 39.95 (ISBN 0-8357-1392-X). Univ Microfilms.

Bien, David D. The Calas Affair: Persecution, Toleration, & Heresy in Eighteenth-Century Toulouse. LC 78-12393. 1979. Repr. of 1960 ed. lib. bdg. 22.50x (ISBN 0-313-21206-6, BICA). Greenwood.

Bien, Joseph, ed. see Ricoeur, Paul.

Bien, Joseph J., tr. see Merleau-Ponty, Maurice.

Bien, Peter. Kazantzakis & Linguistic Revolution in Greek Literature. LC 79-154991. (Essays in Literature Ser.). 1972. 28.00 (ISBN 0-691-06206-4). Princeton U Pr.

--Tempted by Happiness: Razantzakis Post-Christian Christ. 1984. pap. 2.30x (ISBN 0-317-12307-6, 253). Pendle Hill.

Bien, Peter, tr. see Kazantzakis, Nikos.

Bien, Peter, tr. see Myrivilis, Stratis.

Bien, Peter, et al. Workbook for Demotic Greek I: Providing Supplementary Exercises in Writing & Spelling, Complementing the Oral-Aural Emphasis of the Text. 104p. 1973. pap. text ed. 4.00x (ISBN 0-87451-090-2). U Pr of New Eng.

--Demotic Greek I. 4th, rev. ed. LC 83-40009. (Illus.). 387p. 1983. pap. text ed. 13.00x (ISBN 0-87451-262-X). U Pr of New Eng.

--Demotic Greek II: The Flying Telephone Booth. LC 81-51609. (Illus.). 439p. (Orig.). 1982. pap. text ed. 17.50x (ISBN 0-87451-208-5); pap. text ed. 9.00x wkbk. (ISBN 0-87451-209-3); instr's. manual free (ISBN 0-87451-980-2). U Pr of New Eng.

Bienayme, Alain. Systems of Higher Education: France. 144p. 1978. pap. 7.00 (ISBN 0-89192-205-9, Pub. by ICED). Interbk Inc.

Bienbar, Arthur, ed. see Silva, Owen F.

Biene, Susanna & Moneli, illus. Sing Through the Seasons: Ninety-Nine Songs for Children. LC 70-164916. (Illus.). 190p. 1972. 11.95 (ISBN 0-87486-006-7); l.p. record 6.00 (ISBN 0-87486-040-7). Plough.

Bienefeld, Manfred & Godfrey, Martin. The Struggle for Development: National Strategies in an International Context. LC 81-19821. 352p. 1982. 53.95 (ISBN 0-471-10152-4). Wiley.

Bienek, Horst. The Cell. Mahlendorf, tr. from Ger. LC 74-134739. 1973. 15.00 (ISBN 0-87775-024-6); pap. 6.95 (ISBN 0-87775-070-X). Unicorn Pr.

--The First Polka. Read, Ralph R., tr. from German. LC 84-1513. (Gleiwitz Suite Ser.). Orig. Title: Die Erste Polka. 326p. (Orig.). 1984. 15.95 (ISBN 0-940242-08-7); pap. 7.95 (ISBN 0-940242-07-9). Fjord Pr.

Bienen, Henry. Armies & Parties in Africa. LC 77-17796. 280p. 1978. text ed. 35.00x (ISBN 0-8419-0359-X, Africana); pap. text ed. 12.50x (ISBN 0-8419-0386-7). Holmes & Meier.

--Kenya, the Politics of Participation & Control. LC 73-2461. (Center for International Affairs, Harvard University Ser.). 192p. 1974. 24.00 (ISBN 0-691-03096-0). Princeton U Pr.

--Nigeria: Absorbing the Oil Wealth. 153p. 1982. 150.00 (ISBN 0-8002-3412-X). Intl Pubns Serv.

--Tanzania: Party Transformation & Economic Development. enl. ed. LC 71-104098. (Center of International Studies Ser.). 1970. 42.00x (ISBN 0-691-03063-4). Princeton U Pr.

--Violence & Social Change. LC 68-56012. 1968. 6.50x (ISBN 0-226-04760-1); pap. 1.95x (ISBN 0-226-04762-8). U of Chicago Pr.

Bienen, Henry, ed. The Military & Modernization. (Controversy Ser.). 242p. 1971. 11.95x (ISBN 0-202-24044-4); pap. 5.95x (ISBN 0-202-24045-2). Lieber-Atherton.

--The Military Intervenes: Case Studies in Political Development. LC 67-31395. 176p. 1968. 9.95x (ISBN 0-87154-110-6). Russell Sage.

Bienen, Henry & Diejomaoh, V. P., eds. Inequality & Development in Nigeria. LC 81-4145. (The Political Economy of Income Distribution in Developing Countries Ser.). 312p. (Orig.). 1982. pap. text ed. 16.50x (ISBN 0-8419-0710-2). Holmes & Meier.

--The Political Economy of Income Distribution in Nigeria. LC 80-16860. (The Political Economy of Income Distribution in Developing Countries Ser.: No. 2). 520p. 1981. text ed. 55.00x (ISBN 0-8419-0618-1). Holmes & Meier.

Bienen, Henry S., jt. ed. see Foltz, William J.

Bienen, Leigh B., jt. auth. see Feild, Hubert S.

Bienenfeld, Arthur. Beachview Tower: A High-Rise Saga. LC 78-61219. 1978. 10.00 (ISBN 0-89430-029-6). Palos Verdes.

Bienenfeld, Florence. Child Custody Mediation. 1983. 12.95 (ISBN 0-8314-0065-X). Sci & Behavior.

--Helping Your Child Succeed after Divorce. 256p. 1985. Repr. lib. bdg. 24.95x (ISBN 0-89370-571-3). Borgo Pr.

--Helping Your Child Succeed After Divorce. (Illus.). 256p. (Orig.). 1986. pap. 9.95 (ISBN 0-89793-041-X). Hunter Hse.

--My Mom & Dad Are Getting a Divorce. LC 80-10534. (Illus.). 48p. (gr. k-4). 1980. pap. text ed. 3.95 (ISBN 0-88436-753-3, 35292). EMC.

Bienenstock, Arthur, ed. Liquids & Amorphous Materials. (Transactions of the American Crystallographic Association Ser.: Vol. 10). 84p. 1974. pap. 15.00 (ISBN 0-686-60381-8). Polycrystal Bk Serv.

Bienenstock, J. Immunology of the Lung & Upper Respiratory Tract. 348p. 1984. 45.00 (ISBN 0-07-005215-8). McGraw.

Biener, K. Geomedizinische Ergometrie bei Jugendlichen: Vergleichende Ergometrie und Spirographie bei Stadt-, Land- und Hochgebirgskindern. Ritzel, G., ed. (Sozialmedizinische und paedagogische Jungendkunde: Band 11). 1976. 10.25 (ISBN 3-8055-2281-9). S Karger.

Bienert, Wolfgang. Dionysius Von Alexandrien Zur Frage Des Originismus. (Patristische Texte und Studien, 21). 1978. 35.20x (ISBN 3-11-007442-7). De Gruyter.

Bienert, Wolfgang A. Allegoria und Anagoge bei Didymos dem Blinden von Alexandria. (Patristische Texte und Studien Ser.: Vol. 13). xii, 188p. 1972. 23.20x (ISBN 3-11-003715-7). De Gruyter.

Bienkiewicz, Krzysztof J. Physical Chemistry of Leather Making. LC 80-27191. 556p. 1983. 46.50 (ISBN 0-89874-304-4). Krieger.

Bienkowska, B., ed. The Scientific World of Copernicus. Cekalska, K., tr. from Pol. LC 73-85712. 1973. lib. bdg. 29.00 (ISBN 90-277-0353-1, Pub. by Reidel Holland). Kluwer Academic.

Bienkowski, W. Theory & Reality: The Development of Social Systems. (Allison & Busby Motive Ser.). 303p. 1982. 19.95x (ISBN 0-8052-8093-6, Pub. by Allison & Busby England); pap. 9.95 (ISBN 0-8052-8092-8). Schocken.

Biennial, ed. A Guide to COPA Recognized Accrediting Associations. 202p. 9.50 (ISBN 0-318-13852-2). Coun Postsecondary Accredit.

Biennial Conference, Dundee, Great Britain, June 28-July 1, 1977. Numerical Analysis: Proceedings. Watson, G. A., ed. (Lecture Notes in Mathematics Ser.: Vol. 630). 1978. pap. 18.00 (ISBN 0-387-08538-6). Springer-Verlag.

Biennial Seminar of the Canadian Mathematical Congress, 14th Univ. of Western Ontario, August 1973. Optimal Control Theory & Its Applications: Proceedings, 2 pts. Kirby, B. J., ed. (Lecture Notes in Economics & Mathematical Systems Ser.). 1974. Pt. 2. pap. 22.00 (ISBN 0-387-07026-5). Springer-Verlag.

Bienstock, Gregory. Struggle for the Pacific. LC 76-115199. 1971. Repr. of 1937 ed. 21.00x (ISBN 0-8046-1092-4, Pub. by Kennikat). Assoc Faculty Pr.

Bienstock, June K. & Anolik, Ruth B. Careers in Fact & Fiction. LC 84-21551. 165p. 1985. pap. 18.95 (ISBN 0-8389-0424-6). ALA.

Bienvenu, Richard, jt. ed. see Beecher, Jonathan.

Bienvenu, Richard, tr. see Beecher, Jonathan & Bienvenu, Richard.

Bienvenue, Dudley. I'm an Alcoholic, What's Your Excuse? (Illus.). 1983. 7.95 (ISBN 0-533-05229-7). Vantage.

Bienz, D. R. The Why & How of Home Horticulture. LC 79-19915. (Illus.). 513p. 1980. text ed. 25.95 (ISBN 0-7167-1078-1). W H Freeman.

Bier, Jesse. The Rise & Fall of American Humor. xii, 544p. 1980. Repr. of 1968 ed. lib. bdg. 40.00x (ISBN 0-374-90632-7). Octagon.

Bier, Justus. Tilmann Riemenschneider: His Life & Work. LC 80-5171. (Illus.). 272p. 1982. 28.00x (ISBN 0-8131-1428-4). U Pr of Ky.

Bier, Milan, ed. Membrane Processes in Industry & Biomedicine. LC 72-149647. 313p. 1971. 32.50x (ISBN 0-306-30528-3, Plenum Pr). Plenum Pub.

Bier, Norman & Lowther, Gerald. Contact Lens Correction. (Illus.). 1977. 79.95 (ISBN 0-407-00101-8). Butterworth.

Bier, O. G., et al. Fundamentals of Immunology. (Illus.). 442p. 1981. pap. 19.50 (ISBN 0-387-90529-4). Springer-Verlag.

Bier, Olga, jt. auth. see Wolfe, Ken.

Bier, W. C., ed. Adolescent, His Search for Understanding. LC 62-17450. (Pastoral Psychology Ser.: No. 3). x, 246p. 1963. 17.50 (ISBN 0-8232-0480-4). Fordham.
--Aging: Its Challenge to the Individual & to Society. LC 74-84804. (Pastoral Psychology Ser: No. 8). xii, 292p. 1974. 20.00 (ISBN 0-8232-0980-6). Fordham.
--Human Life: Problems of Birth, of Living, & of Dying. LC 77-71939. (Pastoral Psychology Ser.: No. 9). 1977. 20.00 (ISBN 0-8232-1025-1). Fordham.
--Personality & Sexual Problems in Pastoral Psychology. LC 62-16224. (Pastoral Psychology Ser: No. 1). xvi, 256p. 1964. 20.00 (ISBN 0-8232-0585-1). Fordham.
--Privacy: A Vanishing Value? LC 79-56138. (Pastoral Psychology Ser.: No. 10). xiv, 398p. 1980. 25.00 (ISBN 0-8232-1044-8). Fordham.
Bier, W. C., ed. see Academy Of Religion & Mental Health.
Bier, William C., ed. Alienation: Plight of Modern Man? LC 72-75644. (Pastoral Psychology Ser: No. 7). xiv, 271p. 1972. 20.00 (ISBN 0-8232-0950-4). Fordham.
--Marriage: A Psychological & Moral Approach. LC 64-25381. (Pastoral Psychology Ser: No. 4). viii, 280p. 1965. 20.00 (ISBN 0-8232-0605-X). Fordham.
--Woman in Modern Life. LC 68-20626. (Pastoral Psychology Ser.: No. 5). x, 278p. 1968. 20.00 (ISBN 0-8232-0800-1). Fordham.
Bierbaum, Athanasius. Pusillum, 4 vols. 7.50 (ISBN 0-685-10971-2, L38675). Franciscan Herald.
Bierberbach, L. Theorie der Geometrishen Konstruktionen. (Mathematische Rehihe Ser.: No. 13). (Illus.). 162p. (Ger.). 1952. 23.95x (ISBN 0-8176-0030-2). Birkhauser.
Bierbrier, Doreen. Living with Tenants: How to Happily Share Your House with Renters for Profit & Security. 128p. (Orig.). 1983. pap. 7.00x (ISBN 0-9609586-0-6). Housing Connect.
--Managing Your Rental House for Increased Income: A Unique System Designed to Make More Money No Matter What Happens to the Economy. 1985. 17.95 (ISBN 0-07-005232-8). McGraw.
Bierbrier, M. L. Hieroglyphic Texts from Egyptian Stelae etc. in the British Museum, Pt. X. 152p. 1982. 99.00x (ISBN 0-7141-0926-6, Pub. by Brit Mus Pubns England). State Mutual Bk.
--The Late New Kingdom in Egypt(C 1300-664 B.C.) 160p. 1975. text ed. 40.50x (ISBN 0-85668-028-1, Pub. by Aris & Phillips England). Humanities.
Bierbrier, Morris. The Tomb-Builders of the Pharaohs. (Illus.). 160p. 1985. 15.95 (ISBN 0-684-18229-7, ScribT). Scribner.
--Tomb Builders of the Pharoahs. 160p. 1982. 75.00x (ISBN 0-7141-8044-0, Pub. by Brit Mus Pubns England). State Mutual Bk.
Bierce, A. The Collected Writings of Ambrose Bierce. 34.95 (ISBN 0-88411-859-2, Pub. by Aeonian Pr). Amereon Ltd.
Bierce, Ambrose. Can Such Things Be? 314p. 1976. Repr. of 1910 ed. lib. bdg. 17.95x (ISBN 0-89190-195-7, Pub. by River City Pr). Amereon Ltd.
--Can Such Things Be? 1977. pap. 2.95 (ISBN 0-8065-0550-8). Citadel Pr.
--Collected Works, 12 vols. 5000.00 (ISBN 0-87968-884-X). Gordon Pr.
--Collected Works of Ambrose Bierce 1909-1912, 12 Vols. LC 66-14638. Set. 185.00x (ISBN 0-87752-010-0). Gordian.
--Collected Writings of Ambrose Bierce. LC 72-13283. (Biography Index Reprint Ser). Repr. of 1946 ed. 41.00 (ISBN 0-8369-8141-3). Ayer Co Pubs.
--Collected Writings of Ambrose Bierce. 832p. 1983. pap. 9.95 (ISBN 0-8065-0180-4, 70). Citadel Pr.
--The Complete Short Stories of Ambrose Bierce. Hopkins, Ernest J., ed. LC 84-8575. iv, 496p. 1984. pap. 10.95 (ISBN 0-8032-6071-7, BB 896, Bison). U of Nebr Pr.
--The Devil's Dictionary. 376p. Repr. of 1911 ed. lib. bdg. 19.95 (ISBN 0-89190-186-8, Pub. by River City Pr). Amereon Ltd.
--The Devil's Dictionary. 145p. 1911. pap. 2.50 (ISBN 0-486-20487-1). Dover.
--The Devil's Dictionary. 13.50 (ISBN 0-8446-0492-5). Peter Smith.
--The Devil's Dictionary. LC 78-13294. (Illus.). 308p. 1978. 14.95 (ISBN 0-916144-34-8). Stemmer Hse.
--Eyes of the Panther: Tales of Soldiers & Civilians. facsimile ed. LC 76-169541. (Short Story Index Reprint Ser.). Repr. of 1928 ed. 22.00 (ISBN 0-8369-4002-4). Ayer Co Pubs.
--Fantastic Fables. 160p. 1976. Repr. of 1911 ed. lib. bdg. 13.95 (ISBN 0-89190-184-1, Pub. by River City Pr). Amereon Ltd.
--Fantastic Fables. LC 73-92026. 116p. 1970. pap. 2.50 (ISBN 0-486-22225-X). Dover.
--Ghost & Horror Stories. 14.00 (ISBN 0-8446-0493-3). Peter Smith.
--Ghost & Horror Stories of Ambrose Bierce. Bleiler, E. F., ed. (Orig.). 1964. pap. 3.95 (ISBN 0-486-20767-6). Dover.
--Ghost & Horror Stories of Ambrose Bierce. Bleiler, E. F., ed. LC 64-13459. lib. bdg. 10.50x (ISBN 0-88307-019-7). Gannon.
--In the Midst of Life, 2 vols. Incl. Pt. 1. Tales of Soldiers. 215p. lib. bdg. 13.95x; Pt. 2. Tales of Civilians. lib. bdg. 12.95x. 1976. Repr. of 1909 ed (Pub. by River City Pr). Amereon Ltd.
--In the Midst of Life. 1977. pap. 2.95 (ISBN 0-8065-0551-6). Citadel Pr.
--Letters. Pope, B. C., ed. LC 67-30702. 1967. Repr. of 1921 ed. 12.50x (ISBN 0-87752-009-7). Gordian.
--The Monk & the Hangman's Daughter. 143p. 1976. Repr. of 1911 ed. lib. bdg. 12.95x (ISBN 0-89190-183-3, Pub. by River City Pr). Amereon Ltd.
--An Occurrence at Owl Creek Bridge. (Creative's Classics Ser.). (Illus.). 40p. (gr. 4-9). 1980. PLB 8.95 (ISBN 0-87191-770-X). Creative Ed.
--Sardonic Humor of Ambrose Bierce. Barkin, George, ed. 232p. (Orig.). 1963. pap. 3.50 (ISBN 0-486-20768-4). Dover.
--The Sardonic Humor of Ambrose Bierce. Barkin, George, ed. LC 63-19487. lib. bdg. 11.50x (ISBN 0-88307-020-0). Gannon.
--The Stories & Fables of Ambrose Bierce. Wagenknecht, Edward, ed. LC 77-20146. (Illus.). 368p. 1977. 14.95 (ISBN 0-916144-19-4). Stemmer Hse.
--Tales of Horror & Fantasy. 228p. Repr. of 1907 ed. lib. bdg. 14.95x (ISBN 0-89190-187-6, Pub. by River City Pr). Amereon Ltd.
--Tales of Soldiers & Civilians. facs. ed. LC 70-121522. (Short Story Index Reprint Ser). 1891. 21.00 (ISBN 0-8369-3478-4). Ayer Co Pubs.
Bierce, Jane. Building Passion. (Harlequin American Romance Ser.). 256p. 1983. pap. 2.25 (ISBN 0-373-16015-1). Harlequin Bks.
Bierce, Lucius V. Travels in the Southland, 1822-1823. Knepper, George W., ed. LC 66-13719. (Illus.). 153p. 1966. 4.50 (ISBN 0-8142-0075-3). Ohio St U Pr.
Bierds, Linda. Flights of the Harvest-Mare. Boyer, Dale K., ed. LC 84-73272. (Modern & Contemporary Poetry of the West Ser.). 50p. (Orig.). 1984. pap. 3.00 (ISBN 0-916272-27-3). Ahsahta Pr.
Bierens, H. J. Robust Methods & Asymptotic Theory in Nonlinear Econometrics. (Lecture Notes in Economics & Mathematical Systems Ser.: Vol. 192). (Illus.). 198p. 1981. pap. 20.00 (ISBN 0-387-10838-6). Springer-Verlag.
Bierfelder, W. Handwoerterbuch des Oeffentlichen Dienster: Das Personalwesen. 1800p. (Ger.). 1976. 250.00 (ISBN 3-503-01424-1, M-7440, Pub. by E. Schmidt). French & Eur.
Bierhorst, Jane B., ed. see Steig, William.
Bierhorst, John. Four Masterworks of American Indian Literature. LC 84-8462. 371p. 1984. pap. 10.95 (ISBN 0-8165-0886-0). U of Ariz Pr.
--The Hungry Woman: Myths & Legends of the Aztecs. LC 83-25068. (Illus.). 160p. (gr. 5up). 1984. 10.00 (ISBN 0-688-02766-0). Morrow.
--The Monkey's Haircut. (Illus.). 128p. (gr. 7 up). 1985. 13.50 (ISBN 0-688-04269-4). Morrow.
--The Mythology of North America. LC 85-281. (Illus.). 256p. (gr. 9 up). 1985. 13.00 (ISBN 0-688-04145-0, Morrow Junior Books). Morrow.
--A Nahuatl-English Dictionary & Concordance to the "Cantares Mexicanos". With an Analytic Transcription & Grammatical Notes. LC 82-61070. 768p. 1985. 69.50x (ISBN 0-8047-1183-6). Stanford U Pr.
Bierhorst, John, ed. & tr. Black Rainbow: Legends of the Incas & Myths of Ancient Peru. LC 76-19092. 160p. (gr. 7 up). 1976. 9.95 (ISBN 0-374-30829-2). FS&G.
Bierhorst, John, ed. In the Trail of the Wind: American Indian Poems & Ritual Orations. LC 71-144822. (Illus.). 224p. (gr. 7 up). 1971. 6.95 (ISBN 0-374-33640-7). FS&G.
--The Red Swan: Myths & Tales of the American Indians. 386p. 1981. Repr. of 1976 ed. lib. bdg. 31.50x (ISBN 0-374-90633-5). Octagon.
--The Red Swan: Myths & Tales of the American Indians. 386p. 1985. 10.95 (ISBN 0-374-51393-7). FS&G.
--The Ring in the Prairie. LC 70-85546. (A Pied Piper Book). (Illus.). (gr. k-3). 1976. pap. 1.75 (ISBN 0-8037-7455-9). Dial Bks Young.
--The Sacred Path: Spells, Prayers & Power Songs of the American Indians. LC 82-14118. (Illus.). 191p. (gr. 5 up). 1983. PLB 10.75 (ISBN 0-688-01699-5). Morrow.
--The Sacred Path: Spells, Prayers, & Power Songs of the American Indians. LC 83-19460. (Illus.). 192p. 1984. pap. 6.70 (ISBN 0-688-02647-8, Quill). Morrow.
--Songs of the Chippewa. LC 74-6040. (Illus.). 48p. (ps up). 1974. 6.95 (ISBN 0-374-37145-8). FS&G.
Bierhorst, John, tr. from Nahuatl. Cantares Mexicanos: Songs of the Aztecs. LC 82-61071. 576p. 1985. 48.50x (ISBN 0-8047-1182-8). Stanford U Pr.
Bierhorst, John, tr. Spirit Child. LC 84-720. (Illus.). 32p. 1984. 12.00 (ISBN 0-688-02609-5, Morrow Junior Books); PLB 11.04 (ISBN 0-688-02610-9). Morrow.
Bieri, James, et al. Clinical & Social Judgment: The Discrimination of Behavioral Information. LC 75-11944. 288p. 1975. Repr. of 1966 ed. 17.50 (ISBN 0-88275-291-X). Krieger.
Bieri, S. Fiscal Federalism in Switzerland. LC 79-50392. (Centre for Research on Federal Financial Relations - Research Monograph: No. 26). (Orig.). 1979. pap. 8.00 (ISBN 0-7081-1072-X, 0533, Pub. by ANUP Australia). Australia N U P.
Bierlein, Lawrence W. Red Book on Transportation of Hazardous Materials. LC 76-44394. 896p. 1977. 90.00 (ISBN 0-8436-1407-2). Van Nos Reinhold.
Bierley, Paul E. Hallelujah Trombone! 1985. 19.95 (ISBN 0-918048-03-6); pap. 14.95 (ISBN 0-918048-05-2). Integrity.
--Hallelujah Trombone! The Story of Henry Fillmore. LC 82-90686. 1982. pap. 14.95 (ISBN 0-918048-03-6). Integrity.
--The Music of Henry Fillmore & Will Huff. LC 82-81491. (Music Catalog Ser.). 1982. pap. 5.95 (ISBN 0-918048-02-8). Integrity.
--Office Fun! LC 76-39578. (Cartoon Ser.). (Illus., Orig.). pap. 2.00 autographed ed. (ISBN 0-918048-01-X). Integrity.
--The Works of John Philip Sousa. LC 84-80665. 1984. 28.50 (ISBN 0-918048-04-4). Integrity.
Bierma, Lyle D., tr. see Von Harnack, Adolf.
Bierman & Smidt. Financial Management for Decision Making. 1200p. 1986. price not set incl. instr's. manual test bank (ISBN 0-02-310030-3). Macmillan.
Bierman, et al. Practical Oscilloscope Handbook. 2nd ed. 184p. pap. 8.95 (ISBN 0-8104-0851-1). Hayden.
Bierman, A. K. Life & Morals: An Introduction to Ethics. 596p. 1980. pap. text ed. 14.95 (ISBN 0-15-550725-7, HC). HarBraceJ.
Bierman, Alan W. & Guiho, Gerard. Automatic Program Construction Techniques. 500p. 1984. 57.50 (ISBN 0-02-949070-7). Macmillan.
Bierman, Arthur K. Logic: A Dialogue. LC 64-16572. (Illus.). pap. 108.30 (ISBN 0-317-08126-8, 2016286). Bks Demand UMI.
Bierman, Arthur K. & Gould, James A. Philosophy for a New Generation. 4th ed. 1980. pap. write for info. (ISBN 0-02-309640-3). Macmillan.
Bierman, Bob. A Collection of Editorial Cartoons, 1984. (Illus.). 180p. 1983. 14.95 (ISBN 0-919573-08-8, Pub. by New Star Bks BC); pap. 7.95 (ISBN 0-919573-09-6). Flatiron Book Dist.
Bierman, C. Warren & Pearlman, David S., eds. Allergic Diseases of Infancy, Childhood & Adolescence. LC 79-3915. (Illus.). 837p. 1980. text ed. 68.00 (ISBN 0-7216-1726-3). Saunders.
Bierman, Elenore C. There's an Iguana in My Plumbing. Ashton, Sylvia, ed. LC 75-777. 1976. 13.95 (ISBN 0-87949-050-0). Ashley Bks.
Bierman, Gerald J. Factorization Methods for Discrete Sequential Estimation. 1977. 42.50 (ISBN 0-12-097350-2). Acad Pr.
Bierman, Harold, Jr. Decision Making & Planning for the Corporate Treasurer. LC 76-58435. (Systems & Controls for Financial Management Ser.). 195p. 1977. 51.50x (ISBN 0-471-07238-9, Pub. by Ronald Pr). Wiley.
--Financial Management & Inflation. (Illus.). 180p. 1981. 15.95 (ISBN 0-02-903570-8). Free Pr.
--Strategic Financial Planning: A Manager's Guide to Improving Profit Performance. LC 80-1058. (Illus.). 1980. 15.95 (ISBN 0-02-903560-0). Free Pr.
Bierman, Harold, Jr. & Drebin, Allan R. Financial Accounting: An Introduction. 3rd ed. LC 77-75531. (Illus.). 1978. text ed. 31.95x (ISBN 0-7216-1704-2); study guide 12.95x (ISBN 0-7216-1717-4). Dryden Pr.
Bierman, Harold, Jr. & Dyckman, Thomas R. Managerial Cost Accounting. 2nd ed. (Illus.). 480p. 1976. write for info. (ISBN 0-02-309720-5, 30972). Macmillan.
Bierman, Harold, Jr. & Haas, Jerome. An Introduction to Managerial Finance. 1973. text ed. 12.95x (ISBN 0-393-09353-0). Norton.
Bierman, Harold, Jr. & Smidt, Seymour. The Capital Budgeting Decision: Economic Analysis of Investment Projects. 6th ed. 544p. 1984. text ed. write for info. (ISBN 0-02-309940-2). Macmillan.
Bierman, Harold, Jr., et al. Quantitative Analysis for Business Decisions. 6th ed. 1981. 31.95 (ISBN 0-256-02524-X). Irwin.
Bierman, Howard. How to Plan & Install Electronic Burglar Alarms. (gr. 10 up). 1977. pap. 6.50 (ISBN 0-8104-5734-2). Hayden.
Bierman, John. Odyssey. 288p. 1984. 16.95 (ISBN 0-671-50156-9). S&S.
--Righteous Gentile: The Story of Raoul Wallenberg, Missing Hero of the Holocaust. LC 80-52465. (Illus.). 256p. 1981. 12.95 (ISBN 0-670-74924-9). Viking.
--Righteous Gentile: The Story of Raoul Wallenberg, Missing Hero of the Holocaust. 210p. Repr. 12.95 (ISBN 0-686-95084-4). ADL.
Bierman, Judah, jt. ed. see Laszlo, Ervin.
Bierman, Stanley M. The World's Greatest Stamp Collectors. LC 80-70957. (Illus.). 320p. 1981. 17.95 (ISBN 0-8119-0347-8). Fell.
Biermann, Alan W. & Guiho, Gerard. Automatic Program Construction. 1982. write for info. Elsevier.
--Computer Program Synthesis Methodologies. 1982. lib. bdg. 52.50 (ISBN 90-277-1504-1, Pub. by Reidel Holland). Kluwer Academic.
Biermann, Berthold, ed. Goethe's World: As Seen in Letters & Memoirs. LC 77-165616. (Select Bibliographies Reprint Ser.). 1972. Repr. of 1949 ed. 29.00 (ISBN 0-8369-5923-X). Ayer Co Pubs.
Biermann, June & Toohey, Barbara. The Diabetic's Book: All Your Questions Answered. LC 81-50792. (Illus.). 252p. 1981. 10.95 (ISBN 0-87477-197-8); pap. 5.95 (ISBN 0-87477-183-8). J P Tarcher.
--The Diabetic's Sports & Exercise Book: How to Play Your Way to Better Health. LC 76-17894. (Illus.). 1977. pap. 5.95i (ISBN 0-397-01202-0, LP-114). Har-Row.
--The Diabetic's Total Health Book. 1983. pap. 3.95 (ISBN 0-671-50335-9). PB.
--The Peripatetic Diabetic: Good Health, Good Times, & Good Food for the Diabetic Who Wants to Have it All. LC 83-24336. 264p. 1984. o. p. 14.95 (ISBN 0-87477-309-1); pap. 7.95 (ISBN 0-87477-308-3). J P Tarcher.
--The Woman's Holistic Headache Relief Book. 212p. Repr. of 1979 ed. 8.95 (ISBN 0-686-35967-4). Sugarfree.
Bierre, Gustave De La see De La Bierre, Gustave H.
Biers, Jane C. The Great Bath on the Lechaion Road: Corinth, Results of Excavations Conducted by the American School of Classical Studies at Athens, Vol. XVII. (Illus.). 128p. 1985. text ed. 25.00 (ISBN 0-87661-171-4). Am Sch Athens.
Biers, Jane C. & Soren, David, eds. Studies in Cypriote Archaeology. (Monographs: No. XVIII). 189p. 1981. pap. 15.00x (ISBN 0-917956-23-0). UCLA Arch.
Biers, Jane C., et al. Illustrated Museum Handbook: A Guide to the Collections in the Museum of Art & Archaeology, University of Missouri-Columbia. Overby, Osmund, ed. LC 81-69839. (Illus.). 135p. 1982. pap. 10.00x (ISBN 0-8262-0366-3). U of Mo Pr.
Biers, William R. The Archaeology of Greece: An Introduction. LC 79-22070. (Cornell Paperbacks Ser.). (Illus.). 343p. 1980. 42.50x (ISBN 0-8014-1023-1); pap. 17.95x (ISBN 0-8014-9229-7). Cornell U Pr.
Biersack, H. J. & Cox, P. H., eds. Radioisotope Studies in Cardiology. (Developments in Nuclear Medicine Ser.). 1985. lib. bdg. 59.50 (ISBN 0-318-04531-1, Martinus Nijhoff Netherlands). Kluwer Academic.
Bierschwale, Margaret. Fort McKavett, Texas. (Illus.). 1966. 15.00 (ISBN 0-685-05001-7). A Jones.
Biersdorf, John E. Healing of Purpose: God's Call to Discipleship. 192p. (Orig.). 1985. pap. 11.95 (ISBN 0-687-16741-8). Abingdon.
Bierstadt, Edward H. Dunsany the Dramatist. 1919. 20.00 (ISBN 0-8274-2208-3). R West.
Bierstadt, Edward Hale, ed. & intro. by see Walker, Stuart.
Bierstadt, O. A., tr. see Blok, Petrus J.
Bierstedt, K. & Fuchssteiner, B., eds. Functional Analysis III: Surveys & Recent Results, Proceedings of the 3rd Paderborn Conference. (Mathematics Studies: Vol. 90). 382p. 1984. 54.00 (ISBN 0-444-86866-6, I-104-84, North-Holland). Elsevier.
Bierstedt, K. D. Functional Analysis: Surveys & Recent Results, 2. (Mathematical Studies Ser.: Vol. 38). 342p. 1980. 59.75 (ISBN 0-444-85403-7, North Holland). Elsevier.
Bierstedt, Robert. American Sociological Theory: A Critical History. LC 81-10820. 1981. 47.50 (ISBN 0-12-097480-0); pap. 20.00 (ISBN 0-12-097482-7). Acad Pr.
--The Social Order. 4th ed. (Illus.). 544p. 1974. text ed. 34.95 (ISBN 0-07-005253-0). McGraw.
Bierstedt, Robert, ed. see Znaniecki, Florian.
Biersteker, Thomas J. Distortion or Development? Contending Perspectives on the Multinational Corporation. 1978. pap. 9.95x (ISBN 0-262-52065-6). MIT Pr.
Bierwag, G. O. The Primary Market for Municipal Debt: Bidding Rules & the Cost of Long-Term Borrowing, Vol. 29. Altman, Edward I. & Walter, Ingo, eds. LC 80-82480. (Contemporary Studies in Economic & Financial Analysis Ser.). 300p. 1981. 40.00 (ISBN 0-89232-167-9). Jai Pr.
Bierwisch, Manfred. Modern Linguistics, Its Development Methods & Problems. (Janua Linguarum, Ser. Minor: No. 110). 103p. 1971. pap. text ed. 10.40x (ISBN 90-2791-657-8). Mouton.
Bierwisch, Manfred & Heidolph, Karl E., eds. Progress in Linguistics: A Collection of Papers. LC 78-123127. (Janua Linguarum Ser.: No. 43). 1970. text ed. 32.80x (ISBN 90-2790-723-4). Mouton.
Bierwolf, D., et al. Geschwulste-Tumors Two. LC 56-2297. (Handbuch der Allgemeineu Pathologie: Vol. 6, Pt. 6). (Illus.). 908p. 1975. 271.40 (ISBN 0-387-06820-1). Springer-Verlag.
Bies, John & Long, Robert A. Mapping & Topographic Drafting. LC 82-62044. (South-Western Series on Technical Drafting). (Illus.). 264p. 1983. text ed. 18.95 (ISBN 0-538-33330-8); instr's guide avail. SW Pub.
Bies, John D. Sheet Metal Work. (AUDEL Ser.). 472p. 1985. lib. bdg. 17.95 (ISBN 0-8161-1706-3). G K Hall.
Biesalski, E., jt. auth. see Hopfan, H. J.

Biesantz, Hagen & Klingborg, Arne. The Goetheanum: Rudolf Steiner's Architectural Impulse. Schmid, Jean, tr. from Ger. (Illus.). 131p. 1979. pap. 14.95 (ISBN 0-85440-355-8, Pub. by Steinerbooks). Anthroposophic.

Biesanz, John & Biesanz, Mavis. Modern Society with Revisions. 3rd ed. 1971. text ed. 28.95 (ISBN 0-13-597732-0). P-H.

Biesanz, John, jt. auth. see Biesanz, Mavis.

Biesanz, John B. & Biesanz, Mavis. Costa Rican Life. LC 78-12865. (Illus.). 1979. lib. bdg. 24.75x (ISBN 0-313-21125-6, BICR). Greenwood.

Biesanz, John B. & Biesanz, Mavis H. The People of Panama. LC 77-8269. (Illus.). 1977. Repr. of 1955 ed. lib. bdg. 27.50x (ISBN 0-8371-9680-9, BIPP). Greenwood.

Biesanz, Mavis & Biesanz, John. Introduction to Sociology. 3rd ed. (Illus.). 1978. text ed. 27.95 (ISBN 0-13-497412-3); study guide o.p. 8.95 (ISBN 0-13-497404-2). P-H.

Biesanz, Mavis, jt. auth. see Biesanz, John.

Biesanz, Mavis, jt. auth. see Biesanz, John B.

Biesanz, Mavis H., jt. auth. see Biesanz, John B.

Biesanz, Richard, et al. The Costa Ricans. (Illus.). 304p. 1982. pap. 23.95 reference (ISBN 0-13-179606-2). P-H.

Biese, Alfred. The Development of the Feeling for Nature in the Middle Ages & Modern Times. 1964. Repr. of 1905 ed. 26.50 (ISBN 0-8337-0276-9). B Franklin.

Biesele, Igildo. Graphic Design Education. (Illus.). 190p. 1981. 72.50 (ISBN 0-8038-2712-1, Visual Communication). Hastings.

Biesenberger, J. A. Devolatization of Polymers: Fundamentals - Equipment - Application. LC 83-62610. 350p. 1983. text ed. 28.00 (ISBN 0-02-949170-3, Pub. by Hanser International). Macmillan.

Biesenberger, Joseph A. & Sebastain, Donald H. Principles of Polymerization Engineering. 744p. 1983. 54.50 (ISBN 0-471-08616-9). Wiley.

Biest, Van der O. see Van der Biest, O.

Biestek, Felix P. The Casework Relationship. LC 57-9453. 1957. pap. 3.95 (ISBN 0-8294-0224-1). Loyola.

Biestek, Felix P. & Gehrig, Clyde C. Client Self-Determination in Social Work: A Fifty Year History. LC 78-14225. 1978. 7.95 (ISBN 0-8294-0275-6); pap. 5.95 (ISBN 0-8294-0276-4). Loyola.

Biestek, T. & Weber, J. Electrolytic & Chemical Conversion Coatings. 434p. 1981. 85.00x (ISBN 0-901994-78-2, Pub. by Portcullio Pr). State Mutual Bk.

Biester, H. E. & Schwarte, L. H. Diseases of Poultry. 5th ed. 1396p. 1981. 90.00x (ISBN 0-686-72947-1, Pub. by Oxford & IBH India). State Mutual Bk.

Bietak, Manfred. Aavaris & Piramesse: Archaeological Exploration in the Eastern Nile Delta. 1981. 15.50x (ISBN 0-85672-201-4, Pub. by Brit Acad England). State Mutual Bk.

Bietenholz, Peter G. & Deutscher, Thomas B., eds. Contemporaries of Erasmus: A Biographical Register of the Renaissance & Reformation, Vol. 1 (A-E) (Illus.). 480p. 1985. 72.50x (ISBN 0-8020-2507-2). U of Toronto Pr.

Bietti, Giambattista & Werner, Georges H. Trachoma: Prevention & Treatment. (Illus.). 248p. 1967. photocopy ed. 25.50x (ISBN 0-398-00154-5). C C Thomas.

Biever, Bruce F. Religion, Culture & Values: A Cross-Cultural Analysis of Motivational Factors in Native Irish & American Irish Catholicism. LC 76-6322. (Irish Americans Ser). 1976. 62.00 (ISBN 0-405-09319-5). Ayer Co Pubs.

Biever, Dale, et al. Four Pennsylvania German Studies. (Penn. German Ser.: Vol. 3). 1970. 20.00 (ISBN 0-911122-26-5). Penn German Soc.

Biey, Mario & Premoli, Amedeo. Tables for Active Filter Design. 1985. pap. text ed. 55.00 (ISBN 0-89006-159-9). Artech Hse.

Biffle, Christopher. Castle of the Pearl. (Illus.). 196p. (Orig.). 1983. pap. 6.68i (BN 4057). B&N NY.

--Castle of the Pearl. 1983. pap. 6.68 (ISBN 0-06-464057-4). Har-Row.

Biffle, Kent. Texas Sheriffs. (Illus.). 200p. Date not set. write for info. (ISBN 0-939722-22-4). Pressworks.

Big D Unlimited. A Guidebook to the Psilocybin Mushrooms of Mexico. (Illus., Orig.). 1976. pap. 3.00x (ISBN 0-934600-01-5). Mother Duck Pr.

Bigandet, Paul A. The Life, or Legend of Gaudama: The Buddha of the Burmese, 2 vols. 4th ed. LC 77-8749. Repr. of 1912 ed. Set. 52.50 (ISBN 0-404-16800-0). AMS Pr.

Bigane, John E., III. Faith, Christ or Peter: Matthew Sixteen: Eighteen in Sixteenth Century Roman Catholic Exegesis. LC 80-6095. 247p. 1981. lib. bdg. 24.00 (ISBN 0-8191-1524-X); pap. text ed. 12.25 (ISBN 0-8191-1525-8). U Pr of Amer.

Bigar, F., ed. Microsugery Update Nineteen Eighty-Two to Nineteen Eighty-Four. (Developments in Opthamology: Vol. 11). (Illus.). x, 206p. 1985. 54.25 (ISBN 3-8055-4004-3). S Karger.

Bigart, Lois S. You Can Have Joy. 1984. 5.00 (ISBN 0-8062-2414-2). Carlton.

Bigart, Robert, ed. Environmental Pollution in Montana. LC 71-169032. 261p. 1972. O.P. 8.50 (ISBN 0-87842-037-1); pap. 4.95 (ISBN 0-87842-025-8). Mountain Pr.

Bigazzi, M. F. & Greenwood, F. C., eds. Biology of Relaxin & Its Role in the Human: Proceedings of the 1st International Conference on Human Relaxin, Florence, Italy, September 30 - October 2, 1983. (International Congress Ser.: No. 610). xiv, 424p. 1983. 93.75 (ISBN 0-444-90303-8, I-362-83, Excerpta Medica). Elsevier.

Bigazzi, Pierluigi E., jt. ed. see Rose, Noel R.

Bigda, John P., jt. auth. see Cushman, Robert F.

Bigeagle, Duane. Bidato: Ten Mile River Poems. 1975. saddlestitched in wrappers 2.00 (ISBN 0-935388-02-8). Workingmans Pr.

Bigelow, Albert, jt. ed. see Paine, Albert B.

Bigelow, Ann C., tr. see Sadovnikov, D. N.

Bigelow, Donald N. William Conant Church & the Army & Navy Journal. LC 68-59264. (Columbia University Studies in the Social Sciences: No. 576). Repr. of 1952 ed. 21.00 (ISBN 0-404-51576-2). AMS Pr.

Bigelow, Erastus B. The Tariff Policy of England & of the United States Contrasted. (The Neglected American Economists Ser.). 1975. lib. bdg. 61.00 (ISBN 0-8240-1015-9). Garland Pub.

Bigelow, Fran, jt. auth. see Hanson, William A.

Bigelow, Gordon E. Frontier Eden: The Literary Career of Marjorie Kinnan Rawlings. LC 66-26808. (Illus.). xviii, 162p. 1966. pap. 10.00 (ISBN 0-8130-0672-4). U Presses Fla.

--The Poet's Third Eye. LC 76-15706. 1976. 7.50 (ISBN 0-8022-2188-2). Philos Lib.

--Rhetoric & American Poetry of the Early National Period. LC 60-63133. (University of Florida Humanities Monographs: No. 4). 1960. 3.50 (ISBN 0-8130-0022-X). U Presses Fla.

Bigelow, Gordon E. & Monti, Laura V., eds. Selected Letters of Marjorie Kinnan Rawlings. LC 82-2674. (Illus.). vi, 414p. 1983. 30.00 (ISBN 0-8130-0728-3). U Presses Fla.

Bigelow, Henry J. The Mechanism of Dislocations & Fracture of the Hip & Litholapaxy. LC 77-81659. 1977. Repr. of 1900 ed. lib. bdg. 40.00 (ISBN 0-89341-137-X). Longwood Pub Group.

--A Memoir of Henry Jacob Bigelow. LC 77-81657. 1977. Repr. of 1900 ed. lib. bdg. 35.00 (ISBN 0-89341-138-8). Longwood Pub Group.

--Orthopedic Surgery. LC 77-81658. 1977. Repr. of 1900 ed. lib. bdg. 40.00 (ISBN 0-89341-136-1): Longwood Pub Group.

--Surgical Anaesthesia. LC 77-6988. 1977. Repr. of 1900 ed. lib. bdg. 40.00 (ISBN 0-89341-144-2). Longwood Pub Group.

Bigelow, Howard E. Mushroom Pocket Field Guide. (Illus.). 1979. pap. 4.95 (ISBN 0-02-062200-7, Collier). Macmillan.

--North American Species of Clitocybe, Vol. I. (Nova Hedwigia Beiheft Ser.: No. 72). (Illus.). 500p. 1982. text ed. 47.25 (ISBN 3-7682-5472-0). Lubrecht & Cramer.

--North American Species of Clitocybe. Part 2. (Nova Hedwigia, Beiheft: No. 81). 250p. 1985. text ed. 42.00x (ISBN 3-7682-5481-X). Lubrecht & Cramer.

Bigelow, Jacob. The Useful Arts. LC 72-5034. (Technology & Society ser.). (Illus.). 762p. 1972. Repr. of 1840 ed. 42.00 (ISBN 0-405-04687-1). Ayer Co Pubs.

Bigelow, John. The Bible that was Lost & is Found. 4th ed. LC 78-65549. pap. 1.95 (ISBN 0-87785-159-X). Swedenborg.

--Campaign of Chancellorsville. (Illus.). 1983. Repr. 200.00 (ISBN 0-89029-075-X). Pr of Morningside.

--Jamaica in Eighteen-Hundred Fifty: The Effects on Sixteen Years of Freedom on a Slave Colony. LC 72-106880. Repr. of 1851 ed. 17.50x (ISBN 0-8371-3276-2, BIJ&, Pub. by Negro U Pr). Greenwood.

--Principles of Strategy, Illustrated Mainly from American Campaigns. LC 68-54787. Repr. of 1894 ed. lib. bdg. 42.50x (ISBN 0-8371-0312-6, BIPS). Greenwood.

--Toleration, & Other Essays & Studies. facs. ed. LC 78-84298. (Essay Index Reprint Ser). 1927. 14.25 (ISBN 0-8369-1075-3). Ayer Co Pubs.

--William Cullen Bryant. LC 70-125678. (American Journalists Ser.). 1970. Repr. of 1890 ed. 23.53 (ISBN 0-405-01653-0). Ayer Co Pubs.

--William Cullen Bryant. LC 80-19850. (American Men & Women of Letters Ser.). 360p. 1980. pap. 5.95 (ISBN 0-87754-160-4). Chelsea Hse.

--William Cullen Bryant. LC 79-78114. (Library of Lives & Letters Ser.). 1970. Repr. of 1890 ed. 34.00x (ISBN 0-8103-3369-4). Gale.

Bigelow, John & Longstreth, Breck. Going Places: Family Getaways in the Pacific Northwest. LC 85-50342. (Illus.). 160p. (Orig.). 1985. pap. 7.95 (ISBN 0-9614626-0-4). Seattle Child Pub.

Bigelow, John, ed. see Tilden, Samuel J.

Bigelow, Josette, ed. see Berlandier, Jean L., et al.

Bigelow, Lafayette J. Bench & Bar: A Complete Digest of the Wit, Humor, Asperities & Amenities of the Law. Repr. of 1871 ed. 40.00 (ISBN 0-384-04260-0). Johnson Repr.

Bigelow, Mab, tr. see Redi, F.

Bigelow, Marybelle S. Fashion in History: Western Dress, Prehistoric to Present. 2nd ed. LC 78-62539. 1979. text ed. 25.95x (ISBN 0-8087-2800-8). Burgess.

Bigelow, Melville M. History of Procedure in England from the Norman Conquest: The Norman Period (1066-1204) LC 80-2235. Repr. of 1880 ed. 49.50 (ISBN 0-404-18752-8). AMS Pr.

--The Law of Fraud & the Procedure Pertaining to the Redress Thereof. lix, 696p. 1981. Repr. of 1877 ed. lib. bdg. 45.00x (ISBN 0-8377-0317-4). Rothman.

--Papers on the Legal History of Government: Difficulties Fundamental & Artificial. 256p. 1982. Repr. of 1920 ed. lib. bdg. 25.00x (ISBN 0-8377-0326-3). Rothman.

--Placita Anglo - Normannica: Law Cases from William First to Richard First. lxiv, 328p. 1970. Repr. of 1881 ed. text ed. 15.00x (ISBN 0-8377-1928-3). Rothman.

--Placita Anglo-Normannica: Law Cases from William One to Richard One. LC 78-112405. Repr. of 1881 ed. lib. bdg. 27.50x (ISBN 0-678-04539-9). Kelley.

Bigelow, Melville M., intro. by. Centralization & the Law: Scientific Legal Education, an Illustration. LC 72-181856. xx, 296p. 1972. Repr. of 1906 ed. text ed. 16.50x (ISBN 0-8377-2004-4). Rothman.

Bigelow, Paige E., ed. Essays on Unicameralism. 65p. 1972. 0.75 (ISBN 0-318-15798-5). Citizens Forum Gov.

Bigelow, Wilbur W. Z-Cycle: Winning by a Force of a Fourth Type. LC 78-56742. 281p. 1980. 14.95 (ISBN 0-936366-00-1); pap. 9.95 (ISBN 0-936366-01-X). Crown.

Bigelow, William. Strangers in Their Own Country: A Curriculum Guide on South Africa. LC 85-71369. (Illus.). 192p. (Orig.). 1985. pap. text ed. write for info. (ISBN 0-86543-010-1). Africa Res.

Bigelow, William S. Buddhism & Immortality. LC 78-72379. Repr. of 1908 ed. 16.50 (ISBN 0-404-17228-8). AMS Pr.

Bigg, Charles. Christian Platonists of Alexandria: Eight Lectures. LC 75-123764. Repr. of 1886 ed. 27.50 (ISBN 0-404-00799-6). AMS Pr.

--The Church's Task Under the Roman Empire. 1977. lib. bdg. 59.95 (ISBN 0-8490-1629-0). Gordon Pr.

Biggadike, E. Ralph. Corporate Diversification: Entry, Strategy, & Performance. (Harvard Business School Publications, Division of Research Ser.). (Illus.). 1979. 16.00x (ISBN 0-87584-118-X). Harvard U Pr.

Biggane, Cecil. John Masefield: A Study. LC 73-15663. 1924. lib. bdg. 10.00 (ISBN 0-8414-3320-8). Folcroft.

Biggar, Charles R. Sir Oliver Mowat: A Biographical Sketch, 2 vols. LC 71-136404. (BCL Ser. I). Repr. of 1905 ed. Set. 75.00 (ISBN 0-404-00858-5). Vol. I (ISBN 0-404-08021-9). Vol. 2 (ISBN 0-404-08022-7). AMS Pr.

Biggar, H. P. Early Trading Companies of New France. LC 70-136303. (Illus.). 1972. Repr. of 1901 ed. lib. bdg. 27.50x (ISBN 0-678-00822-1). Kelley.

Biggar, H. P. & Litt, B. A. The Early Trading Companies of New France. LC 77-108460. 320p. 1972. Repr. of 1901 ed. 39.00 (ISBN 0-403-00452-7). Scholarly.

Biggar, Myron J. Practical Credit & Collections for Small Business. 120p. 1983. Comb-bound 24.95 (ISBN 0-8436-0887-0). Van Nos Reinhold.

Biggar, W. D., et al. Thymus Involvement in Immunity & Disease. new ed. LC 72-13558. (Illus.). 220p. 1973. text ed. 29.50x (ISBN 0-8422-7068-X); pap. text ed. 9.95x (ISBN 0-8290-1197-8). Irvington.

Biggart, John, tr. see Lewin, Moshe.

Biggart, Nicole W., jt. auth. see Hamilton, Gary G.

Bigge, June L. Teaching Individuals with Physical & Multiple Disabilities. 2nd ed. 424p. 1982. text ed. 24.95 (ISBN 0-675-09928-5). Merrill.

Bigge, L. Morris & Hunt, P. Maurice. Psychological Foundations of Education: An Introduction to Human Motivation, Development & Learning. 3rd ed. LC 79-52. 1980. pap. text ed. 21.75 scp (ISBN 0-06-040681-X, HarpC); instr's. manual avail. (ISBN 0-06-360681-X). Har-Row.

Bigge, Morris L. Learning Theories for Teachers. 4th ed. 356p. 1981. pap. text ed. 14.50 scp (ISBN 0-06-040673-9, HarpC); instr. manual avail. (ISBN 0-06-360682-8). Har-Row.

Bigge, Morris L. & Reynolds, George W. Philosophies for Teachers. 240p. 1982. pap. text ed. 13.95 (ISBN 0-675-09839-4). Merrill.

Bigger, Charles P. Participation: A Platonic Inquiry. LC 68-21802. xvi, 224p. 1968. 22.50x (ISBN 0-8071-0326-8). La State U Pr.

Biggers, Don H. German Pioneers in Texas. (Illus.). 230p. Repr. of 1925 ed. 11.95 (ISBN 0-89015-385-X). Eakin Pubns.

Biggers, Earl D. The Agony Column. 1976. Repr. of 1916 ed. PLB 15.95 (ISBN 0-89966-074-6). Buccaneer Bks.

--Black Camel. 1978. Repr. lib. bdg. 16.95x (ISBN 0-89966-077-0). Buccaneer Bks.

--Charlie Chan Carries on. (Charlie Chan Mysteries Ser.). 1976. Repr. of 1930 ed. lib. bdg. 17.95x (ISBN 0-89966-073-8). Buccaneer Bks.

--Fifty Candles. 1979. Repr. lib. bdg. 14.95 (ISBN 0-89966-079-7). Buccaneer Bks.

--The House Without a Key. 1979. Repr. lib. bdg. 17.95x (ISBN 0-89966-081-9). Buccaneer Bks.

--Seven Keys to Baldpate. 1976. Repr. of 1917 ed. lib. bdg. 18.95x (ISBN 0-89966-076-2). Buccaneer Bks.

Biggers, J., jt. auth. see Hamer, D. W.

Biggers, John. Ananse: The Web of Life in Africa. 1962 ed ed. (Illus.). 131p. 1979. pap. 12.50 (ISBN 0-292-70345-7); limited ed. 100.00 (ISBN 0-292-70346-5). U of Tex Pr.

Biggers, John, et al. Black Art in Houston: The Texas Southern University Experience. LC 77-99276. (Illus.). 122p. 1978. 20.00 (ISBN 0-89096-046-1). Tex A&M Univ Pr.

Biggers, John D., jt. ed. see Mastroianni, Luigi.

Biggers, W. Watts, jt. auth. see Goodman, Joseph I.

Biggerstaff, Knight. Nanking Letters: 1949. (East Asia Papers: No. 23). 110p. 1979. 3.00 (ISBN 0-318-04628-8). Cornell China-Japan Pgm.

--Nanking Letters, 1949. (East Asia Papers: No. 23). 110p. 1979. 3.00 (ISBN 0-318-13817-4). Cornell China-Japan Pgm.

Biggerstaff, Knight, jt. ed. see Teng Ssu-Yu.

Biggerstaff, Ray. Public Health Administration: An Instrument for Evaluation. 123p. 1983. pap. text ed. 8.95x (ISBN 0-89917-382-9). Tichenor Pub.

Bigges, Walter. A Summarie & True Discourse of Sir Francis Drake's West Indian Voyage. LC 72-25571. (English Experience Ser.: No. 128). 52p. 1969. Repr. of 1589 ed. 21.00 (ISBN 90-221-0128-2). Walter J Johnson.

Biggio, G. & Costa, E., eds. Receptors as Surramolecular Entities: Proceedings of the Biannual Capo Bio Conference, Cagliari, Italy, 7-10 June, 1981. (Advances in the Biosciences Ser.: Vol. 44). (Illus.). 480p. 1983. 100.00 (ISBN 0-08-029804-4). Pergamon.

Biggle, Lloyd, Jr. All the Colors of Darkness. 1975. pap. 1.25 (ISBN 0-685-54123-1, LB2956K, Leisure Bks). Dorchester Pub Co.

--The Fury Out of Time. 1975. pap. 1.25 (ISBN 0-685-61045-4, LB318, Leisure Bks). Dorchester Pub Co.

--Watchers of the Dark. 1975. pap. 0.95 (ISBN 0-685-53128-7, LB275NK, Leisure Bks). Dorchester Pub Co.

Biggle, Lloyd, Jr. & Sherred, T. L. Alien Main. LC 84-1503. (Science Fiction Ser.). 192p. 1985. 12.95 (ISBN 0-385-19358-0). Doubleday.

Biggles, Barry. The Copy Catalogue. (Illus.). pap. 9.95 (ISBN 0-394-74900-6). Pantheon.

Biggs, A. G., jt. auth. see Fordam, R.

Biggs, A. K. Matrimonial Proceedings. 1980. 30.00x (ISBN 0-686-97103-5, Pub. by Fourmat England). State Mutual Bk.

Biggs, A. K. & Rogers, A. P. Probate Practice & Procedure. 1981. 40.00x (ISBN 0-686-97111-6, Pub. by Fourmat England). State Mutual Bk.

Biggs, Abraham L. The Layman's Guide to Personal Bookkeeping for Credit Cards, Charge Accounts & Loans. (Illus.). 32p. 1984. 6.95 (ISBN 0-8062-2095-3). Carlton.

Biggs, Barbara E., jt. auth. see Felton, Gary S.

Biggs, Bill. To Believe or Not. LC 82-91011. 61p. 1983. 7.95 (ISBN 0-533-05672-1). Vantage.

Biggs, Bradley. Gavin. (Illus.). 182p. 1980. 17.50 (ISBN 0-208-01748-8, Archon). Shoe String.

Biggs, Bruce, ed. The Complete English-Maori Dictionary. (Eng. & Maori.). 1981. 29.95x (ISBN 0-19-647989-4). Oxford U Pr.

Biggs, Bud & Marshall, Lois. Watercolor Workbook. LC 79-12299. 1979. 22.50 (ISBN 0-89134-018-1). North Light Pub.

Biggs, Charles L., et al. Managing the Systems Development Process. 1980. text ed. 39.95 (ISBN 0-13-550830-4). P-H.

Biggs, Cliff, ed. see Biggs, Marjorie I.

Biggs, Don. How to Avoid Lawyers: A Step by Step Guide to Being Your Own Lawyer in Almost Every Situation. LC 84-18636. 1000p. (Orig.). 1985. pap. 22.95 (ISBN 0-8240-7284-7). Garland Pub.

--Pressure Cooker. (Illus.). 1979. 14.95 (ISBN 0-393-08815-4). Norton.

Biggs, Donald A., jt. auth. see Blocher, Donald H.

Biggs, Donald A., jt. auth. see Williamson, Edmund G.

Biggs, Donald A., jt. ed. see Giroux, Roy F.

Biggs, Edith. Confident Mathematics Teaching Five to Thirteen: INSET in the Classroom. 192p. 1983. 13.00x (ISBN 0-7005-0581-4, Pub. by NFER Nelson UK). Taylor & Francis.

--Teaching Mathematics Seven to Thirteen: Slow Learning & Able Children. 160p. 1984. pap. 14.00x (ISBN 0-7005-0661-6, Pub. by NFER Nelson UK). Taylor & Francis.

Biggs, Elizabeth A. White & Black: A Story of the Southern States, 3 vols. in 2. LC 79-8236. Repr. of 1862 ed. 84.50 set (ISBN 0-404-61780-8); Vol. 1. (ISBN 0-404-61791-3); Vol. 2. (ISBN 0-404-61792-1). AMS Pr.

Biggs, Howard. The River Medway. 160p. 1982. 30.00 (ISBN 0-86138-005-3, Pub. by Terence Dalton England). State Mutual Bk.

--The Sound of Maroons. (Illus.). 1979. 25.00 (ISBN 0-900963-83-2, Pub. by Terence Dalton England). State Mutual Bk.

Biggs, J. B., jt. ed. see Kirby, John R.

Biggs, Janet, jt. auth. see Shuttlewood, Nina.

Biggs, John B. & Collis, Kevin. Evaluating the Quality of Learning: The Solo Taxonomy Structure of the Observed Learning Outcome. LC 81-14885. (Educational Psychology Ser.). 1981. 29.50 (ISBN 0-12-097550-5); pap. 19.00 (ISBN 0-12-097552-1). Acad Pr.

Biggs, John, Jr. The Guilty Mind: Psychiatry & the Law of Homicide. LC 55-10812. (Isaac Ray Award Lectures Ser). 248p. (Orig.). 1967. pap. 4.95x (ISBN 0-8018-0070-6). Johns Hopkins.

Biggs, John M. Introduction to Structural Dynamics. 1964. text ed. 45.00 (ISBN 0-07-005255-7). McGraw.

--Introduction to Structural Engineering: Analysis & Design. (Illus.). 304p. 1986. text ed. 38.95 (ISBN 0-13-501008-X). P-H.

Biggs, John R. Letter Forms & Lettering. 1977. 6.95 (ISBN 0-8008-4724-5, Pentalic). Taplinger.

--Lettercraft. 1982. O.P. 14.95 (ISBN 0-7137-1269-4, +009); pap. 7.95 (ISBN 0-7137-1301-1). Sterling.

Biggs, Margaret K. Magnolias & Such. (Illus.). 1982. 2.50 (ISBN 0-943696-00-3). Red Key Pr.

--Petals from the Womanflower. 20p. (Orig.). 1983. pap. 2.50 (ISBN 0-938566-14-8). Adastra Pr.

--Sister to the Sun. Holley, Barbara, ed. (Earthwise Chapbook Ser.). 32p. 1981. pap. 3.50 (ISBN 0-933494-00-9). Earthwise Pubs.

Biggs, Marjorie I. Madame Alexander "Little People". Biggs, Cliff, ed. LC 79-66461. (Ser. I). (Illus.). 1979. 25.00 (ISBN 0-9603218-0-2). M Biggs.

Biggs, Mary, ed. Publishers & Librarians: A Foundation for Dialogue: Proceedings of the 42nd Annual Conference of the Graduate Library School. LC 83-18124. (Library Science Ser.). 120p. 1984. pap. 5.95 (ISBN 0-226-04847-0). U of Chicago Pr.

Biggs, Mary, jt. ed. see Sklar, Morty.

Biggs, Mouzon, jt. auth. see Allen, Charles L.

Biggs, Mouzon, Jr. Moments to Hold Close. 144p. 1983. 9.95 (ISBN 0-687-27147-9). Abingdon.

Biggs, N. L. Algebraic Graph Theory. LC 73-86042. (Tracts in Mathematics Ser.: No. 67). (Illus.). 180p. 1974. 34.50 (ISBN 0-521-20335-X). Cambridge U Pr.

--Interaction Models. LC 77-80827. (London Mathematical Society Lecture Ser.: No. 30). (Illus.). 1977. 19.95x (ISBN 0-521-21770-9). Cambridge U Pr.

Biggs, Neva, et al. Make Time for This. 70p. 1985. 10.00 (ISBN 0-911051-23-6). Plain View.

Biggs, Norman, et al. Graph Theory: Seventeen Thirty-Six to Nineteen Thirty-Six. (Illus.). 1976. 55.00x (ISBN 0-19-853901-0). Oxford U Pr.

Biggs, P. & Dalwood, C. Les Orleanais ont la Parole. (Illus.). 1977. pap. text ed. 6.95x (ISBN 0-582-33121-8); tchr's ed. 5.00x (ISBN 0-582-33122-6); cassettes 14.00 (ISBN 0-582-37885-0). Longman.

Biggs, P. M., et al, eds. see Christ College Symposium. Cambridge, England, June 20-25, 1971.

Biggs, R. D., jt. ed. see Gibson, M.

Biggs, Robert D. Inscriptions from Al-Hiba-Lagash: The First & Second Seasons. LC 76-47770. (Bibliotheca Mesopotamica Ser.: Vol.3). (Illus.). vi, 47p. 1976. 15.50X (ISBN 0-89003-018-9). Undena Pubns.

--Inscriptions from Tell Abu Salabikh. LC 73-91231. (Oriental Institute Publications Ser: Vol. 99). (Illus.). xiii, 114p. 1974. 50.00x (ISBN 0-226-62202-9). U of Chicago Pr.

Biggs, Robert D., ed. Discoveries from Kurdish Looms. LC 83-19535. (Illus.). 116p. (Orig.). 1983. pap. 22.50 (ISBN 0-941680-02-9). M&L Block.

Biggs, Rosa F. A Tender Reflection. 1985. 10.95 (ISBN 0-533-06660-3). Vantage.

Biggs, Shirley A., jt. auth. see Scales, Alice M.

Biggs, Simon J., jt. ed. see Dowrick, Peter.

Biggs, W. D., jt. auth. see Wainwright, S. A.

Biggs-Davison, John. Tory Lives: From Falkland to Disraeli. 1973. Repr. of 1952 ed. 25.00 (ISBN 0-8274-1480-3). R West.

Bigg-Wither, Thomas P. Pioneering in South Brazil: Three Years of Forest & Prairie Life in the Province of Parana, 2 Vols. LC 68-55177. (Illus.). 1968. Repr. of 1878 ed. Set. lib. bdg. 31.75x (ISBN 0-8371-3792-6, BISB). Greenwood.

Bigham, Clive. The Prime Ministers of Britain, 1721-1924. 1977. 59.95 (ISBN 0-8490-2470-6). Gordon Pr.

Bigham, J. A., ed. Select Discussions of Race Problems. (Atlanta Publication Ser.: No. 20). (Orig.). 1916. pap. 16.00 (ISBN 0-527-03121-6). Kraus Repr.

Bigham, James E. The Genesis Theory of Creation: A Layman's Hypothesis. 108p. (Orig.). 1982. pap. 2.25 (ISBN 0-941556-00-X). Ja-Mar Pubs.

Bigham, John A. Select Discussions of Race Problems. LC 16-11409. (Atlanta University Publications Ser.: No. 20). (Orig.). 1916. pap. 14.00 (ISBN 0-317-17940-3). Kraus Repr.

Bigham, Roger. Southeast England & East Anglia. (Ward Lock Regional Guides Ser.). 160p. (Orig.). 1984. pap. 9.95 (ISBN 0-7063-6226-8, Pub. by Auto Assn-British Tourist Authority England). Merrimack Pub Cir.

Bighami, Muhammad Ibn A. Love & War: Adventures from the Firuz Shah Namah of Sheikh Bighami. LC 74-6039. (Unesco Collection of Representative Works, Oriental Ser.). 224p. 1974. 35.00x (ISBN 0-8201-1126-0). Schol Facsimiles.

Bighorse, Tiana, jt. auth. see Bennett, Noel.

Bigl, Joseph H., et al. Blade Coating Technology. Clark, C. Wells, ed. (TAPPI PRESS Reports). (Illus.). 84p. (Orig.). 1978. pap. 24.95 (ISBN 0-89852-373-7, 01-01-R073). TAPPI.

Bigland, Eileen. In the Steps of George Borrow. 1978. Repr. lib. bdg. 25.00 (ISBN 0-89760-033-9, Telegraph). Dynamic Learn Corp.

--In the Steps of George Borrow. 355p. 1982. Repr. of 1951 ed. lib. bdg. 50.00 (ISBN 0-89760-091-6). Telegraph Bks.

--Ouida, the Passionate Victorian. LC 83-45707. Repr. of 1950 ed. 37.50 (ISBN 0-404-20029-X). AMS Pr.

Bigleon, Albert B. The Arkansas Bear: A Tale of Fanciful Adventure Told in Song & Story. 15.95 (ISBN 0-89190-367-4, Pub. by Am Repr). Amereon Ltd.

Bigler, et al. American Government: Issues & Challenges of the 1980's. 224p. 1982. pap. text ed. 13.95 (ISBN 0-8403-2596-7). Kendall-Hunt.

Bigler, Alexander. Equestrian Facilities: Planning & Design Handbook. 1986. cancelled (ISBN 0-442-20739-5). Van Nos Reinhold.

Bigler, Alexander B., jt. auth. see Koelzer, Victor A.

Bigler, Carole L. & Lloyd-Watts, Valery. Studying Suzuki Piano: More Than Music: A Handbook for Teachers, Parents & Students. LC 78-73088. (Illus., Orig.). 1979. pap. 24.95 (ISBN 0-918194-06-7). Accura.

Bigler, Erin D. Diagnostic Clinical Neuropsychology. (Illus.). 240p. 1984. text ed. 35.00x (ISBN 0-292-71536-6). U of Tex Pr.

Bigler, Lola, et al, eds. Cumulative Index to Society Publications 1918-1955. 10.00; text ed. 5.00 members. Am Ceramic.

Bigler, Robert M. The Politics of German Protestantism: The Rise of the Protestant Church Elite in Prussia, 1815-1848. LC 77-142055. 1972. 38.50x (ISBN 0-520-01881-8). U of Cal Pr.

Bigler, Rodney E., ed. see Brill, A. B., et al.

Bigler, Von R., ed. Pestalozzi in Burgdorf. Ingold, Klara, tr. from Ger. (Monograph Ser: Vol. 9, No. 3). (Illus.). 70p. 1972. pap. 3.50 (ISBN 0-87421-043-7). Utah St U Pr.

Bigley, D. B. & Talbot, R. J., eds. Introduction to Organic Chemistry. (Illus.). 400p. 1971. 20.50 (ISBN 0-444-20036-3, Pub. by Elsevier Applied Sci England). Elsevier.

Bigley, John. Tributaries. (Illus.). 1977. pap. 20.00 (ISBN 0-916908-40-2). Place Herons.

Bigley, Nancy J. Immunologic Fundamentals. 2nd ed. 1980. 20.95 (ISBN 0-8151-0801-X). Year Bk Med.

Bigley, William, jt. auth. see Miles, Darrell.

Biglieu, E. G., jt. auth. see Mantero, F.

Bigman, David. Coping with Hunger: Toward a System of Food Security & Price Stabilization. LC 81-22908. 384p. 1982. prof ref 39.95 (ISBN 0-88410-371-4). Ballinger Pub.

--Food Policies & Food Security under Instability. LC 82-48039. 272p. 1985. 29.00x (ISBN 0-669-05886-6). Lexington Bks.

--The Politics & Economics of Food Trade & Food Aid. LC 82-48039. 272p. 1985. 29.00 (ISBN 0-669-05886-6). Lexington Bks.

Bigman, David, ed. Floating Exchange Rates & the State of World Trade Payments. Taya, Teizo. 336p. 1984. prof. ref. 15.00x (ISBN 0-88410-998-4). Ballinger Pub.

Bigman, David & Taya, Teizo, eds. Exchange Rate & Trade Instability: Causes, Consequences & Remedies. LC 82-22798. 376p. 1983. Prof. Ref. 39.95 (ISBN 0-88410-898-8). Ballinger Pub.

--The Functioning of Floating Exchange Rates: Theory, Evidence & Policy Implications. LC 79-21589. 448p. 1980. prof ref 42.50 (ISBN 0-88410-492-3). Ballinger Pub.

Bigmore, F. C. A Bibliography of Printing. 1982. 75.00x (ISBN 0-87556-157-8). Saifer.

Bigmore, F. C. & Wyman, C. W. A Bibliography of Printing with Notes & Illustrations, 3 vols. in one. (Illus.). xxii, 976p. 1978. Repr. of 1880 ed. 75.00 (ISBN 0-900470-01-1). Oak Knoll.

Bignami, A., et al, eds. Central Nervous System Plasticity & Repair. 198p. 1985. text ed. 43.00 (ISBN 0-88167-050-2). Raven.

Bignami, G., jt. ed. see Anisman, H.

Bignell, James & Donovan, Robert. Digital Electronics. LC 84-23853. 300p. 1985. text ed. 28.00 (ISBN 0-8273-2307-7); instrs. guide 3.00 (ISBN 0-8273-2308-5). Delmar.

Bignell, Merle. First the Spring. (Illus.). 251p. 1971. 15.00x (ISBN 0-85564-048-0, Pub. by U of W Austral Pr). Intl Spec Bk.

--The Fruit of the Country: A History of the Shire of Gnowangerup Western Australia. 1978. 22.50x (ISBN 0-85564-125-8, Pub. by U of W Austral Pr). Intl Spec Bk.

--A Place to Meet: A History of the Shire of Katanning Western Australia. 350p. 1983. 24.50x (ISBN 0-85564-202-5, Pub. by U of W Austral Pr). Intl Spec Bk.

Bignell, Steven. Sex Education: Teacher's Guide & Resource Manual. Rev. ed. Hiatt, Jane & Nelson, Mary, eds. 277p. 1982. 24.95 (ISBN 0-941816-08-7); avail. tchr's guide (ISBN 0-941816-03-6). Network Pubns.

Bignell, Steven, ed. Family Life Education: Curriculum Guide. rev. ed. 396p. 1980. 24.95 (ISBN 0-941816-02-8). Network Pubns.

Bignell, Victor & Fortune, Joyce. Understanding Systems Failures. LC 83-12016. 227p. 1984. pap. 6.50 (ISBN 0-7190-0973-1, Pub. by Manchester Univ Pr). Longwood Pub Group.

Bignell, Victor, et al. Catastrophic Failures. 276p. 1977. pap. 17.00x (ISBN 0-335-00038-X, Pub. by Open Univ Pr). Taylor & Francis.

Bigner, Jerry. Human Development: A Life-Span Approach. 688p. 1983. text ed. write for info. (ISBN 0-02-309810-4). Macmillan.

Bigner, Jerry J. Parent-Child Relation. 448p. 1985. text ed. write for info. (ISBN 0-02-309970-4). Macmillan.

Bigner, Sandra H. & Johnston, William W. Cytopathology of the Central Nervous System. (Masson Monographs on Diagnostic Cytopathology, Vol. 3). 162p. 1983. 52.50. Masson Pub.

Bignon, J. & Scarpa, G. L., eds. Biochemistry, Pathology & Genetics of Pulmonary Emphysema: Proceedings of a Meeting on Emphysema Held at Porto Conte, Sassari (Sardinia), April 27-30, 1980. (Illus.). 430p. 1981. 72.00 (ISBN 0-08-027379-3). Pergamon.

Bignon, Jean P. see Shugrue, Michael F.

Bigon, Mario & Regazzoni, Guido. Morrow's Guide to Knots: For Sailing Fishing, Camping & Climbing. Lyman, Kennie, ed. Piotrowska, Maria, tr. from Ital. LC 82-6308. (Illus.). 258p. 1982. 15.00 (ISBN 0-688-01225-6); pap. 9.70 (ISBN 0-688-01226-4). Morrow.

Bigongiari, Dino, ed. see Thomas Aquinas, Saint.

Bigongiari, Dino, tr. see Gentile, Giovanni.

Bigot, A. The Outrageous Joke Book. 96p. (Orig.). 1983. pap. 3.95 (ISBN 0-943392-25-X). Tribeca Comm.

--The Outrageous Joke Book. (Illus.). 96p. 1984. Repr. of 1983 ed. 3.98 (ISBN 0-943392-62-4, Tripro Pub). Tribeca Comm.

Bigot, Arthur, jt. auth. see Kapp, Marshall B.

Bigot, J. M., jt. auth. see Chermet, J.

Bigsbee, Earle M. Mathematics Tables with Explanations of Tables. (Quality Paperback Ser.: No. 8). (Orig.). 1977. pap. 2.95 (ISBN 0-8226-0008-0). Littlefield.

Bigsby. Approaches to Popular Culture. 1977. 14.95 (ISBN 0-87972-083-2). Bowling Green Univ.

Bigsby, C. Albee. (Writers & Critics Ser.). 120p. 1978. 22.50 (ISBN 0-912378-08-5). Chips.

Bigsby, C., jt. ed. see Ziegler, H.

Bigsby, C. W. A Critical Introduction to Twentieth-Century American Drama, Vol. 2: Tennessee Williams, Arthur Miller, Edward Albee. (Illus.). 369p. 1985. 39.50 (ISBN 0-521-25811-1); pap. 14.95 (ISBN 0-521-27717-5). Cambridge U Pr.

--A Critical Introduction to Twentieth-Century American Drama, Vol. 3: Beyond Broadway. (Illus.). 400p. 1985. 39.50 (ISBN 0-521-26256-9); pap. 14.95 (ISBN 0-521-27896-1). Cambridge U Pr.

--A Critical Introduction to Twentieth Century American Drama: 1900-1940, Vol. 1. LC 81-18000. (Illus.). 340p. 1982. 42.50 (ISBN 0-521-24227-4); pap. 15.95 (ISBN 0-521-27116-9). Cambridge U Pr.

--David Mamet. (Contemporary Writers Ser.). 96p. 1985. pap. 4.95 (ISBN 0-416-40980-6, 9597). Methuen Inc.

--The Second Black Renaissance: Essays in Black Literature. LC 79-7723. (Contributions in Afro-American & African Studies: No. 50). 1980. lib. bdg. 37.50x (ISBN 0-313-21304-6, BNB/). Greenwood.

--Superculture: American Popular Culture & Europe. LC 74-84638. 1975. 13.95 (ISBN 0-87972-070-0); pap. 7.95 (ISBN 0-87972-163-4). Bowling Green Univ.

Bigsby, C. W., ed. Contemporary English Drama. LC 81-81341. (Statford-Upon-Avon Ser.: No. 19). 192p. 1981. text ed. 24.50x; pap. text ed. 13.95x (ISBN 0-8419-0717-X). Holmes & Meier.

Bigsby, Christopher W. Joe Orton. (Contemporary Writers Ser.). 96p. 1982. pap. 4.25x (ISBN 0-416-31690-5, NO. 3558). Methuen Inc.

Bigsby, John J. Shoe & Canoe or Pictures of Travel in the Canadas, 2 Vols. LC 69-19549. 1969. Repr. of 1850 ed. Set. 42.50 (ISBN 0-404-00880-1); 22.00 ea. Vol. 1 (ISBN 0-404-00881-X). Vol. 2 (ISBN 0-404-00882-8). AMS Pr.

Bigsten, Arne. Education & Income Determination in Kenya. LC 84-1539. 163p. 1984. text ed. 32.95 (ISBN 0-566-00703-7). Gower Pub Co.

--Income Distribution & Development: Theory, Evidence & Practice. 192p. (Orig.). 1983. pap. text ed. 15.00x (ISBN 0-435-84087-8). Gower Pub Co.

--Regional Inequality & Development: A Case Study of Kenya. 200p. 1980. text ed. 44.00x (ISBN 0-566-00382-1). Gower Pub Co.

Bigus, A. W. Make Yours in Stocks & Bonds at Little Risk: A Buy-Sell System That Makes the Difference. LC 82-82931. xviii, 287p. 1982. 17.50 (ISBN 0-9609330-1-8). Hampol Pub Co.

Bigwood, E. J. & Gerard, A. Fundamental Principles & Objectives of a Comparative Food Law, 4 vols. Incl. Vol. 1. General Introduction & Field of Application. xii, 128p. 1969. pap. 13.00 (ISBN 3-8055-0669-4); Vol. 2. Elements of Motivation & Elements of Qualification. (Illus.). xiv, 234p. 1968. pap. 25.25 (ISBN 3-8055-0670-8); Vol. 3. Elements of Structure & Institutional Elements. 240p. 1970. pap. text ed. 25.75 (ISBN 3-8055-0671-6); Vol. 4. Elements of Control & Sanction; Conclusion; Suggested Outline of a Modern Food Law. xiv, 329p. 1971. pap. text ed. 37.25 (ISBN 3-8055-1305-4). (Illus.). xxxviii, 803p. Set. pap. text ed. 68.25 (ISBN 3-8055-1332-1). S Karger.

Bigwood, E. J., ed. Protein & Amino Acid Functions. 536p. 1972. text ed. 155.00 (ISBN 0-08-016464-1). Pergamon.

Bigwood, Jean, jt. auth. see Bigwood, Kenneth.

Bigwood, Kenneth & Bigwood, Jean. New Zealand in Colour, Vol. 1. Baxter, James K., ed. (Illus.). 1962. 20.00 (ISBN 0-686-00956-8). Wellington.

Bihalji, Oto & Tomasevic, Nebojsa. World Encyclopedia of Naive Art. LC 84-51455. (Illus.). 740p. 1985. 67.50 (ISBN 0-935748-62-8). Scala Books.

Bihalji, Oto M., et al. Grunewald: The Isenheim Altarpiece. (Illus.). 294p. 1984. 75.00 (ISBN 0-933516-36-3). Alpine Bk Co.

Bihalji-Merin, Oto. Caprichos: Their Hidden Truth. Woods, John E., tr. LC 81-47300. (Helen & Kurt Wolff Bk.). (Illus.). 192p. 1981. 65.00 (ISBN 0-15-133463-3). HarBraceJ.

--Dumont: Art of the Primitives. (Pocket Art Ser.). (Illus.). 304p. 1984. pap. 5.95 (ISBN 0-8120-2185-1). Barron.

Bihalji Merin, Oto see Bihalji, Oto M., et al.

Bihova, Diana & Schrader, Connie. Beauty from the Inside Out: A Woman Doctor's Guide to What to Eat, Do & Use to Have Beautiful Skin, Hair & Nails All Your Life. 256p. 1986. 15.95 (ISBN 0-89256-282-X). Rawson Assocs.

Bihun, Yaroslav, ed. Boomerang: The Works of Valentyn Moroz. LC 74-77633. 1974. 5.75 (ISBN 0-914834-00-2); soft-cover 3.75 (ISBN 0-914834-00-2). Smoloskyp.

Bijlani, L. Eating Scientifically. 188p. 1979. 30.00x (ISBN 0-86125-049-4, Pub. by Orient Longman India). State Mutual Bk.

Bijlmer, Hendricus J. Outlines of the Anthropology of the Timor Archipelago. LC 77-87480. (Illus.). Repr. of 1929 ed. 48.00 (ISBN 0-404-16697-0). AMS Pr.

Bijou, Sidney W. & Baer, Donald M. Behavior Analysis of Child Development. (Child Psychology Ser.). 1978. pap. 12.95 ref. ed. (ISBN 0-13-066712-9). P-H.

--Child Development: Readings in Experimental Analysis. (Century Psychology Ser.). (Illus.). 1982. Repr. of 1967 ed. text ed. 28.50x (ISBN 0-8290-0055-0). Irvington.

Bijou, Sidney W. & Ribes-Inesta, Emilio, eds. Behavior Modification: Issues & Extensions. 1972. 32.00 (ISBN 0-12-097650-1). Acad Pr.

Bijou, Sidney W. & Ruiz, Roberto, eds. Behavior Modification: Contributions to Education. LC 80-278780. 352p. 1981. text ed. 36.00x (ISBN 0-89859-051-5). L Erlbaum Assocs.

Bijou, Sidney W., et al. The Exceptional Child: Conditioned Learning & Teaching Ideas. (Illus.). 217p. 1972. text ed. 34.50x (ISBN 0-8422-7001-9). Irvington.

Bijster, Fred. Dancing Is Pleasure for Two: The Story of Ballroom & Social Dance. 1985. lib. bdg. 78.95 (ISBN 0-8490-3249-0). Gordon Pr.

Bikai, Patricia M. The Pottery of Tyre. 92p. 1978. text ed. 65.50x (ISBN 0-85668-108-3, Pub. by Aris & Phillips England). Humanities.

Bikales, N. M., ed. Encyclopedia Reprints Series, 5 vols. LC 78-172950. 1239p. 1971. Set. pap. 101.95x (ISBN 0-471-07236-2, Pub. by Wiley-Interscience). Wiley.

--Water-Soluble Polymers. LC 73-79431. (Polymer Science & Technology Ser.: Vol. 2). 440p. 1973. 65.00x (ISBN 0-306-36402-6, Plenum Pr). Plenum Pub.

Bikales, Norbert M., ed. Adhesion & Bonding. LC 78-172950. 220p. 1971. 16.00 (ISBN 0-471-07230-3). Krieger.

--Extrusion & Other Plastics Operations. LC 78-172950. (Encyclopedia Reprints Ser). 281p. 1971. pap. 18.00 (ISBN 0-471-07232-X). Krieger.

--Mechanical Properties of Polymers. LC 78-172950. 280p. pap. text ed. 18.00 (ISBN 0-471-07234-6). Krieger.

--Molding of Plastics. LC 78-172950. 230p. pap. text ed. 16.00 (ISBN 0-471-07233-8). Krieger.

Bike World Editors. Traveling by Bike. 96p. 1977. pap. 3.95 (ISBN 0-89037-065-6). Anderson World.

Bikerman, J. J. Physical Surfaces. (Physical Chemistry Ser.: Vol. 20). 1970. 92.50 (ISBN 0-12-097851-2). Acad Pr.

Bikhovsky, Anatoly. Spanish (Ruy Lopez) Chigorin. (Illus.). 128p. 1983. pap. 14.95 (ISBN 0-7134-3626-3, Pub. by Batsford England). David & Charles.

Bikkal, Nicholas L. The Straight Man. 1983. 7.95 (ISBN 0-533-05041-3). Vantage.

Bikkenin, N. B. Socialist Ideology. 1980. pap. 5.95 (ISBN 0-8285-1771-1, Pub. by Progress Pubs USSR). Imported Pubns.

Bikkie, James A. Careers in Marketing. 2d ed. Dorr, Eugene, ed. LC 77-3865. (Occupational Manuals and Projects in Marketing). 1978. pap. text ed. 8.68 (ISBN 0-07-005236-0). McGraw.

Bikle, D. D., ed. Assay of Calcium Regulating Hormones. (Illus.). 290p. 1983. 38.50 (ISBN 0-387-90841-2). Springer-Verlag.

Bikle, George B., Jr. The New Jerusalem: Aspects of Utopianism in the Thought of Kagawa Toyohiko. LC 75-36125. (Association for Asian Studies Monograph: No. 30). 343p. 1976. 8.95x (ISBN 0-8165-0550-0); pap. text ed. 4.95x o. p. (ISBN 0-8165-0531-4). U of Ariz Pr.

Bikle, Nancy. Museum of Westward Expansion: A Photographic Collection. 126p. 1977. pap. 3.95 (ISBN 0-686-95748-2). Jefferson Natl.

Biklen, Douglas. Let Our Children Go. 1974. 3.50 (ISBN 0-937540-02-1, HPP-1). Human Policy Pr.

Biklen, Douglas, jt. auth. see Taylor, Steven J.

Biklen, Douglas & Bailey, Lee, eds. Rudely Stamp'd: Imaginal Disability & Prejudice. LC 81-40278. (Illus.). 134p. (Orig.). 1982. lib. bdg. 22.00 (ISBN 0-8191-1982-2); pap. text ed. 9.50 (ISBN 0-8191-1983-0). U Pr of Amer.

Biklen, Douglas, et al. Achieving the Complete School: Strategies for Effective Mainstreaming. (Special Education Ser.). 1985. text ed. 21.95 (ISBN 0-8077-2773-3); pap. text ed. 15.95x (ISBN 0-8077-2772-5). Tchrs Coll.

Biklen, Douglas P. Community Organizing: Theory & Practice. 336p. 1983. text ed. 27.95 (ISBN 0-13-153676-1). P-H.

Biklen, Sari K. & Branningan, Marilyn. Women & Educational Leadership. LC 79-7748. 288p. 1980. 27.50x (ISBN 0-669-03216-6). Lexington Bks.

Biklen, Sari K., jt. auth. see Bogdan, Robert C.

Biklin, D., et al. The Least Restrictive Alternative: Principles & Practices. Turnbull, H. Rutherford, III, ed. 80p. (Orig.). 1981. pap. 5.50 (ISBN 0-940898-06-3). Am Assn Mental.

Biko, Steve. Black Consciousness in South Africa. Arnold, Millard, ed. LC 78-65570. 1979. 12.95 (ISBN 0-394-50282-5, Vin). Random.

Bikram, Mahendra, et al. Hope & Peace. Browne, Bernadine, ed. (Illus.). 320p. pap. 12.00 (ISBN 0-910555-01-X). Berkshire Pub Co.

Bikson, Tora K. New Technology in the Office: Planning for People. (Studies in Productivity: Highlights of the Literature Ser.: Vol. 40). 1985. 35.00 (ISBN 0-08-029514-2). Work in Amer.

Bila, Dennis, et al. Arithmetic. LC 76-19446. 1976. 9.95x (ISBN 0-87901-058-4). Worth.

--Geometry & Measurement. LC 76-19445. 1976. 9.95 (ISBN 0-87901-059-2). Worth.

--Core Mathematics. LC 74-82696. (Illus.). ix, 603p. (Prog. Bk.). 1975. text ed. 22.95x (ISBN 0-87901-035-5). Worth.

--Intermediate Algebra. LC 74-84642. (Illus.). xvii, 625p. (Prog. Bk.). 1975. text ed. 22.95x (ISBN 0-87901-038-X). Worth.

--Introductory Algebra. LC 74-84641. (Illus.). xviii, 610p. (Prog. Bk.). 1975. text ed. 22.95x (ISBN 0-87901-037-1). Worth.

--Mathematics for Business Occupations. (Orig.). 1978. pap. text ed. 21.95 (ISBN 0-316-09475-7); tchr's. ed. avail. (ISBN 0-316-09477-3); test bank avail. (ISBN 0-316-09476-5). Little.

--Mathematics for Technical Occupations. (Orig.). 1978. pap. text ed. 21.95 (ISBN 0-316-09478-1); tcher's manual o.si. (ISBN 0-316-09481-1); test avail. (ISBN 0-316-09480-3). Little.

--Mathematics for the Health Occupations. (Orig.). 1978. pap. text ed. 19.95 (ISBN 0-316-09472-2); tchr's. manual avail. (ISBN 0-316-09474-9); test bank avail. (ISBN 0-316-09473-0). Little.

Bilan, R. P. The Literary Criticism of F. R. Leavis. LC 78-18089. 1979. 39.50 (ISBN 0-521-22324-5). Cambridge U Pr.

Bilancia, Philip R. Dictionary of Chinese Law & Government: Chinese-English. LC 73-80618. 832p. 1981. 55.00x (ISBN 0-8047-0864-9). Stanford U Pr.

Bilateral U. S.-Japan Seminar in Hydrology, 1st, Honolulu, Jan. 11-17, 1971. Systems Approach to Hydrology: Proceedings. Yevjevich, Vujica, ed. LC 71-168496. 1971. 21.00 (ISBN 0-918334-02-0). WRP.

Bilbao, Jon, jt. auth. see Douglass, William A.

Bilbija, Z. G., jt. auth. see Solomon, Ezra.

Bilby, B. A., et al, eds. Fundamentals of Deformation & Fracture. 630p. 1985. 79.50 (ISBN 0-521-26735-8). Cambridge U Pr.

Bild, Ian. The Jews in Britain. (Communities in Britain Ser.). (Illus.). 72p. (gr. 7-12). 1984. 14.95 (ISBN 0-7134-4217-4, Pub. by Batsford England). David & Charles.

Bild, Ian & Humphries, Stephen. Finding Out about Seaside Holidays. (Finding Out About Ser.). (Illus.). 48p. (gr. 5-8). 1983. 12.50 (ISBN 0-7134-4439-8, Pub. by Batsford England). David & Charles.

Bilder, Richard B. Managing the Risks of International Agreement. LC 80-52288. 320p. 1981. 27.50x (ISBN 0-299-08360-8). U of Wis Pr.

Bilderback, Diana & Patent, Dorothy. Garden Secrets. Halpin, Anne, ed. (Illus.). 320p. 1982. 14.95 (ISBN 0-87857-420-4, 01-760-0). Rodale Pr Inc.

Bilderback, Diane E. & Patent, Dorothy H. Backyard Fruits & Berries. Nelson, Suzanne, ed. (Illus.). 300p. 1984. 17.95 (ISBN 0-87857-509-X). Rodale Pr Inc.

Bilderbeck, James B. Chaucer's Legend of Good Women. LC 78-39441. Repr. of 1902 ed. 14.00 (ISBN 0-404-00859-3). AMS Pr.

Bildersee, A. State Scholarship Students at Hunter College of the City of New York. LC 77-176563. (Columbia University. Teachers College. Contributions to Education: No. 540). Repr. of 1932 ed. 22.50 (ISBN 0-404-55540-3). AMS Pr.

Bildstein, Keith, ed. The Wilson Bulletin. (Illus.). 150p. (J). ann. subscr. 20.00, quarterly (ISBN 0-318-16867-7); 16.00, members (ISBN 0-318-16868-5); back issues avail. special price for quantity orders. Wilson Ornithological.

Bilek, Arthur J. & Klotter, John C. Legal Aspects of Private Security. LC 79-55202. 287p. 1981. text ed. 16.95 (ISBN 0-87084-488-1). Anderson Pub Co.

Bilek, Z., jt. auth. see Buchar, Z.

Bilenky, S. M. Introduction to Feynman Diagrams. LC 73-21657. 1974. text ed. 44.00 (ISBN 0-08-017799-9). Pergamon.

--Introduction to the Physics of Electroweak Interactions. LC 81-15839. (Illus.). 250p. 1982. 66.00 (ISBN 0-08-026502-2). Pergamon.

Biles, Blake A., ed. European Environmental Laws & Regulations. 2nd ed. 455p. 1983. wkbk. 85.00 (ISBN 0-86587-115-9). Gov Insts.

Biles, G. Strategic Human Resource Planning. LC 80-81410. 1980. pap. 10.95 (ISBN 0-913878-20-0). T Horton & Dghts.

Biles, George E. Impact of New Withholding Requirements for Pensions, Annuities & Other Deferred Income Under TEFRA of 1982. LC 84-222581. write for info. Amer Bar Assn.

Biles, Jack I. & Evans, Robert O., eds. William Golding: Some Critical Considerations, David Anderson, Ted E. Boyle, Philippe Tristram, et al. LC 77-73705. pap. 73.80 (ISBN 0-317-26707-8, 2024357). Bks Demand UMI.

--William Golding: Some Critical Considerations. LC 77-73705. 296p. 1978. 27.00x (ISBN 0-8131-1362-8). U Pr of Ky.

Biles, Roger. Big City Boss in Depression & War: Mayor Edward J. Kelly of Chicago. LC 83-19391. 219p. 1984. 20.00 (ISBN 0-87580-098-X). N Ill U Pr.

Biles, William E. & Swain, James J. Optimization & Industrial Experimentation. LC 79-9516. 368p. 1980. 56.95x (ISBN 0-471-04244-7, Pub. by Wiley-Interscience). Wiley.

Biletsy, Platon. Soviet Ukrainian Art: Painting, Sculpture, Graphic Arts. 118p. 1979. 30.00x (Pub. by Collet's). State Mutual Bk.

Bilezikian, Gilbert G. Beyond Sex Roles. 264p. 1985. pap. 9.95 (ISBN 0-8010-0885-9). Baker Bk.

Bilginer, Sadettin. Deutsch-Turkisches Worterbuch Fur Technische Berufe. 2nd ed. 448p. (Ger. & Turkish.). 1966. leatherette 55.00 (ISBN 3-7736-5270-4, M-7348, Pub. by Verlag W. Girardet). French & Eur.

Bilgram, Hugo. The Remedy for Overproduction & Unemployment. 1979. lib. bdg. 39.95 (ISBN 0-87700-287-8). Revisionist Pr.

--A Study of the Money Question. 59.95 (ISBN 0-8490-1157-4). Gordon Pr.

Bilgram, Hugo & Levy, L. The Cause of Business Depressions. 75.00 (ISBN 0-87968-095-4). Gordon Pr.

Bilgrami, K. S. & Dube, H. C. Textbook of Modern Plant Pathology. 1976. 13.50 (ISBN 0-7069-0421-4). Intl Bk Dist.

Bilgrami, K. S. & Dube, R. C. Textbook of Modern Plant Pathology. 6th ed. 1984. pap. text ed. 15.95x (ISBN 0-7069-2630-7, Pub. by Vikas India). Advent NY.

Bilgrami, K. S. & Jamaluddin, eds. Fungi of India: Host Index & Addenda. (Pt. II). 250p. 1981. 30.00 (ISBN 0-88065-060-5, Pub. by Messers Today & Tomorrows Printers & Publishers India). Scholarly Pubns.

--Fungi of India: List & References. (Pt. I). 466p. 1979. 50.00 (ISBN 0-88065-059-1, Pub. by Messers Today & Tomorrows Printers & Publishers India). Scholarly Pubns.

Bilgrami, K. S. & Misra, R. S., eds. Advancing Frontiers of Mycology & Plant Pathology: Prof. K. S. Bhargava Commemoration Volume. (Illus.). xxvi, 330p. 1982. 50.00 (ISBN 0-88065-222-5, Pub. by Messers Today & Tomorrow Printers & Publishers). Scholarly Pubns.

Bilgrami, K. S., ed. see All India Symposium, Jabalpur, Feb. 24-27, 1978.

Bilgrami, K. S., et al. Changes in Nutritional Components of Stored Seeds Due to Fungal Association. (International Bioscience Monograph: No. 9). 90p. 1979. 8.00 (ISBN 0-88065-061-3, Pub. by Messers Today & Tomorrows Printers & Publishers India). Scholarly Pubns.

--Fundamentals of Botany. (Illus.). 1979. text ed. 25.00x (ISBN 0-7069-0775-2, Pub. by Vikas India). Advent NY.

Bilgrami, S. J. International Organization. (Illus.). 1979. text ed. 20.00x (ISBN 0-7069-0548-2, Pub. by Vikas India). Advent NY.

Bilgray, A., jt. ed. see Marcus, J. R.

Bilgrey, Marc. The Sherlock Holmes Cartoon Book. 104p. (Orig.). pap. 5.00 (ISBN 0-9606826-0-0). Cuckoo Bird Pr.

Bilhartz, Terry O., ed. Francis Asbury's America: An Album of Early American Methodism. LC 83-18275. 128p. 1984. 9.95 (ISBN 0-310-44790-9, Pub. by F. Asbury Pr); pap. 6.95 (ISBN 0-310-44791-7). Zondervan.

Bilheimer, Robert S. A Spirituality for the Long Haul: Biblical Risk & Moral Stand. LC 83-48918. 176p. 1984. pap. 8.95 (ISBN 0-8006-1760-6, 1-1760). Fortress.

--What Must the Church Do? facsimile ed. LC 70-134053. (Essay Index Reprints - Interseminary Ser.: Vol. 5). Repr. of 1947 ed. 17.00 (ISBN 0-8369-2384-7). Ayer Co Pubs.

Bilheimer, Robert S., ed. Faith & Ferment: An Interdisciplinary Study of Christian Beliefs & Practices. LC 83-70512. 352p. (Orig.). 1983. pap. 14.95 (ISBN 0-8066-2018-8, 10-2168). Augsburg.

Bilheimer, Robert S., ed. see Chittister, Joan D. & Marty, Martin E.

Bilibin, I. The Frog Princess. (Illus.). 12p. 1979. pap. 2.45 (ISBN 0-8285-1147-0, Pub. by Goznak Pubs USSR). Imported Pubns.

Bilibin, I., jt. auth. see Pushkin, Alexander.

Bilibin, I., illus. Fenist the Falcon. 16p. 1979. pap. 2.45 (ISBN 0-8285-1135-7, Pub. by Goznak Pubs USSR). Imported Pubns.

--Marya Morevna. 12p. 1979. pap. 2.45 (ISBN 0-8285-1200-0, Pub. by Goznak Pubs USSR). Imported Pubns.

--Sister Alyonushka & Brother Ivanushka: Bd. with The White Duck. 16p. 1979. pap. 2.45 (ISBN 0-8285-1227-2, Pub. by Goznak Pubs USSR). Imported Pubns.

--Tale of Tsarevich Ivan, the Firebird & the Grey Wolf. (Illus.). 16p. 1979. pap. 2.45 (ISBN 0-8285-1241-8, Pub. by Goznak Pubs USSR). Imported Pubns.

--Vasilisa the Beautiful. (Illus.). 16p. 1979. pap. 2.45 (ISBN 0-8285-1257-4, Pub. by Goznak Pubs USSR). Imported Pubns.

Bilic, N., et al, eds. Frontiers in Particle Physics 1983: Adriatic Meeting on Particle Physics, IV, Dubrovnik, Yugoslavia, June 6-15, 1983. 550p. 1984. 60.00x (ISBN 9971-950-57-X, Pub. by World Sci Singapore). Taylor & Francis.

Bilich, Marion. Weight Loss from the Inside Out: Help for the Compulsive Eater. LC 83-633. 192p. (Orig.). 1983. pap. 9.95 (ISBN 0-8164-2485-3, Pub. by Seabury). Winston Pr.

Bilik, Dorothy S. Immigrant-Survivors: Post-Holocaust Consciousness in Recent Jewish-American Literature. LC 80-15326. 217p. 1981. 17.50x (ISBN 0-8195-5046-9). Wesleyan U Pr.

Bilik, Jerry H. Learning to Hear. 1965. pap. 3.95 o. o. s. (ISBN 0-87506-002-1, 87506-002-1); LP record 4.25 (ISBN 0-87506-003-X). Campus.

--Learning to Hear. 114p. 1965. 4.25 (ISBN 0-87506-003-X). Campus.

Bilinski, Robert. A Guide to Coin Investment. rev. 4th ed. 1969. pap. 10.00 (ISBN 0-912070-17-X). Bale Bks.

Bilinsky, Yaroslav. Changes in the Central Committee, Communist Party of the Soviet Union, 1961-66. (Monograph Series in World Affairs: Vol. 4, 1966-67, Bk. 4). 54p. (Orig.). 3.95 (ISBN 0-87940-014-5). Monograph Series.

Bilitch, Michael. Manual of Cardiac Arrhythmias. 295p. 1971. spiral bdg. 18.95 (ISBN 0-316-09495-1). Little.

Bilitski, Joan & Taylor, Margaret C., eds. Nursing in the Year Two Thousand. 69p. (Orig.). 1984. pap. 6.00 (ISBN 0-937058-20-3). West Va U Pr.

Bilker, Audrey L., jt. auth. see Bilker, Harvey L.

Bilker, Harvey L. Photographer's Guide to Saving Money: A Complete Cost Control Manual to Help the Photographer Spend Less to Create More. (Illus.). 256p. 1983. cancelled (ISBN 0-8174-5413-6, Amphoto); pap. text ed. 12.95 (ISBN 0-8174-5414-4). Watson-Guptill.

Bilker, Harvey L. & Bilker, Audrey L. Writing Mysteries That Sell. 160p. 1982. pap. 7.95 (ISBN 0-8092-5822-6). Contemp Bks.

Bill. Reasons Two, Sects & Cults with Christian Roots. (Orig.). 1981. pap. text ed. 3.90 (ISBN 0-933140-25-8); tchr's manual, 67 pgs. 3.90 (ISBN 0-933140-26-6). Bd of Pubns CRC.

Bill, A. H. A House Called Morven: Its Role in American History. 1977. 23.00 (ISBN 0-691-04641-7). Princeton U Pr.

Bill, Alfred H. Alas, Poor Yorick. facsimile ed. LC 71-110180. (Short Story Index Reprint Ser). 1927. 18.00 (ISBN 0-8369-3331-1). Ayer Co Pubs.

--Astrophel; or The Life & Death of the Renowned Sir Philip Sidney. 1979. Repr. of 1939 ed. lib. bdg. 40.00 (ISBN 0-8495-0525-9). Arden Lib.

--The Beleaguered City: Richmond, 1861-1865. LC 80-16702. (Illus.). xiv, 313p. 1980. Repr. of 1946 ed. lib. bdg. 32.50x (ISBN 0-313-22568-0, BIBE). Greenwood.

--Campaign of Princeton, Seventeen Seventy-Six to Seventy-Seven. LC 75-7660. (Illus.). 160p. 1976. 16.00x (ISBN 0-691-04510-0); pap. 5.95 (ISBN 0-691-00582-6). Princeton U Pr.

--New Jersey & the Revolutionary War. (New Jersey Historical Ser). (Illus.). 117p. 1970. pap. 8.95 (ISBN 0-8135-0642-5). Rutgers U Pr.

--Rehearsal for Conflict: The War with Mexico, 1846-1848. LC 79-105298. (Illus.). 1970. Repr. of 1945 ed. lib. bdg. 24.50 (ISBN 0-8154-0316-X). Cooper Sq.

--The Wolf in the Garden. 144p. 1972. pap. 0.75 (ISBN 0-87818-008-7). Centaur.

Bill, Brent. David Updegraff: Quaker Holiness Preacher. 90p. 1983. pap. 6.95 (ISBN 0-913408-82-4). Friends United.

Bill, E. G., ed. A Catalogue of Manuscripts in Lambeth Palace Library: MSS 2431-3119. 1983. 63.00x (ISBN 0-19-920135-8). Oxford U Pr.

Bill, E. G., compiled by. Queen Anne Churches: A Catalogue of the Papers in Lambeth Palace Library. 280p. 1979. 40.00 (ISBN 0-7201-0919-1). Mansell.

--The Queen Anne Churches: A Catalogue of the Papers in Lambeth Palace Library of the Commission for Building Fifty New Churches in London & Westminster, 1711-1759. 255p. 1979. 53.00x (ISBN 0-7201-0919-1). Mansell.

Bill, Erastus D. Citizen: An American Boy's Early Manhood Aboard a Sag Harbor Whale-Ship Chasing Delirium & Death Around the World, 1843-1849. LC 78-50525. (World Discovery Bks.). (Illus.). 1978. 10.00 (ISBN 0-930766-01-6); pap. 4.95 (ISBN 0-930766-02-4). O W Frost.

Bill Harris Studios, tr. see Stephens, Richard E.

Bill, J. Brent. Rock & Roll. 160p. (Orig.). 1984. pap. 4.95 (ISBN 0-8007-5156-6, Power Bks). Revell.

--Stay Tuned. (Orig.). 1985. pap. 5.95 (ISBN 0-8007-5202-3). Revell.

Bill, James A. U. S. - Arab Relations: The Iranian Dimension, No. 9. (Orig.). 1984. pap. 5.00 (ISBN 0-916729-06-0). Natl Coun Arab.

Bill, James A. & Hardgrave, Robert L., Jr. Comparative Politics: The Quest for Theory. LC 81-43598. (Illus.). 272p. 1982. lib. bdg. 26.00 (ISBN 0-8191-2089-8); pap. text ed. 10.75 (ISBN 0-8191-2090-1). U Pr of Amer.

Bill, James A., et al. Politics in the Middle East. 2nd ed. 1983. 12.95 (ISBN 0-316-09506-0). Little.

Bill, Shirley, jt. ed. see Gottschalk, Louis.

Bill Thomas, Research Associates, jt. auth. see Warren, Bill.

Bill, Valentine T. The Forgotten Class. LC 75-25485. 1976. Repr. of 1959 ed. lib. bdg. 29.75x (ISBN 0-8371-8426-6, BIFOC). Greenwood.

Billam, Rosemary. Fuzzy Rabbit. LC 83-17637. (Picturebacks Ser.). (Illus.). 32p. (ps-3). 1984. pap. 1.95 (ISBN 0-394-86346-1, BYR); PLB 4.99 (ISBN 0-394-96346-6). Random.

--Fuzzy Rabbit. (Pictureback Book & Cassette Library Ser.). (Illus.). 32p. (ps-1). 1985. pap. 4.95 incl. cassette (ISBN 0-394-87656-3). Random.

Billand, Eva. The World Beyond & You: A Guide to Developing Your Own Spiritual Potential. 174p. 1984. 14.95 (ISBN 0-525-48151-6). Bergh Pub.

Billard, E., ed. Computer Science & Statistics: Proceedings of the Symposium on the Interface, 16th, Atlanta, Georgia, March 1984. 296p. 1985. 43.00 (ISBN 0-444-87725-8, North-Holland). Elsevier.

Billard, Lynne & Steila, Donald. Dictionary of Statistical Terminology. 400p. Date not set. text ed. 30.00x (ISBN 0-86598-131-0). Rowman & Allanheld.

Billard, Ruth S. Ralph Morrill's in Museum Quality Fish Taxidermy: A Guide to Molding with Plaster, Casting with Resin, Painting with an Airbrush. LC 84-70664. (Illus.). 275p. 1984. lib. bdg. 30.00x (ISBN 0-9611112-0-8). Bill Art.

Billardiere, J. J. De La see De La Billardiere, J. J.

Billcliffe, Roger. Architectural Sketches & Flowers Drawings by Charles Rennie Mackintosh. 96p. 1977. 40.00x (ISBN 0-85670-149-1, Pub. by Academy Editions England). State Mutual Bk.

--Mackintosh Furniture. (Illus.). 224p. 1985. 19.95 (ISBN 0-525-24317-8, 01937-580); pap. 10.95 (ISBN 0-525-48175-3, 01063-320). Dutton.

--Mackintosh Textile Designs. LC 82-60358. (Illus.). 80p. 1982. 25.00 (ISBN 0-8008-5059-9). Taplinger.

--Mackintosh Watercolours. LC 78-53795. (Illus.). 144p. 1979. pap. 12.50 (ISBN 0-8008-5043-2). Taplinger.

Billdt, Ruth. Pioneer Swedish-American Culture in Central Kansas. 1965. 25.00 (ISBN 0-934844-05-4). W A Linder.

Billdt, Ruth & Jaderborg, Elizabeth. Smoky Valley in the after Years. 1969. 20.00 (ISBN 0-948444-42-8). W A Linder.

Bille, Donald. Staff Development: A Systems Approach. LC 82-61593. 160p. 1983. 14.50 (ISBN 0-913590-85-1). Slack Inc.

Bille, Donald A. Practical Approaches to Patient Teaching. 1981. pap. text ed. 15.95 (ISBN 0-316-09498-6). Little.

Billeb, Emil W. Mining Camp Days. (Illus.). 231p. Date not set. pap. 10.95. Nevada Pubns.

Billehaug, K. & Oye, H. A. Invert Cathodes & Anodes for Aluminium Electrolysis. (Monograph). 1981. 24.00 (ISBN 0-9900034-8-7, Pub. by Aluminium W Germany). Heyden.

Billen, Andrew & Skipworth, Mark, eds. Oxford Type: The Best of "Isis". 204p. 1984. 17.50 (ISBN 0-86051-213-4, Pub. by Salem Acad). Merrimack Pub Cir.

Biller, Ernest F. Understanding & Guiding the Career Development of Adolescents & Young Adults with Learning Disabilities. 180p. (Orig.). 1985. pap. 18.75x (ISBN 0-398-05113-5). C C Thomas.
Biller, Henry B., jt. auth. see Berlinsky, Ellen B.
Biller, Hugh F., jt. auth. see Bailey, Byron J.
Biller, Martie, jt. auth. see Biller, Tom A.
Biller, Tom A. & Biller, Martie. Simple Object Lessons for Children. (Object Lesson Ser.). 160p. 1980. pap. 4.95 (ISBN 0-8010-0793-3). Baker Bk.
Billerbeck, K. & Yasugi, Y. Private Direct Foreign Investment in Developing Countries. (Working Paper: No. 348). iv, 97p. 1979. 5.00 (ISBN 0-686-36174-1, WP-0348). World Bank.
Billeskov-Jansen, F. J. & Mitchell, P. M., eds. Anthology of Danish Literature: Middle Ages to Romanticism. bilingual ed. LC 72-5610. (Arcturus Books Paperbacks). 272p. 1972. pap. 10.95x (ISBN 0-8093-0596-8). S Ill U Pr.
--Anthology of Danish Literature: Realism to the Present. bilingual ed. LC 72-5610. (Arcturus Books Paperbacks). 349p. 1972. pap. 10.95x (ISBN 0-8093-0597-6). S Ill U Pr.
Billet, F., jt. auth. see Fouchier, J.
Billet, M. L. & Arndt, R. E., eds. International Symposium on Cavitation Noise. 1982. 30.00 (H00231). ASME.
Billet, Michael. Thatching & Thatched Buildings. (Illus.). 208p. 1979. 18.50 (ISBN 0-7091-7205-2). Transatlantic.
Billet, R. Distillation Engineering. Wulfinghoff, M., tr. 1978. 55.00 (ISBN 0-8206-0215-9). Chem Pub.
Billeter, Erika. Lucio Fontana, 1899-1968: A Retrospective. LC 77-88448. (Illus.). 1977. softbound 6.98 (ISBN 0-89207-010-2). S R Guggenheim.
Billett, F. S. EGG Structure & Animal Development. (Contemporary Biology Ser.). 180p. 1984. pap. text ed. write for info. (ISBN 0-7131-2809-7). E Arnold.
Billett, F. S., jt. ed. see Balls, M.
Billett, M. G. A Handbook of Industrial Lubrication. 1979. 33.00 (ISBN 0-08-024232-4). Pergamon.
Billett, Roy O. Improving the Secondary-School Curriculum: A Guide to Effective Curriculum Planning. LC 75-80905. 364p. 1970. text ed. 11.95x (ISBN 0-202-09016-7, Tpp). Lieber-Atherton.
--Preparing Theses & Other Typed Manuscripts. (Quality Paperback Ser.: No. 63). (Orig.). 1968. pap. 3.95 (ISBN 0-8226-0063-3). Littlefield.
--Teaching in Junior & Senior High School. (Quality Paperback Ser.: No. 94). (Illus., Orig.). 1967. pap. 3.45 (ISBN 0-8226-0094-3). Littlefield.
--Teaching in Junior & Senior High School. 327p. 1963. 8.95x (ISBN 0-87471-219-X). Rowman.
Billhartz, Celeste. The Complete Book of Job Hunting, Finding, Changing. (Illus., Orig.). 1980. pap. 7.95 (ISBN 0-935448-01-2). Rainbow Collect.
Billheimer, Paul. Destined to Overcome. 123p. 1982. pap. 3.95 (ISBN 0-87508-044-8). Chr Lit.
--Don't Waste Your Sorrows. 1977. pap. 3.95 (ISBN 0-87508-007-3). Chr Lit.
--Love Covers. 1981. pap. 4.95 (ISBN 0-87508-006-5). Chr Lit.
--The Mystery of God's Providence. 1983. pap. 3.95 (ISBN 0-8423-4664-3). Tyndale.
Billheimer, Paul E. Adventure in Adversity. LC 83-51174. 112p. 1984. pap. 3.95 (ISBN 0-8423-0034-1). Tyndale.
--Destinados a Vencer. 96p. 1984. pap. 2.25 (ISBN 0-88113-048-6). Edit Betania.
--Destined for the Cross. 1982. pap. 3.95 (ISBN 0-8423-0604-8). Tyndale.
--Destined for the Throne. LC 83-15151. 140p. (Orig.). 1983. pap. 3.95 (ISBN 0-87123-309-6). Bethany Hse.
--Destined for the Throne. 1983. pap. 3.95 (ISBN 0-87508-040-5). Chr Lit.
--Destined to Overcome. 123p. 1982. pap. 3.95 (ISBN 0-87123-287-1, 210287). Bethany Hse.
--Don't Waste Your Sorrows. LC 83-15821. 144p. (Orig.). 1983. pap. 3.95 (ISBN 0-87123-310-X). Bethany Hse.
--Love Covers. LC 83-15823. 174p. (Orig.). 1984. pap. 4.95 (ISBN 0-87123-400-9). Bethany Hse.
Billias, George, ed. see Great Britain Historical Manuscripts Commission.
Billias, George, ed. see New York Historical Society.
Billias, George, ed. see Raynal, Guillaume T.
Billias, George, ed. see Society of Gentlemen.
Billias, George, ed. see United Empire Loyalists Centennial Committee.
Billias, George A. The American Revolution: How Revolutionary Was It? 3rd ed. LC 80-16521. 203p. 1980. pap. text ed. 13.95 (ISBN 0-03-054761-X, HoltC). HR&W.
--The Massachusetts Land Bankers of 1740. 1959. pap. 5.95 (ISBN 0-89101-005-X). U Maine Orono.
Billias, George A., jt. auth. see Grob, Gerald N.
Billias, George A., ed. George Washington's Generals. LC 79-28195. (Illus.). 327p. 1980. Repr. of 1964 ed. lib. bdg. 27.50x (ISBN 0-313-22280-0, BIGW). Greenwood.
Billias, George A., ed. see Mackesy, Piers.
Billias, George A., ed. see Vinovskis, Maris A.
Billiau, A. & Finter, N. B., eds. Interferon: General & Applied Aspects, Vol. 1. 400p. 1984. 70.50 (ISBN 0-444-80542-7, Biomedical Pr). Elsevier.
Billick, David J. Jose de Espronceda: An Annotated Bibliography, 1834 to 1978. LC 80-8514. 200p. 1981. lib. bdg. 43.00 (ISBN 0-8240-9470-0). Garland Pub.
Billiet, W. E. Automotive Engines - Maintenance & Repair. 4th ed. (Illus.). 1973. 15.95 (ISBN 0-8269-0062-3). Am Technical.
Billiet, W. E. & Goings, L. F. Automotive Electrical Systems. 3rd ed. (Illus.). 1970. 15.95 (ISBN 0-8269-0040-2). Am Technical.
Billiet, Walter. Automotive Electronic-Electrical Systems: A Beginner's Troubleshooting & Repair Manual. (Illus.). 384p. 1985. 29.95 (ISBN 0-13-054255-5); pap. 18.95 (ISBN 0-13-054248-2). P H.
Billiet, Walter, jt. auth. see Frazee, Irving A.
Billiet, Walter E. Do-It-Yourself Automotive Maintenance & Repair. LC 78-15055. (Illus.). 1979. 17.95 (ISBN 0-13-217190-2, Spec); pap. 7.95 (ISBN 0-13-217182-1). P-H.
--Small Gas Engines & Power Transmission Systems: A Repair & Maintenance Handbook. LC 82-3866. (Illus.). 281p. 1982. 20.95 (ISBN 0-13-814327-7); pap. 12.95 (ISBN 0-13-814319-6). P-H.
Billiet, Walter E. & Alley, Walter. Automotive Suspensions, Steering, Alignment & Brakes. 5th ed. (Illus.). 1974. 15.95 (ISBN 0-8269-0122-0). Am Technical.
Billiet, Walter E., jt. auth. see Venk, Ernest A.
Billig, Donal M. & Kreidberg, Marshall B. The Management of Neonates & Infants with Congenital Heart Disease. LC 72-11559. (A Modern Surgical Monograph). 192p. 1973. 49.00 (ISBN 0-8089-0792-1, 790585). Grune.
Billig, Florence G. A Technique for Developing Content for a Professional Course in Science for Teachers in Elementary Schools. (Columbia University. Teachers College. Contributions to Education: No. 397). Repr. of 1930 ed. 22.50 (ISBN 0-404-55397-4). AMS Pr.
Billig, L., jt. ed. see Yellin, Avinoam.
Billig, M. Social Psychology & Intergroup Relations. (European Monographs in Social Psychology). 1976. 65.00 (ISBN 0-12-097950-0). Acad Pr.
Billig, Michael. Fascists: A Second Psychological View of the National Front. 1979. 55.00 (ISBN 0-12-097940-3). Acad Pr.
Billig, Otto. Flying Saucers: Magic in the Skies. 256p. 1982. 16.95x (ISBN 0-87073-833-X); pap. 9.95 (ISBN 0-87073-940-9). Schenkman Bks Inc.
Billig, Otto & Burton-Bradley, B. G. The Painted Message. LC 77-3293. 1978. cloth 19.50x (ISBN 0-470-99126-7). Halsted Pr.
Billigheimer, C. E., tr. see Polya, G. & Szego, G.
Billigmeier, Jon C.. Kadmos & Danaos: Possibility of a Semitic Presence in Halladic Greece. (No. 6). 1981. pap. text ed. price not set (ISBN 90-6032-110-3). Humanities.
Billigmeier, Robert H. A Crisis in Swiss Pluralism: The Romanisch & Their Relations with the German & the Italian-Swiss in the Perpective of a Millenium. (Contributions to the Sociology of Language Ser.: No. 26). 1979. 38.25x (ISBN 90-279-7577-9). Mouton.
Billigmeier, Robert H. & Picard, Fred A., eds. The Old Land & the New: Journals of Two Swiss Families in America in the 1820's. LC 65-15544. (Illus.). pap. 72.30 (ISBN 0-317-29395-8, 2055844). Bks Demand UMI.
Billing, D. E., ed. see Aylett, B. J.
Billing, Hazel. Practical Procedures for Nurses. 3rd ed. (Illus.). 102p. 1981. pap. 8.50 (ISBN 0-7216-0909-0, Pub. by Bailliere-Tindall). Saunders.
Billing, I. R. More Health Metaphysically. 5.00 (ISBN 0-8062-2267-0). Carlton.
Billinge, Mark, jt. ed. see Baker, Alan R.
Billinge, Mark, et al, eds. Recollections of a Revolution: Geography As Spatial Science. LC 83-19191. 256p. 1984. 25.00 (ISBN 0-312-66587-3). St Martin.
Billingham, J. & Pesek, R., eds. Communication with Extraterrestrial Intelligence. (Astronautica: Vol. 6, Nos. 1-2). 1979. 88.00 (ISBN 0-08-024727-X). Pergamon.
Billingham, John, et al, eds. Life in the Universe. 400p. 1981. pap. text ed. 12.50 (ISBN 0-262-52062-1). MIT Pr.
Billingham, Katherine A. Developmental Psychology for the Health Care Professions: Prenatal Through Adolescent Development, Pt. 1. (Behavioral Sciences for Health Care Professionals Ser.). 128p. (Orig.). 1981. 18.50x (ISBN 0-86531-000-9); pap. 8.95x (ISBN 0-86531-001-7). Westview.
Billingham, N. C. Molar Mass Measurements in Polymer Science. LC 77-2823. 254p. 1977. cloth 59.95x (ISBN 0-470-99125-9). Halsted Pr.
Billingham, R. E., jt. ed. see Montagna, W.
Billingham, Richard & Goodkin, Marie. First Steps to Musicianship. 256p. 1980. pap. text ed. 12.50x (ISBN 0-917974-38-7). Waveland Pr.
Billingham, Stuart & Blanchard, Robert. Social Policy & Social Problems. (Themes & Perspectives in Sociology Ser.). 80p. (Orig.). 1985. pap. text ed. 6.95x (ISBN 0-946183-09-0, Pub. by Causeway Pr Ltd England). Sheridan.
Billinghurst. Chemistry for Nuclear Medicine. 1981. 31.50 (ISBN 0-8151-3295-6). Year Bk Med.
Billinghurst, Mervyn W., ed. Studies of Cellular Function Using Radiotracers. 272p. 1981. 74.50 (ISBN 0-8493-6025-0). CRC Pr.
Billings, Anna H. A Guide to the Middle English Metrical Romances. LC 75-26780. 1973. lib. bdg. 27.50 (ISBN 0-8414-3232-5). Folcroft.
--Guide to the Middle English Metrical Romances. LC 66-27040. 1967. Repr. of 1901 ed. 7.50x (ISBN 0-8462-0972-1). Russell.
Billings, Bradley L. & Schmitz, Henry D. Report Writing in Audiology: A Handbook for Students & Clinicians. 46p. 1980. pap. text ed. 3.95 (ISBN 0-8134-2115-2). Interstate.
Billings, Charlene W. Microchip: Small Wonder. LC 84-10179. (Skylight Bk.). (Illus.). 64p. (gr. 2-5). 1984. PLB 7.95 (ISBN 0-396-08452-4). Dodd.
--Salamanders. LC 80-21838. (A Skylight Bk.). (Illus.). 48p. (gr. 2-5). 1981. 7.95 (ISBN 0-396-07913-X). Dodd.
--Scorpions. LC 82-45994. (A Skylight Bk.). (Illus.). 48p. (gr. 2-5). 1983. PLB 7.95 (ISBN 0-396-08125-8). Dodd.
Billings, Deborah A. An Analysis of Lithic Workshop Debris from Iron Mountain, Union County, Illinois. (Research Papers: No. 47). (Illus.). ix, 63p. (Orig.). 1984. softcover 4.00 (ISBN 0-88104-023-1). Center Archaeo.
Billings, Diane M. & Stokes, Lillian G. Medical-Surgical Approaches Throughout the Life Cycle. LC 81-16856. (Illus.). 1440p. 1982. text ed. 41.95 (ISBN 0-8016-0736-1). Mosby.
Billings, Donald B. & Asmus, E. Barry. Crossroads-The Great American Experiment: The Rise, Decline, & Restoration of Freedom & the Market Economy. LC 84-20962. 420p. (Orig.). 1985. lib. bdg. 26.75 (ISBN 0-8191-4362-6); pap. text ed. 14.25 (ISBN 0-8191-4363-4). U Pr of Amer.
Billings, Donald E. Guide to the Solar Corona. 1966. 61.50 (ISBN 0-12-098550-0). Acad Pr.
Billings, Dwight B., Jr. Planters & the Making of a "New South". Class, Politics, & Development in North Carolina, 1865-1900. LC 78-25952. xiii, 284p. 1979. 27.00 (ISBN 0-8078-1315-X). U of NC Pr.
Billings, Edward C. The Struggle Between the Civilization of Slavery & That of Freedom. facsimile ed. LC 76-164379. (Black Heritage Library Collection). Repr. of 1873 ed. 10.75 (ISBN 0-8369-8838-8). Ayer Co Pubs.
Billings, Grace H. The Art of Transition in Plato. Taran, Leonardo, ed. LC 78-66578. (Ancient Philosophy Ser.: Vol. 2). 110p. 1979. lib. bdg. 18.00 (ISBN 0-8240-9609-6). Garland Pub.
Billings, Harold, compiled by. A Bibliography of Edward Dahlberg. LC 75-633117. (Tower Bibliographical Ser: No. 8). (Illus.). 1971. 10.00 (ISBN 0-87959-037-8). U of Tex H Ransom Ctr.
Billings, Harold, ed. Edward Dahlberg, American Ishmael of Letters: Selected Critical Essays. 1968. 19.50 (ISBN 0-911796-01-0). Beacham.
Billings, Harold C., Jr. Watergrate: How to Train Taxed Prisoners. LC 84-90959. 276p. 1985. pap. 14.95 (ISBN 0-9613642-0-3). H C Billings.
Billings, Henry. The Joys of Cheap Wine: A Spirited Guide to Buying, Serving, & Enjoying the World's Greatest Inexpensive (Cheap) Wines. LC 84-61651. (Illus.). 112p. (Orig.). 1984. pap. 4.95 (ISBN 0-933050-26-7). New Eng Pr VT.
Billings, Henry & Billings, Melissa. Heroes. (Illus.). 160p. (gr. 6 up). 1985. pap. text ed. 7.20x (ISBN 0-89061-450-4). Jamestown Pubs.
--Phenomena. (Illus.). 160p. (gr. 6-8). 1984. pap. text ed. 7.20x (ISBN 0-89061-363-X, 762). Jamestown Pubs.
Billings, J. Andrew. Outpatient Care of Advanced Cancer: Symptom Control, Support & Hospice-in-the-Home. 300p. 1985. text ed. write for info. (ISBN 0-397-50648-1, Lippincott Medical). Lippincott.
Billings, Jean, jt. auth. see Robson, Ralph.
Billings, Jeffrey D., jt. auth. see Larsen, James B.
Billings, John D. Hard Tack & Coffee. 408p. 1973. Repr. of 1888 ed. 18.95 (ISBN 0-87928-038-7). Corner Hse.
--Hardtack & Coffee. LC 81-18207. (Collector's Library of the Civil War). 26.60 (ISBN 0-8094-4208-6, Pub. by Time-Life). Silver.
Billings, John S. History & Literature of Surgery. 1970. Repr. of 1895 ed. 15.00 (ISBN 0-87266-038-9). Argosy.
--Report on the Barracks & Hospitals of the United States Army, No. 4. 1870. 95.00 (ISBN 0-914074-08-3, Pub. by J M C & Co). Amereon Ltd.
--Report on the Hygiene of the United States Army, No. 8. 1875. 95.00 (ISBN 0-317-28315-4, Pub. by J M C & Co). Amereon Ltd.
Billings, John S. & Atwater, Wilbur O. Physiological Aspects of the Liquor Problem, 2 Vols. 37.00 (ISBN 0-8369-6965-0, 7846). Ayer Co Pubs.
Billings, John S., et al, eds. Hospitals, Dispensaries & Nursing: Papers & Discussion in the International Congress of Charities, Correction & Philanthropy. LC 83-49145. (History of American Nursing Ser.). 713p. 1984. Repr. of 1894 ed. lib. bdg. 90.00 (ISBN 0-8240-6502-6). Garland Pub.
Billings, Josh, pseud. Josh Billings, Hiz Sayings. LC 75-39443. (Illus.). Repr. of 1866 ed. 25.00 (ISBN 0-404-00865-8). AMS Pr.
--Josh Billings on Ice & Other Things. (Illus.). Repr. of 1868 ed. 26.50 (ISBN 0-404-00866-6). AMS Pr.
Billings, Karen & Moursund, David. Are You Computer Literate? LC 79-56396. (Illus.). 160p. 1979. pap. 9.95 (ISBN 0-918398-29-0). Dilithium Pr.
Billings, Leon, et al. The Clean Air Act: Prospects for the Nineteen Eighties. 208p. 1984. 23.95x (ISBN 0-03-062758-3). Praeger.
Billings, Marland P. Structural Geology. 3rd ed. (Illus.). 1972. 37.95 (ISBN 0-13-853846-8). P-H.
Billings, Melissa, jt. auth. see Billings, Henry.
Billings, Peggy. Fire Beneath the Frost. LC 83-16525. (Illus.). 88p. (Orig.). 1984. pap. 5.95 (ISBN 0-377-00135-X). Friend Pr.
--Paradox & Promise in Human Rights. (Orig.). 1979. pap. 2.95 (ISBN 0-377-00083-3). Friend Pr.
Billings, Richard, jt. auth. see Donnelly, Honoria.
Billings, Richard N., jt. auth. see Donnelly, Honoria M.
Billings, Roger D., Jr. Handling Automobile Warranty & Repossesion Cases. LC 84-81609. 1984. 67.50 (ISBN 0-318-03858-7). Lawyers Co-Op.
--Prepaid Legal Services. LC 79-92375. 1981. 74.50 (ISBN 0-686-35941-0); Suppl. 1984. 17.50; Suppl. 1983. 16.00. Lawyers Co-Op.
Billings, Roger E. Hydrogen from Coal. 214p. 1983. 37.50x (ISBN 0-87814-210-X, P-4319). Pennwell Bks.
Billings, Rolland G. & Goldman, Errol. Professional Negotiations for Media-Library Professionals: District & School. LC 80-67724. 70p. 1980. pap. 8.50 (ISBN 0-89240-037-4); pap. 6.50 members. Assn Ed Comm Tech.
Billings, S. A., jt. auth. see Harris, C. J.
Billings, S. A., ed. Identification & System Parameter Estimation: Proceedings of the 7th TFAC-IFORS Symposium, York, UK, July 3-7 1985, 2 vol. (IFAC Proceedings Ser.). (Illus.). 1800p. 1985. 450.00 (ISBN 0-08-032560-2). Pergamon.
Billings, S. A. & Gray, J. O., eds. Nonlinear Systems Design. (IEE Control Engineering Ser.: No. 25). 202p. 1984. 38.00 (ISBN 0-317-37229-7). Inst Elect Eng.
Billings, Susan V. Sarah's Awakening. (Orig.). 1979. pap. 2.50 (ISBN 0-89083-536-5). Zebra.
Billings, Thomas H. The Platonism of Philo Judaeus. Taran, Leonardo, ed. LC 78-66560. (Ancient Philosophy Ser.: Vol. 3). 117p. 1979. lib. bdg. 18.00 (ISBN 0-8240-9608-8). Garland Pub.
Billings, Warren M. The Historic Rules of the Supreme Court of Louisiana, 1813-1879. 1985. price not set (ISBN 0-940984-26-1). U of SW LA Ctr LA Studies.
Billings, Warren M., ed. The Old Dominion in the Seventeenth Century: A Documentary History of Virginia, 1606-1689. LC 74-8302. (Institute of Early American History & Culture Ser.). xxiv, 324p. 1975. 27.50 (ISBN 0-8078-1234-X); pap. 7.00x (ISBN 0-8078-1237-4). U of NC Pr.
Billings, William. The Complete Works of William Billings: Vol. 1, the New-England Psalm-Singer. Kroeger, Karl & Crawford, Richard, eds. LC 80-69464. (Illus.). 386p. 1981. 50.00x (ISBN 0-8139-0917-1, Colonial Soc MA). U Pr of Va.
--The Complete Works of William Billings: Volume 2: The Singing Master's Assistant(1778), Music in Miniature (1779) Nathan, William, et al, eds. LC 76-28587. 1977. 50.00x (ISBN 0-8139-0839-6, Colonial Soc MA). U Pr of Va.
--The Psalm Singer's Amusement. LC 73-5100. (Earlier American Music Ser.: Vol. 20). 104p. 1974. Repr. of 1781 ed. lib. bdg. 22.50 (ISBN 0-306-70587-7). Da Capo.
Billingsley, jt. auth. see Huntsberger.
Billingsley, Andrew. Black Families in White America. LC 68-54602. 1968. pap. 4.95 (ISBN 0-13-077453-7, Spec). P-H.
Billingsley, Andrew & Giovannoni, Jeanne M. Children of the Storm: Black Children & American Child Welfare. 263p. 1972. pap. text ed. 10.95 (ISBN 0-15-507271-4, HC). HarBraceJ.
Billingsley, Lloyd. The Generation That Knew Not Josef. LC 84-27362. 1985. 11.95 (ISBN 0-88070-081-5). Multnomah.
Billingsley, Martin. The Pens Excellencie or the Secretaries Delight. LC 77-6852. (English Experience Ser.: No. 849). 1977. Repr. of 1618 ed. lib. bdg. 10.50 (ISBN 90-221-0849-X). Walter J Johnson.
Billingsley, Marvin T. The East Ninth Street Controversy. Date not set. 7.95 (ISBN 0-8062-2399-5). Carlton.
Billingsley, P. Convergence of Probability Measures. (Probability & Mathematical Statistics Tracts: Probability & Statistics Section). 253p. 1968. 41.95x (ISBN 0-471-07242-7, Pub. by Wiley-Interscience). Wiley.
--Weak Convergence of Measures: Applications in Probability. (CBMS-NSF Regional Conference Ser.: No. 5). v, 31p. 1971. pap. text ed. 6.50 (ISBN 0-89871-176-2). Soc Indus-Appl Math.
Billingsley, Patrick. Ergodic Theory & Information. LC 78-2442. 210p. 1978. Repr. of 1965 ed. lib. bdg. 15.00 (ISBN 0-88275-666-4). Krieger.
--Probability & Measure. LC 78-25632. (Probability & Mathematical Statistics Ser.). 515p. 1979. 41.95x (ISBN 0-471-03173-9, Pub. by Wiley-Interscience). Wiley.
--Statistical Inference for Markov Processes. LC 61-8646. (Midway Reprint Ser.). 84p. 1975. pap. text ed. 5.50x (ISBN 0-226-05077-7). U of Chicago Pr.

Billingsley, Richard. Major College Football, the Decade of the Seventies. 512p. 1981. text ed. 19.95 (ISBN 0-918464-39-0). D Armstrong.
--Major College Football-1981. (Illus.). 100p. 1982. pap. 6.95 (ISBN 0-918464-46-3). D Armstrong.
Billington, C. J. & Osborne-Moss, D. M. The Design of Fixed Offshore Structures. 1986. 60.00x (ISBN 0-87201-305-7). Gulf Pub.
Billington, Cecil. Shrubs of Michigan. 2nd ed. LC 44-1024. (Bulletin Ser.: No. 20). (Illus.). 339p. 1949. text ed. 10.00x (ISBN 0-87737-005-2). Cranbrook.
Billington, D. P. Thin Shell Concrete Structures. 1965. 42.50 (ISBN 0-07-005271-9). McGraw.
Billington, David. The Tower & the Bridge: The New Art of Structural Engineering. LC 83-70758. (Illus.). 306p. 1983. 24.95 (ISBN 0-465-08677-2). Basic.
Billington, David P. Robert Maillart's Bridges: The Art of Engineering. LC 78-70279. (Illus.). 1979. 32.50 (ISBN 0-691-08203-0). Princeton U Pr.
--Thin-Shell Concrete Structures. 2nd ed. (Illus.). 432p. 1981. 48.50 (ISBN 0-07-005279-4). McGraw.
--The Tower & the Bridge: The New Art of Structural Engineering. (Illus.). 328p. 1985. pap. 12.95 (ISBN 0-691-02393-X). Princeton U Pr.
Billington, Douglas, et al. Radiation Damage in Solids. LC 60-16414. pap. 115.50 (ISBN 0-317-07756-2, 2000985). Bks Demand UMI.
Billington, E. J., et al, eds. Combinatorial Mathematics IX, Brisbane, Australia: Proceedings, 1981. (Lecture Notes in Mathematics: Vol. 952). 443p. 1982. pap. 25.00 (ISBN 0-387-11601-X). Springer-Verlag.
Billington, E. W. & Tate, A. The Physics of Deformation & Flow. (Illus.). 720p. 1981. text ed. 72.00 (ISBN 0-07-005285-9). McGraw.
Billington, Elizabeth T. Getting to Know Me. LC 81-15952. 144p. (gr. 4-9). 1982. 8.95 (ISBN 0-7232-6206-3). Warne.
--The Move. LC 82-21568. 128p. (gr. 5-9). 1984. 9.95 (ISBN 0-7232-6259-4). Warne.
--The Randolph Caldecott Treasury. LC 76-45308. (Illus.). 1978. 30.00 (ISBN 0-7232-6139-3). Warne.
--Understanding Ecology. rev ed. LC 69-10306. (Illus.). (gr. 5 up). 1971. 6.95 (ISBN 0-7232-6022-2). Warne.
Billington, James H. Fire in the Minds of Men. LC 79-2750. 677p. 1980. pap. 13.50 (ISBN 0-465-02407-6, CN-5096). Basic.
--Icon & the Axe: An Interpretive History of Russian Culture. LC 66-18687. (Illus.). 1970. pap. 9.95 (ISBN 0-394-70846-6, V620, Vin). Random.
Billington, Michael. Alan Ayckbourn. LC 83-49373. (Modern Dramatists Ser.). 224p. 1984. 19.50 (ISBN 0-394-53856-0, GP893); pap. 9.95 (ISBN 0-394-62051-8, E908). Grove.
--Guinness Book of Theatre Facts & Feats. (Guinness Superlatives Ser.). (Illus.). 256p. 1982. 6.98 (ISBN 0-85112-239-6, Pub. by Guinness Superlatives England). Sterling.
--How Tickled I Am: A Celebration of Ken Dodd. (Illus.). 11.95 (ISBN 0-241-89345-3, Pub. by Hamish Hamilton England). David & Charles.
--The Performing Arts: A Guide to Practice & Appreciation. (Illus.). 224p. 1980. 29.95 (ISBN 0-87196-421-X). Facts on File.
Billington, Monroe. Southern Politics since the Civil War. LC 83-23885. 208p. 1984. pap. 7.95 (ISBN 0-89874-673-6). Krieger.
Billington, Monroe L., ed. The South: A Central Theme. LC 76-23223. (American Problem Studies). 122p. 1976. pap. text ed. 5.95 (ISBN 0-88275-410-6). Krieger.
Billington, N. S. & Roberts, B. M. Building Services Engineering: A Review of Its Development. LC 80-42036. (International Ser. on Building Environmental Engineering: Vol. 1). 537p. 1981. 88.00 (ISBN 0-08-026741-6); pap. 24.00 (ISBN 0-08-026742-4). Pergamon.
Billington, Rachel. Occasion of Sin. 320p. 1983. 14.95 (ISBN 0-671-45938-4). Summit Bks.
Billington, Ray. The Westward Movement in the United States. 192p. (Orig.). pap. 6.95 (ISBN 0-442-00037-5). Krieger.
Billington, Ray A. American History Before Eighteen Seventy-Seven. (Quality Paperback Ser.: No. 26). 278p. (Orig.). 1981. pap. 5.95 (ISBN 0-8226-0026-9). Littlefield.
--America's Frontier Culture: Three Essays. LC 77-89510. (Essays on the American West Ser.: No. 3). 100p. 1977. 5.00 (ISBN 0-89096-036-4). Tex A&M Univ Pr.
--America's Frontier Heritage. LC 66-13289. (Histories of the American Frontier). 318p. 1974. pap. 10.95x (ISBN 0-8263-0310-2). U of NM Pr.
--The Far Western Frontier, 1830-1860. LC 56-9665. (New American Nation Ser.). 1956. 16.30i (ISBN 0-06-010330-2, HarpT). Har-Row.
--The Far Western Frontier, 1830-1860. 1962. pap. 5.50 (ISBN 0-06-133012-4, CN). Har-Row.
--Genesis of the Frontier Thesis: A Study in Historical Creativity. LC 74-171108. 315p. 1971. 12.50 (ISBN 0-87328-050-4). Huntington Lib.
--Guide to American History Manuscript Collections in Libraries of the United States. pap. 2.00 (ISBN 0-8446-1077-1). Peter Smith.
--Land of Savagery, Land of Promise: The European Image of the American Frontier in the Nineteenth Century. LC 84-40695. (Illus.). 384p. (Orig.). 1985. pap. 10.95 (ISBN 0-8061-1929-2). U of Okla Pr.
--Land of Savagery,Land of Promise: The European Image of the American Frontier. (Illus.). 1981. 18.95 (ISBN 0-393-01376-6). Norton.
--Limericks Historical & Hysterical: Plagiarized, Arranged, Annotated & Some Written by Ray Allen Billington. 1981. 9.95 (ISBN 0-393-01453-3). Norton.
--The Origins of Nativism in the United States, 1800-1844. LC 73-19129. (Politics & People Ser.). (Illus.). 716p. 1974. Repr. 52.00x (ISBN 0-405-05854-3). Ayer Co Pubs.
--People of the Plains & Mountains: Essays in the History of the West Dedicated to Everett Dick. LC 72-784. (Contr. in American History No. 25). (Illus.). 193p. 1973. lib. bdg. 29.95x (ISBN 0-8371-6358-7, BID/). Greenwood.
--Westward to the Pacific: An Overview of America's Westward Expansion. LC 77-18408. (Illus.). 116p. (Orig.). 1979. pap. 6.95 (ISBN 0-295-96054-X). U of Wash Pr.
Billington, Ray A. & Ridge, Martin. American History after Eighteen Sixty-Five. 9th ed. (Quality Paperback: No. 27). 370p. 1981. pap. text ed. 5.95 (ISBN 0-8226-0027-7). Littlefield.
--Westward Expansion. 5th ed. 1982. text ed. write for info. (ISBN 0-02-309860-0). Macmillan.
Billington, Ray A., ed. The Frontier Thesis: Valid Interpretation of American History? LC 77-9103. (American Problem Studies Ser.). 128p. 1977. pap. 6.95 (ISBN 0-88275-586-2). Krieger.
Billington, Ray A. & Whitehill, Walter M., eds. Dear Lady: The Letters of Frederick Jackson Turner & Alice Forbes Perkins Hooper, 1910-1932. LC 76-134261. (Illus.). 487p. 1970. 15.00 (ISBN 0-87328-046-6). Huntington Lib.
Billington, Ray A., ed. see Forten, Charlotte L.
Billington, Ray A., jt. ed. see Ridge, Martin.
Billington, Sandra. A Social History of the Fool. LC 83-40624. 256p. 1984. 25.00 (ISBN 0-312-73293-7). St Martin.
Billington, W. D., jt. ed. see Isojima, S.
Billinton, R. Power System Reliability Evaluation. 310p. 1970. 52.50 (ISBN 0-677-02870-9). Gordon.
Billinton, R. & Allan, R. N. Reliability Evaluation of Engineering Systems. LC 82-15878. 359p. 1983. 42.50 (ISBN 0-306-41296-9, Plenum Press). Plenum Pub.
Billinton, Roy & Allan, Ronald N., eds. Reliability Evaluation of Power Systems. 435p. 1984. 55.00x (ISBN 0-306-41450-3, Plenum Pr). Plenum Pub.
Billinton, Roy, et al. Power-System Reliability Calculations. (Modern Electrical Technology Ser.: No. 6). 195p. 1973. 32.50x (ISBN 0-262-02098-X). MIT Pr.
Billion, Anna. Kundalini: Secret of the Ancient Yogis. 1982. pap. 4.95 (ISBN 0-686-97516-2, Reward). P-H.
Billionis, Cynthia, jt. auth. see Foster, Sunny.
Billionis, Cynthia, jt. auth. see Horner, Don R.
Billip, K. English-Polish, Polish-English Pocket Dictionary. 1982. pap. 5.00 (ISBN 0-317-18985-9, P508). Vanous.
--Polish Pocket Dictionary: Polish-English & English-Polish Minimum. rev. ed. 1982. 5.00x (ISBN 0-89918-298-4, P-508). Vanous.
Billip, K., jt. auth. see Stanislawski, J.
Billis, jt. auth. see Taylor.
Billis, David. Welfare Bureaucracies: Their Design & Changes in Response to Social Problems. 252p. 1985. pap. text ed. 23.95x (ISBN 0-435-82059-1). Gower Pub Co.
Billis, David, et al. Organising Social Services Departments. 1981. text ed. 26.00x (ISBN 0-435-82085-0). Gower Pub Co.
Billman, Carol. The Secret of the Syndicate: Nancy Drew, the Hardy Boys, & the Stratemeyer Mystery Factory. 250p. 1985. 13.95 (ISBN 0-8044-2055-6); pap. 8.95 (ISBN 0-8044-6052-3). Ungar.
Billman, Kenneth W., ed. Radiation Energy Conversion in Space. LC 78-8566. (Illus.). 670p. 1978. 59.00 (ISBN 0-915928-26-4, PAAS61); members 32.00 (ISBN 0-317-32182-X). AIAA.
Billman, L. S. Advanced Propulsion Concepts: Fourth Symposium. 314p. 1966. 84.75 (ISBN 0-677-11080-4). Gordon.
Billmers, Laura, jt. auth. see Sussman, Julie.
Billmeyer. Colour Seventy Seven. 75.00 (ISBN 0-9960017-5-1, Pub. by A Hilger England). Heyden.
Billmeyer, Fred W. & Kelley, Richard N. Entering Industry: A Guide for Young Professionals. LC 75-22283. pap. 73.80 (ISBN 0-317-10678-3, 2022243). Bks Demand UMI.
Billmeyer, Fred W., Jr. Textbook of Polymer Science. LC 83-19870. 560p. 1984. 34.95x (ISBN 0-471-03196-8, Pub. by Wiley-Interscience). Wiley.
Billmeyer, Fred W., Jr. & Saltzman, Max. Principles of Color Technology. 2nd ed. LC 80-21561. 240p. 1981. 39.50 (ISBN 0-471-03052-X, Pub. by Wiley-Interscience). Wiley.
Billmeyer, Pat. The Complete Encyclopedia of Wild Game & Fish Cleaning & Cooking, 3 Vols. LC 83-50091. 96p. 1983. pap. 9.95 set (ISBN 0-9606262-3-9); Vol. 1. pap. 3.95 (ISBN 0-9606262-4-7); Vol. 2. pap. 3.95 (ISBN 0-9606262-5-5); Vol. 3. pap. 3.95 (ISBN 0-9606262-6-3). Yesnaby Inc.
Billmeyer, Patricia. The Encyclopedia of Wild Game & Fish Cleaning & Cooking. LC 79-54388. 116p. pap. 3.95 (ISBN 0-9606262-0-4). Yesnaby Inc.
Billnitzer, Harold. Before You Divorce. 1978. pap. 0.95 (ISBN 0-933350-12-0). Morse Pr.
--Chances for a Happy Marriage. 1978. pap. 0.95 (ISBN 0-933350-00-7). Morse Pr.
--Chances in a Mixed Marriage. 1978. pap. 1.95 (ISBN 0-933350-11-2). Morse Pr.
--It's Your Death, Make the Most of It. LC 79-88402. 1979. pap. 7.95 (ISBN 0-933350-27-9). wkbk. 0.90 (ISBN 0-933350-28-7). Morse Pr.
Billon, B. M. Death's an End & a Beginning Without. 1981. 15.00x (ISBN 0-7223-1388-8, Pub. by Stockwell). State Mutual Bk.
Billon, Francois De see De Billon, Francois.
Billon, Frederic L. Annals of St. Louis in Its Early Days under the French & Spanish Dominations. LC 72-146373. (First American Frontier Ser). (Illus.). 1971. Repr. of 1886 ed. 27.00 (ISBN 0-405-02824-5). Ayer Co Pubs.
--Annals of St. Louis in Its Territorial Days from 1804 to 1821: Being a Continuation of the Author's Previous Work, the Annals of the French & Spanish Period. LC 76-146374. (First American Frontier Ser). (Illus.). 1971. Repr. of 1888 ed. 26.50 (ISBN 0-405-02825-3). Ayer Co Pubs.
Billot, Michel, tr. see Olsen, Maryann, et al.
Billout, Guy. By Camel or by Car: A Look at Transportation. (Illus.). 32p. 1983. pap. 5.95 (ISBN 0-13-109595-1, Pub. by Treehouse); 8.95 (ISBN 0-13-109603-6). P-H.
--Squid & Spider: A Look at the Animal Kingdom. (Illus.). 32p. (Orig.). (gr. 6 up). 1982. 10.95 (ISBN 0-13-839928-X). P-H.
--Stone & Steel: A Look at Engineering. (Illus.). 1980. 8.95x (ISBN 0-13-846873-7). P-H.
--Thunderbolt & Rainbow: A Look at Greek Mythology. (Illus.). 1981. 9.95 (ISBN 0-13-920637-X). P-H.
Billroth, Theodor. Medical Sciences in the German Universities. 300p. 1983. 32.00 (ISBN 0-941432-06-8); pap. 9.00 (ISBN 0-941432-07-6). Silvergirl Inc.
Bills, Garland D., jt. ed. see Bergen, John J.
Bills, Jay & Bills, Shirley. Home Food Dehydrating: Economical "Do-It Yourself" Methods for Preserving, Storing, & Cooking. 1974. pap. 6.95 (ISBN 0-88290-035-8). Horizon Utah.
Bills, M. A. see Hull, Clark L.
Bills, Paul. Alaska. LC 80-65307. (Illus.). 160p. (Orig.). 1980. pap. 2.50 (ISBN 0-88243-462-4, 02-0462). Gospel Pub.
Bills, Rex E. The Rulership Book: A Directory of Astrological Correspondences. 1984. Repr. of 1979 ed. 15.00 (ISBN 0-88053-759-0). Macoy Pub.
Bills, Robert E. Education for Intelligence or Failure. LC 81-19135. 300p. 1982. 12.50 (ISBN 0-87491-430-2). Acropolis.
--A System for Assessing Affectivity. LC 73-22712. 240p. 1975. 21.75 (ISBN 0-8173-9107-X). U of Ala Pr.
Bills, Robert E., jt. auth. see Nevin, David.
Bills, Scott L., ed. Kent State-May Four: Echoes Through a Decade. LC 82-10102. (Illus.). 316p. 1982. 16.50 (ISBN 0-87338-278-1). Kent St U Pr.
Bills, Shirley, jt. auth. see Bills, Jay.
Bills, Steven H. Lillian Hellman: An Annotated Bibliography. LC 78-68282. 248p. 1979. lib. bdg. 31.00 (ISBN 0-8240-9803-X). Garland Pub.
Billson, Charles J. Popular Poetry of the Finns. (Popular Studies in Mythology, Romance & Folklore: No. 5). Repr. of 1900 ed. 5.50 (ISBN 0-404-53505-4). AMS Pr.
Billson, Janet Mancine, ed. Clinical Sociology Review, Vol. II. 150p. 1984. 24.95 (ISBN 0-930390-56-3); pap. text ed. 12.50 (ISBN 0-942756-01-0). Clin Soc Assn.
Billstein, et al. LOGO: A Problem Solving Approach. LC 84-24229. 1985. text ed. 26.95 (ISBN 0-8053-0860-1). Benjamin-Cummings.
Billstein, R. & Libeskind, S. A Problem-Solving Approach to Mathematics for Elementary School Teachers. 2nd ed. 1984. 29.95 (ISBN 0-8053-0856-3); instr's. resource manual 5.95 (ISBN 0-8053-0857-1). Benjamin-Cummings.
Billstein, R., et al. A Problem Solving Approach to Mathematics for Elementary School Teachers. 1981. text ed. 28.95 (ISBN 0-8053-0851-2); instr.'s manual 5.95 (ISBN 0-8053-0857-1). Addison-Wesley.
Billups, Ann. Discussion Starters for Youth Groups: Ser. 1. (Orig.). 1966. pap. 9.95 (ISBN 0-8170-0351-7). Judson.
--Discussion Starters for Youth Groups: Ser. 2. LC 70-75185. 1969. pap. 9.95 (ISBN 0-8170-0443-2). Judson.
--Discussion Starters for Youth Groups, Ser. 3. LC 70-75185. 224p. 1976. pap. 9.95 (ISBN 0-8170-0687-7). Judson.
--Perspectives: Discussion Starters on Attitudes & Values for Church Groups. 224p. 1981. pap. 11.95 (ISBN 0-8170-0905-1). Judson.
Billy, Christopher, ed. Business & Management Jobs 1985. (Peterson's Annual Guides-Careers Ser.). 226p. (Orig.). 1985. pap. 12.95 (ISBN 0-87866-249-9). Petersons Guides.
--Engineering, Science, & Computer Jobs 1985. 6th ed. (Peterson's Annual Guides-Careers Ser.). 686p. (Orig.). 1984. pap. 14.95 (ISBN 0-87866-248-0). Petersons Guides.
Billy, Christopher & Wells, John, eds. Guide to Independent Secondary Schools 1985-86. 6th ed. (Peterson's Annual Guides Ser.). 1150p. (Orig.). 1985. 13.95 (ISBN 0-87866-301-0). Petersons Guides.
Billy, George J., et al. Sources of Information in Transportation: Part 3, Shipping. 3rd ed. (Public Administration Ser.: Bibliography P-1601). 49p. 1985. pap. 7.50 (ISBN 0-89028-251-X). Vance Biblios.
Billy Graham Center, ed. An Evangelical Agenda: Nineteen Eighty-Four & Beyond. LC 79-15889. 1979. pap. 5.95 (ISBN 0-87808-171-2). William Carey Lib.
Bilmanis, Alfred. History of Latvia. LC 69-13827. Repr. of 1951 ed. lib. bdg. 45.00x (ISBN 0-8371-1446-2, BIHL). Greenwood.
Bilnitzer. Check Your Chances of Success in a Mixed Marriage. pap. 1.75 (ISBN 0-686-12318-2). Christs Mission.
Bilodeau, Edward A., ed. Acquisition of Skill. 1966. 58.50 (ISBN 0-12-099150-0). Acad Pr.
Bilokur, Borys. A Concordance to the Russian Poetry of Fedor I. Tiutchev. LC 75-9419. 357p. 1975. 30.00x (ISBN 0-87057-145-1). U Pr of New Eng.
Biloon, F. Medical Equipment Service Manual: Theory & Maintenance Procedures. LC 77-513. 1978. 31.95 (ISBN 0-13-572644-1). P-H.
Bilotta. Electrical Connection in Electronic Assemblies. (Manufacturing Engineering Ser.). 328p. 1985. price not set (ISBN 0-8247-7319-5). Dekker.
Bilotto, Gerardo & Washam, Veronica. Work Independence & the Severely Disabled: A Bibliography. LC 79-91351. 108p. 1980. 7.50 (ISBN 0-686-38821-6). Human Res Ctr.
Bilovsky, Frank. Lion Country: Inside Penn State Football. LC 82-81802. (Illus.). 192p. 1982. 12.95 (ISBN 0-88011-072-4). Leisure Pr.
Bilovsky, Frank & Westcott, Richard. The Phillies Encyclopedia. LC 82-83945. (Illus.). 500p. 1984. 39.95 (ISBN 0-88011-121-6). Leisure Pr.
Bilsborrow, Richard E. Population in Development Planning: Background & Bibliography. 1976. pap. 5.00 (ISBN 0-89055-048-4). Carolina Pop Ctr.
Bilsborrow, Richard E., et al. Migration Surveys in Low-Income Countries: Guidelines for Survey & Questionnaire Design. LC 84-11354. 560p. 1984. 28.00 (ISBN 0-7099-3266-9, Pub. by Croom Helm Ltd). Longwood Pub Group.
Bilsen, F. A., ed. see International Symposium on Hearing, Fifth, Noordwijkerhout, the Netherlands, April 8-12, 1980.
Bilskey, Lester J. The State Religion of Ancient China, 2vols. (Asian Folklore & Social Life Monograph: No. 70 & 71). 1975. 25.00 set (ISBN 0-89986-067-2). Oriental Bk Store.
Bilski, Audrey. Problems of Your Child's Vital Years. (Illus.). 1977. 10.95 (ISBN 0-285-62188-2, Pub. by Souvenir Pr). Intl Spec Bk.
--The Vital Years & Your Child. 1977. 6.95 (ISBN 0-285-62088-6, Pub. by Souvenir Pr). Intl Spec Bk.
Bilski, R., et al, eds. Can Planning Replace Politics? (The Van Leer Jerusalem Foundation Ser.: No. 11). 338p. 1980. lib. bdg. 41.50 (ISBN 90-247-2324-8, Pub. by Martinus Nijhoff Netherlands). Kluwer Academic.
Bilsky, Lester J., ed. Historical Ecology: Essays on Environment & Social Change. (National University Pubns. Ser.). 1980. 16.95x (ISBN 0-8046-9247-5, Pub. by Kennikat). Assoc Faculty Pr.
Bilson, Elizabeth, jt. ed. see Terzian, Yervant.
Bilson, Frank. Crossbows. rev. ed. (Illus.). 186p. 1983. 14.95 (ISBN 0-88254-701-1). Hippocrene Bks.
Bilson, Geoffrey. A Darkened House: Cholera in Nineteenth Century Canada. (Social History of Canada Ser.). 1980. o. p. 17.50x (ISBN 0-8020-2367-3); pap. 8.50 (ISBN 0-8020-6402-7). U of Toronto Pr.
Bilson, John F. & Marston, Richard C., eds. Exchange Rate Theory & Practice. LC 84-2441. (National Bureau of Economic Research Conference Reports). 464p. 1985. lib. bdg. 58.00x (ISBN 0-226-05096-3). U of Chicago Pr.
Bilson, Thomas. The True Difference Between Christian Subjection & Unchristian Rebellion. LC 70-38154. (English Experience Ser.: No. 434). 854p. 1972. Repr. of 1585 ed. 143.00 (ISBN 90-221-0434-6). Walter J Johnson.
Bilstein, Roger. Flight Patterns: Trends of Aeronautical Development in the United States, 1918-1929. (Illus.). 248p. 18.50 (ISBN 0-8203-0670-3). U of Ga Pr.
Bilstein, Roger & Miller, Jay. Aviation in Texas. Lubeck, Scott, ed. (Illus.). 288p. 1985. 24.95 (ISBN 0-932012-95-7). Texas Month Pr.
Bilstein, Roger E. Flight in America, Nineteen Hundred to Nineteen Eighty-Three: From the Wrights to the Astronauts. LC 83-24822. (Illus.). 356p. 1984. 32.50 (ISBN 0-8018-2973-9). Johns Hopkins.
Bilton, Tony, et al. Introductory Sociology. (Illus.). 750p. 1982. pap. text ed. 16.50x (ISBN 0-333-28205-1). Sheridan.
Bilu, Dalya, tr. see Appelfeld, Aharon.
Bilu, Dalya, tr. see Shabtai, Yaakov.

Bily, M. & Cacko, J. Realtime Simulation of Random Processes. 1981. 28.00 (ISBN 0-9961074-3-6, 996107436S, Pub. by VDI W Germany). Heyden.

Bilyeu, Richard. The Tanelorn Archives: A Primary & Secondary Bibliography of the Works of Michael Moorcock,1949-1979. 160p. 1982. lib. bdg. 15.95x (ISBN 0-919695-04-3); pap. text ed. 7.95x (ISBN 0-919695-05-1). Borgo Pr.

Bilz, H. & Kress, W. Phonon Dispersion Relations in Insulators. (Springer Ser. in Solid-State Sciences: Vol. 10). (Illus.). 1979. 48.00 (ISBN 0-387-09399-0). Springer-Verlag.

Bilz, H., et al. Dynamical Properties of IV-VI Compounds. (Springer Tracts in Modern Physics Ser.: Vol. 99). (Illus.). 115p. 1983. 28.00 (ISBN 0-387-12092-0). Springer-Verlag.

Bilzer, B. Begriffslexikon der Bildenden Kuenste, 2 vols. 320p. (Ger.). 1971. Set. pap. 25.50 (ISBN 3-499-16142-7, M-7305). French & Eur.

Bimala dasi, ed. see Dasa Goswami, Satvarupa.

Bimala dasi, ed. see Das Goswami, Satsvarupa.

Bimala dasi, ed. see Das Goswami, Satvarupa.

Bimba, Anthony. History of the American Working Class. 3rd ed. LC 68-30818. (Illus.). 1968. Repr. of 1936 ed. lib. bdg. 25.00x (ISBN 0-8371-0020-8, BIWC). Greenwood.

--The Molly Maguires. LC 75-15046. 144p. 1970. pap. 2.50 (ISBN 0-7178-0273-6). Intl Pubs Co.

Bimler, Rich & Brokering, Herb. Lord, I Want to Celebrate. 1980. pap. 2.95 (ISBN 0-570-03069-2, 06-1185). Concordia.

Bimler, Richard. Seventy-Seven Ways of Involving Youth in the Church. (Illus.). 1976. pap. 4.50 (ISBN 0-570-03737-9, 12-2641). Concordia.

Bimler, Richard W. Grand Opening. 1983. 3:50 (ISBN 0-89536-589-8). CSS of Ohio.

--The Youth Group Meeting Guide. 254p. (Orig.). 1984. pap. 11.95 (ISBN 0-936664-17-7). Group Bks.

Bimmerman, W. & Hart, M. D. Value Engineering: A Practical Approach for Owners, Engineers & Contractors. 279p. 1981. 38.50 (ISBN 0-318-17683-1); 34.75 (ISBN 0-318-17684-X). Soc Am Value E.

Bimson, John J. Redating the Exodus & Conquest. 2nd ed. 288p. 1981. pap. text ed. 14.95x (ISBN 0-907459-04-8, Pub. by Almond Pr England). Eisenbrauns.

Bin, Bhikshuni Heng, et al, trs. Flower Adornment Sutra, Chapter 22: The Ten Inexhaustible Treasuries Commentary by Tripitka Master Hua. (Illus.). 184p. (Orig.). 1983. pap. 7.00 (ISBN 0-917512-38-3). Buddhist Text.

Bina, Cyrus. The Economics of Oil Crisis: Theories of Oil Crisis, Oil Rent & Internationalization of Capital in the Oil Industry. LC 84-22888. 268p. 1985. 29.95 (ISBN 0-312-23661-1). St Martin.

Binau, Brad. Henry Miller's Thanksgiving Prayer. (Orig.). 1980. pap. 1.95 (ISBN 0-937172-06-5). JLJ Pubs.

Binchy, Maeve. Central Line. 152p. (Orig.). 1980. pap. 4.50 (ISBN 0-7043-3210-8, Pub. by Quartet England). Irish Bk Ctr.

--Dublin Four. (Poolbeg--Ward River Short Stories Ser.). Orig. Title: Maeve Binchy's Dublin Four. 208p. (Orig.). 1982. pap. 4.95 (ISBN 0-907085-18-0, Pub. by Ward River Ireland). Irish Bk Ctr.

--Dublin Four. 208p. 1982. pap. 5.95 (ISBN 0-907085-18-0, Pub. by Ward River Pr Ireland). Irish Bks Media.

--Echoes. 1985. 17.95 (ISBN 0-317-20649-4). Viking.

--Light a Penny Candle. 540p. 1983. 17.75 (ISBN 0-670-42827-2). Viking.

--Light a Penny Candle. 1984. pap. 3.95 (ISBN 0-440-14795-6). Dell.

--The Lilac Bus. 200p. (Orig.). 1984. pap. 7.95 (ISBN 0-907085-79-2, Pub. by Ward River Ireland). Irish Bks Media.

--London Transports. 1986. pap. 3.95 (ISBN 0-440-14870-7). Dell.

--Victoria Line. 154p. (Orig.). 1980. pap. 4.50 (ISBN 0-7043-3342-2, Pub. by Ward River Ireland). Irish Bk Ctr.

Binchy, William. Is Divorce the Answer? An Examination of No-Fault Divorce Against the Background of the Irish Debate. 116p. 1984. pap. 9.00x (ISBN 0-7165-0314-X, BBA 04861, Pub. by Irish Academic Pr Ireland). Biblio Dist.

Bindari, Sami. The House of Power. Bindari, Sami & St. Leger, Muna, trs. from Arabic. LC 79-24665. Orig. Title: Al-Sarayah. 1980. 7.95 (ISBN 0-395-28540-2). HM.

Bindel, Henry J., Jr., jt. ed. see Science & Children Editorial Staff.

Bindeman, Steven L. Heidegger & Wittgenstein: The Poetics of Silence. LC 80-6066. 159p. 1980. lib. bdg. 20.50 (ISBN 0-8191-1350-6); pap. text ed. 9.25 (ISBN 0-8191-1351-4). U Pr of Amer.

Binder, A. & Geis, G. Methods of Research in Criminology & Criminal Justice. 288p. 1983. text ed. 25.95 (ISBN 0-07-005286-7). McGraw.

Binder, Abraham W. Studies in Jewish Music: The Collected Writings of the Noted Musicologist. Heskes, Irene, ed. LC 72-136423. 1971. 15.00x (ISBN 0-8197-0272-2). Bloch.

Binder, Arnold, jt. auth. see Scharf, Peter.

Binder, Bob. The Earthly Pleasure of Wine. (Illus.). 86p. 1984. pap. 4.95 (ISBN 0-89015-423-6). Eakin Pubns.

Binder, David A. & Bergman, Paul. Fact Investigation: From Hypothesis to Proof. LC 84-3676. (American Casebook Ser.). 354p. 1984. text ed. 14.95 (ISBN 0-314-81258-X). West Pub.

Binder, David A. & Price, Susan C. Legal Interviewing & Counseling: A Client-Centered Approach. LC 77-84550. 1977. pap. 6.95 (ISBN 0-685-88127-X). West Pub.

Binder, David F. The Hearsay Handbook. 2nd ed. (Trial Publications). 546p. 1983. write for info. (Pub. By Shepards-McGraw). McGraw.

--The Hearsay Handbook: The Hearsay Rule & Its 40 Exceptions. 2nd ed. LC 83-17600. (Trail Practice Ser.). 1984. 70.00 (ISBN 0-07-005287-5, Shepards-McGraw). McGraw.

Binder, Eando. Menace of the Saucers. 1978. pap. 1.25 (ISBN 0-8439-0576-X, Leisure Bks). Dorchester Pub Co.

Binder, Frederick M. Coal Age Empire: Pennsylvania Coal & Its Utilization to 1860. LC 75-621822. 184p. 1974. 8.95 (ISBN 0-911124-75-6). Pa Hist & Mus.

Binder, George A., et al. Computed Tomography of the Brain in Axial, Coronal, & Sagittal Planes. 1979. 59.95 (ISBN 0-316-09507-9). Little.

Binder, Henry, ed. see Crane, Stephen.

Binder, Henry J., ed. Mechanisms of Intestinal Secretion. LC 79-2066. (Kroc Foundation Ser.: Vol. 12). 320p. 1979. 37.00x (ISBN 0-8451-0302-4). A R Liss.

Binder, Jamie. Planets, Personality & Professions. Lockhart, Julie, ed. 250p. (Orig.). 1985. pap. 12.95 (ISBN 0-914918-69-9). Para Res.

Binder, Jeffrey L., jt. auth. see Strupp, Hans H.

Binder, K., ed. Applications of the Monte Carlo Method in Statistical Physics. (Topics in Current Physics: Vol. 36). (Illus.). 330p. 1984. 34.00 (ISBN 0-387-12764-X). Springer-Verlag.

Binder, Leonard. Ideological Revolution in the Middle East. 2nd ed. LC 77-24596. 424p. 1979. lib. bdg. 25.50 (ISBN 0-88275-593-5). Krieger.

--In a Moment of Enthusiasm: Political Power & the Second Stratum in Egypt. LC 77-15480. (Illus.). 1978. lib. bdg. 37.50x (ISBN 0-226-05144-7). U of Chicago Pr.

--Revolution in Iran. 62p. 4.95 (ISBN 0-317-31966-3). AAAPME.

--The Study of the Middle East: Research & Scholarship in the Humanities & Social Sciences. LC 76-7408. 648p. 1976. cloth 64.00x (ISBN 0-471-07304-0, Pub. by Wiley-Interscience). Wiley.

Binder, Leonard, ed. The Study of the Middle East: Research & Scholarship in the Humanities & the Social Sciences. LC 76-7408. pap. 160.00 (ISBN 0-317-11061-6, 2055412). Bks Demand UMI.

Binder, Leonard, et al, eds. Crises & Sequences in Political Development. LC 79-141952. (Studies in Political Development, 7). 344p. 1971. 35.00 (ISBN 0-691-07523-9); pap. 9.95x (ISBN 0-691-02171-6). Princeton U Pr.

Binder, Louis R. Modern Religious Cults & Society. LC 77-113556. Repr. of 1933 ed. 10.00 (ISBN 0-404-00867-4). AMS Pr.

Binder, M. B. Vidotex & Teletext: New Online Resources for Libraries. (Foundations of Library & Information Science Ser.: Vol. 21). 1985. 47.50 (ISBN 0-89232-612-3). Jai Pr.

Binder, M. H., jt. auth. see Henderson, R. W.

Binder, Otto, ed. see Shelley, Mary.

Binder, Otto, ed. see Verne, Jules.

Binder, Otto, ed. see Wells, H. G.

Binder, Otto O. Flying Saucers Are Watching Us. 1978. pap. 1.50 (ISBN 0-505-51304-8, Pub. by Tower Bks). Dorchester Pub Co.

Binder, R., jt. auth. see Novak, J.

Binder, Raymond C. Fluid Mechanics. 5th ed. (Illus.). 448p. 1973. ref. ed. 38.95 (ISBN 0-13-322594-1). P-H.

Binder, Robert. Application Debugging: An MVS Abend Handbook for COBOL, Assembly, PL-1 & Fortran Programmers. (Illus.). 288p. 1985. text ed. 35.00 (ISBN 0-13-039348-7). P-H.

Binder, Rudolph M., jt. ed. see Bliss, William D.

Binder, V., et al. Modern Therapies. 1976. (Spec); pap. 5.95 (ISBN 0-13-598995-7). P-H.

Binder, Z., ed. see IFAC Symposium, Paris, France, Dec. 1982.

Binding, G. J. About Comfrey-Forgotten Herb. 1981. pap. 4.95x (ISBN 0-317-07291-9, Regent House). B of A.

--About Garlic. 1981. pap. 4.95x (ISBN 0-317-07290-0, Regent House). B of A.

--About Kelp. 1981. pap. 4.95x (ISBN 0-317-07287-0, Regent House). B of A.

--About Pollen. 1982. pap. 4.95x (ISBN 0-317-07289-7, Regent House). B of A.

--About Pollen. 64p. 1985. pap. 1.95 (ISBN 0-7225-0660-0). Thorsons Pubs.

--Vegetables & Herbs with a Difference. 64p. 1972. pap. 3.00x (ISBN 0-8464-1059-1). Beekman Pubs.

--Vegetables & Herbs with a Difference. 1980. 19.50x (ISBN 0-85032-178-6, Pub. by Daniel Co England). State Mutual Bk.

Binding, Paul. Lorca: The Gay Imagintion. 208p. (Orig.). 1985. 25.00 (ISBN 0-907040-37-3, Pub. by GMP England); pap. 8.95 (ISBN 0-907040-36-5). Alyson Pubns.

Binding, Paul, ed. see Stevenson, Robert Louis.

Binding, T. J., ed. Firebird One: Writing Today. 1982. pap. 6.95 (ISBN 0-14-006206-8). Penguin.

Bindler, Norman. The Conservative Court, Nineteen Ten to Nineteen Thirty, 9 vols. LC 84-2810. (Supreme Court in American Life Ser.: Vol. 6). Date not set. 30.00 (ISBN 0-86733-061-9); Set. 230.00x. Assoc Faculty Pr.

Bindley, T. Herbert, ed. The Ecumenical Documents of the Faith: The Creed of Nicea; Three Epistles of Cyril; The Tome of Leo; The Chalcedonian Definition. 4th ed. LC 79-8708. viii, 246p. 1980. Repr. of 1950 ed. lib. bdg. 24.75x (ISBN 0-313-22197-9, BIOD). Greenwood.

Bindloss, H. & Pinnock, J. In the Niger Country, Benin: The Surrounding Country, Inhabitants, Customs, & Trade. 398p. 1968. Repr. of 1898 ed. 32.50x (ISBN 0-7146-1791-1, F Cass Co). Biblio Dist.

Bindman, David. Hogarth. (World of Art Ser.). (Illus.). 216p. 1985. pap. text ed. 9.95 (ISBN 0-500-20182-X). Thames Hudson.

Bindman, David, ed. The Thames & Hudson Encyclopedia of British Art. LC 84-51499. 320p. 1985. 24.95 (ISBN 0-500-23420-5). Thames Hudson.

Bindman, Geoffrey, jt. auth. see Lester, Anthony.

Bindman, Lynn & Lippold, Olof. The Neurophysiology of the Cerebral Cortex. (Illus.). 507p. 1981. text ed. 85.00x (ISBN 0-292-75521-X). U of Tex Pr.

Bindman, Lynn & Loppold, Olof. The Neurophysiology of the Cerebral Cortex. 512p. 1981. 135.00x (ISBN 0-7131-4360-6, Pub. by E Arnold England). State Mutual Bk.

Bindman, Stephen. Love Without Illusions. LC 85-80019. 200p. (Orig.). Date not set. pap. 10.95 (ISBN 0-932385-19-2). Human Futures.

Bindmann. Festkoerperphysik und Elektronische Technik. 1104p. (Eng. & Ger., Dictionary of Solid State Physics and Electrical Engineering). 1972. 83.95 (ISBN 3-87097-055-3, M-7410, Pub. by Brandstetter). French & Eur.

Bindmann, W. Dictionary of Solid State Physics & Electronics Technology: English-German, German-English. (Technical Dictionary). 1973. 31.50x (ISBN 0-685-27547-7). Adlers Foreign Bks.

--Fachwoerterbuch Optik und Optischer Geraetebau. 408p. (Eng. & Ger., Dictionary of Optics and Optical Devices). 1974. 75.00 (ISBN 3-7684-6411-3, M-7402, Pub. by Dausien). French & Eur.

Bindmann, W., ed. Dictionary of Microelectronics: English-German & German-English. 480p. 1985. 105.75 (ISBN 0-444-99619-2, I-187-84). Elsevier.

--Optics & Optical Instrumentation: Dictionary. 450p. (Eng. -Ger.). 1974. 30.60 (ISBN 0-685-42256-9); german-english ed. 30.60x (ISBN 0-686-66956-8). Adlers Foreign Bks.

Bindoff, S. T. Tudor England, Vol. 5. 1950. pap. 4.95 (ISBN 0-14-020212-9, Pelican). Penguin.

Bindoff, S. T. & Boulton, James T. Research in Progress in English & History. LC 75-29642. 1976. 15.00 (ISBN 0-312-67690-5). St Martin.

Bindoff, S. T., ed. The House of Commons 1509-1558: The History of Parliament, 3-Vols. (Parliament Ser.). (700 Pgs. ea. vol.). 1983. Set. 250.00x (ISBN 0-436-04282-7, Pub by Secker & Warburg UK). David & Charles.

Bindon, Kathleen R. Inventories & Foreign Currency Translation Requirements. Farmer, Richard N., ed. LC 82-21729. (Research for Business Decisions: No. 56). 158p. 1983. 39.95 (ISBN 0-8357-1391-1). Univ Microfilms.

Bindra, Dalbir. Motivation: A Systematic Reinterpretation. LC 59-6101. (Illus.). pap. 70.50 (ISBN 0-317-10481-0, 2012559). Bks Demand UMI.

Bindra, Dalbir, ed. The Brain's Mind: A Neuroscience Perspective on the Mind-Body Problem. (Illus.). 128p. 1980. text ed. 18.95x (ISBN 0-89876-003-8). Gardner Pr.

Bindra, Jasjit S. Prostaglandin Synthesis. 1977. 60.00 (ISBN 0-12-099460-7). Acad Pr.

Bindra, Jasjit S. & Bindra, Ranjna. Creativity in Organic Synthesis, Vol. 1. 1975. 45.00 (ISBN 0-12-099450-X). Acad Pr.

Bindra, Jasjit S. & Lednicer, Daniel. Chronicles of Drug Discovery, Vol. 1. LC 81-11471. 283p. 1982. cloth 37.50x (ISBN 0-471-06516-1, Pub. by Wiley-Interscience). Wiley.

--Chronicles of Drug Discovery, Vol. 2. LC 81-11471. 272p. 1983. cloth 48.50 (ISBN 0-471-89135-5, Pub. by Wiley-Interscience). Wiley.

Bindra, Ranjna, jt. auth. see Bindra, Jasjit S.

Bindra, S. S. India & Her Neighbours. 404p. 1984. text ed. 30.50x (ISBN 0-391-03267-4, Pub. by Deep & Deep India). Humanities.

Bindseil, Kenneth R. & Dickey, Imogene B. Effective Writing: Methods & Examples. LC 77-72907. (Illus.). 1978. pap. text ed. 16.50 (ISBN 0-395-24950-3); instr's. manual & suppl. tests 0.50 (ISBN 0-395-24949-X). HM.

Bindslev, N., jt. auth. see Ussing, H. H.

Bines, Harvey E. Law of Investment Management. 1977. 84.00 (ISBN 0-88262-150-5, 77-10130). Warren.

Binet, Alfred. Alterations of Personality. Baldwin, Helen G., tr. from Fr. Bd. with On Double-Consciousness. Repr. of 1890 ed. (Contributions to the History of Psychology Ser., Vol V, Pt. C: Medical Psychology). 1978. Repr. of 1896 ed. 30.00 (ISBN 0-89093-169-0). U Pubns Amer.

--Psychic Life of Micro-Organisms. 1971. Repr. 7.50x (ISBN 0-87556-025-3). Saifer.

--The Psychic Life of Micro-Organisms: A Study in Experimental Psychology. 2nd ed. (Religion of Science Library). 121p. 9.95 (ISBN 0-912050-59-4). Open Court.

Binet, Alfred & Simon, Thomas. The Development of Intelligence in Children. LC 73-2962. (Classics in Psychology Ser.). Repr. of 1916 ed. 23.50 (ISBN 0-405-05135-2). Ayer Co Pubs.

Binet, Alfred see Magendie, Francois.

Binet, Alfred, et al see Stern, William L.

Binet, Hyacinthe. Style de la lyrique courtoise en France aux douzieme et triezieme siecles. 1968. Repr. of 1891 ed. 21.00 (ISBN 0-8337-0278-5). B Franklin.

Binet, J.; see Poirier, J.

Binet, Pere. The Divine Favors Granted to St. Joseph. LC 82-50590. 176p. 1983. pap. 3.00 (ISBN 0-89555-187-X). TAN Bks Pubs.

Binet, Suzanne. Desserts for Diabetics & Dieters. 1977. pap. 6.95 (ISBN 0-7715-9367-8). Vanguard.

--Salads for Diabetics. 1979. pap. 6.95 (ISBN 0-7715-9487-9). Vanguard.

Binfield, Clyde. So Down to Prayers: Studies in English Nonconformity, 1780-1920. (Rowman & Littlefield University Library). 296p. 1977. 20.00x (ISBN 0-87471-959-3). Rowman.

Binford, Henry C. The First Suburbs: Residential Communities on the Boston Periphery, 1815-1860. LC 84-16127. (Illus.). 273p. 1985. lib. bdg. 25.00x (ISBN 0-226-05158-7). U of Chicago Pr.

Binford, Jesse S., Jr. Foundation of Chemistry. 1977. write for info. (ISBN 0-02-309880-5, 30988). Macmillan.

--Foundations of Chemistry. (Illus.). 334p. 1985. pap. text ed. 23.95 (ISBN 0-931541-03-4). Bk Pubs.

Binford, Lewis, ed. For Theory Building in Archaeology: Essays on Faunal Remains, Aquatic Resources, Spatial Analysis & Systematic Modelling. (Studies in Archaeology). 1977. 50.00 (ISBN 0-12-100050-8). Acad Pr.

Binford, Lewis R. Bones: Ancient Men & Modern Myths. LC 80-81776. (Studies in Archaeology). 1981. 37.50 (ISBN 0-12-100035-4). Acad Pr.

--Faunal Remains from Klasies River Mouth: Monograph. LC 83-15909. 1984. 39.50 (ISBN 0-12-100070-2). Acad Pr.

--In Pursuit of the Past: Decoding the Archaeological Record. LC 82-50816. (Illus.). 1983. 18.95f (ISBN 0-500-05042-2). Thames Hudson.

--Nunamuit Ethnoarchaeology. (Studies in Archaeology Ser.). 1978. 50.00 (ISBN 0-12-100040-0). Acad Pr.

--Working at Archaeology. (Studies in Archaeology). 1983. 29.50 (ISBN 0-12-100060-5). Acad Pr.

Bing, Alexander M. War-Time Strikes & Their Adjustment. LC 79-156405. (American Labor Ser., No. 2). 1971. Repr. of 1921 ed. 23.50 (ISBN 0-405-02915-2). Ayer Co Pubs.

Bing, Elisabeth. Moving Through Pregnancy. LC 74-17673. 144p. 1975. pap. 8.95 (ISBN 0-672-52095-8). Bobbs.

--Six Practical Lessons for an Easier Childbirth. 1980. pap. 2.95 (ISBN 0-553-23082-4). Bantam.

Bing, Elisabeth, jt. auth. see Michele, Karen.

Bing, Elizabeth & Coleman, Libby. Having a Baby after Thirty. 1980. pap. 3.95 (ISBN 0-553-24642-9). Bantam.

Bing, Elizabeth, jt. auth. see Michele, Karen.

Bing, Gordon. Corporate Acquisitions. LC 80-22386. 248p. 1980. 19.95x (ISBN 0-87201-009-0). Gulf Pub.

--Corporate Divestment. LC 77-86528. 166p. 1978. 19.95x (ISBN 0-87201-141-0). Gulf Pub.

Bing, Ilse. Numbers in Images: Illuminations of Numerical Meanings. LC 76-5739. (Illus.). 176p. 1976. 10.00 (ISBN 0-916832-00-7). Ilkon Pr.

--Words As Visions: Logograms. LC 73-90744. 216p. 1974. pap. 7.00 (ISBN 0-916832-01-5). Ilkon Pr.

Bing, Janet M. Aspects of English Prosody. (Outstanding Dissertations in Linguistics Ser.). 241p. 1985. lib. bdg. 30.00 (ISBN 0-317-19423-2). Garland Pub.

Bing, John. Handbook of Legal Information Retrieval. LC 84-1177. 1984. 92.75 (ISBN 0-444-87576-X). Elsevier.

Bing, John W., jt. ed. see Kinsey, David C.

Bing, Jon & Harvold, Trygve. Legal Decisions & Information Systems. 1977. 25.00x (ISBN 82-00-05031-9, Dist. by Columbia U Pr). Universitet.

Bing, Jon & Selmer, Knut S. A Decade of Computers & Law. 480p. 1980. pap. 35.00x (ISBN 82-0005-376-8). Universitet.

Bing, Peter, ed. see Burkert, Walter.

Bing, R. H. The Geometric Topology of Three Manifolds. LC 83-14962. (Colloquium Publications Ser.: Vol. 40). 240p. 1983. 54.00 (ISBN 0-8218-1040-5). Am Math.

Bing, R. H., et al, eds. Continua, Decompositions, Manifolds. (Illus.). 279p. 1983. text ed. 35.00x (ISBN 0-292-78061-3). U of Tex Pr.

Bing, Richard J., jt. ed. see Morin, Robert J.

Bing, Samuel. Artistic America, Tiffany Glass & Art Nouveau. (Illus.). 288p. 1970. pap. 9.95 (ISBN 0-262-52025-7). MIT Pr.

Bing, Stephen & Brown, Larry. Standards Relating to Monitoring. LC 77-3939. (IJA-ABA Juvenile Justice Standards Project Ser.). 104p. 1980. prof ref 22.50 (ISBN 0-88410-753-1); pap. 12.50 (ISBN 0-88410-805-8). Ballinger Pub.

Bing, Valetyn & Braet Von Uberfeldt, Jan. Regional Costumes of the Netherlands. (Illus.). 1978. 75.00 (ISBN 0-686-43013-1). Heinman.

Bingaman, Joseph W. Latin America: A Survey of Holdings at the Hoover Institution on War, Revolution & Peace. LC 78-142949. (Library Survey Ser.: No. 5). 96p. 1972. pap. 3.00x (ISBN 0-8179-5052-4). Hoover Inst Pr.

Bingelis, Tony. The Sportplane Builder. rev. ed. Rivers, David A., ed. (Illus.). 320p. 1980. pap. 17.95x (ISBN 0-911721-84-3, Pub. by Bingelis). Aviation.

Bingen, James R. Food Production & Rural Development in the Sahel: Lessons from Mal's Operation Riz-Segou. (Replica Edition-Softcover Ser.). 350p. 1985. pap. 18.50x (ISBN 0-86531-893-X). Westview.

Binger. Lippincott's Guide to Nursing Literature. text ed. 15.25 (ISBN 0-397-54344-1, 64-02861, Lippincott Nursing). Lippincott.

Binger, Jane L., jt. auth. see Huntsman, Ann J.

Binger, Norman H., tr. see Busch, Moritz.

Binggeli, M. H. & Ruckenbauer, E. INIS Input Training Kit. 771p. (Orig.). 1984. pap. 67.25 (ISBN 92-0-179083-X, ISP653, IAEA). Unipub.

Bingham. Ministry of Death. 1985. pap. 2.95 (ISBN 0-8027-3126-0). Walker & Co.

Bingham, et al. Centrifuges. LC 83-161604. (Mud Equipment Manual Ser.: No. 8). 68p. (Orig.). 1983. pap. 17.95x (ISBN 0-87201-620-X). Gulf Pub.

--Challenges. (Junior & Senior High Ser.). 240p. (gr. 8 up). 1984. 12.95 (ISBN 0-317-14808-7). Learning Wks.

--Choices. (Junior & Senior High Ser.). 240p. (gr. 8 up). 1983. 12.95. Learning Wks.

Bingham, Alfred M. & Rodman, Selden, eds. Challenge to the New Deal. facsimile ed. LC 79-156614. (Essay Index Reprint Ser). Repr. of 1934 ed. 24.50 (ISBN 0-8369-2269-7). Ayer Co Pubs.

Bingham, Anne, jt. auth. see MacDonald, Jeffrey.

Bingham, Beverly. Cooking with Fragile Hands. LC 84-73054. (Illus.). 384p. 1985. 18.50 (ISBN 0-9614122-0-8); pap. 15.50 (ISBN 0-9614122-1-6). Creative Cuisine.

Bingham, Bruce. Ferro-Cement: Design, Techniques, & Application. LC 74-4255. (Illus.). 459p. 1984. pap. 28.00 (ISBN 0-87033-317-8). Cornell Maritime.

--The Sailor's Sketchbook. LC 83-531. (Illus.). 144p. 1983. pap. 9.95 (ISBN 0-915160-55-2). Seven Seas.

Bingham, C. T. Hymenoptera: Ants & Cuckoowasps, Vol. 2. (Fauna of British India Ser.). xx, 508p. 1975. Repr. of 1903 ed. 25.00 (ISBN 0-88065-063-X, Pub. by Messers Today & Tomorrows Printers & Publishers India). Scholarly Pubns.

--Hymenoptera: Wasps & Bees, Vol. 1. (Fauna of British India Ser.). xxx, 590p. 1975. Repr. of 1897 ed. 30.00 (ISBN 0-88065-062-1, Pub. by Messers Today & Tomorrows Printers & Publishers India). Scholarly Pubns.

Bingham, Caleb. Young Lady's Accidence. LC 81-5663. (Amer. Linguistics Ser.). 1981. Repr. of 1785 ed. 40.00x (ISBN 0-8201-1360-3). Schol Facsimilies.

Bingham, Chas. W. Wise Sayings & Favorite Passages from the Works of Henry Fielding, Including His Essay on Conversation. LC 74-12102. 1974. Repr. of 1909 ed. lib. bdg. 10.00 (ISBN 0-8414-3211-2). Folcroft.

Bingham, Clifton, jt. auth. see Nister, Ernest.

Bingham, Colin. Wit & Wisdom: A Public Affairs Miscellany. 368p. 1982. 35.00x (ISBN 0-522-84241-0, Pub. by Melbourne U Pr); pap. 21.00x (ISBN 0-522-84255-0). Intl Spec Bk.

Bingham, Denis A. Marriages of the Bourbons, Two Vols, 2 Vols. LC 70-113557. (Illus.). Repr. of 1890 ed. Set. 45.00 (ISBN 0-404-00890-9); 23.00 ea. Vol. 1 (ISBN 0-404-00891-7). Vol. 2 (ISBN 0-404-00892-5). AMS Pr.

Bingham, Doris. Lovers & Liars. 1981. pap. 2.25 (ISBN 0-8439-0905-6, Leisure Bks). Dorchester Pub Co.

Bingham, Earl. Pocketbook for Technical & Professional Writers. 304p. 1981. pap. text ed. 9.95x (ISBN 0-534-01004-0). Wadsworth Pub.

Bingham, Edwin. Oregon! LC 79-2296. (Illus.). 300p. (gr. 4). 1985. text ed. 17.25x (ISBN 0-87905-103-5, Peregrine Smith). Gibbs M Smith.

Bingham, Edwin R. Charles F. Lummis: Editor of the Southwest. LC 73-15058. (Illus.). 218p. 1974. Repr. of 1955 ed. lib. bdg. 24.75x (ISBN 0-8371-7149-0, BICL). Greenwood.

Bingham, Edwin R., ed. California Gold: Selected Source Materials for College Research Papers. LC 81-2001. ix, 117p. 1981. Repr. of 1959 ed. lib. bdg. 19.75x (ISBN 0-313-22776-4, BICAG). Greenwood.

Bingham, Edwin R. & Love, Glen A., eds. Northwest Perspectives: Essays on the Culture of the Pacific Northwest. LC 77-15189. 264p. 1979. 20.00x (ISBN 0-295-95594-5); pap. 9.95x (ISBN 0-295-95805-7). U of Wash Pr.

Bingham, Fred P. Practical Yacht Joinery: Tools, Techniques, Tips. LC 81-81418. (Illus.). 320p. 1983. 32.50 (ISBN 0-87742-140-4). Intl Marine.

Bingham, Hiram. Across South America. (Latin America in the 20th Century Ser.). 1976. Repr. of 1911 ed. lib. bdg. 45.00 (ISBN 0-306-70834-5). Da Capo.

--The Dawnwatchers. 365p. 1984. pap. 6.95 (ISBN 0-9613602-0-8). Triune Bks.

--Elihu Yale: The American Nabob of Queen Square. (Illus.). x, 344p. 1968. Repr. of 1939 ed. 25.00 (ISBN 0-208-00690-7, Archon). Shoe String.

--Lost City of the Incas. LC 48-9227. (Illus.). 1963. pap. text ed. 4.95x (ISBN 0-689-70014-8, 33). Atheneum.

--Lost City of the Incas. LC 81-7196. (Illus.). xviii, 263p. 1981. Repr. of 1948 ed. lib. bdg. 35.00x (ISBN 0-313-22950-3, BILC). Greenwood.

--Machu Pichu: A Citadel of the Incas. LC 79-83881. (Illus.). 1979. Repr. of 1930 ed. lib. bdg. 50.00 (ISBN 0-87817-252-1). Hacker.

--The Monroe Doctrine. (Latin America in the 20th Century Ser.). 1976. Repr. of 1913 ed. lib. bdg. 22.50 (ISBN 0-306-70833-7). Da Capo.

--A Residence of Twenty-One Years in the Sandwich Islands: A Civil, Religious & Political History. rev. 3rd ed. LC 77-83041. 1981. 27.50 (ISBN 0-8048-1252-7). C E Tuttle.

Bingham, Howard R. Living with Teens: A Parent's Handbook. LC 83-72479. 71p. 1983. 5.95 (ISBN 0-87747-956-9). Deseret Bk.

Bingham, J. Pocket Picture Guides for Nurses. 100p. 1984. text ed. 11.95 (ISBN 0-683-00916-8). Williams & Wilkins.

--Sexually Transmitted Diseases. (Pocket Picture Guides to Clinical Medicine Ser.). 100p. 1984. text ed. 11.95 (ISBN 0-683-00915-X). Williams & Wilkins.

Bingham, J., tr. see Aelianus, Tacitus.

Bingham, J., tr. see Aelinaus, Tacitus.

Bingham, J., tr. see Xenophon.

Bingham, J. Elliot. Narrative of the Expedition to China, 2 vols. LC 72-79813. (China Library Ser.). 1972. Repr. of 1842 ed. Set. lib. bdg. 43.00 (ISBN 0-8420-1361-X). Scholarly Res Inc.

Bingham, J. W., jt. auth. see Crolier, M. J.

Bingham, Jane & Scholt, Grayce, eds. Fifteen Centuries of Children's Literature: An Annotated Chronology of British & American Works in Historical Context. LC 79-8584. (Illus.). l, 540p. 1980. lib. bdg. 49.95x (ISBN 0-313-22164-2, BCL/). Greenwood.

Bingham, Janet, jt. ed. see Bingham, Sam.

Bingham, Joan & Riccio, Delores. Rodale's Sensational Desserts. Gerras, Charles, ed. (Illus.). 320p. 1985. 21.95 (ISBN 0-87857-542-1); pap. 12.95 (ISBN 0-87857-585-5). Rodale Pr Inc.

Bingham, Joan & Riccio, Dolores. The Smart Shopper's Guide to Food Buying & Preparation. 320p. 1983. pap. 6.95 (ISBN 0-684-17822-2, ScribT). Scribner.

Bingham, Joan, jt. auth. see Riccio, Dolores.

Bingham, John. The Handbook for Apartment Living. LC 80-70350. 288p. (gr. 11-12). 1981. 13.95 (ISBN 0-8019-6987-5); pap. 8.95 (ISBN 0-8019-6988-3). Chilton.

Bingham, John E. & Davies, Garth W. A Handbook of Systems Analysis. 2nd ed. LC 77-28954. 229p. 1980. pap. 24.95x (ISBN 0-470-26997-9). Halsted Pr.

Bingham, Jonathan B. Shirt-Sleeve Diplomacy. facs. ed. LC 77-133512. (Select Bibliographies Reprint Ser). 1954. 19.00 (ISBN 0-8369-5544-7). Ayer Co Pubs.

Bingham, Julie. One-Two-Three Go. (Illus.). 256p. 1984. pap. 14.38 (ISBN 0-201-13047-5). Addison-Wesley.

Bingham, June. Courage to Change: An Introduction to the Life & Thought of Reinhold Niebuhr. Repr. of 1961 ed. lib. bdg. 27.50x (ISBN 0-678-02766-8). Kelley.

Bingham, Madeleine. The Making of Kew. (Folio Miniature Ser.). 48p. 1975. 4.95 (ISBN 0-7181-1304-7, Pub. by Michael Joseph). Merrimack Pub Cir.

--Masks & Facades: Sir John Vanbrugh, the Man & His Setting. (Illus.). 376p. 1974. 23.50x (ISBN 0-87471-632-2). Rowman.

Bingham, Marie B. & Hoole, W. Stanleycompiled by. A Catalog of the Yucatan Collection on Microfilm in the University of Alabama Libraries. LC 72-4602. 100p. 1972. 11.00 (ISBN 0-8173-9512-1). U of Ala Pr.

Bingham, Marjorie W. & Gross, Susan H. Women in Ancient Greece & Rome. Donaldson, Janet M., ed. LC 83-14016. (Women in World Area Studies). 125p. (Orig.). 1983. 10.95 (ISBN 0-914227-01-7); pap. 6.95 (ISBN 0-914227-00-9). Glenhurst Pubns.

--Women in Latin America: From Pre-Columbian Times to the 20th Century, Vol. I. (Women in World Area Studies). (Illus.). 210p. (Orig.). 1985. pap. 6.95 (ISBN 0-914227-04-1). Glenhurst Pubns.

Bingham, Marjorie W., jt. auth. see Gross, Susan H.

Bingham, Millicent T., ed. see Dickinson, Emily.

Bingham, Mindy & Edmondson, Judy. Choices: A Teen Woman's Journal for Self-Awareness & Personal Planning. Coon, Dennis & Coon, Sevren, eds. LC 82-74535. (Illus.). 240p. (gr. 9-12). 1983. pap. 12.95 (ISBN 0-911655-22-0). Advocacy Pr.

Bingham, Mindy, jt. auth. see Poynter, Dan.

Bingham, Mindy, et al. Challenges: A Young Man's Journal for Self-Awareness & Personal Planning. Greene, Barbara & Peters, Kathleen, eds. LC 84-70108. (Illus.). 240p. (gr. 9-12). 1984. pap. 12.95 (ISBN 0-911655-24-7). Advocacy Pr.

Bingham, Nelson E. Teaching Nutrition in Biology Classes: An Experimental Investigation of High School Biology Pupils in Their Study of the Relation of Food to Physical Well-Being. LC 74-176565. (Columbia University. Teachers College. Contributions to Education: No. 772). Repr. of 1939 ed. 22.50 (ISBN 0-404-55772-4). AMS Pr.

Bingham, Opha & Bingham, Robert E. One Step More, Lord! LC 84-4942. 1984. pap. 7.95 (ISBN 0-8054-5432-2). Broadman.

Bingham, Peregrine. The Law of Infancy & Coverture. 2nd ed. viii, 396p. 1980. Repr. of 1849 ed. lib. bdg. 35.00x (ISBN 0-8377-0311-5). Rothman.

Bingham, Phil. Drive It: The Complete Book of Formula Ford. (Drive it! Ride it ! Ser.). 128p. 9.95 (ISBN 0-85429-434-1, F434). Haynes Pubns.

Bingham, R. C. & Von Schleyer, P. R. Chemistry of Adamantanes: Recent Developments in the Chemistry of Adamantane & Related Polycyclic Hydrocarbons. (Topics in Current Chemistry: Vol. 18). (Illus.). 1971. pap. 32.50 (ISBN 0-387-05387-5). Springer-Verlag.

Bingham, Rebecca. Opals. (Illus.). 48p. 1982. 30.00 (ISBN 0-88014-042-9). Mosaic Pr OH.

Bingham, Richard, et al. Professional Associations & Municipal Innovation. 200p. 1981. 25.00x (ISBN 0-299-08330-6). U of Wis Pr.

Bingham, Richard D. Reapportionment of the Oklahoma House of Representatives: Politics & Process. (Legislative Research Ser: No. 2). 33p. 1972. pap. 1.50 (ISBN 0-686-20792-0). Univ OK Gov Res.

--State & Local Government in an Urban Society. 448p. 1986. text ed. 25.00 (ISBN 0-394-33206-7, RanC). Random.

Bingham, Richard D. & Ethridge, Marcus E. Reaching Decisions in Public Administration: Methods & Applications. LC 81-12427. (Illus.). 416p. 1982. pap. text ed. 21.95x (ISBN 0-582-28248-9). Longman.

Bingham, Richard D., jt. auth. see Gibson, James L.

Bingham, Richard D. & Blair, John P., eds. Urban Economic Development. LC 84-11456. 288p. 1984. 29.95 (ISBN 0-8039-1998-0); pap. 14.95 (ISBN 0-8039-1999-9). Sage.

Bingham, Robert. Fight Back Against Arthritis. LC 84-71312. (Arthritis Patient Information Ser.). (Illus.). 315p. 1984. 14.00x (ISBN 0-317-13112-5). Desert Arthritis.

Bingham, Robert, jt. auth. see Oberman, Joseph.

Bingham, Robert E. Traps to Avoid in Good Administration. LC 78-67265. 1979. pap. 4.25 (ISBN 0-8054-2535-7). Broadman.

Bingham, Robert E., jt. auth. see Bingham, Opha.

Bingham, Robert J. Photogenic Manipulation. LC 72-9182. (The Literature of Photography Ser.). (Illus.). Repr. of 1852 ed. 12.00 (ISBN 0-405-04893-9). Ayer Co Pubs.

Bingham, Sam & Bingham, Janet, eds. Between Sacred Mountains: Navajo Stories & Lessons from the Land. LC 82-82827. (Illus.). 296p. (gr. 4 up). 1982. 30.00 (ISBN 0-910675-00-7); pap. 19.95 (ISBN 0-910675-01-5). U of Ariz Pr.

--Between Sacred Mountains: Navajo Stories & Lessons from the Land. LC 84-121. (Sun Tracks Ser.: No. 11). (Illus.). 287p. 1984. 35.00x (ISBN 0-8165-0855-0); pap. 19.95 (ISBN 0-8165-0856-9). U of Ariz Pr.

Bingham, W. G., ed. Recent Advances in Brain Tumor Research. (Progress in Experimental Tumor Research: Vol. 17). 1972. 59.75 (ISBN 3-8055-1402-6). S Karger.

Bingham, W. Van Dyke see Richardson, Florence.

Bingham-Newman, Ann, jt. auth. see Saunders, Ruth.

Binghurst, Robert, jt. auth. see Reid, Bill.

Bingley, William. Musical Biography, 2 vols. LC 70-127286. (Music Reprint Ser.). 1971. Repr. of 1834 ed. Set. lib. bdg. 85.00 (ISBN 0-306-70032-8). Da Capo.

Bin Gorion, Emanuel, jt. ed. see Bin Gorion, Micha J.

Bin Gorion, Micha J. & Bin Gorion, Emanuel, eds. Mimekor Yisrael: Classical Jewish Folktales, 3 vols. Lask, I. M., tr. from Heb. LC 74-15713. 1666p. 1976. 100.00 (ISBN 0-253-15330-1). Ind U Pr.

Binh, Duong T. Tagmemic Comparison of the Structure of English & Vietnamese Sentences. LC 74-123126. (Janua Linguarum, Ser. Practica: No. 110). (Orig.). 1971. pap. text ed. 35.20x (ISBN 90-2791-598-9). Mouton.

Binh, Vu T., ed. Surface Mobilities on Solid Materials: Fundamental Concepts & Applications. (NATO ASI Series B, Physics: Vol. 86). 598p. 1983. 89.50x (ISBN 0-306-41125-3, Plenum Press). Plenum Pub.

Binham, Philip, jt. ed. see Dauenhauer, Richard.

Binham, Philip, et al. Hotel English. LC 80-42264. (Illus.). 128p. 1981. pap. 4.95 (ISBN 0-08-025340-7). Pergamon.

Binham, Philip, et al, trs. see Friis, Erik J.

Binham, Timothy, tr. see Schildt, Goran.

Binhammer, Robert T., jt. auth. see Crafts, R. C.

Binhorst, Rob A., et al, eds. Children & Exercise XI, Vol. 15. (International Sport Sciences Ser.). 1985. text ed. 27.50x (ISBN 0-87322-019-6, BBIN0019). Human Kinetics.

Bini, Daniela. A Fragrance from the Desert: Poetry & Philosophy in Giacomo Leopardi. (Stanford French & Italian Studies: Vol. 27). 200p. 1983. pap. 25.00 (ISBN 0-915838-10-9). Anma Libri.

Bining, Arthur C. British Regulation of the Colonial Iron Industry. LC 68-55481. Repr. of 1933 ed. 22.50x (ISBN 0-678-00924-4). Kelley.

--Pennsylvania Iron Manufacture in the Eighteenth Century. LC 72-120547. Repr. of 1938 ed. lib. bdg. 22.50x (ISBN 0-678-00678-4). Kelley.

--Pennsylvania Iron Manufacture in the Eighteenth Century. rev. ed. LC 73-623131. (Illus.). 215p. 1973. 9.75 (ISBN 0-911124-72-1); pap. 5.75 (ISBN 0-911124-71-3). Pa Hist & Mus.

Binion, Alice. Antonio & Francesco Guardi: Their Life & Milieu: With a Catalogue of Their Figure Drawings. LC 75-23782. (Outstanding Dissertations in the Fine Arts - 17th & 18th Century). (Illus.). 1976. lib. bdg. 58.00 (ISBN 0-8240-1979-2). Garland Pub.

Binion, R. Hitler among the Germans. 1976. 27.50 (ISBN 0-444-99033-X, BHA/, Pub. by Elsevier). Greenwood.

Binion, Rudolph. Defeated Leaders: The Political Fate of Caillaux, Jouvenel & Tardieu. LC 75-33933. 425p. 1976. Repr. of 1960 ed. lib. bdg. 22.25x (ISBN 0-8371-8539-4, BIDL). Greenwood.

--Hitler among the Germans. LC 84-1198. 207p. 1984. pap. 7.50 (ISBN 0-87580-531-0). N Ill U Pr.

--Soundings: Psychohistorical & Psycholiterary. 164p. 1981. 19.95 (ISBN 0-914434-16-0); pap. 9.95 (ISBN 0-914434-17-9). Psychohistory Pr.

Binkert, Peter J. Generative Grammar Without Transformations. LC 83-27034. viii, 240p. 1984. 37.60x (ISBN 3-11-009720-6). Mouton.

Binkin, Irving & Owings, Mark. Lovecraftiana: A Catalog of the Largest Collection by & on H. P. Lovecraft Currently in Private Hands. (Illus.). 140p. (Orig.). 1974. 7.00 (ISBN 0-88358-122-1); pap. 4.00 (ISBN 0-88358-020-9). Mirage Pr.

Binkin, Martin. America's Volunteer Military. (Studies in Defence Policy). 65p. 1984. pap. 6.95 (ISBN 0-8157-0975-7). Brookings.

--The Military Pay Muddle. (Studies in Defense Policy). 60p. 1975. pap. 6.95 (ISBN 0-8157-0961-7). Brookings.

--Shaping the Defense Civilian Work Force: Economics, Politics, & National Security. LC 78-14897. (Studies in Defense Policy). 1978. pap. 6.95 (ISBN 0-8157-0967-6). Brookings.

--Support Costs in the Defense Budget: The Submerged One-Third. (Studies in Defense Policy). 49p. 1972. pap. 6.95 (ISBN 0-8157-0957-9). Brookings.

--U. S. Reserve Forces: The Problem of the Weekend Warrior. (Studies in Defense Policy). 63p. 1974. pap. 6.95 (ISBN 0-8157-0959-5). Brookings.

Binkin, Martin & Bach, Shirley J. Women & the Military. (Studies in Defense Policy). 1977. 16.95 (ISBN 0-8157-0966-8); pap. 6.95 (ISBN 0-8157-0965-X). Brookings.

Binkin, Martin & Eitelberg, Mark. Blacks & the Military. LC 82-70886. (Studies in Defense Policy). 200p. 1982. 22.95 (ISBN 0-8157-0974-9); pap. 8.95 (ISBN 0-8157-0973-0). Brookings.

Binkin, Martin & Kyriakopoulos, Irene. Paying the Modern Military. LC 80-70080. (Studies in Defense Policy). 100p. 1981. pap. 6.95 (ISBN 0-8157-0971-4). Brookings.

--Youth or Experience? Manning the Modern Military. (Studies in Defense Policy). 1979. pap. 6.95 (ISBN 0-8157-0969-2). Brookings.

Binkin, Martin & Record, Jeffrey. Where Does the Marine Corps Go from Here? LC 75-45068. (Studies in Defense Policy). pap. 26.30 (ISBN 0-317-30403-8, 2024962). Bks Demand UMI.

Binkley, Barbara, jt. auth. see Piaget, Gerald.

Binkley, Harold R. & Byers, Charles W. SOE Programs in Agriculture. (Illus.). 563p. 1984. 17.50x (ISBN 0-8134-2406-2, 2406). Interstate.

Binkley, Harold R. & Tulloch, Rodney W. Teaching Vocational Agriculture-Agribusiness. (Illus.). 250p. 1981. pap. 9.95x (ISBN 0-8134-2153-5). Interstate.

Binkley, Harold R., jt. auth. see Byers, Charles W.

Binkley, Thomas, tr. see Winckel, Fritz.

Binkley, Wilfred E. The Man in the White House: His Powers & Duties. LC 78-16368. 1978. Repr. of 1972 ed. lib. bdg. 22.25x (ISBN 0-313-20536-1, BIMW). Greenwood.

--The Man in the White House: His Powers & Duties. (Johns Hopkins Paperbacks Edition Ser.). pap. 80.00 (ISBN 0-317-09019-4, 2020759). Bks Demand UMI.

Binkley, William C. The Expansionist Movement in Texas, 1836-1850. LC 71-77718. (American Scene Ser). 1970. Repr. of 1925 ed. lib. bdg. 35.00 (ISBN 0-306-71356-X). Da Capo.

--The Texas Revolution. LC 79-63065. 1979. 12.95 (ISBN 0-87611-041-3); pap. 6.50 (ISBN 0-87611-042-1). Tex St Hist Assn.

Binko, C. A., et al. The Ortho Problem Solver. Smith, Michael D., ed. LC 82-82093. (Illus.). 1024p. 1982. 149.95 (ISBN 0-89721-008-5). Ortho.

Binks, Gerald S. Best in Show: Breeding & Exhibiting Budgerigars. (Illus.). 176p. 1985. 12.95 (ISBN 0-668-06282-7). Arco.

Binks, Martin & Coyne, John. The Birth of Enterprise. (Institute of Economic Affairs, Hobart Papers Ser.: No. 98). pap. 7.50 technical (ISBN 0-255-36161-0). Transatlantic.

Binks, Robert, et al. Tables for Use in High Resolution Mass Spectometry. Incl. Chemical Formulae from Mass Determinations. Henneberg, D. & Casper, K.. LC 75-130645. pap. 52.00 (ISBN 0-317-29340-0, 2024031). Bks Demand UMI.

Binmore, K. G. Calculus. LC 82-19728. (London School of Economics Mathematics Ser.). 450p. 1983. 52.50 (ISBN 0-521-24771-3); pap. 19.95 (ISBN 0-521-28952-1). Cambridge U Pr.

--Foundations of Analysis: A Straightforward Introduction: Bk. 1 Logic, Sets & Numbers. LC 79-41790. (Illus.). 200p. 1981. 27.95 (ISBN 0-521-23322-4); pap. 15.95 (ISBN 0-521-29915-2). Cambridge U Pr.

--Foundations of Analysis: A Straightforward Introduction: Bk. 2 Topological Ideas. LC 79-41790. (Illus.). 350p. 1981. 49.50 (ISBN 0-521-23350-X); pap. 19.95 (ISBN 0-521-29930-6). Cambridge U Pr.

--Mathematical Analysis: A Straightforward Approach. 2nd ed. LC 81-21728. 330p. 1983. 34.50 (ISBN 0-521-24680-6); pap. 12.95 (ISBN 0-521-28882-7). Cambridge U Pr.

Binnedyk, H. Frank, jt. auth. see Turino, Jon.

Binnendijk, Leendert. Properties of Double Stars: A Survey of Parallaxes & Orbits. LC 58-8011. pap. 66.40 (ISBN 0-317-08370-8, 2055279). Bks Demand UMI.

Binner, Vinal O. American Folktales One: A Structured Reader. 1966. pap. text ed. 8.95 scp (ISBN 0-690-06704-6, HarpC). Har-Row.

--International Folktales Two: A Structured Reader. (Crowell Contemporary English Ser). 1970. pap. text ed. 8.95 scp (ISBN 0-690-44338-2, HarpC). Har-Row.

Binner, Vinal O., ed. American Folktales Two: A Structured Reader. (Orig.). 1968. pap. text ed. 8.95 scp (ISBN 0-690-06705-4, HarpC). Har-Row.

Binney, Charles C. Life of Horace Binney. LC 72-2577. (Select Bibliographies Reprint Ser). 1972. Repr. of 1903 ed. 26.50 (ISBN 0-8369-6849-2). Ayer Co Pubs.

Binney, Edwin, 3rd. Turkish Treasures from the Collection of Edwin Binney, 3rd. (Illus.). 250p. (Orig.). 1979. pap. 15.00 (ISBN 0-295-96136-8, Pub. by Portland Art Museum). U of Wash Pr.

Binney, Edwin, 3rd & Binney-Winslow, Gail. Homage to Amanda: Two Hundred Years of American Quilts. LC 84-61419. (Illus.). 96p. (Orig.). 1984. pap. 16.95 (ISBN 0-9613708-0-7). R K Press.

Binney, Horace. An Enquiry into the Formation of Washington's Farewell Address. LC 74-98692. (Law, Politics, & History Ser.). 1969. Repr. of 1859 ed. lib. bdg. 37.50 (ISBN 0-306-71840-5). Da Capo.

Binney, James J., jt. auth. see Mihalas, Dimitri M.

Binney, M., ed. see Gilbert & Sullivan.

Binney, Marcus. Sir Robert Taylor: From Rococo to Neo-Classicism. (Genius of Architecture Ser.: No. 4). (Illus.). 152p. 1984. text ed. 19.95x (ISBN 0-04-720028-6); pap. 9.95 (ISBN 0-04-720031-6). Allen Unwin.

Binney, Marcus, jt. ed. see Lowenthal, David.

Binney, William R. The Architectural Characteristics & Types of Spanish Gardens. (The Masterpieces of World Architecture Library). (Illus.). 129p. 1983. 87.45 (ISBN 0-86650-045-6). Gloucester Art.

Binney-Winslow, Gail, jt. auth. see Binney, Edwin, 3rd.

Binnick, Robert I. Modern Mongolian: A Transformational Syntax. 1979. 20.00x (ISBN 0-8020-5422-6). U of Toronto Pr.

Binnie & Parners & EEC Commission. Islands for Offshore Nuclear Power Stations. 160p. 1981. 85.00x (ISBN 0-686-80926-2, Pub. by Graham & Trotman England). State Mutual Bk.

Binnie & Partners. Islands for Offshore Nuclear Power Stations. 167p. 1983. pap. 40.00x (ISBN 0-8448-1423-7). Crane-Russak Co.

Binnie, C. D., et al. A Manual of Electroencephalographic Technology. LC 80-42003. (Techniques in Measurement in Medicine Ser.: No. 6). (Illus.). 300p. 1982. 67.50 (ISBN 0-521-23847-1); pap. 24.95 (ISBN 0-521-28257-8). Cambridge U Pr.

Binnie, Eric. The Theatrical Designs of Charles Ricketts. Beckerman, Bernard, ed. LC 84-23921. (Theater & Dramatics Studies: No. 23). 200p. 1985. 39.95 (ISBN 0-8357-1584-1). UMI Res Pr.

Binnie, F. G., tr. see Metchnikoff, Elie.

Binnie-Clark, Georgina. Wheat & Woman. (Social History of Canada Ser.). 1979. 25.00x (ISBN 0-8020-2354-1); pap. 10.95 (ISBN 0-8020-6386-1). U of Toronto Pr.

Binns, Archie. Lightship. 8.95 (ISBN 0-8323-0109-4). Binford.

--Mighty Mountain. 1951. 8.95 (ISBN 0-8323-0110-8). Binford.

--Mighty Mountain. 440p. 1975. pap. 5.95 (ISBN 0-8323-0259-7). Binford.

--Northwest Gateway: The Story of the Port of Seattle. (Illus.). 1949. 8.95 (ISBN 0-8323-0004-7). Binford.

--Peter Skene Ogden, Fur Trader. LC 67-23627. (Illus.). 1967. 8.95 (ISBN 0-8323-0054-3). Binford.

Binns, Bronwyn & Jones, Ian. Against the Wind: Screenplay. (Australian Theatre Workshop Ser.). 1978. pap. text ed. 8.00x (ISBN 0-686-65307-6, 00538). Heinemann Ed.

Binns, C., jt. auth. see Vincent, A. L.

Binns, David. Beyond the Sociology of Conflict. LC 77-82860. 1978. 26.00 (ISBN 0-312-07784-X). St Martin.

Binns, H. B. Walt Whitman & His Poetry. LC 72-193665. 1915. lib. bdg. 15.00 (ISBN 0-8414-1644-3). Folcroft.

Binns, Harold. Outlines of the World's Literature. 1973. Repr. of 1914 ed. 35.00 (ISBN 0-8274-1473-0). R West.

Binns, Henry B. Life of Walt Whitman. LC 78-92937. (Studies in Whitman, No. 28). 1969. Repr. of 1905 ed. lib. bdg. 49.95x (ISBN 0-8383-1001-X). Haskell.

--Walt Whitman & His Poetry. LC 75-120971. (Poetry & Life Ser.). Repr. of 1915 ed. 7.25 (ISBN 0-404-52502-4). AMS Pr.

Binns, N. E. An Introduction to Historical Bibliography. 1969. 30.00x (ISBN 0-900092-18-1, Pub. by Hill & Son England). State Mutual Bk.

Binns, R. A. & McBryde, I. A Petrological Analysis of Ground-Edge Artifacts from Northern New South Wales. (AIAS Prehistory & Material Culture Ser.: No. 10). (Illus., Orig.). 1972. pap. text ed. 11.50x (ISBN 0-85575-025-1). Humanities.

Binns, Richard. French Leave. (Illus.). 224p. 1982. 6.95 (ISBN 0-89919-101-0). Ticknor & Fields.

--French Leave. 3rd ed. (Illus.). 336p. 1983. 9.95 (ISBN 0-89919-196-7). Ticknor & Fields.

--Richard Binns' Best of Britain. LC 84-45570. (Illus.). 144p. 1985. pap. 8.95 (ISBN 0-689-11522-9). Atheneum.

Binns, Ronald. The Loch Ness Mystery Solved. LC 84-43103. (Science & the Paranormal Ser.). (Illus.). 228p. 1985. 18.95 (ISBN 0-87975-278-5); pap. 9.95 (ISBN 0-87975-291-2). Prometheus Bks.

--Malcolm Lowry. 96p. 1984. pap. 4.75 (ISBN 0-416-37750-5, NO. 9102). Methuen Inc.

Bin-Nun, Aaron. The Language of Faith. LC 78-65723. 1979. 8.95 (ISBN 0-88400-061-3). Shengold.

Bin-Nun, Judy & Cooper, Nancy. Pesach: A Holiday Funtext. (Illus.). 32p. (Orig.). (gr. 1-3). 1983. pap. text ed. 5.00 (ISBN 0-8074-0161-7, 101310). UAHC.

Bin-Nun, Judy & Einhorn, Franne. Rosh Hashana: A Holiday Funtext. (Illus.). 1978. pap. 5.00 (ISBN 0-8074-0010-6, 101300). UAHC.

Binny, J., jt. auth. see Mayhew, Henry.

Binny, John, jt. auth. see Mayhew, Henry.

Binsbergen, Wim M., jt. ed. see Geschiere, Peter.

Binsbergen, Wim M. J. Van see Van Binsbergen, Wim M. J. & Schoffeleers, J. Matthew.

Binsbergen, Wim M. Van see Van Binsbergen, Wim M.

Binsfield, Alfred. A Simple, Thorough & Reliable Course in Pottery Making. (Illus.). 147p. 1984. 67.85 (ISBN 0-86650-115-0). Gloucester Art.

Binsse, Harry L., tr. see Maritain, Jacques.

Binstead, Harry E. The Fully Illustrated Book of Decorative Details from Major Architectural Styles. (Illus.). 157p. Repr. of 1894 ed. 89.45 (ISBN 0-89901-057-1). Found Class Reprints.

Binstead, Herbert E. The Book of Decorative Details for Artists, Architects, Builders, Cabinet & Furniture Makers. (Illus.). 119p. 1983. 87.45x (ISBN 0-86650-074-X). Gloucester Art.

--The Book of Decorative Details for Artists, Upholsterers, Architects, Builders, Cabinet & Furniture Makers. (Illus.). 1979. deluxe ed. 97.50x (ISBN 0-930582-40-3). Gloucester Art.

Binsted, Don. Design for Learning in Management Training & Development: A View. 1981. 79.00x (ISBN 0-86176-099-9, Pub. by MCB Pubns). State Mutual Bk.

Binstock, Richard H., et al, eds. International Perspectives on Aging: Population & Policy Challenges. (Policy Development Studies: No. 7). xvi, 216p. write for info (UNFPA). Unipub.

Binstock, Robert, jt. auth. see Woll, Peter.

Binstock, Robert H. & Shanas, Ethel. Handbook of Aging & the Social Sciences. 2nd ed. (Illus.). 816p. 1985. 65.00 (ISBN 0-442-26480-1). Van Nos Reinhold.

Binstock, Robert H., jt. auth. see Morris, Robert.

Binstock, Robert H., jt. auth. see Woll, Peter.

Binswanger, Barbara & Charlton, James. The Perfect Wedding Planner. 112p. (Orig.). 1986. pap. 3.95 (ISBN 0-440-56889-7, Dell Trade Pbks). Dell.

Binswanger, Hans P. & Rosenzweig, Mark. Contractual Arrangements, Employment, & Wages in Rural Labor Markets in Asia. LC 83-5944. (An Economic Growth Center Publication Ser.). 352p. 1984. text ed. 39.00 (ISBN 0-300-03214-5). Yale U Pr.

Binswanger, Hans P., et al. Induced Innovation: Technology, Institutions & Development. LC 77-23387. (Illus.). 1978. text ed. 38.50x (ISBN 0-8018-2027-8). Johns Hopkins.

Binswanger, Hans P., et al, eds. Rural Household Studies in Asia. 1981. pap. 14.00x (ISBN 9971-69-002-0, 82-93615, Pub. by Singapore U Pr). Ohio U Pr.

Binswanger, Ludwig. Being in the World: Selected Papers of Ludwig Binswanger. Needleman, Jacob, tr. from Ger. 1978. 15.00x (ISBN 0-285-64783-0, Pub. by Souvenir Pr). Intl Spec Bk.

--Uber Ideenflucht. LC 78-66767. (Phenomenology Ser.). 200p. 1980. lib. bdg. 26.00 (ISBN 0-317-28848-2). Garland Pub.

Binswanger, Rotraut, ed. see Congress on Occupational Therapy, 5th International, Zurich, 1970.

Bin Uthman, Ali see Uthman, Ali Bin.

Binyon, C. M., tr. see Blochet, Edgar.

Binyon, Helen. Eric Ravilious: Memoir of an Artist. (Illus.). 144p. 30.00 (ISBN 0-913720-42-9). Beil.

Binyon, Laurence. Asiatic Arts: Sculpture & Paintings. (Illus.). 74p. 1981. Repr. of 1925 ed. text ed. 70.50x (ISBN 0-391-02389-6, Pub. by UBS India). Humanities.

--Followers of William Blake. LC 68-56526. (Illus.). Repr. of 1925 ed. 27.50 (ISBN 0-405-08270-3, Blom Pubns). Ayer Co Pubs.

--The Mind & the Artist. Repr. of 1909 ed. 17.50 (ISBN 0-8482-7401-6). Norwood Edns.

--Tradition & Reaction in Modern Poetry. LC 74-5434. 1926. lib. bdg. 8.50 (ISBN 0-8414-3159-0). Folcroft.

Binyon, Laurence, ed. Golden Treasury of Modern Lyrics. (Poetry Library). 382p. 1985. Repr. of 1924 ed. 37.75x (ISBN 0-89609-246-1). Granger Bk.

--The Letters of Maurice Hewlett to Which Is Added a Diary in Greece, 1914. 294p. lib. bdg. 30.00 (ISBN 0-89984-061-2). Century Bookbindery.

Binyon, Lawrence. Engraved Designs of William Blake. LC 67-25542. (Graphic Art Ser.). 1967. Repr. of 1926 ed. lib. bdg. 65.00 (ISBN 0-306-70956-2). Da Capo.

Binyon, Michael. Life in Russia. LC 83-19377. 1984. 15.45 (ISBN 0-394-53339-9). Pantheon.

--Life in Russia. 304p. 1985. pap. 3.95 (ISBN 0-425-08188-5). Berkley Pub.

Binyon, Pamela M. The Concepts of Spirit & Demon: A Study in the Use of Different Languages Describing the Same Phenomena. (IC-Studies in the International History of Christianity: Vol. 8). 132p. 1977. pap. 19.60 (ISBN 3-261-01787-2). P Lang Pubs.

Binyon, T. J. Swan Song. LC 84-4250. 203p. 1984. 13.95 (ISBN 0-385-27970-1, Dial). Doubleday.

--Swan Song. 1986. Repr. pap. 3.50 (ISBN 0-8125-8095-8). Tor Bks.

Binyons, Lawrence, illus. Examples of Indian Sculpture at the British Museum. (Illus.). 12p. 1978. Repr. of 1923 ed. 12.50 (ISBN 0-89684-151-0). Orient Bk Dist.

Binz, Carl. Doctor Johann Weyer: Ein Rheinischer Arzt der Erste Bekampfer Des Hexenwahns Beitrag Zur Geschicte der Aufklarung und der Heilkunde. rev. 2nd. ed. LC 75-16683. (Classics in Psychiatry Ser.). (Ger.). 1976. Repr. of 1896 ed. 15.00x (ISBN 0-405-07415-8). Ayer Co Pubs.

Binz, E., ed. see Conference Held at Manheim, 21-25 July, 1975.

Binzagr, Safeya. Saudi Arabia: An Artist's View of the Past. (Illus.). 1979. 60.00 (ISBN 2-88001-076-4). Three Continents.

Bioavailability of Drug Products Project. The Bioavailability of Drug Products. LC 77-94131. 1978. 18.00 (ISBN 0-917330-18-8). Am Pharm Assn.

Biochemical Engineering Conference, 2nd, Henniker, New Hampshire, July 13-18, 1980. Biochemical Engineering II. Constantinides, A., et al, eds. (Annals of the New York Academy of Sciences Ser.: Vol. 369). 384p. 1981. 75.00x (ISBN 0-89766-127-3); pap. 75.00x (ISBN 0-89766-128-1). NY Acad Sci.

Biochemical Societies of France, Great Britain, Italy, & the Netherlands. Joint Meeting, Venice, 1976. Phosphorylated Proteins & Related Enzymes: Proceedings. 128p. 1977. 10.00 (ISBN 0-904147-45-2). IRL Pr.

Biogas & Other Rural Energy Resources Workshop. Workshop on Biogas & Other Rural Energy Resources: Proceedings, Roving Seminar on Rural Energy Development, Held at Bangkok, Manila, Tehran & Jakarta. (Energy Resources Development Ser.: No. 19). 152p. 1979. pap. text ed. 10.00 (ISBN 0-686-71072-X, UN79/2F10, UN). Unipub.

Biokinesiology Institute. Muscle Testing Your Way to Health Using Emotions, Nutrition & Massage. (Illus.). 116p. (Orig.). 1982. pap. 5.95 (ISBN 0-937216-07-0). Biokinesiology Institute.

Biokinesiology Institute & Barton, John. Allergies: How to Find & Conquer. (Encyclopedia of Mind & Body: Vol. 1). (Illus.). 280p. 1980. pap. 15.00 (ISBN 0-937216-01-1). Biokinesiology.

--The Atlas. (Encyclopedia of Mind & Body: Vol. 4). (Illus.). 1780p. (Orig.). 1981. pap. 125.00 (ISBN 0-937216-08-9). Biokinesiology.

--Be Your Own Chiropractor: Through Biokinetic Exercises. rev. 2nd ed. (Illus.). 210p. 1979. pap. 11.95 (ISBN 0-937216-03-8). Biokinesiology.

--How to Take Care of Yourselves Naturally. 4th ed. LC 77-80393. Orig. Title: Flow Lines to Health. (Illus.). 158p. 1980. pap. 9.95 (ISBN 0-937216-04-6). Biokinesiology.

--Quick Ready Reference. (Illus.). 250p. (Orig.). 1981. pap. text ed. 25.00 (ISBN 0-937216-06-2). Biokinesiology.

--Which Vitamin - Which Herb Do You Need? 2nd ed. (Illus.). 64p. 1981. pap. 2.00 (ISBN 0-937216-16-X). Biokinesiology.

Bioler, I. & Sternlicht, M. The Psychology of Mental Retardation. LC 77-4137. 800p. 1977. 39.95x (ISBN 0-88437-013-5). Psych Dimensions.

Biological Laboratory, Imperial Household & Sakai, Tune, eds. The Crabs of Sagami Bay: Collected by His Majesty the Emperor of Japan. (Illus.). 1965. 40.00x (ISBN 0-8248-0033-8, Eastwest Ctr). UH Pr.

Biological Science Curriculum Study. Biological Science: Interaction of Experiments & Ideas (BSCS Second Course) 3rd ed. (gr. 10-12). 1977. text ed. 26.64 (ISBN 0-13-076562-7); tchrs. ed. 3.75 (ISBN 0-13-076919-3). P-H.

Biological Sciences Curriculum Study. Biology Teacher's Handbook. 3rd ed. LC 77-27548. 585p. 1978. text ed. 40.95x (ISBN 0-471-01945-3). Wiley.

--Energy & Society: Investigations in Decision Making. (Illus.). (gr. 9-12). 1977. pap. text ed. 3.95 (ISBN 0-8331-1502-2); tchr's manual 7.95 (ISBN 0-8331-1503-0). Hubbard Sci.

--Research Problems in Biology. 2nd ed. (Investigations for Students Ser.: No. 1-2-3). 1976. pap. text ed. 8.95x; Ser. 1. pap. text ed. (ISBN 0-19-502063-4); Ser. 2. pap. text ed. (ISBN 0-19-502064-2); Ser. 3. pap. text ed. (ISBN 0-19-502065-0). Oxford U Pr.

Biology & Agriculture Division. Biochronometry. LC 79-610527. (Illus.). 662p. 1971. text ed. 18.25 (ISBN 0-309-01866-8). Natl Acad Pr.

Biology Colloquium, 22nd, Oregon State University, 1961. Physiology of Reproduction: Proceedings. Hisaw, Frederick L., Jr., ed. LC 52-19235. (Illus.). 1963. 9.95x (ISBN 0-87071-161-X). Oreg St U Pr.

Biology Colloquium, 29th, Oregon State University 1968. Biochemical Coevolution: Proceedings. Chambers, Kenton L., ed. LC 52-19235. (Illus.). 128p. 1970. 9.95x (ISBN 0-87071-168-7). Oreg St U Pr.

Biology Colloquium, 30th, Oregon State University, 1969. Biological Ultrastructure: The Origin of Cell Organelles: Proceedings. Harris, Patricia J., ed. LC 52-19235. (Illus.). 1971. 9.95x (ISBN 0-87071-169-5). Oreg St U Pr.

Biology Colloquium, 32nd, Oregon State University, 1971. The Biology of Behavior: Proceedings. Kiger, John A., Jr., ed. LC 52-19235. (Illus.). 1972. 9.95x (ISBN 0-87071-171-7). Oreg St U Pr.

Biology Colloquium, 33rd, Oregon State University, 1972. The Biology of the Ocean Pacific. Miller, Charles, ed. LC 52-19235. (Illus.). 1974. 9.95 (ISBN 0-87071-172-5). Oreg St U Pr.

Biology Colloquium, 34th, Oregon State University, 1973. The Biology of Tumor Viruses: Proceedings. Beaudreau, George S., ed. LC 52-19235. (Illus.). 144p. 1976. pap. text ed. 9.95x (ISBN 0-87071-173-3). Oreg St U Pr.

Biology Colloquium, 35th,Oregon State University,1974. Chromosomes - from Simple to Complex: Proceedings. Roberts, Paul, ed. LC 76-5880. (Illus.). 96p. 1977. pap. text ed. 9.95x (ISBN 0-87071-174-1). Oreg St U Pr.

Biology Colloquium, 37th, Oregon State University, 1976. Historical Biogeography, Plate Tectonics, & the Changing Environment: Proceedings. Gray, Jane & Boucot, Arthur J., eds. LC 78-31376. (Illus.). 512p. 1979. 69.50x (ISBN 0-87071-176-8). Oreg St U Pr.

Biology Colloquium, 40th, Oregon State University, 1979. Forests: Fresh Perspectives from Ecosystem Analysis: Proceedings. Waring, Richard H., ed. LC 80-14883. (Illus.). 210p. 1979. pap. 15.95x (ISBN 0-87071-179-2). Oreg St U Pr.

Biomechanical & Human Factors Conference (2nd: 1967: Washington, D.C.) Biomechanical & Human Factors Symposium: 1967. Gage, Howard, ed. LC 67-21480. (Illus.). pap. 46.00 (ISBN 0-317-08409-7, 2016814). Bks Demand UMI.

Biomedical Information Corporation. Physicians' Manual for Patients: The Standard Physicians' Source Book of Symptoms, Diagnosis & Treatment. (Illus.). 1984. 19.95 (ISBN 0-8129-1102-4). Times Bks.

Bion, M. Construction & Principle Use of Mathematical Instruments, 1758. Stone, Edmund, tr. from Lat. (Illus.). 55.00 (ISBN 0-87556-159-4). Saifer.

Bion, Wilfred. Second Thoughts. LC 77-11749. 173p. 1984. 20.00x (ISBN 0-87668-330-8). Aronson.

Bion, Wilfred R. Attention & Interpretation. LC 84-45115. 136p. 1983. 20.00 (ISBN 0-87668-675-7). Aronson.

--Elements of Psycho-Analysis. 120p. 1983. 15.00 (ISBN 0-87668-716-8). Aronson.

--Learning from Experience. 128p. 1983. 17.50 (ISBN 0-87668-687-0). Aronson.

--Transformations. 192p. 1983. 17.50 (ISBN 0-87668-723-0). Aronson.

Biondi, Albano, et al, eds. Eresia e Riforma Nell'italia del Cinquecento: Miscellanea I. LC 74-30505. (Corpus Reformatorum Italicorum & Biblioteca Series). 357p. (Ital.). 1974. pap. 30.00 (ISBN 0-87580-520-5). N Ill U Pr.

Biondi, Angelo M., ed. The Creative Process. 72p. 1972. pap. 2.95 (ISBN 0-914634-07-0). DOK Pubs.

Biondi, Lawrence. The Italian American Child: His Sociolinguistic Acculturation. LC 75-38898. 160p. 1975. pap. 7.50 (ISBN 0-87840-208-X). Georgetown U Pr.
Biondo, Norma, jt. auth. see Woodward, Dan.
Biondo, Vincent J. & Hembree, Cecil W., eds. English Is a Happy Thing: A Book of Readings. 269p. 1972. pap. text ed. 8.50x (ISBN 0-8422-0192-0). Irvington.
Biophy, Mary A. see Bottiglia, William F.
Biorci, Giuseppe, ed. Network & Switching Theory. (Electrical Science Ser). 1968. 85.00 (ISBN 0-12-099550-6). Acad Pr.
Biorklund, Elis. International Atomic Policy During a Decade: An Historical-Political Investigation into the Problems of Atomic Weapons During the Period 1945-55. Reed, Albert, tr. LC 78-13715. 1979. Repr. of 1956 ed. lib. bdg. 24.75x (ISBN 0-313-20633-3, BIIA). Greenwood.
Biostim Inc. Clinical & Engineering Research Group & Dunham, Geoffrey. The Advantages of Biostimulation. (Pain Management-Informative Ser.: No. 2). (Illus.). 40p. (Orig.). 1983. pap. 9.95 (ISBN 0-912863-02-1). Biostim.
--The Application of Biostimulation. (Pain Management-Informative Ser.: No. 3). (Illus.). 60p. (Orig.). 1983. pap. 19.95 (ISBN 0-912863-03-X). Biostim.
--Pain Management. Abridged ed. (Informative Ser.). (Illus.). 64p. 1983. pap. write for info (ISBN 0-912863-04-8). Biostim.
--Pain Management-Informative Series. (Informative Ser.: No. 1, 2 & 3). 1983. 60.00 (ISBN 0-912863-00-5). Biostim.
Biostim Inc. Clinical & Engineering Research Group. The Theory of Pain & the Role of Biostimulation. (Pain Management-Informative Ser.: No. 1). (Illus.). 44p. (Orig.). 1983. pap. 19.95 (ISBN 0-912863-01-3). Biostim.
Biotechnology in Energy Product Symposium, 5th & Scott, Charles. Biotechnology & Bioengineering: Proceedings, Vol. 13. 672p. 1983. pap. 89.95x (ISBN 0-471-88173-2, Pub. by Wiley-Interscience). Wiley.
Biotelemetry International Symposium, 2nd, Davos, May, 1974. Proceedings. Neukomm, P. A., et al, eds. 1975. 27.25 (ISBN 3-8055-2103-0). S Karger.
Bioy Casares, Adolfo. Asleep in the Sun. Levine, Suzanne J., tr. from Sp. LC 77-91846. 1978. 8.95 (ISBN 0-89255-030-9). Persea Bks.
--Breve Diccionario del Argentino Exquisito. 162p. (Span.). 1978. 10.50 (ISBN 0-686-56668-8, S-33774). French & Eur.
Bioy-Casares, Adolfo. The Invention of Morel & Other Stories. Simms, Ruth L., tr. from Span. (Texas Pan American Ser.). (Illus.). 246p. 1985. pap. 9.95 (ISBN 0-292-73840-4). U of Tex Pr.
Bioy-Cesares, Adolfo, jt. auth. see Borges, Jorge L.
Bippen, Linda, jt. auth. see Pullis, Joe M.
Bir, G. L. & Pikus, G. E. Symmetry & Strain-Induces Effects in Semiconductors. 484p. 1974. 94.95 (ISBN 0-470-07321-7). Halsted Pr.
Bir, S. S. Aspects of Plant Sciences, Vol. III. 170p. 1980. 15.00 (ISBN 0-88065-172-5, Pub. by Messers Today & Tomorrows Printers & Publishers India). Scholarly Pubns.
--Pteridophytes: Some Aspects of Their Structure & Morphology. (Aspects of Plant Sciences Ser.: Vol. III). 170p. 1980. 15.00 (ISBN 0-88065-064-8, Pub. by Messers Today & Tomorrows Printers & Publishers India). Scholarly Pubns.
Bir, S. S., ed. Aspects of Plant Sciences, Vol. VI. (Illus.). 261p. 1983. 19.00x (ISBN 0-88065-235-7, Pub. by Messers Today & Tomorrow Printers & Publishers). Scholarly Pubns.
Biracree, Tom. How You Rate: Men. (Orig.). 1984. pap. 3.95 (ISBN 0-440-53809-2, Dell Trade Pbks). Dell.
--How You Rate: Women. (Orig.). 1984. pap. 3.95 (ISBN 0-440-53807-6, Dell Trade Pbks). Dell.
--The Red Berets. 352p. 1983. pap. 2.75 (ISBN 0-523-41704-7). Pinnacle Bks.
--The Torch. 240p. 1983. pap. 2.95 (ISBN 0-515-05622-7). Jove Pubns.
Biracree, Tom & Insinger, Wendy. Complete Book of Thoroughbred Horse Racing. LC 80-1650. (Illus.). 380p. 1982. pap. 14.95 (ISBN 0-385-15676-6, Dolp). Doubleday.
Biram, John, tr. see Wegener, Alfred.
Biram, John G., ed. see Levy, Jean-Phillippe.
Biran, Pierre Maine De see Maine De Biran, Pierre.
Birau, N. & Schlott, W., eds. Melatonin - Current Status & Perspectives: Proceedings of an International Symposium on Melatonin, Held in Bremen, F. R. Germany, September 18-30, 1980. (Advances in the Biosciences Ser.: Vol. 29). (Illus.). 420p. 1981. 72.00 (ISBN 0-08-026400-X). Pergamon.
Birbaumer, N. & Kimmel, H. D., eds. Biofeedback & Self-Regulation. 496p. 1976. 49.95x (ISBN 0-89859-428-6). L Erlbaum Assocs.
Birbeck, M. S., jt. auth. see Mercer, E. M.
Birch, jt. auth. see Mauch.
Birch, A. & Tolmie, J. Anesthesia for the Uninterested. (Illus.). 200p. 1976. pap. text ed. 16.00 (ISBN 0-8391-0860-5). Univ Park.
Birch, Alan. Economic History of the British Iron & Steel Industry: 1784-1879. (Illus.). 398p. 1967. 30.00x (ISBN 0-7146-1272-3, F Cass Co). Biblio Dist.
Birch, Alan & Cole, Martin. Captive Christmas: The Battle of Hong Kong December 1941. 179p. (Orig.). 1979. pap. text ed. 8.95 (ISBN 0-686-98158-8). Heinemann Ed.
Birch, Alan, ed. see Endacott, George B.
Birch, Alexander. Anesthesia for the Uninterested. 2nd ed. 1985. pap. text ed. 18.00 (ISBN 0-8391-2062-1, 21741). Univ Park.
Birch, Anthony H. The British System of Government. 6th ed. 298p. 1982. pap. text ed. 7.95x (ISBN 0-04-320154-7). Allen Unwin.
--Political Integration & Disintegration in the British Isles. 1977. text ed. 19.95x (ISBN 0-04-320123-7); pap. text ed. 8.95x (ISBN 0-04-320124-5). Allen Unwin.
Birch, Austin. The Boy's Brigade. 9.50 (ISBN 0-392-07678-0, SpS). Sportshelf.
Birch, B. J., ed. see International Summer School, Univ. of Antwerp, RUCA, July-Aug., 1972.
Birch, B. J, et al, eds. The Collected Works of Harold Davenport, Vol. I. 1978. 69.00 (ISBN 0-12-099301-5). Acad Pr.
Birch, B. J., et al, eds. The Collected Works of Harold Davenport, Vols. 2-4. 1978. 69.50 ea.; Vol. 2. (ISBN 0-12-099302-3); Vol. 3, 1978. (ISBN 0-12-099303-1); Vol. 4. (ISBN 0-12-099304-X); Vol. 1. 69.00 (ISBN 0-12-099301-5). Acad Pr.
Birch, Beverley. Festivals. LC 85-40205. (Let's Look Up Ser.). (Illus.). 32p. (gr. 3-6). PLB 5.95 (ISBN 0-382-09077-2). Silver.
--Let's Look Up Food from Many Lands. LC 85-40203. (Let's Look Up Ser.). (Illus.). 32p. (gr. 3-6). 1985. PLB 5.95 (ISBN 0-382-09078-0). Silver.
Birch, Bruce C. & Rasmussen, Larry L. Bible & Ethics in the Christian Life. LC 76-3856. 208p. 1976. pap. 7.95 (ISBN 0-8066-1524-9, 10-0703, 10-0702). Augsburg.
--The Predicament of the Prosperous. LC 78-18412. (Biblical Perspectives on Current Issues). 212p. 1978. pap. 7.95 (ISBN 0-664-24211-1). Westminster.
Birch, C. Allan, et al. The House Physician's Handbook. 5th ed. (Illus.). 336p. 1980. pap. text ed. 13.75 (ISBN 0-443-02117-1). Churchill.
Birch, C. G. & Parker, K. J., eds. Control of Food Quality & Food Analysis. 320p. 1984. 64.75 (ISBN 0-85334-239-3, 1-525-83, Pub. by Elsevier Applied Sci England). Elsevier.
Birch, Carol L., ed. see New American Foundation.
Birch, Charles & Cobb, John B. The Liberation of Life: From the Cell to the Community. 361p. 1985. pap. 17.95 (ISBN 0-521-31514-X). Cambridge U Pr.
Birch, Claire. Collision Course. (Lucy Hill Mystery Ser.: No. 2). (Orig.). (gr. k-12). 1985. pap. 2.50 (ISBN 0-440-91366-7, LFL). Dell.
--Double Danger. (Lucy Hill Ser.: No. 3). (Orig.). (gr. k-12). 1985. pap. 2.50 (ISBN 0-440-92126-0, LFL). Dell.
--False Lead. (Lucy Hill Mystery Ser.: No. 4). (Orig.). (gr. k-12). 1986. pap. 2.50 (ISBN 0-440-92459-6, LFL). Dell.
--Tight Spot. (Lucy Hill Mystery Ser: No. 1). 160p. pap. 2.50 (ISBN 0-440-98732-6, LFL). Dell.
Birch, Clive. Book of Chesham. 1977. 40.00x (ISBN 0-86023-014-7). State Mutual Bk.
Birch, Clive, jt. auth. see Hope, Valerie.
Birch, Cyril, ed. & intro. by. Studies in Chinese Literary Genres. LC 77-157825. 1975. 32.00x (ISBN 0-520-02037-5). U of Cal Pr.
Birch, Cyril & Keene, Donald, eds. Anthology of Chinese Literature, Vol. 1: From Early Times to the Fourteenth Century. Birch, Cyril, tr. from Chinese. (Illus.). 1965. pap. 17.50 (ISBN 0-394-17252-3, E417, Ever). Grove.
--Anthology of Chinese Literature, Vol. 2. From the Fourteenth Century to the Present. Birch, Cyril, tr. from Chinese. (Illus.). 1972. pap. 12.95 (ISBN 0-394-17766-5, E584, Ever). Grove.
Birch, Cyril, tr. Stories from a Ming Collection. 1968. pap. 5.95 (ISBN 0-394-17308-2, E473, Ever). Grove.
Birch, Cyril, tr. see Birch, Cyril & Keene, Donald.
Birch, Cyril, tr. see Feng Meng-Lung.
Birch, Cyril, tr. see Tang, Xianzu.
Birch, D. Early Reformation English Polemics, No.92: 7. (Salzburg-Elizabethan & Renaissance Ser.). 131p. 1983. pap. text ed. 25.50x (ISBN 0-391-03047-7, Pub. by Salzburg Austria). Humanities.
Birch, D., jt. auth. see Rissover, F.
Birch, David L. Economic Future of City & Suburb. LC 74-127247. 56p. 1970. pap. 1.25 (ISBN 0-87186-230-1). Comm Econ Dev.
Birch, Dorothy. A Book of Short Plays Fifteenth-Sixteenth Centuries. 1940. 10.00 (ISBN 0-8482-0144-2). Norwood Edns.
--Training for the Stage. 1952. 20.00 (ISBN 0-8482-7417-2). Norwood Edns.
Birch, E. M., jt. auth. see Ottoson, H. W.
Birch, Eugenie Ladner, ed. The Unsheltered Woman: Women & Housing in the 80's. (Illus.). 346p. 1985. pap. text ed. 14.95x (ISBN 0-88285-104-7). Transaction Bks.
Birch, G. G. Vitamin C: Recent Aspects of Its Physiological & Technological Importance. (Illus.). 260p. 1974. 46.25 (ISBN 0-85334-606-2, Pub. by Elsevier Applied Sci England). Elsevier.
Birch, G. G. & Blakebrough. Enzymes & Food Processing: An Industry-University Co-Operation Symposium. Reading, England, April 1980. (Illus.). 295p. 1980. 48.00 (ISBN 0-85334-935-5, Pub. by Elsevier Applied Sci England). Elsevier.
Birch, G. G., ed. Analysis of Food Carbohydrate. 288p. 1985. 60.00 (ISBN 0-85334-354-3, Pub. by Elsevier Applied Sci England). Elsevier.
Birch, G. G. & Green, L. F., eds. Molecular Structure & Function of Food Carbohydrate. LC 73-16299. 308p. 1973. 58.95 (ISBN 0-470-07323-3). Halsted Pr.
Birch, G. G. & Lindley, M. G., eds. Alcoholic Beverages. 240p. 1985. 39.00 (ISBN 0-85334-326-8, Pub. by Elsevier Applied Sci England). Elsevier.
Birch, G. G. & Parker, K. J., eds. Dietary Fibre. (Illus.). 304p. 1983. 55.50 (ISBN 0-85334-178-8, Pub. by Elsevier Applied Sci England). Elsevier.
--Food & Health: Science & Technology. (Illus.). xii, 532p. 1976. 76.00 (ISBN 0-85334-875-8, Pub. by Elsevier Applied Sci England). Elsevier.
--Nutritive Sweeteners. (Illus.). 316p. 1982. 57.50 (ISBN 0-85334-997-5, Pub. by Elsevier Applied Sci England). Elsevier.
--Sugar: Science & Technology. (Illus.). 475p. 1979. 89.00 (ISBN 0-85334-805-7, Pub. by Elsevier Applied Sci England). Elsevier.
Birch, G. G. & Shallenberger, R. S., eds. Developments in Food Carbohydrates, Vol. 1. 189p. 1977. 40.75 (ISBN 0-85334-733-6, Pub. by Elsevier Applied Sci England). Elsevier.
Birch, G. G., et al, eds. Food from Waste. (Illus.). 301p. 1976. 70.50 (ISBN 0-85334-659-3, Pub. by Elsevier Applied Sci England). Elsevier.
--Glucose Syrups & Related Carbohydrates. (Illus.). 1970. 18.00x (ISBN 0-444-20103-3, Pub. by Applied Science). Burgess-Intl Ideas.
--Glucose Syrups & Related Carbohydrates. (Illus.). 118p. 1971. 20.50 (ISBN 0-444-20103-3, Pub. by Elsevier Applied Sci England). Elsevier.
--Health & Food. 224p. 1972. 24.00 (ISBN 0-85334-558-9, Pub. by Elsevier Applied Sci England). Elsevier.
--Sweetness & Sweeteners. (Illus.). 176p. 1971. 26.00 (ISBN 0-85334-503-1, Pub. by Elsevier Applied Sci England). Elsevier.
--Sensory Properties of Foods. (Illus.). 326p. 1977. 53.75 (ISBN 0-85334-744-1, Pub. by Elsevier Applied Sci England). Elsevier.
Birch, Gareth. Sixty Smiles an Hour. 1984. 3.25 (ISBN 0-89536-992-3). CSS of Ohio.
Birch, Gordon G., et al. Food Science. 2nd ed. 1977. pap. text ed. 11.25 (ISBN 0-08-021346-4). Pergamon.
Birch, Herbert G. & Gussow, Joan D. Disadvantaged Children: Health, Nutrition & School Failure. LC 78-102443. (Illus.). 320p. 1970. 37.00 (ISBN 0-8089-0643-7, 790590). Grune.
Birch, I., et al. Intergovernmental Relations & Australian Education. LC 79-55415. (Centre for Research on Federal Financial Relations - Research Monograph: No. 29). 107p. (Orig.). 1980. pap. text ed. 8.00 (ISBN 0-908160-46-1, 0566). Australia N U P.
Birch, I. K. The School & the Law. (Second Century in Australian Education Ser.: No. 13). 1976. pap. 7.50x (ISBN 0-522-84103-1, Pub. by Melbourne U Pr). Intl Spec Bk.
Birch, J. R., ed. Fourier Transform Spectroscopy: Proceedings of the International Conference, Durham, U. K., 19-22 September, 1983. 290p. 1984. pap. 64.00 (ISBN 0-08-030265-3). Pergamon.
Birch, Jack, jt. auth. see Sellin, Don.
Birch, Jack W. & Johnstone, B. Kenneth. Designing Schools & Schooling for the Handicapped. (Illus.). 244p. 1975. 22.50x (ISBN 0-398-03362-5). C C Thomas.
Birch, Jack W. & Reynolds, Maynard C., eds. Teaching Exceptional Children in All America's Schools: A First Course for Teachers & Principals. 1977. text ed. 19.95 (ISBN 0-86586-084-X). Coun Exc Child.
Birch, Jeremy, jt. auth. see Loring, Honey.
Birch, Jillian, ed. see International Cancer Congress, 12th, Buenos Aires, 5-11 October.
Birch, John H. Denmark in History. 1976. lib. bdg. 59.95 (ISBN 0-8490-1707-6). Gordon Pr.
--Denmark in History. LC 75-16608. (Illus.). 444p. 1975. Repr. of 1938 ed. lib. bdg. 28.00x (ISBN 0-8371-8254-9, BIDH). Greenwood.
Birch, L. C. & Cobb, J. B. The Liberation of Life: From the Cell to the Community. LC 80-42156. 300p. 1982. 39.50 (ISBN 0-521-23787-4). Cambridge U Pr.
Birch, L. C., jt. auth. see Andrewartha, H. G.
Birch, Martin C. & Haynes, Ken F. Insect Pheromones. (Studies in Biology: No. 147). 64p. 1982. pap. text ed. 8.95 (ISBN 0-7131-2852-6). E Arnold.
Birch, N. H. & Bramson, A. E. The Pilot's Guide to Flight Emergency Procedures. LC 77-91556. (Illus.). 1978. 7.95 (ISBN 0-385-13544-0). Doubleday.
Birch, Neville, jt. auth. see Bramson, Alan.
Birch, R. C. The Shaping of the Welfare State. (Seminar Studies in History). 126p. 1974. pap. text ed. 6.25x (ISBN 0-582-35200-2). Longman.
Birch, Robert L., jt. auth. see Fauver, William.
Birch, Thomas. Court & Times of James the First, 2 Vols. LC 74-113558. Repr. of 1849 ed. Set. 75.00 (ISBN 0-404-00906-9). AMS Pr.
--The History of the Royal Society of London, 4 Vols. Repr. Set. 170.00 (ISBN 0-384-04305-4). Johnson Repr.
--Memoirs of the Reign of Queen Elizabeth, 2 Vols. LC 79-131513. Repr. of 1754 ed. Set. lib. bdg. 85.00 (ISBN 0-404-00909-3). AMS Pr.
Birch, Thomas, ed. see Raleigh, Walter.
Birch, Una. Secret Societies & the French Revolution. 1976. lib. bdg. 59.95 (ISBN 0-8490-2585-0). Gordon Pr.
Birch, W. J. An Inquiry into the Philosophy & Religion of Shakespeare. LC 72-3660. (Studies in Shakespeare, No. 24). 1972. Repr. of 1848 ed. lib. bdg. 59.95x (ISBN 0-8383-1569-0). Haskell.
Birch, Walter D. Index Saxonicus. 140p. Repr. of 1899 ed. 22.00 (ISBN 0-384-04404-2). Johnson Repr.
Birch, Walter D., ed. Cartularium Saxonicum: A Collection of Charters Relating to Anglo-Saxon History, 3 vols. Repr. of 1893 ed. Set. with index. 260.00 (ISBN 0-384-04405-0); sep. index 14.00 (ISBN 0-685-13365-6). Johnson Repr.
Birch, Walter D., ed. & tr. see D'Albuquerque, Alfonso.
Birch, Walter D., ed. see Kemble, John.
Birch, William. Inquiry into the Philosophy & Religion of Shakspeare. LC 76-39446. Repr. of 1848 ed. 15.00 (ISBN 0-404-00868-2). AMS Pr.
Birch, William D., tr. see Birch, Williiam D.
Birch, William G. & Meilach, Dona Z. Doctor Discusses Pregnancy. (Illus.). 1980. pap. 2.99 (ISBN 0-910304-00-9). Budlong.
Birch, Williiam D., ed. Vita Haroldi: The Romance of the Life of Harold, King of England. Birch, William D., tr. LC 80-2232. Repr. of 1885 ed. 36.00 (ISBN 0-404-18753-6). AMS Pr.
Birchall, Christopher, tr. see Holy Transfiguration Monastery.
Birchall, Christopher, tr. see Khrapovitsky, Antony.
Birchall, D. W. & Hammond, V. Tomorrow's Office Today: Managing Technological Change. 202p. 1981. 32.95x (ISBN 0-470-27236-8). Halsted Pr.
Birchall, D. W. & Hammond, V. J. Tomorrow's Office Today: Managing Technological Change. 203p. 1981. 29.95 (ISBN 0-686-98084-0). Telecom Lib.
Birchall, Emily. A Wedding Tour: January to June Eighteen Seventy-Three & Visit to the Vienna Exhibition. Verey, David, ed. (Illus.). 166p. 1985. 25.00 (ISBN 0-312-85998-8). St Martin.
Birchenall, Joan M. Care of the Older Adult. 2nd ed. (Illus.). 288p. 1982. text ed. 12.50 (ISBN 0-397-54271-2, Lippincott Nursing). Lippincott.
Birchenhall, Chris & Grout, Paul. Mathematics for Modern Economics. 424p. 1984. 32.50x (ISBN 0-389-20521-4, BNB-08083); pap. 20.00x (ISBN 0-389-20522-2, BNB-08084). B&N Imports.
Bircher, Martin, ed. see Greiffenberg, Catharina Regina von.
Bircher, Max E., jt. auth. see Bircher-Benner, M.
Bircher-Benner, M. The Bircher-Benner Children's Diet Book. LC 76-58766. 64p. 1977. pap. 2.50 (ISBN 0-87983-141-3). Keats.
Bircher-Benner, M. & Bircher, Max E. The Bircher-Benner Raw Fruits & Vegetables Book. LC 77-72388. (Illus.). 48p. 1977. pap. 2.50 (ISBN 0-87983-142-1). Keats.
Bircher-Benner, Max & Bircher-Benner, Ruth. Bircher-Benner Nutrition Plan for Skin Problems. 1981. pap. 4.95x (ISBN 0-317-07347-8, Regent House). B of A.
Bircher-Benner, Ruth, jt. auth. see Bircher-Benner, Max.
Bircher-Brenner, M. The Prevention of Incurable Disease. LC 78-61330. 1978. pap. 3.95 (ISBN 0-87983-186-3). Keats.
Birchfield, E. & Coolman, J. The Complete Reference Guide to United Nations Sales Publications: 1946-1978, 2 vols. 700p. 1982. 115.00x (ISBN 0-89111-011-9). UNIFO Pubs.
Birchfield, John C. Foodservice Operations Manual. LC 79-15622. 250p. 1979. spiral bd. 59.95 (ISBN 0-8436-2145-1). Van Nos Reinhold.
Birchfield, Marilyn E. Stages of Illness: Guidelines for Nursing Care. (Illus.). 288p. 1985. pap. text ed. 14.95 (ISBN 0-89303-863-6). Brady Comm.
Birchfield, Mary E. Consolidated Catalog of League of Nations Publications Offered for Sale. LC 75-17970. 478p. 1976. 55.00x (ISBN 0-379-00328-7). Oceana.
Birchman, Willis. Faces & Facts, by & About Twenty-Six Contemporary Artists. facs. ed. LC 68-25600. (Essay Index Reprint Ser). 1937. 15.00 (ISBN 0-8369-0211-4). Ayer Co Pubs.
Birck, Sixt. Saemtliche Dramen, Vol. 2. Brauneck, M., ed. (Ausgaben Deutscher Literatur Des 15-18 Jahrhunderts Ser.). 1976. 128.00x (ISBN 3-11-006758-7). De Gruyter.
Birckbichler, Diane W. Creative Activities for the Second Language Classroom. (Language in Education Series No. 48). 98p. (Orig.). 1982. pap. 8.95 (ISBN 0-15-599013-6). Ctr Appl Ling.
Bircks, W., ed. Cardiovascular Surgery. (Illus.). 765p. 1981. 64.00 (ISBN 0-387-10929-3). Springer-Verlag.

Bircks, W., et al, eds. Medical & Surgical Management of Tacharrhythmias. (Illus.). 190p. 1980. pap. 33.00 (ISBN 0-387-09929-8). Springer-Verlag.

Bird, et al. A World View of Art History: Selected Readings. 464p. 1985. pap. text ed. 44.95 (ISBN 0-8403-3503-2). Kendall-Hunt.

Bird, A., et al. Combined Care of the Rheumatic Patient. (Illus.). 320p. 1985. pap. 24.50 (ISBN 0-387-13557-X). Springer-Verlag.

Bird, Adren J., et al. The Craft of Hawaiian Lauhala Weaving. LC 82-4818. (Illus.). 163p. 1982. pap. 12.95 (ISBN 0-8248-0779-0). UH Pr.

Bird, Alan. The Plays of Oscar Wilde. (Critical Studies Ser.). 220p. 1977. 24.50x (ISBN 0-06-490415-6, 06347). B&N Imports.

Bird, Alan F. Structure of Nematodes. 1971. 65.00 (ISBN 0-12-099650-2). Acad Pr.

Bird, Anthony & Hallows, Ian. The Rolls-Royce Motor Car: And the Bentley since 1931. 5th, rev. ed. (Illus.). 328p. 1985. 39.95 (ISBN 0-312-68957-8). St Martin.

Bird, Arthur. Looking Forward: A Dream of the United States of the Americas in 1999. LC 76-154429. (Utopian Literature Ser). 1971. Repr. of 1899 ed. 15.00 (ISBN 0-405-03512-8). Ayer Co Pubs.

Bird, Augusto. Bibliografia Puertorriquena Nineteen Thirty to Nineteen Forty-Five, 4 vols. (Puerto Rican Ser.). 1979. Set. lib. bdg. 600.00 (ISBN 0-8490-2872-8). Gordon Pr.

Bird, B. M. & King, K. G. Power Electronics. 287p. 1983. cloth 49.95 (ISBN 0-471-10430-2, Pub. by Wiley-Interscience); pap. 21.95 (ISBN 0-471-90051-6, Pub. by Wiley-Interscience). Wiley.

Bird, Betsy, jt. auth. see Rand, Peter.

Bird, Bob. Happiness. 220p. (Orig.). 1983. pap. 10.00 (ISBN 0-934804-10-9). Inspiration MI.

--Help Yourself to Happiness. 20p. (Orig.). 1979. pap. 1.50 (ISBN 0-934804-07-9). Inspiration MI.

--You Are a Special Person. 16p. (Orig.). 1974. pap. 1.50 (ISBN 0-934804-06-0). Inspiration MI.

Bird, Brian. Talking with Patients. 2nd ed. LC 73-2804. 365p. 1973. 19.50 (ISBN 0-397-50313-X, 65-00466, Lippincott Medical). Lippincott.

Bird, Byron R., et al. Dynamics of Polymeric Liquids, 2 vols. Incl. Vol. 1. Fluid Mechanics. 576p. 69.45 (ISBN 0-471-07375-X); Vol. 2. Kinetic Theory. 304p. 69.45x (ISBN 0-471-01596-2). LC 76-15408. 1977. Wiley.

Bird, C. F. & Ongkosongo, Otto S. Environmental Changes on the Coasts of Indonesia. 52p. 1981. pap. 10.00 (ISBN 92-808-0197-X, TUNU128, UNU). Unipub.

Bird, C. L. The Theory & Practice of Wool Dyeing. 4th ed. 249p. 1972. 39.00x (ISBN 0-686-91778-2, Pub. by Soc Dyers & Colour). State Mutual Bk.

Bird, C. L. & Boston, W. S. The Theory of Coloration of Textiles. 432p. 1975. 80.00x (ISBN 0-686-98192-8, Pub. by Soc Dyers & Colour). State Mutual Bk.

Bird, C. W. Transition Metal Intermediates in Organic Synthesis. 1967. 62.50 (ISBN 0-12-099750-9). Acad Pr.

Bird, C. W. & Cheeseman, G. W., eds. Aromatic & Heteroaromatic Chemistry, Vols. 1-6. Incl. Vol. 1. 1971-72 Literature. 1973. 42.00 (ISBN 0-85186-753-7); Vol. 2. 1972-73 Literature. 1974. 47.00 (ISBN 0-85186-763-4); Vol. 3. 1973-74 Literature. 1975. 53.00 (ISBN 0-85186-773-1); Vol. 4. 1974-75 Literature. 1976. 70.00 (ISBN 0-85186-783-9); Vol. 5. 1975-76 Literature. 1977. 87.00 (ISBN 0-85186-793-6); Vol. 6. 1976-77 Literature. 1978. 70.00 (ISBN 0-85186-803-7). LC 72-95095 (Pub. by Royal Soc Chem London). Am Chemical.

Bird, Caroline. The Good Years: Your Life in the 21st Century. 288p. 1983. 15.95 (ISBN 0-525-93284-4, 01549-460). Dutton.

--The Two Paycheck Marriage. 1982. pap. 3.50 (ISBN 0-671-45366-1). PB.

Bird, Carolyn J. & Ragan, Mark A., eds. Proceedings of the Eleventh International Seaweed Symposium. (Developments in Hydrobiology Ser.). 1985. lib. bdg. 128.50 (ISBN 90-6193-773-6, Pub. by Junk Pubs Netherlands). Kluwer Academic.

Bird, Charles. The Dialects of Mandekan. LC 81-70547. 423p. (Orig.). 1982. pap. text ed. 20.00 (ISBN 0-941934-09-8). Indiana Africa.

Bird, Charles & Koita, Mamadou. The Songs of Seydou Camara: Volume 1-Kambili. (Occasional Papers in Mande Studies). 120p. (Orig.). 1974. pap. text ed. 5.00 (ISBN 0-941934-12-8). Indiana Africa.

Bird, Charles P. Choose Success: A Personal Competency Guide for the Emerging Manager. (The Business of Business Ser.). (Illus.). 98p. (Orig.). cancelled (ISBN 0-943920-54-X); pap. cancelled (ISBN 0-943920-55-8). Metamorphous Pr.

Bird, Charles S., jt. auth. see Soumaoro, Bourama.

Bird, Charles S., jt. ed. see Karp, Ivan.

Bird, Christopher. The Divining Hand: The 500-Year-Old Mystery of Dowsing. (Illus.). 353p. 1983. pap. 13.50 (ISBN 0-525-48038-2, 01311-390). Dutton.

Bird, Christopher, jt. auth. see Tompkins, Peter.

Bird, David, jt. auth. see Reese, Terence.

Bird, Dorothy M. Granite Harbor. (gr. 5 up). 1967. 4.50g (ISBN 0-02-710670-5). Macmillan.

Bird, E. A. Electronic Data Processing & Computers for Commercial Students. 1979. pap. 9.50 (ISBN 0-434-90142-3, Pub. by W Heinemann Ltd). David & Charles.

Bird, E. J. Ten Tall Tales. LC 84-12086. (Carolrhoda Good Time Library). (Illus.). 96p. (gr. 2-6). 1984. PLB 8.95 (ISBN 0-87614-267-6). Carolrhoda Bks.

Bird, Eric. Coasts. 3rd ed. (Illus.). 320p. 1984. 34.95x (ISBN 0-631-13567-7); pap. 11.95x (ISBN 0-631-13568-5). Basil Blackwell.

Bird, Eric & Dubois, Jean-Paul. The Impacts of Opencast Mining on the Rivers & Coasts of New Caledonia. 52p. 1985. pap. 15.00 (ISBN 92-808-0505-3, TUNU232, TUNU). Unipub.

Bird, Eric C. Coastline Changes: A Global Review. LC 84-22064. 1985. 39.95 (ISBN 0-471-90646-8). Wiley.

--Jakarta Workshop on Coastal Resources Management: Proceedings. Soegiarto, Aprilani, ed. 106p. 1980. pap. 15.00 (TUNU100, UNU). Unipub.

Bird, Eric C. & Schwartz, Maurice L., eds. The World's Coastline. (Illus.). 1184p. 1985. 97.50 (ISBN 0-442-21116-3). Van Nos Reinhold.

Bird, Francis A. Accounting Theory: Conceptual CPA Approach. LC 80-70163. (Accounting Ser.). 389p. 1980. 28.95 (ISBN 0-936328-02-9); text ed. 24.95 (ISBN 0-936328-02-9). Dame Inc.

--Accounting Theory: Conceptual CPA Approach. 1983. text ed. 28.95 (ISBN 0-8359-0046-0). Reston.

--Accounting Theory: Selected Conceptual Readings. 1983. pap. text ed. 19.95 (ISBN 0-8359-0045-2). Reston.

Bird, Francis A., ed. Accounting Theory: Selected Conceptual Readings. LC 81-66817. (Accounting Ser.). 450p. (Orig.). 1981. pap. 26.95 (ISBN 0-936328-09-6); pap. text ed. 17.50 (ISBN 0-936328-09-6). Dame Inc.

Bird, Frank E. Management Guide to Loss Control (IS131) 1981. 80.00x (ISBN 0-686-45797-8, Pub. by RoSPA Can Hse England). State Mutual Bk.

Bird, Frank E., Jr. Management Guide to Loss Control. LC 74-75765. (Illus.). 243p. (Orig.). 1974. pap. text ed. 15.00 (ISBN 0-88061-001-8). Inst Pub Ga.

--Mine Safety & Loss Control: A Management Guide. LC 80-84050. 241p. pap. text ed. 15.00 (ISBN 0-88061-010-7). Inst Pub GA.

Bird, Frank E., Jr. & Germain, George L. Damage Control. LC 66-29722. (Illus.). 176p. 1984. pap. text ed. 12.50 (ISBN 0-88061-006-9). Inst Pub GA.

--Damage Control (IS181) 1981. 60.00x (ISBN 0-686-45784-6, Pub. by RoSPA Can Hse England). State Mutual Bk.

Bird, Frank E., Jr. & Loftus, Robert G. Loss Control Management. LC 76-7279. (Illus.). 574p. 1976. lib. bdg. 24.00 (ISBN 0-88061-000-X). Inst Pub Ga.

--Loss Control Management (IS130) 1981. 85.00x (ISBN 0-686-45796-X, Pub. by RoSPA Can Hse England). State Mutual Bk.

Bird, G., tr. see Wagner, Richard.

Bird, G. A. Molecular Gas Dynamics. (Oxford Engineering & Science Ser.). 1976. text ed. 72.00x (ISBN 0-19-856120-2). Oxford U Pr.

Bird, Gail. Russian Punch Needle Embroidery. 1981. pap. 2.50 (ISBN 0-486-24146-7). Dover.

Bird, Gail B., jt. auth. see Verrall, Harold E.

Bird, George & Stokes, Richard, trs. The Fischer-Dieskau Book of Lieder. LC 76-47955. 448p. 1984. pap. 9.95 (ISBN 0-87910-004-4). Limelight Edns.

Bird, George, tr. see Roubiczek, Paul.

Bird, George, et al, trs. see Dostoyevsky, Fyodor.

Bird, George L. & Merwin, Frederic E., eds. Press & Society: A Book of Readings. rev. ed. LC 79-147215. 1971. Repr. of 1951 ed. lib. bdg. 27.50x (ISBN 0-8371-5980-6, BIPR). Greenwood.

Bird, Glenn, jt. auth. see Kavanagh, Barry.

Bird, Graham. Kant's Theory of Knowledge: An Outline of One Central Argument in the Critique of Pure Reason. (International Library of Philosophy & Scientific Method Ser.). 1973. Repr. of 1962 ed. text ed. 15.50x (ISBN 0-391-00316-X). Humanities.

--World Finance & Adjustment: An Agenda for Reform. 368p. 1985. 32.50 (ISBN 0-312-89125-3). St Martin.

Bird, H. A. & Wright, V. Applied Drug Therapy of the Rheumatic Diseases. (Illus.). 324p. 1982. pap. 31.50 (ISBN 0-7236-0658-7). PSG Pub Co.

Bird, Harriet & Freed, Margaret M. The Warm Fuzzy Song Book. LC 79-90080. (Transactional Analysis for Everybody Ser.). (Illus., Orig.). (gr. k-6). 1980. pap. 4.95 (ISBN 0-915190-14-1). Jalmar Pr.

Bird, Henry. The Narrative of Henry Bird. 14p. 1973. 5.00 (ISBN 0-87770-116-4); pap. 2.50 (ISBN 0-87770-115-6). Ye Galleon.

Bird, Isabella. Golden Chersonese. (Travel Classics Ser.). 384p. 1985. lib. bdg. 23.95 (ISBN 0-317-19639-1, Pub. by Century Pubs UK). Hippocrene Bks.

--Korea & Her Neighbours. (Pacific Basin Bks.). 400p. (Orig.). 1985. pap. 12.95 (ISBN 0-7103-0135-9, Kegan Paul International). Routledge & Kegan.

--A Lady's Life in the Rocky Mountains. LC 60-8748. 1977. pap. 3.50 (ISBN 0-89174-025-2). Comstock Edns.

Bird, Isabella L. Englishwoman in America. 526p. 1966. o. p. 20.00x (ISBN 0-299-03520-4); pap. 9.50x (ISBN 0-299-03524-7). U of Wis Pr.

--Korea & Her Neighbours. (Illus.). 664p. 1985. pap. 11.50 (ISBN 0-8048-1489-9). C E Tuttle.

--Lady's Life in the Rocky Mountains. LC 60-8748. (Western Frontier Library: No. 14). (Illus.). 1969. pap. 4.95 (ISBN 0-8061-1328-6). U of Okla Pr.

--Six Months in the Sandwich Islands. LC 73-77575. (Illus.). 1973. pap. 5.95 (ISBN 0-8048-1112-1). C E Tuttle.

--Unbeaten Tracks in Japan. LC 75-172002. (Illus.). 1971. pap. 6.75 (ISBN 0-8048-1000-1). C E Tuttle.

--Up Long's Peak in 1873 with Rocky Mountain Jim. Jones, William R., ed. (Illus.). 40p. 1977. pap. 1.00 (ISBN 0-89646-023-1). Outbooks.

Bird, Isabelle. A Lady's Life in the Rocky Mountains. 298p. 1983. pap. 8.95 (ISBN 0-86068-267-6, Pub. by Virago Pr). Merrimack Pub Cir.

Bird, J. R., et al. Ion Beam Techniques in Archaeology & the Arts. 172p. 1984. 26.00 (ISBN 3-7186-0188-5). Harwood Academic.

Bird, Jean & Bird, Jim. Birds' Guide to Bargain Shopping. 540p. 1984. pap. 8.95 (ISBN 0-8362-7954-9). Andrews McMeel Parker.

Bird, Jean D. Factory Outlet Shopping Guide for New Jersey & Rockland County 1984. 1983. pap. 3.95 (ISBN 0-913464-70-8). FOSG Pubns.

--Factory Outlet Shopping Guide for New York 1984. 1984. pap. 3.95 (ISBN 0-913464-71-6). FOSG Pubns.

--Factory Outlet Shopping Guide for Pennsylvania 1984. 1984. pap. 3.95 (ISBN 0-913464-72-4). FOSG Pubns.

--Factory Outlet Shopping Guide for Washington, D.C., Maryland, Virginia, Delaware 1984. 1984. pap. 3.95 (ISBN 0-913464-73-2). FOSG Pubns.

Bird, Jim, jt. auth. see Bird, Jean.

Bird, John. Percy Grainger. (Illus.). 360p. 1982. pap. 14.95 (ISBN 0-571-11717-1). Faber & Faber.

Bird, John, ed. Plate Tectonics. rev. ed. (Illus.). 986p. 1980. pap. 25.00 (ISBN 0-87590-223-5). Am Geophysical.

Bird, John B. The Physiography of Artic Canada, with Special Reference to the Area South of Perry Channel. LC 67-16232. pap. 106.80 (ISBN 0-317-19890-4, 2023083). Bks Demand UMI.

Bird, Joseph W. & Bird, Lois F. Freedom of Sexual Love. LC 67-10377. 1970. pap. 3.50 (ISBN 0-385-04341-4, Im). Doubleday.

--Love Is All: Conversations of a Husband & Wife with God. LC 67-22453. 1968. pap. 3.50 (ISBN 0-385-00779-5, Im). Doubleday.

--Marriage Is for Grownups. LC 79-78725. 1971. pap. 4.50 (ISBN 0-385-04256-6, Im). Doubleday.

--Power to the Parents. LC 77-176346. 240p. 1974. pap. 1.95 (ISBN 0-385-08423-4, Im). Doubleday.

Bird, Julio & Maramorosch, Karl, eds. Tropical Diseases of Legumes: Papers Presented at the Rio Piedras Agricultural Experiment Station of the University of Puerto Rico, Mayaguez Campus, June, 1974. 1975. 39.50 (ISBN 0-12-099950-1). Acad Pr.

Bird, Junius B., intro. by. Peruvian Painting by Unknown Artists: 800 B. C. to 1700 A. D. (Illus.). 1973. pap. 3.00 (ISBN 0-913456-20-9, Pub. by Ctr Inter-Am Rel). Interbk Inc.

Bird, Keith W. German Naval History: A Guide to the Literature. Higham, Robin & Kipp, Jacob, eds. LC 83-49084. (Military History Bibliographies Ser.). 1142p. 1984. lib. bdg. 154.00 (ISBN 0-8240-9024-1). Garland Pub.

--Weimar, the German Naval Officer Corps & the Rise of National Socialism. 1977. pap. text ed. 34.75x (ISBN 90-6032-094-8). Humanities.

Bird, Larry & Bischoff, John. Bird on Basketball: How-to Strategies from the Great Celtics Champion. (Illus.). 128p. 1985. pap. 9.95 (ISBN 0-201-10646-9). Addison-Wesley.

Bird, Larry J. & Bischoff, John R. Larry Bird's Basketball Birdwise. McPeek, Bobbi, ed. LC 82-60614. (Illus.). 132p. (Orig.). 1983. pap. 9.95 (ISBN 0-910109-00-1, 900A). Phoenix Projects.

Bird, Leonard. Costa Rica: The Unarmed Democracy. (Illus.). 224p. 1985. 15.00 (ISBN 0-900661-37-2, Sheppard Press Limited England). Seven Hills Bks.

Bird, Lois F., jt. auth. see Bird, Joseph W.

Bird, M. B. The Black Man. facsimile ed. LC 70-164380. (Black Heritage Library Collection). Repr. of 1869 ed. 26.50 (ISBN 0-8369-8839-6). Ayer Co Pubs.

Bird, Malcolm. There Is a Better Way to Manage. 128p. 1985. pap. 17.95 (ISBN 0-89397-207-X). Nichols Pub.

--The Witch's Handbook. (Illus.). 96p. 1985. 10.95 (ISBN 0-312-88458-3). St Martin.

Bird, Michael. Canadian Folk Art: Old Ways in a New Land. (Illus.). 1983. 24.95 (ISBN 0-19-540424-6). Oxford U Pr.

Bird, Michael & Koblayashi, Teruko. A Splendid Harvest: Germanic Folk & Decorative Arts. 240p. 1981. 29.95 (ISBN 0-442-29620-7). Van Nos Reinhold.

Bird, Michael, jt. ed. see May, John R.

Bird, Monroe M., jt. ed. see Pingry, Jack R.

Bird, Nicky. Luggage Labels. (Illus.). 48p. (Orig.). 1984. pap. 6.95 (ISBN 0-905209-28-1, Pub. by Victoria & Albert Mus UK). Faber & Faber.

Bird, Otto. Cultures in Conflict. LC 76-638. 1978. pap. text ed. 6.95 (ISBN 0-268-00724-1, 85-07246). U of Notre Dame Pr.

Bird, Otto, tr. see Bochenski, J. M.

Bird, P. E., ed. Elements of Sport Airplane Design for the Homebuilder. (Illus.). 1977. pap. 11.95 (ISBN 0-911720-25-1, Pub. by Vogel). Aviation.

Bird, Patricia. Blueprint for Love. 1983. 8.95 (ISBN 0-8034-8307-4, Avalon). Bouregy.

--Bright Dreams, Dark Desires. (Orig.). 1980. pap. 2.75 (ISBN 0-8439-8005-2, Tiara Bks). Dorchester Pub Co.

--The Crystal Heart. 1982. 8.95 (ISBN 0-686-84157-3, Avalon). Bouregy.

--Golden Dream. (YA) 1979. 8.95 (ISBN 0-685-95873-6, Avalon). Bouregy.

--Our Foolish Hearts. (YA) 1984. 8.95 (ISBN 0-8034-8438-0, Avalon). Bouregy.

--Peril at Land's End. (Orig.). 1980. pap. 1.75 (ISBN 0-8439-8008-7, Tiara Bks). Dorchester Pub Co.

--Shamrock in the Sun. (YA) 1980. 8.95 (ISBN 0-686-73921-3, Avalon). Bouregy.

--Shipboard Kisses. (YA) 1983. 8.95 (ISBN 0-8034-8317-1, Avalon). Bouregy.

--Sunshine Lost. (YA) 1979. 8.95 (ISBN 0-685-65276-9, Avalon). Bouregy.

--The Tender Dream. (YA) 1984. 8.95 (ISBN 0-8034-8427-5, Avalon). Bouregy.

Bird, Peter. Athletics. 7.50x (ISBN 0-392-08961-0, SpS). Sportshelf.

Bird, Phyllis A. The Bible As the Church's Book. LC 82-7049. (Library of Living Faith: Vol. 5). 118p. 1982. pap. 5.95 (ISBN 0-664-24427-0). Westminster.

Bird, R. The Computer in Experimental Psychology. LC 80-41610. (Computers & People Ser.). 256p. 1981. 47.50 (ISBN 0-12-099760-6). Acad Pr.

Bird, R. B. & Shetter, W. Z. Dutch: Een Goed Begin, a Contemporary Dutch Reader, 2 vols. 2nd ed. 1978. Set. pap. 12.50 (ISBN 9-0247-2073-7). Vol. 1 (ISBN 9-0247-2071-0). Vol. 2 (ISBN 9-0247-2072-9). Heinman.

Bird, R. B., et al. Fundamental Physics of Gases. Donaldson, C. D., ed. (Princeton Aeronautical Paperbacks Ser.: Vol. 7). 1961. pap. 13.95 (ISBN 0-691-07968-4). Princeton U Pr.

Bird, R. Byron, et al. Transport Phenomena. LC 60-11717. 780p. 1960. 49.95x (ISBN 0-471-07392-X). Wiley.

Bird, R. M. & Slack, N. E. Residential Property Tax Relief in Ontario. (Ontario Economic Council Research Studies). 1978. 12.00 (ISBN 0-8020-3355-5). U of Toronto Pr.

Bird, Richard. A General Index of Japanese Art. LC 79-21840. (Heibonsha Survey of Japanese Art Ser.: No. 31). 1980. 17.50 (ISBN 0-8348-1031-X). Weatherhill.

Bird, Richard & Slack, Enid. Urban Public Finance. 160p. 1983. pap. 12.95 (ISBN 0-317-12268-1). Inst Real Estate.

Bird, Richard, compiled by. General Index: The Heibonsha Survey of Japanese Art, Vol. 31. 1980. 17.50 (ISBN 0-8348-1031-X, Pub. by John Weatherhill Inc Tokyo). C E Tuttle.

Bird, Richard & Oldman, Oliver, eds. Readings on Taxation in Developing Countries. 3rd ed. LC 74-24385. (Illus.). 624p. 1975. 30.00x (ISBN 0-8018-1693-9). Johns Hopkins.

Bird, Richard M. Bibliography on Taxation in Developing Countries. LC 68-20366. 198p. (Orig.). 1968. pap. 5.00x (ISBN 0-915506-08-4). Harvard Law Intl Tax.

--Central-Local Fiscal Relations & the Provision of Urban Public Services. LC 79-55416. (Centre for Research on Federal Financial Relations - Research Monograph: No. 30). 57p. (Orig.). 1980. pap. text ed. 8.00 (ISBN 0-908160-47-X, 0580). Australia N U P.

--The Growth of Public Employment in Canada. 190p. 1979. pap. text ed. 12.95x (ISBN 0-920380-17-4, Pub. by Inst Res Pub Canada). Brookfield Pub Co.

--Intergovernmental Finance in Colombia: Final Report of the Mission on Intergovernmental Finance. LC 83-22752. 434p. 1984. pap. 20.00x (ISBN 0-915506-28-9). Harvard Law Intl Tax.

--Taxing Agricultural Land in Developing Countries. LC 73-77991. (Harvard Law School International Tax Program Ser). 384p. 1974. 25.00x (ISBN 0-674-86855-2). Harvard U Pr.

--Taxing Corporations. 65p. 1980. pap. text ed. 6.95 (ISBN 0-686-78519-3, Pub. by Inst Res Pub Canada). Brookfield Pub Co.

Bird, Robert M. Calavar; or The Knight of the Conquest: A Romance of Mexico, 2 vols. LC 78-64061. Repr. of 1834 ed. 75.00 set (ISBN 0-404-17070-6). AMS Pr.

--The City Looking Glass: A Philadelphia Comedy. LC 74-177511. Repr. of 1933 ed. 20.00 (ISBN 0-405-08271-1, Blom Pubns.). Ayer Co Pubs.

--The Hawks of Hawk-Hollow: A Tale of Pennsylvania, 2 vols. LC 78-64062. Repr. of 1835 ed. 75.00 set (ISBN 0-404-17390-X). AMS Pr.

--The Infidel; or the Fall of Mexico. A Romance, 2 vols. LC 78-64064. Repr. of 1835 ed. Set. 75.00 (ISBN 0-404-17150-8). AMS Pr.

--Nick of the Woods. Dahl, Curtis, ed. (Masterworks of Literature Ser.). 1967. New Coll U Pr.

Bird, Roland T. Bones for Barnum Brown: Adventures of a Dinosaur Hunter. Schreiber, V. Theodore, ed. LC 84-24047. (Illus.). 192p. 1985. 29.95 (ISBN 0-87565-007-4); pap. 12.95 (ISBN 0-87565-011-2). Tex Christian.

Bird, Roy. Topeka: A Pictorial History. Friedman, Donna R., ed. LC 80-39669. (Illus.). 208p. pap. 13.95 cancelled (ISBN 0-89865-114-X). Donning Co.

Bird, Roy D. & Wallace, Douglass W. Witness of the Times, a History of Shawnee County. Richmond, Robert W., ed. LC 76-4390. 376p. 1976. 7.95 (ISBN 0-685-72361-5); pap. 8.95 (ISBN 0-916934-03-9). Shawnee County Hist.

Bird, Roy K. Wright Morris: Memory & Imagination. (American University Studies IV (English Language & Literature): Vol. 20). 149p. 1986. text ed. 21.00 (ISBN 0-8204-0181-1). P Lang Pubs.

Bird, Sarah. Do Evil Cheerfully. 192p. 1983. pap. 2.95 (ISBN 0-380-84137-1, 84137-1). Avon.

Bird, Stewart & Robilotta, Peter. The Wobblies. (Orig.). 1980. pap. 3.95 (ISBN 0-918266-13-0). Smyrna.

Bird, Stewart, et al. Solidarity Forever: An Oral History of the I. W. W. LC 84-82491. (Illus.). 256p. 1985. 25.00x (ISBN 0-941702-11-1); pap. 9.95 (ISBN 0-941702-12-X). Lake View Pr.

Bird, Stuart L. Converting to Timex-Sinclair BASIC. 206p. 1983. spiral binding 14.95 (ISBN 0-88006-063-8, BK7396). Green Pub Inc.

Bird, Thomas E., ed. Foreign Language Learning: Research & Development. Incl. The Classroom Revisited. Simches, Seymour O; Innovative Foreign Language Programs. Andrews, Oliver, Jr; Liberated Expression. Edgerton, F. Mills. 118p. 1968. pap. 7.95x (ISBN 0-915432-68-4). NE Conf Teach Foreign.

--Foreign Languages: Reading, Literature, Requirements. Incl. The Teaching of Reading. Moulton, William G; The Times & Places for Literature. Paquette, F. Andre; Trends in Foreign Language Requirements & Placement. Gummere, John F. 124p. 1967. pap. 7.95x (ISBN 0-915432-67-6). NE Conf Teach Foreign.

--Modern Theologians, Christians & Jews. 2nd ed. 1967. 15.95 (ISBN 0-268-00183-9). U of Notre Dame Pr.

Bird, Tom, jt. auth. see Marshall, Merlin.

Bird, Tom, jt. auth. see Stargell, Willie.

Bird, Viola, et al. Order Procedures. (AALL Publications Ser.: No. 2). v, 66p. (Orig.). 1960. pap. 8.50x (ISBN 0-8377-0102-3). Rothman.

Bird, Vivian. Ward Lock Guide: Shakespeare Country & the Cotswolds. 192p. 1982. pap. 9.95 (ISBN 0-7063-6153-9, Pub. by Auto Assn-British Tourist Authority England). Merrimack Pub Cir.

Bird, W. R. The Misadventures of Rufus Burdy. 1975. 7.95 (ISBN 0-07-082240-9). McGraw.

Bird, Wendell R., jt. auth. see Whitehead, John W.

Bird, William. Drawings & Sketches of Oxford. (Illus.). 32p. 1985. 7.95 (ISBN 0-907540-31-7, Pub. by Salamander Pr). Merrimack Pub Cir.

Birdi, K. S., jt. auth. see Chattoraj, D. K.

Birdmann, G. English-German, German, English Solid State Physics & Electronics Dictionary. 1103p. (Eng. & Ger.). 1980. 100.00x (ISBN 0-569-07204-2, Pub. by Collet's). State Mutual Bk.

Birds, John. Reminders for Company Secretaries. 23rd ed. 90.00x (ISBN 0-85308-048-8, Pub. by Jordan & Sons England); Supplement 1980. 20.00x (ISBN 0-85308-056-9). State Mutual Bk.

Birdsall. Plasma Physics via Computer. 512p. 1983. text ed. 45.00 (ISBN 0-07-005371-5). McGraw.

Birdsall, Charles K. & Bridges, William B. Electron Dynamics of Diode Regions. (Electrical Science Ser). 1966. 62.50 (ISBN 0-12-099850-5). Acad Pr.

Birdsall, Clair M. The United States Branch Mint at Dahlonega, Georgia: Its History and Coinage. (Illus.). 122p. 27.50. Southern Hist Pr.

Birdsall, Eric, ed. see Wordsworth, William.

Birdsall, Nancy. Population & Poverty in the Developing World. (Working Paper: No. 404). 96p. 1980. 5.00 (ISBN 0-686-36200-4, WP-0404). World Bank.

Birdsall, Richard D. Berkshire County: A Cultural History. LC 77-18827. (Illus.). 1978. Repr. of 1959 ed. lib. bdg. 31.50x (ISBN 0-313-20218-4, BIBC). Greenwood.

Birdsall, S. S. & Florin, J. W. Regional Landscapes of the United States & Canada. 2nd ed. 497p. 1981. 36.00 (ISBN 0-471-06064-X). Wiley.

Birdsall, Stephen S. Regional Landscapes of the United States & Canada. 3rd ed. Florin, John W., ed. 457p. 1985. 32.95 (ISBN 0-471-88490-1). Wiley.

Birdsall, Steve. The B-17 Flying Fortress. LC 65-16862. (Famous Aircraft Ser.). (Illus.). 1979. pap. 6.95 (ISBN 0-8168-5646-X). Aero.

--B-24 in Action. (Aircraft in Action Ser.). (Illus.). 50p. 1984. pap. 4.95 (ISBN 0-89747-020-6, 1021). Squad Sig Pubns.

--The B-24 Liberator. Gentle, Ernest J., ed. LC 67-14200. (The Famous Aircraft Ser.). (Illus.). 64p. 1985. pap. 7.95 (ISBN 0-8168-5657-5). Aero.

--Superfortress-The Boeing B-29. (Illus.). 1984. pap. 7.95 (ISBN 0-89747-104-0, 6028). Squad Sig Pubns.

Birdsall, Virginia O. Defoe's Perpetual Seekers. LC 83-46154. 208p. 1985. 26.50 (ISBN 0-8387-5076-1). Bucknell U Pr.

Birdsall, William Filfred & Jones, Rufus M. The Literature of American & Our Favorite Authors. 1897. Repr. 50.00 (ISBN 0-8274-2964-9). R West.

Birdsall, William W. & Jones, Rufus, eds. The Literature of America & Our Favorite Authors: Containing the Lives of Our Noted American & Favorite English Authors. 672p. 1983. Repr. of 1983 ed. lib. bdg. 200.00 (ISBN 0-89987-954-3). Darby Bks.

Birdsell, J. B. Human Evolution. 3rd ed. 1981. 29.50 (ISBN 0-395-30784-8); instr's manual 1.50 (ISBN 0-395-30785-6). HM.

Birdsell, J. B., et al, eds. Occasional Papers in Human Biology, Vol. 2. (Illus.). 1979. pap. text ed. 13.00x (ISBN 0-391-00998-2). Humanities.

Birdsell, Sandra. Night Travellers. 192p. 1984. pap. 3.95 (ISBN 0-7736-7068-8). Beaufort Bks NY.

Birdseye, Clarence & Birdseye, Eleanor. Growing Woodland Plants. (Illus.). 1972. pap. 4.50 (ISBN 0-486-20661-0). Dover.

Birdseye, Clarence & Birdseye, Eleanor G. Growing Woodland Plants. (Illus.). 13.00 (ISBN 0-8446-4510-9). Peter Smith.

Birdseye, Eleanor, jt. auth. see Birdseye, Clarence.

Birdseye, Eleanor G., jt. auth. see Birdseye, Clarence.

Birdsong, Craig W., jt. auth. see Stinnett, Nick.

Birdsong, Robert E. Achieving Total Self-Awareness: A Discourse on Discipline. (Aquarian Academy Monograph, Series A: Lecture No. 3). 1975. pap. 1.25 (ISBN 0-917108-09-4). Sirius Bks.

--Adamic Christianity: Questions & Answers, Vol. 1. 1978. pap. 3.75 (ISBN 0-917108-22-1). Sirius Bks.

--The Anatomy of Transition: The Process of Dying & the Mechanics of Death. (Aquarian Academy Monograph, Series E.: Lecture No. 2). 1974. pap. 1.25 (ISBN 0-917108-02-7). Sirius Bks.

--Animatics: The Nature & Function of the Human Soul. (Aquarian Academy Monograph, Series D: Lecture No. 1). 1975. pap. 1.25 (ISBN 0-917108-07-8). Sirius Bks.

--The Challenge of the Aquarian Age. (Aquarian Academy Monograph, Ser. A: Lecture No. 7). 1978. pap. 1.25 (ISBN 0-917108-25-6). Sirius Bks.

--Common Obstacles to Personal Progress. (Aquarian Academy Monograph, Series A: Lecture No. 5). 1976. pap. 1.25 (ISBN 0-917108-15-9). Sirius Bks.

--Constructive Self-Criticism: True & False Values. (Aquarian Academy Monograph, Series E: Lecture No. 3). 1975. pap. 1.25 (ISBN 0-917108-10-8). Sirius Bks.

--Cosmic Cooperation: Aid for the Asking. (Aquarian Academy Monograph: Ser. E, No. 7). 1977. pap. 1.50 (ISBN 0-917108-18-3). Sirius Bks.

--Destination Earth: Re-Entry into Physical Experience. (Aquarian Academy Supplementary Lecture Ser.: No. 4). 1980. pap. 1.25 (ISBN 0-917108-30-2). Sirius Bks.

--Four-Dimensional Values & Their Attainment. (Aquarian Academy Monograph: No. E 5). 17p. (Orig.). 1981. pap. 1.25 (ISBN 0-917108-33-7). Sirius Bks.

--Fundamentals of Adamic Christianity. (Aquarian Academy Monograph, Series A: Lecture No. 1). 1974. pap. 1.25 (ISBN 0-917108-00-0). Sirius Bks.

--The Hermetic Commandments in Today's World. (Aquarian Academy Monograph, Ser. F: Lecture No. 7). 1977. pap. 1.25 (ISBN 0-917108-19-1). Sirius Bks.

--Introspection-Panacea or Pitfall? (Aquarian Academy Supplementary Lecture No. 1: No. 1). 1975. pap. 0.75 (ISBN 0-917108-16-7). Sirius Bks.

--Mission to Mankind: A Cosmic Autobiography. LC 74-18195. 1975. 6.35 (ISBN 0-917108-12-4); pap. 3.50 (ISBN 0-917108-08-6). Sirius Bks.

--Paths to Human Perfection. (Aquarian Academy Supplementary Lecture: No. 3). 1979. pap. 0.75 (ISBN 0-917108-26-4). Sirius Bks.

--Physical Experience & Karmic Liability. (Aquarian Academy Monograph: Ser. A, Lecture No. 6). 38p. 1977. pap. 1.50 (ISBN 0-917108-20-5). Sirius Bks.

--Positive Application of Racial Qualities: Color As a Growth Factor. (Aquarian Academy Monograph: Ser. F, No. 6). 1980. pap. 1.50 (ISBN 0-917108-31-0). Sirius Bks.

--Positive Behavior Patterns. (Aquarian Academy Monography: Suppl. Lecture No. 2). 1978. pap. text ed. 1.00 (ISBN 0-917108-21-3). Sirius Bks.

--Positive Egocentricity: Aquarian Academy Monograph. (Aquarian Academy Monograph). 1978. pap. 1.25x (ISBN 0-917108-23-X). Sirius Bks.

--The Revelations of Hermes: An Exposition of Adamic Christianity. LC 74-84553. (Illus.). 1975. 10.00 (ISBN 0-917108-11-6); pap. 6.95 (ISBN 0-917108-04-3). Sirius Bks.

--Ritual & Reality. (Aquarian Academy Monograph, Series F: Lecture No. 1). 1975. pap. 1.25 (ISBN 0-917108-05-1). Sirius Bks.

--Sapientology: The Nature & Function of the Human Spirit. (Aquarian Academy Monograph, Series C: Lecture No. 1). 1975. pap. 1.25 (ISBN 0-917108-06-X). Sirius Bks.

--Self-Realignment. (Aquarian Academy Monograph, Series E: Lecture No. 1). 1974. pap. 1.25 (ISBN 0-917108-01-9). Sirius Bks.

--Sensory Awareness & Psychic Manifestation. LC 78-65000. (Orig.). 1978. pap. text ed. 4.75 (ISBN 0-917108-24-8). Sirius Bks.

--Soul Mates: The Facts & the Fallacies. (Aquarian Academy Supplementary Lecture Ser.: No. 9). 22p. (Orig.). 1980. pap. 1.25 (ISBN 0-917108-32-9). Sirius Bks.

--Steps on the Path: Daily Words of Wisdom. 1975. pap. 2.75 (ISBN 0-917108-13-2). Sirius Bks.

--To Those Who Seek. (Aquarian Academy Monograph, Series A: Lecture No. 2). 1974. pap. 1.25 (ISBN 0-917108-03-5). Sirius Bks.

--Truth As a Way of Life. (Aquarian Academy Monograph: Ser. F, Lecture No. 3). 1977. pap. 1.50 (ISBN 0-917108-17-5). Sirius Bks.

--Value Analysis. (Aquarian Academy Monograph, Series A: Lecture No. 4). 1975. pap. 1.25 (ISBN 0-917108-14-0). Sirius Bks.

--Way of the Immortal Threefold Self: The Straight Path. (Aquarian Academy Monograph: Ser. E, No. 4). 1980. pap. 1.45 (ISBN 0-917108-29-9). Sirius Bks.

--Way of the Soul: The "Heart Path" to Human Perfection. (Aquarian Academy Monograph: Ser. D, No. 2). 1980. pap. 1.45 (ISBN 0-917108-28-0). Sirius Bks.

--Way of the Spirit: The "Head Path" to Human Perfection, Ser. C, No. 2. (Aquarian Academy Monograph). 1980. pap. 1.45 (ISBN 0-917108-27-2). Sirius Bks.

Birdsong, Sam. Weather or Not: A Study of Weather Control. pap. 3.50 (ISBN 0-918700-09-4). Duverus Pub.

Birdwell, Russell. Mount Horeb. LC 77-187991. (Illus.). 104p. 1972. 8.85 (ISBN 0-8315-0122-7). Speller.

Birdwhistell, Ray L. Kinesics & Context: Essays on Body Motion Communication. LC 77-122379. (Conduct & Communication Ser.: No. 2). 1970. pap. 12.95x (ISBN 0-8122-1012-3, Pa Paperbks). U of Pa Pr.

Birdwhistell, Terry L., ed. see Allen, Susan E.

Birdwood, G., jt. ed. see Beaconsfield, R.

Birdwood, G., ed. see Goblet D'Alviella, Eugene F.

Birdwood, George F., jt. ed. see Elsdon-Dew, Robin W.

Birdwood, Lord. Khaki & Gown. 10.00 (ISBN 0-8315-0041-7). Speller.

Birdzell, L. E., Jr., jt. auth. see Rosenberg, Nathan.

Bireley, Robert S. J. Religion & Politics in the Age of the Counterreformation: Emperor Ferdinand II, William Lamormaini, S.J., & the Formation of Imperial Policy. LC 80-27334. xiii, 311p. 1981. 28.00x (ISBN 0-8078-1470-9). U of NC Pr.

Birenbaum, Arnold. Health Care & Society. LC 80-67092. 272p. 1981. text ed. 29.95x (ISBN 0-916672-57-3). Allanheld.

Birenbaum, Arnold & Cohen, Herbert J. Community Services for the Mentally Retarded. LC 84-15905. (Illus.). 208p. 1985. 29.95x (ISBN 0-86598-151-5). Rowman & Allanheld.

Birenbaum, Barbara. The Gooblins Night. (Holidays Adventure of Kindl Ser.: No. 1). (Illus.). 40p. 1985. PLB 5.95 (ISBN 0-935343-31-8). Peartree.

Birenbaum, Harvey. Tragedy & Innocence. LC 82-23828. (Illus.). 176p. (Orig.). 1983. lib. bdg. 23.50 (ISBN 0-8191-2991-7); pap. text ed. 11.00 (ISBN 0-8191-2992-5). U Pr of Amer.

Birge, E. A. Bacterial & Bacteriophage Genetics: An Introduction. (Springer Ser. in Microbiology). (Illus.). 359p. (Corrected 2nd printing). 1981. 29.50 (ISBN 0-387-90504-9). Springer-Verlag.

Birge, Edward B. History of Public School Music in the United States. 323p. 1985. Repr. of 1937 ed. 9.00 (ISBN 0-686-37916-0, 1020). Music Ed Natl.

Birge, Jack E. Murder Without Death. LC 81-90064. 422p. (Orig.). 1981. pap. 10.95 (ISBN 0-940946-00-9). JEB Pub.

Birge, John K. The Bektashi Order of Dervishes. LC 77-87662. Repr. of 1937 ed. 35.00 (ISBN 0-404-16400-5). AMS Pr.

Birge, Priscilla. Photo Extensions: Selected Work Utilizing Photographic Images. LC 77-80646. (Illus.). 3.50 (ISBN 0-918326-01-X). Art Adventure.

Birger, Boris, illus. Boris Birger: Catalogue, Oil Paintings. (Illus.). 64p. 1975. pap. 5.00 (ISBN 0-88233-081-0). Ardis Pubs.

Birglen, J. H. Van see Van Birglen, J. H. & Hartzuiker, J. Y.

Biringuccio, Vannoccio. Pirotechnia. 1966. pap. 6.95x (ISBN 0-262-52017-6). MIT Pr.

Birjukov, A. P., et al. Sixteen Papers on Number Theory & Algebra. LC 51-5559. (Translations Ser.: No. 2, Vol. 82). 1969. 35.00 (ISBN 0-8218-1782-5, TRANS 2-82). Am Math.

Birjukov, B. V. Two Soviet Studies on Frege. Angelelli, Ignacio, tr. from Rus. (Sovietica Ser.: No. 15). 101p. 1964. lib. bdg. 18.50 (ISBN 90-277-0072-9, Pub by Reidel Holland). Kluwer Academic.

Birk, Ann W., jt. ed. see Bassuk, Ellen L.

Birk, Dorothy D. The World Came to St. Louis: A Visit to the 1904 World's Fair. (Illus.). 1979. 10.95 (ISBN 0-8272-4213-1). CBP.

Birk, Genevieve B., jt. auth. see Birk, Newman P.

Birk, Genevieve G, jt. auth. see Birk, Newman P.

Birk, L. S., jt. ed. see Herglotz, H. K.

Birk, Lance A. The Paphiopedilum Grower's Manual. (Illus.). 208p. 1984. 75.00x (ISBN 0-9612826-0-6). Pisang Pr.

Birk, Lee, ed. Biofeedback: Behavioral Medicine: A "Seminars in Psychiatry" Reprint. 210p. 1974. 42.00 (ISBN 0-8089-0832-4, 790595). Grune.

Birk, Newman P. & Birk, Genevieve B. Practice for Understanding & Using English: Eighty Exercises. 2nd ed. LC 71-189751. 1972. pap. 7.20 scp (ISBN 0-672-63291-8). Odyssey Pr.

--Practice for Understanding & Using English: Eighty Exercises Workbook. 2nd ed. 168p. 1972. pap. text ed. write for info (ISBN 0-02-310090-7). Macmillan.

--Understanding & Using English. 5th ed. LC 71-179751. 1972. scp 18.76 (ISBN 0-672-63214-4). Odyssey Pr.

Birk, Newman P. & Birk, Genevieve G. Understanding & Using English. 5th ed. 1972. pap. text ed. write for info. (ISBN 0-02-310050-8). Macmillan.

Birkbeck, John. Toward Earnestness of Soul. LC 83-80409. 88p. (Orig.). 1983. pap. 4.50 (ISBN 0-8358-0459-3). Upper Room.

Birkbeck, Morris. Letters from Illinois. LC 68-8685. (American Scene Ser). 1970. Repr. of 1818 ed. lib. bdg. 24.50 (ISBN 0-306-71170-2). Da Capo.

--Letters from Illinois & Notes of a Journey in America. 3rd ed. LC 71-119545. Repr. of 1818 ed. 37.50x (ISBN 0-678-00686-5). Kelley.

Birkby, Phyllis, et al, eds. Amazon Expedition: A Lesbian-Feminist Anthology. LC 73-79902. (Illus.). 96p. (Orig.). 1973. 6.50 (ISBN 0-87810-526-3); pap. 3.00 (ISBN 0-87810-026-1). Times Change.

Birke, Adolf M. & Kluxen, Kurt, eds. Church, State & Society in the Nineteenth Century. (Prince Albert Studies: Vol. 2). 130p. 1984. lib. bdg. 24.00 (ISBN 3-598-21402-2). K G Saur.

Birke, L., jt. auth. see Archer, J.

Birke, Lynda & Gardner, Katy. Why Suffer? Periods & Their Problems. 76p. 1983. pap. 3.95 (ISBN 0-86068-284-6, Pub. by Virago Pr). Merrimack Pub Cir.

Birkeland, Joran, tr. see Undset, Sigrid.

Birkeland, Jorgen, jt. ed. see Bowman, Craig T.

Birkeland, Peter W. Soils & Geomorphology. (Illus.). 1984. text ed. 37.50x (ISBN 0-19-503398-1); pap. 22.95x (ISBN 0-19-503435-X). Oxford U Pr.

Birkeland, Peter W. & Larson, Edwin E., eds. Putnam's Geology. 4th ed. (Illus.). 1982. text ed. 27.95x (ISBN 0-19-503002-8); tchr's manual avail. (ISBN 0-19-503004-4); study guide 8.95x (ISBN 0-19-503003-6). Oxford U Pr.

Birkeland, Torger. Echoes of Puget Sound: Fifty Years of Logging & Steamboating. (Shorey Historical Ser.). (Illus.). 252p. pap. 9.95 (ISBN 0-8466-0315-2). Shorey.

Birkelbach, Aubrey W. A Sampler of New England Land Use. 1975. pap. 2.00 (ISBN 0-686-17294-9). Lincoln Inst Land.

Birkelbach, Aubrey W., Jr. & Wassall, Gregory H. The Case Against the Sale of Development Rights of Connecticut's Agricultural Land. 1975. pap. text ed. 1.00 (ISBN 0-686-23012-4). Lincoln Inst Land.

Birkenbihl, Michael. Train the Trainer: In Effective Course Design & Presentation. 201p. 1977. pap. text ed. 19.95x (ISBN 0-86238-045-6, Pub. by Chartwell-Bratt England). Brookfield Pub Co.

Birkenhager, W. H., et al, eds. Control Mechanisms in Essential Hypertension. 2nd, rev., enl. ed. 358p. 1982. 98.75 (ISBN 0-444-80405-6, Biomedical Pr). Elsevier.

--Adrenergic Blood Pressure Regulation: Proceedings of the Symposium Corfu. 22-25 May 1984. (Current Clinical Practice Ser.: Vol 14). 258p. 1985. 68.75 (ISBN 0-444-90408-5, Excerpta Medica). Elsevier.

Birkenhead. Contemporary Personalities. LC 69-17562. (Essay Index Reprint Ser.). 326p. Repr. of 1924 ed. lib. bdg. 16.00 (ISBN 0-8290-0480-7). Irvington.

--Fifty Famous Fights in Fact & Fiction. 1932. Repr. 20.00 (ISBN 0-8274-2344-6). R West.

--John Betjeman's Collected Poems. pap. 8.95 (ISBN 0-318-03135-3, Pub. by Salem Hse Ltd). Merrimack Pub Cir.

Birkenhead, Frederick E. America Revisited. facs. ed. LC 68-16911. (Essay Index Reprint Ser.). 1968. Repr. of 1924 ed. 17.00 (ISBN 0-8369-0212-2). Ayer Co Pubs.

--Contemporary Personalities. facsimile ed. LC 69-17562. (Essay Index Reprint Ser.). 1924. 19.00 (ISBN 0-8369-0061-8). Ayer Co Pubs.

--Last Essays. facsimile ed. LC 78-104996. (Essay Index Reprint Ser.). 1930. 25.50 (ISBN 0-8369-1546-1). Ayer Co Pubs.

--Law, Life & Letters, 2 Vols. facsimile ed. LC 71-10997. (Essay Index Reprint Ser.). Repr. of 1927 ed. 39.50 (ISBN 0-8369-1450-3). Ayer Co Pubs.

--Points of View, 2 Vols. facsimile ed. LC 77-111815. (Essay Index Reprint Ser.). 1923. 36.50 (ISBN 0-8369-1594-1). Ayer Co Pubs.

--Turning Points in History. facsimile ed. LC 78-86730. (Essay Index Reprint Ser). 1930. 24.50 (ISBN 0-8369-1246-2). Ayer Co Pubs.

Birkenhead, Sheila. Against Oblivion, the Life of Joseph Severn. 244p. 1981. Repr. of 1943 ed. lib. bdg. 30.00 (ISBN 0-89984-066-3). Century Bookbindery.

Birkenmaier, Willy, ed. Studies in Descriptive Russian Grammar. (Studies in Descriptive Linguistics: No. 8). iv, 120p. (Orig.). 1983. pap. 15.00x (ISBN 3-87276-246-X, Pub. by J Groos W Germany). Benjamins North Am.

Birkenmayer, Sigmund & Folejewski, Zbigniew. Introduction to the Polish Language: Enlarged. 3rd rev. ed. LC 76-26367. (Illus.). 1978. pap. 8.00 (ISBN 0-917004-11-6). Kosciuszko.

Birker, D., tr. see Kaiser, Artur.

Birkerts, Gunnar. Gunnar Birkerts Buildings, Projects & Thoughts, 1960 to 1985. LC 85-50641. (Illus.). 96p. (Orig.). 1985. pap. 23.50 (ISBN 0-9614792-0-5). U Mich Arch.

Birket, James. Some Cursory Remarks. facs. ed. LC 77-150169. (Select Bibliographies Reprint Ser). 1916. 12.00 (ISBN 0-8369-5682-6). Ayer Co Pubs.

Birket-Smith, Kaj. Anthropological Observations on the Central Eskimos. Calvert, W. E., tr. LC 76-22525. (Thule Expedition, 1921-24: Vol. 3, No. 2). (Illus.). Repr. of 1928 ed. 42.50 (ISBN 0-404-58312-1). AMS Pr.

--The Caribou Eskimos. LC 76-21702. (Thule Expedition Ser.: Vol. 5). Repr. of 1929 ed. 137.50 (ISBN 0-404-58316-4). AMS Pr.

--Contributions to Chipewyan Ethnology. LC 76-21701. (Thule Expedition Ser.: Vol. 6, No. 3). Repr. of 1930 ed. 38.50 (ISBN 0-404-58319-9). AMS Pr.

--Ethnographical Collections from the Northwest Passage. Calvert, W. E., tr. LC 76-21697. (Thule Expedition Ser.: Vol. 6 No. 2). (Illus.). Repr. of 1945 ed. 82.00 (ISBN 0-404-58318-0). AMS Pr.

--Ethnography of the Egedesminde District, with Aspects of the General Culture of West Greenland. LC 74-5827. (Illus.). Repr. of 1924 ed. 73.00 (ISBN 0-404-11630-2). AMS Pr.

--Five Hundred Eskimo Words. LC 76-21770. (Thule Expedition, 5th, 1921-24: Vol. 3, No. 3). Repr. of 1928 ed. 25.00 (ISBN 0-404-58313-X). AMS Pr.

--Geographical Notes on the Barren Grounds. LC 76-21642. (Thule Expedition, 5th, 1921-24: Vol. 1, No. 4). (Illus.). Repr. of 1933 ed. 32.50 (ISBN 0-404-58304-0). AMS Pr.

--Paths of Culture: A General Ethnology. Fennow, Karin, tr. LC 64-8488. (Illus.). 550p. 1965. 27.50x (ISBN 0-299-03381-3). U of Wis Pr.

--The Paths of Culture: A General Ethnology. LC 64-8488. pap. 137.00 (ISBN 0-317-09286-3, 2015354). Bks Demand UMI.

Birket-Smith, Kaj & De Laguna, Frederica. The Eyak Indians of the Copper River Delta, Alaska. LC 74-7932. (Illus.). Repr. of 1938 ed. 42.50 (ISBN 0-404-11817-8). AMS Pr.

Birkett, G. A., ed. see Boronina, E.

Birkett, G. A., ed. see Ehrenburg, Ilya.

Birkett, G. A., ed. see Fedin, Konstantine.

Birkett, G. A., ed. see Gorky, Maxim.

Birkett, Mary E. Lamartine & the Poetics of Landscape. LC 82-82427. (French Forum Monographs: No. 38). 105p. 1982. pap. 10.00x (ISBN 0-917058-37-2). French Forum.

Birkey, Verna. You Are Very Special: A Biblical Guide to Self-Worth. 160p. 1977. pap. 5.95 (ISBN 0-8007-5032-2, Power Bks). Revell.

Birkey, Verna & Turnquist, Jeanette. Building Happy Memories & Family Traditions. (Illus.). 128p. 1983. 4.95 (ISBN 0-8007-5109-4, Power Bks). Revell.

--A Mother's Answer Book. 160p. (Orig.). 1983. pap. 5.95 (ISBN 0-8007-5127-2, Power Bks.). Revell.

--A Mother's Problem Solver. 128p. 1979. pap. 5.95 (ISBN 0-8007-5050-0, Power Bks). Revell.

Birkhaeuser, H. & Fox, W., eds. Advances in Tuberculosis Research, Vol. 20. (Illus.). 1980. 30.00 (ISBN 3-8055-2954-6). S Karger.

Birkhaeuser, H., et al, eds. Advances in Tuberculosis Research, Vol. 17. (Bibliotheca Tuberculosea et Medicinae Thoracalis: No. 26). 1970. 36.75 (ISBN 3-8055-0364-4). S Karger.

--Advances in Tuberculosis Research, Vol. 18. 1972. 41.75 (ISBN 3-8055-1301-1). S Karger.

Birkhauser-Boston Publishing. The Herbst-Readett Three-Language Dictionaries of Commerce, Finance & Law, 3 Vols. (Eng., Ger. & Fr.). 1983. Vol. 1 1979 English-German-French. 98.95 (ISBN 0-686-87520-6); Vol. 2 1982 German-English-French. 98.95 (ISBN 0-686-87521-4); Vol. 3 1983 French-English-German. 98.95 (ISBN 0-686-87522-2). Birkhauser.

--The Herbst-Readett Two-Language Dictionaries of Finance, Commerce & Law, 2 vols. (Eng. & Ger.). 1976. Vol. 1 1975 English-German. 24.95 (ISBN 0-686-87523-0); Vol. 2 1976 German-English. 24.95 (ISBN 3-85942-004-6). Birkhauser.

Birkhauser, Kaspar. Light from the Darkness: Paintings by Peter Birkhauser. Wertenschlag, Eva, ed. (Illus.). 80p. (English, German.). 1980. pap. 20.95x (ISBN 0-8176-1190-8, Dist. by Sigo Pr). Birkhauser.

Birkhead, Alice. Heroes of Modern Europe. facs. ed. LC 67-22073. (Essay Index Reprint Ser.). 1913. 15.00 (ISBN 0-8369-0213-0). Ayer Co Pubs.

--Heroes of Modern Europe. (Essay Index Reprint Ser.). (Illus.). 239p. Repr. of 1913 ed. text ed. 12.00 (ISBN 0-8290-0525-0). Irvington.

Birkhead, Edith. Christina Rossetti & Her Poetry. LC 75-148751. Repr. of 1930 ed. 7.25 (ISBN 0-404-52503-2). AMS Pr.

--Christina Rossetti & Her Poetry. 1978. Repr. of 1930 ed. lib. bdg. 7.50 (ISBN 0-8495-0426-0). Arden Lib.

Birkhead, Tim R., jt. ed. see Nettleship, David N.

Birkhimer, William E. Historical Sketch of the Organization, Administration, Materiel & Tactics of the Artillery, United States Army. LC 68-54788. Repr. of 1884 ed. lib. bdg. 19.75x (ISBN 0-8371-0314-2, BIAR). Greenwood.

Birkhoff, Barbara. As Between Friends: Criticism of Themselves & One Another in the Letters of Coleridge, Wordsworth & Lamb. LC 73-10246. 1930. lib. bdg. 15.00 (ISBN 0-8414-3181-7). Folcroft.

Birkhoff, G., ed. see Society for Industrial & Applied Mathematics-American Mathematical Society Symposia-N.C.-April, 1968.

Birkhoff, G., ed. see Symposium in Applied Mathematics, New York, 1957.

Birkhoff, G., ed. see Symposium in Applied Mathematics-New York-1959.

Birkhoff, Garrett. Hydrodynamics: A Study in Logic, Fact, & Similitude. LC 77-18143. (Illus.). 1978. Repr. of 1960 ed. lib. bdg. 24.75x (ISBN 0-313-20118-8, BIHY). Greenwood.

--The Numerical Solution of Elliptic Equations. (CBMS-NSF Regional Conference Ser.: No. 1). xi, 82p. (Orig.). 1972. pap. text ed. 8.00 (ISBN 0-89871-001-4). Soc Indus-Appl Math.

--A Source Book in Classical Analysis. LC 72-85144. (Source Books in the History of the Sciences Ser). 488p. 1973. text ed. 27.50x (ISBN 0-674-82245-5). Harvard U Pr.

Birkhoff, Garrett & Gian-Carlo Rota. Ordinary Differential Equations. 3rd ed. LC 78-8304. 350p. 1978. text ed. 42.50x (ISBN 0-471-07411-X). Wiley.

Birkhoff, Garrett & Lynch, Robert E. Numerical Solution of Elliptic Problems. LC 84-51823. (SIAM Studies in Applied Mathematics: No. 6). (Illus.). xi, 319p. 1984. text ed. 31.50 (ISBN 0-89871-197-5). Soc Indus Appl Math.

Birkhoff, Garrett & MacLane, Saunders. Survey of Modern Algebra. 4th ed. 1977. text ed. write for info. (ISBN 0-02-310070-2, 31007). Macmillan.

Birkhoff, Garrett & Scheonstadt, Arthur. Elliptic Problem Solvers, No. II: Symposium. 1984. 44.00 (ISBN 0-12-100560-7). Acad Pr.

Birkhoff, Garrett, jt. auth. see MacLane, Saunders.

Birkhoff, Garrett, ed. see Society for Industrial & Applied Mathematics - American Mathematical Society Symposia - New York - March, 1971.

Birkhoff, Garrett D. Dynamical Systems. rev. ed. LC 28-28411. (Colloquium Pubns Ser.: Vol. 9). 313p. 1983. Repr. of 1927 ed. 27.00 (ISBN 0-8218-1009-X, COLL-9). Am Math.

--Lattice Theory. rev. ed. LC 66-23707. (Colloquium Pubns. Ser.: Vol. 25). 418p. 1979. pap. 39.00 (ISBN 0-8218-1025-1, COLL-25). Am Math.

Birkhoff, George D. & Beatley, R. Basic Geometry. 3rd ed. LC 59-7308. (gr. 9-12). 1959. text ed. 12.00 (ISBN 0-8284-0120-9); tchr's. manual 2.50 (ISBN 0-8284-0034-2); answer bk. 1.50 (ISBN 0-8284-0162-4). Chelsea Pub.

Birkin, Stanley J., jt. auth. see Sanders, Donald H.

Birkin, Stanley J., jt. ed. see Walsh, Ruth M.

Birkinshaw, Elsye. Think Slim-Be Slim. rev. ed. LC 80-7115. (Illus.). 144p. (Orig.). 1981. pap. 5.95 (ISBN 0-912800-91-7). Woodbridge Pr.

--Turn off Your Age. LC 79-27693. 1980. pap. 7.95 (ISBN 0-912800-77-1). Woodbridge Pr.

Birkland, Carol. Finding Home: A Guide to Solidarity with the World's Uprooted. (Orig.). 1983. pap. write for info. (ISBN 0-377-00129-5); 4.95. Friend Pr.

Birkle, John & Yearsley, Ronald. Computer Applications in Management. 1975. 90.00 (ISBN 0-286-61861-3, Pub. by MCB Pubns). State Mutual Bk.

Birkmaier, Emma. Foreign Language Education: An Overview. (ACTFL Review Ser.: Vol. 1). 1972. pap. text ed. 10.00 (ISBN 0-8442-9312-1). Natl Textbk.

Birkmayer, J. G. Tumorbiologie. (Illus.). viii, 230p. 1984. 24.25 (ISBN 3-8055-3892-8). S Karger.

Birkmayer, W. Epileptic Siezures-Behaviour-Pain. 372p. 1976. 39.00 (ISBN 3-456-80271-4, Pub. by Holdan Bk Ltd UK). State Mutual Bk.

--Spasticity: A Topical Survey. 218p. 1972. 69.00 (ISBN 3-456-00390-0, Pub. by Holdan Bk Ltd UK). State Mutual Bk.

Birkmayer, W. & Riederer, P. Parkinson's Disease: Biochemistry, Clinical Pathology, & Treatment. Reynolds, G., tr. from Ger. (Illus.). 194p. 1983. 41.00 (ISBN 0-387-81722-0). Springer-Verlag.

Birkmayer, W. & Duvoism, R. C., eds. Extrapyramidal Disorders. (Illus.). 340p. 1983. 55.20 (ISBN 0-387-81756-5). Springer-Verlag.

Birkmire, William H. Skeleton Construction in Buildings. LC 72-5035. (Technology & Society Ser.). (Illus.). 200p. 1972. Repr. of 1894 ed. 19.00 (ISBN 0-405-04688-X). Ayer Co Pubs.

Birkner, Lawrence R. Respiratory Protection Program: A Manual & Guideline. 93p. 1980. 14.00 (ISBN 0-932627-14-5); members 11.50 (ISBN 0-317-32859-X). Am Indus Hygiene.

Birkner, Michael J. Samuel L. Southard: Jeffersonian Whig. LC 82-48517. Date not set. 32.50 (ISBN 0-8386-3160-6). Fairleigh Dickinson.

--Samuel Southard. LC 82-48517. 272p. 1984. Fairleigh Dickinson.

Birkner, Michael J., ed. see Webster, Daniel.

Birkner, Rudolf. Normal Radiologic Patterns & Variances of the Human Skeleton: An X-Ray Atlas of Adults & Children. LC 78-692. (Illus.). 574p. 1978. text ed. 78.00 (ISBN 0-8067-0211-7). Urban & S.

Birkofer, L. Organic Chemistry: Syntheses & Reactivity. (Topics in Current Chemistry Ser.: Vol. 88). (Illus.). 200p. 1980. 61.00 (ISBN 0-387-09817-8). Springer-Verlag.

Birkos, Alexander S. Soviet Cinema: Directors & Films. (Illus.). x, 344p. (Orig.). 1976. 25.00 (ISBN 0-208-01581-7, Archon). Shoe String.

Birkos, Alexander S. & Tambs, Lewis A. Historiography, Method, History Teaching: A Bibliography of Books & Articles in English, 1965-1973. xi, 130p. 1975. 15.00 (ISBN 0-208-01420-9, Linnet). Shoe String.

Birks, C. J. Information Services in the Market Place. 1978. 40.00x (ISBN 0-905984-16-1, Pub. by Brit Lib England). State Mutual Bk.

Birks, H. J. Quaternary Paleoecology. (Illus.). 300p. 1980. text ed. 89.50 (ISBN 0-8391-4127-0). Univ Park.

Birks, H. J. & Gordon, A. D. Numerical Methods in Quarternary Pollen Analysis. Date not set. price not set (ISBN 0-12-101250-6). Acad Pr.

Birks, H. J., jt. auth. see Huntley, Brian.

Birks, H. J. & West, R. G., eds. Quaternary Plant Ecology: Fourteenth Symposium of the British Ecological Society, University of Cambridge, 28-30 March 1972. LC 73-10215. (British Ecological Society Symposia Ser.). 326p. 1974. 84.95x (ISBN 0-470-07534-1). Halsted Pr.

Birks, J. B. & Birks, J. B., eds. Proceedings of the Rutherford Jubilee International Conference-Manchester, 1962. 90.00 (ISBN 0-12-101162-3). Acad Pr.

Birks, J. S. Across the Savannas to Mecca: The Overland Pilgrimage Route from West Africa. (Illus.). 161p. 1978. 29.50x (ISBN 0-7146-6005-1, F Cass Co). Biblio Dist.

Birks, J. S. & Sinclair, C. A. Arab Manpower. LC 80-12416. 450p. 1980. 55.00 (ISBN 0-312-04708-8). St Martin.

--International Migration & Development in the Arab Region. International Labour Office, ed. (Illus.). 175p. (Orig.). 1980. 19.95 (ISBN 9-22-102252-8); pap. 14.25 (ISBN 9-22-102251-X). Intl Labour Office.

--International Migration & Development in the Arab Region. xii, 174p. 1980. pap. 14.25 (ISBN 92-2-102251-X, ILO222, ILO). Unipub.

Birks, John B., ed. Excited States of Biological Molecules: Based on the Proceedings of the International Conference at the Calouste Gulbenkian Foundation Centre, Lisbon, Portugal, on April 18-24, 1974. LC 75-6985. (Wiley Monographs in Chemical Physics). pap. 160.00 (ISBN 0-317-29353-2, 2024005). Bks Demand UMI.

Birks, L. S. Electron Probe Microanalysis. 2nd ed. LC 79-9773. 204p. 1979. Repr. of 1971 ed. lib. bdg. 21.50 (ISBN 0-88275-952-3). Krieger.

--X-Ray Spectrochemical Analysis, Vol. 2. 2nd ed. LC 71-79144. (Illus.). 143p. 1969. text ed. 11.25 (ISBN 0-471-07525-6, Pub. by Wiley). Krieger.

Birks, L. S., et al, eds. Advances in X-Ray Analysis, Vol. 16. LC 58-35928. 410p. 1973. 59.50x (ISBN 0-306-38116-8, Plenum Pr). Plenum Pub.

Birks, N. & Meier, G. H. An Introduction to High Temperature Oxidation of Metals. 208p. 1983. pap. text ed. 29.50 (ISBN 0-7131-3464-X). E Arnold.

Birks, Tony. Basic Pottery. LC 83-51480. (Illus.). 100p. (Orig.). 1984. pap. 6.95 (ISBN 0-8069-7862-7). Sterling.

--Hans Coper. LC 83-49060. (Illus.). 208p. 1984. 36.06 (ISBN 0-06-430390-X, Icon Edus). Har-Row.

--The New Potter's Companion. 168p. 1981. 16.95 (ISBN 0-13-615377-1); pap. 8.95 (ISBN 0-13-615369-0). P-H.

Birks, Tony, ed. see Meyer, Franz.

Birky, C. William, Jr., et al, eds. Genetics & Biogenesis of Mitochondria & Chloroplasts. LC 75-20271. (Ohio State University Biosciences Colloquia: No.1). (Illus.). 371p. 1976. 15.00x (ISBN 0-8142-0236-5). Ohio St U Pr.

Birky, Lela. The Bible Nurture & Reader Ser. (gr. 1-4). 1969. write for info. avail. Span. (ISBN 0-686-05603-5); tchrs' ed. avail. (ISBN 0-686-05604-3). Rod & Staff.

--Developing Better Reading. 1973. write for info. (ISBN 0-686-05586-1); tchrs' ed. avail. (ISBN 0-686-05587-X). Rod & Staff.

--Truth for Life Bible Studies. (gr. 7-9). pap. write for info (ISBN 0-686-15481-9). Rod & Staff.

--We Learn Letter Sounds, U. O. 1977. write for info (ISBN 0-686-23332-8); tchr's. ed. avail. (ISBN 0-686-23333-6). Rod & Staff.

Birky, Lela & Conley, Lucy. The Building Christian English Series. (gr. 3-7). 1973. send for info. (ISBN 0-686-05606-X); tchrs' ed. avail. (ISBN 0-686-05607-8). Rod & Staff.

Birla, G. D. Bapu, A Unique Association: Correspondence with Mahatma Gandhi, 4 vols. 1838p. 1983. Set. 50.00 (ISBN 0-934676-33-X). Greenlf Bks.

Birla Institute. India & the Atom. 1983. 11.00x (ISBN 0-8364-1031-9, Pub. by Allied India). South Asia Bks.

Birla Institute of Scientific Research, Economic Research Division & Agarwal, R. J. Defence Production & Development. (Birla Institute of Scientific Research Ser.). 1978. text ed. 10.00x (ISBN 0-8426-1081-2). Verry.

Birla, Madan. Best of Both Worlds, Career, & Marriage. LC 84-90144. 1984. 11.95 (ISBN 0-533-06209-8). Vantage.

Birlem, Ellen & Wiesendanger, Katherine. Parent: Help Your Child Become a Better Reader. Reed, R., ed. LC 81-83608. (Orig.). 1982. 13.95 (ISBN 0-88247-652-1); pap. 8.95 (ISBN 0-88247-630-0). R & E Pubs.

Birley, A. R., ed. see Syme, Ronald.

Birley, Anthony. Life in Roman Britain. 1976. pap. 14.95 (ISBN 0-7134-7151-X, Pub. by Batsford England). David & Charles.

--Lives of the Later Caesars. (Classics Ser.). 320p. 1976. pap. 4.95 (ISBN 0-14-044308-8). Penguin.

--The People of Roman Britain. LC 79-3604. 240p. 1980. 35.00x (ISBN 0-520-04119-4). U of Cal Pr.

Birley, Anthony, ed. Universal Rome. LC 68-78675. (Selections from History Today Ser.: No. 4). (Illus.). 1969. pap. 5.95 (ISBN 0-05-000020-9). Dufour.

Birley, Anthony R. The Fasti of Roman Britain. 1981. 85.00x (ISBN 0-19-814821-6). Oxford U Pr.

Birley, Arthur W. & Scott, Martyn J. Plastics Materials. 1982. (Pub. by Chapman & Hall); pap. 23.00x (ISBN 0-412-00221-3, NO. 5022). Methuen Inc.

Birley, Eric, et al, eds. see International Congress of Limesforschung, 8th, Cardiff.

Birley, Robert. Sunk Without Trace: Some Forgotten Masterpieces Reconsidered. LC 75-10209. 208p. 1975. Repr. of 1962 ed. lib. bdg. 24.75x (ISBN 0-8371-8170-4, BIST). Greenwood.

Birley, Sue. New Enterprises: A Start-up Case Book. 215p. 1982. pap. 11.95 (ISBN 0-7099-0680-3, Pub. by Croom Helm Ltd); 30.00 (ISBN 0-7099-0614-5). Longwood Pub Group.

Birman, Igor. Secret Incomes of the Soviet State Budget. 330p. 1981. lib. bdg. 78.50 (ISBN 90-247-2550-X, Pub. by Martinus Nijhoff Netherlands). Kluwer Academic.

Birman, J. L. Theory of Crystal Space Groups & Lattice Dynamics: Infra-Red & Raman Optical Processes of Insulating Crystals. (Illus.). 570p. 1984. pap. 35.00 (ISBN 0-387-13395-X). Springer Verlag.

Birman, J. L., et al, eds. Light Scattering in Solids. LC 79-21683. 557p. 1980. 85.00x (ISBN 0-306-40313-7, Plenum Pr). Plenum Pub.

Birman, Joan S. Braids, Links & Mapping Class Groups. LC 74-2961. (Annals of Mathematics Studies: No. 82). 300p. 1974. 27.00x (ISBN 0-691-08149-2). Princeton U Pr.

Birman, M., ed. Spectral Theory. LC 78-93768. (Topics in Mathematical Physics: Vol. 3). pap. 24.80 (ISBN 0-317-12984-8, 2020693). Bks Demand UMI.

Birman, M. S. & Solomjak, M. Z. Quantitative Analysis in Sobolev Imbedding Theorems & Applications to Spectral Theory. (Translations Ser. 2: Vol. 114). 1980. 34.00 (ISBN 0-8218-3064-3, TRANS2-114). Am Math.

Birman, M. S., ed. Topics in Mathematical Physics, 5 vols. Incl. Vol. 1. Spectral Theory & Wave Processes. LC 67-16365. 114p. 1967 (ISBN 0-306-18401-X); Vol. 2. Spectral Theory & Problems in Diffraction. LC 68-28089. 134p. 1968 (ISBN 0-306-18402-8); Vol. 3. Spectral Theory. LC 78-93768. 93p. 1969 (ISBN 0-306-18403-6); Vol. 4. Spectral Theory & Wave Processes. LC 68-28089. 121p. 1971 (ISBN 0-306-18404-4); Vol. 5. Spectral Theory. LC 68-28089. 112p. 1972 (ISBN 0-306-18405-2). 25.00x ea. (Consultants). Plenum Pub.

Birman, M. S., et al. Fifteen Papers on Analysis. LC 51-5559. (Translations Ser.: No. 2, Vol. 54). 1966. 36.00 (ISBN 0-8218-1754-X, TRANS 2-54). Am Math.

Birman, Wendy. Gregory of Rainworth. 296p. 1980. 35.00x (ISBN 0-85564-165-7, Pub by U of W Austral Pr). Intl Spec Bk.

Birmelian, Blair T. The Dead Woman's Sister. LC 84-23511. 256p. 1985. 17.95 (ISBN 0-8052-3971-5). Schocken.

Birmelin, Blair T. The Superintendent. LC 83-40458. 240p. 1984. 17.95 (ISBN 0-8052-3893-X). Schocken.

Birmingham, A. T. Riley. 2nd ed. (Illus.). 272p. 12.95 (ISBN 0-85429-155-5, F155). Haynes Pubns.

Birmingham Alabama News Staff. Remembering Bear. 110p. 1983. 12.95 (ISBN 0-89730-111-0); pap. 4.95 (ISBN 0-89730-108-0). News Bks Intl.

Birmingham & Midland Society for Genealogy & Heraldry, ed. The Registers of Christ Church, Oldbury, Worcs. 1981. 12.50x (ISBN 0-905105-35-4, Pub. by Birmingham-Midland Soc England). State Mutual Bk.

--The Registers of St. George Hockley, Marks. 1981. 13.50x (ISBN 0-905105-32-X, Pub. by Birmingham-Midland Soc England). State Mutual Bk.

--The Registers of Wednesfield, Staffs. 1981. 12.00x (ISBN 0-905105-38-9, Pub. by Birmingham-Midland Soc England). State Mutual Bk.

Birmingham, David. Central Africa to Eighteen-Seventy: Zambezia, Zaire & the South Atlantic. LC 81-9947. (Illus.). 168p. 1982. 32.50 (ISBN 0-521-24116-2); pap. 11.95 (ISBN 0-521-28444-9). Cambridge U Pr.

Birmingham, David & Martin, Phyllis M., eds. History of Central Africa, Vol. 1. (Illus.). 336p. 1983. 55.00 (ISBN 0-582-64673-1); pap. text ed. 16.95 (ISBN 0-582-64674-X). Longman.

--History of Central Africa, Vol. 2. (Illus.). 432p. 1983. 60.00 (ISBN 0-582-64675-8); pap. text ed. 17.95 (ISBN 0-582-64676-6). Longman.

Birmingham, Duncan. The Maya, Aztecs & Incas Pop-up. (Tarquin Pop-up Ser.). (Illus.). 32p. (gr. 3 up). 1985. pap. 7.50 (ISBN 0-906212-37-5). Parkwest Pubns.

Birmingham, Frederic A. John: the Man Who Would Be President. Synhorst, Thomas J., ed. LC 79-93341. (Illus.). 128p. 1979. 9.95 (ISBN 0-89387-040-4, Co-Pub by Sat Eve Post). Curtis Pub Co.

Birmingham, George A. The Red Hand of Ulster. 298p. 1972. Repr. of 1912 ed. text ed. 12.50x (ISBN 0-7165-1800-7, Pub. by Irish Academic Pr Ireland). Biblio Dist.

Birmingham Historical Society, jt. auth. see Blake, Thomas H.

Birmingham, Jacqueline. The Problem-Oriented Record: A Self-Learning Module. (Illus.). 1978. pap. text ed. 19.95 (ISBN 0-07-005385-5). McGraw.

Birmingham, Jacqueline, jt. auth. see Carini, Geraldine.

Birmingham, Jacqueline J. Medical Terminology: A Self-Learning Module. (Illus.). 448p. 1981. pap. text ed. 22.00 (ISBN 0-07-005386-3). McGraw.

Birmingham, Jacqueline J., jt. auth. see Hills, Sally W.

Birmingham, Joan. The Christmas Creatures. 1985. 10.00 (ISBN 0-317-28883-0). Vantage.

Birmingham, Mary & Meissner, Edie, eds. Libraries & the Political Process. (Occasional Papers of the Minnesota Library Association: No. 1). 51p. 1981. pap. 5.00 (ISBN 0-939098-00-8). Minn Library.

Birmingham, Richard. Boat Building Techniques Illustrated. LC 83-81366. (Illus.). 320p. 1984. 28.50 (ISBN 0-87742-176-5, B144). Intl Marine.

Birmingham Shakespeare Library, compiled by. Shakespeare Bibliography: The Catalogue of the Birmingham Shakespeare Library, 7 vols. 4311p. 1971. Set. 445.00x (ISBN 0-7201-0180-8); pap. 191.00. Mansell.

Birmingham, Stephen. The Auerbach Will. 416p. 1983. 16.45i (ISBN 0-316-09646-6). Little.

--The Auerbach Will. (General Ser.). 1984. lib. bdg. 17.95 (ISBN 0-8161-3657-2, Large Print Bks). G K Hall.

--The Auerbach Will. 432p. 1985. pap. 4.50 (ISBN 0-425-08520-1). Berkley Pub.

--Certain People. 1977. 9.95 (ISBN 0-316-09642-3). Little.

--The Golden Dream: Surburbia in the 1970's. LC 76-57891. 1978. 10.00 (ISBN 0-06-010334-5, HarpT). Har-Row.

--The Grandees. 384p. 1985. pap. 4.50 (ISBN 0-425-08390-X). Berkley Pub.

--The Grandes Dames. (General Ser.). 1983. lib. bdg. 18.95 (ISBN 0-8161-3498-7, Large Print Bks). G K Hall.

--Jacqueline Bouvier Kennedy Onassis. (Illus.). 1979. pap. 2.50 (ISBN 0-671-82862-2). PB.

--The LeBaron Secret. 1985. 17.95 (ISBN 0-316-09649-0). Little.

--Life at the Dakota: New York's Most Unusual Address. LC 79-4800. (Illus.). 1979. 12.50 (ISBN 0-394-41079-3). Random.

--Our Crowd: The Great Jewish Families of New York. 528p. 1985. pap. 4.50 (ISBN 0-425-07557-5). Berkley Pub.

--Real Lace: America's Irish Rich. LC 73-4061. (Illus.). 336p. 1973. 12.95i (ISBN 0-06-010336-1, HarpT). Har-Row.

--The Rest of Us: The Rise of America's Eastern European Jews. 384p. 1984. 19.95i (ISBN 0-316-09647-4). Little.

--The Rest of Us: The Rise of America's Eastern European Jews. 432p. 1985. pap. 4.50 (ISBN 0-425-08074-9). Berkley Pub.

--Those Harper Women. 352p. 1985. pap. 3.95 (ISBN 0-425-07384-X). Berkley Pub.

Birn, Donald S. The League of Nations Unions, Nineteen Eighteen to Nineteen Forty-Five. 1981. 55.00x (ISBN 0-19-822650-0). Oxford U Pr.

Birn, Herluf & Winther, Jens E. Manual of Minor Oral Surgery: A Step by Step Atlas. 2nd ed. 132p. 1982. 31.50 (ISBN 0-7216-1737-9). Saunders.

Birn, Randi. Aksel Sandemose: Exile in Search of a Home. LC 83-13034. (Contributions to the Study of World Literature: No. 2). xii, 137p. 1984. lib. bdg. 25.00 (ISBN 0-313-24163-5, BAS/). Greenwood.

Birn, Randi & Gould, Karen, eds. Orion Blinded: Essays on Claude Simon. LC 79-17687. 320p. 1981. 27.50 (ISBN 0-8387-2420-5). Bucknell U Pr.

Birnbach, Lisa. Lisa Birnbach's College Book. (Orig.). 1984. pap. 9.95 (ISBN 0-345-30918-9). Ballantine.

Birnbach, Lisa, ed. The Official Preppy Handbook. LC 80-51892. (Illus.). 224p. (Orig.). 1980. deluxe ed. 9.95 (ISBN 0-89480-195-3, 326); pap. 4.95 (ISBN 0-89480-140-6, 440). Workman Pub.

Birnbach, Martin. Neo-Freudian Social Philosophy. 1961. 22.50x (ISBN 0-8047-0076-1). Stanford U Pr.

Birnbaoum, Philip. Hasiddur Hashalem Daily Prayer Book: Sephardic. 860p. 1969. 17.00 (ISBN 0-88482-053-X). Hebrew Pub.

Birnbaum & Free, eds. Eddy-Current Characterization of Materials & Structures - STP 722. 505p. 1981. 44.50 (ISBN 0-8031-0752-8, 04-722000-22). ASTM.

Birnbaum, Alfred, tr. see Tsuchiya, Yoshio.

Birnbaum, Alfred T., tr. see Miyagawa, Torao, et al.

Birnbaum, Allan R., ed. see Chirgotis, William G.

Birnbaum, Eleazar. Books on Asia from the Near East to the Far East: A Guide for the General Reader. LC 75-151361. pap. 89.30 (ISBN 0-317-10729-1, 2014133). Bks Demand UMI.

Birnbaum, Ervin. Politics of Compromise: State & Religion in Israel. LC 70-92557. 348p. 1970. 27.50 (ISBN 0-8386-7567-0). Fairleigh Dickinson.

Birnbaum, George see Marton, L.

Birnbaum, H., et al, eds. Studia Linguistica Alexandro Vasilii Filio Issatschenko: A Collegis Amicusque Oblata. 517p. (Orig., Eng., Fr., Ger., Rus.). 1978. pap. 62.00x (ISBN 0-686-32343-2). Benjamins North Am.

Birnbaum, Harold F., jt. auth. see Birnbaum, Ruth F.

Birnbaum, Henrik. Linguistic Reconstruction: Its Potentials & Limitations in New Perspective. (Journal of Indo-European Studies Monograph: No.2). (Orig.). 1976. pap. text ed. 20.00 (ISBN 0-941694-26-7). Inst Study Man.

--Lord Novgorod the Great Essays in the History & Culture of a Medieval City State, Pt. 1: The Historical Background. (UCLA Slavic Studies: Vol. 2). (Illus.). 170p. (Orig.). 1981. pap. 10.95 (ISBN 0-89357-088-5). Slavica.

--On Medieval & Renaissance Slavic Writings. LC 73-85243. (Slavistic Printings & Reprintings Ser.: No. 266). 381p. 1974. text ed. 52.00x (ISBN 90-2792-680-8). Mouton.

--Problems of Typological & Genetic Linguistics Viewed in a Generative Framework. LC 70-123298. (Janua Linguarum, Ser. Minor: No. 106). (Orig.). 1970. pap. text ed. 11.20x (ISBN 90-2791-541-5). Mouton.

Birnbaum, Henrik & Eekman, Thomas. Fiction & Drama in Eastern & Southeastern Europe: Evolution & Experiment in the Postwar Period. (UCLA Slavic Studies: Vol. 1). ix, 463p. 1980. 24.95 (ISBN 0-89357-064-8). Slavica.

Birnbaum, Henrik & Merrill, Peter T. Recent Advances in the Reconstruction of Common Slavic (1971 to 1982) vi, 141p. (Orig.). 1985. pap. 11.95 (ISBN 0-89357-116-4). Slavica.

Birnbaum, Henrik & Speros, V. Aspects of the Balkans: Continuity & Change. (Slavistic Printings & Reprintings Ser: No. 27). 1972. text ed. 66.00x (ISBN 90-2792-172-5). Mouton.

Birnbaum, Henrik & Flier, Michael S., eds. Medieval Russian Culture. LC 82-23866. (California Slavic Studies: Vol. 12). 416p. 1984. text ed. 35.00x (ISBN 0-520-04938-1). U of Cal Pr.

Birnbaum, Howard, et al. Public Pricing of Nursing Home Care. (Illus.). 208p. 1982. text ed. 24.00 (ISBN 0-89011-565-6). Abt Bks.

--Public Pricing of Nursing Home Care. (Illus.). 222p. 1984. Repr. of 1981 ed. lib. bdg. 24.50 (ISBN 0-8191-4065-1). U Pr of Amer.

Birnbaum, Hubert C. Amphoto Guide to Cameras. (Illus.). 184p. 1978. (Amphoto); pap. 7.95 (ISBN 0-8174-2117-3). Watson-Guptill.

--Black & White Darkroom Techniques. LC 81-67033. (Kodak Workshop Ser.). (Illus.). 96p. (Orig.). 1981. pap. 8.95 (ISBN 0-87985-274-7, KW-15). Eastman Kodak.

--Photographing with Automatic Cameras. LC 81-67431. (The Kodak Workshop Ser.). (Illus.). 96p. 1981. pap. 8.95 (ISBN 0-87985-270-4, KW-11). Eastman Kodak.

Birnbaum, I. M. & Parker, E. S., eds. Alcohol & Human Memory. 240p. 1977. 24.95x (ISBN 0-89859-423-5). L Erlbaum Assocs.

Birnbaum, Jacob S. The Musculo-Skeletal Manual. LC 82-3878. 1982. 44.00 (ISBN 0-12-788075-5); pap. 44.00 (ISBN 0-12-788074-7). Acad Pr.

Birnbaum, Karl E. The Politics of East-West Communication in Europe. 182p. 1979. text ed. 37.95x (ISBN 0-566-00254-X). Gower Pub Co.

Birnbaum, Karl E., jt. auth. see Andren, Nils.

Birnbaum, Lucia C. Liberazione della Donna: Feminism in Italy. (Illus.). 320p. 25.95 (ISBN 0-8195-5133-3). Wesleyan U Pr.

Birnbaum, Mark & Sickman, John. How to Choose Your Small Business Computer: Popular. LC 82-11665. (Microcomputer Bks.). 176p. 1983. pap. 9.95 (ISBN 0-201-10187-4). Addison-Wesley.

Birnbaum, Martin. Last Romantic. 1960. 13.95x (ISBN 0-8084-0379-6). New Coll U Pr.

Birnbaum, Martin, et al. Ideas for Urban-Rural Gifted-Talented: Case Histories & Program Plans. 94p. 5.25 (ISBN 0-318-02132-3). NSLTIGT.

Birnbaum, Martin, jt. auth. see Sato, Irving S.

Birnbaum, Max, jt. auth. see Benne, Kenneth D.

Birnbaum, Max, jt. auth. see Cass, James.

Birnbaum, Max, jt. auth. see Babad, Elisha Y.

Birnbaum, Michael, jt. auth. see Sonnenburg, David.

Birnbaum, Milton. Aldous Huxley's Quest for Values. LC 71-142146. 230p. 1971. 17.50x (ISBN 0-87049-127-X). Lib Soc Sci.

Birnbaum, Norman. Crisis of Industrial Society. 1969. pap. 4.95 (ISBN 0-19-500794-8, 295, GB). Oxford U Pr.

--Social Structure & the German Reformation. Zuckerman, Harriet & Merton, Robert K., eds. LC 79-8976. (Dissertation on Sociology Ser.). 1980. lib. bdg. 40.00x (ISBN 0-405-12952-1). Ayer Co Pubs.

--Toward a Critical Sociology. 1971. pap. 5.95 (ISBN 0-19-501664-5, GB). Oxford U Pr.

--Toward a Critical Sociology. 1983. 13.25 (ISBN 0-8446-6019-1). Peter Smith.

Birnbaum, Norman, ed. Beyond the Crisis. LC 16-42637. 1977. pap. 4.95 (ISBN 0-19-502198-3, GB 491, GB). Oxford U Pr.

Birnbaum, Philim. Hasiddur Hashalem: Daily Prayer Book. 790p. 1977. pap. 9.95 pocket flexible ed. (ISBN 0-88482-054-8). Hebrew Pub.

Birnbaum, Philip. The Birnbaum Haggadah. (Illus.). 160p. 1976. 5.95 (ISBN 0-88482-908-1); pap. 3.95 (ISBN 0-88482-912-X). Hebrew Pub.

--Encyclopedia of Jewish Concepts. rev. ed. 1979. 19.50 (ISBN 0-88482-876-X, Sanhedrin Pr); pap. 7.95 (ISBN 0-88482-930-8). Hebrew Pub.

--Hasiddur Hashalem (Daily Prayer Book) 790p. 1964. 17.00 (ISBN 0-88482-045-9). Hebrew Pub.

--Mahzor Hashalem: High Holiday Prayer Book, Vol. 1, Rosh Hashahah. 646p. 1960. 14.00 (ISBN 0-88482-246-X). Hebrew Pub.

--Mahzor Hashalem: High Holyday Prayer Book, 5 Vols. 1971. Set. 58.00 (ISBN 0-88482-169-2). Hebrew Pub.

--Mahzor Hashalem: High Holyday Prayer Book, 2 Vols. 1960. Set. 26.50 (ISBN 0-88482-170-6). Hebrew Pub.

--Mahzor Hashalem: High Holyday Prayer Book, 1 Vol. 1042p. 1951. 17.00 (ISBN 0-88482-240-0). Hebrew Pub.

--Mahzor Hashalem: Prayer Book for Pesah, Vol. 4. 459p. 1971. 11.50 (ISBN 0-88482-172-2). Hebrew Pub.

--Mahzor Hashalem: Prayer Book for Shavuot, Vol. 5. 358p. 1971. 11.50 (ISBN 0-88482-173-0). Hebrew Pub.

--Mahzor Hashalem: Prayer Book for Sukkot, Vol. 3. 478p. 1971. 11.50 (ISBN 0-88482-174-9). Hebrew Pub.

--Mahzor Leshalosh Regalim: Prayer Book for Three Festivals. 641p. 1971. 15.00 (ISBN 0-88482-149-8). Hebrew Pub.

--Mazhor Hashalem High Holiday Prayer Book, Vol. 2: Yom Kippur. 770p. 1960. 14.00 (ISBN 0-88482-247-8). Hebrew Pub.

--Siddur Leshabbat Veyom Tov: Prayer Book for Sabbath & Festivals with Torah Readings. 724p. 1950. 14.50 (ISBN 0-88482-062-9). Hebrew Pub.

--The Torah & the Haftarot. 933p. 1983. 19.50 (ISBN 0-88482-456-X). Hebrew Pub.

Birnbaum, Philip, ed. The New Treasury of Judaism. 1977. 15.00 (ISBN 0-88482-410-1, Sanhedrin Pr); pap. 9.95 (ISBN 0-88482-411-X, Sanhedrin Pr). Hebrew Pub.

Birnbaum, Philip, tr. Selihot. 61p. 1952. pap. 1.95 (ISBN 0-88482-344-X). Hebrew Pub.

Birnbaum, Philip, tr. see Maimonides, Moses.

Birnbaum, Phyllis, ed. & tr. Rabbits, Crabs, Etc. LC 82-8365. 156p. 1982. text ed. 15.00x (ISBN 0-8248-0777-4); pap. 7.95 (ISBN 0-8248-0817-7). UH Pr.

Birnbaum, Pierre. The Heights of Power: An Essay on the Power Elite in France. Goldhammer, Arthur, tr. from Fr. LC 81-16101. (Illus.). 168p. 1982. lib. bdg. 17.00x (ISBN 0-226-05202-8). U of Chicago Pr.

Birnbaum, Pierre, jt. auth. see Badie, Bertrand.

Birnbaum, Pierre, et al, eds. Democracy, Consensus & Social Contract. LC 77-84075. (Sage Modern Politics Ser.: Vol. 2). 361p. 1978. 28.00 (ISBN 0-8039-9882-1); pap. 14.00 (ISBN 0-8039-9883-X). Sage.

Birnbaum, Robert. Creative Academic Bargaining: Managing Conflict in the Unionized College & University. LC 80-18806. 288p. 1980. text ed. 20.95x (ISBN 0-8077-2631-1). Tchrs Coll.

--Maintaining Diversity in Higher Education. LC 83-48156. (Higher Education Ser.). 1983. text ed. 17.95x (ISBN 0-87589-574-3). Jossey-Bass.

Birnbaum, Ruth F. & Birnbaum, Harold F. The Prometheus Trilogy. 7.50x (ISBN 0-87291-125-X). Coronado Pr.

Birnbaum, S. A. Yiddish: A Survey & a Grammar. 1979. 42.50x (ISBN 0-8020-5382-3). U of Toronto Pr.

Birnbaum, S. L. & Crawford, G. E. How to Protect Your Company from Product Liability Exposure. 16p. 1984. 2.50x (ISBN 0-317-07504-7, 43057-9). P-H.

Birnbaum, Salomo A. Grammatik der Jiddischen Sprache. 200p. (Orig., Ger.). 1979. pap. 11.00x (ISBN 3-87118-014-9, Pub by Helmut Buske Verlag Hamburg). Benjamins North Am.

--Grammatik der Jiddischen Sprache, Mit einem Woerterbuch und Lesestuecken: Erganzte Auflage. (No. 4). 206p. (Orig., Ger.). 1984. pap. 11.00x (ISBN 3-87118-658-9, Pub. by Helmut Buske Verlag Hamburg). Benjamins North AM.

--Die Jiddische Sprache: Ein Kurzer Ueberblick und Texte aus acht Jahrhunderten. viii, 141p. (Orig., Ger.). 1974. pap. 11.00x (ISBN 3-87118-133-1, Pub by Helmut Buske VerlagHamburg). Benjamins North Am.

Birnbaum, Sheila & Phelan, Richard J. Special Problems in Toxic Substances Litigation after Manville, 1983. LC 83-60146. (Litigation Course Handbook Ser.: No. 220). (Illus.). 552p. 1983. 35.00. PLI.

Birnbaum, Stanley. Credo: A Catholic Catechism. Davies, Benedict, tr. 300p. 1985. pap. 5.95 (ISBN 0-86683-901-1); pap. 3.95 leaders guide (ISBN 0-86683-743-4). Winston Pr.

Birnbaum, Stephen. Birnbaum's Canada, Nineteen Eighty-Six. 1985. pap. 11.95 (ISBN 0-317-31601-X). HM.

--Birnbaum's Caribbean, Nineteen Eighty-Six. 1985. pap. 11.95 (ISBN 0-317-31581-1). HM.

--Birnbaum's Disney World, Nineteen Eighty-Six. 1985. pap. write for info. HM.

--Birnbaum's Europe for Business Travellers, 1986. 1985. pap. write for info. HM.

--Birnbaum's Europe, Nineteen Eighty-Six. 1985. pap. 13.95 (ISBN 0-317-31598-6). HM.

--Birnbaum's France, Nineteen Eighty-Six. 1985. pap. 11.95 (ISBN 0-317-31604-4). HM.

--Birnbaum's Great Britain, Nineteen Eighty-Six. 1985. pap. 11.95 (ISBN 0-317-31599-4). HM.

--Birnbaum's Hawaii, Nineteen-Eighty Six. 1985. pap. 11.95 (ISBN 0-317-31583-8). HM.

--Birnbaum's Mexico, Nineteen Eighty-Six. 1985. pap. 11.95 (ISBN 0-317-31582-X). HM.

--Birnbaum's South America, Nineteen-Eighty Six. 1985. pap. 11.95 (ISBN 0-317-31584-6). HM.

--Birnbaum's U. S. A. for Business Travellers, 1986. 1985. pap. write for info. HM.

--Birnbaum's United States, Nineteen Eighty-Six. 1985. pap. 11.95 (ISBN 0-317-31600-1). HM.

--Canada Nineteen Hundred Six. 688p. 1985. pap. 11.95 (ISBN 0-395-39401-5). HM.

--Caribbean, Bermuda & the Bahamas 1986. 688p. 1985. pap. 11.95 (ISBN 0-395-39406-6). HM.

--Europe. (Get 'em & Go Travel Guide Ser.). 1982. pap. 12.95 (ISBN 0-395-31534-4). HM.

--Europe for Business Travelers 1986. 560p. 1985. pap. 7.95 (ISBN 0-395-39403-1). HM.

--Europe 1986. 1232p. 1985. pap. 13.95 (ISBN 0-395-39398-1). HM.

--France 1986. 784p. 1985. pap. 11.95 (ISBN 0-395-39402-3). HM.

--Great Britain & Ireland Nineteen Eighty-Two. (The Get 'em & Go Travel Guide Ser.). 704p. 1981. pap. 10.95 (ISBN 0-395-31535-2). HM.

--Great Britain & Ireland Nineteen Eighty-Six. 800p. 1985. pap. 11.95 (ISBN 0-395-39399-X). HM.

--Hawaii Nineteen Eighty-Six. 456p. 1985. pap. 11.95 (ISBN 0-395-39396-5). HM.

--Mexico Nineteen Eighty-Six. 528p. 1985. pap. 11.95 (ISBN 0-395-39397-4). HM.

--Mexico 1984. (The Get'em & Go Travel Guide Ser.). 1983. 11.95 (ISBN 0-395-34628-2). HM.

--Mexico, 1985. (Get 'em & Go Travel Guides Ser.). 1984. pap. 11.95 (ISBN 0-395-36520-1). HM.

--South America Nineteen Eighty-Six. 784p. 1985. pap. 11.95 (ISBN 0-395-39397-3). HM.

--South America, 1985. (Get 'em & Go Travel Guides). 1984. pap. 11.95 (ISBN 0-395-36519-8). HM.

--U. S. A. for Business Travelers 1986. 592p. 1985. pap. 7.95 (ISBN 0-395-39408-2). HM.

--United States Nineteen Eighty-Six. 848p. 1985. pap. 11.95 (ISBN 0-395-39400-7). HM.

--United States 1984. 1982. 11.95 (ISBN 0-395-34631-2). HM.

--United States, 1985. (Stephen Birnbaum Travel Guides Ser.). pap. 11.95. HM.

Birnbaum, Steve. Disneyland 1986. 160p. 1985. pap. 5.95 (ISBN 0-395-39405-8). HM.

--Walt Disney World, 1986. 192p. 1985. pap. 6.95 (ISBN 0-395-39404-X). HM.

Birnbaumer, L., jt. ed. see O'Malley, B. W.

Birnbaumer, Lutz, jt. ed. see O'Malley, B. W.

Birnberg, Thomas B. & Resnick, Stephen A. Colonial Development: An Econometric Study. LC 74-20077. (Illus.). 416p. 1975. 36.00x (ISBN 0-300-01821-5). Yale U Pr.

Birner, Herbert A. Marriage Should Be Honored by All. 5.95 (ISBN 0-686-76769-1, 12N1719). Northwest Pub.

Birner, William B., frwd. by. Twenty Plays for Young People. (YA) 1967. 17.50 (ISBN 0-87602-015-5). Anchorage.

Birnes. The Apple Megabook. Date not set. pap. 12.95 (ISBN 0-671-54386-5). S&S.

Birnes, W. J. McGraw-Hill Personal Computer Programming Encyclopedia: Languages & Operating Systems. 712p. 1985. 80.00 (ISBN 0-07-005389-8). McGraw.

Birnes, William. Selling at the Top: The 100 Best Companies to Sell for in America Today. LC 84-48579. (Illus.). 320p. 1985. 17.26i (ISBN 0-06-015424-1, HarpT). Har-Row.

Birnes, William J. Arco Computer Preparation for the SAT. (Designed for the Apple II, Apple Plus & Apple IIe). incl. disk 69.95 (ISBN 0-317-05034-6). Arco.

Birney, Alice L. Satiric Catharsis in Shakespeare: A Theory of Dramatic Structure. LC 79-185976. 1973. 33.00x (ISBN 0-520-02214-9). U of Cal Pr.

Birney, Arthur A. Sun Sight Navigation: Celestial for Sailors. LC 83-46034. (Illus.). 128p. 1984. pap. 12.50 (ISBN 0-87033-318-6). Cornell Maritime.

Birney, C. M. Grimke Sisters-Sarah & Angelina Grimke, the First American Women Advocates of Abolition & Women's Rights. LC 68-24971. (American Biography Ser., No. 32). 1969. Repr. of 1885 ed. lib. bdg. 49.95x (ISBN 0-8383-0912-7). Haskell.

Birney, Catherine H. Grimke Sisters: Sarah & Angelina Grimke, the First American Women Advocates of Abolition & Women's Rights. LC 69-13828. Repr. of 1885 ed. lib. bdg. 15.00x (ISBN 0-8371-1303-2, BIGS). Greenwood.

--Grimke Sisters, Sarah & Angelina Grimke: The First America Women Advocates of Abolition & Women's Rights. LC 70-108461. 1970. Repr. of 1855 ed. 13.00x (ISBN 0-403-00230-3). Scholarly.

Birney, Earle. The Mammoth Corridors. 1980. pap. 5.00 (ISBN 0-936892-07-2). Stone Pr MI.

Birney, Elmer C. Systematics of Three Species of Woodrats (Genus Neotome) in Central North America. (Miscellaneous Publications Ser.: No. 58). 173p. 1973. 9.00 (ISBN 0-317-04956-9). U of KS Mus Nat Hist.

Birney, James G. American Churches: The Bulwarks of American Slavery. LC 79-82174. (Anti-Slavery Crusade in America Ser). 1969. Repr. of 1842 ed. 11.00 (ISBN 0-405-00611-X). Ayer Co Pubs.

--Collection of Valuable Documents, Being Birney's Vindication of Abolitionists. Repr. of 1836 ed. 12.50 (ISBN 0-404-00247-1). AMS Pr.

--Letter on the Political Obligations of Abolitionists, by James G. Birney: With a Reply by William Lloyd Garrison. LC 71-82172. (Anti-Slavery Crusade in America Ser). 1969. Repr. of 1839 ed. 7.50 (ISBN 0-405-00613-6). Ayer Co Pubs.

--Letters: Eighteen Thirty-One to Eighteen Fifty-Seven, 2 vols. Dumond, Dwight L., ed. Set. 24.00 (ISBN 0-8446-1078-X). Peter Smith.

Birney, James G., ed. Correspondence Between the Honorable F. H. Elmore & James G. Birney. LC 75-82173. (Anti-Slavery Crusade in America Ser). 1969. Repr. of 1838 ed. 9.50 (ISBN 0-405-00612-8). Ayer Co Pubs.

Birney, William. James G. Birney & His Times: The Genesis of the Republican Party with Some Account of Abolition Movements in the South Before 1828. LC 71-77190. Repr. of 1890 ed. 20.50x (ISBN 0-8371-1313-X, BIB&, Pub. by Negro U Pr). Greenwood.

Birngruber, R. & Gabel, V. P., eds. Laser Treatment & Photocoagulation of the Eye. (Documenta Ophthalmologica Proceedings Ser.). 1983. lib. bdg. 67.00 (ISBN 90-619-3732-9, Pub. by Junk Pubs Netherlands). Kluwer Academic.

Birnhack, Sarah. Happy Is the Heart: A Year in the Life of a Jewish Girl. (Illus.). (gr. 5-8). 1976. 5.95 (ISBN 0-87306-131-4). Feldheim.

Birnie, Patricia. International Regulation of Whaling, 2 vols. 1985. Vol. 1. lib. bdg. 50.00 (ISBN 0-379-20602-1); Vol. 2. lib. bdg. 50.00 (ISBN 0-379-20605-6); Set. lib. bdg. 100.00. Oceana.

--Legal Measures for the Conservation of Marine Mammals. (Environmental Policy & Law Papers: No. 19). 163p. 1982. in binder 20.00 (ISBN 2-88032-087-9, IUCN115, IUCN). Unipub.

Birnie, Patricia, jt. ed. see Barston, R. P.

Birnkrant, Sam. Mama, Say 'I Do' (Illus.). 58p. 1970. pap. 2.75 (ISBN 0-88680-126-5); royalty 50.00 (ISBN 0-317-03581-9). I E CLark.

Birnkraut, Ruth. Fascinating Facts About Love, Sex & Marriage. 192p. 1982. 10.95 (ISBN 0-517-54289-7); pap. 2.98 (ISBN 0-517-54505-5). Crown.

Birns, Tex, pseud. To Tame a Land. 15.95 (ISBN 0-89190-159-0, Pub. by Am Repr). Amereon Ltd.

Biro. Gumdrop & the Secret Switches. LC 82-14786. (Gumdrop Ser.). 32p. 1982. 8.95 (ISBN 0-89813-051-4). Childrens Bk Co.

--Gumdrop Finds a Friend. LC 82-17688. (Gumdrop Ser.). 32p. 1982. 8.95 (ISBN 0-89813-052-2). Childrens Bk Co.

--Gumdrop Finds a Ghost. LC 82-17686. (Gumdrop Ser.). 32p. 1982. 8.95 (ISBN 0-89813-050-6). Childrens Bk Co.

--Gumdrop Gets His Wings. LC 82-17716. (Gumdrop Ser.). 32p. 1982. 8.95 (ISBN 0-89813-053-0). Childrens Bk Co.

--Gumdrop Has a Birthday. LC 82-14779. (Gumdrop Ser.). 32p. 1982. 8.95 (ISBN 0-89813-055-7). Childrens Bk Co.

--Gumdrop in Double Trouble. LC 82-17687. (Gumdrop Ser.). 32p. 1982. 8.95 (ISBN 0-89813-054-9). Childrens Bk Co.

--Symposium on the Muscle. 1976. 11.50 (ISBN 0-9960001-9-4, Pub. by Akademiai Kaido Hungary). Heyden.

Biro, Charlotte S. Flavors of Hungary. LC 73-81085. (Illus.). 192p. (Orig.). 1973. pap. 6.95 (ISBN 0-912238-37-2). One Hund One Prods.

Biro, Elizabeth De see De Biro, Elizabeth.

Biro, J. I. & Shahan, Robert W. Mind, Brain & Function: Essays in the Philosophy of Mind. LC 81-40296. 208p. 1982. 16.95x (ISBN 0-8061-1783-4). U of Okla Pr.

Biro, J. I., jt. ed. see Shahan, Robert W.

Biro, Lajos & Wimperis, Arthur. The Private Life of Henry VIII. Kupelnick, Bruce S., ed. LC 76-52090. (Classics of Film Literature Ser.). 1978. lib. bdg. 22.00 (ISBN 0-8240-2866-X). Garland Pub.

Biro, Lajos & Cohen, Marc J., eds. The United States in Crisis: Marxist Analyses, Papers from the Third Midwest Marxist Scholars Conference. LC 78-61686. (Studies in Marxism: Vol. 4). 256p. 1979. x 8.95 (ISBN 0-930656-08-3); pap. 3.00 (ISBN 0-930656-07-5). MEP Pubns.

Biro, P., jt. ed. see Salanki, J.

Biro, Val. Gumdrop & the Secret Switches. (Gumdrop Ser.). (Illus.). 32p. (gr. 2-6). PLB 8.95 (ISBN 0-317-31015-1). Creative Ed.

--Gumdrop Finds a Friend. (Gumdrop Ser.). (Illus.). 32p. (gr. 2-6). PLB 8.95 (ISBN 0-317-31014-3). Creative Ed.

--Gumdrop Finds a Ghost. (Gumdrop Ser.). (Illus.). 32p. (gr. 2-6). PLB 8.95 (ISBN 0-317-31016-X). Creative Ed.

--Gumdrop Gets His Wings. (Gumdrop Ser.). (Illus.). 32p. (gr. 2-6). PLB 8.95 (ISBN 0-317-31013-5). Creative Ed.

--Gumdrop Has a Birthday. (Gumdrop Ser.). (Illus.). 32p. (gr. 2-6). PLB 8.95 (ISBN 0-317-31012-7). Creative Ed.

--Gumdrop in Double Trouble. (Gumdrop Ser.). (Illus.). 32p. (gr. 2-6). PLB 8.95 (ISBN 0-317-31018-6). Creative Ed.

--Hungarian Folk Tales. (Illus.). 192p. 1982. 11.95 (ISBN 0-19-274126-8, Pub. by Oxford U Pr Childrens). Merrimack Pub Cir.

--The Magic Doctor. (Illus.). 32p. 1982. 10.95 (ISBN 0-19-279752-2, Pub. by Oxford U Pr Childrens). Merrimack Pub Cir.

--The Magic Doctor. (Illus.). 32p. (ps-2). 1985. pap. 4.95 (ISBN 0-19-272129-1, Pub. by Oxford U Pr Childrens). Merrimack Pub Cir.

--The Pied Piper of Hamelin. LC 84-52469. 30p. (ps-3). 1985. 9.45 (ISBN 0-382-09014-4). Silver.

Biro, Yvette. Profane Mythology: The Savage Mind of the Cinema. Goldstein, Imre, tr. LC 82-48384. 160p. 1982. 22.50 (ISBN 0-253-18010-4); pap. 7.95x (ISBN 0-253-20293-0). Ind U Pr.

Biro, Z., et al, eds. Homeostasis in Injury & Shock: Proceedings of a Satellite Symposium of the 28th International Congress of Physiological Sciences, Budapest, Hungary, 1980. LC 80-42104. (Advances in Physiological Sciences: Vol. 26). (Illus.). 360p. 1981. 44.00 (ISBN 0-08-027347-5). Pergamon.

Birolini, F. A. Critical Maneuvers in Trauma Surgery: A Color Atlas. (Illus.). 204p. 1982. 125.00 (ISBN 0-387-10955-2). Springer-Verlag.

Biron, Armand D. The Letters & Documents of Armand De Gontaut, Baron De Biron, Marshal of France: 1524-1592, 2 vols. Ehrman, Sidney H., ed. LC 76-29405. Repr. of 1936 ed. Set. 57.50 (ISBN 0-404-15351-8). AMS Pr.

Biron, C. & Arioglu, E. Design of Supports in Mines. 248p. 1983. cloth 42.95 (ISBN 0-471-86726-8). Wiley.

--Designs of Supports in Mines. 248p. 1983. 45.95 (ISBN 0-471-86726-8). Wiley.

Biron, Chartres. Sir, Said Dr. Johnson. 1979. Repr. of 1940 ed. lib. bdg. 17.50 (ISBN 0-8414-9843-1). Folcroft.

Biron, Henry C. & Chalmers, Kenneth E. The Law & Practice of Extradition. xv, 432p. 1981. Repr. of 1903 ed. lib. bdg. 36.00x (ISBN 0-8377-0315-8). Rothman.

Biros, Francis J., jt. ed. see Haque, Rizwanel.

Birou see Schlegal, John P., et al.

Birou, Alain. Lexico De Economia. 6th ed. 200p. (Span.). 1977. pap. 8.75 (ISBN 84-7222-751-0, S-50040). French & Eur.

--Lexico De Sociologia. 5th ed. 114p. (Span.). 1975. pap. 8.75 (ISBN 84-7222-753-7, S-50041). French & Eur.

--Vocabulaire Pratique des Sciences Sociales. 384p. (Fr.). 29.95 (ISBN 0-686-57277-7, F-136960). French & Eur.

Birr, C. Aspects of the Merrifield Peptide Synthesis. (Reactivity & Structure Ser.: Vol. 8). (Illus.). 1978. 28.00 (ISBN 0-387-08872-5). Springer-Verlag.

Birr, C., ed. Methods of Peptide & Protein Sequence Analysis: Proceedings of the International Conference on Solid Phase, 3rd, Heidelberg, October 1-4, 1979. 532p. 1980. 92.00 (ISBN 0-444-80218-5, Biomedical Pr). Elsevier.

Birr, Kendall, jt. auth. see Curti, Merle E.

Birr, Shirley, jt. auth. see Rouch, Roger L.

Birrel, Augustine. William Hazlitt: English Men of Letters. 230p. 1979. Repr. lib. bdg. 17.50 (ISBN 0-89987-051-1). Darby Bks.

Birrell, Anne, tr. New Songs from a Jade Terrace: An Anthology of Early Chinese Love Poetry. 374p. 1982. 28.50 (ISBN 0-04-895026-2). Allen Unwin.

Birrell, Augustine. Andrew Marvell. LC 77-39666. (Select Bibliographies Reprint Ser). 1972. Repr. of 1905 ed. 15.50 (ISBN 0-8369-9929-0). Ayer Co Pubs.

--Andrew Marvell. LC 78-14755. 1905. lib. bdg. 15.00 (ISBN 0-8414-1730-X). Folcroft.

--Collected Essays & Addresses, Eighteen Eighty to Nineteen Twenty, 3 vols. facs. ed. LC 68-24844. (Essay Index Reprint Ser.). 1922. Set. 60.50 (ISBN 0-8369-0214-9). Ayer Co Pubs.

--Emerson: A Lecture. 1978. Repr. of 1903 ed. lib. bdg. 8.50 (ISBN 0-8495-0422-8). Arden Lib.

--Emerson: A Lecture. LC 72-193664. 1903. lib. bdg. 8.50 (ISBN 0-8414-9936-5). Folcroft.

--Essays about Men, Women & Books. LC 71-115231. 1970. Repr. of 1894 ed. 21.00 (ISBN 0-403-00451-9). Scholarly.

--Essays & Addresses. facsimile ed. LC 75-104998. (Essay Index Reprint Ser.). 1901. 19.00 (ISBN 0-8369-1451-1). Ayer Co Pubs.

--Et Cetera: A Collection. facsimile ed. LC 72-167310. (Essay Index Reprint Ser). Repr. of 1930 ed. 18.00 (ISBN 0-8369-2453-3). Ayer Co Pubs.

--In the Name of the Bodleian: And Other Essays. LC 70-177952. (Essay Index Reprint Ser.). Repr. of 1905 ed. 17.00 (ISBN 0-8369-2893-8). Ayer Co Pubs.

--Life of Charlotte Bronte. Robertson, E. S., ed. LC 78-148752. Repr. of 1887 ed. 14.00 (ISBN 0-404-08726-4). AMS Pr.

--Life of Charlotte Bronte. 1887. lib. bdg. 17.00 (ISBN 0-8414-9115-1). Folcroft.

--More Obiter Dicta. facs. ed. LC 68-57304. (Essay Index Reprint Ser). 1924. 17.00 (ISBN 0-8369-0062-6). Ayer Co Pubs.

--Obiter Dicta. LC 17-21084. (First & Second Ser.). 1969. Repr. of 1887 ed. 9.00x (ISBN 0-403-00131-5). Scholarly.

--Selected Essays: Eighteen Eighty-four to Nineteen Seven. 383p. 1983. Repr. of 1908 ed. lib. bdg. 30.00 (ISBN 0-89984-098-1). Century Bookbindery.

--Seven Lectures on the Law & History of Copyright in Books. 228p. 1971. Repr. of 1899 ed. 20.00x (ISBN 0-8377-1929-1). Rothman.

--Seven Lectures on the Law & History of Copyright in Books. LC 74-112404. 228p. 1971. Repr. lib. bdg. 25.00x (ISBN 0-678-04538-0). Kelley.

--William Hazlitt. LC 70-98817. Repr. of 1902 ed. lib. bdg. 18.75x (ISBN 0-8371-2848-X, BIWH). Greenwood.

--William Hazlitt. 230p. 1983. Repr. of 1902 ed. text ed. 20.00 (ISBN 0-89984-134-1). Century Bookbindery.

Birrell, Derek & Murie, Alan. Policy & Government in Northern Ireland: Lessons of Devolution. LC 79-53790. 353p. 1980. 32.50x (ISBN 0-389-20019-0, 06348). B&N Imports.

Birrell, Francis. A Letter from a Black Sheep. 1973. Repr. of 1932 ed. 8.50 (ISBN 0-8274-1481-1). R West.

Birrell, Gordon. The Boundless Present: Space & Time in the Literary Fairy Tales of Novalis & Tieck. (Studies in the Germanic Languages & Literatures: No. 95). ix, 163p. 1979. 14.00 (ISBN 0-8078-8095-7). U of NC Pr.

Birrell, J. F. Paediatric Otolaryngology. (Illus.). 216p. 1978. pap. text ed. 31.00 (ISBN 0-7236-0479-7). PSG Pub Co.

Birrell, Murray. Essays about Men, Women & Books. Repr. 8.50 (ISBN 0-8274-2289-X). R West.

Birrell, N. D. & Davies, P. C. Quantum Fields in Curved Space. LC 81-3851. (Cambridge Monographs on Mathematical Physics: No. 7). (Illus.). 340p. 1982. 57.50 (ISBN 0-521-23385-2). Cambridge U Pr.

--Quantum Fields in Curved Space. (Cambridge Monographs in Mathematical Physics). 360p. 1984. pap. 27.95 (ISBN 0-521-27858-9). Cambridge U Pr.

Birrell, N. D. & Ould, M. A. A Practical Handbook for Software Development. (Illus.). 275p. 1985. 34.50 (ISBN 0-521-25462-0). Cambridge U Pr.

Birrell, Robert & Hill, Douglas, eds. Quarry Australia? Social & Environmental Perspectives on Managing the Nations Resources. (Illus.). 1982. text ed. 47.00x (ISBN 0-19-554345-9). Oxford U Pr.

Birrell, Susan, jt. auth. see Hart, Marie.

Birrell, T. A. The Library of John Morris: The Reconstruction of a Seventeenth-Century Collection. 108p. 1980. 50.00x (ISBN 0-7141-0365-9, Pub. by Brit Lib England). State Mutual Bk.

Birrell, Verla. The Textile Arts: A Handbook of Weaving, Braiding, Printing, & Other Textile Techniques. LC 58-8363. (Illus.). 530p. 1973. pap. 8.95 (ISBN 0-8052-0390-7). Schocken.

Birrell, Vivian T. The Psychological Theory of the Sexual Temptations. 1979. deluxe ed. 53.15 (ISBN 0-930582-28-4). Gloucester Art.

Birren, Faber. Color: A Survey in Words & Pictures. (Illus.). 256p. 1984. pap. 14.95 (ISBN 0-8065-0849-3). Citadel Pr.

--Color & Human Response. LC 77-12505. (Illus.). 120p. 1978. pap. 10.95 (ISBN 0-442-20961-4). Van Nos Reinhold.

--Color in Your World. rev. ed. (Illus.). 126p. 1978. pap. 3.95 (ISBN 0-02-075570-8, Collier). Macmillan.

--Color Psychology & Color Therapy. (Illus.). 302p. 1984. 7.95 (ISBN 0-8065-0653-9). Citadel Pr.

--Light, Color, & Environment. rev. ed. 112p. 1969. pap. 16.95 (ISBN 0-442-21270-4). Van Nos Reinhold.

--Principles of Color: A Review of Past Traditions & Modern Theories. 1969. pap. 9.95 (ISBN 0-442-20774-3). Van Nos Reinhold.

Birren, Faber, ed. see Itten, Johannes.

Birren, J. E., ed. Aging: A Challenge to Science & Society; Vol. 3, Behavioral Sciences & Conclusions. (Illus.). 1983. text ed. 74.00x (ISBN 0-19-261256-5). Oxford U Pr.

Birren, James, et al, eds. Human Aging. LC 79-8658. (Growing Old Ser.). (Illus.). 1980. Repr. of 1963 ed. lib. bdg. 30.50x (ISBN 0-405-12776-6). Ayer Co Pubs.

Birren, James E. Psychology of Aging. 1964. text ed. 27.95 (ISBN 0-13-733428-1). P-H.

--Relations of Development & Aging. (Illus.). 308p. 1964. photocopy ed. 24.50x (ISBN 0-398-00155-3). C C Thomas.

Birren, James E., jt. auth. see Welford, A. T.

Birren, James E., jt. auth. see Woodruff, Diana S.

Birren, James E. & Livington, Judy, eds. Cognition, Stress, & Aging. (Illus.). 240p. 1985. text ed. 29.95 (ISBN 0-13-139825-3). P-H.

Birren, James E. & Sloane, R. Bruce, eds. Handbook of Mental Health & Aging. (Illus.). 1980. text ed. 92.00 (ISBN 0-13-380261-2). P-H.

Birren, James E. & Stein, Leon, eds. Relations of Development & Aging. LC 79-8659. (Growing Old Ser.). (Illus.). 1980. Repr. of 1964 ed. lib. bdg. 27.50x (ISBN 0-405-12775-8). Ayer Co Pubs.

Birren, James E., et al. The Process of Aging in the Nervous System. (Illus.). 240p. 1959. photocopy ed. 22.50x (ISBN 0-398-00156-1). C C Thomas.

--Developmental Psychology: A Life-Span Approach. LC 80-82839. (Illus.). 736p. 1981. text ed. 28.50 (ISBN 0-395-29717-6); instr's manual 2.50 (ISBN 0-395-29718-4); test-bank 1.75 (ISBN 0-395-29720-6); study guide 10.50 (ISBN 0-395-29719-2). HM.

--Age, Health & Employment. 192p. 1986. text ed. 29.95 (ISBN 0-13-018524-8). P-H.

Birrer, Christina D., jt. auth. see Birrer, Richard B.

Birrer, Cynthia. Multiple Sclerosis: A Personal View. (Illus.). 304p. 1979. 24.75x (ISBN 0-398-03864-3). C C Thomas.

Birrer, Cynthia & Birrer, William. The Shoemaker & the Elves. LC 83-1145. (Illus.). 32p. (gr. k-3). 1983. 11.75 (ISBN 0-688-01988-9); PLB 11.88 (ISBN 0-688-01989-7). Lothrop.

Birrer, Richard. Sports Medicine for the Primary Care Physician. (Illus.). 400p. 1983. 34.95 (ISBN 0-8385-8651-1). ACC.

Birrer, Richard B. Pathogenetic Mechanisms of Disease: A Primer for the Primary Care Specialist. 186p. 1985. 22.50 (ISBN 0-87527-336-X). Green.

Birrer, Richard B. & Birrer, Christina D. Medical Diagnostic Signs: A Reference Collection of Eponymic Bedside Signs. 118p. 1982. 14.75x (ISBN 0-398-04541-0). C C Thomas.

--Medical Injuries in the Martial Arts. (Illus.). 240p. 1981. 18.75x (ISBN 0-398-04133-4); pap. 12.95x (ISBN 0-398-04134-2). C C Thomas.

Birrer, William, jt. auth. see Birrer, Cynthia.

Birriel, Marta C. & Williams, J. Clifton. Conducta Organizacional. (Span.). 1984. text ed. 18.95 (ISBN 0-538-22760-5, V76). SW Pub.

Birringer, Johannes. Marlowe's "Dr Faustus" & "Tamburlaine". Theological & Theatrical Perspectives. (Trier Studien zur Literatur: Vol. 10). 402p. (Orig.). 1983. pap. text ed. 40.55 (ISBN 0-8204-5421-4). P Lang Pubs.

Birsner, E. Patricia & Balsley, Ronald D. Practical Guide to Customer Service Management & Operation. 224p. 1982. 19.95 (ISBN 0-8144-5673-1). AMACOM.

--Practical Guide to Customer Service Management & Operations. LC 81-69366. pap. 56.00 (ISBN 0-317-26242-4, 2052140). Bks Demand UMI.

Birss, Robert R., jt. auth. see Gerber, Richard.

Birt, David. The Black Death. (Resource Units: Middle Ages, 1066-1485). (Illus.). 24p. 1974. pap. text ed. 12.95x 10 copies & tchr's guide (ISBN 0-582-39383-3). Longman.

--The Black Prince. (Resouces Units: Middle Ages, 1066-1484 Ser.). (Illus.). 24p. 1974. pap. text ed. 12.95x 10 copies & tchr's guide (ISBN 0-582-39382-5). Longman.

--Knights & Tournaments. (Resource Units: Middle Ages 1066-1485 Ser.). (Illus.). 24p. 1974. pap. text ed. 12.95 10 copies & tchr's guide (ISBN 0-582-39374-4). Longman.

--The Medieval Town. (Resource Units: Middle Ages, 1066-1485 Ser.). (Illus.). 24p. (Orig.). 1974. pap. text ed. 12.95 10 copies & tchr's guide (ISBN 0-582-39389-2). Longman.

--The Medieval Village. (Resoource Units: Middle Ages, 1066-1485 Ser.). (Illus.). 24p. 1974. pap. text ed. 12.95 10 copies & tchr's guide (ISBN 0-582-39373-6). Longman.

--The Monastery. (Resource Units: Middle Ages, 1066-1485 Ser.). (Illus.). 1974. pap. text ed. 12.95x 10 copies & tchr's guide (ISBN 0-582-39380-9). Longman.

--The Murder of Becket. (Resource Units: Middle Ages, 1066-1485 Ser.). (Illus.). 24p. 1974. pap. text ed. 12.95 10 copies & tchr's guide (ISBN 0-582-39376-0). Longman.

--The Norman Conquest. (Resource Units: Middle Ages, 1066-1485 Ser.). (Illus.). 24p. 1974. pap. text ed. 12.95 10 copies & tchr's guide (ISBN 0-582-39372-8). Longman.

--Peasants Revolt. (Resource Units: Middle Ages, 1066-1485 Ser.). (Illus.). 24p. 1974. pap. text ed. 12.95 10 copies & tchr's guide (ISBN 0-582-39384-1). Longman.

--Stephen & Matilda. (Resource Units: Middles Ages, 1066-1485 Ser.). (Illus.). 24p. 1974. pap. text ed. 12.95 10 copies & tchr's guide (ISBN 0-582-39375-2). Longman.

Birt, David, jt. auth. see Fletcher, Mark.

Birt, Robert F. Basic Grammar & Punctuation: A Text-Workbook Program. 111p. (Orig.). 1979. pap. text ed. 8.50 (ISBN 0-911593-06-3). Morrison Pub Co.

Birt, Robert F., jt. auth. see Morrison, Leger.

Birt, Robert F., jt. auth. see Morrison, Leger R.

Birta-Probert. Algorithm Design I. 148p. 1983. shrink wrapped 11.95 (ISBN 0-8403-3138-X). Kendall-Hunt.

Birtchnell, J., et al. Effects of Early Parent Death. (Attitudes Toward Death Ser.: Vol. 1). 177p. 1973. text ed. 27.00x (ISBN 0-8422-7145-7). Irvington.

Birth Defects Annual Conference, 10th Memphis, Tenn., June, 1977. Annual Review of Birth Defects, 1977: Proceedings, 3 vols. Summitt, Robert L. & Bergsma, Daniel, eds. Incl. No. 6A. Cell Surface Factors,Immune Deficiencies, Twin Studies. LC 78-17058. 240p. 37.00 (ISBN 0-8451-1020-9); No. 6B. Recent Advances & New Syndromes. LC 78-17056. 400p. 61.00 (ISBN 0-8451-1021-7); No. 6C. Sex Differentiation & Chromosomal Abnormalities. LC 78-17057. 440p. 67.00 (ISBN 0-8451-1022-5). (Birth Defects: Original Article Ser.: Vol. 14, No. 6). (Illus.). 1978. Set. 125.00 (ISBN 0-8451-0951-0). A R Liss.

Birth Defects Conference, Kansas City, Mo., May 1975. Growth Problems & Clinical Advances: Proceedings. Bergsma, Daniel & Schimke, R. Neil, eds. LC 76-21714. (Birth Defects - Original Article Ser.: Vol. 12, No. 6). 340p. 1976. 46.00x (ISBN 0-8451-1005-5). A R Liss.

Birth Defects Conference-1975, Kansas City, Missouri. Cancer & Genetics: Proceedings. Bergsma, Daniel, ed. LC 75-43622. (Birth Defects-Original Article Ser.: Vol. 12, No. 1). 212p. 1976. 31.00x (ISBN 0-8451-1002-0). A R Liss.

Birth Defects Conference, 1975, Kansas City, Missouri. Cytogenetics, Environment & Malformation Syndromes: Proceedings. Bergsma, Daniel & Schimke, R. Neil, eds. LC 76-20510. (Birth Defects Original Article Ser.: Vol. 12, No. 5). 364p. 1976. 46.00x (ISBN 0-8451-1004-7). A R Liss.

Birth Defects Conference, 1978, San Francisco. Risk, Communication, & Decision Making in Genetic Counseling: Proceedings, Annual Review of Birth Defects, 1978, Pt. C. Epstein, Charles J., et al, eds. LC 79-5120. (Birth Defects: Original Article Ser.: Vol. XV, No. 5C). 392p. 1979. 47.00x (ISBN 0-8451-1030-6). A R Liss.

Birtha, Becky. For Nights Like This One: Stories of Loving Women. LC 82-21087. 128p. (Orig.). 1983. pap. 4.75 (ISBN 0-9603628-4-3). Frog in Well.

Birtles, Philip. Planemakers: DeHavilland. (Planemakers Ser.). (Illus.). 160p. 1984. 17.95 (ISBN 0-7106-0303-7). Jane's Pub Inc.

Birtles, T. G., jt. auth. see Menghetti, D.

Birtwell, Charles W., jt. ed. see Spencer, Anna G.

Birtwhistle, John. The Conversion to Oil of the Lots Road London Transport Power Station & Other Poems. 1972. pap. 1.95 (ISBN 0-685-27674-0, Pub. by Anvil Pr); pap. 5.00 signed ltd. ed. (ISBN 0-685-27675-9). Small Pr Dist.

Birtwistle, Graham M. & Dahl, Ole-Johan. Simula Begin. 391p. 1979. pap. text ed. 29.50x (ISBN 91-44-06212-5, Pub. by Chartwell-Bratt England). Brookfield Pub Co.

Biruni, Al. The Chronology of Ancient Nations: An English Version of the Arab Text of Athar-ul-Bakiya of Albiruni. Sachau, Edward C., tr. (Islam Ser.). 1976. lib. bdg. 59.95 (ISBN 0-8490-1624-X). Gordon Pr.

Birx, H. James. Pierre Teilhard De Chardin's Philosophy of Evolution. 192p. 1972. 18.50x (ISBN 0-398-02466-9). C C Thomas.

--Theories of Evolution. 432p. 1984. 39.50x (ISBN 0-398-04902-5). C C Thomas.

Biryukov, N. S. Television in the West & Its Doctrines. 207p. 1981. 5.80 (ISBN 0-8285-2058-5, Pub. by Progress Pubs USSR). Imported Pubns.

Birzea, Cesar, compiled by. Educational Research in Five European Socialist Countries: A Survey, 1972. (Documents on Educational Research: No. 3). 198p. (Orig., Eng. & Fr.). 1973. pap. 5.00 (ISBN 92-820-0001-X, U213, UNESCO). Unipub.

BIS Applied Systems & MacKintosh International. The Local Area Network Reference Guide. Brooks, Tom, ed. (Illus.). 288p. 1985. text ed. 70.00 (ISBN 0-13-539586-0). P-H.

BIS Applied Systems, Inc. Data Base Techniques: Software Selection & Systems Development. LC 80-50100. 562p. 1980. pap. 24.50 (ISBN 0-89435-043-9). QED Info Sci.

BIS-PEDDER Associates Ltd. Computing Marketplace: A Directory of Computing Services & Software Supplies for Word Processors, Micros, Minis, & Mainframes. 2nd ed. (Computing Services for the Eighties). 472p. (Orig.). 1983. pap. text ed. 69.50x (ISBN 0-566-03476-X). Gower Pub Co.

Bisagno, John. God Is. 1981. 3.95 (ISBN 0-88207-345-1). Victor Bks.

--Power of Positive Praying. 1965. pap. 2.50 (ISBN 0-310-21212-X). Zondervan.

Bisagno, John R. Great Mysteries of the Bible. LC 81-67997. 1982. 7.95 (ISBN 0-8054-1952-7). Broadman.

--How to Build an Evangelistic Church. LC 78-178055. 1972. 8.50 (ISBN 0-8054-2524-1). Broadman.

--Life Without Compromise. LC 81-71253. 1983. 3.50 (ISBN 0-8054-1503-3). Broadman.

--Love Is Something You Do. LC 75-9314. 1979. pap. 6.68 (ISBN 0-06-060793-9, RD-238, HarpR). Har-Row.

--Power of Positive Evangelism: How to Hold a Revival. LC 68-26912. 1968. pap. 3.95 (ISBN 0-8054-2503-9). Broadman.

--Power of Positive Living. LC 70-93913. (Orig.). 1970. pap. 3.25 (ISBN 0-8054-1910-1). Broadman.

Bisagno, Juan. El Poder De la Oracion Tenaz. De Lerin, Olivia S. D., tr. from Eng. Orig. Title: The Power of Positive Praying. 96p. (Span.). 1983. pap. 2.15 (ISBN 0-311-40029-9). Casa Bautista.

Bisanz, J., et al, eds. Learning in Children: Progress in Cognitive Development Research. (Springer Series in Cognitive Development). (Illus.). 201p. 1983. 25.00 (ISBN 0-387-90802-1). Springer-Verlag.

Bisanz, Rudolf. The Rene von Schleinitz Collection of the Milwaukee Art Center: Major Schools of German Nineteenth-Century Popular Painting. LC 78-53284. (Illus.). 256p. 1980. 37.50x (ISBN 0-299-07700-4). U of Wis Pr.

Bisanz, Rudolf M. German Romanticism & Philipp Otto Runge: A Study in Nineteenth-Century Art Theory & Iconography. LC 74-98388. (Illus.). 144p. 1970. 17.50 (ISBN 0-87580-013-0). N Ill U Pr.

Bisbee, A. The History & Practice of Daguerreotyping. LC 72-9183. (The Literature of Photography Ser.). Repr. of 1853 ed. 17.00 (ISBN 0-405-04894-7). . Ayer Co Pubs.

Bisbee, Charles A. Harvest. 1984. 12.75 (ISBN 0-8062-2287-5). Carlton.

Bisbee, Eleanor. The New Turks: Pioneers of the Republic, 1920-1950. LC 74-23411. (Illus.). 298p. 1975. Repr. of 1951 ed. lib. bdg. 22.50x (ISBN 0-8371-7868-1, BINT). Greenwood.

Bisbee, Gerald E., Jr. & Vraciu, Robert A. Managing the Finances of Health Care Organizations. 549p. 1980. 15.95 (ISBN 0-914904-51-5, 1140); 28.95 (ISBN 0-914904-50-7, 1142). Healthcare Fin Mgmt Assn.

Bisbee, Kolan K., jt. auth. see Hawkins, Harry M.

Bisbee Press Collective. Second Bisbee Anthology. Dietz, Chris & Gregory, Michael, eds. 56p. (Orig.). 1983. pap. 8.00x (ISBN 0-938196-03-0). Bisbee Pr.

Bisbee Press Collective, ed. The Bisbee Anthology Nineteen Eighty: Poetry. 62p. (Orig.). 1980. pap. 5.00 (ISBN 0-938196-00-6). Bisbee Pr.

Bisby, jt. auth. see Ainsworth.

Bisby, jt. auth. see Ainsworth, G. C.

Bisby, F. A., et al, eds. Chemosystematics: Principles & Practice. LC 80-41428. (Systematic Association Ser.: No. 16). 1981. 85.00 (ISBN 0-12-101550-5). Acad Pr.

Bisby, Frank, jt. auth. see Allkin, Robert.

Bisby, J. R., et al, eds. Electrical Fitting, Vol. 2. (Engineering Craftsmen: No. G23). (Illus.). 1969. spiral bdg. 47.50x (ISBN 0-89563-002-8). Trans-Atlantic.

Bisby's, jt. auth. see Ainsworth.

Bisceglia, Louis. Norman Angell & Liberal Internationalism in Britain 1931-1935. Stanksky, Peter & Hume, Leslie, eds. LC 81-48355. (Modern British History Ser.). 250p. 1982. lib. bdg. 40.00 (ISBN 0-8240-5150-5). Garland Pub.

Bischel, Jon E. & Feinschreiber, Robert. Fundamentals of International Taxation. 2nd ed. 450p. text ed. 70.00 (ISBN 0-317-14136-8, J1-1450). PLI.

Bischel, Jon E., ed. Income Tax Treaties. LC 78-58373. 1978. text ed. 25.00 (ISBN 0-685-65701-9, J3-1412). PLI.

Bischko, Johannes. An Introduction to Acupuncture. Reese-Soltesz, Diana, tr. 1978. pap. 12.95 (ISBN 3-7760-0506-8). Volcano Pr.

Bischler, H. Marchantia I: The New World Species. (Bryophytorum Bibliotheca Ser.: 26). (Illus.). 228p. 1984. text ed. 21.00x (ISBN 3-7682-1401-X). Lubrecht & Cramer.

Bischler, H., ed. see Bonner, C. E. B.

Bischof, P. Placental Proteins. (Contributions to Gynecology & Obstetrics: Vol. 12). (Illus.). viii, 96p. 1984. 28.25 (ISBN 3-8055-3853-7). S Karger.

Bischof, P. & Klopper, A., eds. Proteins of the Placenta. (Illus.). viii, 208p. 1985. 76.25 (ISBN 3-8055-4034-5). S Karger.

Bischoff, jt. auth. see Woodard.

Bischoff, A., jt. ed. see Luthy, F.

Bischoff, Alesia. The Beautiful Puppy. (Little Book Ser). (Illus.). (gr. k-6). 1976. 0.50 (ISBN 0-89409-008-9). Childrens Art.

Bischoff, David. The Crunch Bunch. 144p. 1985. pap. 2.50 (ISBN 0-380-89695-8, Flare). Avon.

--Destiny Dice. (Gaming Magi Ser.: Bk. 1). 1985. pap. 2.95 (ISBN 0-451-13489-3, Sig). NAL.

--Galactic Warriors. (Star Hounds Ser.: No. 2). 160p. 1985. pap. 2.75 (ISBN 0-441-27256-8). Ace Bks.

--The Infinite Battle. (Star Hounds Ser.: No. 1). 176p. 1985. pap. 2.75 (ISBN 0-441-37018-7, Pub. by Ace Science Fiction). Ace Bks.

--The Vampires of the Nightworld. (Orig.). 1981. pap. 2.25 (ISBN 0-345-28763-0, Del Rey). Ballantine.

--War Games. 224p. (Orig.). 1983. pap. 2.95 (ISBN 0-440-19387-7). Dell.

Bischoff, David & Bailey, Dennis. Tin Woodman. 256p. 1982. pap. 2.50 (ISBN 0-441-81292-9). Ace Bks.

Bischoff, David & White, Ted. Forbidden World. 224p. 1985. pap. 2.95 (ISBN 0-445-20017-0, Pub. by Popular Lib). Warner Bks.

Bischoff, David, jt. auth. see Byron Preiss Visual Publications Inc.

Bischoff, David, jt. auth. see Sheffield, Charles.

Bischoff, David, et al. A Personal Demon. 1985. pap. 2.95 (ISBN 0-451-13814-7, Sig). NAL.

Bischoff, David E. & Monteleone, Thomas E. Night of the Dragonstar. 272p. 1985. pap. 2.95 (ISBN 0-425-07963-5). Berkley Pub.

Bischoff, David F. Mandala. 240p. 1983. pap. 2.50 (ISBN 0-425-06275-9). Berkley Pub.

Bischoff, David F. & Bailey, Dennis R. Tin Woodman. 192p. 1985. pap. 2.75 (ISBN 0-441-81293-7). Ace Bks.

Bischoff, David F. & Monteleone, Thomas F. Day of the Dragonstar. 352p. (Orig.). 1985. pap. 2.95 (ISBN 0-425-08172-9). Berkley Pub.

Bischoff, Erich. The Kabbala: An Introduction to Jewish Mysticism & Secret Doctrine. LC 84-52262. 1985. pap. 5.95 (ISBN 0-87728-564-0). Weiser.

Bischoff, Ernst. Microscopic Analysis of the Anastomoses Between the Cranial Nerves. Sachs, Ernst, Jr. & Valtin, Eva W., eds. LC 77-72520. pap. 37.00 (ISBN 0-317-20022-4, 2023231). Bks Demand UMI.

Bischoff, F. A. Kanjur und Seine Kolophone, Pts. 1 & 2. LC 68-19043. 1968. Set. pap. 25.00x (ISBN 0-911706-03-8). Selbstverlag.

Bischoff, J. Comprehensive History of the Woollen & the Worsted Manufacturers, 2 vols. (Illus.). 1968. Repr. of 1842 ed. 75.00x (ISBN 0-7146-1387-8, F Cass Co). Biblio Dist.

Bischoff, J. L. & Piper, D. Z., eds. Marine Geology & Oceanography of the Pacific Manganese Nodule Province. LC 79-12475. (Marine Science Ser.: Vol. 9). 855p. 1979. 89.50x (ISBN 0-306-40187-8, Plenum Pr). Plenum Pub.

Bischoff, John, jt. auth. see Bird, Larry.

Bischoff, John R., jt. auth. see Bird, Larry J.

Bischoff, K. B., jt. auth. see Uhl, A. E.

Bischoff, Kenneth B., jt. auth. see Froment, Gilbert F.

Bischoff, Louis V. New Look at the Bible Tradition. LC 62-21556. 1963. 7.50 (ISBN 0-8022-0132-6). Philos Lib.

Bischoff, Ralph F. Nazi Conquest Through German Culture. LC 78-63651. (Studies in Fascism: Ideology & Practice). Repr. of 1942 ed. 27.50 (ISBN 0-404-16906-6). AMS Pr.

Bischoff, William N., intro. by. We Were Not Summer Soldiers: The Indian War Diary of Plympton J. Kelly 1855-1856. LC 76-11999. (Illus.). 191p. 1976. Repr. 8.75 (ISBN 0-917048-00-8). Wash St Hist Soc.

Biscoe, Eleanor, ed. Planning for Statewide Continuing Education for Library-Information-Media Personnel. 1980. 5.00 (ISBN 0-686-39877-7); 4.25 (ISBN 0-686-39878-5). Clene Pubns.

Bisconte, J. C. & Sklansky, J., eds. Biomedical Images & Computers: St. Pierre de Chartreuse, France 1980, Proceedings. (Lecture Notes in Medical Informatics: Vol. 17). 332p. 1982. pap. 23.00 (ISBN 0-387-11579-X). Springer-Verlag.

Biscuits & Bows. Home Cooking Southern Style. LC 84-17567. 52p. 1984. pap. 2.95 (ISBN 0-87797-089-0). Cherokee.

Bisdom, E. B. Submicroscopy of Soils & Weathered Rocks: First Workshop of the International Working Group on Submicroscopy of Undisturbed Soil Materials, Wageningen, The Netherlands, 1980. 320p. (Eng. & Fr.). 1981. 45.25 (ISBN 90-220-0777-4, PDC235, Pudoc). Unipub.

Bisdom, E. B. & Duclox, J., eds. Submicroscopic Studies of Soils. (Developments in Soil Science Ser.: Vol. 12). 352p. 1983. Repr. 79.00 (ISBN 0-444-42195-5, I-308-83). Elsevier.

Bise, Christopher J., ed. see Stefanko, Robert.

Bise, Gabriel, ed. Medieval Legends. 192p. 1983. 16.95 (ISBN 0-312-52726-8). St Martin.

Bisen, Malini, tr. see Rajneesh, Acharya.

Bisgaard, Erling & Aaron, Tossi. In Canon: Explorations of Familiar Canons for Voices, Recorders & Orff Instruments. 1978. pap. 5.75 (ISBN 0-918812-03-8). MMB Music.

Bisgaard, Erling & Stehouwer, Gulle. Musicbook 0: Songs, Games, Movement Activities for Teaching Music to Young Children. Aaron, Tossi, ed. 1976. pap. 6.50 (ISBN 0-918812-04-6). MMB Music.

Bish, Robert L. Governing Puget Sound. LC 82-2743. (A Puget Sound Bk.). (Illus.). 136p. (Orig.). 1982. pap. 8.95 (ISBN 0-295-95886-3, Pub. by Wash Sea Grant). U of Wash Pr.

Bish, Robert L. & Ostrom, Vincent. Understanding Urban Government: Metropolitan Reform Reconsidered. 1973. pap. 5.25 (ISBN 0-8447-3120-X). Am Enterprise.

Bish, Tommy L. Home Gunsmithing Digest. 3rd ed. 256p. 1984. pap. 11.95 (ISBN 0-910676-71-2). DBI.

Bishay, A. & McGinnies, W. G., eds. Applications of Science & Technology for Desert Development. (Advances in Desert & Arid Land Technology & Development: Vol. 1). 630p. 1979. lib. bdg. 102.95 (ISBN 3-7186-0002-1). Harwood Academic.

Bishay, Adlai, ed. Recent Advances in Science & Technology of Materials, 3 vols. LC 74-17098. 1974. Vol. 1, 419p. 65.00x (ISBN 0-306-37691-1, Plenum Pr); Vol. 2, 449p. 65.00x (ISBN 0-306-37692-X); Vol. 3, 391p. 65.00x (ISBN 0-306-37693-8). Plenum Pub.

Bishay, Adli, ed. Interaction of Radiation with Solids. LC 67-19567. 701p. 1967. 62.50x (ISBN 0-306-30302-7, Plenum Pr). Plenum Pub.

Bishchoff, Heather W., jt. auth. see Woodard, Ed U.

Biship, Neal. Everywhere the Light. Young, Billie, ed. LC 78-14861. 1979. 14.95 (ISBN 0-87949-137-X). Ashley Bks.

Bishirjian, Richard. The Nature of Public Philosophy. LC 82-20170. 62p. 1983. Repr. of 1978 ed. pap. text ed. 4.50 (ISBN 0-8191-2861-9). U Pr of Amer.

Bishko, Charles J. Studies in Medieval Spanish Frontier History. 336p. 1980. 75.00x (ISBN 0-86078-069-4, Pub. by Variorum England). State Mutual Bk.

Bishofs, Maris. Feisty Virginia Woolf. LC 85-1306. (Illus.). 96p. (Orig.). 1985. pap. 9.95 (ISBN 0-915361-17-5, Dist. by Watts). Adama Pubs Inc.

Bishop. The Shirt Look. (Illus.). 116p. (Orig.). 1976. pap. 4.12 (ISBN 0-397-40193-0). Har-Row.

--Staff Development & Instructional Improvement: Plans & Procedures. 1985. 25.95 (ISBN 0-205-05470-6, 225470). Allyn.

--The Tailored Look. (Illus.). 128p. (Orig.). 1976. pap. 4.12 (ISBN 0-397-40246-5). Har-Row.

Bishop & Burns. Lining, Underlining, Interfacing. (Illus.). 72p. (Orig.). 1976. pap. 4.12 (ISBN 0-397-40245-7). Har-Row.

Bishop, jt. auth. see Lee.

Bishop, A., ed. Rutherford B. Hayes, 1822-1893: Chronology, Documents, Bibliographical Aids. LC 69-15394. (Presidential Chronology Ser.: No. 12). 96p. 1969. 8.00 (ISBN 0-379-12062-3). Oceana.

--Thomas Jefferson 1743-1826: Chronology, Documents, Bibliographical Aids. LC 70-140619. (Presidential Chronology Ser). 122p. 1971. 8.00 (ISBN 0-379-12082-8). Oceana.

Bishop, A. A. & Kulacki, F. A., eds. Nuclear Reactor Safety Heat Transfer: Presented at the Winter Meeting of the ASME. LC 77-87329. pap. 20.00 (ISBN 0-317-09185-9, 2016904). Bks Demand UMI.

Bishop, A. A., jt. ed. see Chen, John C.

Bishop, A. A., jt. ed. see Corradini, M. L.

Bishop, A. C., et al. Catalogue of the Rock Collections in the British Museum (Natural History). 2nd ed. 148p. 1984. pap. text ed. 36.00x (ISBN 0-565-00875-7, Pub by Brit Mus Nat Hist England). Sabbot-Natural Hist Bks.

Bishop, A. J. & Nickson, Marilyn. Research on the Social Context of Mathematics Education. 84p. 1983. 10.00x (ISBN 0-7005-0613-6, Pub. by NFER Nelson UK). Taylor & Francis.

Bishop, A. R. & Schneider, T., eds. Solutions & Condensed Matter Physics: Proceedings. rev. ed. (Series in Solid-State Sciences: Vol. 8). (Illus.). 342p. 1978. 35.00 (ISBN 0-387-09138-6). Springer-Verlag.

Bishop, A. R., et al. Nonlinear Problems: Present & Future. (Mathematical Studies: Vol. 61). 484p. 1982. 64.00 (ISBN 0-444-86395-8, North-Holland). Elsevier.

Bishop, A. R., et al, eds. Fronts, Interfaces & Patterns: Proceedings of the 3rd International Conference, Held at the Centre for Non-linear Studies, Los Alamos, NM, 2-6 May, 1983. 436p. 1984. 63.00 (ISBN 0-444-86906-9, North Holland). Elsevier.

Bishop, Ada L. All about the Collie. 2nd ed. (All About Ser.). (Illus.). 144p. 1980. 12.95 (ISBN 0-7207-1215-7, Pub. by Michael Joseph). Merrimack Pub Cir.

Bishop, Adele & Lord, Cile. The Art of Decorative Stenciling. rev. ed. (Handbooks). 192p. 1985. pap. 17.95 (ISBN 0-14-046728-9). Penguin.

Bishop, Alan, ed. see Brittain, Vera.

Bishop, Albert B. Introduction to Discrete-Linear Controls: Theory & Applications. (Operations Research & Industrial Engineering Ser). 1975. 70.00 (ISBN 0-12-101650-1). Acad Pr.

Bishop, Amelia. The Gift & the Giver. LC 84-2796. 1984. 5.95 (ISBN 0-8054-5106-4). Broadman.

Bishop, Ann. Annie O'Kay's Riddle Roundup. (Illus.). 40p. (gr. 2-5). 1981. 8.25 (ISBN 0-525-66727-X, 0801-240). Lodestar Bks.

--Cleo Catra's Riddle Book. (Illus.). (gr. 2-5). 1981. 6.95 (ISBN 0-525-66706-7). Lodestar Bks.

--The Ella Fannie Elephant Riddle Book. LC 74-14931. (Riddle Bk.). (Illus.). 40p. (gr. 1-3). 1974. PLB 7.75 (ISBN 0-8075-1966-9). A Whitman.

--Hello, Mr. Chips: Computer Jokes & Riddles. (Illus.). 64p. (YA) 1982. 9.95 (ISBN 0-525-66775-X, 0966-290); pap. 3.95 (ISBN 0-525-66782-2, 0383-120). Lodestar Bks.

--Merry-Go-Riddle. LC 73-7321. (Riddle Bk.). (Illus.). 40p. (gr. 1-3). 1973. PLB 7.75 (ISBN 0-8075-5072-8). A Whitman.

--Riddle Ages. Rubin, Caroline, ed. LC 77-12828. (Riddle Bk.). (Illus.). (gr. 1-4). 1977. PLB 7.75 (ISBN 0-8075-6965-8). A Whitman.

--Riddle, Raddle, Fiddle Faddle. LC 68-22189. (Riddle Bk.). (Illus.). (gr. 2-4). 1966. PLB 7.75 (ISBN 0-8075-6974-7). A Whitman.

--Wild Bill Hiccup's Riddle Book. Rubin, Caroline, ed. LC 75-33161. (Riddle Bk.). (Illus.). 1975. PLB 7.75 (ISBN 0-8075-9097-5). A Whitman.

Bishop, Anne E. & Simpson, Doris. The Victorian Seaside Cookbook. LC 83-61979. (Illus.). 154p. (Orig.). pap. 8.95 (ISBN 0-911020-09-8). NJ Hist Soc.

Bishop, Anne H. & Scudder, John R., Jr. Caring, Curing, Coping: Nurse, Physician, Patient Relationships. LC 84-8836. 152p. 1985. 13.95 (ISBN 0-8173-0242-5). U of Ala Pr.

Bishop, Arthur C. Outline of Crystal Morphology. 1970. pap. text ed. 10.00x (ISBN 0-09-079423-0). Humanities.

Bishop, Audrey & Bishop, Owen. Handbook of Procedures & Functions for the BBC Micro. (Illus.). 144p. (Orig.). 1984. pap. 13.95 (ISBN 0-246-12415-6, Pub. by Granada England). Sheridan.

--Handbook of Procedures & Functions for the Electron. (Illus.). 151p. (Orig.). 1984. pap. 13.95 (ISBN 0-246-12416-4, Pub. by Granada England). Sheridan.

--Take off with the Electron & BBC Micro. (Illus.). 144p. (Orig.). 1984. pap. 11.95 (ISBN 0-246-12356-7, Pub. by Granada England). Sheridan.

Bishop, Audrey, jt. auth. see Bishop, Owen.

Bishop, B., jt. ed. see Force, R. W.

Bishop, Barbara E. The Maternity Cycle: One Nurse's Reflections. LC 79-13380. (Illus.). 325p. 1980. pap. 15.00x (ISBN 0-8036-0868-3). Davis Co.

Bishop, Beata. My Triumph over Cancer. 270p. Date not set. pap. 9.95 (ISBN 0-87983-380-7). Keats.

Bishop, Beverly. Basic Neurophysiology. 3rd ed. (Illus.). 1982. spiral bdg. 22.50 (ISBN 0-87488-600-7). Med Exam.

--Pain: Its Physiology & Rationale for Management. pap. 3.00 (ISBN 0-912452-23-4). Am Phys Therapy Assn.

--Spasticity: Its Physiology & Management. 1977. pap. 3.00 (ISBN 0-912452-20-X). Am Phys Therapy Assn.

Bishop, Beverly & Craik, Rebecca L. Neural Plasticity. 1982. pap. 5.00 (ISBN 0-912452-38-2). Am Phys Therapy Assn.

Bishop, Billy. Cley Marsh & Its Birds. (Illus.). 134p. 1983. 11.95 (ISBN 0-85115-180-9, Pub. by Boydell & Brewer). Longwood Pub Group.

Bishop, Bob, et al. Apple Visions. 256p. (Orig.). 1985. pap. 39.95 315 bk. disk package (ISBN 0-201-15324-6). Addison-Wesley.

Bishop, C. F. & Maunder, W. F. Potato Mechanisation & Storage. (Illus.). 256p. 22.95 (ISBN 0-85236-109-2, Pub. by Farming Pr UK). Diamond Farm Bk.

Bishop, C. James, jt. auth. see Kopf, David.

Bishop, C. T. see International Union of Pure & Applied Chemistry.

Bishop, Carol. Book of Home Remedies & Herbal Cures. (Octopus Bk.). (Illus.). 1979. 12.50 (ISBN 0-7064-1069-6, Mayflower Bks); pap. 6.95 (ISBN 0-7064-1088-2). Smith Pubs.

--A Critical Edition of Massinger & Fields "The Fatal Dowry". (Salzburg Studies in English Literature, Jacobean Drama Studies: No. 63). 267p. 1976. pap. text ed. 25.50x (ISBN 0-391-01326-2). Humanities.

Bishop, Carolyn, jt. auth. see Rife, Carl B.

Bishop, Carolyn, jt. ed. see Richards, Delphene.

Bishop, Chara, jt. auth. see Mroczkowski, George.

Bishop, Charles, ed. Overview of Blood. LC 74-648008. 1978. pap. 10.00x (ISBN 0-914508-03-2). Blood Info.

Bishop, Claire H. The Five Chinese Brothers. (Illus.). (gr. k-3). 1938. 7.95 (ISBN 0-698-20044-6, Coward). Putnam Pub Group.

--Here Is France. LC 69-20376. (Illus.). 224p. (gr. 7 up). 1969. 10.95 (ISBN 0-374-32970-2). FS&G.

--Twenty & Ten. (Story Bks). (Illus.). 1978. pap. 3.95 (ISBN 0-14-031076-2, Puffin). Penguin.

--Twenty & Ten. (Illus.). 1984. 13.75 (ISBN 0-8446-6168-6). Peter Smith.

Bishop, Claire H., ed. Happy Christmas: Tales for Boys & Girls. LC 56-13330. (Illus.). (gr. 1-8). 1956. text ed. 12.00 (ISBN 0-8044-5111-7, Pub. by Stephen Daye Pr). Ungar.

Bishop, Claude T. How to Edit a Scientific Journal. (The Professional Editing & Publishing Ser.). 138p. 1984. 21.95 (ISBN 0-89495-033-9); pap. 14.95 (ISBN 0-89495-034-7). ISI Pr.

Bishop, Claudia. Irrestible You. (Second Chance at Love Ser.: No. 186). 192p. 1984. pap. 1.95 (ISBN 0-515-07802-6). Jove Pubns.

--Kiss Me Once Again. (Second Chance at Love Ser.). 192p. 1984. pap. 1.95 (ISBN 0-515-08205-8). Jove Pubns.

--That Champagne Feeling. (To Have & to Hold Ser.: No. 26). 192p. 1984. pap. 1.95 (ISBN 0-515-07828-X). Jove Pubns.

--Where the Heart Is. (To Have & to Hold Ser.: No. 36). 192p. 1984. pap. 1.95 (ISBN 0-515-07838-7). Jove Pubns.

Bishop, Coleman. Pictures from English History by the Great Historical Artists. 1977. lib. bdg. 59.95 (ISBN 0-8490-2441-2). Gordon Pr.

Bishop, Cortlandt F. History of Elections in the American Colonies. LC 78-137277. (Columbia University Studies in the Social Sciences: No. 8). Repr. of 1893 ed. 17.00 (ISBN 0-404-51008-6). AMS Pr.

--History of Elections in the American Colonies. (Research & Source Works Ser.: No. 183). 1968. Repr. of 1893 ed. 18.50 (ISBN 0-8337-0296-3). B Franklin.

Bishop, Curtis, et al. America: Ideals & Men. (Illus.). (gr. 8). 1965. text ed. 7.72 (ISBN 0-87443-041-0); tchr's ed. 7.72 (ISBN 0-685-06896-X). Benson.

--Trails to Texas. (Illus.). (gr. 7). 1965. text ed. 7.48 (ISBN 0-87443-039-9); tchrs' ed. 7.48 (ISBN 0-87443-040-2). Benson.

Bishop, D. & Carter, L. P. Crop Science & Food Production. 416p. 1983. text ed. 19.60 (ISBN 0-07-005431-2); activity guide 6.76 (ISBN 0-07-005432-0). McGraw.

Bishop, D. F. & Desnick, R. J., eds. Assays of the Heme Biosynthetic Enzymes. (Journal: Enzyme: Vol. 28, No. 2-3). (Illus.). vi, 144p. 1982. pap. 41.50 (ISBN 3-8055-3573-2). S Karger.

Bishop, D. H. & Compans, R. W., eds. The Replication of Negative Strand Viruses. (Developments in Cell Biology Ser.: Vol. 7). 990p. 1981. 205.00 (ISBN 0-444-00606-0, Biomedical Pr). Elsevier.

Bishop, Dale, jt. ed. see Yarshater, Ehsan.

Bishop, David & Holloway, R. Ross. Wheaton College Collection of Greek & Roman Coins. (Ancient Coins in North American Collections Ser.). (Illus.). 32p. 1981. 30.00 (ISBN 0-89722-190-7). Am Numismatic.

Bishop, David H. Rhabdoviruses, Vol. I. LC 79-20575. 208p. 1979. 59.00 (ISBN 0-8493-5913-9). CRC Pr.

--Rhabdoviruses, 2 vols. 1980. Vol. II, 256 Pgs. 64.00 (ISBN 0-8493-5914-7); Vol. III, 272 Pgs. 69.50 (ISBN 0-8493-5915-5). CRC Pr.

Bishop, David H. & Compans, Richard W., eds. Nonsegmented Negative Strand Viruses: Paramyxoviruses & Rhabodoviruses (Symposium) 1984. 59.00 (ISBN 0-12-102480-6). Acad Pr.

Bishop, David H., jt. ed. see Compans, Richard W.

Bishop, David M. Group Theory & Chemistry. (Illus.). 1973. 49.00x (ISBN 0-19-855140-1). Oxford U Pr.

Bishop, David S. Effective Communication. LC 76-58043. 1977. 5.25 (ISBN 0-87148-285-1); pap. text ed. 4.25 (ISBN 0-87148-286-X). Pathway Pr.

Bishop, Denis, jt. auth. see Ingram, Arthur.

Bishop, Dennis. Cattle of the World. (Illus.). 1978. 12.95 (ISBN 0-7137-0856-5, Pub. by Blandford Pr England). Sterling.

Bishop, Donald G. The Administration of British Foreign Relations. LC 74-3761. 410p. 1974. Repr. of 1961 ed. lib. bdg. 21.50x (ISBN 0-8371-7461-9, BIBF). Greenwood.

--Roosevelt-Litvinov Agreements: The American View. LC 65-15852. 1965. 22.95x (ISBN 0-8156-2077-2). Syracuse U Pr.

Bishop, Doris T., jt. auth. see Blake, Marion E.

Bishop, Dorothy S., et al. Bilingual Fables & Folk Tales. Incl. Perez y Martina (ISBN 0-8442-7167-5, 7167-5); El Pajaro Cu: The Cu Bird (7163-5); Las Manchos del Sapo: How the Toad Lost its Spots (7171-5); Chiquita y Pepita: The City Mouse & the Country Mouse (ISBN 0-8442-7446-1, 7446-1); Tina la Tortuga y Carlos el Conejo: The Tortoise & the Hare (ISBN 0-8442-7444-5, 7444-5); Leonardo el Leon y Ramon el Raton: The Lion & The Mouse (ISBN 0-8442-7445-3, 7445-3); Poniendo el Cascabel el Gato: Belling the Cat (ISBN 0-8442-7282-5, 7282-5); El Muchacho Que Grito EL Lobo!: The Boy Who Cried Wolf (7295-5); La Lechera y Su Cubeta: The Milkmaid & Her Pail (7250-5). (Illus.). 72p. (Span. & Eng.). 1983. pap. 3.95 ea. (Passport Bks.). Natl Textbk.

Bishop, Douglas D. Working in Plant Science. Amberson, Max L. & Chapman, Stephen, eds. (Illus.). (gr. 9-10). 1978. pap. text ed. 13.72 (ISBN 0-07-000835-3). McGraw.

Bishop, Duane S. Behavioral Problems & the Disabled. LC 83-24844. 494p. 1984. Repr. of 1980 ed. lib. bdg. 27.50 (ISBN 0-89874-726-0). Krieger.

Bishop, E. Indicators. 756p. 1973. text ed. 125.00 (ISBN 0-08-016617-2). Pergamon.

Bishop, E. & Bridges, D. Contructive Analysis. (Grundlehren der Mathematischen Wissenschaften: Vol. 279). 500p. 1985. 48.00 (ISBN 0-387-15066-8). Springer-Verlag.

Bishop, E., jt. auth. see Oulton, A. J.

Bishop, Edna B. & Arch, Marjorie S. Super Sewing: The New Bishop-Arch Book. rev. ed. 1974. pap. 10.12i (ISBN 0-397-40192-2). Har-Row.

Bishop, Edward & Cefalo, Robert, eds. Signs & Symptoms in Disorders of Pregnancy. 188p. 1983. text ed. 29.50 (ISBN 0-397-50566-3, 65-07248, Lippincott Medical). Lippincott.

Bishop, Eleanor C. Ponies, Patriots & Powder Monkeys: A History of Children in America's Armed Forces, 1776-1916. (Illus.). 180p. 1983. 12.95 (ISBN 0-911329-00-5). Bishop Pr.

Bishop, Elizabeth. The Collected Prose. Giroux, Robert, ed. LC 83-16418. 278p. 1984. 17.50 (ISBN 0-374-12628-3); pap. 8.95 (ISBN 0-374-51855-6). FS&G.

--The Complete Poems. LC 69-15407. 216p. 1969. pap. 7.95 (ISBN 0-374-51516-6). FS&G.

--The Complete Poems: 1927-1979. 298p. 1983. 17.50 (ISBN 0-374-12747-6); pap. 9.95 (ISBN 0-374-51817-3). FS&G.

--Geography III. 50p. 1976. 7.95 (ISBN 0-374-16135-6); pap. 5.25 (ISBN 0-374-51440-2). FS&G.

Bishop, Elizabeth & Brasil, Emanuel, eds. An Anthology of Twentieth-Century Brazilian Poetry. Blackburn, Paul, et al, trs. from Port. LC 75-184359. 224p. (Orig.). 1972. pap. 8.95 (ISBN 0-8195-6023-5). Wesleyan U Pr.

Bishop, Elizabeth, tr. from Portuguese. The Diary of "Helena Morley". LC 57-12509. (Neglected Books of the Twentieth Century). 1977. pap. 6.95 (ISBN 0-912946-46-6). Ecco Pr.

Bishop, Eric. Dental Insurance: The What, the Why & the How of Dental Benefits. 224p. 1983. 31.95 (ISBN 0-07-005471-1). McGraw.

Bishop, Ernest S. The Narcotic Drug Problem. LC 75-17204. (Social Problems & Social Policy Ser.). 1976. Repr. of 1920 ed. 14.00x (ISBN 0-405-07476-X). Ayer Co Pubs.

Bishop, Errett & Cheng, Henry. Constructive Measure Theory. LC 52-42839. (Memoirs: No. 116). 85p. 1972. pap. 9.00 (ISBN 0-8218-1816-3, MEMO-116). Am Math.

Bishop, Eugene A. The Development of a State School System: New Hampshire. LC 78-176566. (Columbia University. Teachers College. Contributions to Education Ser.: No. 391). Repr. of 1930 ed. 22.50 (ISBN 0-404-55391-5). AMS Pr.

Bishop, Evelyn M. Blake's Hayley: The Life, Works, & Friendships of William Hayley. LC 72-5490. (Biography Index Reprint Ser). 1972. Repr. of 1951 ed. 27.75 (ISBN 0-8369-8133-2). Ayer Co Pubs.

Bishop, Ferman. Allen Tate. (Twayne's United States Authors Ser.). 1967. pap. 5.95x (ISBN 0-8084-0050-9, T124, Twayne). New Coll U Pr.

Bishop, Franklin C. World Hunger: Reality & Challenge. 32p. 1969. pap. 0.50 (ISBN 0-8361-1603-8). Herald Hse.

Bishop, G. Reginald, Jr., ed. Culture in Language & Learning. Incl. An Anthropological Concept of Culture. Friedl, Ernestine; Language As Culture. Welmers, William E; Teaching of Classical Cultures. Kibbe, Doris E; Teaching of Western European Cultures. Wade, Ira; Teaching of Slavic Cultures. Twarog, Leon I. 1960. pap. 7.95x (ISBN 0-915432-60-9). NE Conf Teach Foreign.

--Foreign Language Teaching: Challenges to the Profession. Incl. The Case for Latin. Parker, William R; The Challenge of Bilingualism. Gaarder, A. Bruce; From School to College: The Problem of Continuity. Dufau, Micheline; Study Abroad. Freeman, Stephen A. 158p. 1965. pap. 7.95x (ISBN 0-915432-65-X). NE Conf Teach Foreign.

Bishop, Garth, ed. Master Chefs of the World, Vol. 1: U S A. (Illus.). 1985. pap. 5.95 (ISBN 0-913290-57-2). Camaro Pub.

Bishop, Gavin. Chicken Licken. (Illus.). 32p. (ps). 1985. laminated boards 9.95 (ISBN 0-19-558108-3, Pub. by Oxford U Pr Childrens). Merrimack Pub Cir.

--Mr. Fox. (Illus.). 32p. (ps-1). 1983. bds. 10.95 laminated (ISBN 0-19-558089-3, Pub. by Oxford U Pr Childrens). Merrimack Pub Cir.

--Mrs. McGinty & the Bizarre Plant. (Illus.). 32p. (ps). 1983. bds. 10.95 (ISBN 0-19-558074-5, Pub by Oxford U Pr Childrens). Merrimack Pub Cir.

Bishop, George. John Wayne: The Actor, the Man. (Illus.). 254p. 1979. 16.95 (ISBN 0-89803-009-9, Dist. by Kampmann). Green Hill.

--My Brother, My Enemy. 224p. 1985. pap. 7.95 (ISBN 0-8407-5953-3). Nelson.

Bishop, George, jt. auth. see Linkletter, Art.

Bishop, George F., et al, eds. The Presidential Debates: Media Electoral & Policy Perspective. Meadow, Robert G. & Jackson-Beeck, Marilyn. LC 78-70323. 1978. 49.95 (ISBN 0-03-044271-0); pap. 19.95 (ISBN 0-03-057707-1). Praeger.

Bishop, George W. Barry Jackson & the London Theatre. LC 76-81972. 1933. 22.00 (ISBN 0-405-08272-X, Blom Pubns). Ayer Co Pubs.

--Barry Jackson & the London Theatre. 215p. 1983. Repr. of 1933 ed. text ed. 13.00x cancelled (ISBN 0-8290-1449-7). Irvington.

Bishop, Gerald. New British Science Fiction & Fantasy Books Published During 1970 & 1971. LC 80-20579. 1980. Repr. of 1972 ed. lib. bdg. 19.95x (ISBN 0-89370-057-6). Borgo Pr.

--Science Fiction Books Published in Britain, 1972 & 1973. LC 80-20590. 64p. 1980. Repr. of 1975 ed. lib. bdg. 15.95x (ISBN 0-89370-086-X). Borgo Pr.

--Science Fiction Books Published in Britain: 1974 to 1978. LC 80-20576. 82p. 1980. Repr. of 1979 ed. lib. bdg. 19.95x (ISBN 0-89370-087-8). Borgo Pr.

--Spaniels. (Illus.). 176p. 1984. 18.95 (ISBN 0-7153-8483-X). David & Charles.

Bishop Graphics, Inc. The Design & Drafting of Printed Circuits. 1979. 47.95 (ISBN 0-07-005430-4). McGraw.

Bishop, H. L., jt. ed. see Uys, J. M.

Bishop, Helen G., tr. see Ionesco, Eugene.

Bishop, Hillman, jt. auth. see Hendel, Samuel.

Bishop, Irene S. The Lenten Tree. 12p. 1976. pap. 3.00 (ISBN 0-89536-119-1). CSS of Ohio.

Bishop, Isabella L. The Aspects of Religion in the United States of America. LC 75-38438. (Religion in America, Ser. 2). 200p. 1972. Repr. of 1859 ed. 20.00 (ISBN 0-405-04059-8). Ayer Co Pubs.

Bishop, J. Home Video Production: Getting the Most from Your Video Equipment. (VTX Ser.). 224p. 1985. price not set (ISBN 0-07-005472-X). McGraw.

Bishop, J. A. & Cook, L. M., eds. Genetic Consequences of Man Made Change. LC 81-66391. 1981. 55.00 (ISBN 0-12-101620-X). Acad Pr.

Bishop, J. Dean, ed. see Burke, Kenneth, et al.

Bishop, J. Leander, et al. History of American Manufactures from 1608 to 1860, 3 Vols. 3rd ed. Repr. of 1868 ed. Set. 100.00 (ISBN 0-384-04480-8). Johnson Repr.

Bishop, J. M., jt. auth. see Barron, D. W.

Bishop, J. Michael, et al. Genes & Cancer. LC 84-14407. (UCLA Symposia on Molecular & Cellular Biology, New Ser.: Vol. 17). 710p. 1984. 88.00 (ISBN 0-8451-2616-4). A R Liss.

Bishop, J. R. & Schimmels, Cliff, eds. Sports & Your Child: What Every Parent Must Know. 192p. 1985. pap. 6.95 (ISBN 0-8407-9527-0). Nelson.

Bishop, James. The Illustrated London News Social History of the First World War. 160p. 1982. 42.00x (ISBN 0-207-95951-X, Pub. by Angus & Robertson). State Mutual Bk.

Bishop, James, jt. auth. see Woods, Oliver.

Bishop, James, ed. The Illustrated Counties of England. Date not set. price not set. Facts on File.

Bishop, Jim. The Day Christ Died. LC 57-6125. 1978. pap. 4.72 (ISBN 0-06-060786-6, HJ 38, HarpR). Har-Row.

--Day Christ Died. LC 57-6125. (Illus.). 1957. 12.50i (ISBN 0-06-010345-0, HarpT). Har-Row.

--The Day Christ Was Born. LC 60-13444. 1978. pap. 2.95i (ISBN 0-06-060785-8, HJ 37, HarpR). Har-Row.

--The Day Kennedy Was Shot. LC 83-16608. 1983. 6.98 (ISBN 0-517-43100-9). Outlet Bk Co.

--The Day Lincoln Was Shot. 1964. pap. 3.80i (ISBN 0-06-080005-4, P5, PL). Har-Row.

--This Man & This Woman. 320p. 1975. pap. 1.50 (ISBN 0-532-15161-5, 532-15161-150). Woodhill.

Bishop, Joel P. Commentaries on the Criminal Law, 2 vols. LC 76-156005. (Foundations of Criminal Justice Ser). Repr. of 1882 ed. Set. 125.00 (ISBN 0-404-09105-9). AMS Pr.

Bishop, John. Cabin Twelve: A One Act Play. 1978. pap. 1.85x (ISBN 0-685-60700-3). Dramatists Play.

--Confluence. Bd. with The Skirmishers. pap. 3.35x (ISBN 0-686-81619-6). Dramatists Play.

--The Harvesting. 1984. pap. 3.35x (ISBN 0-317-17217-4). Dramatists Play.

--Methodist Worship: In Relation to Free Church Worship. rev. ed. LC 75-20379. xvii, 173p. 1976. lib. bdg. 6.95 (ISBN 0-89177-001-1). Scholars Studies.

Bishop, John & Wilson, Edmund. Undertaker's Garland. LC 74-14616. 1922. lib. bdg. 20.00 (ISBN 0-8414-0504-2). Folcroft.

Bishop, John L. Colloquial Short Story in China: A Study of the San-Yen Collections. LC 56-7211. (Harvard-Yenching Institute Studies: No. 14). 1956. pap. 4.50x (ISBN 0-674-14200-4). Harvard U Pr.

--History of American Manufactures from 1608 to 1860, 3 vols. 3rd ed. LC 66-122404. Repr. of 1863 ed. 95.00x (ISBN 0-678-00166-9). Kelley.

Bishop, John L., ed. Studies in Chinese Literature. LC 65-13836. (Harvard-Yenching Institute Studies: No. 21). (Orig.). 1965. pap. 8.50x (ISBN 0-674-84705-9). Harvard U Pr.

--Studies of Governmental Institutions in Chinese History. LC 68-17622. (Harvard-Yenching Institute Studies: No. 23). 1968. pap. 8.50x (ISBN 0-674-85110-2). Harvard U Pr.

Bishop, John P. Act of Darkness. LC 83-45709. Repr. of 1935 ed. 32.50 (ISBN 0-404-20031-1). AMS Pr.

Bishop, John P. & Wilson, Edmund. The Undertaker's Garland. LC 74-4263. (American Literature Ser., No. 49). 1974. lib. bdg. 42.95x (ISBN 0-8383-2041-4). Haskell.

Bishop, John Peale. The Collected Essays of John Peale Bishop. Wilson, Edmund, ed. 508p. 1975. Repr. of 1948 ed. lib. bdg. 37.50x (ISBN 0-374-90642-2). Octagon.

--The Collected Poems of John Peale Bishop. Tate, Allen, ed. 277p. 1975. Repr. of 1948 ed. lib. bdg. 23.00x (ISBN 0-374-90644-0). Octagon.

Bishop, Jonathan. The Covenant: A Reading. 458p. (Orig.). 1983. pap. 9.95 (ISBN 0-87243-113-4). Templegate.

--Emerson on the Soul. LC 80-2527. Repr. of 1964 ed. 29.50 (ISBN 0-404-19251-3). AMS Pr.

--Something Else. LC 77-161570. 1972. 8.95 (ISBN 0-8076-0619-7); pap. 2.45 (ISBN 0-8076-0608-1). Braziller.

Bishop, Joseph. Law of Corporate Officers & Directors: Indemnification & Insurance. LC 82-4383. 1982. write for info. Callaghan.

Bishop, Joseph B. Notes & Anecdotes of Many Years. facs. ed. LC 78-128210. (Essay Index Reprint Ser). 1925. 18.00 (ISBN 0-8369-1904-1). Ayer Co Pubs.

Bishop, Joseph B., ed. see Roosevelt, Theodore.

Bishop, Joseph M. Applied Oceanography. LC 83-26091. (Ocean Engineering Ser.: 1-194). 300p. 1984. text ed. 32.95x (ISBN 0-471-87445-0, Pub. by Wiley-Interscience). Wiley.

--A Mariner's Guide to Radiofacsimile Weather Charts. (Illus.). 128p. (Orig.). 1981. pap. 9.95 (ISBN 0-686-32920-1). Alden Electronics.

Bishop, Joseph P. The Eye of the Storm. 128p. (Orig.). 1983. pap. 3.95 (ISBN 0-87123-263-4). Bethany Hse.

Bishop, Lea, jt. auth. see Bailey, Covert.

Bishop, Lee. Border Legend. LC 83-42732. (Western Ser.). 192p. 1983. 12.95 (ISBN 0-8027-4025-1). Walker & Co.

--Davy Crockett: Frontier Fighter. (American Explorer Ser.: No. 11). (Orig.). 1983. pap. 2.95 (ISBN 0-440-01695-9). Dell.

--Gunblaze. 1978. pap. 1.75 (ISBN 0-8439-0604-9, Leisure Bks). Dorchester Pub Co.

Bishop, Leonard. The Everlasting. 480p. (Orig.). 1984. pap. 3.95 (ISBN 0-671-47677-7). PB.

Bishop, Lloyd. In Search of Style: Essays in French Literary Stylistics. LC 82-13370. 224p. 1982. 14.95x (ISBN 0-8139-0957-0). U Pr of Va.

--The Romantic Hero & His Heirs in French Literature. LC 83-49351. (American University Studies II Romance Languages & Literature: Vol. 10). 295p. 1984. text ed. 32.50 (ISBN 0-8204-0096-3). P Lang Pubs.

Bishop, Louis F. Myself When Young: Growing up in New York 1901-1925. LC 85-71005. (Illus.). 160p. 1985. 12.95 (ISBN 0-934025-00-2). Giniger.

Bishop, Marcus see McLaren, A.

Bishop, Mary. The Chill Winds of Ravenhall. 1981. pap. 1.95 (ISBN 0-89083-757-0). Zebra.

Bishop, Mary C. Adult Echocardiography: A Handbook for Technicians. LC 84-62545. (Illus.). 120p. (Orig.). 1985. pap. 14.95 (ISBN 0-931028-60-4). Pluribus Pr.

Bishop, Maurice. In Nobody's Backyard: Maurice Bishop's Speeches: 1979-1983: A Memorial Volume. (Third World Studies). 301p. 1984. bds. 29.50x (ISBN 0-86232-248-0, Pub. by Zed Pr England); pap. 10.75 (ISBN 0-86232-249-9). Biblio Dist.

--Maurice Bishop Speaks: The Grenada Revolution 1979-83. Marcus, Bruce & Taber, Michael, eds. LC 83-63309. (Illus.). 400p. 1983. 30.00 (ISBN 0-87348-611-0); pap. 6.95 (ISBN 0-87348-612-9). Path Pr NY.

Bishop, Michael. Alien Graffiti. Date not set. price not set. Ziesing Mark.

--Ancient of Days. 310p. 1985. 15.95 (ISBN 0-87795-724-X). Arbor Hse.

--Blooded on Arachne. (Illus.). 352p. 1982. 13.95 (ISBN 0-87054-093-9). Arkham.

--Blooded on Arachne. 1983. pap. 3.50 (ISBN 0-671-41978-X, Timescape). PB.

--Eyes of Fire. 1983. pap. 2.95 (ISBN 0-671-46752-2, Timescape). PB.

--No Enemy but Time. 1982. pap. 3.95 (ISBN 0-671-49615-8, Timescape). PB.

--One Winter in Eden. (Illus.). 288p. 1984. 13.95 (ISBN 0-87054-096-3). Arkham.

--Stolen Faces. LC 76-26262. 176p. 1977. 15.00 (ISBN 0-06-010362-0). Ultramarine Pub.

--Who Made Stevie Cry? (Illus.). 325p. 1984. 15.95 (ISBN 0-87054-099-8, Arkham House). Arkham.

Bishop, Michael, ed. The Language of Poetry: Crisis & Solution, Studies in Modern Poetry of French Expression, 1945 to the Present. 268p. 1980. 34.75x (ISBN 90-6203-681-3). Humanities.

--Light Years & Dark. 512p. 1984. pap. 8.95 (ISBN 0-425-07214-2). Berkley Pub.

Bishop, Michael & Watson, Ian, eds. Changes. 320p. (Orig.). pap. 2.75 (ISBN 0-441-10260-3). Ace Bks.

Bishop, Michael L., et al. Clinical Chemistry: Principles, Procedures, Correlations. (Illus.). 624p. 1985. text ed. 42.50 (ISBN 0-397-50662-7, Lippincott Medical). Lippincott.

Bishop, Micheal & Watson, Ian. Under Heaven's Bridge. 224p. 1982. pap. 2.50 (ISBN 0-441-84481-2). Ace Bks.

Bishop, Milo E. Mainstreaming: Practical Ideas for Educating Hearing-Impaired Students. 1979. 10.95 (ISBN 0-88200-126-4). Alexander Graham.

Bishop, Morris. The Best of Bishop: Selected Light Verse from the" New Yorker" & Elsewhere. Reppert, Charlotte P., ed. LC 80-66902. (Illus.). 224p. 1980. 19.95x (ISBN 0-8014-1310-9). Cornell U Pr.

--Champlain: The Life of Fortitude. 1979. Repr. lib. bdg. 27.50x (ISBN 0-374-90642-4). Octagon.

--A Gallery of Eccentrics. 1977. Repr. of 1928 ed. lib. bdg. 30.00 (ISBN 0-8495-0303-5). Arden Lib.

--A Gallery of Eccentrics: Or a Set of Twelve Originals & Extravagants from Elagabalus, the Waggish Emperor to Mr. Professor Porson, the Tipping Philol. 1978. Repr. of 1928 ed. 25.00 (ISBN 0-8492-3567-7). R West.

--History of Cornell. (Illus.). 663p. 1962. 29.50x (ISBN 0-8014-0036-8). Cornell U Pr.

--Middle Ages. abr. ed. LC 70-95728. 1970. pap. 6.95 (ISBN 0-07-005466-5). McGraw.

--The Middle Ages. 1983. 14.25 (ISBN 0-8446-6063-9). Peter Smith.

--The Odyssey of Cabeza de Vaca. LC 70-139123. (Illus.). 306p. 1972. Repr. of 1933 ed. lib. bdg. 20.00x (ISBN 0-8371-5739-0, BICV). Greenwood.

--Pascal, the Life of Genius. LC 68-9538. (Illus.). 1968. Repr. of 1936 ed. lib. bdg. 27.75x (ISBN 0-8371-0021-6, BILG). Greenwood.

--A Survey of French Literature, 2 vols. rev. ed. Incl. Vol. 1. The Middle Ages to 1800. 462p (ISBN 0-15-584963-8, HC); Vol. 2. The Nineteenth & Twentieth Centuries. 462p (ISBN 0-15-584964-6, HC). 1965. text ed. 22.95 ea. (HC). HarBraceJ.

--A Treasury of British Humour. 1977. Repr. of 1942 ed. lib. bdg. 30.00 (ISBN 0-8495-0302-7). Arden Lib.

Bishop, Morris, ed. Treasury of British Humor. facs. ed. (Granger Index Reprint Ser). 1942. 35.00 (ISBN 0-8369-6194-3). Ayer Co Pubs.

Bishop, Morris, tr. see Guicharnaud, Jacques.

Bishop, Morris, tr. see Petrarca, Francesco.

Bishop, Nancy, jt. auth. see Camden, Thomas M.

Bishop, Nathaniel Holmes. Four Months in a Sneak Box: A Boat Voyage of Twenty Six Hundred Miles Down the Ohio & Mississippi Rivers. LC 71-142572. (Illus.). xii, 322p. 1976. Repr. of 1879 ed. 51.00x (ISBN 0-8103-4170-0). Gale.

Bishop of Exeter, jt. auth. see Hardy, Paul E.

Bishop, Olga B. Bibliography of Ontario History, 1867-1976: Cultural, Economic, Political, Social, 2 vols. 1980. 85.00x set (ISBN 0-8020-2359-2). U of Toronto Pr.

--Canadian Official Publications. (Guides to Official Publications Ser.: Vol. 9). 308p. 1980. 48.00 (ISBN 0-08-024697-4). Pergamon.

Bishop, Owen. Adventure with Small Animals. 64p. 1982. 29.00x (ISBN 0-7195-3944-7, Pub. by Murray England). State Mutual Bk.

--Commodore 64 Wargaming. (Illus.). 160p. (Orig.). 1985. pap. 17.95 (ISBN 0-00-383010-1, Pub. by Collins England). Sheridan.

--Electronic Projects for Home Security. 96p. 1981. 9.95 (ISBN 0-408-00535-1). Butterworth.

--Figuring out Facts with a Micro. (Illus.). 160p. 1985. pap. 13.95 (ISBN 0-00-383023-3, Pub. by Collins England). Sheridan.

--Simple Interfacing Projects. (Illus.). 168p. 1983. 17.95 (ISBN 0-13-811091-3); pap. 10.95 (ISBN 0-13-811083-2). P-H.

--Yardsticks of the Universe. LC 83-15782. (Illus.). 130p. 1984. 10.95x (ISBN 0-911745-17-3); pap. 5.95 (ISBN 0-911745-42-4). P Bedrick Bks.

Bishop, Owen & Bishop, Audrey. BBC Micro Wargaming. (Illus.). 170p. (Orig.). 1985. pap. 15.95 (ISBN 0-00-383000-4, Pub. by Collins England). Sheridan.

--Practical Programs for the BBC Micro. (Illus.). 120p. (Orig.). 1983. pap. 13.95 (ISBN 0-246-12405-9, Pub. by Granada England). Sheridan.

Bishop, Owen, jt. auth. see Bishop, Audrey.

Bishop, Paul L. Marine Pollution & Its Control. (Water Resource Engineering Ser.). (Illus.). 384p. 1982. text ed. 45.00 (ISBN 0-07-005482-7). McGraw.

Bishop, Pike. Dead Man's Hand. (Diamondback Ser.: No. 4). 192p. 1984. pap. 2.25 (ISBN 0-523-42200-8). Pinnacle Bks.

--Diamondback. 208p. (Orig.). 1983. pap. 2.25 (ISBN 0-523-41948-1). Pinnacle Bks.

--Judgement at Poisoned Well. (Diamondback Ser.: No. 2). 208p. (Orig.). 1983. pap. 2.25 (ISBN 0-523-41949-X). Pinnacle Bks.

--Old Bone Betrayal. (Diamondback Ser.: No. 7). 192p. (Orig.). 1985. pap. 2.50 (ISBN 0-523-42286-5). Pinnacle Bks.

--River Race Verdict. (Diamondback Ser.: No. 5). 192p. (Orig.). 1984. pap. 2.50 (ISBN 0-523-42201-6). Pinnacle Bks.

--Shroud of Vengeance. (Diamonback Ser.: No. 6). (Orig.). 1985. pap. 2.50 (ISBN 0-523-42202-4). Pinnacle Bks.

--Snake Eyes. (Diamondback Ser.: No. 3). 208p. (Orig.). 1984. pap. 2.25 (ISBN 0-523-42147-8). Pinnacle Bks.

Bishop, R. The Borden Limner & His Contemporaries. 1976. pap. 3.95 (ISBN 0-912303-10-7). Michigan Mus.

Bishop, R. E. Vibration. 2nd ed. LC 79-11172. (Illus.). 1979. 34.50 (ISBN 0-521-22779-8); pap. 13.95 (ISBN 0-521-29639-0). Cambridge U Pr.

Bishop, R. E. & Johnson, D. C. The Mechanics of Vibration. (Illus.). 1979. 125.00 (ISBN 0-521-04258-5). Cambridge U Pr.

Bishop, R. E. & Price, W. G. Hydroelasticity of Ships. LC 78-67297. 1980. 105.00 (ISBN 0-521-22328-8). Cambridge U Pr.

Bishop, R. E., jt. auth. see Clayton, B. R.

Bishop, R. E., et al. The Matrix Analysis of Vibration. (Illus.). 1979. 99.50 (ISBN 0-521-04257-7). Cambridge U Pr.

Bishop, Richard & Goldberg, Samuel. Tensor Analysis on Manifolds. (Illus.). 1980. pap. 5.95 (ISBN 0-486-64039-6). Dover.

Bishop, Richard B. Practical Polymerization for Polystyrene. LC 75-132666. (Illus.). 480p. 1971. 34.95 (ISBN 0-8436-1200-2). Van Nos Reinhold.

Bishop, Richard C. & Anderson, Stephen O. Natural Resource Economics: Selected Papers. 275p. 1985. 22.85x (ISBN 0-8133-0064-9). Westview.

Bishop, Robert. American Folk Sculpture. (Illus.). 392p. 1983. pap. 19.95 (ISBN 0-525-48060-9, 01937-580). Dutton.

--How to Know American Antique Furniture. 1973. pap. 8.25 (ISBN 0-525-47337-8). Dutton.

--Land in the Sky Totem. (Shorey Indian Ser.). 18p. pap. 2.95 (ISBN 0-8466-0179-6, SJS179). Shorey.

--New Discoveries in American Quilts. 128p. 1975. pap. 13.75 (ISBN 0-525-47410-2, 01335-400). Dutton.

Bishop, Robert & Coblentz, Patricia. Furniture One: Prehistoric Through Rococo. Gilchrist, Brenda, ed. LC 78-62733. (Smithsonian Illustrated Library of Antiques). (Illus.). 128p. (Orig.). 1979. 9.95 (ISBN 0-910503-23-0). Cooper-Hewitt Museum.

Bishop, Robert & Safanda, Elizabeth. A Gallery of Amish Quilts: Design Diversity from a Plain People. (Illus.). 1976. pap. 12.50 (ISBN 0-525-47444-7, 01214-360). Dutton.

Bishop, Robert & Secord, William. Quilts, Coverlets, Rugs & Samplers. LC 82-47848. (The Knopf Collector's Guides to American Antiques Ser.). 1982. 13.95 (ISBN 0-394-71271-4). Knopf.

Bishop, Robert, jt. auth. see Safford, Carleton L.

Bishop, Robert, et al. Folk Art: Painting, Sculpture & Country Objects. LC 82-48945. (The Knopf Collectors' Guides to American Antiques Ser.). 1983. 13.95 (ISBN 0-394-71493-8). Knopf.

Bishop, Ron. Basic Microprocessors & Sixty-Eight Hundred. 1979. pap. 17.95 (ISBN 0-8104-0758-2). Hayden.

--Rebuilding the Famous Ford Flathead. (Illus.). 140p. (Orig.). 1981. 9.95 (ISBN 0-8306-9965-1); pap. 7.25 (ISBN 0-8306-2066-4, 2066). TAB Bks.

--Troubleshooting Old Cars. (Illus.). 182p. 1982. 13.95o.p (ISBN 0-8306-3075-9); pap. 9.25 (ISBN 0-8306-2075-3, 2075). TAB Bks.

Bishop, Russell H., jt. auth. see Miller, J. Dale.

Bishop, S. G., jt. ed. see Taylor, P. C.

Bishop, Selma L. Isaac Watts's Hymns & Spiritual Songs (1707) A Publishing History & a Bibliography. LC 73-78316. 1974. 29.50 (ISBN 0-87650-033-5). Pierian.

Bishop, Sharon & Weinzweig, Marjorie. Philosophy & Women. 1979. pap. text ed. write for info. (ISBN 0-534-00609-4). Wadsworth Pub.

Bishop, Sheila. Consequences. 224p. 1981. pap. 1.95 (ISBN 0-449-50208-2, Coventry). Fawcett.

--Penelope Devereux. 1978. pap. 1.75 (ISBN 0-8439-0551-4, Leisure Bks). Dorchester Pub Co.

--Penelope Devereux. (Inflation Fighter Ser.). 192p. 1982. pap. 1.50 (ISBN 0-8439-1094-1, Leisure Bks). Dorchester Pub Co.

--Rosalba. 192p. (Orig.). 1982. pap. 1.50 (ISBN 0-449-50312-7, Coventry). Fawcett.

Bishop, Tania E. Born of the Spirit. LC 68-13394. 1968. 4.50 (ISBN 0-8022-0134-2). Philos Lib.

Bishop, Tom. Gold: The Way to Roadside Riches. 1971. pap. 3.50 (ISBN 0-933472-31-5). Johnson Bks.

Bishop, Vaughn F. & Meszaros, J. William. Comparing Nations: The Developed & the Developing Worlds. 1980. text ed. 20.95 (ISBN 0-669-01142-8). Heath.

Bishop, Vernon S. Cardiac Performance, Vol. 1. Granger, Harris J., ed. (Annual Research Reviews). 1979. 18.00 (ISBN 0-88831-060-9). Eden Pr.

Bishop, Virginia E. Teaching the Visually Limited Child. (Illus.). 224p. 1978. 16.50x (ISBN 0-398-00158-8). C C Thomas.

Bishop, W. D., jt. auth. see Veljanovski, C. G.

Bishop, W. E., et al, eds. Aquatic Toxicology & Hazard Assessment: Sixth Symposium. LC 82-73772. (Special Technical Publications: No. 802). 560p. 1983. text ed. 59.00 (ISBN 0-8031-0255-0, 04-802000-16). ASTM.

Bishop, W. H. Mr. Howells in Beacon Street, Boston, in "Authors at Home," Edited by J. L. & J. B. Gilder. 1888. Repr. 35.00 (ISBN 0-8274-2768-9). R West.

Bishop, Walter W. Geological Background to Fossil Man: Recent Research in the Gregory Rift Valley, East Africa. 1978. 85.00x (ISBN 0-8020-2302-9). U of Toronto Pr.

Bishop, Walter W. & Clark, J. Desmond, eds. Background to Evolution in Africa. LC 66-30212. (Illus.). 1967. 70.00x (ISBN 0-226-05393-8). U of Chicago Pr.

Bishop, Wayne, jt. auth. see Venit, Stewart.

Bishop, Wiley L., jt. auth. see Weaver, Barbara N.

Bishop, William H. Saint Louis in 1884. Jones, William R., ed. (Illus.). 24p. 1977. pap. 2.95 (ISBN 0-89646-024-X). Outbooks.

Bishop, William W. Backs of Books, & Other Essays in Librarianship. facs. ed. LC 68-54328. (Essay Index Reprint Ser.). 1968. Repr. of 1926 ed. 18.00 (ISBN 0-8369-0215-7). Ayer Co Pubs.

--Practical Handbook of Modern Library Cataloging. (Library Science Ser.). 1980. lib. bdg. 59.95 (ISBN 0-8490-3179-6). Gordon Pr.

Bishop, William W. & Keogh, Andrew. Essays Offered to Herbert Putnam by His Colleagues & Friends on His 30th Anniversary As Librarian of Congress, 5 April Nineteen Twenty-Nine. 1929. 20.00x (ISBN 0-686-51379-7). Elliots Bks.

Bishop, William W., Jr. International Law: Cases & Materials. 3rd ed. 1122p. 1971. 31.00 (ISBN 0-316-09664-4). Little.

Bishop Ignatius Brianchianinov. The Arena. Archimandrite Lazarus Moore, tr. from Rus. 300p. (Orig.). 1982. 15.00 (ISBN 0-88465-009-X); pap. 10.00 (ISBN 0-88465-011-1). Holy Trinity.

--Asketitcheskaya Propovjed: Tom 4, Tom 4. 537p. 25.00 (ISBN 0-317-28962-4); pap. 20.00 (ISBN 0-317-28963-2). Holy Trinity.

--Asketitcheskije Opiti, Tom 2. 332p. 20.00 (ISBN 0-317-28949-7); pap. 15.00 (ISBN 0-317-28950-0). Holy Trinity.

--Asketitcheskije Opiti: Tom 1, Tom 1. 468p. Repr. of 1957 ed. 25.00 (ISBN 0-317-28935-7). Holy Trinity.

--Asketitcheskije Opiti, tom 3, Tom 3. 315p. 20.00 (ISBN 0-317-28957-8); pap. 15.00 (ISBN 0-317-28958-6). Holy Trinity.

--Prinoshenije Sovremennomu Monashestvu, Vol. 5. 354p. 20.00 (ISBN 0-317-28966-7); pap. 15.00 (ISBN 0-317-28967-5). Holy Trinity.

Bishop John of Smolensk. Iisus Khristos Pred Sudom Sovemjennogo Razuma. 16p. pap. 1.00 (ISBN 0-317-28988-8). Holy Trinity.

Bishops' Committee on the Bicentennial. Catholics in America - 1776-1976. Trisco, Robert, ed. 1977. 19.95 (ISBN 0-686-18993-0); pap. 7.95 (ISBN 0-686-18994-9). US Catholic.

Bishop Theophan the Recluse. Misli na Kazhdij Den' Goda. 186p. 1982. pap. 7.00 (ISBN 0-317-28912-8). Holy Trinity.

--O Pravoslavii s Predestereshenijami ot Pogreshenij Protiv Hego. 202p. 1962. pap. 7.00 (ISBN 0-317-28919-5). Holy Trinity.

--Psalom 118. 496p. 22.00 (ISBN 0-317-28925-X); pap. 17.00 (ISBN 0-317-28926-8). Holy Trinity.

Bishov, Bertha K., jt. ed. see London, Anne.

Bisignani, J. D. Japan Handbook. LC 82-5805. (Illus.). 520p. (Orig.). 1983. pap. 12.95 (ISBN 0-9603322-2-7). Moon Pubns CA.

Bisignano, Alphonse. Cooking the Italian Way. LC 82-12641. (Easy Menu Ethnic Cookbooks Ser.). (Illus.). 48p. (gr. 5 up). 1982. PLB 8.95 (ISBN 0-8225-0906-7). Lerner Pubns.

Bisignano, Joseph & Bisignano, Judith. Creating Your Future: Level 3. (Illus.). 72p. 1982. workbook 6.95 (ISBN 0-9607366-9-7, KP109). Kino Pubns.

--Creating Your Future: Level 4. (Illus.). 64p. 1983. workbook 6.95 (ISBN 0-910141-01-0, KP115). Kino Pubns.

Bisignano, Judith, jt. auth. see Bisignano, Joseph.

Bisignano, Judith, jt. auth. see Cera, Mary J.

Bisignano, Judith, jt. auth. see Robinson, Marilyn.

Bisignano, Judith, jt. auth. see Bisignano, Joseph.

Bisio, A. & Olson, D. H., eds. Sixth International Zeolite Conference. 1000p. 1984. text ed. 89.95 (ISBN 0-408-22158-5). Butterworth.

Bisio, Attilio. Encyclopedia of Energy Technology. 4000p. 1983. Set. 350.00x (ISBN 0-471-89039-1, Pub. by Wiley-Interscience). Wiley.

Bisio, Attilio & Gastwirt, Lawrence. Turning Research & Development into Profits: A Systematic Approach. LC 78-10239. pap. 71.80 (ISBN 0-317-27063-X, 2023541). Bks Demand UMI.

Bisio, Attilio & Kabel, Robert L. Scaleup in the Chemical Process Industries: Conversion from Laboratory Scale Tests to Successful Commercial Size Design. 704p. 1985. 75.00 (ISBN 0-471-05747-9). Wiley.

Bisio, Attilio, jt. auth. see Herbert, Vernon.

Biskind, Elliot L., ed. see Harvey, David C.

Biskind, Elliott L., jt. auth. see Frumer, Louis R.

Biskind, Elliott L., ed. Boardman's New York Family Law, 2 Vols. rev. ed. LC 64-17549. 1981. Set. looseleaf 110.00 (ISBN 0-87632-058-2). Boardman.

Biskind, Elliott L. & Barasch, Clarence S., eds. Law of Real Estate Brokers, N.Y. LC 70-83769. 1981. 50.00 (ISBN 0-87632-050-7). Boardman.

Biskind, Peter. Seeing Is Believing: How Hollywood Taught Us to Stop Worrying & Love the Fifties. LC 83-47751. (Illus.). 384p. 1983. 22.45 (ISBN 0-394-52729-1); pap. 10.95 (ISBN 0-394-72115-2). Pantheon.

Bisko, W. Mowimy Po Polsku: A Beginner's Text. 1984. 12.00 (ISBN 0-317-18986-7, P519). Vanous.

Bisko, W. & Karolak, S. Mowimy Po Polski: A Beginners Course. 327p. 1979. pap. 12.00x (ISBN 0-89918-519-3, P519). Vanous.

Bisko, Waclaw, et al. A Beginners' Course of Polish. 1976. pap. 5.00 (ISBN 0-686-19943-X). Intl Learn Syst.

--A Beginner's Course of Polish. 329p. (Eng. & Pol.). 1979. pap. 9.95 (ISBN 83-214-0058-2, M-9130). French & Eur.

Biskup, M., jt. ed. see Gabrovska, S.

Biskup, Manfred, et al, eds. The Family & Its Culture: An Investigation in Seven East & West European Countries. 496p. 1984. text ed. 63.50x (ISBN 963-05-3655-2, Pub. by Kultura Hungary). Humanities.

Biskup, Peter, ed. see Mouton, J. B.

Biskupski, B., jt. auth. see Blejwas, S.

Bisland, Elizabeth. At the Sign of the Hobby Horse. 1973. Repr. of 1910 ed. 17.50 (ISBN 0-8274-1471-4). R West.

--The Japanese Letters of Lafcadio Hearn. 1973. Repr. of 1911 ed. 35.00 (ISBN 0-8274-1217-7). R West.

--Three Wise Men. 1973. Repr. of 1930 ed. 30.00 (ISBN 0-8274-1472-2). R West.

Bisland, Elizabeth, ed. The Japanese Letters of Lafcadio Hearn. LC 72-82097. (Japan Library Ser.). (Illus.). 1973. Repr. of 1910 ed. lib. bdg. 36.00 (ISBN 0-8420-1391-1). Scholarly Res Inc.

Bisley, Geoffrey G. A Handbook of Ophthalmology for Developing Countries. 2nd ed. (Illus.). 1981. pap. text ed. 14.95x (ISBN 0-19-261244-1). Oxford U Pr.

Bismarck, Orro Vow. Kaiser vs. Bismarck. Miall, Bernard, tr. LC 75-136405. Repr. of 1921 ed. 14.50 (ISBN 0-404-00869-0). AMS Pr.

Bismarck, Otto von. Gesammelte Werke: Nineteen Twenty-Four to Nineteen Thirty-Five. (Ger.). 869.00 (ISBN 0-686-47439-2). Kraus Repr.

Bismut, Jean-Michel. Large Deviations & the Malliavin Calculus, Vol. 45. (Progress in Mathematics Ser.). 216p. 1984. 17.50 (ISBN 0-8176-3220-4). Birkhauser.

--Theorie probabiliste du controle des diffusions. LC 75-41602. (Memoirs: No. 167). 130p. 1976. pap. 14.00 (ISBN 0-8218-1867-8, MEMO-167). Am Math.

Bismut, Roger, jt. auth. see Maupassant, Guy de.

Bisno, Abraham. Abraham Bisno, Union Pioneer. (Illus.). 262p. 1967. 19.50x (ISBN 0-299-04441-6). U of Wis Pr.

Bisno, Alan, ed. Treatment of Infective Endocarditis. LC 81-7080. 352p. 1981. 44.50 (ISBN 0-8089-1450-2, 790598). Grune.

Bisno, Beatrice. Tomorrow's Bread. LC 74-26096. Repr. of 1938 ed. 21.50 (ISBN 0-404-58407-1). AMS Pr.

Bisnow, Mark. Diary of a Dark Horse: The 1980 Anderson Presidential Campaign. LC 83-329. (Illus.). 352p. 1983. 24.95 (ISBN 0-8093-1114-3). S Ill U Pr.

Bispham, David. A Quaker Singer's Recollections. Farkas, Andrew, ed. LC 76-29927. (Opera Biographies). (Illus.). 1977. Repr. of 1921 ed. lib. bdg. 27.50x (ISBN 0-405-09669-0). Ayer Co Pubs.

Bispham, G. T. Fielding's Jonathan Wild in Eighteenth Century Literary: An Oxford Miscellany. 1909. 12.50 (ISBN 0-8274-2343-8). R West.

Bisplinghoff, Gretchen, jt. auth. see Wexman, Virginia W.

Bisplinghoff, Raymond L. & Ashley, Holt. Principles of Aeroelasticity. 2nd ed. LC 74-20442. (Illus.). 527p. 1975. Repr. of 1962 ed. 10.00 (ISBN 0-486-61349-6). Dover.

Biss, Roderick, jt. ed. see Mitchell, Donald.

Bissantz, ed. see Instructors of Introduction to Language the Ohio State University.

Bisschop, Marijke & Compernolle, Theo. Your Child Can Do It Alone: An Easy Way to Teach Self-Sufficiency. Haasl, Edward, tr. LC 83-2957. (Illus.). 256p. 1983. 16.95 (ISBN 0-13-977090-9); pap. 8.95 (ISBN 0-13-977082-8). P-H.

Bisschop, W. R. Rise of the London Money Market: Sixteen Forty to Eighteen Twenty Six. LC 68-56765. (Research & Source Works Ser: No. 250). 1968. Repr. of 1910 ed. 20.50 (ISBN 0-8337-0297-1). B Franklin.

--Rise of the London Money Market: 1640-1826. 256p. 1968. Repr. of 1826 ed. 30.00x (ISBN 0-7146-1206-5, F Cass Co). Biblio Dist.

Bissel, Richard E. & Crocker, Chester A., eds. South Africa into the Nineteen Eighties. (Special Studies on Africa). 1979. lib. bdg. 31.50x (ISBN 0-89158-373-4). Westview.

Bissell, A. M. & Oertel, E. J. Shipboard Damage Control. (Illus.). 208p. 1976. 15.95 (ISBN 0-87021-627-9); bulk rates avail. Naval Inst Pr.

Bissell, B. The American Indian in English Literature of the 18th Century. 59.95 (ISBN 0-87968-604-9). Gordon Pr.

Bissell, Benjamin H. American Indian in English Literature of the Eighteenth Century. (Yale Studies in English Ser.: No. 68). (Illus.). ix, 223p. 1968. Repr. of 1925 ed. 21.00 (ISBN 0-208-00710-5, Archon). Shoe String.

Bissell, Charles B., III. Letters I Never Wrote, Conversations I Never Had: Dealing with Unresolved Grief & Anger. 58p. (Orig.). 1983. pap. 4.95 (ISBN 0-9612604-0-8). C Bissell.

Bissell, Claude. The Young Vincent Massey. 272p. 1981. 22.50 (ISBN 0-8020-2398-3). U of Toronto Pr.

Bissell, Claude T. Halfway up Parnassus: A Personal Account of the University of Toronto, 1932-1971. LC 74-82289. 1974. 17.50 (ISBN 0-8020-2172-7). U of Toronto Pr.

Bissell, Elaine. As Time Goes By. 400p. (Orig.). 1983. pap. 3.95 (ISBN 0-671-42043-7). PB.

--Family Fortunes. 384p. 1985. 16.95 (ISBN 0-312-28050-5). St Martin.

--Women Who Wait. LC 78-2905. 264p. 1978. 8.95 (ISBN 0-87131-251-4). M Evans.

Bissell, Frederick O. Fielding's Theory of the Novel. LC 68-57713. Repr. of 1933 ed. 15.00 (ISBN 0-8154-0302-X). Cooper Sq.

Bissell, LeClair & Haberman, Paul. Alcoholism in the Professions. 1984. 24.95x (ISBN 0-19-503459-7). Oxford U Pr.

Bissell, LeClair & Watherwax, Richard. The Cat Who Drank Too Much. (Illus.). 48p. (Eng. & Span.). (gr. 4 up). 1982. pap. 4.00 (ISBN 0-911153-00-4). Spanish ed., 03/1984 (ISBN 0-911153-01-2). Bibulophile Pr.

Bissell, Michael E., jt. ed. see McCormick, Gordon H.

Bissell, R. Ward. Orazio Gentileschi & the Poetic Tradition in Caravaggesque Painting. LC 80-11452. (Illus.). 404p. 1982. 59.75x (ISBN 0-271-00263-8). Pa St U Pr.

Bissell, Richard E. South Africa & the United States: The Erosion of an Influence Relationship. LC 81-22663. (Studies of Infleunce in International Relations). 172p. 1982. 29.95 (ISBN 0-03-047026-9); pap. 14.95 (ISBN 0-03-047021-8). Praeger.

Bissell, Richard E. & Radu, Michael, eds. Africa in the Post-Decolonization Era. 250p. 1984. 29.95 (ISBN 0-87855-496-3); pap. 9.95 (ISBN 0-87855-955-8). Transaction Bks.

Bissell, Richard E., jt. auth. see Ayubi, Shaheen.

Bisselle, Walter C., jt. auth. see Sanders, Irwin T.

Bisseret, Noelle. Education, Class Language & Ideology. 1979. 21.95x (ISBN 0-7100-0118-5). Routledge & Kegan.

Bissert, Ellen M. The Immaculate Conception of the Blessed Virgin Dyke. LC 75-27883. (Illus.). 1977. pap. 3.00 (ISBN 0-9601224-1-9). Thirteenth Moon.

Bisset, George, tr. see Skogsberg, Bertil.

Bisset, James & Stephensen, P. R. Sail Ho. LC 58-5447. (Illus.). 1958. 17.95 (ISBN 0-87599-015-0). S G Phillips.

--Tramps & Ladies. LC 59-12193. (Illus.). 1959. 17.95 (ISBN 0-87599-014-2). S G Phillips.

Bisset, N. G., tr. see Frohne, Dietrich & Pfaender, Hans J.

Bisset, Virgil, jt. ed. see Hunting, Constance.

Bissett, D. E., et al, eds. The Printing Ink Manual. 3rd ed. Leach, R. H. & Williams, C. H. (Illus.). 480p. 1984. 49.50 (ISBN 0-442-30600-8). Van Nos Reinhold.

Bissett, Lesley D. Client Finder II. LC 84-9954. 1984. pap. 21.95 (ISBN 0-8359-0765-1). Reston.

Bissett, Ron. Pigeon Fancying: Racing & Exhibiting. (Illus.). 173p. 1985. 13.95 (ISBN 0-7153-8427-9). David & Charles.

Bissex, Glenda. Gnys at Wrk: A Child Learns to Write & Read. LC 80-14558. (Illus.). 235p. 1980. text ed. 17.50x (ISBN 0-674-35485-0). Harvard U Pr.

Bissex, Glenda L. Gnys at Wrk: A Child Learns to Write & Read. 240p. 1985. pap. text ed. 6.95x (ISBN 0-674-35490-7). Harvard U Pr.

Bisshoff, David. Wraith Board. (Gaming Magi Ser.: Bk. 2). 1985. pap. 2.95 (ISBN 0-451-13669-1, Sig). NAL.

Bissing, Hurbert. Songs of Submission: On the Practice of Subud. 180p. (Orig.). 1983. pap. 9.50 (ISBN 0-227-67852-4, Pub. by J Clarke UK). Attic Pr.

Bissland, James, III, jt. auth. see Tolve, Arthur.

Bisson, I. J., ed. see Shakespeare, William.

Bisson, L. A. Proust & Hardy: Incidence or Coincidence in Studies in French Language Literature & History Presented to R. L. Graeme Ritchie. 1949. Repr. 40.00 (ISBN 0-8274-3920-2). R West.

Bisson, T. A. Japan in China. LC 73-4546. 424p. 1973. Repr. of 1938 ed. lib. bdg. 29.00x (ISBN 0-374-90640-8). Octagon.

--Yenan in June 1937: Talks with the Communist Leaders. LC 73-620023. (China Research Monographs: No. 11). 1973. pap. 5.00x (ISBN 0-912966-12-2). IEAS.

--Zaibatsu Dissolution in Japan. LC 76-5412. 314p. 1976. Repr. of 1954 ed. lib. bdg. 21.75x (ISBN 0-8371-8816-4, BIZD). Greenwood.

Bisson, T. N. Assemblies & Representation in Languedoc in the Thirteenth Century. 1964. 36.00x (ISBN 0-691-09201-X). Princeton U Pr.

Bisson, T. N., ed. Medieval Representative Institution: Their Origins & Nature. (European Problem Ser.). 154p. 1973. pap. 5.95 (Pub. by HR&W). Krieger.

Bisson, Thomas A. American Policy in the Far East, 1931-1941. LC 75-30096. (Institute of Pacific Relations). Repr. of 1941 ed. 30.00 (ISBN 0-404-59505-7). AMS Pr.

--America's Far Eastern Policy. LC 75-30095. (Institute of Pacific Relations). Repr. of 1945 ed. 24.50 (ISBN 0-404-59506-5). AMS Pr.

--Japan in China. LC 73-3920. (Illus.). 417p. 1973. Repr. of 1938 ed. lib. bdg. 22.50x (ISBN 0-8371-6858-9, BIJC). Greenwood.

Bisson, Thomas N. Conservation of Coinage: Monetary Exploitation & Its Restraint in France, Catalonia, & Aragon C.1000-1225 A.D. (Illus.). 1979. 54.00x (ISBN 0-19-828275-3). Oxford U Pr.

--Fiscal Accounts of Catalonia under the Early Count-Kings, 1151-1213, 2 vols. LC 81-22000. 663p. 1983. Set. 95.00x (ISBN 0-520-04588-2). Vol. I: Introduction. Vol. II: Accounts, Related Records, & Indices. U of Cal Pr.

Bissonnet, Wilhelm P. & Sagsetter, Brad. Beyond the Limit. 1984. pap. 3.95 (ISBN 0-89896-021-5). Larksdale.

Bissonnette, Georges. Moscow Was My Parish. LC 78-16489. 1978. Repr. of 1956 ed. lib. bdg. 20.75x (ISBN 0-313-20594-9, BIMM). Greenwood.

Bissuel, Henri. Les Touareg de l'ouest. LC 77-87620. (Illus.). Repr. of 1888 ed. 21.00 (ISBN 0-404-16447-1). AMS Pr.

Bisswanger, Hans & Schmincke-Ott, Eva, eds. Multifunctional Proteins. LC 79-16055. 333p. 1980. 84.50 (ISBN 0-471-04270-6, Pub. by Wiley-Interscience). Wiley.

Bist, Umrao S. Jaina Theories of Reality & Knowledge. 1985. 6.50x (ISBN 0-8364-1362-8, Pub. by Eastern). South Asia Bks.

Bister, Feliks J. & Kuhner, Herbert, eds. Carinthian Slovenian Poetry. (Illus.). 216p. (Eng. & Slovenian.). 1985. 12.95 (ISBN 3-85013-029-0). Slavica.

Bistner, Stephen I., jt. auth. see Kirk, Robert W.

Biswas. Terracotta Art Manual of Bengal. (Illus.). 277p. 1982. text ed. 65.00x (ISBN 0-391-02666-6). Humanities.

Biswas, A., jt. auth. see Biswas, S. B.

Biswas, A., et al. New Educational Pattern in India. 1976. 7.50 (ISBN 0-7069-0384-6). Intl Bk Dist.

Biswas, A. K., jt. auth. see Ausebel, J.

Biswas, A. K., jt. ed. see Golubev, G. N.

Biswas, Asit K. Models for Water Quality Management. (M-H Series in Water Resources & Environmental Engineering). (Illus.). 392p. 1981. text ed. 60.00 (ISBN 0-07-005481-9). McGraw.

Biswas, Asit K., jt. auth. see Biswas, Margaret R.

Biswas, Asit K., ed. Climate & Development. (Natural Resources & the Environment Ser.: Vol. 13). (Illus.). 144p. 1984. 19.50 (ISBN 0-907567-36-3, TYP131, TYP); pap. 9.75 (ISBN 0-907567-37-1, TYP130). Unipub.

--The Ozone Layer: Synthesis of Papers Based on the UNEP Meeting on the Ozone Layer, Washington DC, March 1977. LC 79-42879. (Environmental Sciences & Applications Ser.: Vol. 4). 1980. 68.00 (ISBN 0-08-022429-6). Pergamon.

--Systems Approach to Water Management. (Illus.). 1976. text ed. 48.00 (ISBN 0-07-005480-0). McGraw.

--United Nations Water Conference: Summary & Main Documents. new ed. LC 77-30461. 1978. text ed. 50.00 (ISBN 0-08-022392-3). Pergamon.

Biswas, Asit K., jt. ed. see El-Hinnawi, Essam.

Biswas, Asit K., jt. ed. see Zaman, Munir.

Biswas, Asu K. & Dakang, Zuo, eds. Long Distance Water Transfer: A Chinese Case Study & International Experience. (Water Resources Ser.: Vol. 3). 416p. 1983. 48.75 (ISBN 0-907567-52-5, TYP144, TYP); pap. 28.25 (ISBN 0-907567-53-3, TYP143). Unipub.

Biswas, B. B., et al, eds. Control of Transcription. LC 73-20166. (Basic Life Sciences Ser.: Vol. 3). (Illus.). 442p. 1974. 52.50x (ISBN 0-306-36503-0, Plenum Pr). Plenum Pub.

Biswas, D. C. Shakespeare in His Own Time. 1979. text ed. 13.00x (ISBN 0-391-01762-4). Humanities.

Biswas, Dinesh C. Shakespeare's Treatment of His Sources in the Comedies. 1978. Repr. of 1971 ed. lib. bdg. 30.00 (ISBN 0-8414-0093-8). Folcroft.

Biswas, Dipti K. Political Sociology: An Introduction. 1978. 7.00x (ISBN 0-8364-0138-7). South Asia Bks.

Biswas, Jayasee. U. S. - Bangladesh Relations: A Study of the Political & Economic Developments During 1971-1981. 1985. 12.50x (ISBN 0-8364-1309-1). South Asia Bks.

Biswas, Manju. Mentally Retarded & Normal Children: A Comparative Study of Their Family Conditions. 157p. 1980. 19.95x (ISBN 0-940500-50-7, Pub. by Sterling India). Asia Bk Corp.

Biswas, Margaret R. & Biswas, Asit K. Desertification: Associated Case Studies Prepared for the United Nations Conference on Desertification. LC 80-40024. (Environmental Sciences & Applications: Vol. 12). (Illus.). 532p. 1980. 105.00 (ISBN 0-08-023581-6). Pergamon.

Biswas, Nripendra U. Introduction to Logic & Switching Theory. 368p. 1975. 67.25x (ISBN 0-677-02860-1). Gordon.

Biswas, S. B. & Biswas, A. Introduction to Viruses. (Illus.). 1976. 7.50 (ISBN 0-7069-0411-7). Intl Bk Dist.

Bisztray, George. Marxist Models of Literary Realism. LC 77-23833. 247p. 1978. 21.00x (ISBN 0-231-04310-4). Columbia U Pr.

Bisztricsany, E. & Szeidovitz, G., eds. Proceedings: Assembly of European Seismological Commission, 17th, Budapest, 24-29 Aug. 1980. (Developments in Solid Earth Geophysics: Vol. 15). 690p. 1983. 117.00 (ISBN 0-444-99662-1). Elsevier.

Bitar, Sergio. Chile: Experiment in Democracy. LC 84-5618. (Inter-American Politics Ser.: Vol. 6). 350p. 1985. text ed. 33.00 (ISBN 0-89727-062-2). ISHI PA.

Bitel, Jane. Jane Butel's Tex-Mex Cookbook. 224p. 1980. 12.95 (ISBN 0-517-53986-1, Harmony). Crown.

Bitensky, M., et al, eds. see ICN-UCLA Symposium on Transmembrane Signaling, Keystone, Colorado, February, 1978.

Bitha, R. P. Morphological Mechanisms: Lexicalist Analyses of Synthetic Compounding. (Language & Communication Library: Vol. 7). 176p. 1984. 28.00 (ISBN 0-08-031820-7). Pergamon.

Bithell, J. & Yarmolinsky, D. Contemporary German Poetry. 59.95 (ISBN 0-87968-938-2). Gordon Pr.

Bithell, J. F. & Coppi, R., eds. Perspectives in Medical Statistics. LC 81-68973. 1982. 60.00 (ISBN 0-12-102520-9). Acad Pr.

Bithell, Jethro. Life & Writings of Maurice Maeterlinck. LC 71-160743. 1971. Repr. of 1913 ed. 19.50x (ISBN 0-8046-1556-X, Pub. by Kennikat). Assoc Faculty Pr.

Bithell, Jethro, tr. Contemporary French Poetry. 227p. 1981. Repr. of 1912 ed. lib. bdg. 35.00 (ISBN 0-89987-080-5). Darby Bks.

--Contemporary French Poetry. 227p. 1980. Repr. lib. bdg. 20.00 (ISBN 0-89760-041-X). Telegraph Bks.

Bithell, Jethro, tr. see Zweig, Stefan.

Bither, Steve, jt. auth. see Wicked Good Band Staff.

Bitman, Sam & Zalk, Sue R. Expectant Fathers. (Orig.). 1981. pap. 6.95 (ISBN 0-345-28746-0). Ballantine.

Bitner, Harry, jt. auth. see Price, Miles O.

Bitney, James. Bright Intervals: Prayers for Paschal People. 96p. (gr. 9-12). 1982. pap. 5.95 (ISBN 0-86683-669-1). Winston Pr.

Bitney, James L. Sunday's Children. 80p. (Orig.). 1986. pap. 8.95 (ISBN 0-89390-071-0). Resource Pubns.

Bito, L. & Davson, H., eds. The Ocular & Cerebrospinal Fluids: Experimental Eye Research Supplement. 1978. 69.50 (ISBN 0-12-102550-0). Acad Pr.

Bitossi, Sergio. Ferdinand Magellan. LC 84-40405. (Why They Became Famous Ser.). (Illus.). 64p. (gr. 5 up). 1985. 12.96 (ISBN 0-382-06984-6). Silver.

Bitov, Andrei. Pushkinskill Dom. (Rus.). 1978. pap. 8.95 (ISBN 0-88233-351-8). Ardis Pubs.

Bitoy, Earl, ed. see Grayson, David.

Bitros, George C., ed. Selected Economic Writings of Fritz Machlup. LC 75-34675. 603p. 1976. 65.00x (ISBN 0-8147-1004-2). NYU Pr.

Bitsadze, A. V. Equations of Mathematical Physics. 1980. 8.95 (ISBN 0-8285-1809-2, Pub. by Mir Pubs USSR). Imported Pubns.

Bitsadze, A. V. & Kalinichenko, D. F. A Collection of Problems on the Equations of Mathematical Physics. 1980. 9.45 (ISBN 0-8285-1779-7, Pub. by Mir Pubs USSR). Imported Pubns.

Bitsilli, Peter. Chekhov's Art: A Stylistic Analysis. Clyman, Toby & Cruise, Edwina, trs. from Rus. 1983. 25.00; pap. 5.00. Ardis Pubs.

Bitta, Albert J. Della see Loudon, David & Della Bitta, Albert J.

Bittar, E. E., ed. Membrane Structure & Function, Vol. 4. LC 79-14969. (Membrane Structure & Function Ser.: No. 1-447). 304p. 1984. text ed. 69.95x (ISBN 0-471-08908-7, Pub. by Wiley-Interscience). Wiley.

Bittar, E. Edward. Membrane Structure & Function, 3 vols. LC 79-14969. (Membrane Structure & Function Ser.). 1980. Vol. 1, 211p. 43.95 (ISBN 0-471-03816-4, Pub. by Wiley-Interscience); Vol. 2, 373p. 69.50 (ISBN 0-471-03817-2); Vol. 3, 183p. 45.95 (ISBN 0-471-03818-0). Wiley.

Bittar, E. Edward, ed. Cell Biology in Medicine. LC 75-19060. Repr. of 1973 ed. 120.00 (ISBN 0-8357-9853-4, 2012595). Bks Demand UMI.

--Membranes & Ion Transport, Vol. 1. pap. 123.50 (ISBN 0-317-29868-2, 2016176). Bks Demand UMI.

Bittar, Edward E., ed. Membrane Structure & Function, Vol. 5. (Membrane Structure & Function Ser.: 1-447). 1984. text ed. 69.95 (ISBN 0-471-81090-8, Pub. by Wiley-Interscience). Wiley.

Bittar, Neville, ed. see Mackinney, Archie A., Jr.

Bittel, L. R. Business in Action: An Introduction to Business. 432p. 1982. text ed. 26.50 (ISBN 0-07-005456-8). McGraw.

--What Every Supervisor Should Know. 5th ed. 672p. 1984. skills development portfolio 11.70 (ISBN 0-07-005574-2); skills development portfolio 9.95 (ISBN 0-07-005575-0). McGraw.

Bittel, L. R. & Burke, R. S. Sweetco: Business Model & Activity File. 2nd ed. 320p. 1983. 9.90 (ISBN 0-07-005516-5). McGraw.

Bittel, L. R. & Ramsey, J. E. Handbook for Professional Managers. 1088p. 1985. 59.95 (ISBN 0-07-005469-X). McGraw.

Bittel, L. R., et al. Set for the Donut Franchise: A Microcomputer Simulation for Business in Action. 2nd ed. 48p. 1984. TRS S80 Version. 150.00 (ISBN 0-07-079357-3); Apple Version. 199.00. McGraw.

Bittel, Lester. Leadership: The Key to Management Success. 272p. 1984. 15.95 (ISBN 0-531-09577-0). Watts.

Bittel, Lester R. Business in Action: An Introduction to Business. LC 79-9320. 1980. 29.95 (ISBN 0-07-079164-3). McGraw.

--Encyclopedia of Professional Management. (Illus.). 1979. 46.95 (ISBN 0-07-005478-9). McGraw.

--Essentials of Supervisory Management. LC 80-13784. (Illus.). 288p. 1980. 19.55 (ISBN 0-07-005571-8). McGraw.

--What Every Supervisor Should Know: The Basics of Supervisory Management. 4th ed. LC 79-16387. 1980. text ed. 27.65x (ISBN 0-07-005561-0). McGraw.

Bittel, Lester R., jt. auth. see Burke, Ronald S.

Bitter, et al. McGraw-Hill Mathematics, 8 levels. Incl. Level 1. text ed. 8.96 (ISBN 0-07-005761-3); Level 2. text ed. 8.96 (ISBN 0-07-005762-1); Level 3. text ed. 14.08 (ISBN 0-07-005763-X); Level 4. text ed. 14.08 (ISBN 0-07-005764-8); Level 5. text ed. 14.08 (ISBN 0-07-005765-6); Level 6. text ed. 13.28 (ISBN 0-07-005766-4); Level 7. text ed. 17.28 (ISBN 0-07-005767-2); Level 8. text ed. 17.28 (ISBN 0-07-005768-0). 1981. McGraw.

--McGraw-Hill Mathematics Parents Guide to Problem Solving. (McGraw-Hill Mathematics, Ser.). 16p. 1981. 1.12 (ISBN 0-07-005749-4). McGraw.

--Mathematics Classroom Management Guide, Grade 1-8. (Mathematics Ser.). 1981. 1.96 ea. Gr. 1 (ISBN 0-07-006091-6). Gr. 2 (ISBN 0-07-006092-4). Gr. 3 (ISBN 0-07-006093-2). Gr. 4 (ISBN 0-07-006094-0). Gr. 5 (ISBN 0-07-006095-9). Gr. 6 (ISBN 0-07-006096-7). Gr. 7 (ISBN 0-07-006097-5). Gr. 8 (ISBN 0-07-006098-3). McGraw.

Bitter, Francis & Medicus, Heinrich A. Fields & Particles: An Introduction to Electromagnetic Wave Phenomena & Quantum Physics. LC 72-87209. pap. 160.00 (ISBN 0-317-08584-0, 2007763). Bks Demand UMI.

Bitter, G. & Watson, N. IBM PC & PCjR LOGO Primer. 1985. 17.95 (ISBN 0-8359-3180-3). Reston.

Bitter, Gary. Exploring with Computers. (gr. 7up). 4.95 (ISBN 0-671-49884-3). Messner.

--Microcomputer Applications for Calculus. 256p. 1982. pap. text ed. write for info (ISBN 0-87150-378-6, 8010, Prindle). PWS Pubs.

Bitter, Gary & Watson, Nancy. The Apple LOGO Primer. 1983. pap. 16.95 (ISBN 0-8359-0314-1). Reston.

Bitter, Gary, jt. auth. see Watson, Nancy.

Bitter, Gary A. & Watson, Nancy R. Commodore 64 LOGO Primer. 1984. pap. text ed. 16.95 (ISBN 0-8359-0794-5). Reston.

Bitter, Gary G. Computers in Today's World. LC 83-10588. 306p. 1984. pap. text ed. 21.95x (ISBN 0-471-87552-X); tchr's. edition avail. (ISBN 0-471-87206-7); avail. student wkbk. 10.95x (ISBN 0-471-87205-9); BASIC supplement 10.45 (ISBN 0-471-87551-1); Pascal supplement 10.45 (ISBN 0-471-87553-8). Wiley.

--Exploring with Computers. LC 80-29509. (Illus.). 64p. (gr. 4-7). 1981. PLB 9.29 (ISBN 0-671-34034-4). Messner.

--Exploring with Computers. rev. ed. LC 83-7917. (Illus.). 96p. (gr. 4 up). 1983. lib. bdg. 9.29 (ISBN 0-671-47789-7); pap. 4.95 (ISBN 0-671-49884-3). Messner.

Bitter, Gary G. & Camuse, Ruth A. Using a Microcomputer in the Classroom. (gr. k-12). 1983. text ed. 16.95 O.P.; pap. 16.95 (ISBN 0-8359-8144-4). Reston.

Bitter, Gary G. & Cook, Paul M. IBM BASIC for Business. (Illus.). 192p. 1986. pap. text ed. 19.95 (ISBN 0-13-448093-7). P-H.

Bitter, Gary G. & Gateley, Wilson Y. BASIC for Beginners. 2nd ed. (Illus.). 1978. pap. text ed. 22.95 (ISBN 0-07-005492-4). McGraw.

Bitter, Gary G. & Gore, Kay. The Best of Educational Software for Apple II Computers. 300p. 1984. pap. 16.95 (ISBN 0-89588-206-X). SYBEX.

--The Best of Educational Software for the Commodore 64. 250p. 1984. pap. 16.95 (ISBN 0-89588-223-X). SYBEX.

Bitter, Gary G. & Mikesell, Jeraldi L. Activities Handbook for Teaching with the Hand Held Calculator. 1979. text ed. 28.57 scp (ISBN 0-205-06713-1, 236713). Allyn.

Bitter, Gary G. & Watson, Nancy. IBM PC LOGO Primer. (Illus.). 150p. 15.95 (ISBN 0-317-13057-9). P-H.

Bitter, Gary G. & Geer, Charles. Materials for Metric Instruction. 90p. 1975. pap. 2.50 (ISBN 0-317-35361-6, 78). NCTM.

Bitter, Gary G., et al. How to Feel at Home with a Home Computer. LC 83-50901. 264p. 1983. pap. 12.95 (ISBN 0-89512-097-6). Tex Instr Inc.

--One Step at a Time. LC 77-82666. 1977. pap. text ed. 18.00 (ISBN 0-88436-419-4, MAA 103000). EMC.

Bitter, Grant B. Parents in Action. LC 78-58604. 1978. pap. 6.95 (ISBN 0-88200-122-1, I5672). Alexander Graham.

Bitter, James A. & Goodyear, Don L., eds. Rehabilitation Evaluation: Some Application Guidelines. LC 75-9719. 1975. text ed. 29.50x (ISBN 0-8422-5223-1); pap. text ed. 7.95x (ISBN 0-8422-0502-0). Irvington.

Bitter, John. Practical Public Relations for the Public Schools. LC 77-71467. 1977. text ed. 9.95x (ISBN 0-916624-08-0). Troy State Univ.

Bitterman, M. E., et al, eds. Animal Learning: Survey & Analysis. LC 78-9894. (NATO ASI Series A, Life Sciences: Vol. 19). 522p. 1979. 55.00x (ISBN 0-306-40061-8, Plenum Pr). Plenum Pub.

Bitterman, M. E., jt. ed. see Masterton, R. B.

Bittermann, Henry J. The Refunding of International Debt. LC 72-93542. 234p. 1973. 21.00 (ISBN 0-8223-0280-2). Duke.

--State & Federal Grants-In-Aid. Repr. of 1938 ed. 37.00 (ISBN 0-384-04511-1). Johnson Repr.

Bittiger, H. & Schnebli, H. P., eds. Concanavalin A as a Tool. LC 75-37841. (Wiley-Interscience Publication Ser.). pap. 160.00 (ISBN 0-317-26200-9, 2052066). Bks Demand UMI.

Bitting, K. Gastronomic Bibliography. 718p. 1939. 60.00 (ISBN 0-87556-723-1). Saifer.

Bitting, Mary M. Soups on the Piano. 64p. 1984. 6.95 (ISBN 0-89962-341-7). Todd & Honeywell.

Bittinger, Emmet F. Heritage & Promise: Perspectives on the Church of the Brethren. rev. ed. 1983. pap. 6.95 (ISBN 0-87178-357-6). Brethren.

Bittinger, Lucy F. Germans in Colonial Times. LC 68-25064. (Illus.). 314p. 1968. Repr. of 1901 ed. 8.50x (ISBN 0-8462-1225-0). Russell.

Bittinger, M. L. Logic, Proof, & Sets. 2nd ed. LC 81-14913. 144p. 1982. pap. text ed. 8.95 (ISBN 0-201-10384-2). Addison-Wesley.

Bittinger, M. L. & Crown, J. C. Mathematics for Business, Economics & Management. 1982. 31.95 (ISBN 0-201-10104-1); instrs' manual 2.50 (ISBN 0-201-10105-X). Addison-Wesley.

Bittinger, M. L., jt. auth. see Keedy, M. L.

Bittinger, Marvin, jt. auth. see Keedy, Mervin.

Bittinger, Marvin L. Calculus: Modeling Approach. 3rd ed. LC 83-6334. (Illus.). 544p. 1984. 32.95 (ISBN 0-201-11217-5); instr's manual 3.00 (ISBN 0-201-11219-1); student manual 9.95 (ISBN 0-201-11218-3). Addison-Wesley.

Bittinger, Marvin L. & Crown, J. Conrad. Mathematics: A Modeling Approach. 1981. 29.95 (ISBN 0-201-03116-7); instr's. manual 2.50 (ISBN 0-201-03117-5). Addison-Wesley.

Bittinger, Marvin L. & Keedy, Mervin L. Essential Mathematics. 4th ed. 736p. 1984. pap. 25.95 (ISBN 0-201-14806-4). Addison-Wesley.

Bittinger, Marvin L., jt. auth. see Crown, J. Conrad.

Bittinger, Marvin L., jt. auth. see Keedy, Mervin L.

Bittinger, Morton N. & Green, Elizabeth B. You Never Miss the Water till... The Ogallalla Story. LC 80-50167. 1981. 7.00 (ISBN 0-918334-33-0). WRP.

Bittinger, Ross T., jt. auth. see Fowler, Herbert A.

Bittinger, Wayne. Generations. 1974. 7.00 (ISBN 0-87012-173-1). McClain.

Bittker, Boris & Clark, Elias. Federal Estate & Gift Taxation. 5th ed. LC 83-82904. 608p. 1984. text ed. 28.00 (ISBN 0-316-09687-3). Little.

Bittker, Boris & Eustice, James. Fundamentals of Federal Income Taxation of Corporations & Shareholders: Annual Supplement. LC 80-50916. 1980. student ed. 33.50 (ISBN 0-88262-467-9); guide 15.00study (ISBN 0-88262-973-5). Warren.

Bittker, Boris I. Federal Taxation of Income, Estates & Gifts: Cumulative Supplementation, 5 vols., index. LC 80-50773. 1981. 350.00 set (ISBN 0-88262-460-1). Warren.

--Fundamentals of Federal Income Taxation: Annual Supplement. 1983. student ed. 32.50 (ISBN 0-88262-963-8). Warren.

Bittker, Boris I. & Emory, Meade. Federal Income Taxation of Corporations & Shareholders: Forms, Cumulative Supplementation, 2 vols. 1982. 96.50 (ISBN 0-88262-631-0, 75-6129). Warren.

Bittker, Boris I. & Eustice, James S. Federal Income Taxation of Corporations & Shareholders: Cumulative Supplementation. 4th ed. 1979. 96.00 (ISBN 0-88262-288-9); student's ed. 35.50. Warren.

Bittker, Boris I. & Stone, Lawrence M. Federal Income Taxation. 6th ed. LC 83-82839. 987p. 1984. text ed. 31.00 (ISBN 0-316-09693-8); Supplement, 1985. text ed. write for info. (ISBN 0-316-09695-4). Little.

--Federal Income Taxation. 6th ed. 1985. write for info.; Case supplement, 1985. write for info. Little.

Bittker, Boris I., jt. ed. see Goldstein, Gersham.

Bittle, Jerry. Let's Burn That Bridge When We Come to It. (Illus.). 128p. (Orig.). 1985. pap. 6.95 (ISBN 0-8362-1257-6). Andrews McMeel Parker.

Bittles, A. H. & Collins, K. J., eds. The Biology of Human Ageing. (Illus.). 350p. Date not set. price not set (ISBN 0-521-30485-7). Cambridge U Pr.

Bittleston, Adam & Jones, Daniel T., eds. The Golden Blade, 1985. 112p. (Orig.). 1985. pap. 9.95x (ISBN 0-88010-128-8, Pub. by Steinerbooks). Anthroposophic.

Bittleston, Adam, ed. see Steiner, Rudolf.

Bittleston, Adam, tr. see Steiner, Rudolf.

Bittleston, Adam, tr. see Von Goethe, Johann W. & Steiner, Rudolf.

Bittleston, John & Shorter, Barbara. The Book of Business Communications Checklist. 114p. 1981. 34.95x (ISBN 0-470-27307-0). Halsted Pr.

--The Book of Business Communications Checklists. 180p. 1982. 40.00x (ISBN 0-85227-263-4). State Mutual Bk.

Bittleston, R., jt. auth. see Weston, G. F.

Bittlingmayer, George, jt. auth. see Gould, John.

Bittman, Ladislav. The Deception Game. (Espionage Intelligence Library: No. 6). 1981. pap. 2.75 (ISBN 0-345-29808-X). Ballantine.

--KGB-Disinformation: Soviet Active Measures Against the United States. (Illus.). 260p. 1985. 16.90 (ISBN 0-08-031572-0, Pub. by Aberdeen Scotland). Pergamon.

Bittman, Sam & Zalk, Sue. Expectant Fathers. LC 78-54666. 1979. 12.95 (ISBN 0-8015-2444-X, Hawthorn). Dutton.

Bittman, Sam & Satullo, Steven A., eds. Berkshire Seasons of Celebration. (Illus.). 108p. 1982. 25.00 (ISBN 0-910931-01-1); pap. 15.00 (ISBN 0-910931-00-3). Either-Or Pr.

Bittner, Donald F. The Lion & the White Falcon: Britain & Iceland in the World War II Era. (Illus.). xii, 207p. 1983. 25.00 (ISBN 0-208-01956-1, Archon Bks). Shoe String.

Bittner, Egon. The Functions of the Police in Modern Society. LC 79-22154. 1979. text ed. 22.50 o. p. (ISBN 0-89946-007-0); pap. text ed. 12.50 (ISBN 0-89946-006-2). Oelgeschlager.

--Popular Interset in Psychiatric Remedies: A Study in Social Control. Zuckerman, Harriet & Merton, Robert K., eds. LC 79-8977. (Dissertations on Sociology). 1980. lib. bdg. 24.50x (ISBN 0-405-12953-X). Ayer Co Pubs.

Bittner, Egon & Krantz, Sheldon. Standards Relating to Police Handling of Juvenile Problems. LC 77-3376. (IJA-ABA Juvenile Justice Standards Project Ser.). 168p. 1980. prof ref 22.50 (ISBN 0-88410-755-8); pap. 12.50 (ISBN 0-88410-806-6). Ballinger Pub.

Bittner, Egon & Messinger, Sheldon L., eds. Criminology Review Yearbook, Vol. 2. (Illus.). 733p. 1980. 40.00 (ISBN 0-8039-1309-5). Sage.

Bittner, Egon, jt. ed. see Messinger, Sheldon L.

Bittner, F. Rosanne. Arizona Bride. 1985. pap. 3.75 (ISBN 0-8217-1597-6). Zebra.

--Savage Destiny, No. 3: River of Love. 1984. pap. 3.50 (ISBN 0-8217-1373-6). Zebra.

Bittner, J. Broadcasting: An Introduction. 1980. 26.95 (ISBN 0-13-083535-8). P-H.

--Professional Broadcasting: A Brief Introduction. 1981. pap. 19.95 (ISBN 0-13-725465-2). P-H.

Bittner, James W. Approaches to the Fiction of Ursula K. Le Guin. Scholes, Robert, ed. LC 84-8507. (Studies in Speculative Fiction: No. 4). 180p. 1984. 24.95 (ISBN 0-8357-1573-6). UMI Res Pr.

Bittner, John. Broadcast Law & Regulation. (Illus.). 464p. 1982. 35.95 (ISBN 0-13-083592-7). P-H.

Bittner, John R. Broadcasting & Telecommunication: An Introduction. 2nd ed. (Illus.). 544p. 1985. text ed. 26.95 (ISBN 0-13-083551-X). P-H.

--Each Other: An Introduction to Interpersonal Communication. (Illus.). 368p. 1983. text ed. 20.95 (ISBN 0-13-222190-X). P-H.

--Fundamentals of Communication. (Illus.). 560p. 1985. pap. text ed. 18.95 (ISBN 0-13-335217-X). P-H.

--Mass Communication: An Introduction. 3rd ed. (Illus.). 496p. 1983. pap. 21.95 (ISBN 0-13-559286-0). P-H.

--Mass Communication: An Introduction. 4th ed. (Illus.). 528p. 1986. pap. text ed. 21.95 (ISBN 0-13-559246-1). P-H.

Bittner, Melinda J. The Oaks of People's Lives. Date not set. 6.95 (ISBN 0-8062-2349-9). Carlton.

Bittner, Rosanne F. Ride the Free Wind. (Savage Destiny: No. 2). 1984. pap. 3.50 (ISBN 0-8217-1311-6). Zebra.

--Sweet Prairie Passion. (Savage Destiny Ser.: No. 1). 1983. pap. 3.50 (ISBN 0-8217-1251-9). Zebra.

Bittner, Vernon J. Make Your Illness Count: A Hospital Chaplain Shows How God's Healing Power Can Be Released in Your Life. LC 76-3862. 128p. (Orig.). 1976. pap. 5.50 (ISBN 0-8066-1532-X, 10-4260). Augsburg.

--You Can Help with Your Healing: A Guide for Recovering Wholeness in Body, Mind, & Spirit. LC 78-66946. 1979. pap. 5.95 (ISBN 0-8066-1698-9, 10-7411). Augsburg.

Bittner, William C. Frank J. Lausche: A Political Biography. LC 76-361526. (Studia Slovenica, Special Series). 78p. 1975. 5.00 (ISBN 0-686-28389-9). Studia Slovenica.

Bittnger, Marvin L., jt. auth. see Keedy, Mervin L.

Bitton, Davis. French Nobility in Crisis, 1560-1640. LC 69-13177. 1969. 15.00x (ISBN 0-8047-0684-0). Stanford U Pr.

Bitton, Davis, jt. auth. see Arrington, Leonard J.

Bitton, Davis, jt. auth. see Bunker, Gary L.

Bitton, Gabriel. Introduction to Environmental Virology. 326p. 1980. 37.50 (ISBN 0-471-04247-1, BG75, Pub. by Wiley-Interscience). Wiley.

Bitton, Gabriel & Gerba, Charles, eds. Groundwater Pollution Microbiology. LC 83-1475. (Environmental Science & Technology Ser.: No. 1-121). 377p. 1984. 49.95 (ISBN 0-471-09656-3, Pub by Wiley Interscience). Wiley.

Bitton, Gabriel & Marshall, Kevin C., eds. Absorption of Micro-Organisms to Surfaces. LC 79-19482. 439p. 1980. 51.50x (ISBN 0-471-03157-7, Pub. by Wiley-Interscience). Wiley.

Bitton-Jackson, Livia. Madonna or Courtesan: The Jewish Woman in Christian Literature. 160p. 1983. pap. 7.95 (ISBN 0-8164-2440-3, Pub. by Seabury). Winston Pr.

Bitz, Gregory W. Carrots, As We All Know, Do Not Cast Shadows. Bedell, George F. & Fowler, Charles, eds. (Illus.). 1977. pap. 7.95 (ISBN 0-916320-04-9). Red Studio.

Bitz, Gregory W., et al. Dim Lake. LC 75-33554. (Illus.). 1975. 3.95 (ISBN 0-916320-01-4). Red Studio.

Bitzer, Heinrich, ed. Light on the Path: Daily Scripture Readings in Hebrew & Greek. 400p. (Orig.). 1982. pap. 7.95 (ISBN 0-8010-0822-0). Baker Bk.

Bitzer, Lloyd & Rueter, Theodore. Carter vs. Ford: The Counterfeit Debates of Nineteen Seventy-Six. LC 80-5110. 444p. 1980. 35.00x (ISBN 0-299-08280-6); pap. 12.50x (ISBN 0-299-08284-9). U of Wis Pr.

Bivand, Ewa S., jt. auth. see Bivand, Roger.

Bivand, Roger & Bivand, Ewa S. Britain: Continuity & Change. LC 80-40778. (Illus.). 196p. 1981. 6.40 (ISBN 0-08-025312-1). Pergamon.

Bivens, Allison, ed. The High Museum of Art Recipe Collection. (Illus.). 200p. (Orig.). 1981. pap. 10.95 (ISBN 0-939802-14-7). High Mus Art.

Bivens, Gordon E., jt. auth. see Allentuck, Andrew J.

Bivens, John. Art of the Fire-Lock, Twentieth Century: Being a Discourse Upon the Present & Past Practices of Stocking & Mounting the Sporting Fire-Lock Rifle-Gun, 3 vols. (The Longrifle Ser.). 1986. 40.00 (ISBN 0-686-75398-4). Shumway.

Bivens, William E., jt. auth. see Ankner, William.

Biver, Paul. Pere Lamy. O'Connor, John, tr. from Fr. 1973. pap. 5.50 (ISBN 0-89555-055-5). TAN Bks Pubs.

Biviano, Ronald S. Medical Conditions & Terms Made Simple. LC 80-68397. 100p. (Orig.). 1981. pap. 10.00 (ISBN 0-9605476-0-6). Biviano.

Bivin, David. Understanding the Difficult Words of Jesus. LC 83-61850. (Illus.). 172p. (Orig.). 1983. pap. 8.95 (ISBN 0-918873-00-2). Ctr Judaic-Christ Studies.

Bivins, Frank J. The Farmer's Political Economy. facsimile ed. McCurry, Dan C. & Rubenstein, Richard E., eds. LC 74-30619. (American Farmers & the Rise of Agribusiness Ser.). (Illus.). 1975. Repr. of 1913 ed. 13.00 (ISBN 0-405-06766-6). Ayer Co Pubs.

Bivins, John, Jr. The Moravian Potters in North Carolina. LC 70-172396. (Old Salem Ser.). (Illus.). xiii, 303p. 1972. 14.95 (ISBN 0-8078-1191-2). U of NC Pr.

Biwas, Amita & Biwas, S. B. Introduction to Viruses. Rev. ed. (Illus.). 292p. 1983. text ed. 22.50x (ISBN 0-7069-2515-7, Pub by Vikas India). Advent NY.

Biwas, S. B., jt. auth. see Biwas, Amita.

Bix, Cynthia & Dillon, Ann. Contributions of Women: Theater. LC 77-13094. (Contributions of Women Ser.). (Illus.). (gr. 6 up). 1978. PLB 8.95 (ISBN 0-87518-152-X). Dillon.

Bixby, F. Rew. Fire Throne Mountain. 208p. (Orig.). 1982. pap. 2.25 (ISBN 0-505-51723-X, Pub. by Tower Bks). Dorchester Pub Co.

Bixby, Louis W. The Excitement of Learning: The Boredom of Education. LC 76-24282. 1977. 7.95 (ISBN 0-87212-056-2). Libra.

--The Mechanics of Physics: A Rational Approach to Learning Newtonian Physics. 1982. 7.95 (ISBN 0-533-05117-7). Vantage.

--The Problems of Education: With Some Forward Help. 168p. 1981. 7.95 (ISBN 0-8059-2782-4). Dorrance.

Bixler, David, jt. auth. see Melnick, Michael.

Bixler, Herbert E. Railroads: Their Rise & Fall. 115p. (Orig.). 1982. pap. 7.95 (ISBN 0-9610066-0-9). H E Bixler.

Bixler, Julius S. Conversations with an Unrepentant Liberal. LC 72-85298. 128p. 1973. Repr. of 1946 ed. 19.50x (ISBN 0-8046-1713-9, Pub. by Kennikat). Assoc Faculty Pr.

--A Faith That Fulfills. LC 74-138100. 122p. 1972. Repr. of 1951 ed. lib. bdg. 15.00x (ISBN 0-8371-5676-9, BIFF). Greenwood.

--Immortality & the Present Mood. LC 75-3047. Repr. of 1931 ed. 16.00 (ISBN 0-404-59044-6). AMS Pr.

--Religion for Free Minds. LC 75-3048. (Philosophy in America Ser.). 1976. Repr. of 1939 ed. 18.00 (ISBN 0-404-59045-4). AMS Pr.

--Religion in the Philosophy of William James. LC 75-3049. Repr. of 1926 ed. 24.50 (ISBN 0-404-59046-2). AMS Pr.

Bixler, Norma. Burmese Journey. LC 67-11440. pap. 46.80 (ISBN 0-317-11181-7, 2016111). Bks Demand UMI.

Bixler, Paul, ed. The Antioch Review Anthology. (Essay Index Reprint Ser.). 480p. Repr. of 1953 ed. lib. bdg. 24.00 (ISBN 0-8290-0793-8). Irvington.

Bixler, Paul, ed. see American Library Association Committee On Intellectual Freedom-1st Conference-New York-1952.

Bixler, Paul, ed. see Antioch Review.

Bixler, Phyllis. Frances Hodgson Burnett. (English Authors Ser.: No. 373). 1984. lib. bdg. 18.95 (ISBN 0-8057-6859-9, Twayne). G K Hall.

Bixler, Russell. Learning to Know God As Provider. 96p. 1982. pap. 3.50 (ISBN 0-88368-120-X). Whitaker Hse.

Bixler, Susan. Professional Image. (Illus.). 288p. 1985. pap. 8.95 (ISBN 0-399-51115-6, Perigee). Putnam Pub Group.

--The Professional Image: The Total Program for Marketing Yourself Visually. LC 83-24769. (Illus.). 256p. 1984. 16.95 (ISBN 0-399-12954-5, Putnam). Putnam Pub Group.

Biyidi, Alexandre see Beti, Mongo, pseud.

Bizer, Ernst, ed. see Heppe, Heinrich.

Bizer, Linda & Nathan, Beverly. Discovering New Worlds. Lawrence, Leslie & Weingartner, Ronald, eds. (Bright Beginnings I). (Illus.). 48p. (Orig.). (gr. k-2). pap. 1.69 (ISBN 0-88049-023-3, 7386). Milton Bradley Co.

--Learning My Letters. Lawrence, Leslie & Weingartner, Ronald, eds. (Bright Beginnings I). (Illus.). 48p. (Orig.). (gr. k-2). pap. 1.69 (ISBN 0-88049-021-7, 7384). Milton Bradley Co.

--Learning My Numbers. Lawrence, Leslie & Weingartner, Ronald, eds. (Bright Beginnings I). (Illus.). 48p. (Orig.). (gr. k-2). pap. 1.69 (ISBN 0-88049-025-X, 7388). Milton Bradley Co.

--Letter Sounds. Lawrence, Leslie & Weingartner, Ronald, eds. (Bright Beginnings I Ser). (Illus.). 48p. (Orig.). (gr. k-2). pap. 1.69 (ISBN 0-88049-022-5, 7385). Milton Bradley Co.

--Spell Well. Lawrence, Leslie & Weingartner, Ronald, eds. (Bright Beginnings I). (Illus.). 48p. (Orig.). (gr. k-2). pap. 1.69 (ISBN 0-88049-028-4, 7391). Milton Bradley Co.
--Understanding What I Read. Lawrence, Leslie & Weingartner, Ronald, eds. (Bright Beginnings I). (Illus.). 48p. (Orig.). (gr. k-2). pap. 1.69 (ISBN 0-88049-024-1, 7387). Milton Bradley Co.
--Writing My Letters & Numbers. Lawrence, Leslie & Weingartner, Ronald, eds. (Bright Beginnings I). (Illus.). 48p. (Orig.). (gr. k-2). pap. 1.69 (ISBN 0-88049-027-6, 7390). Milton Bradley Co.
Bizer, Linda, jt. auth. see Nathan, Beverly.
Bizer, Linda S. & Markel, Geraldine P. The ABC's of the SAT: A Parent's Guide to College Entrance Exams. LC 82-13858. (Illus.). 160p. (Orig.). 1983. pap. 4.95 (ISBN 0-668-05666-5, 5666). Arco.
Bizet, George. Carmen, No. 13. Nicholas, John, ed. Moody, Nell & Moody, John, trs. from Fr. (English National Opera Guide Ser.: No. 13 Libretto, Articles). 128p. 1982. pap. 4.95 (ISBN 0-7145-3937-6). Riverrun NY.
Bizet, Georges. Bizet's Carmen. (Music Ser.). 96p. (Orig.). 1984. pap. 2.50 (ISBN 0-486-24556-X). Dover.
--Doctor Miracle. Harris, David, tr. 1964. 2.00 (ISBN 0-19-335300-8). Oxford U Pr.
Bizollon, C. A., ed. Monoclonal Antibodies & New Trends in Immunoassays: Proceedings of the 6th International Symposium on Radioimmunology Held in Lyon, France, 12-14 April, 1984. 310p. 1984. 59.25 (ISBN 0-444-80619-9). Elsevier.
--Physiological Peptides & New Trends in Radioimmunology. 370p. 1981. 59.25 (ISBN 0-444-80358-0, Biomedical Pr). Elsevier.
Bizzaro, Patrick. Violence. (Orig.). 1979. pap. 2.00 (ISBN 0-918092-12-4). Tamarack Edns.
Bizzarro, Salvatore. Pablo Neruda: All Poets the Poet. LC 78-24437. 204p. 1979. lib. bdg. 16.50 (ISBN 0-8108-1189-8). Scarecrow.
Bizzell, William B. The Green Rising: An Historical Survey of Agrarianism with Special Reference to the Organized Efforts of the Farmers of the United States to Improve Their Economic & Social Status. LC 72-89078. (Rural America Ser.). 1973. Repr. of 1926 ed. 27.00 (ISBN 0-8420-1475-6). Scholarly Res Inc.
--Judicial Interpretation of Political Theory: A Study of the Relation of the Courts to the American Party System. LC 73-21602. 1974. Repr. of 1914 ed. lib. bdg. 20.00 (ISBN 0-8337-4819-X). B Franklin.
Bizzi, E., ed. see International Congress on Physiological Sciences, 25th, Munich, 1971.
Bizzi, Emilio. Central & Peripheral Mechanisms in Motor Control. Date not set. price not set (ISBN 0-89004-466-X, 521). Raven.
Bizzozero, Julius. On a New Blood Particle & Its Role in Thrombosis & Blood Coagulation. Beck, Eugen A., tr. from Ger. (Illus.). 156p. 1982. pap. text ed. 16.50 (ISBN 3-456-81182-9, Pub. by Hans Huber Switzerland). J K Burgess.
Bjaerevoll, Olav, jt. auth. see Ronning, Olaf.
Bjaerke, Tor & Manum, Svein B. Mesozoic Palynology of Svalbard. (Norsk Polarinstitutt Skrifter: No. 165). (Illus.). 1978. pap. 8.00x (ISBN 82-00-29719-5, Dist. by Columbia U Pr). Universitet.
Bjarkman, Peter C. & Raskin, Victor. The Real-World Linguist. 272p. 1985. text ed. 32.50 (ISBN 0-89391-357-X). Ablex Pub.
Bjarngard, Bengt, jt. ed. see Kase, Kenneth R.
Bjelland, Harley. How to Buy the Right Home. 1980. pap. 3.95 (ISBN 0-346-12438-7). Cornerstone.
--Technical Writing: The Easy Way. LC 81-90026. (Illus.). 116p. (Orig.). 1981. pap. 10.00 (ISBN 0-939648-00-8). Norway Bks.
Bjelle, A., jt. ed. see Munthe, E.
Bjerk, Irid. Boy off the Farm. 272p. 14.95 (ISBN 0-931170-18-4). Ctr Western Studies.
Bjerke, L. & Soraas, H., eds. Norwegian Dictionary: English-Norwegian. 1963. 30.00x (N434). Vanous.
Bjerke, Odd & Motson, Meredith. The Search for Trollhaven. LC 77-77794. (Illus.). (gr. 4-7). 1977. pap. 7.95 (ISBN 0-916238-06-7). R O Beatty Assocs.
Bjerke, Svein. Religion & Misfortune. 240p. 1981. pap. 27.00x (ISBN 82-00-05681-3). Universitet.
Bjerkebek, Helmer. A Pilgrim in the Sky. 1984. 5.95 (ISBN 0-934860-40-8). Adventure Pubns.
Bjerkholt, O. & Offederal, E., eds. Macroeconomic Prospects for a Small Oil Exporting Country. 1985. lib. bdg. 44.50 (ISBN 90-247-3183-6, Pub. by Martinus Nijhoff Netherlands). Kluwer Academic.
Bjerkholt, Olav, et al, eds. Analysis of Supply & Demand of Electricity in the Norwegian Economy. 250p. 1983. pap. 9.00x (ISBN 82-00-09540-1). Universitet.
Bjerkoe, Ethel H. Cabinetmakers of America. 2nd ed. LC 57-7278. (Illus.). 272p. 1978. 22.50 (ISBN 0-916838-14-5). Schiffer.
Bjerre, Andreas. The Psychology of Murder: A Study in Criminal Psychology. Classen, E., tr. from Swedish. (Historical Foundations of Forensic Psychiatry & Psychology Ser.). 164p. 1980. Repr. lib. bdg. 22.50 (ISBN 0-306-76067-3). Da Capo.
Bjerregaard. Scandinavia, Design. 144p. 1983. pap. 13.00x (ISBN 0-89918-754-4). Vanous.
Bjerregaard, C. H. The Great Mother: A Gospel of the Eternally Feminine. 1977. lib. bdg. 59.95 (ISBN 0-8490-1900-1). Gordon Pr.
--The Inner Life. Incl. The Tao-Teh-King. 1977. lib. bdg. 49.00 (ISBN 0-8490-2061-1). Gordon Pr.
--Lectures on Mysticism & Nature Worship. 1977. lib. bdg. 59.95 (ISBN 0-8490-2138-3). Gordon Pr.
Bjerregaard, Ritt, ed. see Marcussen, Ernst, et al.
Bjerregard, Carl H. Jesus: A Poet, Prophet, Mystic & Man of Freedom. 1976. lib. bdg. 59.95 (ISBN 0-8490-2094-8). Gordon Pr.
Bjerreskov, Merete. Llandoverian & Wenlockian Graptolites from Bornholm. (Fossils & Strata: No.8). 1975. pap. text ed. 25.00x (ISBN 8-200-09392-1, Dist. by Columbia U Pr). Universitet.
Bjerring, N., tr. see Basaroff, F.
Bjerring, Nicholas, tr. see Anatolius, Bishop of Mohilew & Mstislaw.
Bjerrum, O. J., ed. Electroimmunochemical Analysis of Membrane Proteins. xiv, 476p. 1983. 106.50 (ISBN 0-444-80461-7, I-158-83, Biomedical Pr). Elsevier.
Bjersby, B. Interpretation of the Cuchulain Legend in the Works of W. B. Yeats. LC 73-16090. 1950. lib. bdg. 20.00 (ISBN 0-8414-9872-5). Folcroft.
Bjorck, Ake & Dahlquist, Germund. Numerical Methods. Anderson, N., tr. (Illus.). 576p. 1974. ref. ed. 42.95 (ISBN 0-13-627315-7). P-H.
Bjorck, Margaret, et al. Now You Know About: Animals, 5 bks. Incl. Animal Coverings. 32p; Animal Homes. 32p; How Animals Stay Alive. 32p; Many Animals. 32p (ISBN 0-87827-091-4); Where Animals Live. 32p (ISBN 0-87827-003-5). (Illus.). (gr. k-3). 1972. 99.00 (ISBN 0-87827-090-6); records, cassetts & tchr's guide avail. (ISBN 0-685-38373-3). Ency Brit Ed.
Bjorck, Svante. A Stratigraphic Study of Late Weichselian Delaciation, Shore Displacement, & Vegetation History in South-Eastern Sweden. 93p. (Orig.). 1982. pap. 22.00x (ISBN 82-00-09526-6). Universitet.
Bjorge, James R. And Heaven & Nature Sings. (Illus.). 1977. pap. 4.95 (ISBN 0-570-03047-1, 6-1172). Concordia.
--Doing the Gospel. 1976. pap. 5.50 (ISBN 0-89536-056-X). CSS of Ohio.
--Forty Ways to Fortify Your Faith. 128p. (Orig.). 1984. pap. 4.95 (ISBN 0-8066-2059-5, 10-2358). Augsburg.
--Forty Ways to Say I Love You. LC 78-52179. 1978. pap. 4.95 (ISBN 0-8066-1654-7, 10-2360). Augsburg.
--Forty Ways to Say Thank You, Lord. LC 80-67802. 96p. (Orig.). 1981. pap. 4.95 (ISBN 0-8066-1864-7, 102361). Augsburg.
--Here Comes Jesus. 100p. (Orig.). 1974. pap. 4.50 (ISBN 0-89536-091-8). CSS of Ohio.
--Living Without Fear. (Orig.). 1977. pap. 5.00 (ISBN 0-89536-144-2). CSS of Ohio.
--Lord of the Waters. 1982. pap. 3.50 (ISBN 0-89536-523-5). CSS of Ohio.
Bjorge, James R. & Bjorge, John R. Girded with Truth. 1981. 3.75 (ISBN 0-89536-493-X). CSS of Ohio.
Bjorge, John R., jt. auth. see Bjorge, James R.
Bjork, Daniel W. The Compromised Scientist: William James in the Development of American Psychology. (Illus.). 224p. 1983. 27.50x (ISBN 0-231-05500-5); pap. 14.00x (ISBN 0-231-05501-3). Columbia U Pr.
Bjork, Gordon C. Life, Liberty & Property: The Economics & Politics of Land-Use Planning & Environmental Controls. LC 80-8038. 160p. 1980. 22.00x (ISBN 0-669-03952-7). Lexington Bks.
--Stagnation & Growth in the American Economy, 1784-1792. Bruchey, Stuart, ed. LC 84-48304. (American Economic History Ser.). 186p. 1985. lib. bdg. 25.00 (ISBN 0-8240-6652-9). Garland Pub.
Bjork, J. E. Rings of Differential Operators. (Mathematical Library: Vol. 21). 360p. 1979. 66.00 (ISBN 0-444-85292-1, North Holland). Elsevier.
Bjork, Kenneth O. West of the Great Divide: Norwegian Migration to the Pacific Coast, 1847-1893. LC 58-4511. (Publications of the Norwegian-American Historical Association Ser.). pap. 160.00 (ISBN 0-317-27953-X, 2056021). Bks Demand UMI.
Bjork, Lennart A. The Literary Notes of Thomas Hardy, Vol. 1 In 2 Pts. (Gothenburg Studies in English: No. 29). 479p. 1975. Set. text ed. 38.50x (ISBN 91-7346-002-8). Humanities.
Bjork, Lennart A., ed. The Literary Notebooks of Thomas Hardy, Vols. I & II. 384p. 1984. Set. 89.00x (ISBN 0-8147-1063-8). Vol. I (ISBN 0-8147-1064-6). NYU Pr.
Bjork, Robert E., tr. see Fridegard, Jan.
Bjork, Robert M. & Fraser, Stewart E. Population, Education, & Children's Futures. LC 80-82683. (Fastback Ser.: No. 150). 1980. pap. 0.75 (ISBN 0-87367-150-3). Phi Delta Kappa.
Bjork, Russell, jt. auth. see Townsley, David.
Bjorkegren, Hans. Aleksandr Solzhenitsyn: A Biography. Eneberg, Kaa, tr. from Swed. LC 72-80185. 1973. pap. 4.95 (ISBN 0-89388-050-7). Okpaku Communications.
Bjorken, J. D., jt. auth. see Atwood, W. B.
Bjorken, James D. & Drell, S. D. Relativistic Quantum Fields. (International Pure & Applied Physics Ser.). 1965. text ed. 44.95 (ISBN 0-07-005494-0). McGraw.
--Relativistic Quantum Mechanics. (International Series in Pure & Applied Physics). 1964. text ed. 40.95 (ISBN 0-07-005493-2). McGraw.
Bjorkland, Gary, jt. auth. see Sparks, Ken.
Bjorklund, A. & Stenvi, U. Neural Grafting in the Mammalian CNS. (Fernstrom Foundation Ser.: Vol. 5). xxi, 728p. Date not set. 157.50 (ISBN 0-444-80622-9). Elsevier.
Bjorklund, A. see Sjolund, B. H.
Bjorklund, A., ed. Geochemical Exploration, 1983: Selected Papers from the International Geochemical Explorational Symposium, 10th, Symposium on Methods of Geochemical Prospecting, 3rd, Held in Espoo, Finland, Aug.29-Sept. 2, 1983. 1984. Repr. 89.00 (ISBN 0-444-42385-0). Elsevier.
Bjorklund, A. & Hokfelt, T., eds. Methods in Chemical Neuroanatomy. (Handbook of Chemical Neuroanatomy Ser.: No. 1). xxvi, 548p. 1983. 140.50 (ISBN 0-444-90281-3, Excerpta Medica). Elsevier.
--Neuropeptides in the CNS. (Handbook of Chemical Neuroanatomy: No. 3). 550p. 1983. 123.50 (ISBN 0-444-90340-2, Biomedical Pr). Elsevier.
Bjorklund, A. & Swanson, L. W., eds. Integrated Systems of the CNS. (Handbook of Chemical Neuroanatomy: No. 4). 1984. write for info. (ISBN 0-444-90353-4, Excerpta Medica). Elsevier.
Bjorklund, A., et al. Classical Transmitters in the CNS, Pt. II. (Handbook of Chemical Neuroanatomy Ser.: Vol. 3, pt. II). 1985. 92.75 (ISBN 0-444-90352-6). Elsevier.
Bjorklund, A., et al, eds. Classical Transmitters in the CNS, Pt. I. (Handbook of Chemical Neuroanatomy Ser.: Vol. 2, pt. I). 1985. 100.00 (ISBN 0-444-90330-5, Excerpta Medica). Elsevier.
Bjorklund, Lavern. The Way to Wellness. 1984. pap. 5.95 (ISBN 0-88207-111-4). Victor Bks.
Bjorklund, Oddvar. Historical Atlas for the World. pap. 6.95 (ISBN 0-06-463249-0, EH 249, EH). B&N NY.
Bjorklund, Oddvar, et al. Historical Atlas of the World. LC 64-26. (Illus.). 132p. 1972. pap. 14.95x (ISBN 0-06-490435-0, 06349). B&N Imports.
Bjorklund, Paul. What is Spirituality? 16p. (Orig.). 1983. pap. 0.95 (ISBN 0-89486-182-4). Hazelden.
Bjorklund, Paul E. An Adventure in Self-Discovery: A Guide to the Fourth Step. 44p. 1981. pap. 2.25 (ISBN 0-89486-118-2). Hazelden.
Bjorkman, Adaline. While It Was Still Dark. (Illus.). 1978. pap. 3.95 (ISBN 0-910452-34-2). Covenant.
Bjorkman, E. Scandinavian Loan-Words in Middle English. LC 68-24897. (Studies in Language, No. 41). 1969. Repr. of 1902 ed. lib. bdg. 49.95x (ISBN 0-8383-0913-5). Haskell.
Bjorkman, Edwin. Gates of Life. LC 75-144882. (Literature Ser). 384p. 1972. Repr. of 1923 ed. 39.00x (ISBN 0-403-00868-9). Scholarly.
--The Soul of a Child. LC 79-144883. (Literature Ser). 322p. 1972. Repr. of 1922 ed. 39.00x (ISBN 0-403-00869-7). Scholarly.
Bjorkman, Edwin, tr. see Christiansen, Sigurd.
Bjorkman, Edwin A. Voices of Tomorrow: Critical Studies of the New Spirit in Literature. LC 74-98818. Repr. of 1913 ed. lib. bdg. 19.75x (ISBN 0-8371-2962-1, BJVT). Greenwood.
--Voices of Tomorrow, Critical Studies of the New Spirit in Literature. Repr. of 1913 ed. 25.00 (ISBN 0-384-04540-5). Johnson Repr.
Bjorkman, Erik. Scandinavian Loan-Words in Middle English. LC 75-107161. 360p. 1972. Repr. of 1900 ed. 14.00 (ISBN 0-403-00450-0). Scholarly.
Bjorkman, James. Changing Division of Labor in South Asia. LC 85-61081. 225p. 1985. 19.00x (ISBN 0-913215-05-8). Riverdale CO.
--Fundamentalism, Revivalists & Violence in South Asia. LC 85-61080. 210p. 1985. 19.00 (ISBN 0-913215-06-6). Riverdale Co.
Bjorkman, James W. Politics of Administrative Alienation in India's Rural Development Programme. 1979. 14.00x (ISBN 0-8364-0341-X). South Asia Bks.
Bjorkman, James W., jt. auth. see Altenstetter, Christa.
Bjorkquist, David C. Supervision in Vocational Education: Management of Human Resources. 1982. 28.95 (ISBN 0-205-07357-3, 237357). Allyn.
Bjorkstein, Ingmar. Patrick White: A General Introduction. Gerson, Stanley, tr. from Swedish. 1976. text ed. 13.00x (ISBN 0-7022-1404-3); pap. text ed. 7.00x (ISBN 0-7022-1214-8). Humanities.
Bjorksten, Oliver J. New Clinical Concepts in Marital Therapy. LC 85-11201. (Clinical Insights Monograph). 100p. 1985. pap. text ed. 12.00X (ISBN 0-88048-074-2, 48-074-2). Am Psychiatric.
Bjorling, Joel. The Baha'i Faith: An Historical Bibliography. Melton, J. G, ed. LC 84-49294. (Reference Library of Social Science- Sects & Cults in America: Bibliographic Guides). 250p. 1985. lib. bdg. 35.00 (ISBN 0-8240-8974-X). Garland Pub.
Bjorn, Eva N. The Impossible Playground (Why) LC 81-80790. (A Trilogy of Play: Why, Where, & How Ser.). (Illus.). 224p. 1981. text ed. 19.95 (ISBN 0-918438-29-2); pap. text ed. 14.95 (ISBN 0-918438-88-8). Leisure Pr.
Bjorn, L. O. Light & Life. LC 76-27618. 247p. 1976. pap. 9.95x (ISBN 0-8448-1006-1). Crane-Russak Co.
Bjorn-Anderson, N., et al, eds. Information Society: For Richer, for Poorer. 320p. 1982. 47.00 (ISBN 0-444-86422-9, North-Holland). Elsevier.
Bjorn-Anderson, Neils, ed. Human Side of Information Processing. 230p. 1980. 42.75 (ISBN 0-444-85415-0, North-Holland). Elsevier.
Bjornard, Reidar B. Thus Says the Lord. 1979. pap. 3.50 (ISBN 0-8170-0827-6). Judson.
Bjorndal, Karen A., ed. Biology & Conservation of Sea Turtles: Proceedings of the World Conference on Sea Turtle Conservation. LC 82-600180. (Illus.). 583p. 1982. pap. text ed. 25.00x (ISBN 0-87474-243-9). Smithsonian.
Bjorner, B. & Oest, O. N., eds. Towards a Formal Description of Ada. (Lecture Notes in Computer Science: Vol. 98). 630p. 1980. pap. 31.00 (ISBN 0-387-10283-3). Springer-Verlag.
Bjorner, D., ed. Abstract Software Specifications. (Lecture Notes in Computer Sciences Ser.: Vol. 86). 567p. 1980. pap. 35.00 (ISBN 0-387-10007-5). Springer-Verlag.
--Formal Description of Programming Concepts, II. 456p. 1983. 55.50 (ISBN 0-444-86619-1, I-173-83, North Holland). Elsevier.
Bjorner, D. & Jones, C. B., eds. The Vienna Development Method: The Meta - Language. (Lectures Notes in Computer Science Ser.: Vol. 61). 1978. pap. 20.00 (ISBN 0-387-08766-4). Springer-Verlag.
Bjorno, L., ed. Underwater Acoustics & Signal Processing. 1981. 87.00 (ISBN 90-277-1255-7, Pub. by Reidel Holland). Kluwer Academic.
Bjornskov, Elizabeth. The Complete Book of American Fish & Shellfish Cookery. LC 83-48847. (Illus.). 1984. 18.95 (ISBN 0-394-53095-0). Knopf.
--The Complete Book of American Fish & Shellfish Cookery. 499p. 1984. 18.95 (ISBN 0-317-03383-2). HM.
Bjornson, Bjornstjerne. Bridal March & Other Stories. facsimile ed. Anderson, Rasmos B., tr. LC 74-98562. (Short Story Index Reprint Ser.). 1882. 17.00 (ISBN 0-8369-3136-X). Ayer Co Pubs.
--Captain Mansana & Other Stories. facsimile ed. Anderson, Rasmos B., tr. LC 79-103494. (Short Story Index Reprint Ser.). 1882. 18.00 (ISBN 0-8369-3236-6). Ayer Co Pubs.
--Synnove Solbakken. Sutter, Julie, tr. LC 79-38341. (Select Bibliographies Reprint Ser.). 1894. 16.00 (ISBN 0-8369-6758-5). Ayer Co Pubs.
--Three Comedies. LC 73-17652. 198p. 1974. Repr. of 1912 ed. lib. bdg. 18.75x (ISBN 0-8371-7259-4, BJTC). Greenwood.
--Three Dramas. Sharp, R. Farquharson, tr. LC 73-17654. 291p. 1974. Repr. of 1914 ed. lib. bdg. 22.50 (ISBN 0-8371-7260-8, BJTD). Greenwood.
Bjornson, Richard. The Picaresque Hero in European Fiction. LC 76-11312. (Illus.). 320p. 1977. 27.50x (ISBN 0-299-07100-6); pap. 11.75x (ISBN 0-299-07104-9). U of Wis Pr.
Bjornson, Richard, ed. Approaches to Teaching Cervantes' Don Quixote. (Approaches to Teaching Masterpieces of World Literature Ser.: No. 3). 204p. 1984. 25.00x (ISBN 0-87352-479-9); pap. 14.50x (ISBN 0-87352-480-2). Modern Lang.
Bjornson, Richard, tr. from French see Beti, Mongo.
Bjornson, Richard, tr. see Philombe, Rene.
Bjornstad, James. Counterfeits at Your Door. LC 78-72864. 160p. 1979. pap. text ed. 2.95 (ISBN 0-8307-0610-0, S124254). Regal.
--The Moon Is Not the Son: A Close Look at the Religion of Rev. Son Myung Moon. LC 76-46208. 128p. 1977. pap. 3.50 (ISBN 0-87123-380-0, 200380). Bethany Hse.
--Sun Myung Moon & the Unification Church. 160p. 1984. pap. 2.50 (ISBN 0-87123-301-0). Bethany Hse.
Bjornstad, James, jt. auth. see Weldon, John.
Bjornvig, Thorkild. The Pact: My Friendship with Isak Dinesen. Schousboe, Ingvar & Smith, William J., trs. from Danish. LC 83-9335. (Illus.). 184p. 1983. 16.95 (ISBN 0-8071-1125-2). La State U Pr.
Bjorov, Malvin, jt. auth. see International Meeting on Organic Geochemistry, Norway, 10th, 1981.
Bjorseth & Randahl. Handbook of Polycyclic Aromatic. 368p. write for info. (ISBN 0-8247-7442-6). Dekker.
Bjorseth, A. & Angeletti, G., eds. Analysis of Organic Micropollutants in Water. 1982. 49.50 (ISBN 90-277-1398-7, Pub. by Reidel Holland). Kluwer Academic.
Bjorseth, A., jt. ed. see Angeletti, G.
Bjorseth, Alf & Dennis, Anthony J., eds. Polynuclear Aromatic Hydrocarbons: Chemistry & Biological Effects. (Illus.). 1097p. 1980. 49.95 (ISBN 0-935470-05-0). Battelle.
Bjurstrom, Per, jt. auth. see Nationalmuseum, Stockholm.
Blaauw, Adriaan & Schmidt, Maarten, eds. Galactic Structure. LC 64-23428. (Stars & Stellar Systems Ser: Vol. 5). (Illus.). 1965. 50.00x (ISBN 0-226-45957-8). U of Chicago Pr.
Blaauw, Gerritt A. Digital System Implementation. (Illus.). 1976. 36.95 (ISBN 0-13-212241-3). P-H.
Blaazer, Caroline & Molyneux, Eric. Supervising the Electronic Office. 202p. 1984. text ed. 29.50x (ISBN 0-566-02448-9). Gower Pub Co.
Blacam, Mark De see De Blacam, Mark.

Blacher, Jan. Severely Handicapped Young Children & Their Families: Research in Review. LC 83-21469. 1984. 29.50 (ISBN 0-12-102750-3). Acad Pr.

Blachere, Regis & Chouemi, Moustafa. Dictionnaire Arabe-Francais-Anglais, 1, Pts. 1-12. (Arabic, Fr. & Eng.). 1967. 350.00 (ISBN 0-686-56918-0, M-6034). French & Eur.

--Dictionnaire Arabe-Francais-Anglais, 2, Pts. 13-24. (Arab., Fr. & Eng.). 1970. 350.00 (ISBN 0-686-56919-9, M-6035). French & Eur.

Blachford, G., jt. auth. see Divine, J. A.

Blachly, Frederick F. & Oatman, Miriam E. Government & Administration of Germany. (Brookings Institution Reprint Ser). Repr. of 1928 ed. lib. bdg. 36.50x (ISBN 0-697-00152-0). Irvington.

Blachly, Paul H. Progress in Drug Abuse. (Illus.). 336p. 1972. 29.75x (ISBN 0-398-02233-X). C C Thomas.

Blachman, Morris J. & Hellman, Ronald G., eds. Terms of Conflict: Ideology in Latin American Politics. LC 76-54814. (Inter-American Politics Ser.: Vol. 1). 288p. 1977. text ed. 9.95 (ISBN 0-915980-05-3). ISHI PA.

Blachman, Nelson M. Noise & Its Effect on Communication. 2nd ed. LC 81-8140. 274p. 1982. lib. bdg. 26.50 (ISBN 0-89874-256-0). Krieger.

Blachon, Roger, et al. Le Vin: French Wine Humor. 100p. 1982. 29.95 (ISBN 0-932664-28-8). Wine Appreciation.

Blachut, T. J., et al. Urban Surveying & Mapping. LC 78-31768. (Illus.). 1979. 39.00 (ISBN 0-387-90344-5). Springer-Verlag.

Black. Cost Accounting. (Plaid Ser.). 1978. pap. 9.95 (ISBN 0-256-01280-6). Dow Jones-Irwin.

--Cost Engineering Management Techniques. (Cost Engineering Ser.). 264p. 1984. 35.00 (ISBN 0-8247-7088-9). Dekker.

--Materials in the Biological Environment. (Biomedical Engineering & Instrumentation Ser.: Vol. 8). 264p. 1981. pap. 45.00 (ISBN 0-8247-7208-3). Dekker.

Black, jt. auth. see Coles, Adlard.

Black, ed. see Fisher, Alan.

Black, A. N., jt. auth. see Coles, K. Adlard.

Black, Al & Manlove, Bill. Attacking Modern Defenses with Belly Option Football. LC 84-26464. 208p. 1984. 17.95 (ISBN 0-13-050188-3). Parker Pub OR.

Black, Alan W. & Glasner, Peter E., eds. Practice & Belief. (Studies in Society). 200p. 1983. text ed. 30.00x (ISBN 0-86861-357-6). Allen Unwin.

Black, Alexander. American Husbands & Other Alternatives. facs. ed. LC 68-57305. (Essay Index Reprint Ser). 1925. 16.25 (ISBN 0-8369-1021-4). Ayer Co Pubs.

Black, Alfred B. & Smith, Robert M. Shakespeare Allusions & Parallels. LC 78-113559. Repr. of 1931 ed. 12.50 (ISBN 0-404-00893-3). AMS Pr.

Black, Algernon D. The People & the Police. LC 75-40991. 246p. 1976. Repr. lib. bdg. 15.75x (ISBN 0-8371-8699-4, BLPP). Greenwood.

Black, Ann N. & Smith, Jo R. Ten Tools of Language-Written. 2nd ed. (Illus.). 166p. (gr. 11-12). 1982. pap. text ed. 12.60x (ISBN 0-910513-00-7). Mayfield Printing.

--Ten Tools of Language-Written: Revised Edition II, Form B. rev. ed. 166p. 1983. pap. text ed. 12.60x (ISBN 0-910513-01-5). Mayfield Printing.

Black, Anthony. An Edition of the Cavendish Irish Parliamentary Diary 1776-1778. LC 84-81378. 750p. Date not set. text ed. 75.00 (ISBN 0-87319-031-9). C Hallberg.

--Monarchy & Community: Political Ideas in the Later Conciliar. LC 72-108101. (Cambridge Studies in Medieval Life & Thought: Vol. 2, 3rd). pap. 50.30 (ISBN 0-317-09416-5, 2022436). Bks Demand UMI.

Black, Antony. Council & Commune: The Conciliar Movement & the Fifteenth-Century Heritage. LC 79-89220. x, 253p. 1979. 25.95x (ISBN 0-915762-08-0). Patmos Pr.

--Guilds & Civil Society in European Political Thought from the Twelfth-Century to the Present. LC 83-72879. 271p. 1984. 32.50x (ISBN 0-8014-1690-6). Cornell U Pr.

Black, Arther. Freedom Poems. 1981. 4.95 (ISBN 0-8062-1807-X). Carlton.

Black, Austin I. The Aquarian Mandate. 1976. pap. 7.00 (ISBN 0-87613-046-5). Suratao.

Black, Barbara. Bulletin Boards to Brag About: Delightfully Dimensional Displays. 1985. pap. 8.95 (ISBN 0-673-18280-0). Scott F.

Black, Bertram J. Principles of Industrial Therapy for the Mentally Ill. LC 73-88017. 200p. 1970. 48.00 (ISBN 0-8089-0062-5, 790600). Grune.

Black, Beth, et al. Songs That Teach. 108p. (Orig.). 10.95x (ISBN 0-941214-20-6, Eden Hill Pub). Signature BKs.

Black, Betty, jt. auth. see Green, Karen.

Black, Bruce, jt. auth. see Rose, Stephen M.

Black, Bruce J. Manufacturing Technology for Level-Three Technicians. 224p. 1981. pap. 18.95x (ISBN 0-7131-3430-5). Intl Ideas.

--Manufacturing Technology for Level-2 Technicians. (Illus.). 183p. 1983. pap. text ed. 18.95x (ISBN 0-7131-3485-2). Intl Ideas.

--Workshop Processes, Practices & Materials. (Illus.). 282p. 1979. pap. 19.95x (ISBN 0-7131-3409-7). Intl Ideas.

Black, C. A. Soil-Plant Relationships. LC 83-17509. 800p. 1984. Repr. of 1957 ed. lib. bdg. 55.50 (ISBN 0-89874-675-2). Krieger.

Black, C. A., ed. Methods of Soil Analysis, 2 Pts. Incl. Pt. 1. (Illus.). 1965. 17.50 (ISBN 0-89118-010-9); Pt. 2. (Illus.). 1982. 36.00 (ISBN 0-89118-072-9). Am Soc Agron.

Black, C. E. & Helmreich, E. C. Twentieth Century Europe. 4th ed. LC 73-152714. 1972. text ed. 28.00 (ISBN 0-394-31638-X, KnopfC). Knopf.

Black, C. E. & Falk, Richard A., eds. The Future of International Legal Order, 4 vols. Incl. Vol. 1. Trends & Patterns. 1969. 50.00 (ISBN 0-691-09215-X); Vol. 2. DP-Report. 1970; Vol. 3. DP-Report. 416p. 1971. 35.00x (ISBN 0-691-09220-6); Vol. 4. The Structure of the International Environment. 600p. 1972. pap. o.p. (ISBN 0-691-10005-5). Princeton U Pr.

Black, Campbell. Letters from the Dead. LC 84-40487. 1985. 15.95 (ISBN 0-394-54277-0). Villard Bks.

--Mr. Apology. 352p. (Orig.). 1984. pap. 3.50 (ISBN 0-345-29411-4). Ballantine.

--Raiders of the Lost Ark. 192p. 1984. pap. 2.50 (ISBN 0-345-29548-X). Ballantine.

Black, Caroline M., jt. auth. see Nauert, Patricia.

Black, Catherine F., jt. auth. see Giza, Joanne.

Black, Cecelia, jt. auth. see Manhold, John H.

Black, Charles. Owls Bay in Babylon. (The American Dust Ser.: No. 13). 90p. 1980. 7.95 (ISBN 0-913218-92-8); pap. 2.95 (ISBN 0-913218-91-X). Dustbooks.

--The Waking Passenger. Cassin, Maxine, ed. (A New Orleans Journal Press Bk.). 80p. 1983. pap. 5.00 (ISBN 0-938498-03-7). New Orleans Poetry.

Black, Charles, jt. auth. see Eckhardt, Bob.

Black, Charles L. Impeachment: A Handbook. LC 74-82692. (Illus.). 90p. 1974. pap. 3.95x (ISBN 0-300-01819-3). Yale U Pr.

--Structure & Relationship in Constitutional Law. LC 69-17621. (Edward Douglass White Lecture Ser.: 1968). pap. 26.80 (ISBN 0-317-28671-4, 2055300). Bks Demand UMI.

--Telescopes & Islands. LC 76-179826. (New Poetry Ser.). Repr. of 1963 ed. 16.00 (ISBN 0-404-56026-1). AMS Pr.

Black, Charles L., Jr. Capital Punishment: The Inevitability of Caprice & Mistake. Rev. ed. 1982. pap. 4.95x (ISBN 0-393-95289-4). Norton.

--Decision According to Law: The 1979 Holmes Lectures. 1981. 12.95 (ISBN 0-393-01452-5). Norton.

--The People & the Court: Judicial Review in a Democracy. LC 77-8076. 238p. 1977. Repr. of 1960 ed. deluxe ed. 20.00x (ISBN 0-8371-9682-5, BLPC). Greenwood.

Black, Charles T. & Worden, Diane D., eds. Michigan Nature Centers & Other Environmental Education Facilities. 64p. 1982. pap. 6.50 (ISBN 0-939294-06-0, LB 1047-M5). Beech Leaf.

Black, Christopher. The Android Invasion. (Star Challenge Ser.: No. 2). (Orig.). (gr. 4-8). 1984. pap. 2.50 (ISBN 0-440-40081-3, YB). Dell.

--The Cosmic Funhouse. (Star Challenge Ser.: No. 3). (Orig.). (gr. 4-8). 1984. pap. 2.50 (ISBN 0-440-41615-9, YB). Dell.

--Dimension of Doom. (Star Challenge Ser.: No. 7). 128p. (Orig.). (gr. k-6). 1985. pap. 2.50 (ISBN 0-440-41859-3, YB). Dell.

--The Exploding Suns. (Star Challenge Ser.: No. 4). (Orig.). (gr. k-6). 1984. pap. 2.50 (ISBN 0-440-42473-9, YB). Dell.

--Galactic Raiders. (Star Challenge Ser.: No. 5). (Illus.). 128p. (gr. 3-7). 1984. pap. 2.50 (ISBN 0-440-42833-5, YB). Dell.

--The Haunted Planet. (Star Challenge Ser.: No. 10). (Orig.). (gr. k-6). 1985. pap. 2.50 (ISBN 0-440-43368-1, YB). Dell.

--The Lost Planet. (Star Challenge Ser.: No. 8). (gr. k-6). 1985. pap. 2.50 (ISBN 0-440-44944-8, YB). Dell.

--Moons of Mystery. (Star Challenge Ser.: No. 9). 128p. (Orig.). (gr. k-6). 1985. pap. 2.50 (ISBN 0-440-45800-5, YB). Dell.

--Planets in Peril. (Star Challenge Ser.: No. 1). (Orig.). (gr. 4-8). 1984. pap. 2.50 (ISBN 0-440-46892-2, YB). Dell.

--Star Challenge: How Do You Rate As a Space Ace? 128p. (gr. 3-7). Date not set. price not set (YB). Dell.

--The Weird Zone. (Star Challenge Ser.: No. 6). (Orig.). (gr. k-6). 1984. pap. 2.50 (ISBN 0-440-49310-2, YB). Dell.

Black, Claudia. It Will Never Happen to Me. LC 59-776. (Illus.). 183p. 1982. text ed. 12.95 (ISBN 0-910223-02-5); pap. 7.95 (ISBN 0-910223-00-9). MAC Print.

--My Dad Loves Me: My Dad Has a Disease. (Illus.). 76p. (gr. 1-12). 1979. 7.00 (ISBN 0-9607940-0-X). MAC Print.

--My Dad Loves Me, My Dad Has a Disease. LC 59-776. (Illus.). 84p. (Orig.). (gr. k-9). Date not set. pap. 7.95 (ISBN 0-9607940-2-6). MAC Print.

--My Dad Loves, My Dad Has a Disease: Workbook for Children Ages 5-14. LC 59-776. (Illus.). 84p. (Orig.). (gr. 1-9). pap. 7.95 (ISBN 0-317-19903-X). MAC Print.

Black, Clayton C., jt. ed. see Burris, Robert H.

Black, Clementina. Married Women's Work. 304p. 1983. pap. 9.95 (ISBN 0-86068-410-5, Pub. by Virago Pr). Merrimack Pub Cir.

--Married Women's Work: Being the Report of an Inquiry Undertaken by the Women's Industrial Council. LC 79-56947. (The Englishworking Class Ser.). 1980. lib. bdg. 33.00 (ISBN 0-8240-0102-8). Garland Pub.

Black, Clyde & Waters, Archie. Secrets of Spanish Pool Checkers, 2 Bks. Bk. 1. pap. 4.50 (ISBN 0-685-20862-1); Bk. 2. pap. 6.00 (ISBN 0-685-20863-X). Univ Place.

Black, Cobey, ed. see Haar, Francis.

Black, Colin. A Handbook of Free Conversation. 1970. pap. text ed. 3.25x (ISBN 0-19-432773-6). Oxford U Pr.

Black, Cyril E. The Establishment of Constitutional Government in Bulgaria. (Princeton Studies in History Ser: Vol. 1). Repr. of 1943 ed. 24.00 (ISBN 0-384-04601-0). Johnson Repr.

Black, Cyril E., ed. Challenge in Eastern Europe. LC 75-118427. (Essay & General Literature Index Reprint Ser). 1971. Repr. of 1954 ed. 22.50x (ISBN 0-8046-1400-8, Pub. by Kennikat). Assoc Faculty Pr.

--Comparative Modernization: A Reader. LC 75-16647. (Perspectives on Modernization Ser). 1976. 19.95 (ISBN 0-02-903530-9). Free Pr.

Black, Cyril E. & Thompson, John M., eds. American Teaching about Russia. LC 59-15377. pap. 47.30 (ISBN 0-317-09481-5, 2005734). Bks Demand UMI.

Black, Cyril E. & Thornton, Thomas P., eds. Communism & Revolution: The Strategic Uses of Political Violence. (Center of International Studies, Princeton Univ.). 1964. 39.00x (ISBN 0-691-08702-4). Princeton U Pr.

Black, Cyril E., ed. see Wallace, Donald M.

Black, Cyril E., et al. Neutralization & World Politics. LC 68-29388. (Center of International Studies, Princeton Univ.). 1968. 23.50 (ISBN 0-691-05639-0); pap. 9.95x (ISBN 0-691-01056-0). Princeton U Pr.

--The Modernization of Japan & Russia. LC 75-8429. (Perspectives on Modernization Ser.). 1975. 22.95 (ISBN 0-02-906850-9). Free Pr.

Black, D. C. & Matthews, Mildred S., eds. Protostars & Planets II. LC 85-11223. 1985. 45.00 (ISBN 0-8165-0950-6). U of Ariz Pr.

Black, David. Gravitations. 1983. 20.00x (ISBN 0-904265-30-7, Pub. by Macdonald Pub UK). State Mutual Bk.

--The Happy Crow. 1983. 20.00x (ISBN 0-904265-31-5, Pub. by Macdonald Pub UK). State Mutual Bk.

--Like Father. LC 78-6841. 237p. 1984. 12.95 (ISBN 0-934878-51-X). Dembner Bks.

--The Macmillan Atlas of Rugs & Carpets. 1985. 29.95 (ISBN 0-02-511120-5). Macmillan.

--Medicine Man: A Young Doctor on the Brink of the Twenty-First Century. 192p. 1985. 14.95 (ISBN 0-531-09702-1). Watts.

--Minds. 1985. 6.95 (ISBN 0-87795-703-7). Arbor Hse.

--Murder at the Met. LC 84-7079. 312p. 1984. 15.95 (ISBN 0-385-27852-7, Dial). Doubleday.

Black, David, ed. The MacMillan Atlas of Rugs & Carpets: A Comprehensive Guide for the Buyer & Collector. (Illus.). 256p. 1985. 29.95 (ISBN 0-02-511120-5). MacMillan.

Black, David A. Paul, Apostle of Weakness: Astheneia & Its Cognates in the Pauline Literature. LC 83-49515. (American University Studies VII (Theology & Religion): Vol. 3). 340p. (Orig.). 1984. pap. text ed. 27.00 (ISBN 0-8204-0106-4). P Lang Pubs.

Black, Davidson. The Human Skeletal Remains from the Sha Kuo T'un Cave Deposits: In Comparison with Those from Yang Shao Tsun & Recent North China Skeletal Material. LC 77-86441. (China. Geological Survey. Palaeontologia Sinica. Ser. D.: Vol. 1, Fasc. 3). Repr. of 1925 ed. 24.00 (ISBN 0-404-16684-9). AMS Pr.

--On a Lower Molar Hominid Tooth from the Chou Kou Tien Deposit. LC 77-86443. (China. Geological Survey. Palaeontologia Sinica. Ser. D.: Vol. 7, Fasc. 1). 1977. 12.50 (ISBN 0-404-16686-5). AMS Pr.

--On an Adolescent Skull of Sinanthropus Pekinensis: In Comparison with an Adult Skull of the Same Species & with Other Hominid Skulls, Recent & Fossil. LC 77-86442. (China. Geological Survey. Palaeontologia Sinica. Ser. D.: Vol. 7, Fasc. 2). Repr. of 1930 ed. 23.00 (ISBN 0-404-16685-7). AMS Pr.

--Selected Paleoanthropological Papers: 1915-1934, 2 vols. LC 78-72689. Repr. 78.50 set (ISBN 0-404-18261-5). AMS Pr.

--A Study of Kansu & Honan Aeneolithic Skulls & Specimens from Later Kansu Prehistoric Sites in Comparison with North China & Other Recent Crania. LC 77-86444. (China. Geological Survey. Palaeontologia Sinica. Ser. D.: Vol. 6., Fasc. 1). Repr. of 1928 ed. 21.00 (ISBN 0-404-16687-3). AMS Pr.

Black, Davidson, ed. Fossil Man in China. LC 73-38049. Repr. of 1933 ed. 32.00 (ISBN 0-404-56903-X). AMS Pr.

Black, Don. South African Bonsai Book. 93p. 1981. cloth 15.95x (ISBN 0-86978-136-7, Pub. by Timmins Africa). Intl Spec Bk.

Black, Donald. The Behavior of Law. 1980. pap. 10.00 (ISBN 0-12-102652-3). Acad Pr.

--The Behavior of Law. 1976. 24.50 (ISBN 0-12-102650-7). Acad Pr.

--The Manners & Customs of the Police. 1980. 35.00 (ISBN 0-12-102880-1); pap. 12.00 (ISBN 0-12-102882-8). Acad Pr.

--Toward a General Theory of Social Control, Vol. 2: Selected Problems. LC 83-11886. (Studies on Law & Social Control). 310p. 1984. 39.50 (ISBN 0-12-102802-X). Acad Pr.

Black, Donald & Mileski, Maureen. Social Organization of Law. LC 72-9998. 1973. 24.50 (ISBN 0-12-785057-0). Acad Pr.

Black, Donald J. Toward a General Theory of Social Control, Vol. 1: Fundamentals. LC 83-11886. (Studies on Law & Social Control). 363p. 1984. 45.00 (ISBN 0-12-102801-1). Acad Pr.

Black, Duncan. Incidence of Income Taxes. 136p. 1965. Repr. of 1939 ed. 29.50x (ISBN 0-7146-1207-3, F Cass Co). Biblio Dist.

Black, Earl. Southern Governors & Civil Rights: Racial Segregation As a Campaign Issue in the Second Reconstruction. 384p. 1976. 25.00x (ISBN 0-674-82510-1). Harvard U Pr.

Black, Edwin. Rhetorical Criticism: A Study in Method. LC 77-91050. 1978. 20.00x (ISBN 0-299-07550-8); pap. text ed. 10.75x (ISBN 0-299-07554-0). U of Wis Pr.

--The Transfer Agreement: The Untold Story of the Secret Pact Between the Third Reich & Jewish Palestine. 416p. 1984. 19.95 (ISBN 0-02-511130-2). Macmillan.

Black, Edwin R. Divided Loyalties: Canadian Concepts of Federalism. 264p. 1975. pap. 7.95 (ISBN 0-7735-0238-6). McGill-Queens U Pr.

Black, Elizabeth, jt. auth. see Fulton, James E.

Black, Esther B. Stories of Old Upland: Early Years Picture Album, Pt. 5. 3rd ed. Orig. Title: Stories of Old Upland for Young Listeners. (Illus.). 124p. 1979. pap. text ed. 7.00 (ISBN 0-9603586-0-9). Chaffey Commun Cult Ctr.

Black, Eugene C. The Association: British Extraparliamentary Political Organization, 1769-1793. LC 63-17195. (Historical Monographs Ser: No. 54). (Illus.). 1963. 22.50x (ISBN 0-674-05000-2). Harvard U Pr.

Black, F. O., et al. Congenital Deafness: A New Approach to Early Detection of Deafness Through a High Risk Register. LC 76-135285. 1971. 14.50x (ISBN 0-87081-005-7). Colo Assoc.

Black, F. William, jt. auth. see Strub, Richard L.

Black, Frank. Epistolary Novel in the Late Eighteenth Century. LC 74-6155. 1940. lib. bdg. 28.50 (ISBN 0-8414-3151-5). Folcroft.

Black, Frank G. The Epostolary Novel in the Late Eighteenth Century. 1978. lib. bdg. 30.00 (ISBN 0-8482-3404-9). Norwood Edns.

Black, G. F. County Folklore, Vol. III, Printed Extracts No. 5, Examples of Printed Folklore Concerning the Orkney & Shetland Islands: Folk-Lore Society, London, vol. 49. Thomas, Northcote W., ed. pap. 18.00 (ISBN 0-317-16270-5). Kraus Repr.

Black, G. J. William Howard Taft, Eighteen Fifty-Seven to Nineteen Thirty: Chronology, Documents, Bibliographical Aids. LC 70-116059. (Presidential Chronology Ser). 89p. 1970. 8.00 (ISBN 0-379-12080-1). Oceana.

Black, G. J., ed. Theodore Roosevelt, Eighteen Fifty-Eight to Nineteen Nineteen: Chronology, Documents, Bibliographical Aids. LC 69-15392. (Presidential Chronology Ser.: No. 8). 128p. 1969. 8.00 (ISBN 0-379-12058-5). Oceana.

Black, Garth. The Holy Spirit. rev. ed. (Way of Life Ser: No. 102). 1967. pap. 3.95 (ISBN 0-89112-102-1). Bibl Res Pr.

Black, George. Guatemala: The Making of a Revolution. (Illus.). 176p. 1984. 24.95xcancelled (ISBN 0-86232-186-7, Pub. by Zed Pr England); pap. 8.95xcancelled (ISBN 0-86232-187-5, Pub. by Zed Pr England). Biblio Dist.

--Sales Engineering: An Emerging Profession. 2nd ed. LC 79-17716. 228p. 1979. 17.95x (ISBN 0-87201-799-0). Gulf Pub.

--Triumph of the People: The Sandinista Revolution in Nicaragua. 340p. 1981. 25.00x (ISBN 0-86232-092-5, Pub. by Zed Pr England); pap. 9.95x (ISBN 0-86232-036-4). Biblio Dist.

Black, George, et al. Garrison Guatemala. 208p. 1984. 25.00 (ISBN 0-85345-665-8); pap. 9.00 (ISBN 0-85345-666-6). Monthly Rev.

Black, George A. History of Municipal Ownership of Land on Manhattan Island to the Beginning of Sales by the Commissioner of the Sinking Fund in 1844. LC 12-28238. (Columbia University Studies in the Social Sciences: No. 3). Repr. of 1891 ed. 16.00 (ISBN 0-404-51003-5). AMS Pr.

Black, George D., et al. On Walt Whitman. LC 76-30545. 1892. lib. bdg. 6.50 (ISBN 0-8414-9948-9). Folcroft.

Black, George F. A Gypsy Bibliography. LC 76-30594. 1977. Repr. of 1914 ed. lib. bdg. 33.50 (ISBN 0-8414-9946-2). Folcroft.

--Gypsy Bibliography. LC 74-149780. 1971. Repr. of 1914 ed. 34.00x (ISBN 0-8103-3708-8). Gale.

--Surnames of Scotland: Their Origin, Meaning & History. new, rev. ed. LC 47-1716. 838p. 1984. Repr. of 1946 ed. 25.00 (ISBN 0-87104-172-3). NY Pub Lib.

Black, George F., ed. Calendar of Cases of Witchcraft in Scotland, 1510-1727. LC 78-137707. (New York Public Library Publications in Reprint Ser.). (Illus.). 1971. Repr. of 1938 ed. 8.00 (ISBN 0-405-01751-0). Ayer Co Pubs.

Black, George W., Jr. American Science & Technology: A Bicentennial Bibliography. LC 78-15820. 172p. 1979. 15.95x (ISBN 0-8093-0898-3). S Ill U Pr.

Black, H. D. Constructing Diagnostic Instruments in Home Economics. 58p. 1983. pap. text ed. 5.75x (Pub. by Scottish Coun Res UK). Humanities.

Black, H. D. & Dockrell, W. B. Diagnostic Assessment in Secondary Schools. (SCRE Ser.: No. 77). 86p. 1980. pap. text ed. 5.25x (ISBN 0-901116-26-2, Pub. by Scottish Coun Res UK). Humanities.

Black, Hallie. Animal Cooperation: A Look at Sociobiology. LC 81-1355. (Illus.). 64p. (gr. 7-9). 1981. 11.25 (ISBN 0-688-00360-5); PLB 11.88 (ISBN 0-688-00361-3). Morrow.

--Dirt Cheap: Evolution of Renewable Resource Management. LC 79-11353. (Illus.). (gr. 4-6). 1979. 12.50 (ISBN 0-688-22184-X); PLB 12.88 (ISBN 0-688-32184-4). Morrow.

Black, Harold. Manual Of Horsemanship. 1978. pap. 5.00 (ISBN 0-87980-359-2). Wilshire.

Black, Harry & Broadfoot, Patricia. Keeping Track of Teaching: Assessment in the Modern Classroom. (Education Bks.). 100p. (Orig.). 1982. pap. 12.95x (ISBN 0-7100-9017-X). Routledge & Kegan.

Black, Harry G. Historic Trails & Tales of Northwest Indiana. LC 84-80304. (Illus.). 60p. (Orig.). 1985. pap. write for info. (ISBN 0-937086-03-7). HMB Pubns.

--The Lost Dutchman Mine: A Short Story of a Tall Tale. LC 75-2825. (Illus.). 110p. 1975. 10.00 (ISBN 0-8283-1613-9). Branden Pub Co.

--Pictorial Americana: The National Road. LC 83-90398. (Illus.). 88p. (Orig.). 1984. pap. 4.95 (ISBN 0-937086-02-9). HMB Pubns.

--Trails to Hoosier Heritage. LC 80-81608. (Illus.). 99p. (Orig.). 1981. pap. 4.95 (ISBN 0-937086-00-2). HMB Pubns.

--Trails to Illinois Heritage. LC 81-85017. (Trails to Ser.). (Illus.). 110p. (Orig.). 1982. pap. 5.50 (ISBN 0-937086-01-0). HMB Pubns.

Black Hawk. Black Hawk: An Autobiography. Jackson, ed. 15.00 (ISBN 0-8446-1685-0). Peter Smith.

Black, Helen. The Great Co-Op Food Book. 200p. 1983. pap. 9.95 (ISBN 0-915950-59-6). Bull Pub.

Black, Helen, ed. The Berkeley Co-Op Food Book. (Orig.). 1980. pap. 9.95 (ISBN 0-915950-43-X). Bull Pub.

--The Berkeley Co-op Food Book. 280p. 1980. 9.95 (ISBN 0-318-15059-X). NASCO.

Black, Helen C. Notable Women Authors of the Day. 1973. Repr. of 1906 ed. 17.50 (ISBN 0-8274-1786-1). R West.

--Notable Women Authors of the Day. 342p. Repr. of 1893 ed. lib. bdg. 39.00 (ISBN 0-932051-27-8). Am Repr Serv.

Black, Henry C. Black's Law Dictionary. 5th ed. Nolan, Joseph R. & Connolly, Michael J., eds. LC 79-12547. 1511p. 1979. text ed. 19.95 (ISBN 0-8299-2041-2); deluxe ed. 40.00 (ISBN 0-8299-2045-5). West Pub.

--Black's Law Dictionary. 5th, abr. ed. Nolan, Joseph R., et al, eds. LC 83-12494. 855p. 1983. pap. text ed. 11.95 (ISBN 0-314-77135-2). West Pub.

--An Essay on the Constitutional Prohibitions Against Legislation Impairing the Obligation of Contracts, & Against Retroactive & Ex Post Facto Laws. xxvi, 355p. 1980. Repr. of 1887 ed. lib. bdg. 32.50x (ISBN 0-8377-0312-3). Rothman.

--The Relation of the Executive Power to Legislation. LC 73-19130. (Politics & People Ser.). 192p. 1974. Repr. 12.00x (ISBN 0-405-05855-1). Ayer Co Pubs.

Black, Hester M. William Butler Yeats: A Catalogue of an Exhibition from P. S. O'Hegarty Collection in the University of Kansas Library. Repr. of 1958 ed. lib. bdg. 10.00 (ISBN 0-8414-1647-8). Folcroft.

Black, Hillel. The Watchdogs of Wall Street. facsimile ed. LC 75-2621. (Wall Street & the Security Market Ser.). 1975. Repr. of 1962 ed. 20.00x (ISBN 0-405-06948-0). Ayer Co Pubs.

Black, Homer A. & Edwards, James D., eds. The Managerial & Cost Accountant's Handbook. LC 78-61201. 1979. 50.00 (ISBN 0-87094-173-9). Dow Jones-Irwin.

Black, Homer A., jt. ed. see Edwards, James D.

Black, Homer A., et al. Accounting in Business Decisions: Theory, Method, & Use. 3rd ed. (Illus.). 752p. 1973. accounting forms o.p 4.95x (ISBN 0-13-001644-6); practice case 4.95x (ISBN 0-13-001230-0). P-H.

Black, Hugh. Lectures on Rhetoric Condensed by Grenville Kleiser. 1973. Repr. of 1911 ed. 8.50 (ISBN 0-8274-1787-X). R West.

Black, Hugh C., et al. The Great Educators: Readings for Leaders in Education. LC 72-88717. 799p. 1972. 29.95x (ISBN 0-911012-48-6). Nelson-Hall.

Black, Ian, et al. Advanced Urban Transport. 226p. 1975. text ed. 44.50x (ISBN 0-347-01081-4). Gower Pub Co.

Black, Ian D. A Gambling Style of Government: The Establishment of Chartered Company Rule in Sabah, 1878-1915. (Illus.). 1982. 26.00x (ISBN 0-19-582535-7). Oxford U Pr.

Black, Ira B., ed. Cellular & Molecular Biology of Neuronal Development. 390p. 1984. 49.50x (ISBN 0-306-41550-X, Plenum Pr). Plenum Pub.

Black, Irma S. Little Old Man Who Could Not Read. LC 68-9115. (Illus.). (gr. k-2). 1968. PLB 9.50 (ISBN 0-8075-4621-6). A Whitman.

Black, Ish. Key to Judo. pap. 2.00 (ISBN 0-87497-078-4). Assoc Bk.

Black, J. British Foreign Policy in the Age of Walpole. 256p. 1985. text ed. 31.00x (ISBN 0-85976-126-6, Pub. by John Donald Scotland). Humanities.

--Liquid Fuels in Australia: A Social Science Research Perspective. 280p. 1983. 37.50 (ISBN 0-08-024834-9); 21.00 (ISBN 0-08-024833-0). Pergamon.

Black, J. & Bradley, J. F. Essential Mathematics for Economists. 2nd ed. LC 79-40826. 316p. 1980. 69.95x (ISBN 0-471-27659-6, Pub. by Wiley-Interscience). Wiley.

Black, J. A., jt. auth. see Blunden, W. R.

Black, J. Anderson & Garland, Madge. A History of Fashion. rev. ed. LC 80-82797. (Illus.). 304p. 1980. 35.00 (ISBN 0-688-03742-9). Morrow.

Black, J. B. Reign of Elizabeth, Fifteen Fifty-Eight to Sixteen Three. 2nd ed. (Oxford History of England Ser.). 1959. 42.00x (ISBN 0-19-821701-3). Oxford U Pr.

Black, J. D., jt. auth. see Mighell, Ronald L.

Black, J. E. & Thompson, K. W., eds. Foreign Policies in a World of Change. (New Reprints in Essay & General Literature Index Ser.). 1975. Repr. of 1963 ed. 58.50 (ISBN 0-518-10196-7, 10196). Ayer Co Pubs.

Black, J. L. Citizens for the Fatherland: Education, Educators, & Pedagogical Ideals in Eighteenth Century Russia. (East European Monographs: No. 53). 273p. 1979. 25.00x (ISBN 0-914710-46-X). East Eur Quarterly.

Black, J. L., ed. Essays on Karamzin: Russian Man of Letters, Political Thinker, Historian, 1766-1826. (Slavistic Printings & Reprints: No.309). 232p. 1975. pap. text ed. 29.60x (ISBN 90-2793-251-4). Mouton.

Black, J. S., jt. ed. see Cheyne, T. K.

Black, J. Thomas & Morina, Michael. Downtown Office Growth & the Role of Public Transit. LC 82-50921. (Illus.). 128p. (Orig.). 1982. 28.00 (ISBN 0-87420-615-4, D31); members 21.00. Urban Land.

Black, J. Thomas, jt. auth. see Priest, Donald E.

Black, J. Thomas & Hoben, James E., eds. Urban Land Markets: Price Indices, Supply Measures, & Public Policy Effects. LC 80-53134. (ULI Research Report: No. 30). (Illus.). 232p. 1980. pap. 19.00 (ISBN 0-87420-593-X); pap. 14.25 members. Urban Land.

Black, J. Thomas, et al. Mixed-Use Development Projects in North America: Project Profiles. LC 82-84338. 70p. (Orig.). 1982. pap. 40.00 (ISBN 0-87420-618-9, M19). Urban Land.

--Downtown Retail Development: Conditions for Success & Project Profiles. LC 83-81784. 90p. (Orig.). 1983. pap. 28.00 (ISBN 0-87420-650-2, D35); pap. 21.00 members. Urban Land.

Black, J. W. Maryland's Attitude in the Struggle for Canada. pap. 9.00 (ISBN 0-384-04605-3). Johnson Repr.

Black, Jack. The Card-Counting Guide to Winning Blackjack. Valente, John, ed. (Illus.). 80p. (Orig.). 1983. 14.95 (ISBN 0-914087-00-2). Consumer Pubn.

--Gold Locations of the United States. LC 77-92557. 176p. 1975. pap. 6.95 (ISBN 0-89632-000-6). Del Oeste.

--Gold Prospectors Handbook. LC 77-92558. (Illus.). 176p. 1980. pap. 6.95 (ISBN 0-89632-001-4). Del Oeste.

Black, Jackie. Autumn Fires. (Candlelight Ecstasy Ser.: No. 152). (Orig.). 1983. pap. 1.95 (ISBN 0-440-10272-3). Dell.

--The Catch of the Season. (Candlelight Ecstasy Ser.: No. 389). (Orig.). 1985. pap. 2.25 (ISBN 0-440-11107-2). Dell.

--Crimson Morning. (Candlelight Ecstasy Ser.: No. 92). (Orig.). 1982. pap. 1.95 (ISBN 0-440-11141-2). Dell.

--Fascination. (Candlelight Ecstasy Supreme Ser.: No. 28). (Orig.). 1984. pap. 2.50 (ISBN 0-440-12442-5). Dell.

--For All Time. (Candlelight Ecstasy Supreme Ser.). (Orig.). 1984. pap. 2.50 (ISBN 0-440-12616-9). Dell.

--From This Day Forward. (Candlelight Supreme Ser.: No. 61). (Orig.). 1985. pap. 2.50 (ISBN 0-440-12740-8). Dell.

--A Little Bit of Warmth. (Candlelight Supreme Ser.: No. 85). 1985. pap. 2.75 (ISBN 0-440-14735-2). Dell.

--Payment in Full. (Candlelight Ecstasy Supreme: No. 16). (Orig.). 1984. pap. 2.50 (ISBN 0-440-16828-7). Dell.

--Promises in the Night. (Candlelight Ecstasy Ser.: No. 170). 192p. (Orig.). 1983. pap. 1.95 (ISBN 0-440-17160-1). Dell.

--Romantic Roulette. (Candlelight Ecstasy Ser.: No. 339). 1985. pap. 2.25 (ISBN 0-440-17486-4). Dell.

--A Time to Love. (Candlelight Ecstasy Romance Ser.: No. 187). (Orig.). 1983. pap. 1.95 (ISBN 0-440-18670-6). Dell.

--Winter Winds. (Candlelight Ecstasy Ser.: No. 39). (Orig.). 1982. pap. 1.75 (ISBN 0-440-19528-4). Dell.

Black, James. The Old Testament: Student Text. LC 82-70087. (Illus.). 160p. (Orig.). (gr. 10-12). 1982. pap. 4.50 (ISBN 0-87793-248-4). Ave Maria.

--The Old Testament: Teacher's Manual. 80p. (Orig.). 1982. tchrs. ed. 2.25 (ISBN 0-87793-249-2). Ave Maria.

Black, James, jt. auth. see Jelen, Frederic C.

Black, James, ed. see Tate, Nahum.

Black, James A. The Sentencing of Sex Offenders. LC 74-28602. 1975. soft bdg. 11.95 (ISBN 0-88247-324-7). R & E Pubs.

Black, James A. & Champion, Dean J. Methods & Issues in Social Research. LC 75-26659. pap. 114.30 (ISBN 0-317-28190-9, 2020187). Bks Demand UMI.

Black, James M. The Basics of Supervisory Management: Mastering the Art of Effective Supervision. 256p. 1975. 36.50 (ISBN 0-07-005513-0). McGraw.

--How to Get Results from Interviewing: A Practical Guide for Operating Management. LC 81-20952. 222p. 1982. Repr. of 1970 ed. 17.50 (ISBN 0-89874-417-2). Krieger.

Black, James W. Maryland's Attitude in the Struggle for Canada. LC 78-63812. (Johns Hopkins University. Studies in the Social Sciences. Tenth Ser. 1892: 7). Repr. of 1892 ed. 11.50 (ISBN 0-404-61075-7). AMS Pr.

Black, Jan & Smart, Pat. Getting Started. (Character Foundation Curriculum Ser.). (gr. k). 1981. pap. 2.95 (ISBN 0-8007-7025-0); tchr's ed. 20.00 (ISBN 0-8007-7026-9). Revell.

Black, Jan K. Latin America: Its Problems & Its Promise, an Introduction. 450p. 1984. 40.00x (ISBN 0-86531-212-5); pap. text ed. 16.95x (ISBN 0-86531-213-3). Westview.

--United States Penetration of Brazil. LC 76-53192. 1977. 22.50x (ISBN 0-8122-7720-1). U of Pa Pr.

Black, Jay & Whitney, Frederick C. Introduction to Mass Communication. 496p. 1983. pap. text ed. write for info (ISBN 0-697-04355-X); instr's. manual avail. (ISBN 0-697-04360-6). Wm C Brown.

Black, Jean, ed. see Weis, Margaret & Hickman, Tracy.

Black, Jeanette. Silent Tears. 1985. 11.95 (ISBN 0-533-06497-X). Vantage.

Black, Jeannette D., ed. The Blathwayt Atlas, Vol. 1, The Maps. LC 78-654217. (Illus.). 1970. Set. unbound boxed 500.00x (ISBN 0-87057-125-7). U Pr of New Eng.

--The Blathwayt Atlas: Vol. II, Commentary. LC 73-7118. 255p. 1975. 25.00x (ISBN 0-87057-139-7). U Pr of New Eng.

Black, Jeannette D., ed. see David, Ebenezer.

Black, Jeff. Extra Credit. 180p. 1985. pap. 5.95 (ISBN 0-932870-70-8). Alyson Pubns.

Black, Jeremy. The British & the Grand Tour. 256p. 1985. 29.00 (ISBN 0-7099-3257-X, Pub. by Croom Helm Ltd). Longwood Pub Group.

Black, Jeremy, ed. Britain in the Age of Walpole. LC 84-15089. 280p. 1985. 27.95 (ISBN 0-312-09826-X). St Martin.

Black, Jim & Bowl, Ric. Social Work in Context. 1983. 31.00 (ISBN 0-422-78270-X, NO. 3964, Pub. by Tavistock). Methuen Inc.

Black, Jim N. Managing the Student Yearbook: A Resource for Modern Yearbook Management & Design. LC 83-3930. (Illus.). 272p. 1983. text ed. 19.95 (ISBN 0-87833-333-9). Taylor Pub.

Black, Joan, jt. ed. see Holloway, John.

Black, John. The Economists of Modern Britain: An Introduction to Macroeconomics. 3rd ed. 281p. 1982. 34.95x (ISBN 0-85520-529-6); pap. 11.95x (ISBN 0-85520-530-X). Basil Blackwell.

--The Italian Romantic Libretto: A Study of Salvatore Commatano. 300p. 1985. 40.00x (ISBN 0-85224-463-0, Pub. by Edinburgh U Pr Scotland). Columbia U Pr.

Black, John, ed. Urban Transport Planning: Theory & Practice. LC 80-8860. (Illus.). 257p. 1981. pap. text ed. 9.95x (ISBN 0-8018-2604-7). Johns Hopkins.

Black, John & Dorrance, Graeme S., eds. Problems of International Finance. LC 83-24747. 188p. 1984. 29.95 (ISBN 0-312-64767-0). St Martin.

Black, John & Dunning, John H., eds. International Capital Movements. 246p. 1983. 32.50 (ISBN 0-8419-5095-4). Holmes & Meier.

Black, John & Hindley, Brian, eds. Current Issues in Commercial Policy & Diplomacy. 1980. 26.00 (ISBN 0-312-17926-X). St Martin.

Black, John & Winters, Alan, eds. Policy & Performance in International Trade. LC 82-23137. 250p. 1983. 25.00 (ISBN 0-312-62003-9). St Martin.

Black, John, tr. see Goldoni, Carlo.

Black, John, tr. see Schlegel, Augustus W.

Black, John, tr. see Von Humboldt, Alexander.

Black, John, tr. see Von Schlegel, Augustus W.

Black, John B. The Art of History: A Study of Four Great Historians of the Eighteenth Century. 1976. lib. bdg. 59.95 (ISBN 0-8490-1452-2). Gordon Pr.

Black, John B., jt. ed. see Britton, Bruce K.

Black, John B., jt. ed. see Graesser, Arthur C.

Black, John D. Parity, Parity, Parity. LC 72-2364. (FDR & the Era of the New Deal Ser.). 367p. 1972. Repr. of 1942 ed. 45.00 (ISBN 0-306-70482-X). Da Capo.

Black, John D., et al. Provocative Perspectives: When We Were 20 & Now That We're 60. LC 82-60220. 137p. 1982. pap. 6.95 (ISBN 0-936988-07-X). Tompson & Rutter.

--Provocative Perspectives. LC 82-60220. 137p. 1982. pap. 6.95 (ISBN 0-936988-07-X, Pub. by Tompson & Rutter). Shoe String.

Black, John G. & Stanley, Delmar S. Practical Accounting. 3rd ed. LC 75-40983. 1980. pap. text ed. 21.70x (ISBN 0-673-16133-1). Scott F.

Black, John W. American Speech for Foreign Students. 2nd ed. (Illus.). 226p. 1983. spiral 28.75x (ISBN 0-398-03999-2). C C Thomas.

--Word Discrimination. 64p. 1985. pap. text ed. 5.75x (ISBN 0-8134-2465-8, 2465). Interstate.

Black, John W. & Moore, Wilbur E. Speech: Code, Meaning, & Communication. LC 72-6686. (Illus.). 430p. 1973. Repr. of 1955 ed. lib. bdg. 24.75x (ISBN 0-8371-6493-1, BLSC). Greenwood.

Black, Jonathan. Biological Performance of Materials: Fundamentals of Biocompatibility. (Biomedical Engineering & Instrumentation Ser.: Vol. 8). (Illus.). 264p. 1981. 45.00 (ISBN 0-8247-1267-6). Dekker.

--Streisand. 1975. pap. 1.50 (ISBN 0-685-57553-5, LB298DK, Leisure Bks). Dorchester Pub Co.

Black, Jonathan & Dumbleton, John. Clinical Biomechanics: A Case History Approach. (Illus.). 416p. 1980. text ed. 50.00 (ISBN 0-443-08022-4). Churchill.

Black, Jonathan, jt. auth. see Dumbleton, John H.

Black, Joseph. Experiments Upon Magnesia Alba, Quicklime & Some Other Alcaline Substances. LC 79-8596. Repr. of 1898 ed. 13.50 (ISBN 0-404-18449-9). AMS Pr.

--Lectures on the Elements of Chemistry, 3 vols. LC 78-72776. Repr. Set. 145.00 (ISBN 0-404-17625-9). AMS Pr.

Black, Joseph, jt. auth. see Watt, James.

Black, Joseph L. Nicholas Karamzin & Russiam Society in the Nineteenth Century: A Study in Russian Political & Historical Thought. LC 75-20146. pap. 70.00 (ISBN 0-317-09272-3, 2055458). Bks Demand UMI.

Black, Judith, tr. see Liebermann, Rolf.

Black, Judith, tr. see Pedretti, Erica.

Black, Judith, tr. see Walser, Martin.

Black, Karen L., ed. A Biobibliographical Handbook of Bulgarian Authors. Matejic, Predrag, tr. from Bulgarian. (Illus.). 347p. (Orig.). 1982. pap. 14.95 (ISBN 0-89357-091-5). Slavica.

Black, Kathleen. Short-Term Counseling for the Helping Professions: A Humanistic Approach. 1983. pap. 14.95 (ISBN 0-201-00073-3, 00073, Med-Nurse). Addison-Wesley.

Black, Kenneth, jt. auth. see Russell, Hugh.

Black, Kenneth, Jr. & Huebner, S. S. Life Insurance. 10th ed. (Illus.). 784p. 1982. 29.95 (ISBN 0-13-535799-3). P-H.

Black, Kitty. Upper Circle. (Theatrical Chronical Ser.). (Illus.). 260p. 1985. text ed. 17.95 (ISBN 0-413-51040-9, 9687). Methuen Inc.

Black, Landbroke. Some Queer People. 1979. Repr. lib. bdg. 30.00 (ISBN 0-8414-9842-3). Folcroft.

--Some Queer People: Margaret Fuller, Poe, Beddoes. 1973. 35.00 (ISBN 0-8274-1477-3). R West.

Black, Larry. It Couldn't Happen Here. LC 84-90462. 1985. 10.95 (ISBN 0-87212-187-9). Libra.

Black, Laura. Albany. 256p. 1984. 11.95 (ISBN 0-312-01708-1). St Martin.

--Albany. (Large Print Books (General Ser.)). 1985. lib. bdg. 17.95 (ISBN 0-8161-3881-8). G K Hall.

--Ravenburn. 464p. 1980. pap. 3.50 (ISBN 0-446-30628-2). Warner Bks.

--Strathgallant. 316p. 1981. 11.95 (ISBN 0-312-76481-2). St Martin.

--Strathgallant. (General Ser.). 1982. lib. bdg. 15.95 (ISBN 0-8161-3361-1, Large Print Bks). G K Hall.

--Strathgallant. 1983. pap. 3.50 (ISBN 0-446-30318-6). Warner Bks.

--Wild Cat. (General Ser.). 454p. 1983. lib. bdg. 17.95 (ISBN 0-8161-3587-8, Large Print Bks). G K Hall.

Black, Leo, tr. see Badura-Skoda, Eva & Badura-Skoda, Paul.

Black, Leo, tr. see Eimert, Herbert & Stockhausen, Karlheinz.

Black, Leo, tr. see Reich, Willi.

Black, Leo, tr. see Stein, Leonard.

Black, Leo, tr. see Webern, Anton.

Black, Leslie. The Builder's Reference Book. 11th ed. 432p. 1981. 40.00x (ISBN 0-7198-2810-4, Pub. by Northwood Bks). State Mutual Bk.

Black, Linda. Pediatric Policy & Procedure Manual. LC 79-19681. 1980. pap. 9.50 (ISBN 0-87125-060-8). Cath Health.

Black, Lionel. Outbreak. 176p. 1984. pap. 2.95 (ISBN 0-8128-8062-5). Stein & Day.

--Ransom for a Nude. 190p. 1982. pap. 2.50 (ISBN 0-8128-7050-6). Stein & Day.

Black, Lowell-Dwight. The Negro Volunteer Militia Units of the Ohio National Guard, 1870-1954: The Struggle for Military Recognition & Equality in the State of Ohio. 422p. 1976. pap. text ed. 35.00x (ISBN 0-89126-031-5). MA-AH Pub.
Black, Lydia, tr. see Pierce, Richard A.
Black, Lydia T. An Ethnohistory of the Western Aleutians. (Illus.). 219p. 1984. 26.00 (ISBN 0-317-30554-9). Limestone Pr.
Black, Lydia T., tr. The Journals of Iakov Netsvetov: The Yukon Years, 1845-1863. 505p. 29.00 (ISBN 0-317-30555-7). Limestone Pr.
Black, M. & Bewley, J. D. Physiology & Biochemistry of Seeds in Relation to Germination: Viability, Dormancy, & Environmental Control, Vol. 2. (Illus.). 380p. 1982. 56.00 (ISBN 0-387-11656-7). Springer-Verlag.
Black, M., jt. auth. see Bewley, D.
Black, M., ed. Christian Palestinian Syriac Horologian (Berlin MS. OR. Oct. 1019) Repr. of 1954 ed. 52.00 (ISBN 0-317-16760-X). Kraus Repr.
Black, M. & Reed, J., eds. Perspectives on the American South: An Annual Review, Vol. 1. 424p. 1981. 38.50 (ISBN 0-677-16260-X). Gordon.
Black, Maggie. Smoking Food at Home. (Illus.). 192p. 1985. 19.95 (ISBN 0-7153-8484-8). David & Charles.
--The Wholesome Food Cookbook. (Illus.). 256p. 1982. 22.50 (ISBN 0-7153-8229-2). David & Charles.
Black, Malcolm. First Reading to First Night: A Candid Look at Stage Directing. LC 75-20336. (Illus.). 102p. 1975. 15.00x (ISBN 0-295-95432-9). U of Wash Pr.
Black, Margaret M. Robert Louis Stevenson. LC 73-12450. 1978. Repr. of 1898 ed. lib. bdg. 20.00 (ISBN 0-8414-3233-3). Folcroft.
Black, Martha L. My Ninety Years. Whyard, Flo, ed. LC 76-3117. (Northern History Library). (Illus.). 1976. pap. 7.95 (ISBN 0-88240-062-2). Alaska Northwest.
Black, Mary. American Advertising Posters of the Nineteenth Century. (Illus., Orig.). 1976. pap. 9.95 (ISBN 0-486-23356-1). Dover.
--American Naive Paintings from NGA. LC 85-4874. (Illus.). 160p. 1985. 20.00 (ISBN 0-89468-083-8). Natl Gallery Art.
--New York City's Gracie Mansion: A History of the Mayor's House. LC 84-15445. (Illus.). 104p. 1984. 17.95 (ISBN 0-9613729-0-7); pap. 10.95 (ISBN 0-9613729-1-5). Pub Ctr Cult Res.
--Old New York in Early Photographs: Eighteen Fifty-Three to Nineteen Hundred & One. (Illus.). 200p. (Orig.). 1973. pap. 9.95 (ISBN 0-486-22907-6). Dover.
Black, Mary, ed. Old New York in Early Photographs, 1853-1901. (Illus.). 13.25 (ISBN 0-8446-5005-6). Peter Smith.
Black, Mary, ed. see Tracy, Berry B.
Black, Mary E. The Key to Weaving. 2nd, rev. ed. (Illus.). 1980. 29.95 (ISBN 0-02-511170-1). Macmillan.
Black, Mathew. Midsummer Night's Dream Notes. (Orig.). 1980. pap. 3.25 (ISBN 0-8220-0057-1). Cliffs.
Black, Matthew. Aramaic Approach to the Gospels & Acts. 3rd ed. 1967. 32.50x (ISBN 0-19-826157-8). Oxford U Pr.
--Romans. (New Century Bible Series). 191p. 1973. 9.50 (ISBN 0-551-00447-9). Attic Pr.
--Romans. rev. ed. (New Century Bible Commentary Ser.). 192p. 1981. pap. 6.95 (ISBN 0-8028-1905-2). Eerdmans.
--The Scrolls & Christian Origins: Studies in the Jewish Background of the New Testament. LC 83-11519. (Brown Judaic Studies). 232p. 1983. pap. 14.00 (ISBN 0-89130-639-0, 14 00 48). Scholars Pr GA.
Black, Matthew & Davidson, Robert. Constantin Von Tischendorf & the Greek New Testament. 81p. 1981. 30.00x (ISBN 0-85261-164-1, Pub. by U of Glasgow Pr Scotland). State Mutual Bk.
Black, Matthew & Rowley, H. H. Peake's Commentary on the Bible. 1962. 34.95 (ISBN 0-8407-5019-6). Nelson.
Black, Matthew, ed. see Best, Ernest.
Black, Matthew, ed. see Bruce, F. F.
Black, Matthew, ed. see Grayston, Kenneth.
Black, Matthew, ed. see Guthrie, Donald.
Black, Matthew, ed. see Mitton, C. Leslie.
Black, Matthew, ed. see Neil, William.
Black, Matthew, ed. see Sidebottom, E. M.
Black, Matthew W. & Shaaber, M. A. Shakespeare's Seventeenth-Century Editors, 1632-1685. LC 38-3681. (MLA.MGS). 1937. 37.00 (ISBN 0-527-08600-2). Kraus Repr.
Black, Matthew W., ed. see Middleton, Thomas.
Black, Matthew W., jt. ed. see Schelling, Felix E.
Black, Matthew W., ed. see Shakespeare, William.
Black, Max. Caveats & Critiques: Philosophical Essays in Language, Logic, & Art. LC 74-25365. (Illus.). 280p. 1975. 25.00x (ISBN 0-8014-0958-6). Cornell U Pr.
--A Companion to Wittgenstein's Tractatus. 466p. 1964. 37.50x (ISBN 0-8014-0039-2). Cornell U Pr.
--Critical Thinking. 2nd ed. 1952. text ed. 22.95 (ISBN 0-13-194092-9). P-H.
--Language & Philosophy: Studies in Method. LC 81-6206. (Illus.). xiii, 264p. 1981. Repr. of 1949 ed. lib. bdg. 27.50x (ISBN 0-313-23082-X, BLLP). Greenwood.
--Models & Metaphors: Studies in Language & Philosophy. 278p. 1962. 27.50x (ISBN 0-8014-0041-4). Cornell U Pr.
--Nature of Mathematics. (Quality Paperback: No. 201). 219p. 1965. pap. 3.95 (ISBN 0-8226-0201-6). Littlefield.
--The Prevalence of Humbug & Other Essays. LC 82-22211. 185p. (Orig.). 1985. 19.95x (ISBN 0-8014-1514-4); pap. 7.95x (ISBN 0-8014-9321-8). Cornell U Pr.
--Problems of Analysis: Philosophical Essays. LC 74-139124. 1971. Repr. of 1954 ed. lib. bdg. 16.25x (ISBN 0-8371-5740-4, BLPA). Greenwood.
Black, Max, ed. Importance of Language. 186p. 1968. pap. 6.95x (ISBN 0-8014-9077-4). Cornell U Pr.
--Philosophical Analysis: A Collection of Essays. facsimile ed. LC 78-152158. (Essay Index Reprint Ser). Repr. of 1950 ed. 27.50 (ISBN 0-8369-2214-X). Ayer Co Pubs.
--Philosophical Analysis: A Collection of Essays. LC 78-152158. (Essay Index Reprint Ser.). 405p. Repr. of 1950 ed. lib. bdg. 39.00 (ISBN 0-8290-0796-2). Irvington.
--Philosophical Analysis: A Collection of Essays. LC 78-152158. (Essay Index Reprint Ser.). 405p. 1984. pap. 14.95 (ISBN 0-8290-1567-1). Irvington.
--The Social Theories of Talcott Parsons: A Critical Examination. LC 75-40325. (Arcturus Books Paperbacks). 384p. 1976. pap. 8.95 (ISBN 0-8093-0759-6). S Ill U Pr.
Black, Max, ed. see Frege, Gottlob.
Black, Max, ed. see Von Wright, Georg H.
Black, Max, ed. see Wertheimer, Roger.
Black, Merle & Reed, John S. Perspectives on the American South. (Perspectives on the American South Ser.: Vol. 2). 288p. 1983. 36.25 (ISBN 0-677-16450-5). Gordon.
Black, Merle, jt. ed. see Beyle, Thad L.
Black, Merle, et al. Political Attitudes in the Nation & the States. (Comparative State Elections Project Monograph Ser.). (Illus.). 210p. 1974. pap. text ed. 5.00 (ISBN 0-89143-004-0). U NC Inst Res Soc Sci.
Black, Michael, jt. ed. see Bewley, J. Derek.
Black, Michael H. Cambridge University Press: Fifteen Eighty-Four to Nineteen Eighty-Four. (Illus.). 250p. 1984. 19.95 (ISBN 0-521-26473-1). Cambridge U Pr.
Black, Michael L. & Black, Nancy B. A History of New York: The Complete Works of Washington Irving. (Critical Editions Program Ser.). 738p. 1984. lib. bdg. 45.00 (ISBN 0-8057-8514-0, Twayne). G K Hall.
Black, Nancy B., jt. auth. see Black, Michael L.
Black, Nancy B. & Weidman, Bette S., eds. White on Red: Images of the American Indian. 1976. 24.50 (ISBN 0-8046-9084-7, Pub. by Kennikat). Assoc Faculty Pr.
Black, Nelson W., ed. see Huttman, Elizabeth D.
Black, O. F., jt. auth. see Igarashi, M.
Black, P. Strength of Materials. 1966. 26.00 (ISBN 0-08-011555-1). Pergamon.
Black, Patsie. Tapestry: A Finespun Grace & Mercy. LC 82-8231. 1982. pap. 6.95 (ISBN 0-930014-92-8). Multnomah.
Black, Patti & Morrison, Ann, eds. Walter Anderson for Children: An Activity Book from the Mississippi State Historical Museum. (Illus.). 64p. (Orig.). pap. 12.95. Mississippi De.
Black, Patti C. The Natchez Trace. (Illus.). 96p. 1985. 25.00 (ISBN 0-87805-226-7). U Pr of Miss.
Black, Patti C., ed. Documentary Portrait of Mississippi: The Thirties. LC 82-4823. (Illus.). 128p. 1982. pap. 15.00 (ISBN 0-87805-166-X). U Pr of Miss.
--Mississippi Patent Models. (Illus.). 24p. 1981. pap. 3.50 (ISBN 0-938896-32-6). Mississippi De.
Black, Patti C. & Freeman, Roland L., eds. Something to Keep You Warm: The Roland Freeman Collection of Black American Quilts from the Mississippi Heartland. (Illus.). 46p. (Orig.). 1981. pap. 6.00 (ISBN 0-938896-31-8). Mississippi De.
Black, Paul H. & Adams, O. Eugene, Jr. Machine Design. 3rd ed. LC 68-13623. 1968. text ed. 45.00 (ISBN 0-07-005524-6). McGraw.
Black, Perry, ed. Brain Dysfunction in Children: Etiology, Diagnosis & Management. 320p. 1981. text ed. 51.00 (ISBN 0-89004-022-2). Raven.
--Drugs & The Brain: Papers on the Action, Use, & Abuse of Psychotropic Agents. LC 68-31642. pap. 104.00 (ISBN 0-317-07918-2, 2001191). Bks Demand UMI.
--Physiological Correlates of Emotion: Based Upon a Symposium. 1970. 55.00 (ISBN 0-12-102850-X). Acad Pr.
Black, Perry O. Pumps. 3rd ed. 464p. 1977. 10.95 (ISBN 0-672-23292-8). Audel.
Black, Perry O. & Scahill. Diesel Engine Manual. 3rd ed. LC 82-20635. (Audel Ser.). 1983. 12.95 (ISBN 0-672-23371-1). Bobbs.
Black, Perry O. & Schahill, William E. Diesel Engine Manual. 4th ed. LC 82-20635. (Illus.). 499p. 1983. 12.95 (ISBN 0-672-23371-1). Audel.
Black, Peter E. Conservation of Water & Related Land Resources. LC 81-21103. 234p. 1982. 29.95x (ISBN 0-03-060419-2). Praeger.
--Environmental Impact Analysis. LC 81-7339. 160p. 1981. 26.95 (ISBN 0-03-059618-1). Praeger.
Black, Peter E., ed. Readings in Environmental Impact. LC 74-13079. 345p. 1974. text ed. 37.50x (ISBN 0-8422-5201-0); pap. text ed. 9.75x (ISBN 0-8422-0451-2). Irvington.
--Readings in Soil & Water Conservation. 275p. 1974. text ed. 38.50x (ISBN 0-8422-5204-5); pap. text ed. 14.95x (ISBN 0-8422-0452-0). Irvington.
Black, Peter E. & Herrington, Lee P., eds. Working with NEPA: Environmental Impact Analysis for the Resource Manager. LC 74-23639. 145p. 1974. pap. text ed. 4.75x (ISBN 0-8422-0483-0). Irvington.
Black, Peter E., jt. ed. see Eschner, Arthur R.
Black, Peter M. The Complete Book of Orchid Growing. 160p. 1981. 40.00x (ISBN 0-7063-5512-1, Pub. by Ward Lock Ed England). State Mutual Bk.
--The Complete Handbook of Orchid Growing. 160p. 1980. 17.65 (ISBN 0-8129-0951-8). Times Bks.
--Orchids. (Illus.). 127p. 1985. 14.95 (ISBN 0-600-36887-4, Pub. by Salem Hse Ltd). Merrimack Pub Cir.
Black, Peter M., et al, eds. Secretory Tumors of the Pituitary Gland. (Progress in Endocrine Research & Therapy Ser.: Vol. 1). 416p. 1984. text ed. 74.50 (ISBN 0-89004-585-2). Raven.
Black, Peter R. Ernst Kaltenbrunner: Ideological Soldier of the Third Reich. LC 83-42550. (Illus.). 352p. 1984. 32.50x (ISBN 0-691-05397-9). Princeton U Pr.
Black, R. & Boden, P., eds. Alkaline Ring Complexes in Africa: Proceedings of the International Conference Held in Zaria, Nigeria, Dec. 6-10, 1983. 286p. 1985. pap. 46.75 (ISBN 0-08-032613-7, Pub by PPL). Pergamon.
Black, R. Collison. Catalogue of Pamphlets on Economic Subjects 1750-1900 & Now Housed in Irish Libraries. LC 79-81989. 1969. 57.50x (ISBN 0-678-08002-X). Kelley.
Black, R. Collison, et al, eds. The Marginal Revolution in Economics: Interpretation & Evaluation. LC 72-91850. 375p. 1973. 21.00 (ISBN 0-8223-0278-0). Duke.
Black, R. D. Economic Thought & the Irish Question, 1817-1870. LC 85-12499. xiv, 299p. 1985. Repr. of 1960 ed. lib. bdg. 47.50x (ISBN 0-313-24946-6, BLET). Greenwood.
Black, R. D., ed. see Longfield, Mountiford.
Black, R. H. Manual of Epidemiology & Epidemiological Services in Malaria Programmes. (Illus.). 223p. 1968. pap. 3.60 (ISBN 92-4-154015-X, 601). World Health.
Black, R. L. The Church of God of Prophecy: Pastor. 1977. 4.25 (ISBN 0-934942-29-3). White Wing Pub.
--Discerning the Body. 98p. (Orig.). 1984. pap. 3.95 (ISBN 0-934942-42-0, 1264). White Wing Pub.
--Holy Ghost & Speaking in Tongues. 180p. (Orig.). 1983. pap. 4.95 (ISBN 0-934942-35-8, 1869). White Wing Pub.
--Is Divorce & Remarriage Sin? Rev. ed. Orig. Title: Pastor, Why Can't I Remarry. 1982. pap. 2.25 (ISBN 0-934942-31-5). White Wing Pub.
--Yet Not I. 1976. pap. 3.50 (ISBN 0-934942-19-6). White Wing Pub.
Black, R. M. A History of Electric Wires & Cables. (IEE History of Technology Series). 304p. 1983. 60.00 (ISBN 0-86341-001-4, HT004). Inst Elect Eng.
Black, Rhona M. Elements of Palaeontology. (Illus.). 1970. 67.50 (ISBN 0-521-07445-2); pap. 21.95 (ISBN 0-521-09615-4). Cambridge U Pr.
Black, Richard L., et al. Ninth Year Mathematics. (Arco's Regents Review Ser.). 288p. (Orig.). 1983. pap. 3.95 (5701). Arco.
Black, Rita B., jt. ed. see Schild, Sylvia.
Black, Rita B., et al. Nursing Management of Epilepsy. LC 81-20524. 188p. 1982. text ed. 36.50 (ISBN 0-89443-675-9). Aspen Systems.
Black, Robert. Benedetto Accolti & the Florentine Renaissance. Date not set. price not set (ISBN 0-521-25016-1). Cambridge U Pr.
--Nutrition of Finches & Other Cagebirds. 362p. 1981. 19.95 (ISBN 0-910631-01-8). Avian Pubns.
--Problems with Finches. (Illus.). 108p. 1980. pap. 9.95 (ISBN 0-910631-00-X). Avian Pubns.
Black, Robert & Blank, Stephen. Multinationals in Contention: Responses at Governmental & International Levels. LC 78-66971. (Report Ser.: No. 749). (Illus.). 233p. 1978. pap. 30.00 (ISBN 0-8237-0185-9); pap. 10.00 member. Conference Bd.
Black, Robert, tr. see Guizot, Francois P.
Black, Robert F., et al, eds. The Wisconsinan Stage. LC 72-89466. (Geological Society of America Memoir Ser.: No. 136). pap. 86.00 (ISBN 0-317-30054-7, 2025030). Bks Demand UMI.
Black, Robert G. Nutrition of Finches & Other Cage Birds. 326p. 1981. 19.95 (ISBN 0-910631-01-8). R G Black.
Black, Ronald E., jt. ed. see Schultz, Julius.
Black, S. Public Relations in the Nineteen Eighties. 46.00 (ISBN 0-08-024065-8). Pergamon.
Black, Sam. Exhibiting Overseas. 1971. 15.95x (ISBN 0-8464-0393-5). Beekman Pubs.
Black, Sam & Sharpe, Melvin A. Practical Public Relations: Common Sense Guidelines for Business & Professional People. 224p. 1983. 16.95 (ISBN 0-13-693531-1); pap. 8.95 (ISBN 0-13-693523-0). P-H.
Black, Samuel. A Journal of a Voyage from Rocky Mountain Portage to the Sources of Finlay's Branch & Northwestward in Summer 1824. Rich, E. E. & Johnson, A. M., eds. (Hudson's Bay Record Society Publication Ser.: Vol. 18). pap. 52.00 (ISBN 0-317-16727-8). Kraus Repr.
Black, Sonia. The Get Along Gang & the New Neighbor. (Get Along Gang Ser.). (Illus.). 32p. (Orig.). (ps-2). 1984. pap. 1.50 (ISBN 0-590-33190-6). Scholastic Inc.
--The Get Along Gang & the Tattletale. (The Get Along Gang Ser.). (Illus.). 32p. (Orig.). (ps-2). 1984. pap. 1.50 (ISBN 0-590-33279-1). Scholastic Inc.
--Ghostbusters Puzzle Fun Book. 64p. 1985. 1.50 (ISBN 0-590-33793-9). Scholastic Inc.
Black, Stanley. The Banking System: A Preface to Public Interest Analysis. LC 75-4049. 458p. 15.00 (ISBN 0-318-16246-6, F-1). Public Int Econ.
Black, Stephen A. Whitman's Journeys into Chaos: A Psychoanalytic Study in the Poetic Process. LC 75-2979. Repr. of 1975 ed. 51.70 (ISBN 0-8357-9516-0, 2010547). Bks Demand UMI.
Black, Sue, as told to see Posserello, Jodie A.
Black, Susan. Crash in the Wilderness. LC 79-21852. (Quest, Adventure, Survival). (Illus.). 46p. (gr. 4-9). 1982. pap. 9.27 (ISBN 0-8172-2054-2). Raintree Pubs.
--Crash in the Wilderness. LC 79-21852. (Quest, Adventure, Survival). (Illus.). (gr. 4-8). 1980. PLB 14.25 (ISBN 0-8172-1553-0). Raintree Pubs.
Black, Theodore M. Straight Talk About American Education. 307p. 1982. 14.95 (ISBN 0-15-185584-6). HarBraceJ.
Black, Thomas. Black's Texas Evidence Manual. LC 85-393. 1985. 100.00 (ISBN 0-317-18308-7). Callaghan.
--Secured Transactions Handbook for the Texas Attorney. LC 81-85831. 171p. 1982. 30.00 (ISBN 0-938160-27-3, 6241). State Bar TX.
--Texas Evidence. Date not set. 100.00. Callaghan.
Black, Thomas F. Why Is PI. 6.95x (ISBN 0-89741-012-2). Roadrunner Tech.
Black, Thomas K. The Biological & Social Analysis of a Mississippian Cemetery from Southeast Missouri: The Turner Site 23b21a. (Anthropological Papers Ser.: No. 68). (Illus.). 170p. (Orig.). 1980. pap. 6.00x (ISBN 0-932206-81-6). U Mich Mus Anthro.
Black, Tyrone & Daniel, Donnie L. Money & Banking: Contemporary Policies & Issues. 2nd ed. 1985. 27.95x (ISBN 0-256-03253-X). Business Pubns.
Black, Virginia M. Tackling Notre Dame. LC 83-82713. (Illus.). 250p. pap. 6.95 (ISBN 0-87319-030-0). C Hallberg.
Black, W. Wayne. An Introduction to On-Line Computers. LC 70-141580. (Illus.). 462p. 1971. 85.75 (ISBN 0-677-02930-6). Gordon.
Black, William. Bella. (Orig.). 1979. pap. 2.50 (ISBN 0-89083-498-9). Zebra.
--Bella's Blessings. (Orig.). 1980. pap. 2.50 (ISBN 0-89083-562-4). Zebra.
--A Daughter of Heth, 3 vols. in 1. LC 79-8237. Repr. of 1871 ed. 44.50 (ISBN 0-404-61781-6). AMS Pr.
--Goldsmith. Morley, John, ed. LC 68-58370. (English Men of Letters). Repr. of 1887 ed. lib. bdg. 12.50 (ISBN 0-404-51702-1). AMS Pr.
--Goldsmith. 1909. lib. bdg. 12.00 (ISBN 0-8414-1648-6). Folcroft.
--Macleod of Dare, 3 vols. in 1. LC 79-8418. Repr. of 1878 ed. 44.50 (ISBN 0-404-61782-4). AMS Pr.
--Magic Ink & Other Stories. facsimile ed. LC 79-37537. (Short Story Index Reprint Ser.). Repr. of 1892 ed. 19.00 (ISBN 0-8369-4096-2). Ayer Co Pubs.
--Maid of Killeena, & Other Stories. facsimile ed. LC 71-152936. (Short Story Index Reprint Ser.). Repr. of 1874 ed. 18.00 (ISBN 0-8369-3794-5). Ayer Co Pubs.
--Penance of John Logan & Two Other Tales. facsimile ed. LC 73-106248. (Short Story Index Reprint Ser.). 1893. 18.00 (ISBN 0-8369-3284-6). Ayer Co Pubs.
Black, William & Hartley, James G. Thermodynamics. 755p. 1984. text ed. 37.50 scp (ISBN 0-06-040732-8, HarpC). Har-Row.
Black, William G. Folk-Medicine: A Chapter in the History of Culture. LC 74-124308. (Research & Source Ser.: No. 486). 1970. Repr. of 1883 ed. 15.00 (ISBN 0-8337-0298-X). B Franklin.
--Folk-Medicine: A Chapter in the History of Culture. (Folk-Lore Society London Monographs: Vol. 12). pap. 24.00 (ISBN 0-317-16719-7). Kraus Repr.
Black, William H. Illustrations of Ancient State & Chivalry. LC 78-63488. Repr. of 1840 ed. 33.50 (ISBN 0-404-17136-2). AMS Pr.
Black, William O. History of Slavery & the Slave Trade, Ancient & Modern. facs. ed. LC 78-83956. (Black Heritage Library Collection Ser). 1857. 28.00 (ISBN 0-8369-8512-5). Ayer Co Pubs.
Black, William R. Railroads for Rent: The Local Rail Assistance Program. LC 84-48546. 352p. 1985. 29.95x (ISBN 0-253-34774-2). Ind U Pr.

Black, William Z., jt. auth. see Kreith, Frank.

Blackaby, F., et al, eds. No-First-Use. LC 84-2467. (Peace Studies). (Illus.). 156p. 1984. 22.00 (ISBN 0-85066-274-5, Pub. by SIPRI); pap. 11.00 (ISBN 0-85066-260-5, Pub. by SIPRI). Taylor & Francis.

Blackaby, F. T. British Economic Policy: Nineteen Sixty to Nineteen Seventy-Four. LC 77-28282. (NIESR Economic & Social Policy Studies: No. 31). (Illus.). 1979. 85.00 (ISBN 0-521-22042-4); pap. 19.95x (ISBN 0-521-29597-1). Cambridge U Pr.

Blackaby, Frank, ed. De-Industrialisation. (Economic Policy Papers). 1979. text ed. 37.50x (ISBN 0-435-84076-2); pap. text ed. 21.50x (ISBN 0-435-84077-0). Gower Pub Co.

--The Future of Pay Bargaining. (Joint Studies in Public Policy). 1981. text ed. 44.00x (ISBN 0-435-83921-7). Gower Pub Co.

Blackaby, Linda, et al. In Focus: A Guide to Using Films. (Cine Information Ser.). 1980. pap. 11.95 (ISBN 0-918432-22-7). NY Zoetrope.

Blackaby, Suzy, ed. see Crabtree, Elizabeth.

Blackaby, Suzy, et al, eds. see Knight, Diane.

Blackadar, Thomas. The Atari 800XL: A Practical Guide. LC 84-50365. (Illus.). 198p. 1984. pap. 9.95 (ISBN 0-89588-125-X). SYBEX.

--The Best of Commodore 64 Software. LC 84-50352. (Illus.). 181p. 1984. pap. 12.95 (ISBN 0-89588-194-2). SYBEX.

--The Best of TI 99-4A Cartridges. LC 83-50716. (Illus.). 150p. (Orig.). 1984. pap. 9.95 (ISBN 0-89588-137-3). SYBEX.

--The Best of VIC-20 Software. LC 83-51188. (Illus.). 173p. (Orig.). 1984. pap. 7.95 (ISBN 0-89588-139-X). SYBEX.

--The Easy Guide to Your Coleco Adam. LC 84-50364. 175p. 1984. pap. 9.95 (ISBN 0-89588-181-0). SYBEX.

--The IBM PCjr: A Practical Guide. 175p. 1984. pap. 12.95 (ISBN 0-89588-217-5). SYBEX.

Blackadder, D. A. & Nedderman, R. M. Handbook of Unit Operations. 1971. 49.50 (ISBN 0-12-102950-6). Acad Pr.

Blackall, E. Faust's Last Speech. (Bithell Memorial Lectures). vi, 14p. 1985. pap. text ed. 3.25x (ISBN 0-85457-126-4, Pub. by Inst Germanic UK). Humanities.

Blackall, Eric A. Goethe & the Novel. LC 75-38426. 344p. 1976. 57.50x (ISBN 0-8014-0978-0). Cornell U Pr.

--The Novels of the German Romantics. LC 82-22104. (Illus.). 320p. 1983. 37.50x (ISBN 0-8014-1523-3); pap. 14.95x (ISBN 0-8014-9885-6). Cornell U Pr.

Blackall, W. E. & Grieve, B. J. How to Know Western Australian Wildflowers, Pt. IIIB: Epacridaceae-Lamiaceae. (Illus.). 45p. 1982. 39.00x (ISBN 0-85564-161-4, Pub. BY U of W Austral Pr). Intl Spec Bk.

Blackall, W. E., jt. auth. see Grieve, B. J.

Blackall, W. E., jt. ed. see Grieve, B. J.

Blackard, M. Kay & Barsh, Elizabeth T. Reaching Out: Achieving Community Involvement with Developmentally Disabled Children. 72p. 1982. pap. text ed. 9.95 (ISBN 0-911227-00-8). Willoughby Wessington.

Blackbeard. Krazy Kats & Gibson Girl. 1985. lib. bdg. 37.00 (ISBN 0-8240-9033-0). Garland pub.

Blackbeard, Bill & Marschall, Rick. Krazy Kat's Kreator: A Biography of George Herriman. 1985. pap. 19.95 (ISBN 0-03-004567-3, Owl Bks). HR&W.

Blackbeard, Bill & Whyte, Malcolm. Great Comic Cats. LC 81-7622. 160p. 1981. pap. 14.95 (ISBN 0-8431-4010-0). Troubador Pr.

Blackbeard, Bill & Williams, Martin, eds. The Smithsonian Collection of Newspaper Comics. LC 77-608090. (Illus.). 1978. pap. 15.95 (ISBN 0-8109-2081-6). Abrams.

--The Smithsonian Collection of Newspaper Comics. LC 77-608090. (Illus.). 336p. 1978. 29.95 (ISBN 0-686-77340-3); pap. 14.95 (ISBN 0-87474-167-X). Smithsonian.

Blackbeard, Bill, ed. see Caniff, Milton.

Blackbeard, Bill, ed. see Crosby, Percy L.

Blackbeard, Bill, ed. see De Beck, Billy.

Blackbeard, Bill, ed. see Dwiggins, Clare V.

Blackbeard, Bill, ed. see Fisher, Harry C.

Blackbeard, Bill, ed. see Godwin, Frank.

Blackbeard, Bill, ed. see Goldberg, Rube.

Blackbeard, Bill, ed. see Herriman, George.

Blackbeard, Bill, ed. see Hershfield, Harry.

Blackbeard, Bill, ed. see McBride, Clifford.

Blackbeard, Bill, ed. see McKay, Winsor.

Blackbeard, Bill, intro. by see McManus, George.

Blackbeard, Bill, ed. see Mager, Gus.

Blackbeard, Bill, ed. see Moores, Dick.

Blackbeard, Bill, ed. see Opper, Frederick B.

Blackbeard, Bill, ed. see Outcault, Richard F.

Blackbeard, Bill, intro. by see Segar, Elzie C.

Blackbeard, Bill, ed. see Sterret, Cliff.

Blackbeard, Bill, ed. see Storm, George.

Blackbeard, Bill, ed. see Tuthill, Harry J.

Blackbeer, Lawrence. Student Earth Scientist Explores the Geologic Past. LC 76-2565. (Student Scientist Ser.). (gr. 7 up). 1976. PLB 8.97 (ISBN 0-8239-0353-2). Rosen Group.

Blackborow, J. R. & Young, D. Metal Vapour Synthesis in Organometallic Chemistry. LC 79-9844. (Reactivity & Structure Ser.: Vol. 9). (Illus.). 1979. 63.00 (ISBN 0-387-09330-3). Springer-Verlag.

Blackbourn, A. & Putnam, R. G. The Industrial Geography of Canada. LC 84-9768. 224p. 1984. 25.00 (ISBN 0-312-41426-9). St Martin.

Blackbourn, David. Class, Religion, & Local Politics: The Centre Party in Wurttemberg Before 1914. LC 80-11878. 288p. 1980. text ed. 45.00x (ISBN 0-300-02464-9). Yale U Pr.

Blackbourn, David & Eley, Geoff. The Peculiarities of German History: Bourgeois Society & Politics in 19th Century Germany. 300p. 1984. 25.95x (ISBN 0-19-873058-6); pap. 10.95x (ISBN 0-19-873057-8). Oxford U Pr.

Blackburn. Enzyme Structure & Function. (Enzymology Ser.: Vol. 3). 1976. 85.00 (ISBN 0-8247-6326-2). Dekker.

--Management of Obesity by Severe Caloric Restriction. 1985. 47.50 (ISBN 0-88416-495-0). PSG Pub Co.

Blackburn, Albert. Now Consciousness: Exploring the World Beyond Thought. LC 83-82540. 168p. 1983. pap. 8.95 (ISBN 0-915520-64-8). Idylwild Bks.

Blackburn, Alex. Writer's Forum, Vol. 1, 1974; Vol. 2, 1985. LC 78-649046. 200p. (Orig.). 1985. Set. pap. 8.95x (ISBN 0-9602992-5-4). U CO at Colorado Springs.

Blackburn, Alex, ed. Writers Forum 10, 1984. LC 78-649046. 1984. pap. 8.95 (ISBN 0-9602992-4-6). U Co At Colorado Springs.

--Writers Forum 7, 1981. LC 78-649046. pap. 8.95 (ISBN 0-686-87317-3). U CO at Colorado Springs.

--Writers Forum 8, 1982. LC 78-649046. pap. 8.95 (ISBN 0-9602992-2-X). U CO at Colorado Springs.

--Writers Forum 9, 1983. LC 78-649046. 1983. pap. 8.95. U CO at Colorado Springs.

Blackburn, Alexander. The Cold War of Kitty Pentecost. LC 78-58533. (A Writers West Bk.). 232p. 1979. 12.95 (ISBN 0-8040-9015-7, 82-87732, Pub by Swallow); pap. 5.95 (ISBN 0-8040-9011-4, 82-87740, Pub by Swallow). Ohio U Pr.

--The Myth of the Picaro: Continuity & Transformation of the Picaresque Novel, 1554-1954. LC 78-23605. x, 267p. 1979. 22.50 (ISBN 0-8078-1334-6). U of NC Pr.

Blackburn, Bill. Understanding Your Feelings. LC 83-70644. 1983. pap. 4.50 (ISBN 0-8054-5215-X). Broadman.

--What You Should Know About Suicide. 154p. 1982. 8.95 (ISBN 0-318-18135-5). Contact Teleministries.

Blackburn, Bill & Blackburn, Deana. Coping with Stress in Marriage. 160p. 1985. 9.95 (ISBN 0-8499-0388-2, 0388-2). Word Bks.

Blackburn, Charles. Needlepoint Designs for Traditional Furniture. LC 79-67255. (Illus.). 160p. 1980. 17.50 (ISBN 0-8149-0815-2); pap. 12.95 (ISBN 0-8149-0835-7). Vanguard.

--The Pillow Book. LC 77-93302. (Illus.). 156p. 1979. pap. 9.95 (ISBN 0-8149-0801-2). Vanguard.

Blackburn, Deana, jt. auth. see Blackburn, Bill.

Blackburn, Emily, jt. auth. see Thomas, Art.

Blackburn, F. Sugar-Cane. (Tropical Agriculture Ser.). (Illus.). 414p. 1984. text ed. 75.00 (ISBN 0-582-46028-X). Longman.

Blackburn, Ferdie. The Chicken Gourmet: Over One Hundred International & Classic Recipes for Family & Festive Occasions. 96p. 1984. pap. 4.95 (ISBN 0-312-13181-X). St Martin.

Blackburn, Forrest R., et al, eds. Kansas & the West: Bicentennial Essays in Honor of Nyle H. Miller. LC 76-20097. (Illus.). 226p. 1976. 8.95 (ISBN 0-87726-002-8). Kansas St Hist.

Blackburn, Francis, et al, eds. see White, Terence.

Blackburn, Francis A., ed. Exodus & Daniel. LC 76-144440. (Belles Lettres Ser., Section I: No. 6). Repr. of 1907 ed. 16.50 (ISBN 0-404-53607-7). AMS Pr.

Blackburn, G. M., III see Brewton, John E.

Blackburn, G. M, III see Brewton, John E.

Blackburn, Gabriele. Science & Art of the Pendulum: A Complete Course in Radiesthesia. LC 83-83220. (Illus.). 96p. (Orig.). 1984. pap. 10.00 (ISBN 0-9613054-1-X). Idylwild Bks.

Blackburn, Gary M., jt. auth. see Bullock, Lyndal M.

Blackburn, George M., ed. Dear Carrie... The Civil War Letters of Thomas N. Stevens. (Illus.). 1984. 17.50 (ISBN 0-916699-10-2). Clarke His.

--The Wandering Regiment: The Diary of Capt. Ralph Ely. (Illus.). 73p. (Orig.). 1965. pap. 5.00 (ISBN 0-317-18874-7, Pub. by Central MI Univ Pr). Hardscrabble Bks.

Blackburn, Gilmer W. Education in the Third Reich: Race & History in Nazi Textbooks. 288p. 1984. 34.95x (ISBN 0-87395-822-5); pap. 14.95x (ISBN 0-87395-823-3). State U NY Pr.

Blackburn, Glenn. The West & World since Nineteen Forty-Five. LC 84-51149. 150p. 1984. pap. text ed. 9.95 (ISBN 0-312-86280-6). St Martin.

Blackburn, Graham. Illustrated Basic Carpentry. LC 77-1669. (Illus.). 1977. pap. 4.95 (ISBN 0-316-09870-1). Little.

--The Illustrated Encyclopedia of Ships, Boats & Vessels. LC 78-16565. (Illus.). 448p. 1978. 35.00 (ISBN 0-87951-082-X); pap. 14.95 (ISBN 0-87951-141-9). Overlook Pr.

--Illustrated Housebuilding. (Illus.). 160p. 1974. 14.95 (ISBN 0-87951-020-X); pap. 7.95. Overlook Pr.

--Illustrated Interior Carpentry. LC 77-12270. (Illus.). 192p. 1980. pap. 7.95 (ISBN 0-87951-092-7). Overlook Pr.

--The Overlook Illustrated Dictionary of Nautical Terms. LC 80-39640. (Illus.). 368p. 1984. 22.50 (ISBN 0-87951-124-9); pap. 9.95 (ISBN 0-87951-950-9). Overlook Pr.

Blackburn, H. Women's Suffrage: A Record of the Women's Sufferage Movement in the British Isles. Repr. of 1902 ed. 28.00 (ISBN 0-527-08680-0). Kraus Repr.

Blackburn, H., jt. auth. see Rose, G. A.

Blackburn, H. P. Hell Fire Ranch. 1978. pap. 1.50 (ISBN 0-8439-0546-8, Leisure Bks). Dorchester Pub Co.

Blackburn, Henry. Art in the Mountains: Story of the Passion Play. LC 77-94544. 1979. Repr. of 1870 ed. lib. bdg. 20.00 (ISBN 0-89341-178-7). Longwood Pub Group.

--Breton Folk. Repr. of 1880 ed. 30.00 (ISBN 0-8482-0145-0). Norwood Edns.

--Breton Folk. 1880. 30.00 (ISBN 0-686-17221-3). Scholars Ref Lib.

--Breton Folk: An Artistic Tour in Brittany. 1880. 30.00 (ISBN 0-8495-6250-3). Arden Lib.

--Measurement in Exercise Electrocardiography: The Ernst Simonson Conference. (Illus.). 516p. 1969. 49.75x (ISBN 0-398-01763-8). C C Thomas.

--Randolph Caldecott. LC 68-21757. 1969. Repr. of 1886 ed. 35.00x (ISBN 0-8103-3490-9). Gale.

Blackburn, Henry, jt. ed. see Prineas, Ronald J.

Blackburn, Jack & Busman, Gloria. Understanding Unions in the Public Sector. (Policy & Practice Publication). 167p. 1977. 6.00 (ISBN 0-89215-079-3). U Cal LA Indus Rel.

Blackburn, Jack E. & Powell, W. Conrad. One at a Time All at Once: The Creative Teacher's Guide to Individualized Instruction Without Anarchy. LC 75-21174. 1976. 14.95 (ISBN 0-673-16404-7); pap. 12.95 (ISBN 0-673-16403-9). Scott F.

Blackburn, James A., ed. Spectral Analysis: Methods & Techniques. 304p. 1970. 65.00 (ISBN 0-8247-1045-2). Dekker.

Blackburn, Jeanne M. & Seniz, Refah. Say It in Turkish. (Orig.). pap. 2.50 (ISBN 0-486-20821-4). Dover.

Blackburn, John, jt. auth. see Dunfee, Thomas.

Blackburn, John D., jt. auth. see Getman, Julius G.

Blackburn, John D., et al. Legal Environment of Business: Public Law & Regulation. 1982. 27.50x (ISBN 0-256-02480-4). Irwin.

Blackburn, Joyce. The Bloody Summer of Seventeen Forty-Two: A Colonial Boy's Journal. (Illus.). 64p. (gr. 5-8). 1985. pap. 4.25 (ISBN 0-930803-00-0). Fort Frederica.

--James Edward Oglethorpe. LC 82-23498. 144p. 1983. Repr. 8.95 (ISBN 0-396-08158-4). Dodd.

Blackburn, Kate & McDonald, Agnes. Four North Carolina Women Poets. Bayes, Ronald H., ed. LC 82-62747. 84p. 1982. pap. 7.95 (ISBN 0-932662-42-0). St Andrews NC.

Blackburn, Keith. Tutor. (Organization in Schools Ser.). 1975. text ed. 16.95x (ISBN 0-435-80079-5); pap. text ed. 11.00x (ISBN 0-435-80080-9). Heinemann Ed.

Blackburn, Laurie & Taylor, Marcus. Pocket Guide: CP-M. (Pitman Programming Pocket Guides Ser.). 64p. (Orig.). 1984. pap. 6.95 (ISBN 0-273-02136-2). Pitman Pub MA.

--Pocket Guide: UNIX. (Pitman Programming Pocket Guides Ser.). 64p. 1984. pap. 6.95 (ISBN 0-273-02106-0). Pitman Pub MA.

Blackburn, Lois H. A Handbook for Planning & Conducting Tennis Tournaments. rev. ed. (Illus.). 1981. pap. 4.50 (ISBN 0-938822-04-7). USTA.

Blackburn, Lois J. Florida Food Fare: & Food for Thought. (Illus.). 120p. (Orig.). 1980. pap. 5.00 (ISBN 0-938910-00-0). Pecalhen.

Blackburn, Lorraine see Brewton, John E.

Blackburn, Lorraine A., jt. ed. see Brewton, John E.

Blackburn, Mark, et al. Early Medieval Coins from Lincoln & Its Shire, c770-1100, Vol. VI. (Archaeology of Lincoln Ser.). 46p. 1983. pap. text ed. 13.00x (ISBN 0-906780-26-8, Pub. by Coun Brit Archaelogy England). Humanities.

Blackburn, Michael, et al, eds. Stand One: Winners of the Stand Magazine Short Story Competition. 208p. 1984. 18.95 (ISBN 0-575-03516-1, Pub. by Gollanez). David & Charles.

Blackburn, N. & Huppert, B. Finite Groups. (Grundlerhen der Mathematischen Wissenschaften Ser.: Vol. 242). 550p. 1982. lib. bdg. 72.00 (ISBN 0-387-10632-4). Springer-Verlag.

Blackburn, N., jt. auth. see Huppert, B.

Blackburn, Norma D. Legal Secretaryship. 2nd ed. (Illus.). 400p. 1981. text ed. 21.95 (ISBN 0-13-528927-0). P-H.

Blackburn, Paul. The Collected Poems of Paul Blackburn. Jarolim, Edith, et al, eds. (Persea Lamplighter Ser.). 400p. 1985. 37.50 (ISBN 0-89255-086-4). Persea Bks.

--Early Selected Y Mas: Collected Poems, 1949-1966. Kelly, Robert, ed. 130p. (Orig.). 1977. pap. 5.00 (ISBN 0-87685-120-0). Black Sparrow.

--Halfway down the Coast. LC 75-20727. (Illus.). 64p. 1975. 6.00 (ISBN 0-913142-10-7); pap. 3.50 (ISBN 0-913142-09-3). Mulch Pr.

--The Journals. Kelly, Robert, ed. 160p. (Orig.). 1977. pap. 5.00 (ISBN 0-87685-239-8). Black Sparrow.

Blackburn, Paul, tr. Peire Vidal. LC 72-83856. (Illus.). 6.00 (ISBN 0-913142-02-6). Mulch Pr.

--Proensa: An Anthology of Troubador Poetry. LC 75-7466. 1978. 29.50x (ISBN 0-520-02985-2). U of Cal Pr.

Blackburn, Paul, tr. see Lorca, Federico G.

Blackburn, Paul, et al, trs. see Bishop, Elizabeth & Brasil, Emanuel.

Blackburn, Phil, et al. Technology, Economic Growth & the Labour Process. LC 84-22849. 272p. 1985. 29.95 (ISBN 0-312-79001-5). St Martin.

Blackburn, R. M., ed. see Stewart, Alexander, et al.

Blackburn, Robert T., jt. auth. see Risenhoover, Morris.

Blackburn, Robert T., jt. ed. see Baldwin, Roger G.

Blackburn, Robin, ed. Explosion in the Subcontinent: India, Pakistan, Bangladesh & Ceylon. 10.00 (ISBN 0-8446-5160-5). Peter Smith.

--Revolution & Class Struggle: A Reader in Marxist Politics. LC 77-1640. 1978. text ed. 25.25x (ISBN 0-391-00712-2). Humanities.

Blackburn, Roderic H. Cherry Hill: The History & Collections of a Van Rensselaer Family. LC 75-44844. (Illus.). 176p. 1976. 15.00 (ISBN 0-943366-00-3); pap. 9.00 (ISBN 0-943366-01-1). Hist-Cherry Hill.

Blackburn, Roderic H., jt. auth. see Piwonka, Ruth.

Blackburn, S., ed. Amino Acid Determination: Methods & Techniques. 1978. 65.00 (ISBN 0-8247-6349-1). Dekker.

Blackburn, Simon. Spreading the Words: Groundings in the Philosophy of Language. (Illus.). 1984. 32.00x (ISBN 0-19-824650-1). Oxford U Pr.

Blackburn, Simon, ed. Meaning, Reference, & Necessity: New Studies in Semantics. LC 74-31785. pap. 55.00 (ISBN 0-317-26065-0, 2024425). Bks Demand UMI.

Blackburn, Stanley. Protein Sequence Determination: Methods & Techniques. LC 77-13046. pap. 75.30 (ISBN 0-317-08354-6, 2055410). Bks Demand UMI.

Blackburn, T. H., jt. auth. see Fenchel, T.

Blackburn, Thomas. The Holy Stone. LC 83-45710. Repr. of 1954 ed. 16.00 (ISBN 0-404-20032-X). AMS Pr.

--The Price of an Eye. LC 73-20900. 170p. 1974. Repr. of 1961 ed. lib. bdg. 24.75x (ISBN 0-8371-5869-9, BLPE). Greenwood.

--Robert Browning: A Study of His Poetry. 210p. 1973. Repr. of 1967 ed. 22.50x (ISBN 0-7130-0083-X, Pub. by Woburn Pr England). Biblio Dist.

Blackburn, Thomas C., jt. auth. see Hudson, Travis.

Blackburn, Thomas C., ed. December's Child: A Book of Chumash Oral Narratives. LC 74-27284. 360p. 1976. 22.50 (ISBN 0-520-02930-5); pap. 5.95 (ISBN 0-520-04088-0). U of Cal Pr.

Blackburn, Thomas C., jt. ed. see Great Basin Foundation.

Blackburn, Vernon, ed. see Steevens, George W.

Blackburn, William. Duke Miscellany: Narrative & Verse of the Sixties. LC 74-142290. Repr. of 1970 ed. cancelled (ISBN 0-8357-9102-5, 2017885). Bks Demand UMI.

Blackburn, William, ed. see Hyman, Mac.

Blackburn, William M. William Farel & the Story of the Swiss Reform. Date not set. Repr. of 1865 ed. 40.00 (ISBN 0-404-19870-8). AMS Pr.

Blackburn, William M., ed. Duke Miscellany: Narrative & Verse of the Sixties. LC 74-142280. viii, 248p. 1970. 16.75 (ISBN 0-8223-0242-X). Duke.

--Under Twenty-Five: Duke Narrative & Verse, 1945-1962: A Collection of Short Stories & Verse by Sixteen Duke Authors. LC 63-9005. 240p. 1963. 10.75 (ISBN 0-8223-0349-3). Duke.

Blackburn, William W. Young Calvin in Paris: Or the Scholar & the Cripple. LC 83-45602. Date not set. Repr. of 1868 ed. 30.00 (ISBN 0-404-19869-4). AMS Pr.

Blackburne, Joseph H. Blackburne's Chess Games. Graham, P. Anderson, ed. (Illus.). 1979. pap. 6.95 (ISBN 0-486-23857-1). Dover.

Blackeney, Jay D. The Children of Anthi. 256p. 1985. pap. 2.75 (ISBN 0-441-10399-5). Ace Bks.

Blacker, Carmen. The Catalpa Bow: A Study of Shamanistic Practices in Japan. 376p. 1982. pap. 9.95 (ISBN 0-04-398006-6). Allen Unwin.

--Japanese Enlightenment. (University of Cambridge Oriental Pubns). 1964. 34.50 (ISBN 0-521-04267-4). Cambridge U Pr.

Blacker, Carmen, jt. ed. see Loewe, Michael.

Blacker, Charles P. Eugenics: Galton & After. LC 78-20452. 1981. Repr. of 1952 ed. 25.00 (ISBN 0-88355-832-7). Hyperion Conn.

Blacker, Coit D., jt. ed. see Bellany, Ian.

Blacker, Coit D., ed. see Stanford Arms Control Group.

Blacker, Frank & Shimmin, Sylvia. Applying Psychology in Organizations. 160p. 1984. pap. 5.95 (ISBN 0-416-33680-9, NO. 9180). Methuen Inc.

Blacker, Harry. Just Like It Was: Memoirs of the Middle East. (Illus.). 192p. 1974. 14.50x (ISBN 0-85303-178-9, Pub. by Vallentine Mitchell England). Biblio Dist.

Blacker, Harry see Nero, pseud.

Blacker, Irwin R., ed. Old West in Fact. 1962. 17.95 (ISBN 0-8392-1081-7). Astor-Honor.

--Old West in Fiction. 1961. 17.95 (ISBN 0-8392-1082-5). Astor-Honor.

Blacker, Terence, jt. auth. see Planner, Nigel.

Blackerby, Hubert C. Blacks in Blue & Gray: Afro-American Service in the Civil War. LC 77-94485. (Illus.). 1979. 10.00 (ISBN 0-916620-15-8). Portals Pr.

Blackert, Wesley J., jt. auth. see Arndt, Heinz W.

Blackett, tr. see Hitler, Adolph.

Blackett, D. W. Elementary Topology: A Combinatorial & Algebraic Approach. 1982. 22.00 (ISBN 0-12-103060-1). Acad Pr.

Blackett, Patrick M. Studies of War: Nuclear & Conventional. LC 78-16364. (Illus.). 1978. Repr. of 1962 ed. lib. bdg. 27.50x (ISBN 0-313-20575-2, BLSW). Greenwood.

Blackett, R. J. Building an Antislavery Wall: Black Americans in the Atlantic Abolitionist Movement, 1830 to 1860. LC 82-21724. 264p. 1983. text ed. 25.00x (ISBN 0-8071-1082-5). La State U Pr.

Blackett, Ruth & Millhollin, Bonnie. Apple Cellar. Shreves, Kathey, ed. (Illus.). 102p. 1981. 5.95 (ISBN 0-940158-05-1). Zucchini Patch.

--Country Cellar. Shreves, Kathey, ed. (Illus.). 114p. 1981. spiral bdg. 5.95 (ISBN 0-940158-01-9). Zucchini Patch.

Blackett, Ruth, ed. see Sherves, Kathey L. & Millhollin, Bonnie.

Blackett-Ord, Mark. Hell-Fire Duke: The Life of the Duke of Wharton. 1983. 17.95 (ISBN 0-946041-02-4, Pub. by Salem Hse Ltd). Merrimack Pub Cir.

Blackey, Robert. Revolutions & Revolutionists: A Comprehensive Guide to the Literature. LC 82-6653. (War-Peace Bibliography Ser.: No. 17). 488p. 1982. lib. bdg. 55.75 (ISBN 0-87436-330-6). ABC-Clio.

Blackey, Robert & Paynton, Clifford. Revolution & the Revolutionary Ideal. 256p. 1976. 14.50x (ISBN 0-87073-986-7). Schenkman Bks Inc.

Blackford, Bland, et al. Bassett Hall: The Williamsburg Home of Mr. & Mrs. John D. Rockefeller, Jr. (Illus.). 48p. (Orig.). 1984. pap. 3.95 (ISBN 0-87935-107-1). Williamsburg.

Blackford, Jason C. Ohio Corporation Law, 2 vols. (Baldwin's Ohio Practice Ser.). 2902p. 1982. Set. annual 135.00 (ISBN 0-8322-0007-7). Banks-Baldwin.

Blackford, Mansel G. Pioneering a Modern Small Business: Wakefield Seafoods & the Alaskan Frontier. Porter, Glenn, ed. LC 77-7794. (Industrial Development & the Social Fabric Ser.: Vol. 6). 222p. 1979. 29.50 (ISBN 0-686-74079-3). Jai Pr.

--The Politics of Business in California, 1890-1920. LC 76-27319. 235p. 1977. 12.50x (ISBN 0-8142-0259-4). Ohio St U Pr.

--A Portrait Cast in Steel: Buckeye International & Columbus, Ohio, 1881-1980. LC 82-6114. (Contributions in Economics & Economic History Ser.: No. 49). (Illus.). xviii, 225p. 1982. lib. bdg. 35.00 (ISBN 0-313-23393-4, BPC/). Greenwood.

Blackhall, David S. This House Had Windows. 1962. 7.95 (ISBN 0-8392-1115-5). Astor-Honor.

Blackham, E. Donnell, jt. auth. see Keeler, J. J.

Blackham, Garth J. & Silberman, Adolph. Modification of Child & Adolescent Behavior. 3rd ed. 1979. pap. text ed. write for info. (ISBN 0-534-00725-2). Wadsworth Pub.

Blackham, H. Moral & Religious Education in County Primary Schools. 6.00x (ISBN 0-85633-115-5, Pub. by NFER Nelson UK). Taylor & Francis.

Blackham, H. J. The Fable As Literature. LC 84-21674. 240p. 1985. 36.00 (ISBN 0-485-11278-7, Pub. by Athlone Pr Ltd). Longwood Pub Group.

--Six Existentialist Thinkers. 179p. 1983. pap. 8.95 (ISBN 0-7100-4611-1). Routledge & Kegan.

Blackham, H. J., et al. Objections to Humanism. LC 73-16796. 128p. 1974. Repr. of 1963 ed. lib. bdg. 15.00x (ISBN 0-8371-7235-7, BLOH). Greenwood.

Blackham, Robert L. Incomparable India: Tradition: Superstitions: Truth. (Illus.). 302p. 1981. Repr. text ed. 36.25x (ISBN 0-391-02438-8, Pub. by Concept India). Humanities.

Black Hawk. Black Hawk: An Autobiography. Jackson, Donald, ed. LC 55-11217. (Illus.). 177p. 1964. pap. 4.95x (ISBN 0-252-72325-2). U of Ill Pr.

Blackhurst, A. Edward & Berdine, William H. An Introduction to Special Education. 2nd ed. text ed. 24.95 (ISBN 0-316-09891-4); tchr's. ed. avail. (ISBN 0-316-09892-2). Little.

Blackhurst, Hector, ed. Africa Bibliography, 1984. rev. ed. 200p. (Orig.). 1985. pap. 22.00 (ISBN 0-7190-1823-4, Pub. by Manchester Univ Pr). Longwood Pub Group.

Blackhurst, Richard & Tumlir, Jan. Trade Relations Under Flexible Exchange Rates. (Studies in International Trade: No. 8). 80p. 1981. pap. 8.00 (ISBN 0-686-69637-9, G143, GATT). Unipub.

Blackhurst, W. E. Afterglow: A Collection of Short Stories & Poems. 1972. 10.00 (ISBN 0-87012-127-8). McClain.

--Mixed Harvest. 1972. 10.00 (ISBN 0-87012-082-4). McClain.

--Of Men & a Mighty Mountain. 1965. 10.00 (ISBN 0-87012-007-7). McClain.

--Riders of the Flood. (Illus.). 1954. 8.00 (ISBN 0-87012-008-5). McClain.

--Sawdust in Your Eyes. 1963. 10.00 (ISBN 0-87012-006-9). McClain.

--Your Train Ride Through History. (Illus.). 1968. pap. 3.00 (ISBN 0-87012-009-3). McClain.

Blackie And Son. Victorian Cabinet-Maker's Assistant. (Illus.). 1970. pap. 10.00 (ISBN 0-486-22353-1). Dover.

Blackie, C. Geographical Etymology: A Dictionary of Place-Names Giving Their Derivations. LC 68-17916. 1968. Repr. of 1887 ed. 35.00x (ISBN 0-8103-3882-3). Gale.

Blackie, John. Inside the Primary School. LC 71-163327. (Illus.). 1971. pap. 2.25 (ISBN 0-8052-0311-7). Schocken.

Blackie, John S. Four Phases of Morals: Socrates, Aristotle, Christianity, Utilitarianism. 59.95 (ISBN 0-8490-0186-2). Gordon Pr.

--The Language & Literature of the Scottish Highlands. 1979. Repr. of 1876 ed. lib. bdg. 40.00 (ISBN 0-8495-0402-3). Arden Lib.

--The Language & Literature of the Scottish Highlands. LC 73-3441. 1973. lib. bdg. 30.00 (ISBN 0-8414-1776-8). Folcroft.

--Life of Burns. LC 75-30844. (English Literature Ser, No. 33). 1975. lib. bdg. 43.95x (ISBN 0-8383-2102-X). Haskell.

--Life of Robert Burns. 1979. Repr. of 1888 ed. lib. bdg. 20.00 (ISBN 0-8495-0389-2). Arden Lib.

--Life of Robert Burns. 1973. Repr. of 1888 ed. 10.00 (ISBN 0-8274-1476-5). R West.

--Scottish Song. LC 70-144563. Repr. of 1889 ed. 24.00 (ISBN 0-404-08579-2). AMS Pr.

--The Wisdom of Goethe. LC 74-1443. 1883. lib. bdg. 30.00 (ISBN 0-8414-9918-7). Folcroft.

Blackie, M. J., jt. auth. see Dent, J. B.

Blackie, M. J. & Dent, J. B., eds. Information Systems for Agriculture. (Illus.). 176p. 1979. 27.75 (ISBN 0-85334-829-4, Pub. by Elsevier Applied Sci England). Elsevier.

Blackie, Margery G. The Patient, Not the Cure: The Challenge of Homeopathy. LC 78-54659. (Illus.). 1978. pap. 4.95 (ISBN 0-912800-49-6). Woodbridge Pr.

Blacking, John. How Musical Is Man? LC 72-6710. (John Danz Lecture Ser). (Illus.). 132p. 1973. 16.00x (ISBN 0-295-95218-0, WP72); pap. 7.95x (ISBN 0-295-95338-1); tapes 17.50 (ISBN 0-295-75510-5); c-60 cassette 17.50 (ISBN 0-295-75517-2). U of Wash Pr.

Blacking, John, ed. The Anthropology of the Body. 1978. 55.00 (ISBN 0-12-103250-7). Acad Pr.

Blacking, John & Kealiinohomoku, Joann W., eds. The Performing Arts: Music & Dance. (World Anthropology Ser.). 1979. text ed. 30.00x (ISBN 90-279-7870-0). Mouton.

Blackistone, Mick, jt. auth. see McLendon, Charles.

Blackith, R. E., tr. see Gabe, M.

Blackledge, David & Hunt, Barry. Sociological Interpretations of Education. LC 85-4145. 352p. 1985. 29.00 (ISBN 0-7099-0647-1, Pub. by Croom Helm Ltd); pap. 13.50 (ISBN 0-7099-0676-5). Longwood Pub Group.

Blackledge, Ethel H. & Blackledge, Walter L. The Job You Want - How to Get It. (gr. 9-12). 1983. text ed. 3.25 wkbk. (ISBN 0-538-11260-3, K26). SW Pub.

Blackledge, Walter L., jt. auth. see Blackledge, Ethel H.

Blackler, F. H. & Brown, C. A. Whatever Happened to Shell's New Philosophy of Management? 192p. 1980. text ed. 27.00x (ISBN 0-566-00306-6). Gower Pub Co.

Blackler, Frank. Social Psychology & Developing Countries. LC 83-6560. 297p. 1984. 39.95x (ISBN 0-471-90192-X, Pub. by Wiley-Interscience). Wiley.

Blackley, Becky. The Autoharp Book. LC 83-81145. (Illus.). 256p. (Orig.). 1983. pap. 19.95x (ISBN 0-912827-01-7). I A D Pubns.

--Pieces of Eight. (Illus.). 52p. (Orig.). 1985. pap. 7.95 (ISBN 0-912827-04-1). I A D Pubns.

Blackley, Becky, ed. The Care & Feeding of the Autoharp, Vol. 1. LC 82-108061. (Illus.). 103p. (Orig.). 1981. pap. 10.00 (ISBN 0-912827-00-9). I A D Pubns.

--The Care & Feeding of the Autoharp, Vol. 2. LC 82-108061. (Illus.). 93p. (Orig.). 1984. pap. 10.00 (ISBN 0-912827-02-5). I A D Pubns.

--The Care & Feeding of the Autoharp, Vol. 3. LC 82-108061. (Illus.). 93p. (Orig.). 1984. pap. 10.00 (ISBN 0-912827-03-3). I A D Pubns.

Blackley, Becky, ed. see Beck, Stevie, et al.

Blackley, D. C. Emulsion Polymerisation: Theory & Practice. (Illus.). 566p. 1975. 48.00 (ISBN 0-85334-627-5, Pub. by Elsevier Applied Sci England). Elsevier.

--Synthetic Rubbers: Their Chemistry & Technology. (Illus.). 372p. 1983. 72.25 (ISBN 0-85334-152-4, I-462-82, Pub. by Elsevier Applied Sci England). Elsevier.

Blacklock, Craig, jt. auth. see Blacklock, Les.

Blacklock, Craig, jt. auth. see Link, Mike.

Blacklock, Fran, et al. Our Minnesota. (Illus.). 128p. 1978. 18.95 (ISBN 0-318-04122-7); pap. 11.95 (ISBN 0-89658-027-X). Voyageur Pr Inc.

Blacklock, Gene W., jt. auth. see Rappole, John H.

Blacklock, Gladys. Modern Winemaking Techniques. (Illus.). 97p. Date not set. pap. 4.95 (ISBN 0-900841-71-0, Pub. by Aztex Corp). Argus Bks.

Blacklock, Les. Ain't Nature Grand. (Illus.). 131p. 1980. 10.95 (ISBN 0-89658-009-1). Voyageur Pr Inc.

--Meet My Psychiatrist. (Illus.). 111p. 1977. pap. 12.95 (ISBN 0-318-04121-9); 7.95 (ISBN 0-89658-003-2). Voyageur Pr Inc.

Blacklock, Les & Blacklock, Craig. Minnesota Wild. (Illus.). 135p. 1983. 29.95 (ISBN 0-89658-029-6). Voyageur Pr Inc.

Blacklock, Thomas. Poems of Thomas Blacklock. 3rd ed. Repr. of 1756 ed. 13.50 (ISBN 0-404-08553-9). AMS Pr.

Blacklow, Robert S., et al, eds. MacBryde's Signs & Symptoms: Applied Pathologic Physiology & Clinical Interpretation. 6th ed. (Illus.). 864p. 1983. text ed. 42.50 (ISBN 0-397-52094-8, 65-00482, Lippincott Medical). Lippincott.

Blackman, Brenda. One Hundred One Ways to Meet Your Lover. 65p. (Orig.). 1985. pap. 5.00 (ISBN 0-9615074-0-3). B Blackman.

Blackman, D. E. & Sanger, J. D., eds. Contemporary Research in Behavioral Pharmacology. LC 77-16206. (Illus.). 520p. 1978. 49.50x (ISBN 0-306-31061-9, Plenum Pr). Plenum Pub.

Blackman, D. E., jt. ed. see Sanger, D. J.

Blackman, Derek. Operant Conditioning: An Experimental Analysis of Behaviour. LC 74-18545. 247p. 1974. pap. 12.50 (ISBN 0-416-81480-8, NO. 2089). Methuen Inc.

Blackman, E. V. Miami & Dade County, Florida: Its Settlement, Progress & Achievement. LC 77-88898. (Florida County History Ser.). (Illus.). 1977. Repr. of 1921 ed. 22.50 (ISBN 0-913122-12-2). Mickler Hse.

Blackman, Edward B, jt. auth. see Abrams, Edwin D.

Blackman, Edwin C. Marcion & His Influence. LC 77-84695. Repr. of 1948 ed. 18.50 (ISBN 0-404-16103-0). AMS Pr.

Blackman, Emily C. History of Susquehanna County, Pennsylvania. LC 78-110486. (Illus.). 685p. 1980. Repr. of 1873 ed. 30.00 (ISBN 0-8063-7979-0). Regional.

Blackman, Everett. Astrology: Worlds Visible & Invisible. 100p. 1974. 5.00 (ISBN 0-86690-059-4, 1104-03). Am Fed Astrologers.

--So You Want to Be President. 88p. 1972. 2.00 (ISBN 0-86690-060-8, 1024-01). Am Fed Astrologers.

Blackman, Irving L. The Book of Tax Knowledge. 2nd ed. LC 82-24369. 595p. 1984. Repr. o. p. 60.00 (ISBN 0-932648-36-3). Boardroom.

--The Complete Guide to Building Your Automobile Deductions - Legally. LC 84-102959. (Special Report Ser.: No. 6). (Illus.). 51p. 1983. pap. 15.00 (ISBN 0-317-13354-3). Blackman Kallick.

--The Complete Guide to Building Your Entertainment Deductions - Legally. LC 84-102962. (Special Report Ser.). Date not set. pap. 15.00 (ISBN 0-317-27337-X). Blackman Kallick.

--The Complete Guide to Building Your Entertainment Deductions Legally. (Special Report Ser.). 43p. 1982. pap. 15.00 (ISBN 0-916181-06-5). Blackman Kallick.

--The Complete Guide to Building Your Travel Deductions: Legally. (BK Special Report Ser.). 46p. 1982. pap. 15.00 (ISBN 0-916181-07-3). Blackman Kallick.

--Divorce, Taxes & You. (Special Report Ser.). 49p. 1982. pap. 17.00 (ISBN 0-916181-04-9). Blackman Kallick.

--Free Life Insurance: For the High-Bracket Taxpayer. (Special Report Ser.). 53p. 1982. pap. 19.00 (ISBN 0-916181-13-8). Blackman Kallick.

--Golden Handcuffs: Executive Riches from Tax Savings. (Special Report Ser.). 57p. 1984. pap. 21.00 (ISBN 0-916181-19-7). Blackman Kallick.

--How IRA Can Make You a Millionaire: A Tax Thriller. (Special Report Ser.). 48p. 1982. pap. 14.00 (ISBN 0-916181-06-5). Blackman Kallick.

--How to Take Money Out of Your Closely Held Corporation. (Special Report Ser.). 53p. 1982. pap. 21.00 (ISBN 0-916181-09-X); cassette 68.00 (ISBN 0-916181-23-5). Blackman Kallick.

--How to Transfer Your Corporation to the Next Generation Tax Free. (Special Report Ser.). 47p. 1982. pap. 19.00 (ISBN 0-916181-10-3). Blackman Kallick.

--How to Value Your Business for Tax Purposes & Win the Tax Game. LC 84-102879. (Special Report Ser.: No. 2). 57p. 1983. pap. 19.00 (ISBN 0-317-13355-1). Blackman Kallick.

--How to Value Your Oil Jobbership for Tax Purposes. 91p. 1981. 65.00 (ISBN 0-318-16169-9, F-4); members 50.00 (ISBN 0-318-16170-2). Petro Mktg Ed Found.

--Investing in Real Estate: Tax Gold. (Special Report Ser.). 45p. 1983. pap. 19.00 (ISBN 0-916181-15-4). Blackman Kallick.

--Investor's Tax Survival Guide. (Special Report Ser.). 80p. 1983. pap. 21.00 (ISBN 0-318-01153-0). Blackman Kallick.

--The New Depreciation Rules: A Tax Gold Mine. (Special Report Ser.). 56p. 1982. pap. 17.00 (ISBN 0-916181-03-0). Blackman Kallick.

--A New Tax Superstar: S Corporation. (Special Report Ser.). 57p. 1983. pap. 17.00 (ISBN 0-916181-16-2). Blackman Kallick.

--Section Four Hundred One (k)...Everybody Wins, Employer & Employee. (BK Special Reports Ser.). 69p. 1984. pap. 23.00 (ISBN 0-916181-25-1). Blackman Kallick.

--Starting a Business: One Hundred Two Tax-Saving Ideas to Make You Rich. (Special Report Ser.). 53p. 1983. pap. 18.00 (ISBN 0-916181-17-0). Blackman Kallick.

--A Tax Bonanza for the Eighties. (Special Reports Ser.). 53p. 1982. pap. 15.00 (ISBN 0-916181-01-4). Blackman Kallick.

--A Tax Roadmap for Home Business Operators. (Special Report Ser.). 57p. 1983. 19.00 (ISBN 0-916181-18-9). Blackman Kallick.

--TEFRA: Opportunities Still Abound. (Special Report Ser.). 45p. 1982. pap. 16.00 (ISBN 0-916181-12-X). Blackman Kallick.

--Your Business-America's Best Tax Shelter. LC 84-102848. (Special Report Ser.: No. 1). 46p. 1981. pap. 21.00 (ISBN 0-916181-00-6). Blackman Kallick.

Blackman, Irving L. & Russ, Donald J., Jr. Pay Zero Estate Tax...The Super Trust Way. (BK Special Reports Ser.). 64p. 1984. pap. 21.00 (ISBN 0-916181-24-3). Blackman Kallick.

Blackman, Irving L., ed. see Wilson, Robert A.

Blackman, Irving L., ed. see Wood, Robert C.

Blackman, Dr. James. Medical Aspects of Developmental Disabilities in Children Birth to Three. Rev. 1st ed. LC 84-11128. 239p. 1984. 18.95 (ISBN 0-89443-553-1). Aspen Systems.

Blackman, John L. Presidential Seizure in Labor Disputes. LC 67-20871. (Wertheim Publications in Industrial Relations Ser). 1967. 20.00x (ISBN 0-674-70201-8). Harvard U Pr.

Blackman, Larry L., ed. Classics of Analytical Metaphysics. 536p. (Orig.). 1984. lib. bdg. 31.25 (ISBN 0-8191-3756-1); pap. text ed. 19.75 (ISBN 0-8191-3757-X). U Pr of Amer.

Blackman, Margaret B. During My Time: Florence Edenshaw Davidson, a Haida Woman. LC 82-8674. (Illus.). 192p. 1985. pap. 8.95 (ISBN 0-295-96219-4). U of Wash Pr.

Blackman, Margaret B. & Davidson, Florence E. During My Time: Florence Edenshaw Davidson, a Haida Woman. LC 82-8674. (Illus.). 192p. 1982. 19.95x (ISBN 0-295-95943-6). U of Wash Pr.

Blackman, Martin E. & Hochberg, Phillip R. Representing Professional Athletes & Teams 1983. (Nineteen Eighty-Two to Eighty-Three Copyrights, Trademarks & Literary Property Course Handbook Ser.). 1051p. 1983. pap. text ed. 35.00 (ISBN 0-686-68830-9, G4-3725). PLI.

Blackman, Maurice. Design of Real Time Applications. Authur Andersen & Co., ed. LC 74-26960. 265p. 1975. 59.95 (ISBN 0-471-07770-4, Pub. by Wiley-Interscience). Wiley.

Blackman, Murray. A Guide to Jewish Themes in American Fiction, 1940-1980. LC 80-24953. 271p. 1981. lib. bdg. 17.50 (ISBN 0-8108-1380-7). Scarecrow.

Blackman, Paul. The Kansas City Trivia Quiz, Vol. 1. Zoglin, Richard, ed. (American Metropolitan Area Trivia Quizzes). (Illus.). 1983. pap. 3.95 (ISBN 0-916399-00-1). Normandy Pubns.

Blackman, Paul H., jt. auth. see Phillips, Kevin P.

Blackman, Philip. Ethics of the Fathers. 166p. 1980. pap. 3.95 (ISBN 0-910818-15-0). Judaica Pr.

Blackman, Philip, tr The Mishnah, 7 vols. with index vol. 4050p. (Eng. & Hebrew.). 1962. 70.00 (ISBN 0-910818-00-2). Judaica Pr.

Blackman, R. B. & Tukey, J. W. Measurement of Power Spectra from the Point of View of Communications Engineering. 1958. pap. 5.00 (ISBN 0-486-60507-8). Dover.

Blackman, R. D. A Dictionary of Foreign Phrases & Classical Quotations. Repr. of 1893 ed. 25.00 (ISBN 0-686-20089-6). Quality Lib.

Blackman, R. D., ed. Composition & Style. 323p. 1981. Repr. of 1931 ed. lib. bdg. 20.00 (ISBN 0-89984-111-2). Century Bookbindery.

Blackman, R. L. & Eastop, V. F. Aphids on the World's Crops: An Identificaton Guide. 470p. 1985. text ed. 75.00x (ISBN 0-471-90426-0, Pub. by Wiley-Interscience). Wiley.

Blackman, R. L., et al. Insect Cytogenetics. LC 80-41700. (Royal Entomological Society of London Symposium Ser.). 278p. 1981. 91.95x (ISBN 0-470-27126-4). Halsted Pr.

Blackman, Richard. Follow the Leaders. 1979. 3.95 (ISBN 0-346-12382-8). Cornerstone.

Blackman, Sheldon, jt. auth. see Goldstein, Kenneth M.

Blackman, William. Seascape Painting. (Illus.). 80p. (Orig.). 1985. pap. price not set (ISBN 0-917121-03-1, 40-101). M F Weber Co.

Blackman, William F. History of Orange County, Florida. LC 73-75939. (Florida County History Ser.,). (Illus.). 460p. 1973. Repr. of 1927 ed. 27.50 (ISBN 0-913122-03-3). Mickler Hse.

--The Making of Hawaii: A Study in Social Evolution. 2nd ed. LC 75-35175. Repr. of 1906 ed. 22.50 (ISBN 0-404-14204-4). AMS Pr.

Blackman, Winifred S. Fellahin of Upper Egypt: Their Religious, Social & Industrial Life. new ed. 332p. 1968. 32.50x (ISBN 0-7146-1637-0, F Cass Co). Biblio Dist.

Blackmar, Charles B., jt. auth. see Devitt, Edward J.

Blackmar, F. Spanish Colonization in the Southwest. 1976. lib. bdg. 59.95 (ISBN 0-8490-2648-2). Gordon Pr.

Blackmar, F. W. Spanish Colonization in the Southwest. pap. 9.00 (ISBN 0-685-92932-9). Johnson Repr.

Blackmar, Frank W. History of Human Society. 1926. 20.00 (ISBN 0-8482-7381-8). Norwood Edns.

--The Life of Charles Robinson: The First State Governor of Kansas. facsimile ed. LC 70-169751. (Select Bibliographies Reprint Ser). Repr. of 1901 ed. 27.50 (ISBN 0-8369-5971-X). Ayer Co Pubs.

--Spanish Colonization in the Southwest. LC 78-63794. (Johns Hopkins University. Studies in the Social Sciences. Eighth Ser. 1890: 4). Repr. of 1890 ed. 11.50 (ISBN 0-404-61059-5). AMS Pr.

--Spanish Institutions of the Southwest. LC 78-64254. (Johns Hopkins University. Studies in the Social Sciences. Extra Volumes: 10). Repr. of 1891 ed. 24.50 (ISBN 0-404-61358-6). AMS Pr.

--Spanish Institutions of the Southwest. (Beautiful Rio Grande Classics Ser.). (Illus.). 460p. 1983. Repr. of 1891 ed. 17.50 (ISBN 0-87380-117-2). Rio Grande.

Blackmer, Donald L. Unity in Diversity: Italian Communism & the Communist World. (Studies in Communism, Revisionism & Revolution). 1968. 35.00x (ISBN 0-262-02030-0). MIT Pr.

Blackmer, Donald L. & Kreigel, Annie. The International Role of the Communist Parties of Italy & France. (Harvard Studies in International Affairs: No. 32). 76p. 1984. pap. text ed. 7.25 (ISBN 0-8191-4041-4). U Pr of Amer.

Blackmer, Donald L. & Tarrow, Sidney, eds. Communism in Italy & France. 492p. 1975. 59.00x (ISBN 0-691-08724-5). Princeton U Pr.

Blackmer, Rollin C. The Lodge & the Craft. 1976. s.p. 7.95 (ISBN 0-88053-043-X). Macoy Pub.

Blackmon, Beverly S. & Dewsnap, James W. Clear Thinking, Clear Writing: Paragraphs under Control. 208p. 1982. pap. text ed. write for info (ISBN 0-534-01071-7). Wadsworth Pub.

Blackmore, ed. see Lawrence Urdang Associates, Ltd.,.

Blackmore, Anauta, jt. auth. see Washburne, Heluiz.

Blackmore, D. K., et al. Some Observations on the Diseases of Brunus Edwardii. (Illus.). 1983. pap. 2.50 (ISBN 0-912184-04-3). Synergistic Pr.

Blackmore, Howard L. English Pistols. (Illus.). 64p. 1985. 12.95 (ISBN 0-85368-712-9, Pub. by Arms & Armour). Sterling.

Blackmore, Jane. Hawkridge. 1976. pap. 1.95 (ISBN 0-441-31930-0). Ace Bks.

--Perilous Waters. 1981. pap. 1.50 (ISBN 0-440-17309-4). Dell.

Blackmore, John. The Gibraltar Dialogues: A Philosophy for the Space Age. LC 80-5527. 249p. 1980. lib. bdg. 22.75 (ISBN 0-8191-1125-2); pap. text ed. 12.00 (ISBN 0-8191-1126-0). U Pr of Amer.

Blackmore, Josiah H. & Weissenberger, Glen. Anderson's Ohio Evidence, 1980-1982: Civil & Criminal, 2 vols. LC 82-238692. 660p. 1984. looseleaf 100.00. Anderson Pub Co.

Blackmore, Michael. Your Book of Watching Wildlife. (gr. 7 up). 1972. 5.25 (ISBN 0-571-08347-1). Transatlantic.

Blackmore, R. D. Lorna Doone. (Puffin Classics Ser.). 272p. 1984. pap. 2.25 (ISBN 0-14-035021-7, Puffin). Penguin.

Blackmore, R. D see Swan, D. K.

Blackmore, R. L. Advice to a Young Poet. LC 79-77089. 216p. 1969. 18.00 (ISBN 0-8386-7348-1). Fairleigh Dickinson.

Blackmore, R. W., tr. Duties of Parish Priests in the Russian Orthodox Church. Repr. of 1845 ed. 15.00 (ISBN 0-686-01291-7). Eastern Orthodox.

Blackmore, Richard. Lorna Doone. 345p. 1981. Repr. PLB 18.95 (ISBN 0-89966-350-8). Buccaneer Bks.

Blackmore, Richard D. Christowell: A Dartmoor Tale, 3 vols in 2. LC 79-3327. Repr. of 1882 ed. 84.50 set (ISBN 0-404-61783-2). AMS Pr.

--Lorna Doone. (Classics Ser). (gr. 8 up). 1967. pap. 2.50 (ISBN 0-8049-0149-X, CL-149). Airmont.

--Lorna Doone. 378p. 1981. Repr. PLB 18.95x (ISBN 0-89967-024-5). Harmony Raine.

--Mary Anerley: A Yorkshire Tale, 3 vols in 2. LC 79-8238. Repr. of 1880 ed. 84.50 set (ISBN 0-404-61786-7). AMS Pr.

--Perlycross: A Tale of the Western Hills, 3 vols. in 1. LC 79-8239. Repr. of 1894 ed. 44.50 (ISBN 0-404-61790-5). AMS Pr.

--Slain by the Doones, & Other Stories. facs. ed. LC 74-86137. (Short Story Index Reprint Ser.). 1895. 17.00 (ISBN 0-8369-3041-X). Ayer Co Pubs.

Blackmore, Robert. Powys to Knight: The Letters of John Cowper Powys to G.R. Wilson Knight. 144p. 1983. text ed. 18.50x (ISBN 0-900821-48-5). Humanities.

Blackmore, Ruth. Index to American Reference Books Annual, 1980-1984: A Cumulative Index to Subjects, Authors, & Titles. 400p. 1984. lib. bdg. 45.00 (ISBN 0-87287-431-1). Libs Unl.

Blackmore, Simon A. The Riddles of Hamlet & the Newest Answers. LC 73-4188. 1973. lib. bdg. 42.50 (ISBN 0-8414-1762-8). Folcroft.

Blackmore, Stephen. Bee Orchids. (Shire Natural History Ser.: No. 3). (Orig.). 1985. pap. 3.95 (ISBN 0-85263-745-4, Pub. by Shire Pubns England). Seven Hills Bks.

--Buttercups. (Shire Natural History Ser.: No. 6). (Orig.). 1985. pap. 3.95 (ISBN 0-85263-763-2, Pub. by Shire Pubns England). Seven Hills Bks.

Blackmore, Stephen, jt. ed. see Tootill, Elizabeth.

Blackmore, Susan J. Beyond the Body. 272p. pap. 5.95 (ISBN 0-586-08428-2, Pub. by Granada England). Academy Chi Pubs.

Blackmore, Thaung. Catalogue of the Burney Parabaiks in the India Office Library. 136p. 1985. 30.00 (ISBN 0-7123-0042-2, Pub. by British Lib). Longwood Pub Group.

Blackmore, Vivian, retold by. Why Corn Is Golden: Stories about Plants. LC 82-17280. (Illus.). (gr. k-3). 1984. 12.45i (ISBN 0-316-54820-0). Little.

Blackmun, Ora. Western North Carolina: Its Mountains & Its People to 1880. 2nd ed. LC 76-53030. (Illus., Orig.). 1977. 12.95 (ISBN 0-913239-32-1); pap. 5.95 (ISBN 0-913239-31-3). Appalach Consortium.

Blackmur, R. P. Dirty Hands; or The True-Born Censor. LC 76-46924. 1930. lib. bdg. 10.00 (ISBN 0-8414-3269-4). Folcroft.

--From Jordan's Delight. LC 73-16284. 1937. lib. bdg. 10.00 (ISBN 0-8414-9883-0). Folcroft.

--Henry Adams. Makowsky, Veronica A., ed. (Quality Paperbacks Ser.). 381p. 1984. pap. 10.95 (ISBN 0-306-80219-8). Da Capo.

--Language As Gesture. LC 80-28610. (Morningside Book Ser.). 448p. 1981. pap. 11.00x (ISBN 0-231-05295-2). Columbia U Pr.

--The Lion & the Honeycomb: Essays in Solicitude & Critique. LC 77-10875. 1977. Repr. of 1955 ed. lib. bdg. 24.75x (ISBN 0-8371-9799-6, BLLH). Greenwood.

--Poems of R. P. Blackmur. Donaghue, Denis, pref. by. LC 76-39598. 1977. 17.50x (ISBN 0-691-06335-4); pap. 6.95 (ISBN 0-691-01337-3). Princeton U Pr.

--Studies in Henry James. Makowsky, Veronica A., ed. LC 82-18911. 256p. 1983. 19.50 (ISBN 0-8112-0863-X); pap. 9.25 (ISBN 0-8112-0864-8, NDP552). New Directions.

Blackmur, R. P., ed. Henry Adams. LC 79-1812. 384p. 1980. 19.95 (ISBN 0-15-139997-2). HarBraceJ.

Blackmur, Richard P. Anni Mirabiles, Nineteen Twenty-One to Twenty-Five. LC 72-13511. 1974. Repr. of 1956 ed. lib. bdg. 12.00 (ISBN 0-8414-1196-4). Folcroft.

--The Double Agent. 11.50 (ISBN 0-8446-1080-1). Peter Smith.

--The Expense of Greatness. 11.50 (ISBN 0-8446-1079-8). Peter Smith.

--Expense of Greatness. Repr. of 1940 ed. 9.00x (ISBN 0-403-04062-0). Somerset Pub.

--Language As Gesture: Essays in Poetry. LC 77-10141. 1977. Repr. of 1952 ed. lib. bdg. 32.50x (ISBN 0-8371-9782-1, BLLG). Greenwood.

Blackmure, R. P. Selected Essays of R. P. Blackmure. Donoghue, Denis, ed. 17.50 (ISBN 0-88001-083-5). Ecco Pr.

Blacknall, Carolyn. Sally Ride: America's First Woman in Space. LC 84-12671. (Taking Part Ser.). (Illus.). 72p. (gr. 3 up). 1984. lib. bdg. 8.95 (ISBN 0-87518-260-7). Dillon.

Blackorby, C. & Primont, D. Duality, Separability & Functional Structure: Theory & Economic Applications. (Dynamic Economics Ser.: Vol. 2). 396p. 1978. 59.00 (ISBN 0-444-00235-9, North-Holland). Elsevier.

Blacksburg Group, ed. see Goldsbrough, Paul.

Blacksell, Mark & Gilg, Andrew. The Countryside: Planning & Change. (Resource Management Ser.: No. 2). (Illus.). 288p. (Orig.). 1981. text ed. 35.00x (ISBN 0-04-711008-2); pap. text ed. 17.95x (ISBN 0-04-711009-0). Allen Unwin.

Blackshaw, Kenneth, jt. auth. see Severinghaus, Sheldon.

Blackshear, P. J. & Klausner, R. D. Key References in Internal Medicine, 8 vols. 1982. pap. text ed. 115.00 (ISBN 0-443-08079-8). Churchill.

Blackshear, Perry J. Key References in Endocrinology: An Annotated Guide. LC 82-14662. (Key References in Internal Medicine Ser.: Vol. 5). 136p. 1982. pap. text ed. 15.00 (ISBN 0-443-08210-3). Churchill.

Blackson, Lorenzo D. The Rise & Progress of the Kingdoms of Light & Darkness. LC 72-78568. Repr. of 1867 ed. lib. bdg. 16.50 (ISBN 0-8398-0166-1). Irvington.

Blackstock, Charity. The Bitter Conquest. 14.95 (ISBN 0-317-27904-1, Pub. by Aeonian Pr). Amereon Ltd.

--Dewey Death. 272p. 1985. pap. 2.95 (ISBN 0-345-32509-5). Ballantine.

--A House Possessed. 222p. 1976. Repr. of 1962 ed. lib. bdg. 14.95x (ISBN 0-89244-077-5, Pub. by Queens Hse). Amereon Ltd.

--The Widow. 1978. pap. 1.95 (ISBN 0-505-51219-X, Pub. by Tower Bks). Dorchester Pub Co.

--The Woman in the Woods. 1978. pap. 1.75 (ISBN 0-8439-0568-9, Leisure Bks). Dorchester Pub Co.

Blackstock, L. S. Ruy Lopez: Breyer System. 1976. pap. 16.95 (ISBN 0-7134-3142-3, Pub. by Batsford England). David & Charles.

Blackstock, L. S., ed. see Korchnoi, Viktor.

Blackstock, Nelson, et al. Cointelpro: The FBI's Secret War on Political Freedom. Perkus, Cathy, ed. LC 75-34818. (Illus.). 160p. 1976. 16.00 (ISBN 0-913460-41-9, Dist. by Path Pr NY). Monad Pr.

Blackstock, Paul W. & Schaf, Frank, Jr. Intelligence, Espionage, Counterespionage & Covert Operations: A Guide to Information Sources. LC 74-11567. (International Relations Information Guide Ser.: Vol. 2). 1978. 60.00x (ISBN 0-8103-1323-5). Gale.

Blackstock, Paul W., tr. see Solzhenitsyn, Aleksandr.

Blackstone Associates. Paralegals & Administrative Assistants. 5.00 (ISBN 0-686-22354-3). Natl Dist Atty.

Blackstone, Bernard. The Consecrated Urn: An Interpretation of Keats in Terms of Growth & Form. LC 78-13773. 1979. Repr. of 1966 ed. lib. bdg. 32.50x (ISBN 0-313-20628-7, BLCU). Greenwood.

--The Lost Travellers: A Romantic Theme with Variations. LC 83-1546. xi, 292p. 1983. Repr. of 1962 ed. lib. bdg. 42.50x (ISBN 0-313-23882-0, BLLT). Greenwood.

--Virginia Woolf. Dobree, Bonamy, et al, eds. Bd. with E. M. Forster. Warner, Rex; Katherine Mansfield. Gordon, Ian A. LC 63-63095. (British Writers & Their Work Ser: Vol. 3). viii, 126p. 1964. pap. 2.35x (ISBN 0-8032-5652-3, BB 452, Bison). U of Nebr Pr.

Blackstone, Harry. Blackstone's Modern Card Tricks. 1974. pap. 3.00 (ISBN 0-87980-282-0). Wilshire.

--Blackstone's Secrets of Magic. pap. 3.00 (ISBN 0-87980-260-X). Wilshire.

--Blackstone's Tricks Anyone Can Do. 240p. 1983. pap. 4.95 (ISBN 0-8065-0862-0). Citadel Pr.

--Secrets of Magic. 2.95x (ISBN 0-685-47574-3). Wehman.

Blackstone, Harry, Jr., et al. The Blackstone Book of Magic & Illusion. (Illus.). 224p. (gr. 7 up). 1985. pap. 19.95 (ISBN 0-937858-45-5). Newmarket.

Blackstone, Michael O. Endoscopic Interpretation: Normal & Pathologic Appearances of the Gastrointestinal Tract. (Illus.). 592p. 1984. text ed. 118.00 (ISBN 0-89004-789-8). Raven.

Blackstone, Orin. Index to Jazz: Jazz Recordings, 1917-1944. LC 77-27076. 1978. Repr. of 1948 ed. lib. bdg. 22.25x (ISBN 0-313-20178-1, BLIJ). Greenwood.

Blackstone, Sandra L. Mineral Severance Taxes in Western States: Economic, Legal, & Policy Considerations, Vol. 75, No. 3. Raese, Jon W., ed. LC 80-29698. (Colorado School of Mines Quarterly Ser.). (Illus.). 39p. 1981. pap. text ed. 8.00 (ISBN 0-317-06078-3). Colo Sch Mines.

Blackstone, T., jt. auth. see Williams, G.

Blackstone, Tessa & Vines, Peter. Social Policy & Administration in Britain: A Bibliography. 130p. 1975. 17.50x (ISBN 0-87471-811-2). Rowman.

Blackstone, Tessa, jt. auth. see Mortimore, Jo.

Blackstone, Tessa, jt. auth. see Williams, Gareth.

Blackstone, William. Commentaries on the Laws of England: A Facsimile of the First Edition of 1765-1769, 4 vols. LC 79-11753. 1979. Set. lib. bdg. 100.00x (ISBN 0-226-05536-1); pap. 15.00. Vol. I (ISBN 0-226-05538-8). Vol. II. 15.00 (ISBN 0-226-05541-8); Vol. III. 15.00 (ISBN 0-226-05543-4); Vol. IV. 15.00 (ISBN 0-226-05545-0). U of Chicago Pr.

--Commentaries on the Laws of England: First Edition with Rare Supplement 1765, 4 vols. 1961. Repr. of 1769 ed. Set. lib. bdg. 250.00 (ISBN 0-89941-359-5). W S Hein.

--Commentaries on the Laws of England: 1765-1769, 4 Vols. 1981. write for info. (ISBN 0-08-027642-3, HE 029); microfiche 155.00 (ISBN 0-686-32111-1). Pergamon.

--Ehrlich's Blackstone. Ehrlich, J. W., ed. LC 72-5652. 987p. 1973. Repr. of 1959 ed. lib. bdg. 39.75x (ISBN 0-8371-6446-X, BLER). Greenwood.

Blackstone, William T., ed. Philosophy & Environmental Crisis. LC 73-90842. 148p. 1974. pap. 6.00x (ISBN 0-8203-0343-7). U of Ga Pr.

Blackstone, William T. & Heslep, Robert D., eds. Social Justice & Preferential Treatment: Women & Racial Minorities in Education & Business. LC 76-28921. 228p. 1977. pap. 9.00x (ISBN 0-8203-0434-4). U of Ga Pr.

Blackwelder, E. United States of North America. 1912. 30.00 (ISBN 0-384-04645-2). Johnson Repr.

Blackwelder, Julia K. Women of the Depression: Caste & Culture in San Antonio, 1929-1939. LC 83-40496. (Texas A&M Southwestern Studies: No. 2). (Illus.). 1984. 22.50x (ISBN 0-89096-177-8). Tex A&M Univ Pr.

Blackwelder, Richard E. Checklist of the Coleopterous Insects of Mexico, Central America, the West Indies, & South America, Pts. 1-6. LC 81-607585. 1492p. 1982. text ed. 29.95x (ISBN 0-87474-244-7). Smithsonian.

--Classification of the Animal Kingdom. LC 62-17618. 99p. 1963. pap. 1.95 (ISBN 0-8093-0096-6). S Ill U Pr.

--Guide to the Taxonomic Literature of Vertebrates. 256p. 1972. 9.50x (ISBN 0-8138-1630-0). Iowa St U Pr.

Blackwelder, Richard E. & Arnett, Ross H., Jr. Checklist of the Beetles of Canada, United States, Mexico, Central America, & the West Indies: Yellow Version, 10 parts. 1977. 20.00 ea.; 200.00 set (ISBN 0-89140-015-X). World Natural Hist.

Blackwelder, Richard E. & Shepherd, Benjamin A., eds. Diversity of Animal Reproduction. 152p. 1981. 59.00 (ISBN 0-8493-6355-1). CRC Pr.

Blackwelder, Sheila K. Science for All Seasons. (Human Science Ser.). (Illus.). 272p. 1980. 11.95 (ISBN 0-13-795286-4, Spec); pap. 5.95 (ISBN 0-13-795278-3). P-H.

Blackwelder, Stephen & Negroni, J. L. The Price of Heaven. (Orig.). 1984. pap. 3.95 (ISBN 0-440-17089-3). Dell.

Blackwell, Albert L., tr. see Wohlfarth, Hannsdieter.

Blackwell, Alice S. Lucy Stone, Pioneer of Woman's Rights. Repr. of 1930 ed. 21.00 (ISBN 0-527-08700-9). Kraus Repr.

Blackwell, Alice S., ed. Armenian Poems. LC 78-14975. 308p. 1978. Repr. of 1917 ed. 25.00x (ISBN 0-88206-022-8). Caravan Bks.

Blackwell, Alice S., ed. see Breshko-Breshkovskaia, Ekaterina K.

Blackwell, Alice S., tr. Some Spanish-American Poets. LC 68-22694. (Eng. & Span.). 1968. Repr. of 1937 ed. 10.00x (ISBN 0-8196-0217-5). Biblo.

--Some Spanish-American Poets. 2nd ed. LC 68-23276. (Illus.). 1968. Repr. of 1937 ed. lib. bdg. 32.50x (ISBN 0-8371-0022-4, BLSP). Greenwood.

Blackwell, Alice S., tr. from Span. Some Spanish-American Poets. 559p. 1982. Repr. of 1937 ed. lib. bdg. 85.00 (ISBN 0-89987-074-0). Darby Bks.

Blackwell, Anna, tr. see Kardec, Allan.

Blackwell, Antoinette B. The Sexes Throughout Nature. LC 75-7714. (Pioneers of the Woman's Movement: an International Perspective Ser.). 240p. 1976. Repr. of 1875 ed. 21.45 (ISBN 0-88355-349-X). Hyperion Conn.

Blackwell, Basil H., jt. auth. see Makower, Stanley V.

Blackwell, Basil H., jt. ed. see Makower, Stanley V.

Blackwell, Betty, jt. auth. see Carlson, Carolyn E.

Blackwell, David A. & Girshick, M. A. Theory of Games & Statistical Decisions. 368p. 1980. pap. 5.50 (ISBN 0-486-63831-6). Dover.

Blackwell, David S. & Rajhans, G. S. Practical Guide to Respirator Usage in Industry. (Illus.). 144p. 1985. pap. text ed. 24.95 (ISBN 0-317-19301-5). Butterworth.

Blackwell, Deborah J. Telecommunications & Education. 1974. pap. 4.00x (ISBN 0-89011-467-6, TEC-103). Abt Bks.

--Telecommunications & Health Services. 1974. pap. 3.50x (ISBN 0-89011-466-8, TEC-104). Abt Bks.

Blackwell, Dianne R. For Tara: A Mother's Journal. (Illus.). 48p. 1983. 6.95 (ISBN 0-89962-297-6). Todd & Honeywell.

Blackwell, E. Harold, jt. auth. see Carlson, Gerald P.

Blackwell, Elizabeth. Essays in Medical Sociology, 2 vols. in 1. LC 73-180555. (Medicine & Society in America Ser). 580p. 1972. Repr. of 1902 ed. 33.00 (ISBN 0-405-03935-2). Ayer Co Pubs.

--The Laws of Life, with Special Reference to the Physical Education of Girls. Rothman, David J. & Rothman, Sheila M., eds. (Women & Children First Ser.). 30.00 (ISBN 0-8240-7652-4). Garland Pub.

Blackwell, Elsie, jt. auth. see Adcock, Mabel.

Blackwell, Gordon W. The Selected Addresses of Gordon W. Blackwell, President of Florida State University, Sept. 16, 1960 to Jan. 31, 1965. LC 65-64028. (Florida State U. Studies: No. 43). 1965. 6.95 (ISBN 0-8130-0481-0). U Presses Fla.

Blackwell, James. The Black Community: Diversity & Unity. 2nd ed. 398p. 1984. pap. text ed. 13.50 scp (ISBN 0-06-040736-0, HarpC). Har-Row.

Blackwell, James E. The Black Community: Diversity & Unity. LC 74-28532. (Illus.). 336p. (Orig.). 1975. pap. text ed. 17.50 scp (ISBN 0-06-040735-2, HarpC). Har-Row.

--Mainstreaming Outsiders: The Production of Black Professionals. LC 81-82121. (Illus.). 345p. 1981. 30.95x (ISBN 0-930390-39-3). Gen Hall.

Blackwell, James E. & Hart, Philip S. Cities, Suburbs & Blacks: A Study of Concerns, Distrust & Alienation. LC 82-80239. 228p. (Orig.). 1982. lib. bdg. 25.95x (ISBN 0-930390-45-8); pap. text ed. 11.95x (ISBN 0-930390-46-6). Gen Hall.

Blackwell, James E. & Janowitz, Morris, eds. Black Sociologists: Historical & Contemporary Perspectives. LC 73-84187. (Heritage of Sociology Ser). xxii, 416p. 1975. Repr. of 1974 ed. 11.00x (ISBN 0-226-05566-3). U of Chicago Pr.

Blackwell, John, jt. auth. see Walton, Alan G.

Blackwell, Kate, jt. auth. see Nader, Ralph.

Blackwell, Kenneth. The Spinozistic Ethics of Bertrand Russell. 192p. 1985. text ed. 20.00x (ISBN 0-04-190008-1). Allen Unwin.

Blackwell, Kenneth, jt. auth. see Eames, Elizabeth.

Blackwell, Leslie. African Occasions: Reminiscences of Thirty Years of Bar, Bench, & Politics in South Africa. LC 76-109319. (Illus.). 287p. Repr. of 1938 ed. 19.75x (ISBN 0-8371-3574-5, BLO&, Pub. by Negro U Pr). Greenwood.

Blackwell, Liz. A Treasury of Crochet Patterns. (Illus.). 1979. 12.95 (ISBN 0-684-16320-9, ScribT). Scribner.

Blackwell, Lyle M. Gauley Bridge: The Town & Its Church. 1980. 17.50 (ISBN 0-87012-382-3). McClain.

Blackwell, Marian. Care of the Mentally Retarded. 1979. 17.95 (ISBN 0-316-09890-6). Little.

Blackwell, Marilyn J., ed. Structures of Influence: A Comparative Approach to August Strindberg. LC 80-29545. (Studies in the Germanic Languages & Literatures: No.98). xiv, 370p. 1982. 26.00x (ISBN 0-8078-8098-1). U of NC Pr.

Blackwell, Marilyn S., jt. auth. see Hill, Ellen C.

Blackwell, Meredith, jt. auth. see Wheeler, Quentin.

Blackwell, Muriel. Peter: The Prince of Apostles. (BibLearn Ser.). (Illus.). (gr. 1-6). 5.95 (ISBN 0-8054-4227-8, 4242-27). Broadman.

Blackwell, Muriel, jt. auth. see Blackwell, William.

Blackwell, Muriel F. Called to Teach Children. LC 82-82954. 1983. 6.50 (ISBN 0-8054-3233-7). Broadman.

--The Dream Lives On. LC 82-73865. 1984. 6.95 (ISBN 0-8054-4808-X, 4248-08). Broadman.

--The Keeping Shelf. 1985. 6.95 (ISBN 0-8054-5023-8). Broadman.

--Potter & Clay. LC 74-33501. 96p. 1975. 7.50 (ISBN 0-8054-5135-8, 4251-35). Broadman.

--The Secret Dream. LC 80-70406. (gr. 5-9). 1981. 7.95 (ISBN 0-8054-4804-7, 4248-04). Broadman.

Blackwell, Oris F., et al. Sanitarian's Examination Review Book. 1977. spiral bdg. 17.50 (ISBN 0-87488-423-3). Med Exam.

Blackwell, Peter. Hearing-Impaired Children in Regular Classrooms: Approaches to Teaching Language Arts. (Language in Education Ser.: No.54). 1983. pap. 3.95 (ISBN 0-15-599014-4). Ctr Appl Ling.

Blackwell, Peter M., et al. Sentences & Other Systems: A Language & Learning Curriculum for Hearing-Impaired Children. LC 78-51922. 1978. pap. text ed. 15.95 (ISBN 0-88200-118-3, C2557). Alexander Graham.

Blackwell, Richard J., compiled by. A Bibliography of the Philosophy of Science; Nineteen Forty-Five to Nineteen Eighty-One. LC 83-5671. xvii, 585p. 1983. lib. bdg. 75.00 (ISBN 0-313-23124-9, BLB/). Greenwood.

Blackwell, Robert, jt. auth. see Pancsofar, Ernest.

Blackwell, Robert B. & Joynt, Robert R. Mainstreaming: What to Expect...What to Do. 1980. 15.95 (ISBN 0-87804-416-7). Mafex.

Blackwell, Robert B. & Joynt, Robert R., eds. Learning Disabilities Handbook for Teachers. 208p. 1976. 20.75x (ISBN 0-398-02234-8). C C Thomas.

Blackwell, Roger D. & Talarzyk, Wayne W. Consumer Attitudes Toward Health Care & Medical Malpractice. LC 77-368622. pap. 27.00 (ISBN 0-317-30122-5, 2025305). Bks Demand UMI.

Blackwell, Roger D., jt. auth. see Engel, James F.

Blackwell, Ruby Chapin. A Girl in Washington Territory. LC 72-619693. (Illus.). 31p. 1973. pap. 2.75 (ISBN 0-917048-13-X). Wash St Hist Soc.

Blackwell, Russell T., jt. auth. see Todd, Charles L.

Blackwell, Thomas. Letters Concerning Mythology. LC 75-27887. (Renaissance & the Gods Ser.: Vol. 42). (Illus.). 1976. Repr. of 1748 ed. lib. bdg. 88.00 (ISBN 0-8240-2091-X). Garland Pub.

Blackwell, Thomas E., ed. College Law Digest, 1935-1970. xi, 256p. (Orig.). 1974. pap. text ed. 12.00x (ISBN 0-8377-0307-7). Rothman.

Blackwell, Vera, tr. see Havel, Vaclav.

Blackwell, Will H. Tides: A Collection of Poems. 1980. 6.95 (ISBN 0-87212-099-6). Libra.

Blackwell, Will H., Jr. Guide to the Woody Plants of the Tri-State Area. (Illus.). 1976. pap. text ed. 7.95 (ISBN 0-8403-1581-3). Kendall-Hunt.

Blackwell, William. Geometry in Architecture. LC 83-10281. 185p. 1984. 37.50x (ISBN 0-471-09683-0, Pub. by Wiley-Interscience). Wiley.

Blackwell, William & Blackwell, Muriel. Working Partners Working Parents. LC 79-51134. 1979. 5.95 (ISBN 0-8054-5637-6). Broadman.

Blackwell, William A. & Grigsby, Leonard L. Introductory Network Theory. 1985. text ed. write for info. (ISBN 0-534-03771-2, 22R2100, Pub. by PWS Engineering). PWS Pubs.

Blackwell, William L. The Industrialization of Russia. 2nd ed. (Europe Since 1500 Ser.). 216p. 1982. pap. 8.95x (ISBN 0-88295-813-5). Harlan Davidson.

Blackwood, jt. auth. see Turner.

Blackwood, A. W. La Preparacion de Sermones Biblicos. Crane, Santiago D., tr. 255p. (Span.). 1981. pap. 3.75 (ISBN 0-311-42030-3). Casa Bautista.

Blackwood, Adam. History of Mary Queen of Scots. MacDonald, Alexander, ed. LC 73-39448. (Maitland Club, Glasgow. Publications Ser.: No. 31). Repr. of 1834 ed. 21.50 (ISBN 0-404-52991-7). AMS Pr.

Blackwood, Alan. The Performing World of the Singer. LC 81-50296. (The Performing World Ser.). 114p. (gr. 7 up). 15.20 (ISBN 0-382-06591-3). Silver.

Blackwood, Algernon. Best Ghost Stories. 14.00 (ISBN 0-8446-5006-4). Peter Smith.

--Best Ghost Stories of Algernon Blackwood. Bleiler, E. F., ed. 396p. (Orig.). 1973. pap. 5.95 (ISBN 0-486-22977-7). Dover.

--The Centaur. Reginald, R. & Menville, Douglas, eds. LC 75-46254. (Supernatlural & Occult Fiction Ser.). 1976. Repr. of 1911 ed. lib. bdg. 26.50x (ISBN 0-405-08113-8). Ayer Co Pubs.

--The Fruit Stoners: Being the Adventures of Maria among the Fruit Stoners. Reginald, R. & Melville, Douglas, eds. LC 77-84200. (Lost Race & Adult Fantasy Ser.). 1978. Repr. of 1935 ed. lib. bdg. 24.50x (ISBN 0-405-10958-X). Ayer Co Pubs.

--The Listener, & Other Stories. facsimile ed. LC 70-150537. (Short Story Index Reprint Ser.). Repr. of 1907 ed. 17.00 (ISBN 0-8369-3834-8). Ayer Co Pubs.

--Lost Valley, & Other Stories. facsimile ed. LC 70-167442. (Short Story Index Reprint Ser.). Repr. of 1914 ed. 21.00 (ISBN 0-8369-3968-9). Ayer Co Pubs.

--Pan's Garden: A Volume of Nature Stories. facsimile ed. LC 74-157772. (Short Story Index Reprint Ser.). Repr. of 1912 ed. 27.50 (ISBN 0-8369-3884-4). Ayer Co Pubs.

--Strange Stories. Reginald, R. & Menville, Douglas, eds. LC 75-46255. (Supernatural & Occult Fiction Ser.). 1976. Repr. of 1929 ed. lib. bdg. 55.00x (ISBN 0-405-08114-6). Ayer Co Pubs.

--Tales of the Uncanny & Supernatural. 432p. Repr. of 1962 ed. lib. bdg. 21.95x (ISBN 0-88411-145-8, Pub. by Aeonian Pr). Amereon Ltd.

--Ten Minute Stories. facsimile ed. LC 72-103495. (Short Story Index Reprint Ser.). 1914. 18.00 (ISBN 0-8369-3237-4). Ayer Co Pubs.

Blackwood, Andrew W. Prayers for All Occasions. (Pocket Pulpit Library). pap. 2.95 (ISBN 0-8010-0557-4). Baker Bk.

Blackwood, Andrew W., Jr. When God Came Down. (Pocket Paperback Library Ser.). 1978. pap. 1.45 (ISBN 0-8010-0753-4). Baker Bk.

Blackwood, B. G. The Lancashire Gentry & the Great Rebellion 1640-60. (Illus.). 1978. text ed. 35.75x (ISBN 0-7190-1334-8). Humanities.

--The Lancashire Gentry & the Great Rebellion, 1640-60. 1978. 24.00 (ISBN 0-7190-1334-8, Pub. by Manchester Univ Pr). Longwood Pub Group.

Blackwood, Beatrice. Both Sides of Buka Passage. LC 76-44691. Repr. of 1935 ed. 44.50 (ISBN 0-404-15907-9). AMS Pr.

Blackwood, Brian, jt. auth. see Blackwood, George.

Blackwood, Brian D. & Blackwood, George H. Apple FORTRAN. LC 81-86556. 240p. 1982. pap. 14.95 (ISBN 0-672-21911-5, 21911). Sams.

--Applesoft Language. 2nd ed. LC 83-60172. 288p. 1983. 14.95 (ISBN 0-672-22073-3, 22073). Sams.

--Disks, Files, & Printers for the Apple II. LC 83-61068. 264p. 1983. pap. text ed. 15.95 (ISBN 0-672-22163-2, 22163). Sams.

--Intimate Instructions in Integer BASIC. LC 81-51551. 160p. 1982. pap. 8.95 (ISBN 0-672-21812-7, 21812). Sams.

Blackwood, C. M. Water Supplies for Fish Processing Plants. (Fisheries Technical Papers: No. 174). 86p. (Eng., Fr. & Span.). 1978. pap. 7.50 (ISBN 92-5-100685-7, F1595, FAO). Unipub.

Blackwood, Cardine. Cornigan. 1985. 15.95 (ISBN 0-670-80420-7). Viking.

Blackwood, Caroline. For All That I Found There. LC 73-92762. 144p. 1974. 6.95 (ISBN 0-8076-0742-8). Braziller.

--On the Perimeter. (Nonfiction Ser.). 128p. 1985. pap. 5.95 (ISBN 0-317-19394-5). Penguin.

Blackwood, Cheryl P. & Slattery, Kathryn. A Bright-Shining Place. (Epiphany Ser.). 240p. 1983. pap. 2.75 (ISBN 0-345-30698-8). Ballantine.

Blackwood, Easley. The Structure of Recognizable Diatonic Tunings. (Illus.). 360p. 1985. text ed. 50.00x (ISBN 0-691-09129-3). Princeton U Pr.

Blackwood, Evelyn. Anthropology & Homosexuality. (Journal of Homosexuality: Vol. 11, No. 3-4). 256p. 1985. 29.95 (ISBN 0-86656-328-8); pap. text ed. 19.95 (ISBN 0-86656-420-9). Haworth Pr.

Blackwood, Evelyn, ed. The Many Faces of Homosexual Behavior: Anthropological Approaches to Homosexual Behavior. 1985. pap. 8.95 (ISBN 0-918393-20-5). Harrington Pk.

Blackwood, Gary L. Attack of the Mushroom People. (Orig.). 1984. pap. 5.00 (ISBN 0-88734-308-2). Players Pr.

--The Lion & the Unicorn. LC 82-90758. 291p. (Orig.). 1983. pap. 5.95 (ISBN 0-910971-00-5). Eagle Bks.

Blackwood, George & Blackwood, Brian. Applesoft for the Apple IIe. LC 83-50833. 304p. 1983. 19.95 (ISBN 0-672-22259-0, 22259). Sams.

Blackwood, George, jt. auth. see Levin, Murray B.

Blackwood, George H., jt. auth. see Blackwood, Brian D.

Blackwood, James R. House on College Avenue: The Comptons at Wooster, 1891-1913. 1968. pap. 6.95x (ISBN 0-262-52026-5). MIT Pr.

Blackwood, R. T., jt. ed. see Herman, A. L.

Blacque-Belair, Alain. Dictionnaire Medicine, Clinique, Pharmacologique et Therapeutique. 2nd ed. 1938p. (Fr.). 1978. 115.00 (ISBN 0-686-56920-2, M-6036). French & Eur.

Blacque-Belair, Alain & Fossey, Bernard M. de. Dictionnaire de Diagnostic Clinique et Topographique. 1250p. (Fr.). 1969. 55.00 (ISBN 0-686-56921-0, M-6037). French & Eur.

Blad, Blaine L., jt. auth. see Rosenberg, Norman J.

Blade, Melinda K. Education of Italian Renaissance Women. rev. ed. LC 83-287. (Woman in History Ser.: Vol. 21B). (Illus.). 86p. 1983. lib. bdg. 15.95 (ISBN 0-86663-070-8); pap. text ed. 10.95 (ISBN 0-86663-072-4). Ide Hse.

Bladel, J. van see Van Bladel, J.

Bladel, J. Van see Van Bladel, J.

Bladen, Ashby. How to Cope with the Developing Financial Crisis. 192p. 1981. pap. 4.95 (ISBN 0-07-005549-1). McGraw.

Bladen, Wilford & Karan, P. P. The Evolution of Geographic Thought in America: A Kentucky Root. 176p. 1983. pap. text ed. 13.95 (ISBN 0-8403-3045-6). Kendall-Hunt.

Bladen, Wilford A. A Geography of Kentucky: A Tropical-Regional Overview. 240p. 1984. pap. text ed. 18.95 (ISBN 0-8403-3320-X). Kendall-Hunt.

Blades, Ann. A Boy of Tache. LC 76-58698. (Illus.). (gr. 1-5). 1973. 11.95 (ISBN 0-88776-023-6); pap. 5.95 (ISBN 0-88776-034-1). Tundra Bks.

--Mary of Mile 18. (Illus.). (gr. 1-4). 1971. 11.95 (ISBN 0-370-01804-4); pap. 7.95 (ISBN 0-88776-059-7). Tundra Bks.

Blades, Dudley. Spiritual Healing. 128p. (Orig.). 1980. pap. 4.95 (ISBN 0-85030-130-0). Newcastle Pub.

Blades, J. Books in Chains. 1976. lib. bdg. 59.95 (ISBN 0-8490-1537-5). Gordon Pr.

--The Enemies of Books. 1976. lib. bdg. 59.95 (ISBN 0-8490-1768-8). Gordon Pr.

Blades, James. Percussion Instruments & Their History. rev. ed. LC 83-20807. (Illus.). 511p. (Orig.). 1984. pap. 32.00 (ISBN 0-571-18081-7). Faber & Faber.

Blades, James & Montagu, Jeremy. Early Percussion Instruments. (Early Music Ser.). (Illus.). 1976. pap. 10.95x (ISBN 0-19-323176-X). Oxford U Pr.

Blades, Joan. Family Mediation: Cooperative Divorce Settlement. (Illus.). 256p. 1985. text ed. 25.95 (ISBN 0-13-302431-8). P-H.

--Mediate Your Divorce: A Guide to Cooperative Custody, Property & Support Agreements. (Illus.). 256p. 1985. pap. 13.95 (ISBN 0-13-572595-X). P-H.

Blades, Joseph D., Jr. A Comparative Study of Selected American Film Critics, 1958-1974. Jowett, Garth S., ed. LC 75-21429. (Dissertations on Film Ser.). 1976. lib. bdg. 18.00x (ISBN 0-405-07532-4). Ayer Co Pubs.

Blades, William. Books in Chains & Other Bibliographical Papers. LC 68-30610. 1968. Repr. of 1892 ed. 35.00x (ISBN 0-8103-3298-1). Gale.

--Shakespeare & Typography: Being an Attempt to Show Shakespeare's Personal Connection with & Technical Knowledge of the Art of Printing. (Illus.). 1969. Repr. of 1872 ed. Set. 11.00 (ISBN 0-8337-0303-X). B Franklin.

--Shakespere & Typography. LC 72-113560. Repr. of 1872 ed. 6.00 (ISBN 0-404-00894-1). AMS Pr.

Blades, William F. Fishing Flies & Flytying. LC 61-17665. (Illus.). 320p. 1980. 24.95 (ISBN 0-8117-0613-3). Stackpole.

Bladon, P., jt. auth. see Wood, E. J.

Bladwin, R. L., et al. Rx for Success. (Illus.). 318p. 1983. 48.00 (ISBN 0-912063-00-9). Vision Pubns.

Blady, Michael. Children at Risk: Making a Difference Through the Court Appointed Special Advocate Project. (Illus.). 318p. 1982. wkbk 7.50 (ISBN 0-686-84113-1). NCJW.

Blaffer, Sarah C. The Black-Man of Zinacantan: A Central American Legend. (Texas Pan American Ser). (Illus.). 210p. 1972. 13.95x (ISBN 0-292-70701-0). U of Tex Pr.

Blagden, C. O. Catalogue of Manuscripts in European Languages Belonging to the Library of the Indian Office: The Mackenzie Collections, Vol. 1. Pt. 1. 334p. 1916. 9.75 (ISBN 0-7123-0601-3, Pub. by British Lib). Longwood Pub Group.

Blagden, Charles O., jt. auth. see Skeat, Walter W.

Blagden, Cyprian. The Stationers' Company: A History, 1403-1959. LC 76-48000. 1960. 27.50x (ISBN 0-8047-0935-1). Stanford U Pr.

Blagden, John. Do We Really Need Libraries? An Assessment of Approaches to the Evaluation of the Performance of Libraries. 160p. 1980. 18.50 (ISBN 0-85157-308-8, Pub. by Bingley England). Shoe String.

Blagden, Nellie & Marshall, Edith P. The Complete Condo & Co-Op Information Book. 1983. pap. 7.50 (ISBN 0-395-32195-6). HM.

Blagg, Thomas M., ed. Index of Wills Proved in the Prerogative Court of Canterbury, Vol. 8: 1657-1660. (British Record Society Index Library Ser.: Vol. 61). Repr. of 1936 ed. 58.00 (ISBN 0-317-16730-8). Kraus Repr.

Blagg, Thomas M. & Moir, Josephine S., eds. An Index of Wills Proved in the Prerogative Court of Canterbury, Vol. 7: 1653-1656. (British Record Society Index Library Ser.: Vol. 54). pap. 59.00 (ISBN 0-317-16728-6). Kraus Repr.

Blagg, Thomas M. & Wadsworth, Arthur, eds. Abstracts of Nottinghamshire Marriage Licences, Vol. 1: Archdeaconry Court, 1577-1700; Peculiar of Southwell, 1588-1754. (British Record Society Index Library: Vol. 58). pap. 52.00 (ISBN 0-317-16398-1). Kraus Repr.

Blagosklonov, K. N., jt. auth. see Astanin, L. P.

Blagowidow, George. Last Train from Berlin. 206p. 7.95 (ISBN 0-385-12339-6, Pub. by Doubleday). Hippocrene Bks.

--Operation Parterre. 286p. 1982. 10.95 (ISBN 0-88254-712-7). Hippocrene Bks.

--Traveler's Trivia Test: One Thousand & One Questions & Answers for the Sophisticated Globetrotter. 100p. (Orig.). 1985. pap. 3.95 (ISBN 0-87052-063-6). Hippocrene Bks.

Blagoy, D. Sacred Lyre. 422p. 1982. 11.95 (ISBN 0-8285-2344-4, Pub. by Progress Pubs USSR). Imported Pubns.

Blagrave, John. The Art of Dyalling in Two Parts. LC 68-27476. (English Experience Ser.: No. 69). (Illus.). 151p. 1968. Repr. of 1609 ed. 21.00 (ISBN 90-221-0069-3). Walter J Johnson.

--Astrolabium Vranicum Generale: Nova Orbis Terrarum Descripto (A Map to Accompany the Astrolabium) LC 78-38156. (English Experience Ser.: No. 435). (Illus.). 69p. 1972. Repr. of 1596 ed. 9.50 (ISBN 90-221-0435-4). Walter J Johnson.

--Baculum Familliare, a Booke of the Making & Use of a Staffe. LC 71-26001. (English Experience Ser.: No. 225). 1970. Repr. of 1590 ed. 11.50 (ISBN 90-221-0225-4). Walter J Johnson.

--The Mathematicall Iewell. LC 74-171735. (English Experience Ser.: No. 294). 1971. Repr. of 1585 ed. 20.00 (ISBN 90-221-0294-7). Walter J Johnson.

Blagrove, Luanna C. Business Problems & Solutions for Proprietors & Partnerships. LC 81-65224. 160p. 1981. 24.95 (ISBN 0-9604466-8-0); pap. 19.95 (ISBN 0-9604466-9-9). Blagrove Pubns.

--How to Have an Ideal Business Client in Four Months. LC 80-70036. (Illus.). 67p. (Orig.). 1981. pap. 9.95 (ISBN 0-9604466-6-4). Blagrove Pubns.

--How to Start & Operate a Business Manual. LC 80-67943. (Illus.). 175p. 1981. 24.95 (ISBN 0-9604466-4-8). Blagrove Pubns.

--Introduction to Proprietor & Partnership Businesses. LC 81-65222. 160p. 1981. 24.95 (ISBN 0-939776-00-6); pap. 19.95 (ISBN 0-939776-01-4). Blagrove Pubns.

--Management for Proprietors & Partnerships. LC 80-70035. (Illus.). 165p. 1981. text ed. 24.95 (ISBN 0-9604466-7-2). Blagrove Pubns.

--The Professional's Business Guide for Proprietor & Partnerships. rev. ed. LC 81-65223. (Illus.). 185p. 1981. 29.95 (ISBN 0-9604466-5-6). Blagrove Pubns.

--Strategy for Minority Businesses. LC 80-67944. 67p. (Orig.). 1980. pap. 5.95 (ISBN 0-686-77585-6). Blagrove Pubns.

--Untapped Profits by Professionals in the Small Business Field. LC 80-67306. (Illus.). 169p. 1980. 29.95 (ISBN 0-9604466-2-1). Blagrove Pubns.

--Untold Facts About the Small Business Game. LC 80-67307. (Illus.). 171p. (Orig.). 1980. 24.95 (ISBN 0-9604466-1-3); pap. 19.95 (ISBN 0-9604466-0-5). Blagrove Pubns.

Blaguy, John. The Foundation of Moral Goodness, 2 vols. in 1. Wellek, Rene, ed. LC 75-11194. (British Philosophers & Theologians of the 17th & 18th Centuries Ser.: Vol. 1). 1976. Repr. of 1729 ed. lib. bdg. 51.00 (ISBN 0-8240-1750-1). Garland Pub.

Blaha, K & Malon, P., eds. Peptides, 1982: Proceedings of the 17th European Peptide Symposium, Prague, Czechoslovakia, August 29-September 3, 1982. (Illus.). 846p. 1982. 112.00 (ISBN 3-11-009574-2). De Gruyter.

Blaharskl, Barbra. International Ticketing. (Illus.). 150p. (Orig.). 1985. pap. text ed. 21.95X (ISBN 0-917063-06-6). Travel Text.

Blahut, Richard E. Fast Algorithms for Digital Signal Processing. 1985. 41.95 (ISBN 0-201-10155-6). Addison-Wesley.

--Theory & Practice of Error Control Codes. LC 82-11441. (Illus.). 512p. 1983. text ed. 35.95 (ISBN 0-201-10102-5). Addison-Wesley.

Blaicher, Guenther. Freie Zeit-Langeweile-Literatur. Studien Zur Therapeutischen Funktion der Englischen Prosaliteratur im 18 Jahrhundert. 1977. 40.80x (ISBN 3-11-006951-2). De Gruyter.

Blaikie, M. P., et al. The Struggle for Basic Needs in Nepal. (Illus.). 100p. (Orig.). 1980. pap. 6.50x (ISBN 92-64-12101-3). OECD.

Blaikie, Piers. The Political Economy of Soil Erosion in Developing Countries. (Development Studies). (Illus.). 256p. 1985. pap. text ed. 14.95 (ISBN 0-582-30089-4). Longman.

Blaikie, W. G. & Law, R. The Inner Life of Christ. 459p. 1982. lib. bdg. 17.25 Smythe Sewn (ISBN 0-86524-156-2, 9515). Klock & Klock.

Blaikie, Walter B. Itinerary of Prince Charles Edward Stuart. 1976. 12.50x (ISBN 0-7073-0103-3, Pub. by Scottish Academic Pr Scotland). Columbia U Pr.

--Origins of the Forty-Five. 1976. 20.00x (ISBN 0-7073-0104-1, Pub. by Scottish Academic Pr Scotland). Columbia U Pr.

Blaikie, William. How to Get Strong & How to Stay So. (Physical Education Reprint Ser). (Illus.). Repr. of 1899 ed. lib. bdg. 27.50x (ISBN 0-697-00100-8). Irvington.

Blaikie, William G. The Book of Joshua. 416p. 1983. lib. bdg. 15.75 (ISBN 0-86524-173-2, 0601). Klock & Klock.

--David, King of Israel. 1981. 17.50 (ISBN 0-86524-054-X, 8401). Klock & Klock.

--First Book of Samuel. 440p. 1983. lib. bdg. 16.50 (ISBN 0-86524-174-0, 0901). Klock & Klock.

--Heroes of Israel. 1982. lib. bdg. 19.50 (ISBN 0-86524-082-5, 0102). Klock & Klock.

--Personal Life of David Livingstone. LC 69-19353. (Illus.). 1880. 22.00x (ISBN 0-8371-0518-8, BLL&). Greenwood.

--The Public Ministry of Christ. 356p. 1984. lib. bdg. 13.25 (ISBN 0-86524-167-8, 9517). Klock & Klock.

--Second Book of Samuel. 400p. 1983. lib. bdg. 15.00 (ISBN 0-86524-175-9, 0903). Klock & Klock.

Blaiklock, D. A., ed. Living Is Now. 1972. pap. 1.50 (ISBN 0-8010-0579-5). Baker Bk.

Blaiklock, E. M. The Archaeology of the New Testament. 2nd, rev. ed. 192p. 1984. pap. 6.95 (ISBN 0-8407-5909-6). Nelson.
--The Bible & I. 128p. (Orig.). 1983. pap. 3.95 (ISBN 0-87123-298-7). Bethany Hse.
--Blaiklock's Handbook to the Bible. 256p. 1981. pap. 6.95 (ISBN 0-8007-5055-1, Power Bks). Revell.
--Commentary on the Psalms. Hitt, Russell T., ed. Incl. Vol. 1. Psalms in Life. LC 77-1122. pap. 4.95 (ISBN 0-87981-080-7); Vol. II. Psalms in Worship. LC 77-2875. pap. 4.95 (ISBN 0-87981-081-5). 1977. pap. Broadman.
--Commentary on the Psalms: Psalms in Life, Vol. I. LC 77-1122. 1982. pap. 4.95 (ISBN 0-8054-1222-0). Broadman.
--Commentary on the Psalms: Vol. II, Psalms in Worship. LC 77-2875. 1982. pap. 4.95 (ISBN 0-8054-1223-9). Broadman.
--The Confessions of St. Augustine. 224p. 1983. pap. 6.95 (ISBN 0-8407-5863-4). Nelson.
--Eight Days in Israel. 128p. 25.00x (ISBN 0-686-75529-4, Pub. by Ark Pub England). State Mutual Bk.
--Hero of the Aeneid: An Address. 1961. Repr. 8.50 (ISBN 0-8274-2491-4). R West.
--Jesus Christ: Man or Myth? 144p. 1984. pap. 4.95 (ISBN 0-8407-5913-4). Nelson.
--The Pastoral Epistles. 128p. 1972. pap. 4.95 (ISBN 0-310-21233-2). Zondervan.
--Understanding the New Testament: Luke. LC 78-9119. 1982. pap. 3.95 (ISBN 0-8054-1329-4). Broadman.
--Understanding the New Testament: Romans. LC 78-9794. 1982. pap. 3.95 (ISBN 0-8054-1332-4). Broadman.
--World of the New Testament. (Bible Study Commentary Ser.). 127p. 1983. pap. 4.50 (ISBN 0-87508-176-2). Chr Lit.
--Zondervan Pictorial Bible Atlas. (Illus.). 1969. 19.95 (ISBN 0-310-21240-5). Zondervan.
Blaiklock, E. M., commentary by. Living Waters: Psalms for Your Quiet Time with God. (Illus.). 256p. 1985. Repr. 10.95 (ISBN 0-687-22378-4). Abingdon.
Blaiklock, E. M., tr. see Lawrence, Brother.
Blaiklock, E. M., tr. see Thomas A'Kempis.
Blaiklock, M., tr. see Rolland, Romain.
Blain, Alexander. Clackshant. Leo, K. R., ed. LC 82-80034. (Orig.). 1982. pap. 5.00 (ISBN 0-9606678-1-4). Sylvan Pubns.
Blain, Beryl B., et al. A Complete Preparation for the MCAT. Braestrup, Angelica & Hassan, Aftab, eds. 1985. Set. pap. text ed. 35.00; Vol. 1, Knowledge & Comprehension of Science. pap. text ed. 19.00 (ISBN 0-317-26390-0); Vol. 2, Skills Development in Reading, Writing & Quantatitive. pap. text ed. 17.00 (ISBN 0-317-26391-9). Betz Pub Co Inc.
--A Complete Preparation for the New MCAT: Skills Development in Reading & Quantitative, Vol. II. (Illus.). 340p. (Orig.). 1982. pap. text ed. 14.00 (ISBN 0-941406-02-4); Set of 2 vols. pap. text ed. 35.00 (ISBN 0-941406-03-2). Betz Pub Co Inc.
Blain, Hugh M. Favorite Huey Long Stories. 1972. 4.95 (ISBN 0-685-08164-8); pap. 1.00 (ISBN 0-685-08165-6). Claitors.
Blain, Nicholas. Industrial Relations in the Air: Australian Airline Pilots. LC 83-6972. (Illus.). 219p. 1984. text ed. 27.50x (ISBN 0-7022-1983-5). U of Queensland Pr.
Blain, Virginia, ed. see Surtees, R. S.
Blaine, Celia, et al. Romance Reader No. Three. 288p. (Orig.). 1985. pap. 4.99 (ISBN 0-8007-1440-7). Revell.
Blaine, Charles G. Federal Regulation of Bank Holding Companies: An Analysis of the Bank Holding Company Act of 1956. LC 73-75982. pap. 124.80 (ISBN 0-317-26768-X, 2024343). Bks Demand UMI.
Blaine, D. & Overeen, J. Van, eds. Railway Mechanical Engineering: A Century of Progress - Car & Locomotive Design. 446p. 1979. 35.00 (ISBN 0-317-33605-3, H00155); members 25.00 (ISBN 0-317-33606-1). ASME.
Blaine, J. C. End of an Era in Space Exploration. Jacobs, H., ed. (Science & Technology: Vol. 42). (Illus.). 1976. 25.00x (ISBN 0-87703-080-4, Pub. by Am Astronaut). Univelt Inc.
Blaine, Laurence. Black Muscle. Rev. ed. (Orig.). 1983. pap. 2.25 (ISBN 0-87067-227-4, BH227). Holloway.
--Sweet Street Blues. rev. ed. (Orig.). 1985. pap. 2.50 (ISBN 0-87067-260-6, BH260). Holloway.
Blaine, Lawrence. Grant Proposals: A Practical Guide to Planning, Funding & Managing. 105p. 1981. pap. text ed. 12.00 (ISBN 0-686-35865-1). Psyon Pubns.
Blaine, M., jt. auth. see Euwe, Max.
Blaine, Marcia S., jt. auth. see Campbell, Catherine H.
Blaine, Martha R. The Ioway Indians. LC 78-21385. (Illus.). 1979. 29.95 (ISBN 0-8061-1527-0). U of Okla Pr.
--Pawnees: A Critical Bibliography. LC 80-8034. (The Newberry Library Center for the History of the American Indian Bibliographical). (Illus.). 128p. 1981. pap. 4.95x (ISBN 0-253-31502-6). Ind U Pr.
Blaine, R. L. & Schoff, C. K., eds. Purity Determinations by Thermal Methods - STP 838. LC 83-72815. 150p. 1984. text ed. 24.00 (ISBN 0-8031-0222-4, 04-838000-40). ASTM.
Blaine, Tom. Goodbye, Allergies. 4.95x (ISBN 0-8065-0639-3). Cancer Control Soc.
Blaine, Tom R. The Easy, Natural Way to Reduce. 1978. pap. text ed. 4.95 (ISBN 0-87983-171-5). Keats.
--Goodbye, Allergies. rev. ed. 1978. pap. 4.95 (ISBN 0-8065-0639-3). Citadel Pr.
--Goodbye, Allergies. 1968. 6.95 (ISBN 0-8065-0348-3); pap. 3.95 (ISBN 0-8065-0139-1, C270). Citadel Pr.
--Mental Health Through Nutrition. 210p. 1974. 5.95 (ISBN 0-8065-0091-3); pap. 3.45 (ISBN 0-8065-0424-2). Citadel Pr.
--Prevent That Heart Attack. 6.95 (ISBN 0-8065-0299-1). Citadel Pr.
Blaine, Veola J. Verse from Veola. 1983. 5.95 (ISBN 0-8062-2037-6). Carlton.
Blaine, Vera & Clark, Scott. Progression. (Educational Dance Score Registry Ser.: No. 3). (Illus.). 194p. 1981. dance score 10.00 (ISBN 0-932582-36-2). Dance Notation.
Blaine, William L., ed. see California Continuing Education of the Bar.
Blainey, Ann. Immortal Boy: A Portrait of Leigh Hunt. LC 84-27582. (Illus.). 256p. 1985. 27.50 (ISBN 0-312-40945-1). St Martin.
Blainey, Geoffrey. The Causes of War. LC 73-2016. 1975. pap. 9.95 (ISBN 0-02-903590-2). Free Pr.
--The Peaks of Lyell. 4th ed. 1979. pap. 13.00x (ISBN 0-522-84164-3, Pub. by Melbourne U Pr). Intl Spec Bk.
--The Rush That Never Ended: A History of Australian Mining. 3rd ed. 1978. pap. 15.00x (ISBN 0-522-84145-7, Pub. by Melbourne U Pr). Intl Spec Bk.
--Triumph of the Nomads: A History of Aboriginal Australia. LC 75-37122. 304p. 1980. 22.95 (ISBN 0-87951-043-9); pap. 9.95 (ISBN 0-87951-084-6). Overlook Pr.
Blair. Forging Links of Co-operation: The Task Force Approach to Consultation. 101p. 1984. 125.00 (ISBN 0-317-36600-9, CS-80); members 25.00 (ISBN 0-317-36601-7). Conference Bd.
Blair & Rubin. Regulating the Professions: A Public-Policy Symposium. LC 79-2272. 336p. 1980. 33.00x (ISBN 0-669-03094-5). Lexington Bks.
Blair, Al. Moosewhopper: A Juicy, Moosey Min-Min-Minnesota Burger Tale. 3rd ed. LC 83-61092. (Illus.). 32p. 1983. pap. 3.95 (ISBN 0-930366-04-2). Northcountry Pub.
Blair, Alain, tr. see Lagerkvist, Par.
Blair, Alan, tr. see Bergman, Ingmar.
Blair, Alan, tr. see Josephson, Lennart.
Blair, Alan, tr. see Sillanpaa, Frans E.
Blair, Alice C. No-Nonsense Principal Handbook for Educators. LC 82-50907. (Illus.). 112p. 1982. 10.95 (ISBN 0-941484-02-5). Urban Res Inst.
Blair, Allen J. Epistles of John: Living Confidently. LC 82-15196. pap. 4.95 (ISBN 0-87213-028-2). Loizeaux.
Blair, Allen M. Minnesota Fortune Cookies: Sayings, Observations, Sentiments, & a Little Jazz from Outstate Minnesota. 24p. (Orig.). 1984. pap. 3.00 (ISBN 0-930366-05-0). Northcountry Pub.
Blair, Alpha. Through Eyes of Evil. 1981. pap. 2.50 (ISBN 0-8439-0865-3, Leisure Bks). Dorchester Pub Co.
Blair, Anne Denton. Hurrah for Arthur: A Mount Vernon Birthday Party. LC 82-10636. (Illus.). 64p. (gr. k-3). 1983. 11.95 (ISBN 0-932020-15-1). Seven Locks Pr.
Blair, Arthur W. & Burton, William H. Growth & Development of the Preadolescent. 1951. 37.00x (ISBN 0-89197-490-3). Irvington.
Blair, B., et al. Introduction to Pressurized Water Reactor Nuclear Power Plants. (Illus.). 276p. 1982. looseleaf 60.00x (ISBN 0-87683-247-8). G P Courseware.
Blair, Bevelyn W. Country Cakes. LC 84-72948. (Illus.). 240p. 1984. 10.95 (ISBN 0-9613709-0-4). Blair Columbus.
Blair, Brenda R. Hospital Employee Assistance Programs. 104p. (Orig.). 1984. text ed. 24.95 (ISBN 0-939450-44-5). AHPI.
Blair, Bruce G. Strategic Command & Control: Redefining the Nuclear Threat. LC 84-73164. 430p. 1985. 32.95 (ISBN 0-8157-0982-X); pap. 12.95 (ISBN 0-8157-0981-1). Brookings.
Blair, C. Masterpieces of Cutlery & the Art of Eating. (Orig.). pap. 3.95 (ISBN 0-317-02536-8, Pub. by Victoria & Albert Mus UK). Faber & Faber.
Blair, Calvin P., frwd. by see Holbik, Karel & Swan, Philip L.
Blair, Carole L. & Salerno, Elizabeth M. The Expanding Family: Childbearing. LC 75-30278. 1976. pap. text ed. 12.95 (ISBN 0-316-09915-5). Little.
Blair, Caroline G. Prayers for Mothers. 1980. pap. 1.95 (ISBN 0-8170-0864-0). Judson.
Blair, Carvel H. Seamanship: A Handbook for Oceanographers. LC 76-56349. (Illus.). 238p. 1977. 9.00x (ISBN 0-87033-228-7). Cornell Maritime.
Blair, Carvel H. & Ansel, Willits D. Chesapeake Bay Notes & Sketches. LC 76-124311. (Illus.). 176p. 1970. pap. 7.95 (ISBN 0-87033-277-5). Tidewater.
--A Guide to Fishing Boats & Their Gear. LC 68-19048. (Illus.). 154p. 1968. pap. 6.00 (ISBN 0-87033-002-0). Cornell Maritime.
Blair, Charles & Sherrill, John. The Man Who Could Do No Wrong. 1982. pap. 3.50 (ISBN 0-8423-4002-5). Tyndale.
Blair, Chauncey J. Heat in the Rig Veda & Atharva Veda. (American Oriental Ser.: Vol. 45). 1961. 8.00x (ISBN 0-940490-45-5). Am Orient Soc.
Blair, Chris, jt. auth. see Cantrell, Charles L.
Blair, Christina. Crystal Destiny. 400p. 1984. pap. 2.95 (ISBN 0-8217-1394-9). Zebra.
Blair, Claude. Arms, Armour, & Base-Metalwork. (The Waddesdon Catalogues Ser.). (Illus.). 532p. 1985. text ed. 45.00 (ISBN 0-7078-0008-0, Pub. by P Wilson Pubs). Sotheby Pubns.
Blair, Claude & Levine, Charles, eds. Pollard's History of Firearms. (Illus.). 560p. 1985. 40.00 (ISBN 0-02-597630-3). Macmillan.
Blair, Clay. Beyond Courage. (War Library). 208p. 1983. pap. 2.50 (ISBN 0-345-30824-7). Ballantine.
--Ridgeway's Paratroopers. LC 85-7065. (Illus.). 600p. 1985. 19.95 (ISBN 0-385-27888-8, Dial). Doubleday.
Blair, Clay, jt. auth. see Bradley, Omar N.
Blair, Clay, jt. auth. see Shepley, James R.
Blair, Clay, Jr. Silent Victory: The U. S. Submarine War Against Japan. LC 74-2005. (Illus.). 1975. 25.75i (ISBN 0-397-00753-1). Har-Row.
Blair, Clay, Jr., jt. auth. see Blair, Joan.
Blair, Clay, Jr., jt. auth. see Crossfield, A. Scott.
Blair, Cynthia. All Our Secrets. 368p. (Orig.). 1985. pap. 3.95 (ISBN 0-345-31873-0). Ballantine.
--The Banana Split Affair. 144p. 1985. pap. 2.50 (ISBN 0-449-70033-X, Juniper). Fawcett.
--Beautiful Dreamer. (Love & Life Romance Ser.). 176p. (Orig.). 1983. pap. 1.75 (ISBN 0-345-30794-1). Ballantine.
--Commitment. (Love & Life Romance Ser.). 176p. (Orig.). 1983. pap. 1.75 (ISBN 0-345-30795-X). Ballantine.
--Forever Rainbows. 224p. 1982. pap. 2.50 (ISBN 0-449-14468-2, GM). Fawcett.
--The Hot Fudge Sunday Affair. 1985. pap. 2.50 (ISBN 0-449-70158-1, Juniper). Fawcett.
--Just Married. 1984. pap. 2.50 (ISBN 0-317-05558-5). Ballantine.
--Once There Was a Fat Girl. 1981. pap. 1.95 (ISBN 0-449-14394-5, GM). Fawcett.
Blair, D. E. Contact Manifold in Riemannian Geometry. (Lecture Notes in Mathematics Ser: Vol. 509). 1976. pap. 13.00 (ISBN 0-387-07626-3). Springer-Verlag.
Blair, Dike. Books & Bedlam. 1962. pap. 1.00 (ISBN 0-911570-04-7). Vermont Bks.
Blair, Dorothy. A History of Glass in Japan. LC 72-94022. 479p. 1973. 60.00 (ISBN 0-87011-196-5). Corning.
--A History of Glass in Japan. LC 72-94022. (Illus.). 480p. 1973. 85.00 (ISBN 0-87011-196-5). Kodansha.
--A History of Glass in Japan. (Illus.). 479p. 1973. 60.00x (ISBN 0-87011-196-5, Corning Museum of Glass). U Pr of Va.
Blair, Dorothy S. African Literature in French: A History of Creative Writing in French from West & Equatorial Africa. LC 75-39374. 348p. (Orig.). 1981. pap. 16.95 (ISBN 0-521-28403-1). Cambridge U Pr.
--Senegalese Literature: A Critical History. (World Authors Ser.: No. 696). 188p. 1984. lib. bdg. 19.95 (ISBN 0-8057-6543-3, Twayne). G K Hall.
Blair, Ectyl H., ed. Chlorodioxins: Origin & Fate. LC 73-84139. (Advances in Chemistry Ser: No. 120). 1973. 24.95 (ISBN 0-8412-0181-1). Am Chemical.
Blair, Edward. Leadville: Colorado's Magic City. (Illus.). 1980. 29.95 (ISBN 0-87108-544-5). Pruett.
--Leadville: Colorado's Magic City. (Illus.). 1984. pap. 14.95 (ISBN 0-87108-665-4). Pruett.
--Palace of Ice: A History of Leadville's Ice Palace, 1895-1896. 1978. 2.00 (ISBN 0-913488-03-8). Timberline Bks.
Blair, Edward & Churchill, E. Richard. Everybody Came to Leadville. 1978. 2.00 (ISBN 0-913488-00-3). Timberline Bks.
Blair, Edward H. Tabor Family Album. 1978. 2.95 (ISBN 0-913488-06-2). Timberline Bks.
Blair, Edward P. Abingdon Bible Handbook. rev. ed. (Illus.). 528p. 1982. pap. 21.95 (ISBN 0-687-00170-6). Abingdon.
--Abingdon Bible Handbook. (Span.). 1982. pap. 12.95 (ISBN 0-687-23170-1). Abingdon.
--Deuteronomy, Joshua. LC 59-10454. (Layman's Bible Commentary Ser: Vol. 5). 1964. pap. 4.95 (ISBN 0-8042-3065-X). John Knox.
--Manual Biblico de Abingdon. LC 81-12774. 400p. (Orig., Span.). 1982. pap. 12.95 (ISBN 0-687-23170-1). Abingdon.
Blair, Eulalia. Breakfast & Brunch Dishes for Food Service Menu Planning. LC 74-34100. (Foodservice Menu Planning Ser.). 272p. 1975. 17.95 (ISBN 0-8436-2057-9). Van Nos Reinhold.
--Dishes for Special Occasions. LC 75-4684. (Foodservice Menu Planning Ser.). 320p. 1975. 17.95 (ISBN 0-8436-2058-7). Van Nos Reinhold.
Blair, Eulalia, ed. see Atkinson, Alta.
Blair, Eulalia C. Casseroles & Vegetables for Foodservice Menu Planning. LC 76-29357. (Cahners Foodservice Menu Planning Ser). 288p. 1976. 17.95 (ISBN 0-8436-2121-4). Van Nos Reinhold.
--Garnishes, Relishes & Sauces for Foodservice Menu Planning. LC 77-3292. (Foodservice Menu Planning Ser.). 320p. 1977. 17.95 (ISBN 0-8436-2173-7). Van Nos Reinhold.
--Luncheon & Supper Dishes for Foodservice Menu Planning. LC 72-92379. (Foodservice Menu Planning Ser.). 1973. 17.95 (ISBN 0-8436-0559-6). Van Nos Reinhold.
--Meat & Poultry Entrees for Foodservice Menu Planning. LC 78-9126. (Foodservice Menu Planning Ser.). (Illus.). 256p. 1978. 17.95 (ISBN 0-8436-2152-4). Van Nos Reinhold.
--Mini Meals for Food Service Menu Planning. LC 76-7073. (Foodservice Menu Planning Ser.). 240p. 1976. 17.95 (ISBN 0-8436-2102-8). Van Nos Reinhold.
--Quick to Fix Desserts. LC 80-13124. (Foodservice Menu Planning Ser.). 309p. 1980. 17.95 (ISBN 0-8436-2183-4). Van Nos Reinhold.
Blair, F. Isadora. 384p. 1985. price not set (ISBN 0-07-005598-X). McGraw.
Blair, F., tr. see Colling, Rex.
Blair, F. Michael. A Spinal Specialist's Guide to Exercise, Fitness & Health. LC 85-1234. (Illus.). 188p. 1985. pap. 12.95 (ISBN 0-932620-41-8). Betterway Pubns.
Blair, Floy, ed. see Blair, W. Charles & McGill, John K.
Blair, Fredrika. Isadora: Portrait of the Artist As a Woman. (Illus.). 1985. 19.95 (ISBN 0-07-005598-X). McGraw.
Blair, G. W. Measurement of Mind & Matter. 1956. 4.50 (ISBN 0-8022-0138-5). Philos Lib.
Blair, George S. Cumulative Voting. LC 75-10210. (Illinois Studies in the Social Sciences: Vol. 45). (Illus.). 145p. 1975. Repr. of 1960 ed. lib. bdg. 15.00x (ISBN 0-8371-8174-7, BLCV). Greenwood.
--Government at the Grass-Roots. 3rd ed. LC 80-84554. (Illus.). 1981. 15.95 (ISBN 0-913530-25-5); pap. 10.95x (ISBN 0-913530-24-7). Palisades Pub.
Blair, Gerry. Predator Caller's Companion. LC 81-497. 280p. 1981. 18.95 (ISBN 0-8329-3362-7, Pub. by Winchester Pr). New Century.
Blair, Gerry, jt. auth. see Musgrove, Bill.
Blair, Glenn M. Mentally Superior & Inferior Children of Junior & Senior High School Age: A Comparative Study of Their Backgrounds, Interests & Ambitions. LC 71-176567. (Columbia University. Teachers College. Contributions to Education: No. 766). Repr. of 1938 ed. 22.50 (ISBN 0-404-55766-X). AMS Pr.
Blair, Glenn M., et al. Educational Psychology. 4th ed. (Illus.). 672p. 1975. pap. text ed. write for info. (ISBN 0-02-310500-3, 31050). Macmillan.
Blair, Graeme. Sulfur in the Tropics. (Technical Bulletin Ser.: T-12). (Illus.). 71p. (Orig.). 1979. pap. 4.00 (ISBN 0-88090-011-3). Intl Fertilizer.
Blair, Guillermo, tr. see Ford, LeRoy.
Blair, Gwenda. Laura Ingalls Wilder. (Beginning Biography Bk.). (Illus.). 64p. (gr. 1-4). 1981. lib. bdg. 6.99 (ISBN 0-399-61139-8, Putnam); pap. 3.95 (ISBN 0-399-20953-0). Putnam Pub Group.
Blair, H., ed. see Nekrasov, V.
Blair, Harry C. & Tarshis, Rebecca. Lincoln's Constant Ally: Life of Col. Edward D. Baker. (Illus.). 234p. 1960. 7.95 (ISBN 0-87595-010-8). Oreg Hist Soc.
Blair, Harry W. The Political Economy of Participation in Local Development Programs: Short-Term Impasse & Long-Term Change in South Asia & the United States from the 1950s to the 1970s. (Monograph Ser.). 180p. (Orig.). 1981. pap. text ed. 10.65 (ISBN 0-86731-055-3). RDC Ctr Intl Stud.
Blair, Hugh. A Critical Dissertation on the Poems of Ossian. LC 78-67648. 1980. Repr. of 1765 ed. 22.50 (ISBN 0-404-17178-8). AMS Pr.
--Lectures on Rhetoric & Belles Lettres. 1824. 50.00 (ISBN 0-8274-1468-4). R West.
--Lectures on Rhetoric & Belles Lettres, 3 vols. 1743. Set. 100.00 (ISBN 0-686-17750-9). Ridgeway Bks.
Blair, I. Taming the Atom: Facing the Future with Nuclear Power. 1983. 27.00 (ISBN 0-9960023-8-3, Pub. by A Hilger England); pap. 11.50 (ISBN 0-9960027-2-3, Pub. by A Hilger England). Heyden.
Blair, I. M., et al. Aspects of Energy Conversion. 800p. 1976. text ed. 97.00 (ISBN 0-08-021175-5). Pergamon.
Blair, Iain. Frankie Goes to Hollywood. (Illus.). 80p. (Orig.). 1985. pap. 4.95 (ISBN 0-8092-5275-9). Contemp Bks.
Blair, Ian. Investigating Rape: A New Approach for Police. LC 84-23802. 110p. 1985. 26.00 (ISBN 0-7099-2098-9, Pub. by Croom Helm Ltd). Longwood Pub Group.
Blair, J. A., jt. auth. see Johnson, R. H.
Blair, J. A., ed. Chemistry & Biology of Pteridines: Pteridines & Folic Acid Derivatives. LC 83-7666. xxxvi, 1070p. 1983. 128.00x (ISBN 3-11-008560-7). De Gruyter.
Blair, J. Allen. Daniel: Living Courageously. LC 70-140898. 1971. pap. 4.95 (ISBN 0-87213-044-4). Loizeaux.
--First Corinthians: Living Wisely. LC 68-58844. 1969. pap. 5.50 (ISBN 0-87213-057-6). Loizeaux.

--Job: Living Patiently. LC 66-25720. 1966. pap. 5.95 (ISBN 0-87213-051-7). Loizeaux.

--John: Living Eternally. LC 77-28529. 1978. pap. 4.95 (ISBN 0-87213-046-0). Loizeaux.

--Jonah: Living Obediently. LC 63-18265. 1963. pap. 3.95 (ISBN 0-87213-050-9). Loizeaux.

--Living Peacefully: First Peter. 1959. pap. 3.50 (ISBN 0-87213-052-5). Loizeaux.

--Living Reliantly: Twenty-Third Psalm. 1958. pap. 2.75 (ISBN 0-87213-054-1). Loizeaux.

--Living Victoriously: Philippians. LC 62-290. 1962. pap. 2.75 (ISBN 0-87213-056-8). Loizeaux.

--Second Peter: Living Faithfully. LC 61-14600. 1961. pap. 4.95 (ISBN 0-87213-047-9). Loizeaux.

Blair, J. Antony & Johnson, Ralph H., eds. Informal Logic: The First International Symposium. LC 80-67674. 175p. (Orig.). 1980. pap. 9.95x (ISBN 0-918528-09-7). Edgepress.

Blair, J. W. Coleccion Navidena, No. 1 & 2. 1980. No. 1. pap. 1.75 (ISBN 0-311-08201-7); No. 2. pap. 1.75 (ISBN 0-311-08202-5). Casa Bautista.

Blair, James, jt. auth. see Toulmin, Harry.

Blair, Joan & Blair, Clay, Jr. Return from the River Kwai. 320p. 1981. pap. 2.75 (ISBN 0-345-29007-0). Ballantine.

Blair, John. Illustrated Discography of Surf Music. rev ed. (Illus.). 1983. pap. 15.95x (ISBN 0-9601880-1-0). J Blair.

--The Illustrated Discography of Surf Music, 1961-1965. 2nd, rev. ed. (Rock & Roll Reference Ser.: No. 15). 1985. (individuals) 19.50 (ISBN 0-87650-174-9); (institutions) 29.50. Pierian.

--Industrial Polarization & the Location of New Manufacturing Firms: An Empirical Application. (Discussion Paper Ser.: No. 89). 1976. pap. 3.25 (ISBN 0-686-32255-X). Regional Sci Res Inst.

Blair, John G. The Confidence Man in Modern Fiction: A Rogue's Gallery of Six Portraits. LC 79-50928. (Critical Studies). 142p. 1979. text ed. 28.50x (ISBN 0-06-490449-0, 06352). B&N Imports.

Blair, John M. The Control of Oil. 1978. pap. 6.95 (ISBN 0-394-72532-8, V-532, Vin). Random.

Blair, John M., et al, eds. see U. S. Smaller War Plants Corporation.

Blair, John P., jt. auth. see Barrett, G. Vincent.

Blair, John P. & Nachmias, David, eds. Fiscal Retrenchment & Urban Policy. LC 79-13695. (Urban Affairs Annual Reviews: Vol.17). 1979. 28.00 (ISBN 0-8039-1242-0); pap. 14.00 (ISBN 0-8039-1243-9). Sage.

Blair, John P., jt. ed. see Bingham, Richard D.

Blair, John S. The Profitable Way: Carbon Plate Steel Specifying & Purchasing Handbook. (Illus.). 194p. 1978. 39.95x (ISBN 0-931690-08-0). Genium Pub.

--The Profitable Way: Carbon Sheet Steel Specifying & Purchasing Handbook. (Illus.). 158p. 1978. 39.95x (ISBN 0-931690-04-8). Genium Pub.

--The Profitable Way: Carbon Strip Steel Specifying & Purchasing Handbook. (Illus.). 194p. 1978. 39.95x (ISBN 0-931690-05-6). Genium Pub.

Blair, Karen. The Clubwoman As Feminist: True Womanhood Redefined, 1868 to 1914. LC 79-26390. 199p. 1980. text ed. 34.50x (ISBN 0-8419-0538-X). Holmes & Meier.

--Cubal Analysis: A Post-Sexist Model of the Psyche. pap. 10.50 (ISBN 0-317-03639-4). Assoc Bk.

Blair, Karin. Meaning in Star Trek. LC 77-7438. (Illus.). 1978. 9.95 (ISBN 0-89012-010-2). Anima Pubns.

Blair, Katherine D. Four Villages-Architecture in Nepal: Studies of Village Life. LC 83-71007. (Illus.). 72p. 1985. pap. 10.00 (ISBN 0-226-05594-9, 05594-9, Pub. by Craft & Folk Art Museum). U of Chicago Pr.

Blair, Kay. Ladies of the Lamplight. pap. 2.50 (ISBN 0-936564-31-8). Little London.

Blair, Kay R. Ladies of the Lamplight. 1978. 2.50 (ISBN 0-913488-01-1). Timberline Bks.

Blair, Lawrence. Rhythms of Vision: The Changing Patterns of Belief. LC 75-34508. (Illus.). 256p. 1976. 8.95 (ISBN 0-8052-3610-4). Schocken.

Blair, Leigh, jt. auth. see Bernstein, Bonnie.

Blair, Leon B. Western Window in the Arab World. (Illus.). 342p. 1970. 17.50x (ISBN 0-292-70083-0). U of Tex Pr.

Blair, Leona. With This Ring. LC 83-10150. 384p. 1984. 16.95 (ISBN 0-385-29274-0). Delacorte.

--With This Ring. 400p. 1985. pap. 3.95 (ISBN 0-440-19709-0). Dell.

--A Woman's Place. 408p. 1981. 13.95 (ISBN 0-385-29156-6). Delacorte.

--A Woman's Place. 1983. pap. 3.95 (ISBN 0-440-19629-9). Dell.

Blair, Louis H., et al. Monitoring the Impacts of Prison & Parole Services: An Initial Examination. 88p. 1977. pap. 6.00x (ISBN 0-87766-201-0, 16900). Urban Inst.

Blair, Lowell, tr. The Essential Rousseau. 320p. (Orig.). 1974. pap. 3.95 (ISBN 0-452-00674-0, Mer). NAL.

Blair, Lowell, tr. see Dumas, Alexandre.

Blair, Lowell, tr. see Rostand, Edmond.

Blair, Marcia. The Final Appointment. (Mystery Puzzlers Ser.: No. 17). (Illus., Orig.). 1979. pap. 1.95 (ISBN 0-89083-452-0). Zebra.

--The Final Fair. (Mystery Puzzler Ser.: No. 21). (Illus., Orig.). 1979. pap. 1.95 (ISBN 0-89083-476-8). Zebra.

--The Final Guest. (Mystery Puzzler Ser.: No. 16). (Illus., Orig.). 1979. pap. 1.95 (ISBN 0-89083-436-9). Zebra.

--The Final Lie. (Mystery Puzzler Ser.: No. 6). (Illus., Orig.). 1978. pap. 1.95 (ISBN 0-89083-409-1). Zebra.

--The Final Pose. (Mystery Puzzler Ser.: No. 10). (Illus.). 1978. pap. 1.95 (ISBN 0-89083-422-9). Zebra.

--The Final Ring. (Mystery Puzzler Ser.: No. 2). (Illus.). 1978. pap. 1.95 (ISBN 0-89083-396-6). Zebra.

Blair, Mary. Mary Blair's Hors d'Oeuvre Cookbook. (Illus.). 302p. 1984. 20.00 (ISBN 0-88191-004-X). Freundlich.

Blair, Maury & Brendel, Doug. Maury: A True Story. LC 82-72580. 123p. (gr. 8-12). 1982. pap. 3.95 (ISBN 0-87123-323-1, 210323). Bethany Hse.

Blair, May. Once Upon the Lagan: The Story of the Lagan Canal. rev. ed. (Illus.). 144p. 1981. pap. 12.95x (ISBN 0-85640-245-1, Pub. by Blackstaff Pr). Longwood Pub Group.

Blair, P. H. An Introduction to Anglo-Saxon England. 2nd ed. LC 77-71404. (Illus.). 1977. 59.50 (ISBN 0-521-21650-8); pap. 15.95 (ISBN 0-521-29219-0). Cambridge U Pr.

Blair, Patricia, ed. Development in the People's Republic of China: A Selected Bibliography. LC 76-53149. (Occasional Papers: No. 8). 94p. 1976. 2.50 (ISBN 0-686-28696-0). Overseas Dev Council.

Blair, Patricia, jt. ed. see Ingle, John I.

Blair, Patricia W., ed. Health Needs of the World's Poor Women. 205p. pap. 17.50 (ISBN 0-941696-00-6). Equity Policy.

Blair, Peter D. Multi-Objective Regional Energy Planning. (Studies in Applied Regional Science: Vol. 14). 1979. lib. bdg. 22.95 (ISBN 0-89838-008-1, Pub. by Martinus Nijhoff Netherlands). Kluwer Academic.

Blair, Peter D., jt. auth. see Miller, Ronald E.

Blair, Peter D., et al. Geothermal Energy: Prospects for Energy Production. LC 81-13139. (Alternate Energy Ser.). 184p. 1982. 36.95x (ISBN 0-471-08063-2, Pub. by Wiley-Interscience). Wiley.

Blair, Peter H. Roman Britain & Early England 55 B. C. to A. D. 871. (Library History of England). (Illus.). 1966. pap. 7.95 (ISBN 0-393-00361-2, Norton Lib). Norton.

Blair, Peter Hunter see Malone, Kemp & Schibsbye, Knud.

Blair, Philip M. Federalism & Judicial Review in West Germany. 1981. 69.00x (ISBN 0-19-827427-0). Oxford U Pr.

Blair, Phillip M. Job Discrimination & Education: An Investment Analysis, a Case Study of Mexican-Americans in Santa Clara County, California. LC 70-180842. (Special Studies in U.S. Economic, Social & Political Issues). 1972. 36.50x (ISBN 0-89197-807-0). Irvington.

Blair, R. & Hunter, David. In Victorian Days & Other Papers. 1979. Repr. of 1939 ed. lib. bdg. 25.00 (ISBN 0-8482-3415-4). Norwood Edns.

Blair, R. D. & Kenny, L. W. Microeconomics for Managerial Decision Making. 1982. 33.95 (ISBN 0-07-005800-8). McGraw.

Blair, Ray, jt. auth. see Wentzel, Fred.

Blair, Rhonda L., jt. ed. see Faulkner, Thomas C.

Blair, Robert. Tales of the Superstitions: Origins of the Lost Dutchman Legend. LC 35-35054. 1975. 8.95 (ISBN 0-910152-07-1); pap. 4.95 (ISBN 0-910152-08-X). AZ Hist Foun.

Blair, Robert W., ed. Innovative Approaches to Language Teaching. 328p. 1982. pap. text ed. 15.95 (ISBN 0-88377-247-7). Newbury Hse.

Blair, Robert W., et al. Mayan Language Dictionary. LC 81-43356. 491p. 1981. lib. bdg. 91.00 (ISBN 0-8240-9277-5). Garland Pub.

Blair, Roger & Kaserman, David. Antitrust Economics. 1985. 27.95x (ISBN 0-256-02807-9). Irwin.

Blair, Roger D. & Kaserman, David L. Law & Economics of Vertical Integration & Control. 1983. 38.00 (ISBN 0-12-103480-1). Acad Pr.

Blair, Roger D. & Lanzillotti, Robert F., eds. The Conglomerate Corporation: An Antitrust Law & Economics Symposium. LC 80-22093. 384p. 1981. text ed. 40.00 (ISBN 0-89946-051-8). Oelgeschlager.

Blair, Ruth. Some Early Tax Digests of Georgia. 316p. 1971. Repr. of 1926 ed. 20.00 (ISBN 0-89308-003-9). Southern Hist Pr.

Blair, Sam, jt. auth. see Trevino, Lee.

Blair, Shannon. Call Me Beautiful. (Sweet Dreams Ser.: No. 69). 176p. (Orig.). pap. 2.25 (ISBN 0-553-24254-7). Bantam.

--Star Struck. (Sweet Dreams Ser.: No. 79). 176p. (gr. 6 up). 1985. pap. 2.25 (ISBN 0-553-24971-1). Bantam.

Blair, Sheila, jt. auth. see Grabar, Oleg.

Blair, Sheri. Eight Moves to a Perfect Body. (Illus.). 96p. (Orig.). 1983. pap. 4.95 (ISBN 0-87491-727-1). Acropolis.

Blair, Skippy. Contemporary Social Dance. (Ballroom Dancing Ser.). 1985. lib. bdg. 70.00 (ISBN 0-87700-860-4). Revisionist Pr.

--Disco to Tango & Back. 1978. 19.95 (ISBN 0-932980-01-5). Golden St Dance Teach Assn.

--Skippy Blair on Contemporary Social Dance. 1978. 19.95 (ISBN 0-932980-00-7). Golden St Dance Teach Assn.

Blair, T. & Fite, R. Weather Elements: Text in Elementary Meteorology. 5th ed. 1965. ref. ed. 35.95 (ISBN 0-13-947721-7). P-H.

Blair, Thomas. Oqua. LC 79-15861. 1985. 9.95 (ISBN 0-87949-163-9). Ashley Bks.

Blair, Thomas L. The International Urban Crisis. 176p. 1974. 6.95 (ISBN 0-8090-5848-0). Hill & Wang.

Blair, Thomas L., ed. Urban Innovation Abroad: Problem Cities in Search of Solutions. 424p. 1984. 55.00x (ISBN 0-306-41492-9, Plenum Pr). Plenum Pub.

Blair, Thomas S. Botanic Drugs: Their Materia Medica, Pharmacology & Therapeutics. 1976. lib. bdg. 134.75 (ISBN 0-8490-1539-1). Gordon Pr.

Blair, Timothy H., jt. auth. see Rupley, William H.

Blair, Timothy R., jt. auth. see Rupley, William H.

Blair, Tom, jt. auth. see Morgan, Neil.

Blair, W. Charles & McGill, John K. Employing Family Members in Your Business: A Tax Bonanza. Blair, Floy & McGill, Meredith, eds. 258p. 1983. pap. 24.95 (ISBN 0-915771-00-4). Blair McGill Co.

Blair, W. Frank. The Rusty Lizard: A Population Study. LC 59-8122. pap. 47.80 (ISBN 0-317-29262-5, 2055521). Bks Demand UMI.

Blair, W. Frank, ed. Evolution in the Genus "Bufo". (Illus.). 467p. 1972. 35.00x (ISBN 0-292-72001-7). U of Tex Pr.

Blair, Walter. Mark Twain & Huck Finn: 1855-1873. Frank, Michael B. & Sanderson, Kenneth M, eds. (California Library Reprint Ser.). 1974. 39.50x (ISBN 0-520-02521-0). U of Cal Pr.

--Mike Fink, King of Mississippi Keelboatmen. LC 74-138143. (Illus.). 1971. Repr. of 1933 ed. lib. bdg. 17.00x (ISBN 0-8371-5600-9, BLMF). Greenwood.

--Native American Humor. 1960. pap. text ed. 12.25 scp (ISBN 0-8102-0044-9, HarpC). Har-Row.

--Native American Humor: 1800-1900. 1979. Repr. of 1937 ed. lib. bdg. 40.00 (ISBN 0-8495-0524-0). Arden Lib.

Blair, Walter & Gerber, John. Repertory. 2nd. ed. 1967. text ed. 20.60x (ISBN 0-673-05240-0). Scott F.

Blair, Walter & Hill, Hamlin. America's Humor: From Poor Richard to Doonesbury. (Galaxy Bks.: No. 609). 1978. pap. 10.95 (ISBN 0-19-502756-6). Oxford U Pr.

Blair, Walter & Franklin, Meine J., eds. Half Horse Half Alligator: The Growth of the Mike Fink Legend. LC 77-70578. (Intenational Folklore Ser.). Repr. of 1956 ed. lib. bdg. 24.50x (ISBN 0-405-10079-5). Ayer Co Pubs.

Blair, Walter & McDavid, Raven I., Jr., eds. The Mirth of a Nation: America's Great Dialect. LC 81-16403. (Illus.). 336p. 1983. 35.00x (ISBN 0-8166-1022-3); pap. 12.95x (ISBN 0-8166-1168-8). U of Minn Pr.

Blair, Walter & Meine, Franklin J., eds. Half Horse Half Alligator: The Growth of the Mike Fink Legend. LC 81-3358. (Illus.). x, 289p. 1981. pap. 6.50 (ISBN 0-8032-6060-1, BB 772, Bison). U of Nebr Pr.

Blair, Walter, ed. see Melville, Herman.

Blair, Walter, ed. see Twain, Mark.

Blair, Walter, et al. The Literature of the United States, 2 vols. 3rd ed. (Heritage printing). 1970. Vol. 2. text ed. 19.50x (ISBN 0-673-07637-7). Scott F.

Blair, Wesley. The Complete Book of Target Shooting. Schnell, Judith, ed. (Illus.). 416p. 1984. 24.95 (ISBN 0-8117-0427-0). Stackpole.

Blair, William. Fire! Survival & Prevention. (Illus.). 192p. (Orig.). 1983. pap. 3.80i (ISBN 0-06-465147-9, P-BN 5147). B&N NY.

--An Inquiry into the State of Slavery Amongst the Romans. LC 72-92417. 1833. 39.00x (ISBN 0-403-00152-8). Scholarly.

Blair, William A. & Clark, W. A. The Historical Sketch of Banking in North Carolina & the History of the Banking Institutions Organized in South Carolina Prior to 1860, 2 vols. 1. Bruchey, Stuart, ed. LC 80-1134. (The Rise of Commercial Banking Ser.). (Illus.). 1981. Repr. of 1922 ed. lib. bdg. 48.00x (ISBN 0-405-13634-X). Ayer Co Pubs.

Blairs. Fear Round About. 1985. pap. 2.95 (ISBN 0-8027-3120-1). Walker & Co.

Blais, Madeleine. They Say You Can't Have a Baby: The Dilemma of Infertility. 1979. 12.95 (ISBN 0-393-01260-3). Norton.

Blais, Marie-Claire. The Day is Dark & Three Travelers. 208p. 1985. pap. 5.95 (ISBN 0-14-007911-4). Penguin.

--Nights in the Underground. 208p. 1983. pap. 3.95 (ISBN 0-7736-7032-7). Beaufort Bks NY.

--St. Lawrence Blues. Manheim, Ralph, tr. from Fr. 229p. 1974. 7.95 (ISBN 0-374-25350-1). FS&G.

--A Season in the Life of Emmanuel. Coltman, Derek, tr. from Fr. 145p. 1966. 10.95 (ISBN 0-374-14628-4); pap. 5.95 (ISBN 0-374-51616-2). FS&G.

Blais, Marie-Claire, jt. ed. see Teleky, Richard.

Blaisdell, Donald C. European Financial Control in the Ottoman Empire. LC 29-15742. Repr. of 1929 ed. 10.00 (ISBN 0-404-00895-X). AMS Pr.

--Government & Agriculture: Growth of Federal Farm Aid. LC 72-2365. (FDR & the Era of the New Deal Ser.). 217p. 1974. Repr. of 1940 ed. lib. bdg. 32.50 (ISBN 0-306-70488-9). Da Capo.

--International Organization. LC 66-16837. pap. 134.80 (ISBN 0-317-09594-3, 2012468). Bks Demand UMI.

Blaisdell, F. William & Lewis, Frank R. Respiratory Distress Syndrome of Shock & Trauma: Post-Traumatic Respiratory Failure. LC 76-19603. (Major Problems in Clinical Surgery: Vol. 21). (Illus.). 1977. text ed. 23.00 (ISBN 0-7216-1715-8). Saunders.

Blaisdell, F. William & Trunkey, Donald D. Abdominal Trauma. LC 81-65553. (Illus.). 272p. 1982. text ed. 42.00 (ISBN 0-86577-011-5). Thieme-Stratton.

Blaisdell, Foster W., Jr. & Kalinke, Marianne E., trs. Erex Saga & Ivens Saga: The Old Norse Versions of Chretien de Troye's "Erec" & "Yvain". LC 77-5395. xxiv, 88p. 1977. 10.95x (ISBN 0-8032-0925-8). U of Nebr Pr.

Blaisdell, Frank. Just Ropes. Dawson, Steve, ed. 95p. 1981. pap. 10.00 (ISBN 0-915926-50-4). Magic Ltd.

--More of Magic. Dawson, Steve, ed. (Illus.). iv, 97p. (gr. 8). 1980. 10.00 (ISBN 0-915926-48-2). Magic Ltd.

Blaisdell, Frank E. Blaisdell's Original Magic. 1976. 20.00 (ISBN 0-915926-19-9). Magic Ltd.

--Magical Fun with Magic Squares. Walker, Barbara, ed. (Illus.). 86p. (Orig.). 1978. pap. 10.00 (ISBN 0-915926-35-0). Magic Ltd.

Blaisdell, Gus. Prose Ocean. (Illus.). 1975. perfect bound in wrappers 3.00 (ISBN 0-685-78877-6, Pub. by Bear Hug). Small Pr Dist.

Blaisdell, Gus, jt. auth. see Baltz, Lewis.

Blaisdell, Gus, ed. see Connell, Evan S.

Blaisdell, Harold F. The Art of Fishing with Worms & Other Live Bait. 1978. 14.50 (ISBN 0-394-40039-9). Knopf.

Blaisdell, Thomas C., Jr. Federal Trade Commission. LC 32-26900. Repr. of 1932 ed. 10.00 (ISBN 0-404-00896-8). AMS Pr.

Blaisdell, William F. & Trunkey, Donald D. Cervicothoracic Trauma. (The Trauma Management Ser.). (Illus.). 256p. 1985. text ed. 42.00 (ISBN 0-86577-129-4). Thieme-Stratton.

Blaise, Clark. Lusts. LC 82-45100. (Illus.). 264p. 1983. 14.95 (ISBN 0-385-15474-7). Doubleday.

--Lusts. (Penguin Fiction Ser.). 272p. 1985. pap. 6.95 (ISBN 0-14-007387-6). Penguin.

Blaise, Clark & Mukherjee, Bharati. Days & Nights in Calcutta. LC 75-40711. 240p. 1977. 8.95 (ISBN 0-385-02895-4). Doubleday.

Blaise, Michael. The Complete Book of Disasters. (Illus.). 192p. 1985. 9.98 (ISBN 0-943392-64-0, Tripro Pub). Tribeca Comm.

Blaisse, Mark. Anwar Sadat: The Last Hundred Days. 76p. 16.95. Vendome.

Blakar, Rolv M. Communication: A Social Perspective on Clinical Issues. 152p. 1984. pap. 18.00x (ISBN 82-00-06742-4). Universitet.

--Studies of Familial Communication & Psychopathology: A Socio-Developmental Approach to Deviant Behavior. 192p. 1980. pap. 18.00x (ISBN 8-20001-999-3). Universitet.

Blake. Hello & Goodbye. 1965. 2.00 (ISBN 0-685-41666-6). Child Study.

Blake, A., ed. The Black Papers on Design: Selected Writings of the Late Sir Misha Black. 260p. 1983. 61.00 (ISBN 0-08-026771-8). Pergamon.

Blake, A. G. A Seminar on Time. LC 79-52756. 1980. 5.95 (ISBN 0-934254-00-1). Claymont Comm.

Blake, Alexander. Design of Curved Members for Machines. LC 79-12202. 288p. 1979. Repr. of 1966 ed. lib. bdg. 18.50 (ISBN 0-88275-970-1). Krieger.

--Handbook of Mechanics, Materials & Structures. (Mechanical Engineering Practice Ser.). 1000p. 1985. 71.95 (ISBN 0-471-86239-8). Wiley.

--Practical Stress Analysis in Engineering Design. (Mechanical Engineering Ser.: Vol. 12). (Illus.). 680p. 1982. 49.50 (ISBN 0-8247-1370-2). Dekker.

Blake, Alma C. Of Life & Love & Things. 1971. 4.95 (ISBN 0-87012-075-1). McClain.

Blake, Amy, illus. The Dance Notebook: An Illustrated Journal with Quotes. (Illus.). 96p. (Orig.). 1984. pap. 4.95 (ISBN 0-89471-275-6); lib. bdg. 12.90 (ISBN 0-89471-276-4). Running Pr.

Blake, Avril. Misha Black. (Design Council Ser.). (Illus.). 108p. (Orig.). 1985. pap. 12.50x (ISBN 0-87663-870-1). Universe.

Blake, B. J. Case Marking in Australian Languages. LC 77-88816. (Linguistic Ser.: No. 23). (Illus.). 1977. pap. text ed. 14.00x (ISBN 0-391-00813-7). Humanities.

Blake, B. J., jt. auth. see Mallinson, G.

Blake, B. J., jt. ed. see Dixon, R. M.

Blake, B. J., jt. ed. see Dixon, R. M. W.

Blake, B. J., et al. Papers on the Languages of Australian Aboriginals. (AIAS Linguistics Ser.: No. 16). (Orig.). 1971. pap. text ed. 14.00x (ISBN 0-85575-017-0). Humanities.

Blake, Ben, ed. Four Soviet Plays. LC 77-174873. Repr. of 1937 ed. 31.00 (ISBN 0-405-08273-8, Blom Pubns). Ayer Co Pubs.

Blake, Benjamin, et al. The Kingston Trio on Record. LC 85-50660. (Illus.). 200p. (Orig.). 1985. pap. 14.95 (ISBN 0-9614594-0-9). Kingston Korner.

Blake, Bud. Tiger. 128p. 1983. pap. 1.75 (ISBN 0-448-15721-7). Ace Bks.
--Tiger Turns On. 1983. pap. 1.75 (ISBN 0-448-15722-5, Tempo). Ace Bks.
Blake, C. D. Fundamentals of Modern Agriculture. 516p. 1974. (Pub. by Sydney U Pr); pap. 21.00x (ISBN 0-424-06930-X, Pub. by Sydney U Pr). Intl Spec Bk.
Blake, C. Fred. Ethnic Groups & Social Change in a Chinese Market Town. LC 80-16978. (Asian Studies at Hawaii: No. 27). 192p. (Orig.). 1981. pap. 10.50x (ISBN 0-8248-0720-0). UH Pr.
Blake, Carla. The Irish Cookbook. (Illus.). 157p. 1983. pap. 4.95 (ISBN 0-85342-233-8, Pub. by Mercier Pr Ireland). Irish Bks Media.
Blake, Charles A. The Pituitary Gland. Head, J. J., ed. LC 83-71203. (Carolina Biology Readers Ser.). (Illus.). 16p. (gr. 10 up). 1984. pap. 1.60 (ISBN 0-89278-318-4, 45-9718). Carolina Biological.
Blake, Christina. Dr. Beautiful. 408p. (Orig.). 1984. pap. 3.50 (ISBN 0-345-31611-8). Ballantine.
Blake, Christopher. Fair, Fair Ladies of Chantres Street. 1965. pap. 3.95 (ISBN 0-87651-203-1). Southern U Pr.
--Red Beans & Ricely Yours. 1974. pap. 2.50 (ISBN 0-317-11781-5). Southern U Pr.
Blake, Claire. Greenhouse Gardening for Fun. (Illus.). 1967. pap. 3.95 (ISBN 0-688-06737-9). Morrow.
Blake, Clarence N. & Martin, Donald F. Quiz Book on Black America. (Illus.). 224p. (gr. 7 up). 1976. 6.95 (ISBN 0-395-24389-0). HM.
--Quiz Book on Black America. (gr. 7 up). 1976. pap. 3.95 o.s. (ISBN 0-395-24974-0, Sandpiper). HM.
Blake, David & Ormerod, Paul. The Economics of Prosperity: Social Priorities in the Eighties. 230p. 1980. 15.00x (ISBN 0-86216-013-8, Pub. by McIntyre England). State Mutual Bk.
Blake, David, jt. auth. see Barnes, Charles.
Blake, David & Travis, Carole, eds. Periodicals from Africa: A Bibliography & Union List of Periodicals Published in Africa, First Supplement. 1984. lib. bdg. 60.00 (ISBN 0-8161-8525-5, Hall Reference). G K Hall.
Blake, David H. & Walters, Robert S. The Politics of Global Economic Relations. 2nd ed. (Illus.). 320p. 1983. pap. 18.95 (ISBN 0-13-684449-9). P-H.
Blake, David H. & Lambert, Richard D., eds. The Multinational Corporation. new ed. LC 72-85688. (The Annals of the American Academy of Political & Social Science: No. 403). 300p. 1972. 15.00 (ISBN 0-87761-154-8); pap. 7.95 (ISBN 0-87761-153-X). Am Acad Pol Soc Sci.
Blake, David H., et al. Social Auditing: Evaluating the Impact of Corporate Programs. LC 76-2901. (Illus.). 176p. 1976. pap. text ed. 16.95 (ISBN 0-275-85710-7). Praeger.
Blake, David P, jt. auth. see Barnes, Charles.
Blake, David P., jt. auth. see Barnes, Charles.
Blake, David P., et al. Making Seventy-Five Rugs by the Square. (Illus.). 1978. 10.95 (ISBN 0-517-52471-6). Crown.
Blake, Dick. Instant Dance. (Ballroom Dance Ser.). 1985. lib. bdg. 75.00 (ISBN 0-87799-859-0). Revisionist Pr.
Blake, Donna J., jt. auth. see Glerum, Richard Z.
Blake, Duane L. Dynamics of Human Relations in Vocational Education: The Development of Self-Confidence & a Sense of Mastery. LC 77-9416. 152p. 1979. pap. 11.00x (ISBN 0-910328-26-9). Carroll Pr.
Blake, Elizabeth. Hello & Goodbye: A Play for Parents About Learning to Love & Let Go. 39p. 1965. pap. 2.30 (ISBN 0-686-12274-7). Jewish Bd Family.
Blake, Elizabeth J. Up & Down. LC 78-144726. (Yale Ser. of Younger Poets: No. 19). Repr. of 1924 ed. 18.00 (ISBN 0-404-53819-3). AMS Pr.
Blake, Emmet R. Manual of Neotropical Birds: Spheniscidae (Penguins) to Laridae (Gulls & Allies, Vol. 1. LC 75-43229. (Illus.). 640p. 1977. lib. bdg. 100.00x (ISBN 0-226-05641-4). U of Chicago Pr.
Blake, Faro. Devil's Gambit. (A Zeke Masters Western Bk.). (Orig.). 1983. pap. 2.25 (ISBN 0-671-49306-X). PB.
Blake, Fay M. The Strike in the American Novel. LC 72-623. 295p. 1972. 16.50 (ISBN 0-8108-0481-6). Scarecrow.
Blake, Fay M. & Newman, H. Morton. Verbis non Factis: Words Meant to Influence Political Choices in the United States, 1800-1980. LC 84-1325. 143p. 1984. 13.50 (ISBN 0-8108-1688-1). Scarecrow.
Blake, Forrester. Johnny Christmas. (ZIA Bks.). 1982. pap. 6.95x (ISBN 0-8263-0608-X, J-10). U of NM Pr.
Blake, Frank R. Grammar of the Tagalog Language, the Chief Native Idiom of the Philippine Islands. (American Oriental Ser.). 1925. 28.00 (ISBN 0-527-02676-X). Kraus Repr.
Blake, G. H. & Lawless, R. I., eds. The Changing Middle Eastern City. LC 80-479247. (Illus.). 273p. 1980. 28.50x (ISBN 0-06-490451-2, 06353). B&N Imports.
Blake, Gary & Bly, Robert W. Creative Careers: Real Jobs in Glamour Fields. LC 84-29093. 256p. 1985. pap. 9.95 (ISBN 0-471-81560-8). Wiley.
--How to Promote Your Own Business. (Illus.). 1983. pap. 10.95 (ISBN 0-452-25456-6, Plume). NAL.
Blake, Gary, jt. auth. see Bly, Robert W.
Blake, Gary, jt. auth. see McGaw, Charles.
Blake, George C. History of Radio Telegraphy & Telephony. LC 74-4667. (Telecommunications Ser). (Illus.). 425p. 1974. Repr. of 1928 ed. 35.50x (ISBN 0-405-06034-3). Ayer Co Pubs.
Blake, Gerald H., jt. auth. see Drysdale, Alasdair.
Blake, Henry. Talking with Horses. 1976. 9.95 (ISBN 0-87690-196-8). Dutton.
Blake, Howard. The Island Self. LC 72-91755. 128p. 1973. 8.50 (ISBN 0-87923-066-5); pap. 5.95 (ISBN 0-87923-089-4). Godine.
Blake, Ian F. Introduction to Applied Probability. LC 78-11360. 528p. 1979. text ed. 47.00x (ISBN 0-471-03210-7). Wiley.
Blake, Ian F. & Mullin, Ronald C. An Introduction to the Mathematical Theory of Coding. 1976. 29.50 (ISBN 0-12-103560-3). Acad Pr.
--The Mathematical Theory of Coding. 1975. 76.00 (ISBN 0-12-103550-6). Acad Pr.
Blake, Ian F., jt. auth. see Walker, B. J.
Blake, Ian F., ed. Algebraic Coding Theory: History & Development. LC 73-9627. (Benchmark Papers in Electrical Engineering & Computer Science: Vol. 3). 413p. 1973. 52.50 (ISBN 0-87933-038-4). Van Nos Reinhold.
Blake, Irving H. A Comparison of the Animal Communities of Coniferous & Deciduous Forests. Repr. of 1927 ed. 15.00 (ISBN 0-384-04665-7). Johnson Repr.
Blake, J. F. Cornbrash Fauna, Pts. 1 & 2. Repr. of 1905 ed. Set. 18.00 (ISBN 0-384-04669-X). Johnson Repr.
Blake, J. G., ed. see Thoreau, Henry.
Blake, James N. Monty Monkey-Shines with Speech Sounds. (Illus.). 80p. 1973. spiral bdg. 12.75x (ISBN 0-398-02791-9). C C Thomas.
--Run Your Car on Sunshine: Using Solar Energy for a Solar Powered Car. LC 80-82734. (Illus.). 64p. 1981. lib. bdg. 12.95 (ISBN 0-915216-64-7); pap. 4.95 (ISBN 0-915216-65-5). Marathon Intl Pub Co.
--Speech Education Activities for Children. (Illus.). 136p. 1970. 14.50x (ISBN 0-398-00165-0). C C Thomas.
--Speech, Language & Learning Disorders: Education & Therapy. (Illus.). 172p. 1971. 12.75x (ISBN 0-398-00166-9). C C Thomas.
--Word Clowns & Sentence Circuses. (Illus.). 48p. 1973. pap. 10.75x spiral (ISBN 0-398-02790-0). C C Thomas.
Blake, James Neal. ABC Phonics & Faces. (Illus.). 84p. 1972. spiral 9.75x (ISBN 0-398-02528-2). C C Thomas.
Blake, Jennifer. Embrace & Conquer. 320p. 1981. pap. 4.95 (ISBN 0-449-90056-8, Columbine). Fawcett.
--Embrace & Conquer. 352p. 1983. pap. 3.50 (ISBN 0-449-12592-0, GM). Fawcett.
--Fierce Eden. LC 84-91681. 384p. 1985. pap. 6.95 (ISBN 0-449-90100-9, Columbine). Fawcett.
--Golden Fancy. 1980. pap. 2.75 (ISBN 0-449-14369-4, GM). Fawcett.
--Midnight Waltz. 384p. 1985. pap. 6.95 (ISBN 0-449-90099-1, Columbine). Fawcett.
--Royal Passion. pap. 7.95. Fawcett.
--Royal Seduction. 1983. pap. 5.95 (ISBN 0-449-90081-9). Fawcett.
--Royal Seduction. 416p. 1985. pap. 3.95 (ISBN 0-449-12979-9, GM). Fawcett.
--The Storm & the Splendor. (Orig.). 1979. pap. 2.95 (ISBN 0-449-14282-5, GM). Fawcett.
--Surrender in Moonlight. 416p. 1984. pap. 6.95 (ISBN 0-449-90082-7, Columbine). Fawcett.
--Tender Betrayal. 416p. 1984. pap. 3.50 (ISBN 0-446-31314-9). Warner Bks.
Blake, Jeri. When Presidents Die: A Sidereal Investigation. LC 80-65776. (Illus.). 224p. (Orig.). 1980. pap. 9.00 (ISBN 0-936560-00-2). DoubLeo Pubns.
Blake, Jim & Ernst, Barbara. The Great Perpetual Learning Machine: A Stupendous Collection of Ideas, Games, Experiments, Activities, & Recommendations for Further Exploration with Tons of Illustrations. LC 76-24124. (YA) 1976. pap. 11.95 (ISBN 0-316-09937-6). Little.
Blake, John. His Satanic Majesty: Mick Jagger. LC 84-47970. (Illus.). 192p. 1986. pap. 10.95 (ISBN 0-03-000744-5, Owl Bks). HR&W.
Blake, John B. Public Health in the Town of Boston, 1630-1822. LC 59-10314. (Historical Studies: No. 72). (Illus.). 1959. 17.50x (ISBN 0-674-72250-7). Harvard U Pr.
Blake, John B. & Roos, Charles, eds. Medical Reference Works, 1679-1966: A Selected Bibliography. LC 67-30664. 1967. 10.00 (ISBN 0-912176-02-4). Med Lib Assn.
Blake, John B., ed. see Conference on the History of Medicinal Drug Control (1968: National Library of Medicine.
Blake, John W. European Beginnings in West Africa, 1454-1578: A Survey of the First Century of White Enterprise in West Africa, with Special Emphasis upon the Rivalry of the Great Powers. LC 72-97393. Repr. of 1937 ed. cancelled (ISBN 0-8371-2671-1, BLB&, Pub. by Negro U Pr). Greenwood.
Blake, John W., ed. Europeans in West Africa, Fourteen Fifty to Fifteen Sixty, 2 vols. in 1, (Hakluyt Society Works Ser.: No. 2, Vols. 86-87). (Illus.). 1941-1942. 62.00 (ISBN 0-317-16497-X). Kraus Repr.
Blake, Judith & Donovan, Jerry J. Western European Censuses, Nineteen Sixty. LC 76-4558. (Population Monograph Ser.: No. 8). 1976. Repr. of 1971 ed. lib. bdg. 48.50 (ISBN 0-8371-8831-8, BLWE). Greenwood.
Blake, Judith, et al. Family Structure in Jamaica: The Social Context of Reproduction. LC 80-12362. (Illus.). x, 262p. 1980. Repr. of 1961 ed. lib. bdg. 24.75x (ISBN 0-313-22448-X, BLFS). Greenwood.
Blake, Katherine. Night Stands at the Door. 240p. 1984. pap. 3.50 (ISBN 0-8128-8055-2). Stein & Day.
Blake, Kathleen. Love & the Woman Question in Victorian Literature: The Art of Self-Postponement. LC 83-11918. 272p. 1983. 29.50x (ISBN 0-389-20425-0, 07311). B&N Imports.
Blake, Kathryn. Educating Exceptional Pupils: An Introduction to Contemporary Practices. LC 80-15222. (Illus.). 528p. 1981. text ed. 24.25 (ISBN 0-201-00083-0); instr's. manual 3.50 (ISBN 0-201-00084-9). Addison-Wesley.
Blake, Kathryn A. College Reading Skills. (Illus.). 304p. 1973. pap. text ed. 16.95 (ISBN 0-13-150003-1). P-H.
Blake, Kathryn A. & McBee, Mary L. Essays. 2nd ed. 1981. pap. text ed. write for info. (ISBN 0-02-472160-3). Macmillan.
Blake, Kathryn A., jt. auth. see Johnson, G. Orville.
Blake, L. S., ed. Civil Engineer's Reference Book. 3rd ed. 1800p. 1977. 119.95 (ISBN 0-408-70475-6). Butterworth.
Blake, Lamont V. Antennas. 425p. 1984. text ed. 55.00 (ISBN 0-89006-154-8). Artech Hse.
--Radar Range-Performance: Analysis. LC 76-16318. (Illus.). 480p. 1980. 43.00x (ISBN 0-669-00781-1). Lexington Bks.
Blake, Laurel. Into the Whirlwind. (Second Chance at Love Ser.: No. 202). 192p. 1984. pap. 1.95 (ISBN 0-515-07818-2). Jove Pubns.
--Stranger in Paradise. 192p. 1983. pap. 1.95 (ISBN 0-515-07242-7). Jove Pubns.
Blake, Leonard, ed. see Phillips, Charles H.
Blake, Liam. Real Ireland: People & Landscape. (Illus.). 112p. 1984. 19.95 (ISBN 0-88162-053-X, Pub. by Salem Hse Ltd). Merrimack Pub Cir.
Blake, M. Mexico. 1976. lib. bdg. 59.95 (ISBN 0-8490-2242-8). Gordon Pr.
Blake, M. B., et al. Education of the Modern Girl. facs. ed. LC 67-30208. (Essay Index Reprint Ser). 1929. 17.00 (ISBN 0-8369-0406-0). Ayer Co Pubs.
Blake, Marion E. Ancient Roman Construction in Italy from the Prehistoric Period to Augustus. (Carnegie Institution Publication Ser.: No. 570). (Illus.). 1968. Repr. of 1947 ed. 44.00 (ISBN 0-527-08850-1). Kraus Repr.
Blake, Marion E. & Bishop, Doris T. Roman Construction in Italy from Nerva Through the Antonines. LC 72-83463. (Memoirs Ser.: Vol. 96). (Illus.). 1973. 20.00 (ISBN 0-87169-096-9). Am Philos.
Blake, Maurice C. & Davis, Wilbur W. Boston Postmarks to Eighteen Ninety. LC 72-85120. (Illus.). 392p. 1974. Repr. of 1949 ed. 35.00x (ISBN 0-88000-040-6). Quarterman.
Blake, Melody, ed. Hollywood Reporter Studio Blu-Book. 258p. 1984. 25.00 (ISBN 0-941140-02-4). Verdugo Pr.
--Hollywood Reporter Studio Blu-Book Directory, 1985. 300p. 1985. 35.00 (ISBN 0-941140-04-0). Verdugo Pr.
Blake, Michael, ed. see Dickson, Murray.
Blake, Michael J., jt. ed. see Kavass, Igor I.
Blake, Michael P. & Mitchell, William S., eds. Vibration & Acoustic Measurement Handbook. (Illus.). 1972. 34.50 (ISBN 0-8104-9195-8). Hayden.
Blake, Mindy. The Golf Swing of the Future. (Illus.). 124p. 1973. 10.95 (ISBN 0-393-08376-4). Norton.
Blake, N. F. The Canterbury Tales. 720p. 1980. text ed. 98.50 (ISBN 0-7131-6217-1). E Arnold.
--The English Language in Medieval Literature. 1979. pap. 9.95x (ISBN 0-416-72470-1, NO.2024). Methuen Inc.
--Non-Standard Language in English Literature. Crystal, David, ed. (Language Library). 217p. 1981. pap. 12.95x (ISBN 0-233-97422-9). Basil Blackwell.
--Shakespeare's Language: An Introduction. 154p. 1984. pap. 9.95 (ISBN 0-312-71430-0). St Martin.
Blake, N. F., jt. auth. see Lewis, R. E.
Blake, N. F., ed. see Caxton, William.
Blake, Neil F. The World of Show Jumping. 1973. Repr. 13.95 (ISBN 0-912830-29-8). Printed Horse.
Blake, Nelson M. Land into Water-Water into Land: A History of Water Management in Florida. LC 79-21836. (Illus.). viii, 344p. 1980. 19.95 (ISBN 0-8130-0642-2). U Presses Fla.
--Novelists' America: Fiction As History, 1910-1940. LC 68-31563. (Illus., Orig.). 1969. pap. 5.95x (ISBN 0-8156-2147-7). Syracuse U Pr.
--The Road to Reno: A History of Divorce in the United States. 1977. Repr. of 1962 ed. lib. bdg. 60.00x (ISBN 0-8371-9797-X, BLRR). Greenwood.
--Water for the Cities: A History of the Urban Water Supply Problem in the United States. (Illus.). 1956. 14.95x (ISBN 0-8156-2017-9). Syracuse U Pr.
Blake, Nelson M., jt. auth. see Barck, Oscar T.
Blake, Nelson M., jt. ed. see Rich, Jane K.
Blake, Nicholas. The Beast Must Die. LC 85-42552. (A Niegel Strangeways Mystery Ser.). 256p. 1985. pap. 3.50 (ISBN 0-06-080781-4, P 781, PL). Har-Row.
--Head of a Traveler. 1976. pap. 2.25i (ISBN 0-06-080398-3, P398, PL). Har-Row.
--Minute for Murder. lib. bdg. 13.95x (ISBN 0-89966-246-3). Buccaneer Bks.
--Minute for Murder. LC 85-42553. (A Nigel Strangeway Mystery Ser.). 256p. 1985. pap. 3.50 (ISBN 0-06-080782-2, P 782, PL). Har-Row.
--The Morning After Death. LC 66-22042. 212p. 1980. pap. 1.95i (ISBN 0-06-080520-X, P 520, PL). Har-Row.
--A Penknife in My Heart. LC 59-6338. 169p. 1980. pap. 2.25i (ISBN 0-06-080521-8, P 521, PL). Har-Row.
--The Private Wound. LC 68-15980. 224p. 1981. pap. 2.25i (ISBN 0-06-080531-5, P 531, PL). Har-Row.
--There's Trouble Brewing. LC 81-47805. 224p. 1982. pap. 3.37i (ISBN 0-06-080569-2, P 569, PL). Har-Row.
--Thou Shell of Death. 1977. pap. 1.95i (ISBN 0-06-080428-9, P428, PL). Har-Row.
Blake, Nigel & Pole, Kay, eds. Dangers of Deterrence: Philosophers on Nuclear Strategy. 169p. (Orig.). 1984. pap. 9.95x (ISBN 0-7100-9885-5). Routledge & Kegan.
--Objections to Nuclear Defence: Philosophers on Deterrence. 208p. (Orig.). 1984. pap. 11.95x (ISBN 0-7102-0249-0). Routledge & Kegan.
Blake, Norman, ed. English Historical Linguistics: Studies in Development, Vol. 1. 256p. 1983. text ed. 30.45x (ISBN 0-86127-007-X, Pub. by Avebury England). Humanities.
Blake, Norman L. The English Language in Medieval Literature. (Rowman & Littlefield University Library). 190p. 1977. 17.50x (ISBN 0-87471-989-5). Rowman.
Blake, O. William & Volp, Anne M. Lead-up Games to Team Sports. (Orig.). 1964. pap. text ed. 17.95 (ISBN 0-13-527028-6). P-H.
Blake, Olive. The Grape Jelly Mystery. new ed. LC 78-18040. (Illus.). 48p. (gr. 2-4). 1979. PLB 8.59 (ISBN 0-89375-096-4); pap. 1.95 (ISBN 0-89375-084-0). Troll Assocs.
--Mystery of the Lost Letter. new ed. LC 78-18037. (Illus.). 48p. (gr. 2-4). 1979. PLB 8.59 (ISBN 0-89375-093-X); pap. 1.95 (ISBN 0-89375-081-6). Troll Assocs.
--Mystery of the Lost Pearl. LC 78-60121. (Illus.). 48p. (gr. 2-4). 1979. PLB 8.59 (ISBN 0-89375-086-7); pap. 1.95 (ISBN 0-89375-074-3). Troll Assocs.
Blake, P., ed. Advanced Manufacturing Technology: Programming Research & Operations Logistics. 480p. 1980. 68.00 (ISBN 0-444-85455-X, North-Holland). Elsevier.
Blake, Patricia, ed. see Hayward, Max.
Blake, Patricia, ed. see Mayakovsky, Vladimir.
Blake, Patricia, ed. see Voznesensky, Andrei.
Blake, Peter. Davis, Brody & Associates. LC 83-43005. (Illus.). 204p. 1985. pap. 25.00 (ISBN 0-8478-0514-X). Rizzoli Intl.
--The Master Builders: Le Corbusier, Mies Van der Rohe, Frank Lloyd Wright. new ed. (Illus.). 432p. 1976. pap. 9.95 (ISBN 0-393-00796-0, N796, Norton Lib). Norton.
Blake, Peter & Sefton, Alan. Blake's Odyssey: The Round the World Race with Ceramco New Zealand. (Illus.). 198p. 1982. 29.95 (ISBN 0-340-27994-X, Pub. by Hodder & Stoughton). Sheridan.
Blake, Quentin. Mister Magnolia. 32p. (gr. k-3). 1980. 8.95 (ISBN 0-224-01612-1, Pub. by Jonathan Cape). Merrimack Pub Cir.
--Patrick. (Illus.). 32p. (gr. 4-7). 1980. 8.95 (ISBN 0-224-61463-0, Pub. by Jonathan Cape). Merrimack Pub Cir.
--Quentin Blake's Nursery Rhyme Book. LC 83-48171. (Illus.). 32p. (gr. k-3). 1984. 7.64i (ISBN 0-06-020533-4); PLB 8.89g (ISBN 0-06-020532-6). HarpJ.
--The Story of the Dancing Frog. LC 84-12222. (Illus.). 32p. (ps-3). 1985. PLB 9.99 (ISBN 0-394-97033-0); pap. 9.95 (ISBN 0-394-87033-6). Knopf.
Blake, R. & Mouton, J. Productivity: The Human Side. 1982. pap. 5.95 (ISBN 0-317-31399-1). AMACOM.
Blake, R., jt. auth. see Ruttkowski, W.
Blake, R. A. The Lutheran Milieu of the Films of Ingmar Bergman. LC 77-22905. (Dissertation on Films Ser.). 1978. lib. bdg. 26.50x (ISBN 0-405-10751-X). Ayer Co Pubs.
Blake, R. R. & Mouton, J. S. Executive Achievement: Making It at the Top. 192p. 1985. price not set (ISBN 0-07-005681-1). McGraw.
Blake, R. W. Fish Locomotion. LC 82-12861. (Illus.). 250p. 1983. 52.50 (ISBN 0-521-24303-3). Cambridge U Pr.
Blake, Randy, jt. auth. see Sekuler, Robert.
Blake, Rebecca. Forbidden Dreams. (Illus.). 176p. 1984. 40.00 (ISBN 0-7043-2475-X, Pub. by Quartet Bks). Merrimack Pub Cir.
Blake, Reed H. & Haroldsen, Edwin O. A Taxonomy of Concepts in Communication. (Humanistic Studies in the Communication Arts). (Illus.). 176p. 1975. pap. text ed. 6.95x (ISBN 0-8038-7155-4). Hastings.
Blake, Reed H., jt. auth. see Harris, John S.

Blake, Richard. Social Work: A Rewarding Career. (Illus.). 136p. 1982. 15.75x (ISBN 0-398-04663-8). C C Thomas.

Blake, Robert. The Decline of Power, Nineteen Fifteen to Nineteen Sixty-Four. (The Paladin History of England Ser.). (Illus.). 400p. 1985. 19.95 (ISBN 0-19-520480-8). Oxford U Pr.

--Disraeli's Grand Tour: Benjamin Disraeli in the Holy Land, 1830-31. (Illus.). 1982. 16.95x (ISBN 0-19-520367-4). Oxford U Pr.

Blake, Robert, jt. auth. see Thorp, Roderick.

Blake, Robert, ed. One Hundred & One Elephant Jokes. (Illus., Orig.). (gr. 6-9). pap. 1.50 (ISBN 0-590-08078-4). Scholastic Inc.

Blake, Robert M. Measured Doses of Data Communications. (Illus.). 320p. (Orig.). 1985. plastic comb bdg. 24.95 (ISBN 0-02-948010-8). Macmillan.

--Measured Doses of dBASE II. 1985. 24.95 (ISBN 0-02-948690-4). Macmillan.

--Measured Doses of Framework. (Illus.). 320p. (Orig.). 1985. plastic comb bdg. 24.95. Macmillan.

Blake, Robert R. & Monroe, George E. Managing the Stress in Your Life. (Illus.). 97p. (Orig.). 1981. pap. 6.95 (ISBN 0-9606788-0-8). Life Mgmt IL.

Blake, Robert R. & Mouton, Jane S. Consultation: A Comprehensive Approach to Individual & Organization Development. 2nd ed. LC 82-6746. (Illus.). 528p. 1983. pap. text ed. 26.95 (ISBN 0-201-10165-3). Addison-Wesley.

--Corporate Excellence Through Grid Organization Development. LC 68-21510. 376p. 1968. 17.95x (ISBN 0-87201-331-6). Gulf Pub.

--Diary of an OD Man. LC 75-18202. 356p. 1976. 19.95x (ISBN 0-87201-169-0). Gulf Pub.

--Grid Approaches for Managerial Leadership in Nursing. Tapper, Mildred, ed. LC 80-21583. (Illus.). 158p. 1980. pap. text ed. 12.95 (ISBN 0-8016-0696-9). Mosby.

--Grid Approaches to Managing Stress. (Illus.). 196p. 1980. 16.50x (ISBN 0-398-04093-1). C C Thomas.

--The Managerial Grid III. 3rd ed. LC 84-10875. 300p. 1984. 15.95x (ISBN 0-87201-470-3). Gulf Pub.

--Productivity: The Human Side. 143p. 1981. 12.95 (ISBN 0-8144-5692-8). AMACOM.

--Productivity: The Human Side: A Social Dynamics Approach. LC 80-69695. pap. 35.80 (ISBN 0-317-09603-6, 2022619). Bks Demand UMI.

--Solving Costly Organizational Conflicts: Achieving Intergroup Trust, Cooperation, & Teamwork. LC 84-47980. (Management Ser.). 1984. 21.95x (ISBN 0-87589-612-X). Jossey-Bass.

--The Versatile Manager: A Grid Profile. 1982. pap. 15.25 (ISBN 0-256-02749-8). Irwin.

Blake, Robert R. & Srygley, Jane. The Secretary Grid: A Program for Increasing Office Synergy. 208p. 1983. 14.95 (ISBN 0-8144-5762-2). AMACOM.

Blake, Robert R. & Srygley-Mouton, Jane. Guideposts for Effective Salesmanship. 2nd ed. LC 81-80671. 256p. 1984. pap. 3.50 (ISBN 0-515-08088-8). Jove Pubns.

Blake, Robert R., jt. auth. see Mouton, Jane S.

Blake, Robert R., et al. Managing Intergroup Conflict in Industry. LC 64-8696. 210p. 1964. 14.95x (ISBN 0-87201-375-8). Gulf Pub.

--The Academic Administrator Grid: A Guide to Developing Effective Management Teams. LC 80-8908. (Higher Education Ser.). 1981. text ed. 19.95x (ISBN 0-87589-492-5). Jossey-Bass.

--The Social Worker Grid. (Illus.). 200p. 1979. 20.50x (ISBN 0-398-03915-1). C C Thomas.

Blake, Roland P. Industrial Safety. 3rd ed. 1963. ref. ed. 24.95 (ISBN 0-13-463133-1). P-H.

Blake, S. F. Geographical Guide to Floras of the World: Annotated List with Special Reference to Useful Plants & Common Plant Names, Pt. II. LC 78-51431. (Landmark Reprints in Plant Science). 1978. Repr. of 1961 ed. text ed. 40.00x (ISBN 0-86598-006-3). Allanheld.

Blake, S. F. & Atwood, A. C. Geographical Guide to the Floras of the World: Western Europe, Finland, Sweden etc, Pt. 2. 742p. 1974. Repr. of 1961 ed. text ed. 49.00X (ISBN 3-87429-060-3). Lubrecht & Cramer.

Blake School Parent Association. The Educated Palate. Nordstam, Lois, ed. (Illus.). 120p. (Orig.). 1985. pap. 10.00 (ISBN 0-933023-00-6). Blake Schools.

Blake, Stephanie. Blaze of Passion. LC 78-50087. (Orig.). 1978. pap. 2.95 (ISBN 0-86721-005-2). Jove Pubns.

--Bride of the Wind. 352p. 1984. pap. 3.95 (ISBN 0-515-07874-3). Jove Pubns.

--Callie Knight. 432p. 1982. pap. 5.95 (ISBN 0-86721-075-3). Jove Pubns.

--Daughter of Destiny. LC 77-79951. 448p. (Orig.). 1977. pap. 2.95 (ISBN 0-86721-121-0). Jove Pubns.

--Fires of the Heart. LC 81-84140. 368p. (Orig.). 1982. pap. 2.95 (ISBN 0-86721-059-1). Jove Pubns.

--Flowers of Fire. LC 76-49400. 448p. 1977. pap. 2.95 (ISBN 0-87216-891-3). Jove Pubns.

--A Glorious Passion. 352p. 1983. pap. 3.50 (ISBN 0-515-07071-8). Jove Pubns.

--Scarlet Kisses. LC 81-80079. 368p. (Orig.). 1981. pap. 2.95 (ISBN 0-87216-847-6). Jove Pubns.

--Secret Sins. LC 80-80982. (Stephanie Blake Ser.). 400p. (Orig.). 1980. pap. 2.75 (ISBN 0-87216-719-4). Jove Pubns.

--So Wicked My Desire. LC 78-70092. (Orig.). 1979. pap. 2.95 (ISBN 0-87216-892-1). Jove Pubns.

--Unholy Desires. LC 80-82849. 368p. (Orig.). 1981. pap. 2.95 (ISBN 0-87216-785-2). Jove Pubns.

--Wicked Is My Flesh. LC 79-89965. 352p. (Orig.). 1984. pap. 2.50 (ISBN 0-86721-044-3). Jove Pubns.

Blake, Stewart P. Managing for Responsive Research & Development. LC 77-26120. (Illus.). 280p. 1978. text ed. 27.95 (ISBN 0-7167-0036-0). W H Freeman.

Blake, Susan. The Haunted Dollhouse. (Twilight Ser.: No. 22). 160p. (Orig.). (gr. 7-12). 1984. pap. 2.25 (ISBN 0-440-93643-8, LFL). Dell.

--The Last Word. (Sweet Dreams Ser.: No. 84). 176p. (Orig.). (gr. 6). 1985. pap. 2.25 (ISBN 0-553-24718-2). Bantam.

--Summer Breezes. (Sweet Dreams Ser.: No. 60). 160p. (Orig.). (gr. 6-8). 1984. pap. text ed. 2.25 (ISBN 0-553-24097-8). Bantam.

Blake, Sylvia & Kaufman, Sy. Keys to Comprehension: Reading Through Cloze. 1984. wkbk. 2.25 (ISBN 0-317-18829-1). Comp Pr.

--Practice Book for the Degrees of Reading Power Test. 1981. 4.50 (ISBN 0-9602800-6-5). Comp Pr.

--Practice Book for the Regents Competency Test in Reading. 103p. 1981. 4.50 (ISBN 0-9602800-0-6). Comp pr.

--Turn on to Reading (All Night Long) 1984. wkbk. 1.00 (ISBN 0-910307-04-0). Comp Pr.

Blake, Ted. The Intermountain Area: A Guide with Points of Interests, Historical Notes, Maps & Sketches. (Illus.). 60p. (Orig.). 1981. pap. 3.75 (ISBN 0-9605840-0-5). Intermntn Arts.

Blake, Thomas H. & Birmingham Historical Society. Birmingham Since 1885. 1972. pap. 5.00 (ISBN 0-87651-202-3). Southern U Pr.

Blake, Thomas M. The Practice of Electrocardiography. LC 80-13084. 1980. 24.00 (ISBN 0-87488-903-0); pap. 14.00 (ISBN 0-87488-997-9). Med Exam.

--The Practice of Electrocardiography. 2nd ed. 1985. pap. text ed. price not set (ISBN 0-87488-897-2). Med Exam.

Blake, Vernon. Art & Craft of Drawing. LC 75-116351. (Illus.). 1971. Repr. of 1927 ed. buckram 35.00 (ISBN 0-87817-039-1). Hacker.

--The Way to Sketch: With Special Reference to Watercolour. (Illus.). 1983. 11.25 (ISBN 0-8446-5878-2). Peter Smith.

--The Way to Sketch: With Special Reference to Water Color. (Illus.). 144p. (Unabridged replication of 2nd ed.). 1981. pap. 3.00 (ISBN 0-486-24119-X). Dover.

Blake, Viola, jt. auth. see Christenson, Evelyn.

Blake, W. A., et al, eds. Spinning. (Engineering Craftsmen: No. D4). (Illus.). 1968. spiral bdg. 37.50x (ISBN 0-85083-009-5). Intl Ideas.

Blake, W. John. West Africa: Quest for God & Gold, 1454-1578. rev. 2nd ed. (Illus.). 246p. 1977. 16.50x (ISBN 0-87471-965-8). Rowman.

Blake, W. O. History of Slavery & the Slave Trade. LC 73-100496. (Studies in Black History & Culture, No. 54). 1970. lib. bdg. 79.95x (ISBN 0-8383-1105-9). Haskell.

Blake, Wendon. Acrylic Painting. (The Artist's Painting Library). (Illus.). 80p. 1979. pap. 6.95 (ISBN 0-8230-0068-0). Watson-Guptill.

--Children's Portraits in Oil. (The Artist's Painting Library). (Illus.). 80p. 1980. pap. 6.95 (ISBN 0-8230-0623-9). Watson-Guptill.

--The Color Book. (Illus.). 256p. 27.50 (ISBN 0-8230-0694-8). Watson-Guptill.

--Color in Acrylic. (Artist's Painting Library). (Illus.). 80p. (Orig.). 1982. pap. 6.95 (ISBN 0-8230-0737-5). Watson-Guptill.

--Color in Oil. (Artist's Painting Library). (Illus.). 80p. (Orig.). 1982. pap. 6.95 (ISBN 0-8230-0739-1). Watson-Guptill.

--Color in Watercolor. (Artist's Painting Library). (Illus.). 80p. (Orig.). 1982. pap. 6.95 (ISBN 0-8230-0744-8). Watson-Guptill.

--Complete Guide to Acrylic Painting. LC 70-154028. (Illus.). 208p. 1971. 22.50 (ISBN 0-8230-0790-1). Watson-Guptill.

--Complete Guide to Landscape Painting in Oil. rev. ed. (Illus.). 192p. (Orig.). 1981. 23.50 (ISBN 0-8230-0808-8). Watson-Guptill.

--Creative Color: A Practical Guide for the Oil Painter. rev. ed. LC 79-1905. (Illus.). 176p. 1972. 23.50 (ISBN 0-8230-1035-X). Watson-Guptill.

--Creative Color for the Oil Painter. (Illus.). 160p. 1983. 23.50 (ISBN 0-8230-1036-8). Watson-Guptill.

--The Drawing Book. (Beginner's Painting Library). (Illus.). 336p. (gr. 9-12). 1980. 27.50 (ISBN 0-8230-1365-0). Watson-Guptill.

--Figure Drawing. (Artist's Painting Library). (Illus.). 80p. (Orig.). 1981. pap. 6.95 (ISBN 0-8230-1696-X). Watson-Guptill.

--Figures in Oil. (The Artist's Painting Library). (Illus.). 80p. 1980. pap. 6.95 (ISBN 0-8230-1698-6). Watson-Guptill.

--Landscape Drawing. (Artist's Painting Library Ser.). (Illus.). 80p. (Orig.). 1981. pap. 6.95 (ISBN 0-8230-2593-4). Watson-Guptill.

--Landscapes in Acrylic. (Artist's Painting Library). (Illus.). 80p. 1980. pap. 6.95 (ISBN 0-8230-2599-3). Watson-Guptill.

--Landscapes in Watercolor. (The Artist's Painting Library). (Illus.). 80p. 1979. pap. 6.95 (ISBN 0-8230-2621-3). Watson-Guptill.

--The Oil Painting Book. (Illus.). 256p. 1979. 27.50 (ISBN 0-8230-3270-1). Watson-Guptill.

--Painting in Alkyd. (Illus.). 96p. 14.95 (ISBN 0-8230-3553-0). Watson-Guptill.

--The Portrait & Figure Painting Book. (Illus.). 256p. 1980. 27.50 (ISBN 0-8230-4095-X). Watson-Guptill.

--Portrait Drawing. (Artist's Painting Library). (Illus.). 80p. (Orig.). 1981. pap. 6.95 (ISBN 0-8230-4094-1). Watson-Guptill.

--Portraits in Oil. (The Artist's Painting Library). (Illus.). 80p. (Orig.). 1980. pap. 6.95 (ISBN 0-8230-4105-0). Watson-Guptill.

--Seascapes in Acrylic. (The Artist's Painting Library). (Illus.). 80p. 1979. pap. 6.95 (ISBN 0-8230-4728-8). Watson-Guptill.

--Seascapes in Oil. (The Artist's Painting Library). (Illus.). 80p. 1980. pap. 6.95 (ISBN 0-8230-4729-6). Watson-Guptill.

--Seascapes in Watercolor. (The Artist's Painting Library). (Illus.). 80p. (Orig.). 1980. pap. 6.95 (ISBN 0-8230-4730-X). Watson-Guptill.

--Starting to Draw. (The Artist's Painting Library). (Illus.). 80p. 1981. pap. 6.95 (ISBN 0-8230-4916-7). Watson-Guptill.

--The Watercolor Painting Book. (Illus.). 1978. 27.50 (ISBN 0-8230-5672-4). Watson-Guptill.

Blake, Wendon & Caddell, Foster. Oil Painting Techniques: Learn How to Master Oil Painting Working Techniques to Create Your Own Successful Paintings. 144p. 1983. pap. 14.95 (ISBN 0-8230-3261-2). Watson-Guptill.

Blake, Wendon & Cherepov, George. Landscapes in Oil. (The Artist's Painting Library). (Illus.). 1979. pap. 6.95 (ISBN 0-8230-2598-5). Watson-Guptill.

--Oil Painting. (The Artist's Painting Library). (Illus.). 80p. 1979. pap. 6.95 (ISBN 0-8230-3271-X). Watson-Guptill.

Blake, Wendon & Croney, Claude. Watercolor Painting. (The Artist's Painting Library). (Illus.). 80p. 1979. pap. 6.95 (ISBN 0-8230-5673-2). Watson-Guptill.

Blake, Wendon & De Reyna, Rudy. The Acrylic Painting Book. (Illus.). 256p. 1978. 27.50 (ISBN 0-8230-0067-2). Watson-Guptill.

Blake, Wendon, ed. see Blockley, John & Bolton, Richard.

Blake, William. Blake: Selected Poems & Letters. Bronowski, J., ed. (Poets Ser.). 1958. pap. 4.95 (ISBN 0-14-042042-8). Penguin.

--Blake's America, a Prophecy, & Europe, a Prophecy: Facsimile Reproductions of Two Illuminated Books, with 35 Plates in Color. (Fine Art Ser.). (Illus.). 48p. 1984. pap. 5.95 (ISBN 0-486-24548-9). Dover.

--Blake's Job: William Blake's Illustrations of the Book of Job. Damon, S. Foster, ed. LC 82-13585. (Illus.). 76p. 1982. pap. 8.95 (ISBN 0-87451-241-7). U Pr of New Eng.

--Blake's Job: William Blake's Illustrations of the Book of Job. Damon, S. Foster, ed. LC 66-13155. (Illus.). 76p. 1966. 20.00x (ISBN 0-87057-096-X). U Pr of New Eng.

--The Book of Thel: A Facsimile & a Critical Text. Bogen, Nancy, ed. LC 74-155857. (Berg Collection Copy). (Illus.). 96p. 1971. 20.00 (ISBN 0-87104-236-3, Co-Pub Brown Univ Press, Dist. by University Press of New England). NY Pub Lib.

--The Book of Thel: A Facsimile & Critical Text. Bogen, Nancy, ed. LC 74-155857. pap. 24.50 (ISBN 0-317-19845-9, 2023011). Bks Demand UMI.

--The Book of Urizen. LC 78-58217. (Illus.). 102p. 1978. pap. 6.95 (ISBN 0-87773-132-2, 73629-X). Shambhala Pubns.

--The Book of Urizen. LC 66-27494. 1966. pap. 6.95x (ISBN 0-87024-065-X). U of Miami Pr.

--Choice of Blake's Verse. Raine, Kathleen, ed. 151p. 1970. pap. 6.95 (ISBN 0-571-09268-3). Faber & Faber.

--The Complete Poetry & Prose of William Blake. rev. ed. Erdman, David V., ed. LC 81-40323. 1000p. 1981. 38.50x (ISBN 0-520-04473-8). U of Cal Pr.

--Complete Writings of William Blake, with Variant Readings. Keynes, Geoffrey. ed. (Oxford Standard Authors Ser.). 1966. 39.95 (ISBN 0-19-254157-9); pap. 9.95x (ISBN 0-19-281050-2). Oxford U Pr.

--Drawings of William Blake: Ninety Two Pencil Studies. Keynes, Geoffrey, ed. LC 74-100545. (Illus., Orig.). 1970. pap. 5.00 (ISBN 0-486-22303-5). Dover.

--Drawings of William Blake: Ninety-two Pencil Studies. Keynes, Geoffrey, intro. by. (Illus.). 17.00 (ISBN 0-8446-0033-4). Peter Smith.

--The Grave: An Illustrated Poem. (Illus.). 38p. 1984. Repr. of 1858 ed. 25.00 (ISBN 0-87556-386-4). Saifer.

--Letters from William Blake to Thomas Butts. LC 72-194986. 1973. lib. bdg. 17.50 (ISBN 0-8414-1649-4). Folcroft.

--The Marriage of Heaven & Hell. facsimile ed. 1975. pap. 8.95 (ISBN 0-19-281167-3, 448, GB). Oxford U Pr.

--The Marriage of Heaven & Hell. LC 63-19483. 1963. pap. 9.95x (ISBN 0-87024-019-6). U of Miami Pr.

--Mary Wollstonecraft's Original Stories. LC 72-10149. 1973. Repr. of 1907 ed. lib. bdg. 30.00 (ISBN 0-8414-0658-8). Folcroft.

--Milton. Russell, A. & Maclagan, E., eds. LC 73-16264. 1907. lib. bdg. 15.00 (ISBN 0-8414-3345-3). Folcroft.

--Observations on the Principles Which Regulate the Course of Exchange & on the Present Depreciated State of the Currency, 2 vols. in 1. Bd. with Observations on the Effects Produced by the Expenditure of Government During the Restriction of Cash Payments. 1969. Repr. of 1823 ed. 26.50 (ISBN 0-8337-0304-8). B Franklin.

--The Pickering Manuscript. (Illus.). 28p. 1972. pap. 3.00 (ISBN 0-87598-036-8). Pierpont Morgan.

--Poems & Prophecies. Plowman, Max, ed. 1978. 9.95x (ISBN 0-460-00792-0, Evman); pap. 3.50x (ISBN 0-460-01792-6, Evman). Biblio Dist.

--The Poems of William Blake. Yeats, W. B., ed. 277p. 1905. pap. 5.50 (ISBN 0-7100-0174-6). Routledge & Kegan.

--Poetical Works. Rosetti, William M., ed. LC 79-13496. Repr. of 1914 ed. 21.50 (ISBN 0-404-07259-3). AMS Pr.

--Portable Blake. Kazin, Alfred, ed. (Portable Library: No. 26). 1977. pap. 7.95 (ISBN 0-14-015026-9, P26). Penguin.

--The Portable Blake. Kazin, Alfred, ed. (Viking Portable Library: No. 26). 1956. 14.95 (ISBN 0-670-17325-8). Viking.

--Prophetic Writings of William Blake, 2 Vols. Sloss, D. J. & Wallis, J. P., eds. (Oxford English Texts Ser). (Illus.). 1926. Set. 85.00x set (ISBN 0-19-811801-5). Oxford U Pr.

--Selected Poems. LC 73-4633. 1973. Repr. of 1947 ed. 17.50 (ISBN 0-8414-7534-2). Folcroft.

--Selected Poems: William Blake. Butter, P. H., ed. (Everyman Library). 302p. 1982. pap. text ed. 6.00x (ISBN 0-460-01125-1, Evman). Biblio Dist.

--Selected Poetry & Prose. Frye, Northrop, ed. (Modern Library College Editions). 1966. pap. text ed. 4.95 (ISBN 0-394-30986-3, T86, RanC). Random.

--Selections from the Symbolical Poems of William Blake. Pierce, F. E., ed. 1915. 49.50x (ISBN 0-686-51308-8). Elliots Bks.

--Songs of Experience. (Fine Arts). 48p. 1984. pap. 3.00 (ISBN 0-486-24636-1). Dover.

--Songs of Innocence. LC 70-165396. 1971. pap. 3.00 (ISBN 0-486-22764-2). Dover.

--Songs of Innocence & of Experience. Todd, Ruthven, ed. LC 72-14319. 1794. lib. bdg. 16.50 (ISBN 0-8414-2525-6). Folcroft.

--Songs of Innocence & of Experience. (Illus.). 1977. pap. 9.95 (ISBN 0-19-281089-8, GB 523, GB). Oxford U Pr.

--William Blake's Design for Edward Young's Night Thoughts: Complete, Vols. 1 & 2. Grant, John E. & Rose, Edward J., eds. (Illus.). 1980. Set. 385.00x (ISBN 0-19-817312-1). Oxford U Pr.

--William Blake's Poetry & Designs. Grant, John E. & Johnson, Mary L., eds. (Critical Editions). (Illus.). 1979. pap. 12.95x (ISBN 0-393-09083-3). Norton.

--William Blake's Works in Conventional Typography. LC 82-10815. 1984. 55.00x (ISBN 0-8201-1388-3). Schol Facsimiles.

--William Blake's Writings, 2 vols. Bentley, G. E., ed. (Oxford English Texts Ser.). (Illus.). 1979. Set. 185.00x (ISBN 0-19-811885-6). Oxford U Pr.

--Works of William Blake, Poetic, Symbolic, & Critical, 3 Vols. LC 79-13496. (Illus.). Repr. of 1893 ed. Set. 145.50 (ISBN 0-404-08990-9); 48.50 ea. Vol. 1 (ISBN 0-404-08961-5). Vol. 2 (ISBN 0-404-08999-2). Vol. 3 (ISBN 0-404-08993-3). AMS Pr.

Blake, William & Young, Edward. Night Thoughts, or the Complaint & the Consolation. LC 74-83141. 128p. (Orig.). 1975. 6.00 (ISBN 0-486-20219-4). Dover.

Blake, William, jt. ed. see Keynes, Geoffrey.

Blake, William D. My Time or Yours? (Orig.). 1979. pap. 1.95 (ISBN 0-532-23286-0). Woodhill.

Blake, William H. A Preliminary Study of the Interpretation of Bodily Expression. LC 75-176568. (Columbia University. Teachers College. Contributions to Education: No. 574). Repr. of 1933 ed. 22.50 (ISBN 0-404-55574-8). AMS Pr.

Blake, William K. Mechanics of Flow-Induced Sound & Vibration, 2 vols. LC 83-3698. (Applied Mathematics & Mechanics Ser.). Date not set. Vol. 1: General Concepts & Elementary Sources. write for info. (ISBN 0-12-103501-8); Vol. 2: Complex Flow-Structure Interactions. write for info. (ISBN 0-12-103502-6). Acad Pr.

Blake, William O. History of Slavery & the Slave Trade: Ancient & Modern. LC 76-92418. 848p. 1857. Repr. 45.00 (ISBN 0-403-00176-5). Scholarly.

Blakeborough, Peter. The Coinage of New Zealand Eighteen Forty to Nineteen Sixty-Three. pap. 5.25x (ISBN 0-392-09186-0, ABC). Sportshelf.

Blakeborough, R. Yorkshire Wit: Character, Folklore & Customs. 1977. Repr. of 1898 ed. lib. bdg. 37.00 (ISBN 0-8495-0301-9). Arden Lib.

Blakeborough, Richard. Legends of Highwaymen & Others. LC 75-154493. (Illus.). 1971. Repr. of 1924 ed. 40.00x (ISBN 0-8103-3373-2). Gale.

--Wit, Character, Folklore & Customs of the North Riding of Yorkshire. (Folklore Ser.). 1898. 27.50 (ISBN 0-8482-7422-9). Norwood Edns.

--Yorkshire Wit, Character, Folklore & Customs. (Folklore Ser). 27.50 (ISBN 0-8482-7424-5). Norwood Edns.

Blakebrough, jt. auth. see Birch, G. G.

Blakebrough, Ken. Fireball Outfit: The 457th Bombardment Group in the Skies Over Europe. LC 68-54881. (World War II Ser.). (Illus.). 1968. pap. 7.95 (ISBN 0-8168-9754-9). Aero.

Blakeley, B. H., jt. auth. see Lewis, R.

Blakeley, Brian L. & Collins, Jacquelin. Documents in English History: Early Times to the Present. 467p. 1975. pap. text ed. 18.95 (ISBN 0-394-34166-X, RanC). Random.

Blakeley, Edward, ed. Community Development Research: Concepts, Issues & Strategies. LC 78-11568. 224p. 1979. text ed. 24.95 (ISBN 0-87705-334-0); pap. text ed. 11.95 (ISBN 0-87705-348-0). Human Sci Pr.

Blakeley, Peggy. What Shall I Be Tomorrow? LC 83-25008. (Illus.). 28p. 1984. 11.95 (ISBN 0-907234-51-8, Pub. by Picture Bk Studio USA). Neugebauer Pr.

Blakeley, Peggy, tr. see Iguchi, Bunshu.

Blakeley, Robert W. The Practice of Speech Pathology: A Clinical Diary. (Illus.). 240p. 1973. 28.50x (ISBN 0-398-02575-4). C C Thomas.

Blakeley, T. J. Soviet Philosophy: A General Introduction to Contemporary Soviet Thought. (Sovietica Ser.: No. 18). 81p. 1964. lib. bdg. 18.50 (ISBN 90-277-0038-9, Pub. by Reidel Holland). Kluwer Academic.

--Soviet Scholasticism. (Sovietica Ser.: No. 6). 176p. 1961. lib. bdg. 18.50 (ISBN 90-277-0039-7, Pub. by Reidel Holland). Kluwer Academic.

--Soviet Theory of Knowledge. (Sovietica Ser.: No. 16). 203p. 1964. lib. bdg. 21.00 (ISBN 90-277-0040-0, Pub. by Reidel Holland). Kluwer Academic.

Blakeley, T. J., ed. Themes in Soviet Marxist Philosophy: Selected Articles from the Sovetskaja Enciklopedija. (Sovietica: No. 37). 230p. 1975. lib. bdg. 39.50 (ISBN 90-277-0637-9, Pub. by Reidel Holland). Kluwer Academic.

Blakeley, T. J., jt. ed. see Bochenski, J. M.

Blakeley, T. J., tr. see Bochenski, J. M.

Blakeley, T. J., tr. see Fleischer, H.

Blakeley, T. J., tr. see Planty-Bonjour, G.

Blakeley, T. J., tr. see Thiel, C.

Blakeley, T. J., tr. see Von Boeselager, Wolfhard.

Blakeley, T. J., tr. see Zinov'ev, A. A.

Blakeley, Thomas J. & O'Rourke, James J. The Varieties of Contemporary Marxism. 1984. lib. bdg. 53.50 (ISBN 90-277-1636-6, Pub. by Reidel Holland). Kluwer Academic.

Blakeley, Thomas J., jt. auth. see Gavin, William J.

Blakeley, Walter R. Calculus for Engineering Technology. LC 67-29017. 441p. 1968. 31.95 (ISBN 0-471-07931-6). Wiley.

Blakelock, John H. Automatic Control of Aircraft & Missiles. LC 65-16402. 348p. 1965. 64.50x (ISBN 0-471-07930-8, Pub. by Wiley-Interscience). Wiley.

Blakely & Wolde. Our United States. Rev. ed. 64p. 1982. 2.65 (ISBN 0-317-35479-5). New Readers.

Blakely, Allison. Russia & the Negro: Blacks in Russian History & Thought. LC 85-5251. (Illus.). 1986. 17.95 (ISBN 0-88258-146-5). Howard U Pr.

Blakely, Caroline. Occupations One. 64p. 1975. 2.25 (ISBN 0-317-35476-0). New Readers.

Blakely, Carolyn. Crossword Puzzles for Skill, Bk. 4. (Laubach Way to Reading Ser.). 32p. (gr. 7-12). 1984. 1.00 (ISBN 0-88336-958-3). New Readers.

Blakely, E. Jordan. The Decline of Common Sense & the Rise of Mental Illness. Nicholas-Wolosuk, Wanda, ed. LC 85-71239. (Illus.). 80p. 1985. pap. 6.95 (ISBN 0-9614582-1-6, 090185-0). Blakely.

--The Work Ethic: Pride, or Mental Illness. Ross, M. Sarah, ed. 1985. pap. 7.95 (ISBN 0-9614582-0-8). Blakely.

Blakely, Edward J., jt. auth. see Bradshaw, Ted K.

Blakely, Henry. A Windy Place. 1974. 6.00 (ISBN 0-910296-84-7); pap. 2.00 (ISBN 0-910296-15-4). Broadside.

Blakely, J. Paul, ed. see International Technical Communication Conference, 27th.

Blakely, James & Bade, David. The Science of Animal Husbandry. 4th ed. 1985. text ed. 24.95 (ISBN 0-8359-6897-9); instr's manual avail. (ISBN 0-8359-6898-7). Reston.

Blakely, James Doc. Doc Blakeley's Handbook of Wit & Pungent Humor. LC 83-61029. 228p. 1983. 20.00 (ISBN 0-9607256-2-8). Rich Pub Co.

Blakely, Jeffry A. & Toombs, Lawrence E. The Tell el-Hesi Field Manual: Joint Archaeological Expedition to Tell el-Hesi: Vol. 1. LC 80-21724. (Excavation Reports Ser.: No. 3). 134p. 1981. text ed. 15.00x (ISBN 0-89757-205-X, Am Sch Orient Res); pap. text ed. 12.00x (ISBN 0-89757-203-3). Eisenbrauns.

Blakely, Mary K., jt. ed. see Kaufman, Gloria.

Blakely, Pat. How Do We Smell? (Creative's Little Question Bks.). (Illus.). 32p. (gr. 3-6). 1982. lib. bdg. 6.95 (ISBN 0-87191-880-3). Creative Ed.

--What's Skin For? (Creative Question & Answer Library). 32p. (gr. 3-4). 1981. PLB 6.95 (ISBN 0-87191-745-9). Creative Ed.

--Why Do We Have Hair? (Creative's Little Question Bks.). (Illus.). 32p. 1982. PLB 6.95 (ISBN 0-87191-881-1). Creative Ed.

Blakely, Peggy, tr. see Kobayashi, Kenzo.

Blakely, R. The New Environment: Questions for Adult Educators. (Occasional Papers Ser: No. 23). 1971. pap. text ed. 2.00 (ISBN 0-87060-004-4, OCP 23). Syracuse U Cont Ed.

--Use of Instructional Television in Adult Education. LC 73-13295. (Occasional Papers Ser.: No. 40). 1974. pap. text ed. 2.00 (ISBN 0-87060-064-8, OCP 40). Syracuse U Cont Ed.

Blakely, R. J. Toward a Homeodynamic Society. 1965. 2.50 (ISBN 0-8156-7028-1, NES 49). Syracuse U Cont Ed.

Blakely, Raymond L. & Benkovic, Stephen J., eds. Folates & Pterins: Chemistry & Biochemistry of Pterins, Vol. 2. (Biochemistry Ser.). 414p. 1984. 89.50x (ISBN 0-471-89121-5). Wiley.

Blakely, Richard. Seeds in the Wind. (Social Political Criticism of Modern America). (Illus.). 80p. 1981. pap. 3.00 (ISBN 0-9607110-1-5). R P Blakely.

Blakely, Robert J. People's Instrument. 1971. pap. 7.00 (ISBN 0-8183-0190-2). Pub Aff Pr.

--To Serve the Public Interest: Educational Broadcasting in the United States. 1979. 18.95x (ISBN 0-8156-2198-1); pap. 7.95x (ISBN 0-8156-0153-0). Syracuse U Pr.

Blakely, Robert J. & Lappin, Ivan M. Knowledge Is Power to Control Power: New Institutional Arrangement & Organizational Patterns for Continuing Education. LC 71-106557. (Notes & Essays Ser.: No. 63). 1969. pap. 2.50 (ISBN 0-87060-027-3, NES 63). Syracuse U Cont Ed.

Blakely, Robert L., ed. Biocultural Adaptation in Prehistoric America. LC 76-49155. (Southern Anthropological Society Ser: No. 11). 144p. 1977. pap. 6.50x (ISBN 0-8203-0417-4). U of Ga Pr.

Blakely, Roger. North From Duluth: Tourist & Hiking Guide for Minnesota's North Shore. LC 81-83882. (Illus.). 96p. 1981. pap. 10.00. New Rivers Pr.

Blakely, T. J., tr. see Kirschenmann, P. K.

Blakely, W. A., ed. American State Papers Bearing on Sunday Legislation. LC 79-122165. (Civil Liberties in American History Ser.). 1970. Repr. of 1911 ed. lib. bdg. 95.00 (ISBN 0-306-71973-8). Da Capo.

Blakeman, J. P., ed. Microbial Ecology of the Phylloplane. LC 80-42354. 1981. 55.00 (ISBN 0-12-103750-9). Acad Pr.

Blakeman, John, et al. IPC: Interpersonal Communication Skills for Correctional Management. 118p. (Orig.). 1977. pap. text ed. 15.00x (ISBN 0-914234-69-2). Human Res Dev Pr.

Blakeman, John D., jt. auth. see Brown, James C.

Blakemore, Colin. Mechanics of the Mind. LC 76-53515. (BBC Reith Lectures: 1976). 1977. 52.50 (ISBN 0-521-21559-5); pap. 13.95 (ISBN 0-521-29185-2). Cambridge U Pr.

Blakemore, Colin, jt. ed. see Gazzaniga, Michael S.

Blakemore, Frances. Japanese Design: Through Textile Patterns. LC 78-2430. (Illus.). 1978. 10.95 (ISBN 0-8348-0132-9). Weatherhill.

--Who's Who in Modern Japanese Prints. LC 74-28174. (Illus.). 268p. 1975. 13.95 (ISBN 0-8348-0101-9). Weatherhill.

Blakemore, Harold. British Nitrates & Chilean Politics 1886-1896: Balmaceda & North. (Institute of Latin American Studies Monographs: No. 4). (Illus.). 260p. 1974. 42.50 (ISBN 0-485-17704-8, Pub. by Athlone Pr Ltd). Longwood Pub Group.

Blakemore, Harold & Smith, Clifford, eds. Latin America: Geographical Perspectives. 2nd ed. LC 82-20877. 576p. 1983. pap. 19.95 (ISBN 0-416-32830-X, NO.3814). Methuen Inc.

Blakemore, Harold, jt. ed. see Collier, Simon.

Blakemore, J. S. Solid State Physics. 506p. Date not set. price not set. (ISBN 0-521-30932-8). Cambridge U Pr.

Blakemore, John & Rasmussen, Henry. Postwar MG & Morgan. (Illus.). 1979. 29.95 (ISBN 0-918506-04-2). Picturama.

Blakemore, John, jt. auth. see Bondurant, Bob.

Blakemore, Kenneth. A Retailer's Guide to Glass & Pottery. (Illus.). 192p. 1984. text ed. 39.95 (ISBN 0-408-01219-6). Butterworth.

Blakemore, Kenneth & Cooksey, Brian. A Sociology of Education for Africa. 256p. 1981. pap. text ed. 12.50x (ISBN 0-04-370105-1). Allen Unwin.

Blakemore, Louis B. Masonic Lodge Methods. 1981. Repr. of 1953 ed. text ed. 11.50 (ISBN 0-88053-027-8, M-76). Macoy Pub.

Blakeney, Ben B., ed. see Togo, Shigenori.

Blakeney, Edward, ed. Horace on the Art of Poetry. facsimile ed. LC 73-119934. (Select Bibliographies Reprint Ser). (Eng. & Lat.). Repr. of 1928 ed. 17.00 (ISBN 0-8369-5377-0). Ayer Co Pubs.

Blakeney, W. Carlyle, Jr., jt. auth. see Neal, William J.

Blaker. Japan's National Security. 128p. 1983. cancelled 6.96 (ISBN 0-03-062003-1). Praeger.

Blaker, Alfred A. Applied Depth of Field. (Illus.). 240p. 1985. pap. 17.95. Butterworth.

--Field Photography: Beginning & Advanced Techniques. LC 75-33382. (Illus.). 451p. 1976. text ed. 37.95 (ISBN 0-7167-0518-4); field supplement incl. W H Freeman.

--Handbook for Scientific Photography. LC 77-24661. (Illus.). 319p. 1977. text ed. 35.95 (ISBN 0-7167-0285-1). W H Freeman.

--Photography: Art & Technique. LC 79-23536. (Illus.). 460p. 1980. text ed. 34.95 (ISBN 0-7167-1115-X); pap. text ed. 19.95 (ISBN 0-7167-1116-8); reference manual incl. W H Freeman.

--Photography: Art & Technique. (Illus.). 460p. (Orig.). 1980. pap. 19.95 (ISBN 0-240-51741-5). Focal Pr.

Blaker, Charles W. The College Matchmaker. LC 80-67604. (Illus.). 56p. (Orig.). (YA) (gr. 11-12). 1980. pap. text ed. 3.50 (ISBN 0-9604614-0-X). Rekalb Pr.

Blaker, Michael. Development Assistance to Southeast Asia: The U. S. & Japanese Approaches. 163p. 1984. pap. 7.00 (ISBN 0-913418-07-2). Columbia U E Asian Inst.

--Japanese International Negotiating Style. LC 77-8056. (Studies of the East Asian Institute). 253p. 1977. 26.00x (ISBN 0-231-04130-6). Columbia U Pr.

--Oil & the Atom: Issues in U. S.-Japan Energy Relations. (Occasional Papers of the East Asian Institute). 100p. 1981. pap. 4.00 (ISBN 0-317-17099-6). Columbia U E Asian Inst.

--The Politics of Trade: U. S. & Japanese Policymaking for the GATT Negotiations. (Occasional Papers of the East Asian Institute). 184p. 1979. pap. 4.00 (ISBN 0-317-17100-3). Columbia U E Asian Inst.

Blaker, Michael K., ed. Japan at the Polls: The House of Councilors Election of 1974. LC 76-23589. 1976. pap. 6.25 (ISBN 0-8447-3213-3). Am Enterprise.

Blaker, R. M., jt. ed. see Rommetveit, R.

Blaker, Richard. The Needle-Watcher: The Will Adams Story, British Samurai. LC 72-89743. 1973. pap. 7.95 (ISBN 0-8048-1094-X). C E Tuttle.

Blakers, C., jt. auth. see Anderson, D. S.

Blakers, Catherine. School & Work. (Education Research Unit Occasional Report Ser: No. 12). 1978. pap. 9.75 (ISBN 0-7081-1061-4, Pub by ANUP Australia). Australia N U P.

Blakers, M., et al. Atlas of Australian Birds. (Illus.). xlvi, 738p. 1984. 60.00 (ISBN 0-522-84285-2, Pub. by Melbourne Pr). Intl Spec Bk.

Blakeslee, A. F. Sexual Reproduction in the Mucorinaeae. (Biblioteca Mycologica Ser: No. 48). 1976. Repr. of 1904 ed. text ed. 14.00 (ISBN 3-7682-1064-2). Lubrecht & Cramer.

Blakeslee, Alton, et al. More FYI: Further Tips for Healthful Living. Brandt, Nat, ed. LC 83-14171. 288p. (Orig.). 1983. 12.95 (ISBN 0-87131-424-X, 01258-370); pap. 7.95 (ISBN 0-87131-420-7, 0772-230). M Evans.

Blakeslee, Berton, ed. The Limb-Deficient Child. (Illus.). 1963. 46.00x (ISBN 0-520-00125-7). U of Cal Pr.

Blakeslee, David W. & Chinn, William G. Introductory Statistics & Probability: A Basis for Decision-Making. (gr. 11-12). 1975. text ed. 20.80 (ISBN 0-395-19992-1); instrs' guide 6.96 (ISBN 0-395-19991-3). HM.

Blakeslee, George H., jt. auth. see Quigley, Harold S.

Blakeslee, Grace. A College Testament. 1984. 9.00 (ISBN 0-8233-0378-0). Golden Quill.

--Wings O'er the Sea. 1980. 5.50 (ISBN 0-8233-0323-3). Golden Quill.

Blakeslee, LeRoy L., et al. World Food Production, Demand, & Trade. facsimile ed. 428p. 1973. 18.20x (ISBN 0-8138-2435-4). Iowa St U Pr.

Blakeslee, Mary E. The Wheelchair Gourmet: A Cookbook for the Disabled. LC 81-4547. 192p. 1981. spiralbound 8.95 (ISBN 0-8253-0063-0). Beaufort Bks NY.

Blakeslee, Richard, et al. Dental Technology: Theory & Practice. LC 80-157. (Illus.). 364p. 1980. text ed. 29.95 (ISBN 0-8016-0695-0). Mosby.

Blakeslee, Thomas. The Right Brain: A New Understanding of the Unconscious Mind & Its Creative Powers. LC 79-26209. (Illus.). 288p. 1980. 14.95 (ISBN 0-385-15099-7, Anchor Pr). Doubleday.

Blakeslee, Thomas R. Digital Design with Standard MSI & LSI: Design Techniques for the Microcomputer Age. 2nd ed. LC 78-24201. 384p. 1979. 28.95 (ISBN 0-471-05222-1, Pub. by Wiley-Interscience). Wiley.

--The Right Brain. LC 82-60690. 288p. 1984. pap. 3.50 (ISBN 0-425-08161-3). Berkley Pub.

Blakey, Fred. The Florida Phosphate Industry: A History of the Development & Use of a Vital Mineral. LC 73-82345. (Wertheim Publications in Industrial Relations Ser.). 1973. text ed. 15.00x (ISBN 0-674-30670-8). Harvard U Pr.

Blakey, George T. Historians on the Homefront: American Propagandists for the Great War. LC 79-132825. 176p. 1970. 15.00x (ISBN 0-8131-1236-2). U Pr of Ky.

Blakey, Leonard S. Sale of Liquor in the South. LC 74-94922. (Columbia University Studies in the Social Sciences: No. 127). Repr. of 1912 ed. 15.00 (ISBN 0-404-51127-9). AMS Pr.

Blakey, Robert. The History of Political Literature from the Earliest Times. 2 vols. (Reprints in History Ser.). Repr. of 1855 ed. Set. lib. bdg. 92.00x (ISBN 0-89197-790-2); Vol. 1. lib. bdg. 48.00x (ISBN 0-697-00029-X); Vol. 2. lib. bdg. 48.00x (ISBN 0-697-00030-3). Irvington.

Blakey, Ronald S. The Man in the Manse, Eighteen Hundred to Nineteen Hundred. 160p. 1979. 10.00x (ISBN 0-905312-05-8, Pub. by Scottish Academic Pr Scotland). Columbia U Pr.

Blakey, Roy G. United States Beet Sugar Industry & the Tariff. LC 77-76717. (Columbia University. Studies in the Social Sciences: No. 119). Repr. of 1912 ed. 22.50 (ISBN 0-404-51119-8). AMS Pr.

Blakey, T. N., ed. English for Maritime Studies Book. (Materials for Language Practice (ESP)). 192p. 1982. pap. 8.50 (ISBN 0-08-028636-4). Pergamon.

Blakey, Walker, jt. auth. see Howe, Joseph.

Blakey, Walker J., jt. auth. see Broun, Kenneth S.

Blakiston. Blakiston's Pocket Medical Dictionary. 4th ed. Gennaro, Alphonso R., ed. 1979. 25.00 (ISBN 0-07-005715-X); text ed. 21.00 (ISBN 0-07-005714-1). McGraw.

Blakiston, Noel. The Roman Question. 360p. 1980. 35.00 (ISBN 0-89453-150-6). M Glazier.

Blakley, Raymond L. & Benkovic, Stephen J., eds. Folates & Pterins: Chemistry & Biochemistry of Folates, Vol. 1. LC 84-3592. (Biochemistry Ser.). 628p. 1984. text ed. 99.50x (ISBN 0-471-87586-4, Pub. by Wiley-Interscience). Wiley.

Blakney, R. B., tr. see Lao Tzu.

Blakstad, Michael. The Risk Business. 144p. 1979. pap. 11.95x (ISBN 0-85072-098-2, Pub. by Design Council England). Intl Spec Bk.

Blalock, Ann B., jt. auth. see Blalock, Hubert M.

Blalock, H. M. Social Statistics. 2nd ed. 1979. 33.95 (ISBN 0-07-005752-4). McGraw.

Blalock, H. M., Jr., ed. Causal Models in Experimental & Panel Designs. LC 84-24276. (Illus.). 287p. 1985. lib. bdg. 49.95x (ISBN 0-202-30315-2); pap. text ed. 24.95x (ISBN 0-202-30316-0). Aldine Pub.

--Causal Models in the Social Sciences. 2nd ed. LC 84-24258. (Illus.). 448p. 1985. lib. bdg. 49.95x (ISBN 0-202-30313-6); pap. text ed. 24.95x (ISBN 0-202-30314-4). Aldine Pub.

--Measurement in the Social Sciences: Theories & Strategies. LC 73-89514. 470p. 1974. pap. text ed. 19.95x (ISBN 0-202-30272-5). Aldine Pub.

Blalock, Hubert M. Race & Ethnic Relations. (Foundations of Modern Sociology Ser.). (Illus.). 160p. 1982. 18.95 (ISBN 0-13-750182-X); pap. 14.95 (ISBN 0-13-750174-9). P-H.

Blalock, Hubert M. & Blalock, Ann B. Introduction to Social Research. 2nd ed. (Illus.). 176p. 1982. 18.95 (ISBN 0-13-496810-7); pap. 14.95 (ISBN 0-13-496802-6). P-H.

Blalock, Hubert M., Jr. Black-White Relations in the Nineteen Eighties: Towards a Long-Term Policy. LC 79-10224. 220p. 1979. 39.95x (ISBN 0-03-050461-9). Praeger.

Blalock, Hubert M., Jr. & Wilken, Paul H. Intergroup Processes: A Micro-Macro Perspective. LC 78-19856. 1979. 28.95 (ISBN 0-02-903620-8). Free Pr.

Blalock, Hubert M., Jr., ed. Conceptualization & Measurement in the Social Sciences. LC 81-23269. (Illus.). 256p. 1982. 22.50 (ISBN 0-8039-1804-6); pap. 14.95 (ISBN 0-8039-2505-0). Sage.

--Sociological Theory & Research: A Critical Appraisal. LC 80-754. (Illus.). 1980. 29.95 (ISBN 0-02-903630-5). Free Pr.

Blalock, Jack E., Jr. It's All There If You Want It: And Here Is the Map. LC 80-69519. 200p. (Orig.). 1981. 12.95 (ISBN 0-9605156-0-7); pap. 10.95 (ISBN 0-9605156-1-5). J Blalock.

Blalock, Joyce. Civil Liability of Law Enforcement Officers. 248p. 1974. 16.75x (ISBN 0-398-02864-8). C C Thomas.

Blalock, Steven, jt. auth. see Ivener, Mark A.

Blalock, Steven F., jt. auth. see North Carolina Bar Association Foundation.

Blamer, Thomas & Shulman, Richard. Dow Three Thousand: The Investment Opportunity of the 1980's. 1982. 13.50 (ISBN 0-671-43224-9, Wyndham Bks). S&S.

Blamey & Fitter. The Wild Flowers of Britain & Europe. pap. 13.95 (ISBN 0-00-219550-X, Pub. by Collins Pub England). Greene.

Blamey, jt. auth. see Fitter.

Blamey, jt. auth. see Grey-Wilson.

Blamey, Marjorie, jt. auth. see Blamey, Philip.

Blamey, Philip & Blamey, Marjorie. Marjorie Blamey's Portraits of Wild Flowers. (Illus.). 80p. 1985. 11.95 (ISBN 0-00-411762-X, Pub. by Salem Hse Ltd). Merrimack Pub Cir.

Blamires, D. David Jones: Artist & Writer. 1978. pap. 8.50 (ISBN 0-7190-0730-5, Pub. by Manchester Univ Pr). Longwood Pub Group.

Blamires, David. Herzog Ernst & the Otherworld Voyage. (Illus.). 118p. 1979. text ed. 16.00 (ISBN 0-7190-1292-9, Pub. by Manchester Univ Pr). Longwood Pub Group.

Blamires, Harry. The Bloomsday Book: A Guide Through Joyce's Ulysses. (Orig.). 1966. pap. 11.95 (ISBN 0-416-69500-0, NO.2092). Methuen Inc.

--The Christian Mind. 1978. pap. 4.95 (ISBN 0-89283-049-2). Servant.

--Cold War in Hell. 204p. 1984. pap. 4.95 (ISBN 0-8407-5930-4). Nelson.

--The Devil's Hunting Grounds. 180p. 1984. pap. 4.95 (ISBN 0-8407-5932-0). Nelson.

--Highway to Heaven. 204p. 1984. pap. 4.95 (ISBN 0-8407-5928-2). Nelson.

--On Christian Truth. 168p. (Orig.). pap. 4.95 (ISBN 0-89283-130-8). Servant.

--A Short History of English Literature. 2nd ed. 512p. 1985. pap. 9.95 (ISBN 0-416-37440-9, NO. 4136). Methuen Inc.

--Twentieth-Century English Literature. Jeffares, A. Norman, ed. LC 82-5749. (History of Literature Ser.). (Illus.). 312p. 1982. 28.50x (ISBN 0-8052-3827-1). Schocken.

--Words Made Flesh: God Speaks to Us in the Ordinary Things of Life. 173p. (Orig.). 1985. pap. 6.95 (ISBN 0-89283-235-5). Servant.

Blamires, Harry, ed. A Guide to Twentieth-Century Literature in English. 325p. 1983. 32.00 (ISBN 0-416-56180-2, NO. 4034); pap. 15.95 (ISBN 0-416-36450-0, NO. 4035). Methuen Inc.

Blamires, Harry, et al. Chosen Vessels: Portraits of Ten Outstanding Christian Men. Turner, Charles, ed. 224p. (Orig.). 1985. 10.95 (ISBN 0-89283-226-6, Pub. by Vine Books). Servant.

Blamires, Henry, ed. Twentieth-Century English Literature. LC 82-5749. (History of Literature Ser.). (Illus.). 312p. 1984. pap. 8.95 (ISBN 0-8052-0772-4). Schocken.

Blampain, R. The Vredeling Proposal. 1983. lib. bdg. 36.00 (ISBN 90-312-0208-8, Pub. by Kluwer Law & Taxation). Kluwer Academic.

Blan, Anna. Tales of Ayrshire. 224p. 1984. 11.50 (ISBN 0-318-04107-3, Pub. by Shepheard-Walwyn); pap. 5.95 (ISBN 0-85683-069-0). Flatiron Book Dist.

Blan, L. B. Special Study of the Incidence of Retardation. LC 79-176569. (Columbia University. Teachers College. Contributions to Education: No. 40). Repr. of 1911 ed. 22.50 (ISBN 0-404-55040-1). AMS Pr.

Blanc, Albert D. So You Have Asthma! (Illus.). 280p. 1966. 29.75x (ISBN 0-398-00168-5). C C Thomas.

Blanc, Andre. F. C. Dancourt (1661-1725) La Comedie Francaise a l'Heure du Soleil Couchant. (Etudes litteraires francaises: No. 29). 408p. (Orig., Fr.). 1984. pap. 40.00x (ISBN 3-87808-729-2, Pub. by G N Verlag Germany). Benjamins North Am.

Blanc, C. Equations Aux Derivees Partielles. (International Ser. of Numerical Mathematics: No. 34). 136p. (Fr.). 1976. pap. 23.95x (ISBN 0-8176-0869-9). Birkhauser.

Blanc, Charles. Art in Ornament & Dress. LC 77-156923. (Tower Bks.). (Illus.). 1971. Repr. of 1876 ed. 43.00x (ISBN 0-8103-3922-6). Gale.

Blanc, Charles Le see Bodde, Derk.

Blanc, Elsie T. The Cooperative Movement in Russia. LC 75-37206. (Russia Studies: Perspectives on the Revolution Ser.). 324p. 1977. Repr. of 1924 ed. lib. bdg. 25.85 (ISBN 0-88355-425-9). Hyperion-Conn.

Blanc, Emile & Egger, Eugrure. Educational Innovations in Switzerland: Traits & Trends. (Experiments & Innovations in Education Ser.: No. 33). (Illus.). 98p. 1978. pap. 5.25 (ISBN 92-3-101504-4, U904, UNESCO). Unipub.

Blanc, Henry. Narrative of Captivity in Abyssinia with Some Account of the Late Emperor Theodore, His Country & People. (Illus.). 410p. 1970. Repr. of 1868 ed. 37.50x (ISBN 0-7146-1792-X, F Cass Co). Biblio Dist.

Blanc, Hippolyte. Bibliographie des corporations ouvrieres avant 1789. LC 68-7209. (Bibliography & Reference Ser.: No. 201). 1968. Repr. of 1885 ed. 20.95 (ISBN 0-8337-0306-4). B Franklin.

Blanc, Jacques Le see LeBlanc, Jacques.

Blanc, Karen. Dear Hilda. (Illus.). 400p. 1983. pap. 9.95 (ISBN 0-937776-01-7). Fowler & Wells.

Blanc, L. Le see Le Blanc, L.

Blanc, Linda-Gay. Fire in Your Home. LC 78-60515. (Illus.). 1978. pap. 1.75 (ISBN 0-87765-131-0, SPP-52). Natl Fire Prot.

Blanc, Louis. Histoire de la Revolution francaise, 12 Vols. LC 79-39452. (Fr). Repr. of 1862 ed. Set. 270.00 (ISBN 0-404-07150-3); 22.50 ea. AMS Pr.

Blanc, M. Francis Le see Le Blanc, Sr. M. Francis.

Blanc, Madame see De Solms, Marie T., pseud.

Blanc, Rufus J. Le see Le Blanc, Rufus J. & Breeding, Julia G.

Blanc, Suzanne. The Green Stone. 192p. 1984. pap. 3.50 (ISBN 0-88184-069-6). Carroll & Graf.

Blance & Cook. Monstruo, 12 bks, Set 2. Incl. Monstruo Compre un Animalito (ISBN 0-8372-3482-4); Monstruo Encuentra Trabajo (ISBN 0-8372-3485-9); Monstruo, la Senorita Monstruo y el Paseo en bicicleta (ISBN 0-8372-3488-3); Monstruo Recorre la Ciudad (ISBN 0-8372-3490-5); Monstruo va al Circo (ISBN 0-8372-3483-2); Monstruo va al Hospital (ISBN 0-8372-3489-1); Monstruo va a la Playa (ISBN 0-8372-3479-4); Monstruo y la Galleta de Sorpresa (ISBN 0-8372-3486-7); Monstruo y la Liquidacion de Juguetes (ISBN 0-8372-3480-8); Monstruo y el Muro (ISBN 0-8372-3487-5); El Plan de la Senorita Monstruo (ISBN 0-8372-3481-6); La Senorita Monstruo ayuda (ISBN 0-8372-3484-0). (Pap. 215.40 set, 5 English & 5 Spanish of title (ISBN 0-8372-3493-x)). (gr. k-4). pap. 1.98 ea.; pap. 24.30 1 of ea. title with tchr's. guide (ISBN 0-8372-3491-3); tchr's. guide 1.98 (ISBN 0-8372-9175-5); filmstrips & tapes avail. Bowmar-Noble.

Blanch, H. J. A Century of Guns: A Sketch of the Leading Types of Sporting & Military Small Arms. (Illus.). 1977. Repr. of 1909 ed. 25.00x (ISBN 0-7158-1156-8). Charles River Bks.

Blanch, Harvey W. & Popoutsakis, E. Terry, eds. Foundations of Biochemical Engineering: Kinetics & Thermodynamics in Biological Systems. LC 82-20694. (ACS Symposium Ser.: No. 207). 522p. 1983. lib. bdg. 54.95x (ISBN 0-8412-0752-6). Am Chemical.

Blanch, Jose M., tr. see Dunnett, W. M.

Blanch, Jose M., tr. see Lebar, Lois & Berg, Miguel.

Blanch, Lesley. Pierre Loti: The Legendary Romantic. (A Helen & Kurt Wolff Book). (Illus.). 336p. 1983. 15.95 (ISBN 0-15-171931-4). HarBraceJ.

--The Sabres of Paradise. 495p. 1984. pap. 9.95 (ISBN 0-88184-042-4). Carroll & Graf.

--The Wilder Shores of Love. 368p. 1983. pap. 8.95 (ISBN 0-88184-055-6, Publishers Group West). Carroll & Graf.

Blanch, Lesly. Pierre Loti: The Legendary Romantic. 336p. 1985. pap. 10.95 (ISBN 0-88184-118-8). Carroll & Graf.

Blanch, Michael. Soldiers. LC 82-50400. (History Eye Witness Ser.). 93p. PLB 15.96 (ISBN 0-382-06664-2). Silver.

Blanch, Miguel, tr. see Collins, Gary.

Blanch, Miguel, tr. see Ladd, George E.

Blanch, Miguel, tr. see Morris, Leon.

Blanch, Robert J. Sir Gawain & the Green Knight: A Reference Guide. 300p. 1984. 22.50x (ISBN 0-87875-244-7). Whitston Pub.

Blanch, Robert J., ed. Style & Symbolism in Piers Plowman: A Modern Critical Anthology. LC 69-20115. (Illus., Orig.). 1969. pap. text ed. 8.95x (ISBN 0-87049-101-6). U of Tenn Pr.

Blanch, Stuart. For All Mankind: A New Approach to the Old Testament. (GB); pap. 4.95 (ISBN 0-19-520025-X). Oxford U Pr.

--Living by Faith. 160p. (Orig.). 1984. pap. 5.95 (ISBN 0-8028-0008-4). Eerdmans.

--The Trumpet in the Morning. 1979. 15.00x (ISBN 0-19-520167-1). Oxford U Pr.

Blanch, Stuart Y. The Burning Bush. 1979. pap. 5.95 (ISBN 0-8192-1260-1). Morehouse.

Blanchan, N. The Fully Illustrated Encyclopedia of American Flower Gardens, 3 vols. (Illus.). 427p. 1985. Repr. of 1909 ed. Set. 187.55 (ISBN 0-89901-221-3). Found Class Reprints.

Blanchard, jt. auth. see Abram.

Blanchard, Adele B. Quickscript: The Fast & Simple Shorthand Method. LC 82-67031. 160p. 1982. pap. 5.95 (ISBN 0-668-05572-3, 5572). Arco.

Blanchard, Alain. Sigles et Abreviations Dans les Papyrus Grecs: Recherches De Paleographie. 59p. 1981. 35.00x (ISBN 0-900587-31-8, Pub. by Inst Class Stud England). State Mutual Bk.

Blanchard, Alain A. Phase-Locked Loops: Application to Coherent Receiver Design. LC 75-30941. 1976. 49.95x (ISBN 0-471-07941-3, Pub. by Wiley-Interscience). Wiley.

Blanchard, B. & Fabrycky, W. Systems Engineering & Analysis. 1981. 34.95 (ISBN 0-13-881631-X). P-H.

Blanchard, B. Everard. A New System of Education. LC 74-23970. 1975. 14.95 (ISBN 0-88280-012-4). ETC Pubns.

Blanchard, Benjamin S. Design & Manage to Life Cycle Cost. LC 77-18875. 1978. 29.95 (ISBN 0-930206-00-2). M-A Pr.

--Engineering Organization & Management. (P-H International Industrial & System Engineering Ser.). (Illus.). 544p. 1976. 30.95 (ISBN 0-13-279430-6). P-H.

--Logistics Engineering & Management. 2nd ed. (P-H Ser. in Industrial & Systems Engineering). (Illus.). 464p. 1981. text ed. 34.95 (ISBN 0-13-540088-0). P-H.

--Logistics Engineering & Management. 3rd ed. (Illus.). 496p. text ed. 34.95 (ISBN 0-13-540238-7). P-H.

Blanchard, Calvin. Art of Real Pleasure: That New Pleasure, for Which an Imperial Reward Was Offered. LC 70-154430. (Utopian Literature Ser). (Illus.). 1971. Repr. of 1864 ed. 18.00 (ISBN 0-405-03513-6). Ayer Co Pubs.

Blanchard, Caroline, jt. ed. see Blanchard, Robert J.

Blanchard, Charles A. Getting Things from God. (Classic Elective Ser.: No. 1). 168p. 1985. pap. 0.95 (ISBN 0-89693-520-5); pap. 0.95. Victor Bks.

Blanchard, Charles E. The Romance of Proctology. LC 75-23684. Repr. of 1938 ed. 23.50 (ISBN 0-404-13237-5). AMS Pr.

Blanchard, Chuck, jt. auth. see Shafer, Dan.

Blanchard, Claude. Journal of Claude Blanchard, Commissary of the French Auxiliary Army Sent to the U. S. During the American Revolution, 1780-1783. Balch, Thomas, ed. Duane, William, tr. LC 76-76241. (Eyewitness Accounts of the American Revolution Ser., No. 2). 1969. Repr. of 1876 ed. 13.50 (ISBN 0-405-01143-1). Ayer Co Pubs.

Blanchard, Duncan C. From Raindrops to Volcanoes: Adventures with Sea Surface Meteorology. LC 80-19134. (Science Study Ser.: Selected Topics in Atmospheric Sciences). (Illus.). xii, 180p. 1980. Repr. of 1967 ed. lib. bdg. 24.75x (ISBN 0-313-22638-5, BLFR). Greenwood.

Blanchard, Edward B. & Andrasik, Frank. Management of Chronic Headaches: A Psychological Approach. (Psychology Practitioner Guidebooks). 200p. 1985. 17.51 (ISBN 0-08-030963-1); pap. 9.91 (ISBN 0-08-030962-3). Pergamon.

Blanchard, Edward B. & Epstein, Leonard H. Biofeedback Primer. LC 76-74321. (Illus.). 218p. 1978. pap. text ed. 11.95 (ISBN 0-394-34759-5, RanC). Random.

Blanchard, Fessenden, jt. auth. see Stone, William T.

Blanchard, Harold F. & Ritchen, Ralph. Motor Auto Engines & Electrical Systems. 7th ed. LC 77-88821. (Illus.). 1977. 14.95 (ISBN 0-910992-73-8). Hearst Bks.

Blanchard, Homer, tr. see Klais, Hans G. & Steinhaus, Hans.

Blanchard, Homer D. The Bach Organ Book. (Illus.). 250p. 1985. 40.00 (ISBN 0-930112-07-5). Praestant.

Blanchard, Homer D., jt. auth. see Lindow, Ch. W.

Blanchard, Homer D., ed. Organs of Our Time. Rev. ed. LC 82-90079. (Illus.). 231p. 1982. 24.00 (ISBN 0-930112-06-7). Praestant.

--Organs of Our Time II. LC 81-185580. (Illus.). 176p. (Orig.). 1981. pap. 16.00 (ISBN 0-930112-05-9). Praestant.

Blanchard, Howard L. Organization & Administration of Pupil Personnel Services. (Illus.). 148p. 1974. 15.75x (ISBN 0-398-03142-8). C C Thomas.

Blanchard, J. Knight Templarism. rev. ed. 8.95x (ISBN 0-685-22013-3). Wehman.

--Standard Freemasonry. 8.95x (ISBN 0-685-22116-4). Wehman.

Blanchard, J., et al. Principles & Perspective in Drug Bioavailability. 1978. 41.75 (ISBN 3-8055-2440-4). S Karger.

Blanchard, J. Richard & Farrell, Lois. Guide to Sources for Agricultural & Biological Research. 672p. 1981. 48.50x (ISBN 0-520-03226-8). U of Cal Pr.

Blanchard, James. Hidden Animal Word Puzzles. (Illus.). 32p. (Orig.). (gr. 1-3). 1983. pap. 1.50 (ISBN 0-590-32837-9). Scholastic Inc.

Blanchard, James, jt. auth. see Ford, Phyllis.

Blanchard, Jay S., jt. auth. see Mason, George E.

Blanchard, Johathan. Debate on Slavery. LC 70-92419. 1845. 18.00x (ISBN 0-403-00153-6). Scholarly.

Blanchard, John. Aceptado Por Dios. 2.95 (ISBN 0-686-12564-9). Banner of Truth.

--Right with God. LC 78-6809. 1978. pap. 2.95 (ISBN 0-8024-7357-1). Moody.

Blanchard, Jonathan & Rice, N. L. Debate on Slavery: Is Slavery in Itself Sinful & the Relation Between Master & Slave a Sinful Relation. LC 72-82175. (Anti-Slavery Crusade in America Ser.). 1969. Repr. of 1846 ed. 21.00 (ISBN 0-405-00614-4). Ayer Co Pubs.

Blanchard, Jonathan & Rice, Nathan L. Debate on Slavery. LC 70-76853. Repr. of 1846 ed. 20.50x (ISBN 0-8371-1178-1, BLD&, Pub. by Negro U Pr). Greenwood.

Blanchard, Kendall. The Economics of Sainthood: Religious Change among the Rimrock Navajos. LC 75-10141. (Illus.). 244p. 1976. 22.50 (ISBN 0-8386-1770-0). Fairleigh Dickinson.

Blanchard, Kendall & Cheska, Alyce. The Anthropology of Sport: An Introduction. (Illus.). 320p. 1984. text ed. 29.95 (ISBN 0-89789-040-X); pap. text ed. 16.95 (ISBN 0-89789-041-8). Bergin & Garvey.

Blanchard, Kendall A. Mississippi Choctaws at Play: The Serious Side of Leisure. LC 80-26527. 248p. 1981. 15.95x (ISBN 0-252-00866-9). U of Ill Pr.

Blanchard, Kenneth & Johnson, Spencer. The One Minute Manager. Golbitz, Pat, ed. LC 82-8106. 112p. 1982. 15.00 (ISBN 0-688-01429-1). Morrow.

--The One Minute Manager. 112p. 1985. pap. 6.95 (ISBN 0-425-08521-X). Berkley Pub.

Blanchard, Kenneth & Lorber, Robert. Putting the One-Minute Manager to Work: How to Turn the Three Secrets into Skills. Golbitz, Pat, ed. LC 83-63021. 112p. 1984. 15.00 (ISBN 0-688-02632-X). Morrow.

--Putting the One-Minute Manager to Work. 112p. 1985. pap. 6.95 (ISBN 0-425-07757-8). Berkley Pub.

Blanchard, Kenneth & Zigarmi, Drea. Leadership & the One Minute Manager. Golbitz, Pat, ed. LC 84-62389. (One Minute Manager Ser.). 112p. 1985. 15.00 (ISBN 0-688-03969-3). Morrow.

Blanchard, Kenneth H., jt. auth. see Hersey, Paul.

Blanchard, Lois J., jt. ed. see Della-Dora, Delmo.

Blanchard, Marc E. Description: Sign, Self, Desire. (Approaches to Semiotics Ser.: No. 43). 1979. text ed. 27.20x (ISBN 0-686-27019-3). Mouton.

--Description: Sign, Self, Desire: Critical Theory in the Wake of Semiotics. (Approaches to Semiotics Ser.: No. 43). 300p. 1980. pap. text ed. 8.00 (ISBN 90-279-3488-6). Mouton.

--In Search of the City: Engels, Baudelaire, Rimbaud. (Stanford French & Italian Studies: Vol. 37). 1985. pap. 25.00 (ISBN 0-915838-53-2). Anma Libri.

Blanchard, Margaret, ed. see Lomax, Walter E., et al.

Blanchard, Margarge, ed. see Lomax, Walter E.

Blanchard, Marjorie. The Home Gardener's Cookbook. LC 73-89129. 192p. 1974. pap. 4.95 (ISBN 0-88266-013-6). Garden Way Pub.

--The Sprouter's Cookbook: For Fast Kitchen Crops. LC 74-83147. (Illus.). 144p. 1975. pap. 5.95 (ISBN 0-88266-041-1). Garden Way Pub.

Blanchard, Marjorie P. Cater from Your Kitchen. 1981. pap. 8.95 (ISBN 0-672-52688-3). Bobbs.

--The Easy Harvest Sauce & Puree Cookbook. rev. ed. LC 82-934. (Illus.). 172p. 1982. pap. 5.95 (ISBN 0-88266-272-4). Garden Way Pub.

--Home Gardener's Month-by-Month Cookbook. rev. ed. LC 73-89129. (Illus.). 192p. 1985. pap. 6.95 (ISBN 0-88266-013-6). Garden Way Pub.

--The Woman's Day Food Processor Cookbook. 160p. 1981. 6.95 (ISBN 0-449-90062-2, Columbine). Fawcett.

Blanchard, Nina. How to Break into Motion Pictures, Television Commercials & Modeling. 1980. pap. 2.50 (ISBN 0-380-47118-3, 47118). Avon.

Blanchard, P. & Streit, L., eds. Dynamics & Processes. (Lecture Notes in Mathematics: Vol. 1031). 213p. 1983. pap. 13.00 (ISBN 0-387-12705-4). Springer-Verlag.

Blanchard, Paul. Southern Italy: From Rome to Calabria. 4th, rev. ed. (Blue Guides Ser.). (Illus.). 1984. pap. 16.95 (ISBN 0-393-30065-X). Norton.

Blanchard, Peter. The Origins of the Peruvian Labor Movement, 1883-1919. LC 81-23102. (Pitt Latin American Ser.). xx, 214p. 1982. 23.95x (ISBN 0-8229-3455-8). U of Pittsburgh Pr.

Blanchard, Phyllis & Manasses, Carlyn. New Girls for Old. 1978. Repr. of 1930 ed. lib. bdg. 25.00 (ISBN 0-8492-3727-0). R West.

Blanchard, Phyllis, jt. auth. see Paynter, Richard H.

Blanchard, Rae, ed. see Steele, Richard.

Blanchard, Ralph R. Bits & Pieces of a Man's Life. LC 84-90196. 56p. 1985. 6.95 (ISBN 0-533-06254-3). Vantage.

Blanchard, Robert & Tattar, Terry. Field & Laboratory Guide to Tree Pathology. 1981. 25.50 (ISBN 0-12-103980-3). Acad Pr.

Blanchard, Robert, jt. auth. see Billingham, Stuart.

Blanchard, Robert G. The First Editions of John Buchan: A Collector's Bibliography. x, 246p. 1982. 32.50 (ISBN 0-208-01905-7, Archon). Shoe String.

Blanchard, Robert J. & Blanchard, Caroline, eds. Advances in the Study of Aggression, Vol. 1. (Serial Publication Ser.). 238p. 1984. 35.00 (ISBN 0-12-037701-2). Acad Pr.

Blanchard, Robert O., ed. Congress & the News Media. (Studies in Public Communication). 1974. 19.95 (ISBN 0-8038-1192-6); pap. text ed. 10.75x (ISBN 0-8038-1194-2). Hastings.

Blanchard, Roberta R. How to Restore & Decorate Chairs in Early American Styles. Orig. Title: How to Restore & Decorate Chairs. (Illus.). 128p. 1981. pap. 4.00 (ISBN 0-486-24177-7). Dover.

--Traditional Tole Painting: With Authentic Antique Designs & Working Diagrams for Stenciling & Brush-Stroke Painting. LC 77-78208. (Illus.). 1977. pap. 3.95 (ISBN 0-486-23531-9). Dover.

--Traditional Tole Painting, with Authentic Antique Designs & Working Diagrams for Stenciling & Brush-Stroke Painting. 13.75 (ISBN 0-8446-5559-7). Peter Smith.

Blanchard, Roderick D. Litigation & Trial Practice for the Legal Paraprofessional. 2nd ed. (Paralegal Ser.). (Illus.). 400p. 1982. text ed. 19.95 (ISBN 0-314-63160-7). West Pub.

Blanchard, Russel W. Graphic Design. (Illus.). 208p. 1984. pap. text ed. 20.95 (ISBN 0-13-363226-1). P-H.

Blanchard, Smoke. Walking Up & Down in the World: Memories of a Mountain Rambler. LC 84-5380. (Illus.). 288p. 1985. 15.95 (ISBN 0-87156-827-6). Sierra.

Blanchard, Tim. A Practical Guide to Finding & Using Your Spiritual Gifts. 1983. pap. 5.95 (ISBN 0-8423-4898-0). Tyndale.

Blanchard, W. O. & Visher, S. S. Economic Geography of Europe. 1979. Repr. of 1931 ed. lib. bdg. 30.00 (ISBN 0-8495-0522-4). Arden Lib.

--Economic Geography of Europe. 1931. 20.00 (ISBN 0-686-17717-7). Quest Edns.

Blanchard, William. Aggression: American Style. LC 77-28051. 1978. pap. 13.25x (ISBN 0-673-16254-0). Scott F.

Blanchard, William H. Revolutionary Morality: A Psychosexual Analysis of Twelve Revolutionists. LC 82-22679. 281p. 1984. lib. bdg. 42.50 (ISBN 0-87436-032-3). ABC Clio.

Blanche, Claude-Pierre. Dictionnaire et Armorial des Noms de Famille de France. 312p. (Fr.). 1974. pap. 55.00 (ISBN 0-686-56922-9, M-6038). French & Eur.

Blanche, Ella. Searching the Shadows. (Contemporary Poets Ser.: No. 1). 48p. (Orig.). 1983. pap. 2.95 (ISBN 0-916982-26-2, RL226). Realities.

Blanche, Jacques-Emile, jt. auth. see Mauriac, Francois.

Blanchet, A. M. Journal of a Catholic Bishop on the Oregon Trail. Kowrach, Edward J., tr. 1979. 18.95 (ISBN 0-87770-166-0). Ye Galleon.

Blanchet, Francis N. Historical Sketches of the Catholic Church in Oregon. 164p. 1983. 14.95 (ISBN 0-87770-306-X). Ye Galleon.

Blanchet, Francis X. Ten Years on the Pacific Coast. 1982. 9.95 (ISBN 0-87770-281-0). Ye Galleon.

Blanchet, Francoise & Doornekamp, Rinke. What to Do with...a Potato. LC 77-85383. (Children's Cookery Ser.). (gr. 3-8). 1979. 3.95 (ISBN 0-8120-5255-2). Barron.

Blanchet, Kevin D. & Switlik, Mary M. The Handbook of Hospital Admitting Management. Date not set. price not set (ISBN 0-87189-121-2). Aspen Systems.

Blanchet, Leon. Campanella Fifteen Sixty-Eight to Sixteen Thirty-Nine. 1964. Repr. of 1920 ed. 32.00 (ISBN 0-8337-0308-0). B Franklin.

Blanchet, Louis-Emile. Comment Presenter Un Texte Philosophique. (Fr.). pap. 41.50 (ISBN 0-317-08034-2, 2022666). Bks Demand UMI.

Blanchet, M. Wylie. Curve of Time. 1977. 7.95 (ISBN 0-88826-071-7). Superior Pub.

Blanchette, Jean-François, jt. auth. see Boily, Lise.

Blanchette, Madeleine H. My Reminder. 1984. 6.50 (ISBN 0-8062-2289-1). Carlton.

Blanchette, Oliva. For a Fundamental Social Ethic. LC 73-77400. 228p. 1973. 7.50 (ISBN 0-8022-2113-0). Philos Lib.

Blanchette, Oliva, tr. see Blondel, Maurice.

Blanchette, Zelda B. & Martin, Clyde I. Around Our Village. (Illus.). (gr. 2). 1958. text ed. 4.44 (ISBN 0-87443-033-X). Benson.

Blanchfield, William C., jt. auth. see Oser, Jacob.

Blanchflower, Danny. Soccer My Way. pap. 6.50x (ISBN 0-392-07454-0, SpS). Sportshelf.

Blanchot, M. Le Ressassement Eternel. (Reimpressions G & B Ser.). 146p. (Fr.). 1970. 26.95 (ISBN 0-677-50425-X, PAP). Gordon.

Blanchot, Maurice. Death Sentence. Davis, Lydia, tr. from French. LC 78-59907. Orig. Title: L' Arret De Mort. 88p. 1978. 10.00 (ISBN 0-930794-05-2); pap. 5.95 (ISBN 0-930794-04-4). Station Hill Pr.

--The Gaze of Orpheus: & Other Literary Essays. Sitney, P. Adams, ed. Davis, Lydia, tr. from Fr. LC 80-27297. 216p. 1981. 20.00 (ISBN 0-930794-37-0); pap. 8.95 (ISBN 0-930794-38-9). Station Hill Pr.

--The Madness of the Day: La Folie du Jour. Davis, Lydia, tr. Orig. Title: La Folie Du Jour. 32p. (Eng. & Fr.). 1981. 8.50 (ISBN 0-930794-39-7); pap. 3.95 (ISBN 0-930794-36-2). Station Hill Pr.

--The Sirens' Song: Selected Essays of Maurice Blanchot. Josipovic, Gabriel, ed. Rabinovitch, Sacha, tr. LC 81-48510. 264p. 1982. 22.50 (ISBN 0-253-35255-X). Ind U Pr.

--The Space of Literature: A Translation of "L'Espace Litteraire". Smock, Ann, tr. from Fr. LC 82-2062. xviii, 276p. 1982. 23.50x (ISBN 0-8032-1166-X). U of Nebr Pr.

--Vicious Circles. Auster, Paul, tr. from Fr. Orig. Title: Le Ressassement Eternel. 96p. (Orig.). 1985. 13.95 (ISBN 0-930794-93-1); pap. 6.95 (ISBN 0-930794-92-3). Station Hill Pr.

--When the Time Comes. Davis, Lydia, tr. from Fr. Orig. Title: Au Moment Voulu. 80p. (Orig.). 1984. 12.95 (ISBN 0-930794-96-6); pap. 5.95 (ISBN 0-930794-95-8). Station Hill Pr.

--The Writing of the Disaster. Smock, Ann, tr. from Fr. & intro. by. LC 85-8562. 150p. 1985. price not set (ISBN 0-8032-1186-4). U of Nebr Pr.

Blanck, Gertrude & Blanck, Rubin. Ego Psychology: Theory & Pratice. LC 73-17287. 394p. 1974. 29.00x (ISBN 0-231-03615-9). Columbia U Pr.

--Ego Psychology Two: Developmental Psychology. LC 78-10956. (Illus.). 264p. 1979. 26.00x (ISBN 0-231-04470-4). Columbia U Pr.

Blanck, Gertrude, jt. auth. see Blanck, Rubin.

Blanck, Jacob, compiled by. Bibliography of American Literature, 7 vols. Incl. Vol. 1. Henry Adams to Donn Byrne. xlix, 474p. 1955. 70.00x (ISBN 0-300-00310-2); Vol. 2. George W. Cable to Timothy Dwight. xix, 534p. 1957. 70.00x (ISBN 0-300-00311-0); Vol. 3. Edward Eggleston to Bret Harte. xxi, 482p. 1959. 70.00x (ISBN 0-300-00312-9); Vol. 4. Nathaniel Hawthorne to Joseph Holt Ingraham. xxii, 495p. 1963. 70.00x (ISBN 0-300-00313-7); Vol. 5. Washington Irving to Henry Wadsworth Longfellow. xxii, 1969p. 1969. 70.00x (ISBN 0-300-01099-0); Vol. 6. Augustus Baldwin Longstreet to Thomas William Parsons. LC 54-5283. 608p. 1973. 55.00x (ISBN 0-300-01618-2); Vol. 7. James Kirke Paulding to Frank Richard Stockton. 700p. text ed. 75.00x (ISBN 0-300-02636-6). LC 54-5283. (Illus.). Yale U Pr.

Blanck, Rubin & Blanck, Gertrude. Marriage & Personal Development. LC 68-9577. 191p. 1968. 21.00x (ISBN 0-231-03150-5). Columbia U Pr.

Blanck, Rubin, jt. auth. see Blanck, Gertrude.

Blanckenburg, F. Von. Literarische Zusatze Zu Johann Sulzers Allgemeiner Theorie der Schonen Kunste: 1796-1798, 3 vols. Repr. of 1798 ed. Set. 260.00 (ISBN 0-384-04670-3). Johnson Repr.

Blanc-LaPierre, A. Mankind & Energy: Needs, Resources, Hopes. (Studies in Environmental Science: Vol. 16). 720p. 1982. 149.00 (ISBN 0-444-99715-6). Elsevier.

Blanc-LaPierre, Andre & Fortet, R. Theory of Random Functions, 2 Vols. LC 65-16343. (Illus.). 810p. 1968. Set. 153.95 (ISBN 0-677-04250-7). Gordon.

Blanco, Alberto. Curso de Obligaciones y Contratos: Contratos en Especie (Explicaciones de Clase, Vol. III. 3rd ed. LC 77-4251. 1978. 15.00 (ISBN 0-8477-3010-7); pap. 12.00 (ISBN 0-8477-3011-5). U of PR Pr.

--Curso de Obligaciones y Contratos: Doctrina General de los Contratos, Vol. II. 3rd, enl. ed. LC 77-4251. (Span.). 1979. 12.00 (ISBN 0-8477-3008-5); pap. 9.00 (ISBN 0-8477-3009-3). U of PR Pr.

--El Regimen De la Propiedad Privada En el Estado Libre Asociado De Puerto Rico (Intervencionismo, Dirigismo, Socializacion) LC 78-1748. (Span.). 1978. pap. 3.50 (ISBN 0-8477-3016-6). U of PR Pr.

Blanco, Amanda, photos by. Ward Ritchie, Printer & Designer. (Illus.). 1985. portfolio 250.00 (ISBN 0-937048-40-2). CSUN.

Blanco, Antonio De Fierro. The Journey of the Flame. 1933. 30.00 (ISBN 0-89984-004-3). Century Bookbindery.

Blanco, Enrique G. Verbos Espanoles Regulares e Irregulares. (Span.). 1966. pap. text ed. 1.30 (ISBN 0-8294-0133-4). Loyola.

Blanco, Hugo. Land or Death: The Peasant Struggle in Peru. LC 73-186689. 192p. 1972. 20.00 (ISBN 0-87348-265-4); pap. 5.95 (ISBN 0-87348-266-2). Path Pr NY.

Blanco, L., jt. auth. see Bassols, C.

Blanco, Lobo F., ed. see Lisboa, Henriqueta.

Blanco, Miquel A., jt. auth. see Watson, E. W.

Blanco, O., tr. see Pendleton, Don.

Blanco, O. J., tr. see Pendleton, Don.

Blanco, Osvaldo J., tr. see Pendleton, Don.

Blanco, Ralph F. Prescriptions for Children with Learning & Adjustment Problems. 2nd ed. 288p. 1982. 19.75x (ISBN 0-398-04511-9). C C Thomas.

Blanco, Ralph F. & Rosenfeld, Joseph G. Case Studies in Clinical & School Psychology. (Illus.). 256p. 1978. 25.75x (ISBN 0-398-03807-4). C C Thomas.

Blanco, Richard L. Rommel the Desert Warrior: The Afrika Korps in World War II. LC 82-2293. 192p. (gr. 7 up). 1982. PLB 9.79 (ISBN 0-671-42245-6); pap. 4.95 (ISBN 0-671-49582-8). Messner.

--The War of the American Revolution: A Selected, Annotated Bibliography of Published Sources. LC 82-49168. (Wars of the U. S.: Vol. 1). 654p. 1983. lib. bdg. 49.00 (ISBN 0-8240-9171-X). Garland Pub.

--Wellington's Surgeon General, Sir James McGrigor. LC 74-75477. pap. 64.30 (ISBN 0-317-28968-3, 2023759). Bks Demand UMI.

Blanco, Richard L., ed. see Beede, Benjamin R.

Blanco, Richard L., ed. see Smith, Myron J.

Blanco, Tomas. The Child's Gifts: A Twelfth Night Tale. LC 75-46530. (Illus.). 32p. (English & Spanish.). 1976. 8.95 (ISBN 0-664-32595-5). Westminster.

--El Prejuicio Racial en Puerto Rico: Racial Prejudice in Puerto Rico, Spanish Text. LC 74-14222. (The Puerto Rican Experience Ser). (Illus.). 90p. 1975. Repr. 11.00x (ISBN 0-405-06212-5). Ayer Co Pubs.

--Prontuario Historico de Puerto Rico. LC 80-67412. (Obras completas de Tomas Blanco). 132p. 1981. pap. 4.25 (ISBN 0-940238-34-9). Ediciones Huracan.

--Vates. LC 80-67415. (Obras completas de Tomas Blanco). 96p. 1981. pap. 3.75 (ISBN 0-940238-43-8). Ediciones Huracan.

Blanco Fombona, Rufino. The Man of Gold. Goldberg, Isaac, tr. 1977. lib. bdg. 59.95 (ISBN 0-8490-2200-2). Gordon Pr.

Blancq, Charles. Sonny Rollins: The Journey of a Jazzman. LC 82-15860. (Music Ser.). (Illus.). 148p. (gr. 10-12). 1982. pap. 19.95 (ISBN 0-8057-9460-3, Twayne). G K Hall.

Bland, Alan, et al. Utilization Potential of Kentucky Coal Refuse. (IMMR Reports). (Illus.). 45p. 1983. pap. 5.00 (ISBN 0-86607-023-0). Inst Mining & Minerals.

Bland, Alden. Behold a Cry. LC 73-18554. Repr. of 1947 ed. 19.50 (ISBN 0-404-11369-9). AMS Pr.

Bland, Alexander. Nureyev Valantino. 1977. pap. 6.95 (ISBN 0-440-56478-6). Dell.

Bland, Alexander & Percival, John. Men Dancing. (Illus.). 192p. 1984. 35.00 (ISBN 0-02-511450-6). Macmillan.

Bland, Brian F. Crop Production: Cereals & Legumes. 1971. 73.50 (ISBN 0-12-104050-X). Acad Pr.

Bland, C. C., tr. The Autobiography of Guibert: Abbot of Nogent-Sous-Coucy. 1979. Repr. of 1925 ed. lib. bdg. 30.00 (ISBN 0-8482-0140-X). Norwood Edns.

Bland, C. C., tr. see De Nogent, Guibert.

Bland, C. Swinton, tr. see Coulton, G. G.

Bland, Carole J. Faculty Development Through Workshops. 232p. 1980. spiral 20.75x (ISBN 0-398-03940-2). C C Thomas.

Bland, Charles. A Vision of Unity: The Bland Family in England & America, 1555-1900. 552p. (Orig.). 1982. 69.95 (ISBN 0-9610804-0-X). C L Bland.

Bland, Charles E., jt. ed. see Couch, John N.

Bland, D. S. Three Revels from the Inns of the Court. 132p. 1982. text ed. 23.50x (ISBN 0-86127-402-4, Pub. by Avebury England). Humanities.

Bland, Glenn. Success: The Glenn Bland Method. 1983. pap. 2.95 (ISBN 0-8423-6689-X). Tyndale.

Bland, J. Men, Manners & Morals in South America. 1976. lib. bdg. 59.95 (ISBN 0-8490-2227-4). Gordon Pr.

Bland, J. O. China under the Empress Dowager. lib. bdg. 79.95 (ISBN 0-87968-485-2). Krishna Pr.

--Houseboat Days in China. lib. bdg. 79.95 (ISBN 0-87968-486-0). Krishna Pr.

Bland, J. O., jt. auth. see Backhouse, E. T.

Bland, Jeffery. Glandular-Based Food Supplements. 1981. pap. 7.95x (ISBN 0-317-07293-5, Regent House). B of A.

--Nutraerobics: The Complete Individualized Nutrition & Fitness Program for Life after 30. LC 83-47716. 320p. 1983. 16.30 (ISBN 0-06-250053-8, HarpR). Har-Row.

Bland, Jeffrey. Bioflavonoids. Mindell, Earl & Passwater, Richard, eds. (Good Health Guides Ser.). 26p. 1984. pap. 1.45 (ISBN 0-87983-330-0). Keats.

--Choline, Lecithin, Inositol. Passwater, Richard, ed. (Good Health Guide Ser.). 1983. pap. 1.45 (ISBN 0-87983-277-0). Keats.

--Digestive Enzymes. Passwater, Richard A. & Mindell, Earl, eds. 1983. pap. 1.45 (ISBN 0-87983-331-9). Keats.

--Hair Tissue Mineral Analysis: An Emergent Diagnostic Technique. 80p. (Orig.). 1984. pap. 5.95 (ISBN 0-7225-0876-X). Thorsons Pubs.

--Nutraerobics. LC 83-47716. 384p. 1985. pap. 16.30 (ISBN 0-06-250054-6, HarpR). Har-Row.

--Octacosanol, Carnitine, & Other "Accessory" Nutrients. Passwater, Richard A. & Mindell, Earl, eds. (Good Health Guide Ser.). 36p. 1982. pap. text ed. 1.45 (ISBN 0-87983-316-5). Keats.

--Your Health under Siege. LC 80-39545. 256p. 1982. pap. 8.50 (ISBN 0-8289-0416-2). Greene.

Bland, Jeffrey, ed. Medical Applications of Clinical Nutrition. LC 82-84365. 250p. 1983. 25.00 (ISBN 0-87983-327-0). Keats.

--The Yearbook of Nutritional Medicine, 1984-1985. 336p. 1985. 39.95 (ISBN 0-87983-359-9). Keats.

Bland, John. Forests of Lilliput: The Realm of Mosses & Lichens. LC 70-143811. (Natural History Ser). (Illus.). 1971. 9.95 (ISBN 0-13-326868-3). P-H.

Bland, John O. China, Japan & Korea. facsimile ed. LC 77-160959. (Select Bibliographies Reprint Ser). Repr. of 1921 ed. 32.00 (ISBN 0-8369-5826-8). Ayer Co Pubs.

--Li Hung-Chang. facsimile ed. LC 77-175688. (Select Bibliographies Reprint Ser). Repr. of 1917 ed. 21.00 (ISBN 0-8369-6603-1). Ayer Co Pubs.

--Recent Events & Present Policies in China. LC 73-865. (China Studies: from Confucius to Mao Ser). (Illus.). xi, 481p. 1973. Repr. of 1912 ed. 33.45 (ISBN 0-88355-061-X). Hyperion Conn.

Bland, Kalman P. Epistle on the Possibility of Conjunction with the Active Intellect by Ibn Rushd with the Commentary of Moses Narboni. LC 81-20788. 314p. 1982. 35.00x (ISBN 0-87334-005-1). Ktav.

Bland, Kalman P., ed. & tr. see Rushd, Ibn.

Bland, Larry I. & Hadsel, Fred L., eds. The Papers of George Catlett Marshall, "The Soldierly Spirit", Vol. I. LC 81-47593. (Illus.). 750p. 1981. text ed. 35.00x (ISBN 0-8018-2552-0). Johns Hopkins.

Bland, Leland D. Sight Singing Through Melodic Analysis. LC 83-8184. 512p. 1983. text ed. 36.95x (ISBN 0-8304-1003-1); pap. text ed. 19.95x (ISBN 0-88229-820-8). Nelson-Hall.

Bland, Margaret. Shadows of Things Past. 51p. 1984. 5.95 (ISBN 0-533-05527-X). Vantage.

Bland, Michael. Employee Communications in the 1980's. 1981. 27.50 (ISBN 0-85038-252-1). Nichols Pub.

--The Executive's Guide to TV & Radio Appearances. LC 79-9607. (Video Bookshelf Ser.). 138p. 1980. professional 14.95 (ISBN 0-914236-53-9, 504-BW). Knowledge Indus.

Bland, Peter. Passing Gods. 1970. pap. 2.00 (ISBN 0-686-02018-9, Pub. by Ferry Pr); pap. 11.00 signed ltd. ed. with holograph poem (ISBN 0-686-02019-7). Small Pr Dist.

Bland, Randall W. Private Pressure on Public Law: The Legal Career of Justice Thurgood Marshall. 220p. 1973. 19.50x (ISBN 0-8046-9035-9, 9035); pap. 11.50x (ISBN 0-8046-9048-0, 9048). Assoc Faculty Pr.

Bland, Randall W., jt. auth. see Pettus, Beryl E.

Bland, Randall W., et al, eds. see Corwin, Edward S.

Bland, Roger G. & Jaques, H. E. How to Know the Insects. 3rd ed. (Pictured Key Nature Ser.). 432p. 1978. wire coil avail. (ISBN 0-697-04752-0). Wm C Brown.

Bland, Salem. New Christianity. LC 72-95815. (Social History of Canada Ser.). 1973. pap. 6.00 (ISBN 0-8020-6179-6). U of Toronto Pr.

Bland, W. B. The Restoration of Capitalism in the Soviet Union. 1984. 22.00x (ISBN 0-317-14524-X, Pub. by Selecteditions). State Mutual Bk.

Bland, William F. & Davidson, R. L. Petroleum Processing Handbook. 1967. 88.95 (ISBN 0-07-005860-1). McGraw.

Bland, William M., Jr. The History of Rocket Technology: Essays on Research, Development, & Utility. Emme, Eugene M., ed. LC 64-17625. pap. 82.80 (ISBN 0-317-09294-4, 2001337). Bks Demand UMI.

Blandau, Richard J. Morphogenesis & Malformation of the Skin. LC 81-8302. (Birth Defects: Original Article Ser.: Vol. 17, No. 2). 286p. 1981. 48.00 (ISBN 0-8451-1042-X). A R Liss.

Blandau, Richard J., ed. The Biology of the Blastocyst. LC 70-128713. pap. 143.50 (ISBN 0-317-28279-4, 2019955). Bks Demand UMI.

Blandau, Richard J. & Moghissi, Kamran, eds. The Biology of the Cervix. LC 72-91429. pap. 115.80 (ISBN 0-317-28276-X, 2019956). Bks Demand UMI.

Blandau, Richard J., ed. see International Conference on Morphogenesis & Malformation, Lake Wilderness, Washington, 3rd, July 1976.

Blandeau, R. J., ed. see International Symposium on Aging Gametes, Seattle, June 1973.

Blandford. The Complete Handbook of Drafting. (Illus.). 322p. 1982. 16.95 (ISBN 0-8306-0049-3). TAB Bks.

--The Master Handbook of Sheetmetalwork-with Projects. 378p. 1981. 16.95 (ISBN 0-8306-9644-X); pap. 9.95 (ISBN 0-8306-1257-2, 1257). TAB Bks.

Blandford, Brian. Winners & Losers: The Pulkington Printouts. LC 84-26709. 1985. pap. 3.95 (ISBN 0-8307-1012-4, S181422). Regal.

Blandford, G. Fielding. Insanity & Its Treatment: Lectures on the Treatment, Medical & Legal, of Insane Patients. LC 75-16684. (Classics in Psychiatry Ser.). 1976. Repr. of 1871 ed. 35.50x (ISBN 0-405-07416-6). Ayer Co Pubs.

Blandford, H. F. A List of the Ferns of Simla & North Western Himalaya. (Illus.). 22p. 1978. Repr. of 1885 ed. 2.00 (ISBN 0-88065-065-6, Pub. by Messers Today & Tomorrows Printers & Publishers India). Scholarly Pubns.

Blandford, Linda. The LSO: Scenes from Orchestra Life. (Illus.). 160p. 1985. 19.95 (ISBN 0-7181-2463-4, Pub. by Michael Joseph). Merrimack Pub Cir.

Blandford, Linda A., tr. Supreme Court of the United States 1789-1980: An Index to Opinions Arranged by Justice. Evans, Patricia R. LC 82-48981. (Orig.). 1983. lib. bdg. 110.00 (ISBN 0-527-27952-8). Kraus Intl.

Blandford, P. W. Working in Canvas. 2nd ed. (Illus.). 74p. 1981. pap. 6.50x (ISBN 0-85174-416-8). Sheridan.

Blandford, Percy. Care & Repair Below Decks. (Illus.). 112p. 1980. 15.00 (ISBN 0-229-11636-1). Sheridan.

--Illustrated History of Small Boats. (Illus.). 1974. 9.50 (ISBN 0-902875-51-5). Transatlantic.

--The Woodturner's Bible. LC 76-8647. (Illus.). 1979. pap. 13.95 (ISBN 0-8306-1044-8, 1044). TAB Bks.

Blandford, Percy W. Building Better Beds. (Illus.). 304p. 1984. pap. 14.50 (ISBN 0-8306-1664-0). TAB Bks.

--Country Craft Tools. LC 73-22569. (Illus.). 240p. 1974. 40.00x (ISBN 0-8103-2011-8). Gale.

--Country Craft Tools. LC 75-27176. (Funk & W Bk.). (Illus.). 240p. 1976. pap. 5.95i (ISBN 0-308-10242-8). T Y Crowell.

--Fifty-Eight Home Shelving & Storage Projects. (Illus.). 288p. (Orig.). 1985. text ed. 25.95 (ISBN 0-8306-0844-3, 1844); pap. 14.95 (ISBN 0-8306-1844-9). TAB Bks.

--Fifty-Three Space-Saving Built-In Furniture Projects. (Illus.). 400p. (Orig.). 1983. pap. 17.50 (ISBN 0-8306-1504-0). TAB Bks.

--The Illustrated Handbook of Woodworking Joints. (Illus.). 352p. 1984. 19.95o.p (ISBN 0-8306-0274-7); pap. 15.95 (ISBN 0-8306-0174-0, 1574). TAB Bks.

--Maps & Compasses: A User's Handbook. (Illus.). 252p. (Orig.). 1984. 15.95 (ISBN 0-8306-0644-0, 1644); pap. 10.95 (ISBN 0-8306-1644-6). TAB Bks.

--Modern Sailmaking. (Illus.). 1978. pap. 7.95 (937). TAB Bks.

--Old Farm Tools & Machinery: An Illustrated History. LC 75-44376. 1976. 36.00x (ISBN 0-8103-2019-3). Gale.

--The Practical Handbook of Blacksmithing & Metalworking. 448p. 11.75 (ISBN 0-318-14891-9, F152). Midwest Old Settlers.

--Practical Knots & Ropework. (Illus., Orig.). 1980. 14.95o.p (ISBN 0-8306-9956-2); pap. 9.95 (ISBN 0-8306-1237-8, 1237). TAB Bks.

--Rigging Sail. (Illus.). 272p. (Orig.). 1983. pap. 15.50 (ISBN 0-8306-1634-9, 1634). TAB Bks.

--Sixty-Six Children's Furniture Projects. (Illus.). 1979. pap. 9.95 (ISBN 0-8306-1188-6, 1188). TAB Bks.

Blandford, Roger D., jt. ed. see Riegler, Guenter R.

Blandford, W. T. & Godwin-Austen, H. N. Mollusca: Testacelldae & Zonitidae, Vol. 1. (Fauna of British India Ser.). xxxii, 332p. 1978. Repr. of 1908 ed. 30.00 (Pub. by Messers Today & Tomorrows Printers & Publishers India). Scholarly Pubns.

Blandi, Joseph G. Maryland Business Corporations, Seventeen Eighty-Three to Eighteen Fifty-Two. LC 78-64155. (Johns Hopkins University. Studies in the Social Sciences. Fifty-Second Ser. 1934: 3). Repr. of 1934 ed. 15.00 (ISBN 0-404-61265-2). AMS Pr.

Blandin, I. M. History of Higher Education of Women in the South Prior to 1860. LC 75-37960. 1976. Repr. of 1909 ed. 17.95 (ISBN 0-89201-024-X). Zenger Pub.

Blanding, Don. Floridays. (Florida Classics Ser.). (Illus., Orig.). 1977. pap. 4.95 (ISBN 0-912451-03-3). Florida Classics.

--Leaves from a Grass House. pap. 2.50 (ISBN 0-912180-17-X). Petroglyph.

--Paradise Loot. (Illus.). 1978. pap. 1.00 (ISBN 0-912180-35-8). Petroglyph.

Blanding, Warren. Practical Handbook of Distribution-Customer Service. Harps, Leslie, ed. (Illus.). 584p. 1985. 40.00 (ISBN 0-87408-033-9). Traffic Serv.

Blandino, Betty. Coiled Pottery: Traditional & Contemporary Ways. LC 84-21470. 112p. 1985. pap. 12.95 (ISBN 0-8019-7601-4). Chilton.

Blandino, Giovanni. Theories on the Nature of Life. LC 66-24445. 1969. 6.00 (ISBN 0-8022-2251-X). Philos Lib.

Blandon, Peter. Soviet Forest Industries. LC 83-10306. (Replica Edition Ser.). 290p. 1983. pap. 26.50x (ISBN 0-86531-960-X). Westview.

Blandy. Transuretheral Resection. 2nd ed. (Illus.). 192p. 1978. text ed. 32.00 (ISBN 0-8391-1325-0). Univ Park.

Blandy, J. P. & Lytton, Bernard. The Prostate: BIMR Urology, Vol. 3. 320p. 1985. text ed. 59.95 (ISBN 0-407-02359-3). Butterworth.

Blandy, John. Lecture Notes on Urology. 3rd ed. (Illus.). 384p. 1982. pap. text ed. 19.95 (ISBN 0-632-00688-9, B 0889-9). Mosby.

Blandy, John P., et al. Tumours of the Testicle. (Illus.). 187p. 1970. 37.00 (ISBN 0-8089-0564-3, 790605). Grune.

Blandy, Richard & Covick, Owen, eds. Understanding Labour Markets. 264p. 1984. 19.95x (ISBN 0-86861-151-4). Allen Unwin.

Blandy, Thomas & Lamoureux, Denis. All Through the House: A Guide to Home Weatherization. (Illus., Orig.). 1980. pap. 7.95 (ISBN 0-07-005871-7). McGraw.

Blandy, William. Castle or Picture of Policy. LC 71-38157. (English Experience Ser.: No. 436). 68p. 1972. Repr. of 1581 ed. 9.50 (ISBN 90-221-0436-2). Walter J Johnson.

Blane, Andrew, ed. The Ecumenical World of Orthodox Civilization: Russia & Orthodoxy, Vol. 3. (Slavistic Printings & Reprintings Ser: No. 260). 1974. text ed. 44.80x (ISBN 90-2792-610-7). Mouton.

Blane, H. T. & Chafetz, M. E., eds. Youth, Alcohol, & Social Policy. LC 79-9094. (Illus.). 450p. 1979. 35.00x (ISBN 0-306-40253-X, Plenum Pr). Plenum Pub.

Blane, Linda. Development of Psycho-Motor Competence: Selected Readings. LC 74-31488. 201p. 1975. 20.00x (ISBN 0-8422-5219-3); pap. text ed. 6.95x (ISBN 0-8422-0443-1). Irvington.

Blane, William N. Excursion Through the United States & Canada During the Years 1822-1823. LC 68-58049. (Illus.). Repr. of 1824 ed. 24.75x (ISBN 0-8371-4978-9, BLA&, Pub. by Negro U Pr). Greenwood.

Blaner, Gideon, jt. ed. see Sund, Blauer.

Blanes Prieto, Joaquin. Diccionario de Terminos Contables. 2nd ed. 388p. (Eng. & Span.). 1972. pap. 21.95 (ISBN 0-686-57342-0, S-28549). French & Eur.

Blaney, D., jt. auth. see May, Ernest.

Blaney, Harry C. Global Challenges. 1979. 12.95; pap. 6.95 (ISBN 0-531-05619-8). Watts.

Blaney, Worth, jt. auth. see Provost, C. Antonio.

Blank, et al see Gratovich.

Blank, Ben & Garcia, Mario R. Professional Video Graphics Design. 188p. 1985. 29.95 (ISBN 0-13-725797-X). P-H.

Blank, C. L., et al, eds. Microwave Fixation of Labile Metabolites: Proceedings of an official Satellite Symposium of the 8th International Congress of Pharmacology Held in Tokyo, Japan, 25 July 1981. (Illus.). 204p. 1983. 60.00 (ISBN 0-08-029829-X). Pergamon.

Blank, Chotsie. California Artists Cookbook. LC 82-6798. (Illus.). 216p. 1982. 25.00 (ISBN 0-89659-246-4). Abbeville Pr.

Blank, David. Ancient Philosophy & Grammar: The Syntax of Appolon·us Dyscolus. LC 82-5751. (American Philological Association, American Classical Studies). 136p. 1982. pap. 11.25 (ISBN 0-89130-580-7, 40 04 10). Scholars Pr GA.

Blank, David E. Venezuela: Politics in a Petroleum Republic. LC 83-24469. (Politics in Latin America Ser.). 240p. 1984. 29.95 (ISBN 0-03-069792-1). Praeger.

Blank, Florence W. & Guertin, Carolyn W. Sound Skill Builder: Use with Sure Steps to Reading & Spelling, 3 bks. Incl. Bk. 1. price not set (ISBN 0-916720-04-7); Bk. 2. price not set (ISBN 0-916720-05-5); Bk. 3. price not set (ISBN 0-916720-06-3). (gr. 1-7). Date not set. Weiss Pub.

Blank, Hannah. Mastering Micros. (Illus.). 300p. 1984. 24.95. Van Nos Reinhold.

Blank, Hannah I. Mastering Micros. (Illus.). 340p. 1983. 24.95x (ISBN 0-89433-207-4). Petrocelli.

Blank, J., et al. Software Engineering: Methods & Techniques. 241p. 1983. 26.95 (ISBN 0-471-88503-7). Wiley.

Blank, Joan. Give Your Whole Self. (Illus.). 96p. (Orig.). 1981. pap. 4.95 (ISBN 0-941374-00-9). Grapetree Prods.

--Laugh Lines. (Illus.). 96p. (Orig.). 1982. pap. 4.95 (ISBN 0-941374-01-7). Grapetree Prods.

Blank, Joan, et al. Career Guidance Resources: A Handbook of Resource Abstracts-Grades K-14 1978 Updates. 179p. 1979. 10.50 (ISBN 0-318-15413-7, RD157). Natl Ctr Res Voc Ed.

Blank, Joani. Good Vibrations: The Complete Guide to Vibrators. 52p. 1982. pap. 4.50 (ISBN 0-940208-05-9). Down There Pr.

--The Kid's First Book about Sex. (Illus.). 48p. (Orig.). (ps-3). 1983. pap. 5.50 (ISBN 0-940208-07-5, Pub. by Yes Pr). Down There Pr.

--Playbook for Kids About Sex. (Illus.). 56p. (gr. 2-6). 1980. pap. 4.75 (ISBN 0-9602324-6-X). Down There Pr.

--Playbook for Men About Sex. rev. ed. 32p. 1981. pap. 4.00 (ISBN 0-9602324-8-6). Down There Pr.

--Playbook for Women About Sex. rev. ed. 32p. 1982. pap. 4.00 (ISBN 0-9602324-0-0). Down There Pr.

Blank, Josef. The Gospel According to St. John, Vol. II. McKenzie, John L., ed. LC 81-605. (The New Testament for Spiritual Reading Ser.). 282p. 1981. pap. 4.95. Crossroad NY.

Blank, Joseph P. Nineteen Steps up the Mountain: The Story of the DeBolt Family. LC 76-22659. (Illus.). 1976. 11.49i (ISBN 0-397-01155-5). Har-Row.

Blank, Leland T. Statistical Procedures for Engineering, Management & Science. (Industrial Engineering & Management Science Ser.). (Illus.). 1980. text ed. 39.95 (ISBN 0-07-005851-2). McGraw.

Blank, Leland T. & Tarquin, Anthony J. Engineering Economy. 2nd ed. (Illus.). 496p. 1983. text ed. 37.95 (ISBN 0-07-062961-7). McGraw.

Blank, Leonard. Age of Shrinks. LC 79-52476. 1979. 10.95 (ISBN 0-686-25248-9). Ewing Pubns.

Blank, Les. Burden of Dreams. Bogan, James, ed. 1984. pap. 12.95 (ISBN 0-938190-17-2); text ed. 25.00. North Atlantic.

Blank, M., ed. Surface Chemistry of Biological Systems. LC 70-110799. (Advances in Experimental Medicine & Biology Ser.: Vol. 7). 352p. 1970. 49.50x (ISBN 0-306-39007-8, Plenum Pr). Plenum Pub.

Blank, Marion. Developmental Discourse Therapy. 192p. 1985. pap. text ed. 18.50 (ISBN 0-8391-2039-7, 21490). Univ Park.

--Teaching Learning in the Preschool: A Dialogue Approach. 2nd ed. LC 83-16884. 334p. 1983. pap. text ed. 14.95 (ISBN 0-914797-06-9). Brookline Book.

Blank, Marion, et al. The Language of Learning: The Preschool Years. 208p. 1978. pap. 30.00 (ISBN 0-8089-1058-2, 790610). Grune.

--Preschool Language Assessment Instrument: Language of Learning in Practice. 116p. 1978. pap. 26.50 (ISBN 0-8089-1072-8, 790611); record forms 16.00 (ISBN 0-8089-1107-4, 790612). Grune.

--Preschool Language Assessment Instrument: Spanish Edition. Berlin, Laura, ed. 124p. 1983. pap. text ed. 36.50 reference ed. (ISBN 0-8089-1562-2, 790613); scoring forms 19.50 (ISBN 0-8089-1576-2, 790615). Grune.

Blank, Marion S., compiled by. Working with People: A Selected Social Casework Bibliography. 2nd ed. LC 81-43789. 126p. 1982. 8.95 (ISBN 0-87304-193-3). Family Serv.

Blank, Martin, ed. Bioelectrochemistry: Ions, Surfaces, Membranes. LC 80-18001. (Advances in Chemistry Ser.: No. 188). 1980. 59.95 (ISBN 0-8412-0473-X). Am Chemical.

Blank, Phillip E., Jr., ed. Lyric Forms in the Sonnet Sequences of Barnabe Barnes. LC 72-94447. (De Proprietatubus Litterarum, Series Practica, No. 18). 162p. (Orig.). 1974. pap. text ed. 18.40x (ISBN 90-2793-062-7). Mouton.

Blank, R. Political Parties: An Introduction. 1980. 27.95 (ISBN 0-13-684761-7). P-H.

Blank, Raymond. Playing the Game. (Ace Business Library Ser.). 224p. 1982. pap. 2.95 (ISBN 0-441-67075-X). Ace Bks.

Blank, Richard. A Christian Passover Celebration. 1981. 2.50 (ISBN 0-89536-477-8). CSS of Ohio.

Blank, Robert H. The Political Implications of Human Genetic Technology. (Special Studies in Science, Technology, & Public Policy). 209p. (Orig.). 1981. lib. bdg. 28.50x (ISBN 0-89158-975-9); pap. text ed. 12.95x (ISBN 0-86531-193-5). Westview.

--Redefining Human Life: Reproductive Technologies & Social Policy. (Special Studies in Science, Technology, & Public Policy-Society). 280p. 1983. lib. bdg. 27.00x (ISBN 0-86531-665-1). Westview.

--Regional Diversity of Political Values: Idaho Political Culture. LC 78-62742. 1978. pap. text ed. 10.50 (ISBN 0-8191-0590-2). U Pr of Amer.

--Torts for Wrongful Life: Individual & Eugenic Implications. 23p. 1982. pap. text ed. 2.00x (ISBN 0-88738-638-5). Transaction Bks.

Blank, Robert H., jt. ed. see Darrough, Masako N.

Blank, S. H. Prophetic Thought: Essays & Addresses. (Jewish Perspectives Ser: Vol. 2). 15.00x (ISBN 0-87820-501-2, HUC Pr). Ktav.

Blank, Sheldon. Jeremiah, Man & Prophet. 1961. 12.50x (ISBN 0-87820-100-9, Pub. by Hebrew Union). Ktav.

--Understanding the Prophets. 144p. 1983. pap. text ed. 4.00 (ISBN 0-8074-0250-8, 382755). UAHC.

Blank, Stephen, jt. auth. see Black, Robert.

Blank, Stephen, jt. auth. see LaPalombara, Joseph.

Blank, Stephen, et al. Assessing the Political Environment: An Emerging Function in International Companies. (Report Ser.: No. 794). (Illus.). viii, 72p. (Orig.). 1980. pap. 75.00 (ISBN 0-8237-0230-8); pap. 15.00 member. Conference Bd.

Blank, Steven. Practical Business Research Methods. (Illus.). 1984. text ed. 27.50 (ISBN 0-87055-455-7). AVI.

Blank, Stuart J., jt. auth. see Hobbs, Donald A.

Blank, Thomas O. A Social Psychology of Developing Adults. LC 81-19835. (Personality Processes Ser.). 325p. 1982. 40.00 (ISBN 0-471-08787-4, Pub. by Wiley-Interscience). Wiley.

Blank, William E. Handbook for Developing Competency-Based Training Programs. (Illus.). 352p. 1982. 24.95 (ISBN 0-13-377416-3). P-H.

Blanke, Fritz. Brothers in Christ. LC 61-6723. 78p. (Orig.). 1961. pap. 2.95 (ISBN 0-8361-1326-8). Herald Pr.

Blanke, Richard. Prussian Poland in the German Empire, 1871-1900. (East European Monograph: No. 86). 268p. 1981. 25.00x (ISBN 0-914710-80-X). East Eur Quarterly.

Blanken. Force of Order & Methods. (Studies in Social Life: Vol. 19). 1976. pap. 24.00 (ISBN 90-247-1849-X, Pub. by Martinus Nijhoff Netherlands). Kluwer Academic.

Blanken, Ann J. Hospital Discharges & Length of Stay: Short-Stay Hospitals, U. S., 1972. LC 75-619408. (Ser. 10: No. 107). 52p. 1976. pap. text ed. 1.25 (ISBN 0-8406-0063-1). Natl Ctr Health Stats.

Blanken, Gary E. Surgical Operations in Short-Stay Hospitals, U. S. 1971. LC 74-6259. (Data from the Hospital Discharge Survey Ser. 13: No. 18). 62p. 1974. pap. text ed. 1.50 (ISBN 0-8406-0017-8). Natl Ctr Health Stats.

Blanken, M. C. Force of Order & Methods... An American View into the Dutch Directed Society. (Studies in Social Life: Vol. 19). 1976. pap. 32.50 (ISBN 9-0247-1849-X). Heinman.

Blankenagel, John C., ed. see Pascal, Blaise.

Blankenbaker, E. Keith. Modern Plumbing. rev. ed. LC 81-4114. (Illus.). 300p. 1981. text ed. 16.00 (ISBN 0-87006-325-1). Goodheart.

Blankenburg, Erhard, ed. Innovations in the Legal Services. LC 79-24923. (Research on Service Delivery, Vol. 1). 336p. 1980. text ed. 35.00 (ISBN 0-89946-010-0). Oelgeschlager.

Blankenburg, Peter von. Agricultural Extension Systems in Some African & Asian Countries. (Economic & Social Development Papers: No. 46). 75p. 1985. pap. 7.50 (ISBN 92-5-101461-2, F2683 5071, FAO). Unipub.

Blankenhorn, Heber. The Strike for Union. LC 75-89718. (American Labor, from Conspiracy to Collective Bargaining Ser., No. 1). 259p. 1969. Repr. of 1924 ed. 19.00 (ISBN 0-405-02104-6). Ayer Co Pubs.

Blankenship, A., jt. auth. see Breen, G.

Blankenship, Albert B. Consumer & Opinion Research. Assael, Henry, ed. LC 78-234. (Century of Marketing Ser.). (Illus.). 1978. Repr. of 1943 ed. lib. bdg. 22.00x (ISBN 0-405-11177-0). Ayer Co Pubs.

Blankenship, Albert B., jt. auth. see Heidingsfield, Myron S.

Blankenship, Albert S. The Accessibility of Rural Schoolhouses in Texas. LC 73-176570. (Columbia University. Teachers College. Contributions to Education: No. 229). Repr. of 1926 ed. 22.50 (ISBN 0-404-55229-3). AMS Pr.

Blankenship, Colleen & Lilly, M. Stephen. Mainstreaming Students with Learning & Behavior Problems. 1981. text ed. 27.95 (ISBN 0-03-046051-4, HoltC). HR&W.

Blankenship, G., et al, eds. Current Concepts in Diagnosis & Treatment of Vitreoretinal Diseases. (Developments in Ophthalmology: Vol. 2). (Illus.). xxviii, 408p. 1981. 125.75 (ISBN 3-8055-1672-X). S Karger.

Blankenship, George E. Early History of Thurston County. (Shorey Historical Ser.). 400p. Repr. of 1914 ed. 29.95 (ISBN 0-8466-9003-9, S284). Shorey.

Blankenship, Jane & Stelzner, Hermann G., eds. Rhetoric & Communication: Studies in the University of Illinois Tradition. LC 75-37621. 282p. 1976. 16.50x (ISBN 0-252-00566-X). U of Ill Pr.

Blankenship, Jayne. In the Center of the Night: Journey Through a Bereavement. LC 84-8356. 320p. 1985. 17.95 (ISBN 0-399-12995-2, Putnam). Putnam Pub Group.

Blankenship, John. The Apple House. LC 83-16052. (Illus.). 160p. 1984. text ed. 22.95 (ISBN 0-13-038729-0); pap. text ed. 14.95 (ISBN 0-13-038711-8). P-H.

--Apple II-IIe Robotic Arm Projects. (Illus.). 192p. 1985. text ed. 21.95 (ISBN 0-13-038324-4); pap. text ed. 16.95 (ISBN 0-13-038316-3). P-H.

--The Gradebook System: Apple II-IIe. (Illus.). 80p. 1984. pap. 14.95 (ISBN 0-13-362526-5); incl. disk 29.95 (ISBN 0-13-362542-7); disk 15.95 (ISBN 0-13-362534-6). P-H.

Blankenship, Judy, illus. Teddy Beddy Bear's Bedtime Songs & Poems. LC 84-4837. (Picturebacks Ser.). (Illus.). 32p. (ps). 1984. pap. 1.95 saddle-stitched (ISBN 0-394-86826-9, Pub. by BYR). Random.

Blankenship, Martha L. & Moer Chen, Barbara D. Home Economics Education. LC 78-69595. (Illus.). 1979. text ed. 27.50 (ISBN 0-395-26700-5); instr's. manual 1.95 (ISBN 0-395-26699-8); self-instruction module 15.95 (ISBN 0-395-26698-X). HM.

Blankenship, Ralph L. The Emerging Organization of a Community Mental Health Center. LC 75-38310. 1976. softbound 12.95 (ISBN 0-88247-397-2). R & E Pubs.

Blankenship, Ralph L., ed. Colleagues in Organization: The Social Construction of Professional Work. LC 80-18149. 442p. 1980. Repr. of 1977 ed. lib. bdg. 25.50 (ISBN 0-89874-233-1). Krieger.

Blankenship, Russell. American Literature As an Expression of the National Mind. LC 72-85845. xvii, 731p. 1973. Repr. of 1949 ed. lib. bdg. 29.50 (ISBN 0-8154-0432-8). Cooper Sq.

Blankenship, William D. Brotherly Love. LC 80-70212. 1981. 12.95 (ISBN 0-87795-301-5). Arbor Hse.

--Brotherly Love. 1983. pap. 3.50 (ISBN 0-671-44765-3). PB.

--The Helix File. 240p. 1974. pap. 1.50 (ISBN 0-532-15138-0). Woodhill.

--The Programmed Man. 272p. 1975. pap. 1.50 (ISBN 0-532-15156-9). Woodhill.

Blankenstein, M. E. Rotary in Baton Rouge 1918-1970. 10.00x (ISBN 0-685-00412-0). Claitors.

Blankenstein, M. Van & Welbergen, U. R. The Development of the Infant: The First Year of Life in Photographs. (Illus.). 1975. pap. 15.00 (ISBN 0-433-03235-9). Heinman.

Blanker, Frederika, ed. & tr. from Scandinavian. The History of the Scandinavian Literatures. LC 75-2692. 407p. 1975. Repr. of 1938 ed. lib. bdg. 22.50x (ISBN 0-8371-8036-8, BLHS). Greenwood.

Blankert, Albert, et al. Gods, Saints & Heroes: Dutch Painting in the Age of Rembrandt. LC 80-20371. (Illus.). pap. 14.95 (ISBN 0-89468-039-0). Natl Gallery Art.

Blanking-Clark, T. & Cross, T. B. The Soft Side of Software: A Management Approach to Producing Documentation. 1985. write for info. (ISBN 0-471-81527-6). Wiley.

Blanks, Sue & Woodis, Carole. The Herpes Manual: The Book for Everyone Concerned about Herpes. 120p. 49.00x (ISBN 0-907070-17-5, Pub. by Settle & Bendall UK); pap. 29.00x (ISBN 0-907070-18-3). State Mutual Bk.

Blankstein, Kirk R., et al, eds. Assessment & Modification of Emotional Behavior. (Advances in the Study of Communication & Affect Ser.: Vol. 6). (Illus.). 235p. 1980. 27.50x (ISBN 0-306-40502-4, Plenum Pr). Plenum Pub.

Blanksten, George I. Peron's Argentina. (Midway Reprint Ser.). pap. 123.50 (ISBN 0-317-26646-2, 2024083). Bks Demand UMI.

Blankstenin, Kirk R., et al, eds. Self-Control & Self-Modification of Emotional Behavior. (Advances in the Study of Communication & Affect Ser.: Vol. 7). 216p. 1982. text ed. 29.50 (ISBN 0-306-40945-3, Plenum Pr). Plenum Pub.

Blanning, T. C. The French Revolution in Germany: Occupation & Resistance in the Rhineland 1792-1802. (Illus.). 1983. 45.00x (ISBN 0-19-822564-4). Oxford U Pr.

Blanpain, Jan, et al. National Health Insurance & Health Resources: The European Experience. LC 77-25818. 1978. 20.00x (ISBN 0-674-26955-1). Harvard U Pr.

Blanpain, R. The Badger Case & the OECD Guidelines for Multinational Enterprises. 1977. lib. bdg. 27.50 (ISBN 90-312-0056-5, Pub. by Kluwer Law Netherlands). Kluwer Academic.

Blanpain, R. & Aaron, Benjamin. Comparative Labour Law & Industrial Relations. 2nd ed. LC 85-10000. Date not set. price not set (ISBN 9-06-544228-6, Pub. by Kluwer Law Netherlands). Kluwer Academic.

Blanpain, R., jt. auth. see Hanami, Tadashi.

Blanpain, R., ed. Bulletin of Comparative Labour Relations, No. 10. 1979. pap. 31.50 (ISBN 90-312-0091-3, Pub. by Kluwer Law Netherlands). Kluwer Academic.

--Bulletin of Comparative Labour Relations: Workers Participation in the European Community, No. 8. 1978. pap. 24.00 (ISBN 90-312-0044-1, Pub. by Kluwer Law Netherlands). Kluwer Academic.

--Bulletin of Comparative Labour Relations, 1980: Job Security & Industrial Relations, No. 11. 249p. 1982. cancelled 26.00 (ISBN 90-312-0147-2, Pub. by Kluwer Law Netherlands). Kluwer Academic.

--Comparative Labour Law & Industrial Relations. 412p. 1982. 26.00 (ISBN 90-31-20179-0). Kluwer Academic.

--Employee Participation at the Level of the Enterprise: Labour Relations at the European Level & in Different Countries. (Bulletin of Comparative Labour Relations Ser.: No. 4). 1973. 12.00 (ISBN 90-31-20020-4). Kluwer Academic.

--Guaranteed Income Funds: Labour Relations at the European Level. (Bulletin of Comparative Labour Relations Ser.: No. 3). 1972. 12.00 (ISBN 90-31-20019-0). Kluwer Academic.

--International Bibliography of Publications in English & French on Labour Law & Labour Relations in Those Countries Where English & French Are Not Official Languages. (Bulletin of Comparative Labour Relations Ser.: No. 6). 1976. 15.00 (ISBN 90-31-20023-9). Kluwer Academic.

--The International Encyclopaedia for Labour Law & Industrial Relations, 9 Vols. 1982. 181.00 (ISBN 0-686-40990-6, Pub. by Kluwer Law, Netherlands). Kluwer Academic.

--Labour Relations in Different Countries: Labour Relations at the European Level; Labour Relations in the Multinational Enterprise. (Bulletin of Comparative Labour Relations Ser.: No. 7). 1976. 22.00 (ISBN 90-31-20024-7). Kluwer Academic.

--Women & Labour. (Bulletin of Comparative Labour Relations Ser.: No. 9). 1978. 26.00 (ISBN 90-31-20077-8). Kluwer Academic.

--Workers' Participation in the European Community. 1984. pap. text ed. 30.00 (ISBN 90-6544-187-5, Pub. by Kluwer Law Netherlands). Kluwer Academic.

Blanpain, Roger. The O E C D Guidelines for Multinational Enterprises & Labour Relations: 1976-1979 Experience & Review. 366p. 1980. lib. bdg. 47.00 (ISBN 90-312-0108-1, Pub. by Kluwer Law Netherlands). Kluwer Academic.

--Public Employee Unionism in Belgium. LC 76-634393. (Comparative Studies in Public Employment Labor Relations Ser.). 1971. 6.50x (ISBN 0-87736-003-0); pap. 2.50x (ISBN 0-87736-004-9). U of Mich Inst Labor.

--Technological Change & Industrial Relations: An International Symposium. Date not set. pap. text ed. 32.00 (ISBN 90-312-0205-3, Pub. by Kluwer Law Netherlands). Kluwer Academic.

Blanpain, Roger, ed. Comparative Labour Law & Industrial Relations. 416p. 1983. text ed. 32.50 (ISBN 0-87179-396-2). BNA.

Blanpain, W. A. R. & Veldkamp, G. M. J. Temporary Work in Modern Society: A Comparative Study II. (Cahier Ser.: No. 20). 51.00 (ISBN 90-312-0155-3, Pub. by Kluwer Law, Netherlands). Kluwer Academic.

Blanpied, John W. Time & the Artist in Shakespeare's English Histories. LC 82-40387. 280p. 1983. 29.50 (ISBN 0-87413-230-4). U Delaware Pr.

Blanpied, W., jt. ed. see Holton, G.

Blanquez. Diccionario Latino-Espanol, Espanol-Latino, 3 vols. 2703p. (Lat. & Span.). Set. leatherette 75.00 (ISBN 84-303-0151-8, S-50419). French & Eur.

Blanqui, Jerome A. & De Girardin, Emile. De la liberte du Commerce et la Protection de l'Industrie. LC 76-146244. (Research & Source Works Ser: No. 857). 1971. Repr. of 1847 ed. lib. bdg. 18.50 (ISBN 0-8337-0310-2). B Franklin.

Blanqui, Jerome-Adolphe. History of Political Economy in Europe. 59.95 (ISBN 0-8490-0344-X). Gordon Pr.

--History of Political Economy in Europe. Leonard, Emily J., tr. LC 67-29494. Repr. of 1880 ed. 45.00x (ISBN 0-678-00407-2). Kelley.

Blansett, Mary L. Put a Frog in Your Pocket. (Illus.). 112p. (gr. 3-6). 1985. guide 7.95 (ISBN 0-86530-085-2). Incentive Pubns.

Blanshard, Audrey. The Fearns of Audley Street. 224p. 1980. pap. 1.75 (ISBN 0-449-50035-7, Coventry). Fawcett.

--The Lydeard Beauty. 1980. pap. 1.75 (ISBN 0-449-50016-0, Coventry). Fawcett.

Blanshard, Brand. Four Reasonable Men: Aurelius, Mill, Renan, Sidgwick. (Illus.). 347p. 1984. 25.95 (ISBN 0-8195-5100-7); pap. 9.95 (ISBN 0-8195-6102-9). Wesleyan U Pr.

--Nature of Thought, 2 Vols. (Muirhead Library of Philosophy). 1964. Set. text ed. 42.50x (ISBN 0-391-00923-0); Vol. 1. text ed. (ISBN 0-685-92789-X); Vol. 2. text ed. (ISBN 0-685-92790-3). Humanities.

--On Philosophical Style. LC 69-13830. Repr. of 1954 ed. lib. bdg. 15.00x (ISBN 0-8371-1975-8, BLPS). Greenwood.

--Reason & Analysis. 2nd ed. LC 62-9576. (Paul Carus Lectures Ser.). 505p. 1962. 29.95x (ISBN 0-87548-104-3). Open Court.

--Reason & Belief. LC 74-13253. 600p. 1975. Yale U Pr.

--The Uses of a Liberal Education, & Other Talks to Students. 436p. 1974. 19.95 (ISBN 0-87548-122-1). Open Court.

Blanshard, Brand, ed. Education in the Age of Science. facs. ed. LC 70-142608. (Essay Index Reprint Ser). 1959. 20.00 (ISBN 0-8369-2144-5). Ayer Co Pubs.

Blanshard, Frances. Frank Aydelotte of Swarthmore. LC 70-108646. (Illus.). 1970. 22.50x (ISBN 0-8195-4023-4). Wesleyan U Pr.

--Portraits of Wordsworth. (Illus.). 208p. 1981. Repr. of 1959 ed. lib. bdg. 30.00 (ISBN 0-89987-077-5). Darby Bks.

--Portraits of Wordsworth. 208p. 1983. Repr. of 1959 ed. lib. bdg. 45.00 (ISBN 0-8495-0616-6). Arden Lib.

--Portraits of Wordsworth. 208p. 1984. Repr. of 1959 ed. lib. bdg. 45.00 (ISBN 0-89760-196-3). Telegraph BKS.

Blanshard, Frances M. Retreat from Likeness in the Theory of Painting. facsimile 2nd ed. LC 72-37913. (Select Bibliographies Reprint Ser). Repr. of 1945 ed. 20.00 (ISBN 0-8369-6733-X). Ayer Co Pubs.

Blanshard, J. M. & Mitchell, J. R. Polysaccharides in Food. new ed. LC 79-40370. (Studies in the Agricultural & Food Sciences). (Illus.). 1979. text ed. 99.95 (ISBN 0-408-10618-2). Butterworth.

Blanshard, Paul. American Freedom & Catholic Power. LC 84-19141. xii, 402p. 1984. Repr. of 1958 ed. lib. bdg. 47.50x (ISBN 0-313-24620-3, BLAF). Greenwood.

--Communism, Democracy, & Catholic Power. LC 75-156175. 340p. 1972. Repr. of 1952 ed. lib. bdg. 35.00x (ISBN 0-8371-6118-5, BLCD). Greenwood.

--The Irish & Catholic Power: An American Interpretation. LC 70-112321. 375p. 1972. Repr. of 1953 ed. lib. bdg. 18.50x (ISBN 0-8371-4708-5, BLIC). Greenwood.

--Some of My Best Friends Are Christians. LC 74-744. 200p. 1974. 14.95 (ISBN 0-87548-149-3). Open Court.

Blanshard, Paul, ed. Classics of Free Thought. LC 77-73846. (Skeptic's Bookshelf Ser.). 190p. 1977. 14.95 (ISBN 0-87975-071-5). Prometheus Bks.

Blanshard, Paul, Jr. The KRC Fund Raiser's Manual. pap. cancelled (ISBN 0-686-24202-5). Public Serv Materials.

Blanshei, J., et al, eds. see Turkevich, John.

Blansit, Frankie C. Fitness Is Fun. (Illus.). 67p. (Orig.). 1980. pap. text ed. 2.95x (ISBN 0-89641-035-8). American Pr.

Blansitt, Edward L., Jr., ed. see Linguistic Association of Canada & the U.S.

Blanton, Alma E. God & Mrs. Adam. (Illus.). 152p. (Orig.). 1978. lib. bdg. 4.95 (ISBN 0-938134-00-0, G-1); pap. 4.95 (ISBN 0-686-73968-X). Loving Pubs.

--Our Gospel's Women. (Illus.). 114p. (Orig.). 1979. pap. 3.00 (ISBN 0-938134-01-9). Loving Pubs.

Blanton, Cherie. A Little Fur in the Meringue Never Really Hurts the Filling. 6.00 (ISBN 0-918544-90-4). Wimmer Bks.

Blanton, J. Neal. Game of the Century. (Illus.). 1970. 12.50 (ISBN 0-8363-0034-3). Jenkins.

Blanton, Linda L. Elementary Composition Practice, Book 2. LC 78-5736. 1979. pap. text ed. 7.95 (ISBN 0-88377-128-4). Newbury Hse.

--Elementary Composition Practice Book 1. 1978. pap. text ed. 7.95 (ISBN 0-88377-112-8). Newbury Hse.

--Intermediate Composition Practice, Bk I. (Illus., Orig.). (gr. 7-12). 1981. pap. text ed. 7.95 (ISBN 0-88377-194-2). Newbury Hse.

Blanton, Mary T. God Made It All! LC 83-7345. (Illus.). 32p. (ps-k). 1983. PLB 4.95 (ISBN 0-89693-209-5). Dandelion Hse.

--Knock on a Door. 32p. 1984. 4.95. Victor Bks.

--Knock on a Door. LC 84-7027. (Illus.). 32p. (ps-k). 1984. lib. bdg. 4.95. Dandelion Hse.

Blanton, Richard, jt. ed. see Flannery, Kent V.

Blanton, Richard E., ed. Monte Alban: Settlement Patterns at the Ancient Zapotec Capital. (Studies in Archaeology). 1978. 50.00 (ISBN 0-12-104250-2). Acad Pr.

Blanton, Richard E., et al. Ancient Mesoamerica: A Comparison of Change in Three Regions. LC 81-3834. (New Studies in Archaeology Ser.). (Illus.). 304p. 1982. 32.50 (ISBN 0-521-22858-1); pap. 12.95 (ISBN 0-521-29682-X). Cambridge U Pr.

Blanton, Smiley & Gordon, Arthur. Now or Never: The Promise of the Middle Years. 192p. 1976. pap. 1.95 (ISBN 0-346-12217-1). Cornerstone.

Blanton, Smiley, jt. auth. see Peale, Norman V.

Blanton, William, et al, eds. Reading Tests for the Secondary Grades. LC 70-190453. (Reading Aids Ser). 1972. 4.00 (ISBN 0-87207-211-8). Intl Reading.

Blanton, William E., et al, eds. Measuring Reading Performance. 1st ed. LC 74-11048. 70p. 1974. pap. 4.50 (ISBN 0-87207-718-7). Intl Reading.

Blanton, Wyndham. Medicine in Virginia in the Seventeenth Century. LC 77-180556. (Medicine & Society in America Ser). (Illus.). 430p. 1972. Repr. of 1930 ed. 25.50 (ISBN 0-405-03936-0). Ayer Co Pubs.

Blanton, Wyndham B. Medicine in Virginia in the Eighteenth Century. LC 80-12669. Repr. of 1931 ed. 64.50 (ISBN 0-404-13238-3). AMS Pr.

Blanton Freedberg, Catherine. The Spanish Pavilion at the Paris World's Fair of 1937, 2 vols. Freedberg, S. J., ed. (Outstanding Dissertations in Fine Arts Ser.). (Illus.). 1200p. 1985. Repr. of 1981 ed. 125.00 (ISBN 0-8240-6865-3). Garland Pub.

Blantz, Thomas E. A Priest in Public Service: Francis J. Haas & the New Deal. LC 81-40452. 384p. 1982. 25.00 (ISBN 0-268-01547-3). U of Notre Dame Pr.

Blanzaco, Andre. VD: Facts You Should Know. LC 78-120168. (Illus.). (gr. 7-12). 1970. 11.25 (ISBN 0-688-41487-7); PLB 11.88 (ISBN 0-688-51487-1). Lothrop.

Blaquier, Jorge A., jt. auth. see DeNicola, Alejandro F.

Blaquiere, A., et al. Quantitative & Qualitative Games. (Mathematics in Science & Engineering Ser.: Vol. 58). 1969. 49.50 (ISBN 0-12-104360-6). Acad Pr.

Blaquiere, A., jt. auth. see Avez, A.

Blaquiere, A., et al, eds. Dynamical Systems & Microphysics. (CISM - International Centre for Mechanical Sciences Courses & Lectures: Vol. 261). (Illus.). ix, 412p. 1980. pap. 48.00 (ISBN 0-387-81533-3). Springer-Verlag.

Blaquiere, Austin. Nonlinear System Analysis. (Electrical Science Ser.). 1966. 75.00 (ISBN 0-12-104350-9). Acad Pr.

Blaquiere, Austin, ed. Topics in Differential Games. LC 73-75528. 460p. 1973. 42.75 (ISBN 0-444-10467-4, North-Holland). Elsevier.

Blaquiere, Edward, ed. Narrative of a Second Visit to Greece, Including Facts Connected with the Last Days of Lord Byron. LC 76-27677. 1976. Repr. of 1825 ed. lib. bdg. 50.00 (ISBN 0-8414-3336-4). Folcroft.

Blaquiere, Goergette. The Grace to Be a Woman. Wild, Robert, tr. from Fr. LC 83-15858. 127p. 1983. pap. 6.95 (ISBN 0-8189-0449-6). Alba.

Blaquriere, Austin & Leitmann, George, eds. Dynamical Systems & Microphysics. 1984. 29.50 (ISBN 0-12-104365-7). Acad Pr.

Blasberg, Robert W. & Bohdan, Carol L. Fulper Art Pottery: An Aesthetic Appreciation 1909-1929. (Illus.). 88p. 1984. pap. 15.00 (ISBN 0-942410-00-9). Jordan-Volpe Gall.

Blasch, Bruce B., jt. ed. see Welsh, Richard L.

Blaschke, W. Analytische Geometrie. 2nd ed. (Mathematics Reihe Ser.: No. 16). 190p. (Ger.). 1954. 23.95x (ISBN 0-8176-0031-0). Birkhauser.

--Einfuehrung in die Goemetrie der Waben. (Elemente der Mathematik Vom Hoeheren Standpunkt Aus: Vol. 4). 108p. (Ger.). 1955. pap. 16.95x (ISBN 0-8176-0033-7). Birkhauser.

--Projektive Geometrie. 3rd ed. (Mathematische Reihe Ser.: No. 17). (Illus.). 197p. 1954. 23.95x (ISBN 0-8176-0032-9). Birkhauser.

Blaschke, W. S. & McGill, J. The Control of Industrial Processes by Digital Techniques: The Organization, Design & Construction of Digital Control Systems. 186p. 1976. 53.25 (ISBN 0-444-41493-2). Elsevier.

Blascoer, Frances. Colored School Children in New York. Johnson, Eleanor H., ed. LC 73-100279. Repr. of 1915 ed. 15.00x (ISBN 0-8371-2935-4, BLC&, Pub. by Negro U Pr). Greenwood.

Blasco Ibanez, Vicente. Blood & Sand. Partridge, Frances, tr. LC 62-12957. pap. 4.95 (ISBN 0-8044-6046-9). Ungar.

Blasco-Ibanez, Vicente. Reeds & Mud. Beberfall, Lester, tr. (Orig.). 1966. pap. 4.00 (ISBN 0-8283-1470-5). Branden Pub Co.

Blasco-Ibanez, Vincente. The Four Horsemen of the Apocalypse. 1982. Repr. lib. bdg. 24.95x (ISBN 0-89966-384-2). Buccaneer Bks.

Blasco-Ibanez, Vincenti. Last Lion & Other Stories. pap. 2.50 (ISBN 0-8283-1444-6, IPL). Branden Pub Co.

Blase, Betty E. de see De Blase, Betty E.

Blase, M., et al. Readings in International & Agricultural Economic Development. 1970. pap. text ed. 7.25x (ISBN 0-8422-0107-6). Irvington.

Blase, Melvin G. Institution Building: A Source Book. 480p. 1985. text ed. 40.00x (ISBN 0-8262-0479-1). U of Mo Pr.

Blasecki. Mechanisms of Immunity to Virus-Induced Tumors. (Immunology Ser.: Vol. 12). 376p. 1981. 57.50 (ISBN 0-8247-1162-9). Dekker.

Blaser, A., ed. see IBM Germany's Informatik Symposium, 6th, Bad Homburg, Sept. 1976.

Blaser, Cathy B. & Rodger, David, eds. The Stage Managers Directory, 1985-86. 180p. 1985. pap. 10.00 (ISBN 0-911747-03-6). Broadway Pr.

Blaser, R. E. Agronomy & Health. 1970. pap. free (ISBN 0-89118-026-5). Am Soc Agron.

Blaser, Robin, ed. see Spicer, Jack.

Blaser, W. Elemental Building Forms. 1982. 43.00 (ISBN 0-9908000-1-6, Pub. by Beton Bks W Germany). Heyden.

Blaser, Werner. Architecture Nineteen Seventy to Nineteen Eighty in Switzerland. 2nd ed. (Illus.). 168p. (Eng. Ger. & Fr.). 1982. 15.95 (ISBN 3-7643-1311-0). Birkhauser.

--Filigree Architecture: Metal & Glass Construction. (Illus.). 216p. (Eng. Fr. & Ger.). 1980. pap. 19.00 (ISBN 0-89192-298-9, Pub. by Wepf & Co). Interbk Inc.

--Folding Chairs, Klappstuehle. 110p. 1982. 18.95 (ISBN 0-8176-1357-9). Birkhauser.

--Mies Van Der Rohe: Continuing the Chicago School of Architecture. (Illus.). 294p. 1981. 31.95 (ISBN 3-7643-1247-5). Birkhauser.

--Mies van der Rohe: Principles & School. 2nd ed. 294p. 1981. 31.95x (ISBN 0-8176-1247-5). Birkhauser.

--Wooden Bridges in Switzerland (Ponts de Bois en Suisse; Schweizer Holzbrucken) 184p. 1982. 52.95 (ISBN 0-8176-1334-X). Birkhauser.

Blaser, Werner, ed. Architecture & Nature. 160p. (Eng., Fr. & Ger.). 1983. text ed. 29.95 (ISBN 3-7643-1524-5). Birkhauser.

--Drawings of Great Buildings. 176p. (Eng., Fr. & Ger.). 1983. 29.95 (ISBN 3-7643-1522-9). Birkhauser.

Blasewitz, A. G. & Davis, John M., eds. Treatment & Handling of Radioactive Wastes. LC 82-22695. 658p. 1983. 65.00 (ISBN 0-935470-14-X). Battelle.

Blasewitz, Robert M. & Stern, Frank. Microcomputer Systems: Hardware-Software Design. 560p. 29.95 (5123). Hayden.

Blashfield, Edwin H. Italian Cities, 2 vols. 1900. 52.00 set (ISBN 0-932062-16-4). Sharon Hill.

Blashfield, Edwin H. & Wilbour, Evangeline. Italian Cities, 2 vols. 1976. lib. bdg. 250.00 (ISBN 0-8490-2085-9). Gordon Pr.

--Italian Cities, 2 vols. Repr. of 1900 ed. Set. 97.50 (ISBN 0-8482-7389-3). Norwood Edns.

Blashfield, Evangeline. Portraits & Backgrounds. facs. ed. LC 73-134054. (Essay Index Reprint Ser.). 1917. 27.50 (ISBN 0-8369-2103-8). Ayer Co Pubs.

Blashfield, Jean. Backward Magic. LC 84-91270. (Dungeons & Dragons Cartoon Show Books Ser.). (Illus.). 80p. (gr. 2-5). 1985. pap. 2.25 (ISBN 0-394-72962-5). Random.

--Ghost Tower. LC 84-91359. (Super Endless Quest Books Ser.). (Illus.). 192p. (gr. 5-7). 1985. pap. 2.50 (ISBN 0-394-73978-7). Random.

--Hellraisers, Heroines, & Holy Women. 256p. 1981. 14.95 (ISBN 0-312-36736-8); pap. 7.95 (ISBN 0-312-36737-6). St Martin.

--Star Rangers & the Spy. LC 83-91422. (Fantasy Forest Adventures Ser.). 80p. (gr. 2-5). 1984. pap. 1.95 (ISBN 0-394-72457-7). Random.

Blashfield, Roger K. The Classification of Psychopathology: Neokraepelinian & Quantitative Approaches. 314p. 1984. 35.00x (ISBN 0-306-41405-8, Plenum Pr). Plenum Pub.

Blashford-Snell, John. Mysteries: Encounters with the Unexplained. 256p. 1984. 16.95 (ISBN 0-370-30479-9, Pub. by the Bodley Head). Merrimack Pub Cir.

Blashko, H., et al. Reviews of Physiology, Biochemistry & Pharmacology, Vol. 98. (Illus.). 260p. 1983. 48.50 (ISBN 0-387-12817-4). Springer-Verlag.

Blasi, Anthony J., et al. The Sociology of Music. LC 83-40597. 224p. 1984. text ed. 15.95 (ISBN 0-268-01710-7, 85-17104). U of Notre Dame Pr.

Blasi, J. R. The Communal Future. 1985. 54.50 (ISBN 0-317-19962-5). Porter.

Blasi, Joseph. Communal Experience of the Kibbutz. 275p. 1985. 24.95 (ISBN 0-88738-056-5); pap. 14.95 (ISBN 0-88738-611-3). Transaction Bks.

Blasi, Joseph, ed. Employee Ownership & Employee Attitudes: Two Case Studies, Vol. 1. (Worker Ownership & Participation Book). 222p. 1984. lib. bdg. 22.50 (ISBN 0-8482-4775-2). Norwood Edns.

Blasi, Joseph, ed. see Rosner, Menachem.

Blasi, Joseph R. The Communal Future: The Kibbutz & the Utopian Dilemma. LC 78-7876. 1978. Repr. lib. bdg. 27.50 (ISBN 0-8482-3425-1). Norwood Edns.

--Work, Ownership, & Participation. 250p. 1987. 24.95 (ISBN 0-88730-065-0). Ballinger Pub.

Blasi, Vincent, ed. The Burger Court: The Counter-Revolution that Wasn't. LC 83-5828. 320p. 1983. 27.50x (ISBN 0-300-02941-1). Yale U Pr.

Blasien, Otto Von St. see Otto, Von St. Blasien.

Blasier, Cole. The Giant's Rival: The USSR & Latin America. LC 83-47826. (Pitt Latin American Ser.). (Illus.). 232p. 1983. 14.95x (ISBN 0-8229-3486-8); pap. text ed. 7.95 (ISBN 0-8229-5355-2). U of Pittsburgh Pr.

--The Hovering Giant: U. S. Responses to Revolutionary Change in Latin America. LC 75-9130. (Pitt Latin American Ser.). (Illus.). 1976. pap. 9.95x (ISBN 0-8229-5264-5). U of Pittsburgh Pr.

Blasier, Cole, ed. Constructive Change in Latin America. LC 68-12724. (Pitt Latin American Ser.). 1968. 18.95x (ISBN 0-8229-3145-1). U of Pittsburgh Pr.

Blasier, Cole & Mesa-Lago, Carmelo, eds. Cuba in the World. LC 78-53598. (Pitt Latin American Ser.). (Illus.). 1979. pap. 9.95x (ISBN 0-8229-5298-X). U of Pittsburgh Pr.

Blasing, Mutlu K. The Art of Life: Studies in American Autobiographical Literature. LC 76-20760. (Illus.). 221p. 1977. text ed. 15.00x (ISBN 0-292-70315-5). U of Tex Pr.

Blasing, Randy. Light Years. LC 77-76621. 1977. pap. 3.95 (ISBN 0-89255-022-8). Persea Bks.

--The Particles. LC 83-10052. 57p. (Orig.). 1983. pap. 5.00 (ISBN 0-914278-40-1). Copper Beech.

--To Continue. 75p. (Orig.). 1983. cancelled 10.95 (ISBN 0-89255-070-8); pap. 5.95 (ISBN 0-89255-071-6). Persea Bks.

Blasing, Randy, tr. see Hikmet, Nazim.

Blasingame, Ike. Dakota Cowboy: My Life in the Old Days. LC 58-11667. (Illus.). 317p. 1964. 23.50x (ISBN 0-8032-0906-1); pap. 6.50 (ISBN 0-8032-5015-0, BB 191, Bison). U of Nebr Pr.

Blasingame, Margaret C. A Selected Bibliography on Employee Attitude Surveys. (Special Report Ser.: No. 2). 42p. 1983. pap. 12.00 (ISBN 0-912879-51-3). Ctr Creat Leader.

Blasingame, Margaret C., et al. Performance Appraisal Bibliography of Recent Publications, 1981. (Special Report Ser.: No. 1). 72p. 1981. pap. 12.00 (ISBN 0-912879-50-5). Ctr Creat Leader.

Blasinsky, Margaret & Russell, George K. Urine Testing for Marijuana Use: Implications for a Variety of Setting. 49p. (Orig.). 1981. pap. 2.50 (ISBN 0-942348-03-6). Am Council Drug Ed.

Blasio, Jose L. Maximilian, Emperor of Mexico. 1934. 49.50x (ISBN 0-686-83620-0). Elliots Bks.

Blasis, Carlo. The Code of Terpsichore. LC 75-9166. (Illus.). 548p. 1975. pap. 10.50 (ISBN 0-87127-055-2). Dance Horiz.

--Elementary Treatise upon the Theory & Practice of the Art of Dancing. 3rd ed. Evans, Mary S., tr. LC 65-26020. Orig. Title: Traite Elementaire Theorique et Pretique De l'Art De La Danse. 1968. pap. 3.95 (ISBN 0-486-21592-X). Dover.

Blasis, Celese De see De Blasis, Celese.

Blasis, Celeste De. Suffer a Sea Change. 1979. pap. 1.95 (ISBN 0-449-23954-3, Crest). Fawcett.

Blasis, Celeste De see De Blasis, Celeste.

Blasis, Celeste de see De Blasis, Celeste.

Blaskovic, D., et al. Studies on Tick-Borne Encephalitis. (Bulletin of WHO: Suppl. No. 1 to Vol. 36). 94p. 1967. pap. 3.60 (ISBN 92-4-068361-5). World Health.

Blasky, Harold P. & Keiser, Henry B. The Architect-Engineer Primer of Federal Government Contracting. LC 83-80818. 234p. 1983. 65.00. Fed Pubns Inc.

Blass, Bill & Hauser, Joan. Dining In-Manhattan. (Dining In Ser.). 210p. 1983. pap. 8.95 (ISBN 0-89716-088-6). Peanut Butter.

Blass, Bill, jt. auth. see Molinsky, Steven J.

Blass, F., ed. see Demosthenes.

Blass, F., ed. see Isocrates.

Blass, Gerhard A. Theoretical Physics. LC 62-8896. (ACC Series in Physics). pap. 112.80 (ISBN 0-317-26225-4, 2055682). Bks Demand UMI.

Blass, Jacqueline, jt. auth. see Hess, Edith.

Blass, Laurie & Durighello, Joy. From Concept to Composition: Reading & Writing for ESL Students. (Illus.). 200p. 1985. pap. text ed. 10.95 (ISBN 0-13-330630-5). P-H.

Blass, Laurie & Pike-Baky, Meredith. English As a Second Language: Writing, Level III-IV. 256p. 1985. pap. text ed. 12.00 ea. (RanC). Level III (ISBN 0-394-33715-8). Level IV (ISBN 0-394-33724-7). Random.

Blass, Thomas, ed. Contemporary Social Psychology: Representative Readings. LC 75-17318. 474p. 1976. pap. text ed. 13.95 (ISBN 0-87581-190-6). Peacock Pubs.

Blass, William E. & Halsey, George. Deconvolution of Absorption Spectra. LC 81-12667. 1981. 29.50 (ISBN 0-12-104650-8). Acad Pr.

Blassie, Richard R. de see De Blassie, Richard R. & Anderson, John.

Blassingame, John W. Black New Orleans, Eighteen Sixty to Eighteen Eighty. LC 72-97664. (Illus.). xviii, 302p. 1976. pap. 4.95x (ISBN 0-226-05708-9, P662). U of Chicago Pr.

--The Slave Community: Plantation Life in the Ante-Bellum South. 2nd rev. enl. ed. (Illus.). 1979. 22.50x (ISBN 0-19-502562-8); pap. text ed. 8.95x (ISBN 0-19-502563-6). Oxford U Pr.

Blassingame, John W. & Henderson, Mae G. Anti-Slavery Newspapers & Periodicals: An Annotated Index of Letters in the Philanthropist Emancipator, Genius of Universal Emancipation, Abolition Intelligencer, African Observer & the Liberator, 1817-1845, Vol. I. 1980. lib. bdg. 73.00 (ISBN 0-8161-8163-2, Hall Reference). G K Hall.

--Antislavery Newspapers & Periodicals: Annotated Index of Letters, 1817 - 1871, Vol. III: 1836-1854. 1981. lib. bdg. 83.50 (ISBN 0-8161-8558-1, Hall Reference). G K Hall.

--Antislavery Newspapers & Periodicals, Vol. II: Annotated Index of Letters in the "Liberator, Anti-Slavery Record, Human Rights & Observer, 1846-1865. 1980. lib. bdg. 73.00 (ISBN 0-8161-8434-8, Hall Reference). G K Hall.

Blassingame, John W., jt. auth. see Berry, Mary F.

Blassingame, John W., ed. Slave Testimony: Two Centuries of Letters, Speeches, Interviews, & Autobiographies. LC 75-18040. (Illus.). xvi, 777p. 1977. 45.00x (ISBN 0-8071-0184-2); pap. 14.95x (ISBN 0-8071-0273-3). La State U Pr.

Blassingame, John W., ed. see Douglass, Frederick.

Blassingame, John W., ed. see Washington, Booker T.

Blassingame, John W., et al. Antislavery Newspapers & Periodicals, Volume IV: Annotated Index of Letters in the National Antislavery Standard, 1840-1860. 592p. 1984. lib. bdg. 125.00 (ISBN 0-8161-8559-X, Hall Reference). G K Hall.

--Antislavery Newspapers & Periodicals, Volume V: Annotated Index of Letters in the National Antislavery Standard, 1861-1871. 504p. 1984. lib. bdg. 125.00 (ISBN 0-8161-8560-3, Hall Reference). G K Hall.

Blassingame, Wyatt. Dan Beard: Scoutmaster of America. LC 72-76325. (Illus.). (gr. 2-5). 1972. PLB 4.47 (ISBN 0-8116-6754-5). Garrard.

--Franklin D. Roosevelt: Four Times President. LC 66-10024. (Discovery Bks.). (Illus.). (gr. 2-5). 1966. PLB 7.47 (ISBN 0-8116-6314-0). Garrard.

--His Kingdom for a Horse. facs. ed. LC 75-81263. (Short Story Index Reprint Ser). 1957. 17.00 (ISBN 0-8369-3015-0). Ayer Co Pubs.

--How Davy Crockett Got a Bearskin Coat. LC 74-180783. (American Folktales Ser.). (Illus.). 36p. (gr. 2-5). 1972. PLB 7.47 (ISBN 0-8116-4035-3). Garrard.

--Jake Gaither: Winning Coach. LC 69-12140. (Americans All Ser.). (Illus.). (gr. 3-6). 1969. PLB 7.98 (ISBN 0-8116-4552-5). Garrard.

--Jim Beckwourth: Black Trapper & Indian Chief. LC 73-5698. (Discovery Ser.). (Illus.). 80p. (gr. 2-5). 1973. PLB 7.47 (ISBN 0-8116-6314-0). Garrard.

--John Henry & Paul Bunyan Play Baseball. LC 72-151138. (American Folktales Ser.). (Illus.). (gr. 2-5). 1971. PLB 7.47 (ISBN 0-8116-4027-2). Garrard.

--Joseph Stalin & Communist Russia. LC 70-153153. (Century Biographies Ser.). (Illus.). (gr. 4-8). 1971. PLB 4.47 (ISBN 0-8116-4753-6). Garrard.

--The Look-It-Up Book of Presidents: Updated, Revised & Newly Illustrated with Photographs & Old Prints. LC 84-2114. (Illus.). 160p. (gr. 5-9). 1984. pap. 8.95 (ISBN 0-394-86839-0, BYR); lib. bdg. 9.99 GLB (ISBN 0-394-96839-5). Random.

--Pecos Bill & the Wonderful Clothesline Snake. LC 77-17972. (American Folktales Ser.). (Illus.). (gr. 2-5). 1978. PLB 7.47 (ISBN 0-8116-4046-9). Garrard.

--Pecos Bill Catches a Hidebehind. LC 76-23336. (American Folktales Ser.). (Illus.). (gr. 2-5). 1977. lib. bdg. 7.47 (ISBN 0-8116-4045-0). Garrard.

--Pecos Bill Rides a Tornado. LC 73-5894. (American Folktales Ser.). (Illus.). (gr. 2-5). 1973. PLB 7.47 (ISBN 0-8116-4038-8). Garrard.

--Porcupines. LC 82-7379. (Skylight Bk.). (Illus.). 64p. (gr. 2-5). 1982. PLB 7.95 (ISBN 0-396-08074-X). Dodd.

--Skunks. LC 80-21555. (A Skylight Bk.). (Illus.). 64p. (gr. 2-5). 1981. PLB 7.95 (ISBN 0-396-07909-1). Dodd.

--Story of the Boy Scouts. LC 68-13593. (American Democracy Ser.). (Illus.). (gr. 3-6). 1968. PLB 7.98 (ISBN 0-8116-6500-3). Garrard.

--Story of the United States Flag. LC 68-10030. (American Democracy Ser.). (Illus.). (gr. 3-6). 1969. PLB 7.98 (ISBN 0-8116-6502-X). Garrard.

--The Strange Armadillo. LC 83-9073. (Skylight Bks.). (Illus.). 64p. (gr. 2-5). 1983. PLB 7.95 (ISBN 0-396-08180-0). Dodd.

--Underwater Warriors. LC 81-787. (Landmark Paperback: No. 11). (Illus.). 160p. (gr. 3-8). 1982. pap. 2.95 (ISBN 0-394-84884-5). Random.

--William Beebe: Underwater Explorer. LC 75-29069. (Americans All Ser.). (Illus.). 96p. (gr. 3-6). 1976. PLB 7.98 (ISBN 0-8116-4584-3). Garrard.

--Wonders of Crows. LC 78-21633. (Wonder Ser.). (Illus.). (gr. 5 up). 1979. 9.95 (ISBN 0-396-07649-1). Dodd.

--Wonders of Egrets, Bitterns, & Herons. (Wonders Ser.). (Illus.). 80p. (gr. 5 up). 1982. PLB 9.95 (ISBN 0-396-08033-2). Dodd.

--Wonders of Frogs & Toads. LC 74-25523. (Wonders Ser.). (Illus.). (gr. 3-7). 1975. PLB 9.95 (ISBN 0-396-07086-8). Dodd.

--Wonders of Raccoons. LC 77-6491. (Wonder Ser). (Illus.). (gr. 4 up). 1977. 9.95 (ISBN 0-396-07485-5). Dodd.

--Wonders of Sharks. (Wonders Ser.). (Illus.). 96p. (gr. 5 up). 1984. PLB 9.95 (ISBN 0-396-08463-X). Dodd.

--Wonders of the Turtle World. (Wonders Ser). (gr. 4 up). 1976. 9.95 (ISBN 0-396-07342-5). Dodd.

Blassingame, Wyatt, jt. auth. see Cottman, Evans W.

Blassneck, Marce. Frankreich Als Vermittler Englisch-Deutscher Einflusse Im Siebzehnten und Achtzehnten Jahrhundert. 1934. 12.00 (ISBN 0-384-04685-1). Johnson Repr.

Blaster, Grandmaster. Rappin'! (Illus.). 64p. (Orig.). 1984. pap. 2.95 (ISBN 0-8092-5315-1). Contemp Bks.

Blatch, Harriet. Challenging Years: Memoirs. LC 74-33933. (Pioneers of the Woman's Movement: an International Perspective Ser). 1976. Repr. of 1940 ed. 23.85 (ISBN 0-88355-256-6). Hyperion Conn.

Blatch, Harriot S. Mobilizing Woman-Power. LC 74-75231. (The United States in World War 1 Ser). (Illus.). iv, 195p. 1974. Repr. of 1918 ed. lib. bdg. 13.95x (ISBN 0-89198-094-6). Ozer.

Blatch, Harriot S., jt. auth. see Stanton, Theodore.

Blatcher, Marjorie. The Court of King's Bench 1450-1550: A Study in Self-Help. (University of London Legal Ser.: No. 12). 181p. 1978. 50.00 (ISBN 0-485-13412-8, Pub. by Athlone Pr Ltd). Longwood Pub Group.

Blatchford, Charles H., ed. Directory of Teacher Preparation Programs in TESOL & Bilingual Education: 1982-1985. 6th ed. 243p. 1982. 6.50 (ISBN 0-318-16638-0). Tchrs Eng Spkrs.

Blatchford, Charles H. & Schacter, Jacquelyn, eds. EFL Policies, Programs, Practices. (On TESOL Ser.: '78). 264p. 1978. 8.00 (ISBN 0-318-16639-9). Tchrs Eng Spkrs.

Blatchford, Claire. All Alone (Except for My Dog Friday) (Pennypincher Bks.). 132p. (gr. 4-7). 1983. 2.25 (ISBN 0-89191-755-1, 57554). Cook.

Blatchford, John. Narrative of John Blatchford Detailing His Sufferings in the Revolutionary War While a Prisoner with the British. LC 70-140855. (Eyewitness Accounts of the American Revolution Ser.: No. 3). (Illus.). 1970. Repr. of 1865 ed. 11.50 (ISBN 0-405-01216-0). Ayer Co Pubs.

Blatchford, Noel. Your Book of Forestry. (Illus.). 48p. (gr. 4 up). 1980. 8.95 (ISBN 0-571-11456-3). Faber & Faber.

Blatchford, Peter, jt. auth. see Curtis, Audrey.

Blatchford, Peter, et al. The First Transition: Home to Pre-school. 192p. 1982. 16.00x (ISBN 0-317-17998-5, Pub. by NFER Nelson UK). Taylor & Francis.

Blatchford, Robert. Dismal England. LC 83-48474. (The World of Labour-English Workers' 1850-1890 Ser.). 240p. 1984. lib. bdg. 30.00 (ISBN 0-8240-5701-5). Garland Pub.

--My Favourite Books. 1973. 12.50 (ISBN 0-8274-1475-7). R West.

Blatchford, William. Grand Horizontal. 256p. 1984. pap. 3.50 (ISBN 0-8128-8103-6). Stein & Day.

Blatchford, William, ed. see Pearl, Cora.

Blate, Michael. First-Aid Using Simple Remedies. (The G-Jo Institute Self-Health Ser.). (Illus.). 196p. (Orig.). 1983. pap. 8.95 (ISBN 0-916878-17-1). Falkynor Bks.

--Five Minutes to Fitness with Acugenics. (The G-Jo Institute Acugenics Ser.). (Illus.). 144p. (Orig.). Date not set. pap. 8.95 (ISBN 0-916878-20-1). Falkynor Bks.

--The G-Jo Institute Manual of Medicinal Herbs. (The G-Jo Institute Self-Health Ser.). (Illus.). 96p. (Orig.). 1983. pap. 6.95 (ISBN 0-916878-19-8). Falkynor Bks.

--The G-Jo Institute Manual of Vitamins & Minerals. (The G-Jo Institute Self-Health Ser.). 96p. (Orig.). 1983. pap. 6.95 (ISBN 0-916878-18-X). Falkynor Bks.

--Help Defuse the Bomb...Now! Easy Effective Ways You Can Help Prevent Nuclear Holocaust. (G-Jo Institute Life Enhancement Ser.). (Illus.). 60p. 1984. pap. 3.95 (ISBN 0-916878-29-5). Falkynor Bks.

--How to Beat Stress with Acugenics. (The G-Jo Institute Acugenics Ser.). (Illus.). 96p. (Orig.). Date not set. pap. 6.95 (ISBN 0-916878-24-4). Falkynor Bks.

--How to Enjoy Sex More with Acugenics. (G-Jo Institute Acugenics Ser.). (Illus.). 96p. (Orig.). Date not set. pap. 6.95 (ISBN 0-916878-25-2). Falkynor Bks.

--How to Heal Yourself Using Foot Acupressure (Foot Reflexology) (The G-Jo Institute Self-Health Ser.). (Illus.). 185p. (Orig.). 1982. pap. 8.95 (ISBN 0-916878-22-8). Falkynor Bks.

--How to Heal Yourself Using Hand Acupressure (Hand Reflexology) (The G-Jo Institute Self-Health Ser.). (Illus.). 195p. (Orig.). 1982. pap. 8.95 (ISBN 0-916878-21-X). Falkynor Bks.

--How to Lose Weight Easily with Acugenics. (The G-Jo Institute Acugenics Ser.). (Illus.). 144p. (Orig.). Date not set. pap. 8.95 (ISBN 0-916878-11-2). Falkynor Bks.

--How to Relieve Arthritis with Acugenics. (The G-Jo Institute Acugenics Ser.). (Illus.). 144p. Date not set. pap. 8.95 (ISBN 0-916878-23-6). Falkynor Bks.

--How to Stop Smoking with Acugenics. (The G-Jo Institute Acugenics Ser.). (Illus.). 96p. (Orig.). Date not set. pap. 6.95 (ISBN 0-916878-26-0). Falkynor Bks.

--The Natural Healer's Acupressure Handbook: Advanced G-Jo, Vol. 2. (The G-Jo Institute Self-Health Ser.). (Illus.). 272p. 1982. case 12.95 (ISBN 0-916878-14-7). Falkynor Bks.

--The Natural Healer's Acupressure Handbook: G-Jo Fingertip Technique, Vol. 1. (G-Jo Institute Self-Health Ser.). (Illus.). 1977. 12.95 (ISBN 0-916878-06-6). Falkynor Bks.

--The Natural Healer's Acupressure Handbook, Vol. 1, revised: Basic G-Jo. (The G-Jo Institute Self-Health Ser.). (Illus.). 224p. 1982. case 12.95 (ISBN 0-916878-28-7). Falkynor Bks.

--The Tao of Health: The Way of Total Well-Being. (Illus., Orig.). 1978. pap. 6.95 (ISBN 0-916878-05-8). Falkynor Bks.

Blate, Michael & Watson, Gail C. A Way of Eating for Pleasure & Health. (The G-Jo Institute Fabulous Foods). 130p. (Orig.). 1983. pap. 6.95 (ISBN 0-916878-15-5). Falkynor Bks.

Blatner, Barbara. The Pope in Space. (Illus.). 20p. (Orig.). 1986. pap. 7.95 (ISBN 0-912767-05-7). Intertxt Ak.

Blatner, Howard A. Acting-In: Practical Applications of Psychodramatic Methods. LC 73-80598. (Illus.). 1973. pap. text ed. 10.95 (ISBN 0-8261-1400-8). Springer Pub.

Blatnick, Srully. The Corporate Steeplechase. (Penguin Nonfiction Ser.). 304p. 1985. pap. 7.95 (ISBN 0-14-008009-0). Penguin.

Blaton, Victor H., jt. ed. see Malinow, M. Rene.

Blatt, A. H. Organic Synthesis Collective Volumes, Vol. 2. 654p. 1943. 42.95 (ISBN 0-471-07986-3). Wiley.

Blatt, A. H., ed. Organic Syntheses: Collective Volumes, Vol. 2. 654p. 1943. Vols. 10-19. 45.95 (ISBN 0-471-07986-3). Wiley.

Blatt, Art. Gun Digest Book of Trap & Skeet Shooting. LC 83-70143. 256p. 1984. pap. 11.95 (ISBN 0-910676-66-6). DBI.

Blatt, Burton. In & Out of Books: Admirations & Rebuttals on Special Education. LC 83-10282. (Illus.). 264p. 1984. 18.00 (ISBN 0-8391-1836-8, 20028). Pro Ed.

--In & Out of Mental Retardation. LC 81-1652. (Illus.). 392p. 1981. pap. 16.00 (ISBN 0-8391-1664-0). Pro Ed.

--In & Out of the University. LC 81-1652. 224p. 1982. pap. 16.00 (ISBN 0-8391-1734-5). Pro Ed.

--Revolt of the Idiots. 1976. 10.95 (ISBN 0-686-84868-3). Exceptional Pr Inc.

Blatt, Burton & Kaplan, Fred. Christmas in Purgatory. 1974. 3.50 (ISBN 0-937540-00-5, HPP-3). Human Policy Pr.

Blatt, Burton & Morris, Richard J. Perspectives in Special Education: Personal Orientations. (The Scott, Foresman Special Eduction Ser.). 1984. text ed. 25.80x (ISBN 0-673-16566-3). Scott F.

Blatt, Elisabeth. Eighty-Eight Musical Keys. 183p. (Orig.). 1985. pap. 6.95 (ISBN 0-9613767-0-8). Billib Press.

Blatt, Ethal S., jt. auth. see Blatt, Sidney J.

Blatt, Frank J. Principles of Physics. 800p. 1983. 42.14 (ISBN 0-205-07588-6, 737588); student manual avail.; instrs. manual avail.; study guide 19.29 (ISBN 0-205-07589-4, 737589). Allyn.

Blatt, Gloria T. It's Your Move: Expressive Movement Activities for the Language Arts Class. LC 81-9014. (Orig.). 1981. text ed. 21.95x (ISBN 0-8077-2687-7); pap. 13.95x (ISBN 0-8077-2640-0). Tchrs Coll.

Blatt, H., et al. Origin of Sedimentary Rock. 2nd ed. 1980. 42.95 (ISBN 0-13-642710-3). P-H.

Blatt, Harvey. Sedimentary Petrology. LC 81-22147. (Illus.). 564p. 1982. text ed. 35.95 (ISBN 0-7167-1354-3). W H Freeman.

Blatt, Harvey, jt. auth. see Ehlers, Ernest G.

Blatt, Irwin B. A Study of Culture Change in Modern Puerto Rico. LC 78-68459. 1979. perfect bdg. 12.00 (ISBN 0-88247-558-4). R & E Pubs.

Blatt, J. & Weisskopf, V. F. Theoretical Nuclear Physics. LC 79-4268. 1979. pap. 44.50 (ISBN 0-387-90382-8). Springer-Verlag.

Blatt, J. & Schroeder, P. A., eds. Thermoelectricity in Metallic Conductors. LC 78-6010. 432p. 1978. 65.00x (ISBN 0-306-40003-0, Plenum Pr). Plenum Pub.

Blatt, J., et al. Thermoelectric Power of Metals. LC 76-20706. (Illus.). 264p. 1976. 55.00x (ISBN 0-306-30907-6, Plenum Pr). Plenum Pub.

Blatt, John M. Dynamic Economic Systems: A Post Keynesian Approach. LC 82-24013. 370p. 1983. pap. 14.95 (ISBN 0-87332-306-8). M E Sharpe.

--Theory of Superconductivity. (Pure and Applied Physics Ser.: Vol. 17). 1964. 69.50 (ISBN 0-12-104950-7). Acad Pr.

Blatt, Martin, ed. The Collected Works of Ezra H. Heywood. 392p. 1985. 35.00x (ISBN 0-87730-013-5). M&S Pr.

Blatt, Max, compiled by. Index to Monthly Review: May 1949-April 1981. LC 81-85233. 1983. 25.00 (ISBN 0-85345-585-6). Monthly Rev.

Blatt, S. R., jt. ed. see Pandeya, R. C.

Blatt, Sidney J. & Blatt, Ethal S. Continuity in Art: The Development of Modes of Representation. 432p. 1984. text ed. 45.00 (ISBN 0-89859-342-5). L Erlbaum Assocs.

Blatt, Sidney J. & Wild, Cynthia. Schizophrenia: A Developmental Analysis. 1976. 37.50 (ISBN 0-12-105050-5). Acad Pr.

Blatteau, John, ed. see D'Espouy, Hector.

Blattenberger, Ruth, ed. see Leach, Robert J.

Blatter, Alfred. Instrumentation-Orchestration. LC 79-17001. (Longman Music Ser.). 1980. pap. text ed. 24.95x (ISBN 0-582-28118-0). Longman.

Blatter, E. Ferns of Bombay. 1979. 15.00x (ISBN 0-89955-261-7, Pub. by Intl Bk Dist). Intl Spec Bk.

--Palms of British India & Ceylon. (Illus.). 1978. Repr. of 1926 ed. 68.75x (ISBN 0-89955-295-1, Pub. by Intl Bk Dist). Intl Spec Bk.

Blatter, E. & McCann, C. The Bombay Grasses. 1982. 75.00x (ISBN 0-686-45800-1, Pub. by United Bk Traders India). State Mutual Bk.

Blatter, George J., tr. see Agreda, Mary.

Blatter, Janet & Milton, Sybil. Art of the Holocaust. 272p. 1981. 29.95 (ISBN 0-8317-0418-7, Rutledge Pr). Smith Pubs.

Blatter, Joerg. Grothendieck Spaces in Approximation Theory. LC 52-42839. (Memoirs: No. 120). 121p. 1972. pap. 9.00 (ISBN 0-8218-1820-1, MEMO-120). Am Math.

Blattner, Barbara. Holistic Nursing. (Illus.). 400p. 1981. text ed. 25.75 (ISBN 0-13-392563-3); pap. text ed. 21.95 (ISBN 0-13-392571-4). P-H.

Blattner, John. Growing in the Fruit of the Spirit. (Living As A Christian Ser.). 96p. 1984. pap. 3.95 (ISBN 0-89283-177-4). Servant.

Blattner, John, jt. auth. see Manney, James.

Blattner, John W., et al. Encyclopedia for the TRS-80, Vol. 5. Putnam, Katherine & Comiskey, Kate, eds. 239p. (Orig.). 1982. 19.95 (ISBN 0-88006-035-2, EN8105); pap. 10.95 (ISBN 0-88006-036-0, EN8085). Green Pub Inc.

Blatty, William P. The Exorcist. 416p. 1972. pap. 3.95 (ISBN 0-553-24769-7). Bantam.

--Exorcist. LC 73-144189. 1971. 9.95i (ISBN 0-06-010365-5, HarpT). Har-Row.

--I'll Tell Them I Remember You. LC 73-5561. 176p. 1973. 5.95 (ISBN 0-393-07479-X). Norton.

--Legion. 256p. 1983. 14.95 (ISBN 0-671-47045-0). S&S.

--Legion. 320p. 1984. pap. 3.95 (ISBN 0-671-50848-2). PB.

Blatz, William E. Collected Studies on the Dionne Quintuplets. LC 74-21401. (Classics in Child Development Ser). (Illus.). 294p. 1975. Repr. 26.00x (ISBN 0-405-06454-3). Ayer Co Pubs.

--Human Security: Some Reflections. LC 66-486. 1966. pap. 36.80 (ISBN 0-317-08110-1, 2014138). Bks Demand UMI.

Blau, Abram. The Master Hand: A Study of the Origin & Meaning of Right & Left Sidedness & Its Relation to Personality & Language. LC 78-72790. (Brainedness, Handedness, & Mental Ability Ser.). Repr. of 1946 ed. 21.50 (ISBN 0-404-60854-X). AMS Pr.

Blau, Clare, ed. see Foulke, Jan.

Blau, Clare, ed. see Worrell, Estelle A.

Blau, David & Freed, Anne O., eds. Mental Health in the Nursing Home: An Educational Approach for Staff. 138p. (Orig.). 1983. pap. text ed. 17.50 (ISBN 0-8236-3362-4, 03362). Intl Univs Pr.

Blau, Eric. The Keys to Billy Tillio. 288p. (Orig.). 1984. pap. 3.50 (ISBN 0-523-42255-5). Pinnacle Bks.

Blau, Esther, ed. The Spice & Spirit of Kosher-Jewish Cooking. LC 77-72116. (Illus.). 1977. 16.95 (ISBN 0-8197-0455-5). Bloch.

Blau, Esther & Deitsch, Cyrel, eds. Spice & pirit of Kosher-Passover Cooking. LC 77-72116. (Lubavitch Women's Organization Ser.). 1981. 7.95 (ISBN 0-317-14690-4). Lubavitch Women.

Blau, Esther, ed. see Lubavitch Womens Organization.

Blau, Eve. Ruskinian Gothic: The Architecture of Deane & Woodward, 1845-1861. LC 81-7302. (Illus.). 350p. 1982. cloth 46.00x (ISBN 0-691-03984-4); pap. 20.00x LPE (ISBN 0-691-10127-2). Princeton U Pr.

Blau, Evenlyn, jt. auth. see Robbins, Jack.

Blau, Fred, jt. auth. see Sheeter, Sean.

Blau, Fredric. One Hundred Years of Experimental Telepathy. 200p. (Orig.). 1984. pap. 9.95 cancelled (ISBN 0-9605378-3-X). Process Pr.

Blau, G. International Commodity Arrangements & Policies. (Commodity Policy Studies: No. 16). 1964. pap. 4.50 (ISBN 0-685-36304-X, F241, FAO). Unipub.

Blau, G. & Music, D. A. Agricultural Commodity Trade & Development: Prospects, Problems & Policies: A Reference Paper. (Commodity Policy Studies: No. 17). (Orig.). 1964. pap. 4.75 (ISBN 0-685-09370-0, F9, FAO). Unipub.

Blau, Gary. Human Resource Accounting. (Studies in Productivity: Highlights of the Literature Ser.: Vol. 6). 55p. 1978. pap. 35.00 (ISBN 0-08-029487-1). Work in Amer.

Blau, Gary E., jt. ed. see Neely, W. Brock.

Blau, Gerda & Ezekiel, Mordecai. Food Aid for Development. 343p. 1985. pap. 28.25 (ISBN 92-5-102180-5, F2747, FAO). Unipub.

Blau, Herbert. Blooded Thought: Occasions of Theatre. LC 82-81976. 1982. 18.95 (ISBN 0-933826-38-9); pap. 6.95 (ISBN 0-933826-39-7). Performing Arts.

--Take Up the Bodies: Theater at the Vanishing Point. LC 81-19774. (Illus.). 328p. 1982. 16.95x (ISBN 0-252-00945-2); pap. 10.95x. U of Ill Pr.

--Take Up the Bodies: Theater at the Vanishing Point. LC 81-19774. (Illus.). 328p. 1985. pap. 10.95x (ISBN 0-252-01245-3). U of Ill Pr.

Blau, J. L., ed. see James, William.

Blau, Joseph L. Judaism in America: From Curiosity to Third Faith. LC 75-5069. (Chicago History of American Religion Ser.). 176p. 1976. 12.95x (ISBN 0-226-05727-5). U of Chicago Pr.

--Judaism in America: From Curiosity to Third Faith. LC 75-5069. (Chicago History of American Religion Ser.). 1978. pap. 4.95 (ISBN 0-226-05728-3, P761, Phoen). U of Chicago Pr.

--Modern Varieties of Judaism. LC 66-10732. (Lectures on the History of Religion Ser.). 217p. 1966. 23.00x (ISBN 0-231-02867-9); pap. 10.00x (ISBN 0-231-08668-7). Columbia U Pr.

--The Story of Jewish Philosophy. 8.95x (ISBN 0-87068-174-5). Ktav.

Blau, Joseph L., ed. Essays on Jewish Life & Thought. LC 57-11757. 458p. 1959. 31.00x (ISBN 0-231-02171-2). Columbia U Pr.

Blau, Joseph L., ed. see Wayland, Francis.

Blau, Joseph L., et al, eds. The Jews of the United States, 1790-1840: A Documentary History, 3 Vols. LC 64-10108. 1034p. 1964. Set. 126.00x (ISBN 0-231-02651-X). Columbia U Pr.

Blau, Joshua. The Renaissance of Modern Hebrew & Modern Standard Arabic: Parallels & Differences in the Revival of Two Semitic Languages. (Publications in Near East Studies: Vol. 18). 1982. 24.00x (ISBN 0-520-09548-0). U of Cal Pr.

Blau, Judith R. Architects & Firms: A Sociological Perspective on Architectural Practices. (Illus.). 200p. (Orig.). 1984. text ed. 19.95x (ISBN 0-262-02209-5). MIT Pr.

Blau, Judith R. & La Gory, Mark E., eds. Professionals & Urban Form. LC 82-10422. 376p. 1983. 44.50x (ISBN 0-87395-675-3); pap. 14.95x (ISBN 0-87395-676-1). State U NY Pr.

Blau, Karl & King, Graham S., eds. Handbook of Derivatives for Chromatography. LC 78-310911. pap. 148.00 (ISBN 0-317-26142-8, 2025195). Bks Demand UMI.

Blau, Lucie R. Relative National Accounts: A Statistical Basebook - 1976 Edition. LC 77-70217. (Report Ser.: No. 708). (Illus.). 79p. (Orig.). 1977. 30.00 (ISBN 0-8237-0142-5); member 10.00. Conference Bd.

--Relative National Accounts: A Statistical Basebook. (Report Ser: No. 620). 77p. (Orig.). 1974. pap. 17.50 (ISBN 0-8237-0048-8); pap. 3.50 member. Conference Bd.

Blau, Melinda. Killer Bees. LC 77-10010. (Great Unsolved Mysteries). (Illus.). (gr. 4-5). 1977. PLB 14.25 (ISBN 0-8172-1055-5). Raintree Pubs.

--Whatever Happened to Amelia Earhart? LC 77-22173. (Great Unsolved Mysteries). (Illus.). (gr. 4-5). 1977. PLB 14.25 (ISBN 0-8172-1057-1). Raintree Pubs.

Blau, Melinda E. Killer Bees. LC 77-11010. (Great Unsolved Mysteries Ser.). (Illus.). 48p. (gr. 4up). 1983. pap. 9.27 (ISBN 0-8172-2159-X). Raintree Pubs.

--Whatever Happened to Amelia Earhart? LC 77-22173. (Great Unsolved Mysteries Ser.). (Illus.). 48p. (gr. 4up). 1983. pap. 9.27 (ISBN 0-8172-2170-0). Raintree Pubs.

Blau, Peter M. Bureaucracy in Modern Society. 2nd ed. (Orig.). 1971. pap. text ed. 7.00 (ISBN 0-394-31452-2, RanC). Random.

--The Dynamics of Bureacracy. 2nd. rev. ed. LC 63-22822. xiv, 322p. 1973. text ed. 6.95x (ISBN 0-226-05726-7, P500, Phoen). U of Chicago Pr.

--Exchange & Power in Social Life. LC 64-23827. 352p. 1964. 38.95x (ISBN 0-471-08030-6). Wiley.

--Exchange & Power in Social Life. 372p. 1985. pap. text ed. 14.95x (ISBN 0-88738-628-8). Transaction Bks.

--Inequality & Heterogeneity: A Primitive Theory of Social Structure. LC 77-70272. (Illus.). 1977. 19.95 (ISBN 0-02-903660-7). Free Pr.

--On the Nature of Organizations. LC 81-19330. 368p. 1983. Repr. of 1974 ed. 29.50 (ISBN 0-89874-463-6). Krieger.

--The Organization of Academic Work. LC 73-6992. 330p. 1973. 25.50 (ISBN 0-471-08025-X). Krieger.

Blau, Peter M. & Duncan, Otis D. The American Occupational Structure. LC 78-50657. 1978. pap. text ed. 14.95 (ISBN 0-02-903670-4). Free Pr.

Blau, Peter M. & Schwartz, Joseph E. Crosscutting Social Circles: Testing a Macrostructural Theory of Intergroup Relations. 1983. 30.00 (ISBN 0-12-105250-8); pap. 15.00 (ISBN 0-12-105252-4). Acad Pr.

Blau, Peter M., ed. Approaches to the Study of Social Structure. LC 75-2809. 1975. 19.95 (ISBN 0-02-903650-X). Free Pr.

Blau, Richard M. The Body Impolitic: A Reading of Four Novels by Herman Melville. 219p. 1979. pap. text ed. 25.50x (ISBN 90-6203-571-X). Humanities.

Blau, Rosalie, et al. Activities for School-Age Child Care. LC 77-91044. (Illus.). 85p. 1977. pap. text ed. 4.00 (ISBN 0-912674-57-1, NAEYC 214). Natl Assn Child Ed.

Blau, Theodore H. The Psychologist As Expert Witness. LC 84-7512. (Health Psychology Ser.: Behavioral Medicine 1-639). 432p. 1984. text ed. 37.95 (ISBN 0-471-87129-X, Pub. by Wiley-Interscience). Wiley.

Blau, Tom. In & Out of Focus. (Illus.). 176p. 1984. 19.95 (ISBN 0-241-11058-0, Pub. by Hamish Hamilton England). David & Charles.

Blau, Ulrich. Die Dreiwertige Logik der Sprache Ihre Syntax, Semantik und Anwendung in der Sprachanalyse. (Grundlagen der Kommunikation). 1977. 25.60x (ISBN 3-11-006989-X). De Gruyter.

Blau, Zena. Aging in a Changing Society. 2nd ed. 288p. 1981. 8.95 (ISBN 0-531-05637-6, New Viewpoints). Watts.

Blau, Zena S. Black Children-White Children: Competence, Socialization & Social Structure. LC 80-1643. 1981. 24.95 (ISBN 0-02-903640-2). Free Pr.

Blauberg, I. V., et al. Systems Theory: Philosophical & Methodological Problems. 318p. 1977. 5.95 (ISBN 0-8285-0440-7, Pub. by Progress Pubs USSR). Imported Pubns.

Blauch, Lloyd E. Federal Cooperation in Agricultural Extension Work, Vocational Education, & Vocational Rehabilitation. LC 76-89150. (American Education: Its Men, Institutions & Ideas, Ser. 1). 1969. Repr. of 1935 ed. 15.00 (ISBN 0-405-01388-4). Ayer Co Pubs.

Blauer, G. & Sund, H., eds. Optical Properties & Structure of Tetrapyrroles: Proceedings of a Symposium, University of Konstanz, West Germany, August 12-17, 1984. (Illus.). xiv, 536p. 1985. 92.00x (ISBN 3-11-010054-1). De Gruyter.

Blauer, Gideon, ed. see Protein-Ligand Interactions Symposium, Univ. of Konstanz, Germany, Sep, 1974.

Blauer, Stephen, jt. auth. see Kushi, Michio.

Blauer, Steven. Satyrday. 1982. pap. 4.95 lg. (ISBN 0-425-05317-2). Berkley Pub.

Blauert, Jens. Spacial Hearing: The Psycho Physics of Human Sound Localization. 1983. 42.50x (ISBN 0-262-02190-0). MIT Pr.

Blaufarb, Douglas S. The Counterinsurgency Era: U. S. Doctrine & Performance 1950 to Present. LC 77-72692. (Illus.). 1977. 14.95 (ISBN 0-02-903700-X). Free Pr.

Blaufox, Donald, jt. ed. see Freeman, Leonard M.

Blaufox, M. Donald & Bianchi, Claudio, eds. Secondary Forms of Hypertension: Current Diagnosis & Management. (Illus.). 352p. 1981. 34.50 (ISBN 0-8089-1384-0, 790614). Grune.

Blaufox, M. Donald & Funck-Brentano, Jean-Louis, eds. Radionuclides in Nephrology: An International Symposium. LC 76-182811. (Illus.). 448p. 1972. 86.50 (ISBN 0-8089-0745-X, 790617). Grune.

Blaufox, M. Donald, jt. ed. see Freeman, Leonard M.

Blaug, M. Economics of Education. 3rd ed. 1978. text ed. 45.00 (ISBN 0-08-020627-1). Pergamon.

--Methodology of Appraisal of Marxian Economics. (Lectures in Economics Ser.: Vol. 3). 82p. 1980. 27.75 (ISBN 0-444-85424-X, North-Holland). Elsevier.

Blaug, Mark. The Cambridge Revolution: Success or Failure. (Institute of Economic Affairs, Hobart Paperbacks Ser.: No. 6). 1975. pap. 5.95 technical (ISBN 0-255-36072-X). Transatlantic.

--Economic Theory in Retrospect. LC 77-7899. 1978. 34.50 (ISBN 0-521-21733-4). Cambridge U Pr.

--Economic Theory in Retrospect. 3rd ed. LC 77-7899. 756p. 1983. pap. 19.95 (ISBN 0-521-27496-6). Cambridge U Pr.

--Economic Theory in Retrospect. 4th ed. (Illus.). 750p. Date not set. price not set (ISBN 0-521-30354-0); pap. price not set (ISBN 0-521-31644-8). Cambridge U Pr.

--Education & the Employment Problem in Developing Countries. 4th ed. 1981. 6.85 (ISBN 92-2-101005-8). Intl Labour Office.

--Education & the Employment Problem in Developing Countries. vii, 89p. (4th Impression). 1981. pap. 7.00 (ISBN 92-2-101005-8, ILO54, ILO). Unipub.

--Great Economists since Keynes: An Introduction to the Lives & Works of One Hundred Economists. LC 84-12443. (Illus.). 280p. 1985. 32.50x (ISBN 0-389-20517-6, BNB-08079). B&N Imports.

--Ricardian Economics. LC 73-9208. 269p. 1973. Repr. of 1958 ed. lib. bdg. 17.75x (ISBN 0-8371-6982-8, BLRE). Greenwood.

Blaug, Mark & Sturges, Paul, eds. Who's Who in Economics: A Biographical Dictionary of Major Economics, 1700-1981. 416p. 1983. 75.00x (ISBN 0-262-02188-9). MIT Pr.

Blaukopf, Herta, ed. Gustav Mahler & Richard Strauss Correspondence, 1888-1911. Jephcott, Edmund, tr. from Ger. LC 84-16473. (Illus.). 240p. 1985. Repr. of 1980 ed. 22.50 (ISBN 0-226-05767-4). U of Chicago Pr.

Blaukopf, K., ed. The Phonogram in Cultural Communications. (Illus.). 180p. 1982. pap. 25.50 (ISBN 0-387-81725-5). Springer-Verlag.

Blaukopf, Kurt. Gustav Mahler. Goodwin, Inge, tr. LC 84-26148. 280p. 1985. 9.95 (ISBN 0-87910-029-X). Limelight Edns.

Blaukopf, Kurt & Desmont, Mark, eds. The Cultural Behaviour of Youth: Towards a Cross-Cultural Survey in Europe & Asia. 1976. pap. 25.00 (ISBN 3-7024-0114-8, 51-26247). Eur-Am Music.

Blaukopf, Kurt, ed. see Bontinck-Kueffel, Irmgard.

Blaum, Rudolph P. E.R.A. Man Era of Error. (Illus.). 220p. pap. 4.50 (ISBN 0-318-12516-1). Am Educ Assn.

Blaun, Randi. The Incredibly Lazy Person's Guide to a Much Better Body (in Only Six Weeks) 1983. 15.95 (ISBN 0-671-47306-9); pap. 6.95 (ISBN 0-671-45484-6). S&S.

Blauner, Robert. Alienation & Freedom: The Factory Worker & His Industry. LC 64-15820. 1967. pap. 6.50x (ISBN 0-226-05811-5). U of Chicago Pr.

--Racial Oppression in America. 1972. pap. text ed. 14.10 scp (ISBN 0-06-040771-9, HarpC). Har-Row.

Blaustein, A., ed. Pathology of the Female Genital Tract. 2nd ed. (Illus.). 940p. 1981. 83.50 (ISBN 0-387-90574-X). Springer-Verlag.

Blaustein, A. P. & Blaustein, E. B. Constitution of Dependencies & Special Sovereignties. 1975. loose-leaf 700.00 (ISBN 0-317-30245-0). Oceana.

Blaustein, Albert & Zangrando, Robert. Civil Rights & the Black American. Orig. Title: Civil Rights & the American Negro. (Orig.). pap. 1.45 (ISBN 0-671-48402-8). WSP.

Blaustein, Albert P. A Bibliography on the Common Law in French. LC 73-21604. 179p. 1974. lib. bdg. 17.00 (ISBN 0-379-00227-2). Oceana.

Blaustein, Albert P. & Ferguson, Clarence C., Jr. Deseregation & the Law: The Meaning of the School Segregation Cases. (Illus.). xiv, 333p. 1985. Repr. of 1957 ed. lib. bdg. 32.50x (ISBN 0-8377-0344-1). Rothman.

Blaustein, Albert P. & Mersky, Roy M. The First One Hundred Justices: Statistical Studies on the Supreme Court of the United States. 210p. 1978. 19.50 (ISBN 0-208-01290-7, Archon). Shoe String.

Blaustein, Albert P. & Paust, Jordon J. The Arab Oil Weapon. LC 77-2937. 1977. 30.00 (ISBN 0-379-00797-5). Oceana.

Blaustein, Albert P. & Porter, Charles O. The American Lawyer: A Summary of the Survey of the Legal Profession. LC 72-5452. 360p. 1972. Repr. of 1954 ed. lib. bdg. 19.50x (ISBN 0-8371-6438-9, BLAL). Greenwood.

Blaustein, Albert P., ed. Fundamental Legal Documents of Communist China. xxix, 603p. 1962. 20.00x (ISBN 0-8377-0300-X). Rothman.

--Manual on Foreign Legal Periodicals & Their Index. LC 62-11757. (Parker School Studies in Foreign & Comparative Law). 137p. 1962. 17.50 (ISBN 0-379-00119-5). Oceana.

Blaustein, Albert P. & Blaustein, Eric B., eds. Constitutions of Dependencies & Special Sovereignties, 6 vols. plus yearly supplements. LC 75-21651. 1975. Suppl. 75.00x ea.; Set. 600.00 (ISBN 0-379-00278-7). Oceana.

Blaustein, Albert P. & Flanz, Gisbert H., eds. Constitutions of the Countries of the World: 1975, Suppl 1; 1976, Suppl 1 & 2; 1977, Suppl 1; 1976, Cummulative Suppl. LC 76-141327. 1971. 75.00 ea.; Set. 1300.00 (ISBN 0-379-00467-4). Oceana.

Blaustein, Albert P., et al. Independence Documents of the World, 2 vols. LC 77-7333. 1977. Set. 85.00. Vol. 1 (ISBN 0-379-00794-0). Vol. 2 (ISBN 0-379-00795-9). Oceana.

Blaustein, Ancel. Interpretation of Endometrial Biopsies. 2nd ed. (Biopsy Interpretation Ser.). (Illus.). 256p. 1985. text ed. 35.00 (ISBN 0-88167-120-7). Raven.

Blaustein, Arthur I., ed. The American Promise: Equal Justice & Economic Opportunity. LC 81-16313. 140p. (Orig.). 1982. pap. 9.95 (ISBN 0-87855-905-1). Transaction Bks.

Blaustein, Bernard D., ed. Chemical Reactions in Electrical Discharges. LC 70-76951. (Advances in Chemistry Ser: No. 80). 1969. 39.95 (ISBN 0-8412-0081-5). Am Chemical.

Blaustein, Bernard D., et al, eds. New Approaches in Coal Chemistry. LC 81-12740. (ACS Symposium Ser.: No. 169). 1981. 41.95 (ISBN 0-8412-0659-7). Am Chemical.

Blaustein, David. Memoirs of David Blaustein: Educator & Communal Worker. facsimile ed. LC 74-27966. (Modern Jewish Experience Ser.). (Illus.). 1975. Repr. of 1913 ed. 29.00x (ISBN 0-405-06696-1). Ayer Co Pubs.

Blaustein, E. B., jt. auth. see Blaustein, A. P.

Blaustein, E. H., et al. Your Environment & You: Understanding Ecology. 1978. write for info. (ISBN 0-379-00803-3). Oceana.

--Your Environment & You: Understanding the Pollution Problem, Level 2. LC 74-5230. 1974. 8.75x (ISBN 0-379-00802-5). Oceana.

Blaustein, Eric B., jt. ed. see Blaustein, Albert P.

Blaustein, Gustav P., ed. see Skinner, Joseph O.

Blaustein, John & Abbey, Edward. The Hidden Canyon: A River Journey. (Large Format Ser.). (Illus.). 1977. pap. 12.95 (ISBN 0-14-004678-X). Penguin.

Blaustein, Mordecai P. & Lieberman, Melvyn, eds. Electrogenic Transport: Fundamental Principles & Physiological Implications. (Society of General Physiologists Ser.: Vol. 38). (Illus.). 416p. 1984. text ed. 71.50 (ISBN 0-89004-959-9). Raven.

Blaustein, Paul H. Learned Hand on Patent Law. LC 82-63003. 350p. 1983. lib. bdg. 50.00 (ISBN 0-9610490-0-6); text ed. 50.00 (ISBN 0-686-88645-3). Pineridge Pub.

Blaustein, Randy B. How to Do Business with the IRS. LC 82-5319. 342p. 39.95 (ISBN 0-13-396168-0, Busn). P-H.

--How to Do Business with the IRS: Taxpayers Edition. 250p. 1984. 17.95 (ISBN 0-13-405507-1); pap. 8.95 (ISBN 0-13-405499-7). P-H.

--Tax Shelters: Shrewd Insights. LC 83-16200. 107p. 1983. 50.00 (ISBN 0-932648-46-0). Boardroom.

Blaustein, Saul J. Job & Income Security for Unemployed Workers: Some New Directions. LC 81-10423. 127p. 1981. text ed. 13.95 (ISBN 0-911558-83-7); pap. text ed. 8.95 (ISBN 0-911558-84-5). W E Upjohn.

--Unemployment Insurance Fund Insolvency & Debt in Michigan. 82p. 1982. pap. 6.95 (ISBN 0-88099-004-X). W E Upjohn.

--Unemployment Insurance Objectives & Issues: An Agenda for Research & Evaluation. 64p. 1968. pap. 0.50 (ISBN 0-911558-35-7). W E Upjohn.

Blaustein, Saul J. & Craig, Isabel. An International Review of Unemployment Insurance Schemes. (Studies in Unemployment Insurance). 1977. pap. 7.95 (ISBN 0-911558-22-5). W E Upjohn.

Blaustein, Saul J. & Kozlowski, Paul J. Interstate Differences in Unemployment Insurance Benefit Cost: A Cross Section Study. 1978. pap. 1.50 (ISBN 0-911558-21-7). W E Upjohn.

Blauth, W. & Schneider-Sickert, F. R. Congenital Deformities of the Hand: An Atlas of Their Surgical Treatment. (Illus.). 394p. 1981. 240.00 (ISBN 0-387-10084-9). Springer-Verlag.

Blauvelt, Carolyn T. & Nelson, Fred. A Manual of Orthopaedic Terminology. 2nd ed. LC 81-4029. (Illus.). 257p. 1981. pap. text ed. 23.95 (ISBN 0-8016-0752-3). Mosby.

Blauvelt, Euan & Durlacher, Jennifer, eds. Sources of African & Middle-Eastern Economic Information, 2 vols. LC 81-4125. 1982. lib. bdg. 150.00 (ISBN 0-313-23058-7, BAF/). Greenwood.

--Sources of Asian Pacific Economic Information, 2 vols. LC 80-28645. 1981. Set. lib. bdg. 150.00 (ISBN 0-313-22963-5, BLS/). Greenwood.

Blauvelt, Peter D. Effective Strategies for School Security. Koerner, Thomas F., ed. 84p. 1981. pap. 6.00 (ISBN 0-88210-129-3). Natl Assn Principals.

Blavatsky, H. P. Collected Writings of H. P. Blavatsky, Vol. 13. De Zirkoff, Boris, ed. LC 75-10528. (Illus.). 465p. 1983. 16.50 (ISBN 0-8356-0229-X). Theos Pub Hse.

--A Modern Panarion. 504p. 1981. Repr. of 1895 ed. 15.00 (ISBN 0-938998-22-6). Theosophy.

--Theosophical Articles: Reprinted from the Theosophist, Lucifer & other Nineteenth-Century Journals, 3 vols. 1692p. 1982. Set. 37.50 (ISBN 0-938998-26-9). Theosophy.

--The Theosophist: Oct. Eighteen Seventy-Nine to Sept. Eighteen Eighty. 2nd ed. (Secret Doctrine Reference Ser.). (Illus.). 320p. 1979. pap. 12.00 (ISBN 0-913510-31-9). Wizards.

Blavatsky, H. P., compiled by. Gems from the East: A Birthday Book of Precepts & Axioms. LC 83-50510. (Illus.). 224p. Repr. of 1890 ed. 8.50 (ISBN 0-911500-12-X). Theos U Pr.

Blavatsky, H. P., et al. Theosophical Articles & Notes. 300p. 1985. Repr. write for info. (ISBN 0-938998-29-3). Theosophy.

Blavatsky, Helena P. Abridgement of the Secret Doctrine. Preston, Elizabeth & Humphreys, Christmas, eds. 1968. pap. 5.50 (ISBN 0-8356-0009-2, Quest). Theos Pub Hse.

--The Caves & Jungles of Hindustan. De Zirkoff, Boris, ed. LC 74-26605. (Illus.). 750p. 1975. 18.50 (ISBN 0-8356-0219-2). Theos Pub Hse.
--The Circle of Wisdom. rev ed. Parley, Winifred A., ed. LC 78-8790. 1978. pap. 3.25 (ISBN 0-8356-0516-7, Quest). Theos Pub Hse.
--Collected Writings of H. P. Blavatsky, Vols. 1-11. Incl. Vol. 1. 1874-1878. rev. ed. 14.50 (ISBN 0-8356-0082-3); Vol. 2. 1879-1880 (ISBN 0-8356-0091-2); Vol. 3. 1881-1882 (ISBN 0-8356-0099-8); Vol. 4. 1882-1883 (ISBN 0-8356-0106-4); Vol. 5. 1883 (ISBN 0-8356-0117-X); Vol. 6. 1883-1884-1885 (ISBN 0-8356-0125-0); Vol. 7. 1886-1887 (ISBN 0-8356-0222-2); Vol. 8. 1887 (ISBN 0-8356-7166-6); Vol. 9. 1888 (ISBN 0-8356-0217-6); Vol. 10. 1888-1889 (ISBN 0-8356-0218-4); Vol. 11. 1889. 16.50 (ISBN 0-686-86789-0). (Illus.). 16.50 ea. Theos Pub Hse.
--Dynamics of the Psychic World: Comments by H. P. Blavatsky on Magic, Mediumship, Psychism, & the Powers of the Spirit. LC 72-78193. 150p. (Orig.). 1972. pap. 1.95 (ISBN 0-8356-0429-2, Quest). Theos Pub Hse.
--Esoteric Writings of H. P. Blavatsky. LC 79-6547. (Illus.). 500p. (Orig.). 1980. pap. 8.75 (ISBN 0-8356-0535-3, Quest). Theos Pub Hse.
--H. P. Blavatsky Collected Writings, Vol. XII. De Zirkoff, Boris, ed. LC 80-53953. (Illus.). 849p. 1981. cloth 16.50 (ISBN 0-8356-0228-1). Theos Pub Hse.
--H. P. Blavatsky to the American Conventions: 1888-1891, with a Historical Perspective. LC 78-74256. 1979. pap. 4.00 (ISBN 0-911500-88-X). Theos U Pr.
--Isis Unveiled, 2 Vols. De Zirkoff, Boris, ed. 1971. Set. 30.00 (ISBN 0-8356-0193-5). Theos Pub Hse.
--Isis Unveiled, 2 vols. LC 72-186521. 1976. Repr. of 1877 ed. Set. 20.00 (ISBN 0-911500-02-2); Set. pap. 14.00 (ISBN 0-911500-03-0). Theos U Pr.
--Isis Unveiled: A Master-Key to the Mysteries of Ancient & Modern Science & Theology, 2 vols. in 1. (Illus.). xlix, 1260p. 1931. Repr. of 1877 ed. 17.00 (ISBN 0-938998-01-3). Theosophy.
--The Key to Theosophy. xii, 310p. 1930. Repr. of 1889 ed. 6.00 (ISBN 0-938998-03-X). Theosophy.
--The Key to Theosophy: Verbatim with 1889 Edition. LC 72-95701. 1972. 9.00 (ISBN 0-911500-06-5); pap. 6.00 (ISBN 0-911500-07-3). Theos U Pr.
--Practical Occultism. 3rd ed. 1967. 2.50 (ISBN 0-8356-7124-0). Theos Pub Hse.
--The Secret Doctrine, 3 vols. 7th ed. De Zirkoff, Boris, ed. (Illus.). 1980. 45.00 ea. (ISBN 0-8356-7525-4). Theos Pub Hse.
--The Secret Doctrine, 2 vols. facsimile reprint of 1888 ed. LC 74-76603. 1977. Set. 20.00 (ISBN 0-911500-00-6); Set. pap. 14.00 (ISBN 0-911500-01-4). Theos U Pr.
--The Secret Doctrine: The Synthesis of Science, Religion, & Philosophy, 2 vols. in 1. xci, 1474p. 1925. Repr. of 1888 ed. 18.50 (ISBN 0-938998-00-5). Theosophy.
--Studies in Occultism. LC 67-18822. 1973. 7.50 (ISBN 0-911500-08-1); pap. 4.00 (ISBN 0-911500-09-X). Theos U Pr.
--The Theosophical Glossary: A Photographic Reproduction of the Original Edition, As First Issued at London, England, 1892. Mead, G. R., ed. & intro. by. vi, 389p. 1930. Repr. of 1892 ed. 8.50 (ISBN 0-938998-04-8). Theosophy.
--Transactions of the Blavatsky Lodge. LC 52-16841. 1946. 6.00 (ISBN 0-911500-10-3). Theos U Pr.
--Transactions of the Blavatsky Lodge of the Theosophical Society. xxiv, 149p. 1923. Repr. of 1890 ed. 5.00 (ISBN 0-938998-05-6). Theosophy.
--Voice of the Silence. LC 73-7619. 1970. pap. 2.50 (ISBN 0-8356-0380-6, Quest). Theos Pub Hse.
--The Voice of the Silence: Verbatim with 1889 ed. LC 76-25345. 1976. 5.00 (ISBN 0-911500-04-9); pap. 2.75 (ISBN 0-911500-05-7). Theos U Pr.
Blavatsky, Helena P., tr. & intro. by. The Voice of the Silence: Chosen Fragments from the Book of the Golden Precepts. iv, 110p. 1928. Repr. of 1889 ed. 3.00 (ISBN 0-938998-06-4). Theosophy.
Blavatsky, Helena P., et al. Karma Lore: One. 71p. (Orig.). 1983. pap. 3.95 (ISBN 0-912181-02-8). East School Pr.
Blavatsky, Helene. The Theophysical Glossary. lib. bdg. 69.95 (ISBN 0-87968-487-9). Krishna Pr.
Blavatsky, Helene P. Complete Works, 10 vols. 4000.00 (ISBN 0-87968-918-8). Gordon Pr.
--The Secret Doctrine, 2 vols. 250.00 (ISBN 0-8490-1010-1). Gordon Pr.
--Theosophical Glossary. LC 74-142546. 1971. Repr. of 1892 ed. 46.00x (ISBN 0-8103-3679-0). Gale.
Blawis, Patricia B. Tijerina & the Land Grants: Mexican Americans in Struggle for Their Heritage. LC 79-175178. (Illus.). 192p. (Orig.). 1971. pap. 2.65 (ISBN 0-7178-0337-6). Intl Pubs Co.
Blaxall, Martha, ed. Women & the Workplace: The Implications of Occupational Segregation. LC 76-10536. 312p. 1976. lib. bdg. 20.00x (ISBN 0-226-05821-2); pap. 8.95x (ISBN 0-226-05822-0). U of Chicago Pr.
Blaxland, G. Cuthbert. Mayflower Essays: On the Story of the Pilgrim Fathers, As Told in Governor Bradford's Ms. History of the Plimoth Plantation. LC 78-39713. (Essay Index Reprint Ser.). Repr. of 1896 ed. 13.00 (ISBN 0-8369-2748-6). Ayer Co Pubs.
Blaxter, J. H., ed. Advances in Marine Biology, Vol. 22. (Serial Publication Ser.). Date not set. 57.00 (ISBN 0-12-026122-7). Acad Pr.
Blaxter, J. H., et al, eds. Advances in Marine Biology, Vol. 17. LC 63-14040. (Serial Publication Ser.). 1980. 85.00 (ISBN 0-12-026117-0). Acad Pr.
--Advances in Marine Biology, Vol. 19. (Serial Publication Ser.). 1982. 75.00 (ISBN 0-12-026119-7). Acad Pr.
--Advances in Marine Biology, Vol. 20. (Serial Publication Ser.). 1982. 75.00 (ISBN 0-12-026120-0). Acad Pr.
--Advances in Marine Biology, Vol. 18. (Serial Publication). 1980. 93.00 (ISBN 0-12-026118-9). Acad Pr.
Blaxter, K., ed. Food Chains & Human Nutrition. (Illus.). 459p. 1980. 64.75 (ISBN 0-85334-863-4, Pub. by Elsevier Applied Sci England). Elsevier.
--Food, Nutrition & Climate. Fowden, L. (Illus.). 422p. 1982. 72.25 (ISBN 0-85334-107-9, Pub. by Elsevier Applied Sci England). Elsevier.
Blaxter, Mildred. The Health of the Children. (SSRC-DHSS Studies in Deprivation & Disadvantages: No. 3). 1982. text ed. 30.00x (ISBN 0-435-82034-6). Gower Pub Co.
Blaxter, Mildred & Paterson, Elizabeth. Mothers & Daughters: A Three-Dimensional Study of Health Attitudes & Behaviour. (SSRC-DHSS Studies in Deprivation & Disadvantages: No. 5). viii, 211p. 1982. text ed. 29.00x (ISBN 0-435-82055-9). Gower Pub Co.
Blaxton, John. The English Usurer: Or, Usury Condemned. LC 73-6102. (English Experience Ser.: No. 578). 80p. 1973. Repr. of 1634 ed. 9.50 (ISBN 90-221-0578-4). Walter J Johnson.
Blay, Cecil J. It Is Written. 1968. pap. text ed. 2.00 (ISBN 0-910424-63-2). Concordant.
--It Is Written. 1968. text ed. 4.00 (ISBN 0-910424-62-4). Concordant.
Blay, Gillian L., jt. auth. see Collins, Garfield L.
Blaydes, Sophia B. & Bordinat, Philip. Sir William Davenant: An Annotated Bibliography. LC 84-45395. (Literature Ser.). 250p. 1985. lib. bdg. 33.00 (ISBN 0-8240-8874-3). Garland Pub.
Blaydes, Sophia B., jt. auth. see Bordinat, Philip.
Blaylock, Enid V. Librespouse. LC 81-7985. 185p. 1984. 10.95 (ISBN 0-87949-202-3). Ashley Bks.
Blaylock, James. The Elfin Ship. 352p. 1982. pap. 2.75 (ISBN 0-345-29491-2, Del Rey). Ballantine.
Blaylock, James P. The Digging Leviathan. 288p. 1984. pap. 2.95 (ISBN 0-441-14800-X). Ace Bks.
--The Disappearing Dwarf. 288p. (Orig.). 1983. pap. 2.75 (ISBN 0-345-30376-8, Del Rey). Ballantine.
Blayne, Diana. Color Love Blue. (Candlelight Ecstacy Supreme Ser.: No. 49). (Orig.). 1984. pap. 2.50 (ISBN 0-440-11341-5). Dell.
--Dark Surrender. (Candlelight Ecstasy Ser.: No. 184). 192p. (Orig.). 1983. pap. 1.95 (ISBN 0-440-11833-6). Dell.
--A Loving Arrangement. (Candlelight Ecstacy Ser.: No. 113). (Orig.). 1983. pap. 1.95 (ISBN 0-440-15026-4). Dell.
--Night of the Unicorn. (Candlelight Supreme Ser.: No. 110). (Orig.). 1986. pap. 2.75 (ISBN 0-440-16382-X). Dell.
--A Waiting Game. (Candlelight Ecstasy Ser.: No. 94). (Orig.). 1982. pap. 1.95 (ISBN 0-440-19570-5). Dell.
--White Sand, Wild Sea. (Candlelight Ecstasy Ser.: No. 138). (Orig.). 1983. pap. 1.95 (ISBN 0-440-19627-2). Dell.
Blayney, Margaret S., ed. see Chartier, Alain.
Blayney, Peter W. The Texts of King Lear & Their Origins, Vol. 1: Nicholas Okes & the First Quarto. LC 77-82485. (New Cambridge Shakespeare Studies & Supplementary Text Ser.). (Illus.). 1983. 99.00 (ISBN 0-521-22634-1). Cambridge U Pr.
Blaze, Francois H. L' Academie Imperiale De Musique: Histoire Litteraire, Musicale, Politique et Galant De Ce Theatre, De 1645 a 1855, 2 vols. LC 80-2258. Repr. of 1855 ed. 95.00 (ISBN 0-404-18804-4). AMS Pr.
--De l'Opera en France, 2 vols. LC 80-2259. Repr. of 1820 ed. Set. 82.50 (ISBN 0-404-18810-9). AMS Pr.
--L' Opera-Italien de 1548 a 1856. LC 80-2260. Repr. of 1856 ed. 52.00 (ISBN 0-404-18807-9). AMS Pr.
Blaze, Wayne & Nero, John. College Degrees for Adults. LC 78-53779. 1979. 16.95x (ISBN 0-8070-3156-9). Beacon Pr.
Blaze De Bury, Ange H. Meyerbeer et Son Temps. LC 80-2257. Repr. of 1865 ed. 40.50 (ISBN 0-404-18813-3). AMS Pr.
Blaze De Bury, Yetta. French Literature of Today. LC 68-8223. 1969. Repr. of 1898 ed. 19.50x (ISBN 0-8046-0103-8, Pub. by Kennikat). Assoc Faculty Pr.
Blazek, Doug. I Advance with a Loaded Rose. 1969. pap. 3.50 (ISBN 0-912136-06-5). Twowindows Pr.
--Skull Juices. (Orig.). 1970. pap. 4.25 (ISBN 0-912136-22-7); pap. 10.00x signed ed. (ISBN 0-685-04867-5). Twowindows Pr.
Blazek, Douglas. Exercises in Memorizing Myself. 1976. pap. 4.75 (ISBN 0-685-79276-5, Pub. by Twowindows Pr). Small Pr Dist.
--Flux & Reflux. pap. 2.50 (ISBN 0-685-04668-0). Oyez.
Blazek, Douglas, ed. A Charles Bukowski Sampler. 3rd ed. 1979. pap. 3.00 (ISBN 0-686-60609-4). Quixote.
Blazek, Ron. Influencing Students Toward Media Center Use: An Experimental Investigation in Mathematics. LC 75-26769. (Studies in Librarianship Ser.: No. 5). 238p. 1975. pap. text ed. 9.00x (ISBN 0-8389-0201-4). ALA.
Blazek, Ron, ed. Achieving Accountability: Readings on the Evaluation of Media Centers. 280p. 1981. pap. text ed. 14.50x (ISBN 0-8389-0349-5). ALA.
Blazer, Dan G., jt. ed. see Busse, Ewald W.
Blazer, Don. Natural Western Riding. 1979. 14.95 (ISBN 0-395-28476-7). HM.
Blazer, Howard A. Angels, Their Origin, Nature, Mission & Destiny. 64p. 1974. pap. 2.50x (ISBN 0-88428-034-9). Parchment Pr.
Blazer, Stuart. Ricochet. 51p. (Orig.). 1983. pap. 4.50 (ISBN 0-914278-39-8). Copper Beech.
Blazi, Peter, jt. auth. see Whiting, Eldene.
Blazier, Kenneth D. Building an Effective Church School: Guide for the Superintendent & Board of Christian Education. LC 75-42018. 64p. 1976. pap. 1.95 (ISBN 0-8170-0708-3). Judson.
--Una Escuela Biblica: A Growing Church School. De Olivieri, Evelyn R., tr. from Eng. 64p. (Span.). 1981. pap. 3.25 (ISBN 0-8170-0928-0). Judson.
--A Growing Church School. 1978. pap. text ed. 2.50 (ISBN 0-8170-0785-7). Judson.
--Workbook for Planning Christian Education. 48p. 1983. pap. 4.95 (ISBN 0-8170-0996-5). Judson.
Blazier, Kenneth D. & Huber, Evelyn M. Planning Christian Education in Your Church. LC 73-19585. 32p. (Orig.). 1974. pap. 1.00 (ISBN 0-8170-0633-8); pap. 2.95 spanish ed (ISBN 0-8170-0685-0). Judson.
Blazier, Kenneth D., ed. The Teaching Church at Work. 64p. 1980. pap. 4.25 (ISBN 0-8170-0879-9). Judson.
Blazier, William H. Lights! Action! Camera! Learn! LC 74-80347. 1974. 10.00 (ISBN 0-686-10561-3). Allison Pubs.
Blazquez, Jose M. Diccionario De las Religiones Prerromanas De Hispania. 192p. (Espn.). 1975. pap. 9.95 (ISBN 84-7090-071-4, S-50058). French & Eur.
Blazynski, George. Flashpoint Poland. 1980. 46.00 (ISBN 0-08-024638-9). Pergamon.
Blazynski, T. Z. Applied Elasto-Plasticity of Solids. (Illus.). 272p. 1984. text ed. 39.50x (ISBN 0-317-18202-1). Scholium Intl.
Blazynski, T. Z., ed. Explosive Welding, Forming & Compaction. LC 82-222627. (Illus.). 402p. 1983. 72.25 (ISBN 0-85334-166-4, I-461-82, Pub. by Elsevier Applied Sci England). Elsevier.
Bleach, Mervyn. CZ125, 175, & 175 Trail '69 - '76. (Owners Workshop Manuals Ser.: No. 185). 1979. 10.50 (ISBN 0-85696-185-X, Pub. by J H Haynes England). Haynes Pubns.
--Garelli Mopeds 'Seventy-Two to 'Seventy-Eight. 10.50 (ISBN 0-85696-189-2, 189). Haynes Pubns.
--Honda C50, C70 & C90 '72 - '81. (Illus.). pap. 10.50 (ISBN 0-85696-324-0, 324). Haynes Pubns.
--Honda Owner's Workshop Manual: XR75 Dirt Bikes '72-78. (Owners Workshop Manuals Ser.: No. 287). 1979. 10.50 (ISBN 0-85696-287-2, Pub. by J H Haynes England). Haynes Pubns.
--Honda XR 75 Dirt Bikes '72 -'78. (Owners Workshop Manual Ser.). 10.50 (ISBN 0-85696-287-2, 287). Haynes Pubns.
--Moped Owners Workshop Manual: Garelli Mopeds '69 Thru '78. new ed. (Owners Workshop Manuals Ser.: No. 189). 1979. 10.50 (ISBN 0-85696-189-2, Pub. by J H Haynes England). Haynes Pubns.
Bleackley, Horace. Ladies Fair & Frail. (Biographical Reference Work Ser.). xiv, 328p. 1985. Repr. of 1909 ed. 39.00 (ISBN 0-932051-26-X). Am Repr Serv.
Bleakley, Alan. Fruits of the Moon Tree: The Medicine Wheel & Transpersonal Psychology. (Illus.). 311p. 1985. 12.95 (ISBN 0-946551-08-1, Pub. by Gateway Bks); pap. 9.95 (ISBN 0-946551-10-3). Interbook.
Bleakley, David. Sadie Patterson: Irish Peacemaker. (Illus.). 118p. 1980. pap. 8.95 (ISBN 0-85640-224-9, Pub. by Blackstaff Pr). Longwood Pub Group.
Bleakley, Horace. The Hangmen of England. (Illus.). 1977. Repr. of 1929 ed. 29.00x (ISBN 0-7158-1184-3). Charles River Bks.
Bleakley, Robert. African Masks. LC 77-95303. (Art for All Ser.). 1978. pap. 5.95 (ISBN 0-312-00970-4). St Martin.
Bleakmore, Mary, jt. auth. see Putter, Eileen.
Bleakney, Thomas. Retirement Systems for Public Employees. 1972. 15.00 (ISBN 0-256-01407-8). Irwin.
Bleaney, B., jt. auth. see Bleaney, B. I.
Bleaney, B. I. & Bleaney, B. Electricity & Magnetism. 3rd ed. (Illus.). 1976. pap. 29.95x (ISBN 0-19-851141-8). Oxford U Pr.
Bleaney, M. Underconsumption Theories: A History & Critical Analysis. pap. text ed. 14.00x (ISBN 0-8464-0945-3). Beekman Pubs.
Bleaney, Michael. The Rise & Fall of Keynesian Economics: An Investigation of Its Contribution to Capitalist Development. LC 84-17746. 256p. 1984. 29.95 (ISBN 0-312-68267-0). St Martin.
Bleaney, Michael F. Underconsumption Theories. LC 76-26935. 262p. 1977. pap. 3.95 (ISBN 0-7178-0476-3). Intl Pubs Co.
Bleasdale, Alan. Are You Lonesome Tonight. LC 85-6988. 80p. (Orig.). 1985. pap. 7.95 (ISBN 0-571-13732-6). Faber & Faber.
Bleasdale, J. K. Plant Physiology in Relation to Horticulture. 1977. text ed. 13.50 (ISBN 0-87055-239-2). AVI.
Bleasdale, J. K., jt. auth. see Salter, P. J.
Bleasdale, J. K., jt. ed. see Salter, P. J.
Bleasdale, John E., et al, eds. Inositol & Phosphoinositides. Eicberg, J. & Hauser, G. LC 84-131. (Experimental Biology & Medicine Ser.). (Illus.). 720p. 1985. 69.50 (ISBN 0-89603-074-1). Humana.
Blease, W. Lyon. The Emancipation of English Women. LC 78-173103. Repr. of 1910 ed. 24.50 (ISBN 0-405-08274-6, Blom Pubns). Ayer Co Pubs.
Bleau, Barbara L. Forgotten Algebra: A Refresher Course. (Barron's Educational Ser.). 1983. pap. text ed. 8.95 (ISBN 0-8120-2438-9). Barron.
Bleazard, G. B. Program Design Methods: Results of an NCC Study. LC 78-314354. 1976. pap. 15.50x (ISBN 0-85012-164-7). Intl Pubns Serv.
--Teleprocessing Monitor Packages for ICL 2903-04. 1978. pap. 34.50x (ISBN 0-85012-197-3). Intl Pubns Serv.
--Why Packet Switching. (Illus.). 174p. (Orig.). 1979. pap. 32.50x (ISBN 0-85012-194-9). Intl Pubns Serv.
Bleby, Henry. Josiah: The Maimed Fugitive. facs. ed. LC 76-89422. (Black Heritage Library Collection Ser.). 1873. 12.00 (ISBN 0-8369-8513-3). Ayer Co Pubs.
Blech, Gustavus M. & Lynch, Charles. Medical Tactics & Logistics. (Illus.). 205p. 1934. 18.50x (ISBN 0-398-04208-X). C C Thomas.
Blecha, Diane, jt. auth. see Timmermann, Tim.
Blecher, Arthur C., ed. see Butwin, Frances.
Blecher, Earl. Advocacy Planning for Urban Development: With Analysis of Six Demonstration Programs. LC 77-146890. (Special Studies in U.S. Economic, Social & Political Issues). 1971. 39.50x (ISBN 0-89197-650-7). Irvington.
Blecher, George, tr. see Kullman, Harry.
Blecher, George, tr. see Lagercrantz, Rose.
Blecher, Lone T., tr. see Kullman, Harry.
Blecher, M. & Gotow, K., eds. Low Energy Tests of Conservation Laws in Particle Physics: Conference Proceedings, Blacksburg, Virginia, 1983. LC 84-71157. (AIP Conference Proceedings: No. 114, Subseries on Particles & Fields No. 33). 322p. 1984. lib. bdg. 40.50 (ISBN 0-88318-313-7). Am Inst Physics.
Blecher, Marc J. & White, Gordon. Micropolitics in Contemporary China: A Technical Unit During & after the Cultural Revolution. LC 79-67176. 136p. 1980. 30.00 (ISBN 0-87332-136-7). M E Sharpe.
Blecher, Melvin, ed. Methods in Receptor Research, Pt. 1. (Methods in Molecular Biology Ser.: Vol. 9). 1976. 69.75 (ISBN 0-8247-6414-5). Dekker.
--Methods in Receptor Research, Pt. 2. (Methods in Molecular Biology Ser.: Vol. 9). 1976. 69.75 (ISBN 0-8247-6415-3). Dekker.
Blechman, Barry. National Security & Strategic Minerals: U. S. Dependence on Foreign Sources of Cobalt. (Westview Special Studies in National Security & Defense Policy). 90p. 1985. softcover 14.50x (ISBN 0-8133-7038-8). Westview.
Blechman, Barry M. The Changing Soviet Navy. (Studies in Defense Policy). 1973. pap. 6.95 (ISBN 0-8157-0995-1). Brookings.
--The Control of Naval Armaments: Prospects & Possibilities. LC 75-5153. (Brookings Institution Studies in Defense Policy Ser.). pap. 27.50 (ISBN 0-317-30180-2, 2025362). Bks Demand UMI.
--National Security & Strategic Minerals. 96p. 1985. 14.50 (ISBN 0-8133-7038-8). CSI Studies.
Blechman, Barry M. & Kaplan, Stephen S. Force Without War: U. S. Armed Forces As a Political Instrument. 1978. 31.95 (ISBN 0-8157-0986-2); pap. 14.95 (ISBN 0-8157-0985-4). Brookings.
Blechman, Barry M., ed. Preventing Nuclear War: A Realistic Approach. LC 84-43115. (Publication Series of the Soviet Union in the 1980s). 224p. 1985. 22.50x (ISBN 0-253-34601-0); pap. 9.95 (ISBN 0-253-20350-3). Ind U Pr.
--Rethinking the U. S. Strategic Posture. LC 82-11436. 320p. 1982. pap. 14.95x prof ref (ISBN 0-88410-910-0). Ballinger Pub.
--Toward a More Effective Defense: Report of the Defense Organization Project. 264p. 1985. ref. ed. 28.00 (ISBN 0-88730-026-X). Ballinger Pub.
Blechman, Barry M. & Luttwak, Edward N., eds. The International Security Yearbook, 1983-1984. 200p. 1984. 29.95 (ISBN 0-312-42340-3); pap. 11.95 (ISBN 0-312-42341-1). St Martin.
--International Security Yearbook: 1984-85. 280p. 1985. 33.00x (ISBN 0-8133-0206-4); pap. text ed. 15.95 (ISBN 0-8133-0207-2). Westview.
Blechman, Barry M., et al. The Soviet Military Buildup & U. S. Defense Spending. LC 77-86492. (Brookings Institution Studies in Defense Policy Ser.). pap. 20.00 (ISBN 0-317-30181-0, 2025363). Bks Demand UMI.
Blechman, Barry M., et al see Pechman, Joseph A.
Blechman, Burt. How Much. 1961. 7.95 (ISBN 0-8392-1050-7). Astor-Honor.
Blechman, Elaine A. Solving Child Behavior Problems at Home & at School. LC 85-61468. 300p. (Orig.). 1985. pap. 15.95 (ISBN 0-87822-247-2). Res Press.

Blechman, Elaine A., ed. Behavior Modification with Women. LC 82-15655. 541p. 1983. text ed. 35.00 (ISBN 0-89862-625-0, 2625). Guilford Pr.

Blechman, Fred. Apple IIc: An Intelligent Guide. 1985. FPT 17.95 (ISBN 0-03-001749-1). CBS Ed.

--Programs for Beginners on the TRS-80. (Illus.). 150p. 1981. pap. 10.95 (ISBN 0-8104-5182-4). Hayden.

Blechman, Fred, et al. Encyclopedia for the TRS-80, Vol. 6. Putnam, Katherine & Comiskey, Kate, eds. (Illus.). 303p. 1982. 19.95 (ISBN 0-88006-040-9, EN8106); pap. 10.95 (ISBN 0-88006-041-7, EN8086). Green Pub Inc.

Blechman, Mark, jt. auth. see Fox, Donna R.

Blechman, R. O. R. O. Blechman: Behind the Lines. LC 80-15191. (Illus.). 188p. 1980. 32.50 (ISBN 0-933920-07-5). Hudson Hills.

Blechmma, Michael D. & Standish, Peter D. Marketing Institute. LC 83-62214. (Corporate Law & Practice Course Handbook: No. 427). 1983. write for info. PLI.

Blechschmidt, E. The Beginnings of Human Life. Transemantics, Inc., tr. from Ger. LC 77-16658. (Heidelberg Science Library). (Illus.). 1977. pap. 17.00 (ISBN 0-387-90249-X). Springer-Verlag.

Blechschmidt, E. & Gasser, R. F. Biokinetics & Biodynamics of Human Differentiation: Principles & Applications. (Illus.). 304p. 1978. photocopy ed. 46.75x (ISBN 0-398-03654-3). C C Thomas.

Blechschmidt, Meinulf. Der Leib und das Heil. (European University Studies: No. 23, Vol. 207). 435p. (Ger.). 1983. 22.10 (ISBN 3-261-03264-2). P Lang Pubs.

Bleck, Eugene E. & Nagel, Donald, eds. Physically Handicapped Children: A Medical Atlas for Teachers. 2nd ed. 560p. 1981. 38.00 (ISBN 0-8089-1391-3, 790623). Grune.

Bleck, Eugene E., et al. Atlas of Plaster Cast Techniques. 2nd ed. (Illus.). 160p. 1974. pap. 26.50 (ISBN 0-8151-0910-5). Year Bk Med.

Bleck, Robert T., jt. auth. see Araoz, Daniel L.

Blecke, Curtis J. & Gotthilf, Daniel L. Financial Analysis for Decision Making. 272p. 1980. 39.95 (ISBN 0-13-315234-0). P-H.

Bleckman, Isaac A. Death & Dying A to Z. LC 80-65302. 1985. 69.00 (ISBN 0-87514-007-6). Croner.

Blecourt, J. J. de see De Blecourt, J. J.

Bledsoe, Albert T. Essay on Liberty & Slavery. facs. ed. LC 72-149864. (Black Heritage Library Collection Ser). 1856. 20.25 (ISBN 0-8369-8746-2). Ayer Co Pubs.

--An Examination of President Edwards' Inquiry into the Freedom of the Will. LC 75-3003. Repr. of 1845 ed. 18.00 (ISBN 0-404-59047-0). AMS Pr.

--The Philosophy of Mathematics. LC 75-3004. Repr. of 1868 ed. 20.00 (ISBN 0-404-59048-9). AMS Pr.

Bledsoe, Brian. Atlas of Paramedic Skills. (Illus.). 352p. 1985. pap. 24.95 (ISBN 0-89303-444-4). Brady Comm.

Bledsoe, Bryan E. Manual of Emergency Drugs. LC 83-10034. (Illus.). 1983. pap. 9.95 (ISBN 0-89303-647-1). Brady Comm.

Bledsoe, Bryan E. & Bosker, Gideon. Prehospital Emergency Pharmacology. LC 83-15893. 336p. pap. text ed. 16.95 (ISBN 0-89303-765-6). Brady Comm.

Bledsoe, Caroline H. Women & Marriage in Kpelle Society. LC 78-66170. (Illus.). 233p. 1980. 22.50x (ISBN 0-8047-1019-8). Stanford U Pr.

Bledsoe, Dennis, jt. ed. see Cutino, Peter.

Bledsoe, Jane K., ed. Anders Zorn Rediscovered. (Orig.). 1984. pap. 10.00 (ISBN 0-936270-23-3). Art Mus Gall.

Bledsoe, Jane K., ed. see Keyes, Roger & Matsudaira, Susumu.

Bledsoe, Jerry. Carolina Curiosities: Jerry Bledsoe's Outlandish Guide to the Dadblamest Things to See & Do in North Carolina. LC 83-49042. 224p. 1984. pap. 7.95 (ISBN 0-88742-007-9). East Woods.

--Just Folks: Visitin' with Carolina People. LC 80-36880. (Illus.). 208p. 1980. 9.95 (ISBN 0-914788-31-0). East Woods.

--Where's Mark Twain When We Really Need Him? 183p. 1982. 9.95 (ISBN 0-9610320-0-6). Grape Hill Pr.

Bledsoe, John T. The Bledsoe Family. LC 73-75223. (Illus.). pap. 74.50 (ISBN 0-317-09105-0, 2050419). Bks Demand UMI.

Bledsoe, Robert L. & Boczek, Boleslaw A. The International Law Dictionary. (Clio Dictionaries in Political Science Ser.: No. 11). 400p. 1986. 40.00 (ISBN 0-87436-406-X). ABC-Clio.

Bledsoe, Samuel T. Indian Land Laws. Bruchey, Stuart, ed. LC 78-53557. (Development of Public Land Law in the U. S. Ser.). 1979. Repr. of 1909 ed. lib. bdg. 47.50x (ISBN 0-405-11369-2). Ayer Co Pubs.

Bledsoe, Shirley, jt. auth. see McKenzie, Joy.

Bledsoe, Shirley, jt. auth. see MacKenzie, Joy.

Bledsoe, Thomas. Meanwhile Back at the Henhouse: A Novel. LC 82-71306. 185p. 1966. 4.95 (ISBN 0-8040-0197-9, Pub by Swallow). Ohio U Pr.

Bledsoe, Thomas, tr. see Usigli, Rodolfo.

Bledsoe, W. W. & Loveland, Donald, eds. Automated Theorem Proving: After 25 Years. LC 84-9226. (Contemporary Mathematics Ser.: Vol. 29). 366p. 1984. pap. 30.00 (ISBN 0-8218-5027-X). Am Math.

Bledsoe, Wayne. The Advent of Civilization. (Problems in European Civilization Ser.). 204p. 1975. pap. text ed. 4.95x (ISBN 0-669-94714-8). Heath.

Bledstein, Burton J. The Culture of Professionalism: The Middle Class & the Development of Higher Education in America. 1976. 12.95 (ISBN 0-393-05574-4, Norton Lib); pap. 7.95x 1978 (ISBN 0-393-00891-6). Norton.

Blee, Ben W. Battleship North Carolina. Conlon, Frank S. & Judd, Amo F., eds. (Illus.). 100p. 1982. 14.95 (ISBN 0-9608538-0-4); pap. 8.95 (ISBN 0-9608538-1-2). USS North Car.

Bleeck, Arthur H. Avesta: The Religious Books of the Parsees. lib. bdg. 79.95 (ISBN 0-87968-133-0). Krishna Pr.

Bleeck, Oliver. The Brass Go-Between. LC 82-48806. 224p. 1983. pap. 2.84i (ISBN 0-06-080645-1, P 645, PL). Har-Row.

--The Highbinders. LC 83-48946. 224p. 1984. pap. 2.84i (ISBN 0-06-080702-4, P 702, PL). Har-Row.

--No Questions Asked. 240p. 1984. pap. 2.84i (ISBN 0-06-080703-2, P 703, PL). Har-Row.

--Protocol for a Kidnapping. LC 82-48807. 256p. 1983. pap. 2.84i (ISBN 0-06-080646-X, P 646, PL). Har-Row.

Bleecker, Ann E. Posthumous Works. LC 70-104419. Repr. of 1793 ed. lib. bdg. 15.00 (ISBN 0-8398-0167-X). Irvington.

Bleecker, D. D., jt. auth. see Booss, B.

Bleecker, Joyce, jt. auth. see Kromer, Thomas.

Bleed, Peter. Archaeology of Petaga Point: The Preceramic Component. LC 75-626260. (Minnesota Prehistoric Archaeology Ser.: No. 2). 51p. 1969. pap. 3.00 (ISBN 0-87351-049-6). Minn Hist.

Bleedorn, Berenice & McKelvey, Sara. Humor: Lessons in Laughter for Learning & Living. (Illus.). 28p. (Orig.). (gr. 3-12). 1984. 3.95 (ISBN 0-88047-042-9, 8407). DOK Pubs.

Bleedorn, Bernice D. Looking Ahead: Tested Ideas in Future Studies. (Illus.). 36p. (Orig.). 1981. pap. text ed. 4.95 (ISBN 0-914634-92-5). DOK Pubs.

Bleehan & Glatstein. Radiation Therapy Planning, Vol. 1. (Fundamentals of Cancer Management). 792p. 1983. 77.50 (ISBN 0-8247-1830-5). Dekker.

Bleehen, N. M., ed. Ovarian Cancer. (Illus.). 180p. 1985. 55.00 (ISBN 0-387-13326-7). Springer-Verlag.

Bleek, Dorothea F. A Bushman Dictionary. (American Oriental Society: Vol. 41). 1956. pap. 11.00x (ISBN 0-940490-41-2). Am Orient Soc.

--The Naron: A Bushman Tribe of the Central Kalahari. LC 76-44692. Repr. of 1928 ed. 10.50 (ISBN 0-404-15908-7). AMS Pr.

Bleek, Oliver. The Procane Chronicle. LC 82-48808. 224p. 1983. pap. 2.84i (ISBN 0-06-080647-8, P 647, PL). Har-Row.

Bleek, Whilhelm H. & Lloyd, Lucy C. Specimens of Bushman Folklore. LC 78-67687. (The Folktale). (Illus.). Repr. of 1911 ed. 37.00 (ISBN 0-404-16056-5). AMS Pr.

Bleek, Wilhelm, jt. auth. see Sontheimer, Kurt.

Bleek, Wilhelm H. Reynard the Fox in South Africa. LC 78-67686. (The Folktale). Repr. of 1864 ed. 17.50 (ISBN 0-404-16055-7). AMS Pr.

Bleeker, G. M., et al, eds. Orbital Disorders. (Illus.). 1978. lib. bdg. 34.00 (ISBN 90-6193-570-9, Pub. by Junk Pubs Netherlands). Kluwer Academic.

Bleeker, G. M., et al, eds. see International Symposium on Orbital Disorders, 2nd, Amsterdam, May 1973.

Bleeker, P. Explanatory Notes to the Land Limitation & Agricultural Land Use Potential Map of Papua New Guinea. (Land Research Ser.: No. 36). (Illus.). 1977. pap. 10.00x (ISBN 0-643-00164-6, Pub. by CSIRO). Intl SPEC Bk.

Bleeker, Pieter. Atlas Ichtyologique des Indes Orientales Neerlandaises. Repr. of 1862 ed. Vol. 1, 168 Pp. 1977 50.00x (ISBN 0-87474-234-X); Vol. 2, 112 Pp. 1979 50.00x (ISBN 0-87474-236-6); Vol. 3, 150 Pp. 1981 50.00x (ISBN 0-87474-237-4). Smithsonian.

--Atlas Ichtyologique des Indes Orientales Neerlandaises, Vol. IV: Murenes, Symbranches, et Leptocephales. 2nd ed. LC 82-80033. (Illus.). 132p. (Fr.). 1985. Repr. of 1862 ed. 50.00x (ISBN 0-87474-226-9, BLA4). Smithsonian.

--Atlas Ichtyologique Indes Orientales Neerlandaises, Vols. 11-14. (Atlas of Fishes of the Dutch East Indies). (Illus.). 200p. 1983. text ed. 250.00x (ISBN 0-87474-240-4). Smithsonian.

Bleeker, Samuel E. The Politics of Architecture: The Buildings of Nelson A. Rockefeller. (Illus.). 256p. 1981. 50.00 (ISBN 0-8317-0389-X, Rutledge Pr). Smith Pubs.

Bleeker, Sonia. The Apache Indians: Raiders of the Southwest. (Illus.). (gr. 4-7). 1951. PLB 10.88 (ISBN 0-688-31046-X). Morrow.

--The Cherokee: Indians of the Mountains. (Illus.). (gr. 3-6). 1952. PLB 10.88 (ISBN 0-688-31160-1). Morrow.

--The Chippewa Indians: Rice Gatherers of the Great Lakes. (Illus.). (gr. 3-6). 1955. PLB 10.88 (ISBN 0-688-31167-9). Morrow.

--The Delaware Indians: Eastern Fishermen & Farmers. (Illus.). (gr. 3-6). 1953. PLB 10.88 (ISBN 0-688-31230-6). Morrow.

--The Sioux Indians: Hunters & Warriors of the Plains. (Illus.). (gr. 3-6). 1962. PLB 10.88 (ISBN 0-688-31457-0). Morrow.

Bleekman, George, et al. Looking at Biology. rev. ed. (Illus.). 180p. 1983. 8.95x (ISBN 0-917962-80-X). Peek Pubns.

Blegen, C. W. & Rawson, M. Palace of Nestor at Pylos in Western Messehia, 3 vols. Incl. Vol. 1. The Buildings & Their Contents, 2 pts. 1966; Vol. 2. The Frescoes. Lang, M. 1969; Vol. 3. Acropolis & Lower Town, Tholois, Grave Circle, & Chamber Tombs, Discoveries Outside the Citadel. 1973. 80.00x (ISBN 0-691-03529-6). LC 65-17131. (Cincinnati Classical Studies Ser.). Princeton U Pr.

Blegen, Carl W., et al, eds. The Palace of Nestor at Pylos in Western Messenia: Acropolis & Lower Town; Tholoi, Grave Circle, & Chamber Tombs; Discoveries Outside the Citadel, Vol. III. LC 65-17131. (Illus.). pap. 91.00 (ISBN 0-317-10667-8, 2013032). Bks Demand UMI.

Blegen, Carl W., et al, eds. see Univerity of Cincinnati, Excavations in the Troad.

Blegen, Theodore. Norwegian Migration to America, 1825-1860, 2 Vols. LC 68-31271. (American History & Americana Ser., No. 47). 1969. Repr. of 1931 ed. lib. bdg. 79.95 (ISBN 0-8383-0330-7). Haskell.

Blegen, Theodore C. Grass Roots History. LC 75-85987. 1969. Repr. of 1947 ed. 22.50x (ISBN 0-8046-0602-1, Pub. by Kennikat). Assoc Faculty Pr.

--Kensington Rune Stone: New Light on an Old Riddle. LC 68-66739. (Illus.). 212p. 1968. 7.50 (ISBN 0-87351-044-5). Minn Hist.

--The Land Lies Open. LC 74-27727. 246p. 1975. Repr. of 1949 ed. lib. bdg. 17.00x (ISBN 0-8371-7912-2, BLLO). Greenwood.

--Minnesota: A History of the State. 2nd ed. LC 75-6116. (Illus.). 713p. 1975. 16.95x (ISBN 0-8166-0754-0). U of Minn Pr.

--Norwegian Migration to America, 1825-1860. LC 69-18759. (American Immigration Collection Ser., No. 1). 1969, Repr. of 1931 ed. 17.50 (ISBN 0-405-00507-5). Ayer Co Pubs.

--The Saga of Saga Hill. (Illus.). 85p. 1971. Repr. of 1970 ed. 6.95 (ISBN 0-87351-068-2). Minn Hist.

Blegen, Theodore C. & Davidson, Sarah A., eds. Iron Face. 1950. 15.00 (ISBN 0-940550-00-8). Caxton Club.

Blegen, Theodore C. & Ruud, Martin B., eds. Norwegian Emigrant Songs & Ballads. LC 78-15211. (Scandinavians in America Ser.). 1979. Repr. of 1936 ed. lib. bdg. 27.50x (ISBN 0-405-11633-0). Ayer Co Pubs.

Blegen, Theodore C., ed. see Heg, Hans C.

Blegen, Theodore C., ed. see Neill, Edward D.

Blegen, Theodore C., ed. & tr. see Rynning, Ole.

Blegvad, B. M., ed. European Yearbook in Law & Sociology. (European Studies in Law & Sociology). 1979. lib. bdg. 39.00 (ISBN 90-247-2158-X, Pub. by Martinus Nijhoff Netherlands). Kluwer Academic.

Blegvad, B. M., et al, eds. European Yearbook in Law & Sociology: 1977. 1977. lib. bdg. 24.00 (ISBN 90-247-2017-6, Pub. by Martinus Nijhoff Netherlands). Kluwer Academic.

Blegvad, Erik, illus. The Three Little Pigs. LC 80-10410. (Illus.). 32p. (ps-4). 1980. 11.95 (ISBN 0-689-50139-0, McElderry Bk); 2.95 (ISBN 0-689-71040-2). Atheneum.

Blegvad, Lenore. Anna Banana & Me. LC 84-457. (Illus.). 32p. (ps-3). 1985. 9.95 (ISBN 0-689-50274-5, McElderry Bk). Atheneum.

Blegvad, Lenore, compiled by. Mittens for Kittens: And Other Rhymes About Cats. LC 74-76269. (Illus.). 32p. (ps-3). 1974. 5.95 (ISBN 0-689-50003-3, McElderry Bk). Atheneum.

Blegvad, Lenore, ed. The Parrot in the Garret & Other Rhymes About Dwellings. LC 81-10859. (Illus.). 32p. (ps-3). 1982. PLB 8.95 (ISBN 0-689-50217-6, Mcelderry Bk). Atheneum.

Blegvad, Lenore, compiled by. This Little Pig-a-Wig: And Other Rhymes about Pigs. LC 78-7015. (Illus.). 32p. (ps-3). 1978. 7.95 (ISBN 0-689-50110-2, McElderry Bk). Atheneum.

Blehar, M. C., jt. auth. see Ainsworth, M. D.

Bleher, Petra, jt. auth. see Vriends, Matthew M.

Bleher, Petra, tr. see Nicolai, Jurgen.

Blehl, Vincent F. John Henry Newman: A Bibliograhical Catalogue of His Writings. LC 77-12141. 148p. 1978. 17.50x (ISBN 0-8139-0738-1). U Pr of Va.

Blei, Norbert. Adventures in an American's Literature. 224p. (Orig.). 1982. pap. 5.95 (ISBN 0-933180-41-1). Ellis Pr.

--Door Steps: The Days, the Seasons. 288p. 1983. 14.95 (ISBN 0-933180-44-6). Ellis Pr.

--Door to Door. 242p. 1985. 14.95 (ISBN 0-933180-73-X). Ellis Pr.

--The Door Way. 320p. 1981. 14.95 (ISBN 0-933180-22-5). Ellis Pr.

--The Second Novel. LC 77-91291. (Illus.). 245p. 1978. pap. 6.00 (ISBN 0-913204-09-9). December Pr.

Blei, R. C. & Sidney, S. J., eds. Lectures in Banach Spaces Harmonic Analysis & Probability Theory. (Lecture Notes in Mathematics: Vol. 995). 173p. 1983. pap. 12.00 (ISBN 0-387-12314-8). Springer-Verlag.

Bleiberg, Aaron H. & Leubling, Harry. Parents Guide to Cleft Palate Habilitation: The Team Approach. 1971. 10.00 (ISBN 0-682-47183-6, University). Exposition Pr FL.

Bleiberg, German. Diccionario de Historia de Espana, 3 vols. 3776p. (Span.). 1979. Set. pap. 70.00 (ISBN 84-206-5997-5, S-50374). French & Eur.

--Diccionario de Historia de Espana, 3 vols. 3776p. (Span.). 1979. Set. 100.00 (ISBN 84-206-5298-9, S-10785). French & Eur.

Bleibreu, John, ed. Interviews with Oscar Ichazo. LC 81-70539. 190p. 1982. 14.95 (ISBN 0-916554-02-3); pap. 8.95 (ISBN 0-916554-03-1). Arica Inst Pr.

Bleibtreu, John, ed. see Ichazo, Oscar.

Bleich, Alan. Exploring Careers in Medicine. (Careers in Depth Ser.). 140p. 1983. lib. bdg. 8.97 (ISBN 0-8239-0613-2). Rosen Group.

Bleich, D. J. Contemporary Halakhic Problems, Vol. I. (The Library of Jewish Law & Ethics: No. 4). 20.00x (ISBN 0-87068-450-7). Ktav.

Bleich, David. Readings & Feelings: An Introduction to Subjective Criticism. LC 74-84482. 114p. 1975. pap. 5.25 (ISBN 0-8141-3921-3). NCTE.

--Subjective Criticism. LC 77-12968. 320p. 1978. text ed. 28.50x (ISBN 0-8018-2032-4); pap. 9.95x (ISBN 0-8018-2093-6). Johns Hopkins.

--Utopia: The Psychology of a Cultural Fantasy. Scholes, Robert, ed. LC 84-2537. (Studies in Speculative Fiction: No. 5). 160p. 1984. 29.95 (ISBN 0-8357-1574-4). UMI Res Pr.

--With Perfect Faith. 1982. 25.00x (ISBN 0-87068-891-X). Ktav.

Bleich, David J. Contemporary Halakhic Problems, Vol.II. 20.00x (ISBN 0-87068-275-X). Ktav.

--Judaism & Healing: Halakhic Perspectives. 1981. pap. 9.95 (ISBN 0-87068-890-1). Ktav.

Bleich, J. David. Contemporary Halakhic Problems, Vol. II. (The Library of Jewish Law & Ethics, Volume X). 423p. 1983. 20.00x (ISBN 0-87068-451-5). Ktav.

Bleich, Sondra. The Xerox 860 Made Easy. 21.95 (ISBN 0-8359-8943-7). Reston.

Bleicher, F. & Hu, W. C. Temmoku: A Study of Pottery & Tea Aesthetics. 1984. write for info (ISBN 0-89344-032-9). Ars Ceramica.

Bleicher, F., et al. Highlights of Pewabic Pottery. LC 77-92628. 1977. pap. 8.50 (ISBN 0-89344-015-9). ARS Ceramica.

Bleicher, Fred, jt. auth. see Bowes, James L.

Bleicher, Fred, jt. auth. see Swallow, Robert W.

Bleicher, Josef. Contemporary Hermeneutics: Hermeneutics As Method, Philosophy & Critique. 224p. 1980. 28.00x (ISBN 0-7100-0551-2); pap. 14.00x (ISBN 0-7100-0552-0). Routledge & Kegan.

--The Hermeneutic Imagination: Outline of a Positive Critique of Scientism & Sociology. 240p. 1982. pap. 9.95 (ISBN 0-7100-9257-1). Routledge & Kegan.

Bleicher, Sheldon, jt. auth. see Brodoff, Bernard N.

Bleick, Roy. Much More Than Giving. 112p. (Orig.). 1985. pap. 6.95 (ISBN 0-570-03951-7, 12-2886). Concordia.

Bleicken, Jochen. Lex Publica: Gesetz und Recht in der roemischen Republik. 1975. 58.00x (ISBN 3-11-004584-2). De Gruyter.

Bleier, Inge J. Bedside Maternity Nursing. 4th ed. LC 78-65374. (Illus.). 362p. 1979. pap. 13.00 (ISBN 0-7216-1743-3); wkbk. 11.95 (ISBN 0-7216-1747-6). Saunders.

Bleier, Rocky & O'Neil, Terry. Fighting Back. rev. ed. LC 75-12865. (Illus.). 240p. 1980. 14.95 (ISBN 0-8128-2767-8). Stein & Day.

--Fighting Back. (Illus.). 288p. 1976. pap. 2.75 (ISBN 0-446-95704-6). Warner Bks.

Bleier, Ruth. The Hypothalmus of the Guinea Pig: A Cytoarchitectronic Atlas. LC 83-47756. (Illus.). 176p. 1984. text ed. 50.00x (ISBN 0-299-09040-X). U of Wis Pr.

--The Hypothalmus of the Rhesus Monkey: A Cytoarchitectonic Atlas. LC 84-40146. (Illus.). 136p. 1984. text ed. 50.00x (ISBN 0-299-09890-7). U of Wis Pr.

--Science & Gender: A Critique of Biology & Its Theories on Women. (Athene Ser.). (Illus.). 250p. 1984. 25.00 (ISBN 0-08-030972-0); pap. 12.50 (ISBN 0-08-030971-2). Pergamon.

Bleier, Ruth, ed. Feminist Approaches to Science. (Athene Ser.). (Illus.). 224p. 1986. 25.00 (ISBN 0-08-032787-7, Pub. by P P I); pap. 11.50 (ISBN 0-08-032786-9). Pergamon.

Bleifeld. Encyclopedia of Biology Terms. 320p. Date not set. 6.95 (ISBN 0-8120-2511-3). Barron.

Bleifeld, Maurice. How to Prepare for the College Board Achievement Test - Biology. 7th ed. LC 81-3892. 352p. 1981. 9.50 (ISBN 0-8120-5416-4); pap. 7.95 (ISBN 0-8120-2345-5). Barron.

--Modern Biology at a Glance. LC 79-11789. 1979. pap. text ed. 4.95 (ISBN 0-8120-2064-2). Barron.

Bleifeld, Maurice, jt. auth. see Johnson, Gaylord.

Bleifeld, Maurice, ed. see Edwards, Gabrielle & Cimmino, Marion.

Bleifeld, W., et al, eds. Evaluation of Cardiac Function by Echocardiography. (Illus.). 210p. 1980. 43.00 (ISBN 0-387-10045-8). Springer-Verlag.

Bleikasten, Andre. Faulkner's As I Lay Dying. Little, Roger, tr. LC 72-79904. (Midland Bks.: No. 159). (Illus.). 192p. 1973. pap. 3.95x (ISBN 0-253-20159-4). Ind U Pr.

--The Most Splendid Failure: Faulkner's the Sound & the Fury. LC 75-22638. 288p. 1976. 12.50x (ISBN 0-253-33877-8). Ind U Pr.

Bleil, D. F., ed. Natural Electromagnetic Phenomena Below Thirty KCS. LC 64-25831. 470p. 1964. 49.50x (ISBN 0-306-30171-7, Plenum Pr). Plenum Pub.

Bleiler, ed. Three Gothic Novels. Bd. with The Vampyre. Polidori, J; The Castle of Otranto. Walpole, H; Vathek. Beckford, W. 14.00 (ISBN 0-8446-3133-7). Peter Smith.

Bleiler, ed. see LeFanu, J. S.

Bleiler, E. F. Essential Japanese Grammar. (Orig.). 1963. pap. 2.75 (ISBN 0-486-21027-8). Dover.

--Mother Goose Melodies. 128p. 1985. pap. 2.50 (ISBN 0-486-22577-1). Dover.

Bleiler, E. F., ed. Five Victorian Ghost Novels. Incl. Uninhabited House. Riddell, Mrs. J. H; Amber Witch. Meinhold, W; Monsieur Maurice. Edwards, A; Phantom Lover. Lee, Vernon; Ghost of Guir House. Beale, C. W. LC 77-102771. (Illus.). 1971. pap. 6.50 (ISBN 0-486-22558-5). Dover.

--Five Victorian Ghost Novels, 5 vols. in 1. Incl. The Uninhabited House. Riddell, J. H; The Amber Witch. Meinhold, W; Monsieur Maurice. Edwards, A. B; A Phantom Lover. Lee, V; The Ghost of Guir House. Beale, C. W. 13.50 (ISBN 0-8446-0034-2). Peter Smith.

--Science Fiction Writers: Critical Studies of the Major Authors from the Early Nineteenth Century to the Present Day. LC 81-51032. 623p. 1982. lib. bdg. 65.00 (ISBN 0-684-16740-9, ScribR). Scribner.

--Supernatural Fiction Writers, 2 vols. 1985. lib. bdg. 130.00 (ISBN 0-684-17808-7, ScribR). Scribner.

--Three Supernatural Novels of the Victorian Period. Bd. with The Haunted Hotel. Collins, Wilkie; The Lost Stradivarius. Falkner, J. Meade; The Haunted House at Latchford. Riddell, Mrs. J. H. Set. 10.75 (ISBN 0-8446-5161-3). Peter Smith.

--Three Victorian Detective Novels. 1978. pap. 5.00 (ISBN 0-486-23668-4). Dover.

Bleiler, E. F. & Dikty, T. E., eds. The Best Science Fiction Stories. 256p. 1980. Repr. lib. bdg. 20.00 (ISBN 0-8492-3582-0). R West.

Bleiler, E. F., ed. see Bierce, Ambrose.

Bleiler, E. F., ed. see Blackwood, Algernon.

Bleiler, E. F., ed. see Bramah, Ernest.

Bleiler, E. F., ed. see Donnelly, Ignatius.

Bleiler, E. F., ed. see Doyle, Arthur Conan.

Bleiler, E. F., ed. see Dunsany, Lord.

Bleiler, E. F., ed. see Freeman, R. Austin.

Bleiler, E. F., ed. see Futrelle, Jacques.

Bleiler, E. F., ed. & intro. by see Hoffman, E. T.

Bleiler, E. F., ed. see Hoffmann, E. T.

Bleiler, E. F., ed. see Le Fanu, J. S.

Bleiler, E. F., ed. see Le Fanu, J. Sheridan.

Bleiler, E. F., ed. see Lovecraft, Howard P.

Bleiler, E. F., ed. see Marmaduke.

Bleiler, E. F., ed. see Meyrink, Gustav & Busson, Paul.

Bleiler, E. F., ed. see Morrison, Arthur.

Bleiler, E. F., ed. see Mother Goose.

Bleiler, E. F., ed. see Richmond.

Bleiler, E. F., ed. see Riddell, Mrs. J. H.

Bleiler, E. F., ed. see Sweerts, Emanuel.

Bleiler, E. F., ed. see Sweerts, Emmanuel.

Bleiler, E. F., ed. see Walpole, Horace.

Bleiler, E. F. see Walpole, Horace.

Bleiler, E. F., ed. see Wells, H. G.

Bleiler, E. F., ed. see Woelcken, Fritz.

Bleiler, E. F., ed. see Wood, H. F.

Bleiler, E. G., ed. see Orczy, Emmuska.

Bleiler, Ellen, ed. & tr. see Donizetti, Gaetano.

Bleiler, Ellen, tr. see Mozart, Wolfgang A.

Bleiler, Ellen, tr. see Puccini, Giacomo.

Bleiler, Ellen H., tr. see Da Ponte, Lorenzo.

Bleiler, Ellen H., tr. see Donizetti, Gaetano.

Bleiler, Ellen H., tr. & see Mozart, Wolfgang A.

Bleiler, Everett. A Treasury of Victorian Ghost Stories. 368p. 1983. pap. 7.95 (ISBN 0-684-17823-0, ScribT). Scribner.

Bleiler, Everett F. The Guide to Supernatural Fiction. LC 82-25477. 736p. 1983. 55.00X (ISBN 0-87338-288-9). Kent St U Pr.

Bleiler, Everett F., jt. auth. see Stern, Guy.

Bleiler, Everett F., ed. A Treasury of Victorian Detective Stories. 416p. 1982. pap. 3.95 (ISBN 0-684-17640-8, ScribT). Scribner.

Bleiler, Everett F., ed. see James, Montague R.

Bleiler, Everett F., ed. see Okakura, Kakuzo.

Bleiman, David, jt. auth. see Keating, Michael.

Bleistein, Norman. Mathematical Methods for Wave Phenomena: Monograph. (Computer Science & Applied Mathematics Ser.). 1984. 55.00 (ISBN 0-12-105650-3). Acad Pr.

Bleiweiss, Robert M., ed. Torah at Brandeis Institute: The Layman Expounds. LC 76-7776. 1976. 8.95 (ISBN 0-916952-00-2). Brandeis-Bardin Inst.

Blejwas, S. & Biskupski, B. Pastor of the Poles: Polish American Essays. 223p. 1982. 15.00 (ISBN 0-317-36706-4). Kosciuszko.

Blejwas, Stanislas, jt. auth. see Slominski, Linda.

Blejwas, Stanislaus A. Realism in Polish Politics: Warsaw Positivism & National Survival in Nineteenth Century Poland. (Yale Russian & East European Publications Ser.: No. 5). xii, 312p. 1984. 27.50 (ISBN 0-936586-05-2). Slavica.

--Realism in Polish Politics: Warsaw Positivism & National Survival in Nineteenth Century Poland. (Yale Russian & East European Publications Ser.: No. 5). 312p. 1984. 27.50 (ISBN 0-936586-05-2). Yale Russian.

Blelloch, A., ed. Measurements of the Impacts of Materials Substitution: A Case Study in the Automobile Industry. 1978. 8.00 (ISBN 0-685-66804-5, H00131). ASME.

Bleloch, William E. New South Africa: Its Value & Development. LC 69-18973. (Illus.). Repr. of 1901 ed. cancelled (ISBN 0-8371-0923-X, BIA&, Pub. by Negro U Pr). Greenwood.

Blench, J. W. Preaching in England in the Late Fifteenth & Sixteenth Centuries. 378p. 1981. Repr. of 1964 ed. lib. bdg. 50.00 (ISBN 0-8495-0604-2). Arden Lib.

Blencowe, jt. auth. see Hanify.

Blendon, E. G. & Nalepa, B. H. Quick Survey Course in Forms Typing. 1967. standard ed. 6.12 (ISBN 0-07-005892-X); facsimile ed. 6.12 (ISBN 0-07-005891-1). McGraw.

Blendon, Robert J. & Moloney, Thomas W., eds. New Approaches to the Medicaid Crisis. (Health Care Economics & Technology Ser.). 480p. 1983. 33.95 (ISBN 0-86621-007-5). F&S Pr.

Blenerhasset, Thomas. A Direction for the Plantation in Ulster. LC 75-38158. (English Experience Ser.: No. 437). 32p. 1972. Repr. of 1610 ed. 7.00 (ISBN 90-221-0437-0). Walter J Johnson.

--A Revelation of the True Minerva. LC 42-5954. 1978. Repr. of 1582 ed. 30.00x (ISBN 0-8201-1196-1). Schol Facsimiles.

Blenerhasset, Thomas, jt. auth. see Higgins, John.

Blenkin & Kelly. Primary Curriculum in Action. 1983. pap. 12.50 (ISBN 0-06-318252-1, Pub. by Har-Row Ltd England). Har-Row.

Blenkinsop, R. J. Silhouettes of the Big Four. 96p. 30.00x (ISBN 0-902888-78-1, Pub. by ORPC Ltd UK). State Mutual Bk.

--The Steam Scene Series, 5 vols. 96p. Set. 100.00x (ISBN 0-317-19252-3, Pub. by ORPC Ltd Uk). State Mutual Bk.

Blenkinsopp, J. Gibeon & Israel: The Role of Gibeon & the Gibeonites in the Political and Religious History of Early Israel. LC 74-171672. (Society for Old Testament Studies Monographs). 1972. 34.50 (ISBN 0-521-08368-0). Cambridge U Pr.

Blenkinsopp, Joseph. A History of Prophecy in Israel. LC 83-10178. 288p. (Orig.). 1983. pap. 16.95 (ISBN 0-664-24479-3). Westminster.

--Prophecy & Canon: A Contribution to the Study of Jewish Origins. LC 76-22411. (University of Notre Dame, Center for the Study of Judaism & Christianity in Antiquity: No. 3). pap. 55.00 (ISBN 0-317-26691-8, 2024370). Bks Demand UMI.

--Wisdom & Law in the Old Testament: The Ordering of Life in Israel & Early Judaism. (The Oxford Bible Ser.). (Orig.). 1983. pap. 9.95 (ISBN 0-19-213253-9). Oxford U Pr.

Blenkinsopp, Joseph & Challenor, John. Pentateuch. Bright, Laurence, ed. LC 71-173033. (Scripture Discussion Commentary Ser.: Pt. 1). 248p. 1971. pap. text ed. 4.50 (ISBN 0-87946-000-8). ACTA Found.

Blenkinsopp, Joseph, tr. see Brox, Norbert.

Blenman, Jonathan. Remarks on Several Acts of Parliament Relating More Especially to the Colonies Abroad. LC 70-141127. (Research Library of Colonial Americana). 1971. Repr. of 1742 ed. 13.00 (ISBN 0-405-03331-1). Ayer Co Pubs.

Blennerhassett, Charlotte J. Sidelights. facs. ed. Gulcher, E., tr. LC 68-54329. (Essay Index Reprint Ser). 1913. 17.00 (ISBN 0-8369-0216-5). Ayer Co Pubs.

Blenner-Hassett, Roland. Study of the Place-Names in Lawman's Brut. LC 50-4808. (Stanford University. Stanford Studies in Language & Literature: No. 1). Repr. of 1950 ed. 18.00 (ISBN 0-404-51817-6). AMS Pr.

Blensly, Douglas L. & Plank, Tom M. Accounting Desk Book. 8th ed. LC 84-21102. 542p. 1985. 59.50 (ISBN 0-87624-011-2). Inst Busn Plan.

Blenz, Beth. The Encyclopedia of Michigan. LC 81-85112. (The Encyclopedia of the U. S. Ser.). (Illus.). 428p. 1981. lib. bdg. 79.00x (ISBN 0-403-09996-X). Somerset Pub.

Blerkom, Jonathan Van & Motta, Pietro. The Cellular Basis of Mammalian Reproduction. LC 78-10230. (Illus.). 263p. 1979. text ed. 42.00 (ISBN 0-8067-2041-7). Urban & S.

Blerkom, Jonathan van see Van Blerkom, Jonathan & Motta, Pietro.

Bles, Arthur, tr. see Weingartner, Felix.

Bleser, Carol. The Hammonds of Redcliffe. (Illus.). 1981. 25.00x (ISBN 0-19-502920-8). Oxford U Pr.

Bleser, Carol K. Promised Land: The History of the South Carolina Land Commission, 1869-1890. LC 78-79127. (Tricentennial Studies: No. 1). 192p. 1969. 19.95x (ISBN 0-87249-148-X). U of SC Pr.

Blesh, Rudi. Classic Piano Rags. (Orig.). 1973. pap. 10.95 (ISBN 0-486-20469-3). Dover.

--Combo, U.S.A. Eight Lives in Jazz. (The Roots of Jazz Ser.). 1979. Repr. of 1971 ed. 25.00 (ISBN 0-306-79568-X). Da Capo.

--Shining Trumpets: A History of Jazz. 2nd, rev. ed. LC 75-31664. (Roots of Jazz Ser.). (Illus.). xxxii, 412p. 1975. lib. bdg. 35.00 (ISBN 0-306-70658-X); pap. 7.95 (ISBN 0-306-80029-2). Da Capo.

Blesh, Rudi & Janis, Harriet. They All Played Ragtime. rev. ed. LC 66-19054. (Illus.). 347p. pap. 9.95 (ISBN 0-8256-0091-X, 000091, Oak). Music Sales.

Bless, Diane M. & Abbs, James H., eds. Vocal Fold Physiology: Contemporary Research & Clinical Issues. LC 83-1899. (Illus.). 482p. 1983. pap. 39.50 (ISBN 0-933014-87-2). College-Hill.

Blesser, William B. A Systems Approach to Biomedicine. LC 80-11717. 632p. 1981. Repr. of 1969 ed. lib. bdg. 36.50 (ISBN 0-89874-146-7). Krieger.

Blessin, Ann M. Sacred Dance with Physically & Mentally Handicapped. Adams, Doug, ed. 1982. pap. 3.00 (ISBN 0-941500-28-4). Sharing Co.

Blessing, Marlene, jt. auth. see Bollen, Constance.

Blessing, Patrick. The British & Irish in Oklahoma. LC 79-6722. (Newcomers to a New Land Ser.: Vol. 3). (Illus.). 96p. (Orig.). 1980. pap. 3.95 (ISBN 0-8061-1672-2). U of Okla Pr.

Blessing, Richard. A Closed Book. LC 80-50865. 80p. 1981. 9.95x (ISBN 0-295-95757-3). U of Wash Pr.

--A Passing Season. LC 82-47912. 228p. (gr. 6 up). 1982. 12.45 (ISBN 0-316-09957-0). Little.

--Poems & Stories. LC 82-22177. 88p. 1983. 14.00 (ISBN 0-937872-12-1); pap. 6.00 (ISBN 0-937872-13-X). Dragon Gate.

--Winter Constellations. 2nd. ed. Boyer, Dale, ed. LC 77-72388. (Modern & Contemporary Poets of the West Ser.). (Orig.). 1977. pap. 3.00 (ISBN 0-916272-05-2). Ahsahta Pr.

Blessing, Richard, ed. see Oberg, Arthur.

Blessing, Richard A. Theodore Roethke's Dynamic Vision. LC 73-15282. 256p. 1974. 20.00x (ISBN 0-253-35910-4). Ind U Pr.

--Wallace Stevens: Whole Harmonium. LC 71-105612. 1970. 15.95x (ISBN 0-8156-2145-0). Syracuse U Pr.

Blessington, Francis C. Paradise Lost & the Classical Epic. 1979. 19.95x (ISBN 0-7100-0160-6). Routledge & Kegan.

Blessington, Francis C. & Rotella, Guy, eds. Motive for Metaphor: Essays on Modern Poetry. LC 82-22280. 175p. 1983. 18.95x (ISBN 0-930350-38-3). NE U Pr.

Blessington, John P. Let My Children Work. LC 72-79377. 200p. 1975. pap. 2.95 (ISBN 0-385-00875-9, Anch). Doubleday.

Blessington, Marguerite P. The Works of Lady Blessington. LC 71-37681. (Women of Letters Ser.). Repr. of 1838 ed. 47.50 (ISBN 0-404-56717-7). AMS Pr.

Blessman, Lyle. The Blessman Approach. LC 78-64483. 1978. 12.95 (ISBN 0-87863-175-5). Farnswth Pub.

Blest Gana, Alberto. Martin Rivas. Whitham, Mrs. Charles, tr. 1977. lib. bdg. 59.95 (ISBN 0-8490-2212-6). Gordon Pr.

Bletter, Rosemarie H., jt. auth. see Robinson, Cervin.

Bletz, Donald F. The Role of the Military Professional in U.S. Foreign Policy. LC 71-170468. (Special Studies in International Politics & Government). 1972. 49.50x (ISBN 0-275-28269-4). Irvington.

Bletzer, June G. The Donning International Encyclopedic Psychic Dictionary. Horwege, Richard A., ed. LC 84-13808. 700p. 1985. 29.95 (ISBN 0-89865-372-X); pap. 12.95 (ISBN 0-89865-371-1). Donning Co.

Bletzer, Keith V. Selected References in Medical Anthropology. (Public Administration Ser.: Bibliography P-551). 59p. 1980. pap. 6.50 (ISBN 0-88066-079-1). Vance Biblios.

Bleuel, Hans P. Deutschlanfs Bekenner: German Men of Knowledge: the Professiate from the Rule of the Kaiser to the Rise of Hitler. Metzger, Walter P., ed. LC 76-55206. (The Academic Profession Ser.). (Illus., Ger.). 1977. Repr. of 1968 ed. lib. bdg. 19.00x (ISBN 0-405-10032-9). Ayer Co Pubs.

Bleuel, William H., Jr. & Patton, Joseph D. Service Management: Principles & Practices. LC 78-55481. (Illus.). 284p. 1978. text ed. 26.95x (ISBN 0-87664-373-X); instr's manual 6.25x (ISBN 0-87664-414-0). Instru Soc.

Bleuler, Eugen. Dementia Praecox or the Group of Schizophrenias. Zinkin, Joseph, tr. (Monograph Ser. on Schizophrenia: No. 1). 548p. 1966. text ed. 35.00 (ISBN 0-8236-1180-9). Intl Univs Pr.

--Textbook of Psychiatry. LC 75-16685. (Classics in Psychiatry Ser.). (Illus.). 1976. Repr. of 1924 ed. 49.50x (ISBN 0-405-07417-4). Ayer Co Pubs.

--The Theory of Schizophrenic Negativism. White, William A., tr. (Nervous & Mental Disease Monograph: No. 11). Repr. of 1912 ed. 14.00 (ISBN 0-384-04705-X). Johnson Repr.

Bleuler, k., ed. Quarks & Nuclear Structure: Proceedings of the Klaus Erkelenz Symposium, 3rd Held at Bad Honnef June 13-16, 1983. (Lecture Notes in Physics Ser.: Vol. 197). viii, 414p. 1984. pap. 22.00 (ISBN 0-387-12922-7). Springer Verlag.

Bleuler, K., et al, eds. Differential Geometrical Methods in Mathematical Physics II: Proceedings, University of Bonn, July 13-16, 1977. (Lecture Notes in Mathematics Ser.: Vol. 676). 1978. pap. 37.00 (ISBN 0-387-08935-7). Springer-Verlag.

Bleuler, Manfred. The Schizophrenic Disorders: Long-Term Patient & Family Studies. Clemens, Siegfried M., tr. LC 75-43303. 1978. 62.00x (ISBN 0-300-01663-8). Yale U Pr.

Bleunard, A. Babylon Electrified. 59.95 (ISBN 0-87968-690-1). Gordon Pr.

Bleustein, Jeffrey L., ed. Mechanics & Sport AMD, Vol. 4. 318p. 1973. pap. text ed. 25.00 (ISBN 0-685-41497-3, H00007). ASME.

Bleustein-Blanchet, Marcel. The Rage to Persuade: Confessions of a French Advertising Man. Boddewyn, Jean, tr. from Fr. LC 82-12954. 156p. 1982. 15.00 (ISBN 0-87754-363-1). Chelsea Hse.

Blevin, Margo & Ginder, Geri. The Low Blood Sugar Cookbook. LC 72-79378. 384p. 1973. 15.95 (ISBN 0-385-05174-3). Doubleday.

Blevins, Audie, Jr., jt. auth. see Minge, David.

Blevins, Dorothy. The Diabetic & Health Care. (Illus.). 1979. text ed. 30.00 (ISBN 0-07-005902-0). McGraw.

Blevins, Dorothy, jt. auth. see Asheervath, Jeyanthi.

Blevins, George, jt. auth. see Gilfond, Henry.

Blevins, James L. Revelation. Hayes, John, ed. LC 84-4387. (Preaching Guides Ser.). 132p. (Orig.). 1984. pap. 6.95 (ISBN 0-8042-3250-4). John Knox.

--Revelation As Drama. LC 84-4986. 1984. pap. 6.95 (ISBN 0-8054-1393-6). Broadman.

Blevins, James L., tr. see Otto, Eckart & Schramm, Tim.

Blevins, Leon W. The Young Voter's Manual: A Topical Dictionary of American Government & Politics. (Quality Paperback: No. 260). 366p. (Orig.). 1975. pap. 5.95 (ISBN 0-8226-0260-1). Littlefield.

Blevins, Richard W. Franz Xaver Kroetz: The Emergence of a Political Playwright. Sander, Volkmar, ed. LC 83-48018. (NYU Ottendorfer Ser.: Vol. 18). 295p. 1983. pap. text ed. 28.40 (ISBN 0-8204-0013-0). P Lang Pubs.

Blevins, Robert D. Applied Fluid Dynamics Handbook. 1984. 49.50 (ISBN 0-442-21296-8). Van Nos Reinhold.

--Flow-Induced Vibration. 380p. 1986. Repr. of 1977 ed. lib. bdg. price not set (ISBN 0-89874-891-7). Krieger.

--Formulas for Natural Frequency & Mode Shape. LC 84-12583. 506p. Repr. of 1979 ed. lib. bdg. 35.50 (ISBN 0-89874-791-0). Krieger.

Blevins, T. F., ed. see Richardson, Robert M.

Blevins, Winfred. Charbonneau. (Frontier Library). 280p. 1985. pap. 7.95 (ISBN 0-915463-16-4, Dist. by Kampmann). Jameson Bks.

--Give Your Heart to the Hawks: A Tribute to the Mountain Men. 328p. 1983. pap. 4.50 (ISBN 0-380-00694-4, 69039-X, Discus). Avon.

--Silk & Shakespeare. (Frontier Library). 250p. 1985. 13.95 (ISBN 0-915463-26-1, Dist. by Kampmann). Jameson Bks.

Blevins, Winfred, ed. Edward Warren. Bart Barbour ed ed. (Classics of the Fur Trade Ser.). 400p. 1985. 24.95 (ISBN 0-87842-183-1); pap. 11.95 (ISBN 0-87842-184-X). Mountain Pr.

Blevins, Winfred, ed. see Victor, Frances F.

Blevins, Winifred. Charbonneau. 15.95 (ISBN 0-8488-0110-5, Pub. by Amereon Hse). Amereon Ltd.

Blew, Genevieve S; see Mead, Robert G., Jr.

Blew, Robert W., ed. see Bose, Johanne C.

Blew, William, ed. Breviarium Aberdonense, 2 Vols. LC 73-39874. (Bannatyne Club, Edinburgh. Publications: No. 96). Repr. of 1854 ed. Set. 170.00 (ISBN 0-404-52844-9). AMS Pr.

Blewett, David. Defoe's Art of Fiction: Robinson Crusoe, Moll Flanders, Colonel Jack, & Roxana. LC 79-12827. 1979. 22.50x (ISBN 0-8020-5447-1). U of Toronto Pr.

Blewett, David, ed. see Defoe, Daniel.

Blewett, George J. The Christian View of the World. 1912. 49.50x (ISBN 0-685-89741-9). Elliots Bks.

Blewett, John, ed. John Dewey: His Thought & Influence. LC 72-8236. (Orestes Brownson Ser. on Contemporary Thought & Affairs). 242p. 1973. Repr. of 1960 ed. lib. bdg. 21.25x (ISBN 0-8371-6543-1, BLJD). Greenwood.

Blewett, Mary H., intro. by. Handbook for the Visitor to Lowell. 46p. 1982. pap. 3.50 (ISBN 0-943730-01-5). Lowell Pub.

Blewett, Mary H., ed. Surviving Hard Times: The Working People of Lowell. LC 81-86362. (Illus.). xii, 178p. (Orig.). 1982. pap. 6.95 (ISBN 0-942472-05-5). Lowell Museum.

Blewitt, Mary. Celestial Navigation for Yachtsmen. LC 67-25097. 1967. 7.95 (ISBN 0-8286-0028-7). J De Graff.

Blewitt, Phyllis, tr. see Zweig, Stefan.

Blewitt, Trevor, tr. see Zweig, Stefan.

Blexrud, Jan. A Toast to Sober Spirits & Joyous Juices: A Collection of Non-Alcoholic Beverage Recipes. LC 76-55449. (Illus.). 1976. pap. 6.95 (ISBN 0-89638-041-6). CompCare.

Bley, Edgar S. Best Singing Games for Children of All Ages. rev. ed. LC 57-1014. (Illus.). (gr. k-6). 1959. 11.95 (ISBN 0-8069-4450-1); PLB 14.49 (ISBN 0-8069-4451-X). Sterling.

--Best Singing Games for Children of All Ages. (Illus.). 96p. (gr. k-3). 1985. pap. 7.95 spiral (ISBN 0-8069-7956-9). Sterling.

Bley, Nancy S. & Thornton, Carol A. Teaching Mathematics to the Learning Disabled. LC 81-3569. 421p. 1981. text ed. 32.00 (ISBN 0-89443-357-1). Aspen Systems.

Bleyer, Willard G. How to Write Special Feature Articles. 1977. Repr. of 1919 ed. lib. bdg. 15.00 (ISBN 0-686-19810-7). Havertown Bks.
--Main Currents in the History of American Journalism. LC 70-77720. (American Scene Ser). (Illus.). v, 464p. 1973. Repr. of 1927 ed. lib. bdg. 59.50 (ISBN 0-306-71358-6). Da Capo.
--Newspaper Writing & Editing. LC 76-144885. 412p. 1923. Repr. 59.00 (ISBN 0-403-00871-9). Scholarly.
Bleyhl, Norris A., compiled by. Indian-White Relationships in Northern California 1849-1920 in the Congressional Set of U.S. Public Documents. 109p. 1978. 12.00 (ISBN 0-686-38930-1). Assn NC Records.
--Some Newspaper References Concerning Indian-White Relationships in Northeastern California 1850-1920. 209p. 1979. 9.00 (ISBN 0-686-38929-8). Assn NC Records.
Bleyker, Merle Den see Hendricks, William C. & Den Bleyker, Merle.
Bleything, Dennis & Hawkins, Susan. Getting off on Ninety-Six & Other Less Traveled Roads. LC 75-9248. (Illus.). 1975. pap. 4.95 (ISBN 0-911518-32-0). Touchstone Pr Ore.
Bleznick, Donald W. Quevedo. 192p. 1984. Repr. of 1972 ed. text ed. 22.50x (ISBN 0-8290-0730-X). Irvington.
--A Sourcebook for Hispanic Literature & Language: A Selected, Annotated Guide to Spanish American Bibliography, Literature, Linguistics, Journals, & Other Source Material. LC 74-77776. 192p. 1974. 14.95 (ISBN 0-87722-036-0). Temple U Pr.
--A Sourcebook for Hispanic Literature & Language: A Selected Annotated Guide to Spanish, Spanish-American, & Chicano Bibliography, Literature, Linguistics, Journals, & Other Source Materials. 2nd ed. LC 83-3060. xii, 304p. 1983. 19.50 (ISBN 0-8108-1616-4). Scarecrow.
--Studies on Don Quijote & Other Cervantine Works. LC 83-51090. 79p. 1984. 12.00x (ISBN 0-938972-07-3). Spanish Lit Pubns.
Bleznick, Donald W., ed. El Ensayo Espanol del Siglo Veinte. 294p. (Span.). pap. text ed. cancelled (ISBN 0-8290-0886-1). Irvington.
Bleznick, Donald W., ed. see Goytisolo, Juan.
Bleznick, Donald W., jt. ed. see Pattison, Walter T.
Bleznick, Donald W., ed. see Vallejo, Antonio B.
Blicher, A. Power Thyristor Physics. (Applied Physics & Engineering Ser.: Vol. 12). 1976. 52.50 (ISBN 0-387-90173-6). Springer-Verlag.
Blicher, Adolph. Field-Effect & Bipolar Power Transistor Physics. 1981. 59.50 (ISBN 0-12-105850-6). Acad Pr.
Blicher, S. S. Twelve Stories. Repr. of 1945 ed. 26.00 (ISBN 0-527-08950-8). Kraus Repr.
Blichfeldt, E. A Mexican Journey. 1976. lib. bdg. 59.95 (ISBN 0-8490-2237-1). Gordon Pr.
Blick, K. E. & Liles, S. M. Principles of Clinical Chemistry. 650p. 1985. 22.95 (ISBN 0-471-88502-9). Wiley.
Blickenstaff, Loren D., jt. auth. see Morris, James M.
Blickenstaff, Robert T., et al. Total Synthesis of Steroids. 1974. 75.00 (ISBN 0-12-105950-2). Acad Pr.
Blickle, Calvin & Corcoran, Frances. Sports: A Multimedia Guide for Children & Young Adults. (Selection Guide Ser.: No. 6). 245p. 1980. 22.95 (ISBN 0-87436-283-0). Neal-Schuman.
Blickle, Katrinka. The Vain & the Vainglorious. LC 80-2324. 360p. 1981. 12.95 (ISBN 0-385-15182-9). Doubleday.
Blickle, Margaret D., jt. auth. see Andrews, Deborah C.
Blickle, Peter. The Revolution of Fifteen Twenty-Five: The German Peasants' War from a New Perspective. Midelfort, H. C. Erik & Brady, Thomas A., Jr., trs. from Ger. LC 81-47603. (Illus.). 272p. 1982. text ed. 26.50x (ISBN 0-8018-2472-9). Johns Hopkins.
--The Revolution of Fifteen Twenty-Five: The German Peasants' War from a New Perspective. Brady, Thomas A., Jr. & Midelfort, H. C., trs. LC 81-47603. 272p. 1985. pap. text ed. 8.95x (ISBN 0-8018-3162-8). Johns Hopkins.
Blicksilver, Edith. The Ethnic American Woman: Problems, Protests, Lifestyle. 1979. pap. text ed. 14.95 (ISBN 0-8403-1951-7, 40195102). Kendall-Hunt.
Blicksilver, Jack. Defenders & Defense of Big Business in the United States, 1880-1900. Bruchey, Stuart, ed. LC 84-48305. (American Economic History Ser.). 430p. 1985. lib. bdg. 50.00 (ISBN 0-8240-6653-7). Garland Pub.
Blicksilver, Jack, ed. Views on U. S. Economic & Business History: Molding the Mixed Enterprise Economy. 350p. 1984. pap. 18.95 (ISBN 0-88406-165-5). Ga St U Busn Pub.
Blicq, Ron. Guidelines for Report Writers: A Complete Manual for On-the-Job Report Writing. (Illus.). 182p. 1982. 17.95 (ISBN 0-13-371435-7); pap. 9.95 (ISBN 0-13-371427-6). P-H.
--On the Move: Communication for Employees. 1976. pap. 16.95 (ISBN 0-13-634212-4). P-H.
Blicq, Ron S. Technically Write! Communicating in a Technological Era. 3rd ed. (Illus.). 416p. 1986. pap. text ed. 19.95 (ISBN 0-13-898750-5). P H.
Blidstein, Gerald. Honor Thy Father & Mother. 15.00x (ISBN 0-87068-251-2). Ktav.
Bliem, C., et al. Ceramic Heat Exchanger Concepts & Materials Technology. LC 85-4914. (Illus.). 385p. 1985. 45.00 (ISBN 0-8155-1030-6). Noyes.
Bliemetzrieder, Franz P. Literarische Polemik zu Beginn des grossen Abendlaendischen Schismas. (Illus.). 14.00 (ISBN 0-384-04715-7). Johnson Repr.
Bliese, Loren. A Generative Grammar of Afar. (SIL Publications on Linguistics Ser. No. 65). 306p. 1981. 10.00 (ISBN 0-88312-083-6); microfiche (4) 4.73x (ISBN 0-88312-483-1). Summer Inst Ling.
Bligh & Woodgate. Pickfords Guide to Business Removals. 1977. 25.00 (ISBN 0-85941-047-1). State Mutual Bk.
Bligh, Alexander. From Prince to King: Royal Succession in the House of Saud in the Twentieth Century. 136p. 1984. 26.00x (ISBN 0-8147-1050-6). NYU Pr.
Bligh, Donald, ed. Accountability or Freedom for Teachers? SRHE Leverhulme VII. 137p. 1982. 15.00 (ISBN 0-900868-88-0). Taylor & Francis.
--Professionalism & Flexibility in Learning: SRHE Leverhulme VI. 167p. 1982. 14.00 (ISBN 0-317-31501-3). Taylor & Francis.
Bligh, Donald A., et al. Methods & Techniques in Post-Secondary Education. (Educational Studies & Documents: No. 31). 138p. 1980. pap. 7.00 (ISBN 92-3-101575-3, U1045, UNESCO). Unipub.
Bligh, E. W. Sir Kenelm Digby & His Venetia. 1932. Repr. 20.00 (ISBN 0-8274-3428-6). R West.
Bligh, Stanley M. The Ability to Converse. 1912. 10.00 (ISBN 0-8274-1810-8). R West.
Bligh, William. An Account of the Mutiny on H. M. S. Bounty. Bowman, Robert, ed. 224p. 1980. text ed. 24.00x (ISBN 0-391-02095-1, Pub. by Alan Sutton England); pap. text ed. 11.00x (ISBN 0-86299-005-X). Humanities.
--Mutiny on Board H. M. S. Bounty. 1962. pap. 2.95 (ISBN 0-451-51879-9, Sig Classics). NAL.
--Mutiny on Board H.M.S. Bounty. (Classics Ser). (gr. 8 up). pap. 1.95 (ISBN 0-8049-0088-4, CL-88). Airmont.
--Mutiny on Board HMS Bounty. (Now Age Illustrated V Ser.). (Illus.). 64p. (gr. 4-12). 1979. text ed. 5.00 (ISBN 0-88301-404-1); pap. text ed. 1.95 (ISBN 0-88301-392-4); student activity bk 1.25 (ISBN 0-88301-416-5). Pendulum Pr.
--The Mutiny on Board HMS Bounty. 486p. 1984. Repr. lib. bdg. 19.95x (ISBN 0-89968-256-1). Lightyear.
--A Voyage to the South Sea. 1980. 29.00 (ISBN 0-09-135440-4, NO. 0219, Pub. by Hutchinson England). Methuen Inc.
--William Bligh's Log of HMS Bounty. ltd. ed. (Illus.). 700p. 1975. hand bound leather 460.00 (ISBN 0-904351-00-9). Genesis Pubns.
Bligh, William & Walters, Stephen. William Bligh's Log of HMS Providence. ltd. ed. (Illus.). 900p. 1976. hand bound leather 376.00 (ISBN 0-904351-01-7). Genesis Pubns.
Bligh, William, jt. auth. see Bowker, R. M.
Bligh, William, ed. A Book of the "Bounty". William Bligh & Others. Mackaness, George, ed. 1981. 12.95x (ISBN 0-460-00950-8, Evman). Biblio Dist.
Blight, John. Holiday Sea Sonnets. LC 84-28076. 100p. 1985. 14.95 (ISBN 0-7022-1865-0). U of Queensland Pr.
Blight, Rose. The Revolting Garden. (Illus.). 80p. 1979. pap. 2.95 (ISBN 0-233-97179-3, Pub. by Private Eye UK). David & Charles.
Blij, Harm J. see De Blij, Harm J.
Blij, Harm J. De, jt. auth. see Best, Alan C.
Blij, Harm J. De see De Blij, Harm J.
Blij, Harm J. de see De Blij, Harm J.
Blij, Harm J. De see De Blij, Harm J. & Martin, Esmond B.
Blik, Tyler, jt. auth. see Baker, Eric.
Blikle, A., ed. see Symposium, 3rd, Jadwisin, June 17-22, 1974.
Blimes, Michael E. & Sproat, Ron. More Dialing, More Dollars: Twelve Steps to Successful Telemarketing for Contributions, Subscriptions & Memberships. (Illus.). 72p. (Orig.). 1985. pap. 7.50 (ISBN 0-915400-47-2). Am Council Arts.
Blimling, Gregory & Miltenberger, Lawrence. The Resident Assistant: Working with College Students in Residence Halls. 272p. 1984. pap. text ed. 13.95 (ISBN 0-8403-3312-9, 40331201). Kendall-Hunt.
Blimling, Gregory S. & Schuh, John H., eds. Increasing the Educational Role of Residence Halls. LC 80-84300. (Student Services Ser.: No.13). 1981. pap. text ed. 8.95x (ISBN 0-87589-861-0). Jossey-Bass.
Blin, J. M. Patterns & Configurations in Economic Science: A Study of Social Decision Processes. LC 72-92525. 148p. 1973. lib. bdg. 26.00 (ISBN 90-277-0302-7, Pub. by Reidel Holland). Kluwer Academic.
Blin, Jean, et al. Flexible Exchange Rates & International Business. LC 81-85396. (British-North American Committee Ser.). 112p. 1981. pap. 8.00 (ISBN 0-89068-058-2). Natl Planning.
Blinc, R., et al. Ferroelectric Liquid Crystals. 500p. 1984. text ed. 130.00 (ISBN 0-677-16595-1). Gordon.
Blinchikoff, Herman J. & Zverev, Anatol I. Filtering in the Time & Frequency Domains. LC 76-120. 494p. 1976. 63.50x (ISBN 0-471-98679-8, Pub. by Wiley-Interscience). Wiley.
Blind, M. George Eliot. 59.95 (ISBN 0-8490-0220-6). Gordon Pr.
--George Eliot. LC 72-3623. (English Literature Ser., No. 33). 1972. Repr. of 1888 ed. lib. bdg. 49.95x (ISBN 0-8383-1586-0). Haskell.
Blind, Mathilde, intro. by. Letters & Journals of Lord Byron. 1886. 10.00 (ISBN 0-8274-2824-3). R West.
Blinder, Alan S. Economic Policy & the Great Stagflation. student ed. 1981. pap. 13.50i (ISBN 0-12-106162-0). Acad Pr.
--Economic Policy & the Great Stagflation. LC 79-22301. (Economic Theory, Econometric & Mathematical Economic Ser.). 1979. 22.50 (ISBN 0-12-106160-4). Acad Pr.
Blinder, Alan S., jt. auth. see Baumol, William J.
Blinder, Alan S. & Friedman, Philip, eds. Natural Resources, Uncertainty, & General Equilibrium System Memory: Essays in Honor of Rafael Lusky. (Economic Theory & Mathematical Economics Ser.). 1977. 55.00 (ISBN 0-12-106150-7). Acad Pr.
Blinder, Alan S., et al. The Economics of Public Finance. (Studies of Government Finance). 26.95 (ISBN 0-8157-0998-6); pap. 9.95 (ISBN 0-8157-0997-8). Brookings.
Blinder, Henriette, jt. auth. see Osman, Betty.
Blinder, Henriette, jt. auth. see Osman, Betty B.
Blinder, Martin. Psychiatry in the Everyday Practice of Law. 2nd ed. LC 72-95085. 1982. 69.50 (ISBN 0-686-05454-7); Suppl. 1984. 19.00; Suppl. 1983. 17.00. Lawyers Co-Op.
Blinder, S. M. Foundations of Quantum Dynamics. 1974. 42.00 (ISBN 0-12-106050-0). Acad Pr.
Blinderman, Abraham. American Writers on Education After 1865. (World Leader Ser.: No. 54). 1976. lib. bdg. 13.50 (ISBN 0-8057-7654-0, Twayne). G K Hall.
Blinderman, Abraham, ed. Critics on Upton Sinclair. LC 74-11470. (Readings in Literary Criticism Ser: No. 24). 1975. 5.95x (ISBN 0-87024-263-6). U of Miami Pr.
Blinderman, Barry, et al. Contemporary Perspectives, Nineteen Eighty-Four. Jacobs, Joseph, ed. (Illus.). 44p. pap. 5.00 (ISBN 0-916279-01-4). Cntr Gallery Buck Univ.
Blinderman, Rita. Pizza: Theme & Variations. LC 79-19115. (Illus., Orig.). 1980. pap. 4.95 (ISBN 0-8289-0357-3). Greene.
Blindheim, Martin. Graffiti in Norwegian Stave Churches. 160p. 1984. 39.00x (ISBN 82-00-07136-7). Universitet.
--Norwegian Romanesque Decorative Sculpture, 1090-1210. (Illus.). 1966. 20.00 (ISBN 0-85458-170-7). Transatlantic.
Bling, M. see Von Wiesner, J. & Von Regel, C.
Blinick, Augusta. Joanna's People. LC 82-61565. 260p. 1983. pap. 9.95 (ISBN 0-910873-00-3). Springtide.
Blinkenberg, A. & Hoybye, P. Dansk-Fransk Ordbog. 2058p. (Danish & Fr.). 1975. leatherette 175.00 (ISBN 0-686-92500-9, M-1278). French & Eur.
Blinkenberg, C. The Thunderweapon in Religion & Folklore. xii, 122p. 1985. Repr. of 1911 ed. lib. bdg. 20.00x (ISBN 0-89241-205-4). Caratzas.
--The Thunderweapon in Religion & Folklore. 1977. lib. bdg. 59.95 (ISBN 0-8490-2749-7). Gordon Pr.
--Timachidas: The Lindian Temple-Chronicle. 80p. 1980. 10.00 (ISBN 0-89005-353-7). Ares.
Blinkert, B. Herder-Lexikon Soziologie. 240p. (Ger.). 23.95 (ISBN 3-451-16468-X, M-7452, Pub. by Herder). French & Eur.
Blinkhorn, Martin. Mussolini & Facist Italy. (Lancaster Pamphlets Ser.). 64p. 1984. pap. text ed. 3.95 (ISBN 0-416-36020-3, NO. 4164). Methuen Inc.
Blinkin, Meir. Stories. Rosenfeld, Max, tr. from Yiddish. (Modern Jewish Literature & Culture Ser.). 166p. 1984. 10.95 (ISBN 0-87395-818-7). State U NY Pr.
Blinkov, S. M. & Smirnov, N. A. Brain Displacements & Deformations. LC 70-107532. 218p. 1971. 29.50x (ISBN 0-306-30447-3, Plenum Pr). Plenum Pub.
Blinkov, Samuil Mikha'ilovich & Smirnov, N. A. Brain Displacements & Deformations. Lindsley, Donald B., ed. Onischenko, George T., tr. from Russian. LC 70-107532. pap. 57.50 (ISBN 0-317-07813-5, 2020705). Bks Demand UMI.
Blinn, D. W., jt. auth. see Czarnecki, D. B.
Blinn, James D., jt. ed. see Cole, Mitchell.
Blinn, James E., jt. auth. see Glenn, Ronald E.
Blinn, Lynn. Making Decisions. LC 79-54910. 1980. pap. 8.80 (ISBN 0-8273-1712-3); instr's. guide 3.00 (ISBN 0-8273-1711-5). Delmar.
--Your Nutrition. 1983. text ed. 13.25 (ISBN 0-538-32600-X, HE60). SW Pub.
Blinn, Walter C., ed. Search for Explanation: Studies in Natural Science Vol. 3. (Illus.). 409p. 1969. text ed. 9.75x (ISBN 0-87013-132-X). Mich St U Pr.
Blinn, William. Brian's Song. (Illus.). 128p. (Orig.). (gr. 6 up). 1972. pap. 2.50 (ISBN 0-553-24072-2). Bantam.
Blinov, G. Russian Folk-Style Figurines: A Collector's Notes. 200p. 1983. 9.95 (ISBN 0-8285-2766-0, Pub. by Raduga Pubs USSR). Imported Pubns.
Blinov, Lev M. Electro-Optical & Magneto-Optical Properties of Liquid Crystals. LC 82-24800. 341p. 1984. 74.95x (ISBN 0-471-10231-8, Pub. by Wiley-Interscience). Wiley.
Bliokh, P. V. & Nikolaenko, A. P. Schumann Resonances in the Earth-Ionosphere Cavity. (IEE Electromagnetic Waves Series: EW009). 176p. 1980. 78.00 (ISBN 0-906048-33-8, EW009). Inst Elect Eng.
Bliokh, P. V., et al. Schumann Resonances in the Earth Ionosphere Cavity. Jones, D. Llanwyn, ed. Chomer, S., tr. (IEE Electromagnetic Waves Ser.). (Illus.). 176p. 1980. softcover casebound 78.00 (ISBN 0-906048-33-8, EW009, Pub. by Peregrinus London). Inst Elect Eng.
Bliquez, Lawrence J. Classical Vases & Containers in the Collection of the Seattle Art Museum. LC 85-50711. (Illus.). 32p. (Orig.). 1985. pap. text ed. 4.95 (ISBN 0-932216-19-6). Seattle Art.
Blish, Helen H., jt. auth. see Bad Heart Bull, Amos.
Blish, James. Anywhen. 144p. 1983. pap. 2.50 (ISBN 0-380-63941-6, 63941-6). Avon.
--Black Easter. 176p. 1982. pap. 2.50 (ISBN 0-380-59568-0, 59568-0). Avon.
--Cities in Flight. 608p. 1982. pap. 3.95 (ISBN 0-380-00998-6, 65623-X). Avon.
--The Day after Judgement. 1982. pap. 2.50 (ISBN 0-380-59527-3, 59527-3). Avon.
--Dr. Mirabilis. 272p. 1982. pap. 2.95 (ISBN 0-380-60335-7, 60335-7). Avon.
--Fallen Star. 192p. 1983. pap. 2.50 (ISBN 0-380-62463-X, 62463-X). Avon.
--Jack of Eagles. 208p. 1982. pap. 2.75 (ISBN 0-380-61150-3, 61150-3). Avon.
--Mission to the Heart Stars. 112p. 1982. pap. 1.95 (ISBN 0-380-57968-5, 57968-5). Avon.
--The Night Shapes. 128p. 1983. pap. 2.50 (ISBN 0-380-64675-7, 64675). Avon.
--Quincunx of Time. 1983. pap. 2.50 (ISBN 0-380-65185-8, 65185-8, Flare). Avon.
--The Seedling Stars-Galactic Cluster. 336p. 1983. pap. 2.95 (ISBN 0-451-12148-1, Sig). NAL.
--Spock Must Die. (Star Trek Ser.). 128p. 1985. pap. 2.95 (ISBN 0-553-24634-8). Bantam.
--Titan's Daughter. 128p. 1981. pap. 1.95 (ISBN 0-380-76929-8, 76929). Avon.
--Welcome to Mars. 160p. 1983. pap. 2.50 (ISBN 0-380-63347-7, 63347-7). Avon.
Blish, James see Atheling, William, Jr., pseud.
Blish, James, Jr. And All the Stars a Stage. 1982. pap. 2.25 (ISBN 0-380-00013-X, 61739-0). Avon.
Blishchenko, I., et al. Terrorism & International Law. Bobrov, Lev, tr. 287p. 1984. pap. 5.95 (ISBN 0-8285-2811-X, Pub. by Progress Pubns USSR). Imported Pubns.
Blishen, Edward. A Cack-Handed War. 224p. 1983. pap. 9.95 (ISBN 0-241-10919-1, Pub. by Hamish Hamilton England). David & Charles.
--Donkey Work. 249p. 1983. 18.95 (ISBN 0-241-11093-9, Pub. by Hamish Hamilton England). David & Charles.
--Lizzie Pye. 224p. 1982. 21.50 (ISBN 0-241-10781-4, Pub. by Hamish Hamilton England). David & Charles.
--A Nest of Teachers. 186p. 1980. 19.95 (ISBN 0-241-10145-X, Pub. by Hamish Hamilton England). David & Charles.
--Shakey Relations. 186p. 1982. 22.50 (ISBN 0-241-10348-7, Pub. by Hamish Hamilton England). David & Charles.
--Sorry, Dad. 217p. 1984. pap. 5.95 (ISBN 0-8052-8209-2, Pub. by Allison & Busby, England). Schocken.
--Uncommon Entrance. 192p. 1983. pap. 9.95 (ISBN 0-241-10920-5, Pub. by Hamish Hamilton England). David & Charles.
Blishen, Edward, ed. Encyclopedia of Education. 1970. 20.00 (ISBN 0-8022-2308-7). Philos Lib.
--Junior Pears Encyclopaedia. 23rd ed. 650p. 1983. 12.95 (ISBN 0-7207-1464-8, Pub. by Michael Joseph). Merrimack Pub Cir.
--Junior Pears Encyclopedia. 24th ed. (Illus.). 1040p. 1984. 12.95 (ISBN 0-7207-1524-5, Pub. by Michael Joseph). Merrimack Pub Cir.
--The Oxford Book of Poetry for Children. LC 83-21500. (Illus.). 168p. (Orig.). 1984. pap. 9.95 (ISBN 0-911745-34-3). P Bedrick Bks.
Bliss. Zero-Base Budgeting: A Management Tool for School Districts. 1978. 5.95 (ISBN 0-910170-04-5). Assn Sch Busn.
Bliss, A. J. A Dictionary of Foreign Words & Phrases in Current English. 400p. 1983. 18.00x (ISBN 0-7100-1092-3); pap. 9.95 (ISBN 0-7100-9521-X). Routledge & Kegan.
--The Metre of Beowulf. 1977. Repr. of 1966 ed. lib. bdg. 20.00 (ISBN 0-8274-4323-4). R West.
Bliss, A. J., ed. Sir Orfeo. (Illus.). 79p. 1981. Repr. of 1954 ed. lib. bdg. 35.00 (ISBN 0-8495-0486-4). Arden Lib.
Bliss, A. J. & Dunning, T. P., eds. The Wanderer. (Old English Ser.). 1969. pap. text ed. 4.95x (ISBN 0-89197-572-1). Irvington.
Bliss, Alan, ed. Spoken English in Ireland Sixteen Hundred to Seventeen Forty: Twenty Seven Representative Texts Assembled & Analysed. (Dolmen Texts: No. 5). 1979. text ed. 37.00x (ISBN 0-391-01119-7, Dolmen Pr). Humanities.
Bliss, Alan, ed. see Tolkien, J. R. R.
Bliss, Alan J. An Introduction to Old English Metre. LC 76-29022. 1976. Repr. of 1962 ed. lib. bdg. 12.50 (ISBN 0-8414-1780-6). Folcroft.

Bliss, Ann & Cohen, Eva. The New Health Professionals: Nurse Practitioners & Physician's Assistants. LC 76-46831. 472p. 1977. 46.50 (ISBN 0-912862-35-1). Aspen Systems.

Bliss, Anne. A Handbook of Dyes from Natural Materials. (Illus.). 192p. 1983. pap. 9.95 (ISBN 0-684-17893-1, ScribT). Scribner.

--North American Dye Plants. (Illus.). 1980. pap. 5.95 (ISBN 0-684-16393-4). Scribner.

--Weeds: A Guide for Dyers & Herbalists. LC 78-59236. (Illus.). 1978. pap. 5.00x (ISBN 0-931870-01-1). Juniper Hse.

Bliss, Anne, jt. auth. see Maxson, Mary Lou.

Bliss, Anne M. & Rigg, J. A., eds. Zambia. (World Bibliographical Ser.: No. 51). 230p. 1984. lib. bdg. 38.00 (ISBN 0-903450-88-7, Pub. by Clio Pr England). ABC-Clio.

Bliss, Austin, jt. auth. see Bliss, Corinne D.

Bliss, B. P. & Johnson, A. G. Aims & Motives in Clinical Medicine: A Practical Approach to Medical Ethics. 150p. 1975. pap. text ed. 12.50x (ISBN 0-8464-0123-1). Beekman Pubs.

Bliss, Beatrice. How Did You Get Where You Are. 1978. 7.95 (ISBN 0-914558-07-2); pap. 3.95 (ISBN 0-914558-08-0). Georgetown Pr.

--The Turk. 1976. 6.95 (ISBN 0-914558-03-X); pap. 3.95 (ISBN 0-914558-06-4). Georgetown Pr.

Bliss, Beatrice L. Mary Vowell Adams: Reluctant Pioneer. LC 70-188685. (Illus.). 1978. pap. 4.95 perfectbound (ISBN 0-9600504-1-8). Bliss.

--Reluctant Pioneer: Mary Vowell Adams. (Illus.). 233p. 1972. pap. 4.95 (ISBN 0-9600504-1-8). Binford.

Bliss, Betsy, jt. auth. see Aherne, Dee Dee.

Bliss, Bill, jt. auth. see Molinsky, Steven J.

Bliss, C. J. & Stern, N. H. Palanpur: The Economy of an Indian Village. (Illus.). 1982. 37.50x (ISBN 0-19-828419-5). Oxford U Pr.

Bliss, Carey S. Julius Firmicus Maternus & the Aldine Edition of the Scriptures Astronomici Veteres. (Illus.). 35p. 1981. limited ed. 125.00x (ISBN 0-931043-00-X). K Karmiole.

Bliss, Carman. The Making of Personality. 375p. 1980. Repr. lib. bdg. 25.00 (ISBN 0-89984-103-1). Century Bookbindery.

Bliss, Christopher. Economic Growth & Resources: Natural Resources, Vol III. LC 79-4430. 1980. 40.00x (ISBN 0-312-23316-7). St Martin.

Bliss, Corinne D. Daffodils or the Death of Love: Short Fiction. LC 82-11048. (Breakthrough Bks.: No.39). 128p. (Orig.). 1983. pap. 6.95 (ISBN 0-8262-0385-X). U of Mo Pr.

Bliss, Corinne D. & Bliss, Austin. That Dog Melly! (Illus.). 32p. (gr. k-4). 1981. 7.95 (ISBN 0-8038-7217-8). Hastings.

Bliss, Dennis C. The Effects of the Juvenile Justice System on Self-Concept. LC 76-55465. 1977. soft bdg. 9.00 (ISBN 0-88247-433-2). R & E Pubs.

Bliss, Dorothy. Shrimps, Lobster, & Crabs: Their Fascinating Life Story. LC 82-7853. (Illus.). 256p. 1982. 14.95 (ISBN 0-8329-0124-5). New Century.

Bliss, Dorothy, ed. The Biology of Crustacea: Vol. 7: Behavior & Ecology of Crustacea. 1983. 47.00 (ISBN 0-12-106407-7). Acad Pr.

Bliss, Dorothy & Abele, Lawrence, eds. Biology of Crustacea: Vols. 1 & 2: Systematic Fossil & Biogeography Record. 1982. Vol. 1. 41.00 (ISBN 0-12-106401-8); Vol. 2: Embryology, Morphology, & Genetics. 53.00 (ISBN 0-12-106402-6). Acad Pr.

Bliss, Dorothy & Atwood, H. L., eds. The Biology of Crustacea: Vol. 3, Structure & Function. 1982. 61.00 (ISBN 0-12-106403-4). Acad Pr.

Bliss, Dorothy & Atwood, Harold, eds. The Biology of Crustacea: Vol. 4, Neural Integration & Behavior. LC 81-22881. 1982. 39.00 (ISBN 0-12-106404-2). Acad Pr.

Bliss, Dorothy E. & Provenzano, Anthony J. Biology of Crustacea, Vol. 10. Date not set. write for info. (ISBN 0-12-106410-7). Acad Pr.

Bliss, Dorothy E. & Mantel, Linda H., eds. The Biology of the Crustacea: Itegument, Pigments, & Hormonal Process, Vol. 9. 1985. 79.00 (ISBN 0-12-106409-3). Acad Pr.

Bliss, Dorothy E. & Provenzano, J., eds. Biology of the Crustacea: Vol. 6, Economic Aspects: Pathobiology, Culture & Fisheries. LC 82-4058. 1983. 42.00 (ISBN 0-12-106406-9). Acad Pr.

Bliss, Dorothy E., jt. ed. see Mantel, Linda H.

Bliss, Edward, Jr. & Patterson, John M. Writing News for Broadcast. 2nd ed. LC 78-17510. 216p. 1978. 21.00x (ISBN 0-231-04372-4). Columbia U Pr.

Bliss, Edward N. Defense Investigation. 336p. 1956. 25.50x (ISBN 0-398-04209-8). C C Thomas.

Bliss, Edwin C. Doing It Now. 224p. 1984. pap. 3.50 (ISBN 0-553-24433-7). Bantam.

--Doing It Now: A Twelve-Step Program for Curing Procrastination & Achieving Your Goals. (Illus.). 192p. 1983. 12.95 (ISBN 0-684-18001-4, ScribT). Scribner.

--Getting Things Done. 1978. pap. 3.50 (ISBN 0-553-24426-4). Bantam.

--Getting Things Done. 144p. 1983. pap. 6.95 (ISBN 0-684-17982-2, ScribT). Scribner.

--Getting Things Done: The ABC's of Time Management. LC 76-1363. (Illus.). 128p. 1976. 9.95 (ISBN 0-684-14644-4, ScribT). Scribner.

Bliss, Elizabeth. Data Processing Mathematics. (Illus.). 176p. 1985. text ed. 24.95 (ISBN 0-13-196155-1). P-H.

Bliss, Eugene, jt. auth. see Bliss, Jonathan.

Bliss, Eugene F., ed. Diary of David Zeisberger: A Missionary Among the Indians of Ohio, 2 vols. LC 73-108557. 1972. Repr. of 1885 ed. 59.00x (ISBN 0-403-00253-2). Scholarly.

Bliss, Eugene L., ed. Roots of Behavior: Genetics, Instinct, & Socialization in Animal Behavior. (Illus.). 1969. Repr. of 1962 ed. 22.95x (ISBN 0-02-841540-X). Hafner.

Bliss, Frederick J. The Development of Palestine Exploration: Being the Ely Lectures for 1903. Davis, Moshe, ed. LC 77-70676. (America & the Holy Land). 1977. Repr. of 1907 ed. lib. bdg. 30.00x (ISBN 0-405-10228-3). Ayer Co Pubs.

--Religions of Modern Syria & Palestine. LC 76-39454. Repr. of 1912 ed. 20.00 (ISBN 0-404-00897-6). AMS Pr.

Bliss, G. A. Algebraic Functions. LC 34-5791. (Colloquium Publications: No. 16). 220p. 1933. 34.90 (ISBN 0-317-32950-2, OP-13796); pap. 29.90 (ISBN 0-317-32951-0). Am Math.

--Fundamental Existence Theorems. LC 14-3157. (Colloquium Publications: No. 3 (1)). 107p. 1913. 34.80 set (ISBN 0-317-32968-5, OP-52182); pap. 29.80 set (ISBN 0-317-32969-3). Am Math.

Bliss, G. A., ed. see Chicago University Department Of Mathematics.

Bliss, George R. see Hovey, Alvah.

Bliss, Gilbert A. Calculus of Variations. (Carus Monograph: No. 1). 189p. 1925. 19.00 (ISBN 0-88385-001-X). Math Assn.

--Lectures on the Calculus of Variations. LC 46-5369. (Midway Reprints Ser.). 304p. 1980. 9.00x (ISBN 0-226-05896-4). U of Chicago Pr.

Bliss, Gilbert A; see Evans, Griffith C.

Bliss, J., ed. see Andrewes, Lancelot.

Bliss, Joan, et al. Qualitative Data Analysis for Educational Research: A Guide to Uses of Systemic Networks. (Illus.). 224p. 1983. 29.00 (ISBN 0-7099-0698-6, Pub. by Croom Helm Ltd). Longwood Pub Group.

Bliss, Jonathan. Merchants & Miners in Utah. 1984. 20.00 (ISBN 0-914740-29-6). Western Epics.

Bliss, Jonathan & Bliss, Eugene. Prism: Andrea's World. LC 84-40721. 288p. 1985. 16.95 (ISBN 0-8128-3022-9). Stein & Day.

Bliss, L. C., jt. auth. see Balbach, M. K.

Bliss, L. C., et al, eds. Tundra Ecosystems. LC 79-50913. (International Biological Programme Ser.: No. 25). (Illus.). 1000p. 1981. 140.00 (ISBN 0-521-22776-3). Cambridge U Pr.

Bliss, Lawrence C., jt. auth. see Balbach, Margaret.

Bliss, Lee. The World's Perspective: John Webster & the Jacobean Drama. 239p. 1983. 22.50x (ISBN 0-8135-0967-X). Rutgers U Pr.

Bliss, Michael. Brian de Palma. LC 83-3306. (Filmakers Ser.: No. 6). 176p. 1983. 15.00 (ISBN 0-8108-1621-0). Scarecrow.

--The Discovery of Insulin. (Illus.). 304p. 1982. lib. bdg. 25.00 (ISBN 0-226-05897-2). U of Chicago Pr.

--The Discovery of Insulin. LC 82-50911. (Illus.). 304p. 1984. pap. 9.95 (ISBN 0-226-05898-0). U of Chicago Pr.

Bliss, P., jt. auth. see Barnes, D.

Bliss, Philip, ed. see Wood, Anthony.

Bliss, Richard. Origins: Two Models. Gish, Duane T. & Moore, John N., eds. LC 76-20178. (Illus.). 1976. 4.95 (ISBN 0-89051-040-7); tchr's guide avail. Master Bks.

Bliss, Richard, et al. Fossils: Key to the Present. 1980. pap. 4.95 (ISBN 0-89051-058-X). Master Bks.

Bliss, Richard B. & Parker, Gary E. Origin of Life. LC 78-58477. (Illus.). 1978. pap. 4.95 (ISBN 0-89051-053-9). Master Bks.

Bliss, Ronald G. Eagle Trap. LC 82-71045. (Illus.). 108p. (gr. 3-5). 1982. 12.95x (ISBN 0-943864-06-2); pap. 4.50x (ISBN 0-943864-05-4). Davenport.

Bliss, Sands & Co. The Magic Moving Picture Book. Orig. Title: The Motograph Moving Picture Book. 32p. (gr. 4 up). 1975. pap. 2.95 (ISBN 0-486-23224-7). Dover.

Bliss, Shepherd, ed. The New Holistic Health Handbook: Living Well in a New Age. (Illus.). 1985. 29.95 (ISBN 0-8289-0560-6); pap. 14.95 (ISBN 0-8289-0561-4). Greene.

Bliss, Steve. Buckeye Football Fitness. LC 83-81212. (Illus.), 352p. (Orig.). 1984. pap. 12.95 (ISBN 0-88011-214-X). Leisure Pr.

Bliss, Sylvester. Memoirs of William Miller. LC 72-134374. Repr. of 1853 ed. 30.00 (ISBN 0-404-08422-2). AMS Pr.

Bliss, Trudy. Jane Welsh Carlyle: A New Selection of Her Letters. 1977. Repr. of 1949 ed. lib. bdg. 20.00 (ISBN 0-8492-0249-3). R West.

Bliss, Trudy, ed. see Carlyle, Thomas.

Bliss, W. D., jt. ed. see Andrews, John B.

Bliss, William D., ed. The Encyclopedia of Social Reform: Including Political Economy, Political Science, Sociology & Statistics. LC 71-88519. vii, 1439p. Repr. of 1897 ed. lib. bdg. 74.50x (ISBN 0-8371-4974-6, BLSR). Greenwood.

Bliss, William D. & Binder, Rudolph M., eds. New Encyclopedia of Social Reform. 3rd ed. LC 77-112524. (Rise of Urban America). 1970. Repr. of 1910 ed. 66.00 (ISBN 0-405-02436-3). Ayer Co Pubs.

Bliss, William R. Side Glimpses from the Colonial Meeting House. LC 70-140410. 1970. Repr. of 1894 ed. 40.00x (ISBN 0-8103-3594-8). Gale.

Blisset, William. The Long Conversation: A Memoir of David Jones. (Illus.). 1981. 29.00x (ISBN 0-19-211778-5). Oxford U Pr.

Blissett, Marlan, jt. auth. see Redford, Emmette S.

Blissett, William. Editing Illustrated Books: Papers Given at the Fifteenth Annual Conference on Editorial Problems, University of Toronto, 2-3 November 1979. LC 80-22003. (Conferences on Editorial Problems Ser.). 133p. 1981. lib. bdg. 22.00 (ISBN 0-8240-2430-3). Garland Pub.

Blissett, William, ed. see MacCallum, Reid.

Blissett, William, et al, eds. A Celebration of Ben Jonson. LC 73-91241. (Illus.). 1974. pap. 7.50 (ISBN 0-8020-6284-9). U of Toronto Pr.

Blissmer, Robert, jt. auth. see Stallings, Warren.

Blissmer, Robert H. Computer Annual: An Introduction to Information Systems 1985-1986. (Wiley Series in Computers & Information Processing Systems for Business). 487p. 1985. pap. text ed. 18.95 (ISBN 0-471-81106-8); tchr's ed. avail. (ISBN 0-471-81105-X); tests avail. (ISBN 0-471-81916-6). Wiley.

Blistein, Elmer H. Comedy in Action. LC 64-22154. pap. 40.50 (ISBN 0-317-20087-9, 2023368). Bks Demand UMI.

Blistein, Elmer M., ed. see Beane, William.

Blitch, John D. How to Become a Civilian & Succeed in Your New Career. LC 79-52695. (Illus., Orig.). 1979. pap. 4.95 (ISBN 0-934206-00-7). CS Pubns.

Blitchington, Evelyn. The Family Devotions Idea Book. LC 82-4252. 139p. (Orig.). 1982. pap. 4.95 (ISBN 0-87123-254-5, 210254). Bethany Hse.

Blitchington, Evelyn, jt. auth. see Blitchington, W. Peter.

Blitchington, Peter & Cruise, Robert J. Understanding Your Temperament: A Self-Analysis with a Christian Viewpoint. 38p. (Orig.). 1979. pap. 2.95 (ISBN 0-943872-67-7). Andrews Univ Pr.

Blitchington, W. Peter. The Christian Woman's Search for Self-Esteem. LC 81-18963. 168p. 1983. pap. 4.95 (ISBN 0-8407-5830-8). Nelson.

--The Energy & Vitality Book. 234p. 1983. pap. 3.50 (ISBN 0-8423-0704-4). Tyndale.

--Sex Roles & the Christian Family. 1983. pap. 5.95 (ISBN 0-8423-5896-X); leader's guide 2.95 (ISBN 0-8423-5897-8). Tyndale.

Blitchington, W. Peter & Blitchington, Evelyn. Understanding the Male Ego. LC 84-2154. 176p. 1984. pap. 10.95 (ISBN 0-8407-5327-6). Nelson.

Blits, Jan H. End of the Ancient Republic: Essays on Julius Caesar. LC 82-73241. 96p. 1983. lib. bdg. 12.95 (ISBN 0-89089-249-0). Carolina Acad Pr.

Blits, Jan H., ed. The American University: Problems, Prospects & Trends. 177p. 1985. 18.95 (ISBN 0-87975-283-1). Prometheus Bks.

Blitsten, Dorothy R. Human Social Development: Psychobiological Roots & Social Consequences. 1972. New Coll U Pr.

Blitt, jt. auth. see Adair, J.

Blitt, Casey D. Catheterization Techniques for Invasive Cardiovascular Monitoring. (Illus.). 144p. 1981. 28.75x (ISBN 0-398-04499-6). C C Thomas.

Blitt, Casey D., ed. Monitoring in Anesthesia & Critical Care Medicine. (Illus.). 750p. 1985. text ed. 79.00 (ISBN 0-443-08277-4). Churchill.

Blitt, Casey D., jt. auth. see Brown, Burnell R.

Blitz, J., et al. Electrical, Magnetic & Visual Methods of Testing Materials. (Illus.). 1970. 12.00 (ISBN 0-8088-8350-X). Davey.

Blitz, John H. An Archaeological Study of the Mississippi Choctaw Indians. LC 85-620004. (Archaeological Reports: No. 16). (Illus.). vi, 116p. (Orig.). 1985. pap. text ed. 7.50 (ISBN 0-938896-44-X). Mississippi De.

Blitz, Mark. Heidegger's "Being & Time" & the Possibility of Political Philosophy. LC 81-3253. 288p. 1981. 24.50x (ISBN 0-8014-1320-6). Cornell U Pr.

Blitz, Michael. Partitions. 50p. (Orig.). 1982. 11.00 (ISBN 0-916258-13-0); pap. 7.50 (ISBN 0-916258-12-2). Volaphon Bks.

Blitz, Rudolph C., tr. see Gossen, Hermann H.

Blitzer, Andrew, et al, eds. Rehabilitation of the Head & Neck Cancer Patient: Psychosocial Aspects. 240p. 1985. 26.75x (ISBN 0-398-05156-9). C C Thomas.

Blitzer, Charles. Immortal Commonwealth: The Political Thought of James Harrington. xv, 344p. 1970. Repr. of 1960 ed. 27.50 (ISBN 0-208-00811-X, Archon). Shoe String.

Blitzer, Charles, jt. auth. see Friedrich, Carl J.

Blitzer, Charles, ed. see Harrington, James.

Blitzer, Charles, et al, eds. Economy-Wide Models & Development Planning. (World Research Bank Publications Ser). (Illus.). 1975. pap. 9.95x (ISBN 0-19-920074-2). Oxford U Pr.

Blitzer, Richard. Basic Electricity for Electronics. LC 73-20102. 727p. 1974. text ed. 31.95x (ISBN 0-471-08160-4). Wiley.

Blitzer, Robert & Gill, Jack C. College Mathematics Review. 2nd ed. LC 84-149402. (Illus.). 266p. (Orig.). 1983. 15.95x (ISBN 0-943202-10-8). H & H Pub.

Blitzer, Wolf. Between Washington & Jerusalem: A Reporter's Notebook. (Illus.). 288p. 1985. 18.95 (ISBN 0-19-503708-1). Oxford U Pr.

Bliven, Bruce. Men Who Make the Future. facs. ed. LC 70-111816. (Essay Index Reprint Ser). 1942. 21.50 (ISBN 0-8369-1643-3). Ayer Co Pubs.

Bliven, Bruce & Mezerik, Avrahm G., eds. What the Informed Citizen Needs to Know. LC 72-1244. (Essay Index Reprint Ser.). Repr. of 1945 ed. 24.50 (ISBN 0-8369-2833-4). Ayer Co Pubs.

Bliven, Bruce, Jr. The American Revolution. LC 80-20813. (Landmark Bks.). (Illus.). 160p. (gr. 5-9). 1981. pap. 2.95 (ISBN 0-394-84696-6). Random.

--American Revolution. (Landmark Ser.: No. 83). (Illus.). (gr. 4-6). 1958. (BYR); PLB 5.99 (ISBN 0-394-90383-8). Random.

--From Casablanca to Berlin. (Landmark Ser, No. 112). (gr. 5-9). 1965. (BYR); PLB 5.99 (ISBN 0-394-90412-5). Random.

--From Pearl Harbor to Okinawa. (Landmark Ser.: No. 94). (Illus.). (gr. 5-9). 1960. PLB 6.99 (ISBN 0-394-90394-3, BYR). Random.

--New York. (States & the Nation Ser.). (Illus.). 1981. 14.95 (ISBN 0-393-05665-1). Norton.

--The Story of D-Day. LC 81-483. (Landmark Paperback Ser.: No. 9). (Illus.). 160p. (gr. 5-9). 1981. pap. 2.95 (ISBN 0-394-84886-1). Random.

--Story of D-Day: June 6, 1944. (Landmark Ser.: No. 94). (Illus.). (gr. 6-8). 1956. (BYR); PLB 5.99 (ISBN 0-394-90362-5). Random.

Bliven, Lorayne. Read English, Bk. 5. (Speak English Ser.). (Illus.). 80p. (Orig.). 1983. pap. text ed. 4.95 (ISBN 0-88499-679-4). Inst Mod Lang.

Blixen, Karen. Winter's Tales. LC 70-169542. (Short Story Index Reprint Ser.). Repr. of 1942 ed. 17.00 (ISBN 0-8369-4003-2). Ayer Co Pubs.

Blixen-Finecke, Hans Von see Von Blixen-Finecke, Hans.

Blixrud, Julia C. A Manual of AACR 2 Examples for Serials. 2nd ed. 1985. pap. 15.00 (ISBN 0-936996-21-8). Soldier Creek.

Blixrud, Julia C. & Swanson, Edward. A Manual of AACR 2 Examples Tagged & Coded Using the MARC Format. 116p. 1982. pap. 12.50x (ISBN 0-936996-13-7). Soldier Creek.

Blixt, S. G., jt. ed. see Vose, P. B.

Blizard, David, jt. ed. see Dimond, Stuart J.

Blizek, William L., ed. The Humanities & Public Life. 1978. pap. 4.95 (ISBN 0-918626-50-1, Pied Pubns). Word Serv.

Blizek, William L., jt. ed. see Cederblom, J. B.

Blizzard, Richard. Blizzard's Wonderful Wooden Toys. LC 83-5080. (Illus.). 224p. (Orig.). 1983. pap. 9.95 (ISBN 0-8069-7798-1). Sterling.

--Making Wooden Toys. (Illus.). 128p. (Orig.). 1982. pap. 7.95 (ISBN 0-8069-7620-9). Sterling.

Blizzard, Roy B., Jr. Let Judah Go up First: A Study in Praise, Prayer, & Worship. 46p. (Orig.). 1984. pap. 2.95 (ISBN 0-918873-01-0). Ctr Judaic-Christ Studies.

Bljach, I. S. & Bagma, B. T. Deutsch-Russisches Okonomisches Worterbuch: Dictionary German-Russian of Economics. 664p. (Ger. & Rus.). 1977. leatherette 24.75 (ISBN 0-686-92495-9, M-9056). French & Eur.

Blobaum, Robert. Feliks Dzierzynski & the Sdkpil: A Study of the Origins of Polish Communism. 256p. 1984. 25.00x (ISBN 0-88033-046-5). East Eur Quarterly.

Blo Bzang, Ye Shes. The Younger Brother, Don Yod: A Tibetan Play, Being the Secret Biography from the Words of the Glorious Lama, the Holy Reverend Blo Bzang Ye Shes. Norbu, Thubten J. & Ekvall, Robert B., trs. LC 74-19623. pap. 39.50 (ISBN 0-317-10095-5, 2050129). Bks Demand UMI.

Bloch. Compressors & Expanders: Selection & Application for the Process Industry. (Chemical Industries Ser.: Vol. 8). (Illus.). 328p. 1982. 49.50 (ISBN 0-8247-1854-2). Dekker.

--Marxism & Anthropology. 194p. 1985. 19.95x (ISBN 0-19-876091-4); pap. 5.95 (ISBN 0-19-285148-9). Oxford U Pr.

Bloch, ed. Journal of Jewish Bibliography, 4 vols. Set. 29.50 (ISBN 0-685-48593-5). Feldheim.

Bloch, A., ed. see Pope John Paul II.

Bloch, A. P. The Biblical & Historical Background of the Jewish Holy Days. 1978. 20.00x (ISBN 0-87068-338-1). Ktav.

Bloch, Abby & Margie, Joyce D. Nutrition & the Cancer Patient. LC 81-70351. 269p. 1983. pap. 11.95 (ISBN 0-8019-7120-9). Chilton.

Bloch, Abraham P. The Biblical & Historical Backround of Jewish Customs & Ceremonies. 1979. 20.00x (ISBN 0-87068-658-5). Ktav.

--A Book of Jewish Ethical Concepts. 1984. 20.00 (ISBN 0-88125-039-2). Ktav.

--Day-by-Day in Jewish History. 1983. 20.00x (ISBN 0-87068-736-0). Ktav.

Bloch, Alexander, ed. Chemistry, Biology, & Clinical Uses of Nucleoside Analogs, Vol. 255. (Annals of the New York Academy of Sciences). 610p. 1975. 71.00x (ISBN 0-89072-009-6). NY Acad Sci.

Bloch, Alfred, ed. The Real Poland: An Anthology of National Self-Perception. LC 82-1559. 224p. 1982. 14.95 (ISBN 0-8264-0060-4). Continuum.

Bloch, Alice. The Law of Return. 206p. 1983. 7.95 (ISBN 0-932870-48-1). Alyson Pubns.

--Lifetime Guarantee. 132p. 1983. pap. 6.95 (ISBN 0-932870-49-X). Alyson Pubns.

Bloch, Arthur. Murphy's Law: And Other Reasons Why Things Go Wrong. (Orig.). 1977. pap. 2.95 (ISBN 0-8431-0428-7). Price Stern.

--Murphy's Law Book Three: And Other Reasons Why Things Continue to Go Wrong. 96p. (Orig.). 1982. pap. 2.95 (ISBN 0-8431-0618-2). Price Stern.
--Murphy's Law Book Two: More Reason's Why Things Go Wrong. 1980. 2.95 (ISBN 0-8431-0674-3). Price Stern.
Bloch, Barbara. If It Doesn't Pan Out: How to Cope With Cooking Disasters. LC 80-26508. 1981. 10.95 (ISBN 0-934878-02-1); pap. 7.95 (ISBN 0-934878-19-6). Dembner Bks.
--Meat Board Meat Book. LC 76-52873. 7.95 (ISBN 0-317-11711-4). Benjamin CO.
Bloch, Barbara, jt. auth. see Ralston Purina Kitchens.
Bloch, Bernard & Hastings, Garth W. Plastics Materials in Surgery. 2nd ed. (Illus.). 284p. 1972. 34.75x (ISBN 0-398-02465-0). C C Thomas.
Bloch, Bernard & Jorden, Eleanor H. Spoken Japanese. LC 74-150406. (Spoken Language Ser.). 387p. (gr. 9-12). 1975. pap. 10.00x Units 1-12 (ISBN 0-87950-140-5); 6 12-inch LP records 50.00x (ISBN 0-87950-143-X); bk. & records 55.00x (ISBN 0-87950-144-8); 6 dual track cassettes 60.00x (ISBN 0-87950-145-6); bk. & cassettes 65.00x (ISBN 0-87950-146-4). Spoken Lang Serv.
Bloch, Carl, illus. Jesus, the Son of Man. (Illus.). 80p. 1983. pap. 12.95 (ISBN 0-87973-652-6, 652). Our Sunday Visitor.
Bloch, Carolyn C. Coal Information Sources & Data Bases. LC 80-22344. 128p. 1981. 24.00 (ISBN 0-8155-0830-1). Noyes.
--Federal Energy Information Sources & Data Bases. LC 79-15543. 1979. 24.00 (ISBN 0-8155-0764-X). Noyes.
Bloch, Chana. The Secrets of the Tribe. LC 80-52193. 80p. 1980. 9.95 (ISBN 0-935296-13-1); pap. 4.95 (ISBN 0-935296-14-X). Sheep Meadow.
--Spelling the Word: George Herbert & the Bible. LC 84-123. 375p. 1985. 30.00x (ISBN 0-520-05121-1). U of Cal Pr.
Bloch, Chana, tr. see Ravikovitch, Dahlia.
Bloch, Charles E. The First Chanukah. LC 56-12405. (Illus.). 1957. pap. 1.75 (ISBN 0-8197-0450-4). Bloch.
Bloch, Donald & Simon, Robert, eds. The Strength of Family Therapy: Selected Papers of Nathan W. Ackerman. LC 82-4285. 460p. 1982. 42.50 (ISBN 0-87630-271-1). Brunner-Mazel.
Bloch, Donald A., ed. Techniques of Family Psychotherapy: A Primer. LC 73-6655. (Seminars in Psychiatry Reprint). 136p. 1973. 28.50 (ISBN 0-8089-0818-9, 790625). Grune.
Bloch, Dorothy. So the Witch Won't Eat Me: Fantasy & the Child's Fear of Infanticide. LC 83-49374. 256p. 1984. pap. 7.95 (ISBN 0-394-62104-2, E909, Ever). Grove.
Bloch, E. Maurice. The Drawings of George Caleb Bingham: With a Catalogue Raissone. LC 75-15613. (Illus.). 272p. 1975. 65.00x (ISBN 0-8262-0180-6). U of Mo Pr.
Bloch, Ernest & Schwartz, Robert A. Impending Changes for Securities Markets: What Role for the Exchanges? Altman, Edward I. & Walter, Ingo, eds. LC 77-7784. (Contemporary Studies in Economic & Financial Analysis: Vol. 14). lib. bdg. 34.50 (ISBN 0-89232-081-8). Jai Pr.
Bloch, Ernst. Essays on the Philosophy of Music. Palmer, P., tr. 300p. Date not set. price not set (ISBN 0-521-24873-6); pap. price not set (ISBN 0-521-31213-2). Cambridge U Pr.
--Natural Law & Human Dignity. Schmidt, Dennis J., tr. from Ger. (Studies in Contemporary German Social Thought Ser.). 408p. 1985. 25.00x (ISBN 0-262-02221-4). MIT Pr.
Bloch, Ernst, et al. Aesthetics & Politics. 1979. 19.25 (ISBN 0-8052-7062-0, Pub. by NLB). Schocken.
Bloch, Farrell, ed. Research in Labor Economics, Supplement 1: Evaluating Manpower Training Programs. 1979. lib. bdg. 42.50 (ISBN 0-89232-046-X). Jai Pr.
Bloch, Frank S. Federal Disability Law & Practice. LC 84-10473. (Federal Practice Ser.). 752p. 1984. text ed. 75.00x (ISBN 0-471-89389-7, 1-703, Pub. by Wiley Law Pubns). Wiley.
Bloch, George. Picasso. (Catalogue of the Printed Graphic Work: Vols. 1 & 2). (Illus.). 1971. 82.50x ea. Vol. 1, 1904-1967 (ISBN 0-8150-0467-2). Vol. 2, 1967-1969 (ISBN 0-8150-0468-0). Wittenborn.
Bloch, George, tr. see Mesmer, Franz A.
Bloch, George J. Body & Self: Elements of Human Biology, Behavior & Health. (Illus.). 320p. (Orig.). 1985. pap. 15.95 (ISBN 0-86576-041-1, 041-1). W Kaufmann.
Bloch, Georges. Pablo Picasso: Catalogue of the Printed Graphic Work 1904-1972, 3 Vols. 911p. 1971-79. 250.00 (ISBN 0-686-87741-1). A Wofsy Fine Arts.
--Picasso Catalogue of the Printed Graphic Work, Vol. 4. (Illus.). 253p. (Eng., Fr. & Ger.). 1979. 82.50x (ISBN 3-8577-3009-9). Wittenborn.
--Picasso Ceramics. (Catalogue of the Printed Graphic Work Ser: Vol. 3, Ceramiques 1949-1971). (Illus., Tri-"lingual). 1972. 145.00x (ISBN 0-8150-0646-2). Wittenborn.
Bloch, H. A. & Prince, M. Social Crisis & Deviance: Theoretical Foundations. 6.25 (ISBN 0-8446-1690-7). Peter Smith.
Bloch, H. P. & Geitner, F. K. Machinery Failure Analysis & Troubleshooting. LC 83-10731. (Practical Machinery Management for Process Plants Ser.: Vol. 2). 656p. 1983. 69.95x (ISBN 0-87201-872-5). Gulf Pub.
Bloch, Heinz P. Improving Machinery Reliability. LC 82-2879. (Process Machinery Management for Process Plants Ser.: Vol. 1). 366p. 1982. 49.95x (ISBN 0-87201-376-6). Gulf Pub.
Bloch, Heinz P. & Geitner, Fred K. Machinery Component Maintenance & Repair. LC 84-15738. (Practical Machinery Management for Process Plants Ser.: Vol. 3). (Illus.). 576p. 1985. 59.95x (ISBN 0-87201-453-3). Gulf Pub.
--Major Process Equipment Maintenance & Repair. LC 84-15782. (Practical Machinery Management for Process Plants Ser.: Vol. 4). (Illus.). 680p. 1985. 74.95x (ISBN 0-87201-454-1). Gulf Pub.
Bloch, Herbert. Monte Cassino in the Middle Ages. 1983. text ed. 100.00x (ISBN 0-674-58655-7). Harvard U Pr.
Bloch, Herbert & Niederhoffer, Arthur. Gang: A Study in Adolescent Behavior. 1958. 6.00 (ISBN 0-8022-0143-1). Philos Lib.
Bloch, Herbert A. Concept of Our Changing Loyalties: An Introductory Study into the Nature of the Social Individual. LC 34-36571. (Columbia University Studies in the Social Sciences: No. 401). Repr. of 1934 ed. 22.50 (ISBN 0-404-51401-4). AMS Pr.
Bloch, Herbert A. & Niederhoffer, Arthur. The Gang: A Study in Adolescent Behavior. LC 76-6517. 1976. Repr. of 1958 ed. lib. bdg. 29.75x (ISBN 0-8371-8865-2, BLTG). Greenwood.
Bloch, Iwan. Anthropological Studies in the Strange Sexual Practices of All Races in All Ages, Ancient & Modern, Oriental & Occidental, Primitive & Civilized. Wallis, Keene, tr. from Ger. LC 72-9615. Repr. of 1933 ed. 15.00 (ISBN 0-404-57410-6). AMS Pr.
--Ethnological & Cultural Studies of the Sex Life in England As Revealed in Its Erotic & Obscene Literature & Art. Deniston, Richard, ed. LC 72-9614. (Illus.). Repr. of 1934 ed. 27.50 (ISBN 0-404-57411-4). AMS Pr.
--Marquis De Sade: The Man & His Age. Bruce, James, tr. LC 72-9613. (Human Sexual Behavior Ser.). Repr. of 1931 ed. 15.00 (ISBN 0-686-74584-1). AMS Pr.
--Odoratus Sexualis: A Scientific & Literary Study of Sexual Scents & Erotic Perfumes. LC 72-9620. Repr. of 1934 ed. 15.00 (ISBN 0-404-57414-9). AMS Pr.
--The Sexual Life of Our Time in Its Relation to Modern Civilization. Paul, M. Eden, tr. LC 72-9619. Repr. of 1910 ed. 47.50 (ISBN 0-404-57415-7). AMS Pr.
Bloch, J. The Formation of the Marathi Language. Chanana, D. R., tr. 1970. 10.95 (ISBN 0-89684-206-1). Orient Bk Dist.
Bloch, Jean De. The Future of War. 59.95 (ISBN 0-8490-0208-7). Gordon Pr.
Bloch, Jean L., jt. auth. see Minton, Michael.
Bloch, Jean-Richard, jt. auth. see Rolland, Romain.
Bloch, Jonathan & Fitzgerald, Patrick. British Intelligence & Covert Action: Africa, Middle East & Europe Since 1945. LC 84-124942. 286p. 1984. pap. 9.95 (ISBN 0-86322-035-5, Pub. by Brandon Bks). Longwood Pub Group.
Bloch, Joseph S. My Reminiscences. LC 73-2188. (The Jewish People; History, Religion, Literature Ser.). Repr. of 1923 ed. 44.00 (ISBN 0-405-05254-5). Ayer Co Pubs.
Bloch, Joshua, et al. Hebrew Printing & Bibliography. Berlin, Charles, ed. LC 72-12075. (Illus.). 1976. text ed. 35.00 (ISBN 0-87104-515-X, Co-Pub by Ktav). NY Pub Lib.
Bloch, Julius M., ed. An Account of Her Majesty's Revenue in the Province of New York, Seventeen Hundred & One to Seventeen Hundred & Nine. (Illus.). 1966. 25.00 (ISBN 0-8398-0059-2). Parnassus Imprints.
Bloch, Konrad, et al, eds. Membranes, Molecules, Toxins, & Cells. LC 80-16595. 350p. 1981. 37.00 (ISBN 0-88416-309-1). PSG Pub Co.
Bloch, Kurt. German Interests & Policies in the Far East. LC 75-30098. (Institute of Pacific Relations). Repr. of 1939 ed. 11.50 (ISBN 0-404-59507-3). AMS Pr.
Bloch, Lawrence W., ed. see Farr, Naunerle.
Bloch, Lawrence W., ed. see Farr, Naunerle & Dostert, Dennis.
Bloch, Leonard W., ed. see Farr, Naunerle.
Bloch, Lolla, tr. see Taubes, Hella.
Bloch, Louis M., Jr. The Gas Pipe Networks: A History of College Radio, 1936-1946. LC 80-70047. (Illus.). 128p. 1981. text ed. 12.95 (ISBN 0-914276-02-6). Bloch & Co OH.
--Overland to California in Eighteen Fifty-Nine: A Guide for Wagon Train Travelers. LC 83-71506. (Illus.). 64p. 1983. lib. bdg. 9.95 (ISBN 0-914276-03-4). Bloch & Co OH.
Bloch, Lucille S., jt. auth. see Margulies, Harold.
Bloch, M. The Historian's Craft. 1954. pap. 7.00 (ISBN 0-7190-0664-3, Pub. by Manchester Univ Pr). Longwood Pub Group.
Bloch, Marc. Feudal Society, 2 Vols. Manyon, L. A., tr. LC 61-4322. 1961. Vol. 1. pap. 7.95 (ISBN 0-226-05978-2, P156, Phoen); Vol. 2. pap. 6.50 (ISBN 0-226-05979-0, P157, Phoen). U of Chicago Pr.
--French Rural History: An Essay on Its Basic Characteristics. Sondheimer, Janet, tr. LC 66-15483. (Illus.). 1966. 40.00x (ISBN 0-520-00127-3); pap. 9.95x (ISBN 0-520-01660-2, CAMPUS28). U of Cal Pr.
--Historian's Craft. 1964. pap. 3.95 (ISBN 0-394-70512-2, V512, Vin). Random.
--The Ile-De-France: The Country Around Paris. Anderson, J. E., tr. LC 70-148715. (Illus.). 175p. 1971. 22.50x (ISBN 0-8014-0640-4). Cornell U Pr.
--Memoirs of War, Nineteen Fourteen to Nineteen Fifteen. Fink, Carole, tr. from Fr. LC 79-6849. Orig. Title: Souvenirs De Guerre. (Illus.). 184p. 1980. 19.95x (ISBN 0-8014-1220-X). Cornell U Pr.
--Strange Defeat. 178p. 1981. Repr. of 1949 ed. lib. bdg. 25.00 (ISBN 0-89987-075-9). Darby Bks.
--Strange Defeat: A Statement of Evidence Written in 1940. Hopkins, Gerard M., tr. 1968. pap. 5.95 (ISBN 0-393-00371-X, Norton Lib). Norton.
Bloch, Marie H. Aunt America. LC 63-7265. (Illus.). 160p. (gr. 3-6). 1963. pap. 0.95 (ISBN 0-689-70300-7, A-4, Aladdin). Atheneum.
Bloch, Marie H., ed. see Dubovy, Andrew.
Bloch, Marie H., tr. see Dubovy, Andrew.
Bloch, Mary H. Footprints in the Swamp. LC 84-21553. (Illus.). 80p. (gr. 4-6). 1985. 12.95 (ISBN 0-689-31085-4). Atheneum.
Bloch, Maurice. Marxist Analyses & Social Anthropology. 2nd ed. (ASA Studies). 256p. 1985. pap. 11.95x (ISBN 0-422-79500-3, 9278, Pub by Tavistock England). Methuen Inc.
--Placing the Dead: Tombs, Ancestral Villages, & Kinship Organization in Madagascar. LC 70-162375. (Seminar Studies in Anthropology). 242p. 1971. 44.00 (ISBN 0-12-785062-7). Acad Pr.
Bloch, Maurice, ed. Political Language & Oratory in Traditional Society. 1975. 39.50 (ISBN 0-12-106850-1). Acad Pr.
Bloch, Maurice & Parry, Jonathan, eds. Death & the Regeneration of Life. LC 82-9467. 256p. 1982. 34.50 (ISBN 0-521-24875-2); pap. 10.95 (ISBN 0-521-27037-5). Cambridge U Pr.
Bloch, N. J., jt. auth. see Michaels, J. G.
Bloch, Norman J. & Michaels, John G. Linear Algebra. (Illus.). 1976. text ed. 33.00 (ISBN 0-07-005906-3). McGraw.
Bloch, Oscar & Wartburg, Walther Von. Dictionnaire Etymologique de la Langue Francaise. 6th ed. 684p. (Fr.). 1975. 83.95 (ISBN 0-686-57293-9, F-C1016). French & Eur.
Bloch, R. F., jt. auth. see Ingram, D.
Bloch, R. Howard. Etymologies & Genealogies: A Literary Anthropology of the French Middle Ages. LC 82-20036. 296p. 1983. lib. bdg. 25.00x (ISBN 0-226-05981-2). U of Chicago Pr.
--Medieval French Literature & Law. LC 76-7754. 1977. 35.00x (ISBN 0-520-03230-6). U of Cal Pr.
Bloch, Ricard I., jt. auth. see Zack, Arnold M.
Bloch, Richard I., jt. auth. see Zack, Arnold M.
Bloch, Robert. Cold Chills. 1978. pap. 1.75 (ISBN 0-8439-0542-5, Leisure Bks). Dorchester Pub Co.
--Cold Chills. 224p. 1982. pap. 2.50 (ISBN 0-505-51863-5, Pub. by Tower Bks). Dorchester Pub Co.
--The Cunning. 1981. pap. 2.50 (ISBN 0-89083-825-9). Zebra.
--Mysteries of the Worm. 1981. pap. 2.95 (ISBN 0-89083-815-1). Zebra.
--The Night of the Ripper. LC 84-4077. 240p. 1984. 14.95 (ISBN 0-385-19422-6). Doubleday.
--Out of the Mouths of Graves. LC 78-53503. 1978. 10.00 (ISBN 0-89296-043-4); limited ed. o.p. 25.00 (ISBN 0-89296-044-2). Mysterious Pr.
--Psycho. Repr. lib. bdg. 16.95x (ISBN 0-88411-077-X, Pub. by Aeonian Pr). Amereon Ltd.
--Psycho II. 224p. 1982. 16.00 (ISBN 0-918372-09-7); signed & slipcased 36.00x (ISBN 0-918372-08-9). Whispers.
--Psycho II. 320p. (Orig.). 1982. pap. 3.50 (ISBN 0-446-90804-5). Warner Bks.
--Robert Bloch's Unholy Trinity. rev. ed. 296p. 1985. Repr. 20.00 (ISBN 0-910489-09-2) (ISBN 0-317-20265-0). Scream Pr.
--Strange Eons. LC 78-66962. (Illus.). 1979. 12.00 (ISBN 0-918372-30-5); signed-slipcased ed 25.00x (ISBN 0-918372-29-1). Whispers.
--There Is a Serpent in Eden. (Orig.). 1979. pap. 2.25 (ISBN 0-89083-514-4). Zebra.
--The Twilight Zone: The Movie. (Orig.). 1983. pap. 2.95 (ISBN 0-446-30840-4). Warner Bks.
Bloch, Robert, et al. The First World Fantasy Convention: Three Authors Remember. 4.95 (ISBN 0-686-31248-1). Necronomicon.
Bloch, Sidney. What Is Psychotherapy? 1982. text ed. 18.95x (ISBN 0-19-219154-3). Oxford U Pr.
--What Is Psychotherapy? 1982. pap. 7.95 (ISBN 0-19-289142-1, GB 734, GB). Oxford U Pr.
Bloch, Sidney & Reddaway, Peter. Psychiatric Terror. LC 77-75238. 1977. 12.95x (ISBN 0-465-06488-4). Basic.
--Soviet Psychiatric Abuse: The Shadow over World Psychiatry. (Illus.). 288p. 1985. 25.00 (ISBN 0-575-03253-7). Westview.
Bloch, Sidney, ed. An Introduction to the Psychotherapies. 1979. pap. text ed. 14.95x (ISBN 0-19-261217-4). Oxford U Pr.
Bloch, Sidney & Chodoff, Paul, eds. Psychiatric Ethics. (Oxford Medical Publications Ser.). (Illus.). 1981. text ed. 32.50x (ISBN 0-19-261182-8); pap. 12.95 (ISBN 0-19-261512-2). Oxford U Pr.
--Psychiatric Ethics. (Oxford Medical Publications Ser.). (Illus.). 365p. 1985. pap. 12.95 (ISBN 0-19-261512-2). Oxford U Pr.
Bloch, Stuart M., ed. Real Estate Timesharing & the Property Tax. (Monograph: No. 85-4). (Illus.). 103p. 1985. pap. text ed. 15.00 (ISBN 0-318-04692-X). Lincoln Inst Land.
Bloch, Stuart M., ed. see Burlingame, et al.
Bloch, Thomas M., et al, eds. Services Marketing in a Changing Environment: Proceedings. LC 84-24307. (Illus.). 138p. (Orig.). 1985. pap. text ed. 16.00 (ISBN 0-87757-174-0). Am Mktg.
Bloch-Dermant, Janine. Le Verre en France, d'Emile Galle a Nos Jours. (Illus.). 312p. (Fr.). 1983. 100.00 (ISBN 2-85917-029-4, Pub. by Editions de l'Amateur FR). Seven Hills Bks.
Blocher, Arlo. Country. LC 75-39817. (Illus.). 32p. (gr. 5-10). 1976. PLB 9.79 (ISBN 0-89375-012-3); pap. 2.50 (ISBN 0-89375-028-X). Troll Assocs.
--Folk. LC 75-39815. (Illus.). 32p. (gr. 5-10). 1976. PLB 9.79 (ISBN 0-89375-013-1); pap. 2.50 (ISBN 0-89375-029-8). Troll Assocs.
--Jazz. new ed. LC 75-39816. (Illus.). 32p. (gr. 5-10). 1976. PLB 9.79 (ISBN 0-89375-014-X); pap. 2.50 (ISBN 0-89375-030-1). Troll Assocs.
--Rock. new ed. LC 75-39819. (Illus.). 32p. (gr. 5-10). 1976. PLB 9.79 (ISBN 0-89375-015-8); pap. 2.50 (ISBN 0-89375-031-X). Troll Assocs.
Blocher, Donald H. Developmental Counseling. 2nd ed. (Illus.). 320p. 1974. 28.95x (ISBN 0-471-06894-2, Pub by Ronald Pr). Wiley.
Blocher, Donald H. & Biggs, Donald A. Counseling Psychology in Community Settings. 304p. 1983. text ed. 23.95 (ISBN 0-8261-3680-X). Springer Pub.
Blocher, E. & Willingham, J. Analytical Review: A Guide to Evaluating Financial Statements. 192p. 1984. 27.50 (ISBN 0-07-005912-8). McGraw.
Blocher, Henri. In the Beginning: The Opening Chapters of Genesis. Preston, David G., tr. from Fr. LC 84-12800. 180p. 1984. pap. 6.95 (ISBN 0-87784-325-2). Inter-Varsity.
Blocher, John, et al, eds. see International Conference on Chemical Vapor Deposition.
Blocher, John M., Jr., ed. see International Conference on Chemical Vapor Deposition.
Blochet, Edgar. Musulman Painting, 12th-17th Century. Binyon, C. M., tr. from Fr. (Illus.). 1975. Repr. of 1929 ed. lib. bdg. 40.00 (ISBN 0-87817-155-X). Hacker.
Bloch-Hoell, Nils. The Pentecostal Movement: Its Origin, Development & Distinctive Character. 1964. text ed. 19.00x (ISBN 8-200-06004-7, Dist. by Columbia U Pr). Universitet.
Blochman, Lawrence G., jt. auth. see Callas, Evangelia.
Blochmann, Henry F. The Prosody of the Persians, According to Saifi, Jami & Other Writers. 1976. lib. bdg. 59.95 (ISBN 0-8490-2487-0). Gordon Pr.
Block, A. The Changing World in Plays & Theatre. LC 73-77721. (Theatre, Film & Literature Ser.). 448p. 1971. Repr. of 1939 ed. lib. bdg. 45.00 (ISBN 0-306-71359-4). Da Capo.
Block, A. A. & Chambliss, W. J. Organizing Crime. xii, 238p. 1981. 28.50 (ISBN 0-444-99079-8). Elsevier.
Block, Adrienne F. The Early French Parody Noel, 2 Vols. Buelow, George, ed. LC 83-1175. (Studies in Musicology: No. 36). 924p. 1983. Set. 89.95 (ISBN 0-8357-1123-4). Vol. 1, 228p (ISBN 0-8357-1437-3). Vol. 2, 696p (ISBN 0-8357-1438-1). UMI Res Pr.
Block, Adrienne F. & Neuls-Bates, Carol, eds. Women in American Music: A Bibliography of Music & Literature. LC 79-7722. (Illus.). 1979. lib. bdg. 39.95x (ISBN 0-313-21410-7, NBW/). Greenwood.
Block, Alan. East Side - West Side: Organizing Crime in New York, 1930-1950. LC 83-4773. 280p. 1983. pap. 9.95 (ISBN 0-87855-931-0). Transaction Bks.
Block, Alan & Scarpitti, Frank. Poisoning for Profit: Organized Crime & Toxic Waste in America. LC 84-62024. 352p. 1985. 17.95. Morrow.
Block, Andrew. The English Novel, Seventeen Forty to Eighteen Fifty: A Catalogue Including Prose Romances, Short Stories, & Translations of Foreign Fiction. rev. ed. LC 81-17868. xv, 349p. 1982. Repr. of 1961 ed. lib. bdg. 42.50x (ISBN 0-313-23224-5, BLEN). Greenwood.
--English Novel, Seventeen Forty to Eighteen Fifty: A Catalogue Including Prose Romances, Short Stories & Translations of Foreign Fiction. LC 62-3325. 349p. 1962. 32.00 (ISBN 0-379-00028-8). Oceana.
--Sir J. M. Barrie: His First Editions, Points & Values. LC 73-15690. 1933. lib. bdg. 15.00 (ISBN 0-8414-3292-9). Folcroft.
Block, Anita R. Love Is a Four Letter Word. facs. ed. LC 73-116940. (Short Story Index Reprint Ser). 1958. 19.00 (ISBN 0-8369-3442-3). Ayer Co Pubs.
Block, Arthur R., jt. auth. see Rebell, Michael A.

Block, Barry H. Foot Talk. 1985. pap. 2.95 (ISBN 0-8217-1613-1). Zebra.
--Foot Talk: A Complete Guide to the Good Health & Care of the Feet. (Illus.). 1984. 13.95 (ISBN 0-87795-522-0). Arbor Hse.
Block, Barry H., jt. auth. see Marcus, Stuart A.
Block, Betsy & Henry, Sue S. Having a Baby in Denver: A Guide to Pregnancy & Early Parenthood. Dority, Kim & Lacey, Marcia, eds. (Illus.). 175p. (Orig.). 1985. pap. 9.95 (ISBN 0-9608012-2-7). Metro Source Pubns.
Block, Bob. The Politics of Projects. (Illus.). 160p. 1983. pap. 18.50 (ISBN 0-917072-35-9). Yourdon.
Block, C., et al. Geillustrerd Woordenboek Voor de Automobieltechniek en Zes Talen. 502p. (Dutch, Rus., Eng., Ger. & Ital.). 1978. 145.00 (ISBN 90-201-1070-5, M-9475). French & Eur.
Block, Carl E. & Roering, Kenneth J. Essentials of Consumer Behavior. 2nd ed. 650p. 1979. 33.95x (ISBN 0-03-041961-1). Dryden Pr.
Block, Carolyn R. Homicide in Chicago: Time Series Analysis by Homicide Type & Offender-Victim Characteristics. 150p. 1985. pap. 6.00 (ISBN 0-911531-16-5). Loyola U Ctr Urban.
Block, Dennis J. & Hoddinott, Alfred H. The Corporate Counsellor's Deskbook. 2nd ed. LC 84-28913. 1984. write for info. (ISBN 0-15-004384-8, Law & Business). HarBraceJ.
Block, Dennis J. & Pitt, Harvey L. Hostile Battles for Corporate Control, 1984, 2 vols. LC 82-63146. (Corporate Law & Practice Course Handbook Ser.). (Illus.). 1984. 35.00. PLI.
Block, Dennis J. & Hoddinott, Alfred H., eds. The Corporate Counsellor's Desk Book. 2nd ed. 1985. Supplements avail. 75.00 (ISBN 0-317-29398-2, #H43848). HarBraceJ.
Block, Dennis J., et al, eds. The Corporate Counsellor's Desk Book. 297p. 1982. 50.00 (ISBN 0-15-100015-8, H42817). HarBraceJ.
Block, Elizabeth. The Effects of Divine Manifestations on the Reader's Perspective in Virgil's "Aneid". rev. ed. Connor, W. R., ed. LC 80-2640. (Monographs in Classical Studies). 1981. lib. bdg. 39.00 (ISBN 0-405-14028-2). Ayer Co Pubs.
Block, Elizabeth J. A Woman's Guide to Credit. 224p. (Orig.). 1982. pap. 3.25 (ISBN 0-441-90785-7). Ace Bks.
Block, Eric, ed. Reactions of Organosulfur Compounds. 1978. 38.50 (ISBN 0-12-107050-6). Acad Pr.
Block, Eugene B. Science vs. Crime. LC 79-21941. (Illus.). 208p. 1980. pap. 6.95 (ISBN 0-89666-010-9). Cragmont Pubns.
--Science vs. Crime. LC 79-21941. (Illus.). 1980. 12.95 (ISBN 0-89666-007-9). Cragmont Pubns.
--When Men Play God: The Fallacy of Capital Punishment. LC 81-15143. 1984. 14.95 (ISBN 0-89666-015-X). Cragmont Pubns.
Block, Francesca. Moon Harvest. (Santa Susana Press Ser.). 1978. pap. 31.00 (ISBN 0-937048-19-4). CSUN.
Block, Fred L. The Origins of International Economic Disorder: A Study of United States International Monetary Policy from World War Two to the Present. LC 75-7190. 1977 pap. 8.95x (ISBN 0-520-03729-4, CAMPUS 214). U of Cal Pr.
--The Origins of International Economic Disorder: A Study of U. S. International Monetary Policy from W.W. II to the Present. 1983. 16.00 (ISBN 0-8446-5971-1). Peter Smith.
Block, Geoffrey D. Allied Aircraft vs. Axis Aircraft. 1970. 6.95 (ISBN 0-87364-225-2). Paladin Pr.
Block, Gertrude. Effective Legal Writing: A Style Book for Law Students & Lawyers. 2nd ed. LC 83-1487. 212p. 1983. pap. text ed. write for info. (ISBN 0-88277-109-4). Foundation Pr.
Block, Gloria & Nolan, Joellen. Health Assessment for Professional Nursing: A Developmental Approach. (Illus.). 362p. 1981. 23.50x (ISBN 0-8385-3660-3). ACC.
Block, Gwendoline H. see Gifford, Edward W.
Block, H. Poly (y-Benzyl-L-Glutamate) (Polymer Monographs: Vol. 9). 215p. 1983. 49.00 (ISBN 0-677-05680-X). Gordon.
Block, Haskell & Shedd, Robert, eds. Masters of Modern Drama. LC 62-10776. 1962. text ed. 35.00 (ISBN 0-394-30084-X, RanC). Random.
Block, Haskell M. Mallarme & the Symbolist Drama. LC 77-9242. (Wayne State University Study of Language & Literature: No. 14). 1977. Repr. of 1963 ed. lib. bdg. 24.75x (ISBN 0-8371-9706-6, BLMS). Greenwood.
Block, Haskell M., ed. see Moliere, Jean B.
Block, Haskell M., ed. see Voltaire, Francois M.
Block, Herbert. Herblock Through the Looking Glass. (Illus.). 1984. 12.95 (ISBN 0-393-01929-2). Norton.
Block, Herbert & Cline, Ray S. The Planetary Product in Nineteen Eighty-Two: World Economic Output, 1970-1982. LC 83-21067. (Significant Issues Ser.: Vol V, No. 8). 31p. 1983. 5.95 (ISBN 0-89206-051-4). CSI Studies.
Block, I. E., et al, eds. Studies in Approximation & Analysis. vi, 195p. 1966. text ed. 15.50 (ISBN 0-89871-156-8). Soc Indus-Appl Math.
Block, Ira, jt. auth. see Smith, Betty.
Block, Irving, ed. Perspectives on the Philosophy of Wittgenstein. (Studies in Contemporary German Social Thought). 224p. 1982. text ed. 32.50x (ISBN 0-262-02173-0); pap. 9.95x (ISBN 0-262-52087-7). MIT Pr.
Block, J. & Labonville, J. English Skills for Technicians. 1971. 20.30 (ISBN 0-07-005910-1). McGraw.
Block, J. Bradford. The Signs & Symptoms of Chemical Exposure. 164p. 1980. spiral bdg. 18.75x (ISBN 0-398-03958-5). C C Thomas.
Block, J. H. Mastery Learning: Theory & Practice. LC 70-147025. 1971. pap. text ed. 10.95 (ISBN 0-03-086073-3, HoltC). HR&W.
Block, J. Richard, jt. auth. see Yuker, Harold E.
Block, Jack. Lives Through Time. LC 70-156597. xxii, 313p. 1971. 19.95x (ISBN 0-9600332-0-3). Bancroft Bks.
--The Q-Sort Method in Personality Assessment & Psychiatric Research. Harrower, Molly, ed. LC 61-10370. 161p. 1978. pap. 13.50x (ISBN 0-89106-000-6, 0791). Consulting Psychol.
--Understanding Historical Research: A Search for Truth. (Illus.). 156p. 1971. pap. text ed. 7.00x (ISBN 0-9600478-0-8). Research Pubns.
Block, Jacqueline, jt. auth. see Martinez, Benjamin.
Block, James H. & Anderson, Lorin W. Mastery Learning & Classroom Instruction. 1975. pap. 7.95x (ISBN 0-02-311000-7, 31100). Macmillan.
Block, Jane. Les XX & Belgian Avant-Gardism, 1868-1894. Foster, Stephen, ed. LC 83-17981. (Studies in the Fine Arts: The Avant-Garde: No. 41). 202p. 1984. 39.95 (ISBN 0-8357-1463-2). UMI Res Pr.
Block, Jean F. Hyde Park Houses: An Informal History, 1856-1910. LC 78-3174. (Illus.). 1978. 12.95 (ISBN 0-226-06000-4). U of Chicago Pr.
--The Uses of Gothic: Planning & Building the Campus of the University of Chicago, 1892-1932. LC 83-6545. (Illus.). xix, 262p. 1985. pap. 19.95 (ISBN 0-226-06004-7, 06004-7). U of Chicago Pr.
Block, Jean L., jt. auth. see Minton, Michael H.
Block, Jean L., jt. auth. see Tanzer, Deborah.
Block, Jeanne H. Sex Role Identity & Ego Development. LC 84-7918. (Social & Behavioral Science Ser.). 1984. 21.95x (ISBN 0-87589-607-3). Jossey-Bass.
Block, Jerome B. Oncology: UCLA Postgraduate Medicine for the Internist. (Illus.). 1981. write for info. (ISBN 0-89289-376-1). Wiley.
Block, Jerome B., ed. Oncology. LC 81-318. 364p. 1982. 42.95 (ISBN 0-471-09511-7). Krieger.
Block, Joel. Friendship: How to Give It, How to Get It. 1981. pap. 4.95 (ISBN 0-02-075590-2). MacMillan.
Block, Joel D. Lasting Love: How to Give It, How to Get It, How to Keep It. 256p. 1982. 13.50 (ISBN 0-02-511800-5). Macmillan.
--The Magic of Lasting Love. 272p. 1983. 7.95 (ISBN 0-346-12589-8). Cornerstone.
Block, Joel D. & Greenberg, Diane. Women & Friendship. 256p. 1985. 16.95 (ISBN 0-531-09707-2). Watts.
Block, Judy. Performance Appraisal on the Job. 1982. pap. 5.95 (ISBN 0-917386-52-3). Exec Ent Inc.
Block, Judy R. Performance Appraisal on the Job: Making It Work. LC 81-65122. 86p. 1982. 9.95 (ISBN 0-13-657080-1); pap. 4.95 (ISBN 0-13-657072-0). P-H.
Block, Julian. Julian Block's Guide to Year-Round Tax Savings, 1985. 220p. 1985. pap. 9.95 (ISBN 0-87094-576-9). Dow Jones-Irwin.
--Julian Block's Guide to Year-Round Tax Savings, 1986. 220p. 1985. pap. 9.95 (ISBN 0-87094-692-7). Dow Jones-Irwin.
--Tax Saving. LC 80-70260. 224p. 1981. 12.95 (ISBN 0-8019-7080-6); pap. 7.95 (ISBN 0-8019-7068-7). Chilton.
--Tax Saving: A Year-Round Guide. rev. & enl. ed. LC 81-69048. 288p. 12.95 (ISBN 0-8019-7227-2); pap. 8.95 (ISBN 0-8019-7228-0). Chilton.
--Tax Saving: A Year Round Guide. 3rd ed. LC 82-73542. 288p. 1983. 12.95; pap. 8.95 (ISBN 0-8019-7362-7). Chilton.
Block, K. S., ed. Ludus Coventriae. (EETS ES Ser.: Vol. 120). Repr. of 1917 ed. 23.00 (ISBN 0-317-16544-5). Kraus Repr.
--Ludus Coventriae, Or, the Place Called Corpus Christi. (Early English Text Society Ser.). 1922. 26.00x (ISBN 0-19-722560-8). Oxford U Pr.
Block, Lawrence. After the First Death. 160p. 1984. pap. 3.95 (ISBN 0-88150-020-8, Foul Play). Countryman.
--A.K.A. Chip Harrison. (Foul Play Press Ser.). 380p. 1983. pap. 5.95 (ISBN 0-88150-001-1, Foul Play Pr). Countryman.
--Ariel. LC 79-87835. 1980. 9.25 (ISBN 0-87795-234-5). Arbor Hse.
--Burglar in the Closet. Date not set. pap. 2.95 (ISBN 0-671-54718-6). PB.
--The Burglar Who Liked to Quote Kipling. 1982. pap. 2.50 (ISBN 0-671-83582-3). PB.
--The Burglar Who Liked to Quote Kipling. 1979. 7.95 (ISBN 0-394-50417-8). Random.
--The Burglar Who Painted Like Mondrian. 217p. 1983. 14.50 (ISBN 0-87795-517-4). Arbor Hse.
--The Burglar Who Studied Spinoza. 1982. pap. 2.95 (ISBN 0-671-43723-2). PB.
--The Canceled Czech. 192p. 1984. pap. 2.95 (ISBN 0-515-08387-9). Jove Pubns.
--Eight Million Ways to Die. LC 81-71689. 1982. 12.95 (ISBN 0-87795-405-4). Arbor Hse.
--The Five Little Rich Girls. 160p. 1984. 13.95 (ISBN 0-8052-8183-5, Pub. by Allison & Busby England). Schocken.
--The Girl with the Long Green Heart. 1985. pap. 3.95 (ISBN 0-88150-042-9). Countryman.
--Here Comes a Hero. 176p. 1985. pap. 2.95 (ISBN 0-515-08420-4). Jove Pubns.
--In the Midst of Death. 192p. 1985. pap. 2.95 (ISBN 0-515-08098-5). Jove Pubns.
--Introducing Chip Harrison: Two Novels: No Score & Chip Harrison Scores Again. 328p. 1984. pap. 5.95 (ISBN 0-88150-019-4, Foul Play). Countryman.
--Like a Lamb to Slaughter. LC 84-9324. 256p. 1984. 15.95 (ISBN 0-87795-526-3). Arbor Hse.
--Like a Lamb to Slaughter. 240p. 1985. pap. 2.95 (ISBN 0-515-08413-1). Jove Pubns.
--Mayday. 336p. 1985. pap. 2.95 (ISBN 0-425-04729-6). Berkley Pub.
--The Sins of the Fathers. 192p. 1985. pap. 2.95 (ISBN 0-515-08157-4). Jove Pubns.
--The Sins of the Fathers. pap. cancelled. Arbor Hse.
--Sometimes They Bite. 304p. 1983. 14.50 (ISBN 0-87795-485-2). Arbor Hse.
--Sometimes They Bite. 288p. 1985. pap. 2.95 (ISBN 0-515-08370-4). Jove Pubns.
--The Specialists. 160p. 1985. pap. 3.95 (ISBN 0-88150-043-7). Countryman.
--A Stab in the Dark. LC 81-66971. 192p. 1981. 10.95 (ISBN 0-87795-340-6). Arbor Hse.
--A Stab in the Dark. 192p. 1985. pap. 2.95 (ISBN 0-515-08158-2). Jove Pubns.
--A Stab in the Dark. pap. cancelled. Arbor Hse.
--Such Men Are Dangerous. 192p. 1985. pap. 2.95 (ISBN 0-515-08170-1). Jove Pubns.
--Tanner's Tiger. 192p. 1985. pap. 2.95 (ISBN 0-515-08328-3). Jove Pubns.
--Tanner's Twelve Swingers. 192p. 1985. pap. 2.95 (ISBN 0-515-08106-X). Jove Pubns.
--Telling Lies for Fun & Profit: A Manual for Fiction Writers. LC 81-66965. 240p. 1981. 13.95 (ISBN 0-87795-334-1). Arbor Hse.
--Telling Lies For Fun & Profit: A Manual for Fiction Writers. LC 81-66965. 1982. pap. 6.95 (ISBN 0-87795-393-7, Pub. by Priam). Arbor Hse.
--The Thief Who Couldn't Sleep. 208p. 1985. pap. 2.95 (ISBN 0-515-08311-9). Jove Pubns.
--Time to Murder & Create. 192p. 1985. pap. 2.95 (ISBN 0-515-08159-0). Jove Pubns.
--The Topless Tulip Caper. 192p. 1984. 13.95 (ISBN 0-8052-8202-5, Pub. by Allison & Busby, England). Schocken.
--Two for Tanner. 192p. 1985. pap. 2.95 (ISBN 0-515-08187-6). Jove Pubns.
--When the Gin Mill Closes. 1986. price not set (ISBN 0-87795-774-6). Arbor Hse.
--Writing the Novel: From Plot to Print. LC 79-10677. 197p. 1979. 10.95 (ISBN 0-911654-67-4). Writers Digest.
--Writing the Novel: From Plot to Print. LC 79-1067. 197p. 1985. pap. 8.95 (ISBN 0-89879-208-8). Writers Digest.
Block, Lee F., ed. Marketing for Hospitals in Hard Times. 200p. 1981. text ed. 18.95 (ISBN 0-931028-16-7); pap. 14.95 (ISBN 0-931028-15-9). Teach'em.
Block, Leonard. Profiting from Your Real Estate License in Good Times & Bad. 174p. 1982. 14.95 (ISBN 0-13-729343-7); pap. 6.95 (ISBN 0-13-729335-6). P-H.
Block, Marguerite. The New Church in the New World. 486p. 12.95 (ISBN 0-87785-126-3). Swedenborg.
Block, Marilyn. Women Over Forty: Visions & Realities. LC 80-20774. (Focus on Women Ser.: No. 4). 176p. 1981. pap. text ed. 13.95 (ISBN 0-8261-3001-1); cloth 20.95 (ISBN 0-8261-3000-3). Springer Pub.
Block, Martin. Gypsies: Their Life & Their Customs. Kuczynski, Barbara & Taylor, Duncan, trs. LC 75-3451. (Illus.). Repr. of 1939 ed. 31.50 (ISBN 0-404-16886-8). AMS Pr.
Block, Marvin A. Alcohol & Alcoholism: Drinking & Dependence. 63p. 1970. pap. 3.50 (ISBN 0-318-15276-2). Natl Coun Alcoholism.
--Alcoholism: Its Facets & Phases. 320p. 1962. 8.95 (ISBN 0-318-15289-4). Natl Coun Alcoholism.
Block, Mary H., jt. auth. see Rubenstein, Hiasaura.
Block, Matthew H. Text-Atlas of Hematology. LC 75-38565. (Illus.). 651p. 1976. text ed. 76.50 (ISBN 0-8121-0014-X). Lea & Febiger.
Block, Michael K., jt. auth. see Clabault, James M.
Block, N. J. & Dworkin, Gerald, eds. The IQ Controversy. LC 75-38113. 1976. pap. 8.95 (ISBN 0-394-73087-9). Pantheon.
Block, Ned, ed. Readings in Philosophy of Psychology, Vol. I. (Language & Thought Ser.). 320p. 1983. pap. text ed. 8.95x (ISBN 0-674-74876-X). Harvard U Pr.
--Readings in Philosophy of Psychology, Vol. 2. (Language & Thought Ser.). 376p. 1985. pap. text ed. 8.95x (ISBN 0-674-74878-6). Harvard U Pr.
--Readings in the Philosophy of Psychology, 2 vols. LC 79-25593. (Language & Thought Ser.). 1980. Vol. 1. 20.00x (ISBN 0-674-74875-1); Vol. 2, 1981. 22.50x (ISBN 0-674-74877-8). Harvard U Pr.
Block, Ned J., ed. Imagery. LC 81-24732. 192p. 1981. text ed. 24.75x (ISBN 0-262-02168-4, Pub. by Bradford); pap. text ed. 9.50x (ISBN 0-262-52072-9). MIT Pr.
Block, Pauline, jt. auth. see Sacks, Rita L.
Block, Peter. Flawless Consulting: A Guide to Getting Your Expertise Used. LC 81-4283. (Illus.). 215p. 1981. text ed. 21.95 (ISBN 0-89384-052-1). Learning Concepts.
Block, Phyllis R. Debuts Litteraires. LC 76-58856. 1977. pap. text ed. 12.95 (ISBN 0-03-015011-6, HoltC). HR&W.
Block, R. W. Handbook of Behavioral Pediatrics. 1981. 16.95 (ISBN 0-8151-0835-4). Year Bk Med.
Block, Richard A., ed. Fundamentals of Loran-C. 42p. (Orig.). 1982. pap. 6.00 (ISBN 0-934114-36-6, BK-267). Marine Educ.
--Radiotelephone Operator. (Illus.). 52p. 1984. pap. 6.00 (ISBN 0-934114-56-0, BK-111). Marine Educ.
--Tankerman-All Grades. rev. "C" ed. (Illus.). 336p. pap. 28.00 (ISBN 0-934114-57-9, BK-106). Marine Educ.
--Understanding T-Boat Regulations. (Illus.). 143p. 1979. pap. text ed. 12.00 (ISBN 0-934114-22-6, BK-115). Marine Educ.
Block, Richard A. & Bramble, C. A., eds. Master & Mate License Preparation Course. rev. "B" ed. (Illus.). 572p. 1984. pap. text ed. 44.00 (ISBN 0-934114-59-5, BK-104). Marine Educ.
--Motorboat, Ocean & Inland Operator License Preparation Course, 2 bks. rev. ed. (Illus.). 841p. 1983. 58.00 (ISBN 0-934114-58-7). Marine Educ.
Block, Richard A. & Collins, Charles B., eds. The M&O Master's Handbook. (Illus.). 271p. (Orig.). 1979. pap. text ed. 15.00 (ISBN 0-934114-16-1, BK-117). Marine Educ.
--Standard Operations Manual for the Marine Transportation Sector of the Offshore Mineral & Oil Industry. 61p. (Orig.). 1979. pap. text ed. 5.00 (ISBN 0-934114-09-9, BK-116). Marine Educ.
Block, Richard A., ed. see Vandegrift, John F., Sr.
Block, Richard A., ed. see Ward, Robert J.
Block, Richard A., ed. see Zee, Thomas E.
Block, Richard A., et al, eds. R. B. - 169: New Unified Navigation Rules for International & Inland Waters Including the Great Lakes & Western Rivers. rev. "A" ed. (Illus.). 194p. 1983. pap. text ed. 14.00 (ISBN 0-934114-46-3, BK-234). Marine Educ.
Block, Richard J. & Bolling, Diana. The Amino Acid Composition of Proteins & Foods: Analytical Methods & Results. 2nd ed. (Illus.). 584p. 1951. 48.50x (ISBN 0-398-04210-1). C C Thomas.
Block, Richard J. & Weiss, Kathryn W. Amino Acid Handbook: Methods & Results of Protein Analysis. (Illus.). 384p. 1956. 32.50x (ISBN 0-398-04211-X). C C Thomas.
Block, Rudolph E. Children of Men. LC 76-103496. (Short Story Index Reprint Ser.). 1903. 19.00 (ISBN 0-8369-3238-2). Ayer Co Pubs.
Block, Russell, et al, trs. see Trotsky, Leon.
Block, Ruth H. Visionary Republic: Millennial Themes in American Thought, 1756-1800. 320p. Date not set. price not set. (ISBN 0-521-26811-7). Cambridge U Pr.
Block, Seymor S., ed. Disinfection, Sterilization & Preservation. 3rd ed. LC 82-24002. (Illus.). 1053p. 1983. text ed. 87.50 (ISBN 0-8121-0863-9). Lea & Febiger.
Block, Stanley, ed. Mechanisms of Phase Transitions. (Transactions of the American Crystallographic Association Ser.: Vol. 7). 154p. 1971. pap. 15.00 (ISBN 0-686-60378-8). Polycrystal Bk Serv.
Block, Stanley B. & Hirt, Geoffrey A. Foundations of Financial Management. 3rd ed. 1982. 29.95 (ISBN 0-256-02498-7). Irwin.
--Introduction to Finance. LC 80-69851. Orig. Title: Foundation of Financial Management. 289p. 1980. Repr. of 1978 ed. text ed. 16.00 (ISBN 0-89463-030-X). Am Inst Property.
Block, Stanley B., jt. auth. see Hirt, Geoffrey A.
Block, Sue. Aerobics Plus: How to Sweat with Class. LC 81-80789. (Illus.). 192p. (Orig.). 1982. pap. text ed. 7.95 (ISBN 0-918438-72-1). Leisure Pr.
Block, Susan. Advertising for Love: How to Play the Personals. (Illus.). 160p. (Orig.). 1983. pap. 5.95 (ISBN 0-688-02644-3, Quill). Morrow.
Block, Thomas. Forced Landing. 320p. 1984. pap. 3.95 (ISBN 0-425-06830-7). Berkley Pub.
--Orbit. 320p. 1983. pap. 3.50 (ISBN 0-425-05740-2). Berkley Pub.
Block, Thomas H. Airship Nine. LC 84-13421. 304p. 1984. 16.95 (ISBN 0-399-12977-4, Putnam). Putnam Pub Group.
--Airship Nine. 288p. 1985. pap. 3.95 (ISBN 0-425-08301-2). Berkley Pub.
--Forced Landing. LC 82-23469. 288p. 1983. 14.95 (ISBN 0-698-11232-6, Coward). Putnam Pub Group.
--Mayday. 336p. 1980. pap. 2.95 (ISBN 0-425-04729-6). Berkley Pub.
Block, Toby, jt. auth. see Riley, Gary F.
Block, Toby F. Experiments in General Chemistry. 240p. 1983. pap. text ed. 11.50 (ISBN 0-8403-3103-7). Kendall-Hunt.
Block, Walter. Defending the Undefendables: The Pimp, Prostitute, Scab, Usurer, Libeler, & Other Scapegoats in the Rogue's Gallery of American Society. LC 74-21359. 1976. 12.95 (ISBN 0-8303-0136-4); pap. 9.50 (ISBN 0-8303-0183-6). Fleet.

Block, Walter D. & Van Goor, Kornelius. Metabolism, Pharmacology & Therapeutic Uses of Gold Compounds. 80p. 1956. 9.75x (ISBN 0-398-04212-8). C C Thomas.

Block, Walter E. Focus: On Discrimination. 80p. 1985. 5.00 (ISBN 0-88975-088-2). Fraser Inst.

Block, Walter E., jt. auth. see Floyd, John E.

Block, Walter E., ed. The Environmentalists versus the Economy. 200p. 1985. avail. (ISBN 0-88975-067-X). Fraser Inst.

Blockcolsky, V. D., et al. Peel & Put Manual for Speech & Language Development. rev. ed. 88p. 1977. pap. 8.95 (ISBN 0-88450-173-6, 2040-B). Communication Skill.

Blockcolsky, Valeda & Frazer, Joan. Peel & Put Reading Manual. 84p. 1980. pap. text ed. 8.95 (ISBN 0-88450-180-9, 3122-B). Communication Skill.

Blockcolsky, Valeda & Frazer, Joan M. Star Trails: Reproducible Carryover Worksheets for R, S, L, TH, SH, CH. rev. & Combined ed. 258p. (gr. k-8). 1983. pap. 24.95 (ISBN 0-88450-862-5, 7029-B). Communication Skill.

Blocker, H. Gene. The Metaphysics of Absurdity. LC 78-78399. 1979. pap. text ed. 11.00 (ISBN 0-8191-0712-3). U Pr of Amer.

--Philosophy of Art. LC 78-10942. 278p. 1979. pap. text ed. 13.95 (ISBN 0-02-310840-1, Pub. by Scribner). Macmillan.

Blocker, H. Gene, jt. auth. see Stewart, David.

Blocker, H. Gene & Smith, Elizabeth H., eds. John Rawls' Theory of Social Justice: An Introduction. LC 80-11272. xxiv, 520p. 1980. 29.95x (ISBN 0-8214-0445-8, 82-83368); pap. text ed. 14.95x (ISBN 0-8214-0593-4, 82-83376). Ohio U Pr.

Blocker, Jack S., Jr. Give to the Winds Thy Fears: The Women Temperance Crusade, 1873-1874. LC 84-15718. (Contributions in Women Studies: No. 55). (Illus.). xix, 280p. 1985. lib. bdg. 35.00 (ISBN 0-313-24556-8, BGW/). Greenwood.

--Retreat from Reform: The Prohibition Movement in the United States, 1890-1913. LC 76-5325. (Contributions in American History: No. 51). 288p. 1976. lib. bdg. 29.95x (ISBN 0-8371-8899-7, BRR/). Greenwood.

Blocker, Jack S., Jr., ed. Alcohol, Reform & Society: The Liquor Issue in Social Context. LC 78-73800. (Contributions in American History: No. 83). (Illus.). 1979. lib. bdg. 29.95x (ISBN 0-313-20889-1, BLA/). Greenwood.

Blocker, Joel, ed. Israeli Stories: A Selection of the Best Contemporary Hebrew Writing. LC 61-14918. 1965. pap. 6.95 (ISBN 0-8052-0108-4). Schocken.

Blocker, William, Jr. & Cardus, David, eds. Rehabilitation in Ischemic Heart Disease. LC 80-22840. (Illus.). 500p. 1983. text ed. 80.00 (ISBN 0-89335-096-6). SP Med & Sci Bks.

Blockey, Harry & Paz, Jaime. Great Western Recipes from Texas. 48p. pap. cancelled (ISBN 0-88409-086-8). Creative Bk Co.

Blockhaus, Arthur P. Grievance Arbitration Case Studies. LC 74-8433. 416p. 1974. 19.95 (ISBN 0-8436-0722-X). Van Nos Reinhold.

Blockhus, Wanda A., jt. auth. see Stewart, Jeffrey R., Jr.

Blocki, Jack. Underwater Gorillas Are Hard to Find. LC 82-91009. 102p. 1984. 10.00 (ISBN 0-533-05674-8). Vantage.

Blockley, D. I. The Nature of Structure-Design & Safety. 365p. 1980. 99.95x (ISBN 0-470-27047-0). Halsted Pr.

Blockley, J., jt. auth. see Fraser, G. M.

Blockley, John. Country Landscapes in Watercolor. (Illus.). 144p. 1982. 22.50 (ISBN 0-8230-1616-1). Watson-Guptill.

--Creative Watercolour Techniques. (Leisure Arts Ser.: Bk. 7). (Illus.). 32p. 1984. pap. 2.95 (ISBN 0-89134-083-1, Pub. by North Light). Writers Digest.

--How To Paint with Pastels. 64p. 1982. pap. 6.95 (ISBN 0-89586-159-3). H P Bks.

Blockley, John & Bolton, Richard. Watercolor Painting Techniques: Learn How to Master Watercolor Working Techniques to Create Your Own Successful Paintings. Blake, Wendon, ed. (Illus.). 144p. 1983. pap. 14.95 (ISBN 0-8230-5669-4). Watson-Guptill.

Blockley, R. C. Ammianus Marcellinus: A Selection. 250p. 30.00x (ISBN 0-906515-07-6, Pub. by Bristol Classical Pr). State Mutual Bk.

Blockley, Rain, ed. see Laborde, Genie Z.

Blocksma, Dewey, jt. auth. see Blocksma, Mary.

Blocksma, Mary. Apple Tree! Apple Tree! LC 82-19852. (Just One More Ser.). (Illus.). 24p. (ps-2). 1983. PLB 9.65 (ISBN 0-516-01584-2); pap. 2.50 (ISBN 0-516-41584-0). Childrens.

--The Best-Dressed Bear. LC 84-9565. (Just One More Ser.). (Illus.). 24p. (ps-2). 1984. lib. bdg. 9.65 (ISBN 0-516-01585-0); pap. text ed. 2.50 (ISBN 0-516-41585-9). Childrens.

--Did You Hear That? LC 82-19877. (Just One More Ser.). (Illus.). 24p. (ps-2). 1983. PLB 9.65 (ISBN 0-516-01581-8); pap. 2.50 (ISBN 0-516-41581-6). Childrens.

--Grandma Dragon's Birthday. LC 82-19851. (Just One More Ser.). (Illus.). 24p. (ps-2). 1983. PLB 9.65 (ISBN 0-516-01582-6); pap. 2.50 (ISBN 0-516-41582-4). Childrens.

--The Marvelous Music Machine: A Story of the Piano. LC 84-4892. (Illus.). 64p. (gr. 3-7). 1984. pap. 10.95 (ISBN 0-13-559410-3). P-H.

--The Pup Went up. LC 82-19862. (Just One More Ser.). (Illus.). 24p. (ps-2). 1983. PLB 9.65 (ISBN 0-516-01583-4); pap. 2.50 (ISBN 0-516-41583-2). Childrens.

--Rub-aDub-Dub: What's in the Tub? LC 84-12139. (Just One More Ser.). (Illus.). 24p. (ps-2). 1984. lib. bdg. 9.65 (ISBN 0-516-01586-9); pap. 2.50 (ISBN 0-516-41586-7). Childrens.

Blocksma, Mary & Blocksma, Dewey. Easy-to-Make Spaceships That Really Fly. (Illus.). 40p. (gr. 2-6). 1985. pap. 4.95 (ISBN 0-13-223199-9). P-H.

--Easy-to-Make Water Toys That Really Work. (Illus.). 64p. (gr. 2-6). 1985. 10.95 (ISBN 0-13-223561-7). P-H.

Blocksman, Mary, et al. Easy to Make Spaceships That Really Fly. LC 83-10986. (Illus.). 48p. (gr. 2-6). 1983. PLB 9.95 (ISBN 0-13-223180-8). P-H.

Blocksom, Claudia. A Child's American Heritage. (Fat Cat Fun Books Ser.). (Illus.). 40p. 1975. pap. 2.95 (ISBN 0-8431-1743-5, 58-2). Troubador Pr.

--It's Your World. (Illus.). 40p. (gr. 1-8). 1979. pap. 2.95 (ISBN 0-8431-1749-4). Troubador Pr.

Blockson, Charles. Pennsylvania's Black History. (Illus.). 1981. pap. 5.95 (ISBN 0-933184-15-8). Flame Intl.

Blockson, Charles L. The Underground Railroad in Pennsylvania. LC 80-69847. (Illus.). 225p. 1981. 13.95 (ISBN 0-933184-21-2); pap. 6.95 (ISBN 0-933184-22-0). Flame Intl.

Blodget, Samuel. Economica: A Statistical Manual for the United States of America. LC 64-17403. Repr. of 1806 ed. 27.50x (ISBN 0-678-00037-9). Kelley.

Blodgett & Swanson. Carmina Burana: Love Lyrics. 1985. lib. bdg. 40.00 (ISBN 0-8240-8779-8). Garland Pub.

Blodgett, Audrey H., jt. auth. see Wheelwright, Joseph B.

Blodgett, Diane, jt. auth. see Bell, C. William.

Blodgett, Diane E. Manual of Pediatric Respiratory Care Procedures. (Illus.). 256p. 1982. pap. text ed. 13.75 (ISBN 0-397-50506-X, 65-006505, Lippincott Medical). Lippincott.

Blodgett, Diane E., ed. Manual of Respiratory Care Procedures. (Illus.). 239p. 1980. pap. text ed. 13.75 (ISBN 0-397-50434-9, 65-05614, Lippincott Medical). Lippincott.

Blodgett, Geoffrey. Oberlin Architechture, College & Town: A Guide to Its Social History. 264p. pap. 9.95 (ISBN 0-317-29657-4). Kent St U Pr.

--Oberlin Architecture, College & Town: A Social History. LC 84-18987. (Illus.). 260p. (Orig.). 1985. pap. 9.95 (ISBN 0-87338-309-5). Kent St U Pr.

Blodgett, George B. Early Settlers of Rowley, MA. LC 81-83875. 472p. 1981. Repr. of 1933 ed. 45.00x (ISBN 0-89725-027-3). NE History.

Blodgett, Harold W. Walt Whitman in England. 59.95 (ISBN 0-8490-1274-0). Gordon Pr.

Blodgett, Harold W., ed. see Whitman, Walt.

Blodgett, Harriet E. Mentally Retarded Children: What Parents & Others Should Know. LC 72-152301. pap. 43.80 (ISBN 0-317-29393-1, 2055845). Bks Demand UMI.

Blodgett, Harriet E. & Warfield, Grace J. Understanding Mentally Retarded Children. LC 59-12295. (Illus., Orig.). 1959. pap. text ed. 4.95x (ISBN 0-89197-457-1). Irvington.

Blodgett, Joan. Metrics the Easy Way. LC 76-20211. (Illus., Orig.). 1976. pap. 1.50 (ISBN 0-912800-35-6). Woodbridge Pr.

Blodgett, Ralph. Hell: Will the Wicked Burn Forever? (Outreach Ser.). 1981. pap. 0.99 (ISBN 0-8163-0375-4). Pacific Pr Pub Assn.

--How Will It End? (Eighty-Five-Miss Ser). 1984. pap. 1.19 (ISBN 0-8163-0567-6). Pacific Pr Pub Assn.

--Millennium. (Outreach Ser.). 1981. pap. 0.99 (ISBN 0-8163-0398-3). Pacific Pr Pub Assn.

Blodgett, Ralph H., jt. auth. see Anderson, Montgomery D.

Blodgett, Richard. Photographs: A Collector's Guide. (Illus.). 1979. 12.95 (ISBN 0-345-27710-4); pap. 6.95 (ISBN 0-345-28272-8). Ballantine.

Blodgett, Richard, ed. see Merrill Lynch.

Blodgett, Richard E. The New York Times Book of Money. rev. ed. LC 78-23467. (Illus.). 224p. 1978. pap. 8.95 (ISBN 0-8129-6308-3). Times Bks.

Blodgett, Terrell. Management Study of the Texas State Auditor's Office. 167p. 1984. 3.00 (ISBN 0-89940-807-9). LBJ Sch Pub Aff.

Blodgett, Terrell & Jordan, Barbara. Local Government Election Systems. LC 84-81908. (Policy Research Project Ser.: No. 62). 174p. 1984. 8.95 (ISBN 0-89940-664-5). LBJ Sch Pub Aff.

Blodgett, Timothy B., jt. ed. see Bursk, Edward C.

Blodgette, George B., jt. auth. see Mighill, Benjamin P.

Blodi, F. C., jt. ed. see Lommatzch, P. K.

Blodi, Frederick, tr. see Bec, Pierre.

Blodi, Frederick, tr. see Hollwich, Fritz.

Blodi, Frederick C., ed. Herpes Simplex Infections of the Eye. (Contemporary Issues in Opthalmology Ser.: Vol. 1). (Illus.). 176p. 1984. text ed. 39.50 (ISBN 0-443-08339-8). Churchill.

Blodi, Frederick C., tr. see Nover, Arno.

Blodi, Frederick C., tr. see Sautter, H. & Straub, W.

Blodi, Fredrick, ed. see Huber, Alfred.

Blodinger. Formulation of Veterinary Dosage Forms. (Drugs & the Pharmaceutical Sciences Ser.). 454p. 1983. 55.00 (ISBN 0-8247-1730-9). Dekker.

Blodnieks, Adolfs. Undefeated Nation. 1959. 9.95 (ISBN 0-8315-0019-0). Speller.

Bloedau, Carl A. Von see Von Bloedau, Carl A.

Bloedel, James, jt. ed. see Davis, Ross.

Bloem, Diane. A Womans Workshop on Proverbs. 1978. leader's manual 3.95 (ISBN 0-310-21371-1); student manual 2.95 (ISBN 0-310-21361-4). Zondervan.

--A Woman's Workshop on the Beautitudes. (Orig.). 1981. Leader's Manual, 160 Pages. pap. 3.95 (ISBN 0-310-42641-3); Student's Manual, 96 Pages. pap. 2.95 (ISBN 0-310-42651-0). Zondervan.

Bloem, Diane B. Growing Godly: A Woman's Workshop on Bible Women. 128p. 1983. pap. 3.95 (ISBN 0-310-23151-5). Zondervan.

Bloem, Diane B. & Bloem, Robert C. A Women's Workshop on Bible Marriages. (Woman's Workshop Series of Study Books). 128p. (Orig.). 1980. pap. 2.95 student's manual (ISBN 0-310-21391-6); pap. 3.95 leader's manual (ISBN 0-310-21401-7). Zondervan.

Bloem, Robert C., jt. auth. see Bloem, Diane B.

Bloembergen, N., ed. Nonlinear Spectroscopy: Proceedings. (Enrico Fermi Internatinal School of Physics Ser.: No. 64). 460p. 1977. 95.75 (ISBN 0-7204-0568-8, North-Holland). Elsevier.

Bloembergen, Nicolaas. Nonlinear Optics. (Frontiers in Physics Ser.: No. 21). 1965. 30.95 (ISBN 0-8053-0938-1). Benjamin-Cummings.

Bloemendal, Hans. Molecular & Cellular Biology of the Eye Lens. LC 80-26815. 469p. 1981. 109.95 (ISBN 0-471-05171-3, Pub. by Wiley-Interscience). Wiley.

Bloesch, Donald. Is the Bible Sexist? LC 81-71344. 128p. (Orig.). 1982. pap. 5.95 (ISBN 0-89107-243-8, Crossway Bks). Good News.

Bloesch, Donald, et al. Christianity Confronts Modernity: A Theological & Pastoral Inquiry by Protestant Evangelicals & Roman Catholics. Perrotta, Kevin, et al, eds. 172p. (Orig.). 1981. pap. 7.95 (ISBN 0-89283-100-6). Servant.

Bloesch, Donald G. Battle for the Trinity: The Debate over Inclusive God-Language. 1985. 10.95 (ISBN 0-89283-230-4, Pub. by Vine Books). Servant.

--Crumbling Foundations. 160p. (Orig.). 1984. pap. text ed. 6.95 (ISBN 0-310-29821-0, 12740P, Pub. by Academie Bks). Zondervan.

--Essentials of Evangelical Theology, Vol. I: God, Authority, Salvation. LC 77-15872. 288p. 1982. pap. 11.49i (ISBN 0-686-81487-8, RD 386, HarpR). Har-Row.

--Essentials of Evangelical Theology, Vol. II: Life, Ministry, & Hope. LC 78-3140. 352p. 1982. pap. 11.49i (ISBN 0-06-060803-X, RD 387, HarpR). Har-Row.

--Jesus Is Victor! Karl Barth's Doctrine of Salvation. LC 76-14360. Repr. of 1976 ed. 33.50 (ISBN 0-8357-9013-4, 2016373). Bks Demand UMI.

Blofeld, John. Bodhisattva of Compassion: The Mystical Tradition of Kuan Yin. LC 77-91352. (Illus.). 155p. 1978. pap. 5.95 (ISBN 0-87773-126-8, 73609-5). Shambhala Pubns.

--The Chinese Art of Tea. LC 84-23661. (Illus.). 200p. (Orig.). 1985. pap. 8.95 (ISBN 0-87773-320-1, 73799-7). Shambhala Pubns.

--Mantras: Sacred Words of Power. (Paperbacks Ser.). (Illus.). 120p. 1977. pap. 6.50 (ISBN 0-04-294097-4). Allen Unwin.

--Taoism: The Road to Immortality. LC 77-90882. 195p. 1978. pap. 9.95 (ISBN 0-87773-116-0, 73582-X). Shambhala Pubns.

Blofeld, John, tr. I Ching, the Book of Change. 1968. pap. 6.95 (ISBN 0-525-47212-6, 0631-190). Dutton.

Blofeld, John, tr. see Huang Po.

Blofeld, John E. The Jewel in the Lotus: Outline of Present Day Buddhism in China. LC 74-10096. (China Studies: from Confucius to Mao Ser). 193p. 1975. Repr. of 1948 ed. 19.25 (ISBN 0-88355-161-6). Hyperion Conn.

Blogg, J. Rowan. The Eye in Veterinary Practice: Extraocular Disease. LC 76-54038. (Illus.). 1980. text ed. 70.00 (ISBN 0-7216-1751-4). Saunders.

Blogg, Rowan & Allan, Eric. Everydog: The Complete Book of Dog Care. LC 83-63599. (Illus.). 312p. 1984. 17.95 (ISBN 0-688-02509-9). Morrow.

Blohincev, D. I., et al. Probability & Physical Problems. (Translations Ser.: No. 1, Vol. 11). 1962. 24.00 (ISBN 0-8218-1611-X, TRANS 1-11). Am Math.

Blohm, Hannelore & Cremer, Hans-Diedrich. Simple & Quick Diet Cookbook: How to Lose Weight & Stay Healthy. 104p. 1985. 8.95 (ISBN 0-8120-5659-0). Barron.

Blohm, Hans & Naske, Claus. Alaska. (Illus.). 1984. 15.00 (ISBN 0-19-540604-4). Skyline Press.

Blohm, Hans & Naske, Claus, illus. Alaska. (Illus.). 1985. pap. 12.95 (ISBN 0-318-12035-6). Skyline Press.

Bloice, Carl. Israel: Image & Reality: a Journalist's First-Hand Report. 48p. 1973. pap. 0.65 (ISBN 0-87898-103-9). New Outlook.

Blois, John T. Gazetteer of the State of Michigan. facsimile ed. LC 75-87. (Mid-American Frontier Ser.). 1975. Repr. of 1838 ed. 31.00x (ISBN 0-405-06855-7). Ayer Co Pubs.

--Michigan Gazetteer. 1838. 418p. 1979. 19.75 (ISBN 0-686-27820-8). Bookmark.

Blois, K. J. & Cowell, D. W. Short Cases in Marketing Management. 1973. text ed. 22.95x (ISBN 0-7002-0207-2). Intl Ideas.

Blois, M. S., ed. Symposium on Free Radicals in Biological Systems. 1961. 75.00 (ISBN 0-12-107550-8). Acad Pr.

Blois, Marsden S. Information & Medicine: The Nature of Medical Descriptions. LC 83-24923. 300p. 1985. 27.50x (ISBN 0-520-04988-8). U of Cal Pr.

Blois, R. E. The American Reputation & Influence of William Blake. 59.95 (ISBN 0-87968-611-1). Gordon Pr.

Blok, Aleksandr. The Twelve & Other Poems. Hollo, Anselm, tr. 1971. pap. 4.00 (ISBN 0-917788-04-4). Gnomon Pr.

Blok, Alexander. Selected Poems: Alexander Blok. 327p. 1981. 9.00 (ISBN 0-8285-1981-1, Pub. by Progress Pubs USSR). Imported Pubns.

--The Spirit of Music. Freiman, I., tr. from Rus. LC 72-14050. (Soviet Literature in English Translation Ser.). (Illus.). 70p. 1973. Repr. of 1946 ed. 8.50 (ISBN 0-88355-001-6). Hyperion Conn.

Blok, C. & Jezewski, W. Dictionnaire Illustre de l'Automobile "Kluwer," en 6 Langues. 504p. (Fr., Eng., Ger., Ital., Rus. & Dutch.). 1979. 145.00 (ISBN 0-686-56923-7, M-6039). French & Eur.

Blok, Czeslaw & Jezewski, Wieslaw. Illustrated Automobile Dictionary. (Illus.). 1978. lib. bdg. 89.00 (ISBN 9-0201-1070-5, Pub. by Kluwer Tech Netherlands). Kluwer Academic.

Blok, D. P., ed. Proceedings of the Eighth International Congress of Onomastic Sciences, Amsterdam, 1963. (Janua Linguarum Series Major: No. 17). 1966. 92.00x (ISBN 90-2790-609-2). Mouton.

Blok, Petrus J. History of the People of the Netherlands, 5 Vols. Bierstadt, O. A. & Putnam, Ruth, trs. LC 76-109911. (Illus.). Repr. of 1912 ed. Set. 125.00 (ISBN 0-404-00900-X); 25.00 ea. AMS Pr.

--The Life of Admiral De Ruyter. Renier, G. J., tr. LC 74-9393. (Illus.). 388p. 1975. Repr. of 1933 ed. lib. bdg. 22.50x (ISBN 0-8371-7666-2, BLAR). Greenwood.

Blokhintsev, D. I. The Philosophy of Quantum Mechanics. LC 68-22439. 132p. 1968. lib. bdg. 24.00 (ISBN 90-277-0105-9, Pub. by Reidel Holland). Kluwer Academic.

--Quantum Mechanics. (Russian Monographs & Texts on the Physical Sciences). 552p. 1966. 115.50 (ISBN 0-677-60080-1). Gordon.

--Quantum Mechanics. Sykes, J. B. & Kearsley, M. J., trs. from Rus. 535p. 1964. lib. bdg. 39.50 (ISBN 90-277-0104-0, Pub. by Reidel Holland). Kluwer Academic.

--Space & Time in the Microworld. Smith, Z., tr. from Rus. LC 72-77871. Orig. Title: Prostranstuo I Uremja V Micromire. 330p. 1973. lib. bdg. 60.50 (ISBN 90-277-0240-3, Pub. by Reidel Holland). Kluwer Academic.

Blokker, Roy & Dearling, Robert. The Music of Dmitri Shostakovich. LC 78-68623. 192p. 1979. 22.50 (ISBN 0-8386-1948-7). Fairleigh Dickinson.

Blokland, J. Continuous Consumer Equivalence Scales. 1976. pap. 17.00 (ISBN 90-247-1847-3, Pub. by Martinus Nijhoff Netherlands). Kluwer Academic.

Blokland, R. Elasticity & Structure of Polyurethane Networks. 120p. 1969. 44.25 (ISBN 0-677-61200-1). Gordon.

Blom, Benjamin. New York: Photographs Eighteen Fifty to Nineteen Fifty. LC 82-71495. (Illus.). 55.00 (ISBN 0-943276-00-4). Amaryllis Pr.

--People Mostly, New York in Photographs 1900-1950. LC 83-71881. (Illus.). 25.00 (ISBN 0-943276-01-2). Amaryllis Pr.

--People Mostly: New York in Photographs, 1900-1950. LC 84-71237. (Illus.). 160p. 1984. pap. 15.00. Amaryllis Pr.

Blom, Dick. Rider's Complete Guide to Motorcycle Touring: How to Have Fun & Worries on your Motorcycle Tours. (Illus.). 213p. 1981. 12.95 (ISBN 0-934798-02-8). TL Enterprises.

Blom, Dorothea. Art & the Changing World: Uncommon Sense in the Twentieth Century. LC 72-80094. (Illus.). 32p. (Orig.). 1972. pap. 5.00x (ISBN 0-87574-183-5, 183). Pendle Hill.

--Art Imagery & the Mythic Process. LC 77-91636. (Illus.). 31p. (Orig.). 1977. pap. 2.30x (ISBN 0-87574-215-7). Pendle Hill.

--Art Responds to the Bible. LC 74-24006. (Illus.). 32p. (Orig.). 1974. pap. 2.30x (ISBN 0-87574-197-5). Pendle Hill.

--Encounters with Art. 1983. pap. 5.00x (ISBN 0-87574-128-2, 128). Pendle Hill.

--Life Journey of a Quaker Artist. LC 80-80916. 32p. (Orig.). 1980. 2.30x (ISBN 0-87574-232-7). Pendle Hill.

--The Prophetic Element in Modern Art. 1983. pap. 5.00x (ISBN 0-87574-148-7, 148). Pendle Hill.

Blom, Edward C. Radio & Electric Power Supply Equipment for Schools. LC 77-176571. (Columbia University. Teachers College. Contributions to Education: No. 409). Repr. of 1930 ed. 22.50 (ISBN 0-404-55409-1). AMS Pr.

Blom, Eric. Beethoven's Pianoforte Sonatas Discussed. LC 68-21092. (Music Ser.). 1968. Repr. of 1938 ed. 27.50 (ISBN 0-306-71059-5). Da Capo.

--Classics: Major & Minor. LC 74-166098. 212p. 1972. Repr. of 1958 ed. lib. bdg. 24.50 (ISBN 0-306-70293-2). Da Capo.

--A General Index to Modern Musical Literature in the English Language: Including Periodicals for the Years 1915-1926. LC 71-108736. (Music Ser.). 1970. Repr. of 1927 ed. lib. bdg. 21.50 (ISBN 0-306-71898-7). Da Capo.

--The Limitations of Music: A Study in Aesthetics. LC 72-80139. Repr. of 1928 ed. 18.00 (ISBN 0-405-08275-4, Blom Pubns). Ayer Co Pubs.

--Mozart. rev. ed. (Master Musicians Ser.: No. M155). (Illus.). 388p. 1978. pap. 7.95 (ISBN 0-8226-0700-X). Littlefield.

--Mozart. rev. ed. (The Master Musicians Ser.). (Illus.). 400p. 1976. Repr. of 1974 ed. 13.00x (ISBN 0-460-03157-0, Pub by J M Dent England). Biblio Dist.

--Music in England. LC 71-181112. 220p. 1942. Repr. 29.00 (ISBN 0-403-01511-1). Scholarly.

--Romance of the Piano. LC 69-15608. (Music Ser). (Illus.). 1969. Repr. of 1928 ed. 27.50 (ISBN 0-306-71060-9). Da Capo.

--Stepchildren of Music. facs. ed. LC 67-28731. (Essay Index Reprint Ser). 1926. 18.00 (ISBN 0-8369-0217-3). Ayer Co Pubs.

--Tchaikovsky: Orchestral Works. LC 70-109711. Repr. of 1927 ed. lib. bdg. 22.50x (ISBN 0-8371-4202-4, BLTC). Greenwood.

Blom, Eric, ed. Grove's Dictionary of Music & Musicians, 10 vols. 5th ed. 1954. Set. 600.00 (ISBN 0-333-19262-1). Groves Dict Music.

Blom, Eric, tr. see Deutsch, Otto E.

Blom, F. The Conquest of Yucatan. 1976. lib. bdg. 59.95 (ISBN 0-8490-1665-7). Gordon Pr.

Blom, Frank S., et al. Focus on a Middle School Belief System. (Illus.). 1979. pap. text ed. 2.50 (ISBN 0-918449-01-4). MI Middle Educ.

Blom, Frans. Conquest of Yucatan. LC 77-164521. 1972. Repr. of 1937 ed. 25.00 (ISBN 0-8154-0390-9). Cooper Sq.

Blom, Gaston E., et al. Stress in Childhood: An Intervention Model for Teachers. (Special Education Ser.). 200p. 1985. pap. text ed. 15.95x (ISBN 0-8077-2780-6). Tchrs Coll.

Blom, Gertrude. Gertrude Blom-Bearing Witness. Harris, Alex & Sartor, Margaret, eds. LC 83-23272. (Illus.). x, 150p. 1984. 32.00 (ISBN 0-8078-1597-7). U of NC Pr.

Blom, Jan B. & Nyhus, Sven, eds. Norwegian Folk Music: Vol. VII, Harding Fiddle Music. 320p. 1981. 65.00x (ISBN 82-00-05508-6). Universitet.

Blom, Jan P., et al, eds. Norwegian Folk Music: Series One: Slattar for the Harding Fiddle. Vol. VI, Springar in 3/4 Time. 1979. 36.00x (ISBN 82-00-08794-8, Dist. by Columbia U. Pr.). Universitet.

Blom, John J. Descartes: His Moral Philosophy & Psychology. LC 78-55241. 1978. 26.00x (ISBN 0-8147-0999-0). NYU Pr.

Blom, Lynne A. & Chaplin, L. Tarin. The Intimate Act of Choreography. LC 82-2056. (Illus.). xx, 230p. 1982. 19.95x (ISBN 0-8229-3463-9); pap. 7.95x (ISBN 0-8229-5342-0). U of Pittsburgh Pr.

Blom, Margaret. Charlotte Bronte. (English Authors Ser.). 1977. lib. bdg. 13.50 (ISBN 0-8057-6673-1, Twayne). G K Hall.

Blom, Margaret H. & Blom, Thomas, eds. Canada Home: Juliana Horatia Ewing's Fredericton Letters, 1867-1869. (Illus.). 448p. 1983. 24.95 (ISBN 0-7748-0174-3, Pub. by U of BC). Intl Spec Bk.

Blom, Paul. Ministry of Welcome: A Guide for Ushers & Greeters. 32p. (Orig.). 1980. pap. 2.50 (ISBN 0-8066-1806-X, 10-4442). Augsburg.

Blom, Thomas, jt. ed. see Blom, Margaret H.

Blombach, Birger & Hanson, Lars A., eds. Plasma Proteins. LC 78-102126. 400p. 1979. 104.95 (ISBN 0-471-99730-7, Pub. by Wiley-Interscience). Wiley.

Bomback, M. & Brakman, P., eds. Synthetic Substrates & Synthetic Inhibitors: The Use of Chromogenic Substrates in Studies of the Haemostatic Mechanism. (Haemostasis: Vol. 7, Nos. 2-3). (Illus.). 1978. pap. 16.25 (ISBN 3-8055-2907-4). S Karger.

Blomberg, Belinda. Material Correlates of Increasing Sedentism: The Black Mesa Navajo. LC 82-72265. (Research Paper: No. 32). (Illus.). v, 65p. 1982. soft cover 5.00 (ISBN 0-88104-002-9). Center Archaeo.

Blomberg, Don W. Good News of the Kingdom. 1985. 8.75 (ISBN 0-317-13203-2). Carlton.

Blomberg, Hans & Ylinen, R. Algebraic Theory for Multivariable Linear Systems. (Mathematics in Science & Engineering Ser.). 1983. 55.00 (ISBN 0-12-107150-2). Acad Pr.

Blomberg, Thomas G. Juvenile Court & Community Corrections. (Illus.). 154p. (Orig.). 1985. lib. bdg. 21.50 (ISBN 0-8191-4260-3); pap. text ed. 10.25 (ISBN 0-8191-4261-1). U Pr of Amer.

Blomberg, Thomas G., jt. ed. see Brantingham, Patricia L.

Blombery, Alec & Rodd, Tony. Palms. (Illus.). 199p. 1983. 24.95 (ISBN 0-207-14848-1, Pub. by Salem Hse Ltd). Merrimack Pub Cir.

Blom-Cooper, Louis, ed. Progress in Penal Reform. 1974. 52.00x (ISBN 0-19-825325-7). Oxford U Pr.

Blom-Cooper, Louis & Drewry, Gavin, eds. Law & Morality: A Reader. 265p. 1976. 40.50x (ISBN 0-7156-0805-3, Pub. by Duckworth England); pap. 13.50x (ISBN 0-7156-0804-5, Pub. by Duckworth England). Biblio Dist.

Blomenberg, Paula, ed. Graduate Programs & Faculty in Reading. 4th ed. 382p. 1981. pap. 15.50 (ISBN 0-87207-928-7). Intl Reading.

Blomfield, Adelaide. The Sound of Breathing. 1977. 6.25 (ISBN 0-941490-15-7). Solo Pr.

Blomfield, Reginald. Three Hundred Years of French Architecture, 1494-1794. facs. ed. LC 70-124233. (Select Bibliographies Reprint Ser). 1936. 16.00 (ISBN 0-8369-5414-9). Ayer Co Pubs.

Blomfield, Reginald T. Formal Garden in England. 3rd ed. LC 77-181912. (BCL Ser. I). Repr. of 1901 ed. 15.00 (ISBN 0-404-00898-4). AMS Pr.

--Six Architects. facs. ed. LC 78-99682. (Essay Index Reprint Ser.). 1935. 18.00 (ISBN 0-8369-1340-X). Ayer Co Pubs.

Blomgren, David K. Bible Survey. (Illus.). 70p. (gr. 9-12). 1979. pap. 6.25 (ISBN 0-914936-39-5). Bible Temple.

--Biblical View of Restoration. (Illus.). 20p. pap. 1.30 (ISBN 0-914936-41-7). Bible Temple.

--The Laying on of Hands & Prophecy of the Presbytery. (Illus.). 100p. 1979. pap. 6.50 (ISBN 0-914936-36-0). Bible Temple.

--The Song of the Lord. 50p. 1978. pap. 3.75 (ISBN 0-914936-31-X). Bible Temple.

Blomguist, Donals S., jt. auth. see Magrab, Edward B.

Blommerde, Anton C. Northwest Semetic Grammar & Job. (Biblica et Orientalia Ser.: Vol. 22). 1969. pap. 13.00 (ISBN 88-7653-322-2). Loyola.

Blommers, Paul J. & Forsyth, Robert A. Elementary Statistical Methods in Psychology & Education. 2nd ed. LC 83-6978. (Illus.). 584p. 1983. pap. text ed. 19.75 (ISBN 0-8191-2684-5). U Pr of Amer.

--Elementary Statistical Methods in Psychology & Education: Study Manual. 2nd ed. (Illus.). 268p. 1984. pap. text ed. 12.50 (ISBN 0-8191-4122-4). U Pr of Amer.

Blomquist, Hugo L., jt. auth. see Greene, Wilhelmina F.

Blomquist, Kathleen B., et al. Community Health Nursing Continuing Education Review. 1979. pap. 13.00 (ISBN 0-87488-401-2). Med Exam.

Blomquist, Lawrence, tr. L' Art D'amours. LC 84-48065. 375p. 1985. lib. bdg. 30.00 (ISBN 0-8240-8915-4). Garland Pub.

Blomstrom, Magus & Hettne, Bjorn. Development Theory in Transition: The Dependency Debate & Beyond: Third World Responses. 224p. 1984. bds. 26.25x (ISBN 0-86232-270-7, Pub. by Zed Pr England); pap. 10.25 (ISBN 0-86232-271-5, Pub. by Zed Pr England). Biblio Dist.

Blomstrom, Robert L., ed. Strategic Marketing Planning in the Hospitality Industry: A Book of Readings. 1983. pap. 23.95 (ISBN 0-86612-013-0). Educ Inst Am Hotel.

Blond, Anne G. & Janusz, Leslye. Spectrum of Visual Arts for Young Children. Radin, Jessica, ed. LC 76-3044. (Illus.). 114p. 1976. pap. 4.95 (ISBN 0-916634-00-0). Double M Pr.

Blond, Anthony. Family Business. LC 77-3784. 1978. 13.41i (ISBN 0-06-010364-7, HarpT). Har-Row.

Blond, Aubrey Le see Le Blond, Aubrey.

Blondal, S. The Varangians of Byzantium. Benedikz, S., tr. LC 77-82486. (Illus.). 1979. 59.50 (ISBN 0-521-21745-8). Cambridge U Pr.

Blonde, Allan. The Complete Guide to Researching & Writing the English Term Paper. LC 78-63036. (Orig.). 1978. pap. text ed. 3.95x (ISBN 0-87936-013-5). Scholium Intl.

Blondel, Jacques. Milton Poete De la Bible Dans le Paradis Perdu. LC 73-13668. 1959. lib. bdg. 12.50 (ISBN 0-8414-3252-X). Folcroft.

Blondel, Jean. The Discipline of Politics. 192p. 1981. text ed. 49.95 (ISBN 0-408-10681-6); pap. text ed. 14.95 (ISBN 0-408-10785-5). Butterworth.

--The Organization of Governments: A Comparative Analysis of Governmental Structures. LC 82-80523. (Political Executives in Comparative Perspective: A Cross-National Empirical Study: Vol. 2). (Illus.). 248p. 1982. 28.00 (ISBN 0-8039-9776-0); pap. 14.00 (ISBN 0-8039-9777-9). Sage.

--World Leaders: Heads of Government in the Postwar Period. LC 79-63826. (Political Executives in Comparative Perspective: A Cross-National Empirical Study: Vol. 1). 282p. 1980. 28.00 (ISBN 0-8039-9830-9). Sage.

Blondel, Jean & Walker, Carol, eds. Directory of European Political Scientists. 3rd rev. ed. LC 79-10686. 461p. 1979. 82.50x (ISBN 0-8419-0498-7). Holmes & Meier.

Blondel, Maurice. Action: Essay on a Critique of Life & a Science of Practice. Blanchette, Oliva, tr. from Fr. LC 83-401133. 448p. 1984. text ed. 29.95 (ISBN 0-268-00605-9, 85-06057). U of Notre Dame Pr.

Blondel De Nesle. Der Lieder Des Blondel De Nesle. LC 80-2157. Repr. of 1904 ed. 35.50 (ISBN 0-404-19023-5). AMS Pr.

Blondheim, S. H., ed. see International Congress of Internal Medicine, 12th, Tel Aviv, 1974.

Blondin, Antoine. To Live in Paris. 264p. 1981. 60.00 (ISBN 2-71910-031-5). Edns Vilo.

Blondis, Marion N. & Jackson, Barbara E. Nonverbal Communication with Patients: Back to the Human Touch. 2nd ed. LC 81-16261. 260p. 1982. pap. 13.50 (ISBN 0-471-08217-1, Pub. by Wiley Med). Wiley.

Blong, R. J. The Time of Darkness: Local Legends & Volcanic Reality in Papua New Guinea. LC 81-11484. (Illus.). 270p. 1982. 27.50x (ISBN 0-295-95880-4). U of Wash Pr.

--Volcanic Hazards: A Sourcebook on the Effects of Eruptions. 440p. 1984. 66.00 (ISBN 0-12-107180-4). Acad Pr.

Blonien, Rodney & Greenfield, Joel I. California Law Manual for the Administration of Justice. (Criminal Justice Ser.). 1979. pap. text ed. 23.50 (ISBN 0-8299-0252-X). West Pub.

Blonigen, Julie A. Teaching the Public About Communication Disorders. 64p. 1985. 12.50x (ISBN 0-8134-2486-0, 2486). Interstate.

Blonk, W. A. Transport & Regional Development. 352p. 1979. text ed. 47.50x (ISBN 0-566-00285-X). Gower Pub Co.

Blonsky, Marshall, ed. On Signs. LC 84-47952. 576p. 1985. 35.00x (ISBN 0-8018-3006-0); pap. 12.95 (ISBN 0-8018-3007-9). Johns Hopkins.

Blonston, Ann, jt. ed. see Waters, Dennis P.

Blonton, Richard E. Monte Alban's Hinterland, Pt. 1: The Prehispanic Settlement Patterns of the Valley of Oaxaca, Mexico. (Prehistory & Human Ecology of the Valley of Oaxaca Ser.: Vol. 7). 1982. pap. 20.00 (ISBN 0-932206-91-3). U Mich Mus Anthro.

Blood, Benjamin P. The Anaesthetic Revelation & the Gist of Philosophy. LC 75-3051. Repr. of 1874 ed. 11.50 (ISBN 0-404-59050-0). AMS Pr.

--Optimism, the Lesson of Ages. LC 75-3055. Repr. of 1860 ed. 18.00 (ISBN 0-404-59053-5). AMS Pr.

--The Philosophy of Justice Between God & Man. LC 75-3056. Repr. of 1851 ed. 20.50 (ISBN 0-404-59054-3). AMS Pr.

--Pluriverse: An Essay in the Philosophy of Pluralism. LC 75-3057. Repr. of 1920 ed. 20.50 (ISBN 0-404-59055-1). AMS Pr.

--Pluriverse: An Essay in the Philosophy of Pluralism. LC 75-36829. (Occult Ser.). 1976. Repr. of 1920 ed. 23.50x (ISBN 0-405-07941-9). Ayer Co Pubs.

--The Poetical Alphabet. (Surrealist Research & Development Monograph). 24p. 1972. pap. 2.50. Black Swan Pr.

Blood, Bob & Blood, Margaret. Marriage. 3rd ed. LC 77-3847. 1978. text ed. 24.95 (ISBN 0-02-904180-5). Free Pr.

Blood, Charles L. American Indian Games & Crafts. (Easy-Read Activity Bks.). (Illus.). 32p. (gr. 1-3). 1981. PLB 8.90 (ISBN 0-531-04304-5). Watts.

Blood, D. C., et al. Veterinary Medicine: A Textbook of the Diseases of Cattle, Pigs, Goats & Horses. 6th ed. (Illus.). 1328p. 1983. 65.00 (ISBN 0-7216-0817-5, Pub. by Bailliere-Tindall). Saunders.

Blood, Donald F. & Budd, William C. Educational Measurement & Evaluation. 1972. pap. text ed. 14.50 scp (ISBN 0-06-041029-9, HarpC). Har-Row.

Blood, F. R., ed. Essays in Toxicology, Vols. 1-7. Incl. Vol. 1. 1969. pap. 24.00 (ISBN 0-12-107651-2); Vol. 2. 1970. 50.00 (ISBN 0-12-107602-4); pap. 24.00 (ISBN 0-12-107652-0); Vol. 3. Hayes, Wayland J., Jr. 1972. 35.00 (ISBN 0-12-107603-2); pap. 24.00 (ISBN 0-12-107653-9); Vol. 4. 1973. 50.00 (ISBN 0-12-107604-0); pap. write for info.; Vol. 5. 1974. 49.00 (ISBN 0-12-107605-9); Vol. 6. 1975. 50.00 (ISBN 0-12-107606-7); Vol. 7. 1976. 60.00 (ISBN 0-12-107607-5). pap. Acad Pr.

Blood-Horse. Auctions of 1981. (The Blood-Horse Annual Supplement Ser.). (Illus.). 300p. (Orig.). 1982. pap. 10.00 (ISBN 0-936032-50-2). Blood-Horse.

Blood-Horse, ed. Principal Winners Abroad of 1979. (Annual Supplement, the Blood-Horse). (Orig.). 1980. pap. 10.00 (ISBN 0-936032-07-3). Blood-Horse.

--Sires of Runners of 1979. (Annual Supplement). 1980. lib. bdg. 20.00 (ISBN 0-936032-19-7); pap. 10.00 (ISBN 0-936032-20-0). Blood-Horse.

Blood Horse, ed. Stallion Register, 1981. (Illus.). 900p. 1980. 20.00 (ISBN 0-936032-33-2); pap. 10.00 (ISBN 0-936032-34-0). Blood-Horse.

Blood-Horse Editors. Principal Winners Abroad of 1980. (Annual Supplement of the Blood-Horse). (Orig.). 1981. pap. 10.00 (ISBN 0-936032-38-3). Blood-Horse.

Blood-Horse Staff. Principal Winners Abroad of 1981. (The Blood-Horse Annual Supplement). 160p. (Orig.). 1982. pap. 10.00 (ISBN 0-936032-47-2). Blood-Horse.

--Stakes Winners of 1981. (Annual Supplement Ser.). 800p. 1982. lib. bdg. 30.00 (ISBN 0-936032-48-0); pap. 20.00 (ISBN 0-936032-49-9). Blood-Horse.

--Thoroughbred Broodmare Records, 1982: Annual Edition. 2724p. 1983. 87.50 (ISBN 0-936032-59-6); leather binding 102.50 (ISBN 0-936032-60-X). Blood-Horse.

--Thoroughbred Broodmare Records 1983. 2800p. 87.50 (ISBN 0-936032-72-3); leather 102.50 (ISBN 0-936032-73-1). Blood Horse.

--Thoroughbred Stallion Records, 1981. 1300p. 1982. lib. bdg. 85.00 (ISBN 0-936032-46-4). Blood-Horse.

--Thoroughbred Stallion Records, 1983. 747p. 1984. 85.00 (ISBN 0-936032-71-5). Blood Horse.

Blood Horse Staff, ed. Principal Winners Abroad of 1982. (Blood-Horse Annual Supplement Ser.). 175p. 1983. pap. 10.00 (ISBN 0-936032-56-1). Blood-Horse.

Blood-Horse Staff, ed. Stakes Winners of 1982. (Annual Supplement to the Blood-Horse Ser.). 900p. 1983. 30.00 (ISBN 0-936032-61-8); pap. 21.50 (ISBN 0-936032-62-6). Blood-Horse.

--Stallion Register, 1983: Annual Supplement to the Blood-Horse. (Illus.). 1200p. 1982. 20.00 (ISBN 0-936032-54-5); pap. 10.00 (ISBN 0-936032-55-3). Blood-Horse.

Blood-Horse-Thoroughbred Owners & Breeders Assn., ed. The Breeder's Guide for 1979. (Bound Supplements of the Blood-Horse). 1980. 51.75 (ISBN 0-936032-01-4). Blood-Horse.

Blood-Horse Thoroughbred Owners & Breeders Assn., ed. The Breeder's Guide for 1981. 1982. 47.50 (ISBN 0-936032-51-0). Blood-Horse.

Blood-Horse-Thoroughbred Owners & Breeders Assn. The Breeder's Guide for 1982, 1 vol. (Bound Supplements of the Blood-Horse). 1983. 52.00 (ISBN 0-936032-58-8). Blood-Horse.

Blood-Horse Thoroughbred Owners & Breeders Assn., ed. Breeder's Guide for 1983: Bound Supplements of The Blood-Horse, All in One Volume. 1984. 53.33 (ISBN 0-936032-68-5). Blood Horse.

Blood, Margaret, jt. auth. see Blood, Bob.

Blood, Marje. Exploring the Oregon Coast by Car. LC 80-25484. (Illus.). 224p. (Orig.). 1980. pap. 6.95 (ISBN 0-916076-41-5). Writing.

Blood, Robert O. & Wolfe, Donald M. Husbands & Wives: The Dynamics of Married Living. LC 78-5734. 293p. 1978. Repr. of 1960 ed. lib. bdg. 25.75x (ISBN 0-313-20453-5, BLHW). Greenwood.

Blood, Robert O., Jr. The Family. LC 71-161235. 1972. text ed. 17.95 (ISBN 0-02-904150-3). Free Pr.

Blood, Robert O., Jr. & Wolfe, D. M. Husbands & Wives: The Dynamics of Married Living. LC 59-6824. 1965. pap. text ed. 7.95 (ISBN 0-02-904070-1). Free Pr.

Bloodboot Collective. The Political Palate: A Feminist Vegetarian Cookbook. LC 80-53521. (Illus.). 325p. (Orig.). 1980. pap. 8.95 (ISBN 0-9605210-0-3). Sanguinaria.

Bloodgood, Ruth S., jt. auth. see Bowler, Alida C.

Bloodroot Collective. The Second Seasonal Political Palate. LC 84-52064. 200p. 1984. pap. 10.95 (ISBN 0-9605210-2-X). Sanguinaria.

Blood-Ryan, H. W., tr. see Goering, H. W.

Bloodstein, Oliver. A Handbook on Stuttering. rev. 1981 ed. 477p. 1975. pap. 10.00 (ISBN 0-317-35137-0, G-19). Natl Easter Seal.

--Speech Pathology: An Introduction. 2nd ed. LC 83-82315. 464p. 1983. text ed. 27.95 (ISBN 0-395-34100-0). HM.

Bloodworth, Bertha E. & Morris, Alton C. Places in the Sun: The History & Romance of Florida Place-Names. LC 77-13754. 1978. 12.50 (ISBN 0-8130-0544-2). U Presses Fla.

Bloodworth, Dennis. The Chinese Looking Glass. rev. ed. 448p. 1980. 15.00 (ISBN 0-374-12241-5); pap. 8.95 (ISBN 0-374-51493-3). FS&G.

--An Eye for the Dragon: Southeast Asia Observed, 1954-1970. LC 70-122826. (Illus.). 414p. 1970. 8.95 (ISBN 0-374-15129-6). FS&G.

Bloodworth, J. M., Jr. Endocrine Pathology: General & Surgical. 2nd ed. (Illus.). 894p. 1982. 99.00 (ISBN 0-683-00854-4). Williams & Wilkins.

Bloodworth, Jessie A. & Greenwood, Elizabeth J. Personal Side. LC 71-137156. (Poverty U.S.A. Historical Record Ser). 1971. Repr. of 1939 ed. 26.50 (ISBN 0-405-03094-0). Ayer Co Pubs.

Bloodworth, Venice. Key to Yourself. 12th ed. 1970. pap. 3.00- (ISBN 0-87516-296-7). De Vorss.

Bloodworth, William, Jr. Upton Sinclair. (United States Authors Ser.). 1977. lib. bdg. 13.90 (ISBN 0-8057-7197-2, Twayne). G K Hall.

Bloom, A. Diabetes Explained. (Illus.). 160p. 1975. text ed. 16.00 (ISBN 0-8391-0577-0). Univ Park.

--Diabetes Explained. 4th ed. (Illus.). 162p. 1982. text ed. 14.95 (ISBN 0-85200-472-9, Pub. by MTP Pr England). Kluwer Academic.

Bloom, A. L. Surface of the Earth. (gr. 10 up). pap. text ed. 15.95 (ISBN 0-13-877944-9). P-H.

Bloom, Alan. Alpines for Your Garden. 128p. 1981. 14.95 (ISBN 0-938804-01-4, Pub. by Floraprint). Intl Spec Bk.

--Perennials for Your Garden. 144p. 1981. 14.95 (ISBN 0-938804-00-6, Pub. by Floraprint). Intl Spec Bk.

--Perennials in Island Beds. (Illus.). 112p. 1977. 9.95 (ISBN 0-571-10892-X). Faber & Faber.

--Plantes vivaces de nos jardins. new ed. Korff, E. & Bossard, R., trs. from Eng. (Collection "Flore"). (Illus.). 144p. (Fr.). 1974. 15.95x (ISBN 2-03-074702-5). Larousse.

--Two Hundred Fifty Years of Steam. 208p. 1981. 45.00x (Pub. by Worlds Work England). State Mutual Bk.

--Two Hundred Fifty Years of Steam. 1981. 24.95 (ISBN 0-437-01400-2, Pub. by Worlds Work). David & Charles.

Bloom, Alexander. Prodigal Sons: The New York Intellectuals & Their World. 448p. 1986. 24.95 (ISBN 0-19-503662-X). Oxford U Pr.

Bloom, Alfred. Shinran's Gospel of Pure Grace. LC 64-8757. (Association for Asian Studies Monograph: No. 20). 97p. 1965. pap. 4.50x (ISBN 0-8165-0405-9). U of Ariz Pr.

--Tannisho: A Resource for Modern Living. LC 80-39523. 112p. (Orig.). 1981. pap. 6.95 (ISBN 0-938474-00-6). Buddhist Study.

Bloom, Alfred, jt. auth. see Baird, Robert D.

Bloom, Alfred H. Linguistic Shaping of Thought: A Study in the Impact of Language on Thinking in China & the West. 128p. 1981. text ed. 19.95x (ISBN 0-89859-089-2). L Erlbaum Assocs.

Bloom, Allan, ed. see Kojeve, Alexandre.

Bloom, Allan, tr. see Rousseau, Jean-Jacques.

Bloom, Allan M., jt. auth. see Lord, Kenniston W., Jr.

Bloom, Allen & Jaffa, Harry V. Shakespeare's Politics. LC 81-10342. 160p. 1981. pap. 6.00x (ISBN 0-226-06041-1). U of Chicago Pr.

Bloom, Anthony. Living Prayer. 1975. pap. 6.95 (ISBN 0-87243-054-5). Templegate.

--Meditations. 3.95 (ISBN 0-87193-010-2). Dimension Bks.

Bloom, Anthony & LeFebvre, George. Courage to Pray. 3rd ed. Livingstone, Dinah, tr. from Fr. 123p. (Orig.). pap. text ed. 3.95 (ISBN 0-88141-031-4). St Vladimirs.

Bloom, Arnold. Toohey's Medicine for Nurses. 13th ed. (Illus.). 1981. pap. text ed. 18.75 (ISBN 0-443-02201-1). Churchill.

Bloom, Arnold & Ireland, John. Color Atlas of Diabetes. (Illus.). 128p. 1980. 55.95 (ISBN 0-8151-0941-5). Year Bk Med.

Bloom, Arnold L. Gas Lasers. LC 77-28278. 184p. 1978. Repr. of 1968 ed. lib. bdg. 14.50 (ISBN 0-88275-659-1). Krieger.

Bloom, Arthur D. & James, L. S. Annual Review of Birth Defects, 1980: The Fetus & the Newborn. LC 81-3745. (Birth Defects: Original Article Ser.: Vol. 17, No. 1). 286p. 1981. 40.00 (ISBN 0-8451-1041-1). A R Liss.

Bloom, Arthur D. & James, L. S., eds. The Fetus & the Newborn. (Alan R. Less, Inc. Ser.: Vol. 17, No.1). 1981. 36.00 (ISBN 0-686-37765-6). March of Dimes.

Bloom, Arthur L. Geomorphology: A Systematic Analysis of Late Cenozoic Landforms. LC 77-25816. (Illus.). 1978. ref. ed. 40.95 (ISBN 0-13-353086-8). P-H.

Bloom, Arthur L. & Thomas, Duncan P., eds. Haemostasis & Throabosis. (Illus.). 868p. 1981. 87.50 (ISBN 0-443-01991-6). Churchill.

Bloom, Barbara. Basic Data on Women Who Use Family Planning Clinics: U. S., 1980. Shipp, Audrey, ed. (Series 13: No. 67). 60p. 1982. pap. text ed. 1.75 (ISBN 0-8406-0263-4). Natl Ctr Health Stats.

--Utilization Patterns & Financial Characteristics of Nursing Homes in the United States: 1977 Nchs. Shipp, Audrey, ed. (Series Thirteen: No. 53). 50p. 1981. pap. 1.75 (ISBN 0-8406-0215-4). Natl Ctr Health Stats.

Bloom, Barbara & Jack, Susan S. Persons with & Without a Regular Source of Medical Care: United States 1978. Cox, Klaudia, ed. (Series Ten: No. 151). 80p. 1985. pap. text ed. 1.50 (ISBN 0-8406-0317-7). Natl Ctr Health Stats.

Bloom, Barbara H. Index to the Journal of Sedimentary Petrology, Volumes 1-26, 1931-1956. (Society of Economic Paleontologists & Mineralogists, Special Publication: No. 6). pap. 20.00 (ISBN 0-317-27107-5, 2024733). Bks Demand UMI.

Bloom, Barry R. & David, John R., eds. In Vitro Methods in Cell-Mediated & Tumor Immunity. 1976. 74.50 (ISBN 0-12-107760-8). Acad Pr.

Bloom, Barry R. & Glade, Philip R., eds. In Vitro Methods in Cell-Mediated Immunity. 1971. 66.00 (ISBN 0-12-107750-0). Acad Pr.

Bloom, Benjamin S. All Our Children Learning: A Primer for Parents, Teachers, & Other Educators. 288p. 1982. pap. 6.95 (ISBN 0-07-006121-1). McGraw.

--Human Characteristics & School Learning. 288p. 1982. pap. 6.95 (ISBN 0-07-006122-X). McGraw.

Bloom, Benjamin S. & Madaus, George F. Evaluation of Student Learning. LC 80-25580. 1981. 29.95 (ISBN 0-07-006109-2). McGraw.

Bloom, Benjamin S., ed. Developing Talent in Young People. LC 84-90809. 448p. (Orig.). 1985. 19.95 (ISBN 0-345-31951-6); pap. 9.95 (ISBN 0-345-31509-X). Ballantine.

Bloom, Benjamin S., et al. Taxonomy of Educational Objectives: Handbook 1: Cognitive Domain. LC 64-12369. 1977. pap. text ed. 13.95x (ISBN 0-582-28010-9). Longman.

Bloom, Bernard, ed. Psychological Stress in the Campus Community. LC 74-6184. (Community Psychology Ser: No. III). 282p. 1975. text ed. 29.95 (ISBN 0-87705-145-3). Human Sci Pr.

Bloom, Bernard L. Changing Patterns of Psychiatric Care. LC 74-8850. 360p. 1975. text ed. 29.95 (ISBN 0-87705-209-3). Human Sci Pr.

--Community Mental Health: A General Introduction. 2nd ed. LC 83-2841. (Psychology-Counseling Ser.). 512p. 1983. text ed. 22.75 pub net (ISBN 0-534-01408-9). Brooks-Cole.

Bloom, Bernard L. & Asher, Shirley J., eds. Psychiatric Patient Rights & Patient Advocacy: Issues & Evidence. LC 81-13165. (Community Psychology Ser.: Vol. VII). 287p. 1982. 29.95 (ISBN 0-89885-056-8). Human Sci Pr.

Bloom, Billy, jt. auth. see Horowitz, Judy.

Bloom, C. O. & Kazarinoff, N. D. Short Wave Radiation Problems in Homogeneous Media: Asymptotic Solutions. (Lecture Notes in Mathematics: Vol. 522). 1976. 13.00 (ISBN 0-387-07698-0). Springer-Verlag.

Bloom, Claire. Limelight & After: The Education of an Actor. 216p. 1983. pap. 3.95 (ISBN 0-14-006529-6). Penguin.

Bloom, D. M. Linear Algebra & Geometry. LC 77-26666. 1979. 41.50 (ISBN 0-521-21959-0); pap. 29.95 (ISBN 0-521-29324-3). Cambridge U Pr.

Bloom, Daniel. Bubbie & Zadie Come to My House. (Illus.). (gr. k-3). 1985. 9.95 (ISBN 0-917657-49-7). D I Fine.

Bloom, Deborah, jt. auth. see Bloom, Frances.

Bloom, Edward & Bloom, Lillian. Addison & Steele: The Critical Heritage. (Critical Heritage Ser.). 1980. 37.50x (ISBN 0-7100-0375-7). Routledge & Kegan.

Bloom, Edward A. & Bloom, Lillian D. Joseph Addison's Sociable Animal: In the Market Place, on the Hustings, in the Pulpit. LC 73-111455. (Illus.). 290p. 1971. 20.00x (ISBN 0-87057-120-6). U Pr of New Eng.

--Satire's Persuasive Voice. LC 78-11668. 305p. 1979. 27.50x (ISBN 0-8014-0839-3). Cornell U Pr.

Bloom, Edward A., ed. Shakespeare 1564-1964: A Collection of Modern Essays by Various Hands. LC 64-17777. 240p. 1964. 20.00x (ISBN 0-87057-083-8). U Pr of New Eng.

Bloom, Edward A., ed. & intro. by see Burney, Fanny.

Bloom, Edward A., ed. see Burney, Fanny.

Bloom, Edward A., et al, eds. The Order of Poetry: An Introduction. (Orig.). 1961. pap. 7.20 scp (ISBN 0-672-63078-8). Odyssey Pr.

--The Order of Poetry: An Introduction. 192p. 1961. pap. text ed. write for info. (ISBN 0-02-311080-5). Macmillan.

Bloom, Edward A., et al, eds. see Burney, Fanny.

Bloom, Elaine. Sell Your Writing. 24p. (Orig.). 1984. pap. 4.00 (ISBN 0-935000-03-8). Bloom Bks.

Bloom, F. Ill-Posed Problems for Integrodifferential Equations in Mechanics & Electromagnetic Theory. LC 80-53713. (SIAM Studies in Applied Mathematics: No. 3). ix, 222p. 1981. 37.50 (ISBN 0-89871-171-1). Soc Indus-Appl Math.

--Modern Differential Geometric Techniques in the Theory of Continuous Distributions of Dislocations. Dold, A. & Eckmann, B., eds. (Lecture Notes in Mathematics: Vol. 733). 1979. pap. 17.00 (ISBN 0-387-09528-4). Springer-Verlag.

Bloom, F. E., ed. Dynamics of Synaptic Modulation. 100p. 1976. pap. text ed. 8.95x (ISBN 0-262-52037-0). MIT Pr.

Bloom, F. E. see International Congress on Pharmacology, 5th, San Francisco, 1972.

Bloom, Floyd, et al. Brain, Mind, & Behavior. 336p. pap. text ed. 23.95 (ISBN 0-7167-1637-2); study guide avail. W H Freeman.

Bloom, Floyd, jt. auth. see Symposium of Beta-Carbolines & Tetrahydroisoquinolines, La Jolla, Ca., December, 12-13, 1981.

Bloom, Floyd E., ed. Peptides: Integrators of Cell & Tissue Function. (Society of General Physiologists Ser.: Vol.35). 274p. 1980. text ed. 36.00 (ISBN 0-89004-485-6). Raven.

Bloom, Floyd E., jt. auth. see Cooper, Jack R.

Bloom, Frances & Bloom, Deborah. Recipe for Spelling. Goin, Kenn & Jaeger, Ina C., eds. 256p. (Orig.). 1984. pap. 16.95 (ISBN 0-8027-8042-3). Walker & Co.

Bloom, Freddy. The Boy Who Couldn't Hear. 30p. 1979. 4.95 (ISBN 0-370-01811-7, Pub. by the Bodley Head). Merrimack Pub Cir.

--Care to Help? 1981. 29.00x (ISBN 0-906549-14-0, Pub. by J Clare Bks England). State Mutual Bk.

--Dear Philip: A Diary of Captivity, Changing, Nineteen Forty-Two-Nineteen Forty-Five. 158p. 1981. 14.95 (ISBN 0-370-30345-8, Pub. by the Bodley Head). Merrimack Pub Cir.

--Face It. 1981. 20.00x (ISBN 0-906549-23-X, Pub. by J Clare Bks England). State Mutual Bk.

--One Hundred & One Questions & Answers about Deaf Children. 1984. 25.00x (ISBN 0-906549-44-2, Pub. by J Clare Bks UK); pap. 12.00x (ISBN 0-906549-45-0, Pub. by J Clare Bks UK). State Mutual Bk.

Bloom, George F. & Harrison, Henry S. Appraising the Single Family Residence. 510p. 1978. 20.00 (ISBN 0-911780-40-8). Am Inst Real Estate Appraisers.

--Appraising the Single Family Residence. 510p. 17.50 (ISBN 0-318-15172-3, 21-1009). Natl Assoc Realtors.

Bloom, George F., et al. Real Estate. 8th ed. LC 81-15933. 738p. 1982. text ed. 36.50 (ISBN 0-471-09398-X); tchr's. manual 16.00 (ISBN 0-471-86234-7). Wiley.

Bloom, Gilbert D., jt. auth. see Newton, George.

Bloom, Gilbert D., jt. auth. see Newton, Grant W.

Bloom, Gordon F. Productivity in the Food Industry: Problems & Potential. 240p. 1972. 25.00x (ISBN 0-262-02088-2). MIT Pr.

Bloom, Gordon F. & Northrup, Herbert R. Economics of Labor Relations. 9th ed. 1981. 28.50 (ISBN 0-256-02490-1). Irwin.

Bloom, Gretchen. The Language of Hospital Services in English. (English for Careers Ser.). (Illus.). (gr. 10 up). 1976. pap. 4.25 (ISBN 0-88345-270-7, 18511). Regents Pub.

--The Language of Medicine in English. (English for Careers Ser.). (gr. 10 up). 1981. pap. text ed. 4.25 (ISBN 0-88345-351-7, 18527). Regents Pub.

Bloom, H. J., et al, eds. Cancer in Children: Clinical Management. LC 75-8910. (Illus.). 500p. (Orig.). 1975. pap. 25.00 (ISBN 0-387-07261-6). Springer-Verlag.

Bloom, Harold. Agon: Towards a Theory of Revisionism. 1982. 25.00x (ISBN 0-19-502945-3). Oxford U Pr.

--Agon: Towards a Theory of Revisionism. 1982. pap. 7.95 (ISBN 0-19-503354-X, GB740, GB). Oxford U Pr.

--Anxiety of Influence: A Theory of Poetry. 1973. pap. 7.95 (ISBN 0-19-501896-6, GB426, GB). Oxford U Pr.

--The Breaking of the Vessels. LC 81-12975. (Wellek Library Lectures). 1982. 10.00x (ISBN 0-226-06043-8); pap. 4.95x (ISBN 0-226-06044-6). U of Chicago Pr.

--Figures of Capable Imagination. LC 75-35826. 1976. 11.95x (ISBN 0-8264-0103-1). Continuum.

--The Flight to Lucifer: A Gnostic Fantasy. 236p. 1979. 9.95 (ISBN 0-374-15644-1). FS&G.

--Kabbalah & Criticism. LC 75-12820. 100p. 1975. 8.95 (ISBN 0-8264-0124-4). Continuum.

--Kabbalah & Criticism. LC 82-4674. 126p. 1983. pap. 7.95 (ISBN 0-8245-0487-9). Crossroad NY.

--A Map of Misreading. 1975. pap. 7.95 (ISBN 0-19-502809-0, GB 623). Oxford U Pr.

--Ringers in the Tower. LC 73-149595. xii, 352p. 1973. pap. 3.45x (ISBN 0-226-06049-7, P536, Phoen). U of Chicago Pr.

--The Visionary Company: A Reading of English Romantic Poetry. rev. ed. LC 73-144032. 506p. 1971. pap. 14.95x (ISBN 0-8014-9117-7, CP117). Cornell U Pr.

--Wallace Stevens: The Poems of Our Climate. 416p. 1980. pap. 9.95 (ISBN 0-8014-9185-1). Cornell U Pr.

--Wallace Stevens: The Poems of Our Climate. LC 76-55482. 1977. 32.00x (ISBN 0-8014-0840-7). Cornell U Pr.

--Yeats. 1972. pap. 8.95 (ISBN 0-19-501603-3, 378, GB). Oxford U Pr.

Bloom, Harold & Munich, Adrienne. Robert Browning: Collection of Critical Essays. 1979. text ed. 12.95 (ISBN 0-13-781484-4, Spec); pap. text ed. 4.95 (ISBN 0-13-781476-3). P-H.

Bloom, Harold, ed. Alfred Lord Tennyson. (Modern Critical Views Ser.). 1985. 17.95x (ISBN 0-87754-615-0). Chelsea Hse.

--Art of the Critic, 11 vols. Set. 660.00x (ISBN 0-87754-493-X). Chelsea Hse.

--Art of the Critic, Vol. 1: Classic & Medieval. 1985. 60.00x (ISBN 0-87754-494-8). Chelsea Hse.

--Art of the Critic, Vol. 10: Contemporary. 1986. 60.00x (ISBN 0-87754-503-0). Chelsea Hse.

--Art of the Critic, Vol. 11: Index, Bibliography & Glossary. 1986. 60.00x (ISBN 0-87754-504-9). Chelsea Hse.

--Art of the Critic, Vol. 2: Early Renaissance. 1985. Set. 60.00x (ISBN 0-87754-495-6). Chelsea Hse.

--Art of the Critic, Vol. 3: Later Renaissance. 1985. 60.00x (ISBN 0-87754-496-4). Chelsea Hse.

--Art of the Critic, Vol. 4: Enlightenment. 1985. 60.00x (ISBN 0-87754-497-2). Chelsea Hse.

--Art of the Critic, Vol. 5: Early Romantic. 1985. 60.00x (ISBN 0-87754-498-0). Chelsea Hse.

--Art of the Critic, Vol. 6: Later Romantic. 1985. 60.00x (ISBN 0-87754-499-9). Chelsea Hse.

--Art of the Critic, Vol. 8: Early Twentieth Century. 1986. 60.00x (ISBN 0-87754-501-4). Chelsea Hse.

--Art of the Critic, Vol. 9: Middle Twentieth Century. 1986. 60.00x (ISBN 0-87754-502-2). Chelsea Hse.

--The Critical Perspective: Twentieth-Century Criticism of British & American Literature to 1904. 10 vols. Set. 500.00x (ISBN 0-87754-789-0). Chelsea Hse.

--The Critical Perspective, Vol. 1: Beowulf Through Sir Philip Sidney. 1985. 50.00x (ISBN 0-87754-790-4). Chelsea Hse.

--The Critical Perspective, Vol. 10: Thomas Carlyle Through Herman Melville. 1986. 50.00x. Chelsea Hse.

--The Critical Perspective, Vol. 2: Edmund Spenser Through William Shakespeare. 1985. 50.00x (ISBN 0-87754-791-2). Chelsea Hse.

--The Critical Perspective, Vol. 3: John Webster Through George Herbert. 1985. 50.00x (ISBN 0-87754-792-0). Chelsea Hse.

--The Critical Perspective, Vol. 4: John Milton Through John Bunyan. 1985. 50.00x (ISBN 0-87754-793-9). Chelsea Hse.

--The Critical Perspective, Vol. 5: John Dryden Through Alexander Pope. 1985. 50.00x (ISBN 0-87754-795-5). Chelsea Hse.

--The Critical Perspective, Vol. 6: Henry Fielding Through Samuel Johnson. 1986. 50.00x. Chelsea Hse.

--The Critical Perspective, Vol. 7: Edmund Burke Through Jane Austen. 1986. 50.00x (ISBN 0-87754-796-3). Chelsea Hse.

--The Critical Perspective, Vol. 8: William Wordsworth Through Edgar Allan Poe. 1986. 50.00x (ISBN 0-87754-798-X). Chelsea Hse.

--The Critical Perspective, Vol. 9: Walt Whitman Through Oscar Wilde. 1986. 50.00x (ISBN 0-87754-799-8). Chelsea Hse.

--Edgar Allan Poe. (Modern Critical Views Ser.). 1985. 17.95x (ISBN 0-87754-602-9). Chelsea Hse.

--Emily Dickinson. (Modern Critical Views Ser.). 1985. 17.95x (ISBN 0-87754-605-3). Chelsea Hse.

--Ernest Hemingway. (Modern Critical Views Ser.). 1985. 17.95x (ISBN 0-87754-616-9). Chelsea Hse.

--Geoffrey Chaucer. (Modern Critical Views Ser.). 1985. 17.95x (ISBN 0-87754-606-1). Chelsea Hse.

--John Keats. (Modern Critical Views Ser.). 1985. 17.95x (ISBN 0-87754-608-8). Chelsea Hse.

--Major Authors Edition of New Moulton's Library Literary Criticism, Vol. 1: Geoffrey Chaucer Through Christopher Marlowe. 1985. 55.00x (ISBN 0-87754-815-3). Chelsea Hse.

--Major Authors Edition of the New Moulton's Library of Literary Criticism, 5 vols. Set. 275.00x (ISBN 0-87754-814-5). Chelsea Hse.

--Major Authors Edition of the New Moulton's Library of Literary Criticism, Vol. 2. 1985. 55.00x (ISBN 0-87754-816-1). Chelsea Hse.

--Major Authors Edition of the New Moulton's Library of Literary Criticism, Vol. 3: John Donne Through Jane Austin. 1985. 55.00x (ISBN 0-87754-817-X). Chelsea Hse.

--Major Authors Edition of the New Moulton's Library of Literary Criticism, Vol. 4: William Blake Through Edgar Allan Poe. 1986. 55.00x (ISBN 0-87754-818-8). Chelsea Hse.

--Major Authors Edition of the New Moulton's Library of Literary Criticism, Vol. 5: Walt Whitman Through Oscar Wilde. 1986. 55.00x (ISBN 0-87754-819-6). Chelsea Hse.

--Modern Critical Views, 129 vols. 200p. Set. 15.55x (ISBN 0-87754-599-5). Chelsea Hse.

--New Moulton's Library of Literary Criticism: British & American Literature 1904, 10 vols. Set. 500.00 (ISBN 0-87754-778-5). Chelsea Hse.

--New Moulton's Library of Literary Criticism, Vol. 1: Beowulf Through Sir Phillip Sidney. 1985. 50.00 (ISBN 0-87754-779-3). Chelsea Hse.

--New Moulton's Library of Literary Criticism, Vol. 2: Edmund Spenser Through William Shakespeare. 1985. 50.00x (ISBN 0-87754-780-7). Chelsea Hse.

--New Moulton's Library of Literary Criticism, Vol. 3: John Webster Through George Herbert. 1985. 50.00x (ISBN 0-87754-781-5). Chelsea Hse.

--New Moulton's Library of Literary Criticism, Vol. 4: John Milton Through John Bunyan. 1985. 50.00 (ISBN 0-87754-782-3). Chelsea Hse.

--New Moulton's Library of Literary Criticism, Vol. 5: John Dryden Through Alexander Pope. 1985. 50.00x (ISBN 0-87754-783-1). Chelsea Hse.

--New Moulton's Library of Literary Criticism, Vol. 6: Henry Fielding Through Samuel Johnson. 1986. 50.00 (ISBN 0-87754-784-X). Chelsea Hse.

--New Moulton's Library of Literary Criticism, Vol. 7: Edmund Burke Through Jane Austen. 1986. 50.00x (ISBN 0-87754-785-8). Chelsea Hse.

--New Moulton's Library of Literary Criticism, Vol. 8: William Wordsworth Through Edgar Allan Poe. 1986. 50.00x (ISBN 0-87754-786-6). Chelsea Hse.

--Oscar Wilde. (Modern Critical Views Ser.). 1985. 17.95x (ISBN 0-87754-611-8). Chelsea Hse.

--Percy Bysshe Shelley. (Modern Critical Views Ser.). 1985. 17.95x (ISBN 0-317-16756-1). Chelsea Hse.

--Ralph Waldo Emerson. (Modern Critical Views Ser.). 1985. 17.95x (ISBN 0-87754-604-5). Chelsea Hse.

--Robert Browning. (Modern Critical Views Ser.). 1985. 17.95x (ISBN 0-87754-614-2). Chelsea Hse.

--The Romantic Tradition in American Literature, 33 bks. 1972. Repr. Set. 891.00 (ISBN 0-405-04620-0). Ayer Co Pubs.

--Romanticism & Consciousness. (Orig.). 1970. pap. text ed. 9.95x (ISBN 0-393-09954-7, NortonC). Norton.

--Selected Poetry & Prose of Shelley. 1978. pap. 7.95 (ISBN 0-452-00659-7, F491, Mer). NAL.

--Selected Writings of Walter Pater. LC 81-17099. (A Morningside Book). 304p. 1982. 30.00x (ISBN 0-231-05480-7); pap. 12.00x (ISBN 0-231-05481-5). Columbia U Pr.

--Sigmund Freud. (Modern Critical Views Ser.). 1985. 17.95x (ISBN 0-87754-600-2). Chelsea Hse.

--T. S. Eliot. (Modern Critical Views Ser.). 1985. 17.95x (ISBN 0-87754-601-0). Chelsea Hse.

--Twentieth-Century American Literature, 7 vols. 1985. Set. 385.00x (ISBN 0-87754-800-5); 55.00x ea. Vol. 1 (ISBN 0-87754-801-3). Vol. 2 (ISBN 0-87754-802-1). Vol. 3 (ISBN 0-87754-803-X). Vol. 4 (ISBN 0-87754-804-8). Vol. 5 (ISBN 0-87754-805-6). Vol. 6 (ISBN 0-87754-806-4). Vol. 7 (ISBN 0-87754-807-2). Chelsea Hse.

--Twentieth-Century British Literature, 5 vols. Set. 275.00x (ISBN 0-87754-808-0); 55.00x ea. Vol. 1 (ISBN 0-87754-809-9). Vol. 2 (ISBN 0-87754-810-2). Vol. 3 (ISBN 0-87754-811-0). Vol. 4 (ISBN 0-87754-812-9). Vol. 5 (ISBN 0-87754-813-7). Chelsea Hse.

--Walt Whitman. (Modern Critical Views Ser.). 1985. 17.95x (ISBN 0-87754-603-7). Chelsea Hse.

--Walter Pater. (Modern Critical Views Ser.). 1985. 17.95x (ISBN 0-87754-612-6). Chelsea Hse.

--William Blake. (Modern Critical Views Ser.). 1985. 17.95x (ISBN 0-87754-610-X). Chelsea Hse.

--William Wordsworth. (Modern Critical Views Ser.). 1985. 17.95x (ISBN 0-87754-613-4). Chelsea Hse.

Bloom, Harold & Trilling, Lionel, eds. Romantic Prose & Poetry. (Anthology of English Literature Ser.). (Illus.). 1973. pap. 16.95x (ISBN 0-19-501615-7). Oxford U Pr.

Bloom, Harold, jt. ed. see Hollander, Joan.

Bloom, Harold, jt. ed. see Trilling, Lionel.

Bloom, Harold, et al. Deconstruction & Criticism. 1979. 16.95 (ISBN 0-8264-0092-2); pap. 8.95x (ISBN 0-8264-0010-8, Continuum). Continuum.

Bloom, Harry. Transvaal Episode. LC 81-51098. 363p. 1981. 16.95 (ISBN 0-933256-32-9); pap. 8.95 (ISBN 0-933256-25-6). Second Chance.

Bloom, Harry, jt. ed. see Gutmann, Felix.

Bloom, Herschel M., jt. auth. see Mills, David W.

Bloom, Ira M., jt. auth. see Gaubatz, John T.

Bloom, Irene, jt. ed. see De Bary, W. Theodore.

Bloom, J. Harvey. Folk Lore, Old Customs & Superstitions in Shakespeare Land. LC 73-2830. viii, 167p. 1973. Repr. of 1930 ed. 31.00x (ISBN 0-8103-3269-8). Gale.

--Folklore, Old Customs & Superstitions in Shakespeare Land. (Folklore Ser). 10.00 (ISBN 0-88305-055-2). Norwood Edns.

Bloom, J. M. & Ekvall, J. C., eds. Probabilistic Fracture Mechanics & Fatigue Methods: Applications for Structural Design & Maintenance - STP 798. LC 82-83518. 215p. 1983. text ed. 36.00 (ISBN 0-8031-0242-9, 04-798000-30). ASTM.

Bloom, James D. The Stock of Available Reality: R. P. Blackmur & John Berryman. LC 83-45489. 216p. 1984. 24.50 (ISBN 0-8387-5066-4). Bucknell U Pr.

Bloom, James H. Shakespeare's Church. LC 73-116790. (Studies in Shakespeare, No. 24). 1971. Repr. of 1902 ed. lib. bdg. 49.95x (ISBN 0-8383-1032-X). Haskell.

Bloom, Joel A. Principles of Intermediate Swimming. (Illus.). 111p. 1978. pap. text ed. 3.95x plastic comb bdg. (ISBN 0-89641-002-1); pap. text ed. 3.95x perfect bdg. (ISBN 0-89641-010-2). American Pr.

Bloom, Joel A., jt. auth. see Fleming, A. William.

Bloom, John & Atkinson, Jim. Evidence of Love. 1985. pap. 3.95 (ISBN 0-317-19268-X). Bantam.

--Evidence of Love: A True Story of Passion & Death in the Suburbs. Rodriguez, Barbara, ed. 224p. 1984. 15.95 (ISBN 0-932012-48-5). Texas Month Pr.

Bloom, Kathleen, ed. Prospective Issues in Infancy Research. LC 80-17479. 208p. 1981. text ed. 19.95x (ISBN 0-89859-059-0). L Erlbaum Assocs.

Bloom, Ken. American Song: The Complete Musical Theatre Companion, 2 vols. LC 84-24728. 1985. Vol. 1, 824p 95.00 (ISBN 0-87196-960-2); Set. Vol. 2, 616p 95.00 (ISBN 0-87196-924-6). Facts on File.

--American Song: The Complete Stage Musical, Vol. I. (Illus.). 500p. 1984. cancelled (ISBN 0-918432-48-0). NY Zoetrope.

Bloom, L. Z., et al. The New Assertive Woman. 1976. pap. 3.50 (ISBN 0-440-16393-5, LE). Dell.

Bloom, Leonard & Riemer, Ruth. Removal & Return: The Socio-Economic Effects of the War on Japanese Americans. LC 49-9867. (University of California Publications in Culture & Society: Vol. 4). pap. 69.00 (ISBN 0-317-29103-3, 2021393). Bks Demand UMI.

Bloom, Lillian, jt. auth. see Bloom, Edward.

Bloom, Lillian D., jt. auth. see Bloom, Edward A.

Bloom, Lillian D., ed. see Burney, Fanny.

Bloom, Lois. One Word at a Time: The Use of Single Word Utterances Before Syntax. LC 72-94445. (Janua Linguarum, Ser. Minor: No. 154). 262p. 1973. pap. text ed. 14.40x (ISBN 90-2793-375-8). Mouton.

Bloom, Lois & Lahey, Margaret. Language Development & Language Disorders. LC 77-21482. (Communication Disorders Ser.). 689p. 1978. text ed. 40.00 (ISBN 0-471-08220-1). Wiley.

Bloom, Lois, ed. Readings in Language Development. LC 77-10717. (Communications Disorders Ser.). 506p. 1978. text ed. 38.00x (ISBN 0-471-08221-X). Wiley.

Bloom, Louise, et al. Victorian Arkansans: How They Lived, Played & Worked. Daggett, Mala, ed. LC 81-67251. (Illus.). 208p. 1981. notebook 17.00 (ISBN 0-686-30547-7). AR Commemorative.

Bloom, Lynda. Fitting & Showing the Halter Horse. LC 79-13615. (Illus.). 1980. 11.95 (ISBN 0-668-04431-4). Arco.

Bloom, Lynn. Strategic Writing. 480p. 1983. text ed. 16.00 (ISBN 0-394-31277-5, RanC). Random.

Bloom, Lynn Z. The Easy Connection. 491p. 1984. pap. text ed. 9.95 (ISBN 0-669-04476-8); student's guide 1.95 (ISBN 0-669-07049-1). Heath.

--Fact & Artifact: Writing Nonfiction. 337p. 1985. pap. text ed. 11.95 (ISBN 0-15-527076-1, HC). HarBraceJ.

Bloom, Lynn Z., ed. see Crouter, Natalie.

Bloom, M. H., ed. see Symposium on Computers in Aerodynamics at the Aerodynamics Laboratories Polytechnic Institute of New York, 1979.

Bloom, Marc. The Marathon: What It Takes to Go the Distance. LC 80-18859. (Illus.). 304p. 1981. pap. 7.95 (ISBN 0-03-059153-8). HR&W.

--Runner's Bible. LC 82-46075. (Outdoor Bible Ser.). (Illus.). 160p. 1986. pap. 6.95 (ISBN 0-385-18874-9). Doubleday.

Bloom, Marc, jt. auth. see Shorter, Frank.

Bloom, Mark, jt. auth. see Barley, Elizabeth G.

Bloom, Martin. Configurations of Human Behavior. 544p. 1984. pap. text ed. write for info. (ISBN 0-02-311010-4). Macmillan.

--Life Span Development: Bases for Preventive & Interventive Helping. 2nd ed. 500p. 1984. pap. 13.50 (ISBN 0-02-311060-0). Macmillan.

--The Paradox of Helping: Introduction to the Philosophy of Scientific Practice. LC 74-13524. 283p. 1975. text ed. 33.95x (ISBN 0-471-08235-X). Wiley.

--Primary Prevention: The Possible Science. (P-H Series in Social Work). (Illus.). 288p. 1981. pap. text ed. 22.95 (ISBN 0-13-700062-6). P-H.

--Research in the Human Services. 710p. 1986. text ed. price not set (ISBN 0-02-311040-6). Macmillan.

Bloom, Martin & Fischer, Joel. Evaluating Practice: Guidelines for the Accountable Professional. (Series in Sociology Work Practice). (Illus.). 512p. 1982. reference 30.95 (ISBN 0-13-292318-1). P-H.

Bloom, Martin, ed. Single-System Research Designs. (Journal of Social Service Research Ser.: Vol. 3, No. 1). 134p. 1979. pap. text ed. 10.00 (ISBN 0-917724-70-4, B70). Haworth Pr.

Bloom, Metropolitan A. Living Prayer. pap. 6.95 (ISBN 0-87243-054-5). Templegate.

Bloom, Michael. Adolescent Parent Separation. 1980. text ed. 23.95 (ISBN 0-89876-035-6). Gardner Pr.

Bloom, Mortimer, jt. auth. see Booth, Verne H.

Bloom, Murray T. The Brotherhood of Money. 365p. 1983. 17.95 (ISBN 0-931960-12-6). BNR Pr.

--Money of Their Own. 2nd ed. (Illus.). 320p. 1983. 17.95 (ISBN 0-931960-09-6). BNR Pr.

Bloom, Paul N., jt. auth. see Kotler, Phillip.

Bloom, Robert. Anatomies of Egotism: A Reading of the Last Novels of H. G. Wells. LC 76-47559. x, 196p. 1977. 15.95x (ISBN 0-8032-0907-X). U of Nebr Pr.

Bloom, Robert & Bebessay, Araya. Inflation Accounting: Reporting of General & Specific Price Changes. LC 83-26973. 334p. 1984. 27.95 (ISBN 0-03-062367-7). Praeger.

Bloom, Robert & Elgers, Pieter T. Accounting Theory & Policy: A Reader. 529p. 1981. pap. text ed. 17.95 (ISBN 0-15-500477-8, HC). HarBraceJ.

Bloom, Robert, et al. Behavioral Accounting: A Reader. 464p. 1982. pap. text ed. 14.95 (ISBN 0-8403-2727-7). Kendall-Hunt.

Bloom, S. R., ed. Gut Hormones. 2nd ed. Polack, J. M. (Illus.). 605p. 1981. text ed. 59.00 (ISBN 0-686-31136-1). Churchill.

Bloom, S. R., jt. ed. see Hodgson, H. J.

Bloom, Samuel W. Doctor & His Patient: A Sociological Interpretation. LC 66-1994. 1965. pap. text ed. 11.95 (ISBN 0-02-903890-1). Free Pr.

Bloom, Solomon F. World of Nations: A Study of the National Implications in the Work of Karl Marx. Repr. of 1941 ed. 16.50 (ISBN 0-404-00899-2). AMS Pr.

Bloom, Stephen R. & Long, R. G. Radioimmunoassay of Gut Regulatory Peptides. 256p. 1982. 35.95 (ISBN 0-03-062116-X). Praeger.

Bloom, Ursula. The Great Tomorrow. 1978. pap. 1.95 (ISBN 0-89083-361-3). Zebra.

Bloom, William & Fawcett, Don W. A Textbook of Histology. 10th ed. LC 73-77935. (Illus.). 1040p. 1975. text ed. 45.95 (ISBN 0-7216-1757-3). Saunders.

Bloom, William L., Jr., et al. Medical Radiographic Technic. 3rd ed. (Illus.). 368p. 1979. photocopy ed. 37.75x (ISBN 0-398-00171-5). C C Thomas.

Bloombaum, Milton, jt. auth. see Gugelyk, Ted.

Bloomberg, Lawrence N. The Investment Value of Goodwill. LC 78-64172. (Johns Hopkins University. Studies in the Social Sciences. Fifty-Sixth Ser. 1938: 3). 1983. Repr. of 1938 ed. 24.50 (ISBN 0-404-61281-4). AMS Pr.

Bloomberg, Marty. Introduction to Public Services for Library Technicians. 3rd ed. LC 81-8210. (Library Science Text Ser.). (Illus.). 323p. 1981. text ed. 28.00 (ISBN 0-87287-257-2); pap. text ed. 20.00 (ISBN 0-87287-263-7). Libs Unl.

--Introduction to Public Services for Library Technicians. 4th ed. LC 84-23369. (Library Science Text). 350p. 1985. lib. bdg. 35.00 (ISBN 0-87287-460-5); pap. text ed. 21.50 (ISBN 0-87287-461-3). Libs Unl.

--The Jewish Holocaust: An Annotated Guide to Books in English. LC 81-21605. (Studies in Judaica & The Holocaust: No. 1). 256p. 1985. lib. bdg. 19.95x (ISBN 0-89370-160-2); pap. 9.95x (ISBN 0-89370-260-9). Borgo Pr.

Bloomberg, Marty & Evans, G. Edward. Introduction to Technical Services for Library Technicians. 4th ed. LC 81-798. (Library Science Text). (Illus.). 363p. 1981. lib. bdg. 28.00 (ISBN 0-87287-228-9); pap. text ed. 20.00 (ISBN 0-87287-248-3). Libs Unl.

Bloomberg, Morton, ed. Creativity: Theory & Research. 1973. 12.95x (ISBN 0-8084-0347-8); pap. 9.95x (ISBN 0-8084-0348-6). New Coll U Pr.

Bloomberg, Warner & Schmandt, Henry J., eds. Power, Poverty & Urban Policy. LC 68-24710. (Urban Affairs Annual Reviews Ser.: Vol. 2). pap. 151.00 (ISBN 0-317-08732-0, 2021871). Bks Demand UMI.

Bloomberg, Warner, Jr., jt. ed. see Schmandt, Henry J.

Bloomenstein, Richard & Finger, Anne L. One Day Plastic Surgery: A Consumer's Guide to Savings & Safety. (Illus.). 144p. 1984. 10.50 (ISBN 0-89962-405-7). Todd & Honeywell.

Bloomenthal, Harold. Securities & Federal Corporate Law, 4 vols. LC 72-90956. (Securities Law Ser.). 1972. looseleaf 285.00 (ISBN 0-87632-086-8). Boardman.

Bloomenthal, Harold S. International Capital Markets & Securities Regulation, 3 vols. LC 82-12959. (Securities Law Ser.). 1982. 210.00 (ISBN 0-87632-357-3). Boardman.

--Securities Law Handbook, 1984. (Securities Law Ser.). (Orig.). 1984. pap. 75.00 (ISBN 0-87632-354-9). Boardman.

--Securities Law in Perspective. 1977. pap. text ed. 10.95 (ISBN 0-316-09988-0). Little.

Bloomenthal, Harold S., et al. Going Public Handbook, 1985. 1985. 62.50 (ISBN 0-87632-460-X). Boardman.

Bloomer, D. C. Life & Writings of Amelia Bloomer. LC 72-78650. 1895. Repr. 39.00 (ISBN 0-403-01994-X). Somerset Pub.

Bloomer, Kent C. & Moore, Charles W. Body, Memory & Architecture. LC 77-76304. (Illus.). 1977. pap. 10.95 (ISBN 0-300-02142-9). Yale U Pr.

Bloomer, M. & Shaw, K. E. Challenge of Education Change: The Content & Organization of Schooling. 1979. pap. 15.75 (ISBN 0-08-022993-X). Pergamon.

Bloomer, O T. & Eakin, B E. Thermodynamic Properties of Methane-Nitrogen Mixtures. (Research Bulletin Ser.: No.21). iv, 51p. (B). 1955. 3.50 (ISBN 0-317-34317-3); supplement 3.50 (ISBN 0-317-34318-1). Inst Gas Tech.

Bloomer, Richard H. Reading Comprehension for Scientists. 228p. 1963. 16.50x (ISBN 0-398-00172-3). C C Thomas.

Bloomfield, Arthur. Arthur Bloomfield's Guide to San Francisco's Restaurants: 1977-1978. 2nd ed. 1977. pap. 2.95 (ISBN 0-89174-023-6). Comstock Edns.

--Before the Last Battle-Armageddon. 192p. 1976. pap. 3.95 (ISBN 0-87123-035-6). Bethany Hse.

--The Changing Climate. LC 77-80427. 128p. 1977. pap. 2.50 (ISBN 0-87123-060-7, 200060). Bethany Hse.

--The San Francisco Opera: 1922-1978. 3rd, rev ed. (Illus.). 1978. pap. 11.95 (ISBN 0-89174-032-5). Comstock Edns.

Bloomfield, Arthur E. All Things New. LC 42-5300. 1959. pap. 6.95 (ISBN 0-87123-007-0); study guide 1.95 (ISBN 0-87123-520-X). Bethany Hse.

--Antes de la Ultima Batalla-Armagedon. 192p. 1977. 3.25 (ISBN 0-88113-003-6). Edit Betania.

--End of the Days. LC 51-9505. 288p. 1961. 6.95 (ISBN 0-87123-122-0, 210122). Bethany Hse.

--El Futuro Glorioso del Planeta Tierra. 256p. 1984. 4.75 (ISBN 0-88113-097-4). Edit Betania.

--How to Recognize the Antichrist. LC 75-29424. 160p. 1975. pap. 3.95 (ISBN 0-87123-225-1, 210225). Bethany Hse.

--Signs of His Coming. LC 57-8724. 160p. 1962. pap. 3.95 (ISBN 0-87123-513-7, 210513). Bethany Hse.

Bloomfield, Arthur I. Capital Imports & the American Balance of Payments, 1934-39. LC 66-23017. (Illus.). Repr. of 1950 ed. 29.50x (ISBN 0-678-00165-0). Kelley.

--Monetary Policy Under the International Gold Standard. Wilkins, Mira, ed. LC 78-3899. (International Finance Ser.). 1978. Repr. of 1959 ed. lib. bdg. 14.00x (ISBN 0-405-11204-1). Ayer Co Pubs.

Bloomfield, B. C. Philip Larkin: A Bibliography. 192p. 1980. 54.95 (ISBN 0-571-11447-4). Faber & Faber.

Bloomfield, B. C. & Mendelson, Edward. W. H. Auden, a Bibliography 1924-1969. 2nd ed. LC 72-77260. 420p. 1973. 25.00x (ISBN 0-8139-0395-5, Bibliographic Society, University of Virginia). U Pr of Va.

Bloomfield, B. C., ed. The Autobiography of Sir James Kay Shuttleworth. 1964. 29.00x (ISBN 0-900008-08-3, Pub. by U of London England). State Mutual Bk.

--Middle East Studies & Libraries: A Felicitation Volume for J. D. Pearson. 244p. 1980. text ed. 51.00x (ISBN 0-7201-1512-4). Mansell.

--Theses on Asia Accepted by Universities in the United Kingdom & Ireland: 1877-1964. 127p. 1967. 25.00x (ISBN 0-7146-1093-3, F Cass Co). Biblio Dist.

Bloomfield, C. D. Adult Leukemias. 1982. 69.50 (ISBN 90-247-2478-3, Pub. by Martinus Nijhoff Netherlands). Kluwer Academic.

Bloomfield, Charles. American Love Letters, Vol. I. 96p. 1983. 6.95 (ISBN 0-916083-00-4). Am Love Letters.

Bloomfield, Clara D., ed. Chronic & Acute Leukemias in Adults. (Cancer Treatment & Research Ser.). 1985. lib. bdg. 69.50 (ISBN 0-89838-702-7, Pub. by Martinus Nijhoff Netherlands). Kluwer-Academic.

Bloomfield, Dennis A., jt. auth. see Simon, Hansjorg.

Bloomfield, Dennis A., ed. Dye Curves: The Theory & Practice of Indicator Dilution. LC 77-356568. pap. 116.50 (ISBN 0-317-26199-1, 2052067). Bks Demand UMI.

Bloomfield, Derek. From Arithmetic to Algebra. 2nd ed. (Illus.). 1976. pap. 19.95 (ISBN 0-8359-2110-7); instrs'. manual avail. (ISBN 0-8359-2111-5). Reston.

--Intermediate Algebra. 1984. text ed. 24.95 (ISBN 0-8359-3132-3). Reston.

--Introductory Algebra. 1983. pap. text ed. 21.95 (ISBN 0-8359-3268-0). Reston.

Bloomfield, G. T. New Zealand: A Handbook of Historical Statistics. LC 83-18365. (International Historical Statistics Ser.). 429p. 1984. lib. bdg. 68.00 (ISBN 0-8161-8168-3, Hall Reference). G K Hall.

Bloomfield, Harold & Felder, Leonard. Making Peace with Your Parents. 220p. 1983. 14.95 (ISBN 0-394-53414-X). Random.

--Making Peace with Your Parents. 240p. 1985. pap. 3.95 (ISBN 0-345-30904-9). Ballantine.

Bloomfield, Harold, et al. How to Survive the Loss of a Love. 1977. pap. 3.50 (ISBN 0-553-25479-0). Bantam.

Bloomfield, Harold H. & Felder, Leonard. The Achilles Syndrome: Transforming Your Weaknesses into Strengths. 1985. 15.95 (ISBN 0-394-54256-8). Random.

Bloomfield, Harold H. & Kory, Robert B. Inner Joy. LC 81-83487. 320p. 1985. pap. 3.95 (ISBN 0-515-08156-6). Jove Pubns.

Bloomfield, Horace R. Female Executives & the Degeneration of Management. (Illus.). 129p. 1983. 79.85x (ISBN 0-86654-063-6). Inst Econ Finan.

--The Negative Factors in the Employment of Women As Corporate Executives. (Illus.). 112p. 1981. 69.85x (ISBN 0-86654-008-3). Inst Econ Finan.

--Negative Factors in the Employment of Women as Corporate Executives. (Illus.). 166p. 1985. 97.75 (ISBN 0-86654-173-X). Inst Econ Finan.

Bloomfield, Irirangi C., jt. auth. see Bloomfield, Lincoln P.

Bloomfield, J. A. Introduction to Organ Imaging. (Medical Outline Ser.). 1984. pap. text ed. write for info. (ISBN 0-87488-072-6). Med Exam.

Bloomfield, J. A., ed. The Lakes of New York State, 2 vols. Incl. Vol. 1. Ecology of the Finger Lakes. 47.50 (ISBN 0-12-107301-7); Vol. 2. The Lakes of Western New York. 43.00 (ISBN 0-12-107302-5). 1978. Acad Pr.

Bloomfield, Jay A., ed. Lakes of New York State, Vol. 3: Ecology of the Lakes of East-Central New York. 1980. 39.50 (ISBN 0-12-107303-3). Acad Pr.

Bloomfield, John A. Pathology for Radiographers & Health Care Professionals. 150p. 1982. 14.95 (ISBN 0-8151-0946-6). Year Bk Med.

Bloomfield, Jonathan. The Passive Revolution: Politics & the Czechoslovak Working Class 1945-48. LC 78-25922. 1979. 27.50x (ISBN 0-312-59788-6). St Martin.

Bloomfield, Julia, ed. Oppositions 27. (Illus.). 144p. pap. 15.00 (ISBN 0-8478-5361-6). Rizzoli Intl.

Bloomfield, Leonard. Colloquial Dutch. LC 74-175102. ix, 284p. 1971. 10.00x (ISBN 0-87950-064-6). Spoken Lang Serv.

--Cree-English Lexicon, 2 vols. (Language & Literature Ser.). 1984. Set. 30.00 (ISBN 0-317-37051-0). HRAFP.

--Fox-English Lexicon. (Language & Literature Ser.). 1984. 15.00 (ISBN 0-317-37052-9). HRAFP.

--Introduction to the Study of Language. (Classics in Psycholinguistics: 3). xxxiii, 335p. 1982. 44.00 (ISBN 90-272-1891-9); pap. 27.00 (ISBN 90-272-1892-7). Benjamins North Am.

--Language. LC 84-8439. x, 564p. 1984. pap. text ed. 12.50x (ISBN 0-226-06067-5). U of Chicago Pr.

--A Leonard Bloomfield Anthology. Hockett, Charles F., ed. LC 78-98981. (History & Theory of Linguistics Ser). 592p. 1970. 32.50x (ISBN 0-253-33327-X). Ind U Pr.

--Linguistic Aspects of Science. (Foundations of the Unity of Science Ser: Vol. 1, No. 4). 1939. pap. 1.95x (ISBN 0-226-57579-9, P403, Phoen). U of Chicago Pr.

--The Menomini Language. 1962. 59.50x (ISBN 0-686-50049-0). Elliots Bks.

--Menomini Texts. LC 73-3548. (American Ethnological Society. Publications: No. 12). Repr. of 1928 ed. 58.00 (ISBN 0-404-58162-5). AMS Pr.

--Plains Cree Texts. LC 73-3552. (American Ethnological Society. Publications Ser.: No. 16). Repr. of 1934 ed. 36.00 (ISBN 0-404-58166-8). AMS Pr.

--Sacred Stories of the Sweet Grass Cree. LC 74-7933. Repr. of 1930 ed. 34.50 (ISBN 0-404-11821-6). AMS Pr.

--Spoken Dutch. LC 75-15107. (Spoken Language Ser.). 266p. (Prog. Bk.). 1975. pap. 10.00x (ISBN 0-87950-054-9); cassettes 5 dual track 60.00x (ISBN 0-87950-060-3); cassettes with course-bk. 65.00x (ISBN 0-87950-061-1). Spoken Lang Serv.

Bloomfield, Leonard & Barnhart, Clarence L. Let's Read, a Linguistic Approach. LC 61-9080. (Illus.). 468p. 1961. 12.50x (ISBN 0-8143-1115-6). Wayne St U Pr.

Bloomfield, Leonard & Hockett, Charles F., eds. Menomini Lexicon. 308p. 1975. 7.50 (ISBN 0-89326-014-2). Milwaukee Pub Mus.

Bloomfield, Leonard, et al. Spoken Russian. bk.I, units 1-12, 1971 481p. 10.00x (ISBN 0-87950-190-1); bk. II, units 13-30, 1971 398p. 10.00x (ISBN 0-87950-191-X); bk.I & cassettes I 65.00x (ISBN 0-87950-197-9); bk.I & cassettes IE 105.00x (ISBN 0-87950-202-9); bk.II & cassettes IIE 100.00x (ISBN 0-87950-203-7); bks.I & II, cassettes IE & IIE 195.00x (ISBN 0-87950-204-5); cassettes I for Bk.I, 6 dual track 60.00x (ISBN 0-87950-196-0); cassettes IE for bk.I, 15 dual track 100.00x (ISBN 0-87950-200-2); cassettes IIE for bk.II, 11 dual track 95.00x (ISBN 0-87950-201-0). Spoken Lang Serv.

Bloomfield, Lincoln P. The Foreign Policy Process: A Modern Primer. (Illus.). 256p. 1982. pap. 16.95 reference (ISBN 0-13-326504-8). P-H.

--The Power to Keep Peace, Today & in a World Without War. pap. 2.95 (ISBN 0-912018-12-7). World Without War.

Bloomfield, Lincoln P. & Bloomfield, Irirangi C. The U. S., Interdependence & World Order. LC 75-36296. (Headline Ser.: 228). (Orig.). 1975. pap. 3.00 (ISBN 0-87124-033-5). Foreign Policy.

Bloomfield, Lincoln P. & Yost, Charles W. What Future for the U. N.? 40p. 1977. pap. 2.00x (ISBN 0-87855-741-5). Transaction Bks.

Bloomfield, Lincoln P., jt. auth. see Yost, Charles W.

Bloomfield, Lincoln P., ed. see American Assembly.

Bloomfield, Lincoln P., et al. Khrushchev & the Arms Race: Soviet Interests in Arms Control & Disarmament 1954-1964. (Illus.). 1966. 25.00x (ISBN 0-262-02017-3). MIT Pr.

Bloomfield, M. Hymns of the Atharva-Veda. (Sacred Books of the East: Vol. 42). 18.00 (ISBN 0-89581-532-X). Asian Human Pr.

Bloomfield, M., tr. Hymns of the Atharva-Veda: Together with Extracts from the Ritual Books & the Commentaries. LC 69-14131. 716p. 1897. Repr. lib. bdg. 32.50x (ISBN 0-8371-1879-4, VEHA). Greenwood.

Bloomfield, Mark A., jt. auth. see Walker, Charls E.

Bloomfield, Mark A., jt. ed. see Walker, Charles E.

Bloomfield, Masse. How to Use a Library. (Illus.). 1970. pap. 4.00x (ISBN 0-87881-000-5). Mojave Bks.

Bloomfield, Maurice. Religion of the Veda. LC 70-94310. (BCL Ser. II). Repr. of 1908 ed. 18.00 (ISBN 0-404-00912-3). AMS Pr.

Bloomfield, Maxwell. American Lawyers in a Changing Society, 1776-1876. (Studies in Legal History). 416p. 1976. 27.50x (ISBN 0-674-02910-0). Harvard U Pr.

Bloomfield, Maxwell & McWilliams, John. Law & American Literature. LC 82-21345. (Borzoi Books in Law & American Society). 1983. text ed. 15.00 (ISBN 0-394-33574-0, KnopfC); pap. text ed. 9.00 (ISBN 0-394-33190-7). Knopf.

Bloomfield, Maxwell, et al. Law & American Literature: A Collection of Essays. (Law & American Society Ser.). 240p. 1983. (RanC); 9.00 (ISBN 0-394-33190-7). Random.

Bloomfield, Meyer. Vocational Guidance of Youth. LC 70-89151. (American Education: Its Men, Institutions & Ideas Ser). 1969. Repr. of 1911 ed. 13.00 (ISBN 0-405-01389-2). Ayer Co Pubs.

Bloomfield, Meyer, ed. Readings in Vocational Guidance. 723p. 1982. Repr. of 1915 ed. lib. bdg. 65.00 (ISBN 0-89987-090-2). Darby Bks.

Bloomfield, Michael, jt. auth. see Summerville, Scott.

Bloomfield, Mike. The Vedic Concordance. 1983. Repr. 90.00 (ISBN 0-89684-336-X). Orient Bk Dist.

Bloomfield, Molly M. Chemistry & the Living Organism. 3rd ed. LC 83-14788. 391p. 1984. text ed. 32.50 (ISBN 0-471-87627-5); write for info. tchr's manual (ISBN 0-471-87892-8); study guide 13.50 (ISBN 0-471-88601-7); lab experiments 18.50 (ISBN 0-471-88599-1); write for info. transparancies (ISBN 0-471-87893-6). Wiley.

Bloomfield, Morton, jt. ed. see Haugen, Einar.

Bloomfield, Morton W. Essays & Explorations: Studies in Ideas, Language, & Literature. LC 70-106956. (Illus.). x, 321p. 1970. 20.00x (ISBN 0-674-26425-8). Harvard U Pr.

Bloomfield, Morton W. & Newmark, Leonard. Linguistic Introduction to the History of English. LC 79-4563. (Illus.). 1979. Repr. of 1963 ed. lib. bdg. 47.50x (ISBN 0-313-20936-7, BLLI). Greenwood.

Bloomfield, Morton W., ed. Allegory, Myth, & Symbol. (Harvard English Studies: 9). 440p. 1982. text ed. 30.00x (ISBN 0-674-01640-8); pap. text ed. 9.95x (ISBN 0-674-01641-6). Harvard U Pr.

Bloomfield, Morton W., et al. Incipits of Latin Works on the Virtues & Vices, 1100-1500 A. D. LC 75-36481. 1979. 75.00x (ISBN 0-910956-65-0). Medieval Acad.

Bloomfield, Paul. Benjamin Disraeli. Dobree, Bonamy, et al, eds. Bd. with William Makepeace Thackeray. Brander, Laurence A; Charles Dickens. Fielding, K. J; Anthony Trollope. Davies, Hugh S. LC 63-63096. (British Writers & Their Work Ser: Vol. 9). viii, 182p. 1965. pap. 3.25x (ISBN 0-8032-5659-0, BB 458, Bison). U of Nebr Pr.

--Imaginary Worlds: Or, the Evolution of Utopia. 59.95 (ISBN 0-8490-0385-7). Gordon Pr.

--William Morris. LC 73-15902. 1934. lib. bdg. 25.00 (ISBN 0-8414-3322-4). Folcroft.

Bloomfield, Peter. Fourier Analysis of Time Series: An Introduction. LC 75-34294. (Probability & Mathematical Statistics Ser.). 258p. 1976. 33.95x (ISBN 0-471-08256-2, Pub. by Wiley-Interscience). Wiley.

Bloomfield, Peter & Steiger, William, eds. Applications of Least Absolute Deviations. (Progress in Probability & Statistics Ser.: Vol. 6). 400p. 1983. 24.95 (ISBN 0-8176-3157-7). Birkhauser.

Bloomfield, Richard J. Puerto Rico: The Search for a National Policy. (WVSS on Latin America & the Caribbean Ser.). 210p. 1985. 30.00x (ISBN 0-8133-0027-4). Westview.

Bloomfield, Robert. Collected Poems, 1800-1822, 5 vols. in 1. Lawson, Jonathan N., ed. & intro. by. LC 79-161927. 704p. 1971. 90.00x (ISBN 0-8201-1088-4). Schol Facsimiles.

Bloomfield, Robert & Chandler, Ted. Pocket Mnemonics for Practitioners. abr. ed. 1983. pap. 4.95 (ISBN 0-9612242-2-3). Harbinger Med Pr NC.

Bloomfield, Robert L. & Chandler, Ted. Mnemonics Rhetoric & Poetics for Medics. 1983. pap. 10.95 (ISBN 0-9612242-1-5). Harbinger Med Pr NC.

Bloomfield, Robert L., jt. auth. see Chandler, E. Ted.

Bloomfield, Stephen, jt. auth. see Theodore, Frederick.

Bloomfield, Valerie. Commonwealth Elections, 1945-1970: A Bibliography. LC 76-24992. 1977. lib. bdg. 45.00x (ISBN 0-8371-9067-3, BCE/). Greenwood.

Bloomfield, William M. The Vocational Action Plan: Targeting Job Success. LC 82-70136. (The Vocational Action Plan Ser.: No. 1). (Illus.). 176p. (Orig.). 1982. pap. 8.50 (ISBN 0-942834-00-3); tchrs.' ed. 8.50 (ISBN 0-942834-01-1). WB&A Pubns.

Bloomflied, Bob. The Mystique of Healing. LC 85-50010. 120p. (Orig.). 1985. pap. 5.95 (ISBN 0-87728-640-X). Weiser.

Bloomgarden, Barry. Your Future in Insurance Careers. (Careers in Depth Ser.). (gr. 7-12). 1978. PLB 8.97 (ISBN 0-8239-0455-5). Rosen Group.

Bloomgarden, Yehoash. The Feet of the Messenger. Davis, Moshe, ed. LC 77-70682. (America & the Holy Land Ser.). 1977. Repr. of 1923 ed. lib. bdg. 26.50x (ISBN 0-405-10229-1). Ayer Co Pubs.

Bloomingdale, L., ed. Attention Deficit Disorders. 240p. 1984. 35.00 (ISBN 0-89335-193-8). SP Med & Sci Bks.

Bloomingdale, Lewis M., ed. Attention Deficit Disorder: Identification, Course, & Rationale. LC 84-25447. 170p. 1985. text ed. 25.00 (ISBN 0-89335-219-5). SP Med & Sci Bks.

Bloomingdale, Teresa. I Should Have Seen It Coming When the Rabbit Died. 208p. 1980. pap. 2.95 (ISBN 0-553-23686-5). Bantam.

--Life Is What Happens When You're Making Other Plans. LC 83-45344. 216p. 1984. 12.95 (ISBN 0-385-18064-0). Doubleday.

--Murphy Must Have Been a Mother! (General Ser.). 1983. lib. bdg. 13.95 (ISBN 0-8161-3505-3, Large Print Bks). G K Hall.

--Murphy Must Have Been a Mother. 192p. 1983. pap. 2.95 (ISBN 0-553-23583-4). Bantam.

--Up a Family Tree. LC 81-43053. 256p. 1981. 11.95 (ISBN 0-385-17032-7). Doubleday.

--Up a Family Tree. (General Ser.). 1982. lib. bdg. 13.95 (ISBN 0-8161-3344-1, Large Print Bks). G K Hall.

Bloomquist, jt. auth. see Kiess.

Bloomquist, Dale S., et al. Surgical Complications: A Self-Instructional Guide, Bk. 4. 3rd, rev. ed. Hooley, James R. & Whitacre, James R., eds. (Illus.). 64p. 1983. pap. 7.95x (ISBN 0-89939-041-2). Stoma Pr.

Bloomquist, Gordon, jt. ed. see McClain, David.

Bloomquist, R., et al. Number-Key Practice for Use on Typewriter, Ten-Key & Keypunch Keyboards. 1975. 8.48 (ISBN 0-07-006105-X). McGraw.

Bloomstein, Charles, ed. see Nesbitt, William A. & Abramowitz, Norman.

Bloomstein, Henry. The Brothers Kresky. 224p. 1983. 10.95 (ISBN 0-912650-04-4). Brookdale Pr.

Bloor, Byron M. Cerebral Hemodynamics in Man & Monkey: Some Considerations in Cerebrovascular Disease, Subarachnoid Hemorrhage, & Intracranial Pressure. (Illus.). 160p. 1981. 19.75x (ISBN 0-398-04066-4). C C Thomas.

Bloor, C. H. Pathology. (Illus.). pap. text ed. write for info. (ISBN 0-443-08073-9). Churchill.

Bloor, Carolyn & Seiberling, Grace. A Vision Exchanged. (Illus.). 48p. (Orig.). 1985. pap. 7.95 (ISBN 0-948107-05-7, Pub. by Victoria & Albert Mus UK). Faber & Faber.

Bloor, Colin M. & Liebow, Averill A. The Pulmonary & Bronchial Circulations in Congenital Heart Disease. (Topics in Cardiovascular Disease Ser.). (Illus.). 293p. 1980. 37.50x (ISBN 0-306-40383-8, Plenum Med Bk). Plenum Pub.

Bloor, Colin M., ed. Comparative Pathophysiology of Circulatory Disturbances. LC 72-76859. (Advances in Experimental Medicine & Biology Ser: Vol. 22). 395p. 1972. 52.50x (ISBN 0-306-39022-1, Plenum Pr). Plenum Pub.

Bloor, Colin M. & Olsson, Ray A., eds. Current Topics in Coronary Research. LC 73-15916. (Advances in Experimental Medicine & Biology Ser.: Vol. 39). 327p. 1973. 45.00x (ISBN 0-306-39039-6, Plenum Pr). Plenum Pub.

Bloor, David. Knowledge & Social Imagery. (Routledge Direct Editions). 168p. 1976. 16.95x (ISBN 0-7100-8377-7). Routledge & Kegan.

--Wittgenstein & Social Science. 250p. 1983. 26.00x (ISBN 0-231-05800-4); pap. 13.00x. Columbia U Pr.

Bloor, R. H. Christianity & the Religious Drama. LC 73-261. 1973. lib. bdg. 8.50 (ISBN 0-8414-1425-4). Folcroft.

--English Novel from Chaucer to Galsworthy. LC 74-9556. 1935. lib. bdg. 15.00 (ISBN 0-8414-3105-1). Folcroft.

Bloore, John. Alternative Views of the Bible. 1978. Repr. of 1925 ed. lib. bdg. 20.00 (ISBN 0-8495-0366-3). Arden Lib.

Blos, Joan. A Gathering of Days: A New England Girl's Journal, 1830-32. LC 79-16898. (gr. 6-8). 1979. 10.95 (ISBN 0-684-16340-3, ScribJ); pap. 3.95 (ISBN 0-689-70750-9). Scribner.

--A Gathering of Days: A New England Girl's Journal, 1830-32. LC 79-16898. 160p. 1982. pap. 3.50 (ISBN 0-689-70750-9, A-126, Aladdin). Atheneum.

--Martin's Hats. LC 83-13389. (Illus.). 32p. (ps-3). 1984. 9.50 (ISBN 0-688-02027-5); PLB 8.59 (ISBN 0-688-02033-X). Morrow.

Blos, Joan W. Brothers of the Heart. LC 85-40293. 176p. (gr. 7 up). 1985. 12.95 (ISBN 0-684-18452-4). Scribner.

Blos, Peter. The Adolescent Passage: Developmental Issues. LC 78-61245. 538p. (Orig.). 1979. 40.00 (ISBN 0-8236-0095-5). Intl Univs Pr.

--On Adolescence: A Psychoanalytic Interpretation. LC 61-14110. 1966. 18.95 (ISBN 0-02-904320-4); pap. 9.95 (ISBN 0-02-904330-1). Free Pr.

--Son & Father: Before & Beyond the Oedipus Complex. 256p. 22.50x (ISBN 0-02-903680-1). Free Pr.

--Young Adolescent. LC 73-125597. 1974. pap. 9.95x (ISBN 0-02-904300-X). Free Pr.

Bloss, Donald F. The Spindle Stage: Principles & Practice. LC 80-21488. (Illus.). 416p. 1981. 79.50 (ISBN 0-521-23292-9). Cambridge U Pr.

Bloss, Donald F., jt. auth. see Jones, Norris W.

Bloss, Esther. Labor Legislation in Czechoslovakia. LC 79-76641. (Columbia University Studies in the Social Sciences: No. 446). Repr. of 1938 ed. 18.50 (ISBN 0-404-51446-4). AMS Pr.

Bloss, F. D. Crystallography & Crystal Chemistry. LC 77-136774. 1971. text ed. 40.95 (ISBN 0-03-085155-6, HoltC). HR&W.

--Introduction to the Methods of Optical Crystallography. LC 61-6759. 1961. text ed. 38.95 (ISBN 0-03-010220-0, HoltC). HR&W.

Bloss, Margaret V. Badminton. 4th ed. (Physical Education Activities Ser.). 112p. 1980. pap. text ed. write for info. (ISBN 0-697-07096-4). Wm C Brown.

Bloss, Margaret V. & Bramall, Norman. Squash Racquets. (Physical Education Activities Ser.). 80p. 1967. pap. text ed. write for info (ISBN 0-697-07027-1); tchrs.' man. o.p. avail. (ISBN 0-697-07224-X). Wm C Brown.

Bloss, Margaret V. & Harrison, J. Rufford. Table Tennis. (Physical Education Activities Ser.). 80p. 1967. pap. text ed. write for info. (ISBN 0-697-07029-8). Wm C Brown.

Bloss, Marjorie E. Guidelines for Union Lists of Serials. 52p. 1982. 12.00 (ISBN 0-317-36990-3); members 10.80 (ISBN 0-317-36991-1). ALA.

Bloss, W. H. & Grassi, G., eds. E. C. Photovoltaic Solar Energy Conference, 4th. 1982. 96.00 (ISBN 90-277-1463-0, Pub. by Reidel Holland). Kluwer Academic.

Blosser, Betsy. English for Adult Living: Competency-Based "Survival Skills" ESL Book 2. Ragan, Lise B. & Weinstein, Amy, eds. (English for Adult Living Ser.). (gr. 9-12). 1979. pap. text ed. 4.95 (ISBN 0-88499-528-3). Inst Mod Lang.

Blosser, Betsy J. English for Adult Living: Competency-Based "Survival Skills" ESL, Bk. 1. Ragan, Lise B., ed. (English for Adult Living Ser.). 1979. pap. text ed. 4.95 (ISBN 0-88499-527-5). Inst Mod Lang.

Blosser, Jean. Let's Talk About It! (Illus.). 1984. binder 9.00x (ISBN 0-8134-2340-6, 2340). Interstate.

Blosser, Jean & De Pompei, Roberta. Let's Listen Today! (Illus.). 1985. binder 9.00x (ISBN 0-8134-2483-6, 2483). Interstate.

Blossey, E. C. & Neckers, D. C., eds. Solid Phase Synthesis. (Benchmark Papers in Organic Chemistry Ser: Vol. 2). 400p. 1975. 66.00 (ISBN 0-12-786165-3). Acad Pr.

Blossfeldt, Karl. Art Forms in the Plant World. (Illus.). 128p. 1985. pap. 7.95 (ISBN 0-486-24990-5). Dover.

Blossom, Aline. My Beloved. 3.00 (ISBN 0-8338-0002-7). M Jones.

Blossom, F. A. La Composition de Salammbo, d'Apres la Correspondance de Flaubert, 1857-62. (Elliott Monographs: Vol. 3.). 1914. 11.00 (ISBN 0-527-02607-7). Kraus Repr.

Blossom, Thomas. Narino, Here of Colombian Independence. LC 66-20661. pap. 60.30 (ISBN 0-317-28632-3, 2055374). Bks Demand UMI.

Blostein, David A., ed. see Marston, John.

Blot, David & Davidson, David. Put It in Writing: Writing Activities for Students of ESL. (Illus.). 104p. (Orig.). 1981. pap. text ed. 5.95 (ISBN 0-88377-175-6). Newbury Hse.

Blot, David, jt. auth. see Davidson, David.

Blot, Pierre. Hand-book of Practical Cookery, for Ladies & Professional Cooks. LC 72-9789. (Cookery Americana Ser). Repr. of 1869 ed. 14.00 (ISBN 0-405-05042-9). Ayer Co Pubs.

Blotner, ed. see Faulkner, William.

Blotner, et al, eds. see Faulkner, Wiliam.

Blotner, et al, eds. see Faulkner, William.

Blotner, J. & McHaney, T., eds. Go Down, Moses: Nineteen Forty-Two, Typescript. Polk, N. (William Faulkner Manuscripts Ser.). 100.00 (ISBN 0-8240-6830-0). Garland Pub.

--The Hamlet: Nineteen Forty, Preliminary Materials. (William Faulkner Manuscripts Ser.). 100.00 (ISBN 0-8240-6820-3). Garland Pub.

Blotner, J., et al, eds. Go Down, Moses: Nineteen Forty-Two, Pre Material. (William Faulkner Manuscripts Ser.). 100.00 (ISBN 0-8240-6822-X). Garland Pub.

--The Hamlet: Nineteen Forty, Typescripts. (William Faulkner Manuscripts Ser.). (Illus.). 100.00 (ISBN 0-8240-6821-1). Garland Pub.

--Intruder in the Dust, 1948. (William Faulkner Manuscripts Ser.). 26.00 (ISBN 0-8240-6838-6). Garland Pub.

Blotner, J., et al, eds. see Faulkner, William.

Blotner, J., et al, eds. see Faulkner, William F.

Blotner, Josef, et al, eds. see Faulkner, William.

Blotner, Joseph. Faulkner: A Biography, 2 vols. (Illus.). 1974. Boxed Set. 30.00 (ISBN 0-394-47452-X). Random.

--Faulkner: A Biography, Vol. 1. LC 83-17663. 778p. 1984. 35.00 (ISBN 0-394-50413-5). Random.

Blotner, Joseph, jt. auth. see Gwynn, Frederick L.

Blotner, Joseph, ed. Selected Letters of William Faulkner. 1978. pap. 4.95 (ISBN 0-394-72505-0, Vin). Random.

Blotner, Joseph, ed. see Faulkner, William.

Blotner, Joseph, et al, eds. Elmer (1925) (William Faulkner Manuscripts Ser.). 100.00 (ISBN 0-8240-6800-9). Garland Pub.

Blotner, Joseph L. The Political Novel. LC 78-9868. 1979. Repr. of 1955 ed. lib. bdg. 22.50x (ISBN 0-313-21228-7, BLPN). Greenwood.

Blotner, Joseph L., jt. ed. see Gwynn, Frederick L.

Blotnick, Elihu. Baby Faces. (Illus.). 64p. (Orig.). 1982. spiral 6.95 (ISBN 0-915090-04-X). Calif Street.

--Blue Turtle Moon Queen. (Illus.). 120p. (gr. 6-12). Date not set. pap. 6.95 (ISBN 0-915090-20-1). Calif Street.

--California Street No. 1. (Illus.). 1980. pap. 9.95 (ISBN 0-915090-21-X). Calif Street.

--The Fog Line. (Mr. Blot Ser.: No. 3). (Illus.). 72p. (gr. 6 up). Date not set. pap. 5.95 (ISBN 0-915090-12-0). Calif Street.

--Glimmins: Children of the Western Woods. (Illus.). 72p. (gr. 1 up). Date not set. pap. 11.95 (ISBN 0-915090-18-X). Calif Street.

--Never Distrust an Asparagus. (Complete Blot Ser.). (Illus.). 1979. pap. 3.95 (ISBN 0-915090-10-4). Calif Street.

--Rio Arriba. (Illus.). 342p. (Orig.). Date not set. pap. 17.95 (ISBN 0-915090-24-4). Calif Street.

--Russian Hill: Storm Year. Fragment, Ariel, ed. 64p. 1983. pap. 7.25 (ISBN 0-915090-17-1). Calif Street.

--Saltwater Flats: A Silent Film. LC 74-18166. (Illus.). 64p. 1975. pap. 12.95 (ISBN 0-915090-00-7). Calif Street.

Blotnick, Elihu & Murray, Linda. Little People. (Illus.). 64p. (Orig.). (gr. 1-8). 1981. pap. 10.00 (ISBN 0-915090-03-1). Calif Street.

--Word Windows: A Language Game, 7 bks. (Illus.). 200p. (gr. 1-6). 1981. Boxed Set. spiral bdg. 70.00 (ISBN 0-915090-07-4). Calif Street.

Blotnick, Elihu & Robinson, Barbara. Free-for-All: The Reds, the Whites & the Blues. (Illus.). 64p. (Orig.). 1981. pap. 8.95 (ISBN 0-915090-02-3). Calif Street.

--Mysterious Mr. Blot. Fragment, Ariel, ed. LC 79-51994. (Illus.). 1979. 4.95 (ISBN 0-915090-09-0). Calif Street.

Blotnick, Elihu, ed. Revolution: A Sixties Album. (Illus.). 224p. Date not set. pap. 27.95 (ISBN 0-915090-23-6). Calif Street.

Blotnick, Elihu, et al. I Saw an Eagle Today: Living Lightly in Nature. (Illus.). 208p. 1984. spiral bound 11.95 (ISBN 0-915090-26-0). Calif Street.

Blotnick, S. Computers Made (Ridiculously) Easy. (Illus.). 198p. 1984. pap. 12.95 (ISBN 0-07-006123-8). McGraw.

Blotnick, Srully. The Corporate Steeplechase: Predictable Crises in a Business Career. 352p. 1984. 17.95 (ISBN 0-87196-840-1). Facts on File.

--Getting Rich Your Own Way. LC 81-86252. 256p. 1982. pap. 2.95 (ISBN 0-86721-130-X). Jove Pubns.

--Otherwise Engaged: The Private Lives of Successful Career Women. Date not set. price not set. Facts on File.

--Winning: The Psychology of Successful Investing. 1978. 29.95 (ISBN 0-07-006119-X). McGraw.

Blotter, P. Thomas. Introduction to Engineering. LC 80-25375. 289p. 1981. 29.45x (ISBN 0-471-04935-2); solutions 10.00 (ISBN 0-471-09947-3). Wiley.

Blottner, Joseph, ed. see Faulkner, William.

Blouch, Ralph I. & Blouch, Ralph I., eds. International Association of Fish & Wildlife Agencies 69th Convention: Proceedings. (Orig.). 1980. 11.00 (ISBN 0-932108-04-0). IAFWA.

Blouet, Brian W. & Blouet, Olwyn M., eds. Latin America: An Introductory Survey. LC 81-7451. 300p. 1982. text ed. 24.95 (ISBN 0-471-08385-2). Wiley.

Blouet, Brian W. & Lawson, Merlin P., eds. Images of the Plains: The Role of Human Nature in Settlement. LC 74-76130. (Illus.). xiv, 214p. 1975. 17.95x (ISBN 0-8032-0839-1). U of Nebr Pr.

Blouet, Brian W. & Luebke, Frederick C., eds. The Great Plains: Environment & Culture. LC 79-1152. (Illus.). xxviii, 246p. 1979. 19.95x (ISBN 0-8032-1155-4). U of Nebr Pr.

Blouet, Brian W. & Stitcher, Teresa L., eds. The Origins of Academic Geography in the United States. xii, 342p. 1981. 37.50 (ISBN 0-208-01881-6, Archon). Shoe String.

Blouet, Olwyn M., jt. ed. see Blouet, Brian W.

Blough, Carman G. Practical Applications of Accounting Standards: A Decade of Comment on Accounting & Auditing Problems. Brief, Richard P., ed. LC 80-1472. (Dimensions of Accounting Theory & Practice Ser.). 1981. Repr. of 1957 ed. lib. bdg. 45.00x (ISBN 0-405-13502-5). Ayer Co Pubs.

Blough, Dorris. The Brass Ring. (Orig.). 1975. pap. 1.25 (ISBN 0-87178-105-0). Brethren.

Blough, Dorris M. Tied to a Leopard. 125p. (Orig.). 1982. pap. 2.75 (ISBN 0-87178-845-4). Brethren.

Blough, Dwight, jt. auth. see Arnold, Heini.

Blough, Glenn O. & Schwartz, Julius. Elementary School Science & How to Teach It. 7th ed. LC 83-22537. 670p. 1984. text ed. 30.95 (ISBN 0-03-062866-0, HoltC). HR&W.

Blough, H. A. & Tiffany, J. M. Cell Membranes & Viral Envelopes, Vol. 1. LC 79-84537. 1980. 95.00 (ISBN 0-12-107201-0). Acad Pr.

Blough, H. A. & Tiffany, J. M., eds. Cell Membranes & Viral Envelopes, Vol. 2. LC 77-84537. 1980. 95.00 (ISBN 0-12-107202-9). Acad Pr.

Blough, H. A., et al. Current Topics in Microbiology & Immunology, Vol. 70. LC 75-12910. (Illus.). 140p. 1975. 40.00 (ISBN 0-387-07223-3). Springer-Verlag.

Blough, J. L., jt. auth. see Hill, Vernon L.

Blough, Roger M. The Washington Embrace of Business. LC 75-12001. (Benjamin Fairless Memorial Lectures Ser.). 161p. 1975. 18.00x (ISBN 0-915604-03-5). Columbia U Pr.

Blough, Roy & Behrman, Jack N. Regional Integration & the Trade of Latin America. LC 68-19545. 184p. 1968. pap. 2.50 (ISBN 0-87186-222-0). Comm Econ Dev.

Blouin, Andree & MacKellar, Jean. My Country, Africa: The Autobiography of the Black Passionaria. LC 82-18888. (Illus.). 302p. 1983. 20.95 (ISBN 0-03-062759-1). Praeger.

Blouin, Francis X., Jr. The Boston Region, 1810-1850: A Study of Urbanization. Berkhofer, Robert, ed. LC 79-28080. (Studies in American History & Culture: No. 10). 234p. 1980. 44.95 (ISBN 0-8357-1077-7). UMI Res Pr.

Blount, Ben G., jt. auth. see Sanches, Mary.

Blount, Ben G. & Sanches, Mary, eds. Sociocultural Dimensions of Language Change. 1977. 65.00 (ISBN 0-12-107450-1). Acad Pr.

Blount, C. H., ed. see Davies, Herbert A.

Blount, Charles. Miscellaneous Works. LC 75-11197. (British Philosophers & Theologians of the 17th & 18th Centuries: Vol. 4). 1979. Repr. of 1695 ed. lib. bdg. 51.00 (ISBN 0-8240-1753-6). Garland Pub.

Blount, Edward. Memoirs of Sir Edward Blount. Wilkins, Mira & Reid, Stuart J., eds. LC 76-29985. (European Business Ser.). (Illus.). 1977. Repr. of 1902 ed. lib. bdg. 25.50x (ISBN 0-405-09717-4). Ayer Co Pubs.

Blount, George. Contemporary Science: The Christian's New Friend. 1977. pap. 3.95 (ISBN 0-916608-03-4). Quill Pubns.

Blount, Henry. A Voyage into Levant. LC 77-6850. (English Experience Ser.: No. 850). 1977. Repr. of 1636 ed. lib. bdg. 13.00 (ISBN 90-221-0850-3). Walter J Johnson.

Blount, Henry C. Looking for Honey. (Illus., Orig.). 1984. 5.00 (ISBN 0-9614047-0-1). McArthur Pub.

Blount, James. Equations. 1981. cancelled 5.75 (ISBN 0-8062-1653-0). Carlton.

Blount, Joe. Diary of a Fatphomaniac. 200p. 1984. pap. 9.95 (ISBN 0-89015-467-8). Eakin Pubns.

Blount, R. E. Mamas, Don't Let Your Babies Grow Up to Play Football. (Illus.). 216p. 1985. 11.95 (ISBN 0-89015-527-5). Eakin Pubns.

Blount, R. E. Peppy. We Band of Brothers. 304p. 1984. 16.95 (ISBN 0-89015-443-0). Eakin Pubns.

Blount, Ray, Jr. What Men Don't Tell Women. (Humor Ser.). 192p. 1985. pap. 5.95 (ISBN 0-14-007788-X). Penguin.

Blount, Raymond N. Housekeeping Procedures for the Small Hospital. 152p. 1978. 19.75x (ISBN 0-398-03693-4). C C Thomas.

Blount, Roy J. One Fell Soup: Or I'm Just a Bug on the Windshield of Life. 255p. 1982. 14.45 (ISBN 0-316-10005-6, An Atlantic-Little, Brown Book). Little.

Blount, Roy, Jr. About Three Bricks Shy of a Load. 1981. pap. 2.75 (ISBN 0-345-29110-7). Ballantine.

--Crackers. 1982. pap. 2.95 (ISBN 0-345-29805-5). Ballantine.

--Not Exactly What I Had in Mind. Davison, Peter, ed. 208p. 1985. 14.95 (ISBN 0-87113-031-9, Pub. by Atlantic Monthly Pr). Little.

--One Fell Soup: Or, I'm Just a Bug on the Windshield of Life. 288p. 1984. pap. 4.95 (ISBN 0-14-006892-9). Penguin.

Blount, Steve. Diving & Snorkeling Guide to the Bahamas: Nassau & New Providence Island. LC 85-582. (Diving & Snorkeling Guides Ser.). (Illus.). 64p. 1985. pap. 8.95 (ISBN 0-86636-030-1). PBC Intl Inc.

Blount, Steve & Taylor, Herb. The Joy of Snorkeling. (Illus.). 112p. 1984. 17.95 (ISBN 0-02-511950-8, 83-63487); pap. 8.95 (ISBN 0-02-028110-2). Macmillan.

Blount, Thomas. Nomo-Lexicon: A Law Dictionary. LC 70-103245. 330p. 1983. Repr. of 1970 ed. lib. bdg. 39.95x (ISBN 0-89370-785-6). Borgo Pr.

Blount, Trevor, ed. see Dickens, Charles.

Blount, W. P. Fractures in Children. LC 76-11. 294p. 1977. Repr. of 1955 ed. 21.50 (ISBN 0-88275-392-4). Krieger.

Blount, Willie. A Catechetical Exposition of the Constitution of the State of Tennessee. LC 74-583. (Tennessee Beginnings Ser.). 1974. 10.00. Reprint.

Bloustein, E. J., ed. Nuclear Policy, Public Policy & the Law. 160p. 1964. 10.00 (ISBN 0-317-30218-3). Oceana.

Bloustein, Edward J. Individual & Group Privacy. LC 77-28972. 100p. 1978. 12.95 (ISBN 0-87855-286-3). Transaction Bks.

Bloustein, Edward J., ed. Nuclear Energy, Public Policy & the Law. LC 64-22787. 114p. 1964. 10.00 (ISBN 0-379-00231-0). Oceana.

Blout, E. R., et al. Peptides, Polypeptides & Proteins. LC 74-22202. 656p. 1974. 38.00 (ISBN 0-471-08387-9). Krieger.

Blow, D. M., jt. auth. see Holmes, K. C.

Blow, John see Arkwright, G. E. P.

Blow, Simon. Fields Elysian: A Portrait of Hunting Society. (Illus.). 160p. 1983. 19.95x (ISBN 0-460-04534-2, BKA-05242, Pub. by J M Dent England). Biblio Dist.

Blow, Suzanne K. A Study of Rhetoric in the Plays of Thomas Dekker. (Salzburg Studies in English Literature, Jacobean Drama Studies: No. 3). 1972. pap. text ed. 25.50x (ISBN 0-391-01327-0). Humanities.

Blower, G. J. Plumbing. (Illus.). 208p. 1982. pap. text ed. 19.95x (ISBN 0-7121-1750-4). Trans-Atlantic.

Blower, J. G., et al. Estimating the Size of Animal Populations. 96p. (Orig.). 1981. text ed. 22.50x (ISBN 0-04-591017-0); pap. text ed. 9.95x (ISBN 0-04-591018-9). Allen Unwin.

Blower, W. E. The MG Workshop Manual: From "M" Type to "T.F. 1500". LC 75-33494. (Illus.). 608p. 1975. pap. 40.00 (ISBN 0-8376-0117-7). Bentley.

Blowers, et al. Urban Change & Conflict. 1982. text ed. 33.00 (ISBN 0-06-318203-3, Pub. by Har-Row Ltd England); pap. text ed. 18.50 (ISBN 0-06-318204-1, Pub. by Har-Row Ltd England). Har-Row.

Blowers, A. Something in the Air. 1984. pap. text ed. 12.50 (ISBN 0-06-318279-3). Har-Row.

Blowers, Andrew. The Limits of Power: The Politics of Local Planning Policy. (Urban & Regional Planning Ser.: Vol. 21). (Illus.). 1980. 28.00 (ISBN 0-08-023016-4). Pergamon.

Blowers, Andrew & Thompson, Grahame, eds. Inequalities, Conflict & Change. 300p. 1977. pap. 13.00x (ISBN 0-335-01961-7, Pub. by Open Univ Pr). Taylor & Francis.

Blowers, G. H., jt. ed. see Dawson, J. L.

Blowers, Margaret G. & Sims, Roberta S. How to Read an ECG. 3rd ed. (Illus.). 70p. 1983. pap. 13.95 spiral bdg. (ISBN 0-87489-307-0). Med Economics.

Blowers, Thomas. The Follow Through on Follow Me. (Orig.). 1977. pap. 4.00 (ISBN 0-89536-072-1). CSS of Ohio.

Bloxam, John R., ed. see Heylyn, Peter.

Bloxham, Christine. The Book of Banbury. 1977. 20.00x (ISBN 0-86023-007-4). State Mutual Bk.

Bloxsom, Peter, jt. auth. see Schollick, Nigel.

Bloxton, Marian W. Pioneers of Faith. 80p. 1984. pap. 7.95 (ISBN 0-8170-1036-X). Judson.

Bloy, Colin. History of Printing Ink. 148p. 1980. 40.00x (ISBN 0-85331-314-8, Pub. by Lund Humphries England). State Mutual Bk.

Bloy, Colin H. A History of Printing Ink, Balls & Rollers: 1440-1850. (Illus.). 147p. 1980. 19.95 (ISBN 0-913720-07-0, Sandstone). Beil.

Bloy, Leon. Pilgrim of the Absolute. 1977. Repr. of 1947 ed. lib. bdg. 35.00 (ISBN 0-8495-0318-3). Arden Lib.

Bloy, Myron B., Jr., et al. The Recovery of Spirit in Higher Education. Rankin, Robert, ed. 1980. 17.50 (ISBN 0-8164-0469-0, Pub. by Seabury). Winston Pr.

Blu, Karen. The Lumbee Problem. LC 79-12908. (Cambridge Studies of Cultural Systems). (Illus.). 1980. 34.50 (ISBN 0-521-22525-6); pap. 10.95 (ISBN 0-521-29542-4). Cambridge U Pr.

Blucher, Judy, jt. auth. see Llewellyn, Jack H.

Bluck, R. S. Plato's Phaedo. 1955. pap. text ed. write for info. (ISBN 0-02-311090-2). Macmillan.

Bluck, R. S., tr. see Plato.

Bludau, August. Die Pilgerreise der Aetheria. pap. 22.00 (ISBN 0-384-04760-2). Johnson Repr.

Bludworth, E. G. Three Hundred Most Abused Drugs. rev. ed. (Illus.). 29p. 1981. 3.50 (ISBN 0-9606732-0-2). MAD Hse.

--Three Hundred Most Abused Drugs. rev. ed. (Illus.). 29p. 1985. 3.50 (ISBN 0-9606732-1-0). MAD Hse.

Blue. Pilgrim Hymnal. 1958. 8.95 (ISBN 0-8298-0460-9). Pilgrim NY.

Blue, Betty. Authentic Mexican Cooking. LC 77-23355. 1977. (Spec); pap. 5.95 (ISBN 0-13-054098-6, Spec). P-H.

Blue, Betty A. Authentic Spanish Cooking. 211p. 1981. 13.95 (ISBN 0-13-054080-3); pap. 7.95 (ISBN 0-13-054072-2). P-H.

Blue, Brantley, frwd. by see Kappler, Charles J.

Blue Cliff Editions Staff, tr. see Zehetmair, Helmut & Steinschaden, Bruno.

Blue, Daniel. Thrilling Narrative of the Adventures, Sufferings & Starvation of Pike's Peak Gold Seekers on the Plains of the West in the Winter & Spring of 1859. 23p. 1968. pap. 2.50 (ISBN 0-87770-032-X). Ye Galleon.

Blue, Elaine. Moods & Works of Blue. 61p. 1985. 7.95 (ISBN 0-533-06239-X, 84-90187). Vantage.

Blue, Frederick J. The Free Soilers: Third Party Politics 1848-54. LC 72-86408. pap. 91.00 (ISBN 0-317-28838-5, 2020231). Bks Demand UMI.

Blue, Gregory, jt. ed. see Abdel-Malek, Anouar.

Blue, Jane. The Madeleine Poems. (Illus.). 55p. 1982. pap. 4.00 (ISBN 0-686-36921-1). Trill Pr.

Blue, John S. History & Tales of a Pioneer. (Illus.). 194p. 1980. 25.00x (ISBN 0-9604474-0-7). Jasper County.

--Hoosier Tales & Proverbs. (Illus.). 93p. 1982. 15.00x (ISBN 0-9604474-1-5). Jasper County.

--Hoosier Wit & Wisdom. Kriebel, Robert C., ed. 20.00 (ISBN 0-317-19889-0). Jasper County.

Blue, Ken, jt. auth. see White, John.

Blue Lake-Deerhaven Cookbook Staff. A Texas Hill Country Cookbook. (Illus.). 406p. 1983. pap. 10.95 (ISBN 0-9609210-0-1). Blue Haven.

Blue, Lionel & Rose, June. A Taste of Heaven: Adventures in Food & Faith. new ed. (Orig.). 1978. pap. 4.50 (ISBN 0-87243-077-4). Templegate.

Blue, Martha, jt. auth. see Davidson, Marion.

Blue Mountain Ranch Commune. January Thaw: People at Blue Mt. Ranch Write About Living Together in the Mountains. LC 74-79106. (Illus.). 160p. (Orig.). (YA) 1974. 8.50 (ISBN 0-87810-530-1); pap. 3.25 (ISBN 0-87810-030-X). Times Change.

Blue Ribbon Commission of the World Jewish Congress. Issues Facing World Jewry. LC 81-53025. Orig. Title: The Implications of Israel-Arab Peace for World Jewry. (Illus.). 144p. 1982. pap. 6.95 (ISBN 0-9607092-0-7). Hershel Shanks Pubs.

Blue, Rose. Bright Tomorrow. 96p. 1983. pap. 7.95 (ISBN 0-88450-858-7, 4687-B). Communication Skill.

--Cold Rain on the Water. (gr. 7 up). 1979. 7.95 (ISBN 0-07-006168-8). McGraw.

--Everybody's Evy. 139p. 1983. pap. 2.25 (ISBN 0-441-21835-0). Ace Bks.

--Grandma Didn't Wave Back. LC 79-189568. 64p. (gr. 3-5). 1972. PLB 8.90 (ISBN 0-531-02557-8). Watts.

--Heart to Heart. (Caprice Ser.: No. 70). 144p. 1985. pap. 2.25 (ISBN 0-441-31996-3). Ace Bks.

--Me & Einstein: Breaking Through the Reading Barrier. (Illus.). (gr. 2 up). 1984. 11.95 (ISBN 0-87705-388-X); pap. 4.95 (ISBN 0-89885-185-8). Human Sci Pr.

--My Mother the Witch. LC 79-23950. (gr. 6-8). 1980. 8.95 (ISBN 0-07-006169-6). McGraw.

--Wishful Lying. LC 79-21806. 32p. 1980. 10.95 (ISBN 0-87705-473-8). Human Sci Pr.

Blue, Terry W. The Teaching & Learning Process. 72p. 1981. 6.95 (ISBN 0-8106-1684-X, 1684-X-06). NEA.

Blue, William F., Jr., jt. auth. see Moore, Charles B.

Blue, William R. The Development of Imagery in Calderons Comedias. LC 82-60939. 222p. 1983. 18.00x (ISBN 0-938972-05-7). Spanish Lit Pubns.

Bluebond-Langner, Myra. The Private Worlds of Dying Children. LC 77-85529. 298p. 1980. 27.50 (ISBN 0-691-09374-1); pap. 8.95 (ISBN 0-691-02820-6). Princeton U Pr.

Blue Cloud, Peter. Back Then Tomorrow. (Illus.). 1978. pap. 3.00 (ISBN 0-942396-27-8). Blackberry ME.

--Sketches in Winter, with Crows. 30p. (Orig.). 1984. pap. 4.00 (ISBN 0-936574-11-9). Strawberry Pr NY.

Bluefarb, Sam. The Escape Motif in the American Novel: Mark Twain to Richard Wright. LC 73-188738. 185p. 1972. 8.00 (ISBN 0-8142-0168-7). Ohio St U Pr.

--Set in L. A. Scenes of the City in Fiction. 128p. 1985. Repr. lib. bdg. 29.95x (ISBN 0-89370-573-X). Borgo Pr.

--Set in L.A. Scenes of the City in Fiction. (Illus.). 128p. (Orig.). 1985. pap. 11.95 (ISBN 0-89793-042-8). Hunter Hse.

Bluefarb, Samuel M. Cutaneous Manifestations of Malignant Lymphomas. (Illus.). 548p. 1959. photocopy ed. 49.50x (ISBN 0-398-00174-X). C C Thomas.

--The Cutaneous Manifestations of the Benign Inflammatory Reticuloses. (Illus.). 428p. 1960. photocopy ed. 32.50x (ISBN 0-398-04213-6). C C Thomas.

--Cutaneous Manifestations of the Reticuloendothelial Granulomas. (Illus.). 456p. 1960. photocopy ed. 37.50x (ISBN 0-398-00177-4). C C Thomas.

--Kaposi's Sarcoma: Multiple Idiopathic Hemorrhagic Sarcoma. (Illus.). 192p. 1957. photocopy ed. 16.50x (ISBN 0-398-00175-8). C C Thomas.

--Leukemia Cutis. (Illus.). 536p. 1960. photocopy ed. 44.50x (ISBN 0-398-00176-6). C C Thomas.

Bluejay, Jana. It's Time: A Nuclear Novel. 224p. (Orig.). pap. cancelled (ISBN 0-933216-10-6). Spinsters Ink.

--It's Time: A Nuclear Novel. 180p. (Orig.). 1985. pap. 7.95 (ISBN 0-9615129-0-3). Tough Dove.

Blue Love. The Challengers. 1982. 8.95 (ISBN 0-533-05446-X). Vantage.

Bluem, A. William, ed. Religious Television Programs: A Study in Relevance. (Communication Arts Bks.). (Illus.). 1968. 5.50 (ISBN 0-8038-6298-9). Hastings.

Blues, Ann & Zerwekh, Joyce. Hospice & Palliative Nursing Care. (Monograph Ser.). 400p. 1983. 39.50 (ISBN 0-8089-1577-0, 790626). Grune.

Blues, Suzie. And the Dogs Breathed Heavily. 44p. 1979. pap. 3.00 (ISBN 0-9604198-0-2). Three Tree Pr.

--Scurrying in Rhythm. 64p. 1982. pap. 6.00 (ISBN 0-9604198-2-9). Three Tree Pr.

--South of Summer. 28p. 1979. pap. 2.50 (ISBN 0-9604198-1-0). Three Tree Pr.

Bluestein, A., ed. Fighters for Freedom: Mollie Steimer & Senya Fleshin. 1984. lib. bdg. 79.95 (ISBN 0-87700-634-2). Revisionist Pr.

Bluestein, Abe, ed. see Steimer, Mollie & Fleshin, Senya.

Bluestein, Bernard R. & Hilton, Clifford L., eds. Amphoteric Surfactants. LC 82-12999. (Surfactant Science Ser.: Vol. 12). (Illus.). 352p. 1982. 55.00 (ISBN 0-8247-1277-3). Dekker.

Bluestein, Bill & Bluestein, Enid. Mom, How Come I'm Not Thin? (Illus.). (gr. 2-5). 1981. 8.95 (ISBN 0-89638-044-0). CompCare.

--The Year Santa Got Thin. (Illus.). 48p. (gr. k-4). 1981. 8.95 (ISBN 0-89638-045-9). CompCare.

Bluestein, Enid, jt. auth. see Bluestein, Bill.

Bluestein, Jane E. The Beginning Teacher's Resource Handbook. 407p. (Orig.). 1982. pap. 24.95 (ISBN 0-915817-00-4). ISS Pubns.

--Rx: Handwriting; An Individualized, Prescriptive System for Painless Managing Handwriting Instruction. (Illus.). 48p. 1983. pap. 5.95 (ISBN 0-915817-01-2). ISS Pubns.

Bluestein, Jane E. & Collins-Fantozzi, Lynn. Parents in a Pressure Cooker. 167p. 1983. pap. 7.95 (ISBN 0-915817-02-0); wkbk. 4.95 (ISBN 0-915817-08-X). ISS Pubns.

Bluestein, Sheldon. Hiking Trails of Southern Idaho. LC 79-52543. (Illus.). 195p. (Orig.). 1981. pap. 7.95 (ISBN 0-87004-280-7). Caxton.

--North Idaho Hiking Trails. (Illus.). 128p. (Orig.). 1982. pap. 6.95 (ISBN 0-9608120-0-8). Challenge Exp.

Bluestien, Abe, tr. see Souchy-Bauer, Agustin.

Blueston, Barry & Harrison, Bennett. The Deindustrialization of America. LC 82-70844. 1982. 19.95 (ISBN 0-465-01590-5). Basic.

Bluestone, Barbara, tr. see Stangerup, Henrik.

Bluestone, Barry & Harrison, Bennet. The Deindustrialization of America. LC 82-70844. 323p. 1984. pap. 8.95 (ISBN 0-465-01591-3, CN 5110). Basic.

Bluestone, Barry & Jordan, Peter. Aircraft Industry Dynamics. LC 81-2118. 208p. 1981. 24.95 (ISBN 0-86569-053-7). Auburn Hse.

Bluestone, Barry, et al. The Retail Revolution: Market Transformation, Investment, & Labor in the Modern Department Store. LC 80-26036. (Illus.). 176p. 1981. 23.00 (ISBN 0-86569-052-9). Auburn Hse.

--Low Wages & the Working Poor. LC 73-620152. (Policy Papers in Human Resources & Industrial Relations Ser.: No. 22). 215p. 1973. 9.95x (ISBN 0-87736-126-6); pap. 4.95x (ISBN 0-87736-127-4). U of Mich Inst Labor.

Bluestone, Charles D. & Klein, Jerome O. Otitis Media in Infants & Children. (Major Problems in Clinical Pediatrics Ser.). (Illus.). 300p. Date not set. price not set (ISBN 0-7216-1759-X). Saunders.

Bluestone, Charles D., ed. Pediatric Otalaryngology, 2 Vols. Stool, Sylvan F. (Illus.). 1728p. 1983. Vol. 1. 90.00 (ISBN 0-7216-1761-1); Vol. 2. 90.00 (ISBN 0-7216-1762-X); Two Vol. Set. 170.00 (ISBN 0-7216-1758-1). Saunders.

Bluestone, George. Novels into Film: The Metamorphosis of Fiction into Cinema. 1957. pap. 3.95 (ISBN 0-520-00130-3, CAL41). U of Cal Pr.

Bluestone, Max. From Story to Stage: The Dramatic Adaptation of Prose Fiction in the Period of Shakespeare & His Contemporaries. (Studies in English Literature: No. 70). 1974. pap. 27.20x (ISBN 90-2792-697-2). Mouton.

Bluestone, Naomi. So You Want to Be a Doctor? The Realities of Pursuing Medicine As a Career. LC 81-2545. 256p. (gr. 7 up). 1981. 13.50 (ISBN 0-688-00739-2). Lothrop.

Bluestone, Rodney, ed. Rheumatology. LC 79-23833. 544p. 1980. 42.95 (ISBN 0-89289-375-3). Krieger.

Bluffield, Robert. Making & Managing a Photographic Studio in Britain. (Illus.). 144p. 1982. 17.95 (ISBN 0-7153-8245-4). David & Charles.

Bluglass, Robert. A Guide to the Mental Health Act, 1983. LC 83-7635. 1983. pap. text ed. 19.00 (ISBN 0-443-03017-0). Churchill.

Bluglass, Robert, jt. ed. see Roth, Martin.

Bluh, Bonnie. The Old Speak Out. LC 78-20302. 1979. 10.95 (ISBN 0-8180-1125-4). Horizon.

Bluh, Bonnie C. Woman to Woman: European Feminists. LC 74-20184. 1974. pap. 5.00 (ISBN 0-9603234-0-6). Starogubski.

Bluhm, Donna L. Teaching the Retarded Visually Handicapped: Indeed They Are Children. LC 68-23679. (Illus.). Repr. of 1968 ed. 26.50 (ISBN 0-8357-9560-8, 2013063). Bks Demand UMI.

Bluhm, Heinz. Luther Translator of Paul: Studies in Romans & Galatians. 580p. 1984. text ed. 49.80 bndg. text (ISBN 0-8204-0186-2). P Lang Pubs.

Bluhm, Heinz, ed. Essays in History & Literature Presented by Fellows of the Newberry Library to Stanley Pargellis. (Illus.). 1965. 15.00 (ISBN 0-911028-12-9). Newberry.

Bluhm, Jeremy S., jt. auth. see Roberts, Marc J.

Bluhm, William. Building an Austrian Nation: The Political Integration of a Western State. LC 72-91288. pap. 69.50 (ISBN 0-317-29592-6, 2021981). Bks Demand UMI.

Bluhm, William T. Force or Freedom? The Paradox in Modern Political Thought. LC 83-51293. 336p. 1984. 26.00x (ISBN 0-300-03087-8). Yale U Pr.

--Theories of the Political System: Classics of Political Thought & Modern Political Analysis. 3rd ed. 1978. ref. ed. 27.95 (ISBN 0-13-913327-5). P-H.

Bluhm, William T., ed. The Paradigm Problem in Political Science: Perspectives from Philosophy & from Practice. LC 81-70433. 227p. 1982. lib. bdg. 19.95 (ISBN 0-89089-218-0); pap. 9.95 (ISBN 0-89089-219-9). Carolina Acad Pr.

Bluhme-Kojima, Taka. Perception Auditive de Certaines Attitudes Psychologiques en Francais une E'tude Intonative et Statisique, Vol. 38. (Hamburger Phonetische Beitrage Ser.). 188p. (Orig.). 1982. pap. text ed. 16.00x (ISBN 3-87118-521-3, Pub. by Helmut Buske Verlag Hamburg). Benjamins North Am.

Blum, jt. auth. see Manzo.

Blum, et al, eds. Pharmaceuticals & Health Policy: An International Perspective on Provision & Control. LC 80-26498. 387p. 1981. text ed. 42.50x (ISBN 0-8419-0682-3). Holmes & Meier.

Blum, A & McHugh, P. Self-Reflection in the Arts & Sciences. 159p. 1984. text ed. 13.45x (ISBN 0-391-02877-4). Humanities.

Blum, A. L., jt. ed. see Kern, F., Jr.

Blum, Alan. Theorizing. 1974. pap. text ed. 16.50x (ISBN 0-435-82071-0). Gower Pub Co.

Blum, Alan & McHugh, Peter, eds. Friends, Enemies, & Strangers: Theorizing in Art, Science, & Everyday Life. LC 79-11397. (Modern Sociology). 1979. text ed. 24.50 (ISBN 0-89391-007-4). Ablex Pub.

Blum, Albert. Government-Sponsored Manpower Research: Its History & Implications. (Working Paper Ser.: No. 3). 48p. 1976. pap. 2.50 (ISBN 0-318-00188-8). LBJ Sch Pub Aff.

Blum, Albert A. A History of the American Labor Movement. LC 72-93038. (AHA Pamphlets: No. 250). 1972. pap. text ed. 1.50 (ISBN 0-87229-008-5). Am Hist Assn.

Blum, Albert A., ed. The Arts: Years of Development, Time of Decision. (Symposia Ser.). 142p. 1976. pap. 3.50 (ISBN 0-89940-403-0). LBJ Sch Pub Aff.

--International Handbook of Industrial Relations: Contemporary Developments & Research. LC 79-8586. (Illus.). xiv, 698p. 1981. 55.00 (ISBN 0-313-21303-8, BLH/). Greenwood.

Blum, Albert A., jt. ed. see Form, William H.

Blum, Alexander. Russkie Perezvony: An Album of Soviet Russian Recordings. LC 71-136569. 155p. 1972. 25.00 (ISBN 0-08-006878-2). Pergamon.

Blum, Andre. The Origin & Early History of Engraving in France. LC 77-73881. (Illus.). 1978. Repr. of 1930 ed. lib. bdg. 50.00 (ISBN 0-87817-216-5). Hacker.

Blum, Ann & Taylor, R. Earnest. An Introduction to Law in Georgia. LC 85-50970. Date not set. price not set (ISBN 0-89854-109-3). U of GA Inst Govt.

Blum, Arlene. Annapurna: A Woman's Place. LC 80-13288. (Illus.). 272p. 1980. 16.95 (ISBN 0-87156-236-7); pap. 9.95 (ISBN 0-87156-806-3). Sierra.

--Annapurna: A Woman's Place. 16.00 (ISBN 0-8446-6130-9). Peter Smith.

Blum, B. I., ed. Information Systems for Patient Care. (Computers & Medicine). (Illus.). 400p. 1984. 27.50 (ISBN 0-387-90912-5). Springer Verlag.

Blum, Barbara L. Psychological Aspects of Pregnancy, Birthing, & Bonding. LC 80-14227. (New Directions in Psychotherapy Ser.: Vol. IV). 380p. (Series editor Paul T. Olsen). 1980. 29.95 (ISBN 0-87705-210-7). Human Sci Pr.

Blum, Bruce, ed. A Framework for Medical Information Science, Vol. 3, 4, & 9. 148p. 1984. pap. 39.00 (ISBN 0-85066-999-5). Taylor & Francis.

Blum, D. Steven. Walter Lippmann: Cosmopolitanism in the Century of Total War. LC 84-7041. 208p. 1984. 19.95x (ISBN 0-8014-1676-0). Cornell U Pr.

Blum, Daniel. Pictorial History of the Silent Screen. 1982. 9.95 (ISBN 0-399-50667-5, G&D). Putnam Pub Group.

--Screen World, 10 vols. 1949, 1951-1959. LC 70-84068. (Illus.). 1969. Set. 165.00x (ISBN 0-8196-0255-8); 18.00x ea. Biblo.

Blum, Daniel & Kobal, John. A New Pictorial History of the Talkies. rev. ed. (Illus.). 384p. 1982. pap. 9.95 (ISBN 0-399-50666-7). Putnam Pub Group.

Blum, David. Casals & the Art of Interpretation. LC 77-1444. 1980. pap. 6.95 (ISBN 0-520-04032-5, CAL 450). U of Cal Pr.

Blum, David, jt. auth. see Tortelier, Paul.

Blum, E., jt. auth. see Blum, J.

Blum, E. K., et al, eds. Mathematical Studies of Information Processing: Proceedings, International Conference, Kyoto, Japan, August 23-26, 1978. (Lecture Notes in Computer Science Ser.: Vol. 75). 1979. pap. 37.00 (ISBN 0-387-09541-1). Springer-Verlag.

Blum, Eleanor. Basic Books in the Mass Media: An Annotated, Selected Booklist Covering General Communications, Book Publishing, Broadcasting, Film, Editorial Journalism, & Advertising. 2nd ed. LC 80-11289. 439p. 1980. 27.50x (ISBN 0-252-00814-6). U of Ill Pr.

--Basic Books in the Mass Media: An Annotated, Selected Booklist Covering General Communications, Book Publishing, Broadcasting, Film, Magazines, Newspapers, Advertising, Indexes, & Scholarly & Professional Periodicals. LC 71-151998. pap. 50.20 (ISBN 0-317-10281-8, 2019052). Bks Demand UMI.

Blum, Ethel. Miami Alive. (Span.). 1981. pap. 5.95 (ISBN 0-935572-06-6). Alive Pubns.

--Miami Alive. (Orig.). 1981. pap. 4.95 (ISBN 0-935572-09-0). Alive Pubns.

--The Total Traveler by Ship: The Cruise Traveler's Handbook. 3rd ed. (The Compleat Traveler's Guides Ser.). (Illus.). 1981. pap. 8.95 (ISBN 0-89102-165-5). B Franklin.

Blum, Etta. The Space My Body Fills. LC 80-26565. 68p. (Orig.). 1980. pap. 4.95 (ISBN 0-913270-93-8). Sunstone Pr.

Blum, Eva, jt. auth. see Blum, Richard H.

Blum, Eva M. & Blum, Richard H. Alcoholism: Modern Psychological Approaches to Treatment. LC 67-13278. (Social & Behavioral Science Ser.). 1967. 23.95x (ISBN 0-87589-005-9). Jossey-Bass.

Blum, Fred. Jean Sibelius: An International Bibliography, 1965. LC 66-3288. (Detroit Studies in Music Bibliography Ser.: No. 8). 1965. pap. 2.00 (ISBN 0-911772-28-6). Info Coord.

Blum, Fred see Van der Waerden, B. L.

Blum, Fred H. Toward a Democratic Work Process. LC 73-11840. 229p. 1974. Repr. of 1953 ed. lib. bdg. 15.00x (ISBN 0-8371-7063-X, BLDW). Greenwood.

Blum, G. Numismatique D'Antinoos. 1979. 20.00 (ISBN 0-916710-60-2). Obol Intl.

Blum, Harold F. Time's Arrow & Evolution. 3rd ed. LC 68-31676. (Illus.). 1968. pap. 8.95x (ISBN 0-691-02354-9). Princeton U Pr.

Blum, Harold P., ed. Defense & Resistance: Historical Perspectives & Current Concepts. 420p. 1985. text ed. 40.00 (ISBN 0-8236-1157-4, 01157). Intl Univs Pr.

--Female Psychology: Contemporary Psychoanalytic Views. LC 76-53908. 454p. 1977. 35.00 (ISBN 0-8236-1890-0). Intl Univs Pr.

--Psychoanalytic Explorations of Technique: Discourse on the Theory of Therapy. LC 79-22349. 468p. 1980. text ed. 35.00 (ISBN 0-8236-5053-7). Intl Univs Pr.

Blum, Henrik L. Expanding Health Care Horizons: From a General Systems Concept of Health to a National Health Policy. LC 82-84707. 256p. 1983. pap. text ed. 7.95x (ISBN 0-89914-011-4). Third Party Pub.

--Planning for Health: Generics for the Eighties. 2nd ed. LC 80-23461. 1981. 34.95 (ISBN 0-89885-013-4). Human Sci Pr.

Blum, Howard. Wanted: The Search for Nazis in America. 1978. pap. 1.95 (ISBN 0-449-23409-6, Crest). Fawcett.

--Wanted! The Search for Nazis in America. LC 76-9689. 1977. 8.95 (ISBN 0-8129-0607-1). Times Bks.

--Wishful Thinking. LC 84-45609. 256p. 1985. 14.95 (ISBN 0-689-11543-1). Atheneum.

Blum, Howard L. The Wines & Vines of Europe. LC 72-97409. (Orig.). 1973. pap. 1.95 (ISBN 0-87502-027-5). Benjamin Co.

Blum, J. & Blum, E. Keypunch, Keytape & Keydisc. 210p. 1975. 33.75 (ISBN 0-677-03950-6). Gordon.

Blum, Jack, et al. A Guide to the Whole Writing Process. LC 83-82316. 336p. 1984. pap. text ed. 15.95 (ISBN 0-395-34113-2); instr's manual 2.00 (ISBN 0-395-34114-0). HM.

Blum, Jakub & Rich, Vera. The Image of the Jew in Soviet Literature. LC 84-12196. 276p. 1985. 25.00 (ISBN 0-88125-062-7). Ktav.

Blum, James D. & Goldstein, Mark S. Business Law: Selected Questions & Unofficial Answers Indexed to Content Specification Outline. LC 84-189048. 1984. write for info. Am Inst CPA.

Blum, James D., ed. see American Institute of Certified Public Accountants.

Blum, Jeffrey. Pseudoscience & Mental Ability: The Origins & Fallacies of the IQ Controversy. LC 77-81371. 240p. 1979. pap. 5.95 (ISBN 0-85345-496-5). Monthly Rev.

Blum, Jerome. The End of the Old Order in Rural Europe. 1978. text ed. 46.00 (ISBN 0-691-05266-2); pap. 20.00 LPE (ISBN 0-691-10067-5). Princeton U Pr.

--Noble Landowners & Agriculture in Austria, 1815-1848: A Study in the Origins of the Peasant Emancipation of 1848. LC 78-64204. (Johns Hopkins University. Studies in the Social Sciences. Sixty-Fifth Ser. 1947: 2). Repr. of 1948 ed. 25.50 (ISBN 0-404-61310-1). AMS Pr.

--Our Forgotten Past: Seven Centuries of Life on the Land. LC 81-85070. (Illus.). 1982. 29.95 (ISBN 0-500-25080-4). Thames Hudson.

Blum, John & Gertman, Paul M. PSROS & the Law. LC 77-70436. 300p. 1977. 34.00 (ISBN 0-912862-39-4). Aspen Systems.

Blum, John, et al, eds. Harbrace History of England, 4 Vols. Incl. Pt. 1. Ancient & Medieval England: Beginnings to 1509. Lander, J. R. 192p. pap. text ed. 10.95 (ISBN 0-15-535107-9); Pt. 2. Renaissance & Reformation England: 1509-1714. Gray, Charles M. 230p. pap. text ed. 10.95 (ISBN 0-15-535108-7); Pt. 3. The Birth & Growth of Industrial England: 1714-1867. Harrison, John. 171p. pap. text ed. 10.95 (ISBN 0-15-535109-5); Pt. 4. England Since 1867: Continuity & Change. Stansky, Peter. 194p. pap. text ed. 10.95 (ISBN 0-15-535110-9). 1973. pap. text ed. 10.95 ea. (HC). HarBraceJ.

Blum, John M. Joe Tumulty & the Wilson Era. (Illus.). xiii, 337p. 1969. Repr. of 1951 ed. 21.50 (ISBN 0-208-00736-9, Archon). Shoe String.

--The Progressive Presidents: Theodore Roosevelt, Woodrow Wilson, Franklin D. Roosevelt, Lyndon B. Johnson. 224p. 1982. pap. 6.95x (ISBN 0-393-00063-X). Norton.

--Republican Roosevelt. 2nd ed. LC 54-5182. 1954. 10.00x (ISBN 0-674-76300-9); pap. 4.95x (ISBN 0-674-76302-5). Harvard U Pr.

--V Was for Victory: Politics & American Culture During World War II. LC 77-3426. 1977. pap. 7.95 (ISBN 0-15-693628-3, Harv). HarBraceJ.

--Woodrow Wilson & the Politics of Morality. (Library of American Biography). 1962. pap. 6.95 (ISBN 0-316-10021-8). Little.

Blum, John M., jt. auth. see Cole, Donald B.

Blum, John M., ed. Public Philosopher: Selected Letters of Walter Lippman. 544p. 1985. 29.95 (ISBN 0-89919-260-2). Ticknor & Fields.

--Public Philosopher: Selected Letters of Walter Lippmann. 544p. 1985. 29.95 (ISBN 0-89919-260-2). HM.

Blum, John M., et al. The National Experience: A History of the United States. 6th ed. 983p. 1985. text ed. 25.95 (ISBN 0-15-565664-3, HC); test manual avail. (ISBN 0-15-565667-8). HarBraceJ.

--The National Experience: A History of the United States since 1865, Pt. II. 6th ed. 595p. 1985. pap. text ed. 17.95 (ISBN 0-15-565666-X, HC); Learning History II. study guide avail. (ISBN 0-15-565669-4). HarBraceJ.

--The National Experience: A History of the United States to 1877, Pt. I. 6th ed. 473p. 1985. pap. text ed. 17.95 (ISBN 0-15-565665-1, HC); Learning History I. study guide avail. (ISBN 0-15-565668-6). HarBraceJ.

Blum, Joseph J. Introduction to Analog Computation. 175p. (Orig.). 1969. pap. text ed. 18.95 (ISBN 0-15-541553-0, HC); solutions manual avail. (ISBN 0-15-541554-9, HC). HarBraceJ.

Blum, Julius. Von der Tarif- zur Effectivlohnstruktur. (European University Studies: No. 5, Vol. 404). 351p. (Ger.). 1983. 38.40 (ISBN 3-8204-7394-7). P Lang Pubs.

Blum, K., ed. Alcohol & Opiates: Neurochemical & Behavioral Mechanisms. 1977. 50.00 (ISBN 0-12-108450-7). Acad Pr.

Blum, Karl. Density Matrix Theory & Applications. LC 81-268. (Physics of Atoms & Molecules Ser.). 230p. 1981. 37.50x (ISBN 0-306-40684-5, Plenum Pr). Plenum Pub.

Blum, Kenneth. Handbook of Abusable Drugs. 1984. 79.95 (ISBN 0-89876-036-4). Gardner Pr.

Blum, Lawrence. Friendship, Altruism & Morality. (International Library of Philosophy). 256p. 1980. 24.95x (ISBN 0-7100-0582-2); pap. 9.95x (ISBN 0-7100-9332-2). Routledge & Kegan.

Blum, Leon. For All Mankind. Pickles, W., tr. 12.00 (ISBN 0-8446-0499-2). Peter Smith.

--Marriage. Wells, Warre B., tr. from Fr. LC 72-9703. (Illus.). Repr. of 1937 ed. 20.00 (ISBN 0-404-57416-5). AMS Pr.

Blum, Leonor, tr. see Fraginals, Manuel M.

Blum, Lucille H. Reading Between the Lines. LC 79-182040. 183p. 1972. text ed. 17.50 (ISBN 0-8236-5770-1); pap. text ed. 10.95 (ISBN 0-8236-8268-4, 25770). Intl Univs Pr.

Blum, Lucille H., et al. Rorschach Workbook. rev. ed. LC 74-10227. 193p. (Orig.). 1975. spiral bdg. 20.00 (ISBN 0-8236-5901-1). Intl Univs Pr.

Blum, M. S. Fundamentals of Insect Physiology. 640p. 40.00 (ISBN 0-471-05468-2). Wiley.

Blum, Marian S. The Day-Care Dilemma: Women & Children First. LC 82-47777. 160p. 1983. 20.00x (ISBN 0-669-05604-9); pap. 9.95x (ISBN 0-669-08960-5). Lexington Bks.

Blum, Marius. Through the Years with Marius. 1984. 8.95 (ISBN 0-533-05813-9). Vantage.

Blum, Mark E. The Austro-Marxists Eighteen Ninety to Nineteen Eighteen: A Psychobiographical Study. LC 84-13036. 304p. 1985. 28.00x (ISBN 0-8131-1515-9). U Pr of KY.

Blum, Martin. Bibliographie Luxembourgeoise: Nineteen Hundred & Two to Nineteen Hundred & Thirty-Two, 2 Vols. in 3. (Ger.). 165.00 (ISBN 0-686-47440-6). Kraus Repr.

Blum, Murray S. & Blum, Nancy A. Insect Pheromones. LC 82-25974. 200p. 1984. 19.95t (ISBN 0-03-056962-1). Praeger.

Blum, Murray S., ed. Chemical Defenses of Arthopods. LC 81-7925. 1981. 66.00 (ISBN 0-12-108380-2). Acad Pr.

Blum, Murray S. & Blum, Nancy A., eds. Sexual Selection & Reproductive Competition in Insects. 1979. 47.50 (ISBN 0-12-108750-6). Acad Pr.

Blum, Nancy A., jt. auth. see Blum, Murray S.

Blum, Nancy A., jt. ed. see Blum, Murray S.

Blum, Odette, et al, trs. see Humphrey, Doris.

Blum, Paul C., tr. see Pezeu-Massabuau, Jacques.

Blum, Paul Von see Von Blum, Paul.

Blum, Peter. Everybody Counts: A T. A. Self-Help Book for Math Aversion. LC 81-80247. 54p. (Orig.). 1981. pap. 6.95 (ISBN 0-9605756-0-X). Math Counsel Inst.

Blum, Peter J. Model Soldier Manual. (Orig.). 1971. pap. 4.95 (ISBN 0-912364-03-3). Imrie-Risley.

Blum, R. L. Discovery & Representation of Causal Relationships from a Large Time-Oriented Clinical Database: The RX Project. (Lecture Notes in Medical Informatics Ser.: Vol. 19). 242p. 1982. pap. 20.00 (ISBN 0-387-11962-0). Springer-Verlag.

Blum, Ralph. The Book of Runes: A Handbook for the Use of an Ancient & Contemporary Oracle. (Illus.). 112p. (Orig.). 1982. pap. 9.95 (ISBN 0-943434-00-9). Oracle Bks.

--The Book of Runes: A Handbook for the Use of an Ancient Oracle: The Viking Runes. 128p. 1983. 14.95 (ISBN 0-312-09002-1); with stones 19.95 (ISBN 0-312-09001-3). St Martin.

--The Book of Runes: A Handbook for the Use of an Ancient Oracle-The Viking Runes. 1984. 22.95 (ISBN 0-312-08999-6). St Martin.

Blum, Ralph, commentary by. Rune Play: A Method of Self-Counseling & a Year-Round Runecasting Recordbook. (Illus.). 160p. 1985. 14.95 (ISBN 0-312-69591-8). St Martin.

Blum, Richard. Television Writing. 2nd ed. (Illus.). 192p. (Orig.). 1984. pap. 12.95 (ISBN 0-240-51737-7). Focal Pr.

Blum, Richard A. American Film Acting: The Stanislavski Heritage. Kirkpatrick, Diane, ed. LC 84-8778. (Studies in Cinema: No. 28). 132p. 1984. 29.95 (ISBN 0-8357-1590-6); pap. text ed. 14.95 (ISBN 0-8357-1609-0). UMI Res Pr.

Blum, Richard H. Deceivers & Deceived: Observations on Confidence Men & Their Victims, Informants & Their Quarry, Political & Industrial Spies & Ordinary Citizens. (Illus.). 340p. 1972. 35.75x (ISBN 0-398-02235-6). C C Thomas.

--Drug Dealers-Taking Action. LC 76-187065. (Jossey-Bass Behavioral Science Ser.). pap. 84.00 (ISBN 0-317-08614-6, 2013858). Bks Demand UMI.

--Offshore Haven Banks, Trusts & Companies: The Business of Crime in the Euromarket. LC 83-27059. 334p. 1984. 29.95 (ISBN 0-03-069629-1). Praeger.

--Police Selection. 272p. 1964. 23.50x (ISBN 0-398-00178-2). C C Thomas.

Blum, Richard H. & Blum, Eva. Health & Healing in Rural Greece. 1965. 25.00x (ISBN 0-8047-0250-0). Stanford U Pr.

Blum, Richard H. & Ezekiel, Jonathan. Clinical Records for Mental Health Services: A Guide to the Study & Development of Clinical Records Systems Including a Manual of Model Forms & Procedures. 176p. 1962. 14.75x (ISBN 0-398-00179-0). C C Thomas.

Blum, Richard H., jt. auth. see Blum, Eva M.

Blum, Richard H., ed. Surveillance & Espionage in a Free Society. LC 72-85979. (Special Studies in U.S. Economic, Social & Political Issues). 1972. 34.00x (ISBN 0-275-28643-6); pap. text ed. 9.95x (ISBN 0-89197-957-3). Irvington.

Blum, Richard H., et al. The Dream Sellers: Perspectives on Drug Dealers. LC 79-184960. (Jossey-Bass Science Ser.). pap. 101.50 (ISBN 0-8357-9316-8, 2013789). Bks Demand UMI.

--Horatio Alger's Children: The Role of the Family in the Origin & Prevention of Drug Risk. LC 72-186580. (Jossey-Bass Behavioral Science Ser.). Repr. of 1973 ed. 86.30 (ISBN 0-8357-9325-7, 2013860). Bks Demand UMI.

--Society & Drugs, Social & Cultural Observations. Incl. Vol. 2. Students & Drugs, College & High School Observations. LC 73-75936. (Social & Behavioral Science Ser.). 1969. 2 vol. set 60.00x (ISBN 0-87589-424-0); Vol. 1. (ISBN 0-87589-033-4); Vol. 2. (ISBN 0-87589-034-2). Jossey-Bass.

Blum, Robert. Adolescent Health Care: Clinical Issues. LC 80-67276. 1981. 39.00 (ISBN 0-12-788080-1). Acad Pr.

Blum, Robert, ed. Chronic Illness & Disabilities in Childhood & Adolescence. 496p. 1984. 49.50 (ISBN 0-8089-1635-1, 790624). Grune.

Blum, Robert S. The Girl from the Emeraline Island. 288p. 1984. pap. 2.95 (ISBN 0-345-30847-6, Del Rey). Ballantine.

Blum, Rochelle. The Chipmunks' Counting Book. LC 83-63491. (Cuddle Shape Bks.). (Illus.). 14p. (ps-1). 1984. bds. 3.95 (ISBN 0-394-86792-0, Pub. by BYR). Random.

Blum, Ronald, jt. auth. see Roller, Duane.

Blum, Ruth C. Von see Von Blum, Ruth C., et al.

Blum, S., ed. see Erte.

Blum, Shirley N. Early Netherlandish Triptychs: A Study in Patronage. LC 68-10902. (California Studies in the History of Art: No. XIII). (Illus.). 1969. 100.00x (ISBN 0-520-01444-8). U of Cal Pr.

Blum, Solomon. Labor Economics. LC 79-89719. (American Labor from Conspiracy to Collective Bargaining, Ser. 1). 579p. 1969. Repr. of 1925 ed. 30.00 (ISBN 0-405-02105-4). Ayer Co Pubs.

Blum, Stella. Eighteenth Century French Fashion Plates in Full Color: 64 Engravings from the "Galerie des Modes", 1778-1787. (Antiques Ser.). (Illus.). 80p. (Orig.). 1982. pap. 9.95 (ISBN 0-486-24331-1). Dover.

--Everyday Fashions of the Twenties as Pictured in Sears & Other Catalogs. (Illus.). 160p. 1982. pap. 8.50 (ISBN 0-486-24134-3). Dover.

--Fashions & Costumes from Godey's Lady's Book: Eight Plates in Full Color. (Antiques Series: Costume). (Illus.). 91p. 1985. pap. 7.95 (ISBN 0-486-24841-0). Dover.

--Victorian Fashions & Costumes from Harper's Bazaar: 1898-1967. (Illus.). 320p. (Orig.). 1974. pap. 9.95 (ISBN 0-486-22990-4). Dover.

Blum, Stella, ed. Everyday Fashions of the Twenties as Pictured in Sears & Other Catalogs. 1982. 19.00 (ISBN 0-8446-5879-0). Peter Smith.

--Paris Fashions of the Eighteen Nineties: A Picture Source Book with 450 Designs, Including 24 in Full Color. (Antiques Ser.). 144p. (Orig.). 1984. pap. 6.95 (ISBN 0-486-24534-9). Dover.

Blum, Stella, ed. see Ackermann.

Blum, Stella, ed. see Ackermann, Rudolph.

Blum, Virgil C. Freedom of Choice in Education. LC 77-8086. 1977. Repr. of 1958 ed. lib. bdg. 22.50x (ISBN 0-8371-9677-9, BLFC). Greenwood.

Blum, W., et al, eds. W. Heisenberg: Gesammelte Werke - Collected Works. 509p. 1984. 39.50 (ISBN 0-387-13020-9). Springer-Verlag.

Blum, Walter & Yerian, C. Theo. Personal Shorthand for the Journalist. 176p. (Orig.). 1980. pap. text ed. 8.85 (ISBN 0-89420-214-6, 242032); optional cassettes recordings 237.20 (ISBN 0-89420-225-1, 242000). Natl Book.

Blum, William & Hogaboom, George B. Principles of Electroplating & Electroforming. 455p. 1949. 32.00 (ISBN 0-318-12556-0); members 24.00 (ISBN 0-318-12557-9). Am Electroplate.

Bluman, G. W. Problem Book for First Year Calculus. (Problem Books in Mathematics Ser.). (Illus.). 350p. 1984. 39.00 (ISBN 0-387-90920-6). Springer-Verlag.

Blumberg. Southern Africa. 1981. 8.90 (ISBN 0-531-04278-2). Watts.

Blumberg, A. E., tr. see Schlick, M.

Blumberg, Abraham S. Criminal Justice: Issues & Ironies. 2nd ed. 1979. pap. 10.95 (ISBN 0-531-05618-X). Watts.

--Current Perspectives on Criminal Behavior. 2nd ed. 442p. 1981. pap. text ed. 12.00 (ISBN 0-394-32156-1, KnopfC). Knopf.

Blumberg, Abraham S., jt. auth. see Niederhoffer, Arthur.

Blumberg, Abraham S., ed. Law & Order: The Scales of Justice. rev. 2nd. ed. LC 72-87667. 188p. 1970. pap. text ed. 6.95x (ISBN 0-87855-543-9). Transaction Bks.

Blumberg, Albert. Logic: A First Course. LC 75-38679. 1976. text ed. 21.00 (ISBN 0-394-31442-5, KnopfC). Knopf.

Blumberg, Arnold B. Zion Before Zionism: 1838-1880. (Illus.). 240p. 1985. text ed. 28.00x (ISBN 0-8156-2336-4). Syracuse U Pr.

Blumberg, Arthur. Current Perspectives. 2nd ed. 1980. text ed. 12.00 (ISBN 0-394-32156-1, RanC). Knopf.

--The School Superintendent: Living with Conflict. 256p. 1985. text ed. 23.95x (ISBN 0-8077-2764-4). Tchrs Coll.

--Sensitivity Training: Processes, Problems & Applications. LC 74-157409. (Notes & Essays Ser No. 68). 1971. pap. 2.50 (ISBN 0-87060-040-0, NES 68). Syracuse U Cont Ed.

--Supervisors & Teachers: A Private Cold War. 2nd ed. LC 79-89771. 1980. 22.75x (ISBN 0-8211-0133-1); text ed. 20.50x in copies of 10. McCutchan.

Blumberg, Arthur & Greenfield, William. The Effective Principal: Perspectives on School Leadership. 280p. 1980. 30.95x (ISBN 0-205-06812-X, 236812, Pub. by Longwood Div). Allyn.

Blumberg, Barbara. The New Deal & the Unemployed: The View from New York City. 332p. 1979. 28.50 (ISBN 0-685-19073-0). Bucknell U Pr.

Blumberg, C., jt. auth. see Hare, L.

Blumberg, Daniel A. Tactical Economics: Investment Strategy in a Changing Economy. LC 83-26141. (Illus.). 1984. 14.95 (ISBN 0-930032-05-5). Consol Cap Comm Grp.

Blumberg, Donald F. & Dooley, Brian J. The IBM PC Guide to Risk & Decision Making: Acting Wisely in An Uncertain World. 320p. 1985. pap. 49.95 incl. disk (ISBN 0-88693-064-2). Banbury Bks.

Blumberg, Harris M. A Program of Sequential Language Development: A Theoretical & Practical Guide for Remediation of Language, Reading & Learning Disorders. (Illus.). 108p. 1975. 15.75x (ISBN 0-398-03320-X). C C Thomas.

Blumberg, Harry & Lewittes, Mordecai. Modern Hebrew: Ivrit Hayah, Vol. 1. 3rd ed. 449p. pap. 8.95x (ISBN 0-88482-718-6). Hebrew Pub.

Blumberg, Harry, ed. see Averroes.

Blumberg, Harry, tr. see Averroes.

Blumberg, Herbert H. & Hare, A. Paul. Small Groups & Social Interactions, Vol. 2. 593p. 1983. 88.95 (ISBN 0-471-90091-5, Pub. by Wiley-Interscience). Wiley.

Blumberg, Herbert H., jt. ed. see Hare, A. Paul.

Blumberg, Herbert H., et al. Small Groups & Social Interaction, Vol. 1. 461p. 1983. 88.95 (ISBN 0-471-10242-3, Pub. by Wiley-Interscience). Wiley.

Blumberg, Janice R. One Voice: Rabbi Jacob M. Rothschild & the Troubled South. LC 84-22723. (Illus.). xi, 240p. 1985. 19.95 (ISBN 0-86554-150-7, MUP H141). Mercer Univ Pr.

Blumberg, Leda. The Horselover's Handbook: An Introduction to Owning, Caring for, & Riding Horses. 112p. (Orig.). (gr. 2-6). 1984. pap. 2.95 (ISBN 0-380-89326-6, Camelot). Avon.

--Pets. (First Bks). (Illus.). 72p. (gr. 4up). PLB 8.90 (ISBN 0-531-04649-4). Watts.

Blumberg, Leda, jt. auth. see Blumberg, Rhoda.

Blumberg, Leonard, et al. Skid Row & Its Alternatives: Research & Recommendations from Philadelphia. LC 72-92877. 350p. 1973. 29.95 (ISBN 0-87722-055-7). Temple U Pr.

Blumberg, Leonard U., et al. Liquor & Poverty: Skid Row As a Human Condition. LC 76-620080. (Rutgers Center of Alcohol Studies: Monograph No. 13). 1978. 12.00 (ISBN 0-911290-46-X). Rutgers Ctr Alcohol.

Blumberg, Melvin. Job Switching in Autonomous Groups: A Descriptive & Exploratory Study in an Underground Coal Mine. LC 78-62234. 1978. soft cover 12.00 (ISBN 0-88247-531-2). R & E Pubs.

Blumberg, Morris B. In Soul. LC 84-28229. 1985. 14.95 (ISBN 0-87949-258-9). Ashley Bks.

Blumberg, Nathan B., jt. ed. see Brier, Warren J.

Blumberg, Nathaniel. The Afternoon of March Thirtieth: A Contemporary Historical Novel. LC 84-90141. 378p. 1984. 15.00 (ISBN 0-9613338-0-4). Wood Fire.

Blumberg, Paul. Inequality in an Age of Decline. (Illus.). 1980. pap. 8.95 (ISBN 0-19-502967-4, GB 649). Oxford U Pr.

Blumberg, Philip. Corporate Groups: Procedural Law. 1983. 70.00i (ISBN 0-316-10025-0). Little.

Blumberg, Phillip. The Law of Corporate Groups: 1984 Supplement. 1984. pap. 30.00 (ISBN 0-316-10035-8). Little.

Blumberg, Phillip I. Law of Corporate Groups: Bankruptcy Law. LC 84-81755. 1985. 75.00i (ISBN 0-316-10033-1). Little.

Blumberg, Rae L. Stratification: Socioeconomic & Sexual Inequality. 128p. 1978. pap. text ed. write for info. (ISBN 0-697-07521-4). Wm C Brown.

Blumberg, Rena. Headstrong: My Story of Conquest & Celebrations... Living with Chemotherapy. 1982. 12.95 (ISBN 0-517-54723-6). Crown.

Blumberg, Rhoda. Commodore Perry in the Land of the Shogun. LC 84-21800. (Illus.). 128p. (gr. 4 up). 1985. 13.00 (ISBN 0-688-03723-2). Lothrop.

--Devils & Demons. (Illus.). 72p. (gr. 4 up). 1982. PLB 8.90 (ISBN 0-531-04392-4). Watts.

--The First Travel Guide to the Bottom of the Sea. LC 82-17938. (Illus.). 74p. (gr. 4 up). 1983. 10.25 (ISBN 0-688-01692-8). Lothrop.

--The First Travel Guide to the Moon. (Illus.). 96p. (gr. 4-6). 1984. pap. 1.95 (ISBN 0-590-33286-4, Apple Paperbacks). Scholastic Inc.

--Monsters. (First Bks). (Illus.). 96p. (gr. 4up). PLB 8.90 (ISBN 0-531-04648-6). Watts.

--More Freaky Facts. (Funnybones Ser.). (Illus.). 64p. (Orig.). (gr. 3-7). 1981. pap. 1.95 (ISBN 0-671-43363-6). Wanderer Bks.

--Sharks. (First Bks.). (Illus.). 72p. (gr. 4 up). 1976. PLB 8.90 (ISBN 0-531-00846-0). Watts.

Blumberg, Rhoda & Blumberg, Leda. The Julian Messner Book of Facts & Fallacies. LC 83-6697. (Illus.). 160p. (gr. 7 up). 1983. 9.59 (ISBN 0-671-47612-2). Childrens.

--The Simon & Schuster Book of Facts & Fallacies. Schwartz, Betty, ed. 160p. (Orig.). (gr. 3-8). 6.95 (ISBN 0-686-45458-8). Wanderer Bks.

--The Simon & Schuster Book of Facts & Fallacies. LC 83-6697. 1983. PLB 9.59 (ISBN 0-671-47612-2). Messner.

--The Simon & Schuster Book of Facts & Fallacies. (gr. 9-12). 1983. lib. bdg. 9.59 (ISBN 0-671-47612-2). S&S.

Blumberg, Rhoda & Dwaraki, Leela. India's Educated Women: Options & Constraints. 172p. 1981. text ed. 13.50x (ISBN 0-391-02420-5, Pub. by Hindustan India). Humanities.

Blumberg, Rhoda G. & Roye, Wendell J., eds. Interracial Bonds. LC 79-63730. 199p. (Orig.). 1979. lib. bdg. 24.95x (ISBN 0-930390-34-2); pap. text ed. 8.95x (ISBN 0-930390-33-4). Gen Hall.

Blumberg, Rhoda L. Civil Rights: The Nineteen Sixties Freedom Struggle. LC 84-3810. (Social Movements Past & Present Ser.). 1984. 18.95 (ISBN 0-8057-9704-1, Twayne); pap. 7.95 (ISBN 0-8057-9708-4, Twayne). G K Hall.

Blumberg, Rhoda L. & Dwarkai, Leela. India's Educated Women. 1982. 16.00x (ISBN 0-8364-0834-9, Pub. by Hindustan). South Asia Bks.

Blumberg, Rhoda L. & Dwarki, Leela. India's Educated Women: Options & Constraints. 172p. 1980. 19.95x (ISBN 0-940500-36-1). Asia Bk Corp.

Blumberg, Rhonda. Sharks. 1980. pap. 2.25 (ISBN 0-380-49247-4, 64980-2, Camelot). Avon.

--UFO. (Illus.). 66p. (gr. 4-7). 1980. pap. 1.95 (ISBN 0-380-49254-7, 55707-X, Camelot). Avon.

Blumberg, Robert S. & Hannum, Hurst. The Fine Wines of California. 3rd ed. LC 83-45091. (Illus.). 432p. 1984. pap. 9.95 (ISBN 0-385-17973-1). Doubleday.

Blumberg, Stephen K. Win-Win Administration. 1983. pap. 10.95 (ISBN 0-913878-26-X). T Horton & Dghts.

Blume, Arthur, jt. ed. see Oxender, Dale.

Blume, August G. California Music Directory, 1985: Northern California Edition. 160p. 1985. pap. 29.95 (ISBN 0-932521-00-2). Blume & Assocs.

Blume, C. & Jakob, W. PASRO Pascal for Robots. (Illus.). 145p. 1985. 22.00 (ISBN 0-387-15120-6). Springer-Verlag.

Blume, Clemens, ed. Hymnodia Gotica. Repr. of 1909 ed. 60.00 ea. Vol. 1. (ISBN 0-384-04766-1); Vol. 2. (ISBN 0-384-04767-X). Johnson Repr.

--Thesauri Hymnologici Hymnarium, 2 Vols. Repr. of 1909 ed. 60.00 ea. Johnson Repr.

--Thesauri Hymnologica Prosarium, 2 Vols in 3. (Illus.). Repr. of 1922 ed. 60.00 ea. Johnson Repr.

--Tropi Graduales, 2 Vols. (Illus.). Repr. of 1906 ed. 60.00 ea. Johnson Repr.

Blume, Dan. Making It In Radio: Your Future in the Modern Medium. LC 83-71022. (Illus.). 176p. (Orig.). 1983. pap. 9.95 (ISBN 0-912349-00-X). Continent Media.

Blume, Dieter. The Sculpture of Anthony Caro, Nineteen Forty-Two to Nineteen Eighty: A Catalogue Raisonne, 4 Vols. (Illus.). 736p. (Orig.). 1983. Set. pap. 85.00 (ISBN 0-8390-0299-8). Abner Schram Ltd.

Blume, Dorothy M. & Cornett, Emily F. Dosages & Solutions. 4th ed. LC 83-7413. (Illus.). 156p. 1983. pap. text ed. 9.95x (ISBN 0-8036-0953-1). Davis Co.

Blume, Eli. Cours Superieur de Francais. (Orig.). (gr. 11-12). 1970. pap. text ed. 7.50 (ISBN 0-87720-460-8); wkbk. 8.67 (ISBN 0-87720-462-4). AMSCO Sch.

--Douze Contes de Maupassant. (Fr.). (gr. 10-12). 1973. pap. text ed. 6.83 (ISBN 0-87720-468-3). AMSCO Sch.

--Review Text in French First Year. 1984. pap. 6.83 (ISBN 0-87720-474-8, 240P); key 1.15 (ISBN 0-317-03316-6). Amsco Sch.

--Review Text in French Three Years. 2nd ed. (Orig.). (gr. 11-12). 1980. pap. text ed. 8.08 (ISBN 0-87720-471-3). AMSCO Sch.

--Review Text in French Two Years. 1982. pap. 7.42 (ISBN 0-87720-456-X, 214P); key 1.40 (ISBN 0-317-03317-4). AMSCO Sch.

--Workbook in French First Year. 3rd ed. (Orig.). (gr. 9-10). 1981. wkbk. 8.83 (ISBN 0-87720-453-5). AMSCO Sch.

--Workbook in French Three Years. 2nd. ed. (Illus., Orig.). (gr. 10-12). 1978. wkbk. 8.67 (ISBN 0-87720-459-4). AMSCO Sch.

--Workbook in French Two Years. 3rd ed. (Orig.). (gr. 10-11). 1979. pap. text ed. 9.67 (ISBN 0-87720-470-5). AMSCO Sch.

Blume, F., ed. Musik in Geschichte und Gegenwart: Allegemeine Enzyklopaedie der Musik, 16 vols. 2380.20 set (ISBN 3-7618-0641-8); 1 index vol. incl. Adlers Foreign Bks.

Blume, Friedrich. Classic & Romantic Music. Norton, M. D., tr. LC 78-77390. 1970. pap. 6.95x (ISBN 0-393-09868-0). Norton.

--Renaissance & Baroque Music, a Comprehensive Survey. Norton, M. Herter, tr. (Illus., Orig.). 1967. pap. 7.95x (ISBN 0-393-09710-2, NortonC). Norton.

--Two Centuries of Bach. Godman, Stanley, tr. (Music Reprint Ser.). 1978. Repr. of 1950 ed. lib. bdg. 18.50 (ISBN 0-306-77567-0). Da Capo.

Blume, Judy. Are You There God? It's Me, Margaret. LC 79-122741. 160p. (gr. 5-7). 1970. 9.95 (ISBN 0-02-710990-9). Bradbury Pr.

--Are You There God? It's Me, Margaret. 156p. (gr. 5-9). 1974. pap. 2.50 (ISBN 0-440-90419-6, LFL). Dell.

--La Ballena. Ada, Alma F., tr. LC 83-2731. 160p. (Span.). (gr. 4-6). 1983. 9.95 (ISBN 0-02-710940-2). Bradbury Pr.

--Blubber. LC 73-94116. 160p. (gr. 4-6). 1974. 9.95 (ISBN 0-02-711010-9). Bradbury Pr.

--Blubber. 144p. (gr. 4-7). 1978. pap. 2.50 (ISBN 0-440-90707-1, LFL). Dell.

--Blubber. pap. 1.75 (ISBN 0-686-74492-6, YB). Dell.

--Blubber. 160p. (gr. 7 up). 1976. pap. 2.50 (ISBN 0-440-40707-9, YB). Dell.

--Deenie. LC 73-80197. 192p. (gr. 6-8). 1973. 9.95 (ISBN 0-02-711020-6). Bradbury Pr.

--Deenie. 144p. 1974. pap. 2.50 (ISBN 0-440-93259-9, LFL). Dell.

--Estas ahi Dios? Soy yo, Margaret. Ada, Alma F., tr. LC 83-2730. 160p. (Span.). (gr. 5-7). 1983. 9.95 (ISBN 0-02-710950-X). Bradbury Pr.

--Forever. LC 74-22850. 216p. (YA) 1975. 10.95 (ISBN 0-02-711030-3). Bradbury Pr.

--Forever. 224p. (Orig.). 1984. pap. 3.50 (ISBN 0-671-53225-1). PB.

--Freckle Juice. (Illus.). 48p. (gr. 2-4). 1978. pap. 1.95 (ISBN 0-440-42813-0, YB). Dell.

--Iggie's House. LC 70-104340. 128p. (gr. 4-6). 1970. 9.95 (ISBN 0-02-711040-0). Bradbury Pr.

--Iggie's House. 128p. (gr. k-6). 1981. pap. 2.50 (ISBN 0-440-44062-9, YB). Dell.

--It's Not the End of the World. (gr. 4-6). 1981. pap. 1.95 (ISBN 0-553-13628-3, Skylark). Bantam.

--It's Not the End of the World. LC 70-181739. 176p. (gr. 5-7). 1972. 9.95 (ISBN 0-02-711050-8). Bradbury Pr.

--It's Not the End of the World. 176p. (gr. 4-7). 1982. pap. 2.50 (ISBN 0-440-94140-7, LFL). Dell.

--The Judy Blume Diary: The Place to Put Your Own Feelings. 192p. (ps up). 1981. 6.95 (ISBN 0-440-44266-4, YB). Dell.

--The One in the Middle Is the Green Kangaroo. LC 80-29664. (Illus.). 40p. (gr. k-3). 1981. 8.95 (ISBN 0-02-711060-5). Bradbury Pr.

--The One in the Middle Is the Green Kangaroo. (Illus.). 48p. (gr. 1-2). 1982. pap. 1.95 (ISBN 0-440-46731-4, YB). Dell.

--Otherwise Known As Sheila the Great. (gr. 3-6). 1972. 9.95 (ISBN 0-525-36455-2, 0966-290). Dutton.

--Otherwise Known as Shelia the Great. 128p. (gr. k-6). 1981. pap. 2.50 (ISBN 0-440-46701-2, YB). Dell.

--The Pain & the Great One. LC 84-11009. (Illus.). 32p. (gr. k-3). 1984. PLB 10.95 (ISBN 0-02-711100-8). Bradbury Pr.

--The Pain & the Great One. (gr. k-12). 1985. pap. 3.95 (ISBN 0-440-46819-1, YB). Dell.

--Smart Women. LC 83-15958. 324p. 1984. 15.95 (ISBN 0-399-12840-9, Putnam). Putnam Pub Group.

--Smart Women. 1985. pap. 3.95 (ISBN 0-671-50268-9). PB.

--Starring Sally J. Freedman As Herself. LC 76-57805. 296p. (gr. 4-7). 1977. 10.95 (ISBN 0-02-711070-2). Bradbury Pr.

--Starring Sally J. Freedman As Herself. 240p. (gr. 4 up). 1978. pap. 2.75 (ISBN 0-440-98239-1, LFL). Dell.

--Superfudge. 176p. (gr. 4-7). 1981. pap. 2.50 (ISBN 0-440-48433-2, YB). Dell.

--Superfudge. LC 80-10439. 176p. (gr. 3-6). 1980. 9.95 (ISBN 0-525-40522-4, 0966-290). Dutton.

--Tales of a Fourth Grade Nothing. 128p. (gr. 3-7). 1981. pap. 2.75 (ISBN 0-440-48474-X, YB). Dell.

--Tales of a Fourth Grade Nothing. LC 70-179050. (Illus.). 128p. (gr. 2-5). 1972. 9.95 (ISBN 0-525-40720-0, 0966-290). Dutton.

--Then Again, Maybe I Won't. LC 77-156548. 176p. (gr. 5-7). 1971. 9.95 (ISBN 0-02-711090-7). Bradbury Pr.

--Then Again, Maybe I Won't. 128p. (gr. 6 up). pap. 2.50 (ISBN 0-440-98659-1, LFL). Dell.

--Then Again, Maybe I Won't. 164p. (gr. 6 up). pap. 2.50 (ISBN 0-440-48659-9, YB). Dell.

--Tiger Eyes. LC 81-6152. 256p. (gr. 7 up). 1981. 10.95 (ISBN 0-02-711080-X). Bradbury Pr.

--Tiger Eyes. 224p. 1982. pap. 2.50 (ISBN 0-440-98469-6, LFL). Dell.

--Wifey. 1983. pap. 3.95 (ISBN 0-671-50189-5). PB.

Blume, K. L. Catalogus van eenige der merkwaardigste zoo in- als uitheemsche Gewassen: te vinden in's land Plantentium te Buitenzorg. 1946. pap. 5.00 (ISBN 0-934454-25-7). Lubrecht & Cramer.

Blume, Karl G. & Petz, Lawrence D., eds. Clinical Bone Marrow Transplantation. (Illus.). 383p. 1983. text ed. 50.00 (ISBN 0-443-08271-5). Churchill.

Blume, Keith. The Presidential Election Show: Nightly News Coverage of the 1984 Campaign. 208p. 1985. 27.95 (ISBN 0-89789-080-9); pap. 12.95 (ISBN 0-89789-081-7). Bergin & Garvey.

Blume, Marshall E. & Friedman, Jack P., eds. The Complete Guide to Investment Opportunities. 1100p. 1984. pap. 19.95 (ISBN 0-02-903710-7). Free Pr.

Blume, Marshall E., et al, eds. Economic Activity & Finance. LC 81-20539. 288p. 1982. prof ref 35.00x (ISBN 0-88410-858-9). Ballinger Pub.

Blume, Philip & Freier, Esther, eds. Enzymology in the Practice of Laboratory Medicine. 1974. 55.00 (ISBN 0-12-107950-3). Acad Pr.

Blume, Stuart S. Perspectives in the Sociology of Science. LC 76-30827. 1977. 56.95 (ISBN 0-471-99480-4, Pub. by Wiley-Interscience). Wiley.

--Toward a Political Sociology of Science. LC 73-5291. 1974. text ed. 18.95 (ISBN 0-02-904350-6). Free Pr.

Blume, Warren T. Atlas of Pediatric Electroencephalography. 344p. 1982. text ed. 108.00 (ISBN 0-89004-564-X). Raven.

Blume, Wilbur & Schneller, Paul. Toward International Tele-Education. (Replica Edition Ser.). 225p. 1984. softcover 19.50x (ISBN 0-86531-829-8). Westview.

Blumenau, Lili. Creative Design in Wall Hangings. (Arts & Crafts Ser). (Illus.). 1966. 9.95 (ISBN 0-517-02559-0). Crown.

Blumenbach, Johann F. The Anthropological Treatises of Johann Blumenbach. LC 77-94627. 1978. Repr. of 1865 ed. lib. bdg. 40.00 (ISBN 0-89341-511-1). Longwood Pub Group.

Blumenberg, Hans. The Legitimacy of the Modern Age. McCarthy, Tom, ed. Wallace, Robert M., tr. from German. (German Social Thought Ser.). 768p. 1985. 40.00x (ISBN 0-262-02184-6); pap. 13.95x (ISBN 0-262-52105-9). MIT Pr.

--Work on Myth. Wallace, Robert M., tr. from Ger. (German Social Thought Ser.). 770p. 1985. text ed. 40.00x (ISBN 0-262-02215-X). MIT Pr.

Blumenberg, Werner. August Bebels Briefwechsel Mit Friedrich Engels. (Quellen und Untersuchungen Zur Geschichte der Deutschenund Osterreichischen Arbeiterbewegung: No. 6). 1965. 84.00x (ISBN 90-2790-155-4). Mouton.

Blumenberg, Werner, jt. auth. see Silberner, Edmund.

Blumenbrg & Kury. Herder-Lexikon Psychologie. 2nd ed. 239p. (Ger.). 1976. pap. 25.95 (ISBN 3-451-16467-1, M-7451, Pub. by Herder). French & Eur.

Blumenfeld, Arthur. Heart Attack: Are You a Candidate. LC 64-17749. 1964. 5.95 (ISBN 0-8397-3200-7). Eriksson.

Blumenfeld, Esther & Alpers, Lynne. The Smile Connection: How to Use Humor in Dealing with People. 300p. 1985. 14.95 (ISBN 0-13-525783-2); pap. 7.95 (ISBN 0-13-525775-1). P-H.

Blumenfeld, Gerry & Blumenfeld, Harold. Naughty but Nice. 1976. pap. 1.25 (ISBN 0-685-69508-5, LB374ZK, Leisure Bks). Dorchester Pub Co.

--Sex Over Lightly. 1976. pap. 1.25 (ISBN 0-685-72355-0, LB381ZK, Leisure Bks). Dorchester Pub Co.

Blumenfeld, Hans. Modern Metropolis: Its Origins, Growth, Characteristics, & Planning, Selected Essays. Spreiregen, Paul, ed. 1971. pap. 5.95x (ISBN 0-262-52028-1). MIT Pr.

Blumenfeld, Hans & Spreiregen, Paul D. Metropolis & Beyond: Selected Essays. LC 78-17955. pap. 108.30 (ISBN 0-317-26259-9, 2055714). Bks Demand UMI.

Blumenfeld, Harold, jt. auth. see Blumenfeld, Gerry.

Blumenfeld, Harold, tr. see Praetorius, Michael.

Blumenfeld, L. A. Physics of Bioenergetics Processes. Haken, H., ed. (Springer Series in Energetics: Vol. 16). (Illus.). 150p. 1983. 33.00 (ISBN 0-387-11417-3). Springer-Verlag.

--Problems of Biological Physics. (Series in Synergetics: Vol. 7). (Illus.). 300p. 1981. 39.00 (ISBN 0-387-10401-1). Springer-Verlag.

Blumenfeld, Milton J. Careers in Photography. LC 79-16299. (Early Career Bks.). (Illus.). (gr. 2-5). 1979. PLB 5.95 (ISBN 0-8225-0338-7). Lerner Pubns.

Blumenfeld, R. D. In the Days of Bicycles & Bustles. 1978. Repr. of 1930 ed. lib. bdg. 30.00 (ISBN 0-8495-0380-9). Arden Lib.

Blumenfeld, Samuel, ed. Property in a Humane Economy. LC 74-22455. 294p. 1974. pap. 9.95 (ISBN 0-87548-340-2). Open Court.

Blumenfeld, Samuel L. Alpha-Phonics: A Primer for Beginning Readers. 172p. (Orig.). 1983. pap. 19.95 (ISBN 0-8159-6916-3). Devin.

--How to Tutor. LC 73-10834. 1977. pap. 4.95 (ISBN 0-915134-21-7). Mott Media.

--Is Public Education Necessary? 272p. 1985. pap. 9.95 (ISBN 0-8159-5826-9). Devin.

--Is Public Education Necessary? 263p. (Orig.). 1985. pap. 9.95 (ISBN 0-914981-10-2). Paradigm ID.

--NEA: Trojan Horse in American Education. 300p. (Orig.). 1984. pap. 9.95 (ISBN 0-914981-03-X). Paradigm ID.

Blumenfeld, Thomas, jt. ed. see Slockbower, Jean.

Blumenfeld, Warren S. Development & Evaluation of Job Performance Criteria: A Procedural Guide. LC 76-18778. (Research Monograph: No. 64). 75p. 1976. spiral bdg. 10.00 (ISBN 0-88406-096-9). Ga St U Busn Pub.

--The Effectiveness of Management Three Hundred Fifty. (Research Monograph: No. 54). 1974. spiral bdg. 5.00 (ISBN 0-88406-020-9). Ga St U Busn Pub.

Blumenfeld, Yorick. Jenny. 1982. 5.95 (ISBN 0-316-10032-3). Little.

Blumenfield, Lenore. Devil & His Devilish Daughter. (Illus.). 28p. (Director's Production Script). 1973. pap. 5.00 (ISBN 0-88680-211-3). I E Clark.

Blumenfield, Michael, ed. Applied Supervision in Psychotherapy. 240p. 1982. 29.00 (ISBN 0-8089-1461-8, 790627). Grune.

Blumenfrucht, Israel & Weiss, Jerold M. Tax Questions & Answers: A Tax Review Handbook for CPA Candidates, Tax Practitioners, Students & Taxpayers. 1979. text ed. 18.95 (ISBN 0-13-885160-3, Spec); pap. 9.95 (ISBN 0-13-885152-2). P-H.

Blumenkrantz, Joseph. Bellevue Behemoth. 1983. 12.95 (ISBN 0-8062-2204-2). Carlton.

Blumenkrantz, Steven J., jt. auth. see Rothenberg, Robert D.

Blumenkranz, Bernhard. Juifs et Chretiens-Patristique et Moyen-Age. 368p. 1977. 60.00x (ISBN 0-86078-014-7, Pub. by Variorum). State Mutual Bk.

Blumensen, Martin. Patton Papers, Eighteen Eighty-Five to Nineteen Forty, Vol. 1. LC 76-156490. (Illus.). 1024p. 1972. 39.50 (ISBN 0-395-12706-8). HM.

--Patton Papers, Nineteen Forty to Nineteen Forty-Five, Vol. 2. LC 74-156490. 912p. 1974. 39.50 (ISBN 0-395-18498-3). HM.

Blumenson, John C. Identifying American Architecture: A Pictorial Guide to Styles & Terms, 1600-1945. rev. ed. (Illus.). 1981. 13.95 (ISBN 0-393-01428-2). Norton.

Blumenson, Martin. Anzio: The Gamble That Failed. LC 77-26027. (Great Battles of History). (Illus.). 1978. Repr. of 1963 ed. lib. bdg. 21.00x (ISBN 0-313-20093-9, BLAN). Greenwood.

--Anzio: The Gamble that Failed. 1986. pap. 3.50 (ISBN 0-440-10353-3). Dell.

--Kasserine Pass. LC 82-60693. 351p. 1983. pap. 3.50 (ISBN 0-515-07618-X). Jove Pubns.

--Liberation. LC 78-21967. (World War II Ser.). (Illus.). (gr. 7 up). 1979. lib. bdg. 22.60 (ISBN 0-8094-2511-4, Pub. by Time-Life). Silver.

--Liberation. (World War Two Ser.). (Illus.). 1979. 14.95 (ISBN 0-8094-2510-6). Time-Life.

--Mark Clark: Last of the Great World War II Commanders. 320p. 1984. 17.95 (ISBN 0-312-92517-4). Congdon & Weed.

--Patton: The Man Behind the Legend - 1885-1945. (Illus.). 1985. 17.95 (ISBN 0-688-06082-X). Morrow.

Blumensow, John J. Identifying American Architecture: A Pictorial Guide to Styles & Terms, 1600-1945. Rev. ed. LC 80-28103. (Illus.). 1981. pap. 8.95 (ISBN 0-910050-50-3). AASLH Pr.

Blumenstein, Barbara J., ed. see Blumenstein, Lynn.

Blumenstein, Lynn. Truly American. Blumenstein, Barbara J., ed. LC 74-113428. (Illus., Orig.). 1970. pap. 1.95 (ISBN 0-911068-06-6). Old Time.

Blumenstengel, A. Twenty-Four Exercises for Violin, Op. 33. (Carl Fischer Music Library: No. 621). 1911. pap. 4.50 (ISBN 0-8258-0082-X, L621). Fischer Inc NY.

Blumenstock, David I. The Ocean of Air. LC 59-7509. pap. 117.80 (ISBN 0-317-11067-5, 2050472). Bks Demand UMI.

Blumenstock, Dorothy, jt. auth. see Lasswell, Harold D.

Blumental, James, jt. auth. see Keefe, Francis.

Blumenthal, Aaron H. If I Am Only for Myself: The Story of Hillel. 1973. 3.75x (ISBN 0-8381-0219-0). United Syn Bk.

Blumenthal, Albert. Moral Responsibility. 1977. 10.00 (ISBN 0-686-20044-6). Rayline.

Blumenthal, Arthur. Giulio Parigi's Stage Designs: Florence & the Early Baroque Spectacle. Freedberg, S. J., ed. (Outstanding Dissertations in Fine Arts Ser.). (Illus.). 500p. 1985. Repr. of 1984 ed. 60.00 (ISBN 0-8240-6874-2). Garland Pub.

Blumenthal, Arthur L. Language & Psychology: Historical Aspects of Psycholinguistics. LC 80-12611. 262p. 1980. Repr. of 1970 ed. lib. bdg. 15.00 (ISBN 0-89874-167-X). Krieger.

Blumenthal, Arthur R. Theater Art of the Medici. LC 80-22452. (Illus.). 248p. 1980. pap. 19.95x (ISBN 0-87451-191-7). U Pr of New Eng.

Blumenthal, D. R. Understanding Jewish Mysticism: A Source Reader, No. I. (Library of Judaic Learning). 20.00x (ISBN 0-87068-334-9). Ktav.

Blumentahl, Daniel S. Introduction to Environmental Health. 272p. 1985. pap. 24.95 (ISBN 0-8261-3900-0). Springer Pub.

Blumenthal, David R. Approaches to Judaism in Medieval Times. LC 83-18886. (Brown Judaic Ser.). 188p. pap. 14.95 (ISBN 0-89130-659-5, 14 00 54). Scholars Pr GA.

Blumenthal, David R., ed. Emory Studies on the Holocaust. LC 84-52494. 178p. (Orig.). 1985. pap. 5.00 (ISBN 0-912313-01-3). Witness Holocaust.

Blumenthal, Eileen. Joseph Chaikin. (Directors in Perspective Ser.). (Illus.). 272p. 1984. 34.50 (ISBN 0-521-24298-3); pap. 11.95 (ISBN 0-521-28589-5). Cambridge U Pr.

Blumenthal, Friedrich. Lord Byron's Mystery "Cain" & Its Relation to Milton's "Paradise Lost" & Gesner's "Death of Abel". LC 77-17808. 1977. Repr. of 1891 ed. lib. bdg. 8.50 (ISBN 0-8414-0456-9). Folcroft.

Blumenthal, G. J. Development of Secure Units in Child Care. 120p. 1985. pap. text ed. write for info. (ISBN 0-566-00868-8). Gower Pub co.

Blumenthal, Gerda. Andre Malraux: The Conquest of Dread. LC 78-12576. 1979. Repr. of 1960 ed. lib. bdg. 22.50x (ISBN 0-313-21194-9, BLAM). Greenwood.

--Thresholds: A Study of Proust. 112p. 1984. 13.95 (ISBN 0-917786-06-8). Summa Pubns.

Blumenthal, H. J. & Markus, R. A., eds. Neoplatonism & Early Christian Thought: Essays in Honour of A. H. Armstrong. 256p. 1981. 60.00x (ISBN 0-86078-085-6, Pub. by Variorum England). State Mutual Bk.

Blumenthal, H. T., ed. The Regulatory Role of the Nervous System in Aging. (Interdisciplinary Topics in Gerontology: Vol. 7). 1970. 22.25 (ISBN 3-8055-0508-6). S Karger.

Blumenthal, H. T., ed. see International Association of Gerontology-5th Congress.

Blumenthal, Henry. American & French Culture, 1800 to 1900: Interchanges in Art, Science, Literature & Society. LC 74-27187. xv, 554p. 1975. 37.50x (ISBN 0-8071-0155-9). La State U Pr.

--A Reappraisal of Franco-American Relations, Eighteen Thirty to Eighteen Seventy-One. LC 79-25197. 255p. 1980. Repr. of 1959 ed. lib. bdg. 24.75x (ISBN 0-313-22138-3, BLRA). Greenwood.

Blumenthal, Herman T. Cowdry's Atheriosclerosis: A Survey of the Problem. 2nd ed. (Illus.). 884p. 1967. photocopy ed. 84.50x (ISBN 0-398-00180-4). C C Thomas.

Blumenthal, Herman T. & Probstein, J. G. Pancreatitis: A Clinico-Pathologic Correlation. (Illus.). 392p. 1959. photocopy ed. 34.50x (ISBN 0-398-04214-4). C C Thomas.

Blumenthal, Herman T., ed. Handbook of the Diseases of Aging. 512p. 1983. 39.50 (ISBN 0-442-21566-5). Van Nos Reinhold.

Blumenthal, Howard J. Everyone's Guide to Personal Computers. 288p. (Orig.). 1983. pap. 8.95 (ISBN 0-345-30218-4). Ballantine.

--The Media Room: Creating Your Own Home Entertainment & Information Center. (Illus.). 256p. (Orig.). 1983. pap. 9.95 (ISBN 0-14-046538-3). Penguin.

Blumenthal, Jay. Revenue Producing Documentation. 1984. write for info. loose-leaf (ISBN 0-935506-24-1). Carnegie Pr.

Blumenthal, John. Anthony Geary. 96p. 1982. pap. 6.95 (ISBN 0-671-44942-7, Wallaby). S&S.

--The Case of the Hardboiled Dicks: A Novel. 1985. 2.95 (ISBN 0-671-55538-3, Pub. by Fireside). S&S.

--The Official Hollywood Handbook. pap. 6.95 (ISBN 0-671-49713-8). S&S.

--The Tinseltown Murders: A Mac Slade Mystery. 1985. pap. 2.95 (Fireside). S&S.

Blumenthal, Joseph. Art of the Printed Book, Fourteen Fifty-Five to Nineteen Fifty-Five. LC 73-82830. (Illus.). 212p. 1973. 50.00 (ISBN 0-87923-082-7); pap. 25.00 (ISBN 0-87923-259-5). Godine.

--Art of the Printed Book, Fourteen Fifty-Five to Nineteen Fifty-Five. LC 73-82830. (Illus.). 1974. pap. 25.00 (ISBN 0-87923-259-5). Godine.

--The Printed Book in America. LC 77-79004. (Illus.). 268p. 1977. 45.00x (ISBN 0-87923-210-2). Godine.

--Robert Frost & His Printers. 85.00x (ISBN 0-318-11686-3). W T Taylor.

--Typographic Years: A Printer's Journey Through a Half Century. LC 82-71904. (Illus.). 153p. 26.50 (ISBN 0-913720-38-0). Beil.

Blumenthal, Joseph C. English 2200: A Programmed Course in Grammar & Usage-College Edition. 3rd ed. 383p. 1981. pap. text ed. 12.95 (ISBN 0-15-522719-X, HC); tests avail. (ISBN 0-15-522720-3); answer key to tests avail. (ISBN 0-15-522721-1). HarBraceJ.

--English 2600: A Programmed Course in Grammar & Usage-College Edition. 5th ed. 448p. 1981. pap. text ed. 12.95 (ISBN 0-15-522716-5, HC); tests avail. (ISBN 0-15-522717-3); answer key to tests avail. (ISBN 0-15-522718-1). HarBraceJ.

--English 3200: A Programmed Course in Grammar & Usage - College Edition. 3rd ed. 550p. 1981. pap. text ed. 13.95 (ISBN 0-15-522711-4, HC); tests avail. (ISBN 0-15-522712-2); answer key to tests avail. (ISBN 0-15-522713-0); alternate tests avail. (ISBN 0-15-522714-9); answer key to alternate tests avail. (ISBN 0-15-522715-7). HarBraceJ.

Blumenthal, Karen & Weinberg, Anita, eds. Establishing Parental Involvement in Foster Care Agencies. 1984. pap. write for info. (ISBN 0-87868-214-7). Child Welfare.

Blumenthal, Karen L., jt. auth. see McGowan, Brenda G.

Blumenthal, Lassor A. The Art of Letter Writing. (The Practical Handbook Ser.). 96p. 1976. pap. 5.95 (ISBN 0-399-50799-X, G&D); PLB 8.45 (ISBN 0-448-13324-5, G&D). Putnam Pub Group.

--Successful Business Writing. 112p. (Orig.). 1985. pap. 5.95 (ISBN 0-399-51146-6, Perigee). Putnam Pub Group.

Blumenthal, Leonard M. A Modern View of Geometry. (Illus.). 1980. pap. text ed. 5.95 (ISBN 0-486-63962-2). Dover.

--Theory & Applications of Distance Geometry. 2nd ed. LC 79-113117. 1970. text ed. 16.95 (ISBN 0-8284-0242-6). Chelsea Pub.

Blumenthal, Leonard M. & Menger, Karl. Studies in Geometry. LC 74-75624. (Illus.). 512p. 1970. text ed. 31.95 (ISBN 0-7167-0437-4). W H Freeman.

Blumenthal, Leonhard Von see Leonhard, Blumenthal Von.

Blumenthal, Marc D., jt. ed. see Ingber, Abie I.

Blumenthal, Margarete. Technik Des Englischen Gegenwartsromanes. pap. 9.00 (ISBN 0-384-04775-0). Johnson Repr.

Blumenthal, Michael. Days We Would Rather Know. 112p. 1984. pap. 9.95 (ISBN 0-14-042328-1). Penguin.

--Days We Would Rather Know. 112p. 1984. 14.95 (ISBN 0-670-77612-2). Viking.

--Laps. LC 84-8601. 54p. 1984. 10.00x (ISBN 0-87023-459-5); pap. 4.95 (ISBN 0-87023-460-9). U of Mass Pr.

--Sympathetic Magic. LC 80-50812. (Illus.). 96p. (Orig.). 1980. 30.00 (ISBN 0-931956-04-8); pap. 7.50 (ISBN 0-931956-03-X); handbound o.p. 60.00 (ISBN 0-686-70197-6). Water Mark.

Blumenthal, Monica D., et al. Justifying Violence: Attitudes of American Men, 1969. 2nd ed. 1978. codebk. write for info. (ISBN 0-89138-995-4). ICPSR.

--Justifying Violence: Attitudes of American Men. LC 74-169101. 380p. 1972. cloth 18.00x (ISBN 0-87944-005-8); pap. 12.00x (ISBN 0-87944-004-X). Inst Soc Res.

--More About Justifying Violence: Methodological Studies of Attitudes & Behavior. LC 74-620136. 416p. 1975. cloth 20.00x (ISBN 0-87944-192-5); pap. 12.00x (ISBN 0-87944-191-7). Inst Soc Res.

Blumenthal, P. J. Slow Train to Cincinnati. 1975. pap. 3.00 (ISBN 0-915572-51-6, Pub by Black Dragon Bks). Panjandrum.

Blumenthal, R., jt. ed. see DeLisi, C.

Blumenthal, Richard L., jt. auth. see Meltzoff, Julian.

Blumenthal, Robert M. Markov Processes & Potential Theory. LC 68-18659. (Pure & Applied Mathematics Ser.: Vol. 29). 1968. 68.50 (ISBN 0-12-107850-7). Acad Pr.

Blumenthal, Shirley. Black Cats & Other Superstitions. LC 77-10623. (Myth, Magic & Superstition). (Illus.). (gr. 4-5). 1977. PLB 14.25 (ISBN 0-8172-1036-9). Raintree Pubs.

--Immigrants from Eastern Europe. LC 81-65504. 224p. (gr. 7 up). 1981. 12.95 (ISBN 0-385-28161-7). Delacorte.

Blumenthal, Shirley & Ozer, Jerome S. Coming to America: Immigrants from the British Isles. LC 80-65841. 192p. (gr. 9-12). 1980. 12.95 (ISBN 0-385-28114-5). Delacorte.

--Coming to America: Immigrants from the British Isles. (gr. 7-9). 1981. pap. 2.25 (ISBN 0-440-91074-9, LE). Dell.

--Immigrants from the British Isles. 192p. pap. 2.25 (ISBN 0-440-91074-9). Dell.

--Immigrants from the British Isles. LC 80-65841. 192p. 1980. 12.95 (ISBN 0-385-28114-5). Delacorte.

Blumenthal, Sidney. The Permanent Campaign. 1983. pap. 6.95 (ISBN 0-671-45341-6, Touchstone Bks). S&S.

--The Permanent Campaign: Inside the World of Elite Political Operatives. LC 79-53755. 1980. 16.95x (ISBN 0-8070-3208-5). Beacon Pr.

Blumenthal, Susan. Understanding & Buying a Small Business Computer. LC 81-86553. 160p. 1982. pap. 9.95 (ISBN 0-672-21890-9, 21890). Sams.

Blumenthal, Susan J., jt. auth. see Osofsky, Howard J.

Blumenthal, Tuvia. Saving in Postwar Japan. LC 78-119071. (East Asian Monographs Ser.: No. 35). 1970. pap. 11.00x (ISBN 0-674-78997-0). Harvard U Pr.

Blumenthal, Uta-Renate, ed. Carolingian Essays: Andrew W. Mellon Lectures in Early Christian Studies. LC 83-14562. 249p. 1983. 25.95x (ISBN 0-8132-0579-4). Cath U Pr.

Blumenthal, Vera De see De Blumenthal, Vera.

Blumenthal, Walter H. American Indians Dispossessed: Fraud in Land Cessions Forced Upon the Tribes. facs. ed. LC 74-30620. (American Farmers & the Rise of Agribusiness Ser.). 1975. Repr. of 1955 ed. 18.00x (ISBN 0-405-06767-4). Ayer Co Pubs.

--Bookmen's Bedlam of Literary Oddities. facs. ed. LC 77-80383. (Essay Index Reprint Ser). 1955. 23.75 (ISBN 0-8369-1022-2). Ayer Co Pubs.

--Brides from Bridewell: Female Felons Sent to Colonial America. LC 73-7307. (Illus.). 139p. 1973. Repr. of 1962 ed. lib. bdg. 15.00x (ISBN 0-8371-6924-0, BLBB). Greenwood.

--Women Camp Followers of the American Revolution. LC 74-3931. (Women in America Ser). 104p. 1974. Repr. of 1952 ed. 13.00 (ISBN 0-405-06077-7). Ayer Co Pubs.

Blumenthal, Warren B. The Creator & Man. LC 80-5843. 139p. 1980. lib. bdg. 20.50 (ISBN 0-8191-1340-9); pap. text ed. 9.25 (ISBN 0-8191-1341-7). U Pr of Amer.

Blumenthal, Y. C., ed. Hamishkan V'keilov. (Illus., Hebrew.). softcover 1.75 (ISBN 0-686-33060-9, B15). Torah Umesorah.

Blumer, Diedrich, jt. ed. see Benson, Frank.

Blumer, Dietrich. Psychiatric Aspects of Epilepsy. LC 84-6236. 352p. 1984. text ed. 24.50x (ISBN 0-88048-024-6, 48-024-6). Am Psychiatric.

Blumer, Dietrich, jt. ed. see Benson, D. Frank.

Blumer, Herbert. Critiques of Research in the Social Sciences: An Appraisal of Thomas & Znaniecki's "the Polish Peasant in Europe & America". (Social Science Classics Ser.). 210p. 1979. text ed. 29.95 (ISBN 0-87855-312-6); pap. text ed. 9.95 (ISBN 0-87855-694-X). Transaction Bks.

--Movies & Conduct. LC 76-124023. (Literature of Cinema Ser.: Payne Fund Studies of Motion Pictures & Social Values). Repr. of 1933 ed. 17.00 (ISBN 0-405-01640-9). Ayer Co Pubs.
--Symbolic Interactionism: Perspective & Method. 1969. text ed. 23.95 (ISBN 0-13-879924-5). P-H.
Blumer, Herbert & Hauser, Philip M. Movies, Delinquency & Crime. LC 70-124024. (Literature of Cinema Ser.: Payne Fund Studies of Motion Pictures & Social Values). Repr. of 1933 ed. 16.00 (ISBN 0-405-01641-7). Ayer Co Pubs.
Blumer, Herbert & Hauset, Philip M. Movies, Delinquency, & Crime. 1933. 30.00 (ISBN 0-8482-3421-9). Norwood Edns.
Blumerthal, David R., ed. And Bring them Closer to Torah: The Life & Work of Robin Aavon H. Blumerthal. 1985. pap. text ed. 11.95 (ISBN 0-88125-082-1). Ktav.
Blumfeld, Samuel L., ed. Property in a Humane Economy: A Selection of Essays Compiled by the Institute for Humane Studies. LC 74-22455. 278p. 1974. pap. 10.00 (ISBN 0-87548-321-6). Inst Humane.
Blumgart, L., jt. auth. see Kennedy, A. C.
Blumgart, L. H., ed. The Biliary Tract. LC 82-4532. (Clinical Surgery International Ser.: Vol. 5). (Illus.). 293p. 1983. text ed. 37.50 (ISBN 0-443-02322-0). Churchill.
Blumhagen, Kathleen O. & Johnson, Walter D., eds. Women's Studies: An Interdisciplinary Collection. (Contributions in Women's Studies: No. 2). 1978. lib. bdg. 25.00 (ISBN 0-313-20028-9, SJW/). Greenwood.
Blumhardt, Christoph. Evening Prayers for Every Day in the Year. Society Of Brothers, ed. LC 73-141948. 1971. 3.50 (ISBN 0-87486-204-3). Plough.
Blumhardt, Christoph see Barth, Karl.
Blumhardt, Christoph, jt. auth. see Blumhardt, Johann C.
Blumhardt, Christoph F., jt. auth. see Blumhardt, Johann C.
Blumhardt, Christopher F., jt. auth. see Blumhardt, Johann C.
Blumhardt, Doreen & Brake, Brian. Craft New Zealand: The Art of the Craftsman. (Illus.). 300p. 1981. text ed. 75.00x (ISBN 0-87663-374-2). Universe.
Blumhardt, J. F. Catalogue of the Bengali & Assamese Manuscripts in the India Office. (Orig.). 1924. pap. 2.25 (ISBN 0-7123-0605-6, Pub. by British Lib). Longwood Pub Group.
--Catalogue of the Gujarati & Rajasthani Manuscripts in the India Office Library. Rev. & Enl. ed. Master, A., ed. (Illus.). 177p. 1954. 11.25 (ISBN 0-19-815409-7, Pub. by British Lib). Longwood Pub Group.
--Catalogue of the Hindustani Manuscripts in the Library of the India Office. 183p. (Orig.). 1926. pap. 8.95 (ISBN 0-317-30594-8, Pub. by British Lib). Longwood Pub Group.
--Catalogue of the Oriya Manuscripts in the Library of the India Office. 26p. (Orig.). 1924. pap. 2.25 (ISBN 0-7123-0607-2, Pub. by British Lib). Longwood Pub Group.
Blumhardt, J. F. & Kanhere, S. G. Catalogue of the Marathi Manuscripts in the India Office Library. 133p. (Orig.). 1950. pap. 8.25 (ISBN 0-317-30617-0, Pub. by British Lib). Longwood Pub Group.
Blumhardt, J. F. & MacKenzie, D. N. Catalogue of Pashto Manuscripts in the Libraries of the British Isles. 160p. 1965. cloth 79.00x (ISBN 0-7141-0625-9, Pub. by Brit Lib England). State Mutual Bk.
--Catalogue of Pashto Manuscripts in the Libraries of the British Isles. 160p. 1965. 30.00 (ISBN 0-7141-0625-9, Pub. by British Lib). Longwood Pub Group.
Blumhardt, Johann C. & Blumhardt, Christoph. Now Is Eternity. LC 76-10251. 1976. 3.95 (ISBN 0-87486-209-4); pap. 2.95 (ISBN 0-87486-219-1). Plough.
Blumhardt, Johann C. & Blumhardt, Christopher F. Thoughts about Children. Hutterian Society of Brothers, tr. from Ger. LC 79-24844. 77p. 1980. pap. 3.25 (ISBN 0-87486-224-8). Plough.
Blumhardt, Johann C. & Blumhardt, Christoph F. Thy Kingdom Come. Eller, Vernard, ed. LC 80-19328. (A Blumhardt Reader Ser.). 180p. 1980. text ed. 5.50 (ISBN 0-8028-3544-9, Pub. by Eerdmans). Plough.
Blumhofer, Edith W. The Assemblies of God: A Popular History. LC 85-70552. (Orig.). 1985. pap. 2.95 (ISBN 0-88243-469-1, 02-0469). Gospel Pub.
Blumin, Leonard. Victorian Decorative Art: A Photographic Study of Ornamental Design in Antique Doorknobs. LC 83-50477. (Illus.). 200p. (Orig.). 1983. pap. 14.95 (ISBN 0-913693-00-6). Victorian Design.
Blumin, Stuart & Durlach, Hansi. The Short Season of Sharon Springs: Portrait of Another New York. (Illus.). 128p. 1980. 25.00 (ISBN 0-8014-1303-6). Cornell U Pr.
Blumin, Stuart M. The Urban Threshold: Growth & Change in a Nineteenth-Century American Community. LC 75-27891. (Heritage of Sociology Ser.). 1976. pap. 10.00x (ISBN 0-226-06170-1, Midway Reprint). U of Chicago Pr.
Blumler, Jay G. & Katz, Elihu. The Uses of Mass Communications: Current Perspectives on Gratifications Research. LC 73-90713. (Annual Reviews of Communication Research: Vol. 3). 320p. 1975. 25.00 (ISBN 0-8039-0340-5); pap. 12.50 (ISBN 0-8039-0494-0). Sage.
Blumner, Hugo. Home Life of the Ancient Greeks. Zimmern, A., tr. LC 66-30007. (Illus.). 548p. Repr. of 1893 ed. 28.50 (ISBN 0-8154-0025-X). Cooper Sq.
--Technologie und Terminologie der Gewerbe und Kunste bei Griechen und Romern, 4 vols. Finley, Moses, ed. LC 79-4963. (Ancient Economic History Ser.). (Illus., Ger.). 1980. Repr. of 1875 ed. Set. lib. bdg. 148.00x (ISBN 0-405-12350-7); 37.00x ea. Vol. 1 (ISBN 0-405-12351-5). Vol. 2 (ISBN 0-405-12352-3). Vol. 3 (ISBN 0-405-12484-8). Vol. 4 (ISBN 0-405-12485-6). Ayer Co Pubs.
Blumner, Hugo, jt. auth. see Buchsenschutz, B.
Blumner, Jack. Your Basic Love Story. 1984. pap. 4.95 (ISBN 0-03-069581-3). HR&W.
Blumrosen, Alfred, et al. Age Discrimination in Employment Act: A Compliance & Litigation Manual for Lawyers & Personnel Practitioners. LC 82-71302. 456p. (Orig.). 1982. pap. 19.95 (ISBN 0-937856-04-5). Equal Employ.
Blumrosen, Alfred W. Black Employment & the Law. 1971. 40.00x (ISBN 0-8135-0682-4). Rutgers U Pr.
Blumstein, Alexandre, ed. Liquid Crystalline Order in Polymers. 1978. 56.50 (ISBN 0-12-108650-X). Acad Pr.
--Mesomorphic Order in Polymers & Polymerization in Liquid Crystalline Media. LC 78-9470. (ACS Symposium Ser.: No. 74). 1978. 30.95 (ISBN 0-8412-0419-5). Am Chemical.
--Polymeric Liquid Crystals. 449p. 1985. 75.00x (ISBN 0-306-41814-2, Plenum Pr). Plenum Pub.
Blumstein, Alfred, jt. auth. see National Research Council Panel on Sentencing Research.
Blumstein, Andree K. Misogyny & Idealization in the Courtly Romance. (Studien zur Germanistik, Anglistik und Komparatistik: Vol. 41). vi, 189p. (Orig.). 1977. pap. 17.00x (ISBN 3-416-01212-7, Pub. by Bouvier Verlag W Germany). Benjamins North Am.
Blumstein, James F. & Martin, Eddie J., eds. The Urban Scene in the Seventies. LC 74-3452. 260p. 1974. 14.95x (ISBN 0-8265-1196-1). Vanderbilt U Pr.
Blumstein, James F. & Walter, Benjamin, eds. Growing Metropolis: Aspects of Development in Nashville. LC 74-32320. 357p. 1975. 17.50x (ISBN 0-8265-1200-3). Vanderbilt U Pr.
Blumstein, Philip & Schwartz, Pepper. American Couples. 1985. pap. 9.95 (ISBN 0-671-52353-8). PB.
--American Couples: Money, Work, & Sex. LC 83-62066. (Illus.). 512p. 1983. text ed. 19.95 (ISBN 0-688-03772-0). Morrow.
Blumstein, Sheila, jt. auth. see Goodglass, Harold.
Blumstein, Sheila E. A Phonological Investigation of Aphasic Speech. (Janua Linguarum Ser. Minor: No. 153). 1973. pap. text ed. 14.00x (ISBN 90-2792-448-1). Mouton.
Blunck, Jurgen. Mars & Its Satellites: A Detailed Commentary on the Nomenclature. 2nd ed. (Illus.). 1982. 10.00 (ISBN 0-682-49777-0, University). Exposition Pr FL.
Blundell. Wild Flowers of Kenya. 29.95 (ISBN 0-00-219317-5, Collins Pub England). Greene.
Blundell, Alan J. Bond Graphs for Modelling Engineering Systems. LC 82-18688. (Electrical & Electronic Engineering Ser.). 151p. 1982. 44.95x (ISBN 0-470-27546-4). Halsted Pr.
Blundell, Derek. The Thin Grey Line. 224p. 1984. 16.95 (ISBN 0-241-11046-7, Pub. by Hamish Hamilton England). David & Charles.
Blundell, J. E. & McArthur, R. A. Obesity and Its Treatment. Horrobin, D. F., ed. (Obesity Research Review Ser.: Vol. I). 104p. 1979. 19.95 (ISBN 0-87705-967-5). Human Sci Pr.
Blundell, John. Physiological Psychology. (Essential Psychology Ser.). 1975. pap. 4.95x (ISBN 0-416-81950-8, NO. 2610). Methuen Inc.
Blundell, Mary. Pastorals of Dorset. facsimile ed. LC 73-160931. (Short Story Index Reprint Ser.). Repr. of 1901 ed. 20.00 (ISBN 0-8369-3910-7). Ayer Co Pubs.
Blundell, Pat. Granma Pritchard's Receipts. 48p. 1982. pap. 5.95 (ISBN 0-933992-23-8). Coffee Break.
Blundell, Susan. Theories of Evolution in Antiquity. 208p. 1985. 29.00 (ISBN 0-7099-3212-X, Pub. by Croom Helm Ltd). Longwood Pub Group.
Blundell, T. L. & Johnson, Louise. Protein Crystallography. (Molecular Biology Ser.). 1976. 87.50 (ISBN 0-12-108350-0). Acad Pr.
Blundell, T. L., jt. auth. see Noble, D.
Blundell, T. L., jt. ed. see Noble, D.
Blunden, Caroline & Elvin, Mark. Cultural Atlas of China. (Cultural Atlas Ser.). (Illus.). 237p. 1983. 35.00 (ISBN 0-87196-132-6, 82-675304). Facts on File.
Blunden, E. Charles Lamb & His Life: Recorded by His Contemporaries. 59.95 (ISBN 0-87968-841-6). Gordon Pr.
--Shelley & Keats As They Struck Their Contemporaries. LC 70-174689. (English Literature Ser., No. 33). 1971. Repr. of 1925 ed. lib. bdg. 32.95x (ISBN 0-8383-1341-8). Haskell.
Blunden, Edmond, ed. English Villages. 48p. 1980. Repr. lib. bdg. 12.50 (ISBN 0-89987-052-X). Darby Bks.
Blunden, Edmund. After the Bombing, & Other Short Poems. facsimile ed. LC 70-164589. (Select Bibliographies Reprint Ser). Repr. of 1949 ed. 10.00 (ISBN 0-8369-5873-X). Ayer Co Pubs.
--Charles Lamb & His Contemporaries. ix, 215p. 1967. Repr. of 1933 ed. 22.50 (ISBN 0-208-00461-0, Archon). Shoe String.
--Charles Lamb: His Life Recorded by His Contemporaries. 1934. Repr. 35.00 (ISBN 0-8274-2039-0). R West.
--Chaucer to B. V. LC 72-194107. lib. bdg. 20.00 (ISBN 0-8414-1056-9). Folcroft.
--Coleridge. LC 73-9668. 1971. Repr. of 1934 ed. lib. bdg. 20.00 (ISBN 0-8414-3164-7). Folcroft.
--Edward Gibbon & His Age. 1978. Repr. of 1935 ed. lib. bdg. 7.50 (ISBN 0-8495-0448-1). Arden Lib.
--The Face of England: In a Series of Occasional Sketches. 178p. Repr. of 1932 ed. lib. bdg. 35.00 (ISBN 0-89760-173-4). Telegraph Bks.
--Favourite Studies in English Literature: Lectures Given at Keio University in 1948 & 1950. 130p. 1980. lib. bdg. 25.00 (ISBN 0-89760-823-2). Telegraph Bks.
--Great Short Stories of the War. Repr. of 1933 ed. 40.00 (ISBN 0-89987-158-5). Darby Bks.
--Keat's Publisher: A Memoir of John Taylor. LC 77-121320. (Illus.). Repr. of 1936 ed. lib. bdg. 27.50x (ISBN 0-678-00683-0). Kelley.
--Nature in English Literature. LC 72-191814. 1929. lib. bdg. 15.00 (ISBN 0-8414-2528-0). Folcroft.
--Nature in English Literature. LC 74-113330. 1970. Repr. of 1929 ed. 15.00x (ISBN 0-8046-0941-1, Pub. by Kennikat). Assoc Faculty Pr.
--On Shelley. LC 72-191827. 1938. lib. bdg. 17.50 (ISBN 0-8414-2529-9). Folcroft.
--On the Poems of Henry Vaughan. LC 74-14681. 1927. lib. bdg. 15.00 (ISBN 0-8414-9869-5). Folcroft.
--The Poems of William Collins. LC 73-11422. 1929. lib. bdg. 30.00 (ISBN 0-8414-3214-7). Folcroft.
--Selected Poems. Marsack, Robyn, ed. 64p. pap. 8.50 (ISBN 0-85635-425-2). Carcanet.
--Shakespeare to Hardy. LC 73-16007. 1948. lib. bdg. 17.50 (ISBN 0-8414-9862-8). Folcroft.
--Shakespeare's Significance. LC 73-9822. 1929. lib. bdg. 12.50 (ISBN 0-8414-3160-4). Folcroft.
--Shelley & Keats As They Struck Their Contemporaries. LC 74-16306. 1925. lib. bdg. 17.50 (ISBN 0-8414-9878-4). Folcroft.
--Shelley's Defence of Poetry & Blunden's Lectures on Defence. LC 73-16387. 1948. lib. bdg. 10.00 (ISBN 0-8414-9852-0). Folcroft.
--Sketches in the Life of John Clare. 1931. lib. bdg. 20.00 (ISBN 0-8414-9932-2). Folcroft.
--Sons of Light: A Series of Lectures on English Writers. LC 74-5382. 1949. lib. bdg. 17.50 (ISBN 0-8414-3148-5). Folcroft.
--Three Young Poets. LC 73-10005. 1959. lib. bdg. 12.50 (ISBN 0-8414-3137-X). Folcroft.
Blunden, Edmund, jt. auth. see Clark, Leonard.
Blunden, Edmund, ed. Favorite Studies in English Literature: Milton, Shelley, Hazlitt, Blake, Wordsworth, Coleridge, Tennyson. 130p. 1983. Repr. of 1950 ed. lib. bdg. 25.00 (ISBN 0-89760-061-4). Telegraph Bks.
--Selected Poems of Tennyson. (The Poetry Bookshelf). 1960. pap. text ed. 5.00x (ISBN 0-435-15029-4). Heinemann Ed.
Blunden, Edmund & Porter, Alan, eds. John Clare Poems: Chiefly from Manuscript. 1920. 25.00 (ISBN 0-8274-2618-6). R West.
Blunden, Edmund, ed. see Lamb, Charles.
Blunden, Edmund C. Edmund Blunden. facs. ed. LC 76-117761. (Essay Index Reprint Ser). 1961. 24.50 (ISBN 0-8369-1743-X). Ayer Co Pubs.
--Edward Gibbon & His Age. LC 74-14702. 1974. Repr. of 1935 ed. lib. bdg. 7.50 (ISBN 0-8414-3287-2). Folcroft.
--Leigh Hunt's Examiner Examined: Comprising Some Accounts of That Celebrated Newspaper's Contents. 1973. Repr. of 1928 ed. 6.95 (ISBN 0-8274-1349-1). R West.
--Mind's Eye: Essays. facs. ed. LC 67-28745. (Essay Index Reprint Ser). 1934. 18.00 (ISBN 0-8369-0218-1). Ayer Co Pubs.
--Votive Tablets: Studies Chiefly Appreciative of English Authors & Books. facs. ed. LC 67-26716. (Essay Index Reprint Ser). 1932. 20.00 (ISBN 0-8369-0219-X). Ayer Co Pubs.
Blunden, Edmund C. & Mellor, Bernard. Wayside Poems of the Early Eighteenth Century: An Anthology. LC 64-54686. pap. 43.50 (ISBN 0-317-28807-5, 2020773). Bks Demand UMI.
Blunden, Godfrey. The Land & People of Australia. rev. ed. LC 73-37234. (Ports. of the Nations Ser.). (Illus.). (gr. 6 up). 1972. lib. bdg. 10.89 (ISBN 0-397-31256-3). Lipp Jr Bks.
Blunden, Godfrey & Blunden, Maria. Impressionists & Impressionism. LC 76-12315. (Illus.). 1976. 50.00 (ISBN 0-8478-0047-4). Rizzoli Intl.
--Impressionists & Impressionism. (Illus.). 1980. pap. 17.50 (ISBN 0-8478-0341-4). Rizzoli Intl.
Blunden, Godfrey, jt. auth. see Blunden, Maria.
Blunden, John. Mineral Resources & Their Management. (Themes in Resource Management Ser.). 352p. 1985. pap. text ed. 17.95 (ISBN 0-582-30058-4). Longman.
Blunden, John & Curry, Nigel, eds. The Changing Countryside. LC 85-5283. (Illus.). 270p. (Orig.). 1985. pap. 16.95 (ISBN 0-7099-3297-9, Pub. by Croom Helm Ltd). Longwood Pub Group.
Blunden, John & Haggett, Peter, eds. Fundamentals of Human Geography: A Reader. 1978. text ed. 22.95 (ISBN 0-06-318065-0, IntlDept); pap. text ed. 13.50 (ISBN 0-06-318064-2, IntlDept). Har-Row.
Blunden, John, et al. Regional Analysis & Development. 1974. pap. 6.80x (ISBN 0-06-318013-8, IntlDept). Har-Row.
Blunden, John R., jt. ed. see McGlashan, Neil.
Blunden, Maria & Blunden, Godfrey. Impressionists & Impressionism. (Illus.). 240p. 1977. 50.00 (ISBN 0-8478-0047-4). Rizzoli Intl.
Blunden, Maria, jt. auth. see Blunden, Godfrey.
Blunden, R. Social Development. (Studies in Developmental Paediatrics). (Illus.). 160p. 1982. text ed. 25.00 (ISBN 0-85200-304-8, Pub. by MTP Pr England). Kluwer Academic.
Blunden, W. R. & Black, J. A. The Land Use-Transport System. 2nd ed. (Urban & Regional Planning Ser.: Vol. 2). (Illus.). 264p. 1984. 40.00 (ISBN 0-08-029836-2); pap. 19.20 (ISBN 0-08-029841-9). Pergamon.
Blundeville, Thomas. The Art of Logike. Plainly Taught in the English Tongue. LC 71-26166. (English Experience Ser.: No. 102). 170p. 1969. Repr. of 1599 ed. 25.00 (ISBN 90-221-0102-9). Walter J Johnson.
--A Briefe Description of Universal Mappes & Cardes. LC 79-38159. (English Experience Ser.: No. 438). 44p. 1972. Repr. of 1589 ed. 7.00 (ISBN 90-221-0438-9). Walter J Johnson.
--M. Blundeville, His Exercises Containing Sixe Treatises. LC 78-171736. (English Experience Ser.: No. 361). (Illus.). 718p. 1971. Repr. of 1594 ed. 64.00 (ISBN 90-221-0361-7). Walter J Johnson.
--A Newe Booke, Containing the Arte of Ryding. LC 75-25640. (English Experience Ser.: No. 118). (Illus.). 232p. 1969. Repr. of 1560 ed. 35.00 (ISBN 90-221-0118-5). Walter J Johnson.
--The True Order & Method of Wryting & Reading Hystories. LC 79-84088. (English Experience Ser.: No. 908). 68p. (Eng.). 1979. Repr. of 1574 ed. lib. bdg. 7.00 (ISBN 90-221-0908-9). Walter J Johnson.
Blunt. The Drawings of Poussin. 1979. 57.00x (ISBN 0-300-01971-8). Yale U Pr.
--Organizational Theory & Behaviour. LC 82-17078. 208p. 1984. pap. text ed. 9.95 (ISBN 0-582-64404-6). Longman.
Blunt, Adrian. Law Librarianship. (Outlines of Modern Librarianship Ser.). 1980. 12.00 (ISBN 0-85157-299-5, Pub. by Bingley England). Shoe String.
Blunt, Anne. Bedouin Tribes of the Euphrates, 2 vols. (Illus.). 1968. Repr. of 1879 ed. 85.00x (ISBN 0-7146-1978-7, F Cass Co). Biblio Dist.
--Pilgrimage to Nejd, 2 vols. (Illus.). 1968. Repr. of 1881 ed. 85.00x (ISBN 0-7146-1979-5, F Cass Co). Biblio Dist.
--Pilgrimage to Nejd. (Century Travel Classics Ser.). 1985. pap. 9.95 (ISBN 0-7126-0989-X, Pub. by Century Pubs UK). Hippocrene Bks.
Blunt, Anthony. Art & Architecture in France: 1500-1700. (Pelican History of Art Ser: No. 4). (Illus.). 1973. pap. 18.95x (ISBN 0-14-056104-8, Pelican). Penguin.
--Art & Architecture in France, 1500-1700. rev. ed. (Pelican History of Art Ser.: No. 4). 1954. 35.00 (ISBN 0-670-13386-8, Pelican). Viking.
--Artistic Theory in Italy, 1450-1600. 1956. 25.00x (ISBN 0-19-817106-4); pap. 7.95x (ISBN 0-19-881050-4, OPB). Oxford U Pr.
--Borromini. LC 78-11320. (Illus.). 1979. text ed. 17.50x (ISBN 0-674-07925-6). Harvard U Pr.
--Francois Mansart & the Origins of French Classical Architecture. LC 42-1541. 1941. Repr. 45.00x (ISBN 0-403-07230-1). Somerset Pub.
--Guide to Baroque Rome. LC 82-47546. (Icon Editions). (Illus.). 256p. 1982. 33.65i (ISBN 0-06-430395-0, HarpT). Har-Row.
Blunt, Anthony & Lockspeiser, Edward. French Art & Music since Fifteen Hundred. 1974. pap. 4.95x (ISBN 0-416-81650-9, NO. 2095). Methuen Inc.
Blunt, Anthony, ed. Treasures from Chatsworth: The Devonshire Inheritance. LC 79-89141. (Illus.). 236p. (Orig.). 1979. soft bdg. 12.00 (ISBN 0-88397-007-4, Pub. by Intl Exhibit Foun). C E Tuttle.
Blunt, Anthony, ed. see De Chantelou, Paul F.
Blunt, Anthony, jt. ed. see Friedlaender, Walter.
Blunt, Anthony F. The Art of William Blake. LC 59-12399. (Bantam Lectures in America). (Illus.). 114p. 1959. 24.00x (ISBN 0-231-02364-2). Columbia U Pr.
Blunt, Sir Anthony, ed. Baroque & Rococo: Architecture & Decoration. LC 78-4446. (Illus.). 1978. 75.00i (ISBN 0-06-010417-1, HarpT). Har-Row.
Blunt, David. Elephant. (Illus.). 260p. 1972. Repr. of 1933 ed. 17.50x (ISBN 0-87556-535-2). Saifer.
Blunt, Hugh F. Great Magdelens. facs. ed. LC 71-86731. (Essay Index Reprint Ser). 1928. 18.50 (ISBN 0-8369-1122-9). Ayer Co Pubs.
--Great Penitents. facs. ed. LC 67-30198. (Essay Index Reprint Ser). 1921. 17.00 (ISBN 0-8369-0220-3). Ayer Co Pubs.

Blunt, J. A Historical Sketch of the Formation of the Confederacy, Particularly with Reference to the Provincial Limits & the Jurisdiction of the General Government Over Indian Tribes & the Public Territory. Repr. of 1825 ed. 15.00 (ISBN 0-527-09000-X). Kraus Repr.

--Stage Dialects. 1968. text ed. 20.95 scp (ISBN 0-8102-0046-5, HarpC); scp reels to accompany text 34.50; scp cassettes to accompany texts o.p. 41.90 (ISBN 0-690-01523-2). Har-Row.

Blunt, J. H., ed. The Myroure of Oure Lady. (EETS, ES Ser.: No. 19). Repr. of 1873 ed. 40.00 (ISBN 0-527-00232-1). Kraus Repr.

Blunt, Jerry. Composite Art of Acting. 1966. text ed. write for info. (ISBN 0-02-311150-X, 31115). Macmillan.

--More Stage Dialects. (Illus.). 1980. text ed. 20.95 scp (ISBN 0-06-040784-0, HarpC); scp cassettes to accompany text 35.50 (ISBN 0-06-040796-4). Har-Row.

Blunt, John H. Dictionary of Sects, Heresies, Ecclesiastical Parties & Schools of Religious Thought. LC 74-9653. 1974. Repr. of 1874 ed. 75.00x (ISBN 0-8103-3751-7). Gale.

Blunt, M. H. The Blood of Sheep: Composition & Function. (Illus.). 250p. 1975. 43.00 (ISBN 0-387-07234-9). Springer-Verlag.

Blunt, Reginald. The Carlyle's Chelsea Home. LC 75-30875. (Studies in Carlyle, No. 53). 1975. lib. bdg. 49.95x (ISBN 0-8383-2079-1). Haskell.

--The Carlyles' Chelsea Home: Being Some Account of Number Five Cheyne Row. 98p. 1982. Repr. of 1895 ed. lib. bdg. 35.00 (ISBN 0-89760-088-6). Telegraph Bks.

--The Carlyles' Chelsea Home, Being Some Account of No. 5 Cheyne Row. 1973. Repr. of 1895 ed. 20.00 (ISBN 0-8274-1469-2). R West.

Blunt, Vernon T. Heart Challenger. 1985. 6.95 (ISBN 0-8062-2471-1). Carlton.

Blunt, W. & Raphael, S. The Illustrated Herbal. 1981. 35.00x (ISBN 0-686-78791-9, Pub. by RHS Ent England). State Mutual Bk.

Blunt, Wilfred. England's Michelangelo: A Biography of George Frederic Watts. (Illus.). 1978. 25.00 (ISBN 0-241-89174-4, Pub. by Hamish Hamilton England). David & Charles.

Blunt, Wilfrid S. The Land War in Ireland. LC 75-28808. (Celtic Ser.). 528p. Repr. of 1912 ed. 49.50 (ISBN 0-404-13801-2). AMS Pr.

--My Diaries: Being a Personal Narrative of Events, 1888-1914. LC 79-26837. 1980. Repr. of 1921 ed. lib. bdg. 69.00x (ISBN 0-374-90691-2). Vol. 1, 419 Pp. Vol. 2, 484 Pp. Octagon.

--Poetical Works of Wilfrid Scawen Blunt, 2 Vols. LC 14-22324. 1968. Repr. of 1914 ed. Set. 59.00 (ISBN 0-403-00110-2). Scholarly.

Bluntschli, J. K. The Theory of the State. 1979. Repr. of 1892 ed. lib. bdg. 65.00 (ISBN 0-8495-0543-7). Arden Lib.

Bluntschli, Johann C. Geschichte des Alligemeinen Staatsrechts und der Politik. Mayer, J. P., ed. LC 78-67333. (European Political Thought Ser.). (Ger.). 1979. Repr. of 1864 ed. lib. bdg. 46.00x (ISBN 0-405-11679-9). Ayer Co Pubs.

Bluntschli, Johann K. Theory of the State. facsimile ed. LC 77-152975. (Select Bibliographies Reprint Ser). Repr. of 1895 ed. 29.00 (ISBN 0-8369-5727-X). Ayer Co Pubs.

Blurton-Jones, N. G., ed. Ethological Studies of Child Behaviour. (Illus.). 416p. 1974. 54.50 (ISBN 0-521-08260-9); pap. 17.95x (ISBN 0-521-09855-6). Cambridge U Pr.

Bluske, Margaret K. & Walther, Elizabeth K. Das Erste Jahr. 4th ed. (Illus.). 1980. text ed. 20.50 scp (ISBN 0-06-040788-3, HarpC); Programmed Assignment Bk. scp 10.40 (ISBN 0-06-040795-6); instructor's manual avail. (ISBN 0-06-360784-0); scp tapes 385.00 (ISBN 0-06-047490-4). Har-Row.

Blusse, L. & Gaastra, F., eds. Companies & Trade: Essays on Overseas Trading During the Ancient Regime. 272p. 1982. 44.00 (ISBN 90-6021-473-0, Pub. by Martinus Nijhoff Netherlands). Kluwer Academic.

Blust, Robert A. The Proto-Oceanic Palatals. 193p. 1979. pap. text ed. 15.00x (ISBN 0-8248-0684-0, Pub. by Polynesian Soc). UH Pr.

Blustain, Harvey. Resource Management & Agricultural Development in Jamaica: Lessons for a Participatory Approach. (Special Series on Resource Management: No. 2). 151p. (Orig.). 1982. pap. text ed. 9.00 (ISBN 0-86731-083-9). RDC Ctr Intl Stud.

Blustain, Harvey & LeFranc, Elsie, eds. Strategies for Organization of Small-Farm Agriculture in Jamaica. 217p. (Orig.). 1981. pap. text ed. 8.00 (ISBN 0-86731-013-8). RDC Ctr Intl Stud.

Blustain, Harvey S., jt. auth. see Goldsmith, Arthur A.

Blustein, Jeffrey. Parents & Children: The Ethics of the Family. 1982. pap. text ed. 9.95x (ISBN 0-19-503073-7). Oxford U Pr.

Blustein, Lotte & Geary, Rosemary J. Writing the Research Paper. rev. ed. 57p. (gr. 7 up). 1981. pap. text ed. 5.50 (ISBN 0-9605248-2-7). Blustein-Geary.

Bluth, B. J. Parsons' General Theory of Action: A Summary of the Basic Theory. LC 82-3408. (Illus.). 131p. (Orig.). 1982. pap. text ed. 9.95 (ISBN 0-937654-02-7). Natl Behavior.

Bluth, B. J. & McNeal, S. R., eds. Update on Space, Vol. 1. LC 80-52460. (Illus., Orig.). 1981. pap. 7.95 (ISBN 0-937654-00-0). Natl Behavior.

Bluth, Brad. The Buddies in a Day for Knights. (Illus.). (ps-k). 1984. 5.95 (ISBN 0-317-16178-4). Ideals PA.

--Siegfried's Silent Night. (Christmas Bks.). (Illus.). 32p. (gr. k-4). 1983. 10.60 (ISBN 0-516-09159-X). Childrens.

Bluth, Brad & Bluth, Toby. Siegfried's Silent Night. 32p. (Orig.). (gr. k-6). 1983. 3.95 (ISBN 0-8249-8059-X). Ideals.

Bluth Brothers. A Day for Knights. (Buddies Ser.). (Illus.). 48p. (gr. k-6). 1984. 5.95 (ISBN 0-8249-8062-X). Ideals.

--Somebody's Hero. (Buddies Ser.). (Illus.). 48p. (gr. k-6). 1984. 5.95 (ISBN 0-8249-8063-8). Ideals.

Bluth, Doug. Football's Twin-I: A Complete Multiple Option Attack. LC 84-3138. 1984. 18.95x (ISBN 0-13-324302-8, Busn). P-H.

Bluth, John V. Concordance to the Doctrine & Covenants. 8.95 (ISBN 0-87747-048-0). Deseret Bk.

Bluth, Thomas F., ed. see Nash, Gerald D., et al.

Bluth, Toby. The Buddies Tenderfoot. (Illus.). 48p. (gr. k-6). 1985. 5.95 (ISBN 0-8249-8088-3). Ideals.

--Little Luv Angel. (Illus.). 48p. (gr. k-6). 1985. 5.95 (ISBN 0-8249-8093-X). Ideals.

--Mark Twain's Tom Sawyer. (Illus.). 48p. (gr. k-6). 1985. 5.95 (ISBN 0-8249-8097-2). Ideals.

Bluth, Toby, jt. auth. see Bluth, Brad.

Bluthardt, O. D. See-Me-Nots: The Reality of the Invisibles. (Illus.). 1982. 8.95 (ISBN 0-533-05249-1). Vantage.

--Universal Energy & Intelligence. 1985. 12.50 (ISBN 0-682-40237-0). Exposition Pr FL.

Bly. The Crucible (Miller) (Book Notes). 1984. pap. 2.50 (ISBN 0-8120-3408-2). Barron.

Bly, et al. Walt Whitman: The Measure of His Song. 1st ed. Perlman, Jim, et al, eds. LC 80-85268. (Illus.). 454p. (Orig.). 1981. 20.00 (ISBN 0-930100-09-3); pap. 10.00 (ISBN 0-930100-08-5). Holy Cow.

Bly, Carol. Backbone: Short Stories. (Milkweed Fiction Ser.). (Illus.). 128p. (Orig.). 1985. pap. 6.95 (ISBN 0-915943-04-2). Milkweed Ed.

--Letters from the Country. 1982. pap. 4.95 (ISBN 0-14-006196-7). Penguin.

Bly, Janet. Hawaiian Computer Mystery. (Making Choices Ser.). (Illus.). 124p. (Orig.). (gr. 4-8). 1985. pap. 2.50 (ISBN 0-89191-954-6, 59543, Chariot Bks). Cook.

Bly, Janet, jt. auth. see Bly, Stephen.

Bly, John. Discovering English Furniture. (Discovering Ser.: No. 223). (Illus.). 95p. (Orig.). 1983. pap. 6.95 (ISBN 0-85263-359-9, Pub. by Shire Pubns England). Seven Hills Bks.

--Discovering Hallmarks on English Silver. 6th ed. (Discovering Ser.: No. 38). (Illus.). 64p. 1983. pap. 3.50 (ISBN 0-85263-657-1, Pub. by Shire Pubns Eng). Seven Hills Bks.

Bly, Mary, jt. auth. see Dizick, Missy.

Bly, Robert. The Eight Stages of Translation. LC 82-60670. (Poetics Ser.: No. 2). 107p. 1983. pap. text ed. 7.95 (ISBN 0-937672-10-6). Rowan Tree.

--Four Ramages. (Illus.). 16p. (Orig.). 1983. pap. 3.95 (ISBN 0-935306-11-0). Barnwood Pr.

--Leaping Poetry: An Idea with Poems & Translations. LC 73-6243. 112p. 1978. pap. 4.95 (ISBN 0-8070-6393-2, BP462). Beacon Pr.

--Light Around the Body. 1967. 8.95 (ISBN 0-06-010388-4, HarpT). Har-Row.

--The Light Around the Body. LC 84-48640. 80p. 1985. pap. 5.72i (ISBN 0-06-090786-X, CN 786, CN). Har-Row.

--Loving a Woman in Two Worlds. LC 84-12704. 96p. 1985. 12.95 (ISBN 0-385-27418-1, Dial). Doubleday.

--The Man in the Black Coat Turns. LC 81-3153. 1981. 10.95 (ISBN 0-385-27186-7, Dial). Doubleday.

--The Man in the Black Coat Turns: Poems. 76p. 1983. pap. 7.95 (ISBN 0-14-042303-6). Penguin.

--The Morning Glory. LC 74-15811. 96p. 1975. 8.95i (ISBN 0-06-010368-X, HarpT); (HarpT). Har-Row.

--Out of the Rolling Ocean & Other Love Poems. LC 84-6442. 1984. Handcased & Signed 30.00x (ISBN 0-915408-29-5); pap. 3.50 (ISBN 0-915408-28-7). Ally Pr.

--Silence in the Snowy Fields. LC 62-18340. (Wesleyan Poetry Program: Vol. 15). (Orig.). 1962. 15.00x (ISBN 0-8195-2015-2); pap. 7.95 (ISBN 0-8195-1015-7). Wesleyan U Pr.

--Sleepers Joining Hands. LC 72-123916. 96p. 1973. 8.95i (ISBN 0-06-010381-7, HarpT). Har-Row.

--Sleepers Joining Hands. LC 84-48642. (Illus.). 80p. 1985. pap. 5.72i (ISBN 0-06-090785-1, CN 785, CN). Har-Row.

--Talking All Morning. (Poets on Poetry Ser.). 316p. 1980. pap. 7.95 (ISBN 0-472-15760-4). U of Mich Pr.

--This Body Is Made of Camphor & Gopherwood. LC 76-47258. (Illus.). 1977. 7.95i (ISBN 0-06-010363-9, HarpT); pap. 7.64i (ISBN 0-06-010414-7, TD-277, HarpT). Har-Row.

--This Tree Will Be Here for a Thousand Years. LC 78-22449. 1979. 8.95i (ISBN 0-06-010358-2, HarpT); pap. 5.72i (ISBN 0-06-090713-4, CN-713, HarpT). Har-Row.

--Waking from Newton's Sleep: Selected Essays of Literary Imagination. 1986. 15.95 (ISBN 0-385-27508-0, DP). Doubleday.

Bly, Robert & Richter, Franz. Old Man Rubbing His Eyes. 4th ed. LC 72-77913. (Illus.). 1975. 15.50 (ISBN 0-87775-050-5); pap. 5.00 (ISBN 0-87775-034-3). Unicorn Pr.

Bly, Robert, ed. Neruda & Vallejo: Selected Poems. 1971. pap. 8.95x (ISBN 0-8070-6421-1, BP376). Beacon Pr.

--News of the Universe: Poems of Twofold Consciousness. LC 79-12812. 312p. 1980. 15.95 (ISBN 0-87156-198-0); pap. 8.95 (ISBN 0-87156-199-9). Sierra.

--Selected Poems of Rainer Maria Rilke: A Translation from the German & Commentary. LC 78-2114. 192p. 1981. 15.34i (ISBN 0-06-010432-5, CN727, HarpT); pap. 8.17i (ISBN 0-06-090727-4). Har-Row.

--Seventies No. 1: An Anthology of Leaping Poetry. pap. 1.50 (ISBN 0-685-31525-8). Eighties Pr.

--Ten Love Poems. 1981. pap. 3.50 (ISBN 0-915408-24-4). Ally Pr.

Bly, Robert, ed. see Ignatow, David.

Bly, Robert, ed. see Jacosen, Rolf.

Bly, Robert, intro. by see Sonnevi, Goran.

Bly, Robert, tr. The Kabir Book: Forty-Four of the Ecstatic Poems of Kabir. LC 76-7737. (Illus.). 1977. pap. 5.95 (ISBN 0-8070-6379-7, BP544). Beacon Pr.

--Times Alone: Selected Poems of Antonio Machado. 176p. 1983. 19.50x (ISBN 0-8195-5087-6); pap. 9.95 (ISBN 0-8195-6081-2). Wesleyan U Pr.

Bly, Robert & Kirkland, Will, trs. Selected Poems & Prose of Antonio Machado. 1983. pap. 5.00 (ISBN 0-934834-34-2). White Pine.

Bly, Robert, tr. see Ekelof, Gunnar.

Bly, Robert, tr. see Hamsun, Knut.

Bly, Robert, tr. see Kabir.

Bly, Robert, tr. see Machado, Antonio.

Bly, Robert, tr. see Rilke, Rainer M.

Bly, Robert, tr. see Rumi.

Bly, Robert, tr. see Transtromer, Tomas.

Bly, Robert W. Computers: Cookies, Marbles & Games. (A First Look Bk.). (Illus.). 96p. (gr. 2-6). 1984. pap. 3.95 (ISBN 0-88693-057-X). Banbury Bks.

--Computers: Pascal, Pong & Pac-Man. (A First Look Bk.). (Illus.). 88p. (gr. 2-6). 1984. pap. 3.95 (ISBN 0-88693-055-3). Banbury Bks.

--The Copywriter's Handbook. 368p. 1985. 17.95 (ISBN 0-396-08546-6); pap. 10.95 (ISBN 0-396-08547-4). Dodd.

--A Dictionary of Computer Words. (Illus.). 160p. (gr. 6-10). 1983. pap. 4.95 (ISBN 0-440-01920-6, Banbury). Dell.

--The Personal Computer in Advertising: Using Technology to Increase Creativity. 256p. 1984. pap. 14.95 (Banbury Bks). Putnam Pub Group.

--The Personal Computer in Advertising: Using Technology to Increase Creativity. 256p. 1984. pap. 14.95 (ISBN 0-88693-003-0). Banbury Bks.

--Ronald's Dumb Computer. (Illus.). 88p. (gr. 6-9). 1983. pap. 3.95 (ISBN 0-440-07486-X, Banbury). Dell.

Bly, Robert W. & Blake, Gary. Dream Jobs: A Guide to Tomorrow's Top Careers. LC 83-6773. (General Trade Bks.: I-581). 240p. 1983. pap. 8.95 (ISBN 0-471-89204-1, Pub. by Wiley Pr). Wiley.

--Technical Writing: Structure, Standards & Style. LC 82-15223. 160p. 1982. 11.95 (ISBN 0-07-006174-2); pap. 6.95 (ISBN 0-07-006173-4). McGraw.

Bly, Robert W., jt. auth. see Blake, Gary.

Bly, Stephen. Quality Living in a Complicated Age. LC 84-47803. 170p. (Orig.). 1984. 3.95 (ISBN 0-89840-071-6). Heres Life.

--Trouble in Quartz Mountain Tunnel. (Making Choices Ser.). (Illus.). 124p. (gr. 4-8). 1985. pap. 2.50 (ISBN 0-89191-979-1, 59790, Chariot Bks). Cook.

Bly, Stephen & Bly, Janet. Devotions with a Difference. LC 82-8304. 128p. (gr. 3 up). 1982. pap. 5.95 (ISBN 0-8024-1789-2). Moody.

--Questions I'd Like to Ask. LC 82-2252. 1982. 3.50 (ISBN 0-8024-7058-0). Moody.

Bly, Stephen A. The President Is Stuck in the Mud. (Making Choices Ser.: No. 4). (Orig.). (gr. 3-8). 1982. pap. 2.50 (ISBN 0-89191-661-X, 56614). Cook.

Bly, Tacey, compiled by. Poems & Hymns of Christ's Sweet Singer: Frances Ridley Havergal. LC 77-86549. 1977. 7.95 (ISBN 0-87983-163-4); pap. 3.95 (ISBN 0-87983-164-2). Keats.

Blyakhman, L. & Shkaratan, O. Man at Work. 306p. 1977. 4.95 (ISBN 0-8285-0242-0, Pub. by Progress Pubs USSR). Imported Pubns.

Blyakhman, L. S., et al. Questions on Economics & Planning of Scientific Research (Collection of Articles) LC 77-136731. 287p. 1969. 34.50 (ISBN 0-403-04487-1). Mgmt Info Serv.

Blyden, Edward W. Black Spokesman. Lynch, Hollis, ed. 354p. 1971. 30.00x (ISBN 0-7146-1745-8, F Cass Co). Biblio Dist.

Blydenburgh, John C., jt. auth. see Rai, Kul B.

Blyiliterature. Developing Successful Sales Literature. 1985. pap. 9.95 (ISBN 0-471-82525-5). Wiley.

Blymire, Lynn, et al. A. C. T. I. (gr. k-4). 1981. pap. 3.00 (ISBN 0-931992-40-0). Penns Valley.

Blyskal, Jeff & Blyskal, Marie. PR-How the Public Relations Industry Writes the News. 252p. 1985. 17.95 (ISBN 0-688-04788-2). Morrow.

Blyskal, Marie, jt. auth. see Blyskal, Jeff.

Blyth, Alan. Development, Experience & Curriculum in Primary Education. LC 84-40036. 208p. 1984. 22.50 (ISBN 0-312-19686-5). St Martin.

--Opera on Record. LC 81-47801. 688p. 1982. pap. 11.06i (ISBN 0-06-090910-2, CN 910, CN). Har-Row.

--Opera on Record. (Illus.). 672p. 1980. 29.95 (ISBN 0-09-139980-7, NO. 0215, Pub. by Hutchinson England). Methuen Inc.

--Opera on Record 3. LC 84-48475. 355p. 1984. 24.95 (ISBN 0-89341-531-6). Longwood Pub Group.

Blyth, Alan, ed. Opera on Record Two. 1984. 24.95 (ISBN 0-8253-0212-9). Beaufort Bks NY.

Blyth, Dale A. & Karnes, Elizabeth L., eds. Philosophy, Policies & Programs for Early Adolescent Education: An Annotated Bibliography. LC 81-4237. 704p. 1981. lib. bdg. 55.00 (ISBN 0-313-22687-3, BEA/). Greenwood.

Blyth, F. G. & De Freitas, M. H. A Geology for Engineers. 6th ed. 557p. 1974. pap. 24.50x (ISBN 0-8448-0612-9). Crane-Russak Co.

Blyth, F. G. & Defreitas, M. H. Geology for Engineers. 7th ed. 1984. 29.50 (ISBN 0-444-00946-9). Elsevier.

Blyth, Hugh F., jt. auth. see Stevenson, Don.

Blyth, Joan. Place & Time with Children: Five to Nine. (Teaching 5-13 Ser.). 192p. 1984. 27.50 (ISBN 0-7099-0661-7, Pub. by Croom Helm Ltd); pap. 13.00 (ISBN 0-7099-0662-5). Longwood Pub Group.

Blyth, John A. English University Adult Education 1908-1958. LC 82-21698. 384p. 1982. 20.00 (ISBN 0-7190-0903-0, Pub. by Manchester Univ Pr). Longwood Pub Group.

Blyth, John W. Whitehead's Theory of Knowledge. LC 73-9672. 112p. 1973. Repr. of 1941 ed. 18.00 (ISBN 0-527-09100-6). Kraus Repr.

Blyth, Mary M. & Blyth, W. John. Telecommunications: Concepts, Development & Management. 352p. 1985. text ed. 30.08 scp (ISBN 0-672-97991-8); scp instr's. guide 7.33 (ISBN 0-672-97992-6). Bobbs.

Blyth, Myrna. Cousin Suzanne. 1976. pap. 1.75 (ISBN 0-380-00668-5, 29082). Avon.

Blyth, R. H. Buddhist Sermons on Christian Texts. 1976. pap. 2.95 (ISBN 0-89346-000-1). Heian Intl.

--Edo Satirical Verse Anthologies. (Illus.). 1961. 29.50 (ISBN 0-89346-015-X, Pub. by Hokuseido Pr.). Heian Intl.

--Haiku, 4 vols. 1981. pap. 11.95 (ISBN 0-89346-184-9). Vol. 1 (ISBN 0-89346-158-X). Vol. 2 (ISBN 0-89346-159-8). Vol. 3 (ISBN 0-89346-160-1). Vol. 4 (ISBN 0-89346-161-X). Set. 47.80. Heian Intl.

--Japanese Life & Character in Senryu. (Illus.). 1960. 39.50 (ISBN 0-89346-069-9, Pub. by Hokuseido Pr). Heian Intl.

--Zen & Zen Classics, Vol. 1. 123p. 1982. pap. 4.95 (ISBN 0-89346-204-7). Heian Intl.

--Zen & Zen Classics, Vol. 2. 211p. 1982. pap. 5.95 (ISBN 0-89346-205-5). Heian Intl.

--Zen in English Literature & Oriental Classics. (Illus.). 460p. Date not set. pap. price not set (ISBN 0-89346-207-1). Heian Intl.

Blyth, Reginald H. Senryu: Japanese Satirical Verses. LC 72-98820. Repr. of 1949 ed. lib. bdg. 18.75x (ISBN 0-8371-2958-3, BLSE). Greenwood.

Blyth, T. S. Module Theory: An Approach to Linear Algebra. (Illus.). 1977. 49.00x (ISBN 0-19-853162-1). Oxford U Pr.

Blyth, T. S. & Janowitz, M. F. Residuation Theory. LC 77-142177. 380p. 1972. text ed. 72.00 (ISBN 0-08-016408-0). Pergamon.

Blyth, W. A. & Derricott, R. The Social Significance of Middle Schools. 1977. 31.50 (ISBN 0-7134-0487-6, Pub. by Batsford England); pap. 17.50 (ISBN 0-7134-0488-4, Pub. by Batsford England). David & Charles.

Blyth, W. John, jt. auth. see Blyth, Mary M.

Blythe, A. R. Electrical Properties of Polymers. LC 77-85690. (Cambridge Solid State Science Ser.). (Illus.). 201p. 1980. pap. text ed. 15.95 (ISBN 0-521-29825-3). Cambridge U Pr.

--Electrical Properties of Polymers. LC 77-85690. (Solid State Science Ser.). 1979. 57.50 (ISBN 0-521-21902-7). Cambridge U Pr.

Blythe, Cheryl, jt. auth. see Sackett, Susan.

Blythe, H. J., ed. see International Symposium on the Decontamination of Nuclear Installations.

Blythe, Hal T., et al. Competencies in Materials Development & Machine Operation, Self Directive Activities: A Functional Approach. 2nd ed. (Illus.). 173p. 1982. pap. text ed. 7.95x (ISBN 0-89641-114-1). American Pr.

Blythe, Ian. History of the Market Research Society. 300p. 1985. text ed. write for info. (ISBN 0-566-05005-6). Gower Pub Co.

Blythe, L. N., ed. see Ebel, Jurgen.

Blythe, L. N., ed. see Hasan, Khaja S.

Blythe, LeGette. William Henry Belk: Merchant of the South. LC 58-14574. xvi, 271p. 1950. 17.50 (ISBN 0-8078-0729-X). U of NC Pr.

Blythe, Leonora. Carolina. 224p. 1981. pap. 1.95 (ISBN 0-449-50205-8, Crest). Fawcett.

--Helene. 1979. pap. 1.75 (ISBN 0-449-50004-7, Coventry). Fawcett.

--Miranda. 1980. pap. 1.75 (ISBN 0-449-50048-9, Coventry). Fawcett.

--Sally, No. 156. 224p. 1981. pap. 1.50 (ISBN 0-449-50229-5, Coventry). Fawcett.

Blythe, Richard. Dragons & Other Fabulous Beasts. LC 79-51211. (Illus.). (gr. 3-7). 1980. 5.95 (ISBN 0-448-16561-9, G&D). Putnam Pub Group.

Blythe, Ronald. The Age of Illusion. 1984. pap. 6.95 (ISBN 0-19-281423-0). Oxford U Pr.

--Akenfield: Portrait of an English Village. (Pantheon Village Ser.). 1980. pap. 5.95 (ISBN 0-394-73847-0). Pantheon.

--Characters & Their Landscapes. LC 83-7890. (A Helen & Kurt Wolff Bk.). Orig. Title: From the Headlands. 1983. 14.95 (ISBN 0-15-116792-3). HarBraceJ.

--Characters & Their Landscapes. (A Helen & Kurt Wolff Bk.). 216p. 1984. pap. 5.95 (ISBN 0-15-616763-8, Harv). HarBraceJ.

--The View in Winter. 288p. 1980. pap. 5.95 (ISBN 0-14-005663-7). Penguin.

--The View in Winter: Reflections on Old Age. Wolff, Helen, ed. LC 79-1813. (Helen & Kurt Wolff Bk.). 1979. 12.95 (ISBN 0-15-193638-2). HarBraceJ.

--The Visitors: The Stories of Ronald Blythe. LC 85-8527. (A Helen & Kurt Wolff Book). 256p. 1985. 16.95 (ISBN 0-317-20396-7). HarBracej.

Blythe, Ronald, ed. Places: An Anthology of Britain. (Illus.). 1981. 19.95x (ISBN 0-19-211575-8). Oxford U Pr.

Blythe, Ronald, ed. see Austen, Jane.

Blythe, Ronald, ed. see Hardy, Thomas.

Blythe, Samuel G. Making of a Newspaper Man. LC 76-95085. Repr. of 1912 ed. lib. bdg. 18.75x (ISBN 0-8371-3075-1, BLNM). Greenwood.

Blythe, William, ed. see Hazlitt, William.

Blythin & Samovar. Communicating Effectively on Television. 1984. write for info (ISBN 0-534-03355-5). Wadsworth Pub.

Blyton, Carey. Bananas in Pyjamas. 28p. 1973. 7.50 (ISBN 0-571-10138-0). Transatlantic.

--Bananas in Pyjamas: A Book of Nonsense. 32p. (Orig.). (ps-5). 1976. pap. 3.95 (ISBN 0-571-10671-4). Faber & Faber.

Blyton, Enid. Enid Blyton's Gift Book of Bedtime Stories. (Illus.). 1985. 3.98 (ISBN 0-517-47134-5). Outlet Bk Co.

--Five Caught in a Treacherous Plot. 188p. (gr. 3-6). 1972. pap. 1.95 (ISBN 0-689-70326-0, B-7, Aladdin). Atheneum.

--Five Fall into Adventure. 188p. (gr. 3-6). 1972. pap. 1.95 (ISBN 0-689-70327-9, B-8, Aladdin). Atheneum.

--Five Find a Secret Way. 190p. (gr. 3-6). 1972. pap. 1.95 (ISBN 0-689-70320-1, B-2, Aladdin). Atheneum.

--Five Go to Demon's Rock. 184p. (gr. 3-6). 1980. pap. 1.95 (ISBN 0-689-70478-X, B-10, Aladdin). Atheneum.

--Five Go to Smuggler's Top. 188p. (gr. 3-6). 1972. pap. 1.95 (ISBN 0-689-70323-6, B-4, Aladdin). Atheneum.

--Five Guard a Hidden Discovery. 188p. (gr. 3-6). 1972. pap. 1.95 (ISBN 0-689-70324-4, B-5, Aladdin). Atheneum.

--Five on a Secret Trail. 184p. (gr. 3-6). 1980. pap. 1.95 (ISBN 0-689-70477-1, B-9, Aladdin). Atheneum.

--Five on a Treasure Island. 189p. (gr. 3-6). 1972. pap. 1.95 (ISBN 0-689-70319-8, B-1, Aladdin). Atheneum.

--Five on the Track of a Spook Train. 188p. (gr. 3-6). 1972. pap. 1.95 (ISBN 0-689-70325-2, B-6, Aladdin). Atheneum.

--Five Run Away to Danger. 190p. (gr. 3-6). 1972. pap. 2.50 (ISBN 0-689-70322-8, B-3, Aladdin). Atheneum.

Blyton, Enid see Swan, D. K.

Blyton, Paul. Changes in Working Time: An International Survey. 192p. 1985. 25.00 (ISBN 0-312-12937-8). St Martin.

BNA Editoral Staff. Labor Relations Yearbook 1981. 516p. 1982. text ed. 30.00 (ISBN 0-87179-381-4). BNA.

BNA EDitorial Staff. Alcoholism & Employee Relations. 22p. 1978. pap. 2.50 (ISBN 0-686-88607-0). BNA.

--BNA's Collective Bargaining Briefing Sessions Workbook 1985. 1985. 15.00. BNA.

--Federal Labor & Employment Laws. 322p. 1985. pap. text ed. 20.00 (ISBN 0-87179-478-0). BNA.

--Grievance Guide. 6th ed. LC 82-4338. 386p. 1982. pap. 17.50 (ISBN 0-87179-382-2). BNA.

--Labor Relations Yearbook 1980. 492p. 1981. text ed. 30.00 (ISBN 0-87179-358-X). BNA.

BNA Editorial Staff, ed. Labor Relations Yearbooks. Incl. 1965. 416p (ISBN 0-87179-028-9); 1966. 546p (ISBN 0-87179-029-7); 1967. 646p (ISBN 0-87179-030-0); 1969. 864p (ISBN 0-87179-032-7); 1970. 546p (ISBN 0-87179-033-5); 1971. 464p (ISBN 0-87179-034-3); 1972 O.P (ISBN 0-87179-035-1); 1973. 422p (ISBN 0-87179-036-X); 1974. 570p (ISBN 0-87179-217-6). LC 66-19726. 30.00 ea. BNA.

BNA Editorial Staff of Construction Labor Report. Construction Craft Jurisdiction Agreements 1979. LC 79-4318. 192p. 1979. pap. 8.00 (ISBN 0-87179-273-7). BNA.

BNA Editorial Staff of Labor Relations Reporter. Labor Relations Yearbook 1976. LC 66-19726. 630p. 1977. 30.00 (ISBN 0-87179-239-7). BNA.

--Labor Relations Yearbook 1977. LC 66-19726. 552p. 1978. 30.00 (ISBN 0-87179-242-7). BNA.

--Labor Relations Yearbook 1978. 556p. 1979. 30.00 (ISBN 0-87179-295-8). BNA.

--Labor Relations Yearbook 1979. 540p. 1980. 30.00 (ISBN 0-87179-334-2). BNA.

B'nai B'rith Leadership Council. B'nai B'rith Community Volunteer Service. 63p. 1978. 4.25 (ISBN 0-318-17184-8, C49). Natl Ctr Cit Involv.

BNA's Business Regualtion & Economic Information Services. Housing & Development Reporter. write for info. BNA.

BNA's Business Regulation & Economic Information Services. Antitrust & Trade Regulation Report. write for info. BNA.

--Corporate Practice Series. write for info. BNA.

--Daily Report for Executives. write for info. BNA.

--Daily Tax Report. write for info. BNA.

--Federal Contracts Report. write for info. BNA.

--International Trade Reporter's Export Shipping Manual. write for info. BNA.

--International Trade Reporter's U. S. Export Weekly. write for info. BNA.

BNA's Business Regulation & Economic Informationn Service. International Trade Reporter's U. S. Import Weekly. write for info. BNA.

BNA's Business Regulation & Economic Information Services. Securities Regulation & Law Report. write for info. BNA.

--Washington Financial Reports. write for info. BNA.

BNA's Environmental & Safety Information Services. Air Pollution. (BNA Policy & Practice Ser.). write for info. BNA.

--Chemical Regulation Reporter. write for info. BNA.

--Chemical Substances Control. (Policy & Practice Ser.). write for info. BNA.

--Energy Users Report. write for info. (ISBN 0-686-88953-3). BNA.

--Environmental Reporter. write for info. BNA.

--Hazardous Materials Transportation. write for info. BNA.

--Index to Government Regulation. write for info. BNA.

--International Environmental Reporter. write for info. BNA.

--Job Safety & Health. (Policy & Practice Ser.). write for info. BNA.

--Loss Prevention & Control. (Policy & Practice Ser.). write for info. BNA.

--Mine Safety & Health Reporter. write for info. BNA.

BNA"s Environmental & Safety Information Services. Noise Regulation Reporter. write for info. BNA.

BNA's Environmental & Safety Information Services. Occupational Safety & Health Reporter. write for info. BNA.

--Product Safety & Liability Reporter. write for info. BNA.

--Sewage Treatment Construction Grants Manual. write for info. BNA.

--Water Pollution Control. (Policy & Practice Ser.). write for info. BNA.

BNA's Labor Information Services. Affirmative Action Compliance Manual. write for info. BNA.

--BNA Pension Reporter. write for info. BNA.

--BNA Policy & Practice Series. write for info. BNA.

--BNA's Labor Relations Reporter: State Laws. write for info. BNA.

--Collective Bargaining Negotiation & Contracts. write for info. BNA.

--Construction Labor Report. write for info. BNA.

--Daily Labor Report. write for info. BNA.

--EEOC Compliance Manual. write for info. BNA.

--Employee Benefits Cases. write for info. BNA.

--Employment & Training Reporter. write for info. BNA.

--Fair Employment Practice Service. write for info. BNA.

--Government Employee Relations Report. write for info. BNA.

--The Government Manager. write for info. BNA.

--Labor Arbitration Reports. write for info. BNA.

--Retail Services Labor Report. write for info. BNA.

--Union Labor Report. write for info. BNA.

--White Collar Report. write for info. BNA.

BNA's Legal Information Services. BNA's Law Reprints. write for info. BNA.

--BNA's Patent, Trademark & Copyright Journal. write for info. BNA.

--The Criminal Law Reporter. write for info. BNA.

--Family Law Reporter. write for info. BNA.

--The Law Officer's Bulletin. write for info. BNA.

--Media Law Reporter. write for info. BNA.

--Specialty Law Digest: Education. write for info. BNA.

--Specialty Law Digest: Health Care. write for info. BNA.

--The United States Law Week. write for info. BNA.

--United States Patents Quarterly. write for info. BNA.

Bo. How to Succeed with Women. LC 76-4236. 1976. 6.95 (ISBN 0-87212-064-3). Libra.

Bo, Dino Del see Del Bo, Dino.

Bo, K. & Tucker, H. A., eds. Eurographics '84: Proceedings of the European Graphics Conference & Exhibit, Copenhagen, Denmark, 12-14 September 1984. 440p. 1985. 59.25 (ISBN 0-444-87617-0, North-Holland). Elsevier.

Bo, Ketil & Lillehagen, Frank M., eds. CAD Systems Framework: Proceedings of the WG 5.2 Working Conference, Roros, June 1982. x, 342p. 1983. 49.00 (ISBN 0-444-86604-3, I-172-83, North Holland). Elsevier.

Bo, Walter J., et al. Basic Atlas of Cross-Sectional Anatomy: A Clinical Approach. (Illus.). 357p. 1980. 44.00 (ISBN 0-7216-1767-0). Saunders.

Boa, Kenneth. Cults, World Religions, & You. 1977. pap. 6.95 (ISBN 0-88207-752-X). Victor Bks.

Boa, Kenneth & Moody, Larry. I'm Glad You Asked. 1982. pap. 6.95 (ISBN 0-88207-354-0). Victor Bks.

Boa, Kenneth & Proctor, William. The Return of the Star of Bethlehem. 224p. (Orig.). 1985. pap. 7.95 (ISBN 0-310-33631-7, Pub. by Zondervan Bks). Zondervan.

Boa, Kenneth, jt. auth. see Livgren, Kerry.

Boa, Kenneth, jt. auth. see Wilkinson, Bruce.

Boada, Francesc, adapted by see Andersen, Hans Christian.

Boada, Francesc, retold by see Grimm, Jacob, et al.

Boadella, David. The Spiral Flame: A Study in the Meaning of D. H. Lawrence. Efron, Arthur & Hoerner, Dennis, eds. 1977. pap. 6.00 (ISBN 0-9602478-2-3). Paunch.

Boadella, David, ed. In the Wake of Reich. LC 77-75314. 1978. 17.95 (ISBN 0-87949-103-5). Ashley Bks.

Boaden, Ann, ed. The Masks of Comedy. LC 79-57417. (Augustana College Library Publications: No. 34). 102p. (Orig.). 1980. pap. 2.50x (ISBN 0-910182-40-X). Augustana Coll.

Boaden, James. Inquiry into the Authenticity of Various Pictures & Prints. 1824. Repr. 8.50 (ISBN 0-8274-2574-0). R West.

--An Inquiry into the Authenticity of Various Pictures & Prints Which, from the Decease of the Poet to Our Own Times Have Been Offered to the Public As Portraits of Shakespeare. LC 70-39458. (Illus.). Repr. of 1824 ed. 12.50 (ISBN 0-404-00915-8). AMS Pr.

--Letter to George Steevens. LC 74-39459. Repr. of 1796 ed. 14.50 (ISBN 0-404-00916-6). AMS Pr.

--Memoirs of the Life of John Philip Kemble, 2 vols. LC 77-89713. 1825. 55.00 (ISBN 0-405-08276-2, Blom Pubns). Ayer Co Pubs.

--On the Sonnets of Shakespeare. LC 79-39460. Repr. of 1837 ed. 14.50 (ISBN 0-404-00917-4). AMS Pr.

--The Plays of James Boaden. Backscheider, P. R. & Cohan, Steven, eds. LC 78-66608. (Eighteenth Century English Drama Ser.). lib. bdg. 73.00 (ISBN 0-8240-3579-8). Garland Pub.

Boaden, P. J. & Seed, R. An Introduction to Coastal Ecology. (Illus.). 192p. 1985. 39.95 (ISBN 0-412-01021-6, 9442); pap. 19.95 (ISBN 0-412-01031-3, 9443). Methuen Inc.

Boaden, P. S. & Seed, R. An Introduction to Coastal Ecology. (Tertiary Level Biology Ser.). 192p. 1985. text ed. 39.95 (ISBN 0-412-01021-6, Pub. by Chapman & Hall); pap. text ed. 19.95 (ISBN 0-412-01031-3, Pub. by Chapman & Hall). Methuen Inc.

Boadt, Lawrence. Jeremiah 1-25. (Old Testament Message Ser.: Vol. 9). 1982. 15.95 (ISBN 0-89453-409-2); pap. 9.95 (ISBN 0-89453-262-6). M Glazier.

--Jeremiah 26-52, Habakkuk, Zephaniah & Nahum. (Old Testament Message Ser.: Vol. 10). 1982. 15.95 (ISBN 0-89453-410-6); pap. 9.95 (ISBN 0-89453-244-8). M Glazier.

--Reading the Old Testament: An Introduction. (Orig.). 1984. pap. 6.95 (ISBN 0-8091-2631-1). Paulist Pr.

Boadt, Lawrence, et al, eds. Biblical Studies: Meeting Ground of Jews & Christians. LC 80-82812. (Stimulus Bk). 232p. (Orig.). 1981. pap. 7.95 (ISBN 0-8091-2344-4). Paulist Pr.

Boadway, R. W. & Treddenick, J. M. The Impact of the Mining Industries on the Canadian Economy. 117p. (Orig.). 1977. pap. text ed. 6.00x (ISBN 0-686-63141-2, Pub. by Ctr Resource Stud Canada). Brookfield Pub Co.

Boadway, Robin & Bruce, Neil. Welfare Economics: Theory & Applications. 336p. 1984. 45.00x (ISBN 0-631-13326-7); pap. 19.95x (ISBN 0-631-13327-5). Basil Blackwell.

Boadway, Robin W., et al. Public Sector Economics. 2nd ed. 1984. 30.95 (ISBN 0-316-10052-8). Little.

Boag, P., ed. see Lack, David.

Boahan, A. Adu see International Scientific Committee for the Drafting of a General History of Africa.

Boahen, A. A., jt. auth. see Webster, J. B.

Boahen, Adu. Topics in West African History. (Africana Forum Ser.). (Orig.). 1977. pap. text ed. 6.00x (ISBN 0-582-64502-6). Humanities.

Boak, Arthur E. Manpower Shortage & the Fall of the Roman Empire in the West. LC 74-11423. (Illus.). 169p. 1974. Repr. of 1955 ed. lib. bdg. 22.50 (ISBN 0-8371-7676-X, BOMAS). Greenwood.

--Two Studies in Later Roman & Byzantine Administration. Repr. of 1924 ed. 37.00 (ISBN 0-384-38814-0). Johnson Repr.

Boak, Arthur E., jt. auth. see Sinnigen, William G.

Boakes, R. A., jt. ed. see Dickinson, A.

Boakes, Robert. From Darwin to Behaviourism: Psychology & the Minds of Animals. LC 83-10091. (Illus.). 300p. 1984. 69.50 (ISBN 0-521-23512-X); pap. 19.95 (ISBN 0-521-28012-5). Cambridge U Pr.

Boal, Alan W. & White, T. M. Idea Transfer: Inside Techniques for Executive Presentations. 131p. (Orig.). 1982. pap. 9.95 (ISBN 0-912441-00-3). Comware Pub.

Boal, Augusto. Theatre of the Oppressed. 1985. pap. 8.95 (ISBN 0-930452-49-6). Theatre Comm.

Boal, Barbara. The Konds: Human Sacrifice & Religious Change. 294p. 1982. pap. text ed. 42.00x (ISBN 0-85668-154-7, Pub. by Aris & Phillips England). Humanities.

Boal, D. H. & Kamal, A. N., eds. Particles & Fields 1. LC 78-2509. 470p. 1978. 55.00 (ISBN 0-306-31147-X, Plenum Pr). Plenum Pub.

Boal, David H. & Woloshyn, Richard M., eds. Short-Distance Phenomena in Nuclear Physics. (NATO ASI Series B, Physics: Vol. 104). 438p. 1983. 62.50x (ISBN 0-306-41494-5, Plenum Pr). Plenum Pub.

Boal, F. W. & Douglas, J. N., eds. Integration & Division: Geographical Perspectives on the Northern Ireland Problem. LC 81-68978. 1982. 44.00 (ISBN 0-12-108080-3). Acad Pr.

Boalt, G., et al, eds. Communication & Communication Barriers in Sociology. LC 75-44623. 163p. 1976. 42.95x (ISBN 0-470-15016-5). Halsted Pr.

Boalt, Gunnar. Sociology of Research. LC 68-25558. (Perspectives in Sociology Ser.). 204p. 1969. 7.95x (ISBN 0-8093-0362-0). S Ill U Pr.

Boalt, Gunnar, et al. Sociologists in Search of Their Intellectual Domain. 1979. text ed. 35.50x (ISBN 0-391-01152-9). Humanities.

Boanes, Phyllis, ed. see Abrams, Irving.

Boar, B. H. Abend Debugging for COBOL Programmers. LC 75-42457. 321p. 1976. 37.50x (ISBN 0-471-08413-1, Pub. by Wiley-Interscience). Wiley.

Boar, Bernard H. Application Prototyping: A Project Management Perspective. (AMA Management Briefings Ser.). 1985. 10.00 (ISBN 0-8144-2312-4). AMACOM.

--Application Prototyping: A Requirements Definition Strategy for the '80's. LC 83-16934. 210p. 1984. 32.50x (ISBN 0-471-89317-X, Pub. by Wiley-Interscience). Wiley.

Boar, Gerard. Sketches for Thirteen Sonnets. 1969. pap. 1.00 (ISBN 0-685-04673-7). Oyez.

Board Members & Managing Directors of Theatre Companies, Dance Companies, Operas & Orchestras. In Art We Trust: The Boards of Trustees in the Performing Arts. Crawford, Robert W., ed. 72p. 1981. pap. text ed. 12.95 (ISBN 0-9602942-3-6). FEDAPT.

Board Of Aldermen. Police in New York City: An Investigation. LC 79-154565. (Police in America Ser). 1971. Repr. of 1913 ed. 27.00 (ISBN 0-405-03382-6). Ayer Co Pubs.

Board Of Christian Service Of The General Conference Mennonite Church. Church, the State & the Offender. 1963. pap. 0.50 (ISBN 0-87303-200-4). Faith & Life.

Board of Cooperative Education Services, Nassau County. Two Hundred Ways to Help Children Learn While You're at It. 1976. 18.95 (ISBN 0-87909-845-7). Reston.

Board of Education & Training. Bringing Life to Microbiology. 1979. 14.00 (ISBN 0-686-95719-9). Am Soc Microbio.

--Directory of Colleges & Universities Granting Degrees in Microbiology, 1980. 1980. 5.00 (ISBN 0-686-95711-3). Am Soc Microbio.

--Fundamentals of Anaerobic Bacteriology as Related to the Clinical Laboratory. (Continuing Education Manual Ser.). 1980. 9.00 (ISBN 0-686-95682-6). Am Soc Microbio.

--Highlights in Microbiology Nineteen Seventy-Nine to Eighty, Vol. 3. (Highlights Ser.). 1981. 5.00 (ISBN 0-686-95718-0). Am Soc Microbio.

--Identification of Aerobic Gram-Positive & Gram-Negative Cocci. 3rd ed. (Continuing Education Manual Ser.). 1981. 9.00 (ISBN 0-686-95651-6). Am Soc Microbio.

--Identification of Glucose-Nonfermenting Gram-Negative Rods. (Continuing Education Manual Ser.). 1977. 12.00 (ISBN 0-686-95697-4). Am Soc Microbio.

--Identification of Saprophytic Fungi Commonly Encountered in a Clinical Environment. (Continuing Education Manual Ser.). (Illus.). 1979. 14.00 (ISBN 0-686-95686-9). Am Soc Microbio.

--Topic Outlines in Microbiology. 1980. 10.00 (ISBN 0-686-95715-6). Am Soc Microbio.

Board of Education & Training Staff. Systemic Mycoses. rev. ed. (Continuing Education Manual Ser.). 1984. 12.00 (ISBN 0-317-16825-8). Am Soc Microbio.

Board of Governers, Federal Reserve System. All-Bank Statistics, United States, 1896-1955. LC 75-22816. (America in Two Centuries Ser). 1976. Repr. of 1959 ed. 98.00x (ISBN 0-405-07688-6). Ayer Co Pubs.

Board of Governors of the Federal Reserve System (U. S.), jt. auth. see Hardy, Charles O.

Boas, Frederich S. Thomas Heywood. LC 75-15587. 159p. 1974. Repr. of 1950 ed. 8.50x (ISBN 0-87753-056-4). Phaeton.

Boas, Frederick, ed. Songs & Lyrics from the English Masques & Light Operas. 175p. 1949. Repr. 15.00x (ISBN 0-403-03693-3). Scholarly.

Boas, Frederick, ed. see Kyd, Thomas.

Boas, Mrs. Frederick. With Milton & the Cavaliers. 1904. Repr. 20.00 (ISBN 0-8274-3732-3). R West.

Boas, Frederick S. American Scenes, Tudor to Georgian, in the English Literary Mirror. LC 74-14790. 1974. Repr. of 1944 ed. lib. bdg. 8.50 (ISBN 0-8414-9873-3). Folcroft.

--From Richardson to Pinero: Some Innovators & Idealists. 292p. 1982. Repr. of 1975 ed. lib. bdg. 30.00 (ISBN 0-89760-082-7). Telegraph Bks.

--An Introduction to Eighteenth Century Drama, 1700-1780. LC 77-27612. 1978. Repr. of 1953 ed. lib. bdg. 27.50x (ISBN 0-313-20193-5, BOEC). Greenwood.

--An Introduction to the Reading of Shakespeare. LC 74-14912. 1974. Repr. of 1927 ed. lib. bdg. 10.00x (ISBN 0-8414-3279-1). Folcroft.

--An Introduction to Tudor Drama. LC 75-41032. (BCL Ser.: II). Repr. of 1933 ed. 14.00 (ISBN 0-404-14509-4). AMS Pr.

--An Introduction to Tudor Drama. LC 76-50079. (Illus.). 1977. Repr. of 1933 ed. lib. bdg. 24.75x (ISBN 0-8371-9073-8, BOIT). Greenwood.

--Ovid & the Elizabethans. (Studies in Shakespeare, No. 24). 1970. pap. 11.95x (ISBN 0-8383-0008-1). Haskell.

--Queen Elizabeth in Drama & Related Studies. facs. ed. LC 78-119954. (Select Bibliographies Reprint Ser). 1950. 19.00 (ISBN 0-8369-5397-5). Ayer Co Pubs.

--Queen Elizabeth in Drama & Related Studies. 212p. 1982. Repr. of 1950 ed. lib. bdg. 13.00 (ISBN 0-8290-0828-4). Irvington.

--Queen Elizabeth in Drama & Related Studies. 212p. 1980. Repr. lib. bdg. 25.00 (ISBN 0-8492-3588-X). R West.

--Queen Elizabeth in Drama & Related Studies. LC 71-158905. 1971. Repr. of 1950 ed. 12.00x (ISBN 0-403-01317-8). Scholarly.

--Queen Elizabeth in Drama & Related Studies. 212p. 1983. Repr. of 1950 ed. lib. bdg. 40.00 (ISBN 0-8495-0635-2). Arden Lib.

--Shakespeare & His Predecessors. LC 68-59404. 1968. Repr. of 1902 ed. 15.00x (ISBN 0-87752-011-9). Gordian.

--Shakespeare & His Predecessors. LC 69-13831. 1969. Repr. of 1904 ed. lib. bdg. 22.50x (ISBN 0-8371-0316-9, BOSH). Greenwood.

--Shakespeare & His Predecessors. 1969. Repr. of 1904 ed. 13.00x (ISBN 0-403-00109-9). Scholarly.

--Sir Philip Sidney: Representative Elizabethan. 1955. lib. bdg. 15.00 (ISBN 0-8414-3153-1). Folcroft.

--Thomas Heywood. LC 74-5032. 1973. lib. bdg. 15.00 (ISBN 0-8414-9938-1). Folcroft.

--Thomas Heywood. Repr. of 1950 ed. 19.00 (ISBN 0-403-02292-4). Somerset Pub.

--University Drama in the Tudor Age. LC 65-20049. (Illus.). 1914. 27.50 (ISBN 0-405-08277-0, Blom Pubns). Ayer Co Pubs.

Boas, Frederick S., ed. The Christmas Prince. LC 82-45783. (Malone Society Reprint Ser.: No. 52). Repr. of 1922 ed. 40.00 (ISBN 0-404-63052-9). AMS Pr.

Boas, Frederick S., intro. by. The Player's Library: The Catalogue of the Library of the British Drama League. 1115p. 1982. Repr. of 1950 ed. lib. bdg. 100.00 (ISBN 0-89987-097-X). Darby Bks.

Boas, Frederick S., ed. Songs & Lyrics from the English Masques & Light Operas. LC 77-14508. 1977. Repr. of 1949 ed. lib. bdg. 19.75x (ISBN 0-8371-9842-9, BOMO). Greenwood.

--Songs & Lyrics from the English Playbooks. Repr. of 1945 ed. 15.00x (ISBN 0-403-04290-9). Somerset Pub.

Boas, Frederick S., ed. see Howard, Edward.

Boas, Frederick S., ed. see Marlowe, Christopher.

Boas, Mrs. Frederick S. Rossetti & His Poetry. LC 72-191813. 1918. lib. bdg. 15.00 (ISBN 0-8414-2531-0). Folcroft.

Boas, George. Challenge of Science. LC 65-23907. (John Danz Lecture Ser.). 116p. 1965. 10.00x (ISBN 0-295-73735-2). U of Wash Pr.

--Critical Analysis of the Philosophy of Emile Meyerson. facsimile ed. LC 70-109616. (Select Bibliographies Reprint Ser). 1930. 17.00 (ISBN 0-8369-5224-3). Ayer Co Pubs.

--The Cult of Childhood. 1966. 25.00x (ISBN 0-686-79323-4, Pub. by U of London England). State Mutual Bk.

--The Cult of Childhood. (Warburg Institute Studies: Vol. 29). 1966. 15.00 (ISBN 0-317-16764-2). Kraus Repr.

--Essays on Primitivism & Related Ideas in the Middle Ages. 1966. lib. bdg. 21.50x (ISBN 0-374-90704-8). Octagon.

--The Heaven of Invention. 394p. 1963. 32.00x (ISBN 0-8018-0078-1). Johns Hopkins.

--The Inquiring Mind: An Introduction to Epistemology. LC 58-6815. (Paul Carus Lectures Ser.). vi, 437p. 1959. 24.95 (ISBN 0-87548-099-3). Open Court.

--Limits of Reason. LC 68-21324. Repr. of 1961 ed. lib. bdg. 15.00x (ISBN 0-8371-0023-2, BOLR). Greenwood.

--The Mind's Road to God: Bonaventura. 1953. pap. text ed. write for info. (ISBN 0-02-311250-6). Macmillan.

--Primer for Critics. LC 68-55100. (Illus.). 1968. Repr. of 1937 ed. lib. bdg. 22.50x (ISBN 0-8371-0318-5, BOPC). Greenwood.

--Primer for Critics. LC 68-59377. 1968. Repr. of 1937 ed. 8.50x (ISBN 0-87753-006-8). Phaeton.

--Rationalism in Greek Philosophy. LC 61-15638. pap. 97.70 (ISBN 0-317-08864-5, 2013173). Bks Demand UMI.

Boas, George, jt. auth. see Lovejoy, Arthur O.

Boas, George, tr. see Bonaventura, Saint.

Boas, George, tr. see Michaud, Regis.

Boas, Guy. An Anthology of Wit. 285p. 1983. Repr. of 1934 ed. lib. bdg. 40.00 (ISBN 0-89760-056-8). Telegraph Bks.

--Lytton Strachey. 1973. Repr. of 1935 ed. 8.50 (ISBN 0-8274-0067-5). R West.

--Modern English Prose. 1977. Repr. of 1933 ed. 10.00 (ISBN 0-89984-046-9). Century Bookbindery.

--Modern English Prose. 260p. 1984. Repr. of 1933 ed. lib. bdg. 25.00 (ISBN 0-918377-09-9). Russell Pr.

--Modern English Prose. 260p. 1984. Repr. of 1935 ed. lib. bdg. 30.00 (ISBN 0-8495-0617-4). Arden Lib.

--Tennyson & Browning. LC 78-1844. 1925. Repr. 15.00 (ISBN 0-8492-3508-1). R West.

--Wordsworth & Coleridge. 1925. 15.00 (ISBN 0-8274-3748-X). R West.

Boas, Hans U. Syntactic Generalizations & Linear Order in Generative Transformational Grammar. (Tuebinger Beitraege Zur Linguistik Ser.: No. 56). 255p. (Orig.). pap. 17.00x (ISBN 3-87808-056-5). Benjamins North Am.

Boas, Henrietta O. Rossetti & His Poetry. LC 74-120979. (Poetry & Life Ser.). Repr. of 1914 ed. 7.25 (ISBN 0-404-52504-0). AMS Pr.

Boas, Jacob. Boulevard des Miseres: The Story of Transit Camp Westerbork. (Illus.). 200p. 1985. lib. bdg. 19.50 (ISBN 0-208-01977-4, Archon Bks). Shoe String.

Boas, Louise, jt. auth. see Boas, Ralph.

Boas, Louise S. A Great Rich Man: The Romance of Sir Walter Scott. 1978. Repr. of 1929 ed. lib. bdg. 35.00 (ISBN 0-8492-3519-7). R West.

--Harriet Shelley: Five Long Years. LC 78-12350. 1979. Repr. of 1962 ed. lib. bdg. 27.50x (ISBN 0-313-21143-4, BOHF). Greenwood.

--Woman's Education Begins: The Rise of the Women's Colleges. LC 74-165705. (American Education Ser., No. 2). 1971. Repr. of 1935 ed. 18.00 (ISBN 0-405-03694-9). Ayer Co Pubs.

Boas, Marie. Robert Boyle & Seventeenth-Century Chemistry. LC 58-4386. Repr. of 1958 ed. 23.00 (ISBN 0-527-09250-9). Kraus Repr.

--Scientific Renaissance, 1450-1630. (Illus.). pap. 7.95xi (ISBN 0-06-130583-9, TB583, Torch). Har-Row.

Boas, Mary L. Mathematical Methods in the Physical Sciences. 2nd ed. LC 83-1226. 793p. 1983. text ed. 39.95 (ISBN 0-471-04409-1); solutions manual avail. (ISBN 0-471-09920-1). Wiley.

Boas, Maurits. It Did Happen. 128p. 1984. 12.95 (ISBN 0-8119-0530-6). Fell.

Boas, Maurits I. Preludes. LC 78-855. 1978. 9.95 (ISBN 0-8119-0305-2). Fell.

Boas, Max & Chain, Steve. Big Mac: The Unauthorized Story of McDonald's. (YA) (RL 10). 1977. pap. 2.95 (ISBN 0-451-62227-8, ME2227, Ment). NAL.

Boas, R. P. Collected Works of Hidehiko Yamabe. (Notes on Mathematics & Its Applications Ser.). 154p. 1967. 38.50 (ISBN 0-677-00610-1). Gordon.

Boas, R. P., tr. see Shiryayev, A. N.

Boas, R. P., Jr. Integrability Theorems for Trigonometric Transforms. (Ergebnisse der Mathematik und Ihrer Grenzgebiete: Vol. 38). 1967. 19.50 (ISBN 0-387-03780-2). Springer-Verlag.

Boas, R. P., Jr. & Buck, R. C. Polynomial Expansions of Analytic Functions. 2nd ed. (Ergebnisse der Mathematik und Ihrer Grenzgebiete: Vol. 19). (Illus.). 1964. 23.10 (ISBN 0-387-03123-5). Springer-Verlag.

Boas, Ralph & Boas, Louise. Cotton Mather, Keeper of the Puritan Conscience. (Illus.). ix, 271p. 1964. Repr. of 1928 ed. 25.00 (ISBN 0-208-00332-0, Archon). Shoe String.

Boas, Ralph, ed. see Polya, George.

Boas, Ralph P. Enjoyment of Literature. 1952. Repr. 20.00 (ISBN 0-8274-2277-6). R West.

--The Study & Appreciation of Literature. 1931. Repr. 20.00 (ISBN 0-8274-3546-0). R West.

--The Study & Appreciation of Literature. 356p. 1982. Repr. of 1931 ed. lib. bdg. 35.00 (ISBN 0-89760-084-3). Telegraph Bks.

--Youth & the New World. 1921. 25.00 (ISBN 0-8482-7450-4). Norwood Edns.

Boas, Ralph P. & Hahn, Barbara M. Social Backgrounds of English Literature. 337p. 1983. Repr. of 1932 ed. lib. bdg. 45.00 (ISBN 0-89760-060-6). Telegraph Bks.

Boas, Ralph P. & Smith, Edwin. An Introduction to the Study of Literature. 1977. Repr. of 1925 ed. lib. bdg. 20.00 (ISBN 0-8492-0344-9). R West.

--An Introduction to the Study of Literature. 454p. 1982. Repr. of 1925 ed. lib. bdg. 25.00 (ISBN 0-89760-085-1). Telegraph Bks.

--An Introduction to the Study of Literature. 454p. 1982. Repr. of 1933 ed. lib. bdg. 30.00 (ISBN 0-89760-097-5). Telegraph Bks.

--An Introduction to the Study of Literature. 454p. 1983. Repr. of 1925 ed. lib. bdg. 35.00 (ISBN 0-89984-099-X). Century Bookbindery.

Boas, Ralph P., et al. An Introduction to the Study of Literature. 454p. 1984. Repr. of 1925 ed. lib. bdg. 45.00 (ISBN 0-89760-998-0). Telegraph Bks.

Boas, Ralph P., Jr. Entire Functions. (Pure & Applied Mathematics Ser.: Vol. 5). 1954. 59.50 (ISBN 0-12-108150-8). Acad Pr.

--A Primer of Real Functions. 3rd ed. LC 81-82669. (Carus Monograph: No. 13). 232p. 1981. 16.50 (ISBN 0-88385-022-2). Math Assn.

Boas, Robert, jt. ed. see Stanton-Hicks, Michael.

Boas, S., jt. auth. see Mungall, S.

Boas, Simone B., tr. see De Maupertuis, Pierre-Louis M.

Boas, Simone B., tr. see Foucher, Alfred C.

Boase, A. M., ed. see Montaigne, Michel de.

Boase, F. Modern English Biography, (6 vols. 1965. Repr. of 1892 ed. Set. 350.00x (ISBN 0-7146-2118-8, BHA-02118, F Cass Co). Biblio Dist.

Boase, Frederic. Modern English Biographies, 4 vols. lib. bdg. 100.00 set (ISBN 0-686-76990-2). Milford Hse.

--Modern English Biography, 6 vols. Set. 650.00 (ISBN 0-8490-0647-3). Gordon Pr.

Boase, Paul H. The Rhetoric of Christian Socialism. 9.00 (ISBN 0-8446-0501-8). Peter Smith.

Boase, Paul H., jt. auth. see Eisenson, Jon.

Boase, Paul H., jt. auth. see Whitman, Richard F.

Boase, Paul H., ed. The Rhetoric of Protest & Reform, 1878-1898. LC 80-11631. viii, 354p. 1980. 18.00x (ISBN 0-8214-0421-0, 82-83137). Ohio U Pr.

Boase, Roger. The Origin & Meaning of Courtly Love: A Critical Study of European Scholarship. (Illus.). 171p. 1977. 23.50x (ISBN 0-87471-950-X). Rowman.

Boase, T. S. Giorgio Vasari: The Man & the Book. LC 74-25631. (Bollinger Ser. XXXV-20: A. W. Mellon Lecture in the Fine Arts). (Illus.). 276p. 1979. 45.00 (ISBN 0-691-09905-7). Princeton U Pr.

Boase, T. S., ed. Cilician Kingdom of Armenia. LC 74-22291. 1979. text ed. 27.50 (ISBN 0-312-13895-4). St Martin.

Boase, Wendy. The Castle. LC 83-62967. (Early Bird Bks.). (Illus.). 32p. (ps-1). 1984. 1.95 (ISBN 0-394-86659-2, Pub. by BYR). Random.

--The Circus. LC 83-62968. (Early Bird Bks.: Hide & Seek Sub-Ser.). (Illus.). (ps-1). 1984. 1.95 (ISBN 0-394-86660-6, Pub. by BYR). Random.

--Fairyland. LC 83-62969. (Early Bird Bks.: Hide & Seek Sub-Ser.). (Illus.). 32p. (ps-1). 1984. 1.95 (ISBN 0-394-86661-4, Pub. by BYR). Random.

--The Folklore of Hampshire & the Isle of Wight. (Folklore of British Isles Ser.). (Illus.). 192p. 1976. 17.50x (ISBN 0-87471-784-1). Rowman.

--Hide & Seek Books. (Early Bird Bks.). (Illus.). (ps-1). pap. 1.95 ea. Random.

--Mealtime. (Time to Talk Ser.). (Illus.). 32p. (ps-2). 1983. 2.50 (ISBN 0-671-47108-2, Little Simon). S&S.

--Toyland. LC 83-62970. (Early Bird Bks.: Hide & Seek Sub-Ser.). (Illus.). 32p. (ps-1). 1984. 1.95 (ISBN 0-394-86662-2, Pub. by BYR). Random.

Boasson, Charles & Nurock, Max, eds. The Changing International Community: Some Problems of Its Laws, Structures, & Peace Research & the Middle East Conflict. (New Babylon Studies in Social Sciences: No. 18). 1973. text ed. 25.60x (ISBN 90-2797-292-3). Mouton.

Boast, Carol, jt. auth. see Foster, Lynn.

Boast, Carol, jt. auth. see Nyberg, Cheryl.

Boat, Jaydee. Dining In-Denver. (Dining in Ser.). 185p. (Orig.). 1981. pap. 7.95 (ISBN 0-89716-036-3). Peanut Butter.

Boateng, E. A. Geography of Ghana. 2nd ed. pap. 8.95x (ISBN 0-521-04273-9). Cambridge U Pr.

--A Political Geography of Africa. LC 77-80828. 1978. 42.50 (ISBN 0-521-21764-4); pap. 17.95 (ISBN 0-521-29269-7). Cambridge U Pr.

Boater, Debbie, jt. auth. see Saint-Pierre, Gaston.

Boatfield, Graham. Farm Crops. 2nd ed. (Illus.). 144p. 1983. pap. write for info. (ISBN 0-85236-129-7, Pub. by Farming Pr UK). Diamond Farm Bk.

--Farm Livestock. 2nd ed. (Illus.). 144p. 1983. pap. 13.95 (ISBN 0-85236-130-0, Pub. by Farming Pr UK). Diamond Farm Bk.

Boatman, Don E. Helps from Hebrews. LC 75-1066. (The Bible Study Textbook Ser.). (Illus.). 1960. 14.30 (ISBN 0-89900-044-4). College Pr Pub.

Boatman, Don E. & Boles, Kenny. Galatians. rev. ed. LC 70-1141. (The Bible Study Textbook Ser.). (Illus.). 1976. 12.20 (ISBN 0-89900-039-8). College Pr Pub.

Boatman, Russel. What the Bible Says about End Time. 3rd ed. LC 79-56542. (What the Bible Says Ser.). 1980. 13.50 (ISBN 0-89900-075-4). College Pr Pub.

Boatner, Mark M. Military Customs & Traditions. LC 75-17189. 176p. 1976. Repr. of 1956 ed. lib. bdg. 22.50x (ISBN 0-8371-8299-9, BOMCT). Greenwood.

Boatner, Mark M., 3rd. The Civil War Dictionary. (Illus., Maps & diagrams). 25.00 (ISBN 0-679-50013-8). McKay.

Boatner, Maxine & Gates, John E. A Dictionary of American Idioms. rev. ed. Makkai, Adam, ed. LC 75-42110. Date not set. 14.95 (ISBN 0-8120-5419-9); pap. 9.95 (ISBN 0-8120-2349-8). Barron.

Boatner, Maxine T. & Gates, John E. A Dictionary of Idioms for the Deaf. 1975. 10.95x (ISBN 0-913072-05-2); pap. 9.95 (ISBN 0-685-56461-4). Natl Assn Deaf.

Boatner, Maxine T., et al. Handbook of Commonly Used Idioms. 224p. 1984. pap. 5.95 (ISBN 0-8120-2816-3). Barron.

Boatright, Kevin, ed. see Stetson, Daniel E.

Boatright, Kevin, ed. see Stetson, Daniel E. & Shamen, Sanford S.

Boatright, Lori. Out of Bounds. 159p. 1982. pap. 1.95 (ISBN 0-449-70028-3, Juniper). Fawcett.

Boatright, M. C. Folk Laughter on the American Frontier. 11.75 (ISBN 0-8446-0035-0). Peter Smith.

Boatright, Mody. Mody Boatright, Folklorist: A Collection of Essays. Speck, Ernest B., ed. LC 73-6908. 224p. 1973. 14.95x (ISBN 0-292-75007-2). U of Tex Pr.

Boatright, Mody C. Folklore of the Oil Industry. LC 63-21186. vii, 228p. 1984. pap. 9.95 (ISBN 0-87074-204-3). SMU Press.

--Gib Morgan: Minstrel of the Oil Fields. LC 46-815. (Texas Folklore Society Publications: No. 20). (Illus.). 1965. Repr. of 1945 ed. 9.95 (ISBN 0-87074-008-3). SMU Press.

--Tall Tales from Texas Cow Camps. (American Folklore Ser.). 108p. 1982. Repr. of 1934 ed. 9.95 (ISBN 0-87074-181-0, A 74613). SMU Press.

Boatright, Mody C. & Owens, William A. Tales from the Derrick Floor: A People's History of the Oil Industry. LC 81-19725. (Illus.). xx, 284p. 1982. 22.50x (ISBN 0-8032-1177-5); pap. 6.50 (ISBN 0-8032-6067-9, BB 804, Bison). U of Nebr Pr.

Boatright, Mody C., ed. Mexican Border Ballads & Other Lore. LC 48-7407. (Texas Folklore Society Publications: No. 21). (Illus.). 1967. Repr. of 1946 ed. 9.95 (ISBN 0-87074-009-1). SMU Press.

--The Sky Is My Tipi. LC 49-1690. (Texas Folklore Society Publications: No. 22). (Illus.). 1966. Repr. of 1949 ed. 9.95 (ISBN 0-87074-010-5). SMU Press.

Boatright, Mody C. & Day, Donald, eds. Backwoods to Border. LC 48-18054. (Texas Folklore Society Publications Ser.: No. 18). (Illus.). 1967. Repr. of 1943 ed. 9.95 (ISBN 0-87074-011-3). SMU Press.

--From Hell to Breakfast. LC 45-1540. (Texas Folklore Society Publications Ser.: No. 19). (Illus.). 1967. Repr. of 1944 ed. 9.95 (ISBN 0-87074-012-1). SMU Press.

Boatright, Mody C., et al, eds. And Horns on the Toads. LC 59-15694. (Texas Folklore Society Publications: No. 29). 1959. 9.95 (ISBN 0-87074-013-X). SMU Press.

--Folk Travelers: Ballads, Tales, & Talk. LC 53-12578. (Texas Folklore Society Publications: No. 25). 1953. 9.95 (ISBN 0-87074-014-8). SMU Press.

--Golden Log. LC 61-17184. (Texas Folklore Society Publications Ser.: No. 31). 1962. 9.95 (ISBN 0-87074-015-6). SMU Press.

--Good Tale & a Bonnie Tune. LC 63-10979. (Texas Folklore Society Publications: No. 32). 1964. 9.95 (ISBN 0-87074-016-4). SMU Press.

--Mesquite & Willow. LC 56-12566. (Texas Folklore Society Publications Ser.: No. 27). 1957. 9.95 (ISBN 0-87074-018-0). SMU Press.

--Singers & Storytellers. LC 60-15894. (Texas Folklore Society Publications: No. 30). 1961. 9.95 (ISBN 0-87074-019-9). SMU Press.

--Texas Folk & Folklore. LC 54-11299. (Texas Folklore Society Publications Ser.: No. 26). (Illus.). 1954. 15.00 (ISBN 0-87074-020-2). SMU Press.

--Madstones & Twisters. LC 58-9269. (Texas Folklore Society Publication Ser.: No. 28). 180p. 1958. 9.95 (ISBN 0-87074-017-2). SMU Press.

Boatwright, Howard. Introduction to the Theory of Music. (Illus.). 1956. 16.95x (ISBN 0-393-02057-6, NortonC). Norton.

Boatwright, Howard, ed. see Ives, Charles.

Boatwright, Victor T., jt. ed. see Sheets, Herman E.

Boaz, David & Crane, Edward H., eds. Beyond the Status Quo: Policy Proposals for America. 292p. 1985. 20.00 (ISBN 0-932790-46-1); pap. 8.95 (ISBN 0-932790-49-6). Cato Inst.

Boaz, Martha. Strategies for Meeting the Information Needs of Society in the Year 2000. LC 81-11751. 197p. 1981. lib. bdg. 25.00 (ISBN 0-87287-249-1). Libs Unl.

Boaz, Martha, ed. Current Concepts in Library Management. LC 79-20734. 289p. 1979. lib. bdg. 27.50x (ISBN 0-87287-204-1). Libs Unl.

--A Living Library. LC 58-8970. 84p. 1957. pap. 2.25 (ISBN 0-88474-006-4). U of S Cal Pr.

Boaz, Noel T., et al. Neogene Paleontology & Geology of Sahabi, Libya. 238p. 1985. write for info. A R Liss.

Bob & Couchman, Win. Ruth & Jonah: People in Process. (Carpenter Studyguide). 80p. 1983. saddle-stiched member's handbk. 1.95 (ISBN 0-87788-736-5); leader's handbook 2.95 (ISBN 0-87788-737-3). Shaw Pubs.

BO'B, ed. see Campbell, Ramsey.

Bob, Arnold. Discount America Guide, Vol. 1. (Illus.). 192p. 1982. looseleaf 20.00 (ISBN 0-942528-01-8). Discount America.

Bob, P., ed. see Wolf, F. A.

Boba, Antonio. Death in the Operating Room. (Illus.). 120p. 1965. 12.75x (ISBN 0-398-00181-2). C C Thomas.

--Hypothermia for the Neurosurgical Patient. (Illus.). 132p. 1960. photocopy ed. 12.75x (ISBN 0-398-00182-0). C C Thomas.

Bobak, Irene, jt. auth. see Jensen, Margaret.

Bobak, Irene M. & Jensen, Margaret D. Essentials of Maternity Nursing. (Illus.). 1072p. 1984. pap. text ed. 33.95 (ISBN 0-8016-2486-X). Mosby.

--A Modular Study Guide to Maternity Care. LC 82-7911. (Illus.). 229p. 1983. pap. text ed. 12.95 (ISBN 0-8016-0738-8). Mosby.

Bobango, Gerald J. Religion & Politics: Bishop Valerian Trifa & His Times. (East European Monograph: No. 92). 299p. 1981. 25.00x (ISBN 0-914710-86-9). East Eur Quarterly.

Bobango, Gerald S. The Emergence of the Romanian Nation State. (East European Monographs: No. 58). 307p. 1979. 25.00x (ISBN 0-914710-51-6). East Eur Quarterly.

Bobart, Henry H. Basketwork Through the Ages. LC 72-171354. 188p. 1971. Repr. of 1936 ed. 35.00x (ISBN 0-8103-3400-3). Gale.

Bobath, B. Abnormal Postural Reflex Activity Caused by Brain Lesions. 2nd ed. (Illus.). 1976. pap. 12.50 (ISBN 0-433-03332-0). Heinman.

--Adult Hemiplegia: Evaluation & Treatment. 2nd, rev. ed. (Illus.). 1978. pap. 15.00 (ISBN 0-433-03334-7). Heinman.

Bobath, B. & Bobath, K. Motor Development in the Different Types of Cerebral Palsy. (Illus.). 1978. pap. 12.50 (ISBN 0-433-03333-9). Heinman.

Bobath, Berta. Abnormal Postural Reflex Activity Caused by Brain Lesions. 2nd ed. 1973. cancelled (ISBN 0-433-03332-0). Intl Ideas.

--Abnormal Postural Reflex Activity Caused by Brain Lesions. LC 84-24451. 113p. Date not set. 21.00 (ISBN 0-87189-091-7, Pub by W Heinemann). Aspen Systems.

Bobath, K., jt. auth. see Bobath, B.

Bobath, Karel. A Neurophysical Basis for the Treatment of Cerebral Palsy. (Clinics in Developmental Medicine Ser.: No. 75). 106p. 1980. 21.00 (ISBN 0-433-03335-5, Pub. by Spastics Intl England). Lippincott.

Bobb, Bernard E. The Viceregency of Antonio Maria Bucareli in New Spain, 1771-1779. (Texas Pan American Ser.). (Illus.). 325p. 1962. 17.50x (ISBN 0-292-73425-5). U of Tex Pr.

Bobb, Dilip & Raina, Ashok. The Great Betrayal: Assassination of Indira Gandhi. 100p. 1985. text ed. 13.95 (ISBN 0-7069-2745-1, Pub. by Vikas India). Advent NY.

Bobbi. Feelings from Within. 1980. 5.00 (ISBN 0-682-49659-6). Exposition Pr FL.

Bobbitt. Indiana Appellate Practice & Procedure, 2 vols. 1972. 75.00, with 1981 cum. (ISBN 0-672-81526-5, Bobbs-Merrill Law); 1981 cum. suppl 15.00 (ISBN 0-672-82813-8). Michie Co.

--Work's Indiana Practice with Forms, 1971-1981, 7 vols. 300.00; latest suppl. incl. Anderson Pub Co.

Bobbitt, Franklin. Curriculum. LC 78-165706. (American Education Ser). 1972. Repr. of 1918 ed. 27.50 (ISBN 0-405-03695-7). Ayer Co Pubs.

Bobbitt, H. R., et al. Organizational Behavior: Understanding & Prediction. 2nd ed. LC 77-25383. 1978. ref. 28.95 (ISBN 0-13-641209-2). P-H.

Bobbitt, Philip. Constitutional Fate: Theory of the Constitution. 1982. 22.95x (ISBN 0-19-503120-2); pap. 8.95x (ISBN 0-19-503422-8). Oxford U Pr.

Bobbitt, Philip, jt. auth. see Calabresi, Guido.

Bobbs, Howard. Bows & Arrows: An Archery Bibliography. 22p. (Orig.). 1974. pap. 2.25 (ISBN 0-913270-27-X). Sunstone Pr.

Bobc, N., et al. H-Cones. (Lecture Notes in Mathematics: Vol. 853). 286p. 1981. pap. 19.00 (ISBN 0-387-10692-8). Springer-Verlag.

Bobe, Bernard. Public Assistance to Industries & Trade Policy in France. LC 83-14827. (World Bank Staff Working Papers: No. 570). 1983. 3.00 (ISBN 0-8213-0200-0). World Bank.

Bober, G. F. Protection & the Law. (Contemporary Consumer Ser.). text ed. 8.68 (ISBN 0-07-006210-2). McGraw.

Bober, Gerald, jt. auth. see Hamill, Ann D.

Bober, Harry, ed. see Male, Emile.

Bober, Mandell M. Karl Marx's Interpretation of History. 2nd rev. ed. LC 48-8857. (Economic Studies: No. 31). 1948. 20.00x (ISBN 0-674-50150-0). Harvard U Pr.

--Karl Marx's Interpretation of History. 1965. pap. 7.45x (ISBN 0-393-00270-5, Norton Lib). Norton.

Bober, Natalie S. Breaking Tradition: The Story of Louise Nevelson. LC 83-15618. (Illus.). 192p. (gr. 7 up). 1984. 12.95 (ISBN 0-689-31036-6). Atheneum.

--A Restless Spirit: The Story of Robert Frost. LC 80-23930. (Illus.). 224p. (gr. 5 up). 1981. PLB 14.95 (ISBN 0-689-30801-9). Atheneum.

Bober, Phyllis P. Drawings after the Antique by Amico Aspertini: Sketchbooks in the British Museum. (Warburg Institute Studies: Vol. 21). Repr. of 1957 ed. 17.00 (ISBN 0-317-16763-4). Kraus Repr.

--Drawings After the Antique by Amico Aspertini. 1957. 30.00x (ISBN 0-686-79066-9, Pub. by U of London England). State Mutual Bk.

Bober, Phyllis P. & Rubenstein, Ruth. Renaissance Artists & Antique Sculpture: A Handbook of Sources. (A Harvey Miller Publication Ser.). (Illus.). 1985. 65.00x (ISBN 0-19-921029-2). Oxford U Pr.

Bober, Stanley. Capital, Distribution & Growth: A Look at Neo-Keynesian Economics. LC 80-5861. 229p. 1980. lib. bdg. 22.75 (ISBN 0-8191-1263-1); pap. 11.75 (ISBN 0-8191-1264-X). U Pr of Amer.

Boberach, Heinz & Franz, Eckjart G., eds. In der Gemeinschaft der Volker Dokumente aus Deutschen Archiven uber die Beziehungen zwischen Deutschen und enderen Nationen in elf Jahrunderten. Zum X Internationalen Archivkongress. 442p. (Ger.). Date not set. lib. bdg. 131.00 (ISBN 3-598-10575-4). K G Saur.

Boberg, ed. Maintenance of Fluency: Proceedings of the Bauff Conference. 284p. 1980. 39.50 (ISBN 0-444-00415-7, Biomedical Pr). Elsevier.

Boberg, Anne-Marie & Svennas, Elsie. Macrame. LC 74-14199. (Illus.). 104p. 1975. lib. bdg. 7.95 o. p. (ISBN 0-668-03753-9); pap. 3.95 (ISBN 0-668-03623-0). Arco.

Bobgan, Deidre, jt. auth. see Bobgan, Martin.

Bobgan, Martin & Bobgan, Deidre. How to Counsel from Scripture. 1985. pap. 8.95 (ISBN 0-8024-0373-5). Moody.

--Hypnosis & the Christian. LC 83-21401. 64p. (Orig.). 1984. pap. 2.50 (ISBN 0-87123-402-5, 210402). Bethany Hse.

--The Psychological Way: the Spiritual Way. LC 79-17884. 224p. 1979. pap. 5.95 (ISBN 0-87123-026-7, 210026). Bethany Hse.

Bobik, Joseph. Aquinas in Being & Essence: A Translation & Interpretation. LC 65-23516. pap. 75.50 (ISBN 0-317-26719-1, 2024364). Bks Demand UMI.

Bobik, Joseph, ed. Nature of Philosophical Inquiry. LC 77-85347. 1970. pap. 5.95x (ISBN 0-268-00482-X). U of Notre Dame Pr.

Bobillier, Marie. Haydn. Leese, C. Leonard, tr. LC 79-39688. (Select Bibliographies Reprint Ser). 1972. Repr. of 1919 ed. 12.75 (ISBN 0-8369-9930-4). Ayer Co Pubs.

Bobillier, Marie see Brenet, Michel, pseud.

Bobillier, P. A., et al. Simulation with Gpss & Gpssv. LC 75-40316. 1976. 37.50 (ISBN 0-13-810549-9). P-H.

Bobinski, George S. Carnegie Libraries: Their History & Impact on American Public Library Development. LC 68-54216. (Illus.). 1969. lib. bdg. 10.00x (ISBN 0-8389-0022-4). ALA.

Bobitt, Franklin. The Curriculum of Modern Education. (Educational Ser.). 1941. Repr. 20.00 (ISBN 0-8482-7351-6). Norwood Edns.

Bobker, Lee R. Elements of Film. 3rd ed. 302p. 1979. pap. text ed. 16.95 (ISBN 0-15-522096-9, HC). HarBraceJ.

--Flight of a Dragon. LC 80-22670. 256p. 1981. 10.95 (ISBN 0-688-03759-3). Morrow.

--Making Movies: From Script to Screen. 304p. 1973. pap. text ed. 13.95 (ISBN 0-15-554630-9, HC). HarBraceJ.

Bobkins, Denk. The Compassionate Deathmakers. (Orig.). 1980. pap. 2.25 (ISBN 0-532-23209-7). Woodhill.

Bobko, Jane, tr. see Loseff, Lev.

Bobley, Roger, ed. Illustrated World Encyclopedia, 21 vols. (gr. 5-9). 1974. Set. goldmark ed. 59.95 (ISBN 0-685-42347-6). Bobley.

Bobley, Roger, intro. by. Illustrated World Encyclopedia. (Illus.). (gr. 5-9). 1977. 39.95 (ISBN 0-685-81847-0). Bobley.

Bobo, Benjamin F. Corporate & Third World Engagement: A Reciprocal Responsibility. cancelled (ISBN 0-88410-063-4). Ballinger Pub.

Bobo, J. B. Modern Coin Magic. (Illus.). 358p. 1982. pap. 6.00 (ISBN 0-486-24258-7). Dover.

Bobon, D. & Baumahn, U., eds. AMDP System in Pharmacopsychiatry. (Modern Problems of Pharmacopsychiatry: Vol. 20). (Illus.). vi, 234p. 1983. 56.25 (ISBN 3-8055-3637-2). S Karger.

Bobon, D. P., et al, eds. The Neuroleptics. (Modern Problems of Pharmacopsychiatry: Vol. 5). 1970. 20.00 (ISBN 3-8055-0530-2). S Karger.

Bobosh, Theodore. Am I Saved? 1984. pap. 3.45 (ISBN 0-937032-38-7). Light&Life Pub Co MN.

Bobrik, Michael A. General Chemistry Laboratory Manual. 94p. 1982. pap. text ed. 8.95 (ISBN 0-8403-2653-X). Kendall-Hunt.

Bobrinskoy, Count. Peacock from Heaven. 32p. 1983. 15.00 (ISBN 0-89756-012-4). Two Rivers.

Bobroba, Raissa, tr. see Raud, Eno.

Bobroff, Arthur. Acne: And Related Disorders of Complexion & Scalp. 136p. 1964. 12.75x (ISBN 0-398-00183-9). C C Thomas.

--Eczema: Its Nature, Cure & Prevention. (Illus.). 264p. 1962. 22.75x (ISBN 0-398-00184-7). C C Thomas.

Bobrov, Lev, tr. see Blishchenko, I., et al.

Bobrov, N., tr. see Raikov, I. B.

Bobrov, Vladimir, tr. see Yuzefovich, Victor.

Bobrova, Raissa, tr. see Dlugolensky, Yakov.

Bobrovskaya, Cecilia. Twenty Years in Underground Russia: Memoirs of a Rank & File Bolshevik. pap. 3.95 (ISBN 0-89380-015-5). Proletarian Pubs.

Bobrow, Daniel G., ed. Qualitative Reasoning about Physical Sciences. 504p. 1985. text ed. 22.50x (ISBN 0-262-02218-4, Pub. by Bradford). MIT Pr.

Bobrow, David B., et al. Understanding Foreign Policy Decisions: The Chinese Case. LC 78-24667. (Illus.). 1979. 22.95 (ISBN 0-02-904410-3). Free Pr.

Bobrow, Edwin E. Selling the Volume Retailer: A Practical Plan for Success. LC 75-1168. 126p. 1975. 15.95 (ISBN 0-86730-511-8). Lebhar Friedman.

Bobrow, Edwin E. & Bobrow, Mark D. Marketing Handbook, 2 vols. LC 85-70439. 1985. 47.50 ea. Vol. I: Marketing Practices (ISBN 0-87094-523-8). Vol. II: Marketing Management (ISBN 0-87094-524-6). Dow Jones-Irwin.

Bobrow, Edwin E. & Wizenberg, Larry, eds. Sales Manager's Handbook. LC 82-71068. 576p. 1983. 50.00 (ISBN 0-87094-240-9). Dow Jones-Irwin.

Bobrow, Ella. Three Brave Snowflakes. (Illus.). 24p. (Orig.). 1982. pap. 3.95 (ISBN 0-88962-204-3, Pub by Mosaic Pr Canada). Flatiron Book Dist.

Bobrow, J. Barron's New Guide to the Law School Admission Test (LSAT) Rev. ed. 640p. 1982. 21.95 (ISBN 0-8120-5420-2); pap. 7.95 (ISBN 0-8120-2362-5). Barron.

Bobrow, Jerry. Barron's How to Prepare for the Law School Admission Test (LSAT) LC 79-12930. 1982. 21.95 (ISBN 0-8120-2362-5); pap. 7.95 (ISBN 0-8120-5420-2). Barron.

--How to Prepare for the Law School Admission Test (LSAT) 3rd ed. 1985. text ed. 23.95 (ISBN 0-8120-5555-1); pap. 8.95 (ISBN 0-8120-2790-6). Barron.

Bobrow, Jerry & Covino, William A. GMAT (Graduate Management Admissions Test) Preparation Guide. (Cliffs Test Preparation Ser.). (Illus.). 1982. pap. text ed. 5.95 (ISBN 0-8220-2006-8). Cliffs.

--PSAT (Preliminary Scholastic Aptitude Test) Preparation Guide. (Cliffs Test Preparation Ser.). (Illus.). (gr. 10-11). 1982. pap. 3.25 (ISBN 0-8220-2002-5). Cliffs.

--SAT (Scholastic Aptitude Test) Preparation Guide. (Cliffs Test Preparation Ser.). (Illus.). (gr. 11-12). 1982. pap. 4.95 wkbk. (ISBN 0-8220-2000-9). Cliffs.

Bobrow, Jerry & Orton, Peter Z. CBEST: California Basic Educational Skills Test Preparation Guide. (Cliffs Test Preparation Ser.). (Illus.). 244p. (Orig.). 1983. pap. text ed. 7.95 (ISBN 0-8220-2030-0). Cliffs.

Bobrow, Jerry, et al. ACT (American College Testing Preparation Guide) (Cliffs Test Preparation Ser.). (Illus.). (gr. 10-12). 1982. pap. 4.95 wkbk. (ISBN 0-8220-2004-1). Cliffs.

--NTE (National Teacher Examinations) Preparation Guide. (Cliffs Test Preparation Ser.). (Illus.). 534p. (Orig.). 1984. 14.95 (ISBN 0-8220-2017-3). Cliffs.

Bobrow, Jill & Jinkins, Dana. Classic Yacht Interiors: A Reissue. (Illus.). 1983. 39.95 (ISBN 0-393-03274-4). Norton.

--St. Vincent & the Grenadines. (Illus.). 1985. 25.00 (ISBN 0-393-03309-0). Norton.

Bobrow, Leonard S. Elementary Linear Circuit Analysis. LC 80-15555. 714p. 1981. text ed. 41.95 (ISBN 0-03-055696-1, HoltC); study manual 19.95 (ISBN 0-03-057687-3). HR&W.

Bobrow, Mark D., jt. auth. see Bobrow, Edwin E.

Bobrow, Mitchell. Habit Breakthrough. 1985. 12.95 (ISBN 0-933705-03-4); pap. 7.95 (ISBN 0-933705-02-6). Loiry-Bonner Pr.

Bobrowski, Johannes. From the Rivers. Mead, Ruth & Mead, Matthew, trs. from Ger. (International Bks.). 72p. pap. 2.50 (ISBN 0-317-04124-X). U of Iowa Pr.

--Lithuanian Pianos. Hoffman, Carl J., tr. from Ger. (Nightsun Ser.). 192p. (Orig.). Date not set. pap. 8.95 (ISBN 0-913623-10-5). Adler Pub Co.

Bobrowski, Robert. Rediscovering the Woodburning Cookstove. LC 76-4680. (Illus.). 98p. 1976. pap. 7.95 (ISBN 0-85699-130-9). Chatham Pr.

Bobula, Ida. Origin of the Hungarian Nation. 1982. 5.00 (ISBN 0-87934-028-2, 82-0724). Danubian.

Bobyn, J. D., jt. auth. see Engh, Charles A.

Boca, Angelo Del see Del Boca, Angelo.

Boca, Frances K. del see Ashmore, Richard D. & Del Boca, Frances K.

Bocaccio, Giovanni. A Pleasant Disport of Divers Noble Personages Entitled Philocopo. LC 71-25579. (English Experience Ser.: No. 277). 116p. 1970. Repr. of 1567 ed. 14.00 (ISBN 90-221-0277-7). Walter J Johnson.

Bocage, Ducarmel. The General Economic Theory of Francois Perroux. 216p. (Orig.). 1985. lib. bdg. 19.75 (ISBN 0-8191-4381-2); pap. text ed. 11.25 (ISBN 0-8191-4382-0). U Pr of Amer.

Bocca, Geoffrey. Amanda in France. (Commander Amanda). 224p. 1976. pap. 1.50 (ISBN 0-89083-170-X). Zebra.

--Amanda in Spain. 1975. pap. 1.50 (ISBN 0-89083-146-7). Zebra.

--Best-Seller: A Nostalgic Celebration of the Less Than Great Books You Have Always Been Afraid to Admit You Loved. 1981. 12.95 (ISBN 0-686-70452-5, Wyndham Bks). S&S.

--You Can Write a Novel. LC 83-13990. 133p. 1983. 12.95 (ISBN 0-13-976845-9); pap. 5.95 (ISBN 0-13-976837-8). P-H.

Boccaccio. Andreuccio de Perugia. (Easy Reader, A). pap. 3.25 (ISBN 0-88436-049-0, 55250). EMC.

--Tales of Ardent & Whimsical Love. (Illus.). 151p. 1984. 147.45 (ISBN 0-89901-189-6). Found Class Reprints.

Boccaccio, Giovanni. Amorosa Visione. Hollander, Robert, et al, eds. LC 85-40488. 236p. (Ital. & Eng.). 1985. Repr. of 1362 ed. 30.00x (ISBN 0-87451-347-2). U Pr of New Eng.

--Amorous Fiammetta. LC 76-98821. Repr. of 1926 ed. lib. bdg. 19.75x (ISBN 0-8371-3026-3, BOAF). Greenwood.

--Chichibo & the Crane. (Illus.). (gr. 1-6). 1961. 5.95 (ISBN 0-8392-3004-4). Astor-Honor.

--The Corbaccio. Cassell, Anthony K., ed. & tr. from It. LC 75-9844. (Illus.). 216p. 1975. 15.95x (ISBN 0-252-00479-5). U of Ill Pr.

--De Casibus Illustrium Virorum. LC 62-7017. 1962. Repr. of 1520 ed. 35.00x (ISBN 0-8201-1005-1). Schol Facsimiles.

--De Casibus Illustrium Virorum: Here Begynneth the Boke Calledde Ioh. Bochas Descriuinge the Falle of Princis. Ludgate, John, tr. LC 76-57358. (English Experience Ser.: No. 777). 1977. Repr. of 1494 ed. lib. bdg. 86.00 (ISBN 90-221-0777-9). Walter J Johnson.

--Decameron, 2 vols. 1973. Repr. of 1930 ed. 8.95x ea. (Evman); Vol. I. (ISBN 0-460-00845-5, Evman); Vol. II. (ISBN 0-460-00846-3, Evman). Biblio Dist.

--Decameron, 2 vols. in 1. 1953. 14.95x (ISBN 0-460-10845-X, Evman). Biblio Dist.

--The Decameron. Musa, Mark & Bondanella, Peter, eds. LC 77-5664. (Norton Critical Editions). 1977. 15.95 (ISBN 0-393-04458-0); pap. 8.95x (ISBN 0-393-09132-5). Norton.

--The Decameron. McWilliam, G. H., tr. from It. (Classics Ser.). (Orig.). 1972. pap. 6.95 (ISBN 0-14-044269-3). Penguin.

--The Decameron. 1982. pap. 5.95 (ISBN 0-451-62134-4, ME2134, Ment). NAL.

--The Decameron. Musa, Mark & Bondanella, Peter, trs. from Ital. 1983. 29.95 (ISBN 0-393-01754-0). Norton.

--The Decameron: A Diplomatic Edition. Singleton, Charles S., ed. LC 72-8892. (Illus.). 688p. (Ital.). 1974. 75.00x (ISBN 0-8018-1465-0). Johns Hopkins.

--The Decameron: A Selection. Speight, Kathleen, ed. LC 83-61667. (The Italian Texts Ser.). 250p. 1984. pap. text ed. 9.50 (ISBN 0-7190-0934-0, Pub. by Manchester Univ Pr). Longwood Pub Group.

--Decameron: Preserved to Posterity, 4 Vols. Hutton, Edward, tr. LC 10-4801. (Tudor Translations, First Ser.: Nos. 41-44). Repr. of 1909 ed. Set. 180.00 (ISBN 0-404-51960-1); 45.00 ea. Vol. 1 (ISBN 0-404-51961-X). Vol. 2 (ISBN 0-404-51962-8). Vol. 3 (ISBN 0-404-51963-6). Vol. 4 (ISBN 0-404-51964-4). AMS Pr.

--Decameron: The John Payne Translation, 3 vols. Singleton, Charles S., rev. by. Payne, John, tr. from Ital. LC 77-83112. (Illus.). 1983. Boxed Set. 125.00 (ISBN 0-520-03557-7). Vol. I, 444 pg. Vol. II, 354 pg. Vol. III, 150 pg. U of Cal pr.

--Filostrato of Giovanni Boccaccio. Griffin, Nathaniel E. & Myrick, Arthur B., trs. LC 72-120232. 1973. Repr. lib. bdg. 40.00x (ISBN 0-374-90730-7). Octagon.

--The Nymph of Fiesole. Donno, Daniel J., tr. LC 74-5781. Orig. Title: Il Ninfale Fiesolano. (Illus.). 149p. 1974. Repr. of 1960 ed. lib. bdg. 24.75x (ISBN 0-8371-7500-3, BONY). Greenwood.

Boccaccio, Giovanni & Aretino, Lionardo B. Earliest Lives of Dante. 1973. Repr. of 1901 ed. 17.50 (ISBN 0-8274-1189-8). R West.

Boccato, Paolo, jt. auth. see Ravetto, Carlo.

Bocchetta, Vittore & Young, Ruth E., eds. New Century Vest-Pocket Italian Dictionary. (Ital.). 1978. 2.95 (ISBN 0-8329-1535-1). New Century.

Bocchetta, Vittore E., ed. New Century World-Wide Italian Dictionary: Italian-English, English-Italian. LC 81-85508. (Orig., Ital. & Eng.). 9.95 (ISBN 0-8329-9696-3). New Century.

--World-Wide Italian Dictionary. (Ital.). 1977. pap. 2.50 (ISBN 0-449-30840-5, Prem). Fawcett.

Bocchi, Achille. Symbolicarum Quaestionum de Universo Genere. Orgel, Stephen, ed. LC 78-68188. (Philosphy of Images Ser: Vol. 5). 1979. lib. bdg. 80.00 (ISBN 0-8240-3679-4). Garland Pub.

Bocchino, Anthony J. & Beal, Ronald L. McLain vs. Barber. 200p. 1984. 12.50 (ISBN 0-318-11882-3). Natl Inst Trial Ad.

Bocchino, Anthony J. & Natali, Louis M. NITA Fire & Casualty Co. vs. Anthony Rubino, d.b.a. Rubino & Son. 88p. 1981. 10.00 (ISBN 0-318-11884-X); tchr's. manual 5.00 (ISBN 0-318-11885-8). Natl Inst Trial Ad.

Bocchino, Anthony J. & Tanford, J. Alexander. North Carolina Trial Evidence Manual. LC 76-29099. 98p. 1976. with 1978 suppl 25.00 (ISBN 0-87215-188-3); 1978 suppl. 7.50 (ISBN 0-87215-277-4). Michie Co.

Bocchino, Anthony J., jt. auth. see Greenberg, Mark S.

Bocchino, William A. Management Information Systems: Tools & Techniques. LC 73-38416. (Illus.). 384p. 1972. ref. ed. O.P. 24.95 (ISBN 0-13-548693-9). P-H.

--Simplified Guide to Microcomputers with Practical Programs & Applications. LC 82-3671. 256p. 1982. 19.95 (ISBN 0-13-810085-3, Busn). P-H.

Boccia & Coehlo. Armi Bianche Italiane. (Illus.). 462p. 1976. 135.00 (ISBN 0-686-14972-6). Arma Pr.

Boccio, Karen C. Inner Sanctions. rev. ed. 35p. (Orig.). 1980. pap. 3.50 (ISBN 0-910829-01-2). First East.

Bochan, Bohdan. The Phenomenology of Freedom in Kleist's Die Familie Schroffenstein & Penthesilea. (German Language & Literature-European University Studies: No. 1, Vol. 490). 195p. 1982. pap. 25.80 (ISBN 3-8204-7092-1). P Lang Pubs.

Bochank, Elizabeth & Krauss, Elissa, eds. Women's Self-Defense Cases: Theory & Practice. 330p. 1981. 27.50 (ISBN 0-87215-354-1). Michie Co.

Boche, Cheryl, et al. Pinetree Fashions: A Flow-of-Work Office Simulation. (gr. 9-12). 1980. 945.00 (ISBN 0-538-25520-X, Y52). SW Pub.

Bochel, Dorothy. Probation & Aftercare. 1976. 17.50x (ISBN 0-7073-0192-0, Pub. by Scottish Academic Pr Scotland). Columbia U Pr.

Bochel, J. M. & Denver, D. T. The Scottish Local Government Elections 1974. 1974. pap. 12.50x (ISBN 0-7073-0111-4, Pub. by Scottish Academic Pr Scotland). Columbia U Pr.

Bochel, J. M., et al, eds. The Referendum Experience, Scotland 1979. (Illus.). 224p. 1981. 20.00 (ISBN 0-08-025734-8, R120). Pergamon.

Bochenski, Innocentius. Contemporary European Philosophy. Nicholl, Donald & Aschenbrenner, Karl, trs. from Ger. LC 82-2987. Orig. Title: Europaische Philosophie der Gegenwart. xviii, 326p. 1982. Repr. of 1956 ed. lib. bdg. 35.00x (ISBN 0-313-23490-6, BOCY). Greenwood.

Bochenski, Innocenty M. History of Formal Logic. 2nd ed. LC 72-113118. 1970. text ed. 24.95 (ISBN 0-8284-0238-8). Chelsea Pub.

Bochenski, J. M. The Dogmatic Principles of Soviet Philosophy (As of 1958) Synopsis of Osnovy Marksistkoj Filosofii. Blakeley, T. J., tr. from Ger. (Sovietica Ser.: No. 14). 78p. 1963. with complete index 16.00 (ISBN 90-277-0042-7, Pub. by Reidel Holland). Kluwer Academic.

--The Methods of Contemporary Thought. Caws, Peter, tr. from Ger. 135p. 1965. lib. bdg. 21.00 (ISBN 90-277-0004-4, Pub. by Reidel Holland). Kluwer Academic.

--Philosophy: An Introduction. Newell, William M., tr. from Ger. 112p. 1963. lib. bdg. 16.00 (ISBN 90-277-0005-2, Pub. by Reidel Holland). Kluwer Academic.

--Precis of Mathematical Logic. (Illus.). 110p. 1962. 27.95 (ISBN 0-677-00070-7). Gordon.

--A Precis of Mathematical Logic. Bird, Otto, tr. from Fr & Ger. (Snthese Library: No.1). 100p. 1959. lib. bdg. 14.50 (ISBN 90-277-0073-7, Pub. by Reidel Holland). Kluwer Academic.

--Soviet Russian Dialectical Materialism. rev. ed. Sollohub, Nicholas, tr. from Ger. 185p. 1963. lib. bdg. 18.50 (ISBN 90-277-0043-5, Pub. by Reidel Holland). Kluwer Academic.

Bochenski, J. M. & Blakeley, T. J., eds. Bibliographie der sowjetischen Philosophie, 7 vols. Incl. Die Voprosy filosophie, 1947-1956. 75p. 1959. 18.50 (ISBN 90-277-0044-3); Buecher, 1947-1956, Buecher und Aufsaetze, 1957-1958, Namenverzeichnis 1947-1958. 109p. 1959. 21.00 (ISBN 90-277-0045-1); Buecher und Aufsaetze, 1959-1960. 73p. 1962. 18.50 (ISBN 90-277-0046-X); Ergaenzungen, Supplement, 1947-1960. 158p. 1963. 24.00 (ISBN 90-277-0047-8); Register, Indices 1947-1960. 144p. 1964. 13.50 (ISBN 90-277-0048-6); Buecher und Aufsaetze 1961-1963. 195p. 1968. 26.00 (ISBN 90-277-0049-4); Buecher und Aufsaetze 1964-1966. 311p. 1968. 39.50 (ISBN 90-277-0050-8). (Sovietica Ser.). (Ger., Pub. by Reidel Holland). Kluwer Academic.

--Studies in Soviet Thought. (Sovietica Ser.: No. 7). 141p. 1961. lib. bdg. 24.00 (ISBN 90-277-0051-6, Pub. by Reidel Holland). Kluwer Academic.

Bochet, Jean-Jacques. Management of Upland Watersheds: Participation of the Mountain Communities. (Conservation Guides: No. 8). 199p. 1984. pap. text ed. 15.50 (F2495, FAO). Unipub.

Bochius, Johannes & Van Der Borcht, Pieter. Descriptio Publicae Gratulationis Spectaculorum Et Ludorum, in Adventu: Ernesti Archiducis Austriae Antiverpiae. LC 68-21207. (Illus., Lat). 1969. Repr. of 1595 ed. 49.50 (ISBN 0-405-08278-9, Blom Pubns). Ayer Co Pubs.

Bochkarev, Y. Soviet Russian Stories of the 1960's & 1970's. 419p. 1977. 7.45 (ISBN 0-8285-0949-2, Pub. by Progress Pubs USSR). Imported Pubns.

Bochkov, A. E. & Zaikov, G. E. Chemistry of the O-Glycosidic Bond: Formation & Cleavage. 1979. 53.00 (ISBN 0-08-022949-2). Pergamon.

Bochkova, O. P. & Shreyder, E. Y. Spectroscopic Analysis of Gaseous Mixtures. 1966. 74.50 (ISBN 0-12-109450-2). Acad Pr.

Bochmann, G. V. Concepts for Distributed System Design. (Illus.). 259p. 1983. pap. 21.00 (ISBN 0-387-12049-1). Springer-Verlag.

Bochner, Felix, et al. Handbook of Clinical Pharmacology. 2nd ed. 352p. 1983. 14.95 (ISBN 0-316-10064-1). Little.

Bochner, Jay. Blaise Cendrars: Discovery & Re-Creation. LC 77-2580. 1978. 32.50x (ISBN 0-8020-5352-1). U of Toronto Pr.

Bochner, S. & Chandrasekharan, K. Fourier Transforms. (Annals of Math Studies). 1949. 15.00 (ISBN 0-527-02735-9). Kraus Repr.

Bochner, S., jt. auth. see Yano, K.

Bochner, Salomon. Einstein Between Centuries. LC 79-66703. (Rice University Studies: Vol. 65, No. 3). 54p. 1979. pap. 5.50x (ISBN 0-89263-242-9). Rice Univ.

--Fouriersche Integrale. LC 49-22695. (Ger). 10.50 (ISBN 0-8284-0042-3). Chelsea Pub.

--Role of Mathematics in the Rise of Science. 1966. 37.50x (ISBN 0-691-08028-3); pap. 10.50 (ISBN 0-691-02371-9). Princeton U Pr.

Bochner, Salomon, et al. History of Analysis. Stanton, R. J., Jr. & Wells, R. O., Jr., eds. (Rice University Studies: Vol. 64, Nos. 2 & 3). 1979. pap. 11.00x (ISBN 0-89263-236-4). Rice Univ.

Bochner, Stephen, ed. Cultures in Contact: Studies in Cross-Cultural Interaction. LC 82-3852. (International Series in Experimental Social Psychology). (Illus.). 280p. 1982. 42.00 (ISBN 0-08-025805-0, K134); pap. 14.95 (ISBN 0-08-028919-3, J125). Pergamon.

--The Meditating Person: Bridges Between Cultures. 334p. 1982. pap. text ed. 13.25x (ISBN 0-87073-893-3). Schenkman Bks Inc.

Bochnovic, John. The Inventive Step: Its Evolution in Canada, the United Kingdom, & the United States. Beier, Freidrich & Schricker, Gerhard, eds. (I I C Studies, Vol. 5). 90p. 1982. pap. 25.30x (ISBN 0-89573-058-8). VCH Pubs.

Bochroch, Albert R. American Cars of the Seventies. (Olyslager Auto Library Photo Ser.). (Illus.). 63p. 1982. 11.95 (ISBN 0-7232-2870-1, Pub. by Warne Pubs England). Motorbooks Intl.

Bock. Guidebook to California Taxes, 1984. 558p. pap. 12.00 (ISBN 0-317-04243-2). Commerce.

Bock, Audie. Japanese Film Directors. LC 77-75968. (Illus.). 1978. 15.50 (ISBN 0-87011-304-6). Kodansha.

--Japanese Film Directors. LC 84-82294. (Illus.). 380p. 1985. pap. 9.95 not set (ISBN 0-87011-714-9). Kodansha.

Bock, Audie, tr. see Kurosawa, Akira.

Bock, Audie E., tr. see Kurosawa, Akira.

Bock, Betty. Antitrust in the Competitive World of the 1980's: Exploring Options. 29p. 1982. 50.00. Conference Bd.

--Line of Business Reporting: Problems in the Formulation of a Data Program. (Report Ser.: No. 654). 109p. (Orig.). 1975. pap. 25.00 (ISBN 0-8237-0073-9); pap. 5.00 member. Conference Bd.

--Restructuring Proposals: Measuring Competition in Numerical Grids. (Report Ser: No. 619). 177p. (Orig.). 1974. pap. 12.50 (ISBN 0-8237-0050-X); pap. 2.50 member. Conference Bd.

--Toward a National Antitrust Policy: Information Problems & Antitrust. (Report No. 696). 108p. 1976. 15.00 (ISBN 0-8237-0130-1); 5.00. Conference Bd.

Bock, Betty, et al, eds. The Impact of the Modern Corporation. (Government & Business Ser.). 400p. 1984. 40.00x (ISBN 0-231-05930-2); pap. 17.50x (ISBN 0-317-03995-4). Columbia U Pr.

Bock, Bruno & Bock, Klaus. Soviet Bloc Merchant Ships. LC 80-81092. (Illus.). 272p. 1981. 29.95 (ISBN 0-87021-669-4). Naval Inst Pr.

--Soviet Bloc Merchant Ships. (Illus.). 256p. 1980. 29.95 (ISBN 0-87021-669-4); bulk rates avail. Naval Inst Pr.

Bock, C. V. London German Studies, I. 165p. 1980. 30.00x (ISBN 0-85457-095-0, Pub. by Inst Germanic Stud England). State Mutual Bk.

Bock, C. V., ed. London German Studies, I. (Publications of the Institute of Germanic Studies: Vol. 26). 165p. 1980. pap. text ed. 17.25x (ISBN 0-85457-095-0, Pub. by Inst Germanic UK). Humanities.

Bock, C. V. & Riley, V. J., eds. Theses in Germanic Studies, 1972-1977. (Publications of the Institute of Germanic Studies: Vol. 27). 57p. 1980. pap. text ed. 11.00x (ISBN 0-85457-081-0, Pub. by Inst Germanic UK). Humanities.

Bock, Carl A. The Head-Hunters of Borneo: A Narrative of Travel up the Mahakkam & Down the Barito. 2nd ed. LC 77-86966. Repr. of 1882 ed. 67.50 (ISBN 0-404-16698-9). AMS Pr.

Bock, Carolyn E; see Levy, Harold L.

Bock, Catherine C. Henri Matisse & Neo-Impressionism, 1898-1908. Foster, Stephen, ed. LC 81-1753. (Studies in the Fine Arts: The Avant-Garde: No. 13). 238p. 1981. 44.95 (ISBN 0-8357-1169-2). UMI Res Pr.

Bock, Cindy. Cindy's Short Stories for Children. 1985. 4.95 (ISBN 0-533-06609-3). Vantage.

Bock, D. L., ed. Finite-Difference Techniques for Vectorized Fluid Dynamics Calculations. (Springer Ser. Computational Physics). (Illus.). 240p. 1981. 38.00 (ISBN 0-387-10482-8). Springer-Verlag.

Bock, David & Wallich, Christine I. Currency Swaps: A Borrowing Technique in a Public Policy Context. (World Bank Staff Working Papers: No. 640). 70p. Date not set. 5.00 (ISBN 0-318-02924-3). World Bank.

Bock, Edward C. Wilhelm Von Ketteler, Bishop of Mainz: His Life, Times & Ideas. 287p. 1977. pap. text ed. 12.25 (ISBN 0-8191-0270-9). U Pr of Amer.

Bock, Felicia G. Classical Learning & Taoist Practices in Early Japan, with Translation of Books XVI & XX of the Engi-Shiki. Bock, Felicia G., tr. from Japanese. & intro. by. (Occasional Paper Arizona State Univ., Center for Asian Studies: No. 17). 102p. 1985. pap. 8.00 (ISBN 0-939252-13-9). ASU Ctr Asian.

Bock, Fred & Leech, Bryan J., eds. The Hymnal Companion. 1979. 12.95 (ISBN 0-89477-004-7). Paragon Assocs.

--Hymns for the Family of God. 1976. 6.95 (ISBN 0-89477-000-4, Dist. by Alexandria House); looseleaf 5.00 (ISBN 0-89477-002-0); pap. 5.00 (ISBN 0-89477-001-2). Paragon Assocs.

Bock, Fred G., jt. ed. see Gori, Gio B.

Bock, Fred G., et al. Carcinogenesis: Recent Investigations. LC 72-6311. (Illus.). 204p. 1972. text ed. 24.50x (ISBN 0-8422-7017-5). Irvington.

Bock, G. De see Vokaer, R. & De Bock, G.

Bock, Glenn H., ed. see Haensel, Phyllis C.

Bock, Glenn N & Hoff, Marshall G., eds. Someone Special. (Living with Kidney Disease). (Illus.). 32p. (gr. k-6). 1981. write for info. (ISBN 0-940210-00-2). Minn Med Found.

Bock, H., jt. auth. see Heilbronner, E.

Bock, Hal. Save: Hockey's Brave Goalies. 1974. pap. 1.25 (ISBN 0-380-00135-7, 20669). Avon.

Bock, Hal, jt. ed. see Hollander, Zander.

Bock, Hans-Michael & Berger, Juergen, eds. Photo: Casparius. (Illus.). 432p. (Orig.). 1981. pap. 29.95 (ISBN 0-918432-37-5). NY Zoetrope.

Bock, Hedwig & Wertheim, Albert, eds. Essays on Contemporary British Drama. 310p. 1981. pap. 10.95x (ISBN 3-19-002214-3, Pub. by Verlag W Germany). Adlers Foreign Bks.

Bock, Hedwig & Werthrim, Albert, eds. Essays on Contemporary American Drama. 302p. (Orig.). 1981. pap. 10.95x (ISBN 3-19-002232-1, Pub. by Verlag W Germany). Adlers Foreign Bks.

Bock, Henning, intro. by. Ronald Searle. LC 79-10375. (Illus.). 1979. 25.00 (ISBN 0-8317-1650-9, Mayflower Bks). Smith Pubs.

Bock, Janet. The Jesus Mystery. 240p. 1981. 15.00x (ISBN 0-686-81454-1, Pub. by Spearman England). State Mutual Bk.

Bock, Janet L. The Jesus Mystery: Of Lost Years & Unknown Travels. LC 80-67420. (Illus.). 231p. (Orig.). 1980. pap. 6.95 (ISBN 0-937736-00-7). Aura Bks.

Bock, Joanne. Pop Wiener: Naive Painter. LC 72-90409. (Illus.). 178p. 1974. lib. bdg. 20.00 (ISBN 0-87023-122-7). U of Mass Pr.

Bock, John & Papagiannis, George, eds. Nonformal Education & National Development: A Critical Assessment of Policy, Research, & Practice. LC 83-4031. (Praeger Special Studies Series in Comparative Education). 414p. 1983. 32.95x (ISBN 0-03-061359-0). Praeger.

Bock, Kenneth. Human Nature & History: A Response to Sociobiology. 192p. 1980. 25.00x (ISBN 0-231-05078-X); pap. 12.00 (ISBN 0-231-05079-8). Columbia U Pr.

Bock, Klaus, jt. auth. see Bock, Bruno.

Bock, M. E., jt. auth. see Judge, G. G.

Bock, Michael, jt. ed. see Rickheit, Gert.

Bock, P. G. & Rothenberg, Irene F. Internal Migration Policy & New Towns: The Mexican Experience. LC 78-31918. 167p. 1980. 14.95x (ISBN 0-252-00744-1). U of Ill Pr.

Bock, Paul. In Search of a Responsible World Society: The Social Teachings of the World Council of Churches. LC 74-9986. 252p. 1974. 10.00 (ISBN 0-664-20708-1). Westminster.

Bock, Paul, ed. Signs of the Kingdom: A Ragaz Reader. 152p. (Orig.). 1984. pap. 7.95 (ISBN 0-8028-1986-9). Eerdmans.

Bock, Philip K. Continuities in Psychological Anthropology: A Historical Introduction. LC 79-23200. (Illus.). 288p. 1980. text ed. 20.95 (ISBN 0-7167-1136-2); pap. text ed. 11.95 (ISBN 0-7167-1137-0). W H Freeman.

--Shakespeare & Elizabethan Culture: An Anthropological View. LC 83-20238. 220p. 1984. 17.25 (ISBN 0-8052-3902-2). Schocken.

Bock, Philip K., ed. Culture Shock: A Reader in Modern Cultural Anthropology. LC 81-40770. 392p. 1981. pap. text ed. 10.25 (ISBN 0-8191-1812-5). U Pr of Amer.

Bock, R., ed. Heavy Ion Collisions, Vol. 3. 674p. 1983. 140.50 (ISBN 0-444-85352-9, North-Holland). Elsevier.

--Heavy Ion Collisions: Heavy Ion Reactors & Microscopic Properties of Nuclear States, Vol. 1. 676p. 1979. 121.50 (ISBN 0-7204-0738-9, North Holland). Elsevier.

--Heavy Ion Collisions: Heavy Ion Reactors & Microscopic Properties of Nuclear States, Vol. 2. 472p. 1980. 102.25 (ISBN 0-444-85295-6, North-Holland). Elsevier.

Bock, R. Darrell & Yates, George R. Multiqual II: Log-linear Analysis of Nominal or Ordinal Qualitative Data by the Method of Maximum Likelihood. 1983. pap. 4.00 (ISBN 0-89498-008-4). Sci Ware.

Bock, Ramond. Vitamin E: Key to Youthful Longevity. 1981. pap. 4.95x (ISBN 0-317-06942-X, Regent House). B of A.

Bock, Richard. Camper Cookery. 1977. pap. 5.95 (ISBN 0-89328-008-9). Lorenz Pr.

--The Galley Guide to Fine Food. 1977. pap. 5.95 (ISBN 0-89328-009-7). Lorenz Pr.

Bock, Richard D. & Jones, Lyle V. The Measurement & Prediction of Judgment & Choice. LC 66-17897. (Holden-Day Series in Psychology). pap. 96.00 (ISBN 0-317-28136-4, 2055743). Bks Demand UMI.

Bock, Rudolf & Marr, Iain L. A Handbook of Decomposition Methods in Analytical Chemistry. LC 78-70559. 444p. 1979. 94.95x (ISBN 0-470-26501-9). Halsted Pr.

Bock, Russell S. Guidebook to California Taxes 1985. 588p. 1984. pap. 13.00 (ISBN 0-317-19221-3, 5895). Commerce.

--Guidebook to California Taxes-1986. 588p. 1985. 14.00 (ISBN 0-317-30592-1, 5896). Commerce.

Bock, S. Allen. Food Allergy: A Primer for People. May, Charles D., intro. by. LC 83-72531. 72p. 1983. pap. 5.00 (ISBN 0-9612332-0-6). AJ Pub Co.

Bock, Walter J., jt. auth. see Richards, Lawrence P.

Bockar, J. A. Primer for the Psychotherapist. 2nd. ed. 149p. 1981. pap. 13.95 (ISBN 0-89335-127-X). SP Med & Sci Bks.

Bockar, Joyce. The Last Best Diet Book. 221p. 1984. pap. 3.50 (ISBN 0-8128-8029-3). Stein & Day.

Bockar, Joyce A. The Last Best Diet Book. LC 79-3710. 192p. 1980. 10.00 (ISBN 0-8128-2594-2). Stein & Day.

Bockarev, S. V. The Method of Averaging in the Theory of Orthogonal Series, & Some Questions in the Theory of Bases. LC 80-26300. (Proceedings of the Steklov Institute of Mathematics: No. 146). 1980. 34.00 (ISBN 0-8218-3045-7). Am Math.

Bockelman, A. E. Practical Guide for Altar Guilds. LC 62-16936. (Illus., Orig.). 1962. pap. 4.95 (ISBN 0-8066-0223-6, 10-5050). Augsburg.

Bockelmann, W. D. Auge, Brille, Auto. (Illus.). xii, 496p. 1982. pap. 46.75 (ISBN 3-8055-3445-0). S Karger.

Bockemuhl, Jochen, et al. Toward a Phenomenology of the Etheric World: Investigations into the Life of Nature & Man. Gardner, Malcolm, et al, eds. Meeks, John, tr. from Ger. (Illus.). 200p. (Orig.). 1985. pap. 16.95 (ISBN 0-88010-115-6). Anthroposophic.

Bockeria, L. A., jt. auth. see Burakovsky, V. I.

Bockett, J. C., et al. Belfast: The Making of the City. (Illus.). 188p. 1983. 25.95 (ISBN 0-86281-100-7, Pub. by Appletree Pr); pap. 11.95 (ISBN 0-86281-119-8). Irish Bks Media.

Bockford, William see Fairclough, Peter.

Bockhoff, K. H., ed. Nuclear Data for Science & Technology. 1983. lib. bdg. 120.00 (ISBN 90-277-1560-2, Pub. by Reidel Holland). Kluwer Academic.

Bockhoff, K. H., ed. see Specialists Meeting Held at the Central Bureau for Nuclear Measurements, Geel, Belgium, 5-8 Dec. 1977.

Bockholt, A. J. World Food & Fiber Crops. 1975. coil bdg. 8.95 (ISBN 0-88252-037-7). Paladin Hse.

Bockhoot, Robert. Social Action & the Law. pap. 2.50 (ISBN 0-686-37042-2). Ctr Respon Psych.

Bockl, George. How Real Estate Fortunes Are Made. 1972. 10.95 (ISBN 0-13-431098-5, Reward); pap. 4.95 (ISBN 0-13-431106-X). P-H.

--How to Find Something Big to Live for: A Spiritual Odyssey. 193p. (Orig.). 1984. pap. 7.95 (ISBN 0-942494-83-0). Coleman Pub.

--Recycling Real Estate: The Number One Way to Make Money in the 80's. LC 82-12244. 237p. 1983. 19.95 (ISBN 0-13-768804-0, Busn). P-H.

Bockle, Franz. War, Poverty, Freedom: The Christian Response. (Concilium Ser.: Vol. 15). 6.95 (ISBN 0-8091-0154-8). Paulist Pr.

Bockle, Franz & Beemer, Theo. Dilemmas of Tomorrow's World. LC 78-86974. (Concilium Ser.: No. 45). 188p. 1965. 6.95 (ISBN 0-8091-0030-4). Paulist Pr.

Bockle, Franz, ed. Moral Problems & Christian Personalism. LC 65-24045. (Concilium Ser.: Vol. 5). 191p. 6.95 (ISBN 0-8091-0099-1). Paulist Pr.

--Social Message of the Gospels. LC 68-31249. (Concilium Ser.: Vol. 35). 188p. 6.95 (ISBN 0-8091-0138-6). Paulist Pr.

--Understanding the Signs of the Times. LC 67-25694. (Concilium Ser.: Vol. 25). 176p. 1967. 6.95 (ISBN 0-8091-0152-1). Paulist Pr.

Bockle, Franz & Pohier, Jean-Marie, eds. Sexuality in Contemporary Catholicism. (Concilium Ser.: Vol. 100). 1977. pap. 6.95 (ISBN 0-8245-0260-4). Crossroad NY.

Bockmon, Guy A. & Starr, William J. Scored for Listening: A Guide to Music. 2nd ed. (Illus.). 213p. (Orig.). 1972. pap. text ed. 13.95 (ISBN 0-15-579055-2, HC); records 13.95 (ISBN 0-15-579056-0). HarBraceJ.

Bockmuehl, Klaus, ed. see Burkhardt, Helmut.

Bockmuehl, Klaus, ed. see Scott, Waldron.

Bocknis, J. O'M. Energy Options Real Economics & the Solar-Hydrogen System. 442p. 1980. cancelled (ISBN 0-85066-204-4). Taylor & Francis.

Bockoven, Georgia. Restless Tide. (Superromances Ser.). 384p. 1983. pap. 2.95 (ISBN 0-373-70082-2). Harlequin Bks.

Bockrath, J. & Dunham, C. W. Contracts, Specifications & Law for Engineers. 4th ed. 544p. 1985. price not set (ISBN 0-07-018237-X). McGraw.

Bockrath, Joseph. Concepts in Environmental Law for Engineers, Scientists & Managers. (Environmental Engineering Ser.). 1976. text ed. 42.00 (ISBN 0-07-006327-3). McGraw.

Bockrath, Joseph T., jt. auth. see Dunham, Clarence W.

Bockris, J., et al. An Introduction to Electrochemical Science. (Wykeham Science Ser.: No.29). 144p. 1974. 9.95x (ISBN 0-8448-1156-4). Crane Russak Co.

Bockris, J. O. Energy: The Solar Hydrogen Alternative. LC 75-19125. 365p. 1975. 44.95x (ISBN 0-470-08429-4). Halsted Pr.

Bockris, J. O. & Khan, S. U. Quantum Electrochemistry. LC 78-11167. 538p. 1978. 69.50 (ISBN 0-306-31143-7, Plenum Pr). Plenum Pub.

Bockris, J. O. & White, J. L., eds. Physicochemical Measurements at High Temperatures. pap. 100.50 (ISBN 0-317-09034-8, 2051332). Bks Demand UMI.

Bockris, J. O., et al, eds. Modern Aspects of Electrochemistry, Vol. 14. LC 54-12732. 678p. 75.00 (ISBN 0-306-40845-7, Plenum Pr). Plenum Pub.

Bockris, J. O'M. & Fredlein, R. A. A Workbook of Electrochemistry. LC 72-83606. 177p. 1973. pap. 25.00x (ISBN 0-306-30590-9, Plenum Pr). Plenum Pub.

Bockris, J. O'M. & Nagy, Zolton. Electrochemistry for Ecologists. LC 73-84003. 200p. 1974. 29.50x (ISBN 0-306-30749-9, Plenum Pr). Plenum Pub.

Bockris, J. O'M. & Razumney, G. A. Fundamental Aspects of Electrocrystallization. LC 66-22123. 155p. 1967. 29.50x (ISBN 0-306-30254-3, Plenum Pr). Plenum Pub.

Bockris, J. O'M. & Reddy, A. K. Modern Electrochemistry, An Introduction to an Interdisciplinary Area, Vol. 1. LC 68-19518. 622p. 1970. text ed. 39.50x (ISBN 0-306-37036-0, Plenum Pr); pap. 17.50x (ISBN 0-306-25001-2). Plenum Pub.

--Modern Electrochemistry, An Introduction to an Interdisciplinary Area, Vol. 2. LC 68-19518. 810p. 1970. 39.50x (ISBN 0-306-37037-9, Plenum Pr); pap. 17.50x (ISBN 0-306-25002-0). Plenum Pub.

Bockris, J. O'M., ed. Electrochemistry of Cleaner Environments. LC 72-179762. 296p. 1972. 39.50x (ISBN 0-306-30560-7, Plenum Pr). Plenum Pub.

--Environmental Chemistry. LC 76-21081. (Illus.). 795p. 1977. 79.50x (ISBN 0-306-30869-X, Plenum Pr). Plenum Pub.

Bockris, J. O'M. & Conway, Brian E., eds. Comprehensive Treatise of Electrochemistry, Vol. 6: Electrodics-Transport. LC 82-13144. 546p. 1982. 72.50x (ISBN 0-306-40942-9, Plenum Pr). Plenum Pub.

Bockris, J. O'M., jt. ed. see Conway, B. E.

Bockris, J. O'M., et al, eds. Comprehensive Treatise of Electrochemistry, Vol. 1: The Double Layer. LC 80-21493. 472p. 1980. 65.00x (ISBN 0-306-40275-0, Plenum Pr). Plenum Pub.

--Comprehensive Treatise of Electrochemistry, Vol. 2: Electrochemical Processing. LC 80-24836. 638p. 1981. 79.50x (ISBN 0-306-40503-2, Plenum Pr). Plenum Pub.

--Comprehensive Treatise of Electrochemistry, Vol. 3: Electrochemical Energy Conversion & Storage. LC 81-2175. 525p. 1981. 75.00x (ISBN 0-306-40590-3, Plenum Pr). Plenum Pub.

--Comprehensive Treatise of Electrochemistry, Vol. 4: Electrochemical Materials Science. LC 81-4780. 586p. 1981. 77.50x (ISBN 0-306-40614-4, Plenum Pr). Plenum Pub.

--Trends in Electrochemistry. LC 79-18318. (Illus.). 408p. 1977. 59.50x (ISBN 0-306-30990-4, Plenum Pr). Plenum Pub.

Bockris, John O. Energy Options: Real Economics & the Solar-Hydrogen System. 441p. 1980. 44.95x (ISBN 0-470-26915-4). Halsted Pr.

Bockris, John O'M. & Reddy, Amulya K. Modern Electrochemistry: An Introduction to an Interdisciplinary Area, 2 vols. LC 73-13712. 1973. pap. text ed. 17.50x ea. (Rosetta). Vol. 1, 622p (ISBN 0-306-25001-2). Vol. 2, 810p (ISBN 0-306-25002-0). Plenum Pub.

Bockris, John O'M., jt. auth. see McGown, Linda B.

Bockris, Victor. With William Burroughs: A Report from the Bunker. LC 80-24905. (Illus.). 256p. 1981. 14.95 (ISBN 0-394-51809-8); pap. 7.95 (ISBN 0-394-17828-9). Seaver Bks.

Bockris, Victor & Malanga, Gerard. Uptight: The Velvet Underground Story. LC 84-62393. (Illus.). 128p. 1985. pap. 7.95 (ISBN 0-688-03906-5, Quill). Morrow.

Bockstiegel, Karl H., jt. auth. see Institute of International Business Law & Practice.

Bockstoce, John. The Archaeology of Cape Nome, Alaska. (University Museum Monographs: No. 38). (Illus.). xiii, 133p. (Orig.). 1979. pap. 19.00x (ISBN 0-934718-27-X). Univ Mus of U PA.

Bockus, Frank. Couple Therapy. LC 80-66923. 300p. 1980. 25.00 (ISBN 0-87668-412-6). Aronson.

Bockus, H. William, Jr. Advertising Graphics. 3rd ed. 1979. pap. write for info. (ISBN 0-02-311490-8). Macmillan.

Bockus, Henry L., ed. Gastroenterology, Vol. 1. 3rd ed. LC 73-91276. (Illus.). 1170p. 1974. text ed. 63.00 (ISBN 0-7216-1773-5). Saunders.

--Gastroenterology, Vol. 2. 3rd ed. LC 73-91276. (Illus.). 1976. text ed. 63.00 (ISBN 0-7216-1774-3). Saunders.

--Gastroenterology, Vol. 3. 3rd ed. LC 73-91276. (Illus.). 1984. Repr. of 1976 ed. text ed. 60.00 (ISBN 0-7216-1775-1). Saunders.

--Gastroenterology, Vol. 4. 3rd ed. LC 73-91276. (Illus.). 1976. text ed. 63.00 (ISBN 0-7216-1776-X). Saunders.

Bockus, William H., Jr. Advertising Graphics. 4th ed. 288p. 1986. pap. price not set (ISBN 0-02-311530-0). Macmillan.

Bocock, Peter, jt. auth. see Cortes, Mariluz.

Bocock, Robert. Freud & Modern Society: An Outline & Analysis of Freud's Sociology. LC 77-19118. 200p. 1978. text ed. 28.50x (ISBN 0-8419-0364-6); pap. text ed. 16.50x (ISBN 0-8419-0365-4). Holmes & Meier.

Bocock, Robert, ed. Sigmund Freud. (Key Sociologists Ser.). 128p. 1983. 11.50 (ISBN 0-85312-511-2, NO. 3888, Tavistock); pap. 4.95 (ISBN 0-85312-580-5, NO. 3754). Methuen Inc.

Bocquet, Gilbert. Revisio Physolychnidum: Silene Subg. Physolychnis. (Phanero Gamarum Monographiae: Vol. 1). (Illus.). 1969. 52.50 (ISBN 3-7682-0624-6). Lubrecht & Cramer.

Bocuse, Paul. Paul Bocuse in Your Kitchen: An Introduction to Classic French Cooking. (Illus.). 351p. 9.98 (ISBN 0-317-18938-7). Smith Pubs.

--Paul Bocuse's French Cooking. Rossant, Colette, tr. LC 77-76511. 1977. 25.00 (ISBN 0-394-40670-2). Pantheon.

Boczek. Taxation in Switzerland. (Harvard Law School World Tax Ser.). 1976. 75.00 (ISBN 0-685-46987-5). Commerce.

Boczek, B. & Boleslaw, A. The Transfer of Marine Technology to Developing Nations in International Law. 79p. 1982. 7.50 (ISBN 0-911189-04-1). Law Sea Inst.

Boczek, Boleslaw A., jt. auth. see Bledsoe, Robert L.

Boda, Yang, jt. auth. see Wan-go Weng.

Bodak, Chuck & Milbert, Neil. Boxing Basics. LC 79-50983. (Illus.). 1979. pap. 6.95 (ISBN 0-8092-7210-5). Contemp Bks.

Bodanis, David. The Body Book: A Fantastic Voyage to the World Within. (Illus.). 312p. 1984. 24.95 (ISBN 0-316-10071-4). Little.

--The Body Book: A Fantastic Voyage to the World Within. 1985. pap. 16.95 (ISBN 0-316-10072-2). Little.

Bodansky, Miklos. Peptide Synthesis. 2nd ed. LC 83-22190. 224p. 1985. Repr. of 1976 ed. lib. bdg. write for info. (ISBN 0-89874-709-0). Krieger.

Bodansky, Oscar. Biochemistry of Human Cancer. 1975. 79.00 (ISBN 0-12-109850-8). Acad Pr.

Bodansky, Oscar see Sobotka, Harry & Stewart, C. P.

Bodanszky, M. Principles of Peptide Synthesis. (Reactivity & Structure Ser.: Vol. 16). (Illus.). 240p. 1984. 49.00 (ISBN 0-387-12395-4). Springer-Verlag.

Bodanszky, M., et al. The Practice of Peptide Synthesis. (Reactivity & Structure, Concepts in Organic Chemistry Ser.: Vol. 21). 240p. 1984. 49.50 (ISBN 0-387-13471-9). Springer-Verlag.

Bodanszky, Miklos O., et al. Peptide Synthesis. 2nd ed. LC 76-16099. (Interscience Monographs on Organic Chemistry). 208p. 1976. 43.50x (ISBN 0-471-08451-4, Pub. by Wiley-Interscience). Wiley.

Bodanza, Mary F. Clinical & Laboratory Procedures in the Physicians Office. LC 81-11573. 313p. 1982. 21.95 (ISBN 0-471-06497-1, Pub. by Wiley Med). Wiley.

Bodart, Joni. Booktalk! LC 80-16461. 246p. 1980. 12.00 (ISBN 0-8242-0650-9). Wilson.

Bodde, D. Shakespeare & the Ireland Forgeries. LC 75-22073. (Studies in Shakespeare, No. 24). 1975. lib. bdg. 40.95x (ISBN 0-8383-2084-8). Haskell.

Bodde, D., tr. see Fung Yu-Lan.

Bodde, D., tr. see Ssu-Ma, Ch'Ien.

Bodde, Derk. Annual Customs & Festivals in Peking. 1977. 24.00 (ISBN 0-89986-001-X). Oriental Bk Store.

--China's Gifts to the West. LC 43-3077. (Asiatic Studies in American Education Ser.: No. 1). pap. 20.00 (ISBN 0-317-10030-0, 2014507). Bks Demand UMI.

--Chinese Ideas in the West. LC 48-8567. (Asiatic Studies in American Education Ser.: No. 3). pap. 20.00 (ISBN 0-317-10034-3, 2014500). Bks Demand UMI.

--Essays on Chinese Civilization. Le Blanc, Charles & Borei, Dorothy, eds. LC 80-8586. (Princeton Ser. of Collected Essays). 504p. 1981. 28.00 (ISBN 0-691-03129-0); pap. 12.50 (ISBN 0-691-00024-7). Princeton U Pr.

--Peking Diary: A Year of Revolution. 1973. lib. bdg. 24.50x (ISBN 0-374-90735-8). Octagon.

--Shakespeare & the Ireland Forgeries. LC 73-15741. 1930. lib. bdg. 15.00 (ISBN 0-8414-3300-3). Folcroft.

--Tolstoy & China. 12.00 (ISBN 0-384-04895-1). Johnson Repr.

Bodde, Derk & Morris, Clarence. Law in Imperial China. (Pennsylvania Paperbacks Ser). 620p. 1973. pap. 12.50x (ISBN 0-8122-1060-3). U of Pa Pr.

Bodden, Ilona, jt. auth. see Poppel, Hans.

Bodden, Thomas A. Selling Tax Shelter & Real Estate Securities: An Introduction to the New NASD Direct Participation Program License. LC 83-5483. (Illus.). 105p. (Orig.). 1983. pap. 14.95 (ISBN 0-88462-446-3, 1970-05, Longman Fin Serv Pub). Longman USA.

Boddewyn, J. Advertising Taxation. 92p. 1983. 25.00 (ISBN 0-318-03441-7); members 15.00. Intl Advertising Assn.

--Advertising to Children. rev. ed. 118p. 1984. 50.00 (ISBN 0-318-14490-5); members 25.00 (ISBN 0-318-14491-3). Intl Advertising Assn.

--Comparison Advertising. (Illus.). 245p. 1978. 12.50 (ISBN 0-318-14492-1); members 9.50 (ISBN 0-318-14493-X). Intl Advertising Assn.

--Consumer Credit & Investment Advertising. 106p. 1982. 14.00 (ISBN 0-318-17388-3); members 5.00 (ISBN 0-318-17389-1). Intl Advertising Assn.

Boddewyn, J. J. Comparison Advertising Update. 60p. 1983. 25.00 (ISBN 0-318-03436-0); members 12.50. Intl Advertising Assn.

--Food Advertising Regulation & Self-Regulation. 58p. 1982. 20.00 (ISBN 0-318-17386-7); members 10.00 (ISBN 0-318-17387-5). Intl Advertising Assn.

--Medicine Avertising Regulation & Self-Regulation in 54 Countries. 128p. 1985. avail. Intl Advertising Assn.

--Outdoor-Billboard Advertising Regulation. 82p. 1979. 15.00 (ISBN 0-318-14503-0); members 7.50 (ISBN 0-318-14504-9). Intl Advertising Assn.

--Premiums, Gifts & Competitions. 78p. 1978. pap. 15.00 (ISBN 0-318-14496-4); pap. 7.50 members (ISBN 0-318-14497-2). Intl Advertising Assn.

Boddewyn, J. J. & Marton, Katherin. Comparison Advertising: A Worldwide Study. (Illus.). 1978. pap. 9.50 (ISBN 0-8038-1249-3). Hastings.

Boddewyn, Jean, tr. see Bleustein-Blanchet, Marcel.

Boddie, Caryn, jt. auth. see Boddie, Peter.

Boddie, John B. Historical Southern Families, 14 vols, Vols. 2, 8, 9, 16-18, 20, 22, 23. LC 67-29833. (Illus.). 1967-80. Repr. of 1957 ed. 15.00 ea. (ISBN 0-8063-0027-2). Genealog Pub.

--Seventeenth Century Isle of Wight County, Virginia. LC 73-2146. (Illus.). 756p. 1980. Repr. of 1938 ed. 28.50 (ISBN 0-8063-0559-2). Genealog Pub.

--Southside Virginia Families, Vol. 1. LC 66-28239. (Illus.). 422p. 1976. Repr. of 1955 ed. 22.50 (ISBN 0-8063-0040-X). Genealog Pub.

Boddie, Peter & Boddie, Caryn. The Hiker's Guide to Colorado. LC 84-80091. (Illus.). 256p. (Orig.). 1984. pap. 8.95 (ISBN 0-934318-36-0). Falcon Pr MT.

Boddin, J. E. see Moore, T. V.

Bodding, Paul O. Santal Folk Tales, 3 vols. LC 78-67688. (The Folktale). Repr. of 1923 ed. Set. 95.00 (ISBN 0-404-16060-3). AMS Pr.

Boddington, Craig. Campfires & Gametrails: Hunting North America's Big Game. 256p. 1985. 19.95 (ISBN 0-8329-0387-6, Pub. by Winchester Pr). New Century.

Boddington, Craig, ed. America: The Men & Their Guns That Made Her Great. 200p. 1981. 19.95 (ISBN 0-8227-3022-7). Petersen Pub.

Boddington, David. Building & Flying Radio-Controlled Model Aircraft. (Illus.). 227p. 1985. pap. 11.95 (ISBN 0-85242-790-5, Pub. by Argus). Aztex.

--Radio Control Primer. (Illus.). 134p. 1985. pap. 9.95 (ISBN 0-85242-378-0, Pub. by Argus). Aztex.

--Scale Model Aircraft Radio Control. (Illus.). 300p. (Orig.). 1984. pap. 19.95 (ISBN 0-85242-810-3, Pub. by ARGUS). Aztex.

Boddington, Harry. University of Spiritualism. 59.95 (ISBN 0-8490-1248-1). Gordon Pr.

Boddy, David, jt. auth. see Buchanan, David A.

Boddy, Joe, jt. auth. see Greeber, Charlotte.

Boddy, John. Brain Systems & Psychological Concepts. LC 77-21203. 461p. 1978. 59.95 (ISBN 0-471-99601-7); pap. 28.95x (ISBN 0-471-99600-9, Pub. by Wiley-Interscience). Wiley.

Boddy, R., jt. auth. see Caulcutt, R.

Bode, Boyd H. How We Learn. LC 77-138204. 308p. 1972. Repr. of 1940 ed. lib. bdg. 20.75x (ISBN 0-8371-5562-2, BOWL). Greenwood.

--Progressive Education at the Crossroads. LC 71-165707. (American Education Ser, No. 2). 1971. Repr. of 1938 ed. 14.00 (ISBN 0-405-03696-5). Ayer Co Pubs.

Bode, Carl. American Lyceum: Town Meeting of the Mind. LC 56-5163. 282p. 1968. Repr. of 1956 ed. lib. bdg. 7.00x (ISBN 0-8093-0318-3). S Ill U Pr.

--American Lyceum: Town Meeting of the Mind. LC 56-5163. (Arcturus Books Paperbacks). 282p. 1968. pap. 2.45 (ISBN 0-8093-0319-1). S Ill U Pr.

--The Anatomy of American Popular Culture, 1840-1861. LC 83-5643. (Illus.). xxi, 292p. 1983. Repr. of 1959 ed. lib. bdg. 35.00 (ISBN 0-313-24005-1, BOAN). Greenwood.

--Half-World of American Culture: A Miscellany. LC 64-20257. (Arcturus Books Paperbacks). 281p. 1967. pap. 2.45 (ISBN 0-8093-0271-3). S Ill U Pr.

--Highly Irregular: The Newspaper Columns of Carl Bode. LC 74-8704. 176p. 1974. 7.95x (ISBN 0-8093-0684-0). S Ill U Pr.

--Maryland. (States & the Nation Ser.). (Illus.). 1978. 14.95 (ISBN 0-393-05672-4, Co-Pub by AASLH). Norton.

--Mencken. LC 72-11997. (Arcturus Books Paperbacks). (Illus.). 474p. 1973. pap. 8.95 (ISBN 0-8093-0627-1). S Ill U Pr.

--The Portable Thoreau. (Viking Portable Library: No. 31). 1980. 14.95 (ISBN 0-670-70417-2). Viking.

--Practical Magic: Poems. LC 80-17597. viii, 54p. 1981. 11.95x (ISBN 0-8040-0362-9, 82-75091, Pub. by Swallow); pap. 6.95 (ISBN 0-8040-0373-4, 82-75109, Pub. by Swallow). Ohio U Pr.

--Sacred Seasons: Poems. LC 75-179807. (New Poetry Ser.). Repr. of 1953 ed. 16.00 (ISBN 0-404-56007-5). AMS Pr.

Bode, Carl, ed. Collected Poems of Henry Thoreau. enl. ed. 432p. 1964. pap. 9.95 (ISBN 0-8018-0082-X). Johns Hopkins.

--Midcentury America: Life in the 1850s. LC 72-181986. (Illus.). 256p. 1972. 15.00x (ISBN 0-8093-0562-3). S Ill U Pr.

Bode, Carl & Cowley, Malcolm, eds. The Portable Emerson. 720p. 1981. 14.95 (ISBN 0-670-29274-5). Viking.

Bode, Carl, ed. see Alger, Horatio, Jr.

Bode, Carl, ed. see Barnum, P. T.

Bode, Carl, ed. see Emerson, Ralph Waldo.

Bode, Carl, ed. see Thoreau, Henry D.

Bode, Charles G. Wines of Italy. (Illus.). 135p. 1974. pap. 2.50 (ISBN 0-486-23003-1). Dover.

--Wines of Italy. 8.25 (ISBN 0-8446-5007-2). Peter Smith.

Bode, Ed C. & Cowley. Emerson, the Portable. (Portable Library). 1981. pap. 6.95 (ISBN 0-14-015094-3). Penguin.

Bode, Elroy. Alone in the World Looking. LC 73-76995. 1973. 8.00 (ISBN 0-87404-046-9). Tex Western.

--Home & Other Moments. LC 75-2744. 1975. 8.00 (ISBN 0-87404-052-3). Tex Western.

--This Favored Place: The Texas Hill Country. (Illus.). 124p. 1983. 13.95 (ISBN 0-940672-09-X). Shearer Pub.

--To Be Alive. (Illus.). 160p. 1979. 10.00 (ISBN 0-87404-064-7). Tex Western.

Bode, Frederick A. Protestantism & the New South: North Carolina Baptists & Methodists in Political Crisis, 1894-1903. LC 75-1289. 171p. 1975. 13.95x (ISBN 0-8139-0597-4). U Pr of Va.

Bode, H. James Brindley. (Clarendon Biography Ser.). (Illus.). 1973. pap. 3.50 (ISBN 0-912728-59-0). Newbury Bks.

Bode, Hans H. & Warshaw, Joseph B., eds. Parenteral Nutrition in Infancy & Childhood. LC 74-6060. (Advances in Experimental Medicine & Biology Ser.: Vol. 46). 318p. 1974. 42.50x (ISBN 0-306-39046-9, Plenum Pr). Plenum Pub.

Bode, Janet. Kids Having Kids. (YA) (gr. 9 up). 1980. PLB 8.90 (ISBN 0-531-02882-8, B19). Watts.

--Rape: Preventing It; Coping with the Legal, Medical, & Emotional Aftermath. (Impact Ser.). (gr. 7 up). 1979. PLB 9.90 s&l (ISBN 0-531-02289-7). Watts.

--View from Another Closet: Exploring Bisexuality in Women. 1977. pap. 1.95 (ISBN 0-671-80972-5). PB.

Bode, Kenneth A. The South Dakota Poll: A Critical Analysis. 1970. write for info. U of SD Gov Res Bur.

Bode, Mabel H. The Pali Literature of Burma. LC 77-87008. Repr. of 1909 ed. 15.00 (ISBN 0-404-16796-9). AMS Pr.

Bode, Sharon, et al. Listening in & Speaking Out: Advanced. (English As a Second Language Bk.). 1981. pap. text ed. 5.75x (ISBN 0-582-79737-3); cassette 11.75 (ISBN 0-582-79738-1); cassette & bk. in plastic tote 15.95x (ISBN 0-582-79780-2). Longman.

--Listening in & Speaking Out: Intermediate. (Listening in & Speaking Out Ser.). (Illus.). 128p. (Orig.). 1980. pap. 5.75x (ISBN 0-582-79735-7); cassette 11.75x (ISBN 0-582-79736-5); bk. & cassette in tote 15.75 (ISBN 0-582-79770-5). Longman.

Bode, Wilhelm. The Italian Bronze Statuettes of the Renaissance. Draper, James D., ed. Gretor, William, tr. LC 80-82165. (Illus.). 1980. 340.00 (ISBN 0-937370-00-2). MAS De Reinis.

Bode, Wilhelm Von see Von Bode, Wilhelm.

Bode, Wilhelm von see Von Bode, Wilhelm & Kuhnel, Ernst.

Bode, Willi & Lito, Mario. Classical Food Preparation & Presentation. (Illus.). 288p. 1984. pap. 19.95 (ISBN 0-7134-4348-0, Pub. by Batsford England). David & Charles.

Bodea, Cornelia & Candea, Virgil. Heritage & Continuity in Eastern Europe: The Transylvanian Legacy in the History of the Romanians. (East European Monographs: No. 117). 160p. 1982. 17.50x (ISBN 0-88033-010-4). East Eur Quarterly.

Bodecker, N. M. Carrot Holes & Frisbee Trees. LC 83-2799. (Illus.). 48p. (gr. 3-6). 1983. 12.95 (ISBN 0-689-50097-1, McElderry Bk). Atheneum.

--Hurry, Hurry, Mary Dear! & Other Nonsense Poems. LC 76-14841. (Illus.). 128p. (gr. 4 up). 1976. 6.95 (ISBN 0-689-50066-1, McElderry Bk). Atheneum.

--It's Raining, Said John Twaining. (Illus.). 1977. pap. 1.95 (ISBN 0-689-70437-2, A-62, Aladdin). Atheneum.

--It's Raining Said John Twaining: Danish Nursery Rhymes. LC 72-85912. (Illus.). 32p. (ps-3). 1973. (McElderry Bk); pap. 1.95 (ISBN 0-689-70437-2). Atheneum.
--Let's Marry, Said the Cherry. (Illus.). pap. 1.95 (ISBN 0-689-70434-8, A-71, Aladdin). Atheneum.
--The Mushroom Center Disaster. (Illus.). (gr. k-3). 1979. pap. 1.95 (ISBN 0-689-70455-0, A-84, Aladdin). Atheneum.
--A Person from Britain Whose Head Was the Shape of a Mitten & Other Limericks. LC 79-22779. (Illus.). 64p. (gr. 3 up). 1980. 7.95 (ISBN 0-689-50152-8, McElderry Bk). Atheneum.
--Pigeon Cubes & Other Verse. LC 82-3954. (Illus.). 80p. (gr. 7up). 1982. 10.95 (ISBN 0-689-50235-4, McElderry). Atheneum.
--Quimble Wood. LC 80-24045. (Illus.). 32p. (ps-4). 1981. 9.95 (ISBN 0-689-50190-0, McElderry Bk). Atheneum.
--Quimble Wood. (Illus.). 48p. (gr. 8-12). 1984. pap. 1.95 (ISBN 0-553-15277-7, Skylark). Bantam.
--Snowman Sniffles & Other Verse. LC 82-13927. (Illus.). 80p. (gr. 4-7). 1983. 9.95 (ISBN 0-689-50263-X, McElderry Bk). Atheneum.
Bodeen, Dewitt, jt. auth. see Ringgold, Gene.
Bodeen, DeWitt, jt. auth. see Ringgold, Gene.
Bodel, John. Roman Brick Stamps in the Kelsey Museum. (Kelsey Museum Ser.). (Illus.). 1983. pap. text ed. 22.50x (ISBN 0-472-08039-3). U of Mich Pr.
Bodel, Sen A., jt. auth. see Vinterberg, H.
Bodell, Bill. The Immortal Spirit. LC 84-12561. 184p. 1984. 13.95 (ISBN 0-912526-36-X). Lib Res.
--The Year I Went to High School with My Parents. (Pennypinchers Ser.). 128p. (gr. 4-9). 1985. pap. 2.25 (ISBN 0-89191-985-6, 59857, Chariot Bks). Cook.
Bodelsen, C. A., jt. auth. see Vinterberg, H.
Bodem, G., ed. see International Symposium, Bonn, Germany, 27-29 Jan. 1977.
Boden, Arthur & Woodside, John. Boden's Beasts. (Illus.). (gr. 1-5). 1964. 6.95 (ISBN 0-8392-3045-1). Astor-Honor.
Boden, Clive & Charter, Angus. The Windsurfing Funboard Handbook. (Illus.). 176p. 1984. 11.95 (ISBN 0-8120-5582-9). Barron.
Boden, Deanna. You & Me. (Illus.). (ps-3). 1979. pap. 3.95 (ISBN 0-87516-290-8). De Vorss.
Boden, Evan H. Guide for the Lay Preacher. 1979. pap. 2.95 (ISBN 0-8170-0836-5). Judson.
Boden, Margaret. Artificial Intelligence & Natural Man. LC 76-8117. (Illus.). 537p. 1981. pap. 15.95x (ISBN 0-465-00453-9, TB-5063). Basic.
Boden, Margaret A. Minds & Mechanism: Philosophical Psychology & Computational Models. 256p. 1981. 32.50x (ISBN 0-8014-1431-8). Cornell U Pr.
--Purposive Explanation in Pschology. LC 73-169858. (Illus.). 432p. 1972. 25.00x (ISBN 0-674-73902-7). Harvard U Pr.
Boden, P., jt. ed. see Black, R.
Boden, Robert. Teen Talks with God. 1980. pap. 3.50 (ISBN 0-570-03812-X, 12-2921). Concordia.
Boden, William E. & Capone, Robert J. Coronary Care. (A Volume in the Saunders Blue Book Ser.). (Illus.). 224p. 1984. pap. 14.95 spiral bound (ISBN 0-7216-1072-2). Saunders.
Bodenham, John. Bodenham's Belvedere or the Garden of the Muses. (Spencer Society Publications Ser.: No. 17). 1966. Repr. of 1600 ed. 32.00 (ISBN 0-8337-0313-7). B Franklin.
Bodenhamer, David J. & Ely, James W., Jr., eds. Ambivalent Legacy: A Legal History of the South. LC 83-25928. 240p. 1984. text ed. 20.00x (ISBN 0-87805-210-0); pap. text ed. 8.95x (ISBN 0-87805-211-9). U Pr of Miss.
Bodenhamer, Greg. Back in Control: How to Get Your Children to Behave. 132p. 1984. pap. 5.95 (ISBN 0-13-056870-8). P-H.
Bodenhamer, Joseph S. Nixon & the Congressional China Lobby, 1946-1952. LC 83-80971. 1984. text ed. 10.95 (ISBN 0-86666-185-9). Natl Lit Guild.
Bodenheim, Maxwell. Against This Age. LC 73-18550. (BCl Ser.: I). Repr. of 1923 ed. 11.50 (ISBN 0-404-11365-6). AMS Pr.
--The King of Spain. LC 73-18551. (BCL Ser.: I). Repr. of 1928 ed. 11.50 (ISBN 0-404-11366-4). AMS Pr.
--Replenishing Jessica. LC 73-18548. (BCL Ser.: II). Repr. of 1949 ed. 16.50 (ISBN 0-404-11363-X). AMS Pr.
--Returning to Emotion. LC 73-18552. (BCL Ser.: I). Repr. of 1927 ed. 11.50 (ISBN 0-404-11367-2). AMS Pr.
--Sixty Seconds. LC 73-18549. (BCL Ser.: I). Repr. of 1929 ed. 16.50 (ISBN 0-404-11364-8). AMS Pr.
Bodenheimer, Aron-Ronald. Doris: The Story of a Disfigured Deaf Child. Basilius, Harold A., tr. from Ger. LC 72-11341. 128p. 1974. 9.95x (ISBN 0-8143-1495-3). Wayne St U Pr.
Bodenheimer, Edgar. Jurisprudence: The Philosophy & Method of the Law. rev. ed. LC 74-77182. 1974. text ed. 32.50x (ISBN 0-674-49001-0). Harvard U Pr.
--Philosophy of Responsibility. x, 147p. 1980. text ed. 18.50x (ISBN 0-8377-0309-3). Rothman.
--Power, Law & Society. LC 73-81049. 211p. 1973. 24.50x (ISBN 0-8448-0215-8). Crane-Russak Co.
Bodenheimer, Edgar, et al. The Anglo-American Legal System,Readings & Cases Introduction to. LC 80-18757. (American Casebook). 185p. 1980. pap. text ed. 8.50 (ISBN 0-8299-2103-6). West Pub.
Bodenheimer, Susanne & Danning, Dave. Yanqui Dollar: The Contribution of U.S. Private Investment to Underdevelopment in Latin America. (Illus.). 64p. 1971. pap. 3.00 (ISBN 0-916024-03-2). NA Cong Lat Am.
Bodenheimer, Thomas see Dixon, Marlene.
Bodenhorn, Diran, jt. auth. see Graham, Pearson.
Bodenstein, Dietrich, ed. Milestones in Developmental Physiology of Insects: Papers in Development & Heredity. LC 70-133194. 231p. 1971. 25.00x (ISBN 0-306-50007-8, Plenum Pr). Plenum Pub.
Boder. Alphabet Tasks Recording Forms. 1982. 10.50 (ISBN 0-8089-1448-0, 790637). Grune.
--Diagnostic Summary Form. 1982. 10.50 (ISBN 0-8089-1449-9, 790639). Grune.
--Spelling Test Form. 1982. 10.50 (ISBN 0-8089-1447-2, 790636). Grune.
Boder, Elena. Further Studies on the Etiology & Significance of Congenital Cranial Osteoporosis. (SRCD.M.). 1948. pap. 14.00 (ISBN 0-527-01544-X). Kraus Repr.
Boder, Elena & Jarrico, Sylvia. The Boder Reading-Spelling Patterns: A Diagnostic Screening Test for the Subtypes of Reading Disability. 1982. complete kit 58.00 (ISBN 0-8089-1445-6, 790634); examiner's recording forms 16.00 (ISBN 0-8089-1446-4, 790635) (ISBN 0-8089-1448-0). Grune.
--Boder Test of Reading-Spelling Patterns. 1984. 25.00 (ISBN 0-317-13524-4, 790640). Grune.
Boderland Sciences Research Foundation Staff. Koch Remedy - Cancer. 4.00x (ISBN 0-686-29868-3). Cancer Control Soc.
Bodey & Rodriquez. Hospital Associated Infections in the Compromised Host. (Handbook on Hospital-Associated Infection Ser.: Vol. 2). 1979. 59.75 (ISBN 0-8247-6785-3). Dekker.
Bodey, Donald. F. N. G. 1985. 16.95 (ISBN 0-670-80724-9). Viking.
Bodey, Gerald P. & Fainstein, Victor, eds. Candidiasis. 294p. 1985. text ed. 50.50 (ISBN 0-88167-046-4). Raven.
Bodey, Hugh. Immigrants & Emigrants. (History in Focus Ser.). (Illus.). 72p. (gr. 7-10). 1982. 14.95 (ISBN 0-7134-3564-X, Pub. by Batsford England). David & Charles.
--Nailmaking. (Shire Album Ser.: No. 87). (Illus.). 32p. pap. 2.95 (ISBN 0-85263-606-7, Pub. by Shire Pubns England). Seven Hills Bks.
--Roman People. (Illus.). 72p. (YA) (gr. 7-12). 1981. 14.95 (ISBN 0-7134-3568-2, Pub. by Batsford England). David & Charles.
Bodey, Hugh & Hallas, Michael. Elementary Surveying for Industrial Archeaologists. (Illus.). 64p. 1978. pap. 5.95 (ISBN 0-85263-375-0, Pub. by Shire Pubns England). Seven Hills Bks.
Bodger, Lorraine. Christmas Tree Ornaments. (Illus.). 168p. 1985. 18.95 (ISBN 0-02-496740-8, Pub by Sedgewood Press). MacMillan.
--Gift Wraps: Elegant, Easy. LC 84-48580. (Illus.). 128p. 1985. pap. 5.72i (ISBN 0-06-091240-5, PL 1240, PL). Har-Row.
--Paper Dreams. LC 76-21221. (Illus.). 1977. 11.95x (ISBN 0-87663-287-8); pap. 6.95 (ISBN 0-87663-964-3). Universe.
Bodger, Lorraine & Ephron, Delia. Crafts for All Seasons. LC 79-6410. (Illus.). 112p. 1980. pap. 6.95 (ISBN 0-87663-996-1). Universe.
Bodha, Daji, ed. see John, Da Free.
Bodhisattva Swami Anand Madyapa, ed. see Rajneesh, Bhagwan S.
Bodian, Nat G. Book Marketing Handbook, Vol. II. 525p. 1983. 59.95 (ISBN 0-8352-1685-3). Bowker.
--Book Marketing Handbook: Tips & Techniques for the Sale & Promotion of Scientific, Technical, Professional, & Scholarly Books & Journals, Vol. I. 482p. 1980. 59.95 (ISBN 0-8352-1286-6). Bowker.
--Copywriters Handbook: A Practical Guide for Advertising & Promotion of Specialized & Scholarly Books & Journals. (The Professional Editing & Publishing Ser.). 277p. 1984. 29.95 (ISBN 0-89495-040-1); pap. 19.95 (ISBN 0-89495-039-8). ISI Pr.
Bodie, Charles A., compiled by. A Guide to Gloucester County, Virginia, Historical Manuscripts, 1651-1865. xvii, 109p. 1976. pap. 5.00 (ISBN 0-88490-070-3). VA State Lib.
Bodie, Idella. Ghost in the Capitol. LC 75-32397. 118p. 1976. pap. 3.95 (ISBN 0-87844-028-3). Sandlapper Pub Co.
--The Mystery of the Pirate's Treasure. LC 72-94930. (Illus.). (gr. 4-8). 1973. 3.95 (ISBN 0-87844-018-6). Sandlapper Pub Co.
--The Mystery of the Pirate's Treasure. LC 72-94930. (Illus.). 136p. (gr. 5-9). 1984. pap. 5.95 (ISBN 0-87844-059-3). Sandlapper Pub Co.
--The Secret of Telfair Inn. LC 79-177909. (Illus.). 98p. (gr. 5-9). 1983. pap. 4.95 (ISBN 0-87844-050-X). Sandlapper Pub Co.
--South Carolina Women: They Dared to Lead. LC 78-64858. (Illus.). 160p. 1978. Clothbound 9.95 (ISBN 0-87844-044-5). Sandlapper Pub Co.
--Stranded! (Illus.). 132p. (Orig.). (gr. 5-9). 1984. pap. 6.95 (ISBN 0-87844-060-7). Sandlapper Pub Co.
Bodie, Idella F. A Hunt for Life's Extras, the Story of Archibald Rutledge. LC 80-50789. (Illus.). 176p. 1982. Clothbound 11.95 (ISBN 0-87844-046-1). Sandlapper Pub Co.
Bodie, Scott & Browne, Corinne. Confessions of a Fish Doctor. LC 76-25474. (Illus.). 311p. 1977. 7.95 (ISBN 0-911104-83-6, 116). Workman Pub.
Bodie, Zvi, et al. Financial Aspects of the United States Pension System. LC 83-9119. (National Bureau of Economic Research-Project Report). 464p. 1984. lib. bdg. 47.00x (ISBN 0-226-06281-3). U of Chicago Pr.
Bodig, Jozsef & Jayne, Benjamin A. Mechanics of Wood & Wood Composites. 736p. 1982. 44.50 (ISBN 0-442-00822-8). Van Nos Reinhold.
Bodily, S. Modern Decision Making: A Guide to Modeling with Decision Support Systems. 448p. 1984. 26.95 (ISBN 0-07-006360-5). McGraw.
Bodin, Fredrik D. The Freelance Photographer's Handbook. LC 81-9803. (Illus.). 160p. (Orig.). 1981. pap. 12.95 (ISBN 0-930764-30-7). Curtin & London.
--How to Get the Best Travel Photographs. (Illus.). 150p. 1982. pap. 14.95 (ISBN 0-930764-40-4). Curtin & London.
Bodin, Harry S., ed. Civil Litigation & Trial Techniques. 1976. text ed. 40.00 (ISBN 0-685-85342-X, H3-2934). PLI.
Bodin, Jean. Colloquium of the Seven About Secrets of the Sublime. Daniels, Marion L., tr. from Lat. & intro. by. LC 73-2453. 480p. 1975. 60.00x (ISBN 0-691-07193-4). Princeton U Pr.
--The Six Bookes of Commonweale. Mayer, J. P., ed. LC 78-67335. (European Political Thought Ser.). 1979. Repr. of 1962 ed. lib. bdg. 66.50x (ISBN 0-405-11680-2). Ayer Co Pubs.
Bodin, Jeanne & Mitelman, Bonnie. Mothers Who Work: Strategies for Coping. LC 82-90834. 320p. (Orig.). 1983. pap. 5.95 (ISBN 0-345-30140-4). Ballantine.
Bodin, John. Method for the Easy Comprehension of History. Reynolds, Beatrice, tr. 402p. 1985. Repr. of 1945 ed. lib. bdg. 75.00 (ISBN 0-918377-76-5). Russell Pr.
Bodin, L. D., jt. auth. see Golden, B. L.
Bodin, S. Very Short-Range Forecasting - Observations, Methods & Systems. (World Weather Watch Planning Reports: No. 38). 56p. (Orig.). 1984. pap. text ed. 13.00 (ISBN 92-63-10621-5, W583, WMO). Unipub.
Bodinat, Henri De see De Bodinat, Henri.
Bodin De Saint-Laurent, Jean De see De Bodin De Saint-Laurent, Jean.
Bodine, A. Aubrey, jt. auth. see Spatz, Don.
Bodine, Jay F., jt. ed. see Probst, Gerhard F.
Bodine, John J. Taos Pueblo: A Walk Through Time. LC 77-73460. 1977. pap. 2.95 (ISBN 0-89016-038-4). Lightning Tree.
Bodine, Walter R. The Greek Text of Judges: Recensional Developments. LC 80-12578. (Harvard Semitic Monographs: No. 23). 15.00x (ISBN 0-89130-400-2, 04-00-23). Scholars Pr GA.
Bodine, William L. Bodine's Reference Book on Juvenile Welfare. 1913. 15.00 (ISBN 0-8482-0143-4). Norwood Edns.
--Bodine's Reference Book on Juvenile Welfare. 1913. 25.00 (ISBN 0-932062-17-2). Sharon Hill.
Bodington, Stephen. Science & Social Action. 192p. 1980. 14.00x (ISBN 0-8052-8027-8, Pub. by Allison & Busby England); pap. 7.95 (ISBN 0-8052-8026-X, Pub. by Allison & Busby England). Schocken.
Bodini, Vittorio. The Hands of the South. Feldman, Ruth & Swann, Brian, trs. LC 80-68879. 1980. 7.50 (ISBN 0-910350-02-7). Charioteer.
Bodinski, Lois H. The Nurse's Guide to Diet Therapy. LC 82-6954. 381p. 1982. pap. 19.50 (ISBN 0-471-08167-1, Pub. by Wiley Med). Wiley.
Bodio, Stephen. A Rage for Falcons. 144p. 1984. 16.50 (ISBN 0-8052-3931-6, Pub. by Nick Lyon Books, NY). Schocken.
Bodis-Wollner, Ivan, intro. by. Evoked Potentials. (Annals of The New York Academy of Sciences Ser.: Vol. 388). 738p. 1982. lib. bdg. 157.00x (ISBN 0-89766-166-4); pap. 157.00x (ISBN 0-89766-167-2). NY Acad Sci.
Bodkin, Maud. Archetypal Patterns in Poetry: Psychological Studies of Imagination. LC 75-28993. (BCL Ser.: Ii). Repr. of 1934 ed. 21.50 (ISBN 0-404-14004-1). AMS Pr.
--Archetypal Patterns in Poetry: Psychological Studies of Imagination. 1978. Repr. of 1934 ed. lib. bdg. 20.00 (ISBN 0-8495-0401-5). Arden Lib.
--Quest for Salvation in an Ancient & a Modern Play. LC 73-15984. 1941. lib. bdg. 7.50 (ISBN 0-8414-3314-3). Folcroft.
--Studies of Type-Images in Poetry, Religion & Philosophy. LC 74-14665. 1951. lib. bdg. 15.00 (ISBN 0-8414-3273-2). Folcroft.
Bodkin, Ronald G. Wage-Price-Productivity Nexus. LC 64-24502. 1966. 10.00x (ISBN 0-8122-7470-9). U of Pa Pr.
Bodky, Erwin. The Interpretation of Bach's Keyboard Works. LC 75-44101. (Illus.). 421p. 1976. Repr. of 1960 ed. lib. bdg. 35.00x (ISBN 0-8371-8720-6, BOBK). Greenwood.
Bodle, David W., et al. Characterization of the Electrical Environment. LC 76-22886. 1976. 30.00x (ISBN 0-8020-2194-8). U of Toronto Pr.
Bodle, Yvonne & Corey, Joseph. Retail Selling. 2nd ed. McGarry, Mary A., ed. (Illus.). (gr. 10-12). 1976. text ed. 18.28 (ISBN 0-07-006371-0). McGraw.
Bodley, John H. Anthropology & Contempory Human Problems. 2nd. ed. 258p. 1985. pap. text ed. 10.95 (ISBN 0-87484-671-4). Mayfield Pub.
--Victims of Progress. 2nd ed. (Illus.). 264p. 1982. pap. 11.95 (ISBN 0-87484-593-9). Mayfield Pub.
Bodley, R. V. Wind in the Sahara. 1944. 25.00 (ISBN 0-686-17222-1). Scholars Ref Lib.
Bodley, Ronald V. Messenger: The Life of Mohammed. LC 70-92296. Repr. of 1946 ed. lib. bdg. 35.00 (ISBN 0-8371-2423-9, BOTM). Greenwood.
Bodley, Temple, ed. Littell's Political Transactions in & Concerning Kentucky. Bd. with Letter of George Nicholas to His Friend in Virginia; General Wilkinson's Memorial. LC 70-146375. (First American Frontier Ser). 322p. 1971. Repr. of 1926 ed. 22.00 (ISBN 0-405-02826-1). Ayer Co Pubs.
Bodman, Jean & Lanzano, Michael. No Hot Water Tonight. 2nd ed. 279p. 1986. pap. text ed. price not set (ISBN 0-02-311600-5). Macmillan.
Bodman, N. C. Spoken Amoy Hokkien. (Spoken Language Ser.). 450p. 1985. pap. 15.00x (ISBN 0-87950-450-1); 16 cassettes 120.00x (ISBN 0-87950-451-X); book & cassettes 130.00x (ISBN 0-87950-452-8). Spoken Lang Serv.
Bodman, N. C. & Su-Chu, Wu. Spoken Taiwanese. (Spoken Language Ser.). 208p. (Taiwanese.). 1980. pap. 10.00x (ISBN 0-87950-460-9); cassettes 9 dual track 100.00x (ISBN 0-87950-461-7); text & cassettes 110.00x (ISBN 0-87950-462-5). Spoken Lang Serv.
Bodman, Nicholas C. Spoken Amoy Hokkien: Units 1-30. (Spoken Language Ser.). 450p. (Amoy Hokkien.). 1985. pap. text ed. 15.00x (ISBN 0-87950-450-1); cassettes, 16 dual track 120.00x (ISBN 0-87950-451-X); bk. & cassettes combined 130.00x (ISBN 0-87950-452-8). Spoken Lang Serv.
Bodmer, Frederick. The Loom of Language. 669p. 1981. text ed. 24.50x (ISBN 0-85036-275-X, Pub. by Merlin England). Humanities.
--The Loom of Language. Hogben, Lancelot, ed. (Illus.). 720p. 1985. pap. 9.95 (ISBN 0-393-30034-X). Norton.
--The Loom of Language. 1985. lib. bdg. 79.95 (ISBN 0-8490-3241-5). Gordon Pr.
Bodmer, Karl. Karl Bodmer's America. Hunt, David, et al, eds. LC 83-27391. (Illus.). xii, 376p. 1984. 65.00 (ISBN 0-8032-1185-6). U of Nebr Pr.
Bodmer, W. F. & Cavalli-Sforza, L. L. Genetics, Evolution, & Man. LC 75-33990. (Illus.). 782p. 1976. 30.95 (ISBN 0-7167-0573-7). W H Freeman.
Bodmer, W. F., ed. Inheritance of Susceptibility to Cancer in Man. (Illus.). 1983. 26.95 (ISBN 0-19-261420-7). Oxford U Pr.
Bodmer, W. F. & Kingman, J. F., eds. Mathematical Genetics. (Proceedings of the Royal Society: Ser. B, Vol. 219). (Illus.). 133p. 1984. Repr. lib. bdg. 30.00x (ISBN 0-85403-219-3, Pub. by Royal Soc London). Scholium Intl.
Bodmer, W. F., compiled by. Genetics of the Cell Surface. LC 79-670277. (Proceedings of the Royal Society). 1978. text ed. 25.00x (ISBN 0-85403-101-4). Scholium Intl.
Bodmer, Walter F., jt. auth. see Cavalli-Sforza, L. L.
Bodnar, Edward W. & Mitchell, Charles. Cyriacus of Ancona's Journeys in the Propontis & the Northern Aegean: 1444-1445. LC 75-35466. (Memoirs Ser.: Vol. 112). 1976. pap. 6.00 (ISBN 0-87169-112-4). Am Philos.
Bodnar, George. Accounting Information Systems. 2nd ed. 520p. 1983. text ed. 37.14 (ISBN 0-205-07929-6, 057929). Allyn.
Bodnar, John. Anthracite People: Families, Unions & Work, 1900-1940. 100p. (Orig.). 1983. pap. 3.50 (ISBN 0-89271-023-3). Pa Hist & Mus.
--Immigration & Industrialization: Ethnicity in an American Mill Town, 1870-1940. LC 77-74549. 1977. 19.95s (ISBN 0-8229-3348-9). U of Pittsburgh Pr.
--The Transplanted: A History of Immigrants in Urban America. LC 84-48041. (Interdisciplinary Studies in History). (Illus.). 320p. 1985. 27.50x (ISBN 0-253-31347-3). Ind U Pr.
--Workers' World: Kinship, Community & Protest in an Industrial Society, 1900-1940. LC 82-6626. (Illus.). 256p. 1982. 24.00x (ISBN 0-8018-2785-X). Johns Hopkins.
Bodnar, John, et al. Lives of Their Own: Blacks, Italians & Poles in Pittsburgh, 1900-1960. LC 81-3382. (The Working Class in American History Ser.). 302p. 1981. 22.95x (ISBN 0-252-00880-4); pap. 8.95 (ISBN 0-252-01063-9). U of Ill Pr.
Bodnar, John E., ed. & intro. by. The Ethnic Experience in Pennsylvania. LC 72-3257. (Illus.). 330p. 1973. 26.50 (ISBN 0-8387-1155-3). Bucknell U Pr.
Bodner, Joan, ed. see American Friends Service Committee of San Francisco.
Bodner, Paul M. U. S. Taxation of Employees Abroad. 50.00 (ISBN 0-686-90411-7, 730604). Am Inst CPA.
Bodo, G., jt. ed. see Surjan, L.

Bodo, John R. Protestant Clergy & Public Issues, Eighteen Twelve to Eighteen Forty-Eight. LC 79-12849. (Perspectives in American History Ser: No. 52). 1980. Repr. of 1954 ed. lib. bdg. 22.50x (ISBN 0-87991-854-3). Porcupine Pr.

Bodo, Murray. Clare: A Light in the Garden. (Orig.). 1979. pap. 2.75 (ISBN 0-912228-54-7). St Anthony Mess Pr.

--Francis: The Journey & the Dream. (Illus.). 1972. pap. 2.95 (ISBN 0-912228-07-5). St Anthony Mess Pr.

--Juniper: Friend of Francis, Fool of God. 90p. pap. text ed. cancelled (ISBN 0-86716-021-7). St Anthony Mess Pr.

--Song of the Sparrow: Meditations & Poems to Pray by. (Illus.). 187p. (Orig.). 1976. pap. 3.95 (ISBN 0-912228-26-1). St Anthony Mess Pr.

--Way of St. Francis: The Challenge of Franciscan Spirituality for Everyone. LC 83-14066. 192p. 1984. 12.95 (ISBN 0-385-19073-5). Doubleday.

--The Way of St. Francis: The Challenge of Franciscan Spirituality for Everyone. LC 83-14066. 1985. 6.95 (ISBN 0-385-19913-9, Im). Doubleday.

Bodolai, Joe & Radlauer, Steven. Special Moments. (Orig.). 1984. pap. 5.95 (ISBN 0-345-31534-0). Ballantine.

Bodoni, Giambattista. Manuale Typografia, 2 Vols. 1960. 200.00x (ISBN 0-87556-035-0). Saifer.

Bodor, G., ed. Orientation Effects in Solid Polymers. 432p. 1984. pap. 44.95 (ISBN 0-471-04658-2). Krieger.

Bodrogligeti, A. J., jt. ed. see Decsy, Gyula.

Bodrova, Valentina & Anker, Richard, eds. Working Women in Socialist Countries: The Fertility Connection. (World Employment Programme Study). 234p. 1985. pap. 15.70 (ISBN 92-2-103910-2, ILO409 5091, ILO). Unipub.

Bodrova, Valentina, ed. see International Labour Office Staff.

Bodson, D., et al, eds. Land Mobile Communications Engineering. LC 83-26564. 1983. 49.95 (ISBN 0-87942-174-6, PC01685). Inst Electrical.

Bodson, Dennis, ed. & frwd. by. Fiberoptics & Lightwave Communications Vocabulary. LC 80-26168. 156p. (Orig.). 1983. pap. text ed. 12.95 (ISBN 0-07-606706-8, R-030). McGraw.

Bodsworth, Colin & Appleton, A. S. Problems in Applied Thermodynamics. LC 66-78638. pap. 55.80 (ISBN 0-317-08450-X, 2003636). Bks Demand UMI.

Bodsworth, Fred. Sparrow's Fall. 1975. pap. 2.25 (ISBN 0-451-09794-7, E9794, Sig). NAL.

Bodtke, Richard. Tragedy & the Jacobean Temper: The Major Plays of John Webster. (Salzburg Studies in English Literature, Jacobean Drama Studies: No. 2). 1972. pap. text ed. 25.50x (ISBN 0-391-01328-9). Humanities.

Bodurtha, Frank T. Industrial Explosion Prevention & Protection. (Illus.). 1980. 31.50 (ISBN 0-07-006359-1). McGraw.

Bodwell, C. E. Evaluation of Proteins for Humans. (Illus.). 1977. lib. bdg. 56.50 (ISBN 0-87055-215-5). AVI.

Bodwell, C. E. & Adkins, J. S. Protein Quality in Humans: Assessment & in Vitro Estimation. (Illus.). 1981. lib. bdg. 56.50 (ISBN 0-87055-388-7). AVI.

Body, E., jt. auth. see De Borhegy, Stephen F.

Body, Jacques, jt. auth. see Giraudoux, Jean.

Body, R., jt. auth. see Evans, D.

Bodyazhina, V. I. Textbook of Obstetrics. 400p. 1984. 12.00 (ISBN 0-8285-2574-9, Pub. by Mir Pubs USSR). Imported Pubns.

Bodzenta, Erich, jt. ed. see Peachey, Paul.

Boe, Alf. From Gothic Revival to Functional Form. (Architecture & Decorative Art Ser.). 1979. Repr. of 1957 ed. 27.50 (ISBN 0-306-77544-1). Da Capo.

Boe, Beverly, jt. auth. see Philcox, Phil.

Boe, Erling E. & Church, Russell M., eds. Punishment: Issues & Experiments. LC 68-23894. (Century Psychology Ser.). (Illus., Orig.). 1968. pap. text ed. 7.95x (ISBN 0-89197-367-2). Irvington.

Boe, Eugene, jt. auth. see Agel, Jerome.

Boe, Lois, ed. see Baudelaire, Charles P.

Boece, Hector. Hectoris Boetii Murthlacensium Et Aberdonensium Episcoporum Vitae, Iterum in Lucem Editae. LC 76-39462. (Bannatyne Club, Edinburgh. Publications: No. 11). Repr. of 1825 ed. 20.00 (ISBN 0-404-52711-6). AMS Pr.

Boeck, P. The Paraganglia. (Handbuch der Mikroskopischen Anatomie Des Menschen: Vol. 1-8). (Illus.). 400p. 1982. 124.70 (ISBN 0-387-10978-1). Springer-Verlag.

Boeck, P., et al. Peroxisomes & Related Particles in Animal Tissues. (Cell Biology Monographs: Vol. 7). (Illus.). 250p. 1980. 86.00 (ISBN 0-387-81582-1). Springer-Verlag.

Boecker, Alexander. Probable Italian Source of Shakespeare's Julius Caesar. Repr. of 1913 ed. 14.50 (ISBN 0-404-00918-2). AMS Pr.

Boecker, Hans J. Law & the Administration of Justice in the Old Testament & Ancient East. Moiser, Jeremy, tr. LC 80-65556. 224p. 1980. pap. 13.50 (ISBN 0-8066-1801-9, 10-3761). Augsburg.

Boeckh, August. Enzyklopaedie und Methodenlehre der Philologischen Wissenschaften. 3rd ed. 247p. (Ger.). 1966. 39.95 (ISBN 3-519-07201-7, M-7079). French & Eur.

Boeckh, Augustus. The Public Economy of Athens: To Which Is Added a Dissertation on the Silver Mines of Laurion. 2nd rev. ed. Lewis, George C., tr. LC 75-13364. (History of Ideas in Ancient Greece Ser.). (Eng.). 1976. Repr. of 1842 ed. 43.00x (ISBN 0-405-07299-6). Ayer Co Pubs.

Boeckh, J. Anthony & Coghlan, Richard T., eds. The Stock Market & Inflation. LC 81-82913. 225p. 1982. 19.95 (ISBN 0-87094-272-7). Dow Jones-Irwin.

Boeckmann, J., tr. see Schill, Gottfried.

Boeckx, R., jt. auth. see Moyer, T.

Boeckx, R., jt. ed. see Moyer, T.

Boeckx, Roger L., jt. auth. see Hicks, Jocelyn M.

Boedeker, Deborah. Descent from Heaven. (American Philological Association, American Classical Studies: No. 13). 154p. 1985. pap. 11.95 (ISBN 0-89130-807-5, 40 04 13). Scholars Pr GA.

Boeder, Robert B. Malawi. (World Bibliographical Ser.: No. 8). 165p. 1979. 28.50 (ISBN 0-903450-22-4). ABC Clio.

--Malawi. (Westview Profiles-Nations of Contemporary Africa Ser.). 135p. 1986. 26.50x (ISBN 0-86531-777-1). Westview.

Boedtker, A. T., ed. Partonopeus de Blois. (EETS, ES Ser.: No. 109). (The Middle English version, 1911). Repr. of 1912 ed. 45.00 (ISBN 0-527-00312-3). Kraus Repr.

Boeft, J. Den. Calcidius on Demons: Commentaries Ch. 127-136. (Philosophia Antiqua Ser.: No. 33). 1977. pap. text ed. 17.50x (ISBN 90-04-05283-6). Humanities.

Boege, F. W. Smollett's Reputation As a Novelist. LC 75-96150. 1970. Repr. of 1947 ed. lib. bdg. 18.50x (ISBN 0-374-90741-2). Octagon.

Boegehold, ed. see Bream, Jon.

Boegehold, ed. see Fisher, Alan.

Boegehold, Betty. Daddy Doesn't Live Here Anymore: A Book about Divorce. (Golden Learn About Living Bks.). (Illus.). 32p. (gr. k-3). 1985. 4.95 (ISBN 0-307-12480-0, 12480, Pub. by Golden Bks). Western Pub.

--Education Before Five. 1978. pap. 9.50x (ISBN 0-8077-2557-9). Tchrs Coll.

--Hurray for Pippa! LC 79-19105. (Illus.). 64p. (gr. k-3). 1980. PLB 5.99 (ISBN 0-394-94067-9). Knopf.

--Pippa Mouse. (Illus.). 64p. (gr. 1-3). 1976. pap. 1.95 (ISBN 0-440-47148-6, YB). Dell.

--Pippa Mouse. (Illus.). (gr. k-2). 1973. PLB 5.99 (ISBN 0-394-92671-4). Knopf.

--Pippa Pops Out! LC 78-12491. (Illus.). 1979. PLB 5.99 (ISBN 0-394-94057-1). Knopf.

--Three to Get Ready. LC 62-8042. (I Can Read Bk.). (Illus.). (gr. k-3). PLB 9.89 (ISBN 0-06-020551-2). HarpJ.

--You Can Say "No". A Book about Protecting Yourself. (Golden Learn about Living Bks.). (Illus.). 32p. (gr. k-3). 1985. 4.95 (ISBN 0-307-12483-5, 12483, Pub. by Golden Bks). Western Pub.

Boegehold, Betty D. Getting Ready to Read. (Band Street College of Education Child Development Ser.). 240p. 1984. pap. 5.95 (ISBN 0-345-30519-1). Ballantine.

Boegli, A. Karst Hydrology & Physical Speleology. (Illus.). 300p. 1980. 41.00 (ISBN 0-387-10098-9). Springer-Verlag.

Boehler, J. P., ed. Mechanical Behavior of Anisotropic Solids. 1983. lib. bdg. 120.00 (ISBN 90-2472-813-4, Pub. by Martinus Nijhoff Netherlands). Kluwer Academic.

Boehler, Jill. Social Interaction Group Therapy: A Speech Language Program for Adult Aphasics. (Illus.). 162p. 1984. spiral 16.75x (ISBN 0-398-04926-2). C C Thomas.

Boehler, Ted. NAUI Professional Resource Organizer. Sleeper, Jeanne B. & Hardy, Jon, eds. (Illus., Prog. Bk.). 1977. tchrs' ed. 50.00 (ISBN 0-916974-26-X). NAUI.

Boehler, Ted, jt. auth. see Galbraith, Robert.

Boehler, Ted, ed. see Miscavich, Ron.

Boehles, H. Infusionsterapie und klinische Ernaehrung in der Kinderheilkunde. (Handbuch der Infusionstherapie und klinische Ernaehrung: Band 6). (Illus.). x, 166p. 1983. 30.25 (ISBN 3-8055-3719-0). S Karger.

Boehlig, Gertrud, ed. Ioannis Caminiatae de expugnatione Thessalonicae. LC 72-83054. (Corpus Fontium Historiae Byzantinae Series Berolinensis: Vol. 4). 1973. 27.60x (ISBN 3-11-002286-9). De Gruyter.

Boehlje, Michael D. & Eidman, Vernon R. Farm Management. 806p. 1984. text ed. 35.95 (ISBN 0-471-04688-4). Wiley.

Boehlke, Neal. Jesus & Bartimaeus. 1982. pap. 0.99 (ISBN 0-570-06156-3, 59-1270). Concordia.

--Zacchaeus Meets the Savior. 1980. pap. 0.99 (ISBN 0-570-06132-6, 59-1250, Arch Bk). Concordia.

Boehlke, Neal A. Man Who Met Jesus at Bethesda. (Arch Bk.). (gr. k-4). 1981. pap. 0.99 (ISBN 0-570-06143-1, 59-1260). Concordia.

Boehm. Vom Gesichtspunkt der Phanomenologie Husserl - Studien. (Phaenomenologica Ser: No. 26). 1968. lib. bdg. 34.00 (ISBN 90-247-0259-3, Pub by Martinus Nijhoff Netherlands); pap. 18.50 (ISBN 90-247-0258-5). Kluwer Academic.

Boehm, A., et al, eds. see Kraus, K.

Boehm, Ann E. & Slater, Barbara R. Cognitive Skills Assessment Battery. 2nd ed. 1981. complete kit 48.95x (ISBN 0-8077-5975-9); refill 8.50x (ISBN 0-8077-5976-7); assesors manual 3.50x (ISBN 0-8077-5977-5); sampler 3.95x (ISBN 0-8077-5978-3). Tchrs Coll.

Boehm, Ann E. & Weinberg, Richard A. The Classroom Observer: Guide to Developing Observation Skills. LC 77-4316. (Illus.). 1977. pap. text ed. 8.95x (ISBN 0-8077-2506-4). Tchrs Coll.

Boehm, Ann E. & White, Mary A. The Parents' Handbook on School Testing. LC 81-16700. (Illus.). 191p. 1982. 14.95 (ISBN 0-8077-2660-5). Tchrs Coll.

Boehm, B. W., et al. Characteristics of Software Quality. (TRW Series on Software Technology: Vol. 1). 166p. 1978. 53.25 (ISBN 0-444-85105-4, North-Holland). Elsevier.

Boehm, Barbara D., tr. see Grodecki, Louis & Brisac, Catherine.

Boehm, Barry W. Software Engineering Economics. (Illus.). 768p. 1981. text ed. 45.00 (ISBN 0-13-822122-7). P-H.

Boehm, Barry W., jt. ed. see Sackman, Harold.

Boehm, C., ed. Calculus & Computer Science Theory: Proceedings of the Symposium Held in Rome, March 25-27, 1975. (Lecture Notes in Computer Science: Vol. 37). xiv, 370p. 1975. pap. 20.00 (ISBN 0-387-07416-3). Springer-Verlag.

Boehm, C., jt. ed. see Astesiano, E.

Boehm, C., jt. ed. see Ausiello, G.

Boehm, Christopher. Blood Revenge: The Anthropology of Feuding in Montenegro & Other Tribal Societies. LC 84-2203. (Illus.). 304p. 1984. 25.00x (ISBN 0-7006-0245-3); pap. text ed. 9.95x (ISBN 0-7006-0246-1). U Pr of KS.

--Montenegrin Social Organization & Values: Political Ethnography of a Refuge Area Tribal Adaptation. LC 77-87156. (Ams Studies in Anthropology: No. 1). 1983. 24.50 (ISBN 0-404-16895-7). AMS Pr.

Boehm, Ellen, jt. auth. see Toole, Amy L.

Boehm, Eric H. We Survived: Fourteen Histories of the Hidden & Hunted of Nazi Germany. 3rd ed. 320p. 1985. lib. bdg. 20.00 (ISBN 0-87436-429-9). ABC-Clio.

Boehm, Eric H., et al, eds. Historical Periodicals Directory: Australia, New Zealand, & Cumulative Subject & Geographical Index, Vols. 1-5. (Clio Historical Periodicals Directory Ser.: No. 5). 550p. 1985. lib. bdg. 89.00 (ISBN 0-87436-022-6). ABC-CLIO.

--Historical Periodicals Directory. LC 81-12892. (Historical Periodicals Directories Ser.). Vol. 1: USA & Canada 180p, 1981. lib. bdg. 87.50 (ISBN 0-87436-018-8); Vol. 2: Europe: West, North, Central & South 597p, 1983. lib. bdg. 95.00 (ISBN 0-87436-019-6); Vol. 3: Europe: East & Southeseast; USSR, 257p, 1984. lib. bdg. 89.00 (ISBN 0-87436-020-X). ABC-Clio.

Boehm, Erika & Berd, Malcolm, eds. Passage Four. LC 74-1564. (Passage Ser.). (Illus.). 1978. pap. 3.95 (ISBN 0-931672-03-1). Triton Coll.

--Passage V-VI. LC 74-1564. 1980. 3.95 (ISBN 0-931672-01-5). Triton Coll.

Boehm, Erika & Semelroth, W. Darrell, eds. Ariel. (Poetry Anthology Ser.). 1983. 2.95 (ISBN 0-931672-05-8). Triton Coll.

--Ariel III. (Poetry Anthology Ser.). 1984. 3.95 (ISBN 0-931672-07-4). Triton Coll.

Boehm, Erika, jt. ed. see Semelroth, W. Darrell.

Boehm, Erika C., jt. ed. see Berd, Malcolm D.

Boehm, George A. & Groner, Alex. The Battelle Story: Science in the Service of Mankind. LC 81-14875. (Illus.). 170p. 1982. 10.00 (ISBN 0-935470-10-7). Battelle.

Boehm, Helen F. & Dunnan, Nancy. With a Little Luck: An American Odyssey. (Illus.). 240p. 1985. 17.95 (ISBN 0-89256-277-3). Rawson Assocs.

Boehm, J. & Hertel, E. Polyedergeometrie in n-dimensionalen Raeumen konstanter Kruemmung. (LMW-MA Ser.: No. 70). 288p. 1980. 51.95x (ISBN 0-8176-1160-6). Birkhauser.

Boehm, Klaus, jt. auth. see Morris, Brian.

Boehm, Laszlo. Modern Music Notation. 1961. pap. 8.95 (ISBN 0-02-870490-8). Schirmer Bks.

Boehm, Margaret D., tr. see Maine De Biran, Pierre.

Boehm, N. see Huth, F., et al.

Boehm, Randolph H. & Heldman, Dan C. Public Employees, Unions, & the Erosion of Civic Trust: A Study of San Francisco in the 1970s. LC 82-51293. 265p. 1982. lib. bdg. 25.00 (ISBN 0-89093-473-8, Aletheia Bks); pap. 9.00 (ISBN 0-89093-499-1, Aletheia Bks). U Pubns Amer.

Boehm, Richard G. Exporting Cotton in Texas: Relationships of Ports & Inland Supply Points. LC 75-40622. (Urban & Regional Studies: No. 2). 1975. pap. 5.00 (ISBN 0-87755-224-X). Bureau Busn UT.

--Latin America: Case Studies. 336p. 1984. pap. text ed. 24.95 (ISBN 0-8403-3278-5). Kendall Hunt.

Boehm, Ronald J. ABC-Clio: A Twenty-Five Year History. 95p. 1981. pap. 9.75 (ISBN 0-87436-325-X). ABC-Clio.

Boehm, Rudolph. Vom Gesichtspunkt der Phanomenologie, No. II. (Phaenomenologica Ser.: No. 83). vii, 262p. 1981. 47.50 (ISBN 90-247-2415-5, Pub. by Martinus Nijhoff Netherlands). Kluwer Academic.

Boehm, Theobald. Flute & Flute-Playing: In Acoustal, Technical & Artistic Aspects. (Illus.). 13.25 (ISBN 0-8446-1697-4). Peter Smith.

Boehm, Theobold. Flute & Flute-Playing in Acoustical, Technical & Artistic Aspects. Miller, Dayton C., tr. (Illus.). 1964. pap. 4.50 (ISBN 0-486-21259-9). Dover.

Boehm, W. Methods of Studying Root Systems. LC 79-9706. (Ecological Studies: Vol. 33). (Illus.). 1979. 45.00 (ISBN 0-387-09329-X). Springer-Verlag.

Boehm, W. M., tr. see Kautzky, R.

Boehm, William D. Glacier Bay. LC 75-17886. (Illus.). 136p. 1975. pap. 11.95 album style (ISBN 0-88240-056-8). Alaska Northwest.

Boehm, Wolfgang, jt. ed. see Barnhill, Robert E.

Boehme, Guenther. Urbanitaet. 116p. (Ger.). 1982. 10.00 (ISBN 3-8204-7025-5). P Lang Pubs.

Boehme, Jacob. A Discourse Between Two Souls. pap. 2.95 (ISBN 0-916411-89-3). Sure Fire.

--Jacob Boehme's "The Way to Christ". Stoudt, John J., tr. LC 78-13976. 1979. Repr. of 1947 ed. lib. bdg. 19.75x (ISBN 0-313-21075-6, BOTW). Greenwood.

--Of the Supersensual Life. pap. 4.95 (ISBN 0-916411-90-7). Sure Fire.

--Signature of All Things: & Other Writings. 307p. 1969. pap. 12.95 (ISBN 0-227-67733-1). Attic Pr.

--Six Theosophic Points & Other Writings. 1958. pap. 7.95 (ISBN 0-472-06017-1, 17, AA). U of Mich Pr.

Boehme, Jakob. The Confessions. 69.95 (ISBN 0-87968-258-2). Gordon Pr.

--Works of Jakob Boehme, 4 vols. 1974. lib. bdg. 1500.00 (ISBN 0-87968-465-8). Gordon Pr.

Boehme, S., ed. Astronomy & Astrophysics Abstracts: Literature, Vol. 32; 1982, Pt. 2. 848p. 1983. 72.00 (ISBN 0-387-12516-7). Springer-Verlag.

--Astronomy & Astrophysics Abstracts, Vol. 29: Literature 1981, Pt. 1. 853p. 1981. 65.00 (ISBN 0-387-11264-2). Springer-Verlag.

--Astronomy & Astrophysics Abstracts, Vol. 3: Literature 1970, Pt. 1. x, 490p. 1970. 50.20 (ISBN 0-387-05314-X). Springer-Verlag.

--Astronomy & Astrophysics Abstracts, Vol. 4: Literature 1970, Pt. 2. x, 562p. 1971. 50.20 (ISBN 0-387-05514-2). Springer-Verlag.

--Astronomy & Astrophysics Abstracts, Vol. 5: Literature 1971, Pt. 1. x, 505p. 1971. 50.20 (ISBN 0-387-05701-3). Springer-Verlag.

--Astronomy & Astrophysics Abstracts, Vol. 6: Literature 1971, Pt. 2. x, 560p. 1972. 50.20 (ISBN 0-387-05888-5). Springer-Verlag.

Boehme, S., et al. Astronomy & Astrophysics Abstracts, Vol. 31: Literature 1982, Pt. 1. x, 776p. 1982. 72.00 (ISBN 0-387-12072-6). Springer-Verlag.

Boehme, S., et al, eds. Astronmomy & Astrophysics Abstracts, Vol. 25: Literature 1979, Pt. 1. x, 871p. 1979. 82.00 (ISBN 0-387-09831-3). Springer-Verlag.

--Astronomy & Abstrophysics Abstracts, Vol. 9: Literature 1973, Pt. 1. vii, 610p. 1973. 50.20 (ISBN 0-387-06560-1). Springer-Verlag.

--Astronomy & Astrophysics Abstracts, Vol. 1: Literature 1969, Part 1. vii, 435p. 1969. 50.20 (ISBN 0-387-04421-3). Springer-Verlag.

--Astronomy & Astrophysics Abstracts: Vol. 23-24. 1127p. 1979. 77.00 (ISBN 0-387-09830-5). Springer-Verlag.

--Astronomy & Astrophysics Abstracts: Literature 1979, Pt. 2, Vol. 26. 794p. 1980. 80.00 (ISBN 0-387-10134-9). Springer-Verlag.

--Astronomy & Astrophysics Abstracts, Vol. 10: Literature 1973, Pt. 2. viii, 661p. 1974. 50.80 (ISBN 0-387-06795-7). Springer-Verlag.

--Astronomy & Astrophysics Abstracts, Vol. 11: Literature 1974, Pt. 1. viii, 579p. 1975. 54.00 (ISBN 0-387-07003-6). Springer-Verlag.

--Astronomy & Astrophysics Abstracts, Vol. 12: Literature 1974. Pt. 2. viii, 699p. 1975. 58.00 (ISBN 0-387-07339-6). Springer-Verlag.

--Astronomy & Astrophysics Abstracts, Vol. 13: Literature 1975, Pt. 1. viii, 632p. 1975. 51.00 (ISBN 0-387-07492-9). Springer-Verlag.

--Astronomy & Astrophysics Abstracts, Vol. 14: Literature 1975, Pt. 2. viii, 747p. 1976. 58.00 (ISBN 0-387-07784-7). Springer-Verlag.

--Astronomy & Astrophysics Abstracts, Vol. 18: Literature 1976, Pt. 2. x, 859p. 1977. 58.00 (ISBN 0-387-08319-7). Springer-Verlag.

--Astronomy & Astrophysics Abstracts, Vol. 19: Literature 1977, Pt. 1. viii, 732p. 1977. 66.00 (ISBN 0-387-08555-6). Springer-Verlag.

--Astronomy & Astrophysics Abstracts, Vol. 15-16: Author & Subject Indexes to Volumes 1-10, Literature 1969-1973. v, 655p. 1976. 58.00 (ISBN 0-387-07905-X). Springer-Verlag.

Boehme, S, et al, eds. Astronomy & Astrophysics Abstracts, Vol. 27: Literature 1980, Pt. 1. 939p. 1980. 80.00 (ISBN 0-387-10479-8). Springer-Verlag.

Boehme, S., et al, eds. Astronomy & Astrophysics Abstracts, Vol. 2: Literature 1969, Pt. 2. x, 516p. 1970. 50.20 (ISBN 0-387-04773-5). Springer-Verlag.

--Astronomy & Astrophysics Abstracts, Vol. 20: Literature 1977, Pt. 2. viii, 786p. 1978. 65.00 (ISBN 0-387-08838-5). Springer-Verlag.

--Astronomy & Astrophysics Abstracts, Vol. 21: Literature 1978, Pt. 1. viii, 834p. 1978. 65.00 (ISBN 0-387-09067-3). Springer-Verlag.

--Astronomy & Astrophysics Abstracts, Vol. 22: Literature 1978, Pt. 2. viii, 849p. 1979. 60.00 (ISBN 0-387-09464-4). Springer-Verlag.

--Astronomy & Astrophysics Abstracts, Vol. 28: Literature 1980, Pt. 2. 841p. 1981. 70.00 (ISBN 0-387-10799-1). Springer-Verlag.

--Astronomy & Astrophysics Abstracts, Vol. 30: Literature, 1981. 792p. 1982. 72.00 (ISBN 0-387-11721-0). Springer-Verlag.

--Astronomy & Astrophysics Abstracts, Vol. 7: Literature 1972, Pt. 1. x, 526p. 1972. 50.20 (ISBN 0-387-06072-3). Springer-Verlag.

--Astronomy & Astrophysics Abstracts, Vol. 8: Literature 1972, Pt. 2. x, 594p. 1973. 50.20 (ISBN 0-387-06352-8). Springer-Verlag.

--Literature Nineteen Seventy Eight, Part 1. (Astronomy & Astrophysics Abstracts Ser.: Vol. 21). 1978. 65.00 (ISBN 0-387-09067-3). Springer-Verlag.

--Literature 1983, Pt. 1. (Astronomy & Astrophysics Asbstracts Ser.: Vol. 33). 815p. 1983. 72.00 (ISBN 0-387-13017-9). Springer Verlag.

Boehme-Brown, M., tr. see Hirt, Franz J.

Boehmer, Eduard. Bibliotheca Wiffeniana: Bibliotheca Wiffeniana: Spanish Reformers of Two Centuries from Fifteen Twenty, 3 Vols. 1964. Repr. of 1904 ed. Set. 62.00 (ISBN 0-8337-0330-7). B Franklin.

Boehmer, H. The Jesuits. 69.95 (ISBN 0-87968-199-3). Gordon Pr.

Boehmer, H. V., et al, eds. T Cell Hybridomas: A Workshop at the Basle Institute for Immunology. (Current Topics in Microbiology & Immunology Ser.: Vol. 100). 262p. 1982. 26.00 (ISBN 0-387-11535-8). Springer-Verlag.

Boehmer, H. Von see Haas, W. & Von Boehmer, H.

Boehmer, Heinrich. Luther & the Reformation in the Light of Modern Research. LC 83-45639. Date not set. Repr. of 1930 ed. 44.50 (ISBN 0-404-19823-6). AMS Pr.

--Luther in the Light of Recent Research. 1977. lib. bdg. 59.95 (ISBN 0-8490-2189-8). Gordon Pr.

Boehmer, M. C. The Micro in Your Library. 50p. (Orig.). 1984. pap. 5.00 (ISBN 0-914677-00-4). Contemp Issues.

Boehmer, Raquel. A Foraging Vacation: Edibles from Maine's Sea & Shore. (Illus.). 150p. (Orig.). 1982. pap. 7.95 (ISBN 0-89272-139-1, PIC488). Down East.

Boehn, Erika C., ed. Passage VII-VIII. LC 74-1564. 1982. 3.95 (ISBN 0-931672-04-X). Triton Coll.

Boehn, Max. Dolls. 1972. pap. 4.95 (ISBN 0-486-22847-9). Dover.

Boehn, Max Von. Miniatures & Silhouettes: Modes & Manners Supplement. LC 70-145772. (Illus.). 1969. Repr. of 1928 ed. 27.50 (ISBN 0-405-08279-7, Blom Pubns). Ayer Co Pubs.

--Modes & Manners: From the Middle Ages to the End of the Eighteenth Century, 4 vols. in 2. LC 68-56493. (Illus.). Repr. of 1932 ed. 50.00 (ISBN 0-405-08280-0, Blom Pubns). Ayer Co Pubs.

--Ornaments--Lace, Fans, Gloves, Walking-Sticks, Parasols, Jewelry & Trinkets: Modes & Manners Supplement. LC 70-148467. (Illus.). Repr. of 1929 ed. 27.50 (ISBN 0-405-08286-X, Blom Pubns). Ayer Co Pubs.

Boehn, Max Von & Fischel, Oskar. Modes & Manners of the Ninteenth Century, 4 Vols in 2. rev. & enl. ed. LC 68-56493. (Illus.). Repr. of 1927 ed. Set. 50.00 (ISBN 0-405-08283-5, Blom Pubns); 25.00 ea. Vol. 1 (ISBN 0-405-08281-9). Vol. 2 (ISBN 0-405-08282-7). Ayer Co Pubs.

Boehn, Max Von see Von Boehn, Max.

Boehne, Patricia J. J. V. Foix. (World Authors Ser.). 1980. 16.95 (ISBN 0-8057-6412-7, Twayne). G K Hall.

Boehner, Philotheus. Conferences for Franciscan Religious. (Spirit & Life Ser). 1966. 2.00 (ISBN 0-686-11571-6). Franciscan Inst.

--Itinerarium Mentis in Deum. (Works of Saint Bonaventure Ser). 1956. 3.50 (ISBN 0-686-11591-0). Franciscan Inst.

--Walter Burleigh De Puritate Artis Logicae Tractus Langios. Incl. Tractatus Brevior. (Text Ser). 1955. 6.00 (ISBN 0-686-17965-X). Franciscan Inst.

Boehner, Philotheus & Buytaert, Eligius M. Collected Articles on Ockham. (Philosophy Ser). 1958. 23.00 (ISBN 0-686-11542-2). Franciscan Inst.

Boehner, Philotheus, ed. The Tractatus De Successivis Attributed to William Ockham. (Philosophy Ser). 1944. 8.00 (ISBN 0-686-11531-7). Franciscan Inst.

Boehner, Philotheus & Brown, Stephen, eds. Guillelmi de Ockham: Opera Philosophica, Vol. 2. 1978. 40.00 (ISBN 0-686-27930-1). Franciscan Inst.

Boehner, Philotheus, et al, eds. Guillelmi de Ockham: Opera Philosophica, Vol. 1, Summa Philosophica. 1974. 52.00 (ISBN 0-686-11530-9). Franciscan Inst.

Boehringer, Christof. Zur Chronologie Mittelhellenistischer Muenzserien 220-160 vor Chr. (Antike Muenzen und Geschnittene Steine Ser.: Vol. 5). (Illus.). 240p. 1972. 71.20 (ISBN 3-11-001763-6). De Gruyter.

Boehringer, Erich, ed. Altertuemer von Pergamon. Incl. Vol. 8, Pt. 3. Die Inschriften des Asklepieions. Habicht, Christian. (Illus.). xii, 202p. 1969. 48.00x (ISBN 3-11-001197-2); Vol. 11, Pt. 1. Das Asklepieion: Der Suedliche Temenosbezirk in Hellenistischer & Fruehroemischer Zeit. Ziegenaus, Oskar & De Luca, Gioia. (Illus.). xii, 188p. 1968. 62.40x (ISBN 3-11-001196-4). (Deutsches Archaeologisches Institut). (Ger.). De Gruyter.

Boehringer, Marie. Everyday Miracles. 1983. 6.50 (ISBN 0-8233-0363-2). Golden Quill.

Boeing & Haeusgen. Herder-Lexikon Kunst. 240p. (Ger.). 1974. pap. 25.95 (ISBN 3-451-16459-0, M-7458, Pub. by Herder). French & Eur.

Boeing Computer Service Co. Staff, jt. auth. see Lines, M. Vardell.

Boeing, G. Herder-Lexikon Wirtschaft. 2nd ed. 256p. (Ger.). 1975. pap. 25.95 (ISBN 3-451-16460-4, M-7462, Pub. by Herder). French & Eur.

Boeing-Haeusgen, Ursula. Diccionario Rioduero: Arte. 620p. (Span.). 1978. leatherette 26.95 (ISBN 84-220-0873-4, S-50170). French & Eur.

Boeke, Julius H. Economics & Economic Policy of Dual Societies, As Exemplified by Indonesia. LC 75-30045. (Institute of Pacific Relations). Repr. of 1953 ed. 31.50 (ISBN 0-404-59508-1). AMS Pr.

--The Structure of the Netherlands Indian Economy. LC 75-30047. (Institute of Pacific Relations). 216p. 1983. Repr. of 1942 ed. 29.50 (ISBN 0-404-59509-X). AMS Pr.

Boeke, W., ed. see International Symposium on Immunology & Immunopathology of the Eye, 1st, Strasbourg, 1974.

Boeker, M. Status of the Beginning Calculus Students in Pre-Calculus College Mathematics: Study Carried Out with Students in Brooklyn College & City College of New York. LC 76-176690. (Columbia University. Teachers College. Contributions to Education: No. 922). Repr. of 1947 ed. 22.50 (ISBN 0-404-55922-0). AMS Pr.

Boekholt, Albert. Puppets & Masks. LC 81-8572. (Illus.). 112p. (gr. 4 up). 1981. 10.95 (ISBN 0-8069-7042-1); PLB 13.29 (ISBN 0-8069-7043-X). Sterling.

Boekman. Surviving Your Parent's Divorce. (gr. 7 up). 1980. PLB 8.90 (ISBN 0-531-02869-0, B51). Watts.

Boele-Woelki, Katharina. Die Effektivitatsprufung der Staatsangehorigkeiten im Niederlandischen Internationalen Familienrecht. 206p. 1983. pap. 34.00 (ISBN 90-65-4411-74). Kluwer Academic.

Boelhower, William, tr. see Gramsci, Antonio.

Boelhower, William Q., tr. see Goldmann, Lucien.

Boella, M. J. Personnel Management in the Hotel & Catering Industry. 3rd ed. 268p. (Orig.). 1983. pap. text ed. 17.00 (ISBN 0-09-150101-6, Hutchinson & Co). Brookfield Pub Co.

Boella, Michael. Working in a Hotel. 1982. 26.00x (ISBN 0-7134-1138-4, Pub. by Careers Con England). State Mutual Bk.

Boeminghaus, Dieter, ed. Pedestrian Areas & Dewing Elements. 288p. 1982. 110.00x (ISBN 0-686-45590-8, Pub. by L Brooks England). State Mutual Bk.

Boemus, Joannes. The Fardle of Facions Conteining the Aunciente Maners of Affrike & Asia. LC 76-25836. (English Experience Ser.: No. 227). 368p. 1970. Repr. of 1555 ed. 28.00 (ISBN 90-221-0227-0). Walter J Johnson.

Boen, F. S., ed. see International Symposium on Peritoneal Dialysis, 1st, Chapala, Jalisco, Mexico, June 25-28, 1978.

Boen, Helen C. Kuhn: Mary Katherine Kuhn & Descendants. (Illus.). 336p. (Orig.). 1985. pap. 40.00 (ISBN 0-915551-00-4). Coalson-Kuhn.

Boen, James R. & Zahn, Douglas A. The Human Side of Statistical Consulting. (Research Methods Ser.). 196p. 1982. 16.95 (ISBN 0-534-97949-1). Lifetime Learn.

Boenau, A. Bruce & Niiro, Katsuyuki, eds. Post-Industrial Society. 508p. (Orig.). 1984. pap. text ed. 19.75 (ISBN 0-8191-3613-1). U Pr of Amer.

Boenau, A. Bruce, jt. ed. see McCardle, Arthur W.

Boenig, Herman V. Plasma Chemistry & Technology. LC 83-51363. 209p. 1983. 45.00 (ISBN 0-87762-337-6). Technomic.

--Plasma Science & Technology. LC 81-15200. 304p. 1982. 39.95x (ISBN 0-8014-1356-7). Cornell U Pr.

Boenig, Herman V., ed. Advances in Low-Temperature Plasma Chemistry, Technology, Applications, Vol. 1. LC 84-51635. 377p. 1984. 55.00 (ISBN 0-87762-373-2). Technomic.

Boenig, Robert, ed. Richard Rolle Biblical Commentaries. (Salzburg - Elizabethan Studies: Vol. 92). 193p. 1984. pap. text ed. 25.50x (ISBN 0-391-03342-5, Pub. by Salzburg Austria). Humanities.

Boening, John, ed. & intro. by. The Reception of Classical German Literature in England, 1760-1860: A Documentary History from Contemporary Periodicals, 10 vols. Incl. Vol. 1. General Introduction & Reviews from 1760 to 1813 (ISBN 0-8240-0990-8); Vol. 2. Reviews from 1813 to 1835 (ISBN 0-8240-0991-6); Vol. 3. Reviews from 1835 to 1860 (ISBN 0-8240-0992-4); Vol. 4. Authors from Bodmer to Klopstock (ISBN 0-8240-0993-2); Vol. 5. Authors from Lavater to Novalis (ISBN 0-8240-0994-0); Vol. 6. The Reception of Early German Romantics: Richter, the Brothers Schlegel, Tieck & Hoffmann (ISBN 0-8240-0995-9); Vol. 7. General Critical Articles on Goethe & Reviews Which Discuss Goethe & Schiller Together, Arranged in Order of Appearance (ISBN 0-8240-0996-7); Vol. 8. Reviews of Werther, Goethe's Early Works, His Poems & Faust (ISBN 0-8240-0997-5); Vol. 9. The Works of Goethe's Midcareer, Wilhelm Meister & Such Works As Dichtung und Wahrheit, Etc (ISBN 0-8240-0998-3); Vol. 10. The English Reception of Specific Works of Schiller, from the Early Plays to the Historical Works (ISBN 0-8240-0999-1). 1977. Set. lib. bdg. 120.00 each (ISBN 0-686-77265-2). Garland Pub.

Boenisch, Edmond W., Jr., jt. auth. see Haney, C. Michele.

Boenneken, M. Wilhelm Raabes Roman Die Akten Des Vogelsangs. pap. 19.00 (ISBN 0-384-04905-2). Johnson Repr.

Boenzi, Joe, tr. see Aubry, Joseph.

Boer, ed. see International Solar Energy Society.

Boer, Bertil H. van see Bengtsson, Ingmar & Van Boer, Bertil H., Jr.

Boer, C. H. De see Harrison, R. G. & DeBoer, C. H.

Boer, Charles, jt. auth. see Hillman, James.

Boer, Charles, tr. from Gr. The Homeric Hymns. rev. ed. (Dunquin Ser.: No. 10). vi, 182p. 1983. pap. 11.50 (ISBN 0-88214-210-0). Spring Pubns.

Boer, Charles, tr. see Ficino, Marsilio.

Boer, Den W. Private Morality in Greece & Rome: Some Historical Aspects. 1980. text ed. 46.25x (ISBN 90-04-05976-8). Humanities.

Boer, E. de see De Boer, E. & Viergever, M. A.

Boer, Germain B. Direct Cost & Contribution Accounting: An Integrated Management Accounting System. LC 73-17324. (Systems & Controls for Financial Managment Ser.). 246p. 1974. 45.95 (ISBN 0-471-08505-7, Pub. by Wiley-Interscience). Wiley.

Boer, H. H., jt. ed. see Lever, J.

Boer, H. J., jt. auth. see McConnell, P. S.

Boer, Harry R. The Bible & Higher Criticism. Orig. Title: Above the Battle. 112p. 1981. pap. 3.95 (ISBN 0-8028-1896-X). Eerdmans.

--The Doctrine of Reprobation in the Christian Reformed Church. 104p. 1983. pap. 4.95 (ISBN 0-8028-1952-4). Eerdmans.

--The Four Gospels & Acts: A Short Introduction. 112p. 1982. pap. 3.95 (ISBN 0-8028-1901-X). Eerdmans.

--A Short History of the Early Church. LC 75-25742. pap. 6.95 (ISBN 0-8028-1339-9). Eerdmans.

Boer, James Den see Den Boer, James.

Boer, James Den see Olson, Charles & Den Boer, James.

Boer, Jan De see De Boer, Jan & Baillie, Thomas W.

Boer, Jan H. Missionary Messengers of Liberation in a Colonial Context: A Case Study of the Sudan United Mission. 542p. 1979. pap. text ed. 52.00x (ISBN 90-6203-561-2). Humanities.

Boer, Janet de see De Boer, Janet.

Boer, John J. De see De Boer, John J.

Boer, Karl W. & Duffie, John A., eds. Advances in Solar Energy: An Annual Review of Research & Development in 1981, Vol. I. (Illus.). 1982. pap. text ed. 95.00x (ISBN 0-89553-040-6). Am Solar Energy.

Boer, Karl W., ed. see International Solar Energy Society, American Section.

Boer, Karl W., ed. see International Solar Energy Society, American Section, Annual Meeting, Denver, 1978.

Boer, P. de see Searle, A. G. & De Boer, P.

Boer, Paul M. De see De Boer, Paul M.

Boer, S. P. De see De Boer, S. P. & Driessen, E. J.

Boer, Theo de see De Boer, Theo.

Boer, Theodore De. The Development of Husserl's Thought. Plantinga, Theodore, tr. (Phaenomenologica Ser.: No. 76). 1978. lib. bdg. 79.00 (ISBN 9-0247-2039-7, Pub. by Martinus Nijhoff Netherlands); pap. 45.00 (ISBN 9-0247-2124-5, Pub. by Martinus Nijhoff Netherlands). Kluwer Academic.

Boer, Tjitze J. De. The History of Philosophy in Islam. LC 70-131638. 216p. 1903. Repr. 39.00x (ISBN 0-403-00525-6). Scholarly.

Boerens, Trice, et al. Of Daydreams & Memories. (Illus.). 32p. (Orig.). 1983. 11.95. Vanessa-Ann Collec.

Boerhave Beekman, W., ed. Elsevier's Wood Dictionary, 3 Vols. (Eng., Fr., Span., Ital., Swedish, Dutch & Ger.). 1964-75. Set. 259.75 (ISBN 0-686-43878-7); Vol. 1. 89.50 (ISBN 0-444-40063-X); Vol. 2. 89.50 (ISBN 0-444-40053-2); Vol. 3. 89.50 (ISBN 0-444-40713-8). Elsevier.

Boer-Hoff, Louise E., tr. see Schuurman, C. J.

Boeri, David. People of the Ice Whale: Eskimos, White Men, & the Whale. LC 83-14072. (Illus.). 284p. 1984. 19.95 (ISBN 0-525-24206-6, 01937-580). Dutton.

--People of the Ice Whale: Eskimos, White Men & the Whale. (Illus.). 300p. 1985. pap. 7.95 (ISBN 0-15-671660-7, Harv). HarBraceJ.

Boericke, Arthur, et al. The Complete Adventures of Olga da Polga. LC 82-72753. (Illus.). 512p. (gr. 4-6). 1983. 16.95 (ISBN 0-440-00981-2). Delacorte.

Boericke, William. Materia Medica with Repertory. 1982. 20.00x (ISBN 0-685-76567-9, Pub. by Boericke & Tafel). Formur Intl.

Boericke, William & Dewey, Willis. The Twelve Tissue Remedies of Schuessler. 7.00 (ISBN 0-89378-065-0, Pub. by Harjeet). Formur Intl.

Boericke, William F. Prospecting & Operating Small Gold Placers. 2nd ed. 144p. 1936. 15.95 (ISBN 0-471-08514-6, Pub. by Wiley-Interscience). Wiley.

Boeringer, James. Organa Britannica, Vol. 1. LC 78-72492. (Illus.). 352p. 1983. 85.00 (ISBN 0-8387-1894-9). Bucknell U Pr.

Boeringer, James, ed. Choral Buch: A-Facsimile of the First Edition of 1784. LC 83-62496. (Illus.). 336p. 1984. 25.00 (ISBN 0-941642-00-3). Moravian NJ.

Boerma, A. H. A Right to Food. 177p. 1976. pap. 13.25 (ISBN 92-5-101642-9, F1146, FAO). Unipub.

Boerma, Conrad. The Rich, the Poor & the Bible. rev. ed. Bowden, John, tr. from Dutch. LC 80-15337. 120p. 1980. pap. 5.95 (ISBN 0-664-24349-5). Westminster.

Boerner, F. Taschenwoerterbuch der Botanischen Pflanzennamem. 2nd ed. 435p. (Ger.). 1966. 39.95 (ISBN 3-489-56322-0, M-7631, Pub. by P. Parey). French & Eur.

Boerner, G., et al. Astrophysics. LC 25-9130. (Springer Tracts in Modern Physics: Vol. 69). (Illus.). iv, 120p. 1973. 46.10 (ISBN 0-387-06376-5). Springer-Verlag.

Boerner, Wolfgang M., et al, eds. Inverse Methods in Electromagnetic Imaging, 2 Vol. Set Only. 1984. Set. lib. bdg. 145.00 (ISBN 90-277-1890-3, Pub. by Reidel Holland). Kluwer Academic.

Boers, Hendrikus. What Is New Testament Theology? The Rise of Criticism & the Problem of a Theology of the New Testament. Via, Dan O., Jr., ed. LC 79-7372. (Guides to Biblical Scholarship: New Testament Ser.). 96p. 1979. pap. 3.95 (ISBN 0-8006-0466-0, 1-466). Fortress.

Boersch, Sabine. Fremdsprachenstudium-Frauenstudium? Subjektive Bedeutung und Funktion des Fremdsprachenerwerbs und. (Studiums fur Studentinnen und Studenten). 208p. 1982. pap. 20.00x (ISBN 3-923721-03-X, 8417, Stauffenberg Verlag Tubingen Netherlands). Benjamins North Am.

Boerschmann, Ernest. Old China in Historic Photographs: Two Hundred Eighty-Eight Views. rev. ed. (Illus.). 304p. 1982. pap. 12.95 (ISBN 0-486-24282-X). Dover.

Boerschmann, Ernst. Old China in Historic Photographs. 1983. 18.50 (ISBN 0-8446-5945-2). Peter Smith.

Boersma, A., jt. auth. see Haq, B. U.

Boersma, Frederic J. & Muir, Walter. Eye Movements & Information Processing in Mentally Retarded Children. (Modern Approaches to the Diagnosis & Instruction of Multi-Handicapped Children Ser.: Vol. 14). 100p. 1975. text ed. 16.00 (ISBN 90-237-4125-0, Pub. by Swets & Zeitlinger Netherlands). Hogrefe Intl.

Boersma, Frederic J., jt. auth. see Chapman, James W.

Boersma, Frederic J., jt. auth. see Wilton, Keri M.

Boersma, J. Amoenissima Civitas. 544p. 1984. text ed. 90.50x (ISBN 90-232-2049-8, Pub. by Van Gorcum Holland). Humanities.

Boersner, Demetrio. The Bolsheviks & the National & Colonial Question, 1917-1928. LC 79-2894. 285p. 1981. Repr. of 1957 ed. 36.50 (ISBN 0-8305-0062-6). Hyperion Conn.

Boerstler, Richard W. Letting Go: A Holistic & Meditative Approach to Living & Dying. LC 81-71653. (Illus.). 112p. (Orig.). 1982. pap. 3.95 (ISBN 0-9607928-0-5). Assocs Thanatology.

Boerstra, M. L., ed. Engineering Databases: Survey of Existing Engineering Database Management Systems, Criteria for Selecting a Database, & Some Practical Experiences in Applying a Database System. (Report of the CIAD Project Group on Engineering Databases). 178p. 1985. 111.00 (ISBN 0-444-42472-5). Elsevier.

Boes, D., et al, eds. Public Production: International Seminar in Public Economics, Bonn, FRG 1981. (Journal of Economics Supplementum: Vol. 2). (Illus.). 222p. 1982. pap. 44.00 (ISBN 0-387-81726-3). Springer-Verlag.

Boesak, Allan. Farewell to Innocence: A Socio-Ethical Study on Black Theology & Black Power. LC 77-5578. 197p. (Orig.). 1977. pap. 6.95 (ISBN 0-88344-130-6). Orbis Bks.

--The Finger of God: Sermons on Faith & Socio-Political Responsibility. Randall, Peter, tr. from Afrikaans. LC 81-16943. 112p. (Orig.). 1982. pap. 5.95 (ISBN 0-88344-135-7). Orbis Bks.

--Walking on Thorns: The Call to Christian Obedience. 80p. (Orig.). 1984. pap. 3.95 (ISBN 0-8028-0041-6). Eerdmans.

Boesak, Allan A. Black & Reformed: Apartheid, Liberation, & the Calvinist Tradition. LC 84-7212. 160p. (Orig.). 1984. pap. 6.95 (ISBN 0-88344-148-9). Orbis Bks.

Boesch, Francis T., ed. Large-Scale Networks: Theory & Design. LC 75-25324. 1976. 36.35 (ISBN 0-87942-063-4, PC00604). Inst Electrical.

Boesche, Roger, ed. Alexis de Tocqueville: Selected Letters on Politics & Society. Toupin, James, tr. 417p. Date not set. 24.95 (ISBN 0-317-27292-6). U of Cal Pr.

Boesche, Roger, ed. see De Tocqueville, Alexis.

Boeschemeyer, Uwe. Die Sinnfrage in Psychotherapie und Theologie: Die Existenzanalyse und Logotherapie Viktor E. Frankls aus theologischer Sicht. (Theologische Bibliothek Toepelmann Ser.: Vol. 32). 1977. 22.80x (ISBN 3-11-006727-7). De Gruyter.

Boeschen, John. Freelance Writing for Profit: A Guide to Selling Nonfiction Articles. (Illus.). 160p. 1982. pap. 6.95 (ISBN 0-312-30440-4). St Martin.

Boeschen, John, jt. auth. see Magid, Lawrence J.

Boeschenstein, Hermann. German Literature in the Nineteenth Century. LC 70-76383. 1969. 19.95 (ISBN 0-312-32585-1). St Martin.

Boeschoten, W. C. & Fase, M. M. The Volume of Payments & the Informal Economy in the Netherlands 1965-82. 1984. pap. 12.50 (ISBN 90-247-3095-3, Pub. by Martinus Nijhoff Netherlands). Kluwer Academic.

Boese, A., ed. Search for the Cause of Multiple Sclerosis & Other Chronic Diseases of the Central Nervous System. (Illus.). 502p. (Orig.). 1980. pap. 67.50x (ISBN 3-527-25875-2). VCH Pubs.

Boese, Jannik, et al. Ujamaa - Socialism from Above. (Scandinavian Institute of African Studies, Uppsala). (Illus.). 186p. 1978. text ed. 25.25x (ISBN 0-8419-9730-6, Africana). Holmes & Meier.

Boese, Johannes. Altmesopotamische Weihplatten: Eine Sumerische Denkmalsgattung des Dritten Jahrtausends v. Chr. (Untersuchungen Zur Assyriologie und Vorderasiatischen Archaeologie Ser.: Vol. 6). (Illus.). 232p. 1971. 70.00x (ISBN 3-11-002484-5). De Gruyter.

Boeselager, Wolfhard Von see Von Boeselager, Wolfhard.

Boesen, Jannik & Mohele, A. T. The "Success Story" of Peasant Tobacco Production in Tanzania. (Centre for Development Research Studies: No. 2). (Illus.). 169p. 1983. pap. text ed. 9.50x (ISBN 0-8419-9757-8, Africana). Holmes & Meier.

Boesiger, Ernest, jt. auth. see Dobzhansky, Theodosius.

Boesing, Martha. Journeys along the Matrix: Three Plays. (Illus.). 1978. pap. 3.75 (ISBN 0-917266-15-3). Vanilla.

Boesky, Ivan F. Merger Mania: Arbitrage-Wall Street's Best-Kept Money-Making Secret. Madrick, Jeffrey, ed. LC 84-25193. 1985. 18.95 (ISBN 0-03-002602-4). HR&W.

Boestamam, Ahmad. Carving the Path to the Summit. Roff, William R., tr. from Malayan. LC 79-11174. (Southeast Asia Translation Ser.: Vol. 2). xxxii, 149p. 1980. 13.95x (ISBN 0-8214-0397-4, 82-82881); pap. 6.50x (ISBN 0-8214-0409-1, 82-82899). Ohio U Pr.

Boetcher-Joeres, Ruth-Ellen, ed. Wally, Die Zweiflerin: A Translation from the German of Karl Gutzkow. (Germanic Studies in America: Vol. 19). 130p. 1974. 19.60 (ISBN 3-261-01086-X). P Lang Pubs.

Boetger, Gary. In Search of Balance. LC 75-42602. 1976. 5.00 (ISBN 0-87212-051-1). Libra.

Boethal, D. J. & Eikenbary, R. D., eds. Pest Management Programs for Deciduous Tree Fruits & Nuts. LC 79-12616. 267p. 1979. 39.50x (ISBN 0-306-40178-9, Plenum Pr). Plenum Pub.

Boethius. The Consolation of Philosophy. Green, Richard H., tr. LC 62-11788. 1962. pap. 5.44 scp (ISBN 0-672-60273-3, LLA86). Bobbs.

--The Consolation of Philosophy. Watts, V. E., tr. (Classics Ser). 192p. 1976. pap. 3.95 (ISBN 0-14-044208-1). Penguin.

--De Consolatione Philosophiae. Walton, John, tr. (EETS,OS Ser.: No. 170). Repr. of 1927 ed. 40.00 (ISBN 0-527-00167-8). Kraus Repr.

--In Isagogen Porphyrii Commenta. (Corpus Scriptorum Ecclesiasticorum Latinorum Ser: Vol. 48). 1906. 50.00 (ISBN 0-384-04925-7). Johnson Repr.

--King Alfred's Anglo-Saxon Version of Beothius De Consolatione Philosophiae. Tupper, Martin F., tr. LC 74-136366. (Bohn's Antiquarian Library). Repr. of 1864 ed. 27.50 (ISBN 0-404-50002-1). AMS Pr.

--On the Consolidation of Philosophy. LC 81-52212. 128p. 1981. pap. 3.95 (ISBN 0-89526-885-X). Regnery-Gateway.

--Theological Tractates. Bd. with Consolation of Philosophy. (Loeb Classical Library: No. 74). 12.50x (ISBN 0-674-99083-8). Harvard U Pr.

Boethius, Anicius. Boecius de Consolacione Philosophie. Chaucer, Geoffrey, tr. LC 74-80164. (English Experience Ser.: No. 644). 1974. Repr. of 1478 ed. 28.00 (ISBN 90-221-0644-6). Walter J Johnson.

Boethius, Axel. Etruscan & Early Roman Architecture. (Pelican History of Art Ser.). (Illus.). 1979. pap. 18.95 (ISBN 0-14-056144-7, Pelican). Penguin.

--Etruscan & Early Roman Architecture. (Pelican History of Art Ser.: No. 44). 1979. 35.00 (ISBN 0-670-29875-1). Viking.

Boethius, Hector. Chronicle of Scotland. LC 77-6858. (English Experience Ser.: No. 851). 1977. Repr. of 1540 ed. lib. bdg. 80.00 (ISBN 90-221-0851-1). Walter J Johnson.

Boethmer, Dietrich Von see Von Boethmer, Dietrich.

Boetie, Etienne de la see De La Boetie, Etienne.

Boettcher, Barbara. Summary Plan Descriptions: No. B359. (Requirements for Qualification of Plans Ser.). 42p. 1979. pap. 6.00 (ISBN 0-317-31167-0). Am Law Inst.

Boettcher, Barry, ed. Immunological Influence on Human Fertility. 370p. 1977. 47.50 (ISBN 0-12-109950-4). Acad Pr.

Boettcher, Carl, jt. auth. see Gumpel, Henry J.

Boettcher, Thomas D. Vietnam: The Valor & the Sorrow. (Illus.). 384p. 1985. 27.00 (ISBN 0-316-10083-8); pap. 14.45i (ISBN 0-316-10081-1). Little.

Boettiger, John R. A Love in Shadow. (Illus.). 1978. 10.95 (ISBN 0-393-07530-3). Norton.

Boettinger, H. M. The Telephone Book: Bell, Watson, Vail & American Life 1876-1983. rev. ed. 216p. 1983. pap. 35.00 (ISBN 0-9612186-0-6). Stearn Pubs.

Boettinger, Henry M. Moving Mountains: Or the Art & Craft of Letting Others See Things Your Way. LC 74-9745. (Illus.). 340p. 1975. pap. 4.95 (ISBN 0-02-079250-6, Collier). Macmillan.

Boettner, Loraine. A Harmony of the Gospels. 1976. kivar 3.95 (ISBN 0-87552-132-0). Presby & Reformed.

--Immortality. 1956. 4.50 (ISBN 0-87552-127-4). Presby & Reformed.

--Millennium. 1983. 7.95 (ISBN 0-87552-128-2). Presby & Reformed.

--Reformed Doctrine of Predestination. 1932. 7.95x (ISBN 0-87552-129-0). Presby & Reformed.

--Roman Catholicism. 7.95 (ISBN 0-8010-0685-6). Baker Bk.

--Roman Catholicism. 1962. 7.95 (ISBN 0-87552-130-4). Presby & Reformed.

--Studies in Theology. 1947. 7.95 (ISBN 0-87552-131-2). Presby & Reformed.

Boetzel, Eric, jt. auth. see Clock, Herbert.

Boeuff, Randall Le see LeBoeuff, Randall, Jr.

Boever, William J., jt. auth. see Wallach, Joel D.

Boevey, James. The Art of Building a Man. 1966. 20.00x (ISBN 0-900008-11-3, Pub. by U of London England). State Mutual Bk.

Boevey, Mateo C. Hora Santa. 1978. plastic 4.00 (ISBN 0-8198-0579-3); pap. 3.00 (ISBN 0-8198-0580-7). Dghtrs St Paul.

--Twenty Holy Hours. 1978. pap. 5.00 (ISBN 0-8198-0563-7). Dghtrs St Paul.

Boewe, Charles, ed. see Fitzpatrick, T. J.

Boewering, Gerhard. The Mystical Vision of Existence in Classical Islam. (Studien zur Sprache, Geschichte und Kultur des islamischen Orients, Beihefte zur "der Islam"). 296p. 1979. text ed. 53.60x (ISBN 3-11-007546-6). De Gruyter.

Boeynaems, J. J. & Dumont, J. E., eds. Outlines of Receptor Theory. 1980. 67.00 (ISBN 0-444-80131-6). Elsevier.

Boeynaems, J. M. & Herman, A. G., eds. Prostaglandins, Prostacyclin, Thromboxanes Measurement. (Developments in Pharmacology Ser.: No. 1.). (Illus.). 209p. 1981. PLB 34.00 (ISBN 90-247-2417-1, Pub. by Martinus Nijhoff Netherlands). Kluwer Academic.

Boff. Handbook of Perception & Human Performance. 1985. Vol. 1. 50.00 (ISBN 0-471-88544-4); write for info. (ISBN 0-471-82957-9). Wiley.

Boff, Clodovis & Boff, Leonardo. Salvation & Liberation: In Search of a Balance between Faith & Politics. Barr, Robert R., tr. from Port. LC 84-7220. 128p. (Orig.). 1984. pap. 6.95 (ISBN 0-88344-451-8). Orbis Bks.

Boff, Leonardo. Church, Charisma, Power: Liberation Theology & the Institutional Church. Dierksmeyer, John, tr. from Span. LC 84-21431. 192p. 1985. 16.95 (ISBN 0-8245-0590-5). Crossroad NY.

--Jesus Christ Liberator: A Critical Christology for Our Time. Hughes, Patrick, tr. from Portuguese. LC 78-969. 335p. (Orig.). 1978. pap. 9.95 (ISBN 0-88344-236-1). Orbis Bks.

--Liberating Grace. Drury, John, tr. from Port. LC 79-4206. 256p. (Orig.). 1979. pap. 8.95 (ISBN 0-88344-282-5). Orbis Bks.

--The Lord's Prayer: The Prayer of Integral Liberation. Morrow, Theodore, tr. from Portuguese. LC 82-18811. 144p. (Orig.). 1983. pap. 6.95 (ISBN 0-88344-299-X). Orbis Bks.

--Saint Francis: A Model for Human Liberation. LC 82-14152. 224p. 1982. 12.95 (ISBN 0-8245-0488-7). Crossroad NY.

--Saint Francis: A Model for Human Liberation. 192p. 1984. pap. 9.95 (ISBN 0-8245-0671-5). Crossroad NY.

--The Way of the Cross: Way of Justice. Drury, John, tr. from Port. LC 79-23776. 144p. (Orig.). 1980. pap. 4.95 (ISBN 0-88344-701-0). Orbis Bks.

Boff, Leonardo, jt. auth. see Boff, Clodovis.

Boff, Leonardo & Elizondo, Virgil, eds. La Iglesia Popular: Between Fear & Hope. (Concilium Ser.: Vol. 176). 128p. pap. 6.95 (ISBN 0-317-31468-8, 30-30056-1902) (ISBN 0-317-31469-6). Fortress.

Boff, Vic. Body Builder's Bible for Men & Women. (Illus.). 160p. 1985. 16.95 (ISBN 0-668-05625-8); pap. 9.95 (ISBN 0-668-05630-4). Arco.

Boffa, M., et al, eds. Logic Colloquium 1978. (Studies in Logic & the Foundations of Mathematics: Vol. 97). 434p. 1979. 70.25 (ISBN 0-444-85378-2, North Holland). Elsevier.

Boffa, P. S., et al. Pathological Effects of Oral Contraceptives. LC 72-13565. (Illus.). 220p. 1973. text ed. 26.00x (ISBN 0-8422-7081-7). Irvington.

Boffey, Julia. Manuscripts of English Courtly Love Lyrics in the Later Middle Ages. Griffiths, Jeremy, ed. (Manuscript Studies). 256p. 1985. 37.50 (ISBN 0-85991-179-9, Pub. by Boydell & Brewer). Longwood Pub Group.

Boffey, T. B. Graph Theory in Operations Research. (Computer Science Ser.). (Illus.). 314p. 1982. text ed. 49.50x (ISBN 0-333-28213-2); pap. text ed. 25.50x (ISBN 0-333-28214-0). Scholium Intl.

Boffi, S. & Passatore, G., eds. Nuclear Optical Model Potential. (Lecture Notes in Physics: Vol. 55). 1976. pap. 17.00 (ISBN 0-387-07864-9). Springer-Verlag.

Boffi, S., et al, eds. Perspectives in Nuclear Physics at Intermediate Energies: Proceedings of a Workshop ICTP, Trieste, Italy, Oct. 10-14, 1983. 560p. 1984. 60.00 (ISBN 9971-966-32-8, Pub. by World Sci Singapore). Taylor & Francis.

Bofill, Ricardo. El Tiempo es el Diablo. (Biblioteca Cubana Contemporanea Ser.). 106p. (Orig., Span.). 1985. pap. 6.00 (ISBN 0-317-28601-3). Ediciones.

Bofinger, V. J. & Wheeler, J. L. Developments in Field Experiment Design & Analysis: Proceedings of Symposium held at the University of New England, Armidale, New South Wales, 3-7 September, 1973. 196p. 1975. 42.00x (ISBN 0-85198-333-2, Pub. by CAB Bks England). State Mutual Bk.

Bofman, Theodora H. The Poetics of the Ramakian. (Special Report Ser.: No. 21). 258p. (Orig.). 1984. pap. 15.00x (ISBN 0-318-03064-0, Ctr SE Asian Stud). Cellar.

Bogach, Susan V. Wood As Fuel: Energy for Developing Countries. LC 84-26640. 176p. 1985. 39.95 (ISBN 0-03-001649-5). Praeger.

Bogad, Carolyn. Fraction Fantasy. (Math Ser.). (gr. 5-7). 1979. pap. 5.50 (ISBN 0-88160-067-9). Learning Wks.

Bogadov, Leonid T., tr. see Noeldeke, Theodor.

Bogaert, Daniel A. Van see Van Bogaert, Daniel A.

Bogan, et al. Pharmacological Basis of Large Animal Medicine. (Illus.). 1983. pap. text ed. 53.95 (ISBN 0-632-01055-X, B0686-1). Mosby.

Bogan, James & Goss, Fred, eds. Sparks of Fire: William Blake in a New Age. (Io: No. 29). (Illus.). 484p. (Orig.). 1982. 35.00 (ISBN 0-913028-89-4); pap. 12.95 (ISBN 0-913028-90-8). North Atlantic.

Bogan, James, ed. see Blank, Les.

Bogan, Louise. The Blue Estuaries: Poems, 1923-1968. LC 76-46175. (American Poetry Ser: Vol. 11). 1977. pap. 7.95 (ISBN 0-912946-37-7). Ecco Pr.

Bogan, Louise & Smith, William J. The Golden Journey: Poems for Young People. 296p. 3.95 (ISBN 0-8092-7963-0). Contemp Bks.

Bogan, Louise, tr. see Goethe, Johann W.

Bogan, Mary Inez. Vocabulary & Style of the Soliloquies & Dialogues of St. Augustine, Vol. 42. (Patristic Studies). 238p. 1984. Repr. of 1935 ed. 28.00x (ISBN 0-939738-27-9). Zubal Inc.

Bogar, Rosa. Black Woman Sorrow. Britts, Maurice W., ed. LC 83-80020. (Illus.). 50p. (Orig.). 1983. pap. 4.25 (ISBN 0-940248-14-X). Guild Pr.

Bogard, Travis. Contour in Time: The Plays of Eugene O'Neill. 1972. 27.50x (ISBN 0-19-501573-8). Oxford U Pr.

--Tragic Satire of John Webster. LC 65-13952. 1965. Repr. of 1955 ed. 18.00x (ISBN 0-8462-0585-8). Russell.

Bogard, Travis, ed. see O'Neill, Eugene.

Bogard, Travis, et al. Revels History of Drama in English, Vol. 8: American Drama. (Illus.). 1978. 55.00x (ISBN 0-416-13090-9, NO. 2101); pap. 19.95x (ISBN 0-416-81400-X, NO. 2102). Methuen Inc.

Bogarde, Dirk. An Orderly Man. LC 83-47784. (Illus.). 288p. 1983. 14.95 (ISBN 0-394-53216-3). Knopf.

--Voices in the Garden. LC 81-47494. 352p. 1981. 12.95 (ISBN 0-394-52156-0). Knopf.

--West of Sunset. 1984. 16.95 (ISBN 0-670-75784-5). Viking.

Bogardi, John L. Sediment Transport in Alluvial Streams. 68.00 (ISBN 9-6305-1826-0). WRP.

Bogardus, Carl R., Jr. Clinical Applications of Physics of Radiology & Nuclear Science. LC 67-26010. (Illus.). 248p. 1969. 15.00 (ISBN 0-87527-002-6). Green.

Bogardus, E. S., ed. see American Sociological Society.

Bogardus, Edgar. Various Jangling Keys. LC 70-144756. (Yale Ser. of Younger Poets: No. 50). Repr. of 1953 ed. 18.00 (ISBN 0-404-53850-9). AMS Pr.

Bogardus, Emory S. The Development of Social Thought. 4th ed. LC 79-9741. 1979. Repr. of 1960 ed. lib. bdg. 42.50x (ISBN 0-313-21261-9, BODS). Greenwood.

--Fundamentals of Social Psychology. LC 73-2963. (Classics in Psychology Ser.). Repr. of 1924 ed. 27.00 (ISBN 0-405-05136-0). Ayer Co Pubs.

--Mexican in the United States. LC 70-129389. (American Immigration Collection, Ser. 2). 1970. Repr. of 1934 ed. 10.00 (ISBN 0-405-00575-X). Ayer Co Pubs.

Bogardus, James, jt. auth. see Badger, D. D.

Bogardus, King J., Jr. Pocket Notes for Personal Success: It's As Easy As ABC. (Illus.). 44p. 1977. pap. 1.00 (ISBN 0-918176-01-8). P & K Ent.

Bogardus, Mary. Crisis in the Catskills. 1976. Repr. of 1892 ed. 6.95 (ISBN 0-685-69662-6). Hope Farm.

Bogardus, Ralph F. Pictures & Texts: Henry James, A. L. Coburn, & New Ways of Seeing in Literary Culture. Kirkpatrik, Diane, ed. LC 84-8844. (Studies in Photography: No. 2). 266p. 1984. 39.95 (ISBN 0-8357-1471-3). UMI Res Pr.

Bogardus, Ralph F. & Hobson, Fred, eds. Literature at the Barricades: Essays on the American Writer in the 1930s. LC 81-3015. 256p. text ed. 22.50 o. p. (ISBN 0-8173-0078-3); pap. text ed. 8.95 (ISBN 0-8173-0079-1). U of Ala Pr.

Bogart, Bonnie. The Ewoks Join the Fight. LC 82-62834. (Illus.). 32p. (ps-4). 1983. PLB 4.99 (ISBN 0-394-95858-6); pap. 1.95 (ISBN 0-394-85858-1). Random.

Bogart, Doris Van De see Van De Bogart, Doris.

Bogart, Ernest L. An Economic History of the United States. 1979. Repr. of 1923 ed. lib. bdg. 40.00 (ISBN 0-8495-0514-3). Arden Lib.

--Financial History of Ohio. (Illus.). Repr. of 1912 ed. 31.00 (ISBN 0-384-04950-8). Johnson Repr.

--War Costs & Their Financing: A Study of the Financing of the War & the After-War Problems of Debt & Taxation. LC 74-75232. (The United States in World War I Ser). xxiv, 510p. 1974. Repr. of 1921 ed. lib. bdg. 23.95x (ISBN 0-89198-095-4). Ozer.

Bogart, Ernest L. & Rawles, William A. Trial Bibliography & Outline of Lectures on the Financial History of the United States. LC 71-75563. Repr. of 1901 ed. lib. bdg. 18.75x (ISBN 0-8371-2157-4, BOTB). Greenwood.

Bogart, Gary L. see Cook, Dorothy E. & Monro, Isabel S.

Bogart, John L. Orthodox & Heretical Perfectionism in the Johannine Community As Evident in the First Epistle of John. LC 77-5447. (Society of Biblical Literature. Dissertation Ser.). 1977. pap. 9.95 (ISBN 0-89130-138-0, 060133). Scholars Pr GA.

Bogart, Kenneth P. Introductory Combinatorics. 400p. 1983. text ed. 29.95 (ISBN 0-273-01923-6). Pitman Pub MA.

Bogart, Leo. Polls & the Awareness of Public Opinion. 250p. 1985. pap. 14.95 (ISBN 0-88738-620-2). Transaction Bks.

--Premises for Propaganda. LC 75-18007. 1976. 12.95 (ISBN 0-02-904390-5). Free Pr.

--The Press & Public: Who Reads What, Where, & Why in American Newspapers. LC 80-18357. 304p. 1981. text ed. 24.95x (ISBN 0-89859-077-9). L Erlbaum Assocs.

--Strategy in Advertising. 2nd ed. LC 84-70447. 406p. 1984. 28.95 (ISBN 0-87251-094-8). Crain Bks.

Bogart, Lois S. Cheerful Thoughts & Promises for Troubled Persons. 1983. 4.95 (ISBN 0-8062-0849-X). Carlton.

Bogart, Louis. The Teachers. 199p. 1984. pap. 5.95 (ISBN 0-317-11799-8). Ramparts.

Bogart, Marcel J. Ammonia Absorption Refrigeration in Industrial Processes. LC 81-197. 474p. 1981. 75.00x (ISBN 0-87201-027-9). Gulf Pub.

Bogart, Margo, ed. see Cichy, Ronald F.

Bogart, Margo, ed. see Troy, David.

Bogart, Max, ed. The Jazz Age. LC 69-11435. (American Character Ser.). (Illus.). 261p. 1969. pap. text ed. 8.95 (ISBN 0-02-311700-1, Pub. by Scribner). Macmillan.

Bogart, Michele & Nevins, Deborah. Fauns & Fountains: American Garden Statuary, 1890-1930. LC 85-60160. (Illus.). 80p. 1985. pap. 16.50 (ISBN 0-943526-13-2). Parrish Art.

Bogart, Ralph. Scientific Farm Animal Production. 2nd ed. 1983. text ed. 26.95x (ISBN 0-8087-4093-8). Burgess.

Bogart, Ralph, ed. Genetics Lectures, Vol. 1. LC 73-87943. (Illus.). 194p. (Orig.). 1969. pap. 9.00x (ISBN 0-87071-431-7). Oreg St U Pr.

--Genetics Lectures, Vol. 2. LC 73-87943. 128p. 1971. pap. 9.00x (ISBN 0-87071-432-5). Oreg St U Pr.

--Genetics Lectures, Vol. 3. LC 73-87943. 192p. 1974. pap. 9.00x (ISBN 0-87071-433-3). Oreg St U Pr.

--Genetics Lectures, Vol. 4. LC 73-87943. (Illus.). 296p. (Orig.). 1975. pap. 12.00x (ISBN 0-87071-434-1). Oreg St U Pr.

--Genetics Lectures, Vol. 5. LC 73-87943. (Illus.). 136p. 1978. pap. 12.00x (ISBN 0-87071-435-X). Oreg St U Pr.

Bogart, T. F. Basic Concepts in Linear Systems: Theory & Experiments. 136p. 1983. pap. 14.95 (ISBN 0-471-87513-9). Wiley.

--Laplace Transforms: Theory & Experiments. 160p. 1983. pap. 14.95 (ISBN 0-471-87509-0). Wiley.

Bogart, Theodore F. Computer Simulation of Linear Circuits & Systems. (Illus.). 255p. 1983. pap. 14.95 (ISBN 0-471-87508-2). Wiley.

--Laplace Transforms & Control Systems Theory for Technology: Including Microprocessor Based Control System. LC 81-14708. (Electronic Technology Ser.). 541p. 1982. 31.95 (ISBN 0-471-09044-1); write for info solutions manual (ISBN 0-471-86325-4). Wiley.

--Linear Integrated Circuits: Applications & Experiments. 245p. 1983. pap. text ed. 14.95x (ISBN 0-471-87512-0). Wiley.

Bogart, Theodore F., Jr. Applied BASIC for Technology. 320p. 1984. pap. text ed. 21.95 (ISBN 0-574-21585-9, 13-4585); instr's guide avail. (ISBN 0-574-21586-7, 13-4586). SRA.

--BASIC Programs for Electrical Circuits Analysis. 1985. pap. 22.95 (ISBN 0-8359-0406-7). Reston.

--Experiments for Electrical Circuit Analysis with BASIC Programming. 288p. 1982. pap. text ed. 18.95 (ISBN 0-574-21565-4, 13-4565); solutions manual avail. (ISBN 0-574-21569-7, 13-4569). SRA.

Bogason, S. O., jt. auth. see Sigurdsson, A.

Bogatyrev, Petr. The Functions of Folk Costume in Moravian Slovakia. LC 78-149915. (Approaches to Semiotics Ser: No. 5). (Illus.). 107p. 1971. text ed. 17.60x (ISBN 90-2791-756-6). Mouton.

Bogdan, jt. auth. see Skalimierski, B.

Bogdan, M., tr. see Popescu, D. R.

Bogdan, R. J., ed. Local Induction. LC 75-34922. (Synthese Library: No. 93). 1975. lib. bdg. 58.00 (ISBN 90-277-0649-2, Pub. by Reidel Holland). Kluwer Academic.

Bogdan, R. J., ed. see International Congress for Logic, Methodology, & Philosophy of Science, 4th, Bucharest, Sept. 1971.

Bogdan, Radu, ed. Henry E. Kyburg, Jr. & Isaac Levi. 1982. 49.50 (ISBN 90-277-1308-1, Pub. by Reidel Netherlands); pap. text ed. 24.50 (ISBN 90-277-1309-X, Pub. by Reidel Holland). Kluwer Academic.

Bogdan, Radu J., ed. D. M. Armstrong. 1984. lib. bdg. 55.00 (ISBN 0-318-00888-2, Pub. by Reidel Holland). Kluwer Academic.

--Patrick Suppes. LC 78-21095. (Profiles 1 Ser.). 1979. lib. bdg. 36.00 (ISBN 9-0277-0950-5, Pub. by Reidel Holland); pap. 9.95 (ISBN 9-0277-0951-3, Pub. by Reidel Holland). Kluwer Academic.

Bogdan, Robert. Participant Observation in Organizational Settings. LC 72-85383. (Segregated Settings & the Problem of Change Ser.: No. 3). 106p. 1972. text ed. 10.00x (ISBN 0-8156-8080-5). Syracuse U Pr.

Bogdan, Robert & Taylor, Steven. Inside Out: The Social Meaning of Mental Retardation. 232p. 1982. 14.95 (ISBN 0-8020-2432-7). U of Toronto Pr.

Bogdan, Robert, jt. auth. see Taylor, Steven J.

Bogdan, Robert C. & Biklen, Sari K. Qualitative Research for Education: An Introduction to Theory & Methods. 350p. 1982. text ed. 31.43 (ISBN 0-205-07695-5, 247695-9). Allyn.

Bogdanaite, E. I., tr. see Zukauskas, A. & Ziugzda, J.

Bogdankevich, O. V. & Nikolayev, F. A. Methods in Bremsstrahlung Research. 1966. 47.00 (ISBN 0-12-110850-3). Acad Pr.

Bogdanoff, A., pseud. A Short Course of Economic Science. Fineberg, J., tr. LC 78-20483. 1980. Repr. of 1923 ed. text ed. 30.25 (ISBN 0-88355-860-2). Hyperion Conn.

Bogdanoff, John L. & Kozin, Frank. Probabilistic Models of Cumulative Damage. LC 84-11799. 341p. 1985. text ed. 53.50 (ISBN 0-471-88180-5, Pub. by Wiley Interscience). Wiley.

Bogdanor, Vernon. Coalition Government in Western Europe. 282p. 1983. text ed. 42.00 (ISBN 0-435-83104-6). Gower Pub Co.

--Devolution. 1979. 17.95x (ISBN 0-19-219128-4). Oxford U Pr.

--Liberal Party Politics. 1983. 37.50x (ISBN 0-19-827465-3). Oxford U Pr.

--Multi-Party Politics & the Constitution. LC 83-1901. 208p. 1983. 39.50 (ISBN 0-521-25524-4). Cambridge U Pr.

--The People & the Party System: The Referendum & Electoral Reform in British Politics. LC 81-3895. 280p. 1981. 47.50 (ISBN 0-521-24207-X); pap. 17.95 (ISBN 0-521-28525-9). Cambridge U Pr.

--Representatives of the People. 350p. 1985. text ed. 38.50 (ISBN 0-566-00878-5). Gower Pub Co.

Bogdanor, Vernon, ed. Parties & Democracy in Britain & America. (American Political Parties & Elections Ser.). 208p. 1984. 27.95 (ISBN 0-03-062599-8). Praeger.

--Science & Politics: The Herbert Spencer Lectures, 1982. (Illus.). 1984. 16.95x (ISBN 0-19-857605-6). Oxford U Pr.

Bogdanor, Vernon & Butler, David, eds. Democracy & Elections: Electoral Systems & Their Political Consequences. LC 82-25300. 280p. 1983. 42.50 (ISBN 0-521-25295-4). Cambridge U Pr.

Bogdanos, Theodore. Pearl, Image of the Ineffable: A Study in Medieval Poetic Symbolism. LC 82-42783. 184p. 1983. 22.50x (ISBN 0-271-00339-1). Pa St U Pr.

Bogdanov, A. A. Bogdanov: Essays in Tektology. Gorelik, George, tr. from Rus. (Systems Inquiry Ser.). 280p. (Orig.). 1980. pap. text ed. 15.95x (ISBN 0-914105-06-X). Intersystems Pubns.

--Krasnaja zvezda, Roman-Utopija: Inzener Menni,Fantast,Roman. (Bibliotheca Russia Ser.: No. Bd.2). 358p. (Orig.). 1979. pap. text ed. 16.00x (ISBN 3-87118-410-1, Pub. by Helmut Buske Verlag Hamburg). Benjamins North Am.

Bogdanov, Alexander. Red Star: The First Bolshevik Utopia. Graham, Loren R. & Stites, Richard, eds. Rougle, Charles, tr. from Rus. LC 83-48637. (Soviet History, Politics, Society & Thought Ser.). (Illus.). 272p. (Orig.). 1984. 22.50x (ISBN 0-253-17350-7); pap. 12.50x (ISBN 0-253-20317-1). Ind U Pr.

Bogdanov, O. V., jt. auth. see Kaliadin, A. N.

Bogdanovich, Peter. John Ford. expanded rev. ed. (Cal Ser.: No. 369). 1978. pap. 4.95 (ISBN 0-520-03498-8). U of Cal Pr.

--The Killing of the Unicorn: Dorothy Stratten 1960-1980. LC 84-5326. (Illus.). 208p. 1984. 12.95 (ISBN 0-688-01611-1). Morrow.

--Pieces of Time: Peter Bogdanovich on the Movies. LC 73-82189. 1973. 7.95 (ISBN 0-87795-069-5). Arbor Hse.

Bogdanowicz, Maureen S. Write, Wrote, Written. (Orig.). 1980. pap. text ed. 7.25 (ISBN 0-8403-3153-3, 40315303). Kendall-Hunt.

Bogden, A. V. Tropical Pasture & Fodder Plants: Grasses & Legumes. LC 76-14977. (Tropical Agriculture Ser.). pap. 122.30 (ISBN 0-317-29850-X, 2019606). Bks Demand UMI.

Bogdonoff, Morton D. Forever Fit: The Exercise Program for Staying Young. (Illus.). 224p. 1983. 16.45i (ISBN 0-316-10085-4). Little.

Bogel, Frederic V. Literature & Insubstantiality in Later Eigteenth Century England. LC 83-43060. 248p. 1984. 22.50x (ISBN 0-691-06597-7). Princeton U Pr.

Bogel, Fredric V. Acts of Knowledge: Pope's Later Poems. LC 78-75194. 248p. 1981. 21.50 (ISBN 0-8387-2380-2). Bucknell U Pr.

Bogelsack, G., et al, eds. Terminology for the Theory of Machines & Mechanisms. 30p. 1983. pap. 10.00 (ISBN 0-08-031140-7). Pergamon.

Bogen, Arthur M. Mind Games. (Burchardt & Decker Mystery Ser.). 128p. (Orig.). 1984. pap. 2.25 (ISBN 0-380-86512-2, 86512, Flare). Avon.

Bogen, Boris D. Jewish Philanthropy: An Exposition of Principles & Methods of Jewish Social Service in the United States. LC 69-16225. (Criminology, Law Enforcement, & Social Problems Ser.: No. 86). (With a new intro. by Harry Lurie). 1969. Repr. of 1917 ed. 17.00x (ISBN 0-87585-086-3). Patterson Smith.

Bogen, David S. Bulwark of Liberty: The Courts & the First Amendment. LC 81-18624. (Multidisciplinary Studies in Law & Jurisprudence). 216p. 1985. 23.50x (ISBN 0-8046-9329-3, Pub. by Kennikat). Assoc Faculty Pr.

Bogen, H. J. see Ruhland, W., et al.

Bogen, J. E., frwd. by see Wigan, A. L.

Bogen, James & McGuire, James E. How Things Are. 1984. lib. bdg. 46.00 (ISBN 90-277-1583-1, Pub. by Reidel Holland). Kluwer Academic.

Bogen, Jules I. & Nadler, Marcus. The Banking Crisis: The End of an Epoch. Bruchey, Stuart, ed. LC 80-1179. (The Rise of Commercial Banking Ser.). 1981. Repr. of 1933 ed. lib. bdg. 18.00x (ISBN 0-405-13670-6). Ayer Co Pubs.

Bogen, Jules I., jt. auth. see Willis, Henry P.

Bogen, Laurel A. Do Iguanas Dance, under the Moonlight. 100p. (Orig.). 1984. pap. 4.95 (ISBN 0-89807-033-3). Illuminati.

--The Great Orange Leonard Scandal. (Tattletales Ser.). 10p. (Orig.). 1984. pap. 1.50 (ISBN 0-89807-121-6). Illuminati.

Bogen, M. Arthur. Barely Undercover. (Burchardt & Decker Mystery Ser.). 112p. (Orig.). 1983. pap. 2.25 (ISBN 0-380-85217-9, 85217-9, Flare). Avon.

--Double Dealing. 160p. 1983. pap. 2.25 (ISBN 0-380-83394-8, 83394-8, Flare). Avon.

Bogen, Nancy. Klytaimnestra, Who Stayed at Home. LC 80-51052. 240p. (Orig.). 1980. pap. 6.95x (ISBN 0-936726-00-8). Twickenham Pr.

Bogen, Nancy, ed. see Blake, William.

Bogenschneider, Duane, ed. A Directory to Collective Bargaining Agreements: Private Sector, 1981. 275p. 1982. reference bk. 100.00 (ISBN 0-667-00643-5). Microfilming Corp.

Bogenschuetz, A. Fachwoerterbuch Fuer Batterien und Energie-Direktumwandlung. 200p. (Ger. & Eng., Dictionary of Batteries and Energy Transformation). 1968. 29.95 (ISBN 3-87097-002-2, M-7395, Pub. by Brandstetter). French & Eur.

Bogenschutz, ed. Technical Dictionary for Batteries & Direct Energy Conservation. 200p. 1968. 11.00 (ISBN 0-9913000-3-3, Pub. by O Brandstetter WG). Heyden.

Bogenschutz, A. F. Surface Technology & Electroplating in the Electronics Industry. 392p. 1981. 70.00x (ISBN 0-901994-50-2, Pub. by Portcullio Pr). State Mutual Bk.

Boger, Donald C. Essentials of Emergency Room Radiology. (Illus.). 200p. pap. price not set (ISBN 0-7216-1799-9). Saunders.

Boger, Gordon, jt. auth. see Mull, J. Alexander.

Boger, H. Batterson, jt. auth. see Boger, Louise.

Boger, Louise & Boger, H. Batterson. Dictionary of Antiques & the Decorative Arts. rev. ed. (Illus.). 1979. 35.00 (ISBN 0-684-10030-4, ScribT). Scribner.

Boger, Louise A. The Complete Guide to Furniture Styles. (Illus.). 512p. 1982. 35.00 (ISBN 0-684-10029-0, ScribT); pap. 22.50 (ISBN 0-684-17641-6). Scribner.

Boger, Robert P., et al, eds. Child Nurturance: Child Nurturing in the 1980s, Vol. 4. 204p. 1984. 29.50x (ISBN 0-306-41505-4, Plenum Pr). Plenum Pub.

Bogert. Trusts & Trustees: Second Edition. write for info. West Pub.

Bogert, George G. & Bogert, George T. Trusts. 5th ed. (Hornbook Ser.). 726p. 1973. 19.95 (ISBN 0-317-00051-9). West Pub.

Bogert, George T. The Law of Trusts. 5th ed. (Hornbook Ser.). 752p. 1985. Repr. of 1973 ed. text ed. 20.95 (ISBN 0-314-28334-X). West Pub.

Bogert, George T., jt. auth. see Bogert, George G.

Bogg, Edmund. From Eden Vale to the Plains of York. 1976. 20.00 (ISBN 0-8495-0360-4). Arden Lib.

Boggan, Tim. Winning Table Tennis. 4.95 (ISBN 0-8092-8151-1). Contemp Bks.

Boggess, Arthur C. Settlement of Illinois, 1778-1830. facs. ed. LC 71-128873. (Select Bibliographies Reprint Ser). 1908. 18.00 (ISBN 0-8369-5493-9). Ayer Co Pubs.

Boggess, Bill & Boggess, Louise. American Brilliant Cut Glass. 1977. 17.95 (ISBN 0-517-52525-9). Crown.

--Identifying American Brilliant Cut Glass. (Illus.). 1984. 19.95 (ISBN 0-517-55009-1); pap. 12.95 (ISBN 0-517-55010-5). Crown.

Boggess, Louis. How to Write Short Stories that Sell. LC 79-26010. 212p. 1984. pap. 7.95 (ISBN 0-89879-139-1). Writers Digest.

Boggess, Louise, jt. auth. see Boggess, Bill.

Boggess, W. R. & Wixson, B. G., eds. Lead in the Environment. (Illus.). 272p. 1979. text ed. 43.00 (ISBN 0-7194-0024-4, Pub. by Castle Hse England). J K Burgess.

Boggio, G. & Gallimore, R., eds. Evaluation of Research & Development. 1982. lib. bdg. 24.50 (ISBN 90-277-1425-8, Pub. by Reidel Holland). Kluwer Academic.

Boggio, Giorgio & Spachis-Papazois, Eleni, eds. Evaluation of Research & Development, Methodologies for R & D Evaluation in the European Community Member States, the United States of America & Japan. 1984. lib. bdg. 27.00 (ISBN 90-277-1759-1, Pub. by Reidel Holland). Kluwer Academic.

Boggs & Dixson. English Step by Step with Pictures. new ed. (gr. 4-12). 1980. pap. text ed. 5.25 (ISBN 0-88345-416-5, 18186). Regents Pub.

Boggs, Carl. Gramsci's Marxism. 145p. (Orig.). 1976. pap. 4.95 (ISBN 0-904383-03-2). Pluto Pr.

--The Impasse of European Communism. LC 81-22005. 181p. 1981. lib. bdg. 27.00x (ISBN 0-89158-784-5); pap. 12.50x (ISBN 0-86531-285-0). Westview.

--The Two Revolutions: Antonio Gramsci & the Dilemmas of Marxism. LC 84-50943. 250p. (Orig.). 1984. 20.00 (ISBN 0-89608-226-1); pap. 9.50 (ISBN 0-89608-225-3). South End Pr.

Boggs, Carl & Plotke, David, eds. The Politics of Eurocommunism: Socialism in Transition. LC 79-66993. 479p. 1980. 15.00 (ISBN 0-89608-052-8); pap. 6.50 (ISBN 0-89608-051-X). South End Pr.

Boggs, Dane R. & Winkelstein, Alan. White Cell Manual. 4th ed. LC 82-23474. (Illus.). 109p. 1983. pap. text ed. 8.95 (ISBN 0-8036-0961-2). Davis Co.

Boggs, Donald L. & Merkel, Robert A. Live Animal Carcass Evaluation & Selection Manual. 208p. (Orig.). 1984. pap. text ed. 12.95 (ISBN 0-8403-3331-5, 40333101). Kendall-Hunt.

Boggs, Edward. Stop Smoking Activity Book. Arena, John, ed. LC 84-28465. (Illus.). 96p. (Orig.). 1985. pap. 7.95 (ISBN 0-87879-464-6). Interbook.

Boggs, George T., jt. ed. see Paxman, John M.

Boggs, Grace L., jt. auth. see Boggs, James.

Boggs, H. Glenn, II, jt. auth. see Lilly, Claude C., III.

Boggs, James. American Revolution: Pages from a Negro Worker's Notebook. LC 63-20103. (Orig.). 1963. pap. 2.95 (ISBN 0-85345-015-3). Monthly Rev.

--Racism & the Class Struggle: Further Pages from a Black Worker's Notebook. LC 74-105314. 164p. 1970. pap. 5.95 (ISBN 0-85345-164-8). Monthly Rev.

Boggs, James & Boggs, Grace L. Revolution & Evolution in the Twentieth Century. LC 73-90076. 288p. 1975. pap. 9.00 (ISBN 0-85345-353-5). Monthly Rev.

Boggs, James, et al. Conversations in Maine. LC 78-55014. 299p. 1978. 15.00 (ISBN 0-89608-009-9); pap. 8.50 (ISBN 0-89608-008-0). South End Pr.

Boggs, Joan M., jt. ed. see Aloia, Roland C.

Boggs, Joseph. The Art of Watching Films. 2nd ed. 1985. pap. 16.95 (ISBN 0-87484-712-5). Mayfield Pub.

Boggs, Juanita & Starr, Carole. Take Time to Focus. (Illus.). 60p. 1983. pap. text ed. 5.50 (ISBN 0-910817-01-4). Collaborative Learn.

Boggs, Juanita, jt. auth. see Strand, Julie.

Boggs, Marion A., ed. The Alexander Letters, 1787-1900. LC 79-5187. (Brown Thrasher Bks.). 394p. 1980. 25.00x (ISBN 0-8203-0492-1); pap. 7.95 (ISBN 0-8203-0493-X). U of Ga Pr.

Boggs, Pamela. Retailing Careers-Pleasure in Store. 126p. 1982. 30.00x (ISBN 0-85225-752-X, Pub. by Careers Con England). State Mutual Bk.

Boggs, Paul, et al, eds. Numerical Optimization Nineteen Eighty-Four. LC 85-50611. xi, 287p. 1985. text ed. 30.50 (ISBN 0-89871-054-5). Soc Indus-Appl Math.

Boggs, R. F. Radiological Safety Aspects of the Operation of Neutron Generators. (Safety Ser.: No. 42). (Illus.). 42p. 1976. pap. 9.25 (ISBN 92-0-123076-1, ISP427, IAEA). Unipub.

Boggs, R. S. & Dixon, J. I. Everyday Spanish Idioms. (Span.). (gr. 9-12). 1978. pap. text ed. 5.95 (ISBN 0-88345-326-6, 18426). Regents Pub.

Boggs, R. S., jt. auth. see Jagendorf, Moritz A.

Boggs, Ralph S. Basic Spanish Pronounciation. (Orig., Span.). (gr. 9-11). 1969. pap. 3.75 (ISBN 0-88345-012-7, 17442); cassettes 60.00 (ISBN 0-685-19785-9). Regents Pub.

--Folklore. 1977. Repr. of 1919 ed. lib. bdg. 10.00 (ISBN 0-8495-0328-0). Arden Lib.

Boggs, Robert F. Shark Man: Master Hunter of the Deep. 1977. 7.95 (ISBN 0-89328-007-0). Lorenz Pr.

Boggs, Robert G. Elementary Structural Analysis. 1984. text ed. 38.95 (ISBN 0-03-063933-6). HR&W.

Boggs, Roy A. Advanced BASIC. 1983. text ed. 24.95 (ISBN 0-8359-0163-7); pap. 17.95 (ISBN 0-8359-0161-0). Reston.

--Advanced BASIC for the IBM PC. 1985. pap. 16.95 (ISBN 0-8359-9142-3). Reston.

--Applied BASIC for Microcomputers. (Illus.). 225p. 1984. 16.95 (ISBN 0-8359-0042-8). Reston.

Boggs, S. A., et al, eds. see Symposium on Underground Cable Thermal Backfill, Toronto, Ont., Canada, Sept. 1981.

Boggs, S. Whittemore. International Boundaries: A Study of Boundary Functions & Problems. LC 40-8082. Repr. of 1940 ed. 14.50 (ISBN 0-404-00919-0). AMS Pr.

Boggs, Stephen T. Speaking, Relating & Learning. 224p. 1985. text ed. 26.50 (ISBN 0-89391-330-8). Ablex Pub.

Boggs, Sue H. All Mine to Give. pap. 2.75 (ISBN 0-89137-433-7). Quality Pubns.

--Is a Job Really Worth It? 1979. pap. 3.50 (ISBN 0-89137-522-8). Quality Pubns.

--The Secret of Hind's Feet. 2.75 (ISBN 0-89137-537-6). Quality Pubns.

Boggs, Thomas H. & Boyce, Katherine R. Corporate Political Activity. LC 85-121299. (Business Law Monographs). (Illus.). Date not set. price not set. Bender.

Boggs, Thomas L. & Zinn, Ben T., eds. Experimental Diagnostics in Combustion of Solids. LC 78-26677. (Illus.). 339p. 1978. 45.00 (ISBN 0-915928-28-0, PAAS63); members 25.00 (ISBN 0-317-32141-2). AIAA.

Boggs, Vernon, et al. The Apple Sliced: Sociological Studies of New York City. (Illus.). 352p. 1983. 34.95x (ISBN 0-03-063213-7). Praeger.

Boggs, Vernon, et al, eds. The Apple Sliced: Studies of New York City. 368p. 1984. text ed. 29.95; pap. 14.95 (ISBN 0-89789-016-7). Bergin & Garvey.

Boggs, Winthrop S. Foundations of Philately. (Illus.). 196p. 1955. 6.00 (ISBN 0-911989-01-3). Philatelic Found.

--The Postage Stamps & Postal History of Canada. LC 74-79893. (Illus.). 896p. 1974. Repr. of 1945 ed. 60.00x (ISBN 0-88000-042-2). Quarterman.

Bog-Hansen, T. C. & Spengler, G. A. Lectins: Biology, Biochemistry, Clinical Biochemistry, Vol.3. (Proceedings of the Fifth Lectin Meeting Bern, May 31-June 5,1982 Ser.). (Illus.). 708p. 1983. 98.00 (ISBN 3-11-009504-1). De Gruyter.

Bog-Hansen, T. C., ed. Lectins: Biology, Biochemistry, Chemical Biochemistry, Vol. 2. (Illus.). 801p. 1982. 99.20x (ISBN 3-11-008680-8). De Gruyter.

--Lectins: Biology, Biochemistry, Clinical Biochemistry, Vol. 1. (Illus.). 1981. 48.00x (ISBN 3-11-008483-X). De Gruyter.

Bogholm, N. Milton & Paradise Lost. LC 74-7116. (Studies in Milton, No. 22). 1974. lib. bdg. 39.95x (ISBN 0-8383-1968-8). Haskell.

Boghurst, William. Loimographia: An Account of the Great Plague of London in 1665. Payne, J. F., ed. LC 75-23686. Repr. of 1894 ed. 14.50 (ISBN 0-404-13239-1). AMS Pr.

Bogin, George. In a Surf of Strangers. LC 80-23965. (University of Central Florida Contemporary Poetry Ser.). vii, 59p. 1981. 8.95 (ISBN 0-8130-0682-1). U Presses Fla.

Bogin, George, tr. see Supervielle, Jules.

Bogin, Magda, tr. see Allende, Isabel.

Bogin, Meg. The Women Troubadours. (Illus.). 192p. 1980. pap. 5.95 (ISBN 0-393-00965-3). Norton.

Bogin, Ruth. Abraham Clark & the Quest for Equality in the Revolutionary Era, 1774 - 1794. LC 81-65872. 219p. 1982. 26.50 (ISBN 0-8386-3100-2). Fairleigh Dickinson.

Bogin, Ruth, jt. ed. see Loewenberg, Bert J.

Boglar-Kovacs. Indian Art from Mexico to Peru. (Illus.). 277p. 40.00 (ISBN 963-13-1325-5). Newbury Bks.

Bogle, Darlene. Long Road to Love. 192p. (Orig.). 1985. pap. 6.95 (ISBN 0-310-60981-X, Pub. by Chosen Bks). Zondervan.

Bogle, Donald. Brown Sugar: Eighty Years of America's Black Female Superstars. (Illus.). 256p. 1980. 6.98 (ISBN 0-517-53637-4, Harmony). Crown.

Bogle, Irma, jt. auth. see Adams, Carolyn E.

Bogle, Margaret L., jt. auth. see Alford, Betty B.

Bogle, Michael. Textile Dyes, Finishes & Auxiliaries. LC 76-25746. (Reference Library of Science & Technology Ser.: Vol. 8). (Illus.). 1977. lib. bdg. 24.00 (ISBN 0-8240-9902-8). Garland Pub.

Bognad, Morris. The Managers' Style Book: How Communication Skills Can Improve Your Performance. 1979. 11.95 (ISBN 0-13-549204-1, Spec); pap. 4.95 (ISBN 0-13-549196-7). P-H.

Bognar. The Early Copper Age Tiszapolgar Culture in Carpathian Basin. 1972. 30.00 (ISBN 0-9960002-7-5, Pub. by Kaido Hungary). Heyden.

--Recent Developments in the Chemistry of Natural Carbon Compounds, Vol. 6. 1975. 14.00 (ISBN 0-9960003-2-1, Pub. by Akademiai Kaido Hungary). Heyden.

Bognar & Szantay. Recent Developments in the Chemistry of Natural Carbon Compounds, Vol. 10. 1984. 21.00 (ISBN 0-9910001-3-7, Pub. by Akademiai Kaido Hungary). Heyden.

Bognar, et al. Recent Developments in the Chemistry of Natural Carbon Compounds, Vol. 9. 420p. 1979. 41.00 (ISBN 0-9960014-2-5, Pub. by Akademiai Kaido Hungary). Heyden.

Bognar, Botond. Contemporary Japanese Architecture: Its Development & Challenge. (Illus.). 304p. 1985. 40.00 (ISBN 0-442-21174-0). Van Nos Reinhold.

Bognar, Desi K. Hungarians in America. LC 72-97113. (East-European Biographies & Studies: No. 3). 240p. 1972. 8.50x (ISBN 0-912460-01-6). Media Forum.

Bognar, J. & Szoekelalvi-Nagy, J. Indefinite Inner Product Spaces. LC 73-10669. (Ergebnisse der Mathematik und Ihrer Grenzgebiete: Vol. 78). 236p. 1974. 31.00 (ISBN 0-387-06202-5). Springer-Verlag.

Bogner, Desi K., ed. Ad Honorem: Reprint from Hungarians in America, Vol. 4 & 5. 48p. Set. pap. 4.50 (ISBN 0-317-17747-8). Media Forum.

Bogner, Norman. Arena. 1980. pap. 3.25 (ISBN 0-440-10369-X). Dell.

--California Dreamers. 1981. 14.95 (ISBN 0-671-42877-2, Wyndham Bks). S&S.

--California Dreamers. 400p. 1982. pap. 3.50 (ISBN 0-345-30266-4). Ballantine.

Bogner, R. E. & Constantinides, A. G., eds. Introduction to Digital Filtering. LC 74-4924. 198p. 1975. 45.95 (ISBN 0-471-08590-1, Pub. by Wiley-Interscience). Wiley.

Bogoch, Samuel, ed. The Future of the Brain Sciences: Proceedings of a Conference Held at the New York Academy of Medicine, May 2-4, 1968. LC 75-79571. pap. 160.00 (ISBN 0-317-07812-7, 2020704). Bks Demand UMI.

Bogojavlensky, Marianna. Russian Review Grammar. 450p. (Orig.). 1982. pap. text ed. 15.95 (ISBN 0-89357-096-6). Slavica.

Bogojavlensky, Marrianne. Reflections on Nikolai Gogol. 69p. 1968. pap. 3.00 (ISBN 0-317-30452-6). Holy Trinity.

Bogolepov, Alexander. Church Reforms in Russia, 1905-1918. 59p. 1966. pap. 1.95 (ISBN 0-913836-01-X). St Vladimirs.

--Orthodox Hymns of Christmas, Easter, & Holy Week. LC 65-16177. 78p. 1965. pap. 1.95 (ISBN 0-913836-02-8). St Vladimirs.

Bogolepov, N. N. Ultrastructure of the Brain in Hypoxia. Burov, Michael, tr. 208p. 1983. 8.95 (ISBN 0-8285-2573-0, Pub. by Mir Pubs USSR). Imported Pubns.

Bogoliubov, N. M. & Mitropolsky, Y. A. Asymptotic Methods in the Theory of Non-Linear Oscillations. 548p. 1961. 131.95 (ISBN 0-677-20050-1). Gordon.

Bogoliubov, N. N. Lectures on Quantum Statistics, 2 vols. 252p. 1970. Vol. 1. 69.50 (ISBN 0-677-20030-7); Vol. 2. 48.50 (ISBN 0-677-20570-8). Gordon.

Bogoliubov, N. N. & Shirkov, D. V. Introduction to the Theory of Quantized Fields. 3rd ed. LC 79-17919. 616p. 1980. 83.50 (ISBN 0-471-04223-4, Pub. by Wiley-Interscience). Wiley.

--Quantum Fields. 403p. 1982. text ed. 48.95 (ISBN 0-8053-0983-7). Benjamin-Cummings.

Bogoliubov, N. N., ed. Theory of Superconductivity. (International Science Review Ser.). (Illus.). 370p. 1968. 56.75 (ISBN 0-677-00080-4). Gordon.

Bogolubov, N. N. & Bogolubov, N. N., Jr. Introduction to Quantum Statistical Mechanics. viii, 300p. 1982. 33.00x (ISBN 9971-950-31-6, Pub. by World Sci Singapore); pap. 19.00x (ISBN 9971-950-04-9, Pub. by World Sci Singapore). Taylor & Francis.

Bogolubov, Nikolai N., et al. Introduction to Axiomatic Quantum Field Theory. Fulling, Stephen & Popova, Ludmila G., trs. from Rus. LC 72-5554. (Mathematical Physics Monographs: No. 18). 700p. 1975. text ed. 71.95 (ISBN 0-8053-0982-9). Benjamin-Cummings.

Bogolyubov, N. N. Analytic Number Theory, Mathematical Analysis & Their Applications. LC 84-265. (Trudy Steklov Ser.: No.158). 248p. 1983. pap. 74.00 (ISBN 0-8218-3077-5). Am Math.

Bogolyubov, N. N. & Mardzhanishvili, K. K. Theory of Numbers, Mathematical Analysis & Their Applications. LC 83-22405. (Proceedings of the Steklov Institute of Mathematics: Vol. 157). 248p. 1983. pap. 71.00 (ISBN 0-8218-3076-7, STEKL 157). Am Math.

Bogolyubov, N. N., ed. Particles & Nuclei. Incl. Vol. 1, Pt. 1. 189p (ISBN 0-306-17191-0); Vol. 1, Pt. 2. 191p (ISBN 0-306-17192-9); Vol. 2, Pt. 1. 171p (ISBN 0-306-17193-7); Vol. 2, Pt. 2. 138p (ISBN 0-306-17194-5); Vol. 2, Pt. 3. 178p (ISBN 0-306-17195-3); Vol. 2, Pt. 4. 178p (ISBN 0-306-17196-1). LC 72-83510. 1972. 45.00x ea. (Consultants). Plenum Pub.

Bogolyubov, N. N., et al, eds. Analytic Number Theory, Mathematical Analysis & Their Applications: Proceedings of the Steklov Institute of Math, No. 143. LC 80-14363. (Proceedings of the Steklov Institute of Mathematics). 220p. 1977. 71.00 (ISBN 0-8218-3044-9). Am Math.

--Theory of Numbers, Mathematical Analysis & Their Applications. LC 79-20552. (Proceedings of the Steklov Institute: No. 142). 1979. 84.00 (ISBN 0-8218-3042-2, STEKLO 142). Am Math.

Bogolyubov, Nikolai N., ed. Structure of Complex Nuclei. LC 69-12510. pap. 56.30 (ISBN 0-317-09191-3, 2020679). Bks Demand UMI.

Bogolyubov, Sergei & Voinov, Alexander. Engineering Drawing. (Illus.). 340p. text ed. cancelled (ISBN 0-8290-1489-6). Irvington.

Bogomolny, R. L., et al. A Handbook on the 1970 Federal Drug Act: Shifting the Perspective. (Illus.). 192p. 1975. 21.00x (ISBN 0-398-03190-8). C C Thomas.

Bogomolny, Robert L., ed. Human Experimentation. LC 76-10649. 148p. (Orig.). 1976. pap. 9.95 (ISBN 0-87074-155-1). SMU Press.

Bogomolov, A., et al. Cuba: Experiencia del Desarrollo Social. 299p. (Span.). 1983. 5.95 (ISBN 0-317-07238-2, Pub. by Progress Pubs USSR). Imported Pubns.

Bogomolov, Vladimir. Aching in My Heart. Isaacs, Bernard, et al, trs. from Rus. 635p. 1982. 12.95 (ISBN 0-8285-2524-2, Pub. by Progress Pubs USSR). Imported Pubns.

Bogomolov, Yu. G. & Zhabin, V. F., eds. Effect of Reclamation on Hydrogeological Conditions. Erastov, Konstantin, tr. from Rus. 300p. 1983. 101.95 (ISBN 0-677-06070-X). Gordon.

Bogorad, L. & Weil, J. H., eds. Nucleic Acids & Protein Synthesis in Plants. LC 77-23267. (NATO ASI Series A, Life Sciences: Vol. 12). 429p. 1977. 55.00x (ISBN 0-306-35612-0, Plenum Pr). Plenum Pub.

Bogoraz, Vladimir G. The Chukchee. LC 73-3527. (Jessup North Pacific Expedition. Publications: No. 7). Repr. of 1909 ed. 75.00 (ISBN 0-404-58107-2). AMS Pr.

--Chukchee. (Landmarks in Anthropology). 1969. Repr. of 1904 ed. 55.00 (ISBN 0-384-04955-9). Johnson Repr.

--Chukchee Mythology. LC 73-3528. (Jessup North Pacific Expedition. Publications: Vol. 8, Pt. 1). Repr. of 1910 ed. 27.50 (ISBN 0-404-58108-0). AMS Pr.

--The Eskimo of Siberia. LC 73-3530. (Jessup North Pacific Expedition. Publications: Vol. 8, Pt. 3). Repr. of 1913 ed. 15.00 (ISBN 0-404-58126-9). AMS Pr.

--Koryak Texts. LC 73-3540. (American Ethnological Society. Publications: No. 5). Repr. of 1917 ed. 25.00 (ISBN 0-404-58155-2). AMS Pr.

--Tales of Yukaghir, Lamut & Russianized Natives of Eastern Siberia. LC 78-67689. (The Folktale). Repr. of 1918 ed. 17.50 (ISBN 0-404-16057-3). AMS Pr.

Bogorodskii, N. The Doctrine of St. John Damascene on the Procession of the Holy Spirit. LC 80-2351. Repr. of 1879 ed. 28.50 (ISBN 0-404-18903-2). AMS Pr.

Bogoslovski, V., jt. auth. see Solodovnikov, V.

Bogoslovsky, B. B. The Technique of Controversy: Principles of Dynamic Logic. 1977. lib. bdg. 59.95 (ISBN 0-8490-1180-9). Gordon Pr.

Bogoslovsky, V. V., jt. auth. see Solodovnikov, V. J.

Bogot, Howard. Yoni. 1982. pap. 4.00 (ISBN 0-686-82564-0). UAHC.

Bogot, Howard, jt. auth. see Kipper, Lenore.

Bogovski, P., et al, eds. see Working Conference, International Agency for Research on Cancer. Lyon, France. October 2-6, 1972.

Bogovski, P., et al, eds. see Working Conference. International Agency for Research on Cancer. Lyon, France Oct. 17-20, 1973.

Bogovski, P., et al, eds. see Working Conference.Deutsches Krebsforschungszentrum, Heidelberg, Germany.Oct. 13-15, 1971.

Bogoyavlensky, O. I. Methods in the Qualitative Theory of Dynamical Systems in Astrophysics & Gas Dynamics. Gokhman, D., tr. from Russ. (Soviet Mathematics Ser.). (Illus.). 320p. 1985. 49.00 (ISBN 0-387-13614-2). Springer-Verlag.

Bograd, Larry. Bad Apple. LC 82-15727. 152p. (gr. 7 up). 1982. 10.95 (ISBN 0-374-30472-6). FS&G.

--The Better Angel. LC 85-42613. 256p. (YA) (gr. 7 up). 1985. 12.45i (ISBN 0-397-32126-0); PLB 12.89g (ISBN 0-397-32127-9). Lipp Jr Bks.

--The Kolokol Papers. LC 81-15313. 176p. (gr. 7 up). 1981. 10.95 (ISBN 0-374-34277-6). FS&G.

--The Kolokol Papers. 160p. (YA) (gr. 7 up). 1983. pap. 2.25 (ISBN 0-440-94552-6, LFL). Dell.

--Los Alamos Light. LC 83-11638. 168p. (gr. 7 up). 1983. 11.95 (ISBN 0-374-34656-9). FS&G.

--Lost in the Store. LC 81-4038. (Illus.). 32p. (gr. k-3). 1981. 9.95 (ISBN 0-02-710980-1). Macmillan.

Bogue, Allan G. Clio & the Bitch Goddess: Quantification in American Political History. (New Approaches to Social Science History Ser.: Vol. 3). 280p. 1983. 28.00 (ISBN 0-8039-2089-X); pap. 14.00 (ISBN 0-8039-2090-3). Sage.

--The Earnest Men: Republicans of the Civil War Senate. LC 81-67176. (Illus.). 368p. 1981. 34.95x (ISBN 0-8014-1357-5). Cornell U Pr.

--Money at Interest: The Farm Mortgage on the Middle Border. LC 55-1350. x, 293p. 1969. pap. 4.50x (ISBN 0-8032-5018-5, BB 396, Bison). U of Nebr Pr.

Bogue, Allan G. & Taylor, Robert, eds. The University of Wisconsin: One Hundred & Twenty-Five Years. LC 74-27306. (Illus.). 302p. 1975. 15.00x (ISBN 0-299-06840-4). U of Wis Pr.

Bogue, Donald J. Population of the United States. LC 59-12184. 1959. 25.00 (ISBN 0-02-904480-4). Free Pr.

--The Population of the United States: Historical Trends & Future Projections. Rev. ed. LC 84-18688. 704p. 1985. 70.00x (ISBN 0-02-904700-5). Free Pr.

Bogue, Donald J. & Biehler, Susan. Techniques for Making Functional Population Projections. LC 79-53201. (Orig.). 1979. pap. text ed. 4.00 (ISBN 0-89836-013-7). Comm & Family.

Bogue, Donald J. & Bogue, Elizabeth J. Comparative Birth Interval Analysis. LC 79-56503. 150p. 1980. pap. 3.00 (ISBN 0-89836-028-5). Comm & Family.

Bogue, Donald J., jt. auth. see Amy Ong Tsui.

Bogue, Donald J. & White, Michael J., eds. Essays in Human Ecology, Vol. 2. 173p. (Orig.). 1984. pap. text ed. 6.00 (ISBN 0-89836-017-X). Comm & Family.

Bogue, Donald J., jt. ed. see Burgess, Ernest W.

Bogue, Donald J., ed. see Community & Family Study Center.

Bogue, Donald J., et al. Communicating to Combat VD: The Los Angeles Experiment, 2 vols. Incl. Vol. I. LC 78-74099. 1979. pap. text ed. 5.00 (ISBN 0-89836-008-0); Vol. II. LC 79-51309. 1979. pap. text ed. 4.00 (ISBN 0-89836-009-9). Set. pap. text ed. 7.50 (ISBN 0-89836-007-2). Comm & Family.

--Techniques of Estimating Net Migration. 112p. 1981. pap. 8.00 (ISBN 0-89836-018-8). Comm & Family.

Bogue, Elizabeth J., jt. auth. see Bogue, Donald J.

Bogue, Lucile. Dancers on Horseback: The Perry-Mansfield Story. (Illus.). 256p. (Orig.). 1984. pap. 9.95 (ISBN 0-89407-058-4). Strawberry Hill.

--Salt Lake. 352p. (Orig.). 1982. pap. 2.95 (ISBN 0-523-41319-X). Pinnacle Bks.

Bogue, Lucille M. Typhoon, Typhoon: An Illustrated Haiku Sequence. LC 75-94026. (Illus.). 1969. pap. 1.25 (ISBN 0-8048-0605-5). C E Tuttle.

Bogue, Margaret B. Around the Shores of Lake Michigan: A Guide to Historic Sites. LC 84-40490. (Illus.). 1985. 35.00 (ISBN 0-299-10000-6); pap. text ed. 19.95 (ISBN 0-299-10004-9). U of WIS PR.

--Patterns from the Sod. Bruchey, Stuart, ed. LC 78-56691. (Management of Public Lands Law in the U. S. Ser.). (Illus.). 1979. Repr. of 1959 ed. lib. bdg. 24.50x (ISBN 0-405-11318-8). Ayer Co Pubs.

--Patterns from the Sod: Land Use & Tenure in the Grand Prairie, 1850-1900. (Illinois Historical Collections Ser.: Vol. 34). 1959. 2.50 (ISBN 0-912154-14-4). Ill St Hist Lib.

Bogue, Margaret B. & Palmer, Virginia A. Around the Shores of Lake Superior: A Guide to Historic Sites. LC 79-65184. (Illus.). 186p. 1979. pap. 7.95 (ISBN 0-299-97013-2). U of Wis Pr.

Bogue, Margaret B., ed. The New American State Papers: Public Lands Subject Set, 8 vols. LC 72-95582. 1972. Set. lib. bdg. 500.00 (ISBN 0-8420-1643-0). Scholarly Res Inc.

Bogue, Robert H. The Dawn of Christianity. 1985. 15.00 (ISBN 0-533-06545-3). Vantage.

--There Is a Tide: The Downbeat of Pristine Christianity. 1983. 11.95 (ISBN 0-533-05592-X). Vantage.

Bogue, Ted. Cutting Prices: A Guide to Washington Area Surgeon's Fees. 69p. 1979. 3.50 (ISBN 0-317-35662-3). Pub Citizen Inc.

--How to Compile a Consumer's Directory of Doctors & their Fee. 69p. 1979. 3.50. Pub Citizen Inc.

Bogumill, George F. & Schwamm, Harry A. Orthopaedic Pathology: A Synopsis with Clinical & Radiographic Correlation. (Illus.). 784p. 1984. 75.00 (ISBN 0-7216-1169-9). Saunders.

Bogus, Ronald, jt. ed. see Landau, Sidney.

Bogus, SDiane. Her Poems: An Anniversaric Chronology. (Illus., Orig.). 1980. 200.00 (ISBN 0-934172-02-1). WIM Pubns.

--I'm Off to See the Goddamn Wizard, Alright! 63p. 1980. pap. 4.00 (ISBN 0-934172-00-5). WIM Pubns.

--Sapphire's Sampler. LC 81-90217. (Illus.). 228p. (Orig.). 1982. 10.00 (ISBN 0-934172-07-2); pap. 7.00 (ISBN 0-934172-06-4). WIM Pubns.

--Woman in the Moon. (Illus.). 58p. 1979. pap. 6.00 (ISBN 0-934172-01-3). WIM Pubns.

Bogus, SDiane, ed. see Sebastian, Adele.

Boguslaski, Robert C., et al, eds. Clinical Immunochemistry: Principles of Methods & Applications. 296p. 1984. text ed. 39.50 (ISBN 0-316-10087-0). Little.

Boguslavskii, Leonid I. & Vannikov, Anatolii V. Organic Semiconductors & Biopolymers. LC 72-75452. (Monographs in Semiconductor Physics Ser.: Vol. 6). 221p. 1970. 32.50x (ISBN 0-306-30433-3, Plenum Pr). Plenum Pub.

Boguslavsky, B. M., et al. A B C of Dialectical & Historical Materialism. 398p. 1976. 4.95 (ISBN 0-8285-0188-2, Pub. by Progress Pubs USSR). Imported Pubns.

Boguslavsky, M. U. S. S. R. & International Copyright Protection. 303p. 1979. 8.45 (ISBN 0-8285-1919-6, Pub. by Progress Pubs USSR). Imported Pubns.

Boguslavsky, M. M. Copyright in International Relations: International Protection of Literary & Scientific Works. Catterns, David, ed. Poulet, N., tr. from Rus. 224p. 1979. 30.00x (ISBN 0-9595513-0-1, Pub. by Australian Copyright Council Australia). Rothman.

Boguslaw, Robert. New Utopians: A Study of System Design & Social Change. enl. ed. LC 80-18602. 1981. pap. text ed. 9.95x (ISBN 0-8290-0115-8). Irvington.

--Systems Analysis & Social Planning: Human Problems of Post-Industrial Society. 1982. text ed. 29.50x (ISBN 0-8290-0111-5). Irvington.

Boguslaw, Robert, jt. auth. see Berg, William M.

Boguslawski, Dorothy B. Guide for Establishing & Operating Day Care Centers for Young Children. LC 66-18695. 1966. pap. 6.50 (ISBN 0-87868-032-2, J-52). Child Welfare.

Bohak, Zvi & Sharon, Nathan, eds. Biotechnological Application of Proteins & Enzymes. 1977. 65.00 (ISBN 0-12-110950-X). Acad Pr.

Bohall, Vesta R. The Loom of Life. (Illus.). 80p. 1984. 6.95 (ISBN 0-8059-2925-8). Dorrance.

Bohan, Anthony. Rheumatology Continuing Education Review. 1978. spiral bdg. 21.00 (ISBN 0-87488-333-4). Med Exam.

Bohan, Peter & Hammerslough, Philip. Early Connecticut Silver, 1700-1840. LC 76-82543. (Illus.). 1970. 45.00x (ISBN 0-8195-4008-0). Wesleyan U Pr.

Bohan, Ruth L. The Societe Anonyme's Brooklyn Exhibition: Katherine Dreier & Modernism in America. Foster, Stephen, ed. LC 82-7006. (Studies in the Fine Arts: The Avant-Garde: No. 20). 282p. 1982. 39.95 (ISBN 0-8357-1294-X). UMI Res Pr.

Bohanan, Robert D. Dwight D. Eisenhower: A Selected Bibliography of Periodical & Dissertation Literature. LC 81-3139. 162p. (Orig.). 1981. pap. 3.25 (ISBN 0-9605728-0-5). Eisenhower Lib.

Bohannan, Harry M. see Morris, Alvin L.

Bohannan, Laura & Bohannan, Paul. The Tiv of Central Nigeria. (Ethnographic Survey of Africa Ser.; Western Africa). pap. 25.80 (ISBN 0-317-11266-X, 2055382). Bks Demand UMI.

Bohannan, Lawa, jt. auth. see Bohannan, Paul.

Bohannan, P. All the Happy Families: Exploring the Varieties of Family Life. 224p. 1984. 16.95 (ISBN 0-07-006432-6). McGraw.

Bohannan, Paul. Tiv Farm & Settlement. pap. 10.00 (ISBN 0-384-04959-1). Johnson Repr.

Bohannan, Paul & Bohannan, Lawa. Tiv Economy. LC 66-17013. (Northwestern University African Studies: No. 20). pap. 53.10 (ISBN 0-317-27800-2, 2015288). Bks Demand UMI.

Bohannan, Paul & Curtin, Philip. Africa & Africans. rev. ed. LC 79-139006. 1971. 6.50 (ISBN 0-385-08231-2, AMS). Natural Hist.

Bohannan, Paul & Glazer, Mark. High Points in Anthropology. 1973. text ed. 15.00 (ISBN 0-394-31672-X, KnopfC). Knopf.

Bohannan, Paul, jt. auth. see Bohannan, Laura.

Bohannan, Paul, ed. Law & Warfare: Studies in the Anthropology of Conflict. (Texas Press Sourcebooks: No. 1). 455p. 1976. pap. 11.95x (ISBN 0-292-74617-2). U of Tex Pr.

Bohannan, Paul, ed. see Tylor, Edward B.

Bohannon, Cynthia. The North & South Nodes: The Guideposts of the Spirit. LC 79-55867. 1979. pap. 4.95 (ISBN 0-932782-02-7). Arthur Pubns.

Bohannon, Laura, ed. see Pettengill, Samuel B.

Bohannon, M. A., ed. see Braithwaite, Gary M., et al.

Bohannon, Paul, jt. ed. see Gruter, Margaret.

Bohannon Wilson Co. Locks Catalog. (Illus.). Repr. of 1911 ed. 15.00 (ISBN 0-87556-350-3). Saifer.

Bohanon, Mary. Strictly Personal: Black Vignettes. LC 76-56031. 1977. 7.95 (ISBN 0-87881-058-7). Mojave Bks.

Bohart, G. E. & Gressitt, J. L. Filth-Inhabiting Flies of Guam. (BMB). 1951. 22.00 (ISBN 0-527-02312-4). Kraus Repr.

Bohart, R. M. & Kimsey, Lynn S. A Synopsis of the Chrysididae in America North of Mexico: Memoir 33. (Illus.). 266p. 1982. 26.00x (ISBN 0-686-40423-8). Am Entom Inst.

Bohart, R. M. & Menke, A. S. Sphecid Wasps of the World: A Generic Revision. 1976. 90.00x (ISBN 0-520-02318-8). U of Cal Pr.

Bohart, R. M. & Washino, R. K. Mosquitoes of California. 3rd ed. LC 77-84551. 1978. pap. 6.00x (ISBN 0-931876-15-X, 4084). Ag & Nat Res.

Bohatta, Ida. All of the Birds. Head, June, ed. (Illus.). 18p. (gr. 3-5). 1981. PLB 3.95 (ISBN 0-86724-012-1). Ars Edition.
--Barli the Ice Bear. Theobald, John, tr. from Ger. (Illus.). 18p. (gr. 3-5). 1981. PLB 3.95 (ISBN 0-86724-007-5). Ars Edition.
--Bow Wow. Head, June, tr. from Ger. (Illus.). 18p. (gr. 3-5). 1981. PLB 3.95 (ISBN 0-86724-001-6). Ars Edition.
--The Brown Family. Head, June, tr. from Ger. (Illus.). 18p. (gr. 3-5). 1981. 3.95 (ISBN 0-86724-011-3). Ars Edition.
--The Busy Savers. Theobald, Mary L., tr. from Ger. (Illus.). 18p. (gr. k up). 1981. 3.95 (ISBN 0-86724-020-2). Ars Edition.
--The Cloud Kitchen. Head, June, tr. from Ger. (Illus.). 18p. (gr. 3-5). 1981. PLB 3.95 (ISBN 0-86724-009-1). Ars Edition.
--A Day with Heinzel. Theobald, John, tr. from Ger. (Illus.). 26p. (gr. 3-5). 1981. PLB 3.95 (ISBN 0-86724-008-3). Ars Edition.
--Doctor Allsgood. Head, June, tr. from Ger. (Illus.). 18p. (gr. 3-5). 1981. PLB 3.95 (ISBN 0-86724-002-4). Ars Edition.
--Flipp & Flirr. Theobald, John, tr. from Ger. (Illus.). 18p. (gr. k up). 1981. 3.95 (ISBN 0-86724-017-2). Ars Edition.
--The Hardworking Bee. Head, June, tr. from Ger. (Illus.). 18p. (gr. k up). 1981. 3.95 (ISBN 0-86724-018-0). Ars Edition.
--Heinzel the Innkeeper. Head, June, tr. from Ger. (Illus.). 18p. (gr. 3-5). 1981. PLB 3.95 (ISBN 0-86724-003-2). Ars Edition.
--The Helpful Dwarfs. Kummer, Pia, tr. from Ger. (Illus.). 26p. (gr. k up). 1981. 3.95 (ISBN 0-86724-015-6). Ars Edition.
--Ice Men. Theobald, John, tr. from Ger. (Illus.). 18p. (gr. k up). 1981. 3.95 (ISBN 0-86724-021-0). Ars Edition.
--The Little Advent Book. Theobald, John, tr. from Ger. (Illus.). 18p. (gr. kup). 1981. 3.95 (ISBN 0-86724-022-9). Ars Edition.
--Little Men Underground. Theobald, John, tr. from Ger. (Illus.). 18p. (gr. k up). 1981. 3.95 (ISBN 0-86724-019-9). Ars Edition.
--The Merry Hoppers. Theobald, John, tr. from Ger. (Illus.). 18p. (gr. 3-5). 1981. PLB 3.95 (ISBN 0-86724-004-0). Ars Edition.
--Raindrops. Theobald, John, tr. from Ger. (Illus.). 18p. (gr. k up). 1981. 3.95 (ISBN 0-86724-016-4). Ars Edition.
--Saint Nicholas. Theobald, John, tr. from Ger. (Illus.). 18p. (gr. 2-5). 1981. 3.95 (ISBN 0-86724-024-5). Ars Edition.
--Shooting Stars. Theobald, John, tr. from Ger. (Illus.). 18p. (gr. 3-5). 1981. PLB 3.95 (ISBN 0-86724-005-9). Ars Edition.
--Velvet Paws. Theobald, Mary L., tr. from Ger. (Illus.). 18p. (gr. 3-5). 1981. PLB 3.95 (ISBN 0-86724-010-5). Ars Edition.
--Winter House. Theobald, John, tr. from Ger. (Illus.). 18p. (gr. k up). 1981. 3.95 (ISBN 0-86724-023-7). Ars Edition.
--Wixi the Easter Rabbit. Theobald, John, tr. from Ger. (Illus.). 18p. (gr. 2-5). 1981. 3.95 (ISBN 0-86724-014-8). Ars Edition.
--Wulli & Susi. Theobald, John, tr. from Ger. (Illus.). 18p. (gr. k up). 1981. 3.95 (ISBN 0-86724-013-X). Ars Edition.
Bohatta, Ida & Theobald, John. The Misjudged Mushroom. (Illus.). 26p. (gr. 3-5). 1981. PLB 3.95 (ISBN 0-86724-006-7). Ars Edition.
Bohdan & Szuprowicz, Maria. Doing Business with the People's Republic of China. 449p. 24.95 (ISBN 0-317-35808-1, 504). Soc Intercult Ed Train & Res.
Bohdan, Carol L., jt. auth. see Blasberg, Robert W.
Bohdanecky, M. & Kovar, J. Viscosity of Polymer Solutions. (Polymer Science Library: No. 2). 286p. 1982. 76.75 (ISBN 0-444-42066-5). Elsevier.
Bohen, Halcyone H. & Viveros-Long, Anamaria. Balancing Jobs & Family Life: Do Flexible Work Schedules Help? (Family Impact Seminar Ser.). (Illus.). 360p. 1981. 32.95 (ISBN 0-87722-199-5). Temple U Pr.
Bohen, Halcyone H., jt. auth. see Aspen Institute for Humanistic Studies.
Bohensky, Fred. Photo Manual & Dissection Guide of the Shark. (Avery's Anatomy Ser.). (Illus.). 144p. (Orig.). 1981. pap. text ed. 7.95 (ISBN 0-89529-140-1). Avery Pub.
--Photo Manual & Dissection Guide of the Rat. (Avery's Anatomy Ser.). (Illus.). 140p. (Orig.). 1985. lab manual 6.95 (ISBN 0-89529-213-0). Avery Pub.
--Photo Manual & Dissection Guide of the Frog. (Avery's Anatomy Ser.). (Illus.). 88p. (Orig.). 1982. lab manual 5.95x (ISBN 0-89529-162-2). Avery Pub.
--Photo Manual & Dissection Guide of the Fetal Pig: With Sheep Heart, Brain, Eye. (Illus.). 1978. 6.95 (ISBN 0-89529-058-8). Avery Pub.
--Photo Manual of the Cat: With Sheep Heart, Brain, Eye. (Illus.). 1977. lab manuel 6.95 (ISBN 0-89529-019-7). Avery Pub.
Bohere, G. Profession Journalist: A Study of the Working Conditions of Journalists. International Labour Office Staff, ed. Orig. Title: Fr. ix, 117p. 1984. pap. 14.95 (ISBN 92-2-103531-X). Intl Labour Office.
Bohi, Charles, jt. auth. see Grant, H. Roger.
Bohi, Douglas R. Analyzing Demand Behavior: A Study of Energy Elasticities. LC 81-47616. (Resources for the Future: Economics of Natural Resources Ser.). 192p. 1981. text ed. 19.50x (ISBN 0-8018-2705-1). Johns Hopkins.
Bohi, Douglas R. & Montgomery, David. Oil Prices, Energy Security, & Import Policy. LC 82-15083. 224p. 1983. text ed. 25.00x (ISBN 0-8018-2821-X). Johns Hopkins.
Bohi, Douglas R. & Quandt, William B. Energy Security in the Nineteen Eighties: Economic & Political Perspectives. 67p. 1984. pap. 6.95 (ISBN 0-8157-1001-1). Brookings.
Bohi, Douglas R & Russell, Milton. Limiting Oil Imports: An Economic History & Analysis. 376p. 1978. 28.50 (ISBN 0-8018-2106-1). Resources Future.
Bohi, Douglas R. & Toman, Michael A. Analyzing Nonrenewable Resource Supply. LC 83-43264. 180p. 1984. lib. bdg. 25.00x (ISBN 0-915707-05-5); pap. text ed. 10.00x (ISBN 0-915707-06-3). Resources Future.
Bohigas, Oriol, et al. Miguel Angel Roca. 2nd, rev. ed. (Academy Architecture Ser.). (Illus.). 176p. 1984. pap. 24.95 (ISBN 0-312-53229-6). St Martin.
Bohigas Rosell, Mauricio. Diccionario Ingles-Espanol, Spanish-English. 1370p. (Eng. & Span.). 1974. 7.95 (ISBN 84-7183-007-8, S-12385). French & Eur.
Bohigian, Haig. Master Track & Field Indoor Record Book. 48p. (Orig.). 1983. pap. 4.00 (ISBN 0-933390-07-6). Gazette Pr.
--Track & Field Masters Ranking Book 1982: Men & Women Ages 30-89, U.S.A., Canada Mexico. 96p. (Orig.). 1981. pap. 10.00 (ISBN 0-686-91816-9). Gazette Pr.
--Track & Field Masters Ranking Book 1981: Men & Women Ages 30-89; U.S.A., Canada & Mexico. 104p. (Orig.). 1980. pap. 6.00 (ISBN 0-933390-06-8). Gazette Pr.
Bohigian, Haig E. The Foundations & Mathematical Models of Operations Research with Extensions to the Criminal Justice System. LC 75-186274. (Illus.). xxiii, 282p. (Orig.). 1972. pap. 12.95 (ISBN 0-933390-01-7). Gazette Pr.
Bohigian, Valerie. How to Make Your Home-Based Business Grow: Getting Bigger Profits from Your Products. LC 84-6900. 288p. 1984. pap. 7.95 (ISBN 0-452-25620-8, Plume). NAL.
--Real Money from Home: How to Start, Manage, & Profit from a Home-Based Service Business. Date not set. pap. 9.95 (ISBN 0-452-25661-5, Plume). NAL.
Bohinski, Robert C. Modern Concepts in Biochemistry. 4th ed. 1983. text ed. 44.64 (ISBN 0-205-07905-9, 6879055); solution's manual 3.60 (688158). Allyn.
Bohl, E., et al, eds. Numerik und Anwendungen von Eigenwertaufgaben und Verzweigungsproblemen. (International Series of Umerical Mathematics: No. 38). 218p. (Ger.). 1977. pap. 36.95x (ISBN 0-8176-0938-5). Birkhauser.
Bohl, Marilyn. Computer Concepts. LC 75-101499. (Illus.). 1970. text ed. 24.95 (ISBN 0-574-16080-9, 13-0751); instr's guide avail. (ISBN 0-574-16082-5, 13-0753); problems & exercises 10.95 (ISBN 0-574-16081-7, 13-0752). SRA.
--Flowcharting Techniques. 208p. 1971. pap. text ed. 11.95 (ISBN 0-574-16096-5, 13-1440). SRA.
--A Guide for Programmers. LC 77-14982. (Illus.). 1978. ref. 17.95x (ISBN 0-13-370551-X); pap. text ed. 15.95 (ISBN 0-13-370544-7). P-H.
--Information Processing. 4th ed. xxx, 609p. 1984. pap. text ed. 24.95 (ISBN 0-574-21445-3, 13-4445). SRA.
--Information Processing: With PASCAL. 3rd ed. 1982. text ed. 21.95 (ISBN 0-574-21390-2, 13-4390). instr. guide avail. (ISBN 0-574-21391-0, 13-4391). SRA.
--Introduction to IBM Direct Access Storage Devices. 224p. 1981. text ed. 20.95 (ISBN 0-574-21140-3, 13-4140). SRA.
--Tools for Structured Design. LC 77-13704. 1978. pap. text ed. 12.95 (ISBN 0-574-21170-5, 13-4170). SRA.
Bohl, Marilyn & Walter, Arline. Introduction to PL-1 Programming & PL-C. LC 72-92560. (Computer Science Ser.). (Illus.). 280p. 1973. pap. text ed. 15.95 (ISBN 0-574-17075-8, 13-0075). SRA.
Bohl, Marilyn, ed. Information Processing with BASIC. 4th ed. 688p. 1984. 25.95 (ISBN 0-574-21465-8, 13-4465); study guide o.p. 9.95 (ISBN 0-574-21448-8, 13-4448); study guide 9.95 (ISBN 0-574-21447-X); telecourse study guide avail. (ISBN 0-574-21448-8, 13-4448); transparencies avail. (ISBN 0-574-21449-6, 13-4449); test bank avail. (ISBN 0-574-21466-6, 13-4466); instr's guide avail. (ISBN 0-574-21446-1, 13-4446). SRA.
Bohlander, George. Flextime: A New Face on the Work Clock. (Policy & Practice Publication). 138p. 1977. 6.00 (ISBN 0-89215-080-7). U Cal LA Indus Rel.
Bohlander, George W. Impact of Third-Party Payors on Collective Bargaining in the Health Care Industry. (Monograph & Research Ser.: No. 26). 106p. 1980. 6.50 (ISBN 0-89215-109-9). U Cal LA Indus Rel.
Bohle, Bruce W., ed. Human Life: Controversies & Concerns. (Reference Shelf Ser.). 1979. 8.00 (ISBN 0-8242-0636-3). Wilson.
Bohle, Robert H. From News to Newsprint: Producing a Student Newspaper. (Illus.). 288p. 1984. pap. 17.95 (ISBN 0-13-330829-4). P-H.
Bohlen, Charles E. Transformation of American Foreign Policy. 1969. 3.95x (ISBN 0-393-05385-7, NortonC). Norton.
Bohlen, E. Crop Pests in Tanzania & Their Control. 2nd rev. ed. (Illus.). 142p. 1978. lib. bdg. 34.00 (ISBN 3-489-65126-X). Parey Sci Pubs.
Bohlen, H. David. Annotated Checklist of the Birds of Illinois. (Popular Science Ser.: Vol. IX). 154p. 1978. pap. 3.00 (ISBN 0-89792-071-6). Ill St Museum.
Bohlen, James. The New Pioneer's Handbook: Getting Back to the Land in an Energy-Scarce World. LC 75-7767. (Illus.). 256p. 1975. 8.95x (ISBN 0-8052-3591-4); pap. 4.95 (ISBN 0-8052-0581-0). Schocken.
Bohlen, John R. How to Rule the World: Seek First the Kingdom of God. LC 81-90513. (Illus.). 271p. 1982. pap. 3.95 (ISBN 0-9607702-0-8). Kingdom God.
Bohlender, Dorothy G. & McCallum, Frances T. H. P. N. Gammel. 15.00 (ISBN 0-317-20887-X). Texian.
Bohler, Jorg, jt. auth. see Bohler, Lorenz.
Bohler, Lorenz & Bohler, Jorg. The Treatment of Fractures: Supplement Vol. 1966. with 406pp. 131.50 (ISBN 0-8089-0063-3). Grune.
Bohler, Lorenz, et al. The Treatment of Fractures. LC 55-5445. (Illus.). 1956-58. Vol. 2, 450pps. 1957. 63.00 (ISBN 0-8089-0065-X, 790633); Vol. 3, 816pps, 1958. 93.00 (ISBN 0-8089-0066-8). Grune.
Bohlig, H. Lung & Pleura. 1980. 15.50 (ISBN 0-8151-1016-2). Year Bk Med.
Bohlin, Diane D. Prints & Related Drawings by the Carracci Family. LC 78-31551. (Illus.). pap. 8.00 (ISBN 0-89468-047-1). Natl Gallery Art.
Bohlin, Raymond G., jt. auth. see Lester, Lane.
Bohlin, William H. Modern Approach: Flower Painting. 4.97 (ISBN 0-87505-059-X); pap. 1.95 (ISBN 0-87505-234-7). Borden.
--Modern Approach to Drawing & Painting: Landscapes-Seascapes. 4.97 (ISBN 0-87505-235-5); pap. 1.95 (ISBN 0-87505-236-3). Borden.
Bohlin, William L. Flower Painting: Modern Approach. 1967. treasure trove bdg. 4.97 (ISBN 0-87505-059-X); pap. 1.95 (ISBN 0-87505-234-7). Borden.
Bohlinger, Maryanne Smith. Merchandise Buying: A Practical Guide. 2nd ed. 560p. 1983. pap. text ed. write for info. (ISBN 0-697-08086-2); instrs.' manual avail. (ISBN 0-697-08076-5). Wm C Brown.
Bohlke, Eugenia B. Catalog of Type Specimens in the Ichthyological Collection of the Academy of Natural Sciences of Philadelphia. (Special Publication: No. 14). 246p. 1984. pap. 15.00 (ISBN 0-910006-41-5). Acad Nat Sci Phila.
Bohlmann, F., et al. Naturally Occurring Acetylenes. 1973. 98.00 (ISBN 0-12-111150-4). Acad Pr.
Bohlmann, Otto. Yeats & Nietzsche: An Exploration of Major Nietzschean Echoes in the Writings of William Butler Yeats. (Illus.). 240p. 1982. 28.50x (ISBN 0-389-20065-4, 06835). B&N Imports.
Bohlmann, Ralph A. Principles of Biblical Interpretations in the Lutheran Confessions. rev. ed. 192p. 1983. pap. 8.95 (ISBN 0-570-03910-X, 12-2991). Concordia.
Bohlool, Janet. Library Orientation: Syllabus. 2nd ed. 1975. pap. text ed. 5.80 (ISBN 0-89420-080-1, 216788); cassette recordings 101.70 (ISBN 0-89420-161-1, 140800). Natl Book.
Bohm & MacDonald. Power: Mechanics of Energy Control. 2nd ed. 1983. 18.64 (ISBN 0-87345-256-9). McKnight.
Bohm, A. Dinoflagellates of the Coastal Waters of the Western Pacific. (BMB). 1936. pap. 10.00 (ISBN 0-527-02243-8). Kraus Repr.
--Distribution & Variability of Ceratium in the Northern & Western Pacific. (BMB). 1931. pap. 8.00 (ISBN 0-527-02193-8). Kraus Repr.
--Quantum Mechanics. (Texts & Monographs in Physics). (Illus.). 1979. 39.00 (ISBN 0-387-08862-8). Springer-Verlag.
Bohm, David. Causality & Chance in Modern Physics. LC 57-28894. 1971. pap. 8.95x (ISBN 0-8122-1002-6, Pa Paperbks). U of Pa Pr.
--Fragmentation & Wholeness: An Inquiry into the Function of Language & Thought. (The Van Leer Jerusalem Foundation Ser.). 1976. text ed. 5.50x (ISBN 0-391-00397-6). Humanities.
--Quantum Theory. 1951. ref. ed. 42.95 (ISBN 0-13-747873-9). P-H.
--Wholeness & the Implicate Order. 224p. 1980. 25.00x (ISBN 0-7100-0366-8); pap. 6.95 (ISBN 0-7448-0000-5). Routledge & Kegan.
--Wholeness & the Implicate Order. 240p. (Orig.). 1983. pap. 6.95 (ISBN 0-7448-0000-5, Ark Paperbacks). Routledge & Kegan.
Bohm, David, jt. auth. see Krishnamurti, J.
Bohm, Dorothy, jt. auth. see Norrie, Ian.
Bohm, Ewald. Textbook in Rorschach Test Diagnosis for Psychologists, Physicians & Teachers. LC 55-6011. 336p. 1958. 47.50 (ISBN 0-8089-0067-6, 790638). Grune.
Bohm, Fred C. & Swartout, Robert R., Jr., eds. Naval Surgeon in Yi Korea: The Journal of George W. Woods. (Korea Research Monographs: No. 10). (Illus.). 150p. (Orig.). 1984. pap. text ed. 12.00x (ISBN 0-912966-68-8). IEAS.
Bohm, G. J. & Cloud, R. L., eds. Pressure Vessels & Piping: Design & Analysis - A Decade of Progress, 4 vols. Incl. Vol. 1. Analysis. 780p; Vol. 2. Components & Structural Dynamics. 812p. 1972. 35.00 ea. (G00019, G00020). ASME.
Bohm, G. J., et al, eds. Components & Structural Dynamics, Vol II. 812p. 1972. 35.00 (ISBN 0-317-33458-1, G00020); members 17.50 (ISBN 0-317-33459-X). ASME.
Bohm, J. Electrostatic Precipitators. (Chemical Engineering Monographs: Vol. 14). 366p. 1982. 78.75 (ISBN 0-444-99764-4). Elsevier.
Bohm, Manfred, jt. auth. see Becher, Peter.
Bohm, Peter. Deposit-Refund Systems: Theory & Applications to Environmental, Conservation, and Consumer Policy. LC 81-47617. (Resources for the Future: Economics of Natural Resources Ser.). 192p. 1981. text ed. 22.00x (ISBN 0-8018-2706-X). Johns Hopkins.
--Social Efficiency: A Concise Introduction to Welfare Economics. LC 73-9379. 150p. 1975. pap. 18.95x (ISBN 0-470-08636-X). Halsted Pr.
Bohm, Peter & Kneese, Allen V. The Economics of Environment: Papers from Four Nations. LC 73-178244. 1972. 22.50 (ISBN 0-312-23240-3). St Martin.
Bohm, Robert. Kali Yuga. 1976. pap. 3.00 (ISBN 0-89924-003-8). Lynx Hse.
--Notes on India. 220p. 1982. 20.00 (ISBN 0-89608-126-5); pap. 7.50 (ISBN 0-89608-125-7). South End Pr.
Bohm, Robert A., et al, eds. Toward an Efficient Energy Future: Proceedings of the III International Energy Symposium III-May 23-27, 1982. Energy, Environment, & Resources Center,the University of Tennessee. (International Energy Symposia Ser.). 352p. 1983. prof. ref. 39.95 (ISBN 0-88410-878-3). Ballinger Pub.
--World Energy Production & Productivity: Proceedings of the International Energy Symposium I-October 14, 1980. Energy, Environment, & Resource Center, the University of Tennessee. (International Energy Symposia Ser.). 448p. 1981. prof ref 28.50x (ISBN 0-88410-649-7). Ballinger Pub.
Bohm, Ronald J. & Templeton, Lee. The Executive Guide to Video Teleconferencing. 150p. 1984. text ed. 40.00 (ISBN 0-89006-148-3). Artech Hse.
Bohman, James, tr. see Peukert, Helmut.
Bohman, Svante. What Is Intelligence? 148p. 1981. pap. text ed. 28.50x (Pub. by Almqvist & Wiksell Sweden). Humanities.
Bohman, Sven-Olof, jt. ed. see Mandal, Anil K.
Bohm-Bawerk, Eugen & Hilferding, Rudolph. Karl Marx & the Close of His System: Bohm-Bawerk's Criticism of Marx. Sweezy, Paul M., ed. xxx, 224p. 1984. pap. 9.95x (ISBN 0-87991-250-2). Orion Ed.
Bohm-Bawerk, Eugen V. The Positive Theory of Capital. facsimile ed. Smart, William, tr. LC 70-175689. (Select Bibliographies Reprint Ser). Repr. of 1891 ed. 26.50 (ISBN 0-8369-6604-X). Ayer Co Pubs.
Bohm-Bawerk, Eugen Von. Capital & Interest, 3 vols. Incl. Vol. 1. History & Critique of Interest Theories. 490p (ISBN 0-910884-09-9); Vol. 2. Positive Theory of Capital. 466p (ISBN 0-910884-10-2); Vol. 3. Further Essays on Capital & Interest. 246p (ISBN 0-910884-11-0). LC 58-5555. 1959. 3 vols. 47.50 (ISBN 0-910884-07-2). Libertarian Press.
--Karl Marx & the Close of His System. Sweezy, Paul M., ed. LC 73-8804. Repr. of 1949 ed. lib. bdg. 25.00x (ISBN 0-678-00140-5). Kelley.
--Shorter Classics of Bohm-Bawerk: Five Essays. Incl. The Austrian Economists; Control or Economic Law; Ultimate Standard of Value; Unresolved Contradiction in the Marxian Economic System; Whether Legal Rights & Relationships Are Economic Goods. LC 60-11663. 376p. 1962. 15.95 (ISBN 0-910884-12-9). Libertarian Press.
Bohme, Frederick G. A History of the Italians in New Mexico. LC 74-17920. (Italian American Experience Ser). (Illus.). 304p. 1975. 21.00x (ISBN 0-405-06393-8). Ayer Co Pubs.
Bohme, H. & Viehe, H. G. Imminium Salts in Organic Chemistry. LC 76-16155. (Advances in Organic Chemistry Ser.: Vol. 9, Pt. 2). 238p. 1979. 145.00 (ISBN 0-471-90693-X, Pub. by Wiley-Interscience). Wiley.
Bohme, H. & Viehe, H. G., eds. Iminium Salts in Organic Chemistry. LC 76-16155. (Advances in Organic Chemistry Ser: Vol. 9, Pt. 1). 631p. 1976. 127.00 (ISBN 0-471-90692-1, Pub. by Wiley-Interscience). Wiley.
Bohme, Helmut. An Introduction to the Social & Economic History of Germany. Lee, W. R., tr. from Ger. LC 78-18913. 1978. 26.00 (ISBN 0-312-43315-8). St Martin.
Bohme, Klaus-Richard. The Defense Policies of the Nordic Countries, Nineteen Eighteen to Nineteen Thirty-Nine. Krosby, H. Peter, tr. from Swedish. 80p. (Orig.). 1979. pap. 7.00x (ISBN 0-89126-073-0). MA-AH Pub.

Bohme, S., et al, eds. Astronomy & Astrophysics Abstracts, Vol. 37. Schmadel, L. D., tr. (Literature 1984: Pt. 1). 920p. 1984. 68.50 (ISBN 0-387-13937-0). Springer-Verlag.

--Literature Nineteen Eighty-Three, Pt. 2. (Astronomy & Astrophysics Abstracts Ser.: Vol. 34). 960p. 1984. 68.50 (ISBN 0-387-13485-9). Springer-Verlag.

--Literature, 1984, Pt. 2. Heinrich, I. & Hofmann, W. Zech, G., tr. (Astronomy & Astrophysics Abstracts Ser.: Vol. 38). 920p. 1985. 69.50 (ISBN 0-387-15562-7). Springer-Verlag.

Bohmer, Gunter. Wonderful World of Puppets. LC 76-107968. (Illus.). 1971. 12.95 (ISBN 0-8238-0084-9). Plays.

Bohmer, K. & Stetter, H. J., eds. Defect Correction Methods. (Computing Ser.: Supplementum 5). (Illus.). 240p. 1984. 20.00 (ISBN 0-387-81832-4). Springer-Verlag.

Bohmer, K., et al, eds. Spline Functions. (Lectures in Mathematics: Vol. 501). 1976. pap. 23.00 (ISBN 0-387-07543-7). Springer-Verlag.

Bohmont, Bert L. The New Pesticide User's Guide. 1983. text ed. 23.95 (ISBN 0-8359-4890-0); instr's. manual free (ISBN 0-8359-4891-9). Reston.

Bohn & Petschek. Kinsey: Photographer. ltd. ed. (Illus.). 320p. 1980. hand bound leather 550.00 (ISBN 0-904351-19-X). Genesis Pubns.

Bohn, et al. Soil Chemistry. 2nd ed. 1985. write for info. (ISBN 0-471-82217-5). Wiley.

Bohn, Dave. East of These Golden Shores: Architecture of the Earlier Days in Contra Costa & Alameda Counties. (Illus.). 124p. 1971. pap. 7.50 (ISBN 0-937106-00-3). Ross Valley.

--Glacier Bay: The Land & the Silence. 2nd ed. Bower, David, ed. (Illus.). 160p. pap. 3.00 (ISBN 0-686-32834-5). Alaska Natural.

--Rambles Through an Alaskan Wild: Katmai & the Valley of the Smokes. LC 79-14527. (Illus.). 176p. 1979. 20.00 (ISBN 0-88496-125-7, Noel Young Bk). Capra Pr.

Bohn, Dave & Jett, Stephen C. House of Three Turkeys: Anasazi Redoubt. LC 77-15013. (Noel Young Bks.). (Illus.). 1977. pap. 3.95 (ISBN 0-88496-115-X). Capra Pr.

Bohn, Dave & Petschek, Rodolfo. Kinsey, Photographer. LC 78-1029. (Illus.). 320p. 1984. 50.00 (ISBN 0-87701-287-3). Chronicle Bks.

--Kinsey, Photographer: A Half Century of Negatives by Darius & Tabitha May Kinsey. (Illus.). 320p. 1975. boxed set 150.00 (ISBN 0-685-52668-2, Pub. by Scrimshaw Calif); Vol. 1. (ISBN 0-937106-01-1); Vol. 2. (ISBN 0-937106-02-X). Ross Valley.

Bohn, Dave & Petschek, Rodolpho. Kinsey, Photographer: The Locomotive Portraits, Vol. 3. 144p. 1984. 35.00 (ISBN 0-87701-319-5). Chronicle Bks.

Bohn, Henry G. Biography & Bibliography of Shakespeare. LC 74-38033. Repr. of 1863 ed. 12.50 (ISBN 0-404-00920-4). AMS Pr.

--The Biography & Bibliography of Shakespeare. (Illus.). 2368p. 1981. lib. bdg. 100.00 (ISBN 0-8495-0489-9). Arden Lib.

--A Catalogue of Books: The Famous "Guinea Catalogue". LC 74-8717. Repr. of 1841 ed. 137.50 (ISBN 0-404-11610-8). AMS Pr.

--A Guide to the Knowledge of Pottery & Porcelain Monograms & Marks & Other Objects di Virtu. (Illus.). 101p. 1984. 77.45 (ISBN 0-86650-120-7). Gloucester Art.

--Handbook of Proverbs. LC 68-55795. (Bohn's Antiquarian Library Ser). Repr. of 1855 ed. 18.00 (ISBN 0-404-50003-X). AMS Pr.

--Polyglot of Foreign Proverbs. LC 68-55796. (Bohn's Antiquarian Library Ser.). Repr. of 1857 ed. 12.50 (ISBN 0-404-50004-8). AMS Pr.

--A Polyglot of Foreign Proverbs: Comprising French, Italian, German, Dutch, Spanish, Portuguese & Danish with English Translations. 579p. 1983. Repr. of 1889 ed. lib. bdg. 85.00 (ISBN 0-8495-0613-1). Arden Lib.

Bohn, Henry G., ed. Hand-book of Games. LC 73-84610. 1969. Repr. of 1850 ed. 43.00x (ISBN 0-8103-3570-0). Gale.

--Polyglot of Foreign Proverbs - with English Translations. LC 67-23915. (Polyglot Ser.). 1968. Repr. of 1857 ed. 40.00x (ISBN 0-8103-3197-7). Gale.

Bohn, Henry G., tr. see Von Humboldt, Alexander.

Bohn, Hinrich L., et al. Soil Chemistry. LC 79-14515. 329p. 1979. 29.95x (ISBN 0-471-04082-7, Pub. by Wiley-Interscience). Wiley.

Bohn, John T., jt. auth. see Polmar, Norman.

Bohn, Ralph C., jt. auth. see Silvius, G. Harold.

Bohn, Raymond J. & Wool, John D. Useful Arithmetic, Vol. 1. rev. ed. 1981. pap. 3.00x (ISBN 0-88323-164-6, 251); tchr's. key 1.00x (ISBN 0-88323-167-0, 252). Richards Pub.

Bohn, Raymond J., jt. auth. see Wool, John D.

Bohn, Robert F. Budget Book & Much More: Your Money, Goals, Time, Assets, Vital Records. 2nd ed. 128p. pap. text ed. 6.95 (ISBN 0-8403-2185-6). Kendall-Hunt.

Bohne, Harald & Van Ierssel, Harry. Publishing: The Creative Business. LC 72-96455. pap. 25.00 (ISBN 0-317-10315-6, 2020456). Bks Demand UMI.

Bohner, Charles. Bold Journey: West with Lewis & Clark. LC 84-19328. 192p. (gr. 5 up). 1985. 11.95 (ISBN 0-395-36691-7). HM.

--Robert Penn Warren. rev. ed. (United States Authors Ser.). 1981. lib. bdg. 13.95 (ISBN 0-8057-7345-2, Twayne). G K Hall.

Bohner, Charles H. Robert Penn Warren. (Twayne's United States Authors Ser.). 1964. pap. 5.95x (ISBN 0-8084-0268-4, T69, Twayne). New Coll U Pr.

Bohner, H. O., ed. Light Metal 1985. 1525p. 1985. 80.00 (ISBN 0-89520-488-6); students 24.00 (ISBN 0-317-37220-3). Metal Soc.

--Light Metals, 1985. LC 84-29479. (Illus.). 1527p. 1985. 80.00 (ISBN 0-89520-488-6). Metal Soc.

Bohner, Philotheus. Medieval Logic: An Outline of Its Development from 1250 to c. 1400. LC 78-59007. 1979. Repr. of 1952 ed. 14.50 (ISBN 0-88355-682-0). Hyperion Conn.

Bohnert, Herbert G. Logic: Its Use & Basis. 1977. pap. text ed. 13.75 (ISBN 0-8191-0265-2). U Pr of Amer.

Bohning, I., ed. Autonome Architekur und Partizipatorisches Bauen. 356p. (Ger.). 1981. text ed. 28.95x (ISBN 0-8176-1260-2). Birkhauser.

Bohning, W. R. Studies in International Labor Migration. LC 83-40607. 350p. 1984. 32.50 (ISBN 0-312-77092-8). St Martin.

Bohning, W. R., ed. Black Migration to South Africa: A Selection of Policy-Oriented Research. viii, 184p. (Orig.). 1981. 17.10 (ISBN 92-2-102758-9); pap. 11.40 (ISBN 92-2-102759-7). Intl Labour Office.

Bohny, Barbara, jt. auth. see Aurigemma, Ann.

Boholm, A. Swedish Kinship. (Goteburg Studies in Social Anthropology: No. 5). 252p. 1983. pap. text ed. 26.00x (ISBN 91-7346-127-X, Pub. by Acta Universitatis Sweden). Humanities.

Bohonek, Jan B. & Bohonek, Stan B. How Peter Molar Looked for a Smile. LC 83-73507. (Illus.). 32p. (gr. 1-3). 1984. PLB 9.95 (ISBN 0-914827-00-6). Adonis Studio.

Bohonek, Stan B., jt. auth. see Bohonek, Jan B.

Bohr, A. Elementary Modes of Excitation in Nuclei. (Enrico Fermi Summer Institute Ser.: Vol. 69). 548p. 1978. 117.00 (ISBN 0-444-85153-4, North-Holland). Elsevier.

Bohr, A. & Mottelson, B. R. Nuclear Structure, Vol. 3: Nucleonic Correlations. Date not set. (ISBN 0-8053-1017-7, Adv Bk Prog). Benjamin-Cummings.

Bohr, D. F., ed. see U. S.-Japan Cooperative Symposium.

Bohr, Ellen, ed. see Mees, L. F.

Bohr, Harald. Almost Periodic Functions. LC 47-5500. 1980. 7.95 (ISBN 0-8284-0027-X). Chelsea Pub.

Bohr, Niels. Atomic Theory & the Description of Nature. LC 75-41033. 1976. Repr. of 1934 ed. 12.50 (ISBN 0-404-14737-2). AMS Pr.

--Niels Bohr Collected Works, Vol. 1: Early Work, 1905-1911. Nielsen, J. R., ed. 608p. 1973. 125.75 (ISBN 0-444-10003-2, North-Holland). Elsevier.

--Niels Bohr Collected Works, Vol 2: Work on Atomic Physics, 1912-1917. Hoyer, V., ed. 648p. 1982. 125.75 (ISBN 0-444-86132-7, North Holland). Elsevier.

--Niels Bohr Collected Works, Vol. 3: The Correspondence 1918-1923, Vol. 3. Nielsen, J. Rud, ed. 1976. 136.25 (ISBN 0-7204-1803-8, North-Holland). Elsevier.

--Niels Bohr Collected Works, Vol. 4: The System, 1920-23. Nielsen, J. Rud, ed. 766p. 1977. 149.00 (ISBN 0-7204-1804-6, North-Holland). Elsevier.

--Niels Bohr, Collected Works, Vol. 5: The Emergence of Quantum Mechanics, 1924-1926. Stolzenberg, K. & Rudinger, E., eds. 600p. 1985. 92.75 (ISBN 0-444-86501-2, North-Holland). Elsevier.

Bohr, Paul R. Famine in China & the Missionary: Timothy Richard As Relief Administrator & Advocate of National Reform, 1876-1884. LC 72-75828. (East Asian Monographs Ser: No. 48). (Illus.). 1972. pap. 11.00x (ISBN 0-674-29425-4). Harvard U Pr.

Bohr, Paula, jt. auth. see Furgeson, Michael D.

Bohr, Peter, ed. Road & Track's Used Car Classics. (Illus.). 1985. pap. 10.95 (ISBN 0-912528-44-3). John Muir.

Bohra, R., jt. auth. see Mehrotra, R. C.

Bohren, Craig F. & Huffman, Donald R. Absorption & Scattering of Light by Small Particles. 530p. 1983. 51.95 (ISBN 0-471-05772-X, Pub. by Wiley-Interscience). Wiley.

Bohrer, Dick. Bill Borden: The Finished Course -- The Unfinished Task. (Golden Oldies Ser.). 1984. pap. 3.95 (ISBN 0-8024-0390-5). Moody.

--They Called Him Shifta. LC 95-28. 320p. 1981. pap. 4.95 (ISBN 0-8024-7910-3). Moody.

Bohrer, Dick, jt. auth. see Newton, John.

Bohrer, Stanley P. & Alavi, Abass. Bone Ischaemia & Infarction in Sickle Cell Disease. (Illus.). 349p. 1981. 44.50 (ISBN 0-87527-188-X). Green.

Bohrmann, Hans. NS-Presseanweisungen der Vorkriegszeit Edition und Dokumentation, Vol. 1. 480p. 1984. lib. bdg. 60.00 (ISBN 3-598-10552-5). K G Saur.

Bohrmann, Hans, ed. Presseanweisungen der Vorkriegszeit Edition und Dokumentation, Bd. 3. 800p. 1986. lib. bdg. 60.00 (ISBN 3-598-10554-1). K G Saur.

Bohrmann, Hans & Englert, Marianne, eds. Handbuch der Pressearchive. 250p. (Ger.). 1984. lib. bdg. 42.00 (ISBN 0-317-13858-8). K G Saur.

Bohrmann, Harns, ed. Presseanweisungen der Vorkriegszeit Edition und Dokumentation, Bd. 2. 800p. 1985. lib. bdg. 60.00 (ISBN 3-598-10553-3). K G Saur.

Bohrn, Harold, jt. auth. see Assarsson-Rizzi, Kerstin.

Bohrnstedt, George W. & Knoke, David. Statistics for Social Data Analysis. LC 81-82889. 530p. 1982. text ed. 27.50 (ISBN 0-87581-275-9). Peacock Pubs.

Bohrnstedt, George W. & Borgatta, Edgar F., eds. Social Measurement: Current Issues, 3 pts. (Illus.). 256p. 1981. 28.00 (ISBN 0-8039-1595-0); pap. 14.00 (ISBN 0-8039-1596-9). Sage.

Bohrnstedt, George W., jt. ed. see Borgatta, Edgar F.

Bohrod, Aaron. Decade of Still Life. (Illus.). 312p. 1966. 45.00 (ISBN 0-299-04121-2). U of Wis Pr.

Bohrod, Aaron, jt. auth. see Gard, Robert E.

Bohrs, Mary A. Getting Ready for Christmas. 32p. 1976. pap. 2.95 (ISBN 0-8170-0722-9). Judson.

Bohse, August. Die Lebenswuerdige Europaerin Constantine. 660p. Repr. of 1698 ed. 60.00 (ISBN 0-384-04962-1). Johnson Repr.

Bohstedt, John. Riots & Community Politics in England & Wales, 1790-1810. (Illus.). 336p. 1983. text ed. 30.00x (ISBN 0-674-77120-6). Harvard U Pr.

Bohusch, Otmar. Lexikon der Grammatischen Terminologie. (Ger.). 1972. 27.50 (ISBN 3-403-00298-5, M-7254). French & Eur.

Bohuslov, Ronald L. Analytic Geometry: A Precalculus Approach. (Illus.). 1970. text ed. write for info. (ISBN 0-02-311810-5, 31181). Macmillan.

--Basic Mathematics for Technical Occupations. (Illus.). 480p. 1976. 26.95 (ISBN 0-13-063396-8). P-H.

Boiangiu, Suri, jt. auth. see Keylin, Arleen.

Boice, J. C., Jr., jt. ed. see Day, N. E.

Boice, J. Montgomery. God & History. LC 80-24457. (Foundations of the Christian Faith: Vol 4). 292p. (Orig.). 1981. pap. 7.95 (ISBN 0-87784-746-0). Inter-Varsity.

Boice, James M. The Christ of Christmas. 1983. 9.95 (ISBN 0-8024-0337-9). Moody.

--The Christ of the Empty Tomb. 1985. 9.95 (ISBN 0-8024-1303-X). Moody.

--Does Inerrancy Matter? 1980. pap. 2.95 (ISBN 0-8423-0653-6). Tyndale.

--The Epistles of John. 224p. 1983. pap. 7.95 (ISBN 0-310-21531-5). Zondervan.

--Genesis. 352p. 1982. 16.95 (ISBN 0-310-21540-4). Zondervan.

--Genesis: Expositional Commentary. 352p. 1985. 16.95 (ISBN 0-310-21560-9, Pub. by Minister Res Lib). Zondervan.

--The Gospel of John: Peace in Storm, Vol. IV. 496p. 1983. pap. 9.95 (ISBN 0-310-21461-0). Zondervan.

--How to Live the Christian Life. LC 81-18839. 128p. 1982. pap. 3.95 (ISBN 0-8024-3666-8). Moody.

--The Minor Prophets: An Expositional Commentary (Hosea-Jonah, Vol. 1. 272p. 1983. 12.95 (ISBN 0-310-21550-1). Zondervan.

--Ordinary Men Called by God: Abraham, Moses, & David. 160p. 1982. pap. 3.50 (ISBN 0-88207-224-2). Victor Bks.

--The Parables of Jesus. 1983. pap. 6.95 (ISBN 0-8024-0163-5). Moody.

--Philippians: An Expositional Commentary. 320p. 1982. pap. 9.95 (ISBN 0-310-21501-3). Zondervan.

--The Sermon on the Mount. 328p. (Orig.). 1981. pap. 8.95 (ISBN 0-310-21511-0). Zondervan.

--The Sovereign God. LC 77-14879. (Foundations of the Christian Faith: Vol. 1). 1978. pap. 7.95 (ISBN 0-87784-743-6). Inter-Varsity.

--Standing on the Rock: The Importance of Biblical Inerrancy. (Orig.). 1984. leader's guide 2.95 (ISBN 0-8423-6604-0); pap. 4.95 (ISBN 0-8423-6603-2). Tyndale.

--Witness & the Revelation in the Gospel of John. 192p. 1970. pap. 4.95 (ISBN 0-85364-099-8). Attic Pr.

Boice, James M., ed. Our Savior God: Man, Christ, & the Atonement. 192p. 1980. pap. 6.95 (ISBN 0-8010-0790-9). Baker Bk.

Boice, James M., et al. The Foundation of Biblical Authority. (International Council on Biblical Inerrancy Ser.: Vol. 1). 1978. pap. 6.95 (ISBN 0-310-21521-8). Zondervan.

Boice, John D., Jr. & Fraumeni, Joseph F., Jr., eds. Radiation Carcinogenesis: Epidemiology & Biological Significance. (Progress in Cancer Research & Therapy Ser.: Vol. 26). 510p. 1984. text ed. 91.00 (ISBN 0-89004-907-6). Raven.

Boice, L. Peter. Encountering a City: The Spatial Learning Process of Urban Newcomers. 1977. 5.00 (ISBN 0-686-19119-6, 1264). CPL Biblios.

Boichenko, M. S., et al. Continuous Casting of Steel in the Soviet Union. LC 58-25475. pap. 20.00 (ISBN 0-317-10510-8, 2020645). Bks Demand UMI.

Boidman, Nathan & Ducharme, Bruno. Taxation in Canada. 300p. 1983. 62.00 (ISBN 0-686-41019-X). Kluwer Academic.

--Taxation in Canada: Implications for Foreign Investment. LC 84-15430. 1984. write for info. (Pub. by Kluwer Law Netherlands). Kluwer Academic.

Boies & Verkuil. Cases & Materials on the Public Control of Business. 1977. 29.95 (ISBN 0-316-10090-0). Little.

Boies, Henry M. Prisoners & Paupers: A Study of the Abnormal Increase of Criminals & the Public Burden of Pauperism in the United States; the Causes & Remedies. LC 72-5478. (Select Bibliographies Reprint Ser.). 1972. Repr. of 1893 ed. 25.00 (ISBN 0-8369-6897-2). Ayer Co Pubs.

Boies, Jack J. The Lost Domain: Avatars of the Earthly Paradise in Western Literature. LC 81-40923. 244p. (Orig.). 1982. lib. bdg. 24.25 (ISBN 0-8191-2387-0); pap. text ed. 12.25 (ISBN 0-8191-2388-9). U Pr of Amer.

Boies, Janice. Learning to Love. (Caprice Ser.: No. 71). 144p. 1985. pap. 2.25 (ISBN 0-441-47722-4). Ace Bks.

Boijsen, E. Computed Topography in Orthopedic Radiology. (Illus.). 64p. 1983. 34.00 (ISBN 0-86577-103-0). Thieme-Stratton.

Boikess, Robert, et al. Elements of Chemistry: General, Organic & Biological. (Illus.). 704p. 1986. text ed. 35.95 (ISBN 0-13-263583-6). P-H.

Boikess, Robert S. & Edelson, Edward. Chemical Principles. 3rd ed. 866p. 1985. text ed. 36.50 scp (ISBN 0-06-040805-7, HarpC); instr's. manual avail. (ISBN 0-06-360795-6); solutions manual avail. (ISBN 0-06-040813-8); answer book avail. (ISBN 0-06-360796-4). Har-Row.

Boikess, Robert S. & Sorum, C. Harvey. How to Solve General Chemistry Problems. 6th ed. (Illus.). 1981. pap. text ed. 17.95 (ISBN 0-13-434126-0). P-H.

Boikess, Robert S., et al. Chemical Principles. 2nd ed. (Illus.). 1981. text ed. 33.95 scp (ISBN 0-06-040808-1, HarpC); pap. text ed. 18.50 scp lab manual (ISBN 0-06-040811-1); study guide scp 8.50 (ISBN 0-06-040809-X); scp solutions manual 6.75 (ISBN 0-06-040812-X); instr. manual avail. (ISBN 0-06-360792-1); ans. bk. avail. (ISBN 0-06-360793-X). Har-Row.

Boiko, Claire. Children's Plays for Creative Actors. 384p. (gr. 3-7). 1985. pap. 10.95 (ISBN 0-8238-0267-1). Plays.

--Dramatized Parodies of Familiar Stories. (gr. 7-12). 1980. 12.00 (ISBN 0-8238-0240-X). Plays.

--Plays & Programs for Girls & Boys. (gr. 3-6). 1972. 12.00 (ISBN 0-8238-0134-9). Plays.

Boileau, Michel, jt. auth. see Johnson, Douglas.

Boileau, Nicolas. Art Poetique: Univers des Lettres Bordas. (Illus.). 1963. pap. 3.95 (ISBN 0-685-11015-X). French & Eur.

--Oeuvres, 2 tomes. Incl. Tome I. Satires, Le Lutrin. Vercruysse, ed; Tome II. Epitres, Oeuvres Diverses. Menant, ed. (Coll. GF). 3.95 ea. French & Eur.

--Oeuvres Completes. (Bibl. De la Pleiade). 1966. 42.95 (ISBN 0-685-11441-4). French & Eur.

Boileau, Richard A., ed. Advances in Pediatric Sport Sciences: Biological Issues, Vol. 1. (Advances in Pediatric Sport Sciences Ser.). 224p. 1984. text ed. 22.00x (ISBN 0-931250-71-4, BBOI0071). Human Kinetics.

Boileau-Despreaux, Nicolas. Selected Criticism. Dilworth, Ernest, tr. from Fr. LC 65-26530. 1965. pap. text ed. 7.95x (ISBN 0-672-60471-X). Irvington.

Boillin, Mary L. Determination of the Interrelations, Partial & Multiple, Between Various Anthropometric Measurements of College Women. LC 74-176573. (Columbia University. Teachers College. Contributions to Education Ser.: No. 450). Repr. of 1930 ed. 22.50 (ISBN 0-404-55450-4). AMS Pr.

Boillot, G. Geology of the Continental Margins. Scarth, Alwyn, tr. from Fr. (Illus.). 160p. 1981. pap. text ed. 11.95x (ISBN 0-582-30036-3). Longman.

Boillot, Michel. Understanding BASIC in Business. 1978. pap. text ed. 22.95 (ISBN 0-8299-0206-6). West Pub.

--Understanding FORTRAN. 2nd ed. (Illus.). 520p. 1981. pap. text ed. 21.95 (ISBN 0-8299-0355-0). West Pub.

--Understanding FORTRAN. 3rd ed. (Illus.). 600p. 1985. pap. text ed. 20.95 (ISBN 0-314-85219-0). West Pub.

--Understanding FORTRAN-77 with Structured Problem Solving. (Illus.). 320p. 1984. pap. text ed. 23.95 (ISBN 0-314-77845-4); write for info. instr's guide (ISBN 0-314-77846-2). West Pub.

Boillot, Michel & Boillot, Mona. BASIC: Concepts & Structured Problem Solving. (Illus.). 500p. 1984. pap. text ed. 21.95 (ISBN 0-314-77843-8); intr's. manual avail. (ISBN 0-314-77844-6). West Pub.

--Understanding FORTRAN-77 with Structured Problem Solving. International ed. 525p. 1984. 17.00 (ISBN 0-314-77847-0). West Pub.

--Understanding Structured COBOL. (Illus.). 600p. 1982. pap. text ed. 24.95 (ISBN 0-314-63161-5). West Pub.

Boillot, Michel & Horn, L. Wayne. BASIC. 3rd ed. (Illus.). 375p. 1983. pap. text ed. 20.95 (ISBN 0-314-69636-9). West Pub.

Boillot, Michel H. & Shingles, Carol R. Understanding WATFIV. (Illus.). 1980. pap. text ed. 22.95 (ISBN 0-8299-0232-5). West Pub.

Boillot, Michel H., et al. Essentials of Flowcharting. 4th. ed. 176p. 1985. pap. text ed. write for info. (ISBN 0-697-00420-1). Wm C Brown.

Boillot, Mona, jt. auth. see Boillot, Michel.

Boily, Lise & Blanchette, Jean-Francois. The Bread Ovens of Quebec. (Illus.). 1979. pap. 8.95 (ISBN 0-660-00120-9, 56284-0, Pub. by Natl Mus Canada). U of Chicago Pr.

Boim, L. & Morgan, G. G., eds. The Soviet Procuracy Protests: 1937-1973. (Law in Eastern Europe Ser.: No. 21). 324p. 1978. 95.00x (ISBN 90-286-0138-4). Sijthoff & Noordhoff.

Boime, Albert. Thomas Couture & the Eclectic Vision. LC 79-23507. (Illus.). 704p. 1980. 95.00x (ISBN 0-300-02158-5). Yale U Pr.

Bois, Guy. The Crisis of Feudalism: Economy & Society in Eastern Normandy c. 1300-1500. LC 83-7882. (Past & Present Publications Ser.). 392p. 1984. 59.50 (ISBN 0-521-25483-3). Cambridge U Pr.

Bois, J. Samuel. The Art of Awareness: A Textbook on General Semantics & Epistemics. 3rd ed. 432p. 1978. pap. text ed. write for info. (ISBN 0-697-04279-0). Wm C Brown.

--Epistemics: The Science-Art of Innovating. LC 71-93028. 165p. 1972. pap. text ed. 5.50x (ISBN 0-918970-09-1). Intl Gen Semantics.

--Explorations in Awareness. 212p. 1984. 6.50 (ISBN 0-918970-32-6); members 5.50 (ISBN 0-317-36917-2). Intl Gen Semantics.

Bois, Mario. Iannis Xenakis, the Man & His Music: A Conversation with the Composer & a Description of His Works. LC 80-12638. (Illus.). 40p. 1980. Repr. of 1967 ed. lib. bdg. 25.00x (ISBN 0-313-22415-3, BOIX). Greenwood.

Bois, Pene du see Du Bois, Pene.

Bois, W. E. B. Du see Du Bois, W. E. B.

Bois, W. E. Du see Du Bois, W. E.

Bois, W. E. Du see Du Bois, W. E. B.

Bois, W. E. Du see Du Bois, W. E.

Bois, W. E. Du see DuBois, W. E.

Bois, William E. Du see Dubois, William E.

Bois, William E. Du see Du Bois, William E.

Bois, William P. Du see Du Bois, William P.

Bois, William Pene Du see Pene Du Bois, William.

Bois, William Pene Du see Pene du Bois, William.

Bois, William Pene Du see Strand, Mark.

Boisard, Marcel. Humanism in Islam. Quinlan, Hamid, ed. Al-Jarrahi, Abdussamad, tr. from Fr. LC 82-70456. 200p. (Orig.). Date not set. pap. 8.00 (ISBN 0-89259-035-1). Am Trust Pubns.

Boisclair, Joan, ed. Capital Campaign Resource Guide. 1100p. (Orig.). 1985. 345.00x (ISBN 0-916664-36-8). Public Management.

Boisdeffre, Pierre De see Alberes, Rene M. & De Boisdeffre, Pierre.

Boise, Otis B. Music & Its Masters. LC 73-39464. (Illus.). Repr. of 1902 ed. 14.00 (ISBN 0-404-08367-6). AMS Pr.

Boiselle, Arthur H., et al. Using Mathematics in Business. LC 80-16710. (Illus.). 384p. 1981. pap. 21.95 (ISBN 0-201-00098-9); tests 3.00 (ISBN 0-201-00041-5); instr's. manual 10.95 (ISBN 0-201-00099-7). Addison-Wesley.

Boisen, Anton T. Exploration of the Inner World: A Study of Mental Disorder and Religious Experience. 1971. pap. 11.95x (ISBN 0-8122-1020-4, Pa Paperbks). U of Pa Pr.

Boisen, Anton T. & Leary, John. Religion in Crisis & Custom: A Sociological & Psychological Study. LC 72-10977. 271p. 1973. Repr. of 1955 ed. lib. bdg. 22.50x (ISBN 0-8371-6642-X, BORC). Greenwood.

Boisits, jt. auth. see Maibach.

Boisot, Max. Intangible Factors in Japanese Corporate Strategy. (Atlantic Papers: No. 50). 55p. 1983. pap. 5.00 (ISBN 0-318-01100-X). Rowman & Allanheld.

Boissard, Janine. Christmas Lessons. Feeney, Mary, tr. from Fr. 252p. 1984. 15.45i (ISBN 0-316-10097-8). Little.

--A Matter of Feeling. 256p. 1981. pap. 2.25 (ISBN 0-449-70001-1, Juniper). Fawcett.

--A Matter of Feeling. 1980. 8.45i (ISBN 0-316-10098-6). Little.

--A New Woman. 1982. 11.95 (ISBN 0-316-10099-4). Little.

--A New Woman. 192p. 1983. pap. 2.50 (ISBN 0-449-20338-7, ROHO, Crest). Fawcett.

--A Question of Happiness. 224p. 1985. pap. 2.50 (ISBN 0-449-70133-6, Juniper). Fawcett.

--A Time to Choose. Feeney, Mary, tr. 196p. 1985. 15.95 (ISBN 0-316-10102-8). Little.

Boisselle, Bea, ed. see West Pasco Genealogical Society Staff.

Boissevain, Gideon M. Monetary Question. Warner, G. T., tr. LC 75-75564. Repr. of 1891 ed. lib. bdg. 15.00x (ISBN 0-8371-1080-7, BOMQ). Greenwood.

Boissevain, Jan G. Rulamort Castle. (Illus.). 160p. 1984. 12.95 (ISBN 0-89962-397-2). Todd & Honeywell.

Boissevain, Jeremy. The Italians of Montreal. LC 74-17921. (Italian American Experience Ser). (Illus.). 104p. 1975. Repr. 11.50x (ISBN 0-405-06394-6). Ayer Co Pubs.

--A Village in Malta. LC 79-21054. 136p. 1980. pap. text ed. 9.95 (ISBN 0-03-053411-9, HoltC). HR&W.

Boissevain, Jeremy & Mitchell, J. Clyde, eds. Network Analysis: Studies in Human Interaction. LC 72-77471. (Change & Continuity in Africa Monographs). 1973. 16.80x (ISBN 90-2797-187-0). Mouton.

Boissier, Gaston. Cicero & His Friends: A Study of Roman Society in the Time of Caesar. Jones, Adnah D., tr. from Fr. LC 75-114085. 1970. Repr. of 1897 ed. lib. bdg. 25.00 (ISBN 0-8154-0318-6). Cooper Sq.

--Great French Writers: Madame De Sevigne. 154p. 1980. Repr. of 1887 ed. lib. bdg. 25.00 (ISBN 0-8495-0476-7). Arden Lib.

--Madame De Sevigne. Williams, Henry L., tr. LC 79-38341. (Select Bibliographies Reprint Ser.). 1887. 14.00 (ISBN 0-8369-6794-1). Ayer Co Pubs.

--Madame De Sevigne. 205p. 1981. Repr. of 1889 ed. lib. bdg. 30.00 (ISBN 0-89984-079-5). Century Bookbindery.

--Madame De Sevigne. Williams, Henry L., tr. 1973. Repr. of 1887 ed. 20.00 (ISBN 0-8274-0068-3). R West.

--Rome & Pompeii: Archaeological Rambles. Fisher, D. Havelock, tr. LC 77-39193. 435p. Repr. of 1896 ed. lib. bdg. 28.00 (ISBN 0-8290-0505-6). Irvington.

--Rome & Pompeii: Archeological Rambles. Fisher, D. Havelock, tr. LC 77-39193. (Select Bibliographies Reprint Ser.). (Illus.). 1896. 29.00 (ISBN 0-8369-6795-X). Ayer Co Pubs.

Boissier, J. R., et al, eds. Differential Psychopharmacology on Anxiolytics & Sedatives. (Modern Problems of Pharmacopsychiatry: Vol. 14). (Illus.). 1977. 23.00 (ISBN 3-8055-2777-2). S Karger.

--International Congress of Pharmacology, 7th, Paris, 1978: Abstracts. 1979. text ed. 175.00 (ISBN 0-08-023768-1). Pergamon.

Boissiere, Ralph de see De Boissiere, Ralph.

Boissiere, Robert. The Hopi Way: An Odyssey. LC 84-16256. 96p. (Orig.). 1985. pap. 8.95 (ISBN 0-86534-055-2). Sunstone Pr.

--Po Pai Mo: The Search for White Buffalo Woman. LC 83-4668. (Illus.). 96p. (Orig.). 1983. pap. 8.95 (ISBN 0-86534-024-2). Sunstone Pr.

Boisson, M., jt. ed. see Chalazonitis, N.

Boissoneau, Robert. Continuing Education in the Health Professions. LC 80-19748. 322p. 1981. text ed. 34.50 (ISBN 0-89443-325-3). Aspen Systems.

Boissonet, V. D. Dictionnaire Alphabetico-Methodique des Ceremonies et des Rites Sacres, 3 vols. Migne, J. P., ed. (Encyclopedie Theologique Ser.: Vols. 15-17). 1986p. (Fr.). Repr. of 1847 ed. lib. bdg. 252.00x (ISBN 0-89241-237-2). Caratzas.

--Dictionnaire Dogmatique, Moral, Historique, Canonique, Liturgigue et Disciplinaire des Decrets des Diverse Congregations Romaines. Migne, J. P., ed. (Nouvelle Encyclopedie Theologique Ser.: Vol. 26). 646p. (Fr.). Repr. of 1852 ed. lib. bdg. 82.50x (ISBN 0-89241-269-0). Caratzas.

Boissonnade, Prosper. Les Etudes Relatives a l'Histoire Economique de l'Espagne et Leurs Resultats. (Publications de la Revue de Synthese Historique). 1964. Repr. of 1913 ed. 22.50 (ISBN 0-8337-0329-3). B Franklin.

--Etudes Relatives a l'Histoire Economique de la Revolution Francaise. 1967. Repr. of 1906 ed. 22.50 (ISBN 0-8337-0331-5). B Franklin.

--Life & Work in Medieval Europe: The Evolution of Medieval Economy from the Fifth to the Fifteenth Century. Power, Eileen, tr. from Fr. LC 82-11818. (Illus.). 395p. 1982. Repr. of 1964 ed. lib. bdg. 37.75x (ISBN 0-313-23566-X, BOLW). Greenwood.

Boisvert, R. F., jt. auth. see Rice, J.

Boisvert, Real. What You Really Ought to Know about Those Big Bucks One-Armed-Bandits. 1984. pap. 5.00 (ISBN 0-935810-12-9). Primer Pubs.

Boit, H. G., ed. see Beilstein Institute for Literature of Organic Chemistry.

Boit, John. The Log of the Union: John Boit's Remarkable Voyage to the Northwest Coast 7 Around the World 1974-1976. Hayes, Edmund, Sr., ed. LC 80-83181. (North Pacific Studies: No. 6). (Illus.). 176p. 1981. 19.95 (ISBN 0-87595-097-3); pap. 12.95 (ISBN 0-87595-089-2); deluxe boxed set 50.00 (ISBN 0-87595-097-3). Oreg Hist Soc.

Boitani, Peiro. Chaucer & the Italian Trecento. (Illus.). 322p. Date not set. pap. price not set (ISBN 0-521-31350-3). Cambridge U Pr.

Boitani, Piero. Chaucer & the Imaginary World of Fame. LC 84-412. (Chaucer Studies: Vol. XI). 264p. 1984. 53.50x (ISBN 0-389-20476-5, 08036). B&N Imports.

--Chaucer & the Italian Trecento. LC 82-17772. 312p. 1983. 49.50 (ISBN 0-521-23998-2). Cambridge U Pr.

--English Medieval Narrative in the Thirteenth & Fourteenth Centuries. Hall, Joan, tr. LC 81-17081. 328p. 1982. 47.50 (ISBN 0-521-23562-6). Cambridge U Pr.

Boitani, Piero & Torti, Anna, eds. Literature in Fourteenth Century England: The J. A. W. Bennett Memorial Lectures, Perugia, 1981-1982. (Tuebinger Beitraege zur Anglistik: No. 5). 220p. (Orig.). 1983. pap. 27.00x (ISBN 3-87808-590-7, Pub by GN Verlag Germany). Benjamins North Am.

--Medieval & Pseudo-Medieval Literature: The J.A.W. Bennett Memorial Lectures Perugia, 1982-1983. (Tuebinger Beitraege zur Anglistik: No. 6). 198p. (Orig.). 1984. pap. 27.00x (ISBN 3-87808-600-8, Pub. by G N Verlag Germany). Benjamins North Am.

--Medieval & Pseudo-Medieval Literature. 198p. 1985. 25.00 (ISBN 0-85991-177-2, Pub. by Boydell & Brewer). Longwood Pub Group.

Boite, R. Network Theory. 588p. 1972. 131.95 (ISBN 0-677-14170-X). Gordon.

Boite, R. & De Wilde, P. Circuit Theory & Design: Proceedings of the 1st European Conference. 1090p. 1982. 117.00 (ISBN 0-444-86307-9, North-Holland). Elsevier.

Boite, R. & Neirynck, J. Analyse des Circuits Lineaires. LC 73-135122. (Cours & Dcuments de Mathematiques & de Physique Ser.). (Illus.). 374p. (Fr.). 1971. 93.75 (ISBN 0-677-50350-4). Gordon.

Boiteau, Dieudonne A. Les Traites de commerce. (Research & Source Works Ser., History, Economics & Social Science). 1971. Repr. of 1863 ed. 32.50 (ISBN 0-8337-0332-3). B Franklin.

Boiteux, Henri, jt. auth. see Mavrodineanu, Radu.

Boiti, M., et al, eds. Nonlinear Evolution Equations & Dynamical Systems. (Lecture Notes in Physics: Vol. 120). 368p. 1980. pap. 29.00 (ISBN 0-387-09971-9). Springer-Verlag.

Boito, Camilo, ed. The Basilica of St. Mark in Venice Illustrated from the Points of View of Art & History by Venetian Writers. Scott, William, tr. 1976. lib. bdg. 125.95 (ISBN 0-8490-1477-8). Gordon Pr.

Bojar, Johan. A Pilgrimage. Muir, Jessie, tr. 246p. 1981. Repr. of 1924 ed. lib. bdg. 20.00 (ISBN 0-89987-081-3). Darby Bks.

Bojarski, Richard. The Films of Bela Lugosi. 1980. pap. 9.95 (ISBN 0-8065-5071-6). Citadel Pr.

Bojarski, Richard & Beale, Kenneth. The Films of Boris Karloff. LC 71-147832. (Illus.). 256p. 1974. 12.00 (ISBN 0-8065-0396-3). Citadel Pr.

Bojarsky, Richard & Beale, Kenneth. The Films of Boris Karloff. (Illus.). 288p. 1984. pap. 9.95 (ISBN 0-8065-0906-6). Citadel Pr.

Boje, Axel. Open Plan Offices. 212p. 1971. 17.95x (ISBN 0-8464-1160-1). Beekman Pubs.

--Open Plan Offices. 212p. 1971. 17.95x (ISBN 0-317-06177-1). Beekman Pubs.

Boje, R. & Tomczak, M., eds. Upwelling Ecosystems. (Illus.). 1978. pap. 34.00 (ISBN 0-387-08822-9). Springer-Verlag.

Bojer, Johan. The Emigrants. Jayne, A. G., tr. 351p. 1981. lib. bdg. 20.00 (ISBN 0-89987-072-4). Darby Bks.

--The Emigrants. Jayne, A. G., tr. LC 73-21338. 351p. 1974. Repr. of 1925 ed. lib. bdg. 24.75x (ISBN 0-8371-6194-0, BOTE). Greenwood.

--The Emigrants. Jayne, A. G., tr. from Norwegian. LC 78-9813. xviii, 355p. 1978. pap. 8.95 (ISBN 0-8032-6051-2, BB 673, Bison). U of Nebr Pr.

--The Great Hunger. 17.95 (ISBN 0-88411-064-8, Pub. by Aeonian Pr). Amereon Ltd.

--The New Temple. Archer, C., tr. 1979. Repr. of 1928 ed. lib. bdg. 15.00 (ISBN 0-8492-3571-5). R West.

Bojorge, Horacio. The Image of Mary: According to the Evangelists. Owen, Aloysius, tr. from Span. LC 77-15516. (Illus.). 1978. pap. 4.00 (ISBN 0-8189-0362-7). Alba.

Bojrab, M. Joseph, ed. Current Techniques in Small Animal Surgery. 2nd ed. LC 82-24929. (Illus.). 811p. 1983. text ed. 85.00 (ISBN 0-8121-0862-0). Lea & Febiger.

--Pathophysiology in Small Animal Surgery. LC 80-25780. (Illus.). 906p. 1981. text ed. 75.00 (ISBN 0-8121-0696-2). Lea & Febiger.

Bojtar, Endre. Slavic Structuralism in Literary Science. (Linguistic & Literary Studies in Eastern Europe: 11). 150p. 1986. 30.00x (ISBN 90-272-1507-3). Benjamins North Am.

Bojtech, O. T., compiled by. Organic Coolants & Moderators. (Bibliographical Ser.: No. 17). 173p. 1975. pap. 11.25 (ISBN 92-0-054065-1, IDC70, IAEA). Unipub.

Bok, Bart J. & Bok, Priscilla F. The Milky Way. 5th ed. LC 80-22544. (Harvard Books on Astronomy Ser.). (Illus.). 384p. 1981. text ed. 25.00 (ISBN 0-674-57503-2). Harvard U Pr.

Bok, Bart J. & Jerome, Lawrence E. Objections to Astrology. LC 75-29798. (Science & the Paranormal Ser.). 62p. 1975. pap. 6.95 (ISBN 0-87975-059-6). Prometheus Bks.

Bok, Curtis. Star Wormwood. LC 84-45877. 1983. Repr. of 1959 ed. 30.00 (ISBN 0-404-62402-2, 8675). AMS Pr.

Bok, Derek. Beyond the Ivory Tower: Social Responsibilities of the Modern University. 328p. 1984. pap. 7.95 (ISBN 0-674-06898-X). Harvard U Pr.

Bok, Derek C. Beyond the Ivory Tower: Social Responsibilities of the Modern University. LC 81-20278. 336p. 1982. 18.00x (ISBN 0-674-06899-8). Harvard U Pr.

Bok, Derek C., jt. auth. see Cox, Archibald.

Bok, Edward. The Americanization of Edward Bok: An Autobiography. 1920. Repr. 30.00 (ISBN 0-8482-0135-3). Norwood Edns.

--Dollars Only. 1926. Repr. 20.00 (ISBN 0-8482-7355-9). Norwood Edns.

--A Dutch Boy Fifty Years After. 1920. Repr. 20.00 (ISBN 0-8482-7356-7). Norwood Edns.

--A Man from Maine. 1922. Repr. 30.00 (ISBN 0-8482-7396-6). Norwood Edns.

--Successward. 1895. Repr. 20.00 (ISBN 0-8482-7413-X). Norwood Edns.

--Twice Thirty. 1895. Repr. 20.00 (ISBN 0-8482-7418-0). Norwood Edns.

Bok, Gordon. Time & the Flying Snow. LC 77-80648. 88p. 1977. pap. 8.95 (ISBN 0-938702-03-3). Folk-Legacy.

Bok, Hannes, jt. auth. see Merritt, A.

Bok, Priscilla F., jt. auth. see Bok, Bart J.

Bok, Sissela. Lying: Moral Choice in Public & Private Life. LC 78-21949. 1979. pap. 3.95 (ISBN 0-394-72804-1, Vin). Random.

--Lying: Moral Choice in Public Life. LC 77-88779. 1978. 10.95 (ISBN 0-394-41370-9). Pantheon.

--Secrets: On the Ethics of Concealment & Revelation. 1983. 16.45 (ISBN 0-394-51581-1). Pantheon.

--Secrets: On the Ethics of Concealment & Revelation. 1984. pap. 5.95 (ISBN 0-394-72142-X, Vin). Random.

Bok, Sissela, jt. ed. see Callahan, Daniel.

Bokenham, O. Legendys of Hooly Wummen. (EETS, OS Ser.: No. 206). Repr. of 1938 ed. 22.00 (ISBN 0-527-00206-2). Kraus Repr.

Bokenkotter, Thomas. A Concise History of the Catholic Church. LC 78-20269. 1979. pap. 6.50 (ISBN 0-385-13015-5, Im). Doubleday.

Bokenkotter, Thomas, tr. Essential Catholicism. LC 84-13631. 432p. 1985. 19.95 (ISBN 0-385-18357-7). Doubleday.

Boker, Carlos. Joris Ivens, Film-Maker: Facing Reality. Kirkpatrick, Diane, ed. LC 81-4697. (Studies in Cinema: No. 1). 222p. 1981. 39.95 (ISBN 0-8357-1182-X). UMI Res Pr.

Boker, Dea. Alike-but Unalike. 32p. 1974. pap. text ed. 0.50 (ISBN 0-8134-1635-3, 1635). Interstate.

Boker, George H. Plays & Poems, 2 vols. Repr. of 1856 ed. Set. 37.50 (ISBN 0-404-00930-1). AMS Pr.

--Poems of the War. LC 72-4949. (The Romantic Tradition in American Literature Ser.). 204p. 1972. Repr. of 1864 ed. 25.50 (ISBN 0-405-04623-5). Ayer Co Pubs.

Boker, H. Boker Tree Brand Knives: Everything in Fine Cutlery. (Illus.). 96p. pap. text ed. 10.00 (ISBN 0-911881-03-4). Am Blade Bk Serv.

Boker, John J., Jr., et al. Anphilex '71 Anniversary Philatelic Exhibition Commemorating the 75th Year of the Collectors Club of New York. (Illus.). 1971. 12.50 (ISBN 0-912574-28-3). Collectors.

Boker, W., jt. auth. see Hafner, H.

Bokhari, R. H. Subvention Policy & Practices for Public Enterprises. (ICPE Monograph). 59p. 1982. pap. 10.00x (ISBN 92-9038-903-6, Pub. by Intl Ctr Pub Yugoslavia). Kumarian Pr.

Bokhoven, W. M. Van see Van Bokhoven, W. M. & Jess, J.

Boklage, Cecilia, jt. auth. see Veitch, Carol.

Boklund, G. The Sources of the White Devil. (Essays & Studies on English Language & Literature: Vol. 17). pap. 24.00 (ISBN 0-317-16717-0). Kraus Repr.

Boklund, Gunnar. Sources of the White Devil, John Webster. LC 68-1396. (Studies in Comparative Literature, No. 35). 1969. Repr. of 1957 ed. lib. bdg. write for info. (ISBN 0-8383-0648-9). Haskell.

Bokoli, Madeleine, jt. auth. see Ray, Juliana.

Bokonyi, S. Animal Husbandary & Hunting in Tac-Gorsium. (Studia Archaeologica: No. 8). 237p. 1984. text ed. 39.75x (ISBN 963-05-3152-6, Pub. by Akademiai Kiado Hungary). Humanities.

Bokor, Selma, ed. see Patent, Arnold M.

Bokor-Szego, H. The Role of the United States in International Legislation. 192p. 1979. 47.00 (ISBN 0-444-85041-4, North Holland). Elsevier.

Bokov, Nikolai. Nobody. Fitzlyon, April, tr. from Rus. 1979. 9.95 (ISBN 0-7145-3502-8); pap. 4.95 (ISBN 0-7145-3551-6). Riverrun NY.

Boksenbaum, Howard, jt. ed. see Commoner, Barry.

Bokser, Baruch M. History of Judaism: The Next Ten Years. Neusner, Jacob, ed. LC 80-25501. (Brown Judaic Studies). 1980. 15.00 (ISBN 0-89130-450-9, 14-00-21); pap. 10.50 (ISBN 0-89130-451-7). Scholars Pr GA.

--The Origins of the Seder: The Passover Rite & Early Rabbinic Judaism. LC 83-17932. (Illus.). 160p. 1984. 19.95 (ISBN 0-520-05006-1). U of Cal Pr.

--Post Mishnaic Judaism in Transition: Samuel in Berakhot & the Beginnings of Gemara. LC 80-19702. (Brown Judaic Studies). 543p. 1980. 19.50 (ISBN 0-89130-432-0, 14 00 17); pap. 15.00 (ISBN 0-89130-433-9). Scholars Pr GA.

Bokser, Ben. Hasiddur: The Prayer Book. 842p. 1957. pap. 9.00 pocket flexible ed. (ISBN 0-88482-069-6). Hebrew Pub.

Bokser, Ben Z. The Jewish Mystical Tradition. LC 80-27627. 280p. 1981. 14.95 (ISBN 0-8298-0435-8); pap. 9.95 (ISBN 0-8298-0451-X). Pilgrim NY.

--Pharisaic Judaism in Transition. LC 73-2189. (The Jewish People; History, Religion, Literature Ser.). Repr. of 1935 ed. 18.00 (ISBN 0-405-05255-3). Ayer Co Pubs.

Bokser, Ben Z., tr. Minhah & Maariv Service. 45p. 1958. pap. 6.50 (ISBN 0-88482-125-0). Hebrew Pub.

Bokser, Ben Z., tr. from Hebrew. The Prayer Book. 430p. 1983. pap. text ed. 11.95 (ISBN 0-87441-372-9). Behrman.

Bokser, Ben-Zion. The Gifts of Life & Love. 193p. 1975. 7.00 (ISBN 0-88482-894-8). Hebrew Pub.

Bokser, Ben Zion. The Jewish Mystical Tradition. 1980. 15.00 (ISBN 0-88482-922-7); pap. 6.95 (ISBN 0-88482-923-5). Hebrew Pub.

--Judaism & Modern Man. 1958. 5.00 (ISBN 0-8022-0148-2). Philos Lib.

Bokser, Ben Zion, tr. Abraham Isaac Kook: The Lights of Penitance, Lights of Holiness. the Moral Principles. Essays, Letters & Poems. LC 78-70465. (Classics of Western Spirituality Ser.). 448p. 1978. 11.95 (ISBN 0-8091-0278-1); pap. 9.95 (ISBN 0-8091-2159-X). Paulist Pr.

Bokshtein, S. Z., ed. Diffusion Processes Structure & Properties of Metals. LC 65-10718. 135p. 1965. 35.00x (ISBN 0-306-10698-1, Consultants). Plenum Pub.

Bokstein, M. F., et al. Four Papers on Topology. LC 51-5559. (Translations Ser.: No. 2, Vol. 11). 1964. Repr. of 1959 ed. 32.00 (ISBN 0-8218-1711-6, TRANS 2-11). Am Math.

Bol, L. J. Adriaen Coorte: A Unique Late Seventeenth Century Dutch Still-Life Painter. (Illus.). 1977. text ed. 26.25x (ISBN 90-232-1516-8). Humanities.

--The Bosschaert Dynasty: Painters of Flowers & Fruits. 112p. 1981. 60.00x (ISBN 0-85317-650-7, Pub. by Lewis Pubs). State Mutual Bk.

Bol, Laurens J. & Keyes, George S., eds. Netherlandish Paintings & Drawings from the Collection of F. C. Butot: By Little-Known & Rare Masters of the Seventeenth Century. (Illus.). 264p. 35.00 (ISBN 0-85667-103-7). Sotheby Pubns.

Bol, Laurens J., et al. Netherlandish Paintings & Drawings from the Collection of F. C. Butot: By Little-Known & Rare Masters of the Seventeenth Century. (Illus.). 264p. 1981. 50.00x (ISBN 0-85667-103-7, Pub. by Sotheby Pubns England). Biblio Dist.

Bol, Peter C. Grossplastik aus Bronze in Olympia. (Olympische Forschungen: Vol. 14). 1978. 58.00x (ISBN 3-11-006701-3). De Gruyter.

Bol, Peter R. The Winner's Guide on Retail Selling. LC 84-72669. 128p. (Orig.). 1985. pap. text ed. 6.95 (ISBN 0-9613917-0-7). Dynamic Comm.

Bola Publications. Bola Glossary of Civil Procedural Law: Spanish-English & English-Spanish. LC 82-72320. (Bola Glossary Ser.: Vol. 2). 100p. (Orig., Span. & Eng.). 1986. pap. 19.95 (ISBN 0-943118-01-8). Bola Pubns.

Bolado, Victor H. Management Terminology: English-Spanish & Spanish-English. 192p. (Eng. & Span.). 1981. 9.95 (ISBN 0-89962-034-5). Todd & Honeywell.

Bolam, A. G. The Trans-Australian Wonderland. 1979. 21.00x (ISBN 0-85564-139-8, Pub. by U of W Austral Pr). Intl Spec Bk.

Bolam, R., et al. LEA Advisers & the Mechanisms of Innovation. 256p. 1979. 18.00x (ISBN 0-85633-175-9, Pub. by NFER Nelson UK). Taylor & Francis.

Bolam, Ray, ed. School-Focussed In-Service Training. (Heinemann Organization in Schools Ser.). x, 246p. 1983. text ed. 25.00x (ISBN 0-435-80090-6). Heinemann Ed.

Bolan, Mack. Dirty War. 384p. 1984. pap. 3.95 (ISBN 0-317-31361-4). S&S.

Boland, Bill, ed. Annals Index, 1960-1974, Vol. 289. (Annals of the New York Academy of Sciences). 581p. 1977. 47.00x (ISBN 0-89072-035-5). NY Acad Sci.

Boland, Bill, et al, eds. Annals Index. (Annals of The New York Academy of Sciences Ser.: Vol. 391). 154p. 1982. lib. bdg. 30.00x (ISBN 0-89766-172-9); pap. 30.00x (ISBN 0-89766-173-7). NY Acad Sci.

Boland, Bill M. & Cullinan, Justine, eds. Annals Index 1975-1977. (Annals of the New York Academy of Sciences: Vol. 331). 226p. 1979. 41.00x (ISBN 0-89766-041-2). NY Acad Sci.

Boland, Bridget & Boland, Maureen. Gardener's Magic & Other Old Wives' Lore. (Illus.). 64p. 1977. 5.95 (ISBN 0-374-16034-1). FS&G.

--Old Wives' Lore for Gardeners. (Illus.). 64p. 1977. pap. 3.95 (ISBN 0-374-51639-1). FS&G.

Boland, Bridget, jt. ed. see Byrne, Muriel S.

Boland, Bridget, jt. ed. see Byrne, Muriel St. C.

Boland, Charles M. Ring in the Jubilee: The Story of America's Liberty Bell. LC 72-80407. (Illus.). 96p. (gr. 6 up). 1973. pap. 5.95 (ISBN 0-85699-055-8). Chatham Pr.

Boland, D. J. & Brooker, M. I. Eucalyptus Seed. 204p. 1980. 32.50 (ISBN 0-643-02586-3, C058, CSIRO). Unipub.

Boland, D. J., et al. Eucalyptus Seed. (Illus.). 191p. 1980. pap. 22.00x (ISBN 0-643-02586-3). Sabbot-Natural Hist Bks.

--Eucalyptus Seed. (Illus.). 191p. 1980. 25.00x. Intl Spec Bk.

--Eucalyptus Seed. 204p. 1984. 55.00x (Pub. by CSIRO Australia). State Mutual Bk.

Boland, Eavan. Introducing Eavan Boland: Poems. LC 80-84833. (Ontario Review Press Poetry Ser.). 72p. 1981. 10.95 (ISBN 0-86538-009-0); pap. 6.95 (ISBN 0-86538-010-4). Ontario Rev NJ.

Boland, Ian, tr. Within the Whirlwind. 448p. 1985. pap. 8.95 (ISBN 0-15-697649-8). HarBraceJ.

Boland, Ian, tr. see Ginzburg, Eugenia.

Boland, Jack. Master Mind Goal Achiever's Journal, 1985. 206p. 1984. 12.95 (ISBN 0-88152-020-9). Master Mind.

Boland, James F. Nuclear Reactor Instrumentation (In-Core) LC 76-101310. 230p. 1970. 12.50 (ISBN 0-677-02420-7, 450015). Am Nuclear Soc.

Boland, James P., jt. auth. see Berry, Ralph E.

Boland, John C. Wall Street's Insiders: How You Can Watch Them & Profit. LC 84-62023. (Illus.). 226p. 1985. 16.95 (ISBN 0-688-03872-7). Morrow.

Boland, John J. Federal Income Taxation of Securities. 4th ed. 273p. 1977. pap. 15.00 (ISBN 0-317-30782-7, B288). Am Law Inst.

Boland, Kevin. The Rise & Decline of Fianna Fail. 150p. 1982. pap. 5.50 (ISBN 0-85342-683-X, Pub. by Mercier Pr Ireland). Irish Bks Media.

Boland, Lawrence A. The Foundations of Economic Method. 200p. 1982. text ed. 29.50x (ISBN 0-04-330328-5); pap. text ed. 10.95x (ISBN 0-04-330329-3). Allen Unwin.

--A Methodology for a New Microeconomics. 224p. 1985. text ed. 28.50x (ISBN 0-04-330351-X). Allen Unwin.

Boland, Margaret M. Cleomades: A Study in Architectonic Patterns. LC 74-19101. (Romance Monographs: No. 11). 1975. 12.00x (ISBN 0-686-17920-X); pap. 10.00x (ISBN 84-399-2791-6). Romance.

Boland, Maureen, jt. auth. see Boland, Bridget.

Boland, Peter. New Healthcare Market: A Guide to PPOs for Purchasers, Payors & Providers. LC 84-71429. 1985. 65.00 (ISBN 0-87094-534-3). Dow Jones-Irwin.

Boland, Richard, jt. auth. see Tricker, R. I.

Bolande, Robert P. Cellular Aspects of Developmental Pathology. LC 67-19136. (Illus.). Repr. of 1967 ed. 95.80 (ISBN 0-8357-9398-2, 2014526). Bks Demand UMI.

Bolande, Robert P., jt. ed. see Rosenberg, Harvey S.

Bolander, B. O. Instant Medical Dictionary. (Career Institute Instant Reference Library). 1970. 4.95 (ISBN 0-531-02009-6). Watts.

--The Instant Quotation Dictionary. (Career Institute Instant Reference Library). 314p. 1969. 4.95 (ISBN 0-531-02006-1). Watts.

--Instant Synonyms & Antonyms. (Career Institute Instant Reference Library). 314p. 1970. 4.95 (ISBN 0-531-02008-8). Watts.

Bolander, D. O., jt. auth. see Semmelmeyer, Madeline.

Bolander, Donald O., et al. Instant Quotation Dictionary. LC 74-104786. 320p. 1969. 4.95 (ISBN 0-911744-05-3). Career Pub IL.

--Instant Spelling Medical Dictionary. LC 77-124400. 320p. 1970. 4.95 (ISBN 0-911744-35-5). Career Pub IL.

--Instant Synonyms & Antonyms. LC 75-113518. 320p. 1970. 4.95 (ISBN 0-911744-06-1). Career Pub IL.

Bolander, Steven F., et al, eds. Manufacturing Planning & Control in Process Industries. LC 81-68512. 162p. 1981. pap. 13.50 (ISBN 0-935406-04-2). Am Prod & Inventory.

Bolandis, Jerry. Hospital Finance: A Comprehensive Approach. LC 81-20506. 284p. 1982. text ed. 35.50 (ISBN 0-89443-377-6). Aspen Systems.

Bolas, Gerald D. An Illustrated Checklist of the Washington University Collection. (Illus.). 80p. 1981. pap. 5.00 (ISBN 0-936316-01-2). Wash U Gallery.

Bolas, Gerald D., ed. An Illustrated Checklist of the Collection: Washington University Gallery of Art, St. Louis. (Illus.). 80p. 1981. pap. 5.00 (ISBN 0-936316-01-2). Wash U Gallery.

Bolay, Karl H. I Seek an Island. (Illus.). 48p. 1982. 5.00 (ISBN 0-682-49784-3). Exposition Pr FL.

Bolc, L., ed. The Design of Interpreters, Compilers, & Editors, for Augmented Transition Networks. (Symbolic Computation). (Illus.). 214p. 1983. 31.00 (ISBN 0-387-12789-5). Springer-Verlag.

--Natural Language Communication with Computers. (Lecture Notes in Computer Science: Vol. 63). 1978. pap. 17.00 (ISBN 0-387-08911-X). Springer-Verlag.

--Natural Language Communication with Pictorial Information Systems. (Symbolic Computation: Artificial Intelligence Ser.). (Illus.). 340p. 1984. 31.00 (ISBN 0-387-13478-6). Springer-Verlag.

Bolc, L. & Kulpa, Z., eds. Digital Image Processing Systems: Proceedings. (Lecture Notes in Computer Science Ser.: Vol. 109). 353p. 1981. pap. 22.00 (ISBN 0-387-10705-3). Springer-Verlag.

Bolc, Leonhard, ed. Speech Communication with Computers. 1978. pap. 29.00x (ISBN 3-4461-2650-3). Adlers Foreign Bks.

Bolce, William J., ed. see Hysom, John L.

Bolch, Judith & Miller, Kay. Investigative & in-Depth Reporting. 1978. 9.95 (ISBN 0-8038-3413-6); pap. text ed. 4.95x (ISBN 0-8038-3414-4). Hastings.

Bolch, Judy, ed. see Goldstein, Helen H.

Bolchazy, L. J. Hospitality in Early Rome: Livy's Concept of Its Humanizing Force. 1977. 15.00 (ISBN 0-89005-212-3). Ares.

Bolcom, William, jt. auth. see Kimball, Robert.

Bolcom, William, ed. see Rochberg, George.

Bold. A Scottish Poetry Book. 10.95 (ISBN 0-19-916029-5, Pub. by Oxford U Pr Childrens). Merrimack Pub Cir.

--A Scottish Poetry Book. pap. 4.95 (ISBN 0-19-916030-9, Pub. by Oxford U Pr Childrens). Merrimack Pub Cir.

Bold, Alan. The Ballad. (Critical Idiom Ser.). 1979. 19.95x (ISBN 0-416-70890-0, NO.2035). Methuen Inc.

--Drink to Me Only: The Prose & Cons of Drinking. 184p. 1983. 11.95 (ISBN 0-86072-058-6, Pub. by Quartet Bks). Merrimack Pub Cir.

--George Mackay Brown. (Modern Writers Ser). 117p. 1978. text ed. 17.50x (ISBN 0-06-490569-1, 06354). B&N Imports.

--In This Corner. 1983. 30.00x (ISBN 0-86334-022-9, Pub. by Macdonald Pub UK). State Mutual Bk.

--Introduction to Modern Scottish Literature. LC 82-8956. 352p. 1983. pap. text ed. 13.95x (ISBN 0-582-49064-2). Longman.

--MacDiarmid: The Terrible Crystal. LC 83-3075. 252p. 1984. 22.50x (ISBN 0-7100-9493-0). Routledge & Kegan.

Bold, Alan, ed. Byron: Wrath & Rhyme. LC 83-3734. (Critical Studies). 216p. 1983. text ed. 28.50x (ISBN 0-389-20373-4, 07245). B&N Imports.

--Harold Pinter: You Never Heard Such Silence. LC 84-20357. (Critical Studies). 184p. 1984. 27.50x (ISBN 0-389-20535-4, BNB-08097). B&N Imports.

--The Letters of Hugh MacDiarmid. LC 84-8723. 910p. 1985. 30.00x (ISBN 0-8203-0735-1). U of Ga Pr.

--Muriel Spark: An Odd Capacity for Vision. LC 84-2830. (Critical Studies). 208p. 1984. 27.50x (ISBN 0-389-20482-X, 08044). B&N Imports.

--The Sexual Dimension in Literature. LC 82-13894. (Critical Studies Ser.). 224p. 1983. text ed. 28.50x (ISBN 0-389-20314-9, 07152). B&N Imports.

--Sir Walter Scott: The Long Forgotten Melody. LC 83-2792. (Critical Studies). 224p. 1983. text ed. 28.50x (ISBN 0-389-20371-8, 07243). B&N Imports.

--Smollett: Author of the First Distinction. (Critical Studies). 240p. 1982. text ed. 28.50x (ISBN 0-389-20240-1, 07097). B&N Imports.

--W. H. Auden: The Far Interior. (Critical Studies). 222p. 1985. 27.50x (ISBN 0-389-20573-7). B&N Imports.

Bold, Alan, ed. see MacDiarmid, Hugh.

Bold, Alan, ed. see MacDonald, Hugh.

Bold, Benjamin. Famous Problems of Geometry & How to Solve Them. (Illus.). 128p. 1982. pap. 3.00 (ISBN 0-486-24297-8). Dover.

Bold, Claire H. Blindsight & Other Stories. 1985. 8.95 (ISBN 0-8062-2442-8). Carlton.

Bold, Ellyn, ed. see Menorah Medical Center Auxiliary Cookbook Committee.

Bold, H. C., jt. auth. see Cox, E. R.

Bold, Harold C. & Hundell, C. L. The Plant Kingdom. 4th ed. (Foundation of Modern Biology Ser.). (Illus.). 1977. pap. 19.95 (ISBN 0-13-680389-X). P-H.

Bold, Harold C. & Wynne, Michael. Introduction to the Algae. 2nd ed. (Illus.). 848p. 1985. text ed. 44.95 (ISBN 0-13-477746-8). P-H.

Bold, Harold C. & Wynne, Michael J. Introduction to the Algae: Structure & Reproduction. (P-H Biology Ser.). (Illus.). 1978. ref. ed. o.p. 36.95 (ISBN 0-13-477786-7). P-H.

Bold, Harold C., jt. auth. see Alexopoulos, Constantine J.

Bold, Harold C., et al. Morphology of Plants & Fungi. 4th ed. (Illus.). 1980. text ed. 35.95 scp (ISBN 0-06-040848-0, HarpC). Har-Row.

Boldan, Ruth. Sammy Robin Learns to Flý. 1984. 4.95 (ISBN 0-934860-38-6). Adventure Pubns.

Boldea, I., jt. auth. see Nasar, S. A.

Bolden, C. E. Appellate Opinion Preparation: A Selective Bibliography & Survey. 1978. 25.00 (ISBN 0-686-28391-0). Natl Judicial Coll.

Bolden, Theodore E., et al. Dental Hygiene Examination Review, Vol. 1. 4th ed. 1982. 18.50 (ISBN 0-87488-461-6). Med Exam.

Boldereff, Frances M. Hermes to His Son Thoth: Joyce's Use of Giordano Bruno in Finnegans Wake. LC 68-21486. (Illus.). 1968. 10.50 (ISBN 0-9606540-0-3); pap. 4.95 (ISBN 0-9606540-1-1). Classic Nonfic.

Bolding, Amy. Brief Welcome Speeches & Other Helps for Speakers. (Pocket Pulpit Library). 1979. pap. 4.50 (ISBN 0-8010-0856-5). Baker Bk.

--Cheerful Devotions to Give. (Amy Bolding Library). 96p. 1984. pap. 4.50 (ISBN 0-8010-0868-9). Baker Bk.

--Dynamic Fingertip Devotions. (Paperback Program Ser). 1977. pap. 3.95 (ISBN 0-8010-0708-9). Baker Bk.

--Easy Devotions to Give. (Paperback Program Ser.). 96p. (Orig.). 1981. pap. 3.95 (ISBN 0-8010-0794-1). Baker Bk.

--Fingertip Devotions. 1970. 3.95 (ISBN 0-8010-0798-4). Baker Bk.

--I'll Be Glad to Give a Devotion. (Paperback Program Ser). 1978. pap. 3.95 (ISBN 0-8010-0709-7). Baker Bk.

--Inspiring Devotions for Church Groups. 144p. 1985. pap. 5.95 (ISBN 0-8010-0889-1). Baker Bk.

--Installation Services for All Groups. 1984. pap. 4.50 (ISBN 0-8010-0863-8). Baker Bk.

--Please Give a Devotion. 1963. 3.95 (ISBN 0-8010-0819-0). Baker Bk.

--Please Give a Devotion for Active Teens. (Direction Bks). 1974. pap. 3.95 (ISBN 0-8010-0827-1). Baker Bk.

--Please Give a Devotion for All Occasions. 1967. pap. 4.45 (ISBN 0-8010-0519-1). Baker Bk.

--Please Give a Devotion for Church Groups. (Paperback Program Ser.). pap. 3.95 (ISBN 0-8010-0623-6). Baker Bk.

--Please Give a Devotion: For Women's Groups. (Paperback Program Ser.). 108p. 1976. pap. 3.95 (ISBN 0-8010-0583-3). Baker Bk.

--Please Plan a Program. (Paperback Program Ser). (Orig.). 1971. pap. 3.95 (ISBN 0-8010-0527-2). Baker Bk.

--Simple Welcome Speeches & Other Helps. (Pocket Pulpit Library). 1973. pap. 4.50 (ISBN 0-8010-0612-0). Baker Bk.

--Words of Comfort. (Bolding Library). 132p. 1984. pap. 3.95 (ISBN 0-8010-0860-3). Baker Bk.

--Words of Welcome. (Preaching Helps Ser.). (Orig.). 1965. pap. 3.95 (ISBN 0-8010-0550-7). Baker Bk.

Boldman, Bob. Walking with the River. 32p. 1980. 10.00 (ISBN 0-913719-15-3); pap. 3.50 (ISBN 0-913719-14-5). High-Coo Pr.

Boldman, Craig, jt. auth. see Erskine, Jim.

Boldman, Robert. Eating a Melon. 52p. 1982. pap. 3.00 (ISBN 0-941190-00-5). Wind Chimes.

Boldrewood, Rolf. The Miner's Right. (Australian Literary Reprints Ser.). 407p. 1973. 18.00x (ISBN 0-424-06670-X, Pub. by Sydney U Pr); pap. 10.00x (ISBN 0-424-06680-7, Pub. by Sydney U Pr). Intl Spec Bk.

Boldrini, M. Scientific Truth & Statistical Method. 1971. 20.25 (ISBN 0-02-841610-4). Hafner.

Boldt, Christine, ed. AIS New Car Cost Guide, Nineteen Eighty-Six Edition. 1986. 73.00 (ISBN 0-88098-076-1). H M Gousha.

Boldt, Jeanine, jt. ed. see Jones, Michael P.

Boldt, Joe, jt. auth. see Miner, Joshua L.

Boldt, Marjorie A. Acute Coronary Care. LC 83-42587. (Series in Critical Care Nursing). (Illus.). 196p. (Orig.). 1983. pap. text ed. 16.95 (ISBN 0-471-88802-8). Wiley.

Boldt, Menno, et al. The Quest for Justice: Aboriginal Peoples & Aboriginal Rights. 432p. 1985. 45.00x (ISBN 0-8020-2572-2); pap. 17.50 (ISBN 0-8020-6589-9). U of Toronto Pr.

Bolduc, Henry. Create Your Own Destiny Through Self-Hypnosis. Friedman, Robert, ed. 200p. (Orig.). pap. cancelled (ISBN 0-89865-338-X, Unilaw). Donning Co.

Bolduc, Jean B. Mission of the Columbia. 1979. 14.95 (ISBN 0-87770-216-0). Ye Galleon.

Boldy & Heuman. Housing for the Elderly: Planning & Policy Formation in Western Europe & North America. LC 82-10684. 224p. 1982. 27.50 (ISBN 0-312-39349-0). St Martin.

Boldy, Duncan, ed. Operational Research Applied to Health Services. 1981. 32.50x (ISBN 0-312-58682-5). St Martin.

Boldy, Stephen. The Novels of Julio Cortazar. LC 79-41579. (Cambridge Iberian & Latin American Studies). 320p. 1980. 34.50 (ISBN 0-521-23097-7). Cambridge U Pr.

Boldyrev, V. V., et al, eds. Control of the Reactivity of Solids. (Studies in Surface Science & Catalysts: Vol. 2). 226p. 1979. 64.00 (ISBN 0-444-41800-8). Elsevier.

Bole, A. G. & Jones, K. D. Automatic Radar Plotting Aids Manual. LC 81-71212. (Illus.). 150p. 1982. text ed. 16.00x (ISBN 0-87033-285-6). Cornell Maritime.

Bole, John A. The Harmony Society: A Chapter in German American Culture History. LC 72-2981. Repr. of 1904 ed. 14.50 (ISBN 0-404-10744-3). AMS Pr.

--The Harmony Society: A Chapter in German American Culture History. 1976. lib. bdg. 59.95 (ISBN 0-8490-1933-8). Gordon Pr.

Bole, Thorwald. Grow Your Own Vegetables. 1981. pap. 4.95x (ISBN 0-317-06948-9, Regent House). B of A.

--Value of Foods. 1981. pap. 4.95x (ISBN 0-317-06963-2, Regent House). B of A.

Boleach, Jim. Stenciling with Style. LC 84-18714. (Illus.). 192p. 1985. 16.95 (ISBN 0-385-18542-1). Doubleday.

Boleat, Mark. The Building Society Industry. 224p. 1982. text ed. 29.50x (ISBN 0-04-332086-4); pap. text ed. 15.95x (ISBN 0-04-332087-2). Allen Unwin.

--National Housing Finance Systems: A Comparative Study. 490p. 1984. 50.00 (ISBN 0-7099-3249-9, Pub. by Croom Helm Ltd). Longwood Pub Group.

Bolek, Francis, ed. Who's Who in Polish America: A Biographical Directory of Polish-American Leaders & Distinguished Poles Resident in the Americas. LC 75-129390. (American Immigration Collection, Ser. 2). 1970. Repr. of 1943 ed. 31.50 (ISBN 0-405-00545-8). Ayer Co Pubs.

Bolek, Raymond W., jt. auth. see Berkery, Michael J.

Bolek, Raymond W., et al. Touche Ross Government Executives' Guide to Selecting a Small Computer. LC 84-4726. 244p. 1984. 49.95 (ISBN 0-13-925611-3, Busn). P-H.

Bolemon, Jay S. Physics: An Introduction. (Illus.). 692p. 1985. text ed. 24.95 (ISBN 0-13-672221-0). P-H.

Bolen, Dick. Chosen: The Incredible Story of Benji Clark. LC 81-83109. 120p. (Orig.). 1981. pap. 4.95 (ISBN 0-940958-00-7). Mitzi Bks.

Bolen, Eric G. & Rylander, Michael K. Whistling-ducks: Zoogeography, Ecology, Anatomy. (Special Publications of the Museum, Texas Tech University: No. 20). (Illus.). 67p. 1983. pap. 12.00 (ISBN 0-89672-111-6). Tex Tech Pr.

Bolen, Eric G., jt. auth. see Robinson, William L.

Bolen, Frances E. Irony & Self-Knowledge in the Creation of Tragedy. (Salzburg Studies in English Literature, Elizabethan & Renaissance Studies: No. 18). 379p. 1973. pap. text ed. 25.50x (ISBN 0-391-01330-0). Humanities.

Bolen, Jean S. Goddesses in Everywoman: A New Psychology of Women. LC 83-48990. 334p. 1984. 15.34 (ISBN 0-06-250082-1, HarpR). Har-Row.

--Goddesses in Everywoman: A New Psychology of Women. LC 83-48990. 352p. 1985. pap. 7.95 (ISBN 0-06-091291-X, PL 1291, PL). Har-Row.

--The Tao of Psychology: Synchronicity. LC 79-1778. 1979. (HarpR); pap. 6.68 (CN-4024). Har-Row.

Bolen, William. Contemporary Retailing. 2nd ed. 528p. 1982. text ed. 28.95 (ISBN 0-13-170266-1). P-H.

Bolen, William H. Advertising. 2nd ed. LC 83-21695. 649p. 1984. text ed. 33.50 (ISBN 0-471-86348-3). Wiley.

Bolender, John, jt. auth. see Arman, Mike.

Bolenius, Emma M. Teaching Literature in the Grammar Grades & High School. (Educational Ser.). 1915. Repr. 20.00 (ISBN 0-8482-7414-8). Norwood Edns.

--The Teaching of Oral English. (Educational Ser.). 1914. Repr. 20.00 (ISBN 0-8482-7415-6). Norwood Edns.

Boles, Donald E. Bible, Religion & the Public Schools. 3rd ed. 408p. 1965. 8.95x (ISBN 0-8138-0200-8). Iowa St U Pr.

Boles, H. Leo. Eldership of the Churches of Christ. 1978. pap. 1.50 (ISBN 0-89225-179-4). Gospel Advocate.

--The Holy Spirit. 10.95 (ISBN 0-89225-102-6). Gospel Advocate.

Boles, H. Leo see Gospel Advocate.

Boles, Harold W. & Davenport, James A. Introduction to Educational Leadership. rev. ed. LC 82-17516. (Illus.). 518p. 1984. lib. bdg. 32.25 (ISBN 0-8191-2777-9); pap. text ed. 18.75 (ISBN 0-8191-2778-7). U Pr of Amer.

Boles, Harold W., et al. Multidisciplinary Readings in Educational Leadership. LC 75-44465. 442p. 1976. pap. text ed. 12.95x (ISBN 0-8422-0461-X). Irvington.

Boles, John B. Black Southerners, Sixteen Nineteen to Eighteen Sixty-Nine. LC 83-10177. (New Perspectives on the South Ser.). 256p. 1983. 24.00 (ISBN 0-8131-0303-7); pap. 9.00 (ISBN 0-8131-0161-1). U Pr of Ky.

--The Great Revival, Seventeen-Eighty Seven-Eighteen Hundred Five: The Origins of the Southern Evangelical Mind. LC 77-183349. pap. 63.00 (ISBN 0-317-26703-5, 2024358). Bks Demand UMI.

--Great Revival, Seventeen Eighty-Seven to Eighteen Five: The Origins of the Southern Evangelical Mind. LC 77-183349. (Illus.). 260p. 1972. 24.00x (ISBN 0-8131-1260-5). U Pr of Ky.

--Religion in Antebellum Kentucky. LC 76-4434. (Kentucky Bicentennial Bookshelf Ser.). 160p. 1976. 6.95 (ISBN 0-8131-0227-8). U Pr of Ky.

Boles, John B., ed. Dixie Dateline: A Journalistic Portrait of the Contemporary South. LC 83-60523. (New Ser.: No. 1). 182p. 1983. 12.95 (ISBN 0-89263-251-8); pap. 7.95 (ISBN 0-89263-252-6). Rice Univ.

--Maryland Heritage: Five Baltimore Institutions Celebrate the Bicentennial. LC 76-10079. (Illus.). 1976. 15.00 (ISBN 0-938420-10-0); pap. 7.50 (ISBN 0-686-16684-1). Md Hist.

Boles, Kenny. Thirteen Lessons on Ephesians. (Bible Student Study Guides). 1978. pap. 2.95 (ISBN 0-89900-159-9). College Pr Pub.

--Thirteen Lessons on Galatians. (Bible Student Study Guides). 1978. pap. 2.95 (ISBN 0-89900-158-0). College Pr Pub.

--Thirteen Lessons on Philippians, Colossians & Philemon. LC 79-53714. (Bible Student Study Guides). (Orig.). 1979. pap. 2.95 (ISBN 0-89900-163-7). College Pr Pub.

Boles, Kenny, jt. auth. see Boatman, Don E.

Boles, Leo H. Manual for Teachers. pap. 2.25 (ISBN 0-89225-120-4). Gospel Advocate.

Boles, M. Ann. A Sign Language Manual. (Illus.). 472p. 1984. pap. 29.75x spiral (ISBN 0-398-04943-2). C C Thomas.

Boles, Paul D. Night Watch. LC 80-8778. (Illus.). 32p. 1980. 1.00 (ISBN 0-931948-15-0). Peachtree Pubs.

--Storycrafting. LC 84-15182. 243p. 1984. 14.95 (ISBN 0-89879-147-2). Writers Digest.

Bolesch, Herman O., et al. Guten Tag wie geht's: Bilder aus der Bundesrepublik Deutschland. (Illus.). 172p. 1972. 3.00 (ISBN 0-685-56863-6). Intl Film.

Boleslavsky, Richard. Acting: The First Six Lessons. 1949. 9.95 (ISBN 0-87830-000-7). Theatre Arts.

Boleslaw & Mastai, Marie-Louise D. The Stripes & Stars. pap. 8.95 (ISBN 0-88360-001-3, Dist. by Univ. of Texas Pr.). Amon Carter.

Boleslaw, A., jt. auth. see Boczek, B.

Bolet, Adela & Ebinger, Charles, eds. Forecasting U. S. Electricity Demand: Trends & Methodologies. (CSIS Energy Research Ser.). 230p. 1985. pap. 23.50x (ISBN 0-8133-7036-1). Westview.

Bolet, Adela M., et al. Ethanol: National Security Implications. LC 83-23919. (Significant Issues Ser.: Vol. 5, No. 7). 64p. 1983. 6.95 (ISBN 0-89206-050-6). CSI Studies.

Boley, B. A., ed. see International Union of Theoretical & Applied Mechanics Symposium, Glasgow, 1968.

Boley, B. A., jt. ed. see Jaeger, T. A.

Boley, B. A., jt. ed. see Rastoin, J.

Boley, Bruno A. Crossfire in Professional Education. LC 76-47033. 1977. 16.50 (ISBN 0-08-021429-0). Pergamon.

Boley, Bruno A. & Weiner, Jerome H. Theory of Thermal Stresses. LC 84-19404. 602p. 1985. Repr. of 1960 ed. lib. bdg. write for info. (ISBN 0-89874-806-2). Krieger.

Boley, G. E. Liberia: The Rise & Fall of the First Republic. LC 84-40340. 225p. 1985. 27.50 (ISBN 0-312-48352-X). St Martin.

Boley, Jack. A Guide to Effective Industrial Safety. LC 76-23915. 120p. 1977. 12.95x (ISBN 0-87201-798-2). Gulf Pub.

Bolgan, Anne C. What the Thunder Really Said: A Retrospective Essay on the Making of "The Waste Land". 204p. 1973. 17.50x (ISBN 0-7735-0165-7). McGill-Queens U Pr.

Bolgar, R. R. The Classical Heritage & Its Beneficiaries. LC 54-13284. 1977. 80.00 (ISBN 0-521-04277-1); pap. 22.95 (ISBN 0-521-09812-2). Cambridge U Pr.

Bolgar, R. R., ed. Classical Influences on European Culture, 1500-1700 A. D. (Illus.). 300p. 1976. 69.50 (ISBN 0-521-20840-8). Cambridge U Pr.

--Classical Influences on European Culture, 500-1500 A. D. LC 77-113599. (Illus.). 1971. 62.50 (ISBN 0-521-07842-3). Cambridge U Pr.

--Classical Influences on Western Thought, 1650-1870 A. D. LC 77-91078. 1979. 69.50 (ISBN 0-521-21964-7). Cambridge U Pr.

Bolge, Richard, jt. auth. see Gerlach, Joel.

Bolger, A. W., ed. Counselling in Britain. (Illus.). 1982. pap. 19.95 (ISBN 0-7134-3702-2, Pub. by Batsford England). David & Charles.

Bolger, Dermot. Night Shift. 144p. 1985. pap. 5.95 (ISBN 0-86322-067-3, Pub. by Brandon Bks). Longwood Pub Group.

Bolger, Francis W., et al. Spirit of Place: Lucy Maud Montgomery & Prince Edward Island. (Illus.). 1983. 14.95 (ISBN 0-19-540389-4). Oxford U Pr.

Bolger, Philip C. One Hundred Small-Boat Rigs. LC 84-47753. (Illus.). 272p. (Orig.). 1984. pap. 17.95 (ISBN 0-87742-182-X, H450). Intl Marine.

--Thirty-Odd Boats. LC 82-80403. (Illus.). 224p. 1982. 22.50 (ISBN 0-87742-152-8). Intl Marine.

Bolger, Philip G. Bolger Boats: Combining Small Boats & the Folding Schooner. LC 82-84548. (Illus.). 400p. 1983. Intl Marine.

Bolger, Philip H., ed. Space Rescue & Safety 1974. (Science & Technology Ser.: Vol. 37). (Illus.). 294p. 1975. lib. bdg. 25.00x (ISBN 0-87703-073-1, Pub. by Am Astronaut). Univelt Inc.

--Space Rescue & Safety, 1975. New ed. (Science & Technology Ser: Vol. 41). (Illus.). 1976. lib. bdg. 25.00x (ISBN 0-87703-077-4, Pub. by Am Astronaut). Univelt Inc.

Bolger, Philip H., ed. see Goddard Memorial Symposium, Twelfth.

Bolger, Stephen G. The Irish Character in American Fiction, 1830-1860. LC 76-6323. (Irish Americans Ser.). 1976. 19.00 (ISBN 0-405-09320-9). Ayer Co Pubs.

Bolger, Steve, et al, eds. Towards Socialist Welfare Work: Working in the State. (Critical Texts in Social Work & the Welfare State). 176p. 1980. text ed. 25.50x (ISBN 0-333-28905-6); pap. text ed. 10.50x (ISBN 0-333-28906-4). Humanities.

Bolger, William F., intro. by. All about Letters. Rev. ed. LC 82-600601. (Illus.). 64p. (gr. 9-12). 1982. pap. 2.50x (ISBN 0-8141-0113-5, 01135). USPS.

--P. S. Write Soon! All about Letters. LC 82-600641. (Illus.). 64p. (Orig.). (gr. 4-8). 1982. pap. 2.50x (ISBN 0-8141-3796-2, 37962). USPS.

Bolich, Gregory G. Authority & the Church. LC 81-40935. 228p. 1982. lib. bdg. 26.00 (ISBN 0-8191-2322-6); pap. text ed. 12.25 (ISBN 0-8191-2323-4). U Pr of Amer.

--Karl Barth & Evangelicalism. (Orig.). 1979. pap. 6.95 (ISBN 0-87784-615-4). Inter-Varsity.

Bolick, James H. Sermon Outlines from the Word. (Sermon Outline Ser.). (Orig.). 1980. pap. 1.95 (ISBN 0-8010-0528-0). Baker Bk.

Boliek, Caroline B. Celebrity Witness. LC 84-71119. 184p. 1984. pap. 4.95 (ISBN 0-88270-572-5). Bridge Pub.

Bolin, B. Climatic Changes & Their Effects on the Biosphere. 49p. (4th IMO Lecture). 1980. pap. 30.00 (ISBN 92-63-10542-1, W481, WMO). Unipub.

Bolin, B. & Cook, R. B., eds. The Major Biogeochemical Cycles & Their Interactions. (SCOPR Ser. (Scientific Committee on Problems of the Environment): Report 21). 532p. 1983. 79.95 (ISBN 0-471-10522-8, 1-409, Pub. by Wiley-Interscience). Wiley.

Bolin, B., et al, eds. The Global Carbon Cycle. LC 78-16261. (SCOPE Ser. (Scientific Committee on Problems of the Environment): Report 13). 491p. 1979. pap. 69.95 (ISBN 0-471-99710-2, Pub. by Wiley-Interscience). Wiley.

Bolin, Bert. The Global Atmospheric Research Programme: A Co-Operative Effort to Explore the Weather Climate of Our Planet. 28p. (Eng. & Fr., WMO-ICSU Publication). 1971. pap. 2.00 (W351, WMO). Unipub.

Bolin, Bert, ed. The Atmosphere & the Sea in Motion. LC 59-14858. (Illus.). 512p. 1960. 10.00x (ISBN 0-87470-000-0). Rockefeller.

--Carbon Cycle Modelling-Scope Report 16. (SCOPE Ser. (Scientific Committe on Problems of the Environment): Vol. 16). 390p. 1981. 57.95 (ISBN 0-471-10051-X, Pub. by Wiley-Interscience). Wiley.

Bolin, Daniel L. Ohio Valley History. 1976. 17.50 (ISBN 0-686-20887-0). Polyanthos.

Bolin, Robert B., et al. Advances in Blood Substitute Research. LC 83-918. (Progress in Clinical & Biological Research Ser.: Vol. 122). 500p. 1983. 56.00 (ISBN 0-8451-0122-6). A R Liss.

Bolin, T. D., jt. auth. see Davis, A. E.

Boling, Joseph E., jt. auth. see Frederick, C. Schwan.

Boling, Katharine. A Piece of the Fox's Hide. LC 72-86903. 1972. 8.50 (ISBN 0-87844-013-5). Sandlapper Pub Co.

--A Piece of the Fox's Hide. LC 72-86903. 376p. pap. 7.50 (ISBN 0-87844-054-2). Sandlapper Pub Co.

Boling, Robert, jt. ed. see Campbell, Edward F., Jr.

Boling, Robert G. & Wright, Ernest. Joshua, Vol. 6. LC 79-6583. (Anchor Bible Ser.). (Illus.). 432p. 1982. 18.00 (ISBN 0-385-00034-0). Doubleday.

Boling, Robert G., tr. & intro. by. Judges, Vol. 6A. LC 72-96229. (Anchor Bible Ser). (Illus.). 360p. 1975. 16.00 (ISBN 0-385-01029-X). Doubleday.

Boling, T. Edwin, et al. Nursing Home Management: A Humanistic Approach. (Illus.). 376p. 1983. 30.75x (ISBN 0-398-04823-1). C C Thomas.

Bolingbroke. Lord Bolingbroke: Historical Writings. Kramnick, Isaac & Clive, John, eds. LC 72-75608. (Classics of British Historical Literature Ser). liv, 344p. 1974. pap. 3.45x (ISBN 0-226-06346-1, P491, Phoen). U of Chicago Pr.

--Political Writings of Viscount Bolingbroke. Kramnick, Isaac, ed. LC 78-91459. (Crofts Classics Ser.). 1970. pap. text ed. 1.25x (ISBN 0-88295-015-0). Harlan Davidson.

Bolingbroke, Henry S. Works of Lord Bolingbroke, 4 Vols. LC 67-16351. Repr. of 1844 ed. 175.00x (ISBN 0-678-05028-7). Kelley.

Bolingbroke, Henry Viscount. The Philosophical Works, 5 vols. Wellek, Rene, ed. LC 75-11198. (British Philosophers & Theologians of the 17th & 18th Centuries: Vol. 5). 1976. Repr. of 1777 ed Set. lib. bdg. 231.00 (ISBN 0-8240-1754-4); lib. bdg. 254.00. Garland Pub.

Bolingbroke, Lord. Works, 4 vols. 1967. Repr. of 1844 ed. Set. 185.00x (ISBN 0-7146-1011-9, F Cass Co). Biblio Dist.

Bolinger, Dwight. Degree Words. (Janua Linguarum, Ser. Major: No. 53). 1972. text ed. 35.20x (ISBN 0-686-22528-7). Mouton.

--Intonation & Its Parts: Melody in Spoken English. LC 83-40698. 400p. 1985. 38.50x (ISBN 0-8047-1241-7). Stanford U Pr.

--Language: The Loaded Weapon. (Longman Linguistics Library). (Illus.). 240p. 1980. pap. text ed. 11.95x (ISBN 0-582-29108-9). Longman.

--That's That. (Janua Linguarum, Ser. Minor: No. 155). 79p. (Orig.). 1972. pap. text ed. 8.80x (ISBN 90-2792-319-1). Mouton.

Bolinger, Dwight & Sears, Donald A. Aspects of Language. 3rd ed. 352p. 1981. pap. text ed. 14.95 (ISBN 0-15-503872-9, HC). HarbraceJ.

Bolinger, Dwight L. Interrogative Structures of American English (the Direct Question) (Publications of the American Dialect Society: No. 28). 184p. 1957. pap. 9.65 (ISBN 0-8173-0628-5). U of Ala Pr.

Bolinger, Judith & English, Jane. Water Child. 64p. 1985. Repr. of 1980 ed. lib. bdg. 19.95x (ISBN 0-89370-592-6). Borgo Pr.

--Waterchild. LC 80-80650. (Orig.). 1980. pap. 6.95 (ISBN 0-89793-023-1). Hunter Hse.

Bolinger, Robert E. Endocrinology: New Directions in Therapy. 2nd ed. 1982. 42.50 (ISBN 0-87488-678-3). Med Exam.

Bolinger, Willeta R. You & Your World. (gr. 7-12,RL 2.3). 1964. pap. 5.00 (ISBN 0-8224-7650-9); tchrs' manual free (ISBN 0-8224-7651-7). Pitman Learning.

Bolino, August C. Ellis Island Source Book. (Illus.). 224p. 1983. 15.00 (ISBN 0-89962-331-X). Todd & Honeywell.

Bolis, L., et al. Comparative Physiology of Sensory Systems. LC 83-14457. 450p. 1984. 99.50 (ISBN 0-521-25002-1). Cambridge U Pr.

Bolis, L., et al, eds. Comparative Physiology: Locomotion, Respiration, Transport & Blood: Proceedings of the International Congress Held in Acquasparta, 1972. 1973. 42.75 (ISBN 0-444-10556-5); pap. 25.75 (ISBN 0-686-44058-7). Elsevier.

--Toxins, Drugs & Pollutants in Marine Animals. (Proceedings in Life Sciences Ser.). (Illus.). vi, 200p. 1984. 34.00 (ISBN 0-387-13643-6). Springer-Verlag.

Bolis, Lian, jt. ed. see Karnovsky, Manfred L.

Bolis, Liana, jt. ed. see Nistico, Giuseppe.

Bolis, Liana, et al, eds. Membranes & Disease. LC 75-30235. 424p. 1976. 57.00 (ISBN 0-89004-082-6). Raven.

--Peptide Hormones, Biomembranes & Cell Growth. 304p. 1985. 49.50x (ISBN 0-306-41816-9, Plenum Pr). Plenum Pub.

Bolis, Liana C., et al. Information & Energy Transduction in Biological Membranes. LC 84-12545. (Progress in Clinical & Biological Research Ser.: Vol. 164). 472p. 1984. 94.00 (ISBN 0-8451-5014-6). A R Liss.

Bolitho, A. R. & Sandler, P. L. Learn English for Science. (English As a Second Language Bk.). 108p. 1977. pap. text ed. 4.95x student bk. (ISBN 0-582-55247-8); pap. text ed. 2.95x tchr's bk. (ISBN 0-582-55482-9). Longman.

--Study English for Science. (English As a Second Language Bk.). 104p. 1980. pap. text ed. 4.95x (ISBN 0-582-55248-6); tchr's ed. 2.95x (ISBN 0-582-74821-6). Longman.

Bolitho, H. Meiji Japan. LC 76-54130. (Cambridge Introduction to the History of Mankind Ser.). (Illus.). 1977. 4.50 (ISBN 0-521-20922-6). Cambridge U Pr.

Bolitho, Harold. Meiji Japan. LC 80-7448. (Cambridge Topic Bks.). (Illus.). (gr. 5-10). 1980. PLB 7.95 (ISBN 0-8225-1219-X). Lerner Pubns.

Bolitho, Harold, ed. A Northern Prospect: Australian Papers on Japan. Rix, Alan. 200p. 1981. pap. text ed. 6.95 (ISBN 0-9594391-0-2, 0099, Pub. by ANUP Australia). Australia N U P.

Bolitho, Hector. Beside Galilee. 206p. 1981. Repr. of 1933 ed. lib. bdg. 25.00 (ISBN 0-89987-076-7). Darby Bks.

--Jinnah: Creator of Pakistan. LC 81-13249. (Illus.). x, 244p. 1982. Repr. of 1964 ed. lib. bdg. 27.50x (ISBN 0-313-23052-8, BOJI). Greenwood.

--Older People: Shaw, Lawrence, Maurice Baring. 1973. Repr. of 1935 ed. 25.00 (ISBN 0-8274-1466-8). R West.

--Twelve Jews. 1934. Repr. 25.00 (ISBN 0-8274-3655-6). R West.

Bolitho, Hector & Mulgan, John. Emigrants. facsimile ed. LC 70-108635. (Essay Index Reprint Ser.). 1939. 18.00 (ISBN 0-8369-1547-X). Ayer Co Pubs.

--The Emigrants: Early Travellers to the Antipodes. (Essay Index Reprint Ser.). 223p. 1982. Repr. of 1939 ed. lib. bdg. 15.00 (ISBN 0-686-79687-X). Irvington.

Bolitho, Hector, ed. Twelve Jews. facs. ed. LC 67-23179. (Essay Index Reprint Ser). 1934. 20.00 (ISBN 0-8369-0223-8). Ayer Co Pubs.

Bolitho, Hector, ed. see Victoria, Queen.

Bolitho, Rod & Tomlinson, Brian. Discover English. (Orig.). 1980. pap. text ed. 8.95x (ISBN 0-435-28991-8). Heinemann Ed.

Bolitho, William. Murder for Profit. LC 82-61435. 332p. 1982. 14.95 (ISBN 0-910395-02-0); pap. 7.95 (ISBN 0-910395-03-9). Marlboro Pr.

Bolivar, Josefa V., ed. see Bolivar, Jossy Ann.

Bolivar, Jossy Ann. With Love, from Jo. Bolivar, Josefa V., ed. LC 80-13999. (Illus.). 120p. (Orig.). 1980. pap. 5.95 (ISBN 0-914598-01-5). Padre Prods.

Boliver, David E. Basic Mathematical Skills for College Students. 224p. 1981. pap. text ed. 11.95 (ISBN 0-8403-2470-7). Kendall-Hunt.

Bolker, Ethan D. Using Algebra. 1983. text ed. 25.95 (ISBN 0-316-10114-1). Little.

Bolker, Henry. Natural & Synthetic Polymers: An Introduction. 712p. 1974. 95.00 (ISBN 0-8247-1060-6). Dekker.

Bolkestein, A. M. Problems in the Description of Modal Verbs: An Investigation of Latin. (Studies in Greek & Latin Linguistics). 180p. 1980. pap. text ed. 21.50x (ISBN 90-232-1764-0). Humanities.

Bolkestein, A. M., et al. Predication & Expression of Functional Grammar. LC 81-68966. 1982. 46.00 (ISBN 0-12-111350-7). Acad Pr.

Bolkestein, Hendrik. Wonnltatigkeit und Armenpflege Im Vorchristlichen Altertum. Vlastos, Gregory, ed. LC 78-15858. (Morals & Law in Ancient Greece Ser.). 1979. Repr. of 1939 ed. lib. bdg. 37.00x (ISBN 0-405-11531-8). Ayer Co Pubs.

Bolkestein, Hendrik, jt. auth. see Bolkestein, Johanna C.

Bolkestein, Johanna C. & Bolkestein, Hendrik. Hosios en Eusebes & Thecphrasts' Charakter der Deisidaimonia ais Religionsgeschichtliche, 2 vols. in one. Vlastos, Gregory, ed. LC 78-14605. (Morals & Law in Ancient Greece Ser.). (Dutch, Gr. Fr. & Ger.). 1979. Repr. of 1936 ed. lib. bdg. 25.50x (ISBN 0-405-11575-X). Ayer Co Pubs.

Bolkhovitinov, Nikolai. The Beginnings of Russian-American Relations, 1775-1815. Levin, Elena, tr. 576p. 1976. 37.50x (ISBN 0-674-06455-0). Harvard U Pr.

--Russia & the American Revolution. Smith, C. Jay, tr. from Russian. LC 74-42220. 277p. 1976. 29.70 (ISBN 0-910512-20-5). Diplomatic IN.

Bolkosky, Sidney, jt. auth. see Lipson, Greta.

Bolkstein, F. Modern Liberalism: Conversations with Liberal Politicians. 292p. 1982. 19.25 (ISBN 0-444-86484-9, I-345-82, North-Holland). Elsevier.

Boll. Erzahlungen. (Easy Reader, D). pap. 4.25 (ISBN 0-88436-108-X, 45275). EMC.

Boll, Carl R. Executive Jobs Unlimited: Updated Edition. 1980. 12.95 (ISBN 0-02-512790-X). Macmillan.

Boll, Eleanor, jt. auth. see Bossard, James.

Boll, Eleanor S., jt. auth. see Bossard, James H.

Boll, Eleanor S., jt. ed. see Bossard, James H.

Boll, Heinrich. Adam & the Train. Vennewitz, Leila, tr. from Ger. Bd. with The Train. LC 71-127920. 288p. 1974. pap. 4.95 (ISBN 0-07-006409-1). McGraw.

--And Never Said a Word. Vennewitz, Leila, tr. LC 77-18123. 1978. 8.95 (ISBN 0-07-006428-8). McGraw.

--And Never Said a Word. Vennewitz, Leila, tr. 1978. pap. 5.95 (ISBN 0-07-006421-0). McGraw.

--Billiards at Half-Past Nine. 1975. pap. 3.95 (ISBN 0-380-00280-9, 62471-0, Bard). Avon.

--Billiards at Half-Past Nine. LC 62-15141. 288p. 1973. pap. 5.95 (ISBN 0-07-006401-6). McGraw.

--Billiards at Half-Past Nine. 1983. 12.50 (ISBN 0-8446-6056-6). Peter Smith.

--Children Are Civilians Too. Vennewitz, Leila, tr. LC 79-86086. 1977. pap. 5.95 (ISBN 0-07-006430-X). McGraw.

--The Clown. 1975. pap. 4.95 (ISBN 0-380-00333-3, 69534, Bard). Avon.

--Clown. Vennewitz, Leila, tr. from Ger. LC 64-7935. 1971. pap. 5.95 (ISBN 0-07-006420-2). McGraw.

--The Collected Stories of Heinrich Boll. Janeway, Carol B., ed. Vennewitz, Leila, tr. LC 85-40392. 1986. 25.00 (ISBN 0-394-51405-X). Knopf.

--Eighteen Stories. Vennewitz, Leila, tr. from Ger. 1966. pap. 5.95 (ISBN 0-07-006416-4). McGraw.

--Group Portrait with Lady. 1974. pap. 4.50 (ISBN 0-380-00020-2, 60106-0, Bard). Avon.

--Group Portrait with Lady. Vennewitz, Leila, tr. from Ger. LC 72-8835. 320p. 1973. 8.95 (ISBN 0-07-006423-7). McGraw.

--Irish Journal. Vennewitz, Leila, tr. from Ger. 1967. pap. 4.95 (ISBN 0-07-006415-6). McGraw.

--The Lost Honor of Katharina Blum. Vennewitz, Leila, tr. from Ger. LC 74-28138. (McGraw-Hill Paperbacks). 1976. pap. 5.95 (ISBN 0-07-006429-6). McGraw.

--Missing Persons. Vennewitz, Leila, tr. from German. LC 77-9351. 1977. 9.95 (ISBN 0-07-006424-5). McGraw.

--The Safety Net. LC 81-47513. 1982. 13.95 (ISBN 0-394-51404-1). Knopf.

--The Safety Net. Vennewitz, Leila, tr. from Ger. 1983. pap. 4.95 (ISBN 0-14-006468-0). Penguin.

--A Soldier's Legacy. Vennewitz, Lelia, tr. LC 84-40724. 144p. 1985. 12.95 (ISBN 0-394-53603-7). Knopf.

--What's to Become of the Boy? Vennewitz, Leila, tr. LC 83-49087. 96p. 1984. 11.95 (ISBN 0-394-53016-0). Knopf.

--What's to Become of the Boy. (Fiction Ser.). 96p. 1985. pap. 4.95 (ISBN 0-317-19375-9). Penguin.

Boll, Heinrich, et al. New Writing & Writers, No. 15. 1980. pap. 6.00 (ISBN 0-7145-3561-3); 12.95 (ISBN 0-7145-3554-0). Riverrun NY.

Boll, John J. Introduction to Cataloging, Vol. 2: Entry Headings with Emphasis on Cataloging Process & Personal Names. new ed. (Library Education Ser). (Illus.). 448p. 1974. 35.95 (ISBN 0-07-006412-1). McGraw.

Boll, John J., ed. Reader Services in Libraries: A Day in Honor of Margaret E. Monroe. 64p. 1982. pap. 4.00 (ISBN 0-936442-09-3). U Wis Lib Sch.

Boll, Lawrence L. Relation of Diu Krone to La Mule Sanz Frain. LC 77-140018. (Catholic University Studies in German Ser.: No. 2). Repr. of 1929 ed. 18.00 (ISBN 0-404-50222-9). AMS Pr.

Boll, Michael M. Cold War in the Balkans: American Foreign Policy & the Emergence of Communist Bulgaria, 1943-1947. LC 84-7438. 264p. 1984. 25.00x (ISBN 0-8131-1527-2). U Pr of KY.

Boll, R. Soft Magnetic Materials. 348p. 1979. 49.95 (ISBN 0-471-25600-5, Pub. by Wiley Heyden). Wiley.

Boll, Richard Henry. Tables of Light-Scattering Functions: Relative Indices of Less Than Unity & Infinity. LC 57-7175. pap. 93.00 (ISBN 0-317-08493-3, 2011234). Bks Demand UMI.

Boll, Theophilus E. M. Miss May Sinclair: A Biographical & Critical Introduction. LC 72-414. 332p. 1973. 29.50 (ISBN 0-8386-1156-7). Fairleigh Dickinson.

Boll, Thomas J., jt. ed. see Filskov, Susan B.

Boll, Tom. Teach Me Tonight. LC 83-50560. 58p. (Orig.). 1984. pap. 4.95 (ISBN 0-912393-01-7). Mercury Pr.

Bolla, M., ed. Endometrial Cancers. (Illus.). x, 190p. 1986. 64.00 (ISBN 3-8055-4211-9). S Karger.

Bollabas, Bela. Extreme Graph Theory. (L. M. S. Monogrphs). 1978. 65.00 (ISBN 0-12-111750-2). Acad Pr.

Bollabas, Bela, ed. Graph Theory & Combinatorics. 1984. 50.00 (ISBN 0-12-111760-X). Acad Pr.

Bollack, C. & Cinqualbre, J., eds. Recent Advances in Renal Cell Carcinoma. (Progress in Surgery: Vol. 17). (Illus.). viii, 160p. 1983. bound 55.00 (ISBN 3-8055-3621-6). S Karger.

Bollack, C. & Clavert, A., eds. Seminal Vesicles & Fertility. (Progress in Reproductive Biology & Medicine: Vol. 12). (Illus.). x, 182p. 1984. 63.50 (ISBN 3-8055-3907-X). S Karger.

Bollack, C. G. & Clavert, A., eds. Epididymis & Fertility: Biology & Pathology. (Progress in Reproductive Biology: Vol. 8). (Illus.). x, 174p. 1981. 50.75 (ISBN 3-8055-2157-X). S Karger.

Bollan, William. Coloniae Anglicanae Illustratae: Or, the Acquest of the Dominion.., Pt. 1. LC 75-31082. Repr. of 1762 ed. 14.00 (ISBN 0-404-13501-3). AMS Pr.

--Continued Corruption, Standing Armies, & Popular Discontents Considered. LC 75-31083. Repr. of 1768 ed. 21.00 (ISBN 0-404-13502-1). AMS Pr.

--The Freedom of Speech & Writing upon Public Affairs Considered. LC 75-107346. (Civil Liberties in American History Ser). 1970. Repr. of 1766 ed. lib. bdg. 25.00 (ISBN 0-306-71878-2). Da Capo.

--The Importance & Advantage of Cape Breton. Repr. of 1698 ed. 14.00 (ISBN 0-384-04965-6). Johnson Repr.

--A Succint View of the Origin of Our Colonies. LC 75-31084. 1976. Repr. of 1766 ed. 21.00 (ISBN 0-404-13503-X). AMS Pr.

Bolland, John, et al. Hampstead Psychoanalytic Index: A Study of the Psychoanalytic Case Material of a Two-Year-Old Boy. LC 65-23575. (Psychoanalytic Study of the Child Monographs: No. 1). 205p. 1966. text ed. 22.50 (ISBN 0-8236-2280-0). Intl Univs Pr.

Bolland, Kathleen A. Vocational Education Outcomes: An Evaluative Bibliography of Empirical Studies. 127p. 1979. 7.75 (ISBN 0-318-15595-8, BB 49). Natl Ctr Res Voc Ed.

Bolland, O. Nigel. Belize: A New Nation in Central America. (Profiles - Nations of Contemporary Latin America Ser.). 125p. 1986. 26.50x (ISBN 0-8133-0005-3). Westview.

--The Formation of a Colonial Society: Belize, from Conquest to Crown Colony. LC 76-47377. (Studies in Atlantic History & Culture). (Illus.). 256p. 1977. 24.50x (ISBN 0-8018-1887-7). Johns Hopkins.

Bollard, Alan. Agricultural Project Design & Evaluation in an Island Community. (Development Studies Centre - Monograph: No. 15). (Illus., Orig.). 1980. pap. 8.00 (ISBN 0-7081-1071-1, 0537, Pub. by ANUP Australia). Australia N U P.

--Just for Starters: A Handbook of Small-Scale Business Opportunities. (Illus.). 197p. 24.50 (ISBN 0-903031-94-9, Pub. by Intermediate Tech England). Intermediate Tech.

--Small Beginnings: New Roles for British Businesses. (Illus.). 335p. 1983. 28.50x (ISBN 0-903031-91-4, Pub. by Intermediate Tech England). Intermediate Tech.

Bolle, H. J., ed. Radiation in the Atmosphere: Proceedings. LC 77-5205. (Illus.). 1977. lib. bdg. 62.00 (ISBN 0-89500-002-4). Sci Pr.

--Remote Sounding of the Atmosphere from Space: Proceedings of the Committee on Space Research, 21st Plenary Meeting, Innsbruck, Austria, 1978. (Illus.). 1979. 69.00 (ISBN 0-08-023419-4). Pergamon.

Bolle, Kees W. Freedom of Man in Myth. LC 68-8564. 1968. 5.00 (ISBN 0-8265-1125-2). Vanderbilt U Pr.

--The Freedom of Man in Myth. LC 68-8564. pap. 53.30 (ISBN 0-317-27618-2, 2025066). Bks Demand UMI.

Bolle, Kees W., ed. Mythology Series, 39 vols. (Illus.). 1978. Set. lib. bdg. 1807.50x (ISBN 0-405-10529-0); Set. lib. bdg. 669.00 (ISBN 0-405-18984-2). Ayer Co Pubs.

--Reading in Mythology: An Original Anthology. LC 77-139. (Mythology Ser.). (Ger., Fr.). 1978. lib. bdg. 14.00x (ISBN 0-405-10573-8). Ayer Co Pubs.

--Studies of A. J. Wensinck: An Original Arno Press Anthology. LC 77-82275. (Mythology Ser.). 1978. lib. bdg. 17.00x (ISBN 0-405-10567-3). Ayer Co Pubs.

Bolle, Kees W., ed. see Creuzer, Georg F.

Bolle, Kees W., ed. see David-Neel, Alexandra & Yongden, Lama.

Bolle, Kees W., ed. see De Gubernatis, Angelo.

Bolle, Kees W., ed. see De Rebecque, Constant & Benjamin, Henri.

Bolle, Kees W., ed. see De Vries, Jan.

Bolle, Kees W., ed. see Dumezil, Georges.

Bolle, Kees W., ed. see Ehrenreich, Paul.

Bolle, Kees W., ed. see Gorres, Joseph.

Bolle, Kees W., ed. see Jensen, Adolf E.

Bolle, Kees W., jt. ed. see Jensen, Adolf E.

Bolle, Kees W., ed. see Krappe, Alexandre H.

Bolle, Kees W., ed. see Langer, Fritz.

Bolle, Kees W., ed. see Leenhardt, Maurice.

Bolle, Kees W., ed. see Lessmann, Heinrich.

Bolle, Kees W., ed. see Liebert, Arthur.

Bolle, Kees W., ed. see Lipps, Gottlob F.

Bolle, Kees W., ed. see Mannhardt, Wilhelm.

Bolle, Kees W., ed. see Meyer, Richard M.

Bolle, Kees W., ed. see Muller, Friedrich M.

Bolle, Kees W., ed. see Muller, Karl O.

Bolle, Kees W., ed. see Mus, Paul.

Bolle, Kees W., ed. see Nestle, Wilhelm.

Bolle, Kees W., ed. see Oppert, Gustav.

Bolle, Kees W., ed. see Otto, Walter F.

Bolle, Kees W., jt. ed. see Pettazzoni, Raffaele.

Bolle, Kees W., ed. see Pettazzoni, Rattaele.

Bolle, Kees W., ed. see Pigott, Grenville.

Bolle, Kees W., ed. see Preller, Ludwig.

Bolle, Kees W., ed. see Siecke, Ernst.

Bolle, Kees W., ed. see Vignoli, Tito.

Bolle, Kees W., ed. see Wirz, Paul.

Bolle, Kees W., ed. see Zeitlin, Ida.

Bolle, Kees W., ed. see Ziegler, Leopold.

Bolle, Kees W., tr. from Sanskrit. The Bhagavadgita: A New Translation. LC 78-59451. 1979. 21.95 (ISBN 0-520-03741-3). U of Cal Pr.

Bolle, Kees W., tr. & intro. by see De Vries, Jan.

Bolle, M., et al. Working Time in West Germany. 200p. 1982. 62.00x (ISBN 0-905492-34-X, Pub. by Anglo-German Found England). State Mutual Bk.

Bolleme, Genevieve. Les Almanachs Populaires aux XVIIe et XVIIIe Siecles: Essai d'Histoire Sociale. (Livre et Societes: No. 3). 1969. pap. 11.20x (ISBN 90-2796-265-0). Mouton.

Bollen, Constance & Blessing, Marlene. One Potato, Two Potato: A Cookbook. 1983. 7.95 (ISBN 0-914718-82-7). Pacific Search.

Bollen, J. D. Protestantism & Social Reform in New South Wales 1890-1910. (Illus.). 200p. 1972. 20.00x (ISBN 0-522-84023-X, Pub. by Melbourne U Pr). Intl Spec Bk.

Bollen, Peter D. A Handbook of Great Labor Quotations. LC 83-90292. (Illus.). 128p. (Orig.). 1983. pap. 5.95 (ISBN 0-9611350-0-X). Hillside Bks.

--Nuclear Voices: A Book of Quotations & Perspectives. LC 85-60616. (Illus.). 192p. (Orig.). 1985. pap. 6.95x (ISBN 0-9611350-1-8). Hillside Bks.

Bollenback, G. N., jt. auth. see Hoynak, P. X.

Bollens, John C. Appointed Executive Local Government: The California Experience. LC 52-12988. (Illus.). xi, 233p. Repr. of 1952 ed. lib. bdg. 15.00x (ISBN 0-8371-8068-6, BOAE). Greenwood.

--How to be a Successful Student. LC 82-60386. 125p. 1982. pap. 6.95 (ISBN 0-913530-30-1). Palisades Pub.

--Special District Governments in the United States. LC 77-26250. 1978. Repr. of 1957 ed. lib. bdg. 22.00x (ISBN 0-313-20065-3, BOSD). Greenwood.

Bollens, John C. & Geyer, Grant B. Yorty: Politics of a Constant Candidate. LC 72-95289. 250p. 1973. 6.95 (ISBN 0-913530-00-X). Palisades Pub.

Bollens, John C. & Schmandt, Henry J. The Metropolis: Its People, Politics & Economic Life. 4th ed. 461p. 1981. text ed. 19.50 scp (ISBN 0-06-040794-8, HarpC). Har-Row.

--Political Corruption: Power, Money, & Sex. LC 79-88114. 1979. 9.95 (ISBN 0-913530-17-4). Palisades Pub.

Bollens, John C. & Williams, G. Robert. Jerry Brown: In a Plain Brown Wrapper. LC 78-53641. (Illus.). 1978. 9.95 (ISBN 0-913530-12-3). Palisades Pub.

Bollens, John C., jt. auth. see Berman, David R.

Boller, Francois & Frank, Ellen. Sexual Dysfunction in Neurological Disorders: Diagnosis, Management & Rehabilitation. 108p. 1982. text ed. 16.50 (ISBN 0-89004-500-3). Raven.

Boller, Francois & Dennis, Maureen, eds. Auditory Comprehension: Clinical & Experimental Studies with the Token Test. LC 79-22510. 1979. 32.00 (ISBN 0-12-111650-6). Acad Pr.

Boller, Henry A. Among the Indians: Four Years on the Upper Missouri, 1858-1862. Quaife, Milo M., ed. LC 76-100810. (Illus.). xvi, 370p. 1972. pap. 6.95 (ISBN 0-8032-5714-7, BB 514, Bison). U of Nebr Pr.

Boller, Paul F. & Story, Ronald. A More Perfect Union: Documents in U. S. History. LC 83-81880. 250p. 1984. Vol. 1, to 1877. pap. text ed. 13.50 (ISBN 0-395-34936-2); Vol. 2, Since 1865. pap. text ed. 13.50 (ISBN 0-395-34357-7). HM.

Boller, Paul F., Jr. American Thought in Transition: The Impact of Evolutionary Naturalism, 1865-1900. LC 80-6210. 285p. 1981. lib. bdg. 24.75 (ISBN 0-8191-1550-9); pap. text ed. 12.00 (ISBN 0-8191-1551-7). U Pr of Amer.

--Freedom & Fate in American Thought: From Edwards to Dewey. LC 78-5813. (Bicentennial Series in American Studies: No. 7). 1978. 17.50 (ISBN 0-87074-169-1). SMU Press.

--George Washington & Religion. LC 63-9755. 1963. 12.95 (ISBN 0-87074-021-0). SMU Press.

--Presidential Anecdotes. LC 80-27092. 1981. 17.95 (ISBN 0-19-502915-1). Oxford U Pr.

--Presidential Anecdotes. 1982. pap. 6.95 (ISBN 0-14-006349-8). Penguin.

--Presidential Campaigns. LC 83-25047. 1984. 16.95 (ISBN 0-19-503420-1). Oxford U pr.

--Presidential Campaigns. 432p. 1985. pap. 6.95 (ISBN 0-19-503722-7). Oxford U Pr.

--Quotemanship: The Use & Abuse of Quotations for Polemical & Other Purposes. LC 66-29652. 1967. 17.50 (ISBN 0-87074-022-9). SMU Press.

Bolles, Albert S. Financial History of the United States, 3 vols. Incl. Vol. 1. From 1774 to 1789. 4th ed. Repr. of 1896 ed (ISBN 0-678-04033-8); Vol. 2. From 1789 to 1860. 4th ed. Repr. of 1894 ed (ISBN 0-678-04034-6); Vol. 3. From 1861-1885. 2nd ed. LC 68-22311. Repr. of 1894 ed (ISBN 0-678-04035-4). LC 68-22371. Set. 125.00x (ISBN 0-678-00465-X); 50.00 ea. Kelley.

--Industrial History of the United States. 3rd ed. LC 66-21655. (Illus.). 1881. 57.50x (ISBN 0-678-00180-4). Kelley.

--The National Bank Act & Its Judicial Meaning. Bruchey, Stuart, ed. LC 80-1135. (The Rise of Commercial Banking Ser.). 1981. Repr. of 1892 ed. lib. bdg. 38.00x (ISBN 0-405-13635-8). Ayer Co Pubs.

--Pennsylvania, Province & State, 2 Vols. LC 74-147140. (Research & Source Work Ser.: No. 652). 1971. Repr. of 1890 ed. Set. 51.50 (ISBN 0-8337-0333-1). B Franklin.

--Practical Banking. Bruchey, Stuart, ed. LC 80-1136. (The Rise of Commercial Banking Ser.). 1981. Repr. of 1884 ed. lib. bdg. 28.00x (ISBN 0-405-13627-7). Ayer Co Pubs.

Bolles, Blair. Tyrant from Illinois. LC 73-16641. 248p. 1974. Repr. of 1951 ed. lib. bdg. 22.50x (ISBN 0-8371-7205-5, BOTI). Greenwood.

Bolles, Edmund B. The Penguin Adoption Handbook: A Guide to Creating Your New Family. 244p. (Orig.). 1984. pap. 8.95 (ISBN 0-14-046548-0). Penguin.

--The Penguin Adoption Handbook: A Guide to Creating Your New Family. LC 83-23750. 224p. 1984. 17.95 (ISBN 0-670-10510-4). Viking.

--So Much to Say. (Illus.). 288p. 1982. 16.95 (ISBN 0-312-73120-5); pap. 9.95 (ISBN 0-312-73121-3). St Martin.

--Who Owns America? (Illus.). 288p. 1984. pap. 8.95 (ISBN 0-87131-450-9). M Evans.

Bolles, Frank. A Collection of Important English Statutes. 3rd ed. 189p. 1978. Repr. of 1888 ed. lib. bdg. 35.00 (ISBN 0-89941-141-X). W S Hein.

Bolles, M. Marjorie, jt. auth. see Landis, Carney.

Bolles, Richard. Tea Leaves: A New Look at Resumes. 1976. pap. 0.50x (ISBN 0-913668-72-9). Ten Speed Pr.

Bolles, Richard H. The Quick Job-Hunting Map. (Orig.). 1976. pap. 1.25x (ISBN 0-913668-60-5). Ten Speed Pr.

Bolles, Richard N. The Quick Job-Hunting Map: Advanced Version Trade. 1982. pap. 1.50 (ISBN 0-89815-008-6). Ten Speed Pr.

--The Three Boxes of Life: And How to Get Out of Them. LC 78-17000. (Illus.). 480p. 1981. 14.95 (ISBN 0-913668-52-4); pap. 8.95 (ISBN 0-913668-58-3). Ten Speed Pr.

--What Color Is Your Parachute? 2nd, rev. & enl. ed. LC 81-50471. 384p. 1984. 15.95 (ISBN 0-89815-144-9); pap. 8.95 (ISBN 0-89815-143-0). Ten Speed Pr.

Bolles, Richard N. & Zenoff, Victoria B. Quick Job-Hunting Map for Beginners. 1977. pap. 1.25x (ISBN 0-913668-59-1). Ten Speed Pr.

Bolles, Richard N., jt. auth. see Crystal, John C.

Bolles, Robert. Learning Theory. 2nd ed. LC 78-2768. 1979. text ed. 29.95 (ISBN 0-03-019306-0, HoltC). HR&W.

Bollet, A. J., ed. see Pretest Service Inc.

Bollet, Alfred J., ed. Harrison's Principles of Internal Medicine Patient Management Cases PreTest Self-Assessment & Review. (Illus.). 248p. (Orig.). 1981. 35.00 (ISBN 0-07-051647-2). McGraw Pretest.

Bollet, Alfred J. & Bruckheim, Allan H., eds. Mediquiz, Vol. 2. (Illus.). 1984p. 75.00 (ISBN 0-935466-04-5). Pierson Pubs.

Bollettieri, Nick. Tennis Your Way. (Illus.). 160p. (Orig.). 1984. pap. text ed. 6.95 (ISBN 0-87670-066-0, Dist. by Sterling). Athletic Inst.

Bollettieri, Nick & McDermott, Barry. Nick Bollettieri's Junior Tennis. LC 84-10618. (Illus.). 256p. 1984. 17.95 (ISBN 0-671-50840-7). S&S.

Bollettieri, Nick, jt. auth. see Anthony, Julie.

Bollettino. Giovanni Boccaccio: The Life of. (Library Medieval Literature). 1985. lib. bdg. 15.00 (ISBN 0-8240-8873-5). Garland Pub.

Bolli, Hans & Saunders, John B., eds. Plankton Stratigraphy. (Earth Science Ser.). (Illus.). 800p. 1984. 125.00 (ISBN 0-521-23576-6). Cambridge U Pr.

Bollier, David. How to Appraise & Improve Your Daily Newspaper. 1980. pap. 5.00 (ISBN 0-686-36550-X). Ctr Responsive Law.

--Liberty & Justice for Some: Defending a Free Society from the Radical Right's Holy War on Democracy. LC 82-51019. 336p. (Orig.). 1982. pap. 8.95 (ISBN 0-8044-6060-4, Co-pub. by People for Amer Way). Ungar.

Bollier, John A. The Literature of Theology: A Guide for Students & Pastors. LC 78-10962. 208p. 1979. pap. 5.95 (ISBN 0-664-24225-1). Westminster.

Bollig, Richard Joseph. History of Catholic Education in Kansas: 1836-1932. 131p. 1984. 24.00x (ISBN 0-939738-22-8). Zubal Inc.

Bolliger, A. Get Fit for Tennis: Practical Advice for Every Tennis Player. (Illus.). 176p. 1982. 12.95 (ISBN 0-7207-1350-1, Pub. by Michael Joseph). Merrimack Pub Cir.

Bolliger, Hans, intro. by. Picasso's Vollard Suite. (Illus.). 1985. pap. 9.95 (ISBN 0-500-27100-3). Thames Hudson.

Bolliger, Markus. Die Gattung Pulmonaria in Westeuropa. (Phanerogamarum Monographiae VIII). 250p. (Orig., Ger.). 1982. text ed. 47.25x (ISBN 3-7682-1338-2). Lubrecht & Cramer.

Bolliger, Max. The Lonely Prince. LC 81-66439. (Illus.). 32p. (ps-3). 1981. PLB 12.95 (ISBN 0-689-50215-X, McElderry Bk). Atheneum.

--The Most Beautiful Song. (Illus.). (ps-3). 1981. 8.95 (ISBN 0-316-10117-6). Little.

--Noah & the Rainbow: An Ancient Story. Bulla, Clyde R., tr. LC 72-76361. (Illus.). (gr. k-3). 1972. pap. 9.95 (ISBN 0-690-58448-2). Crowell Jr Bks.
Bolling, Diana, jt. auth. see Block, Richard J.
Bolling, Landrum. Lands of the Bible Today. 208p. 1985. write for info. (ISBN 0-8499-0483-8, 0483-8). Word Bks.
Bolling, Landrum R. Reporters under Fire: U. S. Media Coverage of Conflicts in Lebanon & Central America. (Replica Edition-Softcover Ser.). 170p. 1985. pap. 17.00x (ISBN 0-8133-7006-X). Westview.
Bolling, Landrum R. & Smith, Craig. Private Foreign Aid: U. S. Philanthropy in Relief & Development. LC 82-1867. (Illus.). 330p. 1982. pap. 29.50x (ISBN 0-86531-393-8). Westview.
Bolling, Patricia, jt. auth. see Harding, Anne D.
Bolling, Robert. A Memoir of a Portion of the Bolling Family in England & Virginia. LC 9-7487. (Illus.). 68p. Repr. of 1868 ed. write for info. (ISBN 0-685-65058-8). Va Bk.
Bollinger, A., jt. ed. see Reneman, R. S.
Bollinger, C. Grog's Own Country. (Illus.). 15.00 (ISBN 0-392-03162-0, ABC). Sportshelf.
Bollinger, Donald E. Band Director's Complete Handbook. (Illus.). 1979. 22.95x (ISBN 0-13-055442-1, Parker). P-H.
Bollinger, Edward E. The Cross & the Floating Dragon: The Gospel in Ryukyu. LC 82-23540. (Illus.). 368p. 1983. pap. 10.95 (ISBN 0-87808-190-9). William Carey Lib.
Bollinger, Edward T. Rails That Climb: A Narrative History of the Moffat Road. Jones, William C., ed. LC 79-14634. (Illus.). 1979. 24.95 (ISBN 0-918654-29-7). CO RR Mus.
Bollinger, Edward T. & Bauer, Frederick. The Moffat Road. LC 62-12397. (Illus.). 359p. 1981. Repr. of 1967 ed. 22.95 (ISBN 0-8214-0665-5, 82-84341). Ohio U Pr.
Bollinger, G. A. Blast Vibration Analysis. LC 79-22421. (Illus.). 149p. 1980. pap. 6.95x (ISBN 0-8093-0951-3). S Ill U Pr.
Bollinger, John G., jt. auth. see Harrison, Howard L.
Bollinger, L. E. & Goldsmith, M., eds. Liquid Rockets & Propellants. LC 60-16913. (Illus.). 682p. 1970. 34.00 (ISBN 0-317-36836-2); members 17.50 (ISBN 0-317-36837-0). AIAA.
Bollinger, Lee C., jt. auth. see Jackson, John H.
Bollinger, Rick L. Communication Management of the Geriatric Patient. 48p. 1977. pap. text ed. 2.25x (ISBN 0-8134-1940-9, 1940). Interstate.
Bollinger, Theresa & Cramer, Patricia. The Baby Gear Guide: How to Make Smart Choices in Essential Baby Equipment. (Illus.). 320p. 1985. 21.95 (ISBN 0-201-10637-X); pap. 12.95 (ISBN 0-201-10636-1). Addison-Wesley.
Bollinger, William H., et al. Project Design & Recommendations for Watershed Reforestation & Fuelwood Development in Sri Lanka. (Illus.). 122p. 1979. pap. 15.00 (ISBN 0-936130-03-2). Intl Sci Tech.
Bollioud-Mermet, Louis. De la Corruption du Goust dans la Musique Francaise. LC 76-43907. (Music & Theatre in France in the 17th & 18th Centuries). Repr. of 1746 ed. 15.00 (ISBN 0-404-60150-2). AMS Pr.
Bollmann, W. Crystal Defects & Crystalline Interfaces. LC 77-124069. (Illus.). 1970. 69.00 (ISBN 0-387-05057-4). Springer-Verlag.
--Crystal Lattices, Interfaces, Matrices: An Extension of Crystallography. (Illus.). 360p. 1982. 45.00 (ISBN 2-88105-000-X). Polycrystal Bk Serv.
Bollobas. Graph Theory & Combinatorics. 1984. 50.00 (ISBN 0-12-111760-X). Acad Pr.
Bollobas, B. Graph Theory: An Introductory Course. (Graduate Texts in Mathematics Ser.: Vol. 63). (Illus.). 1979. 24.00 (ISBN 0-387-90399-2). Springer-Verlag.
Bollobas, B., ed. Advances in Graph Theory. (Annals of Discrete Mathematics Ser.: Vol. 3). 296p. 1978. 70.25 (ISBN 0-444-85075-9, North-Holland). Elsevier.
--Graph Theory: Proceedings of the Conference on Graph Theory, Cambridge. (Mathematics Studies: Vol. 62). 202p. 1982. 42.75 (ISBN 0-444-86449-0, North Holland). Elsevier.
Bollobas, B., tr. see Boltjansky, Vladimir G., et al.
Bollobas, Bella, ed. Survey in Combinatorics. LC 79-51596. (London Mathematical Society Lecture Note Ser.: No. 38). 1979. pap. 27.95x (ISBN 0-521-22846-8). Cambridge U Pr.
Bollon, Arthur P. Recombinant DNA Products: Insulin-Interferon-Growth Hormone. 208p. 1984. 70.00 (ISBN 0-8493-5542-7). CRC Pr.
Bolloten, Burnett. La Revolucion Espanola. 335p. (Sp.). 1964. pap. 3.00 (ISBN 0-912098-01-5). Cal Inst Intl St.
--The Spanish Revolution: The Left & the Struggle for Power During the Civil War. LC 78-5011. xxvi, 665p. 1980. pap. 9.95x (ISBN 0-8078-4077-7). U of NC Pr.
Bollow, Ludmillow. One Acts & Monologues for Women. (Illus.). 96p. 1983. pap. 4.00 (ISBN 0-88145-008-1). Broadway Play.
Bolls, Imogene. Glass Walker. (Cleveland Poets Ser.: No. 33). 29p. (Orig.). 1983. pap. 3.50 (ISBN 0-914946-37-4). Cleveland St Univ Poetry Ctr.
Bollum, Fred J., jt. ed. see Bertazzoni, Umberto.
Bolman, Frederick D., Jr., tr. see Von Schelling, Friedrich.
Bolman, Lee G. & Deal, Terrence E. Modern Approaches to Understanding & Managing Organizations. LC 83-49257. (Management Ser.). 1984. text ed. 18.95x (ISBN 0-87589-592-1). Jossey-Bass.
Bolman, Wm. M., ed. Child Psychiatry in ASEAN Countries: A Book of Readings. Maretzki, Thos W. 1979. pap. 8.00x (ISBN 0-686-26671-4, Pub. by New Day Pub). Cellar.
Bolmeier, Edward C. Judicial Excerpts Governing Students & Teachers. 1977. 14.50 (ISBN 0-87215-199-9). Michie Co.
--Legality of Student Disciplinary Practices. 200p. 1976. 14.50 (ISBN 0-87215-186-7). Michie Co.
Bolner, James, ed. Lousiana Politics: Festival in a Labyrinth. 352p. 1982. text ed. 35.00x (ISBN 0-8071-0983-5); pap. text ed. 9.95x (ISBN 0-8071-0984-3). La State U Pr.
Bolner, Mary, ed. Planning & Developing a Library Orientation Program: Proceedings. LC 75-676. (Library Orientation Ser.: No. 3). 1975. 19.50 (ISBN 0-87650-061-0). Pierian.
Bolocan, David. JAZZ! 1985. 24.95 (ISBN 0-8306-0978-4, 1978); pap. 17.95 (ISBN 0-8306-1978-X). TAB Bks.
--Lotus 1-2-3 Simplified. (Illus.). 128p. 1984. 16.95 (ISBN 0-8306-0748-X, 1748); pap. 10.25 (ISBN 0-8306-1748-5). TAB Bks.
--Mastering Symphony. (Illus.). 224p. 1985. 22.95 (ISBN 0-8306-0948-2, 1948); pap. 16.95 (ISBN 0-8306-1948-8). TAB Bks.
--The WORD Book. LC 85-2528. (Illus.). 240p. (Orig.). 1985. 24.95 (ISBN 0-8306-0958-X, 1958); pap. 16.95 (ISBN 0-8306-1958-5). TAB Bks.
Bolocan, David & Microtrend, Inc. Visi-On on the IBM PC. (Microtrend Ser.). 1984. 14.95 (ISBN 0-13-942301-X). P-H.
Bolodeau, Michel L., jt. auth. see Mackenzie, Brian W.
Bologh, Roslyn W. Dialectical Phenomenology: Marx's Method. (International Library of Phenomenology & Moral Sciences). 1979. 25.00x (ISBN 0-7100-0335-8). Routledge & Kegan.
Bologna, Ferdinando, 1st. I Pittori Ala Corte Angionina Di Napoli, 1266-1414. Briganti, Giuliano, ed. LC 79-106768. (Saggi E Studi Di Storia Dell'arte). (Illus.). 802p. (It.). 1970. 87.50x (ISBN 0-271-00117-8). Pa St U Pr.
Bologna, G. & Vincelli, M., eds. Data Acquisition in High Energy Physics: Proceedings of the International School of Physics "Enrico Fermi," Course LXXXIV, Varenna, Italy, July 28-Aug. 7, 1981. (Enrico Fermi International Summer School of Physics Ser.: Vol. 84). 400p. 1984. 75.00 (ISBN 0-444-86520-9, I-081-84, North Holland). Elsevier.
Bologna, Gianfranco. The World of Birds. Pleasance, Simon, tr. LC 79-1190. (Abbeville Press Encyclopedia of Natural Science). (Illus.). 256p. 1979. 13.95 (ISBN 0-89659-034-8). Abbeville Pr.
Bologna, Jack. Corporate Fraud: The Basics of Prevention & Detection. 220p. 1984. text ed. 19.95 (ISBN 0-409-95129-3). Butterworth.
Bolognese, Don. Drawing Dinosaurs & Other Prehistoric Animals. (How to Draw Ser.). (Illus.). 72p. (gr. 4 up). 1982. PLB 8.90 (ISBN 0-531-04398-3). Watts.
--Drawing Horses & Foals. (How to Draw Ser.). (gr. 4-6). 1977. PLB 8.90 (ISBN 0-531-00379-5). Watts.
--Drawing Spaceships & Other Spacecraft. (How to Draw Ser.). (Illus.). 64p. (gr. 4-6). 1982. PLB 8.90 (ISBN 0-531-04470-X). Watts.
Bolognese, Don & Raphael, Elaine. Drawing Fashions. (How to Draw Ser.). (Illus.). 64p. (gr. 7-12). 1985. lib. bdg. 10.90 (ISBN 0-531-10049-9). Watts.
Bolognese, Don & Thornton, Robert. Drawing & Painting with a Computer. (How to Draw Ser.). (Illus.). 72p. (gr. 4-6). PLB 8.90 (ISBN 0-531-04653-2); pap. 4.95 (ISBN 0-531-03593-X). Watts.
Bolognese, Don, jt. auth. see Raphael, Elaine.
Bolooki, H. Thoracic Surgery. 3rd ed. (Medical Examination Review Book: Vol. 18). 1981. 27.95 (ISBN 0-87488-118-8). Med Exam.
Bolooki, Hooshang, ed. Clinical Application of Intra-Aortic Balloon Pump. rev. ed. 500p. 1984. 59.50 (ISBN 0-87993-184-1). Futura Pub.
Bolotin, Norm. Klondike Lost: A Decade of Photographs by Kinsey & Kinsey. LC 79-25687. (Illus.). 1980. album style 12.95 (ISBN 0-88240-130-0). Alaska Northwest.
Bolotin, V. V. Random Vibrations of Elastic Systems. (Mechanics of Elastic Stability: No. 8). 480p. 1984. lib. bdg. 86.00 (ISBN 90-247-2981-5, Pub. by Martinus Nijhoff Netherlands). Kluwer Academic.
Bolotnik, Anthony S., et al. Recreation Facilities. Moore, Gary T., ed. (Illus.). vii, 118p. 1985. write for info. (ISBN 0-938744-34-8). U of Wis Ctr Arch-Urban.
Bolotoff, George P. The Man That Walks Like a Bear. Ashton, Sylvia, ed. LC 77-80277. 1979. 14.95 (ISBN 0-87949-082-9). Ashley Bks.
Bolsby, Clare E., jt. auth. see Berglund, Berndt.
Bolsche, Wilhelm. The Evolution of Man. Untermann, Ernest, tr. from Ger. (Science for the Workers Ser.). (Illus.). 160p. 1984. lib. bdg. 7.95 (ISBN 0-88286-084-4). C H Kerr.
--The Triumph of Life. Simons, May W., tr. from Ger. (Science for the Workers Ser.). (Illus.). 157p. 1984. 7.95 (ISBN 0-88286-085-2). C H Kerr.
Bolshakoff, Serge. Russian Nonconformity: The Story of Unofficial Religion in Russia. Repr. of 1950 ed. 10.00 (ISBN 0-404-00933-6). AMS Pr.
Bolshakoff, Sergius. Russian Mystics. (Cistercian Studies: No. 26). Orig. Title: I Mistici Russi. 303p. 1981. pap. 6.95 (ISBN 0-87907-926-6). Cistercian Pubns.
Bolshakoff, Sergius & Pennington, M. Basil. In Search of True Wisdom: Visits to Eastern Spiritual Fathers. LC 78-20029. 1979. 8.95 (ISBN 0-385-14791-0). Doubleday.
Bolshakov, V. This Whole Human Rights Business. 327p. 1985. pap. 2.95 (ISBN 0-8285-2973-6, Pub. by Progress Pubs USSR). Imported Pubns.
Bolster, John. Lotus Elan & Europa: A Collector's Guide. (Collector's Guide Ser.). (Illus.). 138p. 1980. 18.95 (ISBN 0-900549-48-3, Pub. by Motor Racing England). Motorbooks Intl.
--Rolls-Royce Silver Shadow. (AutoHistory Ser.). (Illus.). 1979. 14.95 (ISBN 0-85045-324-0, Pub. by Osprey Pubns. England). Motorbooks Intl.
Bolsterli, Margaret J. The Early Community at Bedford Park: The Pursuit of "Corporate Happiness" in the First Garden Suburb. LC 76-8299. (Illus.). xii, 133p. 1977. 14.00x (ISBN 0-8214-0224-2, 82-82295). Ohio U Pr.
Bolt, et al. Today's Busperson. (Restaurant Training Manuals Ser). (Illus., Prog. Bk.). 1979. pap. 3.50 (ISBN 0-912016-22-1); supervisor's manual avail. (ISBN 0-912016-23-X). Lebhar Friedman.
--Today's Cocktail Waitress. (Restaurant Training Manuals Ser.). (Illus.). 216p. (Prog. Bk.). 1979. pap. 3.50 (ISBN 0-912016-35-3, 086730233). Lebhar Friedman.
--Today's Dishwashing Machine Operator. (Restaurant Training Manual Ser.). (Illus., Prog. Bk.). 1979. pap. 3.50 (ISBN 0-912016-24-8); supervisor's manual avail. (ISBN 0-912016-25-6). Lebhar Friedman.
--Today's Waiter & Waitress. (Restaurant Training Manuals Ser). (Illus., Prog. Bk.). 1979. pap. 3.50 (ISBN 0-912016-20-5, 086730220); supervisor's manual avail. (ISBN 0-912016-21-3). Lebhar Friedman.
Bolt, Alice De see De Bolt, Alice.
Bolt, B. A., jt. auth. see Bullen, K. E.
Bolt, B. A., et al. Geological Hazards. LC 74-32049. (Illus.). 450p. 1977. 29.50 (ISBN 0-387-90254-6). Springer-Verlag.
Bolt, Brian. The Amazing Mathematical Amusement Arcade. (Illus.). 128p. 1984. pap. 7.95 (ISBN 0-521-26980-6). Cambridge U Pr.
--More Mathematical Activities: A Further Resource Book for Teachers. (Illus.). 160p. Date not set. price not set. Cambridge U Pr.
Bolt, Bruce A. Earthquakes: A Primer. LC 77-12908. (Geology Ser.). (Illus.). 241p. 1978. pap. text ed. 12.95 (ISBN 0-7167-0057-3). W H Freeman.
--Inside the Earth: Evidence From Earthquakes. LC 81-17431. (Illus.). 191p. 1982. text ed. 24.95 (ISBN 0-7167-1359-4); pap. text ed. 12.95 (ISBN 0-7167-1360-8). W H Freeman.
--Nuclear Explosions & Earthquakes: The Parted Veil. LC 75-28295. (Illus.). 309p. 1976. text ed. 26.95 (ISBN 0-7167-0276-2). W H Freeman.
Bolt, Bruce A., intro. by. Earthquakes & Volcanoes: Readings from Scientific American. LC 79-21684. (Illus.). 154p. 1980. text ed. 20.95 (ISBN 0-7167-1163-X); pap. text ed. 10.95 (ISBN 0-7167-1164-8). W H Freeman.
Bolt, Bruce A. see Alder, B., et al.
Bolt, Bruce A., et al see Alder, B., et al.
Bolt, Christine & Dresher, Seymour. Anti-Slavery, Religion & Reform. xi, 377p. 1980. 27.50 (ISBN 0-208-01783-6, Archon). Shoe String.
Bolt, Christine, jt. auth. see Barbrook, Alec.
Bolt, Ernest C., Jr. Ballots Before Bullets: The War Referendum Approach to Peace in America, 1914-1941. LC 77-680. 206p. 1977. 16.95x (ISBN 0-8139-0662-8). U Pr of Va.
Bolt, G. H. & Bruggenwert, M. G. Soil Chemistry, Pt. A: Basic Elements. (Developments in Soil Science Ser.: Vol. 5A). 282p. 1976. 30.00 (ISBN 0-444-41435-5). Elsevier.
Bolt, G. H., ed. Soil Chemistry, Pt. B: Physico-Chemical Models. 2nd, rev. ed. (Developments in Soil Science Ser.: Vol. 5B). 538p. 1982. 76.75 (ISBN 0-444-42060-6). Elsevier.
Bolt, John, ed. see Buchanan, Annette M. & Martin, Kay A.
Bolt, Joseph W. De see De Bolt, Joseph W.
Bolt, Martin & Myers, David G. The Human Connection. LC 83-20420. 168p. (Orig.). 1984. pap. 4.95 (ISBN 0-87784-913-7). Inter-Varsity.
Bolt, Nancy M., ed. State Aid Nineteen Eighty Three: A Survey Report. 88p. 1984. 20.00 (ISBN 0-8389-6766-3); members 18.00 (ISBN 0-318-17734-X). ASCLA.
Bolt, Peter. A Way of Loving. LC 73-86798. 64p. (Orig.). 1973. 3.50x (ISBN 0-8358-0292-2). Upper Room.
Bolt, Richard A. The Human Interface: Where People & Computers Meet. (Computer Science Ser.). (Illus.). 192p. 1984. 28.00 (ISBN 0-534-03380-6); pap. 16.95 (ISBN 0-534-03387-3). Lifetime Learn.
--The Human Interface: Where People & Computers Meet. (Illus.). 114p. 1984. 22.95 (ISBN 0-534-03380-6); pap. 16.95 (ISBN 0-534-03387-3). Van Nos Reinhold.
Bolt, Robert. Man for All Seasons. 1962. 10.95 (ISBN 0-394-40623-0). Random.
--Man for All Seasons. 1966. pap. 2.95 (ISBN 0-394-70321-9, V321, Vin). Random.
--State of Revolution. (National Theatre Plays Ser.). 1977. pap. text ed. 7.50x (ISBN 0-435-23131-6). Heinemann Ed.
--The Thwarting of Baron Bolligrew. 1966. pap. text ed. 3.00x (ISBN 0-435-23103-0). Heinemann Ed.
--Vivat! Vivat! Regina! (Hereford Plays Ser.). 1974. pap. text ed. 3.50x (ISBN 0-435-22104-3). Heinemann Ed.
Bolt, Robert J., et al. The Digestive System. LC 82-10906. 429p. 1983. pap. 27.50x (ISBN 0-471-92207-2, Pub. by Wiley Med). Wiley.
Bolt, Sydney. Preface to James Joyce. LC 79-41169. (Preface Bks.). (Illus.). 1981. text ed. 13.50x (ISBN 0-582-35194-4); pap. text ed. 8.95x (ISBN 0-582-35195-2). Longman.
Boltanski, Luc. Prime Education et Morale De Classe. (Cahiers Du Centre De Sociologie Europeenne: No. 5). 1969. pap. 8.40x (ISBN 90-2796-255-3). Mouton.
Boltax, Robert S., jt. auth. see Krat, Siegfried J.
Bolte, Carl E. Secrets of Successful Songwriting. LC 84-6391. 208p. (Orig.). 1984. pap. 7.95 (ISBN 0-668-06170-7, 6170-7). Arco.
Bolte, Charles, ed. Portrait of a Woman Down East: Selected Writings of Mary Bolte. 1981. 7.95 (ISBN 0-89272-129-4). Down East.
Bolte, Charles G. Libraries & the Arts & Humanities. pap. 14.50 (ISBN 0-915794-13-6). Gaylord Prof Pubns.
Bolte, H. D. Myocardial Biopsy: Diagnostic Significance. (Illus.). 180p. 1980. 33.00 (ISBN 0-387-10063-6). Springer-Verlag.
Bolte, H. D., ed. Viral Heart Disease. (Illus.). 190p. 1984. pap. 29.00 (ISBN 0-387-13112-4). Springer Verlag.
Bolten, Johannes. Imago Clipeata, Ein Beitrag Zur Portrait Und Typengeschichte. pap. 12.00 (ISBN 0-384-04915-X). Johnson Repr.
Bolten, Steven E. Managerial Finance: Principles & Practice. LC 75-31036. (Illus.). 896p. 1976. text ed. 32.50 (ISBN 0-395-20462-3); instr's. manual 2.15 (ISBN 0-395-20461-5). HM.
Bolten, Steven E. & Conn, Robert L. Essentials of Managerial Finance: Principles & Practice. LC 80-80961. (Illus.). 800p. 1981. text ed. 30.50 (ISBN 0-395-29638-2); instr's. manual 2.50 (ISBN 0-395-29639-0); test-bank 2.50 (ISBN 0-395-30359-1); study guide 12.50 (ISBN 0-395-30089-4). HM.
Bolter, J. David. Turing's Man: Western Culture in the Computer Age. LC 83-6942. (Illus.). xii, 264p. 1984. 19.95 (ISBN 0-8078-1564-0); pap. 8.95 (ISBN 0-8078-4108-0). U of NC Pr.
Boltho, Andrea. The European Economy: Growth & Crisis. (Illus.). 1982. 49.00x (ISBN 0-19-877119-3); pap. 19.95 (ISBN 0-19-877118-5). Oxford U Pr.
--Japan: An Economic Survey 1953-1973. (Economies of the World). (Illus.). 1975. 32.50x (ISBN 0-19-877036-7). Oxford U Pr.
Boltianski, V. G. La Envolvente. 88p. (Span.). 1977. pap. 1.95 (ISBN 0-8285-1452-6, Pub. by Mir Pubs USSR). Imported Pubns.
Boltianskii, Vladimir G. Optimal Control of Discrete Systems. LC 78-67814. 392p. 1978. 89.95x (ISBN 0-470-26530-2). Halsted Pr.
Boltjansky, Vladimir G., et,al. Results & Problems in Combinatorial Geometry. Bollobas, B. & Harris, A., trs. (Illus.). 112p. Date not set. price not set (ISBN 0-521-26298-4); pap. price not set (ISBN 0-521-26923-7). Cambridge U Pr.
Boltman, Brigid. Cook-Freeze Catering Systems. (Illus.). 247p. 1978. 39.00 (ISBN 0-85334-768-9, Pub. by Elsevier Applied Sci England). Elsevier.
Bolton. Santa Fe in a Day. (Illus.). 56p. 1981. pap. 4.95 (ISBN 0-937050-24-5). Stonehenge.
Bolton, B. Electromagnetism & Its Applications. 1980. 28.50 (ISBN 0-442-30243-6). Van Nos Reinhold.
--A Revision of Six Minor Genera of Myrmicinae (Hymenoptera; Formicidae) in the Ethiopian Zoogeographical Region. 40.00x (ISBN 0-686-78662-9, Pub. by Brit Mus Pubns England). State Mutual Bk.
Bolton, B., jt. ed. see Chantry, G. W.
Bolton, Barbara & Smith, Charles. Creative Bible Learning for Children, Grades 1-6. LC 77-74532. 192p. 1977. pap. 3.95 (ISBN 0-8307-0478-7, 9100105). Regal.
Bolton, Brenda. Medieval Reformation. (Foundations of Medieval History). (Illus.). 112p. 1983. text ed. 19.75x (ISBN 0-8419-0879-6); pap. text ed. 11.75x (ISBN 0-8419-0835-4). Holmes & Meier.
Bolton, Brett, ed. Edgar Cayce Speaks. 1969. pap. 4.95 (ISBN 0-380-00553-0, 60130-3). Avon.
Bolton, Brian. Rehabilitation Counseling Research. (Illus.). 323p. 1979. pap. text ed. 10.00 (ISBN 0-8391-1501-6). Pro Ed.
--Vocational Adjustment of Disabled Persons. LC 82-7058. 272p. 1982. pap. 14.00 (ISBN 0-8391-1722-1). Pro Ed.
Bolton, Brian & Cook, Daniel W. Rehabilitation Client Assessment. LC 79-23871. (Illus.). 336p. 1980. pap. 10.00 (ISBN 0-8391-1546-6). Pro Ed.
Bolton, Brian, jt. auth. see Hinman, Suki.
Bolton, Brian, jt. auth. see Hinman, Sukit.
Bolton, Brian, ed. Rehabilitation Counseling: Theory & Practice. LC 77-18287. (Illus.). 303p. 1978. pap. 10.00 (ISBN 0-8391-1199-1). Pro Ed.

Bolton, Brian & Cooper, Paul G., eds. Readings in Rehabilitation Counseling Research. LC 80-18055. (Illus.). 272p. 1980. pap. 10.00 (ISBN 0-8391-1603-9). Pro Ed.

Bolton, Brian & Jacques, Madeline E., eds. The Rehabilitation Client. LC 79-12258. (Illus.). 256p. 1979. pap. 10.00 (ISBN 0-8391-1603-9). Pro Ed.

Bolton, Carole. The Good-Bye Year. 192p. (gr. 5-9). 1982. 10.95 (ISBN 0-525-66787-3, 01063-320). Lodestar Bks.

--Never Jam Today. LC 76-134805. (Illus.). 256p. (gr. 5-9). 1963. pap. 0.95 (ISBN 0-689-70355-4, A-26, Aladdin). Atheneum.

Bolton, Charles D. & Kammeyer, Kenneth C. The University Student: A Study of Behavior & Values. 1967. 12.95x (ISBN 0-8084-0307-9); pap. 9.95x (ISBN 0-8084-0308-7). New Coll U Pr.

Bolton, Charles K. The Founders: Portraits of Persons Born Abroad Who Came to the Colonies in North America Before the Year 1701, 3 vols. in 2. LC 75-29181. (Illus.). 1103p. 1976. Repr. of 1919 ed. Set. 50.00 (ISBN 0-8063-0692-0). Genealog Pub.

--Marriage Notices, 1785-1795, for the Whole United States from the Massachusetts Centinel & the Columbian Centinel. LC 65-28304. 139p. 1985. Repr. of 1900 ed. 12.50 (ISBN 0-317-31637-0). Genealog Pub.

--The Private Soldier Under Washington. (Illus.). 258p. 1976. Repr. of 1902 ed. 16.95 (ISBN 0-87928-072-7). Corner Hse.

Bolton, Charles S. Southern Anglicanism: The Church of England in Colonial South Carolina. LC 81-6669. (Contributions to the Study of Religion: No. 5). (Illus.). 248p. 1982. lib. bdg. 29.95 (ISBN 0-313-23090-0, BOS/). Greenwood.

Bolton, Christopher R., jt. auth. see Peterson, David A.

Bolton, Clyde. Alabama Football: The Crimson Tide. LC 72-91388. (College Sports Ser.). 1982. 10.95 (ISBN 0-87397-235-X). Strode.

--The Basketball Tide: A Story of Alabama Basketball. LC 76-45925. (College Sports Ser.). (Illus.). 1977. 9.95 (ISBN 0-87397-110-8). Strode.

--Bolton's Best: Stories of Auto Racing. LC 74-28643. 1975. 7.95 (ISBN 0-87397-060-8). Strode.

--The Crimson Tide: Alabama Football. (College Sports Ser.: Football). 1982. 10.95 (ISBN 0-87397-235-X). Strode.

--Unfogettable Days in Southern Football. (Sports Ser.). (Illus.). 255p. 1974. 9.95 (ISBN 0-87397-057-8). Strode.

--War Eagle: A Story of Auburn Football. Rev. & enl. ed. LC 73-83502. (College Sports Ser.). 1979. 9.95 (ISBN 0-87397-023-3). Strode.

Bolton Conference, 5th. Weldments: Physical Metallurgy & Failure Phenomena - Proceedings. Christoffel, R. J., et al, eds. LC 79-14269. (Illus.). 436p. 1979. 55.75 (ISBN 0-931690-07-2). Genium Pub.

Bolton, D., tr. see Saurat, Denis.

Bolton, Dale. Selection & Evaluation of Teachers. LC 72-10648. 260p. 1973. 22.00x (ISBN 0-8211-0123-4); text ed. 19.75x 10 or more copies. McCutchan.

Bolton, Dale L. Evaluating Administrative Personnel in School Systems. LC 79-21121. 1980. 16.95x (ISBN 0-8077-2572-2). Tchrs Coll.

Bolton, Derek. An Approach to Wittgensteins' Philosophy. 1979. text ed. 28.00x (ISBN 0-391-01036-0). Humanities.

Bolton, Dianne. Nationalization: A Road to Socialism, the Case of Tanzania. (Illus.). 240p. 1984. pap. 9.95 (ISBN 0-86232-162-X, Pub. by Zed Pr England). Biblio Dist.

--Nationalization: A Road to Socialism? The Lessons of Tanzania. 190p. 1985. 26.25x (ISBN 0-86232-377-0, Pub. by Zed Pr England). Biblio Dist.

Bolton, Dorothy G., jt. auth. see Bolton, Robert.

Bolton, Douglas. Garden or Wilderness. 202p. 1980. 12.50 (ISBN 0-87073-890-9). Schenkman Bks Inc.

Bolton, Edmund. The Cities Advocate: Whether Apprentiship Extinguisheth Gentry? LC 74-28834. (English Experience Ser.: No. 715). 1975. Repr. of 1629 ed. 7.00 (ISBN 90-221-0715-9). Walter J Johnson.

--The Elements of Armories. LC 73-38160. (English Experience Ser.: No. 363). 356p. 1971. Repr. of 1610 ed. 32.50 (ISBN 90-221-0363-3). Walter J Johnson.

Bolton, Edward R. Oils, Fats & Fatty Foods: Their Practical Examination. 4th ed. Williams, K. A., ed. LC 67-73132. pap. 124.00 (ISBN 0-317-09891-8, 2004594). Bks Demand UMI.

Bolton, Elizabeth. Case of the Wacky Cat. LC 84-8725. (Illus.). 48p. (gr. 2-4). 1985. PLB 9.29 (ISBN 0-8167-0400-7); pap. text ed. 1.95 (ISBN 0-8167-0401-5). Troll Assocs.

--Ghost in the House. LC 84-20530. 48p. (gr. 2-4). 1985. PLB 9.29 (ISBN 0-8167-0418-X); pap. 1.95 (ISBN 0-8167-0419-8). Troll Assocs.

--Secret of the Ghost Piano. LC 84-8745. (Illus.). 48p. (gr. 2-4). 1985. PLB 9.29 (ISBN 0-8167-0410-4); pap. text ed. 1.95 (ISBN 0-8167-0411-2). Troll Assocs.

--Secret of the Magic Potion. LC 84-8881. (Illus.). 48p. (gr. 2-4). 1985. PLB 9.29 (ISBN 0-8167-0420-1); pap. text ed. 1.95 (ISBN 0-8167-0421-X). Troll Assocs.

--The Tree House Detective Club. LC 84-8762. (Illus.). 48p. (gr. 2-4). 1985. PLB 9.29 (ISBN 0-8167-0404-X); pap. text ed. 1.95 (ISBN 0-8167-0405-8). Troll Assocs.

Bolton, Elizabeth & Goodwin, Diana. Pool Exercises. 4th ed. (Illus.). 1974. pap. 3.75x (ISBN 0-443-01126-5). Churchill.

Bolton, Ethel S. Immigrants to New England, 1700-1775. LC 66-28669. 235p. 1979. Repr. of 1931 ed. 15.00 (ISBN 0-8063-0047-7). Genealog Pub.

--Wax Portraits & Silhouettes. LC 71-164115. 88p. 1974. Repr. of 1914 ed. 40.00x (ISBN 0-8103-3168-3). Gale.

Bolton, Ethel S., ed. see Topliff, Samuel.

Bolton, Evelyn. Dream Dancer. LC 74-9571. (Evelyn Bolton's Horse Stories Ser). (Illus.). 32p. (gr. 3-7). 1974. PLB 7.95 (ISBN 0-87191-371-2); pap. 3.95 (ISBN 0-89812-128-0). Creative Ed.

--Goodbye Charlie. LC 74-9572. (Evelyn Bolton's Horse Stories Ser). (Illus.). 32p. (gr. 2-6). 1974. PLB 7.95 (ISBN 0-87191-369-0); pap. 3.95 (ISBN 0-89812-127-2). Creative Ed.

--Lady's Girl. LC 74-9528. (Evelyn Bolton's Horse Stories Ser). (Illus.). 32p. (gr. 3-7). 1974. PLB 7.95 (ISBN 0-87191-372-0); pap. 3.95 (ISBN 0-89812-125-6). Creative Ed.

--Ride When You're Ready. LC 74-9763. (Evelyn Bolton's Horse Stories Ser). (Illus.). 32p. (gr. 3-7). 1974. PLB 7.95 (ISBN 0-87191-373-9); pap. 3.95 (ISBN 0-89812-130-2). Creative Ed.

--Stable of Fear. LC 74-9704. (Evelyn Bolton's Horse Stories Ser). (Illus.). 32p. (gr. 3-7). 1974. PLB 7.95 (ISBN 0-87191-370-4); pap. 3.95 (ISBN 0-89812-129-9). Creative Ed.

--The Wild Horses. LC 74-9530. (Evelyn Bolton's Horse Stories Ser). (Illus.). 32p. (gr. 3-7). 1974. PLB 7.95 (ISBN 0-87191-374-7); pap. 3.95 (ISBN 0-89812-126-4). Creative Ed.

Bolton, Frank G., Jr. The Pregnant Adolescent: Problems of Premature Parenthood. LC 79-27082. (Sage Library of Social Research: Vol. 100). (Illus.). 247p. 1980. 24.00 (ISBN 0-8039-1433-4); pap. 12.00 (ISBN 0-8039-1434-2). Sage.

--When Bonding Fails: Clinical Assessment of High Risk Families, Vol. 151. (Sage Library of Social Research). 224p. 1983. 28.00 (ISBN 0-8039-2079-2); pap. 14.00 (ISBN 0-8039-2080-6). Sage.

Bolton, Frederick E. Principles of Education. (Educational Ser.). 1910. Repr. 15.00 (ISBN 0-8482-3446-4). Norwood Edns.

Bolton, G. C. Fine Country to Starve in. LC 72-86808. 1972. 18.00x (ISBN 0-85564-061-8, Pub. by U of W Austral Pr). Intl Spec Bk.

Bolton, G. C., ed. Everyman in Australia. (Octagon Lectures, 1970). 1970. 5.00x (ISBN 0-85564-062-6, Pub. by U of W Austral Pr). Intl Spec Bk.

Bolton, G. M. Interviewing for Selection Decisions. (The NFER-Nelson Personnel Library). 32p. 1983. pap. 5.00x (ISBN 0-7005-0556-3, Pub. by NFER Nelson UK). Taylor & Francis.

Bolton, Geoffrey. Spoils & Spoilers: Australians Make their Environment 1788-1980. (Australian Experience Ser.: No. 3). (Illus.). 200p. 1982. pap. text ed. 12.50x (ISBN 0-86861-226-X). Allen Unwin.

Bolton, George W., jt. auth. see Bolton, Mimi D.

Bolton, Guy, jt. auth. see Wodehouse, P. G.

Bolton, H. The Insects of the British Coal Measures, Pts. 1-2. Repr. of 1922 ed. Set. 28.00 (ISBN 0-384-04980-X). Johnson Repr.

Bolton, H. C. A Select Bibliography of Chemistry. Incl. 1492-1892. 1893. 128.00 (ISBN 0-527-09400-5); First Supplement, 1492-1897, Section 1-7. 1899. 35.00 (ISBN 0-527-09420-X); First Supplement, 1492-1897, Section 8: Academic Dissertations. 1901. 35.00 (ISBN 0-527-09426-9); Second Supplement, 1492-1902. 1904. 35.00 (ISBN 0-527-09432-3). (Smithsonian Miscellaneous Collections Ser: No. 36). Kraus Repr.

Bolton, Henry C. Catalogue of Scientific & Technical Periodicals. 1665-1895. 2nd ed. Repr. of 1897 ed. 72.00 (ISBN 0-384-04985-0). Johnson Repr.

--Counting-out Rhymes of Children. LC 68-23139. 1969. Repr. of 1888 ed. 30.00x (ISBN 0-8103-3475-5). Gale.

--The Counting-out Rhymes of Children. 59.95 (ISBN 0-87968-950-1). Gordon Pr.

Bolton, Herbert E. Bolton & the Spanish Borderlands. Bannon, John F., ed. 1974. pap. 9.95 (ISBN 0-8061-1150-X). U of Okla Pr.

--Coronado: Knight of Pueblos & Plains. LC 64-17854. 491p. 1981. pap. 12.95 (ISBN 0-8263-0007-3). U of NM Pr.

--Coronado, Knight of Pueblos & Plains. LC 64-17854. 1964. pap. 8.95 (ISBN 0-8263-0007-3). U of NM Pr.

--Fray Juan Crespi, Missionary Explorer on the Pacific Coast, 1769-1774. LC 78-158616. Repr. of 1927 ed. 29.50 (ISBN 0-404-01838-6). AMS Pr.

--Guide to Materials for the History of the United States in the Principal Archives of Mexico. 1913. 41.00 (ISBN 0-527-00698-X). Kraus Repr.

--History of the Americas. (Illus.). 1980. Repr. of 1935 ed. lib. bdg. 32.50x (ISBN 0-8371-5273-9, BOHA). Greenwood.

--Padre on Horseback. LC 63-13248. (Illus.). 1963. Repr. of 1962 ed. 3.00 (ISBN 0-8294-0003-6). Loyola.

--Rim of Christendom: A Biography of Eusebio Francisco Kino, Pacific Coast Pioneer. LC 84-8814. 644p. 1984. Repr. of 1960 ed. 40.00x (ISBN 0-8165-0863-1). U of Ariz Pr.

--Spanish Borderlands. 1921. 8.50x (ISBN 0-686-83780-0). Elliots Bks.

--Texas in the Middle Eighteenth Century: Studies in Spanish Colonial History & Administration. 1977. Repr. of 1915 ed. 44.00 (ISBN 0-527-00941-5). Kraus Repr.

--Texas in the Middle Eighteenth Century: Studies in Spanish Colonial History & Administration. (Texas History Paperbacks Ser.: No. 8). 511p. 1970. pap. 10.95 (ISBN 0-292-70034-2). U of Tex Pr.

--Wider Horizons of American History. 1967. pap. 5.95x (ISBN 0-268-00301-7). U of Notre Dame Pr.

Bolton, Herbert E. & Marshall, Thomas M. The Colonization of North America, 1492-1783. (Illus.). 1971. Repr. of 1920 ed. 28.50x (ISBN 0-02-841590-6). Hafner.

Bolton, Herbert E see Johnson, Allen & Nevins, Allan.

Bolton, Herbert E., ed. Spanish Exploration in the Southwest, 1542-1706. (Original Narratives). 486p. 1976. Repr. of 1908 ed. 21.50x (ISBN 0-06-480088-1, 06355). B&N Imports.

Bolton, J. L. The Medieval English Economy: Eleven Fifty to Fifteen Hundred. LC 80-503599. (Rowman & Littlefield University Library). (Illus.). 400p. 1980. 25.00x (ISBN 0-8476-6234-9); pap. 16.00x (ISBN 0-8476-6235-7). Rowman.

Bolton, James. Ancient Crete & Mycenae. Reeves, Marjorie, ed. (Then & There Ser.). (Illus.). 96p. (YA) (gr. 7-12). 1968. pap. text ed. 3.40x (ISBN 0-582-20415-1). Longman.

Bolton, John R. Legislative Veto: Unseparating the Powers. 109p. 1977. pap. 4.25 (ISBN 0-8447-3245-1). Am Enterprise.

Bolton, Joseph S. Melanthe: A Latin Pastoral Play of the Early Seventeenth Century Written by Samuel Brooke. (Yale Studies in English Ser.: No. 79). vi, 206p. 1972. Repr. of 1928 ed. 17.50 (ISBN 0-208-01123-4, Archon). Shoe String.

Bolton, Joyce & Wilson, Yvonne. To Discover, to Delight: A Book on Creative Activities for Young Children. (LC- A-898861). 1977. 6.95 (ISBN 0-9602368-1-3). D J Bolton.

Bolton Landing Conference. Ordered Alloys. 1970. 20.00x. Claitors.

Bolton, Leonard. China Call. LC 83-82301. 256p. 1984. pap. text ed. 4.95 (ISBN 0-88243-509-4, 02-0509). Gospel Pub.

Bolton, Lyndon. An Introduction to the Theory of Relativity. 1976. lib. bdg. 69.95 (ISBN 0-8490-2075-1). Gordon Pr.

Bolton, Malcolm. A Guide to Soil Mechanics. LC 80-14875. 439p. 1980. 52.95x (ISBN 0-470-26929-4). Halsted Pr.

Bolton, Mimi D. & Bolton, George W. Wilhelmina's Inheritance. LC 84-51420. (Illus.). 147p. 1984. 10.95 (ISBN 0-9614274-0-X). Wisla Pubs.

Bolton, Muriel R. The Golden Porcupine. 1977. pap. 1.95 (ISBN 0-380-01657-5, 33258). Avon.

Bolton, Neil. Concept Formation. 1977. text ed. 14.75 o. p. (ISBN 0-08-021493-2); pap. text ed. 8.25 (ISBN 0-08-021494-0). Pergamon.

--The Psychology of Thinking. 325p. 1976. pap. 11.95x (ISBN 0-416-70450-6, NO. 2607). Methuen Inc.

Bolton, P. M. Civil Rights. 7th ed. 228p. 1984. 8.95 (ISBN 0-88908-581-1). Self Counsel Pr.

--Criminal Procedure in Canada. 6th ed. 160p. 1983. 12.95 (ISBN 0-88908-556-0). Self Counsel Pr.

Bolton, R., jt. auth. see De la Mare, P. B.

Bolton, R. & Mayer, E., eds. Andean Kinship & Marriage. 1977. 7.50 (ISBN 0-686-36559-3). Am Anthro Assn.

Bolton, R. P., jt. ed. see Losowsky, M. S.

Bolton, R. P., et al. Action Chemistry, 9 units. Incl. Unit 1. Matter. pap. 4.44 (ISBN 0-03-001471-9); Unit 2. Solutions. pap. 4.44 (ISBN 0-03-001481-6); Unit 3. Acids, Bases, & Salts. pap. 4.44 (ISBN 0-03-001486-7); Unit 4. The "Why" of Chemical Behavior. pap. 4.44 (ISBN 0-03-001491-3); Unit 5. Chemical Reactions. pap. 4.44 (ISBN 0-03-001496-4); Unit 6. Organic Chemistry & Biochemistry. pap. 4.44 (ISBN 0-03-001501-4); Unit 7. Chemistry in the Home. pap. 4.44 (ISBN 0-03-001506-5); Unit 8. Chemistry in the Environment. pap. 4.44 (ISBN 0-03-001511-1); Unit 9. Chemistry in Industry. pap. 4.44 (ISBN 0-03-001516-2). 1973. text for use with all units 20.84 (ISBN 0-03-086072-5, HoltE); lab manuals for units 1-9 3.84 ea.; magazines to accompany units 1-5 3.84 ea. HR&W.

Bolton, Ralph. Systems Contracting. 1979. pap. 7.50 (ISBN 0-8144-2236-5). AMACOM.

Bolton, Ralph, tr. see Flores-Ochoa, Jorge A.

Bolton, Reg. Circus in a Suitcase. (Illus.). 94p. 1982. pap. 7.95 (ISBN 0-932720-08-0). New Plays Bks.

Bolton, Reginald P. New York City in Indian Possession. 2nd ed. (Illus.). 1975. soft cover 6.00 (ISBN 0-934490-02-3). Mus Am Ind.

Bolton, Reginald P., jt. auth. see Calver, William L.

Bolton, Richard. Painting Weathered Textures in Watercolor. (Illus.). 144p. 1982. 22.50 (ISBN 0-8230-3876-9). Watson-Guptill.

--Weathered Texture Workshop. (Illus.). 144p. 1984. 24.95 (ISBN 0-8230-5697-X). Watson-Guptill.

Bolton, Richard, jt. auth. see Blockley, John.

Bolton, Robert. A Discourse About the State of True Happinesse. LC 79-84089. (English Experience Ser.: No. 909). 184p. 1979. Repr. of 1611 ed. lib. bdg. 14.00 (ISBN 90-221-0909-7). Walter J Johnson.

--A Guide to New Rochelle & Its Vicinity: Pelham, West Chester, West Farms, Morrisania, Fordham, Yonkers, East Chester, White Plains, Mamaroneck & Rye. Weigold, Marilyn, ed. LC 76-6922. (Illus.). 1976. pap. 2.95 (ISBN 0-916346-22-6). Harbor Hill Bks.

Bolton, Robert & Bolton, Dorothy G. Social Style-Management Style. LC 83-45959. 192p. 1984. 19.95 (ISBN 0-8144-5703-7); pap. 9.95 (ISBN 0-8144-7617-1). AMACOM.

Bolton, Robert H. People Skills: How to Assert Yourself, Listen to Others & Resolve Conflicts. (Illus.). 1979. 13.95 (ISBN 0-13-655779-1, Spec); pap. 5.95 (ISBN 0-13-655761-9). P-H.

Bolton, Robert L. & Musarra, Russ. The Chameleon's Mask. LC 85-80050. 350p. (Orig.). 1985. pap. 3.95 (ISBN 0-932909-02-7). SNB Pub.

--Sleep with the Angels. LC 84-52601. 344p. (Orig.). 1985. pap. 3.95 (ISBN 0-932909-00-0). SNB Pub.

Bolton, Sanford. Pharmaceutical Statistics: Practical & Clinical Applications. (Drugs & the Pharmaceutical Sciences Ser.: Vol. 25). (Illus.). 544p. 1984. 75.00 (ISBN 0-8247-7218-0); text ed. 39.75. Dekker.

Bolton, Sarah K. Famous American Authors. 1887. Repr. 25.00 (ISBN 0-8274-2333-0). R West.

--Famous English Statesmen: Of Queen Victoria's Reign. LC 78-39705. (Essay Index Reprint Ser.). Repr. of 1891 ed. 27.50 (ISBN 0-8369-2749-4). Ayer Co Pubs.

--Famous European Artists. LC 74-39676. (Essay Index Reprint Ser.). Repr. of 1890 ed. 24.00 (ISBN 0-8369-2750-8). Ayer Co Pubs.

--Famous European Artists. 1976. lib. bdg. 59.95 (ISBN 0-8490-1801-3). Gordon Pr.

--Famous Givers & Their Gifts. facsimile ed. LC 76-37129. (Essay Index Reprint Ser). Repr. of 1896 ed. 25.00 (ISBN 0-8369-2484-3). Ayer Co Pubs.

--Famous Leaders Among Women. facsimile ed. LC 76-38745. (Essay Index Reprint Ser). Repr. of 1895 ed. 19.50 (ISBN 0-8369-2639-0). Ayer Co Pubs.

--Famous Men of Science. 4th ed. Cline, Barbara L., rev. by. LC 61-6133. (Illus.). (gr. 7-11). 1960. Crowell Jr Bks.

--Famous Types of Womanhood. facsimile ed. LC 74-37123. (Essay Index Reprint Ser). Repr. of 1892 ed. 23.00 (ISBN 0-8369-2485-1). Ayer Co Pubs.

--Famous Voyagers & Explorers. LC 70-39659. (Essay Index Reprint Ser.). Repr. of 1893 ed. 33.00 (ISBN 0-8369-2751-6). Ayer Co Pubs.

--How Success is Won. 14.75 (ISBN 0-8369-7209-0, 8008). Ayer Co Pubs.

--Lives of Poor Boys Who Became Famous. rev. ed. Wilson, Margaret, ed. LC 62-5076. (Illus.). (gr. 5-11). 1962. Crowell Jr Bks.

--Lives of Poor Boys Who Became Famous: Samuel Johnson, Oliver Goldsmith. 1885. Repr. 25.00 (ISBN 0-8274-2977-0). R West.

--Ralph Waldo Emerson. LC 73-15752. 1973. lib. bdg. 10.00 (ISBN 0-8414-3304-6). Folcroft.

--Social Studies in England. 11.00 (ISBN 0-8369-7210-4, 8009). Ayer Co Pubs.

--Successful Women: With Portraits. LC 74-936. (Essay Index Reprint Ser.). (Illus.). Repr. of 1888 ed. 15.75 (ISBN 0-518-10143-6). Ayer Co Pubs.

Bolton, Theodore. Early American Portrait Draughtsmen in Crayons. LC 74-77724. (Library of American Art Ser). (Illus.). 1970. Repr. of 1923 ed. lib. bdg. 29.50 (ISBN 0-306-71362-4). Da Capo.

Bolton, Theodore & Cortelyou, Irwin F. Ezra Ames of Albany. LC 55-27077. (Illus.). xix, 398p. (Supplement included). 1955. 8.50x (ISBN 0-685-73898-1, New York Historical Society). U Pr of Va.

Bolton, Urgil, ed. see Minnesota Trade Office.

Bolton, W. F. Alcuin & Beowulf: An Eighth-Century View. 1978. 22.50 (ISBN 0-8135-0865-7). Rutgers U Pr.

--The Language of Nineteen Eighty-Four: Orwell's English & Ours. LC 83-21671. 252p. 1984. text ed. 19.95x (ISBN 0-87049-412-0). U of Tenn Pr.

--A Short History of Literary English. 2nd ed. (Quality Paperback: No. 266). 86p. 1973. pap. 1.50 (ISBN 0-8226-0266-0). Littlefield.

Bolton, W. F. & Crystal, D. J. English Language, 2 vols. Incl. Vol. 1. 1490-1839. 44.50 (ISBN 0-521-04280-1); pap. 15.95 (ISBN 0-521-09379-1); Vol. 2. 1858-1964. 1965. pap. 17.95x (ISBN 0-521-09545-X). 1966. pap. Cambridge U Pr.

Bolton, W. F., ed. see Jonson, Ben.

Bolton, Whitney F. Beowulf. LC 72-86666. 1982. text ed. 16.95 (ISBN 0-312-07561-8). St Martin.

--A Living Language: The History & Structure of English. 512p. 1982. 28.00 (ISBN 0-394-32280-0, RanC). Random.

Bolton-Smith, Robin. Portrait Miniatures in the National Museum of American Art. LC 84-2692. (CVL Ser.: No. 46). (Illus.). 88p. 1984. 60.00 (ISBN 0-226-68857-7). U of Chicago Pr.

Boltovskoy, E., et al, eds. Atlas of Benthic Shelf Foraminifera of the Southwest Atlantic. (Illus.). v, 153p. 1980. lib. bdg. 58.00 (ISBN 90-6193-604-7, Pub. by Junk Pubs Netherlands). Kluwer Academic.

Boltwood, Bertram B., jt. auth. see Rutherford, Ernest.

Boltwood, Lucius M. Genealogies of Hadley Families Embracing the Early Settlers of the Towns of Hatfield, South Hadley, Amherst & Granby. LC 79-52942. 205p. 1979. Repr. of 1905 ed. 12.50 (ISBN 0-8063-0848-6). Genealog Pub.

Boltyanskii, V. G. & Postnikov, M. M. Two Papers on Homotopy Theory of Continuous Mappings. LC 51-5559. (Translation Ser.: No. 2, Vol. 7). 1957. 27.00 (ISBN 0-8218-1707-8, TRANS 2-7). Am Math.

Boltyanskii, V. G., et al. Topology & Topological Algebra. (Translations Ser.: No. 1, Vol. 8). 1962. 24.00 (ISBN 0-8218-1608-X, TRANS 1-8). Am Math.

--Twenty Papers on Analytic Functions & Ordinary Differential Equations. LC 51-5559. (Translations Ser.: No. 2, Vol. 18). 1961. 30.00 (ISBN 0-8218-1718-3, TRANS 2-18). Am Math.

Boltyanskii, Vladimir G. & Gokhberg, Izrail T. The Decomposition of Figures into Smaller Parts. Christoffers, Henry & Branson, Thomas P., trs. from Rus. LC 79-10382. (Popular Lectures in Mathematics). 1980. pap. text ed. 6.00x (ISBN 0-226-06357-7). U of Chicago Pr.

Boltyansky, V. G. Differentiation Explained. 63p. 1977. pap. 1.95 (ISBN 0-8285-0716-3, Pub. by Mir Pubs USSR). Imported Pubns.

Boltz, C. W. How Electricity Is Made. Date not set. price not set. Facts on File.

Boltz, Carol & Seyler, Dorothy. Language Power. 303p. 1982. pap. text ed. 11.00 (ISBN 0-394-32715-2, RanC). Random.

Boltz, Carol, jt. auth. see Seyler, Dorothy.

Boltz, David F. & Howell, James A. Colorimetric Determination of Nonmetals. 2nd ed. LC 77-12398. (Chemical Analysis Ser.: Vol. 8). 543p. 1978. 92.00 (ISBN 0-471-08750-5, Pub by Wiley-Interscience). Wiley.

Boltzius, John M. & Gronau, Israel Christian. Detailed Reports on the Salzburger Emigrants Who Settled in America, 1736, Vol. 3. Jones, George F., ed. LC 67-27137. 368p. 1972. 20.00x (ISBN 0-8203-0278-3). U of Ga Pr.

Boltzius, John M & Gronau, Israel Christian. Detailed Reports on the Salzburger Emigrants Who Settled in America, 1737, Vol. 4. Jones, George F. & Wilson, Renate, eds. LC 67-27137. 264p. 1976. 17.00x (ISBN 0-8203-0400-X). U of Ga Pr.

--Detailed Reports on the Salzburger Emigrants Who Settled in America, 1738, Vol. 5. Jones, George F. & Wilson, Renate, eds. LC 67-27137. 374p. 1980. 20.00x (ISBN 0-8203-0482-4). U of Ga Pr.

Boltzius, John M. & Gronau, Israel Christian. Detailed Reports on the Salzburger Emigrants Who Settled in America, Vol. 6. Jones, George F. & Wilson, Renate, eds. LC 67-27137. 1739p. 1981. 27.50x (ISBN 0-8203-0512-X). U of Ga Pr.

Boltzius, John Martin & Gronau, Israel Christian. Detailed Reports on the Salzburger Emigrants Who Settled in America, Vol. 7, 1740. Jones, George F. & Savelle, Don, eds. LC 67-27137. (Wormsloe Foundation Ser.). 328p. 1983. 25.00x (ISBN 0-8203-0664-9). U of Ga Pr.

Boltzmann, Ludwig. Theoretical Physics & Philosophical Problems: Selected Writings. McGuinness, Brian, ed. Foulke, Paul, tr. from Ger. LC 74-79571. (Vienna Circle Collection: No. 5). 270p. 1974. lib. bdg. 46.00 (ISBN 90-277-0249-7, Pub. by Reidel Holland); pap. 24.00 (ISBN 90-277-0250-0). Kluwer Academic.

--Wissenschaftliche Abhandlungen, 3 Vols. Hasenohrl, Fritz, ed. LC 66-26524. (Ger). 1969. Set. 99.50 (ISBN 0-8284-0215-9). Chelsea Pub.

Bolvers, Stanely J. & Staton, Janet L., eds. National tax Association-Tax Institute of America 77th Annual Conference: Proceedings. 400p. 1984. 20.00 (ISBN 0-318-17673-4); members free. Natl Tax.

Bolweg, Joep F. Job Design & Industrial Democracy. (Studies in the Quality of Working Life: No. 3). 1976. lib. bdg. 20.50 (ISBN 90-207-0634-9, Pub. by Martinus Nijhoff Netherlands). Kluwer Academic.

Bolwell, Robert W. Life & Works of John Heywood. LC 21-22336. Repr. of 1921 ed. 18.50 (ISBN 0-404-00934-4). AMS Pr.

Bolyard, Charles W., jt. auth. see Barkhaus, Robert S.

Bolyard, Judith L. Medicinal Plants & Home Remedies of Appalachia. (Illus.). 206p. 1981. 18.50x (ISBN 0-398-04180-6). C C Thomas.

Bolz, J. Arnold. Portage into the Past: By Canoe along the Minnesota-Ontario Boundary Waters. (Illus.). 1960. 8.95 (ISBN 0-8166-0218-2); pap. 4.95 (ISBN 0-8166-0919-5). U of Minn Pr.

Bolz, Ray E. & Tuve, George L., eds. Handbook of Tables for Applied Engineering Science, CRC. 2nd ed. (Handbook Ser.). 1184p. 1973. 49.95 (ISBN 0-8493-0252-8). CRC Pr.

Bolz, Roger W. Manufacturing Automation Management: A Productivity Handbook. 220p. 1985. 27.50 (ISBN 0-412-00731-2, NO. 9094, Pub. by Chapman & Hall England). Methuen Inc.

--Production Processes: The Productivity Handbook. 5th ed. 1089p. 1981. 48.00 (ISBN 0-8311-1088-0). Indus Pr.

Bolz, Roger W., jt. auth. see Tver, David F.

Bolza, Eleanor, jt. auth. see Keating, W. G.

Bolza, Eleanor, jt. auth. see Benni, C. A.

Bolza, Oskar. Lectures on the Calculus of Variations. 3rd ed. LC 73-16324. 12.95 (ISBN 0-8284-0145-4). Chelsea Pub.

--Vorlesungen Ueber Variationsrechnung. LC 62-8228. 23.95 (ISBN 0-8284-0160-8). Chelsea Pub.

Bolza, Oskar, et al. Festschrift Schwarz. LC 73-20209. Orig. Title: Mathematische Abhandlungen. viii, 451p. 1974. Repr. text ed. 25.00 (ISBN 0-8284-0275-2). Chelsea Pub.

Bolzano, Bernhard. The Theory of Science, (Die Wissenschaftslehre Oder Versuch Einer Neuen Darstellung der Logik) George, Rolf, ed. & tr. LC 71-126765. 1972. 48.50x (ISBN 0-520-01787-0). U of Cal Pr.

Bom, N. Echocardiology. 1977. lib. bdg. 53.00 (ISBN 90-247-2009-5, Pub. by Martinus Nijhoff Netherlands). Kluwer Academic.

Boman, Thorleif. Hebrew Thought Compared with Greek. Moreau, Jules L., tr. from Ger. 1970. pap. 4.95 (ISBN 0-393-00534-8, Norton Lib). Norton.

Bomani, Paul, jt. auth. see Ensminger, Douglas.

Bomans, Godfried. The Wily Witch & All the Other Fairy Tales & Fables. Crampton, Patricia, tr. from Dutch. LC 76-54196. (Illus.). 208p. (gr. 3 up). 1977. 9.95 (ISBN 0-916144-09-7). Stemmer Hse.

Bomar, George W. Texas Weather. (Illus.). 277p. 1983. 22.50 (ISBN 0-292-78052-4); pap. 9.95 (ISBN 0-292-78053-2). U of Tex Pr.

Bomar, Suzanne K., jt. auth. see Sager, Diane P.

Bomar, Willie M. The Education of Homemakers for Community Activities. LC 78-176574. (Columbia University. Teachers College. Contributions to Education: No. 477). Repr. of 1931 ed. 22.50 (ISBN 0-404-55477-6). AMS Pr.

Bombace, G. Preliminary Report on Fish Distribution & Marketing in Sicily. (General Fisheries Council of the Mediterranean (GFCM): Studies & Reviews: No. 28). 28p. (Eng. & Fr.). 1966. pap. 7.50 (ISBN 92-5-101946-0, F1789, FAO). Unipub.

Bombal, Maria L. New Islands & Other Stories. Cunningham, Richard, tr. from Span. 112p. 1982. 12.95 (ISBN 0-374-22118-9). FS&G.

Bombardieri, Merle. The Baby Decision: How to Make the Most Important Choice of Your Life. 1981. 13.95 (ISBN 0-89256-138-6); pap. 2.95 (ISBN 0-89256-175-0). Rawson Assocs.

Bombaugh, Charles C. Facts & Fancies for the Curious: From the Harvest-Fields of Literature. 1979. Repr. of 1905 ed. lib. bdg. 65.00 (ISBN 0-8482-3414-6). Norwood Edns.

--Gleanings for the Curious from Literature. 59.95 (ISBN 0-8490-0237-0). Gordon Pr.

--Gleanings for the Curious from the Harvest Fields of Literature: A Melange of Excerpta. LC 68-23465. 1970. Repr. of 1875 ed. 54.00x (ISBN 0-8103-3086-5). Gale.

--Oddities & Curiosities of Words & Literature. Gardner, M., ed. Orig. Title: Gleanings for the Curious. 1961. pap. 5.95 (ISBN 0-486-20759-5). Dover.

Bombaugh, Charles C., ed. Facts & Fancies for the Curious from the Harvest-Fields of Literature. LC 68-23464. 1968. Repr. of 1905 ed. 38.00x (ISBN 0-8103-3085-7). Gale.

Bombaugh, Charles D., ed. Facts & Fancies for the Curious from The Harvest Fields of Literature: A Melange of Excerpta. 647p. 1984. Repr. of 1934 ed. lib. bdg. 100.00 (ISBN 0-89987-966-7). Darby Books.

Bombeck, Erma. At Wit's End. LC 67-19068. 1967. 8.95 (ISBN 0-385-08333-5). Doubleday.

--At Wit's End. 1984. pap. 2.95 (ISBN 0-449-20760-9, Crest). Fawcett.

--At Wit's End (from "Giant Economy Size") Large Print ed. LC 83-18090. 260p. 1984. Repr. of 1983 ed. 13.95 (ISBN 0-89621-510-5). Thorndike Pr.

--Aunt Erma's Cope Book. 1984. pap. 2.95 (ISBN 0-449-20758-7, Crest). Fawcett.

--Aunt Erma's Cope Book: How to Get from Monday to Friday in Twelve Days. 1979. 8.95 (ISBN 0-07-006452-0). McGraw.

--Aunt Erma's Cope Book: How to Get from Monday to Friday...in Twelve Days. (General Ser.). 1980. lib. bdg. 13.95 (ISBN 0-8161-3054-X, Large Print Bks). G K Hall.

--Four of a Kind. 1985. 17.95 (ISBN 0-07-006456-3). McGraw.

--The Grass Is Always Greener Over the Septic Tank. (General Ser.). 1977. lib. bdg. 12.95 (ISBN 0-8161-6502-5, Large Print Bks). G K Hall.

--The Grass Is Always Greener Over the Septic Tank. LC 76-20645. 1976. 6.95 (ISBN 0-07-006450-4). McGraw.

--The Grass Is Always Greener over the Septic Tank. 1985. pap. 2.95 (ISBN 0-449-20759-5, Crest). Fawcett.

--I Lost Everything in the Post-Natal Depression. LC 72-97269. 168p. 1973. 8.95 (ISBN 0-385-02904-7). Doubleday.

--I Lost Everything in the Post-Natal Depression. 1978. pap. 2.25 (ISBN 0-449-23785-0, Crest). Fawcett.

--I Lost Everything in the Post-Natal Depression. large print ed. LC 84-106. 252p. 1984. Repr. of 1983 ed. 13.95 (ISBN 0-89621-528-8). Thorndike Pr.

--If Life Is a Bowl of Cherries, What Am I Doing in the Pits? 1979. pap. 2.50 (ISBN 0-449-23894-6, Crest). Fawcett.

--If Life Is a Bowl of Cherries-What Am I Doing in the Pits? (General Ser.). 1978. lib. bdg. 12.95 (ISBN 0-8161-6613-7, Large Print Bks). G K Hall.

--If Life Is a Bowl of Cherries, What Am I Doing in the Pits. LC 77-17344. 1978. 7.95 (ISBN 0-07-006451-2). McGraw.

--Just Wait Till You Have Children of Your Own! large print ed. LC 84-8580. (Illus.). 221p. 1984. Repr. of 1983 ed. 12.95. Thorndike Pr.

--Laugh along with Erma Bombeck. 1984. Boxed Set. pap. 11.40 (ISBN 0-449-28108-6). Fawcett.

--Motherhood: The Second Oldest Profession. (General Ser.). 1984. lib. bdg. 13.95 (ISBN 0-8161-3602-5, Large Print Bks). G K Hall.

--Motherhood: The Second Oldest Profession. 1984. 12.95 (ISBN 0-07-006454-7). McGraw.

--Motherhood: The Second Oldest Profession. 192p. 1984. pap. 3.95 (ISBN 0-440-15900-8). Dell.

Bombeck, Erma & Keane, Bil. Just Wait till You Have Children of Your Own! 1979. pap. 2.50 (ISBN 0-449-23786-9, Crest). Fawcett.

Bombelles, Joseph T. Economic Development of Communist Yugoslavia, 1947-1964. LC 68-28098. (Publications Ser.: No. 73). (Illus., Orig.). 1968. 9.95x (ISBN 0-8179-1731-4); pap. 6.95 (ISBN 0-8179-1732-2). Hoover Inst Pr.

Bombelli, R. Osteoarthritis of the Hip: Classification & Pathogenesis-the Role of Osteotomy As Consequent Therapy. 2nd, rev. & enl ed. (Illus.). 386p. 1983. 170.00 (ISBN 0-387-11422-X). Springer-Verlag.

Bomberger, Audery S. & Dannenfelser, Betty A. Radiation & Health. 272p. 1984. 29.95 (ISBN 0-89443-586-8). Aspen Systems.

Bombieri, Enrico. Seminar on Minimal Submanifolds. LC 82-61356. (Annals of Mathematics Studies: No. 103). 500p. 1983. 45.00 (ISBN 0-691-08324-X); pap. 15.00 (ISBN 0-691-08319-3). Princeton U Pr.

Bombin, Luis M. Plant Protection Legislation. (Legislative Study Ser.: No. 28). 165p. 1985. pap. 12.50 (ISBN 92-5-101460-4, F2732, FAO). Unipub.

Bombin-Bombin, Luis M. Seed Legislation. (Legislative Studies: No. 16). 121p. (Eng., Fr. & Span.). 1978. pap. 8.25 (ISBN 92-5-100832-9, F2083, FAO). Unipub.

Bomely, Steven. Glory to God: A Candlelight Service for Christmas. 1983. pap. 2.25 (ISBN 0-89536-625-8). CSS of Ohio.

Bomer, Hildegard, tr. see Mayer-Skumanz, Lene.

Bomers, Gerald B. & Peterson, Richard B. Conflict Management & Industrial Relations. 1982. lib. bdg. 40.00 (ISBN 0-89838-068-5). Kluwer-Nijhoff.

Bomford, G. Geodesy. 4th ed. 1980. 119.00x (ISBN 0-19-851946-X). Oxford U Pr.

Bomgren, Marilyn J. Godparents, Why? 1981. 2.50 (ISBN 0-89536-473-5). CSS of Ohio.

Bomhard, Allan R. Toward Proto-Nostratic: A New Approach to the Comparison of Proto-Indo-European & Proto-Asiatic. (Current Issues in Linguistic Theory Ser.: Vol. 27). 356p. 1984. 40.00 (ISBN 90-272-3519-8). Benjamins North Am.

Bomhard, Allan R., jt. ed. see Arbeitman, Yoel L.

Bomhoff, E. J. Monetary Uncertainty. 1983. 32.00 (ISBN 0-444-86734-1, I-405-83). Elsevier.

Bommarito, James W., jt. auth. see Johnson, Orval G.

Bommel, W. J. Van see Van Bommel, W. J. & DeBoer, J. B.

Bommer, C. M. & Symonds, D. A. Skeletal Structures: Matrix. 106p. 1968. 38.50 (ISBN 0-677-61120-X). Gordon.

Bommer, Michael R. & Chorba, Ronald W. Decision Making for Library Management. LC 81-17160. (Professional Librarian Ser.). 178p. 1982. pap. text ed. 27.50 professional (ISBN 0-86729-000-5, 208-BW). Knowledge Indus.

Bompa, Tudor. Fitness & Body Development Exercises. 224p. 1981. pap. text ed. 12.95 (ISBN 0-8403-2388-3). Kendall-Hunt.

Bompa, Tudor O. Theory & Methodology of Training: The Key to Athletic Performance. 352p. 1983. pap. text ed. 18.95 (ISBN 0-8403-2934-2). Kendall-Hunt.

Bompas, Cecil H., tr. see Dorson, Richard M.

Bompas, George C. The Problem of the Shakespeare Plays. 1902. lib. bdg. 20.00 (ISBN 0-8414-3282-1). Folcroft.

Bompois, H. F. Examen Chronologique des Monnais Frappes par la Communaute des Macedoniens Avant, Pendant et Apes la Conquete Romaine. (Illus.). 102p. (Fr.). 20.00 (ISBN 0-916710-77-7). Obol Intl.

--Monnaies De Koinon Makedonon. 1985. Repr. of 1896 ed. 20.00 (ISBN 0-89005-393-6). Ares.

Bompray, Augustine C. The Ignorant Man's Guide to the Mysteries of Philosophy. (Illus.). 87p. (Orig.). 1984. pap. 19.75 (ISBN 0-89266-454-1). Am Classical Coll Pr.

Bomse, Marguerite D. Practical Spanish Dictionary & Phrasebook. new ed. (Span.). 1978. pap. text ed. 7.50 (ISBN 0-08-023020-2). Pergamon.

--Practical Spanish Grammar. 1978. pap. 7.50 (ISBN 0-08-021859-8). Pergamon.

Bomse, Marguerite D. & Alfaro, Julian H. Practical Spanish for Medical & Hospital Personnel. 2nd ed. 1978. pap. text ed. 6.55 (ISBN 0-08-023001-6). Pergamon.

--Practical Spanish for School Personnel, Firemen, Policemen & Community Agencies. 2nd ed. 1978. pap. text ed. 6.55 (ISBN 0-08-023002-4). Pergamon.

Bomze, Henry D. Treasury of American Turf. 1967. 10.00 (ISBN 0-685-13754-6). Landau.

Bomze, Howard. Programming Digital's Personal Computer: BASIC. 1986. text ed. 17.75 (ISBN 0-03-063729-5). HR&W.

Bon & Hart. Linking Canada's New Solitudes: The Executive Interchange Program & Business-Government Relations. 55p. 1983. 125.00 (ISBN 0-317-36604-1, CS-77); members 25.00 (ISBN 0-317-36605-X). Conference Bd.

Bon Appetit, ed. Beef, Veal, Lamb & Pork. 144p. 1985. 12.95 (ISBN 0-517-55467-4). Knapp Pr.

Bon Appetit Editors, ed. The Bon Appetit Dinner Party Cookbook. 1983. 25.00 (ISBN 0-89535-118-8). Knapp Pr.

--Bon Appetit Too Busy to Cook? LC 81-5959. (Illus.). 224p. 1981. 19.95 (ISBN 0-89535-049-1). Knapp Pr.

Bon Appetit Magazine Editors. The Best of Bon Appetit, Vol 1. (Illus.). 1985. 9.95 (ISBN 0-89535-164-1). Knapp Pr.

--The Best of Bon Appetit, Vol. 2. (Illus.). 1985. 9.95 (ISBN 0-89535-165-X). Knapp Pr.

--Cooking with Bon Appetit: Appetizers. (Illus.). 144p. 1984. 12.95 (ISBN 0-89535-105-6). Knapp Pr.

--Cooking with Bon Appetit: Beef, Veal, Lamb & Pork. (Illus.). 1985. 12.95 (ISBN 0-89535-138-2). Knapp Pr.

--Cooking with Bon Appetit: Breads. (Illus.). 120p. 1985. 12.95 (ISBN 0-89535-168-4). Knapp Pr.

--Cooking with Bon Appetit: Breakfasts & Brunches. (Illus.). 144p. 1984. 12.95 (ISBN 0-89535-115-3, Dist. by C N Potter). Knapp Pr.

--Cooking with Bon Appetit: Buffets. (Illus.). 1985. 12.95 (ISBN 0-89535-139-0). Knapp Pr.

--Cooking with Bon Appetit: Light Desserts. (Illus.). 144p. 1984. 12.95 (ISBN 0-89535-135-8). Knapp Pr.

--Cooking with Bon Appetit: Pasta & Pizza. (Illus.). 1985. 12.95 (ISBN 0-89535-167-6). Knapp Pr.

--Cooking with Bon Appetit: Poultry. (Illus.). 1984. 12.95 (ISBN 0-89535-134-X, Dist. by C N Potter). Knapp Pr.

--Cooking with Bon Appetit: Seafood. (Illus.) 144p. 1984. 12.95 (ISBN 0-89535-120-X). Knapp Pr.

--Cooking with Bon Appetit: Soups & Salads. (Illus.). 144p. 1984. 12.95 (ISBN 0-89535-116-1). Knapp Pr.

--Cooking with Bon Appetit: Vegetables. (Illus.). 144p. 1984. 12.95 (ISBN 0-89535-119-6). Knapp Pr.

--New York's Master Chefs. Sax, Richard, ed. (Illus.). 1985. 9.95 (ISBN 0-89535-090-4). Knapp Pr.

Bon Appetit Magazine Editors, ed. The Best of Bon Appetit. LC 79-2384. (Illus.). 1979. 19.95 (ISBN 0-89535-008-4). Knapp Pr.

--Cooking with Bon Appetit: American. (Illus.). 1985. 12.95 (ISBN 0-89535-169-2). Knapp Pr.

--Cooking with Bon Appetit: Special Occasion Desserts. (Illus.). 1986. 12.95 (ISBN 0-89535-170-6). Knapp Pr.

Bon, Daniel Le see Jackins, Harvey.

Bon, Gustave Le see Le Bon, Gustave.

Bon, Gustave Le see LeBon, Gustave.

Bon, Gustave Le see Le Bon, Gustave.

Bon Viveur. An ABC of Wine Drinking. 1974. lib. bdg. 69.95 (ISBN 0-685-51377-7). Revisionist Pr.

Bona, C., et al, eds. see CISM (International Center for Mechanical Sciences), Dept. for General Mechanics, 1972, et al.

Bona, Constantin. Idiotypes & Lymphocytes. LC 81-10759. (Immunology: An International Series of Monographs & Treatise). 1981. 35.00 (ISBN 0-12-112950-0). Acad Pr.

Bona, Constantin & Cazenave, Pierre-Andre. Lymphocytic Regulation by Antibodies. LC 80-17399. 324p. 1981. 79.50 (ISBN 0-471-05693-6, Pub. by Wiley-Interscience). Wiley.

Bona, Constantin A. & Kohler, Heinz, eds. Immune Networks, Vol. 418. 80.00x (ISBN 0-89766-230-X); pap. 80.00x (ISBN 0-89766-231-8). NY Acad Sci.

Bona, Maurice De see De Bona, Maurice, Jr.

Bona, Mercy. Sleeping Obsessions. LC 75-44680. 64p. 1976. pap. 2.00 (ISBN 0-913722-09-X, Pub. by Release). Small Pr Dist.

Bonachea, Ramon L. & Martin, Marta S. The Cuban Insurrection, 1952-1959. LC 72-94546. (Social History Ser). 450p. 1974. pap. 12.95 (ISBN 0-87855-576-5). Transaction Bks.

Bonachea, Rolando, ed. see Castro, Fidel.

Bonacich, Edna & Modell, John. The Economic Basis of Ethnic Solidarity: Small Business in the Japanese Community. LC 80-51233. 1980. 24.00x (ISBN 0-520-04155-0). U of Cal Pr.

Bonacich, Edna, jt. ed. see Cheng, Lucie.

Bonacina, Conrad M., tr. see Von Lefort, Gertrud F.

Bonacina, Conrad R., tr. see Von Le Fort, Gertrud.

Bonacker, Wilhelm. Karten-Woerterbuch. (Ger.). 1970. 39.95 (ISBN 3-7812-0704-8, M-7493, Pub. by Kirschbaum). French & Eur.

Bonadonna, G., jt. ed. see Veronesi, U.

Bonadonna, G., et al, eds. Adjuvant Therapies & Markers of Post-Surgical Minimal Residual Disease One: Markers & General Problems. (Recent Results in Cancer Research Ser.: Vol. 67). (Illus.). 1979. 33.00 (ISBN 0-387-09291-9). Springer-Verlag.

--Adjuvant Therapies & Markers of Post-Surgical Minimal Residual Disease Two: Adjuvant Therapies. (Recent Results in Cancer Research: Vol. 68). (Illus.). 1979. 63.00 (ISBN 0-387-09360-5). Springer-Verlag.

Bonadonna, Gianni, ed. Breast Cancer: Diagnosis & Treatment. (Cancer Investigation & Management Ser.: 1-690). 347p. 1984. text ed. 38.95 (ISBN 0-471-90193-8, Pub by Wiley Med). Wiley.

Bonafide, John, jt. auth. see Franks, Lloyd.

Bonaforte, Lisa. I Can Draw Dinosaurs. (I Can Draw Ser.). (Illus.). 64p. (Orig.). (gr. 2-7). 1984. pap. 3.50 (ISBN 0-671-52756-8). Wanderer Bks.

Bonafoux, Pascal. Rembrandt Self-Portraits. LC 85-42921. (Illus.). 140p. 1985. 50.00 (ISBN 0-8478-0629-4). Rizzoli Intl.

Bonafoux, Pascal & Skira-Rizzoli. Portraits of the Artist: The Self-Portrait in Painting. 158p. 1985. 35.00 (ISBN 0-8478-0586-7). Rizzoli Intl.

Bonaiuti, Andrea. A Critical & Historical Corpus of Florentine Painting Section IV: Richard Offneri, Vol. VI. LC 58-15756. 1979. 120.00 (ISBN 0-685-71939-1). J J Augustin.

Bonal, Denise. Family Portrait. Johns, Timothy, tr. (Ubu Repertory Theater Publications Ser.: No. 10). (Orig.). 1985. pap. text ed. 7.25 (ISBN 0-913745-11-1, Dist. by Publishing Center for Cultural Resources). Ubu Repertory.

Bonal, Joaquin & Poston, J. W., eds. Clinical Pharmacy Education & Patient Education: Proceedings of the European Symposium on Clinical Pharmacy, 12th, Barcelona, 1983. (Progress in Clinical Pharmacy Ser.: No. 6). 322p. 1984. 49.50 (ISBN 0-521-26610-6). Cambridge U Pr.

Bonando, Wanda. Stitches, Patterns & Projects for Crocheting. LC 83-48327. (Illus.). 256p. 1984. pap. 9.57i (ISBN 0-06-091095-X, CN 1095, CN). Har-Row.

--Stitches, Patterns & Projects for Knitting. LC 83-48328. (Illus.). 256p. 1984. pap. 9.57i (ISBN 0-06-091094-1, CN 1094, CN). Har-Row.

Bonando, Wanda & Nava, Marinella. Stitches, Patterns & Projects for Needlecraft. LC 83-48329. (Illus.). 256p. 1984. pap. 9.57i (ISBN 0-06-091096-8, CN 1096, CN). Har-Row.

Bonanni, Filippo. Antique Musical Instruments & Their Players. rev. ed. (Illus.). 1923. pap. 5.95 (ISBN 0-486-21179-7). Dover.

Bonanno, Antonio C. & Matlins, Antoinette L. The Complete Guide to Buying Gems: How to Buy Diamonds & Colored Gemstones with Confidence & Knowledge. LC 83-10056. (Illus.). 1984. 17.95 (ISBN 0-517-54792-9). Crown.

Bonanno, Diane, jt. auth. see Dougherty, Neil J.

Bonanno, Ellen, jt. auth. see Mechlin, Stuart.

Bonanno, Joseph. A Man of Honor: The Autobiography of Joseph Bonanno. 1984. pap. 3.95 (ISBN 0-671-50042-2). PB.

Bonanno, Joseph & Lalli, Sergeo. A Man of Honor: The Autobiography of Joseph Bonanno. 416p. 1983. 17.95 (ISBN 0-671-46747-6). S&S.

Bonanno, Margaret W. A Certain Slant of Light. 1980. pap. 2.75 (ISBN 0-671-83057-0). PB.

--Dwellers in the Crucible. (Star Trek Ser.: No. 25). 1985. pap. 3.50 (ISBN 0-671-60373-6). PB.

Bonansea, B. M. Man & His Approach to God in John Duns Scotus. 258p. (Orig.). 1983. lib. bdg. 26.75 (ISBN 0-8191-3299-3); pap. text ed. 13.25 (ISBN 0-8191-3300-0). U Pr of Amer.

Bonansea, Berbardine, ed. see Bettoni, Efrem.

Bonansea, Bernardine M., ed. see Ryan, John K.

Bonansea, Bernardino M. Tommaso Campanella: Renaissance Pioneer of Modern Thought. LC 78-76125. 421p. 1969. 19.95x (ISBN 0-8132-0263-9). Cath U Pr.

Bonaparte, Beverly. Gastrointestinal Care: A Guide for Patient Education. (Patient Education Ser.). (Illus.). 132p. 1981. pap. 18.95 (ISBN 0-8385-3096-6). ACC.

Bonaparte, Josephine & Redoute, Pierre-Joseph. Roses for an Empress. (Illus.). 118p. 1984. 17.95 (ISBN 0-283-98983-1, Pub. by Sidgwick & Jackson). Merrimack Pub Cir.

Bonaparte, Marie. Female Sexuality. 225p. (Orig.). 1956. text ed. 27.50 (ISBN 0-8236-1900-1); pap. 7.95 (ISBN 0-8236-8050-9, 021900). Intl Univs Pr.

Bonaparte, Marie, et al, eds. see Freud, Sigmund.

Bonaparte, Marion, ed. see Logan, Thaddeus.

Bonaparte, Napoleon. Code Napoleon. 1960. Repr. of 1841 ed. 15.00x (ISBN 0-685-08158-3). Claitors.

Bonaparte, T. H. & Franzen, William L. Instructional Innovations: Ideals, Issues, Impediments. 165p. 1977. 9.95 (ISBN 0-88737-207-4, 16-1687). Natl League Nurse.

Bonar, A. A. Robert Murray McCheyne: A Biography. 224p. 1983. pap. 5.95 (ISBN 0-310-44701-1, Clarion Class). Zondervan.

Bonar, Andrew. Andrew Bonar Life & Diary. 535p. 1984. Repr. of 1893 ed. 12.95 (ISBN 0-85151-432-4). Banner of Truth.

--Leviticus. (Banner of Truth Geneva Series Commentaries). 1978. 15.95 (ISBN 0-85151-086-8). Banner of Truth.

--The Life of R. M. M'Cheyne. 1978. pap. 3.45 (ISBN 0-85151-085-X). Banner of Truth.

Bonar, Andrew, jt. auth. see Tyler, Bennet.

Bonar, Andrew A. Memoir & Remains of R. M. M'cheyne. 1978. 15.95 (ISBN 0-85151-084-1). Banner of Truth.

--The Visitor's Book of Texts: The Word Brought Nigh to the Sick & Sorrowful. (Summit Bks.). 248p. 1982. pap. 3.95 (ISBN 0-8010-0817-4). Baker Bk.

Bonar, Ann. How to Book of Basic Gardening. Daniels, Gilbert, ed. (How to Bks.). (Illus.). 96p. 1982. pap. 3.95 (ISBN 0-7137-1287-2, Pub. by Blandford Pr England). Sterling.

--How to Book of Flower Gardening. Daniels, Gilbert, ed. (How to Bks.). (Illus.). 96p. (Orig.). 1983. pap. 3.95 (ISBN 0-7137-1289-9, Pub. by Blandford Pr England). Sterling.

--How to Book of Herbs & Herb Gardening. (How-To Ser.). (Illus.). 96p. (Orig.). 1982. pap. 3.95 (ISBN 0-7137-1290-2, Pub. by Blandford Pr England). Sterling.

--How to Book of Vegetable Gardening. (How to Bks.). (Illus.). 96p. (Orig.). 1982. pap. 3.95 (ISBN 0-7137-1288-0, Pub. by Blandford Pr England). Sterling.

--The Macmillan Treasury of Herbs. 144p. 1985. 14.95 (ISBN 0-02-513470-1). Macmillan.

Bonar, Ann & MacCarthy, Daphne. How to Grow & Use Herbs. (Orig.). 1980. pap. 6.95x (ISBN 0-8464-1024-9). Beekman Pubs.

Bonar, Clayton. Beacon Small-Group Bible Studies, Deuteronomy: Following God's Directions. Wolf, Earl C., ed. 96p. (Orig.). 1986. pap. 2.50 (ISBN 0-8341-0959-X). Beacon Hill.

Bonar, D. D. On Annular Functions. (Math. Forschungsberichte, No.24). (Illus.). 1971. pap. 15.00x (ISBN 0-685-37412-2). Adlers Foreign Bks.

Bonar, Horatius. Thoughts on Genesis. LC 79-2516. 1979. 11.95 (ISBN 0-8254-2235-3). Kregel.

--When God's Children Suffer. LC 80-84441. (Shepherd Illustrated Classics Ser.). (Illus.). 144p. 1981. pap. 5.95 (ISBN 0-87983-221-5). Keats.

--Words to Winners of Souls. (Summit Bks.). 1979. pap. 2.50 (ISBN 0-8010-0773-9). Baker Bk.

Bonar, James. Letters of David Ricardo to Thomas Robert Malthus. 1887. 30.00 (ISBN 0-686-17718-5). Quest Edns.

--Malthus & His Work. 2nd ed. 438p. 1966. Repr. of 1924 ed. 30.00x (ISBN 0-7146-1273-1, F Cass Co). Biblio Dist.

--Tables Turned. LC 70-107918. Repr. of 1931 ed. 22.50x (ISBN 0-678-00633-4). Kelley.

--Theories of Population from Raleigh to Arthur Young. 253p. 1966. Repr. of 1931 ed. 30.00x (ISBN 0-7146-1274-X, BHA-01274, F Cass Co). Biblio Dist.

Bonar, James, ed. Catalogue of the Library of Adam Smith. 2nd ed. LC 66-15561. Repr. of 1932 ed. 25.00x (ISBN 0-678-00188-X). Kelley.

--Letters of David Ricardo to Thomas Robert Malthus: 1810-1823. 1978. Repr. of 1887 ed. lib. bdg. 40.00 (ISBN 0-8492-2272-9). R West.

Bonar, James, tr. see Knapp, Georg F.

Bonar, Jeanne R. Diabetes: A Clinical Guide. 2nd ed. (Medical Outline Ser.). 1980. 26.00 (ISBN 0-87488-710-0). Med Exam.

Bonar, John A. Goliaths of the World. Beasley, James, ed. 89p. 1981. pap. 7.00 (ISBN 0-936204-22-2). Jelm Mtn.

Bonar, Lore S., et al. Say It in Another Language: Phrases in Spanish, French, Japanese, Swahili, & German. 16p. (YA) 1976. pap. text ed. 3.25 pkg. of 20 (ISBN 0-88441-414-0, 26-814). GS.

Bonarius, Han, et al, eds. Personal Construct Psychology. 300p. 1981. 32.50x (ISBN 0-312-60228-6). St Martin.

Bonaschi, Alberto C. Italian Currents & Curiosities in the English Literature from Chaucer to Shakespeare. LC 73-6949. 1937. lib. bdg. 10.00 (ISBN 0-8414-3118-3). Folcroft.

Bonasco, Beatriz see Alexandria, Betty, pseud.

Bonatti, Luigi. Uncertainty: Studies in Philosophy, Economics & Socio-Political Theory. (Bochumer Studien zur Philosophie Ser.: Vol. 2). 132p. 1984. 24.00x (ISBN 90-6032-230-4, Pub. by B R Gruener Netherlands). Benjamins North Am.

Bonatti, Walter. Magic of Mont Blanc. (Illus.). 208p. 1985. 55.00 (ISBN 0-575-03560-9, Pub. by Gollancz England). David & Charles.

Bonatz, E., tr. see Pichlmayr, I., et al.

Bonaventura. The Problem of God & the Emotional Equilibrium of Man. (Illus.). 78p. 1984. pap. 23.75 (ISBN 0-89266-490-8). Am Classical Coll Pr.

Bonaventura, Saint The Mind's Road to God. Boas, George, tr. 1953. pap. 3.56 scp (ISBN 0-672-60195-8, LLA32). Bobbs.

Bonaventure, Saint Bonaventure, Rooted in Faith: Homilies to a Contemporary World. Schumacher, Marigwen, tr. from Lat. 1974. 5.95 (ISBN 0-8199-0465-1). Franciscan Herald.

Bonaventure, St. The Mind's Journey to God (Itinerarium Mentis Ad Deum) Cunningham, Lawrence S., tr. 1979. 6.95 (ISBN 0-8199-0765-0). Franciscan Herald.

--The Works of St. Bonaventure: Collations on the Six Days, Vols. 1-5. De Vinck, Jose, tr. (Works of St. Bonaventure Ser.). 1972. 7.50 ea. Franciscan Herald.

Bonavia, David. China Unknown. LC 84-40121. (Illus.). 144p. 1985. 24.95 (ISBN 0-8129-1141-5). Times Bks.

--The Chinese. LC 80-7873. (Illus.). 288p. 1980. 14.37i (ISBN 0-690-01996-3). Har-Row.

--The Chinese. rev. ed. 1983. pap. 5.95 (ISBN 0-14-022394-0, Pelican). Penguin.

--Tibet. LC 82-6914. (Illus.). 128p. 1982. 50.00 (ISBN 0-86565-021-7). Vendome.

--Verdict in Peking: The Trial of the Gang of Four. 336p. 1984. 17.95 (ISBN 0-399-12803-4, Putnam). Putnam Pub Group.

Bonavia, Duccio. Mural Painting in Ancient Peru. Lyon, Patricia J., tr. from Span. LC 84-47883. (Illus.). 208p. 1985. 57.50 (ISBN 0-253-33940-5). Ind U Pr.

Bonavia, E. The Cultivated Oranges & Lemons Etc. of India & Ceylon: With Researches into Their Origin & the Derivation of Their Names, & Other Useful Information, 2 vols. 1978. Repr. Set. 75.00x (ISBN 0-89955-258-7, Pub. by Intl Bk Dist). Intl Spec Bk.

Bonavia, Ferruccio. Verdi. LC 78-66902. (Illus.). 1980. Repr. of 1947 ed. 16.50 (ISBN 0-88355-726-6). Hyperion Conn.

Bonavia, Ferruccio, ed. Musicians on Music. LC 78-66892. (Encore Music Editions Ser.). 1979. Repr. of 1956 ed. 23.75 (ISBN 0-88355-725-8). Hyperion Conn.

Bonavia, Michael. Twilight of British Rail. (Illus.). 176p. 1985. 18.95 (ISBN 0-7153-8625-5). David & Charles.

Bonavia, Michael R. British Rail: The First Twenty-Five Years. LC 80-68687. (Illus.). 208p. 1981. 21.00 (ISBN 0-7153-8002-8). David & Charles.

--The Four Great Railways. LC 79-91498. (Illus.). 1980. 17.95 (ISBN 0-7153-7842-2). David & Charles.

--Railway Policy Between the Wars. 160p. 1982. 15.00 (ISBN 0-7190-0826-3, Pub. by Manchester Univ Pr). Longwood Pub Group.

Bonavia-Hunt, Noel A. Modern Organ Stops. (Illus.). 1976. pap. 10.00x (ISBN 0-913746-05-3). Organ Lit.

Bonazza, Blaze O., et al. Studies in Fiction. enl. 3rd ed. 880p. 1982. pap. text ed. 10.50 scp (ISBN 0-06-040832-4, HarpC); instructors manual avail. (ISBN 0-06-360849-9); scp wkbk. 7.95 (ISBN 0-06-040842-1); instr's manual wkbk. avail. (ISBN 0-06-360851-0). Har-Row.

Bonazzi, Robert. Fictive Music. 1979. pap. 4.00 (ISBN 0-930324-12-9). Wings Pr.

--Living the Borrowed Life. 1974. signed 10.00 (ISBN 0-685-79005-3); 5.00 (ISBN 0-685-79006-1); sewn in wrappers 2.50 (ISBN 0-685-79007-X). New Rivers Pr.

Bonazzi, Robert, ed. Making a Break. (Illus.). 243p. 1975. 7.50 (ISBN 0-685-78968-3); sewn in wrappers 4.50 (ISBN 0-685-78969-1). Latitudes Pr.

Bonbright, James C. Principles of Public Utility Rates. LC 61-6569. 433p. 1961. 40.00x (ISBN 0-231-02441-X). Columbia U Pr.

--Public Utilities & the National Power Policies. LC 73-172007. (FDR & the Era of the New Deal Ser.). 1972. Repr. of 1940 ed. lib. bdg. 19.50 (ISBN 0-306-70424-2). Da Capo.

--Railroad Capitalization. LC 70-78003. (Columbia University Studies in the Social Sciences: No. 215). Repr. of 1920 ed. 24.50 (ISBN 0-404-51215-1). AMS Pr.

--Valuation of Property, 2 Vols. 1965. Repr. 60.00 (ISBN 0-87215-014-3). Michie Co.

Bonbright, James C. & Means, Gardiner C. Holding Company: Its Public Significance & Its Regulation. LC 68-55486. Repr. of 1932 ed. 35.00x (ISBN 0-678-00502-8). Kelley.

Bonch-Bruevich, et al. Domain Electrical Instabilities in Semiconductors. (Studies in Soviet Science: Physical Sciences Ser.). (Illus.). 400p. 1975. 55.00 (ISBN 0-306-10911-5, Consultants). Plenum Pub.

Bonchek, Lawrence I. & Brooks, Harold L. Office Management of Medical & Surgical Heart Disease: A Concise Guide for Non-Cardiologists. 1981. text ed. 27.50 (ISBN 0-316-10121-4). Little.

Bonchev, Danail. Information Theoretic Indices for Characterization of Chemical Structures. (Chemotrics Research Studies Ser.). 264p. 1983. 58.95 (ISBN 0-471-90087-7, Pub. by Res Stud Pr). Wiley.

Boncompagno, Signa Da see Boncompagno da Signa.

Boncompagno da Signa. Rota Veneris. Purkart, Josef, ed. LC 74-18250. 128p. 1975. Repr. of 1474 ed. lib. bdg. 25.00x (ISBN 0-8201-1137-6). Schol Facsimiles.

Boncore Di Santa Vittoria. Boncore Di Santa Victoria Novus Liber Hymnorum Ac Orationum. Repr. of 1903 ed. 60.00 (ISBN 0-384-12867-X). Johnson Repr.

Bonczek, Robert H., et al. Foundations of Decision Support Systems. LC 80-1779. (Operations Research & Industrial Engineering Ser.). 1981. 44.00 (ISBN 0-12-113050-9). Acad Pr.

--Micro Data Base Management. 1984. 37.50 (ISBN 0-12-113060-6). Acad Pr.

Bond. Machine Intelligence. (Infotech Computer State of the Art Reports). 407p. 1981. 405.00 (ISBN 0-08-028556-2). Pergamon.

--Modern Polargraphic Methods in Analytical Chemistry. (Monographs in Electroanalytical Chemistry & Electrochemistry: Vol.4). 536p. 1980. 69.75 (ISBN 0-8247-6849-3). Dekker.

Bond, A. C. & Faget, M. A. Technologies of Manned Space Flight. 132p. 1965. 38.50 (ISBN 0-677-01250-0). Gordon.

Bond, A. M., jt. auth. see Rand, D. A.

Bond, A. M. & Hefter, G. T., eds. Critical Survey of Stability Constants & Related Thermodynamic Data of Flouride Complexes in Aqueous Solution. (Chemical Data Ser.: No. 27). 80p. 1980. pap. text ed. 29.00 (ISBN 0-08-022377-X). Pergamon.

Bond, Adrienne Moore. Eugene W. Stetson. LC 83-8292. x, 200p. 1983. 12.95x (ISBN 0-86554-069-1, H65). Mercer Univ Pr.

Bond, Alec. North of Sioux Falls. 24p. 1983. pap. 3.00 (ISBN 0-933180-58-6). Spoon Riv Poetry.

--Poems for an Only Daughter. 24p. 1982. pap. 2.50 (ISBN 0-933180-39-X). Spoon Riv Poetry.

Bond, Anatole. German Loanwords in the Russian Language of the Petrine Period: Slavonic Languages & Literatures, Vol. 5. (European University Studies: Ser. 16). 180p. 1974. pap. 18.25 (ISBN 3-261-01377-X). P Lang Pubs.

--A Study of the English & the German Translations of Alexander I. Solzhenitsyn's 'The Gulag Archipelago, Vol. 1. (Slavonic Languages & Literatures-European University Studies: No. 16, Vol. 28). 331p. 1983. pap. 34.20 (ISBN 3-261-03317-7). P Lang Pubs.

Bond, Anita W. & Mordarski, Sheila W. Dental Hygiene Care of the Special Needs Patient. 66p. 1983. 49.00 (ISBN 0-318-17797-8); members 39.00 (ISBN 0-318-17798-6). Am Dental Hygienists.

Bond, Ann S. Adam & Noah & the Cops. LC 82-21181. (Illus.). 160p. (gr. 3-6). 1983. 8.95 (ISBN 0-395-33225-7). HM.

--Saturdays in the City. (gr. 3-6). 1979. 8.95 (ISBN 0-395-28376-0). HM.

Bond, Augustus, ed. see Fletcher, Giles.

Bond, Austin D. An Experiment in the Teaching of Genetics with Special Reference to the Objectives of General Education. LC 71-176575. (Columbia University. Teachers College. Contributions to Education: No. 797). Repr. of 1940 ed. 22.50 (ISBN 0-404-55797-X). AMS Pr.

Bond, B., Jr. see Wittke, Carl.

Bond, Beverley W. Civilization of the Old Northwest. LC 71-88787. (BCL Ser.: Ii). Repr. of 1934 ed. 12.50 (ISBN 0-404-00935-2). AMS Pr.

--The Monroe Mission to France, 1794-1796. LC 78-63920. (Johns Hopkins University. Studies in the Social Sciences. Twenty-Fifth Ser. 1907: 2-3). Repr. of 1907 ed. 14.50 (ISBN 0-404-61171-0). AMS Pr.

--The Quit-Rent System in the American Colonies. 1919. 11.75 (ISBN 0-8446-1082-8). Peter Smith.

Bond, Beverley W., Jr. Civilization of the Old Northwest. facs. ed. LC 73-124226. (Select Bibliographies Reprint Ser). 1934. 20.00 (ISBN 0-8369-5415-7). Ayer Co Pubs.

Bond, Beverly W. State Government in Maryland, 1777-1781. LC 78-63907. (Johns Hopkins University. Studies in the Social Sciences. Twenty-Third Ser. 1905: 3-4). Repr. of 1905 ed. 15.50 (ISBN 0-404-61159-1). AMS Pr.

Bond, Bob. The Handbook of Sailing. LC 79-3496. (Illus.). 1980. 22.50 (ISBN 0-394-50838-6). Knopf.

--The Rya Sailing Manual. (Illus.). 174p. 11.95 (ISBN 0-7207-1131-2, Pub. by Michael Joseph). Merrimack Pub Cir.

Bond, Bob & Sleight, Steve. Cruising Boat Sailing: The Basic Guide. LC 82-48882. (Illus.). 1983. 14.95 (ISBN 0-394-52447-0). Knopf.

--Small Boat Sailing: The Basic Guide. LC 82-48883. (Illus.). 1983. 14.95 (ISBN 0-394-52446-2). Knopf.

Bond, Brian. British Military Policy Between the Two World Wars. 1980. 52.00x (ISBN 0-19-822464-8). Oxford U Pr.

--France & Belgium, Nineteen Thirty-Nine to Nineteen Forty. Frankland, Noble & Dowling, Christopher, eds. LC 79-52237. (The Politics & Strategy of the Second World War Ser.). 208p. 1979. 18.50 (ISBN 0-87413-157-X). U Delaware Pr.

--War & Society in Europe, Eighteen Seventy to Nineteen Seventy. LC 83-40281. 256p. 1984. 25.00 (ISBN 0-312-85547-8). St Martin.

Bond, Brian, ed. Chief of Staff: The Diaries of Lieutenant General Sir Henry Pownall Vol. 2, 1940-1944. (Illus.). xviii, 216p. (Orig.). 1974. 25.00 (ISBN 0-208-01462-4, Archon). Shoe String.

--Chief of Staff: The Diaries of Lieutenant General Sir Henry Pownall, Vol. 1, 1933-40. (Illus.). xxxii, 399p. 1973. 27.50 (ISBN 0-208-01326-1, Archon). Shoe String.

Bond, Brian & Roy, Ian, eds. War & Society: A Yearbook of Military History, 2 vols. LC 75-23095. Vol. 1 (1976) 255p. text ed. 29.50x (ISBN 0-8419-0230-5); Vol. 2 (1977) 196p. text ed. 35.00x (ISBN 0-8419-0293-3). Holmes & Meier.

Bond, Carl E. Biology of Fishes. LC 77-84665. (Illus.). 1979. text ed. 37.95 (ISBN 0-7216-1839-1). HR&W.

Bond, Carrie J. Old Melodies of the South. 59.95 (ISBN 0-8490-0760-7). Gordon Pr.

Bond, Charles A., Jr. & Anderson, Terry H. A Flying Tiger's Diary. LC 83-40497. (The Centennial Series of the Association of Former Students: No. 15). (Illus.). 264p. 1984. 17.50 (ISBN 0-89096-178-6). Tex A&M Univ Pr.

Bond, Clara-Beth Y., et al. The Low Fat, Low Cholesterol Diet. rev. ed. LC 84-1665. (Illus.). 528p. 1984. 17.95 (ISBN 0-385-18879-X). Doubleday.

Bond, Courtney C. Ottawa, Ont. Meet: Where Rivers Meet. (Illus.). 190p. 1984. 24.95 (ISBN 0-89781-111-9). Windsor Pubns Inc.

Bond, Creina & Siegried, Roy. Antarctica: No Single Country, No Single Sea. (Illus.). 1979. 27.50 (ISBN 0-8317-0380-6, Mayflower Bks). Smith Pubs.

Bond, D., jt. auth. see Shearer, R.

Bond, D. A., ed. Vicia Faba: Feeding Value, Processing & Viruses. (World Crops: Production, Utilization, & Description: Vol. 3). x, 424p. 1980. lib. bdg. 50.00 (ISBN 9-0247-2362-0, Pub. by Martinus Nijhoff Netherlands). Kluwer Academic.

Bond, D. J. & Chandley, A. C. Aneuploidy. (OMMG Ser.). (Illus.). 1983. 69.00x (ISBN 0-19-261376-6). Oxford U Pr.

Bond, David. The Fiction of Andre Pieyre de Mandiargues. LC 82-5894. 176p. 1982. text ed. 22.00x (ISBN 0-8156-2265-1); pap. text ed. 12.95x (ISBN 0-8156-2283-X). Syracuse U Pr.

--The Guinness Guide to Twentieth-Century Homes. (Illus.). 224p. 1985. 24.95 (ISBN 0-85112-413-5, Pub. by Guinness Superlatives England). Sterling.

--Twentieth Century Fashion. (A Guinness Superlatives Guide Ser.). (Illus.). 224p. 1981. 24.95 (ISBN 0-85112-234-5, Pub. by Guinness Superlatives England). Sterling.

Bond, Donald F., compiled by. Age of Dryden. LC 72-118855. (Goldentree Bibliographies in Language & Literature Ser). (Orig.). 1970. pap. 13.95x (ISBN 0-88295-502-0). Harlan Davidson.

Bond, Donald F., ed. see Addison, Joseph.

Bond, Donald F., ed. see Steele, Richard.

Bond, Donald F., compiled by. The Eighteenth Century. LC 74-28590. (Goldentree Bibliographies in Language & Literature Ser.). (Orig.). 1975. pap. 13.95x (ISBN 0-88295-547-0). Harlan Davidson.

Bond, Dorothy. Crazy Quilt Stitches. (Illus.). 112p. (Orig.). 1981. pap. 10.00 (ISBN 0-9606086-0-5). D Bond.

Bond, E. J. Manual of Fumigation for Insect Control. Rev. ed. (Plant Production & Protection Papers: No. 54). (Illus.). 432p. 1985. pap. 31.75 (ISBN 92-5-101483-3, F2674, FAO). Unipub.

--Reason & Value. LC 82-4564. (Cambridge Studies in Philosophy). 220p. 1983. 32.50 (ISBN 0-521-24571-0); pap. 10.95 (ISBN 0-521-27079-0). Cambridge U Pr.

Bond, Earl D. & Komora, Paul O. Thomas W. Salmon: Psychiatrist. Grob, Gerald N., ed. LC 78-22550. (Historical Issues in Mental Health Ser.). (Illus.). 1979. Repr. of 1950 ed. lib. bdg. 17.00x (ISBN 0-405-11904-6). Ayer Co Pubs.

Bond, Edward. A-A-America! & Stone. rev. ed. 115p. 1982. pap. 6.95 (ISBN 0-413-48320-7, NO. 3512). Methuen Inc.

--Bingo & the Sea: Two Plays. 124p. 1975. 10.00 (ISBN 0-8090-3030-6). Hill & Wang.

--Bond - Plays One: Saved, Early Morning, The Pope's Wedding. 312p. 1983. pap. 4.50 (ISBN 0-413-45410-X, NO.3942). Methuen Inc.

--The Bundle. 98p. 1978. pap. 6.95 (ISBN 0-413-39360-7, NO.2986). Methuen Inc.

--Derek & Choruses from "After the Assassinations". (Methuen Theatrescript Ser.). 48p. 1984. pap. 4.95 (ISBN 0-413-54700-0, NO. 4104). Methuen Inc.

--Early Morning. 1980. pap. 4.95 (ISBN 0-7145-0207-3). Riverrun NY.

--The Fool & We Come to the River. 122p. 1976. pap. 6.95 (ISBN 0-413-34770-2, NO. 2984). Methuen Inc.

--Human Cannon. (Methuen New Theatrescripts Ser.). 48p. (Orig.). 1985. pap. 4.95 (ISBN 0-413-57250-1, 9380). Methuen Inc.

--Narrow Road to the Deep North: A Play. 65p. 1981. pap. 6.95 (ISBN 0-413-30840-5, NO. 2592). Methuen Inc.

--The Pope's Wedding. 111p. 1971. pap. 6.95 (ISBN 0-416-09210-1, NO. 2983). Methuen Inc.

--Restoration & the Cat. 2nd ed. 128p. 1982. pap. 7.95 (ISBN 0-413-49920-0, NO. 3638). Methuen Inc.

--Saved. (Metheun Modern Plays Ser.). 123p. 1984. pap. 6.95 (ISBN 0-413-31360-3, NO. 9049). Methuen Inc.

--Summer & Fables. (Modern Plays Ser.). 100p. 1983. pap. 6.95 (ISBN 0-413-50970-2, NO. 3789). Methuen Inc.

--Theatre Poems & Songs. 145p. 1978. pap. 6.95 (ISBN 0-413-45430-4, NO. 2988). Methuen Inc.

--War Plays: A Trilogy. (Methuen New Theatrescripts Ser.). 56p. (Orig.). 1985. pap. 4.95 (ISBN 0-413-57240-4, 9381). Methuen Inc.

--The Worlds: Includes the Activists Papers. 176p. 1980. pap. 6.95 (ISBN 0-413-46610-8, NO. 2085). Methuen Inc.

Bond, Edward, tr. see Wedekind, Frank.

Bond, Edward A., ed. Chronica Monasterii de Melsa, a Fundatione Usque ad Annum 1396: Auctiore Thoma de Burton, Abbate, 3 vols. (Rolls Ser.: No. 43). Repr. of 1868 ed. Set. 132.00 (ISBN 0-317-16690-5). Kraus Repr.

Bond, Elden A. Tenth-Grade Abilities & Achievements. LC 79-176577. (Columbia University. Teachers College. Contributions to Education: No. 813). Repr. of 1940 ed. 22.50 (ISBN 0-404-55813-5). AMS Pr.

Bond, Elias A. The Professional Treatment of the Subject Matter of Arithmetic for Teacher-Training Institutions. LC 75-176576. (Columbia University. Teachers College. Contributions to Education: No. 525). Repr. of 1934 ed. 22.50 (ISBN 0-404-55525-X). AMS Pr.

--Short Method Arithmetic. pap. 1.00 (ISBN 0-685-19500-7). Powner.

Bond, Evagene H., ed. La Comunidad: Design, Development, & Self-Determination in Hispanic Communities. LC 81-83365. (Illus.). 64p. 1982. pap. 7.50 (ISBN 0-941182-02-9). Partners Livable.

--La Comunidad: Design, Development, & Self-Determination in Hispanic Communities. (Illus.). 54p. 1982. pap. 7.50 (ISBN 0-941182-02-9). Pub Ctr Cult Res.

Bond, Evelyn. Bride of Terror. 272p. 1975. pap. 1.25 (ISBN 0-532-12308-5). Woodhill.

--The Clouded Mirror. 288p. 1975. pap. 1.25 (ISBN 0-532-12297-6). Woodhill.

--House of Shadows. 256p. 1975. pap. 1.25 (ISBN 0-532-12284-4). Woodhill.

--Ventian Secret. 1977. pap. 1.50 (ISBN 0-532-15242-5). Woodhill.

Bond, F. Fraser. Breaking into Print. 1977. Repr. of 1933 ed. lib. bdg. 15.00 (ISBN 0-686-19798-4). Havertown Bks.

--How to Write & Sell Nonfiction. (Illus.). 262p. 1981. Repr. of 1938 ed. lib. bdg. 40.00 (ISBN 0-8495-0487-2). Arden Lib.

Bond, Felicia. Christmas in the Chicken Coop. LC 82-45918. (Illus.). 32p. (ps-3). 1983. 4.76i (ISBN 0-690-04332-5); PLB 9.89g (ISBN 0-690-04333-3). Crowell Jr Bks.

--Four Valentines in a Rainstorm. LC 82-45586. (Illus.). 32p. (ps-3). 1983. 4.76i (ISBN 0-690-04306-6); PLB 9.89g (ISBN 0-690-04307-4). Crowell Jr Bks.

--The Halloween Performance. LC 82-45920. (Illus.). 32p. (ps-3). 1983. 4.76i (ISBN 0-690-04308-2); PLB 9.89g (ISBN 0-690-04309-0). Crowell Jr Bks.

--Mary Betty Lizzie McNutt's Birthday. (Illus.). (ps-3). 1983. 4.76i (ISBN 0-690-04255-8); lib. bdg. 7.89g (ISBN 0-690-04256-6). Crowell Jr Bks.

--Poinsettia & Her Family. LC 81-43035. (Illus.). 32p. (ps-3). 1981. 9.57i (ISBN 0-690-04144-6); PLB 9.89g (ISBN 0-690-04145-4). Crowell Jr Bks.

--Poinsettia & Her Family. LC 81-43035. (Trophy Picture Bk.). (Illus.). 32p. (ps-3). 1985. pap. 2.84i (ISBN 0-06-443076-5, Trophy). HarpJ.

--Poinsettia & the Firefighters. LC 83-46169. (Illus.). 32p. (ps-3). 1984. 10.10i (ISBN 0-690-04400-3); PLB 9.89g (ISBN 0-690-04401-1). Crowell Jr Bks.

Bond, Floyd A., ed. Technological Change & Economic Growth: Proceedings, C. I. C. Conference, 1964. (Michigan Business Papers: No. 41). 1965. pap. 1.00 (ISBN 0-87712-090-0). U Mich Busn Div Res.

Bond, Floyd A., et al. The Newly Promoted Executive: A Study in Corporate Leadership 1982-1983. 30p. pap. 2.00 (ISBN 0-87712-230-X). U Mich Busn Div Res.

--The Newly Promoted Executive: A Study in Corporate Leadership 1983-84. 30p. pap. 2.00 (ISBN 0-87712-236-9). U Mich Busn Div Res.

Bond, Francis. Gothic Architecture in England. LC 70-39656. (Select Bibliographies Reprint Ser). 1972. Repr. of 1905 ed. 71.50 (ISBN 0-8369-9931-2). Ayer Co Pubs.

--An Introduction to English Church Architecture: From the 11th to the 16th Century. LC 77-94546. 1979. Repr. of 1908 ed. lib. bdg. 25.00 (ISBN 0-89341-225-2). Longwood Pub Group.

Bond, Francis, jt. auth. see Zimmerman, Isidore.

Bond, Frederic D. Stock Movements & Speculation. 2nd ed. LC 75-871. (Wall Street & the Security Market Ser.). 1975. Repr. of 1930 ed. 23.50x (ISBN 0-405-07248-1). Ayer Co Pubs.

Bond, Frederick W. The Negro & the Drama: The Direct & Indirect Contribution Which the American Negro Has Made to Drama & the Legitimate Stage. 10.00 (ISBN 0-405-18492-1). Ayer Co Pubs.

Bond, G. C. Heterogeneous Catalysis: Principles & Applications. new ed. (Oxford Chemistry Ser). 1978. pap. text ed. 12.95x (ISBN 0-19-855412-5). Oxford U Pr.

Bond, George, et al, eds. African Christianity: Patterns of Religious Continuity. LC 79-51668. (AP Studies in Anthropology Ser.). 1979. 34.00 (ISBN 0-12-113450-4). Acad Pr.

Bond, George C. The Politics of Change in a Zambian Community. LC 75-12228. (Illus.). 232p. 1976. lib. bdg. 18.00x (ISBN 0-226-06408-5). U of Chicago Pr.

Bond, George D., jt. auth. see Carter, John R.

Bond, George R. & Crosby, Harry H., eds. The Shape of Thought: An Analytical Anthology. LC 83-5800. 340p. 1983. pap. text ed. 10.00 (ISBN 0-8191-3090-7). U Pr of Amer.

Bond, Gerald A., ed. The Poetry of Duke William IX of Aguitaine (Guilhem of Poitiers) (The Garland Library of Medieval Literature). 1981. lib. bdg. 44.00 (ISBN 0-8240-9441-7). Garland Pub.

Bond, Gladys B. Little Stories. (Illus.). 80p. 1.95 (ISBN 0-686-95005-4). ADL.

Bond, Godfrey W., ed. see Euripides.

Bond, Guy L. The Auditory & Speech Characteristics of Poor Readers. LC 72-176578. (Columbia University. Teachers College. Contributions to Education Ser.: No. 657). Repr. of 1935 ed. 22.50 (ISBN 0-404-55657-4). AMS Pr.

Bond, Guy L., et al. Reading Difficulties: Their Diagnosis & Correction. 5th ed. (Illus.). 368p. 1984. 26.95 (ISBN 0-13-754960-1). P-H.

Bond, Harold. The Way It Happens to You. LC 79-50730. 1979. 6.95 (ISBN 0-933706-08-1); pap. 3.95 (ISBN 0-933706-09-X). Ararat Pr.

Bond, Harold, ed. see Sheohmelian, O.

Bond, Harold L. The Literary Art of Edward Gibbon. LC 75-4977. 167p. 1975. Repr. of 1960 ed. lib. bdg. 15.00x (ISBN 0-8371-8050-3, BOLA). Greenwood.

Bond, Harold Lewis. An Encyclopedia of Antiques. LC 74-31297. (Illus.). 389p. 1975. Repr. of 1945 ed. 60.00x (ISBN 0-8103-4206-5). Gale.

Bond, Helen J. Trends & Needs in Home Management: An Analytical Study of Home Management in Higher Institutions, in Order to Ascertain Trends & to Formulate Policies. LC 77-176922. (Columbia University. Teachers College. Contributions to Education: No. 365). Repr. of 1929 ed. 22.50 (ISBN 0-404-55365-6). AMS Pr.

Bond, Horace M. Black American Scholars: A Study of Their Beginnings. LC 72-78234. 210p. 1972. 8.95 (ISBN 0-913642-01-0); pap. 3.95 (ISBN 0-913642-04-5). Balamp Pub.

--Negro Education in Alabama. 1969. Repr. of 1939 ed. lib. bdg. 22.00x (ISBN 0-374-90780-3). Octagon.

--Negro Education in Alabama: A Study in Cotton & Steel. LC 39-18307. (Studies in American Negro Life Ser). 1969. pap. 3.45 (ISBN 0-689-70019-9, NL17). Atheneum.

Bond, Horatio, ed. Fire & the Air War. 139p. 1946. pap. text ed. 14.00x (ISBN 0-89126-004-8). MA-AH Pub.

Bond, Howard. Light Motifs. LC 84-119081. (Illus.). 30p. 1984. pap. 19.50 (ISBN 0-9612734-1-0). Goodrich Pr.

Bond, J. Mark. The Gold Seekers. 432p. 1984. pap. 3.75 (ISBN 0-8439-2183-8, Leisure Bks). Dorchester Pub Co.

--Half a Treasure. 1978. pap. 1.50 (ISBN 0-8439-0544-1, Leisure Bks). Dorchester Pub Co.

Bond, J. T., jt. auth. see Lambie, D. A.

Bond, J. T., jt. auth. see Weikart, D. P.

Bond, James. Birds of the West Indies. (Illus.). 1971. 14.95 (ISBN 0-395-07431-2). HM.

Bond, James E. Plea Bargaining & Guilty Pleas. 2nd ed. LC 82-4125. 1982. looseleaf 65.00 (ISBN 0-87632-105-8). Boardman.

--The Rules of Riot: Internal Conflict & the Law of War. LC 72-5390. 240p. 1974. 28.50x (ISBN 0-691-05651-X). Princeton U Pr.

Bond, James O. Walk Cheerfully over the Earth. (Illus.). 275p. 1985. text ed. 22.00 (ISBN 0-9608520-1-8). J O Bond.

--We Held Hands Within the Dark. Bond, Lydia S., ed. LC 82-90272. 182p. (Orig.). 1982. pap. 5.95 (ISBN 0-9608520-0-X). J O Bond.

Bond, Jenny T., et al, eds. Infant & Child Feeding. (Nutrition Foundation Ser.). 1981. 59.50 (ISBN 0-12-113350-8). Acad Pr.

Bond, John J. Handy-Book of Rules & Tables for Verifying Dates with the Christian Era. LC 66-29473. 1966. Repr. of 1889 ed. 10.00x (ISBN 0-8462-1795-3). Russell.

Bond, Jules. Recipes from Around the World. (Easy Cooking Ser.). (Illus.). 64p. 1984. pap. 4.95 (ISBN 0-8120-5604-3). Barron.

Bond, Julian. Julian Bond: Black Candidates. (Southern Campaign Experience). write for info. Voter Ed Proj.

Bond, Lydia S., ed. see Bond, James O.

Bond, Lynne A. & Joffe, Justin M., eds. Facilitating Infant & Early Childhood Development. LC 81-69944. (Primary Prevention of Psychopathology Ser.: Vol. 6). (Illus.). 586p. 1982. 45.00x (ISBN 0-87451-205-0). U Pr of New Eng.

Bond, Lynne A. & Rosen, James C., eds. Competence & Coping During Adulthood. LC 79-56776. (Primary Prevention of Psychopathology Ser.: Vol. 4). (Illus.). 396p. 1980. 35.00x (ISBN 0-87451-159-3). U Pr of New Eng.

Bond, Marjorie N. Twentieth-Century American Literature. 1977. Repr. of 1933 ed. lib. bdg. 10.00 (ISBN 0-8495-0325-6). Arden Lib.

Bond, Marshall, Jr. Adventures with Peons, Princes & Tycoons. (Illus.). 251p. 1983. pap. 8.95 (ISBN 0-932458-14-9). Star Rover.

Bond, Mary W. Far Afield in the Caribbean. LC 75-140150. (Illus.). 1971. 4.95 (ISBN 0-915180-13-8). Harrowood Bks.

--Far Afield in the Caribbean: Migratory Flights of a Naturalist's Wife. (Illus.). 1971. 4.95 (ISBN 0-915180-13-8). Livingston.

--To James Bond with Love. LC 80-17134. (Illus.). 224p. 1980. 10.95 (ISBN 0-915010-28-3). Sutter House.

Bond, Michael. Bear Called Paddington. LC 60-9096. (Illus.). 128p. (gr. 3-7). 1968. pap. 2.50 (ISBN 0-440-40483-5, YB). Dell.

--Bear Called Paddington. (Illus.). 128p. (gr. 1-5). 1960. 9.95 (ISBN 0-395-06636-0). HM.

--Book of Bears. (Puffin Story Bks.). 1974. pap. 3.95 (ISBN 0-14-030662-5, Puffin). Penguin.

--Fire Like the Sun. 526p. 1985. 14.95 (ISBN 0-312-29195-7, Pub. by Marek). St Martin.

--The Hilarious Adventures of Paddington, 5 bks. Incl. A Bear Called Paddington; More about Paddington; Paddington at Large; Paddington at Work; Paddington Helps Out. (Illus.). pap. 10.00 boxed set (ISBN 0-440-43668-0). Dell.

--J. D. Polson & the Liberty Head Dime. (Illus.). 48p. 1980. 6.95 (ISBN 0-7064-1381-4, Mayflower Bks). Smith Pubs.

--M. Pamplemousse & the Secret Mission: A Gastronomic Mystery. 208p. 1986. 13.95 (ISBN 0-8253-0301-X). Beaufort Bks NY.

--Monsieur Pamplemousse: A Gastronomic Mystery. 192p. 1985. 13.95 (ISBN 0-8253-0267-6). Beaufort Bks NY.

--More About Paddington. (Illus.). 128p. (gr. 3-7). 1970. pap. 1.75 (ISBN 0-440-45825-0, YB). Dell.

--More About Paddington. (Illus.). (gr. 4-6). 1962. 9.95 (ISBN 0-395-06640-9). HM.

--Olga Carries on. 144p. (Orig.). (gr. 3-7). 1983. pap. 2.25 (ISBN 0-440-46541-9, YB). Dell.

--Olga Counts Her Blessings. LC 77-10685. (Olga Da Polga Ser.). (Illus.). (gr. k-3). 1977. pap. text ed. 1.45 (ISBN 0-88436-458-5, ELA 010054). EMC.

--Olga Makes a Friend. LC 77-10684. (Olga Da Polga Ser.). (Illus.). (gr. k-3). 1977. pap. text ed. 1.45 (ISBN 0-88436-462-3, ELA 011054). EMC.

--Olga Makes a Wish. LC 77-10683. (Olga Da Polga Ser.). (Illus.). (gr. k-3). 1977. pap. text ed. 1.45 (ISBN 0-88436-456-9, ELA 010052). EMC.

--Olga Makes Her Mark. LC 77-10713. (Olga Da Polga). (Illus.). (gr. k-3). 1977. pap. text ed. 1.45 (ISBN 0-88436-459-3). EMC.

--Olga Meets Her Match. (gr. 1 up). 1973. pap. 2.95 (ISBN 0-14-030600-5, Puffin). Penguin.

--Olga Meets Her Match. 128p. (Orig.). (gr. k-6). 1983. pap. 2.25 (ISBN 0-440-46622-9, YB). Dell.

--Olga Meets Her Match: More Tales of Olga Da Polga. (Illus.). 128p. (Orig.). (gr. 3-6). 1975. 7.95 (ISBN 0-8038-5377-7). Hastings.

--Olga Takes a Bite. LC 77-21321. (Olga Da Polga Ser.). (Illus.). (gr. k-3). 1977. pap. text ed. 1.45 (ISBN 0-88436-460-7, ELA 010055). EMC.

--Olga Takes Charge. 128p. (Orig.). (gr. 3-7). 1983. pap. 2.25 (ISBN 0-440-46620-2, YB). Dell.

--Olga's New Home. LC 77-10476. (Olga Da Polga Ser.). (Illus.). (gr. k-3). 1977. pap. text ed. 1.45 (ISBN 0-88436-457-7, ELA 010053). EMC.

--Olga's Second Home. LC 77-10477. (Olga Da Polga Ser.). (Illus.). (gr. k-3). 1977. pap. text ed. 1.45 (ISBN 0-88436-461-5, ELA 011053). EMC.

--Olga's Special Day. LC 77-10714. (Olga Da Polga Ser.). (Illus.). (gr. k-3). 1977. pap. text ed. 1.45 (ISBN 0-88436-463-1, ELA 011055). EMC.

--Paddington Abroad. (Illus.). 128p. (gr. 2-6). 1974. pap. 1.25 (ISBN 0-440-47352-7, YB). Dell.

--Paddington Abroad. LC 72-2753. (Illus.). 128p. (gr. 1-5). 1972. 9.95 (ISBN 0-395-14331-4). HM.

--Paddington & the Knickerbocker Rainbow. (Paddington Bks.). (Illus.). 32p. (gr. k-2). 1985. 4.95 (ISBN 0-399-21202-7, Putnam). Putnam Pub Group.

--Paddington at Large. (Illus.). 128p. (gr. 3-7). 1970. pap. 1.75 (ISBN 0-440-46801-9, YB). Dell.

--Paddington at Large. (Illus.). (gr. 1-5). 1963. 9.95 (ISBN 0-395-06641-7). HM.

--Paddington at the Circus. LC 74-4279. (The Paddington Picture Bks). (Illus.). 36p. (ps-2). 1974. (BYR). Random.

--Paddington at the Fair. (Paddington Ser.). (Illus.). 32p. (ps-2). 1986. 4.95 (ISBN 0-399-21271-X, G&D). Putnam Pub Group.

--Paddington at the Seaside. LC 77-90190. (ps-3). 1978. 4.95 (ISBN 0-394-83801-7, BYR); PLB 4.99 (ISBN 0-394-93801-1). Random.

--Paddington at the Tower. LC 77-90189. (ps-3). 1978. 4.95 (ISBN 0-394-83802-5, BYR); PLB 4.99 (ISBN 0-394-93802-X). Random.

--Paddington at the Zoo. (Paddington Bks.). (Illus.). 32p. (gr. k-2). 1985. 4.95 (ISBN 0-399-21201-9, Putnam). Putnam Pub Group.

--Paddington at the Zoo. (Illus.). 32p. pap. 4.94 (ISBN 0-317-31369-X). Putnam Pub Group.

--Paddington at Work. 128p. (gr. k-8). 1971. pap. 1.75 (ISBN 0-440-40797-4, YB). Dell.

--Paddington at Work. LC 67-20372. (Illus.). (gr. 1-5). 1967. 9.95 (ISBN 0-395-06637-9). HM.

--Paddington Bear. (Illus.). (ps-2). 1973. 4.95 (ISBN 0-394-82642-6, BYR); PLB 4.99 (ISBN 0-394-92642-0). Random.

--Paddington Goes to Town. 128p. (gr. 2-5). 1972. pap. 2.50 (ISBN 0-440-46793-4, YB). Dell.

--Paddington Goes to Town. LC 68-28043. (Illus.). (gr. 1-5). 1968. 9.95 (ISBN 0-395-06635-2). HM.

--Paddington Helps Out. 128p. (gr. 3-7). 1970. pap. 1.75 (ISBN 0-440-46802-7, YB). Dell.

--Paddington Helps Out. (Illus.). (gr. 4-6). 1961. 9.95 (ISBN 0-395-06639-5). HM.

--Paddington Marches On. (Illus.). 128p. (gr. 2-6). 1971. pap. 2.50 (ISBN 0-440-46799-3, YB). Dell.

--Paddington Marches On. (Illus.). (gr. 4-6). 1965. 9.95 (ISBN 0-395-06642-5). HM.

Bone, Robert C. American Government. LC 76-52828. 306p. 1977. pap. 5.95 (ISBN 0-06-460170-6, CO 170, COS). B&N NY.

Bone, Robert W. Maverick Guide to Australia: 1984-1985. (Maverick Guide Ser.). 336p. (Orig.). 1984. pap. 10.95 (ISBN 0-88289-435-8). Pelican.

--Maverick Guide to Australia, 1986-87. (Maverick Guide Ser.). 336p. 1985. pap. 10.95 (ISBN 0-88289-492-7). Pelican.

--Maverick Guide to Hawaii, 1985. (Maverick Guide Ser.). 456p. 1985. pap. 10.95 (ISBN 0-88289-469-2). Pelican.

--Maverick Guide to Hawaii, 1986. (Maverick Guide Ser.). 448p. (Orig.). 1985. pap. 10.95 (ISBN 0-88289-491-9). Pelican.

--Maverick Guide to New Zealand, 1985-1986. (Maverick Guide Ser.). 320p. (Orig.). 1985. pap. 11.95 (ISBN 0-88289-470-6). Pelican.

Bone, Roger C. Pulmonary Disease Reviews. (Pulmonary Disease Ser.: Vol. 2). 642p. 1981. 60.00x (ISBN 0-471-09047-6, Pub. by Wiley Med). Wiley.

--Pulmonary Disease Reviews. (Pulmonary Disease Ser.: Vol. 4). 688p. 1983. 60.00 (ISBN 0-471-89158-4, Pub. by Wiley Med). Wiley.

--Pulmonary Disease Reviews. (Pulmonary Disease Ser.: Vol. 6). 1985. 69.00 (ISBN 0-471-82574-3). Wiley.

--Pulmonary Disease Reviews, Vol. 1. (Pulmonary Disease Review Ser.). 581p. 1980. 60.00 (ISBN 0-471-05736-3, Pub. by Wiley Med). Wiley.

--Pulmonary Disease Reviews, Vol. 5. (Pulmonary Disease Review Ser.). 828p. 1984. 69.00x (ISBN 0-471-80433-9). Wiley.

Bone, Roger C., ed. Critical Care: A Comprehensive Approach. Date not set. text ed. price not set (ISBN 0-89004-786-3). Raven.

--Critical Care: A Comprehensive Approach. 1984. text ed. 49.95 (ISBN 0-317-07722-8). Am Chest Phys.

--Pulmonary Disease Reviews, 2 Vols. LC 80-648256. Vol. 1. pap. 145.30 (ISBN 0-317-28954-3, 2055984); Vol. 2. pap. 160.00 (ISBN 0-317-28955-1). Bks Demand UMI.

Bone, Roger C., jt. ed. see Murphy, Marvin L.

Bone, Woutrina A. Children's Stories & How to Tell Them. LC 75-28363. (Illus.). xviii, 200p. 1975. Repr. of 1924 ed. 40.00x (ISBN 0-8103-3747-9). Gale.

Bonebakker, Seeger A., jt. auth. see Rowson, Everett K.

Bonebreak, Robert L. Practical Techniques of Electronic Circuit Design. LC 81-11394. 306p. 1982. 39.95 (ISBN 0-471-09612-1, Pub. by Wiley Interscience). Wiley.

Bonelli, Robert A. The Executive Handbook to Minicomputers. (Illus.). text ed. 16.00 (ISBN 0-89433-090-X). Petrocelli.

--Increasing Profitability with Minicomputers. (Illus.). 256p. 1981. text ed. 17.50 (ISBN 0-89433-175-2). Petrocelli.

Bonello, Frank J. The Formulation of Expected Interest Rates. LC 71-627748. 1969. 8.00 (ISBN 0-87744-092-1). Mich St U Pr.

Bonello, Frank J., jt. auth. see Davisson, William I.

Bonello, Frank J. & Swartz, Thomas R., eds. Alternative Directions in Economic Policy. LC 77-17422. 1978. 3.95x (ISBN 0-268-00584-2); pap. 3.95 (ISBN 0-268-00585-0). U of Notre Dame Pr.

Bonem, Gilbert W., jt. auth. see Wollman, Nathaniel.

Bonenko, Allen. Pacific Salmon Fishing. LC 78-75298. (Illus.). 1980. 19.95 (ISBN 0-498-02326-5). A S Barnes.

Boneparth, Ellen. Women, Power & Policy. (Pergamon Policy Studies on Social Policy). 300p. 1982. 39.00 (ISBN 0-08-028048-X); pap. 10.95 (ISBN 0-08-028047-1). Pergamon.

Boner, C. J. Modern Lubricating Greases. LC 75-18294. (Illus.). 250p. 1976. ref. ed. 40.00x (ISBN 0-87936-002-X). Scholium Intl.

Boner, Charles. Transylvania: Its Products & Its People. LC 77-87531. (Illus.). Repr. of 1865 ed. 55.00 (ISBN 0-404-16601-6). AMS Pr.

Boner, Charles, tr. see Andersen, Hans Christian.

Boner, Marian. A Reference Guide to Texas Law & Legal History: Sources & Documentation. LC 75-19408. 118p. 1976. 12.50x (ISBN 0-292-77007-3). U of Tex Pr.

Bones, Jim. Rio Grande: Mountains to the Sea. Winkler, Suzanne, ed. (Illus.). 224p. 1985. 35.00 (ISBN 0-87719-008-9). Texas Month Pr.

--Texas Earth Surfaces: A Photographic Essay. (Illus.). 1970. 15.00 (ISBN 0-88426-016-X). Encino Pr.

Bones, Jim, Jr. Texas West of the Pecos. LC 81-40397. (Louise Lindsey Merrick Texas Environment Ser.: No. 4). (Illus.). 138p. 1981. 29.95 (ISBN 0-89096-117-4). Tex A&M Univ Pr.

Bones, Jim, Jr. & Graves, John. Texas Heartland: A Hill Country Year. LC 75-16352. (Illus.). 104p. 1975. 24.95 (ISBN 0-89096-002-X). Tex A&M Univ Pr.

Bones, R. Concise Encyclopedia Dictionary of Telecommunications. Date not set. 15.00 (ISBN 0-444-99955-8). Elsevier.

Bones, R. A., ed. Dictionary of Telecommunications. (Illus.). 1970. 15.00 (ISBN 0-8022-2309-5). Philos Lib.

Bonesteel, Georgia. Lap Quilting with Georgia Bonesteel. LC 81-83054. (Illus.). 128p. 1982. 19.18i (ISBN 0-8487-0524-6). Oxmoor Hse.

--More Lap Quilting with Georgia Bonesteel. LC 84-60287. (Illus.). 128p. 1985. 18.22i (ISBN 0-8487-0634-X). Oxmoor Hse.

Bonet, Alieke A., jt. auth. see Van der Beek, Jan M.

Bonet, C., jt. ed. see Bell, A. T.

Bonett, Emery, jt. auth. see Bonett, John.

Bonett, John & Bonett, Emery. A Banner for Pegasus. LC 81-47806. 240p. 1982. pap. 2.40i (ISBN 0-06-080554-4, P 554, PL). Har-Row.

--Dead Lion. LC 81-47807. 240p. 1982. pap. 2.40i (ISBN 0-06-080563-3, P 563, PL). Har-Row.

--Not in the Script. Barzun, J. & Taylor, W. H., eds. LC 81-47396. (Crime Fiction 1950-1975 Ser.). 187p. 1982. 18.00 (ISBN 0-8240-4963-2). Garland Pub.

--The Sound of Murder. LC 82-48809. 224p. 1983. pap. 2.84i (ISBN 0-06-080642-7, P 642, PL). Har-Row.

Bonevac, Daniel A. Reduction in the Abstract Sciences. 184p. 1982. 18.50 (ISBN 0-915145-14-6). Hackett Pub.

Bonewit, Kathy. Clinical Competencies for the Medical Assistant. 359p. 1981. 14.95x (ISBN 0-8036-0963-9). Davis Co.

--Clinical Procedures for Medical Assistants. 1979. text ed. 19.95 (ISBN 0-7216-1846-4). Saunders.

--Clinical Procedures for Medical Assistants. 2nd ed. (Illus.). 545p. 1984. 24.95 (ISBN 0-7216-1269-5). Saunders.

Bonewits, P. E. Real Magic. 3rd ed. LC 70-146087. (Illus.). 300p. 1979. pap. 7.95 (ISBN 0-916870-19-7). Creative Arts Bk.

Bonewitz, Ra. Cosmic Crystals: Crystal Consciousness & the New Age. 176p. 1984. pap. 9.95 (ISBN 0-85500-205-0). Newcastle Pub.

Boney, A. D. Phytoplankton. (Studies in Biology: No. 52). 124p. 1975. pap. text ed. 8.95 (ISBN 0-7131-2476-8). E Arnold.

Boney, C. D. Study of Library Reading in the Primary Grades. LC 76-176579. (Columbia University. Teachers College. Contributions to Education: No. 578). Repr. of 1933 ed. 22.50 (ISBN 0-404-55578-0). AMS Pr.

Boney, Elaine E. Rainer Maria Rilke: German Text with English Translation & Commentary. (Studies in the Germanic Languages & Literatures: No. 81). xi, 150p. 1975. 13.00 (ISBN 0-8078-8081-7). U of NC Pr.

Boney, F. N. A Pictorial History of the University of Georgia. LC 83-18078. (Illus.). 272p. 1984. 27.50 (ISBN 0-8203-0711-4). U of Ga Pr.

--Sotherner's All. x, 218p. 1985. pap. 12.95 (ISBN 0-86554-189-2, MUP-P19). Mercer Univ Pr.

--Southerners All. LC 84-9127. x, 218p. 1984. 16.95 (ISBN 0-86554-114-0, MUP/H105). Mercer Univ Pr.

Boney, William J. & Igleheart, Glenn, eds. Baptists & Ecumenism. 1980. pap. 6.95 (ISBN 0-8170-0893-4). Judson.

Bonfante, Guillano & Bonfante, Larissa. The Etruscan Language: An Introduction. (Illus.). 176p. 1983. 35.00x (ISBN 0-8147-1047-6). NYU Pr.

Bonfante, Larissa. Etruscan Dress. LC 75-11344. (Illus.). 256p. 1976. 25.00x (ISBN 0-8018-1640-8). Johns Hopkins.

Bonfante, Larissa, jt. auth. see Bonfante, Guillano.

Bonfield, Lloyd. Marriage Settlements, Sixteen Hundred One to Seventeen Forty: The Adoption of the Strict Settlement. LC 82-19828. (Cambridge Studies in English Legal History). (Illus.). 152p. 1983. 37.50 (ISBN 0-521-25021-8). Cambridge U Pr.

Bonfiglio, Thomas A. Cytopathologic Interpretation of Transthoracic Fine-Needle Biopsies. (Masson Monographs in Diagnostic Cytopathology, Vol. 4). 206p. 1983. 57.50 (ISBN 0-89352-197-3). Masson Pub.

Bonfils Templer, Margherita De see Templer, Margherita D.

Bonfonte, Larissa. Etruscan Life & Afterlife. (Illus.). 380p. 40.00 (ISBN 0-8143-1772-3). Wayne St U Pr.

Bonforte, John. The Rebellious Galilean. LC 81-82691. 1982. 9.95 (ISBN 0-8022-2391-5). Philos Lib.

Bonforte, Lisa, illus. Farm Animals. LC 80-53106. (Board Bks.). (Illus.). 14p. (ps). 1981. boards 3.50 (ISBN 0-394-84767-9). Random.

--Who Lives on the Farm? (Golden Storytime Bks.). (Illus.). (ps). 1980. 1.95 (ISBN 0-307-11985-8, Golden Pr). Western Pub.

Bonforte, Lisa, photos by. Fifty Favorite Birds Coloring Book. (Illus.). 48p. (Orig.). (gr. 3 up). 1982. pap. 2.50 (ISBN 0-486-24261-7). Dover.

Bong, Carl & O'Conner, Mike. Rule the Air: The Story of Dick Bong, America's Ace of Aces. 1985. cancelled. Champlin Museum.

Bong, Carl & O'Connor, Mike. Ace of Aces: The Dick Bong Story. 170p. 1985. 14.95 (ISBN 0-912173-06-8). Champlin Museum.

Bonga, J. M. & Durzan, D. J. Tissue Culture in Forestry. 1982. lib. bdg. 49.50 (ISBN 90-247-2660-3, Pub. by Martinus Nijhoff Netherlands). Kluwer Academic.

Bongaarts, John & Potter, Robert G., eds. Fertility, Biology & Behavior: An Analysis of the Proximate Determinants (Monograph) (Studies in Population). 216p. 1983. 29.50 (ISBN 0-12-114380-5). Acad Pr.

Bongar, Emmet. Theatre Student: Practical Stage Lighting. LC 70-125194. (Theatre Student Ser). (Illus.). (gr. 9 up). 1971. PLB 15.00 (ISBN 0-8239-0224-2). Rosen Group.

Bongard-Levin, G. M. The Origin of Aryans. 124p. 1981. text ed. 11.25x (ISBN 0-391-02193-1, Pub. by Heinemann India). Humanities.

Bongartz, Roy. Dollarwise Guide to the Southwest. 456p. 1985. pap. 10.95 (ISBN 0-671-50620-X). Frommer-Pasmantier.

Bonge, Dusti. Dusti Bonge: The Life of an Artist. Longnecker, Nancy, ed. LC 82-4804. (Mississippi Art Ser.). (Illus.). 128p. (Orig.). 1982. pap. 17.50 (ISBN 0-87805-160-0). U Pr of Miss.

Bonge, Lyle. The Photographs of Lyle Bonge. 32.50 (ISBN 0-912330-53-8). Jargon Soc.

Bonger, Willem A. Race & Crime. Hordyk, Margaret M., tr. LC 69-14912. (Criminology, Law Enforcement, & Social Problems Ser.: No. 34). 1969. 10.00x (ISBN 0-87585-034-0); pap. 5.00x (ISBN 0-87585-907-0). Patterson Smith.

Bongers, C. Standardization: Mathematical Methods in Assortment Determination. 265p. 1980. lib. bdg. 24.00 (ISBN 0-89838-029-4, Pub. by Martinus Nijhoff Netherlands). Kluwer Academic.

Bongert, Yvonne. Recherches Sur les Cours Laiques Du Xe Au XIIIe Siecle. LC 80-1996. 1981. Repr. of 1949 ed. 38.50 (ISBN 0-404-18554-1). AMS Pr.

Bonghan, Kim, et al. Acupuncture: The Scientific Evidence & Far-Eastern Medicine. Rev. ed. (Illus.). 1984. pap. 7.50 (ISBN 0-916508-15-3). Happiness Pr.

Bongie, Laurence L., ed. Etienne Bonnot de Condillac: Les Monades. 216p. 1981. 100.00x (ISBN 0-7294-0242-8, Pub. by Voltaire Found). State Mutual Bk.

Bongio, Enrico P. Principles of Industrial Welding. 1978. text ed. 6.50 (ISBN 0-686-24289-0); text ed. 5.85 (ISBN 0-686-26120-8). Lincoln Arc Weld.

Bongiorno, Andrew, tr. from Ital. Castelvetro on the Art of Poetry: An Abridged Translation of Castelvetro's Poetica d'Aristotele, Vulgarizzata et Sposta. LC 83-17386. (Medieval & Rennaissance Texts & Studies: Vol. 29). 432p. 1984. 26.00 (ISBN 0-86698-063-6). Medieval & Renaissance NY.

Bongiorno, Andrew, tr. see Pareto, Vilfredo.

Bongiorno, Benedetto & Garland, Robert R. Real Estate Accounting & Reporting Manual. 1983. text ed. 72.00 (ISBN 0-88262-965-4). Warren.

Bongiovanni, Alfred M., ed. Adolescent Gynecology: A Guide for Clinicians. 276p. 1983. 32.50x (ISBN 0-306-41203-9, Plenum Pr). Plenum Pub.

Bongiovanni, G. Manual of Clinical Gastroenterology. 598p. 1982. 17.95 (ISBN 0-07-006471-7). McGraw.

Bongiovanni, Gail. Medical Spanish. (Span.). 1977. pap. text ed. 15.95 (ISBN 0-07-006470-9). McGraw.

Bonham, Audrey R. & Paye, Burrall. Secrets of Winning Fast Break Basketball. LC 84-6997. 211p. 1984. 17.95 (ISBN 0-13-798745-5, Busn). P-H.

Bonham, Barbara. Bittersweet. 288p. 1984. pap. 3.50 (ISBN 0-515-07601-5). Jove Pubns.

--Dance of Desire. LC 78-54991. 416p. (Orig.). 1978. pap. 1.95 (ISBN 0-87216-470-5). Jove Pubns.

--Green Willow. LC 82-80212. 400p. (Orig.). 1982. pap. 3.50 (ISBN 0-86721-143-1). Jove Pubns.

--Passion's Price. LC 77-73928. 320p. (Orig.). 1982. pap. 2.95 (ISBN 0-86721-152-0). Jove Pubns.

Bonham, Frank. Blood on the Land. 208p. 1983. pap. 2.25 (ISBN 0-441-06751-4). Ace Bks.

--Bold Passage. 192p. 1984. pap. 2.50 (ISBN 0-441-06991-6). Ace Bks.

--Break for the Border. 176p. 1984. pap. 2.50 (ISBN 0-441-07876-1). Ace Bks.

--Cast a Long Shadow. 192p. 1984. pap. 2.25 (ISBN 0-441-09246-2). Ace Bks.

--Defiance Mountain. 176p. 1984. pap. 2.25 (ISBN 0-441-14237-0). Ace Bks.

--Durango Street. 160p. (gr. 7 up). 1972. pap. 2.50 (ISBN 0-440-92183-X, LFL). Dell.

--Durango Street. (gr. 7 up). 1967. 10.95 (ISBN 0-525-28950-X, 01063-320). Dutton.

--The Feud at Spanish Ford. 176p. 1983. pap. 2.25 (ISBN 0-441-23356-2). Ace Bks.

--The Forever Formula. LC 79-11381. (Illus.). (gr. 5-9). 1979. 11.95 (ISBN 0-525-30025-2, 01160-350). Dutton.

--Fort Hogan. 176p. 1984. pap. 2.25 (ISBN 0-441-24856-X). Ace Bks.

--The Friends of the Loony Lake Monster. (gr. 3-6). 1972. 8.95 (ISBN 0-525-30205-0). Dutton.

--Gimme an H, Gimme an E, Gimme an L, Gimme a P. 24p. (gr. 7 up). 1982. pap. 1.95 (ISBN 0-590-32136-6). Scholastic Inc.

--Gimme an H, Gimme an E, Gimme an L, Gimme a P. LC 80-23926. 192p. (gr. 7 up). 1980. 10.95 (ISBN 0-684-16717-4, ScribJ). Scribner.

--Hardrock. 192p. 1984. pap. 2.50 (ISBN 0-441-31741-3). Ace Bks.

--Last Stage West. 160p. 1981. pap. 1.95 (ISBN 0-425-04947-7). Berkley Pub.

--Last Stage West. 160p. 1984. pap. 2.25 (ISBN 0-441-47194-3). Ace Bks.

--Logan's Choice. 176p. 1981. pap. 1.95 (ISBN 0-425-05223-0). Berkley Pub.

--Logan's Choice. 192p. 1984. pap. 2.50 (ISBN 0-441-48829-3, Pub. by Charter Bks). Ace Bks.

--Lost Stage Valley. 192p. 1984. pap. 2.25 (ISBN 0-441-49513-3). Ace Bks.

--The Missing Persons League. (gr. 7 up). 1983. pap. 1.95 (ISBN 0-590-05387-6, Vagabond). Scholastic Inc.

--Mystery of the Fat Cat. 160p. (gr. 5-9). 1971. pap. 2.50 (ISBN 0-440-46226-6, YB). Dell.

--Night Raid. 192p. 1984. pap. 2.25 (ISBN 0-441-57586-2). Ace Bks.

--Premonitions. LC 84-3844. (gr. 8 up). 1984. 11.95 (ISBN 0-03-071306-4). HR&W.

--The Rascals from Haskell's Gym. (gr. 4-6). 1977. 9.95 (ISBN 0-525-38070-1, 0966-290). Dutton.

--Rawhide Guns. rev. ed. (Orig.). 1981. pap. 1.95 (ISBN 0-425-04815-2). Berkley Pub.

--Rawhide Guns. 176p. 1985. pap. 2.50 (ISBN 0-441-70820-X). Ace Bks.

--Snaketrack. 176p. 1985. pap. 2.50 (ISBN 0-441-77197-1). Ace Bks.

--Sound of Gunfire. 192p. 1984. pap. 2.50 (ISBN 0-441-77596-9). Ace Bks.

--Tough Country. 1981. pap. 1.95 (ISBN 0-425-04851-9). Berkley Pub.

--Tough Country. 176p. 1983. pap. 2.25 (ISBN 0-441-81850-1). Ace Bks.

--Trago. 192p. 1981. pap. 1.95 (ISBN 0-425-05041-6). Berkley Pub.

--Trago. 192p. 1984. pap. 2.25 (ISBN 0-441-82096-4). Ace Bks.

--Viva Chicano. 160p. (gr. 7 up). 1971. pap. 1.95 (ISBN 0-440-99400-4, LFL). Dell.

Bonham, George W. Education for a Global Century: Handbook of Exemplary International Programs. LC 80-69769. 157p. (Orig.). 1981. pap. 7.95 (ISBN 0-915390-29-9, Pub. by Change Mag). Transaction Pubs.

Bonham, George W., et al. Colleges & Money: A Faculty Guide to Academic Economics. LC 76-2872. 1976. pap. 4.95 (ISBN 0-915390-04-3, Pub. by Change Mag). Transaction Pubs.

--The Communications Revolution & the Education of Americans. LC 80-66849. 64p. (Orig.). 1980. pap. 6.95 (ISBN 0-915390-24-8, Pub. by Change Mag). Transaction Pubs.

--The Future of Foundations: Some Reconsiderations. LC 78-65580. 79p. 1978. pap. 6.95 (ISBN 0-915390-20-5, Pub. by Change Mag). Transaction Pubs.

--How to Succeed As a New Teacher: A Handbook for Teaching Assistants. LC 78-56237. 63p. 1978. pap. 4.95 (ISBN 0-915390-16-7, Pub. by Change Mag). Transaction Pubs.

Bonham, Gordon S. Content & Instruments of the National Medical Care Utilization & Expenditure Survey. Michael, Geraldine, ed. 60p. 1982. pap. text ed. 1.85 (ISBN 0-8406-0256-1). Natl Ctr Health Stats.

Bonham, Hilledge L. British Consuls in the Confederacy. LC 11-31660. (Columbia University Studies in the Social Sciences: No. 111). Repr. of 1911 ed. 12.50 (ISBN 0-404-51111-2). AMS Pr.

Bonham, John. The Middle Class Vote. LC 74-11985. (Illus.). 210p. 1974. Repr. of 1954 ed. lib. bdg. 22.50x (ISBN 0-8371-7709-X, BOMI). Greenwood.

Bonham, Tal D. Another Treasury of Clean Jokes. LC 82-73643. (Orig.). 1983. pap. 3.95 (ISBN 0-8054-5706-2). Broadman.

--The Treasury of Clean Business Jokes. 1985. pap. 2.95 (ISBN 0-8054-5712-7). Broadman.

--The Treasury of Clean Jokes. LC 80-67639. (Orig.). 1981. pap. 3.95 (ISBN 0-8054-5703-8). Broadman.

--The Treasury of Clean Teenage Jokes. (gr. 7 up). 1985. pap. 2.95 (ISBN 0-8054-5713-5, 4257-13). Broadman.

Bonham, Thomas. The Chyrgeons: Or, an Antidotarie Chyrurgicall. Poeton, E., ed. LC 68-54619. (English Experience Ser.: No. 31). 360p. 1968. Repr. of 1630 ed. 49.00 (ISBN 90-221-0031-6). Walter J Johnson.

Bonham-Carter, Graeme, jt. auth. see Harbaugh, John W.

Bonham-Carter, Victor. Authors by Profession, Vol. II. LC 79-314171. 336p. 16.95 (ISBN 0-86576-071-3). W Kaufmann.

--Authors by Profession, Vol. 1. 256p. 1978. 14.95x (ISBN 0-913232-59-9). W Kaufmann.

--Land & Environment: The Survival of the English Countryside. LC 72-3522. (Illus.). 240p. 1973. 22.50 (ISBN 0-8386-1195-8). Fairleigh Dickinson.

Bonheim, Helmut. A Lexicon of the German in "Finnegans Wake". LC 65-21267. (California Library Reprint Ser.: No. 126). 176p. 1985. Repr. 18.50 (ISBN 0-520-05355-9). U of Cal Pr.

--The Narrative Modes: Techniques of the Short Story. 197p. 1982. text ed. 30.00 (ISBN 0-85991-086-5, BAB-04697, Pub. by Boydell & Brewer). Longwood Pub Group.

Bonheur, Gaston. To Live in France. 272p. 1981. 60.00 (ISBN 2-71910-125-7). Edns Vilo.

Bonhoeffer, Dietrich. Act & Being. 192p. 1983. Repr. of 1962 ed. 18.50 (ISBN 0-88254-869-7). Octagon.

--Christ the Center: A New Translation. new ed. LC 78-4747. (Harper's Ministers Paperback Library Ser.). 1978. pap. 7.64 (ISBN 0-06-060815-3, RD 285, HarpR). Har-Row.

--The Cost of Discipleship. 1983. 13.50 (ISBN 0-8446-5960-6). Peter Smith.
--Cost of Discipleship. 1963. pap. 4.95 (ISBN 0-02-083850-6, Collier). Macmillan.
--Creation & Fall. Bd. with Temptation. 1965. pap. 3.95 (ISBN 0-02-083890-5, 08389). Macmillan.
--Creation & Fall: Temptation. 1983. 13.00 (ISBN 0-8446-5962-2). Peter Smith.
--Ethics. Bethge, Eberhard, ed. 1965. pap. 3.95 (ISBN 0-02-083870-0). Macmillan.
--Ethics. 1983. 12.00 (ISBN 0-8446-5963-0). Peter Smith.
--Fiction from Prison: Gathering up the Past. Green, Clifford, tr. from Ger. LC 80-2378. 224p. 1981. 15.95 (ISBN 0-8006-0663-9, 1-663). Fortress.
--Letters & Papers from Prison. enl. ed. 1972. pap. 5.95 (ISBN 0-02-083920-0). Macmillan.
--Life Together. LC 54-6901. 128p. 1976. pap. 6.68i (ISBN 0-06-060851-X, RD292, HarpR). Har-Row.
--The Martyred Christian: One Hundred & Sixty Readings. Brown, Joan W., ed. 288p. 1985. pap. 5.95 (ISBN 0-02-084020-9, Collier). Macmillan.
--Prayers from Prison. Hampe, Johann C., tr. from Ger. LC 77-15228. 1978. pap. 4.95 (ISBN 0-8006-1334-1, 1-1334). Fortress.
--Spiritual Care. Rochelle, Jay C., tr. LC 85-47711. 128p. 1985. pap. 4.95 (ISBN 0-8006-1874-2). Fortress.

Bonhote, J. Lewis. Birds of Britain & Their Eggs. Repr. of 1907 ed. 35.00 (ISBN 0-686-20650-9). Lib Serv Inc.

Bonhote, J. M. Samuel Mareschal: Melodiae Suaves. (Wissenschaftliche Abhandlngen-Musicological Studies Ser.: Vol. 25). 36p. (Fr.). 1976. pap. 6.00 (ISBN 0-912024-77-1). Inst Mediaeval Mus.

Boni, Ada. Talisman Italian Cook Book. La Rosa, Mathilde, tr. (International Cook Book Ser). 1955. 9.95 (ISBN 0-517-50387-5, Harmony). Crown.

Boni, Sylvain. The Self & the Other in the Ontologies of Sartre & Buber. LC 82-20130. 202p. (Orig.). 1983. lib. bdg. 24.75 (ISBN 0-8191-2852-X); pap. text ed. 12.50 (ISBN 0-8191-2853-8). U Pr of Amer.

Bonic. The Picture Life of Pope John Paul II. Date not set. lib. bdg. 9.90 (ISBN 0-531-04806-3). Watts.

Bonic, Robert, et al. Freshman Calculus. 2nd ed. 1976. text ed. 27.95 (ISBN 0-669-96727-0). Heath.

Bonic, Robert A. Linear Functional Analysis. (Notes on Mathematics & Its Applications Ser.). 138p. 1969. 44.25 (ISBN 0-677-02050-3). Gordon.

Bonica, J. J., jt. ed. see Ng, L. K.

Bonica, John J., ed. Pain. (Association for Research in Nervous & Mental Disease Publications Ser.: Vol. 58). 424p. 1980. text ed. 54.50 (ISBN 0-89004-376-0). Raven.

Bonica, John J. & Ventafridda, Vittorio, eds. International Symposium on Pain of Advanced Cancer. LC 78-55811. (Advances in Pain Research & Therapy Ser.: Vol. 2). 734p. 1979. text ed. 96.00 (ISBN 0-89004-271-3). Raven.

Bonica, John J., ed. see World Conference on Pain, 3rd Edinburgh, et al.

Bonica, John J., et al, eds. Management of Superior Pulmonary Sulcus Syndrome, Pancoast Syndrome. (Advances in Pain Research & Therapy Ser.: Vol. 4). 256p. 1982. text ed. 51.50 (ISBN 0-89004-770-7). Raven.
--Recent Advances on Pain: Pathophysiology & Clinical Aspects. (Illus.). 352p. 1974. photocopy ed. 32.50x (ISBN 0-398-02964-4). C C Thomas.

Boniface, Jean-Michel & Jeudy, Jean-Gabriel. GMC Six by Six & DUKW. (Illus.). 1979. 19.95 (ISBN 0-87938-072-1). Motorbooks Intl.

Boniface, Saint Letters of Saint Boniface. Emerton, Ephraim, ed. 1967. lib. bdg. 21.50x (ISBN 0-374-92584-4). Octagon.

Boniface, St., et al. English Correspondence of Saint Boniface & His Friends in England. Kylie, Edward, tr. LC 66-30729. (Medieval Library). (Illus.). 209p. 1966. Repr. of 1926 ed. 22.50 (ISBN 0-8154-0028-4). Cooper Sq.

Bonifacio, Andes see Craig, Austin.

Bonifacio, R. & Lugiato, L. A., eds. Dissipative Systems in Quantum Optics. (Topics in Current Physics Ser.: Vol. 27). (Illus.). 160p. 1982. 23.00 (ISBN 0-387-11062-3). Springer-Verlag.

Bonifacius, Saint Winfrid. Briefe des Heiligen Bonifatius. pap. 23.00 (ISBN 0-384-05025-5). Johnson Repr.

Bonifazi, Conrad. The Soul of the World: An Account of Inwardness of Things. LC 78-64826. 1978. pap. text ed. 13.00 (ISBN 0-8191-0638-0). U Pr of Amer.
--A Theology of Things. LC 76-7549. 1976. Repr. of 1967 ed. lib. bdg. 17.00x (ISBN 0-8371-8838-5, BOTT). Greenwood.

Bonifazi, Flavian. Yearning of a Soul. 1979. 4.95 (ISBN 0-8198-0614-5); pap. 3.50 (ISBN 0-8198-0615-3). Dghtrs St Paul.

Bonifer & Weaver. Out of Bounds: An Anecdotal History of Notre Dame Football. LC 78-60060. (Illus.). 1978. 15.00 (ISBN 0-87832-043-1). Piper.

Bonifer, Michael. The Making of Tron. (Illus.). 96p. (Orig.). (gr. 1-4). 1982. pap. 7.95 (ISBN 0-671-45575-3, Little Simon). S&S.

Bonikowska, Halina. Pod Sztandarem Z Gwiazd. LC 85-61376. 112p. (Orig., Polish.). 1985. pap. text ed. 8.00 (ISBN 0-930401-01-8). Serpent Pub Co.

Bonilla, C. F., ed. Fifth Symposiums on Thermophysical Properties. 503p. 1970. 19.00 (ISBN 0-317-33510-3, G0068); members 9.50 (ISBN 0-317-33511-1). ASME.

Bonilla, Frank & Silva-Michelena, Jose A. The Politics of Change in Venezuela, 3 vols. Incl. Vol. 1. A Strategy for Research on Social Policy. 1967; Vol. 2. The Failure of Elites. 1970. 35.00x (ISBN 0-262-02058-0); Vol. 3. The Illusion of Democracy in Dependent Nations. 1971. 32.50x (ISBN 0-262-19069-9). MIT Pr.

Bonilla, Plutarco. Los Milagros Tambien Son Parabolas. LC 78-59240. 166p. (Orig., Span.). 1978. pap. 3.95 (ISBN 0-89922-114-9). Edit Caribe.

Bonime, Walter. The Clinical Use of Dreams. (Psychoanalysis Examined & Re-Examined Ser.). 343p. 1982. Repr. of 1962 ed. lib. bdg. 27.50 (ISBN 0-306-79710-0). Da Capo.

Bonin, Edmond, ed. see St. Cyprian of Carthage.

Bonin, Edmond, tr. see Evely, Louis.

Bonin, Gerhardt Von. The Evolution of the Human Brain. LC 63-13062. (Midway Reprint Ser.). 1975. pap. 6.95x (ISBN 0-226-06436-0). U of Chicago Pr.

Bonin, Gerhardt von see Von Bonin, Gerhardt.

Bonin, Helene, tr. see Champsaur, Paul & Milleron, Jean-Claude.

Bonin, Jane. Mario Fratti. (World Authors Ser.). 1982. lib. bdg. 18.95 (ISBN 0-8057-6498-4, Twayne). G K Hall.

Bonin, John P., tr. see Champsaur, Paul & Milleron, Jean-Claude.

Bonin, Serge. Le Traitement Graphique D'une Information Hydrometeorologique Relative a L'espace Maritime Du Nord Sovietique, 2 vols. Incl. Vol. 1. Les Documents Graphiques. (Illus.); Vol. 2. Analyses et Commentaires. 2200p. (Contributions Du Centre D' Etudes Antiques: No. 11). (Illus., Fr.). 1974. Set. pap. text ed. 34.80x (ISBN 0-686-22587-2). Mouton.

Bonine, John E. & McGarity, Thomas O. The Law of Environmental Protection. LC 84-2246. (American Casebook Ser.). 1076p. 1984. text ed. 31.95 (ISBN 0-314-79309-7); July 1984, 197 pgs. pap. write for info. tchr's. man. (ISBN 0-314-86678-7). West Pub.

Bonine, Michael E. & Keddie, Nikki R., eds. Continuity & Change in Modern Iran. LC 80-19468. 225p. 1981. pap. text ed. 12.95x (ISBN 0-87395-466-1). State U NY Pr.
--Modern Iran: The Dialectics of Continuity & Change. LC 80-19463. 400p. 1981. 39.50x (ISBN 0-87395-465-3); pap. 19.95x (ISBN 0-87395-641-9). State U NY Pr.

Boning, Richard A. Alone. (Incredible Ser). (Illus.). (gr. 5-11). 1975. PLB 7.50 (ISBN 0-87966-108-9, Pub. by Dexter & Westbrook). B Loft.
--Blondin: Hero of Niagara. (Incredible Ser). (Illus.). (gr. 5-11). 1972. PLB 7.50 (ISBN 0-87966-101-1, Pub. by Dexter & Westbrook). B Loft.
--The Cardiff Giant. (Incredible Ser.). (Illus.). (gr. 5-11). 1972. PLB 7.50 (ISBN 0-87966-102-X, Pub. by Dexter & Westbrook). B Loft.
--Developing Key Concepts in Comprehension. (gr. 1-10). 1983. 3.65 (ISBN 0-8484-1000-9). B Loft.
--Escape. (Incredible Ser.). (Illus.). (gr. 5-11). 1975. PLB 7.50 (ISBN 0-87966-109-7, Pub. by Dexter & Westbrook). B Loft.
--Horror Overhead. (Incredible Ser). (Illus.). (gr. 5-11). 1973. PLB 7.50 (ISBN 0-87966-105-4, Pub. by Dexter & Westbrook). B Loft.
--Joshua James. (The Incredible Ser.). (Illus.). 48p. (gr. 5-11). 1972. PLB 7.50 (ISBN 0-87966-104-6, Pub. by Dexter & Westbrook). B Loft.
--The Long Search. (The Incredible Ser). (Illus.). 48p. (gr. 5-11). 1972. PLB 7.50 (ISBN 0-87966-103-8, Pub. by Dexter & Westbrook). B Loft.
--Multiple Skills Series: Levels Picture Level Through I. Incl. E1 (ISBN 0-8484-0041-0); E2 (ISBN 0-8484-0042-9); E3 (ISBN 0-8484-0043-7); E4 (ISBN 0-8484-0044-5); F1 (ISBN 0-8484-0045-3); F2 (ISBN 0-8484-0046-1); F3 (ISBN 0-8484-0047-X); F4 (ISBN 0-8484-0048-8). (Also available in span. edition-levels picture through f). (YA) 1976. pap. 24.50 set (ISBN 0-685-69056-3); pap. 2.65 ea. B Loft.
--Picto-Cabulary Series, 7 sets. Incl. Basic Word Set-A. (gr. 1-2). 104.45 (ISBN 0-87965-409-0); Words to Eat. (gr. 4-6). 77.95 (ISBN 0-87965-401-5); Words to Wear. (gr. 4-6). 77.95 (ISBN 0-87965-402-3); Words to Meet. (gr. 4-6). 77.95 (ISBN 0-87965-403-1); Descriptive Words. (gr. 5-9). 77.95 (ISBN 0-87965-421-X); Words Around the House. (gr. 4-6). 77.95 (ISBN 0-87965-405-8); Words Around the Neighborhood. (gr. 4-6). 77.95 (ISBN 0-87965-404-X). 1980. B Loft.
--The Red Baron. (Incredible Ser.). (Illus.). 1975. 7.50 (ISBN 0-87966-111-9, Pub. by Dexter & Westbrook). B Loft.
--Seventeen Minutes to Live. (Incredible Ser.). (Illus.). 48p. (gr. 5-11). 1973. PLB 7.50 (ISBN 0-87966-106-2, Pub. by Dexter & Westbrook). B Loft.
--Soldier Girl. (Incredible Ser.). (Illus.). 1975. 7.50 (ISBN 0-87966-110-0, Pub. by Dexter & Westbrook). B Loft.
--Specific Skill Reading Series: New 1982. Incl. Detecting the Sequence, 14 bks. (gr. 1-12); Drawing Conclusions, 14 bks. (gr. 1-12); Following Directions, 14 bks. (gr. 1-12); Getting the Facts, 14 bks. (gr. 1-12); Getting the Main Idea, 14 bks. (gr. 1-12); Locating the Answer, 14 bks. (gr. 1-12); Using the Context, 14 bks. (gr. 1-12); Working with Sounds, 14 bks. (gr. 1-12). bk. 2.50 ea.; tchr's manuals 3.80 ea.; Set. spirit masters 8.80 (ISBN 0-87965-798-7); complete elementary set 161.35 (ISBN 0-87965-824-X); complete midway set (4-9) 125.20 (ISBN 0-87965-826-6); complete secondary set (7-12) 125.20 (ISBN 0-87965-825-8). B Loft.
--Titanic. (Incredible Ser.). (Illus.). 48p. (gr. 5-11). 1974. PLB 7.50 (ISBN 0-87966-107-0, Pub. by Dexter & Westbrook). B Loft.
--The Tom Thumb Book. (gr. k-3). 1971. 4.95 (ISBN 0-87966-100-3, Pub. by Dexter & Westbrook). B Loft.
--We Study Word Shapes, Bks. K-A. (gr. k-1). 1969. 3.75 ea. (Pub. by Dexter & Westbrook); Bk. K. (ISBN 0-87966-056-2); Bk. A. (ISBN 0-87966-057-0). B Loft.
--Word Theater Series: Nineteen Seventy-Eight to Nineteen Seventy-Nine, 12 sets ea. level, Levels 3-6. Set. 7.95 ea. (ISBN 0-686-65402-1); Complete Set Of 48. 378.00 (ISBN 0-87965-358-2). B Loft.

Bonington, Chris. I Chose to Climb. (Illus.). 210p. 1985. pap. 9.95 (ISBN 0-575-03590-0, Pub. by Gollancz England). David & Charles.
--Kongur: China's Elusive Summit. (Illus.). 1983. 19.95 (ISBN 0-393-01762-1). Norton.
--Quest for Adventure. (Illus.). 448p. 1982. 30.00 (ISBN 0-517-54696-5). Crown.

Bonington, Chris & Clarke, Charles. Everest: The Unclimbed Ridge. (Illus.). 1984. 24.95 (ISBN 0-393-01875-X). Norton.

Bonington, Chris see Allen, W. S.

Bonington, Chris, et al. Everest -- the Hard Way. 1977. 14.95 (ISBN 0-394-40786-5). Random.

Bonini, Charles P. Computer Models for Decision Analysis. (Illus.). 148p. (Orig.). 1980. pap. text ed. 15.00x (ISBN 0-89426-042-1); tchrs'. ed. 15.00x (ISBN 0-89426-043-X). Scientific Pr.

Bonini, Charles P., jt. auth. see Spurr, William A.

Bonini, Don Severo. Severo Bonini's Discorsi e Regole: A Bilingual Edition. Bonino, MaryAnn, ed. & tr. from Italian. LC 77-18514. (Illus.). 1979. text ed. 24.95x (ISBN 0-8425-0997-6). Brigham.

Bonini, William E., et al, eds. The Caribbean-South American Plate Boundary & Regional Tectonics. (Memoir Ser.: No. 162). (Illus.). 1984. 47.50. Geol Soc.

Bonino, Jose M. Doing Theology in a Revolutionary Situation. Lazareth, William H., ed. LC 80-424. 208p. 1975. pap. 5.50 (ISBN 0-8006-1451-8, 1-1451). Fortress.
--Room to Be People: An Interpretation of the Message of the Bible for Today's World. Leach, Vickie, tr. from Span. LC 78-14662. 80p. 1979. pap. 4.50 (ISBN 0-8006-1349-X, 1-1349). Fortress.
--Toward a Christian Political Ethics. LC 82-48541. 144p. 1983. pap. 6.95 (ISBN 0-8006-1697-9, 1-1697). Fortress.

Bonino, MaryAnn, ed. & tr. see Bonini, Don Severo.

Bonior, David E., et al. The Vietnam Veteran: A History of Neglect. 208p. 1984. 21.95 (ISBN 0-03-070279-8). Praeger.

Bonis, L. J., ed. see Symposium on Fundamental Phenomena in the Materials Science, 1st, 1963, Boston.

Bonis, L. J., et al, eds. Fracture of Metals, Polymers & Glasses. (Fundamental Phenomena in the Materials Science Ser.: Vol. 4). 310p. 1967. 32.50x (ISBN 0-306-38604-6, Plenum Pr). Plenum Pub.

Bonito, Grace. Medical Office Management Handbook. rev. ed. McFadden, S. Michele & Hawkins, Mary, eds. (Illus.). 352p. 1981. pap. text ed. 19.50x (ISBN 0-89262-048-X). pegboard kit 16.50 (ISBN 0-686-78759-5, CA-118). Career Pub.
--Medical Office Management Workbook. rev. ed. McFadden, S. Michele, ed. 1981. 15.00x (ISBN 0-89262-049-8); guide 50.00 (ISBN 0-89262-050-1). Career Pub.

Bonjean, C. M., et al. Community Politics: A Behavioral Approach. LC 72-136273. 1971. pap. text ed. 7.95 (ISBN 0-02-904440-5). Free Pr.

Bonjean, Charles M., jt. ed. see Schneider, Louis.

Bonjean, Charles M., et al, eds. Social Science in America: The First Two Hundred Years. 229p. 1976. 14.95x (ISBN 0-292-77530-X); pap. 7.95 (ISBN 0-292-77531-8). U of Tex Pr.

Bonjour, Adrien. Coleridge's Hymn Before Sunrise. 1978. Repr. of 1942 ed. lib. bdg. 30.00 (ISBN 0-8495-0442-2). Arden Lib.
--Coleridge's Hymn Before Sunrise. LC 73-9666. 1942. lib. bdg. 17.50 (ISBN 0-8414-3156-6). Folcroft.

Bonjour, Adrien, ed. Dialogue De Saint-Julien et Son Disciple. 1949. pap. 10.00 (ISBN 0-384-11690-6). Johnson Repr.

Bonjour, Edgar, et al. A Short History of Switzerland. LC 84-25253. viii, 388p. 1985. Repr. of 1952 ed. lib. bdg. 49.75x (ISBN 0-313-24675-0, BOSZ). Greenwood.

BonJour, Laurence. The Structure of Empirical Knowledge. 312p. 1985. text ed. 22.50x (ISBN 0-674-84380-0). Harvard U Pr.

Bonk, Jon. Ethiopian Orthodox Church. LC 84-10547. (ATLA Bibliography Ser.: No. 11). 132p. 1984. 15.00 (ISBN 0-8108-1710-1). Scarecrow.

Bonk, U. E. Biopsie und Operationspraeparat. (Illus.). viii, 134p. 1983. pap. 9.50 (ISBN 3-8055-3702-6). S Karger.

Bonk, Wallace J. Michigan's First Bookstore. (School of Library Science Ser.). (Illus.). 36p. 1957. pap. 3.00 (ISBN 0-87506-036-6). Campus.

Bonk, Wallace J. & Magrill, Rose M. Building Library Collections. 5th ed. LC 79-11151. 390p. 1979. 14.50 (ISBN 0-8108-1214-2). Scarecrow.

Bonke, Felix I. The Sinus Node: Structure, Function, & Clinical Relevance. 1978. lib. bdg. 55.00 (ISBN 90-247-2064-8, Pub. by Martinus Nijhoff Netherlands). Kluwer Academic.

Bonkovsky, Frederick O. International Norms & National Policy. LC 79-21206. pap. 58.50 (ISBN 0-317-07962-X, 2020839). Bks Demand UMI.

Bonn, E. W, et al, eds. Guidelines for Striped Bass Culture. American Fisheries Society Southern Division. 117p. 1976. pap. 10.00 (ISBN 0-913235-20-2). Am Fisheries Soc.

Bonn, Franz. The Children's Theatre: A Reproduction of the Antique Pop-up Book. LC 79-5071. (Illus.). (gr. k-3). 1979. 10.95 (ISBN 0-670-21773-5, Co-Pub. by Kestrel Bks). Viking.

Bonn, George S., ed. Information Resources in the Environmental Sciences. LC 73-75784. (Allerton Park Institute Ser.: No. 18). 238p. 1973. 7.00x (ISBN 0-87845-037-8). U of Ill Lib Info Sci.

Bonn, George S. & Faibisoff, Sylvia G., eds. Changing Times: Changing Libraries. LC 78-1283. (Allerton Part Institutes Ser.: No. 22). 166p. 1978. 8.00x (ISBN 0-87845-047-5). U of Ill Lib Info Sci.

Bonn, Thomas. Paperback Primer: A Guide for Collectors. LC 81-84454. 64p. 1981. lib. bdg. 14.95x (ISBN 0-941858-00-6). Borgo Pr.

Bonn, Thomas L. Paperback Primer: A Guide for Collectors. LC 81-84454. 70p. 1982. 9.95 (ISBN 0-941858-00-6). Paperback Quarterly.

Bonnaffe, Edmond. Dictionnaire des Amateurs Francais au Dix-Septieme Siecle. (Bibliography & Reference Ser.: No. 138). (Fr.). 1968. Repr. of 1884 ed. 26.50 (ISBN 0-8337-0335-8). B Franklin.

Bonnar, J. Pregnancy Hypertension. (Illus.). 620p. 1980. text ed. 49.50 (ISBN 0-8391-4122-X). Univ Park.

Bonnar, J., jt. auth. see Hathaway, William E.

Bonnar, J., jt. auth. see Harrison, R. F.

Bonnar, J., et al, eds. Research in Family Planning. (Studies in Fertility & Sterility Ser.). 1985. lib. bdg. 60.25 (ISBN 0-318-04476-5, Pub. by MTP Pr England). Kluwer-Academic.

Bonnard, H., et al. Modern French Usage: A Student Guide. 1971. write for info. (ISBN 0-02-312100-9). Macmillan.

Bonnardot, Alfred. Essai sur l'Art de Restaurer les Estampes et les Livres, 2 vols. in 1. Incl. De la reparation des vieilles reliures. LC 78-7009. LC 74-7008. 352p. 1858. Repr. 25.50 (ISBN 0-8337-0336-6). B Franklin.

Bonnardot, F., ed. see D' Anglure, Ogier.

Bonnassieux, Louis J. Grandes Compagnies de Commerce: Etude pour Servir a l'Histoire de la Colonisation. LC 68-57900. (Research & Source Works Ser.: No. 296). (Fr) 1968. Repr. of 1892 ed. 29.00 (ISBN 0-8337-0337-4). B Franklin.

Bonnat, jt. auth. see Haivaux.

Bonne, A., jt. auth. see D'Allessandro, M.

Bonne, Alfred. The Economic Development of the Middle East: An Outline of Planned Reconstruction after the War. LC 79-51856. 1981. Repr. of 1945 ed. 19.25 (ISBN 0-88355-949-8). Hyperion Conn.
--State & Economics in the Middle East. LC 72-11325. (Illus.). 452p. 1973. Repr. of 1955 ed. lib. bdg. 35.00x (ISBN 0-8371-6661-6, BOSE). Greenwood.
--Studies in Economic Development: With Special Reference to Conditions in the Underdeveloped Areas of Western Asia & India. LC 77-27500. 1978. Repr. of 1957 ed. lib. bdg. 21.50x (ISBN 0-313-20183-8, BOED). Greenwood.

Bonneau, B. Lee & Smith, Billy A. Astronomy Illustrated. 3rd ed. 1980. wire coil bdg. 15.95 (ISBN 0-8403-2168-6). Kendall Hunt.

Bonneau, M & Hennessen, W., eds. Herpes Virus of Man & Animal: Standardization of Immunological Procedures. (Developments in Biological Standardization: Vol. 52). (Illus.). x, 574p. 1983. pap. 55.50 (ISBN 3-8055-3636-4). S Karger.

Bonneau, Maurice & Souchier, B., eds. Constituents & Properties of Soils. LC 81-68957. 1982. 67.00 (ISBN 0-12-114550-6). Acad Pr.

Bonnechose, Emile de. The Reformers Before the Reformation. Mackenzie, Campbell, tr. LC 78-63194. (Heresies of the Early Christian & Medieval Era: Second Ser.). Repr. of 1844 ed. 27.50 set (ISBN 0-404-16190-1). AMS Pr.

Bonnechose, Emile de see Bonnechose, Emile de.

Bonnefoi, Alexandre. Woerterbuch des Arbeits und Sozialrechtd. (Ger. & Fr.). 1975. 55.00 (ISBN 3-19-006293-5, M-6938). French & Eur.

Bonnefoy, Claude, et al. Dictionnaire de Litterature Francais Contemporaine. 411p. (Fr.). 1977. 39.95 (ISBN 0-686-56924-5, M-6042). French & Eur.

Bonnefoy, Yves. Poems, Nineteen Fifty-Nine to Nineteen Seventy-Five. Pevear, Richard, tr. 1985. 7.95 (ISBN 0-394-73956-6, Vin). Random.

--Words in Stone: Pierre Ecrite. Lang, Susanna, tr. LC 75-32481. 160p. (Eng. & Fr.). 1976. lib. bdg. 13.00x (ISBN 0-87023-203-7). U of Mass Pr.

Bonnel, Peter & Sedwick, Frank. Conversation in French: Points of Departure. 4th ed. 128p. 1985. pap. text ed. 11.95 (ISBN 0-8384-1274-2). Heinle & Heinle.

Bonnell, Allen T., ed. see American Association For The Advancement Of Science.

Bonnell, F. C. & Bonnell, F. W. Conrad Aiken: A Bibliography. LC 82-9241. 291p. 1983. 45.00 (ISBN 0-87328-118-7). Huntington Lib.

Bonnell, F. W., jt. auth. see Bonnell, F. C.

Bonnell, Henry H. Charlotte Bronte, George Eliot & Jane Austin: Studies in Their Works. LC 74-5002. 1902. lib. bdg. 35.00 (ISBN 0-8414-9930-6). Folcroft.

--Charlotte Bronte, George Eliot, Jane Austen. 1978. Repr. of 1902 ed. lib. bdg. 40.00 (ISBN 0-8495-0430-9). Arden Lib.

Bonnell, Pamela G. Fund Raising for the Small Library. 1982. 1.00 (ISBN 0-8389-5604-1). Library Admin.

Bonnell, Peter & Sedwick, Frank. Conversation in German: Points of Departure. 4th ed. 128p. 1985. pap. text ed. 12.95 (ISBN 0-8384-1275-0). Heinle & Heinle.

Bonnell, Victoria E. Roots of Rebellion: Workers' Politics & Organizations in St. Petersburg & Moscow, 1900-1914. LC 83-1084. 528p. 1983. text ed. 38.50x (ISBN 0-520-04740-0, CAMPUS 316); pap. 10.95x (ISBN 0-520-05114-9). U of Cal Pr.

Bonnell, Victoria E., ed. The Russian Worker: Life & Labor under the Tsarist Regime. LC 83-47856. 240p. 1983. text ed. 32.50x (ISBN 0-520-04837-7, CAL 673); pap. 9.95 (ISBN 0-520-05059-2). U of Cal Pr.

Bonnellan, Thomas K. How to Grow People into Self-Starters. 238p. 40.00 (ISBN 0-318-15131-6); members 32.00 (ISBN 0-318-15132-4); commodity line association members 36.00 (ISBN 0-318-15133-2). Natl Assn Wholesale Dists.

Bonnelle, C. & Mande, C., eds. Advances in X-Ray Spectroscopy: A Reference Text in Honour of Professor Y. Cauchois. LC 82-12300. (Illus.). 400p. 1982. 88.00 (ISBN 0-08-025266-4). Pergamon.

Bonnelle, J. P. & Delmon, B., eds. Surface Properties & Catalysis by Non-Metals. 1983. lib. bdg. 69.50 (ISBN 90-2771-607-2, Pub. by Reidel Holland). Kluwer Academic.

Bonnemann, K. H., et al, eds. Ionic Liquids, Molten Salts, & Polyelectrolytes: Berlin (West), 1982 Proceedings. (Lecture Notes in Physics: Vol. 172). 253p. 1982. pap. 17.00 (ISBN 0-387-11952-3). Springer-Verlag.

Bonnenberg, F., et al see Hellwege, K. H.

Bonner. Kate Chopin Dictionary. 1985. lib. bdg. 20.00 (ISBN 0-8240-9076-4). Garland Pub.

--Two-Way Pitcher. PLB 6.19 (ISBN 0-8313-0008-6). Lantern.

Bonner & Hall. Care of the Surgical Patient with Acute Respiratory Failure. 1984. 27.50 (ISBN 0-8016-0862-7). Mosby.

Bonner, Amy, et al, eds. Poetry Society of America Anthology. facsimile ed. LC 76-75709. (Granger Index Reprint Ser). 1946. 20.00 (ISBN 0-8369-6003-3). Ayer Co Pubs.

Bonner, Ann & Bonner, Roger. Earlybirds...Earlywords. LC 72-89449. (Illus.). 32p. (ps-2). 1973. 6.95 (ISBN 0-87592-013-6). Scroll Pr.

Bonner, Anthony, ed. Selected Works of Ramon Llull, 1232-1316, 2 vols. (Illus.). 1330p. 1985. text ed. 150.00x (ISBN 0-691-07288-4). Princeton U Pr.

Bonner, C. E. Index Hepaticarum: An Index to the Liverworts of the World. Incl. Pt. 2. Achiton to Balantiopsis. 26.25 (ISBN 3-7682-0092-2); Pt. 3. Barbilophozia to Ceranthus. 26.25 (ISBN 3-7682-0093-0); Pt. 4. Ceratolejeunea to Crystolejeunea. 26.25 (ISBN 3-7682-0094-9); Pt. 5. Delavayella to Geothallus. 35.00 (ISBN 3-7682-0095-7); Pt. 6. Goebelliella to Jubula. 26.25 (ISBN 3-7682-0096-5). 1963-66. Lubrecht & Cramer.

--Index Hepaticarum, Index to the Liverworts of the World Part 7A: Supplement, Additions & Corrections to Parts 2-4. 1977. pap. text ed. 21.00 (ISBN 3-7682-0097-3). Lubrecht & Cramer.

--Index Hepaticarum. Index to the Liverworts of the World Part 8: Jungermannia. 1976. pap. text ed. 42.00. Lubrecht & Cramer.

--Index Hepaticarum. Part 9: Jungermanniopsis-Lejeunea. 1978. pap. 35.00x. Lubrecht & Cramer.

Bonner, C. E. B. Index Hepaticarum: Lembidium to Mytilopsis, Vol. 10. Geissler, P. & Bischler, H., eds. 352p. 1985. lib. bdg. 52.50 (ISBN 3-7682-1100-2). Lubrecht & Cramer.

Bonner, Charles D. The Team Approach to Hemiplegia. (Illus.). 304p. 1969. photocopy ed. 24.50x (ISBN 0-398-00187-1). C C Thomas.

Bonner, Charles W. A Rocky Road: The Pilgrimage of the Grape. 2nd ed. 172p. 1984. 11.95 (ISBN 0-914330-61-6). Panorama West.

Bonner, Cleon R. A Black Principal's Struggle to Survive. 1982. 8.95 (ISBN 0-686-76760-8). Vantage.

Bonner, Clint. Hymn Is Born. LC 59-9694. 1959. 10.95 (ISBN 0-8054-6801-3). Broadman.

Bonner, David, jt. auth. see Curry, Jess, Jr.

Bonner, David M., jt. ed. see Curry, Jess W., Jr.

Bonner, Deborah, tr. see Manila, Gabriel J.

Bonner, Deborah, tr. see Valenzuela, Luisa.

Bonner, Dismas, jt. auth. see Coyle, Alcuin.

Bonner, Dismas, jt. ed. see Mathis, Marcian.

Bonner, Fred. Atlanta Area Jobhunter's Companion. 80p. (Orig.). 1984. pap. 2.95 (ISBN 0-9613020-0-3). Jobhunter's Comp.

Bonner, G. A. British Transport Law by Road & Rail. 1974. 11.50 (ISBN 0-7153-6000-0). David & Charles.

Bonner, Geraldian. St. Augustine of Hippo: Life & Controversies. LC 82-45807. 1985. Repr. of 1963 ed. 42.50 (ISBN 0-404-62376-X). AMS Pr.

Bonner, J. T., ed. Evolution & Development. (Dahlem Workshop Reports Ser.: Vol. 22). (Illus.). 357p. 1982. 29.00 (ISBN 0-387-11331-2). Springer-Verlag.

Bonner, James. The World's People & the World's Food Supply. Head, J. J., ed. (Carolina Biology Readers Ser.). (Illus.). 16p. (YA) (gr. 10 up). 1980. pap. 1.60 (ISBN 0-89278-322-2, 45-9722). Carolina Biological.

Bonner, James, jt. auth. see McMahon, Thomas.

Bonner, James & Varner, Joseph, eds. Plant Biochemistry. 3rd ed. 1976. text ed. 42.50 (ISBN 0-12-114860-2). Acad Pr.

Bonner, James C. Georgia's Last Frontier: The Development of Carroll County. LC 77-156040. 246p. 1971. 17.00 (ISBN 0-8203-0303-8). U of Ga Pr.

--Milledgeville: Georgia's Antebellum Capital. (Illus.). 307p. 1985. Repr. of 1978 ed. 19.95 (ISBN 0-86554-167-1, MUP-H157). Mercer Univ Pr.

Bonner, Jeffrey P. Land Consolidation & Economic Development in India: A Study of Two Haryana Villages. LC 85-61149. (Illus.). 170p. 1985. 15.20 (ISBN 0-913215-07-4); text ed. 14.25 (ISBN 0-317-19575-1). Riverdale Co.

Bonner, John T. Cells & Societies. 1955. 25.00x (ISBN 0-691-07919-6). Princeton U Pr.

--On Development: The Biology of Form. LC 73-88053. (Commonwealth Fund Publications Ser). 337p. 1977. text ed. 17.50x (ISBN 0-674-63410-1); pap. 7.95x (ISBN 0-674-63412-8). Harvard U Pr.

--Size & Cycle: An Essay on the Structure of Biology. (Illus.). 1965. 25.00x (ISBN 0-691-08033-X). Princeton U Pr.

Bonner, John T., ed. see Thompson, D'Arcy W.

Bonner, John T., Jr. The Evolution of Culture in Animals. LC 79-3190. (Illus.). 225p. 1980. 23.00 (ISBN 0-691-08250-2); pap. 9.95x (ISBN 0-691-02373-5). Princeton U Pr.

Bonner, Jordan, ed. see Campbell, Carolyn.

Bonner, Jordon, ed. see Campbell, Carolyn & Thompson, Pat.

Bonner, Kathleen, ed. see California-International Arts Foundation Staff.

Bonner, Mary G. Spray Hitter. (Illus.). (gr. 4-7). 1956. PLB 6.19 (ISBN 0-8313-0011-6). Lantern.

Bonner, Miller, jt. auth. see Nelson, Mark.

Bonner, Nigel. Whales. (Illus.). 248p. 1980. 24.95 (ISBN 0-7137-0887-5, Pub. by Blandford Pr England). Sterling.

Bonner, Phillip. Kings, Commoners & Concessionaires: The Evolution & Dissolution of the Nineteenth-Century Swazi State. LC 82-4234. (African Studies: No. 31). (Illus.). 352p. 1983. 49.50 (ISBN 0-521-24270-3). Cambridge U Pr.

Bonner, R., et al. The Visually Limited Child. 1970. pap. text ed. 9.95x (ISBN 0-8422-0061-4). Irvington.

Bonner, Raymond. Weakness & Deceit: U. S. Policy & El Salvador. LC 83-45921. (Illus.). 408p. 1984. 16.95 (ISBN 0-8129-1108-3). Times Bks.

Bonner, Raymond E. & Pryor, T. Allan, eds. Computerized Interpretation of the Electrocardiogram VI. LC 82-82657. 224p. 1982. pap. write for info. (ISBN 0-939204-16-9, 81-12). Eng Found.

Bonner, Robert J. Lawyers & Litigants in Ancient Athens: The Genesis of the Legal Profession. LC 68-57185. Repr. of 1927 ed. 22.00 (ISBN 0-405-08289-4, Blom Pubns). Ayer Co Pubs.

Bonner, Robert J. & Harrell, Hansen C. Evidence in Athenian Courts & Public Arbitration in Athenian Law, 2 vols. in one. Vlastos, Gregory, ed. LC 78-14610. (Morals & Law in Ancient Greece Ser.). (Eng. & Gr.). 1979. Repr. of 1936 ed. lib. bdg. 14.00x (ISBN 0-405-11586-5). Ayer Co Pubs.

Bonner, Robert J. & Smith, Gertrude E. Administration of Justice from Homer to Aristotle, 2 Vols. LC 69-13832. (Illus.). 1969. Repr. of 1938 ed. Set. lib. bdg. 32.50x (ISBN 0-8371-0320-7, BOAJ). Greenwood.

Bonner, Robert J. & Smith, Gertrude S. The Administration of Justice from Homer to Aristotle, 2 vols. LC 70-101917. (BCL Ser.: I). Repr. of 1938 ed. Set. 60.00 (ISBN 0-404-00650-7). AMS Pr.

Bonner, Roger, jt. auth. see Bonner, Ann.

Bonner, S. F. Roman Declamation in the Late Republic & Early Empire. 184p. 1969. 35.00x (ISBN 0-85323-250-4, Pub. by Liverpool Univ England). State Mutual Bk.

Bonner, Sabine M. Chateaux of the Loire. (Illus.). 144p. 1984. english ed. 29.95 (ISBN 2-03-523106-X); french ed. 29.95 (ISBN 2-03-523105-1). Larousse.

Bonner, Sherwood. Dialect Tales. facsimile ed. LC 70-38640. (Black Heritage Library Collection). Repr. of 1883 ed. 17.75 (ISBN 0-8369-8998-8). Ayer Co Pubs.

--Suwanee River Tales. facsimile ed. LC 73-38641. (Black Heritage Library Collection). Repr. of 1884 ed. 20.25 (ISBN 0-8369-8999-6). Ayer Co Pubs.

Bonner, Stanley F. Education in Ancient Rome: From the Older Cato to the Younger Pliny. LC 76-52023. (Illus.). 1977. pap. 11.95x (ISBN 0-520-03501-1). U of Cal Pr.

Bonner, T., et al. Hazardous Waste Incineration Engineering. LC 81-14223. (Pollution Technology Review Ser.: No. 88). (Illus.). 432p. 1982. 45.00 (ISBN 0-8155-0877-8). Noyes.

Bonner, T. D. Life & Adventures of James P. Beckwourth. 1965. Repr. 12.50 (ISBN 0-87018-003-7). Ross.

--The Life & Adventures of James P. Beckwourth. Rev. ed. (Illus.). 400p. 1977. Repr. of 1892 ed. 18.50 (ISBN 0-87928-085-9). Corner Hse.

--The Life & Adventures of James P. Beckwourth, 2 vols. 537p. Date not set. Repr. lib. bdg. 69.00 (ISBN 0-932051-88-X). Am Repr Serv.

Bonner, T. D., ed. Life & Adventures of James P. Beckwourth, Mountaineer, Scout & Pioneer & Chief of the Crow Nation of Indians. LC 69-18563. (American Negro: His History & Literature Ser., No. 2). 1969. Repr. of 1856 ed. 21.00 (ISBN 0-405-01850-9). Ayer Co Pubs.

Bonner, Terry N. The Defiant. (New South Wales Ser.: No. 9). 320p. (Orig.). 1983. pap. 3.50 (ISBN 0-440-01863-3, Emerald). Dell.

--The Free Woman. (The Australians Ser.: No. 3). 352p. (Orig.). 1983. pap. 3.50 (ISBN 0-440-01072-1, Emerald). Dell.

--The Pioneers. (New South Wales Ser.: No. 4). (Orig.). 1983. pap. 3.50 (ISBN 0-440-07166-6). Dell.

--Rum Colony. 352p. 1982. pap. 3.50 (ISBN 0-440-07469-X, Emerald). Dell.

--The Seekers. (New South Wales Ser.). 320p. 1983. pap. 3.50 (ISBN 0-440-07663-3, Emerald). Dell.

--The Unvanquished. 320p. 1983. pap. 3.50 (ISBN 0-440-09257-4, Emerald). Dell.

Bonner, Thomas D., jt. auth. see Beckwourth, James P.

Bonner, Thomas, Jr. & Falcon, Guillermo N. William Faulkner, the William B. Wisdom Collection: A Descriptive Catalog. LC 79-26556. (Illus.). 1980. pap. 13.00 (ISBN 0-9603212-2-5). Tulane Univ.

Bonner, Tricia K., et al. The New York Corporate Handbook: Nineteen Eighty-Three to Nineteen Eighty-Four Cumulative Supplement. Merritt, Raymond W. & Ennico, Clifford R., eds. 100p. (Orig.). 1985. pap. 20.00 (ISBN 0-942954-07-6). NYS Bar.

Bonner, W. N. & Berry, R. J., eds. Ecology in the Antarctic. (Linnean Society of London). 1981. 30.00 (ISBN 0-12-114950-1). Acad Pr.

Bonner, W. Nigel. Seals & Man: A Study of Interactions. LC 81-69684. (Illus.). 184p. (Orig.). 1982. pap. 9.95x (ISBN 0-295-95890-1, Pub. by Wash Sea Grant). U of Wash Pr.

Bonner, William H. Communicating Clearly: The Effective Message. 384p. 1980. pap. text ed. 14.95 (ISBN 0-574-20605-1, 13-3605); instr's. guide avail. (ISBN 0-574-20606-X, 13-3606). SRA.

--De Quincey at Work. LC 73-9715. 1936. lib. bdg. 15.00 (ISBN 0-8414-3162-0). Folcroft.

Bonner, William H. & Voyles, Jean. Communicating in Business: Key to Success, Vol. 1. 3rd. ed. LC 82-721522. (Illus.). 551p. 1983. text ed. 25.95x (ISBN 0-931920-42-6); study guide 7.95 (ISBN 0-686-63215-X); letter writing wkbk. o.p. 4.50 (ISBN 0-686-63216-8); report writing wkbk. o.p. 3.95 (ISBN 0-686-63217-6). Dame Pubns.

Bonnerjea, Biren. Dictionary of Superstitions & Mythology. LC 69-17755. 1969. Repr. of 1927 ed. 43.00x (ISBN 0-8103-3572-7). Gale.

Bonnerjea, Lucy, jt. auth. see Ashworth, Georgina.

Bonnerot, Luce. L' Oeuvre de Walter de la Mare: Une Aventure Spirituelle. 530p. (Fr.). 1983. Repr. of 1969 ed. lib. bdg. 100.00 (ISBN 0-686-47423-6). Century Bookbindery.

Bonners, Susan. Panda. LC 78-50404. (gr. k-3). 1978. 12.95; PLB 12.95 (ISBN 0-385-28775-5). Delacorte.

--Panda. LC 78-50404. (Illus.). 32p. (ps-3). 1978. 12.95 (ISBN 0-385-28772-0); PLB 12.95 (ISBN 0-385-28775-5). Delacorte.

--A Penguin Year. LC 79-53595. (Illus.). 48p. (ps-3). 1981. 11.95; PLB 12.95 (ISBN 0-385-28022-X). Delacorte.

Bonnesen, T. & Fenchel, W. Theorie der Konvexen Koerper. LC 49-29452. (Ger). 6.95 (ISBN 0-8284-0054-7). Chelsea Pub.

Bonnet, ed. see Breton, Andre.

Bonnet, Alain. Artificial Intelligence. (Illus.). 272p. 1986. pap. text ed. 19.95 (ISBN 0-13-048869-0). P-H.

Bonnet, Alfred, tr. see Pareto, Vilfredo.

Bonnet, Alfred, tr. see Salvioli, G.

Bonnet, F. P. Adipose Tissue in Childhood. 192p. 1981. 69.00 (ISBN 0-8493-5771-3). CRC Pr.

Bonnet, Gerard, jt. auth. see Bonnet, Monique.

Bonnet, Hans. Reallexikon der aegyptischen Religionsgeschichte. 2nd ed. (Illus., Ger.). 1981. 71.20x (ISBN 3-11-003365-8). De Gruyter.

Bonnet, Jules, ed. see Calvin, Jean.

Bonnet, Jules, ed. see Calvin, John.

Bonnet, L. & Schroeder, A. Epistolas De Pablo Tomo III. Cativiela, A., tr. from Fr. (Comentario del Nuevo Testamento). 538p. 1983. pap. 12.95 (ISBN 0-311-03052-1). Casa Bautista.

Bonnet, L., jt. auth. see Schroeder, A.

Bonnet, L., jt. auth. see Schrolder, A.

Bonnet, Marcel, ed. see Rutz-Rees, Carolina.

Bonnet, Marguerite & Chenieux-Gendron, Jacqueline. Revues Surrealistes Francaises Autour d'Andre Breton, 1948-1972. LC 82-14045. 294p. (Orig.). 1982. lib. bdg. 40.00 (ISBN 0-527-09750-0). Kraus Intl.

Bonnet, Mireille. Microsurgery of Retinal Detachment. (Illus.). 1980. text ed. 33.00x (ISBN 0-89352-067-5). Masson Pub.

Bonnet, Monique & Bonnet, Gerard. Feeding Your Baby: A Parent's Guide to Practical Nutrition. (Illus.). 128p. 1983. 12.95 (ISBN 0-13-314054-7); pap. 6.95 (ISBN 0-13-314047-4). P-H.

Bonnet, Pierre. Bibliographia Araneorum: Analyse Methodique De Toute la Litterature Araneologique Jusqu'en 1939. LC 57-57845. 832p. 1968. Repr. 40.00 (ISBN 0-686-09299-6). Entomol Soc.

Bonnet, Pierre see Janequin, Clement, et al.

Bonnet, R. & Dupree, A., eds. Solar Phenomena in Stars & Stellar Systems. 1981. 69.50 (ISBN 90-277-1275-1, Pub. by Reidel Holland). Kluwer Academic.

Bonne-Tamir, Batsheva & Cohen, Tirza, eds. Human Genetics, Part A: The Unfolding Genome. LC 82-17230. (Progress in Clinical & Biological Research Ser.: Vol. 103A). 584p. 1982. 88.00 (ISBN 0-8451-0168-4). A R Liss.

--Human Genetics, Part B: Medical Aspects. LC 82-17230. (Progress in Clinical & Biological Research Ser.: Vol. 103B). 654p. 1982. 98.00 (ISBN 0-8451-0169-2). A R Liss.

Bonnett, Aubrey W. Group Identification Among Negroes: An Examination of the Soul Concept in the Unites States of America. LC 79-93304. 130p. 1980. 10.95 (ISBN 0-86548-001-X). R & E Pubs.

--Institutional Adaptation of West Indian Immigrants to America: An Analysis of Rotating Credit Associations. LC 80-69054. 160p. 1981. lib. bdg. 21.50 (ISBN 0-8191-1500-2); pap. text ed. 9.50 (ISBN 0-8191-1501-0). U Pr of Amer.

Bonnett, Harold. Traction Engines. (Shire Album Ser.: No. 143). (Orig.). 1985. pap. 3.50 (ISBN 0-85263-738-1, Pub. by Shire Pubns England). Seven Hills Bks.

Bonnett, Kendra, jt. auth. see Digit Magazine Editors.

Bonnett, Penelope, jt. auth. see Gill, Don.

Bonnett, S., ed. see Ingram, H. E.

Bonnett, Theodore. The Mudlark. 19.95 (ISBN 0-88411-063-X, Pub by Aeonian Pr). Amereon Ltd.

Bonnett, Wayne, ed. see DeNevi, Don & Moulin, Thomas.

Bonnett, Wayne, ed. see Tracy, Jack.

Bonnette, Jeanne. Three Friends. (Read-to-Me Coloring Bks.). (ps-2). 1982. pap. 1.95 (ISBN 0-89992-066-7). Coun India Ed.

Bonnette, Jeanne D. Leaf Change. 1979. 8.00 (ISBN 0-8233-0305-5). Golden Quill.

Bonnett-Sanderson. Earth Materials: A Laboratory Manual for Physical Geology. 128p. 1983. pap. text ed. 8.95 (ISBN 0-8403-3236-X). Kendall-Hunt.

Bonneville, Douglas. Diderot's "Vie De Seneque". A Swan Song Revised. LC 66-63483. (University of Florida Humanities Monographs: No. 19). 1966. 3.50 (ISBN 0-8130-0024-6). U Presses Fla.

Bonneville, Georges, jt. auth. see Beaumarchais, Pierre.

Bonneville, J. F., et al. Radiology of the Sella Turcica. (Illus.). 262p. 1981. 180.00 (ISBN 0-387-10319-8). Springer-Verlag.

Bonneville, Mary A., jt. auth. see Porter, Keith R.

Bonney, Charles C. World's Congress Addresses. 88p. pap. 6.95 (ISBN 0-912050-48-9). Open Court.

Bonney, E. A. Aerodynamics, Propulsion, Structures, & Design Practice. LC 56-9727. 595p. 1956. 29.50 (ISBN 0-442-00896-1, Pub. by Van Nos Reinhold). Krieger.

Bonney, Lorraine, jt. auth. see Bonney, Orin H.

Bonney, Lorraine, jt. auth. see Bonney, Orrin H.

Bonney, Lorraine G., jt. auth. see Bonney, Orrin H.

Bonney, Lorraine G., jt. ed. see Bonney, Orrin H.

Bonney, M. & Yong, Y. F., eds. Robot Safety. 300p. 1985. 40.00x (ISBN 0-903608-69-3, Pub. by IFS Pubns UK). Air Sci Co.

--Robot Safety. (International Trends in Manufacturing Technology Ser.). 300p. 1985. 39.50 (ISBN 0-387-15484-1). Springer-Verlag.

Bonney, Meta. Goatkeeping. (Illus.). 4.95 (ISBN 0-317-11566-9). Diamond Farm Bk.

Bonney, Orin H. & Bonney, Lorraine. Guide to the Wyoming Mountains & Wilderness Areas. 3rd ed. LC 74-132584. 701p. 1977. 24.95 (ISBN 0-8040-0537-0, 82-72734, Pub. by Swallow). Ohio U Pr.

Bonney, Orrin H. & Bonney, Lorraine. Battle Drums & Geysers: The Life & Journals of Lt. Gustavus Cheyney Doane. LC 70-91169. (Illus.). 1970. Three Volumes. pap. write for info. Bonney.

--Field Book. Incl. The Teton Range & the Gros Ventre Range: Climbing Routes & Back Country. rev., 2nd ed. LC 76-189201. 263p. pap. 7.95 (ISBN 0-8040-0578-8, 82-73096); Yellowstone Park: Absaroka Range. rev. 2nd ed. LC 70-189202. 162p. pap. 7.95 (ISBN 0-8040-0579-6, 82-73104); Big Horn Range. LC 72-132589. 172p. pap. 7.95 (ISBN 0-8040-0536-2, 82-72726). (Illus.). 1977. (SB). Ohio U Pr.

Bonney, Orrin H. & Bonney, Lorraine G. Bonney's Guide to Grand Teton National Park & Jackson's Hole. rev. ed. (Illus.). 1983. pap. 4.45 (ISBN 0-931620-00-7). Bonney.

--Field Book Wind River Range. rev. ed. (Illus.). 1968. pap. 5.95 with 1975 supp. (ISBN 0-931620-01-5). Bonney.

Bonney, Orrin H. & Bonney, Lorraine G., eds. Battle Drums & Geysers, 3 vols. Incl. Vol. I. Lt. Gustavus C. Doane: His Life & Remarkable Military Career. pap. 2.95 (ISBN 0-931620-03-1); Vol. II. Exploration of Yellowstone Park, Lt. Doane's Yellowstone Journal. pap. 3.95 (ISBN 0-931620-04-X); Vol. III. Lt. G. C. Doane's Snake River Journal of 1876. pap. 2.95 (ISBN 0-931620-05-8). (Illus.). 1978. Vols. I, II & III. pap. 8.95 (ISBN 0-931620-02-3). Bonney.

Bonney, Richard. The King's Debts: Finance & Politics in France 1589-1661. 1981. 57.00x (ISBN 0-19-822563-6). Oxford U Pr.

--Political Change in France under Richelieu & Mazarin, 1624-1661. (Illus.). 1977. text ed. 59.00x (ISBN 0-19-822537-7). Oxford U Pr.

Bonney, T. G., et al. Abbeys & Churches of England & Wales. LC 77-23529. 1977. Repr. of 1890 ed. lib. bdg. 40.00 (ISBN 0-89341-203-1). Longwood Pub Group.

Bonney, William W. Thorns & Arabesques: Contexts for Conrad's Fiction. LC 80-13308. 272p. 1980. text ed. 24.50x (ISBN 0-8018-2345-5). Johns Hopkins.

Bonnice, J. G. & Rosenberg, R. Business Law Thirty. 3rd. ed. 1982. 10.88 (ISBN 0-07-006472-5). McGraw.

Bonnice, Joseph & Bannister, Rosella. Developing Consumer Attitudes. 1985. text ed. 12.50 (ISBN 0-538-32400-7, HE40). SW Pub.

Bonnice, Joseph G., jt. auth. see Rosenberg, R. Robert.

Bonnici, Peter. The Festival. LC 84-15597. (Arjuna Bks.). (Illus.). (ps-3). 1985. PLB 8.95 (ISBN 0-87614-229-3). Carolrhoda Bks.

--The First Rains. LC 84-14979. (Arjuna Bks.). (Illus.). 24p. (ps-3). 1985. PLB 8.95 (ISBN 0-87614-228-5). Carolrhoda Bks.

Bonnici, Roberta L. I'm Scared to Witness! (Discovery Bks.). (Illus.). 48p. (Orig.). (YA) (gr. 9-12). 1979. pap. 1.50 (ISBN 0-88243-931-6, 02-0931); tchr's ed 3.95 (ISBN 0-88243-330-X, 02-0330). Gospel Pub.

--Your Right to Be Different. (Discovery Bks.). 48p. (YA) (gr. 9-12). 1982. pap. text ed. 1.50 (ISBN 0-88243-842-5, 02-0842); tchr's ed 3.95 (ISBN 0-88243-333-4, 02-0333). Gospel Pub.

Bonnici, Virginia. Conversations. 80p. 1985. 10.00 (ISBN 0-682-40245-1). Exposition Pr FL.

Bonnicksen, Andrea L. Civil Rights & Liberties: Principles of Interpretation. LC 81-81279. 311p. 1981. pap. 11.95 (ISBN 0-87484-476-2). Mayfield Pub.

Bonnie, Richard J. Marijuana Use & Criminal Sanctions: Essays in the Theory & Practice of Decriminalization. 264p. 1980. 25.00 (ISBN 0-87215-244-8). Michie Co.

Bonnie, Richard J. & Whitebread, Charles H. The Marihuana Conviction: A History of Marihuana Prohibition in the United States. LC 73-89907. pap. 96.00 (ISBN 0-317-29046-0, 2020322). Bks Demand UMI.

Bonniere, G. De Beaumont de la see De Beaumont de la Bonniere, G. & De Tocqueville, Alexis.

Bonnifield, Mathew P. Oklahoma Innovator: The Life of Virgil Browne. LC 75-41452. (Oklahoma Trackmaker Ser: Vol. 2). (Illus.). 190p. 1976. 14.95 (ISBN 0-8061-1326-X). U of Okla Pr.

Bonnifield, Paul. The Dust Bowl: Men, Dirt, & Depression. LC 78-55706. (Illus.). 1979. 14.95 (ISBN 0-8263-0485-0). U of NM Pr.

Bonnin, Gertrude. American Indian Stories. (Illus.). 216p. 1985. pap. 5.95 (ISBN 0-8032-9902-8). U of Nebr Pr.

--Old Indian Legends. LC 85-8639. (Illus.). 212p. (Orig.). 1985. 16.95x (ISBN 0-8032-4905-5); pap. 5.95 (ISBN 0-8032-9903-6). U of Nebr Pr.

Bonnin, Reggie. Music of Maine. Jack, Susan, ed. (Illus.). 200p. cancelled (ISBN 0-930096-48-7, Tales of the Sea). G Gannett.

Bonnington, S. T. & King, A. L., eds. Jet Pumps & Ejectors: A State of the Art Review & Bibliography. 2nd ed. (BHRA Fluid Engineering Ser.: Vol. 1). 1977. pap. 40.50x (ISBN 0-900983-63-9, Dist. by Air Science Co.). BHRA Fluid.

Bonnivier, Carlene S. Reading Attack Skills for Adults. (Illus.). 208p. 1984. pap. text ed. 9.95 (ISBN 0-13-753955-X). P-H.

Bonniwell, William R. The Life of Blessed Margaret of Castello. LC 83-70524. 113p. (gr. 8). 1983. pap. 4.00 (ISBN 0-89555-213-2). TAN Bks Pubs.

Bonnley, Brian H. Cell Biology Level II. (Illus.). 256p. 1982. pap. text ed. 18.50x (ISBN 0-7121-0389-9). Trans-Atlantic.

Bonno, Gabriel D. La Constitution britannique devant l'opinion francaise de Montesquieu a Bonaparte. LC 71-157163. (Research & Source Work Ser.). 324p. (Fr.). 1972. Repr. of 1932 ed. 21.50 (ISBN 0-8337-3995-6). B Franklin.

Bonno, John A. & Fields, Kent T. Introduction to COBOL. 1982. pap. 18.95 (ISBN 0-256-02287-9). Business Pubns.

Bonnor, W. B., et al, eds. Classical General Relativity. 275p. 1984. 44.50 (ISBN 0-521-26747-1). Cambridge U Pr.

Bonnot, Bernard R. Pope John Twenty-Third: A Clever, Pastoral Leader. LC 79-1770. 1980. 9.95 (ISBN 0-8189-0388-0). Alba.

Bonnot De Condillac, Etienne see Condillac, Etienne Bonnot de.

Bonnot de Condillac, Etienne, tr. see Albury, W. R.

Bonny, jt. ed. see Bastenie, P. A.

Bonnycastle, Richard H. Canada in Eighteen Forty-One, 2 Vols. Repr. of 1841 ed. Set. 50.00 (ISBN 0-384-05080-8). Johnson Repr.

Bono, Barbara J. Literary Transvaluation: From Vergilian Epic to Shakespearean Tragicomedy. LC 83-1069. 375p. 1984. lib. bdg. 32.00x (ISBN 0-520-04743-5). U of Cal Pr.

Bono, E. De see De Bono, E.

Bono, Edward De see De Bono, Edward.

Bono, Edward de see De Bono, Edward.

Bono, F. English Cathedrals. 1976. lib. bdg. 234.95 (ISBN 0-8490-1771-8). Gordon Pr.

Bono, Saverio G., jt. auth. see Kovacik, Robert.

Bonola, Roberto. Non-Euclidean Geometry. Carslaw, H. S., ed. 1954. pap. 7.00 (ISBN 0-486-60027-0). Dover.

Bonoma, Thomas V. Managing Marketing: Text Cases & Reading. 512p. 1984. text ed. 27.50 (ISBN 0-02-903720-4). Free Pr.

--The Marketing Edge: Making Strategies Work. 240p. 1985. 20.95 (ISBN 0-02-904200-3). Free Pr.

Bonoma, Thomas V. & Shapiro, Benson. Segmenting the Industrial Market. LC 82-49325. 144p. 1983. 22.00 (ISBN 0-669-06578-1); pap. 11.00 (ISBN 0-669-09469-2). Lexington Bks.

Bonomi, G. & Erseus, C., eds. Aquatic Oligochaeta. (Developments in Hydrobiology Ser.). 1984. lib. bdg. 68.50 (ISBN 90-6193-775-2, Pub. by Junk Pubs Netherlands). Kluwer Academic.

Bonomi, Ivanoe. From Socialism to Fascism: A Study of Contemporary Italy. LC 78-63652. (Studies in Fascism: Ideology & Practice). 168p. Repr. of 1924 ed. 22.50 (ISBN 0-404-16907-4). AMS Pr.

Bonomi, Patricia, et al, eds. The American Constitutional System under Strong & Weak Parties. LC 80-39659. 158p. 1981. 28.95x (ISBN 0-03-059041-8). Praeger.

Bonomi, Patricia U. A Factious People: Politics & Society in Colonial New York. LC 74-156803. 342p. 1971. 30.00x (ISBN 0-231-03509-8); pap. 13.00x (ISBN 0-231-08329-7). Columbia U Pr.

Bonomi, Patricia U., ed. Party & Political Opposition in Revolutionary America. LC 80-13480. 176p. 1980. text ed. 17.50 (ISBN 0-912882-39-5). Sleepy Hollow.

Bonomini, V. & Chang, T. M., eds. Hemoperfusion. (Contributions to Nephrology: Vol. 29). (Illus.). vi, 150p. 1982. pap. 38.00 (ISBN 3-8055-3421-3). S. Karger.

Bonomini, V., ed. see International Congress, 6th, Florence, June 1975.

Bonomo, J. Improve Your Dancing. (Ballroom Dance Ser.). 1985. lib. bdg. 77.00 (ISBN 0-87700-858-2). Revisionist Pr.

Bonomo, Joe. Barbell Training Routines. 1981. pap. 8.95x (ISBN 0-317-07346-X, Regent House). B of A.

Bonomo, Michael, jt. auth. see Finacchiaro, Mary.

Bononcini, Antonio M. Griselda. Brown, Howard M., ed. LC 76-21051. (Italian Opera 1640-1770 Ser.). 1978. lib. bdg. 83.00 (ISBN 0-8240-2620-9). Garland Pub.

Bononcini, Giovanni. Il Trionfo Di Camilla, Regina De 'Volsci. Brown, Howard M., ed. LC 76-21029. (Italian Opera 1640-1770 Ser.: Vol. 17). 1978. lib. bdg. 77.00 (ISBN 0-8240-2616-0). Garland Pub.

Bonosky, Phillip. Washington's Secret War Against Afghanistan. LC 84-19139. 360p. (Orig.). 1985. pap. 6.95 (ISBN 0-7178-0617-0). Intl Pubs Co.

Bonotto, S., jt. ed. see Brachet, Jean.

Bonotto, Silvano, et al, eds. Biology & Radiobiology of Anucleate Systems, 2 vols. 1972. Vol. 1. 42.00 (ISBN 0-12-115001-1); Vol. 2. 46.00 (ISBN 0-12-115002-X). Acad Pr.

Bonpland, Aime, jt. auth. see Von Humboldt, Alexander.

Bonsal, Philip W. Cuba, Castro, & the United States. LC 72-151505. (Pitt Latin American Ser.). 1971. 24.95 (ISBN 0-8229-3225-3). U of Pittsburgh Pr.

Bonsal, Stephen. The American Mediterranean. 1977. lib. bdg. 69.95 (ISBN 0-8490-1415-8). Gordon Pr.

--Suitors & Suppliants: The Little Nations at Versailles. LC 68-26226. 1969. Repr. of 1946 ed. 23.50x (ISBN 0-8046-0033-3, Pub. by Kennikat). Assoc FAculty Pr.

--When the French Were Here. LC 68-26261. 1968. Repr. of 1945 ed. 22.00x (ISBN 0-8046-0034-1, Pub. by Kennikat). Assoc Faculty Pr.

Bonsall, Crosby. And I Mean It, Stanley. LC 73-14324. (Trophy I Can Read Bk.). (Illus.). 32p. (ps-1). 1984. pap. 2.40i (ISBN 0-06-444046-X, Trophy). HarpJ.

--The Case of the Cat's Meow. (I Can Read Bk.). (Illus.). 1978. pap. 2.84 (ISBN 0-06-444017-6, Trophy). HarpJ.

--The Case of the Double Cross. LC 80-7768. (A Trophy I Can Read Bk.). (Illus.). 64p. (gr. k-3). 1982. pap. 2.84i (ISBN 0-06-444029-X, Trophy). HarpJ.

--The Case of the Dumb Bells. LC 66-8267. (A Trophy I Can Read Bk.). (Illus.). 64p. (gr. k-3). 1982. pap. 2.84i (ISBN 0-06-444030-3, Trophy). HarpJ.

--The Case of the Hungry Stranger. LC 63-17947. (I Can Read Bk.). (Illus.). 64p. (gr. k-3). 1980. pap. 2.95 (ISBN 0-06-444026-5, Trophy). HarpJ.

--The Case of the Hungry Stranger. LC 63-17947. (Trophy I Can Read Book & Cassette Set). (Illus.). 64p. (ps-3). 1985. pap. 5.98 incl. cassette (ISBN 0-694-00001-9, Trophy). HarpJ.

--The Case of the Scaredy Cats. LC 75-159039. (A Trophy I Can Read Bk.). (Illus.). 64p. (ps-3). 1984. pap. 2.84i (ISBN 0-06-444047-8, Trophy). HarpJ.

--The Goodbye Summer. (gr. 4-6). 1980. pap. 1.95 (ISBN 0-671-44145-0). Archway.

--Goodbye Summer. LC 78-23245. 160p. (gr. 4-7). 1979. PLB 11.88 (ISBN 0-688-84202-X). Greenwillow.

--Mine's the Best. LC 72-9863. (A Trophy Early I Can Read Bk.). (Illus.). 32p. (gr. k-3). 1984. pap. 2.40i (ISBN 0-06-444054-0, Trophy). HarpJ.

--Twelve Bells for Santa. LC 76-58714. (A Trophy I Can Read Bk.). (Illus.). 64p. (gr. k-3). 1985. pap. 2.84i (ISBN 0-06-444086-9, Trophy). HarpJ.

--What Spot? LC 63-8005. (I Can Read Bk.). (Illus.). 64p. (gr. k-3). 1980. pap. 2.95 (ISBN 0-06-444027-3, Trophy). HarpJ.

--Who's Afraid of the Dark? LC 79-2700. (Trophy Early I Can Read Bk.). (Illus.). 32p. (ps-2). 1985. pap. 2.40i (ISBN 0-06-444071-0, Trophy). HarpJ.

Bonsall, Crosby & Reed, E. Let Papa Sleep. (Easy Readers Ser.). (gr. k-3). 1.50 (ISBN 0-8431-4311-8). Wonder.

Bonsall, Crosby N. And I Mean It, Stanley. LC 73-14324. (Early I Can Read Bk.). (Illus.). 32p. (gr. k-3). 1974. PLB 9.89 (ISBN 0-06-020568-7). HarpJ.

--Case of the Cat's Meow. LC 65-11451. (I Can Read Mystery Bk.). (Illus.). 64p. (gr. k-3). 1965. PLB 9.89 (ISBN 0-06-020561-X). HarpJ.

--The Case of the Double Cross. LC 80-7768. (I Can Read Mystery Bk.). (Illus.). 64p. (gr. k-3). 1980. 8.61i (ISBN 0-06-020602-0); PLB 9.89 (ISBN 0-06-020603-9). HarpJ.

--Case of the Dumb Bells. LC 66-8267. (I Can Read Mystery Bk.). (Illus.). 64p. (gr. k-3). 1966. PLB 9.89 (ISBN 0-06-020624-1). HarpJ.

--Case of the Hungry Stranger. LC 63-17947. (I Can Read Mystery Bk.). (Illus.). 64p. (gr. k-3). 1963. PLB 9.89 (ISBN 0-06-020571-7). HarpJ.

--Case of the Scaredy Cats. LC 75-159039. (I Can Read Mystery Bk.). (Illus.). 64p. (gr. k-3). 1971. PLB 9.89 (ISBN 0-06-020566-0). HarpJ.

--Caso el Forastero Hambriento. Belpre, Pura, tr. LC 69-14449. (Spanish I Can Read Bk.). Orig. Title: Case of the Hungry Stranger. (Illus., Span.). (gr. k-3). 1969. PLB 9.89 (ISBN 0-06-020574-1). HarpJ.

--The Day I Had to Play with My Sister. LC 72-76507. (Early I Can Read Bk.). (Illus.). 32p. (ps-2). 1972. PLB 8.89 (ISBN 0-06-020576-8). HarpJ.

--It's Mine. LC 64-11839. (Illus.). 32p. (gr. k-3). 1964. PLB 9.89 (ISBN 0-06-020586-5). HarpJ.

--Mine's the Best. LC 72-9863. (Early I Can Read Bk.). (Illus.). 32p. (ps-2). 1973. PLB 8.89 (ISBN 0-06-020578-4). HarpJ.

--Piggle. LC 73-5478. (I Can Read Bk.). (Illus.). 64p. (gr. k-3). 1973. 8.64i (ISBN 0-06-020579-2); PLB 9.89 (ISBN 0-06-020580-6). HarpJ.

--Tell Me Some More. LC 61-5773. (I Can Read Bk.). (Illus.). 64p. (gr. k-3). 1961. PLB 9.89 (ISBN 0-06-020601-2). HarpJ.

--Twelve Bells for Santa. LC 76-58714. (I Can Read Bk.). (Illus.). 64p. (ps-3). 1977. PLB 9.89 (ISBN 0-06-020582-2). HarpJ.

--What Spot? LC 63-8005. (I Can Read Bk.). (Illus.). 64p. (gr. k-3). 1963. PLB 9.89 (ISBN 0-06-020611-X). HarpJ.

--Who's a Pest? LC 62-13310. (I Can Read Bks.). (Illus.). 64p. (gr. k-3). 1962. PLB 9.89 (ISBN 0-06-020621-7). HarpJ.

--Who's Afraid of the Dark? LC 79-2700. (Early I Can Read Bks). (Illus.). 32p. (ps-3). 1980. 7.64i (ISBN 0-06-020598-9); PLB 8.89 (ISBN 0-06-020599-7). HarpJ.

Bonsall, F. F. & Duncan, J. Complete Normed Algebras. Hilton, P. J., ed. (Ergenbnisse der Mathematik und Ihrer Grenzgebiete: Vol. 80). 208p. 1973. 45.00 (ISBN 0-387-06386-2). Springer Verlag.

--Numerical Ranges of Operators on Normed Spaces & of Elements of Normed Algebras. LC 71-128498. (London Mathematical Society Lecture Note Ser.: No. 2). 1971. 17.95x (ISBN 0-521-07988-8). Cambridge U Pr.

Bonsall, George. Weather. (How & Why Wonder Books Ser.). (gr. 4-6). pap. 1.25 (ISBN 0-8431-4266-9). Wonder.

Bonsall, Thomas. Dodge Cars, Nineteen Forty-Six to Nineteen Eighty-Five. (ID Guide Ser.). (Illus.). 96p. 1985. pap. 8.95 (ISBN 0-934780-66-8). Bookman Dan.

--Eldorado. (Classic Source Bks.). (Illus.). 144p. 1984. pap. 12.95 (ISBN 0-934780-40-4). Bookman Dan.

--GTO, Vol. II. (Source Bks.). (Illus.). 144p. 1984. pap. 12.95 (ISBN 0-934780-50-1). Bookman Dan.

--Muscle Buicks. (Muscle Car Ser.). (Illus.). 96p. 1985. pap. 8.95 (ISBN 0-934780-65-X). Bookman Dan.

--Muscle Chevys. (Muscle Car Ser.). (Illus.). 96p. 1985. pap. 8.95 (ISBN 0-934780-56-0). Bookman Dan.

--Muscle Dodges. (Muscle Car Ser.). (Illus.). 96p. 1985. pap. 8.95 (ISBN 0-934780-60-9). Bookman Dan.

--Muscle Fords. (Muscle Car Ser.). (Illus.). 96p. 1985. pap. 8.95 (ISBN 0-934780-52-8). Bookman Dan.

--Muscle Mercurys. (Muscle Car Ser.). (Illus.). 96p. 1984. pap. 8.95 (ISBN 0-934780-48-X). Bookman Dan.

--Muscle Mopars. (Muscle Car Ser.). (Illus.). 96p. 1985. pap. 8.95 (ISBN 0-934780-63-3). Bookman Dan.

--Muscle Oldsmobiles. (Muscle Car Ser.). (Illus.). 96p. 1985. pap. 8.95 (ISBN 0-934780-59-5). Bookman Dan.

--Muscle Plymouths. (Muscle Car Ser.). (Illus.). 96p. 1984. pap. 8.95 (ISBN 0-934780-49-8). Bookman Dan.

--Muscle Pontiacs. (Muscle Car Ser.). (Illus.). 96p. 1984. pap. 8.95 (ISBN 0-934780-44-7). Bookman Dan.

Bonsall, Thomas E. Big Pontiacs: A Source Book. (Source Book Ser.). (Illus.). 144p. (Orig.). 1984. pap. 12.95 (ISBN 0-934780-26-9). Bookman Dan.

--Chrysler Three Hundred: A Source Book. (Illus.). 144p. (Orig.). 1981. pap. 12.95 (ISBN 0-934780-09-9). Bookman Dan.

--Couger: A Source Book. (Illus.). 144p. (Orig.). 1983. pap. 12.95 (ISBN 0-934780-22-6). Bookman Dan.

--Firebird: A Source Book. (Illus.). 144p. (Orig.). (YA) 1981. pap. 12.95 (ISBN 0-934780-07-2). Bookman Dan.

--The Lincoln Motorcar: Sixty Years of Excellence. (Illus.). 325p. 1981. 32.95 (ISBN 0-934780-05-6). Bookman Dan.

--Mark Lincoln: A Classic Source Book. (Classic Source Book Ser.). (Illus.). 144p. (Orig.). 1984. pap. 12.95 (ISBN 0-934780-27-7). Bookman Dan.

--Mercury & Edsel Identification Guide, 1939-1969. (Identification Guide Ser.). (Illus.). 96p. 1982. pap. 8.95 (ISBN 0-934780-15-3). Bookman Dan.

--Muscle Plymouths: The Story of a Supercar. (Muscle Bks.). 96p. 1985. pap. 8.95 (ISBN 0-934780-71-4). Bookman Dan.

--Pontiac Identification Guide, 1926-1966. (Identification Guide Ser.). (Illus.). 96p. (Orig.). 1982. pap. 8.95 (ISBN 0-934780-14-5). Bookman Dan.

--Pontiac: The Complete History, 1926-1986. Date not set. price not set. Bookman Dan.

--Trans-Am: A Source Book. (Illus.). 144p. (Orig.). 1983. pap. 12.95 (ISBN 0-934780-23-4). Bookman Dan.

Bonsall, Thomas E., ed. GTO: A Source Book. (Illus.). 142p. (Orig.). 1980. pap. 12.95 (ISBN 0-934780-03-X). Bookman Dan.

--New Series Muscle Pontiacs: The Years of Excitement. (Muscle Bks). (Illus.). 96p. 1985. pap. 8.95 (ISBN 0-934780-68-4). Bookman Dan.

Bonsanti, G. Caravaggio. LC 84-50554. (Illus.). 80p. (Orig.). 1984. pap. 12.50 (ISBN 0-935748-60-1). Scala Books.

Bonsdorff, Bertel Von see Von Bonsdorff, Bertel.

Bonse, U. & Rauch, H., eds. Neutron Interferometry. (Illus.). 1979. 59.00x (ISBN 0-19-851947-8). Oxford U Pr.

Bonsells, Waldemar. An Indian Journey. 273p. Date not set. Repr. of 1928 ed. lib. bdg. 30.00 (ISBN 0-918377-44-7). Russell Pr.

Bonsels, Waldemar. An Indian Journey. 1977. Repr. of 1928 ed. lib. bdg. 20.00 (ISBN 0-8492-0300-7). R West.

--An Indian Journey. 1928. 20.00 (ISBN 0-686-17223-X). Scholars Ref Lib.

Bonser, Frederick G. The Reasoning Ability of Children in the Fourth, Fifth, & Sixth School Grades. LC 70-176580. (Columbia University. Teachers College. Contributions to Education: No. 37). Repr. of 1910 ed. 22.50 (ISBN 0-404-55037-1). AMS Pr.

Bonser, W. & Stephens, T. A. Proverb Literature. 59.95 (ISBN 0-8490-0908-1). Gordon Pr.

Bonser, Wilfred & Stephens, T. A. Proverb Literature. LC 74-26578. 1930. 52.00 (ISBN 0-8414-3317-8). Folcroft.

Bonser, Wilfred, ed. see Stephens, Thomas A.

Bonser, Wilfrid. Anglo-Saxon & Celtic Bibliography 450-1078, 2 Vols. LC 73-16314. 1957. Set. lib. bdg. 250.00 (ISBN 0-8414-9850-4). Folcroft.

--A Bibliography of Folklore as Contained in the First Eighty Years of the Publications of the Folklore Society. (Folklore Society London Monographs: Vol. 121). 1961. 24.00 (ISBN 0-317-16725-1). Kraus Repr.

--A Prehistoric Bibliography. Troy, June, ed. 442p. 1976. 75.00x (ISBN 0-631-17090-1). Basil Blackwell.

--Romano-British Bibliography: 55B.C.-449A.D, Vol. 1 & 2. 1964. Set. 75.00 (ISBN 0-631-18980-7). Vol. 1 (ISBN 0-631-08370-7). Vol. 2 (ISBN 0-631-08380-4). Basil Blackwell.

Bonsett, Charles A. Studies of Pseudohypertrophic Muscular Dystrophy. (Illus.). 168p. 1969. photocopy ed. 18.75x (ISBN 0-398-00188-X). C C Thomas.

Bonsignore, G. & Cumming, G., eds. The Lung in Its Environment. LC 81-12004. (Ettore Majorana International Science Ser., Life Sciences: Vol. 6). 526p. 1981. 69.50x (ISBN 0-306-40742-6, Plenum Pr). Plenum Pub.

Bonsignore, G., jt. ed. see Cumming, G.

Bonsignore, Giovanni, jt. ed. see Cumming, Gordon.

Bonsignore, John J., et al. Before the Law: An Introduction to the Legal Process. 3rd ed. LC 83-81678. 450p. 1984. pap. text ed. 20.95 (ISBN 0-395-34317-8). HM.

Bonsor, N. C. Transportation Rates & Economic Development in Northern Ontario. 1977. pap. 6.00 (ISBN 0-8020-3343-1). U of Toronto Pr.

Bonstingl, John J. Introduction to the Social Sciences. (gr. 7-12). 1980. text ed. 20.80 (ISBN 0-205-05886-8, 8058865); tchrs'. guide 22.40 (ISBN 0-205-05887-6). Allyn.

Bonta, I. & Cats, A., eds. Connective Tissue Changes in Rheumatoid Arthritis & the Use of Penicillamine: Proceedings of a Review Symposium Held in Rotterdam. (Agents & Actions Supplements Ser.: No. 5). 183p. 1979. pap. text ed. 33.95x (ISBN 0-8176-1127-4). Birkhauser.

Bonta, I. L., ed. Recent Developments in the Pharmacology of Inflammatory Mediators. (Agents & Actions Suplements: No. 2). 178p. 1977. pap. 33.95x (ISBN 0-8176-0914-8). Birkhauser.

Bonta, I. L. & Bray, M. A., eds. The Pharmacology of Inflammation. (Handbook of Inflammation Ser.: No. 5). 1985. 89.00 (ISBN 0-444-90312-7, Excerpta Medica). Elsevier.

Bonta, I. L., et al, eds. Inflammation Mechanisms & Their Impact on Therapy. (Agents & Actions Supplements: No. 3). (Illus.). 192p. 1977. pap. text ed. 69.95x (ISBN 0-8176-0913-X). Birkhauser.

Bonta, Juan P. Architecture & Its Interpretation: A Study of Expressive Systems in Architecture. 272p. 1980. 45.00x (ISBN 0-85331-335-0, Pub. by Lund Humphries England). State Mutual Bk.

Bonta, Robert & Spencer, Horace A. Stockton's Historic Public Schools. LC 81-52977. (Illus.). xii, 115p. 1981. 15.00 (ISBN 0-9607134-0-9). Stockton Unified Schl Dist.

Bonta, Robert J. Del see Del Bonta, Robert J. & Berkson, Carmel.

Bonta, Stephen, jt. auth. see Lincoln, Harry.

Bonta, Stephen, jt. auth. see Lincoln, Harry B.

Bonta, Stephen, ed. The Instrumental Music of Giovanni Legrenzi. (Harvard Publications in Music Ser.: No. 14). 224p. 1985. pap. text ed. 30.00x (ISBN 0-674-45620-3). Harvard U Pr.

Bonte, Pierre, jt. auth. see Galaty, John.

Bontecou, Eleanor. The Federal Loyalty-Security Program. LC 73-17628. 377p. 1974. Repr. of 1953 ed. lib. bdg. 18.75x (ISBN 0-8371-7256-X, BOFL). Greenwood.

Bontecou, Eleanor, ed. see Edgerton, Henry.

Bontemps, Arna. The Old South: A Summer Tragedy & Other Stories of the Thirties. LC 73-2136. 200p. 1973. 6.95 (ISBN 0-396-06788-3). Dodd.

--One Hundred Years of Negro Freedom. LC 61-11716. (Illus.). (gr. 9 up). 1961. pap. 2.95 (ISBN 0-396-05520-6). Dodd.

--Personals. 2nd ed. (Heritage Ser). 1974. pap. 2.50x (ISBN 0-685-42539-8). Broadside.

Bontemps, Arna & Conroy, Jack. Fast Sooner Hound. (Illus.). 32p. (gr. 4-8). 1942. PLB 10.95 (ISBN 0-395-18657-9). HM.

Bontemps, Arna, ed. American Negro Poetry. rev. ed. (American Century Ser.). 232p. 1974. 6.25; pap. 6.25 (ISBN 0-8090-0108-X). Hill & Wang.

--Black Thunder. LC 68-31383. 1968. pap. 9.95x (ISBN 0-8070-6429-7, Pub. by Ariadne Bks., BP305). Beacon Pr.

--Great Slave Narratives. LC 77-84792. 1969. pap. 8.95x (ISBN 0-8070-5473-9, BP331). Beacon Pr.

--The Harlem Renaissance Remembered: Essays Edited with a Commentary by Arna Bontemps. 256p. 1984. pap. 9.95 (ISBN 0-396-08432-X). Dodd.

Bontemps, Arna, intro. by see Handy, W. C.

Bontemps, Arna, jt. ed. see Hughes, Langston.

Bontemps, Arna, et al, eds. Five Black Lives: The Autobiographies of Venture Smith, James Mars, William Grimes, the Rev. G. W. Offley, & James L. Smith. LC 74-108647. 1971. 17.50x (ISBN 0-8195-4036-6). Wesleyan U Pr.

Bontemps, Arna W. God Sends Sunday. LC 74-148531. Repr. of 1931 ed. 10.00 (ISBN 0-404-00137-8). AMS Pr.

--One Hundred Years of Negro Freedom. LC 80-10828. xi, 276p. 1980. Repr. of 1961 ed. lib. bdg. 35.00x (ISBN 0-313-22218-5, BOOY). Greenwood.

Bontier, Pierre & Le Verrier, Jean. The Canarian; or Book of the Conquest & Conversion of the Canarians, in the Year 1402, by Messire Jean de Bethencourt. Major, Richard H., ed. LC 70-286234. (Hakluyt Society Ser.: No. 46). 300p. 1972. lib. bdg. 32.00 (ISBN 0-8337-2188-7). B Franklin.

Bontinck, Irmgard, ed. New Patterns of Musical Behaviour of the Young Generation in Industrial Societies. 1974. 34.00 (ISBN 3-7024-0057-5, 51-26246). Eur-Am Music.

Bontinck-Kueffel, Irmgard. Opern Auf Schallplatten Nineteen Hundred to Nineteen Sixty-Two. Blaukopf, Kurt & Wagner, Manfred, eds. (Ger.). 1974. pap. 18.75 (ISBN 3-7024-0014-1, 51-26205). Eur-Am Music.

Bonting, S. L. & De Pont, J. J., eds. Membrane Transport. (New Comprehensive Biochemistry Ser.: Vol. 2). 1981. 64.25 (ISBN 0-444-80307-6). Elsevier.

Bontrager, Ernest J. & Bontrager, Ida, eds. Rudiments of Music. 1968. pap. 1.00x (ISBN 0-87813-102-7). Park View.

--Songs That Live. 1966. 2.95x (ISBN 0-87813-100-0). Park View.

Bontrager, Frances. Church & the Single Person. (Family Life Ser). 32p. (Orig.). 1969. pap. 0.50 (ISBN 0-8361-1575-9). Herald Pr.

Bontrager, G. Edwin. Divorce & the Faithful Church. LC 78-4671. 224p. 1978. 7.95 (ISBN 0-8361-1850-2); pap. 5.95 (ISBN 0-8361-1851-0). Herald Pr.

Bontrager, Ida, jt. ed. see Bontrager, Ernest J.

Bontrager, Ida B. Ozark Parson. 1978. 5.55 (ISBN 0-686-30827-1). Christian Light.

--Under God's Arrest. 1974. 11.50 (ISBN 0-87813-508-1). Christian Light.

Bontrager, Kenneth L. & Anthony, Barry T. Textbook of Radiographic Positioning & Related Anatomy. LC 81-82006. (Illus.). 560p. (Orig.). 1982. text ed. 49.95x (ISBN 0-940122-01-4). Multi Media CO.

Bonus, Thaddeus, ed. Improving Internal Communications. 130p. 1984. 14.50 (ISBN 0-89964-228-4). Coun Adv & Supp Ed.

Bonvalot, Marie. Le Vocabulaire Medical De Base, 2 vols. 447p. (Fr.). 1972. Set. pap. 45.00 (ISBN 0-686-56925-3, M-6043). French & Eur.

Bonventre, Joseph V. Key References in Nephrology: An Annotated Guide. LC 82-14658. (Key References in Internal Medicine Ser.: Vol. 3). 108p. 1982. pap. text ed. 12.50 (ISBN 0-443-08205-7). Churchill.

Bonventura, Celia, jt. auth. see Bonventura, Joseph.

Bonventura, Joseph & Bonventura, Celia. Physiology & Biology of Horseshoe Crabs: Studies on Normal & Environmentally Stressed Animals, Vol.81. LC 82-188. (Progress in Clinical & Biological Research Ser.: Vol. 81). 334p. 1982. 48.00 (ISBN 0-8451-0081-5). A R Liss.

Bonventure, Peter, jt. auth. see Cosell, Howard.

Bonvillain, Nancy, jt. ed. see Levine, Gaynell S.

Bonville, W. J. Footnotes to a Fairytale: A Study in the Nature of Expression in the Arts. 192p. 1979. 15.00 (ISBN 0-87527-192-8). Green.

Bonwick, Colin. English Radicals & the American Revolution. LC 76-12641. xxii, 362p. 1977. 29.00 (ISBN 0-8078-1277-3). U of NC Pr.

Bonwick, G. Automation on Shipboard. 1969. 35.00 (ISBN 0-312-06195-1). St Martin.

Bonwick, James. Daily Life & Origin of the Tasmanians. (Illus.). Repr. of 1870 ed. 35.00 (ISBN 0-384-05090-5). Johnson Repr.

--Irish Druids & Old Irish Religions. LC 75-36830. (Occult Ser.). 1976. Repr. of 1894 ed. 25.50x (ISBN 0-405-07942-7). Ayer Co Pubs.

--The Last of the Tasmanians; or, the Black War of Van Diemen's Land. (Landmarks in Anthropology Ser). Repr. of 1870 ed. lib. bdg. 35.00 (ISBN 0-384-05093-X). Johnson Repr.

--The Lost Tasmanian Race. (Landmarks in Anthropology). Repr. of 1884 ed. 25.00 (ISBN 0-384-05105-7). Johnson Repr.

Bony, Jean. French Gothic Architecture of the Twelfth & Thirteenth Centuries. LC 74-82842. (California Studies in the History of Art: Vol. 20). (Illus.). 640p. 1983. 115.00 (ISBN 0-520-02831-7, CAL 757); pap. 39.95 (ISBN 0-520-05586-1). U of Cal Pr.

Bonynge, David B. MicroMansion: Using Your Apple II-IIe Computer to Have a Safer, More Convenient Home. (Illus.). 176p. (Orig.). 1985. pap. 11.95 (ISBN 0-8306-1916-X, 1916). TAB Bks.

--MicroMansion: Using Your Commodore 64 Computer to Have a Safer, More Convenient Home. (Illus.). 176p. (Orig.). 1985. pap. 11.95 (ISBN 0-8306-1936-4, 1936). TAB Bks.

--MicroMansion: Using Your IBM-PC Computer to Have a Safer, More Convenient Home. (Illus.). 176p. (Orig.). 1985. pap. 11.95 (ISBN 0-8306-1926-7, 1926). TAB Bks.

Bonzanigo, Rocco. Canadian Taxation of Business & Investment Income of Non-Residents. (European University Studies, Series 2, Law: Vol. 77). 100p. 1973. 18.25 (ISBN 3-261-01040-6). P Lang Pubs.

Boobis, et al. Microsomes & Drug Oxidations. 420p. 1985. 80.00 (ISBN 0-85066-282-6). Taylor & Francis.

Booch, Grady. Software Engineering with Ada. 1983. text ed. 25.95 (ISBN 0-8053-0600-5); transparency masters o.p. 50.95 (ISBN 0-8053-0601-3). Benjamin-Cummings.

Boochever, Florence & Jackson, Raymond, eds. Writings from the Beaver Trail. (Illus.). 291p. (Orig.). 1979. pap. 5.50 (ISBN 0-9605090-0-3). Albany Pub Lib.

Boockholdt, James L., jt. auth. see Liad, Woody M.

Boocock, Sarane, jt. ed. see Demos, John.

Boocock, Sarane S. Sociology of Education: An Introduction. 2nd ed. LC 79-88445. (Illus.). 1980. text ed. 26.95 (ISBN 0-395-28524-0). HM.

--Sociology of Education: An Introduction. 2nd ed. LC 84-19607. (Illus.). 374p. 1985. pap. text ed. 16.50 (ISBN 0-8191-4333-2). U Pr of Amer.

Boocock, Sarane S. & Schild, E. O., eds. Simulation Games in Learning. LC 68-21913. 279p. 1978. pap. 14.95 (ISBN 0-8039-1002-9). Sage.

Boodberg, Peter A. Selected Works of Peter A. Boodberg. Cohen, Alvin P., ed. LC 76-24580. 1979. 38.50x (ISBN 0-520-03314-0). U of Cal Pr.

Boodin, J. E. Cosmic Evolution: Outlines of Cosmic Idealism. Repr. of 1925 ed. 21.00 (ISBN 0-527-09800-0). Kraus Repr.

Boodin, John E. God & Creation, 2 vols. LC 75-3058. Repr. of 1934 ed. 52.00 set (ISBN 0-404-59057-8). AMS Pr.

--Religion of Tomorrow. LC 75-3062. Repr. of 1943 ed. 14.00 (ISBN 0-404-59061-6). AMS Pr.

--The Social Mind: Foundations of Social Philosophy. LC 75-3063. (Philosophy in America Ser.). Repr. of 1939 ed. 43.00 (ISBN 0-404-59062-4). AMS Pr.

--Time & Reality. LC 75-3064. (Philosophy in America Ser.). Repr. of 1904 ed. 16.50 (ISBN 0-404-59063-2). AMS Pr.

Boodle, Adelaide A. R. L. S. & His Sina Qua Non. 1926. Repr. 25.00 (ISBN 0-8274-3286-0). R West.

Boodley, James W. The Commercial Greenhouse. LC 78-74806. (Agriculture Ser.). 568p. 1981. 22.80 (ISBN 0-8273-1719-0); instr's. guide 3.60 (ISBN 0-8273-1718-2). Delmar.

Boody, Bertha M. Psychological Study of Immigrant Children at Ellis Island. LC 79-129391. (American Immigration Collection, Ser. 2). 1970. Repr. of 1926 ed. 13.00 (ISBN 0-405-00546-6). Ayer Co Pubs.

--A Psychological Study of Immigrant Children at Ellis Island. 1970. Repr. of 1926 ed. 14.00 (ISBN 0-88247-010-8). R & E Pubs.

Boogher, William F. Gleanings of Virginia History: An Historical & Genealogical Collection, Largely from Original Sources. LC 64-20825. 443p. 1976. Repr. of 1903 ed. 22.50 (ISBN 0-8063-0048-5). Genealog Pub.

Boogman, J. C. & Van Der Plaat, G. N., eds. Federalism: History & Current Significance of a Form of Government. (Illus.). 307p. 1980. pap. 17.00 (ISBN 90-247-9003-4, Pub. by Martinus Nijhoff Netherlands). Kluwer Academic.

Booher, Dianna. How to Write Your Way to Success in Business. 144p. 1985. pap. 4.76i (ISBN 0-06-463597-X, EH 597). B&N NY.

--The Last Caress. (Orig.). 1981. pap. 2.50 (ISBN 0-89083-722-8). Zebra.

--Send Me a Memo: A Handbook of Model Memos. 224p. 1984. 16.95 (ISBN 0-87196-906-8). Facts on File.

--Would You Put That in Writing? How to Write Your Way to Success in Business. LC 82-1529. 224p. 1983. 12.95 (ISBN 0-87196-650-6). Facts on File.

Booher, Dianna D. Coping-When Your Family Falls Apart. LC 79-17342. 192p. (gr. 7 up). 1979. PLB 9.29 (ISBN 0-671-33083-7); pap. 4.95. Messner.

--Getting along with People Who Don't Get Along. LC 83-14406. (Orig.). 1984. pap. 3.25 (ISBN 0-8054-5209-5). Broadman.

--Help! We're Moving. LC 83-42784. (Teen Survival Library). 144p. (gr. 7 up). 1983. PLB 9.29 (ISBN 0-671-46057-9). Messner.

--Love. 160p. (gr. 7 up). 1985. PLB 9.29 (ISBN 0-671-54401-2). Messner.

--Making Friends with Yourself & Other Strangers. LC 82-60650. (Teen Survival Library). 192p. (gr. 7 up). 1982. PLB 9.79 (ISBN 0-671-45878-7). Messner.

--Not Yet Free. LC 80-69005. (YA) (gr. 9 up). 1981. 7.50 (ISBN 0-8054-7315-7, 4273-15). Broadman.

--Rape: What Would You Do If...? LC 81-914. 128p. (gr. 7 up). 1981. PLB 9.79 (ISBN 0-671-42201-4); pap. 4.95. Messner.

Booher, L. J. Surface Irrigation. (Land & Water Development Documents: No. 3). (Illus.). 160p. (Orig.). 1974. pap. 8.00 (ISBN 92-5-100081-6, F455, FAO). Unipub.

Booher, Lee. How to Improve Reading Skills: A New Way with 420 Sight Words in Phonic Pattern Lessons. (Illus.). 68p. (Orig.). (gr. 1-4). 1984. 3.98 (ISBN 0-911975-00-4). Am Pub Today.

Booij, G. E. Dutch Morphology: A Study of Word Formation in Generative Grammar. (Illus.). x, 181p. (Orig.). 1977. pap. 16.00x (ISBN 90-316-0150-0). Benjamins North Am.

Book, Albert C. & Cary, Norman D. The Radio & Television Commercial. LC 78-529597. 1978. 9.95x (ISBN 0-87251-038-7). Crain Bks.

Book, Albert C., jt. auth. see Schick, C. Dennis.

Book, Cassandra, jt. auth. see Galvin, Kathleen M.

Book, Cassandra L., et al. Human Communication: Principles, Contexts, & Skills. 325p. (Orig.). 1980. pap. text ed. 15.95 (ISBN 0-312-39849-2); write for info. instructor's manual. St Martin.

Book, Fredrik. Hans Christian Andersen: A Biography. Schoolfield, George C., tr. LC 62-10765. pap. 71.00 (ISBN 0-317-08231-0, 2004748). Bks Demand UMI.

Book Industry Systems Advisory Committee, jt. auth. see Joint Committee of the Book Industry Study Group.

Book of the Dead. The Chapters of Coming Forth by Day, 3 vols. LC 73-18833. Repr. of 1910 ed. 49.50 set (ISBN 0-404-11303-6). AMS Pr.

Book Review Committee. Family Life & Child Development: Selective Bibliography Cumulative Through 1979. (Jewish Board of Family & Children Services). 1979. pap. 3.45 (ISBN 0-87183-187-2). Jewish Bd Family.

Book, Ronald V., ed. Formal Language Theory: Perspectives & Open Problems. 1980. 37.50 (ISBN 0-12-115350-9). Acad Pr.

Book, Stephen A. Statistics: Basic Techniques for Solving Problems. new ed. (Illus.). 1976. text ed. 30.95 (ISBN 0-07-006493-8). McGraw.

Book, Stephen A. & Epstein, Marc J. Statistical Analysis in Business. 1982. text ed. 32.55x (ISBN 0-673-16002-5). Scott F.

Book, Susan W.. The Chinese in Butte County, California, 1860-1920. LC 75-36573. 1976. perfect bdg. softcover 10.95 (ISBN 0-88247-373-5). R & E Pubs.

Book University of the New Song, ed. & illus. see Theriault, Harry.

Book University of the New Song & Academy of Letters & Arts in America, ed. see Theriault, Harry.

Book, W. J., jt. ed. see Hardt, D. E.

Book, Wayne J., ed. see American Society of Mechanical Engineers.

Book, Wayne J., ed. see ASME Winter Annual Meeting, Phoenix, Ariz., Nov. 1982.

Bookbinder, Albert I. Computer-Assisted Investment Handbook. LC 82-61048. (Illus.). 220p. 1983. pap. text ed. 19.95 (ISBN 0-916106-03-9). Prog Pr.

--Investment Decision Making. LC 67-29760. (Illus.). 145p. 1968. 9.95 (ISBN 0-916106-00-4). Prog Pr.

--Security Options Strategy. LC 76-46120. 201p. 1976. 15.00 (ISBN 0-916106-01-2). Prog Pr.

Bookbinder, Bernie. Long Island: People & Places, Past & Present. (Illus.). 256p. 1983. 30.00 (ISBN 0-8109-1259-7). Abrams.

Bookbinder, Robert. The Films of Bing Crosby. (Illus.). 1977. 14.95 (ISBN 0-8065-0598-2). Citadel Pr.

--The Films of the Seventies. LC 82-1285. (Illus.). 288p. 1982. 18.95 (ISBN 0-8065-0790-X). Citadel Pr.

--The Films of the Seventies. (Illus.). 288p. 1984. pap. 9.95 (ISBN 0-8065-0927-9). Citadel Pr.

Bookbinder, Susan R. Mainstreaming: What Every Child Needs to Know About Disabilities, The Meeting Street School Curriculum Guide for Grades 1-4. Schleifer, Maxwell J. & Griffin, John, eds. 1978. pap. 6.95 (ISBN 0-930958-02-0). Exceptional Parent.

Bookchin, Murray. The Ecology of Freedom: The Emergence & Dissolution of Hierarchy. LC 81-21745. 1982. 19.95 (ISBN 0-917352-09-2); pap. 11.50 (ISBN 0-917352-10-6). Cheshire.

--The Limits of the City. LC 73-17852. 192p. (Orig.). 1974. pap. 4.50xi (ISBN 0-06-131944-9, TB 1944, Torch). Har-Row.

--The Limits of the City. 11.25 (ISBN 0-8446-5847-2). Peter Smith.

Bookchin, Murray, et al. Hip Culture: Six Essays on Its Revolutionary Potential. (Orig.). 1971. pap. 1.25 (ISBN 0-87810-010-5). Times Change.

Booker & Jarnagin. Financial Accounting Standards: Explanation & Analysis, 1983. 5th ed. 975p. pap. 22.00 (ISBN 0-317-04278-5). Commerce.

Booker, Christopher. The Seventies: The Decade That Changed the Future. LC 80-5389. 350p. 1980. 16.95 (ISBN 0-8128-2757-0). Stein & Day.

Booker, Frank. The Great Western Railway. (Illus.). 206p. 1985. 19.95 (ISBN 0-946537-16-X); pap. 10.95 (ISBN 0-946537-21-6). David & Charles.

--The Industrial Archeology of the Tamar Valley. (Industrial Archeology of the British Isles Ser.). (Illus.). 303p. 7.50 (ISBN 0-7153-5172-9). David & Charles.

Booker, H. G. Energy in Electromagnetism. (IEE Electromagnetic Waves Ser.: No. 13). 384p. 1982. casebound 82.50 (ISBN 0-906048-59-1, EW013, Pub. by Peregrinus England). Inst Elect Eng.

Booker, Henry G. Cold Plasma Waves. LC 84-9018. 1984. lib. bdg. 59.50 (ISBN 90-247-2977-7, Pub. by Martinus Nijhoff Netherlands). Kluwer Academic.

Booker, J. Florence. Seven Letters to My Love. (Orig.). 1984. pap. 2.95 (ISBN 0-89221-130-X, Pub. by Sonlife Intl). New Leaf.

Booker, John. The Dutch Oracle. (Illus.). 224p. 1981. pap. 5.95 (ISBN 0-931116-01-5). Ralston-Pilot.

Booker, John M. A Middle English Bibliography. LC 72-18988. Repr. of 1912 ed. lib. bdg. 15.00 (ISBN 0-8414-1137-9). Folcroft.

Booker, John M., ed. The Winston Archives. 541p. 1975. 80.00x (ISBN 0-686-75545-6, Pub. by W Sussex Rec off). State Mutual Bk.

Booker, Jon A., jt. auth. see Jarnagin, Bill D.

Booker, Louise. Tar Heel Stories. (Illus.). 1968. 7.50 (ISBN 0-930230-34-5). Johnson NC.

Booker, Malcolm R. Last Quarter: The Next 25 Years in the Asia & the Pacific. 1978. 22.00x (ISBN 0-522-84151-1, Pub. by Melbourne U Pr Australia). Intl Spec Bk.

Booker, Marjorie M. To Hell with Male Chauvinism! 1985. 7.95 (ISBN 0-533-05707-8). Vantage.

Booker, Marjorie McLachlan. Treasures of My Heart. 112p. 1978. 7.95 (ISBN 0-87881-068-4). Mojave Bks.

Booker, Mary. Music in the Twentieth Century. 1981. 18.00x (ISBN 0-7223-1397-7, Pub. by Stockwell). State Mutual Bk.

Booker, P. J. Three Dimensional Projection Drawing. (Illus.). 64p. 1985. pap. 2.95 (ISBN 0-85242-143-5, Pub. by Argus). Aztex.

Booker, Richard. Come & Dine. LC 82-73508. 1983. pap. 4.95 (ISBN 0-88270-540-7). Bridge Pub.

--Intimacy with God. LC 84-70055. 196p. 1983. pap. 4.95 (ISBN 0-88270-552-0). Bridge Pub.

--The Miracle of the Scarlet Thread. LC 80-84802. (Orig.). (YA) 1981. pap. 4.95 (ISBN 0-88270-499-0, Pub. by Logos). Bridge Pub.

Booker, Stephen T. Waves & Licence. 65p. (Orig.). pap. 4.00 (ISBN 0-912678-55-0). Greenfld Rev Pr.

Bookhout, Theodore A., ed. Waterfowl & Wetlands: An Integrated Review. 152p. 1979. pap. text ed. 3.50 (ISBN 0-932547-03-6). N Central Sect Wildlife.

Bookl, George. How to Use Leverage to Make Money in Local Real Estate. 1965. pap. 4.95 (ISBN 0-13-436212-8, Reward). P-H.

Bookman. Swift Issue. 1973. Repr. of 1907 ed. 25.00 (ISBN 0-8274-0069-1). R West.

--Tennyson Number. 1902. Repr. 25.00 (ISBN 0-8274-3584-3). R West.

Bookman, Barbara, jt. auth. see Chapman, Betsy.

Bookman Publishing Staff. Review-Preview 85-86. (Yearbook Ser.). (Illus.). 96p. 1985. pap. 8.95 (ISBN 0-934780-72-2). Bookman Dan.

Bookman, Ralph. The Dimensions of Clinical Allergy. (Illus.). 158p. 1985. 27.50x (ISBN 0-398-05103-8). C C Thomas.

Books Americana. North American Indian Points. 2nd ed. (Illus.). 208p. (Orig.). 1984. pap. 7.95 (ISBN 0-89689-044-9). Bks Americana.

Books, Cyrus, tr. see Kastner, Erich.

Books, Kathryn J. Michigan Studies Program: Activity Manual. 227p. (gr. 4). 1983. duplicating masters 54.00 (ISBN 0-943068-85-1). Graphic Learning.

--Michigan Studies Program: Teacher's Guide. 28p. (gr. 4). 1983. tchr's guide 6.60 (ISBN 0-943068-86-X). Graphic Learning.

--Michigan Studies Program: Work-A-Text. 1983. pap. 4.10 (ISBN 0-87746-013-2). Graphic Learning.

Books, Kathryn J., ed. see Sayers, Martha & Zick, Kathy.

Books, Kathryn J., et al, eds. see Zola, John.

Books on Tape, Inc., ed. Books on Tape Catalog, 1985. 1985. 5.00 (ISBN 0-913369-02-0). Bks On Tape.

Bookspan, Martin. One Hundred One Masterpieces of Music & Their Composers. rev. ed. LC 72-84961. 480p. 1973. pap. 8.95 (ISBN 0-385-05721-0, Dolp). Doubleday.

Bookspan, Martin & Yockey, Ross. Zubin: The Zubin Mehta Story. LC 77-11822. (Illus.). 1978. 10.00i (ISBN 0-06-120400-5, HarpT). Har-Row.

Bookspan, Rochelle, ed. Santa Barbara by the Sea. (Illus.). 236p. pap. 10.00 (ISBN 0-87461-036-2). McNally.

Bookstaber, Philip D. Judaism & the American Mind: In Theory & Practice. LC 78-26404. 1979. Repr. of 1939 ed. lib. bdg. 24.75x (ISBN 0-313-20875-1, BOJU). Greenwood.

Bookstaber, R. & Clarke, R. Option Strategies for Institutional Investment Management: A Guide for Improving Portfolio Performance. 1983. text ed. 25.95 (ISBN 0-201-03118-3). Addison-Wesley.

Bookstaber, Richard. The Complete Investment Book: Trading Stocks, Bonds & Options with Computer Applications. 416p. 1985. pap. 19.95 (ISBN 0-673-15952-3). Scott F.

Bookstaber, Richard M. Option Pricing & Strategies in Investing. LC 80-15013. 256p. 1981. text ed. 19.95 (ISBN 0-201-00123-3). Addison-Wesley.

Bookstein, Abraham, jt. ed. see Swanson, Don R.

Bookstein, Abraham, et al, eds. Prospects for Change in Bibliographic Control. (University of Chicago Studies in Library Science). 1977. lib. bdg. 10.00x (ISBN 0-226-06365-8). U of Chicago Pr.

Bookstein, F. L. The Measurement of Biological Shape & Shape Change. LC 78-15923. (Lecture Notes in Biomathematics Ser.: Vol. 24). 1978. pap. 14.00 (ISBN 0-387-08912-8). Springer-Verlag.

Bookstein, F. L., et al. Morphometrics in Evolutionary Biology: The Geometry of Size & Shape Change with Examples from Fishes. (Special Publications: No. 15). (Illus.). 250p. 1985. lib. bdg. 22.00 (ISBN 0-910006-47-4); pap. 14.00 (ISBN 0-910006-48-2). Acad Nat Sci Phila.

Bookstein, Joseph J. & Clark, Richard L. Renal Microvascular Disease. 1980. text ed. 52.50 (ISBN 0-316-10237-7). Little.

Bookwalter, John. Siberia & Central Asia. LC 76-27541. (Illus.). 1976. Repr. of 1899 ed. lib. bdg. 55.00 (ISBN 0-89341-041-1). Longwood Pub Group.

Boole, George. Investigation of the Laws of Thought. 16.00 (ISBN 0-8446-1699-0). Peter Smith.

--Laws of Thought. 1953. pap. 7.95 (ISBN 0-486-60028-9). Dover.

--Logical Works, 2 Vols. Incl. Vol. 1. Studies in Logic & Probability. 500p. 29.95x (ISBN 0-87548-038-1); Vol. 2. Laws of Thought. xvi, 464p. 29.95x (ISBN 0-87548-039-X). 1952. Open Court.

--Miscellany. Barry, Patrick D., ed. 1969. pap. 4.00x (ISBN 0-8426-1173-8). Verry.

--Treatise on the Calculus of Finite Differences. 5th ed. LC 76-119364. text ed. 13.95 (ISBN 0-8284-1121-2). Chelsea Pub.

Boole, Mary E. The Preparation of the Child for Science. 157p. 1978. pap. text ed. 5.00x (ISBN 0-918970-24-5). Intl Gen Semantics.

Boolootian, Richard A. Elements of Human Anatomy & Physiology. LC 76-3681. 550p. 1976. text ed. 22.95 (ISBN 0-8299-0086-1); instrs.' manual avail. (ISBN 0-8299-0460-3). West Pub.

--Zoology: An Introduction to the Study of Animals. (Illus.). 1979. text ed. 23.95 (ISBN 0-02-312030-4); student study guide avail.; instrs'. manual avail.; lab. manual avail. Macmillan.

Boolootian, Richard A. & Heyneman, Donald. Illustrated Laboratory Text in Zoology. 4th ed. LC 74-15605. 1980. pap. text ed. 22.95 (ISBN 0-03-051176-3, HoltC). HR&W.

--An Illustrated Laboratory Text in Zoology. brief ed. LC 76-30722. 253p. 1977. pap. text ed. 19.95x (ISBN 0-03-019021-5, HoltC). HR&W.

--An Illustrated Laboratory Text in Zoology. 4th ed. 1980. pap. text ed. 22.95 (ISBN 0-03-051176-3, CBS C). SCP.

Boolootian, Richard A. & Stiles, Karl A. College Zoology. 10th ed. (Illus.). 768p. 1981. text ed. write for info. (ISBN 0-02-311990-X). Macmillan.

Boolos, G. The Unprovability of Consistency. LC 77-85710. (Illus.). 1979. 37.50 (ISBN 0-521-21879-9). Cambridge U Pr.

Boolos, G. S. & Jeffrey, R. C. Computability & Logic. 2nd ed. LC 77-85710. (Illus.). 280p. 1981. 47.50 (ISBN 0-521-23479-4); pap. 16.95 (ISBN 0-521-29967-5). Cambridge U Pr.

Boom. Don't Wrestle, Just Nestle. 7.95 (ISBN 0-318-18172-X). WCTU.

--Each New Day. 2.95 (ISBN 0-318-18177-0). WCTU.

--This Day is the Lord's Day. 2.75 (ISBN 0-318-18182-7). WCTU.

Boom, B. K., jt. auth. see Ouden, P.

Boom, Corrie T. Amazing Love. 1964. pap. 2.50 (ISBN 0-87508-018-9). Chr Lit.

--Amazing Love. (Orig.). 1982. pap. 2.50 (ISBN 0-515-06735-0). Jove Pubns.

--Amor, Asombroso Amor. Orig. Title: Amazing Love. 112p. 1980. pap. 2.25 (ISBN 0-311-40035-3, Edit Mundo). Casa Bautista.

--Common Sense Not Needed. 1969. pap. 1.25 (ISBN 0-87508-020-0). Chr Lit.

--Defeated Enemies. 1962. pap. 1.25 (ISBN 0-87508-021-9). Chr Lit.

--Each New Day. (Christian Library). 1985. Repr. of 1980 ed. 5.99 (ISBN 0-916441-20-2). Barbour & Co.

--Marching Orders for the End Battle. 1970. pap. 1.95 (ISBN 0-87508-024-3). Chr Lit.

--Not Good If Detached. 1966. pap. 1.95 (ISBN 0-87508-022-7). Chr Lit.

--Plenty for Everyone. 1967. pap. 2.95 (ISBN 0-87508-023-5). Chr Lit.

--Prisoner & Yet. 1964. pap. 3.50 (ISBN 0-87508-019-7). Chr Lit.

--A Prisoner & Yet. (Orig.). 1982. pap. 2.50 (ISBN 0-515-06736-9). Jove Pubns.

--This Day Is the Lord's. 1982. pap. 2.75 (ISBN 0-515-06734-2). Jove Pubns.

--Tramp for the Lord. 1974. pap. 3.50 (ISBN 0-87508-028-6); pap. 2.25 (ISBN 0-87508-017-0). Chr Lit.

--Tramp for the Lord. 1976. pap. 2.50 (ISBN 0-515-06486-6). Jove Pubns.

Boom, Corrie ten. Prayers & Promises for Every Day: With Corrie Ten Boom. Shaw, Luci, ed. LC 77-92352. (Day Star Devotional). 144p. 1977. pap. 2.95 (ISBN 0-87788-689-X). Shaw Pubs.

Boom, Corrie Ten see Graham, Billy & Ten Boom, Corrie.

Boom, Corrie Ten see Ten Boom, Corrie.

Boom, Corrie Ten see Ten Boom, Corrie & Sherrill, John.

Boom, G., jt. ed. see Brederoo, P.

Boom, Michael. Everything You Can Do with Your Atari Computer. (Everything You Can Do with Your... Ser.). 1984. pap. cancelled (ISBN 0-88284-277-3). Alfred Pub.

--How to Use Atari Computers. (An Alfred Handy Guide Ser.). 64p. 1983. 3.50 (ISBN 0-88284-235-8). Alfred Pub.

--How to Use Atari Computers. 1984. pap. 2.95 cancelled (ISBN 0-317-13948-7). Alfred Pub.

--Understanding Atari Graphics. LC 82-18463. (An Alfred Handy Guide Ser.). 48p. 1982. pap. 3.50 (ISBN 0-88284-224-2). Alfred Pub.

Boomer, Garth. Fair Dinkum Teaching & Learning: Reflections on Literacy & Power. LC 84-21670. 192p. (Orig.). 1985. pap. text ed. 9.50x (ISBN 0-317-19854-8). Boynton Cook Pubs.

Boomer, Garth & Spender, Dale. The Spitting Image: Reflections on Language, Education & Social Class. 160p. (Orig.). 1976. pap. 9.25x (ISBN 0-7270-0162-0). Boynton Cook Pubs.

Boomer, Percy. On Learning Golf. (Illus.). 1946. 13.95 (ISBN 0-394-41008-4). Knopf.

Boomkamp, M. van Leeuwen see Kapteyn, P. J., et al.

Boon. Computer Design. (Infotech Computer State of the Art Reports). 666p. 1974. 85.00 (ISBN 0-08-028496-5). Pergamon.

--Management Information Systems. (Infotech Computer State of the Art Reports). 661p. 1974. 310.00s (ISBN 0-08-028554-6). Pergamon.

--Microprogramming & Systems Architecture. (Infotech Computer State of the Art Reports). 644p. 1975. 85.00 (ISBN 0-08-028547-3). Pergamon.

--Montaigne, Gentilhomme et Essayiste. 18.50 (ISBN 0-685-34192-5). French & Eur.

--The New Technologies. (Infotech Computer State of the Art Reports). 486p. 1971. 85.00 (ISBN 0-08-028524-4). Pergamon.

Boon, Emilie. Belinda's Balloon. LC 84-21771. (Illus.). 32p. (ps-1). 1985. PLB 8.99 (ISBN 0-394-97342-9); pap. 8.95 (ISBN 0-394-87342-4). Knopf.

--Peterkin Meets a Star. LC 83-9691. (Illus.). 32p. (gr. k-2). 1984. PLB 6.99 (ISBN 0-394-96284-2, BYR); 4.95 (ISBN 0-394-86284-8). Random.

--Peterkin Meets a Star: Random House Picturebacks Ser. LC 84-29810. (Illus.). 32p. (ps-1). 1985. pap. 1.95 (ISBN 0-394-87505-2). Random.

--Peterkin's Wet Walk. LC 83-8937. (Illus.). 32p. (gr. k-2). 1984. 4.95 (ISBN 0-394-86285-6); PLB 6.99 (ISBN 0-394-96285-0). Random.

Boon, G. K. Technology & Sector Choice in Economic Development. 324p. 1978. 40.00x (ISBN 90-286-0068-X). Sijthoff & Noordhoff.

Boon, George C. Silchester: The Roman Town of Calleva. 1974. 12.50 (ISBN 0-7153-6339-5). David & Charles.

Boon, Gerard K. Technology & Employment in Footwear Manufacturing: A Study Prepared for the Int'l Labour Office Within the Framework of the World Employment Programme. LC 80-50458. 232p. 1980. 45.00x (ISBN 90-286-0170-8). Sijthoff & Noordhoff.

--Technology Transfer in Fibres, Textile & Apparel. 600p. 1981. 166.25 (ISBN 90-286-0520-7). Sijthoff & Noordhoff.

Boon, James A. The Anthropological Romance of Bali 1597-1972. LC 76-19626. (Geertz Ser.). (Illus.). 1977. 44.50 (ISBN 0-521-21398-3); pap. 12.95 (ISBN 0-521-29226-3). Cambridge U Pr.

--Other Tribes, Other Scribes: Symbolic Anthropology in the Comparative Study of Cultures, Histories, Religions & Texts. LC 82-9516. (Illus.). 320p. 1983. 37.50 (ISBN 0-521-25081-1); pap. 11.95 (ISBN 0-521-27197-5). Cambridge U Pr.

Boon, Jean P. & Yip, Sidney. Molecular Hydrodynamics. (Illus.). 440p. 1979. text ed. 86.95 (ISBN 0-07-006560-8). McGraw.

Boon, K. G., jt. ed. see Kok, J. Filedt.

Boon, Louis P. Chapel Road. Dixon, Adrienne, tr. (International Studies & Translations Ser.). lib. bdg. 8.50 (ISBN 0-8057-3410-4, Twayne). G K Hall.

Boon, Mathilde E. Gynaecological Cytology. (Illus.). 278p. 1980. pap. 37.50 (ISBN 0-8391-4105-X). Univ Park.

Boone, Bruce, jt. tr. see Gluck, Robert.

Boone, Charles W. Increase Your Personal Effectiveness. (Illus.). 1982. 8.95 (ISBN 0-533-05052-9). Vantage.

Boone, Clinton C. Liberia As I Know It. LC 73-106867. (Illus.). Repr. of 1929 ed. 17.50x (ISBN 0-8371-3284-3, BOL&, Pub. by Negro U Pr). Greenwood.

Boone, Daniel. An Adult Has Aphasia. 1983. pap. 1.75x (ISBN 0-8134-2342-2). Interstate.

Boone, Daniel R. The Voice & Voice Therapy. 3rd ed. (Illus.). 320p. 1983. 27.95 (ISBN 0-13-943118-7). P-H.

Boone, Debby & Baker, Dennis. So Far. 224p. 1982. pap. 2.95 (ISBN 0-515-06323-1). Jove Pubns.

Boone, Donna, ed. Focus on Low Back Pain. (Monograph). 1979. pap. 4.00 (ISBN 0-912452-00-5). Am Phys Therapy Assn.

Boone, Donna C. Comprehensive Management of Hemophilia. LC 76-18109. 185p. 1976. text ed. 11.95x (ISBN 0-8036-1000-9). Davis Co.

Boone, Edgar J. Developing Programs in Adult Education. (Illus.). 320p. 1985. text ed. 23.95 (ISBN 0-13-204694-6). P-H.

Boone, Edgar J., et al. Serving Personal & Community Needs Through Adult Education. LC 79-9664. (Higher Education Ser.). 1980. text ed. 18.95x (ISBN 0-87589-451-8). Jossey-Bass.

Boone, Edna, jt. auth. see Boone, Tom.

Boone, Elizabeth H., jt. auth. see Nuttal, Zelia.

Boone, Elizabeth H., ed. Ritual Human Sacrifice in Mesoamerica: A Conference at Dumbarton Oaks, October 13 & 14, 1979. LC 83-14059. (Illus.). 256p. 1984. 18.50x (ISBN 0-88402-120-3). Dumbarton Oaks.

Boone, F. R., ed. Experiences with Three Tillage Systems on a Marine Loam Soil II: 1976-1979: A Joint Study of the Westmaas Research Group on New Tillage Systems, Carried Out on the Westmaas Experimental Husbandry Farm. (Agricultural Research Reports: No. 925). (Illus.). 263p. 1985. pap. 28.00 (ISBN 90-220-0855-X, PDC280, Pudoc). Unipub.

Boone, Gene. Writing to Be Published. 1984. pap. 4.95x (ISBN 0-317-11581-2, Pub. by Exploits Pub Ltd Canada). R S V P Press.

Boone, Gladys. Women's Trade Union Leagues in Great Britain & United States of America. LC 68-58549. (Columbia University Studies in the Social Sciences: No. 489). Repr. of 1942 ed. 21.00 (ISBN 0-404-51489-8). AMS Pr.

Boone, J. Allen. Kinship with All Life. LC 54-6901. 160p. 1976. pap. 6.68 (ISBN 0-06-060912-5, RD128, HarpR). Har-Row.

Boone, Julia R. Getting to Know Your Bible. LC 81-69259. 176p. 1984. pap. 8.95 (ISBN 0-8054-1140-2). Broadman.

Boone, L. V, et al. Producing Farm Crops. 3rd ed. 1981. 19.00 (ISBN 0-8134-2151-9); text ed. 14.25x (2151). Interstate.

Boone, Lalia P. From A to Z in Latah County, Idaho: A Place Name Dictionary. 127p. pap. 7.95 (ISBN 0-9612758-0-4). L Boone.

Boone, Louis E. Classic in Consumer Behavior. 441p. 1977. pap. text ed. write for info. (ISBN 0-02-312110-6). Macmillan.

Boone, Louis E. & Bowen, Donald D. Great Writing in Management. 475p. 1979. pap. text ed. write for info. (ISBN 0-02-312130-0). Macmillan.

Boone, Louis E. & Hackleman, Edwin C. Marketing Strategy: A Marketing Decision Game. 2nd ed. LC 74-27870. (Illus.). 224p. 1975. pap. text ed. 16.50 (ISBN 0-675-08713-9). Additional supplements may be obtained from publisher. Merrill.

Boone, Louis E. & Johnson, James C. Marketing Channels. 2nd ed. 578p. 1977. pap. text ed. write for info. (ISBN 0-02-312150-5). Macmillan.

Boone, Louis E. & Kurtz, David. Contemporary Personal Finance. 576p. 1985. text ed. 26.95 (ISBN 0-394-34282-8, RanB). Random.

Boone, Louis E. & Kurtz, David L. Contemporary Business. 4th ed. 1985. text ed. 28.95 (ISBN 0-03-071413-3); study guide 13.95 (ISBN 0-03-071414-1). Dryden Pr.

--Contemporary Marketing. 4th ed. 656p. 1983. text ed. 32.95x (ISBN 0-03-062638-2); instr's. manual 20.00 (ISBN 0-03-062639-0); study guide 13.95 (ISBN 0-03-062641-2); transparencies 250.00 (ISBN 0-03-062644-7); test bank 100.00 (ISBN 0-03-062643-9). Dryden Pr.

--Management. 2nd ed. Donnelly, Paul S., ed. (Random House Business Division Ser.). 1984. text ed. 26.95 (ISBN 0-394-33625-9, RanC). wkbk. 10.95 (ISBN 0-394-33622-4). Random.

Boone, Louis E., jt. auth. see Kurtz, David L.

Boone, Louis E., et al. The Sales Management Game. 2nd ed. 1978. pap. text ed. write for info. (ISBN 0-02-312170-X). Macmillan.

Boone, Michele L., ed. Southern Appalachian Resource Catalog, Vol. III. (Illus.). 108p. 1982. 6.00 (ISBN 0-937208-02-7). S Appalachian Res.

--Southern Appalachian Resource Catalog, Vol. I. rev. ed. (Illus.). 84p. 1980. pap. 4.00 (ISBN 0-937208-00-0). S Appalachian Res.

--Southern Applachian Resource Catalog, Vol. II. (Illus.). 76p. 1981. 5.00 (ISBN 0-937208-01-9). S Appalachian Res.

Boone, Pat. My Brothers Keeper? Orig. Title: Dr. Balaam's Talking Mule. 1975. pap. 1.75 (ISBN 0-89129-028-1). Jove Pubns.

--Pat Boone's Favorite Bible Stories for the Very Young. LC 84-6837. (Illus.). 64p. (ps-3). 1984. 7.95 (ISBN 0-394-85891-3, Pub. by BYR); lib. bdg. 9.99 GLB (ISBN 0-394-95891-8). Random.

Boone, Pat & Boone, Shirley. The Marriage Game. LC 84-61912. 120p. 1984. pap. 5.95 (ISBN 0-89221-114-8). New Leaf.

Boone, Richard G. Education in the United States. (Educational Ser.). 1894. Repr. 10.00 (ISBN 0-8482-7360-5). Norwood Edns.

--Education in the United States. 402p. 1981. Repr. of 1894 ed. lib. bdg. 30.00 (ISBN 0-89760-049-5). Telegraph Bks.

--Education in the U. S. Its History from the Earliest Settlements. facsimile ed. (Select Bibliographies Reprint Ser). Repr. of 1889 ed. 22.00 (ISBN 0-8369-5924-8). Ayer Co Pubs.

Boone, Robert, jt. ed. see McGee, Leo.

Boone, Robert S., jt. auth. see Flanigan, Michael C.

Boone, Shirley, jt. auth. see Boone, Pat.

Boone, Thomas, jt. auth. see Nygaard, Gary.

Boone, Thomas H., jt. auth. see Nygaard, Gary.

Boone, Tom & Boone, Edna. Prayer & Action. 1974. pap. 1.25x (ISBN 0-8358-0309-0). Upper Room.

Boone, William T. Better Gymnastics: How to Spot the Performer. LC 78-368. (Illus.). 225p. 1979. pap. 10.00 (ISBN 0-89037-127-X). Anderson World.

Boone-Harris. Rhetoric, Argument & Communication. 224p. 1984. pap. text ed. 16.95 (ISBN 0-8403-3443-5). Kendall-Hunt.

Boone-Thomas, Del. For Kids Who Are Coming of Age: Talking to Teenagers in Language They Understand. LC 84-91735. (Illus.). 57p. (Orig.). (gr. 7-12). 1983. pap. 7.95x (ISBN 0-9611780-0-0). Boone-Thomas.

Boonin, Joseph M. An Index to the Solo Songs of Robert Franz. (Music Indexes & Bibliographies: No. 4). 1970. pap. 1.75 (ISBN 0-913574-04-X). Eur-Am Music.

Boor, C. De see De Boor, C.

Boor, Carl G. De see Nicephorus.

Boor, Helmut De & Wisniewski, Roswitha. Mittelhochdeutsche Grammatik. 9th ed. (Sammlung Goeschen 2209). 1984. 4.90x (ISBN 3-11-010191-2). De Gruyter.

Boor, Jacklyn, jt. auth. see Collins, Dennis.

Boor, John, Jr. Ziegler-Natta Catalysts & Polymerizations. 1979. 80.00 (ISBN 0-12-115550-1). Acad Pr.

Boor, W. De see De Boor, W. & Grossarth-Maticek, R.

Boor, W. De see De Boor, W. & Kohlmann, G.

Booraem, Hendrick. The Formation of the Republican Party in New York: Politics & Conscience in the Antebellum North. LC 83-3995. 1983. 42.50x (ISBN 0-8147-1045-X). NYU Pr.

Boord, W. Arthur, ed. Sun Artists (Original Series, Nos. 1-8. LC 72-9184. (The Literature of Photography Ser.). Repr. of 1891 ed. 44.00 (ISBN 0-405-04895-5). Ayer Co Pubs.

Boore, Jennifer R., jt. auth. see Moghissi, K.

Boorer, Michael. Animals. LC 83-50388. (Silver Burdett Color Library). 48p. (gr. 4 up). 1983. 14.00 (ISBN 0-382-06725-8). Silver.

--The Life of Monkeys & Apes. LC 78-56603. (Easy Reading Edition of Introduction to Nature Ser.). (Illus.). 1978. PLB 12.68 (ISBN 0-382-06188-8). Silver.

--The Life of Strange Mammals. LC 78-56571. (Easy Reading Edition of Introduction to Nature Ser.). (Illus.). 1978. PLB 12.68 (ISBN 0-382-06192-6). Silver.

Boorkman, C. J. Chicano Bibliography. 1974. 59.95 (ISBN 0-87968-398-8). Gordon Pr.

Boorkman, JoAnne, jt. auth. see Roper, Fred.

Boorman, Howard L. & Howard, Richard C., eds. Biographical Dictionary of Republican China, 4 vols. Incl. Vol. 1. Ai-Ch'u. 1967. 54.00x (ISBN 0-231-08955-4); Vol. 2. Dalai-Ma. 1968. 54.00x (ISBN 0-231-08956-2); Vol. 3. Mao-Wu. 1970. 54.00x (ISBN 0-231-08957-0); Vol. 4. Yang-Bibliography. 1971. 54.00x (ISBN 0-231-08958-9). LC 67-12006. Columbia U Pr.

Boorman, Howard L. & Krompart, Janet, eds. Biographical Dictionary of Republican China: A Personal Name Index, Vol. 5. 1979. 54.00x (ISBN 0-231-04558-1). Columbia U Pr.

Boorman, John. The Emerald Forest Diary. (Illus.). 180p. 1985. 14.95 (ISBN 0-374-14769-8). FS&G.

--Money into Light: A Diary. (Illus.). 208p. 1985. pap. 9.95 (ISBN 0-571-13772-5). Faber & Faber.

Boorman, John T., jt. auth. see Havrilesky, Thomas M.

Boorman, John T. see Havrilesky, Thomas M., et al.

Boorman, John T., jt. ed. see Havrilesky, Thomas M.

Boorman, Kathleen E., et al. Blood Group Serology. 5th ed. 1977. text ed. 43.75 (ISBN 0-443-01475-2). Churchill.

Boorman, Linda. The Drugstore Bandit of Horseshoe Bend. 120p. 1982. pap. 2.95 (ISBN 0-88207-492-X). Victor Bks.

--The Giant Trunk Mystery. 96p. (gr. 6-12). 1981. pap. 2.95 (ISBN 0-686-69419-8). Victor Bks.

--The Mystery Man of Horseshoe Bend. LC 79-55320. 100p. (gr. 4-7). 1980. pap. 2.95 (ISBN 0-88207-488-1). Victor Bks.

Boorman, Scott A. Protracted Game: A Wei-Ch'i Interpretation of Maoist Revolutionary Strategy. LC 70-83039. 1969. 22.50x (ISBN 0-19-500490-6). Oxford U Pr.

--Protracted Game: A Wei-Ch'i Interpretation of Maoist Revolutionary Strategy. (Illus.). 1969. pap. 7.95 (ISBN 0-19-501493-6, GB). Oxford U Pr.

Boorman, Scott A. & Levitt, Paul R. The Genetics of Altruism. LC 79-52792. 1980. 35.00 (ISBN 0-12-115650-8). Acad Pr.

Boorman, Stanley. Studies in the Performance of Late Medieval Music. LC 83-2058. 350p. 1984. 49.50 (ISBN 0-521-24819-1). Cambridge U Pr.

Boorsch, S., jt. ed. see Scalini, M.

Boorsch, Suzanne, et al. Giorgio Ghisi: The Engravings. (Illus.). 208p. 1985. 35.00 (ISBN 0-87099-396-8); pap. 25.00 (ISBN 0-87099-397-6). Metro Mus Art.

Boorstein, Edward. Allende's Chile: An Inside View. LC 77-4894. 288p. 1977. pap. 4.25 (ISBN 0-7178-0488-7). Intl Pubs Co.

--Economic Transformation of Cuba. LC 68-13652. 306p. 1969. pap. 5.95 (ISBN 0-85345-095-1). Monthly Rev.

--What's Ahead?... the U. S. Economy. 240p. 1984. 15.00 (ISBN 0-7178-0613-8); pap. 5.95 (ISBN 0-7178-0614-6). Intl Pubs Co.

Boorstein, Seymour & Speeth, Kathleen, eds. Explorations in Transpersonal Psychotherapy. LC 80-51704. 1980. 19.95 (ISBN 0-8314-0060-9). Sci & Behavior.

Boorstin, Daniel. The Exploring Spirit: America & the World, Then & Now. LC 77-4454. (YA) 1977. pap. 2.45 (ISBN 0-394-72423-2, V-423, Vin). Random.

Boorstin, Daniel J. America & the Image of Europe: Reflections on American Thought. 11.25 (ISBN 0-8446-1703-2). Peter Smith.

--The Americans, 3 vols. Incl. Vol. 1. The Colonial Experience. 1958. 24.95 (ISBN 0-394-41506-X); Vol. 2. The Democratic Experience. 1973. 24.95 (ISBN 0-394-48724-9); Vol. 3. The National Experience. 1965. 24.95 (ISBN 0-394-41453-5). Set. 77.85 (ISBN 0-394-49588-8). Random.

--The Americans, 1: The Colonial Experience. (YA) 1985. pap. 6.95 (ISBN 0-394-70513-0, V513, Vin). Random.

--The Americans, 2: The National Experience. (YA) 1985. pap. 8.95 (ISBN 0-394-70358-8, V-358, Vin). Random.

--The Americans, 3: The Democratic Experience. LC 74-3298. (YA) 1984. pap. 7.95 (ISBN 0-394-71011-8, V-11, Vin). Random.

--Decline of Radicalism: Reflections of America Today. 192p. 1969. 5.95 (ISBN 0-394-42184-1, Vin). Random.

--Democracy & Its Discontents: Reflections on Everyday America. 1974. 5.95 (ISBN 0-394-49146-7). Random.

--Democracy & Its Discontents: Reflections on Everyday America. LC 74-20812. (YA) pap. 2.45 (ISBN 0-394-71501-2, V-501, Vin). Random.

--The Discoverers: A History of Man's Search to Know His World & Himself. 768p. 1985. pap. 9.95 (ISBN 0-394-72625-1, Vin). Random.

--The Exploring Spirit: America & the World, Then & Now. 1976. 6.95 (ISBN 0-394-40602-8). Random.

--Genius of American Politics. LC 53-9434. (Walgreen Foundation Lectures Ser.). 1958. pap. 7.00x (ISBN 0-226-06491-3, P27, Phoen). U of Chicago Pr.

--Genius of American Politics, Nineteen Fifty-eight. (Walgreen Foundation Lectures). 10.50x (ISBN 0-226-06490-5, Phoen). U of Chicago Pr.

--Image: A Guide to Pseudo-Events in America. LC 62-7936. Orig. Title: What Happened to the American Dream. 1962. pap. text ed. 4.95x (ISBN 0-689-70280-9, 173). Atheneum.

--The Image: A Guide to Pseudo-Events in America. 1984. 13.75 (ISBN 0-8446-6122-8). Peter Smith.

--Lost World of Thomas Jefferson. 15.25 (ISBN 0-8446-1701-6). Peter Smith.

--The Lost World of Thomas Jefferson. LC 80-26835. 320p. 1981. pap. 10.95 (ISBN 0-226-06496-4). U of Chicago Pr.

--Portraits from the Americans: The Democratic Experience. 1975. pap. 6.95 (ISBN 0-394-73105-0). Random.

Boorstin, Daniel J., ed. America in Two Centuries: An Inventory. 1976. 3571.50 (ISBN 0-405-07666-5). Ayer Co Pubs.

--American Primer. 1968. pap. 6.95 (ISBN 0-452-00760-7, Mer). NAL.

--An American Primer, 2 vols. LC 66-20576. (Collector's Edition Ser.). 1969. boxed set 25.00 (ISBN 0-226-06494-8). U of Chicago Pr.

--Technology & Society, 53 bks. 1972. Repr. Set. 1502.50 (ISBN 0-405-04680-4). Ayer Co Pubs.

Boorstin, Daniel J., ed. see Ellis, John T.

Boorstin, Paul & Boorstin, Sharon. The Glory Hand. 304p. (Orig.). pap. 2.95 (ISBN 0-425-05861-1). Berkley Pub.

Boorstin, Sharon, jt. auth. see Boorstin, Paul.

Boorstyn, Neil. Copyright Law, Vol. I. 1981. 79.50 (ISBN 0-686-31142-6); Suppl. 1984. 17.50; Suppl. 1983. 16.00. Lawyers Co Op.

Boos, jt. auth. see Jancura.

Boos, Florence & Miller, Lynn F., eds. Bibliography of Women & Literature. 450p. 1985. text ed. 75.00x (ISBN 0-8419-0693-9). Holmes & Meier.

Boos, Florence S. The Juvenilia of William Morris. vi, 90p. 1983. 6.00x (ISBN 0-931332-06-0); pap. 4.00x (ISBN 0-931332-05-2). Wedgestone Pr.

--The Poetry of Dante G. Rossetti: A Critical Reading & Source Study. (Studies in English Literature: No. 104). 1976. text ed. 32.00x (ISBN 90-2793-471-1). Mouton.

Boose, Jeanne, jt. auth. see Witt, Beth.

Booser, E. R., ed. CRC Handbook of Lubrication: Theory & Practice of Tribology, Vol. II. 704p. 1984. 115.00 (ISBN 0-8493-3902-2). CRC Pr.

Boos-Hamburger, H. Creative Power of Colour. 1973. lib. bdg. 79.95 (ISBN 0-87968-488-7). Krishna Pr.

Booss, B. & Bleecker, D. D. Topology & Analysis. Mader, A., tr. from Ger. (Universitext Ser.). (Illus.). xvi, 451p. 1985. 34.00 (ISBN 0-387-96112-7). Springer-Verlag.

Booss, Bernhelm & Niss, Mogens. Mathematics & the Real World: Proceedings of an International Workshop, Dennmark. (Interdisciplinary Systems Research: No. 68). 136p. 1979. pap. 25.95x (ISBN 0-8176-1079-0). Birkhauser.

Booss, C., ed. Works of Louisa May Alcott. (Avenel Readers Library). (Illus.). 800p. 1982. 7.98 (ISBN 0-517-37167-7, Avenel); jacketed ed. 7.98 (ISBN 0-517-37146-4). Outlet Bk Co.

Booss, C. & Horowitz, P., eds. Jack London Series II. (Avenel Readers Library). (Illus.). 720p. 1982. 6.98 (ISBN 0-517-38720-4, Avenel); jacketed ed. 6.98 (ISBN 0-517-38581-3). Outlet Bk Co.

Boot, F. Illustrations of the Genus Carex: 1858-1867, 4 pts. in 1. (Illus.). 1968. 112.00 (ISBN 3-7682-0553-3). Lubrecht & Cramer.

Boot, H. M. The Commercial Crisis of Eighteen Forty-Seven. (Occasional Papers in Economic & Social History: No. 11). 105p. 1984. pap. text ed. 16.25x (ISBN 0-85958-442-9, Pub. by U Hull England). Humanities.

Boot, Kelvin. The Nocturnal Naturalist. (Illus.). 208p. 1985. 17.50 (ISBN 0-7153-8421-X). David & Charles.

Boot, R. L., et al. Behavioural Sciences for Managers. 1977. 35.00x (ISBN 0-7131-3382-1); pap. 21.00x (ISBN 0-7131-3383-X). Intl Ideas.

Boot, William. Carrot Cake Cookbook: Forty-Five Varieties. 24p. 1981. pap. 3.00 (ISBN 0-938592-01-7). Harriets Kitchen.

--Harriet's Sugar-Free Cookbook. 48p. 1984. pap. 5.95 (ISBN 0-938592-00-9). Harriets Kitchen.

--Harriet's Zucchini Lovers' Cookbook. (Illus.). 260p. 1983. pap. 6.95 (ISBN 0-938592-03-3). Harriet's Kitchen.

Booth. Nurses Handbook of Investigations. 224p. 1982. pap. text ed. 12.95 (ISBN 0-06-318235-1, Pub. by Har-Row Ltd England). Har-Row.

--Omnibooth: The Best of George Booth. (Illus.). 256p. 1984. pap. 18.95 (ISBN 0-312-92613-8). Congdon & Weed.

Booth, jt. auth. see Roderman.

Booth, A. E. Ministry of Peter, John & Paul. 1982. pap. 1.25 (ISBN 0-88172-004-6). Believers Bkshelf.

Booth, Abrh. The Reign of Grace. 5.95 (ISBN 0-685-88390-6). Reiner.

Booth, Ada. Get More from Your IBM-PC & PCjr & Save Money. (Illus.). 224p. 1984. pap. 8.95 (ISBN 0-86582-163-1, EN79215). Enrich.

Booth, Alan & Higgins, Douglas. Human Service Planning & Evaluation for Hard Times. 214p. 1984. 23.50x (ISBN 0-398-04979-3). C C Thomas.

Booth, Alan, jt. ed. see Edwards, John.

Booth, Alan R. Swaziland: Tradition & Change in a Southern African Kingdom. LC 83-6511. (Profiles-Nations of Contemporary Africa). 144p. 1984. lib. bdg. 22.00x (ISBN 0-86531-233-8). Westview.

Booth, Andrew B., compiled by. Records of Louisiana Confederate Soldiers & Louisiana Confederate Commands, 3 vols. LC 84-22844. 1985. Repr. of 1920 ed. Set. 187.50 (ISBN 0-87152-400-7). Vols. I & II (ISBN 0-87152-401-5). Vol. III, Bk. I (ISBN 0-87152-402-3). Vol. III, Bk. II (ISBN 0-87152-403-1). Reprint.

Booth, Anne & Sundrum, R. M. Labor Absorption in Agriculture. (Illus.). 1984. 29.95x (ISBN 0-19-877205-X); pap. 13.95x (ISBN 0-19-877204-1). Oxford U Pr.

Booth, Bradford & Jones, C. E. Concordance to the Poetical Works of Edgar Allen Poe. 19.00 (ISBN 0-8446-1083-6). Peter Smith.

Booth, Bradford A. Anthony Trollope: Aspects of His Life & Art. LC 77-18822. 1978. Repr. of 1958 ed. lib. bdg. 24.75x (ISBN 0-313-20203-6, BOAT). Greenwood.

Booth, Bradford A., ed. see Trollope, Anthony.

Booth, C. Fusarium: A Laboratory Guide to the Identification of the Major Species. 58p. 1977. 32.75x (ISBN 0-85198-383-9, Pub. by CAB Bks England). State Mutual Bk.

--The Genus Fusarium. 237p. 1971. 59.00x (ISBN 0-85198-395-2, Pub. by CAB Bks England). State Mutual Bk.

Booth, C., jt. ed. see Johnston, A.

Booth, Carlton. On the Mountain Top. 224p. 1984. pap. 6.95 (ISBN 0-8423-4743-7). Tyndale.

Booth, Catherine. The Story. pap. 3.95 (ISBN 0-686-27773-2). Schmul Pub Co.

Booth, Charles. The Aged Poor in England & Wales. LC 79-56948. (The English Working Class Ser.). 1980. lib. bdg. 53.00 (ISBN 0-8240-0103-6). Garland Pub.

Booth, Charles & Esche, Sharon. How to Cut, Curl & Care for Your Hair. Friedman, Arlene, ed. (Illus.). 113p. 1985. pap. 8.95 (ISBN 0-02-079450-9, Collier). Macmillan.

Booth, Charles, et al. Life & Labour of the People in London, 1890-1900, 17 vols. LC 76-113561. Repr. of 1904 ed. Set. 502.50 (ISBN 0-404-00940-9); write for info. AMS Pr.

Booth, Chris, et al. The Birds of Orkney. 298p. 60.00x (ISBN 0-907618-07-3, Pub. by Orkney Pr Uk). State Mutual Bk.

Booth, Christopher C., ed. see Fothergill, John.

Booth, Cindy. Getting Your Child into TV Commercials. Rev. ed. LC 79-26106. 39p. 1982. pap. 2.95 (ISBN 0-87576-087-2). Pilot Bks.

Booth, D. A., ed. Hunger Models: Computable Theory of Feeding Control. 1978. 76.00 (ISBN 0-12-115950-7). Acad Pr.

Booth, David & Sorj, Bernardo, eds. Military Reformism & Social Classes: The Peruvian Experience, 1968-80. LC 82-23152. 225p. 1983. 25.00 (ISBN 0-312-53238-5). St Martin.

Booth, Don & Booth, Jonathan. Sun-Earth Buffering & Superinsulation. LC 83-72283. (Illus.). 1983. 19.95 (ISBN 0-9604422-4-3); pap. 12.95 (ISBN 0-9604422-3-5). Comm Builders.

Booth, Don, et al. Sun-Earth Buffering & Superinsulation. Wolf, Ray, ed. (Illus.). 232p. 1984. pap. 12.95 (ISBN 0-9604422-3-5). Rodale Pr Inc.

Booth, Dorothy, jt. auth. see Williams, Margaret.

Booth, E. Donald, jt. ed. see Locke, William N.

Booth, Edward. Aristotelian Aporetic Ontology in Islamic & Christian Thinkers. LC 82-22068. (Cambridge Studies in Medieval Life & Thought: No. 20). 368p. 1984. 69.50 (ISBN 0-521-25254-7). Cambridge U Pr.

Booth, Edward C. Miss Parkworth, & Three Short Stories. facs. ed. LC 72-125204. (Short Story Index Reprint Ser). 1924. 17.00 (ISBN 0-8369-3571-3). Ayer Co Pubs.

Booth, Edward T. God Made the Country. facsimile ed. LC 77-134055. (Essay Index Reprint Ser). Repr. of 1946 ed. 23.50 (ISBN 0-8369-2486-X). Ayer Co Pubs.

--God Made the Country: Lady Mary Wortley, William Cowper, Wordsworth, Carlyle, Emerson, Thoreau, Melville. 1946. Repr. 25.00 (ISBN 0-8274-2417-5). R West.

Booth, Edwin. The Colorado Gun. 224p. pap. 2.25 (ISBN 0-8439-2296-6, Leisure Bks). Dorchester Pub Co.

--Leadville. (Orig.). 1981. pap. 1.95 (ISBN 0-505-51643-8, Pub. by Tower Bks). Dorchester Pub Co.

--Leadville. 192p. 1986. pap. 2.25 (ISBN 0-8439-2327-X, Leisure Bks). Dorchester Pub Co.

--Rebel's Return. (Orig.). 1981. pap. 1.95 (ISBN 0-505-51686-1, Pub. by Tower Bks). Dorchester Pub Co.

Booth, Edwin & Ruggles, Eleanor. Prince of Players. 20.95 (ISBN 0-89190-565-0, Pub. by Am Repr). Amereon Ltd.

Booth, Elizabeth M., jt. auth. see Dickerson, John W.

Booth, Emmons R. History of Osteopathy, & Twentieth Century Medical Practice: Memorial Edition. LC 74-29281. Repr. of 1924 ed. 60.00 (ISBN 0-404-13401-7). AMS Pr.

Booth, Ernest S. Field Record for Birds. (YA) (gr. 7 up). 1960. pap. 2.00 (ISBN 0-911080-03-1). Outdoor Pict.

--How to Know the Mammals. 4th ed. (Picture Key Nature Ser.). 220p. 1982. wire coil write for info. (ISBN 0-697-04781-4). Wm C Brown.

--Life List for Birds. (YA) (gr. 7 up). 1969. pap. 2.00 (ISBN 0-911080-04-X). Outdoor Pict.

Booth, Ernest S., jt. auth. see Chiasson, Robert B.

Booth, Eugene. At the Beach. LC 77-7659. (A Raintree Spotlight Book). (Illus.). (gr. k-3). 1977. PLB 12.85 (ISBN 0-8393-0111-1). Raintree Pubs.

--At the Beach. LC 77-7659. (Spotlight Ser.). (Illus.). 24p. (gr. k-3). 1985. pap. 9.27 (ISBN 0-8393-0161-8). Raintree Pubs.

--At the Circus. LC 77-7946. (A Raintree Spotlight Book). (Illus.). (gr. k-3). 1977. PLB 12.85 (ISBN 0-8393-0112-X). Raintree Pubs.

--At the Circus. LC 77-7946. (Spotlight Ser.). (Illus.). 24p. (gr. k-3). 1985. pap. 9.27 (ISBN 0-8393-0162-6). Raintree Pubs.

--At the Fair. LC 77-7961. (A Raintree Spotlight Book). (Illus.). (gr. k-3). 1977. PLB 12.85 (ISBN 0-8393-0114-6). Raintree Pubs.

--At the Fair. LC 77-7961. (Spotlight Ser.). (Illus.). 24p. (gr. k-3). 1985. pap. 9.27 (ISBN 0-8393-0163-4). Raintree Pubs.

--At the Zoo. LC 77-7627. (A Raintree Spotlight Book). (Illus.). (gr. k-3). 1977. PLB 12.85 (ISBN 0-8393-0107-3). Raintree Pubs.

--At the Zoo. LC 77-76287. (Spotlight Ser.). (Illus.). 24p. (gr. k-3). 1985. pap. 9.27 (ISBN 0-8393-0164-2). Raintree Pubs.

--In the Air. LC 77-7984. (A Raintree Spotlight Book). (Illus.). (gr. k-3). 1977. PLB 12.85 (ISBN 0-8393-0105-7). Raintree Pubs.

--In the Air. LC 77-7984. (Spotlight Ser.). (Illus.). 24p. (gr. k-3). 1985. pap. 9.27 (ISBN 0-8393-0165-0). Raintree Pubs.

--In the City. LC 77-7949. (A Raintree Spotlight Book). (Illus.). (gr. k-3). 1977. PLB 12.85 (ISBN 0-8393-0109-X). Raintree Pubs.

--In the City. LC 77-7949. (Spotlight Ser.). (Illus.). 24p. (gr. k-3). 1985. pap. 9.27 (ISBN 0-8393-0166-9). Raintree Pubs.

--In the Garden. LC 77-7628. (A Raintree Spotlight Book). (Illus.). (gr. k-3). 1977. PLB 12.85 (ISBN 0-8393-0115-4). Raintree Pubs.

--In the Garden. LC 77-7628. (Spotlight Ser.). (Illus.). 24p. (gr. k-3). 1985. pap. 9.27 (ISBN 0-8393-0167-7). Raintree Pubs.

--In the Jungle. LC 77-7947. (A Raintree Spotlight Book). (Illus.). (gr. k-3). 1977. PLB 12.85 (ISBN 0-8393-0104-9). Raintree Pubs.

--In the Jungle. LC 77-7947. (Spotlight Ser.). (Illus.). 24p. (gr. k-3). 1985. pap. 9.27 (ISBN 0-8393-0168-5). Raintree Pubs.

--In the Park. LC 77-7622. (A Raintree Spotlight Book). (Illus.). (gr. k-3). 1977. PLB 12.85 (ISBN 0-8393-0106-5). Raintree Pubs.

--In the Park. LC 77-7622. (Spotlight Ser.). (Illus.). 24p. (gr. k-3). 1985. pap. 9.75g (ISBN 0-8393-0169-3). Raintree Pubs.

--On the Farm. LC 77-7965. (A Raintree Spotlight Book). (Illus.). (gr. k-3). 1977. PLB 12.85 (ISBN 0-8393-0113-8). Raintree Pubs.

--On the Farm. LC 77-7965. (Spotlight Ser.). (Illus.). 24p. (gr. k-3). 1985. pap. 9.27 (ISBN 0-8393-0170-7). Raintree Pubs.

--Under the Ground. LC 77-8037. (A Raintree Spotlight Book). (Illus.). (gr. k-3). 1977. PLB 12.85 (ISBN 0-8393-0110-3). Raintree Pubs.

--Under the Ground. LC 77-8037. (Spotlight Ser.). (Illus.). 24p. (gr. k-3). 1985. pap. 9.27 (ISBN 0-8393-0171-5). Raintree Pubs.

--Under the Ocean. LC 77-7983. (A Raintree Spotlight Book). (Illus.). (gr. k-3). 1977. PLB 12.85 (ISBN 0-8393-0108-1). Raintree Pubs.

--Under the Ocean. LC 77-7983. (Spotlight Ser.). (Illus.). 24p. (gr. k-3). 1985. pap. 9.27 (ISBN 0-8393-0172-3). Raintree Pubs.

Booth, Evelyn. All about the Cavalier King Charles Spaniel. (All About Ser.). (Illus.). 176p. 1984. 14.95 (ISBN 0-7207-1452-4). Merrimack Pub Cir.

Booth, Frank. It's Easy to Play Ballet Music. 1983. pap. 4.95 (ISBN 0-7119-0287-9). Music Sales.

--It's Easy to Play Opera. pap. 4.95 (ISBN 0-8256-2242-5). Music Sales.

--It's Easy to Play Ragtime. 1981. pap. 4.95 (ISBN 0-8256-2240-9). Music Sales.

Booth, Frank V., jt. auth. see Dean, J. Michael.

Booth, Gavin. Alexander Coachbuilders. 192p. 1981. 45.00x (ISBN 0-903839-38-5, Pub. by Transport). State Mutual Bk.

Booth, George. Consideration upon the Institution of Marriage. LC 83-48617. (Marriage, Sex & the Family in England Ser.). 228p. 1985. lib. bdg. 30.00 (ISBN 0-8240-5906-9). Garland Pub.

--Pussycats Need Love, Too. 128p. 1981. pap. 6.95 (ISBN 0-380-55533-6, 55533-6). Avon.

--Rehearsal's Off! (Illus.). 1977. pap. 5.95 (ISBN 0-380-01719-9, 60574-0). Avon.

--Think Good Thoughts about a Pussycat. (Illus.). 1976. pap. 5.95 (ISBN 0-380-00762-2, 60582-1). Avon.

Booth, George, jt. auth. see Morgan, Henry.

Booth, George, et al, eds. Animals Animals Animals. LC 79-1653. (Illus.). 1979. 12.50i (ISBN 0-06-010429-5, HarpT). Har-Row.

Booth, George C. The Food & Drink of Mexico. LC 75-39349. (Cookbook Ser.). (Illus.). 192p. 1976. pap. 3.50 (ISBN 0-486-23314-6). Dover.

--The Food & Drink of Mexico. 12.75 (ISBN 0-8446-5481-7). Peter Smith.

--Mexico's School-Made Society. LC 71-94601. Repr. of 1941 ed. lib. bdg. 15.00x (ISBN 0-8371-2546-4, BOMS). Greenwood.

Booth, Gotthard. The Cancer Epidemic: Shadow of the Conquest of Nature. LC 59-7362. (Illus.). 277p. 1980. 49.95x (ISBN 0-88946-625-4). E Mellen.

Booth, Grayce M. The Design of Complex Information Systems: Common Sense Methods for Success. (Illus.). 288p. 1983. 32.95 (ISBN 0-07-006506-3). McGraw.

--The Distributed System Environment: Some Practical Approaches. (Illus.). 288p. 1980. 32.95 (ISBN 0-07-006507-1). McGraw.

Booth, Henry. Account of the Liverpool & Manchester Railway. (Illus.). 104p. 1969. Repr. of 1830 ed. 25.00x (ISBN 0-7146-1433-5, F Cass Co). Biblio Dist.

Booth, Howard J. Edwin Diller Starbuck: Pioneer in the Psychology of Religion. LC 80-5731. 304p. 1981. lib. bdg. 29.75 (ISBN 0-8191-1702-1); pap. text ed. 15.25 (ISBN 0-8191-1703-X). U Pr of Amer.

Booth, I. Pediatrics. (Pocket Picture Guides for Nurses Ser.). 100p. 1984. text ed. 11.95 (ISBN 0-683-00922-2). Williams & Wilkins.

Booth, J., ed. see Ovid.

Booth, J. E. Textile Mathematics, Vol. 1. 162p. 1975. 40.00x (ISBN 0-686-63802-6). State Mutual Bk.

--Textile Mathematics, Vol. 2. 213p. 1975. 40.00x (ISBN 0-686-63803-4). State Mutual Bk.

--Textile Mathematics, Vol. 3. 144p. 1977. 40.00x (ISBN 0-686-63804-2). State Mutual Bk.

Booth, J. R., ed. One Banana Step... (Language Patterns Impressions). (gr. 5). 1978. text ed. 7.44 (ISBN 0-03-923084-8, Pub. by HR&W Canada); Tchr's Resource Bk. tchr's ed. 11.25 (ISBN 0-03-923087-2); Skills Bk. 3.75 (ISBN 0-03-923093-7); Idea Bk. 4.37 (ISBN 0-03-923090-2). HR&W.

--One Potato, Two Potato... (Language Patterns Impressions). (gr. 6). 1978. text ed. 7.44 (ISBN 0-03-923085-6, Pub by HR&W Canada); Tchr's Resource Bk. 11.25 (ISBN 0-03-923088-0); Skills Bk. 3.75 (ISBN 0-03-923094-5); Idea Bk. 4.38 (ISBN 0-03-923091-0). HR&W.

--Ready or Not. (Language Patterns Impressions). (gr. 4). 1978. text ed. 7.44 (ISBN 0-03-923083-X, Pub. by HR&W Canada); Tchr's Resource Bk. 11.25 (ISBN 0-03-923086-4); Skills Bk. 3.75 (ISBN 0-03-923092-9); Idea Bk. 4.38 (ISBN 0-03-923089-9). HR&W.

Booth, Jack, ed. Inside Outside. (Language Patterns Impressions). (Illus.). 1978. text ed. 9.00 (ISBN 0-03-920023-X, HR&W Canada); reading skill 4.25 (ISBN 0-03-920027-2); tchr's ed 11.88 (ISBN 0-03-920029-9); language skills wkbk. 4.10 (ISBN 0-03-920025-6). HR&W.

Booth, James. Alternative Health Care & Labor Force Protection. 60p. 4.20 (ISBN 0-318-16241-5). Public Int Econ.

--Taxonomy of Incentive Approaches for Stimulating Innovation. 82p. 7.00 (ISBN 0-318-16306-3, E-11). Public Int Econ.

--Writers & Politics in Nigeria. LC 80-17670. (Writers & Politics Ser.). 128p. 1981. text ed. 27.50x (ISBN 0-8419-0650-5, Africana); pap. text ed. 16.50x (ISBN 0-8419-0651-3). Holmes & Meier.

Booth, James & Ferguson, Allen. An Evaluation of Trends in Hospital Utilization & Nurse Staffing for Estimating the Parameters "Alpha" & "Beta" of the SOAR Model. 98p. 8.00 (ISBN 0-318-16270-9, C-17). Public Int Econ.

Booth, James, jt. auth. see Buchanan, Steve.

Booth, James, jt. auth. see Cook, Zena.

Booth, Janine, tr. see Scheller, William G.

Booth, Jeanette H., et al. Creative Museum Methods & Educational Techniques. (Illus.). 170p. 1982. 18.50x (ISBN 0-398-04694-8). C C Thomas.

Booth, Joan, tr. Ovid: Amores, Bk. II. 220p. 1983. text ed. 29.50x (ISBN 0-85668-174-1, 41067, Pub. by Aris & Phillips England); pap. text ed. 15.00x. Humanities.

Booth, John. Psychic Paradoxes. LC 84-60005. (Illus.). xviii, 243p. 1984. casebound 33.50 (ISBN 0-943230-02-0). Ridgeway Pr.

Booth, John A. The End & the Beginning: The Nicaraguan Revolution. 2nd ed. LC 82-2690. (Latin America & the Caribbean Special Studies). 277p. 1985. 38.50x (ISBN 0-89158-939-2); pap. 14.95x (ISBN 0-86531-148-X). Westview.

Booth, John A. & Walker, Thomas W. Understanding Central America. 130p. 1986. lib. bdg. 26.50x (ISBN 0-8133-0002-9); pap. text ed. 12.95x (ISBN 0-8133-0003-7). Westview.

Booth, John A. & Seligson, Mitchell A., eds. Political Participation in Latin America: Citizen & State, Vol. 1. LC 77-16666. 260p. 1978. 34.50x (ISBN 0-8419-0334-4); pap. text ed. 14.00x (ISBN 0-8419-0376-X). Holmes & Meier.

--Political Participation in Latin America: Vol. 2, Politics & the Poor. LC 77-16666. 262p. 1979. 34.50 (ISBN 0-8419-0405-7); pap. 14.00 (ISBN 0-8419-0406-5). Holmes & Meier.

Booth, John A., jt. ed. see Seligson, Mitchell A.

Booth, John N. Booths in History: Their Roots & Lives, Encounters & Achievements. LC 82-5421. (Illus.). 243p. 1982. text ed. 28.95x (ISBN 0-943230-00-4); pap. text ed. 16.95x (ISBN 0-943230-01-2). Ridgeway Pr.

Booth, Jonathan, jt. auth. see Booth, Don.

Booth, Julianne. Bible Verses to Remember. (gr. 2-5). 1982. pap. 2.95 (ISBN 0-570-04061-2, 56-1364). Concordia.

--Books of the New Testament. (Arch Book Supplement Ser.). 1981. pap. 0.99 (ISBN 0-570-06150-4, 59-1305). Concordia.

--Parables of Jesus. (Arch Bks.). 1982. pap. 0.99 (ISBN 0-570-06163-6, 59-1309). Concordia.

Booth, K. M., ed. Dictionary of Refrigeration & Air Conditioning. 315p. 1971. 27.75 (ISBN 0-444-20069-X, Pub. by Elsevier Applied Sci England). Elsevier.

Booth, Kellogg S., jt. auth. see Beatty, John C.

Booth, Ken. Law, Force & Diplomacy at Sea. 250p. 1985. 25.00x (ISBN 0-04-341027-8); pap. text ed. 12.50 (ISBN 0-04-341028-6). Allen Unwin.

--Navies & Foreign Policies. LC 79-2254. 1979. text ed. 29.50x (ISBN 0-8419-0518-5). Holmes & Meier.

--Strategy & Ethnocentrism. LC 78-24526. 191p. 1979. text ed. 32.50x (ISBN 0-8419-0467-7). Holmes & Meier.

Booth, Ken & Wright, Moorhead, eds. American Thinking about Peace & War: New Essays on American Thought & Attitudes. LC 78-24393. 240p. 1978. text ed. 28.50x (ISBN 0-06-490581-0, 06356). B&N Imports.

Booth, L. Venchael, ed. Crowned with Glory & Honor: The Life of Rev. Lacey Kirk Williams. 1978. 8.00 (ISBN 0-682-48939-5). Exposition Pr FL.

Booth, Larry, jt. auth. see Weinstein, Robert A.

Booth, Leo. Walking on Water. 180p. (Orig.). 1985. pap. 8.95 (ISBN 0-932194-28-1). Health Comm.

Booth, Leseley R. Children's Strategies & Errors: Algebra. 156p. 1984. pap. 18.00X (ISBN 0-7005-0636-5, Pub. by NFER Nelson UK). Taylor & Francis.

Booth, Lesley R. Algebra: Children's Strategies & Errors. 156p. 1984. 20.00 (ISBN 0-7005-0636-5). Taylor & Francis.

Booth, Letha & Dutton, Joan P. Williamsburg Cookbook. rev. ed. (Illus.). 1976. 9.95 (ISBN 0-03-086704-5, Pub by Williamsburg). HR&W.

--Williamsburg Cookbook. enl. & rev. ed. LC 75-2328. (Illus.). 172p. (Orig.). 1975. pap. 6.95 (ISBN 0-910412-92-8). Williamsburg.

Booth, M. L., tr. from Fr. Marble Workers' Manual. (Illus.). 295p. 1984. pap. text ed. 25.00 (ISBN 0-87556-352-X). Saifer.

Booth, M. L., tr. see Cochin, Augustin.

Booth, M. R., et al. Revels History of Drama in English, Vol. 6: 1750-1880. LC 74-15178. (Illus.). 250p. 1975. 19.95x (ISBN 0-416-13070-4, NO. 2103). Methuen Inc.

Booth, Marcella, ed. A Catalogue of the Louis Zukofsky Manuscript Collection. LC 70-38572. (Tower Bibliographical Ser.: No. 11). (Illus.). 1975. 18.50 (ISBN 0-87959-038-6). U of Tex H Ransom Ctr.

Booth, Mark, ed. Christian Short Stories: A Contemporary Anthology. 224p. 1984. 16.95 (ISBN 0-8245-0673-1); pap. 9.95 (ISBN 0-8245-0674-X). Crossroad NY.

Booth, Mark, ed. see Auden, W. H., et al.

Booth, Mark Haworth, intro. by. Photographs By Bill Brandt. (Illus.). 16p. 1980. pap. 4.25 (ISBN 0-88397-035-X). Intl Exhibit Foun.

Booth, Mark W. American Popular Music: A Reference Guide. LC 82-21062. (American Popular Culture Ser.). xvi, 212p. 1983. lib. bdg. 29.95 (ISBN 0-313-21305-4, BPM/). Greenwood.

--The Experience of Songs. LC 81-972. (Illus.). 226p. 1981. 21.00x (ISBN 0-300-02622-6). Yale U Pr.

Booth, Martin. Brevities. 1974. pap. 6.00 (ISBN 0-685-40884-1). Elizabeth Pr.

--British Poetry Nineteen Sixty-Four to Nineteen Eighty-Four: Driving Through the Barricades. 288p. 1985. 23.95x (ISBN 0-7100-9606-2). Routledge & Kegan.

--Devil's Wine. 112p. 1980. text ed. 16.75x (ISBN 0-86140-044-5); pap. text ed. 9.00x. Humanities.

--The Knotting Sequence. 1977. bound in boards, slipcased 16.00 (ISBN 0-685-88988-2); in wraps 8.00 (ISBN 0-685-88989-0). Elizabeth Pr.

--Stalks of Jade. 1976. pap. 2.00 (ISBN 0-685-79257-9, Pub. by Menard Pr). Small Pr Dist.

--Yogh. new ed. 20p. 1975. nos. 1-50 signed 10.00x (ISBN 0-915408-04-X); nos. 50-150 unsigned 2.50 (ISBN 0-915408-03-1); ltd. to 250 unsigned & unnumbered 1.50 (ISBN 0-915408-02-3). Ally Pr.

Booth, Martin, jt. ed. see MacBeth, George.

Booth, Martin, et al. Bismarck. Yapp, Martin & Killingray, Margaret, eds. (World History Ser.). (Illus.). 32p. (gr. 10). 1980. lib. bdg. 6.95 (ISBN 0-89908-048-0); pap. text ed. 2.45 (ISBN 0-89908-023-5). Greenhaven.

Booth, Mary L., tr. see Cochin, Augustin.

Booth, Mary L., tr. see De Gasparin, Agenor.

Booth, Mary L., tr. see Mace, Jean.

Booth, Meyrick, tr. see Hess, Ilse & Hess, Rudolf.

Booth, Michael. T. W. Robertson: Six Plays. 323p. 1981. text ed. 21.50x (ISBN 0-906399-16-5, Pub. by Amber Lane England). Humanities.

Booth, Michael R. Prefaces to English Nineteenth-Century Theatre. 231p. 1981. text ed. 33.00x (ISBN 0-7190-0813-1, Pub. by Manchester England). Humanities.

Booth, Michael R., ed. English Plays of the Nineteenth Century, 5 vols. Incl. Vol. 3. Comedians. 49.00 (ISBN 0-19-812465-1); Vol. 4. Farces, 1973. 55.00x (ISBN 0-19-812466-X). (Illus.). 1969. Oxford U Pr.

Booth, N., ed. Acoustical Holography, Vol. 6. LC 69-12533. 771p. 1975. 95.00x (ISBN 0-306-37726-8, Plenum Pr). Plenum Pub.

Booth, Newell S. African Religions: A Symposium. LC 73-88062. 390p. 1977. text ed. 21.50x (ISBN 0-88357-012-2). Nok Pubs.

Booth, Nicholas H. & McDonald, Leslie E. Veterinary Pharmacology & Therapeutics. 5th ed. (Illus.). 1134p. 1982. text ed. 61.95x (ISBN 0-8138-1740-4). Iowa St U Pr.

Booth, Norman & Hiss, James. Residential Site Design. 1985. text ed. 21.95 (ISBN 0-8359-6651-8). Reston.

Booth, Norman K. Basic Elements of Landscape Architectural Design. 315p. 1983. 42.00 (ISBN 0-444-00766-0). Elsevier.

Booth, Nyla. Room for One More. 160p. 1984. 3.50 (ISBN 0-8423-5711-4). Tyndale.

Booth, P. H. W. The Financial Administration of the Lordship & County of Chester, 1272-1377. 192p. 1982. 20.00 (ISBN 0-7190-1337-2, Pub. by Manchester Univ Pr). Longwood Pub Group.

Booth, Pat. Palm Beach. 1985. 14.95 (ISBN 0-517-55844-0). Crown.

--Self Portrait. (Illus.). 128p. 1984. 30.00 (ISBN 0-7043-2398-2, Pub. by Quartet Bks). Merrimack Pub Cir.

Booth, Pat, ed. Master Photographers: The World's Great Photographers on Their Art & Technique. (Illus.). 1983. 25.00 (ISBN 0-517-55011-3, C N Potter Bks); pap. 14.95 (ISBN 0-517-55012-1). Crown.

Booth, Philip. Available Light. LC 75-38875. 84p. 1976. 9.95 (ISBN 0-670-14310-3). Viking.

--Before Sleep. 96p. 1980. 12.95 (ISBN 0-670-15529-2). Viking.

--Social Security in America. LC 73-620091. (Policy Papers in Human Resources & Industrial Relations Ser.: No. 19). 180p. 1973. 9.50x (ISBN 0-87736-119-3); pap. 4.50x (ISBN 0-87736-120-7). U of Mich Inst Labor.

Booth, Philip, ed. see Social Security Conference, 6th.

Booth, Philip, ed. see Social Security Conference, 7th.

Booth, R. G., jt. ed. see Herzka, A.

Booth, Richard. Book Collecting. LC 76-19637. (Collector Ser.). 300p. 1976. 15.00 (ISBN 0-87637-336-8). Hse of Collectibles.

Booth, Robert. Boston's Freedom Trail. LC 81-81853. (Illus.). 104p. (Orig.). pap. 6.95 (ISBN 0-87106-954-7). Globe Pequot.

Booth, Robert E., et al, eds. Culturally Disadvantaged: A Keyword-Out-Of-Context Index. LC 66-2791. 813p. 1967. 30.00x (ISBN 0-8143-1304-3). Wayne St U Pr.

Booth, S., et al, eds. Inspection & Measurement. (Engineering Craftsmen: No. H26). (Illus.). 1969. spiral bdg. 39.95x (ISBN 0-89563-008-7). Intl Ideas.

Booth, Sally S. Seeds of Anger: Revolts in America, 1670-1771. 1977. 10.95 (ISBN 0-8038-6742-5). Hastings.

--Women of Seventy-Six. (gr. 4 up). 1974. 9.95g (ISBN 0-8038-8066-9). Hastings.

Booth, Stanley. A Centenary Tribute to Sir Alfred Munnings 1878-1959: An Appreciation of the Artist & a Selection of His Paintings. (Illus.). 218p. 1978. 120.00 (ISBN 0-85667-043-X, Pub. by Sotheby Pubns England). Biblio Dist.

--Dance with the Devil: The Rolling Stones & Their Times. LC 84-42517. (Illus.). 379p. 1984. 16.45 (ISBN 0-394-53488-3). Random.

--The True Adventures of the Rolling Stones. 600p. 1985. 4.95 (ISBN 0-394-74110-2, Vin). Random.

Booth, Stephen. King Lear, Macbeth, Indefinition, & Tragedy. LC 83-42875. 176p. 1983. 18.00x (ISBN 0-300-02850-4). Yale U Pr.

Booth, Stephen, commentary by. Shakespeare's Sonnets. LC 76-56161. 1977. 45.00x (ISBN 0-300-01959-9); pap. 14.95 (ISBN 0-300-02495-9). Yale U Pr.

Booth, Sterling & Vance, Robert W., eds. Applications of Cryogenic Technology, Vol. 8. LC 68-57815. (Cryogenic Society of America Applications of Cryogenic Technology Ser.). (Illus.). 1976. text ed. 30.00x (ISBN 0-87936-010-0). Scholium Intl.

Booth, Sterling H., ed. see Conference of the Cryogenic Society of America, 1973.

Booth, Sterling R., Jr. Allergy Cures Your Allergist Never Mentioned. LC 80-20698. 1985. 16.95 (ISBN 0-87949-191-4). Ashley Bks.

Booth, Steve. Championship Enduro. (Illus.). 128p. 1977. pap. 6.95 (ISBN 0-941178-00-5). Paragon Prods.

Booth, Taylor. Introduction to Computer Engineering: Hardware & Software Design. 3rd ed. LC 84-2252. 656p. 1984. 34.95 (ISBN 0-471-87321-7). Wiley.

Booth, Taylor L. & Chien, Yi-Tzuu. Computing: Fundamentals & Applications. LC 73-20157. 497p. 1974. 40.95x (ISBN 0-471-08847-1). Wiley.

Booth, Ted. High Water over the Road: Seven Generations of an American Family. LC 68-56355. (Illus.). pap. 59.00 (ISBN 0-317-09106-9, 2012910). Bks Demand UMI.

Booth, Thornton Y. Mastering the Event: Commitment to Fact in George Meredith's Fiction. 66p. (Orig.). 1967. pap. 3.50 (ISBN 0-87421-033-X). Utah St U Pr.

Booth, Tim. Home Truths. 220p. 1985. pap. text ed. write for info. (ISBN 0-566-00975-7). Gower Pub Co.

Booth, Tony. Growing Up in Society. (Essential Psychology Ser.). 1975. pap. 4.50x (ISBN 0-416-81900-1, NO. 2606). Methuen Inc.

Booth, Tony & Potts, Patricia, eds. Integrating Special Education. 224p. 1984. 34.95x (ISBN 0-631-13195-7); pap. 14.95x (ISBN 0-631-13196-5). Basil Blackwell.

Booth, Tony & Statham, June, eds. The Nature of Special Education: People, Places & Change. 464p. 1982. pap. 12.00 (ISBN 0-7099-0657-9, Pub. by Croom Helm Ltd). Longwood Pub Group.

Booth, V. Hartley. British Extradition Law & Procedure, Vol. II. 604p. 1981. 35.00 (ISBN 90-286-0079-5). Sijthoff & Noordhoff.

Booth, Verne H. & Bloom, Mortimer. Physical Science: A Study of Matter & Energy. 3rd ed. (Illus.). 800p. 1972. text ed. write for info. (ISBN 0-02-312280-3, 31228). Macmillan.

Booth, Vernon. Communicating in Science: Writing & Speaking. 80p. 1985. pap. 6.95 (ISBN 0-521-27771-X). Cambridge U Pr.

--Writing a Scientific Paper & Speaking at Scientific Meetings. 5th ed. 1981. 25.00x (ISBN 0-686-81318-9, Pub. by Biochemical England). State Mutual Bk.

Booth, Victor. We Piano Teachers. rev. ed. 135p. 1984. pap. 9.95 (ISBN 0-09-106191-1, Pub. by Hutchinson Educ). Longwood Pub Group.

Booth, W. Edwin. The Colorado Gun. (Orig.). 1981. pap. 1.75 (ISBN 0-505-51614-4, Pub. by Tower Bks). Dorchester Pub Co.

Booth, W. L. Police Management of Traffic Accident Prevention Programs. (Illus.). 384p. 1980. photocopy ed. 35.50x (ISBN 0-398-04008-7). C C Thomas.

Booth, Wayne C. Critical Understanding: The Powers & Limits of Pluralism. LC 78-15107. 1979. 22.50x (ISBN 0-226-06554-5, Phoen); pap. 8.95x (ISBN 0-226-06555-3). U of Chicago Pr.

--Modern Dogma & the Rhetoric of Assent. LC 73-89786. xviii, 236p. 1974. pap. 10.00x (ISBN 0-226-06572-3, P595, Phoen). U of Chicago Pr.

--Modern Dogma & the Rhetoric of Assent. LC 73-21601. (Ward-Phillips Lecture Ser.: Vol. 5). 240p. 1974. text ed. 19.95x (ISBN 0-268-00506-0, 85-05067). U of Notre Dame Pr.

--Now Don't Try to Reason with Me: Essays & Ironies for a Credulous Age. LC 73-12359. 1970. 9.50x (ISBN 0-226-06579-0, Phoen); pap. 2.95x (ISBN 0-226-06580-4, P461). U of Chicago Pr.

--Rhetoric of Fiction. 2nd ed. LC 82-13592. 1983. pap. 30.00x (ISBN 0-226-06556-1, Phoen). U of Chicago Pr.

--The Rhetoric of Fiction. 2nd ed. 576p. 1983. pap. 12.95x (ISBN 0-226-06558-8). U of Chicago Pr.

--A Rhetoric of Irony. LC 73-87298. xviii, 292p. 1975. 20.00x (ISBN 0-226-06552-9); pap. 11.00x (ISBN 0-226-06553-7, P641). U of Chicago Pr.

Booth, Wayne C. & Gregory, Marshall. The Harper & Row Reader. 752p. 1984. pap. text ed. 12.50 scp (ISBN 0-06-040845-6, HarpC); inst. manual avail. (ISBN 0-06-360850-2). Har-Row.

Booth, Wayne C., ed. Knowledge Most Worth Having. LC 66-23684. 1967. pap. 3.95x (ISBN 0-226-06576-6). U of Chicago Pr.

Booth, William. How to Preach. 84p. (Orig.). 1979. pap. 2.95 (ISBN 0-89216-026-8). Salvation Army.

--In Darkest England & the Way Out. LC 76-108240. (Patterson Smith Series in Criminology, Law Enforcement, & Social Problems: Publication No.142). 10.00x (ISBN 0-87585-142-8). Patterson Smith.

Booth, William D. Upgrading & Refurnishing the Older Fiberglass Sailboat. LC 84-46109. (Illus.). 352p. 1985. 24.50 (ISBN 0-87033-335-6). Cornell Maritime.

Booth, Zilpha M. Mommy, Don't Cry. (Orig.). 1982. pap. 9.00 (ISBN 0-914562-11-8). Merriam-Eddy.

Boothby, Daniel W. The Determinants of Earnings & Occupation for Young Women. LC 79-52687. (Outstanding Dissertations in Economics Ser.). 1983. lib. bdg. 24.00 (ISBN 0-8240-4150-X). Garland Pub.

Boothby, Guy. Dr. Nikola Returns. LC 80-22358. (Dr. Nikola, Master of Occult Mystery: No. 2). 256p. 1980. Repr. of 1976 ed. lib. bdg. 14.95x (ISBN 0-89370-634-5). Borgo Pr.

--Dr. Nikola Returns. (Dr. Nikola, Master of Occult Mystery No. 2). 256p. 1976. pap. 4.95 (ISBN 0-87877-034-8, X-34). Newcastle Pub.

--Enter Dr. Nikola! LC 80-22357. (Dr. Nikola, Master of Occult Mystery: No. 1). 256p. 1980. Repr. of 1975 ed. lib. bdg. 12.95x (ISBN 0-89370-632-9). Borgo Pr.

--Enter Dr. Nikola! (Dr. Nikola Ser: No. 1). 256p. 1975. pap. 4.95 (ISBN 0-87877-032-1, X-32). Newcastle Pub.

--Pharos, the Egyptian. Reginald, R. & Menville, Douglas, eds. LC 75-46256. (Supernatural & Occult & Fiction Ser.). (Illus.). 1976. Repr. of 1899 ed. lib. bdg. 30.00x (ISBN 0-405-08115-4). Ayer Co Pubs.

Boothby, William M. An Introduction to Differentiable Manifolds & Riemannian Geometry. (Pure & Applied Mathematics Ser.). 424p. 1975. Acad Pr.

Boothby, William M., et al, eds. Symmetric Spaces: Short Courses Presented at Washington University. LC 74-182213. (Pure & Applied Mathematics: No. 8). (Illus.). pap. 125.50 (ISBN 0-317-08008-3, 2021506). Bks Demand UMI.

Booth-Clibborn, Edward, ed. American Illustration III. 3rd ed. (Illus.). 292p. 1984. 40.00 (ISBN 0-8109-1821-8). Abrams.

--American Illustration, IV. (Illus.). 292p. 1985. 40.00 (ISBN 0-8109-1829-3). Abrams.

--American Illustration, 1982-1983. (Illus.). 292p. 1983. 37.50 (ISBN 0-8109-1802-1). Abrams.

--American Photography One. (Illus.). 228p. 1985. 40.00 (ISBN 0-8109-1830-7). Abrams.

--European Illustration. 10th ed. (Illus.). 192p. 1984. 45.00 (ISBN 0-8109-0869-7). Abrams.

--European Illustration. 11th ed. (Illus.). 248p. 1985. 45.00 (ISBN 0-8109-0871-9). Abrams.

--European Photography: 1983-84. (Illus.). 176p. 1985. 45.00 (ISBN 0-8109-0872-7). Abrams.

Boothe, J. H., jt. auth. see Hlavka, J. J.

Boothe, Norris, jt. auth. see CEP.

Boothe, Viva B. The Political Party As a Social Process. LC 73-19131. (Politics & People Ser.). (Illus.). 130p. 1974. Repr. 11.00 (ISBN 0-405-05856-X). Ayer Co Pubs.

Boothe, Viva B., ed. Women in the Modern World: (the Annals of the American Academy of Political & Social Science, Vol. 143, May, 1929) LC 74-3929. (Women in America Ser.). (Illus.). 404p. 1974. Repr. of 1929 ed. 29.00x (ISBN 0-405-06078-5). Ayer Co Pubs.

Boothrod, Rodney. Home Winemaking Techniques & Recipes. 160p. 1985. pap. 8.95 (ISBN 0-8052-8232-7, Pub. by Allison & Busby England). Schocken.

Boothroyd. Automatic Assembly. (Mechanical Engineering Ser.: Vol. 6). 352p. 1982. 45.00 (ISBN 0-8247-1531-4). Dekker.

Boothroyd & Poli. Applied Engineering Mechanics: Statistics & Dynamics. (Mechanical Engineering Ser.: Vol. 5). 472p. 1980. 32.75 (ISBN 0-8247-6945-7). Dekker.

Boothroyd, jt. auth. see Roberts.

Boothroyd, Arthur. Hearing Impairments in Young Children. (Illus.). 266p. 1982. 26.95 (ISBN 0-13-384701-2). P-H.

Boothroyd, Carl W., jt. auth. see Roberts, Daniel A.

Boothroyd, H. Articulate Intervention. 154p. 1978. cancelled (ISBN 0-85066-171-4). Taylor & Francis.

Boothroyd, Rodney, jt. auth. see Hughes, Beatrix.

Boothroyd, Ronald, tr. see Lemoisne, Paul A.

Booth-Tucker, Frederick. The Salvation Army in America: Selected Reports, 1899-1903. LC 79-38439. (Religion in America, Ser. 2). 212p. 1972. Repr. of 1972 ed. 19.00 (ISBN 0-405-04060-1). Ayer Co Pubs.

Bootle, Roger. Index-Linked Gilts: A Practical Investment Guide. LC 84-17417. 92p. 1985. 33.00 (ISBN 0-85941-289-X, Pub. by Woodhead-Faulkner). Longwood Pub Group.

Bootman, Tyler. Myself in the Street: Poems. (Orig.). 1966. 4.50 (ISBN 0-8079-0087-7); pap. 1.95 (ISBN 0-8079-0088-5). October.

Boots, B., jt. auth. see Getis, A.

Bootsma, G. A. & Geus, J. W., eds. The Solid-Vacuum Interface: Proceedings Symposium on Surface Physics, 3rd, June 26-28, 1974. 422p. 1975. Repr. 53.25 (ISBN 0-444-10828-9, North-Holland). Elsevier.

Booty, John E. The Church in History. (Church's Teaching Ser.: Vol. 3). 320p. 1979. 5.95 (ISBN 0-8164-0420-8, Pub. by Seabury); pap. 3.95 (ISBN 0-8164-2216-8); user guide 0.95 (ISBN 0-8164-2223-0). Winston Pr.

--Meditating on Four Quartets. 66p. (Orig.). 1983. pap. 5.00 (ISBN 0-936384-15-8). Cowley Pubns.

--The Servant Church: Diaconal Ministry & the Episcopal Church. LC 82-81429. (Orig.). 1982. pap. 7.95 (ISBN 0-8192-1316-0). Morehouse.

--Three Anglican Divines on Prayer: Jewel, Andrewes & Hooker. vii, 48p. (Orig.). 1978. pap. 3.00 (ISBN 0-936384-00-X). Cowley Pubns.

--What Makes Us Episcopalians? 48p. 1982. pap. 2.95 (ISBN 0-8192-1302-0, 82-80468). Morehouse.

Booty, John E., ed. The Divine Drama in History & Liturgy: Essays Presented to Horton Davies on His Retirement from Princeton University. (Pittsburgh Theological Monographs: New Ser. 10). 1984. pap. 19.50 (ISBN 0-915138-67-0). Pickwick.

--The Godly Kingdom of Tudor England: Great Books of the English Reformation. LC 81-80626. (Illus.). 288p. 1981. 15.95 (ISBN 0-8192-1287-3). Morehouse.

Booty, John E. & Hooker, Richard, eds. Of the Laws of Ecclesiastical Polity: Attack & Response, Vol. IV. (The Folger Library Edition of the Works of Richard Hooker). (Illus.). 320p. 1981. text ed. 45.00 (ISBN 0-674-63216-8). Harvard U Pr.

Booty, John E., ed. see Jewel, John.

Bootz, John, ed. The Book of Common Prayer. LC 75-29330. 1976. 24.95 (ISBN 0-918016-58-4). Folger Bks.

Bootzin, et al. Psychology Today. 5th ed. LC 82-20450. 1982. text ed. 28.00 (ISBN 0-394-32581-8, RanC); study guide 9.00 (ISBN 0-394-33182-6). Random.

Bootzin, David & Muffley, Harry C., eds. Biomechanics. LC 69-16519. 185p. 1969. 35.00x (ISBN 0-306-30392-2, Plenum Pr). Plenum Pub.

Bootzin, Richard, et al. Psychology Today: An Introduction. 6th ed. 736p. 1986. text ed. 27.95 (ISBN 0-394-34359-X, RanC); price not set wkbk. (ISBN 0-394-35496-6). Random.

Bootzin, Richard R. Behavior Modification & Therapy: An Introduction. (Orig.). 1975. pap. text ed. 11.95 (ISBN 0-316-10260-1). Little.

Bootzin, Richard R. & Acocella, Joan. Abnormal Psychology: Current Perspectives. 4th ed. 1984. text ed. 28.00 (ISBN 0-394-33424-8, RanC). Random.

Bootzin, Richard R., jt. ed. see Reiss, Steven.

Booy, Derrick M. Rock of Exile. 10.00 (ISBN 0-8159-6711-X). Devin.

Booy, Theodoor N. De see De Booy, Theodoor N.

Booysen, P. de V. see De V. Booysen, P. & Tainton, N. M.

Booz & Allen. Coping with Inflation: Experiences of Financial Executives in the U. K., West Germany & Brazil. LC 81-706. 1982. 5.00. Finan Exec.

Booz, Allen & Booz, Hamilton. Organization & Staffing of the Libraries of Columbia University: A Case Study. 210p. 1973. 12.00 (ISBN 0-318-16081-1). OMS.

Booz, Allen & Hamilton. An Economic Analysis of Imported LNG in Selected End-Use Markets. 65p. 1978. pap. 3.00 (ISBN 0-318-12601-X, F00685). Am Gas Assn.

Booz, Allen & Hamilton & Association of National Advertisers. Management & Advertising Problems in the Advertiser-Agency Relationship. 138p. 1965. 10.00 (ISBN 0-318-13463-2, 15). Assn Natl Advertisers.

Booz, Gretchen & Holmes, Reed M. Kendra. LC 79-12285. 1979. 4.25 (ISBN 0-8309-0234-1). Herald Hse.

Booz, Hamilton, jt. auth. see Booz, Allen.

Booz, J. & Ebert, H. G., eds. Microdosimetry, 6th Symposium, Vols. 1 & 2. (Commission of the European Community Symposium). 1978. lib. bdg. 68.25 ea. Vol. 1, 701p (ISBN 0-906346-02-9). Vol. 2, 589p (ISBN 0-906346-03-7). Harwood Academic.

Booz, J., jt. ed. see Ebert, H. G.

Booz, Paddy, et al. A Guide to Canton, Guilin, & Guangdong. (China Guide Ser.). (Illus.). 207p. (Orig.). 1985. pap. 9.95 (ISBN 0-8351-1433-3). China Bks.

Boozer, William. William Faulkner's First Book: The Marble Faun Fifty Years Later. LC 75-6916. (Illus.). 1975. 7.50 (ISBN 0-686-12125-2). Pigeon Roost Pr.

Boozhie, E. X. The Outlaw's Bible: How to Evade the System Using Constitutional Strategy. (Illus.). 220p. (Orig.). 1985. pap. 11.95 (ISBN 0-9614415-1-8). Circle-A Pubs.

Bopp, James, Jr., ed. Human Life & Health Care Ethics. 420p. 1984. 27.50x (ISBN 0-89093-573-4). U Pubns Amer.

Bopp, Stephen, jt. auth. see Zaccaria, Joseph.

Bopp, William J. Crises in Police Administration. 168p. 1984. 19.75x (ISBN 0-398-05014-7). C C Thomas.

--O. W. O. W. Wilson & the Search for a Police Profession. (National University Publications Interdisciplinary Urban Ser.). 1977. 16.50x (ISBN 0-8046-9179-7, Pub. by Kennikat); pap. 9.95x (ISBN 0-8046-9201-7). Assoc Faculty Pr.

--O.W. O.W. Wilson & the Search for a Police Profession. 168p. 1977. 16.50x (ISBN 0-317-08100-4, 9179); pap. 9.95 (ISBN 0-317-08101-2, 9201). Assoc Faculty Pr.

--The Police Rebellion: A Quest for Blue Power. 228p. 1971. 19.75x (ISBN 0-398-00189-8). C C Thomas.

Bopp, William J. & Schultz, Donald O. A Short History of American Law Enforcement. (Illus.). 192p. 1977. photocopy ed. spiral 17.75x (ISBN 0-398-02479-0). C C Thomas.

Bopp, William J. & Whisenand, Paul M. Police Personnel Administration. 280p. 1980. 28.00 (ISBN 0-205-06923-1, 826923). Allyn.

Bopp, William J., ed. Police-Community Relationships: An Introductory Undergraduate Reader. 464p. 1972. pap. 39.75x spiral (ISBN 0-398-02461-8). C C Thomas.

Boppart, H., jt. ed. see Wachter, P.

Boquist, jt. auth. see Engler.

Bor, Josef. The Terezin Requiem. 1978. pap. 1.95 (ISBN 0-380-01673-7, 33449-6, Bard). Avon.

Bor, Michael, jt. auth. see Franklin, Myrtle.

Bor, N. L. Grasses of India, Burma & Ceylon: Excluding Bambuseae. (Illus.). 1973. Repr. of 1960 ed. 77.00 (ISBN 3-87429-043-3). Lubrecht & Cramer.

Bor, Walter. Making of Cities. (Illus.). 1972. 35.00x (ISBN 0-249-44071-7). Intl Ideas.

Bor, Wout van den see Van den Bor, Wout.

Bora, Ben. Voyagers. 400p. 1985. pap. 3.50 (ISBN 0-553-25145-7). Bantam.

Bora, K. C., et al, eds. Chemical Mutagenesis: Progress in Mutation Research, Vol. 3. 360p. 1982. 87.25 (ISBN 0-444-80352-1, Biomedical Pr). Elsevier.

Bora, P. M. Food Administration in India. 1982. 24.00x (ISBN 0-8364-0883-7, Pub. by Ajanta). South Asia Bks.

Boraas, Roger S. & Geraty, Lawrence T. Heshbon 1974: The Fourth Campaign at Tell Hesban: A Preliminary Report. (Andrews University Monographs, Studies in Religion: Vol. IX). (Illus.). xii, 232p. 1976. 7.95 (ISBN 0-943872-09-X). Andrews Univ Pr.

--Heshbon 1976: The Fifth Campaign at Tell Hesban: A Preliminary Report. (Andrews University Monographs, Studies in Religion: Vol. X). (Illus.). xi, 328p. 1978. 11.95 (ISBN 0-943872-10-3). Andrews Univ Pr.

Boraas, Roger S. & Horn, Siegfried H. Heshbon 1968: The First Campaign at Tell Hesban: A Preliminary Report. (Andrews University Monographs, Studies in Religion: Vol. II). (Illus.). viii, 239p. 1969. 7.95. Andrews Univ Pr.

--Heshbon 1971: The Second Campaign at Tell Hesban: A Preliminary Report. (Andrews University Monographs, Studies in Religion: Vol. VI). (Illus.). viii, 160p. 7.95 (ISBN 0-943872-06-5). Andrews Univ Pr.

--Heshbon 1973: The Third Campaign at Tell Hesban: A Preliminary Report. (Andrews University Monographs, Studies in Religion: Vol. VIII). (Illus.). viii, 288p. 1975. 7.95 (ISBN 0-943872-08-1). Andrews Univ Pr.

Borack, Barbara. Gooney. LC 67-18552. (Illus.). 32p. (gr. k-3). 1968. PLB 10.89 (ISBN 0-06-020630-6). HarpJ.

--Grandpa. LC 67-2764. (Illus.). 32p. (gr. k-3). 1967. PLB 12.89 (ISBN 0-06-020628-4). HarpJ.

Borah, Mary. Elephants & Donkeys. LC 76-14107. 152p. 1976. 3.95 (ISBN 0-89301-032-4). U Pr of Idaho.

Borah, William E. American Problems: A Selection of Speeches & Prophecies. Green, Horace, ed. LC 77-111472. (BCL Ser.: I). Repr. of 1924 ed. 15.00 (ISBN 0-404-00624-8). AMS Pr.

--American Problems: A Selection of Speeches & Prophecies. 1971. Repr. of 1924 ed. 13.00x (ISBN 0-403-00874-3). Scholarly.

Borah, William E., jt. auth. see Baumbach, Richard O.

Borah, William E., jt. auth. see Baumbach, Richard O., Jr.

Borah, Woodrow. Justice by Insurance: The General Indian Court of Colonial Mexico & the Legal Aides of the Half Real. LC 82-20177. 496p. 1983. text ed. 45.00x (ISBN 0-520-04845-8). U of Cal Pr.

--New Spain's Century of Depression. LC 73-16181. 1951. lib. bdg. 12.50 (ISBN 0-8414-3347-X). Folcroft.

Borah, Woodrow, jt. auth. see Cook, Sherburne F.

Boraks, Jagna, tr. see Busza, Andrzej.

Boralevi, Lea Campos see Campos-Boralevi, Lea.

Boram, Clifford. How to Get Parts Cast for Your Antique Stove: Dealing with Foundry Is Easier than You May Think. (Illus.). 52p. 1982. 5.00 (ISBN 0-9612204-0-6). Autonomy Hse.

--What Is My Antique Stove Worth? 5p. Repr. 2.00 (ISBN 0-9612204-3-0). Autonomy Hse.

Borasio, I. & Garibaldi, F. Illustrated Glossary of Rice-Processing Machines. (Agricultural Services Bulletins: No. 37). (Illus.). 104p. (Eng., Fr., Span., Ger. & Ital.). 1979. pap. 7.50 (ISBN 92-5-000784-1, F1854, FAO). Unipub.

Boratav, Pertev N. & Eberhard, Wolfram. Turkische Volkserzahlung und Die Erzahlerkunst, 2 vols. (Asian Folklore & Social Life Monograph: No. 73 & 74). (Ger.). 1975. Set. 25.00 (ISBN 0-89986-069-9). Oriental Bk Store.

Borawski, Walta. Sexually Dangerous Poet. 1984. pap. 5.00 (ISBN 0-915480-16-6). Good Gay.

Borba, Craig & Borba, Michele. The Good Apple Guide to Learning Centers. (gr. k-6). 1978. 11.95 (ISBN 0-916456-33-1, GA86). Good Apple.

Borba, Craig, jt. auth. see Borba, Michele.

Borba, Michele & Borba, Craig. Self-Esteem: A Classroom Affair, Vol. 1. 140p. 1978. pap. 8.95 (ISBN 0-86683-612-8, AY8939). Winston Pr.

--Self-Esteem: A Classroom Affair, Vol.2. 144p. (Orig.). 1982. pap. 9.95 (ISBN 0-86683-675-6, AY8210). Winston Pr.

Borba, Michele & Ungaro, Dan. Bookends. (gr. 1-4). 1982. 8.95 (ISBN 0-86653-065-7, GA 432). Good Apple.

--The Complete Letter Book. (ps-3). 1980. 7.95 (ISBN 0-916456-80-3, GA 182). Good Apple.

--Imagineering the Reading Process. (ps-4). 1980. 10.95 (ISBN 0-916456-81-1, GA 171). Good Apple.

Borba, Michele, jt. auth. see Borba, Craig.

Borba de Moraes, Ruben see De Moraes, Ruben B.

Borbas, Margit, tr. see McCullough, Colleen.

Borbe, Tasso, ed. Semiotics Unfolding, 3 vols. LC 83-13439. (Approaches to Semiotics Ser.: No. 68). 1983. Set. 189.00x (ISBN 3-11-009779-6). Mouton.

Borbely, A. & Valatx, J., eds. Sleep Mechanisms. (Experimental Brain Research Ser.: Suppl. 8). (Illus.). 330p. 1984. 35.00 (ISBN 0-387-13146-9). Springer-Verlag.

Borbely, James A., jt. auth. see Schemel, George J.

Borceux, F. & Van Den Bossche, G. Algebra in a Localic Topos with Applications to Ring Theory. (Lecture Notes in Mathematics Ser.: Vol. 1038). 240p. 1983. pap. 13.00 (ISBN 0-387-12711-9). Springer Verlag.

Borch, C. & Mossiv, Jan, eds. Risk & Uncertainty. LC 68-29940. (International Economic Assn. Ser). (Illus.). 1969. 35.00 (ISBN 0-312-68460-6). St Martin.

Borch, Karl. Economic Theory of Insurance. LC 82-48575. 1984. write for info. (ISBN 0-669-06321-5). Lexington Bks.

Borch, Karl H. Economics of Uncertainty. LC 68-10503. (Princeton Studies in Mathematical Economics: Vol. 2). 1968. 32.00x (ISBN 0-691-04124-5). Princeton U Pr.

Borchard, David C., et al. Your Career: Choices, Chances, Changes. 304p. 1984. pap. text ed. 16.95 (ISBN 0-8403-3343-9, 40334301). Kendall-Hunt.

Borchard, E. & Wynne, W. H. State Insolvency & Foreign Bondholders, 2 vols. LC 82-48295. (The World Economy Ser.). 1033p. 1983. Set. lib. bdg. 121.00 (ISBN 0-8240-5350-8). Garland Pub.

Borchard, E. M. Diplomatic Protection of Citizens Abroad; or, The Law of International Claims. Repr. of 1915 ed. 44.00 (ISBN 0-527-09900-7). Kraus Repr.

Borchard, Edwin & Lage, William P. Neutrality for the United States. 1937. 18.50x (ISBN 0-317-27528-3). Elliots Bks.

Borchard, Edwin M. Convicting the Innocent: Errors of Criminal Justice. LC 74-107406. (Civil Liberties in American History Ser). 1970. Repr. of 1932 ed. lib. bdg. 39.50 (ISBN 0-306-71886-3). Da Capo.

--Guide to the Law & Legal Literature of Argentina, Brazil, & Chile. (Latin America Ser.). 1979. lib. bdg. 75.00 (ISBN 0-8490-2931-7). Gordon Pr.

Borchard, Edwin M. & Lage, William P. Neutrality for the U. S. LC 78-153305. (BCL Ser.: li). Repr. of 1940 ed. 20.00 (ISBN 0-404-04644-4). AMS Pr.

Borchard, Edwin M., jt. auth. see Lage, William.

Borchard, Ruth. John Stuart Mill: The Man. 156p. 1983. Repr. of 1957 ed. lib. bdg. 35.00 (ISBN 0-89987-096-1). Darby Bks.

Borchardt, Ann, tr. see Wiesel, Elie.

Borchardt, Anne, tr. see Wiesel, Elie.

Borchardt, D. H. Australia: Bibliographic Library Science. (International Bibliographical & Library Ser.). Date not set. price not set (ISBN 0-12-785070-8). Acad Pr.

--Early Printing in Australia. Clair, Colin, ed. LC 76-78404. (Spread of Printing Ser). (Illus., Orig.). 1969. pap. 9.75 (ISBN 0-8390-0024-3). Abner Schram Ltd.

Borchardt, D. H. & Francis, R. D. How to Find Out in Psychology: A Guide to the Literature & Methods of Research. (How to Find Out Ser.). 155p. 1985. 21.00 (ISBN 0-08-031280-2). Pergamon.

Borchardt, D. H. & Thawley, J. D. Guide to the Availability of Theses. (IFLA Publications 17 Ser.). 443p. 1982. 38.00 (ISBN 3-598-20378-0). K G Saur.

Borchardt, Donald A. Think Tank Theatre: Decision Making Applied. 350p. (Orig.). 1985. pap. text ed. 18.50 (ISBN 0-8191-4337-5, Co-pub by Am Theat Assn). U Pr of Amer.

Borchardt, Frank L. German Antiquity in Renaissance Myth. LC 75-166484. pap. 92.00 (ISBN 0-317-20472-6, 2022999). Bks Demand UMI.

Borchardt, Glenn. The Scientific Worldview. (Illus.). xiii, 343p. (Orig.). 1984. 49.95 (ISBN 0-917929-01-2); pap. 29.95 (ISBN 0-917929-00-4). Progressive Sci Inst.

Borchardt, Gordon C., jt. auth. see Beighey, Clyde.

Borchardt, R. T., jt. ed. see Usdin, E.

Borchardt, Ronald T., et al, eds. Directed Drug Delivery. LC 85-2291. (Experimental Biology & Medicine Ser.). (Illus.). 384p. 1975. 59.50 (ISBN 0-89603-089-X). Humana.

Borchelt, J., ed. Masonry: Materials, Properties & Performance- STP 778. 277p. 1982. 28.50 (ISBN 0-8031-0610-6, 04-778000-07). ASTM.

Borchelt, Peter, et al, eds. Animal Behavior & Thanatology. (Current Thanatology Ser.). 100p. 1986. pap. 13.95 (ISBN 0-930194-37-3). Ctr Thanatology.

Borcherding, K., et al. Research Perspectives on Decision Making under Uncertainty. 1984. Repr. 50.00 (ISBN 0-444-87574-3). Elsevier.

Borcherding, Thomas E., ed. Budgets & Bureaucrats: The Sources of Government Growth. LC 75-30407. 291p. 1977. 21.00 (ISBN 0-8223-0352-3). Duke.

Borcherds, Petrus B. Autobiographical Memoir of Petrus Borchardus Borcherds. LC 72-5526. (Black Heritage Library Collection). 1972. Repr. of 1861 ed. 29.25 (ISBN 0-8369-9135-4). Ayer Co Pubs.

Borchers, jt. auth. see Oppenheimer, S. L.

Borchers, Elisabeth. Dear Sarah. Shub, Elizabeth, tr. from Ger. LC 80-14512. (Illus.). 32p. (gr. k-3). 1981. 13.00 (ISBN 0-688-80277-X); PLB 12.88 (ISBN 0-688-84277-1). Greenwillow.

Borchers, Elizabeth see Siddons, Suzy & Price, Matthew.

Borchers, Elizabeth S. Nebraska Legal Forms: Family Law. 1982. looseleaf 27.50 (ISBN 0-86678-022-X). Butterworth MN.

Borchers, Hans, ed. Charles Brockden Brown, Memoirs of Stephen Calvert. (Studien und Texte zur Amerikanistik: Vol. 2). xxvii, 215p. 1978. pap. 14.20. P Lang Pubs.

Borchert, Donald M. & Stewart, David. Exploring Ethics. 639p. 1986. price not set (ISBN 0-02-312430-X). Macmillan.

Borchert, Donald M. & Stewart, David, eds. Being Human in a Technological Age. LC 79-4364. viii, 168p. 1979. 16.95x (ISBN 0-8214-0399-0, 82-82915); pap. 8.95x (ISBN 0-8214-0427-X, 82-82923). Ohio U Pr.

Borchert, Gerald L. & Lester, Andrew D., eds. Spiritual Dimensions of Pastoral Care: Witness to the Ministry of Wayne E. Oates. LC 84-19581. 152p. (Orig.). 1985. pap. 11.95 (ISBN 0-664-24562-5). Westminster.

Borchert, James. Alley Life in Washington: Family, Community, Religion, & Folklife in the City, 1850-1970. LC 80-12375. (Blacks in the New World Ser.). (Illus.). 352p. 1980. 18.95x (ISBN 0-252-00689-5); pap. 9.95x (ISBN 0-252-01003-5). U of Ill Pr.

Borchert, John R., et al. Legacy of Minneapolis: Preservation Amid Change. (Illus.). 195p. 1983. pap. 14.95 (ISBN 0-89658-047-4). Voyageur Pr Inc.

Borchert, Wolfgang. The Man Outside. rev. ed. Porter, A. D., tr. from Ger. LC 76-145929. 1971. pap. 6.95 (ISBN 0-8112-0011-6, NDP319). New Directions.

--The Sad Geraniums. LC 73-11251. 1973. 5.95 (ISBN 0-912946-10-5). Ecco Pr.

Borchgrave, Arnaud de see De Borchgrave, Arnaud & Moss, Robert.

Borchgrave, Arnaud de see Moss, Robert & De Borchgrave, Arnaud.

Borchgrevink, C. E. First on the Antarctic Continent. (Illus.). 333p. 1980. Repr. of 1901 ed. 49.00x (ISBN 0-7735-0515-6). McGill-Queens U Pr.

Borchgrevink, Hans, jt. auth. see Butenschon, Sine.

Borch-Johansen, Alison, tr. see Rordam, Thomas.

Borchling, C. & Claussen, B. Niederdeutsche Bibliographie: Gesamtverzeichnis der Niederduetschen Drucke Bis Zum Jahre 1800, 2 vols. 1100p. 1976. Repr. of 1936 ed. Set. 147.00x (ISBN 90-6194-231-4). Benjamins North Am.

Borcht, Pieter Van Der see Bochius, Johannes & Van Der Borcht, Pieter.

Borck, Jim S., ed. The Eighteenth Century: A Current Bibliography, New Series, 7 vols. 1985. 67.50 ea. (ISBN 0-404-62200-3). AMS Pr.

--The Eighteenth Century: A Current Bibliography, Vol. 7. Annual ed. 750p. 1985. Set. 67.50. AMS Pr.

Borck, Leslie E. & Fawcett, Stephen B. Learning Counseling & Problem-Solving Skills. LC 82-2916. 160p. (Orig.). 1982. text ed. 26.00 (ISBN 0-917724-30-5, B30); pap. text ed. 13.95 (ISBN 0-917724-35-6, B35). Haworth Pr.

Borcoman, James. Eugene Atget Eighteen Fifty-Seven to Nineteen Twenty-Seven. (National Gallery of Canada Ser.). (Illus.). 140p. 1984. 35.00 (ISBN 0-88884-510-3, 56273-5, Pub. by Natl Mus Canada). U of Chicago Pr.

Bord, Colin, jt. auth. see Bord, Janet.

Bord, Janet. Paths: Astral Projection. 1981. pap. 7.95x (ISBN 0-317-06951-9, Regent House). B of A.

Bord, Janet & Bord, Colin. Earth Rites Fertility Practices in Pre-Industrial Britain. (Illus.). 274p. 1983. 15.95 (ISBN 0-246-11431-2, Pub. by Salem Acad). Merrimack Pub Cir.

--Earth Rites: Fertility Practices in Pre-Industrial Britain. (Illus.). 288p. pap. 7.95 (ISBN 0-586-08452-5, Pub. by Granada England). Academy Chi Pubs.

--Evidence for Bigfoot & Other Manbeasts. (Illus.). 160p. (Orig.). 1984. pap. 5.95 (ISBN 0-85030-363-X, Pub. by Aquarian Pr England). Sterling.

--A Guide to Ancient Sites in Britain. (Illus.). 183p. 1981. pap. 7.95 (ISBN 0-586-08309-X, Pub. by Granada England). Academy Chi Pubs.

--Mysterious Britain. (Illus.). 287p. 1981. pap. 5.95 (ISBN 0-586-08157-7, Pub. by Granada England). Academy Chi Pubs.

--The Secret Country. (Illus.). 247p. 1981. pap. 5.95 (ISBN 0-586-08267-0, Pub. by Granada England). Academy Chi Pubs.

--The Secret Country. 1977. 9.95 (ISBN 0-8027-0559-6). Walker & Co.

Bord, Richard J. & Faulkner, Joseph E. The Catholic Charismatics: Anatomy of a Modern Religious Movement. LC 82-42782. 160p. 1983. 19.95x (ISBN 0-271-00340-5). Pa St U Pr.

Borda, Orlando F. The Challenge of Social Change. 1985. 21.50 (ISBN 0-8039-9709-4). Sage.

Bordalo, O., ed. European Pancreatic Club, (EPC), 16th Meeting, Cascais, Sept. 1984. (Journal: Digestion: Vol. 30, No. 2). (Illus.). 66p. 1984. pap. 24.75 (ISBN 3-8055-3956-8). S Karger.

Bordas, Carl W. Premeditated Success Through Hypnotism. 168p. (Orig.). 1981. pap. 4.50x (ISBN 0-935648-07-0). Halldin Pub.

Bordas, Herve. Venice. LC 75-11393. (This Beautiful World Ser.: Vol. 55). (Illus.). 120p. (Orig.). 1975. pap. 4.95 (ISBN 0-87011-259-7). Kodansha.

Borde, Andrew. The Breuiary of Helthe, for All Maner of Syckenesses & Diseases, the Whiche May Be in Man, or Woman Deth Folowe, 2 pts. LC 71-38106. (English Experience Ser.: No. 362). 356p. 1971. Repr. of 1547 ed. Set. 50.00 (ISBN 90-221-0362-5). Walter J Johnson.

--The Pryncyples of Astronamye in Maner a Pronosticacyon to Worldes End. LC 73-6101. (English Experience Ser.: No. 570). 61p. 1973. Repr. of 1542 ed. 6.00 (ISBN 90-221-0570-9). Walter J Johnson.

Bordeau, Annette & Battaini, Andre. Mechanical Dolles of Monte-Carlo. (Illus.). 240p. 1985. 45.00 (ISBN 0-8478-0679-0). Rizzoli Intl.

Bordeau, Sanford P. Volts to Hertz: The Rise of Electricity. LC 82-17702. (Illus.). 308p. 1982. 18.95 (ISBN 0-8087-4908-0). Burgess.

Bordeaux, Henry. Georges Guynemer, Knight of the Air. LC 73-169405. (Literature & History of Aviation Ser.). 1972. Repr. of 1918 ed. 18.00 (ISBN 0-405-03751-1). Ayer Co Pubs.

Bordeaux, Jean, jt. auth. see LeCron, Leslie.

Bordeaux, Jean, jt. auth. see LeCron, Leslie M.

Bordeaux, Jean-Luc, et al. Unstretched Surfaces: Los Angeles-Paris. Schwartz, Emmanuelle, tr. (Illus.). 48p. (Orig., Eng. & Fr.). 1977. pap. write for info. (ISBN 0-911291-02-4). Fellows Cont Art.

Bordeaux, Norma N. Dewdrops on A Lotus Leaf. (Illus.). 28p. 1974. pap. 2.75 (ISBN 0-89564-076-7). IBS Intl.

Bordeaux, Norma N., jt. auth. see Szekely, Edmond B.

Bordeleau, J. Alex. Star Spangled Love. 226p. 1984. 8.68 (ISBN 0-89697-203-8). Intl Univ Pr.

Bordelon, Abbe L. A History of the Ridiculous Extravagancies of Monsieur Oufle Occasion'd by His Reading Books Treating of Magick, the Black-Art Demoniacks... & Other Superstitious Practices. LC 76-170524. (Foundations of the Novel Ser.: Vol. 17). 1973. lib. bdg. 61.00 (ISBN 0-8240-0529-5). Garland Pub.

Borden. Arab Horse. 9.50 (ISBN 0-87505-112-X). Borden.

Borden, Arthur R., Jr. A Comprehensive Old-English Dictionary. LC 81-40837. 1612p. 1982. lib. bdg. 114.50 (ISBN 0-8191-2254-8). U Pr of Amer.

Borden, Beatrice B. Wild Animals of Africa. (Illus.). 48p. (ps-2). 1982. PLB 6.99 (ISBN 0-394-95306-1); pap. 5.95 (ISBN 0-394-85306-7). Random.

Borden, Carla M., jt. ed. see Jackman, Jarrell C.

Borden, Emanuel, ed. Hand in Art. (Master Draughtsman Ser). (Illus.). 1963. treasure trove bdg. 9.95x (ISBN 0-87505-044-1); pap. 4.95 (ISBN 0-87505-197-9). Borden.

--More Drawings of Ingres. (Master Draughtsman Ser). (Illus.). 48p. treasure trove bdg. 9.95x (ISBN 0-87505-053-0); pap. 4.95 (ISBN 0-87505-206-1). Borden.

Borden, Gale, jt. auth. see Benjamin, Ben.

Borden, George A. Human Communication Systems. (Illus.). 314p. (Orig.). 1985. pap. text ed. 14.95x (ISBN 0-89641-148-6). American Pr.

Borden, Gloria J. & Harris, Katherine S. Speech Science Primer: Physiology, Acoustics & Perception of Speech. 2nd ed. (Illus.). 302p. 1984. text ed. 28.50 cased (ISBN 0-683-00942-7). Williams & Wilkins.

Borden, Janet. Presentation: Recent Portrait Photography. Meyer, Ruth K., intro. by. (Illus.). 20p. (Orig.). 1983. pap. 3.50 (ISBN 0-915577-02-X). Taft Museum.

Borden, Lester, ed. Management of the Infected Total Knee & Hip. (Techniques in Orthopaedics Ser.). (Illus.). 1985. text ed. 40.00 (ISBN 0-8391-2066-4, 21792). Univ Park.

Borden, Morton. Federalism of James A. Bayard. LC 68-59262. (Columbia University Studies in the Social Sciences: No. 584). Repr. of 1954 ed. 21.00 (ISBN 0-404-51584-3). AMS Pr.

--Jews, Turks, & Infidels. LC 83-19863. xii, 163p. 1984. 17.95x (ISBN 0-8078-1592-6). U of NC Pr.

--Parties & Politics in the Early Republic, 1789-1815. LC 67-14298. (American History Ser.). (Orig.). 1967. pap. 6.95x (ISBN 0-88295-704-X). Harlan Davidson.

Borden, Morton & Graham, Otis. The American Profile. 2nd ed. 1978. pap. text ed. 18.95x (ISBN 0-669-84822-0). Heath.

Borden, Morton & Graham, Otis L. Speculations on American History. 1977. pap. text ed. 7.95x (ISBN 0-669-00488-X). Heath.

Borden, Morton & Borden, Penn, eds. The American Tory. LC 73-168739. (Great Lives Observed). 160p. 1972. 8.95 (ISBN 0-13-031385-8, Spec). P-H.

Borden, Neil H. Advertising in Our Economy. Assael, Henry, ed. LC 78-239. (Century of Marketing Ser.). 1978. Repr. of 1945 ed. lib. bdg. 24.50x (ISBN 0-405-11172-X). Ayer Co Pubs.

--The Economic Effects of Advertising. LC 75-39233. (Getting & Spending: the Consumer's Dilemma). 1976. Repr. of 1942 ed. 77.00x (ISBN 0-405-08010-7). Ayer Co Pubs.

Borden, Neil H., Jr. Acceptance of New Food Products by Supermarkets. LC 68-15544. 248p. 1969. pap. 3.00 (ISBN 0-87005-000-1). Fairchild.

Borden, Penn, jt. ed. see Borden, Morton.

Borden, R. S. A Course in Advanced Calculus. 388p. 1982. 34.00 (ISBN 0-444-00638-9, North-Holland). Elsevier.

Borden, Thomas A., jt. ed. see Crawford, E. David.

Borden, Weston T. Diradicals. LC 82-8604. 343p. 1982. 49.50 (ISBN 0-471-08661-4, Pub. by Wiley-Interscience). Wiley.

Borden, William S. The Pacific Alliance: United States Foreign Economic Policy & Japanese Trade Recovery, 1947-1955. LC 83-14541. 352p. 1984. text ed. 25.00x (ISBN 0-299-09550-9). U of Wis Pr.

Bordenave, Juan E. Communication & Rural Development. (Illus.). 109p. (2nd Printing 1979). 1977. pap. 7.00 (ISBN 92-3-101370-X, U77, UNESCO). Unipub.

Border, Barbara. Food Safety & Sanitation. (Careers in Home Economics Ser.). (Illus.). 1979. pap. text ed. 12.92 (ISBN 0-07-006511-X). McGraw.

Border, Kim C. Fixed Point Theorems with Applications to Economics & Game Theory. (Illus.). 128p. 1985. 29.95 (ISBN 0-521-26564-9). Cambridge U Pr.

Border, Ross. Church & State in Australia, 1788-1872: A Constitutional Study of the Church of England in Australia. LC 64-56989. 1962. text ed. 15.00x (ISBN 0-8401-0226-7). A R Allenson.

Borders. The Adventure Companion. 1985. 12.95 (ISBN 0-8104-6675-9). Hayden.

Borders, Earl, Jr. The Bus Trip Handbook. LC 84-60654. (Illus.). 112p. (Orig.). 1985. pap. 8.95 (ISBN 0-917125-00-2). Home Run Pr.

Borders, Karl. Village Life Under the Soviets. LC 72-12699. (Select Bibliographies Reprint Ser). 1973. Repr. of 1927 ed. 16.00 (ISBN 0-8369-7131-0). Ayer Co Pubs.

--Village Life Under the Soviets. 200p. Repr. of 1927 ed. lib. bdg. 15.00 (ISBN 0-8290-0812-8). Irvington.

Bordes, Charles, ed. Anthologie Des Maitres Religieux Primirties Des XV, XVI & XVII Siecles, 6 vols. (Music Ser.). 1981. Repr. of 1893 ed. Set. lib. bdg. 225.00 (ISBN 0-306-76089-4); Vol. 1; IV, 184 Pp. lib. bdg. 42.50 (ISBN 0-306-76114-9); Vol. 2; VIII, 194 Pp. lib. bdg. 42.50 (ISBN 0-306-76115-7); Vol. 3; IV, 184 Pp. lib. bdg. 42.50 (ISBN 0-306-76116-5); Vol. 4; IV, 190 Pp. lib. bdg. 42.50 (ISBN 0-306-76117-3); Vol. 5; II, 190 Pp. lib. bdg. 42.50 (ISBN 0-306-76118-1); Vol. 6; II, 202 Pp. lib. bdg. 42.50 (ISBN 0-306-76119-X). Da Capo.

Bordes, Francois. Old Stone Age. (Illus., Orig.). 1968. pap. 3.95 (ISBN 0-07-006500-4). McGraw.

Bordes, Gerard. La Grande Encyclopedie Alpha des Sciences et des Techniques, 20 vols. (Fr.). 1976. Set. 1225.00 (ISBN 0-686-57311-0, M-6290). French & Eur.

--Grande Encyclopedie Atlas de la Medecine, 9 vols. 320p. (Fr.). 1976. Set. 595.00 (ISBN 0-686-57312-9, M-6291). French & Eur.

Bordet, E., jt. auth. see Vaquez, H.

Bordewijk, P., jt. auth. see Bottcher, C. J.

Bordewijk, P., ed. see Bottcher, C. J., et al.

Bordewyk, H. W., et al. Netherlands & the World War: Studies in the War History of a Neutral: Volume 4-Effect of the War upon Banking & Currency-War Finances in the Netherlands, 1918-1922-Costs of the War. (Economic & Social History of the World War Ser.). 1928. 75.00x (ISBN 0-686-83642-1). Elliots Bks.

Bordia, A., jt. ed. see Carron, G.

Bordicks, Katherine J. Patterns of Shock: Implications for Nursing Care. 2nd ed. (Illus.). 1980. text ed. write for info. (ISBN 0-02-312450-4). Macmillan.

Bordignon Favero, Giampaolo. The Villa Emo at Fanzolo. LC 73-139113. (Corpus Palladianum, Vol. 5). (Illus.). 56.00x (ISBN 0-271-01153-X). Pa St U Pr.

Bordillon, Henri, ed. see Jarry, Alfred.

Bordin, Edward S. Research Strategies in Psychotheraphy. LC 74-11272. (Wiley Series on Personality Processes). pap. 71.00 (ISBN 0-317-08426-7, 2051569). Bks Demand UMI.

Bordin, Ruth. Woman & Temperance: The Quest for Power & Liberty, 1873 to 1900. LC 80-21140. (American Civilization Ser.). 225p. 1980. 27.95 (ISBN 0-87722-157-X). Temple U Pr.

Bordin, Ruth B. University of Michigan: A Pictorial History. LC 66-17029. (Illus.). 1967. 6.50 (ISBN 0-472-16400-7). U of Mich Pr.

Bordinat, Philip & Blaydes, Sophia B. Sir William Davenant. (English Authors Ser.). 1981. lib. bdg. 14.50 (ISBN 0-8057-6795-9, Twayne). G K Hall.

Bordinat, Philip, jt. auth. see Blaydes, Sophia B.

Bordley, James, III & Harvey, A. McGehee. Two Centuries of American Medicine: 1776-1976. LC 75-19841. (Illus.). 750p. 1976. text ed. 42.00 (ISBN 0-7216-1873-1). Saunders.

Bordley, James, 3rd, jt. auth. see Harvey, A. McGehee.

Bordley, John B. A Summary View of the Courses of Crops in the Husbandry of England & Maryland. LC 72-89075. (Rural America Ser.). 1973. Repr. of 1784 ed. 7.00 (ISBN 0-8420-1477-2). Scholarly Res Inc.

Bordley, John E., et al. Ear, Nose & Throat Disorders in Children. 416p. 1985. 49.50 (ISBN 0-89004-324-8). Raven.

Bordman, Gerald. American Musical Comedy: From Adonis to Dreamgirls. (Illus.). 1982. 22.50 (ISBN 0-19-503104-0). Oxford U Pr.

--American Musical Revue: From the Passing Show to Sugar Babies. (Illus.). 192p. 1985. 17.95 (ISBN 0-19-503630-1). Oxford U Pr.

--American Musical Theatre: A Chronicle. 1978. 45.00x (ISBN 0-19-502356-0). Oxford U Pr.

--American Operetta: From H.M.S. Pinafore to Sweeney Todd. (Illus.). 1981. 19.95 (ISBN 0-19-502869-4). Oxford U Pr.

--Days To Be Happy, Years To Be Sad: The Life & Music of Vincent Youmans. (Illus.). 1982. 22.50x (ISBN 0-19-503026-5). Oxford U Pr.

--Jerome Kern: His Life & Music. (Illus.). 1980. 29.95x (ISBN 0-19-502649-7). Oxford U Pr.

--The Oxford Companion to the American Theatre. (Oxford Companion Ser.). 1984. 49.95 (ISBN 0-19-503443-0). Oxford U Pr.

Bordman, Marcia B., et al. Practical English Structure, Vol. 2. LC 80-85299. (Practical English Structure Ser.). (Illus.). xi, 223p. 1981. text ed. 14.95x (ISBN 0-913580-67-8). Gallaudet Coll.

--Practical English Structure, Vol. 3. LC 80-85299. (Practical English Structure Ser.). (Illus.). xi, 219p. 1981. text ed. 14.95x (ISBN 0-913580-68-6). Gallaudet Coll.

--Practical English Structure, Vol. 4. LC 80-85299. (Practical English Structure Ser.). (Illus.). xiii, 217p. 1981. text ed. 14.95 (ISBN 0-913580-69-4). Gallaudet Coll.

--Practical English Structure, Vol. 5. LC 80-85299. (Practical English Structure Ser.). (Illus.). xi, 335p. 1982. text ed. 14.95 (ISBN 0-913580-70-8). Gallaudet Coll.

Bordman, Marcia Beth, et al. Practical English Structure, Vol. 1. LC 80-85299. (Practical English Structure Ser.). (Illus.). xi, 199p. 1981. text ed. 14.95x (ISBN 0-913580-66-X). Gallaudet Coll.

Bordne, Erich F. Water Resources of a Western New York Region: A Case Study of Water Resources & Use in the Genesee Valley & Western Lake Ontario Basin. LC 60-9945. (Illus.). 149p. (Orig.). 1960. pap. 12.50 (ISBN 0-89366-007-8). Ultramarine Pub.

Bordner, Diane C. & Petersen, David M. Campus Policing: The Nature of University Police Work. 274p. (Orig.). 1983. lib. bdg. 25.50 (ISBN 0-8191-3361-2); pap. text ed. 13.75 (ISBN 0-8191-3362-0). U Pr of Amer.

Bordo, Michael D. & Schwartz, Anna J., eds. A Retrospective on the Classical Gold Standard: 1821-1931. LC 84-2440. (NBER Conference Report Ser.). 704p. 1984. lib. bdg. 65.00x (ISBN 0-226-06590-1). U of Chicago Pr.

Bordow, Allan, ed. The Worker in Australia: A Behavioral Science Perspective. (Illus.). 1978. text ed. 24.95x (ISBN 0-7022-1473-6); pap. text ed. 14.95x (ISBN 0-7022-1474-4). U of Queensland Pr.

Bordow, Joan W. The Ultimate Loss: Coping with the Death of a Child. LC 81-18182. 192p. 1982. 12.95 (ISBN 0-8253-0091-6). Beaufort Bks NY.

Bordow, Richard, et al, eds. Manual of Clinical Problems in Pulmonary Medicine. (Spiral Manual Ser.). 16.95 (ISBN 0-316-10264-4, Little Med Div). Little.

Bordow, Sita, compiled by. The Master's Touch: Disciples' Stories. LC 84-28857. 1984. pap. 4.95 (ISBN 0-932040-26-8). Integral Yoga Pubns.

Bordwell, David. The Films of Carl-Theodor Dreyer. (Illus.). 251p. 1981. 29.50 (ISBN 0-520-03987-4, CAL 517); pap. 11.95 (ISBN 0-520-04450-9). U of Cal Pr.

--French Impressionist Cinema. Jowett, Garth S., ed. LC 79-6668. (Dissertations on Film, 1980 Ser.). 1980. lib. bdg. 33.00x (ISBN 0-405-12902-5). Ayer Co Pubs.

--Narration in the Fiction Film. LC 84-40491. (Illus.). 320p. 1985. text ed. 37.50x (ISBN 0-299-10170-3). U of Wis Pr.

Bordwell, David & Thompson, Kristin. Film Art: An Introduction. (Illus.). 230p. 1979. text ed. 17.95 (ISBN 0-394-34964-4, RanC). Random.

--Film Art: An Introduction. 2nd ed. 416p. 1986. pap. text ed. 16.95 (ISBN 0-394-35237-8, KnopfC). Knopf.

Bordwell, David, et al. The Classical Hollywood Cinema: Film Style & Mode of Production to 1960. 640p. 1985. 49.50x (ISBN 0-231-06054-8). Columbia U Pr.

Bordwell, S., jt. auth. see Sussman, L.

Bordwell, Sally, jt. auth. see Sussman, Les.
Bordwell, Sally, jt. auth. see Sussman, Lesley.
Borecky, L. & Lackovic, V., eds. Physiology & Pathology of Interferon System. (Beitraege zur Onkologie Contributions to Oncology Ser.: Vol. 20). (Illus.). x, 390p. 1984. 33.75 (ISBN 3-8055-3839-1). S Karger.
Boreham, D. A. Narrow Gauge Railway Modelling. (Illus.). 144p. 1985. 10.95 (ISBN 0-85242-611-9, Pub. by Argus). Aztex.
Boreham, Frank W. A Frank Boreham Treasury. 1984. pap. 4.95 (ISBN 0-8024-0364-6). Moody.
Boreham, G., et al. Money & Banking. 2nd ed. 1979. text ed. 14.95 (ISBN 0-03-920006-X, Pub. by HR&W Canada). HR&W.
Boreham, Paul, et al, eds. The State, Class & the Recession. LC 83-2915. 335p. 1983. 35.00x (ISBN 0-312-75609-7). St Martin.
Borei, Dorothy, ed. see Bodde, Derk.
Borek, Carmia & Williams, Gary M., eds. Differentiation & Carcinogenesis in Liver Cell Cultures. LC 80-20918. (Annals of the New York Academy of Sciences: Vol. 349). 429p. 1980. 85.00x (ISBN 0-89766-087-0); pap. 85.00x (ISBN 0-89766-088-9). NY Acad Sci.
Borek, Ernest. The Atoms Within Us. rev. ed. LC 80-19010. 272p. 1980. 29.00x (ISBN 0-231-04386-4); pap. 11.00x (ISBN 0-231-04387-2). Columbia U Pr.
--The Sculpture of Life. LC 73-6831. (Illus.). 181p. 1973. pap. 24.00x (ISBN 0-231-03425-3). Columbia U Pr.
Borek, Ernest, jt. ed. see Monod, Jacques.
Borel, A. Oevres- Collected Papers, 3 Vols. 2240p. 1983. Set. 150.00 (ISBN 0-387-12126-9). Springer-Verlag.
Borel, A. & Wallach, N. Continuous Cohomology, Discrete Subgroups, & Representation of Reductive Groups. LC 79-19858. (Annals of Mathematics Studies: 94). 352p. 1980. 35.00x (ISBN 0-691-08248-0); pap. 16.50 (ISBN 0-691-08249-9). Princeton U Pr.
Borel, A., ed. Automorphic Forms, Representations & L-Functions, 2 vols. LC 78-21184. (Proceedings of Symposia in Pure Mathematics Ser.: Vol. 33). 1980. pap. 44.00 set (ISBN 0-686-52415-2, PSPUM-33); Pt. 1. 25.00 (ISBN 0-8218-1435-4); Pt. 2. pap. 25.00 (ISBN 0-8218-1437-0). Am Math.
Borel, A., ed. see Symposium in Pure Mathematics-Boulder, 1965.
Borel, A., jt. auth. see Seminar on Complex Multiplication, Institute for Advanced Study, Princeton.
Borel, Armand, et al. Intersection Cohomology. (Progress in Mathematics Ser.: No. 50). 235p. 1984. text ed. 19.95 (ISBN 0-8176-3274-3). Birkhauser.
--Lie Algebras & Lie Groups. LC 52-42839. (Memoirs: No. 14). 54p. 1972. pap. 10.00 (ISBN 0-8218-1214-9, MEMO-14). Am Math.
Borel, B., jt. auth. see De Valuy, A.
Borel, Emile. Elemente der Mathematik, 2 vols. in 1. Staeckel, Paul, ed. (Bibliotheca Mathematica Teubneriana Ser: No. 42). Repr. of 1920 ed. 70.00 (ISBN 0-384-05115-4). Johnson Repr.
Borel, Jacques, jt. auth. see Verlaine, Paul.
Borel, Marie-Jeanne, et al. Essai de Logique Naturelle. (Sciences pour la Communication: Vol. 4). 241p. (Fr.). 1983. 21.60 (ISBN 3-261-05073-X). P Lang Pubs.
Borel, Pierre, jt. auth. see Devoluy, Pierre.
Borell, Ulf, et al. The Diagnosis of Hydatidiform Mole, Malignant Hydatiform Mole & Choriocarcinoma with Special Reference to the Diagnosti Value of Pelvic Arteriography. (Illus.). 128p. 1966. photocopy ed. 14.50x (ISBN 0-398-00190-1). C C Thomas.
Borella, Anne. The Home-Canning Handbook. 128p. 1975. Repr. 1.95 (ISBN 0-346-12194-9). Cornerstone.
--The Home Canning Handbook: A Guide to Preserving Food at Home. pap. 1.95 (ISBN 0-87502-040-2). Benjamin Co.
--How to Book: Canning, Freezing, Drying. 1977. 1.95 (ISBN 0-87502-051-8). Benjamin Co.
Borelli, Luigi & Borelli, Mary. Leggende e Racconti Italiani e Quindici Canzoni Popolaei Tradizionali: An Easy Reader for Beginners. 1985. pap. 5.50x (ISBN 0-913298-03-4). S F Vanni.
Borelli, Marianne. Therapeutic Touch: A Book of Readings. Heidt, Patricia, ed. LC 80-14109. 1981. pap. text ed. 14.95 (ISBN 0-8261-3111-5). Springer Pub.
Borelli, Mary, jt. auth. see Borelli, Luigi.
Borello, Robert A. How to Be Successful Selling Yourself in Real Estate. (Illus.). 272p. 1981. text ed. 13.95 (ISBN 0-13-402354-4). P-H.
Boreman, Thomas, ed. A Description of Three Hundred Animals. (Illus.). Repr. of 1786 ed. 18.00 (ISBN 0-384-05125-1). Johnson Repr.
Boren, et al. Apple Tree: Pre-Post Test Booklet. 52p. (gr. 1 up). 1972. 4.95 (ISBN 0-86575-026-2). Dormac.
Boren, Gary. Qualified Deferred Compensation Plans: Treatise, 1 vol. LC 83-23912. 1446p. 1983. 80.00 (ISBN 0-317-11357-7). Callaghan.
Boren, Henry. Roman Society. (Civilization & Society Ser.). 1977. pap. text ed. 9.95x (ISBN 0-669-84681-3). Heath.
Boren, Henry C. The Ancient World: An Historical Perspective. (Illus.). 384p. 1976. ref. ed. 25.95 (ISBN 0-13-036442-8). P-H.
--The Ancient World: An Historical Perspective. 2nd ed. (Illus.). 416p. 1986. pap. text ed. 19.95 (ISBN 0-13-036450-9). P-H.
--The Roman Republic. 192p. (Orig.). pap. 6.95 (ISBN 0-686-47408-2). Krieger.
Boren, James H. The Bureaucratic Zoo: The Search for the Ultimate Mumble. LC 76-39967. (Illus.). 1976. 6.95 (ISBN 0-914440-14-4). EPM Pubns.
--Fuzzify! Borenwords & Strategies for Bureaucratic Success. LC 82-1388. (Illus.). 200p. 1982. 9.95 (ISBN 0-914440-53-5). EPM Pubns.
Boren, Kerry R. Empty Honor: A Pay Dirt of Outlaw History. Bason, M. L. & Hughey, Roberta, eds. LC 84-50711. (Illus.). 200p. (Orig.). 1984. pap. write for info. (ISBN 0-9611028-4-5). Salt Warrior Pr.
Boren, Kerry R., jt. auth. see Rhoades, Gale R.
Boren, Sharon. An Apple in the Classroom. rev. ed. 90p. (gr. 3-8). 1983. pap. 9.95 activity wkbk. (ISBN 0-88056-120-3); tchr's manual 14.95 (ISBN 0-88056-118-1); write for info. (ISBN 0-88056-119-X). Dilithium Pr.
--A Commodore 64 for Kids. (Illus.). 160p. (gr. 4-8). 1985. pap. 9.95 (ISBN 0-88056-355-9). Dilithium Pr.
--A PET for Kids. (Illus.). 1983. pap. 7.95 (ISBN 0-88056-106-8). Dilithium Pr.
Boren, Sharon, et al. An Atari for Kids. 148p. (gr. 3-8). 1984. pap. 9.95 (ISBN 0-88056-123-8). Dilithium Pr.
--An Atari in the Classroom: Activity Workbook. 175p. (gr. 3-8). 1984. pap. 14.95 tchr's guide (ISBN 0-88056-109-2); pap. 5.95 wkbk (ISBN 0-88056-124-6). Dilithium Pr.
Borenius, Tancred & Tristram, Ernest W. English Medieval Painting. LC 75-11051. 1976. Repr. of 1929 ed. lib. bdg. 50.00 (ISBN 0-87817-167-3). Hacker.
Borenstein, Audrey. Chimes of Change & Hours: Views of Older Women in Twentieth-Century America. LC 82-48159. 520p. 1983. 49.50 (ISBN 0-8386-3170-3). Fairleigh Dickinson.
--Older Women in Twentieth Century America: A Selected Annotated Bibliography. LC 82-6082. (Women Studies, Facts & Issues: Vol. 3). 351p. 1982. 48.00 (ISBN 0-8240-9396-8). Garland Pub.
--Redeeming the Sin: Social Science & Literature. LC 78-9332. 269p. 1978. 26.00x (ISBN 0-231-04430-5). Columbia U Pr.
Borenstein, Emily. Cancer Queen. LC 78-71898. 1979. 12.95 (ISBN 0-87929-054-4). Barlenmir.
Borenzweig, Herman. Jung & Social Work. 226p. (Orig.). 1984. lib. bdg. 22.75 (ISBN 0-8191-4135-6); pap. text ed. 12.00 (ISBN 0-8191-4136-4). U Pr of Amer.
Borer. Instrumentation & Process Control for the Process Industries. 1985. 58.50 (ISBN 0-85334-342-X, Pub. by Elsevier Applied Sci England). Elsevier.
Borer, J. S., ed. Non-Invasive Techniques in Cardiology Journal: Cardiology, Vol. 71, No. 2-3, 1984. (Illus.). 112p. 1984. pap. 34.25 (ISBN 3-8055-3886-3). S Karger.
Borer, Katarina T., et al, eds. Frontiers of Exercise Biology. LC 83-81601. (Big Ten Body of Knowledge Symposium Ser.: Vol. 13). 304p. 1983. text ed. 31.95x (ISBN 0-931250-49-8, BB0R0049). Human Kinetics.
Borer, Mary C. London Walks & Legends. (Walks & Legends Ser.). (Illus.). 224p. 1982. pap. 4.95 (ISBN 0-583-13308-8, Pub. by Granada England). Academy Chi Pubs.
--Two Villages: Story of Chelsea & Kensington. (Illus.). 288p. 1974. 12.50 (ISBN 0-491-01061-3). Transatlantic.
Boreshkov. Application of Zeolites in Catalysis. 1981. 17.00 (ISBN 0-9960014-9-2, Pub. by Akademiai Kaido Hungary). Heyden.
Boresi, Arthur P. & Sidebottom, Omar. Advanced Mechanics of Materials. 4th ed. LC 84-883921. 763p. 1985. pap. text ed. 39.95x (ISBN 0-471-88392-1); write for info. (ISBN 0-471-81933-6). Halsted Pr.
Boresi, Arthur P., et al. Advanced Mechanics of Materials. 3rd ed. LC 77-28283. 696p. 1978. text ed. 44.50x (ISBN 0-471-08892-7). Wiley.
Borestone Mountain Poetry Awards, ed. Best Poems of 1958: Borestone Mountain Poetry Awards 1959, Vol. 11. LC 49-49262. 1959. 8.95 (ISBN 0-87015-095-2). Pacific Bks.
--Best Poems of 1960: Borestone Mountain Poetry Awards 1961, Vol. 13. LC 49-49262. 1961. 8.95 (ISBN 0-87015-105-3); pap. 4.95 (ISBN 0-87015-106-1). Pacific Bks.
--Best Poems of 1963: Borestone Mountain Poetry Awards 1964, Vol. 16. LC 49-49262. 1964. 8.95 (ISBN 0-87015-126-6); pap. 4.95 (ISBN 0-87015-127-4). Pacific Bks.
--Best Poems of 1964: Borestone Mountain Poetry Awards 1965, Vol. 17. LC 49-49262. 1965. 8.95 (ISBN 0-87015-142-8). Pacific Bks.
--Best Poems of 1966: Borestone Mountain Poetry Awards 1967, Vol. 19. LC 49-49262. 1967. 8.95 (ISBN 0-87015-157-6). Pacific Bks.
--Best Poems of 1967: Borestone Mountain Poetry Awards, 1968, Vol. 20. LC 49-49262. 1968. 8.95 (ISBN 0-87015-171-1). Pacific Bks.
--Best Poems of 1968: Borestone Mountain Poetry Awards 1969, Vol. 21. LC 49-49262. 1969. 8.95 (ISBN 0-87015-179-7). Pacific Bks.
--Best Poems of 1969: Borestone Mountain Poetry Awards 1970, Vol. 22. LC 49-49262. 1970. 8.95 (ISBN 0-87015-186-X). Pacific Bks.
--Best Poems of 1970: Borestone Mountain Poetry Awards 1971, Vol. 23. LC 49-49262. 1971. 8.95 (ISBN 0-87015-195-9). Pacific Bks.
--Best Poems of 1971: Borestone Mountain Poetry Awards 1972, Vol 24. LC 49-49262. 1972. 8.95 (ISBN 0-87015-200-9). Pacific Bks.
--Best Poems of 1972: Borestone Mountain Poetry Awards 1973, Vol. 25. LC 49-49262. 1973. 8.95 (ISBN 0-87015-208-4). Pacific Bks.
--Best Poems of 1973: Borestone Mountain Poetry Awards 1974, Vol. 26. LC 49-49262. 1974. 8.95 (ISBN 0-87015-217-3). Pacific Bks.
--Best Poems of 1974: Borestone Mountain Poetry Awards 1975, Vol. 27. LC 49-49262. 1975. 8.95 (ISBN 0-87015-219-X). Pacific Bks.
--Best Poems of 1975: Borestone Mountain Poetry Awards 1976, Vol. 28. LC 49-49262. 1976. 8.95 (ISBN 0-87015-223-8). Pacific Bks.
--Best Poems of 1976: Borestone Mountain Poetry Awards 1977, Vol.29. LC 49-49262. 1977. 8.95 (ISBN 0-87015-227-0). Pacific Bks.
Boreta, Anne & Cashel, Sue. Gummy Bear Goes to Camp. LC 82-50668. (Illus.). 48p. (Orig.). 1982. pap. 3.95 (ISBN 0-89815-075-2). Ten Speed Pr.
Boretos, John W. Concise Guide to Biomedical Polymers: Their Design, Fabrication & Molding. (Illus.). 208p. 1973. photocopy ed. 27.50x (ISBN 0-398-02674-2). C C Thomas.
Boretos, John W. & Eden, Murray, eds. Contemporary Biomaterials: Material & Host Response, Clinical Applications, New Technology & Legal Aspects. LC 84-3997. (Illus.). 673p. 1984. 84.00 (ISBN 0-8155-0980-4). Noyes.
Boretti, Giovanni A. Ercole in Tebe. Brown, Howard M., ed. LC 76-20968. (Italian Opera 1640-1770 Ser.). 1978. lib. bdg. 77.00 (ISBN 0-8240-2605-5). Garland Pub.
Boretz, Benjamin. Language, As a Music: Six Marginal Pretexts for Composition. LC 80-80807. (Illus.). 88p. 1980. lib. bdg. 13.95 (ISBN 0-939044-20-X). Lingua Pr.
--Talk: If I Am a Musical Thinker. 56p. (Orig.). 1985. pap. 5.95 (ISBN 0-88268-002-1). Station Hill Pr.
Boretz, Benjamin & Cone, Edward T., eds. Perspectives on Contemporary Music Theory. 304p. (Orig.). 1972. pap. 5.95 (ISBN 0-393-00548-8, Norton Lib). Norton.
--Perspectives on Schoenberg & Stravinsky. LC 83-12964. x, 284p. 1983. Repr. of 1972 ed. lib. bdg. 35.00x (ISBN 0-313-23204-0, BOPR). Greenwood.
Boreus, Lars O. Fetal Pharmacology. 445p. 1973. text ed. 43.50 (ISBN 0-911216-32-4). Raven.
Boreus, Lars O., ed. Principles of Pediatric Pharmacology. (Monographs in Clinical Pharmacology: Vol. 6). (Illus.). 1982. text ed. 32.00 (ISBN 0-443-08006-2). Churchill.
Borewicz, S. J. & Safarewic, I. R. Zahlentheorie. (Mathematische Reihe Ser.: No. 32). (Illus.). 468p. (Ger.). 1966. 57.95x (ISBN 0-8176-0039-6). Birkhauser.
Borg, Albert J. & De Waard, Jan. A Study of Aspect in Maltese. xvi, 188p. 1981. 15.50 (ISBN 0-89720-042-X); pap. 10.50 (ISBN 0-89720-043-8). Karoma.
Borg, Daniel R. The Old-Prussian Church & the Weimar Republic: A Study in Political Adjustment, 1917-1927. LC 83-40559. (Illus.). 388p. 1984. 35.00x (ISBN 0-87451-292-1). U Pr of New Eng.
Borg, Dorothy. Historians & American Far Eastern Policy. (Occasional Papers of the East Asian Institute). 41p. 1966. pap. 2.00 (ISBN 0-317-17105-4). Columbia U E Asian Inst.
Borg, Dorothy & Heinrichs, Waldo, eds. Uncertain Years: Chinese-American Relations, 1947-1950. LC 79-28297. (Studies of the East Asian Institute). 1980. 26.00x (ISBN 0-231-04738-X). Columbia U Pr.
Borg, I. Y. & Smith, D. K. Calculated X-Ray Powder Patterns for Silicate Minerals. LC 72-110814. (Gelological Society of America Memoir Ser.: No. 122). pap. 160.00 (ISBN 0-317-28991-8, 2023730). Bks Demand UMI.
Borg, I. Y., jt ed. see Heard, H. C.
Borg, John. Descriptive Flora of the Maltese Islands Including the Ferns & Flowering Plants. 846p. 1976. pap. text ed. 69.30 (ISBN 3-87429-104-9). Lubrecht & Cramer.
Borg, Marcus J. Conflict, Holiness & Politics in the Teachings of Jesus. LC 84-9029. (Studies in the Bible & Early Christianity: Vol. 5). 410p. 1984. 59.95x (ISBN 0-88946-603-3). E Mellen.
Borg, Nan, ed. see American Association of Critical Care Nurses.
Borg, Nicholas & David, Leonard. Arson: A Multi-Dimensional Problem. 1976. 2.50 (ISBN 0-686-17606-5, TR 76-4). Society Fire Protect.
Borg, S. F. Earthquake Engineering: Damage Assessment & Structural Design. (Methods & Applications in Civil Engineering Ser.). 110p. 1983. 24.95 (ISBN 0-471-26261-7). Wiley.
Borg, Seth A. & Rosenthal, Susan. Handbook of Cancer Diagnosis & Staging: A Clinical Atlas. LC 83-14597. 271p. 1984. 32.00x (ISBN 0-471-87073-0, Pub. by Wiley-Medical). Wiley.
Borg, Susan O. & Lasker, Judith. When Pregnancy Fails: Families Coping with Miscarriage, Stillbirth, & Infant Death. LC 80-28898. 224p. 1981. 14.95x (ISBN 0-8070-3226-3); pap. 8.95 (ISBN 0-8070-3227-1, BP613). Beacon Pr.
Borg, Walter R. Applying Educational Research: A Practical Guide for Teachers. LC 80-24854. 368p. 1981. text ed. 23.45x (ISBN 0-582-28145-8). Longman.
Borg, Walter S. & Gall, Meredith D. Educational Research. 4th ed. LC 82-20849. (Illus.). 768p. 1983. text ed. 29.95x (ISBN 0-582-28246-2). Longman.
Borgaonkar, Digamber S. Chromosomal Variation in Man: A Catalog of Chromosomal Variants & Anomalies. 4th ed. LC 83-25526. 1002p. 1984. 95.00 (ISBN 0-8451-0231-1). A R Liss.
Borgatello, Diego, tr. see Lemoyne, G. B., et al.
Borgatta, Edgar F. & Bohrnstedt, George W., eds. Sociological Methodology 1970. LC 74-110635. (Social & Behavioral Science Ser.). 1970. 32.95x (ISBN 0-87589-070-9). Jossey-Bass.
Borgatta, Edgar F. & Jackson, David J., eds. Aggregate Data: Analysis & Interpretation. LC 79-23909. 192p. 1980. 25.00 (ISBN 0-8039-1428-8); pap. 12.50 (ISBN 0-8039-1429-6). Sage.
Borgatta, Edgar F. & McCluskey, Neil G., eds. Aging & Society: Current Research & Policy Perspectives. LC 79-25727. (Sage Focus Editions: Vol. 18). (Illus.). 216p. 1980. 24.00 (ISBN 0-8039-1181-5); pap. 12.00 (ISBN 0-8039-1182-3). Sage.
Borgatta, Edgar F., jt. ed. see Bohrnstedt, George W.
Borgatta, Edgar F., jt. ed. see Jackson, David J.
Borgatta, Edgar F., jt. ed. see McCluskey, Neil G.
Borgatta, Edgar F., et al. Social Workers' Perceptions of Clients: A Study of the Caseload of a Social Agency. LC 80-27204. 92p. 1981. Repr. of 1960 ed. lib. bdg. 19.25x (ISBN 0-313-22812-4, BOSW). Greenwood.
Borge, Amy. The Monkey Business Payoff. 1983. 4.95 (ISBN 0-317-01470-6). Carlton.
--Santee Sam. (gr. 5 up). Date not set. 5.95 (ISBN 0-8062-2356-1). Carlton.
Borge, J. & Viasnoff, N. The Dakota: A Celebration of the DC3. LC 81-66412. (Illus.). 200p. 1982. 25.95 (ISBN 0-86710-007-9). Edns Vilo.
Borge, Jacques & Viasnoff, Nicolas. The Dakota: The DC3 Story. 192p. 1982. 60.00x (ISBN 0-7232-2963-5, Pub. by F Warne England). State Mutual Bk.
Borge, Tomas. Carlos, the Dawn Is No Longer Beyond Our Reach. Randall, Margaret, tr. from Span. (Illus.). 96p. 1984. lib. bdg. 11.95 (ISBN 0-919573-24-X); pap. 5.95 (ISBN 0-919573-25-8). Left Bank.
Borge, Tomas, et al. The Sandinistas Speak: Speeches & Writings of Nicaragua's Leaders. Taber & Reissner, trs. from Span. 250p. 1982. PLB 15.00 (ISBN 0-87348-618-8); pap. 4.95 (ISBN 0-87348-619-6). Path Pr NY.
Borgen, Johan. Lillelord. Moen, Elizabeth B. & Peterson, Ronald E., trs. from Norwegian. LC 81-14216. 384p. 1982. 16.00 (ISBN 0-8112-0826-5); pap. 7.95 (ISBN 0-8112-0827-3, NDP531). New Directions.
--The Red Mist. 1981. 9.95 (ISBN 0-7145-0896-9). Riverrun NY.
Borgen, William A. & Rudner, Howard L. Psychoeducation for Children: Theory, Programs & Research. (Illus.). 160p. 1981. 18.75x (ISBN 0-398-04441-4). C C Thomas.
Borgenicht, Miriam. Fall from Grace. 224p. 1984. 12.95 (ISBN 0-312-27978-7). St Martin.
--False Colors. 192p. 1985. 12.95 (ISBN 0-312-28011-4). St Martin.
--True or False? 144p. 1982. 10.95 (ISBN 0-312-82055-0). St Martin.
Borger, E., et al, eds. Logic & Machines-Decision Problems & Complexity: Proceedings of the Symposium "Rekursive Kompinatorik" Held from May 23-28, 1983 at the Institut fur Mathematische Logik und Grundlagenfroschung der Universitat Munster-Westfalen. (Lecture Notes in Computer Science Ser.: Vol. 171). vi, 456p. 1984. pap. 20.40. Springer-Verlag.
Borger, Gary A. Naturals. LC 79-23099. 224p. 1980. 17.95 (ISBN 0-8117-1006-8). Stackpole.
--Nymphing: A Basic Book. LC 78-11358. (Illus.). 192p. 1979. 14.95 (ISBN 0-8117-1010-6). Stackpole.
Borger, Mona M. Chinas, Dolls for Study & Admiration. LC 83-91074. (Illus.). 160p. 1983. 21.95 (ISBN 0-9611838-0-2). Borger Pubns.
Borger, R. & Cioffi, F., eds. Explanation in the Behavioural Sciences. LC 71-105497. 1970. 60.00 (ISBN 0-521-07820-2); pap. 24.95 (ISBN 0-521-09905-6). Cambridge U Pr.
Borger, Robert & Seaborne, A. E. The Psychology of Learning. rev. ed. 1982. pap. 5.95 (ISBN 0-14-080443-9, Pelican). Penguin.
Borger, Rykle. Handbuch der Keilschriftliteratur, Vol. 1: Repertorium. (Ger). 1977. 38.40x (ISBN 3-11-000125-X). De Gruyter.

--Handbuch der Keilschriftliteratur, Vol. 2: Anhang-Zur Kuyunjick-Sammlung. new ed. xxxii, 395p. (Ger.). 1975. 33.60x (ISBN 3-11-005960-6). De Gruyter.

--Handbuch der Keilschriftliteratur, Vol. 3: Inhaltliche Ordnung der sumerischen und akkadischen Texte. viii, 168p. (Ger.). 1975. 20.80x (ISBN 3-11-002487-X). De Gruyter.

Borgerhoff, Joseph L., ed. Nineteenth Century French Plays. (Fr). 1978. Repr. of 1931 ed. 49.50x (ISBN 0-89197-319-2). Irvington.

--Nineteenth Century French Plays. (Fr.). 1982. pap. text ed. 24.50x (ISBN 0-8290-1150-1). Irvington.

Borgerson, M. J. Advanced BASIC Programming Set. (General Trade Books). 1985. incl. disk 22.90 (ISBN 0-471-89547-4). Wiley.

Borgerson, Mark J. A BASIC Programmer's Guide to Pascal. LC 81-16281. 118p. 1982. pap. text ed. 11.95 (ISBN 0-471-09293-2, Pub. by Wiley Pr). Wiley.

Borgert, U. H. & Nylan, A. C. German Reference Grammar. 296p. 1975. 38.00x (ISBN 0-424-00010-5, Pub. by Sydney U Pr); pap. 22.00x (ISBN 0-424-00011-3, Pub. by Sydney U Pr). Intl Spec Bk.

Borges, Albert F. Elective Incisions & Scar Revision. 1973. 49.95 (ISBN 0-316-10269-5). Little.

Borges, Jorge L. The Aleph & Other Stories Nineteen Thirty-Three to Nineteen Sixty-Nine. 1979. pap. 5.95 (ISBN 0-525-47539-7, 0578-170). Dutton.

--Book of Imaginary Beings. Di Giovanni, Norman T., tr. (Illus.). 1979. pap. 3.95 (ISBN 0-525-47538-9). Dutton.

--The Book of Sand. Di Giovanni, Norman T., tr. 1979. pap. 5.95 (ISBN 0-525-47540-0, 0578-170). Dutton.

--Dr. Brodie's Report. 1979. pap. 2.50 (ISBN 0-525-47541-9). Dutton.

--Dreamtigers. Boyer, Mildred & Morland, Harold, trs. from Span. (Texas Pan American Ser.). (Illus.). 96p. 1985. pap. 6.95 (ISBN 0-292-71549-8). U of Tex Pr.

--Dreamtigers. Boyer, Mildred & Morland, Harold, trs. (Texas Pan American Ser.). (Illus.). 96p. 1985. pap. 6.95 (ISBN 0-292-71549-8). U of Tex Pr.

--Evaristo Carriego. Di Giovanni, Norman, tr. LC 83-1605. 192p. 1984. 16.95 (ISBN 0-525-24164-7, 01646-490); pap. 8.95 (ISBN 0-525-48085-4, 0869-290). Dutton.

--Ficciones. Kerrigan, Anthony, ed. & intro. by. 1962. pap. 6.95 (ISBN 0-394-17244-2, E368, Ever). Grove.

--In Praise of Darkness. Di Giovanni, Norman T., tr. LC 73-79553. 1974. pap. 5.95 (ISBN 0-525-03635-0). Dutton.

--Introduction to American Literature. Evans, Robert O. & Keating, L. Clark, eds. Evans, Robert O. & Keating, L. Clark, trs. from Span. LC 73-147854. 108p. 1971. Repr. of 1967 ed. 10.00x (ISBN 0-8131-1247-8). U Pr of Ky.

--Labyrinths: Selected Short Stories & Other Writings. Yates, Donald A. & Irby, James E., eds. LC 83-42700. 251p. 8.95 (ISBN 0-394-60449-0). Modern Lib.

--Labyrinths, Selected Stories & Other Writings. Yates, Donald A. & Irby, James E., eds. LC 64-25440. (Fr). 1969. pap. 6.95 (ISBN 0-8112-0012-4, NDP186). New Directions.

--Other Inquisitions. Simms, Ruth L., tr. from Span. (Texas Pan American Ser.). Orig. Title: Otros inquisiciones. 223p. 1964. 14.95 (ISBN 0-292-73322-4); pap. 7.95 (ISBN 0-292-76002-7). U of Tex Pr.

--A Personal Anthology. Kerrigan, Anthony, ed. & frwd. by. 1967. pap. 6.95 (ISBN 0-394-17270-1, E472, Ever). Grove.

--Seven Nights. Weinberger, Eliot, tr. from Span. LC 84-1018. Orig. Title: Siete Noches. 128p. 1984. 14.00 (ISBN 0-8112-0904-0); pap. 5.95 (ISBN 0-8112-0905-9, NDP576). New Directions.

--A Universal History of Infamy. Di Giovanni, Norman T., tr. 1979. pap. 2.95 (ISBN 0-525-47546-X). Dutton.

Borges, Jorge L. & Alifano, Roberto. Argentine Short Stories. 1984. write for info (ISBN 0-911441-04-2); text ed. write for info (ISBN 0-911441-05-0). Altamira Lascaux.

Borges, Jorge L. & Bioy-Cesares, Adolfo. Six Problems for Don Isidro Parodi. Di Giovanni, Norman T., tr. 160p. 1983. pap. 4.95 (ISBN 0-525-48035-8, 0481-140). Dutton.

Borges, Jorge L., et al. Dante Studies, Vol. I: Dante in the Twentieth Century. 1982. 15.00 (Dante U Am); lea. 25.00; leather ltd. ed. 50.00. Branden Pub Co.

Borges, Jorge Luis, et al. Dante Studies: Dante in the Twentieth Century, Vol. 1. 1982. 15.00 (ISBN 0-937832-16-2); leather 25.00 (ISBN 0-937832-17-0); limited 50.00 (ISBN 0-937832-18-9). Dante U Am.

Borges, Jorges L. Atlas. Kerrigan, Anthony, tr. (Illus.). 1985. 14.95 (ISBN 0-525-24344-5, 01258-370). Dutton.

Borges, Ricardo, tr. see Pesce, Celestino.

Borgese, Elisabeth M. The Mines of Neptune: Minerals & Metals from the Sea. (Illus.). 1985. 35.00 (ISBN 0-8109-1322-4). Abrams.

Borgese, Elisabeth M. & Ginsburg, Norton, eds. Ocean Yearbook, No. 5. LC 79-642855. 600p. 1985. lib. bdg. 49.00x est. (ISBN 0-226-06606-1). U of Chicago Pr.

--Ocean Yearbook: 2. LC 79-642855. 1981. 40.00x (ISBN 0-226-06603-7). U of Chicago Pr.

--Ocean Yearbook: 4. LC 79-642855. 620p. 1984. text ed. 49.00x (ISBN 0-226-06605-3). U of Chicago Pr.

Borgese, Elizabeth, tr. see Falassi, Alessandro & Catoni, Guiliano.

Borgese, Elizabeth M. & Ginsburg, Norton. Ocean Yearbook: 3. LC 79-642855. 672p. 1982. lib. bdg. 49.00x (ISBN 0-226-06604-5). U of Chicago Pr.

Borgese, Elizabeth M. & Ginsburg, Norton, eds. Ocean Yearbook: 1. 1979. 30.00x (ISBN 0-226-06602-9). U of Chicago Pr.

Borgese, Elizabeth M., tr. see Schenker, Heinrich.

Borgese, Guiseppe A. Goliath: The March of Fascism. LC 78-14102. 1979. Repr. of 1938 ed. 35.75 (ISBN 0-88355-776-2). Hyperion Conn.

Borgeson, Bet. Color Drawing Workshop. (Illus.). 144p. 1984. 24.95 (ISBN 0-8230-0721-9). Watson-Guptill.

--The Colored Pencil: Key Concepts for Handling the Medium. (Illus.). 144p. 1983. 23.50 (ISBN 0-8230-0742-1). Watson-Guptill.

Borgeson, Frithiof C. The Administration of Elementary & Secondary Education in Sweden. LC 74-176581. (Columbia University. Teachers College. Contributions to Education: No. 278). Repr. of 1927 ed. 22.50 (ISBN 0-404-55278-1). AMS Pr.

Borgeson, Griffith. Errett Lobban Cord, His Empire, His Motor Cars: Auburn-Cord-Duesenberg. (Illus.). 280p. 1983. 395.00 (ISBN 0-915038-35-8). Auto Quarterly.

--Golden Age of the Italian Racing Car. write for info. (ISBN 0-393-08583-X). Norton.

Borgeson, Paul, tr. see Jones, E. Stanley.

Borgeson, Paul, tr. see Sangster, W. E.

Borgeson, Paul W., tr. see Cardenal, Ernesto.

Borghesani, W. H., Jr. The Law & Inter-Corporate Trucking by Conglomerates. 1.00 (ISBN 0-686-31449-2). Private Carrier.

Borghese, Anita. The Down to Earth Cookbook. Rev. ed. LC 80-21483. (Illus.). 128p. (gr. 3 up). 1980. 9.95 (ISBN 0-684-16618-6, ScribJ). Scribner.

--The Great Year-Round Turkey Cookbook. LC 79-13605. (Illus.). 1979. 12.95 (ISBN 0-8128-2673-6). Stein & Day.

--The Great Year-Round Turkey Cookbook. LC 79-13605. (Illus.). 288p. 1982. pap. 8.95 (ISBN 0-8128-6168-X). Stein & Day.

--Just Desserts. 1979. Repr. of 1977 ed. 12.95 (ISBN 0-8128-2346-X). Stein & Day.

--Just Desserts. LC 77-8596. 1977. 12.95 (ISBN 0-8128-2346-X). Stein & Day.

Borghi, Armando. Mussolini: Red & Black. LC 73-20389. (Studies in Political Science, No. 94). 1974. lib. bdg. 42.95x (ISBN 0-8383-1765-0). Haskell.

Borghi, Luigi. Masters of the Violin, Vol. 1. Banat, Gabriel, ed. 75.00. Johnson Repr.

Borgin, Karl & Corbett, Kathleen. The Destruction of a Continent: Africa & International Aid. LC 82-47677. 216p. 1982. 14.95 (ISBN 0-15-125308-0). HarBraceJ.

Borgioli, A. & Cappelli, G. The Living Swamp. (Illus.). 120p. 1985. 14.95 (ISBN 0-85613-012-5, Pub. by Salem Hse Ltd). Merrimack Pub Cir.

Borglum, Lincoln & DenDooven, Gweneth R. Mount Rushmore: The Story Behind the Scenery. LC 76-57455. (Illus.). 1977. 8.95 (ISBN 0-916122-45-X); pap. 3.75 (ISBN 0-916122-20-4). KC Pubns.

Borglum, Lincoln, jt. auth. see Zeitner, June C.

Borgman, Albert. Technology & the Character of Contemporary Life: A Philosophical Inquiry. LC 84-8639. 342p. 1985. lib. bdg. 25.00x (ISBN 0-226-06628-2). U of Chicago Pr.

Borgman, Albert S. The Life & Death of William Mountfort. (Harvard Studies in English Ser: Vol. 15). Repr. of 1935 ed. 23.00 (ISBN 0-384-05135-9). Johnson Repr.

--The Life & Death of William Mountfort. 221p. 1983. Repr. of 1935 ed. lib. bdg. 50.00 (ISBN 0-89760-053-3). Telegraph Bks.

--Thomas Shadwell: His Life & Comedies. LC 68-56540. 1968. Repr. of 1929 ed. 15.00 (ISBN 0-405-08289-4, Blom Pubns). Ayer Co Pubs.

Borgman, Harry. Advertising Layout: A Step-by-Step Guide for Print & T.V. (Illus.). 144p. 1983. 23.50 (ISBN 0-8230-0154-7). Watson-Guptill.

--Art & Illustration Techniques. (Illus.). 1979. 22.50 (ISBN 0-8230-0272-1). Watson-Guptill.

--Drawing in Ink. (Illus.). 160p. 1977. 17.95 (ISBN 0-8230-1385-5). Watson-Guptill.

--Drawing in Pencil. (Illus.). 160p. 1981. 19.95 (ISBN 0-8230-1387-1). Watson-Guptill.

--The Pen & Pencil Technique Book. (Illus.). 176p. 1984. 27.50 (ISBN 0-8230-3989-7). Watson-Guptill.

Borgman, Jim. Smorgasborgman. Borgman, Lynn G., ed. (Illus.). 160p. (Orig.). 1982. pap. 6.95 (ISBN 0-9609632-0-0). Armadillo Pr.

Borgman, Lynn G., ed. see Borgman, Jim.

Borgman, Paul. TV: Friend or Foe? LC 78-73003. 1979. pap. 3.95 (ISBN 0-89191-072-7). Cook.

Borgnine, Tova & Trebek, Elaine C. The Tova Difference: Tova Borgnine's Beauty Book. (Illus.). 160p. (Orig.). 1984. pap. 9.95 (ISBN 0-671-50032-5, Fireside). S&S.

Borgnis, Mervin E. We Had a Shore Fast Line. (Illus.). 246p. 1979. 20.00 (ISBN 0-682-49411-9). Exposition Pr FL.

Borgo, S. Del see Del Borgo, S.

Borgos, Seth, jt. auth. see Adamson, Madeleine.

Borgstedt, H. V., ed. Material Behavior & Physical Chemistry in Liquid Metal Systems. LC 82-3680. 562p. 1982. 79.50x (ISBN 0-306-40917-8, Plenum Pr). Plenum Pub.

Borgstrom, B. & Brockman, H. L. Lipases. 500p. 1984. 123.00 (ISBN 0-444-80526-5, I-208-84, Biomedical Pr). Elsevier.

Borgstrom, Bengt-Erik. The Patron & the Panca. 184p. 1980. text ed. 17.50x (ISBN 0-7069-0997-6, Pub. by Vikas India). Advent NY.

Borgstrom, G. Harvesting the Earth. (Illus.). 1973. 11.49i (ISBN 0-200-71974-2). Har-Row.

Borgstrom, G., ed. Fish As Food, 4 vols. Incl. Vol. 1. Production, Biochemistry & Microbiology. 1961. 90.00 (ISBN 0-12-118501-X); Vol. 2. Nutrition, Sanitation & Utilization. 1962. 85.00 (ISBN 0-12-118502-8); Vol. 3. Processing, Part 1. 1965. 75.00 (ISBN 0-12-118503-6); Vol. 4. Processing, Part 2. 1965. 75.00 (ISBN 0-12-118504-4). Acad Pr.

Borgwardt, Barbara N. The No Milk Cookbook: For Mothers of Children with Milk Allergy. (Illus.). 75p. 1982. pap. 7.95 (ISBN 0-9608398-0-1). Parkway Pubns.

Borham, Gordon S. & Leaverton, Paul E. Use Habits of Cigarettes, Coffee, Aspirin & Sleeping Pills--United States, 1976. Cox, Klaudia, ed. (Series 10: No. 131). 1979. pap. text ed. 1.95 (ISBN 0-8406-0163-8). Natl Ctr Health Stats.

Borhegy, Stephen F. de see De Borhegy, Stephen F. & Body, E.

Borhegyi, Stephan F. Pre-Columbian Ballgames: A Pan-Mesoamerican Tradition. (Illus.). 48p. 1979. 6.95 (ISBN 0-89326-049-5). Milwaukee Pub Mus.

Borhek, James T. & Curtis, Richard F. A Sociology of Belief. LC 80-12472. 216p. 1983. Repr. of 1975 ed. lib. bdg. 13.50 (ISBN 0-89874-177-7). Krieger.

Borhek, Mary V. Coming Out to Parents: A Two-Way Survival Guide for Lesbians & Gay Men & Their Parents. LC 83-3971. 224p. 1983. pap. 9.95 (ISBN 0-8298-0665-2). Pilgrim NY.

--My Son Eric. LC 79-16161. (Orig.). 1979. 8.95 (ISBN 0-8298-0372-6). Pilgrim NY.

--My Son Eric. 160p. (Orig.). 1984. pap. 7.95 (ISBN 0-8298-0729-2). Pilgrim NY.

Borho, W., et al. Lebendige Zahlen - Fuenf Exkhursionen. (Mathematical Miniatures Ser.: Vol. 1). 116p. 1981. 13.95x (ISBN 0-8176-1203-3). Birkhauser.

Borich, Gary & Jemelka, Ron. Programs & Systems: An Evaluation Perspective. LC 81-17539. (Educational Technology Ser.). 1981. 35.00 (ISBN 0-12-118620-2). Acad Pr.

Borich, Gary, jt. auth. see Kubiszyn, Thomas.

Borich, Gary D. & Madden, Susan K. Evaluating Classroom Instruction: A Source-Book of Instruments. LC 76-2953. 1977. text ed. 21.90 (ISBN 0-201-00842-4, Sch Div). Addison-Wesley.

Borich, Gary D., jt. auth. see Kash, Marilynn M.

Borich, Gary D., ed. Evaluating Educational Programs & Products. LC 74-1298. 520p. 1974. 29.95 (ISBN 0-87778-070-6). Educ Tech Pubns.

Borich, Michael. The Black Hawk Songs. LC 74-23379. 86p. 1975. 10.00x (ISBN 0-252-00471-X); pap. 5.95 (ISBN 0-252-00528-7). U of Ill Pr.

--A Different Kind of Love. LC 84-22492. (gr. 6 up). 1985. 11.95 (ISBN 0-03-003249-0). HR&W.

--Nana's Ark. LC 83-13256. 288p. 1984. pap. 6.95 (ISBN 0-8407-5855-3). Nelson.

Borick, Paul M., ed. Chemical Sterilization. LC 73-4967. (Benchmark Papers in Microbiology Ser.: Vol. 1). 352p. 1973. 49.95 (ISBN 0-87933-036-8). Van Nos Reinhold.

Borie, E., tr. see Straumann, N.

Borie, Lou. Bugby Hole, St. Croix, U.S. Virgin Islands: A Land Use Plan. 49p. 1979. 7.50 (ISBN 0-318-14611-8). Isl Resources.

Borie, Marcia, jt. auth. see Wilkerson, Tichi.

Bories, J., ed. The Diagnostic Limitations of Computerised Axial Tomography. (Illus.). 1978. pap. 36.00 (ISBN 0-387-08593-9). Springer-Verlag.

Boring, E. G. see Rand, Gertrude.

Boring, Edwin G. History of Experimental Psychology. 2nd ed. 1950. 40.95 (ISBN 0-13-390039-8). P-H.

--Sensation & Perception in the History of Experimental Psychology. (Century Psychology Ser). 1977. 49.50x (ISBN 0-89197-491-1); pap. text ed. 24.50x (ISBN 0-89197-933-6). Irvington.

Boring, Edwin G. & Lindzey, Gardner, eds. History of Psychology in Autobiography, Vol. 5. LC 30-20129. (Century Psychology Ser.). (Illus.). 1967. 34.50x (ISBN 0-89197-216-1); pap. text ed. 18.95x (ISBN 0-89197-217-X). Irvington.

Boring, Edwin G., jt. ed. see Herrnstein, Richard J.

Boring, Edwin G., Vol et al, eds. History of Psychology in Autobiography, Vol 4. LC 68-10902. 1968. Repr. of 1952 ed. 15.00x (ISBN 0-8462-1098-3). Russell.

Boring, Holland, ed. Songs of Hope. 1979. pap. 2.75 (ISBN 0-88027-059-4). Firm Foun Pub.

Boring, Holland, Sr. & Cox, Bill. Gems for His Crown. 1977. pap. 2.25 (ISBN 0-88027-054-3). Firm Foun Pub.

Boring, M. Eugene. Sayings of the Risen Jesus: Christian Prophecy in the Synoptic Tradition. LC 81-18022. (Society for New Testament Studies Monograph: No. 46). (Illus.). 310p. 1981. 44.50 (ISBN 0-521-24117-0). Cambridge U Pr.

Boring, M. Eugene, tr. see Lohse, Eduard.

Boring, Mel. Incredible Constructions & the People Who Built Them. 96p. (gr. 4 up). 1985. PLB 13.85 (ISBN 0-8027-6560-2). Walker & Co.

--Sealth. LC 77-25470. (Story of an American Indian Ser.). (Illus.). (gr. 5 up). 1978. PLB 7.95 (ISBN 0-87518-155-4). Dillon.

--Wovoka. LC 80-24003. (Story of an American Indian Ser.). (Illus.). 64p. (gr. 5 up). 1981. PLB 7.95 (ISBN 0-87518-179-1). Dillon.

Boring, Phyllis Z. Victor Ruiz Iriarte. (World Authors Ser.). 1980. lib. bdg. 16.95 (ISBN 0-8057-6382-1, Twayne). G K Hall.

Boring, W. Eugene. Truly Human-Truly Divine: Christological Language & the Gospel Form. Lambert, Herbert, ed. 144p. 1984. pap. 11.95 (ISBN 0-8272-3625-5). CBP.

Bo Rin Ra. Bo Yin Ra: About My Books, Concerning My Name, & Other Texts. Reichenbach, Bodo A., tr. from Ger. LC 76-27910. 1977. pap. 1.75 (ISBN 0-915034-00-X). Kober Pr.

Borins, Sandford F. The Language of the Skies: The Bilingual Air Traffic Control Conflict in Canada. (Canadian Public Administration Series: IPAC). 352p. 1983. 30.00x (ISBN 0-7735-0402-8); pap. 12.95 (ISBN 0-7735-0403-6). McGill-Queens U Pr.

Boris, Constance M. & Krutilla, John V. Water Rights & Energy Development in the Yellowstone River. LC 79-3741. (Resources for the Future Ser.). 1980. text ed. 25.00x (ISBN 0-8018-2368-4). Johns Hopkins.

Boris, Constance M & Krutilla, John V. Water Rights & Energy Development in the Yellowstone River Basin: An Integrated Analysis. 296p. 1980. 25.00 (ISBN 0-8018-2368-4). Resources Future.

Boris, Edna Z. Shakespeare's English Kings, the People & the Law: A Study in the Relationship Between the Tudor Constitution & the English History Plays. LC 76-19838. 261p. 1978. 24.50 (ISBN 0-8386-1990-8). Fairleigh Dickinson.

Boris, Eileen. Art & Labor: Ruskin, Morris, & the Craftsman Ideal in America. (American Civilization Ser.). 288p. 1985. 37.95 (ISBN 0-87722-384-X). Temple U Pr.

Boris, Martin. Woodbridge, 1946. 288p. 1981. pap. 3.25 (ISBN 0-441-90865-9). Ace Bks.

Boris, Robert, jt. auth. see Hannibal, Edward.

Borisenko, A. I. & Tarapov, I. E. Vector & Tensor Analysis with Applications. LC 79-87809. 1979. pap. 6.00 (ISBN 0-486-63833-2). Dover.

Borisenko, Leonid F. Scandium: Its Geochemistry & Mineralogy. LC 62-15551. pap. 20.50 (ISBN 0-317-10633-3, 2003358). Bks Demand UMI.

Borish, Irvin M. Clinical Refraction, 2 vols. 3rd ed. LC 70-132836. 1970. leatherette 60.00 (ISBN 0-87873-008-7). Prof Press.

Borish, Irving, jt. auth. see Brooks, Clifford F.

Borishanskii, V. M., jt. auth. see Kutateladze, Samson S.

Borisoff. Walkie Talkie Patrol. (Mystery & Adventure Ser.). (Illus.). 32p. (gr. 2-4). PLB 7.95 (ISBN 0-317-31036-4). Creative Ed.

--Who's There? (Mystery & Adventure Ser.). (Illus.). 32p. (gr. 2-4). PLB 7.95 (ISBN 0-317-31038-0). Creative Ed.

Borisoff, Alexander. How to Write a Melody. 119p. 1981. pap. 9.95 (ISBN 0-938170-01-5). Wimbledon Music.

Borisoff, Deborah & Merrill, Lisa. The Power to Communicate: Gender Differences As Barriers. 100p. (Orig.). 1985. pap. text ed. 4.95x (ISBN 0-88133-130-9). Waveland Pr.

Borisoff, Norman. Bewitched & Bewildered: A Spooky Love Story. 112p. (Orig.). (gr. 7-11). 1982. pap. 1.95 (ISBN 0-440-90905-8, LFL). Dell.

--Bird Seed & Lightning. LC 72-75125. (Mystery & Adventure Ser.). (gr. 2-4). 1973. PLB 7.95 (ISBN 0-87191-206-6). Creative Ed.

--Don't Give up. LC 72-75126. (Mystery & Adventure Ser.). (gr. 2-4). 1973. PLB 7.95 (ISBN 0-87191-207-4). Creative Ed.

--Unknown Avenues. LC 72-77224. (Mystery & Adventure Ser.). (gr. 2-4). 1973. PLB 7.95 (ISBN 0-87191-205-8). Creative Ed.

--Who's There. LC 72-75123. (Mystery & Adventure Ser.). (gr. 2-4). 1973. PLB 7.95 (ISBN 0-87191-098-5). Creative Ed.

Borisov, et al. Diccionario de Economia Politica. 2nd ed. 256p. (Span.). 1977. pap. 6.95 (ISBN 84-253-0610-8, S-50074). French & Eur.

--Diccionario de Economia Politica. 264p. (Span.). 1975. pap. 6.95 (ISBN 84-7339-060-1, S-50150). French & Eur.

Borisov, C. B. & Dubinin, Y. V. Modern Diplomacy of Capitalist Powers. (World Leaders Speeches & Writings Ser.). 396p. 1983. 50.00 (ISBN 0-08-028173-7). Pergamon.

Borisov, O. The Soviet Union & the Manchurian Revolutionary Base 1945-1949. 276p. 1977. pap. 1.50 (ISBN 0-8285-0502-0, Pub. by Progress Pubs USSR). Imported Pubns.

Borisov, O. B. & Koloskov, B. T. Soviet-Chinese Relations, 1945-1970. Petrov, Vladimir, ed. LC 74-31443. 384p. 1975. 17.50x (ISBN 0-253-35410-2). Ind U Pr.

Borisov, P. Can Man Change the Climate? 175p. 1973. pap. 3.45 (ISBN 0-8285-0816-X, Pub. by Progress Pubs USSR). Imported Pubns.

Borisov, S. N., et al. Organosilicon Derivatives of Phosporus & Sulphur. LC 74-159028. 338p. 1971. 45.00x (ISBN 0-306-30511-9, Plenum Pr). Plenum Pub.

--Organosilicon Heteropolymers & Heterocompounds. LC 69-13393. (Monographs in Inorganic Chemistry Ser.). 633p. 1970. 55.00x (ISBN 0-306-30379-5, Plenum Pr). Plenum Pub.

Borisova, Y. S., et al. Outline History of the Soviet Working Class. 387p. 1975. 18.00x (ISBN 0-8464-0695-0). Beekman Pubs.

Borisova, Z. U. Glassy Semiconductors. Adashko, J. George, tr. from Rus. LC 81-17734. 516p. 1981. 85.00x (ISBN 0-306-40609-8, Plenum Pr). Plenum Pub.

Borisovich, Y. G. & Gliklikh, Y. E., eds. Global Analysis Studies & Applications I. (Lecture Notes in Mathematics Ser.: Vol. 1108). v, 301p. 1984. pap. text ed. 16.00 (ISBN 0-387-13910-9). Springer-Verlag.

Borissov, M., ed. Optical & Acoustic Waves in Solids-Modern Topics: Proceedings of the International School on Condensed Matter Physics, 2nd, Varna, Bulgaria Sept. 23-30, 1982. vi, 484p. 1983. 67.00x (ISBN 9971-950-61-8, Pub. by World Sci Singapore). Taylor & Francis.

Borisy, Gary G., et al, eds. Molecular Biology of the Cytoskeleton. LC 84-17566. 576p. 1984. 58.00 (ISBN 0-87969-174-3). Cold Spring Harbor.

Boritz, J. Efrim. Planning for the Internal Audit Function. Holman, Richard, ed. (Illus.). 339p. 1983. text ed. 37.50 (ISBN 0-89413-107-9, 522). Inst Inter Aud.

Borja, Corinne & Borja, Robert. Making Chinese Paper Cuts. Tucker, Kathleen, ed. LC 79-18358. (Crafts Bks.). (Illus.). (gr. 3-8). 1980. PLB 11.25 (ISBN 0-8075-4948-7). A Whitman.

Borja, Robert, jt. auth. see Borja, Corinne.

Borjas, George J. Union Control of Pension Funds: Will the North Rise Again? LC 79-66581. 41p. 1979. pap. 2.00 (ISBN 0-917616-36-7). ICS Pr.

--Wage Policy in the Federal Bureaucracy. 1980. pap. 4.25 (ISBN 0-8447-3410-1). Am Enterprise.

Borjas, George J. & Tienda, Marta, eds. Hispanics in the U. S. Economy. (Institute for Research on Poverty Monograph Ser.). 1985. 29.50 (ISBN 0-12-118640-7). Acad Pr.

Bork, A., ed. Computer Assisted Learning in Physics Education. LC 80-41129. (Illus.). 80p. 1980. 36.00 (ISBN 0-08-025812-3). Pergamon.

Bork, Albert, tr. see De Andrade, Oswald.

Bork, Alfred. Learning with Computers. (Illus.). 286p. 1981. 28.00 (ISBN 0-932376-11-8, EY-AX014-DP). Digital Pr.

--Personal Computers for Education. 179p. 1985. pap. text ed. 24.95 scp (ISBN 0-06-040868-5, HarpC). Har-Row.

Bork, B. A., ed. Researchers in Powder Metallurgy, Vol. 1. Michalewicz, Z. S., tr. from Rus. LC 66-15306. pap. 39.00 (ISBN 0-317-10429-2, 2020675). Bks Demand UMI.

Bork, E. & Kaper, E. Dansk-Tysk Ordbog. 626p. (Danish & Ger.). 1981. 24.95 (ISBN 87-01-93141-5, M-1283). French & Eur.

--Tysk-Dansk Ordbog. 550p. (Ger. & Danish.). 1981. 24.95 (ISBN 0-686-92483-5, M-1282). French & Eur.

Bork, Hans. Chronologische Studien Zu Otfrids Evangelienbuch. 27.00 (ISBN 0-685-02224-2); pap. 22.00 (ISBN 0-685-02225-0). Johnson Repr.

Bork, Paul F. The World of Moses. LC 78-5022. (Horizon Ser.). 1978. pap. 5.95 (ISBN 0-8127-0166-6). Review & Herald.

Bork, Robert H. The Antitrust Paradox: A Policy at War with Itself. LC 77-74573. 462p. 1980. pap. 11.95x (ISBN 0-465-00370-2, TB-5086). Basic.

Bork, Robert H., et al. Welfare Reform: Why? LC 76-25672. 1976. pap. 3.75 (ISBN 0-8447-2087-9). Am Enterprise.

Borka, H., jt. ed. see Slamecka, V.

Borkat, Roberta F., ed. see Cumberland, Richard.

Borkenau, Franz. End & Beginning: On the Generations of Cultures & the Origins of the West. Lowenthal, Richard, ed. 560p. 1981. 30.00x (ISBN 0-231-05066-6); pap. 14.95x (ISBN 0-231-05067-4). Columbia U Pr.

--Pareto. LC 78-20454. 1980. Repr. of 1936 ed. 19.00 (ISBN 0-88355-833-5). Hyperion Conn.

--Spanish Cockpit. 1963. pap. 6.95 (ISBN 0-472-06077-5, 77, AA). U of Mich Pr.

--The Totalitarian Enemy. LC 78-63654. (Studies in Fascism: Ideology & Practice). 256p. Repr. of 1940 ed. 29.50 (ISBN 0-404-16914-7). AMS Pr.

--Der Ubergang Vom Feudalen Zum Burgerlichen Weltbild. LC 74-25740. (European Sociology Ser.). 574p. 1974. Repr. 43.00x (ISBN 0-405-06496-9). Ayer Co Pubs.

Borkin, Ann. Form & Function. Ross, John R. & Lakoff, George, eds. LC 82-11417. (Language & Being Ser.). 192p. 1984. 27.50 (ISBN 0-89391-116-X). Ablex Pub.

Borkin, Joseph. The Crime & Punishment of I. G. Farben. LC 78-430. 1978. 16.95 (ISBN 0-02-904630-0). Free Pr.

--The Crime & Punishment of I. G. Farben. 1979. pap. 2.75 (ISBN 0-671-82755-3). PB.

Borkin, Joseph, jt. auth. see Waldrop, Frank.

Borkin, Sheldon A. Data Models: A Semantic Approach for Database Systems. (Illus.). 275p. 1980. 37.50x (ISBN 0-262-02151-X). MIT Pr.

Borking, John J. Third Party Protection of Software & Firmware: Direct Protection of Zeros & Ones. LC 84-24752. 522p. 1985. 74.00 (ISBN 0-444-87677-4, North-Holland). Elsevier.

Borkland, Elmer, ed. Contemporary Literary Critics. 2nd ed. (Contemporary Literary Critics Ser.). 600p. 1982. 64.00x (ISBN 0-8103-0443-0). Gale.

Borklund, Elmer, ed. Contemporary Literary Critics. 550p. 1978. 30.00x (ISBN 0-312-16678-8). St Martin.

Borko, Harold. Automated Language Processing. LC 66-26735. 386p. 1967. 23.50 (ISBN 0-471-08950-8, Pub. by Wiley). Krieger.

Borko, Harold & Bernier, C. L. Abstracting Concepts & Methods. (Library & Information Science Ser.). 250p. 1975. 25.00 (ISBN 0-12-118650-4). Acad Pr.

Borko, Harold & Bernier, Charles L. Indexing Concepts & Methods. (Library & Information Science). 1978. 20.00 (ISBN 0-12-118660-1). Acad Pr.

Borko, Harold, ed. Targets for Research in Library Education. LC 72-9923. pap. 63.30 (ISBN 0-317-26362-5, 2024223). Bks Demand UMI.

Bor-Komorowski, Tadeusz. The Secret Army. (Allied Forces Ser.: No. 2). (Illus.). 408p. 1984. Repr. of 1951 ed. 18.95x (ISBN 0-89839-082-6). Battery Pr.

Borkovec, A. B. & Kelly, T. J., eds. Insect Neurochemistry & Neurophysiology. 496p. 1984. 69.50x (ISBN 0-306-41511-9, Plenum Pr). Plenum Pub.

Borkovec, Thomas D., jt. auth. see Bernstein, Douglas A.

Borkowski, John G. & Anderson, D. Chris. Experimental Psychology: Tactics of Behavioral Research. 1977. pap. 16.85x (ISBN 0-673-15085-2). Scott F.

Borkowski, John G., jt. auth. see Anderson, D. Chris.

Borkowski, Piotr. English-Polish Dictionary of Idioms & Phrases. 206p. (Orig., Eng. & Pol.). 1982. pap. 6.95 (ISBN 0-903705-46-X). Hippocrene Bks.

Borland, Barbara D., ed. see Borland, Hal.

Borland, D. W., et al, eds. Physics of Materials. LC 79-67059. 1980. 42.00x (ISBN 0-643-02449-2, Pub by CSIRO). Intl Spec Bk.

Borland, Douglas. Homeopathy in Practice. reprint ed. LC 82-84366. 1983. pap. 9.95 (ISBN 0-87983-326-2). Keats.

Borland, Georgia O. Light upon the Path. 1984. 8.95 (ISBN 0-533-06050-8). Vantage.

Borland, Hal. Country Editor's Boy. LC 78-103597. 1970. 9.57 (ISBN 0-397-00640-3). Har-Row.

--A Countryman's Flowers. LC 80-2698. (Illus.). 208p. 1981. 22.50 (ISBN 0-394-51893-4). Knopf.

--The Golden Circle: A Book of Months. LC 77-23560. (Illus.). (gr. 5 up). 1977. 12.98i (ISBN 0-690-03803-8). Crowell Jr Bks.

--Hal Borland's Book of Days. 1985. pap. 9.95 (ISBN 0-393-30281-4). Norton.

--Hal Borland's Twelve Moons of the Year. Borland, Barbara D., ed. LC 79-2164. (Illus.). 1979. 15.00 (ISBN 0-394-50496-8). Knopf.

--Hal Borland's Twelve Moons of the Year. (Nonfiction Ser.). 1985. pap. 9.95 (ISBN 0-8398-2867-5). G K Hall.

--High, Wide & Lonesome: Growing up on the Colorado Frontier. 1984. pap. 6.95 (ISBN 0-8398-2850-0). G K Hall.

--The History of Wildlife in America. Bourne, Russell & MacConomy, Alma D., eds. LC 75-15494. (Illus.). 208p. 1975. 14.95 (ISBN 0-912186-20-8). Natl Wildlife.

--How to Write & Sell Non-Fiction. LC 72-7972. 223p. 1973. Repr. of 1956 ed. lib. bdg. 19.75x (ISBN 0-8371-6558-X, BONF). Greenwood.

--When the Legends Die. 224p. (YA) (gr. 6-12). 1972. pap. 2.75 (ISBN 0-553-24696-8). Bantam.

Borland, Hal & Line, Les. A Countryman's Woods. LC 83-47943. 1983. 25.00 (ISBN 0-394-52724-0). Knopf.

Borland, Hal G. When the Legends Die. LC 63-11753. (gr. 10 up). 1963. 9.95i (ISBN 0-397-00303-X). Har-Row.

Borland, Harriet. Soviet Literary Theory & Practice During the First Five-Year Plan, 1928-1932. LC 69-13833. Repr. of 1950 ed. lib. bdg. 27.50x (ISBN 0-8371-1075-0, BOSL). Greenwood.

Borland, R. Yarrow: Its Poets & Poetry. 1890. Repr. 25.00 (ISBN 0-8274-3779-X). R West.

Borlaug, Norman, jt. auth. see Hanson, Haldore.

Borlaug, Norman E. & Bente, Paul F., Jr. Land Use, Food, Energy & Recreation. 15p. (Orig.). 1983. pap. 6.00 (ISBN 0-940222-07-8). Bio Energy.

Borle, Marie, tr. see Armstrong, Virginia W.

Borman, Denis. The Queen's Brigade. 1984. 6.95 (ISBN 0-8062-2415-0). Carlton.

Borman, Ernest, et al. Interpersonal Communication in the Modern Organization. 2nd ed. (Illus.). 304p. 1982. text ed. 26.95 (ISBN 0-13-475061-6). P-H.

Borman, Gilbert, Jr. Nineteen Eighty Four Notes. (Orig.). 1984. pap. 3.25 (ISBN 0-8220-0899-8). Cliffs.

Borman, J. B. & Gotsman, M. S., eds. Rheumatic Valvular Disease in Children. (Illus.). 240p. 1980. pap. 57.90 (ISBN 0-387-10079-2). Springer-Verlag.

Borman, Joseph, ed. Recent Trends in Cardiovascular & Thoracic Surgery. 222p. 1975. 49.50 (ISBN 0-8089-0870-7, 790642). Grune.

Borman, Joseph B., jt. auth. see Kaplitt, Martin J.

Borman, K. M. The Social Life of Children in a Changing Society. (Illus.). 320p. 1982. text ed. 29.95x (ISBN 0-89859-187-2). L Erlbaum Assoc.

Borman, Kathryn, et al, eds. Women in the Workplace. LC 84-2941. (Modern Sociology Ser.). 268p. 1984. text ed. 29.50 (ISBN 0-89391-166-6). Ablex Pub.

Borman, Kathryn M., ed. The Social Life of Children in a Changing Society. LC 82-11557. 320p. 1982. text ed. 32.50 (ISBN 0-89391-165-8). Ablex Pub.

Borman, Leonard D., et al, eds. Helping People to Help Themselves: Self-Help & Prevention. LC 82-924. (Prevention in Human Services Ser.: Vol. 1, No. 3). 129p. 1982. text ed. 22.95 (ISBN 0-917724-67-4, B67). Haworth Pr.

Borman, Stuart A., ed. Instrumentation in Analytical Chemistry, Vol. 2. LC 72-95641. (Other Technical Bks.). 1982. 34.95x (ISBN 0-8412-0726-7); pap. 24.95x (ISBN 0-8412-0738-0). Am Chemical.

Bormann, Allen G., jt. auth. see Babbush, H. Edward.

Bormann, Ernest. Communication Theory. LC 79-24333. 264p. 1980. pap. text ed. 25.95 (ISBN 0-03-019086-X, HoltC). HR&W.

Bormann, Ernest & Bormann, Nancy C. Speech Communication: A Basic Approach. 3rd ed. 278p. 1981. pap. text ed. 14.50 scp (ISBN 0-06-040865-0, HarpC); instructors manual avail. (ISBN 0-06-360848-0). Har-Row.

Bormann, Ernest G. Discussion & Group Methods: Theory & Practice. 2nd ed. (Auer Ser.). 395p. 1975. text ed. 23.50 scp (ISBN 0-06-040863-4, HarpC); instructor's manual avail. (ISBN 0-06-360845-6). Har-Row.

Bormann, Ernest G. & Bormann, Nancy C. Effective Small Group Communication. 3rd ed. LC 80-65172. 1980. pap. text ed. 10.95x (ISBN 0-8087-4028-8). Burgess.

Bormann, Ernest G., jt. auth. see Howell, William S.

Bormann, F. H. & Likens, G. E. Pattern & Process in a Forested Ecosystem: Disturbance, Development & the Steady State Based on the Hubbard Brook Ecosystem Study. LC 78-6015. (Illus.). 1984. 24.50 (ISBN 0-387-90321-6). Springer-Verlag.

Bormann, Henry H. Unit Costs of School Building. LC 78-176582. (Columbia University. Teachers College. Contributions to Education: No. 842). Repr. of 1941 ed. 22.50 (ISBN 0-404-55842-9). AMS Pr.

Bormann, J., ed. Programming Languages & System Design. 252p. 1984. 32.75 (ISBN 0-444-86794-5, I-535-83, Pub. by North Holland). Elsevier.

Bormann, Martin. The Bormann Letters. Trevor-Roper, H. R., ed. Stevens, R. H., tr. LC 78-63655. (Studies in Fascism: Ideology & Practice). (Illus.). 232p. Repr. of 1954 ed. 24.50 (ISBN 0-404-16908-2). AMS Pr.

Bormann, Nancy C., jt. auth. see Bormann, Ernest.

Bormann, Nancy C., jt. auth. see Bormann, Ernest G.

Bormaster, Jeffrey S. & Treat, Carol L. Talking, Listening, Communicating. 120p. (Orig.). 1982. pap. text ed. 15.00x (ISBN 0-936104-26-0, 072). Pro Ed.

Borms, J., et al, eds. Human Growth & Development. 952p. 1984. 125.00x (ISBN 0-306-41518-6, Plenum Pr). Plenum Pub.

--The Female Athlete. (Medicine & Sport: Vol. 15). (Illus.). xiv, 218p. 1981. 53.00 (ISBN 3-8055-2739-X). S Karger.

--Women & Sport. (Medicine & Sport Ser.: Vol. 14). (Illus.). xiv, 234p. 1981. 53.00 (ISBN 3-8055-2725-X). S Karger.

Bormuth, John R. On the Theory of Achievement Test Items. LC 70-102071. 1970. 10.50x (ISBN 0-226-06630-4). U of Chicago Pr.

Bormuth, Robert, jt. auth. see Usher, Michael.

Bormuth, Robert, jt. auth. see Usher, Michael A.

Born, Ann R., tr. see Brandt, Frithiof.

Born, Anne. South Devon: Combe, Tor & Seascape. (Illus.). 192p. 1985. 16.95 (ISBN 0-575-03249-9, Pub. by Gollancz England). David & Charles.

Born, Anne, tr. see Dinesen, Isak.

Born, Betram De see De Born, Bertran.

Born, David O., jt. auth. see Pozoz, Robert S.

Born, Dorothy. Diabetes in the Family. LC 81-18024. (Illus.). 1982. 12.95 (ISBN 0-89303-067-8); pap. 9.95 (ISBN 0-89303-075-9). Brady Comm.

Born, E. The New Architecture in Mexico. 1976. lib. bdg. 59.95 (ISBN 0-8490-0719-4). Gordon Pr.

Born, Erhard. Lexikon Fuer Eisenbahnfreunde. (Ger.). 1977. pap. 39.95 (ISBN 3-7658-0238-7, M-7200). French & Eur.

Born, Ernest. Book of California Wine. (Broadsheet Ser.). 75.00 (ISBN 0-317-26981-X). U of Cal Pr.

Born, Ernest, et al. This Is a Printing Office Broadsheet. (Broadsheet Ser.: Issue 1). 1984. 75.00 (ISBN 0-520-05360-5). U of Cal Pr.

Born, Ernst. Lexikon Fuer Die Graphische Industrie. 2nd ed. (Ger.). 95.00 (ISBN 3-87641-184-X, M-7201). French & Eur.

Born, G. V., jt. auth. see Bagge, U.

Born, G. V. & Vane, J. R., eds. Interactions Between Platelets & Vessel Walls: Proceedings. (Royal Society of London Ser.). (Illus.). 196p. 1982. lib. bdg. 62.00x (ISBN 0-85403-164-2, Pub. by Royal Soc London). Scholium Intl.

Born, Gustav R. V., et al, eds. Factors in Formation & Regression of the Atherosclerotic Plaque. (NATO ASI Series A, Life Sciences: Vol. 51). 274p. 1982. 39.50x (ISBN 0-306-41035-4, Plenum Pr). Plenum Pub.

Born, Juergen, ed. see Kafka, Franz.

Born, K. E. International Banking in the 19th & 20th Centuries. 360p. 1984. pap. text ed. 14.75x (ISBN 0-907582-04-4, Pub. by Berg Pubs UK). Humanities.

Born, Karl B. International Banking in the 19th & 20th Centuries. Berghahn, Volker R., tr. LC 82-42715. 360p. 1983. 35.00 (ISBN 0-312-41975-9). St Martin.

Born, Lester K., tr. see Erasmus, Desiderius.

Born, M. Physics in My Generation. 2nd rev. ed. LC 68-59281. (Heidelberg Science Lib: Vol. 7). (Illus.). 1969. pap. 12.95 (ISBN 0-387-90008-X). Springer-Verlag.

Born, M. & Wolf, E. Principles of Optics: Electromagnetic Theory of Propagation, Interference & Diffraction of Light. 6th ed. (Illus.). 808p. 1980. 59.00 (ISBN 0-08-026482-4); pap. 29.50 (ISBN 0-08-026481-6). Pergamon.

Born, Max. Atomic Physics. 8th, rev. ed. Dougal, John, tr. LC 84-16503. (Illus.). 1969. 21.95x (ISBN 0-02-841650-3). Hafner.

--Einstein's Theory of Relativity. rev. ed. 376p. 1962. pap. 5.00 (ISBN 0-486-60769-0). Dover.

--Einstein's Theory of Relativity. rev. ed. 14.50 (ISBN 0-8446-1705-9). Peter Smith.

--My Life: Recollections of a Nobel Laureate. 308p. 1978. cancelled (ISBN 0-85066-174-9). Taylor & Francis.

--Restless Universe. 2nd ed. (Illus.). viii, 315p. 1951. pap. 6.00 (ISBN 0-486-20412-X). Dover.

Born, Max & Huang, Kun. Dynamical Theories of Crystal Lattics. (The International Series of Monographs on Physics). pap. cancelled (ISBN 0-317-08962-5, 2051181). Bks Demand UMI.

Born, R., ed. see Broers, A. & Smit, J.

Born, Warren C., ed. The Foreign Language Teacher in Today's Classroom Environment. 1979. pap. 7.95x (ISBN 0-915432-79-X). NE Conf Teach Foreign.

--Goals Clarification: Curriculum, Teaching, Evaluation. 1975. pap. 7.95x (ISBN 0-686-71010-X). NE Conf Teach Foreign.

--Language: Acquisition, Application, Appreciation. Incl. Language Acquisition. Cintas, Pierre F; Language Application. Elaster, Kenneth; Language Appreciation. Bure, Germaine. 1977. pap. 7.95x (ISBN 0-915432-77-3). NE Conf Teach Foreign.

--Language & Culture: Heritage & Horizons. 1976. pap. 7.95x (ISBN 0-915432-76-5). NE Conf Teach Foreign.

Born, Warren C. & Geno, Thomas H., eds. New Contents, New Teachers, New Publics. 1978. pap. 7.95x (ISBN 0-915432-78-1). NE Conf Teach Foreign.

Born, Wolfgang. American Landscape Painting: An Interpretation. LC 71-100222. Repr. of 1948 ed. lib. bdg. 27.50x (ISBN 0-8371-3253-3, BOAL). Greenwood.

Bornand, Odette, ed. see Rossetti, W. M.

Bornat, Joanna, et al. A Manifesto for Old Age. 128p. (Orig.). 1985. pap. 5.25 (ISBN 0-7453-0000-6, Pub. by Pluto Pr). Longwood Pub Group.

Borne, Lawrence R. Dude Ranching: A Complete History. LC 82-14773. (Illus.). 288p. 1983. 24.95x (ISBN 0-8263-0684-5). U of NM Pr.

Borne, Mortimer. Meet Moses: Fifty-Four Drawings in Color. LC 77-74180. (Illus.). 1981. 18.50 (ISBN 0-913870-39-0). Abaris Bks.

--The Visual Bible. LC 76-10438. (Illus.). 1977. 12.50 (ISBN 0-913870-15-3). Abaris Bks.

Bornecque. Les Annees d'Apprentissage d'Alphonse Daudet. 17.50 (ISBN 0-685-34890-3). French & Eur.

Bornecque, ed. see Dumas, Alexandre.

Bornecque, Henri & Cauet, Fernand. Dictionnaire Latin-Francais. 560p. (Fr. & Lat.). 1953. 39.95 (ISBN 0-686-56926-1, M-6044). French & Eur.

Borneman, Walter & Lampert, Lyndon J. Climbing Guide to Colorado's Fourteeners. LC 78-5947. (Illus.). 1978. pap. 8.95 (ISBN 0-87108-519-4). Pruett.

Borneman, Walter R. Marshall Pass: Denver & Rio Grande Gateway to the Gunnison Country. new ed. (Illus.). 160p. 1980. 22.95 (ISBN 0-937080-00-4). Century One.

Bornemann, Bernd. A. Paul Weber. (European University Studies Twenty-Eight: Vol. 19). 229p. (Ger.). 1982. 30.00 (ISBN 3-8204-6952-4). P Lang Pubs.

Bornemisza, Elmer & Alvarado, Alfredo. Soil Management in Tropical America. 1978. Set. lib. bdg. 250.00 (ISBN 0-8490-2622-9). Gordon Pr.

Bornet, E. & Flahault, C. Revision Des Noostocacees Heterocystees: Contocacees Dans les Principaux Herbiers De France, Vol. 1. 1969. 21.00 (ISBN 3-7682-0002-7). Lubrecht & Cramer.

Bornet, E. & Thuret, G. Notes Algologiques: Recueil D'observation Sur les Algues, 2 parts in 1 vol. (Bibl. Phyco.: Vol. 9). (Illus.). 1969. 70.00 (ISBN 3-7682-0601-7). Lubrecht & Cramer.

Bornet, Vaughn D. The Presidency of Lyndon B. Johnson. LC 83-12560. (American Presidency Ser.). 1984. 25.00x (ISBN 0-7006-0237-2); pap. 14.95 (ISBN 0-7006-0242-9). U Pr of KS.

Bornet, Vaughn D., jt. auth. see Robinson, Edgar E.

Bornheimer, Deane G., et al. The Faculty in Higher Education. LC 73-75889. xvi, 213p. 1973. text ed. 7.75 (ISBN 0-8134-1561-6). Interstate.

Bornhoeft, Theodore P. Prayers Responsively: Responsive Prayers for the Three-Year Lectionary. 1984. pap. 8.95 (ISBN 0-570-03922-3, 12-2861). Concordia.

Bornholdt, Laura. Baltimore & Early Pan-Americanism: A Study in the Background of the Monroe Doctrine. LC 49-10098. (Studies in History: No. 34). 1949. pap. 6.00 (ISBN 0-87391-002-8). Smith Coll.

Borning, Bernard C. The Political & Social Thought of Charles A. Beard. LC 84-703. xxv, 315p. 1984. Repr. of 1962 ed. lib. bdg. 45.00x (ISBN 0-313-24462-6, BOPS). Greenwood.

Bornkamm, Gunther. Jesus of Nazareth. LC 61-5256. 240p. 1975. pap. 8.61i (ISBN 0-06-060932-X, RD113, HarpR). Har-Row.

--The New Testament: A Guide to Its Writings. Fuller, Reginald H. & Fuller, Ilse, trs. from Ger. LC 73-79009. 176p. (Orig.). 1973. pap. 4.95 (ISBN 0-8006-0168-8, 1-168). Fortress.

--Paul. Stalker, D. M., tr. from Ger. LC 70-85068. 1971. short disc 15.95xi (ISBN 0-06-060933-8, HarpR). Har-Row.

Bornkamm, Gunther, et al. Tradition & Interpretation in Matthew. LC 63-10495. 308p. 1963. 13.95 (ISBN 0-664-20453-8). Westminster.

Bornkamm, Heinrich. Luther in Mid-Career, 1521-1530. Bachmann, E. Theodore, tr. from German. LC 82-48591. 736p. 1983. 36.95 (ISBN 0-8006-0692-2, 1-692). Fortress.

Bornkamm, R., et al. Urban Ecology. (Illus.). 384p. 1982. text ed. 55.00x (ISBN 0-632-00943-8). Blackwell Sci.

Bornoff, George & Wilson, Don, eds. Fiddler's Holiday. (Illus.). 63p. 1949. pap. 7.50 (ISBN 0-8258-0168-0, 0-3663). Fischer Inc NY.

Borns, Harold W., Jr., et al, eds. Late Pleistocene History of NE New England & Adjacent Quebec. (Special Paper Ser.: No. 197). (Illus.). 160p. 1985. 22.50 (ISBN 0-8137-2197-0). Geol Soc.

Bornschier, Volker & Chase-Dunn, Christopher. Multinational Corporations & Underdevelopment. 192p. 1985. 29.95 (ISBN 0-03-070542-8). Praeger.

Bornstein. Functional Signs: A New Approach from Simple to Complex. (Illus.). 384p. 1983. 22.00 (ISBN 0-8391-1839-2). Pro Ed.

Bornstein, Arthur. Memory: Arthur Bornstein's Memory Training Course. Orig. Title: Bornstein's Miracle Memory Course. (Illus.). 1979. Repr. of 1969 ed. 22.50 (ISBN 0-686-26172-0). Bornstein Memory Schls.

Bornstein, C. & Soucek, P. The Meeting of Two Worlds: The Crusades & the Mediterranean Context. 1981. pap. 15.00 (ISBN 0-912303-24-7). Michigan Mus.

Bornstein, Diane. The Lady in the Tower: Medieval Courtesy. 152p. 1983. lib. bdg. 15.00 (ISBN 0-208-01995-2, Archon). Shoe String.

--Mirrors of Courtesy. (Illus.). 158p. 1975. 18.50 (ISBN 0-208-01501-9, Archon). Shoe String.

Bornstein, Diane, jt. auth. see Fisher, John H.

Bornstein, Diane D. An Introduction to Transformational Grammar. LC 84-5125. 272p. 1984. pap. text ed. 11.50 (ISBN 0-8191-3905-X). U Pr of Amer.

Bornstein, George. Tranformations of Romanticism in Yeats, Eliot & Stevens. LC 75-43241. 1976. lib. bdg. 25.00x (ISBN 0-226-06643-6). U of Chicago Pr.

--Yeats & Shelley. LC 73-92050. 1970. 20.00x (ISBN 0-226-06645-2). U of Chicago Pr.

Bornstein, George, ed. Ezra Pound among the Poets. LC 85-1076. (Illus.). 256p. 1985. 15.00x (ISBN 0-226-06640-1). U of Chicago Pr.

--Romantic & Modern: Revaluations of Literary Tradition. LC 76-6658. 1976. 22.95x (ISBN 0-8229-3322-5). U of Pittsburgh Pr.

Bornstein, George & Finneran, Richard J., eds. Yeats; an Annual of Critical & Textual Studies, Vol. III-1985: A Special Issue on Yeats & Modern Poetry. LC 83-640488. 272p. 1985. text ed. 35.00x (ISBN 0-317-19689-8). Cornell U Pr.

Bornstein, Harry. All by Myself. (Signed English Ser.). 18p. 1975. pap. 2.50 (ISBN 0-913580-43-0). Gallaudet Coll.

--At Night: A Book of Prepositions. (Signed English Ser.). 32p. (Orig.). 1976. pap. 3.50 (ISBN 0-913580-57-0). Gallaudet Coll.

--Baby's Animal Book. (Signed English Ser.). 18p. 1973. pap. 2.50 (ISBN 0-913580-21-X). Gallaudet Coll.

--Be Careful. (Signed English Ser.). 32p. 1976. pap. 3.50 (ISBN 0-913580-55-4). Gallaudet Coll.

--Bobby Visits the Dentist. (Signed English Ser.). 48p. 1975. pap. 4.00 (ISBN 0-913580-38-4). Gallaudet Coll.

--A Book about Me. (Signed English Ser.). 18p. 1973. pap. 2.50 (ISBN 0-913580-19-8). Gallaudet Coll.

--Cars & Trucks & Things. (Signed English Ser.). 36p. 1974. pap. 3.50 (ISBN 0-913580-25-2). Gallaudet Coll.

--Circus Time. (Signed English Ser.). 18p. 1976. pap. 2.50 (ISBN 0-913580-51-1). Gallaudet Coll.

--The Clock Book. (Signed English Ser.). 36p. 1975. pap. 4.00 (ISBN 0-913580-48-1). Gallaudet Coll.

--Count & Color. (Signed English Ser.). 18p. 1973. pap. 2.50 (ISBN 0-913580-20-1). Gallaudet Coll.

--Fireman Brown. (Signed English Ser.). 18p. 1976. pap. 2.50 (ISBN 0-913580-50-3). Gallaudet Coll.

--The Gingerbread Man. (Signed English Ser.). 48p. 1976. pap. 4.00 (ISBN 0-913580-52-X). Gallaudet Coll.

--Good Manners. (Signed English Ser.). 40p. 1976. pap. 4.00 (ISBN 0-913580-58-9). Gallaudet Coll.

--Hansel & Gretel. (Signed English Ser.). 66p. 1975. pap. 4.50 (ISBN 0-913580-08-2). Gallaudet Coll.

--Happy Birthday Carol. (Signed English Ser.). 48p. 1973. pap. 4.00 (ISBN 0-913580-18-X). Gallaudet Coll.

--The Holiday Book. (Signed English Ser.). 48p. 1974. pap. 4.50 (ISBN 0-913580-30-9). Gallaudet Coll.

--How to. (Signed English Ser.). 48p. 1975. pap. 4.00 (ISBN 0-913580-36-8). Gallaudet Coll.

--I Am a Kitten. (Signed English Ser.). 18p. 1975. pap. 2.50 (ISBN 0-913580-44-9). Gallaudet Coll.

--I Want to Be a Farmer. (Signed English Ser.). 48p. 1975. pap. 4.50 (ISBN 0-913580-14-7). Gallaudet Coll.

--Jack & the Beanstalk. (Signed English Ser.). 64p. 1975. pap. 4.75 (ISBN 0-913580-47-3). Gallaudet Coll.

--Julia Goes to School. (Signed English Ser.). 48p. 1974. pap. 4.00 (ISBN 0-913580-34-1). Gallaudet Coll.

--Little Lost Sally. (Signed English Ser.). 40p. 1975. pap. 4.00 (ISBN 0-913580-40-6). Gallaudet Coll.

--Little Poems for Little People. (Signed English Ser.). 56p. 1974. pap. 4.50 (ISBN 0-913580-31-7). Gallaudet Coll.

--Matthew's Accident. (Signed English Ser.). 32p. 1975. pap. 3.50 (ISBN 0-913580-45-7). Gallaudet Coll.

--Mealtime at the Zoo. (Signed English Ser.). 48p. 1973. pap. 4.00 (ISBN 0-913580-11-2). Gallaudet Coll.

--Mouse's Christmas Eve. (Signed English Ser.). 44p. 1974. pap. 4.00 (ISBN 0-913580-28-7). Gallaudet Coll.

--My Toy Book. (Signed English Ser.). 16p. 1973. pap. 2.50 (ISBN 0-913580-22-8). Gallaudet Coll.

--The Night Before Christmas. (Signed English Ser.). 56p. 1976. pap. 4.50 (ISBN 0-913580-15-5). Gallaudet Coll.

--Night-Day, Work-Play. (Signed English Ser.). 48p. 1974. pap. 4.00 (ISBN 0-913580-23-6). Gallaudet Coll.

--Nursery Rhymes from Mother Goose. (Signed English Ser.). 56p. 1972. pap. 4.75 (ISBN 0-913580-07-4). Gallaudet Coll.

--Oliver in the City. (Signed English Ser.). 56p. 1975. pap. 4.50 (ISBN 0-913580-49-X). Gallaudet Coll.

--The Pet Shop. (Signed English Ser.). 16p. 1976. pap. 2.50 (ISBN 0-913580-54-6). Gallaudet Coll.

--Policeman Jones. (Signed English Ser.). 17p. 1976. pap. 2.50 (ISBN 0-913580-53-8). Gallaudet Coll.

--Questions & More Questions. (Signed English Ser.). 52p. 1973. pap. 4.50 (ISBN 0-913580-24-4). Gallaudet Coll.

--Sand, Sea, Shells & Sky. (Signed English Ser.). 36p. 1974. pap. 4.00 (ISBN 0-913580-32-5). Gallaudet Coll.

--Signed English for the Classroom. LC 75-2974. (Signed English Ser.). 70p. 1979. pap. 5.50 (ISBN 0-913580-37-6). Gallaudet Coll.

--Signed English for the Residence Hall. (Signed English Ser.). 100p. 1979. pap. 6.50 (ISBN 0-913580-61-9). Gallaudet Coll.

--Songs in Signed English. (Signed English Ser.). 44p. 1973. pap. 7.00 Book & Record (ISBN 0-913580-12-0). Gallaudet Coll.

--Spring Is Green. (Signed English Ser.). 52p. 1973. pap. 4.50 (ISBN 0-913580-17-1). Gallaudet Coll.

--Stores. (Signed English Ser.). 56p. 1974. pap. 4.50 (ISBN 0-913580-33-3). Gallaudet Coll.

--Tale of Peter Rabbit. (Signed English Ser.). 64p. 1975. pap. 4.75 (ISBN 0-913580-39-2). Gallaudet Coll.

--The Things I Like to Do. (Signed English Ser.). 18p. 1975. pap. 2.50 (ISBN 0-913580-41-4). Gallaudet Coll.

--Three Billy Goats Gruff. (Signed English Ser.). 56p. 1976. pap. 4.50 (ISBN 0-913580-56-2). Gallaudet Coll.

--Three Little Kittens. (Signed English Ser.). 32p. 1974. pap. 3.50 (ISBN 0-913580-16-3). Gallaudet Coll.

--Three Little Pigs. (Signed English Ser.). 44p. 1972. pap. 4.00 (ISBN 0-913580-09-0). Gallaudet Coll.

--Tommy's Day. (Signed English Ser.). 48p. 1973. pap. 4.00 (ISBN 0-913580-10-4). Gallaudet Coll.

--The Ugly Duckling. (Signed English Ser.). 48p. 1974. pap. 4.00 (ISBN 0-913580-29-5). Gallaudet Coll.

--We're Going to the Doctor. (Signed English Ser.). 28p. 1974. pap. 3.50 (ISBN 0-913580-26-0). Gallaudet Coll.

--When I Grow up. (Signed English Ser.). 46p. 1974. pap. 4.00 (ISBN 0-913580-35-X). Gallaudet Coll.

--With My Legs. (Signed English Ser.). 18p. (ps). 1975. pap. 2.50 (ISBN 0-913580-42-2). Gallaudet Coll.

Bornstein, Harry & Saulnier, Karen L. The Signed English Starter. (Signed English Ser.). (Illus.). xxii, 208p. (ps-6). pap. text ed. 11.95 (ISBN 0-913580-82-1). Gallaudet Coll.

Bornstein, Harry & Saulnier, Karen L., eds. The Comprehensive Signed English Dictionary. LC 82-21044. (Illus.). x, 454p. 1983. 25.95 (ISBN 0-913580-81-3). Gallaudet Coll.

Bornstein, Jerry. Unions in Transition. LC 81-13996. 192p. (gr. 7 up). 1981. PLB 10.79 (ISBN 0-671-41913-7); pap. 4.95. Messner.

Bornstein, Jerry, jt. auth. see Bornstein, Sandy.

Bornstein, M. H. & Kessen, W., eds. Psychological Development from Infancy: Image to Intention. 416p. 1979. 39.95x (ISBN 0-89859-229-1). L Erlbaum Assocs.

Bornstein, Marc H., ed. Comparative Methods in Psychology. LC 79-27558. (Crosscurrents in Contemporary Psychology Ser.). (Illus.). 320p. 1980. text ed. 29.95x (ISBN 0-89859-037-X). L Erlbaum Assocs.

--Psychology & Its Allied Disciplines: Psychology & the Humanities, Vol. I. 352p. 1984. 24.95 (ISBN 0-89859-320-4). L Erlbaum Assocs.

--Psychology & Its Allied Disciplines: Psychology & the Natural Sciences, Vol. III. 1984. pap. 24.95 (ISBN 0-89859-322-0). L Erlbaum Assocs.

--Psychology & Its Allied Disciplines. (Cross Currents in Contemporary Psychology Bornstein Ser.). 992p. 1984. lib. bdg. 74.95 (ISBN 0-89859-318-2). L Erlbaum Assocs.

--Psychology & Its Allied Disciplines: The Social Sciences, Vol. II. 304p. 1984. 24.95 (ISBN 0-89859-321-2). L Erlbaum Assocs.

Bornstein, Marc H. & Kessen, William, eds. Psychological Development from Infancy: Image to Intention. LC 78-27566. (Crosscurrents in Contemporary Psychology Ser). 404p. 1979. 24.95x (ISBN 0-470-26603-1). Halsted Pr.

Bornstein, Marcy T., jt. auth. see Bornstein, Philip H.

Bornstein, Morris, ed. Comparative Economic Systems: Models & Cases. 4th ed. 1979. 25.50x (ISBN 0-256-02152-X). Irwin.

--Economic Planning, East & West. LC 75-20470. 416p. 1975. prof. ref. 28.00 (ISBN 0-88410-283-1). Ballinger Pub.

Bornstein, Morris, intro. by. Plan & Market: Economic Reform in Eastern Europe. LC 72-91289. (Yale Russian & East European Studies Ser.: No. 12). (Illus.). pap. 106.00 (ISBN 0-317-09696-6, 2021982). Bks Demand UMI.

Bornstein, Morris, ed. The Soviet Economy: Continuity & Change. LC 80-21159. 381p. (Orig.). 1981. lib. bdg. 36.50x (ISBN 0-89158-958-9); pap. text ed. 13.95x (ISBN 0-89158-959-7). Westview.

Bornstein, Morris, et al, eds. East West Relations & the Future of Eastern Europe Politics & Economics. (Illus.). 288p. 1981. text ed. 28.50x (ISBN 0-04-330317-X). Allen Unwin.

Bornstein, N. Marc & Lamb, Michael E. Developmental Psychology: An Advanced Textbook. 616p. 1984. text ed. 29.95 (ISBN 0-89859-376-X). L Erlbaum Assocs.

Bornstein, Philip & Kazdin, Alan E., eds. Handbook of Clinical Behavior Therapy with Children. LC 84-71430. (Dorsey Professional Bks.). 1985. 55.00 (ISBN 0-256-03485-0). Dorsey.

Bornstein, Philip H. & Bornstein, Marcy T. Marital Therapy: A Behavioral-Communications Approach. (Psychology Practitioner Guidebooks). (Illus.). 160p. 1985. 17.50 (ISBN 0-08-031615-8, Pub. by P P I); pap. 9.95 (ISBN 0-08-031614-X). Pergamon.

Bornstein, Richard, jt. ed. see Yarbro, John.

Bornstein, Robert G., ed. Range & Transposition Guide to Two Hundred Fifty Musical Instruments. LC 64-22747. (Illus.). 1964. pap. 5.00 (ISBN 0-910736-01-4). Holly-Pix.

Bornstein, Ruth. Annabelle. LC 77-20059. (Illus.). (gr. k-1). 1978. o. p. 4.95i (ISBN 0-690-03804-6); PLB 8.89 (ISBN 0-690-03810-0). Crowell Jr Bks.

--The Dream of the Little Elephant. LC 76-27748. (Illus.). 32p. (ps-3). 6.95 (ISBN 0-395-28771-5, Clarion). HM.

--Jim. LC 77-12712. (Illus.). 32p. (ps-3). 1978. 7.95 (ISBN 0-395-28772-3, Clarion). HM.

--Little Gorilla. LC 75-25508. (Illus.). 32p. (ps-3). 1976. 9.95 (ISBN 0-395-28773-1, Clarion). HM.

--Of Course a Goat. LC 79-2015. (Illus.). 32p. (ps-3). 1980. PLB 9.89 (ISBN 0-06-020609-8). HarpJ.

Bornstein, Ruth L. I'll Draw a Meadow. LC 78-22481. (Illus.). (ps-1). 1979. PLB 9.89 (ISBN 0-06-020613-6). HarpJ.

Bornstein, Sandy & Bornstein, Jerry. New Frontiers in Genetics. LC 83-23758. (Illus.). 160p. (YA) 1984. PLB 10.79 (ISBN 0-671-45245-2). Messner.

Bornstein, Scott. Vocabulary Mastery. (Illus.). 272p. (YA) (gr. 9-12). 1982. 22.50 (ISBN 0-9602610-1-X); pap. 14.95 (ISBN 0-9602610-2-8). Bornstein Memory.

Bornstein, Stephen, et al, eds. The State in Capitalist Europe: A Casebook. (Casebook Series on European Politics & Society: No. 3). 208p. 1984. text ed. 37.50x (ISBN 0-04-350058-7); pap. text ed. 14.95x (ISBN 0-04-350059-5). Allen Unwin.

Bornstein, Susan B. Parents of Newborns. LC 80-5950. 153p. 1980. 12.95 (ISBN 0-86618-000-1). Family Serv.

Borochov, Ber. Class Struggle & the Jewish Nation: Selected Essays in Marxist Zionism. Cohen, Mitchell, ed. LC 83-4695. 358p. 1983. 29.95 (ISBN 0-87855-479-3). Transaction Bks.

--Nationalism & the Class Struggle. LC 70-97268. 205p. 1972. Repr. of 1937 ed. lib. bdg. 15.00x (ISBN 0-8371-2590-1, BONA). Greenwood.

Borodin, Leonid. The Year of Miracle & Grief. (Illus.). 186p. 1984. 13.95 (ISBN 0-7043-2447-4, Pub. by Quartet Bks). Merrimack Pub Cir.

Borodulina, T., ed. Marx, Engels & Lenin on Historical Materialism. 751p. 1972. 8.95 (ISBN 0-8285-0034-7, Pub. by Progress Pubs USSR). Imported Pubns.

Boroff, Edith. An Introduction to Elisabeth Claude Jacquet De la Guerre. (Wissenschaftliche Abhandlngen-Musicological Studies Ser.: Vol. 12). 140p. (Eng.). 1969. lib. bdg. 24.00 (ISBN 0-912024-82-8). Inst Mediaeval Mus.

Boroff, Marie. Pearl: A New Verse Translation. 1977. 7.95x (ISBN 0-393-04456-4); pap. 1.95x (ISBN 0-393-09144-9). Norton.

Boroffka, Alexander. Benedict Nta Tanka's Commentary & Dramatized Ideas on Disease & Witchcraft in Our Society: A Schreber Case from Cameroon African on His Mental Illness. (Medical Care in Developing Countries Ser.: Vol. 7). 150p. 1980. 19.45 (ISBN 3-8204-6901-X). P Lang Pubs.

Borok, B. A., ed. Researches in Powder Metallurgy, Vols. 1 & 2. Incl. Vol. 1. 148p. 1966 (ISBN 0-306-10774-0); Vol. 2. 126p. 1972 (ISBN 0-306-10775-9). LC 66-15306. 39.50x ea. (Consultants). Plenum Pub.

Borok, V. M., et al. Eight Papers on Functional Analysis & Partial Differential Equations. LC 51-5559. (Translations, Ser.: No. 2, Vol. 5). 1957. 29.00 (ISBN 0-8218-1705-1, TRANS 2-5). Am Math.

Borome, Joseph. Toussaint Louverture: A Life with Letters. 1986. pap. write for info. (ISBN 0-89874-572-1). Krieger.

Boron, Krystina, tr. see Lesmian, Boreslaw.

Boron, L. L., tr. see Zeidler, E.

Boron, Leo F., ed. see Natanson, I. P.

Boron, Leo F., tr. see Gramain, Andre.

Boron, Leo F., tr. see Natanson, I. P.

Boron, Leo F., tr. see Reidemeister, Kurt.

Boron, Leo. F, tr. see Riesz, Frigyes & Sz-Nagy, Bela.

Boron, Leon F., tr. see Gnedenko, Boris V. & Khinchin, Alexander Y.

Boronina, E. Siberian Forest Adventure. Birkett, G. A., ed. LC 66-25018. (Rus.). 1966. pap. text ed. 1.75x (ISBN 0-89197-485-7). Irvington.

Borooah, Anundoram. Ancient Geography of India. 120p. 1971. pap. 7.50x (ISBN 0-89684-367-X). Orient Bk Dist.

Borooah, Vani K. & Van der Ploeg, Frederick. Political Aspects of the Economy. LC 83-7738. (Cambridge Department of Applied Economics Ser.). 180p. 1984. 29.95 (ISBN 0-521-25841-3). Cambridge U Pr.

Boros, A. Electrical Measurements in Engineering: Studies in Electrical & Electronic Engineering Seventeen. 352p. 1985. 78.00 (ISBN 0-444-99582-X). Elsevier.

Boros, D. L. & Yoshida, T., eds. Basic & Clinical Aspects of Granulomatous Diseases. 348p. 1981. 75.00 (ISBN 0-444-90037-3, Biomedical Pr). Elsevier.

Boros, Julius. Swing Easy, Hit Hard. 192p. 1968. pap. 2.95 (ISBN 0-346-12305-4). Cornerstone.

Boros, L. The Hidden God. 132p. 1973. 5.95 (ISBN 0-8245-0313-9). Crossroad NY.

Boros, Ladislaus. Angels & Men. 1976. 6.95 (ISBN 0-8245-0201-9). Crossroad NY.

--Being a Christian Today. Davies, M. Benedict, tr. LC 79-13607. 124p. 1979. 7.95 (ISBN 0-8245-0202-7). Crossroad NY.

--Christian Prayer. 1976. 5.95 (ISBN 0-8245-0208-6). Crossroad NY.

--The Closeness of God. 1978. pap. 3.95 (ISBN 0-8245-0210-8). Crossroad NY.

--God's Image & Faith. Cunningham, Robert, tr. 1983. 6.00 (ISBN 0-8199-0858-4). Franciscan Herald.

--The Mystery of Death. 216p. 1973. pap. 3.95 (ISBN 0-8245-0330-9). Crossroad NY.

--Pain & Providence. 132p. 1975. pap. 2.95 (ISBN 0-686-85825-5). Crossroad NY.

Boros, Ladislaus, S.J Living in Hope. 120p. 1973. pap. 1.45 (ISBN 0-385-00133-9, Im). Doubleday.

Boros, Ladislav J. Flagorama: Exploring Our World with Flags. LC 73-84143. (gr. 3-10). 1973. pap. 4.50 (ISBN 0-915236-02-8). Focus Quality.

Borosage, Vera, jt. ed. see Morrison, Eleanor S.

Boroson, Warren. How to Buy or Sell Your Home in a Changing Market. 250p. 1983. softcover 16.95 (ISBN 0-87489-278-3). Med Economics.

--Physician's Guide to Professional & Personal Advisers. 1984. pap. 16.95 professional (ISBN 0-87489-355-0). Med Economics.

Boross, L., jt. auth. see Kremmer, T.

Borotto, A. V. Basic Flight Operations & Air Traffic Procedures for Pilots. LC 78-64346. 209p. 1978. pap. 9.95 (ISBN 0-87762-258-2). Technomic.

Borough, John. Notes of the Treaty Carried on at Ripon Between King Charles First & the Covenanters of Scotland, A. D. 1640. Bruce, John, ed. (Camden Society, London. Publications, First Ser.: No. 100). Repr. of 1869 ed. 19.00 (ISBN 0-404-50200-8). AMS Pr.

--Notes of the Treaty Carried on at Ripon Between King Charles First & the Covenanters of Scotland, A. D. 1640. 1869. 19.00 (ISBN 0-384-05145-6). Johnson Repr.

Borough, Rube, jt. auth. see Lindsey, Ben B.

Borough, William. A Discourse of the Variation of the Cumpas. LC 73-6102. (English Experience Ser.: No. 571). 60p. 1973. Repr. of 1581 ed. 21.00 (ISBN 90-221-0571-7). Walter J Johnson.

Boroumand, Jahangir, jt. auth. see Hicks, Norman.

Boroush, M. A., et al, eds. Technology Assessment: Creative Futures. (Systems Science & Engineering Ser.: Vol. 5). 406p. 1980. 58.50 (ISBN 0-444-00328-2, North-Holland). Elsevier.

Borover, William. Opticianry: The Practice & the Art. (The Science of Opticianry Ser.: Vol. II). 300p. 1982. Soft Cover 48.00 (ISBN 0-9606398-2-9). Gracie Ent.

Borover, William A. Opticianry: the Practice & the Art: Introduction to Dispensing, Vol. I. (Illus.). 259p. 1981. softcover perfect bound 48.00 (ISBN 0-9606398-0-2). Gracie Ent.

Borover, Wm. A. Opticianry: The Practice & the Art-Vol. IV-The Business of Opticianry. (Illus.). 1984. pap. text ed. write for info. (ISBN 0-9606398-4-5). Gracie Ent.

--Opticianry: The Practice & the Art-Vol. III-The Dynamics of Dispensing. (Illus.). 1983. pap. text ed. 48.00 (ISBN 0-9606398-3-7). Gracie Ent.

Borovik, G., jt. auth. see Ignatiev, O.

Borovik, Yehuda. Israeli Air Force: Nineteen Forty-Eight to the Present. (Illus.). 72p. 1984. pap. 7.95 (ISBN 0-85368-620-3, Pub. by Arms & Armour Pr). Sterling.

Borovits, Israel. Management of Computer Operations. (Illus.). 288p. 1984. 35.95 (ISBN 0-13-549493-1). P-H.

Borovkov, A. A. Asymptotic Methods in Queuing Theory. LC 83-12557. (Probability & Mathematical Statistics-Probability & Mathematical Statistics: 1-345). 276p. 1984. 47.95x (ISBN 0-471-90286-1, Pub. by Wiley-Interscience). Wiley.

--Stochastic Processes in Queueing Theory. LC 75-43242. (Applications of Math Ser.: Vol. 4). (Illus.). 1976. pap. 46.00 (ISBN 0-387-90161-2). Springer-Verlag.

Borovkov, A. A., ed. Advances in Probability: Limit Theorems & Related Problems. 500p. 1984. pap. 48.00 (ISBN 0-387-90945-1). Springer-Verlag.

Borovkov, A. A., et al. Nineteen Papers on Statistics & Probability. LC 61-9803. (Selected Translations on Mathematical Statistics & Probability Ser.: Vol. 2). 1962. 23.00 (ISBN 0-8218-1452-4, STAPRO-2). Am Math.

Borovsky, A. The Soviet Theatrical Poster. 1977. 30.00x (ISBN 0-317-14301-8, Pub. by Collet's). State Mutual Bk.

Borovsky, Natasha. A Daughter of the Nobility. LC 84-22453. 512p. 1985. 16.95 (ISBN 0-03-003294-6). HR&W.

Borow, Maxwell. Body Function in Health & Disease. 3rd ed. 1983. pap. text ed. 23.50 (ISBN 0-87488-758-5). Med Exam.

Borowiec, Andrew. The Mediterranean Feud. LC 82-16624. 206p. 1983. 32.95 (ISBN 0-03-061847-9). Praeger.

--Yugoslavia After Tito. LC 77-83466. (Praeger Special Studies). 138p. 1977. 38.95 (ISBN 0-03-040916-0). Praeger.

Borowiec, Wlayer A., et al. Ethnic Politics in Urban America: The Polish Experience in Four Cities. Pienkos, Angela T., ed. (Illus.). 1978. pap. 7.00 (ISBN 0-9602162-1-9). Polish American.

Borowiecki, M., et al, eds. Graph Theory. (Lecture Notes in Mathematics: Vol. 1018). 289p. 1983. pap. 17.00 (ISBN 0-387-12687-2). Springer Verlag.

Borowik, Ann. Lions Three, Christians Nothing. 192p. 1975. pap. 1.25 (ISBN 0-532-12273-9). Woodhill.

Borowitz, Albert. A Gallery of Sinister Perspectives: Ten Crimes & a Scandal. LC 81-19352. 175p. 1982. pap. 5.75 (ISBN 0-87338-271-4). Kent St U Pr.

--The Woman Who Murdered Black Satin: The Bermondsey Horror. LC 80-39756. (Illus.). 347p. 1981. 17.50 (ISBN 0-8142-0320-5). Ohio St U Pr.

Borowitz, Andy, et al. Square Pegs. Sharmat, Marjorie, adapted by. 128p. (YA) (gr. 5 up). pap. 2.25 (ISBN 0-440-97984-6, LFL). Dell.

Borowitz, Eugene. Liberal Judaism. LC 83-17997. 468p. (Orig.). 1984. pap. 8.95 (ISBN 0-8074-0264-8, 306050). UAHC.

--Understanding Judaism. 1979. 6.00 (ISBN 0-8074-0027-0, 341800). UAHC.

Borowitz, Eugene B. Choices in Modern Jewish Thought. 352p. 1983. pap. text ed. 9.95x (ISBN 0-87441-343-5). Behrman.

--Choosing a Sex Ethic: A Jewish Inquiry. LC 73-79123. (gr. 10-12). 1970. pap. 5.95 (ISBN 0-8052-0276-5). Schocken.

--Contemporary Christologies: A Jewish Response. LC 80-81051. 208p. (Orig.). 1980. pap. 7.95 (ISBN 0-8091-2305-3). Paulist Pr.

--Reform Judaism Today. 800p. 1983. pap. text ed. 9.95x (ISBN 0-87441-364-8). Behrman.

Borowitz, Eugene B., ed. see Rossel, Seymour.

Borowitz, Helen O. The Impact of Art on French Literature: From Scudery to Proust. LC 83-40317. (Illus.). 248p. 1985. 35.00 (ISBN 0-87413-249-5). U Delaware Pr.

Borowitz, Sidney. Essentials of Physics: A Text for Students of Science & Engineering. LC 70-131201. (Addison-Wesley Series in Physics). pap. 144.00 (ISBN 0-317-07995-6, 2052044). Bks Demand UMI.

Borowkow, A. A. Wahrscheinlichkeitstheorie. (Mathematische Reihe Ser.: No. 53). 264p. (Ger.). 1976. 32.95 (ISBN 0-8176-0788-9). Birkhauser.

Borowski, Harry R. A Hollow Threat: Strategic Air Power & Containment Before Korea. LC 81-4228. (Contributions in Military History Ser.: No. 25). xiii, 242p. 1982. lib. bdg. 29.95 (ISBN 0-313-22235-5, BHT/). Greenwood.

Borowski, Karol. Attempting an Alternative Society: A Sociology Study of a Selected Communal-Revitalization Movement in the United States. LC 84-16583. (Communal Societies & Utopian Studies Book Ser.). 281p. 1984. lib. bdg. 29.50 (ISBN 0-8482-7453-9). Norwood Edns.

Borowski, M. & Murch, M. Marital Violence: The Community Responses. 1983. pap. 10.95 (ISBN 0-422-78130-4, NO. 3777, Pub. by Tavistock). Methuen Inc.

Borowski, Tadeusz. This Way for the Gas, Ladies & Gentlemen. 1976. pap. 5.95 (ISBN 0-14-004114-1). Penguin.

Borowsky, Irvin J. Handbook for Color Printing. LC 74-15717. 1974. 35.00 (ISBN 0-912920-37-8). North Am Pub Co.

Borowsky, Philip, jt. auth. see Larson, Lex K.

Borradaile, G. J., et al, eds. Atlas of Deformational & Metamorphic Rock Fabrics. (Illus.). 530p. 1982. 64.00 (ISBN 0-387-11278-2). Springer-Verlag.

Borradaile, L. A. & Potts, F. A. Invertebrata. 4th ed. 1961. text ed. 44.50 (ISBN 0-521-04285-2). Cambridge U Pr.

Borras, A. A., ed. The Theatre & Hispanic Life: Essays in Honour of Neale H. Taylor. 97p. 1982. text ed. 12.00x (ISBN 0-88920-129-3, Pub. by Wilfred Laurier U Pr Canada). Humanities.

Borras, F. M. Russian Syntax: Aspects of Modern Russian Syntax & Vocabulary. 2nd ed. 1971. pap. 19.95x (ISBN 0-19-872029-7). Oxford U Pr.

Borras, F. M. & Christian, R. F. Russian Prose Composition: Annotated Passages for Translation into Russian. 1964. 12.95x (ISBN 0-19-815646-4). Oxford U Pr.

Borras, Jose. El Inmenso Amor De Dios. 96p. (Span.). 1981. pap. 3.95 (ISBN 0-311-43038-4). Casa Bautista.

Borras, Maria L. Picabia. LC 85-42540. (Illus.). 552p. 1985. 75.00 (ISBN 0-8478-0603-0). Rizzoli Intl.

Borras, Thomas Garcia see Garcia-Borras, Thomas.

Borregaard, Meta C. The Epithet in English & Scottish, Spanish & Danish Popular Ballads. LC 76-29622. 1976. Repr. of 1933 ed. lib. bdg. 12.50 (ISBN 0-8414-1758-X). Folcroft.

Borrego, Jose M., jt. ed. see Mortenson, Kenneth E.

Borrel, Eugene. L' Interpretation de la musique francaise: De Lully a la revolution. LC 76-43908. (Music & Theatre in France in the 17th & 18th Centuries). Repr. of 1934 ed. 24.00 (ISBN 0-404-60151-0). AMS Pr.

Borrell, Alexander. Mamiya M645 Book. 128p. 1983. pap. 9.95 (ISBN 0-240-51197-2). Focal Pr.

Borrelli, John, et al, eds. Advances in Irrigation & Drainage: Surviving External Pressures. LC 83-71586. 568p. 1983. pap. 44.00x (ISBN 0-87262-370-X). Am Soc Civil Eng.

Borrelli, Suzanne. Susanna. (Orig.). 1979. pap. 2.25 (ISBN 0-532-22154-0). Woodhill.

Borrello, Alfred. An E. M. Forster Glossary. LC 74-188548. 335p. 1972. 16.50 (ISBN 0-8108-0475-1). Scarecrow.

--H. G. Wells: Author in Agony. LC 77-180627. (Crosscurrents-Modern Critiques Ser.). 156p. 1972. 6.95 (ISBN 0-8093-0541-0). S Ill U Pr.

Borremans, Gary & Taylor, Chuck. The Hevil in Del City & Plant Your Head in an Iron Glee. 24p. 1982. pap. 2.50 (ISBN 0-941720-06-3). Slough Pr TX.

Borren, Charles V. Sources of Keyboard Music in England. Matthew, James E., tr. LC 78-106714. Repr. of 1914 ed. lib. bdg. 22.50x (ISBN 0-8371-3444-7, BOKM). Greenwood.

Borren, Charles van den see De Monte, Philippe.

Borren, Charles Van Den see Van Den Borren, Charles.

Borrer, William, jt. auth. see Turner, Dawson.

Borresen, Kari E. Subordination & Equivalence: The Nature & Role of Women in Augustine & Thomas Aquinas. Talbot, Charles H., tr. from Fr. & Ital. LC 80-67199. 390p. 1981. lib. bdg. 26.25 (ISBN 0-8191-1681-5); pap. text ed. 15.00 (ISBN 0-8191-1682-3). U Pr of Amer.

Borri, Christoforo. Cochin-China: Containing Many Admirable Rarities of That Countrey. LC 71-25710. (English Experience Ser.: No. 223). 1970. Repr. of 1633 ed. 9.50 (ISBN 90-221-0223-8). Walter J Johnson.

Borrie, John. Management of Thoracic Emergencies. 3rd ed. (Illus.). 500p. 1980. 46.50 (ISBN 0-8385-6124-1). ACC.

Borrie, M. S., jt. auth. see Burghes, D. N.

Borrie, W. D., ed. see International Union for the Scientific Study of Population.

Borriello, S. P., ed. Antibiotic Associated Diarrhoea & Colitis. (Developments in Gastroenterology Ser.). 188p. 1984. text ed. 35.50 (ISBN 0-89838-623-3, Pub. by Martinus Nijhoff Netherlands). Kluwer Academic.

--Clostridia in Gastrointestinal Disease. 256p. 1985. 77.00 (ISBN 0-8493-5656-3). CRC Pr.

Borrman, Axel & Stegger, Manfred. The European Community's Generalized System of Preferences. 276p. 1981. lib. bdg. 59.50 (ISBN 90-247-2547-X, Pub. by Martinus Nijhoff Netherlands). Kluwer Academic.

Borrmann, Axel, et al. The EC's Generalized System of Preferences. 276p. 1981. 56.00 (ISBN 90-286-2111-3). Sijthoff & Noordhoff.

Borrmans, M. Statut Personnel et Famille Au Maghreb De 1940 a Nos Jours. 56.00x (ISBN 90-279-7713-5). Mouton.

Borroff, Edith. Music in Europe & the United States: A History. (Illus.). 1971. text ed. 28.95 (ISBN 0-13-608083-9). P-H.

--The Music of the Baroque. LC 77-17401. (Music Reprint Ser.: 1978). (Illus.). 1978. Repr. of 1970 ed. lib. bdg. 25.00 (ISBN 0-306-77438-0). Da Capo.

--Notations & Editions. (Music Reprint Ser.). 1977. Repr. of 1974 ed. lib. bdg. 27.50 (ISBN 0-306-70867-1). Da Capo.

Borroff, Edith & Irvin, Marjory. Music in Perspective. (Illus.). 310p. (Orig.). 1976. pap. text ed. 17.95 (ISBN 0-15-564883-7, HC); 6 record set 24.95 (ISBN 0-15-564884-5). HarBraceJ.

Borroff, Edith, ed. see De Mondonville, Jean-Joseph C.

Borroff, Marie. Language & the Poet: Verbal Artistry in Frost, Stevens, & Moore. LC 78-14567. (Illus.). 1979. lib. bdg. 18.00x (ISBN 0-226-06651-7). U of Chicago Pr.

Borroff, Marie, tr. Sir Gawain & the Green Knight. (Orig.). 1967. pap. 2.95x (ISBN 0-393-09754-4, NortonC). Norton.

Borror, Donald & Glitz, Maurice L. Florida Bird Songs. 1980. pap. 4.95 record & booklet (ISBN 0-486-23956-X). Dover.

Borror, Donald J. Bird Song & Bird Behavior. 1971. pap. 5.95 booklet with record (ISBN 0-486-22779-0). Dover.

--Common Bird Songs. (Orig.). 1963. pap. 5.95 booklet with record (ISBN 0-486-21829-5). Dover.

--Common Bird Songs. 64p. 1984. pap. 7.95 manual & cassette (ISBN 0-486-99911-4). Dover.

--Dictionary of Word Roots & Combining Forms. LC 60-15564. 134p. 1960. pap. 5.95 (ISBN 0-87484-053-8). Mayfield Pub.

--Songs of Eastern Birds. pap. 5.95 booklet with record (ISBN 0-486-22378-7). Dover.

--Songs of Eastern Birds. 64p. 1984. pap. 7.95 incl. cassette (ISBN 0-486-99912-2). Dover.

--Songs of Western Birds. 1970. pap. 4.95 booklet with record (ISBN 0-486-22765-0). Dover.

--Songs of Western Birds. 64p. 1984. pap. 7.95 incl. cassette (ISBN 0-486-99913-0). Dover.

Borror, Donald J. & White, Richard E. Field Guide to the Insects of America North of Mexico. (Peterson Field Guide Ser). 1970. 15.95 (ISBN 0-395-07436-3). HM.

--A Field Guide to the Insects of America North of Mexico. LC 70-80420. (Peterson Field Guide Ser.). 1974. pap. 10.95 (ISBN 0-395-18523-8). HM.

Borror, Donald J., et al. An Introduction to the Study of Insects. 5th ed. text ed. 41.95 (ISBN 0-03-043531-5, CBS C). SCP.

Borrow. Qualitative Reasoning about Physical Systems. Date not set. price not set (ISBN 0-444-87670-7). Elsevier.

Borrow, G. The Songs of Scandinavia. 59.95 (ISBN 0-8490-1085-3). Gordon Pr.

Borrow, George. Celtic Bards, Chiefs & Kings. 1928. ltd. ed. 40.00 (ISBN 0-8482-0286-4). Norwood Edns.

--Romano Lavo-Lil: A Book of the Gypsy. 192p. 1982. pap. text ed. 6.75x (ISBN 0-86299-024-6, Pub. by Alan Sutton England). Humanities.

--Romany Rye. 1969. text ed. 8.95x (ISBN 0-460-00120-5, Evman); pap. text ed. 3.95x (ISBN 0-460-01120-0, Evman). Biblio Dist.

--The Romany Rye. 1984. pap. 7.95x (ISBN 0-19-281406-0). Oxford U Pr.

--Works, 16 vols. Shorter, Clement, ed. LC 24-5080. Repr. of 1924 ed. Set. 300.00 (ISBN 0-404-00970-0); 20.00 ea. AMS Pr.

Borrow, George H. Celtic Bards, Chiefs, & Kings. LC 76-13038. 1976. Repr. of 1928 ed. lib. bdg. 45.00 (ISBN 0-8414-3313-5). Folcroft.

--Welsh Poems & Ballads. LC 78-72620. (Celtic Language & Literature: Goidelic & Brythonic). Repr. of 1915 ed. 20.00 (ISBN 0-404-17537-6). AMS Pr.

Borrow, Margaret. Women Eighteen Seventy to Nineteen Twenty-Eight: A Select Guide to Printed & Archival Sources in the United Kingdom. 1981. lib. bdg. 73.00 (ISBN 0-8240-9450-6). Garland Pub.

Borrowman, Merle L. The Liberal & Technical in Teacher Education: A Historical Survey of American Thought. LC 77-24026. 1977. Repr. of 1956 ed. lib. bdg. 22.50x (ISBN 0-8371-9737-6, BOLT). Greenwood.

Borrowman, Merle L., ed. Teacher Education in America: A Documentary History. LC 65-17004. Repr. of 1965 ed. 66.00 (ISBN 0-8357-9609-4, 2016925). Bks Demand UMI.

Borrows, F. The Dancers Guide to the 1980's. (Ballroom Dance Ser.). 1985. lib. bdg. 79.95 (ISBN 0-87700-862-0). Revisionist Pr.

--History of Ballroom Dancing: The Dancing Master. (Ballroom Dance Ser.). 1985. lib. bdg. 79.95 (ISBN 0-87700-865-5). Revisionist Pr.

--Theory & Technique of Latin-American Dancing. (Ballroom Dance Ser.). 1985. lib. bdg. 66.00 (ISBN 0-87700-727-6). Revisionist Pr.

Borrup, Roger. Hartford & Wethersfield Horse Railway Co. (Transportation Bulletin: No. 77). (Illus.). 1970. 5.00 (ISBN 0-910506-02-7). De Vito.

--Plattsburgh (N.Y.) Traction Co. (Illus.). 51p. 1971. 5.00 (ISBN 0-910506-14-0). De Vito.

Borrup, Roger & Smith, Carl L. Hyde Park Division. (Transportation Bulletin Ser.: No. 82). (Illus.). 1977. 7.50 (ISBN 0-910506-18-3). De Vito.

Borrup, Roger, ed. see DeVito, Michael C.

Borrus, Michael, et al. U. S.-Japanese Competition in the Semiconductor Industry: A Study in International Trade & Technological Development. LC 82-81106. (Policy Papers in International Affairs Ser.: No. 17). (Illus.). x, 155p. 1982. pap. 7.50x (ISBN 0-87725-517-2). U of Cal Intl St.

Borrutto, Franco, et al, eds. Fetal Ultrasonography: The Secret Prenatal Life. 144p. 1982. 32.00x (ISBN 0-471-10162-1). Wiley.

Bors, Wolf, et al, eds. Oxygen Radicals in Chemistry & Biology: Proceedings-Third International Conference. LC 84-1691. xix, 1029p. 1984. 114.00x (ISBN 3-11-009704-4). De Gruyter.

Borsch, Frederick H. Christian & Gnostic Son of Man. LC 77-131585. (Studies in Biblical Theology, 2nd Ser.: No. 14). (Orig.). 1970. pap. text ed. 10.00x (ISBN 0-8401-3064-3). A R Allenson.

--Coming Together in the Spirit. 1981. pap. 1.10 (ISBN 0-8358-0426-7). Upper Room.

--Introducing the Lessons of the Church Year: A Guide for Lay Readers & Congregations. 240p. (Orig.). 1984. pap. 8.95 (ISBN 0-8164-2496-9, 6102, Seabury). Winston Pr.

Borsch, Frederick H. & Napier, Davie. Advent-Christmas. Achtemeier, Elizabeth, et al, eds. LC 79-7377. (Proclamation 2: Aids for Interpreting the Lessons of the Church Year, Ser. A). 64p. (Orig.). 1980. pap. 3.50 (ISBN 0-8006-4091-8, 1-4091). Fortress.

Borsch, Frederick H., ed. Anglicanism & the Bible. LC 83-62717. (Anglican Studies). (Orig.). 1984. pap. 8.95 (ISBN 0-8192-1337-3). Morehouse.

Borse. FORTRAN 77 & Numerical Methods for Engineers. 1985. text ed. write for info. (ISBN 0-534-04638-X, 22R2105, Pub. by PWS Engineering). PWS Pubs.

Borsellino, A. & Cervetto, L., eds. Photoreceptors. (NATO Series A, Life Sciences: Vol. 75). 368p. 1984. 55.00x (ISBN 0-306-41629-8, Plenum Pr). Plenum Pub.

Borsellino, Antonio, et al, eds. Developments in Biophysical Research. LC 80-25985. 378p. 1981. 55.00x (ISBN 0-306-40627-6, Plenum Pr). Plenum Pub.

Borsenik, Frank D. The Management of Maintenance & Engineering Systems in Hospitality Industries. LC 78-13677. (Service Management Ser.). 494p. 1979. text ed. 29.95 (ISBN 0-471-03213-1). Wiley.

--Property Management. (Illus.). 210p. (Orig.). 1974. 15.95 (ISBN 0-86612-003-3). Educ Inst Am Hotel.

Borsh, Frederick H. Power in Weakness: New Hearing for Gospel Stories of Healing & Discipleship. LC 82-15997. 160p. 1983. pap. 8.95 (ISBN 0-8006-1703-7, 1-1703). Fortress.

Borshchak, Il'Ko. Velykyi Mazepynets' Hryhor Orlyk. (Ukra.). 1972. text ed. 20.00 (ISBN 0-918884-20-9). Slavia Lib.

Borsheim, Roger M. Earth Watch. 168p. 1980. 8.00 (ISBN 0-682-49634-0). Exposition Pr FL.

Borsi, Franco. Bernini. LC 83-42931. (Illus.). 382p. 1985. 75.00 (ISBN 0-8478-0509-3). Rizzoli Intl.

--Leon Battista Alberti: The Complete Works. LC 75-23870. (Illus.). 1977. boxed 55.00i (ISBN 0-06-010411-2, HarpT). Har-Row.

Borsi, Franco & Godoli, Ezio. Vienna Nineteen Hundred. LC 85-42812. (Illus.). 320p. 1985. 45.00 (ISBN 0-8478-0616-2). Rizzoli Intl.

Borsi, Franco & Portoghesi, Paolo. Victor Horta. 104p. 1982. 40.00x (ISBN 0-85670-383-4, Pub. by Academy Editions England). State Mutual Bk.

Borsodi, Ralph. The Distribution Age: A Study of the Economy of Modern Distribution. LC 75-39235. (Getting & Spending: the Consumer's Dilemma). (Illus.). 1976. Repr. of 1927 ed. 26.50x (ISBN 0-405-08011-5). Ayer Co Pubs.

--Education & Living, 2 vols. 1980. Set. lib. bdg. 99.50 (ISBN 0-87700-288-6). Revisionist Pr.

--Inflation Is Coming. 1979. lib. bdg. 59.95 (ISBN 0-87700-289-4). Revisionist Pr.

Borsody, Stephen. The Tragedy of Central Europe. rev. ed. LC 80-51032. (Yale Russian & East European Publications Ser.: No. 2). (Illus.). xviii, 274p. 1981. 18.50 (ISBN 0-936586-01-X). Slavica.

--The Tragedy of Central Europe: Nazi & Soviet Conquest & Aftermath. (Russian & East European Publications Ser.: No. 2). 274p. 1980. 18.50 (ISBN 0-936586-01-X). Yale Russian.

Borsody, Stephen, ed. Hungary & the Hungarians: The Partition of a State & a Nation. LC 85-50189. (Yale Russian & East European Publications Ser.: No. 7). 1985. write for info. (ISBN 0-936586-07-9). Yale Russian.

Borsody, Stephen, tr. from Hungar see Janics, Kalman.

Borsoi, Edward E., jt. auth. see Cressey, William W.

Borsook, Eve. Companion Guide to Florence. (Illus.). 400p. 1983. 16.95 (ISBN 0-13-154484-5); pap. 8.95 (ISBN 0-13-154476-4). P-H.

--The Mural Painters of Tuscany: From Cimabue to Andrea Del Sarto. 2nd ed. (Oxford Studies in the History of Art & Architecture Ser.). (Illus.). 1981. 150.00x (ISBN 0-19-817301-6). Oxford U Pr.

Borsook, Henry. Vitamins: What They Are. (Orig.). pap. 2.50 (ISBN 0-515-05834-3). Jove Pubns.

Borsos, Tibor, jt. auth. see Rapp, Herbert J.

Borssuck, B. Ninety-Seven Needlepoint Alphabets. LC 74-19792. (Illus.). 128p. 1975. pap. 6.95 (ISBN 0-668-03655-9). Arco.

--One Thousand One Designs for Needlepoint & Cross Stitch. LC 77-1701. (Illus.). 1979. pap. 9.95 (ISBN 0-668-04222-2). Arco.

Borst, Bill. Baseball in a Nutshell. (Illus.). 32p. 1975. pap. 1.95 (ISBN 0-940056-04-6). Krank Pr.

--The Brooklyn Dodgers: A Fan's Memoir, 1953-1957. 106p. (Orig.). 1982. pap. 5.95 (ISBN 0-686-46429-X). Krank Pr.

--A Fan's Memoir: The Brooklyn Dodgers 1953-1957. 106p. (Orig.). 1982. pap. 5.95 (ISBN 0-940056-09-7). Chapter & Cask.

--The Pride of St. Louis: A Cooperstown Gallery. (Illus.). 96p. (Orig.). 1984. pap. 6.95 (ISBN 0-9612260-0-5). Krank Pr.

Borst, Bill & Riley, Pat. World Series Trivia, 1982. 2nd ed. (The Suds Ser.). (Illus.). 48p. 1982. pap. text ed. 3.95 (ISBN 0-686-47437-6). Krank Pr.

Borst, C. V., ed. Mind-Brain Identity Theory. LC 70-106388. (Controversies in Philosophy Ser). 1970. pap. text ed. 14.95 (ISBN 0-312-53305-5). St Martin.

Borst, Diane, jt. ed. see Montana, Patrick H.

Borst, James. Contemplative Prayer: A Guide for Today's Catholic. 1979. pap. 1.50 (ISBN 0-89243-106-7). Liguori Pubns.

Borst, Karen G., jt. ed. see Ford, Patrick K.

Borst, Raymond R. Henry David Thoreau: A Descriptive Bibliography. LC 81-50638. (Pittsburgh Series in Bibliography). (Illus.). 248p. 1981. 32.95x (ISBN 0-8229-3445-0). U of Pittsburgh Pr.

Borst, William A. Baseball Through a Knothole. (Illus.). 120p. (Orig.). (YA) 1981. pap. 4.95 (ISBN 0-940056-05-4). Krank Pr.

--Baseball Through a Knothole. (Illus., Orig.). 1980. pap. 5.95 (ISBN 0-940056-05-4). Chapter & Cask.

--Lord Byron's First Pilgrimage. LC 69-15679. (Yale Studies in English Ser.: No. 109). xxiv, 179p. 1969. Repr. of 1948 ed. 19.50 (ISBN 0-208-00773-3, Archon). Shoe String.

Borstein, Susan B. Parents of Newborns. LC 80-5950. 153p. 1980. 14.95 (ISBN 0-86618-000-1). Family Serv.

Borsuk, Karol. Theory of Shape. LC 76-359585. 379p. 1975. 37.50x (ISBN 0-8002-2343-8). Intl Pubns Serv.

Bort, Barry D., jt. auth. see Marks, Alfred H.

Bort, John & Helms, Mary. Panama in Transition: Local Reactions to Development Policies. (Monograph in Anthropology: No. 6). (Illus.). 189p. 1983. pap. 9.50 (ISBN 0-913134-75-9). Mus Anthro MO.

Borten, Helen. Halloween. LC 65-16184. (Holiday Ser.). (Illus.). (gr. 1-3). 1965. PLB 10.89 (ISBN 0-690-36314-1). Crowell Jr Bks.

Borth, Christy. Modern Chemists & Their Work. 410p. Repr. of 1943 ed. lib. bdg. 40.00 (ISBN 0-89984-024-8). Century Bookbindery.

Borthakur, D. N., jt. auth. see Poehlam, J. M.

Borthick, David & Britton, Jack L. Medals, Military & Civilian of the United States. LC 83-50563. (Illus.). 1984. 21.95 (ISBN 0-912958-25-1); spiral bound 14.95 (ISBN 0-912958-26-X). MCN Pr.

Borthwick, Bruce M. Comparative Politics of the Middle East: An Introduction. 1980. pap. text ed. 18.95 (ISBN 0-13-154088-2). P-H.

Borthwick, J. S. The Case of the Hook-Billed Kites. 256p. 1982. 12.95 (ISBN 0-312-12335-3). St Martin.

--The Case of the Hook-Billed Kites. 256p. 1983. pap. 3.50 (ISBN 0-14-006785-X). Penguin.

--The Down East Murders: A Mystery Set on the Coast of Maine. 288p. 1985. 14.95 (ISBN 0-312-21855-9). St Martin.

Borthwick, M., tr. see Key, Ellen.

Borthwick, Meredith. The Changing Role of Women in Bengal: 1849-1905. LC 83-43061. (Illus.). 450p. 1984. 40.00x (ISBN 0-691-05409-6). Princeton U Pr.

--Keshub Chunder Sen: A Search for Cultural Synthesis in India. 1978. 13.50x (ISBN 0-88386-904-7). South Asia Bks.

Borthwick, R. L. & Spence, J. E., eds. British Politics in Perspective. LC 83-40608. 243p. 1984. 27.50 (ISBN 0-312-10508-8). St Martin.

Borthwick, Sally. Education & Social Change in China: The Beginnings of the Modern Era, No. 268. LC 81-83853. (Publication Ser.). (Illus.). 182p. 1983. lib. bdg. 21.95 (ISBN 0-8179-7681-7). Hoover Inst Pr.

Bortin, Mortimer, ed. Alien Histocompatibility Antigens in Cancer: Biologic Significance & Potential Usefulness in Prevention, Diagnosis, & Treatment, Vol. 2. (A "Transplantation Proceedings" Reprint Ser.). 244p. 1982. 57.50 (ISBN 0-8089-1492-8, 790645). Grune.

Bortin, Mortimer M. & Truitt, Robert L., eds. Alien Histocompatibility Antigens in Cancer: Biologic Significance & Potential Usefulness in Prevention, Diagnosis & Treatment. 240p. 1980. 42.50 (ISBN 0-8089-1295-X, 790644). Grune.

Bortin, V. G. Image of a Man. 1984. pap. 3.95 (ISBN 0-440-14110-9). Dell.

--Image of a Man: A Novel of the Shroud of Turin. LC 83-1989. 432p. 1983. 16.95 (ISBN 0-385-29264-3). Delacorte.

Bortin, Virginia. Publicity for Volunteers: A Handbook. LC 81-50233. 128p. 1981. 10.95 (ISBN 0-8027-0685-1); pap. 6.95 (ISBN 0-8027-7176-9). Walker & Co.

--Publicity for Volunteers: A Handbook. 159p. 1981. pap. 7.50 (ISBN 0-318-17151-1, C81). Natl Ctr Cit Involv.

Bortner, Doyle M. Public Relations for Public Schools. LC 79-183947. 434p. 1983. 11.95 (ISBN 0-87073-509-8). Schenkman Bks Inc.

Bortner, M. A. Inside a Juvenile Court: The Tarnished Ideal of Individualized Justice. 328p. 1982. 45.00x (ISBN 0-8147-1062-X); pap. 15.00x. NYU Pr.

Borton, Hugh. American Presurrender Planning for Postwar Japan. (Occasional Papers of the East Asian Institute). 37p. 1967. pap. 2.00 (ISBN 0-317-17102-X). Columbia U E Asian Inst.

--Japan Since Nineteen Thirty-One, Its Political & Social Developments. LC 73-3922. 168p. 1973. Repr. of 1940 ed. lib. bdg. 15.00x (ISBN 0-8371-6859-7, BOJA). Greenwood.

--Japan's Modern Century: From Perry to 1970. 2nd ed. LC 70-110544. pap. 155.00 (ISBN 0-317-27964-5, 2055758). Bks Demand UMI.

Borton, Hugh, et al. Japan Between East & West. LC 76-40008. 1976. Repr. of 1957 ed. lib. bdg. 21.50x (ISBN 0-8371-9102-5, BOJE). Greenwood.

Borton, Hugh, et al, eds. Selected List of Books & Articles on Japan in English, French & German. rev. & enl. ed. LC 53-5055. (Harvard-Yenching Institute Publications Ser). 1954. 17.50x (ISBN 0-674-79800-7). Harvard U Pr.

Borton, Lady see Lady Borton.

Borton, Mark C. Vassar: A Photographic Celebration. (Illus.). 112p. 1984. 30.00 (ISBN 0-930527-01-1); pap. 20.00 (ISBN 0-930527-00-3). Embassy Imp.

Borton, Samuel L., tr. see Steiner, Rudolf.

Bortoni-Ricardo, Stella. The Urbanization of Rural Dialect Speakers: A Sociolinguistic Study in Brazil. (Cambridge Studies in Linguistics: Supplementary Volumes). 350p. Date not set. price not set. (ISBN 0-521-30404-0). Cambridge U Pr.

Borts, George H. & Stein, Jerome L. Economic Growth in a Free Market. LC 64-13735. 235p. 1964. 30.00x (ISBN 0-231-02666-8). Columbia U Pr.

Bortstein, Larry. After Olympic Glory: The Lives of Ten Outstanding Medalists. LC 76-6779. (Illus.). (gr. 5 up). 1978. 6.95 (ISBN 0-7232-6135-0). Warne.

Bortz. Handbook for Developing Occupational Curricula. 1985. 25.95 (ISBN 0-205-07118-X, 467118). Allyn.

Bortz, A. Robotics: A Decision-Makers Guide. 1986. cancelled. Van Nos Reinhold.

Bortz, John, jt. auth. see Mader, Chris.

Bortz, Paul. Getting More Heat from Your Fireplace. LC 81-13389. (Illus.). 156p. 1982. pap. 7.95 (ISBN 0-88266-254-6). Garden Way Pub.

Bortz, Seymour A., jt. ed. see Acquaviva, Samuel J.

Bortz, W. M., jt. ed. see Holmes, W. L.

Boruch, Behn. Coat of Many Colors. 1959. 3.95 (ISBN 0-88482-728-3). Hebrew Pub.

--In the Beginning. 1958. 4.00 (ISBN 0-88482-727-5). Hebrew Pub.

--The Patriarchs. 28p. 1959. 3.95 (ISBN 0-88482-729-1). Hebrew Pub.

Boruch, Robert F. & Cecil, Joe S. Assuring the Confidentiality of Social Research Data. LC 78-65113. (Illus.). 1979. 27.50x (ISBN 0-8122-7761-9). U of Pa Pr.

Boruch, Robert F., jt. auth. see Riecken, Henry W.

Boruch, Robert F. & Cecil, Joe S., eds. Solutions to Ethical & Legal Problems in Social Research: Symposium. LC 83-2697. (Quantitative Studies in Social Relations). 335p. 1983. 31.50 (ISBN 0-12-118680-6). Acad Pr.

Boruch, Robert F., et al. Reanalyzing Program Evaluations: Policies & Practices for Secondary Analysis of Social & Educational Programs. LC 81-2841. (Social & Behavioral Science Ser.). 1981. text ed. 35.00x (ISBN 0-87589-495-X). Jossey-Bass.

Borujerdi, J., tr. see Khomeini, Ayatollah.

Borum, Poul. Danish Literature: A Short Critical Survey. LC 80-501886. (Danes of the Present & Past Ser.). (Illus.). 140p. 1979. pap. text ed. 9.95 (ISBN 87-7429-030-4, Pub. by Det Danske Selskab Denmark). Nordic Bks.

Borun, Minda, et al. Women's Liberation: An Anthropological View. 1971. pap. 2.00 (ISBN 0-912786-19-1). Know Inc.

Borunda, Alfredo, tr. see Harshberger, Claudette.

Borus, Michael. Measuring the Impact of Employment-Related Social Programs: A Primer on the Evaluation of Employment & Training, Vocational Education, Vocational Rehabilitation & Other Job-Oriented Programs. 139p. 1979. pap. 7.95 (ISBN 0-911558-63-2). W E Upjohn.

Borus, Michael E. Measuring the Impact of Employment Related Social Programs: A Primer on the Evaluation of Employment & Training, Vocational Education, Vocational Rehabilitation, Other Job Oriented Programs. LC 79-13151. 1979. pap. text ed. 7.95 (ISBN 0-911558-63-2). W E Upjohn.

--Tomorrow's Workers. LC 82-17154. 208p. 1982. 28.50x (ISBN 0-669-06090-9). Lexington Bks.

Borus, Michael E. & Tash, William R. Measuring the Impact of Manpower Programs: A Primer. LC 73-633548. (Policy Papers in Human Resources & Industrial Relations Ser.: No. 17). (Orig.). 1970. pap. 2.50x (ISBN 0-87736-117-7). U of Mich Inst Labor.

Borus, Michael E., et al. Evaluating the Impact of Health Programs: A Primer. 160p. 1982. 22.50x (ISBN 0-262-02178-1); pap. text ed. 9.95x (ISBN 0-262-52075-3). MIT Pr.

Boruvka, O. Foundations of the Theory of Groupoids & Groups. 216p. 1975. 39.95x (ISBN 0-8176-0780-3). Birkhauser.

Borwick, John. The Gramophone Guide to Hi-Fi Stereo. (Illus.). 192p. 1982. 31.50 (ISBN 0-7153-8231-4). David & Charles.

--Sound Recording Practice. 2nd ed. 1980. 55.00x (ISBN 0-19-311920-X). Oxford U Pr.

Borwick, Robin. The Book of the Donkey. (Illus.). 256p. 1983. 17.95 (ISBN 0-7207-1362-5, Pub. by Michael Joseph). Merrimack Pub Cir.

Bory, Jean-Francois, ed. Once Again: Concrete Poetry. LC 68-15878. (Illus.). 1968. 4.50 (ISBN 0-8112-0251-8); pap. 1.50 (ISBN 0-8112-0010-8, NDP256). New Directions.

Bory, Jean-Louis, jt. auth. see Hermann, Bernard.

Boryczka, Raymond & Cary, Lorin L. No Strength Without Union: An Illustrated History of Ohio Workers, 1803-1980. (Illus.). 328p. 19.95 (ISBN 0-318-00987-0). Ohio Hist Soc.

Boryczka, Raymond, jt. auth. see Ohio Labor History Project Staff.

Borys, Jurij. The Russian Communist Party & the Sovietization of Ukraine: A Study in the Communist Doctrine of the Self-Determination of Nations. LC 79-2895. 374p. 1981. Repr. of 1960 ed. 55.50 (ISBN 0-8305-0063-4). Hyperion Conn.

Borysenko, Myrin & Beringer, Theodore. Functional Histology. 2nd ed. 400p. 1984. pap. text ed. 24.95 (ISBN 0-316-10304-7). Little.

Borysewicz, Edward, et al. Bicycle Road Racing: The Complete Program for Training & Competition. LC 84-52282. (Illus.). 288p. (Orig.). 1985. pap. 22.50 (ISBN 0-941950-07-7). VELO-NEWS.

Borza, E. N., ed. The Impact of Alexander the Great. LC 73-2091. (European Problem Ser.). 182p. 1974. pap. 6.95 (ISBN 0-686-86254-6, Pub. by HR&W). Krieger.

Borza, Eugene N., jt. ed. see Adams, W. Lindsay.

Borza, Eugene N., ed. see Wilcken, Ulrich.

Borza, Eugene N., et al. Studies in the History of Art 1982: Macedonia & Greece in Late Classical & Early Hellenistic Times, Vol. 10. Barr-Sharrar, Beryl, ed. LC 72-600309. (Illus.). 268p. 1982. pap. text ed. 18.95x (ISBN 0-89468-005-6, Dist. by U Pr of New Eng). Natl Gallery Art.

Borzak, Lenore, ed. Field Study: A Sourcebook for Experiential Learning. LC 81-2492. (Illus.). 320p. 1981. pap. 12.50 (ISBN 0-8039-0050-3). Sage.

--Field Study: A Sourcebook for Experiential Learning. LC 81-2492. (Illus.). 320p. 1981. 25.00 (ISBN 0-8039-1614-0). Sage.

Borzsonyi, M., et al, eds. Models, Mechanisms & Etiology of Tumor Promotion. (International Agency for Research on Cancer Scientific Publications: No. 56). 1985. 40.00x (ISBN 0-19-723058-X). Oxford U Pr.

Bos, A., ed. see De Mondeville, Henri.

Bos, A. P. On the Elements: Aristotle's Early Cosmology. 168p. 1972. text ed. 21.75x (ISBN 90-232-1027-1). Humanities.

Bos, Alfred. Simple Minds: The Race is the Prize. 128p. 1986. pap. 10.95 (ISBN 0-88715-014-4). Putnam Pub Group.

Bos, Alphonse, ed. see Guillaume De Berneville.

Bos, Beverley J. Before the Basics: Creating Conversations with Children. LC 82-74059. (Illus.). 1983. pap. 12.50 (ISBN 0-931540-01-1). Turn The Page.

--Don't Move the Muffin Tins: A Hands-off Guide to Art for the Young Child. LC 78-53276. (Illus.). 1982. pap. 7.50 (ISBN 0-931540-00-3). Turn The Page.

Bos, Carole D., jt. auth. see Buchanan, John C.

Bos, Charles Du see Du Bos, Charles.

Bos, D. Public Enterprise Economics: Theory & Applications. 1985. write for info. (North-Holland). Elsevier.

Bos, D., et al, eds. Entrepreneurship. (Zeitschrift fur Nationalokonomie Supplementum: 4). (Illus.). 220p. 1984. pap. 38.70 (ISBN 0-387-81830-8). Springer-Verlag.

Bos, D. J. Schoolkeuze-Adviezen: Resultatencontrole Na Vijf Jaar. 1974. 18.80x (ISBN 90-2797-302-4). Mouton.

Bos, Egbert P. Marsilius of Inghen. 1983. lib. bdg. 49.50 (ISBN 90-277-1343-X, Pub. by Reidel Holland). Kluwer Academic.

Bos, H. C. Spatial Dispersion of Economic Activity. 110p. 1965. 44.25 (ISBN 0-677-61510-8). Gordon.

Bos, H. C., et al. Private Foreign Investment in Developing Countries: A Quantitative Study on the Evaluation of Its Macro-Economic Impact. LC 73-91763. (International Studies in Economics & Econometrics: No. 7). 300p. 1974. lib. bdg. 53.00 (ISBN 90-277-0410-4, Pub. by Reidel Holland); pap. text ed. 28.00 (ISBN 90-277-0439-2, Pub. by Reidel Holland). Kluwer Academic.

Bos, H. J., et al, eds. see Symposium on the Life & Work of Christiaan Huygens, Amsterdam, 22-25 August 1979.

Bos, J. The Isolating Effect of Greenhouses on Anthropod Pests & Its Significance for Integrated Pest Management. 92p. 1984. pap. text ed. 12.25 (ISBN 90-220-0839-8, PDC266, Pudoc). Unipub.

Bos, L. Introduction to Plant Virology. LC 82-12679. 158p. 1983. 14.95x (ISBN 0-582-44680-5). Longman.

--Symptoms of Virus Diseases in Plants: With Index of Names & Symptoms. 3rd ed. (Illus.). 225p. (Eng., Ital., Span. & Dutch.). 1978. 21.00 (ISBN 90-220-0658-1, PDC6, Pudoc). Unipub.

Bos, Lambert Van Den. Position of the "Roode En Witte Roos" in the Saga of "King Richard Third". Campbell, Oscar J., ed. LC 72-131494. Repr. of 1919 ed. 16.50 (ISBN 0-404-01375-9). AMS Pr.

Bos, M. G., ed. Long-Throated Flumes & Broad-Crested Weirs. 1984. lib. bdg. 34.50 (ISBN 90-247-3113-5, Pub. by Martinus Nighoff Netherlands). Kluwer Academic.

Bos, Maarten. Methodology of International Law. 1984. 69.25 (ISBN 0-444-86847-X, I-242-84). Elsevier.

Bos, Marinus G. & Replogle, John A. Flow Measuring Flumes for Open Channel Systems. LC 84-7401. 321p. 1984. text ed. 42.95x (ISBN 0-471-80637-4, Pub. by Wiley-Interscience). Wiley.

Bos, Theodore, jt. auth. see Newbold, Paul.

Bos, V. T., jt. ed. see Hajnal, A.

Bosak, Steven. Gammon. 1985. 13.95 (ISBN 0-312-31629-1, Pub. by Marek). St Martin.

Bosanquet, B. Meeting of Extremes in Contemporary Philosophy. Repr. of 1921 ed. 15.00 (ISBN 0-527-10030-7). Kraus Repr.

--The Psychological Substance of Political Communities in Their Peaceful & Violent Expressions & the Objective of History, 2 vols. 1985. Set. 187.85 (ISBN 0-89920-086-9). Am Inst Psych.

Bosanquet, Bernard. The Aesthetic Consciousness Throughout the Middle Ages & Its Influence upon the History of Mankind. 149p. 1985. 88.25 (ISBN 0-89266-512-2). Am Classical Coll Pr.

--The Approach of the German Philosophers to the Theory of the Beautiful. 153p. 1985. 87.85 (ISBN 0-89901-218-3). Found Class Reprints.

--A Companion to Plato's Republic. LC 76-40128. 1895. Repr. 49.50 (ISBN 0-8414-1786-5). Folcroft.

--Croce's Aesthetic. 1974. lib. bdg. 59.95 (ISBN 0-87968-969-2). Gordon Pr.

--The Education of the Young in the Republic of Plato. 1917. lib. bdg. 27.00 (ISBN 0-8414-3224-4). Folcroft.

--The Education of the Young in the Republic of Plato. 198p. 1980. Repr. of 1917 ed. lib. bdg. 30.00 (ISBN 0-8492-2197-8). R West.

--Essays & Addresses. 12.50 (ISBN 0-8369-7211-2, 8010). Ayer Co Pubs.

--Essentials of Logic: Being Ten Lectures on Judgment & Inference. LC 4-3994. 1968. Repr. of 1895 ed. 14.00 (ISBN 0-527-10006-4). Kraus Repr.

--The Greek Theory of the Beautiful As a Social Force Capable to Achieve the Perfection of the Collective Body. 167p. 1985. 88.25 (ISBN 0-86650-144-4). Gloucester Art.

--Implication & Linear Inference. LC 20-20435. 1968. Repr. of 1920 ed. 15.00 (ISBN 0-527-10012-9). Kraus Repr.

--Knowledge & Reality. LC 14-924. 1968. Repr. of 1892 ed. 23.00 (ISBN 0-527-10018-8). Kraus Repr.

--Logic: Or, The Morphology of Knowledge, 2 vols. in 1. 2nd ed. LC 12-12390. 1968. Repr. of 1911 ed. 46.00 (ISBN 0-527-10024-2). Kraus Repr.

--The Modern Philosophy of Aesthetics & Its Unresolved Problems. 129p. 1985. 87.45 (ISBN 0-89901-217-5). Found Class Reprints.

--The Philosophy of Idealism in Its Structure & Objectives. 121p. 1985. 84.65 (ISBN 0-89266-513-0). Am Classical Coll Pr.

--Principle of Individuality & Value. LC 12-14490. (Gifford Lectures Ser.). 1968. Repr. of 1912 ed. 24.00 (ISBN 0-527-10036-6). Kraus Repr.

--Social & International Ideals: Being Studies in Patriotism. facs. ed. LC 67-23181. (Essay Index Reprint Ser). 1967. Repr. of 1917 ed. 19.00 (ISBN 0-8369-0225-4). Ayer Co Pubs.

--Social & International Ideals: Being Studies in Patriotism. LC 17-28213. 1968. Repr. of 1917 ed. 23.00 (ISBN 0-527-10042-0). Kraus Repr.
--Social Conditions in Provincial Towns. Lees, Lynn H. & Lees, Andrew, eds. LC 84-48280. (The Rise of Urban Britian Ser.). 82p. 1985. lib. bdg. 20.00 (ISBN 0-8240-6282-5). Garland Pub.
--Some Suggestions in Ethics. LC 18-21566. 1968. Repr. of 1918 ed. 17.00 (ISBN 0-527-10048-X). Kraus Repr.
--Three Chapters on the Nature of Mind. Bosanquet, Helen, ed. LC 23-2356. 1968. Repr. of 1923 ed. 14.00 (ISBN 0-527-10054-4). Kraus Repr.
--Three Lectures on Aesthetics Delivered at University College, London, 1914. LC 15-26508. 1968. Repr. of 1915 ed. 12.00 (ISBN 0-527-10060-9). Kraus Repr.
--Value & Destiny of the Individual. LC 13-6278. (Gifford Lectures 1912). 1968. Repr. of 1913 ed. 24.00 (ISBN 0-527-10066-8). Kraus Repr.
--What Religion Is. LC 78-12709. 1979. Repr. of 1920 ed. lib. bdg. 18.75x (ISBN 0-313-21202-3, BOWR). Greenwood.
Bosanquet, Bernard, ed. Aspects of the Social Problem by Various Writers. LC 9-5797. 1968. Repr. of 1895 ed. 23.00 (ISBN 0-527-10000-5). Kraus Repr.
Bosanquet, Bernard, tr. see Hegel, Georg W.
Bosanquet, Charles B. London: Some Account of Its Growth, Charitable Agencies & Wants. LC 83-48474. (The World of Labour-English Workers 1850-1890 Ser.). 323p. 1984. lib. bdg. 50.00 (ISBN 0-8240-5702-3). Garland Pub.
Bosanquet, Edward G. The Imaginative Way to Conduct Psychoanalytical Seances. (Illus.). 103p. 1984. 77.85 (ISBN 0-89920-073-7). Am Inst Psych.
Bosanquet, Eustace F. English Printed Almanacks & Prognostications: A Bibliographical History to the Year 1600. LC 18-6815. (Bibliographical Society, London, Illustrated Monographs: No. 17). pap. 66.00 (ISBN 0-317-29843-7, 2051920). Bks Demand UMI.
Bosanquet, Helen. The Family. 1906. 20.00 (ISBN 0-686-17692-8). Quality Lib.
--The Strength of the People: A Study in Social Economics. 2nd ed. LC 79-56950. (The English Working Class Ser.). 365p. 1980. lib. bdg. 40.00 (ISBN 0-8240-0104-4). Garland Pub.
Bosanquet, Helen, ed. see Bosanquet, Bernard.
Bosanquet, N. & Townsend, P. Labour & Equality. 1980. text ed. 22.00x (ISBN 0-435-83105-4). Gower Pub Co.
Bosanquet, T. Henry James at Work. (Studies in Henry James, No. 17). 1970. pap. 11.95x (ISBN 0-8383-0009-X). Haskell.
--Paul Valery. 59.95 (ISBN 0-8490-0809-3). Gordon Pr.
--Paul Valery. LC 74-6412. (Studies in French Literature, No. 45). 1974. lib. bdg. 47.95x (ISBN 0-8383-1969-6). Haskell.
--Paul Valery. 12.50 (ISBN 0-8274-3109-0). R West.
Bosanquet, Theodora. Harriet Martineau. 1973. Repr. of 1927 ed. 25.00 (ISBN 0-8274-1332-7). R West.
--Harriet Martineau: An Essay in Comprehension. LC 74-16320. Repr. of 1927 ed. lib. bdg. 30.00 (ISBN 0-8414-9940-3). Folcroft.
--Henry James at Work. LC 76-13030. 1976. Repr. of 1924 ed. lib. bdg. 10.00 (ISBN 0-8414-3340-2). Folcroft.
Bosar, Gary J., ed. see Technical Association of the Pulp & Paper Industry.
Bosc, Jacques du see Du Bosc, Jacques.
Boscana, Geronimo. Chinigchinich. LC 77-93183. 1978. 25.00 (ISBN 0-939046-12-1). Malki Mus Pr.
Bosch. Fachwoerterbuch Kraftfahrtechnik, 2 vols, Vol. 1. 354p. (Ger. & Eng., Technical Dictionary for Automotive Engineering). 1976. 85.00 (ISBN 3-18-419044-7, M-7638, Pub. by VDI Verlag GMBH). French & Eur.
--Fachwoerterbuch Kraftfahrtechnik, 2 vols, Vol. 2. 369p. (Ger. & Eng., Technical dictionary of automotive engineering). 1977. 59.95 (ISBN 3-18-419046-3, M-7639, Pub. by VDI Verlag GMBH). French & Eur.
Bosch, Anna. A Handbook of the Creek Language. 35p. (Orig., Muscogee.). 1984. pap. 5.00 (ISBN 0-940392-15-1). Indian U Pr Ok.
Bosch, David J. A Spirituality of the Road. LC 79-10856. (Mennonite Missionary Fellowship: No. 6). 104p. 1979. pap. 3.95 (ISBN 0-8361-1889-8). Herald Pr.
--A Spirituality of the Road. LC 79-10856. 104p. 1979. pap. 3.95. Herald Hse.
Bosch, Donald & Bosch, Eloise. Seashells of Oman. LC 81-14236. (Illus.). 1982. text ed. 35.00x (ISBN 0-582-78309-7). Longman.
Bosch, Eloise, jt. auth. see Bosch, Donald.
Bosch, H. G., jt. auth. see DeHaan, Martin R.
Bosch, Helmut. Die Nurnberger Hausmaler Emailfarbendekor Auf Glasern und Fayencen der Barockzeit. (Illus.). 600p. (Ger.). 1985. 150.00 (ISBN 3-7814-0220-7, Pub. by Klinkhardt & Biermann WG). Seven Hills Bks.
Bosch, Henry G. The Gift of a Thorn. (Solace Ser.). 1984. pap. 1.25 (ISBN 0-8010-0866-2). Baker Bk.
--Rainbows for God's Children in the Storm. 1984. pap. 4.95 (ISBN 0-8010-0870-0). Baker Bk.
--When Burdens Become Bridges. (Solace Ser.). 1984. pap. 1.25 (ISBN 0-8010-0867-0). Baker Bk.
Bosch, Henry G., jt. ed. see De Haan, Richard W.
Bosch, Juan. Hostos el sembrador. (Norte Ser.). 208p. 1976. pap. 3.75 (ISBN 0-940238-19-5). Ediciones Huracan.
Bosch, Klaus & Weede, Ursula. Encyclopedia of Amazon Parrots. Lambrich, Annemarie, tr. (Illus.). 208p. 1984. 24.95 (ISBN 0-87666-871-6, H-1055). TFH Pubns.
Bosch, Paul. The Paschal Cycle. 1979. pap. 6.75 (ISBN 0-570-03796-4, 12-2778). Concordia.
Bosch, Peter. Agreement & Anaphora: A Study of the Roles of Pronouns in Syntax & Discourse. (Cognitive Science Ser.). 1983. 39.00 (ISBN 0-12-118820-5). Acad Pr.
Bosch, R., ed. Technical Dictionary for Automotive Engineering, 2 vols. (Eng. & Ger.). 1976. 68.00 (ISBN 0-9961072-5-8, Pub. by VDI W Germany). Heyden.
Bosch, R. J. van den see Van den Bosch, R. J.
Bosch, Robert van den see Flint, Mary L. & Van Den Bosch, Robert.
Bosch, Robert van den see Van Den Bosch, Robert, et al.
Bosch, S., et al. Non-Archimedean Analysis. (Grundlehren der Mathematischen Wissenschaften Ser.: Vol. 261). 450p. 1984. 59.00 (ISBN 0-387-12546-9). Springer-Verlag.
Bosch, Ten. Dutch-English-French-German Engineering Dictionary. 11th ed. (Dutch, Eng., Fr. & Ger.). 45.00 (ISBN 90-2010-132-3). Heinman.
Bosch, Vanden, et al. Urban Watershed Management: Flooding & Water Quality. Bedient, Philip B. & Rowe, Peter G., eds. (Rice University Studies: Vol. 65, No. 1). 205p. 1979. pap. 10.00x (ISBN 0-89263-240-2). Rice Univ.
Bosch, William. College Algebra. LC 83-18953. (Mathematics Ser.). 450p. 1983. text ed. 21.50 pub net (ISBN 0-534-02866-7). Brooks-Cole.
Boschan, Charlotte, jt. auth. see Bry, Gerhard.
Bosche, H Vanden, et al, eds. Chemotherapy of Gastrointestinal Helminths. (Handbook of Experimental Pharmacology Ser.: Vol. 77). 720p. 1985. 198.00 (ISBN 0-387-13111-6). Springer-Verlag.
Bosche, Susanne. Jenny Lives with Eric & Martin. 52p. (Orig.). (gr. k-6). 1983. pap. 5.50 (ISBN 0-907040-22-5, Pub. by GMP England). Alyson Pubns.
Boschen, Lothar & Barth, Jurgen. The Porsche Book: A Definitive Illustrated History. Frere, Paul, tr. LC 78-695. (Illus.). 1978. 29.95 (ISBN 0-668-04576-0, 4576). Arco.
--The Porsche Book: A Definitive Illustrated History. 2nd ed. LC 83-9257. (Illus.). 584p. 1984. 39.95 (ISBN 0-668-06003-4). Arco.
Boschetti, Norma, tr. see Smelser, G. K., et al.
Boschi, E., jt. ed. see Dziewonski, A.
Boschini, Henny & Boschini, Luciano. Chasing Whales off Norway. LC 72-90690. (Illus.). 32p. (gr. k-4). 1973. 6.95 (ISBN 0-87592-010-1). Scroll Pr.
Boschini, Luciano, jt. auth. see Boschini, Henny.
Boschke, F., ed. Cosmochemistry. LC 51-5479. (Topics in Current Chemistry: Vol. 44). (Illus.). 200p. 1974. 31.00 (ISBN 0-387-06457-5). Springer-Verlag.
--Dynamic Chemistry. LC 51-5497. (Topics in Current Chemistry: Vol. 45). (Illus.). 250p. 1974. 38.00 (ISBN 0-387-06471-0). Springer-Verlag.
--Inorganic & Analytical Chemistry. LC 51-5497. (Topics in Current Chemistry: Vol. 26). (Illus.). 125p. 1972. pap. 26.00 (ISBN 0-387-05589-4). Springer-Verlag.
--Molecular Orbitals. LC 51-5497. (Topics in Current Chemistry: Vol. 23). 1971. pap. 28.40 (ISBN 0-387-05504-5). Springer-Verlag.
--New Concepts One. LC 51-5497. (Topics in Current Chemistry: Vol. 41). (Illus.). 150p. 1973. 31.00 (ISBN 0-387-06333-1). Springer-Verlag.
--New Methods in Chemistry. LC 51-5497. (Topics in Current Chemistry Ser.: Vol. 36). (Illus.). 127p. 1973. pap. 23.60 (ISBN 0-387-06098-7). Springer-Verlag.
--Photochemistry. (Topics in Current Chemistry Ser.: Vol. 46). (Illus.). iv, 236p. 1974. 45.00 (ISBN 0-387-06592-X). Springer-Verlag.
--Reactive Intermediates. LC 51-5497. (Topics in Current Chemistry: Vol. 16, Pt. 1). (Illus.). 1970. pap. 48.40 (ISBN 0-387-05103-1). Springer-Verlag.
--Silicon Chemistry One. LC 51-5497. (Topics in Current Chemistry: Vol. 50). (Illus.). 180p. 1974. 33.00 (ISBN 0-387-06714-0). Springer-Verlag.
--Silicon Chemistry Two. LC 51-5497. (Topics in Current Chemistry Ser.: Vol. 51). (Illus.). 140p. 1974. 30.00 (ISBN 0-387-06722-1). Springer-Verlag.
--Stereo- & Theoretical Chemistry. LC 51-5497. (Topics in Current Chemistry: Vol. 31). (Illus.). 160p. 1972. pap. 27.20 (ISBN 0-387-05841-9). Springer-Verlag.
--Stereochemistry One: In Memory of van't Hoff. LC 51-5497. (Topics in Current Chemistry: Vol. 47). (Illus.). 150p. 1974. 39.00 (ISBN 0-387-06648-9). Springer-Verlag.
--Stereochemistry Two: In Memory of van't Hoff. LC 51-5497. (Topics in Current Chemistry: Vol. 48). (Illus.). 160p. 1974. 33.00 (ISBN 0-387-06682-9). Springer-Verlag.
Boschke, F., ed. see Fluck, E., et al.
Boschke, F., ed. see Kompa, K. L.
Boschke, F., et al, eds. Nuclear Quadrupole Resonance. Boschke, F. (Topics in Current Chemistry: Vol. 30). (Illus.). 180p. (Eng. & Ger.). 1972. pap. 29.50 (ISBN 0-387-05781-1). Springer-Verlag.
--Structure & Transformations of Organic Molecules. (Topics in Current Chemistry: Vol. 32). (Illus.). 110p. 1972. pap. 29.50 (ISBN 0-387-05936-9). Springer-Verlag.
Boschke, F. L., ed. Analytical Problems. (Topics in Current Chemistry Ser.: Vol. 95). (Illus.). 210p. 1981. 59.00 (ISBN 0-387-10402-X). Springer-Verlag.
--Aspects of Molybdenum & Related Chemistry. LC 78-13469. (Topics in Current Chemistry Ser.: Vol. 76). (Illus.). 1979. 47.00 (ISBN 0-387-08986-1). Springer-Verlag.
--Bioactive Organo-Silicon Compounds. LC 79-12799. (Topics in Current Chemistry Ser.: Vol. 84). (Illus.). 1979. 57.00 (ISBN 0-387-09347-8). Springer-Verlag.
--Biochemistry. (Topics in Current Chemistry Ser.: Vol. 83). (Illus.). 1979. 56.00 (ISBN 0-387-09312-5). Springer-Verlag.
--Biochemistry I. (Topics in Current Chemistry Ser.: Vol. 78). (Illus.). 1979. 57.00 (ISBN 0-387-09218-8). Springer-Verlag.
--Bonding & Structure. (Topics in Current Chemistry: Vol. 63). (Illus.). 160p. 1976. 42.00 (ISBN 0-387-07605-0). Springer-Verlag.
--Inorganic & Physical Chemistry. (Topics in Current Chemistry Ser.: Vol. 77). (Illus.). 1978. 59.00 (ISBN 0-387-08987-X). Springer-Verlag.
--Inorganic Chemistry. (Topics in Current Chemistry Ser.: Vol. 96). (Illus.). 155p. 1981. 52.00 (ISBN 0-387-10425-9). Springer-Verlag.
--Inorganic Ring Systems. (Topics in Current Chemistry Ser.: Vol. 102). (Illus.). 240p. 1982. 43.00 (ISBN 0-387-11345-2). Springer-Verlag.
--Instrumental Inorganic Chemistry. LC 79-14180. (Topics in Current Chemistry: Vol. 85). (Illus.). 1979. 58.00 (ISBN 0-387-09338-9). Springer-Verlag.
--Large Amplitude Motion in Molecules One. (Topics in Current Chemistry: Vol. 81). (Illus.). 1979. 58.00 (ISBN 0-387-09310-9). Springer-Verlag.
--Large Amplitude Motion in Molecules Two. (Topics in Current Chemistry: Vol. 82). (Illus.). 1979. 53.00 (ISBN 0-387-09311-7). Springer-Verlag.
--Medicinal Chemistry. LC 77-24573. (Topics in Current Chemistry: Vol. 72). (Illus.). 1977. 43.00 (ISBN 0-387-08366-9). Springer-Verlag.
--Micelles. (Topics in Current Chemistry: Vol. 87). (Illus.). 1980. 56.00 (ISBN 0-387-09639-6). Springer-Verlag.
--New Trends in Chemistry. (Topics in Current Chemistry Ser.: Vol. 100). (Illus.). 213p. 1982. 48.00 (ISBN 0-387-11287-1). Springer-Verlag.
--Organic Chemistry. (Topics in Current Chemistry: Vol. 92). 190p. 1980. 60.00 (ISBN 0-387-10048-2). Springer-Verlag.
--Organic Chemistry. LC 77-14137. (Topics in Current Chemistry: Vol. 73). 1978. 63.00 (ISBN 0-387-08480-0). Springer-Verlag.
--Organic Chemistry & Theory. (Topics in Current Chemistry Ser.: Vol. 75). (Illus.). 1978. 47.00 (ISBN 0-387-08834-2). Springer-Verlag.
--Organotin Compounds. (Topics in Current Chemistry Ser.: Vol. 104). (Illus.). 150p. 1982. 36.00 (ISBN 0-387-11542-0). Springer-Verlag.
--Syntheses of Natural Products. (Topics in Current Chemistry Ser.: Vol. 91). 118p. 1980. 45.00 (ISBN 0-387-09827-5). Springer-Verlag.
--Van der Waals Systems. (Topics in Current Chemistry: Vol. 93). (Illus.). 140p. 1980. 42.00 (ISBN 0-387-10058-X). Springer-Verlag.
Boschke, F. L., jt. ed. see Voegtle, F.
Boschke, G., et al. PI Complexes of Transition Metals. (Topics in Current Chemistry: Vol. 28). (Illus.). 205p. 1972. pap. 27.20 (ISBN 0-387-05728-5). Springer-Verlag.
Boschken, Herman L. Land Use Conflicts: Organizational Design & Resource Management. LC 81-7443. (Illus.). 288p. 1982. text ed. 21.95x (ISBN 0-252-00901-0). U of Ill Pr.
Boschloo, A. W. Annibale Caracci in Bologna: Visible Reality in Art After the Council of Trent, 2 vols. (Illus.). 1974. Set. 65.00 (ISBN 0-8390-0138-X). Abner Schram Ltd.
Boschman, LaMar. The Prophetic Song. (Orig.). 1985. pap. price not set (ISBN 0-938612-12-3). Revival Press.
Boschmann, E. & Wells, N. Chemistry in Action: A Laboratory Manual for General, Organic, & Biological Chemistry. 2nd ed. 320p. 1984. 17.95 (ISBN 0-07-006529-2). McGraw.
Boschmann, Erwin. Dear Chris: A Letter of Advice on How to Study in College. (Illus.). 1981. write for info. (ISBN 0-930116-04-6). Sci Ent.
Boschmann, Erwin, jt. auth. see Welcher, Frank J.
Boschmann, Roger. Hong Kong by Night. (Asia by Night Ser.). (Illus.). 64p. (Orig.). 1981. pap. 4.95 (ISBN 962-7031-07-0, Pub. by CFW Pubns Hong Kong). C E Tuttle.
Boschot, ed. see Gautier, Theophile.
Boschot, Adolphe. La Jeunesse d'un Romantique: Hector Berlioz, 1803-1831, d'Apres de Nombreux Documents Inedits. LC 74-24046. Repr. of 1906 ed. 32.50 (ISBN 0-404-12869-6). AMS Pr.
Bosco, Dominick. The People's Guide to Vitamins & Minerals: From A to Zinc. 336p. 1980. pap. 8.95 (ISBN 0-8092-7139-7). Contemp Bks.
Bosco, James J. & Robin, Stanley S. The Hyperactive Child & Stimulant Drugs. LC 76-57934. 1977. 20.00x (ISBN 0-226-06661-4). U of Chicago Pr.
Bosco, James J., jt. auth. see Robin, Stanley S.
Bosco, James S. & Gustafson, William F. Measurement & Evaluation in Physical Education, Fitness & Sports. (Illus.). 384p. 1983. 26.95 (ISBN 0-13-568352-1). P-H.
Bosco, St. John. St. Dominic Savio. rev. ed. Aronica, Paul, tr. from Ital. LC 78-67221. (Illus.). 1979. pap. 2.95 (ISBN 0-89944-037-1). Don Bosco Multimedia.
Bosco, Rocco Lo see Lo Bosco, Rocco.
Bosco, Ronald A., ed. Lessons for the Children of Godly Ancestors. LC 82-5844. (Sermon in America Ser.). 1982. 60.00x (ISBN 0-8201-1381-6). Schol Facsimiles.
--Puritan Sermon in America, 1630-1750, 4 vols. LC 78-114749. (Sermon in America Ser.). 1978. Repr. 200.00x set (ISBN 0-8201-1320-4). Schol Facsimiles.
Bosco, Ronald A., ed. see Mather, Cotton.
Boscolo, Renucio. Nostradamus-Key to the Future. Mogey, Richard, ed. Sgolombis, Alexandra, tr. from Ital. (Illus.). 220p. (Orig.). 1984. pap. 7.95 (ISBN 0-911533-00-1). Key Found.
Boscovich, Roger J. Theory of Natural Philosophy. (Illus.). 1966. pap. 7.95x (ISBN 0-262-52003-6). MIT Pr.
Bose. The Gentle Craft of Revision in Thomas Dekker's Last Plays. (Salzburg Studies in Elizabethan Literature: Jacobean Drama Studies: No. 87). 1980. pap. text ed. 25.50x (ISBN 0-391-01878-7). Humanities.
Bose, A. & Desai, P. Studies in Social Dynamics of Primary Health Care. (Studies in Economic Development & Planning: No. 29). 1983. text ed. 18.50x (ISBN 0-391-02959-2, Pub. by Hindustan India). Humanities.
Bose, A., et al. Population in India's Development, 1947-2000. 1974. 18.00 (ISBN 0-686-20289-9). Intl Bk Dist.
Bose, A K. see Bernstein, Jeremy, et al.
Bose, Abinash C. Three Mystic Poets: A Study of W. B. Yeats, A. E. & Rabindrath Tagore. LC 72-187263. 1945. lib. bdg. 10.00 (ISBN 0-8414-2534-5). Folcroft.
Bose, Ajoy, jt. auth. see Dayal, John.
Bose, Amalendu. The Early Victorian Verse-Novel. 1978. Repr. of 1959 ed. lib. bdg. 8.50 (ISBN 0-8495-0408-2). Arden Lib.
--The Early Victorian Verse-Novel. LC 73-4863. 1974. Repr. of 1959 ed. lib. bdg. 10.00 (ISBN 0-8414-3109-4). Folcroft.
Bose, Arun. Marx on Exploitation & Inequality: An Essay in Marxian Analytical Economics. 1980. text ed. 15.95x (ISBN 0-19-561149-7). Oxford U Pr.
Bose, Ashish, et al, eds. Social Statistics: Health & Education. 375p. 1982. text ed. 40.00x (ISBN 0-7069-1083-4, Pub. by Vikas India). Advent NY.
Bose, Aurobindo, tr. Later Poems of Tagore. (Orient Paperbacks Ser.). 142p. 1978. pap. 3.00 (ISBN 0-86578-077-3). Ind-US Inc.
Bose, Aurobindo, tr. see Tagore, Rabindranath.
Bose, Bimal K., ed. Adjustable Speed AC Drive Systems. LC 80-27789. 460p. 1981. 41.55 (ISBN 0-87942-145-2, PC01404). Inst Electrical.
Bose, Buddladeva. Rain Through the Night. Seely, Clinton B., tr. from Bengali. (Orient Paperbacks). 139p. 1974. pap. 1.80 (ISBN 0-88253-285-5). Ind-US Inc.
Bose, Charles M. A View of Washington Bottom: A Glance at Blennerhassett Island. write for info. (ISBN 0-9612606-0-2). McClain.
Bose, D. N. Tantras: Their Philosophy & Occult Secrets. rev. 3rd ed. 1981. Repr. of 1956 ed. 12.00x (ISBN 0-8364-0737-7, Pub. by Mukhopadhyay). South Asia Bks.
--The Yoga Vasistha Ramayana. rev. ed. 1984. Repr. of 1954 ed. 12.50x (ISBN 0-8364-1181-1, Pub. by Mukhopadhyaya India). South Asia Bks.
Bose, Johanne C. Farewell to Durango: A German Lady's Diary in Mexico, 1910-1911. Blew, Robert W., ed. Bose, John C., tr. from Ger. LC 78-50471. (A Western Americana Bk.). (Illus., Orig.). 1978. pap. 5.50 (ISBN 0-913626-41-4). S S S Pub Co.
Bose, John C., tr. see Bose, Johanne C.
Bose, Keith W. Video Security Systems. 2nd ed. 210p. 1982. 19.95 (ISBN 0-409-95057-2). Butterworth.
Bose, M. L. British Policy in the North-East Frontier Agency. 1980. text ed. 24.00x (ISBN 0-391-01833-7). Humanities.
Bose, M. L., ed. Historical & Constitutional Documents of North Eastern India. 1980. text ed. 21.00x (ISBN 0-391-01867-1). Humanities.
Bose, Mandakranta. Supernatural Intervention in the Tempest & Sakuntala. (Salzburg-Jacobean Drama Studies: No. 99). 71p. 1980. pap. text ed. 25.50x (ISBN 0-391-02567-8, Pub. by Inst Eng Lit Austria). Humanities.
Bose, N. K. Adjustable Speed AC Drive Systems. LC 80-27789. 449p. 1981. 39.95 (ISBN 0-471-09395-5, Pub. by Wiley-Interscience); pap. 25.95 (ISBN 0-471-09396-3, Pub. by Wiley-Interscience). Wiley.

--Multidimensional Systems: Theory & Applications. (IEEE Reprint Ser.). 295p. 1979. 39.95x (ISBN 0-471-05214-0); (Pub. by Wiley-Interscience). Wiley.
Bose, Nemai. Indian National Movement: An Outline. 3rd rev. ed. 1983. 8.50x (ISBN 0-8364-0961-2, Pub. by Mukhopadhyay India). South Asia Bks.
--Racism, Struggle for Equality & Indian Nationalism. 1982. 18.00x (ISBN 0-8364-0839-X, Pub. By Mukhopadhyay). South Asia Bks.
Bose, Nemai S., ed. India in the Eighties. 1983. 14.00x (ISBN 0-8364-1002-5, Pub. by Mukhopadhyay India). South Asia Bks.
Bose, Nirmal K. Applied Multidimensional System Theory. (Electrical-Computer Science & Engineering Ser.). 350p. 1982. 32.50 (ISBN 0-442-27214-6). Van Nos Reinhold.
Bose, Nirmal K., ed. Multidimensional Systems: Theory & Applications. LC 78-55096. 1979. 41.55 (ISBN 0-87942-109-6, PC01107). Inst Electrical.
Bose, P. K. & Sanyal, B. C. Graduate Employment & Higher Education in West Bengal. (Illus.). 288p. (Co-published with Wiley Eastern Ltd., New Delhi). 1983. pap. text ed. 30.00 (ISBN 92-803-1101-8, U1288, UNESCO). Unipub.
Bose, Prabodh C. Introduction to Juristic Psychology. (Historical Foundations of Forensic Psychiatry & Psychology Ser.). 426p. 1980. Repr. of 1917 ed. lib. bdg. 42.50 (ISBN 0-306-76062-2). Da Capo.
Bose, Pradip K. Classes in a Rural Society: A Sociological Study of Some Bengal Villages. 1985. 28.00x (ISBN 0-8364-1285-0, Pub. by Ajanta). South Asia Bks.
Bose, R. C. & Manuel, B. Introduction to Combinatorial Theory. (Probability & Mathmatical Statistics Ser.: 1-345). 237p. 1984. 29.95x (ISBN 0-471-89614-4, 1-345, Pub by Wiley Interscience). Wiley.
Bose, R. K., jt. auth. see Joshi, M. C.
Bose, R. K., illus. More Legends from Northern India. (Illus.). 77p. 1981. 7.25 (ISBN 0-89744-242-3). Auromere.
--More Stories from the Panchatantra. (Illus.). 96p. 1982. 7.25 (ISBN 0-89744-245-8). Auromere.
Bose, Sajal. Underground Literature During the Emergency, India. 1978. 10.00x (ISBN 0-8364-0034-8). South Asia Bks.
Bose, Sudhindra. Fifteen Years in America. LC 73-13121. (Foreign Travelers in America, 1810-1935 Ser.). (Illus.). 528p. 1974. Repr. of 1920 ed. 37.50 (ISBN 0-405-05444-0). Ayer Co Pubs.
Bose, Walter B. Los Origenes del Correo Terrestre en Guatemala. (No. 1). pap. 3.75x (ISBN 0-913129-03-8). La Tienda.
Bosel, T. K. & Bhattacharjee, S. K. Garden Plants. 282p. 1980. 50.00x (ISBN 0-686-84453-X, Pub. by Oxford & I B H India). State Mutual Bk.
Boselovic, Len, ed. see Benedict, John T.
Boselovic, Len, ed. see Consumer Liaison Committee of the Council.
Boselovic, Len, jt. ed. see Perica, Lou.
Boseman, G., jt. auth. see Schellenberger, R.
Boseman, Glenn, jt. auth. see Schellenberger, Robert E.
Boseman, Glenn & Powell, Kay, eds. Managing Sales Professionals. LC 83-73552. (Illus.). 406p. 1984. text ed. 25.00 (ISBN 0-317-03523-1). Amer College.
Boserup, Anders & Mack, Andrew. War Without Weapons: Non-Violence in National Defense. LC 74-26920. 192p. 1975. 6.50x (ISBN 0-8052-3581-7); pap. 3.95 (ISBN 0-8052-0484-9). Schocken.
Boserup, Dan & Gouge, Gerald. The Case Management Model: Concept, Implementation & Training. rev. ed. 178p. 1980. 6.00 (ISBN 0-318-16342-X, B2). Regional Inst Social Welfare.
Boserup, Ester. Conditions of Agricultural Growth: The Economics of Agrarian Change Under Population Pressure. LC 65-19513. 1965. lib. bdg. 14.95x (ISBN 0-202-07003-4). Aldine Pub.
--Population & Technological Change: A Study of Long-Term Trends. LC 80-21116. (Illus.). 256p. 1981. pap. 9.00x (ISBN 0-226-06674-6). U of Chicago Pr.
--Women's Role in Economic Development. 1974. 10.95 (ISBN 0-312-88655-1). St Martin.
Boserup, Ester & Sachs, Ignacy, eds. Foreign Aid to Newly Independent Countries. bi-lingual ed. LC 70-129142. (European Coordination Centre for Research & Documentation in the Social Sciences Publications Ser). 184p. (Eng. & Fr.). 1971. text ed. 11.20x (ISBN 90-2796-907-8). Mouton.
Bosha, Francis J. John Cheever: A Reference Guide. (Reference Books Ser.). 1981. 23.00 (ISBN 0-8161-8447-X, Hall Reference). G K Hall.
Bosha, Francis J., ed. William Faulkner's Soldier's Pay: A Bibliographical Study. LC 80-54205. 542p. 1982. 42.50x (ISBN 0-87875-211-0). Whitston Pub.
Boshart-McCleary, Jane, jt. auth. see Fleming, Louise.
Boshear, Walton C. & Albrecht, Karl G. Understanding People: Models & Concepts. LC 75-41686. (Illus.). 275p. 1977. pap. 13.50 (ISBN 0-88390-115-3). Univ Assocs.
Boshell, Buris R. Diabetes Mellitus Case Studies. 2nd ed. 1981. spiral bdg. 24.00 (ISBN 0-87488-031-9). Med Exam.
--Diabetic at Work & Play. 2nd ed. (Illus.). 200p. 1979. 12.75x (ISBN 0-398-03921-6). C C Thomas.
--Your Miniature Pinscher. LC 69-19733. (Your Dog Book Ser). (Illus.). 1969. 12.95 (ISBN 0-87714-024-3). Denlingers.
Boshell, Buris R. & Kansal, Prakash C. Diabetes Mellitus Case Studies. 3rd ed. 1984. pap. text ed. write for info (ISBN 0-87488-400-4). Med Exam.
Boshes, Louis D. & Gibbs, Frederic A. Epilepsy Handbook. 2nd ed. (Illus.). 206p. 1972. 22.75x (ISBN 0-398-02194-5). C C Thomas.
Boshkoff, Douglass. Bankruptcy. (Sum & Substance Ser.). 1977. 10.95 (ISBN 0-686-23342-5). Josephson-Kluwer Legal Educ Ctrs.
Boshman, LaMar. The Rebirth of Music. 96p. pap. 3.95 (ISBN 0-938612-04-2). Revival Press.
Boshtchanovsky, Basil. Uroki po Pastirskomu Bogosloviju. 100p. 1961. pap. text ed. 5.00 (ISBN 0-317-30267-1). Holy Trinity.
Bosi, Roberto. The Lapps. Cadell, James, tr. LC 75-32455. 1976. Repr. of 1960 ed. lib. bdg. 22.50x (ISBN 0-8371-8545-9, BOTL). Greenwood.
Bosisio, Gina B., jt. auth. see Cretti, Luciano.
Bosk, Beth & Thompson, Gary, eds. Mendocino Rust. (Illus.). 88p. (Orig.). 1981. pap. 9.99 (ISBN 0-9604100-0-7). Albion Albums.
Bosk, Charles L. Forgive & Remember: Managing Medical Failure. LC 78-16596. 1979. 18.00x (ISBN 0-226-06679-7). U of Chicago Pr.
--Forgive & Remember: Managing Medical Failure. LC 78-16596. 248p. 1981. pap. 8.00x (ISBN 0-226-06680-0). U of Chicago Pr.
Boske, Leigh B. Federal Regulatory Reform Programs & the Use of Cost-Benefit Analysis. LC 84-82015. (Policy Research Project Ser.: No. 64). 97p. 1984. 8.00 (ISBN 0-89940-666-1). LBJ Sch Pub Aff.
Boske, Leigh B. & Hilger, Barbara A. An Evaluation of Traffic Accident Records Systems in Texas & Other States. LC 84-82016. (Policy Research Project Ser.: No. 65). 227p. 1984. 10.00 (ISBN 0-89940-667-X). LBJ Sch Pub Aff.
Bosker, A. Literary Criticism in the Age of Johnson. rev. ed. LC 73-16258. 1971. lib. bdg. 42.50 (ISBN 0-8414-9866-0). Folcroft.
Bosker, Aisso. Literary Criticism in the Age of Johnson. 2nd rev. ed. LC 79-128185. 1970. Repr. of 1953 ed. text ed. 15.00x (ISBN 0-87752-133-6). Gordian.
Bosker, Gideon & Schwartz, George. Geriatric Emergencies. LC 83-15573. (Illus.). 320p. 1984. pap. text ed. 19.95 (ISBN 0-89303-482-7). Brady Comm.
Bosker, Gideon, jt. auth. see Bledsoe, Bryan E.
Bosker, Gideon, ed. see Gangeness, David E. & White, Roger D.
Boskey, James B. & Hughes, Susan C. Teaching about Aging: Religious & Advocacy Perspectives. LC 82-17589. 184p. (Orig.). 1983. lib. bdg. 23.50 (ISBN 0-8191-2802-3); pap. text ed. 11.25 (ISBN 0-8191-2803-1). U Pr of Amer.
Boskin, Joseph. Humor & Social Change in Twentieth-Century America. pap. 8.00 (ISBN 0-89073-061-X). Boston Public Lib.
--Into Slavery: Racial Decisions in the Virginia Colony. LC 79-5347. 1979. pap. text ed. 9.25 (ISBN 0-8191-0868-5). U Pr of Amer.
--Urban Racial Violence, in the Twentieth Century. 2nd ed. 1976. pap. write for info. (ISBN 0-02-470890-9). Macmillan.
Boskin, Joseph & Rosenstone, Robert A., eds. Seasons of Rebellion: Protest & Radicalism in Recent America. LC 79-9678. 349p. 1980. text ed. 24.75 (ISBN 0-8191-0976-2); pap. text ed. 13.25 (ISBN 0-8191-0977-0). U Pr of Amer.
Boskin, Michael, et al. The Impact of Inflation on U.S. Productivity & International Competitiveness. LC 80-83144. (Committee on Changing International Realities Ser.). 80p. 1980. 7.00 (ISBN 0-89068-055-8). Natl Planning.
Boskin, Michael J. Reaganomics Examined: Successes, Failures, Unfinished Agenda. 300p. 1985. 25.95 (ISBN 0-917616-79-0); pap. 10.95 (ISBN 0-917616-80-4). ICS Pr.
Boskin, Michael J., ed. Economic & Human Welfare. (Economic Theory Econometrics & Mathematical Economics Ser.). 1979. 58.00 (ISBN 0-12-118850-7). Acad Pr.
--The Economy in the Nineteen Eighties: A Program for Growth & Stability. LC 80-80647. 462p. (Orig.). 1980. text ed. 17.95 (ISBN 0-87855-399-1); pap. text ed. 7.95 (ISBN 0-917616-39-1). Transaction Bks.
Boskin, Michael J. & Wildavsky, Aaron, eds. The Federal Budget, Economics & Politics. LC 81-86378. 416p. 1982. pap. text ed. 8.95 (ISBN 0-917616-48-0). ICS Pr.
Boskin, Michael J., jt. ed. see Aaron, Henry J.
Boskind-White, Marlene & White, William C., Jr. Bulimarexia: The Binge-Purge Cycle. 1983. 16.95 (ISBN 0-393-01650-1). Norton.
Boskovits, Miklos. Early Italian Panel Paintings. (Illus.). 25.00 (ISBN 0-8283-1118-8). Branden Pub Co.
--Italian Panel Paintings. (Illus.). 12.50x (ISBN 0-89918-309-3, H309). Vanous.
--The Martello Collection: Paintings, Drawings & Miniatures from the XIVth to the XVIIIth Centuries. (Illus.). 182p. 1985. 45.00 (ISBN 0-295-96284-4). U of Wash Pr.
Bosl, Karl. Biographisches Woerterbuch zur Deutschen Geschichte, 3 vols. 1st ed. (Ger.). 1973. Set. 425.00 (ISBN 3-7720-1082-2, M-7312, Pub. by Francke). French & Eur.
Bosley, Elizabeth C. Techniques for Articulatory Disorders. 166p. 1981. 18.50x (ISBN 0-398-04139-3). C C Thomas.
Bosley, Jo Ann. Strangest Summer. LC 75-140970. (gr. 6 up). 1970. PLB 2.98 (ISBN 0-910244-58-8). Blair.
Bosley, Judith, jt. auth. see Bosley, Stacy.
Bosley, Judith, ed. The Big Fat Red Juicy Apple Cook Book. (Illus.). 112p. (Orig.). 1985. pap. 5.95 (ISBN 0-930809-00-9). Grand Bks Inc.
Bosley, Judith A. Lady in Pink. (Sundown Fiction Ser.). 64p. (gr. 3). 1984. 2.25 (ISBN 0-88336-754-8). New Readers.
Bosley, Keith. Dark Summer. 1976. pap. 1.50 (ISBN 0-685-79256-0, Pub. by Menard Pr). Small Pr Dist.
Bosley, Keith, ed. Poetry of Asia: Five Millenniums of Verse from Thirty Languages. 1979. 17.50 (ISBN 0-8348-0139-6). Weatherhill.
Bosley, Keith, tr. see De la Ceppede, Jean.
Bosley, Keith, tr. see Jouve, Pierre J.
Bosley, Keith, tr. see Leino, Eino.
Bosley, Richard. On Truth: A Neo-Pragmatist Treatise in Logic, Metaphysics & Epistemology. LC 81-43800. 244p. (Orig.). 1982. lib. bdg. 25.00 (ISBN 0-8191-2568-7); pap. text ed. 12.50 (ISBN 0-8191-2569-5). U Pr of Amer.
Bosley, Stacy & Bosley, Judith. Grandmother Soup. (Illus.). 36p. (Orig.). 1985. pap. 5.95 (ISBN 0-930809-01-7). Grand Bks Inc.
Boslooper, Thomas. Image of Woman. LC 79-57637. (Illus.). 228p. Date not set. 19.95 (ISBN 0-932894-04-6, Pub. by New Era Bks). Paragon Hse.
--Image of Woman. LC 79-57637. (Illus.). 288p. 1980. 19.95x (ISBN 0-932894-04-6). Rose Sharon Pr.
Boslough, John. Stephen Hawking's Universe. LC 84-4673. (Illus.). 160p. 1984. 12.95 (ISBN 0-688-03530-2). Morrow.
Boslund, Lois, jt. auth. see Bruno, William.
Bosly, Caroline. Rugs to Riches: An Insider's Guide to Buying Oriental Rugs. (Illus.). 1985. pap. 12.95 (ISBN 0-394-73957-4). Pantheon.
--Rugs to Riches: An Insider's Guide to Oriental Rugs. (Illus.). 1980. 17.45 (ISBN 0-394-50039-3). Pantheon.
Bosma, James F. Anatomy of the Infant Head. LC 84-20099. (Contemporary Medicine & Public Health Ser.). (Illus.). 480p. 1985. text ed. 115.00x (ISBN 0-8018-2936-4). Johns Hopkins.
--Oral Sensation & Perception: Second Symposium. (Illus.). 580p. 1970. photocopy ed. 54.50x (ISBN 0-398-00194-4). C C Thomas.
--Symposium on Oral Sensation & Perception. (Illus.). 376p. 1967. photocopy ed. 39.50x (ISBN 0-398-00193-6). C C Thomas.
--Third Symposium on Oral Sensation & Perception: The Mouth of the Infant. (Illus.). 484p. 1972. 58.75x (ISBN 0-398-02238-0). C C Thomas.
Bosmajian, C. Perry & Bosmajian, Linda S. Personalized Guide to Stress Evaluation. Snyder, Thomas L. & Felmeister, Charles J., eds. LC 82-8182. (Dental Practice Management Ser.). (Illus.). 103p. 1983. pap. text ed. 12.95 (ISBN 0-8016-4724-X). Mosby.
Bosmajian, Haig. Justice Douglas & Freedom of Speech. LC 79-26635. 377p. 1980. lib. bdg. 19.50 (ISBN 0-8108-1276-2). Scarecrow.
--Language of Oppression. 1974. pap. 9.00 (ISBN 0-8183-0136-8). Pub Aff Pr.
Bosmajian, Haig A. The Language of Oppression. LC 83-5866. 164p. 1983. 11.00 (ISBN 0-8191-3186-5). U Pr of Amer.
--The Principles & Practice of Freedom of Speech. 2nd ed. LC 82-23739. 424p. 1983. pap. text ed. 17.75 (ISBN 0-8191-2962-3). U Pr of Amer.
Bosmajian, Haig A., compiled by. Censorship, Libraries, & the Law. 234p. 1983. 29.95 (ISBN 0-918212-54-5). Neal-Schuman.
Bosmajian, Haig A., ed. Dissent, Symbolic Behavior & Rhetorical Strategies. LC 79-25821. 328p. 1980. Repr. of 1972 ed. lib. bdg. 32.50x (ISBN 0-313-22253-3, BODI). Greenwood.
Bosmajian, Hamida. Metaphors of Evil: Contemporary German Literature & the Shadow of Nazism. LC 79-22758. (Illus.). 288p. 1979. 23.00x (ISBN 0-87745-093-5); pap. 8.75 (ISBN 0-87745-096-X). U of Iowa Pr.
Bosmajian, Linda S., jt. auth. see Bosmajian, C. Perry.
Bosman, Richard & Greenwald, Ted. Exit the Face. (Illus.). 72p. 1982. pap. 10.00 (ISBN 0-87070-671-3). Museum Mod Art.
Bosman, William. New & Accurate Description of the Coast of Guinea: 1705. 4th. rev. ed. (Illus.). 577p. 1967. 45.00x (ISBN 0-7146-1793-8, F Cass Co). Biblio Dist.
Bosnia, Nella, jt. auth. see Turin, Adela.
Bosniak, Morton, jt. auth. see Evans, John A.
Bosniak, S., ed. Advances in Ophthalmic Plastic & Reconstructive Surgery: The Lacrimal System, Vol. 3. (Illus.). 400p. 1984. 60.00 (ISBN 0-08-030930-5). Pergamon.
--Advances in Ophthalmnic Plastic & Reconstructive Surgery: The Aging Face, Vol. 2. (Advances in Ophthalmic Plastic & Reconstructive Surgery Ser.). (Illus.). 324p. 1983. 60.00 (ISBN 0-08-030931-3). Pergamon.
Bosniak, Stephen L. Advances in Ophthalmic Plastic & Reconstructive Surgery, Vol. 1. Smith, Byron C., ed. (Illus.). 278p. 1983. 60.00 (ISBN 0-08-029656-4). Pergamon.
Bosnjak, V. Early Child Care in Yugoslavia. (International Monographs on Early Child Care). Date not set. price not set (ISBN 0-677-05460-2). Gordon.
Bosque County History Book Committee, ed. Bosque County, Texas: Land & People. (Illus.). 800p. 1985. 55.00 (ISBN 0-88107-029-7). Natl ShareGraphics.
Bosque, Gloria. Strange Meat, Poems Nineteen Sixty-Eight to Nineteen Seventy-Four. LC 74-23345. 2.00 (ISBN 0-914134-03-5). Sipapu-Konocti.
Bosquet, Alain. Instead of Music: Poems. Frawley, William, tr. LC 79-16523. xix, 43p. 1980. text ed. 12.95x (ISBN 0-8071-0584-8). La State U Pr.
--Selected Poems. Beckett, Samuel, et al, trs. from Fr. & Eng. LC 71-181687. 189p. 1972. 12.95 (ISBN 0-8214-0111-4, 82-81149); pap. 7.95 (ISBN 0-8214-0112-2, 82-81156). Ohio U Pr.
Bosquet, Michel. Capitalism in Crisis & Everyday Life. (Marxist Theory & Contemporary Capitalism: No. 6). 1977. text ed. 23.25x (ISBN 0-391-00670-3); pap. text ed. 9.75x (ISBN 0-391-01061-1). Humanities.
Bosqui & Co. Grapes & Grapevines of California. LC 81-4775. (Illus.). 64p. 1981. 29.95 (ISBN 0-15-136786-8). HarBraceJ.
Bosredon de Ransijat, Chevalier. The Seven Year Balance Sheet of the Sovereign, Military & Hospitaller Order of St. John of Jerusalem, of Rhodes & of Malta: From May 1st, 1778 to end of April 1785. Dingli-Attard-Inguanez, Marcel V., ed. (Illus.). 79p. (Orig.). 1985. pap. 10.00 (ISBN 0-9610740-2-7). U Intel Data Bank.
Boss, Andrew. Meat on the Farm: Butchering, Keeping & Curing. facs. ed. (Shorey Lost Arts Ser.). 52p. pap. 2.95 (ISBN 0-8466-6040-7, U40). Shorey.
Boss, Barbara D., et al, eds. Monoclonal Antibodies in Cancer: Symposium. 1984. 40.00 (ISBN 0-12-118880-9). Acad Pr.
Boss, Benjamin, et al, eds. see Carnegie Institution Of Washington - Dept. Of Meridian Astronomy.
Boss, Jim. Ambush at Vermejo. (Living Books). 320p. (Orig.). 1985. pap. 3.95 (ISBN 0-317-27087-7). Tyndale.
Boss, Judy. Garden of Joy. 1974. pap. 3.95 (ISBN 0-87542-082-6). Llewellyn Pubns.
--In Silence They Return. (Illus.). 1972. pap. 5.95 (ISBN 0-87542-080-X). Llewellyn Pubns.
--In Silence They Return. 224p. 1974. pap. 1.25 (ISBN 0-532-12239-9). Woodhill.
Boss, Laura. Stripping. LC 82-4192. (Illus.). 52p. (Orig.). 1982. pap. 5.00 (ISBN 0-941608-01-8). Chantry Pr.
Boss, Medard. I Dreamt Last Night. 1977. 23.95 (ISBN 0-89876-073-9). Gardner Pr.
--Psychoanalysis & Daseinsanalysis. (Psychoanalysis Examined & Re-Examined Ser.). 295p. 1982. Repr. of 1963 ed. lib. bdg. 25.00 (ISBN 0-306-79708-9). Da Capo.
Boss, Medard, ed. Existential Foundation of Medicine & Psychology. LC 84-2822. 303p. 1983. 30.00x (ISBN 0-87668-667-6). Aronson.
Boss, Peter. On the Side of the Child: An Australian Perspective on Child Abuse. 166p. pap. 5.95x (ISBN 0-00-636042-4, Pub. by W Collins Australia). Intl Spec Bk.
Boss, Richard & Raikes, Deborah. Developing Microform Reading Facilities. (Meckler Publishing Series on Library Micrographics Management). 175p. 1981. 38.95 (ISBN 0-913672-09-2). Microform Rev.
Boss, Richard W. Automating Library Acquisitions: Issues & Outlook. LC 82-8941. (Professional Librarian Ser.). 135p. 1982. pap. 27.50 (ISBN 0-86729-006-4, 202-BW). Knowledge Indus.
--Grant Money & How to Get It: A Handbook for Librarians. 1st ed. 138p. 1980. 19.95 (ISBN 0-8352-1274-2). Bowker.
--The Library Manager's Guide to Automation. 2nd ed. LC 83-19886. (Professional Librarian). 169p. 1984. 36.50 (ISBN 0-86729-052-8, 217-BW); pap. 27.50 (ISBN 0-86729-051-X). Knowledge Indus.
--Telecommunications for Library Management. LC 84-26140. (Professional Librarian Ser.). 184p. 1985. 36.50 (ISBN 0-86729-126-5); pap. text ed. 28.50 (ISBN 0-86729-125-7, 241-BW). Knowledge Indus.
Boss, Richard W. & Maranjian, Lorig. Fee-Based Information Services: A Study of a Growing Industry. (Information Management Ser.). 199p. 1980. 24.95 (ISBN 0-8352-1287-4). Bowker.
Boss, Richard W., et al. Telecommunications - Making Sense out of New Technology & New Legislation: Proceedings of the 21st Annual Clinic on Library Applications of Data Processing. Divilbiss, J. L., ed. 1985. text ed. 15.00 (ISBN 0-87845-072-6). U of Ill Lib Info Sci.

Boss, Valentine. Newton & Russia: The Early Influence, 1698-1796. LC 73-188352. (Russian Research Center Studies: No. 69). (Illus.). 563p. 1972. 22.50x (ISBN 0-674-62275-8). Harvard U Pr.

Bossa, Francesco, et al, eds. Structure & Function Relationships in Biochemical Systems. (Advances in Experimental Medicine & Biology Ser.: Vol. 148). 396p. 1982. 55.00x (ISBN 0-306-41034-6, Plenum Pr). Plenum Pub.

Bossard, James & Boll, Eleanor. Ritual in Family Living. LC 75-45454. 228p. 1976. Repr. of 1950 ed. lib. bdg. 19.75x (ISBN 0-8371-8678-1, BORF). Greenwood.

Bossard, James H. Children in a Depression Decade. facsimile ed. LC 74-1667. (Children & Youth Ser.). 302p. 1974. Repr. of 1940 ed. 24.50x (ISBN 0-405-05948-5). Ayer Co Pubs.

--Social Change & Social Problems. 1934. 30.00 (ISBN 0-8482-7407-5). Norwood Edns.

Bossard, James H. & Boll, Eleanor S. Family Situations: An Introduction to the Study of Child Behavior. LC 69-10071. 1969. Repr. of 1943 ed. lib. bdg. 15.50x (ISBN 0-8371-0024-0, BOCB). Greenwood.

--The Large Family System. LC 74-25536. 325p. 1975. Repr. of 1956 ed. lib. bdg. 17.50x (ISBN 0-8371-7871-1, BOLF). Greenwood.

Bossard, James H. & Dewhurst, J. Frederic. University Education for Business. LC 73-1993. (Big Business; Economic Power in a Free Society Ser.). Repr. of 1931 ed. 36.50 (ISBN 0-405-05076-3). Ayer Co Pubs.

Bossard, James H. & Boll, Eleanor S., eds. Adolescents in Wartime. facsimile ed. LC 74-1668. (Children & Youth Ser.). 180p. 1974. Repr. of 1944 ed. 18.00x (ISBN 0-405-05947-7). Ayer Co Pubs.

Bossard, James H., jt. ed. see Murphy, J. Prentice.

Bossard, R., tr. see Bloom, Alan.

Bossart, Donald E. Creative Conflict in Religious Education & Church Administration. LC 80-12704. 284p. (Orig.). 1980. pap. 12.95 (ISBN 0-89135-048-9). Religious Educ.

Bossart, H., ed. see International Symposium, Basel, March 1978.

Bossart, H., et al. Perinatal Medicine. 399p. 1973. 129.00 (ISBN 3-456-00333-1, Pub. by Holdan Bk Ltd UK). State mutual Bk.

Bossche, Edmond Van Den see Steenbergen, G. J. & Grooten, Johan.

Bossche, G. Van Den see Borceux, F. & Van Den Bossche, G.

Bosscher, Marcia V., jt. auth. see Grills, Norma J.

Bosschere, Jean de & Morris, M. C. Christmas Tales of Flanders. (Illus.). 7.75 (ISBN 0-8446-4516-8). Peter Smith.

Bosse, Abraham. Sentimens sur la distinction des divers es manieres de peinture, dessein et graveure. (Documents of Art & Architectural History Series 2: Vol. 5). 142p. (Fr.). 1981. Repr. of 1649 ed. 27.50x (ISBN 0-89371-205-1). Broude Intl Edns.

Bosse, Malcolm. Fire in Heaven: A Novel. 1986. 18.95. S&S.

--The Seventy Nine Squares. 192p. (YA) pap. 1.95 (ISBN 0-440-98901-9, LE). Dell.

--The Warlord. LC 82-19696. 717p. 1983. 17.95 (ISBN 0-671-44332-1). S&S.

--The Warlord. Grey, Linda, ed. 768p. (Orig.). 1984. pap. 3.95 (ISBN 0-553-24184-2). Bantam.

Bosse, Malcolm J. Cave Beyond Time. LC 79-7818. 192p. (gr. 7 up). 1980. PLB 11.89 (ISBN 0-690-04076-8). Crowell Jr Bks.

--Ganesh. LC 80-2453. 192p. (gr. 7 up). 1981. 11.06i (ISBN 0-690-04102-0); PLB 11.89i (ISBN 0-690-04103-9). Crowell Jr Bks.

--The Seventy-Nine Squares. LC 79-7591. (gr. 7 up). 1979. PLB 10.89 (ISBN 0-690-04000-8). Crowell Jr Bks.

Bosse, Raymond & Rose, Charles L. Smoking & Aging. LC 81-48002. 272p. 1984. 30.00x (ISBN 0-669-05230-2). Lexington Bks.

Bosselman, Beulah C. Neurosis & Psychosis. 3rd ed. 216p. 1969. 14.75x (ISBN 0-398-00195-2). C C Thomas.

--Psychiatry in Theory & Practice. 158p. 1957. 14.50x (ISBN 0-398-00196-0). C C Thomas.

--Self-Destruction: A Study of the Suicidal Impulse. 120p. 1961. 13.75x (ISBN 0-398-00197-9). C C Thomas.

Bosselman, Beulah C., et al. Introduction to Developmental Psychiatry. 148p. 1965. 14.50x (ISBN 0-398-00198-7). C C Thomas.

Bosselman, Fred, et al. The Permit Explosion: Coordination of the Proliferation. LC 76-55844. (Management & Control of Growth Ser.). 86p. 1976. pap. 16.00 (ISBN 0-87420-570-0, P04); pap. 12.00 members. Urban Land.

Bosselman, Fred P. In the Wake of the Tourist: Managing Special Places in Eight Countries. LC 78-65196. (Illus.). 1978. 15.00 (ISBN 0-89164-051-7). Conservation Foun.

Bosselman, Fred P., jt. auth. see Babcock, Richard F.

Bossen, Howard S. Henry Holmes Smith: Man of Light. Kirkpatrick, Diane, ed. LC 83-9208. (Studies in Photography: No. 1). 204p. 1983. 39.95 (ISBN 0-8357-1459-4). Univ Microfilms.

Bossen, Laurel H. The Redivision of Labor: Women & Economic Choice in Four Guatemalan Communities. LC 83-426. (SUNY Series in the Anthropology of Work). (Illus.). 368p. 1983. 46.50x (ISBN 0-87395-740-7); pap. 16.95x (ISBN 0-87395-741-5). State U NY Pr.

Bossen, Nathan. The Prescription for Tax Reform in Canada: An Appraisal, 5 Pts. (The White Paper on Taxation Ser.). 50p. 1971. 2.00 (ISBN 0-88806-078-5); Set. 8.00 (ISBN 0-317-34273-8). Inst C D Howe.

Bosserman, Phillip, tr. see Gurvitch, G.

Bossert, Gustav. Quellen zur Geshichte der Wiedertaufer. 90.00 (ISBN 0-384-05276-2); pap. 84.00 (ISBN 0-384-05275-4). Johnson Repr.

Bossert, Jill, ed. The New Illustration. 160p. 1985. pap. 24.95 (ISBN 0-942604-06-7). Madison Square.

Bossert, Thomas J., jt. ed. see Klaren, Peter F.

Bossert, William H., jt. auth. see Wilson, Edward O.

Bossewell, John. Workes of Armorie, 3 bks. LC 72-173. (English Experience Ser.: No. 145). 1969. Repr. of 1572 ed. 39.00 (ISBN 90-221-0145-2). Walter J Johnson.

Bosshard, B. Holzkunde: Mikroskopie und Makroskopie des Holzes, Vol. 1. 225p. 28.95x (ISBN 0-8176-1328-5). Birkhauser.

Bossi, E., ed. Praktische Neonatologie. (Paediatrische Fortbildungskurse fuer die Praxis Series: Vol. 57). (Illus.). xii, 208p. 1983. pap. 41.75 (ISBN 3-8055-3657-7). S Karger.

Bossing, Ed & Bossing, Elsie. Handbook of Favorite Dances. (Illus.). 168p. 1955. write for info. (ISBN 0-912222-10-7); pap. 5.00 (ISBN 0-912222-01-8). FitzSimons.

Bossing, Elsie, jt. auth. see Bossing, Ed.

Bosson, James E. Treasury of Aphoristic Jewels: The Subhasitaratnanidhi of Sa Skya Pandita in Tibetan & Mongolian. (Uralic & Altaic Ser: Vol. 92). 1969. pap. text ed. 12.50x (ISBN 0-87750-080-0). Res Ctr Lang Semiotic.

Bosson, Rex & Varon, Bension. The Mining Industry & the Developing Countries. (A World Bank Research Publication Ser.). 1977. 29.50x (ISBN 0-19-920096-3); pap. 14.95x (ISBN 0-19-920099-8). Oxford U Pr.

Bossone, Richard M. English Proficiency: Developing Your Reading & Writing Power, Bk. 2. (gr. 10-12). 1979. pap. text ed. 10.48 (ISBN 0-07-006591-8). McGraw.

Bossone, Richard M. & Ashe, Amy E. English Proficiency: Developing Your Reading & Writing Power, Bk. 1. 320p. (gr. 7-9). 1980. 14.80 (ISBN 0-07-006589-6). McGraw.

Bossong, Ken. A Guide to Community Energy Self-Reliance, Vol. 1. (Illus.). 70p. (Orig.). 1981. pap. 3.25 (ISBN 0-89988-023-1). Citizens Energy.

--Passive Solar Retrofit for Homeowners & Apartment Dwellers. (Illus.). 80p. (Orig.). 1981. pap. text ed. 6.00 (ISBN 0-89988-068-1). Citizens Energy.

Bossong, Ken & Denman, Scott. Nuclear Power & Civil Liberties: Can We Have Both? 2nd ed. 177p. 1981. 9.50 (ISBN 0-89988-071-1). Citizens Energy.

Bossong, Ken & Pilarski, Jan. National Passive Solar Directory. (Illus.). 60p. 1983. pap. text ed. 4.50 (ISBN 0-89988-100-9). Citizens Energy.

Bossong, Ken & Simpson, Jan. Appropriate Community Technologies Sourcebook, Vol. I. (Illus., Orig.). 1980. pap. 3.00 (ISBN 0-89988-056-8). Citizens Energy.

--Appropriate Community Technologies Sourcebook, Vols. 1 & 2. (Illus.). 80p. (Orig.). 1980. pap. text ed. 4.25 (ISBN 0-89988-055-X). Citizens Energy.

Bossong, Ken, et al. Solar Compendium, Vol. 1. (Illus.). 115p. 1980. 6.50 (ISBN 0-89988-013-4). Citizens Energy.

--A Solar Critique: Solar Compendium, Vol. II. 80p. (Orig.). 1981. 5.00 (ISBN 0-89988-070-3). Citizens Energy.

--Pioneers of Alcohol Fuels, 2 vols. 125p. (Orig.). 1981. 7.50 (ISBN 0-89988-067-3). Citizens Energy.

--Solar Energy & Big Business: Solar Compendium, Vol. III. (Illus.). 50p. (Orig.). 1983. pap. text ed. 4.00 (ISBN 0-89988-082-7). Citizens Energy.

Bossons, John, et al. Regulation by Municipal Licensing. (Ontario Economic Council Research Studies: No. 30). 120p. 1984. pap. 6.50 (ISBN 0-8020-3390-3). U of Toronto Pr.

Boss-Ribs, Mary C. & Running-Crane, Jenny. Stories of Our Blackfeet Grandmothers. (Indian Culture Ser.). (Orig.). (gr. 1-6). 1984. pap. 1.45 (ISBN 0-89992-096-9). Coun India Ed.

Bosstick, Maurice & Cable, John L. Patterns in the Sand: An Exploration in Mathematics. 2nd ed. (Illus.). 1975. text ed. write for info. (ISBN 0-02-471960-9); ans. bk free (ISBN 0-02-471970-6). Macmillan.

Bossu, Pere Rene Le see LeBossu, Pere Rene.

Bossuet. Sermons. new ed. (Documentation thematique). (Illus., Fr.). 1975. pap. 2.95 (ISBN 0-685-65684-5, 41). Larousse.

Bossuet, Jacques B. History of the Variations of the Protestant Churches, 2 vols. LC 83-45603. Date not set. Repr. of 1845 ed. Set. 75.00 (ISBN 0-404-19872-4). AMS Pr.

Bossuet, Jacques-Benigne. Discourse on Universal History. Ranum, Orest, intro. by. LC 75-9062. (Classic European Historians Ser). 424p. 1976. lib. bdg. 35.00x (ISBN 0-226-06708-4). U of Chicago Pr.

--Oeuvres. Velat & Champailler, eds. Incl. Oraisons Funebres; Discours sur l'Histoire Universelle; Sermons; Relations sur le Quietisme. (Bibl. de la Pleiade). 1936. 42.95 (ISBN 0-685-36054-7). French & Eur.

--Oraison Funebres. (Class. Hatier). pap. 3.50 (ISBN 0-685-34206-9). French & Eur.

--Oraisons funebres. new ed. (Nouveaux Classiques Larousse Ser.). (Illus.). 168p. (Fr.). 1975. pap. 2.95 (ISBN 0-685-62360-2, 33). Larousse.

Bossuk, Sidney S. Bank. 1983. 7.95 (ISBN 0-533-05716-7). Vantage.

Bossuyt, A. & Deconinck, F. Amplitude-Phase Patterns in Dynamic Scintigraphic Imaging. (Developments in Nuclear Medicine Ser.). 1984. lib. bdg. 42.00 (ISBN 0-89838-641-1, Pub. by Martinus Nijhoff Netherlands). Kluwer Academic.

Bossy, John. The English Catholic Community, 1570-1850. (Illus.). 1976. 37.00x (ISBN 0-19-519847-6); pap. 5.95x (ISBN 0-19-285148-9). Oxford U Pr.

Bossy, John, ed. Disputes & Settlements: Law & Human Relations in the West. LC 83-2010. (Past & Present Publications Ser.). 1984. 49.50 (ISBN 0-521-25283-0). Cambridge U Pr.

Bossy, John & Jupp, Peter, eds. Essays Presented to Michael Roberts: Sometime Professor of Modern History in the Queen's University of Belfast. 188p. 1976. 11.25 (ISBN 0-85640-085-8, Pub. by Blackstaff Pr). Longwood Pub Group.

Bost, James. Monarchs of the Mimic World. 1977. 20.00 (ISBN 0-89101-033-5). U Maine Orono.

Bosta, Diana, jt. auth. see Allen, Bud.

Bostaph, Charles, jt. auth. see Moore, Marti.

Bostetter, Edward E. Romantic Ventriloquists: Wordsworth, Coleridge, Keats, Shelley, Byron. rev. ed. LC 63-10795. 372p. 1975. 15.00x (ISBN 0-295-73918-5); pap. 6.95x (ISBN 0-295-95318-7). U of Wash Pr.

Bostian, Charles W., jt. auth. see Krauss, Herbert L.

Bosticco, Isabel L. Personal Letters for Business People. 290p. 1986. text ed. price not set (ISBN 0-566-02593-0). Gower Pub Co.

Bostick & Echaoce. Planning Healthy Meals. (Illus.). 80p. 1985. 14.95 (ISBN 0-88102-034-6). Janus Bks.

Bostick, W. F. Jesus & Socrates. 59.95 (ISBN 0-8490-0443-8). Gordon Pr.

Bostick, W. H., et al, eds. Energy Storage, Compression, & Switching, Vol. 1. LC 75-42405. 537p. 1976. 75.00x (ISBN 0-306-30892-4, Plenum Pr). Plenum Pub.

Bostick, William A. A Manual on the Acquiring of a Beautiful & Legible Handwriting. rev., 2nd ed. (Illus.). 1980. pap. 9.95 (ISBN 0-9606630-0-2). La Stampa Calligrafica.

Bostock, Anna, tr. see Lukacs, Georg.

Bostock, C. J. & Summer, A. The Eukaryotic Chromosome. xviii, 526p. 1978. 89.75 (ISBN 0-444-80003-4, Biomedical Pr). Elsevier.

Bostock, D. E. Neoplasia in the Cat, Dog & Horse. (Illus.). 1975. 68.50 (ISBN 0-8151-1079-0). Year Bk Med.

Bostock, David. Logic & Arithmetic, Vol. I: Natural Numbers. 1974. 45.00x (ISBN 0-19-824366-9). Oxford U Pr.

--Logic & Arithmetic, Vol. II: Rational & Irrational Numbers. (Illus.). 1979. 49.50x (ISBN 0-19-824591-2). Oxford U Pr.

Bostock, E. H. Menageries, Circuses & Theatres. LC 72-80140. (Illus.). Repr. of 1927 ed. 22.00 (ISBN 0-405-08290-8, Blom Pubns). Ayer Co Pubs.

Bostock, J. Knight. A Handbook on Old High German Literature. 2nd ed. King, K. C. & McLintock, D. R., eds. (Illus.). 1976. 64.00x (ISBN 0-19-815392-9). Oxford U Pr.

Bostok, Anna, tr. see Ehrenburg, Ilya.

Boston. Short Narrative of the Horrid Massacre in Boston. facsimile ed. LC 71-150170. (Select Bibliographies Reprint Ser). Repr. of 1849 ed. 17.00 (ISBN 0-8369-5683-4). Ayer Co Pubs.

Boston Area Music Libraries. The Boston Composers Project: A Bibliography of Contemporary Music. 400p. 1983. text ed. 55.00x (ISBN 0-262-02198-6). MIT Pr.

Boston Association for Childbirth Education. Handbook in Prepared Childbirth. 2nd ed. Magnacca, Sandy & Murphy, Gail, eds. (Avery's Childbirth Education Ser.). (Illus.). 96p. 1981. pap. 4.95 (ISBN 0-89529-137-1). Avery Pub.

Boston Athenaeum. Index of Obituaries in Boston Newspapers, 1704-1800, 3 Vols. 1968. Set. 156.00 (ISBN 0-8161-0761-0, Hall Library). G K Hall.

--The Work of J. Gregory Wiggins, Woodcarver: Catalogue of an Exhibition Held in February & March 1951. LC 51-7239. (Robert Charles Billings Fund Publications Catalogue Ser.: No. 2). (Illus.). xi, 17p. (Orig.). 1951. pap. 1.50 (ISBN 0-934552-20-7). Boston Athenaeum.

Boston Athenaeum Staff. The Boston Athenaeum: A Reader's Guide. 2nd, rev. ed. 30p. 1981. pap. 0.50 (ISBN 0-934552-39-8). Boston Athenaeum.

Boston Bar Association, jt. auth. see Green, Eric D.

Boston, Bernard. History of the Three Hundred Ninety-Eighth Infantry Regiment in World War II. (Combat Arms Ser.: No. 7). (Illus.). 208p. 1982. Repr. of 1947 ed. 20.00 (ISBN 0-89839-063-X). Battery Pr.

Boston, Bruce. All the Clocks Are Melting. (Illus.). 40p. (Orig.). 1984. pap. 3.00 (ISBN 0-930231-00-7). Velocities.

--Jackbird. 88p. (Orig.). 1976. pap. 3.00 (ISBN 0-917658-05-1). BPW & P.

--She Comes When You're Leaving. 64p. (Orig.). 1982. pap. 3.95 (ISBN 0-917658-14-0). BPW & P.

Boston, Bruce O. The American High School: Time for Reform. 33p. 1982. pap. 3.00 (ISBN 0-317-20289-8). Coun Basic Educ.

--Education Policy & the Education for all Handicapped Children Act (P.L. 94-142) (Policy Paper Ser.: No. 3). 88p. 1977. 4.00 (ISBN 0-318-03025-X). Inst Educ Lead.

--Education Policy & the Education for All Handicapped Children Act (Pl 94-142) (Policy Paper: No. 3). ix, 78p. 1977. 2.50 (ISBN 0-318-14396-8). Inst Educ Lead.

Boston, Bruce O., ed. Apples of Our Eye. 1985. pap. price not set (ISBN 0-935012-07-9). Edit Experts.

Boston, Carol A. The Pennypincher's Guide to Landscaping. LC 84-17775. 192p. 1984. 17.95 (ISBN 0-13-655937-9, Busn); pap. 7.95 (ISBN 0-13-655929-8). P-H.

Boston Children's Medical Center. Child Health Encyclopedia. 1978. 15.00 (ISBN 0-385-28150-1). Delacorte.

--Child Health Encyclopedia. 608p. 1978. pap. 14.95 (ISBN 0-385-28148-X, Delta). Dell.

Boston Children's Medical Center Staff, jt. auth. see Gregg, Elizabeth.

Boston Children's Museum, illus. Antique Fashion Paper Dolls of the 1890s in Full Color. (Paper Dolls Ser.). 32p. 1984. pap. 3.50 (ISBN 0-486-24622-1). Dover.

Boston City Council. Memorial of Crispus Attucks, Samuel Maverick, James Caldwell, Samuel Gray & Patrick Carr, from the City of Boston. facs. ed. LC 71-79022. (Black Heritage Library Collection Ser). 1889. 8.75 (ISBN 0-8369-8515-X). Ayer Co Pubs.

Boston, David M. Pre-Columbian Pottery of the Americas. Charleston, Robert J., ed. LC 78-55079. (Masterpieces of Western & Near Eastern Ceramics Ser.: Vol. 3). (Illus.). 318p. 1980. 250.00 (ISBN 0-87011-344-5). Kodansha.

Boston, L. M. The Children of Green Knowe. LC 77-4506. (Illus.). (gr. 4-7). 1977. pap. 2.95 (ISBN 0-15-616870-7, VoyB). HarBraceJ.

--An Enemy at Green Knowe. LC 78-71151. (Illus.). (gr. 4-7). 1979. pap. 3.95 (ISBN 0-15-628792-7, VoyB). HarBraceJ.

--An Enemy at Green Knowe. (Illus.). 1984. 12.75 (ISBN 0-8446-6152-X). Peter Smith.

--River at Green Knowe. LC 59-8950. (Illus.). 153p. (gr. 4-6). 1966. pap. 2.95 (ISBN 0-15-677701-0, VoyB). HarBraceJ.

--The River at Green Knowe. (Illus.). 1984. 12.50 (ISBN 0-8446-6153-8). Peter Smith.

--The Stones of Green Knowe. LC 75-44143. (Illus.). 128p. (gr. 5-9). 1976. 7.95 (ISBN 0-689-50058-0, McElderry Bk). Atheneum.

--The Treasure of Green Knowe. LC 77-16689. (Illus.). (gr. 4-7). 1978. pap. 1.95 (ISBN 0-15-691302-X, VoyB). HarBraceJ.

Boston, Leslie P. Approaches to Professional Writing. 184p. 1981. pap. text ed. 10.95 (ISBN 0-8403-2532-0). Kendall-Hunt.

Boston, Lucy M. Nothing Said. LC 70-137756. (Illus.). (gr. 2-5). 1971. 4.95 (ISBN 0-15-257580-4, HJ). HarBraceJ.

--Sea Egg. LC 67-10200. (Illus.). (gr. 2-5). 1967. 8.95 (ISBN 0-15-271050-7, HJ). HarBraceJ.

--Stranger at Green Knowe. LC 61-10108. (Illus.). (gr. 4-6). 1961. 9.95 (ISBN 0-15-281752-2, HJ). HarBraceJ.

--A Stranger at Green Knowe. LC 78-71150. (Illus.). (gr. 4-7). 1979. pap. 4.95 (ISBN 0-15-685657-3, VoyB). HarBraceJ.

Boston, Mary & Szur, Rolene, eds. Psychotherapy with Severely Deprived Children. 176p. (Orig.). 1983. pap. 10.95X (ISBN 0-7100-9536-8). Routledge & Kegan.

Boston Medical Commission. The Sanitary Condition of Boston: The Report of a Medical Commission. Rosenkrantz, Barbara G., ed. LC 76-25655. (Public Health in America Ser.). 1977. Repr. of 1875 ed. lib. bdg. 17.00x (ISBN 0-405-09808-1). Ayer Co Pubs.

Boston Medical Library, jt. auth. see Harvard Medical Library.

Boston Museum of Fine Arts. Bulletin of the Boston Museum of Fine Arts, 1903-1942, 8 vols. & index. LC 71-119596. (Illus.). 1971. Repr. of 1903 ed. Set. 401.00 (ISBN 0-405-01242-X); 44.00 ea.; index 49.50 (ISBN 0-685-03214-0). Ayer Co Pubs.

Boston Museum of fine Arts, Department of Classical Art. Romans & Barbarians. LC 76-55539. (Illus.). 1978. pap. 12.00 (ISBN 0-87846-110-8, Pub. by Mus Fine Arts Boston). C E Tuttle.

Boston, Pamela, jt. ed. see Moller, Aage R.

Boston, Penelope J., ed. The Case for Mars. (Science & Technology Ser.: Vol. 57). 348p. 1984. lib. bdg. 45.00x (ISBN 0-87703-197-5, Pub. by Am Astro Soc); pap. text ed. 25.00x (ISBN 0-87703-198-3). Univelt Inc.

Boston Public Library. Canadian Manuscripts in the Boston Public Library: A Descriptive Catalog. 1971. lib. bdg. 69.00 (ISBN 0-8161-0930-3, Hall Library). G K Hall.
--Catalog of the Defoe Collection in the Boston Public Library. 1966. 69.00 (ISBN 0-8161-0731-9, Hall Library). G K Hall.
--Catalogue of the Spanish Library, & of the Portuguese Books Bequeathed by George Ticknor to the Boston Public Library. 1970. lib. bdg. 78.00 (ISBN 0-8161-0865-X, Hall Library). G K Hall.
--Cumulative Film Catalog Supplement. 1978. 2.50 (ISBN 0-685-59551-X). Boston Public Lib.
--Dictionary Catalog of the Music Collection, Boston Public Library, 20 vols. 15617p. 1972. Set. lib. bdg. 1976.00 (ISBN 0-8161-0956-7, Hall Library); lib. bdg. 440.00 1st suppl., 4 vols. 1977 (ISBN 0-8161-1014-X). G K Hall.
--Film Catalog. 1982. 15.00 (ISBN 0-89073-005-9). Boston Public Lib.
--Manuscripts of the American Revolution in the Boston Public Library: A Descriptive Catalog. 1968. 69.00 (ISBN 0-8161-0825-0, Hall Library). G K Hall.
--Typography & Design. 10.00 (ISBN 0-685-60072-6). Boston Public Lib.
--Young Adult Catalog of the Boston Public Library, 2 vols. 1112p. 1972. Set. lib. bdg. 200.00 (ISBN 0-8161-1028-X, Hall Library). G K Hall.
Boston Publishing Co., ed. see Doyle, Edward & Lipsman, Samuel.
Boston Publishing Company & Manning, Robert, eds. Tools of War: Technology in Vietnam, 1965-1973. (Illus.). 192p. 1985. 16.95 (ISBN 0-201-11269-8). Addison-Wesley.
Boston Publishing Company, ed. see Dougan.
Boston Publishing Company Editors, ed. see Morrocco, John.
Boston Publishing Company Editors, ed. see Weiss, Stephen & Doyle, Edward.
Boston, Ray. British Chartists in America, 1839-1900. (Illus.). 110p. 1971. 12.50x (ISBN 0-87471-025-1). Rowman.
Boston Registry Department. Records Relating to the Early History of Boston, 39 vols. LC 74-19611. Repr. of 1909 ed. Set. 1170.00 (ISBN 0-404-12343-0); 30.00 ea. AMS Pr.
Boston, Richard. Baldness Be My Friend. 1978. 14.95 (ISBN 0-241-89732-7, Pub. by Hamish Hamilton England). David & Charles.
Boston, Robert E. How to Write & Use Performance Objectives to Individualize Instruction, 4 vols. 376p. 1972. 27.95 (ISBN 0-87778-040-4). Educ Tech Pubns.
Boston Society of Architects Staff. Architecture Boston. (Illus.). 1976. 12.95 (ISBN 0-517-52501-1, C N Potter Bks); pap. 7.95 (ISBN 0-517-52502-X). Crown.
Boston Symphony Orchestra. The Boston Symphony Cookbook. 1983. 18.95 (ISBN 0-395-33118-8). HM.
Boston, Thomas. The Complete Works of the Late Rev. Thomas Boston, Ettrick: Including His Memoirs, Written by Himself, 12 vols. M'Millan, Samuel, ed. (Puritan Library). (Illus.). 1980. Repr. of 1853 ed. Set. lib. bdg. 225.00 (ISBN 0-686-32100-6). R O Roberts.
--Crook in the Lot. (Summit Books). 1978. pap. 1.95 (ISBN 0-8010-0751-8). Baker Bk.
Boston University Center for Banking Law Studies Staff, ed. Annual Review of Banking Law. 2nd ed. 1984. 72.00 (ISBN 0-88712-129-2). Warren.
Boston University Libraries. Index to the Classed Catalog of the Boston University Libraries, 2 vols. 3rd. rev ed. 1187p. 1972. Set. lib. bdg. 200.00 (ISBN 0-8161-1029-8, Hall Library). G K Hall.
--List of French Doctoral Dissertations on Africa, 1884-1961. 1966. 69.00 (ISBN 0-8161-0742-4, Hall Library). G K Hall.
Boston University Library. Catalog of African Government Documents. 3rd, rev. ed. 1976. lib. bdg. 75.00 (ISBN 0-8161-0036-5, Hall Library). G K Hall.
Boston University School of Medicine see Shapiro, Eileen C. & Lowenstein, Leah M.
Boston Urban Gardeners. A Handbook of Community Gardening. Naimark, Susan, ed. (Illus.). 1982. (ScribT); pap. 7.95 (ISBN 0-684-17843-5). Scribner.
Boston Urban Study Group. Who Rules Boston? A Citizen's Guide to Reclaiming the City. (Illus.). 116p. (Orig.). 1984. pap. write for info. (ISBN 0-9613009-0-6). Inst Dem Socialism.
Boston, W. S., jt. auth. see Bird, C. L.
Boston Women's Health Book Collective. The New Our Bodies, Ourselves. rev. ed. (Illus.). 647p. 1985. 19.95 (ISBN 0-671-46087-0); pap. 12.95 (ISBN 0-671-46088-9). S&S.
--Our Bodies, Ourselves. rev. 2nd ed. (Illus.). 352p. 1976. pap. 10.95 (ISBN 0-671-22146-9). S&S.
Boston Women's Health Book Collective, Inc. Ourselves & Our Children: A Book by & for Parents. 1978. 12.95 (ISBN 0-394-41060-2); pap. 11.95 (ISBN 0-394-73304-5). Random.
Boston's Children's Hospital Staff. A Parent's Guide to Child Nutrition. 1986. write for info. (ISBN 0-201-05729-8). Addison-Wesley.
Bostrom, Alice. David Livingstone, Missionary to Africa. (Children's Missionary Library: Bk. 7). (Illus.). 32p. (Orig.). 1982. pap. 1.50 (ISBN 0-89323-027-8). Bible Memory.
--Search the Word Bible Puzzles. (Illus.). 48p. 1983. pap. 1.95 (ISBN 0-87239-589-8, 2787). Standard Pub.
Bostrom, Bert N. Talent, Truth Energy: The Society of Professional Journalists, Sigma Delta Chicago 75 Years of Service to Journalism. LC 84-50424. (Illus., Orig.). 1984. pap. 19.95 (ISBN 0-9613340-0-2). Soc Pro.
Bostrom, Carol, jt. auth. see Burns, Jim.
Bostrom, Christopher J. Philosophy of Religion. 1962. 42.50x (ISBN 0-685-69791-6). Elliots Bks.
Bostrom, Otto H. Alternative Readings in the Hebrew of the Books of Samuel. LC 18-8964. (Augustana College Library Publication Ser.: No. 8). 60p. 1918. pap. 0.75 (ISBN 0-910182-05-1). Augustana Coll.
Bostrom, Roald. Cameras. LC 80-17413. (A Look Inside). (Illus.). 48p. (gr. 4-12). 1981. PLB 15.52 (ISBN 0-8172-1404-6). Raintree Pubs.
Bostrom, Robert N. Persuasion. (Illus.). 320p. 1983. text ed. 25.95 (ISBN 0-13-661157-5). P-H.
Bostrom, Robert N., ed. Communication Yearbook: An Annual Review Published for the International Communication Association, No. 7. 928p. 1983. 45.00 (ISBN 0-8039-2000-8). Sage.
Bostrom, Ronald. Cameras. LC 80-17413. (A Look Inside Ser.). (Illus.). 48p. (gr. 4-12). 1985. pap. 9.27 (ISBN 0-8172-1427-5). Raintree Pubs.
Bostwick, A. E. Classics of American Librarianship, 8 vols. 1500.00 (ISBN 0-87968-879-3). Gordon Pr.
Bostwick, Arthur E. Earmarks of Literature. facs. ed. LC 67-22074. (Essay Index Reprint Ser.). 1914. 17.00 (ISBN 0-8369-1319-1). Ayer Co Pubs.
--Librarian's Open Shelf: Essays on Various Subjects. facs. ed. LC 67-23182. (Essay Index Reprint Ser). 1920. 20.00 (ISBN 0-8369-0226-2). Ayer Co Pubs.
--Library Essays. facs. ed. LC 71-84299. (Essay Index Reprint Ser). 1920. 22.00 (ISBN 0-8369-1076-1). Ayer Co Pubs.
Bostwick, Arthur E., ed. Library & Society. facs. ed. LC 68-54330. (Essay Index Reprint Ser). 1921. 19.50 (ISBN 0-8369-0227-0). Ayer Co Pubs.
Bostwick, B. E. One Hundred Eleven Proven Techniques & Strategies for Getting the Job Interview. 285p. 1983. pap. 9.95 (ISBN 0-471-88981-4). Wiley.
Bostwick, Burdette. One Hundred Eleven Proven Techniques & Strategies for Getting the Job Interview. LC 80-26454. 285p. 1981. 15.95 (ISBN 0-471-07762-3, Pub. by Wiley-Interscience). Wiley.
Bostwick, Burdette E. How to Find the Job You've Always Wanted. 2nd ed. LC 79-15567. 292p. 1980. pap. 9.95 (ISBN 0-471-87116-8). Wiley.
--Resume Writing: A Comprehensive How-To-Do-It Guide. 3rd ed. 352p. 1985. 15.95 (ISBN 0-471-81693-0); pap. 9.95 (ISBN 0-471-81683-3). Wiley.
Bostwick, Burdette E., ed. Resume Writing: A Comprehensive How-to-Do-It Guide. 2nd ed. LC 80-18100. 314p. 1982. 15.95 (ISBN 0-471-08067-5, Pub. by Wiley-Interscience); pap. 8.95 (ISBN 0-471-09943-0). Wiley.
Bostwick, Fran, jt. auth. see Berko, Roy M.
Bostwick, Jeri. Hawaii 1985. Fisher, Robert C., ed. (Fisher Annotated Travel Guides Ser.). 258p. 1984. 12.95 (ISBN 0-8116-0024-6, Fisher). NAL.
Bostwick, John, III. Aesthetic & Reconstructive Breast Surgery. LC 82-8306. (Illus.). 742p. 1983. text ed. 155.00 (ISBN 0-8016-0731-0). Mosby.
Bostwick, John, III, jt. auth. see Berger, Karen.
Bostwick, Prudence, jt. auth. see Davidson, Levette J.
Boswell, Barbara. Sensuous Perception. (Loveswept Ser.: No. 78). 208p. 1985. pap. 2.25 (ISBN 0-553-21688-0). Bantam.
Boswell, Barbara, ed. Little Consequences. (Loveswept Ser.: No. 53). 192p. (Orig.). 1984. pap. 2.25 (ISBN 0-553-21654-6). Bantam.
Boswell, Charles S. An Irish Precursor of Dante. (Grimm Library: No. 18). Repr. of 1908 ed. 12.50 (ISBN 0-404-53561-5). AMS Pr.
Boswell, David M., ed. The Handicapped Person in the Community. Wingrove, Janet M. 1974. pap. 17.95x (ISBN 0-422-74760-2, NO. 2605, Pub. by Tavistock England). Methuen Inc.
Boswell, Eleanore, ed. Edmond Ironside: Or, War Hath Made All Friends. LC 82-45791. (Malone Society Reprint Ser.: No. 61). Repr. of 1927 ed. 40.00 (ISBN 0-404-63061-8). AMS Pr.
Boswell, Fred & Boswell, Jeanetta. What Men or Gods Are These? A Genealogical Approach to Classical Mythology. LC 80-13780. 324p. 1980. 22.50 (ISBN 0-8108-1314-9). Scarecrow.
Boswell, G. G., jt. auth. see Faires, R. A.
Boswell, J. S. Social & Business Enterprises. (Economics & Society Ser.). 1976. text ed. 22.50x (ISBN 0-04-338078-6). Allen Unwin.
Boswell, Jackson C. Milton's Library. LC 74-22095. (Reference Library of the Humanities: No. 1). 300p. 1975. lib. bdg. 39.00 (ISBN 0-8240-1057-4). Garland Pub.
Boswell, James. Boswell's Journal of a Tour to the Hebrides with Samuel Johnson. (Oxford Standard Authors Ser.). 1930. pap. 6.95x (ISBN 0-19-281072-3). Oxford U Pr.
--Boswell's Life of Johnson. Brady, F., ed. 1968. pap. 3.95 (ISBN 0-452-00752-6, Mer). NAL.
--Boswells' Life of Samuel Johnson. abr. ed. Brady, Frank, ed. 1981. pap. 3.50 (ISBN 0-451-51507-2, CE1507, Sig Classics). NAL.
--Boswell's London Journey. 1960. pap. 6.95 (ISBN 0-07-006603-5). McGraw.
--Dorando. Hunting, Robert S., ed. LC 73-78276. 1973. 3.50 (ISBN 0-913006-05-X). Puckerbrush.
--Dorando: A Spanish Tale. LC 72-189745. 1973. lib. bdg. 16.50 (ISBN 0-8414-2535-3). Folcroft.
--Everybody's Boswell: Being the Life of Samuel Johnson. abr. ed. Morley, Frank, ed. (Illus.). xvii, 665p. 1981. 24.95x (ISBN 0-7135-1237-7, 82-87708). Ohio U Pr.
--Hypochondriack, 2 Vols. Bailey, Margery, ed. LC 78-39512. Repr. of 1928 ed. Set. 85.00 (ISBN 0-404-07654-8); 42.50 ea. Vol. 1 (ISBN 0-404-07655-6). Vol. 2 (ISBN 0-404-07656-4). AMS Pr.
--The Journal of a Tour to the Hebrides with Samuel Johnson. Powell, Lawrence F., ed. 1979. Repr. of 1958 ed. 12.95x (ISBN 0-460-00387-9, Evman). Biblio Dist.
--A Letter to the People of Scotland of the Present State of the Nation. 59.95 (ISBN 0-8490-0509-4). Gordon Pr.
--Letters, 2 vols. Repr. of 1924 ed. Set. 59.00x (ISBN 0-403-04137-6). Somerset Pub.
--Life of Johnson, 6 vols. Hill, George B. & Powell, L. F., eds. Bd. with Boswell's Journal of a Tour to the Hebrides. Boswell, James; Johnson's Diary of a Journey into North Wales. Johnson, Samuel. Vol. 1-4. 1934 ed. 195.00x (ISBN 0-19-811304-8). Oxford U Pr.
--Life of Johnson. (English Library Ser.). 1979. pap. 3.95 (ISBN 0-14-043116-0). Penguin.
--Life of Johnson. Chapman, R. W. & Fleeman, J. E., eds. (World's Classics Ser.). 1982. pap. 12.95 (ISBN 0-19-281537-7). Oxford U Pr.
--Life of Samuel Johnson, 2 vols. in 1. 1978. Repr. of 1976 ed. 17.95x (ISBN 0-460-00001-2, Evman). Biblio Dist.
--Life of Samuel Johnson. (Modern Library College Editions). 1964. pap. text ed. 3.95 (ISBN 0-394-30962-6, T62, RanC). Random.
Boswell, James, jt. auth. see Johnson, Samuel.
Boswell, James, ed. see Shakespeare, William.
Boswell, Jeanetta. Herman Melville & the Critics: A Checklist of Criticism, 1900-1978. LC 80-25959. (Author Bibliographies Ser.: No. 53). 259p. 1981. 20.00 (ISBN 0-8108-1385-8). Scarecrow.
--Nathaniel Hawthorne & the Critics: A Checklist of Criticism, 1900-1978. LC 81-9398. (The Scarecrow Author Bibliographies Ser.: No. 57). 283p. 1982. 20.00 (ISBN 0-8108-1471-4). Scarecrow.
--Past Ruined Ilion... A Bibliography of English & American Literature Based on Greco-Roman Mythology. LC 82-5541. 333p. 1982. text ed. 22.50 (ISBN 0-8108-1549-4). Scarecrow.
--Ralph Waldo Emerson & the Critics: A Checklist of Criticism, 1900-1977. LC 79-4670. (Author Bibliographies Ser.: No. 39). 1979. 17.50 (ISBN 0-8108-1211-8). Scarecrow.
--The Schoolroom Poets: A Bibliography of Bryant, Holmes, Longfellow, Lowell & Whittier with Selective Annotation. LC 83-19276. 311p. 1983. 18.50 (ISBN 0-8108-1659-8). Scarecrow.
--Walt Whitman & the Critics: A Checklist of Criticism, 1900-1978. LC 80-20528. (The Scarecrow Author Bibliographies Ser.: No. 51). 270p. 1980. 20.00 (ISBN 0-8108-1355-6). Scarecrow.
Boswell, Jeanetta & Crouch, Sarah. Henry David Thoreau & the Critics: A Checklist of Criticism 1900-1978. LC 81-929. (Author Bibliographies Ser.: No. 56). 215p. 1981. 17.50 (ISBN 0-8108-1416-1). Scarecrow.
Boswell, Jeanetta, jt. auth. see Boswell, Fred.
Boswell, John. Christianity, Social Tolerance, & Homosexuality: Gay People in Western Europe from the Beginning of the Christian Era to the Fourteenth Century. LC 79-11171. (Illus.). xviii, 424p. 1980. 35.00x (ISBN 0-226-06710-6); pap. 12.95 (ISBN 0-226-06711-4). U of Chicago Pr.
--The Royal Treasure: Muslim Communities under the Crown of Aragon in the Fourteenth Century. LC 77-76303. 1977. 43.00x (ISBN 0-300-02090-2). Yale U Pr.
Boswell, John & Brown, Patty. Chuck & Di Have a Baby. 1982. write for info. (Wallaby). S&S.
Boswell, John, jt. auth. see Fitzgerald, Jim.
Boswell, John & Fitzgerald, James, eds. The U. S. Armed Forces First Aid Manual. 1982. 5.95 (ISBN 0-89256-192-0); pap. 2.95 (ISBN 0-89256-201-3). Rawson Assocs.
Boswell, John & Reiger, George, eds. The U. S. Armed Forces Survival Manual. rev. ed. 1981. 14.95 (ISBN 0-686-30974-X). Rawson Assocs.
Boswell, Jonathan S. Business Policies in the Making: Three Steel Companies Compared. 248p. 1983. text ed. 29.50x (ISBN 0-04-330335-8). Allen Unwin.
Boswell, Katharine Cumming, tr. see Penck, Walther.
Boswell, Kathryn, jt. auth. see O'Connor, Francine M.
Boswell, L. F., ed. Platform Superstructures: Design & Construction. (Illus.). 300p. 1984. text ed. 65.00x (ISBN 0-246-12524-1, Pub. by Granada England). Sheridan.
Boswell, Laurence F. Dynamics of Structural Systems. 200p. 1984. 40.00x (ISBN 0-246-11269-7, Pub. by Granada England). Sheridan.
Boswell, Nelson. Inner Peace, Inner Power. 192p. (Orig.). 1985. pap. 2.95 (ISBN 0-449-12716-8, GM). Fawcett.
Boswell, Sharon. Perception. LC 85-50092. (Illus.). 74p. 1985. 9.95 (ISBN 0-938232-71-1). Winston-Derek.
Boswell, Thomas. How Life Imitates the World Series. (Penguin Sports Library). 296p. 1983. pap. 5.95 (ISBN 0-14-006469-9). Penguin.
--How Life Imitates the World Series: An Inquiry into the Game. LC 81-43286. (Illus.). 360p. 1982. 14.95 (ISBN 0-385-17595-7). Doubleday.
--Why Time Begins on Opening Day. LC 82-46029. 312p. 1984. 14.95 (ISBN 0-385-18409-3). Doubleday.
Boswell, Thomas D. & Curtis, James R. The Cuban-American Experience: Culture, Images' & Perspectives. LC 83-16042. 214p. 1984. text ed. 34.50x (ISBN 0-86598-116-7). Rowman & Allanheld.
Boswell-Stone, W. G. Shakespeare's Holinshed. LC 66-29420. 1967. Repr. of 1909 ed. 30.00 (ISBN 0-405-08291-6, Blom Pubns). Ayer Co Pubs.
Boswick, John A., Jr. Emergency Care. (Illus.). 224p. 1981. pap. text ed. 9.95 (ISBN 0-7216-1876-6). Saunders.
Boswick, John A., Jr., ed. Current Concepts in Hand Surgery. LC 82-24897. (Illus.). 287p. 1983. text ed. 37.50 (ISBN 0-8121-0881-7). Lea & Febiger.
Boswick, John R. The Art & Science of Burn Care. 1985. text ed. 50.00 (ISBN 0-8391-2056-7). Univ Park.
--Upper Extremity Surgery & Rehabilitation. 1985. tchr's. ed. 50.00 (ISBN 0-8391-2055-9, 21679). Univ Park.
Boswirth, L., jt. auth. see Plint, M. A.
Bosworth, A. B. A Historical Commentary on Arrian's History of Alexander, Vol. I: Bks. I-III. 1980. 95.00x (ISBN 0-19-814828-3). Oxford U Pr.
Bosworth, A. S. History of Randolph County. 1975. Repr. of 1916 ed. 25.00 (ISBN 0-87012-214-2). McClain.
Bosworth, Allan R. America's Concentration Camps. (Illus.). 1967. 15.95x (ISBN 0-393-05338-5). Norton.
Bosworth, Barry, et al. Capital Needs in the Seventies. LC 75-5157. pap. 24.30 (ISBN 0-317-30182-9, 2025364). Bks Demand UMI.
Bosworth, Barry P. Tax Incentives & Economic Growth. LC 84-9625. 229p. 1984. 26.95 (ISBN 0-8157-1036-4); pap. 9.95 (ISBN 0-8157-1035-6). Brookings.
Bosworth, Barry P. & Lawrence, Robert Z. Commodity Prices & the New Inflation. LC 81-70467. 250p. 1982. 26.95 (ISBN 0-8157-1034-8); pap. 9.95 (ISBN 0-8157-1033-X). Brookings.
Bosworth, Bruce. Business Programming Projects with BASIC. 256p. 1984. pap. text ed. 17.95 (ISBN 0-574-21480-1, 13-4480); tchr's ed. (ISBN 0-574-21481-X, 13-4481). SRA.
--Codes, Ciphers, & Computers: An Introduction to Information Security. 1982. pap. 16.50 (5149). Hayden.
--Programs in BASIC, a Lecture Notebook. 2nd ed. 1978. pap. text ed. 6.50 (ISBN 0-8403-1210-5). Kendall-Hunt.
--A User's Guide to Statistics Programs: The Rapidata Timesharing System. 1977. pap. text ed. 6.95 (ISBN 0-89529-018-9). Avery Pub.
Bosworth, C. E. The Islamic Dynasties. 243p. 1980. pap. 10.00 (ISBN 0-85224-402-9, Pub. by Edinburgh U Pr Scotland). Columbia U Pr.
--Medieval Arabic Culture & Administration: Sixteen Studies in English 1963-81. 358p. 1982. 75.00x (ISBN 0-86078-113-5, Pub. by Variorum England). State Mutual Bk.
--The Medieval History of Iran, Afghanistan & Central Asia. 374p. 1980. 75.00x (ISBN 0-86078-000-7, Pub. by Variorum England). State Mutual Bk.
Bosworth, C. E., ed. Iran & Islam. 574p. 1972. 35.00x (ISBN 0-85224-085-6, Pub. by Edinburgh U Pr Scotland). Columbia U Pr.
Bosworth, C. E., ed. see Barthold, W.
Bosworth, C. E., jt. ed. see Schacht, Joseph.
Bosworth, Clifford. The Ghaznavids. (Arab Background Ser.). 1973. 18.00x (ISBN 0-86685-005-8). Intl Bk Ctr.
Bosworth, Clifford E. The Later Ghaznavids: Splendor & Decay, the Dynasty in Afganistan & Northern India. LC 77-7879. 196p. 1977. text ed. 26.00x (ISBN 0-231-04428-3). Columbia U Pr.
Bosworth, David. The Death of Descartes. LC 81-50637. (Drue Heinz Literature Prize Winners Ser.). 191p. 1981. 12.95 (ISBN 0-8229-3448-5). U of Pittsburgh Pr.
Bosworth, Derek L. & Dawkins, Peter J. Work Patterns: An Economic Analysis. 276p. 1981. text ed. 47.50x (ISBN 0-566-00310-4). Gower Pub Co.
Bosworth, Derek L., ed. see European Production Study Group Meeting, Loughborough Univ., 1981.
Bosworth, Duane, jt. auth. see Foster, Albert B.
Bosworth, E. & Hillenbrand, Carole, eds. Qajar Iran, Eighteen Hundred to Nineteen Twenty-Five: Political, Social & Cultural Change. LC 84-673453. 414p. 1983. 34.00x (ISBN 0-85224-459-2, Pub. by Edinburgh U Pr Scotland). Columbia U Pr.
Bosworth, F. F. Christ the Healer. 241p. pap. 6.95 (ISBN 0-8007-5124-8, Power Bks). Revell.

Bosworth, Halliam. Technique in Dramatic Art. 1975. Repr. of 1929 ed. 30.00 (ISBN 0-8274-4104-5). R West.

Bosworth, J. A. Neknus & Other Poems. LC 83-90808. 1984. 10.00 (ISBN 0-533-05817-1). Vantage.

Bosworth, Joseph. A Compendious Anglo-Saxon & English Dictionary. 1979. Repr. of 1860 ed. lib. bdg. 30.00 (ISBN 0-89341-478-6). Longwood Pub Group.

Bosworth, Joseph, et al, eds. An Anglo-Saxon Dictionary. (Anglo-Saxon & Eng.). 1972. 115.00x (ISBN 0-19-863101-4); 1921 supplement & addenda 90.00x (ISBN 0-19-863112-X). Oxford U Pr.

Bosworth, Louise M. The Living Wage of Women Workers: Study of Incomes & Expenditures of 450 Women in the City of Boston. LC 75-16459. (Social Problems & Social Policy Ser.). 1976. Repr. of 1911 ed. 11.00x (ISBN 0-405-07477-8). Ayer Co Pubs.

Bosworth, Patricia. Diane Arbus. 464p. 1985. pap. 8.95 (ISBN 0-380-69927-3). Avon.

--Diane Arbus: A Biography. LC 83-48849. (Illus.). 321p. 1984. 17.95 (ISBN 0-394-50404-6). Knopf.

Bosworth, R. J. Italy: The Least of the Great Powers. LC 78-18090. (Illus.). 532p. 1980. 79.50 (ISBN 0-521-22366-0). Cambridge U Pr.

Bosworth, Richard. Italy & the Approach of the First World War. LC 82-16841. (The Making of the Twentieth Century Ser.). 174p. 1984. 22.50x (ISBN 0-312-43924-5). St Martin.

Bosworth, Seymour. Handbook of Banking & Automation. 1986. cancelled (ISBN 0-87094-565-3). Dow Jones-Irwin.

Bosworth, Sheila. Almost Innocent. 320p. 1984. 15.95 (ISBN 0-671-50365-0). S&S.

Boszany. Bracketing of Eigenfrequencies of Continuous Structures. 1981. 55.00 (ISBN 0-9960071-2-1, Pub. by Akademiai Kaido Hungary). Heyden.

Boszormenyi-Nagy, Ivan & Spark, Geraldine M. Invisible Loyalties. LC 83-26300. 408p. 1984. Repr. of 1965 ed. 29.50 (ISBN 0-87630-359-9). Brunner-Mazel.

Bota, Liviu, jt. auth. see Babansky, Yuri K.

Botang, Wen. Sports & Public Health. (China Handbook Ser.). (Illus.). 176p. (Orig.). 1983. pap. 4.95 (ISBN 0-8351-0990-9). China Bks.

Botchek, Charles M. VLSI: Basi Mos Engineering, Vol. 1. LC 83-61990. (Illus.). 368p. 1983. text ed. 36.50 (ISBN 0-913727-00-8). Pacific Tech.

Botchie, G. Employment & Multinational Enterprises in Export Processing Zones: The Cases of Liberia & Ghana. International Labour Office Staff, ed. (Working Papers: No. 30). iv, 74p. (Orig.). 1984. pap. 8.95 (ISBN 92-2-103770-3). Intl Labour Office.

Botein, Bernard. Trial Judge: The Candid, Behind the Bench Story of Justice Bernard Botein. (American Constitutional & Legal History Ser.). 337p. 1974. Repr. of 1952 ed. lib. bdg. 39.50 (ISBN 0-306-70630-X). Da Capo.

Botein, M., et al. Development & Regulation of New Communication Technologies: Cable Television, Subscription Television, Multipoint Distribution Service & Direct Broadcast Satellites. 140p. 1980. pap. 50.00 (ISBN 0-941888-03-7). Comm Media.

Botein, Michael. Videotape in Legal Education: A Study of Its Implications & a Manual for its Users. 70p. 1979. 20.00 (ISBN 0-941888-10-X). Comm Media.

Botein, Michael & Pearce, Alan. Videotex & Electronic Publishing: A Legal, Regulatory & Economic Analysis. 56p. (Orig.). 1982. pap. text ed. write for info. Comm Media.

Botein, Michael & Robb, Scott. Competition vs. Regulation: The Case of the Mass Media. 213p. 1978. pap. 40.00 (ISBN 0-941888-02-9). Comm Media.

Botein, Michael, jt. auth. see Friedlander, Rena.

Botein, Michael & Rice, David, eds. Network Television & the Public Interest: A Preliminary Inquiry. LC 79-1751. 320p. 1980. 27.00x (ISBN 0-669-02927-0). Lexington Bks.

Botein, Stephen. Early American Law & Society. LC 82-17158. (Borozi Books in Law & American Society). 1983. text ed. 15.00 (ISBN 0-394-33582-1, KnopfC); pap. text ed. 7.00 (ISBN 0-394-33252-0). Knopf.

Botein, Stephen, et al, eds. Experiments in History Teaching. LC 77-148. pap. 4.75 (ISBN 0-916704-03-3). Langdon Assocs.

Botel, Morton. Multi-Level Speller for Grades 3-12. (gr. 3-12). pap. 3.20 (ISBN 0-931992-16-8). Penns Valley.

--Multi-Level Speller Guidebook for Teachers. 1961. 2.85 (ISBN 0-931992-17-6). Penns Valley.

--Primary Multi-Level Speller & First Dictionary. (gr. k-2). 1959. pap. 3.10 (ISBN 0-931992-14-1). Penns Valley.

Botel, Morton, jt. auth. see Preston, Ralph C.

Boteler, Alexander R., et al. John Brown's Raid at Harpers Ferry, West Virginia, 1859. (Illus.). 1980. pap. 2.00 (ISBN 0-89646-055-X). Outbooks.

Boteler, Alison. The Children's Party Cookbook. (Illus.). 244p. 1985. 14.95 (ISBN 0-8120-5636-1). Barron.

Botella-Llusia, Jose. Obstetrical Endocrinology. (Illus.). 140p. 1961. 14.50x (ISBN 0-398-00199-5). C C Thomas.

Botermans, Jack. Paper Flight: Forty-Eight Models Ready for Take-Off. Ogle, Deborah, tr. from Dutch. 1984. pap. 9.95 (ISBN 0-03-070506-1, Owl Bks). HR&W.

Botero, Giovanni. The Traveller's Breviant, or an Historical Description of the Most Famous Kingdomes. LC 72-175. (English Experience Ser.: No. 143). 180p. 1969. Repr. of 1601 ed. 21.00 (ISBN 90-221-0143-6). Walter J Johnson.

--A Treatise, Concerning the Causes of the Magnificence & Greatness of Cities. LC 79-84090. (English Experience Ser.: No. 910). 128p. (Eng.). 1979. Repr. of 1606 ed. lib. bdg. 13.00 (ISBN 90-221-0910-0). Walter J Johnson.

Botez, M. I. & Reynolds, E. H., eds. Folic Acid in Neurology, Psychiatry, & Internal Medicine. LC 78-57243. 550p. 1979. text ed. 71.00 (ISBN 0-89004-338-8). Raven.

Botez, Mihai C. & Celac, Mariana. Undesirable Versus Desirable Societies. (Project on Goals, Processes & Indicators of Development). 74p. 1983. pap. text ed. 5.00 (ISBN 92-808-0450-2, TUNU215, UNU). Unipub.

Botfield, Beriah. Notes on the Cathedral Libraries of England. LC 68-23138. 1969. Repr. of 1849 ed. 65.00x (ISBN 0-8103-3174-8). Gale.

Botha, Colin G. Public Archives of South Africa, Sixteen Fifty-Two to Nineteen Hundred Ten. LC 70-82015. 1969. Repr. of 1928 ed. lib. bdg. 19.50 (ISBN 0-8337-0340-4). B Franklin.

Botha, J. F. & Pinder, G. F. Fundamental Concepts in the Numerical Solution of Differential Equations. LC 83-1213. 202p. 1983. 26.95 (ISBN 0-471-87546-5, Pub. by Wiley-Interscience). Wiley.

Botha, Rudolf B. Methodological Status of Grammatical Argumentation. LC 79-126050. (Janua Linguarum Ser.Maior: No. 105). (Orig.). 1970. pap. text ed. 8.80x (ISBN 90-2790-714-5). Mouton.

Botha, Rudolf P. The Justification of Linguistic Hypotheses. (Janua Linguarum Series Maior: No. 84). 1973. text ed. 39.20x (ISBN 90-2792-542-9). Mouton.

Botha, Rudolph P. Methodological Aspects of Transformational Generative Phonology. (Janua Linguarum, Ser. Minor: No. 112). 266p. 1971. pap. text ed. 16.80x (ISBN 90-2791-761-2). Mouton.

Botham, C. N. Audio-Visual Aids for Cooperative Education & Training. (Agricultural Development Papers: No. 86). 99p. (Orig., 4th Printing 1975). 1967. pap. 11.00 (F52, FAO). Unipub.

Botham, Mary & Sharrad, L. Manual of Wigmaking. (Illus.). 112p. 1983. 10.95 (ISBN 0-434-90164-4, Pub. by W Heinemann Ltd). David & Charles.

Bothe, H. & Trebst, A., eds. Biology of Inorganic Nitrogen & Sulfur Metabolism. (Proceedings in Life Sciences Ser.). (Illus.). 370p. 1981. 52.00 (ISBN 0-387-10486-0). Springer-Verlag.

Bothe, M., et al. New Rules for Victims of Armed Conflict. 1982. lib. bdg. 145.00 (ISBN 90-247-2537-2, Pub. by Martinus Nijhoff Netherlands). Kluwer Academic.

Bothe, Michael. Trends in Environmental Policy & Law. (Environmental Policy & Law Papers: No. 15). 404p. 1980. pap. 27.50 (ISBN 2-88032-085-2, IUCN94, IUCN). Unipub.

Botheroyd, Paul F. Ich und Er: First & Third-Person Self-Reference & Problems of Identity in Three Contemporary German-Language Novels. (De Proprietatibus Litterarum Series Practica: No.67). 143p. (Orig.). 1976. pap. text ed. 19.20x (ISBN 90-2793-214-X). Mouton.

Botheroyd, Thomas J., ed. see Rice, John R.

Bothma, Guido H. Madhres...or Survival. 222p. 1985. 12.95 (ISBN 0-533-06309-4). Vantage.

Bothmer, B., ed. see De Meulenaere, Herman & MacKay, P.

Bothmer, Bernard, ed. see Holz, R., et al.

Bothmer, Dietrich Von see Moore, Mary B. & Von Bothmer, Dietrich.

Bothmer, Dietrich von see Von Bothmer, Dietrich.

Bothmer, Dietrich Von see Von Bothmer, Dietrich & Frel, Jiri.

Bothmer, Dietrich Von see Von Bothmer, Dietrich & Mertens, Joan R.

Bothmer, Gerry, tr. see Hansson, Carola, et al.

Bothmer, Gerry, tr. see Lindgren, Astrid.

Bothmer, Gerry, tr. see Lundgren, Astrid.

Bothner, Gerry, tr. see Lindgren, Astrid.

Bothra, Pushpa. Jaina Theory of Perception. 1976. 8.50 (ISBN 0-89684-229-0). Orient Bk Dist.

Bothwell, Dick. Alligators. LC 62-52731. (Orig.). pap. 3.95 (ISBN 0-8200-0302-6). Great Outdoors.

Bothwell, Etta K. Alienation in the Jewish American Novel of the Sixties. LC 78-3559. 1979. pap. 10.00 (ISBN 0-8477-3191-X). U of PR Pr.

Bothwell, H. Roger. My First Book about Baptism. (My Church Teaches Ser.). (Illus.). (ps). 1978. pap. 1.95 (ISBN 0-8127-0179-8). Review & Herald.

--My First Book About Communion. (My Church Teaches Ser.). (Illus.). (ps). 1978. pap. 1.95 (ISBN 0-8127-0180-1). Review & Herald.

Bothwell, James H. Affaires du conte de Boduel. LC 71-39513. (Bannatyne Club, Edinburgh. Publications: No. 29). Repr. of 1829 ed. 17.50 (ISBN 0-404-52735-3). AMS Pr.

Bothwell, Jean. The Onion Cookbook. LC 75-35403. (Illus.). 180p. 1976. pap. 3.50 (ISBN 0-486-23312-X). Dover.

--The Onion Cookbook. 7.75 (ISBN 0-8446-5482-5). Peter Smith.

Bothwell, Lawrence. Broome County Heritage: An Illustrated History. (Illus.). 176p. 1983. 24.95 (ISBN 0-89781-061-9). Windsor Pubns Inc.

Bothwell, Lawrence B., ed. see Stein, Roger B.

Bothwell, Lin K. The Art of Leadership: Skill-Building Techniques that Produce Results. (Illus.). 255p. 1983. 18.95 (ISBN 0-13-047100-3); pap. 9.95 (ISBN 0-13-047092-9). P-H.

Bothwell, Sr. Mary D. We Believe. (Christ Our Life Ser.). (Illus.). (gr. 4). 1981. pap. text ed. 4.20 (ISBN 0-8294-0367-1); tchr's ed. 9.95 (ISBN 0-8294-0368-X). Loyola.

--We Worship. (Christ Our Life Ser.). (Illus.). (gr. 5). 1982. text ed. 4.20 (ISBN 0-8294-0391-4); tchrs. ed. 9.95 (ISBN 0-8294-0392-2). Loyola.

Bothwell, Mary O. The Church. (Christ Our Life Ser.). (Illus.). (gr. 8). 1976. pap. text ed. 3.80 (ISBN 0-8294-0241-1); tchr's ed. 5.95 (ISBN 0-8294-0242-X). Loyola.

Bothwell, Sr. Mary. God Guides Us. (Christ Our Life Ser). (Illus.). (gr. 3). 1981. pap. text ed. 4.20 (ISBN 0-8294-0365-5); tchr's ed. 9.95 (ISBN 0-8294-0366-3). Loyola.

Bothwell, Ralph S. Anatomy of the Economic Forces Dominating the Business & the Political World. (Illus.). 1980. deluxe ed. 63.50x (ISBN 0-918968-59-3). Inst Econ Finan.

Bothwell, Reece B. La Ciudadania en Puerto Rico. 2nd ed. LC 78-24031. (Sp.). 1979. pap. 1.85 (ISBN 0-8477-2451-4). U of PR Pr.

--Manual De Procedimiento Parlamentario. 5th, rev. ed. 6.25 (ISBN 0-8477-3005-0). U of PR Pr.

--Puerto Rico: Cien Anos de Lucha Politica, 4 vols. LC 77-10904. 1980. 100.00 (ISBN 0-8477-2444-1). U of PR Pr.

--Trasfondo Constitucional De Puerto Rico: Primera Parte, 1887-1914. 3rd ed. pap. 2.15 (ISBN 0-8477-0821-7). U of PR Pr.

Bothwell, Reece B. & Cruz Monclava, Lidio. Los Documentos "Que Dicen". pap. 6.85 (ISBN 0-8477-0820-9). U of PR Pr.

Bothwell, Robert. Eldorado: Canada's National Uranium Company. (Illus.). 512p. 1984. 24.95 (ISBN 0-8020-3414-4). U of Toronto Pr.

Bothwell, Robert, et al. Canada Since Nineteen Forty-Five: Power, Politics, & Provincialism. 502p. 1981. pap. 15.95c (ISBN 0-8020-6478-7). U of Toronto Pr.

Bothwell, Roger. For the Umpteenth Time. (Outreach Ser.). 16p. 1983. pap. 0.95 (ISBN 0-8163-0538-2). Pacific Pr Pub Assn.

Botifoll, Luis J., et al. Forjadores de la Conciencia Nacional Cubana. (Illus.). 108p. (Orig., Span.). 1984. pap. 5.00 (ISBN 0-89729-366-5). Ediciones.

Botkin, B. A. A Treasury of New England Folklore. 9.98 (ISBN 0-517-10918-2). Crown.

Botkin, B. A., ed. A Civil War Treasury of Tales. 29.95 (ISBN 0-88411-860-6, Pub. by Aeonian Pr). Amereon Ltd.

--Treasury of American Folklore. 960p. 1984. 7.98 (ISBN 0-517-42057-0, Bonanza). Outlet Bk Co.

Botkin, Benjamin A. New York City Folklore: Legends, Tall Tales, Anecdotes, Stories, Sagas, Heroes & Characters, Customs, Traditions & Sayings. LC 76-43977. (Illus.). 1976. Repr. of 1956 ed. lib. bdg. 28.75x (ISBN 0-8371-9310-9, BONC). Greenwood.

--Sidewalks of America: Folklore, Legends, Sagas, Traditions, Customs, Songs, Stories, & Sayings of City Folk. LC 76-44361. (Illus.). 1976. Repr. of 1954 ed. lib. bdg. 34.75x (ISBN 0-8371-9312-5, BOSA). Greenwood.

Botkin, Daniel B. & Keller, Edward A. Environmental Studies. 480p. 1982. text ed. 27.95 (ISBN 0-675-09813-0). Additional supplements may be obtained from publisher. Merrill.

Botkin, James & Dimancescu, Dan. Global Stakes: The Future of High Technology in America. LC 82-8747. 248p. 1982. prof. ref. 19.95 (ISBN 0-88410-886-4). Ballinger Pub.

Botkin, James, et al. Global Stakes: The Future of High Technology in America. 240p. 1984. pap. 7.95 (ISBN 0-14-007039-7). Penguin.

--The Innovators: Re-discovering America's Creative Energy. LC 83-48783. 224p. 1984. 16.30i (ISBN 0-06-015285-0, HarpT). Har-Row.

Botkin, James W. & Dimancescu, Dan. The New Strategists: America's New R&D Consortia. 240p. 1986. prof. ref. 24.95x (ISBN 0-88730-046-4). Ballinger Pub.

Botkin, James W., et al. No Limits to Learning: Bridging the Human Gap: the Club of Rome Report. LC 79-40911. 1979. 18.25 (ISBN 0-08-024705-9); pap. 7.75 (ISBN 0-08-024704-0). Pergamon.

Botkin, Kenneth E., jt. auth. see Luzadder, Warren J.

Botkin, William E., et al. Union Pacific Three-Nine-Eight-Five. LC 85-9929. (Illus.). 64p. 1985. pap. 9.95 (ISBN 0-918654-36-X). CO RR Mus.

Botman, J. J. Dynamics of Housing & Planning: A Regional Simulation Model. x, 246p. 1982. 44.00 (ISBN 90-6021-473-0, Pub. by Martinus Nijhoff Netherlands). Kluwer Academic.

Botner, J., et al, eds. see Faulkner, William.

Botnick, Diane, jt. auth. see Grove, Nancy.

Botoman, Rodica C., et al. Imi Place Limba Romana: A Romanian Reader. (Illus.). iii, 199p. 1982. pap. text ed. 9.95 (ISBN 0-89357-087-7). Slavica.

Botombele, Bokonga E. Cultural Policy in the Republic of Zaire. (Studies & Documents on Cultural Policies). (Illus.). 112p. 1976. pap. 5.25 (ISBN 92-3-101317-3, U140, UNESCO). Unipub.

Botsch, Robert E. We Shall Not Overcome: Populism & Southern Blue-Collar Workers. LC 80-11567. xv, 237p. 1981. 19.50x (ISBN 0-8078-1444-X). U of NC Pr.

Botsford, George W. A Brief History of the World. (Illus.). 518p. 1980. Repr. of 1917 ed. lib. bdg. 35.00 (ISBN 0-8492-3591-X). R West.

--The Development of the Athenian Constitution. Repr. of 1893 ed. 27.00 (ISBN 0-384-05285-1). Johnson Repr.

--A History of the Ancient World. 1919. 35.00 (ISBN 0-8274-3932-6). R West.

--A History of the Orient & Greece. 1902. 35.00 (ISBN 0-8274-3933-4). R West.

--A Source Book of Ancient History. 1929. 40.00 (ISBN 0-8274-3934-2). R West.

Botsford, Shirley. Making Gifts for Men. LC 84-24660. (Illus.). 224p. 1985. 16.95 (ISBN 0-385-18543-X). Doubleday.

Botsford, Thomas W. & Wilson, Richard E. The Acute Abdomen: An Approach to Diagnosis & Management. 2nd ed. LC 76-20075. 1977. pap. text ed. 15.00 (ISBN 0-7216-1886-3). Saunders.

Botsford, Thomas W., jt. auth. see Dunphy, J. Englebert.

Botsford, Ward, adapted by see Gilbert & Sullivan.

Bott, Alan. Our Fathers (Eighteen Seventy to Nineteen Hundred) 249p. 1980. Repr. lib. bdg. 35.00 (ISBN 0-89987-061-9). Darby Bks.

--Our Fathers: Manners & Customs of the Ancient Victorians. LC 75-160614. (Illus.). 119p. 1976. pap. 5.25 ... 27.50 (ISBN 0-405-08292-4, Blom Pubns). Ayer Co Pubs.

Bott, Alan & Clephane, Irene. Our Mothers. LC 73-81813. (Illus.). 27.50 (ISBN 0-405-08293-2, Blom Pubns.). Ayer Co Pubs.

Bott, Alan, ed. Our Mothers. 220p. 1980. Repr. of 1932 ed. lib. bdg. 30.00 (ISBN 0-8495-0461-9). Arden Lib.

Bott, Alan J. see Contact, pseud.

Bott, D. H. A Nepos Selection. 1970. text ed. 6.95 (ISBN 0-312-56420-1). St Martin.

Bott, Elizabeth. Family & Social Network: Roles, Norms & External Relationships. 2nd ed. LC 71-161235. (Illus.). 1972. pap. text ed. 12.95 (ISBN 0-02-904510-X). Free Pr.

--Tongan Society at the Time of Captain Cook's Visits: Discussions with Her Majesty Queen Salote Tupou. 187p. 1983. pap. text ed. 15.00x (ISBN 0-8248-0864-9). UH Pr.

Bott, J. F., jt. auth. see Gross, R. W.

Bott, M. H. Interior of the Earth: Its Structure, Constitution & Evolution. 2nd ed. 404p. 1982. 37.00 (ISBN 0-444-00723-7). Elsevier.

Bott, Martin H. & Saxov, Svend, eds. Structure & Development of the Greenland-Scotland Ridge: New Methods & Concepts. (NATO Conference Ser. IV, Marine Sciences: Vol. 8). 696p. 1982. 95.00x (ISBN 0-306-41019-2, Plenum Pr). Plenum Pub.

Bott, R. Fouling of Heat Exchange Surfaces. Date not set. write for info. Elsevier.

Bott, R. & Tu, L. W. Differential Forms in Algebraic Topology. (Graduate Texts in Mathematics Ser.: Vol. 82). (Illus.). 288p. 1982. 33.00 (ISBN 0-387-90613-4). Springer-Verlag.

Bott, Raymond & Morrison, Stanley. Discovering Chess. 1975. 10.00 (ISBN 0-571-04834-X). Transatlantic.

Bott, T. R. Fouling of Heat Exchangers. 1984. write for info. Elsevier.

Bott, T. Reg. Chemical Engineering-Beating Pollution. 129p. 1982. 30.00x (ISBN 0-85225-747-3, Pub. by Careers Con England). State Mutual Bk.

Bott, Victor. Anthroposophical Medicine: Spiritual Science & the Art of Healing. 208p. (Orig.). 1984. pap. 8.95 (ISBN 0-7225-0958-8). Thorsons Pubs.

Botta, Ann C. Handbook of Universal Literature from the Best & Latest Authorities. 575p. 1984. Repr. of 1886 ed. lib. bdg. 65.00 (ISBN 0-89760-198-X). Telegraph Bks.

Botta, Charles. History of the War of the Independence of the United States of America, 2 Vols. 9th ed. Otis, George A., tr. from It. LC 75-120868. (American Bicentennial Ser). 1970. Repr. of 1845 ed. Set. 67.50x (ISBN 0-8046-1261-7, Pub. by Kennikat). Assoc Faculty Pr.

Bottcher, Betty & Davis, Mel. Wasatch Trails. (Illus.). 77p. 1973. pap. 2.00 (ISBN 0-915272-00-8). Wasatch Pubs.

Bottcher, C. J. & Bordewijk, P. Theory of Electric Polarization, Vol. 2: Dielectrics in Time Dependent Fields. 2nd ed. 562p. 1978. 127.75 (ISBN 0-444-41579-3). Elsevier.

Bottcher, C. J., et al. Theory of Electric Polarization, Vol. 1: Dielectrics in Static Fields. 2nd ed. Van Belle, O.. C. & Bordewijk, P., eds. LC 72-83198. 396p. 1973. 106.50 (ISBN 0-444-41019-8). Elsevier.

Botteghe Oscure. Anthology of New Italian Writers. Caetani, Marquerite, ed. LC 72-110822. Repr. of 1950 ed. lib. bdg. 24.75x (ISBN 0-8371-3211-8, BOIW). Greenwood.

Bottema, O. & Roth, B. Theoretical Kinematics. (Applied Mathematics & Mechanics: Vol. 24). 558p. 1979. 110.75 (ISBN 0-444-85124-0, North-Holland). Elsevier.

Bottenstein, Jane E. & Sato, Gordon, eds. Cell Culture in the Neurosciences. (Current Topics in Neurobiology Ser.). 404p. 1985. 49.50x (ISBN 0-306-41942-4, Plenum Pr). Plenum Pub.

Botterbusch, Karl F. A Comparison of Commercial Vocational Evaluation Systems. 2nd, rev. ed. 133p. 1982. pap. 12.50x (ISBN 0-916671-09-7). Material Dev.

--A Comparison of Computerized Job Matching Systems. (Illus.). 170p. (Orig.). 1984. pap. 16.50x (ISBN 0-916671-01-1). Material Dev.

--Functional Job Analysis. 120p. (Orig.). 1985. pap. price not set (ISBN 0-916671-55-0). Material Dev.

--A Guide to Job Site Evaluation. (Illus.). 52p. (Orig.). 1978. pap. 4.25x (ISBN 0-916671-07-0). Material Dev.

--A Manual of DOT Related Codes. 130p. (Orig.). 1984. pap. 10.00x (ISBN 0-916671-48-8). Material Dev.

--Psychological Testing in Vocational Evaluation. 96p. (Orig.). 1978. pap. 4.75x (ISBN 0-916671-21-6). Material Dev.

--Revised MDC Behavior Identification Form. rev. ed. 227p. (Orig.). 1985. pap. 12.50 (ISBN 0-916671-49-6). Material Dev.

--Short Term Vocational Evaluation. (Illus.). 163p. (Orig.). 1983. pap. 16.25x (ISBN 0-916671-05-4). Material Dev.

--The Use of Psychological Tests for Indviduals Who are Severely Disabled. 70p. (Orig.). 1976. pap. 4.75x (ISBN 0-916671-31-3). Material Dev.

--Work Sample Norms, Reliability & Validity. (Illus.). 83p. (Orig.). 1981. pap. 11.75x (ISBN 0-916671-28-3). Material Dev.

Botterbusch, Karl F. & Hotz, John. Situational Assessment. 180p. (Orig.). 1985. pap. write for info. (ISBN 0-916671-64-X). Material Dev.

Botterbusch, Karl F. & Michaels, Nancy. Psychological Testing in Vocational Evaluation. rev. ed. 150p. (Orig.). 1985. pap. 10.00x (ISBN 0-916671-54-2). Material Dev.

Botterbusch, Karl F., jt. auth. see Lytel, Robert B.

Botterill, A. E. Systems Engineering for Materials Processing. 1986. cancelled (ISBN 0-08-029974-1); pap. price not set (ISBN 0-08-029973-3). Pergamon.

Botterill, Cal, jt. auth. see Orlick, Terry.

Botterill, G. S., jt. auth. see Harding, T. D.

Botterill, G. S., jt. auth. see Keene, R. D.

Botterill, G. S., ed. British Chess. (Chess Ser.). (Illus.). 300p. 1983. 29.95 (ISBN 0-08-024134-4). Pergamon.

Botterill, Steven, tr. see Cattin, Giulio.

Botterweck, C. Michael. Issues: Exercises in Political & Social Decision-Making. 246p. (Orig.). 1980. pap. 9.95 (ISBN 0-911541-01-2). Gregory Pub.

--A Test of Faith: Challenges of Modern Day Christians. 304p. (Orig.). 1983. pap. 8.95 (ISBN 0-911541-01-2). Gregory Pub.

Botterweck, G. Johannes. Diccionario Teologico del Antiguo Testamento, 4 vols. 1116p. (Espn.). 1978. Set. pns (S-50106). French & Eur.

Botterweck, G. Johannes & Ringgren, Helmer. Theological Dictionary of the Old Testament, Vol. V. Green, David E., tr. 528p. 1985. 27.50 (ISBN 0-8028-2329-7). Eerdmans.

Botterweck, G. Johannes & Ringgren, Helmer, eds. Theological Dictionary of the Old Testament, 4 vols. Incl. Vol. I. (ISBN 0-8028-2325-4); Vol. II. (ISBN 0-8028-2326-2); Vol. III. (ISBN 0-8028-2327-0); Vol. 4. Theological Dictionary of the Old Teatament, Botterweck, G. Johannes & Ringgren, Helmer, eds. 560p. 22.50 (ISBN 0-8028-2328-9). 1978. 25.00ea; Set. 100.00 (ISBN 0-8028-2338-6). Eerdmans.

Botterweck, Michael. Issues: Exercises in Social Decision-Making. 120p. (Orig.). 1980. pap. 6.95 (ISBN 0-911541-02-0). Gregory Pub.

Botti, M., et al. Basic Education in the Sahel Countries: A Study Prepared for the International Bank of Reconstruction & Development. (UIE Monographs: UNESCO Institute for Education: No. 6). 130p. 1978. pap. 5.25 (ISBN 92-820-1011-2, U836, UNESCO). Unipub.

Botticelli, Sandro. Botticelli Drawings. (Illus.). 48p. 1982. pap. 2.95 (ISBN 0-486-24248-X). Dover.

Botticelli, Sondra. Illustrations for the Divine Comedy (1482-1490) write for info. (ISBN 0-384-05290-8). Johnson Repr.

Bottiger, K. A. Literarische Zustande und Zeitgenossen. Repr. of 1838 ed. 80.00 (ISBN 0-384-05290-8). Johnson Repr.

Bottigheimer, Karl S. Ireland & the Irish. (Illus.). 256p. 1982. 22.00x (ISBN 0-231-04610-3); pap. 11.95x (ISBN 0-231-04611-1). Columbia U Pr.

Bottiglia, William F., ed. Current Issues in Language Teaching. Incl. Linguistics & Language Teaching. Hall, Robert A., Jr; Programmed Learning. Hayes, Alfred S; A Survey of FLES Practices. Alkons, Nancy V. & Biophy, Mary A.. 1962. 7.95x (ISBN 0-915432-62-5). NE Conf Teach Foreign.

--The Language Classroom. Incl. The Drop-Out of Students After the Second Year. Fulton, Renee J; The Philosophy of the Language Laboratory. Archer, John B; The Place of Grammar & the Use of English in the Teaching of Foreign Languages. Grew, James H; Spoken Language Tests. Brooks, Nelson; Teaching Aids & Techniques. Pleasants, Jeanne V; Teaching Literature for Admission to College with Advanced Standing. Price, Blanche A. 84p. 1957. pap. 7.95x (ISBN 0-915432-57-9). NE Conf Teach Foreign.

--Language Learning: The Intermediate Phase. Incl. The Continuum: Listening & Speaking. Belasco, Simon; Reading for Meaning. Sherer, George; Writing an Expression. Prochoroff, Marina. 85p. 1963. pap. 9.95 (ISBN 0-915432-63-3). NE Conf Teach Foreign.

Botting, C. G., jt. auth. see Hillard, A. E.

Botting, D. The Second Front. Time-Life Books, ed. (World War II). (Illus.). 1979. 14.95 (ISBN 0-8094-2498-3). Time-Life.

Botting, Douglas. The Aftermath: Europe. LC 82-10324. (World War II Ser.). 1983. lib. bdg. 22.60 (ISBN 0-8094-3412-1, Pub. by Time-Life). Silver.

--The Aftermath: Europe. (World War II Ser.). (Illus.). 208p. 1983. 14.95 (ISBN 0-8094-3411-3). Time Life.

--Dragons. LC 84-2646. (Enchanted World Ser.). 1984. lib. bdg. 22.60 (ISBN 0-8094-5209-X, Pub. by Time-Life). Silver.

--From the Ruins of the Reich: Germany 1945-1949. 1985. 17.95 (ISBN 0-517-55865-3). Crown.

--The Pirates. new ed. Time-Life Books, ed. (Seafarers Ser.). (Illus.). 1978. 13.95 (ISBN 0-8094-2650-1). Time-Life.

--The Second Front. LC 78-3405. (World War II Ser.). (Illus.). (gr. 7 up). 1978. lib. bdg. 22.60 (ISBN 0-8094-2499-1, Pub. by Time-Life). Silver.

--The U-Boats. Time-Life Books, ed. (The Seafarers Ser.). (Illus.). 1980. 13.95 (ISBN 0-8094-2723-0). Time-Life.

Botting, Douglas, jt. auth. see Time-Life Books Editors.

Botting, Gary, jt. auth. see Botting, Heather.

Botting, Heather & Botting, Gary. The Orwellian World of Jehovah's Witnesses. (Illus.). 224p. 1984. 25.00x (ISBN 0-8020-2537-4); pap. 9.95 (ISBN 0-8020-6545-7). U of Toronto Pr.

Botting, T., tr. Mitten. 31p. (ps-3). 1983. pap. 1.95 (ISBN 0-8285-2526-9, Pub. by Malysh Pubs USSR). Imported Pubns.

Bottino, Joseph C., et al, eds. Liver Cancer. (Developments in Oncology Ser.). 1985. lib. bdg. 82.50 (ISBN 0-89838-713-2, Pub. by Martinus Nijhoff Netherlands). Kluwer Academic.

Bottke, Karl G., ed. see Bernard, Jean-Jacques.

Bottle, E. K. Fractional Horse-Power Electric Motors: A Guide to Types & Applications. 209p. 1948. 10.95x (ISBN 0-85264-051-X, Pub. by Griffin England). State Mutual Bk.

Bottner, Barbara. Big Boss! Little Boss! LC 78-3281. (An I AM READING Bk.). (Illus.). (gr. 1-4). 1978. PLB 7.99 (ISBN 0-394-93939-5). Pantheon.

--Dumb Old Casey Is a Fat Tree. LC 78-19474. (Illus.). 48p. (gr. 1-4). 1979. PLB 9.89 (ISBN 0-06-020617-9). HarpJ.

--Mean Maxine. LC 79-18587. (Illus.). 32p. (ps-3). 1980. PLB 5.99 (ISBN 0-394-94219-1). Pantheon.

--Myra. LC 78-10417. (Illus.). (gr. k-3). 1979. 8.95 (ISBN 0-02-711740-5). Macmillan.

--The World's Greatest Expert on Absolutely Everything... Is Crying. LC 83-49487. (Illus.). 160p. (gr. 3-6). 1984. 11.06i (ISBN 0-06-020588-1); PLB 10.89g (ISBN 0-06-020589-X). HarpJ.

Botto, Louis. At This Theatre: Playbill Magazine's Informal History of Broadway Theatres. (Illus.). 288p. 1984. 29.95 (ISBN 0-396-08468-0). Dodd.

Bottom Line Personal, Experts, ed. The Book of Inside Information. LC 82-9408. 500p. 1985. 50.00 (ISBN 0-932648-64-9). Boardroom.

Bottom, Norman R. & Kostanoski, John. Security & Loss Control. 1st ed. 352p. 1983. write for info. (ISBN 0-02-312700-7). Macmillan.

Bottom, Norman R., Jr. & Gallati, Robert R. Industrial Espionage: Intelligence Techniques & Countermeasures. (Illus.). 352p. 1983. text ed. 25.95 (ISBN 0-409-95108-0). Butterworth.

Bottom, Virgil E. Introduction to Quartz Crystal Unit Design. (VNR Electrical Computer Serverice & Engineering Ser.). 272p. 1982. 28.50 (ISBN 0-442-26201-9). Van Nos Reinhold.

Bottome, Edgar. The Balance of Terror: A Guide to the Arms Race. LC 73-16225. 288p. 1972. pap. 2.95x (ISBN 0-8070-0545-2, BP417). Beacon Pr.

Bottome, Edgar M. Missile Gap: A Study of the Formulation of Military & Political Policy. LC 77-129964. 265p. 1971. 24.50 (ISBN 0-8386-7734-7). Fairleigh Dickinson.

Bottome, Phyllis. From the Life. facsimile ed. LC 70-134056. (Essay Index Reprint Ser). Repr. of 1944 ed. 13.00 (ISBN 0-8369-2215-8). Ayer Co Pubs.

--Man & Beast. facs. ed. LC 79-122689. (Short Story Index Reprint Ser). 1953. 12.00 (ISBN 0-8369-3523-3). Ayer Co Pubs.

Bottomley, A. Keith. Criminology in Focus: Past Trends & Future Prospects. LC 78-24393. 181p. 1979. text ed. 28.50x (ISBN 0-06-490583-7, 06357). B&N Imports.

--Prison Before Trial. 117p. 1970. pap. text ed. 5.00 (ISBN 0-7135-1816-2, Pub. by Bedford England). Brookfield Pub Co.

Bottomley, Alan, ed. The Southwold Diary of James Maggs: Vol. II 1848-1876. (Suffolk Records Society Ser.: No. XXVI). (Illus.). 160p. 1984. 19.95 (ISBN 0-85115-411-5, Pub. by Boydell & Brewer). Longwood Pub Group.

--The Southwold Diary of James Maggs: Vol. 1 1818-1848. (Suffolk Records Society Ser.: No. XXV). (Illus.). 160p. 1984. 19.95 (ISBN 0-85115-185-X, Pub. by Boydell & Brewer). Longwood Pub Group.

Bottomley, Frank. The Abbey Explorer's Guide to England, Scotland & Wales. 1981. pap. 9.95 (ISBN 0-7182-1280-0, Pub. by Kaye & Ward). David & Charles.

--Attitudes to the Body in Western Christendom. 272p. 1980. 24.00x (ISBN 0-86019-032-3, Pub. by Kimpton). State Mutual Bk.

--The Castle Explorer's Guide to England, Scotland, & Wales. 1979. pap. 8.95 (ISBN 0-7182-1219-3, Pub. by Kaye & Ward). David & Charles.

--The Church Explorer's Guide to England, Scotland, & Wales. 1978. pap. 4.95 (ISBN 0-7182-1187-1, Pub. by Kaye & Ward). David & Charles.

--The Inn Explorer's Guide. (Illus.). 250p. 1984. 14.95 (ISBN 0-7182-1800-0, Pub. by Kaye & Ward). David & Charles.

Bottomley, Gill & De Lepervanche, Marie M., eds. Ethnicity, Class & Gender in Australia. 232p. 1984. text ed. 29.95x (ISBN 0-86861-704-0); pap. text ed. 13.50x (ISBN 0-86861-712-1). Allen Unwin.

Bottomley, Gill, jt. ed. see Burns, Ailsa.

Bottomley, Gillian. After the Odyssey. (Studies in Society & Culture). 1980. 24.95x (ISBN 0-7022-1399-3). U of Queensland Pr.

Bottomley, Gordon. Gruach & Britain's Daughter: Two Plays. LC 79-50018. (One-Act Plays in Reprint Ser.). 1980. Repr. of 1921 ed. 17.50x (ISBN 0-8486-2042-9). Core Collection.

Bottomley, Jim. Paper Projects for Creative Kids of All Ages. 160p. 1983. 12.45i (ISBN 0-316-10348-9); pap. 9.70i (ISBN 0-316-10349-7). Little.

Bottomley, Keith & Coleman, Clive. Understanding Crime Rates: Police & Public Roles in the Production of Official Statistics. 180p. 1981. 20.00 (ISBN 0-566-00309-0, 03294-8, Pub. by Gower Pub Co England). Lexington Bks.

Bottomley, Keith A. Decisions in the Penal Process. (Law in Society Ser.). 270p. 1973. text ed. 11.75x (ISBN 0-8377-1935-6). Rothman.

Bottomley, Michael H. Personnel Management. 196p. 1983. pap. text ed. 21.00x (ISBN 0-7121-1765-2). Trans-Atlantic.

Bottomley, Tom. Boatman's Handbook. rev. ed. LC 84-81082. (Illus.). 316p. (Orig.). 1984. pap. 10.95 (ISBN 0-688-03925-1, Hearst Marine Bk). Morrow.

--Practical Celestial Navigation. (Illus.). 256p. (Orig.). 1983. pap. 12.95 (ISBN 0-8306-1386-2, 1386). TAB Bks.

--Practical Piloting. (Illus.). 182p. (Orig.). 1983. pap. 10.25 (ISBN 0-8306-0619-X, 1619). TAB Bks.

Bottomley, Tom, jt. auth. see Whiting, John.

Bottomley, Tom, jt. ed. see Gladstone, Bernard.

Bottomly, Frank. Attitudes to the Body in Western Christendom. 257p. 1980. 21.00 (ISBN 0-86019-032-3). Transatlantic.

Bottomore, Mary, tr. see Aron, Raymond.

Bottomore, T. The Frankfurt School & Critical Theory. 1984. 11.50x (ISBN 0-85312-458-2, NO.4158); pap. 4.50x (ISBN 0-85312-468-X, NO. 3752). Methuen Inc.

Bottomore, T. B. Classes in Modern Society. (Orig.). 1968. pap. 2.45 (ISBN 0-394-70414-2, V414, Vin). Random.

Bottomore, Thomas, tr. see Aron, Raymond.

Bottomore, Tom. Marxist Sociology. LC 75-5986. 66p. 1975. text ed. 9.50x (ISBN 0-8419-0201-1); pap. text ed. 5.50x (ISBN 0-8419-0203-8). Holmes & Meier.

--Political Sociology. LC 79-3043. 176p. 1980. 14.37i (ISBN 0-06-010438-4, HarpT). Har-Row.

--Sociology & Socialism. LC 83-22930. 212p. 1984. 25.00 (ISBN 0-312-74004-2); pap. text ed. 11.95 (ISBN 0-312-74005-0). St Martin.

Bottomore, Tom, jt. auth. see Hilferding, Rudolf.

Bottomore, Tom, ed. A Dictionary of Marxist Thought. 544p. 1983. 35.00 (ISBN 0-674-20525-1). Harvard U Pr.

--A Dictionary of Marxist Thought. 544p. 1985. pap. 9.95 (ISBN 0-674-20526-X). Harvard U Pr.

--Karl Marx. 200p. 1979. pap. 9.95 (ISBN 0-631-11061-5). Basil Blackwell.

--Modern Interpretations of Marx. 224p. 1981. pap. 9.95x (ISBN 0-631-12708-9). Basil Blackwell.

Bottomore, Tom & Goode, Patrick, eds. Austro-Marxism. 1978. text ed. 39.95x (ISBN 0-19-827229-4); pap. text ed. 10.95x (ISBN 0-19-827230-8). Oxford U Pr.

--Readings in Marxist Sociology. 1983. text ed. 27.95x (ISBN 0-19-876108-2); pap. text ed. 12.95x (ISBN 0-317-06241-7). Oxford U Pr.

Bottomore, Tom & Nisbet, Robert, eds. A History of Sociological Analysis. 717p. 1981. pap. text ed. 10.95x (ISBN 0-465-03024-6). Basic.

--A History of Sociological Analysis. LC 77-20429. 1978. 32.50x (ISBN 0-465-03023-8). Basic.

Bottomore, Tom & Nowak, Stefan, eds. Sociology: The State of the Art. 382p. 1982. 27.50 (ISBN 0-8039-9790-6); pap. 12.95 (ISBN 0-8039-9791-4). Sage.

Bottomore, Tom, ed. see Lowith, Karl.

Bottomore, Tom, tr. see Hilferding, Rudolf.

Bottomore, Tom, tr. see Simmel, Georg.

Bottoms, A. E., jt. auth. see McClintock, F. H.

Bottoms, Anthony E. & Stelman, Andrew. Rethinking Social Enquiry Reports. (Community Care Practice Handbooks). 110p. 1986. text ed. price not set (ISBN 0-566-05068-4). Gower Pub Co.

Bottoms, Anthony E., ed. The Coming Crisis in British Penology. 224p. 1980. pap. 12.50x (ISBN 0-7073-0265-X, Pub. by Scottish Academic Pr Scotland). Columbia U Pr.

Bottoms, David. In a U-Haul North of Damascus. LC 82-22938. 59p. 1983. 9.70 (ISBN 0-688-02067-4). Morrow.

--In a U-Haul North of Damascus. LC 82-23125. 59p. 1983. pap. 5.70 (ISBN 0-688-01743-6, Quill). Morrow.

--Shooting Rats at the Bibb Co. Dump. LC 79-25724. 64p. 1980. 7.95 (ISBN 0-688-03609-0). Morrow.

--Shooting Rats at the Bibb Co. Dump. 64p. 1980. pap. 3.95 (ISBN 0-688-08609-8, Quill). Morrow.

Bottoms, David, jt. ed. see Smith, Dave.

Bottone, Edward J., ed. Yersinia Enterocolitica. 240p. 1981. 76.00 (ISBN 0-8493-5545-1). CRC Pr.

Bottoni, Lois & Reynolds, Patti, eds. Getting Ready for Math & Reading. (Golden Step Ahead Workbks.). (Illus.). 36p. 1984. 1.95 (ISBN 0-307-23538-6, Golden Bks). Western Pub.

--Letters & Sounds. (Golden Step Ahead Workbks.). (Illus.). 36p. 1984. wkbk. 1.95 (ISBN 0-307-23536-X, 3536, Golden Bks). Western Pub.

--Numbers One-Ten. (Golden Step Ahead Workbks.). (Illus.). 36p. 1984. wkbk. 1.95 (ISBN 0-307-23537-8, 3537, Golden Bks). Western Pub.

Bottorff, Leslie. A Thin Volume of Hate. 1973. pap. 2.95 (ISBN 0-913270-15-6). Sunstone Pr.

Bottorff, William K. James Lane Allen. (Twayne's United States Authors Ser.). 1964. pap. 5.95x (ISBN 0-8084-0171-8, T56, Twayne). New Coll U Pr.

--James Lane Allen. LC 63-20615. (United States Authors Ser.). 1964. lib. bdg. 15.95 (ISBN 0-89197-806-2); pap. text ed. 2.95x (ISBN 0-89197-987-5). Irvington.

Bottorff, William K., ed. see Allen, James L.

Bottrail, Ronald. Poems Nineteen Fifty Five-Nineteen Seventy Three. 1974. 10.00 (ISBN 0-685-78875-X, Pub. by Anvil Pr); sewn in wrappers 6.95 (ISBN 0-685-78876-8). Small Pr Dist.

Bottral, Ronald. Against a Setting Sun: Poems, 1974-1983. 160p. 1984. pap. 8.95 (ISBN 0-8052-8173-8, Pub. by Allison & Busby England). Schocken.

Bottrall, Margaret & Bottrall, Ronald, eds. Collected English Verse. facsimile ed. LC 68-59366. (Granger Index Reprint Ser). 1946. 16.00 (ISBN 0-8369-6050-5). Ayer Co Pubs.

Bottrall, Margaret S. Every Man a Phoenix: Studies in Seventeenth-Century Autobiography. LC 72-3301. (Essay Index Reprint Ser.). Repr. of 1958 ed. 15.00 (ISBN 0-8369-2894-6). Ayer Co Pubs.

Bottrall, Ronald, jt. ed. see Bottrall, Margaret.

Bottrell, Dale G. Guidelines for Integrated Control of Maize Pests. (Plant Production & Protection Papers: No. 18). (Illus.). 98p. (Eng. & Fr.). 1978. pap. 14.50 (ISBN 92-5-100875-2, F1942, FAO). Unipub.

Bottrell, Donna, ed. see Wine Advisory Board.

Bottrell, Donna, et al, eds. see California Winemakers.

Botts, Hank. Encounter Time: Metro-Act & the Sores of Discontent. LC 81-66545. 205p. (Orig.). 1981. pap. 5.00 (ISBN 0-9606020-0-3). Edward Pr.

Botts, Ricky J. A Complete Identification Guide to the Wurlitzer Jukebook. LC 83-82604. (Illus.). 114p. (Orig.). 1984. pap. 12.95 (ISBN 0-912789-01-8). Jukebox Coll New.

--Jukebox Restoration: Restoration Articles-Tips & Techniques Taken from Jukebox Collector Newsletter & Victory Glass Newsletter. LC 83-80797. (Illus.). 88p. (Orig.). 1983. pap. 11.95 (ISBN 0-912789-00-X). Jukebox Coll New.

Botts, Ricky J., ed. see Rudolph Wurlitzer Co. Staff.

Botume, Elizabeth H. First Days Amongst the Contrabands. LC 68-28986. (American Negro: His History & Literature, Ser. 1). 1968. Repr. of 1893 ed. 14.00 (ISBN 0-405-01805-3). Ayer Co Pubs.

Botvinnik & Estrin. The Gruenfeld Defense. LC 75-17385. pap. 12.95 (ISBN 0-89058-017-0). R H M Pr.

Botvinnik, M. M. Achieving the Aim. LC 80-40437. (Pergamon Russian Chess Ser.). (Illus.). 230p. 1981. text ed. 19.00 (ISBN 0-08-024120-4). Pergamon.

--Half a Century of Chess. (Pergamon Russian Chess Ser.). (Illus.). 300p. 1984. 22.50 (ISBN 0-08-026919-2); pap. 14.25 (ISBN 0-08-029739-0). Pergamon.

--Selected Games Nineteen Sixty-Seven to Nineteen Seventy. Neat, K. P., tr. (Pergamon Russian Chess Ser.). (Illus.). 150p. 1981. 29.00 (ISBN 0-08-024124-7); pap. 13.95 (ISBN 0-08-024123-9). Pergamon.

--Solving Inexact Search Problems. Brown, A. A., tr. (Symbolic Computation). (Illus.). 255p. 1984. 25.00 (ISBN 0-387-90869-2). Springer-Verlag.

Botvinnik, Mikhael M. Anatoly Karpov: His Road to the World Championship. Neat, Kenneth P., tr. LC 77-30655. 1978. text ed. 16.25 (ISBN 0-08-021139-9); pap. text ed. 8.95 (ISBN 0-08-021138-0). Pergamon.

Botvinnik, Mikhail M. Fifteen Games & Their Stories. Marfia, Jim, tr. from Russian. (Illus.). 76p. (Orig.). 1982. pap. 4.95 (ISBN 0-931462-15-0). Chess Ent Inc.

--One Hundred Selected Games. (Illus.). pap. 4.50 (ISBN 0-486-20620-3). Dover.

Botwin, Carol. Is There Sex after Marriage? 320p. 1985. 16.95 (ISBN 0-316-10350-0). Little.

Botwinick, Aryeh. Epic Political Theorists & the Conceptualization of the State: An Essay in Political Philosophy. LC 81-43865. 50p. (Orig.). 1982. pap. text ed. 5.75 (ISBN 0-8191-2353-6). U Pr of Amer.

--Ethics, Politics & Epistemology: A Study in the Unity of Hume's Thought. LC 80-5809. 197p. 1980. lib. bdg. 22.50 (ISBN 0-8191-1288-7); pap. text ed. 11.00 (ISBN 0-8191-1289-5). U Pr of Amer.

--Hobbes & Modernity: Five Exercises in Political Philosophical Exegesis. LC 83-6536. 78p. (Orig.). 1983. lib. bdg. 18.75 (ISBN 0-8191-3210-1); pap. text ed. 7.50 (ISBN 0-8191-3211-X). U Pr of Amer.

--Wittgenstein & Historical Understanding. LC 80-5968. 65p. (Orig.). 1981. pap. text ed. 6.25 (ISBN 0-8191-1431-6). U Pr of Amer.

--Wittgenstein, Skepticism & Political Participation: An Essay in the Epistemology of Democratic Theory. 52p. (Orig.). 1985. pap. text ed. 5.25 (ISBN 0-8191-4816-4). U Pr of Amer.

Botwinick, Jack. Aging & Behavior: A Comprehensive Integration of Research Findings. 3rd ed. 448p. 1984. text ed. 24.95 (ISBN 0-8261-1443-1). Springer Pub.

--We Are Aging. 1981. pap. text ed. 11.95 (ISBN 0-8261-3380-0). Springer Pub.

Botwinick, Jack & Storandt, Martha. Memory, Related Functions & Age. (Illus.). 208p. 1974. 22.50x (ISBN 0-398-03143-6). C C Thomas.

Botwinik, Berl. Lead Pencil: Stories & Sketches by Berl Botwinik. Klukoff, Philip J., tr. from Yiddish. LC 83-19848. (Illus.). 164p. 1984. 12.95 (ISBN 0-8143-1745-6). Wayne St U Pr.

Botz, Myrna, jt. auth. see King, Pat.

Botz, Paschal. Runways to God. LC 79-24756. 346p. (Orig.). 1979. pap. 3.50 (ISBN 0-8146-1059-5). Liturgical Pr.

Botz, Paschal, et al. Prayers Before & after Communion. 24p. 1981. pap. 0.50 (ISBN 0-8146-1213-X). Liturgical Pr.

Botzow, Hermann S. Auto Fleet Management. LC 67-30632. pap. 52.80 (ISBN 0-8357-9842-9, 2012354). Bks Demand UMI.

Boua, Chanthou, jt. ed. see Kiernan, Ben.

Bouazis, Charles, jt. ed. see Escarpit, Robert.

Boubat, Edward. Woman. LC 72-86679. (Illus.). 143p. 1973. 15.00 (ISBN 0-8076-0664-2). Braziller.

Boublik, et al. Statistical Thermodynamics of Simple Liquids & Their Mixtures. (Studies in Physical & Chemistry: Vol. 2). 146p. 1980. 40.50 (ISBN 0-444-99784-9). Elsevier.

Boublik, T., et al. Vapor Pressures of Pure Substances. 2nd, rev. ed. (Physical Sciences Data Ser.: Vol. 17). 1984. 173.00 (ISBN 0-444-42266-8, I-478-83). Elsevier.

Bouce, Paul-Gabriel, ed. Sexuality in Eighteenth-Century Britain. LC 82-8785. (Illus.). 274p. 1982. text ed. 28.50x (ISBN 0-389-20313-0, 07151). B&N Imports.

Bouce, Paul-Gabriel, ed. see Smollet, Tobias.

Bouce, Paul-Gabriel, ed. see Smollett, Tobias.

Bouch, Charles M. & Jones, G. P. Short Economic & Social History of the Lake Counties, 1500-1830. LC 67-8870. (Illus.). 1962. 35.00x (ISBN 0-678-06786-4). Kelley.

Bouchard, Claude, jt. auth. see Malina, Robert M.

Bouchard, Constance B. Spirituality & Administration: The Role of the Bishop in Twelfth-Century Auxerre. LC 78-55889. 1979. 11.00x (ISBN 0-910956-79-0, SAM5); pap. 5.00x (ISBN 0-910956-67-7). Medieval Acad.

Bouchard, Donald F., ed. see Foucault, Michel.

Bouchard, Donald F., ed. & tr. see Foucault, Michel.

Bouchard, Eric. Radiology Management: An Introduction. LC 82-22355. (Illus.). 310p. (Orig.). 1983. pap. 18.95X (ISBN 0-940122-04-9). Multi Media CO.

Bouchard, Harry, jt. auth. see Moffitt, Francis H.

Bouchard, Jean J. Radiation Therapy of Tumors & Diseases of the Nervous System. LC 66-23233. (Illus.). pap. 46.40 (ISBN 0-317-07855-0, 2014527). Bks Demand UMI.

Bouchard, Leon. Systeme financier de l'ancienne monarchie. 1971. Repr. of 1891 ed. lib. bdg. 29.00 (ISBN 0-8337-0341-2). B Franklin.

Bouchard, M. Angeline, tr. see Simonet, Andre.

Bouchard, R., et al. Childhood Epilepsy: A Pediatric-Psychiatric Approach. LC 76-46814. 136p. 1977. 17.50 (ISBN 0-8236-0774-7). Intl Univs Pr.

Bouchard, Rene, ed. Culture Populaire et Litteratures au Quebec. (Stanford French & Italian Studies: Vol. 19). vi, 310p. (Fr.). 1980. pap. 25.00 (ISBN 0-915838-20-6). Anma Libri.

Bouchard, Robert. Let's Play the Recorder. 5.00 (ISBN 0-8283-1471-3). Branden Pub Co.

Bouchard, Robert F., jt. ed. see Franklin, Justin D.

Bouchard, Ronald. Personnel Practices for Small Colleges. Welzenbach, Lanora F., ed. LC 80-11868. 179p. 1980. pap. text ed. 20.00 (ISBN 0-915164-08-6). Natl Assn Coll.

Bouchard, Rosemary & Owens, Norma F. Nursing Care of the Cancer Patient. 4th ed. LC 80-21708. (Illus.). 503p. 1981. pap. text ed. 24.95 (ISBN 0-8016-0720-5). Mosby.

Bouchard, S., jt. auth. see Fruehling, R. T.

Bouchard, Sharon, jt. auth. see Fruehling, Rosemary T.

Bouche, Claude. Lautreamont: Du lieu commun a la parodie. new ed. (Collection themes et textes). 253p. (Orig.). 1974. pap. 6.75 (ISBN 2-03-035024-9, 2615). Larousse.

Bouche, F. American Footprints in Paris. 59.95 (ISBN 0-87968-600-6). Gordon Pr.

Bouche, Henri, jt. auth. see Dollfus, Charles.

Bouche, Therese M. la see La Bouche, Therese M.

Bouche-Leclercq, Auguste. Histoire De la Divination Dans L'antiquite, 4 vols. in two. LC 75-7305. (Roman History Ser.). (Fr.). 1975. Repr. Set. 122.00x (ISBN 0-405-07182-5); 60.50x ea. Vols. 1-2 (ISBN 0-405-07183-3). Vols. 3-4 (ISBN 0-405-07184-1). Ayer Co Pubs.

--Les Pontifes de L'Ancienne Rome: Etudes Historique sur les Institutions Religieuses de Rome. facsimile ed. LC 75-10630. (Ancient Religion & Mythology Ser.). (Fr.). 1976. Repr. of 1871 ed. 33.00x (ISBN 0-405-07006-3). Ayer Co Pubs.

Bouchelle, Joan H. With Tennyson at the Keyboard: A Victorian Songbook. (Reference Library of the Humanities). 256p. 1985. lib. bdg. 40.00 (ISBN 0-8240-8872-7). Garland Pub.

Boucher, Alan, et al, trs. see Friis, Erik J.

Boucher, Anthony. The Case of the Baker Street Irregulars. 1980. lib. bdg. 12.50 (ISBN 0-8398-2655-9, Gregg). G K Hall.

--Unearthly Neighbors. LC 84-1875. 1984. 8.95 (ISBN 0-517-55294-9). Crown.

Boucher, Anthony, ed. Four & Twenty Bloodhounds. 260p. 1985. pap. 3.95 (ISBN 0-88184-081-5). Carroll & Graf.

Boucher, Barbara, jt. auth. see Winter, Jacki.

Boucher, Brian, et al. Handbook & Catalog for Instructional Media Selection. LC 72-11983. 214p. 1973. pap. 26.95 (ISBN 0-87778-045-5). Educ Tech Pubns.

Boucher, Carl O., et al. Prosthodontic Treatment for Edentulous Patients. 7th ed. LC 75-13048. 1975. text ed. 29.50 (ISBN 0-8016-0724-8). Mosby.

Boucher, Doug A., ed. The Biology of Mutualism: Ecology & Evolution. 400p. 1985. 49.95 (ISBN 0-19-520483-2). Oxford U Pr.

Boucher, E. A., jt. auth. see Murrell, J. N.

Boucher, I. A., ed. see Advanced Medicine Symposia, 7th, 1971.

Boucher, J., jt. auth. see Mendoz, G.

Boucher, John & Paris, Robert L. Debuts. (Orig.). (gr. 10-12). 1975. text ed. 20.00 (ISBN 0-205-04148-5, 3641481); tchrs'. guide 7.48 (ISBN 0-205-04149-3, 364149X); wkbk. 7.44 (ISBN 0-205-04150-7, 3641503); cassettes o. p. 476.00 (ISBN 0-205-04151-5, 3641511); tests-dup masters o. p. 64.00 (ISBN 0-205-05402-1, 3654028). Allyn.

Boucher, John G. & Hurtgen, Andre O. Encore. (Allyn & Bacon French Program Ser.). (gr. 9-12). 1976. text ed. 24.00 (ISBN 0-205-04903-6, 3649032); tchrs'. guide 8.00 (ISBN 0-205-04904-4, 3649040). Allyn.

--Reprise. (Orig.). (gr. 10-12). 1975. text ed. 20.32 (ISBN 0-205-04171-X, 3641716); tchrs'. guide 7.48 (ISBN 0-205-04172-8, 3641724); wkbk. 7.44 (ISBN 0-205-04173-6, 3641732); cassettes 407.20 (ISBN 0-205-04174-4, 3641740); dup. masters 60.36 (ISBN 0-205-05404-8, 3654044). Allyn.

Boucher, Louis J. & Renner, Robert P. Treatment of Partially Edentulous Patients. LC 81-19016. (Illus.). 352p. 1982. pap. text ed. 38.95 (ISBN 0-8016-0821-X). Mosby.

Boucher, Madeleine. The Mysterious Parable: A Literary Study. LC 76-51264. (Catholic Biblical Quarterly Monographs: No. 6). ix, 101p. 1977. pap. 2.50 (ISBN 0-915170-05-1). Catholic Biblical.

Boucher, Madeleine I. The Parables. (New Testament Message Ser.: Vol. 7). 10.95 (ISBN 0-89453-195-6); pap. 6.95 (ISBN 0-89453-130-1). M Glazier.

Boucher, Michel. Transformations. (Illus.). 56p. (gr. 1 up). 1985. pap. cancelled (ISBN 0-88138-046-6, Star & Elephant Bks.). Green Tiger Pr.

Boucher, Philip P. The Shaping of the French Colonial Empire: A Bio-Bibliography of the Careers of Richelieu, Fouquet, & Colbert. Casada, James, ed. LC 83-49295. (Themes in European Expansion Ser.). 250p. 1985. lib. bdg. 35.00 (ISBN 0-8240-8973-1). Garland Pub.

Boucher, R. The Kingdom of Fife, Its Ballads & Legends. (Folklore Ser). 15.00 (ISBN 0-8482-7391-5). Norwood Edns.

Boucher, Robin C. Decreasing Classroom Conflict. (Illus.). 80p. (Orig.). 1985. pap. text ed. 8.00 (ISBN 0-87562-082-5). Spec Child.

Boucher, Sandy. Heartwomen: An Urban Feminist's Odyssey Home. (Illus.). 276p. 1982. 12.45i (ISBN 0-06-250095-3, HarpT). Har-Row.

--Heartwomen: An Urban Feminist's Odyssey Home. LC 81-48204. 224p. 1983. pap. 7.64 (ISBN 0-06-250096-1, CN 4072, HarpR). Har-Row.

--The Notebooks of Leni Clare & Other Short Stories. LC 82-2542. 150p. (Orig.). 1982. 17.95 (ISBN 0-89594-077-9); pap. 7.95 (ISBN 0-89594-076-0). Crossing Pr.

Boucher, Sharon, jt. auth. see Burchard, Florence.

Boucher, T. O., jt. auth. see Elsayed, E. A.

Boucher, Theresa, jt. ed. see McCuen, Gary E.

Boucher, Therese. Becoming a Sensuous Catechist: Using the Arts in Religion Classes. (Illus.). 80p. 1984. pap. 5.95 (ISBN 0-89622-216-0). Twenty-Third.

Boucher, Virginia. Interlibrary Loan Practices Handbook. LC 83-21359. 207p. 1984. pap. text ed. 20.00x (ISBN 0-8389-3298-3). ALA.

Boucher De Crevecoeur De Perthes, Jacques. Antiquites celtiques et antediluviennes, 3 vols. LC 77-86420. Repr. of 1864 ed. 135.00 set (ISBN 0-404-16620-2). AMS Pr.

Bouchet, Jean. Epistres Morales Et Familieres Du Traverseur. (French Renaissance Classics Ser). Repr. of 1545 ed. 35.00 (ISBN 0-384-05295-9). Johnson Repr.

--Epistres Morales et Familieres Du Traverseur (Poitiers, 1545) (Classiques De la Renaissance En France: No. 4). 1970. 24.40x (ISBN 90-2796-345-2). Mouton.

Bouchet, Philippe, et al. Seashells of Western Europe. Picton, B. E., tr. from Fr. (Illus.). 1979. 5.95 (ISBN 0-915826-05-4). Am Malacologists.

Bouchette, Joseph. British Dominions in North America, 2 Vols. LC 68-56073. Repr. of 1831 ed. Set. 155.00 (ISBN 0-404-00936-0). Vol. 1 (ISBN 0-404-00937-9). Vol. 2 (ISBN 0-404-00938-7). AMS Pr.

Bouchey, L. Francis, ed. Perils of Disorder. 288p. 1984. 18.95 (ISBN 0-89526-612-1). Regnery-Gateway.

Bouchey, Stuart, ed. see Rae, John B.

Bouchey, Stuart, ed. see U. S. House of Representatives.

Bouchez, L. J., et al, eds. Netherlands Yearbook of International Law: State Immunity from Attachment & Execution, Vol. X. 650p. 1980. 40.00x (ISBN 90-286-0710-2). Sijthoff & Noordhoff.

Bouchier, David. The Feminist Challenge: The Movement for Women's Liberation in Britain & the USA. LC 83-14296. 268p. 1984. 18.95 (ISBN 0-8052-3881-6). Schocken.

--Idealism & Revolution: New Ideologies of Liberation in Britain & the United States. LC 78-17007. 1979. 27.50 (ISBN 0-312-40439-5). St Martin.

Bouchier, E. S., ed. see Arnold, William T.

Bouchier, Ian A. Gastroenterology. 3rd ed. (Illus.). 388p. 1982. pap. 24.95 (ISBN 0-7216-0706-3, Pub. by Bailliere-Tindall). Saunders.

Bouchier, Ian A., jt. auth. see Bateson, Malcolm C.

Bouchier, Ian A., ed. Recent Advances in Gastroenterology, No. 5. (Illus.). 293p. 1980. text ed. 39.00 (ISBN 0-443-02461-8). Churchill.

Bouchier, Ian A. & Morris, J. S., eds. Clinical Skills. 2nd ed. (Illus.). 735p. 1982. pap. 24.75 (ISBN 0-7216-1893-6). Saunders.

Bouchier, Ian A., et al. Textbook of Gastroenterology. (Illus.). 1600p. Date not set. price not set (Pub. by Bailliere-Tindall). Saunders.

Bouchier, Pierre J., jt. auth. see Reilly, Robert T.

Bouchner, Miroslav. Birds of Prey of Britain & Europe. (Concise Guide in Colour Ser.). (Illus.). 1978. 7.95 (ISBN 0-686-89165-1). Transatlantic.

Boucicault, Dion. Octoroon: Or, Life in Louisiana: A Play in Five Acts. facs. ed. LC 77-93418. (Black Heritage Library Collection Ser). 1861. 8.75 (ISBN 0-8369-8521-4). Ayer Co Pubs.

--Plays by Dion Boucicault. Thomson, Peter, ed. LC 83-7856. (British & American Playwrights Ser., 1750 to 1920). (Illus.). 230p. 1984. 44.50 (ISBN 0-521-23997-4); pap. 15.95 (ISBN 0-521-28395-7). Cambridge U Pr.

Boucot, A. J. Evolution & Extinction Rate Controls. (Developments in Palaeontology & Stratigraphy Ser.: Vol. 1). 428p. 1975. 98.00 (ISBN 0-444-41182-8). Elsevier.

Boucot, Arthur. Principles of Benthic Marine Paleo-Ecology. LC 79-8535. 1981. 66.50 (ISBN 0-12-118980-5). Acad Pr.

Boucot, Arthur J., ed. see Biology Colloquium, 37th, Oregon State University, 1976.

Boucourechliev, Andre. Schumann. Boyars, Arthur, tr. LC 75-28923. (Illus.). 192p. 1976. Repr. of 1959 ed. lib. bdg. 26.50x (ISBN 0-8371-8475-4, BOSC). Greenwood.

Boucourschlierev, Andre. Schumann. (Illustrated Composer Ser.). (Illus.). 1986. 5.95 (ISBN 0-7145-3592-3). Riverrun NY.

Boud, David. Reflection: Turning Experience into Learning. 200p. 1985. 25.00 (ISBN 0-89397-202-9). Nichols Pub.

Boud, David, ed. Developing Student Autonomy in Learning. 200p. 1981. 32.50x (ISBN 0-89397-102-2). Nichols Pub.

Boudard, J. B. Iconologie. LC 75-27888. (Renaissance & the Gods Ser.: Vol. 43). (Illus.). 1976. Repr. of 1766 ed. lib. bdg. 80.00 (ISBN 0-8240-2092-8). Garland Pub.

Boudarel, R., et al. Dynamic Programming & Its Applications to Optimal Control. (Mathematics in Science & Engineering Ser.: Vol. 81). 1971. 70.00 (ISBN 0-12-118950-3). Acad Pr.

Boudart, M. see Anderson, J. R.

Boudart, M., jt. ed. see Anderson, J. R.

Boudart, Michel & Djega-Mariadassou, G. Kinetics of Heterogeneous Catalytic Reactions. LC 83-43062. (Physical Chemistry: Science & Engineering). (Illus.). 243p. 1984. 35.00x (ISBN 0-691-08346-0); pap. 13.50 (ISBN 0-691-08347-9). Princeton U Pr.

Boudart, Michel, tr. see Semenov, Nikolai N.

Boudeaux, Michael. Risen Indeed: Lessons of Faith from the U. S. S. R. (Orig.). 1983. pap. text ed. 4.95 (ISBN 0-88141-021-7). St Vladimirs.

Boudet De Puymaigre, T. J. Romanceiro: choix de vieux chants portugais. LC 78-20109. (Collection de contes et de chansons populaires: No. 2). Repr. of 1881 ed. 21.50 (ISBN 0-404-60352-1). AMS Pr.

Boudeville, J. R. Le Complexe Agricole. Bd. with La Resolution Mathematique des Problemes d'Economie Regionale en U. R. S. S. Analyse, Planification, Optimisation. Nowicki, A; Le Commerce du 5e Quartier a Lyon. Grawitz, M; Structure Economique et Niveau de Revenu des Departements Francais. Maurel, E. (Economies et Societes Series L: No. 12). 1963. pap. 11.00 (ISBN 0-317-16179-2). Kraus Repr.

--Contribution a L'Etude des Poles de Croissance Bresiliens: Une Industrie Motriee - La Siderurgie du Minas Gerais. (Economies et Societes Series F: No. 10). 1957. pap. 11.00 (ISBN 0-317-16835-5). Kraus Repr.

--L' Economie Regionale, Espace Operationnel. (Economies et Societes Series L: No. 3). 1958. pap. 11.00 (ISBN 0-317-16149-0). Kraus Repr.

Boudewyns, Patrick A. & Shipley, Robert H., eds. Flooding & Implosive Therapy: Direct Therapeutic Exposure in Clinical Practice. 230p. 1983. 24.50x (ISBN 0-306-41155-5, Plenum Pr). Plenum Pub.

Boudhiba, Abdelwahab. La Sociologie Du Developpement Africain: Tendances Actuelles De la Recherche et Bibliographie. (Current Sociology: No. 18/2). 1972. pap. 7.20x (ISBN 90-2796-948-5). Mouton.

Boudier, J. F. & Luquet, F. M. Dictionnaire Laitier: French-English-French. 220p. (Fr. & Eng.). 1981. leatherette 69.95 (ISBN 2-85206-092-2, M-9627). French & Eur.

Boudin, H. L., et al, eds. see De Crevecoeur, St. John.

Boudin, Jean. Some of the Parts. LC 83-60718. 84p. 1983. pap. 8.95 (ISBN 0-915192-08-X). Pomegranate.

Boudin, Louis B. Socialism & War. LC 73-147507. (Library of War & Peace; Labor, Socialism & War). 1972. lib. bdg. 46.00 (ISBN 0-8240-0302-0). Garland Pub.

Boudinot, Elias. Journal of Historical Recollections of American Events During the Revolutionary War. LC 67-29029. (Eyewitness Accounts of the American Revolution Ser., No. 1). 1968. Repr. of 1894 ed. 11.00 (ISBN 0-405-01106-7). Ayer Co Pubs.

--The Life & Public Services, Addresses & Letters of Elias Boudinot, President of the Continental Congress, 2 Vols. Boudinot, Jane J., ed. LC 72-119059. (Era of the American Revolution Ser). 1971. Repr. of 1896 ed. Set. lib. bdg. 95.00 (ISBN 0-306-71946-0). Da Capo.

--Star in the West: A Humble Attempt to Discover the Long Lost Ten Tribes of Israel. facs. ed. LC 79-121499. (Select Bibliographies Reprint Ser). 1816. 17.00 (ISBN 0-8369-5457-2). Ayer Co Pubs.

Boudinot, Jane J., ed. see Boudinot, Elias.

Boudon, Philippe. Lived-In Architecture: Le Corbusier's Pessac Revisited. Onn, Gerald, tr. (Illus.). 1972. pap. 6.95x (ISBN 0-262-52053-2). MIT Pr.

Boudon, Raymond. The Logic of Social Action: An Introduction to Sociological Analysis. Silverman, David, tr. from Fr. 208p. 1981. 21.95X (ISBN 0-7100-0857-0); pap. 9.95x (ISBN 0-7100-0858-9). Routledge & Kegan.

--The Unintended Consequences of Social Action. LC 81-21372. 240p. 1982. 27.50x (ISBN 0-312-83303-2). St Martin.

Boudon, Raymond & Lazarsfeld, Paul, eds. L' Analyse Empirique De la Causalite. 3rd ed. (Methodes De la Sociologie: No. 2). 1976. pap. 14.00x (ISBN 90-2796-158-1). Mouton.

Boudoris, James. Prisons & Kids: Programs for Inmate Parents. (Illus.). 60p. (Orig.). 1985. pap. 17.95 (ISBN 0-942974-70-0). Am Correctional.

Boudout, ed. see Hugo, Victor.

Boudreau, Albert. The Born-Again Catholic. (Illus., Orig.). 1979. pap. 4.95 (ISBN 0-914544-26-8). Living Flame Pr.

Boudreau, Amy. Mighty Mississippi. 1967. pap. 3.00 (ISBN 0-685-08193-1). Claitors.

--Story of the Acadians. (Illus.). 38p. 1971. pap. 2.50 (ISBN 0-911116-30-3). Pelican.

--Story of the Christian Year. 1971. 4.50 (ISBN 0-685-27196-X). Claitors.

Boudreau, Eugene. Making the Adobe Brick. (Illus.). 1972. pap. 6.95 (ISBN 0-394-70617-X, Dist. by Random). Bookworks.

--Trails of the Sierra Madre. 80p. 1973. pap. 4.95 (ISBN 0-912264-68-3). Capra Pr.

Boudreau, Eugene H. Move Over, Don Porfiro: Tales from the Sierra Madre. LC 75-35308. (Illus.). 96p. 1975. pap. 3.00 (ISBN 0-686-10963-5). Pleasant Hill.

--Ways of the Sierra Madre: Crafts of the Sierra Madre. LC 74-22999. (Illus.). 96p. 1974. 6.00 (ISBN 0-686-10332-7). Pleasant Hill.

Boudreau, Eugene H., ed. see Grisby, Robert F.

Boudreau, H. L. & Gonzalez-del-Valle, Luis T., eds. Studies in Honor of Sumner M. Greenfield. 220p. 1985. pap. 25.00 (ISBN 0-89295-030-7). Society Sp & Sp-Am.

Boudreau, J. The Happiness of Heaven. LC 83-51548. 258p. 1984. pap. 6.00 (ISBN 0-89555-232-9). TAN Bks Pubs.

Boudreau, James C., ed. Food Taste Chemistry. LC 79-26461. (ACS Symposium Ser.: No. 115). 1979. 29.95 (ISBN 0-8412-0526-4); pap. 19.95 (ISBN 0-8412-0645-7). Am Chemical.

Boudreau, Martina, ed. Apple Magic. LC 84-50105. 56p. (Orig.). 1984. pap. 2.95 (ISBN 0-942320-09-3). WRC Pub.

Boudreau, Martina, ed. see Kaufman, Sheilah.

Boudreaux, Edward A. Elementary Aspects of Chemical Periodicity. 1976. coil bdg. 2.95 (ISBN 0-88252-061-X). Paladin Hse.

Boudreaux, Florentin. God Our Father. LC 65-36485. pap. 55.00 (ISBN 0-317-10042-4, 2001664). Bks Demand UMI.

Boudreaux, H. Bruce. Anthropod Phylogeny. LC 84-3960. 328p. 1985. Repr. of 1979 ed. lib. bdg. write for info. (ISBN 0-89874-746-5). Krieger.

Boudreaux, Patricia D., jt. auth. see Johnson, Barry L.

Boudrot, Thomas E. Byte-Sized Activities: The Generic Word Processing Book. 1985. pap. 5.95 (ISBN 0-673-18175-8). Scott F.

Boudwin, et al. Childyank Over the Rainbow: 1918. 2nd ed. (Illus.). 1977. pap. 5.95 (ISBN 0-912522-62-3). Aero-Medical.

Boufjaily, Vance. The End of My Life. 1984. pap. 6.95 (ISBN 0-87795-603-0). Arbor Hse.

Bougainville, Louis A. A Voyage Around the World... in the Years Seventeen Sixty-Six to Seventeen Sixty-Nine. 1968. Repr. of 1772 ed. 26.50 (ISBN 0-8398-0169-6). Parnassus Imprints.

Bougeau, Art. Murder at the Cheatin' Heart Motel. 192p. 1985. pap. 2.95 (ISBN 0-317-31723-7) (ISBN 0-317-31724-5). Ace Bks.

Bougerol, Christian. Larousse des oiseaux de cage et de voliere. (Larousse des animaux familiers). (Illus.). 120p. 1975. 26.00x (ISBN 2-03-014853-9). Larousse.

Bougerol, Guy J. Introduction to the Works of St. Bonaventure. 1964. 7.50 (ISBN 0-8199-0525-9). Franciscan Herald.

Bough, Max E. & Hamm, Russell L., eds. The American Intermediate School: A Book of Readings. LC 73-88718. 210p. 1974. pap. 4.95x (ISBN 0-8134-1620-5, 1620). Interstate.

Bough, Max E., jt. ed. see Hamm, Russell L.

Boughey. The Insights of Sociology: An Introduction. 1985. 17.14 (ISBN 0-205-06011-0, 816011). Allyn.

Boughey, Arthur S. Ecology of Populations. 2nd ed. (Illus.). 192p. 1973. pap. text ed. write for info. (ISBN 0-02-312730-9, 31273). Macmillan.

--Man & the Environment. 2nd ed. (Illus.). 480p. 1975. pap. text ed. write for info. (ISBN 0-02-312770-8, 31277). Macmillan.

Boughner, Daniel C. Braggert in Renaissance Comedy: A Study in Comparative Drama from Aristophanes to Shakespeare. LC 75-100223. Repr. of 1954 ed. lib. bdg. 24.75x (ISBN 0-8371-3006-9, BOBR). Greenwood.

--Devil's Disciple. LC 67-24571. 1968. 5.95 (ISBN 0-8022-0159-8). Philos Lib.

--The Devil's Disciple: Ben Jonson's Debt to Machiavelli. LC 73-16606. 264p. 1975. Repr. of 1968 ed. lib. bdg. 19.75x (ISBN 0-8371-7183-0, BODD). Greenwood.

Boughton, Brian. Building & Civil Engineering Construction, Vol. 1. 192p. 1983. pap. 10.00x (ISBN 0-246-11966-7, Pub. by Granada England). Sheridan.

--Building & Civil Engineering Construction, Vol. 2. 173p. 1983. pap. 10.00x (ISBN 0-246-11967-5, Pub. by Granada England). Sheridan.

--Reinforced Concrete Detailer's Manual. 2nd ed. (Illus.). 136p. 1971. text ed. 14.95x (ISBN 0-8464-0788-4). Beekman Pubs.

--Reinforced Concrete Detailer's Manual. 1979. pap. text ed. 14.75x (ISBN 0-258-97128-2, Pub. by Granada England). Brookfield Pub Co.

--Reinforced Concrete Detailer's Manual. 3rd ed. 136p. 1979. pap. 14.00x (ISBN 0-246-11336-7, Pub. by Granada England). Sheridan.

Boughton, Brian & Ballard, Peter. Construction Mathematics, Vol. 1. (Illus.). 160p. 1984. pap. 10.00x (ISBN 0-246-12125-4, Pub. by Granada England). Sheridan.

--Construction Mathematics, Vol. 2. (Illus.). 160p. 1985. pap. 10.00x (ISBN 0-00-383035-7, Pub. by Collins England). Sheridan.

Boughton, Brian & Goodfellow, Denis. Construction Science, Vol. 1. 160p. 1984. pap. 10.00x (ISBN 0-246-12127-0, Pub. by Granada England). Sheridan.

--Construction Science, Vol. 2. 160p. 1984. pap. 10.00x (ISBN 0-246-12128-9, Pub. by Granada England). Sheridan.

Boughton, Brian W. Building & Civil Engineering Construction, Vol. 2. 168p. 1983. pap. text ed. 12.50x (Pub. by Granada England). Brookfield Pub Co.

Boughton, Donald C. Reality Embraced. 132p. 1983. 14.95 (ISBN 0-87975-225-4). Prometheus Bks.

Boughton, James M. Monetary Policy & the Federal Funds Market. LC 74-172018. 230p. 1972. 16.25 (ISBN 0-8223-0287-X). Duke.

Boughton, Pat, jt. auth. see Meagher, Jack.

Boughton, Patricia & Hughes, Martha E. The Buyer's Guide to Cosmetics. 1981. pap. 6.95 (ISBN 0-394-74859-X). Random.

Boughton, Rutland. The Reality of Music. LC 72-80495. Repr. of 1934 ed. 15.50 (ISBN 0-405-08294-0, Blom Pubns). Ayer Co Pubs.

Boughton, Viv. Black Gospel: An Illustrated History of the Gospel Sound. (Illus.). 160p. 1985. 16.95 (ISBN 0-7137-1530-8, Pub. by Blandford Pr England); pap. 8.95 (ISBN 0-7137-1540-5, Pub. by Blandford Pr England). Sterling.

Bougie, Stanley J. & Newkirk, David A. Red Wing Dinnerware & Price Guide. 88p. 1985. pap. 11.95 (ISBN 0-317-29291-9, 99081). Wallace-Homestead.

Bougis, P., ed. Marine Plankton Ecology. 1976. 106.50 (ISBN 0-444-11033-X, North-Holland). Elsevier.

Bougle, Alfred, jt. auth. see Chalres, Celestin.

Bougle, Celestin. Bilan De la Sociologie Francaise Contemporaine: Balance Sheet of Contemporary French Sociology. LC 74-25741. (European Sociology Ser.). 184p. 1975. Repr. 14.00x (ISBN 0-405-06497-7). Ayer Co Pubs.

Bougle, Celestin C. Essays on the Caste System. LC 79-154506. (European Understanding of India Ser.). pap. 61.00 (ISBN 0-317-27545-3, 2024508). Bks Demand UMI.

--Evolution of Values. LC 78-97976. Repr. of 1926 ed. 29.50x (ISBN 0-678-00542-7). Kelley.

--La Sociologie De Proudhon. Mayer, J. P., ed. LC 78-67336. (European Political Thought Ser.). (Fr.). 1979. Repr. of 1911 ed. lib. bdg. 25.50x (ISBN 0-405-11681-0). Ayer Co Pubs.

Bouguer, Pierre. Pierre Bouguer's Optical Treatise on the Gradation of Light. Middleton, W. E., tr. LC 61-19105. pap. 66.00 (ISBN 0-317-08928-5, 2014140). Bks Demand UMI.

Bouhabib, Abdallah R. The Long-Run of New Reserves of Crude Oil in the U. S., 1966-1973. Bruchey, Stuart, ed. LC 78-22665. (Energy in the American Economy Ser.). (Illus.). 1979. lib. bdg. 17.00x (ISBN 0-405-11968-2). Ayer Co Pubs.

Bouhdiba, Abdelwahab. Exploitation of Child Labour. 44p. 1983. pap. text ed. 6.00 (ISBN 0-686-46321-8, UN82/14/2, UN). Unipub.

--Exploitation of Child Labour: Final Report. iv, 44p. 1982. 6.00 (ISBN 0-686-89224-0). UN.

--Sexuality in Islam. 288p. 1985. 42.50x (ISBN 0-7100-9608-9). Routledge & Kegan.

Bouhours, Dominique. Art of Criticism. LC 81-8900. 1981. Repr. of 1705 ed. 50.00x (ISBN 0-8201-1364-6). Schol Facsimiles.

Bouhuys, Arend. Breathing: Physiology, Environment & Lung Disease. LC 74-1283. (Illus.). 510p. 1974. 68.50 (ISBN 0-8089-0758-1, 790648). Grune.

Bouhuys, Arend, ed. Airway Dynamics: Physiology & Pharmacology. (Illus.). 360p. 1970. photocopy ed. 54.50x (ISBN 0-398-00200-2). C C Thomas.

--The Physiology of Breathing: A Textbook for Medical Students. LC 76-46724. (Illus.). 368p. 1977. 30.00 (ISBN 0-8089-0984-3, 790647). Grune.

Bouillane De Lacoste, Henry D. Rimbaud et le probleme des Illuminations. LC 77-10253. Repr. of 1949 ed. 23.50 (ISBN 0-404-16308-4). AMS Pr.

Bouillon, Antoine, jt. auth. see Archer, Robert.

Bouillon, Jean-Paul. Art Nouveau Eighteen Seventy to Nineteen Fourteen. (Illus.). 248p. 1985. 60.00 (ISBN 0-8478-0627-8). Rizzoli Intl.

Bouillon, Jo, jt. auth. see Baker, Josephine.

Bouillon, Joan. Principles of College Chemistry. 160p. 1984. study guide 8.95x (ISBN 0-8087-4920-X). Burgess.

Bouis, Antonia W., tr. see Chernyonok, Mikhail.

Bouis, Antonia W., tr. see Volkov, Solomon.

Bouis, Antonina, tr. see Kopelev, L.

Bouis, Antonina, tr. see Yevtushenko, Yevgeny.

Bouis, Antonina W., tr. see Petrovsky, Boris.

Bouis, Antonina W., tr. see Sarianidi, Viktor.

Bouis, Antonina W., tr. see Shostakovich, Dmitri.

Bouis, Antonina W., tr. see Troyepolsky, Gavriil.

Bouis, Antonina W., tr. see Volkov, Solomon.

Bouis, Nina, tr. see Kraselshchik, S.

Bouissac, Paul. Circus & Culture: A Semiotic Approach. Deely, John & Williams, Brooke, eds. LC 85-9040. (Sources in Semiotics Ser.: Vol. III). (Illus.). 220p. (Orig.). 1985. pap. text ed. 12.75 (ISBN 0-8191-4713-3, Sources Semiotics). U Pr of Amer.

--La Mesure Des Gestes: Prolegomenes a la Semiotique Gestuelle. (Approaches to Semiotics, Paperback Ser.: No. 3). 1973. pap. 28.80x (ISBN 90-279-2377-9). Mouton.

Bouisson, Maurice. Magic: Its History & Principal Rites. Almayrac, G., tr. from Fr. LC 79-8094. (Satanism Ser.). (Illus.). 320p. 1985. Repr. of 1961 ed. 36.00 (ISBN 0-404-18405-7). AMS Pr.

Boukema, H. J. Good Law: Toward a Rational Lawmaking Process, Vol. 2. (Salzburger Schriften zur Rechts-, Staats - und Sozial Philosophie). 156p. 1982. 20.00 (ISBN 3-8204-7020-4). P Lang Pubs.

--Judging: Towards a Rational Judicial Process. 183p. 1982. pap. 27.00 cancelled (ISBN 90-2711-727-6, Pub. by Kluwer Law Netherlands). Kluwer Academic.

Boukli, Noureddine. Mostaganem Institute of Agricultural Technology: An Educational Innovation. (Experiments & Innovations in Education Ser.: No. 19). 46p. 1975. pap. 5.00 (ISBN 92-3-101309-2, U391, UNESCO). Unipub.

Boukydis, C. F., jt. ed. see Lester, Barry M.

Boulaich, Abdeslam, et al. Five Eyes. Bowles, Paul, ed. 125p. 1979. 14.00 (ISBN 0-87685-409-9); pap. 5.00 o. p. (ISBN 0-87685-408-0). Black Sparrow.

Boulanger, Nadia. Songs. (Women Composers Ser.: No. 16). 85p. 1985. Repr. of 1922 ed. lib. bdg. 25.00 (ISBN 0-306-76233-1). Da Capo.

Boulay, F. R. see Du Boulay, F. R.

Boulay, Harvey. The Twilight Cities: Political Conflict, Development, & Decay in Five Communities. LC 81-18609. 173p. 1983. 17.00x (ISBN 0-8046-9311-0, Natl U). Assoc Faculty Pr.

Boulay, J., jt. auth. see Desrosiers, G.

Boulay, Laure, jt. auth. see Jaudel, Francoise.

Boulay, Shirley du see Du Boulay, Shirley.

Boulaye, G. & Lewin, Douglas, eds. Computer Architecture. (NATO Advanced Study Institute Ser. C, Math & Physical Sciences: No. 32). (Illus.). 1977. lib. bdg. 37.00 (ISBN 90-277-0803-7, Pub. by Reidel Holland). Kluwer Academic.

Boulby, Mark. Hermann Hesse: His Mind & Art. 352p. 1967. 32.50x (ISBN 0-8014-0046-5). Cornell U Pr.

--Uwe Johnson. LC 73-82315. (Literature and Life Ser.). 1974. 12.95 (ISBN 0-8044-2062-9). Ungar.

Bould, C., et al, eds. Plant Analysis & Fertilizer Problems, Vol. 4. 1964. 7.50 (ISBN 0-934454-68-X). Lubrecht & Cramer.

Boulden, James. I Am All. (Illus.). 72p. 1982. pap. 2.95 (ISBN 0-87516-481-1). De Vorss.

--We Are One. LC 79-54181. (Illus.). 180p. 1980. pap. 5.95 (ISBN 0-87516-382-3). De Vorss.

Boulder Conference on High Energy Physics. Proceedings. Mahanthappa, K. T., et al, eds. LC 71-115692. (Illus.). 1970. 19.50x (ISBN 0-87081-002-2). Colo Assoc.

Bouldin, D. R., jt. ed. see Barber, S. A.

Bouldin, Dolores J. A Touch of Thots Seasoned with Scriptures. 5.75 (ISBN 0-8062-2494-0). Carlton.

Boulding, Elise. Born Remembering. LC 74-30805. 32p. (Orig.). 1975. pap. 5.00x (ISBN 0-87574-200-9, 200). Pendle Hill.

--Children & Solitude. 1983. pap. 2.30x (ISBN 0-87574-125-8, 125). Pendle Hill.

--Children's Rights & the Wheel of Life. LC 78-62890. 179p. 1979. 10.95 (ISBN 0-87855-295-2). Transaction Bks.

--The Family as a Way into the Future. 1983. pap. 5.00x (ISBN 0-87574-222-X, 222). Pendle Hill.

--From a Monastery Kitchen. LC 76-9973. (Illus.). 128p. 1976. pap. 9.57i (ISBN 0-06-060980-X, RD173, HarpR). Har-Row.

--My Part in the Quaker Adventure. (FGC). 146p. (gr. 8-12). 1964. 1.00 (ISBN 0-318-14150-7). Friends Genl Conf.

--The Underside of History: A View of Women Through Time. LC 75-30558. 750p. 1976. pap. 20.00x (ISBN 0-89158-056-5). Westview.

--Women: The Fifth World. LC 80-65602. (Headline Ser.: No. 248). (Illus.). 64p. (Orig.). 1980. pap. 3.00 (ISBN 0-87124-059-9). Foreign Policy.

Boulding, Elise, et al. Bibliography on World Conflict & Peace. (Special Studies in Peace, Conflict & Conflict Resolution). 1979. softcover 24.50x (ISBN 0-89158-374-2). Westview.

Boulding, Elise, jt. auth. see Chen, Robert S.

Boulding, Kenneth. New Nations for Old. 1983. pap. 5.00x (ISBN 0-87574-017-0, 017). Pendle Hill.

Boulding, Kenneth E. Beasts, Ballads, & Bouldingisms. Beilock, Richard P., ed. LC 79-65223. 200p. 1980. 12.95 (ISBN 0-87855-339-8). Transaction Bks.

--Beyond Economics: Essays on Society, Religion, & Ethics. 1970. pap. 4.95 (ISBN 0-472-06167-4, 167, AA). U of Mich Pr.

--Collected Papers of Kenneth E. Boulding, Vol. 3: Political Economy. Singell, Larry D., ed. LC 77-135288. 465p. 1973. text ed. 19.50x (ISBN 0-87081-046-4). Colo Assoc.

--Collected Papers of Kenneth E. Boulding, Vol. 4: Toward a General Social Science. Singell, Larry D., ed. LC 77-135288. 1974. text ed. 19.50x (ISBN 0-87081-053-7). Colo Assoc.

--Collected Papers of Kenneth E. Boulding, Vol. 5: International Systems. Singell, Larry D., ed. LC 77-135288. 500p. 1975. 19.50x (ISBN 0-87081-062-6). Colo Assoc.

--Ecodynamics: A New Theory of Societal Evolution. LC 77-27282. (Illus.). 384p. 1978. 27.50 (ISBN 0-8039-0945-4). Sage.

--Ecodynamics: A New Theory of Societal Evolution. LC 77-27282. (Illus.). 384p. 1981. pap. 14.95 (ISBN 0-8039-1683-3). Sage.

--The Economics of Human Betterment. 264p. 1984. lib. bdg. 34.50x (ISBN 0-87395-925-6); pap. text ed. 12.95x (ISBN 0-87395-926-4). State U NY Pr.

--Economics of Peace. LC 72-5620. (Essay Index Reprint Ser). 1972. Repr. of 1945 ed. 18.00 (ISBN 0-8369-2982-9). Ayer Co Pubs.

--Evolutionary Economics. LC 81-8953. (Illus.). 192p. 1981. 22.00 (ISBN 0-8039-1648-5). Sage.

--Evolutionary Economics. LC 81-8953. (Illus.). 192p. 1981. pap. 10.95 (ISBN 0-8039-1649-3). Sage.

--The Evolutionary Potential of Quakerism. 1983. pap. 5.00x (ISBN 0-87574-136-3, 136). Pendle Hill.

--Human Betterment. 1985. 25.00 (ISBN 0-8039-2419-4). Sage.

--The Image: Knowledge in Life & Society. 1956. pap. 6.95 (ISBN 0-472-06047-3, AA). U of Mich Pr.

--The Impact of the Social Sciences. (Brown & Haley Lecture Ser.). 1966. 15.00x (ISBN 0-8135-0525-9). Rutgers U Pr.

--The Organizational Revolution: A Study in the Ethics of Economic Organization. LC 84-15695. xxxiv, 286p. 1984. Repr. of 1953 ed. lib. bdg. 37.50x (ISBN 0-313-24371-9, BOOR). Greenwood.

--A Preface to Grants Economics: The Economy of Love & Fear. 160p. 1981. 26.95 (ISBN 0-03-059661-0). Praeger.

--Sonnets from the Interior Life & Other Autobiographical Verse. LC 75-289. 176p. 1975. pap. 14.50x (ISBN 0-87081-064-2). Colo Assoc.

--Stable Peace. LC 78-617. 155p. 1978. pap. 5.95 (ISBN 0-292-76448-0). U of Tex Pr.

--The World as a Total System. 1985. 25.00 (ISBN 0-8039-2443-7). Sage.

Boulding, Kenneth E. & Mayer, Milton. Mayer Boulding Dialogue on Peace Research. Murphy, Carol, ed. LC 67-23313. (Orig.). 1967. pap. 2.30x (ISBN 0-87574-153-3). Pendle Hill.

Boulding, Kenneth E. & Stahr, Elvis J. Economics of Pollution. LC 70-179973. (The Charles C. Moskowitz Lectures). 158p. 1971. 12.50x (ISBN 0-8147-0967-2). NYU Pr.

Boulding, Kenneth E., ed. Peace & the War Industry. rev. 2nd. ed. LC 72-77664. 159p. 1975. pap. text ed. 6.95x (ISBN 0-87855-545-5) (ISBN 0-87855-052-6). Transaction Bks.

Boulding, Kenneth E. & Mukerjee, Tapan, eds. Economic Imperialism: A Book of Readings. LC 74-146490. 1972. 10.00 (ISBN 0-472-16830-4); pap. 4.95x (ISBN 0-472-08170-5). U of Mich Pr.

Boulding, Kenneth E. & Senesh, Lawrence, eds. The Optimum Utilization of Knowledge: Making Knowledge Serve Human Betterment. (Academy of Independent Scholars Forum Ser.). (Illus.). 330p. 1983. 19.50x (ISBN 0-86531-544-2). Westview.

Boulding, Kenneth E. & Wilson, Thomas F., eds. Redistribution Through the Financial System: The Grants Economics of Money & Credit. LC 78-18017. 336p. 1978. 49.95 (ISBN 0-03-045341-0). Praeger.

Boulding, Kenneth E., jt. ed. see Benoit, Emile.

Boulding, Maria. The Coming of God. 224p. 1983. pap. text ed. 9.00 (ISBN 0-8146-1278-4). Liturgical Pr.

Boulding, Maria, ed. A Touch of God: Eight Monastic Journeys. LC 82-24055. 1983. pap. 7.95x (ISBN 0-932506-26-7). St Bedes Pubns.

Boulding, Russell. The Lost Harvest: A Study of the Surface Mining Act's Failure to Reclaim Prime Farmland in the Midwest- Executive Summary. Mavrolas, Pamela & Sheketoff, Chuck, eds. (Illus., Orig.). 1984. pap. 5.00 (ISBN 0-943724-04-X). Illinois South.

--The Lost Harvest: A Study of the Surface Mining Act's Failure to Reclaim Prime Farmland in the Midwest. (Illus.). 1984. pap. 15.00 (ISBN 0-943724-05-8). Illinois South.

--Prime Farmland Restoration. Mavrolas, Pamela & Sheketoff, Chuck, eds. (Your Rights in the Coalfields Ser.). 1984. pap. 3.00 (ISBN 0-943724-06-6). Illinois South.

--A Technical Guide for Reviewing Prime Farmland Restoration Plans in the Midwest. (Illus.). 1984. pap. 5.00 (ISBN 0-943724-07-4). Illinois South.

Bould-Vantil, Sally. Work & the Culture of Poverty: The Labor Force Activity of Poor Men. LC 75-38300. 1976. pap. 12.00 (ISBN 0-88247-409-X). R & E Pubs.

Boule, Marcellin. Fossil Men: Elements of Human Paleontology. LC 78-72691. Repr. of 1923 ed. 69.50 (ISBN 0-404-18262-3). AMS Pr.

--L' Homme Fossile de la Chapelle aux Saints. LC 78-72692. Repr. of 1913 ed. 46.50 (ISBN 0-404-18263-1). AMS Pr.

Bouleau, Charles. The Painter's Secret Geometry: A Study of Composition in Art. LC 79-91815. 268p. 1980. Repr. of 1963 ed. lib. bdg. 35.00 (ISBN 0-87817-259-9). Hacker.

Boulenger, ed. see Rabelais, Francois.

Boulenger, G. A. Catalogue of the Batrachia Gradienta S. Caudata & Batrachia Apoda: Collection of the British Museum. 2nd ed. (Illus.). 1966. 14.00 (ISBN 3-7682-0289-5). Lubrecht & Cramer.

--Catalogue of the Batrachia Salienta S. Ecaudata: Collection of the British Museum. (Illus.). 1966. 47.60 (ISBN 3-7682-0291-7). Lubrecht & Cramer.

--Catalogue of the Chelonians, Rhynchocephalians, & Crocodiles in the British Museum. new ed. (Illus.). 1966. 26.60 (ISBN 3-7682-0443-X). Lubrecht & Cramer.

--Catalogue of the Lizards in the British Museum, 3 vols. in 2. (Illus.). 1964. 168.00 (ISBN 3-7682-0239-9). Lubrecht & Cramer.

--Fishes of the Nile. 1964. Repr. of 1907 ed. 129.50 (ISBN 3-7682-0241-0). Lubrecht & Cramer.
Boulenger, George A. Monograph of the Lacertidae, 2 Vols. (Illus.). 1920-1921. Set. 75.00 (ISBN 0-384-05305-X). Johnson Repr.
--The Tailless Batrachians of Europe, 2 parts in one. Sterling, Keir B., ed. LC 77-81096. (Biologists & Their World Ser.). (Illus.). 1978. Repr. of 1898 ed. lib. bdg. 38.50x (ISBN 0-405-10679-3). Ayer Co Pubs.
Boulenger, Jacques R. Seventeenth Century. LC 70-181913. (National History of France: No. 4). Repr. of 1933 ed. 30.00 (ISBN 0-404-50794-8). AMS Pr.
Boulestin, X. Marcel. Boulestin's Round-the-Year Cookbook. 256p. 1975. pap. 3.50 (ISBN 0-486-23214-X). Dover.
Boulestin, Xavier M. Best of Boulestin. Firuski, Elvia & Firuski, Maurice, eds. 6.95 (ISBN 0-685-12177-1). Housatonuc.
Boulet, Jean. Magoumaz: Pays Mafa (Nord Cameroun) (Etude D'un Terroir De Montagne) (Atlas des Structures Agraires au Sud de Shara: No. 11). (Illus.). 92p. (Fr.). 1975. pap. text ed. 23.20x (ISBN 90-279-7575-2). Mouton.
Bouley, Allan. From Freedom to Formula: The Evolution of the Eucharistic Prayer from Oral Improvisation to Written Texts. LC 80-19716. (Studies in Christian Antiquity: Vol. 21). 302p. 1981. 27.95x (ISBN 0-8132-0554-9). Cath U Pr.
Boulez, Pierre. Boulez on Music Today. Bradshaw, Susan & Bennett, Richard R., trs. 144p. 1979. pap. 3.95 (ISBN 0-571-10587-4). Faber & Faber.
--Conversations with Celestin Deliege. (Eulenburg Music Ser.). 123p. 1985. pap. 15.00 (ISBN 0-903873-22-2). Da Capo.
Boulgarides, James & Fischer, Mary. Are You in the Right Job? 128p. 1984. pap. 7.95 (ISBN 0-671-50222-0). Monarch Pr.
Boulger, Demetrius C. History of China, 2 vols. LC 77-39406. (Select Bibliographies Reprint Ser.). 1972. Repr. of 1898 ed. 59.00 (ISBN 0-8369-9902-9). Ayer Co Pubs.
--The History of China, 2 vols. lib. bdg. 200.00 (ISBN 0-87968-489-5). Krishna Pr.
Boulger, George S., jt. auth. see Hawks, Ellison.
Boulger, James D. The Calvinistic Temper in English Poetry. (De Proprietatibus Litterarum, Ser. Major: No. 21). 1980. text ed. 54.00x (ISBN 90-279-7575-2). Mouton.
Boulind, Richard. Cambridge Libraries: An Illustrated Directory. (Reference Bks.: Vol. 5). (Illus.). 220p. 1985. 21.00 (ISBN 0-906672-95-3). Oleander Pr.
Boulind, Richard, tr. see Didier, Charles.
Boullata, Issa, ed. Critical Perspectives on Modern Arabic Literature. LC 78-13851. 384p. (Orig.). 1980. 26.00x (ISBN 0-89410-007-6); pap. 15.00x (ISBN 0-89410-008-4). Three Continents.
Boullata, Issa, ed. & tr. from Arabic. Modern Arab Poets, 1950-1975. LC 76-222. 1976. cased 20.00 (ISBN 0-914478-37-0); pap. 10.00 (ISBN 0-914478-38-9). Three Continents.
Boullata, Kamal, ed. & tr. Women of the Fertile Crescent: An Anthology of Arab Women's Poems. LC 77-3834. (Illus., Orig.). 1978. 20.00 (ISBN 0-914478-41-9); pap. 10.00 (ISBN 0-914478-42-7). Three Continents.
Boullata, Kamal & Ghossein, Mirene, eds. The World of Rashid Hussein: A Palestinian Poet in Exile. LC 78-62611. (Monograph: No. 12). 208p. (Orig.). 1979. pap. 6.50 (ISBN 0-937694-07-X). Assn Arab-Amer U Grads.
Boulle, Laurence J. Constitutional Reform & Apartheid: Legitimacy, Consociationalism & Control in South Africa. LC 84-40000. 278p. 1984. 27.50 (ISBN 0-312-16543-9). St Martin.
Boulle, Pierre. Aux Sources de la Riviere Kwai. 6.95 (ISBN 0-686-54096-4). French & Eur.
--Le Bon Leviathan. 224p. 1978. 14.95 (ISBN 0-686-54097-2). French & Eur.
--Le Bourreau. 208p. 1954. 3.95 (ISBN 0-686-54098-0). French & Eur.
--Bridge over the River Kwai. (YA) (gr. 8 up). 1970. pap. 2.95 (ISBN 0-553-24850-2). Bantam.
--Bridge over the River Kwai. LC 54-11508. 224p. 11.95 (ISBN 0-8149-0072-0). Vanguard.
--The Bridge over the River Kwai. 11.95 (ISBN 0-89190-571-5, Pub. by Am Repr). Amereon Ltd.
--Desperate Games. Wolf, Patricia, tr. from Fr. LC 73-83035. Orig. Title: Les Jeux De L'esprit. 214p. 1973. 10.95 (ISBN 0-8149-0731-8). Vanguard.
--L' Etrange Croisade de Frederic II. 9.95 (ISBN 0-686-54099-9). French & Eur.
--Executioner. LC 61-15474. 1961. 10.95 (ISBN 0-8149-0065-8). Vanguard.
--La Face. 244p. 1953. 3.95 (ISBN 0-686-54100-6). French & Eur.
--Garden on the Moon. LC 65-10229. 1964. 10.95 (ISBN 0-8149-0063-1). Vanguard.
--The Good Leviathan. LC 78-57255. 1979. 10.95 (ISBN 0-8149-0807-1). Vanguard.
--Histoires Charitables. 296p. 1965. 4.95 (ISBN 0-686-54101-4). French & Eur.
--Histoires Perfides: Six Nouvelles. 1976. 14.95 (ISBN 0-686-54102-2). French & Eur.
--Le Jardin De Kanashima. 320p. 1964. 7.95 (ISBN 0-686-54103-0); pap. 4.95 (ISBN 0-686-54104-9). French & Eur.
--Le Jeux de l'Esprit. 256p. 1971. 9.95 (ISBN 0-686-54105-7). French & Eur.
--The Marvelous Palace & Other Stories. LC 77-77035. 1978. 10.95 (ISBN 0-8149-0788-1). Vanguard.
--Un Metier de Seigneur. 240p. 1973. 4.95 (ISBN 0-686-54106-5). French & Eur.
--My Own River Kwai. LC 67-29216. 1967. 10.95 (ISBN 0-8149-0061-5). Vanguard.
--Noble Profession. LC 60-15063. 1960. 10.95 (ISBN 0-8149-0066-6). Vanguard.
--Not the Glory. 1955. 10.95 (ISBN 0-8149-0071-2). Vanguard.
--Not the Glory. 2nd ed. 240p. 1977. pap. 1.25 (ISBN 0-532-12461-8). Woodhill.
--Les Oreilles de Jungle. 240p. 1972. 12.95 (ISBN 0-686-54107-3). French & Eur.
--Le Photographe. 188p. 1974. 9.95 (ISBN 0-686-54108-1); pap. 3.95 (ISBN 0-686-54109-X). French & Eur.
--Photographer. Fielding, Xan, tr. LC 68-8085. 1968. 10.95 (ISBN 0-8149-0060-7). Vanguard.
--Planet of the Apes. (RL 7). 1968. pap. 1.95 (ISBN 0-451-12318-2, AJ2318, Sig). NAL.
--Planet of the Apes. LC 63-21843. 224p. 1963. 11.95 (ISBN 0-8149-0064-X). Vanguard.
--La Planete des Singes. 3.95 (ISBN 0-686-54110-3). French & Eur.
--Le Pont de la Riviere Kwai. (Illus.). 290p. 1961. 12.95 (ISBN 0-686-54111-1); pap. 3.95 (ISBN 0-686-54112-X). French & Eur.
--Quia Absurdum: Sur la Terre Comme au Ciel. 224p. 1970. 7.95 (ISBN 0-686-54113-8). French & Eur.
--Le Sacrilege Malais. 1967. 9.95 (ISBN 0-686-54114-6). French & Eur.
--Test. LC 57-12252. 10.95 (ISBN 0-8149-0069-0). Vanguard.
--Time Out of Mind. LC 66-26792. 1966. 10.95 (ISBN 0-8149-0062-3). Vanguard.
--Trouble in Paradise. Wolfe, Patricia, tr. from Fr. 192p. 1985. 12.95 (ISBN 0-8149-0897-7). Vanguard.
--Les Vertus de l'Enfer. 272p. 1976. 14.95 (ISBN 0-686-54115-4); pap. 4.50 (ISBN 0-686-54116-2). French & Eur.
--The Virtues of Hell. Wolf, Patricia, tr. from Fr. LC 74-81811. 224p. 1974. 10.95 (ISBN 0-8149-0744-X). Vanguard.
--Les Voies du Salut. 256p. 1958. 4.95 (ISBN 0-686-54117-0). French & Eur.
--The Whale of the Victoria Cross. Wolf, Patricia, tr. from Fr. 192p. 1983. 12.95 (ISBN 0-8149-0873-X). Vanguard.
--William Conrad. 284p. 1972. 9.95 (ISBN 0-686-54118-9); pap. 3.95 (ISBN 0-686-54119-7). French & Eur.
Boullemier, Leo. The Checklist of Species, Hybrids & Cultivars of the Genus Fuchsia. (Illus.). 352p. 1985. 17.95 (ISBN 0-7137-1594-4, Pub. by Blandford Pr England). Sterling.
Boullemier, Leo B. Growing & Showing Fuchsias. (Growing & Showing Ser.). (Illus.). 64p. 1985. 9.95 (ISBN 0-7153-8592-5). David & Charles.
Boullin, David J. Cerebral Vasospasm. LC 79-40735. 337p. 1980. 71.95 (ISBN 0-471-27639-1, Pub. by Wiley-Interscience). Wiley.
--Cerebral Vasospasm. LC 79-40735. (Wiley-Interscience Publication Ser.). pap. 86.80 (ISBN 0-317-26198-3, 2052068). Bks Demand UMI.
Boullin, David J., ed. Serotonin in Mental Abnormalities. LC 77-1828. pap. 82.00 (ISBN 0-317-07778-3, 2019207). Bks Demand UMI.
Boullion, Thomas L. & Odell, Patrick L. Generalized Inverse Matrices. LC 79-149768. 116p. 1971. 15.00 (ISBN 0-471-09110-3, Pub. by Wiley). Krieger.
Boulmetis, John. Job Competency: Adult Vocational Instruction. LC 80-82711. (CBE Forum Ser.: Bk.2). 1981. pap. 6.95 (ISBN 0-8224-4014-8). Pitman Learning.
Boulmetis, John & Purnell, Richard. An Introduction & Guide to Word Processing. 196p. 1983. pap. 11.20x (ISBN 0-89702-043-X). PAR Inc.
Bouloiseau, Marc. The Jacobin Republic 1792-1794. Mandelbaum, Jonathan, tr. LC 83-5293. (The French Revolution Ser.: No. 2). 248p. 1984. 39.50 (ISBN 0-521-24726-8); pap. 13.95 (ISBN 0-521-28918-1). Cambridge U Pr.
Boulos, Jawad. Les Peuples et les Civilisations du Proche-Orient: Essai d'une Histoire Comparee, des Origines a nos Jours, Tomes II-V. Incl. Tome II. De 1600 a 64 Avant J.-C. 430p. 1962. pap. text ed. 21.60x (ISBN 0-686-27788-0); Tome III. De la Conquete Romaine a l'Expansion Arabo-Islamique (64 av. J.-C. to 640 ap. J.-C.) 400p. 1964. pap. text ed. 21.60x (ISBN 0-686-27789-9); Tome IV. De l'Expansion Arabo-Islamique a la Conquete Turco-Ottomane (640-1517) 550p. 1964. pap. text ed. 27.20 (ISBN 0-686-27790-2); Le Proche-Orient Ottoman (1517-1918) et Postottoman (1918-1930) 300p. 1968. pap. text ed. 16.80 (ISBN 0-686-27791-0). pap. Mouton.
Boulos, Loutfy. Medicinal Plants of North Africa. Ayensu, Edward S., ed. LC 82-20412. (Medicinal Plants of the World Ser.: No. 3). (Illus.). 300p. 1983. 39.95 (ISBN 0-917256-16-6). Ref Pubns.
Boulos, Loutfy & El-Hadidi, M. Nabil. The Weed Flora of Egypt: A Practical Guide. 1985. pap. 12.50x (ISBN 977-424-038-3, Pub. by Am Univ Cairo Pr). Columbia U Pr.
Boulougouris, John C. Learning Theory Approaches to Psychiatry. 256p. 1982. 64.95x (ISBN 0-471-28042-9, Wiley-Interscience, Pub. by Wiley-Interscience). Wiley.
Boulougouris, John C. & Rabalivas, Andreas D., eds. The Treatment of Phobic & Obsessive Compulsive Disorders. 1977. text ed. 28.00 (ISBN 0-08-021472-X). Pergamon.
Boulpaep, Emele L., ed. Current Topics in Membranes & Transport: Vol. 13, Cellular Mechanisms of Renal Tubular Ion Transport. LC 70-117091. (Serial Publication). 1980. 61.50 (ISBN 0-12-153313-1). Acad Pr.
Boult, Adrian. Boult on Music: Words from a Lifetime's Communication. 196p. 1985. text ed. 15.00x (ISBN 0-87663-483-8). Universe.
Boult, Adrian C. A Handbook on the Technique of Conducting. 7th rev. ed. LC 75-181113. 1951. Repr. 29.00 (ISBN 0-403-01512-X). Scholarly.
--My Own Trumpet: The Memoirs of Sir Adrian Boult. (Sir). (Illus.). 213p. 1979. 18.95 (ISBN 0-241-02445-5, Pub. by Hamish Hamilton England). David & Charles.
Boult, Katharine F., tr. see Berlioz, Hector.
Boult, Pamela, ed. see Newhouse, Flower A.
Boulter, Bruce. Woodturning in Pictures. (Illus.). 144p. (Orig.). 1983. pap. 12.95 (ISBN 0-8069-7742-6). Sterling.
Boulter, C. G., et al, eds. Lectures in Memory of Louise Taft Semple: Classical Studies, Second Series, 1966-1970. LC 72-9256. (Illus.). 410p. 1974. pap. 12.95 (ISBN 0-8061-1178-X). U of Okla Pr.
Boulter, Cedric G. Corpus Vasorum Antiquorum, Cleveland Museum of Art, Fasc. 15. LC 70-148348. (Corpus Vasorum Antiquorm Ser.: Fascicule 1, U.S.A.). (Illus.). 1971. 38.00 (ISBN 0-691-03540-7). Princeton U Pr.
Boulter, D., ed. Nucleic Acids & Proteins in Plants I: Structure, Biochemistry & Physiology of Proteins. (Encyclopedia of Plant Physiology: Vol. 14A). (Illus.). 760p. 1982. 130.00 (ISBN 0-387-11008-9). Springer-Verlag.
Boulter, D., jt. ed. see Parthier, B.
Boulter, Eric, jt. auth. see Dobree, John H.
Boulter, V. M., jt. auth. see Toynbee, Arnold J.
Boulting, William. Giordano Bruno: His Life, Thought & Martyrdom. LC 72-5438. (Select Bibliographies Reprint Ser.). 1372. Repr. of 1914 ed. 20.00 (ISBN 0-8369-6898-0). Ayer Co Pubs.
--Giordano Bruno: His Life, Thought, & Martyrdom. 1976. lib. bdg. 59.95 (ISBN 0-8490-1890-0). Gordon Pr.
--Tasso & His Times. LC 68-24953. (World History Ser., No. 48). 1969. Repr. of 1907 ed. lib. bdg. 54.95x (ISBN 0-8383-0915-1). Haskell.
--Woman in Italy: From the Introduction of the Chivalrous Service of Love to the Appearance of the Professional Actress. LC 79-2932. (Illus.). 356p. 1981. Repr. of 1910 ed. 27.50 (ISBN 0-8305-0099-5). Hyperion Conn.
Boulton, A., et al, eds. Neuromethods, Vol. 1. 512p. 1985. 59.50 (ISBN 0-317-26923-2). Humana.
--Neuromethods, Vol. 2. (Neuromethods Ser.). 500p. 1985. 59.50 (ISBN 0-89603-076-8). Humana.
Boulton, A. A., et al, eds. Neurobiology of the Trace Amines. LC 84-626. (Experimental & Clinical Neuroscience Ser.). (Illus.). 624p. 59.50 (ISBN 0-89603-063-6). Humana.
Boulton, A. J. see Katritzky, A. R.
Boulton, A. J., jt. ed. see Katritzky, A. R.
Boulton, Carolyn. Birds. LC 84-50015. (Action Science Ser.). (Illus.). 32p. (gr. 2-4). 1984. PLB 9.90 (ISBN 0-531-04634-6). Watts.
--Trees. LC 84-50016. (Action Science Ser.). (Illus.). 32p. (gr. 2-4). 1984. PLB 9.90 (ISBN 0-531-04635-4). Watts.
Boulton, David, ed. Voices from the Crowd, Against the H Bomb. LC 65-25493. 1964. 9.95 (ISBN 0-8023-1012-5). Dufour.
Boulton, David K., jt. auth. see Pickett, Kathleen G.
Boulton, J. T., ed. see Lawrence, D. H.
Boulton, James T. The Language of Politics in the Age of Wilkes & Burke. LC 74-33503. 282p. 1975. Repr. of 1963 ed. lib. bdg. 22.50x (ISBN 0-8371-7969-6, BOLP). Greenwood.
Boulton, James T., jt. auth. see Bindoff, S. T.
Boulton, James T., ed. Johnson: The Critical Heritage. 1978. 38.00x (ISBN 0-7100-7030-6). Routledge & Kegan.
Boulton, James T., ed. see Burke, Edmund E.
Boulton, James T., ed. see Lawrence, D. H.
Boulton, Jane & Boulton, Peter. Psychic Beam to Beyond. LC 82-74522. 144p. 1983. pap. 6.95x (ISBN 0-87516-514-1). De Vorss.
Boulton, Jane & Whitely, Opal. Opal: The Journey of an Understanding Heart. 196p. 1984. 12.95 (ISBN 0-935382-52-6). W Kaufmann.
Boulton, Majorie. The Anatomy of Poetry. Rev. ed. 1983. pap. 6.95 (ISBN 0-7100-9087-0). Routledge & Kegan.
Boulton, Marjorie. The Anatomy of Poetry. 189p. 1981. Repr. of 1953 ed. lib. bdg. 22.50 (ISBN 0-89760-077-0). Telegraph Bks.
Boulton, Mary G. On Being a Mother. LC 83-9150. 240p. 1984. 30.00x (ISBN 0-422-78540-7, NO. 4005); pap. 15.95x (ISBN 0-422-78550-4, NO. 4006). Methuen Inc.
Boulton, Peter, jt. auth. see Boulton, Jane.
Boulton, Roger, et al. Canada Coast to Coast. (Illus.). 1982. 35.00x (ISBN 0-19-540388-6). Oxford U Pr.
Boulton, W. H. Pageant of Transport Through the Ages. LC 77-81514. (Illus.). 22.00 (ISBN 0-405-08296-7, Blom Pubns). Ayer Co Pubs.
--The Pageant of Transport Through the Ages. 1976. lib. bdg. 344.95 (ISBN 0-8490-2398-X). Gordon Pr.
Boulton, Wayne G. Is Leagalism a Heresy? The Legacy of the Pharisees in Christian Ethics. LC 81-85386. 160p. (Orig.). 1982. pap. 6.95 (ISBN 0-8091-2431-9). Paulist Pr.
Boulton, William. Complete History of Alpena County, Michigan. (Local History Reprints Ser.). (Illus.). 1965. pap. 3.25 (ISBN 0-916699-01-3). Clarke His.
Boulton, William R. Business Policy: The Art of Strategic Management. (Illus.). 864p. 1984. text ed. write for info. instr's manual (ISBN 0-02-312840-2, Instructor's Manual). Macmillan.
Boulton, WilliamB. Amusements of Old London, 2 Vols. in 1. LC 75-82820. (Illus.). 1901. 33.00 (ISBN 0-405-08295-9, Blom Pubns). Ayer Co Pubs.
Boulton-Jones, J. M., et al. Diagnosis & Management of Renal & Urinary Disorders. (Illus.). 312p. 1982. pap. text ed. 21.95 (ISBN 0-632-00677-3, B0895-3). Mosby.
Boulton-Jones, M. Acute & Chronic Renal Failure. (Topics in Renal Disease Ser.). 116p. 1982. 17.95 (ISBN 0-85200-420-6, Pub. by MTP Pr England). Kluwer Academic.
Boultwood, Alban. Christ in Us: Reflections on Redemption. LC 81-8371. 144p. (Orig.). 1981. pap. 5.50 (ISBN 0-8146-1234-2). Liturgical Pr.
Boultwood, M. E., jt. auth. see Curtis, S. J.
Boulware, Lemuel R. The Truth about Boulwarism: Trying to Right Voluntarily. LC 77-91413. pap. 48.00 (ISBN 0-317-29423-7, 2024305). Bks Demand UMI.
Boulware, Marcus. Snoring. LC 73-94369. 1974. 6.95 (ISBN 0-912834-02-1). Am Faculty Pr.
Boulware, Marcus H. Oratory of Negro Leaders: Nineteen Hunderd - Nineteen Sixty-Eight. LC 72-90794. 1969. lib. bdg. 35.00 (ISBN 0-8371-1849-2, BOO&). Greenwood.
Bouma, Arnold H. Methods for the Study of Sedimentary Structures. LC 78-11914. 476p. 1979. Repr. of 1969 ed. lib. bdg. 29.50 (ISBN 0-88275-760-1). Krieger.
Bouma, Arnold H., ed. Shell Dredging & Its Influence on Gulf Coast Environments. LC 75-39416. 464p. 1976. 38.95x (ISBN 0-87201-805-9). Gulf Pub.
Bouma, Donald H. The Dynamics of School Integration: Problems & Approaches in a Northern City. LC 68-20582. pap. 39.50 (ISBN 0-317-07888-7, 2012959). Bks Demand UMI.
Bouma, Hans. An Eye on Israel. LC 77-10641. pap. 36.00 (ISBN 0-8357-9128-9, 2012728). Bks Demand UMI.
Bouma, Herman & Bouwhuis, Don G. Attention & Performance X: Control of Language Processes. (Attention & Performance Ser.). 584p. 1984. text ed. 59.95 (ISBN 0-86377-005-3). L Erlbaum Assocs.
Bouma, J., jt. ed. see Nielsen, D. R.
Bouma, J. J., jt. ed. see Tromp, S. W.
Bouma, J. L. The Avenging Gun. 1978. pap. 1.50 (ISBN 0-505-51327-7, Pub. by Tower Bks). Dorchester Pub Co.
--Beyond Vengeance. 1979. pap. 1.75 (ISBN 0-8439-0703-7, Leisure Bks). Dorchester Pub Co.
--Beyond Vengeance. 192p. 1986. pap. 2.25 (ISBN 0-8439-2326-1, Leisure Bks). Dorchester Pub Co.
--Border Vengeance. 1978. pap. 1.25 (ISBN 0-8439-0605-7, Leisure Bks). Dorchester Pub Co.
--Burning Valley. 1976. pap. 0.95 (ISBN 0-685-69511-5, LB378NK, Leisure Bks). Dorchester Pub Co.
--Burning Valley. 160p. 1981. pap. 1.75 (ISBN 0-8439-0992-7, Leisure Bks). Dorchester Pub Co.
--Hell on Horseback. 1981. pap. 1.75 (ISBN 0-8439-0893-9, Leisure Bks). Dorchester Pub Co.
--Longrider. 1978. pap. 1.50 (ISBN 0-8439-0597-2, Leisure Bks). Dorchester Pub Co.
--Mediterranean Caper. 1981. pap. 2.25 (ISBN 0-8439-0873-4, Leisure Bks). Dorchester Pub Co.
--Ride to Violence. 1978. pap. 1.50 (ISBN 0-8439-0596-4, Leisure Bks). Dorchester Pub Co.
--Texas Spurs. 1981. pap. 1.95 (ISBN 0-505-51731-0, Pub. by Tower Bks). Dorchester Pub Co.
--Vengeance. 160p. 1981. pap. 1.75 (ISBN 0-8439-0991-9, Leisure Bks). Dorchester Pub Co.
Bouma, Lowell. The Semantics of the Modal Auxiliaries in Contemporary German. (Janua Linguarum Ser. Practica: No. 146). 1973. pap. text ed. 19.20x (ISBN 90-279-2390-6). Mouton.
Bouma, Mary L. The Creative Homemaker. LC 73-17234. 192p. 1973. pap. 2.95 (ISBN 0-87123-078-X, 200084). Bethany Hse.
Bouma, Mary La G. Divorce in the Parsonage. LC 79-16157. 160p. 1979. pap. 3.95 (ISBN 0-87123-109-3, 210109). Bethany Hse.
Bouman, F. Development of Ovule & Seed Coat Structure in Angiosperms. (International Bioscience Monographs: No. 6). 80p. 1978. 7.50 (ISBN 0-88065-067-2, Pub. by Messers Today & Tomorrows Printers & Publishers India). Scholarly Pubns.

Bouman, H. J., tr. Luther's Works, Vol. 10. 1981. 16.95 (ISBN 0-570-06410-4, 15-1752). Concordia.
Bouman, Helen H., tr. see Chander, Krishan.
Bouman, Herbert, tr. see Schlink, Edmund.
Bouman, Herbert J., tr. Law & Gospel: Selected Writings of C.F.W. Walther. 1981. 12.95 (ISBN 0-570-08275-7, 15-2733). Concordia.
--Luther's Works, Vol. 16. 1968. 14.95 (ISBN 0-570-06416-3, 15-1758). Concordia.
Bouman, Herbert J., tr. see Luther, Martin.
Bouman, Herbert J., tr. see Von Loewenich, Walter.
Bouman, Herbert J., tr. see Walther, C. F.
Bouman, L. N. & Jongsma, H. J. Cardiac Rate & Rhythm. 1982. lib. bdg. 82.50 (ISBN 90-247-2626-3, Pub. by Martinus Nijhoff Netherlands). Kluwer Academic.
Boumans, G. Grain Handling & Storage. (Developments in Agricultural Engineering Ser.: Vol. 4). 442p. 1985. 94.50 (ISBN 0-444-42439-3). Elsevier.
Boumans, P. W. Atomic Absorption Spectroscopy-Past, Present & Future: To Commemorate the 25th Anniversary of Alan Walsh's Landmark Paper in Spectrochimica Acta. 248p. 1981. pap. 35.00 (ISBN 0-08-026267-8). Pergamon.
--Line Coincidence Tables for Inductively Coupled Plasma Atomic Emission Spectrometry, 2 vols. LC 80-41344. (Illus.). 941p. 1984. 275.00 set (ISBN 0-08-031404-X). Pergamon.
--Line Coincidence Tables for Inductively Coupled Plasma Atomic Emission Spectrometry, 2 vols. 2nd ed. LC 84-6402. (Illus.). 944p. 1984. Set. 235.00 (ISBN 0-08-031404-X). Pergamon.
Boumans, P. W., ed. Analytical Spectroscopy: A Polychrome Branch of Science: Proceedings of the Twenty-third Colloquim International, including the 10th International Conference on Atomic Spectroscopy, Amsterdam, 26 June-1 July 1983. 12/1983 ed. 224p. pap. 55.00 (ISBN 0-08-031403-1). Pergamon.
--Atomic Absorption Spectroscopy: Past, Present & Future, Pt. 2: To Commemorate the 25th Anniversary of Alan Walsh's Landmark Paper in Spectrochimica Acta. (Spectrochimica Acta B: Vol. 36, No. 5). iv, 92p. 1981. pap. 17.50 (ISBN 0-08-026287-2). Pergamon.
--Line Coincidence Tables for Inductively Coupled Plasma Atomic Emission Spectrometry, 2 vols. (Illus.). 941p. (Fr.). 1981. 250.00 (ISBN 0-08-026269-4). Pergamon.
--Line Coincidence Tables for Inductively Coupled Plasma Atomic Emission Spectrometry, 2 vols. (Illus.). 941p. (Span.). 1981. 250.00 (ISBN 0-08-026270-8). Pergamon.
Boumans, P. W., et al, eds. A Profile of Current Developments in Atomic Spectroscopy: Dedicated to Kurt Laqua on the Occasion of His 65th Birthday. 400p. 1985. 82.50 (ISBN 0-08-031447-3). Pergamon.
Boumans, Paul W. Theory of Spectrochemical Excitation. LC 66-27686. 383p. 1966. 42.50x (ISBN 0-306-30281-0, Plenum Pr). Plenum Pub.
--Theory of Spectrochemical Excitation. LC 66-27686. pap. 98.50 (ISBN 0-317-27891-6, 2055791). Bks Demand UMI.
Boumelha, Penny. Thomas Hardy & Women: Sexual Ideology & Narrative Form. LC 81-22903. 188p. 1982. text ed. 28.50x (ISBN 0-389-20259-2, 07077). B&N Imports.
Bounds, E. M. The Best of E. M. Bounds. (Best Ser.). 256p. (Orig.). 1981. pap. 4.95 (ISBN 0-8010-0808-5). Baker Bk.
--Catching a Glimpse of Heaven. 150p. 1985. pap. text ed. 3.50 (ISBN 0-88368-167-6). Whitaker Hse.
--The Essentials of Prayer. (Direction Bks Ser.). 1979. pap. 2.45 (ISBN 0-8010-0756-9). Baker Bk.
--Heaven: A Place, a City, a Home. (Direction Bks). 152p. 1975. pap. 3.50 (ISBN 0-8010-0648-1). Baker Bk.
--The Necessity of Prayer. (Direction Bks). 144p. 1976. pap. 2.95 (ISBN 0-8010-0659-7). Baker Bk.
--The Necessity of Prayer. 144p. 1984. pap. 3.50 (ISBN 0-88368-139-0). Whitaker Hse.
--Obtaining Answers to Prayer. 144p. 1984. pap. 3.50 (ISBN 0-88368-142-0). Whitaker Hse.
--The Possibilities of Prayer. (Direction Bks Ser.). 1979. pap. 2.45 (ISBN 0-8010-0757-7). Baker Bk.
--Power Through Prayer. 112p. 1983. pap. text ed. 3.50 (ISBN 0-88368-117-X). Whitaker Hse.
--Power Through Prayer. (Moody Classics Ser.). 1985. pap. text ed. 2.95 (ISBN 0-8024-6729-6). Moody.
--Prayer & Praying Men. (Direction Bks). 1977. pap. 2.95 (ISBN 0-8010-0721-6). Baker Bk.
--Reality of Prayer. (Direction Bks). 1978. pap. 3.50x (ISBN 0-8010-0739-9). Baker Bk.
--Satan: His Personality, Power & Overthrow. (Direction Bks). 1972. pap. 2.95 (ISBN 0-8010-0586-8). Baker Bk.
--A Treasury of Prayer. LC 53-9865. 192p. 1981. pap. 4.95 (ISBN 0-87123-543-9, 210543). Bethany Hse.
--The Weapon of Prayer. (Direction Bks). 57p. 1975. pap. 2.95 (ISBN 0-8010-0634-1). Baker Bk.
--Winning the Invisible War. 160p. 1984. pap. 3.50 (ISBN 0-88368-145-5). Whitaker Hse.
Bounds, Edward M. Power Through Prayer. (Direction Bks). 1972. pap. 2.45 (ISBN 0-8010-0584-1). Baker Bk.
--Power Through Prayer. pap. 2.50 (ISBN 0-310-21612-5). Zondervan.
--Purpose in Prayer. (Direction Bks). 1978. pap. 2.95 (ISBN 0-8010-0738-0). Baker Bk.
--Purpose in Prayer. (E.M. Bound Ser.). pap. 2.95 (ISBN 0-8024-6949-3). Moody.
Bounds, Sarah. No-Salt Cooking: Wholesome Recipes for Low-Sodium Eating. 128p. (Orig.). 1984. pap. 6.95 (ISBN 0-7225-0896-4). Thorsons Pubs.
Bouquard, Thomas J. Arson Investigation: The Step-by-Step Procedure. 132p. 1983. 17.50x (ISBN 0-398-04839-8). C C Thomas.
Bouquerel, F. Innovation Commercialisation au Service de l'Enterprise. cancelled (ISBN 0-08-027063-8); 22.00 (ISBN 0-08-027062-X). Pergamon.
Bouquet, A. C. Everyday Life in New Testament Times. (Hudson River Editions). (Illus.). 1953. lib. rep. ed. 20.00 (ISBN 0-684-14833-1, ScribT). Scribner.
Bouquet, Alan C. The Christian Faith & Non-Christian Religions. LC 76-13920. 1976. Repr. of 1958 ed. lib. bdg. 30.00x (ISBN 0-8371-7974-2, BOCF). Greenwood.
--Religious Experience: Its Nature, Types, & Validity. LC 75-40997. 140p. 1976. Repr. of 1968 ed. lib. bdg. 22.50x (ISBN 0-8371-8714-1, BORL). Greenwood.
Bour, Daniele. The House from Morning to Night. LC 84-21873. (Illus.). 16p. (ps-3). 1985. 8.95 (ISBN 0-916291-01-4). Kane Miller Bk.
Bourassa, Andre G. Surrealism & Quebec Literature: History of a Cultural Revolution. Czarnecki, Mark, tr. (University of Toronto Romance Ser.: 50). 416p. 1984. 45.00x (ISBN 0-8020-2336-3); 20.00 (ISBN 0-8020-6528-7). U of Toronto Pr.
Bourassa, Robert. James Bay. LC 74-169569. (Regional Canadian Ser.). pap. 31.00 (ISBN 0-317-28282-4, 2022286). Bks Demand UMI.
Bourasse, J. J. Dictionnaire d'Archeologie Sacree, 2 vols. Migne, J. P., ed. (Nouvelle Encyclopedie Theologique Ser.: Vols. 11-12). 1236p. (Fr.). Repr. of 1852 ed. lib. bdg. 157.00x (ISBN 0-89241-261-5). Caratzas.
--Dictionnaire d'Epigraphie Chretienne, 2 vols. Migne, J. P., ed. (Nouvelle Encyclopedie Theologique Ser.: Vols. 30-31). 1262p. (Fr.). Repr. of 1852 ed. lib. bdg. 161.00x (ISBN 0-89241-273-9). Caratzas.
Bourbaki, N. Functions of a Real Variable. 1982. text ed. write for info. (ISBN 0-201-00640-5). Addison-Wesley.
Bourbourg, Charles E. Brasseru De see Brasseur De Bourbourg, Charles E.
Bourchier, J., tr. see Froissart, Jean.
Bourchier, John, tr. see Froissart, Jean.
Bourchier, John, tr. see Lee, S. H.
Bourchier, John, tr. see Steele, Robert.
Bourcier, Georges. History of the English Language. Clark, Cecily, tr. 232p. 1981. 59.00x (ISBN 0-85950-482-4, Pub. by S Thornes Pubs England). State Mutual Bk.
Bourdais, Donnat M. le see Le Bourdais, Donat M.
Bourdeaux, Kenneth J. & Long, Hugh W. The Basic Theory of Corporate Finance. LC 76-27895. (Illus.). 1977. pap. text ed. 30.95 (ISBN 0-13-069435-5). P-H.
Bourdette, Robert E. Richard Bentley: A Descriptive, Annotated Bibiography. LC 84-45392. 275p. 1985. lib. bdg. 37.00 (ISBN 0-8240-8849-2). Garland Pub.
Bourdette, Robert E., Jr. & Cohen, Michael. The Poem in Question. 485p. 1983. pap. text ed. 12.95 (ISBN 0-15-570654-3, HC). HarBraceJ.
Bourdier, Jean-Paul & Minh-ha, Trinh T. African Spaces: Designs for Living in Upper Volta. (Illus.). 275p. 1985. text ed. 59.50x (ISBN 0-8419-0890-7, Africana). Holmes & Meier.
Bourdieu, P. Algeria Nineteen Sixty. LC 78-4237. (Studies in Modern Capitalism). (Illus.). 1979. 29.95 (ISBN 0-521-22090-4). Cambridge U Pr.
--Outline of a Theory of Practice. LC 76-11073. (Studies in Social Anthropology: No. 16). (Illus.). 1977. 44.50 (ISBN 0-521-21178-6); pap. 14.95 (ISBN 0-521-29164-X). Cambridge U Pr.
Bourdieu, Pierre. Distinction: A Social Critique of the Judgement of Taste. Nice, Richard, tr. (Illus.). 640p. (Fr.). 1984. 29.50 (ISBN 0-674-21280-0). Harvard U Pr.
Bourdieu, Pierre & Passeron, J. C. Les Etudiants et Leurs Etudes. Eliard, Michel, ed. (Cahiers Du Centre De Sociologie Europeenne: No. 1). 1964. pap. 9.20x (ISBN 90-279-6069-0). Mouton.
Bourdieu, Pierre & Passeron, Jean-Claude. The Inheritors: French Students & Their Relation to Culture with a New Epilogue, 1979. Nice, Richard, tr. from Fr. LC 78-31532. (Illus.). 1979. lib. bdg. 15.00x (ISBN 0-226-06739-4). U of Chicago Pr.
--Reproduction: In Education, Society & Culture. LC 76-55922. (Studies in Social & Educational Change: Vol. 5). 254p. 1977. 25.00 (ISBN 0-8039-9994-1); pap. 12.50 (ISBN 0-8039-9995-X). Sage.
Bourdieu, Pierre J., et al, eds. Le Metier De Sociologue: Prealables Epistemologiques. 4th ed. (Textes De Sciences Sociales: No. 1). 1983. pap. 16.40x (ISBN 0-686-20919-2). Mouton.
Bourdillon, F. W., ed. Cest Oaucasi & De Nicolete. LC 80-2241. (Illus.). Repr. of 1896 ed. 17.50 (ISBN 0-404-19036-7). AMS Pr.
Bourdillon, J. F. Spinal Manipulation. 3rd ed. 240p. 1982. pap. 24.95 (ISBN 0-8385-8641-4). ACC.
Bourdillon, M. F. C. & Fortes, M. Sacrifices. 1980. 39.00 (ISBN 0-12-119040-4). Acad Pr.
Bourdo, Eric, jt. ed. see Edin, Herbert L.
Bourdon, Clinton C. & Levitt, Raymond E. Union & Open-Shop Construction: Compensation, Work Practices, & Labor Markets. LC 79-1724. (Illus.). 176p. 1980. 25.50x (ISBN 0-669-02918-1). Lexington Bks.
Bourdon, J. Growth & Properties of Metal Clusters: Application to Catalysis & the Photographic Process. (Studies in Surface Science & Catalysis: Vol. 4). 550p. 1980. 95.75 (ISBN 0-444-41877-6). Elsevier.
Bourdon, L. P. Elements of Algebra. 59.95 (ISBN 0-8490-0101-3). Gordon Pr.
Bourdon, Sylvia. Love Is a Feast. Wright, Barbara, tr. from Fr. 192p. 1983. 11.95 (ISBN 0-7145-3648-2). Riverrun NY.
Bourdot, H. & Galzin, A. Hymenomycetes De France: Heterobasidies-Homobasidies Gymnocarpes. (Biblio. Myco. Ser.: No.23). 1969. Repr. of 1927 ed. 42.00 (ISBN 3-7682-0655-6). Lubrecht & Cramer.
Bourdreaux, Martina, ed. see Lambourne, Cherie.
Bouret, J. Bardone. (Illus.). 1977. 55.00 (ISBN 0-912728-51-5). Newbury Bks.
Bourg, George Du see DuBourg, George.
Bourgain, J. New Classes of LP-Spaces. (Lecture Notes in Mathematics Ser.: Vol. 889). 143p. 1981. pap. 12.00 (ISBN 0-387-11156-5). Springer-Verlag.
Bourgeacq, Jacques A., jt. auth. see Limouzy, Pierre.
Bourgeade, Pierre. The Passport & the Door. Zeig, Sande, tr. from Fr. (Repertory Theatre Publications Ser.: No.7). 120p. (Orig.). 1984. pap. text ed. 6.25 (ISBN 0-913745-06-5, Dist. by Publishing Center for Cultural Resources). Ubu Repertory.
Bourgeau, Art. The Elvis Murders. 224p. 1985. pap. 2.95 (ISBN 0-441-20431-7, Pub. by Charter Bks). Ace Bks.
--Murder at the Cheatin' Heart Motel. 1985. pap. 2.95 (ISBN 0-317-19741-X, Pub. by Charter Bks). Ace Bks.
Bourgeois, Andre, et al. Studies in French Literature. (Rice University Studies: Vol. 57, No. 2). 127p. 1971. pap. 10.00x (ISBN 0-89263-208-9). Rice Univ.
Bourgeois, Bernard, ed. see Hegel, Georg W. F.
Bourgeois, E. History of Modern France, Eighteen Fifteen to Nineteen Thirteen, 2 vols. 1972. lib. bdg. 57.50x (ISBN 0-374-90847-8). Octagon.
Bourgeois, G. Patrick, et al. Walker's Quantity Surveying & Basic Construction Estimating. Frank R. Walker Company, ed. (Illus.). 128p. 1981. pap. 12.95 (ISBN 0-911592-75-X). F R Walker.
Bourgeois, Henri. On Becoming Christian. 2nd ed. 160p. 1985. pap. 6.95 (ISBN 0-89622-270-5). Twenty-Third.
Bourgeois, J., jt. ed. see Fairbridge, R. W.
Bourgeois, J. P., illus. Starlettes. (Illus.). 80p. 1984. pap. 13.95 (ISBN 0-88715-004-7). Delilah Comm.
Bourgeois, Jean-Francois. Los Ninos de la Biblia. Maecha, Alberto, ed. Orig. Title: Les Enfants de la Bible. 40p. (Span.). (gr. 3-5). 1984. pap. write for info. (ISBN 0-942504-11-9). Overcomer Pr.
Bourgeois, M. John Millington Synge & the Irish Theatre. LC 68-906. (Studies in Irish Literature, No. 16). 1969. Repr. of 1913 ed. lib. bdg. 49.95x (ISBN 0-8383-0511-3). Haskell.
Bourgeois, Maurice. John Millington Synge & the Irish Theatre. LC 65-16228. (Illus.). 1913. 22.00 (ISBN 0-405-08297-5, Pub. by Blom). Ayer Co Pubs.
Bourgeois, Patrick L. & Rosenthal, Sandra B. Thematic Studies in Phenomenology & Pragmatism. 206p. (Orig.). 1983. pap. 18.00x (ISBN 90-6032-238-X). Benjamins North Am.
Bourgeois, Patrick L., jt. auth. see Rosenthal, Sandra R.
Bourgeous, Virginia. Quest for Love & Self-Esteem: New Insights from Psychology & Religion. LC 76-29301. (Illus., Orig.). 1976. pap. 3.95 (ISBN 0-88290-070-6). Horizon Utah.
Bourgeron, J. P. & Balbo, P. J. Nude Nineteen Twenty-Five. LC 78-70678. (Illus.). 64p. 1978. pap. 7.50 (ISBN 0-87100-154-3, 2154). Morgan.
Bourgeron, J. P., ed. Nude Nineteen Hundred. 64p. 1980. pap. 7.50 (ISBN 0-87100-169-1, 2169). Morgan.
Bourges, Hector, jt. ed. see Velazques, Antonio.
Bourget, Paul, jt. ed. see Arnot, Robert.
Bourget, Paul C. Antigone: And Other Portraits of Women. facsimile ed. Marchant, William, tr. LC 71-150469. (Short Story Index Reprint Ser.). Repr. of 1898 ed. 18.00 (ISBN 0-8369-3809-7). Ayer Co Pubs.
--Domestic Dramas: (Drames De Famille) facsimile ed. Marchant, William, tr. LC 76-37259. (Short Story Index Reprint Ser.). Repr. of 1900 ed. 21.00 (ISBN 0-8369-4070-9). Ayer Co Pubs.
--Monica & Other Stories. facsimile ed. Marchant, William, tr. LC 77-106249. (Short Story Index Reprint Ser.). 1902. 18.00 (ISBN 0-8369-3286-2). Ayer Co Pubs.
Bourget-Besnier, Elizabeth, jt. auth. see Huysmans, Joris-Karl.
Bourghei, S. R., et al. Piety. Tavakoli, Amir, tr. from Persian. 1980. pap. 1.00 (ISBN 0-318-03827-7). Book-Dist-Ctr.
Bourgin, Georges. Histoire De La Commune. 1907. 10.00 (ISBN 0-404-07549-5). AMS Pr.
Bourgin, H. DeJaures a Blum: L'ecole Normale et la Republique. 524p. (Fr.). 1970. pap. 85.75 (ISBN 0-677-50375-X). Gordon.
Bourgin, R. D. Geometric Aspects of Convex Sets with the Radon-Nikodym Property. (Lecture Notes in Mathematics: Vol. 993). 474p. 1983. pap. 24.00 (ISBN 0-387-12296-6). Springer-Verlag.
Bourgoignie, jt. auth. see Fontaine.
Bourgoin, Edward. Foreign Languages & Your Career. rev. 3rd ed. i, 100p. 1984. pap. text ed. 7.95 (ISBN 0-9604126-2-X). Columbia Lang Serv.
Bourgoin, J. Arabic Geometrical Pattern & Design. (Illus.). 224p. 1973. pap. 6.50 (ISBN 0-486-22924-6). Dover.
--Design Discovery Coloring Book. (Illus.). 1976. pap. 2.95 (ISBN 0-486-23390-1). Dover.
Bourgoin, J. & Lannoo, M. Point Defects in Semiconductors II: Experimental Aspects. (Springer Series in Solid-State Sciences: Vol. 35). (Illus.). 295p. 1983. 37.00 (ISBN 0-387-11515-3). Springer-Verlag.
Bourgoin, J., jt. auth. see Lannoo, M.
Bourgoing, Jean De see Franz Joseph, I.
Bourgue, R., jt. auth. see Green, C.
Bourguignon, Erika. Possession. LC 76-524. (Cross-Cultural Themes Ser.). 96p. 1976. pap. text ed. 5.95x (ISBN 0-88316-524-4). Chandler & Sharp.
--Psychological Anthropology: An Introduction to Human Nature & Cultural Differences. LC 78-27125. 1979. text ed. 31.95 (ISBN 0-275-56620-X, HoltC). HR&W.
Bourguignon, Erika & Greenbaum, Lenora. Diversity & Homogeneity in World Societies. LC 73-86218. (Comparative Studies). (Illus.). 208p. 1973. 14.50 (ISBN 0-87536-329-6); pap. 7.00x (ISBN 0-87536-330-X). HRAFP.
Bourguignon, Erika, ed. Religion, Altered States of Consciousness, & Social Change. LC 72-8448. (Illus.). 399p. 1973. 12.50 (ISBN 0-8142-0167-9). Ohio St U Pr.
--A World of Women: Anthropological Studies of Women in the Societies of the World. LC 79-11844. 384p. 1980. 39.95 (ISBN 0-03-051221-2); pap. 17.95 (ISBN 0-03-051226-3). Praeger.
--A World of Women: Anthropological Studies of Women in the Societies of the World. 384p. 1980. 29.95x (ISBN 0-686-92297-2); pap. 14.95x (ISBN 0-686-98501-X). Bergin & Garvey.
Bourguignon, Henry J. The First Federal Court: The Federal Appellate Prize Court of the American Revolution, 1775-1787. LC 77-79209. (Memoirs Ser.: Vol. 122). 1977. 12.00 (ISBN 0-87169-122-1). Am Philos.
Bourguina, A. M. Russian Social Democracy: The Menshevik Movement - a Bibliography. LC 68-21035. (Bibliographical Ser.: No. 36). (Rus). 1968. 13.95x (ISBN 0-8179-2361-6). Hoover Inst Pr.
Bourhill, E. J. & Drake, J. B. Fairy Tales from South Africa. LC 78-67690. (The Folktale). (Illus.). Repr. of 1908 ed. 25.50 (ISBN 0-404-16058-1). AMS Pr.
Bouriant, M. U. Memoires: Publies par les Membres de la Mission Archeologique Francaise au Caire, 2 Vols. (French & Arabic.). 1979. 80.00x set (ISBN 0-86685-333-2). Intl Bk Ctr.
Bourinot, J. G. Federal Government in Canada. pap. 18.00 (ISBN 0-384-05312-2). Johnson Repr.
--Local Government in Canada: A Historical Study. pap. 9.00 (ISBN 0-384-05311-4). Johnson Repr.
--The Story of Canada. 1896. 45.00 (ISBN 0-932062-25-3). Sharon Hill.
Bourinot, John G. Federal Government in Canada. LC 78-63791. (Johns Hopkins University. Studies in the Social Sciences. Seventh Ser. 1889: 10-12). Repr. of 1889 ed. 13.25 (ISBN 0-404-61056-0). AMS Pr.
--Local Government in Canada: An Historical Study. LC 78-63771. (Johns Hopkins University. Studies in the Social Sciences. Fifth Ser. 1887: 5-6). Repr. of 1887 ed. 11.50 (ISBN 0-404-61038-2). AMS Pr.
--Parliamentary Procedure & Practice in the Dominion of Canada. 816p. 1971. Repr. of 1884 ed. 75.00x (ISBN 0-7165-2021-4, Pub. by Irish Academic Pr). Biblio Dist.
Bourjaily, Vance. Confessions of a Spent Youth. 1986. price not set (ISBN 0-87795-775-4). Arbor Hse.
--The Unnatural Enemy. LC 84-8640. (Illus.). 181p. 1984. pap. 6.95 (ISBN 0-8165-0884-4). U of Ariz Pr.
Bourjault, Alain. Realisation d'un Systeme Hybride de Simulation Dynamique en Temps Reel des Phenomenes Acoustiques au Sein du Conduit Vocal. (Hamuger Phonetische beitrage (HBP) Sers: 31). 120p. (Ger.). 1979. pap. 12.00x (ISBN 3-87118-407-1). Benjamins North AM.
Bourke, D. O. French-English Horticultural Dictionary. 196p. 1974. 59.00x (ISBN 0-85198-308-1, Pub. by CAB Bks England). State Mutual Bk.
--Horticultural Dictionary: French-English. (Fr. & Eng.). 1974. 49.95 (ISBN 0-85198-308-1, M-9713). French & Eur.
Bourke, Dale H. You Can Make Your Dreams Come True. 160p. 1984. 8.95 (ISBN 0-8007-1216-1). Revell.
Bourke, John. Baroque Churches of Central Europe. (Illus.). 1978. pap. 10.95 (ISBN 0-571-10689-7). Faber & Faber.

Bourke, John G. General Crook in the Indian Country. Bd. with A Scout with the Buffalo Soldiers. Remington, Frederic. LC 78-11630. (Wild & Woolly West Ser.: No. 27). (Illus.). 44p. 1973. 8.00 (ISBN 0-910584-36-2); pap. 1.50 (ISBN 0-910584-70-2). Filter.
--The Medicine Men of the Apache. LC 71-175003. (Illus.). 150p. 13.50 (ISBN 0-87026-049-9). Westernlore.
--The Medicine Men of the Apache: A Paper from the Ninth Annual Report of the Bureau of American Ethnology 1887-1888. LC 77-135517. (Beautiful Rio Grande Classics Ser.). (Illus.). 187p. 1983. Repr. of 1892 ed. casebound 20.00 (ISBN 0-87380-050-8). Rio Grande.
--On the Border with Crook. LC 74-155699. viii, 491p. 1971. pap. 10.95 (ISBN 0-8032-5741-4, BB 535, Bison). U of Nebr Pr.
--Scatalogic Rites of All Nations. Repr. of 1891 ed. 26.00 (ISBN 0-384-05310-6). Johnson Repr.
--The Snake-Dance of the Moquis of Arizona. LC 84-16379. (Illus.). 371p. 1984. pap. 10.95 (ISBN 0-8165-0872-0). U of Ariz Pr.
Bourke, Julia, ed. Ritual: Thematic Studies in Architecture. (Princeton Journal: Vol. 1). 192p. 1983. pap. text ed. 15.00 (ISBN 0-910413-02-9). Princeton Arch.
Bourke, Myles M. Job. (Bible Ser.). Pt. 1. pap. 1.00 (ISBN 0-8091-5073-5); Pt. 2. pap. 1.00 (ISBN 0-8091-5074-3). Paulist Pr.
Bourke, P. Climatic Aspects of the Possible Establishment of the Japanese Beetle in Europe. (Technical Note Ser.: No. 41). 9p. 1961. pap. 11.00 (ISBN 0-685-57275-7, W16, WMO). Unipub.
Bourke, P. Austin. Forecasting from Weather Data of Potato Blight & Other Plant Diseases & Pests. (Technical Note Ser.). 1955. pap. 4.00 (ISBN 0-685-22304-3, W4, WMO). Unipub.
Bourke, Richard S. St. Petersburg & Moscow: A Visit to the Court of the Czar. LC 70-115508. (Russia Observed, Series 1). 1970. Repr. of 1846 ed. 29.00 (ISBN 0-405-03005-3). Ayer Co Pubs.
Bourke, V., ed. see Aquinas, Thomas.
Bourke, Vernon J. Saint Thomas & the Greek Moralists. (Aquinas Lecture). 1947. 7.95 (ISBN 0-87462-111-9). Marquette.
Bourke, Vernon J., compiled by. Thomistic Bibliography: 1920-1940. 312p. 1945. lib. bdg. 25.00 (ISBN 0-915144-96-4). Hackett Pub.
Bourke, Vernon J., commentary by see Augustine, Saint.
Bourke, Vernon J., jt. ed. see Miethe, Terry L.
Bourke, Vernon J. see Thomas Aquinas, St.
Bourke-White, M. & Caldwell, E. Say, Is This the U. S. A. LC 77-9598. (Photography Ser.). (Illus.). 1977. lib. bdg. 32.50 (ISBN 0-306-77434-8); pap. 8.95 (ISBN 0-306-80071-3). Da Capo.
Bourke-White, Margaret. Eyes on Russia. LC 79-39515. 1968. Repr. of 1931 ed. 27.50 (ISBN 0-404-00939-5). AMS Pr.
Bourke-White, Margaret, jt. auth. see Caldwell, Erskine.
Bourland, Caroline B. The Short Story in Spain in the Seventeenth Century, with a Bibliography of the Novela from 1576-1700. LC 73-170183. 1927. 21.00 (ISBN 0-8337-4498-4). B Franklin.
Bourland, Gary N. An Executive Primer: The Management Club. 13p. 1983. saddle-stapled 5.95x (ISBN 0-9609350-0-2). Management Club.
--Help for Drug & Alcohol Abuse: Dallas Area Directory, 1986. 1985. price not set (ISBN 0-9609350-1-0, Pub. by Bourland Publishing). Management Club.
Bourland, George. Refugees from Nowhere. pap. 0.75 (ISBN 0-912136-04-9); pap. 5.00x signed ed. (ISBN 0-685-01070-8). Twowindows Pr.
Bourland, W. George. Who Gets the Antelope's Liver? 12.95 (ISBN 0-686-37633-1). Harp & Thistle.
Bourl'Honne, P. George Eliot: Essai de Biographie Intellectuelle et Morale, 1819-1854. LC 76-148754. Repr. of 1933 ed. 12.50 (ISBN 0-404-08727-2). AMS Pr.
Bourliere, F. Assessment of Biological Age in Man. (Public Health Papers Ser: No. 37). 67p. 1970. pap. 2.80 (ISBN 92-4-130037-X, 60). World Health.
--Tropical Savannas. (Ecosystems of the World Ser.: Vol. 13). 730p. 1983. 198.00 (ISBN 0-444-42035-5). Elsevier.
Bourman, Anatole. Tragedy of Nijinsky. LC 70-98822. Repr. of 1936 ed. lib. bdg. 29.75x (ISBN 0-8371-2965-6, BOTN). Greenwood.
Bourn, Colin. Developments in American Adult & Continuing Education. 1982. 30.00x (ISBN 0-686-45702-1, Pub. by Natl Inst Adult Ed England). State Mutual Bk.
Bourn, Grant L. Advertiser's Copy Prompter. 28p. 1985. pap. 5.00 (ISBN 0-931061-07-5). Mail Trade.
Bourn, Michael, jt. auth. see Stoney, P. J.
Bourne, jt. auth. see Green.
Bourne, jt. auth. see Newberger.
Bourne, A., jt. ed. see Steele, F.
Bourne, A. J., jt. auth. see Green, A. E.
Bourne, Bill & Bourne, Marjorie. Europe A La Carte. Svendsen, Etta, ed. LC 83-23359. (Illus.). 224p. 1984. pap. 9.95 (ISBN 0-915243-02-4). Volare Bks.
Bourne, C. B., ed. The Canadian Yearbook of International Law; Annuaire Canadien de Droit International, 1982, Vol. XX. 432p. (Eng., Fr.). 1983. 45.00 (Pub. by U of BC). Intl Spec Bk.
Bourne, Caroline. On Rapture's Wing. pap. 3.75 (ISBN 0-8217-1352-3). Zebra.
--Wild Southern Rose. 1985. pap. 3.75 (ISBN 0-8217-1603-4). Zebra.
Bourne, D. & Kendall, P. Vector Analysis. 1982. pap. 19.95 (ISBN 0-442-30743-8). Van Nos Reinhold.
Bourne, Douglas J., ed. New Uses of Sulfur-II. LC 78-1004. (Advances in Chemistry Ser.: No. 165). 1978. 29.95 (ISBN 0-8412-0391-1). Am Chemical.
Bourne, Edward E. The History of Wells, & Kennebunk, Maine. 832p. 1984. 55.00 (ISBN 0-917890-43-4). Heritage Bk.
Bourne, Edward G. Essays in Historical Criticism. facs. ed. LC 67-23183. (Essay Index Reprint Ser). 1901. 21.00 (ISBN 0-8369-0228-9). Ayer Co Pubs.
--History of the Surplus Revenue of Eighteen Thirty-Seven. LC 68-58463. (Research & Source Ser.: No. 327). 1969. Repr. of 1885 ed. 16.50 (ISBN 0-8337-0342-0). B Franklin.
Bourne, Edward G., ed. Narratives of the Career of Hernando De Soto in the Conquest of Florida As Told by a Knight of Elvas, 2 Vols. Smith, Buckingham, tr. LC 72-2823. (American Explorers Ser.). (Illus.). Repr. of 1922 ed. Set. 60.00 (ISBN 0-404-54901-2). AMS Pr.
Bourne, Edward G., jt. ed. see Olson, Julius E.
Bourne, Eulalia. Nine Months Is a Year-At Baboquivari School. LC 68-57760. (Southwest Chronicles Ser). 270p. 1968. 7.50 (ISBN 0-8165-0067-3). U of Ariz Pr.
--Woman in Levi's. LC 66-27382. pap. 56.00 (ISBN 0-317-28054-6, 2025552). Bks Demand UMI.
Bourne, F. J., ed. The Mucosal Immune System: Proceedings of a Seminar in the EEC Program of Agricultural Research on Protection of the Young Animal Against Perinatal Diseases. 568p. 1981. 73.00 (ISBN 90-247-2528-3, Pub. by Martinus Nijhoff Netherlands). Kluwer Academic.
Bourne, F. J. & Gorman, N. T., eds. Advances in Veterinary Immunology, 1983. (Developments in Animal & Veterinary Sciences Ser.: Vol. 16). 260p. 1985. 66.75 (ISBN 0-444-42367-2). Elsevier.
Bourne, Frank C. History of the Romans. 1966. text ed. 21.95 (ISBN 0-669-22483-9). Heath.
Bourne, Frank C., abridged by see Gibbon, Edward.
Bourne, G. H. & Danielli, J. F. International Review of Cytology. Incl. Vol. 1. 1952. 85.00 (ISBN 0-12-364301-5); Vol. 2. 1953. 85.00 (ISBN 0-12-364302-3); Vol. 3. 1954. 85.00 (ISBN 0-12-364303-1); Vol. 4. 1955. 85.00 (ISBN 0-12-364304-X); Vol. 5. 1956. 85.00 (ISBN 0-12-364305-8); Vol. 6. 1957. 85.00 (ISBN 0-12-364306-6); Vol. 7. 1958. 85.00 (ISBN 0-12-364307-4); Vol. 8. 1959. 85.00 (ISBN 0-12-364308-2); Vol. 9. 1960. 85.00 (ISBN 0-12-364309-0); Vol. 10. 1961. 85.00 (ISBN 0-12-364310-4); Vol. 11. 1961. 85.00 (ISBN 0-12-364311-2); Vol. 12. 1962. 85.00 (ISBN 0-12-364312-0); Vol. 13. 1962. 85.00 (ISBN 0-12-364313-9); Vol. 14. 1963. 85.00 (ISBN 0-12-364314-7); Vol. 15. 1963. 85.00 (ISBN 0-12-364315-5); Vol. 16. 1964. 85.00 (ISBN 0-12-364316-3); Vol. 17. 85.00 (ISBN 0-12-364317-1); Vol. 18. 1965. 85.00 (ISBN 0-12-364318-X); Vol. 19. 1966. 85.00 (ISBN 0-12-364319-8); Vol. 20. 1966. 85.00 (ISBN 0-12-364320-1); Vol. 21. 1967. 85.00 (ISBN 0-12-364321-X); Vol. 22. Jeon, K., ed. 1967. 85.00 (ISBN 0-12-364322-8); Vol. 23. 1968. 85.00 (ISBN 0-12-364323-6); Vol. 24. 1968. 85.00 (ISBN 0-12-364324-4); Vol. 25. 1969. 85.00 (ISBN 0-12-364325-2); Vol. 26. 1969. 85.00 (ISBN 0-12-364326-0); Vol. 27. 1970. 85.00 (ISBN 0-12-364327-9); Vol. 28. 1970. 85.00 (ISBN 0-12-364328-7); Vol. 29. 1970. 85.00 (ISBN 0-12-364329-5). Acad Pr.
--International Review of Cytology. Incl. Vol. 30. 1971. 85.00 (ISBN 0-12-364330-9); Vol. 31. 1971. 85.00 (ISBN 0-12-364331-7); Vol. 32. 1972. 85.00 (ISBN 0-12-364332-5); Vol. 33. 1972. 85.00 (ISBN 0-12-364333-3); Vol. 34. 1973. 85.00 (ISBN 0-12-364334-1); Vol. 35. 1973. 85.00 (ISBN 0-12-364335-X); Vol. 36. 1973. 85.00 (ISBN 0-12-364336-8); Vol. 37. 1974. 85.00 (ISBN 0-12-364337-6); Vol. 38. 1974. 85.00 (ISBN 0-12-364338-4); Vol. 39. 1974. 85.00 (ISBN 0-12-364339-2); Vol. 40. Jones, R. N., ed. 1975. 85.00 (ISBN 0-12-364340-6); Vol. 41. Leibowitz, Paul J. & Schaechter, Moselio, eds. 1975. 85.00 (ISBN 0-12-364341-4); Vol. 42. Lozzio, Bismarck B. & Lozzio, Carmen, eds. 1975. 85.00 (ISBN 0-12-364342-2); Vol. 43. Mahler, Henry R. & Raff, Rudolf A., eds. 1976. 85.00 (ISBN 0-12-364343-0); Vol. 44. 1976. 85.00 (ISBN 0-12-364344-9); Vol. 45. 85.00 (ISBN 0-12-364345-7); Vol. 46. 1976. 85.00 (ISBN 0-12-364346-5); Vol. 47. 1976. 85.00 (ISBN 0-12-364347-3); Vol. 48. 1977. 85.00 (ISBN 0-12-364348-1); Vol. 49. 1977. 85.00 (ISBN 0-12-364349-X); Vol. 50. 1977. 85.00 (ISBN 0-12-364350-3). Acad Pr.
--International Review of Cytology, Vol. 69. (Serial Publications Ser.). 1981. 65.00 (ISBN 0-12-364469-0). Acad Pr.
--International Review of Cytology, Vol. 86. (Serial Publication). 1984. 49.50 (ISBN 0-12-364486-0). Acad Pr.
--International Review of Cytology, Vol. 87. (Serial Publication). 1984. 49.50 (ISBN 0-12-364487-9). Acad Pr.
--International Review of Cytology, Vol. 88. (Serial Publication). 1984. 60.00 (ISBN 0-12-364488-7). Acad Pr.
--International Review of Cytology, Vol. 89. (Serial Publication). 1984. 49.50 (ISBN 0-12-364489-5). Acad Pr.
--International Review of Cytology Supplement, No. 16. (Serial Publication). 1983. 44.00 (ISBN 0-12-364377-5). Acad Pr.
Bourne, G. H., ed. Aspects of Human & National Nutrition. (World Review of Nutrition & Dietetics: Vol. 41). (Illus.). xii, 260p. 1983. 100.00 (ISBN 3-8055-3591-0). S Karger.
--Aspects of Human Nutrition & Food Contaminants. (World Review of Nutritional Dietetics: Vol. 34). (Illus.). 1979. 70.75 (ISBN 3-8055-3069-2). S Karger.
--Chimpanzee: A Series of Volumes on the Chimpanzee, 6 vols. Incl. Vol. 1. Anatomy, Behavior, & Diseases of Chimpanzees. 1969. 58.75 (ISBN 3-8055-0721-6); Vol. 2. Physiology, Behavior, Serology, & Diseases of Chimpanzees. 1970. 58.75 (ISBN 3-8055-0722-4); Vol. 3. Immunology, Infections, Hormones, Anatomy, & Behavior. 1970. 58.75 (ISBN 3-8055-0723-2); Vol. 4. Behavior, Growth, & Pathology of Chimpanzees. 1971. 51.25 (ISBN 3-8055-1147-7); Vol. 5. Histology, Reproduction, & Restraint. 1972. 42.75 (ISBN 3-8055-1250-3); Vol. 6. Anatomy & Pathology with General Subject Index & Condensed Bibliographic Index. 1973. 51.50 (ISBN 3-8055-1403-4). (Illus.). Set. 292.00 (ISBN 3-8055-1631-2). S Karger.
--Human & Animal Nutrition. (World Review of Nutrition & Dietetics: Vol. 32). (Illus.). 1978. 63.00 (ISBN 3-8055-2855-8). S Karger.
--Human & Veterinary Nutrition. (World Review of Nutrition & Dietetics: Vol. 26). (Illus.). 1977. 70.75 (ISBN 3-8055-2392-0). S Karger.
--Human & Veterinary Nutrition, Biochemical Aspects of Nutrients. (World Review of Nutrition & Dietetics: Vol. 30). (Illus.). 1978. 63.00 (ISBN 3-8055-2789-6). S Karger.
--Human Nutrition & Animal Feeding. (World Review of Nutrition & Dietetics: Vol. 37). (Illus.). xii, 292p. 1981. 105.25 (ISBN 3-8055-2143-X). S Karger.
--Human Nutrition & Diet. (World Review of Nutrition & Dietetics: Vol. 36). (Illus.). x, 226p. 1981. 81.75 (ISBN 3-8055-1347-X). S Karger.
--Human Nutrition & Nutrition & Pesticides in Cattle. (World Review of Nutrition & Dietetics: Vol. 35). (Illus.). 238p. 1980. 81.75 (ISBN 3-8055-0442-X). S Karger.
--Minerals in Food & Nutritional Topics. (World Review of Nutrition & Dietetics: Vol. 46). (Illus.). xii, 260p. 1985. 93.75 (ISBN 3-8055-4058-2). S Karger.
--Nutrients & Energy. (World Review of Nutrition & Dietetics: Vol. 42). (Illus.). xii, 228p. 1983. 84.25 (ISBN 3-8055-3710-7). S Karger.
--Nutrition Education & Modern Concepts of Food Assimilation. (World Review of Nutrition & Dietetics: Vol. 40). (Illus.). xii, 192p. 1982. 69.50 (ISBN 3-8055-3519-8). S Karger.
--Nutrition in Disease & Development. (World Review of Nutrition & Dietetics: Vol. 39). (Illus.). x, 194p. 1982. 68.25 (ISBN 3-8055-3459-0). S Karger.
--Nutritional Considerations in a Changing World. (World Review of Nutrition & Dietetics: Vol. 44). (Illus.). x, 218p. 1984. 70.25 (ISBN 3-8055-3837-5). S Karger.
--Nutritional Problems & Education: Selected Topics. (World Review of Nutrition & Dietetics: Vol. 47). (Illus.). viii, 250p. 1986. 64.00 (ISBN 3-8055-4214-3). S Karger.
--Physiology & Social Nutrition & Nutritional Education. (World Review of Nutrition & Dietetics: Vol. 38). (Illus.). x, 230p. 1982. 69.50 (ISBN 3-8055-3048-X). S Karger.
--World Nutritional Determinants. (World Review of Nutrition & Dietetics: Vol. 45). (Illus.). x, 226p. 1984. 84.25 (ISBN 3-8055-3948-7). S Karger.
--World Review of Nutrition & Dietetics, Vol. 12. 1970. 81.75 (ISBN 3-8055-0663-5). S Karger.
--World Review of Nutrition & Dietetics, Vol. 13. 1971. 41.75 (ISBN 3-8055-1180-9). S Karger.
--World Review of Nutrition & Dietetics, Vol. 14. 1972. 57.25 (ISBN 3-8055-1282-1). S Karger.
--World Review of Nutrition & Dietetics, Vol. 15. (Illus.). 300p. 1972. 48.75 (ISBN 3-8055-1397-6). S Karger.
--World Review of Nutrition & Dietetics, Vol. 17. (Illus.). 300p. 1973. 61.50 (ISBN 3-8055-1336-4). S Karger.
--World Review of Nutrition & Dietetics, Vol. 18. 1973. 99.00 (ISBN 3-8055-1458-1). S Karger.
--World Review of Nutrition & Dietetics, Vol. 19. (Illus.). 319p. 1974. 70.25 (ISBN 3-8055-1589-8). S Karger.
--World Review of Nutrition & Dietetics, Vol. 20. (Illus.). 350p. 1975. 80.50 (ISBN 3-8055-1841-2). S Karger.
--World Review of Nutrition & Dietetics, Vol. 21. (Illus.). x, 327p. 1975. 81.00 (ISBN 3-8055-2133-2). S Karger.
--World Review of Nutrition & Dietetics, Vol. 22. (Illus.). 1975. 84.25 (ISBN 3-8055-2135-9). S Karger.
--World Review of Nutrition & Dietetics, Vol. 23. (Illus.). xii, 315p. 1975. 75.75 (ISBN 3-8055-2243-6). S Karger.
--World Review of Nutrition & Dietetics, Vol. 24. (Illus.). 250p. 1976. 64.75 (ISBN 3-8055-2344-0). S Karger.
--World Review of Nutrition & Dietetics, Vol. 25. (Illus.). 300p. 1976. 73.25 (ISBN 3-8055-2363-7). S Karger.
--World Review of Nutrition & Dietetics, Vol. 37: Human Nutrition & Animal Feeding. (Illus.). xii, 292p. 1981. 105.25 (ISBN 3-8055-2143-X). S Karger.
--World Review of Nutrition & Dietetics, Vol. 38: Physiology & Social Nutrition & Nutritional Education. (Illus.). x, 230p. 1981. 69.50 (ISBN 3-8055-3048-X). S Karger.
Bourne, G. H. & Cama, H. R., eds. Vitamin & Carrier Functions of Polyprenoids. (World Review of Nutrition & Dietetics: Vol. 31). (Illus.). 1978. 58.75 (ISBN 3-8055-2801-9). S Karger.
Bourne, G. H. & Danielli, J. F., eds. International Review of Cytology, Vol. 71. 1981. 65.00 (ISBN 0-12-364471-2). Acad Pr.
--International Review of Cytology, Vol. 78. 360p. 1982. 55.00 (ISBN 0-12-364478-X). Acad Pr.
--International Review of Cytology, Vol. 79. 315p. 1982. 49.50 (ISBN 0-12-364479-8). Acad Pr.
--International Review of Cytology, Vol. 80. 322p. 1982. 49.50 (ISBN 0-12-364480-1). Acad Pr.
--International Review of Cytology, Vol. 84. (Serial Publication). 1983. 55.00 (ISBN 0-12-364484-4). Acad pr.
--International Review of Cytology, Vol. 85. (Serial Publication). 1983. 46.00 (ISBN 0-12-364485-2). Acad Pr.
--International Review of Cytology, Vol. 90. (Serial Publication). 1984. 52.50 (ISBN 0-12-364490-9). Acad Pr.
--International Review of Cytology: Supplements. Incl. Suppl. 1. Microbodies & Related Particles. Hruban, Z. & Rechcigl, M. 1969. 60.00 (ISBN 0-12-364361-9); Suppl. 2. Cellular Mechanisms of Chromosome Distribution. Luykx, Peter, ed. 1970. 60.00 (ISBN 0-12-364362-7); Suppl. 3. Spindle Dynamics & Chromosome Movements. Bajer, Andrew S. & Mole-Bajer, J. 1972. 70.00 (ISBN 0-12-364363-5). Acad Pr.
--International Review of Cytology, Vol. 91: Membranes. (Serial Publications). 1984. 36.50 (ISBN 0-12-364491-7). Acad Pr.
--International Review of Cytology, Vol. 92. (Serial Publications). 1984. 36.50 (ISBN 0-12-364492-5). Acad Pr.
Bourne, G. H. & Muggleton-Harris, Audrey L., eds. International Review of Cytology: Supplement 12. (Serial Publication). 1981. 65.00 (ISBN 0-12-364373-2). Acad Pr.
Bourne, Geoffrey, ed. The Biochemistry & Physiology of Bone, 4 vols. 2nd ed. Vol. 1 1972. 70.00 (ISBN 0-12-119201-6); Vol. 2 1972. 70.00 (ISBN 0-12-119202-4); Vol. 3 1972. 75.00 (ISBN 0-12-119203-2); Vol. 4 1976. 80.00 (ISBN 0-12-119204-0). Acad Pr.
--International Review of Cytology, Vol. 96. (Serial Publication). Date not set. price not set (ISBN 0-12-364496-8). Acad Pr.
Bourne, Geoffrey & Danielli, J. F., eds. International Review of Cytology, Vol. 83. (Serial Publication). 1983. 47.50 (ISBN 0-12-364483-6). Acad Pr.
Bourne, Geoffrey & Danielli, James, eds. International Review of Cytology. LC 52-5203. (Serial Publication). 1982. 55.00 ea. Vol. 74 (ISBN 0-12-364474-7). Vol. 75 (ISBN 0-12-364475-5). Acad Pr.
--International Review of Cytology, Vol. 72. (Serial Publication). 1981. 65.00 (ISBN 0-12-364472-0). Acad Pr.
--International Review of Cytology Supplement, No. 14. (Serial Publication). 1983. 46.50 (ISBN 0-12-364375-9). Acad Pr.
Bourne, Geoffrey & Giles, Kenneth, eds. International Review of Cytology: Supplement 13, Biology of Rhizobiaceae. (Serial Publication). 1981. 52.50 (ISBN 0-12-364374-0). Acad Pr.
Bourne, Geoffrey H., ed. Hearts & Heart-Like Organs: Comparative Anatomy & Development, Vol. I. LC 80-760. 1980. 67.50 (ISBN 0-12-119401-9). Acad Pr.
--Hearts & Heart-Like Organs, Vol. 2: Physiology. LC 80-18121. 1980. 77.00 (ISBN 0-12-119402-7). Acad Pr.
--Hearts & Heart-Like Organs: Vol. 3, Physiology. 1980. 75.00 (ISBN 0-12-119403-5). Acad Pr.
--Human & National Nutrition. 282p. 1983. 139.00. Transaction Bks.
--Non-Human Primates & Medical Research. 1973. 70.00 (ISBN 0-12-119150-8). Acad Pr.
--Nutritional Considerations in a Changing World. 218p. 1985. 99.00. Transaction Bks.
--Some Aspects of Human & Veterinary Nutrition. (World Review of Nutrition & Dietetics: Vol. 28). 1978. 68.75 (ISBN 3-8055-2672-5). S Karger.
--Some Special Aspects of Nutrition. (World Review of Nutrition & Dietetics: Vol. 33). (Illus.). 1979. 67.25 (ISBN 3-8055-2942-2). S Karger.

--The Structure & Function of Nervous Tissue. Incl. Vol. 1. 1968. 95.00 (ISBN 0-12-119281-4); Vol. 2. 1969. 95.00 (ISBN 0-12-119282-2); Vol. 3. 1969. 95.00 (ISBN 0-12-119283-0); Vol. 4. 1972. 95.00 (ISBN 0-12-119284-9); Vol. 5. 1972. 95.00 (ISBN 0-12-119285-7); Vol. 6. 1972. 95.00 (ISBN 0-12-119286-5). Acad Pr.

--World Nutritional Determinants. 237p. 1985. 118.75. Transaction Bks.

Bourne, Geoffrey H. & Danielli, James F., eds. International Review of Cytology, Vol. 58. 1979. 70.00 (ISBN 0-12-364358-9). Acad Pr.

--International Review of Cytology, Vol. 59. LC 52-5203. 1979. 65.00 (ISBN 0-12-364359-7). Acad Pr.

--International Review of Cytology, Vol. 60. 1979. 65.00 (ISBN 0-12-364360-0). Acad Pr.

--International Review of Cytology, Vol. 61. LC 52-5203. 1979. 75.00 (ISBN 0-12-364461-5). Acad Pr.

--International Review of Cytology, Vol. 62. LC 52-5203. (Serial Publication). 1980. 75.00 (ISBN 0-12-364462-3). Acad Pr.

--International Review of Cytology, Vol. 63. LC 52-5203. (Serial Publication). 1980. 75.00 (ISBN 0-12-364463-1). Acad Pr.

--International Review of Cytology, Vol. 64. LC 52-5203. 1980. 75.00 (ISBN 0-12-364464-X). Acad Pr.

--International Review of Cytology, Vol. 65. 1980. 65.00 (ISBN 0-12-364465-8). Acad Pr.

--International Review of Cytology, Vol. 66. (Serial Pub.). 1980. 65.00 (ISBN 0-12-364466-6). Acad Pr.

--International Review of Cytology, Vol. 67. (Serial Publication). 1980. 65.00 (ISBN 0-12-364467-4). Acad Pr.

--International Review of Cytology, Vol. 68. 1980. 65.00 (ISBN 0-12-364468-2). Acad Pr.

--International Review of Cytology, Vol. 70. (Serial Publication). 1981. 65.00 (ISBN 0-12-364470-4). Acad Pr.

--International Review of Cytology, Vol. 77. 284p. 1982. 47.50 (ISBN 0-12-364477-1). Acad Pr.

--International Review of Cytology, Vol. 97. (Serial Publication). Date not set. price not set (ISBN 0-12-364497-6). Acad Pr.

Bourne, Geoffrey H., jt. ed. see Sandler, Maurice.

Bourne, Geoffrey H., et al. International Review of Cytology, Vol. 82. (Serial Publication). 1983. 47.50 (ISBN 0-12-364482-8). Acad Pr.

Bourne, Geoggrey H. & Danielli, James F., eds. International Review of Cytology, Vol. 81. 1983. 43.50 (ISBN 0-12-364481-X). Acad Pr.

Bourne, George. Book & Slavery Irreconcilable. LC 76-82176. (Anti-Slavery Crusade in America Ser). 1969. Repr. of 1816 ed. 14.00 (ISBN 0-405-00615-2). Ayer Co Pubs.

--Picture of Slavery in the United States. LC 74-92420. (Illus.). 228p. 1972. Repr. of 1834 ed. 29.00 (ISBN 0-403-00179-X). Scholarly.

--Slavery Illustrated in Its Effects Upon Woman & Domestic Society. LC 72-6480. (Black Heritage Library Collection Ser). 1972. Repr. of 1837 ed. 13.50 (ISBN 0-8369-9174-5). Ayer Co Pubs.

Bourne, George, ed. Spirit of the Public Journals Or, Beauties of the American Newspapers. LC 74-125679. (American Journalists Ser). 1970. Repr. of 1806 ed. 18.00 (ISBN 0-405-01654-9). Ayer Co Pubs.

Bourne, Gordon, jt. ed. see Stallworthy, John.

Bourne, H. & Danielli, James F., eds. International Review of Cytology, Vol. 73. LC 52-52033. 1981. 65.00 (ISBN 0-12-364473-9). Acad Pr.

Bourne, H. C., ed. Some Aspects of Human Nutrition. (World Review of Nutrition & Dietetics: Vol. 27). 1977. 48.75 (ISBN 3-8055-2393-9). S Karger.

Bourne, H. R. English Merchants: Memoirs in Illustration of the Progress of British Commerce, 2 Vols. in 1. LC 14-5863. 1866. 51.00 (ISBN 0-527-10400-0). Kraus Repr.

--Sir Philip Sidney: Type of English Chivalry in the Elizabethan Age. 1973. Repr. of 1889 ed. 30.00 (ISBN 0-8274-0070-5). R West.

Bourne, Henry R. Sir Philip Sidney. LC 73-14433. (Heroes of the Nation Ser.). Repr. of 1901 ed. 30.00 (ISBN 0-404-58252-4). AMS Pr.

Bourne, Joanna W. Her Ladyship's Companion. (Regency Romance Ser.). 224p. 1983. pap. 2.75 (ISBN 0-380-81596-6, 81596-6). Avon.

Bourne, John C. History & Description of the Great Western Railway. LC 78-83361. (Illus.). Repr. of 1846 ed. lib. bdg. 50.00x (ISBN 0-678-05507-6). Kelley.

Bourne, John R. Laboratory Minicomputing. LC 80-70668. (Notes & Reports in Computer Science & Applied Mathematics Ser.: Vol. I). 1981. 31.00 (ISBN 0-12-119080-3). Acad Pr.

Bourne, K. Palmerston. (Illus.). 750p. 1982. 24.95 (ISBN 0-02-903740-9). Macmillan.

Bourne, K. & Watt, D. C., eds. Studies in International History. 460p. 1967. 28.00 (ISBN 0-208-00406-8, Archon). Shoe String.

Bourne, Kenneth. Palmerston: The Early Years, Seventeen Eighty-Four to Eighteen Forty-One. 1982. 24.95 (ISBN 0-02-903740-9). Free Pr.

Bourne, Kenneth, ed. The Letters of the Third Viscount Palmerston to Laurence & Elizabeth Sulivan: 1804-1863. (Royal Historical Society: Camden Society Fourth Ser.: Vol. 23). 350p. 1979. 20.00x (ISBN 0-8476-3306-3). Rowman.

--The Letters of the Third Viscount Palmerston to Laurence & Elizabeth Sulivan 1804-1863. (Royal Historical Society: Camden Fourth: Vol. 23). 350p. 1979. 15.00 (ISBN 0-901050-55-5, BAB 03306, Pub. by Boydell & Brewer). Longwood Pub Group.

Bourne, Kenneth, et al, eds. British Documents on Foreign Affairs: Reports & Papers from the Foreign Office Confidential Print-Russia, 1859-1914, 6 Vols. LC 82-21722. 2285p. 1983. Set. 420.00 (ISBN 0-89093-600-5). U Pubns Amer.

Bourne, L. S. Urban Systems-Strategies for Regulation. (Illus.). 1975. pap. 15.95x (ISBN 0-19-874055-7). Oxford U Pr.

Bourne, L. S., jt. ed. see Dziewonski, K.

Bourne, Larry S. Geography of Housing. LC 80-19908. (Scripta Series in Geography). 288p. 1981. 49.95x (ISBN 0-470-27058-6); pap. 24.95x (ISBN 0-470-27059-4). Halsted Pr.

--Private Redevelopment of the Central City: Spacial Processes of Structural Change in the City of Toronto. LC 66-30638. (Research Papers Ser.: No. 112). 199p. 1967. pap. 10.00 (ISBN 0-89065-020-9). U Chicago Dept Geog.

Bourne, Larry S., ed. Internal Structure of the City: Readings on Urban Growth, Form, & Policy. 2nd ed. (Illus., Orig.). 1982. pap. text ed. 15.95x (ISBN 0-19-503032-X). Oxford U Pr.

Bourne, Larry S. & Hitchcock, John R., eds. Urban Housing Markets: Recent Directions in Research & Policy. (Orig.). 1979. pap. 17.50x (ISBN 0-8020-2339-8). U of Toronto Pr.

Bourne, Larry S. & Simmons, James W., eds. Systems of Cities: Readings on Structure Growth & Policy. (Illus.). 1978. pap. text ed. 15.95x (ISBN 0-19-502264-5). Oxford U Pr.

Bourne, Larry S., et al, eds. Urban Futures for Central Canada: Perspectives on Forecasting Urban Growth & Form. LC 73-92297. pap. 94.00 (ISBN 0-317-26899-6, 2023595). Bks Demand UMI.

Bourne, Lyle E., et al. Cognitive Processes. 2nd ed. (Illus.). 464p. 1986. text ed. 28.95 (ISBN 0-13-139627-7). P-H.

Bourne, M., et al. El Espanol: La Teoria y la Practica. 2nd ed. 1978. pap. text ed. 19.95 (ISBN 0-03-022421-7). HR&W.

Bourne, Malcolm. Food Texture Seven Viscosity: Concepts & Measurement. (Food Science & Technology). 312p. 1982. 39.00 (ISBN 0-12-119060-9). Acad Pr.

Bourne, Marjorie, jt. auth. see Bourne, Bill.

Bourne, Miriam A. The Ladies of Castine. (Illus.). 224p. 1986. 19.50 (ISBN 0-87795-729-0). Arbor Hse.

--Raccoons Are for Loving. LC 68-23660. (Illus.). (ps-4). 1968. PLB 5.39 (ISBN 0-394-91556-9). Random.

--Uncle George Washington & Harriot's Guitar. (Illus.). 64p. (gr. 3-6). 1983. pap. 8.95 (ISBN 0-698-20573-1, Coward). Putnam Pub Group.

Bourne, Miriam Anne. White House Children. 69p. 3.95 (ISBN 0-317-34940-6). Mt Vernon Ladies.

Bourne, Nina, ed. see Millhauser, Steven.

Bourne, P. G., ed. Psychology & Physiology of Stress. 1969. 50.50 (ISBN 0-12-119550-3). Acad Pr.

Bourne, Peter D., ed. Acute Drug Abuse Emergencies: A Treatment Manual. 1976. 49.50 (ISBN 0-12-119560-0). Acad Pr.

Bourne, Peter G. & Fox, Ruth. Alcoholism: Progress in Research & Treatment. 439p. 1973. 34.50 (ISBN 0-318-15290-8). Natl Coun Alcoholism.

Bourne, Peter G., ed. Addiction. 1974. 50.50 (ISBN 0-12-119535-X). Acad Pr.

--Water Resource Development: Economic & Sociological Perspectives. 1984. 45.00 (ISBN 0-12-119580-5). Acad Pr.

Bourne, Peter G. & Fox, Ruth, eds. Alcoholism: Progress in Research & Treatment. 1973. 65.00 (ISBN 0-12-119540-6). Acad Pr.

Bourne, Randolph. History of a Literary Radical & Other Essays. LC 69-17713. 1969. Repr. of 1920 ed. 12.00x (ISBN 0-8196-0225-6). Biblo.

--Youth & Life. 59.95 (ISBN 0-8490-1346-1). Gordon Pr.

Bourne, Randolph S. Youth & Life. facs. ed. LC 67-23184. (Essay Index Reprint Ser). 1913. 21.50 (ISBN 0-8369-0229-7). Ayer Co Pubs.

--Youth & Life. LC 75-147143. (Philosophy Monographs: No. 74). 1971. Repr. of 1913 ed. lib. bdg. 21.00 (ISBN 0-8337-0343-9). B Franklin.

Bourne, Richard & Levin, Jack. Social Problems: Causes, Consequences, Interventions. (Illus.). 500p. 1983. text ed. 20.95 (ISBN 0-314-69661-X); tchrs.' manual avail. (ISBN 0-314-71081-7). West Pub.

Bourne, Richard & MacArthur, Brian. Struggle for Education. LC 79-136012. 1971. 20.00 (ISBN 0-8022-2041-X). Philos Lib.

Bourne, Richard & Newberger, Eli H., eds. Critical Perspectives on Child Abuse. LC 77-18565. (Illus.). 1979. 25.00x (ISBN 0-669-02109-1). Lexington Bks.

Bourne, Richard B., et al. Artificial Insemination. LC 72-13433. (Illus.). 220p. 1972. text ed. 21.50x (ISBN 0-8422-7077-9). Irvington.

Bourne, Russell, ed. see Arundel, Jocelyn.

Bourne, Russell, ed. see Borland, Hal.

Bourne, Russell, ed. see D'Aulaire, Emily & D'Aulaire, Ola.

Bourne, Russell, ed. see Johnson, Fred.

Bourne, Russell, ed. see Wright, Louis B.

Bourne, Stanford. Under the Doctor-Studies in the Psychological Problems of Physiotherapists, Patients & Doctors. 211p. 1981. text ed. 38.50x (ISBN 0-86127-601-9, Pub. by Avebury England); pap. text ed. 23.50x (ISBN 0-86127-602-7). Humanities.

Bourne, T. W., jt. auth. see Twells, H. N.

Bourne, William. The Arte of Shooting in Great Ordnaunce. LC 77-25950. (English Experience Ser.: No. 117). 96p. 1969. Repr. of 1587 ed. 13.00 (ISBN 90-221-0117-7). Walter J Johnson.

--A Booke Called the Treasure for Travellers. LC 77-25950. (English Experience Ser.: No. 911). 276p. 1979. Repr. of 1578 ed. lib. bdg. 26.00 (ISBN 0-686-71071-1). Walter J Johnson.

Bourne, William O. History of the Public School Society of the City of New York. LC 79-165733. (American Education Ser, No. 2). 1971. Repr. of 1870 ed. 36.00 (ISBN 0-405-03601-9). Ayer Co Pubs.

Bournell, Clive & Thubron, Colin. The Royal Opera House: Covent Garden. 1984. pap. 17.95 (ISBN 0-241-11188-9, Pub. by Hamish Hamilton England). Merrimack Pub Cir.

Bourneuf, Jacques, jt. auth. see Domart, Andre.

Bourneuf, Jacques see Domart, Andre.

Bourneuf, Jacques, jt. ed. see Domart, Andre.

Bournonville, August. My Theatre Life. McAndrew, Patricia, tr. LC 78-27349. (Illus.). 1979. 40.00x (ISBN 0-8195-5035-3). Wesleyan U Pr.

Bournot, K. see Von Wiesner, J. & Von Regel, C.

Bournoutian, George A. Eastern Armenia in the Last Decade of Persian Rule, 1807-1828. (Studies in Near Eastern Culture & Society Ser., Vol. 5). 315p. 1982. osi 34.50x (ISBN 0-89003-123-1); pap. 29.00x (ISBN 0-89003-122-3). Undena Pubns.

Bourns, Phillips, jt. auth. see Casagrande, Louis B.

Bouros, Michael P. Getting into VSAM: An Introduction & Technical Reference. 456p. 1985. text ed. 34.95x (ISBN 0-471-81237-4, Pub. by Wiley-Interscience). Wiley.

Bourque, Edward H., ed. see American Association of Teachers of French.

Bourque, Janet, jt. auth. see LaChapelle, Dolores.

Bourque, Nina. The Best Trade of All. LC 83-7352. (Imagination Bks.). (Illus.). 32p. (gr. k-3). 1983. PLB 14.65g (ISBN 0-940742-33-0). Raintree Pubs.

--The Best Trade of All. LC 83-7352. (Imagination Clippers Ser.). (Illus.). 32p. (gr. k-3). 1984. PLB 27.97 (ISBN 0-8172-2280-4); cassette only 14.00 (ISBN 0-317-19659-6). Raintree Pubs.

Bourque, Susan C. & Divine, Donna R. Women Living Change. LC 84-25277. (Women in the Political Economy Ser.). 288p. 1985. 29.95 (ISBN 0-87722-369-6). Temple U Pr.

Bourque, Susan C. & Warren, Kay B. Women of the Andes. (Women & Culture Ser.; Patriarchy & Social Change in Two Peruvian Towns). 320p. 1981. text ed. 18.50x (ISBN 0-472-06330-8); pap. text ed. 9.50x (ISBN 0-472-09330-4). U of Mich Pr.

Bourquin, David R. The Work of Bruce McAllister: An Annotated Bibliography & Guide. (Bibliographies of Modern Authors: No. 10). 50p. 1985. lib. bdg. 19.95x (ISBN 0-89370-389-3); pap. text ed. 9.95x (ISBN 0-89370-489-X). Borgo Pr.

Bourrelly, P. Recherches Sur les Chrysophycees: Morphologie, Phylogenie, Systematique. (Illus.). 1971. Repr. of 1957 ed. 28.00 (ISBN 3-7682-0703-X). Lubrecht & Cramer.

Bourret, F. M. Ghana: The Road to Independence, 1919-1957. rev. ed. 1960. 20.00x (ISBN 0-8047-0400-7). Stanford U Pr.

Bourricaud, Francis. The Sociology of Talcott Parsons. Goldhammer, Arthur, tr. LC 81-1348. xvi, 326p. 1984. pap. 12.50x (ISBN 0-226-06756-4). U of Chicago Pr.

Bourrienne, Louis A. de see De Bourrienne, Louis A.

Boursin, Jean-Louis. DEMO: Dictionnaire Elementaire de Mathematiques Modernes. 320p. (Fr.). 1972. 21.95 (ISBN 0-686-56927-X, M-6045). French & Eur.

Bourso-Leland, Natalia, tr. see Flint, V. E., et al.

Bousard, Lorraine, jt. auth. see Wardell, Sandra.

Bouscaren, Anthony. Tshombe. 1967. pap. 0.95 (ISBN 0-912080-05-1). Guild Bks.

Bouscaren, Anthony J. Imperial Communism. LC 75-1341. 256p. 1975. Repr. of 1953 ed. lib. bdg. 27.50x (ISBN 0-8371-8009-0, BOIC). Greenwood.

Bouscaren, Anthony T. Government in American Society. Rev. ed. LC 82-11006. 402p. 1982. pap. text ed. 16.25 (ISBN 0-8191-2615-2). U Pr of Amer.

--The Security Aspects of Immigration Work. LC 59-12044. 1959. 10.95 (ISBN 0-87462-453-3). Marquette.

Bouscaren, Anthony T., ed. All Quiet on the Eastern Front: The Death of South Vietnam. LC 76-18443. 1976. 12.00 (ISBN 0-8159-5018-7); pap. 7.95 (ISBN 0-8159-5019-5). Devin.

Bousefield, Paul & Bousfield, W. R. The Mind & Its Mechanism with Special Reference to Ideo-Motor Action, Hypnosis, Habit & Instinct & the Lamarckian Theory of Evolution. 224p. 1982. Repr. of 1927 ed. text ed. 40.00 (ISBN 0-8495-0610-7). Arden Lib.

Bousfield, A. K. Homological Localization Towers for Groups & Pi-Modules. LC 77-3716. (Memoirs: No. 186). 68p. 1977. pap. 13.00 (ISBN 0-8218-2186-5, MEMO-186). Am Math.

Bousfield, A. K. & Gugenheim, V. K. On PL DeRham Theory & Rational Homotopy Type. LC 76-44398. (Memoirs: No. 179). 94p. 1976. pap. 13.00 (ISBN 0-8218-2179-2, MEMO-179). Am Math.

Bousfield, D., ed. Neurotransmitters in Action: Collection of Articles from Trends in NeuroScience. 346p. 1985. 21.00 (ISBN 0-444-80671-7). Elsevier.

Bousfield, E. L. Shallow-Water Gammaridean Amphipoda of New England. 17.50 (ISBN 0-8014-0726-5). Brown Bk.

Bousfield, I. J. & Callely, A. G., eds. Coryneform Bacteria. (Special Publication of the Society for General Microbiology). 1979. 37.50 (ISBN 0-12-119650-X). Acad Pr.

Bousfield, Shirley, jt. auth. see Wallace, Arthur.

Bousfield, W. R., jt. auth. see Bousefield, Paul.

Boush, G. Mallory, jt. ed. see Matsumara, Fumio.

Boushahla, Jo J. & Reidel-Geubtner, Virginia. The Dream Dictionary: The Key to Your Unconscious. 192p. 1983. 16.95 (ISBN 0-8298-0695-4); pap. 9.95 (ISBN 0-8298-0696-2). Pilgrim NY.

Bouska, V. Geochemistry of Coal. (Coal Science & Technology Ser.: Vol. 1). 1982. 64.00 (ISBN 0-444-99738-5). Elsevier.

Bousquet, Georges H. A French View of the Netherlands Indies. Lilienthal, Philip E., tr. from Fr. LC 75-30048. (Institute of Pacific Relations). Repr. of 1940 ed. 12.50 (ISBN 0-404-59510-3). AMS Pr.

Bousquet, M., jt. auth. see Maral, G.

Bousquet-Lefevre, Laure M. Recherches sur la condition de la femme Kabyle: La coutume et l'oeuvre francaise. LC 77-87660. Repr. of 1939 ed. 18.50 (ISBN 0-404-16404-8). AMS Pr.

Boussard, Jacques. Civilization of Charlemagne. (World University Library Ser.). (Illus., Orig.). 1968. pap. 3.95 (ISBN 0-07-006710-4). McGraw.

Boussel. History of Pharmacy. 1983. 75.00 (ISBN 0-686-43177-4). Thieme-Stratton.

Boussel, Patrice. Leonardo da Vinci. (Illus.). 195p. 1984. 65.00 (ISBN 0-933516-93-2). Alpine Bk Co.

Bousset, Wilhelm. The Antichrist Legend: A Chapter in Christian & Jewish Folklore. LC 79-8095. (Satanism Ser.). 344p. Repr. of 1896 ed. 37.50 (ISBN 0-404-18406-5). AMS Pr.

--The Antichrist Legend: A Chapter in Christian & Jewish Folklore. 1977. lib. bdg. 59.95 (ISBN 0-8490-1439-5). Gordon Pr.

Boussinot, R. L' Encyclopedie du Cinema: A-H, Vol. 1. (Fr.). 85.00 (ISBN 0-686-92236-0, F-79450). French & Eur.

--L' Encyclopedie du Cinema: I-Z, Vol. II. (Fr.). 85.00 (ISBN 0-686-92242-5, F-79451). French & Eur.

Bousson, Terry & Coulter, Philip B. Policy Evaluation for Local Governments. LC 84-93706. (Policy Studies Organization Series Publication). 264p. Date not set. 26.00. Assoc Faculty Pr.

Boustead, Alan. Writing Down Music. (Illus.). 1975. pap. 15.00 (ISBN 0-19-317104-X). Oxford U Pr.

Boustead, Hugh. The Wind of Morning. (Illus.). 240p. 1979. 9.95 (ISBN 0-7011-1314-6, Pub. by Chatto & Windus). Merrimack Pub Cir.

Boustead, I. & Hancock, G. F. Energy & Packaging. LC 81-6978. 519p. 1981. 117.95x (ISBN 0-470-27269-4). Halsted Pr.

--Handbook of Industrial Energy Analysis. LC 78-40636. 422p. 1979. 99.95x (ISBN 0-470-26492-6). Halsted Pr.

Boustead, I. & Lidgren, K., eds. Problems in Packaging: The Environmental Issue. LC 83-3743. (Series in Energy & Fuel Science: 1-624). 174p. 1984. text ed. 44.95x (ISBN 0-470-20068-5). Halsted Pr.

Boutas, V., ed. Women in Islam: Social Attitudes & Historical Perspectives. 224p. 1983. 30.00x (ISBN 0-7007-0154-0, Pub. by Curzon England). State Mutual Bk.

Boutell, C. R., jt. ed. see North, Sterling.

Boutell, Wayne S. Accounting for Anyone. (Illus.). 240p. 1982. pap. 17.95 (ISBN 0-13-001602-0). P-H.

Boutelle, Ann E. Thistle & Rose: A Study of Hugh MacDiamid's Poetry. LC 81-65859. 259p. 1981. 25.00 (ISBN 0-8387-5023-0). Bucknell U Pr.

Bouten, J. Mary Wollstonecraft & the Beginnings of Female Emancipation in France & England. 75.00 (ISBN 0-8490-0589-2). Gordon Pr.

Bouten, Jacob. Mary Wollstonecraft & the Beginnings of Female Emancipation in France & England. LC 75-33666. (Perspectives in European History Ser.: No. 2). 184p. 1975. Repr. of 1922 ed. lib. bdg. 19.50x (ISBN 0-87991-608-7). Porcupine Pr.

Bouterse, Wesley. Scriptural Light on Speaking in Tongues. 1980. pap. 1.25 (ISBN 0-86544-010-7). Salvation Army.

Bouterwek, Frederick. History of Spanish & Portugese Literature, 2 vols. 1823. Repr. 100.00 (ISBN 0-8274-2518-X). R West.

--History of Spanish Literature. 1847. Repr. 40.00 (ISBN 0-8274-2519-8). R West.

Bouterwek, K. W. Cademon's Des Angelsachsen Biblishce Dictungen, 2 Vols. 393p. 1983. Repr. of 1854 ed. Set. lib. bdg. 400.00 (ISBN 0-8495-0636-0). Arden Lib.

Boutet De Monvel, Louis B. & Guillemin, Victor. The Spectral Theory of Toeplitz Operators. LC 80-8538. (Annals of Mathematics Studies: No. 99). 222p. 1981. 20.00x (ISBN 0-691-08284-7); pap. 9.50x (ISBN 0-691-08279-0). Princeton U Pr.

Boutet de Monvel, Maurice. Joan of Arc. LC 80-5169. (Illus.). 64p. (gr. 7). 1980. Repr. of 1897 ed. 14.95 (ISBN 0-670-40735-6, Studio). Viking.

Boutette, M. & Karch, G. E. Charcoal: Small Scale Production & Use. 60p. pap. 6.50 (ISBN 3-528-02009-1, 990400298, Pub. by Vieweg & Sohn Germany). Heyden.

Bouthillette, Guy. Tidal Zones: A Guide to Plants & Animals Where the Sea Meets the Shore. Feller-Roth, Barbara, ed. (Maine Geographic Ser.). (Illus.). 48p. 1983. pap. 2.95 (ISBN 0-89933-053-3). DeLorme Pub.

Bouthillier, Patrick H. Hydraulic Tables for Water Supply & Drainage. LC 81-69115. (Illus.). 150p. 1981. pap. text ed. 17.50 (ISBN 0-250-40517-2). Butterworth.

Boutiere, Jean & Schutz, Alexander H., eds. Biographies des Troubadors, Textes Provencaux des 13e et 14e Siecles. (Fr). 1950. 29.00 (ISBN 0-8337-4000-8). B Franklin.

Boutiere, Jean, ed. see Albertet de Sestero.

Boutilier, James A., et al, eds. Mission, Church, & Sect in Oceania. (Asao Monograph: No. 6). (Illus.). 514p. 1984. lib. bdg. 34.50 (ISBN 0-8191-3837-1, Assoc Soc Anthro Oceania); pap. text ed. 20.50 (ISBN 0-8191-3838-X, Assoc Soc Anthro Oceania). U Pr of Amer.

Boutilier, Mary A. & SanGiovanni, Lucinda F. The Sporting Woman. LC 82-83147. 306p. 1983. text ed. 22.95x (ISBN 0-931250-35-8, BBOU0035). Human Kinetics.

Boutilier, Mary A., jt. auth. see Kelly, Rita M.

Boutin, Henri & Yip, Sidney. Molecular Spectroscopy with Neutrons. LC 68-22823. 1968. 27.50x (ISBN 0-262-02042-4). MIT Pr.

Boutin, Otto. The Gold Maker. (Orig.). 1981. pap. 1.95 (ISBN 0-8439-0923-4, Leisure Bks). Dorchester Pub Co.

Boutin, Otto J. A Catfish in the Bodoni: The Golden Age of Tramp Printer's. LC 70-141186. (Illus.). 1971. 4.00 (ISBN 0-87839-004-9). North Star.

Boutis, Victoria. Katy Did It. LC 81-1034. (Illus.). 96p. (gr. 3-5). 1982. 11.75 (ISBN 0-688-00688-4); PLB 11.88 (ISBN 0-688-00689-2). Greenwillow.

Boutman, Herbert J., et al, trs. see Stiller, Gunther.

Boutmy, E. J. & Danthine, A., eds. Teleinformatics Seventy-Nine: Proceedings of the International Cenference, Paris, June '79. 316p. 1979. 64.00 (ISBN 0-444-85349-9, North Holland). Elsevier.

Boutmy, Emile. Studies in Constitutional Law: France-England-United States. 2nd ed. Dicey, E. M., tr. xiv, 183p. 1982. Repr. of 1891 ed. lib. bdg. 22.50x (ISBN 0-8377-0332-8). Rothman.

Bouton, Bobbie & Marshall, Nancy. Home Games: Two Baseball Wives Speak Out. 272p. 1984. pap. 6.95 (ISBN 0-312-38847-0). St Martin.

Bouton, Jim. Ball Four, Plus Ball Five. rev. ed. LC 80-6165. 432p. 1981. 14.95 (ISBN 0-8128-2771-6). Stein & Day.

--Ball Four Plus Ball Five. 496p. 1984. pap. 3.95 (ISBN 0-8128-8016-1). Stein & Day.

--Ball Four Plus Ball Five: An Update, 1970-1980. LC 80-6165. (Illus.). 489p. 1982. pap. 10.95 (ISBN 0-8128-6146-9). Stein & Day.

Bouton, Marshall M. Agrarian Radicalism in South India. LC 85-3411. (Illus.). 336p. 1985. pap. 42.00x (ISBN 0-691-07686-3). Princeton U PR.

Bouton, Nathaniel, ed. see New Hampshire State Legislature.

Bouton, Thomas, jt. ed. see Henderson, J. Neil.

Boutros, Labib. Phoenician Sports - Their Influence on the Origin of the Olympic Games. (Semitohellenica Ser.). 150p. 1981. 19.00x (ISBN 90-70265-13-3, Pub. by Gieben Holland). Humanities.

Boutroux, Emile. The Contingency of the Laws of Nature. Rothwell, Fred, tr. 196p. 24.95 (ISBN 0-912050-50-0). Open Court.

--Science & Religion in Contemporary Philosophy. Nield, Jonathan, tr. 1979. Repr. of 1909 ed. lib. bdg. 35.00 (ISBN 0-8495-0540-2). Arden Lib.

--Science & Religion in Contemporary Philosophy. LC 70-102563. 1970. Repr. of 1909 ed. 31.50x (ISBN 0-8046-0723-0, Pub. by Kennikat). Assoc Faculty Pr.

Boutwell, George S. Reminiscences of Sixty Years in Public Affairs, 2 Vols. LC 68-28618. 1968. Repr. of 1902 ed. Set. lib. bdg. 37.50x (ISBN 0-8371-0322-3, BORS). Greenwood.

Boutwell, Jeffrey D. & Doty, Paul, eds. The Nuclear Confrontation in Europe. 233p. 1985. 27.95 (ISBN 0-86569-128-2). Auburn Hse.

Bouty, Michel. Dictionnaire des Oeuvres et Des Themes de la Litterature Francaise. 351p. (Fr.). 1972. pap. 14.95 (ISBN 0-686-56855-9, M-6633). French & Eur.

Bouuaert, Ignace C. Tax Problems of Cultural Foundations & of Patronage in the European Community. 128p. 1976. lib. bdg. 26.00 (ISBN 90-200-0474-3, Pub. by Kluwer Law Netherlands). Kluwer Academic.

Bouvard, Marguerite. The Intentional Community Movement: Building a New Moral World. LC 74-80593. 1975. 19.50x (ISBN 0-8046-9100-2, Pub. by Kennikat). Assoc Faculty Pr.

--Voices from an Island. LC 85-3831. 70p. 1985. 14.95 (ISBN 0-932576-25-7); pap. 6.95 (ISBN 0-932576-26-5). Breitenbush Bks.

Bouvard, Marguerite G., ed. Landscape & Exile. LC 84-61569. 152p. (Orig.). 1985. pap. 9.95 (ISBN 0-937672-16-5). Rowan Tree.

Bouve, Edward T. Centuries Apart. LC 76-42719. (Communal Societies in America Ser.). Repr. of 1894 ed. 28.50 (ISBN 0-404-60054-9). AMS Pr.

Bouve, Pauline C. Their Shadows Before: A Story of the Southampton Insurrection. facs. ed. LC 72-39078. (Black Heritage Library Collection). Repr. of 1899 ed. 16.50 (ISBN 0-8369-9016-1). Ayer Co Pubs.

Bouveresse, Jacques, jt. ed. see Parret, H. H.

Bouverot, P. Adaptation to Altitude-Hypoxia in Vertebrates. (Zoophysiology Ser.: Vol. 16). (Illus.). 195p. 1985. 35.00 (ISBN 0-387-13602-9). Springer-Verlag.

Bouvet, Francis. Bonnard: The Complete Graphic Work. (Illus.). 352p. 1981. 95.00 (ISBN 0-915346-74-5). A Wofsy Fine Arts.

Bouvier, Jean & Girault, Rene. L' Imperialisme Francais d'Avant 1914: Recueil De Textes. (Savoir Historique Ser.: No. 10). (Fr.). 1976. pap. text ed. 23.50x (ISBN 90-279-7992-8). Mouton.

Bouvier, Jean, et al. Le Mouvement Du Profit En France Au XIXe Siecle: Materiaux et Etudes. (Industrie et Artisanat: No. 1). 1965. pap. 27.60x (ISBN 90-279-6132-8). Mouton.

Bouvier, John. Bouvier's Law Dictionary & Concise Encyclopedia, 2 Vols. 8th ed. 3532p. 1984. Repr. of 1914 ed. lib. bdg. 95.00 (ISBN 0-89941-335-8). W S Hein.

Bouvier, Kathleen. To Jack, with Love. (Orig.). 1979. pap. 2.50 (ISBN 0-89083-528-4). Zebra.

Bouvier, Leon & Rao, Sethu. Socioreligious Factors in Fertility Decline. LC 75-26602. 224p. 1975. text ed. 25.00 prof ref (ISBN 0-88410-352-8). Ballinger Pub.

Bouvier, Leon F., jt. auth. see Weller, Robert H.

Bouvier, Nicolas. The Scorpion-Fish. Marsack, Robyn, tr. from Fr. 144p. 1985. 14.95 (ISBN 0-85635-551-8). Carcanet.

Bouvier Verlag Herbert Grundmann, ed. The Turn of the Century: German Literature & Art 1890-1915. 1982. 36.00x (ISBN 3-416-01588-6, Pub. by Bouvier Verlag Ger). State Mutual Bk.

Bouvier, Virginia M. Alliance or Compliance: Implications of the Chilean Experience for the Catholic Church in Latin America. LC 83-960. (Foreign & Comparative Studies Program, Latin American Ser.: No. 3). (Orig.). 1983. pap. text ed. 5.00x (ISBN 0-915984-94-6). Syracuse U Foreign Comp.

Bouwer, Herman. Groundwater Hydrology. (Environment Water & Resources Ser). (Illus.). 1978. text ed. 45.00x (ISBN 0-07-006715-5). McGraw.

Bouwhuis, Don G., jt. auth. see Bouma, Herman.

Bouwman, Vern. Telephone Plant Records. 7.00 (ISBN 0-317-06286-7). Telephony.

Bouwsma, O. K. Philosophical Essays. LC 82-70014. (Landmark Ed. Ser.). x, 209p. 1982. Repr. of 1965 ed. 18.95x (ISBN 0-8032-1179-1). U of Nebr Pr.

--Toward a New Sensibility: Essays of O. K. Bouwsma. Craft, J. L. & Hustwit, Ronald E., eds. LC 81-16117. xxii, 277p. 1982. 21.50x (ISBN 0-8032-1170-8). U of Nebr Pr.

--Without Proof or Evidence: Essays of O. K. Bouwsma. Craft, J. L. & Hustwit, Ronald E., eds. LC 83-10269. xvi, 161p. 1984. 19.50X (ISBN 0-8032-1174-0). U of Nebr Pr.

Bouwsma, Ward D. & Corle, Clyde G. Basic Mathematics For Elementary Teachers. LC 67-11887. pap. 88.00 (ISBN 0-317-08422-4, 2012448). BKs Demand UMI.

Bouwsma, William J. Concordia Mundi: The Career & Thought of Guillaume Postel, 1510-1581. LC 57-8622. (Historical Monographs Ser: No. 33). 1957. 20.00x (ISBN 0-674-15950-0). Harvard U Pr.

--The Culture of Renaissance Humanism. LC 73-75444. (AHA Pamphlets: No. 401). 60p. (Orig.). 1973. pap. text ed. 1.50 (ISBN 0-87229-013-1). Am Hist Assn.

--Venice & the Defense of Republican Liberty: Renaissance Values in the Age of the Counter Reformation. LC 68-14642. (Illus.). 1968. 47.50x (ISBN 0-520-00151-6). U of Cal Pr.

--Venice & the Defense of Republican Liberty: Renaissance Values in the Age of the Counter Reformation. (Cal Ser.: No. 694). (Illus.). 686p. 1984. pap. 11.95 (ISBN 0-520-05221-8). U of Cal Pr.

Bouyer, L. & Cawley, M. Christology. LC 83-4420. (Word & Spirit Ser.: Vol. V). 1983. pap. 7.00 (ISBN 0-932506-28-3). St Bedes Pubns.

Bouyer, Louis. The Church of God. Quinn, Charles U., tr. 1983. 25.00 (ISBN 0-686-45823-0). Franciscan Herald.

--Diccionario De Teologia. 4th ed. 672p. (Span.). 1977. 25.50 (ISBN 84-254-0377-4, S-14671). French & Eur.

--The Eternal Son. Inkel, Simone, Sr. & Laughlin, John F., trs. from Fr. LC 77-92090. 431p. 1980. pap. 6.95 (ISBN 0-87973-621-6, 621). Our Sunday Visitor.

--Eucharist: Theology & Spirituality of the Eucharist Prayer. Quinn, Charles U., tr. LC 68-17064. 1968. pap. 13.95 (ISBN 0-268-00498-6). U of Notre Dame Pr.

--A History of Christian Spirituality, 3 vols. 1977. pap. write for info. (ISBN 0-8164-2369-5, Pub. by Seabury). Winston Pr.

--A History of Christian Spirituality, Vol. 3. 1977. pap. write for info. (ISBN 0-8164-2374-1, Pub. by Seabury). Winston Pr.

--Liturgical Piety. (Liturgical Studies Ser). 1965. 10.95x (ISBN 0-268-00158-8). U of Notre Dame Pr.

--Liturgy & Architecture. 1967. 6.95x (ISBN 0-268-00159-6). U of Notre Dame Pr.

--Orthodox Spirituality & Protestant & Anglican Spirituality. (A History of Christian Spirituality Ser.: Vol. 3). 232p. 1982. pap. 9.95 (ISBN 0-8164-2374-1, Pub. by Seabury). Winston Pr.

--Rite & Man: Natural Sacredness & Christian Liturgy. Costelloe, Joseph, tr. 224p. 1985. pap. text ed. 12.00 (ISBN 0-8191-4340-5). U Pr of Amer.

--The Spirituality of the New Testament & the Fathers. (A History of Christian Spirituality Ser.: Vol. 1). 560p. 1982. pap. 13.95 (ISBN 0-8164-2372-5, Pub. by Seabury). Winston Pr.

--Woman in the Church. Teichert, Marilyn, tr. from Fr. LC 79-84878. Orig. Title: Mystere et Ministeres de la femme dans l'Eglise. 132p. (Orig.). 1979. pap. 7.95 (ISBN 0-89870-002-7). Ignatius Pr.

Bouygues, Claude, jt. auth. see Frautschi, Richard L.

Bouza, Anthony J. Police Intelligence: The Operations of an Investigative Unit. LC 75-8667. (AMS Studies in Criminal Justice: No. 2). 200p. 1976. 27.50 (ISBN 0-404-13138-7). AMS Pr.

Bouzek, J. The Aegean, Anatolia & Europe: Cultural Interrelations in the Second Millennium B.C. (Studies in Mediterranean Archaeology: Vol. xxix). 271p. 1985. pap. 67.75x (ISBN 0-317-18911-5, Pub. by Paul Astroms Sweden). Humanities.

Bouzinac, J. Les Doctrines economiques au dix-huitieme siecle, Jean-Francois Melon, economiste. LC 70-121597. (Research & Source Ser.: No. 499). (Fr). 1970. Repr. of 1906 ed. lib. bdg. 18.50 (ISBN 0-8337-0344-7). B Franklin.

Bova. Out of the Sun. 2.95 (ISBN 0-317-31878-0). Tor Bks.

--Winds of Alter. 6.95 (ISBN 0-317-31915-9). Tor Bks.

Bova & Dickson. Gremlins Go Home. pap. 2.75 (ISBN 0-317-31853-5). Tor Bks.

Bova, Ben. As on a Darkling Plain. 288p. 1985. pap. 2.95 (ISBN 0-8125-3200-7). Tor Bks.

--Assured Survival: How to Stop the Nuclear Arms Race. 341p. 1984. 15.95 (ISBN 0-395-36405-1). HM.

--The Astral Mirror. 288p. (Orig.). 1985. pap. 2.95 (ISBN 0-8125-3217-1, Dist. by Warner Pub Services & St. Martin). Tor Bks.

--City of Darkness. 176p. 1982. pap. 2.50 (ISBN 0-425-05774-7). Berkley Pub.

--Colony. 1983. pap. 3.95 (ISBN 0-671-46514-7, Timescape). PB.

--The Dueling Machine. 256p. 1984. pap. 2.50 (ISBN 0-425-06466-2). Berkley Pub.

--Escape Plus. 288p. (Orig.). 1984. pap. 2.95 (ISBN 0-8125-3212-0). Tor Bks.

--The Exiles Trilogy. 1983. pap. 2.95 (ISBN 0-425-07037-9). Berkley Pub.

--The High Road. 1983. pap. 3.95 (ISBN 0-671-45805-1). PB.

--Millenium. 304p. 1982. pap. 2.75 (ISBN 0-345-30248-6, Del Rey). Ballantine.

--Millennium. 1976. 8.95 (ISBN 0-394-49421-0). Random.

--Notes to a Science Fiction Writer. 1981. pap. 5.95 (ISBN 0-395-30521-7). HM.

--Orion. 432p. 1985. pap. 3.50 (ISBN 0-8125-3215-5). Tor Bks.

--Out of the Sun-Escape. 288p. (Orig.). 1984. pap. 2.95 (ISBN 0-8125-3210-4, Pinnacle Bks). Tor Bks.

--Privateers. 1985. 15.95 (ISBN 0-312-93604-4). Tor Bks.

--The Starcrossed. 224p. 1984. pap. 2.50 (ISBN 0-441-78046-6). Ace Bks.

--Viewpoint. (Boskone Bk.). (Illus.). 1977. 10.00 (ISBN 0-915368-14-5); finebound, 3/4 leather o.p. 43.00x (ISBN 0-915368-79-X). New Eng SF Assoc.

--The Weathermakers. 256p. 1979. pap. 1.95 (ISBN 0-441-87690-0, Pub. by Charter Bks). Ace Bks.

--The Winds of Altair. 320p. (Orig.). 1983. pap. 6.95 (ISBN 0-523-48583-2). Pinnacle Bks.

Bova, Ben & Dickson, Gordon R. Gremlins Go Home. 256p. (Orig.). 1983. pap. 2.75 (ISBN 0-8125-3221-X, Pinnacle Bks). Tor Bks.

Bova, Ben, ed. The Science Fiction Hall of Fame, Vol. 2A. 1974. pap. 3.95 (ISBN 0-380-00038-5, 58750-5). Avon.

--The Science Fiction Hall of Fame, Vol. 2B. 1974. pap. 3.95 (ISBN 0-380-00054-7, 60194-X). Avon.

Bovaird, Tony, et al, eds. Recreation Management & Pricing: The Effects of Charging Policy on Demand at Countryside Recreation Sites. LC 84-10151. 182p. 1984. text ed. 32.95x (ISBN 0-566-00671-5). Gower Pub Co.

Bovarsky, Abraham & Sarna, Lazar, eds. Canadian Yiddish Writings. LC 77-362060. pap. 37.50 (ISBN 0-317-10945-6, 2022287). Bks Demand UMI.

Bovay, H. E., Jr., ed. Handbook of Mechanical & Electrical Systems for Buildings. (Illus.). 864p. 1981. 62.50 (ISBN 0-07-006718-X). McGraw.

Bovbjerg, Dana, jt. auth. see Iggers, Jeremy.

Bovbjerg, Randall R. & Holahan, John. Medicaid in the Reagan Era: Federal Policy & State Choices. LC 82-83893. (Changing Domestic Priorities Ser.). 72p. (Orig.). 1982. pap. 7.95 (ISBN 0-87766-319-X). Urban Inst.

Bove, A., et al. Propagation of Sincularities for Fuchsian Operators. (Lecture Notes in Mathematics: Vol. 984). 161p. 1983. pap. 13.00 (ISBN 0-387-12285-0). Springer-Verlag.

Bove, Alexander, jt. auth. see Rosales, Benjamin.

Bove, Alexander A. Joint Property. LC 82-5497. 224p. 1982. pap. 8.95 (ISBN 0-671-44967-2, Fireside). S&S.

Bove, Alfred A., ed. Exercise Medicine: Physiological Principles & Clinical Applications. Lowenthal, David T. LC 83-7095. 1983. 47.00 (ISBN 0-12-119720-4). Acad Pr.

Bove, Alfred A., jt. ed. see Santamore, William P.

Bove, Anthony & Rhodes, Cheryl. Pocket Guide to WordStar. (Micro Computer Ser.). 1983. pap. 6.95 (ISBN 0-201-07754-X). Addison-Wesley.

Bove, Anthony L. & Finkel, LeRoy. The TRS-80 Model III User's Guide. LC 82-11051. 252p. 1983. pap. 12.95 (ISBN 0-471-86242-8, Pub. by Wiley Pr). Wiley.

Bove, Arthur. First over Germany: A Story of the 306th Bombardment Group. LC 80-69557. (Aviation Ser.: No. 4). (Illus.). 138p. 1982. Repr. 25.00 (ISBN 0-89839-038-9). Battery Pr.

Bove, F. J. Story of Ergot. 1970. 33.75 (ISBN 3-8055-0770-4). S Karger.

Bove, Linda. Sesame Street Sign Language ABC with Linda Bove. LC 85-1845. (Picturebacks). (Illus.). 32p. (gr. 3-8). 1985. pap. 1.95 (ISBN 0-394-87516-8, BYR); PLB 4.99 (ISBN 0-394-97516-2). Random.

Bove, Paul A. Destructive Poetics: Heidegger & Modern American Poetry. 1980. 22.00x (ISBN 0-231-04690-1). Columbia U Pr.

Bove, Susan B. The Early Italian Immigrants to Seneca Falls, New York (1884-1930) (Illus.). 70p. (Orig.). 1983. pap. write for info. (ISBN 0-9611720-0-2). S B Bove.

Bove, Tony & Rhodes, Cheryl. InfoWorld's Essential Guide to CP-M Systems. (InfoWorld's Essential Guides Ser.). 250p. (Orig.). 1984. pap. 16.95 (ISBN 0-06-669003-X). Har Row.

--The User's Guide to CP-M Systems. (Orig.). 1984. pap. 8.95 (ISBN 0-671-55921-4, Pub. by Baen Books). PB.

Bove, Vincent. And on the Eighth Day God Created the Yankees. LC 81-80696. (Illus.). 176p. (Orig.). 1981. pap. 4.95 (ISBN 0-88270-514-8, Pub. by Haven Bks). Bridge Pub.

--Playing His Game. LC 84-70985. 1984. pap. 5.95 (ISBN 0-88270-570-9). Bridge Pub.

Bovee, Cortland L. & Thill, John V. Business Communication Today. 1986. text ed. 25.95 (ISBN 0-394-35137-1, RanC); pap. 11.95 (ISBN 0-394-35430-3). Random.

Bovee, Courtland L. Better Business Writing for Bigger Profits. 1970. text ed. 10.00 (ISBN 0-682-47127-5, University). Exposition Pr FL.

--Business Writing Workshop. rev. ed. (Illus.). 225p. 1981. pap. text ed. 15.95x (ISBN 0-935732-04-7). Roxbury Pub Co.

--Techniques of Writing Business Letters, Memos & Reports. rev. ed. 90p. 1978. 7.95 (ISBN 0-935732-02-0); pap. 5.95 (ISBN 0-935732-03-9). Roxbury Pub Co.

--Techniques of Writing Business Letters, Memos, & Reports. 1978. 5.95 (ISBN 0-317-17271-9). Banner Pr AL.

Bovee, Courtland L. & Arens, William F. Contemporary Advertising. 1982. 31.95x (ISBN 0-256-02736-6); ill. student supp. 9.95x (ISBN 0-256-02779-X). Irwin.

Bovee, Kenneth C. Canine Nephrology. LC 83-12872. (Illus.). 818p. 1983. text ed. 58.95 (ISBN 0-932036-12-0). Harwal Pub Co.

Bovee, Marvin H. Christ & the Gallows: Or, Reasons for the Abolition of Capital Punishment. LC 82-45656. 1983. Repr. of 1869 ed. 40.00 (ISBN 0-404-62403-0). AMS Pr.

Boven, Theodore Van see Van Boven, Theodore.

Bovet, David & Unnevehr, Laurian. Agricultural Pricing in Togo. (Working Paper: No. 467). 76p. 1981. 5.00 (ISBN 0-686-36094-X, WP-0467). World Bank.

Bovet, Eric D. Stagflation: The Penalty of Speculative Production in a Multi-Stage Economy. LC 82-48021. 208p. 1983. 24.00x (ISBN 0-669-05883-1). Lexington Bks.

Bovet, Lucien. Psychiatric Aspects of Juvenile Delinquency, a Study. LC 74-98747. Repr. of 1951 ed. lib. bdg. 15.00x (ISBN 0-8371-3019-0, BOPA). Greenwood.

Bovet, Richard. Pandaemonium: Or the Devil's Cloyster. 1976. Repr. 18.00x (ISBN 0-7158-1136-3). Charles River Bks.

Bovey, F. A. & Winslow, F. H., eds. Macromolecules: Student Edition. 576p. 1982. pap. 23.00 (ISBN 0-12-119756-5). Acad Pr.

Bovey, Frank & Winslow, F. H., eds. Macromolecules: An Introduction to Polymer Science. LC 78-20041. 1979. 49.00 (ISBN 0-12-119755-7). Acad Pr.

Bovey, Frank, jt. ed. see Woodward, Arthur E.

Bovey, Frank A. High Resolution NMR of Macromolecules. 1972. 73.50 (ISBN 0-12-119740-9). Acad Pr.

--NMR Data Tables for Organic Compounds, Vol. 1. LC 67-20258. pap. 117.70 (ISBN 0-8357-9943-3, 2016474). Bks Demand UMI.

--Polymer Conformation & Configuration. (Current Chemical Concepts Monographs). 1969. 49.50 (ISBN 0-12-119760-3). Acad Pr.

Bovey, Frank A. & Jelinski, Lynn W., eds. Chain Structure & Conformation of Macromolecules. LC 82-20779. (Monograph). 1982. 23.50 (ISBN 0-12-119780-8). Acad Pr.

Bovey, John. Desirable Aliens Stories. LC 80-18596. (Illinois Short Fiction Ser.). 183p. 1980. 11.95x (ISBN 0-252-00837-5); pap. 5.95 (ISBN 0-252-00838-3). U of Ill Pr.

Bovey, Rodney W. & Young, Alvin L. The Science of Two, Four, Five-T & Associated Phenoxy Herbicides. (Environmental Science & Technology: A Wiley-Interscience Series of Texts & Monographs). 462p. 1980. 61.95 (ISBN 0-471-05134-9, Pub. by Wiley-Interscience). Wiley.

Bovie, Palmer, ed. & frwd. by. The Complete Comedies of Terrence: Modern Verse Translations. 420p. 1975. pap. 15.00x (ISBN 0-8135-0805-3). Rutgers U Pr.

Bovie, Smith P., tr. see Horace.

Bovie, Smith P., tr. see Virgil.

Bovill, Diana. Tutorial Therapy: Teaching Neurotics to Treat Themselves. (Illus.). 200p. 1982. text ed. 25.00 (ISBN 0-85200-451-6, Pub. by MTP Pr England). Kluwer Academic.

Bovill, E. W., ed. Missions to the Niger. 406p. 1964. 20.00x (ISBN 0-686-79456-7, Pub. by Hakluyt Soc England). State Mutual Bk.

--Missions to the Niger, 3 vols. in 2. (Hakluyt Society Works Series II: Vols. 128-130). Repr. of 1966 ed. 63.00 (ISBN 0-317-16520-8). Kraus Repr.

Bovill, Edward W. & Hallet, Robin. Golden Trade of the Moors. 2nd ed. (Oxford Paperback Ser.). 1968. pap. 7.95x (ISBN 0-19-285045-8). Oxford U Pr.

Bovin, Murray. Centrifugal or Lost Wax Jewelry Casting for Schools, Tradesmen, Craftsmen. LC 71-135667. (Illus.). 1977. 16.50 (ISBN 0-910280-06-1); pap. 12.95 (ISBN 0-910280-05-3). Bovin.

--Jewelry Making for Schools, Tradesmen, Craftsmen. enl. ed. LC 67-20040. (Illus.). 1979. 18.50 (ISBN 0-910280-02-9); pap. 14.95 (ISBN 0-910280-01-0). Bovin.

--Silversmithing & Art Metal for Schools, Tradesmen, Craftsmen. LC 64-2766. (Illus.). 1977. 16.50 (ISBN 0-910280-04-5); pap. 12.95 (ISBN 0-910280-03-7). Bovin.

Boving, A. G. & Craighead, F. C. An Illustrated Synopsis of the Principal Larval Forms of the Order Coleoptera. (Illus.). 1953. 12.50 (ISBN 0-934454-49-3). Lubrecht & Cramer.

Bovis, Edmond de see De Bovis, Edmond.

Bovis, H. Eugene. Jerusalem Question: 1917-1968. LC 73-149796. (Studies Ser.: No. 29). (Illus.). 175p. 1971. 9.95x (ISBN 0-8179-3291-7). Hoover Inst Pr.

Bovit, Judith B. Le see LeBovit, Judith B.

Bovon, Francois & Rouiller, Gregoire, eds. Exegesis: Problems of Method & Exercises in Reading. Miller, Donald G, tr. from Fr. LC 78-27622. (Pittsburgh Theological Monographs: No. 21). Orig. Title: Exegesis; Problemes de Methode et Exercices de Lecture. 1978. pap. 19.25 (ISBN 0-915138-25-5). Pickwick.

Bow. Pattern Recognition & Picture Processing. (Electrical Engineering & Electronics Ser.). 304p. 1984. 37.50 (ISBN 0-8247-7176-1). Dekker.

Bow & Arrow Magazine Staff & Lewis, Jack, eds. Archery Equipment Illustrated. LC 84-71762. (Illus.). 256p. (Orig.). 1984. pap. 10.95 (ISBN 0-910676-79-8). DBI.

Bow, Fredric Du see Podolefsky, Aaron & DuBow, Fredric.

Bow, J. B. De see De Bow, J. B.

Bow, Paul, et al. The State in Northern Ireland: Political Forces & Social Classes. LC 79-13020. 1980. 26.00x (ISBN 0-312-75608-9). St Martin.

Bowcitch, Charles P., tr. see Seler, Eduard, et al.

Bowcock, Philip & Rose, J. J. Valuing with a Pocket Calculator. 160p. 1981. 35.00x (ISBN 0-686-99796-4, Pub. by Tech Pr). State Mutual Bk.

Bowden. Economics: The Science of Common Sense. 1986. pap. text ed. price not set (ISBN 0-538-08980-6, H98). SW Pub.

Bowden, Aberdeen O. Consumers Uses of Arithmetic: An Investigation to Determine the Actual Uses Made of Arithmetic in Adult Social Life. LC 71-176583. (Columbia University. Teachers College. Contributions to Education: No. 340). Repr. of 1929 ed. 22.50 (ISBN 0-404-55340-0). AMS Pr.

Bowden, Betsy. Performed Literature: Words & Music by Bob Dylan. LC 81-47774. 256p. 1982. 22.50x (ISBN 0-253-34347-X). Ind U Pr.

Bowden, C. M., et al, eds. Cooperative Effects in Matter & Radiation. LC 77-21591. 388p. 1977. 59.50x (ISBN 0-306-31078-3, Plenum Pr). Plenum Pub.

Bowden, Calvin. Trail of the Butterfly. 222p. 1984. 8.95 (ISBN 0-89697-191-0). Intl Univ Pr.

Bowden, Charles. Killing the Hidden Waters. (Illus.). 186p. 1977. pap. 7.95 (ISBN 0-292-74306-8). U of Tex Pr.

Bowden, Charles, et al. Street Signs Chicago: Neighborhood & Other Illusions of Big City Life. (Illus.). 200p. 1981. 12.95 (ISBN 0-914091-05-0); pap. 7.95 (ISBN 0-914091-06-9). Chicago Review.

Bowden, Charles H., ed. Short Dictionary of Catholicism. 1958. 5.00 (ISBN 0-8022-0161-X). Philos Lib.

Bowden, Charles L. & Griffen, Martin B. Psychopharmacology for Primary Care Physicians. LC 77-27297. 92p. (Orig.). pap. 8.95 (ISBN 0-683-01005-0). Krieger.

Bowden, Charles M., et al, eds. Optical Bistability. LC 81-2559. 626p. 1981. 89.50x (ISBN 0-306-40722-1, Plenum Pr). Plenum Pub.

--Optical Bistability Two. 526p. 1984. 69.50x (ISBN 0-306-41628-X, Plenum Pr). Plenum Pub.

Bowden, Charles R. Psychopharmacology for Non-Physician. (Dorsey Professional Bks.). Date not set. cancelled (ISBN 0-256-03489-3). Dow Jones-Irwin.

Bowden, David K. The Execution of Isaac Hayne. new ed. LC 76-20850. (Illus.). 104p. 1977. 5.95 (ISBN 0-87844-037-2). Sandlapper Pub Co.

Bowden, Douglas, tr. see Luria, A. R.

Bowden, Douglas M. Aging in Nonhuman Primates. (Primate Behavior & Development Ser.). 1979. 32.50 (ISBN 0-442-20734-4). Van Nos Reinhold.

Bowden, E. The Imitation of Buddha: Quotations from Buddhist Literature for Each Day. 59.95 (ISBN 0-8490-0386-5). Gordon Pr.

Bowden, Edwin, compiled by. The First Hundred Publications of the Humanities Research Center. LC 70-631002. (Illus.). 1971. 8.00 (ISBN 0-87959-013-0). U of Tex H Ransom Ctr.

Bowden, Edwin T., compiled by. James Thurber: A Bibliography. LC 68-20365. (Illus.). 365p. 1969. 10.00 (ISBN 0-8142-0025-7). Ohio St U Pr.

Bowden, Edwin T., ed. The Satiric Poems of John Trumbull: "The Progress of Dulness" & "M'Fingal". LC 61-15829. 230p. 1971. Repr. of 1962 ed. 14.50x (ISBN 0-292-73366-6). U of Tex Pr.

Bowden, Edwin T. & Farmer, David, eds. The Holy Bible at the University of Texas. rev. ed. Orig. Title: The Holy Bible, an Exhibit. (Illus.). 1967. 8.00 (ISBN 0-87959-027-0). U of Tex H Ransom Ctr.

Bowden, Edwin T., ed. see Irving, Washington.

Bowden, Edwin T., compiled by. Peter De Vries: A Bibliography Nineteen Thirty-Four to Nineteen Seventy-Seven. LC 76-620049. (Tower Bibliographical Ser.: No. 14). 1978. 12.95 (ISBN 0-87959-079-3). U of Tex H Ransom Ctr.

Bowden, Elbert & Holbert, Judith. Revolution in Banking. 2nd ed. 1984. pap. text ed. 14.95 (ISBN 0-8359-6682-8). Reston.

Bowden, Elbert V. Economic Evolution: Principles, Issues, Idea-Through the Looking Glass of Time. 1985 ed. 1985. 8.95 (ISBN 0-538-08071-X, H07). SW Pub.

--Principles of Economics: Abridged. 1983. text ed. 14.95 (ISBN 0-538-08970-9, H97). SW Pub.

--Principles of Economics: Theories, Problems, Policies. 1983. text ed. 24.2501057854e (ISBN 0-538-08960-1, H96). SW Pub.

--Revolution Banking. LC 80-67370. 203p. (Orig.). pap. 15.00 (ISBN 0-936328-01-0); pap. text ed. 9.95 (ISBN 0-686-83171-3). Dame Inc.

Bowden, Elizabeth. Anthony Trollope. 1946. Repr. 10.00 (ISBN 0-8274-3793-5). R West.

Bowden, Frank P. & Tabor, David. Friction: An Introduction to Tribology. LC 82-110. 192p. 1982. Repr. of 1973 ed. lib. bdg. 12.50 (ISBN 0-89874-474-1). Krieger.

Bowden, Frank P. & Yoffa, A. D. Fast Reactions in Solids. pap. 44.00 (ISBN 0-317-09010-0, 2051338). Bks Demand UMI.

Bowden, Gregory H. More Morgan: A Pictorial History of the Morgan Sports Car. (Illus.). 18.95 (ISBN 0-85614-059-7, F404). Haynes Pubns.

--Morgan: First & Last of the Real Sports Cars. rev. ed. 18.95 (ISBN 0-85614-013-9, F403). Haynes Pubns.

Bowden, Henry L. Boards of Trustees: Their Organization & Operation at Private Colleges & Universities. LC 82-7991. 58p. 1982. 8.95x (ISBN 0-86554-040-3). Mercer Univ Pr.

Bowden, Henry S., ed. see Simpson, Richard.

Bowden, Henry W. American Indians & Christian Missions: Studies in Cultural Conflict. LC 80-27840. (Chicago History of American Religion Ser.). 1981. 14.95x (ISBN 0-226-06811-0). U of Chicago Pr.

--American Indians & Christian Missions: Studies in Cultural Conflict. LC 84-27840. (Chicago History of American Religion Ser). xx, 256p. 1985. pap. 7.95 (ISBN 0-226-06812-9). U of Chicago Pr.

--Dictionary of American Religious Biography. Gaustad, Edwin S., ed. LC 76-5258. (Orig.). 1976. lib. bdg. 45.00x (ISBN 0-8371-8906-3, BAR/). Greenwood.

Bowden, Henry W., ed. see Eliot, John.

Bowden, J. H. Peter De Vries. (United States Authors Ser.). 1983. lib. bdg. 16.95 (ISBN 0-8057-7388-6, Twayne). G K Hall.

Bowden, J. J. The Exodus of Federal Forces from Texas, 1861. (Illus.). 140p. 1985. 11.95 (ISBN 0-89015-522-4). Eakin Pubns.

--The Ponce de Leon Land Grant. (Southwestern Studies: No. 24). 1969. pap. 3.00 (ISBN 0-87404-136-8). Tex Western.

--Spanish & Mexican Land Grants in the Chihuahuan Acquisition. 1971. 12.00 (ISBN 0-87404-031-0). Tex Western.

--Surveying the Texas & Pacific Land Grant West of the Pecos River. (Southwestern Studies Ser.: No. 46). 1975. 3.00 (ISBN 0-87404-104-X). Tex Western.

Bowden, James. The History of the Society of Friends in America, 2 vols. in 1. LC 73-38440. (Religion in America, Ser. 2). 870p. 1972. Repr. of 1854 ed. 58.50 (ISBN 0-405-04061-X). Ayer Co Pubs.

Bowden, Joan. Why the Tides Ebb & Flow. (gr. k-3). 1979. PLB 12.95 (ISBN 0-395-28378-7). HM.

Bowden, Joan C. Strong John. LC 79-20689. (Ready-to-Read Ser.). (Illus.). (gr. 1-4). 1980. PLB 6.95 (ISBN 0-02-711790-1). Macmillan.

Bowden, Joan Chase. The Bean Boy. LC 78-12150. 64p. (gr. 1-4). 1979. 6.95x (ISBN 0-02-711800-2). Macmillan.

Bowden, John. Archeology & the Bible. 24p. 1982. pap. 3.00 (ISBN 0-910309-00-0). Am Atheist.

--Bible Absurdities. 24p. 1982. pap. 3.00 (ISBN 0-911826-45-9). Am Atheist.

--The Bible Contradicts Itself. 36p. 1982. pap. 3.00. Am Atheist.

--Edward Schillebeeckx: In Search of the Kingdom of God. 160p. 1983. pap. 8.95 (ISBN 0-8245-0610-3). Crossroad NY.

--Herbert Armstrong & His Worldwide Church of God: An Exposure & an Indictment. 64p. 1982. pap. 3.00 (ISBN 0-911826-24-6). Am Atheist.

Bowden, John, jt. ed. see Richardson, Alan.

Bowden, John, tr. see Beyerlin, Walter.

Bowden, John, tr. see Boerma, Conrad.

Bowden, John, tr. see Grollenberg, Lucas.

Bowden, John, tr. see Gunneweg, A. H.

Bowden, John, tr. see Hengel, Martin.

Bowden, John, tr. see Herrmann, Siegfried.

Bowden, John, tr. see Houtepen, Anton.

Bowden, John, tr. see Jagersma, Henk.

Bowden, John, tr. see Rendtorff, Rolf.

Bowden, John, tr. see Reventlow, Henning G.

Bowden, John, tr. see Schillebeeckx, Edward.

Bowden, John, tr. see Soggin, J. Albert.

Bowden, John, tr. see Soggin, J. Alberto.

Bowden, John, tr. see Theissen, Gerd.

Bowden, John, tr. see Witvliet, Theo.

Bowden, John, et al, trs. see Jeremias, Joachim.

Bowden, John S., tr. see Grillmeier, Aloys.

Bowden, Julie D., jt. auth. see Gravitz, Herbert L.

Bowden, K. F. The Physical Oceanography of Coastal Waters. 302p. 1983. 71.95x (ISBN 0-470-27505-7). Halsted Pr.

Bowden, Kathi, jt. ed. see Brazinsky, Terri C.

Bowden, Ken, jt. auth. see Jacobs, John.

Bowden, Ken, jt. auth. see Nichlaus, Jack.

Bowden, Ken, jt. auth. see Nicklaus, Jack.

Bowden, Ken, jt. ed. see Wilson, Mark.

Bowden, Leon, jt. auth. see Shiffer, M. M.

Bowden, M. L. & Feller, I., eds. The Psycho-Social Aspects of a Severe Burn: A Review of the Literature. Jones, C. A. LC 79-89259. 1979. 16.00 (ISBN 0-917478-34-7). Natl Inst Burn.

Bowden, M. L., et al. Progress in Rehabilitation: A Review of Three Studies. Jones, C., ed. LC 80-83417. (Illus.). 1983. cancelled (ISBN 0-917478-35-5). Natl Inst Burn.

Bowden, Malcolm. Ape-Men. 1979. pap. 8.95 (ISBN 0-9506042-0-8). Master Bks.

--Rise of the Evolution Fraud. 1982. pap. 8.95 (ISBN 0-89051-085-7). Master Bks.

Bowden, Marjorie. Tennyson in France. LC 72-192406. 1930. lib. bdg. 20.00 (ISBN 0-8414-2536-1). Folcroft.

Bowden, Mary W. Philip Freneau. (United States Authors Ser.). 1976. lib. bdg. 13.50 (ISBN 0-8057-7161-1, Twayne). G K Hall.

--Washington Irving. (United States Authors Ser.). 1981. lib. bdg. 13.50 (ISBN 0-8057-7314-2, Twayne). G K Hall.

Bowden, Muriel. A Reader's Guide to Geoffrey Chaucer. 1971. lib. bdg. 18.50x (ISBN 0-88254-860-3). Octagon.

Bowden, Peter J. Wool Trade in Tudor & Stuart England. new ed. 242p. 1971. 27.50x (ISBN 0-7146-1275-8, F Cass Co). Biblio Dist.

Bowden, Phyllis. North Rhine-Westphalia: North West England Regional Development in Action. 127p. 1980. 33.00x (ISBN 0-905492-17-X, Pub. by Anglo-German Found England). State Mutual Bk.

Bowden, R. J. The Econometrics of Disequilibrium. (Studies in Mathematical & Managerial Economics: Vol. 26). 324p. 1978. 55.50 (ISBN 0-444-85251-4, North Holland). Elsevier.

Bowden, R. J. & Turkington, D. A. Instrumental Variables. (Econometric Society Monographs in Quantitative Economics). 252p. 1985. 34.50 (ISBN 0-521-26241-0). Cambridge U Pr.

Bowden, Robert C. Boss Wheels: End of the Supercar Era. (Modern Automotive Ser.). (Illus.). 1979. 9.95 (ISBN 0-8306-9838-8); pap. 7.95 (ISBN 0-8306-2050-8, 2050). TAB Bks.

Bowden, Robert D. Boies Penrose: Symbol of an Era. facsimile ed. LC 75-175690. (Select Bibliographies Reprint Ser). Repr. of 1937 ed. 21.00 (ISBN 0-8369-6605-8). Ayer Co Pubs.

--In Defense of Tomorrow. facs. ed. LC 77-121450. (Essay Index Reprint Ser). 1931. 18.00 (ISBN 0-8369-1697-2). Ayer Co Pubs.

Bowden, Russell, ed. Library Education Programmes in Developing Countries with Special References to Asia. (IFLA Pub. Ser: 20). 221p. 1982. lib. bdg. 28.00 (ISBN 3-598-20383-7). K G Saur.

Bowden, S. Industrial Society in England Towards the End of the Eighteenth Century. 2nd. rev ed. 343p. 1965. 27.50x (ISBN 0-7146-1276-6, F Cass Co). Biblio Dist.

Bowden, Scott. Armies at Waterloo. LC 83-80946. (Armies of the Napoleonic Wars Research Ser.). (Illus.). 356p. 1983. 34.95 (ISBN 0-913037-02-8). Empire Games Pr.

Bowden, Scott & Tarbox, Charles. Armies on the Danube. LC 80-65117. (Armies of the Napoleonic Wars Research Ser.). (Illus.). 198p. 1980. 19.95 (ISBN 0-913037-00-1). Empire Games Pr.

Bowden, Tom. Army in the Service of the State. 168p. 1976. 11.50 (ISBN 0-87855-219-7). Transaction Bks.

--The Breakdown of Public Security: The Case of Ireland. LC 76-56682. (Sage Studies in 20th Century History: Vol. 8). pap. 89.00 (ISBN 0-317-29606-X, 2021872). Bks Demand UMI.

Bowden, William L. Presbyterian Higher Institutions in North Carolina. 669p. (Orig.). 1981. pap. 3.00. Synod NC Church.

Bowden, William R. English Dramatic Lyric, 1603-42: A Study in Stuart Dramatic Technique. LC 69-15680. (Yale Studies in English Ser.: No. 118). xiii, 219p. 1969. Repr. of 1951 ed. 19.50 (ISBN 0-208-00776-8, Archon). Shoe String.

Bowden, Witt. The Industrial History of the United States. 1979. Repr. of 1930 ed. lib. bdg. 35.00 (ISBN 0-8495-0513-5). Arden Lib.

--Industrial History of the United States. LC 77-114825. (Adelphia Economic Ser.). 1970. Repr. of 1930 ed. lib. bdg. 21.50 (ISBN 0-8337-0345-5). B Franklin.

--Industrial History of the United States. LC 67-19583. Repr. of 1930 ed. 39.50x (ISBN 0-678-00238-X). Kelley.

Bowden, Witt, et al. Economic History of Europe Since 1750. LC 75-111686. (BCL Ser. I). 1970. Repr. of 1937 ed. 16.00 (ISBN 0-404-00962-X). AMS Pr.

Bowder, Diana. The Age of Constantine & Julian. (Illus.). 230p. 1978. text ed. 32.50x (ISBN 0-06-490601-9, 06359). B&N Imports.

--Who Was Who in the Greek World. 1984. pap. 8.95 (ISBN 0-671-50159-3). WSP.

--Who Was Who in the Roman World. 1984. pap. 8.95 (ISBN 0-671-50160-7). WSP.

Bowder, Diana, ed. Who Was Who in the Greek World. 240p. 1982. 32.50x (ISBN 0-8014-1538-1). Cornell U Pr.

--Who Was Who in the Roman World. LC 80-67821. (Illus.). 256p. 1980. 32.50x (ISBN 0-8014-1358-3). Cornell U Pr.

Bowdich, T. E. Mission from Cape Coast to Ashantee. new ed. 595p. 1966. 57.50x (ISBN 0-7146-1794-6, F Cass Co). Biblio Dist.

Bowdich, T. E., ed. see Mollien, G.

Bowdich, Thomas E. An Account of the Discoveries of the Portuguese in the Interior of Angola & Mozambique. LC 74-15013. Repr. of 1824 ed. 21.00 (ISBN 0-404-12008-3). AMS Pr.

Bowditch, Charles P. Mexican & Central American Antiquities, Calendar Systems, & History. LC 74-20883. (Smithsonian Institution, Bureau of American Ethnology, Bulletin Ser.: No. 28). (Illus.). 808p. 1975. Repr. of 1904 ed. 45.00 (ISBN 0-87917-042-5). Ethridge.

Bowditch, Charles P., tr. see Cano, Fray A.

Bowditch, Henry I. Consumption in New England: Locality, One of Its Chief Causes & Is Consumption Contagious, or Communicated by One Person to Another in Any Manner, 2 vols. in 1. Rosenkrantz, Barbara G., ed. LC 76-25653. (Public Health in America Ser.). (Illus.). 1977. Repr. of 1864 ed. lib. bdg. 14.00x (ISBN 0-405-09806-5). Ayer Co Pubs.

--Public Hygiene in America. LC 70-180557. (Medicine & Society in America Ser). (Illus.). 415p. 1972. Repr. of 1877 ed. 27.00 (ISBN 0-405-03937-9). Ayer Co Pubs.

Bowditch, Henry P. The Life & Writings of Henry Pickering Bowditch, Vol. 2. 40.00 (ISBN 0-405-12536-4). Ayer Co Pubs.

--The Life & Writings of Henry Pickering Bowditch: An Original Anthology, 2 vols. Cohen, I. Bernard, ed. LC 79-7950. (Three Centuries of Science in America Ser.). (Illus.). 1980. Set. lib. bdg. 80.00x (ISBN 0-405-12531-3). Ayer Co Pubs.

Bowditch, James & Buono, Anthony. Quality of Work Life Assessment: A Survey-Based Approach. 224p. 1982. 23.00 (ISBN 0-86569-067-7). Auburn Hse.

Bowditch, James L. & Buono, Anthony F. A Primer in Organizational Behavior. 320p. 1985. pap. text ed. 18.95 (ISBN 0-471-88030-2). Wiley.

Bowditch, James L., jt. auth. see Huse, Edgar F.

Bowditch, John & Ramsland, Clement, eds. Voices of the Industrial Revolution: Selected Readings from the Liberal Economists & Their Critics. 1961. pap. 7.95 (ISBN 0-472-06053-8, 53, AA). U of Mich Pr.

Bowditch, Nancy. George De Forest Brush: A Joyous Painter. 1970. 16.00 (ISBN 0-87233-008-7). Bauhan.

Bowditch, Nathaniel. The American Practical Navigator; Being an Epitome of Navigation, 2 vols. 1977. Repr. 89.00x (ISBN 0-403-08994-8, Regency). Scholarly.

--Bowditch for Yachtsmen: Piloting. abridged ed. (Illus.). 270p. 1976. 9.95 (ISBN 0-679-50603-9). McKay.

--Bowditch for Yachtsmen: Piloting. 1980. pap. 9.95 (ISBN 0-679-50930-5). McKay.

Bowditch, Nathaniel I. A History of the Massachusetts General Hospital to August 5, 1851. 2nd ed. LC 74-180558. (Medicine & Society in America Ser). (Illus.). 768p. 1972. Repr. of 1872 ed. 45.50 (ISBN 0-405-03938-7). Ayer Co Pubs.

Bowditch, Vincent Y. Life & Correspondence of Henry Ingersoll Bowditch, 2 vols. LC 72-121501. (Select Bibliographies Reprint Ser.). 1972. Repr. of 1902 ed. Set. 40.00 (ISBN 0-8369-5459-9). Ayer Co Pubs.

Bowdle, Donald N., ed. The Promise & the Power. 332p. 1980. 14.95 (ISBN 0-87148-706-3). Pathway Pr.

--La Redencion Lograda y Aplicada. 126p. (Span.). 1979. pap. 3.95 (ISBN 0-87148-521-4). Pathway Pr.

Bowdle, Donald W. Redemption Accomplished & Applied. 1972. 5.25 (ISBN 0-87148-726-8); pap. 4.25 (ISBN 0-87148-727-6). Pathway Pr.

Bowdler, George A., jt. auth. see Cotter, Patrick.

Bowdler, Lucy. The Difficult Patient. 1984. 8.95 (ISBN 0-8034-8451-8, Avalon). Bouregy.

--Nurse Sandra's Choice. (YA) 1978. 8.95 (ISBN 0-685-85781-6, Avalon). Bouregy.

Bowdler, Roger. Queen's Bedfellow. 1975. 11.95x (ISBN 0-8464-0775-2). Beekman Pubs.

Bowdler, Sandra, ed. Coastal Archaeology in Eastern Australia. 151p. (Orig.). 1982. pap. text ed. 10.00 (ISBN 0-86784-015-3, 1185, Pub. by ANUP Australia). Australia N U P.

Bowdoin, James, et al. A Short Narrative of the Horrid Massacre in Boston. 122p. 1973. Repr. of 1849 ed. 13.50 (ISBN 0-87928-039-5). Corner Hse.

Bowdon, Susan J., jt. auth. see Munger, Evelyn M.

Bowe, Forrest & Daniels, Mary F., eds. French Literature in Early American Translation: A Bibliographical Survey of Books & Pamphlets Printed in the United States from 1668 Through 1820. (Reference Library of the Humanities: Vol. 77). (Illus., LC 76-052680). 1977. lib. bdg. 76.00 (ISBN 0-8240-9893-5). Garland Pub.

Bowe, Frank. Comeback: Six Remarkable People Who Triumphed Over Disability. LC 80-8195. 172p. 1981. 13.41i (ISBN 0-06-010489-9, HarpT). Har-Row.

--Handicapping America. 1978. 14.95 (ISBN 0-317-05962-9). Har-Row.

--Handicapping America: Barriers to Disabled People. LC 77-11816. 1978. 15.34i (ISBN 0-06-010422-8, HarpT). Har-Row.

--Rehabilitating America. 1980. 14.95x (ISBN 0-317-05963-7). Har-Row.

--Rehabilitating America: Toward Independence for Disabled & Elderly People. LC 79-1654. 1980. 13.41i (ISBN 0-06-010436-8, HarpT). Har-Row.

Bowe, Frank & Sternberg, Martin L. I'm Deaf Too: Twelve Deaf Americans. 1973. pap. 1.95 (ISBN 0-913072-06-0). Natl Assn Deaf.

Bowe, Frank G. Personal Computers & Special Needs. 175p. 1984. pap. 9.95 (ISBN 0-89588-193-4). SYBEX.

Bowe, Kate. Love's Glittering Web. (Superromances Ser.). 384p. 1982. pap. 2.50 (ISBN 0-373-70028-8, Pub. by Worldwide). Harlequin Bks.

Bowe, Nicola G. Harry Clarke: His Graphic Art. (Illus.). 160p. 1983. text ed. 38.50x (ISBN 0-85105-359-9, Dolmen Pr). Humanities.

Bowe, Patrick, jt. auth. see Malins, Edward.

Bowe, Richard J. Pictorial History of Florida. 3rd ed. 1970. 10.00 (ISBN 0-913122-14-9). Mickler Hse.

Bowe, William J. & Parker, Douglas H. Page on the Law of Wills, 1965-1976: Bowe-Parker Revision, 8 vols. 7732p. 1983. Includes supplement. text ed. 425.00 (ISBN 0-87084-682-5); 1984 suppl. incl. Anderson Pub Co.

Bowen & Behr. The Logical Design of Multiple Microprocessor Systems. (Illus.). 272p. 1980. text ed. 37.50 (ISBN 0-13-539908-4). P-H.

Bowen, jt. auth. see Crowe.

Bowen, A., ed. Passive & Low Energy Ecotechniques: Proceedings of the Third International PLEA Conference, Mexico City, Mexico, 6-11 August 1984. (Illus.). 1140p. 1985. 175.00 (ISBN 0-08-031644-1). Pergamon.

Bowen, A. & Vagner, R., eds. Passive & Low Energy Alternatives I: The First International PLEA Conference, Bermuda, September 13-15, 1982. (Illus.). 475p. 1982. 86.00 (ISBN 0-08-029405-7). Pergamon.

Bowen, Alyce. Dangerous Promise. (Superromances Ser.). 384p. 1982. pap. 2.50 (ISBN 0-373-70032-6, Pub. by Worldwide). Harlequin Bks.

Bowen, Angela. The Diabetic Gourmet. rev. ed. (Illus.). 196p. 1981. pap. 4.76i (ISBN 0-06-463526-0, EH 526, EH). B&N NY.

--The Diabetic Gourmet. rev ed. LC 79-1655. (Illus.). 1980. 13.41i (ISBN 0-06-010437-6, HarpT). Har-Row.

Bowen, Anne M. The Sources & Text of Richard Wagner's Opera "Die Meistersinger Von Nuernberg". LC 74-24047. Repr. of 1897 ed. 10.00 (ISBN 0-404-12870-X). AMS Pr.

Bowen, Anthony, ed. Advanced Latin Unseens: Drawn from the Collection of Cook & Merchant. 100p. 1980. 20.00x (ISBN 0-906515-54-8, Pub. by Bristol Classical Pr). State Mutual Bk.

Bowen, Anthony, ed. see Cook & Marchant.

Bowen, Arthur, et al. Passive Cooling. 1200p. 1982. pap. text ed. 150.00x (ISBN 0-89553-033-3). Am Solar Energy.

Bowen, B. A. & Brown, W. R. VLSI Systems Design for Digital Signal Processing, Vol. 1: Signal Processing & Signal Processors. (Illus.). 256p. 1982. text ed. 39.95 (ISBN 0-13-942706-6). P-H.

Bowen, B. A. & Brown, William R. Systems Design: VLSI for Digital Signal Processing, Vol. II. (Illus.). 432p. 1985. text ed. 40.00 (ISBN 0-317-20146-8). P-H.

Bowen, Barbara C. Age of Bluff: Paradox & Ambiguity in Rabelais & Montaigne. LC 71-165041. (Studies in Language & Literature Ser: No. 62). 176p. 1972. 14.95x (ISBN 0-252-00212-1). U of Ill Pr.

--Words & the Man in French Renaissance Literature. LC 83-80027. (French Forum Monographs: No. 45). 163p. (Orig.). 1983. pap. 12.50x (ISBN 0-917058-45-3). French Forum.

Bowen, Barbara M. Strange Scriptures That Perplex the Western Mind. 1940. pap. 3.95 (ISBN 0-8028-1511-1). Eerdmans.

Bowen, Bob & Clemence, B. J. Golf Everyone. (Illus.). 154p. (Orig.). 1981. pap. text ed. 5.95x (ISBN 0-88725-002-5). Hunter Textbks.

Bowen, Bruce D. & Weisberg, Herbert F. An Introduction to Data Analysis. LC 79-27870. (Illus.). 213p. 1980. text ed. 20.95 (ISBN 0-7167-1173-7); pap. text ed. 11.95 (ISBN 0-7167-1174-5). W H Freeman.

Bowen, Bruce D., jt. auth. see Weisberg, Herbert F.

Bowen, Carol. Glorious Desserts. 128p. 1983. 13.95 (ISBN 0-8120-5535-7). Barron.

--Suppers & Snacks. 80p. 1985. pap. 4.95 (ISBN 0-89586-345-6). H P Bks.

Bowen, Carol & Spencer, Jill. Good & Easy Cookbook. LC 82-84729. (Illus.). 224p. 1983. 24.95 (ISBN 0-88332-315-X, 8038). Larousse.

Bowen, Carolyn C. Angling for Words. (Angling for Words Ser.). 1972. study bk 6.00 (ISBN 0-87879-047-0); wkbk 3.00 (ISBN 0-87879-048-9). Acad Therapy.

Bowen, Catherine. Biography: The Craft & the Calling. LC 77-19110. 1978. Repr. of 1969 ed. lib. bdg. 22.50x (ISBN 0-313-20219-2, BOBI). Greenwood.

Bowen, Catherine & Von Meck, Barbara. Beloved Friend: The Story of Tchaikowsky & Nadejda Von Meck. LC 73-3923. 1976. Repr. of 1961 ed. lib. bdg. 45.00x (ISBN 0-8371-6861-9, BOBF). Greenwood.

Bowen, Catherine D. The Lion & the Throne: The Life & Times of Sir Edward Coke. 1957. (Pub. by Atlantic Monthly Pr); pap. 9.95 (ISBN 0-316-10393-4, LB29). Little.

Bowen, Charles & Peyton, David. How to Get the Most Out of Compuserve. 288p. (Orig.). 1984. pap. 14.95 (ISBN 0-553-34240-1). Bantam.

Bowen, Charles E., jt. auth. see Schneider, J. Stewart.

Bowen, Sir Charles. Virgil in English Verse. 1889. Repr. 35.00 (ISBN 0-8274-3676-9). R West.

Bowen, D. K., et al. Application of Synchrotron Radiation X-Rays in Materials Science. 1984. write for info. Elsevier.

Bowen, D. Keith, jt. ed. see Tanner, Brian K.

Bowen, D. Michael, ed. Air Pollution. LC 72-97720. (ACS Reprint Collection). 1973. Repr. 9.95 (ISBN 0-8412-0160-9). Am Chemical.

Bowen, D. Q. Inqua Field Guides, 16 vols. Incl. Vol. 1. East Anglia. West, R. G., ed; Vol. 2. The English Midlands. Shotton, F. W., ed; Vol. 3. The Isle of Man: Lancashire Coast & Lake District. Tooley, M. J., ed; Vol. 4. South East England & the Thames Valley. Shepherd-Thorn, E. R. & Wymer, J. J., eds.; Vol. 5. Yorkshire & Lincolnshire. Catt, J. A., ed; Vol. 6. South West England. Mottershead, D. N., ed; Vol. 7. Wales & the Cheshire Shropshire Lowland. Bowen, D. Q., ed; Vol. 8. Mid & North Wales. Watson, E., ed; Vol. 9. The Northern Highlands of Scotland. Clapperton, C. M., ed; Vol. 10. The Scottish Highlands. Sissons, J. B., ed; Vol. 11. Western Scotland I. Price, R. J., ed; Vol. 12. Western Scotland II. Dickson, J. H., ed; Vol. 13. South East Ireland. Huddart, D., ed; Vol. 14. South & Southwest Ireland. Lewis, C. A., ed; Vol. 15. Western Ireland. Finch, T; Vol. 16. Southern Shores of the North Sea. Paepe, R., ed. 1980. Set. pap. text ed. 112.00 (ISBN 0-686-64925-7, Pub. by GEO Abstracts England); pap. text ed. 8.00 ea. State Mutual Bk.

Bowen, D. Q., ed. Quaternary Science Reviews, Vol. 1. (Illus.). 340p. 1984. 84.00 (ISBN 0-08-031491-0). Pergamon.

--Quaternary Science Reviews, Vol. 2. (Illus.). 328p. 1984. 96.00 (ISBN 0-08-031736-7). Pergamon.

Bowen, Dana T. Lore of the Lakes. 1940. 9.75 (ISBN 0-912514-12-4). Freshwater.

--Memories of the Lakes. 1946. 9.75 (ISBN 0-912514-14-0). Freshwater.

--Shipwrecks of the Lakes. 1952. 9.75 (ISBN 0-912514-21-3). Freshwater.

Bowen, David. Picture Book of San Antonio. 32p. (English & Spanish.). 1978. pap. 2.50 (ISBN 0-931722-02-0). Corona Pub.

Bowen, David & Bowen, Margareta. Steps to Consecutive Interpretation. Rev. ed. (Illus.). 76p. (Orig.). 1984. pap. text ed. 7.95x (ISBN 0-9605686-2-X). Pen & Booth.

Bowen, Desmond. The Idea of the Victorian Church: A Study of the Church of England 1833-1889. 1968. 20.00x (ISBN 0-7735-0033-2). McGill-Queens U Pr.

--Paul Cardinal Cullen & the Shaping of Modern Irish Catholicism. 311p. 1983. text ed. 17.75x (ISBN 0-88920-136-6, Pub. by Wilfrid Laurier Canada). Humanities.

--The Protestant Crusade in Ireland, 1800-70: A Study of Protestant-Catholic Relations Between the Act of Union & Disestablishment. 1978. 27.50x (ISBN 0-7735-0295-5). McGill-Queens U Pr.

Bowen, Donald D., jt. auth. see Boone, Louis E.

Bowen, Donald J., jt. auth. see Marquez, Ely.

Bowen, Douglas, jt. ed. see Kaylin, Arleen.

Bowen, Douglas J., jt. ed. see Keylin, Arlene.

Bowen, E. Grasslands & Tundra. LC 84-28072. (Planet Earth Ser.). 1985. lib. bdg. 19.94 (ISBN 0-8094-4521-2, Pub. by Time-Life). Silver.

Bowen, E. G. Saints Seaways & Settlements in the Celtic Lands. 2nd ed. 277p. 1983. pap. text ed. 13.00x (ISBN 0-7083-0650-0, Pub. by Univ of Wales Pr). Humanities.

Bowen, E. G. Dewi Sant. Saint David-Patron Saint of Wales. (St. David's Day Bilingual). 90p. 1983. pap. text ed. 6.75x (ISBN 0-7083-0839-2, Pub. by Univ Wales Pr England). Humanities.

Bowen, E. K. & Starr, M. K. Basic Statistics for Business & Economics. 1983. 34.50x (ISBN 0-07-006725-2); study guide 12.95 (ISBN 0-07-006727-9). McGraw.

Bowen, Earl K. Mathematics: With Applications in Management & Economics. 5th ed. 1980. 27.95x (ISBN 0-256-02349-2). Irwin.

Bowen, Edward. Thoroughbreds of 1976. 1979. 46.25 (ISBN 0-936032-14-6). Blood-Horse.

--Thoroughbreds of 1978. 1979. 36.25 (ISBN 0-936032-15-4). Blood-Horse.

--Thoroughbreds of 1979. 1980. 36.25 (ISBN 0-936032-16-2). Blood-Horse.

Bowen, Edward L., jt. auth. see Wharton, Mary E.

Bowen, Elbert R. Theatrical Entertainments in Rural Missouri Before the Civil War. LC 59-15636. 140p. 1959. 15.00x (ISBN 0-8262-0541-0). U of Mo Pr.

Bowen, Elbert R., et al. Communicative Reading. 4th ed, (Illus.). 1978. write for info. (ISBN 0-02-313000-8). Macmillan.

Bowen, Elenore S. Return to Laughter. 1964. 5.50 (N36, Anchor). Natural Hist.

--Return to Laughter. 1964. 5.50 (ISBN 0-385-05312-6). Doubleday.

Bowen, Eli. The United States Post-Office Guide. LC 75-22802. (America in Two Centuries Ser). 1976. Repr. of 1851 ed. 27.50x (ISBN 0-405-07674-6). Ayer Co Pubs.

Bowen, Elizabeth. Ann Lee's & Other Stories. facsimile ed. LC 70-103497. (Short Story Index Reprint Ser.). 1926. 16.00 (ISBN 0-8369-3239-0). Ayer Co Pubs.

--Bowen's Court. LC 64-19368. (Neglected Books of the Twentieth Century). (Illus.). (gr. 10-12). 1979. pap. 6.95 (ISBN 0-912946-67-9). Ecco Pr.

--The Collected Stories of Elizabeth Bowen. LC 80-8729. 784p. 1981. 20.00 (ISBN 0-394-51666-4). Knopf.

--The Collected Stories of Elizabeth Bowen. LC 81-52874. 784p. 1982. pap. 8.95 (ISBN 0-394-75296-1, Vin). Random.

--The Death of the Heart. 352p. (YA) Date not set. 15.45 (ISBN 0-394-42172-8, Vin). Random.

--The Death of the Heart. LC 83-22136. 1984. 8.95 (ISBN 0-394-60504-7). Modern Lib.

--The Death of the Heart. 1984. pap. 8.95 (ISBN 0-394-60504-7, Vin). Random.

--Death of the Heart. 320p. 1985. pap. 5.95 (ISBN 0-14-001690-2). Penguin.

--Friends & Relations. 192p. (YA) 1980. pap. 2.25 (ISBN 0-380-49601-1, 49601-1). Avon.

--Good Tiger. (Illus.). (gr. k-3). 1965. PLB 4.69 (ISBN 0-394-91204-7). Knopf.

--Heat of the Day. 258p. 1981. Repr. lib. bdg. 16.95 (ISBN 0-89966-259-5). Buccaneer Bks.

--The House in Paris. 1979. pap. 2.50 (ISBN 0-380-44602-2, 44602-2). Avon.

--Joining Charles & Other Stories. 1971. Repr. of 1929 ed. 29.00 (ISBN 0-403-00527-2). Scholarly.

--The Little Girls. 240p. 1985. pap. 5.95 (ISBN 0-14-005785-4). Penguin.

--Selected Stories. LC 83-45415. Repr. of 1946 ed. 20.00 (ISBN 0-404-20037-0). AMS Pr.

--Seven Winters. 72p. 1971. Repr. of 1942 ed. 12.50x (ISBN 0-7165-1397-8, BBA 02047, Pub. by Cuala Press Ireland). Biblio Dist.

--Why Do I Write? 57p. 1980. Repr. of 1948 ed. lib. bdg. 10.00 (ISBN 0-8492-3776-9). R West.

Bowen, Elizabeth & Burgess, Anthony. The Heritage of British Literature. LC 82-50818. (Illus.). 1983. 24.95f (ISBN 0-500-01303-9). Thames Hudson.

Bowen, Elizabeth, jt. auth. see Pritchett, V.

Bowen, Elizabeth, ed. see Mansfield, Katherine.

Bowen, Elizabeth, jt. ed. see Ryan, A. P.

Bowen, Ezra. Hypothesis of Population Growth. LC 68-58550. (Columbia University, Studies in the Social Sciences: No. 343). Repr. of 1931 ed. 20.00 (ISBN 0-404-51343-3). AMS Pr.

--Knights of the Air. LC 79-9398. (Epic of Flight Ser.). (gr. 7 up). 21.27 (ISBN 0-8094-3251-X, Pub. by Time-Life). Silver.

--Knights of the Air. Time-Life Books, ed. (Epic of Flight Ser.). (Illus.). 1980. 14.95 (ISBN 0-8094-3250-1). Time-Life.

Bowen, F. The Sea: Its History & Romance, 4 vols. 1977. lib. bdg. 400.00 (ISBN 0-8490-2581-8). Gordon Pr.

Bowen, F. C. Wooden Walls in Action: The History of Ships from 1340 to 1866. 1977. lib. bdg. 69.95 (ISBN 0-8490-2841-8). Gordon Pr.

Bowen, Francis. American Political Economy. LC 79-75565. Repr. of 1870 ed. lib. bdg. 24.25x (ISBN 0-8371-1801-8, BOPE). Greenwood.

--Gleanings from a Literary Life: 1838-1880. 1880. Repr. 45.00 (ISBN 0-8274-2414-0). R West.

--The Principles of Political Economy, Applied to the Condition, the Resources, & the Institutions of the American People. (The Neglected American Economists Ser.). 1974. lib. bdg. 61.00 (ISBN 0-8240-1011-6). Garland Pub.

Bowen, Francis, tr. see DeTocqueville, Alexis.

Bowen, Francis A. A Bride's Guide to a Christian Wedding. LC 78-73642. (Illus.). 1979. text ed. 2.95 (ISBN 0-9602830-0-5). F A Bowen.

--How to Produce a Church Newspaper... & Other Ways Churches Communicate. (Illus.). 1974. 5.00 (ISBN 0-9602830-1-3). F A Bowen.

Bowen, Frank M. & Lee, Eugene C. Limiting State Spending: The Legislature or the Electorate. LC 79-10327. (Research Report: No. 79-4). 1979. pap. 5.00x (ISBN 0-87772-265-X). Inst Gov Stud Berk.

Bowen, Frank M., jt. auth. see Lee, Eugene C.

Bowen, Gary. My Village, Sturbridge. LC 77-10059. (Illus.). 64p. (ps-3). 1977. 8.95 (ISBN 0-374-35110-4). FS&G.

Bowen, Glen. Collectible Fountain Pens: Parker, Sheaffer, Wahl-Eversharp, Waterman. LC 82-90494. (Illus.). 320p. (Orig.). 1982. pap. 16.95 (ISBN 0-910173-00-1). G Bowen Comm.

Bowen, Glyn D. & Nambiar, E. K. Nutrition in Forest Trees in Plantations. 1985. 75.00 (ISBN 0-12-120980-6). Acad Pr.

Bowen, H. Courthope. Froebel & Education Through Self-Activity. (Educational Ser.). 1909. Repr. 15.00 (ISBN 0-8482-7377-X). Norwood Edns.

Bowen, H. J. Environmental Chemistry of the Elements. 1979. 50.00 (ISBN 0-12-120450-2). Acad Pr.

Bowen, Harold. The Life & Times of Ali Ibn Isa: The Good Vizier. LC 77-180320. (Mid-East Studies Ser.). Repr. of 1928 ed. 37.50 (ISBN 0-404-56215-9). AMS Pr.

Bowen, Howard. Toward Social Economy. LC 76-43973. (Political & Social Economy Ser.). 367p. 1977. Repr. of 1948 ed. 22.50x (ISBN 0-8093-0813-4). S Ill U Pr.

Bowen, Howard R. The Costs of Higher Education: How Much Do Colleges & Universities Spend per Student & How Much Should They Spend? LC 80-8321. (Higher Education Ser.). 1980. text ed. 17.95x (ISBN 0-87589-485-2). Jossey-Bass.

--Investment in Learning: The Individual & Social Value of American Higher Education. LC 77-82069. (Higher Education Ser.). 1977. text ed. 19.95x (ISBN 0-87589-341-4). Jossey-Bass.

--The State of the Nation & the Agenda for Higher Education. LC 81-20746. (Higher Education Ser.). 1982. text ed. 16.95x (ISBN 0-87589-515-8). Jossey-Bass.

Bowen, Howard R. & Schuster, Jack H. American Professors: A National Resource Imperiled. (Illus.). 304p. 1986. 24.95 (ISBN 0-317-28536-X). Oxford U Pr.

Bowen, I. & Lockshin, R. Cell Death in Biology & Pathology. (Illus.). 450p. 1981. 75.00x (ISBN 0-412-16010-2, NO.6491, Pub. by Chapman & Hall). Methuen Inc.

Bowen, Ian. Economics & Demography. LC 76-373793. (Studies in Economics: 10). pap. 42.00 (ISBN 0-317-20053-4, 2023272). Bks Demand UMI.

--Inflation & Social Justice. 35p. 1977. pap. 3.00x (ISBN 0-85564-056-1, Pub. by U of W Austral Pr). Intl Spec Bk.

Bowen, J. C. Poems from the Persian. 119p. 1964. Repr. of 1948 ed. text ed. 8.50x (Pub. by Aris & Phillips England). Humanities.

Bowen, J. Donald. Patterns of English Pronunciation. LC 75-24702. 1975. pap. 11.95 (ISBN 0-88377-044-X). Newbury Hse.

--Spoken Tagalog. LC 65-25321. (Spoken Language Ser.). 551p. (Orig.). 1982. pap. text ed. 20.00x (ISBN 0-87950-465-X); Cassettes I, Units 1-12. 6 dual track cassettes 90.00x (ISBN 0-87950-466-8); bk. & cassettes 100.00x. Spoken Lang Serv.

Bowen, J. Donald & Stockwell, Robert P. Patterns of Spanish Pronunciation: A Drill Book. LC 60-16841. (Orig.). 1960. pap. 4.50x (ISBN 0-226-06831-5). U of Chicago Pr.

Bowen, J. Donald, jt. auth. see Stockwell, Robert P.

Bowen, J. Donald, ed. Beginning Tagalog: A Course for Speakers of English. LC 65-25321. (Orig.). 1965. pap. 27.50x (ISBN 0-520-00156-7). U of Cal Pr.

--Intermediate Readings in Tagalog. LC 66-22702. (Orig.). 1968. pap. 23.00x (ISBN 0-520-00157-5). U of Cal Pr.

Bowen, J. Donald, tr. see Cabrera, Neonetta C. & Cunanan, Augustina S.

Bowen, J. R., et al. Flames, Lasers & Reactive Systems. 45.00 (ISBN 0-915928-77-9). AIAA.

--Shock Waves, Explosions & Detonations. 45.00 (ISBN 0-915928-76-0). AIAA.

Bowen, J. R., et al, eds. Gasdynamics of Detonations & Explosions. LC 81-1010. (Illus.). 446p. 1981. 55.00 (ISBN 0-915928-46-9, PAAS75); members 35.00 (ISBN 0-317-32145-5). AIAA.

Bowen, J. W., ed. see Congress On Africa.

Bowen, James. A History of Western Education: Civilization of Europe Sixth to Sixteenth Century, Vol. 2. LC 79-185251. (Illus.). 536p. 1975. 30.00 (ISBN 0-312-38745-8). St Martin.

--A History of Western Education: The Ancient World- Orient & Mediterranean 2000 B.C. - A.D. 1054, Vol. 1. LC 79-185251. 1972. 27.50 (ISBN 0-312-38710-5). St Martin.

--A History of Western Education: The Modern West, Europe & the New World, Vol.3. 1981. 35.00 (ISBN 0-312-38780-6). St Martin.

--Soviet Education: Anton Makarenko & the Years of Experiment. 244p. 1962. pap. 8.50x (ISBN 0-299-02644-2). U of Wis Pr.

Bowen, James, jt. ed. see Fernig, Leo.

Bowen, James A., jt. auth. see Graham, Charles E.

Bowen, James K. & Van Der Beets, Richard, eds. American Short Fiction: Readings & Criticism. LC 74-115055. (Orig.). 1970. pap. 13.92 scp (ISBN 0-672-60648-8). Bobbs.

--American Short Fiction: Readings & Criticism. 476p. 1970. pap. text ed. write for info. (ISBN 0-02-313010-5). Macmillan.

Bowen, Joe. Stiltwalk. LC 81-90324. (Illus.). 157p. 1981. 10.95 (ISBN 0-9606834-0-2); pap. 6.95 (ISBN 0-9606834-1-0). JMB Pubns.

Bowen, John. The McGuffin. LC 84-45817. 160p. 1985. 13.95 (ISBN 0-87113-018-1). Atlantic Monthly.

--A Ship Model Maker's Manual. 192p. 1982. 42.00x (ISBN 0-85177-235-8, Pub. by Conway Maritime England). State Mutual Bk.

--Squeak: A Love Story. 128p. 1984. 12.95 (ISBN 0-670-66617-3). Viking.

--These Primal Years. 213p. 1981. 10.00 (ISBN 0-682-49719-3). Exposition Pr FL.

Bowen, John, ed. Scale Model Sailing Ships. (Illus.). 1978. 12.95 (ISBN 0-8317-7700-1, Mayflower Bks). Smith Pubs.

--Scale Model Warships. LC 78-25641. (Illus.). 1979. 12.95 (ISBN 0-8317-7702-8, Mayflower Bks). Smith Pubs.

Bowen, John W., ed. see Negro Young People's Christian & Educational Congress Atlanta 1902.

Bowen, K. C. Research Games. 126p. 1978. 16.00x (ISBN 0-85066-169-2). Taylor & Francis.

Bowen, K. C., ed. Management Science in Defence. 105p. 1985. pap. 40.50 (ISBN 0-08-032658-7, Pub. by Aberdeen Scotland). Pergamon.

Bowen, Kenneth A. Speaking Pascal: A Computer Language Primer. 236p. (Orig.). 1981. pap. 14.50 (ISBN 0-8104-5164-6). Hayden.

Bowen, Kernochan. Four-Harness Weaving. (Illus.). 1978. 19.50 (ISBN 0-8230-1889-X). Watson-Guptill.

Bowen, Kurt. Protestants in a Catholic State: Ireland's Privileged Minority. 240p. 1983. 27.50x (ISBN 0-7735-0412-5). McGill-Queens U Pr.

Bowen, M. This Shining Woman: Mary Wollstonecraft. 1972. lib. bdg. 59.95 (ISBN 0-8490-1196-5). Gordon Pr.

Bowen, Margareta, jt. auth. see Bowen, David.

Bowen, Margarita. Empiricism & Geographical Thought: From Francis Bacon to Alexander von Humboldt. LC 80-42058. (Cambridge Geographical Studies: No. 15). 336p. 1981. 59.50 (ISBN 0-521-23653-3). Cambridge U Pr.

Bowen, Marjorie. Kecksies & Other Twilight Tales. 1976. 8.95 (ISBN 0-87054-077-7). Arkham.

--Sundry Great Gentlemen. 359p. 1980. Repr. lib. bdg. 30.00 (ISBN 0-89984-056-6). Century Bookbindery.

--Sundry Great Gentlemen: Some Essays in Historical Biography. facs. ed. LC 68-29192. (Essay Index Reprint Ser). 1968. Repr. of 1928 ed. 20.00 (ISBN 0-8369-0230-0). Ayer Co Pubs.

--Viper of Milan. LC 65-25494. (gr. 4-8). 1965. 8.50 (ISBN 0-8023-1014-1). Dufour.

Bowen, Marjorie, ed. Some Famous Love Letters. LC 78-14213. 1978. Repr. of 1937 ed. lib. bdg. 30.00 (ISBN 0-8414-1659-1). Folcroft.

Bowen, Mary, jt. auth. see Petty, Walter T.

Bowen, Mary E. & Mazzeo, J. A., eds. Writing about Science. (Illus.). 1979. pap. text ed. 9.95x (ISBN 0-19-502476-1). Oxford U Pr.

Bowen, Meirion. Michael Tippett. (The Contemporary Composers Ser.). 192p. 1982. text ed. 15.00x (ISBN 0-87663-385-8). Universe.

Bowen, Murray. Family Therapy in Clinical Practice. LC 77-94096. 565p. 1978. 30.00x (ISBN 0-87668-334-0). Aronson.

Bowen, Norman L. The Evolution of Igneous Rocks. 1928. pap. 6.50 (ISBN 0-486-60311-3). Dover.

Bowen, Oliver E., Jr. Rocks & Minerals of the San Francisco Bay Region. (California Natural History Guides: No. 5). (Illus.). 1962. pap. 2.85 (ISBN 0-520-00158-3). U of Cal Pr.

Bowen, Owen. Tales from the Mabinogion. LC 78-155665. (Illus.). 1974. 6.95 (ISBN 0-8149-0706-7). Vanguard.

Bowen, P., jt. auth. see Bell, G.

Bowen, Patrick G. The Sayings of the Ancient One. lib. bdg. 79.95 (ISBN 0-87968-490-9). Krishna Pr.

Bowen, R., ed. Geology in Engineering. (Illus.). 416p. 1984. 48.00 (ISBN 0-85334-234-2, I-215-84, Pub. by Elsevier Applied Sci England). Elsevier.

Bowen, R. L. The Early Arabian Necropolis of Ain Jawan: A Pre-Islamic & Early Islamic Site on the Persian Gulf. (American Schools of Oriental Research, Supplementary Studies: Vols. 7-9). 70p. 1950. text ed. 3.50x (ISBN 0-89757-309-9, Am Sch Orient Res). Eisenbrauns.

--Obsolete Banknotes & Scrip of Michigan, 2 bks. LC 84-70009. (Illus.). 1984. Repr. of 1954 ed. lib. bdg. 45.00 (ISBN 0-942666-37-2). S J Durst.

Bowen, R. M. & Wang, C. C. Introduction to Vectors & Tensors, 2 vols. Incl. Vol. 1. Linear & Multilinear Algebra. 241p. 29.50x (ISBN 0-306-37508-7); Vol. 2. Vector & Tensor Analysis. 192p. 29.50x (ISBN 0-306-37509-5). LC 75-28115. (Mathematical Concepts & Methods in Science & Engineering Ser.: Vols. 1 & 2). 1976 (Plenum Pr). Plenum Pub.

Bowen, Ralph, tr. see Diderot, Denis.

Bowen, Ralph H., ed. A Frontier Family in Minnesota: Letters of Theodore & Sophie Bost, 1851-1920. LC 81-10401. (Illus.). 419p. 1981. 25.00 (ISBN 0-8166-1032-0); pap. 12.95 (ISBN 0-8166-1035-5). U of Minn Pr.

Bowen, Ray. The Novels of Ferdinand Fabre. 1977. lib. bdg. 59.95 (ISBN 0-8490-2362-9). Gordon Pr.

Bowen, Ray P. The Dramatic Construction of Balzac's Novels. 1940. pap. 1.00 (ISBN 0-87114-000-4). U of Oreg Bks.

Bowen, Rich & Fay, Dick. Hot Dog Chicago: A Native's Dining Guide. 150p. 1983. pap. 3.95 (ISBN 0-914091-27-1). Chicago Review.

Bowen, Richard L. Early Rehoboth, Vol. 4. 1950. 10.00 (ISBN 0-685-67655-2). RI Hist Soc.

--Index to the Early Records of the Town of Providence. 1949. pap. 3.00 (ISBN 0-685-67657-9). RI Hist Soc.

--The Providence Oath of Allegiance & Its Signers, 1651-2. 1943. 7.50 (ISBN 0-917012-46-1). RI Hist Soc.

--Some Factors Affecting Employee Motivation at the University of South Dakota. 1982. write for info. U of SD Gov Res Bur.

Bowen, Richard L. & Albright, Frank. Archaeological Discoveries in South Arabia. LC 57-12447. (American Foundation for the Study of Man Publications Ser.: Vol. 2). pap. 85.50 (ISBN 0-317-08832-7, 2001863). Bks Demand UMI.

Bowen, Robert. Geothermal Resources. LC 79-41547. 243p. 1979. 79.95x (ISBN 0-470-26917-0). Halsted Pr.

--Grouting in Engineering Practice. 2nd ed. LC 81-1015. 285p. 1981. 51.95x (ISBN 0-470-27147-7). Halsted Pr.

--Paleotemperature Analysis. (Methods in Geochemistry & Geophysics Ser.: Vol. 2). 265p. 1966. 74.50 (ISBN 0-444-40074-5). Elsevier.

--Surface Water. 290p. 1982. 60.95x (ISBN 0-471-87418-3, Pub. by Wiley-Interscience). Wiley.

Bowen, Robert & Gunatilaka, Ananda. Copper: Its Geology & Economics. LC 77-5877. 366p. 1977. 124.95x (ISBN 0-470-99156-9). Halsted Pr.

Bowen, Robert A. Call of the Sea & Other Verse. (Illus.). 1969. pap. 2.00x (ISBN 0-912462-01-9). Foun Hist Rest.

--Footfalls & Echoes: Verses About Old Pendelton. (Illus.). 1964. pap. 2.00x (ISBN 0-912462-02-7). Foun Hist Rest.

--When Sweet Birds Sing. (Illus.). 1967. pap. 2.00x (ISBN 0-912462-03-5). Foun Hist Rest.

Bowen, Robert G., Jr. My Philosophy: Why My Paintings are Signed "A Friend of Civilization". LC 81-69045. (Orig.). 1982. black & white ed. 30.00 (ISBN 0-9607512-1-1); color ed. 30.00 (ISBN 0-9607512-3-8); pap. 4.00 black & white ed. (ISBN 0-9607512-0-3); pap. 6.00 color ed. (ISBN 0-9607512-2-X). R G Bowen.

Bowen, Robert M., jt. auth. see Pfeiffer, Glenn M.

Bowen, Robert S. Infield Flash. LC 69-14320. (gr. 7-12). 1969. PLB 10.88 (ISBN 0-688-51007-8). Lothrop.

Bowen, Robert T., jt. auth. see Manjone, Joseph A.

Bowen, Roger. Inga. LC 79-52903. 1979. 9.95 (ISBN 0-9602986-1-4). Normandie.

Bowen, Roger, ed. see Spencer, Bernard.

Bowen, Roger W. Rebellion & Democracy in Meiji Japan: A Study of Commoners in the Popular Rights Movement. LC 78-51755. 450p. 1980. 38.50x (ISBN 0-520-03665-4). U of Cal Pr.

--Rebellion & Democracy in Meiji Japan: A Study of Commoners in the Popular Rights Movement. LC 78-51755. (Campus Ser.: No. 321). (Illus.). 382p. 1984. pap. text ed. 14.95x (ISBN 0-520-05230-7). U of Cal Pr.

Bowen, Roger W., ed. E. H. Norman: His Life & Scholarship. 192p. 1984. 24.95 (ISBN 0-8020-2505-6). U of Toronto Pr.

Bowen, T. J. Adventures & Missionary Labours in Several Countries in the Interior of Africa from 1849-1856. 2nd rev. ed. 359p. 1968. Repr. of 1857 ed. 32.50x (ISBN 0-7146-1863-2, F Cass Co). Biblio Dist.

Bowen, Tang, jt. ed. see Stockwell, Foster.

Bowen, Thomas. Seri Prehistory: The Archaeology of the Central Coast of Sonora, Mexico. LC 74-29360. (Anthropological Papers: No. 27). 120p. 1976. pap. 4.95x (ISBN 0-8165-0358-3). U of Ariz Pr.

Bowen, Thomas J. Central Africa: Adventures & Missionary Labors in Several Countries in the Interior of Africa, from 1849-1856. LC 75-79819. (Illus.). Repr. of 1857 ed. 25.00x (ISBN 0-8371-1540-X, BOC&, Pub. by Negro U Pr). Greenwood.

Bowen, Van S. A Vestry Member's Guide. rev. ed. 80p. 1983. pap. 3.95 (ISBN 0-8164-2464-0, Pub. by Seabury). Winston Pr.

Bowen, W. G., jt. auth. see Finegan, T. A.

Bowen, W. R., compiled by. Turfgrass Pests. 60p. 1980. pap. 6.00 (ISBN 0-931876-39-7, 4053). Ag & Nat Res.

Bowen, William. Biology: A Laboratory Experience. 176p. 1984. pap. text ed. 5.95 (ISBN 0-8403-3492-3). Kendall-Hunt.

--Wage Behavior in the Postwar Period. LC 73-10582. (Princeton University Industrial Relations Ser.). (Illus.). 137p. 1973. Repr. of 1960 ed. lib. bdg. 22.50x (ISBN 0-8371-7013-3, BOWB). Greenwood.

Bowen, William A. Willamette Valley: Migration & Settlement on the Oregon Frontier. LC 77-15183. (Illus.). 134p. 1979. 22.50x (ISBN 0-295-95590-2). U of Wash Pr.

Bowen, William G. Wage-Price Issue: A Theoretical Analysis. LC 72-90471. Repr. of 1960 ed. lib. bdg. 22.00x (ISBN 0-8371-2286-4, BOWP). Greenwood.

Bowen, William G., jt. auth. see Baumol, William G.

Bowen, William G. & Ashenfelter, Orley, eds. Labor & the National Economy. rev. ed. (Problems of the Modern Economy Ser). 1975. 8.95x (ISBN 0-393-05456-X); pap. 4.95x (ISBN 0-393-09996-2). Norton.

Bowen, William, Jr. Globalism: America's Demise. LC 84-80408. 222p. (Orig.). 1984. 8.95 (ISBN 0-910311-24-2); pap. 6.95 (ISBN 0-910311-12-9). Huntington Hse Inc.

Bowen, William M., IV & Ganucheau, Frank P., III. The Investor's Equation: Creating Wealth Through Undervalued Stocks. 232p. 19.95 (ISBN 0-917253-00-0). Probus Pub Co.

Bowen, William R. & Baxter, William D. Experimental Cell Biology: An Integrated Laboratory Guide & Text. 2nd ed. (Illus.). 1980. pap. text ed. write for info. (ISBN 0-02-312940-9). Macmillan.

Bowen, York. Pedalling the Modern Pianoforte. 1936. pap. 9.50x (ISBN 0-19-322105-5). Oxford U Pr.

Bowen, Zack. Irish Renaissance Annual IV. LC 80-644275. (Illus.). 176p. 1983. 18.00 (ISBN 0-87413-236-3). U Delaware Pr.

--Mary Lavin. LC 73-126002. (Irish Writers Ser.). 77p. 1975. 4.50 (ISBN 0-8387-7762-7); pap. 1.95 (ISBN 0-8387-7701-5). Bucknell U Pr.

--Padraic Colum: A Biographical-Critical Introduction. LC 77-83665. (Crosscurrents-Modern Critiques Ser.). 175p. 1970. 6.95 (ISBN 0-8093-0412-0). S Ill U Pr.

Bowen, Zack, ed. Irish Renaissance Annual I. (Irish Renaissance Annual Ser.). 192p. 1980. 15.00 (ISBN 0-87413-168-5). U Delaware Pr.

--Irish Renaissance Annual II. 192p. 1981. 15.00 (ISBN 0-87413-185-5). U Delaware Pr.

Bowen, Zack R. Musical Allusions in the Works of James Joyce: Early Poetry Through "Ulysses". LC 74-13314. 1974. 44.50x (ISBN 0-87395-248-0). State U NY Pr.

Bowen, Zack R. & Carens, James F., eds. A Companion to Joyce Studies. LC 83-1479. (Illus.). 832p. 1984. lib. bdg. 65.00 (ISBN 0-313-22832-9, BJS/). Greenwood.

Bowen Cooke, C. J. British Locomotives, Eighteen Ninety-Four. 396p. 1980. 35.00x (ISBN 0-905418-72-7, Pub. by Gresham England). State Mutual Bk.

Bowen-Jones, H., jt. auth. see Clarke, J. I.

Bower & Smith. Nursing Administrators Handbook. 1982. text ed. 17.95 (ISBN 0-8359-5030-1). Reston.

Bower, Alan W., ed. see Arbuthmot, John.

Bower, Anthony, tr. see Camus, Albert.

Bower, B. M. Cabin Fever. 290p. 1981. Repr. of 1918 ed. PLB 16.35x (ISBN 0-89966-017-7). Buccaneer Bks.

--Chip, of the Flying U. 1975. lib. bdg. 16.95x (ISBN 0-89966-012-6). Buccaneer Bks.

--Flying U Ranch. 280p. 1981. Repr. PLB 16.95x (ISBN 0-89966-018-5). Buccaneer Bks.

--The Flying U's Last Stand. 1975. lib. bdg. 16.95x (ISBN 0-89966-020-7). Buccaneer Bks.

--Lonesome Land. 1975. lib. bdg. 16.95x (ISBN 0-89966-022-3). Buccaneer Bks.

Bower, Bill, jt. auth. see Werner, David.

Bower, Blair T., jt. auth. see Brady, Gordon L.

Bower, Blair T., jt. auth. see Kneese, Allen V.

Bower, Blair T., ed. Regional Residuals Environmental Quality Management Modeling. LC 77-92413. (Resources for the Future, RFF Research Paper Ser.: NO. R-7). pap. 61.00 (ISBN 0-317-26044-8, 2023786). Bks Demand UMI.

Bower, Blair T., jt. ed. see Basta, Daniel J.

Bower, Blair T., jt. ed. see Kneese, Allen V.

Bower, Blair T., et al. Incentives in Water Quality Management: France & the Ruhr Area. LC 81-4732. (Resources for the Future Research Paper: R-24). (Illus.). 320p. 1981. pap. text ed. 14.00x (ISBN 0-8018-2661-6). Johns Hopkins.

Bower, C. M., ed. The Composite Materials Glossary. 68p. pap. 18.00 (ISBN 0-317-30186-1). T-C Pubns CA.

--Composites Materials Glossary. 2nd ed. 68p. 1985. 18.00 (ISBN 0-938648-22-5). T-C Pubns CA.

Bower, Carol E. The Basic Marine Aquarium: A Simplified, Modern Approach to the Care of Saltwater Fishes. (Illus.). 290p. 1983. pap. 14.95 (ISBN 0-398-04736-7). C C Thomas.

Bower, Cynthia E. & Rhoads, Mary L., eds. EPA Index: A Key to U. S. Environmental Protection Agency Reports & Superintendent of Documents & NTIS Numbers. LC 82-73733. 392p. 1983. lib. bdg. 45.00x (ISBN 0-89774-032-7). Oryx Pr.

Bower, David, ed. see Bohn, Dave.

Bower, Donald E. The Professional Writers Guide. LC 83-63233. 1984. pap. 12.95 (ISBN 0-88100-038-8). Natl Writ Pr.

Bower, Donald E., jt. ed. see Edwards, Janet M.

Bower, E. M. Early Identification of Emotionally Handicapped Children in School. 3rd ed. (Illus.). 320p. 1982. 26.75 (ISBN 0-398-04604-2). C C Thomas.

Bower, Eli M., jt. auth. see Shears, Loyda M.

Bower, Eli M., ed. The Handicapped in Literature. 407p. 1980. pap. text ed. 18.95 (ISBN 0-89108-098-8). Love Pub Co.

Bower, Fay L. The Process of Planning Nursing Care: A Theoretical Model. 3rd ed. LC 81-14164. (Illus.). 207p. 1982. pap. text ed. 12.95 (ISBN 0-8016-0721-3). Mosby.

Bower, Fay L. & Scott Brown, Marie. Health Maintenance. LC 79-25269. (Wiley Nursing Concept Module Ser.). 252p. 1980. pap. 22.00x (ISBN 0-471-03782-6, Pub. by Wiley Med). Wiley.

Bower, Fay L. & Wheeler, Robinetta T., eds. Nursing Assessment. LC 77-5160. (Wiley Nursing Concept Modules). 167p. 1977. pap. 22.00x (ISBN 0-471-02167-9, Pub. by Wiley Med). Wiley.

Bower, Frank A. & Ward, Richard B., eds. Stratospheric Ozone & Man, Vol. I: Stratospheric Ozone. 232p. 1981. 74.50 (ISBN 0-8493-5753-5). CRC Pr.

--Stratospheric Ozone & Man, Vol. II: Man's Interactions & Concerns. 280p. 1981. 79.50 (ISBN 0-8493-5755-1). CRC Pr.

Bower, Frederick O. Botany of the Living Plant. 4th ed. LC 84-1800. (Illus.). 1969. Repr. of 1947 ed. 23.95x (ISBN 0-02-841800-X). Hafner.

Bower, G. H., jt. auth. see Anderson, J. R.

Bower, G. H., jt. auth. see Trabasso, T.

Bower, G. H. see Spence, Kenneth W., et al.

Bower, George. The Jordons. 1984. 15.95 (ISBN 0-87795-523-9). Arbor Hse.

Bower, Gordon & Bower, Sharon. Asserting Yourself: A Practical Guide for Positive Change. LC 76-5077. (Illus.). 244p. 1976. pap. 7.95 (ISBN 0-201-00838-6); o. p. 2.50. Addison-Wesley.

Bower, Gordon, ed. Human Memory: Basic Processes. 1977. 35.00 (ISBN 0-12-121050-2). Acad Pr.

Bower, Gordon & Lang, Albert R., eds. The Psychology of Learning & Motivation, Vol. 15. (Serial Publication Ser.). 1981. 42.50 (ISBN 0-12-543315-8). Acad Pr.

Bower, Gordon H. Psychology of Learning & Motivations: Advances in Research & Theory, Vol. 16. 1982. 39.50 (ISBN 0-12-543316-6). Acad Pr.

Bower, Gordon H. & Hilgard, Ernest J. Theories of Learning. 5th ed. (Illus.). 640p. 1981. text ed. 32.95 (ISBN 0-13-914432-3). P-H.

Bower, Gordon H., jt. auth. see Anderson, John R.

Bower, Gordon H., ed. The Psychology of Learning & Motivation: Advances in Research & Motivation, Vol. 13. LC 66-30104. (Serial Publication Ser.). 1979. 59.50 (ISBN 0-12-543313-1). Acad Pr.

Bower, Herbert M. The Elevation & Procession of the Ceri at Gubbio. (Folk-Lore Society London Monographs: Vol. 39). pap. 14.00 (ISBN 0-317-16720-0). Kraus Repr.

Bower, Herbert M, tr. see Parini, Guiseppe.

Bower, James B. & Langenderfer, Harold Q. Personal Income Tax Procedures. (Orig.). 1985. pap. text ed. 11.25 wkbk. (ISBN 0-538-01417-2, A415-2). SW Pub.

Bower, James B., et al. Computer-Oriented Accounting Systems. 1985. text ed. 22.35 (ISBN 0-538-01740-6, A74). SW Pub.

Bower, John. Waterline Ship Models. 130p. 1980. 20.00x (ISBN 0-85177-050-9, Pub. by Conway Maritime England). State Mutual Bk.

Bower, Joseph. The Two Faces of Management. 1984. pap. 4.50 (ISBN 0-451-62331-2, Ment). NAL.

Bower, Joseph L. The Two Faces of Management: An American Approach to Leadership in Business & Management. LC 83-141. 288p. 1983. 19.95 (ISBN 0-395-33119-6). HM.

Bower, Joseph L. & Christenson, Charles J. Public Management: Text & Cases. 1978. 27.95x (ISBN 0-256-02070-1). Irwin.

Bower, Julia W. Mathematics: A Creative Art. LC 72-83241. pap. 83.30 (ISBN 0-317-09165-4, 2016333). Bks Demand UMI.

Bower, June, jt. auth. see Heller, Dorothy.

Bower, Muriel. Foil Fencing. 5th. ed. 128p. 1985. write for info. (ISBN 0-697-00369-8). Wm C Brown.

Bower, Peter L. Bicyclist's Guide to Arizona. (Illus.). 86p. 1980. pap. 4.95 (ISBN 0-914778-36-6). Phoenix Bks.

Bower, Ray L. Tactical Airlift: Office of Air Force History, United States Air Force. LC 82-14256. 899p. 1983. 14.00. Off Air Force.

Bower, Robert K. Administering Christian Education. LC 64-22018. 1964. pap. 4.95 (ISBN 0-8028-1559-6). Eerdmans.

Bower, Robert T. The Changing Television Audience in America. 160p. 1985. 20.00 (ISBN 0-231-06114-5). Columbia U Pr.

Bower, Roger. Seasons of Mind. LC 82-90178. (Illus.). 73p. 1982. 8.95 (ISBN 0-9608748-0-1). Marcourt Pr.

Bower, Sharon, jt. auth. see Bower, Gordon.

Bower, Sharon A. Painless Public Speaking. (Illus.). 272p. 1981. 12.95 (ISBN 0-13-647933-2, Spec); pap. 6.95 (ISBN 0-13-647925-1). P-H.

Bower, Stephen & Nyden, Bruce. Diving & Snorkeling Guide to the Virgin Islands. LC 84-1063. (Diving & Snorkeling Guides Ser.). (Illus.). 96p. 1984. pap. 8.95 (ISBN 0-86636-032-8). PBC Intl Inc.

Bower, T. G. Development in Infancy. 2nd ed. LC 81-12544. (Illus.). 304p. 1982. text ed. 27.95 (ISBN 0-7167-1301-2); pap. text ed. 13.95x (ISBN 0-7167-1302-0). W H Freeman.

--Human Development. LC 78-27223. (Psychology Ser.). (Illus.). 473p. 1979. text ed. 25.95 (ISBN 0-7167-0058-1). W H Freeman.

--The Perceptual World of the Child. Bruner, Jerome, et al, eds. (Developing Child Ser.). (Illus.). 1977. 7.95x (ISBN 0-674-66193-1); pap. 3.95 (ISBN 0-674-66192-3). Harvard U Pr.

Bower, T. G. R. Development in Infancy. LC 73-19995. (Psychology Ser.). (Illus.). 258p. 1974. text ed. 22.95x (ISBN 0-7167-0777-2); pap. text ed. 11.95x (ISBN 0-7167-0776-4). W H Freeman.

Bower, Tom. Blind Eye to Murder: Britain, America & the Purging of Nazi Germany - A Pledged Betrayed. (Illus.). 544p. 1983. pap. 8.95 (ISBN 0-89733-098-6, Pub. by Granada England). Academy Chi Pubs.

--Klaus Barbie: The Butcher of Lyons. (Illus.). 248p. 1984. 15.45 (ISBN 0-394-53359-3). Pantheon.

Bower, William C. The Curriculum of Religious Education. (Educational Ser.). 1930. Repr. 30.00 (ISBN 0-8482-7353-2). Norwood Edns.

Bower, William C., ed. Church at Work in the Modern World. facs. ed. LC 67-26717. (Essay Index Reprint Ser). 1935. 18.00 (ISBN 0-8369-0231-9). Ayer Co Pubs.

Bower, Wilma & Willard, Hildegard. Growing & Thinking Slim. 2nd expd. ed. (Illus., Orig.). 1978. pap. text ed. 10.00 (ISBN 0-9606810-0-0). Willard-Bower.

Bowering, David J., ed. Secondary Analysis of Available Data Bases. LC 83-82735. (Program Evaluation Ser.: No. 22). (Orig.). 1984. pap. text ed. 8.95x (ISBN 0-87589-783-5). Jossey-Bass.

Bowering, George, ed. & intro. by see McFadden, David.

Bowerman, Bill, jt. auth. see Moore, Bobbie.

Bowerman, Bruce & O'Connell, Richard. Forecasting & Times Series: An Applied Approach. LC 78-20869. 1979. text ed. 19.95 (ISBN 0-87150-389-1, Duxbury Pr). PWS Pubs.

Bowerman, Bruce L. & O'Connell, Richard. Linear Statistical Models: An Applied Approach. 614p. 1985. text ed. 33.75 (ISBN 0-87150-904-0, 36G8200, Duxbury Pr). PWS Pubs.

Bowerman, Charles E., et al. Unwed Motherhood: Personal & Social Consequences. 419p. 1966. pap. text ed. 4.00 (ISBN 0-89143-059-8). U NC Inst Res Soc Sci.

Bowerman, George F. Censorship & the Public Library, with Other Papers. facs. ed. LC 67-30199. (Essay Index Reprint Ser). 1931. 18.00 (ISBN 0-8369-0232-7). Ayer Co Pubs.

Bowerman, Guy E., Jr. The Compensations of War: The Diary of an Ambulance Driver during the Great War. Carnes, Mark C., ed. LC 82-23846. (Illus.). 200p. 1983. 9.95 (ISBN 0-292-71074-7). U of Tex Pr.

Bowerman, John S. The Civil War Almanac. 400p. 7.98 (ISBN 0-8317-4005-1). Smith Pubs.

Bowerman, Melissa. Early Syntactic Development: A Cross-Linguistic Study with Special Reference to Finnish. (Cambridge Studies in Linguistics: No. 11). pap. 15.95 (ISBN 0-521-09797-5). Cambridge U Pr.

--Early Syntactic Development: A Cross-linguistic Study with Special Reference to Finnish. LC 72-83596. (Cambridge Studies in Linguistics: 11). pap. 78.50 (ISBN 0-317-26062-6, 2024424). Bks Demand UMI.

Bowerman, Walter. Studies in Genius. 5.00 (ISBN 0-8022-0163-6). Philos Lib.

Bowerman, William J. Coaching Track & Field. 1974. text ed. 29.50 (ISBN 0-395-17834-7). HM.

Bowers, Anna M., tr. see Meyer, Adolf.

Bowers, Arden C., jt. auth. see Thompson, June M.

Bowers, B. A History of Electric Light & Power. (IEE History of Technology Ser.: No. 3). 304p. 1982. 80.00 (ISBN 0-906048-68-0); pap. 50.00 (ISBN 0-906048-71-0). Inst Elect Eng.

Bowers, Beth B. Invisible Threads. 1983. pap. 2.50 (ISBN 0-934834-39-3). White Pine.

Bowers, C. A. Cultural Literacy for Freedom: An Existential Perpective on Teaching, Curriculum, & School Policy. 2nd ed. LC 56-5277. 190p. 1974. pap. 6.75 (ISBN 0-9603272-0-7). Elan NW Pubs.

Bowers, Carolyn. Taxing Insurers: The Revolution Ahead. Hadley, Richard D., ed. 508p. 1983. pap. text ed. 63.00 (ISBN 0-914176-24-2). Wash Busn Info.

Bowers, Carolyn O., et al. Judging & Coaching Women's Gymnastics. 2nd ed. (Illus.). 363p. 1981. text ed. 20.95 (ISBN 0-87484-391-X). Mayfield Pub.

Bowers, Cathy, jt. auth. see Newman, Anne.

Bowers, Christine, jt. auth. see Bowers, Q. David.

Bowers, Claude. Party Battles of the Jackson Period. 1965. lib. bdg. 37.50x (ISBN 0-374-90855-9). Octagon.

Bowers, Claude G. Chile Through Embassy Windows, Nineteen Thirty-Nine to Nineteen Fifty-Three. LC 76-56739. 1977. Repr. of 1958 ed. lib. bdg. 22.00x (ISBN 0-8371-9435-0, BOCH). Greenwood.

--Jefferson & Hamilton. LC 75-144890. (Illus.). 542p. 1972. Repr. of 1925 ed. 69.00 (ISBN 0-403-14489-2). Scholarly.

--The Tragic Era: The Revolution after Lincoln. LC 83-45716. Repr. of 1929 ed. 57.50 (ISBN 0-404-20039-7). AMS Pr.

Bowers, Claude G. & Browder, Earl. The Heritage of Jefferson. Franklin, Francis, ed. LC 82-24251. 48p. 1983. Repr. of 1944 ed. lib. bdg. 19.75x (ISBN 0-313-23839-1, BOHE). Greenwood.

Bowers, D., jt. auth. see Bennet, S.

Bowers, D., jt. auth. see Burkitt, B.

Bowers, D. & Ruddy, J., illus. United States Half Cents. LC 83-51003. (Illus.). 1984. soft cover 10.00 (ISBN 0-317-27384-1). S J Durst.

Bowers, D. F. Foreign Influences in American Life. (Illus.). 11.50 (ISBN 0-8446-1084-4). Peter Smith.

Bowers, David. Systems of Organization: Management of the Human Resource. LC 75-31052. 1977. pap. text ed. 9.95x (ISBN 0-472-08173-X). U of Mich Pr.

Bowers, David & Plasterer, Nicholas N. On the News Desk: Practical Exercises in Copy Editing. LC 72-94148. viii, 232p. 1973. pap. text ed. 8.95x (ISBN 0-8071-0219-9). La State U Pr.

Bowers, David A. An Introduction to Business Cycles & Forecasting. LC 84-16786. 432p. 1985. text ed. 28.95 (ISBN 0-201-10163-7). Addison-Wesley.

Bowers, David F., ed. Foreign Influences in American Life: Essays & Critical Biographies. (Princeton Studies in American Civilization: Vol. 2). 1944. pap. 9.95 (ISBN 0-691-02802-8). Princeton U Pr.

Bowers, David G., jt. auth. see Taylor, James C.

Bowers, Dennis. Records Management Projects. 1982. pap. text ed. 12.00 (ISBN 0-8359-6613-5). Reston.

Bowers, Dorothy W. The Irwins & the Harrisons. 1973. 10.00 (ISBN 0-686-05443-1, 73-88914). Irwinton.

Bowers, Edgar. The Form of Loss. LC 78-179813. (New Poetry Ser.). Repr. of 1956 ed. 16.00 (ISBN 0-404-56013-X). AMS Pr.

--Living Together: New & Selected Poems. LC 73-81061. 88p. 1973. pap. 5.95 88p. (ISBN 0-87923-104-1); 96p. 7.95x (ISBN 0-87923-075-4). Godine.

--Witnesses. 22p. (Orig.). 1981. s & l wrappers 22.50 (ISBN 0-936576-05-7). Symposium Pr.

Bowers, Edison L., et al. Financing Unemployment Compensation: Ohio's Experience. 1957. 4.00x (ISBN 0-87776-089-6, R89). Ohio St U Admin Sci.

Bowers, Ellen & Hummel, Judythe. Factors Related to the Underrepresentation of Women in Vocational Education Administration: A Literature Review. 96p. 1979. 6.75 (ISBN 0-318-15475-7, RD152). Natl Ctr Res Voc Ed.

Bowers, Ethel M., jt. auth. see Solomon, Ben.

Bowers, Faubion. Dance in India. LC 78-181075. (BCL Ser. I). Repr. of 1953 ed. 12.50 (ISBN 0-404-00963-8). AMS Pr.

--Japanese Theatre. LC 76-46. (Illus.). 294p. 1976. Repr. of 1952 ed. lib. bdg. 24.75x (ISBN 0-8371-8659-5, BOJT). Greenwood.

--Japanese Theatre: Origin Noh Drama, Puppets, Kabuki Spectacle, Three Kabuki Plays in Translation, Actors & Playwrights, Present-Day Trends. LC 73-90231. (Illus.). 1974. pap. 6.95 (ISBN 0-8048-1131-8). C E Tuttle.

--Theatre in the East. LC 79-7753. (Dance Ser.). (Illus.). 1980. Repr. of 1956 ed. lib. bdg. 53.00x (ISBN 0-8369-9278-4). Ayer Co Pubs.

--The World of Asif Currimbhoy. 4.80 (ISBN 0-89253-664-0); flexible cloth 3.00 (ISBN 0-89253-665-9). Ind-US Inc.

Bowers, Fredson. Elizabethan Revenge Tragedy. 1958. 11.75 (ISBN 0-8446-1085-2). Peter Smith.

--Essays in Bibliography, Text & Editing. LC 74-18055. 1975. 35.00x (ISBN 0-8139-0586-9, Bibliographic Society, University of Virginia). U Pr of Va.

--Studies in Bibliography, Vo. XXXVI. LC 49-3353. 271p. 1983. text ed. 20.00 (ISBN 0-8139-0987-2). U Pr of Va.

Bowers, Fredson, jt. auth. see Hinman, Charlton.

Bowers, Fredson, ed. The Dramatic Works in the Beaumont & Fletcher Canon, 4 vols. LC 74-16999. 1976. Vol. 1. 95.00 (ISBN 0-521-04289-5); Vol. 2. 95.00 (ISBN 0-521-07253-0); Vol. 3. 99.50 (ISBN 0-521-20730-4); Vol. 4. 125.00 (ISBN 0-521-20060-1). Cambridge U Pr.

--The Dramatic Works in the Beaumont & Fletcher Canon, Vol. VI. 730p. 1985. 95.00 (ISBN 0-521-25941-X). Cambridge U Pr.

--The Red Badge of Courage: A Facsimile of the Manuscript. 1973. deluxe ed. 150.00 boxed (ISBN 0-89723-035-3). Bruccoli.

--Studies in Bibliography, Vol. XXXVII. 312p. 1984. text ed. 20.00x (ISBN 0-8139-1029-3). U Pr of Va.

--Studies in Bibliography, Vol. XXXVIII. 380p. 1985. lib. bdg. 25.00x (ISBN 0-8139-1065-X). U Pr of Va.

--Studies in Bibliography, Vol. 32. LC 49-3353. (Illus.). 285p. 1979. 20.00x (ISBN 0-8139-0817-5). U Pr of Va.

--Studies in Bibliography, Vol. 33. LC 49-3353. 282p. 1980. 20.00x (ISBN 0-8139-0860-4). U Pr of Va.

--Studies in Bibliography, Vol. 34. LC 49-3353. 276p. 1981. 20.00x (ISBN 0-8139-0898-1). U Pr of Va.

--Studies in Bibliography, Vol. 35. LC 49-3353. 339p. 1982. 20.00x (ISBN 0-8139-0948-1). U Pr of Va.

--Whitman's Manuscripts: Leaves of Grass (1860): A Parallel Text. LC 55-7313. pap. 85.50 (ISBN 0-317-26648-9, 2024084). Bks Demand UMI.

Bowers, Fredson & Beaurline, L. A., eds. Studies in Bibliography: Papers of the Bibliographical Society of the University of Virginia, Vols. 1-31. Incl. Vol. 1. 1948-49. 204p (ISBN 0-8139-0032-8); Vol. 2. 1949-50. 211p (ISBN 0-8139-0033-6); Vol. 3. 1950-51. 306p (ISBN 0-8139-0034-4); Vol. 4. 1951-52. 237p (ISBN 0-8139-0035-2); Vol. 5. 1952-53. 230p (ISBN 0-8139-0036-0); Vol. 6. 1953-54. 288p (ISBN 0-8139-0037-9); Vol. 7. 1955. 240p (ISBN 0-8139-0038-7); Vol. 8. 1956. 272p (ISBN 0-8139-0039-5); Vol. 9. 1957. 268p (ISBN 0-8139-0040-9); Vol. 10. 1957. 192p; Vol. 11. 1958. 295p (ISBN 0-8139-0042-5); Vol. 12. 1959. 259p (ISBN 0-8139-0043-3); Vol. 13. 1960 (ISBN 0-8139-0044-1); Vol. 14. 1961. 290p (ISBN 0-8139-0045-X); Vol. 15. 1962. 311p (ISBN 0-8139-0046-8); Vol. 16. 1963. 276p (ISBN 0-8139-0047-6); Vol. 17. 1964. 258p (ISBN 0-8139-0048-4); Vol. 18. 1965. 312p (ISBN 0-8139-0049-2); Vol. 19. 1966. 282p (ISBN 0-8139-0050-6); Vol. 20. 1967. 298p (ISBN 0-8139-0051-4); Vol. 21. 1968. 290p (ISBN 0-8139-0052-2); Vol. 22. 1969. 341p (ISBN 0-8139-0053-0); Vol. 23. 1970. 280p (ISBN 0-8139-0309-2); Vol. 24. 1971. 240p (ISBN 0-8139-0331-9); Vol. 25. 1972. (ISBN 0-8139-0404-8); Vol. 26. 1973. (ISBN 0-8139-0468-4); Vol. 27. 1974. (ISBN 0-8139-0580-X); Vol. 28. 1975 (ISBN 0-8139-0636-9). Vol. 29 1976. (ISBN 0-8139-0687-3); Vol. 30 1977. (ISBN 0-8139-0717-9); Vol. 31. 1977. (ISBN 0-8139-0687-3). LC 49-3353. 20.00 ea. U Pr of Va.

Bowers, Fredson, ed. see Beaumont, Francis & Fletcher, John.

Bowers, Fredson, ed. see Crane, Stephen.

Bowers, Fredson, ed. see Dekker, Thomas.

Bowers, Fredson, ed. see Dryden, John.

Bowers, Fredson, ed. see Fielding, Henry.

Bowers, Fredson, ed. see Hoy, Cyrus.

Bowers, Fredson, ed. see Marlowe, Christopher.

Bowers, Fredson, ed. see Nabokov, Vladimir.

Bowers, Fredson, ed. see Shakespeare, William.

Bowers, Fredson, jt. ed. see Hale, Nancy.

Bowers, Fredson, ed. see James, William.

Bowers, Fredson T. Textual & Literary Criticism. (Sanders Lectures in Bibliography: 1957-58). pap. 49.00 (ISBN 0-317-26059-6, 2024423). Bks Demand UMI.

Bowers, G. M. The Faith & Doctrines of the Early Church. LC 78-60521. 1978. pap. 4.95 (ISBN 0-917182-09-X). Triumph Pub.

Bowers, George K. The ABC's of the Parables. 1983. 5.50 (ISBN 0-89536-963-X). CSS of Ohio.

Bowers, Hazel. Cricket Voices. 1970. 4.00 (ISBN 0-8233-0152-4). Golden Quill.

Bowers, J. K. & Cheshire, P. C. Agriculture, the Countryside & Land Use: An Economic Critique. LC 83-13069. 224p. 1983. pap. 11.95 (ISBN 0-416-31830-4, NO. 3925). Methuen Inc.

Bowers, J. Z., jt. ed. see Warren, K. S.

Bowers, Joan S. Psychopharmacology for Non-Medical Therapists: A Manual for Psychologists, Social Workers, Counselors & Nurses. 53p. 1981. pap. 5.45 (ISBN 0-910707-02-2). Ohio Psych Pub.

Bowers, John. In the Land of Nyx. 180p. (Orig.). 1985. pap. 7.95 (ISBN 0-88184-163-3). Carroll & Graf.

--In the Land of Nyx: Night & Its Inhabitants. LC 83-14061. 192p. 1984. 13.95 (ISBN 0-385-19196-0, Anchor Pr). DoubledaY.

Bowers, John B. The Midwife Murder Case: The Rosalie Tarpening Story. (Illus.). 300p. (Orig.). pap. 7.95 (ISBN 0-917982-24-X). Cougar Bks.

Bowers, John D. Save Thousands When You Buy or Sell Your Home. new ed. 132p. (Orig.). 1974. pap. 3.95. J D Bowers.

Bowers, John M. The Crisis of Will in Piers Plowman. 300p. 1986. 29.95 (ISBN 0-8132-0614-6). Cath U Pr.

Bowers, John S. Grammatical Relations. Hankamer, Jorge, ed. (Outstanding Dissertations in Linguistics Ser.). 820p. 1985. 90.00 (ISBN 0-8240-5445-8). Garland Pub.

--The Theory of Grammatical Relations. LC 80-21018. 304p. 1981. 35.00x (ISBN 0-8014-1079-7). Cornell U Pr.

Bowers, John W. & Courtright, John A. Communication Research Methods. 1984. text ed. 27.10x (ISBN 0-673-15468-8). Scott F.

Bowers, John W. & Ochs, Donovan J. The Rhetoric of Agitation & Control. 152p. 1971. pap. text ed. 8.95 (ISBN 0-394-34965-2, RanC). Random.

Bowers, John W., jt. auth. see Arnold, Carroll C.

Bowers, John Z. Western Medical Pioneers in Feudal Japan. LC 73-86098. (Josiah Macy Foundation Ser). 256p. 1970. 24.00x (ISBN 0-8018-1081-7). Johns Hopkins.

--When the Twain Meet: The Rise of Western Medicine in Japan. LC 80-22356. (Henry E. Sigerist Supplement to the Bulletin of the History of Medicine Ser.: No. 5). 192p. 1981. text ed. 18.00x (ISBN 0-8018-2432-X). Johns Hopkins.

Bowers, John Z. & Purcell, Elizabeth F., eds. Advances in American Medicine, 2 vols. LC 76-3162. (Essays at the Bicentennial). (Illus.). 918p. 1976. 25.00 (ISBN 0-914362-17-8). J Macy Foun.

Bowers, Kathleen R. At This Very Minute. (Illus.). 32p. (gr. k-3). 1983. PLB 13.45i (ISBN 0-316-10400-0); pap. 5.70i (ISBN 0-316-10401-9). Little.

Bowers, Kenneth. Hypnosis for the Seriously Curious. 1983. pap. text ed. 9.95x (ISBN 0-393-95339-4). Norton.

Bowers, Kenneth S. & Meichenbaum, Donald. The Unconscious Reconsidered. LC 84-5201. (Personality Processes Ser. (1-341)). 311p. 1984. text ed. 33.95x (ISBN 0-471-87558-9, Pub. by Wiley-Interscience). Wiley.

Bowers, Larry D., jt. auth. see Carr, Peter.

Bowers, Malcolm B., Jr. Retreat from Sanity: The Structure of Emerging Psychosis. LC 73-20296. 245p. 1974. 26.95 (ISBN 0-87705-134-8). Human Sci Pr.

Bowers, Margaretta, et al. Counseling the Dying. LC 74-33146. 192p. 1975. 17.50x (ISBN 0-87668-198-4). Aronson.

Bowers, Mary C. Best Nurse in Missouri. 1982. 8.95 (ISBN 0-686-84167-0, Avalon). Bouregy.

--The Loves of Nurse Rachel. (YA) 1981. 8.95 (ISBN 0-686-74797-6, Avalon). Bouregy.

--Nurse Becky's New World. 1982. 8.95 (ISBN 0-686-84184-0, Avalon). Bouregy.

--Nurse Carrie's Roses. 1984. 8.95 (ISBN 0-8034-8401-1, Avalon). Bouregy.

--Nurse Charly's New Love. 1982. 8.95 (ISBN 0-686-84742-3, Avalon). Bouregy.

--Nurse Heather's Choice. 1983. 8.95 (ISBN 0-317-17553-X, Avalon). Bouregy.

--Nurse Jamie's Surprise. 1982. 8.95 (ISBN 0-686-84172-7, Avalon). Bouregy.

--Nurse Jill's Perfect Man. (YA) 1984. 8.95 (ISBN 0-8034-8416-X, Avalon). Bouregy.

--Nurse Overseas. (YA) 1984. 8.95 (ISBN 0-8034-8431-3, Avalon). Bouregy.

--Nurse Sarah's Confusion. (YA) 1983. 8.95 (ISBN 0-8034-8306-6, Avalon). Bouregy.

--Nurse Stacy's Puzzle. (YA) (gr. 9-12). 8.95 (ISBN 0-8034-8506-9, Avalon). Bouregy.

Bowers, Melvyn K. Easy Bulletin Boards - Number 2. LC 73-21798. (Illus.). 209p. 1974. 15.00 (ISBN 0-8108-0695-9). Scarecrow.

--Library Instruction in the Elementary School. LC 72-155283. 170p. 1971. 15.00 (ISBN 0-8108-0391-7). Scarecrow.

Bowers, Michael, ed. Gas Phase Ion Chemistry. 1979. Vol. 1. 49.50 (ISBN 0-12-120801-X); Vol. 2. 52.50 (ISBN 0-12-120802-8). Acad Pr.

Bowie, S. H., ed. Mineral Deposits of Europe: Vol. 1-Northwest Europe. 362p. 1979. 86.25x (ISBN 0-900488-44-1). IMM North Am.

Bowie, S H. & Thornton, I., eds. Environmental Geochemistry & Health. 1985. lib. bdg. 27.50 (ISBN 90-277-1879-2, Pub. by Reidel Holland). Kluwer Academic.

Bowie, S. H., ed. see Royal Society of London, et al.

Bowie, S. H., et al, eds. Uranium Prospecting Handbook. 346p. 1977. pap. text ed. 49.00x (ISBN 0-900488-15-8). IMM North Am.

Bowie, Theodore. The Drawings of Hokusai. LC 78-12135. 1979. Repr. of 1964 ed. lib. bdg. 32.50x (ISBN 0-313-21074-8, BODH). Greenwood.

Bowie, Theodore, ed. Langdon Warner Through His Letters. LC 66-63378. pap. 59.30 (ISBN 0-317-10184-6, 2005735). Bks Demand UMI.

Bowie, Theodore & Thimme, Diether, eds. The Carrey Drawings of the Parthenon Sculptures. LC 77-155287. (Illus.). 112p. 1971. 50.00x (ISBN 0-253-31320-1). Ind U Pr.

Bowie, Theodore, ed. see De Honnecourt, Villard.

Bowie, Theodore, et al. Art of the Surimono. LC 81-126210. 192p. 1981. 42.50x (ISBN 0-253-30474-1); pap. 22.50x (ISBN 0-253-30475-X). Ind U Pr.

Bowie, Theodore, et al, eds. The Sculpture of Thailand. LC 74-27410. (Asia Society Ser.). (Illus.). 1975. Repr. 33.00x (ISBN 0-405-06559-0). Ayer Co Pubs.

Bowie, Theodore R. East-West in Art: Patterns of Cultural & Aesthetic Relationships. LC 66-12723. (Indiana University International Studies). (Illus.). pap. 47.80 (ISBN 0-317-10444-6, 2051862). Bks Demand UMI.

Bowie, Tom. Jamie, The Adventures of. LC 78-62815. (Illus.). 1978. 14.95 (ISBN 0-932508-00-6); pap. 4.95 (ISBN 0-932508-01-4). Seven Oaks.

--Three Plays for Reading. LC 79-64092. 1979. 14.95 (ISBN 0-932508-04-9); pap. 4.95 (ISBN 0-932508-05-7). Seven Oaks.

Bowin, Carl. Caribbean Gravity Field & Plate Tectonics. LC 76-16261. (Geological Society of America Special Papers: No. 169). pap. 33.80 (ISBN 0-317-29080-0, 2023738). Bks Demand UMI.

Bowker. Prison Victimization: A Gruesome Catalog of Unintended Punishment. 232p. 1980. 26.00 (ISBN 0-444-99077-1); pap. 16.50 (ISBN 0-444-00551-X). Elsevier.

Bowker, Albert & Lieberman, Gerald. Engineering Statistics. 2nd ed. (Illus.). 608p. 1972. ref. ed. 31.95 (ISBN 0-13-279455-1). P-H.

Bowker, Alfred, ed. see Harrison, Frederic.

Bowker, Gordon & Carrier, John, eds. Race & Ethnic Relations: Sociological Readings. LC 76-12586. 400p. 1976. text ed. 29.50x (ISBN 0-8419-0231-3); pap. text ed. 14.50x (ISBN 0-8419-0233-X). Holmes & Meier.

Bowker, Joan P., ed. Education for Primary Prevention in Social Work. LC 83-73055. 92p. (Orig.). 1983. pap. text ed. 6.95 (ISBN 0-87293-002-5). Coun Soc Wk Ed.

Bowker, John. Jesus & the Pharisees. 240p. 1973. 42.50 (ISBN 0-521-20055-5). Cambridge U Pr.

--Problems of Suffering in the Religions of the World. LC 77-93706. 1975. 47.50 (ISBN 0-521-07412-6); pap. 10.95x (ISBN 0-521-09903-X). Cambridge U Pr.

--The Religious Imagination & the Sense of God. 1978. text ed. 32.50x (ISBN 0-19-826646-4). Oxford U Pr.

--Targums & Rabbinic Literature. LC 71-80817. 1969. 62.50 (ISBN 0-521-07415-0). Cambridge U Pr.

Bowker, Lee see Dinan, Joan.

Bowker, Lee, jt. auth. see Zastrow, Charles.

Bowker, Lee H. Beating Wife-Beating. LC 82-48603. 176p. 1983. 22.00x (ISBN 0-669-06345-2). Lexington Bks.

--Drug Use Among American Women, Old & Young: Sexual Oppression & Other Themes. LC 76-55964. 1977. soft bdg. 10.00 (ISBN 0-88247-434-0). R & E Pubs.

--Drug Use at a Small Liberal Arts College. LC 75-38309. 1976. softbound 10.95 (ISBN 0-88247-398-0). R & E Pubs.

--Ending the Violence: A Guide for Battered Women. 128p. (Orig.). 1985. pap. text ed. 9.95 (ISBN 0-918452-86-4). Learning Pubns.

--Humanizing Institutions for the Aged. LC 81-47977. (Illus.). 128p. 1982. 19.50x (ISBN 0-669-05209-4). Lexington Bks.

--Women & Crime in America. 1981. pap. text ed. write for info. (ISBN 0-02-476830-8). Macmillan.

Bowker, Margaret. The Henrician Reformation: The Diocese of Lincoln Under John Longland 1521-1547. LC 80-41655. (Illus.). 256p. 1981. 49.50 (ISBN 0-521-23639-8). Cambridge U Pr.

Bowker, R. M. The Channel Handbook, Vol. 1: Central Section. 2nd ed. 90p. 1982. 75.00x (ISBN 0-686-45563-0, Pub. by Bowker & Bertram UK). State Mutual Bk.

--The Channel Handbook, Vol. 2: The West Country. (Illus.). 90p. 1984. 75.00x (ISBN 0-317-19804-1, Pub. by Bowker & Bertram UK). State Mutual Bk.

--The Channel Handbook, Vol. 3: Harwich to Ushant. (Illus.). 90p. 1982. 75.00x (ISBN 0-317-19805-X, Pub. by Bowker & Bertram UK). State Mutual Bk.

Bowker, R. M. & Bligh, William. Mutiny!! Abroad HM Armand Transport 'Bounty' in 1789. 400p. 1981. 35.00x (ISBN 0-686-79246-7, Pub. by Bowker & Bertram UK). State Mutual Bk.

Bowker, R. M. & Budd, S. A. Make Your Own Sails. rev. ed. LC 61-3835. (Illus.). 1976. pap. 6.95 (ISBN 0-312-50505-1). St Martin.

--Make Your Own Sails. 152p. 1982. 15.00x (ISBN 0-333-17906-4, Pub. by Nautical England). State Mutual Bk.

Bowker, R. M., ed. see Clark, Marcus.

Bowker, Richard. Forbidden Sanctuary. 240p. 1985. pap. 2.50 (ISBN 0-345-32874-4, Del Rey). Ballantine.

Bowl, Ric, jt. auth. see Black, Jim.

Bowlby, J. Maternal Care & Mental Health. 2nd ed. (Monograph Ser.: No. 2). 194p. (Eng, Fr, & Span.). 1952. 7.20 (ISBN 92-4-140002-1). World Health.

Bowlby, John. Attachment. 2nd ed. LC 83-71445. 425p. 1983. pap. 10.95x (ISBN 0-465-00543-8, TB-5087). Basic.

--Loss. LC 79-2759. 1982. pap. 10.95x (ISBN 0-465-04238-4, TB-5102). Basic.

--The Making & Breaking of Affectional Bonds. 1979. (Pub. by Tavistock England); pap. 9.25x (ISBN 0-422-76860-X, NO. 2052). Methuen Inc.

Bowlby, Rachel. Just Looking: Consumer Culture in Dreiser, Gissing & Zola. 160p. 1985. 25.00 (ISBN 0-416-37800-5, 9477); pap. 9.95 (ISBN 0-416-37810-2, 9478). Methuen Inc.

Bowle, John. A History of Europe: A Cultural & Political Survey. xii, 626p. 1981. lib. bdg. 35.00x (ISBN 0-226-06856-0, Pub. by Secker & Warburg). U of Chicago Pr.

--Hobbes & His Critics: A Study in Seventeenth Century Constitutionalism. 1969. Repr. of 1951 ed. 32.50x (ISBN 0-7146-1548-X, F Cass Co). Biblio Dist.

--Unity of European History: A Political & Cultural Survey. rev. ed. 1970. pap. 6.95 (ISBN 0-19-501249-6, GB329, GB). Oxford U Pr.

Bowle, John & Bradford, John, eds. Concise Encyclopedia of World History. LC 74-9041. (Illus.). 511p. 1975. Repr. of 1958 ed. lib. bdg. 44.50x (ISBN 0-8371-7608-5, BOWH). Greenwood.

Bowle, John, ed. see Evelyn, John.

Bowler, Alida C. & Bloodgood, Ruth S. Institutional Treatment of Delinquent Boys. Rothman, David J. & M, Sheila, eds. (Women & Children First Ser.). 60.00 (ISBN 0-8240-7653-2). Garland Pub.

Bowler, Christine, et al. New Writers, No. 8. 1980. pap. 6.00 (ISBN 0-7145-0015-1); 12.95 (ISBN 0-7145-0014-3). Riverrun NY.

--Red Dust One: New Writing. LC 78-127954. 180p. 1971. 5.25 (ISBN 0-87376-016-6); pap. 3.00 (ISBN 0-87376-017-4). Red Dust.

Bowler, I. R. Government & Agriculture: A Spatial Perspective. LC 79-40129. (Topics in Applied Geography). pap. 30.30 (ISBN 0-317-30103-9, 2025271). Bks Demand UMI.

Bowler, Ian R. Agriculture under the Common Agriculture Policy: A Geography. LC 84-25041. 240p. 1985. 27.50 (ISBN 0-7190-1095-0, Pub. by Manchester Univ Pr). Longwood Pub Group.

Bowler, Dr. M. G. Lectures in Statistical Mechanics. (International Series in Natural Philosophy). (Illus.). 208p. 1982. 22.00 (ISBN 0-08-026516-2); pap. 11.00 (ISBN 0-08-026515-4). Pergamon.

Bowler, Michael. Aston Martin V-8. (High Performance Ser.). (Illus.). 176p. 1985. 16.95 (ISBN 0-668-06428-5). Arco.

Bowler, Peter. Superior Persons Book of Words. LC 84-48326. 128p. 1985. 8.95 (ISBN 0-87923-556-X). Godine.

Bowler, Peter, jt. auth. see Hughes, Denis.

Bowler, Peter J. The Eclipse of Darwinism: Anti-Darwinian Evolution Theories in the Decades Around 1900. LC 82-21170. 304p. 1983. text ed. 25.00x (ISBN 0-8018-2932-1). Johns Hopkins.

--Evolution: The History of an Idea. LC 83-5909. (Illus.). 413p. 1984. 29.95 (ISBN 0-520-04880-6, CAL 695); pap. 10.95 (ISBN 0-520-04890-3). U of Cal Pr.

Bowler, Printer & Schaffer, Mac. Wheat Flowers Edition III. 3rd ed. LC 83-83012. 94p. pap. 6.95 (ISBN 0-915945-00-2). Heartland Image.

Bowler, R. Arthur. Logistics & the Failure of the British Army in America, 1775-1783. 320p. 1975. 30.00x (ISBN 0-691-04630-1). Princeton U Pr.

Bowler, Rosemary F., ed. Annals of Dyslexia. 1983. 9.75. Orton Dyslexia.

Bowler, T. D. General Systems Thinking: Its Scope & Applicability. (General Systems Research Ser.: Vol. 4). 234p. 1981. 39.25 (ISBN 0-444-00420-3, North-Holland). Elsevier.

Bowler, Vivien, ed. Forty-Four String & Nail Art Projects. (Illus.). 96p. 1975. 6.95 (ISBN 0-517-51887-2). Crown.

Bowles. Microcomputer Problem Solving Using Pascal. 2nd ed. 500p. 1984. 17.95 (ISBN 0-387-90822-6). Springer-Verlag.

Bowles & Carver. Catchpenny Prints: One Hundred Sixty-Three Popular Engravings from the 18th Century. LC 79-103068. (Pictorial Archives Ser). (Illus., Orig.). 1970. pap. 5.95 (ISBN 0-486-22569-0). Dover.

Bowles, Chester. Africa's Challenge to America. LC 78-100280. (Illus.). Repr. of 1956 ed. 15.00x (ISBN 0-8371-2918-4, BOCA, Pub. by Negro U Pr). Greenwood.

--The Conscience of a Liberal. LC 74-15558. 351p. 1975. Repr. of 1962 ed. lib. bdg. 22.50x (ISBN 0-8371-7826-6, BOCO). Greenwood.

--Ideas, People & Peace. LC 74-12627. 151p. 1974. Repr. of 1958 ed. lib. bdg. 15.00x (ISBN 0-8371-7731-6, BOIP). Greenwood.

--The New Dimensions of Peace. LC 74-1512. (Illus.). 391p. 1974. Repr. of 1955 ed. lib. bdg. 20.50x (ISBN 0-8371-7388-4, BOND). Greenwood.

--View from New Delhi: Selected Speeches & Writings. (Illus.). 1969. 22.50x (ISBN 0-300-01233-0). Yale U Pr.

Bowles, D. Richard. Make Way for Metrication. LC 72-13331. (Math Concepts Bks.). (Illus.). 56p. (gr. 6-10). 1975. PLB 4.95g (ISBN 0-8225-0583-5). Lerner Pubns.

Bowles, Edward A. My Garden in Spring. LC 78-178004. (Illus.). 1971. Repr. of 1914 ed. 12.50 (ISBN 0-685-61145-0). Theophrastus.

Bowles, Ella S. About Antiques. LC 70-174011. (Tower Bks). (Illus.). 1971. Repr. of 1929 ed. 40.00x (ISBN 0-8103-3921-8). Gale.

--Homespun Handicrafts. LC 75-183343. Repr. of 1931 ed. 20.00 (ISBN 0-405-08298-3, Blom Pubns). Ayer Co Pubs.

Bowles, G. Strategies for Women's Studies in the Eighties. 100p. 1984. pap. 17.50 (ISBN 0-08-031320-5). Pergamon.

Bowles, George. Pages from the Virginia Story. (Illus.). 128p. (Orig.). 1979. pap. 8.95 (ISBN 0-9605688-1-6). Maiden Lane.

Bowles, Gloria & Duelli-Klein, Renate, eds. Theories of Women's Studies. 270p. (Orig.). 1983. pap. 9.95x (ISBN 0-7100-9488-4). Routledge & Kegan.

Bowles, Gordon T., jt. ed. see Count, Earl W.

Bowles, J. Foundation Analysis & Design. 3rd ed. 1982. 45.00x (ISBN 0-07-006770-8). McGraw.

Bowles, J. B., jt. auth. see Vichnevetsky, R.

Bowles, J. E. Engineering Properties of Soils & Their Measurement. 3rd ed. 464p. 1985. pap. price not set (ISBN 0-07-006754-6). McGraw.

Bowles, Jacqueline. The I of My Needle. (Masterworks Ser). 1976. pap. 1.25 (ISBN 0-916982-13-0). Realities.

Bowles, Jane. My Sister's Hand in Mine: An Expanded Edition of the Collected Works of Jane Bowles. LC 77-71329. (Neglected Books of the Twentieth Century). 1978. pap. 9.95 (ISBN 0-912946-44-X). Ecco Pr.

--Two Serious Ladies. (Obelisk Ser.). 208p. 1984. pap. 7.95 (ISBN 0-525-48136-2, 0772-230). Dutton.

Bowles, Jerry & Bowles, Suzanne. The Collector's Guide to New England. 160p. 1985. pap. 7.95 (ISBN 0-345-31503-0). Ballantine.

--The Collector's Guild to New England. (Illus.). 160p. (Orig.). 1985. pap. 7.95 (ISBN 0-345-31503-0). World Almanac.

Bowles, John B. Distribution & Biogeography of Mammals of Iowa. (Special Publications Ser.: No. 9). (Illus.). 184p. (Orig.). 1975. pap. 8.00 (ISBN 0-89672-034-9). Tex Tech Pr.

Bowles, Joseph E. Engineering Properties of Soils & Their Measurements. 2nd ed. (Illus.). 1978. pap. text ed. 35.95 (ISBN 0-07-006752-X). McGraw.

--Physical & Geotechnical Properties of Soils. (Illus.). 560p. 1979. text ed. 38.95 (ISBN 0-07-006760-0). McGraw.

--Structural Steel Design. (Illus.). 1980. text ed. 44.00 (ISBN 0-07-006765-1). McGraw.

Bowles, K. L., et al. Problem Solving Using UCSD Pascal. 2nd ed. (Illus.). 350p. 1984. pap. 17.95 (ISBN 0-387-90822-6). Springer Verlag.

Bowles, Ken. Beginner's Manual for the UCSD Pascal System. (Orig.). 1980. pap. 14.95 (ISBN 0-07-006745-7, BYTE Bks). McGraw.

Bowles, Larry L., jt. auth. see Brumgardt, John R.

Bowles, Michael. The Art of Conducting. LC 74-23419. (Music Ser.). 210p. 1975. Repr. of 1959 ed. lib. bdg. 25.00 (ISBN 0-306-70718-7). Da Capo.

Bowles, Patrick, tr. see Beckett, Samuel.

Bowles, Patrick, tr. see Castelain, Daniel.

Bowles, Patrick, tr. see Durrenmatt, Friedrich.

Bowles, Patrick, tr. see Petit, Pierre.

Bowles, Paul. Aperture, No. 94. (Illus.). 80p. 1984. pap. 12.50 (ISBN 0-89381-137-8). Aperture.

--Collected Stories of Paul Bowles. 420p. 1983. 17.50 (ISBN 0-87685-397-1); pap. 10.00 (ISBN 0-87685-396-3). Black Sparrow.

--The Delicate Prey. LC 72-80780. (Neglected Bks of the 20th Century). 307p. 1981. pap. 7.95 (ISBN 0-912946-01-6). Ecco Pr.

--A Hundred Camels in the Courtyard. (Orig.). 1962. pap. 2.00 (ISBN 0-87286-002-7). City Lights.

--Let It Come Down. 300p. 1980. 14.00 (ISBN 0-87685-480-3); pap. 8.50 (ISBN 0-87685-479-X). Black Sparrow.

--Midnight Mass. 176p. 1983. 14.00 (ISBN 0-87685-477-3); pap. 7.50 (ISBN 0-87685-476-5). Black Sparrow.

--Next to Nothing: Collected Poems 1926-1977. 77p. (Orig.). 1981. 14.00 (ISBN 0-87685-505-2); pap. 5.00 (ISBN 0-87685-504-4). Black Sparrow.

--Points in Time. LC 83-16571. 96p. 1984. 12.50 (ISBN 0-88001-044-4). Ecco Pr.

--The Sheltering Sky. LC 49-11888. (Neglected Books of the 20th Century Ser). 1978. pap. 7.95 (ISBN 0-912946-43-1). Ecco Pr.

--The Spider's House. rev. ed. 410p. 1982. 17.50 (ISBN 0-87685-546-X); pap. 10.00 (ISBN 0-87685-545-1). Black Sparrow.

--Their Heads Are Green & Their Hands Are Blue. LC 83-16577. 208p. 1984. pap. 8.50 (ISBN 0-88001-043-6). Ecco Pr.

--Three Tales. LC 75-18063. 24p. (Minimum order: 3 copies). 1975. pap. 3.50 (ISBN 0-916228-10-X). Phoenix Bk Shop.

--Up above the World. LC 82-2357. (Neglected Books of the 20th Century). 223p. 1982. pap. 7.95 (ISBN 0-88001-008-8). Ecco Pr.

--Without Stopping. Halpern, Daniel, ed. LC 72-175258. (Illus.). 379p. pap. 9.50 (ISBN 0-88001-061-4). Ecco Pr.

Bowles, Paul, ed. see Boulaich, Abdeslam, et al.

Bowles, Paul, ed. & tr. see Mrabet, Mohammed.

Bowles, Paul, tr. She Woke Me Up So I Killed Her. LC 82-71550. 100p. 1985. signed ltd. ed 20.00 (ISBN 0-317-02696-8); pap. 7.95. Cadmus Eds.

Bowles, Paul, tr. see Choukri, Mohamed.

Bowles, Paul, tr. see Eberhardt, Isabelle.

Bowles, Paul, tr. see Mrabet, Mohammed.

Bowles, Paul, tr. see Rey-Rosa, Rodrigo.

Bowles, Robert N. How to Buy Gold for Thirty Percent Below Market: And to Avoid Confiscation by the Government. 1981. 45.00 (ISBN 0-940372-00-2). Berot Bk.

Bowles, Roger A. & Whynes, David K. Macroeconomic Planning. (Studies in Economics). (Illus.). 1979. text ed. 25.00x (ISBN 0-04-330294-7). Allen Unwin.

Bowles, Roger A., jt. auth. see Whynes, David K.

Bowles, Rosewell P. The Operation & Effect of a Single Salary Schedule. LC 75-176584. (Columbia University. Teachers College. Contributions to Education: No. 518). Repr. of 1932 ed. 22.50 (ISBN 0-404-55518-7). AMS Pr.

Bowles, Samuel. Life & Times of Samuel Bowles, 2 Vols. Merriam, George S., ed. LC 75-87417. (American Scene Ser). 1970. Repr. of 1885 ed. Set. lib. bdg. 95.00 (ISBN 0-306-71562-7). Da Capo.

--Our New West: Records of Travel Between the Mississippi & the Pacific Ocean. LC 72-9429. (The Far Western Frontier Ser.). (Illus.). 528p. 1973. Repr. of 1869 ed. 32.00 (ISBN 0-405-04960-9). Ayer Co Pubs.

--Planning Educational Systems for Economic Growth. LC 78-82293. (Economic Studies: No. 133). (Illus.). 1969. 16.50x (ISBN 0-674-67090-6). Harvard U Pr.

Bowles, Samuel & Edwards, Richard. Understanding Capitalism: Competition, Command & Change in the U. S. Economy. 419p. 1985. pap. 17.50 scp (ISBN 0-06-040897-9, HarpC). Har-Row.

Bowles, Samuel & Gintis, Herbert. Schooling in Capitalist America: Educational Reform & the Contradictions of Economic Life. LC 75-7267. 320p. 1976. pap. 9.95x (ISBN 0-465-09718-9, TB-5041). Basic.

Bowles, Stephen E. An Approach to Film Study: A Selected Booklist & Bibliography. (Cinema Ser.). 1974. 59.95 (ISBN 0-87700-206-1). Revisionist Pr.

--Index to Critical Film Reviews: Nineteen Seventy-Two to Nineteen Seventy-Six, Vol. IV. 1979. lib. bdg. 32.50x (ISBN 0-89102-123-X). B Franklin.

--Sidney Lumet: A Guide to References & Resources. (Reference Books). 1979. lib. bdg. 18.50 (ISBN 0-8161-7938-7, Hall Reference). G K Hall.

Bowles, Stephen E., ed. Index to Critical Film Reviews in British & American Film Periodicals, 3 vols in 2. new ed. LC 74-12109. x, 900p. 1975. Set. 35.00 (ISBN 0-89102-040-3). B Franklin.

Bowles, Suzanne, jt. auth. see Bowles, Jerry.

Bowles, William A. Authentic Memoirs of William Augustus Bowles, Esquire, Ambassador from the United Nations of Creeks & Cherokees, to the Court of London. LC 73-146376. (First American Frontier Ser.). 1971. Repr. of 1791 ed. 13.00 (ISBN 0-405-02827-X). Ayer Co Pubs.

Bowles, William E. A Daily Key for Today's Christians: 365 Key Texts of the New Testament. 372p. 1984. 14.95 (ISBN 0-13-196113-6); pap. 6.95 (ISBN 0-13-196105-5). P-H.

Bowley, A. L. & Burnett-Hurst, A. R. Livelihood & Poverty: A Study in the Economic Conditions of Working-Class Households in Northampton, Warrington, Stanley, & Reading. LC 79-59651. (The English Working Class Ser.). 1980. lib. bdg. 29.00 (ISBN 0-8240-0105-2). Garland Pub.

Bowley, A. L. & Hogg, M. Has Poverty Diminished? Leventhal, F. M., ed. (English Workers & the Coming of the Welfare State, 1918 - 1945 Ser.). 236p. 1985. lib. bdg. 30.00 (ISBN 0-8240-7601-X). Garland Pub.

Bowley, Agatha H. Guiding the Normal Child. 176p. 1981. Repr. of 1943 ed. lib. bdg. 25.00 (ISBN 0-89987-079-1). Darby Bks.

Bowley, Agatha H. & Gardner, Leslie. The Handicapped Child. 4th ed. (Illus.). 1980. pap. text ed. 19.75 (ISBN 0-443-02084-1). Churchill.

Bowley, Arthur L. F. Y. Edgeworth's Contributions to Mathematical Statistics. LC 68-24161. Repr. of 1928 ed. 19.50x (ISBN 0-678-00889-2). Kelley.

--Mathematical Groundwork of Economics. LC 65-16995. Repr. of 1924 ed. 15.00x (ISBN 0-678-00075-1). Kelley.

--Some Economic Consequences of the Great War. LC 79-1573. 1980. Repr. of 1930 ed. 19.75 (ISBN 0-88355-879-3). Hyperion Conn.

--Wages in the United Kingdom in the Nineteenth Century. LC 68-55489. Repr. of 1900 ed. 22.50x (ISBN 0-678-00870-1). Kelley.

Bowley, C. C., et al, eds. Blood Transfusion: A Guide to the Formation & Operation of a Transfusion Service. 132p. 1971. pap. 5.60 (ISBN 92-4-154013-3, 196). World Health.

Bowley, M. E. British Building Industry. 1966. 59.50 (ISBN 0-521-04292-5). Cambridge U Pr.

Bowley, Marian. Housing & the State: Nineteen Nineteen to Nineteen Thirty-Four. 283p. 1985. lib. bdg. 35.00. Garland Pub.

--Nassau Senior & Classical Economics. 1968. lib. bdg. 27.50x (ISBN 0-374-90874-5). Octagon.

--Studies in the History of Economic Theory Before 1870. 1973. text ed. 25.50x (ISBN 0-391-00321-6). Humanities.

Bowley, R. L. The Fortunate Islands: The Story of the Isles of Scilly. 7th ed. 1980. 29.00x (ISBN 0-686-45443-X, Pub. by Bowley Pubns England). State Mutual Bk.

--Teaching Without Tears. 204p. 1973. pap. 6.95x (ISBN 0-8464-0909-7). Beekman Pubs.

--Teaching Without Tears. 1968. 6.00 (ISBN 0-8022-0165-2). Philos Lib.

Bowlin, Oswald D., et al. Guide to Financial Analysis. LC 78-27412. (Illus.). 1979. 23.50 (ISBN 0-07-006781-3); pap. 17.95x (ISBN 0-07-006780-5). McGraw.

Bowlin, William R., ed. A Book of Living Poems. LC 72-3088. (Granger Index Reprint Ser.). Repr. of 1934 ed. 17.75 (ISBN 0-8369-8233-9). Ayer Co Pubs.

--A Book of Treasured Poems. LC 72-3090. (Granger Index Reprint Ser.). Repr. of 1928 ed. 19.25 (ISBN 0-8369-8234-7). Ayer Co Pubs.

Bowling, Ann. Delegation in General Practice: A Study of Doctors & Nurses. 250p. 1981. 23.00x (ISBN 0-422-77490-1, NO.3474, Pub. by Tavistock). Methuen Inc.

Bowling, Ann & Cartwright, Ann. Life after a Death: A Study of the Elderly Widowed. 239p. 1982. 29.95x (ISBN 0-422-78230-0, NO. 3712, Pub. by Tavistock). Methuen Inc.

Bowling, David L. & Bowling, Patricia H. Dirty Dingy Daryl. Martz, John, ed. LC 81-83120. (Dirty Dingy Daryl Ser.). (Illus.). 24p. 1981. 4.95 (ISBN 0-939700-00-X); pap. 2.95 (ISBN 0-939700-01-8). I D I C P.

--Dirty Dingy Daryl for President. Martz, John, ed. LC 83-82273. (Dirty Dingy Daryl Ser.). (Illus.). 40p. 1983. 4.95 (ISBN 0-939700-02-6); pap. 2.95 (ISBN 0-939700-03-4). I D I C P.

Bowling, G. A. A History of Ayrshire Cattle in the United States. 1975. 10.00 (ISBN 0-87012-211-8). McClain.

Bowling, Patricia H., jt. auth. see Bowling, David L.

Bowling, Sue A., jt. auth. see Weller, Gunter.

Bowling, T. W. The Life, Works & Literary Career of Loaisel de Treogate. 1980. 120.00x (ISBN 0-7294-0261-4, Pub. by Volt Found Taylor Inst England). State Mutual Bk.

Bowling, W Kerby & Loving, Waldon. Management Fumbles & Union Recoveries. 232p. 1982. pap. text ed. 12.95 (ISBN 0-8403-2775-7). Kendall-Hunt.

Bowlt, John. Russian Art of the Avant Garde. (Documents of Twentieth Century Art Ser). 400p. 1976. 20.00 (ISBN 0-670-61257-X). Viking.

--The Silver Age: Russian Art in the Early Twentieth Century & the World Art Group. 2nd ed. (Illus.). 456p. 1982. 28.00 (ISBN 0-89250-063-8). Orient Res Partners.

Bowlt, John E. Russian Art Eighteen Seventy-Five to Nineteen Seventy-Five: A Collection of Essays. LC 76-28405. 213p. 1976. pap. 6.95x (ISBN 0-8422-0547-0). Irvington.

Bowlt, John E., jt. auth. see Misler, Nicoletta.

Bowlt, John E., intro. by. Russian Theater & Costume Designs from the Fine Arts Museums of San Francisco. LC 79-55788. (Illus.). 64p. 1979. pap. 6.95 (ISBN 0-88401-033-3). Fine Arts Mus.

Bowlt, John E., ed. see Livshits, Benedikt.

Bowlt, John E., tr. see Krasovskaya, Vera.

Bowlt, John E., tr. see Sizov, E. S.

Bowlt, John E. see Sarabianov, Dmitri Vladimirovich.

Bowly, Devereux, Jr. The Poorhouse: Subsidized Housing in Chicago, 1895-1976. LC 77-28271. (Illus.). 267p. 1978. 15.00 (ISBN 0-8093-0831-2). S Ill U Pr.

Bowman. Handbook of Carcinogens & Hazardous Substances. 766p. 1982. 99.50 (ISBN 0-8247-1683-3). Dekker.

Bowman & McQueen. Corporations: Formation with Forms. (The Law in Georgia Ser.). incl. latest pocket part supplement 24.95 (ISBN 0-686-90387-0); separate pocket part supplement, 1982 5.45 (ISBN 0-686-90388-9). Harrison Co GA.

Bowman, et al. Corporations: Formation with Forms. (The Law in Tennessee Ser.). incl. latest pocket part supplement 24.95 (ISBN 0-686-91000-1); separate pocket part supplement, 1982 6.45 (ISBN 0-686-91001-X). Harrison Co GA.

Bowman, Alan P. Index to the 1850 Census of the State of California. LC 70-148609. 605p. 1972. 30.00 (ISBN 0-8063-0484-7). Genealog Pub.

Bowman, Albert H. The Struggle for Neutrality: Franco-American Diplomacy During the Federalist Era. LC 73-21917. 1974. 29.75x (ISBN 0-87049-152-0). U of Tenn Pr.

Bowman, Alfred C. Zones of Strain: A Memoir of the Early Cold War. (Publications Ser.: P-273). 175p. 1982. 19.95 (ISBN 0-8179-7731-7). Hoover Inst Pr.

Bowman, Andrew L. Being Human. (Orig.). 1970. pap. 3.45 (ISBN 0-930254-01-5). Alethes.

Bowman, Ann, jt. ed. see Lester, James P.

Bowman, Arthur G. & Bond, Robert J. California Real Estate Principles. 3rd ed. 1982. text ed. 29.90x (ISBN 0-673-16010-6). Scott F.

Bowman, Arthur G. & Milligan, W. D. Real Estate Law in California. new, 6th ed. (Illus.). 368p. 1982. 29.95 (ISBN 0-13-764035-8). P-H.

Bowman, Arthur G., jt. auth. see Bond, Robert J.

Bowman, Arthur G., jt. auth. see Milligan, W. D.

Bowman, Arthur G., jt. auth. see Ogden, Melvin B.

Bowman, Bruce. Ideas: How to Get Them. LC 84-60971. 100p. (Orig.). 1985. pap. text ed. 9.95 (ISBN 0-88247-740-4). R & E Pubs.

Bowman, C. E., jt. auth. see Griffiths, D. A.

Bowman, Claude C. The College Professor in America: An Analysis of Articles Published in the General Magazines, 1890-1938. Metzger, Walter P., ed. LC 76-55170. (The Academic Profession Ser.). 1977. Repr. of 1938 ed. lib. bdg. 16.00x (ISBN 0-405-10001-9). Ayer Co Pubs.

Bowman, Claude C., ed. Humanistic Sociology: Readings. LC 72-13116. 1973. pap. text ed. 6.95x (ISBN 0-89197-221-8). Irvington.

Bowman, Craig T. & Birkeland, Jorgen, eds. Alternative Hydrocarbon Fuels: Combustion & Chemical Kinetics. LC 78-7278. (Illus.). 463p. 1978. 45.00 (ISBN 0-915928-25-6, PAAS62); members 25.00 (ISBN 0-317-32130-7). AIAA.

Bowman, Craig T., jt. ed. see Zinn, Ben T.

Bowman, Daniel J. The CAD-CAM Primer. LC 84-50904. 14.95 (ISBN 0-672-22187-X). Sams.

Bowman, David, jt. auth. see Shivers, Lynne.

Bowman, Dee. Southwestern Cooking Recipes. 16p. pap. 2.00x (ISBN 0-943462-05-3). CaseCo.

Bowman, Derek. Life into Autobiography: A Study of Goethe's "Dichtung und Wahrheit". (Germanic Studies in America: Vol. 5). 162p. 1972. 19.60 (ISBN 3-261-00311-1). P Lang Pubs.

Bowman, Derek, ed. The Diary of David Rubinowicz. 128p. 1982. 10.95 (ISBN 0-938106-03-1). Creative Options.

Bowman, Derek, tr. see Braker, Ulrich.

Bowman, Dicy V., ed. A Guide to Genealogical Resources in Escambia County. (Illus.). 32p. (Orig.). 1983. pap. 2.85 (ISBN 0-939566-03-6). Pensacola Hist.

Bowman, Don. Reunion in Rome. LC 84-61321. 1984. pap. 5.95 (ISBN 0-86666-377-0). Natl Lit Guild.

Bowman, Eldon. A Guide to the General Crook Trail. (Illus.). 1978. pap. 2.50 (ISBN 0-89734-045-0). Mus Northern Ariz.

Bowman, Ethel, jt. auth. see Palmer, Marjorie.

Bowman, Forest J. The Dentists Guide to Tax Shelters. LC 84-25380. 216p. 1985. 35.00 (ISBN 0-87814-276-2). Pennwell Bks.

Bowman, Frank. Introduction to Bessel Functions. (Illus.). 1958. pap. 3.00 (ISBN 0-486-60462-4). Dover.

Bowman, Fred Q. Landholders of Northeastern New York, 1739-1802. LC 83-80308. 228p. 1983. 20.00 (ISBN 0-8063-1026-X). Genealog Pub.

--Ten Thousand Vital Records of Western New York, 1809-1850. LC 84-81870. 318p. 1985. 22.50 (ISBN 0-8063-1099-5). Genealog Pub.

Bowman, G. With Lewis & Clark Through the Rockies. (Illus.). (gr. 7 up). 13.75x (ISBN 0-392-01900-0). Sportshelf.

Bowman, George M. Don't Let Go! An Exposition of Hebrews. 170p. 1982. pap. 4.95 (ISBN 0-87552-121-5). Presby & Reformed.

--How to Be an Effective Teacher. 1982. pap. 3.95 (ISBN 0-87552-120-7). Presby & Reformed.

--How to Succeed with Your Money. pap. 3.95 (ISBN 0-8024-3656-0). Moody.

Bowman, Gerald. With Amundsen at the North Pole. (Illus.). (gr. 7 up). 13.75x (ISBN 0-392-01847-0). Sportshelf.

Bowman, H. B. Handbook of Precision Sheet, Strip & Foil. 1980. 103.00 (ISBN 0-87170-091-3). ASM.

Bowman, Harold M. Administration of Iowa: A Study in Centralization. LC 70-82248. (Columbia University, Studies in the Social Sciences Ser.: No. 46). Repr. of 1903 ed. 18.50 (ISBN 0-404-51046-9). AMS Pr.

Bowman, Herbert J., tr. see Oswald, Hilton.

Bowman, Isaiah. The Andes of Southern Peru. LC 68-23277. (Illus.). Repr. of 1916 ed. lib. bdg. 22.25x (ISBN 0-8371-0025-9, BOAP). Greenwood.

--The Andes of Southern Peru. Repr. of 1916 ed. 25.00 (ISBN 0-8482-0136-1). Norwood Edns.

--Desert Trails of Atacama. LC 76-111776. (BCL Ser. I). Repr. of 1924 ed. 18.50 (ISBN 0-404-00964-6). AMS Pr.

--Desert Trails of Atacama. Repr. of 1924 ed. 25.00 (ISBN 0-8482-7354-0). Norwood Edns.

--Design for Scholarship. facs. ed. LC 71-152159. (Essay Index Reprint Ser). 1936. 15.00 (ISBN 0-8369-2181-X). Ayer Co Pubs.

--Forest Physiography: Physiography of the United States & Principles of Soils in Relation to Forestry. LC 78-125732. (American Environmental Studies). 1970. Repr. of 1911 ed. 52.00 (ISBN 0-405-02659-5). Ayer Co Pubs.

--The Pioneer Fringe. facsimile ed. LC 71-160960. (Select Bibliographies Reprint Ser.). Repr. of 1931 ed. 38.50 (ISBN 0-8369-5828-4). Ayer Co Pubs.

Bowman, Isaiah, ed. Limits of Land Settlement: A Report on Present-Day Possiblities. facs. ed. LC 67-30200. (Essay Index Reprint Ser). 1937. 24.50 (ISBN 0-8369-0233-5). Ayer Co Pubs.

Bowman, Isiah. The Andes of Southern Peru. 1916. 25.00 (ISBN 0-8495-0471-6). Arden Lib.

--Desert Trails of Atacama. 1924. 45.00 (ISBN 0-8495-0480-5). Arden Lib.

Bowman, Isobel, ed. A Theatre of Natures: Some XVIII Century Character Writings. (Illus.). 115p. 1983. Repr. of 1955 ed. lib. bdg. 35.00 (ISBN 0-89984-125-2). Century Bookbindery.

Bowman, J. C. & Susmel, P., eds. The Future of Beef Production in the European Community. (Current Topics in Veterinary Medicine & Animal Science: No. 5). 1979. lib. bdg. 79.00 (ISBN 90-247-2234-9, Pub. by Martinus Nijhoff Netherlands). Kluwer Academic.

Bowman, J. E., ed. Distribution & Evolution of Hemoglobin & Globin Loci: Proceedings of the Comprehensive Sickle Cell Center Symposium, Fourth Annual, University of Chicago, Oct. 10-12, 1982. (The University of Chicago Sickle Cell Center Hemoglobin Symposia Ser.: No. 4). 618p. 1983. 86.00 (ISBN 0-444-00793-8, Biomedical Pr). Elsevier.

Bowman, J. M., ed. Molecular Collision Dynamics. (Topics in Current Physics Ser.: Vol. 33). (Illus.). 158p. 1983. 22.00 (ISBN 0-387-12014-9). Springer-Verlag.

Bowman, J. N. & Heizer, Robert F. Anza & the Northwest Frontier of New Spain. 182p. 1967. 12.50 (ISBN 0-916561-04-6). Southwest Mus.

Bowman, J. S. The Proletarian Novel in America. 59.95 (ISBN 0-8490-0897-2). Gordon Pr.

Bowman, James, ed. see Huddleston, Mark W.

Bowman, James, ed. see McKerns, Joseph P.

Bowman, James C. Contemporary American Criticism. 330p. 1980. Repr. of 1926 ed. lib. bdg. 35.00 (ISBN 0-8495-0457-0). Arden Lib.

--Pecos Bill. LC 37-27327. (Folklore Ser). (Illus.). (gr. 5 up). 1964. PLB 9.25 (ISBN 0-8075-6384-6). A Whitman.

Bowman, James P., Jr. The Muscle Spindle & Neural Control of the Tongue: Implications for Speech. (Illus.). 176p. 1971. photocopy ed. 19.50x (ISBN 0-398-00207-X). C C Thomas.

Bowman, James S., jt. auth. see Rabin, Jack.

Bowman, James S., ed. Essentials of Management: Ethical Values, Attitudes, & Actions. LC 83-3712. 217p. 1983. 22.50x (ISBN 0-8046-9316-1, Natl U). Assoc Faculty Pr.

Bowman, James S., et al. Professional Ethics: Dissent in Organizations, an Annotated Bibliography & Resource Guide. Bowman, James S., ed. LC 82-48768. (Public Affairs & Administration Ser.: Vol. 2). 325p. 1984. lib. bdg. 43.00 (ISBN 0-8240-9217-1). Garland Pub.

Bowman, James T. & Graves, W. H. Placement Services & Techniques. 1976. pap. 9.20x (ISBN 0-87563-124-X). Stipes.

Bowman, Jayne, compiled by. Messages of Faith from the Bible. 1982. 4.95 (ISBN 0-8378-2029-4). Gibson.

--The World of Friendship. (Illus.). 1983. 8.00 (ISBN 0-8378-1801-X). Gibson.

Bowman, Jim, jt. ed. see Kierstead, Fred.

Bowman, Jim R., jt. auth. see Pulliam, John P.

Bowman, Joel, jt. auth. see Branchaw, Bernadine.

Bowman, Joel P. & Branchaw, Bernadine. Understanding & Using Communications in Business. 1977. text ed. 17.50 scp (ISBN 0-06-453709-9, HarpC). Har-Row.

Bowman, Joel P. & Branchaw, Bernadine B. Effective Business Correspondence. 1978. pap. text ed. 13.50 scp (ISBN 0-06-453713-7, HarpC); instructor's manual avail. (ISBN 0-06-453734-X). Har-Row.

Bowman, Joel P. & Branchaw, Bernadine P. Business Report Writing. 496p. 1984. text ed. 29.95x (ISBN 0-03-062793-1); instr's. manual w/transparency acetates & masters 19.95 (ISBN 0-03-062794-X). Dryden Pr.

Bowman, John. De Valera & the Ulster Question, Nineteen Seventeen to Nineteen Seventy-three. 1982. 29.95x (ISBN 0-19-822681-0); pap. 13.95x (ISBN 0-19-822776-0). Oxford U Pr.

--The Fourth Gospel & the Jews: A Study of R. Akiba, Esther, & the Gospel of John. LC 75-40461. (Pittsburgh Theological Monographs: No. 8). 1975. pap. 9.00 (ISBN 0-915138-10-7). Pickwick.

--The Samaritan Problem: Studies in the Relationship of Samaritanism, Judaism, & Early Christianity. Johnson, Alfred M., Jr., tr. from Ger. LC 75-20042. (Pittsburgh Theological Monographs: No. 4). 1975. pap. 8.75 (ISBN 0-915138-04-2). Pickwick.

--The Travellers' Guide to Crete. 5th ed. LC 78-327931. (Travellers' Guide Ser.). (Illus.). 328p. 1979. 13.95 (ISBN 0-224-01951-1, Pub. by Jonathan Cape). Merrimack Pub Cir.

--The Traveller's Guide to Crete. Rev. ed. 320p. 1985. pap. 11.95 (ISBN 0-224-02285-7, Pub. by Jonathan Cape). Merrimack Pub Cir.

Bowman, John & O'Donoghue, Ronan. Portraits: Belvedere College, 1832-1982. 1982. 75.00x (ISBN 0-7171-1235-7, Pub. by Gill & Macmillan Ireland). State Mutual Bk.

Bowman, John, ed. & tr. Samaritans Documents Relating to Their History, Religion & Life. LC 77-4949. (Pittsburgh Original Texts & Translations Ser.: No. 2). 1977. pap. 11.50 (ISBN 0-915138-27-1). Pickwick.

Bowman, John C. Introduction to Animal Breeding. 2nd ed. (Sudies in Biology: No. 46). 88p. 1984. pap. text ed. 8.95 (ISBN 0-7131-2880-1). E Arnold.

Bowman, John S. The Vietnam War: An Almanac. (Illus.). 512p. 1985. 24.95 (ISBN 0-911818-85-5, Bison Books). World Almanac.

Bowman, John S., ed. The Civil War Almanac. LC 82-15514. (Illus.). 400p. 1983. 19.95 (ISBN 0-87196-640-9). Facts on File.

--The Civil War Almanac. LC 82-61819. (Illus.). 400p. pap. 10.95 (ISBN 0-911818-36-7). World Almanac.

--The Civil War Almanac. 1983. pap. 10.95 (ISBN 0-911818-36-7, World Almanac). Newspaper Ent.

Bowman, John S., jt. ed. see Ferrell, Robert H.

Bowman, John W. Hebrews-Second Peter. LC 59-10454. (Layman's Bible Commentary Ser: Vol. 24). 1962. pap. 4.95 (ISBN 0-8042-3084-6). John Knox.

--Unless I See. LC 76-42859. (Illus.). 1977. pap. 5.00 (ISBN 0-89430-002-4). Palos Verdes.

Bowman, Kathleen. New Women in Art & Dance. LC 76-5457. (New Women Ser.). (Illus.). (gr. 4-12). 1976. PLB 8.95 (ISBN 0-87191-512-X). Creative Ed.

--New Women in Entertainment. LC 76-4940. (New Women Ser.). (Illus.). (gr. 4-12). 1976. PLB 8.95 (ISBN 0-87191-510-3). Creative Ed.

--New Women in Media. LC 76-6061. (New Women Ser.). (Illus.). (gr. 4-12). 1976. PLB 8.95 (ISBN 0-87191-511-1). Creative Ed.

--New Women in Medicine. LC 76-4873. (New Women Ser.). (Illus.). (gr. 4-12). 1976. PLB 8.95 (ISBN 0-87191-508-1). Creative Ed.

--New Women in Politics. LC 76-5513. (New Women Ser.). (Illus.). (gr. 4-12). 1976. PLB 8.95 (ISBN 0-87191-507-3). Creative Ed.

--New Women in Social Sciences. LC 76-5508. (New Women Ser.). (Illus.). (gr. 4-12). 1976. PLB 8.95 (ISBN 0-87191-509-X). Creative Ed.

Bowman, Kenneth J., jt. auth. see Lovie-Kitchin, Jan E.

Bowman, Kimiko O., jt. auth. see Shenton, Leonard R.

Bowman, Larry G. Captive Americans: Prisoners During the American Revolution. LC 75-36984. viii, 146p. 1976. 9.00x (ISBN 0-8214-0215-3, 82-82204); pap. 4.50x (ISBN 0-8214-0229-3, 82-82212). Ohio U Pr.

Bowman, Larry W. Politics in Rhodesia: White Power in an African State. LC 73-75057. 224p. 1973. text ed. 15.00x (ISBN 0-674-68786-8). Harvard U Pr.

--South Africa's Outward Strategy: A Foreign Policy Dilemma for the United States. LC 72-183388. (Papers in International Studies: Africa Ser.: No. 13). (Illus.). 32p. 1971. pap. 3.25x (ISBN 0-89680-046-6, 82-91643, Ohio U Ctr Intl). Ohio U Pr.

--South Africa's Outward Strategy: A Foreign Policy Dilemma for the United States. LC 72-183388. (Papers in International Studies. Africa Ser.: No. 13). pap. 20.00 (ISBN 0-317-11331-3, 2007421). Bks Demand UMI.

Bowman, Larry W. & Clark, Ian, eds. The Indian Ocean in Global Politics. LC 80-18298. (Westview Special Studies in International Relations). 272p. 1980. lib. bdg. 30.00x (ISBN 0-86531-038-6); pap. 13.50x (ISBN 0-86531-191-9). Westview.

Bowman, Lea, jt. auth. see Stringer, Leslea.

Bowman, Leonard, ed. Itinerarium: The Idea of Journey. (Salzburg-Elizabethan Studies: No. 92). 234p. 1983. pap. text ed. 25.50x (ISBN 0-391-03063-9, Pub. by Salzburg). Humanities.

Bowman, LeRoy E. The American Funeral: A Study in Guilt, Extravagance, & Sublimity. LC 72-14083. 181p. 1973. Repr. of 1959 ed. lib. bdg. 22.50x (ISBN 0-8371-6749-3, BOFU). Greenwood.

Bowman, Locke E., Jr. Teaching Today: The Church's First Ministry. LC 79-25901. 212p. 1980. pap. 8.95 (ISBN 0-664-24303-7). Westminster.

Bowman, Lynn. Los Angeles: Epic of a City. LC 74-16723. (Illus.). 400p. 1974. 10.00 (ISBN 0-8310-7109-5). Howell-North.

Bowman, M. A. & Allen, D. I. Stress & Women Physicians. (Illus.). 160p. 1985. 27.50 (ISBN 0-387-96117-8). Springer-Verlag.

Bowman, M. C., ed. Analysis of Pesticides by Chromatographic Methods. new ed. 1976. 25.00 (ISBN 0-912474-08-4). Preston Pubns.

Bowman, M. G., jt. auth. see Hausner, H. H.

Bowman, Malcolm. Carcinogens & Related Substances: Analytical Chemistry for Toxicological Research. 1979. 65.00 (ISBN 0-8247-6885-X). Dekker.

Bowman, Martin W. Castles in the Air: The Story of the B-17 Flying Fortress Crews of the U. S. Eighth Air Force. (Illus.). 210p. (Orig.). 1985. 19.95 (ISBN 0-85059-675-0, Pub. by PSL P Stephens England); pap. 12.95 (ISBN 0-85059-786-2). Sterling.
--Fields of Little America. (Illus.). 120p. 16.95 (Pub. by P Stephens England). Motorbooks Intl.
Bowman, Mary A. Library & Information Science Journals & Serials: An Analytical Guide. LC 84-15787. (Annotated Bibliographies of Serials Series-A Subject Approach: No. 1). xiii, 140p. 1985. lib. bdg. 29.95 (ISBN 0-313-23807-3, BLF/). Greenwood.
Bowman, Mary A., compiled by. Western Mysticism: A Guide to the Basic Sources. LC 78-18311. 120p. 1979. pap. 9.00x (ISBN 0-8389-0266-9). ALA.
Bowman, Mary Ann & Stamas, Joan D. Written Communication in Business: A Selective Bibliography. 104p. (Orig.). 1980. pap. 6.60 (ISBN 0-931874-09-2). Assn Busn Comm.
Bowman, Mary Ann, compiled by. Gemstones: Daily Reflections for Positive Living. 76p. (Orig.). 1982. pap. 5.50 (ISBN 0-942228-00-6). Leonine Pr.
Bowman, Mary J. Collective Choice in Education. (Studies in Public Choice). 1982. lib. bdg. 30.00 (ISBN 0-89838-091-X). Kluwer-Nijhoff.
--Educational Choice & Labor Markets in Japan. LC 80-25557. 320p. 1981. lib. bdg. 30.00x (ISBN 0-226-06923-0). U of Chicago Pr.
Bowman, Mary J. & Haynes, W. Warren. Resources & People in East Kentucky: Problems & Potentials of a Lagging Economy. LC 83-11766. (Resources for the Future, Inc. Publications). 480p. Repr. of 1963 ed. 78.50 (ISBN 0-404-60328-9). AMS Pr.
Bowman, Mary J., jt. auth. see Plunkett, H. Dudley.
Bowman, Michael. A Guide to Nurse Management: A Conceptual Approach. 192p. (Orig.). 1985. pap. 15.50 (ISBN 0-7099-3234-0, Pub. by Croom Helm Ltd). Longwood Pub Group.
Bowman, Ned A. Handbook of Technical Practice for the Performing Arts, 2 pts. 1975. 34.95x (ISBN 0-913868-05-1); Pt. 1. perfect bdg. 12.95 (ISBN 0-913868-02-7); Pt. 2. binder 12.95x (ISBN 0-913868-04-3). Scenographic.
Bowman, Ned A., et al. Recent Publications on Theatre Architecture. 1972. acco bdg. 5.95x (ISBN 0-913868-07-8). Scenographic.
--Planning for the Theatre. 1965. spiral bdg. 4.95x (ISBN 0-913868-08-6). Scenographic.
Bowman, Norman H. Publicity in Print. LC 74-30822. (Illus.). 1974. pap. 8.40x (ISBN 0-915716-01-1). Publicity.
Bowman, Norman H., et al. The Grandparenting Book. LC 82-72106. (Illus.). 128p. (Orig.). 1982. pap. 6.95 (ISBN 0-939894-01-7). Blossom Valley.
Bowman, Pasco M., et al. Missouri Corporations-Formation: With Forms. LC 83-234970. (Illus.). vii, 168p. 1983. 34.95. Harrison Co GA.
Bowman, Pat & Ellis, Nigel. Manual of Public Relations. 1977. pap. 12.50 (ISBN 0-434-90170-9, Pub. by W Heinemann Ltd). David & Charles.
Bowman, Princess M. & Johnston, Percy. Georgetown-Foggy Bottom Heritage Trail. (Richardson Foundation History Ser.). 24p. (Orig.). (gr. k-12). 1984. pap. text ed. 6.95 (ISBN 0-915833-83-2); 1.50 (ISBN 0-915833-33-6). Drama Jazz Hse Inc.
--Howard Heritage Trail. (Richardson Foundation History Ser.). 24p. (Orig.). (gr. k-12). 1984. pap. 6.95 (ISBN 0-915833-82-4); 1.50 (ISBN 0-915833-32-8). Drama Jazz Hse Inc.
Bowman, Ralph. Secret Symbols in the Book of Revelation: A Metaphysical Interpretation. (Illus.). 259p. 1972. pap. 4.95 (ISBN 0-917200-09-8). ESPress.
Bowman, Ray, ed. Church Building Sourcebook Two. 264p. 1982. 39.95 (ISBN 0-8341-0759-7). Beacon Hill.
Bowman, Raymond A. Aramaic Ritual Texts from Persepolis. LC 65-55148. (Oriental Institute Pubns. Ser: No. 91). 1970. 35.00x (ISBN 0-226-62194-4). U of Chicago Pr.
Bowman, Richard E., jt. auth. see Kircher, John F.
Bowman, Robert. Basic Financial Accounting. 440p. 1983. pap. text ed. 18.95x (ISBN 0-7131-0729-4). Intl Ideas.
Bowman, Robert, ed. see Bligh, William.
Bowman, Robert I., et al, eds. Patterns of Evolution in Galapagos Organisms. 568p. (Orig.). 1983. 32.50 (ISBN 0-934394-05-9). AAASPD.
Bowman, Robert P., jt. auth. see Myrick, Robert D.
Bowman, Rufus D. Church of the Brethren & the War, 1788-1914. LC 75-147667. (Library of War & Peace; Relig. & Ethical Positions on War). 1972. 46.00 (ISBN 0-8240-0425-6). Garland Pub.
Bowman, Russell. Couponing & Rebates: Profits on the Dotted Line. LC 80-52786. 1980. 14.95 (ISBN 0-86730-508-8). Lebhar Friedman.
--From Chicago. Pace Gallery Publications, ed. (Illus.). 15p. (Orig.). 1982. fold out brochure 6.00 (ISBN 0-938608-20-7). Pace Gallery Pubns.
Bowman, Ruth. Murals Without Walls: Arshile Gorky's Aviation Murals Rediscovered. LC 78-13898. 1978. soft cover 7.95 (ISBN 0-932828-01-9). Newark Mus.
Bowman, S. D. Modern Methods of Pipe Fabrication. rev. ed. 1966. 4.00 (ISBN 0-87511-008-8). Claitors.
--Ordinates for Eight Hundred Pipe Intersections. 3rd ed. 1974. 3.50 (ISBN 0-87511-008-8). Claitors.
--Piping Problems. 1970. 4.00 (ISBN 0-87511-009-6). Claitors.
Bowman, Sara. A Fashion for Extravagance: Parisian Fabric & Fashion Designs from the Art Deco Period. (Illus.). 128p. 1985. 17.95 (ISBN 0-525-24358-5, 01743-520). Dutton.
Bowman, Sarah & Vardey, Lucinda. Pigs: A Troughful of Treasures. 1983. 7.95 (ISBN 0-02-040340-2). Macmillan.
Bowman, Sarah Y., et al. Public Personnel Administration: An Annotated Bibliography. LC 82-49150. (Public Affairs & Administration Ser.). 1985. lib. bdg. 42.00 (ISBN 0-8240-9151-5). Garland Pub.
Bowman, Steven B. The Jews of Byzantium: Twelve Four to Fourteen Fifty-Three. LC 83-17230. (Judaic Studies Ser.). (Illus.). 400p. 1985. 42.50 (ISBN 0-8173-0198-4). U of Ala Pr.
Bowman, Sylvia. Year Two Thousand: A Critical Biography of Edward Bellamy. 1979. Repr. of 1958 ed. lib. bdg. 29.00x (ISBN 0-374-90879-6). Octagon.
Bowman, Sylvia E., ed. see Howe, Edgar W.
Bowman, Sylvia E., et al. Edward Bellamy Abroad. 1962. 15.95x (ISBN 0-8084-0371-0). New Coll U Pr.
Bowman, Thomas, et al. Finding Your Best Place to Live in America. 416p. 1983. pap. 3.95 (ISBN 0-446-30586-3). Warner Bks.
Bowman, Thomas E. & Tareen, Inam U. Cymothoidae from Fishes of Kuwait (Arabian Gulf)(Crustacea: Isopoda) LC 83-600096. (Smithsonian Contributions to Zoology Ser.: No. 382). pap. 20.00 (ISBN 0-317-29613-2, 2021865). Bks Demand UMI.
Bowman, Thomas F. & Giuliani, George A. Finding Your Best Place to Live in America. 416p. 1982. pap. 9.95 (ISBN 0-940162-02-4). Red Lion.
Bowman, Thomas F., et al. Finding Your Best Place to Live in America. LC 81-51506. (Illus.). 352p. (Orig.). 1981. pap. 9.95 (ISBN 0-940162-00-8). Red Lion.
Bowman, Thomas H., Jr., ed. see Real Estate Education Company.
Bowman, W. C. Pharmacology of Neuromuscular Function. (Illus.). 200p. 1981. text ed. 21.00 (ISBN 0-8391-4144-0). Univ Park.
Bowman, W. C., ed. Pharmacology & Therapeutics, Vol. 12, No. 1. LC 77-25743. (Illus.). 283p. 1981. pap. 66.00 (ISBN 0-08-026854-4). Pergamon.
--Pharmacology & Therapeutics, Vol. 12, No. 2. (Illus.). 190p. 1981. pap. 66.00 (ISBN 0-08-026855-2). Pergamon.
Bowman, W. Dodgson. Charlie Chaplin: His Life & Art. LC 74-1090. (American Biography Ser., No. 32). 1974. lib. bdg. write for info. (ISBN 0-8383-1841-X). Haskell.
Bowman, Walter P. & Ball, Robert H. Theatre Language, a Dictionary. LC 60-10495. 1976. pap. 4.95 (ISBN 0-87830-551-3). Theatre Arts.
Bowman, Ward S., Jr. Patent & Antitrust Law: A Legal & Economic Appraisal. 1973. 25.00x (ISBN 0-226-06925-7). U of Chicago Pr.
Bowman, William D. Story of Surnames. LC 68-8906. 1968. Repr. of 1932 ed. 38.00x (ISBN 0-8103-3110-1). Gale.
Bowman, William J. Graphic Communication. LC 67-29931. (Wiley Series on Human Communication). (Illus.). pap. 55.50 (ISBN 0-317-10397-0, 2051238). Bks Demand UMI.
Bowmann, Jeanne. Secret of the Forest. (Contemporary Teens Ser.). 224p. (Orig.). 1981. pap. 2.25 (ISBN 0-89531-146-1, 0146-96). Sharon Pubns.
Bowmen, M. R. & Whitmore, T. C. A Second Look at Agathis. 1980. 30.00x (ISBN 0-85074-053-3, Pub. by For Lib Comm England). State Mutual Bk.
Bown, Colin. China, Nineteen Forty-Nine to Nineteen Seventy-Six. 1977. text ed. 16.95x (ISBN 0-435-32011-4); pap. text ed. 10.00x (ISBN 0-435-32009-2). Heinemann Ed.
--The People's Republic of China. (History Broadsheets Ser.). 1974. pap. text ed. 8.50x (ISBN 0-435-31091-7). Heinemann Ed.
Bown, Colin & Mooney, Peter. Cold War to Detente. 2nd ed. 1981. pap. 10.00x (ISBN 0-435-32132-3). Heinemann Ed.
Bown, Jane, photos by. The Gentle Eye. (Illus., Orig.). 1982. pap. text ed. 12.95 (ISBN 0-500-27204-2). Thames Hudson.
Bown, Lalage. Two Centuries of African English. (African Writers Ser.). 1973. pap. text ed. 6.50x (ISBN 0-435-90132-X). Heinemann Ed.
Bownas, Geoffrey, jt. ed. see Norbury, Paul.
Bownas, Geoffrey & Thwaite, Anthony, trs. The Penguin Book of Japanese Verse. (Orig.). 1964. pap. 5.95 (ISBN 0-14-042077-0). Penguin.
Bownas, Geoffrey, tr. see Akutagawa, Ryunosuke.
Bowne, Alan. Forty-Deuce. LC 83-50309. 96p. (Orig.). 1983. pap. 5.95 (ISBN 0-933322-13-5). Sea Horse.
Bowne, B. P. Theory of Thought & Knowledge. 1897. 22.00 (ISBN 0-527-10460-4). Kraus Repr.
Bowne, Borden O. The Philosophy of Herbert Spencer. 59.95 (ISBN 0-8490-0827-1). Gordon Pr.
Bowne, Borden P. The Christian Revelation. LC 75-3069. Repr. of 1898 ed. 11.00 (ISBN 0-404-59068-3). AMS Pr.
--The Essence of Religion. LC 75-3070. Repr. of 1910 ed. 20.50 (ISBN 0-404-59069-1). AMS Pr.
--The Immanence of God. LC 75-3071. Repr. of 1905 ed. 18.50 (ISBN 0-404-59070-5). AMS Pr.
--Introduction to Psychological Theory. LC 75-3072. (Philosophy in America Ser.). Repr. of 1887 ed. 22.50 (ISBN 0-404-59071-3). AMS Pr.
--Kant & Spencer, a Critical Exposition. LC 66-25898. Repr. of 1912 ed. 14.50x (ISBN 0-8046-0037-6, Pub. by Kennikat). Assoc Faculty Pr.
--Metaphysics... rev. ed. LC 75-948. (Philosophy in America Ser.). Repr. of 1898 ed. 31.50 (ISBN 0-404-59072-1). AMS Pr.
--Personalism. LC 75-949. Repr. of 1908 ed. 22.50 (ISBN 0-404-59073-X). AMS Pr.
--The Principles of Ethics. LC 75-3073. (Philosophy in America Ser.). Repr. of 1892 ed. 28.00 (ISBN 0-404-59074-8). AMS Pr.
--Representative Essays of Borden Parker Bowne. Steinkraus, Warren E., ed. LC 80-82504. 1980. 12.50 (ISBN 0-86610-066-0). Meridian Pub.
--Studies in Christianity. LC 75-3074. Repr. of 1909 ed. 28.50 (ISBN 0-404-59075-6). AMS Pr.
--Studies in Theism. LC 7-25071. 1968. Repr. of 1907 ed. 28.00 (ISBN 0-527-10450-7). Kraus Repr.
--Theism... Comprising the Deems Lectures for 1902. LC 75-3075. (Philosophy in America Ser.). Repr. of 1902 ed. 22.50 (ISBN 0-404-59076-4). AMS Pr.
Bowne, Eliza S. A Girl's Life Eighty Years Ago: Selection from the Letters of Eliza Southgate Bowne. LC 74-3933. (Women in America Ser). (Illus.). 280p. 1974. Repr. of 1888 ed. 21.00x (ISBN 0-405-06079-3). Ayer Co Pubs.
--A Girl's Life Eighty Years Ago: Selections from the Letters of Eliza Southgate Bowne. 239p. 1980. Repr. of 1887 ed. 16.00 (ISBN 0-87938-105-1). Corner Hse.
Bowne, Ford. Drygulchers. 1977. pap. 1.25 (ISBN 0-532-12504-5). Woodhill.
--Rangeland Marshall. (Orig.). 1977. pap. 1.25 (ISBN 0-532-12509-6). Woodhill.
Bowne, John. The Bowne Journal. 1976. 5.00 (ISBN 0-686-20856-0). Polyanthos.
Bownes, Mary, jt. ed. see Balls, Michael.
Bowness, Alan, ed. The Complete Sculpture of Barbara Hepworth 1960-69. 224p. 1980. 50.00x (ISBN 0-85331-271-0, Pub. by Lund Humphries England). State Mutual Bk.
Bowness, Alan, intro. by. Marcel Broodthaer's. (Illus.). 126p. pap. 11.95 (ISBN 0-905005-32-5, Pub. by Salem Hse Ltd). Merrimack Pub Cir.
--St. Ives: Nineteen Thirty-Six to Nineteen Sixty-Four. (Illus.). 247p. 1985. pap. 14.95 (ISBN 0-946590-20-6, Pub. by Salem Hse Ltd). Merrimack Pub Cir.
--The Tate Gallery Collections. 8th ed. 373p. pap. 19.95 (ISBN 0-946590-00-1, Pub. by Salem Hse Ltd). Merrimack Pub Cir.
Bowness, C. The Practice of Meditation 1971. rev. ed. (Paths to Inner Power Ser.). 1979. pap. 2.50 (ISBN 0-87728-151-3). Weiser.
Bowood, Richard. Great Inventions. (Illus.). (gr. 4 up). 2.50 (ISBN 0-7214-0132-5). Merry Thoughts.
--Story of Clothes & Costume. (Illus.). (gr. 4 up). 2.50 (ISBN 0-7214-0137-6). Merry Thoughts.
--Story of Flight. (Illus.). (gr. 4 up). 2.50 (ISBN 0-7214-0131-7). Merry Thoughts.
--Story of Houses & Homes. (Illus.). (gr. 4 up). 2.50 (ISBN 0-7214-0136-8). Merry Thoughts.
--Story of Ships. (Illus.). (gr. 4 up). 2.50 (ISBN 0-7214-0134-1). Merry Thoughts.
--Underwater Exploration. (Illus.). (gr. 4 up). 2.50 (ISBN 0-7214-0140-6). Merry Thoughts.
Bowood, Richard, jt. auth. see Newing, F. E.
Bowra, C. M. The Background of Modern Poetry. LC 75-22207. (Studies in Poetry, No. 38). 1975. lib. bdg. 22.95x (ISBN 0-8383-2075-9). Haskell.
--The Lyrical Poetry of Thomas Hardy. LC 75-22227. (Studies in Thomas Hardy, No. 14). 1975. lib. bdg. 22.95x (ISBN 0-8383-2098-8). Haskell.
Bowra, C. M., ed. see Pindar.
Bowra, C. M., tr. see Pindar.
Bowra, C. M., jt. tr. see Wade, Ger H.
Bowra, C. Maurice. Pindar. 1964. 32.50x (ISBN 0-19-814338-9). Oxford U Pr.
--The Romantic Imagination. (Oxford Paperbook Bks). 1961. pap. 9.95x (ISBN 0-19-281006-5). Oxford U Pr.
Bowra, Cecil M. Edith Sitwell. LC 73-14922. 1947. lib. bdg. 8.50 (ISBN 0-8414-3270-8). Folcroft.
--Edith Sitwell. LC 75-38540. (Studies in Poetry: No. 38). 1976. lib. bdg. 22.95x (ISBN 0-8383-2114-3). Haskell.
--Greek Experience. pap. 4.95 (ISBN 0-451-62392-4, Ment). NAL.
--In General & Particular. LC 72-156615. (Essay Index Reprint Ser.). Repr. of 1964 ed. 19.00 (ISBN 0-8369-2752-4). Ayer Co Pubs.
--Inspiration & Poetry. facsimile ed. LC 77-106407. (Essay Index Reprint Ser.). 1955. 19.00 (ISBN 0-8369-1452-X). Ayer Co Pubs.
--Inspiration & Poetry. LC 73-15750. 1955. lib. bdg. 12.00 (ISBN 0-8414-3316-X). Folcroft.
--Lyrical Poetry of Thomas Hardy. LC 73-2719. 1946. lib. bdg. 7.50 (ISBN 0-8414-1787-3). Folcroft.
--Simplicity of Racine. LC 74-14552. 1956. lib. bdg. 10.00 (ISBN 0-8414-9876-8). Folcroft.
Bowra, Cecil M., ed. A Second Book of Russian Verse. LC 73-114472. xvii, 153p. Repr. of 1948 ed. lib. bdg. 22.50x (ISBN 0-8371-4814-6, BORW). Greenwood.
Bowra, Sir Cecil M. Tradition & Design in the Iliad. LC 77-3065. 1977. Repr. of 1930 ed. lib. bdg. 29.75x (ISBN 0-8371-9561-6, BOTD). Greenwood.
Bowra, Maurice. The Simplicity of Racine. 1978. Repr. of 1956 ed. lib. bdg. 10.00 (ISBN 0-8495-0421-X). Arden Lib.
Bowrey, Thomas. A Geographical Account of Countries Round the Bay of Bengal, 1669-1679. Temple, Richard C., ed. (Hakluyt Society Works Ser.: No. 2, Vol. 12). Repr. of 1903 ed. 52.00 (ISBN 0-317-16484-8). Kraus Repr.
Bowring, Clara & Monro, Alida. The Poodle. 11th ed. (Popular Dog Ser.). (Illus.). 1979. 9.95 (ISBN 0-09-124890-6, Pub. by Hutchinson). Merrimack Pub Cir.
Bowring, Dave. Bowhunting for Whitetails: Your Best Methods for Taking North America's Favorite Deer. Fish, Chet, ed. (Illus.). 320p. 1985. 24.95 (ISBN 0-8117-0289-8). Stackpole.
--How to Fish Streams. LC 77-1863. (Illus.). 1977. 14.95 (ISBN 0-8329-3630-8, Pub. by Winchester Pr). New Century.
--Largemouth, Smallmouth & Close Kin. LC 82-1922. 176p. (Orig.). 1982. pap. 12.95 (ISBN 0-8329-3630-8, Pub. by Winchester Pr). New Century.
Bowring, E. A., et al, trs. see Goethe, Johann W.
Bowring, G. L., jt. auth. see Pryer, G. A.
Bowring, Jean. New Cake Decorating Book. LC 76-113947. (Illus.). 1977. 10.95 (ISBN 0-668-04343-1, 4343). Arco.
Bowring, John. The Kingdom & People of Siam, 2 vols. LC 70-179172. (South & Southeast Asia Studies Ser.). (Illus.). Repr. of 1857 ed. Set. 70.00 (ISBN 0-404-54802-4). AMS Pr.
--Minor Morals for Young People, 2 vols. 1934. 50.00 set (ISBN 0-932062-23-7). Sharon Hill.
--Report on the Commercial Statistics of Syria. LC 73-6271. (The Middle East Ser.). Repr. of 1840 ed. 15.00 (ISBN 0-405-05326-6). Ayer Co Pubs.
Bowring, Nona, jt. auth. see Chester, D. N.
Bowring, R. J. Mori Ogai & the Modernization of Japanese Culture. LC 76-11074. (Oriental Publications Ser.: No. 28). (Illus.). 1979. 49.50 (ISBN 0-521-21319-3). Cambridge U Pr.
Bowring, Richard. Murasaki Shikibu: Her Diary & Poetic Memoirs, a Translation & Study. LC 84-47908. (Library of Asian Translations). 320p. 1985. pap. 10.50x (ISBN 0-691-01416-7). Princeton U Pr.
Bowring, Richard, tr. from Japanese. Murasaki Shikibu: Her Diary & Poetic Memoirs. LC 81-47908. (Princeton Library of Asian Translations). (Illus.). 304p. 1982. 29.00 (ISBN 0-691-06507-1). Princeton U Pr.
Bowron, Bernard R., Jr. Henry B. Fuller of Chicago. LC 70-140915. (Contributions in American Studies, No. 11). (Illus.). 1974. lib. bdg. 29.95x (ISBN 0-8371-5820-6, BHF/). Greenwood.
Bowron, Edgar P. Renaissance Bronzes in the Walters Art Gallery. (A Walters Art Gallery Picture Book). (Illus.). 1978. pap. 4.00 (ISBN 0-911886-16-8). Walters Art.
Bowron, Edgar P., ed. The North Carolina Museum of Art: Introduction to the Collections. LC 82-21982. (Illus.). xvi, 295p. 1983. pap. 19.95x (ISBN 0-8078-4097-1). U of NC Pr.
Bowron, Edgar P., ed. see Clark, Anthony M.
Bowron, P. & Stephenson, F. W. Active Filters for Communication & Instrumentation. (Illus.). 320p. 1979. text ed. 27.00 (ISBN 0-07-084086-5). McGraw.
Bowry, T. R. Immunology Simplified. 2nd ed. (Illus.). 1984. pap. 12.50x (ISBN 0-19-261340-5). Oxford U Pr.
Bowser, Arthur M. What Every Jehovah's Witness Should Know. 1975. micro book 1.45 (ISBN 0-916406-34-2). Accent Bks.
Bowser, Benjamin P. & Hunt, Raymond G. Impacts of Racism on White Americans. LC 81-9111. (Sage Focus Editions: Vol. 36). (Illus.). 288p. 1981. 28.00 (ISBN 0-8039-1593-4); pap. 14.00 (ISBN 0-8039-1594-2). Sage.
Bowser, Benjamin P., et al, eds. Census Data with Maps for Small Areas of New York City 1910-1960: A Guide to the Microfilm Collection. 35p. 1981. 20.00 (ISBN 0-89235-028-8). Res Pubns Conn.
Bowser, Eileen, ed. Biograph Bulletins: 1908-1912. 1973. lib. bdg. 40.00x (ISBN 0-374-90638-6). Octagon.
Bowser, Ellen, jt. auth. see Barry, Iris.
Bowser, Frederick P. The African Slave in Colonial Peru, 1524-1650. LC 73-80619. (Illus.). 456p. 1974. 30.00x (ISBN 0-8047-0840-1). Stanford U Pr.
Bowser, James. Starring Elvis. 1977. pap. 1.95 (ISBN 0-440-18241-7). Dell.
Bowser, Milton. Back to Normal (Re: Back Problems) 120p. (Orig.). 1980. pap. 5.00 (ISBN 0-940178-01-X). Sitare Inc.
--Chemical Hair Straightening. (Illus.). 130p. 1979. softbound 5.00 (ISBN 0-940178-00-1). Sitare Inc.
--Everybody's Buddy. MacLean, Mary M., ed. (Illus.). 100p. 1984. pap. 5.00 (ISBN 0-940178-15-X). Sitare Inc.

--Machinery. LC 74-40419. (Illus.). 58p. (gr. 6-12). 1956. pap. 1.00x (ISBN 0-8395-3337-3, 3337). BSA.
--Masonry. LC 80-131483. (Illus.). 64p. (gr. 6-12). 1980. pap. 1.00x (ISBN 0-8395-3339-X, 3339). BSA.
--Metals Engineering. LC 19-600. (Illus.). 64p. (gr. 6-12). 1972. pap. 1.00x (ISBN 0-8395-3269-5, 3269). BSA.
--Model Design & Building. LC 19-600. (Illus.). 44p. (gr. 6-12). 1964. pap. 1.00x (ISBN 0-8395-3280-6, 3280). BSA.
--Sea Explorer Advanced Seamanship Instructor's Guide. 34p. 1966. pap. 2.00 (ISBN 0-8395-6660-3, 6660). BSA.
--Sea Exploring Manual. LC 66-19112. 456p. (gr. 6-12). 1966. flexible bdg. 5.95x (ISBN 0-8395-3229-6, 3229). BSA.
--Stamp Collecting. LC 19-600. (Illus.). 48p. (gr. 6-12). 1974. pap. 1.00x (ISBN 0-8395-3359-4, 3359). BSA.
--Swimming. LC 80-200995. (Illus.). 48p. (gr. 6-12). 1980. pap. 1.00x (ISBN 0-8395-3299-7, 3299); tchr's guide avail. (ISBN 0-8395-8231-5); Troop leader's can-do-kit 1977 avail. (ISBN 0-8395-8211-0). BSA.
--Textile. LC 19-600. 64p. (gr. 6-12). 1972. pap. 1.00x (ISBN 0-8395-3344-6, 3344). BSA.
--Theater. LC 70-93030. 64p. (gr. 6-12). 1968. pap. 1.00x (ISBN 0-8395-3328-4, 3328). BSA.
--Woodwork. LC 19-600. (Illus.). 48p. (gr. 6-12). 1970. pap. 1.00x (ISBN 0-8395-3316-0, 3316). BSA.
Boy Scouts of America Staff. Camping Guide. 0.65 (ISBN 0-686-96385-7). BSA.
Boyajian, James C. Portuguese Bankers at the Court of Spain, 1626-1650. 300p. 1983. 35.00 (ISBN 0-8135-0962-9). Rutgers U Pr.
Boyajian, N. R., jt. auth. see Collins, Henry H., Jr.
Boyajian, Ned R., jt. auth. see Collins, Henry H.
Boyak, Kenneth. A Parish Guide to Adult Initiation. LC 79-91001. 112p. (Orig.). 1980. pap. 3.95 (ISBN 0-8091-2282-0). Paulist Pr.
Boyan, A. Stephen, Jr., ed. Constitutional Aspects of Watergate: Documents & Materials, 5 Vols., (Including Index Volume) LC 75-45440. 1976-1979. 45.00 ea. (ISBN 0-379-10069-X); Set. 225.00. Oceana.
Boyan, Douglas R., ed. Open Doors: 1982-83. 150p. 1984. pap. text ed. 22.95 (ISBN 0-87206-125-6). Inst Intl Educ.
--Profiles: The Foreign Student in the United States. rev. ed. 179p. 1983. pap. text ed. 22.95 (ISBN 0-87206-118-3). Inst Intl Educ.
Boyan, Lee. Successful Cold Call Selling. LC 83-45211. 208p. 1983. 15.95 (ISBN 0-8144-5771-1). AMACOM.
--Successful Cold Call Selling. LC 83-45211. 213p. 1985. pap. 9.95 (ISBN 0-8144-7639-2). AMACOM.
Bo Yang. Secrets & Eight Other Stories. Deterding, David, tr. 293p. (Chinese.). 1984. 6.95 (ISBN 0-88727-037-9). Cheng & Tsui.
Boyang, Zuo, tr. see Stockwell, Foster & Bowen, Tang.
Boyanus, S. C. Spoken Russian: A Practical Course. Jopson, N. B., ed. 366p. 1980. lib. bdg. 35.00 (ISBN 0-89987-055-4). Darby Bks.
Boyard, Alexis. Savage Embrace. (Orig.). 1982. pap. 3.50 (ISBN 0-8217-1069-9). Zebra.
Boyarin, Jonathan, jt. auth. see Kugelmass, Jack.
Boyarin, Jonathan, jt. ed. see Kugelmass, Jack.
Boyars, Arthur, tr. see Boucourechliev, Andre.
Boyars, Arthur, tr. see Yevtushenko, Yevgeny.
Boyars, Carl & Klager, Karl, eds. Propellants Manufacture, Hazards, & Testing. LC 75-87208. (Advances in Chemistry Ser.: No. 88). 1969. 34.95 (ISBN 0-8412-0089-0). Am Chemical.
Boyars, Marion, ed. see Meyer, Ernst H.
Boyars, Marion, ed. see Schmidt, Arno.
Boyarsky, Saul, ed. Urodynamics: Hydrodynamics of the Ureter & Renal Pelvis. 1971. 91.50 (ISBN 0-12-121250-5). Acad Pr.
Boyarsky, Saul & Polakoski, Kenneth, eds. Goals in Male Reproductive Research: Proceedings of Conference on Future Goals in Reproductive Medicine & Surgery, 20 September, 1979, Bethesda, Md. 144p. 1981. 33.00 (ISBN 0-08-025910-3). Pergamon.
Boyarsky, Saul, et al. Care of the Patient with Neurogenic Bladder. 1979. text ed. 16.95 (ISBN 0-316-10420-5). Little.
Boyatzis, Richard E. The Competent Manager: A Model for Effective Performance. LC 81-13113. 308p. 1982. 32.50x (ISBN 0-471-09031-X, Pub. by Wiley-Interscience). Wiley.
Boyce, et al. Metropolitan Plan Making. (Monograph: No. 4). 10.00 (ISBN 0-686-32165-0). Regional Sci Res Inst.
Boyce, A. J. Chromosome Variation in Human Evolution. LC 75-25643. (Symposia for the Study of Human Biology Ser: Vol. 14). 131p. 1976. 34.95x (ISBN 0-470-09330-7). Halsted Pr.
Boyce, A. J., ed. Chromosome Variations in Human Evolution. (Symposia of the Society for the Study of Human Biology Ser.: Vol. 14). 136p. 1975. cancelled (ISBN 0-85066-081-5). Taylor & Francis.
--Migration & Mobility. (Symposia of the Society for the Study of Human Biology Ser.: Vol. 23). 378p. 1983. 36.00x (ISBN 0-85066-243-5). Taylor & Francis.
Boyce, Allen. Public Trust, Public Property, & Private Property. 1985. 12.00 (ISBN 0-8183-0255-0). Pub Aff Pr.
Boyce, B. Mercury Systems Inc. Practice Set in Word-Information Processing for Conventional & Text-Editing Typewriters. 1981. 8.24 (ISBN 0-07-006901-8). McGraw.
Boyce, B. & Popyk, M. Developing Word Processing Concepts. 1985. pap. 9.60 (ISBN 0-07-006922-0). McGraw.
Boyce, B. & Popyk, M. K. The Electronic Office & You: Word Processing Concepts. 192p. 1984. 8.44 (ISBN 0-07-006921-2). McGraw.
Boyce, Benjamin. Benevolent Man: A Life of Ralph Allen of Bath. LC 67-11667. (Illus.). 1967. 20.00x (ISBN 0-674-06650-2). Harvard U Pr.
--Polemic Character, 1640-1661. 1969. lib. bdg. 18.00x (ISBN 0-374-90893-1). Octagon.
--Tom Brown of Facetious Memory: Grub Street in the Age of Dryden. (Harvard Studies in English Ser: Vol. 21). Repr. of 1939 ed. 23.00 (ISBN 0-384-05315-7). Johnson Repr.
Boyce, Bryl N. & Kinnard, William N. Appraising Real Property. LC 74-16935. 544p. 1984. 24.00x (ISBN 0-669-83097-6). Lexington Bks.
Boyce, Byrl N., ed. Real Estate Appraisal Terminology. rev ed. LC 80-23713. 384p. 1981. 29.95 (ISBN 0-88410-597-0). Ballinger Pub.
Boyce, D. E., ed. see De Lynn, Eileen.
Boyce, D. George. Nationalism in Ireland. LC 81-13731. 448p. 1982. text ed. 37.50x (ISBN 0-8018-2736-1). Johns Hopkins.
--Nationalism in Ireland. 1982. 70.00x (ISBN 0-7171-1219-5, Pub. by Gill & Macmillan Ireland). State Mutual Bk.
Boyce, David E. Equilibrium Solutions to Combined Urban Residential Location, Modal Choice, & Trip Assignment Models. (Discussion Paper Ser.: No. 98). 1977. pap. 3.25 (ISBN 0-686-32264-9). Regional Sci Res Inst.
Boyce, David E., et al. A Computer Program for Optimal Regression Analysis. (Discussion Paper Ser.: No. 28). 1969. pap. 5.75 (ISBN 0-686-32197-9). Regional Sci Res Inst.
--The Development of a Planning Oriented Method for Estimating the Value of Development Easements on Agricultural Land. (Discussion Paper Ser.: No. 105). 1978. pap. 3.25 (ISBN 0-686-32271-1). Regional Sci Res Inst.
Boyce, Eugene M. The Coming Revolution in Education: Basic Education & the New Theory of Schooling. 98p. (Orig.). 1983. lib. bdg. 17.75 (ISBN 0-8191-3406-6); pap. text ed. 7.50 (ISBN 0-8191-3407-4). U Pr of Amer.
Boyce, Everett R., ed. see Hooper, Ben W.
Boyce, Frederick F. The Role of the Liver in Surgery. (Illus.). 365p. 1941. photocopy ed. 34.75x (ISBN 0-398-04217-9). C C Thomas.
Boyce, George A. When Navajos Had Too Many Sheep: The 1940's. Henry, Jeannette, ed. LC 73-93691. (Illus.). 288p. 1974. pap. 5.00 (ISBN 0-913436-13-5). Indian Hist Pr.
Boyce, George A., ed. Some People Are Indians. LC 75-190224. (Illus.). (gr. 4-6). 1974. 6.95 (ISBN 0-8149-0714-8). Vanguard.
Boyce, Gray C., compiled by. Literature of Medieval History: 1930-1975: a Supplement to Louis John Paetow's "Guide to the Study of Medieval History", 5 vols. LC 80-28773. 1981. lib. bdg. 595.00 (ISBN 0-527-10462-0). Kraus Intl.
Boyce, H. Spurgeon. Let's Remember. 1982. 5.95 (ISBN 0-533-05194-0). Vantage.
Boyce, J. S. Host Relationships & the Distribution of Conifer Rusts in the United States & Canada. (Connecticut Academy of Arts & Sciences Transactions Ser.: Vol. 35). 1943. 19.50 (ISBN 0-317-03796-X). Shoe String.
Boyce, James, jt. auth. see Hartmann, Betsy.
Boyce, James K., jt. auth. see Hartman, Betsy.
Boyce, James K., jt. auth. see Hartmann, Betsy.
Boyce, Jean. What Every Mother Knows. (Illus.). 48p. 1984. 6.95 (ISBN 0-8378-5064-9). Gibson.
Boyce, Jefferson. Digital Logic: Operation & Analysis. 2nd ed. (Illus.). 464p. 1982. 32.95 (ISBN 0-13-214619-3). P-H.
--Microprocessor & Microcomputer Basics. (Illus.). 1979. text ed. 29.95 (ISBN 0-13-581249-6). P-H.
--Understanding Microcomputer Concepts: A Guide for Beginners & Hobbyists. LC 83-62030. (Illus.). 336p. 1984. pap. text ed. 14.95 (ISBN 0-13-936956-2). P-H.
Boyce, Jefferson C. Digital Computer Fundamentals. LC 76-11768. (Illus.). 1977. 32.95 (ISBN 0-13-214114-0). P-H.
--Modern Electronics: A Survey of the New Technology. Zuredjian, George Z., ed. (Illus.). 256p. 1982. 18.25x (ISBN 0-07-006915-8). McGraw.
--Operational Amplifiers for Technicians. 1983. text ed. write for info. (ISBN 0-534-01243-4, Pub. by Breton Pubs). Wadsworth Pub.
Boyce, Jefferson C., jt. auth. see Shrader, Robert L.
Boyce, John, et al. Mathematics for Technical & Vocational Students. 7th ed. LC 81-2686. 561p. 1982. 26.95 (ISBN 0-471-05182-9); students study guide 10.95 (ISBN 0-471-09266-5). Wiley.
Boyce, Katherine R., jt. auth. see Boggs, Thomas H.
Boyce, Mary. Zoroastrians: Their Religious Beliefs & Practices. (Library of Beliefs & Practices). 1979. pap. 9.95 (ISBN 0-7102-0156-7). Routledge & Kegan.
--Zoroastrians: Their Religious Beliefs & Practices. (Library of Religious Beliefs & Practices). 220p. 1985. pap. 9.95 (ISBN 0-7102-0156-7). Routledge & Kegan.
Boyce, Mary, ed. Zoroastrianism. LC 84-383. (Textual Sources for the Study of Religion Ser.). 176p. 1984. 23.50x (ISBN 0-389-20478-1, 08040). B&N Imports.
Boyce, Meherwan P. Gas Turbine Engineering Handbook. LC 82-6158. 604p. 1982. 69.95x (ISBN 0-87201-878-4). Gulf Pub.
Boyce, Nancy L. & Larson, Vicki L. Adolescents' Communication: Development & Disorders. 250p. 1983. three-ring binder 24.95 (ISBN 0-9610370-0-8); pap. 19.95x (ISBN 0-9610370-5-9). Thinking Pubns.
Boyce, Neith. Folly of Others. facs. ed. LC 73-122690. (Short Story Index Reprint Ser). 1904. 14.00 (ISBN 0-8369-3511-X). Ayer Co Pubs.
Boyce, P. J. Foreign Affairs for New States: Some Questions of Credentials. LC 77-87169. 1978. 27.50x (ISBN 0-312-29837-4). St Martin.
Boyce, P. J., jt. ed. see Angel, J. R.
Boyce, P. R. Human Factors in Lighting. (Illus.). xiii, 420p. 1981. 52.00x (ISBN 0-686-28903-X). Burgess-Intl Ideas.
--Human Factors in Lighting. (Illus.). 421p. 1981. text ed. 45.00x (ISBN 0-02-949250-5). Macmillan.
Boyce, Ronald N., jt. auth. see Perkins, Rollin M.
Boyce, Ronald R. The Bases of Economic Geography. 2nd ed. LC 77-21382. 1978. text ed. 25.95 (ISBN 0-03-019496-2, HoltC). HR&W.
--Geographic Perspectives on Global Problems: An Introduction to Geography. LC 81-11639. 362p. 1982. text ed. 33.00 (ISBN 0-471-09336-X); tchrs'. manual 5.50 (ISBN 0-471-86928-7); study guide avail. (ISBN 0-471-09337-8). Wiley.
Boyce, Ronald R., ed. see Ullman, Edward L.
Boyce, Terry. Car Interior Restoration. 3rd ed. LC 81-9175. (Illus.). 144p. 1983. pap. 7.95 (ISBN 0-8306-2102-4, 2102). TAB Bks.
--V-Eight Chevys. (Illus.). 176p. 1985. 29.95 (ISBN 0-9606148-2-6). Dragonwyck Pub.
Boyce, Terry V. Chevy Super Sports: 1961-1976. (Illus.). 1981. pap. 14.95 (ISBN 0-87938-096-9). Motorbooks Intl.
Boyce, Timothy J. & Turner, Ronald. Fair Representation the NLRB, & the Courts. LC 84-48291. (Labor Relations & Public Policy Ser.: No. 18). 194p. 1984. pap. 20.00 (ISBN 0-89546-045-9). Indus Res Unit-Wharton.
Boyce, Tommy. How to Write a Hit Song & Sell It. 1974. pap. 7.00 (ISBN 0-87980-291-X). Wilshire.
Boyce, Violet & Harmer, Mabel. Upstairs to a Mine. LC 76-28980. 189p. 1977. 7.95 (ISBN 0-87421-085-2). Utah St U Pr.
Boyce, W. Illustrated South America, 2 vols. 1976. lib. bdg. 250.00 (ISBN 0-8490-2037-9). Gordon Pr.
Boyce, W. E. & Diprima, R. C. Elementary Differential Equations. 3rd ed. 391p. (Arabic.). 1983. pap. 15.40 (ISBN 0-471-09414-5). Wiley.
--Elementary Differential Equations & Boundary Value Problems. 4th ed. 1985. pap. text ed. write for info. (ISBN 0-471-87096-X). Wiley.
Boyce, W. E., ed. Case Studies in Mathematical Modelling. LC 80-14252. (Applicable Mathematics Ser.). 432p. 1980. text ed. 51.95 (ISBN 0-273-08486-0). Pitman Pub MA.
Boyce, W. Scott. Economic & Social History of Chowan County, N.C. 1880-1915. LC 73-76716. (Columbia University Studies in the Social Sciences: No. 179). Repr. of 1917 ed. 18.50 (ISBN 0-404-51179-1). AMS Pr.
Boyce, William D. & Jensen, Larry C. Moral Reasoning: A Psychological-Philosophical Integration. LC 78-5935. xii, 291p. 1978. 22.50x (ISBN 0-8032-0982-7). U of Nebr Pr.
Boyce, William E. & Di Prima, Richard C. Elementary Differential Equations. 3rd ed. LC 75-35565. 497p. 1977. text ed. 32.95 (ISBN 0-471-09339-4). Wiley.
Boyce, William E. & DiPrima, Richard C. Elementary Differential Equations & Boundary Value Problems. 3rd ed. LC 75-45093. 638p. 1977. 35.45 (ISBN 0-471-09334-3); student manual avail. (ISBN 0-471-04707-4). Wiley.
--Introduction to Differential Equations. 310p. 1970. text ed. 31.00x (ISBN 0-471-09338-6). Wiley.
Boyce-Gibson, W. R., tr. see Husserl, Edmund.
Boycott, Rosie. Batty, Bloomers & Boycott: A Little Etymology of Eponymous Words. LC 83-71477. 128p. 1983. 8.95 (ISBN 0-911745-12-2). P Bedrick Bks.
--A Nice Girl Like Me: A Story of the Seventies. 256p. 1985. 14.95 (ISBN 0-7011-2665-5, Pub. by Chatto & Windus). Merrimack Pub Cir.
Boyd. Alessandro Scarlatti. (Italian Cantata in the 17th Century Ser.). 1985. text ed. 60.00 (ISBN 0-8240-8887-5). Garland Pub.
--Toys. (Plumpy Shape Board Bks.). Date not set. 2.95 (ISBN 0-671-54751-8). S&S.
Boyd, jt. auth. see Garrard.
Boyd, jt. auth. see Kastrup.
Boyd & Ramsauer, eds. Career Connections: A Guide to Career Planning Services Throughout Massachussetts. 186p. (Orig.). 1983. pap. 9.95 (ISBN 0-937860-32-8). Adams Inc MA.
Boyd, et al, eds. see Aden, et al.
Boyd, A. An Atlas of World Affairs. 7th ed. LC 83-675921. (Illus.). 200p. 1983. 17.95 (ISBN 0-416-32370-7, NO. 3923); pap. 8.95 (ISBN 0-416-32380-4, NO. 3922). Methuen Inc.
Boyd, A., jt. auth. see Kimber, Richard T.
Boyd, A. F. Aspects of the Russian Novel. 134p. 1972. 8.50x (ISBN 0-87471-097-9). Rowman.
Boyd, A. J. Old Colonials. 308p. 1974. 21.00x (ISBN 0-424-06900-8, Pub. by Sydney U Pr). Intl Spec Bk.
Boyd, A. W., ed. Radiation Chemistry in Nuclear Reactor Technology. 70p. 1983. pap. 22.60 (ISBN 0-08-029156-2). Pergamon.
Boyd, Alan. PC-DOS, MS-DOS: User's Guide to the Most Popular Operating System for Personal Computers. 352p. (Orig.). 1985. pap. 18.95 (ISBN 0-553-34231-2). Bantam.
--Techniques of Interactive Computer Graphics. 240p. 1985. pap. text ed. 25.95x (ISBN 0-86238-024-3, Pub. by Chartwell-Bratt England). Brookfield Pub Co.
--Things That IBM Never Told You: Unveiling the Mysteries of PC-DOS 1.1 & 2.0. 1984. pap. text ed. 24.95 (ISBN 0-88701-001-6). Softalk Pub.
Boyd, Alan, ed. see Buchanan, George.
Boyd, Alexander. England's Wealthiest Son. 1983. 60.00X (ISBN 0-900000-59-7, Pub. by Centaur Pr England). State Mutual Bk.
Boyd, Andrew. Northern Ireland: Who Is to Blame? 132p. (Orig.). 1984. pap. 5.95 (ISBN 0-85342-708-9, Pub. by Mercier Pr Ireland). Irish Bks Media.
--Rise of the Irish Trade Unions. rev. ed. 160p. 1985. pap. 7.95 (ISBN 0-900068-21-3, Pub. by Anvil Pr Ireland). Irish Bks Media.
Boyd, Ann. The Devil with James Bond. LC 73-15312. 123p. 1975. Repr. of 1967 ed. lib. bdg. 24.75x (ISBN 0-8371-7182-2, BOJB). Greenwood.
Boyd, Anne. Life in a Fifteenth Century Monastery. LC 76-22452. (Cambridge Topic Bks). (Illus.). (gr. 5-10). 1978. PLB 7.95 (ISBN 0-8225-1208-4). Lerner Pubns.
--The Monks of Durham. LC 74-14438. (Introduction to the History of Mankind Ser). (Illus.). 48p. (gr. 6-11). 1975. text ed. 4.50 (ISBN 0-521-20647-2). Cambridge U Pr.
Boyd, B. Management-Minded Supervision. 3rd ed. 384p. 1984. 21.55 (ISBN 0-07-006946-8). McGraw.
Boyd, Beverly. Chaucer & the Medieval Book. LC 73-77021. (Illus.). 165p. 1973. 12.50 (ISBN 0-87328-060-1). Huntington Lib.
Boyd, Blanche. The Redneck Way of Knowledge: Down-Home Tales. LC 81-48138. 160p. 1982. 10.95 (ISBN 0-394-51050-X). Knopf.
Boyd, Blanche M. The Redneck Way of Knowledge. 176p. 1983. pap. 4.95 (ISBN 0-14-006725-6). Penguin.
Boyd, Bradford B., compiled by. Supervisory Training Approaches & Methods. 162p. 8.25 (ISBN 0-318-13287-7, BOSTP); members 6.50 (ISBN 0-318-13288-5). Am Soc Train & Devel.
Boyd, Brendan & Engel, Louis. How to Buy Stocks. 1983. 15.45i (ISBN 0-316-10439-6). Little.
Boyd, Brendan, jt. auth. see Engel, Louis.
Boyd, Brian. Nabokov's Ada: The Place of Consciousness. 255p. 1985. 22.95 (ISBN 0-88233-906-0). Ardis Pubs.
Boyd, C. E. Water Quality Management for Pond Fish Culture. (Developments in Aquaculture & Fisheries Science Ser.: Vol. 9). 318p. 1982. 64.00 (ISBN 0-444-42054-1). Elsevier.
Boyd, Candy D. Breadsticks & Blessing Places. LC 84-43021. 209p. (gr. 5-9). 1985. 11.95 (ISBN 0-02-709290-9). Macmillan.
--Circle of Gold. 128p. (Orig.). (gr. 4-6). 1948. pap. 1.95 (ISBN 0-590-32464-0, Apple Paperbacks). Scholastic Inc.
Boyd, Carl. The Extraordinary Envoy: General Hiroshi Oshima & Diplomacy in the Third Reich 1934-1939. LC 79-9600. 246p. 1980. text ed. 23.50 (ISBN 0-8191-0957-6); pap. text ed. 12.25 (ISBN 0-8191-0958-4). U Pr of Amer.
Boyd, Carolyn P. Praetorian Politics in Liberal Spain. LC 79-300. xvii, 376p. 1979. 30.00 (ISBN 0-8078-1368-0). U of NC Pr.
Boyd, Charles E. At Liberty on Bear Creek, 1835-1985. 1984. 14.95; pap. 9.95 (ISBN 0-317-13825-1). Banner Pr AL.
--Devil's Den, at Gettysburg: Forty-Fourth Alabama Regiment (Confederate), Its Action, Roster, & Family Connections. 1985. 30.00. Banner Pr AL.
--Haysop: A Church, A Community, A People of Bibb County, Alabama. (Illus.). 1979. pap. 8.50 (ISBN 0-317-13831-6). Banner Pr AL.
Boyd, Charles W., ed. see Chamberlain, J.
Boyd, Claude E. Water Quality in Warmwater Fish Ponds. (Illus.). 359p. 1979. pap. 9.95 (ISBN 0-8173-0055-4, Pub. by Ag Experiment). U of Ala Pr.
Boyd, Cyrus F. The Civil War Diary of Cyrus F. Boyd, Fifteenth Iowa Infantry 1861-1863. LC 76-44635. 1977. 18.00 (ISBN 0-527-17540-4). Kraus Repr.

Boyd, D. P. Elites & Their Education. (Social Issues Ser.). 11.00x (ISBN 0-85633-025-6, Pub. by NFER Nelson UK). Taylor & Francis.

Boyd, Dallas. Denver in a Day. (Illus.). 62p. 1980. pap. 4.95 (ISBN 0-937050-08-3). Stonehenge.

Boyd, Daniel R. & Lewis, Stephen D. Secretarial Administration & Management. (Illus.). 550p. 1985. text ed. 27.95 (ISBN 0-13-798265-8); wkbk. 9.95 (ISBN 0-13-798315-8). P-H.

Boyd, David R., et al. Systems Approach to Emergency Medical Care. 544p. 1983. 48.00 (ISBN 0-8385-8792-5). ACC.

Boyd, Don & Sedano, Maruja. Master Catechist Guide for the Catechist Formation Book. LC 82-60853. 1982. pap. 3.95 (ISBN 0-8091-2471-8). Paulist Pr.

Boyd, Doug. Rolling Thunder. 288p. 1976. pap. 8.95 (ISBN 0-385-28859-X, Delta). Dell.

Boyd, Douglas. Broadcasting in the Arab World: A Survey of Radio & Television in the Middle East. (International & Comparative Broadcasting Ser.). 306p. 1982. 34.95 (ISBN 0-87722-237-1). Temple U Pr.

Boyd, E. H. L. Mencken. LC 74-1446. (American Literature Ser., No. 49). 1974. lib. bdg. 46.95x (ISBN 0-8383-2038-4). Haskell.

--Indigo. (Illus.). 1962. pap. 1.25 (ISBN 0-89013-055-8). Museum NM Pr.

Boyd, Edith. The Growth of the Surface Area of the Human Body. LC 75-14249. (Univ. of Minnesota, the Institute of Child Welfare Monograph: No. 10). (Illus.). 145p. 1975. Repr. of 1935 ed. lib. bdg. 25.00x (ISBN 0-8371-8069-4, CWBS). Greenwood.

--Origins of the Study of Human Growth. Bhim Sen Savara & Schilke, John F., eds. (Illus.). 700p. 1981. 70.00 (ISBN 0-686-30702-X). Oregon Hlth Sci Univ.

Boyd, Edward M. Wolf Trail Lodge. 120p. 1985. 5.95 (ISBN 0-88240-271-4). Alaska Northwest.

Boyd, Eldon. Respiratory Tract Fluid. (Illus.). 336p. 1972. 29.75x (ISBN 0-398-02239-9). C C Thomas.

Boyd, Eldon M. Toxicity of Pure Foods. (Uniscience Ser). 260p. 1973. 56.00 (ISBN 0-8493-5026-3). CRC Pr.

Boyd, Elizabeth F. Bloomsbury Heritage: Their Mothers & Their Aunts. LC 76-422. (Illus.). 1976. 10.50 (ISBN 0-8008-0821-5). Taplinger.

--Byron's Don Juan: A Critical Study. 1975. Repr. of 1945 ed. 13.00x (ISBN 0-391-00439-5). Humanities.

Boyd, Elizabeth N. A Diagnostic Study of Student's Difficulties in General Mathematics in First Year College Work. LC 79-176585. (Columbia University. Teachers College. Contributions to Education: No. 798). Repr. of 1940 ed. 22.50 (ISBN 0-404-55798-8). AMS Pr.

Boyd, Eric F. see Forbes-Boyd, Eric.

Boyd, Ernest. Guy de Maupassant: A Biographical Study. 1973. Repr. of 1926 ed. 30.00 (ISBN 0-8274-0071-3). R West.

--H. L. Mencken. LC 73-16171. 1927. 16.50 (ISBN 0-8414-9860-1). Folcroft.

--Studies from Ten Literatures. LC 68-16289. 1968. Repr. of 1925 ed. 23.75x (ISBN 0-8046-0038-4, Pub. by Kennikat). Assoc Faculty Pr.

Boyd, Ernest, ed. see Maupassant, Guy De.

Boyd, Ernest, tr. see Maupassant, Guy De.

Boyd, Ernest, tr. see Verneuil, Louis.

Boyd, Ernest A. Appreciations & Depreciations: Irish Literary Studies. facs. ed. LC 68-16913. (Essay Index Reprint Ser). 1918. 15.00 (ISBN 0-8369-0235-1). Ayer Co Pubs.

--Literary Blasphemies. LC 76-90472. Repr. of 1927 ed. lib. bdg. 15.00x (ISBN 0-8371-2516-2, BOLB). Greenwood.

--Portraits. facsimile ed. LC 79-93318. (Essay Index Reprint Ser.). 1924. 19.00 (ISBN 0-8369-1274-8). Ayer Co Pubs.

--Portraits: Real & Imaginary. LC 77-126702. (BCL Ser. I). Repr. of 1924 ed. 9.50 (ISBN 0-404-00965-4). AMS Pr.

--Portraits: Real & Imaginary. LC 71-131641. 1970. Repr. of 1924 ed. 8.00x (ISBN 0-403-00528-0). Scholarly.

--Studies from Ten Literatures. facs. ed. LC 68-20287. (Essay Index Reprint Ser). 1925. 20.00 (ISBN 0-8369-0236-X). Ayer Co Pubs.

--Studies from Ten Literatures. (English Literary Reference Ser.). Repr. of 1927 ed. 17.00 (ISBN 0-384-05330-0). Johnson Repr.

Boyd, F. R., ed. The Mantle Sample: Inclusions in Kimberlites & Other Volcanics. (Illus.). 424p. 1979. 25.00 (ISBN 0-87590-213-8). Am Geophysical.

Boyd, F. R. & Meyer, H. O., eds. Kimberlites, Diatremes, & Diamonds: Their Geology, Petrology & Geochemistry. LC 78-72025. (Illus.). 408p. 1979. 25.00 (ISBN 0-87590-212-X, SP0024). Am Geophysical.

Boyd, Frank M. Ages & Dispensations. 112p. 1955. pap. 1.50 (ISBN 0-88243-463-2, 02-0463). Gospel Pub.

Boyd, G. W. The Will to Live: Five Steps to Officer Survival. (Illus.). 144p. 1980. photocopy ed. 15.75x (ISBN 0-398-04020-6). C C Thomas.

Boyd, Gavin. Region Building in the Pacific. (Pergamon Policy Studies on International Politics). 280p. 1982. 33.00 (ISBN 0-08-025985-5). Pergamon.

Boyd, Gavin, ed. Regionalism & Global Security. LC 82-48481. 208p. 1984. 25.00x (ISBN 0-669-06153-0). Lexington Bks.

Boyd, Gavin & Pentland, Charles, eds. Issues in Global Politics. LC 80-69282. 1981. pap. text ed. 16.95 (ISBN 0-02-904470-7). Free Pr.

Boyd, George, ed. see Mann, Thomas.

Boyd, Gertrude A. Linguistics in the Elementary School. LC 75-17319. 170p. 1976. pap. text ed. 9.95 (ISBN 0-87581-154-X). Peacock Pubs.

Boyd, Greg. The Masked Ball. (Illus.). 60p. (Orig.). 1985. 17.50 (ISBN 0-87775-184-6); pap. 7.00 (ISBN 0-87775-183-8). Unicorn Pr.

Boyd, Hamish. Introduction to Homeopathic Medicine. LC 82-84367. 1983. pap. 14.95 (ISBN 0-87983-324-6). Keats.

Boyd, Harper W., jt. auth. see Britt, Steuart H.

Boyd, Harper W., Jr., et al. Marketing Research: Text & Cases. 5th ed. 1981. 28.95x (ISBN 0-256-02530-4). Irwin.

Boyd, Harry, Jr. A Creative Approach to Controlling Photography. LC 73-92364. (Illus.). 289p. 1974. 12.95 (ISBN 0-913206-02-4). Heidelberg Pubs.

Boyd, Helen M. The True Horoscope of the U. S. LC 75-7188. 1975. 7.25 (ISBN 0-88231-007-0). Asi Pubs Inc.

Boyd, Herb. Former Portugese Colonies. LC 80-24752. (First Bks.). (gr. 4 up). 1981. PLB 8.90 (ISBN 0-531-04273-1). Watts.

Boyd, Howard P. Checklist of Cicindelidae: The Tiger Beetles. (Checklist of the Beetles of Canada, United States, Mexico, Central America, & the West Indies). 40p. (Orig.). 1982. pap. 10.00x (ISBN 0-937548-01-4). Plexus Pub.

Boyd, I. A. & Gladden, M. H. The Muscle Spindle. (Illus.). 360p. 1985. 80.00x (ISBN 0-943818-10-9). Stockton Pr.

Boyd, Mrs. Ima G. The Guthery Family of Cullman County, Alabama. rev. ed. 1979. pap. 10.00 (ISBN 0-9600502-0-5). Ima Boyd.

Boyd, Ina C. Cocktails & Hors D'Oeuvres. Walsh, Jackie, ed. LC 77-93841. (Illus.). 1978. pap. 5.95 (ISBN 0-911954-45-7). Nitty Gritty.

Boyd, J., jt. auth. see O'Connor, J. J.

Boyd, J. D. Biophysical Control of Microfibril Orientation in Plant Cell Walls. (Forestry Sciences Ser.). 1985. lib. bdg. 42.00 (ISBN 90-247-3101-1, Pub. by Martinus Nijhoff Netherlands). Kluwer Academic.

Boyd, J. Morton. Fraser Darling's Islands. 208p. 1986. 25.00x (ISBN 0-85224-514-9, Pub. by Edinburgh U Pr Scotland). Columbia U Pr.

Boyd, J. P., et al, eds. see Jefferson, Thomas.

Boyd, Jack. Leading the Lord's Singing. 1981. pap. 5.95 (ISBN 0-89137-603-8). Quality Pubns.

--Rehearsal Guide for the Choral Director. LC 77-2051. 1977. pap. text ed. 9.95 (ISBN 0-916656-03-9, MF278). Mark Foster Mus.

--Teaching Choral Sight Reading. LC 75-12658. 210p. 1982. pap. text ed. 10.95 (ISBN 0-916656-17-9). Mark Foster Mus.

Boyd, James. Goethe's Knowledge of English Literature. LC 72-6894. (Studies in German Literature, No. 13). 320p. 1972. Repr. of 1932 ed. lib. bdg. 49.95x (ISBN 0-8383-1637-9). Haskell.

--Marching On. 426p. Date not set. Repr. of 1927 ed. lib. bdg. 30.00 (ISBN 0-8482-7455-5). Norwood Edns.

--Ulrich Fuetrer's Parzival: Material & Sources. 1977. lib. bdg. 59.95 (ISBN 0-8490-2782-9). Gordon Pr.

Boyd, James, jt. auth. see Anderson, Jack.

Boyd, James, ed. see Kames, Henry.

Boyd, James P. Boyd's Bible Dictionary. Orig. Title: Vest Pocket Bible Dictionary, Orig. pap. 3.75 (ISBN 0-87981-087-4). Holman.

Boyd, James R. Elements of Criticism. lib. bdg. 25.00 (ISBN 0-8482-9976-0). Norwood Edns.

Boyd, James S. Building for Small Acreages: Farm, Ranch & Recreation. LC 77-80716. 1978. text ed. 13.35 (ISBN 0-8134-1966-2); pap. text ed. 10.00x. Interstate.

--Practical Farm Buildings: A Text & Handbook. 2nd ed. LC 78-179872. 1979. 13.00 (ISBN 0-8134-2054-7, 2054); text ed. 9.75x. Interstate.

Boyd, James W., jt. auth. see Kotwal, Firoze M.

Boyd, James W., jt. ed. see Kotwal, Firoze M.

Boyd, Jesse L., III, jt. ed. see Godfrey, W. Robert.

Boyd, John. Collected Plays One. 272p. (Orig.). 1981. pap. 14.95 (ISBN 0-85640-250-8, Pub. by Blackstaff Pr). Longwood Pub Group.

--Collected Plays Two. 176p. (Orig.). 1982. pap. 14.95 (ISBN 0-85640-250-8, Pub. by Blackstaff Pr). Longwood Pub Group.

--Out of My Class. 192p. (Orig.). 1985. pap. 7.50 (ISBN 0-85640-337-7, Pub. by Blackstaff Pr). Longwood Pub Group.

--Sir George Etienne Cartier, Bart. His Life & Times. facsimile ed. LC 74-164590. (Select Bibliographies Reprint Ser.). Repr. of 1914 ed. 44.00 (ISBN 0-8369-5874-8). Ayer Co Pubs.

--Understanding the Primary Curriculum. LC 84-3835. 191p. 1984. 15.75 (ISBN 0-09-156680-0, Pub. by Hutchinson Educ); pap. 7.95 (ISBN 0-09-156681-9). Longwood Pub Group.

Boyd, John & Boyd, Mary A. Before Book One. (Illus.). (gr. 9-12). pap. text ed. 3.75 (ISBN 0-88345-492-0, 20660). Regents Pub.

Boyd, John, jt. auth. see Grieger, Russell.

Boyd, John, et al. Counselor Supervision: Approaches, Preparation, Practices. LC 78-53069. (Illus.). 552p. 1978. pap. text ed. 15.45x (ISBN 0-915202-15-8). Accel Devel.

Boyd, John D. A College Poetics. 348p. (Orig.). 1983. lib. bdg. 27.75 (ISBN 0-8191-3380-9); pap. text ed. 11.00 (ISBN 0-8191-3381-7). U Pr of Amer.

--The Function of Mimesis & Its Decline. 2nd ed. LC 68-28691. xviii, 317p. 1980. pap. 10.00 (ISBN 0-8232-1046-4). Fordham.

Boyd, John R. & Boyd, Mary A. Alice Blows a Fuse: Fifty Strip Stories in American English. (ESL Ser.). (Illus.). 208p. 1980. pap. text ed. 11.95 (ISBN 0-13-022228-3). P-H.

--Connections. 112p. (gr. 9-12). 1981. pap. text ed. 4.95 (ISBN 0-88345-435-1, 18376); tchrs. ed 5.95 (ISBN 0-88345-444-0, 18377); cassettes 45.00 (ISBN 0-686-86686-X, 58378). Regents Pub.

Boyd, Julian P. Anglo-American Union: Joseph Galloway's Plans to Preserve the British Empire, 1774-1788. LC 76-120233. 1970. Repr. lib. bdg. 18.50x (ISBN 0-374-90900-8). Octagon.

--Number Seven: Alexander Hamilton's Secret Attempts to Control American Foreign Policy. 1964. 21.00x (ISBN 0-691-04529-1). Princeton U Pr.

Boyd, Julianne, jt. auth. see Silver, Joan M.

Boyd, K., ed. The Ethics of Resource Allocations. 152p. 1980. 15.00x (ISBN 0-85224-368-5, Pub. by Edinburgh U Pr Scotland). Columbia U Pr.

Boyd, K. T. ATP-FAR 135: Airline Transport Pilot. (Illus.). 168p. 1983. pap. 17.50 (ISBN 0-8138-0510-4). Iowa St U Pr.

Boyd, K. T. & Downs, Gary E. ATP: Airline Transport Pilot. 2nd ed. (Illus.). 164p. 1978. pap. text ed. 14.50 (ISBN 0-8138-0075-7). Iowa St U Pr.

Boyd, Kenneth M. Scottish Church Attitudes to Sex, Marriage & the Family 1850-1914. 410p. 1980. text ed. 47.50x (ISBN 0-85976-056-1). Humanities.

Boyd, L. M. Boyd's Book of Odd Facts. 1980. pap. 3.50 (ISBN 0-451-11966-5, AE1966, Sig). NAL.

--Clancy's Treasure Book for Children. 166p. (Orig.). 1981. pap. 5.00 (ISBN 0-941620-34-4). H G Carson Ent.

Boyd, L. M. & Carson, H. G. Colorado Ghost Town Atlas, Vol. 2. (Illus.). 150p. (Orig.). 1985. pap. text ed. 15.95 (ISBN 0-941620-35-2). Cache Pr.

--Colorado Ghost Town Atlas, Vol. 1. (Illus.). 134p. (Orig.). 1984. pap. text ed. 12.95 (ISBN 0-941620-19-0). H G Carson Ent.

Boyd, Lawrence H. & Iversen, Gudmund R. Contextual Analysis: Concepts & Statistical Techniques. 1979. text ed. write for info. (ISBN 0-534-00693-0). Wadsworth Pub.

Boyd, Leanne C., illus. Horse Show: Paper Dolls. 32p. 1985. pap. 3.95 (ISBN 0-8431-1756-7, Troubador Pr). Price Stern.

Boyd, Lizzie, ed. British Cookery: A Complete Guide to Culinary Practice in England, Scotland, Ireland & Wales. LC 78-60775. (Illus.). 640p. 1979. 37.95 (ISBN 0-87951-087-0). Overlook Pr.

Boyd, Lois A. & Brackenridge, R. Douglas. Presbyterian Women in America: Two Centuries of a Quest for Status. LC 82-15845. (Contributions to the Study of Religion: No. 9). 416p. 1983. lib. bdg. 35.00 (ISBN 0-313-23678-X, BOY/). Greenwood.

Boyd, Lyle G., jt. auth. see Jones, Bessie Z.

Boyd, M., tr. see Beraud, Henri.

Boyd, Malcolm. Bach. (Illus.). 290p. 1983. 19.50x (ISBN 0-460-04466-4, Pub. by J M Dent England). Biblio Dist.

--Harmonizing Bach Chorales. 40p. 1984. pap. 3.95 (ISBN 0-214-65956-9, Pub. by Hutchinson Educ). Longwood Pub Group.

--Look Back in Joy: Celebration of Gay Lovers. 128p. (Orig.). 1981. 20.00 (ISBN 0-917342-85-2); pap. 6.95 (ISBN 0-917342-77-1). Gay Sunshine.

--Take off the Masks. 178p. 1984. lib. bdg. 24.95 (ISBN 0-86571-048-1); pap. 7.95 (ISBN 0-86571-047-3). New Soc Pubs.

Boyd, Marcia. Curriculum Guide for Nuclear Medicine Technologists. McKeown, Joan A., et al, eds. LC 82-50338. 336p. 1982. 65.00 (ISBN 0-932004-12-1). Soc Nuclear Med.

Boyd, Margaret A. Catalog Sources for Creative People. LC 81-82827. 1981. 7.95 (ISBN 0-89586-130-5). H P Bks.

--Directory of Shop-By-Mail Bargain Sources. LC 77-17778. 61p. 1982. pap. 3.50 (ISBN 0-87576-063-5). Pilot Bks.

--The Sew & Save Source Book. 208p. 1985. pap. 9.95 (ISBN 0-932620-23-X). Wallace-Homestead.

--The Sew & Save Source Book: Your Guide to Supplies for Creative Sewing. LC 83-11888. (Illus.). 216p. (Orig.). 1984. pap. 9.95 (ISBN 0-932620-23-X). Betterway Pubns.

Boyd, Margaret A. & Scott-Martin, Sue. Where-to-Sell-It Directory. rev. ed. LC 78-31582. 79p. 1985. pap. 3.95 (ISBN 0-87576-078-3). Pilot Bks.

Boyd, Marilyn S. Women's Liberation Ideology & Union Participation: A Study. LC 79-65257. 135p. 1981. perfect bdg. 10.95 (ISBN 0-86548-024-9). R & E Pubs.

Boyd, Marion. Say It Graciously. 1984. pap. 2.50 s.p. (ISBN 0-88053-321-8). Macoy Pub.

Boyd, Marion M. Silver Wands. LC 70-144724. (Yale Ser. of Younger Poets: No. 17). Repr. of 1923 ed. 18.00 (ISBN 0-404-53817-7). AMS Pr.

Boyd, Martin. Lucinda Brayford. (Fiction Ser.). 1985. pap. 5.95 (ISBN 0-14-007231-4). Penguin.

--Nuns in Jeopardy. LC 74-17476. 217p. 1975. pap. 2.95 (ISBN 0-15-667820-9, Harv). HarBraceJ.

Boyd, Mary A., jt. auth. see Boyd, John.

Boyd, Mary A., jt. auth. see Boyd, John R.

Boyd, Maurice. Kiowa Voices, Vol. I: Ceremonial Dance, Ritual & Song. Worcester, Donald, ed. LC 81-50977. (Kiowa Voices Ser.). (Illus.). 164p. 1981. 29.95 (ISBN 0-912646-67-5). Tex Christian.

--Kiowa Voices, Vol. II: Myths, Legends & Folktales. Worcester, Donald & Pattie, Jane, eds. LC 81-50977. (Kiowa Voices Ser.). (Illus.). 356p. 1983. 39.95x (ISBN 0-912646-76-4). Tex Christian.

Boyd, Michael. The Reflexive Novel. LC 81-72029. 320p. 1983. 22.50 (ISBN 0-8387-5029-X). Bucknell U Pr.

Boyd, Minnie C. Alabama in the Fifties: A Social Study. LC 31-33199. (Columbia University Studies in the Social Sciences: No. 353). Repr. of 1931 ed. 21.00 (ISBN 0-404-51353-0). AMS Pr.

Boyd, Morrison C. Elizabethan Music & Music Criticism. LC 73-1837. 392p. 1974. pap. 9.95x (ISBN 0-8122-1071-9). U of Pa Pr.

--Elizabethan Music & Musical Criticism. LC 73-1837. (Illus.). 363p. 1973. Repr. of 1962 ed. lib. bdg. 29.75 (ISBN 0-8371-6805-8, BOEL). Greenwood.

Boyd, Nancy. Three Victorian Women Who Changed Their World: Josephine Butler, Octavia Hill, Florence Nightingale. 1982. 22.95x (ISBN 0-19-520271-6). Oxford U Pr.

Boyd, Nancy L. The Pine Cone Book. LC 83-62035. (Illus.). 80p. 1983. 12.95 (ISBN 0-941526-01-1); pap. 7.95 (ISBN 0-941526-02-X). Prospect Hill.

Boyd, Neva L. Handbook of Recreational Games. LC 75-13385. 128p. 1975. pap. 2.75 (ISBN 0-486-23204-2). Dover.

--Hospital & Bedside Games. (Illus.). 72p. 1945. 4.95 (ISBN 0-912222-03-4, R532712). FitzSimons.

Boyd, Mrs. Orsemus B. Cavalry Life in Tent & Field. LC 81-19772. (Illus.). xvi, 370p. 1982. 25.95x (ISBN 0-8032-1176-7); pap. 7.50 (ISBN 0-8032-6063-6, BB 793, Bison). U of Nebr Pr.

Boyd, Patricia, jt. auth. see Mee, A. J.

Boyd, Patricia R. The Furry Wind. (Illus.). 28p. (gr. 2-3). 1982. pap. 2.25 (ISBN 0-9603840-4-9). Andrew Mtn Pr.

Boyd, Patti, jt. auth. see Schlachter, Rita.

Boyd, Pauline, jt. auth. see Boyd, Selma.

Boyd, Peggy. The Silent Wound: A Startling Report on Breast Cancer & Sexuality. LC 84-12448. 1985. 14.95 (ISBN 0-201-10135-1). Addison-Wesley.

Boyd, Preston, jt. auth. see Babcock, Dennis.

Boyd, R. F., jt. auth. see Massey, H. S.

Boyd, Robert & Richerson, Peter J. Culture & the Evolutionary Process. LC 84-24125. (Illus.). 400p. 1985. lib. bdg. 29.95x (ISBN 0-226-06931-1). U of Chicago Pr.

Boyd, Robert, jt. auth. see Modell, Michael.

Boyd, Robert D., et al. Redefining the Discipline of Adult Education. LC 80-8006. (Higher Education Ser.). 1980. text ed. 19.95x (ISBN 0-87589-482-8). Jossey-Bass.

Boyd, Robert F. General Microbiology. (Illus.). 960p. 1984. pap. text ed. 31.95 (ISBN 0-8016-0900-3). Mosby.

Boyd, Robert F. & Hoerl, Bryan G. Basic Medical Microbiology. 2nd ed. 1981. text ed. 26.95 (ISBN 0-316-10433-7); lab manual 8.95 (ISBN 0-316-10434-5). Little.

Boyd, Robert F. & Marr, J. Joseph. Medical Microbiology. 1980. text ed. 29.95 (ISBN 0-316-10432-9). Little.

Boyd, Robert H., ed. & tr. see Westermann, Claus.

Boyd, Robert H., tr. see Westermann, Claus.

Boyd, Robert N. Sex Behind Bars: A Novella, Short Stories & True Accounts. 240p. (Orig.). 1983. pap. 10.00 (ISBN 0-917342-34-8). Gay Sunshine.

Boyd, Robert N., jt. auth. see Morrison, Robert T.

Boyd, Robert T. Boyd's Bible Handbook. LC 82-81088. 800p. 1983. 24.95 (ISBN 0-89081-352-3). Harvest Hse.

--A Pictorial Guide to Biblical Archaeology. rev. ed. LC 75-94696. (Illus.). 224p. 1981. pap. 8.95 (ISBN 0-89081-303-5). Harvest Hse.

Boyd, Robert W. Radiometry & the Detection of Optical Radiation. LC 82-20222. (Pure & Applied Optics Ser.). 254p. 1983. 39.95x (ISBN 0-471-86188-X, Pub. by Wiley-Interscience). Wiley.

Boyd, Robin. New Directions in Japanese Architecture. LC 68-29665. (New Directions in Architecture Ser). (Orig.). 7.95 (ISBN 0-8076-0481-X). Braziller.

--Victorian Modern. write for info. (ISBN 0-522-84156-2, Pub. by Melbourne U Pr). Intl Spec Bk.

Boyd, Rogene & Schumacher, Margaret. Wyoming's People Activity Book. 1978. 4.00x (ISBN 0-933472-37-4). Johnson Bks.

Boyd, Roger N., jt. auth. see Federal Publications Inc.

Boyd, Rosalind E., ed. see Barrett, Stanley R.

Boyd, Rosamonde R. & McConatha, Douglas, eds. Gerontological Practice: Issues & Perspectives. LC 81-40706. 242p. (Orig.). 1982. lib. bdg. 25.00 (ISBN 0-8191-2110-X); pap. text ed. 12.25 (ISBN 0-8191-2111-8). U Pr of Amer.

Boyd, S. M., jt. auth. see Trooboff, P.

Boyd, Selma & Boyd, Pauline. Footprints in the Refrigerator. LC 82-7112. (Easy-Read Story Bks.). (Illus.). (gr. k-3). 1982. 3.95 (ISBN 0-531-03554-9); PLB 8.60 (ISBN 0-531-04450-5). Watts.

--The How: Making the Best of a Mistake. LC 80-13513. (Illus.). 32p. 1981. 10.95 (ISBN 0-87705-176-3). Human Sci Pr.

--I Met a Polar Bear. LC 82-10103. (Illus.). 32p. (gr. k-3). 1983. 10.25 (ISBN 0-688-01881-5); PLB 10.88 (ISBN 0-688-01885-8). Lothrop.

Boyd, Shylah. American Made. 416p. 1975. 10.00 (ISBN 0-374-10416-6). FS&G.

Boyd, Stephen D. & Renz, Mary A. Organization & Outlining: A Workbook for Students in a Basic Speech Course. 58p. 1985. pap. text ed. 4.96 scp (ISBN 0-672-61634-3). Bobbs.

Boyd, Stephen D. & Renz, Mary Anne. Organization & Outlining. 1985. pap. text ed. write for info. (ISBN 0-02-313160-8). Macmillan.

Boyd, Sterling. The Adam Style In America. Freedberg, S. J., ed. (Outstanding Dissertations in America Ser.). (Illus.). 780p. 1985. Repr. of 1964 ed. 75.00 (ISBN 0-8240-6864-5). Garland Pub.

Boyd, Sterling M; see O'Neal, William B.

Boyd, Steven R., ed. The Whiskey Rebellion: Past & Present Perspectives. LC 84-22437. (Contributions in American History Ser.: No. 109). (Illus.). 240p. 1985. lib. bdg. 35.00 (ISBN 0-313-24534-7, BWH/). Greenwood.

Boyd, Susan J., ed. see Hurst, Jane.

Boyd, T. Gardner. Metal Working. LC 81-6741. (Illus.). 1978. text ed. 6.40 (ISBN 0-87006-396-0). Goodheart.

Boyd, T. Munford & Graves, Edward S. Virginia Civil Procedure. 738p. 1982. 65.00 (ISBN 0-87215-424-6). Michie Co.

Boyd, T. Munford & Koontz, William W. Burk's Pleading & Practice. 4th ed. 1952. with 1961 Suppl. 50.00 (ISBN 0-87215-074-7); 1961 Suppl. 15.00 (ISBN 0-87215-273-1). Michie Co.

Boyd, Theo E. Poetic Reflections from the Dust. LC 78-12714. 1979. 5.50 (ISBN 0-8309-0224-4). Herald Hse.

Boyd, Thomas. Poor John Fitch: Inventor of the Steamboat. facsimile ed. LC 75-150171. (Select Bibliographies Reprint Ser). 1972. Repr. of 1935 ed. 20.00 (ISBN 0-8369-5684-2). Ayer Co Pubs.

--Shadow of the Long Knives. 10.25 (ISBN 0-8446-1086-0). Peter Smith.

--Shadow of the Long Knives. 354p. Date not set. Repr. of 1928 ed. lib. bdg. 30.00 (ISBN 0-8482-7454-7). Norwood Edns.

--Shadow of the Long Knives. 18.95 (ISBN 0-88411-861-4, Pub. by Aeonian Pr). Amereon Ltd.

--Through the Wheat: A Novel. LC 77-11635. (Lost American Fiction Ser.). 286p. 1978. Repr. of 1923 ed. 8.95 (ISBN 0-8093-0855-X). S Ill U Pr.

Boyd, Thomas, jt. auth. see Korn, S. Winton.

Boyd, Thomas A. In Time of Peace. LC 74-22769. Repr. of 1935 ed. 17.50 (ISBN 0-404-58408-X). AMS Pr.

--Points of Honor. LC 72-5859. (Short Story Index Reprint Ser.). 1972. Repr. of 1925 ed. 22.00 (ISBN 0-8369-4192-6). Ayer Co Pubs.

--Professional Amateur: The Biography of Charles Franklin Kettering. LC 72-5036. (Technology & Society Ser.). (Illus.). 242p. 1972. Repr. of 1957 ed. 18.00 (ISBN 0-405-04689-8). Ayer Co Pubs.

Boyd, W. E. Control of Formation Pressure. (Well Servicing & Workover: Lesson 9). (Illus.). 44p. (Orig.). 1971. pap. text ed. 4.50 (ISBN 0-88698-065-8, 3.70910). PETEX.

--Fishing Tools & Techniques. (Well Servicing & Workover Ser.: Lesson 10). (Illus.). 48p. (Orig.). 1971. pap. text ed. 4.50 (ISBN 0-88698-066-6, 3.71010). PETEX.

Boyd, W. Harland. Stagecoach Heyday. (Illus.). 1983. 12.00 (ISBN 0-943500-10-9). Kern Historical.

Boyd, W. Harland, ed. Kern Country Wayfarers. 72p. 1977. pap. 4.00 (ISBN 0-943500-03-6). Kern Historical.

Boyd, W. Harland & Ludeke, John, eds. Inside Historic Kern. (Illus.). 1982. 16.95 (ISBN 0-943500-09-5). Kern Historical.

Boyd, W. J. Aldred's Marginalia. 62p. 1975. pap. text ed. 13.00x (ISBN 0-85989-036-8, Pub. by U Exeter England). Humanities.

Boyd, W. T. Fiber Optics Communications: Experiments & Projects. LC 82-50650. 224p. 1982. pap. 15.95 (ISBN 0-672-21834-8). Sams.

Boyd, William. Emile of Jean Jacques Rousseau. (Classics in Education Ser.). 1962. text ed. 11.00 (ISBN 0-8077-1110-1); pap. text ed. 6.00x (ISBN 0-8077-1107-1). Tchrs Coll.

--A Good Man in Africa. LC 81-11041. 1982. 14.50 (ISBN 0-688-00820-8). Morrow.

--A Good Man in Africa. 312p. 1983. pap. 4.95 (ISBN 0-14-005887-7). Penguin.

--The History of Western Education. (Educational Ser.). 1928. Repr. 17.50 (ISBN 0-8482-7382-6). Norwood Edns.

--An Ice-Cream War. LC 82-20813. 352p. 1983. 17.95 (ISBN 0-688-01904-8). Morrow.

--An Ice-Cream War: A Tale of the Empire. 384p. 1984. pap. 4.95 (ISBN 0-14-006571-7). Penguin.

--The Montessori System of Motor Education. (An Intimate Life of Man Library). (Illus.). 131p. 1982. 96.45 (ISBN 0-89920-046-X). Am Inst Psych.

--On the Yankee Station. LC 84-60480. 216p. 1984. Repr. of 1981 ed. 12.95 (ISBN 0-688-03111-0). Morrow.

--On the Yankee Station: Stories. (Fiction Ser.). 192p. 1985. pap. 4.95 (ISBN 0-317-19398-8). Penguin.

--Principles of Drilling Fluid Control. (Illus.). 215p. 1978. pap. text ed. 8.00 (ISBN 0-88698-096-8). Petex.

--The Spontaneous Regression of Cancer. 112p. 1966. photocopy ed. 12.75x (ISBN 0-398-00209-6). C C Thomas.

--Stars & Bars. LC 84-27368. 288p. 1985. 16.95 (ISBN 0-688-02599-4). Morrow.

Boyd, William & King, Edmund J. The History of Western Education. 11th ed. LC 65-789. 517p. 1980. pap. 14.50x (ISBN 0-389-20131-6, 06360). B&N Imports.

Boyd, William D., tr. see Buzas, Ladislaus.

Boyd, William E. Secured Transactions in Arizona: A Lawyer's Guide to Article Nine of the UCC. 106p. 1984. 3 ring binder 18.20 (ISBN 0-910039-10-0). Az Law Inst.

Boyd, William H. The Shasta Route, 1863 to 1887: The Railroad Link Between the Sacremento & the Columbia. Bruchey, Stuart, ed. LC 80-1276. (Railroads Ser.). 1981. lib. bdg. 15.00x (ISBN 0-405-13751-6). Ayer Co Pubs.

Boyd, William H. & Rodgers, Glendon J. San Joaquin Vignettes: The Reminiscences of Captain John Barker. (Illus.). 121p. 1955. 3.50 (ISBN 0-943500-08-7). Kern Historical.

Boyd, William H., ed. Kern County Tall Tales: Selected Folk History. (Illus.). 38p. 1980. pap. 5.00 (ISBN 0-943500-01-X). Kern Historical.

--Minor Educational Writings of Jean-Jacques Rousseau. LC 62-21561. (Classics in Education Ser.). 1962. pap. text ed. 4.50x (ISBN 0-8077-1113-6). Tchrs Coll.

Boyd, William K. Ecclesiastical Edicts of the Theodosian Code. LC 70-77991. (Columbia University. Studies in the Social Sciences: No. 63). Repr. of 1905 ed. 14.50 (ISBN 0-404-51063-9). AMS Pr.

--Some Eighteenth Century Tracts Concerning North Carolina. LC 73-2625. 516p. 1973. Repr. of 1927 ed. 30.00 (ISBN 0-87152-127-X). Reprint.

Boyd, William L., jt. ed. see Immegart, Glenn L.

Boyd, William P., Jr., jt. auth. see Sodeman, William A., Jr.

Boyd, William Y. The Gentle Infantryman. 284p. 1985. 15.95 (ISBN 0-312-32099-X). St Martin.

Boyda, Ellen K. Respiratory Problems, Vol. 5. (RN Assessment Ser.). 180p. 1985. pap. 12.95 (ISBN 0-87489-282-1). Med Economics.

Boyd-Barrett, O. Approaches to Past School Management. 1983. pap. text ed. 15.50 (ISBN 0-06-318263-7). Har-Row.

Boyd-Barrett, Oliver. The International News Agencies. LC 80-51779. (Constable Communication & Society Ser.: Vol. 13). (Illus.). 284p. 1980. 29.95 (ISBN 0-8039-1511-X); pap. 14.95 (ISBN 0-8039-1512-8). Sage.

Boyd-Bowman, Peter. From Latin to Romance in Sound Charts. 134p. 1980. pap. text ed. 8.95 (ISBN 0-87840-077-X). Georgetown U Pr.

--Lexico Hispanoamericano del Siglo XIX. (Spanish Ser.: No. 17). 20p. 1984. incl.13 microfiches 10.00x (ISBN 0-318-02837-9). Hispanic Seminary.

--Lexico Hispanoamericano del Siglo XVII. (Spanish Ser.: No. 11). 14p. 1983. incl. 8 microfiches 10.00x (ISBN 0-942260-33-3). Hispanic Seminary.

--Lexico Hispanoamericano del Siglo XVIII. (Spanish Ser.: No. 5). 26p. 1982. 8 microfiches 10.00xincl. (ISBN 0-942260-21-X). Hispanic Seminary.

--Self-Instructional Language Programs: A Handbook for Faculty & Students. (FAMC Occasional Publication Ser.: No. 20). 51p. (Orig.). 1973. pap. text ed. 2.50x (ISBN 0-936876-08-5). Learn Res Intl Stud.

Boyde, Patrick. Dante, Philomythes & Philosopher: Man in the Cosmos. LC 80-40551. (Illus.). 520p. 1981. 74.50 (ISBN 0-521-23598-7). Cambridge U Pr.

--Dante Philomythes & Philosopher: Man in the Cosmos. LC 80-40551. (Cambridge Paperback Library). 408p. 1983. pap. 17.95 (ISBN 0-521-27390-0). Cambridge U Pr.

--Night Thoughts on Italian Poetry & Art. 32p. 1985. pap. 3.95 (ISBN 0-521-31675-8). Cambridge U Pr.

Boyde, Patrick, jt. ed. see Foster, Kenelm.

Boydell & Brewer Editors, ed. John Constable: Further Correspondence & Documents. 1980. 60.00x (ISBN 0-686-87346-7, Pub. by Boydell & Brewer). State Mutual Bk.

--John Constable's Correspondence II: Early Friends & Maria Bicknell, (Mars Constable) 1981. 42.00x (ISBN 0-686-87333-5, Pub. by Boydell & Brewer). State Mutual Bk.

--John Constable's Correspondence IV: Patrons, Dealers & Fellow Artists. 1980. 50.00x (ISBN 0-686-87335-1, Pub. by Boydell & Brewer). State Mutual Bk.

--John Constable's Correspondence V: Various, Friends, with Charles Boner & the Artist's Children. 1980. 37.00x (ISBN 0-686-87340-8, Pub. by Boydell & Brewer). State Mutual Bk.

--John Constable's Correspondence VI: The Fishes. 1980. 50.00x (ISBN 0-686-87337-8, Pub. by Boydell & Brewer). State Mutual Bk.

--John Constable's Discourses. 1980. 35.00x (ISBN 0-686-87342-4, Pub. by Boydell & Brewer). State Mutual Bk.

--John's Constable's Correspondence III: Correspondence with C. R. Leslie, R. A. 1980. 39.00x (ISBN 0-686-87332-7, Pub. by Boydell & Brewer). State Mutual Bk.

Boydell, Deanne. The Primary Teacher in Action. 135p. 1978. 26.00x (ISBN 0-7291-0177-0, Pub. by Open Bks England). State Mutual Bk.

Boydell, John, ed. Boydell Shakespeare Prints. LC 68-21362. (Illus.). 1968. Repr. of 1805 ed. 44.00 (ISBN 0-405-08299-1, Blom Pubns). Ayer Co Pubs.

Boydell, Mary. Irish Glass. (Irish Heritage Ser.). (Illus.). 26p. 1983. pap. 3.95 (ISBN 0-900346-09-4, Pub. by Salem Hse Ltd). Merrimack Pub Cir.

Boydell, Tom, jt. auth. see Pedler, Mike.

Boydell, Tom & Pedler, Mike, eds. Management Self-Development: Concepts & Practices. 270p. 1981. text ed. 41.00x (ISBN 0-566-02194-3). Gower Pub Co.

Boyden, D. D., ed. see Geminiani, Francesco.

Boyden, David D. History of Violin Playing, from Its Origins to 1761 & Its Relationship to the Violin & Violin Music. (Illus.). 1965. 89.00x (ISBN 0-19-316315-2). Oxford U Pr.

Boyden, Edward A., jt. auth. see Levin, S. I.

Boyden, S., et al. The Ecology of a City & Its People. LC 81-65024. 437p. (Orig.). 1981. pap. text ed. 17.50 (ISBN 0-7081-1095-9, 1079, Pub. by ANUP Australia). Australia N U P.

Boyden, Stephen. An Integrative Ecological Approach to the Study of Human Settlements: Prepared in Cooperation with UNEP. (MAB Technical Notes: No. 12). (Illus.). 87p. 1979. pap. 10.50 (ISBN 92-3-101689-X, U944, UNESCO). Unipub.

Boydston, Jo Ann. John Dewey's Personal & Professional Library: A Checklist. LC 81-18393. (Bibliographic Contributions Ser.). 128p. (Orig.). 1982. pap. 8.00x (ISBN 0-8093-1068-6). S Ill U Pr.

Boydston, Jo Ann, ed. Guide to the Works of John Dewey. LC 70-112383. (Arcturus Books Paperbacks). 413p. 1972. pap. 7.95 (ISBN 0-8093-0561-5). S Ill U Pr.

--The Poems of John Dewey. LC 77-4718. 220p. 1977. 14.95x (ISBN 0-8093-0800-2). S Ill U Pr.

Boydston, Jo Ann & Andresen, Robert L., eds. John Dewey: A Checklist of Translations, 1900-1967. LC 69-15324. 155p. 1969. 7.00x (ISBN 0-8093-0369-8). S Ill U Pr.

Boydston, Jo Ann & Poulos, Kathleen, eds. Checklist of Writings About John Dewey, 1887-1977. 2nd, enl. ed. LC 77-17136. 488p. 1978. 19.95x (ISBN 0-8093-0842-8). S Ill U Pr.

Boydston, Jo Ann, ed. see Dewey, John.

Boydston, Jo Ann, et al, eds. see Dewey, John.

Boye, Alan. A Guide to the Ghosts of Lincoln. (Illus.). 75p. (Orig.). 1983. pap. 3.95 (ISBN 0-913473-07-3). Saltillo Pr.

Boye, Arthur R. Cup of Sunshine. (Illus.). 36p. (Orig.). 1979. pap. 3.50 (ISBN 0-933992-08-4). Coffee Break.

Boye, David. Step-by-Step Knifemaking. LC 77-22383. 1977. pap. 10.95 (ISBN 0-87857-181-7). Rodale Pr Inc.

Boye, Fred, jt. auth. see Louden, Louise.

Boye, Henry. The Headless Horseman Rides Again. LC 75-182949. (Illus.). (gr. 5-10). 1972. text ed. 5.00 (ISBN 0-912472-14-6). Miller Bks.

--Joop Joop, Jeep Jeep & Jopamo: Three Visitors from Jupiter. (Illus.). (gr. 1-4). 1972. pap. 1.50 (ISBN 0-912472-13-8). Miller Bks.

Boye, Karin. Kallocain. Lannestock, Gustaf, tr. from Swedish. (Nordic Translation Ser.). 220p. 1966. Repr. of 1940 ed. 17.50x (ISBN 0-299-03891-2). U of Wis Pr.

--Kallocain: A Novel. 216p. 1985. pap. 7.95 (ISBN 0-88064-050-2). Fromm Intl Pub.

Boye, Richard E. Affirming Life. 1979. pap. 4.50 (ISBN 0-89536-364-X). CSS of Ohio.

Boyeldieu, Pascal. La Langue Lua ("Niellim") (Descriptions de Langues et Monographies Ethnolinguistiques). 585p. Date not set. price not set (ISBN 0-521-27069-3). Cambridge U Pr.

Boyen, John L. Thermal Energy Recovery. 2nd ed. LC 79-19704. 346p. 1980. 49.50x (ISBN 0-471-04981-6, Pub. by Wiley-Interscience). Wiley.

Boyenga, Kirk W. & O'Dell, Gene J. Marketing Your Services to Business & Industry: Fundamentals for Winning Revenues. (Illus.). 100p. 1982. wkbk. 93.00 (ISBN 0-9606362-1-8). Burrell Ctr Inc.

Boyer. Accident Kids. LC 73-93019. (Safety Ser.). (Illus.). (gr. 2-5). 1974. PLB 9.26 (ISBN 0-87783-119-X); pap. 3.94 deluxe ed. (ISBN 0-87783-120-3). cassettes 7.94x (ISBN 0-87783-175-0). Oddo.

--A History of Mathematics. pap. 12.50 (ISBN 0-691-02391-3). Princeton U Pr.

--Let's Walk Safely. LC 80-82953. (Oddo Safety Ser.). (Illus.). (gr. 1-6). 1981. PLB 9.26 (ISBN 0-87783-159-9). Oddo.

--Lucky Bus. LC 73-87801. (Safety Ser.). (Illus.). (gr. k-2). 1974. PLB 10.67 (ISBN 0-87783-131-9); pap. 3.94 deluxe ed. (ISBN 0-87783-132-7); cassette 7.94x (ISBN 0-87783-193-9). Oddo.

--Oddo Safety Series. (Illus.). (ps-6). Set of 4 vols. PLB 39.86 (ISBN 0-87783-170-X); Set of 3 vols. pap. 11.82 deluxe ed. (ISBN 0-87783-171-8); three cassettes 23.82x (ISBN 0-87783-235-8). Oddo.

--Safety on Wheels. LC 73-87802. (Safety Ser.). (Illus.). (gr. k-5). 1974. 10.67 (ISBN 0-87783-133-5); pap. 3.94 deluxe ed. (ISBN 0-87783-134-3); cassette 7.94x (ISBN 0-87783-199-8). Oddo.

Boyer, A. L. Dictionnaire de Physiologie. Migne, J. P., ed. (Troisieme et Derniere Encyclopedie Theologique Ser.: Vol. 58). 776p. (Fr.). Repr. of 1861 ed. lib. bdg. 98.50x (ISBN 0-89241-324-7). Caratzas.

Boyer, Alice J. A Guide to Junior Showmanship Competition. LC 75-20789. (Other Dog Book). (Illus.). 1975. 4.95 (ISBN 0-87714-037-5). Denlingers.

--Your Old English Sheepdog. LC 75-41985. (Your Dog Bk.). (Illus.). 1978. 12.95 (ISBN 0-87714-048-0). Denlingers.

Boyer, Arline, tr. see Dostoyevsky, Fyodor.

Boyer, Barry B., jt. auth. see Gellhorn, Ernest.

Boyer, Bill. Inferno. 1985. 10.95 (ISBN 0-8062-2472-X). Carlton.

Boyer, Blanche, ed. see Abailard, P.

Boyer, Bruce H. see Weingartner, Fannia.

Boyer, Bryce, jt. ed. see Muensterberger, Werner L.

Boyer, Bryce L., jt. auth. see Giovachinni, Peter.

Boyer, Calvin J. & Eaton, Nancy L. Book Selection Policies of American Libraries. (Applications of Library Science: Vol. 3). 211p. 1971. pap. 6.45 (ISBN 0-912556-00-5). Armadillo Pr.

Boyer, Carl B. History of Mathematics. LC 68-16506. 717p. 1968. 40.45x (ISBN 0-471-09374-2). Wiley.

--A History of Mathematics. 732p. 12.50 (ISBN 0-691-02391-3). Princeton U Pr.

--History of the Calculus & Its Conceptual Development. Orig. Title: Concepts of Calculus. 1959. pap. 5.95 (ISBN 0-486-60509-4). Dover.

--The History of the Calculus & Its Conceptual Development. LC 59-9673. 1959. lib. bdg. 15.00x (ISBN 0-88307-623-3). Gannon.

Boyer, Carl, III, jt. auth. see Jacobus, Donald L.

Boyer, Carl, 3rd. Ancestral Lines Revised. LC 81-68273. 666p. 1981. 42.00 (ISBN 0-936124-05-9). C Boyer.

--How to Publish & Market Your Family History. 2nd ed. (Illus.). 160p. 1985. pap. 14.00 (ISBN 0-936124-08-3). C Boyer.

--Ship Passenger Lists: National & New England (1600-1825) LC 76-37355. 270p. 1977. text ed. 22.00 (ISBN 0-936124-00-8). C Boyer.

--Ship Passenger Lists: New York & New Jersey (1600-1825) LC 78-52617. 333p. 1978. text ed. 22.00 (ISBN 0-936124-01-6). C Boyer.

--Ship Passenger Lists: Pennsylvania & Delaware (1641-1825) LC 79-57204. 289p. 1980. text ed. 22.00 (ISBN 0-936124-02-4). C Boyer.

--Ship Passenger Lists: The South (1538-1825) LC 78-52618. 314p. 1979. text ed. 22.00 (ISBN 0-936124-03-2). C Boyer.

Boyer, Carl, 3rd, et al. Brown Families of Bristol Counties, Massachusetts & Rhode Island & Descendants of Jared Talbot. LC 80-68755. (New England Colonial Families Ser.: Vol. 1). 219p. 1982. 22.00 (ISBN 0-936124-04-0). C Boyer.

Boyer, Dale, ed. see Blessing, Richard.

Boyer, Dale, ed. see Crews, Judson.

Boyer, Dale, ed. see Partridge, Dixie.

Boyer, Dale, ed. see Romeo, Leo.

Boyer, Dale, ed. see Taggard, Genevieve.

Boyer, Dale K., ed. see Bierds, Linda.

Boyer, Dale K., ed. see Hales, Corrinne.

Boyer, Dale K., ed. see Wright, Carolyne L.

Boyer, David L., et al, eds. The Philosopher's Annual, 1981, Vol. IV. xii, 250p. (Orig.). 1981. lib. bdg. 24.00x (ISBN 0-917930-75-4); pap. 8.50x (ISBN 0-917930-61-4). Ridgeview.

--The Philosopher's Annual, 1978, Vol. 1. 223p. 1978. 25.00x (ISBN 0-8476-6105-9); pap. 12.50x (ISBN 0-8476-6106-7). Rowman.

--The Philosopher's Annual, 1979, Vol. 2. 231p. 1979. 25.00x (ISBN 0-8476-6202-0). Rowman.

--The Philosopher's Annual 1980, Vol. III. xii, 225p. (Orig.). 1980. lib. bdg. 24.00x (ISBN 0-917930-38-X); pap. text ed. 8.50x (ISBN 0-917930-18-5). Ridgeview.

Boyer, Deena. The Two Hundred Days of Eight & a Half. Kupelnick, Bruce S., ed. LC 76-52091. (Classics of Film Literature Ser.). 1978. lib. bdg. 31.00 (ISBN 0-8240-2867-8). Garland Pub.

Boyer, Donald A., jt. auth. see Russell, Marion J.

Boyer, Dwight. Ghost Ships of the Great Lakes. (Illus.). 320p. 1984. pap. 9.95 (ISBN 0-396-08346-3). Dodd.

--Great Stories of the Great Lakes. (Illus.). 272p. 1985. pap. 9.95 (ISBN 0-396-08596-2). Dodd.

--True Tales of the Great Lakes. (Illus.). 352p. 1984. pap. 9.95 (ISBN 0-396-08348-X). Dodd.

Boyer, E. Gil, jt. ed. see Simon, Anita.

Boyer, E. Marcia. Basic Statistical Concepts & Techniques Applied in Dental Health. (Illus.). 83p. (Orig.). 1981. pap. 6.95 (ISBN 0-89529-128-2). Avery Pub.

Boyer, Edie. As-a-Land. 68p. 1982. pap. 6.95 (ISBN 0-932298-19-2). Copple Hse.

Boyer, Elizabeth. A Colony of One. LC 83-50742. (Illus.). 1983. 22.00 (ISBN 0-915964-05-8). Veritie Pr.

--The Elves & the Otterskin. 1981. pap. 2.50 (ISBN 0-345-29212-X, Del Rey). Ballantine.

--Freydis & Gudrid. LC 76-23353. (Illus., Orig.). 1976. 9.95 (ISBN 0-915964-02-3). Veritie Pr.

--Marguerite De la Roque: A Story of Survival. LC 75-20805. 1975. 9.95 (ISBN 0-915964-01-5). Veritie Pr.

--The Thralls of the Dragon's Heart. 304p. 1982. pap. 2.75 (ISBN 0-345-30236-2, Del Rey). Ballantine.

Boyer, Ernest, Jr. A Way in the World: Family Life as Spiritual Discipline. LC 83-48983. 192p. 1984. 12.45i (ISBN 0-06-061032-8, HarpR). Har-Row.

Boyer, Ernest L. High School: A Report of the Carnegie Foundation for the Advancement of Teaching. LC 83-47528. 256p. 1983. 16.30 (ISBN 0-06-015193-5, HarpT). Har-Row.

Boyer, Ernest L. & Hechinger, Fred. Higher Learning in the Nation's Service. LC 81-70738. 69p. 1981. pap. 6.50 (ISBN 0-931050-20-0). Carnegie Found Adv Teach.

Boyer, Ernest L. & Kaplan, Martin. Educating for Survival. LC 77-72982. 1977. pap. 6.95 (ISBN 0-915390-12-4, Pub. by Change Mag). Transaction Pubs.

Boyer, Ernest L. & Levine, Arthur. A Quest for Common Learning: The Aims of General Education. LC 81-66307. 68p. 1981. pap. 6.95 (ISBN 0-931050-18-9). Carnegie Found Adv Teach.

Boyer, Ernest L., jt. auth. see Carnegie Foundation for the Advancement of Teaching.

Boyer, G. Bruce. Elegance: A Guide to Quality in Menswear. 1985. 18.95 (ISBN 0-393-01878-4). Norton.

Boyer, G. G. The Guns of Morgette. large print ed. LC 84-2507. 339p. 1984. Repr. of 1982 ed. 12.95 (ISBN 0-89621-541-5). Thorndike Pr.

--Morgette in the Yukon. 1983. 11.95 (ISBN 0-8027-4020-0). Walker & Co.

--Morgette in the Yukon. large print ed. LC 84-8747. 269p. 1984. Repr. of 1983 ed. 12.95 (ISBN 0-89621-562-8). Thorndike Pr.

--Morgette on the Barbary Coast. LC 83-40422. 192p. 1984. 12.95 (ISBN 0-8027-4033-2). Walker & Co.

--Return of Morgette. LC 85-7153. (Morgette Ser.). 1985. 14.95 (ISBN 0-8027-4049-9). Walker & Co.

Boyer, Glenn C. The Guns of Morgette. LC 81-71192. 197p. 1982. 11.95 (ISBN 0-8027-4007-3). Walker & Co.

Boyer, Glenn G., ed. see Earp, Josephine.

Boyer, Glenn G., ed. see Earp, Wyatt S.

Boyer, Golda N. Mean Jeans Manufacturing Co. A Business Community Simulation. (gr. 9-12). 1983. 58.00 (ISBN 0-538-07100-1, G10). SW Pub.

Boyer, Harriet, jt. ed. see Cabrera, Vicente.

Boyer, Howard E., jt. ed. see Unterweiser, Paul M.

Boyer, James B. & Boyer, Joe L. Curriculum & Instruction after Desegregation. 1975. pap. 5.00 (ISBN 0-686-00371-3). AG Pr.

Boyer, James L. For a World Like Ours: Studies in I Corinthians. pap. 4.95 (ISBN 0-88469-057-1). BMH Bks.

--A Manual of Greek Forms. pap. 4.95 (ISBN 0-88469-007-5). BMH Bks.

--Prophecy, Things to Come. pap. 4.95 (ISBN 0-88469-006-7). BMH Bks.

Boyer, Jill, et al. Blacksongs, Series I: Four Poetry Broadsides by Black Women. 1977. pap. 2.50x (ISBN 0-916418-15-4). Lotus.

Boyer, Jill W. Breaking Camp. LC 83-82772. (Illus.). 61p. 1984. pap. 6.00x perf. bnd. (ISBN 0-916418-52-9). Lotus.

Boyer, Jill W., ed. The Broadside Annual, 1973. 1973. pap. 1.50 (ISBN 0-910296-91-X). Broadside.

Boyer, Joe L., jt. auth. see Boyer, James B.

Boyer, John W. Political Radicalism in Late Imperial Vienna: Origins of the Christian Social Movement, 1848-1897. LC 80-17302. (Illus.). 1981. lib. bdg. 40.00x (ISBN 0-226-06957-5). U of Chicago Pr.

Boyer, L. B. The Regressed Patient. LC 82-24363. 346p. 1983. 25.00 (ISBN 0-87668-626-9). Aronson.

Boyer, L. Bryce. Childhood & Folklore: A Psychoanalytic Study of Apache Personality. 1979. 16.95 (ISBN 0-914434-07-1); pap. 8.95 (ISBN 0-914434-09-8). Psychohistory Pr.

Boyer, L. Bryce, jt. ed. see Giovacchini, Peter.

Boyer, Linda. God Made Me. LC 81-50677. (A Happy Day Bk.). (Illus.). 24p. (Orig.). (ps-1). 1981. pap. 1.39 (ISBN 0-87239-464-6, 3597). Standard Pub.

Boyer, M. & Kihlstrom, R. E, eds. Bayesian Models in Economic Theory. (Studies in Bayesian Econometrics: Vol. 5). 320p. 1984. 63.50 (ISBN 0-444-86502-0, I-544-83, North-Holland). Elsevier.

Boyer, M. Christine. Dreaming the Rational City: The Myth of American City Planning. 400p. 1983. 27.50x (ISBN 0-262-02186-2). MIT Pr.

Boyer, M. Christine. Manhattan Manners: Architecture & Style 1850-1900. LC 85-42966. (Illus.). 256p. 1985. 30.00 (ISBN 0-8478-0650-2). Rizzoli Intl.

Boyer, Marjorie N. Medieval French Bridges: A History. LC 75-36478. 1976. 12.00x (ISBN 0-910956-58-8). Medieval Acad.

Boyer, Martha. Japanese Lacquers in the Walters Art Gallery. (Illus.). 1970. bds. 30.00 (ISBN 0-911886-11-7). Walters Art.

Boyer, Mary. Arizona in Literature. LC 78-129967. (American History & Americana Ser.: No. 47). 1970. Repr. of 1935 ed. lib. bdg. 62.95x (ISBN 0-8383-1168-7). Haskell.

Boyer, Mildred, jt. auth. see Andersson, Theodore.

Boyer, Mildred, ed. The Texas Collection of Comedias Sueltas: A Descriptive Bibliography. (Reference Publications Ser.). 1978. lib. bdg. 68.50 (ISBN 0-8161-8117-9, Hall Reference). G K Hall.

Boyer, Mildred, tr. see Borges, Jorge L.

Boyer, Natalie R. A Virginia Gentleman & His Family. 1978. Repr. of 1939 ed. lib. bdg. 35.00 (ISBN 0-8492-3712-2). R West.

Boyer, Nicodemus E. Adolf Hitler, the Black Horseman, & the Millennium in 2000. (Dr. M. Nostradamus: 1999, the Seventh Month Ser.: Vol. 1). (Illus.). 482p. 1985. 35.00 (ISBN 0-933569-00-9). Studeophile Pub.

Boyer, Patricia A., et al. A Guide for the Family Therapist: The Family As an International Kaleidoscope. LC 83-3799. 176p. (Orig.). 1984. 20.00 (ISBN 0-87668-637-4). Aronson.

Boyer, Paul. Urban Masses & Moral Order in America, 1820-1920. LC 78-15973. 1978. 25.00x (ISBN 0-674-93109-2). Harvard U Pr.

Boyer, Paul & Nissenbaum, Stephen. Salem Possessed: The Social Orgins of Witchcraft. LC 73-84399. 320p. 1974. 17.50x (ISBN 0-674-78525-8); pap. 5.95 (ISBN 0-674-78526-6). Harvard U Pr.

Boyer, Paul & Nissenbaum, Stephen, eds. The Salem Witchcraft Papers: Verbatim Transcripts, 3 vols. (Civil Liberties in American History Ser.). 1977. Set. lib. bdg. 145.00 (ISBN 0-306-70655-5). Da Capo.

Boyer, Paul D., ed. The Enzymes. Incl. Vol. 1. Enzyme Structure, Control. 3rd. ed. 1970. 80.00 (ISBN 0-12-122701-4); Vol. 2. Kinetics, Mechanisms. 3rd. ed. 1970. 75.00 (ISBN 0-12-122702-2); Vol. 3. Peptide Bond Hydrolysis. 3rd ed. 1971. 90.00 (ISBN 0-12-122703-0); Vol. 4. 1971. 90.00 (ISBN 0-12-122704-9); Vol. 5. 1971. 90.00 (ISBN 0-12-122705-7); Vol. 6. 1972. 88.00 (ISBN 0-12-122706-5); Vol. 7. 1972; Vol. 8. 1973. 83.50 (ISBN 0-12-122708-1); Vol. 9. 1973. 80.00 (ISBN 0-12-122709-X); Vol. 10. 1974. 90.00 (ISBN 0-12-122710-3); Vol. 11. 1975. 88.00 (ISBN 0-12-122711-1); Vol. 12. 1975. 88.00 (ISBN 0-12-122712-X); Vol. 13. 1976. 85.00 (ISBN 0-12-122713-8). student ed. 1973 24.00i (ISBN 0-12-122750-2). Acad Pr.

--The Enzymes, Vol. 14. 3rd ed. LC 75-117107. 1981. 82.50 (ISBN 0-12-122714-6). Acad Pr.

--The Enzymes: Lipid Enzymology: Fatty Acids, Glycerides, Phospholipids, Sphingolipids, Glycolipids, Cholesterol, Special Topics, Vol. 16. 3rd ed. 1983. 79.00 (ISBN 0-12-122716-2). Acad Pr.

--The Enzymes: Nucleic Acids, Vol. 15, Pt. B. 3rd ed. 1982. 79.50 (ISBN 0-12-122715-4). Acad Pr.

Boyer, Pierre. Enciclopedia del Cine Amateur. 2nd ed. 416p. (Espn.). 1976. 37.50 (ISBN 84-279-4513-2, S-14382). French & Eur.

Boyer, R. & Keinath, S., eds. Molecular Motion in Polymers by ESR. (MMI Press Symposium Ser.: Vol. 1). 352p. 1980. lib. bdg. 62.50 (ISBN 3-7186-0012-9). Harwood Academic.

Boyer, R. R. & Roseberg, H. W., eds. Beta Titanium Alloys in the 1980's. LC 84-60323. (Illus.). 505p. 1984. 63.00 (ISBN 0-89520-476-2). Metal Soc.

Boyer, Ralph E. Survey of the Law of Property. 3rd ed. 766p. 1981. text ed. 19.95 (ISBN 0-8299-2128-1). West Pub.

Boyer, Raymond F., ed. Technological Aspects of the Mechanical Behavior of Polymers. LC 74-181576. (Applied Polymer Symposia: No. 24). Repr. of 1974 ed. 23.00 (ISBN 0-8357-9378-8, 2007371). Bks Demand UMI.

Boyer, Reba B. McMinn County Tennessee, Marriages, 1820-1870. (Orig.). 1983. pap. 22.50 (ISBN 0-89308-330-5). Southern Hist Pr.

--Monroe County, Tennessee, Records, 1820-1870, Vol. 1. 198p. 1983. pap. 22.50 (ISBN 0-89308-329-1). Southern Hist Pr.

--Monroe County Tennessee Records, 1820-1870, Vol. 2. 198p. 1983. pap. 22.50 (ISBN 0-89308-327-5). Southern Hist Pr.

Boyer, Rebe B. Wills & Estate Records of McMinn Co. Tennessee, 1820-1870. 202p. 1983. pap. 22.50 (ISBN 0-89308-328-3). Southern Hist Pr.

Boyer, Regis. Les Vikings et Leur Civilisation: Probleme Actuels. (Bibliotheque Arctique et Antartique: No. 5). (Illus.). 1976. pap. text ed. 21.60x (ISBN 90-279-7944-8). Mouton.

Boyer, Regis, notes by. Livre de la Colonisation de l'Islande (Landnamabok), le. (Contributions Du Centre D'etudes Arctiques: No. 10). 1973. pap. 14.00x (ISBN 90-279-2690-5). Mouton.

Boyer, Richard & Morais, Herbert. Labor's Untold Story. 380p. 1955. 5.50 (ISBN 0-916180-01-8). United Elec R&M.

Boyer, Richard & Savageau, David. Places Rated Almanac: Your Guide to Finding the Best Places to Live in America. 2nd ed. (Illus.). 450p. 1985. 24.95 (ISBN 0-528-81091-X); pap. 14.95 (ISBN 0-528-88008-X). Rand.

--Places Rated Retirement Guide. 192p. 1983. pap. 9.95 (ISBN 0-528-88070-5). Rand.

Boyer, Richard, jt. auth. see London, Barbara.

Boyer, Rick. Billingsgate Shoal. 288p. 1982. 11.95 (ISBN 0-395-32041-0). HM.

--Billingsgate Shoal. 1985. pap. 3.50 (ISBN 0-446-32739-5). Warner Bks.

--The Penny Ferry. 1984. 13.95 (ISBN 0-395-35288-6). HM.

Boyer, Robert D., compiled by. Realism in European Theater & Drama, Eighteen Seventy to Nineteen Twenty: A Bibliography. LC 78-19934. 1979. lib. bdg. 35.00x (ISBN 0-313-20607-4, BOR/). Greenwood.

Boyer, Robert E. Oceanography Fact Book. LC 74-1649. (Fact Bks.). (Illus.). 48p. (gr. 7-12). 1974. pap. text ed. 5.95 (ISBN 0-8331-1707-6). Hubbard Sci.

Boyer, Robert E. & Snyder, P. B. Geology. 2nd ed. (Illus.). 48p. (gr. 4-7). 1986. pap. text ed. price not set (ISBN 0-8331-0572-8). Hubbard Sci.

--Geology Fact Book. LC 75-138627. (Fact Books). (Illus.). (gr. 7 up). 1972. pap. text ed. 5.95 (ISBN 0-8331-1700-9). Hubbard Sci.

Boyer, Robert H. & Zahorski, Kenneth J. Fantasists on Fantasy. 304p. (Orig.). 1984. pap. 3.95 (ISBN 0-380-86553-X, 86553, Discus). Avon.

Boyer, Robert H., jt. auth. see Zahorski, Kenneth J.

Boyer, Robert H. & Zahorski, Kenneth J., eds. The Fantastic Imagination, Vol. II. (YA) 1978. pap. 2.50 (ISBN 0-380-41533-X, 41533). Avon.

Boyer, Robert M. & Zahorski, Kenneth J., eds. The Fantastic Imagination. (YA) 1977. pap. 2.25 (ISBN 0-380-00956-0, 32326-5). Avon.

Boyer, Robert S. & Moore, J. Strother. The Correctness Problem in Computer Science. LC 81-67887. (International Lecture in Computer Science Ser.). 1982. 39.50 (ISBN 0-12-122920-3). Acad Pr.

Boyer, Robert S. & Moore, J. Strother, eds. A Computational Logic. LC 79-51693. (ACM Monograph Ser.). 1979. 35.00 (ISBN 0-12-122950-5). Acad Pr.

Boyer, Roy. Soc. LC 82-90597. 128p. 1983. 7.95 (ISBN 0-533-05518-0). Vantage.

Boyer, Ruth. Be Gentle With Yourself: You Have a Right to be Happy! LC 81-85421. 125p. 1982. pap. 6.95 (ISBN 0-88247-656-4). R & E Pubs.

--Be Gentle With Yourself: Your Feelings & the Bad Guys. LC 81-85503. 125p. 1982. pap. 6.95 (ISBN 0-88247-657-2). R & E Pubs.

Boyer, Ruth G. The Happy Adolescent. LC 81-51457. 109p. 1981. perfect bound 8.95 (ISBN 0-88247-591-6). R & E Pubs.

Boyer, Theodore, jt. auth. see Ingleby, Steven L.

Boyer, Thomas D., jt. auth. see Zakim, David.

Boyer, Walter E., et al. Songs along the Mahantonga: Pennsylvania Dutch Folksongs. 231p. 1964. Repr. of 1951 ed. 35.00x (ISBN 0-8103-5002-5). Gale.

Boyer, William. Education for Annihilation. O'Connell, Patrick, ed. (Illus.). 1973. pap. 3.25 (ISBN 0-685-56831-8). Hogarth.

Boyer, William H. America's Future: Transition to the 21st Century. LC 83-27021. 188p. 1984. 29.95 (ISBN 0-03-071121-5). Praeger.

Boyer, William W. America's Virgin Islands: A History of Human Rights & Wrongs. LC 82-72559. 418p. 1983. lib. bdg. 27.75 (ISBN 0-89089-239-3); pap. text ed. 13.75 (ISBN 0-89089-240-7). Carolina Acad Pr.

--Bureaucracy on Trial: Policy Making by Government Agencies. LC 63-16942. 1964. 19.95x (ISBN 0-672-51129-0). Irvington.

Boyer Argens, Jean Baptiste De see Baptiste De Boyer Argens, Jean.

Boyers, A., jt. auth. see Eckerlin, H.

Boyers, Peggy, jt. ed. see Boyers, Robert.

Boyers, Robert. Atrocity & Amnesia: The Political Novel Since 1945. 275p. 1985. 24.95 (ISBN 0-19-503620-4). Oxford U Pr.

--Excursions: Selected Literary Essays. (Literary Criticism Ser). 1976. 21.50x (ISBN 0-8046-9148-7, Pub. by Kennikat). Assoc Faculty Pr.

--F. R. Leavis: Judgment & the Discipline of Thought. LC 78-54704. (Literary Frontiers Editions). 128p. 1978. pap. 7.95x (ISBN 0-8262-0254-3). U of Mo Pr.

--Lionel Trilling: Negative Capability & the Wisdom of Avoidance. LC 77-7322. (Literary Frontiers Editions). 78p. 1977. pap. 7.95x (ISBN 0-8262-0228-4). U of Mo Pr.

--R. P. Blackmur, Poet-Critic: Toward a View of Poetic Objects. LC 80-15414. (Literary Frontiers Editions). 128p. 1980. pap. text ed. 7.95x (ISBN 0-8262-0315-9). U of Mo Pr.

Boyers, Robert & Boyers, Peggy, eds. The Salmagundi Reader. LC 82-49294. 672p. 1983. 25.00x (ISBN 0-253-35060-3). Ind U Pr.

Boyers, Robert & Orrill, Robert, eds. R. D. Laing & Anti-Psychiatry. 304p. 1974. Repr. of 1971 ed. lib. bdg. 21.50x (ISBN 0-374-90906-7). Octagon.

Boyes, G. T. The Diaries & Letters of G. T. W. B. Boyes, Vol. 1. Chapman, Peter, ed. (Illus.). 384p. 1985. 98.00x (ISBN 0-19-554454-4). Oxford U Pr.

Boyes, Geoffrey, ed. Synchro & Resolver Conversion. (Illus.). 196p. (Orig.). 1980. pap. 11.50 (ISBN 0-916550-06-0). Analog Devices.

Boyes, J; see Institute of Marine Engineers.

Boyes, Janet. Making Paper Costumes. (Illus.). 88p. 1974. 10.95 (ISBN 0-8238-0147-0). Plays.

Boyes, John & Russell, Ronald. The Canals of Eastern England. 1977. 22.50 (ISBN 0-7153-7415-X). David & Charles.

Boyes, Jon L. & Andriole, Stephen J., eds. Issues in C3I Program Management: Requirements, Systems & Operations. (AFCEA-Signal Magazine C3I Ser.: Vol. I). (Illus.). 420p. 1984. 29.95 (ISBN 0-916159-02-7); Set. write for info. (ISBN 0-916159-01-9). AFCEA Intl Pr.

Boyes, Lindy. Pilot's Weather Guide. 2nd ed. pap. text ed. 7.95 (ISBN 0-8306-2288-8, 2288). TAB Bks.

Boyes, R. G. Structural & Cut-off Diaphragm Walls. (Illus.). 181p. 1975. 40.75 (ISBN 0-85334-607-0, Pub. by Elsevier Applied Sci England). Elsevier.

Boyes, William E. Jigs & Fixtures. LC 79-64915. pap. 69.50 (ISBN 0-317-08498-4, 2019119). Bks Demand UMI.

Boyes, William E., ed. Jigs & Fixtures. LC 79-64915. pap. 69.50 (ISBN 0-317-27706-5, 2024171). Bks Demand UMI.

Boyes, William J. Macroeconomics: The Dynamics of Theory & Policy. 1984. text ed. 24.25 (ISBN 0-538-08700-5, H70). SW Pub.

Boyesen, Hjalmar H. Essays on German Literature. LC 74-37509. (Essay Index Reprint Ser.). Repr. of 1892 ed. 19.50 (ISBN 0-8369-2536-X). Ayer Co Pubs.

--Essays on Scandinavian Literature. LC 72-80496. Repr. of 1911 ed. 22.00 (ISBN 0-405-08300-9, Blom Pubns). Ayer Co Pubs.

--Essays on Scandinavian Literature. 59.95 (ISBN 0-8490-0129-3). Gordon Pr.

--Ilka on the Hill-Top. facs. ed. LC 78-142259. (Short Story Index Reprint Ser). 1881. 17.00 (ISBN 0-8369-3743-0). Ayer Co Pubs.

--The Mammon of Unrighteousness. LC 78-104421. Repr. of 1891 ed. lib. bdg. 16.00 (ISBN 0-8398-0169-6). Irvington.

--The Modern Vikings: Stories of Life & Sport in the Norseland. 21.00 (ISBN 0-8369-4266-3, 6065). Ayer Co Pubs.

--Queen Titania. facs. ed. LC 77-122691. (Short Story Index Reprint Ser). 1881. 17.00 (ISBN 0-8369-3524-1). Ayer Co Pubs.

--The Story of Norway. 1886. 40.00 (ISBN 0-8482-7412-1). Norwood Edns.

--Tales from Two Hemispheres. facsimile ed. LC 78-98563. (Short Story Index Reprint Ser.). 1877. 18.00 (ISBN 0-8369-3137-8). Ayer Co Pubs.

Boyet, Howard. HERO 1: Advanced Programming Experiments. rev. ed. Johnson, Ron, ed. LC 84-10722. (Illus.). 305p. 1984. Repr. of 1983 ed. lab manual 24.95 (ISBN 0-87119-036-2, EB-1802). Heathkit-Zenith Ed.

Boyett, Rose-Marie. The Adventures of Tiger. (Illus.). 36p. (YA) 1982. pap. 4.95 (ISBN 0-9609566-0-3). Ro-Mar.

Boyett, Steven R. Ariel: A Book of the Change. 336p. 1983. pap. 2.95 cancelled (ISBN 0-441-02920-5, Pub. by Ace Science Fiction). Ace Bks.

Boyette, Tanya, et al. Ceramics & Glass at the Essex Institute. LC 85-71260. (E.I. Museum Booklet Ser.). (Illus.). 64p. 1985. pap. 5.95 (ISBN 0-88389-088-7). Essex Inst.

Boyington, Pappy. Baa Baa Black Sheep. 16.00 (ISBN 0-933458-00-2). J B Wilson.

--Tonya. 15.00 (ISBN 0-933458-01-0). J B Wilson.

Boyink, Betty. Baskets for Quilters. 52p. (Orig.). 1982. softcover 9.50 (ISBN 0-9612608-0-7). B Boyink.

--Child's Play for Quilters. 60p. (Orig.). 1984. soft cover 9.50 (ISBN 0-9612608-3-1). B Boyink.

--Flower Gardens & Hexagons for Quilters. 60p. (Orig.). 1984. pap. 9.50 (ISBN 0-9612608-4-X). B Boyink.

--Trees & Leaves for Quilters. 60p. (Orig.). 1982. softcover 9.50 (ISBN 0-9612608-1-5). B Boyink.

Boyink, Betty & Splitstone, Milly. Michigan Quilters & Their Designs. 52p. (Orig.). 1983. softcover 9.50 (ISBN 0-9612608-2-3). B Boyink.

Bo Yin Ra. The Book on Life Beyond. Reichenbach, Bodo A., tr. from Ger. LC 78-51633. 1978. pap. 3.50 (ISBN 0-915034-02-6). Kober Pr.

--The Wisdom of St. John. Reichenbach, Bodo A., tr. from Ger. LC 74-15272. 112p. 1975. 5.00 (ISBN 0-915034-01-8). Kober Pr.

Boykin, A. Wade, et al, eds. Research Directions of Black Psychologists. Franklin, Anderson J. & Yates, J. Frank. LC 79-7348. 440p. 1980. 20.00x (ISBN 0-87154-254-4). Russell Sage.

Boykin, James H. Black Jews. LC 81-90626. iv, 98p. (Orig.). 1982. pap. 3.25x (ISBN 0-9603342-1-1). Boykin.

--Financing Real Estate. LC 77-205. (Special Series in Real Estate & Urban Land Economics). (Illus.). 1979. 33.00x (ISBN 0-669-01449-4); instr's manual avail. (ISBN 0-669-03998-5). Lexington Bks.

--Foreign Divorce. LC 64-19177. 79p. (Orig.). 1964. pap. 2.00x (ISBN 0-9603342-3-8). Boykin.

--Inter-Ethnic Death Rate Differential in Florida. (Illus.). 41p. (Orig.). 1976. pap. 3.75x (ISBN 0-9603342-5-4). Boykin.

--Thank God for Black Power. LC 83-90000. 172p. 1983. pap. 8.95x (ISBN 0-9603342-2-X). Boykin.

--World Blacks: Self Help & Achievement. LC 79-53631. ix, 193p. 1979. pap. 6.25x (ISBN 0-9603342-0-3). Boykin.

Boykin, James H., jt. auth. see Epley, Donald R.

Boykin, James H., ed. see Ventolo, William L. & Williams, Martha R.

Boykin-Smith, Lorraine & Williams, Barbara K., eds. A Comprehensive Review of Food Preparation & Storage Application. LC 82-50386. 124p. 1982. pap. 14.95x (ISBN 0-938860-04-6). Westville Pub Co.

Boykin-Stith, Lorraine & D'Angelo, Rosemary. A Comprehensive Review of Clinical Nutrition. LC 81-50667. 121p. 1981. pap. 14.95x (ISBN 0-938860-02-X). Westville Pub Co.

Boykin-Stith, Lorraine & Williams, Barbara K. A Basic Primer of Food Service Administration. LC 82-50566. 260p. 1982. pap. 19.95x (ISBN 0-938860-04-6). Westville Pub Co.

--A Comprehensive Review of Food Service Administration. LC 81-50668. 138p. 1981. pap. 14.95x (ISBN 0-938860-01-1). Westville Pub Co.

--A Comprehensive Review of Nutrition. LC 80-54647. 155p. (Orig.). 1980. pap. 14.95x (ISBN 0-938860-00-3). Westville Pub Co.

--A Comprehensive Review of Organization & Management. LC 81-52902. 124p. 1981. pap. 14.95x (ISBN 0-938860-03-8). Westville Pub Co.

Boyko, P. America Latina: Expansion del Imperialismo y Crisis de la Via Capitalista de Desarrollo. 259p. (Span.). 5.45 (ISBN 0-8285-1412-7, Pub. by Progress Pubs USSR). Imported Pubns.

Boyko, Walter N. Guidebook for the Smart Investor: How to Analyze Real Estate Investment Returns. Rand, Elizabeth H., ed. LC 80-52879. (Illus.). 64p. (Orig.). 1981. pap. 4.95 (ISBN 0-914488-24-4). Rand-Tofua.

Boylan, Bernard. Development of the Long-Range Escort Fighter. (USAF Historical Studies: No. 136). 321p. 1955. pap. text ed. 35.00x (ISBN 0-89126-141-9). MA-AH Pub.

Boylan, Brian R., jt. auth. see Weller, Charles.

Boylan, Claire. Holy Pictures. 208p. 1983. 14.95 (ISBN 0-671-46750-6). Summit Bks.

Boylan, Clare. Holy Pictures. 224p. 1984. pap. 3.95 (ISBN 0-14-006811-2). Penguin.

--A Nail on the Head. (Fiction Ser.). 192p. 1985. pap. 3.95 (ISBN 0-14-006823-6). Penguin.

Boylan, Eleanor. Holiday Plays for Puppets or People. 94p. 1974. pap. 4.00 (ISBN 0-932720-33-1). New Plays Bks.

Boylan, Eugene D. Difficulties in Mental Prayer. 128p. 1984. pap. 6.95 (ISBN 0-87061-105-4). Chr Classics.

Boylan, Henry. A Dictionary of Irish Biography. LC 78-67791. 385p. 1978. text ed. 28.50x (ISBN 0-06-490620-5, 06361). B&N Imports.

--Wolfe Tone. (Gill's Irish Lives Ser.). 145p. 1981. 15.95 (ISBN 0-7171-1090-7, Gill & Mcmillan Ireland); pap. 5.95 (ISBN 0-7171-1091-5). Irish Bk Ctr.

Boylan, James. The New Deal Coalition & the Election of 1946. Freidel, Frank, ed. LC 80-8471. (Modern American History Ser.). 233p. 1982. lib. bdg. 36.00 (ISBN 0-8240-4850-4). Garland Pub.

Boylan, Leona D. Spanish Colonial Silver. (Illus.). 216p. 1975. 16.95 (ISBN 0-89013-065-5); pap. 11.00 (ISBN 0-89013-066-3). Museum NM Pr.

Boylan, M. Eugene. This Tremendous Lover. 1957. pap. 4.95 (ISBN 0-8091-1702-9). Paulist Pr.

Boylan, Michael. Method & Practice in Aristotle's Biology. LC 82-23708. (Illus.). 300p. (Orig.). 1983. lib. bdg. 25.50 (ISBN 0-8191-2952-6); pap. text ed. 13.25 (ISBN 0-8191-2953-4). U Pr of Amer.

Boylan, P. Thoth: The Hermes of Egypt. 215p. 1979. 12.50 (ISBN 0-89005-280-8). Ares.

Boylan, R. D., tr. see Goethe, Johann W.

Boylar, R. D., ed. & tr. see Goethe, Johann W.

Boyle, A. C. Color Atlas of Rheumatology. 2nd ed. (Year Book Color Atlas Ser.). 1980. 49.95 (ISBN 0-8151-1126-6). Year Bk Med.

Boyle, A. Raymond, jt. auth. see Peuquet, Donna J.

Boyle, Andrew. Rejected Addresses. LC 74-11000. 1929. 25.00 (ISBN 0-8414-3124-8). Folcroft.

--Rejected Addresses or the Theatrum Poetarum. 1973. Repr. of 1929 ed. 30.00 (ISBN 0-8274-1457-9). R West.

--Trenchard: Man of Vision. 1962. 35.00 (ISBN 0-685-56054-6). Beachcomber Bks.

Boyle, Andrew, tr. see De Spinoza, Benedictus.

Boyle, Ann. Moon Shadows. 1978. pap. 1.50 (ISBN 0-532-15351-0). Woodhill.

--Never Say Never. 176p. 1984. pap. 1.95 (ISBN 0-441-56971-4). Ace Bks.

Boyle, Ann K., jt. auth. see Goodearl, K. R.

Boyle, C., et al. People, Science & Technology: A Guide to Advanced Industrial Society. LC 83-24368. 278p. 1984. 26.50x (ISBN 0-389-20455-2, 08016). B&N Imports.

Boyle, Charles. House of Cards. 64p. 1982. pap. text ed. 7.50x (ISBN 0-85635-426-0, 61049, Pub. by Carcanet New Pr England). Humanities.

Boyle, Charles A. Deliver a Better Speech with Confidence. LC 81-82439. (Illus.). 182p. 1981. pap. 4.95 (ISBN 0-89709-026-8). Liberty Pub.

--Speak Out with Clout. LC 77-17265. 196p. 1977. 6.95 (ISBN 0-89709-020-9). Liberty Pub.

Boyle, Constance. Little Owl & the Tree House. (Illus.). 32p. 1985. 3.95 (ISBN 0-8120-5677-9). Barron.

--Little Owl & the Weed. 32p. 1985. 3.95 (ISBN 0-8120-5639-6). Barron.

--Little Owl's Favorite Uncle. (Illus.). 32p. 1985. 3.95 (ISBN 0-8120-5675-2). Barron.

--The Story of Little Owl. 32p. 1985. 3.95 (ISBN 0-8120-5638-8). Barron.

Boyle, Coraghessan T. Greasy Lake & Other Stories. (Fiction Ser.). 276p. 1985. 16.95 (ISBN 0-670-80542-4). Viking.

Boyle, Danny, et al. The Filmmakers-Filmlovers Survival Trivia Cookbook. Edgars, Susan, ed. (Illus.). 124p. 1984. pap. 4.95 (ISBN 0-930959-00-0). B Movie.

Boyle, Darl M. Where Lilith Dances. LC 70-144713. (Yale Ser. of Younger Poets: No. 6). Repr. of 1920 ed. 18.00 (ISBN 0-404-53806-1). AMS Pr.

Boyle, David H. How to Succeed in Big Time Trucking. (Illus.). 1977. pap. 7.95 (ISBN 0-685-88578-X). Apple Hut.

--How to Succeed in Big Time Trucking. LC 77-70986. (Orig.). 1977. pap. 6.95 (ISBN 0-913668-97-4). Ten Speed Pr.

Boyle, Deirdre, ed. Expanding Media. LC 77-23335. (A Neal-Schuman Professional Bk). 368p. 1977. lib. bdg. 35.00 (ISBN 0-912700-03-3). Oryx Pr.

Boyle, Denis & Braddick, Bill. The Challenge of Change: Developing Business Leaders for the 1980s. 64p. 1981. pap. text ed. 10.00x (ISBN 0-566-02283-4). Gower Pub Co.

Boyle, Desmond. Energy. LC 82-50390. (Visual Science Ser.). 48p. (gr. 6 up). 1982. PLB 13.72 (ISBN 0-382-06658-8). Silver.

Boyle, Donzella C. Quest of a Hemisphere. LC 71-113036. (Illus.). (gr. 7 up). 1970. PLB 18.00 (ISBN 0-88279-218-0). Western Islands.

Boyle, Edward. Biographical Essays, 1790-1890. facs. ed. LC 68-54331. (Essay Index Reprint Ser). 1936. 18.00 (ISBN 0-8369-0237-8). Ayer Co Pubs.

Boyle, Edward, jt. ed. see Wong, C. S.

Boyle, Elisabeth L. & Delbridge, Pauline N. Spoken Cantonese, Bk I. 410p. 1980. pap. 15.00x (ISBN 0-87950-675-X); cassettes I 15 dual track 100.00x (ISBN 0-87950-677-6); book I & cassettes I 105.00x (ISBN 0-87950-679-2). Spoken Lang Serv.

--Spoken Cantonese, Bk. II. 410p. 1980. pap. 15.00x (ISBN 0-87950-676-8); cassettes II 15 dual track 100.00x (ISBN 0-87950-678-4); bk. II & cassettes II 105.00x; bks. I & II & cassettes I & II 200.00x (ISBN 0-87950-681-4). Spoken Lang Serv.

Boyle, Elizabeth L., et al. FSI Cantonese Basic Course: Units 16-30. 1970. pap. text ed. 9.50x (ISBN 0-686-10706-3); 15 cassettes 90.00x (ISBN 0-686-10707-1). Intl Learn Syst.

Boyle, Francis A. World Politics & International Law. (Policy Studies). 416p. 1985. 32.50 (ISBN 0-8223-0609-3); pap. 14.75 (ISBN 0-8223-0655-7). Duke.

Boyle, Gayle M. & Kauffman, Barbara K. Family Councils in Nursing Homes: A Guide to Development. 63p. (Orig.). 1982. pap. 5.75 (ISBN 0-938846-14-0). Ebenezer Ctr.

Boyle, Godfrey. Living on the Sun: Harnessing Renewable Energy for an Equitable Society. (Ideas in Progress Ser.). (Illus.). 128p. 1978. (Dist by Scribner); pap. 6.95 (ISBN 0-7145-0862-4). M Boyars.

Boyle, Hugh, ed. see Lloyd, Llewelyn.

Boyle, J. A. The Mongol World Empire, 1206-1370. 316p. 1980. 79.00x (ISBN 0-86078-002-3, Pub. by Variorum England). State Mutual Bk.

Boyle, J. David, jt. auth. see Radocy, Rudolf E.

Boyle, J. W., ed. Leaders & Workers. (Thomas Davis Lecture Ser.). 95p. 1978. pap. 4.50 (ISBN 0-85342-334-2, Pub. by Mercier Pr Ireland). Irish Bk Ctr.

Boyle, Jack. Boston Blackie. 1979. lib. bdg. 10.50 (ISBN 0-8398-2536-6, Gregg). G K Hall.

Boyle, James T. & Spence, John. Stress Analysis for Creep. 307p. 1983. 59.95 (ISBN 0-408-01172-6). Butterworth.

Boyle, Joe, intro. by. The Federal Way with Words. 1982. 15.00 (ISBN 0-9609194-0-6). Twain Pub.

Boyle, John A. Persian-English Dictionary, Romanized. (Persian & Eng.). 24.50 (ISBN 0-87557-057-7, 057-7). Saphrograph.

Boyle, John A., tr. from Pers. The Successors of Glengis. LC 70-135987. (Illus.). 372p. 1971. 30.00x (ISBN 0-231-03351-6). Columbia U Pr.

Boyle, John H. China & Japan at War, 1939-1945: The Politics of Collaboration. LC 76-183886. (Illus.). 456p. 1972. 30.00x (ISBN 0-8047-0800-2). Stanford U Pr.

Boyle, Joseph M., Jr., jt. auth. see Grisez, Germain.

Boyle, Joseph M., Jr., et al. Free Choice: A Self-Referential Argument. LC 76-645. 232p. 1976. text ed. 15.95x (ISBN 0-268-00940-6). U of Notre Dame Pr.

Boyle, Judith, jt. auth. see Saia, Mary J.

Boyle, Karl, jt. auth. see Smith, Patrick.

Boyle, Kay. Fifty Stories. 648p. 1981. pap. 7.95 (ISBN 0-14-005922-9). Penguin.

--Monday Night. 1977. Repr. of 1938 ed. 10.00x (ISBN 0-911858-35-0). Appel.

--Three Short Novels. 1982. pap. 5.95 (ISBN 0-14-006109-6). Penguin.

--Three Short Novels. Incl. The Crazy Hunter; The Bridgegroom's Body; Decison. 1958. pap. 3.00 (ISBN 0-685-29982-5). Small Pr Dist.

--Wedding Day: And Other Stories, Vol. 1. LC 72-4420. (Short Story Index Reprint Ser). Repr. of 1929 ed. 15.00 (ISBN 0-8369-4171-3). Ayer Co Pubs.

--Words That Must Somehow Be Said: The Selected Essays of Kay Boyle, 1927-1983. LC 84-62301. 288p. 1985. 16.50 (ISBN 0-86547-187-8). N Point Pr.

Boyle, Kay & McAlmon, Robert. Being Geniuses Together: Nineteen Twenty to Nineteen Thirty. (Illus.). 416p. (Orig.). 1984. pap. 13.50 (ISBN 0-86547-149-5). N Point Pr.

Boyle, Kay, tr. see Crevel, Rene.

Boyle, Kevin, et al. Law & State: The Case of Northern Ireland. LC 75-10914. 206p. 1975. lib. bdg. 15.00x (ISBN 0-87023-197-9). U of Mass Pr.

--Ten Years on in Northern Ireland. 1980. 15.00x (ISBN 0-900137-16-9, Pub. by NCCL England). State Mutual Bk.

Boyle, L & Sykes, T. Gore-Brown on Companies. 45rd ed. text ed. 390.00x (ISBN 0-85308-043-7, Pub. by Jordan & Sons); 2nd supplement 125.00 (ISBN 0-686-86767-X). State Mutual Bk.

Boyle, Leonard E. Pastoral Care, Clerical Education & Canon Law, 1200-1400. 362p. 1981. 60.00x (ISBN 0-86078-081-3, Pub. by Variorum). State Mutual Bk.

Boyle, Marjorie O. Christening Pagan Mysteries: Erasmus in Pursuit of Wisdom. (Erasmus Studies). 168p. 1981. 22.50x (ISBN 0-8020-5525-7). U of Toronto Pr.

--Erasmus on Language & Method in Theology. LC 77-2606. (Erasmus Studies: No. 2). pap. 70.30 (ISBN 0-317-26938-0, 2023596). Bks Demand UMI.

--Rhetoric & Reform: Erasmus' Civil Dispute with Luther. (Harvard Historical Monographs: No. 71). 240p. 1983. text ed. 24.00x (ISBN 0-674-76870-1). Harvard U Pr.

Boyle, Mary E., tr. see Breuil, Henri.

Boyle, Michael J., ed. Boyle's Connecticut Almanac & Guide: 1983. (Illus.). 96p. (Orig.). 1982. pap. 2.95 (ISBN 0-911097-00-7). M Boyle Pub.

Boyle, P. R. Molluscs & Man. (Studies in Biology: No. 134). 64p. 1981. pap. text ed. 8.95 (ISBN 0-7131-2824-0). E Arnold.

Boyle, Patrick. The Port Wine Stain: Partick Boyle's Best Short Stroies. Fallon, Peter, ed. (Classic Irish Fiction Ser.). 236p. 1983. 13.75. Devin.

Boyle, Patrick J. Trigonometry with Applications. 372p. 1983. text ed. 23.50 scp (ISBN 0-06-040898-7, HarpC); instr's. manual avail. (ISBN 0-06-360869-3). Har-Row.

Boyle, Patrick J., jt. auth. see Smith, Karl J.

Boyle, Peter, ed. Cephalopod Life Cycles, Vol. 1. 1984.. 120.00 (ISBN 0-12-123001-5). Acad Pr.

Boyle, Peter G. & Snell, J. Laurie. Random Walks & Electric Networks. 173p. 1984. 24.00 (ISBN 0-88385-024-9, CAM-22); 18.50 (ISBN 0-317-37233-5). Math Assn.

Boyle, R. Alexander, jt. auth. see Boyle, Robert H.

Boyle, R. W. Geochemical Prospecting for Thorium & Uranium. (Developments in Economic Geology Ser.: Vol. 16). 498p. 1983. 85.00 (ISBN 0-444-42070-3). Elsevier.

Boyle, Richard. Flower of the Dragon: The Breakdown of the U. S. Army in Vietnam. LC 72-75812. (Illus.). 282p. 1972. 7.95 (ISBN 0-87867-020-3); pap. 4.95 (ISBN 0-87867-036-X). Ramparts.

Boyle, Richard J. American Impressionism. (Illus.). 240p. 1974. 45.00 (ISBN 0-8212-0597-8, 036730); pap. 19.45 (ISBN 0-8212-1500-0, 036684). NYGS.

--John Twachtman. (Illus.). 88p. (Orig.). 1982. pap. 12.95 (ISBN 0-8230-2568-3). Watson-Guptill.

Boyle, Robert. Experiments & Considerations Touching Colours. (Illus.). Repr. of 1664 ed. 25.00 (ISBN 0-384-05350-5). Johnson Repr.

--James Joyce's Pauline Vision: A Catholic Exposition. LC 78-18901. 133p. 1978. 10.95x (ISBN 0-8093-0861-4). S Ill U Pr.

--Origine & Virtues of Gems. LC 78-181434. (Contributions to the History of Geology Ser: Vol. 7). 1972. Repr. of 1672 ed. 22.95x (ISBN 0-02-841710-0). Hafner.

--Robert Boyle on Natural Philosophy: An Essay with Selections from His Writings by Marie Boas Hall. LC 80-12187. (Illus.). ix, 406p. 1980. Repr. of 1965 ed. lib. bdg. 42.50x (ISBN 0-313-22394-7, BOON). Greenwood.

--Selected Philosophical Papers of Robert Boyle. Stewart, M. A., ed. LC 79-53051. (Philosophical Classics Ser.). 256p. 1979. text ed. 28.50x (ISBN 0-06-490625-6). B&N Imports.

Boyle, Robert H. The Hudson River: A Natural & Unnatural History. LC 68-10877. (Illus.). 1969 o.p. 7.95 (ISBN 0-393-05379-2, N844, Norton Lib); pap. 6.95 1979 (ISBN 0-393-00844-4). Norton.

Boyle, Robert H. & Boyle, R. Alexander. Acid Rain. LC 82-21410. 128p. (Orig.). 1983. 14.95 (ISBN 0-8052-3854-9); pap. 8.95 (ISBN 0-8052-0746-5). Schocken.

Boyle, Robert H. & Ciampi, Elgin. Bass. (Illus.). 144p. 1980. 27.50 (ISBN 0-393-01379-0). Norton.

Boyle, Robert H., jt. auth. see Environmental Defense Fund.

Boyle, Robert H., jt. auth. see Leiser, Eric.

Boyle, Robert H. & Whitlock, Dave, eds. Fly Tyers Almanac. LC 83-3522. (Illus.). 220p. 1983. pap. 14.95 (ISBN 0-8329-0332-9, Pub. by Winchester Pr). New Century.

Boyle, Rosalie. Silver Swimmer: Poems. LC 74-33990. 1975. pap. 5.00 (ISBN 0-914562-01-0). Merriam-Eddy.

Boyle, Russell, jt. auth. see Kilpatrick, S. J., Jr.

Boyle, Sallie. Beginning Reading (Basic Sight Words & Picture Stories) (Let's Learn Ser.). (Illus.). 32p. (ps-1). 1984. pap. 1.79 (ISBN 0-88724-092-5, CD-7031). Carson-Dellos.

Boyle, Sallie, et al. Blends, Digraphs & Counting by Twos, Fives, Tens. (Stick-Out-Your-Neck Ser.). (Illus.). 32p. (ps-3). 1984. pap. 1.98 (ISBN 0-88724-162-X, CD-0920). Carson-Dellos.

Boyle, Sarah P. The Desegregated Heart. Baxter, Annette K., ed. LC 79-8777. (Signal Lives Ser.). 1980. Repr. of 1962 ed. lib. bdg. 38.00x (ISBN 0-405-12826-6). Ayer Co Pubs.

Boyle, Sarah-Patton. The Desert Blooms: A Personal Adventure in Growing Old Creatively. 208p. (Orig.). 1983. pap. 6.95 (ISBN 0-687-10484-X). Abingdon.

Boyle, Sean O. The Irish Song Tradition. 2nd ed. (Illus.). 1976. 10.95 (ISBN 0-9505173-0-5). Irish Bk Ctr.

Boyle, T. Coraghessan. Budding Prospects. (Contemporary American Fiction Ser.). 336p. 1985. pap. 6.95 (ISBN 0-14-008151-8). Penguin.

--Budding Prospects: A Pastoral. 320p. 1984. 16.95 (ISBN 0-670-19439-5). Viking.

--Descent of Man & Other Stories. 228p. 1980. pap. 4.95 (ISBN 0-07-006956-5). McGraw.

--Water Music. (Contemporary American Fiction Ser.). 496p. 1983. pap. 6.95 (ISBN 0-14-006550-4). Penguin.

Boyle, Ted E. Brendan Behan. (English Authors Ser.: No. 91). lib. bdg. 13.50 (ISBN 0-8057-1036-1, Twayne). G K Hall.

Boyle, Terence P., ed. Validation & Predictability of Laboratory Methods for Assessing the Fate & Effects of Contaminants in Aquatic Ecosystems - STP 865. LC 85-5985. (Illus.). 242p. 1985. text ed. 34.00 (ISBN 0-8031-0433-2, 04-865000-16). ASTM.

Boyle, Thomas. The Cold Stove League. 221p. 1983. 11.95 (ISBN 0-89733-080-3). Academy Chi Pubs.

--Only the Dead Know Brooklyn. LC 84-48753. 288p. 1985. 15.95 (ISBN 0-87923-565-9). Godine.

Boyle, Thomas A. FORTRAN 77 PDQ. LC 85-4183. (Computer Science Ser.). 145p. 1985. pap. text ed. 11.00 pub net (ISBN 0-534-04938-9). Brooks-Cole.

Boyle, Timm, jt. auth. see Masterson, Dave.

Boyle, Virginia A. ZAS! (Musical Children's Theatre Playscript Ser.). 1979. pap. 2.50x (ISBN 0-88020-005-7). Coach Hse.

Boyle, Virginia F. Brokenburne: A Southern Auntie's War Tale. facsimile ed. LC 77-38642. (Black Heritage Library Collection). (Illus.). Repr. of 1897 ed. 14.75 (ISBN 0-8369-9000-5). Ayer Co Pubs.

--Devil Tales. facsimile ed. LC 70-38643. (Black Heritage Library Collection). Repr. of 1900 ed. 21.50 (ISBN 0-8369-9001-3). Ayer Co Pubs.

Boyle, William C. Designing Production Safety Systems. 264p. 1979. 39.95 (ISBN 0-87814-096-4). Pennwell Bks.

Boylen, R. D. see Hedge, F. H. & Noa, L.

Boyles, Allan. Acoustic Waveguides: Applications to Oceanic Science. LC 83-17000. 321p. 1984. 46.95x (ISBN 0-471-88771-4, Pub. by Wiley Interscience). Wiley.

Boyles, David T. Bio-Energy: Technology, Thermodynamics & Costs. LC 84-4647. (Energy & Fuel Science Ser.: 1-624). 225p. 1984. text ed. 49.95 (ISBN 0-470-20085-5). Halsted Pr.

Boyles, Denis. Maxine's Flattery. (Illus.). 1977. 6.50 (ISBN 0-931848-05-9). Dryad Pr.

Boyles, Marcia V., et al. The Health Professions. LC 77-11331. (Illus.). 465p. 1982. pap. 17.95 (ISBN 0-7216-1904-5). Saunders.

Boyles, Margaret. American Indian Needlepoint Workbook. (Illus.). 96p. 1976. pap. 4.95 (ISBN 0-02-011160-6, Collier). Macmillan.

--The Margaret Boyles Book of Needle Art. LC 77-73064. (Illus.). 1978. pap. 9.95 (ISBN 0-15-657964-2, Harv). HarBraceJ.

--Margaret Boyles' Designs for Babies. 1983. 17.95 (ISBN 0-671-43902-2). S&S.

--Margaret Boyles' Designs for Babies. 144p. 1984. pap. 8.95 (ISBN 0-671-53028-3, Fireside). S&S.

Boyles, Richard. Severing the Cause; or, Wandering Mindless Through Reindeer Passes. 56p. 1975. 5.50 (ISBN 0-87881-022-6). Mojave Bks.

Boyles, William & Nuwer, Hank. The Bounty Hunter, Bk. 1: Deadliest Profession. LC 80-83561. (Bounty Hunter Ser.). 224p. (Orig.). 1981. pap. 2.50 (ISBN 0-87216-804-2). Jove Pubns.

--The Bounty Hunter, Bk. 2: A Killing Trade. LC 81-81398. (Bounty Hunter Ser.). 224p. (Orig.). 1981. pap. 2.50 (ISBN 0-87216-902-2). Jove Pubns.

--The Bounty Hunter, Bk. 3: The Wild Ride. LC 81-82965. (Bounty Hunter Ser.). 224p. (Orig.). 1982. pap. 2.50 (ISBN 0-87216-996-0). Jove Pubns.

--The Bounty Hunter, Bk. 4: Blood Mountain. LC 82-80020. (Bounty Hunter Ser.). 224p. (Orig.). 1982. pap. 2.50 (ISBN 0-86721-127-X). Jove Pubns.

Boylestad, Robert & Nashelsky, Louis. Electricity, Electronics, & Electromagnetics: Principles & Applications. 2nd ed. (Illus.). 544p. 1983. 31.95 (ISBN 0-13-248146-4). P-H.

--Electronic Devices & Circuit Theory. 3rd ed. (Illus.). 768p. 1982. 34.95 (ISBN 0-13-250324-7). P-H.

Boylestad, Robert, jt. auth. see Nashelsky, Louis.

Boylestad, Robert L. Introductory Circuit Analysis. 4th ed. 800p. 1982. text ed. 29.95 (ISBN 0-675-09938-2); student guide 11.95 (ISBN 0-675-09856-4); experiments 16.95x (ISBN 0-675-09858-0). Additional supplements may be obtained from publisher. Merrill.

Boylestad, Robert L., jt. auth. see Nashelsky, Louis.

Boylston, Helen D. Clara Barton, Founder of American Red Cross. (Landmark Ser.: No. 58). (Illus.). (gr. 4-6). 1955. PLB 6.99 (ISBN 0-394-90358-7, BYR). Random.

--Sue Barton, Rural Nurse. 1984. pap. 2.25 (ISBN 0-451-13193-2, Sig). NAL.

--Sue Barton, Senior Nurse. 1984. pap. 2.25 (ISBN 0-451-13130-4, Sig). NAL.

--Sue Barton, Student Nurse. 1984. pap. 2.25 (ISBN 0-451-13103-7, Sig). NAL.

--Sue Barton, Visiting Nurse. 1984. pap. 2.25 (ISBN 0-451-13159-2, Sig). NAL.

Boylston, Helen D., jt. auth. see Lane, Rose W.

Boylston, Samuel L. From Horses to Horse Power with S. C. Trucking. Dickey, Gary, ed. LC 81-86366. (Illus.). 366p. (Orig.). pap. write for info. MTASC.

Boyne, Colin & Wright, Lance. The Best of Architect's Working Details, Vol. 1: External. 240p. 1982. 36.50 (ISBN 0-89397-142-1). Nichols Pub.

--Best of Architect's Working Details, Vol. 2: Internal. 200p. 1982. 36.50 (ISBN 0-89397-143-X). Nichols Pub.

Boyne, Gil, ed. Hypnosis: New Tool in Nursing Practice. 197p. 1982. 20.00 (ISBN 0-930298-12-8). Westwood Pub Co.

Boyne, Walter. Boeing B-52: A Documentary History. (Illus.). 158p. 1982. 22.50 (ISBN 0-87474-246-3, Pub. by Janes England). Smithsonian.

--Boeing B-52: A Documentary History. (Illus.). 160p. 1982. 19.95 (ISBN 0-86720-550-4). Jane's Pub Inc.

Boyne, Walter J. The Aircraft Treasures of Silver Hill. 22.95 (ISBN 0-89256-216-1). Rawson Assocs.

--De Havilland DH-4: From Flaming Coffin to Living Legend. LC 84-1391. (Famous Aircraft of the National Air & Space Museum Ser.). (Illus.). 160p. 1984. pap. 8.95 (ISBN 0-87474-277-3, BODHP). Smithsonian.

--The Messerschmitt ME 262: Arrow to the Future. LC 80-607090. (Illus.). 192p. (Orig.). 1980. 19.95 (ISBN 0-87474-276-5); pap. 10.95 (ISBN 0-87474-275-7). Smithsonian.

--Phantom in Combat. LC 84-52013. (Illus.). 176p. 1985. text ed. 22.50 (ISBN 0-87474-280-3, BOPC). Smithsonian.

Boyne, Walter J. & Lopez, Donald S., eds. The Jet Age: Forty Years of Jet Aviation. LC 79-20216. (Illus.). 190p. 1979. 19.95 (ISBN 0-87474-248-X); pap. 10.95 (ISBN 0-87474-247-1). Smithsonian.

--Vertical Flight: The Age of the Helicopter. (Illus., Orig.). 1984. pap. 15.00 (ISBN 0-87474-279-X). Smithsonian.

Boyne, William. Trade Tokens Issued in the Seventeenth Century in England, Wales, Ireland, by Corporations, Merchants, Etc, 2 vols. Williamson, George C., ed. LC 77-80246. 1970. Repr. of 1889 ed. Set. 57.50 (ISBN 0-8337-0348-X). B Franklin.

Boynes, Cyril H. Freedom Through the Balisier. LC 83-40235. 148p. (Orig.). 1984. pap. 4.75 (ISBN 0-8356-0584-1, Quest). Theos Pub Hse.

Boynes, Wynta. East Africa: Development Assistance Abroad in 1984: A TAICH Regional Directory of U.S. Non-profit Organizations in Overseas Development Assistance. 186p. (Orig.). 1984. pap. 14.50 (ISBN 0-932140-05-X, TAICH106, TAICH). Unipub.

Boynes, Wynta & Lowenstein, Florence M., eds. TAICH Directory 1983: U.S. Nonprofit Organizations in Development Assistance Abroad. 8th. ed. 584p. 1983. pap. 24.50 (ISBN 0-932140-02-5, TAICH100, TAICH). Unipub.

Boynthon, Elizabeth. King Cole: A Picture of Sir Henry Cole KCB. (Illus.). 76p. (Orig.). 1984. pap. 9.95 (ISBN 0-905209-19-2, Pub. by Victoria & Albert Mus UK). Faber & Faber.

Boynton, A., jt. auth. see Higginson, T. W.

Boynton, Alton L. & Leffert, Hyam L., eds. Control of Animal Cell Proliferation, Vol. 1. Edited Treatise ed. Date not set. price not set (ISBN 0-12-123061-9). Acad Pr.

Boynton, Alton L. & McKeehan, Wallace L., eds. Ions, Cell Proliferation & Cancer. LC 82-20786. 1982. 50.00 (ISBN 0-12-123050-3). Acad Pr.

Boynton, Bea. That Hilarious First Year. LC 75-109541. (Illus.). 1971. pap. 2.50 (ISBN 0-87004-203-3). Caxton.

--A Very Amateur Guide to Antique Bottle Collecting. LC 65-22367. (Illus.). 1967. pap. 1.50 (ISBN 0-87004-017-0). Caxton.

Boynton, Charles E., IV & Campbell, Alan D., eds. Bibliography of Extractive Industries Accounting 1960-1982. LC 84-80466. 147p. 1984. pap. 9.50 (ISBN 0-940966-05-0). N Texas St U Pro Devel Inst.

Boynton, Damon, jt. ed. see Whyte, William F.

Boynton, Edward C. History of West Point. facs. ed. LC 71-126233. (Select Bibliographies Reprint Ser.). 1863. 32.00 (ISBN 0-8369-5458-0). Ayer Co Pubs.

Boynton, Edward C., ed. see United States Army, Continental Army.

Boynton, G. R. & Kim, Chong Lim. Legislative Systems in Developing Countries. LC 75-13342. 288p. 1975. 18.75 (ISBN 0-8223-0344-2). Duke.

Boynton, Henry, jt. auth. see Smith.

Boynton, Henry W. Bret Harte. LC 70-133513. (Select Bibliographies Reprint Ser.). 1972. Repr. of 1903 ed. 10.00 (ISBN 0-8369-5545-5). Ayer Co Pubs.

--World's Leading Poets. facs. ed. LC 68-8439. (Essay Index Reprint Ser). 1912. 18.00 (ISBN 0-8369-0238-6). Ayer Co Pubs.

Boynton, John. Aims & Means. LC 64-8214. (Background Ser). (Illus.). 1964. 7.95 (ISBN 0-8023-1015-X). Dufour.

--Love Is Lasting. 96p. (Orig.). 1971. pap. 3.50 (ISBN 0-917814-01-0). Astroart Ent.

--Love Is Radiant. (Illus.). 64p. 1972. pap. 2.60 (ISBN 0-917814-02-9). Astroart Ent.

--Love Is Touching. (Illus.). 48p. 1972. pap. 2.95 (ISBN 0-917814-03-7). Astroart Ent.

Boynton, John F., ed. see Barzun, Jacques & Graff, Henry F.

Boynton, Judy. Guardian of Innocence. (Orig.). 1980. pap. 1.25 (ISBN 0-440-11862-X). Dell.

Boynton, Percy H. American Literature: A Textbook for Secondary Schools. 1923. Repr. 30.00 (ISBN 0-8274-1848-5). R West.

--American Literature: Textbook for Secondary Schools. 1977. Repr. of 1923 ed. lib. bdg. 20.00 (ISBN 0-8495-0323-X). Arden Lib.

--History of American Literature. LC 77-120559. Repr. of 1919 ed. 18.00 (ISBN 0-404-00967-0). AMS Pr.

--A History of American Literature. 1919. Repr. 17.50 (ISBN 0-8274-3844-3). R West.

--Literature & American Life: For Students of American Literature. 1936. Repr. 39.00 (ISBN 0-8274-2950-9). R West.

--London in English Literature. 346p. 1980. Repr. of 1913 ed. lib. bdg. 30.00 (ISBN 0-8414-9906-3). Folcroft.

--London in English Literature. 1913. Repr. 35.00 (ISBN 0-8274-2979-7). R West.

--Milestones in American Literature. 1923. Repr. 20.00 (ISBN 0-8274-2734-4). R West.

--More Contemporary Americans. facs. ed. LC 67-26718. (Essay Index Reprint Ser). 1927. 18.00 (ISBN 0-8369-0239-4). Ayer Co Pubs.

--More Contemporary Americans. LC 75-131642. 1970. Repr. of 1927 ed. 16.00x (ISBN 0-403-00529-9). Scholarly.

--Principles of Composition. Repr. of 1915 ed. 25.00 (ISBN 0-686-19877-8). Ridgeway Bks.

--Rediscovery of the Frontier. LC 75-118636. 184p. 1970. Repr. of 1931 ed. lib. bdg. 20.00 (ISBN 0-8154-0327-5). Cooper Sq.

--Rediscovery of the Frontier. LC 31-28011. (Illus.). 1969. Repr. of 1931 ed. lib. bdg. 18.75x (ISBN 0-8371-0480-7, BORE). Greenwood.

--Some Contemporary Americans. LC 66-23516. 1924. 10.00x (ISBN 0-8196-0181-0). Biblo.

Boynton, Richard W., tr. see Loisy, Alfred F.

Boynton, Robert. Human Color Vision. new ed. LC 78-26443. 1979. text ed. 38.95 (ISBN 0-03-084682-X, HoltC). HR&W.

Boynton, Robert E., ed. see Shakespeare, William.

Boynton, Robert S. Chemistry & Technology of Lime & Limestone. 2nd ed. LC 79-16140. 578p. 1980. 90.00 (ISBN 0-471-02771-5, Pub. by Wiley-Interscience). Wiley.

Boynton, Robert W. & Mack, Maynard. Introduction to the Play: In the Theater of the Mind. rev., 2nd ed. 1976. pap. text ed. 9.25x (ISBN 0-8104-5731-8); tchr's guide 1.75 (ISBN 0-686-77110-9, 6048). Boynton Cook Pubs.

--Introduction to the Poem. 3rd ed. 240p. 1985. pap. text ed. 9.25x (ISBN 0-86709-143-6). Boynton Cook Pubs.

--Introduction to the Short Story. rev. 3rd ed. 288p. (gr. 10-12). 1985. pap. text ed. 9.25x (ISBN 0-86709-143-6); tchr's. guide 1.75. Boynton Cook Pubs.

Boynton, Robert W., ed. see Shakespeare, William.

Boynton, Rose W., et al. Manual of Ambulatory Pediatrics. (Little, Brown Spiral Manual Ser.). 405p. 1983. spiral bdg. 16.95 (ISBN 0-316-10490-6). Little.

Boynton, Sandra. A Is for Angry: An Animal & Adjective Alphabet. LC 83-40038. (Illus.). 48p. 1983. 9.95 (ISBN 0-89480-453-7). Workman Pub.

--But Not the Hippopotamus. Klimo, Kate, ed. (Sandra Boynton Board Bks.). (Illus.). 14p. (ps-k). 1982. bds. 3.50 (ISBN 0-671-44904-4, Little Simon). S&S.

--Chloe & Maude. (ps-3). 1985. 12.95 (ISBN 0-316-10492-2); pap. 4.95 (ISBN 0-316-10493-0). Little.

--Chocolate: The Consuming Passion. LC 81-43781. (Illus.). 112p. 1982. 8.95 (ISBN 0-89480-197-X, 338); pap. 5.95 (ISBN 0-89480-199-6, 485). Workman Pub.

--The Going to Bed Book. Klimo, Kate, ed. (Sandra Boynton Board Bks.). (Illus.). 14p. (ps-k). 1982. bds. 3.50 (ISBN 0-671-44902-8, Little Simon). S&S.

--Good Night, Good Night. (Illus.). 40p. (ps-1). 1985. PLB 7.99 (ISBN 0-394-97285-6, BYR); pap. 6.95 (ISBN 0-394-87285-1). Random.

--Hester in the Wild. LC 78-67026. (Illus.). 32p. (ps-3). 1979. 10.53i (ISBN 0-06-020631-4); PLB 11.89 (ISBN 0-06-020654-3). HarpJ.

--Hey! What's That. LC 84-61557. (Illus.). 14p. (ps). 1985. pap. 4.95 (ISBN 0-394-87208-8, BYR). Random.

--Hippos Go Berserk. LC 79-16134. (Illus.). 32p. (gr. 1-3). 1979. 7.95 (ISBN 0-316-10488-4); pap. 3.95 (ISBN 0-316-10489-2). Little.

--If at First... (Illus.). 32p. (ps-1). 1980. 8.95 (ISBN 0-316-10487-6); pap. 3.95 (ISBN 0-316-10486-8). Little.

--Moo Baa La La La. Klimo, Kate, ed. (Boynton Board Bks.). (Illus.). 14p. 1982. 3.50 (ISBN 0-671-44901-X, Little Simon). S&S.

--Opposites. Klimo, Kate, ed. (Sandra Boynton Board Bks.). (Illus.). (ps-k). 1982. bds. 3.50 (ISBN 0-671-44903-6, Little Simon). S&S.

Boys, C. V. Soap-Bubbles: Their Colours & the Forces Which Mold Them. LC 59-14223. 1959. lib. bdg. 11.50x (ISBN 0-88307-632-2). Gannon.

Boys, Charles V. Soap Bubbles. 3rd ed. (Illus.). 1959. pap. 3.50 (ISBN 0-486-20542-8). Dover.

Boys Club of America, et al. Alternatives to Delinquency: Thrity-Six Tested Youth Develpoment Programs. (Illus.). 5.00 (ISBN 0-318-00480-1). Boys Clubs.

Boys' Clubs of America, et al. Alcohol Abuse Prevention: A Comprehensive Guide for Youth Organization. (Illus., Orig.). pap. 10.00 (ISBN 0-9604288-0-1). Boys Clubs.

Boys, Don. Liberalism: A Rope of Sand. 1979. 4.95 (ISBN 0-686-25591-7). Freedom Univ-FSP.

--Pilgrims, Puritans & Patriots: Our Christian Heritage. 1983. pap. 9.00x (ISBN 0-686-40717-2). Freedom Univ-FSP.

--A Time to Laugh. 1980. pap. 7.50x (ISBN 0-686-40716-4). Freedom Univ-FSP.

--Your Health: How to Feel Better, Look Younger, Live Longer. 1980. pap. 7.50x (ISBN 0-686-40718-0). Freedom Univ-FSP.

Boys, J. V., jt. auth. see Prendergast, E. D.

Boys, Mary C., ed. Ministry & Education in Conversation. LC 80-53204. 160p. (Orig.). 1981. pap. 6.95 (ISBN 0-88489-126-7). St Mary's.

Boys, Michael. The Book of Nude Photography. LC 81-47485. 1981. 16.50 (ISBN 0-394-52108-0). Knopf.

--The Book of Nude Photography. 168p. 1982. 39.00x (ISBN 0-85223-208-X, Pub. by Ebury Pr England). State Mutual Bk.

Boyse, John W., jt. ed. see Pickett, Mary S.

Boyson, Rhodes. The Crisis in Education. 160p. 1975. pap. 18.50x (ISBN 0-7130-0142-9, Pub. by Woburn Pr). Biblio Dist.

Boysson-Bardies, Benedicte De. Negation et Performance Linguistique. (Connaissance et Langage Ser.: No. 4). (Fr.). 1977. pap. text ed. 9.60x (ISBN 90-2796-442-4). Mouton.

Boyt & Copperfield. Alternative Sources of Energy, Wind, Hydro, No. 55. 56p. (Orig.). 1982. pap. 3.50 (ISBN 0-917328-45-0). ASEI.

Boyt, David, jt. ed. see Talbot, Mike.

Boyte, Harry C. The Backyard Revolution: Understanding the New Citizen Movement. 271p. 1981. pap. 9.95 (ISBN 0-87722-229-0). Temple U Pr.

--The Backyard Revolution: Understanding the New Citizen Movement. 288p. 1980. 29.95 (ISBN 0-87722-192-8). Temple U Pr.

--The Backyard Revolution: Understanding the New Citizen Movement. 271p. 1980. pap. 10.50 (ISBN 0-318-17177-5, C63). Natl Ctr Cit Involv.

--Community Is Possible: Repairing America's Roots. LC 84-47558. 224p. 1984. 14.42i (ISBN 0-06-015335-0, HarpT). Har-Row.

--Community Is Possible: Repairing America's Roots. LC 84-47558. 224p. 1984. pap. 6.68i (ISBN 0-06-091157-3, CN). Har-Row.

Boyte, Harry C., ed. Voices of the American Revolution. 2nd ed. 224p. Date not set. pap. 6.95 (ISBN 0-8298-0478-1). Pilgrim NY.

Boytinck, P. Anthony Burgess, Bibliography. 1985. 54.50 (ISBN 0-317-19957-9). Porter.

Boytinck, Paul. Anthony Burgess: A Reference Guide. LC 82-49268. (Reference Library of the Humanities). 600p. 1984. lib. bdg. 62.00 (ISBN 0-8240-9135-3). Garland Pub.

--C. P. Snow: A Reference Guide. 1980. lib. bdg. 28.50 (ISBN 0-8161-8357-0, Hall Reference). G K Hall.

Boytnick, Paul. Anthony Burgess: A Bibliography. 1978. Repr. of 1977 ed. lib. bdg. 22.50 (ISBN 0-8492-3549-9). R West.

Boyum, et al. California Government in National Perspective. 1984. pap. text ed. 8.95 (ISBN 0-8403-3409-5). Kendall-Hunt.

Boyum, Burton H. Saga of Iron Mining in Michigan's Upper Peninsula. 1977. pap. 5.95 (ISBN 0-938746-03-0). Marquette Cnty.

Boyum, Burton H., ed. The Mather Mine, Negaunee & Ishpeming Michigan. LC 79-89638. 87p. 1979. 18.95 (ISBN 0-938746-04-9). Marquette Cnty.

Boyum, Joy G. Double Exposure: Fiction into Film. (Illus.). 335p. 1985. 19.95 (ISBN 0-87663-486-2). Universe.

Bozan, Jian, et al. A Concise History of China. 264p. (Orig.). 1981. pap. 5.95 (ISBN 0-8351-0942-9). China Bks.

Bozanic, Nick. Wood, Birds, Water, Stone. 8p. (Orig.). 1983. pap. 2.95 (ISBN 0-935306-20-X). Barnwood Pr.

Bozanich, Tony L. Captain Flounder, His Sole Brothers & Friends. Isaksen, Lisa A., ed. (Illus.). 16p. (ps-4). 1984. pap. 4.95 (ISBN 0-930655-00-1). Antarctic Pr.

Bozarth, George S., ed. see Brahms, Johannes.

Bozarth, J. & Rubin, S. Facilitative Management in Rehabilitation Counseling. 1972. pap. 8.40x (ISBN 0-87563-053-7). Stipes.

Bozarth, M. A., ed. Methods of Assessing the Reinforcing Properties of Abused Drugs. (Illus.). 470p. 1984. 40.00 (ISBN 0-940090-04-X). Haer Inst.

Bozarth, Rene & Bozarth-Campbell, Alla. Sparrow Songs. 98p. (Orig.). 1981. 6.00 (ISBN 0-932560-02-4); pap. 3.00 (ISBN 0-932560-03-2). Wisdom House.

Bozarth-Campbell, Alla. Life Is Goodbye-Life Is Hello: Grieving Well Through All Kinds of Loss. LC 82-8064. (Illus.). 160p. 1982. 10.95 (ISBN 0-89638-060-2); pap. 7.95 (ISBN 0-89638-061-0). CompCare.

--Womanpriest: A Personal Odyssey. 229p. 1978. 9.95 (ISBN 0-8091-0243-9). Wisdom House.

--The Word's Body: An Incarnational Aesthetic of Interpretation. LC 79-111. 189p. 1980. 18.75 (ISBN 0-8173-0009-0). U of Ala Pr.

Bozarth-Campbell, Alla, jt. auth. see Bozarth, Rene.

Boze, Arthur. Black Words. pap. 1.00 (ISBN 0-910296-80-4). Broadside.

Bozeat, Nicholas, jt. auth. see Rose, Edgar.

Bozeck, H., et al. Fifteen Papers on Algebra. LC 51-5559. (Translations Ser.: No. 2, Vol. 45). 1965. 24.00 (ISBN 0-8218-1745-0, TRANS 2-45). Am Math.

Bozell, Patricia, jt. auth. see Whelan, James R.

Bozeman, Adda B. Conflict in Africa: Concepts & Realities. limited ed. LC 75-30187. 1976. text ed. 46.00 (ISBN 0-691-03104-5); pap. 18.00x limited ed. (ISBN 0-691-10044-6). Princeton U Pr.

--Future of Law in a Multicultural World. LC 78-131127. 1971. pap. 12.95 (ISBN 0-691-01060-9). Princeton U Pr.

--Regional Conflicts Around Geneva. LC 49-10185. (Augustana College Library Ser.: No. 20). 432p. 1949. 7.00x (ISBN 0-910182-15-9). Augustana Coll.

Bozeman, Barry. Public Management & Policy Analysis. LC 78-65247. 1979. text ed. 26.95x (ISBN 0-312-65471-5). St Martin.

Bozeman, Barry & Link, Albert N. Investments in Technology: Corporate Strategies & Public Policy Alternatives. 160p. 1983. 24.95 (ISBN 0-03-062412-6). Praeger.

Bozeman, Barry & Straussman, Jeffrey. New Directions in Public Administration. LC 83-26210. (Public Administration Ser.). 512p. 1984. pap. text ed. 13.00 pub net (ISBN 0-534-03266-4). Brooks-Cole.

Bozeman, Barry, et al, eds. Strategic Management of Industrial R & D. LC 83-49526. 256p. 1984. 25.00x (ISBN 0-669-08269-4). Lexington Bks.

Bozeman, Theodore D. Protestants in an Age of Science: The Baconian Ideal & Antebellum Religious Thought. LC 76-25962. xv, 240p. 1977. 20.00 (ISBN 0-8078-1299-4). U of NC Pr.

Bozeman, William C. Computers & Computing in Education: An Introduction. (Illus.). 180p. 1985. pap. text ed. 14.95 (ISBN 0-89787-407-2). Gorsuch Scarisbrick.

Bozhilov, Bozhidar. American Pages. Bozhilova, Cornelia, tr. LC 80-83427. (International Poetry: Vol. 5). 40p. 1981. 11.95x (ISBN 0-8214-0596-9, 82-83848); pap. 6.95 (ISBN 0-8214-0597-7, 82-83855). Ohio U Pr.

Bozhilova, Cornelia, tr. see Bozhilov, Bozhidar.

Bozic, Patricia. The Sweet Dreams Makeup Workbook: A Guide to Glowing Skin & a Prettier You. 176p. (Orig.). 1984. pap. 2.25 (ISBN 0-553-24165-6). Bantam.

--Thirty Days to Beautiful Nails. 64p. (Orig.). 1984. pap. 3.50 (ISBN 0-446-38028-8). Warner Bks.

Bozic, S. M. Digital & Kalman Filtering: An Introduction to Discrete - Time Filtering & Optimum Linear Estimation. 157p. 1980. pap. 26.95x (ISBN 0-470-26924-3). Halsted Pr.

Bozik. Fundamentals of Speech. 80p. 1984. pap. 5.95 (ISBN 0-8403-3428-1). Kendall-Hunt.

Bozman, John L. The History of Maryland: Its First Settlement, in 1633, to the Restoration, in 1660, 2 vols. Incl. Vol. 1. LC 68-30883. 314p. 12.00 (ISBN 0-87152-048-6); Vol. 2. LC 68-30883. 728p. 20.00 (ISBN 0-87152-049-4). (Illus.). 1968. Repr. of 1837 ed. Set. 40.00 (ISBN 0-87152-324-8). Reprint.

Bozman, M. M., tr. see Bekker, Paul.

Bozman, M. M., tr. see Mersmann, Hans.

Bozman, M. M., tr. see Mozart, Wolfgang A.

Bozo, Dominique, jt. ed. see Rubin, William.

Bozollo, Angelo, jt. auth. see Tisdale, Caroline.

Bozon, Nicole. Les Contes Moralises. 34.00 (ISBN 0-384-05360-2); pap. 28.00 (ISBN 0-384-05361-0). Johnson Repr.

Bozza, Charles M. Criminal Investigation. LC 77-9876. (Justice Administration Ser.). 435p. 1977. 26.95x (ISBN 0-88229-183-1). Nelson-Hall.

Bozzay, George D. Von see Von Bozzay, George D. & Fuller.

Bozzetti, F. & Dionigi, R., eds. Nutrition in Cancer & Trauma-Sepsis. (Illus.). viii, 204p. 1985. pap. 31.50 (ISBN 3-8055-3959-2). S Karger.

Bozzi, jt. auth. see Bent, Bob.

Bozzi, Ed. High Solids Coatings Buyer's Guide. 1982. pap. text ed. 21.00 (ISBN 0-936840-01-3). Tech Marketing.

Bozzini, A. see Silano, V., et al.
Bozzini, David M. & Leksan, Michael K. Beer & Games. 1985. pap. 5.95 (ISBN 0-317-15017-0). MYM Pub Co.
Bozzo, Maxine Z. Toby in the Country, Toby in the City. LC 81-7274. (Illus.). 24p. (ps-1). 1982. 11.75 (ISBN 0-688-00916-6); PLB 11.88 (ISBN 0-688-00917-4). Greenwillow.
Bozzoli, Belinda. The Political Nature of a Ruling Class Capital & Ideology in South Africa, 1890-1933. (International Library of Sociology). 356p. 1981. 40.00x (ISBN 0-7100-0722-1). Routledge & Kegan.
Bozzoli, Belinda, ed. Town & Countryside in the Transvaal: Capitalist Penetration & Popular Response. (Illus.). 466p. 1983. pap. text ed. 19.95x (ISBN 0-86975-139-5, Pub. by Ravan Pr). Ohio U Pr.
Bra, Lemuel De see De Bra, Lemuel.
Braach, Marvin E., jt. auth. see Page, Lawrence M.
Braak, E. On the Structure of the Human Striate Area. (Advances in Anatomy, Embryology & Cell Biology Ser.: Vol. 77). (Illus.). 87p. 1982. pap. 25.00 (ISBN 0-387-11512-9). Springer-Verlag.
Braak, H. Architectonics of the Human Telencephalic Cortex. (Studies of Brain Functions: Vol. 4). (Illus.). 147p. 1980. 31.00 (ISBN 0-387-10312-0). Springer-Verlag.
Braake, Alex L. Ter. Mining in the Netherlands East Indies. Wilkins, Mira, ed. LC 76-29762. (European Business Ser.). (Illus.). 1977. Repr. of 1944 ed. lib. bdg. 14.00x (ISBN 0-405-09777-8). Ayer Co Pubs.
Braakhekke, W. G. On Coexistence: A Casual Approach to Diversity & Stability in Grassland Vegetation. (Agricultural Research Reports: No. 902). 176p. 1980. pap. 25.75 (ISBN 90-220-0747-2, PDC217, PUDOC). Unipub.
Braaksma, B. L., et al, eds. Dynamical Systems & Bifurcations. (Lecture Notes in Mathematics: Vol. 1125). v, 129p. 1985. pap. 9.80 (ISBN 0-387-15233-4). Springer Verlag.
Braam, Geert P. Influence of Business Firms on Government. Braam, Geert P., tr. from Dutch. (New Babylon Studies in the Social Sciences). 320p. 1981. 23.20 (ISBN 90-279-3457-6). Mouton.
Braasch, Marvin E. & Page, Lawrence M. Systematic Studies of Darters of the Subgenus Catonotus (Percidae), with the Description of a New Species from Caney Fork, Tennessee. (Occasional Papers: No. 78). 10p. 1979. 1.25 (ISBN 0-317-04822-8). U of KS Mus Nat Hist.
Braasch, Marvin E., jt. auth. see Page, Lawrence M.
Braasch, Theodor. Vollstaendiges Woerterbuch Zur Sogenannten Caedmonschen Genesis. (Ger.). 1933. 17.95 (ISBN 3-533-00946-7, M-7682, Pub. by Carl Winter). French & Eur.
Braasch, William F. Early Days in the Mayo Clinic. (Illus.). 152p. 1969. 14.75x (ISBN 0-398-00211-8). C C Thomas.
Braaten, Carl E. The Apostolic Imperative: Nature & Aim of the Church's Mission & Ministry. 224p. (Orig.). 1985. pap. 10.95 (ISBN 0-8066-2168-0, 10-0410). Augsburg.
--Principles of Lutheran Theology. LC 82-16542. 160p. 1983. pap. 8.95 (ISBN 0-8006-1689-8). Fortress.
--Stewards of the Mysteries: Sermons for Festivals & Special Occasions. LC 82-72639. 128p. (Orig.). 1983. pap. 5.95 (ISBN 0-8066-1945-7, 10-6004). Augsburg.
Braaten, Carl E., ed. The New Church Debate: Issues Facing American Lutheranism. LC 83-48008. 176p. 1984. pap. 7.95 (ISBN 0-8006-1715-0, 1-1715). Fortress.
Braaten, Carl E. & Jenson, Robert W., eds. Christian Dogmatics, 2 vols. LC 83-48007. 1984. Volume 1. 24.95 (ISBN 0-8006-0703-1); Volume 2. 24.95 (ISBN 0-8006-0704-X); Set. 45.95 (ISBN 0-8006-0712-0). Fortress.
Braatoy, Bjarne. Labour & War: The Theory of Labour Action to Prevent War. LC 77-147508. (Library of War & Peace; Labor, Socialism & War). 1973. lib. bdg. 46.00 (ISBN 0-8240-0303-9). Garland Pub.
Brabander, Guido L. De see De Brabander, Guido L.
Brabander, M. De see De Brabander, M., et al.
Brabans, J. & Nedelec, C. Bottom Trawls for Small-Scale Fishing. (Fisheries Technical Papers: No. 189). 44p. (Eng., Fr. & Span.). 1979. pap. 9.00 (ISBN 92-5-100727-6, F1899, FAO). Unipub.
Brabant, J. C. & Nedelec, C. Bottom Trawls for Small-Scale Fishing: Adaptation for Pair Trawling. (Fisheries Technical Papers: No. 189). (Illus.). 27p. (Eng. & Fr.). 1983. pap. text ed. 7.50 (ISBN 92-5-101235-0, F2420, FAO). Unipub.
Brabant, J. M. Van see Van Brabant, J. M.
Brabazon, Francis. Four & Twenty Blackbirds. (Illus.). 52p. 1975. pap. 2.25 (ISBN 0-913078-22-0). Sheriar Pr.
--In Dust I Sing. 150p. 1974. 8.95 (ISBN 0-940700-08-5); pap. 4.95 (ISBN 0-940700-07-7). Meher Baba Info.
--The Silent Word. new ed. 1978. text ed. 9.95 (ISBN 0-913078-34-4); pap. text ed. 6.95 (ISBN 0-913078-35-2). Sheriar Pr.
--The Word at World's End. 88p. 1971. 5.95 (ISBN 0-940700-04-2); pap. 3.45 (ISBN 0-940700-03-4). Meher Baba Info.
Brabazon, James. Dorothy L. Sayers. 344p. 1982. pap. 3.95 (ISBN 0-380-58990-7, 58990-7, Discus). Avon.
--Dorothy L. Sayers: A Biography. (Illus.). 320p. 1981. Encore 4.50 (ISBN 0-684-16864-2, ScribT). Scribner.
--Dorothy L. Sayers: The Life of a Courageous Woman. 328p. 1981. 20.00x (ISBN 0-575-02728-2, Pub. by Gollancz England). State Mutual Bk.
Brabb, George. Computers & Information Systems in Business. 2nd ed. LC 79-88716. (Illus.). 1980. text ed. 27.50 (ISBN 0-395-28671-9); instr's. manual 1.00 (ISBN 0-395-28670-0). HM.
Brabb, George J. & McKean, Gerald. Business Data Processing: Concepts & Practices. LC 81-82556. 1982. 27.50 (ISBN 0-395-31684-7); instr's manual 2.00 (ISBN 0-395-31685-5); study guide 11.50 (ISBN 0-395-31686-3); test bank 2.00 (ISBN 0-395-31687-1); practice set 5.95 (ISBN 0-395-32018-6). HM.
Brabbs, Derry. English Country Churches. 1985. 24.00 (ISBN 0-670-80736-2). Viking.
Brabder, K. M. The Effect of Two-Hundred Mile Limits on Fisheries Management in the Northeast Atlantic. (Fisheries Technical Papers: No. 183). 26p. (Eng., Fr. & Span.). 1978. pap. 7.50 (ISBN 92-5-100592-3, F1470, FAO). Unipub.
Brabec, Barbara. Creative Cash: How to Sell Your Crafts, Needlework, Designs & Know-How. LC 81-82826. 1981. 7.95 (ISBN 0-89586-129-1). H P Bks.
--Homemade Money: The Definitive Guide to Success in a Home Business. LC 83-21483. (Illus.). 272p. (Orig.). 1984. pap. 12.95 (ISBN 0-932620-31-0). Betterway Pubns.
Braben, Eddie. The Best of Morecambe & Wise. (Entertainers Ser.). (Illus.). 144p. 1974. 8.50x (ISBN 0-7130-0133-X, Pub. by Woburn Pr England). Biblio Dist.
Brabner, Wendy, jt. auth. see Barrett, Gerlad R.
Brabson, G. Dana. Introductory Organic & Biochemistry Experiments for Students in the Health Professions. 1984. pap. text ed. 10.95 (ISBN 0-89917-429-9). Tichenor Pub.
Brabyn, Howard. Daumier's Hunting & Fishing. (Illus.). 140p. 1975. 12.98 (ISBN 0-8148-0642-2). L Amiel Pub.
Brabyn, Howard, tr. see Sorlier, Charles.
Bracanga, Aquino de see De Branganca, Aquino.
Bracchi, G. & Lockemann, P. C., eds. Information Systems Methodology: Proceedings, 2nd Conference of the European Cooperation in Informatics, Venice, Oct. 10-12, 1978. LC 78-12358. (Lecture Notes in Computer Science: Vol. 65). 1978. pap. 37.00 (ISBN 0-387-08934-9). Springer-Verlag.
Bracciolini, Francisco, tr. Alceste: The Tradgeie of Alceste & Eliza. LC 79-84082. (English Experience Ser.: No. 902). 80p. 1979. Repr. of 1638 ed. lib. bdg. 9.00 (ISBN 90-221-0902-X). Walter J Johnson.
Bracciolini, Poggio, ed. see Hammond, Lincoln D. & De Varthema, Ludovico.
Bracco. Stratified Charge Engines, Vol. 2. 112p. 1976. pap. 56.75 (ISBN 0-677-05355-X). Gordon.
Bracco, F. V. Stratified Charge Engines, Vol. 1. 104p. 1973. pap. 46.25 (ISBN 0-677-05165-4). Gordon.
Brace, Arthur William & Allen, F. A. Magnesium Casting Technology. LC 58-821. (Illus.). pap. 43.50 (ISBN 0-317-11125-6, 2051325). Bks Demand UMI.
Brace, Betty L. & Croghan, Tonita. Understanding Adolescents & Safety at Home & on the Job. LC 79-21803. (Lifeworks Ser.). (Illus.). 1980. pap. text ed. 8.00 (ISBN 0-07-060912-8). McGraw.
Brace, Beverly W. The Humboldt Years, 1930-39. 1977. pap. 4.50 (ISBN 0-686-19169-2). B W Brace.
Brace, C. The Stages of Human Evolution. 2nd ed. 1979. pap. 17.95 (ISBN 0-13-840140-3). P-H.
Brace, C. L., et al. Atlas of Human Evolution. 2nd ed. LC 78-27723. 178p. 1979. pap. text ed. 17.95 (ISBN 0-03-045021-7, HoltC). HR&W.
Brace, C. Loring & Metress, James F., eds. Man in Evolutionary Perspective. LC 72-14184. Repr. of 1973 ed. 121.50 (ISBN 0-8357-9926-3, 2012618). Bks Demand UMI.
Brace, Charles L. The Dangerous Classes of New York. LC 73-84256. (NASW Classics Ser.). (Illus.). 448p. 1973. pap. text ed. 6.95x (ISBN 0-87101-061-5). Natl Assn Soc Wkrs.
--Dangerous Classes of New York & Twenty Years's Work among Them. 3rd ed. LC 67-26666. (Criminology, Law Enforcement, & Social Problems Ser.: No. 3). 1967. Repr. of 1880 ed. 17.00x (ISBN 0-87585-003-0). Patterson Smith.
--The Racial Foundation of the History of Mankind, 3 vols. (Illus.). 445p. 1985. 178.75 (ISBN 0-86722-097-X). Inst Econ Pol.
Brace, Edward R. Devils to Ourselves. LC 81-82189. (Illus.). 91p. (Orig.). 1981. pap. write for info. (ISBN 0-9606276-0-X). Jam Jar.
--The Pediatric Guide to Drugs & Vitamins. 1982. pap. 6.95 (ISBN 0-440-57246-0, Dell Trade Pbks). Dell.
--The Pediatric Guide to Drugs & Vitamins. LC 82-1580. 256p. 1982. 13.95 (ISBN 0-385-28828-X). Delacorte.
Brace, Edward R. & Pacanowski, John P. Childhood Symptoms: Every Parent's Guide to Childhood Illness. LC 84-47974. 1985. 22.50 (ISBN 0-06-181098-3, CN); pap. 10.95 (ISBN 0-06-091152-2). Har-Row.
Brace, Emma. The Life of Charles Loring Brace: Chiefly Told in His Own Letters. LC 75-17205. (Social Problems & Social Policy Ser.). (Illus.). 1976. Repr. of 1894 ed. 37.50x (ISBN 0-405-07478-6). Ayer Co Pubs.
Brace, Geoffrey. Something to Play. (Resources of Music Ser). 5.95 (ISBN 0-521-07753-2). Cambridge U Pr.
--Something to Sing, 4 Bks. Bk. 1 Piano Ed. 9.95 (ISBN 0-521-04296-8); Bk. 1 Melody Ed. text ed. 4.50 (ISBN 0-521-04295-X); Bk. 2 Piano. 8.95 (ISBN 0-521-04298-4); Bk. 2 Melody Ed. 4.50 (ISBN 0-521-04297-6); Bk. 3. 5.50 (ISBN 0-521-04299-2); Bk. 4. 5.95 (ISBN 0-521-04300-X). Cambridge U Pr.
--Something to Sing at Assembly. (Resources of Music Ser). Music. 5.50 (ISBN 0-521-07570-X). Cambridge U Pr.
Brace, Geoffrey & Burton, I. Listen! Music & Nature. (Illus.). (gr. 5-8). 1976. pap. 7.50 (ISBN 0-521-20706-1). Cambridge U Pr.
Brace, George. Story of Music. (Illus.). (gr. 5 up). 1968. 2.50 (ISBN 0-7214-0217-8). Merry Thoughts.
Brace, Gerald, jt. auth. see Moreau, M.
Brace, Gerald, jt. ed. see Moureau, Magdaleine.
Brace, Gerald W. The Department. LC 83-1197. (Phoenix Fiction Ser.). 290p. 1968. pap. 6.95 (ISBN 0-226-06968-0). U of Chicago Pr.
--Garretson Chronicle. 1964. pap. 1.65x (ISBN 0-393-00272-1, Norton Lib). Norton.
--The Stuff of Fiction. LC 71-77391. 1969 o.p. 4.50 (ISBN 0-393-04312-6, Norton Lib); pap. 1.95x 1972 (ISBN 0-393-00648-4). Norton.
--Wind's Will. 1964. 4.50 (ISBN 0-393-08435-3). Norton.
--Winter Solstice. 1960. 3.95 (ISBN 0-393-08488-4). Norton.
Brace, Paul K., et al. Reporting of Service Efforts & Accomplishments. LC 80-84887. (The Financial Accounting Standards Board Research Report). (Illus.). 114p. (Orig.). 1980. pap. 6.50 (ISBN 0-910065-09-8). Finan Acct.
Brace, Reginald, jt. auth. see King, Billie J.
Bracebridge, C. Holte. Shakespeare No Deerstealer. LC 76-39517. Repr. of 1862 ed. 14.00 (ISBN 0-404-00921-2). AMS Pr.
Bracegirdle & Miles. Atlas de Estructura Vegetal. 126p. (Span.). 1975. pap. 13.95 (ISBN 0-686-92568-8, S-37583). French & Eur.
Bracegirdle, jt. auth. see Freeman.
Bracegirdle, Brian. The Archaeology of the Industrial Revolution. LC 73-8287. (Illus.). 207p. 1973. 50.00 (ISBN 0-8386-1424-8). Fairleigh Dickinson.
--A History of Microtechnique. LC 77-78658. (Illus.). 375p. 1978. 57.50x (ISBN 0-8014-1117-3). Cornell U Pr.
Bracegirdle, Brian & Miles, Patricia H. An Atlas of Chordate Structure. (Heinemann Biology Atlases Ser.). 1978. text ed. 15.50x (ISBN 0-435-60316-7). Heinemann Ed.
--An Atlas of Plant Structure, 2 vols. 1971. Vol. 1. text ed. 15.50x (ISBN 0-435-60312-4); Vol. 2. text ed. 15.50x (ISBN 0-435-60314-0). Heinemann Ed.
--Thomas Telford. (Great Engineers & Their Works Ser). (Illus.). 112p. 1973. 14.95 (ISBN 0-7153-5933-9). David & Charles.
Bracegirdle, Brian, jt. auth. see Freeman, W. H.
Bracegirdle, Joe. The Border Canary. (Illus.). 160p. 1981. 13.50 (ISBN 0-904558-95-9). Saiga.
Braceland, Lawrence C., tr. see Gilbert.
Braceland, Lawrence C., tr. see Gilbert Of Hoyland.
Bracewell, R. The Fourier Transform & Its Applications. 2nd ed. (Electrical Engineering Ser.). (Illus.). 1978. text ed. 48.00 (ISBN 0-07-007013-X). McGraw.
Bracewell, Ronald N. The Galactic Club: Intelligent Life in Outer Space. (Illus.). 160p. 1979. pap. text ed. 3.95x (ISBN 0-393-95022-0). Norton.
Bracewell, Ronald N., ed. Paris Symposium on Radio Astronomy. (Illus.). 1959. 50.00x (ISBN 0-8047-0571-2). Stanford U Pr.
Bracewell-Milnes, Barry. Eastern & Western European Economic Integration. LC 76-6671. (Illus.). 300p. 1976. 27.50 (ISBN 0-312-22470-2). St Martin.
--The Economics of International Tax Avoidance: Political Power vs. Economic Law. (International Taxation Ser.: No. 2). 120p. 1980. lib. bdg. 29.00 (ISBN 90-2000-633-9, Pub. by Kluwer Law & Taxation Publishers). Kluwer Academic.
--Land & Heritage. (Institute of Economic Affairs, Hobart Papers Ser.: No. 93). pap. 10.95 technical (ISBN 0-255-36151-3). Transatlantic.
Bracewell-Milnes, J. B. & Huiskamp, J. C. Investment Incentives. (International Series of the Fiscal-Economic Institute, Erasmus Univ., Rotterdam). 1977. pap. 25.00 (ISBN 90-200-0499-9, Pub. by Kluwer Law Netherlands). Kluwer Academic.
Bracey, et al. Basic Management. 3rd ed. 1985. pap. write for info. (ISBN 0-256-03411-7). Business Pubns.
Bracey, Audrey. Resolution of the Dominican Crisis, 1965: A Study in Mediation. LC 80-27239. 64p. (Orig.). 1980. pap. 3.50 (ISBN 0-934742-04-9, Inst Study Diplomacy). Geo U Sch For Serv.
Bracey, Doris C. The Tale of Two Towns. (Illus.). 64p. 1984. 5.50 (ISBN 0-682-40168-4). Exposition Pr FL.
Bracey, Dorothy H. Baby-Pros: Preliminary Profiles of Juvenile Prostitutes. (Criminal Justice Center Monographs). 1979. pap. text ed. 3.00x (ISBN 0-89444-024-1). John Jay Pr.
Bracey, Dorothy H., intro. by see Letman, Sloan T.
Bracey, Howard E. In Retirement: Pensioners in Great Britain & the United States. LC 67-10607. xvi, 296p. 1966. 30.00x (ISBN 0-8071-0330-6). La State U Pr.
--Neighbours: Subdivision Life in England & the United States. LC 64-15877. xii, 208p. 1964. 22.50x (ISBN 0-8071-0329-2). La State U Pr.
Bracey, Hyler J., et al. Basic Management: An Experience Based Approach. rev. ed. 1981. pap. 17.95x (ISBN 0-256-02572-X). Business Pubns.
Bracey, Lucius H. & Rogers, Walter R. Wills: A Virginia Law Practice System. 342p. 1982. looseleaf with forms 75.00 (ISBN 0-87215-511-0). Michie Co.
Bracey, Lucius H., Jr. & Rogers, Walter R., Jr. Administration of Estates: A Virginia Law Practice System. (Law Practice Systems Ser.). 354p. 1984. looseleaf 75.00 (ISBN 0-87215-769-5, 69660). Michie Co.
Bracey, Robert. Eighteenth Century Studies & Other Papers. LC 74-19208. 1974. Repr. of 1925 ed. lib. bdg. 15.00 (ISBN 0-8414-3305-4). Folcroft.
Bracher, Frederick, ed. see Etherege, Sir George.
Bracher, Frederick G. The Novels of James Gould Cozzens. LC 72-6187. 306p. 1972. Repr. of 1959 ed. lib. bdg. 22.50x (ISBN 0-8371-6448-6, BRJC). Greenwood.
Bracher, Karl D. The Age of Ideologies: A History of Political Thought in the Twentieth Century. Osers, Ewald, tr. from Ger. LC 84-15104. 276p. 1984. 25.00 (ISBN 0-312-01229-2). St Martin.
--The Age of Ideologies: A History of Political Thought in the Twentieth Century. Osers, Ewald, tr. from Ger. 305p. 1985. pap. 11.95 (ISBN 0-312-01230-6). St Martin.
--The German Dictatorship: The Origins, Structure, & Effects of National Socialism. Steinberg, Jean, tr. from German. LC 70-95662. Orig. Title: Die Deutsche Diktatur: Enstehung, Struktur, & Folgen Des Nationalsozialismus. 553p. 1972. pap. text ed. 15.95 (ISBN 0-275-83780-7). HR&W.
Bracher, Mark. Being Form'd: Thinking Through Blake's "Milton". 288p. (Orig.). 1985. 22.50 (ISBN 0-88268-013-7, Pub. by Clinamen Studies); pap. 9.95 (ISBN 0-88268-012-9). Station Hill Pr.
Bracher, Michael D. Are Australian Families Getting Smaller? A Study of Patterns & Determinants of Fertility in Melbourne. (Australian Family Formation Project Monograph: No. 8). 282p. 1981. pap. text ed. 6.95 (ISBN 0-909409-09-9, 1129, Pub. by ANUP Australia). Australia N U P.
Brachet, J., jt. ed. see Abercrombie, M.
Brachet, J., jt. ed. see Delrio, Giovanni.
Brachet, Jean. Molecular Cytology, Vol. 1: The Cell Cycle. 1985. price not set (ISBN 0-12-123370-7). Acad Pr.
--Molecular Cytology, Vol. 2: Cell Interactions. 1985. price not set (ISBN 0-12-123371-5). Acad Pr.
Brachet, Jean & Bonotto, S., eds. Biology of Acetabularia: Proceedings. 1970. 55.00 (ISBN 0-12-123360-X). Acad Pr.
Brachet, Jean & Mirsky, A. E., eds. The Cell: Biochemistry, Physiology, Morphology, 6 vols. Incl. Vol. 1. Methods: Problems of Cell Biology. 1959. 97.50 (ISBN 0-12-123301-4); Vol. 2. Cells & Their Component Parts. 1961. 97.50 (ISBN 0-12-123302-2); Vol. 3. Meiosis & Mitosis. 1961. 74.50 (ISBN 0-12-123303-0); Vol. 4. Specialized Cells, Part 1. 1960. 80.50 (ISBN 0-12-123304-9); Vol. 5. Specialized Cells, Part 2. 1961. 87.00 (ISBN 0-12-123305-7); Vol. 6. Supplementary Volume. 1964. 87.00 (ISBN 0-12-123306-5). Acad Pr.
Brachin, P., et al, eds. Dutch Studies, Vol. 3. 1978. 28.50 (ISBN 90-247-1996-8, Pub. by Martinus Nijhoff Netherlands). Kluwer Academic.
Brachman, Philip S., jt. auth. see Bennett, John.
Bracht, Neil F. Social Work Administration in Health Care: A Guide to Professional Practice. LC 78-7881. 346p. 1978. 26.95 (ISBN 0-917724-04-6, B4); pap. 14.95 (ISBN 0-917724-05-4, B5). Haworth Pr.
Brack, Edith. Modern Flower Arranging. (Illus.). 144p. 1982. 19.95 (ISBN 0-7134-3893-2, Pub. by Batsford England). David & Charles.
Brack, O. M., ed. Studies in Eighteenth Century Culture, Vol. 13. LC 74-25572. 320p. 1984. text ed. 25.00x (ISBN 0-299-09560-6). U of Wis Pr.
--Studies in Eighteenth-Century Culture, Vol. 15. LC 75-648277. 320p. 1985. text ed. price not set (ISBN 0-299-10430-3). U of Wis Pr.
Brack, O. M., ed. see Smollet, Tobias.
Brack, O. M., Jr. & Barnes, Warner. Bibliography & Textual Criticism: English & American Literature, Seventeen Hundred to the Present. LC 74-92463. (Patterns of Literary Criticism Ser). 1969. pap. 3.45x (ISBN 0-226-06985-0, PLC8). U of Chicago Pr.
Brack, O M, Jr., jt. auth. see Kelley, Robert E.

Brack, O. M., Jr., ed. American Humor: Essays Presented to John C. Gerber. 1977. pap. text ed. 3.95 (ISBN 0-9602148-1-X). Arete Pubns.

Brack, O M, Jr. & Kelley, Robert E., eds. The Early Biographies of Samuel Johnson. LC 73-77385. 377p. 1974. text ed. 30.00x (ISBN 0-87745-038-2). U of Iowa Pr.

Brackbill, Jeremiah U. & Cohen, Bruce I., eds. Multiple Time Scales. (Computational Techniques Ser.). Date not set. 75.00 (ISBN 0-12-123420-7). Acad Pr.

Brackbill, Yvonne. Infancy & Early Childhood. LC 67-15056. 1967. text ed. 14.95 (ISBN 0-02-904520-7). Free Pr.

Brackbill, Yvonne & Rice, June. Birth Trap. LC 84-27114. 1985. pap. 8.95 (ISBN 0-446-38219-1). Warner Bks.

Brackbill, Yvonne, et al. Medication in Maternity: Infant Exposure & Maternal Information. (International Academy for Research in Learning Disabilities Monographs). 160p. 1985. pap. text ed. 8.95x (ISBN 0-472-08059-8). U of Mich Pr.

--Birth Trap: The Legal Lowdown on High-Tech Birthing Practices. 244p. 1984. pap. 9.95 (ISBN 0-317-02792-1). Mosby.

Bracke, P., et al. Inorganic Fibres & Composite Materials: A Survey of Recent Developments. (EPO Applied Technology Ser.: Vol. 3). (Illus.). 192p. 1984. 50.00 (ISBN 0-08-031145-8). Pergamon.

Brackelsberg, Phyllis, ed. see Iowa Home Economics Association.

Bracken. Animal Crackers. (Platt & Munk Cricket Bks.). (Illus.). 24p. (ps-3). 1979. (G&D); PLB 3.59 (ISBN 0-448-13071-8). Putnam Pub Group.

Bracken, et al. Women of the Word: Contemporary Sermons by Women Clergy. Hackett, Charles, ed. LC 84-52656. (Illus.). 144p. (Orig.). 1985. pap. 7.95 (ISBN 0-932419-00-3). Susan Hunter.

Bracken, Carol, illus. The Baby Moses. (Tuck-A-Toy Bks.). (Illus.). 7p. (ps). 1985. 3.95 (ISBN 0-8407-6663-7). Nelson.

Bracken, Carolyn. Little Teddy Bear. (Shaggies Ser.). (Illus.). 12p. (ps-2). 1982. board 3.95 (ISBN 0-671-42550-1, Little Simon). S&S.

--Peter Rabbit's Pockets. (Illus.). 8p. (ps). 1982. 3.95 (ISBN 0-671-44528-6, Little Simon). S&S.

--Super Stickers for Kids: One Hundred & Twenty-Eight Fun Labels. (Illus.). 16p. (Orig.). 1981. pap. 2.50 (ISBN 0-486-24092-4). Dover.

Bracken, Carolyn, illus. The Baby Bear. (Tuck-A-Toy Bks.). 7p. (ps). 1985. 3.95 (ISBN 0-8407-6664-5). Nelson.

--The Baby Jesus. (Tuck-A-Toy Bks.). (Illus.). 7p. (ps). 1985. 3.95 (ISBN 0-8407-6666-1). Nelson.

--Baby Strawberry Shortcake's First Book of Rhymes. LC 83-63391. (Baby Strawberry Shortcake Cuddle Bks.). (Illus.). 14p. (ps). 1984. bds. 1.95 (ISBN 0-394-86718-1, Pub. by BYR). Random.

--Baby Strawberry Shortcake's Playtime Words. LC 83-63319. (Baby Strawberry Shortcake Cuddle Bks.). (Illus.). 14p. (ps). 1984. bds. 1.95 (ISBN 0-394-86717-3, Pub. by BYR). Random.

--Bunny. (Floppies Ser.). (Illus.). 6p. (ps-k). 1981. cloth ed. 2.50 (ISBN 0-671-42531-5, Little Simon). S&S.

--Fast Rolling Fire Trucks. (Fast Rolling Bks.). (Illus.). (ps). 1984. 4.95 (ISBN 0-448-09876-8, G&D). Putnam Pub Group.

--Panda. (Floppies Ser.). (Illus.). 6p. (ps-k). 1981. 2.50 (ISBN 0-671-42530-7, Little Simon). S&S.

--Santa's Pockets. (Illus.). (ps). 1983. 3.95 (ISBN 0-671-47660-2, Little Simon). S&S.

--The Special Baby. (Tuck-A-Toy Ser.). (Illus.). 7p. (ps). 1985. 3.95 (ISBN 0-8407-6665-3). Nelson.

--Teddy Bear's Pockets. (Illus.). 8p. (ps). 1983. washable 3.95 (ISBN 0-671-46448-5, Little Simon). S&S.

Bracken, Carolyn & Barbaresi, Nina, illus. Baby Seal. (Bubble Shape Bks.). (ps). 2.95 (ISBN 0-671-50031-7, Little Simon). S&S.

--Duckling. (Bubble Shape Bks.). (ps). 2.95 (ISBN 0-671-50030-9, Little Simon). S&S.

--Farmhouse. (Busy Bubble Bks.). (ps). 2.95 (ISBN 0-671-47670-X, Little Simon). S&S.

Bracken, Dorothy K. & Redway, Maurine W. Early Texas Homes. LC 56-12565. (Illus.). 1956. 17.50 (ISBN 0-87074-023-7). SMU Press.

Bracken, Harry M. Berkeley. LC 74-15569. 176p. 1975. 19.95 (ISBN 0-312-07595-2). St Martin.

Bracken, Ian. Urban Planning Methods: Research & Policy Analysis. LC 81-13013. 420p. 1981. 37.00x (ISBN 0-416-74860-0, NO. 3564); pap. 17.95x (ISBN 0-416-74870-8, NO. 3563). Methuen Inc.

Bracken, Jeanne & Wigutoff, Sharon, eds. Books for Today's Children: An Annotated Bibliography of Non-Stereotyped Picture Books. 35p. 1979. pap. 3.95x (ISBN 0-912670-53-3). Feminist Pr.

Bracken, Jeanne, et al. Books for Today's Young Readers: An Annotated Bibliography of Recommended Fiction for Ages 10-14. 52p. (Orig.). (gr. 4-7). 1981. 4.95 (ISBN 0-935312-03-X). Feminist Pr.

Bracken, Jerome & Schliefer, Arthur. Tables for Normal Sampling with Unknown Variances: The Student Distribution & Economically Optimal Sampling Plans. LC 64-13716. pap. 52.00 (ISBN 0-317-08675-8, 2002196). Bks Demand UMI.

Bracken, John. Great Plants for Cool Places. LC 80-5406. (Illus.). 192p. (Orig.). 1980. 14.95 (ISBN 0-8128-2721-X); pap. 9.95 (ISBN 0-8128-6064-0). Stein & Day.

Bracken, Joseph A. The Triune Symbol: Persons, Process & Community. (Studies in Religion: No. 1). 216p. (Orig.). 1985. lib. bdg. 22.50 (ISBN 0-8191-4440-1, College Theo Soc); pap. text ed. 11.75 (ISBN 0-8191-4441-X). U Pr of Amer.

--What Are They Saying about the Trinity? LC 78-70819. 1979. pap. 2.45 (ISBN 0-8091-2179-4). Paulist Pr.

Bracken, Michael B. Perinatal Epidemology. (Illus.). 550p. 1984. 55.00x (ISBN 0-19-503389-2). Oxford U Pr.

Bracken, Paul. The Command & Control of Nuclear Forces. LC 83-42874. 288p. 1983. 25.00x (ISBN 0-300-02946-2). Yale U Pr.

--The Command & Control of Nuclear Forces. LC 83-42874. 264p. 1985. pap. 7.95 (ISBN 0-300-03398-2, Y-522). Yale U Pr.

--On Theater Warfare. 52p. 1979. 15.00 (ISBN 0-318-14351-8, HI3036P). Hudson Inst.

Bracken, Peg. Appendix to the I Hate to Cook Book. (Illus.). 1977. pap. 1.95 (ISBN 0-449-24174-2, Crest). Fawcett.

--The I Hate to Cook Almanack. 1977. pap. 2.50 (ISBN 0-449-23370-7, Crest). Fawcett.

--I Hate to Cook Book. 1978. pap. 2.50 (ISBN 0-449-23874-1, Crest). Fawcett.

--I Hate to Cook Book. LC 60-10919. (Illus.). 1960. 6.95 (ISBN 0-15-139263-3). HarBraceJ.

--A Window over the Sink. 256p. 1982. pap. 2.95 (ISBN 0-380-58149-3, 58149-3). Avon.

Bracken, Susan. Canadian Almanac & Directory 1982. Rev., 135 ed. 1122p. 1981. 42.00x (ISBN 0-8103-1189-5, Pub. by Copp Clark Pitman). Gale.

--Canadian Almanac & Directory 1984. 137th ed. 1191p. 1984. 59.00x (Pub. by Copp Clark Pitman). Gale.

Bracken, Susan, ed. Canadian Almanac & Directory, 1982. 135th ed. LC 7-24314. 1122p. 1982. 60.00x (ISBN 0-7730-4046-3). Intl Pubns Serv.

--Canadian Almanac & Directory, 1983. 136th ed. LC 7-24314. 1156p. 1983. 65.00x (ISBN 0-7730-4048-X). Intl Pubns Serv.

--Canadian Almanac & Directory 1985. 1100p. 1985. 64.00x (ISBN 0-7730-4053-6, Pub. by Copp Clark Pitman). Gale.

Brackenbridge, Hugh H. Incidents of the Insurrection. Marder, Daniel, ed. (Masterworks of Literature Ser). 1972. 8.95x (ISBN 0-8084-0014-2); pap. 5.95x (ISBN 0-8084-0015-0). New Coll U Pr.

Brackenbury, A. Breaking Ground. 147p. 1984. pap. text ed. 11.00x (ISBN 0-85635-503-8, Pub. by Carcanet New Pr England). Humanities.

Brackenbury, Alison. Dreams of Power & Other Poems. 128p. (Orig.). 1981. pap. text ed. 9.00x (ISBN 0-85635-352-3, Pub. by Carcanet New Pr England). Humanities.

Brackenbury, H. Ashanti War, 2 vols. 1968. Set. 85.00x (ISBN 0-7146-1795-4, F Cass Co). Biblio Dist.

Brackenbury, Mark. Baltic Southwest Pilot. 1983. 40.00x (ISBN 0-540-07414-4, Pub. by Stanford Maritime England). State Mutual Bk.

--Frisian Pilot: Den Helder to Brunsbuttel & the Kiel Canal. 151p. 1983. 39.00x (ISBN 0-540-07185-4, Pub. by Stanford Maritime England). State Mutual Bk.

--Normandy & Channel Islands Pilot: Calais to St. Malo. 5th ed. (Adlard Coles Pilotage Ser.). (Illus.). 186p. 1983. 35.00 (ISBN 0-229-11697-3, Pub. by Adlard Coles). Sheridan.

--Scottish West Coast Pilot. 144p. 1983. 40.00x (ISBN 0-540-07195-1, Pub. by Stanford Maritime England). State Mutual Bk.

Brackenbury, Mark, tr. see Gree, Alain.

Brackenridge, Celia. Women's Lacrosse. LC 77-93733. (gr. 9-12). 1978. 4.95 (ISBN 0-8120-5152-1). Barron.

Brackenridge, H. M. Journal of a Voyage up the River Missouri. 1976. Repr. of 1815 ed. 18.00 (ISBN 0-527-10510-4). Kraus Repr.

--Voyage to South America, 2 vols. 250.00 (ISBN 0-8490-1269-4). Gordon Pr.

Brackenridge, Henry M. History of the Western Insurrection in Western Pennsylvania, Commonly Called the Whiskey Insurrection, 1794. LC 72-90167. (Mass Violence in America). Repr. of 1859 ed. 17.00 (ISBN 0-405-01302-7). Ayer Co Pubs.

--Voyage to South America, 2 vols. in 1. LC 70-128425. Repr. of 1820 ed. 27.50 (ISBN 0-404-00922-0). AMS Pr.

Brackenridge, Hugh H. A Collection. LC 72-78651. Repr. cancelled (ISBN 0-686-01726-9). Somerset Pub.

--Law Miscellanies: Containing an Introduction to the Study of the Law. LC 73-37967. (American Law: The Formative Years). 600p. 1972. Repr. of 1814 ed. 35.50 (ISBN 0-405-03994-8). Ayer Co Pubs.

--Modern Chivalry. Leary, Lewis, ed. (Masterworks of Literature Ser). 1965. pap. 7.95x (ISBN 0-8084-0221-8, M4). New Coll U Pr.

--Modern Chivalry. 1977. Repr. of 1937 ed. lib. bdg. 40.00 (ISBN 0-8492-0303-1). R West.

Brackenridge, Hugh H. & Freneau, Philip. Father Bombo's Pilgrimage to Mecca, 1770. Bell, Michael D., ed. LC 75-5391. (Illus.). 129p. 1975. 10.00 (ISBN 0-87811-020-8). Princeton Lib.

Brackenridge, R. D. Medical Selection of Life Risks. 2nd ed. 800p. 1985. 100.00x (ISBN 0-943818-07-9). Stockton Pr.

Brackenridge, R. Douglas. Beckoning Frontiers: A Biography of James Woodin Laurie. LC 75-27591. (Illus.). 199p. 1976. 10.00 (ISBN 0-911536-61-2). Trinity U Pr.

--Voice in the Wilderness: A History of the Cumberland Presbyterian Church in Texas. LC 68-20136. (Illus.). 192p. 1968. 4.00 (ISBN 0-911536-03-5). Trinity U Pr.

Brackenridge, R. Douglas & Garcia-Treto, Francisco O. Iglesia Presbiteriana: A History of Presbyterians & Mexican Americans in the Southwest. LC 74-76777. (Illus.). 262p. 1974. 8.00 (ISBN 0-911536-53-1). Trinity U Pr.

Brackenridge, R. Douglas, jt. auth. see Boyd, Lois A.

Brackenridge, W. D. see Wilkes, Charles.

Bracker, William & Nabors, James J. The Third National Cone Box Show Catalog. (Illus.). 64p. (Orig.). 1980. pap. text ed. 10.95 (ISBN 0-8403-2181-3). Kendall-Hunt.

Brackert, Helmut, ed. see Grimm, Jacob & Grimm, Wilhelm K.

Bracket, Hilda. One Little Maid. 1980. 14.95 (ISBN 0-434-08525-1, Pub. by W Heinemann Ltd). David & Charles.

Bracket, Leigh. The Halfling & Other Stories. 1983. pap. 2.75 (ISBN 0-441-31597-6, Pub. by Ace Science Fiction). Ace Bks.

Brackett, Albert G. History of the United States Cavalry. LC 68-54789. Repr. of 1865 ed. lib. bdg. 18.75x (ISBN 0-8371-0323-1, BRHC). Greenwood.

--History of the United States Cavalry, from the Formation of the Federal Government to the 1st of June 1863. facs. ed. LC 74-133514. (Select Bibliographies Reprint Ser). 1865. 18.00 (ISBN 0-8369-5546-3). Ayer Co Pubs.

Brackett, Anna C. & Eliot, Ida M. Poetry for Home & School. facsimile ed. LC 79-38593. (Granger Index Reprint Ser.). Repr. of 1876 ed. 19.00 (ISBN 0-8369-6325-3). Ayer Co Pubs.

Brackett, Anna C., tr. see Rosenkrantz, Johann K.

Brackett, Anna C., tr. see Rosenkranz, Johann K.

Brackett, Babette & Lash, MaryAnn. The Wild Gourmet: A Forager's Guide to Finding & Cooking Wild Foods. LC 74-25953. (Illus.). 144p. 1975. 17.95 (ISBN 0-87923-132-7); pap. 8.95 (ISBN 0-87923-142-4). Godine.

Brackett, Benjamin, et al, eds. New Technologies in Animal Breeding. LC 81-20556. 1982. 49.50 (ISBN 0-12-123450-9). Acad Pr.

Brackett, Bruce, jt. ed. see Paget, Kathleen.

Brackett, Cindi L. Leap into Learning. 1985. 4.95 (ISBN 0-8062-2310-3). Carlton.

Brackett, Frederick S., ed. see American Association For The Advancement Of Science - New York - 1949.

Brackett, Isaac P., jt. auth. see Moncur, John P.

Brackett, J. R. Notes on the Progress of the Colored People of Maryland Since the War. pap. 11.00 (ISBN 0-686-86230-9). Johnson Repr.

Brackett, Jeffrey R. Negro in Maryland. facs. ed. LC 69-18529. (Select Bibliographies Reprint Ser). 1889. 19.00 (ISBN 0-8369-5000-3). Ayer Co Pubs.

--The Negro in Maryland: A Study of the Institution of Slavery. LC 78-64250. (Johns Hopkins University. Studies in the Social Sciences. Extra Volumes: 6). Repr. of 1889 ed. 12.00 (ISBN 0-404-61354-3). AMS Pr.

--Negro in Maryland: A Study of the Institution of Slavery. LC 69-16585. Repr. of 1889 ed. 17.50x (ISBN 0-8371-1549-3, BRM&, Pub. by Negro U Pr). Greenwood.

--Notes on the Progress of the Colored People of Maryland Since the War. LC 78-63796. (Johns Hopkins University. Studies in the Social Sciences. Eighth Ser. 1890). Repr. of 1890 ed. 11.50 (ISBN 0-404-61061-7). AMS Pr.

--Notes on the Progress of the Colored People of Maryland Since the War. facsimile ed. LC 76-170689. (Black Heritage Library Collection). Repr. of 1890 ed. 14.25 (ISBN 0-8369-8879-5). Ayer Co Pubs.

--Supervision & Education in Charity. 222p. 1974. Repr. of 1903 ed. lib. bdg. 25.00 (ISBN 0-87821-275-2). Milford Hse.

Brackett, L. & Richards, W. Games & Activities that Serve a Purpose. 114p. (Orig.). 1984. pap. text ed. 5.00x (ISBN 0-87563-251-3). Stipes.

Brackett, Leigh. Eric John Stark: Outlaw of Mars. 208p. 1982. pap. 2.25 (ISBN 0-345-30515-9, Del Rey). Ballantine.

--Follow the Free Wind. 224p. (Orig.). 1980. pap. 1.75 (ISBN 0-345-29008-9). Ballantine.

--The Ginger Star. (Orig.). 1979. pap. 1.95 (ISBN 0-345-28514-X). Ballantine.

--The Long Tomorrow. 272p. 1986. pap. 2.95 (ISBN 0-345-32926-0, Del Rey). Ballantine.

--The Starmen of Llyrdis. 176p. 1976. pap. 1.95 (ISBN 0-345-28483-6). Ballantine.

--The Sword of Rhiannon. 1979. lib. bdg. 11.95 (ISBN 0-8398-2522-6, Gregg). G K Hall.

Brackett, Michael H. Developing Data Structured Information Systems. LC 82-62821. (Illus.). 184p. (Orig.). 1983. pap. 20.00 (ISBN 0-9605884-1-8). Orr & Assocs.

Brackett, Oliver. English Furniture. 79p. 1980. Repr. lib. bdg. 15.00 (ISBN 0-89760-042-8). Telegraph Bks.

Brackett, Peter, jt. auth. see Sedra, Adel.

Brackin, I. L. & Fitzgerald, W. Darts. 176p. 1984. pap. 5.95 (ISBN 0-671-53239-1, Fireside). S&S.

Brackin, Ivan L. & Fitzgerald, William. All about Darts. (Illus.). 176p. 1976. pap. 7.95 (ISBN 0-8092-7303-9). Contemp Bks.

Brackman, Arnold. Communist Collapse in Indonesia. LC 70-77399. 1969. 6.95 (ISBN 0-393-05377-6). Norton.

Brackman, Arnold C. Indonesian Communism: A History. LC 75-25486. 336p. 1976. Repr. of 1963 ed. lib. bdg. 22.50x (ISBN 0-8371-8419-3, BRIC). Greenwood.

--The Search for the Gold of Tutankhamen. 1979. pap. 2.50 (ISBN 0-671-83027-9). PB.

Brackman, Henriett. The Perfect Portfolio. (Illus.). 144p. 1984. 24.95 (ISBN 0-8174-5400-4); pap. 16.95 (ISBN 0-8174-5401-2). Watson-Guptill.

Brackman, Rita. Vybor V Adu: Zhizneutverzhdenie solzhenitsynskikh geroev. LC 83-26381. 144p. (Rus.). 1984. pap. 7.50 (ISBN 0-938920-20-0). Hermitage.

Brackmann, Derald E., ed. Neurological Surgery of the Ear & Skull Base. 424p. 1982. text ed. 89.00 (ISBN 0-89004-691-3). Raven.

Brackner, Joey, jt. auth. see Willett, E. Henry.

Brackner, Joey, jt. auth. see Willett, Henry.

Brackney, William, ed. Baptist Life & Thought: Sixteen Hundred to Nineteen Eughty. 448p. 1983. 25.00 (ISBN 0-8170-0959-0). Judson.

Brackt, F. & Delanghe, R. Clifford Analysis. (Research Notes in Mathematics Ser.: No. 76). 200p. 1982. pap. text ed. 25.95 (ISBN 0-273-08535-2). Pitman Pub MA.

Brackway, Edith. San Jose Reflections. 1977. 10.25 (ISBN 0-912314-18-4); pap. 4.25 (ISBN 0-912314-17-6). Academy Santa Clara.

Bracton, Henry de. Bracton on the Laws & Customs of England, Vols. 1-4. Thorne, Samuel E., ed. LC 68-28697. Orig. Title: Legibus et Consuetudinibus Angliae. 1400p. 1968. Vols. 1 & 2. 65.00x (ISBN 0-674-08035-1, Belknap Pr); Vols. 3 & 4. 90.00x (ISBN 0-674-08038-6, Belknap Pr). Harvard U Pr.

--De Legibus et Consuetudinibus Angliae. Woodbine, G. E., ed. 1942. Vol. 4. 100.00x (ISBN 0-686-51370-3). Elliots Bks.

Bracuti, Albert E., jt. auth. see Christie, George N.

Bracy, Isabel, ed. see Tuttle, William H.

Bracy, Jane, et al. Read to Succeed. 2nd ed. (Illus.). 192p. 1980. pap. text ed. 18.95x (ISBN 0-07-007035-0). McGraw.

Bracy, Norma M. Light Bulbs. (Illus.). 22p. (gr. k up). 1984. pap. text ed. 2.00 (ISBN 0-915783-01-0). Book Binder.

--Rule of Gold. (Illus.). 20p. (gr. k-12). 1983. pap. text ed. 2.00g (ISBN 0-915783-00-2). Book Binder.

Bracy, William. The Merry Wives of Windsor. 154p. 1981. Repr. of 1952 ed. lib. bdg. 30.00 (ISBN 0-89987-067-8). Darby Bks.

Bradac, G. B. & Oberson, R. Angiography & Computed Tomography in Cerebroarterial Occlusive Diseases. (Illus.). 290p. 1983. 70.00 (ISBN 0-387-11453-X). Springer-Verlag.

Bradac, James J., jt. auth. see Berger, Charles R.

Bradach, Wilfred, jt. auth. see Johnson, Thomas M.

Bradach, Wilfrid, tr. see Johnson, Thomas M.

Bradbard, Marilyn, jt. auth. see Endsley, Richard.

Bradbeer, Grace. The Land Changed Its Face: The Evacuation of Devon's South Hams 1943-44. (Illus.). 152p. 1973. 4.95 (ISBN 0-7153-5781-6). David & Charles.

Bradbeer, Robin. Learning to Use the Dragon 32 Computer: A Gower Read-out Publication. (Learning to Use Computer Ser.). (Illus.). 112p. (Orig.). 1983. pap. text ed. 12.00x (ISBN 0-566-03494-8). Gower Pub Co.

--Learning to Use the ZX Spectrum. (Learning to Use Computer Series, A Gower Read-Out Publication). 96p. (Orig.). 1982. pap. text ed. 12.00x (ISBN 0-566-03481-6). Gower Pub Co.

--Learning to Use the ZX-81 Computer. (Learning to Use Computer Series, A Gower Read-Out Publication). 86p. (Orig.). 1982. pap. text ed. 12.00x (ISBN 0-566-03451-4). Gower Pub Co.

--Robin Bradbeer's Personal Computer Book. 3rd ed. 288p. 1984. text ed. 23.50x (ISBN 0-566-03507-3). Gower Pub Co.

Bradbeer, Robin & Allason, Julian. Choosing & Using a Business Microcomputer. 176p. 1982. text ed. 32.50x (ISBN 0-566-03405-0). Gower Pub Co.

Bradbeer, Robin, jt. auth. see Bawtree, Michael.

Bradbeer, Robin & Gale, Harold, eds. The Times Book of Computer Puzzles & Games for the Commodore 64. (Illus.). 144p. 1985. pap. 11.95 (ISBN 0-283-99163-1, Pub. by Sidgwick & Jackson). Merrimack Pub Cir.

Bradbeer, Robin, et al. The Beginner's Guide to Computers: Everything You Need to Know about the New Technology. (Illus.). 208p. 1982. pap. 10.95 (ISBN 0-201-11209-4). Addison-Wesley.

Bradbery, Jean, jt. auth. see Service, Alastair.

Bradbrook, F. W., ed. see Austen, Jane.

Bradbrook, Frank W. Jane Austen & Her Predecessors. 1966. 39.50 (ISBN 0-521-04304-2). Cambridge U Pr.

--Jane Austen & Her Predecessors. LC 66-10245. pap. 46.80 (ISBN 0-317-28011-2, 2025577). Bks Demand UMI.

Bradbrook, M. C. Artist & Society in Shakespeare's England. LC 82-6645. (The Collected Papers: Vol. 1). 188p. 1982. text ed. 26.75x (ISBN 0-389-20294-0, 07129). B&N Imports.

--Shakespeare & Elizabethan Poetry: A Study of His Earlier Work in Relation to the Poetry of the Time. 1978. Repr. of 1961 ed. lib. bdg. 30.00 (ISBN 0-8492-3520-0). R West.

--T. S. Eliot. Dobree, Bonamy, et al, eds. Bd. with W. H. Auden. Hoggart, Richard; Dylan Thomas. Fraser, G. S. LC 64-17226. (British Writers & Their Work Ser: Vol. 5). vi, 160p. 1965. pap. 2.95x (ISBN 0-8032-5655-8, BB 454, Bison). U of Nebr Pr.

--Women & Literature: Seventeen Seventy-Nine to Nineteen Eighty-Two. LC 82-13914. (The Collected Papers of Muriel Bradbrook: Vol. II). 182p. 1983. text ed. 26.75x (ISBN 0-389-20295-9, 07130). B&N Imports.

Bradbrook, M. C., jt. auth. see Coghill, Nevill.

Bradbrook, M. C., ed. The Queen's Garland. 74p. 1983. 65.00 (ISBN 0-317-18879-8, Pub. by Boydell & Brewer). Longwood Pub Group.

Bradbrook, Muriel. Muriel Bradbrook on Shakespeare. LC 84-6273. 176p. 1984. 26.50x (ISBN 0-389-20487-0, 08049); pap. 11.95x (ISBN 0-389-20488-9, 08050). B&N Imports.

Bradbrook, Muriel C. Aspects of Dramatic Forms in the English & the Irish Renaissance. LC 83-6014. (Collected Papers of Muriel Bradbrook: Vol. 3). 204p. 1983. text ed. 26.75x (ISBN 0-389-20296-7, 07131). B&N Imports.

--The Growth & Structure of Elizabethan Comedy. LC 79-2313. (History of Elizabethan Drama Ser.: Vol. 2). 1979. pap. 12.95 (ISBN 0-521-29526-2). Cambridge U Pr.

--John Webster. 230p. 1980. 24.00x (ISBN 0-231-05162-X). Columbia U Pr.

--The Living Monument: Shakespeare & the Theatre of His Time. LC 79-2317. (History of Elizabethan Drama Ser.: Vol. 6). (Illus.). 1976. 39.50 (ISBN 0-521-21255-3); pap. 11.95 (ISBN 0-521-29530-0). Cambridge U Pr.

--The Rise of the Common Player. LC 79-2314. (History of Elizabethan Drama Ser.: Vol. 3). (Illus.). 1979. pap. 12.95 (ISBN 0-521-29527-0). Cambridge U Pr.

--Shakespeare & the Elizabethan Poetry. LC 79-2315. (History of Elizabethan Drama Ser.: Vol. 4). (Illus.). 1979. pap. 12.95 (ISBN 0-521-29528-9). Cambridge U Pr.

--Shakespeare the Craftsman. LC 79-2316. (History of Elizabethan Drama Ser.: Vol. 5). (Illus.). 1979. pap. 11.95 (ISBN 0-521-29529-7). Cambridge U Pr.

--Shakespeare: The Poet in His World. LC 78-7611. 272p. 1978. 26.00x (ISBN 0-231-04648-0); pap. 11.00x (ISBN 0-231-04649-9). Columbia U Pr.

--Themes & Conventions of Elizabethan Tragedy. 2nd ed. (A History of Elizabethan Drama Ser.). 270p. 1980. 49.50 (ISBN 0-521-22770-4); pap. 16.95 (ISBN 0-521-29695-1). Cambridge U Pr.

Bradburn, Frances B., jt. ed. see Hodges, Gerald.

Bradburn, Norman M. Structure of Psychological Well-Being. LC 67-27388. (NORC Monographs in Social Research Ser.: No. 15). (Illus.). 1969. 12.95x (ISBN 0-202-25029-6). NORC.

Bradburn, Norman M. & Caplovitz, David. Reports on Happiness: A Pilot Study of Behavior Related to Mental Health. LC 64-15605. (NORC Monographs in Social Research Ser.: No. 3). 1965. 9.95x (ISBN 0-202-30020-X). NORC.

Bradburn, Norman M. & Sudman, Seymour. Improving Interview Method & Questionnaire Design: Response Effects to Threatening Questions in Survey Research. LC 79-83569. (Social & Behavioral Science Ser.). (Illus.). 1979. text ed. 18.95x (ISBN 0-87589-402-X). Jossey-Bass.

Bradburn, Norman M., jt. auth. see Sudman, Seymour.

Bradburn, Norman M, et al. Racial Integration in American Neighborhoods: A Comparative Study. (Report Ser: No. IIIB). 6.50x (ISBN 0-932132-08-1). NORC.

Bradburn, Norman M., et al. Side by Side. 208p. pap. 2.95 (ISBN 0-686-74895-6). ADL.

Bradbury, A. J. Adventure Games for the Commodore 64. 194p. 1985. pap. 10.95 (ISBN 0-13-014002-3). P H.

Bradbury, Bianca. The Girl Who Wanted Out. 192p. (Orig.). (gr. 7 up). 1981. pap. 1.95 (ISBN 0-590-32122-6, Wishing Star Bks). Scholastic Inc.

--The Loving Year. 160p. (Orig.). (gr. 7 up). 1982. pap. 1.95 (ISBN 0-590-32174-9, Wishing Star Bks). Scholastic Inc.

--Mixed-up Summer. (gr. 7 up). 1979. 7.95 (ISBN 0-395-27816-3). HM.

Bradbury, D. E., jt. ed. see Thrower, Norman J.

Bradbury, E. M. & Javaherian, K., eds. The Organization & Expression of the Eukaryotic Genome. 1977. 78.00 (ISBN 0-12-123550-5). Acad Pr.

Bradbury, E. Morton & Maclean, Norman. DNA, Chromatin & Chromosomes. Mathews, H., ed. LC 81-3321. 281p. 1981. 29.95x (ISBN 0-470-27173-6); pap. 32.95. Halsted Pr.

Bradbury, F., ed. Technology Transfer Practice on International Firms. 324p. 1978. 37.50x (ISBN 9-0286-0377-8). Sijthoff & Noordhoff.

Bradbury, F. P. & Jervis, R., eds. Transfer Processes in Technical Change. 290p. 1978. 40.00x (ISBN 90-286-0347-6). Sijthoff & Noordhoff.

Bradbury, Frances. Antique Lace Patterns. (International Design Library). (Illus.). 48p. 1985. pap. 3.50 (ISBN 0-88045-070-3). Stemmer Hse.

Bradbury, Frances M. English Crewel Designs: Sixteenth to Eighteenth Centuries. (The International Design Library). (Illus.). 56p. (Orig.). 1982. pap. 3.50 (ISBN 0-88045-015-0). Stemmer Hse.

--Faience Designs. (International Design Library). (Illus.). 48p. (Orig.). 1984. pap. 3.50 (ISBN 0-88045-056-8). Stemmer Hse.

Bradbury, Frederick. Bradbury's Book of Hallmarks. Rev. ed. 108p. (Orig.). pap. 5.50 (ISBN 0-901100-11-0, Pub by JW Northend England). Seven Hills Bks.

--History of Old Sheffield Plate. (Illus.). 539p. 1983. Repr. of 1912 ed. 65.00 (ISBN 0-901100-03-X, Pub by JW Northend England). Seven Hills Bks.

Bradbury, J. S., et al, eds. Turbulent Shear Flows, Two. (Illus.). 480p. 1980. 78.00 (ISBN 0-387-10067-9). Springer-Verlag.

Bradbury, Jim. The Medieval Archer. (Illus.). 192p. 1985. cancelled (ISBN 0-85115-194-9, Pub. by Boydell & Brewer). Longwood Pub Group.

--The Medieval Archer. (Illus.). 179p. 1985. 29.95 (ISBN 0-312-52665-2). St Martin.

--Shakespeare & His Theatre. Reeves, Marjorie, ed. (Then & There Ser.). (Illus.). 95p. (Orig.). (gr. 7-12). 1977. pap. text ed. 3.75 (ISBN 0-582-20539-5). Longman.

Bradbury, John M. The Fugitives. 1958. pap. 7.95x (ISBN 0-8084-0139-4). New Coll U Pr.

Bradbury, John P. Diatom Stratigraphy & Human Settlement in Minnesota. LC 75-21066. (Geological Society of America Special Papers: No. 171). pap. 20.00 (ISBN 0-317-29090-8, 2023739). Bks Demand UMI.

Bradbury, Katharine L. & Downs, Anthony. Energy Costs, Urban Development, & Housing. new ed. LC 83-46033. 296p. 1984. 31.95 (ISBN 0-8157-1050-X); pap. 11.95 (ISBN 0-8157-1049-6). Brookings.

Bradbury, Katharine L., ed. Do Housing Allowances Work? Downs, Anthony. LC 81-6689. (Studies in Social Experimentation). 430p. 1981. 29.95 (ISBN 0-8157-1052-6); pap. 12.95 (ISBN 0-8157-1051-8). Brookings.

Bradbury, Katherine, et al. Futures for a Declining City: Simulations for the Cleveland Area. LC 81-10857. (Studies in Urban Economics). 1981. 35.00 (ISBN 0-12-123580-7). Acad Pr.

Bradbury, Katherine L. & Downs, Anthony. Urban Decline & the Future of American Cities. LC 82-70888. 309p. 1982. 29.95 (ISBN 0-8157-1054-2); pap. 11.95 (ISBN 0-8157-1053-4). Brookings.

Bradbury, L. J. & Durst, F., eds. Turbulent Shear Flows Four. (Illus.). 370p. 1985. 58.00 (ISBN 0-387-13744-0). Springer-Verlag.

Bradbury, L. J., et al. Turbulent Shear Flow 3rd: University of California, Selected Papers, 1981. (Illus.). 321p. 1982. 69.00 (ISBN 0-387-11817-9). Springer-Verlag.

Bradbury, M. & Palmer, D., eds. American Theatre. (Stratford-Upon-Avon Studies: No. 10). 228p. 1967. pap. text ed. 11.75x (ISBN 0-8419-5816-5). Holmes & Meier.

Bradbury, Malcolm. All Dressed Up & Nowhere to Go. 192p. 1983. 14.95 (ISBN 0-907516-16-5, Pub. by Michael Joseph). Merrimack Pub Cir.

--The Modern American Novel. 1983. 22.00x (ISBN 0-19-212591-5); pap. 7.95x (ISBN 0-19-289044-1). Oxford U Pr.

--Rates of Exchange. 320p. 1985. pap. 6.95 (ISBN 0-14-007631-X). Penguin.

--Saul Bellow. (Contemporary Writers Ser.). 96p. 1982. pap. 4.75x (ISBN 0-416-31650-6, NO. 3559). Methuen Inc.

Bradbury, Malcolm & McFarlane, James. Modernism. (Pelican Ser.). 1978. pap. 5.95 (ISBN 0-14-021933-1, Pelican). Penguin.

Bradbury, Malcolm & Palmer, David, eds. Contemporary Criticism. (Stratford-Upon-Avon Studies: No. 12). 219p. 1979. pap. text ed. 14.25x (ISBN 0-8419-5818-1). Holmes & Meier.

--The Contemporary English Novel. LC 79-20447. (Stratford-Upon-Avon Studies: No. 18). 214p. 1980. text ed. 31.75x (ISBN 0-8419-0570-3); pap. text ed. 15.50x (ISBN 0-8419-0571-1). Holmes & Meier.

--Contemporary Theatre. (Stratford-Upon-Avon Studies: No. 4). 208p. 1979. pap. text ed. 15.00x (ISBN 0-8419-5811-4). Holmes & Meier.

--Medieval Drama. (Stratford-Upon-Avon Studies: No. 16). 254p. 1973. text ed. 27.50x (ISBN 0-8419-5824-6); pap. text ed. 19.50 (ISBN 0-8419-5823-8). Holmes & Meier.

--Metaphysical Poetry. (Stratford-Upon-Avon Studies: No. 11). 280p. 1970. text ed. 19.50x (ISBN 0-8419-5817-3). Holmes & Meier.

--Shakespearean Tragedy. LC 84-81206. (Stratford-upon-Avon Ser.: Vol. 20). 192p. 1984. text ed. 32.50x (ISBN 0-8419-0981-4); Oct. 1984. pap. text ed. 13.95x (ISBN 0-8419-0982-2). Holmes & Meier.

--Shakespearian Comedy. (Stratford-Upon-Avon Studies: No. 14). 247p. 1979. pap. text ed. 11.50x (ISBN 0-8419-5820-3). Holmes & Meier.

--Victorian Poetry. (Stratford-Upon-Avon Studies: No. 15). 304p. 1979. pap. text ed. 12.50x (ISBN 0-8419-5821-1). Holmes & Meier.

Bradbury, Malcolm & Temperley, Howard, eds. Introduction to American Studies. LC 79-42620. (Illus.). 352p. (Orig.). 1981. pap. text ed. 12.50x (ISBN 0-582-48904-0). Longman.

Bradbury, Malcolm, ed. see Twain, Mark.

Bradbury, Malcom. The History Man. (Fiction Ser.). 240p. 1985. pap. 6.95 (ISBN 0-14-007630-1). Penguin.

Bradbury, Michael. The Concept of a Blood-Brain Barrier. LC 79-16764. 465p. 1979. 99.95x (ISBN 0-471-99688-2, Pub. by Wiley-Interscience). Wiley.

Bradbury, Nicola. Henry James: The Later Novels. 1979. text ed. 42.00x (ISBN 0-19-812096-6). Oxford U Pr.

Bradbury, R. E. The Benin Kingdom & the Edo-Speaking Peoples of South-Western Nigeria. (Ethnographic Survey of Africa, Western Africa Ser.: Pt. 13). pap. 53.80 (ISBN 0-317-28626-9, 2055383). Bks Demand UMI.

--Benin Studies. Morton-Williams, Peter, intro. by. (International African Institute Ser). (Illus.). 1973. pap. 18.95x (ISBN 0-19-724198-0). Oxford U Pr.

Bradbury, Ray. The Art of Playboy. LC 85-40100. (Illus.). 176p. 1985. 27.50 (ISBN 0-912383-19-4). Van der Marck.

--The Complete Poems of Ray Bradbury. 288p. 1982. pap. 2.95 (ISBN 0-345-30556-6, Del Rey). Ballantine.

--Dandelion Wine. (gr. 6 up). 1969. pap. 2.95 (ISBN 0-553-25236-4). Bantam.

--Dandelion Wine. 1975. 14.95 (ISBN 0-394-49605-1). Knopf.

--Death is a Lonely Business. Nicholas, Nancy, ed. LC 85-40221. 320p. 1985. 15.95 (ISBN 0-394-54702-0). Knopf.

--Dinosaur Tales. 144p. 1984. pap. 2.50 (ISBN 0-553-24614-3). Bantam.

--Fahrenheit Four Fifty-One. (Orig.). 1979. pap. 2.25 (ISBN 0-345-29234-0). Ballantine.

--Fahrenheit Four Fifty One. 176p. 1981. pap. 5.95 (ISBN 0-345-29466-1, Del Rey). Ballantine.

--Fahrenheit Four Fifty-One. 1967. 15.95 (ISBN 0-671-23977-5). S&S.

--Forever & the Earth. LC 84-1896. 43p. 1984. 40.00, ltd. to 300 signed, numbered copies (ISBN 0-912348-12-7). Croissant & Co.

--Golden Apples of the Sun. LC 76-135242. (Illus.). 1971. Repr. of 1953 ed. lib. bdg. 25.00x (ISBN 0-8371-5160-0, BRGA). Greenwood.

--The Halloween Tree. 192p. (gr. 7 up). 1982. pap. 2.75 (ISBN 0-553-25108-2). Bantam.

--The Haunted Computer & the Android Pope. LC 80-2724. 128p. 1981. 8.95 (ISBN 0-394-51444-0). Knopf.

--I Sing the Body Electric. 1976. pap. 3.50 (ISBN 0-553-25308-5). Bantam.

--I Sing the Body Electric. LC 75-88745. (YA) 1969. 13.50 (ISBN 0-394-42985-0). Knopf.

--Illustrated Man. (gr. 6-12). 1969. pap. 2.95 (ISBN 0-553-25483-9). Bantam.

--Illustrated Man. (Science Fiction Ser.). 1958. 7.95 (ISBN 0-385-04218-3). Doubleday.

--Kaleidoscope. 15.95 (ISBN 0-89190-886-2, Pub. by Am Repr). Amereon Ltd.

--The Last Circus. 50p. 1980. 15.00 (ISBN 0-935716-03-3); deluxe signed ed. 50.00 (ISBN 0-935716-04-1). Lord John.

--The Last Good Kiss. 1984. 400.00 (ISBN 0-937048-35-6). CSUN.

--Long After Midnight. 1976. 16.95 (ISBN 0-394-47942-4). Knopf.

--The Love Affair. 40p. 1983. DEC Limited signed ed. 35.00 (ISBN 0-935716-17-3). Lord John.

--Martian Chronicles. 192p. (gr. 9-12). 1974. pap. 2.95 (ISBN 0-553-24691-7). Bantam.

--The Martian Chronicles. LC 58-8207. (Science Fiction Ser.). 1958. 14.95 (ISBN 0-385-05060-7). Doubleday.

--The Martian Chronicles. 15.95 (ISBN 0-88411-862-2, Pub. by Aeonian Pr). Amereon Ltd.

--A Memory of Murder. (Orig.). 1984. pap. 2.95 (ISBN 0-440-15559-2). Dell.

--October Country. 1985. pap. 2.95 (ISBN 0-345-32448-X). Ballantine.

--October Country. (YA) 1970. 12.50 (ISBN 0-394-43892-2). Knopf.

--One Timeless Spring. 17.95 (ISBN 0-89190-345-3, Pub. by Am Repr). Amereon Ltd.

--R Is for Rocket. (gr. 9-12). 1969. pap. 2.95 (ISBN 0-553-25040-X). Bantam.

--Something Wicked This Way Comes. (gr. 6-12). pap. 2.95 (ISBN 0-553-23620-2). Bantam.

--Something Wicked This Way Comes. LC 82-48732. 1983. 15.95 (ISBN 0-394-53041-1). Knopf.

--The Stories of Ray Bradbury. LC 80-7655. 928p. 1980. 20.00 (ISBN 0-394-51335-5). Knopf.

--Twice Twenty-Two. LC 66-10615. (Science Fiction Ser.). 1966. 14.95 (ISBN 0-385-05594-3). Doubleday.

--Vintage Bradbury. 1965. pap. 2.95 (ISBN 0-394-74059-9, Vin, V294). Random.

--When Elephants Last in Dooryard Bloomed. 1973. 8.95 (ISBN 0-394-47931-9). Knopf.

--Where Robot Mice & Robot Men Run Round in Robot Towns. 1977. 6.95 (ISBN 0-394-42206-6). Knopf.

Bradbury, Ray, jt. auth. see West Light Staff.

Bradbury, Ray see Nolan, William F.

Bradbury, Ronald. The Romantic Theories of Architecture of the 19th Century, in Germany, England & France. LC 75-28994. Repr. of 1934 ed. 11.50 (ISBN 0-404-14005-X). AMS Pr.

Bradbury, Samuel, ed. see American Society for Metals.

Bradbury, Savile. An Introduction to the Optical Microscope. (Royal Microscopical Society Handbooks Ser.). (Illus.). 1984. pap. 7.95x (ISBN 0-19-856401-5). Oxford U Pr.

--Optical Microscope in Biology. (Studies in Biology: No. 59). 80p. 1976. pap. text ed. 8.95 (ISBN 0-7131-2533-0). E Arnold.

Bradbury, Ted C. Mathematical Methods with Applications to Problems in the Physical Sciences. LC 84-3530. 702p. 1984. text ed. 39.95 (ISBN 0-471-88639-4, Pub. by Wiley). Wiley.

--Theoretical Mechanics. LC 80-23957. 656p. 1981. Repr. of 1968 ed. text ed. 36.50 (ISBN 0-89874-235-8). Krieger.

Bradbury, William & Guild, Courtenay. History of the Handel & Haydn Society, Vol. 2. (Music Reprint Ser.). 1979. Repr. of 1893 ed. lib. bdg. 45.00 (ISBN 0-306-79506-X). Da Capo.

Bradbury, William C. Mass Behaviour in Battle & Captivity: The Communist Soldier in the Korean War. Meyers, Samuel M., ed. LC 68-16705. pap. 101.80 (ISBN 0-317-08308-2, 2020034). Bks Demand UMI.

Bradby, David. Modern French Drama, Nineteen Forty to Nineteen Eighty. (Illus.). 304p. 1984. 49.50 (ISBN 0-521-26247-X); pap. 15.95 (ISBN 0-521-27881-3). Cambridge U Pr.

--The Theatre of Roger Planchon. (Theatre in Focus Ser.). (Illus.). 56p. 1984. pap. 55.00 incl. 50 slides (ISBN 0-85964-153-8). Chadwyck-Healey.

Bradby, David & McCormick, John. People's Theatre. 179p. 1978. 16.00x (ISBN 0-8476-6073-7). Rowman.

Bradby, David, et al. Studying Drama: A Handbook. 287p. 1984. 36.50x (ISBN 0-7099-0650-1, Pub. by Salem Acad). Merrimack Pub Cir.

Bradby, David, et al, eds. Performance & Politics in Popular Drama: Aspects of Popular Entertainment in Theatre, Film & Television, 1800-1976. LC 79-12036. (Illus.). 1980. 37.50 (ISBN 0-521-22755-0). Cambridge U Pr.

--Performance & Politics in Popular Drama: Aspects of Popular Entertainment in Theatre, Film & Television 1800-1976. LC 79-12036. (Illus.). 360p. 1982. pap. 14.95 (ISBN 0-521-28524-0). Cambridge U Pr.

Bradby, Edward, ed. University Outside Europe. facsimile ed. LC 71-107684. (Essay Index Reprint Ser.). 1939. 20.00 (ISBN 0-8369-1548-8). Ayer Co Pubs.

Bradby, G. About Shakespeare & His Plays. LC 76-51373. (Studies in Shakespeare: No. 24). 1977. lib. bdg. 33.95x (ISBN 0-8383-2121-6). Haskell.

--Short Studies in Shakespeare. LC 76-30728. (Studies in Shakespeare, No. 24). 1977. lib. bdg. 42.95x (ISBN 0-8383-2169-0). Haskell.

Bradby, G. F. About Shakespeare & His Plays. 1978. Repr. of 1926 ed. lib. bdg. 10.00 (ISBN 0-8482-3390-5). Norwood Edns.

--Problems of Hamlet. (Studies in Shakespeare, No. 24). 1970. pap. 22.95x (ISBN 0-8383-0006-5). Haskell.

--Short Studies in Shakespeare. 1978. Repr. of 1929 ed. lib. bdg. 20.00 (ISBN 0-8482-3391-3). Norwood Edns.

Bradby, Godfrey F. About English Poetry. LC 76-43990. 1976. Repr. of 1932 ed. lib. bdg. 10.00 (ISBN 0-8414-1766-0). Folcroft.

--About English Poetry. 1932. Repr. 10.00 (ISBN 0-8274-1812-4). R West.

--Brontes, & Other Essays. facs. ed. LC 67-30176. (Essay Index Reprint Ser). 1932. 15.00 (ISBN 0-8369-0240-8). Ayer Co Pubs.

Braddick, Bill, jt. auth. see Boyle, Denis.

Braddick, Henderson B. Germany, Czechoslovakia, & the "Grand Alliance" in the May Crisis, 1938. (Monographs Series in World Affairs: Vol. 6, 1968-69, Bk. 2). 49p. (Orig.). 1969. 4.95 (ISBN 0-87940-019-6). Monograph Series.

Braddick, O. J. & Sleigh, A. C., eds. Physical & Biological Processing of Images: London, England, 1982, Proceedings. (Springer Series in Information Sciences: Vol. 11). (Illus.). 403p. 1983. 36.00 (ISBN 0-387-12108-0). Springer-Verlag.

Braddock, D. W. The Campaigns in Egypt & Libya: Nineteen Forty to Forty-Two. 1964. pap. 3.95 (ISBN 0-685-56055-4). Beachcomber Bks.

Braddock, David. Opening Closed Doors: The Deinstitutionalization of Disabled Individuals. LC 77-72050. 1977. pap. text ed. 3.75 (ISBN 0-86586-059-9). Coun Exc Child.

Braddock, Karen S., jt. auth. see Guthrie, Helen A.

Braddon, M. E. Lady Audley's Secret. (Illus.). 320p. 1974. pap. 5.00 (ISBN 0-486-23011-2). Dover.

Braddon, Russell. Japan Against the World. 304p. 1984. 16.95 (ISBN 0-8128-2941-7); pap. 3.95 (ISBN 0-8128-8102-8). Stein & Day.
--Japan Against the World, 1941-2041: The One Hundred Year War for Supremacy. LC 83-40078. 256p. 1983. 16.95 (ISBN 0-8128-2941-7). Stein & Day.
--The Thirteenth Trick. LC 73-665. 168p. 1973. 5.95 (ISBN 0-393-08375-6). Norton.
Braddy, Haldeen. Chaucer & the French Poet Graunson. LC 68-16278. 1968. Repr. of 1947 ed. 15.00x (ISBN 0-8046-0039-2, Pub. by Kennikat). Assoc Faculty Pr.
--Chaucer's Parlement of Foules. LC 78-84176. 1969. Repr. of 1932 ed. lib. bdg. 16.50x (ISBN 0-374-90931-8). Octagon.
--Mexico & the Old Southwest: People, Palaver, & Places. LC 71-141307. 1971. 16.50x (ISBN 0-8046-9001-4, Pub. by Kennikat); pap. 9.50 (ISBN 0-8046-9046-4). Assoc Faculty Pr.
--The Paradox of Pancho Villa. Antone, E. H., ed. (Illus.). 1978. 10.00 (ISBN 0-87404-059-0). Tex Western.
--Pershing's Mission in Mexico. LC 66-26835. 1979. 10.00 (ISBN 0-87404-008-6). Tex Western.
--Three Dimensional Poe. LC 73-75915. 1973. 10.00 (ISBN 0-87404-045-0). Tex Western.
Braddy, Nella, ed. Standard Book of British & American Verse: Preface by Christopher Morley. facsimile ed. LC 72-38594. (Granger Index Reprint Ser.). Repr. of 1932 ed. 34.00 (ISBN 0-8369-6326-1). Ayer Co Pubs.
Brade, W., et al. Proceedings of the International Vinca Alkaloid Symposium: Vindesine. Nagel, G. & Seeber, S., eds. (Beitraege zur Onkologie, Contributions to Oncology: Vol. 6). xii, 460p. 1981. 33.75 (ISBN 3-8055-2501-X). S Karger.
Bradeen, D., ed. Louise Taft Semple Lectures, First Series, 1961-65. (Cincinnati Classical Studies Ser., Vol. 1). 1967. 36.00x (ISBN 0-691-03827-9). Princeton U Pr.
Bradeen, Donald W. Inscriptions: The Funerary Monuments. LC 75-332165. (The Athenian Agora Ser.: Vol. 17). (Illus.). 1974. 25.00x (ISBN 0-87661-217-6). Am Sch Athens.
Bradeen, Donald W. & McGregor, Malcolm F. Studies in Fifth-Century Attic Epigraphy. LC 72-9258. (Illus.). 150p. 1974. 14.95x (ISBN 0-8061-1064-3); pap. 7.95x (ISBN 0-8061-1364-2). U of Okla Pr.
Braden, Beatrice. Sex Was More Fun When... rev. ed. 80p. 1973. pap. 1.75 (ISBN 0-8431-0210-1). Price Stern.
Braden, C. The Focus & Limits of Community Health Nursing. 496p. 1983. 29.95 (ISBN 0-8385-2633-0). ACC.
Braden, C. S. Religious Aspects of the Conquest of Mexico. 1976. lib. bdg. 59.95 (ISBN 0-8490-2510-9). Gordon Pr.
Braden, Carrie J., et al. Community Health: A Systems Approach. 291p. 1976. pap. 14.95. ACC.
Braden, Charles see Carroll, John M.
Braden, Charles S. Christian Science Today: Power, Policy, Practice. LC 58-11399. 1958. 19.95 (ISBN 0-87074-024-5). SMU Press.
--Religious Aspects of the Conquest of Mexico. LC 74-181914. Repr. of 1930 ed. 37.50 (ISBN 0-404-00925-5). AMS Pr.
--Spirits in Rebellion: The Rise & Development of New Thought. LC 63-13245. 584p. 1963. pap. 15.95 (ISBN 0-87074-025-3). SMU Press.
Braden, Charles S., ed. Varieties of American Religion. facsimile ed. LC 76-156616. (Essay Index Reprint Ser). Repr. of 1936 ed. 15.50 (ISBN 0-8369-2307-3). Ayer Co Pubs.
Braden, Dennis. In Things Completed. (Illus.). 32p. 1985. write for info. (ISBN 0-916906-29-9); pap. write for info. (ISBN 0-916906-28-0). Konglomerati.
Braden, Gordon. The Classics & English Renaissance Poetry: Three Case Studies. LC 77-10888. (Studies in English Ser.: No. 187). 1978. 30.00x (ISBN 0-300-02154-2). Yale U Pr.
--Renaissance Tragedy & the Senecan Tradition: Anger's Privilege. LC 84-21029. 256p. 1985. text ed. 21.00x (ISBN 0-300-03253-6). Yale U Pr.
Braden, John. Barbie Dream Vacation. (Illus.). 32p. (Orig.). 1984. 8.98 (ISBN 0-87660-002-X). I J E Bk Pub.
--Dear Poochie. 32p. (Orig.). 1984. 8.98 (ISBN 0-87660-015-1). I J E Bk Pub.
--G. I. Joe: Operation Outer Space. (Illus.). 32p. (Orig.). 1984. 8.98 (ISBN 0-87660-001-1). I J E Bk Pub.
--G. I. Joe: Operation Sandstory. (Illus.). 32p. (Orig.). 1984. 8.98 (ISBN 0-87660-010-0). I J E Bk Pub.
--Mr. Potato Head Meets the Creepers. (Illus.). 32p. (Orig.). 1984. 8.98 (ISBN 0-87660-006-2). I J E Bk Pub.
--My Little Pony Adventure Book. (Illus.). 32p. (Orig.). 1984. 8.98 (ISBN 0-87660-009-7). I J E Bk Pub.
Braden, Patricia L. Technological Entrepreneurship: The Allocation of Money & Effort in Technology-Based Firms. (Michigan Business Reports: No. 62). (Illus.). 1977. pap. 5.00 (ISBN 0-87712-187-7). U Mich Busn Div Res.
Braden, Tom. Eight Is Enough. 1977. pap. 2.25 (ISBN 0-449-23002-3, Crest). Fawcett.
Braden, Vic & Bruns, Bill. Teaching Children Tennis the Vic Braden Way. (A Sports Illustrated Bk). (Illus.). 1980. pap. 10.95 (ISBN 0-316-10513-9). Little.
--Vic Braden's Tennis for the Future. 1977. 24.45i (ISBN 0-316-10510-4); pap. 12.45 (ISBN 0-316-10511-2). Little.
Braden, Waldo see Braden, Waldo W. & Peterson, Owen.
Braden, Waldo W. The Oral Tradition in the South. LC 82-20827. 152p. 1983. text ed. 17.50x (ISBN 0-8071-1093-0). La State U Pr.
Braden, Waldo W., ed. Oratory in the New South. LC 78-25909. x, 296p. 1979. 27.50x (ISBN 0-8071-0472-8). La State U Pr.
Braden, Waldo W. & Peterson, Owen, eds. Representative American Speeches. Incl. 1966-1967. Thonssen, Lester, ed. 197p. 1969; 1968-1969. Thonssen, Lester, ed. 200p. 1969; 1969-1970 up to 1979-1989. Braden, Waldo, ed. 1970 (ISBN 0-8242-0412-3); 1970-1971. Braden, Waldo W., ed. 200p. 1971; 1971-1972. 200p. 1972 (ISBN 0-8242-0467-0); 1972-1973. 1973 (ISBN 0-8242-0507-3); 1973-1974. 1974 (ISBN 0-8242-0524-3); 1974-1975. 1975 (ISBN 0-8242-0572-3); 1975-1976. 1976 (ISBN 0-8242-0598-7); 1976-1977. 1977; 1977-78. 1978 (ISBN 0-8242-0625-8); 1978-1979. 1979 (ISBN 0-8242-0634-7); 1979-1980. 1980 (ISBN 0-8242-0648-7); 1980-1981. Peterson, Owen, ed. LC 81-16070. 1981 (ISBN 0-8242-0657-6); 1981-1982. Peterson, Owen, ed. 1982. 8.00 (ISBN 0-8242-0669-X). LC 38-27962. (Reference Shelf Ser.). 8.00x ea. Wilson.
Braden, Waldo W., ed. see Channing, Edward T.
Brader, Norma. Settling the Score. (Candlelight Ecstasy Ser.: No. 244). 192p. (Orig.). 1984. pap. 1.95 (ISBN 0-440-17660-3). Dell.
Bradfield, Byron. White River Pete Sez. 1978. pap. 4.50 (ISBN 0-917624-08-4). Lame Johnny.
Bradfield, Cecil D. Neo-Pentecostalism: A Sociological Assessment. LC 79-66228. 1979. pap. text ed. 8.00 (ISBN 0-8191-0809-X). U Pr of Amer.
Bradfield, E. G., ed. Franklin in Numismatics: An Anthology. (Illus.). 1982. pap. 8.00 (ISBN 0-942666-05-4). S J Durst.
Bradfield, Keith, tr. from Swedish. The Testament of Cain. Bradfield, Kieth. cancelled (ISBN 0-86538-019-8); pap. cancelled (ISBN 0-686-32482-X). Ontario Rev NJ.
Bradfield, Kieth see Bradfield, Keith.
Bradfield, Maitland. Birds of the Hopi Region, Their Hopi Names, & Notes on Their Ecology. (MNA Bulletin Ser.: No. 48). 1974. pap. 7.50 (ISBN 0-89734-006-X). Mus Northern Ariz.
Bradfield, Nancy. Costume in Detail. 1983 ed. (Illus.). 391p. 1983. 24.95 (ISBN 0-8238-0260-4). Plays.
Bradfield, R. The Changing Pattern of Hopi Agriculture. 1971. 40.00x (ISBN 0-686-98307-6, Pub. by Royal Anthro Ireland). State Mutual Bk.
Bradfield, Richard M. Natural History of Associations: A Study in the Meaning of Community. LC 73-5577. (Vol. 1 LC 73-5577; vol. 2, LC 73-5578). 1973. Set. text ed. 60.00x (ISBN 0-8236-8403-2). Vol. 1, 428p (ISBN 0-8236-3495-7). Vol. 2, 596p (ISBN 0-8236-3496-5). Intl Univs Pr.
Bradfield, Robert, ed. Advertiser's Annual, 1979. 54th ed. LC 49-14603. 1979. 47.50x (ISBN 0-610-00519-7). Intl Pubns Serv.
--Who's Who in Education. 926p. 1974. 37.50x (ISBN 0-686-15410-X, BMA 02235, Pub by Intl Biog). Biblio Dist.
Bradfield, Roger. Jolly Roger Bradfield Storybooks. Incl. Flying Hockey Stock (ISBN 0-528-82415-5); Giants Come in Different Sizes (ISBN 0-528-82414-7); Benjamin Dilley's Thirsty Camel (ISBN 0-528-82417-1); Pickle-Chiffon Pie (ISBN 0-528-82416-3). (Illus.). 64p. (gr. 4-7). 7.95 ea. Rand.
Bradfield, Valerie J. Information Sources in Architecture. (Butterworths Guide to Information Sources Ser.). 419p. 1983. 75.00 (ISBN 0-408-10763-4). Butterworth.
Bradfield, Wesley. Cameron Creek Village, a Site in the Mimbres Area in Grant County, New Mexico. LC 32-4291. (Illus.). 244p. 1973. Repr. of 1931 ed. 27.00 (ISBN 0-527-10570-8). Kraus Repr.
Bradford, jt. auth. see Manchester.
Bradford, et al. International Protocols in Cancer Management. 1981. 22.50x (ISBN 0-934740-01-1). Cancer Control Soc.
Bradford, Alden. Speeches of the Governors of Massachusetts from 1765 to 1775. LC 71-119048. (Era of the American Revolution Ser). 1971. Repr. of 1818 ed. 59.50 (ISBN 0-306-71947-9). Da Capo.
Bradford, Angier, jt. auth. see Bradford, Vena.
Bradford, Ann & Gezi, Kal. The Mystery at the Tree House. LC 80-15654. (The Maple Street Five Ser.). (Illus.). 32p. (gr. 3-6). 1980. 10.35 (ISBN 0-516-06494-0). Childrens.
--The Mystery at the Tree House. LC 80-15654. (Mystery Ser.). (Illus.). 32p. (gr. k-4). 1980. PLB 7.45 (ISBN 0-89565-148-3). Childs World.
--The Mystery of the Blind Writer. LC 80-12395. (The Maple Street Five Ser.). (Illus.). 32p. (gr. 3-6). 1980. 10.35 (ISBN 0-516-06493-2). Childrens.
--The Mystery of the Midget Clown. LC 80-72513. (Mystery Ser.). (Illus.). 32p. (gr. k-4). 1980. PLB 7.45 (ISBN 0-89565-146-7). Childs World.
--The Mystery of the Missing Dogs. LC 80-10436. (Mystery Ser.). (Illus.). 32p. (gr. k-4). 1980. PLB 7.45 (ISBN 0-89565-143-2). Childs World.
Bradford, Ann, jt. auth. see Gezi, Kal.
Bradford, Barbara T. Hold the Dream: A Sequel to A Woman of Substance. LC 84-25993. 648p. 1985. 17.95 (ISBN 0-385-18128-0). Doubleday.
--Luxury Designs for Apartment Living. LC 77-16899. (Illus.). 352p. 1981. 29.95 (ISBN 0-385-12769-3). Doubleday.
--Voice of the Heart. LC 81-47863. 744p. 1983. 17.95 (ISBN 0-385-15323-6). Doubleday.
--Voice of the Heart. 784p. 1984. pap. 4.50 (ISBN 0-553-23920-1). Bantam.
--A Woman of Substance. 832p. 1983. pap. 3.95 (ISBN 0-380-49163-X, 60008-0). Avon.
--A Woman of Substance. LC 77-9231. 1984. 17.95 (ISBN 0-385-12050-8). Doubleday.
Bradford, Brick, ed. Healing for the Homosexual. 64p. 1983. 2.00x (ISBN 0-318-04137-5). Presby Ref Ren.
Bradford, Charles E. The God Between. Coffen, Richard W., ed. 96p. 1984. pap. 4.95 (ISBN 0-8280-0243-6). Review & Herald.
Bradford, Clyde M., ed. Lawyer Humor: A Collection of Humorous Stories, Definitions & Comments Relating to Lawyers & Their Work. 1981. pap. 4.95 (ISBN 0-932364-02-0). Ann Arbor Bk.
Bradford, Colin I., Jr. Forces for Change in Latin America: U. S. Policy Implications. LC 70-181831. (Monographs: No. 5). 80p. 1971. 2.00 (ISBN 0-686-28690-1). Overseas Dev Council.
Bradford, Curtis B. Yeats at Work. LC 78-5630. (Abr.). (gr. 10-12). 1978. pap. 5.95 (ISBN 0-912946-60-1). Ecco Pr.
Bradford, Curtis B., compiled by. W. B. Yeats: The Writing of "The Player Queen". LC 73-18798. 483p. 1977. 35.00 (ISBN 0-87580-048-3). N Ill U Pr.
Bradford, Daniel, ed. Solo in the City: A Sourcebook for Singles in Metropolitan Denver. 150p. (Orig.). 1985. pap. 6.95 (ISBN 0-9608012-3-5). Metro Source Pubns.
Bradford, David. VD in Australia. 224p. (Orig.). 1981. pap. 7.50x (ISBN 0-522-84225-9, Pub. by Melbourne U Pr Australia). Intl Spec Bk.
Bradford, David F. & U. S. Treasury Tax Policy Staff. Blueprints for Basic Tax Reform. 2nd rev. ed. 194p. 1984. pap. text ed. 12.50 (ISBN 0-918255-00-7). Tax Analysts.
Bradford, David L. & Cohen, Allan R. Managing for Excellence: The Guide to Developing High Performance in Contemporary Organizations. LC 83-19784. (Wiley Management Series on Problem Solving, Decision Making & Strategic Thinking: 1-578). 301p. 1984. 18.95 (ISBN 0-471-87176-1, 1-578, Pub. by Wiley-Interscience). Wiley.
Bradford, David S. & Hensinger, Robert. The Pediatric Spine. (Illus.). 544p. 1985. text ed. 80.00 (ISBN 0-86577-126-X). Thieme Stratton.
Bradford, David S., jt. auth. see Dickson, RA.
Bradford, David T. The Experience of God: Portraits in the Phenomenological Psychopathology of Schizophrenia. LC 84-47697. (American University Studies VIII (Psychology): Vol. 4). 331p. 1985. text ed. 36.00 (ISBN 0-8204-0126-9). P Lang Pubs.
Bradford, Debra, jt. auth. see Clark, Deborah B.
Bradford, Dennis E. The Concept of Existence: A Study of Nonexistent Particulars. LC 80-5526. 142p. 1980. lib. bdg. 21.75 (ISBN 0-8191-1124-4). U Pr of Amer.
Bradford, E. Hannibal: The General from Carthage. 288p. 1981. 14.95 (ISBN 0-07-007064-4). McGraw.
Bradford, Elizabeth A., ed. see Pick, Michael R.
Bradford, Ernie. The Battle for the West - Thermopylae 480. 1979. 12.95 (ISBN 0-07-007062-8). McGraw.
--The Story of the Mary Rose. (Illus.). 1982. 24.95 (ISBN 0-393-01620-X). Norton.
--Ulysses Found. (Century Seafares Ser.). 256p. 1985. pap. 9.95 (ISBN 0-7126-0844-3, Pub. by Century Pubs UK). Hippocrene Bks.
Bradford, Ernle. Companion Guide to the Greek Islands. (Illus.). 320p. 1983. 15.95 (ISBN 0-13-154500-0); pap. 7.95 (ISBN 0-13-154492-6). P-H.
--Julius Caesar: The Pursuit of Power. LC 84-16500. 1984. 17.95 (ISBN 0-688-03931-6). Morrow.
Bradford, G. Samuel Pepys. LC 75-42291. (English Biography Ser., No. 31). 1974. lib. bdg. 52.95x (ISBN 0-8383-2061-9). Haskell.
Bradford, Gamaliel. American Portraits: Eighteen Seventy-Five to Nineteen Hundred. LC 71-85994. (Essay & General Literature Index Reprint Ser). (Illus.). 1969. Repr. of 1922 ed. 21.00x (ISBN 0-8046-0539-4, Pub by Kennikat). Assoc Faculty Pr.
--As God Made Them. LC 74-85992. (Essay & General Literature Index Reprint Ser). 1969. Repr. of 1929 ed. 22.50x (ISBN 0-8046-0540-8, Pub by Kennikat). Assoc Faculty Pr.
--Bare Souls. LC 24-23738. 1968. Repr. of 1924 ed. 16.00 (ISBN 0-527-10600-3). Kraus Repr.
--Biography & the Human Heart. LC 68-58772. (Essay Index Reprint Ser). 1932. 18.50 (ISBN 0-8369-1023-0). Ayer Co Pubs.
--Daughters of Eve. LC 72-85989. (Essay & General Literature Index Reprint Ser.). 1969. Repr. of 1930 ed. 24.50x (ISBN 0-8046-0542-4, Pub. by Kennikat). Assoc Faculty Pr.
--Elizabethan Women. facs. ed. White, Harold O., ed. LC 75-75505. (Select Bibliographies Reprint Ser). 1936. 20.00 (ISBN 0-8369-5001-1). Ayer Co Pubs.
--Portraits & Personalities. facs. ed. Bessey, M. A., ed. LC 68-8440. (Essay Index Reprint Ser). 1933. 19.00 (ISBN 0-8369-0242-4). Ayer Co Pubs.
--Portraits of Women. facsimile ed. LC 75-90611. (Essay Index Reprint Ser). 1916. 18.00 (ISBN 0-8369-1247-0). Ayer Co Pubs.
--Portraits of Women. LC 75-90611. (Essay Index Reprint Ser.). (Illus.). 202p. Repr. of 1916 ed. lib. bdg. 15.00 (ISBN 0-8290-0469-6). Irvington.
--A Prophet of Joy. facsimile ed. LC 77-179506. (Select Bibliographies Reprint Ser.). Repr. of 1920 ed. 17.00 (ISBN 0-8369-6635-X). Ayer Co Pubs.
--Quick & the Dead. LC 70-85991. (Essay & General Literature Index Reprint Ser). 1969. Repr. of 1931 ed. 22.50x (ISBN 0-8046-0544-0, Pub By Kennikat). Assoc Faculty Pr.
--Samuel Pepys. 1924. Repr. 15.00 (ISBN 0-8274-3323-9). R West.
--Soul of Samuel Pepys. LC 75-85993. 1969. Repr. of 1924 ed. 19.50x (ISBN 0-8046-0603-X, Pub. by Kennikat). Assoc Faculty Pr.
--Union Portraits. facs. ed. LC 68-29194. (Essay Index Reprint Ser). 1916. 18.00 (ISBN 0-8369-0243-2). Ayer Co Pubs.
--Union Portraits. 1978. Repr. of 1916 ed. lib. bdg. 25.00 (ISBN 0-8492-3524-3). R West.
--Wives. LC 72-2591. (American Women Ser.: Images & Realities). 328p. 1972. Repr. of 1925 ed. 22.00 (ISBN 0-405-04448-8). Ayer Co Pubs.
Bradford, Gigi & Moos, Michael, eds. Sixteen Toes: Anthology. (Illus.). (gr. 2-7). 1978. pap. 2.50 (ISBN 0-930970-00-4). O'Neill Pr.
Bradford, H. F., ed. Neurotransmitter Interaction & Compartmentation. (NATO ASI Series A, Life Sciences: Vol. 48). 852p. 1982. 95.00x (ISBN 0-306-41015-X, Plenum Pr). Plenum Pub.
Bradford, H. F. & Marsden, C. D., eds. Biochemistry & Neurology. 304p. 1976. pap. 47.50 (ISBN 0-12-123750-8). Acad Pr.
Bradford, Harry F. Chemical Neurobiology. LC 85-7037. (Illus.). 416p. 1985. text ed. write for info. (ISBN 0-7167-1694-1); study guide 8.95 (ISBN 0-7167-1641-0). W H Freeman.
Bradford, James C., ed. Command Under Sail: Makers of Naval Traditon. (Illus.). 288p. 1985. 24.95 (ISBN 0-87021-137-4). Naval Inst Pr.
Bradford, James N. Escape Route: Surviving the Earth Changes. 180p. 1985. pap. 10.00 (ISBN 0-89540-135-5, SB-135). Sun Pub.
Bradford, John. Ancient Landscapes: Studies in Field Archaeology. LC 80-23204. (Illus.). xvii, 297p. 1980. Repr. of 1957 ed. lib. bdg. 55.00x (ISBN 0-313-22849-3, BRAL). Greenwood.
--A Sermon of Repentance. LC 74-28835. (English Experience Ser.: No. 716). 1975. Repr. of 1553 ed. 6.00 (ISBN 90-221-0716-7). Walter J Johnson.
--Writings of Bradford. 1979. Set. 29.95 (ISBN 0-85151-359-X). Vol. 1 (ISBN 0-85151-283-6). Vol. 2 (ISBN 0-85151-284-4). Banner of Truth.
--Writings of John Bradford...Martyr, 1555, 2 Vols. Repr. of 1853 ed. Set. 92.00 (ISBN 0-384-05440-4). Johnson Repr.
Bradford, John, jt. ed. see Bowle, John.
Bradford, Kate C., ed. see Shabon, Anwar M. & Zeytinoglu, Isik U.
Bradford, Larry J., ed. Physiological Measures of the Audiovestibular System. 1975. 63.00 (ISBN 0-12-123650-1). Acad Pr.
Bradford, Larry J. & Hardy, William G., eds. Hearing & Hearing Impairment. 672p. 1979. 68.50 (ISBN 0-8089-1145-7, 790652). Grune.
Bradford, Leland & Bradford, Martha. Retirement: Coping with Emotional Upheavals. LC 79-4101. 1979. 18.95x (ISBN 0-88229-564-0). Nelson-Hall.
Bradford, Leland P. Making Meetings Work: A Guide for Leaders & Group Members. LC 76-16886. 121p. 1976. pap. 15.95 (ISBN 0-88390-122-6). Univ Assocs.
--Preparing for Retirement: A Program for Survival - A Participant's Workbook. LC 80-52897. 106p. 1981. pap. 9.00 (ISBN 0-88390-160-9). Univ Assocs.
--Preparing for Retirement: A Program for Survival - A Trainer's Kit. LC 80-52897. 196p. 1981. pkg. with looseleaf notebook & wkbk. 45.00 (ISBN 0-88390-161-7). Univ Assocs.
Bradford, Leland P., ed. Group Development. 2nd, rev, enl. ed. LC 78-51283. 234p. 1978. pap. 14.50 (ISBN 0-88390-144-7). Univ Assocs.
Bradford, Leroy. Staying Awake: More Fun Than Sleeping. LC 81-90342. 54p. (Orig.). 1981. 12.50 (ISBN 0-686-32459-5); pap. 9.00x (ISBN 0-686-36897-5). L Bradford.
Bradford, Lowell W., jt. auth. see Kirk, Paul L.
Bradford, Lyle. Building Relationships Through Pastoral Visitation. 64p. 1984. pap. 4.95 (ISBN 0-8170-1006-8). Judson.
Bradford, M. E. A Better Guide Than Reason: Studies in the American Revolution. 242p. pap. 6.95 (ISBN 0-89385-011-X). Sugden.
--Generations of the Faithful Heart: On the Literature of the South. 216p. (Orig.). 1983. pap. 7.95 (ISBN 0-89385-023-3). Sugden.
--Remembering Who We Are: Observations of a Southern Conservative. LC 84-22225. 178p. 1985. 15.95 (ISBN 0-8203-0766-1). U of Ga Pr.

--A Worthy Company: Brief Lives of the Framers of the Constitution. 250p. 1982. 8.95 (ISBN 0-942516-00-1). Plymouth Rock Found.

Bradford, M. E., ed. The Form Discovered: Essays on the Achievement of Andrew Lytle. LC 73-86315. 128p. 1973. 1.00 (ISBN 0-87805-050-7). U Pr of Miss.

Bradford, M. G. & Kent, W. A. Human Geography: Theories & Their Applications. (Science in Geography Ser.). (Illus.). 1977. pap. 9.95x (ISBN 0-19-913227-5). Oxford U Pr.

Bradford, M. Gerald, ed. see Santucci, James A.

Bradford, Martha, jt. auth. see Bradford, Leland.

Bradford, Mary E. Make Your Dreams Come True, No. 1: Angie's Choice. 208p. (Orig.). 1984. pap. 1.95 (ISBN 0-446-30730-0). Warner Bks.

Bradford, Mary-Ellen. Make Your Dreams Come True, No. 7: Language of Love. 160p. (Orig.). 1985. pap. 2.25 (ISBN 0-446-32384-5). Warner Bks.

Bradford, Mary L., ed. Mormon Women Speak. LC 82-62366. 1982. 9.95 (ISBN 0-913420-94-8). Olympus Pub Co.

Bradford, Michelle see Mistral, pseud.

Bradford, Montse, jt. auth. see Bradford, Peter.

Bradford, Murray & Davis, Glenn B. Personal & Business Tax & Financial Planning for Psychiatrists. LC 84-6189. (Private Practice Monograph). 192p. 1984. pap. text ed. 15.00x (ISBN 0-88048-102-1, 48-102-1). Am Psychiatric.

Bradford, Peter & Bradford, Montse. Cooking with Sea Vegetables: A Collection of Naturally Delicious Recipes Using to the Full the Bountiful Harvest of the Oceans. 128p. (Orig.). 1985. pap. 6.95 (ISBN 0-7225-1115-9). Thorsons Pubs.

Bradford, R. The Last Ditch. 272p. pap. 8.95 (ISBN 0-85640-259-1, Pub. by Blackstaff Pr). Longwood Pub Group.

Bradford, R. & Culbert, M. Metabolic Management of Cancer (Protocols) 25.00x (ISBN 0-934740-00-3). Cancer Control Soc.

Bradford, Richard. Red Sky at Morning. LC 68-11272. 1968. 12.45i (ISBN 0-397-00549-0). Har-Row.

--Red Sky at Morning. 1983. pap. 3.50 (ISBN 0-671-50440-1). PB.

--Red Sky at Morning. 1974. pap. 3.50 (ISBN 0-671-50440-1). WSP.

Bradford, Richard H. The Virginius Affair. LC 20-520000. 1980. 17.50x (ISBN 0-87081-080-4). Colo Assoc.

Bradford, Roark. John Henry. facs. ed. LC 77-116941. (Short Story Index Reprint Ser.). 1931. 18.00 (ISBN 0-8369-3443-1). Ayer Co Pubs.

--Let the Band Play Dixie, & Other Stories. facs. ed. LC 70-128721. (Short Story Index Reprint Ser). 1934. 19.00 (ISBN 0-8369-3612-4). Ayer Co Pubs.

Bradford, Robert. Mathematics for Carpenters. LC 75-19525. 1975. pap. 14.80 (ISBN 0-8273-1116-8); instr's. guide 4.20 (ISBN 0-8273-1117-6). Delmar.

Bradford, Robert W., jt. ed. see Watt, William W.

Bradford, Sarah. Disraeli. LC 82-42728. 464p. 1983. 19.95 (ISBN 0-8128-2899-2). Stein & Day.

--Harriet Tubman. 150p. 1974. pap. 4.95 (ISBN 0-8065-0415-3). Citadel Pr.

--Harriet Tubman: The Moses of Her People. 11.25 (ISBN 0-8446-1717-2). Peter Smith.

--Princess Grace. LC 83-40360. (Illus.). 272p. 1984. 17.95 (ISBN 0-8128-2958-1). Stein & Day.

Bradford, Sarah H. Scenes in the Life of Harriet Tubman. facs. ed. LC 70-154071. (Black Heritage Library Collection). 1869. 19.00 (ISBN 0-8369-8782-9). Ayer Co Pubs.

Bradford, Standish, Jr., jt. auth. see Young, G. Richard.

Bradford, T. C. Bibliographers Manual of American History, 5 vols. 600.00 (ISBN 0-87968-732-0). Gordon Pr.

Bradford, T. G., tr. see Chevalier, Michael.

Bradford, Thomas L. Bibliographer's Manual of American History, 5 Vols. Henkels, Stan V., ed. LC 67-14023. 1968. Repr. of 1907 ed. Set. 134.00x (ISBN 0-8103-3319-8). Gale.

Bradford, Tony. Caravanning. (Illus.). 96p. 10.25 (ISBN 0-902280-63-5, P963). Haynes Pubns.

Bradford Town History Committee, ed. Two Hundred Plus: History of Bradford, New Hampshire. LC 76-26494. (Illus.). 1976. 20.00x (ISBN 0-914016-31-8). Phoenix Pub.

Bradford, Vena & Bradford, Angier. Wilderness Wife. 1977. pap. 2.95 (ISBN 0-02-058230-7, 05823, Collier). Macmillan.

Bradford, W. M. & Davis, Glenn B. Business Tax Deduction Master Guide: Strategies for Business & Professional People. LC 83-19211. 1983. 24.95 (ISBN 0-13-108282-5); pap. write for info. (ISBN 0-13-108274-4). P-H.

Bradford, W. Murray & Davis, Glenn B. Business Tax Deduction Master Guide. 2nd ed. 320p. 1983. 24.95 (ISBN 0-13-108282-5); pap. 14.95 (ISBN 0-13-108274-4). P-H.

--Business Tax Deduction Master Guide: Strategies for Business & Professional People. LC 84-24815. Date not set. price not set (ISBN 0-13-108424-0). P-H.

Bradford, William. History of Plymouth Plantation, 1620-1647, 2 Vols. Adams, Charles F., et al, eds. LC 68-10904. (Illus.). 1968. Repr. of 1912 ed. Set. 50.00x (ISBN 0-8462-1118-1). Russell.

--Of Plymouth Plantation: The Pilgrims in America. 18.00 (ISBN 0-8446-1718-0). Peter Smith.

--Of Plymouth Plantation: 1620-1647. Morison, Samuel E., ed. (The American Past Ser). (Illus.). (YA) 1952. 19.95 (ISBN 0-394-43895-7). Knopf.

--Of Plymouth Plantation: 1620-1647. Murphy, Francis, ed. LC 80-22753. (Modern Library College Editions). 1981. pap. text ed. 6.95 (ISBN 0-394-32602-4, RanC). Random.

Bradford, William & Winslow, Edward. Mourt's Relation. 1972. Repr. of 1865 ed. lib. bdg. 22.50 (ISBN 0-8422-8008-1). Irvington.

--Mourt's Relation. LC 72-78652. 1865. Repr. 25.00 (ISBN 0-686-01725-0). Somerset Pub.

Bradford, William, jt. auth. see Bates, Timothy.

Bradford, William, ed. Correspondence of the Emperor Charles Fifth. Repr. of 1850 ed. 27.50 (ISBN 0-404-00926-3). AMS Pr.

Bradford, William & Talberg, Val, illus. Aperture, No. 90. (Illus.). 80p. 1983. pap. 12.50 (ISBN 0-89381-119-X). Aperture.

Bradford, William D. Mergers in the Savings & Loan Industry. (Business Reports: No. 59). 1977. pap. 5.00 (ISBN 0-87712-178-8). U Mich Busn Div Res.

Bradford, Zeb B., Jr. & Brown, Frederic J. The United States Army in Transition. (Armed Forces & Society Ser.). 256p. 1973. 25.00 (ISBN 0-8039-0211-5). Seven Locks Pr.

Bradgate Centennial Committee. Bradgate 1882-1982. 91p. 1983. pap. write for info. Bradgate Cent.

Bradie, Michael & Sayre, Kenneth. Reason & Decision: Bowling Green Studies in Applied Philosophy, Vol. III. 134p. 1981. text ed. 15.00 (ISBN 0-935756-04-3). BGSU Dept Phil.

Bradie, Michael & Brand, Myles, eds. Action & Responsibility. (Bowling Green Studies in Applied Philosophy: Vol. 2). 149p. 1980. text ed. 15.00 (ISBN 0-935756-02-7); pap. text ed. 10.00 (ISBN 0-935756-03-5). BGSU Dept Phil.

Bradie, Michael & Braybrooke, David, eds. Social Justice. (Studies in Applied Philosophy: Vol. IV). 170p. 1982. 15.00 (ISBN 0-935756-05-1). BGSU Dept Phil.

Bradie, Michael, et al, eds. The Applied Turn in Contemporary Philosophy. (Studies in Applied Philosophy: Vol. V). 1983. 15.00 (ISBN 0-935756-06-X). BGSU Dept Phil.

Brading, D. A. Haciendas & Ranchos in the Mexican Bajio Leon 1700-1860. LC 77-90203. (Cambridge Latin American Studies: No. 32). (Illus.). 1979. 49.50 (ISBN 0-521-22200-1). Cambridge U Pr.

--Miners & Merchants in Bourbon Mexico, 1763-1810. LC 74-123666. (Cambridge Latin American Studies: No. 10). (Illus.). 1971. 57.50 (ISBN 0-521-07874-1). Cambridge U Pr.

Brading, D. A., ed. Caudillo & Peasant in the Mexican Revolution. LC 79-16593. (Cambridge Latin American Studies: No. 38). 1980. 54.50 (ISBN 0-521-22997-9). Cambridge U Pr.

Bradish, Norman C. John Sergeant: A Forgotten Critic of Descartes & Locke. 65p. 1929. 6.95 (ISBN 0-87548-363-1). Open Court.

Bradkin, Cheryl G. The Seminole Patchwork Book. (Illus.). 48p. 1980. pap. 7.50 (ISBN 0-932946-03-8). Yours Truly.

Bradlaugh, Charles. Champion of Liberty. 59.95 (ISBN 0-87968-833-5). Gordon Pr.

--Jesus, Shelley, & Malthus. 1978. Repr. of 1877 ed. lib. bdg. 10.00 (ISBN 0-8495-0441-4). Arden Lib.

--Labor & Law. LC 68-55490. Repr. of 1891 ed. 25.00x (ISBN 0-678-00888-4). Kelley.

--Selection of the Political Pamphlets of Charles Bradlaugh 1865-1891. LC 77-104611. 1970. lib. bdg. 45.00x (ISBN 0-678-00604-0). Kelley.

Bradlee, Benjamin C. Conversations with Kennedy. (Illus.). 256p. 1984. pap. 8.95 (ISBN 0-393-30189-3). Norton.

Bradlee, Dick. Instant Tennis. 1963. pap. 2.50 (ISBN 0-346-12353-4). Cornerstone.

--Instant Tennis. (Illus.). 124p. (gr. 7 up). 1962. 6.95 (ISBN 0-8159-5811-0). Devin.

Bradley, A. C. Poetry for Poetry's Sake. LC 73-15728. 1901. lib. bdg. 10.00 (ISBN 0-8414-3306-2). Folcroft.

--The Reaction Against Tennyson. 59.95 (ISBN 0-87968-139-X). Gordon Pr.

--Shakespearean Tragedy. 1977. pap. 2.95 (ISBN 0-449-30817-0, Prem). Fawcett.

--Shakespearean Tragedy: Lectures on Hamlet, Othello, King Lear & Macbeth. 432p. 1905. 25.00 (ISBN 0-312-71470-X). St Martin.

--Shakespearean Tragedy: Lectures on Hamlet, Othello, King Lear, Macbeth. 2nd ed. 456p. 1985. 32.50 (ISBN 0-312-71427-0). St Martin.

Bradley, A. C., ed. see Green, Thomas H.

Bradley, A. G. Fight with France for North America. LC 77-146377. (First American Frontier Ser). (Illus.). 1971. Repr. of 1900 ed. 25.50 (ISBN 0-405-02828-8). Ayer Co Pubs.

Bradley, A. G., ed. see Smith, John.

Bradley, Alfred & Bond, Michael. Paddington on Stage. LC 76-62497. (Illus.). (gr. 2-5). 1977. 9.95 (ISBN 0-395-25155-9). HM.

Bradley, Alfred, jt. auth. see Bond, Michael.

Bradley, Amos D. The Geometry of Repeating Design & Geometry of Design for High Schools. LC 72-176586. (Columbia University. Teachers College. Contributions to Education: No. 549). Repr. of 1933 ed. 22.50 (ISBN 0-404-55549-7). AMS Pr.

Bradley, Andrew C. English Poetry & German Philosophy in the Age of Wordsworth. LC 73-16150. 1909. lib. bdg. 12.50 (ISBN 0-8414-3324-0). Folcroft.

--Ideals of Religion. LC 77-27218. (Gifford Lectures: 1907). Repr. of 1940 ed. 24.00 (ISBN 0-404-60463-3). AMS Pr.

--Miscellany. facs. ed. LC 72-76894. (Essay Index Reprint Ser). 1929. 19.00 (ISBN 0-8369-0005-7). Ayer Co Pubs.

--The Reaction Against Tennyson. 1978. Repr. of 1917 ed. lib. bdg. 10.00 (ISBN 0-8495-0437-6). Arden Lib.

--Reaction Against Tennyson. LC 74-1188. 1917. lib. bdg. 10.00 (ISBN 0-8414-3290-2). Folcroft.

Bradley, Anne. Take Note of College Study Skills. 1983. pap. text ed. 14.15x (ISBN 0-673-15578-1). Scott F.

Bradley, Anthony. William Butler Yeats. LC 77-6953. (Literature and Life Ser.). 306p. 1980. 21.50 (ISBN 0-8044-2068-8). Ungar.

Bradley, Anthony, ed. Contemporary Irish Poetry: An Anthology. LC 76-50244. 1980. 19.95 (ISBN 0-520-03389-2). U of Cal Pr.

Bradley, Anthony & Smith, Terry, eds. Australian Art & Architecture. (Illus.). 1980. 80.00x (ISBN 0-19-550588-3). Oxford U Pr.

Bradley, Ardyth. Inside the Bones Is Flesh. LC 78-20985. 45p. 1978. 3.50 (ISBN 0-87886-103-3). Ithaca Hse.

Bradley, Arthur, jt. auth. see Fibonacci, Leonardo.

Bradley, Arthur G. Owen Glyndwr. LC 73-14435. (Heroes of the Nation Ser.). Repr. of 1901 ed. 30.00 (ISBN 0-404-58253-2). AMS Pr.

--The United Empire Loyalists. LC 75-136413. (BCL Ser. I). Repr. of 1932 ed. 16.50 (ISBN 0-404-00927-1). AMS Pr.

Bradley, B. J., ed. see Fisher, Jay M.

Bradley, Bert. Fundamentals of Speech Communication: The Credibility of Ideas. 4th ed. 432p. 1984. pap. text ed. write for info (ISBN 0-697-04247-2); instr's manual avail. (ISBN 0-697-04249-9). Wm C Brown.

Bradley, Bert E., et al. Workbook for Fundamentals of Speech Communication. 144p. 1981. spiral bdg. 8.95 (ISBN 0-8403-2383-2). Kendall-Hunt.

Bradley, Beverly H. Toward the Setting of the Sun. 1985. 7.95 (ISBN 0-533-06500-3). Vantage.

Bradley, Bill. The Fair Tax. (Orig.). 1984. pap. 3.95 (ISBN 0-671-46544-9). PB.

--The Last of the Great Stations. Walker, Jim, ed. LC 79-84387. (Special Ser.: No. 72). (Illus.). 1979. pap. 11.95 (ISBN 0-916374-36-X). Interurban.

Bradley, Bill, ed. Commercial Los Angeles, Nineteen Twenty-Five to Nineteen Forty-Seven. (Special Ser.: No.X-8). (Illus.). 144p. 1981. pap. 14.95 (ISBN 0-916374-45-9). Interurban.

Bradley, Bill, ed. see Perles, Anthony.

Bradley, Bill, ed. see Steinheimer, Richard & Benson, Ted.

Bradley, Bill, ed. see Steinheimer, Richard & Sims, Donald.

Bradley, Bruce. James Joyce's Schooldays. LC 81-23341. 1982. 16.95 (ISBN 0-312-43978-4). St Martin.

Bradley, Bruce A., jt. auth. see Frison, George C.

Bradley, C. C. High-Pressure Methods in Solid State Research. 184p. 1969. 15.00x (ISBN 0-306-30693-X, Plenum Pr). Plenum Pub.

Bradley, C. Henry. A Linguistic Sketch of Jicaltepec Mixtec. (Publications in Linguistics & Related Fields Ser.: No. 25). 97p. 1970. pap. 3.75x (ISBN 0-88312-027-5); microfiche (2) 2.86x (ISBN 0-88312-536-6). Summer Inst Ling.

Bradley, C. Paul. Electoral Politics in Israel: The Knesset Election of 1981. LC 81-84251. viii, 79p. (Orig.). 1981. pap. text ed. 4.95 (ISBN 0-936988-05-3). Tompson & Rutter.

--Electoral Politics in Israel: The Kresser Elections of 1981. 79p. 1981. pap. 4.95 (ISBN 0-936988-05-3, Pub. by Tompson & Rutter). Shoe String.

--Parliamentary Elections in Israel: Three Case Studies. LC 85-1150. 208p. (Orig.). 1985. pap. text ed. 10.00 (ISBN 0-936988-11-8, Dist. by Shoe String). Tompson & Rutter.

--Recent United States Policy in the Persian Gulf (1971-82) LC 82-16049. 148p. (Orig.). 1982. pap. text ed. 6.95 (ISBN 0-936988-08-8). Tompson & Rutter.

Bradley, Carol. Music Collections in American Libraries: A Chronology. LC 81-2907. (Detroit Studies in Music Bibliography Ser.: No. 46). 1981. 18.50 (ISBN 0-89990-002-X). Info Coord.

Bradley, Carol June, ed. Reader in Music Librarianship. LC 73-82994. 340p. 1973. 28.50 (ISBN 0-313-24044-2, ZRL/). Greenwood.

Bradley, Charles O. High Pressure Methods in Solid State Research. LC 68-58922. pap. 45.80 (ISBN 0-317-28019-8, 2055799). Bks Demand UMI.

Bradley, Curtis, jt. auth. see Friedenberg, Joan.

Bradley, Curtis H. & Friedenberg, Joan E. Foundations & Strategies for Bilingual Vocational Education. 128p. 1982. pap. 10.95x (ISBN 0-15-599016-0). Ctr Appl Ling.

Bradley, Cuthbert. Fox Hunting from Shire to Shire with Many Noted Packs. (Illus.). 1979. Repr. of 1912 ed. lib. bdg. 75.00 (ISBN 0-8492-3729-7). R West.

Bradley, D & Milton, David. Picture History of the Somerset & Dorset Locomotive History. (Illus.). 1973. 15.95 (ISBN 0-7153-5956-8). David & Charles.

Bradley, D. C., et al. Metal Alkoxides. 1979. 83.50 (ISBN 0-12-124250-1). Acad Pr.

Bradley, D. J., et al. Ultra-Short Laser Pulses. (Phil. Strans. Ser. A: Vol. 298). (Illus.). 204p. 1981. text ed. 60.00x (ISBN 0-85403-147-2, Pub. by Royal Soc London). Scholium Intl.

Bradley, D. L. Drummond Greyhounds of the LSWR. 1977. 15.95 (ISBN 0-7153-7329-3). David & Charles.

Bradley, David. Assembly Language Programming for the IBM Personal Computer. LC 83-8638. (Illus.). 416p. 1983. text ed. 26.95 (ISBN 0-13-049189-6); 21.95 (ISBN 0-13-049171-3). P-H.

--The Chaneysville Incident. LC 80-8225. 480p. 1981. 14.37i (ISBN 0-06-010491-0, HarpT). Har-Row.

--The Chaneysville Incident. 456p. 1982. pap. 3.95 (ISBN 0-380-58586-3, 60142-7). Avon.

--Dartmouth: A Visual Remembrance. Patrick, James B., ed. 144p. 1982. 35.00 (ISBN 0-940078-06-6). Foremost Pubs.

--Lahu Dialects. LC 79-52679. (Faculty of Asian Studies Oriental Monograph: No. 23). (Illus., Orig.). 1980. pap. text ed. 6.95 (ISBN 0-7081-1077-0, 0309, Pub. by ANUP Australia). Australia N U P.

--Proto-Lolish. (Scandanavian Institute of Asian Studies Monograph: No. 39). (Orig.). 1980. pap. text ed. 18.50x (ISBN 0-7007-0128-1). Humanities.

Bradley, David, jt. auth. see Coles, Adland.

Bradley, David, jt. auth. see Jones, Dewitt.

Bradley, David J. No Place to Hide Nineteen Forty-Six to Nineteen Eighty-Four. 240p. 1983. 18.00 (ISBN 0-87451-274-3); pap. 8.95 (ISBN 0-87451-275-1). U Pr of New Eng.

--No Place to Hide: 1946-1984. rev. ed. LC 83-40013. (Illus.). 241p. 1983. 18.00x (ISBN 0-87451-274-3); pap. 8.95 (ISBN 0-87451-275-1). U Pr of New Eng.

Bradley, David J., jt. auth. see Feachem, Richard G.

Bradley, Dick. On Board with Bradley. LC 83-81219. (Illus.). 192p. 1983. FPT 15.95 (ISBN 0-688-02483-1, Pub. by Hearst Bks). Morrow.

Bradley, Donald. The Parallax Problem in Astrology. 60p. 1983. soft cover 4.00 (ISBN 0-87542-042-7, L-042). Llewellyn Pubns.

--Stock Market Prediction. (Illus.). 58p. 1982. pap. 4.00 (ISBN 0-87542-046-X). Llewellyn Pubns.

Bradley, Donald A. Picking Winners. 30p. 1981. pap. 2.00 (ISBN 0-87542-043-5). Llewellyn Pubns.

--Solar & Lunar Returns. (Illus.). 123p. 1975. pap. 3.95 (ISBN 0-87542-045-1). Llewellyn Pubns.

Bradley, Duane. Design It, Sew It, & Wear It: How to Make Yourself a Super Wardrobe Without Commercial Patterns. LC 76-55732. (Illus.). (gr. 7 up). 1979 (ISBN 0-690-01297-7). PLB 11.89plb. (ISBN 0-690-03839-9). Crowell Jr Bks.

Bradley, E. R. Selected Readings in Modern World History. 1970. pap. text ed. 9.95 (ISBN 0-8290-1188-9). Irvington.

Bradley, E. S. Henry Charles Lea. 59.95 (ISBN 0-8490-0293-1). Gordon Pr.

Bradley, Edward. The White Wife, with Other Stories Supernatural, Romantic, & Legendary. LC 76-49836. 1976. Repr. of 1865 ed. lib. bdg. 28.50 (ISBN 0-8414-1757-1). Folcroft.

Bradley, Edward J. The Child & Family Genealogy Reporting System. 2nd ed. 1981. 9.95 (ISBN 0-935202-01-3). Child & Family Ent.

Bradley, Edward L., frwd. by. Perspectives in Nursing, 1983-1985. 224p. 1983. pap. 24.95 (ISBN 0-88737-346-1, 41-1935). Natl League Nurse.

Bradley, Edward L., III. Complications of Pancreatitis: Medical & Surgical Management. (Illus.). 336p. 1982. 42.95 (ISBN 0-7216-1907-X). Saunders.

Bradley, Edward S. George Henry Boker. LC 68-57753. (Illus.). 1969. Repr. of 1927 ed. 24.50 (ISBN 0-405-08301-7, Blom Pubns). Ayer Co Pubs.

--George Henry Boker, Poet & Patriot. LC 70-94467. (BCL Ser. I). (Illus.). Repr. of 1927 ed. 12.50 (ISBN 0-404-00928-X). AMS Pr.

Bradley, Edward S., jt. auth. see Teweles, Richard J.

Bradley, Elihu F., ed. Source Book on Materials for Elevated-Temperature Applications. 1979. 54.00 (ISBN 0-87170-081-6). ASM.

Bradley, Eliza. An Authentic Narrative of the Shipwreck & Sufferings of Mrs. Eliza Bradley. Date not set. price not set. Ye Galleon.

Bradley, F., tr. see Briner, Andreas.

Bradley, F. W; see Pound, L.

Bradley, F. W; see Reed, D. W.

Bradley, F. W., et al. Word Lists from South Carolina & Florida. (Publications of the American Dialect Society Ser.: No. 14). 81p. 1950. pap. 5.50 (ISBN 0-8173-0614-5). U of Ala Pr.

Bradley, Francis H. Appearance & Reality: A Metaphysical Essay. 2nd ed. 1930. Repr. of 1897 ed. 42.00x (ISBN 0-19-824109-7). Oxford U Pr.

--Collected Essays, 2 Vols. facs. ed. LC 68-54333. (Essay Index Reprint Ser). 1968. Repr. of 1935 ed. 40.00 (ISBN 0-8369-0244-0). Ayer Co Pubs.

--Collected Essays, 2 Vols. LC 73-98212. Repr. of 1935 ed. Set. lib. bdg. 31.75x (ISBN 0-8371-3255-X, BRCE). Greenwood.

--Public Stake in Union Power. LC 59-11490. x, 382p. 1959. 10.00x (ISBN 0-8139-0054-9). U Pr of Va.

Bradley, Phillips, ed. see De Tocqueville, Alexis.

Bradley, Phillips, ed. see Tocqueville, Alexis De.

Bradley, R., et al. Case Studies in Mathematical Modelling: A Course Book for Engineers & Scientists. 250p. 1981. 39.95x (ISBN 0-470-27235-X). Halsted Pr.

Bradley, R. M. Basic Oral Physiology. 1981. 24.50 (ISBN 0-8151-1183-5). Year Bk Med.

Bradley, R. N. Racial Origins of English Character. LC 72-118461. 1971. Repr. of 1926 ed. 19.00x (ISBN 0-8046-1210-2, Pub by Kennikat). Assoc Faculty Pr.

Bradley, R. S., ed. Advances in High Pressure Research, 4 vols. Vol. 1 1966. 75.00 (ISBN 0-12-021201-3); Vol. 2 1969. 60.00 (ISBN 0-12-021202-1); Vol. 3 1969. 70.00 (ISBN 0-12-021203-X); Vol. 4 1974. 52.00 (ISBN 0-12-021204-8). Acad Pr.

Bradley, Raymond & Swartz, Norman. Possible Worlds: An Introduction to Logic & Its Philosophy. LC 79-51037. (Illus.). 424p. 1979. lib. bdg. 25.00 (ISBN 0-915144-60-3); pap. text ed. 14.50 (ISBN 0-915144-59-X). Hackett Pub.

Bradley, Raymond S. Quaternary Paleoclimatology: Methods of Paleoclimatic Reconstruction. (Illus.). 1985. text ed. 50.00x (ISBN 0-04-551067-9); pap. text ed. 24.95x (ISBN 0-04-551068-7). Allen Unwin.

Bradley, Raymond T. Charisma & Social Structures: A Rational Analysis of Power & Communion in Communes. Date not set. price not set. Paragon Hse.

Bradley, Richard. The Country Housewife & Lady's Director. 504p. 1980. Repr. of 1736 ed. 37.50x (ISBN 0-907325-01-7, Pub. by Prospect England). U Pr of Va.

--The Social Foundations of Prehistoric Britain: Themes & Variation in the Archaeology of Power. (Archaeology Ser.). (Illus.). 224p. 1984. pap. text ed. 17.95 (ISBN 0-582-49164-9). Longman.

Bradley, Richard E., ed. Canine Heartworm Disease: The Current Knowledge. LC 72-2054. 1972. 12.00 (ISBN 0-8130-0357-1). U Presses Fla.

Bradley, Richard W., jt. auth. see Amble, Bruce R.

Bradley, Ritamary & Lagorio, Valerie M. The Fourteenth Century English Mystics: A Comprehensive Annotated Bibliography. LC 79-7922. (Garland Reference Library of the Humanities). 300p. 1981. lib. bdg. 36.00 (ISBN 0-8240-9535-9). Garland Pub.

Bradley, Robert A. Husband Coached Childbirth. 3rd ed. LC 80-8683. (Illus.). 256p. 1981. 13.41i (ISBN 0-06-014850-0, HarpT). Har-Row.

Bradley, Robert F. & Michell, R. B. Eight Centuries of French Literature: Chanson de Roland to Sartre. (Fr., Fr). 1951. 42.95x (ISBN 0-89197-134-3); pap. text ed. 22.50x (ISBN 0-8290-0372-X). Irvington.

Bradley, Rodger P. The Standard Steam Locomotives of British Railways. (Illus.). 112p. 1984. 18.95 (ISBN 0-7153-8384-1). David & Charles.

Bradley, Ronald, jt. ed. see Smythies, John.

Bradley, Ronald J., jt. auth. see Smythies, John R.

Bradley, Ronald J., jt. ed. see Smythies, John R.

Bradley, Ruth, tr. see Arrupe, Pedro S. J.

Bradley, S. A., ed. Anglo-Saxon Poetry. (Everyman Library). 586p. 1982. pap. text ed. 9.95x (ISBN 0-460-11794-7, Evman). Biblio Dist.

Bradley, S. E. & Purcell, E. F., eds. The Parcellular Pathway. LC 82-81100. (Illus.). 382p. 1982. pap. 15.00 (ISBN 0-914362-38-0). J Macy Foun.

Bradley, Sam. Manspell-Godspell. 1975. pap. 5.00 (ISBN 0-685-27676-7, Pub. by Anvil Pr). Small Pr Dist.

--Men, in Good Measure. 1966. 3.00 (ISBN 0-8233-0009-9). Golden Quill.

Bradley, Sculley, ed. see Clemens, Samuel L.

Bradley, Sculley, ed. see Whitman, Walt.

Bradley, Sculley, et al, eds. The American Tradition in Literature. 5th ed. 1981. Vol. 1., 2075p. pap. text ed. 15.00 (ISBN 0-394-32619-9, 32619-9); Vol. 2, 2175p. pap. text ed. 15.00 (ISBN 0-394-32620-2, 32620-2); Short Ed., 2006p. pap. text ed. 17.00 (ISBN 0-394-32624-5). Random.

Bradley, Sculley, et al, eds. see Hawthorne, Nathaniel.

Bradley, Sculley, et al, eds. see Whitman, Walt.

Bradley, Stephen P. & Crane, Dwight B. Management of Bank Portfolios. LC 75-23030. 299p. 1975. 55.95 (ISBN 0-471-09522-2, Pub. by Wiley-Interscience). Wiley.

Bradley, Stephen P., et al. Applied Mathematical Programming. LC 76-10426. (Illus.). 1977. text ed. 37.95 (ISBN 0-201-00464-X). Addison-Wesley.

Bradley, T. J. Hospital Pharmacy & the Patient. 250p. 1983. text ed. 25.00 (ISBN 0-85200-485-0, Pub. by MTP Pr England). Kluwer Academic.

Bradley, T. J. & Miller, T. A., eds. Measurement of Ion Transport & Metabolic Rate in Insects. (Springer Series in Experimental Entomology). (Illus.). 290p. 1984. 41.00 (ISBN 0-387-90855-2). Springer-Verlag.

Bradley, Ute. Applied Market & Social Research. 1982. 42.50 (ISBN 0-442-30437-4). Van Nos Reinhold.

Bradley, Van Allen. New Gold in Your Attic. LC 58-13607. (Illus.). 1968. 10.95 (ISBN 0-8303-0063-5). Fleet.

Bradley, Virginia. Bend to the Willow. LC 79-52036. (gr. 7 up). 1979. 6.95 (ISBN 0-396-07718-8). Dodd.

--Holidays on Stage: A Festival of Special-Occasion Plays. 288p. (gr. 5 up). 1981. PLB 10.95 (ISBN 0-396-07993-8). Dodd.

--Is There An Actor in the House? Dramatic Material from Pantomime to Play. (Illus.). 320p. (gr. 4 up). 1985. pap. 10.95 (ISBN 0-396-07193-7); pap. 4.95 (ISBN 0-396-08637-3). Dodd.

--Who Could Forget the Mayor of Lodi? 192p. (gr. 6 up). 1985. 11.95 (ISBN 0-396-08504-0). Dodd.

Bradley, W. B., et al, eds. Emerging Energy Technologies: 1978. 1978. 20.00 (ISBN 0-685-66797-9, G00141). ASME.

Bradley, W. F. & Hanson, Harold P., eds. Machine Interpretations of Patterson Functions & Alternative Direct Approaches & the Austin Symposium on Gas Phase Molecular Structure. (Transactions of the American Crystallographic Association Ser.: Vol. 2). 1966. pap. 15.00 (ISBN 0-686-60373-7). Polycrystal Bk Serv.

Bradley, Will. Will Bradley: His Graphic Art. Hornung, Clarence & Wong, Roberta W., eds. (Illus.). pap. 6.50 (ISBN 0-486-20701-3). Dover.

Bradley, William. Early Poems of Walter Savage Landor. LC 72-192844. 1914. lib. bdg. 15.00 (ISBN 0-8414-3195-7). Folcroft.

Bradley, William A. Dutch Landscape Etchers of the Seventeenth Century. (Illus.). 1919. 39.50x (ISBN 0-685-89748-6). Elliots Bks.

--William Cullen Bryant. 1978. lib. bdg. 20.00 (ISBN 0-8495-0447-3). Arden Lib.

--William Cullen Bryant. LC 73-11373. 1972. Repr. lib. bdg. 28.50 (ISBN 0-8414-3200-7). Folcroft.

Bradley, William A., tr. see Hemon, Louis.

Bradley, William G., Jr., et al. Magnetic Resonance Imaging of the Brain, Head & Neck: A Text-Atlas. 144p. 1985. 65.00 (ISBN 0-87189-094-1). Aspen Systems.

Bradley, William J. CB Fact Book & Language Dictionary. (Illus.). pap. 1.95 (ISBN 0-89552-011-7). DMR Pubns.

Bradley, William L. Siam Then: The Foreign Colony in Bangkok Before & After Anna. LC 81-12196. (Illus.). 232p. (Orig.). 1981. pap. 9.95 (ISBN 0-87808-185-2). William Carey Lib.

Bradley, William W., jt. auth. see Burns, Robert M.

Bradley-Andrews, Patricia. Basic Public Speaking. 160p. 1985. 10.95scp (ISBN 0-06-040925-8, HarpC). Har-Row.

Bradley-Birt, F. B. Bengal Fairy Tales. 1976. lib. bdg. 59.95 (ISBN 0-8490-1487-5). Gordon Pr.

Bradley-Johnson, Sharon & Lesiak, Judi. Assessment of Written Expression: A Critique of Procedures & Instruments. 82p. 1982. pap. 9.95 (ISBN 0-88422-016-8). Clinical Psych.

Bradley-Johnson, Sharon, jt. auth. see Lesiak, Judi.

Bradley-Johnson, Sharon, ed. New Approaches to Infant Assessment. (Special Issue Ser.: Vol. 3, No.4). 96p. 1984. 9.95 (ISBN 0-686-47625-5). Human Sci Pr.

Bradley-Payne. Humanities & Technologies: An Interdisciplinary Approach. 216p. 1983. pap. text ed. 14.95 (ISBN 0-8403-3083-9). Kendall-Hunt.

Bradlley, A. G. Pembrokeshire & South West Wales. 1930. 20.00 (ISBN 0-89984-006-X). Century Bookbindery.

Bradlow, Daniel D. & Jourdin, Willis W., Jr., eds. International Borrowing: Negotiation & Renegotiation, 2 vols. 1116p. (Orig.). 1984. 125.00 (ISBN 0-935328-27-0). Intl Law Inst.

Bradlow, Edna. Here Comes the Alabama. (Illus., Orig.). 1958. 9.95 (ISBN 0-87651-204-X). Southern U Pr.

Bradner, Enos. Fish-on! LC 76-182889. 3.95 (ISBN 0-87564-610-7). Superior Pub.

--Northwest Angling. 2nd ed. LC 70-81629. (Illus.). 1969. 9.95 (ISBN 0-8323-0125-6). Binford.

Bradner, John. Symbols of Church Seasons & Days. (Illus.). 1977. pap. 6.95 (ISBN 0-8192-1228-8). Morehouse.

Bradner, Leicester. Edmund Spenser & the Faerie Queene. LC 48-6359. 1948. pap. text ed. 16.00x (ISBN 0-226-07051-4). U of Chicago Pr.

--Musae Anglicanae: A History of Anglo-Latin Poetry, 1500-1925. (MLA Mono. General Ser.). 1940. 32.00 (ISBN 0-527-10650-X). Kraus Repr.

Bradner, Leicester, ed. see Elizabeth I.

Bradner, Leicester, ed. see More, St. Thomas, et al.

Bradner, W. T., jt. auth. see Crooke, Stanley T.

Brado, Edward. Cattle Kingdom: Early Ranching in Alberta. (Illus.). 298p. 1985. 18.95 (ISBN 0-88894-445-4, Pub by Salem Hse Ltd). Merrimack Pub Cir.

Brado, Juliana. The Nativity. (Golden Storytime Bks.). (Illus.). 24p. (ps-1). 1982. 1.95 (ISBN 0-307-11960-2, Golden Bks.). Western Pub.

Bradon, Russel, et al. River Journeys. (Illus.). 208p. 1985. 19.95 (ISBN 0-87052-140-3). Hippocrene Bks.

Bradosky, John F. & Joyce, Jon L. Stories We Love. (Orig.). 1981. pap. 12.95 (ISBN 0-937172-21-9). JLJ Pubs.

Bradshaw. Brain CT: An Introduction. 1986. price not set (ISBN 0-7236-0855-5). PSG Pub Co.

Bradshaw, A. D. & Chadwick, M. J. The Restoration of the Land: The Ecology & Reclamation of Derelict & Degraded Land. LC 79-64658. (Blackwell Ecology Ser.: Vol. 6). 1981. 30.00 (ISBN 0-520-03961-0). U of Cal Pr.

Bradshaw, A. D. & McNeilly, D. T. Evolution & Pollution. (Studies in Biology: No. 130). 80p. 1981. pap. text ed. 8.95 (ISBN 0-7131-2818-6). E Arnold.

Bradshaw, Annette & Franson, Gwyn. Forever Families. 48p. (Orig.). pap. write for info. (ISBN 0-88290-180-X, 2804). Horizon Utah.

--The Twelve Days of Christmas. 48p. (Orig.). 1981. pap. 4.95 (ISBN 0-88290-151-6, 2803). Horizon Utah.

Bradshaw, Annette, jt. auth. see Franson, Gwyn.

Bradshaw, Brendan. The Irish Constitutional Revolution in the Sixteenth Century. LC 78-58785. 1979. 47.50 (ISBN 0-521-22206-0). Cambridge U Pr.

Bradshaw, C. M., et al, eds. Quantification of Steady State Operant Behavior. 1981. 70.25 (ISBN 0-444-80298-3). Elsevier.

Bradshaw, Charles. Patriot Souvenir Edition, Eighteen Ninety-Six. 76p. 1976. 3.00 (ISBN 0-686-27518-7). E S Cunningham.

Bradshaw, Charles E. Profile of Faith. 9.95 (ISBN 0-911866-01-9). Advocate.

Bradshaw, David N. & Hahn, Catherine, eds. World Photography Sources. 515p. 40.00 (ISBN 0-9607992-1-4). Directories.

Bradshaw, Emily, ed. Directory of Member Agencies, 1985. rev. ed. 112p. 1985. pap. 16.00 incl. bimonthly updates (ISBN 0-87304-213-1). Family Serv.

Bradshaw, George. Bradshaw's July 1938 Railway Guide. LC 68-24743. (Illus.). Repr. of 1938 ed. 50.00x (ISBN 0-678-05750-8). Kelley.

--Souffles, Quiches, Mousses & the Random Egg. LC 78-156508. 1971. 11.49i (ISBN 0-06-010451-1, HarpT). Har-Row.

Bradshaw, Gillian. In Winter's Shadow. 1983. pap. 2.95 (ISBN 0-451-12276-3, Sig). NAL.

--Kingdom of Summer. 1981. 12.95 (ISBN 0-671-25472-3). S&S.

--Kingdom of Summer. 1982. pap. 3.50 (ISBN 0-451-13553-9, Sig). NAL.

Bradshaw, H. Bradshaw's Life of St. Werburge of Chester. Horstmann, C., ed. (EETS, OS Ser.: No. 88). Repr. of 1887 ed. 20.00 (ISBN 0-527-00085-X). Kraus Repr.

Bradshaw, Henry. Holy Life & History of Saynt Werburg. Repr. of 1848 ed. 28.00 (ISBN 0-384-05450-1). Johnson Repr.

--The Skeleton of Chaucer's Canterbury Tales. LC 70-39518. Repr. of 1871 ed. 16.00 (ISBN 0-404-00929-8). AMS Pr.

Bradshaw, J., ed. The Women's Liberation Movement: Europe & North America. 100p. 1982. 19.00 (ISBN 0-08-028932-0). Pergamon.

Bradshaw, J. D., jt. auth. see Hancock, Barry W.

Bradshaw, Jack L. Laboratory Microbiology. 3rd ed. 1979. pap. text ed. 19.95 (ISBN 0-7216-1909-6, CBS C). SCP.

Bradshaw, Jim. Homework: Helping Students Achieve. 16p. (Orig.). 1985. pap. write for info. (ISBN 0-87652-103-0). Am Assn Sch Admin.

Bradshaw, John. A Concordance to the Poetical Works of John Milton. LC 77-13457. 1977. Repr. of 1894 ed. lib. bdg. 20.00 (ISBN 0-89341-452-2). Longwood Pub Group.

--A Concordance to the Poetical Works of John Milton. LC 70-144894. 412p. 1972. Repr. of 1894 ed. 27.00 (ISBN 0-403-00833-6). Scholarly.

--Greenberg's Guide to Kusan, AMT, & Auburn Trains. Greenberg, Linda, ed. 1985. pap. write for info. (ISBN 0-89778-073-6). Greenberg Pub Co.

Bradshaw, John, ed. The Letters of Philip Dorner, Stanhope Earl of Chesterfield with the Characters Edited with Introduction, Notes & Index, 3 vols. 1453p. 1985. Repr. of 1892 ed. Set. lib. bdg. 450.00 (ISBN 0-8414-1687-7). Folcroft.

Bradshaw, John L. & Nettleton, Norman. Human Cerebral Asymmetry. (Century Psychology Ser.). (Illus.). 352p. 1983. text ed. 31.95 (ISBN 0-13-444646-1). P-H.

Bradshaw, Jon. Dreams That Money Can Buy: The Tragic Life of Libby Holman. (Illus.). 416p. 1984. 17.95 (ISBN 0-688-01158-6). Morrow.

Bradshaw, Jon, jt. auth. see Cooke, Barclay.

Bradshaw, Jonathan & Piachaud, David. Child Support in the European Community. 144p. 1980. pap. text ed. 17.25 (ISBN 0-7199-1045-5, Pub. by Bedford England). Brookfield Pub Co.

Bradshaw, Jonathan & Harris, Toby, eds. Energy & Social Policy. 208p. (Orig.). 1983. pap. 13.95x (ISBN 0-7100-9503-1). Routledge & Kegan.

Bradshaw, Kenneth & Pring, David. Parliament & Congress. 9.95 (ISBN 0-7043-3353-8, Pub. by Quartet England). Charles River Bks.

Bradshaw, L. Jack. Introduction to Molecular Biological Techniques. 1966. pap. 17.95 ref. ed. (ISBN 0-13-489187-2). P-H.

Bradshaw, Lois E. & Mazlen, Roger G. Nutrition in Health Care. LC 79-89882. 1979. pap. 6.95 (ISBN 0-917634-06-3). Creative Infomatics.

--Nutrition in Health Care. 1979. vinyl 6.95 (ISBN 0-686-59813-X). Interfacia Inc.

Bradshaw, M. Royal Society Artists (Members Exhibiting 1824-1962) Vol. 2, 1893-1910. 116p. 1975. text ed. 30.50x (ISBN 0-85317-033-9, Pub. by A & C Black England). Humanities.

--Royal Society of British Artists (Members Exhibiting 1824-1962) Vol. 1, 1824-1892. 113p. 1973. text ed. 30.50x (ISBN 0-85317-026-6, Pub. by A & C Black England). Humanities.

--Royal Society of British Artists (Members Exhibiting 1824-1962) Vol. 3, 1911-1930. 99p. 1975. text ed. 30.50x (ISBN 0-85317-042-8, Pub. by A & C Black England). Humanities.

--Royal Society of British Artists (Members Exhibiting 1824-1962) Vol. 4, 1931-1946. 80p. 1976. text ed. 30.50x (ISBN 0-85317-044-4, Pub. by A & C Black England). Humanities.

--Royal Society of British Artists (Members Exhibiting 1824-1962) Vol. 5, 1947-1962. 64p. 1977. text ed. 30.50x (ISBN 0-85317-048-7, Pub. by A & C Black England). Humanities.

Bradshaw, Marion J. Philosophical Foundations of Faith. LC 78-99248. Repr. of 1941 ed. 10.00 (ISBN 0-404-00968-9). AMS Pr.

Bradshaw, Michael, jt. auth. see Guinness, Paul.

Bradshaw, Michael, ed. Management for Small-to-Medium-Sized Restaurants. (New York Restaurant School Ser.). 450p. 1982. 50.00 (ISBN 0-943368-00-6). Hutchinsons.

Bradshaw, Michael J. Earth: The Living Planet. LC 77-946. 302p. 1977. text ed. 32.95x (ISBN 0-470-99107-0). Halsted Pr.

Bradshaw, P. Engineering Calculation Methods for Turbulent Flow. 1981. 49.50 (ISBN 0-12-124550-0). Acad Pr.

--An Introduction to Turbulance & Its Measurements. Woods, W. A., ed. 218p. 1971. pap. text ed. 19.25 (ISBN 0-08-016621-0). Pergamon.

Bradshaw, P., jt. auth. see Cebeci, T.

Bradshaw, P., ed. Turbulence. 2nd. rev ed. (Topics in Applied Physics Ser.: Vol. 12). (Illus.). 1978. pap. 27.00 (ISBN 0-387-08864-4). Springer-Verlag.

Bradshaw, Paul F. Daily Prayer in the Early Church: A Study of the Origins & Early Development of the Divine Office. 1982. 24.50x (ISBN 0-19-520394-1); pap. 8.95x (ISBN 0-19-520395-X). Oxford U Pr.

Bradshaw, Pete. The Management of Self-Esteem: How People Can Feel Good About Themselves & Better About Their Organizations. (Illus.). 368p. 1981. 10.95 (ISBN 0-13-549535-0, Spec); pap. 4.95 (ISBN 0-13-549527-X). P-H.

Bradshaw, Peter. English Eighteenth Century Porcelain Figures. (Illus.). 320p. (Reprint of 1929 edition). 1980. 62.50 (ISBN 0-902028-83-9). Antique Collect.

--Personal Power: How to Build Self-Esteem & Improve Performance. (Illus.). 144p. 1983. 11.95 (ISBN 0-13-658153-6); pap. 5.95 (ISBN 0-13-658146-3). P-H.

Bradshaw, Ralph & Schneider, Diana, eds. Proteins of the Nervous System. 2nd ed. 407p. 1980. 64.50 (ISBN 0-89004-327-2). Raven.

Bradshaw, Ralph A. Evolution of Hormone-Receptor Systems. LC 83-16185. (UCLA Symposia on Molecular & Celular Biology Ser.: Vol. 6). 526p. 1983. 88.00 (ISBN 0-8451-2605-9). A R Liss.

Bradshaw, Ralph A. & Wessler, Sanford, eds. Heparin: Structure, Function, & Clinical Implications. LC 74-28408. (Advances in Experimental Medicine & Biology Ser.: Vol. 52). 432p. 1975. 55.00x (ISBN 0-306-39052-3, Plenum Pr). Plenum Pub.

Bradshaw, Ralph A., et al, eds. Proteins in Biology & Medicine. 1983. 41.00 (ISBN 0-12-124580-2). Acad Pr.

--Surface Membrane Receptors: Interface Between Cells & Their Environment. LC 76-25821. (NATO ASI Series A, Life Sciences: Vol. 11). 493p. 1976. 62.50x (ISBN 0-306-35611-2, Plenum Pr). Plenum Pub.

Bradshaw, Reagan, jt. auth. see Smith, Griffin, Jr.

Bradshaw, Reagan, photos by. The Great State of Texas. LC 85-71191. (Illus.). 160p. (Text by Griffin Smith Jr.). 1985. 37.50 (ISBN 0-912856-96-3). Graphic Arts Ctr.

Bradshaw, Susan, tr. see Boulez, Pierre.

Bradshaw, Ted K. & Blakely, Edward J. Rural Communities in Advanced Industrial Society: Development & Developers. LC 78-19736. 202p. 1979. 34.95 (ISBN 0-03-041626-4). Praeger.

Bradshaw, Vaughn. Building Control Systems. 624p. 1985. 32.95 (ISBN 0-471-87166-4); slides avail. (ISBN 0-471-82652-9). Wiley.

Bradshaw, Vittoria. From Pure Silence to Impure Dialogue: A Survey of Post-War Italian Poetry, 1945-1965. 1971. 16.50 (ISBN 0-913298-61-1). S F Vanni.

Bradshaw, William R. The Goddess of Atvatabar: History of the Discovery of the Interior World & Conquest of Atvatabar. LC 74-15954. (Science Fiction Ser.). (Illus.). 318p. 1975. Repr. of 1892 ed. 25.50x (ISBN 0-405-06279-6). Ayer Co Pubs.

Bradshaw, William S., Jr. The Big Yellow Bus Is a Good Friend of Mine. LC 80-54535. (Illus.). 24p. (gr. k-5). 1981. pap. 6.95 (ISBN 0-935054-03-0). Webb-Newcomb.

Bradshaw-Smith, Gillian. Adventures in Toy-Making. LC 75-903. (Illus.). 128p. 1976. 9.95 (ISBN 0-8008-0102-4); pap. 5.95 (ISBN 0-8008-0103-2). Taplinger.

Bradsher, Earl L. Mathew Carey: Editor, Author & Publisher. LC 78-181915. (BCL Ser. I). Repr. of 1912 ed. 12.00 (ISBN 0-404-00969-7). AMS Pr.
Bradsher, Frances. The Preacher had Ten Kids. 1980. pap. 3.50 (ISBN 0-8423-4886-7). Tyndale.
Bradsher, Henry S. Afghanistan & the Soviet Union. LC 82-21015. (Duke Press Policy Studies). (Illus.). 336p. 1983. 32.50 (ISBN 0-8223-0496-1); pap. 12.75 (ISBN 0-8223-0563-1). Duke.
--Afghanistan & the Soviet Union. 2nd, expanded ed. (Policy Studies). (Illus.). 330p. 1985. pap. 12.95 (ISBN 0-8223-0690-5). Duke.
Bradsma, L. & Verkruijsse, H. D. Synthesis of Acetylenes, Allenes & Cumulenes: A Laboratory Manual. (Studies in Organic Chemistry: Vol. 8). 276p. 1981. 70.25 (ISBN 0-444-42009-6). Elsevier.
Bradstreet, Anne. Tenth Muse. LC 65-10345. Repr. of 1650 ed. 45.00x (ISBN 0-8201-1006-X). Schol Facsimiles.
--Works in Prose & Verse. Ellis, ed. 18.00 (ISBN 0-8446-1087-9). Peter Smith.
Bradstreet, Anne & Hensley, Jeannie. The Works of Anne Bradstreet. LC 67-17312. (The John Harvard Library Ser.). 368p. 1981. pap. 7.95x (ISBN 0-674-95999-X, Belknap Pr). Harvard U Pr.
Bradstreet, Anne D. The Poems of Mrs. Anne Bradstreet (1612-1672) 1976. Repr. 59.00x (ISBN 0-685-71977-4, Regency). Scholarly.
--The Works of Anne Bradstreet in Prose and Verse. 1976. Repr. 59.00x (ISBN 0-403-08995-6, Regency). Scholarly.
Bradstreet, Valerie. The Fortune Wheel. 160p. 1981. pap. 2.25 (ISBN 0-380-78303-7, 78303-7). Avon.
--The Ivory Fan. 160p. (Orig.). 1982. pap. 2.25 (ISBN 0-380-79244-3, 79244-3). Avon.
Bradt, George. South America River Trips, Vol. I. LC 80-69523. (Illus.). 108p. (Orig.). 1981. pap. 8.95 (ISBN 0-933982-13-5). Bradt Ent.
Bradt, George & Bradt, Hilary. Backpacking in Venezuela, Colombia & Equador. (Backpacking Ser.). (Illus.). 131p. 1980. pap. 7.95 (ISBN 0-9505797-5-0). Bradt Ent.
Bradt, George, jt. auth. see Bradt, Hilary.
Bradt, George N., jt. auth. see Bradt, Hilary J.
Bradt, H., ed. see International Astronomical Union Symposium, 55, Madrid, May 11-13, 1972.
Bradt, Hilary. Backpacker's Africa. 2nd ed. (Backpacker's Guide Ser.). (Illus.). 193p. 1983. pap. 11.95 (ISBN 0-9505797-9-3). Bradt Ent.
Bradt, Hilary & Bradt, George. Backpacking & Trekking in Peru & Bolivia. 3rd, rev. & enl. ed. LC 80-115. (Backpacker Guide Ser.). (Illus.). 1980. pap. 8.95 (ISBN 0-9505797-6-9). Bradt Ent.
--Backpacking in Mexico & Central America: Nicaragua, Colombia, Costa Rica, Panama, Mexico, Belize, Guatemala, El Salvador, Honduras. LC 81-24201. (Backpacker Guide Ser.). (Illus.). 247p. 1982. pap. 9.95 (ISBN 0-9505797-8-5). Bradt Ent.
Bradt, Hilary & Pilkington, John. Backpacking & Trekking in Chile & Argentina. LC 80-68116. (Backpacker Guide Ser.). (Illus.). 144p. 1980. pap. 7.95 (ISBN 0-9505797-7-7). Bradt Ent.
Bradt, Hilary, jt. auth. see Bradt, George.
Bradt, Hilary J. & Bradt, George N. Backpacking in North America: The Great Outdoors. (Backpacker Guide Ser.). (Illus.). 1980. pap. 7.95 (ISBN 0-9505797-4-2). Bradt Ent.
Bradt, Patricia T., jt. auth. see Pritchard, Hayden N.
Bradt, R. C. & Evans, A. G., eds. Fracture Mechanics of Ceramics, Vol. 5: Surface Flaws, Statistics, & Microcracking. 765p. 1983. 89.50x (ISBN 0-306-41021-4, Plenum Pr). Plenum Pub.
--Fracture Mechanics of Ceramics, Vol. 6: Measurements, Transformations & High Temperature Fracture. 655p. 1983. 89.50x (ISBN 0-306-41022-2, Plenum Pr). Plenum Pub.
Bradt, Richard C. & Tressler, Richard E., eds. Deformation of Ceramic Materials. LC 75-4945. 577p. 1975. 85.00x (ISBN 0-306-30839-8, Plenum Pr). Plenum Pub.
Bradt, Richard C., jt. ed. see Tressler, Richard E.
Bradt, Richard C., et al, eds. Fracture Mechanics of Ceramics, 4 vols. Incl. Vol. 1. Concepts, Flaws & Fractography. 471p. 1974. 75.00x (ISBN 0-306-37591-5); Vol. 2. Microstructure, Materials & Applications. 504p. 1974. 75.00x (ISBN 0-306-37592-3); Vol. 3. Flaws & Testing. 528p. 1978. 75.00x (ISBN 0-306-37593-1); Vol. 4. Crack Growth & Microstructure. 504p. 1978. 75.00x (ISBN 0-306-37594-X). LC 73-20399 (Plenum Pr). Plenum Pub.
Bradway, B. M. & Frenzel, M. A. Strategic Marketing: A Handbook for Entrepreneurs & Managers. LC 81-3638. 1982. text ed. 29.95 (ISBN 0-201-00079-2). Addison-Wesley.
Bradway, Bruce M. & Pritchard, Robert E. Protecting Profits During Inflation & Recession. 130p. 1981. pap. text ed. 7.95 (ISBN 0-201-00074-1). Addison-Wesley.
Bradway, John S. How to Practice Law Effectively. LC 58-9193. 96p. 1958. 8.50 (ISBN 0-379-00039-3). Oceana.
--Progress in Family Law. Lambert, Richard D., ed. LC 71-81088. (Annals Ser.: No. 383). 1969. 15.00 (ISBN 0-87761-116-5); pap. 7.95 (ISBN 0-87761-115-7). Am Acad Pol Soc Sci.
Bradway, K. & Signell, K. Sandplay Studies. Hill, Gareth, ed. 238p. 1981. 16.00 (ISBN 0-932630-03-0). C G Jung Frisco.
Bradway, Katherine. Villa of Mysteries: Pompeii Initiation Rites of Women. pap. 4.00 (ISBN 0-317-13541-4). C G Jung Frisco.
Bradway, Lauren C. A Systems Approach to Handicapped Children: Helping Children Grow. (Illus.). 242p. 1984. 24.75x (ISBN 0-398-05025-2). C C Thomas.
Bradwell, Stephen. Physick for the Sickness, Commonly Called the Plague. LC 77-6859. (English Experience Ser.: No. 852). 1977. Repr. of 1636 ed. lib. bdg. 8.00 (ISBN 90-221-0852-X). Walter J Johnson.
Bradwin, Edmund W. Bunkhouse Man: A Study of Work & Play in the Camps of Canada, 1903-1914. LC 68-57564. (Columbia University Studies in the Social Sciences: No. 296). Repr. of 1928 ed. 12.50 (ISBN 0-404-51296-8). AMS Pr.
Brady. General Chemistry: Principles & Structure, Vol. 2. 2nd ed. 500p. 1985. pap. text ed. write for info. (ISBN 0-471-89534-2). Wiley.
--L' Oeuvre d'Emil Zola. 39.95 (ISBN 0-685-37146-8). French & Eur.
Brady & Richardson. BASIC Programming Language. rev. ed. (Plaid Ser.). 1981. 9.95 (ISBN 0-256-02124-4). Dow Jones-Irwin.
Brady, jt. auth. see Rich.
Brady, Alexander. William Huskisson & Liberal Reform. 2nd ed. 177p. 1967. 28.50x (ISBN 0-7146-1456-4, F Cass Co). Biblio Dist.
Brady, Alexander & Scott, Francis R., eds. Canada after the War. facs. ed. LC 75-128212. (Essay Index Reprint Ser). 1944. 21.50 (ISBN 0-8369-1867-3). Ayer Co Pubs.
Brady, Anna, et al, eds. Union List of Film Periodicals: Holdings of Selected American Collections. LC 83-22585. xxvi, 316p. 1984. 35.00 (ISBN 0-313-23702-6, BRL/). Greenwood.
Brady, Anne & Cleeve, Brian. A Biographical Dictionary of Irish Writers. LC 85-40074. 480p. 1985. 35.00 (ISBN 0-312-07871-4). St Martin.
Brady, B. H. & Brown, E. T. Rock Mechanics: For Underground Mining. (Illus.). 550p. 1985. text ed. 60.00x (ISBN 0-04-622004-6); pap. text ed. 29.95x (ISBN 0-04-622005-4). Allen Unwin.
Brady, Ben. The Keys to Writing for Television & Films. 4th ed. 1982. text ed. 19.95 (ISBN 0-8403-3280-7, 40328002). Kendall-Hunt.
Brady, C., et al, eds. Industrial-Commercial Refrigeration Maintenance. (Illus.). 226p. 1982. spiral bdg. 45.00x (ISBN 0-85083-528-3). Intl Ideas.
Brady, Caroline A. Eormanric of the Widsith. LC 73-16225. 1937. lib. bdg. 10.00 (ISBN 0-8414-3349-6). Folcroft.
Brady, Charles. A Spark of Goodness. LC 82-11949. 372p. 1983. 14.95 (ISBN 0-395-31257-4). HM.
Brady, Christine. Cooking in Season. (Illus.). 1978. 16.95 (ISBN 0-241-89451-4, Pub. by Hamish Hamilton England). David & Charles.
Brady, Constance. Right Where You Live. (Illus.). 188p. (Orig.). 1982. pap. 9.95 (ISBN 0-686-35975-5). Conarc.
Brady, Cyrus T. Indian Fights & Fighters. LC 74-156373. (Illus.). xx, 475p. 1971. 29.50x (ISBN 0-8032-1152-X); pap. 8.95 (ISBN 0-8032-5743-0, BB 538, Bison). U of Nebr Pr.
--Little Book for Christmas. facsimile ed. LC 73-167443. (Short Story Index Reprint Ser). Repr. of 1917 ed. 17.00 (ISBN 0-8369-3969-7). Ayer Co Pubs.
--Northwestern Fights & Fighters. 373p. 1974. Repr. of 1907 ed. 16.95 (ISBN 0-685-56786-9). Corner Hse.
--Northwestern Fights & Fighters. LC 79-15171. (Illus.). xxii, 373p. 1979. 25.95x (ISBN 0-8032-1156-2); pap. 6.95 (ISBN 0-8032-6053-9, BB 713, Bison). U of Nebr Pr.
--Sir Henry Morgan, Buccaneer. 445p. Repr. of 1903 ed. lib. bdg. 22.95x (ISBN 0-88411-175-X, Pub. by Aeonian Pr). Amereon Ltd.
--Stephen Decatur. 1978. Repr. of 1900 ed. lib. bdg. 17.50 (ISBN 0-8492-3713-0). R West.
--Woven with the Ship. facs. ed. LC 73-128722. (Short Story Index Reprint Ser). 1902. 20.00 (ISBN 0-8369-3613-2). Ayer Co Pubs.
Brady, D. Guide to Publicity & Public Relations. 1986. cancelled (ISBN 0-442-24657-9). Van Nos Reinhold.
Brady, Darlene. Le Corbusier: An Annotated Bibliography. LC 82-49267. (Reference Library of the Humanities). 320p. 1985. lib. bdg. 60.00 (ISBN 0-8240-9134-5). Garland Pub.
Brady, Darlene & Serban, William, eds. Stained Glass: A Guide to Information Sources. LC 79-23712. (Art & Architecture Information Guide Ser.: Vol. 10). 1980. 60.00x (ISBN 0-8103-1445-2). Gale.
Brady, David. Congressional Voting in a Partisan Era: A Study of the McKinley Houses & a Comparison to the Modern House of Representatives. LC 72-87822. 273p. 1973. 25.00x (ISBN 0-7006-0098-1). U Pr of KS.
Brady, Donald. Logic of the Scientific Method. LC 73-15697. 92p. 1973. pap. text ed. 6.95x (ISBN 0-8422-0361-3). Irvington.
Brady, Donald, ed. Philosophy in the Flesh: A Reader. 149p. 1975. pap. text ed. 6.95x (ISBN 0-8422-0492-X). Irvington.
Brady, Edward M. Marine Salvage Operations. LC 59-12836. (Illus.). 250p. 1960. 12.00x (ISBN 0-87033-051-9). Cornell Maritime.
--Tugs, Towboats & Towing. LC 67-17537. (Illus.). 242p. 1967. 15.00x (ISBN 0-87033-127-2). Cornell Maritime.
Brady, Enid J. The Exciting World of a Psychic. 2nd ed. 117p. 1973. pap. 2.95 (ISBN 0-917200-04-7). ESPress.
Brady, Esther W. The Toad on Capitol Hill. LC 77-15861. 144p. (gr. 3-5). 1978. 6.95 (ISBN 0-517-53319-7). Crown.
Brady, F., ed. see Boswell, James.
Brady, Frank. James Boswell: The Later Years, 1769-1795. LC 83-9400. (Illus.). 640p. 1984. 24.95 (ISBN 0-07-050558-6). McGraw.
--A Singular View: The Art of Seeing with One Eye. 3rd, rev. ed. (Illus.). 129p. 1985. pap. 12.50 (ISBN 0-9614639-0-2). Brady.
Brady, Frank, ed. An Essay on Man: Pope. 1965. pap. text ed. write for info. (ISBN 0-02-313460-7). Macmillan.
--Twentieth Century Interpretations of Gulliver's Travels. LC 68-23699. 9.95 (ISBN 0-13-371575-2, Spec); pap. 1.25 (ISBN 0-13-371567-1, Spec). P-H.
Brady, Frank & Price, Martin, eds. Poetry Past & Present. 527p. (Orig.). 1974. pap. text ed. 13.95 (ISBN 0-15-570682-9, HC). HarBraceJ.
Brady, Frank & Wimsatt, W. K., eds. Samuel Johnson: Selected Poetry & Prose. 1978. 40.00x (ISBN 0-520-02929-1, CAL 378); pap. 9.95 (ISBN 0-520-03552-6). U of Cal Pr.
Brady, Frank, ed. see Boswell, James.
Brady, Frank, ed. see Pope, Alexander.
Brady, Frank, ed. see Wels, Byron G.
Brady, G. S. Monograph of the Free & Semi-Parasitic Copepoda of the British Islands, 3 Vols. Repr. of 1880 ed. Set. 46.00 (ISBN 0-384-05470-6). Johnson Repr.
Brady, G. S. & Claus, H. R. Materials Handbook. 12th ed. 1056p. 1985. price not set (ISBN 0-07-007071-7). McGraw.
Brady, G. S. & Clauser, H. Materials Handbook. 11th ed. 1977. 52.50 (ISBN 0-07-007069-5). McGraw.
Brady, Gene F. & Helmich, Donald L. Executive Succession: Toward Excellence in Corporate Leadership. 256p. 1984. 18.95 (ISBN 0-13-294273-9); pap. 9.95 (ISBN 0-13-294265-8). P-H.
Brady, Gene P. A Master Plan for Winning in Wall Street. 1976. 39.95 (ISBN 0-685-61028-4). Windsor.
Brady, George K. Samuel Daniel: A Critical Study. LC 73-9725. 1973. lib. bdg. 10.00 (ISBN 0-8414-3158-2). Folcroft.
Brady, Gerald P. & Miller, Richard L. CPA Liability: A CPE Guide. 584p. 1985. 45.00 (ISBN 0-471-88751-X). Wiley.
--CPA Liability: CPE Approach. LC 85-12334. Date not set. price not set (ISBN 0-471-88751-X). Wiley.
Brady, Gerald P., jt. auth. see Thompson, George C.
Brady, Gordon L. & Bower, Blair T. Air Quality Management: Qualifying Benefits. LC 81-17478. (East-West Environment & Policy Institute Research Report Ser.: No. 7). v, 25p. (Orig.). 1981. pap. text ed. 3.00 (ISBN 0-86638-029-9). E W Center HI.
Brady, H., jt. auth. see Brady, M.
Brady, Haldeen. Pancho Villa at Columbus: The Raid of Nineteen-Sixteen. (Southwestern Studies Ser.: No. 9). 1965. pap. 3.00 (ISBN 0-87404-132-5). Tex Western.
Brady, Howard, jt. auth. see Brady, Marion.
Brady, Ignatius, tr. see Clausen, Sophronius.
Brady, Ignatius C., jt. ed. see Armstrong, Regis J.
Brady, Irene. America's Horses & Ponies. LC 70-86298. (Illus.). 202p. (gr. 4 up). 1969. 12.95 (ISBN 0-395-06659-X). HM.
--America's Horses & Ponies. (Illus.). 202p. (gr. 4 up). 1976. pap. 6.95 (ISBN 0-395-24050-6, Sandpiper). HM.
--Doodlebug. LC 77-4168. (Illus.). 40p. (gr. 1-5). 1977. PLB 10.95 (ISBN 0-395-25782-4). HM.
--A Horse Named Doodlebug. (gr. 4-6). 1979. pap. 1.50 (ISBN 0-590-12092-1). Scholastic Inc.
--Wild Babies: A Canyon Sketchbook. (Illus.). (gr. 1-12). 1979. PLB 8.95 (ISBN 0-395-27464-8). HM.
Brady, Ivan A., ed. Transactions in Kinship: Adoption & Fosterage in Oceania. LC 76-10342. (Association for Social Anthropology in Oceania Monograph: No.4). 320p. 1976. text ed. 20.00x (ISBN 0-8248-0478-3). UH Pr.
Brady, Ivan A., jt. ed. see Laughlin, Charles D., Jr.
Brady, J. & Nauta, W. J. Principles, Practices & Positions in Neuropsychiatric Research. 320p. 1972. text ed. 79.00 (ISBN 0-08-017007-2). Pergamon.
Brady, J., ed. Biological Timekeeping. LC 81-15506. (Society for Experimental Biology Seminar: No. 14). 220p. 1982. 44.50 (ISBN 0-521-23307-0); pap. 19.95 (ISBN 0-521-29899-7). Cambridge U Pr.
Brady, J. D., jt. auth. see Beyersdorf, Eunice.
Brady, J. E. & Humiston, J. R. General Chemistry: Principles & Structure, 2 vols. 2nd ed. 900p. (Bahasa-Malaysia.). 1985. Set. text ed. write for info. (ISBN 0-471-80156-9); Vol. 1, 500p. pap. text ed. 16.00 (ISBN 0-471-86617-2); Vol. 2, 500p. pap. text ed. 16.00 (ISBN 0-471-86618-0). Wiley.
Brady, J. M. The Theory of Computer Science: A Programming Approach. 1977. pap. 9.95 (ISBN 0-412-15040-9, NO. 6040, Pub. by Chapman & Hall). Methuen Inc.
Brady, J. P., ed. Justice & Politics in People's China: Legal Order of Continuing Revolution. 1983. 37.50 (ISBN 0-12-124750-3). Acad Pr.
Brady, James. Holy Wars. 1983. 15.95 (ISBN 0-671-42589-7). S&S.
--On-Highway Trucks: Power Trains & Suspension Systems. 624p. 1981. text ed. 28.95 (ISBN 0-8359-5232-0). Reston.
Brady, James & Essner, Warren. Accounting & Auditing Problems in Employee Benefit Plans: No. B364. (Rules for Operation of Qualified Plans Ser.). 23p. 1978. pap. 6.00 (ISBN 0-317-31186-7). Am Law Inst.
Brady, James E. & Holum, John R. Fundamentals of Chemistry. 2nd ed. LC 83-21796. 960p. 1984. text ed. 39.50 (ISBN 0-471-87548-1); write for info. tchr's lab (ISBN 0-471-87894-4); study guide 15.50 (ISBN 0-471-87891-X); lab. manual 20.50 (ISBN 0-471-89007-3); sol. manual 13.95 (ISBN 0-471-87947-9); write for info. transparency (ISBN 0-471-87946-0). Wiley.
Brady, James E. & Humiston, Gerard E. General Chemistry: Principles & Structure. 3rd ed. 831p. 1982. 38.50 (ISBN 0-471-07806-9); text ed. 35.95 SI version (ISBN 0-471-86739-X); exam manager 10.95 (ISBN 0-471-80509-2); solutions manual 12.95 (ISBN 0-471-09964-3); solutions manual, SI version 9.50 (ISBN 0-471-86968-6); study guide 13.95 (ISBN 0-471-08354-2). Wiley.
--General Chemistry: Principles & Structure. 2nd ed. LC 77-11045. 800p. 1978. text ed. 27.95 (ISBN 0-471-01910-0). wkbk. 8.25x (ISBN 0-471-03498-3). Wiley.
Brady, Jeremiah D. Sylloge of Coins of the British Isles: Ancient British, Anglo-Saxon & Norman Coins in American Collections. (British Academy Ser.). (Illus.). 1982. 65.00x (ISBN 0-19-726011-X). Oxford U Pr.
Brady, Jo, jt. auth. see Muszynski, Sam.
Brady, Joan. The Imposter. LC 78-24642. 214p. 1979. 7.95 (ISBN 0-8076-0915-3). Braziller.
Brady, Joan, jt. auth. see Koplik, William.
Brady, John. The Craft of Interviewing. LC 77-76543. (YA) 1977. pap. 4.95 (ISBN 0-394-72469-0, Vin). Random.
--The Craft of Interviewing. LC 75-33133. 244p. 1975. 9.95 (ISBN 0-911654-44-5). Writers Digest.
--The Craft of the Screenwriter. 1981. 20.25 (ISBN 0-671-25229-1). S&S.
--The Craft of the Screenwriter. 1982. 8.25 (ISBN 0-671-25230-5). S&S.
--The Unmaking of a Dancer: An Unconventional Life. 1983. pap. 3.95 (ISBN 0-671-46817-0). WSP.
Brady, John & White, Brian. Fifty Hikes in Massachusetts: Hikes & Walks from the Top of the Berkshires to the Tip of Cape Cod. LC 83-6003. (Fifty Hikes Ser.). (Illus.). 224p. 1983. pap. 8.95 (ISBN 0-942440-11-0). Backcountry Pubns.
Brady, John & Hall, James, eds. Sports Literature. (Patterns in Literary Art Ser.). 276p. (gr. 9-12). 1974. pap. text ed. 11.04 (ISBN 0-07-007085-7). McGraw.
Brady, John P. Classics of American Psychiatry Eighteen-Ten to Nineteen Thirty-Four. LC 72-85641. (Illus.). 336p. 1975. 17.50 (ISBN 0-87527-093-X). Green.
Brady, John P., et al, eds. Controversy in Psychiatry. LC 77-77097. pap. 160.00 (ISBN 0-317-26427-3, 2024983). Bks Demand UMI.
Brady, John T. The Heisman: A Symbol of Excellence. Walsh, John A., ed. LC 84-45033. (Illus.). 224p. 1984. 29.95 (ISBN 0-689-11497-4). Atheneum.
Brady, Joseph H. Rome & the Neapolitan Revolution of 1820-1821. 1971. lib. bdg. 20.50x (ISBN 0-374-90933-4). Octagon.
Brady, Joseph V., jt. auth. see Meyer, Eugene.
Brady, Jules, ed. An Augustine Treasury: Selections from the Writings of St. Augustine. 1981. 5.00 (ISBN 0-8198-0706-0); pap. 4.00 (ISBN 0-686-73823-3). Dghtrs St Paul.
Brady, Jules M. A Philosopher's Search for the Infinite. 96p. 1983. 10.00 (ISBN 0-8022-2410-5). Philos Lib.
Brady, June P., jt. auth. see Hirata, Toshiko.
Brady, Katherine. Father's Days. 1981. pap. 3.95 (ISBN 0-440-12475-1). Dell.
Brady, Kathleen. Ida Tarbell: Portrait of a Muckraker. LC 83-27176. 288p. 1984. 17.95 (ISBN 0-399-31023-1). Putnam Pub Group.
Brady, Kristin. The Short Stories of Thomas Hardy. LC 81-5665. 200p. 1982. 22.50x (ISBN 0-312-72219-2). St Martin.
Brady, L. W. T. P. O'Connor & the Liverpool Irish. (Royal Historical Society, Studies: Vol. 39). 296p. 1983. text ed. 42.50x (ISBN 0-391-02957-6, Pub. by Swiftbks. England). Humanities.
Brady, L. W., et al. Ovarian Tumors. (Oncologic Ser.: Vol. 20). (Illus.). 232p. 1984. pap. 100.00 (ISBN 0-08-027472-2). Pergamon.
Brady, Larry G. How to Get the Most from Your Marriage Without a Therapist: Guidelines for Intimate Relationships. 170p. 1985. write for info.; pap. write for info. Larry G Brady.

Brady, Lillian. Saga of a Whitetail Deer. LC 77-77113. (Illus.). 182p. 1981. 12.50 (ISBN 0-86533-004-2). Bk Pools.

Brady, Lloyd. Dick Whittington & His Cat. (Children's Theatre Playscript Ser.). 1963. pap. 2.25x (ISBN 0-88020-026-X). Coach Hse.

Brady, Luther W., ed. Radiation Sensitizers: Their Use in the Clinical Management of Cancer. LC 80-81987. (Masson Cancer Management Ser.: Vol. 5). (Illus.). 544p. 1980. 69.50x (ISBN 0-89352-112-4). Masson Pub.

Brady, M. & Brady, H. Idea & Action in American History. 1977. 21.12 (ISBN 0-13-448548-3). P-H.

Brady, M., ed. Computer Vision. (Journal: Artifical Intelligence Ser.: Vol. 17). 1984. pap. 30.00 (ISBN 0-444-87511-5). Elsevier.

Brady, M., et al, eds. Robotics & Artificial Intelligence. (NATO ASI Ser.: Series F: No. 11). xviii, 694p. 1984. 62.50 (ISBN 0-387-12888-3). Springer-Verlag.

Brady, M. Michael. Nordic Touring & Cross Country Skiing. 5th, rev. ed. (Illus.). 92p. (Orig.). 1979. pap. 5.00x (ISBN 82-09-01781-0, N395). Vanous.

Brady, Sr. M. Rosalie. Thought & Style in the Works of Leon Bloy. LC 70-94176. (Catholic Universtiy of America Studies in Romance Languages & Literatures Ser: No. 30). Repr. of 1945 ed. 19.00 (ISBN 0-404-50330-6). AMS Pr.

Brady, Margaret K. Some Kind of Power: Navajo Children's Skinwalker Narratives. 224p. 1984. 14.95 (ISBN 0-87480-238-5). U of Utah Pr.

Brady, Mari. Please Remember Me. (gr. 7-9). 1978. pap. 1.75 (ISBN 0-671-43137-4). Archway.

Brady, Marion & Brady, Howard. Idea & Action in World Cultures. 1977. text ed. 21.72; Skills & Evaluation Package. 58.08. P-H.

Brady, Mary A. Herbal Lore: Healing Plants of Southern Colorado from Indian, Spanish & Other Settler's Sources. (Orig.). 1986. pap. write for info. (ISBN 0-915617-09-9). Pueblo Co Hist Soc.

Brady, Matthew B., jt. auth. see Elson, Henry W.

Brady, Maureen. Folly: A Novel. LC 82-17235. 198p. 1982. 17.95 (ISBN 0-89594-091-4); pap. 7.95 (ISBN 0-89594-090-6). Crossing Pr.

--Give Me Your Good Ear. LC 78-66097. 1979. pap. 4.50. Spinsters Ink.

Brady, Maxine. The Monopoly Book. (Illus.). (gr. 7 up). 1976. pap. 4.95 (ISBN 0-679-14401-3). McKay.

Brady, Michael. The Complete Ski Cross-Country. LC 81-15131. 288p. 1982. (Dial); pap. 12.95 (ISBN 0-385-27677-X, Dial). Doubleday.

--Cross-Country Ski Gear. 1983. 14.00 (ISBN 0-8446-6048-5). Peter Smith.

--Waxing & Care of Cross-Country Skis. LC 84-52654. (Illus.). 112p. (Orig.). Date not set. pap. 5.95 (ISBN 0-89997-048-6). Wilderness Pr.

Brady, Michael & Skjemstad, Lorns. Waxing for Cross-Country Skiing. 6th ed. LC 81-52038. (Illus.). 48p. (Orig.). 1981. pap. 2.50 (ISBN 0-89997-013-3). Wilderness Pr.

Brady, Michael, jt. auth. see Caldwell, John.

Brady, Michael, ed. Computer Vision. (Journal of Artificial Intelligence Ser.: Vol. 17). vi, 508p. 1982. 64.00 (ISBN 0-444-86343-5, North-Holland). Elsevier.

Brady, Michael & Berwick, Robert C., eds. Computational Models of Discourse. (Artificial Intelligence Ser.). 403p. 1982. 37.50x (ISBN 0-262-02183-8). MIT Pr.

Brady, Michael & Paul, Richard, eds. International Symposium of Robotics Research. LC 83-25592. (Artificial Intelligence Ser.). (Illus.). 600p. 1984. text ed. 65.00x (ISBN 0-262-02207-9). MIT Pr.

--Robotics Research: First International Symposium. 1984. 65.00x (ISBN 0-262-02207-9). MIT Pr.

Brady, Michael, tr. see Bergh, Ulf.

Brady, Michael, tr. see Flemmen, Asbjorn & Grosvold, Olav.

Brady, Michael, et al. Robot Motion: Planning & Control. (Artificial Intelligence Ser.). (Illus.). 585p. 1982. 39.50x (ISBN 0-262-02182-X). MIT Pr.

Brady, Michael J. Infinite Horizons: A Psychic Experience. LC 81-19592. 112p. 1982. pap. 5.95 (ISBN 0-89865-042-9). Donning Co.

Brady, Michael M. & Skjenstad, Lorns O. Ski Cross-Country. LC 81-15131. (Illus.). 192p. 1974. 12.95 (ISBN 0-385-27677-X). Dial.

Brady, Michael P. & Gunter, Philip L., eds. Integrating Moderately & Severely Handicapped Learners: Strategies That Work. 328p. 1985. 34.75x (ISBN 0-398-05127-5). C C Thomas.

Brady, N. C., ed. Advances in Agronomy, Vol. 28. 1976. 75.00 (ISBN 0-12-000728-2). Acad Pr.

--Advances in Agronomy, Vol. 29. 1977. 75.00 (ISBN 0-12-000729-0). Acad Pr.

--Advances in Agronomy, Vol. 30. LC 50-5598. 1979. 65.00 (ISBN 0-12-000730-4). Acad Pr.

--Advances in Agronomy, Vol. 31. LC 50-5598. (Serial Publication Ser.). 1980. 60.00 (ISBN 0-12-000731-2). Acad Pr.

--Advances in Agronomy, Vol. 33. 1980. 65.00 (ISBN 0-12-000733-9). Acad Pr.

--Advances in Agronomy, Vol. 34. 1981. 75.00 (ISBN 0-12-000734-7). Acad Pr.

--Advances in Agronomy, Vol. 35. (Serial Publication Ser.). 1982. 50.00 (ISBN 0-12-000735-5). Acad Pr.

--Advances in Agronomy, Vol. 36. (Serial Publication Ser.). 1983. 50.00 (ISBN 0-12-000736-3). Acad Pr.

Brady, N. C. see Norman, A. G.

Brady, N. C., et al, eds. Food for Peace. (Illus.). 1963. pap. 1.00 (ISBN 0-89118-019-2). Am Soc Agron.

Brady, Nicholas. Bad Guy. 1977. pap. 1.50 (ISBN 0-505-51202-5, Pub. by Tower Bks). Dorchester Pub Co.

--The Homecoming. 1977. pap. 1.50 (ISBN 0-505-51216-5, Pub. by Tower Bks). Dorchester Pub Co.

--Inside Job. 1978. pap. 1.95 (ISBN 0-8439-0571-9, Leisure Bks). Dorchester Pub Co.

Brady, Nick. The Doom Platoon. 1978. pap. 1.75 (ISBN 0-505-51302-1, Pub. by Tower Bks). Dorchester Pub Co.

Brady, Nyle C., ed. Advances in Agronomy, Vol. 37. 1984. 49.50 (ISBN 0-12-000737-1). Acad Pr.

Brady, Patricia A., jt. ed. see Jarett, Irwin M.

Brady, Patrick. Structuralist Perspectives in Criticism of Fiction. (European University Studies: Series 18, Comparative Literature Vol. 16). 236p. 1978. pap. 26.85 (ISBN 3-261-03032-1). P Lang Pubs.

Brady, Patrick, jt ed. see Garvin, Harry R.

Brady, Patrick G., jt. ed. see Nord, H. J.

Brady, Peggy, jt. auth. see Martin, Paul.

Brady, R. J. Anatomy & Physiology: A Programmed Approach, 15 bks. Incl. The Cell. 1972. pap. 6.95 (ISBN 0-87618-031-4); The Cardiovascular System. 1970. pap. 6.95 (ISBN 0-87618-037-3); The Digestive System. 1972. pap. 6.95 (ISBN 0-87618-040-3); The Endocrine System. 1972; The Lymphatic & Reticuloendothelial System. 1973; The Muscular System. 1972. pap. 6.95 (ISBN 0-87618-034-9); The Nervous System. 1972. pap. 6.95 (ISBN 0-87618-035-7); Nutrition, Metabolism, Fluid, & Electrolyte Balance. 1972; Reproduction in Humans. 1973; The Reproductive System. 1972; The Respiratory System. 1972. pap. 6.95 (ISBN 0-87618-039-X); The Skeletal System. 1972. pap. 6.95 (ISBN 0-87618-033-0); The Skin. 1972. pap. 6.95 (ISBN 0-87618-032-2); The Special Senses. 1972. pap. 6.95 (ISBN 0-87618-036-5); The Urinary System. 1974. (Illus.). Brady Comm.

Brady, Robert. Electric & Electronic Systems for Automobiles & Trucks. 1983. text ed. 30.95 (ISBN 0-8359-1610-3); solutions manual free (ISBN 0-8359-1611-1). Reston.

Brady, Robert A. Business As a System of Power. LC 76-167311. (Essay Index Reprint Ser.). Repr. of 1943 ed. 23.50 (ISBN 0-8369-2753-2). Ayer Co Pubs.

Brady, Robert N. Automotive & Small Truck Fuel Injection Systems: Gas & Diesel. 1985. text ed. 32.95 (ISBN 0-8359-0315-X). Reston.

--Diesel Fuel Systems. (Illus.). 640p. 1981. text ed. 29.95 (ISBN 0-8359-1293-0). soln. manual avail. (ISBN 0-8359-1294-9). Reston.

--Servicing Diesel Engines. 1985. text ed. 29.95 (ISBN 0-8359-6996-7). Reston.

Brady, Roscoe O., jt. ed. see Barranger, John A.

Brady, Stephen W. & Farmer, Gale E. The Function Plotter: A Calculus Primer, Apple II Version. 1984. pap. text ed. 23.95 (ISBN 0-471-80189-5). Wiley.

Brady, Thomas A. Sarapis & Isis: Collected Essays. Mitchel, Fordyce, ed. 1978. 25.00 (ISBN 0-89005-253-0). Ares.

Brady, Thomas A., Jr., tr. see Blickle, Peter.

Brady, Thomas, Jr. Turning Swiss: Cities & Empire, 1450-1550. (Cambridge Studies in Early Modern History). 288p. Date not set. price not set. (ISBN 0-521-30525-X). Cambridge U Pr.

Brady, U. Eugene, et al. Pheromones: Current Research, 2 vols, Vol. 2. 157p. 1974. text ed. 28.50x (ISBN 0-8422-7212-7). Irvington.

Brady, Upton, ed. see Balling, L. Christian.

Brady, Upton, ed. see Cole, John & Wing, Cha.

Brady, Upton, ed. see Hazel, Paul.

Brady, Upton, ed. see Searle, Ronald.

Brae, Andrew E. Collier, Coleridge & Shakespeare. LC 70-113562. Repr. of 1860 ed. 16.00 (ISBN 0-404-01061-X). AMS Pr.

Braeman, John. Albert J. Beveridge: American Nationalist. LC 75-142041. 1971. 30.00x (ISBN 0-226-07060-3). U of Chicago Pr.

Braeman, John, et al, eds. Twentieth-Century American Foreign Policy. LC 78-141495. (Modern America: No. 3). 577p. 1971. 10.00 (ISBN 0-8142-0151-2). Ohio St U Pr.

Braemer & Scheurmann. Tropical Fish. (Pet Care Ser.). 1983. pap. 3.95 (ISBN 0-8120-2686-1). Barron.

Braendegaard, Asger, tr. see Steiner, Jurg.

Braendegaard, Barbara, tr. see Steiner, Jurg.

Braendli, H. Stochastische Fehler Prozesse und Treffwahrscheinlichkeitein. (Illus.). 206p. (Ger.). 1972. 50.95x (ISBN 0-8176-0655-6). Birkhauser.

--Die Theories des Mehrfach-Schusses. (Illus.). 200p. (Ger.). 1950. 29.95x (ISBN 0-8176-0042-6). Birkhauser.

--Treffwahrscheinlichkeit und Autokorrelations Funktionen. 2nd, exp. ed. (Illus.). 154p. (Ger.). 1970. 35.20x (ISBN 0-8176-0044-2). Birkhauser.

Braestrup, Angelica, ed. see Blain, Beryl B., et al.

Braestrup, Carl B. & Wyckoff, Harold O. Radiation Protection. (Illus.). 382p. 1958. 32.50x (ISBN 0-398-04219-5). C C Thomas.

Braestrup, Peter. Big Story: American Press & Television Reported & Interpreted the Crisis of Tet 1968 in Vietnam & Washington. LC 82-11041. 632p. 1983. text ed. 27.50x (ISBN 0-300-02953-5); pap. 9.95x (ISBN 0-300-02807-5, Y-446). Yale U Pr.

Braestrup, Peter, ed. Vietnam As History: Ten Years after the Paris Peace Accords. LC 83-21748. (Wilson Center Conference Report Ser.). (Illus.). 208p. (Orig.). 1984. lib. bdg. 17.75 (ISBN 0-8191-3653-0); pap. text ed. 9.25 (ISBN 0-8191-3654-9). U Pr of Amer.

Braetter, P. & Schramel, P., eds. Trace Element Analytical Chemistry in Medicine & Biology, Vol. 3: Proceedings of the 3rd International Workshop. LC 80-26803. (Illus.). xvi, 763p. 1984. 109.00X (ISBN 3-11-009821-0). De Gruyter.

Braetter, Peter & Schramel, Peter, eds. Trace Element Analytical Chemistry in Medicine & Biology, Vol. 2. 1189p. 1983. 112.00 (ISBN 3-11-008681-6). De Gruyter.

Braet Von Uberfeldt, Jan, jt. auth. see Bing, Valetyn.

Braeuning, Christiane, jt. ed. see Huth, K.

Braeunlich, P., ed. Thermally Stimulated Relaxation in Solids. (Topics in Applied Physics Ser.: Vol. 37). (Illus.). 1979. 59.00 (ISBN 0-387-09595-0). Springer-Verlag.

Braeutigam, Ronald, jt. auth. see Owen, Bruce M.

Brafield, Alan E. Life in Sandy Shores. (Studies in Biology: No. 89). 64p. 1978. pap. text ed. 8.95 (ISBN 0-7131-2682-5). E Arnold.

Brafield, Alan E. & Llewellyn, Michael J. Animal Energetics. (Tertiary Level Biology Ser.). 176p. 1982. (Pub. by Chapman & Hall); pap. 18.95x (ISBN 0-412-00031-8, NO. 5004). Methuen Inc.

Brafman, Morris & Schimel, David. Trade for Freedom. LC 75-26371. 96p. 1975. 4.95 (ISBN 0-88400-043-5). Shengold.

Braga, James. Como Preparar Mensajes Biblicos. 296p. (Span.). 1985. pap. 7.95 (ISBN 0-8254-1072-X). Kregel.

--How to Prepare Bible Messages. rev. ed. LC 81-14132. 1982. pap. 6.95 (ISBN 0-930014-71-5). Multnomah.

--How to Study the Bible. LC 82-6420. (Orig.). 1982. pap. 6.95 (ISBN 0-930014-72-3). Multnomah.

Braga, Joseph & Braga, Laurie. Children & Adults: Activities for Growing Together. (Human Development Bks.). (Illus.). 1976. 12.95 (ISBN 0-13-130351-1, Spec); pap. 10.95 (ISBN 0-13-130344-9). P-H.

Braga, Laurie, jt. auth. see Braga, Joseph.

Braga, Meg. Cosas Que Hacer para Navidad. (Editorial Mundo Hispano). (YA) 1981. Repr. of 1980 ed. 3.25 (ISBN 0-311-26607-X). Casa Bautista.

Braga, Thomas J. Portingales. LC 81-86483. 64p. (Orig.). 1981. pap. 3.50 (ISBN 0-943722-01-2). Gavea-Brown.

Bragadin, Marc'Antonio. The Italian Navy in World War II. Hoffman, Gale, tr. LC 79-6102. (Navies & Man Ser.). (Illus.). 1980. Repr. of 1957 ed. lib. bdg. 32.50x (ISBN 0-405-13031-7). Ayer Co Pubs.

Bragadir, Sabine, jt. auth. see Dioudonnat, Pierre-Marie.

Braganca, Aquino de see De Braganca, Aquino.

Braganca-Cunha, Vincente. Revolutionary Portugal. 1976. lib. bdg. 59.95 (ISBN 0-8490-2521-4). Gordon Pr.

Braganti, Nancy & Devine, Elizabeth. Travelers' Guide to European Customs & Manners. Delagran, Louise, ed. LC 83-23700. (Illus.). 273p. (Orig.). 1984. pap. 5.95 (ISBN 0-88166-009-4). Meadowbrook.

Bragaw, Louis K. Managing a Federal Agency: The Hidden Stimulus. LC 79-27702. 320p. 1980. lib. bdg. 30.00x (ISBN 0-8018-2265-3). Johns Hopkins.

Bragaw, Louis K., jt. auth. see Allen, William R.

Bragdon, Allen & Fellows, Len. Diabolical Diversions. LC 79-7487. (Illus.). 1980. 9.95 (ISBN 0-385-15152-7). Doubleday.

Bragdon, Allen D. A Country Christmas Treasury. 192p. 1985. 24.95 (ISBN 0-668-05931-1). Wallace-Homestead.

--The Gingerbread Book. (Illus.). 168p. 1985. 17.95 (ISBN 0-916410-08-0). Wallace-Homestead.

--The Homeowner's Complete Manual of Repair & Improvement. LC 82-18184. (Illus.). 576p. 1984. pap. 14.95 (ISBN 0-668-05749-1). Arco.

Bragdon, Allen D., ed. Basic Car Care Illustrated. 2nd ed. (Illus.). 528p. 1980. 19.95 (ISBN 0-87851-523-2); pap. 9.95 (ISBN 0-87851-520-8). Hearst Bks.

--Built-Ins, Storage & Spacemaking. LC 83-71279. (Illus.). 192p. 1983. 16.95 (ISBN 0-668-05919-2); pap. 10.95 (ISBN 0-668-05923-0). Arco.

--Country Christmas Treasury. LC 83-11776. 192p. 1983. 24.95 (ISBN 0-668-05931-1). Arco.

--A Country Treasury. (Illus.). 192p. 1985. pap. 13.95 (ISBN 0-916410-25-0). Bragdon A.

--A Country Treasury. (Illus.). 192p. 1985. pap. 13.95 (ISBN 0-916410-25-0). Dodd.

--The Gingerbread Book. (Illus.). 168p. 1984. 17.95 (ISBN 0-668-06254-1, 6254-1). Arco.

--The Homeowner's Complete Manual of Repair & Improvement. LC 82-18184. (Illus.). 576p. 1983. 19.95 (ISBN 0-668-05737-8, 5737). Arco.

Bragdon, Charles R. Metal Decorating from Start to Finishes. LC 61-17350. (Illus.). 1969. 5.95 (ISBN 0-87027-065-6). Cumberland Pr.

Bragdon, Claude. The Arch Lectures: Eighteen Discourses on a Great Variety of Subjects. LC 77-92505. (Essay Index in Reprint Ser.). (Illus.). 1978. Repr. 19.75x (ISBN 0-8486-3000-9). Core Collection.

--Architecture & Democracy. 59.95 (ISBN 0-87968-654-5). Gordon Pr.

--The Beautiful Necessity. new ed. LC 77-17454. (Illus.). 1978. pap. 3.75 (ISBN 0-8356-0507-8, Quest). Theos Pub Hse.

--More Lives Than One. 368p. 1980. Repr. of 1938 ed. lib. bdg. 35.00 (ISBN 0-89984-063-9). Century Bookbindery.

--The New Image. 1928. Repr. 20.00 (ISBN 0-8274-3021-3). R West.

Bragdon, Claude F. Frozen Fountain. facs. ed. LC 75-127589. (Essay Index Reprint Ser). 1932. 16.00 (ISBN 0-8369-1784-7). Ayer Co Pubs.

Bragdon, Clifford R. Coping with the Barking Dog Noise Problem. 40p. 1978. pap. text ed. 35.00x (ISBN 0-89671-013-0). SEAI Tech Pubns.

--Municipal Noise Legislation. text ed. 45.00 (ISBN 0-89671-018-1). SEAI Tech Pubns.

--Noise Pollution: The Unquiet Crisis. LC 70-157049. (Illus.). 1972. 22.50x (ISBN 0-8122-7638-8). U of Pa Pr.

Bragdon, Clifford R., ed. Noise Pollution: A Guide to Information Sources. LC 73-17535. (Man & the Environment Information Guide Ser.: Vol. 5). 600p. 1979. 60.00x (ISBN 0-8103-1345-6). Gale.

Bragdon, H. D. Counseling the College Student. pap. 19.00 (ISBN 0-384-05490-0). Johnson Repr.

Bragdon, H. W. Woodrow Wilson: The Academic Years. LC 67-27081. (Illus.). 1967. 32.50x (ISBN 0-674-95595-1, Belknap Pr). Harvard U Pr.

Bragdon, Henry W. & Eliot, Thomas H. The Bright Constellation: Documents of American Democracy. rev. ed. (Illus.). 277p. (gr. 10-12). 1980. pap. text ed. 6.75x (ISBN 0-88334-129-8). Ind Sch Pr.

Bragdon, L. M. York Vital Records, 2 vols. LC 84-72332. 390p. 1985. 40.00 (ISBN 0-941216-72-1); 09/1985 65.00 (ISBN 0-941216-18-7). Cay Bel.

Bragdon, Lillian J. The Land & People of France. rev. ed. LC 78-37605. (Portraits of the Nations Ser.). (Illus.). (gr. 6 up). 1972. lib. bdg. 10.89i (ISBN 0-397-31297-0). Har-Row.

Brager & Perrin, eds. Effects of Radiation on Materials: 11th International Symposium, STP 782. 1225p. 1982. 69.50 (ISBN 0-8031-0753-6, 04-782000-35). ASTM.

Brager, George & Holloway, Stephen. Changing Human Service Organizations: Politics & Practice. LC 77-87572. 1978. text ed. 16.95 (ISBN 0-02-904620-3). Free Pr.

Brager, George & Specht, Harry. Community Organizing. (Social Work & Social Issues Ser). 1973. 22.00x (ISBN 0-231-03393-1). Columbia U Pr.

Brager, George A. & Purcell, Francis P., eds. Community Action Against Poverty: Readings from the Mobilization Experience. 1967. 13.95x (ISBN 0-8084-0087-8); pap. 9.95x (ISBN 0-8084-0088-6). New Coll U Pr.

Bragg. Year Book of Diagnostic Radiology, 1984. 1984. 44.95 (ISBN 0-8151-1133-9). Year Bk Med.

--Year Book of Diagnostic Radiology, 1985. 1985. 44.95 (ISBN 0-8151-1134-7). Year Bk Med.

Bragg, Addison. The Best of Bragg. Wesnick, Richard J., ed. (Illus., Orig.). 1985. pap. 9.95 (ISBN 0-913311-01-4). Unicorn Comm.

Bragg, Alicia, jt. auth. see McLellan, Tom.

Bragg, Bernard & Bergman, Eugene. Tales from the Clubroom. LC 81-81925. (Illus.). xxii, 118p. (Orig.). 1981. 3.00 (ISBN 0-913580-73-2). Gallaudet Coll.

Bragg, Bette J. Bragg about Your House. 12.50 (ISBN 0-8283-1343-1). Branden Pub Co.

Bragg, Bill. Enemy in Sight. (Orig.). 1980. pap. 1.75 (ISBN 0-505-51530-X, Pub. by Tower Bks). Dorchester Pub Co.

--Enemy in Sight. 208p. 1985. pap. 2.25 (ISBN 0-8439-2204-4, Leisure Bks). Dorchester Pub Co.

--The War Horses. (Orig.). 1980. pap. 1.75 (ISBN 0-505-51511-3, Pub. by Tower Bks). Dorchester Pub Co.

Bragg, Charles. Charles Bragg on Medicine. (Illus.). 80p. (Orig.). 1984. pap. 7.95 (ISBN 0-446-38059-8). Warner Bks.

--Charles Bragg on the Law. (Illus.). 80p. (Orig.). 1984. pap. 7.95 (ISBN 0-446-38057-1). Warner Bks.

Bragg, D. G. Yearbook of Diagnostic Radiology, 1983. 1983. 44.95 (ISBN 0-8151-1132-0). Year Bk Med.

Bragg, D. G., et al, eds. Oncologic Imaging. (Illus.). 650p. 1985. 95.00 (ISBN 0-08-031967-X). Pergamon.

Bragg, David & Hendee, William, eds. Tumor Imaging. (Illus.). 160p. 1982. pap. 29.95 (ISBN 0-8385-9042-X). ACC.

Bragg, Emma W. Backround Factors: A Study of Work Motivation of Urban & Rural Apparel Workers in Tennessee. LC 77-15832. 1977. write for info. (ISBN 0-8357-0282-0). E W Bragg.

--The Prediction of Job Behavior from Attitudes of Work Motivation & Demographic Characteristics among Apparel Workers: A Summary. LC 79-19302. 1979. write for info. (ISBN 0-8357-0464-5). E W Bragg.

--Profile of Work Motivation Attitudes of Apparel Workers. LC 79-17776. 1979. write for info. (ISBN 0-8357-0460-2). E W Bragg.
--The Relationship Between Work Motivation Attitudes & Demographic Characteristics among Apparel Workers: A Summary. 1979. write for info. (ISBN 0-8357-0474-2). E W Bragg.
--A Study of Work Motivation Attitudes of Apparel Workers: Power Needs Construct. LC 83-61829. (Illus.). 105p. (Orig.). 1985. 14.95 (ISBN 0-9611930-1-8). E W Bragg.
--Work Motivation Attitudes of Apparel Workers: Methodology Used in the Study. LC 83-61829. (Illus.). 186p. 1983. pap. 24.75 (ISBN 0-9611930-0-X). E W Bragg.
Bragg, Felicia. Rent Control: Strategies for Defense. 53p. 1979. pap. 27.00 (ISBN 0-317-12704-7); pap. 6.75 (ISBN 0-86718-035-8). Natl Assn Home.
Bragg, Gail. An Historiography of American Slave Women. LC 84-1811. (CompuBibs Ser.: No. 6). 24p. 1984. pap. 8.50x (ISBN 0-914791-00-1). Vantage Info.
--An Historiography of the American Woman Suffrage Movement. LC 84-1810. (CompuBibs Ser.: No. 5). 26p. 1984. pap. 8.50x (ISBN 0-914791-01-X). Vantage Info.
Bragg, George F., Jr. History of the Afro-American Group of the Episcopal Church. (Basic Afro-American Reprint Library). (Illus.). Repr. of 1922 ed. 17.00 (ISBN 0-384-05495-1). Johnson Repr.
Bragg, Gordon M. & Strauss, Jennifer. Strauss' Air Pollution Control, Vol. 4. LC 79-28773. (Environmental Science & Technology: A Wiley-Interscience Series of Texts & Monographs). 356p. 1981. 75.00x (ISBN 0-471-07957-X, Pub. by Wiley-Interscience). Wiley.
Bragg, Lawrence. The Development of X-Ray Analysis. Phillips, David, ed. (Illus.). 1975. 21.95x (ISBN 0-02-841880-8). Hafner.
Bragg, Linda B. Rainbow Roun' Mah Shoulder. 135p. (Orig.). 1984. pap. 6.00 (ISBN 0-932112-20-X). Carolina Wren.
Bragg, Marvin. From Gottsched to Goethe: Changes in the Social Function of the Poet & Poetry. LC 84-47682. (American University Studies I (Germanic Languages & Literature): Vol. 32). 157p. (Orig.). 1984. 27.25 (ISBN 0-8204-0132-3). P Lang Pubs.
Bragg, Melvin. Laurence Olivier. 160p. 1985. 19.95 (ISBN 0-312-47523-3). St Martin.
Bragg, Melvyn. Autumn Manoeuvres. 1978. 11.50 (ISBN 0-436-06703-X, Pub. by Secker & Warburg UK). David & Charles.
--For Want of a Nail. 318p. 1965. 16.95 (ISBN 0-436-06700-5, Pub. by Secker & Warburg UK). David & Charles.
--Hired Man. 1969. 15.95 (ISBN 0-436-06705-6, Pub. by Secker & Warburg UK). David & Charles.
--Josh Lawton. 224p. 1972. 16.95 (ISBN 0-436-06708-0, Pub. by Secker & Warburg UK). David & Charles.
--Kingdom Come. 1980. 16.95 (ISBN 0-436-06714-5, Pub. by Secker & Warburg UK). David & Charles.
--Land of the Lakes. (Illus.). 1984. 24.95 (ISBN 0-393-01834-2). Norton.
--A Place in England. 256p. 1983. 16.95 (ISBN 0-436-06706-4, Pub. by Secker & Warburg UK). David & Charles.
--Second Inheritance. 1966. 16.95 (ISBN 0-436-06701-3, Pub. by Secker & Warburg UK). David & Charles.
--The Silken Net. 400p. 1974. 16.95 (ISBN 0-436-06709-9, Pub. by Secker & Warburg UK). David & Charles.
--Speak for England. 512p. 1976. 19.95 (ISBN 0-436-06712-9, Pub. by Secker & Warburg UK). David & Charles.
Bragg, Melvyn, ed. see Clarke, Mary, et al.
Bragg, Melvyn, ed. see Cook, Phillip.
Bragg, Melvyn, ed. see Osborne, Charles.
Bragg, Melvyn, ed. see Scannell, Vernon.
Bragg, Michael, jt. auth. see Garfield, Leon.
Bragg, Pat, jt. auth. see Bragg, Paul.
Bragg, Patricia & Johnson, Bob. The Complete Triathlon Endurance Training Manual: Swim, Bike, Run. rev. ed. LC 84-82236. (Illus.). 600p. 1985. 24.95 (ISBN 0-87790-036-1); pap. 16.95 (ISBN 0-87790-028-0). Health Sci.
Bragg, Patricia, jt. auth. see Bragg, Paul C.
Bragg, Paul. Health Food Cookbook. 6.95x (ISBN 0-87790-001-9). Cancer Control Soc.
--Hi-Protein, Meat-Less Health Recipes. 4.95x (ISBN 0-87790-030-2). Cancer Control Soc.
--Nature's Healing System for Better Eyesight. Date not set. 4.95x (ISBN 0-87790-037-X). Cancer Control Soc.
--Toxicless Diet - Purification. 1.75x (ISBN 0-686-29873-X). Cancer Control Soc.
Bragg, Paul & Bragg, Pat. How to Have Strong Healthy Feet. 1981. pap. 4.95x (ISBN 0-317-07299-4, Regent House). B of A.
--Philosophy of Super Health. 1981. pap. text ed. 4.95x (ISBN 0-317-06952-7, Regent House). B of A.
Bragg, Paul C. & Bragg, Patricia. Bragg Apple Cider Vinegar System. 33rd ed. LC 84-62772. pap. 2.95 (ISBN 0-87790-016-7). Health Sci.
--Bragg Gourmet Health Recipes: For Life Extension & Vital, Healthy Living to 120. rev. ed. LC 84-82080. 448p. 1984. pap. 6.95 (ISBN 0-87790-031-0). Health Sci.
--Bragg Philosophy of Super Health. 10th ed. pap. 1.75 (ISBN 0-87790-022-1). Health Sci.
--Bragg Vegetarian Gourmet Recipes. 6th ed. LC 74-15983. pap. 4.95 (ISBN 0-87790-030-2). Health Sci.
--Building Health & Youthfulness. 11th ed. pap. 1.75 (ISBN 0-87790-017-5). Health Sci.
--Building Powerful Nerve Force. 10th ed. LC 79-76538. pap. 4.95 (ISBN 0-87790-003-5). Health Sci.
--Building Strong Feet. 10th ed. pap. 1.75 (ISBN 0-87790-013-2). Health Sci.
--Complete Gourmet Health Recipes. LC 84-82080. 448p. 1984. pap. 6.95 (ISBN 0-87790-031-0). Health Sci.
--Fitness Program with Spine Motion. 11th ed. pap. 1.95 (ISBN 0-87790-020-5). Health Sci.
--Golden Keys to Internal Physical Fitness. 10th ed. LC 66-30394. pap. 2.95 (ISBN 0-87790-006-X). Health Sci.
--Healthful Eating Without Confusion. 11th ed. LC 71-152392. pap. 4.95 (ISBN 0-87790-024-8). Health Sci.
--How to Keep the Heart Healthy Fit. 11th ed. LC 68-24215. pap. 4.95 (ISBN 0-87790-004-3). Health Sci.
--Miracle of Fasting. 34th ed. LC 84-62771. pap. 4.95 (ISBN 0-87790-035-3). Health Sci.
--Natural Method of Physical Culture. 8th ed. pap. 1.75 (ISBN 0-87790-018-3). Health Sci.
--Natural Way to Reduce. 16th ed. LC 84-62770. pap. 4.95 (ISBN 0-87790-040-X). Health Sci.
--Nature's Way to Health: Health System for Living 100 Years. 10th ed. pap. 1.75 (ISBN 0-87790-019-1). Health Sci.
--New Science of Health. 7th ed. pap. 1.75 (ISBN 0-87790-021-3). Health Sci.
--Salt Free Health Sauerkraut Cook Book. 8th ed. LC 74-32638. pap. 2.95 (ISBN 0-87790-025-6). Health Sci.
--Shocking Truth About Water. 24th ed. LC 77-101348. pap. 4.95 (ISBN 0-87790-000-0). Health Sci.
--South Sea Culture of the Abdomen. 11th ed. LC 74-19923. pap. 1.75 (ISBN 0-87790-023-X). Health Sci.
--Super Brain Breathing. 18th ed. LC 74-32637. pap. 1.75 (ISBN 0-87790-014-0). Health Sci.
--Your Health & Your Hair. 13th, rev. ed. LC 84-82235. pap. 4.95 (ISBN 0-87790-034-5). Health Sci.
Bragg, R. J. & Turner, Roy. Parachute Badges & Insignia of the World. (Illus.). 1979. 12.95 (ISBN 0-7137-0882-4, Pub. by Blandford Pr England). Sterling.
Bragg, S. L., frwd. by. Engineering Challenges in the 1980's, Vol. 2. (Proceedings of the Engineering Section of the British Association for the Advancement of Science Ser.). (Illus.). 103p. 1982. text ed. 79.95 (ISBN 0-89116-349-2, Pub. by Cambridge Info & Res Serv England). Hemisphere Pub.
Bragg, W. F. Buckskin Rider. 1981. pap. 1.75 (ISBN 0-8439-0881-5, Leisure Bks). Dorchester Pub Co.
--Bullet Proof. 1981. pap. 1.95 (ISBN 0-8439-0909-9, Leisure Bks). Dorchester Pub Co.
--Bullet Song. 1981. pap. 1.75 (ISBN 0-8439-0880-7, Leisure Bks). Dorchester Pub Co.
--Buzzard's Roost. 1980. pap. 1.75 (ISBN 0-8439-0805-X, Pub. by Nordon Pubns). Dorchester Pub Co.
--Ghost Mountain Guns. 1981. pap. 1.75 (ISBN 0-8439-0896-3, Leisure Bks). Dorchester Pub Co.
--Guns of Roaring Fork. 1980. pap. 1.75 (ISBN 0-8439-0851-3, Pub. by Nordon Pubns). Dorchester Pub Co.
--Legacy of a Gunfighter. 1980. pap. 1.75 (ISBN 0-8439-0790-8, Pub. by Nordon Pubns). Dorchester Pub Co.
--Maverick Showdown. 1981. pap. 1.75 (ISBN 0-8439-0910-2, Leisure Bks). Dorchester Pub Co.
--Mountain Maverick. 1980. pap. 1.75 (ISBN 0-8439-0804-1, Pub. by Nordon Pubns). Dorchester Pub Co.
--Range Camp. 1980. pap. 1.75 (ISBN 0-8439-0852-1, Pub. by Nordon Pubns). Dorchester Pub Co.
--Shotgun Gap. 1981. pap. 1.75 (ISBN 0-8439-0895-5, Leisure Bks). Dorchester Pub Co.
--Starr of Wyoming. 1981. pap. 2.25 (ISBN 0-8439-0860-2, Leisure Bks). Dorchester Pub Co.
--Texas Fever. 1981. pap. 1.75 (ISBN 0-8439-0864-5, Leisure Bks). Dorchester Pub Co.
Bragg, Wayne G., jt. ed. see Ingerson, Earl.
Bragg, William F. Wyoming: Rugged but Right. LC 79-3527. 1980. 12.95 (ISBN 0-87108-539-9); pap. 7.95 (ISBN 0-87108-540-2). Pruett.
--Wyoming: Wild & Wooly. (Illus.). 168p. 1983. 14.95 (ISBN 0-87108-628-X); pap. 6.95 (ISBN 0-87108-631-X). Pruett.
Bragg, William H. Creative Knowledge. facs. ed. LC 74-134057. (Essay Index Reprint Ser). 1926. 33.00 (ISBN 0-8369-2104-6). Ayer Co Pubs.
Bragg, William L. & Porter, George, eds. Physical Sciences: The Royal Institution Library of Science, 10 vols. plus index. (Illus.). 5300p. 1971. Set. 185.00 (ISBN 0-444-20048-7, Pub. by Elsevier Applied Sci England); Set. pap. 74.00 (ISBN 0-85334-615-1). Elsevier.
Bragger, J. & Rice, D. Allons-y: Le francais par Etapes. 1984. text ed. 25.95 (ISBN 0-8384-1171-1); wkbk. 10.95 (ISBN 0-317-00350-X); cassettes 125.00x (ISBN 0-8384-1174-6). Heinle & Heinle.
Bragger, Jeannette & Ariew, Robert. Chere Francoise: Revision de la Grammaire Francaise. 2nd ed. LC 83-81324. 368p. (Fr.). 1984. pap. text ed. 23.95 (ISBN 0-395-34435-2); lab manual 10.50 (ISBN 0-395-34437-9); reel to reel 200.00 (ISBN 0-395-34439-5); instr's guide 3.50; cassettes 15.95 (ISBN 0-395-34440-9). HM.
--Le Monde Francais. 2nd ed. LC 83-81339. 288p. 1984. pap. text ed. 15.95 (ISBN 0-395-34434-4). HM.
Bragger, Jeannette & Shupp, Robert P. First-Year French: Debuts Culturels. LC 77-433. 1977. pap. text ed. 7.50 (ISBN 0-03-015016-7, HoltC). HR&W.
Braght, Thieleman J. Van see Van Braght, Thieleman J.
Braginsky, B. M. & Braginsky, D. D. Mainstream Psychology: A Critique. LC 74-2157. 1974. pap. text ed. 8.95 (ISBN 0-03-089514-6, HoltC). HR&W.
Braginsky, Benjamin M., et al. Methods of Madness: The Mental Hospital As a Last Resort. LC 81-40099. (Illus.). 238p. 1982. pap. text ed. 12.25 (ISBN 0-8191-2400-1). U Pr of Amer.
Braginsky, D. D., jt. auth. see Braginsky, B. M.
Braginsky, V. B. & Manukin, A. B. Measurement of Weak Forces in Physics Experiments. Douglass, David H., ed. LC 76-22953. (Illus.). 1977. lib. bdg. 11.00x (ISBN 0-226-07070-0). U of Chicago Pr.
Braginsky, V. B., et al. Systems with Small Dissipation. Gliner, Erast, tr. (Illus.). 152p. 1985. lib. bdg. 28.00x (ISBN 0-226-07072-7); pap. 12.00x (ISBN 0-226-07073-5). U of Chicago Pr.
Bragonier, Reg & Fisher, David. What's What: A Visual Glossary of the Physical World. LC 81-7149. (Illus.). 576p. 1981. 30.00 (ISBN 0-8437-3329-2). Hammond Inc.
Bragonier, Reg, jt. auth. see Fisher, David.
Bragonier, Reginald, Jr., jt. ed. see Fisher, David.
Bragstad, Bernice J. & Stumpf, Sharyn M. A Guidebook for Teaching Study Skills & Motivation. 312p. 1982. pap. 29.95x (ISBN 0-205-07737-4, 237737, Pub. by Longwood Div). Allyn.
Bragt, Jan Van, tr. see Nishitani, Keiji.
Braham, Alan. Paintings of the High Renaissance in Italy. (Illus.). 128p. 1984. pap. 14.95 (ISBN 0-00-217402-2, Pub. by Salem Hse Ltd). Merrimack Pub Cir.
Braham, Allan. The Architecture of the French Enlightenment. 1980. 60.00 (ISBN 0-520-04117-8). U of Cal Pr.
Braham, Allan & Hager, Hellmut. Carlo Fontana: The Drawings at Windsor Castle. (Studies in Architecture: Vol. 18). (Illus.). 1978. 100.00 (ISBN 0-8390-0221-1). Abner Schram Ltd.
Braham, J. R. Night Fighter. 240p. (Orig.). 1984. pap. 2.95 (ISBN 0-553-24127-3). Bantam.
Braham, Jeanne. A Sort of Columbus: The American Voyages of Saul Bellow's Fiction. LC 83-10539. 168p. 1984. 15.00x (ISBN 0-8203-0690-8). U of Ga Pr.
Braham, Mark. Aspects of Education. LC 80-42315. 215p. 1982. 74.95x (ISBN 0-471-28019-4, Pub. by Wiley Interscience); pap. 25.95x (ISBN 0-471-28022-4). Wiley.
Braham, Randolph L. Genocide & Retribution. 1983. lib. bdg. 39.50 (ISBN 0-89838-146-0). Kluwer Nijhoff.
--The Hungarian Jewish Catastrophe: Selected & Annotated Bibliography. 501p. 1984. 45.00x (ISBN 0-88033-054-6). East Eur Quarterly.
--The Hungarian Labor Service System, 1939-1945. (East European Monographs: No. 31). 159p. 1977. 20.00x (ISBN 0-914710-24-9). East Eur Quarterly.
--Perspectives on the Holocaust. (Holocaust Studies). 1983. lib. bdg. 20.00 (ISBN 0-89838-124-X). Kluwer Nijhoff.
--The Politics of Genocide: The Holocaust in Hungary, 2 vols. LC 80-11096. (Illus.). 1116p. 1980. Set. 100.00x (ISBN 0-231-04496-8). Columbia U Pr.
Braham, Randolph L., ed. Contemporary Views on the Holocaust. 1983. lib. bdg. 31.50 (ISBN 0-89838-141-X). Kluwer Nijhoff.
--Documents on Major European Governments. 11.25 (ISBN 0-8446-1723-7). Peter Smith.
--Human Rights: Contemporary Domestic & International Issues & Conflicts. 170p. 1980. 17.95 (ISBN 0-8290-0232-4); pap. 9.95 (ISBN 0-8290-1552-3). Irvington.
--Social Justice. 192p. 1981. lib. bdg. 15.00 (ISBN 0-89838-063-4, Pub. by Martinus Nijhoff Netherlands). Kluwer Academic.
Braham, Randolph L. & Vago, Bela, eds. The Holocaust in Hungary: Forty Years Later. 256p. 1985. 25.00x (ISBN 0-88033-083-X, Dist. by Columbia U Pr). East Eur Quarterly.
Braham, Raymond L. Textbook of Pediatric Dentistry. 660p. 1985. 38.00 (ISBN 0-683-01014-X). Williams & Wilkins.
Braham, Rhodes. Discrimination & Disadvantage. 330p. 1982. text ed. 31.50 (ISBN 0-06-318193-2, Pub. by Har-Row Ltd England); pap. text ed. 18.50 (ISBN 0-06-318194-0, Pub. by Har-Row Ltd). Har-Row.
Brahce, Carl I. Preretirement Planning: Individual, Institutional, & Social Perspectives. 49p. 1983. 4.95 (ISBN 0-318-17789-7, IN264). Natl Ctr Res Voc Ed.
Brahe, Tycho. Learned Tico Brahe His Astronomical Conjecture of the New & Much Admired Star Which Appeared in the Year 1572. LC 74-6157. (English Experience Ser.: No. 86). 28p. 1969. Repr. of 1632 ed. 14.00 (ISBN 90-221-0086-3). Walter J Johnson.
Brahic, Andre, jt. ed. see Greenberg, Richard.
Brahm, John G. De see De Brahm, William G.
Brahma, Swami, jt. auth. see Verner, Alexander.
Brahmachari, Dhirenda. Yoga: Yogic Suksma Vyayama. (Illus.). 232p. 1975. 8.95 (ISBN 0-88253-802-0). Ind-US Inc.
Brahmanand, ed. see Narayan, Jayaprakash.
Brahmananda, Swami, ed. see Ramakrishna, Sri.
Brahmanda, P. R., et al, eds. Indian Economic Development & Policy: Essays in Honour of Professor V. L. D'souza. 352p. 1979. 26.00x (ISBN 0-7069-0683-7, Pub. by Vikas India). Advent NY.
Brahms, jt. auth. see Latham, Peter.
Brahms, Caryl & Simon, S. J. A Bullet in the Ballet. LC 84-80237. 159p. 1984. pap. 4.95 (ISBN 0-930330-12-9). Intl Polygonics.
Brahms, Johannes. Alto Rhapsody: Opus Fifty-Three for Contralto, Men's Chorus, & Orchestra (Text from Goethe's Harzreise im Winter); a Facsimile Edition from the Composer's Autograph Manuscript. LC 82-25959. (Illus.). 76p. 1983. 50.00 (ISBN 0-87104-283-5). NY Pub Lib.
--Complete Chamber Music for Strings & Clarinet Quintet. Gal, Hans, ed. 1968. pap. 7.95 (ISBN 0-486-21914-3). Dover.
--Complete Chamber Music for Strings & Clarinet Quintet. Gal, Hans, ed. (Vienna Gesellscaft der Musikfreunde Ed.). 9.00 (ISBN 0-8446-1724-5). Peter Smith.
--Complete Concerti in Full Score. Orig. Title: Johannes Brahms, Samtliche Werke. 352p. 1981. pap. 10.95 (ISBN 0-486-24170-X). Dover.
--Complete Piano Transcriptions, Cadenzas & Exercises. Mandyczewski, Eusebius, ed. LC 72-116826. 1970. pap. 7.00 (ISBN 0-486-22652-2). Dover.
--Complete Piano Works for Four Hands. Mandyczewski, Eusebius, ed. LC 75-27674. 224p. 1976. pap. 6.95 (ISBN 0-486-23271-9). Dover.
--Complete Piano Works for Four Hands. Mandyczewski, Eusebius, ed. 12.00 (ISBN 0-8446-5458-2). Peter Smith.
--Complete Shorter Works for Piano. Mandyczewski, Eusebius, ed. LC 70-116828. 1970. pap. 6.50 (ISBN 0-486-22651-4). Dover.
--Complete Sonatas & Variations for Solo Piano. Mandyczewski, Eusebius, ed. LC 68-11096. 1970. pap. 7.50 (ISBN 0-486-22650-6). Dover.
--Complete Songs for Solo Voice & Piano: Series I. Appelbaum, Stanley, tr. from Ger. LC 79-50615. 1979. pap. 7.50 (ISBN 0-486-23820-2). Dover.
--Complete Songs for Solo Voice & Piano: Series II. Appelbaum, Stanley, tr. from Ger. LC 79-50615. 1979. pap. 7.50 (ISBN 0-486-23821-0). Dover.
--Complete Songs for Solo Voice & Piano. Mandyczewski, Eusebius, ed. Appelbaum, Stanley, tr. (Series III). 224p. 1980. pap. 7.50 (ISBN 0-486-23822-9). Dover.
--Complete Songs for Solos Voice & Piano, Ser. IV. Mandyczewski, ed. Appelbaum, Stanley, tr. from Ger. 224p. 1980. pap. 7.50 (ISBN 0-486-23823-7). Dover.
--Complete Symphonies in Full Orchestral Score. Gal, Hans, ed. LC 73-92635. 352p. 1974. pap. 9.95 (ISBN 0-486-23053-8). Dover.
--Complete Symphonies in Full Orchestral Score: The Vienna Gesellschaft der Musikfreunde Edition. Gal, Hans, ed. 16.50 (ISBN 0-8446-5010-2). Peter Smith.
--Johannes Brahms Autographs. Bozarth, George S. & Webster, James, eds. LC 83-16582. (Music in Facsimile Ser.). 1984. lib. bdg. 138.00 (ISBN 0-8240-5950-6). Garland Pub.
--Johannes Brahms: The Herzogenberg Correspondences. Kalbeck, Max, ed. Bryant, Hannah, tr. LC 72-5395. (Select Bibliographies Reprint Ser.). (Illus.). 1972. Repr. of 1909 ed. 23.00 (ISBN 0-8369-6899-9). Ayer Co Pubs.
--Johannes Brahms: The Herzogenberg Correspondence. Kalbeck, Max, ed. Bryant, Hannah, tr. LC 78-163787. 425p. 1972. Repr. of 1909 ed. 50.00x (ISBN 0-8443-0011-X). Vienna Hse.
--Three Orchestral Works in Full Score: Academic Festival Overture, Tragic Overture, & Variation on a Theme by Haydn. (Music Scores & Music to Play). 112p. 1984. pap. 5.95 (ISBN 0-486-24637-X). Dover.
Brahms, Johannes, jt. auth. see Schumann, Clara J.
Braibanti, Antonio. Bioenergetics & Thermodynamics: Model Systems. (NATO Advanced Study Ser. C. Mathematical & Physical Sciences: No. 55). 483p. 1980. lib. bdg. 58.00 (ISBN 90-277-1115-1, Pub. by Reidel Holland). Kluwer Academic.
Braibanti, Ralph, ed. see Spengler, Joseph J., et al.

Braibanti, Ralph J. Research on the Bureaucracy of Pakistan: A Critique of Sources, Conditions, Issues, with Appended Documents. LC 66-14888. (Duke Univrsity, Commonwealth-Studies Center, Publication: No. 26). pap. 152.50 (ISBN 0-317-20091-7, 2023371). Bks Demand UMI.
Braibanti, Ralph J., ed. Political & Administrative Development. LC 75-79965. (Commonwealth Studies Center: No. 36). xii, 700p. 1969. 28.75 (ISBN 0-8223-0022-2). Duke.
Braibanti, Ralph J., et al. Administration & Economic Development in India. Spengler, Joseph J., ed. LC 63-9006. (Duke University, Commonwealth-Studies Center, Publication: No. 18). pap. 80.00 (ISBN 0-317-20089-5, 2023369). Bks Demand UMI.
--Asian Bureaucratic Systems Emergent from the British Imperial Tradition. LC 66-27487. (Duke University, Commonwealth-Studies Center, Publication: No. 28). pap. 160.00 (ISBN 0-317-20090-9, 2023370). Bks Demand UMI.
Braid, James. Neurypnology. LC 75-16688. (Classics in Psychiatry Ser.). 1976. Repr. of 1843 ed. 21.00x (ISBN 0-405-07418-2). Ayer Co Pubs.
Braidfoot, Larry. The Bible & America. LC 82-73371. 1983. 3.95 (ISBN 0-8054-5519-1). Broadman.
Braidwood, Linda S., et al, eds. Prehistoric Archeology along the Zagros Flanks. LC 81-85896. (Oriental Institute Publications (OIP): Vol. 105). (Illus.). ix, 695p. 1983. 110.00x (ISBN 0-918986-36-2). Oriental Inst.
Braidwood, Robert J. Prehistoric Men. 8th ed. LC 74-82642. 1975. pap. text ed. 10.95 (ISBN 0-394-33356-X, RanC). Random.
Braidwood, Robert J. & Howe, Bruce. Prehistoric Investigations in Iraqi Kurdistan. LC 60-8969. (Illus.). 1960. pap. 14.00x (ISBN 0-226-62404-8, SAOC31). U of Chicago Pr.
Braidwood, Robert J., jt. auth. see Cambel, Halet.
Braier, L. Diccionario Enciclopedico de Medicina. (Span.). 1980. leather 35.00 (ISBN 84-7092-205-X, S-33099). French & Eur.
Braiker, Harriet B., ed. see Polich, J. Michael & Armor, David J.
Brail, Richard K., et al. Transportation Services for the Disabled & Elderly. LC 76-40102. 1976. pap. 10.00 (ISBN 0-88285-039-3). Ctr Urban Pol Res.
Brailey, Nigel. Thailand & the Fall of Singapore: A Frustrated Asian Revolution. (Special Studies Ser.). 1985. pap. 28.00 (ISBN 0-8133-0301-X). Westview.
Brailoiu, Constantin. Problems of Ethnomusicology. Lloyd, A. L., ed. LC 83-15224. (Illus.). 400p. 1984. 49.50 (ISBN 0-521-24528-1). Cambridge U Pr.
Brailovsky, Vladimiro, jt. ed. see Barker, T. S.
Brailow, Michele. Cellars & Attics. 48p. 1981. 6.95 (ISBN 0-87881-099-4). Mojave Bks.
Brailsford, D. F. & Walker, A. N. Introductory ALGOL Sixty-Eight Programming. LC 79-40241. (Computers & Their Applications Ser.). 281p. 1979. 58.95x (ISBN 0-470-26746-1). Halsted Pr.
Brailsford, Edward J. The Spiritual Sense in Sacred Legend. 288p. 1983. Repr. of 1910 ed. lib. bdg. 47.50 (ISBN 0-89987-957-8). Darby Bks.
Brailsford, H. N. Macedonia: Its Races & Their Future. LC 78-135796. (Eastern Europe Collection Ser). 1970. Repr. of 1906 ed. 27.50 (ISBN 0-405-02738-9). Ayer Co Pubs.
Brailsford, H. N., et al. The Living Wage. (English Workers & the Coming of the Welfare State Ser., 1918-1945). 295p. 1985. lib. bdg. 35.00 (ISBN 0-8240-7604-4). Garland Pub.
Brailsford, Henry, ed. see Nevinson, Henry.
Brailsford, Henry N. Socialism for Today. Leventhal, F. M., ed. (English Workers & the Coming of the Welfare State Ser., 1918-1945). 142p. 1985. lib. bdg. 25.00 (ISBN 0-8240-7603-6). Garland Pub.
--Voltaire. 256p. 1981. Repr. of 1935 ed. lib. bdg. 20.00 (ISBN 0-8495-0473-2). Arden Lib.
--Voltaire. (Oxford Paperbacks Ser). 1963. pap. 4.95x (ISBN 0-19-281021-9, OX74). Oxford U Pr.
--The War of Steel & Gold: A Study of the Armed Peace. 3rd ed. (The Development of the Industrial Society Ser.). 340p. 1971. Repr. of 1915 ed. 25.00x (ISBN 0-7165-1767-1, Pub. by Irish Academic Pr). Biblio Dist.
--Why Capitalism Means War. LC 70-147494. (Library of War & Peace; the Political Economy of War). 1972. lib. bdg. 46.00 (ISBN 0-8240-0287-3). Garland Pub.
Brailsford, John. Canoeing. (Illus.). 96p. 8.95 (ISBN 0-902280-59-7, P941). Haynes Pubns.
Brailsford, Mabel R. Making of William Penn. facs. ed. LC 77-124227. (Select Bibliographies Reprint Ser.). 1930. 22.00 (ISBN 0-8369-5416-5). Ayer Co Pubs.
Brailsford, Mabel R., tr. see Pinnow, Hermann.
Braimbridge, M. V. Postoperative Cardiac Intensive Care. 3rd. ed. (Illus.). 240p. 1983. pap. text ed. 24.95 (ISBN 0-632-00233-6, B 0781-7). Mosby.
Brain. Brain's Diseases of the Nervous System. 9th ed. Walton, John N., ed. (Illus.). 704p. 1985. text ed. 59.00x (ISBN 0-19-261438-X). Oxford U Pr.
Brain & Brain. TRS-80 Color Computer Games Master. 1985. 12.95. Hayden.
Brain, et al. Respiratory Defense Mechanisms, Pt. 2. (Lung Biology in Health & Disease Ser.: Vol. 5). 1977. 99.50 (ISBN 0-8247-6532-X). Dekker.
--Respiratory Defense Mechanisms, Pt. 1. (Lung Biology in Health & Disease Ser.: Vol. 5). 1977. 75.00 (ISBN 0-8247-6381-5). Dekker.
Brain Bank. The BASIC Conversions Handbook for Apple, Commodore, TRS-80, & Atari Users. write for info. Hayden.
Brain, C. K. The Hunters or the Hunted? An Introduction to African Cave Taphonomy. LC 79-28104. 1981. lib. bdg. 40.00x (ISBN 0-226-07089-1); pap. 17.50x (ISBN 0-226-07090-5). U of Chicago Pr.
Brain, David, et al. The BASIC Conversions Handbook for Apple, TRS-80 & PET Users. 80p. (Orig.). 1982. pap. 9.95 (ISBN 0-8104-5534-X). Hayden.
Brain, Elizabeth, ed. see Smith, E. Kinsey.
Brain, Elizabeth A., jt. auth. see Hirsh, Jack.
Brain, J. D., jt. ed. see Witschi, H.
Brain, James L. Basic Structure of Swahili, Pt. II. (Foreign & Comparative Studies Program, African Special Publications: No. 2). (Orig.). 1969. pap. text ed. 3.50x (ISBN 0-686-74010-6). Syracuse U Foreign Comp.
--Basic Structure of Swahili. (Foreign & Comparative Studies Program, African Special Publications: No. 1). 151p. (Orig.). 1977. pap. text ed. 6.00x (ISBN 0-915984-58-X). Syracuse U Foreign Comp.
--A Short Dictionary of Social Science Terms for Swahili Speakers. (Foreign & Comparative Studies Program, African Special Publications: No. 4). 70p. (Orig., Swahili.). 1969. pap. text ed. 4.50x (ISBN 0-686-74011-4). Syracuse U Foreign Comp.
--A Social Science Vocabulary of Swahili. (Foreign & Comparative Studies Program, African Special Publications: No. 3). (Orig., Swahili.). 1968. pap. text ed. 3.50x (ISBN 0-686-74012-2). Syracuse U Foreign Comp.
Brain, Jeffrey P. Tunica Treasure. LC 79-57107. (Peabody Museum Papers: Vol. 71). (Orig.). 1981. pap. 35.00x (ISBN 0-87365-196-0). Peabody Harvard.
Brain, Jeffrey P., jt. auth. see Williams, Stephen.
Brain, Joy. Christian Indians in Natal, Eighteen Sixty to Nineteen Eleven. (Illus.). 1983. 21.00x (ISBN 0-19-570297-2). Oxford U Pr.
Brain, K. R., jt. auth. see Ross, M. S.
Brain, Michael C. & McCulloch, Peter B. Current Therapy in Hematology-Oncology 1983-1984: 1983 to 1984. LC 82-83696. 326p. 1983. text ed. 44.00 (ISBN 0-941158-05-5, D07809). Mosby.
Brain, P. F. & Denton, D., eds. Multidisciplinary Approaches to Aggression Research. 550p. 1981. 135.75 (ISBN 0-444-80317-3, Biomedical Pr). Elsevier.
Brain, Paul F. Hormones & Aggression. Horrobin, D. F., ed. (Hormone Research Review Ser.: Vol. I). 126p. 1977. Repr. of 1977 ed. 22.95 (ISBN 0-87705-963-2). Human Sci Pr.
--Hormones & Aggression, Vol. 2. Horrobin, D. F., ed. (Hormones Research Reviews Ser.). 205p. 1979. Repr. of 1979 ed. 24.95 (ISBN 0-87705-964-0). Human Sci Pr.
Brain, Paul F., ed. Hormones, Drugs & Aggression. (Hormone Research Review Ser.: Vol. 3). 173p. 1980. Repr. of 1979 ed. 24.95 (ISBN 0-87705-959-4). Human Sci Pr.
Brain, R., tr. see Godelier, M.
Brain, Robert. Art & Society in Africa. (Illus.). 1981. text ed. pap. text ed. 19.95x (ISBN 0-582-64579-4). Longman.
--Bangwa Kinship & Marriage. LC 70-166945. (Illus.). 1972. 34.50 (ISBN 0-521-08311-7). Cambridge U Pr.
--The Decorated Body. LC 78-20156. (Illus.). 1979. 17.50i (ISBN 0-06-010458-9, HarpT). Har-Row.
Brain, Robert, tr. see Mauss, Marcel.
Brain, Robert, tr. see Simenon, Georges.
Braina, Annie M. The Evolution of Public Health Nursing. (History of American Nursing Ser.). 454p. 1985. lib. bdg. 55.00 (ISBN 0-8240-6503-4). Garland Pub.
Brainard, C. A. & Wirth, M. Respiratory Care: National Board Review. (Illus.). 512p. 1984. pap. 24.95 (ISBN 0-89303-816-4). Brady Comm.
Brainard, Jack, jt. auth. see Phinny, Peter.
Brainard, Joe. I Remember. LC 75-23153. 1975. 17.95 (ISBN 0-916190-02-1); pap. 6.95 (ISBN 0-916190-03-X). Full Court NY.
--Selected Writings. pap. 3.50 (ISBN 0-686-09752-1). Kulchur Foun.
Brainard, John B. Control of Migraine. 1979. pap. 6.95 (ISBN 0-393-00933-5). Norton.
--Control of Migraine. 1977. 10.95 (ISBN 0-393-06421-2). Norton.
Brainard, John G. Letters Found in the Ruins of Fort Braddock, Including an Interesting American Tale. LC 78-64065. Repr. of 1824 ed. 37.50 (ISBN 0-404-17057-9). AMS Pr.
Brainard, Maurice W. Modern Conservative. 1967. pap. 1.00 (ISBN 0-911956-00-X). Constructive Action.
Brainard, Morgan. Men in Low Cut Shoes. (Illus.). 176p. 1985. 11.95 (ISBN 0-89962-474-X). Todd & Honeywell.
Brainard, Newton C. The Hartford State House of Seventeen Ninety-Six. (Illus.). 68p. 1964. 4.00x (ISBN 0-940748-22-3); pap. 2.00x (ISBN 0-940748-23-1). Conn Hist Soc.
Brainard, Sandy. Path to the Brightest Star. (Illus.). 104p. (Orig.). 1984. pap. 6.00 (ISBN 0-942494-54-7). Coleman Pub.
Brainard, Willard T. Aggression, II: Medical Analysis with Research Bibliography. LC 85-47870. 150p. 1985. 29.95 (ISBN 0-88164-028-X); pap. 21.95 (ISBN 0-88164-029-8). ABBE Pubs Assn.
--Aggression: Psychological, Behavioral & Medical Subject Analysis with Research Index & Bibliography. LC 83-71647. 141p. 1984. 29.95 (ISBN 0-88164-028-X); pap. 21.95 (ISBN 0-88164-029-8). ABBE Pubs Assn.
--Diagnosis of Brain Diseases: Medical Analysis Index with Reference Bibliography. 150p. 1985. 29.95 (ISBN 0-88164-388-2); pap. 21.95 (ISBN 0-88164-389-0). ABBE Pubs Assn.
Brainard, Williard T. Injuries of the Spinal Cord: Medical Subject Analysis & Research Guide With Bibliography. LC 83-45535. 150p. 1985. 29.95 (ISBN 0-88164-106-5); pap. 21.95 (ISBN 0-88164-107-3). ABBE Pubs Assn.
Brainbridge, C. G. Teach Yourself Welding. (Teach Yourself Ser.). 192p. 1981. pap. 4.95 (ISBN 0-679-10495-X). McKay.
Braine, John. J. B. Priestley. (Illus.). 163p. 1979. text ed. 24.50x (ISBN 0-06-490642-6, 06363). B&N Imports.
--Life at the Top. LC 79-24779. 1980. pap. 3.95 (ISBN 0-416-00591-8, NO. 0185). Methuen Inc.
--Waiting for Sheila. LC 79-24757. 1977. 9.95 (ISBN 0-416-00571-3, NO. 0183). Methuen Inc.
--Writing a Novel. 224p. 1975. pap. 5.95 (ISBN 0-07-007112-8). McGraw.
Brainen, Howard, jt. auth. see Markowitz, Elysa.
Brainerd, Alvah. A Pioneer History of the Township of Grand Blanc. (Local History Reprints Ser.). 73p. 1965. pap. 3.25 (ISBN 0-916699-00-5). Clarke His.
Brainerd, C. J., ed. Children's Logical & Mathematical Cognition: Progress in Cognitive Developmental Research. (Springer Series in Cognitive Development). (Illus.). 216p. 1982. 26.50 (ISBN 0-387-90635-5). Springer-Verlag.
Brainerd, C. J. & Pressley, M., eds. Basic Processes in Memory Development. (Springer Series in Cognitive Development). (Illus.). 365p. 1985. 39.00 (ISBN 0-387-96064-3). Springer-Verlag.
--Verbal Processes in Children: Progress in Cognitive Developmental Research. (Springer Series in Cognitive Development). (Illus.). 289p. 1982. 30.00 (ISBN 0-387-90648-7). Springer-Verlag.
Brainerd, C. J., jt. ed. see Pressley, M.
Brainerd, Carol P., jt. auth. see Palmer, Gladys L.
Brainerd, Charles J. The Origins of the Number Concept. LC 78-21223. 240p. 1979. 39.95 (ISBN 0-275-24310-9). Praeger.
Brainerd, Charles J., ed. Recent Advances in Cognitive-Developmental Theory, Progress in Cognitive Developmental Research. (Springer Series in Cognitive Development). (Illus.). 270p. 1983. 32.00 (ISBN 0-387-90767-X). Springer-Verlag.
Brainerd, David. David Brainerd's Personal Testimony. (Summit Bks.). pap. 3.50 (ISBN 0-8010-8159-9). Baker Bk.
--The Life of David Brainerd: Chiefly Extracted from His Diary. (Summit Books). 1978. 5.95 (ISBN 0-8010-0726-7). Baker Bk.
Brainerd, David, ed. Memoirs of the Reverend David Brainerd: Missionary to the Indians on the Border of New York, New Jersey & Pennsylvania. LC 70-108477. (American Indian History Sers). 1970. Repr. of 1822 ed. 49.00x (ISBN 0-403-00233-8). Scholarly.
Brainerd, Eleanor. Concerning Belinda. facs. ed. LC 78-86138. (Short Story Index Reprint Ser). 1905. 17.00 (ISBN 0-8369-3042-8). Ayer Co Pubs.
Brainerd, George W. The Maya Civilization. LC 76-43669. Repr. of 1954 ed. 12.50 (ISBN 0-404-15503-0). AMS Pr.
--The Maya Civilization. (Illus.). 1963. Repr. of 1954 ed. 3.00 (ISBN 0-916561-52-6). Southwest Mus.
Brainerd, George W., jt. auth. see Morley, Sylvanus G.
Brainerd, J. Grist, ed. The Ultimate Consumer: A Study in Economic Illiteracy. LC 75-39236. (Getting & Spending: the Consumer's Dilemma). 1976. Repr. of 1934 ed. 20.00x (ISBN 0-405-08012-3). Ayer Co Pubs.
Brainerd, John. Nature Touring: A Guidebook for Travelers & Naturalists. 224p. 1985. 16.95 (ISBN 0-13-610338-3); pap. 7.95 (ISBN 0-13-610320-0). P-H.
Brainerd, Walter S. & Landweber, Lawrence H. Theory of Computation. LC 73-12950. 336p. 1974. 41.50x (ISBN 0-471-09585-0). Wiley.
Brainerd, Walter S., et al. FORTRAN 77 Fundamentals & Style. (Programming Language Ser.). (Illus.). 448p. 1985. pap. text ed. 21.00 (ISBN 0-87835-143-4); write for info. tchr's. manual (ISBN 0-87835-146-9). Boyd & Fraser.
--Pascal Programming: A Spiral Approach. LC 82-70213. 597p. (Orig.). 1982. pap. text ed. 25.00x (ISBN 0-87835-122-1); solutions manual avail. Boyd & Fraser.
Braiotta, Louis, Jr. The Audit Director's Guide. LC 84-3902. 320p. 1984. Repr. of 1981 ed. lib. bdg. 28.50 (ISBN 0-89874-745-7). Krieger.
Braisted, William R. Meiroku: Journal of the Japanese Enlightenment. 1976. 32.50x (ISBN 0-674-56467-7). Harvard U Pr.
--United States Navy in the Pacific, 1897-1909. LC 70-90473. (Illus.). 1958. text ed. 13.00x (ISBN 0-8290-0373-8); pap. text ed. 9.95x (ISBN 0-89197-971-9). Irvington.
--The United States Navy in the Pacific, 1897-1909. LC 57-12530. 294p. 1977. pap. text ed. 17.50x (ISBN 0-292-78505-4). U of Tex Pr.
--The United States Navy in the Pacific, 1909-1922. 753p. 1971. 35.00x (ISBN 0-292-70037-7). U of Tex Pr.
Braitenbach, E. H., tr. from Ger. On the Texture of Brains: An Introduction to Neuroanatomy for the Cybernetically Minded. LC 77-21851. (Illus.). 1977. pap. 14.00 (ISBN 0-387-08391-X). Springer-Verlag.
Braitenberg, Valentino. Vehicles: Experiments in Synthetic Psychology. (Illus.). 144p. 1984. 14.95 (ISBN 0-262-02208-7). MIT Pr.
Braithewaite, John, ed. see Fisse, Brent.
Braithewaite, William S., ed. The Book of Georgian Verse, Vol. 2. LC 76-98076. (Granger Index Reprint Ser.). 1313p. Repr. of 1908 ed. lib. bdg. 35.00 (ISBN 0-8290-0488-2). Irvington.
Braithwait, Richard. The English Gentlewoman Drawne Out to the Full Body, Expressing What Habilliments Do Best Attire Her. LC 70-25509. (English Experience Ser.: No. 215). 222p. 1970. Repr. of 1631 ed. 35.00 (ISBN 90-221-0215-7). Walter J Johnson.
Braithwaite, Bruce. The Films of Jack Nicholson. Castell, David, ed. (The Films of...Ser.). (Illus.). (gr. 7-12). 1978. Repr. PLB 6.95 (ISBN 0-912616-76-8). Greenhaven.
--The Films of Marlon Brando. Castell, David, ed. (The Films of...Ser.). (Illus.). (gr. 7-12). 1978. Repr. of 1974 ed. PLB 6.95 (ISBN 0-912616-86-5). Greenhaven.
Braithwaite, C. The Second Period of Quakerism: To about 1725. 1979. 50.00x (ISBN 0-686-87291-6, Pub. by W Sessions). State Mutual Bk.
Braithwaite, E. R. To Sir, with Love. (gr. 9-12). 1973. pap. 2.75 (ISBN 0-515-07853-0). Jove Pubns.
--To Sir With Love. 1982. pap. 1.75 (ISBN 0-451-11533-3, AE1533, Sig). NAL.
Braithwaite, Errol. Companion Guide to Westland. (Illus.). 1982. pap. 12.95x (ISBN 0-00-216967-3, Pub. by W Collins New Zealand). Intl Spec Bk.
Braithwaite, Gary M., et al. Up Front: The U. S. A. Bumpersticker Catalog. Bohannon, M. A. & Castagnasso, J. M., eds. LC 84-90675. (Illus.). 244p. (Orig.). 1984. pap. 8.95 (ISBN 0-932405-05-3). Nowadays Co.
Braithwaite, George, tr. see Takekoshi, Yosaburo.
Braithwaite, Henry W. The Conductor's Art. (Illus.). 1978. Repr. of 1952 ed. lib. bdg. 19.75x (ISBN 0-313-20058-0, BRCAR). Greenwood.
Braithwaite, John. Corporate Crime in the Pharmaceutical Industry. 500p. 1984. 45.00x (ISBN 0-7102-0049-8). Routledge & Kegan.
--History of the Revolutions in the Empire of Morocco, upon the Death of the Late Emperor, Muley Ishmael. facs. ed. LC 74-88541. (Black Heritage Library Collection Ser.). 1729. 17.25 (ISBN 0-8369-8522-2). Ayer Co Pubs.
--Prisons, Education & Work: Towards a National Employment Strategy for Prisoners. (Illus.). 240p. 1980. text ed. 8.95 (ISBN 0-7022-1524-4). U of Queensland Pr.
--To Punish or Persuade: The Enforcement of Coal Mine Safety. LC 84-2671. 1985. 34.50x (ISBN 0-87395-931-0); pap. 12.95x (ISBN 0-87395-932-9). State U NY Pr.
Braithwaite, John, jt. ed. see Wilson, Paul R.
Braithwaite, John M. & King, Edward J. Multiple-Class Teaching (UNESCO) (Education Studies & Documents: No. 12). pap. 16.00 (ISBN 0-317-16708-1). Kraus Repr.
Braithwaite, Lee F. Graptolites from the Lower Ordovician Pogonip Group of Western Utah. LC 75-31373. (Special Paper: No. 166). (Illus., Orig.). 1976. pap. 9.75 (ISBN 0-8137-2166-0). Geol Soc.
--Graptolites from the Lower Ordovician Pogonip Group of Western Utah. LC 75-31373. (Geological Society of America Ser.: No. 166). pap. 28.00 (ISBN 0-317-28373-1, 2025454). Bks Demand UMI.
Braithwaite, Lee F., jt. auth. see Beck, D Elden.
Braithwaite, William. Removal & Retirement of Judges in Missouri: A Field Study. 57p. (Reprinted from 1968 Washington University Law Quarterly 378). 1969. 2.00 (ISBN 0-317-33354-2). Amer Bar Assn.
Braithwaite, William C. The Beginnings of Quakerism. (Illus.). 562p. 1981. Repr. of 1923 ed. lib. bdg. 65.00 (ISBN 0-8495-0625-5). Arden Lib.
Braithwaite, William S. Anthology of Magazine Verse & Year Book of American Poetry, 6 vols. text ed. 127.75 (ISBN 0-8369-9358-6, 19729). Ayer Co Pubs.
--The Bewitched Parsonage. 1950. 35.00 (ISBN 0-8274-2170-2). R West.
--Book of Georgian Verse, 2 vols. facsimile ed. LC 76-98076. (Granger Index Reprint Ser.). 1908. Set. 52.00 (ISBN 0-8369-6069-6). Ayer Co Pubs.

Bramlette, Carl A., Jr. & Mescon, Michael H., eds. Individual & the Future of Organizations, Vol. 1. LC 72-619550. (Franklin Foundation Lecture Ser.). Orig. Title: Man & the Future of Organizations. 1972. pap. 6.50 (ISBN 0-88406-003-9). Ga St U Busn Pub.
--Individual & the Future of Organizations, Vol. 2. LC 72-619550. (Franklin Foundation Lecture Ser.). Orig. Title: Man & the Future of Organizations. 57p. (Orig.). 1973. pap. 6.50 (ISBN 0-88406-004-7). Ga St U Busn Pub.
Bramlette, Carl A., Jr. & Mescon, Michael H., Jr., eds. The Individual & the Future of Organizations, Vol. 7. LC 72-619550. (Franklin Foundation Lecture Ser.). 1978. pap. 6.50 (ISBN 0-88406-121-3). Ga St U Busn Pub.
Bramlette, Carl A., Jr., jt. ed. see Mescon, Michael.
Bramlette, Carl A., Jr., jt. ed. see Mescon, Michael H.
Bramlette, Carl A., Jr., et al, eds. Individual & the Future of Organizations, Vol. 5. LC 72-619550. (Franklin Foundation Lecture Series). Orig. Title: Man & the Future of Organizations. 46p. 1976. pap. 6.50 (ISBN 0-88406-109-4). Ga St U Busn Pub.
Bramley, Gerald. Apprentice to Graduate: A History of Library Education in the United Kingdom. 220p. 1981. 20.00 (ISBN 0-85157-343-6, Pub. by Bingley England). Shoe String.
--Outreach: Library Services for the Institutionalized, the Elderly, & the Physically Handicapped. 232p. 1978. 17.50 (ISBN 0-208-01663-5, Linnet). Shoe String.
--World Trends in Library Education. 234p. 1975. 19.50 (ISBN 0-208-01368-7, Linnet). Shoe String.
Bramley, Wyn. Group Tutoring. 1979. 27.50 (ISBN 0-89397-059-X). Nichols Pub.
Brammell, P. Roy. Brother Harvey. new ed. (Illus.). 47p. (Orig.). 1976. pap. 1.50 (ISBN 0-87178-120-4). Brethren.
Brammer, A. J. & Taylor, W. Vibration Effects on the Hand & Arm in Industry: A Collection of Papers from the Third International Symposium on Hand-Arm Vibration. LC 82-24819. 376p. 1983. 42.95 (ISBN 0-471-88954-7, Pub. by Wiley-Interscience). Wiley.
Brammer, Billy L. The Gay Place. LC 83-48039. 544p. 1984. pap. 5.95 (ISBN 0-394-72223-X, Vin). Random.
Brammer, Lawrence & Humberger, Frank. Outplacement & Inplacement Counseling. (Illus.). 160p. 1984. text ed. 20.95 (ISBN 0-13-645227-2). P-H.
Brammer, Lawrence M. The Helping Relationship: Process & Skills. 3rd ed. 208p. 1985. pap. text ed. 14.95 (ISBN 0-13-386061-2). P-H.
Brammer, Lawrence M. & Shostrum, Everett L. Therapeutic Psychology: Fundamentals of Counseling & Psychotherapy. 4th ed. (Illus.). 480p. 1982. 27.95 (ISBN 0-13-914614-8). P-H.
Brammer, Lawrence M., jt. auth. see Bamman, Henry A.
Brammer, Lawrence M., et al. Joys & Challenges of Middle Age. LC 82-3524. 232p. 1982. text ed. 18.95x (ISBN 0-88229-703-1). Nelson-Hall.
Brammer, William. The Gay Place. 1978. 11.95 (ISBN 0-932012-05-1). Texas Month Pr.
Bramnick, Lea & Simon, Anita. The Parents' Solution Book. 320p. 1983. 14.95 (ISBN 0-531-09881-8). Watts.
--The Parents' Solution Book: Your Child from Five to Twelve. 1984. pap. 9.95 (ISBN 0-399-51076-1, Perigee). Putnam Pub Group.
Brams, S. J. Superior Beings-If They Exist, How Would We Know? Game-Theoretic Implications of Omniscience, Immortality, & Incomprehensibility. (Illus.). 192p. 1983. 23.00 (ISBN 0-387-91223-1); pap. 11.95 (ISBN 0-387-90877-3). Springer-Verlag.
Brams, Stephen & Fishburn, Peter. Approval Voting. LC 82-17849. 224p. 1983. pap. 14.95 (ISBN 0-8176-3124-0). Birkhauser.
Brams, Steven J. Biblical Games: A Strategic Analysis of Stories in the Old Testament. 1980. text ed. 22.00x (ISBN 0-262-02144-7); pap. 7.95 (ISBN 0-262-52074-5). MIT Pr.
--Game Theory & Politics. LC 74-15370. (Illus.). 1975. pap. text ed. 14.95 (ISBN 0-02-904550-9). Free Pr.
--Paradoxes in Politics: An Introduction to the Nonobvious in Political Science. LC 75-28568. (Illus.). 1976. pap. text ed. 11.95 (ISBN 0-02-904590-8). Free Pr.
--The Presidential Election Game. LC 78-5815. 1978. 27.50x (ISBN 0-300-02254-9); pap. 6.95x (ISBN 0-300-02296-4). Yale U Pr.
--Spatial Models of Election Competition. (UMAP Monographs). 94p. 1979. pap. text ed. 6.95x (ISBN 0-8176-3014-7). Birkhauser.
--Superpower Games: Applying Game Theory to Superpower Conflict. LC 84-21876. (Illus.). 192p. 1985. text ed. 22.50x (ISBN 0-300-03323-0, Y-529); pap. 6.95x (ISBN 0-300-03364-8). Yale U Pr.
Bramsback, B. Folklore & W. B. Yeats: The Function of Folklore Elements in Three Early Plays. (Studia Anglistica Upsaliensia Ser.: No. 51). 178p. 1984. pap. text ed. 20.25x (ISBN 91-554-1502-4, Pub. by Almquist & Wiksell Sweden). Humanities.
Bramsback, Birgit. James Stephens: A Literary & Bibliographical Study. LC 73-7744. 1959. lib. bdg. 20.00 (ISBN 0-8414-3121-3). Folcroft.
Bramsch, Joan. At Nightfall. (Loveswept Ser.: No. 88). 208p. (Orig.). 1985. pap. 2.25 (ISBN 0-553-21702-X). Bantam.
--A Kiss to Make It Better. (Loveswept Ser.: No. 64). 208p. 1984. pap. 2.25 (ISBN 0-553-21670-8). Bantam.
--The Light Side. (Loveswept Ser.: No. 81). 208p. 1985. pap. 2.25 (ISBN 0-553-21685-6). Bantam.
--Teach Me, I'm Yours. LC 79-88155. (Illus.). 1979. spiral-bound 12.95 (ISBN 0-934334-00-5). Libty Comm Hse.
Bramscher, Cynthia S. Holiday Music Activities for the Entire School Year. LC 82-6414. 224p. 1982. 14.50 (ISBN 0-13-392613-3). P-H.
Bramsen, Bo & Wain, Kathleen. The Hambros Seventeen Seventy-Nine to Nineteen Seventy-Nine. (Illus.). 448p. 1980. 33.00 (ISBN 0-7181-1852-9, Pub. by Michael Joseph). Merrimack Pub Cir.
Bramsen, Michele B. A Portrait of Elie Halevy. 1978. pap. text ed. 29.00x (ISBN 90-6032-100-6). Humanities.
Bramsen, Michelle B., jt. ed. see Tinker, Irene.
Bramson, jt. auth. see Selub.
Bramson, A. E., jt. auth. see Birch, N. H.
Bramson, Alan. Be a Better Pilot. LC 80-13401. (Illus.). 256p. 1980. 11.95 (ISBN 0-668-04901-4, 4901-4). Arco.
--The Book of Flight Tests. LC 83-25751. (Illus.). 240p. 1984. 21.95 (ISBN 0-668-06152-9, 6152-9). Arco.
Bramson, Alan & Birch, Neville. The Tiger Moth Story. 352p. 1982. 69.00x (ISBN 0-906393-19-1, Pub. by Airlife England). State Mutual Bk.
Bramson, Ann. Soap. 2nd ed. LC 75-7286. 1975. pap. 4.95 (ISBN 0-911104-57-7, 073). Workman Pub.
Bramson, Leon. Political Context of Sociology. 1961. pap. 8.95 (ISBN 0-691-02804-4). Princeton U Pr.
Bramson, Leon, ed. see MacIver, Robert.
Bramson, M. A. Infrared Radiation: A Handbook for Applications. LC 66-26812. (Optical Physics & Engineering Ser.). 623p. 1968. 85.00x (ISBN 0-306-30274-8, Plenum Pr). Plenum Pub.
Bramson, Maury. Convergence of Solutions of the Kolmogorov Equation to Travelling Waves. LC 83-6437. (Memoirs of the American Mathematical Society: No. 285). pap. 16.00 (ISBN 0-8218-2285-3). Am Math.
Bramson, Morris. Algebra: An Introductory Course. (gr. 9 up). 1978. 9.25 (ISBN 0-87720-240-0). AMSCO Sch.
--Algebra: An Introductory Course, Vol. 2. (gr. 7-8). 1983. pap. 8.42 (ISBN 0-87720-254-0, 269W); key 0.65 (ISBN 0-317-03298-4). Amsco Sch.
--College Board Achievement Test in Mathematics: Level I. 128p. pap. 3.95 (ISBN 0-668-05319-4). Arco.
--College Board Achievement Test in Mathematics: Level II. 128p. pap. 4.95 (ISBN 0-668-05646-0). Arco.
--Graduate Record Examination in Mathematics. 3rd ed. LC 82-16384. 144p. 1983. pap. 6.95 (ISBN 0-668-05675-4, 5675). Arco.
--Mathematics: Level I. 4th ed. LC 81-3540. 128p. (Orig.). 1981. pap. 3.95 (ISBN 0-668-05319-4, 5319). Arco.
--Mathematics: Level II College Board Achievement Test. LC 82-8882. 128p. 1983. pap. 4.95 (ISBN 0-668-05646-0, 5646). Arco.
Bramson, Morris, jt. auth. see Gruber, Edward C.
Bramson, Morris, jt. auth. see Solomon, Lawrence.
Bramson, Rober M., jt. auth. see Harrison, Allen F.
Bramson, Robert M. Coping with Difficult People. LC 80-2319. 240p. 1981. 14.95 (ISBN 0-385-17362-8, Anchor Pr). Doubleday.
Bramson, Robert M. & Bramson, Susan. Stressless Home: A Step by Step Guide to Turning Your Home into the Haven You Deserve. LC 82-45390. (Illus.). 240p. 1985. 15.95 (ISBN 0-385-18289-9, Anchor Pr). Doubleday.
Bramson, Robert M., jt. auth. see Harrison, Allen F.
Bramson, Robert N. Coping with Difficult People. 176p. 1982. pap. 2.75 (ISBN 0-345-30084-X). Ballantine.
Bramson, Susan, jt. auth. see Bramson, Robert M.
Bramsted, Ernest. Aristocracy & the Middle-Classes in Germany: Social Types in German Literature, 1830-1900. rev. ed. LC 64-15031. (Orig.). 1964. pap. 2.95x (ISBN 0-226-07107-3, P163, Phoen). U of Chicago Pr.
Bramsted, Ernest K. Aristocracy & the Middle-Classes in Germany: Social Types in German Literature, 1830-1900. LC 64-15031. pap. 97.00 (ISBN 0-317-28210-7, 2020035). Bks Demand UMI.
Bramstedt, Ernest K. Dictatorship & Political Police: The Technique of Control by Fear. LC 75-41034. Repr. of 1945 ed. 17.50 (ISBN 0-404-14510-8). AMS Pr.
Bramstedt, Wayne G. North American Indians in Towns & Cities: A Bibliography. (Public Administration Ser.: No. P-234). 1979. pap. 7.50 (ISBN 0-88066-019-8). Vance Biblios.
Bramston, John. Autobiography. Repr. of 1845 ed. 46.00 (ISBN 0-384-05515-X). Johnson Repr.
--Autobiography of Sir John Bramston. LC 10-2212. (Camden Society, London. Publications. First Ser.: No. 32). Repr. of 1845 ed. 46.00 (ISBN 0-404-50132-X). AMS Pr.
Bramwell, A. R. Helicopter Dynamics. 416p. 1976. text ed. 65.00 (ISBN 0-7131-3353-8). E Arnold.
Bramwell, Amy. The Training of Teachers in the United States of America. 1976. lib. bdg. 59.95 (ISBN 0-8490-2756-X). Gordon Pr.
Bramwell, Barbara. Decision: A Novel. LC 75-39859. 1976. 7.50 (ISBN 0-916510-01-8). Survey Pub Co.
Bramwell, D. Plants & Islands. LC 79-50299. 1980. 66.00 (ISBN 0-12-125460-7). Acad Pr.
Bramwell, Dana G. The Tragedy of King Richard: Shakespearean Watergate. new ed. LC 74-27927. 96p. 1974. pap. 3.35 (ISBN 0-685-52670-4). Survey Pub Co.
Bramwell, Fitzgerald B., et al. Investigations in General Chemistry: Quantitative Techniques and Basic Principles. 1977. spiral bdg. 14.95x (ISBN 0-8087-2803-2). Burgess.
Bramwell, J. M. Hypnosis & Treatment by Suggestion. (Hypnosis & Altered States of Consciousness Ser.). 230p. 1982. Repr. lib. bdg. 25.00 (ISBN 0-306-76164-5). Da Capo.
Bramwell, James. Lost Atlantis. LC 80-19561. 288p. 1980. Repr. of 1974 ed. lib. bdg. 14.95x (ISBN 0-89370-623-X). Borgo Pr.
--Lost Atlantis. 288p. 1974. pap. 4.95 (ISBN 0-87877-023-2, P-23). Newcastle Pub.
Bramwell, L. E. Formula for Death. (Orig.). 1981. pap. 2.25 (ISBN 0-505-51710-8, Pub. by Tower Bks). Dorchester Pub Co.
Bramwell, M, jt. auth. see Cork, B.
Bramwell, Martin. Oceans. LC 84-51227. (Picture Atlas Ser.). (Illus.). 38p. (gr. 4-6). 1984. PLB 10.90 (ISBN 0-531-04835-7). Watts.
Bramwell, Ruby P. City on the Move: The Story of Salina Kansas. 1969. 20.00 (ISBN 0-934844-01-1). W A Linder.
--Kansas Story of Salina. LC 79-10825. (Illus.). 280p. 6.50 (ISBN 0-685-42141-4). Survey Pub Co.
Branagan, Thomas. The Excellency of the Female Character Vindicated: Being an Investigation Relative to the Cause & Effects of the Encroachments of Men Upon the Rights of Women, & the Too Frequent Degradation & Consequent Misfortunes of the Fair Sex. 2nd ed. LC 72-2592. (American Women Ser: Images & Realities). (Illus.). 326p. 1972. Repr. of 1808 ed. 22.00 (ISBN 0-405-04449-6). Ayer Co Pubs.
--Preliminary Essay on the Oppression of the Exiled Sons of Africa. LC 70-82177. (Anti-Slavery Crusade in America Ser). 1969. Repr. of 1804 ed. 12.00 (ISBN 0-405-00616-0). Ayer Co Pubs.
Branagan, Thomas & Ames, Julius R. The Guardian Genius of the Federal Union & the Beauties of Philanthropy. 18.50 (ISBN 0-8369-9159-1, 9034). Ayer Co Pubs.
Branam, George C. Eighteenth-Century Adaptations of Shakespearean Tragedy. 1979. Repr. of 1956 ed. lib. bdg. 25.00 (ISBN 0-8482-3436-7). Norwood Edns.
Branan, Carl. FLEXCURV (TM) Curvefitting Utility. 40p. 1985. incl. floppy disk 95.00x (ISBN 0-87201-240-9). Gulf Pub.
--The Fractionator Analysis Pocket Handbook. LC 77-84383. 96p. (Orig.). 1978. pap. 9.95x (ISBN 0-87201-296-4). Gulf Pub.
Branan, Carl & Mills, John. Process Evaluation & Economic Analysis. LC 76-1680. (Process Engineer's Pocket Handbook Ser.: Vol. 3). 200p. (Orig.). 1984. pap. 12.95x (ISBN 0-87201-715-X). Gulf Pub.
Branan, Carl R. Process Engineer's Pocket Handbook, Vol. 1. LC 76-1680. 136p. (Orig.). 1976. pap. 9.95x (ISBN 0-87201-712-5). Gulf Pub.
Brana-Shute, G. On the Corner: Male Social Life in a Paramaribo Creole Neighborhood. (Studies of Developing Countries: No. 21). 1979. pap. text ed. 14.00x (ISBN 90-232-1605-9). Humanities.
Brana-Shute, Gary, jt. ed. see Brana-Shute, Rosemary.
Brana-Shute, Rosemary & Brana-Shute, Gary, eds. Crime & Punishment in the Caribbean. LC 80-21078. (Illus.). x, 146p. 1981. pap. 6.00 (ISBN 0-8130-0685-6). U Presses Fla.
Branbsby, Carlos, tr. from Eng. Concordancia Tematica De la Biblia. 199p. 1981. pap. 3.50 (ISBN 0-311-42043-5). Casa Bautista.
Branca, Glenn, jt. ed. see Ess, Barbara.
Branca, Margherita, et al. Immune Complexes & Their Role in the Pathogenesis of Various Diseases. LC 72-10434. (Illus.). 220p. 1973. text ed. 23.50x (ISBN 0-8422-7058-2). Irvington.
Branca, Patricia. Women in Europe Since Seventeen Fifty. LC 77-20202. 1978. 25.00x (ISBN 0-312-88739-6). St Martin.
Branca, Vittore. Boccaccio: The Man & His Works. McCauliffe, Dennis J., ed. & tr. from Ital. LC 71-81830. 341p. 1976. 32.50x (ISBN 0-8147-0953-2); pap. 15.00x (ISBN 0-8147-1055-7). NYU Pr.
Brancaforte, Benito. Defensa De la Poesia: A Seventeenth-Century Anonymous Spanish Translation of Philip Sidney's "Defence of Poesie". (Studies in the Romance Languages & Literatures: No. 186). 80p. (Orig.). 1977. pap. 6.00x (ISBN 0-8078-9186-X). U of NC Pr.
--Guzman de Alfarache: Conversion o Proceso de Degradacion? vi, 230p. 1980. 11.00x (ISBN 0-942260-14-7). Hispanic Seminary.
Brancaforte, Charlotte L., ed. Fridericus Berghius' Partial Latin Translation of Lazarillo de Tormes & its Relationship to the Early Lazarillo Translations in Germany. 112p. 1983. 18.50x (ISBN 0-942260-32-5). Hispanic Seminary.
Brancale, Ralph, jt. auth. see Ellis, Albert.
Brancaleone, Jim. Man with a Broken Heart. (Orig., LC 77-072049). 1977. pap. 3.50 (ISBN 0-9601186-1-6). Brancaleone Educ.
--Success Made Fun. LC 81-90660. (Orig.). 1981. pap. 9.95 (ISBN 0-9601186-2-4). Brancaleone Educ.
Brancatelli, Robert. The Maiden Ape. 1986. 10.95 (ISBN 0-916515-02-8). Mercury Hse Inc.
Brancati, Vitaliano. Bell'Antonio. Hochman, Stanley, tr. LC 77-6960. 256p. 1978. 12.95 (ISBN 0-8044-2069-6); pap. 5.95 (ISBN 0-8044-6058-2). Ungar.
Brancato, Robin. Blinded by the Light. LC 78-4583. (YA) 1978. 7.95 (ISBN 0-394-83721-5); PLB 7.99 (ISBN 0-394-93721-X). Knopf.
--Come Alive at 505. LC 79-19144. 224p. (gr. 7 up). 1980. 8.95 (ISBN 0-394-84294-4); 8.99 (ISBN 0-394-94294-9). Knopf.
--Facing Up. 192p. (YA) (gr. 7 up). 1985. pap. 2.50 (ISBN 0-590-33280-5, Point). Scholastic Inc.
--Something Left to Lose. LC 75-30699. 192p. (gr. 7 up). 1976. 6.95 (ISBN 0-394-83183-7). Knopf.
--Sweet Bells Jangled Out of Tune. LC 81-14283. 224p. 1982. PLB 10.99 (ISBN 0-394-94809-2); 10.95 (ISBN 0-394-84809-8). Knopf.
--Sweet Bells Jangled out of Tune. 192p. (gr. 7 up). 1983. pap. 2.25 (ISBN 0-590-33737-8, Point). Scholastic Inc.
--Winning. (gr. 9-12). 1978. pap. 2.50 (ISBN 0-553-25031-0). Bantam.
Brancato, Robin F. Facing Up. LC 83-18708. (Borzoi Bks.). 192p. 1984. 9.95 (ISBN 0-394-85488-8); PLB 9.99 (ISBN 0-394-95488-2). Knopf.
Brancazio, Peter J. Sportscience: Physical Laws & Optimum Performance. LC 83-20152. 400p. 1984. 18.95 (ISBN 0-671-45584-2). S&S.
Brancazio, Peter J. & Cameron, A. G., eds. Infrared Astronomy: Proceedings of a Conference Held at Goddard Space Center, 1968. LC 69-19544. (Illus.). 258p. 1968. 69.50 (ISBN 0-677-11980-1). Gordon.
--Supernovae & Their Remnants: Proceedings of a Conference Held at Goddard Space Center, 1967. (Illus.). 248p. 1969. 69.50 (ISBN 0-677-13290-5). Gordon.
Branch & Swann. The Wage & Hour Law Handbook for the Lodging & Food Service Industry. LC 80-65115. 1980. 34.95 (ISBN 0-86730-236-4). Lebhar Friedman.
Branch, Alan E. Economics of Shipping Practice & Management. (Illus.). 250p. 1982. (Pub. By Chapman & Hall England); pap. 14.95x (ISBN 0-412-16350-0, 6690). Methuen Inc.
--Elements of Export Marketing & Management. 1984. pap. 16.95 (ISBN 0-412-23150-6, Pub. by Chapman & Hall England, NO. 6838). Methuen Inc.
--Elements of Export Practice. 400p. 1977. pap. 16.95 (ISBN 0-412-15610-5, NO.6042, Pub. by Chapman & Hall England). Methuen Inc.
--Elements of Shipping. 5th ed. 238p. 1982. 28.00x (ISBN 0-412-23700-8, NO.6634, Pub. by Chapman & Hall England); pap. 16.95x (ISBN 0-412-23710-5, NO.6633). Methuen Inc.
Branch, Allen E. The Elements of Export Practice. 2nd ed. 360p. 1985. pap. 17.95 (ISBN 0-412-27000-5, 9460, Pub. by Chapman & Hall England). Methuen Inc.
Branch, Anna H. Shoes That Danced & Other Poems. LC 77-89722. (One-Act Plays in Reprint Ser.). 1977. Repr. of 1905 ed. 19.50x (ISBN 0-8486-2027-5). Core Collection.
Branch, Ben. Investments: A Practical Approach. LC 84-26237. 608p. 1985. text ed. 29.95 (ISBN 0-88462-608-3, 4106-01, Pub. by Longman Fin Serv Pub). Longman USA.
Branch, Christine. Nathan & the Law of the Harvest. (Illus.). 24p. (gr. k-6). 1981. pap. 1.95 (ISBN 0-87747-870-8). Deseret Bk.
Branch, Douglas. Cowboy & His Interpreters. LC 62-7732. (Illus.). 277p. 1961. Repr. of 1926 ed. 25.00 (ISBN 0-8154-0030-6). Cooper Sq.
Branch, E. Douglas. Hunting of the Buffalo. LC 62-8408. (Illus.). xxxviii, 270p. 1962. pap. 6.95x (ISBN 0-8032-5021-5, BB 130, Bison). U of Nebr Pr.
--Westward: The Romance of the American Frontier. LC 76-92485. 626p. Repr. of 1930 ed. 28.50 (ISBN 0-8154-0311-9). Cooper Sq.
Branch, Edgar M. A Bibliography of James T. Farrell's Writings, 1921-1957. LC 58-10532. pap. 37.00 (ISBN 0-317-10905-7, 2051184). Bks Demand UMI.
--James T. Farrell. (Pamphlets on American Writers Ser: No. 29). (Orig.). 1963. pap. 1.25x (ISBN 0-8166-0303-0, MPAW29). U of Minn Pr.
--Mark Twain's Letters in the Muscatine Journal. 1978. Repr. of 1942 ed. lib. bdg. 15.00 (ISBN 0-8495-0409-0). Arden Lib.
--Mark Twain's Letters in the Muscatine Journal. LC 73-11355. 1942. lib. bdg. 15.00 (ISBN 0-8414-3212-0). Folcroft.
Branch, Edgar M., ed. Clemens of the Call: Mark Twain in San Francisco. 1969. 32.50x (ISBN 0-520-01385-9). U of Cal Pr.
Branch, Edgar M., ed. see Twain, Mark.
Branch, Kristi & Hooper, Douglas A. Guide to Social Impact Assessment. LC 84-50793. (Social Impact Assessment Ser.: No. 11). 270p. 1984. softcover 28.00x (ISBN 0-86531-717-8). Westview.

Branch, Mary. Tell Me a Story. LC 78-53210. (Stories That Win Ser.). 1978. pap. 0.99 (ISBN 0-8163-0210-3, 20079-0). Pacific Pr Pub Assn.
--Tell Me a Story 2. (Outreach Ser.). 31p. (ps-4). 1982. pap. 0.99 (ISBN 0-8163-0477-7). Pacific Pr Pub Assn.
Branch, Melville C. Comparative Urban Design-Rare Engravings: 1830-1843. 108p. 49.50 (ISBN 0-686-69145-8, Co Pub by U of Cal Pr). Ayer Co Pubs.
--Comprehensive City Planning. LC 85-70970. (Illus.). 238p. 1985. pap. 21.95 (ISBN 0-918286-41-7). Planners Pr.
--Comprehensive Planning: General Theory & Principles. LC 83-61680. (Illus.). 1983. text ed. 12.95x (ISBN 0-913530-32-8). Palisades Pub.
--Continuous City Planning: Integrating Municipal Management & City Planning. 181p. 1980. 31.95x (ISBN 0-471-08943-5, Pub. by Wiley-Interscience). Wiley.
--Urban Air Traffic & City Planning: Case Study of Los Angeles County. LC 73-1090. (Special Studies in U.S. Economic, Social & Political Issues). 1973. 49.50x (ISBN 0-275-28701-7). Irvington.
Branch, Melville C. & Mazza, Eliane G. Selected Annotated Bibliography on New Town Planning & Development. (Architecture Ser.: Bibliography A-216). 133p. 1980. pap. 14.00 (ISBN 0-88066-061-9). Vance Biblios.
Branch, Michael, ed. Kalevala. Kirby, W. F., tr. LC 84-21619. 650p. 1985. 36.00 (ISBN 0-485-11258-2, Pub. by Athlone Pr Ltd); pap. 14.95 (ISBN 0-485-12048-8). Longwood Pub Group.
Branch, Newton, ed. This Britain. facsimile ed. LC 79-90612. (Essay Index Reprint Ser.). 1951. 35.50 (ISBN 0-8369-1549-6). Ayer Co Pubs.
Branch, Newton, tr. see Defourneaux, Marcelin.
Branch, Paul R., Jr., ed. The Siege of Fort Macon. (Illus.). 105p. (Orig.). 1982. pap. 5.00 (ISBN 0-9614000-0-5). P Branch.
Branch, Rene O., Jr., jt. auth. see Stigum, Marcia.
Branch, Taylor, jt. auth. see Propper, Eugene M.
Branch, Tom. The Photographer's Build-It-Yourself Book. (Illus.). 160p. (Orig.). 1982. 18.95 (ISBN 0-8174-5406-3, Amphoto); pap. text ed. 9.95 (ISBN 0-8174-5407-1). Watson-Guptill.
Branch, Watson G., ed. Melville: The Critical Heritage. (The Critical Heritage Ser.). 1985. 38.00x (ISBN 0-7100-7774-2); 15.00 (ISBN 0-7102-0513-9). Routledge & Kegan.
Branch, William T. Office Practice of Medicine. (Illus.). 1318p. 1982. 79.00 (ISBN 0-7216-1914-2). Saunders.
Branchaw, B. English Made Easy. 2nd ed. 208p. 1985. 9.00 (ISBN 0-07-007174-8). McGraw.
Branchaw, Bernadine & Bowman, Joel. Office Procedures for the Professional Secretary. 630p. 1984. text ed. 23.95 (ISBN 0-574-20640-X, 13-3640); write for info. (ISBN 0-574-20641-8, 13-3641). SRA.
Branchaw, Bernadine, jt. auth. see Bowman, Joel P.
Branchaw, Bernadine B., jt. auth. see Bowman, Joel P.
Branchaw, Bernadine P. English Made Easy. (gr. 9-12). 1979. pap. 9.00 (ISBN 0-07-007171-3). McGraw.
Branchaw, Bernadine P., jt. auth. see Bowman, Joel P.
Brancken, Mary. Veterinary Surgery: All Creatures Great & Small. 131p. 1982. 26.00x (ISBN 0-85225-743-0, Pub. by Careers Con England). State Mutual Bk.
Brand, A. Bibliography for Fishermen's Training. (Fisheries Technical Papers: No. 184). 185p. 1978. pap. 13.50 (ISBN 92-5-100663-6, F1539, FAO). Unipub.
Brand, Alice. As It Happens. 64p. 1983. pap. 5.95 (ISBN 0-931694-23-X). Wampeter Pr.
Brand, Alice G. Therapy in Writing: A Psycho-Educational Enterprise. LC 79-2790. (Illus.). 240p. 1980. 29.00 (ISBN 0-669-03232-8). Lexington Bks.
Brand, C. F. Roman Military Law. 262p. 1968. 15.00x (ISBN 0-292-73393-3). U of Tex Pr.
Brand, C. P. Ariosto. 206p. 1974. 15.00x (ISBN 0-85224-246-8, Pub. by Edinburgh U Pr Scotland). Columbia U Pr.
Brand, Carl F. The British Labour Party: A Short History. rev. ed. LC 73-85103. (Publications Ser.: No. 136). 424p. 1974. 13.95x (ISBN 0-8179-6361-8). Hoover Inst Pr.
Brand, Charles M., tr. see Kinnamos, John.
Brand, Christianna. The Brides of Aberdar. 256p. 1983. 11.95 (ISBN 0-312-09548-1). St Martin.
--Cat & Mouse. 1985. pap. 4.95 (ISBN 0-930330-18-8). Intl Polygonics.
--Fog of Doubt. 272p. 1984. pap. 3.50 (ISBN 0-88184-065-3). Carroll & Graf.
--Green for Danger. LC 81-47091. 256p. 1981. pap. 2.50i (ISBN 0-06-080551-X, P 551, PL). Har-Row.
Brand, Dennis J., Jr., tr. from Span. The Book of Causes. (Mediaeval Philosophical Texts in Translation Ser.). 56p. 1984. pap. 7.95 (ISBN 0-87462-225-5). Marquette.
Brand, Donald, jt. auth. see Sauer, Carl O.
Brand, Donald D. Quiroga, a Mexican Municipio. LC 76-44693. Repr. of 1951 ed. 22.50 (ISBN 0-404-15853-6). AMS Pr.
--Quiroga: A Mexican Municipio. 1976. lib. bdg. 59.95 (ISBN 0-8490-2494-3). Gordon Pr.
Brand, E. W. & Brenner, R. P., eds. Soft Clay Engineering. (Developments in Geotechnical Engineering Ser.: Vol. 20). 780p. 1982. 134.00 (ISBN 0-444-41784-2). Elsevier.
Brand, Eileen, ed. see Lumiere, Cornel.
Brand, Eileen, ed. see Lundberg, Ferdinand.
Brand, Eileen, ed. see National Conference on Rational Psychotherapy,1st.
Brand, F. J., tr. see Linnaeus, Carl.
Brand, Gerd. Welt, Geschichte, Mythos, Politik. 1978. 30.40 (ISBN 3-11-007505-9). De Gruyter.
Brand, H. W. The Fecundity of Mathematical Methods in Economic Theory. Holmstrom, E., tr. from Ger. 56p. 1961. lib. bdg. 10.50 (ISBN 90-277-0092-3, Pub. by Reidel Holland). Kluwer Academic.
Brand, Irene. A Change of Heart. (Promise Romance Ser.: No. 3). 192p. (Orig.). 1984. pap. 2.25 (ISBN 0-8407-7352-8). Nelson.
--Meet Mary & Martha. 144p. 1985. pap. 4.95 (ISBN 0-87239-899-4, 2978). Standard Pub.
--A Mighty Flame. (Promise Romances Ser.: No. 24). 192p. 1985. pap. 2.25 (ISBN 0-8407-7383-8). Nelson.
--A Year of Programs for Today's Women. 96p. (Orig.). 1984. pap. 3.95 (ISBN 0-87239-744-0, 2975). Standard Pub.
Brand, Irene B. Only a Clay Vessel. 120p. (Orig.). 1985. pap. 5.00 (ISBN 0-9615285-0-8). Brand.
Brand, J. J., jt. auth. see Reason, J. T.
Brand, J. P. Cretaceous of Llano Estacado of Texas. (Illus.). 59p. 1953. 0.70 (ISBN 0-686-29330-4, RI 20). Bur Econ Geology.
Brand, Jack. Local Government Reform in England, 1888-1974. 176p. 1974. 19.50 (ISBN 0-208-01480-2, Archon). Shoe String.
Brand, Janet & Tolins, Stephen. The Nursing Student's Guide to Surgery. 1979. 17.95 (ISBN 0-316-10635-6). Little.
Brand, Jeanne L. Doctors & the State: The British Medical Profession & Government Action in Public Health, 1870-1912. LC 65-27326. pap. 84.80 (ISBN 0-317-19887-4, 2023085). Bks Demand UMI.
Brand, Jeanne L., jt. auth. see Mora, George.
Brand, Jeffry, jt. auth. see Gladstone, Nancy.
Brand, John. Observations on the Popular Antiquities of Great Britain, 3 Vols. 3rd ed. Ellis, Henry, ed. LC 71-136368. (Bohn's Antiquarian Library Ser). Repr. of 1849 ed. Set. 37.50 (ISBN 0-404-50005-6); 12.50 ea. Vol. 1 (ISBN 0-404-50011-0). Vol. 2 (ISBN 0-404-50012-9). Vol. 3 (ISBN 0-404-50013-7). AMS Pr.
--Observations on the Popular Antiquities of Great Britain: Chiefly Illustrating the Origin of Our Vulgar & Provincial Customs, Ceremonies & Superstitions, 3 vols. LC 67-23896. 1969. Repr. of 1849 ed. Set. 68.00x (ISBN 0-8103-3256-6). Gale.
Brand, John R. Handbook of Electronic Formulas, Symbols, & Definitions. 1979. 22.95 (ISBN 0-442-20999-1). Van Nos Reinhold.
Brand, Katarzyna Mroczkowska see Kapuscinski, Ryszard.
Brand, Kim. Common C Functions. LC 84-61392. 292p. 1985. 17.95 (ISBN 0-88022-069-4, 148); disk 49.95. Que Corp.
Brand, L., jt. auth. see Morse, P.
Brand, Marvine, ed. Security for Libraries: People, Buildings, Collections. LC 84-455. 144p. 1984. pap. 12.00x (ISBN 0-8389-0409-2). ALA.
Brand, Max. Ambush at Torture Canyon. 1981. pap. 1.95 (ISBN 0-671-41557-3). PB.
--Bandit of the Black Hills. Repr. of 1976 ed. lib. bdg. 15.95 (ISBN 0-88411-512-7, Pub. by Aeonian Pr). Amereon Ltd.
--THe Bandit of the Black Hills. 1983. pap. 2.50 (ISBN 0-671-47432-4). PB.
--The Big Trail. 1976. Repr. of 1934 ed. lib. bdg. 15.95 (ISBN 0-88411-513-5, Pub. by Aeonian Pr). Amereon Ltd.
--Black Jack. 208p. 1983. pap. 2.50 (ISBN 0-671-41575-1). PB.
--Black Jack. (General Ser.). 1984. lib. bdg. 13.95 (ISBN 0-8161-3533-9, Large Print). G K Hall.
--Blood on the Trail. 1982. pap. 1.95 (ISBN 0-671-44714-9). PB.
--The Blue Jay. 1984. pap. 2.50 (ISBN 0-671-54087-4). PB.
--Border Bandit. (Illus.). 272p. 1982. pap. 2.50 (ISBN 0-441-07078-7, Pub. by Charter Bks). Ace Bks.
--Brothers of the Trail. 1976. Repr. of 1934 ed. lib. bdg. 14.95 (ISBN 0-88411-514-3, Pub. by Aeonian Pr). Amereon Ltd.
--Bull Hunter. (General Ser.). 1981. lib. bdg. 13.95 (ISBN 0-8161-3308-5, Large Print Bks). G K Hall.
--Calling Doctor Kildare. 1978. 18.00 (ISBN 0-86025-135-7). State Mutual Bk.
--Dan Barry's Daughter. 1976. Repr. of 1959 ed. lib. bdg. 18.95 (ISBN 0-88411-516-X, Pub. by Aeonian Pr). Amereon Ltd.
--Danger Trail. 1976. Repr. of 1940 ed. lib. bdg. 16.95 (ISBN 0-88411-517-8, Pub. by Aeonian Pr). Amereon Ltd.
--Dead or Alive. 1976. Repr. of 1939 ed. lib. bdg. 17.95x (ISBN 0-88411-518-6, Pub. by Aeonian Pr). Amereon Ltd.
--Destry Rides Again. 1976. Repr. of 1930 ed. lib. bdg. 16.95 (ISBN 0-88411-515-1, Pub. by Aeonian Pr). Amereon Ltd.
--Destry Rides Again. 208p. 1984. pap. 2.50 (ISBN 0-671-83660-9). PB.
--Devil Horse. 202p. Repr. of 1922 ed. lib. bdg. 13.95 (ISBN 0-88411-522-4, Pub. by Aeonian Pr). Amereon Ltd.
--Dr. Kildare Takes Charge. 160p. Repr. of 1940 ed. lib. bdg. 13.95 (ISBN 0-88411-531-3, Pub. by Aneonian Pr). Amereon Ltd.
--Dr. Kildare's Trial. 174p. Repr. of 1941 ed. lib. bdg. 12.95 (ISBN 0-88411-532-1, Pub. by Aneonian Pr). Amereon Ltd.
--The Dude. 1976. Repr. of 1940 ed. lib. bdg. 16.95 (ISBN 0-88411-519-4, Pub. by Aeonian Pr). Amereon Ltd.
--The False Rider. 100p. 1984. pap. 2.25 (ISBN 0-671-41572-7). PB.
--Fightin' Fool. 1984. pap. 2.25 (ISBN 0-671-41579-4). PB.
--Flaming Irons. large print ed. LC 84-8767. 433p. 1984. Repr. of 1976 ed. 13.95 (ISBN 0-89621-564-4). Thorndike Pr.
--The Gambler. 1976. Repr. of 1954 ed. lib. bdg. 18.95 (ISBN 0-88411-520-8, Pub. by Aeonian Pr). Amereon Ltd.
--The Gentle Desperado: A Silver Star Western. 224p. 1985. 14.95 (ISBN 0-396-08715-9). Dodd.
--The Gentle Gunman. (General Ser.). 1984. lib. bdg. 13.95 (ISBN 0-8161-3534-7, Large Print Bks). G K Hall.
--Ghost Rider. 212p. Repr. of 1920 ed. lib. bdg. 13.95 (ISBN 0-88411-521-6, Pub. by Aeonian Pr). Amereon Ltd.
--Ghost Rider. 208p. 1984. pap. 2.50 (ISBN 0-671-50360-X). PB.
--The Gun Tamer. 1983. pap. 2.25 (ISBN 0-671-41580-8). PB.
--Gunfighter's Return. (General Ser.). 1980. lib. bdg. 12.95 (ISBN 0-8161-3055-8, Large Print Bks). G K Hall.
--Gunmen's Feud. (Silver Star Western Ser.). 192p. 1982. 9.95 (ISBN 0-396-08053-7). Dodd.
--Gunmen's Feud. (General Ser.). 265p. 1983. lib. bdg. 13.95 (ISBN 0-8161-3522-3, Large Print Bks). G K Hall.
--The Hair-Trigger Kid. 1983. pap. 2.50 (ISBN 0-671-41570-0). PB.
--Hired Guns. 1980. pap. 1.75 (ISBN 0-671-83469-X). PB.
--Hunted Riders. 1979. pap. 1.75 (ISBN 0-671-82894-0). PB.
--The Jackson Trail. 1978. pap. 1.50 (ISBN 0-671-81756-6). PB.
--King of the Range. 1982. pap. 2.25 (ISBN 0-671-46405-1). PB.
--Laramee's Ranch. 1981. pap. 1.95 (ISBN 0-671-41558-1). PB.
--The Last Showdown. 240p. 1984. pap. 2.25 (ISBN 0-671-41587-5). PB.
--Lawless Land. 256p. 1983. 11.95 (ISBN 0-396-08204-1). Dodd.
--Lawless Land. 192p. 1984. pap. 2.50 (ISBN 0-446-32414-0). Warner Bks.
--The Longhorn Feud. 1985. pap. 2.50 (ISBN 0-671-41559-X). PB.
--The Making of a Gunman. LC 82-19940. 1983. 11.95 (ISBN 0-396-08128-2). Dodd.
--The Making of a Gunman. (General Ser.). 308p. 1983. lib. bdg. 12.95 (ISBN 0-8161-3585-1, Large Print Bks). G K Hall.
--The Making of a Gunman. 193p. 1984. pap. 2.50 (ISBN 0-446-32412-4). Warner Bks.
--Max Brand's Best Western Stories. Nolan, William, ed. 240p. 1983. pap. 2.25 (ISBN 0-446-30232-5). Warner Bks.
--Max Brand's Best Western Stories. (Vol. II). 182p. 1985. 13.95 (ISBN 0-396-08500-8). Dodd.
--Max Brand's Best Western Stories, Vol. 1. Nolan, William F., ed. LC 81-3204. 1981. 8.95 (ISBN 0-396-07984-9). Dodd.
--Mountain Guns: A Silver Western. 224p. 1985. 14.95 (ISBN 0-396-08691-8). Dodd.
--The Night Horseman. 1980. pap. 1.75 (ISBN 0-671-83418-5). PB.
--On the Trail of Four. 1982. pap. 1.95 (ISBN 0-671-44709-2). PB.
--The Outlaw. rev. ed. 1980. pap. 1.75 (ISBN 0-671-83416-9). PB.
--The Outlaw. large print ed. LC 83-24279. 382p. 1984. Repr. of 1974 ed. 13.95 (ISBN 0-89621-518-0). Thorndike Pr.
--Pillar Mountain. 1978. pap. 1.50 (ISBN 0-671-81758-2). PB.
--Pleasant Jim. 1978. pap. 1.50 (ISBN 0-671-81759-0). PB.
--The Rangeland Avenger. 228p. 1985. 13.95 (ISBN 0-396-08562-8). Dodd.
--Rawhide Justice. 1985. pap. 2.50 (ISBN 0-671-41589-1). PB.
--Rawhide Justice. (General Ser.). 1984. lib. bdg. 14.95 (ISBN 0-8161-3532-0, Large Print Bks). G K Hall.
--The Reward. 1979. pap. 1.75 (ISBN 0-671-82892-4). PB.
--Ride the Wild Trail. 1981. pap. 1.75 (ISBN 0-671-41556-5). PB.
--Ride the Wild Trail. (General Ser.). 1983. lib. bdg. 13.95 (ISBN 0-8161-3435-9, Large Print Bks). G K Hall.
--Rider of the High Hills. 240p. 1985. pap. 2.50 (ISBN 0-446-32971-1). Warner Bks.
--Riders of the Plain. 1978. pap. 1.50 (ISBN 0-671-81760-4). PB.
--Rippon Rides Double. 176p. 1975. pap. 2.25 (ISBN 0-671-80053-1). PB.
--Rogue Mustang. 192p. 1984. 11.95 (ISBN 0-396-08311-0). Dodd.
--Rogue Mustang. 176p. 1985. pap. 2.50 (ISBN 0-446-32686-0). Warner Bks.
--Rogue Mustang. (General Ser.). 1985. lib. bdg. 13.95 (ISBN 0-8161-3784-6, Large Print Bks). G K Hall.
--The Secret of Dr. Kildare. 180p. Repr. of 1939 ed. lib. bdg. 12.95x (ISBN 0-88411-530-5, Pub. by River City Pr). Amereon Ltd.
--Silvertip's Search. 1978. pap. 1.50 (ISBN 0-671-81762-0). PB.
--Silvertip's Search. 144p. 1982. 15.00x (ISBN 0-7278-0446-4, Pub. by Severn Hse). State Mutual Bk.
--Silvertip's Trap. 1979. pap. 1.50 (ISBN 0-671-81763-9). PB.
--Singing Guns. 1983. pap. 2.25 (ISBN 0-671-41571-9). PB.
--Single Jack. 1980. pap. 1.75 (ISBN 0-671-83417-7). PB.
--Smoking Land: A Novel of Super-Science & Amazing Adventure. LC 80-17333. (Max Brand Popular Classics Ser.). 112p. 1980. pap. 5.95 (ISBN 0-88496-155-9). Capra Pr.
--South of Rio Grando. 1981. pap. 2.25 (ISBN 0-671-83368-5). PB.
--Steve Train's Ordeal. 1980. pap. 1.75 (ISBN 0-671-41489-5). PB.
--Steve Train's Ordeal. large print ed. LC 82-859. 341p. 1982. Repr. of 1924 ed. 11.95 (ISBN 0-89621-351-X). Thorndike Pr.
--The Stingaree. LC 81-38512. 224p. 1982. Repr. of 1968 ed. 12.50x (ISBN 0-8376-0461-3). Bentley.
--The Stingaree. 1983. pap. 2.25 (ISBN 0-671-41564-6). PB.
--Stolen Stallion. 1979. pap. 1.75 (ISBN 0-671-83023-6). PB.
--Storm on the Range. (General Ser.). 1983. PLB 13.95 (ISBN 0-8161-3436-7, Large Print Bks). G K Hall.
--The Streak. 176p. 1984. pap. text ed. 2.25 (ISBN 0-671-41576-X). PB.
--Three on the Trail. 256p. 1984. 12.95 (ISBN 0-396-08387-0). Dodd.
--Three on the Trail. 208p. 1985. pap. 2.50 (ISBN 0-446-32688-7). Warner Bks.
--Three on the Trail. (Large Print Books (General Ser.)). 1985. lib. bdg. 13.95 (ISBN 0-8161-3851-6). G K Hall.
--Thunder Moon. 160p. 1982. pap. 1.95 (ISBN 0-671-41567-0). PB.
--Thunder Moon. 160p. 1982. 15.00x (ISBN 0-7278-0443-X, Pub. by Severn Hse). State Mutual Bk.
--Thunder Moon. Large Print ed. LC 83-18289. 263p. 1983. Repr. of 1975 ed. 12.95 (ISBN 0-89621-496-6). Thorndike Pr.
--Thunder Moon Strikes. LC 82-5087. (Silver Star Western Ser.). 1982. 12.95 (ISBN 0-396-08081-2). Dodd.
--Thunder Moon Strikes. 224p. 1984. pap. 2.50 (ISBN 0-446-32074-9). Warner Bks.
--Thunder Moon's Challenge. LC 82-5023. (Silver Star Western Ser.). 1982. 11.95 (ISBN 0-396-08077-4). Dodd.
--Thunder Moon's Challenge. 224p. 1984. pap. 2.50 (ISBN 0-446-32050-1). Warner Bks.
--Tragedy Trail. 1982. pap. 2.25 (ISBN 0-671-41563-8). PB.
--The Trail to San Triste. 228p. 1983. 11.95 (ISBN 0-396-08206-8). Dodd.
--Trail to San Triste. 192p. 1985. pap. 2.50 (ISBN 0-446-32416-7). Warner Bks.
--The Trail to San Triste. (Hall Large Print Bk.). 1985. lib. bdg. 13.95 (ISBN 0-8161-3653-X, Large Print Bks). G K Hall.
--Trouble in Timberline. 258p. 1984. 12.95 (ISBN 0-396-08473-7). Dodd.
--Trouble Kid. 1979. pap. 1.75 (ISBN 0-671-83028-7). PB.
--The Trouble Kid. 1985. pap. 2.50 (ISBN 0-671-41582-4). PB.
--The Untamed. 1983. pap. 2.25 (ISBN 0-671-41578-6). PB.
--Valley of the Vanishing Men. 1981. pap. 1.95 (ISBN 0-671-83310-3). PB.
--Valley Thieves. 1981. pap. 1.95 (ISBN 0-671-41583-2). PB.
--Vengeance Trail. 1981. pap. 2.25 (ISBN 0-671-41584-0). PB.
--War Party. LC 81-38502. 224p. 1982. Repr. of 1972 ed. 12.50x (ISBN 0-8376-0460-5). Bentley.
--Way of the Lawless. 1980. pap. 2.50 (ISBN 0-446-32665-8). Warner Bks.
--Wild Freedom. (General Ser.). 1982. 12.95 (ISBN 0-8161-3305-0, Large Print Bks). G K Hall.
--Wild Freedom. 240p. 1983. pap. 2.50 (ISBN 0-446-32769-7). Warner Bks.
--Wine on Desert. 1976. Repr. of 1940 ed. lib. bdg. 16.95x (ISBN 0-88411-511-9, Pub. by Aeonian Pr). Amereon Ltd.
--Young Dr. Kildare. 13.95 (ISBN 0-89190-212-0, Pub. by Am Repr). Amereon Ltd.
Brand, Max see Evans, Evan, pseud.
Brand, May. Six-Gun Country. 208p. 1981. pap. 1.95 (ISBN 0-671-41516-6). PB.

Brand, Mildred. Candy & Candy Molding. (Illus.). 64p. 1982. pap. 3.50 (ISBN 0-8249-3015-0). Ideals.
--Candy Cookbook. Kuse, James A., ed. (Illus.). 1979. pap. 3.50 (ISBN 0-89542-615-3). Ideals.
--Easy Cake Decorating. (Illus., Orig.). 1980. pap. 3.50 (ISBN 0-89542-622-6). Ideals.
Brand, Millen. Peace March. 222p. 1980. 10.95 (ISBN 0-914378-64-3); pap. 7.95 (ISBN 0-914378-63-5). Countryman.
Brand, Myles. Intending & Acting: Toward a Naturalized Action Theory. 320p. 1984. text ed. 30.00x (ISBN 0-262-02202-8). MIT Pr.
Brand, Myles, ed. Action Theory: Proceedings. LC 76-6882. (Synthese Library: No. 97). 1976. PLB 55.00 (ISBN 90-277-0671-9, Pub. by Reidel Holland). Kluwer Academic.
--The Nature of Causation. LC 76-110. 372p. 1976. 17.50x (ISBN 0-252-00407-8). U of Ill Pr.
Brand, Myles, jt. ed. see Bradie, Michael.
Brand, Norman & White, John O. Legal Writing: The Strategy of Persuasion. LC 75-38015. 300p. 1976. text ed. 17.95 (ISBN 0-312-47810-0); instr's manual avail. St Martin.
Brand, Oscar. The Ballad Mongers: Rise of the Modern Folk Song. LC 78-60137. 1979. Repr. of 1962 ed. lib. bdg. 22.50x (ISBN 0-313-20555-8, BRBM). Greenwood.
--Songs of Seventy Six: A Folksinger's History of the Revolution. LC 72-83733. (Illus.). 176p. 1972. 10.00 (ISBN 0-87131-092-9); pap. 4.95 (ISBN 0-87131-170-4). M Evans.
Brand, Paul & Yancey, Philip. Fearfully & Wonderfully Made. (Illus.). 224p. 1980. 10.95 (ISBN 0-310-35450-1). Zondervan.
--In His Image. 224p. 1984. 12.95 (ISBN 0-310-35500-1). Zondervan.
Brand, Paul & Yancey, Phillip. La Obra Maestra de Dios. 224p. 1984. 3.75 (ISBN 0-88113-224-1). Edit Betania.
Brand, Ralph. Simplified Techniques of Counseling. 1972. 4.50 (ISBN 0-89114-050-6); pap. 2.50 (ISBN 0-89114-049-2). Baptist Pub Hse.
Brand, Raymond J. About This & That. LC 84-90173. 114p. 1985. 8.95 (ISBN 0-533-06231-4). Vantage.
Brand, Renee. The Experiment. pap. 3.00 (ISBN 0-317-13550-3). C G Jung Frisco.
Brand, Richard W. & Isselhard, Donald E. Anatomy of Orofacial Structures. 2nd ed. LC 81-14103. (Illus.). 405p. 1982. pap. text ed. 20.95 (ISBN 0-8016-0857-0). Mosby.
Brand, Robert H. Union of South Africa. LC 76-76493. Repr. of 1909 ed. 17.50x (ISBN 0-8371-1090-4, BRU&). Greenwood.
Brand, Roy E. De see De Brand, Roy E.
Brand, Sandra. Between Two Worlds. LC 82-60204. 128p. 1982. 7.95 (ISBN 0-88400-083-4); pap. 3.95 (ISBN 0-88400-084-2). Shengold.
Brand, Stewart. Whole Earth Software Catalog. LC 84-15096. 208p. 1984. pap. 17.50 (ISBN 0-385-19166-9, Quantum Pr). Doubleday.
--Whole Earth Software Catalog, Vol. 2. 1985. pap. 17.50 (ISBN 0-385-23301-9, Quantum Pr). Doubleday.
Brand, Stewart, ed. Next Whole Earth Catalog. 2nd ed. (Illus.). 608p. 1982. pap. 16.00 (ISBN 0-394-70776-1). Point Calif.
--The Next Whole Earth Catalog. 608p. 1981. 14.00 (ISBN 0-317-32273-7). Alternatives.
--Next Whole Earth Catalog. 2nd ed. (Illus.). 608p. (Orig., Pub. by Point Fdn., dist. by Random House). 1981. Repr. of 1980 ed. pap. 16.00 (ISBN 0-394-70776-1). Point Found.
--Space Colonies. 1977. pap. 5.00 (ISBN 0-14-004805-7). Penguin.
Brand, Stewart & Kleiner, Art, eds. News That Stayed News: Ten Years of Coevolution Quarterly. 256p. 1986. 25.00 (ISBN 0-86547-201-7); pap. 10.50 (ISBN 0-86547-202-5). N Point Pr.
Brand, Stewart, jt. ed. see Baldwin, J.
Brand, Susan. Shadows on the Tor. (General Ser.). 1978. lib. bdg. 12.50 (ISBN 0-8161-6589-0, Large Print Bks). G K Hall.
Brand, William R., tr. see Kapuscinski, Ryszard.
Brand, William R., tr. see Micewski, Andrzej.
Branda, Eldon S. see Webb, Walter P. & Carroll, H. Bailey.
Brandabur, Edward. A Scrupulous Meanness: A Study of Joyce's Early Work. LC 71-131057. pap. 49.30 (ISBN 0-317-28998-5, 2020241). Bks Demand UMI.
Brandal, W. Commutative Rings Whose Finitely Generated Modules Decompose. (Lecture Notes in Mathematics: Vol. 723). 1979. pap. 13.00 (ISBN 0-387-09507-1). Springer-Verlag.
Brandall, William S. The Secret of the Universe: New Discoveries on God, Man & the Eternity of Life. (Illus.). 119p. 1985. 127.45 (ISBN 0-89266-535-1). Am Classical Coll Pr.
Brandane, John. The Treasure Ship; Rory Aforesaid; the Happy War: Three Plays. LC 79-50019. (One-Act Plays in Reprint Ser.). 1980. Repr. of 1928 ed. 21.50x (ISBN 0-8486-2043-7). Core Collection.
Brandao, Ignacio D. And Still the Earth. 384p. 1985. pap. 4.95 (ISBN 0-380-89874-8). Avon.
Brandav, R. & Lippold, H. Dermal & Transdermal Absorption. (First International Symposium from 12-14 Jnauary, 1981, Munich). 257p. 1982. 49.00 (ISBN 0-9909000-0-2, Pub. by Wissenschaftliche W Germany). Heyden.
Brande, Dorothea. Becoming a Writer. LC 80-53146. 192p. 1981. pap. 5.95 (ISBN 0-87477-164-1). J P Tarcher.
--Wake up & Live. (Orig.). 1980. pap. 3.95 (ISBN 0-346-12415-8). Cornerstone.
Brandeis, Ann. Color Processing & Printing. (Masterclass Photography Ser.). (Illus.). 176p. 1983. 12.95 (ISBN 0-13-152207-8). P-H.
Brandeis, Arthur, ed. Jacob's Well, an English Treatise on the Cleansing of Man's Conscience, Pt. 1. (EETS, OS Ser.: No. 115). Repr. of 1900 ed. 54.00 (ISBN 0-527-00114-7). Kraus Repr.
Brandeis, Irma, tr. see Rostand, Jean.
Brandeis, Louis D. Brandeis on Zionism. LC 75-6425. (The Rise of Jewish Nationalism & the Middle East Ser.). 156p. 1975. Repr. of 1942 ed. 17.60 (ISBN 0-88355-312-0). Hyperion Conn.
--Business: A Profession. LC 68-55491. Repr. of 1914 ed. 27.50x (ISBN 0-678-00855-8). Kelley.
--Letters of Louis D. Brandeis. Urofsky, Melvin L. & Levy, David W., eds. Incl. Vol. 1. 1870-1907; Urban Reformer. 1971. 49.50x (ISBN 0-87395-078-X); Vol. 2. 1907-1912; People's Attorney. 1972. 49.50x (ISBN 0-87395-091-7); Vol. 3. 1913-1915; Progressive & Zionist. 1973. 49.50x (ISBN 0-87395-231-6); Vol. 4. 1916-1921: Mr. Justice Brandeis. 1975. 49.50x (ISBN 0-87395-297-9); Vol. 5. 1922-1941: Elder Statesman. 1978. 49.50x (ISBN 0-87395-330-4). LC 73-129640. (Illus.). State U NY Pr.
--Other People's Money & How the Bankers Use It. 2nd ed. LC 79-156937. Repr. of 1932 ed. lib. bdg. 25.00x (ISBN 0-678-00856-6). Kelley.
--Other People's Money & How the Bankers Use It. 1977. Repr. of 1932 ed. lib. bdg. 20.00 (ISBN 0-8482-3382-4). Norwood Edns.
--Scientific Management & Railroads. Bd. with Higher Railroad Rates vs. Scientific Management. Bullock, Harry A. (Management History Ser.: No. 82). xii, 178p. 1980. lib. bdg. 20.00 (ISBN 0-87960-101-9); pap. 12.95 (ISBN 0-87960-120-5). Hive Pub.
Brandeis, Louis D. & Goldmark, Josephine. Women in Industry. LC 73-89720. (American Labor, from Conspiracy to Collective Bargaining Ser., No. 1). 121p. 1969. Repr. of 1907 ed. 12.00 (ISBN 0-405-02106-2). Ayer Co Pubs.
Brandeis University - Poses Institute of Fine Arts, ed. Art Criticism in the Sixties. 1965. pap. 3.25 (ISBN 0-8079-0008-7). October.
Brandejs, J. F., ed. Computer Assisted Physicians Offices. (Health Communications & Informatics: Vol. 5, No. 2, 1979). (Illus.). 1979. softcover 8.25 (ISBN 3-8055-3063-3). S Karger.
Brandejs, Jan F. & Pace, Graham. Physician's Primer on Computers: Private Practice. LC 75-39315. 208p. 1979. 23.50 (ISBN 0-669-00431-6). Lexington Bks.
Brandejs, Jan F., jt. ed. see Day, Stacey B.
Brandel, Marc. A Life of Her Own. 468p. 1984. 17.95 (ISBN 0-395-37724-2). HM.
--Murder in the Family. 160p. 1985. pap. 2.95 (ISBN 0-380-89869-1). Avon.
--The Mystery of the Kidnapped Whale. LC 83-3008. (The Three Investigators Mystery Ser.: No.35). (Illus.). 192p. (gr. 4-7). 1983. pap. 1.95 (ISBN 0-394-85841-7); PLB 5.99 (ISBN 0-394-95841-1). Random.
--The Mystery of the Rogues Reunion. LC 84-13395. (The Three Investigators Mystery Ser.: No. 40). (Illus.). 192p. (gr. 4-7). 1985. PLB 5.99 (ISBN 0-394-96920-0, BYR); pap. 1.95 (ISBN 0-394-86920-6). Random.
--The Mystery of the Two-Toed Pigeon. LC 83-21174. (The Three Investigators Mystery Ser.: No. 37). (Illus.). 160p. (gr. 4-7). 1984. pap. 1.95 (ISBN 0-394-85976-6, BYR); PLB 5.99 (ISBN 0-394-95976-0). Random.
--Survivor. 1977. pap. 1.50 (ISBN 0-380-00953-6, 32292). Avon.
Brandel, Roland E., et al. Truth in Lending: A Comprehensive Guide. LC 84-22423. 850p. 1985. Supplements avail. 85.00 (ISBN 0-15-004372-4, #H43724, Law & Business). HarBraceJ.
Brandel, Rose. The Music of Central Africa. (Music Reprint Ser.). xii, 272p. 1983. Repr. of 1973 ed. lib. bdg. 35.00 (ISBN 0-306-76222-6). Da Capo.
Brandell, Gunnar. Freud-A Man of His Century. White, Iain, tr. LC 78-5347. 1979. text ed. 18.75x (ISBN 0-391-00871-4). Humanities.
--Strindberg in Inferno. Jacobs, Barry, tr. from Swedish. LC 73-90851. 352p. 1974. 22.50x (ISBN 0-674-84325-8). Harvard U Pr.
Brandel-Syrier, Mia. Reeftown Elite: Social Mobility in a Black African Community on the Johannesburg Reef. LC 70-151968. 335p. 1971. text ed. 32.50x (ISBN 0-8419-0072-8, Africana). Holmes & Meier.
Branden, F. Van Den see Van Den Branden, F. & Hartsell, Thomas L.
Branden, Michael. The Country Divine. 206p. 1981. 29.00x (ISBN 0-7152-0492-0, Pub. by St Andrew Pr England). State Mutual Bk.
Branden, Nathaniel. The Disowned Self. 256p. 1973. pap. 3.95 (ISBN 0-553-24557-0). Bantam.
--Honoring the Self: Personal Integrity & the Heroic Potentials of Human Nature. 288p. 1984. 15.95 (ISBN 0-87477-270-2). J P Tarcher.
--If You Could Hear What I Cannot Say: Learning to Communicate with the Ones You Love. 1983. pap. 9.95 (ISBN 0-553-34218-5). Bantam.
--A Nathaniel Branden Anthology. 1980. 17.50 (ISBN 0-686-65215-0). HM.
--Nathaniel Branden Anthology: The Psychology of Self-Esteem, Breaking Free, The Disowned Self. LC 80-51879. 721p. 1980. 17.50 (ISBN 0-87477-142-0). J P Tarcher.
--The Psychology of Romantic Love. 288p. 1981. pap. 3.95 (ISBN 0-553-25309-3). Bantam.
--The Psychology of Romantic Love. LC 79-91763. 210p. 1980. 10.00 (ISBN 0-87477-124-2). J P Tarcher.
--Psychology of Self-Esteem. 1971. pap. 3.95 (ISBN 0-553-23449-8). Bantam.
--To See What I See & Know What I Know: A Guide to Self-Discovery. LC 85-47792. 224p. 1985. pap. 7.95 (ISBN 0-553-34235-5). Bantam.
Branden, Thomas, jt. auth. see Alsop, Stewart.
Brandenberg, Franz. Aunt Nina & Her Nephews & Nieces. LC 82-12004. (Illus.). 32p. (gr. k-3). 1983. PLB 10.51 (ISBN 0-688-01870-X); 11.50 (ISBN 0-688-01869-6). Greenwillow.
--Aunt Nina's Visit. LC 83-16531. (Illus.). 32p. (gr. k-3). 1984. 11.50 (ISBN 0-688-01764-9); PLB 10.51 (ISBN 0-688-01766-5). Greenwillow.
--Everyone Ready? LC 78-13744. (Greenwillow Read-Alone Bks.). (Illus.). 56p. (gr. 1-3). 1979. 8.75 (ISBN 0-688-80198-6); PLB 8.88 (ISBN 0-688-84198-8). Greenwillow.
--The Hit of the Party. LC 84-25913. (Illus.). 32p. (gr. k-3). 1985. 11.75 (ISBN 0-688-04240-6); lib. bdg. 11.88 (ISBN 0-688-04241-4). Greenwillow.
--I Wish I Was Sick, Too. LC 75-46610. (Illus.). 32p. (gr. k-3). 1976. PLB 11.88 (ISBN 0-688-84047-7). Greenwillow.
--I Wish I Was Sick Too! (Illus.). 1978. pap. 3.95 (ISBN 0-14-050292-0, Puffin). Penguin.
--It's Not My Fault. LC 79-24157. (Greenwillow Read-Alone Bks.). (Illus.). 64p. (gr. 1-3). 1980. 8.75 (ISBN 0-688-80235-4); PLB 8.88 (ISBN 0-688-84235-6). Greenwillow.
--Leo & Emily. LC 80-19657. (Read-Alone Bks.). (Illus.). 56p. (gr. 1-3). 1981. 8.75 (ISBN 0-688-80292-3); PLB 8.88 (ISBN 0-688-84292-5). Greenwillow.
--Leo & Emily & the Dragon. LC 83-14091. (Read-Alone Bks.). (Illus.). 56p. (gr. 1-3). 1984. 8.75 (ISBN 0-688-02531-5); PLB 7.92 (ISBN 0-688-02532-3). Greenwillow.
--Leo & Emily's Big Ideas. LC 81-6424. (Read-Alone Bks.). (Illus.). 56p. (gr. 1-3). 1982. 9.25 (ISBN 0-688-00754-6); PLB 8.88 (ISBN 0-688-00755-4). Greenwillow.
--Nice New Neighbors. LC 77-1651. (Read-Alone Bks.). (Illus.). 56p. (gr. 1-4). 1977. PLB 10.88 (ISBN 0-688-84105-8). Greenwillow.
--Otto Is Different. LC 84-13654. (Illus.). 24p. (gr. k-3). 1985. 11.75 (ISBN 0-688-04253-8); PLB 11.88 (ISBN 0-688-04254-6). Greenwillow.
--A Picnic, Hurrah! LC 77-3950. (Greenwillow Read-Alone Bks.). (Illus.). 56p. (gr. 1-4). 1978. 8.75 (ISBN 0-688-80115-3). Greenwillow.
--A Secret for Grandmother's Birthday. LC 75-10606. (Illus.). 32p. (ps-3). 1975. 9.55 (ISBN 0-688-84012-4); PLB 10.32. Greenwillow.
--A Secret for Grandmother's Birthday. LC 75-10606. (Illus.). 32p. (gr. k-3). 1985. 10.25 (ISBN 0-688-05781-0); lib. bdg. 10.88 (ISBN 0-688-05782-9). Greenwillow.
--Six New Students. LC 77-24883. (Greenwillow Read-Alone Bks.). (Illus.). 56p. (gr. 1-4). 1978. 8.75 (ISBN 0-688-80124-2); PLB 8.88 (ISBN 0-688-84124-4). Greenwillow.
--What Can You Make of It? LC 76-44406. (Greenwillow Read-Alone Bks.). (Illus.). 56p. (gr. 1-4). 1977. PLB 8.88 (ISBN 0-688-84083-3). Greenwillow.
Brandenberg, P. & McLean, R. J., eds. A Swedish Reader. 174p. 1953. 19.50 (ISBN 0-485-11013-X, Pub. by Athlone Pr Ltd). Longwood Pub Group.
Brandenberger, E. & Stattmann, F. Nuclear Power Dictionary, Vol. 63. 456p. (Eng. & Ger.). 1978. pap. 52.50 (ISBN 3-521-06112-4, M-7572, Verlag Karl Thiemig). French & Eur.
Brandenburg, D., ed. Insulin: Chemistry, Structure & Function of Insulin & Related Hormones. text ed. 68.00 (ISBN 3-11-008156-3). De Gruyter.
Brandenburg, Erich. From Bismark to the World War: A History of German Foreign Policy 1870-1914. Adams, Annie E., tr. LC 83-45416. Repr. of 1927 ed. 49.50 (ISBN 0-404-20041-9). AMS Pr.
Brandenburg, Hans. The Meek & the Mighty. Matchett, Kathy, tr. (Eng.). 1977. 15.95x (ISBN 0-19-519914-6). Oxford U Pr.
Brandenburg, M. M., tr. see Baegert, Johann J.
Brandenburg, Robert O., ed. Office Cardiology. LC 79-19973. (Cardiovascular Clinics Ser.: Vol. 10, No. 3). (Illus.). 308p. 1980. text ed. 37.50x (ISBN 0-8036-1118-8). Davis Co.
Brandenburger, W. Parasitische Pilze an Gefaesspflanzen in Europe. (Illus.). 1248p. 1985. lib. bdg. 112.00x (ISBN 3-437-30433-X). Lubrecht & Cramer.
--Vademekum zum Sammeln Parasitischer Pilze. (Ger.). 1963. pap. 14.95 (ISBN 3-8001-3412-8, M-7136). French & Eur.
Brandenderg. Nice New Neighbors. (ps-3). 1980. pap. 1.95 (ISBN 0-590-30070-9). Scholastic Inc.
Brandenstein, C. Von & Thomas, A. P., trs. Taruru: Aboriginal Song Poetry from the Pilbara. 150p. 1975. 9.00x (ISBN 0-8248-0363-9). UH Pr.
Brander, G. C., et al. Veterinary Applied Pharmacology & Therapeutics. 4th ed. (Illus.). 582p. 1982. 56.00 (ISBN 0-7216-0780-2, Pub. by Bailliere-Tindall). Saunders.
Brander, Harry. What Rhymes With Cancer? LC 82-81363. (Illus.). 54p. 1982. pap. 3.00 (ISBN 0-89823-038-1). New Rivers Pr.
Brander, Laurence A; see Bloomfield, Paul.
Brander, Michael. The Making of the Highlands. (Illus.). 234p. 1981. 16.95 (ISBN 0-312-50739-9). St Martin.
--The Perfect Victorian Hero: The Life & Times of Sir Samuel White Baker. 176p. 1982. 30.00x (ISBN 0-906391-24-5, Pub. by Mainstream). State Mutual Bk.
--The Roughshotter's Dog. 198p. 1981. 18.00x (ISBN 0-85614-000-7, Pub. by Jupiter England). State Mutual Bk.
Brandes, David, ed. Male Accessory Sex Organs: Structure & Function in Mammals. 1974. 82.50 (ISBN 0-12-125650-2). Acad Pr.
Brandes, Eric A., ed. Smithells Metals Reference Book. 6th ed. 1664p. 1983. text ed. 199.95 (ISBN 0-408-71053-5). Butterworth.
Brandes, G. Impressions of Russia. 7.75 (ISBN 0-8446-1728-8). Peter Smith.
--Lord Beaconsfield. 12.00 (ISBN 0-8446-1729-6). Peter Smith.
Brandes, Georg. Henrik Ibsen. LC 64-14698. 1899. 14.00 (ISBN 0-405-08302-5, Blom Pubns). Ayer Co Pubs.
--Michelangelo: His Life, His Times, His Era. Norden, Heinz, tr. LC 67-31052. (Illus.). 1967. 20.00 (ISBN 0-8044-2071-8). Ungar.
Brandes, Georg M. Creative Spirits of the Nineteenth Century. facs. ed. Anderson, R. B., tr. LC 67-26719. (Essay Index Reprint Ser). 1923. 27.50 (ISBN 0-8369-0245-9). Ayer Co Pubs.
--Hellas: Travels in Greece. facs. ed. Hartmann, J. W., tr. LC 72-90613. (Essay Index Reprint Ser). 1926. 17.00 (ISBN 0-8369-1203-9). Ayer Co Pubs.
Brandes, George. Don Quixote & Hamlet. 59.95 (ISBN 0-8490-0056-4). Gordon Pr.
--Friedrich Nietzsche. LC 72-2133. (Studies in German Literature, No. 13). 1972. Repr. of 1914 ed. lib. bdg. 49.95x (ISBN 0-8383-1463-5). Haskell.
--Main Currents in Nineteenth Century Literature, 6 vols. LC 72-3577. (Studies in European Literature, No. 56). 1972. Repr. of 1923 ed. Set. lib. bdg. 375.00x (ISBN 0-8383-1574-7). Haskell.
--Reminiscences of My Childhood & Youth. facsimile ed. LC 74-27967. (Modern Jewish Experience Ser.). 1975. Repr. of 1906 ed. 34.50x (ISBN 0-405-06697-X). Ayer Co Pubs.
--Wolfgang Goethe, 2 vols. 1973. Repr. of 1925 ed. 45.00 set (ISBN 0-8274-0073-X). R West.
Brandes, Joel R. Equitable Distribution Case Law. 368p. 1983. text ed. 50.00 (ISBN 0-942954-03-3). NYS Bar.
Brandes, Joseph. Herbert Hoover & Economic Diplomacy. LC 75-26622. (Illus.). 237p. 1975. Repr. of 1962 ed. lib. bdg. 22.50x (ISBN 0-8371-8362-6, BRHH). Greenwood.
Brandes, Joseph & Douglas, Martin. Immigrants to Freedom: Jewish Communities in Rural New Jersey Since 1882. LC 76-122384. 1971. 25.00x (ISBN 0-8122-7620-5). U of Pa Pr.
Brandes, Norman S., jt. auth. see Gardner, Malcolm L.
Brandes, Ove, jt. ed. see Farley, John U.
Brandes, Ray, tr. see Costanso, Miguel.
Brandes, Stanley. Metaphors of Masculinity: Sex & Status in Andalusian Folklore. LC 79-5258. (American Folklore Society Ser.). 224p. 1980. 27.50x (ISBN 0-8122-7776-7); pap. 11.95x (ISBN 0-8122-1105-7). U of Pa Pr.
Brandes, Stanley H. Forty: The Age & the Symbol. LC 84-29920. 164p. 1985. 12.95 (ISBN 0-87049-463-5). U of Tenn Pr.
--Migration, Kinship & Community: Tradition & Transition in a Spanish Village. 1975. 44.00 (ISBN 0-12-125750-9). Acad Pr.
Brandes, Stuart D. American Welfare Capitalism, Eighteen Eighty to Nineteen Forty. LC 75-20886. x, 210p. 1984. lib. bdg. 20.00x (ISBN 0-226-07121-9); pap. 7.95x (ISBN 0-226-07122-7). U of Chicago Pr.
Brandeth, Gielgud. John Geilgud: A Celebration. LC 83-83217. (Illus.). 186p. 1984. 14.45i (ISBN 0-316-10634-8). Little.
Brandewie, Ernest. Wilhelm Schmidt & the Origin of the Idea of God. 352p. (Orig.). 1983. lib. bdg. 27.00 (ISBN 0-8191-3363-9); pap. text ed. 15.25 (ISBN 0-8191-3364-7). U Pr of Amer.
Brandewyne, Rebecca. And Gold Was Ours. 544p. (Orig.). 1984. pap. 3.95 (ISBN 0-446-30614-2). Warner Bks.
--Forever My Love. 560p. (Orig.). 1982. pap. 3.95 (ISBN 0-446-32130-3). Warner Bks.
--No Gentle Love. 1984. pap. 3.95 (ISBN 0-446-30619-3). Warner Bks.
--Rose of Rapture. 480p. (Orig.). 1985. pap. 3.95 (ISBN 0-446-30613-4). Warner Bks.
Brandham, P. E. & Bennett, M. D., eds. Kew Chromosome Conference, Vol. II. 408p. 1983. text ed. 35.00x (ISBN 0-04-575022-X). Allen Unwin.

Brandi, Herman A. Di see Di Brandi, Herman A.

Brandi, John. Diary from a Journey to the Middle of the World. 1979. signed 10.00 (ISBN 0-685-99724-3); pap. 4.00 (ISBN 0-685-99725-1). Figures.

--Diary from Baja California. (Illus.). 1978. wrappers 4.00 (ISBN 0-87922-103-8). Christopher's Bks.

--Poems from Four Corners. 3.00 (ISBN 0-686-15301-4). Great Raven Pr.

--Poems on the Edge of Day. 1984. 4.50 (ISBN 0-934834-37-7). White Pine.

--Rite for the Beautification of All Beings. LC 83-4774. (Illus.). 24p. 1983. (Pub. by Toothpaste); pap. 7.50 (ISBN 0-915124-65-3). Coffee Hse.

--That Back Road In. (Illus.). 156p. (Orig.). 1985. pap. 7.95 (ISBN 0-914728-43-1). Wingbow Pr.

--That Crow That Visited Was Flying Backwards. (Illus.). 56p. 1982. pap. 6.00 (ISBN 0-940510-05-7). Tooth of Time.

Brandi, John, ed. see Crews, Judson.

Brandi, John, ed. see Inmates of the New Mexico State Penitentiary.

Brandi, John, et al, trs. see Lamadrid, Enrique.

Brandi, Karl. Emperor Charles V: The Growth & Destiny of a Man & of a World-Empire. 1968. pap. text ed. 15.45x (ISBN 0-224-60916-5). Humanities.

--The Emperor Charles V: The Growth & Destiny of a Man & of a World-Empire. Wedgwood, C. V., tr. from Ger. 655p. 1980. Repr. lib. bdg. 35.00 (ISBN 0-8492-3751-3). R West.

--The Emperor Charles V: The Growth & Destiny of a Man & of a World-Empire. Wedgwood, C. V., tr. from Ger. 655p. 1981. Repr. of 1939 ed. lib. bdg. 40.00 (ISBN 0-89760-081-9). Telegraph Bks.

Brandies, Monica M. Sprouts & Saplings: Gardening with a Difference. (Illus.). 240p. (Orig.). 1986. pap. 9.95 (ISBN 0-89407-066-5). Strawberry Hill.

Brandin, Louis, tr. see Sighele, Scipio.

Brandis, Dietrich. The Forest Flora of North-West & Central India: A Handbook of the Indigenous Trees & Shrubs of Those Countries, 2 vols. 1978. Repr. of 1874 ed. Set. 50.00x (ISBN 0-89955-276-5, Pub. by Intl Bk Dist). Intl Spec Bk.

Brandis, Dietrich & Stewart, J. Lindsay. Illustrations of the Forest Flora of North-West & Central India. (Illus.). 1978. Repr. 37.50x (ISBN 0-89955-285-4, Pub. by Intl Bk Dist). Intl Spec Bk.

Brandis, G., et al, eds. Liberals Face the Future. 352p. 1984. pap. 19.95 (ISBN 0-19-554505-2). Oxford U Pr.

Brandis, Henry, Jr. Brandis on North Carolina Evidence: With 1983 Supplement, 2 vols. 1232p. 1982. 90.00 (ISBN 0-87215-447-5); Suppl. 1983. 20.00 (ISBN 0-87215-782-2). Michie Co.

Brandl, Albert. Modern Riding: Walk, Trot, Canter Gallop. (EP Sports Ser.). (Illus.). 1973. 6.95 (ISBN 0-7158-0580-0). Charles River Bks.

Brandl, Alois. Samuel Taylor Coleridge & the English Romantic School. LC 68-757. (Studies in Coleridge, No. 7). 1969. Repr. of 1887 ed. lib. bdg. 49.95 (ISBN 0-8383-0512-1). Haskell.

Brandl, Alois & Zippel, O. Middle English Literature. 2nd ed. LC 48-3315. 1980. 14.95. Chelsea Pub.

Brandl, E. J. Australian Aboriginal Paintings in Western & Central Arnhem Land: Temporal Sequences & Elements of Style in Cadell River & Deaf Adder Creek Art. (AIAS & Material Culture Ser.: No. 9). (Illus.). 1973. text ed. 25.75x (ISBN 0-85575-029-4). Humanities.

Brandl, John, jt. ed. see Reynolds, Maynard.

Brandl, Leopold. Erasmus Darwin's Botanic Garden. pap. 25.00 (ISBN 0-384-05530-3). Johnson Repr.

--Erasmus Darwin's Temple of Nature. pap. 25.00 (ISBN 0-384-05535-4). Johnson Repr.

Brandler, Richard, et al. Patterns of Hypnotic Techniques of Milton H. Erickson, M. D, Vol. 2. LC 75-24584. 1977. 17.95x (ISBN 0-916990-02-8). Meta Pubns.

Brandling, Redvers. A Book of Practical Ideas for the Primary School. (Ward Lock Educational Ser.). 29.00x (ISBN 0-7062-3884-2, Pub. by Ward Lock Educational England). State Mutual Bk.

--Christmas in the Primary School. (Ward Lock Educational Ser.). 29.00x (ISBN 0-7062-4068-5, Pub. by Ward Lock Educational England). State Mutual Bk.

--Festive Occassions in the Primary School. (Ward Lock Educational Ser.). 29.00x (ISBN 0-7062-3746-3, Pub. by Ward Lock Educational England). State Mutual Bk.

--A Year in the Primary School. (Ward Lock Educational Ser.). 29.00x (ISBN 0-7062-4152-5, Pub. by Ward Lock Educational England). State Mutual Bk.

Brandly, C. A. & Cornelius, C. E., eds. Advances in Veterinary Science & Comparative Medicine, Vol. 23. 1979. 60.00 (ISBN 0-12-039223-2). Acad Pr.

--Advances in Veterinary Science & Comparative Medicine, Vol. 24. (Serial Publication Ser.). 1980. 60.00 (ISBN 0-12-039224-0). Acad Pr.

Brandly, C. A. & Jungherr, E. L., eds. Advances in Veterinary Science. Incl. Vol. 1. 1953. 80.00 (ISBN 0-12-039201-1); Vol. 2. 1955. 80.00 (ISBN 0-12-039202-X); Vol. 3. 1957. 80.00 (ISBN 0-12-039203-8); Vol. 4. 1958. 80.00 (ISBN 0-12-039204-6); Vol. 5. 1959. 80.00 (ISBN 0-12-039205-4); Vol. 6. 1961. 80.00 (ISBN 0-12-039206-2); Vol. 7. 1962. 80.00 (ISBN 0-12-039207-0); Vol. 8. 1964. 80.00 (ISBN 0-12-039208-9); Vol. 9. 1964. 80.00 (ISBN 0-12-039209-7); Vol. 10. 1965. 80.00 (ISBN 0-12-039210-0); Vol. 11. Brandly, C. A. & Cornelius, C. A., eds. 1967. 80.00 (ISBN 0-12-039211-9); Vol. 12. 1968. 80.00 (ISBN 0-12-039212-7). Acad Pr.

--Advances in Veterinary Science, Vol. 26. 332p. 1982. 55.00 (ISBN 0-12-039226-7). Acad Pr.

--Advances in Veterinary Science, Vol. 28. 1984. 69.00 (ISBN 0-12-039228-3). Acad Pr.

--Advances in Veterinary Science & Comparative Medicine. Incl. Vol. 13. 1969. 80.00 (ISBN 0-12-039213-5); Vol. 14. 1970. 80.00 (ISBN 0-12-039214-3); Vol. 15. 1971. 80.00 (ISBN 0-12-039215-1); Vol. 16. 1972. 80.00 (ISBN 0-12-039216-X); Vol. 17. 1973. 85.00 (ISBN 0-12-039217-8); Vol. 18. 1974. 70.00 (ISBN 0-12-039218-6); Vol. 19. 1976. 70.00 (ISBN 0-12-039219-4); Vol. 20. 1976. 75.00 (ISBN 0-12-039220-8); Vol. 21. 1977. 80.00 (ISBN 0-12-039221-6); Vol. 22. 1978. 80.00 (ISBN 0-12-039222-4). LC 53-7098. Acad Pr.

Brandner, Gary. Billy Lives. 1976. pap. 1.95 (ISBN 0-532-19120-X). Woodhill.

--The Brain-Eaters. 288p. 1985. pap. 2.95 (ISBN 0-449-12711-7, GM). Fawcett.

--Hellborn. 224p. (Orig.). 1981. pap. 2.50 (ISBN 0-449-14414-3, GM). Fawcett.

--The Howling. 1981. pap. 2.50 (ISBN 0-449-13824-0, GM). Fawcett.

--The Howling III. 256p. 1985. pap. 3.50 (ISBN 0-449-12834-2, GM). Fawcett.

--The Howling Two. 1982. pap. 2.75 (ISBN 0-449-12400-2, GM). Fawcett.

--Walkers. 1980. pap. 2.50 (ISBN 0-449-14319-8, GM). Fawcett.

Brandner, John H. Mammoth Vehicles of the World: Land-Sea-Air. (Illus.). 1982. pap. 15.95 (ISBN 0-89404-009-X). Aztex.

Brando, Anna K. & Stein, E. P. Brando for Breakfast. 1980. pap. 2.75 (ISBN 0-425-04698-2). Berkley Pub.

Brandom, Robert, jt. auth. see Rescher, Nicholas.

Brandon, Belinda B., ed. Effect of the Demographics of Individual Households on Their Telphone Usage. LC 80-27158. 432p. 1981. prof ref 45.00x (ISBN 0-88410-695-0). Ballinger Pub.

Brandon, Brumsic, Jr. Luther's Got Class. LC 75-16502. (Illus.). 96p. 1976. pap. 3.95 (ISBN 0-8397-5668-2). Eriksson.

--Outta Sight, Luther. LC 77-170318. (Illus.). 1972. pap. 1.95 (ISBN 0-8397-6481-2). Eriksson.

Brandon, D. Management Standards for Data Integrity. 1986. cancelled (ISBN 0-442-26709-6). Van Nos Reinhold.

Brandon, D. H. Management Standards for Data Processing. 413p. 1963. 20.00 (ISBN 0-685-72294-5, Pub. by Van Nos Reinhold). Krieger.

Brandon, Dick H. Data Processing Cost Reduction & Control. (Computer Science Ser.). (Illus.). 234p. 1978. text ed. 23.95 (ISBN 0-442-21032-9). Van Nos Reinhold.

Brandon, Dick H. & Gray, Max. Project Control Standards. LC 79-23471. 214p. 1980. Repr. of 1970 ed. lib. bdg. 14.50 (ISBN 0-89874-039-8). Krieger.

Brandon, Dick H. & Segelstein, Sidney. Boardroom's Complete Guide to Microcomputers. LC 83-15450. 302p. 1983. 50.00 (ISBN 0-932648-45-2). Boardroom.

Brandon, Dick H., et al. Data Processing Management: Methods & Standards. new ed. 1975. 34.50 (ISBN 0-02-468150-4). Macmillan Info.

--Data Processing Contracts: Structure, Contents, & Negotiations. 2nd ed. LC 83-5842. 1983. 44.50 (ISBN 0-442-21034-5). Van Nos Reinhold.

Brandon, Dorothy & Scheider, Alfred F. Max Schling Book of Indoor Gardening. (Illus.). 1963. 15.00 (ISBN 0-8392-1065-5). Astor-Honor.

Brandon, Heather. Casualties: Death in Vietnam, Anguish & Survival in America. (Illus.). 357p. 1984. 15.95 (ISBN 0-312-12358-2). St Martin.

Brandon, J., ed. The Records of the Town of Cambridge Massachusetts 1630-1703. 397p. 1985. Repr. of 1901 ed. 30.00 (ISBN 0-917890-50-7). Heritage Bk.

Brandon, James. The Forgotten Steps (Steps Six & Seven) 16p. 1981. pap. 0.70 (ISBN 0-89486-128-X). Hazelden.

Brandon, James, ed. see Langhans, Edward A.

Brandon, James R. Brandon's Guide to Theater in Asia. LC 75-37506. 178p. 1976. pap. 3.95 (ISBN 0-8248-0369-8). UH Pr.

--Kabuki: Five Classic Plays. LC 74-82192. (Illus.). 448p. 1975. 27.50x (ISBN 0-674-30485-3). Harvard U Pr.

--Theater in Southeast Asia. LC 67-14338. (Illus.). 370p. 1974. pap. 8.95x (ISBN 0-674-87587-7). Harvard U Pr.

Brandon, James R., jt. auth. see Baumer, Rachel.

Brandon, James R., ed. Chushingura: Studies in Kabuki & the Puppet Theatre. LC 82-1921. (Illus.). 243p. 1982. text ed. 30.00x (ISBN 0-8248-0793-6). UH Pr.

--On Thrones of Gold: Three Javanese Shadow Plays. LC 73-88802. (Illus.). 1970. 25.00x (ISBN 0-674-63775-5). Harvard U Pr.

--Theatre Perspectives One: Asian Theatre. 198p. 1980. 10.00x (ISBN 0-940528-16-9). Am Theatre Assoc.

Brandon, James R., et al. Studies in Kabuki: Its Acting, Music, & Historical Context. LC 77-5336. 198p. 1978. pap. 8.50x (ISBN 0-8248-0452-X, Eastwest Ctr). UH Pr.

Brandon, Jim. The Rebirth of Pan. LC 83-80550. (Illus.). 301p. (Orig.). 1983. pap. 10.00 (ISBN 0-912019-01-8). Firebird Pr.

Brandon, JoAnna. All the Right Moves. (Candlelight Ecstasy Supreme Ser.: No. 59). (Orig.). 1985. pap. 2.50 (ISBN 0-440-11273-7). Dell.

--The Devil's Playground. (Candlelight Ecstasy Ser.: No. 66). (Orig.). 1982. pap. 1.95 (ISBN 0-440-11985-5). Dell.

--Just a Kiss Away. (Candlelight Ecstasy Ser.: No. 332). 192p. (Orig.). 1985. pap. 2.25 (ISBN 0-440-14402-7). Dell.

--Lingering Laughter. (Ecstasy Ser.: No. 401). (Orig.). 1986. pap. 2.25 (ISBN 0-440-14602-X). Dell.

--Love, Bid Me Welcome. (Candlelight Ecstasy Ser.: No. 237). (Orig.). 1984. pap. 1.95 (ISBN 0-440-15002-7). Dell.

--Sing to Me of Love. (Candlelight Ecstacy Ser.: No. 112). (Orig.). 1983. pap. 1.95 (ISBN 0-440-18119-4). Dell.

Brandon, Joyce. The Lady & the Outlaw. 384p. (Orig.). 1985. pap. 3.50 (ISBN 0-345-31872-2). Ballantine.

Brandon, Kathleen M., jt. auth. see Brandon, Larry L.

Brandon, Kylene B. & Cohen, Sherry S. Southern Beauty. (Illus.). 160p. (Orig.). 1984. pap. 9.95 (ISBN 0-346-16011-1). Cornerstone.

Brandon, Larry L. & Brandon, Kathleen M. The Brandon Maintenance Log. 356p. (Orig.). 1982. looseleaf 49.95 (ISBN 0-934114-38-2, BK-284). Marine Educ.

Brandon, Lewis. The Crime of Moscow in Vynnytsia: The Murder of 9,439 Ukranians by the Soviet NKVD. 1981. lib. bdg. 59.95 (ISBN 0-686-73179-4). Revisionist Pr.

Brandon, Lewis, pref. by. The Crime of Moscow in Vynnytsia. (Illus.). 48p. 1980. pap. 3.00 (ISBN 0-911038-90-6). Inst Hist Rev.

Brandon, Lewis, ed. see Barnes, Harry E.

Brandon, M., tr. see Monin, J. P., et al.

Brandon, Milan L. Corticosteroids in Medical Practice. (Illus.). 608p. 1962. 48.50x (ISBN 0-398-00215-0). C C Thomas.

Brandon, Mitzi. The Best Little Sex Book in Print. Williamson, Randall, ed. 150p. (Orig.). 1983. pap. write for info. (ISBN 0-913315-00-1). S Wing Pub.

Brandon, P. F. & Millman, R. N., eds. Historic Landscapes: Observer's & Recorder's Handbook. 1981. 90.00x (ISBN 0-86127-306-0, Pub. by Avebury Pub England). State Mutual Bk.

Brandon, Peter. A History of Surrey. (The Darwen County History Ser.). (Illus.). 128p. 1978. 17.75x (ISBN 0-8476-2310-6). Rowman.

Brandon, Peter & Millman, Roger, eds. Recording Historic Landscapes: Principles & Practice. 224p. 1982. text ed. 38.50x (ISBN 0-86127-305-2, Pub. by Avebury England); pap. text ed. 23.50x (ISBN 0-86127-306-0). Humanities.

Brandon, Peter S., jt. auth. see Ferry, Douglas J.

Brandon, Peter S. & Moore, Geoffrey, eds. Microcomputers in Building Appraisal. 336p. 1983. pap. 29.50 (ISBN 0-89397-147-2). Nichols Pub.

Brandon, Peter S. & Powell, James A, eds. Quality & Profit in Building Design. 400p. 1985. 52.00 (ISBN 0-419-13390-9, NO. 9191, Pub. by E & FN Spon England). Methuen Inc.

Brandon, Peter S., et al. Computer Programs for Building Cost Appraisal. 200p. (Orig.). 1985. pap. text ed. 25.00x (ISBN 0-00-383043-8, Pub. by Collins England). Sheridan.

Brandon, Robert M., et al. Tax Politics: How They Make You Pay & What You Can Do About It. 297p. 1976. 6.95 (ISBN 0-394-49847-X). Tax Reform Res.

Brandon, Robert N. & Burian, Richard M., eds. Genes, Organisms, Populations: Controversies over the Units of Selection. (Illus.). 300p. 1984. text ed. 32.50x (ISBN 0-262-02205-2, Pub. by Bradford Bks). MIT Pr.

Brandon, Robin. East Spain Pilot, Chapter I: Introduction & Information. 620p. 1983. 50.00x (ISBN 0-85288-056-1, Pub. by Imray Laurie Norie & Wilson UK). State Mutual Bk.

--East Spain Pilot, Chapter II: Costa del Sol. 620p. 1982. 50.00x (ISBN 0-85288-079-0, Pub. by Imray Laurie Norie & Wilson UK). State Mutual Bk.

--East Spain Pilot, Chapter III: Costa Blanca. 620p. 1984. 50.00x (ISBN 0-317-14444-8, Pub. by Imray Laurie Norie & Wilson UK). State Mutual Bk.

--East Spain Pilot, Chapter IV: Costa del Azahar. 620p. 1977. 50.00x (ISBN 0-85288-059-6, Imray Laurie Norie & Wilson UK). State Mutual Bk.

--East Spain Pilot, Chapter V: Costa Dorada. 620p. 1977. 50.00x (ISBN 0-85288-060-X, Pub. by Imray Laurie Norie & Wilson UK). State Mutual Bk.

--East Spain Pilot, Chapter VI: Costa Brava. 620p. 1981. 50.00x (ISBN 0-85288-075-8, Pub. by Imray Laurie Norie & Wilson UK). State Mutual Bk.

--East Spain Pilot, Chapter VII: Islas Baleares. 620p. 1980. 50.00x (ISBN 0-85288-070-7, Pub. by Imray Laurie Norie & Wilson UK). State Mutual Bk.

--The Good Crewman. 1979. 12.95x (ISBN 0-8464-0077-4). Beekman Pubs.

--South Biscay Pilot: The Gironde Estuary to La Coruna. (Illus.). 388p. 1977. 59.95x (ISBN 0-8464-1273-X). Beekman Pubs.

--South England Pilot, Vol. I: North Foreland to Selsey Bill. 1984. 60.00x (ISBN 0-317-14446-4, Pub. by Imray Laurie Norie & Wilson UK). State Mutual Bk.

--South England Pilot, Vol. II: Selsey Bill to Hengistbury Head & the Isle of Wight. 1984. 60.00x (ISBN 0-317-14448-0, Pub. by Imray Laurie Norie & Wilson UK). State Mutual Bk.

--South England Pilot, Vol. III: Hengistbury Head to Start Point. 1983. 60.00x (ISBN 0-85288-080-4, Pub. by Imray Laurie Norie & Wilson UK). State Mutual Bk.

--South England Pilot, Vol. IV: Start Point to Land's End. 160p. 1979. 60.00x (ISBN 0-85288-067-7, Pub. by Imray Laurie Norie & Wilson UK). State Mutual Bk.

--South France Pilot, Chapter I: Introduction & Information. 640p. 1983. 50.00x (ISBN 0-85288-088-X, Pub. by Imray Laurie Norie & Wilson UK). State Mutual Bk.

--South France Pilot, Chapter II: Languedoc-Roussillon. 640p. 1984. 50.00x (ISBN 0-317-14450-2, Pub. by Imray Laurie Norie & Wilson UK). State Mutual Bk.

--South France Pilot, Chapter III: West Cote d'Azur. 640p. 1984. 50.00x (ISBN 0-317-14451-0, Pub. by Imray Laurie Norie & Wilson UK). State Mutual Bk.

--South France Pilot, Chapter IV: East Cote d'Azur. 640p. 1982. 50.00x (ISBN 0-85288-077-4, Pub. by Imray Laurie Norie & Wilson UK). State Mutual Bk.

--South France Pilot, Chapter V: The Riviera. 640p. 1982. 50.00x (ISBN 0-85288-078-2, Pub. by Imray Laurie Norie & Wilson UK). State Mutual Bk.

--South France Pilot, Chapter VI: Corsica. 640p. 1983. 75.00x (ISBN 0-85288-054-5, Pub. by Imray Laurie Norie & Wilson UK). State Mutual Bk.

--Yachtsman's Pilots, Vol. V: The Scilly Isles. 40p. 1983. 40.00x (ISBN 0-85288-090-1, Pub. by Imray Laurie Norie & Wilson UK). State Mutual Bk.

Brandon, Ruth. The Spiritualists: The Passion for the Occult in the Nineteenth & Twentieth Centuries. LC 83-47853. 896p. 1983. 16.95 (ISBN 0-394-52740-2). Knopf.

--The Spiritualists: The Passion for the Occult in the Nineteenth & Twentieth Centuries. LC 83-47853. (Science & the Paranormal Ser.). (Illus.). 315p. 1984. pap. 11.95 (ISBN 0-87975-269-6). Prometheus Bks.

Brandon, Ruth & Davies, Christie. Wrongful Imprisonment, Mistaken Convictions & Their Consequences. 296p. 1973. 22.50 (ISBN 0-208-01337-7, Archon). Shoe String.

Brandon, S. G. Dictionary of Comparative Religions. LC 76-11390. 1970. lib. bdg. 50.00 (ISBN 0-684-15561-3, ScribT). Scribner.

--Time & Mankind: An Historical & Philosophical Study of Mankind's Attitude to the Phenomena of Change. 1977. lib. bdg. 59.95 (ISBN 0-8490-2751-9). Gordon Pr.

--The Trial of Jesus of Nazareth. LC 68-9206. (Illus.). 1979. pap. 4.95 (ISBN 0-8128-6018-7). Stein & Day.

Brandon, S. G. see Sharpe, Eric J. & Hinnells, John R.

Brandon, S. G. F. Diccionario de Religiones Comparadas, 2 vols. 1553p. (Span.). 1975. Set. 49.95 (ISBN 8-4705-7188-5). French & Eur.

Brandon, Samuel. Virtuous Octavia. LC 73-133641. (Tudor Facsimile Texts. Old English Plays: No. 81). Repr. of 1912 ed. 49.50 (ISBN 0-404-53381-7). AMS Pr.

--The Virtuous Octavia. LC 82-45749. (Malone Society Reprint Ser.: No. 15). Repr. of 1909 ed. 40.00 (ISBN 0-404-63015-4). AMS Pr.

Brandon, Samuel G., ed. The Saviour God: Comparative Studies in the Concept of Salvation Presented to Edwin Oliver James. LC 80-14924. xxii, 242p. 1980. Repr. of 1963 ed. lib. bdg. 24.75x (ISBN 0-313-22416-1, BRSG). Greenwood.

Brandon, Sue. Buttonhooks & Shoehorns. (Shire 'Album' Ser.: No. 122). (Illus.). 32p. 1985. pap. 2.95 (ISBN 0-85263-696-2, Pub. by Shire Pubns England). Seven Hills Bks.

Brandon, William. Indians. LC 85-13435. (The American Heritage Library). (Illus.). 350p. 1985. pap. 8.95. Am Heritage.

--Indians. (Illus.). 350p. 1985. pap. 8.95 (ISBN 0-8281-0301-1). HM.

--Manual of Concealed Image Response Techniques. 1978. 5.95 (ISBN 0-915474-02-6). Effective Learn.

--The Men & the Mountain: Fremont's Fourth Expedition. LC 73-20901. (Illus.). 337p. 1974. Repr. of 1955 ed. lib. bdg. 18.25x (ISBN 0-8371-5873-7, BRME). Greenwood.

--New Worlds for Old: Reports from the New World & Their Effect on the Development of Social Thought in Europe, 1500-1800. 285p. 1985. text ed. 26.95x (ISBN 0-8214-0818-6); pap. text ed. 13.95x (ISBN 0-8214-0819-4). Ohio U Pr.
Brandon, William, ed. American Heritage Book of the Indians. 384p. 1964. pap. 3.95 (ISBN 0-440-30113-0, LFL). Dell.
Brandon-Cox, Hugh. Summer of a Million Wings: Arctic Quest for the Sea-Eagle. LC 74-10365. (Illus.). 184p. 1975. 8.95 (ISBN 0-8008-7492-7). Taplinger.
Brandon-Jones, David. Practical Palmistry. 1983. pap. text ed. 5.95x (ISBN 0-7069-1835-5, Pub. by Vikas India). Advent NY.
Brandon-Thomas, Jevan. Practical Stagecraft for Amateurs. 17.50 (ISBN 0-8482-3445-6). Norwood Edns.
Brandow, Gregg. Imperial County, California, Earthquake, October 15, 1979. Leeds, David J., ed. 200p. 1980. 9.00 (ISBN 0-318-16320-9). Earthquake Eng.
Brandow, James C. Genealogies of Barbados Families from Caribbeana & the Journal of the Barbados Museum & Historical Society. LC 82-83586. (Illus.). 753p. 1983. 40.00 (ISBN 0-8063-1004-9). Genealog Pub.
--Omitted Chapters from Hotten's Original Lists of Persons of Quality: Census Returns, Parish Registers, & Militia Rolls from the Barbados Census of 1679-80. LC 81-86305. 245p. 1983. 16.00 (ISBN 0-8063-0954-7). Genealog Pub.
Brandow, Karen & McDonnell, Jim. No Bosses Here: A Manual on Working Collectively & Cooperatively. 115p. 1981. 5.75 (ISBN 0-318-17039-6). NASCO.
Brandow, Karen, jt. auth. see Vocations for Social Change.
Brandreth, Gyles. Amazing Facts about Animals. LC 80-1086. (Amazing Facts Bks.). (Illus.). 32p. (gr. 5-8). 1981. pap. 2.95 (ISBN 0-385-17017-3). Doubleday.
--Amazing Facts about Our Earth. LC 80-1087. (Amazing Facts Bks.). (Illus.). 32p. (gr. 5-8). 1981. pap. 2.95 (ISBN 0-385-17016-5). Doubleday.
--Amazing Facts about Your Body. LC 80-1088. (Amazing Facts Bks.). (Illus.). 32p. (gr. 5-8). 1981. pap. 2.95 (ISBN 0-385-17018-1). Doubleday.
--Bedroom Bloopers. 1985. 2.95 (ISBN 0-517-55732-0). Crown.
--Biggest Tongue Twister Book in the World. LC 78-7784. (Illus.). 123p. (gr. 4 up). 1980. 7.95 (ISBN 0-8069-4594-X); PLB 9.99 (ISBN 0-8069-4595-8); pap. 3.50 (ISBN 0-8069-8972-6). Sterling.
--The Book of Solo Games. LC 85-42555. (Illus.). 224p. 1985. pap. 5.72i (ISBN 0-06-097004-9, PL 7004, PL). Har-Row.
--The Complete Puzzler. 192p. 1982. pap. 6.95 (ISBN 0-312-15839-4). St Martin.
--Game-a-Day Book. LC 80-91386. (Illus.). 192p. (gr. 2-10). 1984. pap. 3.95 (ISBN 0-8069-7878-3). Sterling.
--The Great Book of Optical Illusions. LC 85-9898. (Illus.). 96p. (Orig.). (gr. 2 up). 1985. pap. 3.50 (ISBN 0-8069-6258-5). Sterling.
--Great Theatrical Disasters. 160p. 1983. 8.95 (ISBN 0-312-34677-8). St Martin.
--A Guide to Playing the Scrabble Brand Crossword Game: How to Improve Your Skills & Strategies. 192p. 1985. pap. 6.95 (ISBN 0-671-50652-8, Fireside). S&S.
--A Joke-a-Day Book. LC 78-66298. (Illus.). 128p. (gr. 3 up). 1983. 7.95 (ISBN 0-8069-4598-2); pap. 3.50 (ISBN 0-8069-7796-5). Sterling.
--The Joy of Lex. LC 80-82360. (Illus.). 288p. 1980. 12.45 (ISBN 0-688-03709-7). Morrow.
--The Joy of Lex. LC 82-22434. 320p. 1983. pap. 7.95 (ISBN 0-688-01397-X, Quill). Morrow.
--Numberplay. 256p. 1984. 14.95 (ISBN 0-89256-257-9); pap. 8.95 (ISBN 0-89256-267-6). Rawson Assocs.
--Pears Book of Words. 204p. 1981. 13.95 (ISBN 0-7207-1186-X, Pub. by Michael Joseph). Merrimack Pub Cir.
--Pears Round the World Quiz Book. (Illus.). 1979. pap. 7.95 (ISBN 0-7207-1110-X). Transatlantic.
--The Scrabble Brand Puzzle Book. (Illus.). 240p. 1984. pap. 7.95 (ISBN 0-671-50536-X, Fireside). S&S.
--Seeing Is Not Believing. LC 79-91401. (Illus.). 96p. (gr. 2 up). 1980. 8.95 (ISBN 0-8069-4614-8). Sterling.
--The Super Joke Book. (Illus.). 128p. (gr. 3 up). 1985. 3.50 (ISBN 0-8069-6200-3); PLB 10.99 (ISBN 0-8069-4673-3); pap. 8.95 (ISBN 0-8069-4672-5). Sterling.
--This Is Your Body. 1981. text ed. 19.95x (ISBN 0-317-06962-4, Regent House). B of A.
--The Worlds Best Indoor Games. LC 81-48342. (Illus.). 304p. 1982. pap. 6.95 (ISBN 0-394-71001-0). Pantheon.
--Writing Secret Codes & Sending Hidden Messages. LC 83-24230. (Illus.). 128p. (gr. 2-5). 1984. 7.95 (ISBN 0-8069-4690-3); PLB 9.99 (ISBN 0-8069-4691-1). Sterling.
Brandreth, Gyles & Moran, George. More Joy of Lex: An Amusing & Amazing Z to A & A to Z of Words. LC 82-8127. (Illus.). 310p. 1982. 13.00 (ISBN 0-688-01338-4). Morrow.
Brandreth, Gyles, ed. The Puzzle Mountain. LC 81-4003. (Illus.). 256p. (Orig.). 1981. pap. 7.95 (ISBN 0-688-00686-8, Quill). Morrow.
Brandrup, Johannes & Immergut, E. H., eds. Polymer Handbook. 2nd ed. LC 74-11381. 1408p. 1975. 89.50x (ISBN 0-471-09804-3, Pub. by Wiley-Interscience). Wiley.
Brandsma, Jeff, jt. auth. see Farrelly, Frank.
Brandsma, Jeffrey M. Outpatient Treatment of Alcoholism. (Illus.). 224p. 1979. pap. text ed. 21.00 (ISBN 0-8391-1393-5). Univ Park.
Brandsma, Jeffrey M., jt. auth. see Ables, Billie S.
Brandstadt, Wayne, jt. ed. see Zackler, Jack.
Brandstatter, Hermann & Davis, James, eds. Group Decision Making. LC 81-66398. (European Monographs in Social Psychology: No. 25). 1982. 49.50 (ISBN 0-12-125820-3). Acad Pr.
Brandstatter, Hermann, et al, eds. Dynamics of Group Decisions. LC 78-19143. (Sage Focus Editions: Vol. 5). 276p. 1978. 28.00 (ISBN 0-8039-0872-5); pap. 14.00 (ISBN 0-8039-0873-3). Sage.
Brandstein, C. G. Von see Von Brandenstein, C. G.
Brandt. Metallurgy Fundamentals. 1985. 16.00 (ISBN 0-87006-475-4). Goodheart.
Brandt, A., et al. Cost-Sharing in Health Care: Proceedings. (Illus.). 184p. 1981. pap. 20.00 (ISBN 0-387-10325-2). Springer-Verlag.
Brandt, A. von. Fish Catching Methods of the World. 3rd ed. (Illus.). 418p. 1984. 66.00 (ISBN 0-85238-125-5, FN106, FNB). Unipub.
Brandt, Allan M. No Magic Bullet: A Social History of Venereal Disease in the United States Since 1880. (Illus.). 1985. 19.95 (ISBN 0-19-503469-4). Oxford U Pr.
Brandt, Andres Von see Von Brandt, Andres.
Brandt, Anne, jt. auth. see Trussel, Patricia.
Brandt, Barbara, jt. auth. see Fellman, Gordon.
Brandt, Bill. Bill Brandt: Portraits. (Illus.). 116p. 1982. 37.50 (ISBN 0-292-70740-1). U of Tex Pr.
--Shadow of Light. LC 76-52463. (Quality Paperback Ser.). (Illus.). 1977. lib. bdg. 29.50 o. p. (ISBN 0-306-70858-2); pap. 14.50 (ISBN 0-306-80066-7). Da Capo.
Brandt, Bill & Haworth-Booth, Mark, eds. The Land: Twentieth Century Landscape Photographs. LC 75-30640. 1976. 18.50 (ISBN 0-306-70753-5); pap. 7.95 o. p. (ISBN 0-306-80026-8). Da Capo.
Brandt, Bill, photos by. Bill Brandt Nudes: 1945-1980. 1980. 37.50 (ISBN 0-8212-1097-1, 106410). NYGS.
--London in the Thirties. 22.45 (ISBN 0-394-53565-0). Pantheon.
Brandt, C. D., jt. auth. see Loecherer, K. H.
Brandt, Carl & Roemer, Clinton. Standardized Chord Symbol Notation: A Uniform System for the Music Profession. 2nd ed. 45p. 1976. pap. text ed. 5.95 (ISBN 0-9612684-2-5). Roerick Music.
Brandt, Carol, jt. ed. see Higham, Robin.
Brandt, Catharine. God Bless Grandparents. LC 78-52189. (Illus.). 1978. pap. 5.50 (ISBN 0-8066-1658-X, 10-2559). Augsburg.
--Still Time to Pray. LC 82-72648. 96p. (Orig.). 1983. pap. 5.50 (ISBN 0-8066-1955-4, 10-6007). Augsburg.
--Still Time to Sing: Prayers & Praise for Late in Life. LC 80-65547. 96p. (Orig.). 1980. pap. 5.50 (ISBN 0-8066-1792-6, 10-6010). Augsburg.
--You're Only Old Once: Devotions in Large Print. large type ed. LC 76-27085. 1977. pap. 5.95 (ISBN 0-8066-1570-2, 10-7495). Augsburg.
Brandt, Catharine, jt. auth. see Stoll, Irma.
Brandt Commission. Common Crisis North-South: Cooperation for World Recovery. 184p. 1983. pap. 4.95 (ISBN 0-262-52085-0). MIT Pr.
Brandt, David. Is That All There Is? 1985. pap. 3.95 (ISBN 0-317-55650-9). PB.
--Is That All There Is? Overcoming Disappointment in an Age of Diminished Expectations. 1984. 14.50 (ISBN 0-671-45892-2, Poseidon). PB.
Brandt, Diana, ed. Being Brothers & Sisters. LC 83-83062. (Illus.). 115p. 1984. pap. 7.95 (ISBN 0-87303-091-5). Faith & Life.
Brandt, Edith, jt. auth. see Brandt, Leslie.
Brandt, Frans M. J. The Way to Wholeness: A Guide to Christian Self-Counseling. LC 84-70657. 208p. 1984. pap. 6.95 (ISBN 0-89107-316-7, Crossway Bks). Good News.
Brandt, Frederick, jt. auth. see Preston, John.
Brandt, Frederick R. American Marine Painting. LC 76-28711. (Illus.). 152p. 1976. pap. 8.95x (ISBN 0-917046-01-3). VA Mus Arts.
--Paintings-Prints-Drawings: Allan D'Arcangelo. (Illus.). 1979. pap. 4.00 (ISBN 0-917046-07-2). VA Mus Arts.
Brandt, Frithiof. Kierkegaard, Soren, His Life - His Works. Born, Ann R., tr. (Danes of the Present & Past). (Illus.). 117p. (Danish.). 1963. pap. text ed. 7.95 (ISBN 0-933748-05-1). Nordic Bks.
Brandt, G. W., tr. see Calderon.
Brandt, Geeraert. History of the Reformation & Other Ecclesiastical Transactions in, & about, the Low Countries, from the Beginning of the Eighth Century down to the End of the Famous Synod of Dort, 4 Vols. in 2. LC 70-130625. Repr. of 1733 ed. Set. 285.00 (ISBN 0-404-07960-1). AMS Pr.
Brandt, George, ed. British Television Drama. LC 80-41031. (Illus.). 300p. 1981. 49.50 (ISBN 0-521-22186-2); pap. 16.95 (ISBN 0-521-29384-7). Cambridge U Pr.
Brandt, Harry, ed. see Dyer, Lorna.
Brandt, Hartmut. Work Capacity Restraints in Tropical Agricultural Development. (Medical Care in Developing Countries Ser.: Vol. 8). 278p. 1980. 28.90 (ISBN 3-8204-6900-1). P Lang Pubs.
Brandt, Henry & Landrum, Phil. I Want Happiness Now! 1978. pap. 5.95 (ISBN 0-310-21641-9). Zondervan.
--I Want My Marriage to Be Better. 1976. pap. 5.95 (ISBN 0-310-21621-4). Zondervan.
--I Want to Enjoy My Children. 160p. 1975. pap. 5.95 (ISBN 0-310-21631-1). Zondervan.
Brandt, Henry R. The Struggle for Inner Peace. rev. ed. 136p. 1984. pap. 3.95 (ISBN 0-88207-245-5). Victor Bks.
Brandt, J. C. & McElroy, M. E. Atmosphere of Venus & Mars. 296p. (Orig.). 1968. 80.95 (ISBN 0-677-11590-3). Gordon.
Brandt, Jane. Drinks Without Liquor. LC 82-40504. (Illus.). 192p. 1983. pap. 5.95 (ISBN 0-89480-358-1, 358). Workman Pub.
Brandt, Jane L. La Chingada. 1981. pap. 3.50 (ISBN 0-671-83494-0). PB.
--Firebrand. 1983. pap. 3.75 (ISBN 0-8217-1246-2). Zebra.
Brandt, Jobst. The Bicycle Wheel. (Illus.). 139p. 6.00 (ISBN 0-9607236-0-9). Avocet Inc.
Brandt, Johanna. The Grape Cure. 2.00x (ISBN 0-686-29874-8). Cancer Control Soc.
--The Grape Cure. 192p. 1971. pap. 2.95 (ISBN 0-87904-002-5). Lust.
Brandt, John C. Introduction to the Solar Wind. LC 75-89919. (Illus.). 199p. 1970. text ed. 22.95 (ISBN 0-7167-0328-9). W H Freeman.
--Our Changing Universe. (Physical Science Ser.). 1976. pap. text ed. 9.95 (ISBN 0-675-08574-8). Additional supplements may be obtained from publisher. Merrill.
Brandt, John C. & Chapman, Robert D. Introduction to Comets. LC 76-47207. (Illus.). 256p. 1981. 52.50 (ISBN 0-521-23906-0). Cambridge U Pr.
--Introduction to Comets. LC 76-47207. 256p. 1982. pap. 13.95 (ISBN 0-521-27218-1). Cambridge U Pr.
Brandt, John C. & Maran, Stephen P. New Horizons in Astronomy. 2nd ed. LC 78-11717. (Illus.). 614p. 1979. text ed. 25.95 (ISBN 0-7167-1043-9). W H Freeman.
Brandt, John C., jt. auth. see Chapman, Robert D.
Brandt, John C., ed. Comets: Readings from Scientific American. LC 81-4562. (Illus.). 92p. 1981. text ed. 17.95 (ISBN 0-7167-1319-5); pap. text ed. 10.95 (ISBN 0-7167-1320-9). W H Freeman.
Brandt, John C. & Maran, Stephen P., eds. The New Astronomy & Space Science Reader. LC 76-54316. (Illus.). 371p. 1977. text ed. 23.95 (ISBN 0-7167-0350-5); pap. text ed. 12.95 (ISBN 0-7167-0349-1). W H Freeman.
Brandt, Jorgen G. Selected Longer Poems. 80p. (Orig.). 1983. pap. 6.00 (ISBN 0-915306-36-0). Curbstone.
--Tete-a-Tete: Poems. Brandt, Jorgen G. & Taylor, Alexander, trs. LC 77-18968. pap. 3.00 (ISBN 0-915306-06-9). Curbstone.
Brandt, Joseph. Gus Hall Bibliography. 181p. 1981. 9.95 (ISBN 0-87898-148-9); pap. 4.95 (ISBN 0-87898-149-7). New Outlook.
Brandt, Joseph A. Toward the New Spain: The Spanish Revolution of 1868 & the First Republic. LC 76-54695. (Illus.). xii, 435p. 1977. Repr. of 1933 ed. lib. bdg. 35.00x (ISBN 0-87991-607-9). Porcupine Pr.
Brandt, K. & Apstein, C., eds. Nordisches Plankton: 1911-42, 7 vols. 1964. 372.00 (ISBN 90-6123-110-8). Lubrecht & Cramer.
Brandt, Keith. Abe Lincoln: The Young Years. LC 81-23172. (Illus.). 48p. (gr. 4-6). 1982. PLB 7.89 (ISBN 0-89375-750-0); pap. text ed. 1.95 (ISBN 0-89375-751-9). Troll Assocs.
--Air. LC 84-2608. (Illus.). 32p. (gr. 2-6). 1985. PLB 7.59 (ISBN 0-8167-0130-X); pap. text ed. 1.95 (ISBN 0-8167-0131-8). Troll Assocs.
--Ancient Rome. LC 84-2684. (Illus.). 32p. (gr. 2-6). 1985. PLB 7.59 (ISBN 0-8167-0298-5); pap. text ed. 1.95 (ISBN 0-8167-0299-3). Troll Assocs.
--Babe Ruth, Home Run Hero. LC 85-1091. (Illus.). 48p. (gr. 4-6). 1985. lib. bdg. 8.79 (ISBN 0-8167-0553-4); pap. text ed. 1.95 (ISBN 0-8167-0554-2). Troll Assocs.
--Case of the Missing Dinosaur. LC 81-7620. (Easy-To-Read Mystery Ser.). (Illus.). 48p. (gr. 2-4). 1982. PLB 8.59 (ISBN 0-89375-586-9); pap. text ed. 1.95 (ISBN 0-89375-587-7). Troll Assocs.
--Caves. LC 84-2573. (Illus.). 32p. (gr. 2-6). 1985. PLB 7.59 (ISBN 0-8167-0142-3); pap. text ed. 1.95 (ISBN 0-8167-0143-1). Troll Assocs.
--Daniel Boone: Frontier Adventures. LC 82-15915. (Illus.). 48p. (gr. 4-6). 1983. PLB 7.89 (ISBN 0-89375-843-4); pap. text ed. 1.95 (ISBN 0-89375-844-2). Troll Assocs.
--Deserts. LC 84-8623. (Illus.). 32p. (gr. 2-6). 1985. PLB 7.59 (ISBN 0-8167-0262-4); pap. text ed. 1.95 (ISBN 0-8167-0263-2). Troll Assocs.
--Discovering Trees. LC 81-7522. (Illus.). 32p. (gr. 2-4). 1982. PLB 9.89 (ISBN 0-89375-566-4); pap. text ed. 1.95 (ISBN 0-89375-567-2). Troll Assocs.
--Earth. LC 84-8444. (Illus.). 32p. (gr. 2-6). 1985. PLB 7.59 (ISBN 0-8167-0250-0); pap. text ed. 1.95 (ISBN 0-8167-0251-9). Troll Assocs.
--Electricity. LC 84-2705. (Illus.). 32p. (gr. 2-6). 1985. PLB 7.59 (ISBN 0-8167-0198-9); pap. text ed. 1.95 (ISBN 0-8167-0199-7). Troll Assocs.
--Five Senses. LC 84-2633. (Illus.). 32p. (gr. 2-6). 1985. PLB 7.59 (ISBN 0-8167-0168-7); pap. text ed. 1.95 (ISBN 0-8167-0169-5). Troll Assocs.
--George Washington. LC 84-8624. (Illus.). 32p. (gr. 2-6). 1985. PLB 7.59 (ISBN 0-8167-0256-X); pap. text ed. 1.95 (ISBN 0-8167-0257-8). Troll Assocs.
--Indian Crafts. LC 84-2588. (Illus.). 32p. (gr. 2-6). 1985. lib. bdg. 7.59 (ISBN 0-8167-0132-6); pap. text ed. 1.95 (ISBN 0-8167-0133-4). Troll Assocs.
--Indian Festivals. LC 84-2644. (Illus.). 32p. (gr. 2-6). 1985. PLB 7.59 (ISBN 0-8167-0182-2); pap. text ed. 1.95 (ISBN 0-8167-0183-0). Troll Assocs.
--Indian Homes. LC 84-2650. (Illus.). 32p. (gr. 2-6). 1985. PLB 7.59 (ISBN 0-8167-0126-1); pap. text ed. 1.95 (ISBN 0-8167-0127-X). Troll Assocs.
--Insects. LC 84-2659. (Illus.). 32p. (gr. 2-6). 1985. PLB 7.59 (ISBN 0-8167-0184-9); pap. text ed. 1.95 (ISBN 0-8167-0185-7). Troll Assocs.
--John Paul Jones: Hero of the Seas. LC 82-16045. (Illus.). 48p. (gr. 4-6). 1983. PLB 7.89 (ISBN 0-89375-849-3); pap. text ed. 1.95 (ISBN 0-89375-850-7). Troll Assocs.
--Lou Gehrig, Pride of the Yankees. LC 85-1075. (Illus.). 48p. (gr. 4-6). 1985. lib. bdg. 8.79 (ISBN 0-8167-0549-6); pap. text ed. 1.95 (ISBN 0-8167-0550-X). Troll Assocs.
--Marie Curie: Brave Scientist. LC 82-16092. (Illus.). 48p. (gr. 4-6). 1983. PLB 7.89 (ISBN 0-89375-855-8); pap. text ed. 1.95 (ISBN 0-89375-856-6). Troll Assocs.
--Mexico & Central America. LC 84-2668. (Illus.). 32p. (gr. 2-6). 1985. PLB 7.59 (ISBN 0-8167-0264-0); pap. text ed. 1.95 (ISBN 0-8167-0265-9). Troll Assocs.
--Mountains. LC 84-2577. (Illus.). 32p. (gr. 2-6). 1985. PLB 7.59 (ISBN 0-8167-0154-7); pap. text ed. 1.95 (ISBN 0-8167-0155-5). Troll Assocs.
--Paul Revere: Son of Liberty. LC 81-23147. (Illus.). 48p. (gr. 4-6). 1982. PLB 7.89 (ISBN 0-89375-766-7); pap. text ed. 1.95 (ISBN 0-89375-767-5). Troll Assocs.
--Planets & the Solar System. LC 84-2714. (Illus.). 32p. (gr. 2-6). 1985. PLB 7.59 (ISBN 0-8167-0300-0); pap. text ed. 1.95 (ISBN 0-8167-0301-9). Troll Assocs.
--President. LC 84-2652. (Illus.). 32p. (gr. 2-6). 1985. PLB 7.59 (ISBN 0-8167-0268-3); pap. text ed. 1.95 (ISBN 0-8167-0269-1). Troll Assocs.
--Robert E. Lee. LC 84-2687. (Illus.). 32p. (gr. 2-6). 1985. PLB 7.59 (ISBN 0-8167-0278-0); pap. text ed. 1.95 (ISBN 0-8167-0279-9). Troll Assocs.
--Sound. LC 84-2632. (Illus.). 32p. (gr. 2-6). 1985. PLB 7.59 (ISBN 0-8167-0128-8); pap. text ed. 1.95 (ISBN 0-8167-0129-6). Troll Assocs.
--Sun. LC 84-2715. (Illus.). 32p. (gr. 2-6). 1985. PLB 7.59 (ISBN 0-8167-0190-3); pap. text ed. 1.95 (ISBN 0-8167-0191-1). Troll Assocs.
--Transportation. LC 84-2584. (Illus.). 32p. (gr. 2-6). 1985. PLB 7.59 (ISBN 0-8167-0172-5); pap. text ed. 1.95 (ISBN 0-8167-0173-3). Troll Assocs.
--What Makes It Rain? LC 81-7495. (Illus.). 32p. (gr. 2-4). 1982. PLB 9.89 (ISBN 0-89375-582-6); pap. text ed. 1.95 (ISBN 0-89375-583-4). Troll Assocs.
--Wonders of the Seasons. LC 81-7411. (Illus.). 32p. (gr. 2-4). 1982. PLB 9.89 (ISBN 0-89375-580-X); pap. text ed. 1.95 (ISBN 0-89375-581-8). Troll Assocs.
Brandt, L. Meditations on a Loving God. LC 12-2812. 1983. 10.95 (ISBN 0-570-03858-8). Concordia.
Brandt, Lawrence J. Gastrointestinal Disorders of the Elderly. (Illus.). 640p. 1984. text ed. 75.00 (ISBN 0-89004-987-4). Raven.
Brandt, Leonore. Raccoon Family Pets. pap. 2.95 (ISBN 0-87666-216-5, AP-7500). TFH Pubns.
Brandt, Leslie. Jesus Now. 1978. 8.50 (ISBN 0-570-03268-7, 15-2714). Concordia.
--Psalms-Now. LC 73-78108. 1973. 8.50 (ISBN 0-570-03230-X, 15-2125). Concordia.
--Psalms of Strength. (Psalms Now Gift Books). 1977. pap. 1.95 (ISBN 0-570-07450-9, 12-2684). Concordia.
Brandt, Leslie & Brandt, Edith. Growing Together: Prayers for Married People. LC 75-2830. 96p. (Orig.). 1975. pap. 4.95 (ISBN 0-8066-1476-5, 10-2903). Augsburg.
Brandt, Leslie, tr. Psalms of Comfort. (Psalms Now Gift Books). 1977. pap. 1.95 (ISBN 0-570-07452-5, 12-2686). Concordia.
--Psalms of Joy. (Psalms Now Gift Books). 1977. pap. 1.95 (ISBN 0-570-07451-7, 12-2685). Concordia.
--Psalms of Praise. (Psalms Now Gift Books). 1977. pap. 1.95 (ISBN 0-570-07453-3, 12-2687). Concordia.
Brandt, Leslie F. Bible Reading for the Retired. LC 83-72117. 112p. (Orig.). 1984. pap. 3.75 (ISBN 0-8066-2061-7, 10-0683). Augsburg.
--Bible Readings for Troubled Times. 112p. (Orig.). 1984. pap. 3.75 (ISBN 0-8066-2130-3, 10-0686). Augsburg.
--Book of Christian Prayer. LC 73-88603. 96p. (Orig.). 1974. pap. 3.95 (ISBN 0-8066-1406-4, 10-0785). Augsburg.
--Book of Christian Prayer: Gift Edition. rev. ed. LC 73-88603. 160p. 1980. 7.50 (ISBN 0-8066-1751-9, 10-0786). Augsburg.

--Christ in Your Life. 1980. 7.50 (ISBN 0-570-03292-X, 15-2729). Concordia.

--Epistles Now. LC 75-38711. 176p. 1976. 8.50 (ISBN 0-570-03258-X, 15-2166). Concordia.

--God Is Here-Let's Celebrate. LC 73-89877. 1969. pap. 2.95 (ISBN 0-570-03102-8, 12-2320). Concordia.

--Prophets Now. 1979. 8.50 (ISBN 0-570-03278-4, 15-2722). Concordia.

Brandt, Lilian. Five Hundred Seventy Four Deserters & Their Families: A Descriptive Study of Their Characteristics & Circumstances. Bd. with Family Desertion & Non-Support Laws. Baldwin, William H. LC 72-169374. (Family in America Ser). 210p. 1972. Repr. of 1904 ed. 20.00 (ISBN 0-405-03850-X). Ayer Co Pubs.

Brandt, Linda, ed. Taste the Seasons. LC 85-51259. (Illus.). 136p. 1985. 18.95x (ISBN 0-9615260-0-9). Woodside-Atherton.

Brandt, Louis, jt. auth. see Love, W. W.

Brandt, Louis W. Psychologists Caught: A Psycho-Logic of Psychology. 248p. 1982. 40.00x (ISBN 0-8020-5539-7); pap. 14.95 (ISBN 0-8020-6508-2). U of Toronto Pr.

Brandt, Lucile. The Flame Tree. new ed. 96p. 1973. pap. 2.95 (ISBN 0-87178-275-8). Brethren.

Brandt, N. B. & Chudinov, S. M. Electronic Structure of Metals. 336p. 1973. 6.45 (ISBN 0-8285-0778-3, Pub. by Mir Pubs USSR). Imported Pubns.

Brandt, Nat, ed. see Blakeslee, Alton, et al.

Brandt, Patricia, ed. OSU Theses & Dissertations, 1960-65. (Bibliographic Ser: No. 8). 1967. pap. 4.95x (ISBN 0-87071-128-8). Oreg St U Pr.

Brandt, Patricia & Guilford, Nancy, eds. Oregon Biography Index. (Bibliographic Ser.: No. 11). 140p. 1976. pap. 5.95x (ISBN 0-87071-131-8). Oreg St U Pr.

Brandt, Paul. Sittengeschichte Griechenlands. Lewandowski, Herbert, ed. LC 78-22297. (The Gay Experience). (Illus.). Repr. of 1959 ed. 32.50 (ISBN 0-404-61521-X). AMS Pr.

Brandt, Paul see Licht, Hans, pseud.

Brandt, R. A., tr. Come Not, Lucifer! A Romantic Anthology. 267p. Repr. of 1984 ed. lib. bdg. 40.00 (ISBN 0-918377-47-1). Russell Pr.

Brandt, R. L. Charismatics: Are We Missing Something? LC 81-81367. 1981. pap. 4.95 (ISBN 0-88270-523-7). Bridge Pub.

Brandt, R. M. & Perkins, H. V. Research Evaluating a Child Study Program. (SRCD.M). 1956. pap. 15.00 (ISBN 0-527-01566-0). Kraus Repr.

Brandt, Reinhard, ed. John Locke: Symposium Wolfenbuttel, Nineteen Hundred Seventy-Nine. 288p. 1980. text ed. 27.20x (ISBN 3-11-008266-7). De Gruyter.

Brandt, Rhonda, jt. auth. see Reece, Barry L.

Brandt, Richard B. Philosophy of Schleiermacher: The Development of His Theory of Scientific & Religious Knowledge. LC 68-19265. 1968. Repr. of 1941 ed. lib. bdg. 18.50x (ISBN 0-8371-0027-5, BRPS). Greenwood.

--A Theory of the Good & the Right. 1979. 27.50x (ISBN 0-19-824550-5); pap. 12.95x (ISBN 0-19-824744-3). Oxford U Pr.

Brandt, Richard B., jt. auth. see Alston, William P.

Brandt, Richard M. Public Education under Scrutiny. LC 80-6080. 197p. 1981. lib. bdg. 22.75 (ISBN 0-8191-1566-5); pap. text ed. 11.00 (ISBN 0-8191-1567-3). U Pr of Amer.

--Studying Behavior in Natural Settings. LC 81-40189. (Illus.). 416p. 1981. lib. bdg. 30.50 (ISBN 0-8191-1829-X); pap. text ed. 17.50 (ISBN 0-8191-1830-3). U Pr of Amer.

Brandt, Richard M., jt. ed. see Beegle, Charles W.

Brandt, Robert L. One Way. LC 77-75601. (Radiant Life Ser.). 128p. 1977. pap. 1.50 (ISBN 0-88243-909-X, 02-0909); teacher's ed 2.50 (ISBN 0-88243-179-X, 32-0179). Gospel Pub.

--Pentecostal Promise. (Charismatic Bks.). 47p. 1972. pap. 0.69 (ISBN 0-88243-920-0, 02-0920). Gospel Pub.

Brandt, Robert S. Tennessee Hiking Guide. LC 81-19664. (Illus.). 32p. (Orig.). 1982. pap. 1.95 (ISBN 0-87049-343-4). U of Tenn Pr.

Brandt, Roger & Jorgensen, Dan. Family Hiking Trails in South Dakota. 104p. 1981. pap. 3.50 (ISBN 0-931170-13-3). Ctr Western Studies.

Brandt, Ronald S., ed. Partners: Parents & Schools. LC 79-90730. 1979. pap. text ed. 4.75 (ISBN 0-87120-096-1, 611-79168). Assn Supervision.

Brandt, Ronald S. & Modrak, Nancy, eds. Applied Strategies for Curriculum Evaluation. LC 81-68494. (Illus.). 119p. 1981. 5.75 (ISBN 0-87120-108-9). Assn Supervision.

Brandt, Ronald S., ed. see Remy, Richard C.

Brandt, S. Statistical & Computational Methods in Data Analysis. 2nd, rev. ed. 416p. 1976. 51.00 (ISBN 0-7204-0334-0, North Holland); pap. 28.00 (ISBN 0-444-86615-9). Elsevier.

Brandt, S. & Dahmen, H. D. The Picture Book of Quantum Mechanics. 320p. 1985. 26.95 (ISBN 0-471-81776-7). Wiley.

Brandt, Steven A., jt. ed. see Clark, J. Desmond.

Brandt, Steven C. Entrepreneuring in Established Companies: Managing Toward the Year 2000. 250p. 1985. 19.95 (ISBN 0-87094-664-1). Dow Jones-Irwin.

--Entrepreneuring: The Ten Commandments for Building a Growth Company. LC 82-1660. 225p. 1982. 12.95 (ISBN 0-201-10382-6). Addison-Wesley.

--Entrepreneuring: The Ten Commandments for Building a Growth Company. 1983. pap. 3.95 (ISBN 0-451-62198-0, ME2198, Ment). NAL.

--Strategic Planning in Emerging Companies. (Illus.). 192p. 1981. text ed. 19.95 (ISBN 0-201-00942-0). Addison-Wesley.

Brandt, Sue R. Facts About the Fifty States. rev. ed. (First Bks.). (Illus.). (gr. 4 up). 1979. PLB 8.90 s&l (ISBN 0-531-02899-2). Watts.

Brandt, Susan, jt. auth. see Cantacuzino, Sherban.

Brandt, Vincent S. A Korean Village Between Farm & Sea. LC 73-162857. (East Asian Ser: No. 65). (Illus.). Repr. of 1971 ed. 50.80 (ISBN 0-8357-9163-7, 2017013). Bks Demand UMI.

Brandt, W., et al. Craft of Writing. 1969. pap. text ed. 11.95 (ISBN 0-13-188797-1). P-H.

Brandt, W. H. The Student's Guide to Optical Microscopes. LC 75-23251. (Illus.). 67p. 1976. pap. 4.95x (ISBN 0-913232-22-X). W Kaufmann.

Brandt, Walter I. & Lehmann, Helmut T., eds. Luther's Works: The Christian in Society II, Vol. 45. LC 55-9893. 1962. 19.95 (ISBN 0-8006-0345-1, 1-345). Fortress.

Brandt, William, et al. The Comprehensive Study of Music: Anthology of Music from Monteverdi Through Mozart. 1977. pap. text ed. 14.50 scp (ISBN 0-06-161417-3, HarpC). Har-Row.

--The Comprehensive Study of Music: Anthology of Music from Plainchant Through Gabrieli. 1979. pap. text ed. 14.50 scp (ISBN 0-06-161411-4, HarpC). Har-Row.

Brandt, William J. The Rhetoric of Argumentation. LC 68-24165. 1984. 34.50x (ISBN 0-672-60673-9); pap. text ed. 14.50x (ISBN 0-89197-921-2). Irvington.

Brandt, Willy & Sampson, Anthony, eds. North-South: A Program for Survival (The Brandt Report) 320p. (Orig.). 1980. pap. text ed. 5.95 (ISBN 0-262-52059-1). MIT Pr.

Brandt, Winston. U2. 160p. (Orig.). 1986. pap. 2.95 (ISBN 0-345-32892-2). Ballantine.

Brandt Corstius, H., ed. Grammars for Number Names. (Foundations of Language Supplementary Ser: No. 7). 123p. 1968. lib. bdg. 21.00 (ISBN 90-277-0023-0, Pub. by Reidel Holland). Kluwer Academic.

Brandts, Lois. Word Wowzers. (Language Arts Ser.). 48p. (gr. 4-8). 1982. 4.95 (ISBN 0-317-14740-4, LW 228). Learning Wks.

Brandts, Robert. As We Drifted & Other Poems. LC 72-87039. 1972. pap. 3.00 (ISBN 0-87922-013-9). Christopher's Bks.

Brandtt, W. & Dupasquier, A., eds. Positron Solid State Physics: Proceedings of the International School of Physics, Enrico Fermi, Course LXXXIII, Varenna, Italy July 14-24, 1981. (Enrico Fermi International Summer School of Physics Ser.: No. 83). 716p. 1984. 129.00 (ISBN 0-444-86521-7, I-082-84, North-Holland). Elsevier.

Brandvold, D. C. Water Treatment: Industrial-Commercial-Municipal. 2nd ed. (Illus.). 1982. pap. 5.00 (ISBN 0-9610178-0-5). Branchemco.

Brandwein & MacNeice. The Group House Handbook: How to Live with Others (and love it). LC 82-16475. 1982. pap. 6.95 (ISBN 0-87491-090-0). Acropolis.

Brandwein, Paul F. The Gifted Student as Future Scientist. (Perspective Through a Retrospective Ser.: Vol. 3). 107p. Repr. of 1955 ed. 5.95 (ISBN 0-318-02147-1). NSLTIGT.

--The Gifted Student As Future Scientist: A Perspective Through a Retrospective, Vol. 3. 107p. 5.95 (ISBN 0-318-16005-6, 29). NSLTIGT.

--The Humanities: A Permanent Human Agenda. 50p. 8.95 (ISBN 0-318-02205-2). NSLTIGT.

Brandwein, Paul F. see Tcherikover, Victor A.

Brandwein, Peter, jt. ed. see Danzig, Allison.

Brandwein, Yehuda. Tikune Zohar: Hebrew Text, Vol. 1. 1973. 25.00 (ISBN 0-943688-27-2). Res Ctr Kabbalah.

Brandy Advisory Board. California Brandy Drinks, Cocktails, Punches, Coffee, & Hot Drinks. Hebert, Malcolm P., ed. (Illus.). 160p. 1981. 4.95 (ISBN 0-932664-21-0). Wine Appreciation.

Brandys, Kazimierz. Letters to Mrs. Z. Edelson, Morris, tr. 1985. pap. 5.00 (ISBN 0-317-17750-8). Quixote.

--A Warsaw Dairy: Nineteen Seventy-Eight to Nineteen Eighty-One. LC 84-40052. 272p. 1984. pap. 8.95 (ISBN 0-394-72622-7, Vin). Random.

--A Warsaw Diary. Lourie, Richard, tr. LC 83-42782. 1984. 17.95 (ISBN 0-394-52856-5, Vin); pap. 8.95. Random.

Branegan, Gladys A. Home Economics Teacher Training Under the Smith-Huges Act 1917-1927. LC 76-176587. (Columbia University. Teachers College. Contributions to Education: No. 350). Repr. of 1929 ed. 22.50 (ISBN 0-404-55350-8). AMS Pr.

Branemark, Per-Ingvar. Intravascular Anatomy of Blood Cells in Man. (Illus.). 1971. 41.00 (ISBN 3-8055-0773-9). S Karger.

Branemark, Per-Ingvar, et al. Tissue-Integrated Prostheses. (Illus.). 352p. 1985. pap. text ed. 88.00 (ISBN 0-86715-129-3). Quint Pub CO.

Branfield, John. Brown Cow. 160p. (gr. 6-8). 1985. 10.95 (ISBN 0-575-03223-5, Pub. by Gollancz England). David & Charles.

--The Fox in Winter. LC 81-10793. 168p. (gr. 7 up). 1982. PLB 11.95 (ISBN 0-689-50219-2, McElderry Bk). Atheneum.

--The Poison Factory. 1979. pap. 1.50 (ISBN 0-448-17044-2, Pub. by Tempo). Ace Bks.

--The Poison Factory. LC 72-83225. 176p. (gr. 7 up). 1972. PLB 11.89 (ISBN 0-06-020647-0). HarpJ.

--Thin Ice. 160p. (gr. 6-8). 1985. 10.95 (ISBN 0-575-03350-9, Pub. by Gollancz England). David & Charles.

Branford, Jean. A Dictionary of South African English. 2nd ed. 1980. 22.50x (ISBN 0-19-570177-1). Oxford U Pr.

Branford, Kester A. A Study of Jean-Jacques Bernard's Theatre De L'inexprime. LC 76-58424. (Romance Monographs: No. 24). 1977. 20.00x (ISBN 84-399-6422-6). Romance.

Branford, Susan & Glock, Oriel. The Last Frontier: Fighting for Land in the Amazon. 304p. 1985. 30.95x (ISBN 0-86232-395-9, Pub. by Zed Pr); pap. 12.25 (ISBN 0-86232-396-7). Biblio Dist.

Brang, Peter & Zullig, Monika. Kommentierte Bibliographie Zur Slavischen Soziolinguistik, Vol. 17. (Slaveca Helvetica). 1639p. (Ger.). 1982. 73.70 (ISBN 3-261-04958-8). P Lang Pubs.

Brang, Peter, et al, eds. Schweizerische Beitraege zum IX Internationalen Slavistenkongress in Kiev: 1983. (Slavica Helvetica: Vol. 22). 245p. (Ger.). 1983. 23.15 (ISBN 3-261-03240-5). P Lang Pubs.

Brangham, Norman. The South of France: A Visitor's Guide. 160p. 1984. pap. text ed. 9.95 (ISBN 0-86190-113-4, Pub. by Moorland Pr UK). Bradt Ent.

--The South of France: Visitor's Guide. 142p. (Orig.). 1984. 17.95 (ISBN 0-86190-112-6, Pub. by Moorland Pr UK); pap. 9.95 (ISBN 0-317-19900-5, Pub. by Moorland Pr UK). Bradt Ent.

Brangwyn, Frank & Preston, Hayter. Windmills. LC 70-176821. (Illus.). 126p. 1975. Repr. of 1923 ed. 43.00x (ISBN 0-8103-4077-1). Gale.

Branham, Levi. My Life & Travels. 64p. 1985. pap. 3.95 (ISBN 0-87797-107-2). Cherokee.

Branham, Richard L. & Stuhr, David D. A Language of Form: The Isometric Theory. LC 80-82996. 496p. 1980. pap. text ed. 24.95 (ISBN 0-8403-2291-7). Kendall-Hunt.

Branham, V. C., ed. see Roheim, Geza.

Branica, M., ed. see International Experts Discussion on Lead Occurrence, Fate & Pollution in the Marine Environment, Rovinj, Yugoslavia, 18-22 October 1977.

Branick, Vincent P. Mary, the Spirit & the Church. LC 80-82856. 128p. (Orig.). 1981. pap. 4.95 (ISBN 0-8091-2343-6). Paulist Pr.

--Wonder in a Technical World: An Introduction to the Method & Writers of Philosophy. LC 80-67205. 256p. 1980. lib. bdg. 12.25 (ISBN 0-8191-1248-8). U Pr of Amer.

Branigan, Edward. Point of View in the Cinema: A Theory of Narration & Subjectivity in Classical Film. (Approaches to Semiotics Ser.: No. 66). xvi, 246p. 1984. 34.95x (ISBN 90-279-3079-1); pap. 14.95 (ISBN 90-279-3139-9). Mouton.

Branigan, Keith. Atlas of Ancient Civilizations. LC 75-22115. (John Day Bk.). (Illus.). 1976. 12.95i (ISBN 0-381-98284-X). T Y Crowell.

--The Atlas of Archaeology. 240p. 1982. 60.00x (ISBN 0-356-06253-8, Pub. by MacDonald & Co Pubs England). State Mutual Bk.

--Copper & Bronze Working in Early Bronze Age Crete. (Studies in Mediterranean Archaeology: No. XIX). 1968. pap. text ed. 21.50x (ISBN 0-391-01968-6). Humanities.

--Prehistory. LC 84-50696. (History As Evidence Ser.). (Illus.). 37p. (gr. 5-8). 1984. PLB 10.90 (ISBN 0-531-03745-2). Watts.

Branigan, Keith, ed. The Atlas of Archaeology. LC 82-61698. (Illus.). 240p. 1982. 25.00 (ISBN 0-312-05957-4). St Martin.

Branin, M. Lelyn. The Early Potters & Potteries of Maine. LC 78-16070. 1978. 22.00x (ISBN 0-8195-5022-1). Wesleyan U Pr.

Branks, Judith & Sanchez, Juan B. The Drama of Life: Guambiano Life Cycle Customs. (Museum of Anthropology Publications: No. 4). 107p. 1978. pap. 5.00 (ISBN 0-88312-153-0); microfiche (2) 2.86x (ISBN 0-88312-239-1). Summer Inst Ling.

Brankston, A. D. Early Ming Wares of Chingtechen. (Oxford Asia Studies in Ceramics). 1982. Repr. of 1938 ed. 24.95 (ISBN 0-19-581522-X). Oxford U Pr.

Branley, F., et al. Astronomy. 1975. text ed. 21.95 scp (ISBN 0-690-00760-4, HarpC). Har-Row.

Branley, Franklyn M. Age of Aquarius: You & Astrology. LC 78-22511. (Illus.). 1979. 11.06i (ISBN 0-690-03987-5); PLB 11.89 (ISBN 0-690-03988-3). Crowell Jr Bks.

--Air Is All Around You. LC 62-7738. (A Let's-Read-& Find-Out Science Bk). (Illus.). (gr. k-3). 1962. PLB 11.89 (ISBN 0-690-05356-8). Crowell Jr Bks.

--Big Dipper. LC 62-10999. (A Let's-Read-&-Find-Out Science Bk.). (Illus.). (gr. k-3). 1962. PLB 11.89 (ISBN 0-690-01116-4). Crowell Jr Bks.

--Big Tracks, Little Tracks. LC 60-6251. (A Let's-Read-&-Find-Out Science Bk.). (Illus.). (gr. k-3). 1960. PLB 11.89 (ISBN 0-690-14371-0). Crowell Jr Bks.

--A Book of Flying Saucers for You. LC 72-78278. (Illus.). (gr. 3-6). 1973. PLB 11.89 (ISBN 0-690-15189-6). Crowell Jr Bks.

--Book of Moon Rockets for You. rev. ed. LC 76-101921. (Illus.). (gr. 4-6). 1970. PLB 9.89 (ISBN 0-690-15437-2). Crowell Jr Bks.

--Book of Planets for You. rev. ed. LC 66-16919. (Illus.). (gr. 3-6). 1966. Crowell Jr Bks.

--Book of Stars for You. LC 67-18509. (Illus.). (gr. 3-6). 1967. Crowell Jr Bks.

--Book of Venus for You. LC 73-78256. (Illus.). (gr. 3-6). 1969. Crowell Jr Bks.

--Color: From Rainbows to Lasers. LC 76-46304. (Illus.). (gr. 6 up). 1978. PLB 11.89 (ISBN 0-690-03847-X). Crowell Jr Bks.

--Comets. LC 83-46161. (A Let's-Read-&-Find-Out Science Bk.). (Illus.). 32p. (ps-3). 1984. 11.06i (ISBN 0-690-04414-3); PLB 11.89g (ISBN 0-690-04415-1). Crowell Jr Bks.

--Comets. LC 85-42739. (A Trophy Let's-Read-&-Find-Out Bk.). (Illus.). 32p. (gr. k-3). 1985. pap. 3.80i (ISBN 0-06-445017-1, Trophy). HarpJ.

--Dinosaurs, Asteroids, & Superstars. LC 81-43880. (Illus.). 96p. (gr. 5 up). 1982. 11.06i (ISBN 0-690-04211-6); PLB 11.89 (ISBN 0-690-04212-4). Crowell Jr Bks.

--The Earth: Planet Number Three. LC 66-12668. (Exploring Our Universe Ser.). (Illus.). (gr. 7 up). 1966. Crowell Jr Bks.

--Eclipse: Darkness in Daytime. LC 73-3492. (A Let's-Read-&-Find-Out Science Bk). (Illus.). (gr. k-3). 1973. PLB 11.89 (ISBN 0-690-25414-8). Crowell Jr Bks.

--The Electromagnetic Spectrum: Key to the Universe. LC 77-26591. (Exploring Our Universe Ser.). (Illus.). (gr. 7 up). 1979. 11.06i (ISBN 0-690-03868-2); PLB 11.89 (ISBN 0-690-03869-0). Crowell Jr Bks.

--The End of the World. LC 72-13264. (Illus.). (gr. 5 up). 1974. PLB 11.89 (ISBN 0-690-26608-1). Crowell Jr Bks.

--Energy for the Twenty First Century. LC 74-31144. (Illus.). 96p. (gr. 5 up). 1975. 11.49i (ISBN 0-690-00756-6). Crowell Jr Bks.

--Feast or Famine? The Energy Future. LC 79-7817. (Illus.). 128p. (gr. 5 up). 1980. 11.49i (ISBN 0-690-04040-7); PLB 11.89 (ISBN 0-690-04041-5, TYC-J). Crowell Jr Bks.

--Flash, Crash, Rumble, & Roll. rev. ed. LC 84-45333. (A Let's-Read-&-Find-Out Science Bk.). (Illus.). 32p. (ps-3). 1985. 11.06i (ISBN 0-690-04424-0); PLB 11.89g (ISBN 0-690-04425-9). Crowell Jr Bks.

--Flash, Crash, Rumble, & Roll. rev. ed. LC 84-48532. (Trophy Let's-Read-&-Find-Out Bk.). (Illus.). 32p. (ps-3). 1985. pap. 3.80i (ISBN 0-06-445012-0, Trophy). HarpJ.

--Floating & Sinking. LC 67-15396. (A Let's Read & Find Out Science Bk). (Illus.). (gr. k-3). 1967. PLB 11.89 (ISBN 0-690-30918-X). Crowell Jr Bks.

--Gravity Is a Mystery. LC 70-101922. (A Let's-Read-and-Find-Out Science Bk). (Illus.). (gr. k-3). 1970. PLB 11.89 (ISBN 0-690-35072-4). Crowell Jr Bks.

--Halley: Comet 1986. (Illus.). 96p. (gr. 7 up). 1983. 10.95 (ISBN 0-525-66780-6, 01063-320). Lodestar Bks.

--High Sounds, Low Sounds. LC 67-23662. (A Let's-Read-&-Find-Out Science Bk.). (Illus.). (gr. k-3). 1967. PLB 11.89 (ISBN 0-690-38018-6). Crowell Jr Bks.

--High Sounds Low Sounds. LC 67-23662. (Crocodile Paperback Ser.). (Illus.). 40p. (gr. k-3). 1975. pap. 1.45 (ISBN 0-690-00638-1). Crowell Jr Bks.

--Hurricane Watch. LC 85-47534. (A Let's-Read-&-Find-Out Science Bk.). (Illus.). 32p. (ps-3). 1985. 11.06i (ISBN 0-690-04470-4); PLB 11.89g (ISBN 0-690-04471-2). Crowell Jr Bks.

--Is There Life in Outer Space? LC 83-45057. (A Let's-Read-&-Find-Out Science Bk.). (Illus.). 32p. (ps-3). 1984. 11.06i (ISBN 0-690-04374-0); PLB 11.89g (ISBN 0-690-04375-9). Crowell Jr Bks.

--Jupiter: King of the Gods, Giant of the Planets. (Illus.). 96p. (gr. 7 up). 1981. 10.95 (ISBN 0-525-66739-3, 01063-320). Lodestar Bks.

--Measure with Metric. LC 74-4056. (Young Math Ser.). (Illus.). 40p. (gr. k-3). 1975. PLB 11.89 (ISBN 0-690-01117-2); (TYC-J). Crowell Jr Bks.

--Moon Seems to Change. LC 60-8796. (A Let's-Read-&-Find-Out Science Bk.). (Illus.). (gr. k-3). 1960. PLB 10.89 (ISBN 0-690-55485-0). Crowell Jr Bks.

--Mysteries of Outer Space. (Mysteries of the Universe Ser.). (Illus.). 96p. (gr. 5-9). 1985. 10.95 (ISBN 0-525-67149-8, 01063-320). Lodestar Bks.

--Mysteries of the Universe. LC 83-25302. (Illus.). 96p. (gr. 5-9). 1984. 10.95 (ISBN 0-525-66914-0, 01063-320). Lodestar Bks.

--Mystery of Stonehenge. LC 69-11823. (Illus.). (gr. 5 up). 1969. 11.89 (ISBN 0-690-57046-5). Crowell Jr Bks.

--The Nine Planets. rev. ed. LC 77-26604. (Illus.). (gr. 6 up). 1978. 9.89 (ISBN 0-690-03848-8); PLB 11.89 (ISBN 0-690-03849-6). Crowell Jr Bks.

--Oxygen Keeps You Alive. LC 73-139093. (A Let's Read & Find Out Science Bks.). (Illus.). (gr. k-3). 1971. 111.49i (ISBN 0-690-60702-4); PLB 11.89 (ISBN 0-690-60703-2). Crowell Jr Bks.

--Oxygen Keeps You Alive. LC 73-139093. (Crocodile Paperbacks Ser.). (Illus.). 33p. (gr. k-3). 1972. pap. 2.95 (ISBN 0-690-60708-3). Crowell Jr Bks.

--Pieces of Another World: The Story of Moon Rocks. LC 71-158684. (Illus.). (gr. 5-8). 1972. PLB 11.89 (ISBN 0-690-62566-9). Crowell Jr Bks.

--The Planets in Our Solar System. LC 79-7894. (A Let's Read & Find Out Science Bk.). (Illus.). 40p. (gr. k-3). 1981. 11.49i (ISBN 0-690-04025-3); PLB 11.89 (ISBN 0-690-04026-1). Crowell Jr Bks.

--The Planets in Our Solar System. LC 79-7894. (A Trophy Let's-Read-and-Find-out Science Bk.). (Illus.). 40p. (gr. k-3). 1983. pap. 3.80i (ISBN 0-06-445001-5, Trophy). HarpJ.

--Rain & Hail. LC 83-45058. (Let's Read-&-Find-Out Science Bk.). (Illus.). 40p. (gr. k-3). 1983. 11.06 (ISBN 0-690-04352-X); PLB 11.89g (ISBN 0-690-04353-8). Crowell Jr Bks.

--Roots Are Food Finders. LC 74-23924. (A Let's Read & Find Out Science Bk) (Illus.). 40p. (gr. k-3). 1975. PLB 11.89 (ISBN 0-690-00703-5). Crowell Jr Bks.

--Saturn. LC 81-43890. (Illus.). 64p. (gr. 3-6). 1983. 12.45i (ISBN 0-690-04213-2); PLB 12.89g (ISBN 0-690-04214-0). Crowell Jr Bks.

--Shakes, Quakes & Shifts: Earth Tectonics. LC 73-18059. 40p. (gr. 5 up). 1974. 8.95 (ISBN 0-690-00422-2). Crowell Jr Bks.

--Shivers & Goose Bumps: How We Keep Warm. LC 82-45921. (Illus.). 96p. (gr. 5 up). 1984. 11.49i (ISBN 0-690-04334-1); PLB 11.89g (ISBN 0-690-04335-X). Crowell Jr Bks.

--The Sky Is Full of Stars. LC 81-43037. (A Let's-Read-&-Find-Out Science Bk.). (Illus.). 40p. (gr. k-3). 1981. 11.49i (ISBN 0-690-04122-5); PLB 11.89i (ISBN 0-690-04123-3). Crowell Jr Bks.

--The Sky Is Full of Stars. LC 81-43037. (A Trophy Let's Read-&-Find-Out Science Bk.). (Illus.). 40p. (gr. k-3). 1983. pap. 3.80i (ISBN 0-06-445002-3, Trophy). HarpJ.

--Snow Is Falling. LC 63-15084. (A Let's-Read-&-Find-Out Science Bk). (Illus.). (gr. k-3). 1963. PLB 11.89 (ISBN 0-690-74300-9). Crowell Jr Bks.

--Space Colony: Frontier of the 21st Century. (Illus.). 128p. (gr. 7 up). 1982. 10.95 (ISBN 0-525-66741-5, 01063-320). Lodestar Bks.

--Space Telescope. LC 84-45341. (Illus.). 96p. (gr. 3-6). 1985. 11.06i (ISBN 0-690-04433-X); PLB 10.89g (ISBN 0-690-04434-8). Crowell Jr Bks.

--Sun Dogs & Shooting Stars: A Skywatcher's Calendar. (Illus.). (gr. 5 up). 1980. 6.95 (ISBN 0-395-29520-3). HM.

--Sun: Our Nearest Star. LC 60-13241. (A Let's-Read-&-Find-Out Science Bk). (Illus.). (gr. k-3). 1961. PLB 11.89 (ISBN 0-690-79483-5). Crowell Jr Bks.

--Sunshine Makes the Seasons. rev. ed. LC 85-47540. (A Let's-Read-&-Find-Out Science Bk.). (Illus.). 32p. (ps-3). 1985. 11.06i (ISBN 0-690-04481-X); PLB 11.89g (ISBN 0-690-04482-8). Crowell Jr Bks.

--Sunshine Makes the Seasons. rev. ed. LC 85-42750. (A Trophy Let's-Read-&-Find-Out Bk.). (Illus.). 32p. (gr. k-3). 1985. pap. 3.80i (ISBN 0-06-445019-8, Trophy). HarpJ.

--Think Metric! LC 72-78279. (Illus.). (gr. 3-6). 1973. PLB 11.89 (ISBN 0-690-81862-9). Crowell Jr Bks.

--Volcanoes. LC 84-45344. (A Let's-Read-&-Find-Out Science Bk.). (Illus.). 32p. (ps-3). 1985. 11.06i (ISBN 0-690-04451-8); PLB 11.89g (ISBN 0-690-04431-3). Crowell Jr Bks.

--Water for the World. LC 81-43321. (Illus.). 96p. (gr. 5 up). 1982. 11.06i (ISBN 0-690-04172-1); PLB 11.89 (ISBN 0-690-04173-X). Crowell Jr Bks.

--Weight & Weightlessness. LC 70-132292. (Let's-Read-&-Find-Out Science Bks.). (Illus.). (gr. k-3). 1972. PLB 11.89 (ISBN 0-690-87329-8). Crowell Jr Bks.

--What Makes Day & Night. LC 60-8258. (A Let's-Read-&-Find-Out Science Bks.). (Illus.). (gr. k-3). 1961. PLB 11.89 (ISBN 0-690-87790-0). Crowell Jr Bks.

--What Makes Day & Night. LC 60-8258. (Crocodile Paperbacks Ser.). (Illus.). 33p. (gr. k-3). 1972. pap. 2.95 (ISBN 0-690-87791-9). Crowell Jr Bks.

--What the Moon Is Like. LC 63-8479. (A Let's-Read-&-Find-Out Science Bk). (Illus.). (gr. k-3). 1963. pap. 2.95 (ISBN 0-690-00203-3); lib. bdg. 11.89 (ISBN 0-690-87860-5). Crowell Jr Bks.

Branley, Franklyn M. & Vaughan, Eleanor K. Rusty Rings a Bell. LC 57-7492. (Illus.). (gr. k-3). 1957. PLB 10.89 (ISBN 0-690-71602-8). Crowell Jr Bks.

Branley, Franklyn M. & Vaughn, Eleanor K. Mickey's Magnet. (Illus.). (gr. k-3). pap. 1.50 (ISBN 0-590-02334-9). Scholastic Inc.

Branley, Franklyn M., jt. auth. see Beeler, Nelson F.

Brann, D., jt. auth. see Palmer, K.

Brann, Donald. How to Transform a Garage into Living Space: Create Rental Income. rev. ed. LC 84-82349. 194p. 1985. pap. 9.95 (ISBN 0-87733-884-1). Easi-Bild.

Brann, Donald R. Brann's Guide to Home Improvement. LC 63-9605. (Illus.). 1963. 10.95 (ISBN 0-8303-0053-8). Fleet.

--Bricklaying Simplified. rev. ed. LC 77-140968. (Illus.). 1976. lib. bdg. 5.95 (ISBN 0-87733-068-9). Easi-Bild.

--Bricklaying Simplified. LC 77-140968. 1979. pap. 6.95 (ISBN 0-87733-668-7). Easi-Bild.

--Carpeting Simplified. LC 72-91055. (Illus.). 1980. pap. 6.95 (ISBN 0-87733-683-0). Easi-Bild.

--Concrete Work Simplified. rev. ed. LC 66-24876. 1974. lib. bdg. 5.95 (ISBN 0-87733-017-4). Easi-Bild.

--Concrete Work Simplified. LC 66-24876. 1980. pap. 7.95 (ISBN 0-87733-617-2). Easi-Bild.

--Easi-Bild Simplifies Electrical Repairs. rev. ed. LC 70-95701. 1970. lib. bdg. 5.95 (ISBN 0-87733-094-8). Easi-Bild.

--Electrical Repairs Simplified. LC 70-95701. 1979. pap. 5.95 (ISBN 0-87733-694-6). Easi-Bild.

--Forms, Footings, Foundations, Framings, Stair Building, Bk. 697. rev. ed. LC 70-105687. (Illus.). 210p. 1980. pap. 7.95 (ISBN 0-87733-697-0). Easi-Bild.

--How to Add an Extra Bathroom. rev. ed. LC 68-18108. 1976. lib. bdg. 5.95 (ISBN 0-87733-082-4); pap. 6.95 (ISBN 0-87733-682-2). Easi-Bild.

--How to Build a Kayak. LC 75-2652. 1978. pap. 7.95 (ISBN 0-87733-757-8). Easi-Bild.

--How to Build a Low Cost House - Above or Below Ground. LC 81-69857. 226p. 1982. pap. 7.95 (ISBN 0-87733-832-9). Easi-Bild.

--How to Build a One Car Garage-Carport-Stable. rev. ed. LC 72-88709. 1973. lib. bdg. 5.95 (ISBN 0-87733-800-0); pap. 6.95 (ISBN 0-87733-680-6). Easi-Bild.

--How to Build a One or Two Story Garage with Apartment. LC 83-81875. 224p. 1984. pap. 9.95 (ISBN 0-87733-863-9). Easi-Bild.

--How to Build a Patio, Porch, & Sundeck. LC 78-55238. 1979. pap. 6.95 (ISBN 0-87733-781-0). Easi-Bild.

--How to Build a Stable & a Red Barn Tool House. LC 72-88710. (Illus.). 1973. lib. bdg. 5.95 (ISBN 0-87733-079-4); pap. 7.95 (ISBN 0-87733-679-2). Easi-Bild.

--How to Build a Two Bedroom Ranch House. LC 82-90748. 272p. 1984. pap. 9.95 (ISBN 0-87733-831-0). Easi-Bild.

--How to Build a Two Car Garage. rev. ed. LC 65-27707. 1968. lib. bdg. 5.95 (ISBN 0-87733-063-8). Easi-Bild.

--How to Build a Two Car Garage, Lean-to Porch Cabana. LC 65-27707. 1979. pap. 6.95 (ISBN 0-87733-663-6). Easi-Bild.

--How to Build a Two Car Garage with Apartment Above. new ed. LC 76-29213. 1977. pap. 6.95 (ISBN 0-87733-763-2). Easi-Bild.

--How to Build a Vacation or Retirement House. rev ed. LC 68-54905. 1975. lib. bdg. 6.95 (ISBN 0-87733-032-8); pap. 5.95 (ISBN 0-87733-632-6). Easi-Bild.

--How to Build an Addition. rev. ed. LC 63-16211. Orig. Title: How to Add-a-Room. 1978. lib. bdg. 5.95 (ISBN 0-87733-009-3); pap. 7.95 (ISBN 0-87733-609-1). Easi-Bild.

--How to Build Bars. rev. ed. LC 67-15263. 1976. lib. bdg. 5.95 (ISBN 0-87733-090-5). Easi-Bild.

--How to Build Bars. LC 67-15263. 1979. pap. 6.95 (ISBN 0-87733-690-3). Easi-Bild.

--How to Build Bars, Bk. No. 890. LC 84-80979. 194p. 1984. pap. 7.95 (ISBN 0-87733-890-6). Easi Bild.

--How to Build Bookcases & Stereo Cabinets. LC 79-56769. (Illus.). 194p. 1980. pap. 6.95 (ISBN 0-87733-804-3). Easi-Bild.

--How to Build Collectors' Display Cases. LC 78-57773. (Illus.). 194p. 1979. pap. 6.95 (ISBN 0-87733-792-6). Easi-Bild.

--How to Build Colonial Furniture. LC 74-24602. 1982. pap. 7.95 (ISBN 0-87733-761-6). Easi-Bild.

--How to Build Dollhouses & Furniture, Bk. 753. LC 75-32052. (Illus.). 210p. 1980. lib. bdg. 6.95 (ISBN 0-87733-053-0); pap. 7.95 (ISBN 0-87733-753-5). Easi-Bild.

--How to Build Fences, Gates & Outdoor Projects. LC 74-28771. (Orig.). 1975. pap. 3.50 (ISBN 0-87733-607-5). Easi-Bild.

--How to Build Greenhouses-Sun Houses. rev ed. LC 72-91056. (Illus.). 1976. lib. bdg. 5.95 (ISBN 0-87733-011-5); pap. 3.50 (ISBN 0-87733-611-3). Easi-Bild.

--How to Build Greenhouses-Walk-in, Window, Sun House, Garden Tool House. LC 80-67650. 210p. 1980. pap. 7.95 (ISBN 0-87733-811-6). Easi-Bild.

--How to Build Kitchen Cabinets, Room Dividers & Cabinet Furniture. rev. ed. LC 65-27708. 1978. lib. bdg. 5.95 (ISBN 0-87733-058-1); pap. 3.50 (ISBN 0-87733-658-X). Easi-Bild.

--How to Build Outdoor Furniture. LC 76-14045. 1983. pap. 7.95 (ISBN 0-87733-754-3). Easi-Bild.

--How to Build Outdoor Projects. LC 81-65039. 210p. 1981. pap. 7.95 (ISBN 0-87733-807-8). Easi-Bild.

--How to Build Pet Housing, Bk. 751. LC 75-269. 1978. pap. 6.95 (ISBN 0-87733-751-9). Easi-Bild.

--How to Build Sportman's Revolving Storage Cabinet. rev. ed. LC 67-14312. 1974. lib. bdg. 5.95 (ISBN 0-87733-300-9); pap. 3.50 (ISBN 0-87733-630-X). Easi-Bild.

--How to Build Workbenches. rev. ed. LC 66-30452. 1974. lib. bdg. 5.95 (ISBN 0-87733-072-7). Easi-Bild.

--How to Build Workbenches. LC 66-30452. 1979. pap. 6.95 (ISBN 0-87733-672-5). Easi-Bild.

--How to Construct Built in & Sectional Bookcases. rev. ed. LC 67-27731. 1978. lib. bdg. 5.95 (ISBN 0-87733-064-6); pap. 3.50 (ISBN 0-87733-664-4). Easi-Bild.

--How to Create Room at the Top. LC 77-15691. 1978. pap. 6.95 (ISBN 0-87733-773-X). Easi-Bild.

--How to Find a Job, Start a Business, Learn to Offer What Others Want to Buy. LC 80-68578. 210p. 1981. pap. 7.95 (ISBN 0-87733-850-7). Easi-Bild.

--How to Install a Fireplace, Bk. 674. LC 67-15264. (Illus.). 1978. pap. 7.95 (ISBN 0-87733-674-1). Easi-Bild.

--How to Install Paneling, Make Valances, Cornices. LC 65-25756. 1979. pap. 6.95 (ISBN 0-87733-605-9). Easi-Bild.

--How to Install Paneling, Make Valances, Cornices. rev. ed. LC 65-25756. 1977. lib. bdg. 5.95 (ISBN 0-87733-005-0). Easi-Bild.

--How to Install Protective Alarm Devices. rev ed. LC 72-89141. (Illus.). 1975. lib. bdg. 5.95 (ISBN 0-87733-095-6); pap. 5.95 (ISBN 0-87733-695-4). Easi-Bild.

--How to Install Protective Alarm Devices, Bk. No. 895. rev. ed. LC 83-83077. 176p. 1984. pap. 7.95 (ISBN 0-87733-895-7). Easi-Bild.

--How to Lay Ceramic Tile. rev. ed. LC 66-23067. 1978. pap. 3.50 (ISBN 0-87733-606-7). Easi-Bild.

--How to Modernize a Basement. rev. ed. LC 66-22941. 98p. 1978. lib. bdg. 5.95 (ISBN 0-87733-015-8); pap. 3.50 (ISBN 0-87733-615-6). Easi-Bild.

--How to Modernize a Kitchen, Build Base & Wall Cabinets. LC 79-54720. 210p. 1980. pap. 7.95 (ISBN 0-87733-758-6). Easi-Bild.

--How to Modernize an Attic. rev ed. LC 67-28571. 1974. pap. 3.50 (ISBN 0-87733-665-2). Easi-Bild.

--How to Rehabilitate an Abandoned Building, Bk. L85. LC 73-87513. 258p. 1974. lib. bdg. 6.95 (ISBN 0-87733-085-9). Easi-Bild.

--How to Remodel Buildings. LC 78-55239. 258p. 1978. pap. 7.95 (ISBN 0-87733-585-0). Easi-Bild.

--How to Repair, Refinish, Reupholster. LC 81-68677. 178p. 1982. pap. 6.95 (ISBN 0-87733-823-X). Easi-Bild.

--How to Transform a Garage into Living Space, Bk. 684. LC 72-92125. (Illus.). 128p. 1974. lib. bdg. 5.95 (ISBN 0-87733-084-0); pap. 6.95 (ISBN 0-87733-684-9). Easi-Bild.

--Plumbing Repairs Simplified. rev. ed. LC 67-27691. 1976. lib. bdg. 5.95 (ISBN 0-87733-750-0). Easi-Bild.

--Plumbing Repairs Simplified. LC 82-70274. 1983. pap. 7.95 (ISBN 0-87733-875-2). Easi-Bild.

--Roofing Simplified. LC 81-65487. 176p. 1983. pap. 6.95 (ISBN 0-87733-896-5). Easi-Bild.

--Roofing Simplified. rev. ed. LC 71-99939. 1977. lib. bdg. 5.95 (ISBN 0-87733-096-4). Easi-Bild.

--Roofing Simplified. LC 71-99939. 1979. pap. 5.95 (ISBN 0-87733-696-2). Easi-Bild.

--Scroll Saw Projects, Bk. 756. LC 75-3911. 1975. lib. bdg. 5.95 (ISBN 0-87733-056-5); pap. 5.95 (ISBN 0-87733-756-X). Easi-Bild.

--Stereo Installation Simplified. rev ed. LC 66-28495. Orig. Title: How to Build a Hi-Fi Music Wall. 1975. lib. bdg. 5.95 (ISBN 0-87733-120-0); pap. 3.50 (ISBN 0-87733-612-1). Easi-Bild.

--Toymaking & Children's Furniture Simplified. XRev ed. LC 77-89943. 1982. pap. 7.95 (ISBN 0-87733-771-3). Easi-Bild.

Brann, Eva T. Late Geometric & Protoattic Pottery, Mid Eighth to Late Seventh Century B.C. LC 75-322663. (Athenian Agora Ser: Vol. 8). (Illus.). 1971. Repr. of 1962 ed. 15.00x (ISBN 0-87661-208-7). Am Sch Athens.

--Paradoxes of Education in a Republic. LC 78-10228. 1979. 12.95x (ISBN 0-226-07135-9). U of Chicago Pr.

Brann, M. & Elbogen, I. Festschrift zu Israel Lewy's Siebzigstem Geburtstag. Katz, Steven, ed. LC 79-7157. (Jewish Philosophy, Mysticism & the History of Ideas Ser.). (Ger. & Hebrew.). 1980. Repr. of 1911 ed. lib. bdg. 51.50x (ISBN 0-405-12242-X). Ayer Co Pubs.

Brann, M. & Rosenthal, F. Gedenkbuch zur Erinnerung an David Kaufmann. Katz, Steven, ed. LC 79-7142. (Jewish Philosophy, Mysticism & History of Ideas Ser.). 1980. Repr. of 1900 ed. lib. bdg. 68.50x (ISBN 0-405-12292-6). Ayer Co Pubs.

Brann, William C. Brann, the Iconoclast: Collected Writings, 2 vols. Set. 250.00 (ISBN 0-87968-782-7). Gordon Pr.

--Brann's "Scrap Book". LC 71-104422. Repr. of 1898 ed. lib. bdg. 12.50 (ISBN 0-8398-0171-8). Irvington.

--Complete Works, 12 vols. 2000.00 (ISBN 0-8490-1658-4). Gordon Pr.

Brannan, Carl. Process Systems Development. LC 76-1680. (The Process Engineer's Pocket Handbook Ser.: Vol. 2). 102p. (Orig.). 1983. pap. 9.95x (ISBN 0-87201-713-3). Gulf Pub.

Brannan, D. A. & Clunie, J. G., eds. Aspects of Contemporary Complex Analysis. LC 80-40887. 1981. 75.00 (ISBN 0-12-125950-1). Acad Pr.

Brannan, John, ed. Official Letters of the Military & Naval Officers of the United States, During the War with Great Britain in the Years 1812, 13, 14, & 15: With Some Additional Letters & Documents Elucidating the History of That Period. LC 70-146378. (First American Frontier Ser). 1971. Repr. of 1823 ed. 27.00 (ISBN 0-405-02829-6). Ayer Co Pubs.

Brannan, Joseph D. & Beutel, Frederick K. Beutel's Brannan Negotiable Instruments Law. 7th ed. LC 74-92297. xiii, 1628p. 1971. Repr. of 1948 ed. Set. lib. bdg. 58.75x (ISBN 0-8371-3076-X, BRNI). Greenwood.

Brannen, Jonathan. Approaching the Border. LC 81-11775. (Illus.). 66p. 1982. 30.00 (ISBN 0-916906-42-6); pap. 15.95 (ISBN 0-916906-43-4). Konglomerati.

Brannen, Julia & Collard, Jean. Marriages in Trouble: The Process of Seeking Help. 320p. 1982. 28.00 (ISBN 0-422-78100-2, NO. 3788, Pub. by Tavistock England). Methuen Inc.

Brannen, Noah, jt. auth. see Thorlin, Eldora.

Brannen, Noah S., ed. see Fujiwara, Yoichi.

Brannen, Peter. Authority & Participation in Industry. LC 83-16151. 168p. 1984. 22.50 (ISBN 0-312-06123-4). St Martin.

Brannen, William H. Advertising & Sales Promotion: Cost Effective Techniques for Your Small Business. (Illus.). 247p. 1983. 19.95 (ISBN 0-13-015024-X); pap. 9.95 (ISBN 0-13-015016-9). P-H.

--Practical Marketing for Your Small Retail Business. (Illus.). 272p. 1981. 16.95 (ISBN 0-13-692764-5, Spec); pap. 7.95 (ISBN 0-13-692756-4). P-H.

--Small Business Marketing: A Selected & Annotated Bibliography. LC 78-15082. (American Marketing Association, Bibliography Ser.: No. 31). pap. 21.80 (ISBN 0-317-20070-4, 2023352). Bks Demand UMI.

--Successful Marketing for Your Small Business. LC 78-1116. (Illus.). 1978. 16.95 (ISBN 0-13-863399-1, Spec); pap. 8.95 (ISBN 0-13-863381-9, Spec). P-H.

Branner, H. C. The Story of Borge. Planck, Kristi, tr. from Danish. LC 73-1593. (Library of Scandinavian Literature). 1973. lib. bdg. 27.50x (ISBN 0-8057-3359-0). Irvington.

--Two Minutes of Silence. Vance, Vera L., tr. 244p. 1966. 17.50x (ISBN 0-299-04161-1). U of Wis Pr.

Branner, John C., tr. see Herculano, Alexandre.

Branner, Noah S., tr. see Elliot, William I.

Branner, Robert. Gothic Architecture. LC 61-13690. (Great Ages of World Architecture Ser). 1961. pap. 7.95 (ISBN 0-8076-0332-5). Braziller.

--Manuscript Painting in Paris During the Reign of St. Louis. LC 73-78514. (Studies in the History of Art: Vol. 18). (Illus.). 1977. 90.00x (ISBN 0-520-02462-1). U of Cal Pr.

Branner, Robert, ed. Chartres Cathedral. (Norton Critical Studies in Art History). (Illus.). 1969. pap. 8.95x (ISBN 0-393-09851-6, NortonC). Norton.

Brannigan, Augustine. The Social Basis of Scientific Discoveries. 228p. 1981. 29.95 (ISBN 0-521-23695-9); pap. 11.95 (ISBN 0-521-28163-6). Cambridge U Pr.

Brannigan, Augustine & Goldenberg, Sheldon, eds. Social Responses to Technological Change. LC 84-27934. (Contributions in Sociology Ser.: No. 56). (Illus.). 320p. 1985. lib. bdg. 35.00 (ISBN 0-313-24727-7, BNT/). Greenwood.

Brannigan, Francis, Jr. Fire Hazards in the Construction of Garden Apartments & Town Houses. Tuck, Charles A., ed. LC 76-16714. (Illus.). 1976. incl. tapes & slides 65.00 (ISBN 0-685-73836-1). Natl Fire Prot.

Brannigan, Francis L. Building Construction for the Fire Service: A Fire Officer's Guide. McKinnon, Gordon, ed. (Get Ahead Ser). (Illus.). 87p. 1973. 8.50 (ISBN 0-87765-017-9, FSP-33). Natl Fire Prot.

--Building Construction for the Fire Service. 2nd ed. McKinnon, Gordon P. & Matson, Debra, eds. LC 78-178805. (Illus.). 392p. 1982. text ed. 20.00 (ISBN 0-87765-227-9, FSP-33A). Natl Fire Prot.

Brannigan, Francis L., et al, eds. Fire Investigation Handbook. (National Bureau of Standards Handbook Ser.: No. 134). (Illus.). 197p. 1980. pap. 9.50 (ISBN 0-318-11719-3). Gov Printing Office.

Brannigan, Gary, jt. auth. see Tolor, Alexander.

Brannin, Marilyn. Your Body in Mind. 192p. 1983. pap. 2.95 (ISBN 0-345-29787-3). Ballantine.

Branningan, Marilyn, jt. auth. see Biklen, Sari K.

Brannon. Cincinnati Reds. LC 82-16225. (Baseball Today Ser.). 48p. 1982. 8.95 (ISBN 0-87191-858-7). Creative Ed.

--Cleveland Indians. LC 82-14917. (Baseball Today Ser.). 48p. 1982. 8.95 (ISBN 0-87191-859-5). Creative Ed.

--Los Angeles Dodgers. LC 82-12730. (Baseball Today Ser.). 48p. 1982. 8.95 (ISBN 0-87191-863-3). Creative Ed.

--San Francisco Giants. LC 82-16177. (Baseball Today Ser.). 48p. 1982. 8.95 (ISBN 0-87191-873-0). Creative Ed.

Brannon, Charles. SpeedScript: The Word Processor for the Commodore 64 & VIC-20. Compute Editors, ed. 160p. (Orig.). 1985. pap. 9.95 (ISBN 0-942386-94-9). Compute Pubns.

--SpeedScript: The Word Processor for the Atari. Compute Editors, ed. (Orig.). 1985. pap. 9.95 (ISBN 0-87455-003-3). Compute Pubns.

Brannon, Charles & Martin, Kevin. SpeedScript: The Word Processor for Apple Personal Computers. Compute Editors, ed. (Orig.). 1985. pap. 9.95 (ISBN 0-87455-000-9). Compute Pubns.

Brannon, E., ed. see Larsen, Judith L. & Gull, Carol W.

Brannon, E., ed. see Weinberg, Julia.

Brannon, Emma C. Wayside Blossoms. 77p. 1979. 5.00 (ISBN 0-682-49390-2). Exposition Pr FL.

Brannon, Joan G. North Carolina Sheriffs' Civil Duties: Handling Writs of Execution. 122p. 1980. 5.00 (ISBN 0-686-39455-0). U of NC Inst Gov.

Brannon, Joan G. & Farb, Robert L., eds. Arrest Warrant Forms. 312p. 1984. 16.00 (ISBN 0-686-39456-9). U of NC Inst Gov.

Brannon, Johnnie. Brief Encounters: Short Stories by Johnnie Brannon. LC 83-71996. (Illus.). 110p. (Orig.). 1983. pap. 5.95 (ISBN 0-938232-35-5, Dist. by Baker & Taylor). Winston-Derek.

Brannon, Lil & Knight, Melinda. Writers Writing. LC 82-14587. 192p. (Orig.). 1982. pap. text ed. 9.00x (ISBN 0-86709-045-6). Boynton Cook Pubs.

Brannon, Lil, jt. auth. see Knoblauch, C. H.

Brannon, Robert, jt. auth. see David, Deborah S.

Brannon, Selden. Historic Hampshire: A Symposium of Hampshire County & Its People, Past & Present. 1976. Repr. of 1978 ed. 25.00 (ISBN 0-87012-236-3). McClain.

Brannstrom, Martin. Dentin & Pulp in Restorative Dentistry. (Illus.). 128p. 1982. text ed. 45.00x (ISBN 0-7234-0793-2, Pub. by Wolfe Medical England). Sheridan.

Branover, H., et al, eds. Liquid-Metal & Magnetohydrodynamics. 45.00 (ISBN 0-915928-70-1). AIAA.

Branquart, P., et al. An Analytical Description of CHILL, the CCITT High Level Language. (Lectur Notes in Computer Science Ser.: Vol. 128). 277p. 1982. pap. 19.00 (ISBN 0-387-11196-4). Springer-Verlag.

--An Optimized Translation Process & Its Application to ALGOL 68. LC 75-45092. (Lecture Notes in Computer Science: Vol. 38). 1976. pap. 20.00 (ISBN 0-387-07545-3). Springer-Verlag.

Brans, J. P. Operational Research '84. 1984. 95.00 (ISBN 0-444-87561-1). Elsevier.

Brans, J. P., ed. Operational Research, 1981. 984p. 1982. 127.75 (ISBN 0-444-86223-4, North-Holland). Elsevier.

Branscheid, V., jt. auth. see Bentvelsen, C. L.

Branscombe, Peter, ed. Austrian Life & Literature, Seventeen Eighty to Nineteen Thirty-Eight: Eight Essays. 93p. 1978. 15.00x (ISBN 0-8476-6006-0). Rowman.

Branscombe, Peter, jt. ed. see Badura-Skoda, Eva.

Branscum, Robbie. The Adventures of Johnny May. LC 83-49464. (Illus.). 128p. (gr. 4-7). 1984. 11.06i (ISBN 0-06-020614-4); PLB 10.89g (ISBN 0-06-020615-2). HarpJ.

--Cheater & Flitter Dick. LC 83-5768. 112p. (gr. 3-7). 1983. 10.95 (ISBN 0-670-21350-0, Viking Kestrel). Viking.

--Me & Jim Luke. (YA) (gr. 8-10). 1975. pap. 1.75 (ISBN 0-380-00354-6, 52688-3). Avon.

--The Murder of Hound Dog Bates. LC 82-1911. 96p. (gr. 3-7). 1982. 9.95 (ISBN 0-670-49521-2). Viking.

--The Saving of P.S. 128p. (gr. 6 up). 1979. pap. 1.25 (ISBN 0-440-49099-5, YB). Dell.

--Spud Tackett & the Angel of Doom. 128p. (gr. 3-8). 1983. 11.50 (ISBN 0-670-66582-7). Viking.

--Toby Alone. 96p. 1980. pap. 1.75 (ISBN 0-380-50781-1, 50781-1, Flare). Avon.

--Toby & Johnny Joe. 80p. 1981. pap. 1.75 (ISBN 0-380-52670-0, 52670-0, Flare). Avon.

--Toby, Granny & George. (YA) (gr. 7 up). 1977. pap. 1.75 (ISBN 0-380-01686-9, 56325-8, Flare). Avon.

Bransden, B. H. Atomic Collision Theory. 2nd ed. (Illus.). 500p. 1970. text ed. 39.95 (ISBN 0-8053-1181-5). Benjamin-Cummings.

Bransden, B. H. & Joachain, C. J. Physics of Atoms & Molecules. LC 80-41903. (Illus.). 690p. (Orig.). 1982. pap. text ed. 26.00x (ISBN 0-582-44401-2). Longman.

Bransden, B. H. & Moorhouse, R. Gordon. The Pion-Nucleon System. (Illus.). 552p. 1973. 52.00x (ISBN 0-691-08115-8); pap. 15.50x (ISBN 0-691-08129-8). Princeton U Pr.

Bransford, J., jt. ed. see Shaw, R.

Bransford, Jim, jt. auth. see Baca, Leonard.

Bransford, John D. Human Cognition: Learning, Understanding & Remembering. 1979. pap. text ed. write for info. (ISBN 0-534-00699-X). Wadsworth Pub.

Bransford, John D. & Stein, Barry S. The Ideal Problem Solver: A Guide to Improving Thinking, Learning, & Creativity. (Illus.). 150p. 16.95 (ISBN 0-7167-1668-2); pap. 8.95 (ISBN 0-7167-1669-0). W H Freeman.

Bransford, Kent. The No-Nonsense Guide to Get You into Medical School. LC 78-11160. 1979. pap. 3.95 (ISBN 0-671-18353-2). Monarch Pr.

Bransford, Stephen. Riders of the Long Road. LC 84-7984. 312p. 1984. 15.95 (ISBN 0-385-19399-8). Doubleday.

Bransom, James S. Tragedy of King Lear. LC 71-153306. Repr. of 1934 ed. 10.50 (ISBN 0-404-01063-6). AMS Pr.

Bransom, Paul. All Unplanned: Memoirs of the Golden Age of Illustration. LC 83-81645. (Illus.). 287p. (Orig.). 1984. pap. 7.00 (ISBN 0-9611798-0-5). H I Hays.

Branson. Macroeconomica. 2nd ed. 436p. (Span.). 1981. pap. text ed. write for info. (Pub. by HarLA Mexico). Har-Row.

--Rangeland Hydrology. 2nd ed. 340p. 15.00 (ISBN 0-318-16600-3). Soc Range Mgmt.

Branson, Branley A. & Batch, Donald L. Fishes of the Red River Drainage, Eastern Kentucky. LC 73-80459. (Illus.). 76p. 1974. pap. 5.00x (ISBN 0-8131-1295-8). U Pr of Ky.

Branson, Dorothy. Methods in Clinical Bacteriology: A Manual of Tests & Procedures. 240p. 1972. spiral bdg. 14.75x (ISBN 0-398-02241-0). C C Thomas.

--Microbiology for the Small Laboratory. (Illus.). 80p. 1972. spiral 10.50x (ISBN 0-398-02576-2). C C Thomas.

--Procedure Manual for Clinical Bacteriology: Annotated. 368p. 1982. spiral 39.75x (ISBN 0-398-04660-3). C C Thomas.

Branson, Farrel A. Vegetation Changes on Western Rangelands. (Range Monographs: No. 2). (Illus.). 1985. avail. (ISBN 0-9603692-2-8). Soc Range Mgmt.

Branson, Farrell A., et al. Rangeland Hydrology. 2nd ed. 352p. 1981. pap. text ed. 15.00 (ISBN 0-8403-2408-1). Kendall-Hunt.

Branson, Gary D. Home Maintenance & Repair: Walls, Ceilings, & Floors. (Illus.). 1979. pap. 6.95 (ISBN 0-672-23281-2, 23281). Audel.

Branson, Joan C. & Lenox, Margaret. Hotel, Hostel & Hospital Housekeeping. 4th ed. 310p. 1982. pap. 18.95X (ISBN 0-7131-0581-X). Intl Ideas.

Branson, John J., III. Home Word Processing Start-Up Guide: How to Start Your Own Business. (Illus.). 160p. 1985. pap. 11.95 (ISBN 0-13-392986-8). P H.

Branson, Margaret & Coombs, Fred. Civics for Today. (Illus.). (gr. 7-9). 1980. text ed. 18.92 (ISBN 0-395-26201-1); tchr's ed. 21.92 (ISBN 0-395-26202-X); wkbk. 5.76 (ISBN 0-395-26203-8). HM.

Branson, Margaret S. & Torney-Purta, Judith, eds. International Human Rights, Society, & the Schools. LC 82-60695. (Illus.). 111p. (Orig.). pap. 7.25 (ISBN 0-87986-044-8). Nat Coun Soc Studies.

Branson, Mark L., ed. The Reader's Guide to the Best Evangelical Books. LC 82-48205. 208p. (Orig.). 1982. pap. 5.72i (ISBN 0-06-061046-8, RD-388, HarpR). Har-Row.

Branson, Mark L., ed. see Aune, David E.

Branson, Mark L., ed. see Goldingay, John.

Branson, Mary K. It's Not Easy Being Small. LC 81-65823. (ps). 1981. bds. 5.95 (ISBN 0-8054-4160-3, 4241-60). Broadman.

Branson, Noreen. History of the Communist Party of Great Britain, 1927-1941. 350p. 1985. 27.00 (ISBN 0-85315-611-5, Pub. by Salem Acad). Merrimack Pub Cir.

Branson, O. T. Apache Indian Color Book. 32p. 1983. pap. 1.95 (ISBN 0-918080-13-4). Treasure Chest.

--Fetishes & Carvings of the Southwest. (Illus.). 1976. pap. 7.95 (ISBN 0-918080-04-5). Treasure Chest.

--Indian Dancer Color Book. 32p. 1982. pap. 1.95 (ISBN 0-918080-03-7). Treasure Chest.

--Indian Pueblo Color Book. 32p. 1984. pap. 1.95 (ISBN 0-918080-10-X). Treasure Chest.

--Kachina Color Book. 32p. 1982. pap. 1.95 (ISBN 0-918080-02-9). Treasure Chest.

--Navajo Color Book. 32p. 1983. pap. 1.95 (ISBN 0-918080-06-1). Treasure Chest.

--Papaco Color Book. 32p. 1983. pap. 1.95 (ISBN 0-918080-09-6). Treasure Chest.

--Turquoise: The Gem of the Centuries. (Illus.). 1975. 12.95 (ISBN 0-918080-00-2); pap. 7.95 (ISBN 0-918080-01-0). Treasure Chest.

--What You Need to Know about Your Gold & Silver. (Illus.). 56p. (Orig.). 1980. pap. 4.95 (ISBN 0-918080-44-4). Treasure Chest.

Branson, Oscar T. Indian Jewelry Making, Vol. 1. (Illus.). 1977. pap. 8.95 (ISBN 0-918080-15-0). Treasure Chest.

--Indian Jewelry Making, Vol. 2. (Illus.). 1979. pap. 8.95 (ISBN 0-918080-17-7). Treasure Chest.

Branson, Robert. Beacon Small-Group Bible Studies, Genesis, Pt. I: How It All Began. Wolf, Earl C., ed. 96p. (Orig.). 1984. pap. 2.50 (ISBN 0-8341-0935-2). Beacon Hill.

--Beacon Small-Group Bible Studies, Isaiah: Preparing the Way of the Lord. Wolf, Earl C., ed. 96p. (Orig.). 1985. pap. 2.50 (ISBN 0-8341-0961-1). Beacon Hill.

--God's Word in Man's Language. 83p. (Orig.). 1980. pap. 2.75 (ISBN 0-8341-0659-0). Beacon Hill.

Branson, Robert E. & Norvell, Douglas G. Introduction to Agricultural Marketing. (Illus.). 544p. 1983. text ed. 35.95 (ISBN 0-07-007241-8). McGraw.

Branson, Roy, jt. ed. see Veatch, Robert M.

Branson, Thomas P., tr. see Boltyanskii, Vladimir G. & Gokhberg, Izrail T.

Branson, Thomas P., tr. see Fomin, S. V.

Branson, Thomas P., tr. see Solodovnikov, A. S.

Branson, William H. Macroeconomic Theory & Policy. 2nd ed. (Illus.). 1979. text ed. 30.50 scp (ISBN 0-06-040936-3, HarpC). Har-Row.

Branson, William H. & Litvack, James M. Macroeconomics. 2nd ed. 407p. 1981. text ed. 27.50 scp (ISBN 0-06-040937-1, HarpC); Instr's. manual avail. (ISBN 0-06-360895-2). Har-Row.

Branstatter, H., jt. ed. see Hiebsch, H.

Bransten, Richard, jt. auth. see McKenney, Ruth.

Branster, Mark, jt. auth. see Prahl, Earl J.

Branston, Brian. Gods & Heroes from Viking Mythology. LC 81-14540. (World Mythologies Ser.). (Illus.). 156p. 1982. 15.95 (ISBN 0-8052-3794-1). Schocken.

--Gods of the North. (Illus.). 1980. pap. 8.95 (ISBN 0-500-27177-1). Thames Hudson.

--The Lost Gods of England. (Illus.). 278p. 1984. pap. 10.95f (ISBN 0-500-27321-9). Thames Hudson.

Brant, jt. auth. see Kravitz, W.

Brant & Fuller, eds. Memorial Record of Alabama: A Concise Account of the State's Political, Military,Professional & Industrial Progress, Together with the Personal Memoirs of Many of Its People, 2 vols. LC 75-45434. (Illus.). 1976. Repr. of 1893 ed. 37.50 ea. Vol. 1 (ISBN 0-87152-227-6). Vol. 2 (ISBN 0-87152-228-4). Set. 75.00 (ISBN 0-87152-309-4). Reprint.

Brant, Beth. Mohawk Trail. 96p. 1985. 13.95 (ISBN 0-932379-03-6); pap. 6.95 (ISBN 0-932379-02-8). Firebrand Bks.

Brant, Beth, ed. A Gathering of Spirit: Writing & Art by North American Indian Women. (Illus.). 240p. (Orig.). 1984. pap. 7.95 (ISBN 0-931103-00-2). Sinister Wisdom Bks.

Brant, Billy G. The College Radio Handbook. (Illus.). 1981. 14.95 (ISBN 0-8306-9763-2, 763). TAB Bks.

Brant, Carroll A. Electronics for Communication. 800p. 1983. text ed. 31.95 (ISBN 0-574-21575-1, 13-4575); instr's. guide avail. (ISBN 0-574-21576-X, 13-4576). SRA.

Brant, Charles S. Jim Whitewolf: The Life of a Kiowa Apache. LC 67-25596. 144p. (Orig.). 1969. pap. 3.75 (ISBN 0-486-22015-X). Dover.

Brant, David A., ed. Solution Properties of Polysaccharides. LC 81-236. (ACS Symposium Ser.: No. 150). 1981. 57.95 (ISBN 0-8412-0609-0). Am Chemical.

Brant, George. Introductory Animal Science. 1980. perfect binding 9.95 (ISBN 0-88252-112-8). Paladin Hse.

Brant, H. A. Childbirth for Men. (Illus.). 200p. 1985. pap. 7.95 (ISBN 0-19-261450-9). Oxford U Pr.

Brant, Michelle. Timeless Walks in San Francisco: A Historical Walking Guide to the City. 4th rev. ed. (Illus.). 90p. 1985. pap. 5.95 (ISBN 0-9611346-0-7). Brant.

Brant, Roxanne. Ministering to the Lord. 80p. (Orig.). 1973. pap. 3.95 (ISBN 0-89228-031-X). Impact Bks MO.

Brant, Russ. Coal Resources of the Big Sandy District, Kentucky. (Energy Resource Ser.). (Illus., Orig.). 1983. pap. text ed. 5.00 (ISBN 0-86607-020-6). Inst Mining & Minerals.

--Coal Resources of the Hazard District, Kentucky. (Energy Resource Ser.). 60p. 1983. pap. text ed. 5.00 (ISBN 0-86607-019-2). Inst Mining & Minerals.

--Coal Resources of the Licking River District, Kentucky. (Energy Resource Ser.). (Illus.). 60p. 1983. pap. text ed. 10.00 (ISBN 0-86607-018-4). Inst Mining & Minerals.

--Coal Resources of the Upper Cumberland District, Kentucky. Pettit, Rhonda & Weber, Camille, eds. (Energy Resource Ser.). (Illus.). 65p. 1983. pap. text ed. 5.00 (ISBN 0-86607-021-4, IMMR83-088). Inst Mining & Minerals.

Brant, Russell A. Coal Resources of the Princess District, Kentucky. Pettit, Rhonda & Cobb, James, eds. (Energy Resource Ser.). (Illus.). 50p. (Orig.). 1982. pap. text ed. 10.00 (ISBN 0-86607-011-7). Inst Mining & Minerals.

Brant, Sandra & Cullman, Elissa. Small Folk: A Celebration of Childhood in America. (Illus.). 192p. 1981. 29.95 (ISBN 0-525-93131-7). Dutton.

Brant, Sebastian. Narrenschiff. Von Geodeke, Karl, ed. LC 71-181916. (BCL Ser. II). Repr. of 1872 ed. 17.50 (ISBN 0-404-01064-4). AMS Pr.

--Ship of Fools, 2 Vols. Jamieson, T. H., ed. Barclay, Alexander, tr. LC 14-11937. Repr. of 1874 ed. 75.00 (ISBN 0-404-01065-2). AMS Pr.

--Shyp of Folys of the Worlde. Barcley, Alexander, tr. LC 74-25743. (English Experience Ser.: No. 229). 1970. Repr. of 1509 ed. 76.00 (ISBN 90-221-0229-7). Walter J Johnson.

--Tugent Spyl: Nach der Ausgabe des Magister Johann Winckel von Strassburg. Roloff, Hans G., ed. (Ausgaben Deutscher Literatur des 15 bis 18 Jahrh). (Ger). 1968. 23.60x (ISBN 3-11-000350-3). De Gruyter.

Brantenberg, Gerd. Egalia's Daughters. Mackay, Louis, tr. from Norwegian. 270p. (Orig.). 1985. 15.95 (ISBN 0-931188-35-0); pap. 8.95 (ISBN 0-931188-34-2). Seal Pr Feminist.

Branthwaite, M. A., jt. auth. see Gothard, J. W.

Brantingham, Patricia, jt. auth. see Brantingham, Paul J.

Brantingham, Patricia L. & Brantingham, Paul J. Environmental Criminology. (Sage Focus Editions). (Illus.). 288p. 1981. 28.00 (ISBN 0-686-75623-1); pap. 14.00 (ISBN 0-8039-1678-7). Sage.

Brantingham, Patricia L. & Blomberg, Thomas G., eds. Courts & Diversion: Policy & Operations Studies. (Sage Research Progress Ser. in Criminology: Vol. 14). (Illus.). 144p. 1979. 20.00 (ISBN 0-8039-1321-4); pap. 9.95 (ISBN 0-8039-1322-2). Sage.

Brantingham, Paul J. & Brantingham, Patricia. Patterns in Crime. (Illus.). 448p. 1984. text ed. write for info. (ISBN 0-02-313520-4). Macmillan.

Brantingham, Paul J., jt. auth. see Brantingham, Patricia L.

Brantingham, Paul J., jt. auth. see Faust, Frederic L.

Brantingham, Paul J. & Kress, Jack M., eds. Structure, Law, & Power: Essays in the Sociology of Law. LC 79-18127. (Sage Research Progress Ser. in Criminology: Vol. 13). (Illus.). 160p. 1979. 20.00 (ISBN 0-8039-1318-4); pap. 9.95 (ISBN 0-8039-1319-2). Sage.

Brantl, George. Catholicism. LC 61-15501. (Great Religions of Modern Man Ser). 1961. 8.95 (ISBN 0-8076-0162-4). Braziller.

Brantley & Haught. Probate, Brantley & Haught's, Arkansas. 149p. 1984. 29.95 (ISBN 0-317-18683-3). Harrison Co GA.

Brantley, Cynthia. The Giriama & Colonial Resistance in Kenya, 1800-1920. LC 81-524. 216p. 1982. 36.00x (ISBN 0-520-04216-6). U of Cal Pr.

Brantley, Jill, jt. ed. see Maiolo, Joseph.

Brantley, Richard E. Locke, Wesley & the Method of English Romanticism. LC 83-26026. 311p. 1984. 30.00 (ISBN 0-8130-0783-6). U Presses Fla.

--Wordsworth's "Natural Methodism". LC 74-20078. 224p. 1975. 22.00x (ISBN 0-300-01834-7). Yale U Pr.

Brantley, W. H., Jr. Battle of Horseshoe Bend. (Illus.). 1955. pap. 3.75 (ISBN 0-87651-205-8). Southern U Pr.

Brantley, William H. Three Capitals: A Book About the First Three Capitals of Alabama-St. Stephens, Huntsville, & Cahawba, 1818-1826. LC 76-28483. (A Bicentennial Bk.). (Illus.). 256p. 1976. Repr. of 1947 ed. 13.95 (ISBN 0-8173-5231-7). U of Ala Pr.

Brantley, William H., ed. see Soldano, B. A.

Brantlinger, Patrick. Bread & Circuses: Theories of Mass Culture As Social Decay. LC 83-45134. 312p. (Orig.). 1985. 26.95x (ISBN 0-8014-1598-5); pap. text ed. 9.95x (ISBN 0-8014-9338-2). Cornell U Pr.

--The Spirit of Reform: British Literature & Politics, 1832-1867. 1977. 17.50x (ISBN 0-674-83315-5). Harvard U Pr.

Brantly, J. E. History of Oil Well Drilling. LC 78-149757. (Illus.). 1548p. 1971. 59.95x (ISBN 0-87201-634-X). Gulf Pub.

Brantner, John, jt. auth. see Good, Patricia K.

Brantome, Pierre B. De see De Brantome, Pierre B.

Brantome, Pierre D. Oeuvres Completes de Pierre De Bourdeille, 11 Vols. Set. 415.00 (ISBN 0-384-05542-7); Set. pap. 350.00 (ISBN 0-384-05545-1). Johnson Repr.

Branton, P. E., et al. Polyoma Virus: Current Research, Vol. 2. LC 73-8643. (Oncogenic Viruses Ser.). 160p. 1973. text ed. 27.50x (ISBN 0-8422-7118-X). Irvington.

Branton, Thomas M. How to Incorporate Your Texas Business. LC 83-22634. (Illus.). 112p. (Orig.). 1984. pap. 8.95x (ISBN 0-87201-423-1). Gulf Pub.

Brants, Victor. Economie Politique au Moyen-Age: Esquisse des Theories Economiques Professees par les Ecrivains des Treisieme et Quatorzieme Siecles. LC 75-123598. (Research & Source Ser.: No. 510). (Fr). 1970. Repr. of 1895 ed. lib. bdg. 23.50 (ISBN 0-8337-0354-4). B Franklin.

Branyan, Lawrence, et al. Worcester Blue & White Porcelain, 1751-1790. (Illus.). 367p. 1981. 105.00 (ISBN 0-09-144060-2, Pub. by Barrie & Jenkins England). Seven Hills Bks.

--Worchester Blue & White Porcelain: 1751-1890. (Illus.). 364p. 1982. 100.00 (ISBN 0-8390-0288-2). Abner Schram Ltd.

Branyan, Robert L. The Eisenhower Administration, Nineteen Fifty-Three to Nineteen Sixty-One: A Documentary History, 2 vols. LC 71-164935. 1971. Set. lib. bdg. 95.00 (ISBN 0-313-20126-9, BREAD). Greenwood.

Branyon, Alexandra, jt. auth. see Lee, Karen.

Branyon, Brenda. Outstanding Women Who Promoted the Concept of the Unified School Library & Audio Visual Program. 375p. 1981. 27.50x (ISBN 0-931510-08-2). Hi Willow.

Branzi, Andrea. The Hot House: Italian New Wave Design. LC 84-7929. (Illus.). 160p. 1984. 25.00 (ISBN 0-262-02211-7). MIT Pr.

Braodbent, Donald, jt. ed. see Pribram, Karl.

Braque, George, jt. auth. see Prevert, Jacques.

Braque, Georges. Catalog Raisonne, 1882-1963: An American Tribute. Richardson, J. R., ed. 22.00 (ISBN 0-686-91878-9). Newbury Bks.

--Illustrated Notebooks, 1917-1955. Appelbaum, Stanley, tr. Orig. Title: Cahier De Georges Braque. (Illus., Fr.). 1971. pap. 6.00 (ISBN 0-486-20232-1). Dover.

Braque, Georges, et al, illus. Hommage a Georges Braque. (Illus.). 1964. deluxe ed. 300.00x (ISBN 0-915346-34-6). A Wofsy Fine Arts.

Braquet, P., et al, eds. Prostaglandins & Membrane Ion Transport. (Advances in Ion Transport Regulation Ser.). (Illus.). 430p. 1985. text ed. 59.50 (ISBN 0-88167-052-9). Raven.

Brara, J. S. The Political Economy of Rural Development. 274p. 1983. text ed. 14.25x (ISBN 0-391-02981-9, Pub. by Allied Pub India). Humanities.

Braren, Ken, jt. auth. see Griffith, Roger.

Braroe, Niels W. Indian & White: Self-Image & Interaction in a Canadian Plains Community. LC 74-25927. (Illus.). 1975. 17.50x (ISBN 0-8047-0877-0); pap. 5.95 (ISBN 0-8047-1028-7, SP-152). Stanford U Pr.

Bras, Monique. Your Guide to French Pronunciation. (Illus.). 231p. 1975. pap. text ed. 14.50 (ISBN 2-03-043101-X, 3819). Larousse.

Bras, Rafael & Rodriquez-Itube, I. Hydraulic Analysis & Synthesis. 704p. 1985. text ed. 42.95 (ISBN 0-201-05865-0). Addison-Wesley.

Brasch, Charles. Charles Brasch Collected Poems. Roddick, Alan, ed. (Illus.). 1984. 32.50x (ISBN 0-19-558105-9). Oxford U Pr.

--Indirections. (Illus.). 1980. 35.00x (ISBN 0-19-558050-8). Oxford U Pr.

Brasch, Ila W. & Brasch, Walter M. A Comprehensive Annotated Bibliography of American Black English. LC 73-83908. pap. 75.80 (ISBN 0-317-10312-1, 2051635). Bks Demand UMI.

Brasch, James D. & Sigman, Joseph. Hemingway's Library: A Composite Record. LC 80-8488. 1981. lib. bdg. 91.00 (ISBN 0-8240-9499-9). Garland Pub.

Brasch, Walter M. Black English & the Mass Media. LC 81-2762. 376p. 1981. lib. bdg. 25.00x (ISBN 0-87023-335-1). U of Mass Pr.

--Black English & the Mass Media. 376p. 1984. pap. text ed. 13.50 (ISBN 0-8191-3978-5). U Pr of Amer.

--Cartoon Monikers: An Insight into the Animation Industry. LC 83-72011. (Illus.). 150p. 1983. 21.95 (ISBN 0-87972-243-6); pap. 9.95 (ISBN 0-87972-244-4). Bowling Green Univ.

--Columbia County Place Names. (Illus.). 232p. 1982. 15.00 (ISBN 0-88023-028-2). Columbia County Hist Soc.

Brasch, Walter M., jt. auth. see Brasch, Ila W.

Brascho, Donn J. & Shawker, Thomas H. Abdominal Ultrasound in the Cancer Patient. LC 80-15838. (Diagnostic & Therapeutic Radiology Ser.). 414p. 1980. 65.00 (ISBN 0-471-01742-6, Pub. by Wiley Med). Wiley.

Brase, Charles & Brase, Corinne. Understandable Statistics: Concepts & Methods. 1983. text ed. 22.95 (ISBN 0-669-05387-2); instrs'. manual with tests 1.95 (ISBN 0-669-05388-0); computer applications to accompany understandable stat. 8.95 (ISBN 0-669-07543-4). Heath.

Brase, Charles H. & Brase, Corrine P. College Algebra. 544p. 1982. text ed. 22.95 (ISBN 0-669-02432-5); instr's guide 1.95 (ISBN 0-669-02433-3). Heath.

Brase, Charles H., jt. auth. see Brase, Corrinne P.

Brase, Corrine P., jt. auth. see Brase, Charles H.

Brase, Corrinne, jt. auth. see Brase, Charles.

Brase, Corrinne P. & Brase, Charles H. Basic Algebra for College Students. LC 75-26093. (Illus.). 480p. 1976. text ed. 24.95 (ISBN 0-395-20656-1); instructional options guide & solutions manual 1.90 (ISBN 0-395-20655-3). HM.

Braselle, Keefe. Cannibals. 1971. pap. 1.25 (ISBN 0-380-01084-4, 08979). Avon.

Brasfield, Philip & Elliot, Jeffrey M. Deathman Pass Me by: Two Years on Death Row. LC 82-4126. (Borgo Bioviews Ser.: No. 3). (Illus.). 96p. 1983. lib. bdg. 13.95x (ISBN 0-89370-164-5); pap. text ed. 5.95x (ISBN 0-89370-264-1). Borgo Pr.

Brash, Donald T. American Investment in Australian Industry. LC 66-31366. 1966. 22.50x (ISBN 0-674-02500-8). Harvard U Pr.

Brashear, H. Robert & Raney, R. Beverly. Shands' Handbook of Orthopaedic Surgery. 9th ed. LC 78-65. 548p. 1978. text ed. 43.95 (ISBN 0-8016-4082-2). Mosby.

Brashear, William R. The Gorgon's Head: A Study in Tragedy & Despair. LC 76-49155. 176p. 1977. 14.00x (ISBN 0-8203-0417-4). U of Ga Pr.

--Living Will: A Study of Tennyson & 19th Century Subjectivism. (Studies in English Literature: No. 52). (Orig.). 1969. text ed. 12.00x (ISBN 0-686-22445-0). Mouton.

Brashears, Deya. Dribble Drabble: Art Experiences for Young Children. rev. ed. (Illus.). 120p. pap. 9.95 (ISBN 0-9614717-0-0). Deya Brashears.

Brasher, John L., ed. see Warren, J. S., Jr.

Brasher, Nell. Daddy Poured the Coffee. LC 77-28503. 1978. pap. 4.95 (ISBN 0-88289-156-1). Pelican.

Brasher, Ruth E. & Garrison, Carolyn L. Modern Household Equipment. 512p. 1982. text ed. write for info. (ISBN 0-02-340500-7). Macmillan.

Brasher, Thomas L. Whitman As Editor of the Brooklyn Daily Eagle. LC 70-91872. 265p. 1970. 12.95x (ISBN 0-8143-1408-2). Wayne St U Pr.

Brasher, Thomas L., ed. see Whitman, Walt.

Brashers, Charles. Creative Writing Handbook. 1984. pap. 6.95 (ISBN 0-933362-04-8). Assoc Creative Writers.

--A Snug Little Purchase: How Richard Henderson Bought Kaintuckee from the Cherokees in 1775. LC 78-74150. (Illus.). 1979. 7.95 (ISBN 0-933362-01-3); pap. 4.95 (ISBN 0-933362-02-1). Assoc Creative Writers.

--Whatta Ya Mean, "Get Outa That Dirty Hole"? I Live Here! (Orig.). 1974. pap. 1.50 (ISBN 0-930866-00-2). Helix Hse.

Brashers, H. C. Other Side of Love: Two Novellas. LC 63-11820. 88p. (Orig.). 1963. pap. 3.50 (ISBN 0-8040-0237-1, 82-71611, Pub. by Swallow). Ohio U Pr.

Brashers, Kerstin. Sing the Cows Home: Folklore of Swedish Mountain Dairy Farms. (Illus.). 248p. (Orig.). 1982. pap. 10.00 (ISBN 0-933362-08-0). Assoc Creative Writers.

Brashier, D. LIX. 248p. 1985. 12.95 (ISBN 0-8059-2963-0). Dorrance.

Brasholz, Anton. Lexikon der Anstrichtechnik, Vol. 2. (Ger.). 1975. 52.50 (ISBN 3-7667-0338-2, M-7280). French & Eur.

Brasier, M. D. Microfossils. (Illus., Orig.). 1980. text ed. 30.00x (ISBN 0-04-562001-6); pap. text ed. 15.95x (ISBN 0-04-562002-4). Allen Unwin.

Brasier, M. D., jt. auth. see Neale, J. M.

Brasier, Virginia. Sand Watcher. 1974. 5.00 (ISBN 0-8233-0211-3). Golden Quill.

Brasil, Emanuel, ed. Brazilian Poetry, Nineteen Fifty to Nineteen Eighty. Smith, William J. 160p. 1983. 25.00x (ISBN 0-8195-5075-2); pap. 9.95 (ISBN 0-8195-6083-9). Wesleyan U Pr.

Brasil, Emanuel, jt. ed. see Bishop, Elizabeth.

Brasil, JoAnne. Escape from Billy's Bar-B-Que. 140p. 1985. 14.95 (ISBN 0-931125-01-4); pap. 8.95 (ISBN 0-931125-02-2). Wild Trees Press.

Brasillach, Robert. Youth Goes Over. 59.95 (ISBN 0-8490-1347-X). Gordon Pr.

Brasillach, Robert, jt. auth. see Bardeche, Maurice.

Braskamp, Larry. Evaluating Teaching Effectiveness. LC 84-9942. 136p. 1984. 17.95 (ISBN 0-8039-2341-4); pap. 8.95 (ISBN 0-8039-2342-2). Sage.

Braslow, jt. auth. see Goldberg.

Brasmer, Timothy H. The Acutely Traumatized Small Animal Patient. (Major Problems in Veterinary Medicine Ser.: Vol. 2). (Illus.). 192p. 1984. 29.50 (ISBN 0-7216-1917-7). Saunders.

Brasnett, Clive. English for Engineers. 1969. pap. 6.95x (ISBN 0-423-84130-0, NO.2140). Methuen Inc.

--English for Medical Students. 1976. pap. 6.95x (ISBN 0-423-49760-X, NO. 2771). Methuen Inc.

Brasol, Boris. Elements of Crime: Psycho-Social Interpretation. 2nd ed. LC 69-16226. (Criminology, Law Enforcement, & Social Problems Ser.: No. 93). 1969. Repr. of 1931 ed. 20.00x (ISBN 0-87585-093-6). Patterson Smith.

--The World at the Crossroads. 75.00 (ISBN 0-8490-1333-X). Gordon Pr.

Brasol, Boris, tr. see Dostoievsky, Feodor.

Brass, George A., jt. auth. see Castaldi, Cosmo R.

Brass, L. J., et al. Plants Collected by the Vernay Nyasaland Expedition of 1946: Introduction: Musi, Pteridophyta, Gymnospermae, Angiospermae, Vol. 8(3) (Memoirs of the New York Botanical Garden Series). 96p. 1953. 10.00 (ISBN 0-317-35521-X). NY Botanical.

Brass, Paul. Caste, Faction & Party in Indian Politics, Vol. 1: Faction & Party. 1985. 28.50x (ISBN 0-8364-1299-0, Pub. by Chanakya India). South Asia Bks.

Brass, Paul, ed. Ethnic Groups & the State. LC 84-15688. (Illus.). 352p. 1985. 27.50x (ISBN 0-389-20528-1, 08090). B&N Imports.

Brass, Paul R. & Franda, Marcus F., eds. Radical Politics in South Asia. (Studies in Communism, Revisionism, & Revolution: No.19). 475p. 1973. 30.00x (ISBN 0-262-02099-8). MIT Pr.

Brass, Richard J., ed. see National Council of Staff, Program & Organizational Development.

Brassai. The Secret Paris of the Thirties. Miller, Richard, tr. LC 76-9976. 1977. pap. 16.95 (ISBN 0-394-73384-3). Pantheon.

Brassai, photos by. Jean Rhys: The Complete Novels. 1985. 25.00 (ISBN 0-393-02226-9). Norton.

Brasseaux, Carl A., jt. auth. see Conrad, Glenn R.

Brasseaux, Carl A., ed. see De Villiers du Terrage, Marc.

Brassel, Helen. The Natural Foods Recipe Book: 800 Low Calorie Dishes to Help You Lose Weight. LC 83-12314. 320p. 1983. 16.95 (ISBN 0-668-05626-6); pap. 9.95 (ISBN 0-668-05631-2). Arco.

Brassell, Tim. Tom Stoppard: An Assessment. LC 83-40126. 220p. 1985. 19.95 (ISBN 0-312-80888-7). St Martin.

Brasselle, Keefe. The Barracudas. 1975. pap. 1.50 (ISBN 0-380-01040-2, 14639). Avon.

Brasser, Ted J. Bo'jou, Neejee: Profiles of Canadian Indian Art. (Illus.). 1976. pap. 16.95 (ISBN 0-660-00008-3, 56283-2, Pub. by Natl Mus Canada). U of Chicago Pr.

Brasseur, Guy & Solomon, Susan. Aeronomy of the Middle Atmosphere: Chemistry & Physics of the Stratosphere & Mesophere. (Atmospheric Sciences Library). 464p. 1984. lib. bdg. 44.00 (ISBN 90-277-1767-2, Pub. by Reidel Holland). Kluwer Academic.

Brasseur De Bourbourg, Charles E. Histoire Du Canada, De Son Eglise et De Ses Missions Depuis la Decouverte De L'Amerique Jusqu'a Nos Jours, 2 vols. (Canadiana Before 1867 Ser). (Fr). Repr. of 1852 ed. Set. 50.00 (ISBN 0-384-05570-2). Johnson Repr.

Brasseur De Bourbourg, E. Ch. Histoire De Canada, De Son Eglise et De Ses Missions. (Canadiana Avant 1867: No. 4). 1968. 44.40x (ISBN 90-2796-333-9). Mouton.

Brassey. A Voyage in the Sunbeam. (Travel Classics Ser.). 324p. 1985. lib. bdg. 19.95 (ISBN 0-7126-0336-0, Pub. by Century Pubs UK). Hippocrene Bks.

Brassey, Thomas A. Problems of Empire. 2nd ed. LC 75-118478. 1971. Repr. of 1913 ed. 21.00x (ISBN 0-8046-1227-7, Pub. by Kennikat). Assoc Faculty Pr.

Brassington, William S. Shakespeare's Homeland. LC 75-39522. Repr. of 1903 ed. 15.00 (ISBN 0-404-01068-7). AMS Pr.

Brassley, Paul. Agricultural Economy of Northumberland & Durham in the Period 1640-1750. LC 84-45996. (British Economic History Ser.). 230p. 1985. lib. bdg. 25.00 (ISBN 0-8240-6676-6). Garland Pub.

Brassy, Thomas. Jack Gould. (Claredon Biography Ser.). (Illus.). pap. 3.50 (ISBN 0-912729-15-5). Newbury Bk.

Brastow, Lewis O. Representative Modern Preachers. facs. ed. LC 68-57306. (Essay Index Reprint Ser). 1904. 20.00 (ISBN 0-8369-0101-0). Ayer Co Pubs.

Brastow, Virginia, rev. by see Neville, Amelia R.

Brasunas, Anton De see De Brasunas, Anton & Stansbury, E. E.

Braswell, David, jt. auth. see Logan, Gerald E.

Braswell, George W., Jr. Understanding World Religions. LC 81-65828. (Orig.). 1983. pap. 7.95 (ISBN 0-8054-6605-3). Broadman.

Braswell, J. & Petersen, N. An Investigation of Item Obsolescence in the Scholastic Aptitude Test. 1977. 5.00 (ISBN 0-87447-054-4, 251706). College Bd.

Braswell, James S. & Owens, Douglas T. Mathematics Tests Available in the United States & Canada. 32p. 1981. 2.50 (ISBN 0-87353-197-3). NCTM.

Braswell, Laurel N. Western Manuscripts from Classical Antiquity to the Renaissance: A Handbook. LC 79-7908. 404p. 1985. lib. bdg. 61.00 (ISBN 0-8240-9541-3). Garland Pub.

Braswell, Lauren, jt. auth. see Kendall, Philip C.

Braswell, Mary F. The Medieval Sinner: Confession & Characterization in the Literature of the English Middle Ages. LC 81-69040. 220p. 1983. 22.50 (ISBN 0-8386-3117-7). Fairleigh Dickinson.

Braswell, Michael & Fletcher, Tyler. Cases in Corrections. LC 79-25043. 1980. pap. text ed. 8.95 (ISBN 0-394-33366-7, RanC). Random.

--Cases in Corrections. 2nd ed. 179p. (Orig.). 1985. pap. 9.95x (ISBN 0-88133-125-2). Waveland Pr.

Braswell, Michael & Seay, Thomas. Approaches to Counseling & Psychotherapy. 2nd ed. 310p. 1984. pap. text ed. 10.95 (ISBN 0-88133-085-X). Waveland Pr.

Braswell, Michael, jt. auth. see Taylor, William.

Braswell, Michael C., jt. auth. see Miller, Larry S.

Braswell, Ronald. Financial Management for Not-For-Profit Organizations. 419p. 1984. text ed. 29.95X (ISBN 0-471-84214-1, Pub. by Grid). Wiley.

Braswell, William. Melville's Religious Thought. LC 73-324. ix, 154p. 1973. Repr. lib. bdg. 18.00x (ISBN 0-374-90945-8). Octagon.

Brata, Sashthi. A Search for Home. 152p. 1975. pap. 2.50 (ISBN 0-88253-771-7). Ind-US Inc.

Brata, Sasthi. India: A Journalist Reveals the Enigmas & Glories of His Native Land. Golbitz, Pat, ed. LC 85-11509. (Illus.). 352p. 1985. 19.95 (ISBN 0-688-04780-7). Morrow.

Bratchell, D. F. The Impact of Darwinism. (Orig.). 1981. pap. text ed. 19.50 (ISBN 0-86127-204-8, Pub. by Avebury England). Humanities.

--Robert Greene's Planetomachia & the Text of the Third Tragedy: A Bibliographical Explanation & a New Edition of the Text. 82p. 1979. text ed. 23.50x (ISBN 0-86127-201-3, Pub. by Avebury England). Humanities.

Bratcher, E. B. The Walk-on-Water Syndrome: Dealing with Professional Hazards in the Ministry. 288p. 1984. 12.95 (ISBN 0-8499-0430-7, 0430-7). Word Bks.

Bratcher, James T. Analytical Index to Publications of the Texas Folklore Society, Vols. 1-36. LC 72-97597. 344p. 1973. 15.95 (ISBN 0-87074-135-7). SMU Press.

Bratcher, R. G. Translator's Guide to Paul's First Letter to the Corinthians. LC 82-6951. (Helps for Translators Ser.). 1982. pap. 2.75x (ISBN 0-8267-0185-X, 08566). Am Bible.

--Translator's Guide to the Gospel of Luke. (Helps for Translators Ser.). 388p. 1982. pap. 4.30x (ISBN 0-8267-0181-7, 08712). Am Bible.

--A Translator's Guide to the Revelation to John. LC 84-8670. (Helps for Translators Ser.). viii, 204p. 1984. flexible bdg. 2.40x (ISBN 0-8267-0195-7, 08790, Pub. by United Bible). Am Bible.

Bratcher, R. G. & Nida, E. A. Translator's Handbook on the Gospel of Mark. LC 61-19352. (Helps for Translators Ser.). 534p. Repr. of 1961 ed. soft cover 5.90x (ISBN 0-8267-0135-3, 08501, Pub. by United Bible). Am Bible.

Bratcher, R. G., ed. Marginal Notes for the New Testament. 125p. 1980. softcover 2.30x (ISBN 0-8267-0026-8, 08558, Pub. by United Bible). Am Bible.

--Marginal Notes for the Old Testament. 186p. 1980. softcover 3.05x (ISBN 0-8267-0025-X, 08557, Pub. by United Bible). Am Bible.

--New Testament Index. 37p. 1963. pap. 1.10x (ISBN 0-8267-0003-9, 08507, Pub. by United Bible). Am Bible.

--Short Bible Reference System. 148p. 1961. soft cover 4.65x (ISBN 0-8267-0030-6, 08506, Pub. by United Bible). Am Bible.

Bratcher, R. G. & Thompson, J. A., eds. Bible Index. 136p. 1970. pap. 2.15x (ISBN 0-8267-0005-5, 08511, Pub. by United Bible). Am Bible.

Bratcher, Robert G. A Translator's Guide to Paul's Letters to Timothy & to Titus. LC 83-4823. (Helps for Translators Ser.). viii, 138p. 1983. softcover 2.30x (ISBN 0-8267-0190-6, 08781, Pub. by United Bible). Am Bible.

--Translator's Guide to Paul's Second Letter to the Corinthians. LC 83-1383. (Helps for Translators Ser.). vii, 160p. 1983. pap. 2.40x (ISBN 0-8267-0186-8, 08571, Pub. by United Bible). Am Bible.

--A Translator's Guide to the Gospel of Mark. (Helps for Translators Ser.). 236p. 1981. pap. 3.30x (ISBN 0-8267-0180-9, 08711, Pub. by United Bible). Am Bible.

--A Translator's Guide to the Gospel of Matthew. LC 82-213977. (Helps for Translators Ser.). 388p. 1981. pap. 4.10x (ISBN 0-8267-0179-5, 08710, Pub. by United Bible). Am Bible.

--A Translator's Guide to the Letters from James, Peter, & Jude. LC 83-18159. (Helps for Translators Ser.). viii, 200p. 1984. softcover 2.25x (ISBN 0-8267-0192-2, 08572, Pub. by United Bible). Am Bible.

Bratcher, Robert G. & Nida, Eugene A. Manuel du Traducteur pour l'Evangile de Marc. Weber, C., tr. (Auxiliaires Du Traducteur Ser.). 542p. 1963. pap. 7.05x (ISBN 0-8267-0250-3, 51972, Pub. by United Bible). Am Bible.

--A Translator's Handbook on Paul's Letters to the Colossians & to Philemon. (Helps for Translators Ser.). 149p. soft cover 2.85x (ISBN 0-8267-0145-0, 08529, Pub. by United Bible). Am Bible.

--A Translator's Handbook on Paul's Letter to the Ephesians. LC 81-19691. (Helps for Translators Ser.). viii, 199p. 1982. pap. 3.15x (ISBN 0-8267-0143-4, 08780, Pub. by United Bible). Am Bible.

Bratcher, Robert G., ed. Old Testament Quotations in the New Testament. 2nd, rev. ed. LC 84-8493. (Helps for Translators Ser.). xii, 80p. 1984. flexible bdg. 2.60x (ISBN 0-8267-0029-2, 08530, Pub. by United Bible). Am Bible.

Brateau, Paul, jt. auth. see Tardy.

Brater, D. Craig. Drug Use in Renal Disease. 184p. 1983. 28.00 (ISBN 0-683-10003-3). Williams & Wilkins.

Brater, E. F. Handbook of Hydraulics. 6th ed. (Handbook Ser.). 1976. 51.50 (ISBN 0-07-007243-4). McGraw.

Brater, E. F., jt. auth. see Wisler, Chester O.

Braterman, P. S. Metal Carbonyl Spectra. 1975. 65.00 (ISBN 0-12-125850-5). Acad Pr.

Braterman, P. S., et al. Spectra & Chemical Interactions. LC 67-11280. (Structure & Bonding: Vol. 26). 1976. 36.00 (ISBN 0-387-07591-7). Springer-Verlag.

Brath, Stanley De see Geley, Gustave.

Brath, Stanley De see Richet, Charles.

Brathwait, Richard. The English Gentleman: Containing Sundry Excellent Rules-How to Demeane or Accomodate Himselfe in the Manage of Publike or Private Affairs. LC 74-28836. (English Experience Ser.: No. 717). 1975. Repr. of 1630 ed. 35.00 (ISBN 90-221-0717-5). Walter J Johnson.

Brathwaite. DOS to OS Conversions. 1985. price not set (ISBN 0-471-82578-6). Wiley.

Brathwaite, Ashton J. see Kwamdela, Odimumba, pseud.

Brathwaite, Cyril A. Therapies, Myths & Cosmic Powers. 1985. 6.95 (ISBN 0-533-06522-4). Vantage.

Brathwaite, Edward. The Arrivants. (Orig.). 1981. pap. 8.95x (ISBN 0-19-911103-0). Oxford U Pr.

--The Development of Creole Society in Jamacia, 1770-1820. (Illus.). pap. 14.95x (ISBN 0-19-823195-4). Oxford U Pr.

--Mother Poem. 1977. pap. text ed. 10.95x (ISBN 0-19-211859-5). Oxford U Pr.

Brathwaite, Edward K. Sun Poem. (Orig.). 1982. pap. 11.95x (ISBN 0-19-211945-1). Oxford U Pr.

Brathwaite, Ken S. Selected Topics in Data Adminstration & Data Management: With Emphasis on Aspects of Data Control & Monitoring. 248p. 1985. 31.95x (ISBN 0-471-80923-3, Pub. by Wiley-Interscience). Wiley.

Brathwaite, Sheila. Quest of the Sea Eagle South: Africa's Swim Story. 12.50 (ISBN 0-392-09222-0, SpS). Sportshelf.

Bratkowsky, Joan G. Yiddish Linguistics: A Multilingual Bibliography, 1959-1973. 1984. lib. bdg. 50.00 (ISBN 0-8240-9804-8). Garland Pub.

Bratley, P., et al. A Guide to Simulation. (Illus.). 384p. 1983. 29.50 (ISBN 0-387-90820-X). Springer-Verlag.

Braton, N. R., jt. auth. see Lindberg, R. A.

Braton, Norman R. Cryogenic Recycling & Processing. 256p. 1980. 78.00 (ISBN 0-8493-5779-9). CRC Pr.

Bratos, S. & Pick, R. M., eds. Vibrational Spectroscopy of Molecular Liquids & Solids. LC 80-12174. (NATO ASI Series B, Physics: Vol. 56). 475p. 1980. 69.50x (ISBN 0-306-40445-1, Plenum Pr). Plenum Pub.

Bratt, David. Tom Stoppard: A Reference Guide. 1982. lib. bdg. 36.50 (ISBN 0-8161-8576-X, Hall Reference). G K Hall.

Bratt, I. M., ed. see Immortal Bard.

Bratt, James D. Dutch Calvinism in Modern America: A History of a Conservative Subculture. (Illus.). 368p. (Orig.). 1984. pap. 13.95 (ISBN 0-8028-0009-2). Eerdmans.

Bratt, John. Trails of Yesterday. LC 79-26411. xx, 322p. 1980. 24.95x (ISBN 0-8032-1157-0); pap. 6.50 (ISBN 0-8032-6055-5, BB 723, Bison). U of Nebr Pr.

Bratt, John H. Final Curtain. (Contemporary Discussion Ser.). 1978. pap. 1.95 (ISBN 0-8010-0748-8). Baker Bk.

--Springboards for Discussion. (Contemporary Discussion Ser). (Orig.). 1970. pap. 1.65 (ISBN 0-8010-0510-8). Baker Bk.

--Springboards for Discussion 2. (Contemporary Discussion Ser.). (Orig.). 1974. pap. 1.45 (ISBN 0-8010-0627-9). Baker Bk.

Brattain, Michael G., jt. ed. see Mastromarino, Anthony J.

Bratteli, O. & Robinson, D. W. Operator Algebras & Quantum Statistical Mechanics: Vol. I: C & W-Algebras. Symmerty Groups. Decomposition of States. (Texts & Monographs in Physics). 1979. 47.50 (ISBN 0-387-09187-4). Springer-Verlag.

Bratteli, O. & Jorgensen, P. E., eds. Positive Semigroups of Operators, & Applications. 1984. lib. bdg. 24.50 (ISBN 90-277-1839-3, Pub. by Reidel Holland). Kluwer Academic.

Bratteli, O. & Robinson, D. W., eds. Operators Algebra & Quantum Statistical Mechanics, Vol. II: Equilibrium States; Models. (Texts & Monographs in Physics Ser.). 496p. 1979. 51.00 (ISBN 0-387-09187-4). Springer-Verlag.

Bratten, Thomas A. Florida Criminal Procedure: Florida Practice Systems Library Selection. LC 80-80175. 87.50; Suppl. 1984. 28.00; Suppl. 1983. 24.00. Lawyers Co-Op.

Bratter, Thomas E. & Forrest, Gary G., eds. Alcoholism & Substance Abuse: Strategies for Intervention. 640p. 1985. 40.00x (ISBN 0-02-904260-7). Free Pr.

Brattin, Joel J. & Hornback, Bert G. Our Mutual Friend: An Annotated Bibliography. DeVries, Duane, ed. LC 83-49325. (Dickens Bibliographies Ser.). 250p. 1984. lib. bdg. 37.00 (ISBN 0-8240-8986-3). Garland Pub.

Bratton, Fred G. The Legacy of the Liberal Spirit: Men & Movements in the Making of Modern Thought. 10.75 (ISBN 0-8446-0508-5). Peter Smith.

Bratton, Grace, jt. auth. see Tompkins, John.

Bratton, J. S. The Impact of Victorian Children's Fiction. 230p. 1981. 27.50x (ISBN 0-389-20210-X, 06992). B&N Imports.

--The Victorian Popular Ballad. 275p. 1975. 19.50x (ISBN 0-87471-760-4). Rowman.

Bratton, Jacqueline S. Wilton's Music Hall. (Theatre in Focus Ser.). (Illus.). 44p. (Orig.). 1980. pap. text ed. 55.00x incl. 50 slides (ISBN 0-85964-061-2). Chadwyck-Healey.

Bratton, Jacqueline S. & Traies, Jane. Astley's Amphitheatre. (Theatre in Focus Ser.). 65p. (Orig.). 1980. pap. text ed. 55.00 incl. slides (ISBN 0-85964-059-0). Chadwyck-Healey.

Bratton, Joseph C. How to Retire in Hawaii, on a Lot Less Than You'd Think. LC 83-50149. (Illus.). 112p. 1983. pap. 9.95 (ISBN 0-912921-00-5). Pau Hana Pr.

--Low-Moderate Housing in Hawaii. (Illus.). 112p. 1984. pap. cancelled (ISBN 0-912921-01-3). Pau Hana Pr.

Bratton, Joseph C., jt. auth. see Robertin, Hector.

Bratton, Michael. The Local Politics of Rural Development: Peasant & Party State in Zambia. LC 79-56775. (Illus.). 348p. 1980. 30.00x (ISBN 0-87451-178-X). U Pr of New Eng.

Bratty, Norman. So You Want to Be an Artist! 1984. 6.95 (ISBN 0-8062-2328-6). Carlton.

Bratus, B. V. Russian Intonation. LC 78-82443. 149p. 1972. text ed. 33.00 (ISBN 0-08-012535-2). Pergamon.

Bratz, Gary. Follow Me. 1972. pap. 3.25 (ISBN 0-89536-067-5). CSS of Ohio.

Bratz, Gary C. The Trial. (Orig.). 1975. pap. 3.75 (ISBN 0-89536-236-8). CSS of Ohio.

Bratzler, L. J., ed. Cross Sectional Muscle Nomenclature of the Beef Carcass. (Illus.). 1952. pap. text ed. 4.95x (ISBN 0-87013-001-3). Mich St U Pr.

Brau, E., et al. Recent Multilateral Debt Restructurings with Official & Bank Creditors. (Occasional Papers: No. 25). 43p. 1983. pap. 5.00 (ISBN 0-317-04022-7). Intl Monetary.

Brau, Jean-Louis & Weaver, Helen. Larousse Encyclopedia of Astrology. 1982. pap. 7.95 (ISBN 0-452-25330-6, Plume). NAL.

Brau, Salvador. History of Puerto Rico. (Puerto Rico Ser.). 1979. lib. bdg. 75.95 (ISBN 0-8490-2936-8). Gordon Pr.

Brauch, Hans G. From "Star Wars" to Strategic Defense Initiative. 280p. 1986. 27.50 (ISBN 0-312-30786-1). St Martin.

Brauch, Hans G. & Clarke, Duncan L., eds. Decision Making for Arms Limitation in the 1980's: Assessments & Prospects. LC 82-22773. 368p. 1983. prof ref 35.00x (ISBN 0-88410-864-3). Ballinger Pub.

Braucher, Antoinette. In Search of Mrs. Barrows. 60p. (Orig.). 1985. pap. 5.95 (ISBN 0-933858-07-8). Kennebec River.

Braucher, Robert, jt. auth. see Riegert, Robert A.

Braude, jt. auth. see Vesell.

Braude, Abraham I. Antimicrobial Drug Therapy. LC 75-19842. (Major Problems in Internal Medicine Ser.: Vol. 8). (Illus.). 240p. 1976. text ed. 18.95 (ISBN 0-7216-1918-5). Saunders.

--Medical Microbiology & Infectious Diseases. Samiy, A. H., et al, eds. (International System of Medicine Ser.: Vol. 2). 2000p. 1981. text ed. 79.00 (ISBN 0-7216-1919-3). Saunders.

--Microbiology: Basic Science & Medical Applications. LC 81-40588. (Illus.). 845p. 1982. pap. text ed. 24.95 (ISBN 0-7216-1920-7). Saunders.

Braude, Abraham I. & McCutchan, J. Allen. Review of Medical Microbiology. (Illus.). 208p. 1983. pap. 14.50 (ISBN 0-7216-1183-4). Saunders.

Braude, Beatrice & Coste, Brigitte. Engagements: Prises de Positions Litteraires et Culturelles. 299p. 1981. pap. text ed. 9.95 (ISBN 0-15-522604-5, HC). HarBraceJ.

Braude, Benjamin & Lewis, Bernard, eds. Christians & Jews in the Ottoman Empire: The Functioning of a Plural Society, 2 vols. LC 80-11337. 1982. Set. text ed. 85.00x. Vol. 1, The Central Lands, 450p (ISBN 0-8419-0519-3). Vol. 2, The Arabic-speaking Lands, 248p (ISBN 0-8419-0520-7). Holmes & Meier.

Braude, Jacob M. Braude's Handbook of Stories for Toastmasters & Speakers. 1967. 14.95 (ISBN 0-13-081315-X, Reward); pap. 6.95 (ISBN 0-13-081323-0). P-H.

--Braude's Treasury of Wit & Humor. 1964. 14.95 (ISBN 0-13-081448-2, Reward); pap. 5.95 (ISBN 0-13-081380-X). P-H.

--Complete Speaker's & Toastmaster's Library, 8 Vols. 1965. 49.95 (ISBN 0-13-164616-8). P-H.

Braude, Lee. A Sense of Sociology. rev. ed. LC 79-20785. 160p. 1981. pap. 7.50 (ISBN 0-89874-016-9). Krieger.

--Work & Workers: A Sociological Analysis. rev. ed. LC 79-20996. 240p. 1983. pap. text ed. 8.95 (ISBN 0-89874-017-7). Krieger.

Braude, M., et al, eds. Narcotic Antagonists. 1973. 38.00 (ISBN 0-7204-7507-4). Elsevier.

Braude, Michael. Butcher, Baker, Epigram Maker: A Random Who's Who. (Illus.). 64p. 1984. 9.95 (ISBN 0-02-514610-6). Macmillan.

--The First Thirty Odd Years. 224p. 1976. 8.95 (ISBN 0-8180-0228-X). Horizon.

--A Question of Identitiy. 11.95 (ISBN 0-317-07057-6). Lieber-Atherton.

--A Question of Identity. LC 76-4203. 1976. 6.95 (ISBN 0-88311-900-5). Horizon.

Braude, Monique C. & Szara, Stephen, eds. Pharmacology of Marihuana, 2 vols. LC 75-14562. (National Institute on Drug Abuse Monograph). 901p. 1976. Set. 98.50 (ISBN 0-89004-067-2). Raven.

Braude, Stephen E. ESP & Psychokinesis: A Philosophical Examination. (Philosophical Monographs: 3rd Ser.). 300p. 1979. 29.95 (ISBN 0-87722-163-4). Temple U Pr.

Braude, William G., tr. Midrash on Psalms, 2 Vols. (Judaica Ser.: No. 13). 1959. Set. 80.00x (ISBN 0-300-00322-6). Yale U Pr.

--Pesikta De-Rab Kahana. Kapstein, Israel J. LC 74-6563. 594p. 1975. 23.95 (ISBN 0-8276-0051-8, 365). Jewish Pubns.

--Pesikta Rabbati: Homiletical Discourses for Festal Days & Special Sabbaths, 2 Vols. LC 68-27748. (Judaica Ser.: No. 18). (Illus.). 1968. Set. 80.00x (ISBN 0-300-01071-0). Yale U Pr.

Braude, William G. & Kapstein, Israel J., trs. from Heb. Tanna Debe Eliyyahu. LC 80-10805. 660p. 1980. 27.50 (ISBN 0-8276-0174-3, 455). Jewish Pubns.

Braudel, Fernand. Afterthoughts on Material Civilization & Capitalism. Ranum, Patricia M., tr. from Fr. LC 76-47368. (Symposia in Comparative History Ser). (Illus.). 136p. 1977. pap. 5.95x (ISBN 0-8018-2217-3). Johns Hopkins.

--Capitalism & Material Life, 1400-1800. (Illus.). 1974. pap. 8.95xi (ISBN 0-06-131836-1, TB1836, Torch). Har-Row.

--Capitalism & Material Life, 1400-1800. Kochan, Miriam, tr. from Fr. LC 72-9747. (Illus.). 478p. 1973. 14.95i (ISBN 0-06-010454-6, HarpT). Har-Row.

--The Mediterranean & the Mediterranean World in the Age of Philip Second, 2 vols. rev. 2nd ed. Reynolds, Sian, tr. from Fr. (Illus.). 1418p. 1976. Vol. 1. pap. 12.45i (ISBN 0-06-090566-2, CN566, CN); Vol. 2. pap. 12.02i (ISBN 0-06-090567-0, CN567, CN). Har-Row.

--On History. Matthews, Sarah, tr. from Fr. LC 80-11201. 1982. pap. 8.50 (ISBN 0-226-07151-0). U of Chicago Pr.

--The Perspective of the World: Fifteenth to Eighteenth Century, Vol. III. Reynolds, Sian, tr. LC 81-47653. (Civilization & Capitalism Ser.). (Illus.). 704p. 1984. 33.65 (ISBN 0-06-015317-2, HarpT). Har-Row.

--Structures of Everyday Life. LC 81-47653. (Illus.). 623p. 1982. 33.65i (ISBN 0-06-014845-4, HarpT). Har-Row.

--The Structures of Everyday Life, Vol. 1: Civilization & Capitalism 15th-18th Century. LC 81-47653. (Illus.). 624p. 1985. pap. 16.95 (ISBN 0-06-091294-4, PL 1294, PL). Har-Row.

--The Wheels of Commerce: Civilization & Capitalism, 15th-18th Century Vol. 2. Reynolds, Sian, tr. from Fr. LC 82-48109. (Illus.). 720p. 1983. 33.65i (ISBN 0-06-015091-2, HarpT). Har-Row.

Braudel, Fernand, pref. by. Conjoncture Economique, Structure Sociales: Hommage a Ernest Labrousse. (Civilisations & Societes: No. 47). (Illus.). 1974. pap. 46.00x (ISBN 90-2797-318-0). Mouton.

Braudel, Francoise, tr. see Venturi, Franco.

Braudes, R A. Me 'ayin U-Le'An: Whence & Whither. (Literaria Judaica Section Ser.: No. 7). 21.50 (ISBN 0-404-13860-8). AMS Pr.

--Shete Ha'Qesawot: The Two Extremes Novel. 2nd ed. (Literaria Judaica Section 2 Ser.: No. 5). Repr. of 1888 ed. 29.50 (ISBN 0-404-13861-6). AMS Pr.

Braudy, Leo. Narrative Form in History & Fiction: Hume, Fielding & Gibbon. LC 69-18052. pap. 82.00 (ISBN 0-317-09631-1, 2010538). Bks Demand UMI.

--The World in a Frame: What We See in Films. LC 84-225. xii, 274p. 1984. pap. 9.95x (ISBN 0-226-07155-3). U of Chicago Pr.

Braudy, Leo, ed. Norman Mailer: A Collection of Critical Essays. 1972. pap. 1.95 (ISBN 0-13-545541-3, STC101, Spec). P-H.

Braudy, Leo & Dickstein, Morris, eds. Great Film Directors: A Critical Anthology. 1978. pap. text ed. 10.95x (ISBN 0-19-502312-9). Oxford U Pr.

Braudy, Susan. What the Movies Made Me Do. LC 85-40117. 256p. 1985. 15.95 (ISBN 0-394-53246-5). Knopf.

--Who Killed Sal Mineo? 1982. 14.95 (ISBN 0-671-61009-0, Wyndham Bks). S&S.

--Who Killed Sal Mineo? 1984. pap. 3.95 (ISBN 0-671-46736-0). PB.

Braue, Donald A. Maya in Radhakrishnan's Thought: Six Meanings Other Than Illusion. 1985. 15.00x (ISBN 0-8364-1129-3). South Asia Bks.

Braue, Frederick, jt. auth. see Hugard, Jean.

Brauer, A. Die Suesswasserfauna Deutchlands. (Illus.). 1961. Repr. of 1909 ed. 122.50 (ISBN 3-7682-0045-0). Lubrecht & Cramer.

Brauer, Alan P., et al. ESO: How You & Your Lover Can Give Each Other Hours of Extended Sexual Orgasm. LC 82-50863. (Illus.). 228p. (Orig.). 1983. 13.50 (ISBN 0-446-51270-2); pap. 7.95 (ISBN 0-446-38026-1). Warner Bks.

Brauer, Barbara S. Ground Beef Favorites. Herbert, Susan H., ed. LC 81-83356. (Illus.). 64p. 1981. pap. 2.95 (ISBN 0-915942-19-4). SF Design.

--Steam Cooking Now! LC 80-82174. (Illus.). 1980. pap. 2.95 (ISBN 0-915942-15-1). SF Design.

Brauer, Carl M. John F. Kennedy & the Second Reconstruction. LC 76-57686. (Contemporary American History Ser.). 396p. 1977. 29.00x (ISBN 0-231-03862-3); pap. 13.00x (ISBN 0-231-08367-X). Columbia U Pr.

Brauer, Donna, jt. auth. see Brauer, Ralph.

Brauer, Erich. Ethnologie der Jemenitischen Juden. LC 77-87611. Repr. of 1934 ed. 30.00 (ISBN 0-404-16435-8). AMS Pr.

Brauer, George C. The Education of a Gentleman. 1959. pap. 7.95x (ISBN 0-8084-0115-7). New Coll U Pr.

Brauer, George C., Jr. The Age of the Soldier Emperors: Imperial Rome, A.D. 244-284. LC 75-13569. (Illus.). 288p. 1975. 15.00 (ISBN 0-8155-5036-7, NP). Noyes.

Brauer, George, Jr. Taras: Its History & Coinage. (Illus.). 336p. 1985. lib. bdg. 52.50 (ISBN 0-89241-377-8). Caratzas.

Brauer, H. & Varma, Y. B. Air Pollution Control Equipment. (Illus.). 388p. 1981. 105.00 (ISBN 0-387-10463-1). Springer-Verlag.

Brauer, H., ed. & intro. by see Rehm, H. J. & Reed, G.

Brauer, Jerald C. Protestantism in America: A Narrative History. rev. ed. LC 66-12686. 320p. 1972. pap. 8.95 (ISBN 0-664-24956-6). Westminster.

Brauer, Jerald C., ed. The Impact of the Church Upon Its Culture: Reappraisals of the History of Christianity. Breen, Quirinus & Drake, George A. LC 67-30155. (Essays in Divinity: Vol. 2). pap. 101.50 (ISBN 0-317-26159-2, 2024085). Bks Demand UMI.

--Westminster Dictionary of Church History. LC 69-11071. 900p. 1971. 27.50 (ISBN 0-664-21285-9). Westminster.

Brauer, Jerald C., ed. see Tillich, Paul.

Brauer, Kinley J. Cotton Versus Conscience. 1967. 8.75 (ISBN 0-87018-071-1). Ross.

Brauer, Ralph & Brauer, Donna. The Horse, the Gun & the Piece of Property: Changing Images of the TV Western. LC 75-15289. 1975. 10.00 (ISBN 0-87972-111-1); pap. 4.00 (ISBN 0-87972-110-3). Bowling Green Univ.

Brauer, Richard. Richard Brauer: Collected Papers, 3 vols. Wong, Warren J. & Fong, Paul, eds. 1980. Vol. 1. 75.00x (ISBN 0-262-02135-8); Vol. 2. 75.00x (ISBN 0-262-02148-X); Vol. 3. 75.00x (ISBN 0-262-02149-8). MIT Pr.

Brauer, Roger L. Facilities Planning: User Requirements Method. LC 85-47679. 250p. 1986. 55.00 (ISBN 0-8144-5624-3). AMACOM.

Brault, Gerald J., ed. Celestine: A Critical Edition of the First French Translation, 1527, of the Spanish Classic La Celestina. LC 62-15071. 271p. (Orig.). 1963. pap. 9.95x (ISBN 0-8143-1207-1). Wayne St U Pr.

Brault, Gerard, tr. see Brault, Gerard J.

Brault, Gerard J. La Chanson de Roland: Oxford Text & English Translation. LC 83-43223. 276p. 1984. pap. text ed. 12.95x student ed. (ISBN 0-271-00375-8). Pa St U Pr.

--Eight Thirteenth-Century Rolls of Arms in French & Anglo-Norman Blazon. LC 72-1065. 148p. 1973. 22.50x (ISBN 0-271-01115-7). Pa St U Pr.

Brault, Gerard J., ed. The Song of Roland: An Analytical Edition, 2 vols. Brault, Gerard, tr. (Illus.). 1978. Vol. 1. Introduction & Commentary 27.50x (ISBN 0-271-00516-5); Vol. 2. Oxford text & English Translation 19.50x (ISBN 0-271-00204-2). Pa St U Pr.

Braum, Helga. The Survival of Helga Braun: A Memoir. 1985. 11.95 (ISBN 0-317-28953-5). Vantage.

Braum, Myron, jt. auth. see Jacobs, Jack.

Braum, Robert Love, ed. Southwest Africa Under Mandate. 1976. lib. bdg. 34.95x (ISBN 0-89712-017-5). Documentary Pubns.

Brauman, Ken & Taylor, Ken. The American Method of Sprinting & Relay Racing. 64p. (Orig.). 1981. pap. 4.95 (ISBN 0-317-14600-9). Championship Bks.

Braumiller, Tanya. Visiting Gig Harbor. (Color-a-Story Ser.). (Illus., Orig.). (gr. 1-4). 1983. pap. 2.75 (ISBN 0-933992-28-9). Coffee Break.

Braun. A. J. Foyt. (Sports Superstars Ser.). (Illus.). 32p. (gr. 3-9). 7.95 (ISBN 0-317-31240-5). Creative Ed.

--Nadia Comaneci. (Sports Superstars Ser.). (Illus.). 32p. (gr. 3-9). 7.95 (ISBN 0-317-31237-5). Creative Ed.

Braun & Schneider. Historic Costume in Pictures. 2nd ed. LC 74-12532. (Pictorial Archives Ser.). (Illus.). 256p. 1975. pap. 7.50 (ISBN 0-486-23150-X). Dover.

--Historic Costumes in Pictures: 1450 Costumes on 125 Plates. (Illus.). 15.25 (ISBN 0-8446-5163-X). Peter Smith.

Braun, jt. auth. see Wackenheim, A.

Braun, et al, eds. Practical Macromolecular Organic Chemistry. (MMI Press Polymer Monographs). 344p. 1984. text ed. 96.00 (ISBN 3-7186-0059-5). Harwood Academic.

Braun, A. C., ed. Plant Tumor Research. (Progress in Experimental Tumor Research: Vol. 15). 1972. 26.50 (ISBN 3-8055-1262-7). S Karger.

Braun, Anne R. Incomes Policies & Inflation in Industrial Countries. 1986. write for info. (ISBN 0-939934-36-1). Intl Monetary.

Braun, Armin C. Cancer Problem: A Critical Analysis & Modern Synthesis. LC 77-90432. (Molecular Biology Ser). (Illus.). 209p. 1969. 34.00x (ISBN 0-231-02938-1). Columbia U Pr.

Braun, Aurel. Small-State Security in the Balkans. LC 82-6639. (Studies in Russian & East European History). 346p. 1983. text ed. 25.00x (ISBN 0-389-20288-6, 07110). B&N Imports.

Braun, D. The Indian Ocean: Region of Conflict or "Peace Zone"? LC 83-9680. 250p. 1983. 29.95 (ISBN 0-312-41396-3). St Martin.

Braun, D., et al. Practical Macromolecular Organic Chemistry. Ivin, Kenneth J., tr. from Ger. (MMI Press Polymer Monograph: Vol. 4). 1984. 96.00 (ISBN 3-7186-0059-5). Harwood Academic Pubs.

Braun, Daniel C., jt. auth. see Gross, Paul.

Braun, David P. & Griffin, James B. Contribution Eight in Research Reports in Archaeology: The Snyders Mound & Five Other Mound Groups in Calhoun County, Illinois. (Technical Report Ser: No. 13). (Illus.). 178p. (Orig.). 1982. pap. 7.50x (ISBN 0-932206-90-5). U Mich Mus Anthro.

Braun, Dietrich. Identification of Plastics. 1982. pap. text ed. 14.50 (ISBN 0-02-949260-2). Macmillan.

--Identification of Plastics: Qualitative Analysis of Plastics Using Simple Methods. (Illus.). 100p. 1982. 21.00 (ISBN 0-686-48113-5, 1901). T-C Pubns CA.

Braun, Dietrich & Cherdron, Harald. Techniques of Polymer Syntheses & Characterization. LC 79-148168. pap. 74.00 (ISBN 0-317-08665-0, 2011967). BKs Demand UMI.

Braun, E. L. Deciduous Forests of Eastern North America. 1967. Repr. of 1950 ed. 31.95x (ISBN 0-02-841910-3). Hafner.

--The Woody Plants of Ohio. 1969. 39.95x (ISBN 0-02-841890-5). Hafner.

Braun, E. Lucy. An Ecological Survey of the Vegetation of Fort Hill State Memorial. 1969. 6.50 (ISBN 0-86727-059-4). Ohio Bio Survey.

--Monocotyledoneae: Cat-Tails to Orchids. LC 66-25170. (Vascular Flora of Ohio: Vol. 1). (Illus.). 474p. 1967. 10.00 (ISBN 0-8142-0028-1). Ohio St U Pr.

--The Vegetation of the Mineral Springs Region of Adams County, Ohio. 1928. 3.00 (ISBN 0-86727-014-4). Ohio Bio Survey.

Braun, Earnest & Brown, Vinson. Exploring Pacific Coast Tide Pools. (Illus.). 56p. (gr. 4 up). 1966. 10.95 (ISBN 0-911010-67-X); pap. 4.95 (ISBN 0-911010-66-1). Naturegraph.

Braun, Edmund. Wissenschaftstheoretisches Lexikon. (Ger.). 1977. 79.95 (ISBN 3-222-10953-2, M-7688, Pub. by Styria). French & Eur.

Braun, Edward. The Director & the Stage: From Naturalism to Grotowski. LC 82-1043. (Illus.). 218p. 1982. text ed. 19.75x (ISBN 0-8419-0800-1); pap. text ed. 12.50x (ISBN 0-8419-0801-X). Holmes & Meier.

--The Theatre of Meyerhold: Revolution on the Modern Stage. LC 78-11864. (Illus.). 304p. 1979. pap. text ed. 10.00x (ISBN 0-89676-004-9). Drama Bk.

Braun, Edward L. Digital Computer Design: Its Logic, Circuitry, & Synthesis. 1963. 85.00 (ISBN 0-12-127250-8). Acad Pr.

Braun, Ernest & Macdonald, Stuart. Revolution in Miniature: The History & Impact of Semiconductor Electronics Re-Explored. 2nd ed. LC 82-1117. (Illus.). 250p. 1982. 27.95 (ISBN 0-521-24701-2); pap. 10.95 (ISBN 0-521-28903-3). Cambridge U Pr.

Braun, Ernest, photos by. Portrait of the San Francisco-Oakland Bay Area. LC 81-81323. (Portrait of America Ser.). (Illus.). 80p. (Orig., Text by Lee Foster). 1981. pap. 6.95 (ISBN 0-912856-69-6). Graphic Arts Ctr.

Braun, Ernst. Wayward Technology. LC 83-22586. (Contributions in Sociology Ser.: No. 48). xi, 224p. 1984. lib. bdg. 27.50 (ISBN 0-313-24398-0, BWT/). Greenwood.

Braun, Eunice. From Strength to Strength: The First Half Century of the Formative Age of the Baha'i Faith. LC 78-9424. 1978. pap. 5.95 (ISBN 0-87743-125-6, 332-030). Baha'i.

--The March of the Institutions: A Commentary on the Interdependence of Rulers & Learned. 112p. 7.50 (ISBN 0-85398-182-5); pap. 3.50 (ISBN 0-85398-183-3). G Ronald Pub.

Braun, Eunice & Chance, Hugh E. A Crown of Beauty: The Baha'i Faith & the Holy Land. (Illus.). 104p. 14.75 (ISBN 0-85398-139-6); pap. 9.75 (ISBN 0-85398-140-X). G Ronald Pub.

Braun, Evalynne V., et al. National Boards Examination Review: Basic Sciences, Pt. I. 1984. pap. text ed. write for info. Med Exam.

Braun, Frank X. English Grammer for Language Students. 1947. pap. text ed. 1.00x (ISBN 0-914004-03-4). Ulrich.

Braun, Frederick A. Margaret Fuller & Goethe. LC 72-195018. 1910. lib. bdg. 15.00 (ISBN 0-8414-2537-X). Folcroft.

Braun, George, et al. General Electric: Nickel-Cadmium Battery Application Handbook. 3rd ed. (Orig.). Date not set. price not set (ISBN 0-931690-17-X). G E Company FL.

Braun, Gerhard. Planning & Engineering of Shortwave Links. 252p. 1982. 44.95 (ISBN 0-471-26213-7, Pub. by Wiley Heyden). Wiley.

Braun, Goetz. Norm und Geschichtlichkeit der Dichtung: Klassisch-romantische Aethetik und moderne Literatur. 312p. 1983. write for info. (ISBN 3-11-008238-1). De Gruyter.

Braun, Hans-Gert, et al, eds. The European Economy in the Nineteen Eighties: Proceedings. 257p. 1983. text ed. 44.95x (ISBN 0-566-00478-X). Gower Pub Co.

Braun, Harold A., et al. Introduction to Respiratory Physiology. 2nd ed. 1980. pap. 14.95 (ISBN 0-316-10699-2). Little.

Braun, Henry. Vergil Woods. LC 68-17383. (Orig.). 1968. pap. 2.45 (ISBN 0-689-10045-0). Atheneum.

Braun, Herbert. The Assassination of Gaitan: Public Life & Urban Violence in Columbia. LC 85-40362. (Illus.). 1985. text ed. 32.50x (ISBN 0-299-10360-9). U of Wis Pr.

Braun, Herbert, et al. God & Christ: Existence & Province. Funk, Robert W. & Ebeling, Gerhard, eds. lib. bdg. 17.50x (ISBN 0-88307-042-1). Gannon.

Braun, Hugh. Elements of English Architecture. (Illus.). 212p. 1980. Repr. 21.50 (ISBN 0-7153-5775-1). David & Charles.

--Parish Churches: Their Architectural Development in England. 1970. 12.50 (ISBN 0-571-09045-1). Transatlantic.

--A Short History of English Architecture. (Illus.). 240p. 1978. pap. 9.95 (ISBN 0-571-10714-1). Faber & Faber.

Braun, Hugo, jt. auth. see Page, Daniel.

Braun, Irwin. Building a Successful Professional Practice with Advertising. LC 81-66214. pap. 75.30 (ISBN 0-317-26844-9, 2023499). Bks Demand UMI.

Braun, J., et al. Die Behandlung von Herzrhythmusstoerungen bei Nierenkranken. (Illus.). viii, 248p. 1984. pap. 21.50 (ISBN 3-8055-3917-7). S Karger.

Braun, J. D., et al. Microstructural Science, Vol. 5. 508p. 1977. 105.00 (ISBN 0-444-00204-9). Elsevier.

Braun, J. R. The Consequences of Sexual Freedom. 150p. (Orig.). 1980. pap. text ed. 2.95 (ISBN 0-933656-04-1). Trinity Pub Hse.

--Is This My Neighbor? The Union Gospel Mission. (Illus.). 60p. (Orig.). 1980. pap. text ed. 8.95 (ISBN 0-933656-08-4). Trinity Pub Hse.

--Male Sexual Fantasies: The Destruction of the Feminine Personality; The Christian Mandate Against Pornography. 48p. (Orig.). 1980. pap. 1.95 (ISBN 0-933656-05-X). Trinity Pub Hse.

--The Meaning of Sexual Pleasure: A Christian Understanding of Sexuality. 203p. (Orig.). 1976. pap. 4.95 (ISBN 0-933656-02-5). Trinity Pub Hse.

Braun, J. R. & Braun, Janine. The Girl the Boys Pretended to Love. (Illus.). 24p. (ps-4). 1980. pap. text ed. 3.95 (ISBN 0-933656-10-6). Trinity Pub Hse.

--The Land of Feel Good. (Illus.). 24p. (Orig.). (ps-3). 1980. pap. text ed. 3.95 (ISBN 0-933656-11-4). Trinity Pub Hse.

Braun, Jack, jt. auth. see Becker, Nancy.

Braun, Janine, jt. auth. see Braun, J. R.

Braun, Janine S. Bible Stories for Little Girls. (Illus.). 66p. (Orig.). (ps-3). 1979. pap. 4.95 (ISBN 0-933656-01-7). Trinity Pub Hse.

Braun, Johannes. Shenandoah Valley Family Data 1799-1813. Wust, Klaus, ed. & tr. from Ger. 1978. pap. 7.75 (ISBN 0-917968-05-0). Shenandoah Hist.

Braun, John A. By His Grace. 1983. pap. 7.95 (ISBN 0-8100-0161-6, 06N0560). Northwest Pub.

Braun, Julian H. How to Play Winning Blackjack. (Illus.). 172p. 1980. 12.95 (ISBN 0-935822-00-3). Data Hse.

Braun, K., et al. Deutsch Als Fremdsprache: Ein Unterrichtswerk Fuer Auslaender. Incl. Pt. 1. Grundkurs. text ed. 11.50x lehrbuch (ISBN 3-12-554100-X); strukturuebungen und tests 8.95x (ISBN 3-12-554150-6); dialogische uebungen 10.25x (ISBN 3-12-554160-3); glossar deutsch-englisch 2.75x (ISBN 3-12-556110-8); sprechuebungen fuer das elektronische klassenzimmer, textband. 8.60x, 8 tonbaender, 9.5 cm/s, tapes, 405.00x (ISBN 3-12-554120-4); 4 schallplatten, lektion 1-19 des grundkurses, 17 cm, 33 1/3 rpm, records 16.95x (ISBN 3-12-554110-7); compact-cassette, lektion 1-19 des grundkurses 16.65x (ISBN 0-685-47448-8); 16 tonba 200.00x (ISBN 0-685-47449-6); Pt. 1B. Ergaenzungskurs. text ed. 11.50x lehrbuch (ISBN 3-12-554500-5); glossar deutsch-englisch 2.75x (ISBN 3-12-556510-3); schallplatten, records 16.65x (ISBN 0-685-47450-X); Pt. 2. Aufbaukurs. text ed. 9.25x lehrbuch (ISBN 3-12-554200-6); strukturuebungen und tests 7.25x (ISBN 0-686-66995-9); dialogische uebungen 8.60x (ISBN 0-686-66996-7); glossar deutsch-englisch 2.20x (ISBN 3-12-556210-4); 3 schallplatten, lektion 1-17 des aufbaukurses,17 cm, 33 1/3 rpm, records 16.65x (ISBN 3-12-554210-3); compact-cassette, lektion 1-17 des aufbaukurses 16.65x (ISBN 0-685-47451-8); 12 tonbaender, dialoge und hoer-sprechuebungen, 9.5 cm/s, tapes 221.00x (ISBN 3-12-990430-1). Schoenhof.

Braun, Katherine M. Saga of the Bluebird. (Illus.). 62p. 1982. pap. 7.00 (ISBN 0-682-49913-7). Exposition Pr FL.

Braun, Kirk. Rajneeshpuram: The Unwelcome Society-"Cultures Collide in a Quest for Utopia". 256p. 1984. pap. 7.95 (ISBN 0-930219-00-7). Scout Creek Pr.

Braun, Kurt. Labor Disputes & Their Settlement. LC 73-13320. 343p. 1974. Repr. of 1955 ed. lib. bdg. 18.25x (ISBN 0-8371-7121-0, BRDS). Greenwood.

Braun, Lev. Witness of Decline - Albert Camus: Moralist of the Absurd. LC 72-11082. 283p. 1974. 26.50 (ISBN 0-8386-1246-6). Fairleigh Dickinson.

Braun, Lionel. The Drink Directory. LC 82-4239. 1982. pap. 5.95 (ISBN 0-672-52705-7). Bobbs.

Braun, Louis, et al, illus. Costumes Through the Ages. LC 82-60208. (Illus.). 256p. 1982. 45.00 (ISBN 0-8478-0465-8). Rizzoli Intl.

Braun, M. Differential Equations & Their Applications: An Introduction to Applied Mathematics. 3rd ed. (Applied Mathematical Sciences: Vol. 15). (Illus.). 546p. 1983. pap. 28.00 (ISBN 0-387-90806-4). Springer-Verlag.

--Differential Equations & their Applications. 335p. 1983. 23.50 (ISBN 0-387-90847-1). Springer-Verlag.

Braun, Mathew. El Paso. 1981. pap. 1.95 (ISBN 0-671-44013-6). PB.

Braun, Matt. Bloodstorm. 256p. (Orig.). 1984. pap. 3.50 (ISBN 0-523-42388-8). Pinnacle Bks.

--Bloody Hand. 384p. (Orig.). 1985. pap. 3.50 (ISBN 0-523-42381-0). Pinnacle Bks.

--Buck Colter. 1981. pap. 1.95 (ISBN 0-671-44011-X). PB.

--Indian Territory. 256p. (Orig.). 1985. pap. 3.50 (ISBN 0-523-42389-6). Pinnacle Bks.

--The Judas Tree, No. 7. 1982. pap. 2.25 (ISBN 0-671-41994-3). PB.

--Jury of Six. (Orig.). 1981. pap. 1.95 (ISBN 0-671-43804-2). PB.

--Kinch. 192p. 1985. pap. 2.95 (ISBN 0-523-42427-2). Pinnacle Bks.

--The Manhunter, No. 5. (Orig.). 1981. pap. 1.95 (ISBN 0-671-41992-7). PB.

--Mattie Silks. 320p. (Orig.). 1985. pap. 2.95 (ISBN 0-523-42459-0). Pinnacle Bks.

--Noble Outlaw. 2nd ed. 288p. (Orig.). 1985. pap. 2.95 (ISBN 0-523-42456-6). Pinnacle Bks.

--The Spoilers. 224p. (Orig.). 1981. pap. 1.95 (ISBN 0-671-82034-6). PB.

--The Spoilers. 208p. 1985. pap. 2.95 (ISBN 0-317-27077-X). Pinnacle Bks.

--Tombstone. 224p. 1981. pap. 1.95 (ISBN 0-671-82033-8). PB.

--Tombstone. 208p. (Orig.). 1985. pap. 2.95 (ISBN 0-523-42457-4). Pinnacle Bks.

Braun, Matthew. Black Fox. 1981. pap. 1.95 (ISBN 0-671-44010-1). PB.

--Cimarron Jordon. 1981. pap. 2.25 (ISBN 0-671-44012-8). PB.

--Deadwood, No. 6. (Orig.). 1981. pap. 2.25 (ISBN 0-671-41993-5). PB.

--Noble Outlaw. (Orig.). 1981. pap. 2.25 (ISBN 0-671-43805-0). PB.

--The Savage Land. 1981. pap. 2.25 (ISBN 0-671-44015-2). PB.

--The Save-Your-Life Defense Handbook. (Illus.). 1977. pap. 9.95 (ISBN 0-8159-5712-2). Devin.

--This Loving Promise. 1984. pap. 3.75 (ISBN 0-8217-1404-X). Zebra.

Braun, Mercedes. The New Complete Basset Hound. 4th ed. LC 79-4465. (Complete Breed Book Ser.). (Illus.). 352p. 1982. 15.95 (ISBN 0-87605-021-6). Howell Bk.

Braun, Micheline T., jt. ed. see Dorenlot, Francoise.

Braun, Montgomery W. The Life & Loves of Queen Anne & the History of Great Britain. (Illus.). 139p. 1984. 67.45x (ISBN 0-89266-435-5). Am Classical Coll Pr.

Braun, O. International Trade & Imperialism. Da Silva Araquen, Endaldo, tr. from Span. 124p. 1984. text ed. 13.45x (ISBN 0-391-02906-1, Pub. by Inst Social Studies). Humanities.

Braun, Otto. A Comintern Agent in China, Nineteen Thirty-Two to Nineteen Thirty-Nine. Moore, Jeanne, tr. from Ger. LC 81-85452. (Illus.). 294p. 1982. 27.50x (ISBN 0-8047-1138-0). Stanford U Pr.

Braun, P. C., ed. The Big Book of Favorite Horse Stories. (Illus.). 336p. (YA) (gr. 7 up). 1982. 7.95 (ISBN 0-448-42641-2, G&D). Putnam Pub Group.

Braun, R. D. Introduction to Chemical Analysis. 544p. 1982. 31.95x (ISBN 0-07-007280-9). McGraw.

Braun, Rainer. Kohelet und die fruehhellenistische Popularphilosphie. LC 72-76043. (Beiheft 130 Zur Zeitschrift Fuer Die Alttestamentliche Wissenschaft Ser.: No. 130). 187p. 1973. text ed. 33.60x (ISBN 3-11-004050-6). De Gruyter.

Braun, Richard, tr. see Sophocles.

Braun, Richard E. Bad Land. LC 70-79736. 1971. pap. 4.00 (ISBN 0-912330-08-2, Dist. by Inland Bk). Jargon Soc.

--Children Passing. LC 62-62491. (Tower Poetry Ser: No. 2). (Illus.). 1962. 5.95 (ISBN 0-87959-000-9). U of Tex H Ransom Ctr.

--The Foreclosure Poems. LC 75-174780. 78p. 1972. 10.00 (ISBN 0-252-00230-X); pap. 5.95 (ISBN 0-252-00231-8). U of Ill Pr.

Braun, Richard E., tr. Persius: Satires. 1983. 12.50x (ISBN 0-87291-139-X). Coronado Pr.

Braun, Richard E., tr. see Euripides.

Braun, Robert D. & Walters, Fred H. Applications of Chemical Analysis: Lab Manual. 384p. 1982. text ed. 19.95 (ISBN 0-07-007282-5). McGraw.

Braun, S., ed. MSA - Mechanical Signature Analysis. 88p. 1983. pap. text ed. 24.00 (ISBN 0-317-02630-5, G00236). ASME.

Braun, Shirley W. Life in English. 206p. 1984. pap. text ed. 9.95 (ISBN 0-15-550735-4, HC). HarBraceJ.

Braun, Sidney D. Andre Suares: Hero among Heroes. 96p. 1978. 9.95. Summa Pubns.

Braun, Sidney D., ed. Dictionary of French Literature. LC 70-138576. (Illus.). 1971. Repr. of 1958 ed. lib. bdg. 24.75x (ISBN 0-8371-5775-7, BRDF). Greenwood.

Braun, Simon, jt. auth. see Sheldon, Huntington.

Braun, Susan, jt. ed. see Kitching, Jessie.

Braun, T. & Bujdoso, E., eds. Radiochemical Separation Methods: Proceedings of the 7th Radio Chemical Conference Czechoslovakia 1973. 591p. 1975. Repr. 66.00 (ISBN 0-444-99873-X). Elsevier.

Braun, T. & Ghersini, G., eds. Extraction Chromatography. (Journal of Chromatography Library: Vol. 2). 592p. 1975. 76.75 (ISBN 0-444-99878-0). Elsevier.

Braun, T., et al, eds. Polyurethane Foam Sorbents in Separation Science & Tech. 224p. 1985. 70.00 (ISBN 0-8493-6597-X). CRC Pr.

Braun, Theodore, jt. auth. see Barrette, Paul.

Braun, Thom. Disraeli the Novelist. 176p. 1981. text ed. 15.00x (ISBN 0-04-809017-4). Allen Unwin.

Braun, Thom, ed. see Disraeli, Benjamin.

Braun, Thomas. Franco Harris. (Creative Superstars Ser.). (Illus.). (gr. 3-9). 1975. PLB 7.95 (ISBN 0-87191-473-5). Creative Ed.

--On Stage with Flip Wilson. (gr. 6-12). 1975. pap. 3.95 (ISBN 0-89812-149-3). Creative Ed.

--Sonny & Cher. (Rock 'n Pop Stars Ser.). (Illus.). (gr. 4-12). 1978. pap. 3.95 (ISBN 0-685-81994-9). Creative Ed.

Braun, Thomas, ed. see Rosenthal-Schneider, Ilse.

Braun, Thomas B., et al, eds. In Place Resource Inventories: Principles & Practices. LC 82-61437. 1101p. (Orig.). 1982. pap. 20.00 (ISBN 0-939970-17-1, SAF 82-02). Soc Am Foresters.

Braun, W. & Ungar, J., eds. Non-Specific Factors Influencing Host Resistance: A Reexamination. (Illus.). 1973. 57.25 (ISBN 3-8055-1598-7). S Karger.

Braun, W., ed. see International Symposium on Molecular Biology, 4th, 1970.

Braun, W., jt. ed. see Landy, Maurice.

Braun, W., et al, eds. see Symposium on Cyclic AMP, Cell Growth, & the Immune Response, Marco Island, Fla., 1973.

Braun, Walter. Cruel & the Meek. Meyer, N., tr. (Illus.). 1968. 6.00 (ISBN 0-8184-0024-2). Lyle Stuart.

Braun, Walter O. Asbestos & Asbestosis: A Medical Subject Analysis & Research Index with Bibliography. LC 83-70090. 140p. 1983. 29.95 (ISBN 0-941864-84-7); pap. 21.95 (ISBN 0-941864-85-5). ABBE Pubs Assn.

Braun, Wernher Von see Von Braun, Wernher.

Braun, Wernher Von see Von Braun, Wernher & Ordway, Frederick I., 3rd.

Braun, Wernher von see Von Braun, Wernher, et al.

Braun, Wilhelm A. Types of Weltschmerz in German Poetry. LC 5-33195. (Columbia University. Germanic Studies, Old Ser.: No. 6). Repr. of 1905 ed. 14.50 (ISBN 0-404-50406-X). AMS Pr.

Braun, William E. HLA & Disease: A Comprehensive Review. 160p. 1979. 46.00 (ISBN 0-8493-5795-0). CRC Pr.

Braun, Wolfgang. Die Kalkflachmoore. (Illus.). 1968. 14.00 (ISBN 3-7682-0580-0). Lubrecht & Cramer.

Braunagel, Judith S., jt. auth. see Jahoda, Gerald.

Braunbeck, Oscar A., jt. auth. see Wilkinson, Robert H.

Braunbek, Werner. Pursuit of the Atom. 1959. 9.95 (ISBN 0-87523-115-2). Emerson.

Braun-Blanquet, J. Plant Sociology: The Study of Plant Communities. Fuller, George D. & Conard, Henry S., trs. (Illus.). 439p. 1983. Repr. of 1932 ed. lib. bdg. 33.60X (ISBN 3-87429-208-8). Lubrecht & Cramer.

Braund, David. Rome & the Friendly King: The Character of Client Kingship. LC 83-40184. 224p. 1984. 22.95 (ISBN 0-312-69210-2). St Martin.

Braund, David C. Augustus to Nero: A Sourcebook on Roman History 31 B.C.-A.D. 68. LC 84-20368. 348p. 1985. 28.95x (ISBN 0-389-20536-2, 08098). B&N Imports.

Braund, Katherine. Dog Obedience Training Manual, Vol. 1. LC 81-90017. (Illus.). 64p. 1982. pap. 9.95 (ISBN 0-87714-098-7). Denlingers.

Braund, Kathryn. Dog Obedience Training Manual, Vol. 2. LC 81-17353. (Illus.). 80p. 1983. pap. 9.95 (ISBN 0-87714-100-2). Denlingers.

--The Uncommon Dog Breeds. LC 74-14202. (Illus.). 352p. 1975. 9.95 (ISBN 0-668-03621-4). Denlingers.

Braund, Kathryn & Miller, Deyanne F. The Complete Portuguese Water Dog. (Illus.). 288p. 1985. 16.95 (ISBN 0-87605-262-6). Howell Bk.

Braune & Fischer. On the Centre of Gravity of the Human Body. Maquet, P. G., et al, trs. from Ger. (Illus.). 115p. 1985. 29.00 (ISBN 0-387-13216-3). Springer-Verlag.

Brauneck, M., ed. see Birck, Sixt.

Brauneck, Martin, ed. Spieltexte der Wanderbuehne, 4 vols. Incl. Vol. 1. Engelische Comedue und Tragedean. 1970. 72.00 (ISBN 3-11-002695-3); Vol. 2. Liebeskampf. 1975. 135.00x (ISBN 3-11-005716-6); Vol. 3. Schau-Buehne Englischen und Frantzosischer Comoedianten: 1670. 1970. 90.00x (ISBN 3-11-004685-7); Schau-Buehne Englischen und Frantzosischer Comoedianten: 1670. 1972. Vol. 4. 87.20x (ISBN 3-11-004001-8). (Ausgaben Deutscher Literatur Des XV Bis XVIII Jahrhunderts). De Gruyter.

Brauner, R. A., ed. Shiv'im: Essays & Studies in Honor of Ira Eisenstein. 20.00x (ISBN 0-87068-442-6). Ktav.

Braun-Falco, O. & Lukacs, S. Dermatologic Radiotherapy. Goldschmidt, H., tr. from Ger. (Illus.). 1976. 29.00 (ISBN 0-387-90186-8). Springer-Verlag.

Braun-Falco, O., jt. auth. see Burg, G.

Braunfels, Wolfgang. Monasteries of Western Europe: The Architecture of the Orders. LC 73-2472. (Illus.). 263p. 1973. 52.50 (ISBN 0-691-03896-1); pap. 16.50 (ISBN 0-691-00313-0). Princeton U Pr.

Braungart, Richard, ed. Research in Political Sociology, Vol. 1. 1985. 49.50 (ISBN 0-89232-557-7). Jai Pr.

Braunig, M. Wine Service Procedures. 1974. 19.95 (ISBN 0-911202-20-X). Radio City.

Braunlein, John H. Colonial Long Island Folklife. (Illus.). 38p. (Orig.). 1976. pap. 2.50 (ISBN 0-943924-00-6). Mus Stony Brook.

Braunlich, Tom. Pente Strategy. 144p. 1985. pap. 4.95 (ISBN 0-446-38236-1). Warner Bks.

Braunlin, Walter A., jt. auth. see Chenevert, Martin.

Braunmuller, A. R. George Peele. (English Authors Ser.). 154p. 1983. lib. bdg. 18.95 (ISBN 0-8057-6842-4, Twayne). G K Hall.

Braunmuller, A. R., ed. The Captive Lady. LC 83-71731. (Malone Society Reprint Ser.: No. 142). Repr. of 1982 ed. 40.00 (ISBN 0-404-63142-8). AMS Pr.

Braunmuller, A. R., commentary by. A Seventeenth-Century Letter-Book: A Facsimile Editon of Folger MS V.A. 321. LC 81-50652. 464p. 1983. 60.00 (ISBN 0-87413-201-0). U Delaware Pr.

Braun-Ronsdorf, M. A History of the Handkerchief. (Illus.). 1967. text ed. 25.00x (ISBN 0-85317-011-8, Pub. by A & C Black England). Humanities.

Braunrot, Bruno. L' Imagination Poetique Chez du Bartas: Elements de Sensibilite Baroque dans la "Creation du Monde.". (Studies in the Romance Languages & Literatures: No. 135). 159p. 1973. pap. 9.00x (ISBN 0-8078-9135-5). U of NC Pr.

Brauns, Dorothy A., jt. auth. see Brauns, Friedrich E.

Brauns, Friedrich E. & Brauns, Dorothy A. Chemistry of Lignin: Supplementary Volume Covering Literature for 1949-58. 1960. 90.00 (ISBN 0-12-127861-1). Acad Pr.

Brauns, Robert & Slater, Sarah W. Bankers Desk Reference, 1984. Cox, Edwin B., ed. LC 80-648848. 352p. 1984. 45.00 (ISBN 0-88712-082-2, 78-50154). Warren.

Braunstein, Baruch. The Chuetas of Majorca. rev. ed. 1971. 25.00x (ISBN 0-87068-147-8). Ktav.

Braunstein, Bruce. The Daily Plan-It R. 180p. (Orig.). 1980. pap. 6.95 (ISBN 0-686-27615-9). Tetragrammaton.

--Intergalactic Polish: We Wax the Cars of the Stars. (Orig.). 1980. pap. 10.00 (ISBN 0-686-27616-7). Tetragrammaton.

Braunstein, Daniel N., jt. auth. see Ungson, Gerardo R.

Braunstein, H. Terry. Windows. LC 82-4292. (Artist Bk.). (Illus.). 32p. 1982. 25.00 (ISBN 0-89822-024-6). Visual Studies.

--Windows. 32p. 1982. 25.00 (ISBN 0-942868-01-3). W Blake Pr.

Braunstein, Helen, ed. Biomass Energy Systems & the Environment. (Illus.). 189p. 1981. 16.50 (ISBN 0-08-027194-4). Pergamon.

Braunstein, Herbert. Outlines of Pathology. 1st ed. LC 81-14145. (Illus.). 605p. 1982. pap. text ed. 21.95 (ISBN 0-8016-0869-4). Mosby.

Braunstein, J., jt. ed. see Mamantov, Glen.

Braunstein, J., et al. Advances in Molten Salt Chemistry, 4 vols. Incl. Vol. 1. 296p. 1971. 45.00x (ISBN 0-306-39701-3); Vol. 2. 270p. 1973. 45.00x (ISBN 0-306-39702-1); Vol. 3. 469p. 1975. 69.50x (ISBN 0-306-39703-X). LC 78-131884 (Plenum Pr). Plenum Pub.

Braunstein, Jonathan J. & Toister, Richard P. Medical Applications of the Behavioral Sciences. (Illus.). 634p. 1981. 34.95 (ISBN 0-8151-1194-0). Year Bk Med.

Braunstein, Joseph. Musica Aeterna: Program Notes, 1961-1967. LC 72-8420. (Music Ser). 332p. 1973. Repr. of 1968 ed. lib. bdg. 39.50 (ISBN 0-306-70554-0). Da Capo.

Braunstein, Jules, ed. North American Oil & Gas Fields. LC 76-258. (American Association of Petroleum Geologists, Memoir: 24). pap. 92.50 (ISBN 0-317-20511-0, 2022878). Bks Demand UMI.

Braunstein, Mark. Radical Vegetarianism: A Dialectic of Diet & Ethic. 176p. (Orig.). 1983. 14.95 (ISBN 0-915572-52-4); pap. 6.95 (ISBN 0-915572-37-0). Panjandrum.

Braunstein, Mark L. & James, John D. A Symptom-Oriented Guide to Adverse Drug Reactions. 560p. 1983. pap. 15.95x (ISBN 0-07-032252-X). McGraw.

Braunstein, Mark M., jt. ed. see Cashman, Norine D.

Braunthal, Alfred. Salvation & the Perfect Society: The Eternal Quest. LC 79-4705. 448p. 1979. lib. bdg. 25.00x (ISBN 0-87023-273-8). U of Mass Pr.

Braunthal, Gerard. Socialist Labor & Politics in Weimar Germany: The General Federation of German Trade Unions. (Illus.). 253p. 1978. 25.00 (ISBN 0-208-01740-2, Archon). Shoe String.

--The West German Social Democrats, 1969-1982: Profile of a Party in Power. LC 82-3464. (Replica Edition Ser.). 350p. 1983. softcover 27.00x (ISBN 0-86531-958-8). Westview.

Braunwald, Eugene. Heart Disease: A Textbook of Cardiovascular Medicine, 2 Vols. 2nd ed. (Illus.). 1968p. 1984. Single Vol. 89.00 (ISBN 0-7216-1938-X); Two Vol. Set. 99.00 (ISBN 0-7216-1941-X); Vol. 1. 49.50 (ISBN 0-7216-1939-8); Vol. 2. 49.50 (ISBN 0-7216-1940-1). Saunders.

Braunwald, Eugene, ed. Protection of the Ischemic Myocardium. LC 76-1517. (AHA Monograph: No. 48). 1976. 6.00 (ISBN 0-87493-049-9, 73-034A). Am Heart.

--Symposium on Myocardial Metabolism. (AHA Monograph: No. 44). 1974. 6.00 (ISBN 0-87493-042-1, 73-031A). Am Heart.

Braunwald, Eugene & Mock, Michael B., eds. Congestive Heart Failure: Current Research & Clinical Applications. LC 82-908. 400p. 1982. 49.00 (ISBN 0-8089-1469-3, 790657). Grune.

Braunwald, Eugene & Swan, Harold J., eds. Cooperative Study on Cardiac Catheterization. (AHA Monograph Ser.: Vol. 20). 112p. Repr. of 1968 ed. cancelled (ISBN 0-87493-018-9, 73-013A). Am Heart.

Brause, B., et al. Musculoskeletal Infections: Recognition, Prevention & Management-Antimicrobial Prophylaxis in Musculoskeletal Surgery. Fitzgerald, Robert, Jr., ed. 44p. 1983. write for info. (ISBN 0-911741-02-X). Advanced Thera Comm.

Brause, Dorsey. Expanded Ministry to Adults: Program Guidelines. 1979. pap. 3.50 (ISBN 0-89367-030-8). Light & Life.

Brautigam, Patsy, jt. auth. see Morris, Leslie R.

Brautigam, W., et al, eds. First Steps in Psychotherapy. 200p. 1985. pap. 24.00 (ISBN 0-387-15042-0). Springer-Verlag.

Brautigam, Walter, ed. see European Conference on Psychosomatic Research, 11th, Heidelberg, September 14-17, 1976.

Brautigan, Richard. Abortion. (gr. 10-12). 1979. pap. 2.25 (ISBN 0-671-82797-9). PB.

--Dreaming of Babylon. 1978. pap. 6.95 (ISBN 0-385-28221-4, Delta). Dell.

--The Hawkline Monster. 1981. pap. 2.95 (ISBN 0-671-43786-0). PB.

--In Watermelon Sugar. 176p. (gr. 9 up). 1973. pap. 1.95 (ISBN 0-440-34026-8). Dell.

--June Thirtieth, June Thirtieth. 1978. pap. 3.95 (ISBN 0-385-28491-8, Delta). Dell.

--The Pill Versus the Springhill Mine Disaster. 128p. 1973. pap. 1.95 (ISBN 0-440-36956-8, LE). Dell.

--Revenge of the Lawn. (gr. 10 up). 1980. pap. 2.95 (ISBN 0-671-41852-1). PB.

--Rommel Drives on Deep into Egypt. 1973. pap. 3.50 (ISBN 0-440-37496-0). Dell.

--So the Wind Won't Blow It All Away. 160p. 1982. 12.95 (ISBN 0-385-28967-7, Sey Lawr). Delacorte.

--So the Wind Won't Blow It All Away. 144p. 1983. pap. 6.95 (ISBN 0-385-29287-2, Delta). Dell.

--The Tokyo-Montana Express. 1981. pap. 5.95 (ISBN 0-385-29025-X, Delta). Dell.

--Trout Fishing in America. 182p. 1971. pap. 3.95 (ISBN 0-440-39125-3). Dell.

--Willard & His Bowling Trophies. (gr. 10 up). 1978. pap. 1.95 (ISBN 0-671-82043-5). PB.

Brava, J. S. The Political Economy of Rural Development. 1983. 15.00x (ISBN 0-8364-1012-2, Pub. by Allied India). South Asia Bks.

Bravais, A. On the Systems Formed by Points Regularly Distributed on a Plane or in Space. (American Crystallographic Association Monograph: Vol. 4). 113p. 1969. pap. 3.00 (ISBN 0-686-60370-2). Polycrystal Bk Serv.

Bravard, Robert S., jt. auth. see Peplow, Michael W.

Bravard, Wyman N. Delaware Corporation Formation Package & Minute Book. (Successful Business Library). 250p. 1983. 3-ring binder 33.95 (ISBN 0-916378-26-8). PSI Res.

--Florida Corporation Formation Package & Minute Book. (Successful Business Library). 250p. 1984. 3-ring binder 33.95 (ISBN 0-916378-29-2). PSI Res.

--R & D Limited Partnerships: An Emerging Method for Funding Research & Development. 400p. (Orig.). 1985. 125.00x (ISBN 0-916483-00-2). Market Res Co.

--Texas Corporation Formation Package & Minute Book. (Successful Business Library). 200p. 1984. 3-ring binder 33.95 (ISBN 0-916378-28-4). PSI Res.

Bravard, Wyman N., jt. auth. see Frigstad, David B.

Brave, John R. Uncle John's Original Bread Book. 2nd ed. 1965. 7.50 (ISBN 0-682-46876-2, Banner). Exposition Pr FL.

--Uncle John's Original Bread Book. 1984. pap. 2.25 (ISBN 0-515-05830-0). Jove Pubns.

Braveboy-Wagner, Jacqueline A. The Venezuela-Guyana Border Dispute: Britain's Colonial Legacy in Latin America. (Replica Edition Ser.). 200p. 1984. softcover 27.50x (ISBN 0-86531-953-7). Westview.

Braver, J. C., ed. see Meland, Bernard E.

Braver, John M., jt. auth. see Jones, Bronwyn.

Braverman, Avishay, et al. Alternative Agricultural Pricing Policies in the Republic of Korea: Their Implications for Government Deficits, Income Distribution, & Balance of Payments. (Staff Working Paper No. 621). 174p. 1983. 5.00 (ISBN 0-8213-0275-2, WP 0621). World Bank.

Braverman, Harry. Labor & Monopoly Capital: The Degradation of Work in the Twentieth Century. LC 74-7785. 448p. 1975. 12.50 (ISBN 0-85345-340-3). Monthly Rev.

--Labor & Monopoly Capital: The Degradation of Work in the Twentieth Century. LC 74-7785. (Illus.). 1976. pap. 8.00 (ISBN 0-85345-370-5). Monthly Rev.

Braverman, Harvey. Precalculus Mathematics: Algebra, Trigonometry, Analytic Geometry. LC 83-11298. 546p. 1983. Repr. of 1975 ed. text ed. 26.50 (ISBN 0-89874-653-1). Krieger.

Braverman, Irwin M. Skin Signs of Systematic Disease. (Illus.). 965p. 1981. text ed. 89.00 (ISBN 0-7216-1927-4). Saunders.

Braverman, Jack R., ed. see Educational Research Council of America.

Braverman, Jack R., ed. see Educational Research Council of America Staff.

Braverman, Jay. Jerome's Commentary on Daniel: A Study of Comparative Jewish & Christian Interpretations of the Hebrew Bible. LC 78-55726. (Catholic Biblical Quarterly Monographs: No. 7). xvi, 162p. 1978. 4.00 (ISBN 0-915170-06-X). Catholic Biblical.

Braverman, Jerome D. Maximizing Profits in Small & Medium-Sized Businesses. 256p. 1983. 24.95 (ISBN 0-442-21268-2). Van Nos Reinhold.

Braverman, Jordan. A Consumer's Book of Health: Advice on Stretching Your Health Care Dollar. 1981. o. p. 11.95 (ISBN 0-03-059079-5); pap. 7.95 (ISBN 0-03-059078-7). HR&W.

--Crisis in Health Care. rev. ed. LC 80-17755. 1980. pap. 7.95 (ISBN 0-87491-299-7). Acropolis.

Braverman, L. E. see Robbins, J.

Braverman, Mimi, jt. ed. see Cochran, Wendell.

Braverman, Miriam. Youth, Society & the Public Library. LC 78-17267. 1979. lib. bdg. 20.00x (ISBN 0-8389-0260-X). ALA.

Braverman, Sydell, jt. auth. see Chevigny, Hector.

Bravery, H. E. Successful Winemaking at Home. rev. ed. LC 62-12119. (Illus.). 1967. pap. 2.95 (ISBN 0-668-00861-X, 843). Arco.

Bravmann, Rene A. African Islam. LC 83-21174. (Illus.). 120p. 1984. 25.00 (ISBN 0-87474-282-X, BRAI); pap. 15.00 (ISBN 0-87474-281-1). Smithsonian.

--Islam & Tribal Art in West Africa. (African Studies: No. 11). (Illus.). 204p. 1980. pap. 11.95 (ISBN 0-521-29791-5). Cambridge U Pr.

--Islam & Tribal Art in West Africa. (African Studies: No. 11). (Illus.). 180p. 1974. 42.50 (ISBN 0-521-20192-6). Cambridge U Pr.

--The Poetry of Form: Hans & Thelma Lehmann Collection of African Art. LC 82-83027. (Illus.). 80p. (Orig.). 1982. 14.95 (ISBN 0-935558-09-8); pap. 9.95 (ISBN 0-935558-12-8). Henry Art.

Bravo, R., jt. auth. see Celis, Julio E.

Brawer, Catherine C., ed. Many Trails: Indians of the Lower Hudson Valley. LC 82-84435. (Illus.). 112p. 1983. pap. 12.50 (ISBN 0-686-40394-0). Katonah Gal.

--Many Trails: Indians of the Lower Hudson Valley. (Illus.). 112p. 1983. pap. 12.50. Pub Ctr Cult Res.

Brawer, Florence B. New Perspectives on Personality Development in College Students. LC 73-7150. (Jossey-Bass Higher Education Ser.). Repr. of 1973 ed. 48.30 (ISBN 0-8357-9338-9, 2013794). Bks Demand UMI.

Brawer, Florence B., jt. auth. see Cohen, Arthur M.

Brawick, Theodore. Teacher As World Citizen: A Scenario of the 21st Century. (Education Futures Ser.: No. 5). 1976. 9.95 (ISBN 0-88280-042-6); pap. 5.95 (ISBN 0-88280-043-4). ETC Pubns.

Brawley, Benjamin. Doctor Dillard of the Jeanes Fund. facsimile ed. LC 73-168511. (Black Heritage Library Collection). Repr. of 1930 ed. 15.50 (ISBN 0-8369-8864-7). Ayer Co Pubs.

--Early American Negro Writers. Foner, Philip S., ed. (Black Rediscovery Ser). 1970. pap. 6.00 (ISBN 0-486-22623-9). Dover.

--Early Negro American Writers: Selections with Biographical & Critical Introductions. 14.25 (ISBN 0-8446-0509-3). Peter Smith.

--Negro Builders & Heroes. xiii, 315p. 1937. 14.95 (ISBN 0-8078-0241-7). U of NC Pr.

--Short History of the English Drama. facsimile ed. LC 71-102227. (Select Bibliographies Reprint Ser). 1921. 24.50 (ISBN 0-8369-5112-3). Ayer Co Pubs.

Brawley, Benjamin C. The Negro in Literature & Art in the U. S. 1981. lib. bdg. 39.00 (ISBN 0-403-00531-0). Scholarly.

Brawley, Benjamin G. Early Negro American Writers. facs. ed. LC 68-25601. (Essay Index Reprint Ser). 1968. Repr. of 1935 ed. 24.50 (ISBN 0-8369-0246-7). Ayer Co Pubs.

--Negro Genius. LC 66-17517. 1966. Repr. of 1937 ed. 10.00x (ISBN 0-8196-0184-5). Biblo.

--Negro in Literature & Art in the United States. 3rd ed. LC 75-144586. (BCL Ser. I). Repr. of 1930 ed. 14.50 (ISBN 0-404-00139-4). AMS Pr.

--A Social History of the American Negro. LC 70-37233. Repr. of 1921 ed. 12.50 (ISBN 0-404-00138-6). AMS Pr.

--Social History of the American Negro: Being a History of the Negro Problem in the United States. (Basic Afro-American Reprint Library). Repr. of 1921 ed. 30.00 (ISBN 0-384-05580-X). Johnson Repr.

Brawley, Edward A. Mass Media & Human Services: Getting the Message Across. (Sourcebooks for Improving Human Services: Vol. 2). 240p. 1983. 28.00 (ISBN 0-8039-1975-1); pap. 14.00 (ISBN 0-8039-1976-X). Sage.

Brawley, Edward M., ed. Negro Baptist Pulpit. facs. ed. LC 74-154072. (Black Heritage Library Collection Ser). 1890. 19.25 (ISBN 0-8369-8783-7). Ayer Co Pubs.

Brawley, Ernest. The Alamo Tree. 432p. 1984. 17.95 (ISBN 0-671-45088-3). S&S.

Brawley, James S. Rowan County: A Brief History. (Illus.). xiv, 177p. 1977. pap. 3.00 (ISBN 0-86526-129-6). NC Archives.

Brawn, Peter N. Interpretation of Bladder Biopsies. LC 83-21320. (Biopsy Interpretation Ser.). (Illus.). 222p. 1984. text ed. 48.00 (ISBN 0-89004-258-6). Raven.

--Interpretation of Prostate Biopsies. (Biopsy Interpretation Ser.). (Illus.). 144p. 1983. text ed. 43.50 (ISBN 0-89004-864-9). Raven.

Brawne, Michael. Arup Associates: Biography of an Architectural Office. (Illus.). 200p. 1985. 39.50x (ISBN 0-8390-0347-1). Abner Schram Ltd.

--The Museum Interior: Temporary & Permanent Display Techniques. (Illus.). 1982. 33.95 (ISBN 0-8038-9500-3). Architectural.

Brawner, C. O., ed. Stability in Surface Mining, Vol. 3. LC 81-70690. 872p. 1982. 39.00x (ISBN 0-89520-292-1). Soc Mining Eng.

--Stability in Underground Mining. LC 82-73915. (Illus.). 1071p. 1983. 45.00 (ISBN 0-89520-405-3). Soc Mining Eng.

Brawner, C. O., ed. see International Mine Drainage Symposium, 1st, Denver, Colorado May 1979.

Brawner, C. O., ed. see International Symposium on Stability in Coal Mining, First, Vancouver, B. C., Canada, 1978.

Brawner, C. O., jt. ed. see Radforth, Norman.

Brawner, C. O., jt. ed. see Szwilski, A. B.

Brawner, Carroll O., ed. First International Conference on Uranium Mine Waste Disposal. LC 80-69552. (Illus.). 626p. 1980. 25.00x (ISBN 0-89520-279-4). Soc Mining Eng.

Brawner, Charles O. & Charlotte Hall-Meier, eds. Investment Strategies for Financial Security. LC 84-60701. (Illus.). 220p. 1984. softcover 19.95. Meier & Assocs.

Brawner, Felix. Fantasia in Sonnets. 1983. 5.95 (ISBN 0-8062-2007-4). Carlton.

Brawner, Julianne R., et al. The Kudzu-Ivy Guide to Southern Colleges. LC 81-82293. 580p. (Orig.). 1982. pap. 10.95 (ISBN 0-9605142-1-X). Kudzu-Ivy.

Brawner, Mina R. Woman in the Word. 1.25 (ISBN 0-89985-105-3). Christ Nations.

Brax, Ralph S. The First Student Movement: Student Activism in the United States During the Nineteen Thirties. (National University Publications, Political Science Ser.). 1981. 17.50x (ISBN 0-8046-9266-1, Pub. by Kennikat). Assoc Faculty Pr.

Braxton, Hank. The Committee. (Orig.). 1979. pap. 2.25 (ISBN 0-89083-484-9). Zebra.

Braxton, Virginia A. A Very Important Person's Workbook. (Illus.). 16p. (gr. 1-5). 1980. pap. 1.75 (ISBN 0-935322-08-6). C J Frompovich.

Bray. Boileau, l'Homme et l'Oeuvre. pap. 7.95 (ISBN 0-685-34205-0). French & Eur.

--Sainte-Beuve a l'Academie de Lausanne: Chronique du Cours sur Port-Royal (1837-1838) 9.95 (ISBN 0-685-34976-4). French & Eur.

Bray & Moodie. Defense Technology & the Atlantic Alliance: Competition or Collaboration. 1977. pap. 5.00 (IFPA3, IFPA). Unipub.

Bray, Alan. Homosexuality in Renaissance England. 132p. (Orig.). 1982. pap. 7.50 (ISBN 0-907040-13-6). Gay Mens Pr.

--Homosexuality in Renaissance England. 149p. (Orig.). 15.00 (ISBN 0-907040-16-0, Pub. by GMP England); pap. 7.50 (ISBN 0-907040-13-6). Alyson Pubns.

Bray, Barbara, tr. see Caillois, Roger.

Bray, Barbara, tr. see Caron, Francois.

Bray, Barbara, tr. see Chagall, Bella.

Bray, Barbara, tr. see Chandernagor, Francoise.

Bray, Barbara, tr. see Crebillon, Claude P.

Bray, Barbara, tr. see Duby, Georges.

Bray, Barbara, tr. see Duras, Marguerite.

Bray, Barbara, tr. see Ladurie, Emmanuel L.

Bray, Barbara, tr. see Nadeau, Maurice.

Bray, Barbara, tr. see Schwartz-Bart, Simone.

Bray, Barbara, tr. see Schwarz-Bart, Simone.

Bray, Barbara, tr. see Starobinski, Jean.

Bray, Barbara, tr. see Tournier, Michel.

Bray, Barbara, tr. see Trefusis, Violet.

Bray, Bonita. Afghans: Traditional & Modern. (Illus.). 1977. pap. 2.98 (ISBN 0-517-53105-4). Crown.

Bray, C. M. Nitrogen Metabolism in Plants. LC 82-8942. 176p. 1983. 14.95 (ISBN 0-582-44640-6). Longman.

Bray, Caroline, jt. auth. see Morgan, Roger.

Bray, Charles W. Psychology & Military Proficiency. LC 69-13837. Repr. of 1948 ed. lib. bdg. 18.75x (ISBN 0-8371-1444-6, BRMI). Greenwood.

Bray, D., ed. see Royal Society of London.

Bray, Denys. The Original Order of Shakespeare's Sonnets. LC 76-30699. (Studies in Shakespeare, No. 24). 1977. lib. bdg. 39.95x (ISBN 0-8383-2140-2). Haskell.

Bray, Douglas W., et al. Formative Years in Business: A Long Term AT&T Study of Managerial Lives. LC 78-25609. 256p. 1979. Repr. of 1974 ed. text ed. 19.50 (ISBN 0-88275-824-1). Krieger.

Bray, Edmund C. & Bray, Martha C., eds. Joseph N. Nicollet on the Plains & Prairies: The Expeditions of 1838-39 with Journals, Letters, & Notes on the Dakota Indians. LC 76-3673. (Illus.). 294p. 1976. 14.50 (ISBN 0-87351-098-4). Minn Hist.

Bray, F. C. The World of Myths: A Dictionary of Universal Mythology. 75.00 (ISBN 0-8490-1335-6). Gordon Pr.

Bray, F. E., jt. ed. see Hurst, C. V.

Bray, F. Sewell. The Interpretation of Accounts. LC 79-22380. 232p. 1979. Repr. of 1957 ed. text ed. 13.00 (ISBN 0-914348-29-9). Scholars Bk.

Bray, Frank S. The Accounting Mission. LC 73-84525. 1973. Repr. of 1951 ed. text ed. 13.00 (ISBN 0-914348-01-9). Scholars Bk.

--Precision & Design in Accountancy. Brief, Richard P., ed. LC 80-1473. (Dimensions of Accounting Theory & Practice Ser.). 1981. Repr. of 1947 ed. lib. bdg. 16.00x (ISBN 0-405-13503-3). Ayer Co Pubs.

Bray, Frank T. & Moodie, Michael. Defense Technology & the Atlantic Alliance: Competition or Collaboration? LC 77-80297. (Foreign Policy Report Ser.). 42p. 1977. 5.00 (ISBN 0-89549-000-5). Inst Foreign Policy Anal.

Bray, Gary, ed. see Pokrass, David.

Bray, George A. Recent Advances in Obesity Research, No. II. LC 78-64353. 510p. 1978. 29.00 (ISBN 0-87762-259-0). Technomic.

Bray, George A., jt. ed. see Hershman, Jerome M.

Bray, Gerald. Creeds, Councils & Christ. LC 83-26443. 220p. 1984. pap. 6.95 (ISBN 0-87784-969-2). Inter-Varsity.

Bray, Gerald L. Holiness & the Will of God: Perspectives on the Theology of Tertullian. LC 79-5211. (New Foundations Theological Library). (Peter Toon & Ralph Martin series editors). 1980. 3.25 (ISBN 0-8042-3705-0). John Knox.

Bray, Grady P. & Clark, Gary S. A Stroke Family Guide & Resource. (Illus.). 192p. 1984. pap. 14.50x (ISBN 0-398-04856-8). C C Thomas.

Bray, Hazel V. The Potter's Art in California: 1885-1955. LC 78-73120. (Illus.). 88p. (Orig.). 1980. pap. 12.95 (ISBN 0-295-96200-3). U of Wash Pr.

Bray, Henry G. & Deskins, W. E. Between Nilpotent & Solvable. LC 82-539. 240p. 1982. 22.00x (ISBN 0-936428-06-6). Polygonal Pub.

Bray, Howard. Pillars of the Post: The Making of a News Empire. 1980. 7.95 (ISBN 0-393-01313-8); pap. write for info. (ISBN 0-393-30020-X). Norton.

Bray, J. & Sanchez, Gomez. Spanish in the Office. 128p. (Span.). 1980. pap. text ed. 5.95x (ISBN 0-582-35236-3). Longman.

Bray, J. W. A History of English Critical Terms. 345p. 1979. Repr. of 1898 ed. 35.00 (ISBN 0-8414-9844-X). Folcroft.

--A History of English Critical Terms. 59.95 (ISBN 0-8490-0325-3). Gordon Pr.

--A History of English Critical Terms. 1977. lib. bdg. 59.95 (ISBN 0-8490-1974-5). Gordon Pr.

Bray, J. W., jt. auth. see Hoek, E.

Bray, Jean & Wright, Sheila, eds. The Use of Technology in the Care of the Elderly & the Disabled. LC 80-17847. xii, 267p. 1980. lib. bdg. 35.00 (ISBN 0-313-22616-4, BTC). Greenwood.

Bray, Jeremy. Production, Purpose & Structure. LC 82-42603. 1982. 19.95x (ISBN 0-312-64778-6). St Martin.

--Production, Purpose & Structure: Towards a Socialist Theory of Production. 187p. 1983. pap. 7.45 (ISBN 0-86187-264-9). F Pinter Pubs.

Bray, John, jt. auth. see Barker, John N.

Bray, John F. Labour's Wrongs & Labour's Remedy. LC 66-21656. Repr. of 1839 ed. 22.50x (ISBN 0-678-00283-5). Kelley.

Bray, Lys de. Lys De Bray's Manual of Old-Fashioned Flowers. (Illus.). 272p. 15.95 (ISBN 0-902280-91-0, P991). Haynes Pubns.

Bray, Lys De see De Bray, Lys.

Bray, Lys de see De Bray, Lys.

Bray, M. A., jt. ed. see Bonta, I. L.

Bray, Mark. Educational Planning in a Decentralized System: The Papua New Guinean Experience. (Illus.). 159p. (Orig.). 1985. pap. text ed. 10.00 (ISBN 0-424-00109-8, Pub. by Sydney U Pr). Intl Spec Bk.

--Universal Primary Education in Nigeria: A Study of Kano State. 272p. (Orig.). 1981. pap. 17.50x (ISBN 0-7100-0933-X). Routledge & Kegan.

Bray, Martha C. Joseph Nicollet & His Map. LC 79-54278. (Memoirs Ser.: Vol. 140). 1980. 22.00 (ISBN 0-87169-140-X). Am Philos.

Bray, Martha C., ed. Journals of Joseph N. Nicollet. Fertey, Andre, tr. 288p. 1970. 16.50 (ISBN 0-87351-062-3). Minn Hist.

Bray, Martha C., jt. ed. see Bray, Edmund C.

Bray, Maynard. Mystic Seaport Museum Watercraft. (Illus.). 282p. 1979. 25.00 (ISBN 0-913372-16-1). Mystic Seaport.

Bray, N. N. Shifting Sands. LC 70-180321. Repr. of 1934 ed. 16.00 (ISBN 0-404-56216-7). AMS Pr.

Bray, Natalie. Dress Fitting. 2nd ed. (Illus.). 120p. 1982. pap. text ed. 17.00 (ISBN 0-246-11849-0, Granada England). Brookfield Pub Co.

--Dress Fitting. 2nd Metric ed. 120p. 1982. pap. 14.00x (ISBN 0-246-11849-0, Pub. by Granada England). Sheridan.

--Dress Pattern Designing: Basic Principles of Cut & Fit, Metric System. (Illus.). 160p. 1974. 17.95x (ISBN 0-8464-0343-9). Beekman Pubs.

--Dress Pattern Designing: Basic Principles of Cut & Fit. 4th metric ed. 160p. 1981. pap. 14.00x (ISBN 0-246-11716-8, Pub. by Granada England). Sheridan.

--Dress Pattern Designing: The Basic Principles of the Cut & Fit. 4th ed. (Illus.). 144p. 1982. pap. text ed. 14.50 (ISBN 0-246-11716-8, Granada England). Brookfield Pub Co.

--More Dress Pattern Designing. 3rd ed. (Illus.). 184p. 1982. pap. text ed. 17.00 (ISBN 0-246-11848-2, Granada England). Brookfield Pub Co.

--More Dress Pattern Designing. 3rd, metric ed. 184p. 1982. pap. 14.00x (ISBN 0-246-11848-2, Pub. by Granada England). Sheridan.

--More Dress Pattern Designing: Metric System. (Illus.). 184p. 1974. 17.95x (ISBN 0-8464-0643-8). Beekman Pubs.

Bray, Olin H. Distributed Database Management Systems. LC 79-3185. 176p. 1981. 23.00x (ISBN 0-669-03396-0). Lexington Bks.

Bray, Olin H. & Freeman, Harry A. Data-Base Computers. LC 78-24765. 192p. 1979. 27.00x (ISBN 0-669-02834-7). Lexington Bks.

Bray, Olive, ed. & tr. Elder or Poetic Edda. LC 76-43949. (Viking Society for Northern Research: Translation Ser.: Vol. 2). (Illus.). 416p. Repr. of 1908 ed. 49.00 (ISBN 0-404-60012-3). AMS Pr.

Bray, R. A. see McIvor, J. G.

Bray, R. A., jt. auth. see McIvor, J. G.

Bray, R. A., jt. ed. see McIvor, J. G.

Bray, R. C., et al, eds. Flavins & Flavoproteins: Proceedings of the Eighth International Symposium, Brighton, England, July 9-13, 1984. (Illus.). xxxiv, 923p. (Orig.). 1985. 130.00x (ISBN 3-11-009879-2). De Gruyter.

Bray, R. J. & Loughhead, R. E. Sunspots. (Illus.). 1979. pap. 9.50 (ISBN 0-486-63731-X). Dover.

--Sunspots. (Illus.). 15.25 (ISBN 0-8446-5738-7). Peter Smith.

Bray, R. J., et al. The Solar Granulation. 2nd ed. LC 83-1881. (Cambridge Astrophysics Ser.: No. 4). 1984. 54.50 (ISBN 0-521-24714-4). Cambridge U Pr.

Bray, R. N. Dredging: A Handbook for Engineers. 288p. 1979. pap. text ed. 65.00 (ISBN 0-7131-3412-7). E Arnold.

Bray, Reginald A. Boy Labour & Apprenticeship. LC 79-56952. (The English Working Class Ser.). 259p. 1980. lib. bdg. 29.00 (ISBN 0-8240-0106-0). Garland Pub.

Bray, Robert, jt. auth. see Kerr, Norbert.

Bray, Robert C. Rediscoveries: Literature & Places in Illinios. LC 81-3353. 184p. 1982. 16.95 (ISBN 0-252-00911-8). U of Ill Pr.

Bray, Robert C. & Bushnell, Paul E., eds. The Diary of a Common Soldier in the American Revolution, 1775-1783: An Annotated Edition of the Military Journal of Jeremiah Greenman. LC 77-18528. (Illus.). 333p. 1978. pap. 9.00 (ISBN 0-87580-528-0). N Ill U Pr.

Bray, Robert T., ed. The Missouri Archaeologist, Vol. 44. LC 44-14121. (Illus.). 134p. (Orig.). 1983. pap. 7.00 (ISBN 0-943414-24-5). MO Arch Soc.

Bray, Robert T., ed. see Schmit, Larry J., et al.

Bray, Rodney A., jt. auth. see Prudhoe, Stephen.

Bray, Ruth G. De, tr. see Reymond, Arnold.

Bray, S., jt. auth. see Goodman, G. T.

Bray, Sewell F. Four Essays in Accounting Theory Bound with Some Accounting Terms & Concepts. LC 82-48352. (Accountancy in Transition Ser.). 160p. 1982. lib. bdg. 22.00 (ISBN 0-8240-5305-2). Garland Pub.

Bray, Sharon, jt. auth. see Rothman, Jay.

Bray, Thomas. Reverend Thomas Bray: His Life & Selected Works Relating to Maryland. Steiner, Bernard C., ed. LC 72-14420. (Maryland Historical Society. Fund-Publications Ser.: No. 37). Repr. of 1901 ed. 15.00 (ISBN 0-404-57637-0). AMS Pr.

Bray, W. & Trump, D. Lexikon der Archaeologie. 2 vols. (Ger.). 1975. Set. pap. 29.95 (ISBN 3-499-16187-7, M-7276). French & Eur.

Bray, Warwick & Trump, David. Diccionario de Arqueologia. 276p. (Span.). 1976. pap. 17.95 (ISBN 84-335-9301-3, S-50363). French & Eur.

Bray, Wayne D. Common Law Zone in Panama: A Case Study in Reception. LC 76-23354. (Illus.). 150p. 1976. 20.00 (ISBN 0-913480-35-5). Inter Am U Pr.

Bray, William, ed. see Evelyn, John.

Braybon, Gail. Women Workers in the First World War: The British Experience. 244p. 1981. 28.50x (ISBN 0-389-20100-6, 06874). B&N Imports.

Braybrook, Patrick. Some Thoughts on Hilaire Belloc: Ten Studies. 1973. 17.50 (ISBN 0-8274-1717-9). R West.

Braybrook, Roy. The Aircraft Encyclopedia. (Reference Ser.). (Illus.). 192p. (gr. 4 up). 1985. 9.79 (ISBN 0-671-55338-0); pap. 5.95 (ISBN 0-671-55337-2). Messner.

--British Aerospace Harrier & Sea Harrier. (Illus.). 192p. 1984. 19.95 (ISBN 0-85045-561-8, Pub. by Osprey England). Motorbooks Intl.

--British Aerospace Hawk. (Illus.). 168p. 1984. pap. 16.95 (ISBN 0-85045-580-4, Pub. By Osprey England). Motorbooks Intl.

Braybrooke, David. Ethics in the World of Business. LC 82-18547. (Philosophy & Society Ser.). 506p. 1983. text ed. 34.50x (ISBN 0-8476-7069-4); pap. text ed. 13.95x (ISBN 0-8476-7107-0). Rowman & Allanheld.

Braybrooke, David & Lindblom, Charles E. A Strategy of Decision: Policy Evaluation As a Social Process. LC 63-13537. 1970. pap. text ed. 11.95 (ISBN 0-02-904610-6). Free Pr.

Braybrooke, David, jt. ed. see Bradie, Michael.

Braybrooke, E. Hardy & His Philosophy. LC 73-9581. (Studies in Thomas Hardy, No. 14). 1973. lib. bdg. 39.95x (ISBN 0-8383-1716-2). Haskell.

Braybrooke, Marcus. Inter-Faith Organizations 1893-1979: An Historical Directory. LC 79-91620. (Texts & Studies in Religion: Vol. 6). xiv, 228p. 1980. 49.95x (ISBN 0-88946-971-7). E Mellen.

Braybrooke, Neville, ed. T. S. Eliot: A Symposium for His Seventieth Birthday. facsimile ed. LC 68-58773. (Essay Index Reprint Ser). Repr. of 1958 ed. 20.00 (ISBN 0-8369-0100-2). Ayer Co Pubs.

Braybrooke, P. Some Catholic Novelists: Their Art & Outlook. 59.95 (ISBN 0-8490-1075-6). Gordon Pr.

--The Subtlety of Shaw. LC 72-2125. (English Literature Ser., No. 33). 1972. Repr. of 1930 ed. lib. bdg. 49.95x (ISBN 0-8383-1465-1). Haskell.

Braybrooke, Patrick. The Amazing Mr. Noel Coward. LC 73-13664. 1973. lib. bdg. 23.50 (ISBN 0-8414-3250-3). Folcroft.

--Considerations of Edmund Gosse. Repr. 20.00 (ISBN 0-8274-2092-7). R West.

--G. K. Chesterton. LC 72-6491. (English Biography Ser., No. 31). 130p. 1972. Repr. of 1922 ed. lib. bdg. 35.95x (ISBN 0-8383-1616-6). Haskell.

--Genius of Bernard Shaw. LC 74-8078. 1925. lib. bdg. 22.50 (ISBN 0-8414-3190-6). Folcroft.

--J. M. Barrie: A Study in Fairies & Mortals. LC 75-174693. (English Biography Ser., No. 31). 1972. Repr. of 1924 ed. lib. bdg. 39.95x (ISBN 0-8383-1349-3). Haskell.

--Kipling & His Soldiers. LC 72-3229. (English Literature Ser., No. 33). 1972. Repr. of 1926 ed. lib. bdg. 39.95x (ISBN 0-8383-1506-2). Haskell.

--Lord Morley: Writer & Thinker. Repr. 17.50 (ISBN 0-8274-3862-1). R West.

--Novelists: We Are Seven. facs. ed. LC 67-22075. (Essay Index Reprint Ser). 1926. 18.00 (ISBN 0-8369-1320-5). Ayer Co Pubs.

--Oscar Wilde: A Study. LC 72-194984. 1929. lib. bdg. 27.50 (ISBN 0-8414-2539-6). Folcroft.

--Peeps at the Mighty. facs. ed. LC 67-22076. (Essay Index Reprint Ser.). 1927. 17.00 (ISBN 0-8369-1321-3). Ayer Co Pubs.

--Philosophies in Modern Fiction. facs. ed. LC 67-22077. (Essay Index Reprint Ser.). 1929. 14.00 (ISBN 0-8369-1322-1). Ayer Co Pubs.

--Some Catholic Novelists. facs. ed. LC 67-22078. (Essay Index Reprint Ser.). 1931. 19.00 (ISBN 0-8369-1323-X). Ayer Co Pubs.

--Some Celebrities in Verse. Repr. 15.00 (ISBN 0-8274-3451-0). R West.

--Some Goddesses of the Pen. facs. ed. LC 67-22079. (Essay Index Reprint Ser.). 1928. 17.00 (ISBN 0-8369-1324-8). Ayer Co Pubs.

--Some Thoughts on Hilaire Belloc: Ten Studies. LC 68-1140. (Studies in Irish Literature, No. 16). 1969. Repr. lib. bdg. 48.95x (ISBN 0-8383-0649-7). Haskell.

--Some Victorian & Georgian Catholics. facs. ed. LC 67-22080. (Essay Index Reprint Ser.). 1932. 18.00 (ISBN 0-8369-1325-6). Ayer Co Pubs.

--Subtlety of George Bernard Shaw. LC 73-12607. 1930. lib. bdg. 27.50 (ISBN 0-8414-3227-9). Folcroft.

Braybrooke, Susan, ed. Design for Research: Principles of Laboratories. 1985. 25.00 (ISBN 0-471-06260-X). Wiley.

Brayer, Herbert O. Pueblo Indian Land Grants of the "Rio Abajo", New Mexico. Bruchey, Stuart, ed. LC 78-56700. (Management of Public Lands in the U. S. Ser.). 1979. Repr. of 1938 ed. lib. bdg. 12.00x (ISBN 0-405-11320-X). Ayer Co Pubs.

Brayer, Kenneth, ed. Data Communications via Fading Channels. LC 74-33060. 529p. 1975. 36.35 (ISBN 0-87942-047-2, PC00422); pap. 17.45 (PP00430). Inst Electrical.

Brayer, Yves & Faxon, Alicia. Jean-Louis Forain: Artist, Realist, Humanist. Walker, Janet, ed. Grasselli, Margaret M., tr. from Fr. LC 82-82968. (Illus.). 60p. (Orig.). 1982. pap. 10.00 (ISBN 0-88397-042-2). Intl Exhibit Foun.

Braymer, Daniel H. & Roe, A. C. Rewinding Small Motors. 3rd ed. LC 80-29580. 432p. 1983. Repr. of 1949 ed. lib. bdg. 29.50 (ISBN 0-89874-291-9). Krieger.

Braymer, Marjorie. Atlantis: The Biography of a Legend. LC 82-16727. (Illus.). 256p. (YA) (gr. 7 up). 1983. 13.95 (ISBN 0-689-50264-8, McElderry Bk). Atheneum.

--Walls of Windy Troy: A Biography of Heinrich Schliemann. LC 60-6207. (gr. 7 up). 1966. pap. 1.45 (ISBN 0-15-694201-1, VoyB). HarBraceJ.

Braynard, F. O. World's Greatest Ship: The Story of the S. S. Leviathan, Vol. III. Hamshar, Walter, ed. (Illus.). 400p. 1976. 30.00 (ISBN 0-9606204-2-7). F O Braynard.

Braynard, Frank, jt. auth. see Renick, Charles.

Braynard, Frank O. Fifty Famous Liners. (Illus.). 1982. 24.95 (ISBN 0-393-01611-0). Norton.

--World's Greatest Ship: The Story of the SS Leviathan, Vol. IV. Hamshar, Walter, ed. (Illus.). 424p. 1978. 45.00 (ISBN 0-9606204-3-5). F O Braynard.

--World's Greatest Ship: The Story of the S. S. Leviathan, Vol. VI. (Illus.). 448p. 1983. 59.00 (ISBN 0-9606204-5-1). F O Braynard.

--Worlds Greatest Ship: The Story of the S. S. Leviathan, Vol. I. Hamshar, Walter, ed. (Illus.). 288p. 1972. 50.00 (ISBN 0-9606204-0-0). F O Braynard.

--World's Greatest Ship: The Story of the S. S. Leviathan, Vol. II. Hamshar, Walter, ed. (Illus.). 382p. 1974. 30.00 (ISBN 0-9606204-1-9). F O Braynard.

--World's Greatest Ship: The Story of the S. S. Leviathan, Vol. V. Hamshar, Walter, ed. (Illus.). 424p. 1980. 45.00 (ISBN 0-9606204-3-5). F O Braynard.

Braynard, Frank O. & Miller, William H. Fifty Famous Liners, Vol. 2. (Illus.). 1985. 24.95 (ISBN 0-393-01947-0). Norton.

Braynard, Frank O., frwd. by. A Descriptive Catalogue of the Marine Collection to Be Found at India House. 2nd ed. LC 73-7088. (Illus.). 280p. 1973. 100.00x (ISBN 0-8195-4065-X). Wesleyan U Pr.

Brayton, Abbott A. & Landwehr, Stephana J. The Politics of War & Peace: A Survey of Thought. LC 80-67206. 320p. (Orig.). 1981. lib. bdg. 25.00 (ISBN 0-8191-1726-9); pap. text ed. 12.75 (ISBN 0-8191-1727-7). U Pr of Amer.

Brayton, Alice. The Burying Place of Gov. Arnold: An Account of the Establishment, Destruction & Restoration of the Burying Place of Benedict Arnold. (Illus.). 135p. (Orig.). 1960. pap. 4.75 (ISBN 0-917012-21-6). Preserv Soc Newport.

Brayton, R. & Spence, R. Sensitvity & Optimization. (Computer-aided Design of Electronic Circuits Ser.: No. 2). xii, 368p. 1980. 24.75 (ISBN 0-444-41929-2). Elsevier.

Brayton, R. K., et al. Modern Network Theory: An Introduction. Moschytz, G. S. & Neirynck, J., eds. 1978. text ed. 42.00 (ISBN 2-604-00034-2). Brookfield Pub Co.

Brayton, Robert K., et al. Logic Minimization Algorithms for VLSI Synthesis. (The Kluwer International Series in Engineering & Computer Science). 1984. lib. bdg. 32.50 (ISBN 0-89838-164-9). Kluwer Academic.

Brazeau, Peter. Parts of a World: Wallace Stevens Remembered. 1983. 19.95 (ISBN 0-394-52734-8). Random.

--Parts of a World: Wallace Stevens Remembered. 368p. 1985. 12.50 (ISBN 0-86547-190-8). N Point Pr.

Brazee, Edward, ed. Index to the Sierra Club Bulletin, 1950-1976. (Bibliographic Ser.: No. 16). 60p. 1978. pap. 5.95x (ISBN 0-87071-136-9). Oreg St U Pr.

Brazell, D. Edmunds. Licensing Check Lists. 49p. (Orig.). 1981. pap. 12.50x (ISBN 0-911378-37-5). Sheridan.

Brazell, James. Shelley & the Concept of Humanity: A Study of His Moral Vision. (Salzburg Studies in English Literature, Romantic Reassessment: No. 7). 1972. pap. text ed. 25.50x (ISBN 0-391-01331-9). Humanities.

Brazell, Karen, jt. auth. see Bethe, Monica.

Brazell, Karen, tr. from Jap. The Confessions of Lady Nijo. 320p. 1973. 22.50x (ISBN 0-8047-0929-7); pap. 9.50 (ISBN 0-8047-0930-0, SP 140). Stanford U Pr.

Brazelton, Louise. Guide to Selecting a Group Tour. LC 84-3234. 32p. 1984. pap. 3.50 (ISBN 0-87576-111-9). Pilot Bks.

Brazelton, T. B. & Lester, B., eds. New Approaches to Developmental Screening of Infants. 350p. 1984. 32.50 (ISBN 0-444-00816-0, Biomedical Pr). Elsevier.

Brazelton, T. Berry. Infants & Mothers: Differences in Development. rev. ed. 1983. pap. 12.95 (ISBN 0-385-29209-0, Delta). Dell.

--Infants & Mothers: Differences in Development. rev. ed. 1983. 19.95 (ISBN 0-385-29231-7, Sey Lawr). Delacorte.

--Neonatal Behavioral Assessment Scale. 2nd ed. (Clinics in Developmental Medicine Ser.: No. 88). 125p. 1984. text ed. 16.50 (ISBN 0-632-01263-3). Lippincott.

--On Becoming a Family: The Growth of Attachment. 1981. 14.95 (ISBN 0-385-28760-7, Sey Lawr). Delacorte.

--To Listen to a Child: Understanding the Normal Problems of Growing Up. 224p. 1984. 15.95 (ISBN 0-201-10617-5). Addison-Wesley.

--Toddlers & Parents. 272p. 1976. pap. 10.95 (ISBN 0-385-29034-9, Delta). Dell.

Brazelton, T. Berry, jt. auth. see Vaughan, Victor C.

Brazelton, T. Berry, jt. ed. see Kobayashi, Noboru.

Brazer, Esther S. Early American Decoration: A Comprehensive Treatise Revealing the Technique Involved in the Art of Early American Decoration of Furniture, Walls, Tinware, etc... 2nd ed. LC 83-45718. (Illus.). Repr. of 1947 ed. 74.50 (ISBN 0-404-20042-7). AMS Pr.

Brazer, Harvey E. Michigan's Fiscal & Economic Structure: A Summary of Findings & Policy Options. condensed ed. LC 81-22028. 1982. pap. 2.95 net (ISBN 0-472-08008-3). U of Mich Pr.

Brazer, Harvey E. & Laren, Deborah S., eds. Michigan's Fiscal & Economic Structure. LC 81-22028. 976p. 1982. text ed. 30.00x (ISBN 0-472-10022-X); pap. text ed. 14.95x (ISBN 0-472-08027-X). U of Mich Pr.

Brazer, Marjorie C. Cruising Guide to the Great Lakes & Their Connecting Waterways. (Illus.). 496p. 1985. 19.95 (ISBN 0-8092-5415-8). Contemp Bks.

--The Sweet Water Sea: A Guide to Lake Huron's Georgian Bay. LC 84-992. (Illus.). 208p. 1984. 16.95 (ISBN 0-931850-03-7). Peach Mount Pr.

--Well-Favored Passage: A Guide to Lake Huron's North Channel. rev ed. LC 82-6454. (Illus.). 170p. 1982. 14.95 (ISBN 0-931850-02-9). Peach Mount Pr.

Brazier, A. B, jt. ed. see Crandall, B. F.

Brazier, David, jt. auth. see Hewitt, Edward.

Brazier, L. R., et al, eds. Die & Mould Making. (Engineering Craftsmen: No. H22). (Illus.). 1970. spiral bdg. 42.50x (ISBN 0-85083-126-1). Trans-Atlantic.

Brazier, M. A., ed. Growth & Development of the Brain: Nutritional, Genetic, & Environmental Factors. LC 75-14565. (International Brain Research Organization Ser.: Vol. 1). 412p. 1975. 57.00 (ISBN 0-89004-037-0). Raven.

Brazier, M. A., ed. see Conferences on Brain & Behavior, Los Angeles.

Brazier, Mary, jt. auth. see Cooper, Edwin.

Brazier, Mary, jt. ed. see Honrubia, Vicente.

Brazier, Mary, jt. ed. see Sigman, David S.

Brazier, Mary A. The Electrical Activity of the Nervous System. 4th ed. 260p. 1977. 19.50 (ISBN 0-272-79403-1). Krieger.
--The Neurophysiological Background for Anesthesia. (Illus.). 144p. 1972. 18.50x (ISBN 0-398-02567-3). C C Thomas.
Brazier, Mary A. & Coceani, Flavio. Brain Dysfunction in Infantile Febrile Convulsions. LC 75-14564. (International Brain Research Organization Monograph: Vol. 2). 384p. 1976. 54.00 (ISBN 0-89004-068-0). Raven.
Brazier, Mary A., jt. auth. see Meisami, Esmail.
Brazier, Mary A. & Petsche, Hellmuth, eds. Architectonics of the Cerebral Cortex. LC 77-83694. (International Brain Research Organization (IBRO) Monograph: Vol. 3). 502p. 1978. 68.50 (ISBN 0-89004-140-7). Raven.
Brazier, Mary A., jt. ed. see Buchwald, Nathaniel A.
Brazier, Mary A., jt. ed. see Hobson, J. Allan.
Brazier, Mary A., ed. see Symposium of the Austrian Academy of Sciences, Vienna, 1971.
Brazier, Mary A. B. A History of Neurophysiology in the 17th & 18th Centuries: From Concept to Experiment. (Illus.). 244p. 1984. text ed. 79.00 (ISBN 0-89004-553-4). Raven.
Brazier, Nicolas. Histoire des petits theatres de Paris depuis leur origine, 2 vols in 1. LC 68-56773. (Research & Source Works Ser.: No. 258). 1969. Repr. of 1838 ed. lib. bdg. 26.50 (ISBN 0-8337-0358-7). B Franklin.
Brazil, Diane. South Bay Bargain Guide II. LC 84-370. (Orig.). 1984. pap. 4.95 (ISBN 0-87701-294-6). Chronicle Bks.
Brazil, James, jt. auth. see Koch, Carl.
Brazil, K. L. Can We Preach Philosophy. 1968. 5.00 (ISBN 0-8022-0171-7). Philos Lib.
Brazil, Wayne D. Settling Civil Suits: Litigators' Views About Appropriate Roles & Effective Techniques for Federal Judges. LC 84-72690. (Illus.). 170p. Date not set. price not set (ISBN 0-89707-153-0). Amer Bar Assn.
Brazil, Wayne D., et al. Managing Complex Litigation: A Practical Guide to the Use of Special Masters. Sikes, Bette, ed. xiii, 349p. 1983. 25.00 (ISBN 0-910059-03-9). Am Bar Foun.
Brazini, Luigi. The Europeans. 304p. 1983. 14.95 (ISBN 0-671-24578-3). S&S.
Brazinsky, Terri C. & Bowden, Kathi, eds. Santa Catalina Cookbook, Vol. I. 2nd rev. ed. Santa Catalina Students & Faculty, tr. (Illus.). 293p. 1983. 15.50 (ISBN 0-9612300-0-2). Santa Catalina.
--Santa Catalina Cookbook, Vol. 2. (Illus.). 400p. 1983. 17.50 (ISBN 0-9612300-1-0). Santa Catalina.
Brazleton, T. Berry. On Becoming a Family. 320p. 1983. pap. 8.95 (ISBN 0-385-28759-3, Delta). Dell.
Brazziel, William F. Quality Education for All Americans: An Assessment of Gains of Black Americans with Proposals for Program Development in American Schools & Colleges for the Next Quarter Century. LC 73-88966. 264p. 1974. 10.95 (ISBN 0-88258-007-8). Howard U Pr.
Brcic, V. Application of Holography & Hologram Interferometry to Photoelasticity. 2nd ed. (CISM, International Centre for Mechanical Sciences, Courses & Lectures: Vol. 14). (Illus.). 58p. 1975. pap. 10.00 (ISBN 0-387-81163-X). Springer-Verlag.
Brcic, V., ed. see CISM (International Center for Mechanical Sciences), Dept. for Mechanics of Deformable Bodies, 1970.
Brea, Juan, jt. auth. see Low, Mary.
Breach, N., jt. auth. see Fishman, W. J.
Breadmore, R. G. Organization & Methods. (Teach Yourself Ser.). 1973. pap. 4.95 (ISBN 0-679-10509-3). McKay.
Bready, John W. England, Before & after Wesley: The Evangelical Revival & Social Reform. LC 72-139906. (Illus.). 463p. 1971. Repr. of 1938 ed. 17.00x (ISBN 0-8462-1533-0). Russell.
Break, George F. Federal Lending & Economic Stability. LC 79-28549. (Illus.). x, 185p. 1980. Repr. of 1965 ed. lib. bdg. 22.50x (ISBN 0-313-22285-1, BRFS). Greenwood.
--Financing Government in a Federal System. (Studies of Government Finance). 1980. 22.95 (ISBN 0-8157-1068-2); pap. 8.95 (ISBN 0-8157-1067-4). Brookings.
Break, George F.. & Break, George F. Federal Tax Reform: The Impossible Dream? (Studies of Government Finance). 142p. 1975. 16.95 (ISBN 0-8157-1072-0); pap. 7.95 (ISBN 0-8157-1071-2). Brookings.
Break, George F. & Committee on Taxation, Resources & Economic Development. State & Local Finance: The Pressures of the 80's. LC 83-47757. 1984. 25.00x (ISBN 0-299-09340-9). U of Wis Pr.
Break, George F., jt. auth. see Break, George F..
Break, George F., ed. Metropolitan Financing: Principles & Practice. LC 77-77437. (Illus.). 346p. 1978. 27.50x (ISBN 0-299-07280-0). U of Wis Pr.
Breakefield, X. O., ed. Neurogenetics: Genetic Approaches to the Nervous System. 378p. 1979. 43.95 (ISBN 0-444-00295-2, Biomedical Pr). Elsevier.
Breakey, Gail F. & Voulgaropoulos, Emmanuel. Laos Health Survey: Mekong Valley, 1968-1969. LC 76-14. 140p. 1976. pap. text ed. 10.00x (ISBN 0-8248-0378-7). UH Pr.
Breakstone, et al. The Vietnam Era: A Guide to Teaching Resources. (Illus.). 105p. (Orig.). (gr. 9-12). 1978. pap. text ed. 5.00 (ISBN 0-9607794-1-8). Indochina Curriculum Grp.
Breakstone, et al, eds. Front Lines: Soliders' Writings from Vietnam. (Illus.). 135p. (gr. 9-12). 1975. pap. text ed. 2.00 (ISBN 0-9607794-0-X). Indochina Curriculum Grp.
Breakstone, David & Jochnowitz, Cindy, eds. The Israel Experience Book. LC 76-56985. (Illus.). 240p. 1985. pap. 8.95 (ISBN 0-8197-0021-5). Bloch.
Breakwell & Rowett. Social Work: The Social Psychological Approach. 1982. 51.95 (ISBN 0-442-30519-2); pap. 23.95 (ISBN 0-442-30520-6). Van Nos Reinhold.
Breakwell, Glynis M. Threatened Identities. LC 82-8451. 269p. 1982. 44.95x (ISBN 0-471-10233-4, Pub. by Wiley-Interscience). Wiley.
Breal, Auguste. Velazquez. Bussy, Madame Simon, tr. 1978. Repr. of 1904 ed. lib. bdg. 25.00 (ISBN 0-8495-0337-X). Arden Lib.
Breal, Michel J. Semantics: Studies in the Science of Meaning. 1977. lib. bdg. 69.95 (ISBN 0-8490-2592-3). Gordon Pr.
Brealey, Richard. An Introduction to Risk & Return. 2nd, rev. ed. (Illus.). 192p. 1983. 14.95 (ISBN 0-262-02187-0). MIT Pr.
Brealey, Richard & Myers, Stewart. Principles of Corporate Finance. 2nd ed. (Finance Ser.). 864p. 1984. text ed. 35.95x (ISBN 0-07-007383-X). McGraw.
Brealey, Richard A. Security Prices in a Competitive Market: More About Risk & Return from Common Stocks. 1971. 24.75x (ISBN 0-262-02077-7). MIT Pr.
Brealey, T. B. & Newton, P. W. Living in Remote Communities in Tropical Australia: The Hedland Study. 100p. 1981. 20.00x (ISBN 0-643-02279-1, Pub. by CSIRO Australia). State Mutual Bk.
Brealy, John, jt. auth. see Ainworth, Maryan W.
Brealy, Richard, jt. auth. see Lorie, James.
Bream, Howard N., et al, eds. A Light unto My Path: Old Testament Studies in Honor of Jacob M. Myers. LC 73-85042. (Gettysburg Theological Studies, No. 4). 576p. 1974. 27.95 (ISBN 0-87722-026-3). Temple U Pr.
Bream, Jon. Prince: Inside the Purple Reign. Lippman & Boegehold, eds. (Illus.). 112p. 1984. pap. 8.95 (ISBN 0-02-060410-6, Collier). Macmillan.
Brean, Herbert. How to Stop Smoking. rev. ed. 1984. pap. 2.95 (ISBN 0-671-52460-7). PB.
Brean, Joel. Rebels United: James Dean the Enduring Reality. (Illus.). 140p. (Orig.). Date not set. pap. 6.95 (ISBN 0-318-11857-2). Brean-Jones Pub.
Brearley, Alan & Treadle, John. The Worsted Industry. 198p. 1982. 59.00x (ISBN 0-686-87182-0). State Mutual Bk.
Brearley, Alan & Tredale, John A. The Woolen Industry. 154p. 1982. 40.00x (ISBN 0-686-87180-4). State Mutual Bk.
Brearley, H. C. Homicide in the United States. LC 69-14913. (Criminology, Law Enforcement, & Social Problems Ser.: No. 36). 1969. Repr. of 1932 ed. 15.00x (ISBN 0-87585-036-7). Patterson Smith.
Brearley, Joan. The Book of the Bulldog. (Illus.). 320p. 1984. 29.95 (ISBN 0-86622-027-5, H-1071). TFH Pubns.
Brearley, Joan M. Book of the Afghan Hound. (Illus.). 1978. 29.95 (ISBN 0-87666-665-9, H-991). TFH Pubns.
--The Book of the Akita. (Illus.). 272p. 1985. text ed. 29.95 (ISBN 0-86622-053-4, H-1075). TFH Pubns.
--The Book of the Yorkshire Terrier. (Illus.). 352p. 1984. 29.95 (ISBN 0-87666-940-2, H-1066). TFH Pubns.
--This Is the Afghan Hound. (Illus.). 1965. 12.95 (ISBN 0-87666-231-9, PS-639). TFH Pubns.
--This Is the Alaskan Malamute. (Illus.). 415p. 1975. 19.95 (ISBN 0-87666-650-0, PS-737). TFH Pubns.
Brearley, Joan McD. All about Himalayan Cats. (Illus.). 96p. (Orig.). 1976. 6.95 (ISBN 0-87666-756-6, PS-736). TFH Pubns.
--The Book of the Cocker Spaniel. (Illus.). 300p. 1982. 29.95 (ISBN 0-87666-737-X, H-1034). TFH Pubns.
--The Book of the Doberman Pinscher. (Illus.). 1976. 17.95 (ISBN 0-87666-658-6, H-968). TFH Pubns.
--Book of the Maltese. (Illus.). 320p. 1984. 29.95 (ISBN 0-87666-563-6, H-1067). TFH Pubns.
--The Book of the Pug. (Illus.). 320p. 1980. 14.95 (ISBN 0-87666-683-7, H-1021). TFH Pubns.
--Ibizan Hounds. (Illus.). 128p. 1980. 4.95 (ISBN 0-87666-694-2, KW-060). TFH Pubns.
--This Is the Irish Setter. (Illus.). 480p. 1975. 19.95 (ISBN 0-87666-655-1, H-952). TFH Pubns.
--This Is the Lhasa Apso. (Illus.). 1977. text ed. 14.95 (ISBN 0-87666-663-2, PS-744). TFH Pubns.
--This Is the Samoyed. (Illus.). 384p. 1975. 17.95 (ISBN 0-87666-379-X, H-954). TFH Pubns.
Brearley, Joan McD. & Easton, Allen. Book of the Shih Tzu. (Illus.). 304p. 1980. 24.95 (ISBN 0-87666-664-0, H-996). TFH Pubns.
Brearley, Joan McD. & Nicholas, Anna K. This Is the Skye Terrier. (Illus.). 560p. 1975. 19.95 (ISBN 0-87666-396-X, PS-708). TFH Pubns.
Brearley, Joan McD., jt. auth. see Anderson, Marlene.
Brearley, Joan McD., jt. auth. see Nicholas, Anna K.
Brearley, K. & McBride, R. Nouvelles Du Quebec. 2nd ed. (Fr). 1977. pap. text ed. 11.95 (ISBN 0-13-625467-5). P-H.
Brearley, P., et al. Admission to Residential Care. 1980. 25.00x (ISBN 0-422-76930-4, NO.2019, Pub. by Tavistock). Methuen Inc.
Brearley, Paul, et al. Leaving Residential Care. 220p. 1982. (Pub. by Tavistock); pap. 9.50 (ISBN 0-422-77930-X, NO. 3775). Methuen Inc.
Brearley, Paul C. & Hall, M. R. P. Risk & Aging. (Hazards & Helping). 250p. (Orig.). 1982. pap. 9.95x (ISBN 0-7100-9080-3). Routledge & Kegan.
Brearly, Joan McD. This Is the Siberian Husky. (Illus.). 543p. 1974. 17.95 (ISBN 0-87666-392-7, PS-707). TFH Pubns.
Brearly, Joan McD. & Nicholas, Anna K. This Is the Bichon Frise. (Illus.). 1973. 14.95 (ISBN 0-87666-247-5, PS-700). TFH Pubns.
Breasted, Charles. Pioneer to the Past: The Story of James Henry Breasted, Archaeologist. 1977. pap. 5.95x (ISBN 0-226-07186-3, P710, Phoen). U of Chicago Pr.
Breasted, James H. The Dawn of Conscience. LC 76-19114. 1933. lib. rep. ed. 25.00 (ISBN 0-684-14741-6, ScribT). Scribner.
--Development of Religion & Thought in Ancient Egypt. LC 58-7111. 406p. 1972. pap. 10.95x (ISBN 0-8122-1045-X, Pa Paperbks). U of Pa Pr.
--History of Egypt. (Illus.). 1909. lib. bdg. 27.50x (ISBN 0-684-14510-3, ScribT). Scribner.
--A History of Egypt: From the Earliest Times to the Persian Conquest. 634p. 1983. Repr. of 1916 ed. lib. bdg. 150.00 (ISBN 0-89987-958-6). Darby Bks.
Breasted, Mary. I Shouldn't Be Telling You This. LC 82-48141. 384p. 1983. 15.34i (ISBN 0-06-015092-0, HarpT). Har-Row.
--I Shouldn't Be Telling You This. 384p. (Orig.). 1984. pap. 3.95 (ISBN 0-440-13930-9). Dell.
Breathed, Berke. Bloom County: Loose Tails. (Illus.). 160p. (Orig.). 1983. pap. 6.70i (ISBN 0-316-10710-7). Little.
--Penguin Dreams: And Stranger Things. (Illus.). 120p. 1985. pap. 6.95 (ISBN 0-316-10725-5). Little.
--Toons for Our Times: A Bloom County Book. (Orig.). 1984. pap. 6.70i (ISBN 0-316-10709-3). Little.
Breathett, George, ed. The Catholic Church in Haiti 1704-1785: Selected Letters, Memoirs & Documents. 1983. 27.95x (ISBN 0-89712-103-1). Documentary Pubns.
Breathitt, Edward T. The Public Papers of Governor Edward T. Breathitt, 1963-1967. LC 83-25968. (The Public Papers of the Governors of Kentucky). 632p. 1984. 28.00x (ISBN 0-8131-0603-6). U Pr of KY.
Breathnach, A. S., jt. auth. see Stolinski, C.
Breathnach, A. S., ed. Frazer's Anatomy of the Human Skeleton. 6th ed. 1965. 18.50x (ISBN 0-7000-1135-8). Churchill.
Breathnach, Breandan. Folk Music & Dances of Ireland. 152p. 1983. pap. 5.95 (ISBN 0-85342-509-4, Pub. by Mercier Pr Ireland). Irish Bks Media.
Breau Armand De, Quatrefages De see Quatrefages de Breau, Armand de.
Breault, Joseph. Seeking Purity of Heart: The Gift of Ourselves to God. (Illus.). 96p. (Orig.). 1975. pap. 2.95 (ISBN 0-914544-07-1). Living Flame Pr.
Breault, Judith C. The Odyssey of a Humanitarian: Emily Howland, 1827-1929. 35.00 (ISBN 0-405-14076-2). Ayer Co Pubs.
Breault, William. Under the Fig Tree. LC 79-56689. (Illus.). 96p. (Orig.). 1980. pap. 2.75 (ISBN 0-87793-199-2). Ave Maria.
--A Voice over the Water. LC 84-73051. 128p. (Orig.). 1985. pap. 4.95 (ISBN 0-87793-281-6). Ave Maria.
Breaux, Adele. Saint-Exupery in America, 1942-1943: A Memoir. LC 70-99322. (Illus.). 166p. 1971. 16.50 (ISBN 0-8386-7610-3). Fairleigh Dickinson.
Breazeale, Daniel. Philosophy & Truth: Selections from Nietzsche's Notebooks of the Early 1870s. LC 76-53746. 1979. text ed. 20.45x (ISBN 0-391-00686-X). Humanities.
Breazeale, J. W. Life As It Is. LC 74-17309. 1969. Repr. of 1842 ed. 20.00 (ISBN 0-918450-00-4). C Elder.
Breazile, James E., ed. Textbook of Veterinary Physiology. LC 71-135683. (Illus.). 573p. 1971. text ed. 22.50 (ISBN 0-8121-0327-0). Lea & Febiger.
Brebbia, C. Boundary Element Techniques in Engineering. new ed. (Illus.). 1980. text ed. 39.95 (ISBN 0-408-00340-5). Butterworth.
Brebbia, C., ed. Boundary Element Methods: Proceedings. (Illus.). 622p. 1981. 61.00 (ISBN 0-387-10816-5). Springer-Verlag.
Brebbia, C. A. Boundary Element Techniques. (Illus.). 510p. 1984. 78.00 (ISBN 0-387-12484-5). Springer-Verlag.
--Computational Hydraulics. 1982. text ed. 49.95. Butterworth.
--Dynamic Analysis of Offshore Structures. (Illus.). 1979. 69.95 (ISBN 0-408-00393-6). Butterworth.
--Finite Element Systems. 3rd, rev. ed. 770p. 1980. 85.00 (ISBN 0-387-15116-8). Springer Verlag.
--Progress in Bondary Element Methods. LC 81-6454. 325p. 1981. 58.95x (ISBN 0-470-27223-6). Halsted Pr.
Brebbia, C. A. & Connor, J. J. Numerical Methods in Fluid Dynamics. LC 74-83628. 576p. 1974. 42.50x (ISBN 0-8448-0524-6). Crane-Russak Co.
Brebbia, C. A. & Ferrante, A. J. Computational Methods for the Solution of Engineering Problems. LC 76-53093. 354p. 1977. 34.50x (ISBN 0-8448-1079-7). Crane-Russak Co.
Brebbia, C. A., jt. auth. see Adey, R. A.
Brebbia, C. A., ed. Applied Numerical Modeling: Proceedings of the First International Conference, Held at the University of Southampton, 11-15 July, 1977. LC 77-11141. 713p. 1978. 64.95x (ISBN 0-470-99271-9). Halsted Pr.
--Basic Principles & Applications. (Topics in Boundary Elements Research Ser.: Vol. 3). (Illus.). 280p. 1984. 49.50 (ISBN 0-387-13097-7). Springer-Verlag.
--Boundary Element Methods in Engineering, Southampton, England 1982: Proceedings. (Illus.). 649p. 1982. 66.00 (ISBN 0-387-11819-5). Springer-Verlag.
--Boundary Element Techniques in Computer-Aided Engineering. LC 84-16710. 1984. lib. bdg. 58.50 (ISBN 90-247-3065-1, Pub. by Martinus Nijhoff Netherlands). Kluwer Academic.
--Boundary Elements VI. 900p. 1984. 55.50 (ISBN 0-387-13420-4). Springer-Verlag.
--Finite Element Systems: A Handbook. (Illus.). 500p. 1983. 78.50 (ISBN 0-387-12118-8). Springer-Verlag.
--Time-Dependent & Vibration Problems. (Topics in Boundary Element Research Ser.: Vol. 2). (Illus.). 280p. 1985. 59.00 (ISBN 0-387-13993-1). Springer-Verlag.
Brebbia, C. A. & Keramidas, G. A., eds. Computational Methods & Experimental Measurements: Proceedings of the 2nd International Conference, on Board the Liner, the Queen Elizabeth 2, New York to Southhampton, June-July 1984. 800p. 76.60 (ISBN 0-387-13419-0). Springer-Verlag.
Brebbia, C. A., et al. Vibrations of Engineering Structures. (Lecture Notes in Engineering Ser.: Vol. 10). 300p. 1985. pap. 21.00 (ISBN 0-387-13959-1). Springer-Verlag.
Brebbia, C. A., et al, eds. Boundary Elements. 104p. 1983. 112.00 (ISBN 0-387-12803-4). Springer-Verlag.
--Environmental Forces on Engineering Structures. LC 79-16733. 564p. 1979. 74.95x (ISBN 0-470-26820-4). Halsted Pr.
--Hydrosoft '84; Hydraulic Engineering Software: Proceedings of the International Conference, Protoroz, Yugoslavia, Sept. 10-14, 1984. 1984. 129.75 (ISBN 0-444-99607-9). Elsevier.
Brebion, Antoine. Bibliographie des voyages dans l'Indochine francaise du 9e au 19e siecle. LC 78-132542. (Bibliography & Reference Ser.: No. 395). (Geography & Discovery Ser., No. 8). 1971. Repr. of 1910 ed. lib. bdg. 24.00 (ISBN 0-8337-0359-5). B Franklin.
--Livre d'Or du Cambodge de la Cochinchine & de l'Annam, 1625-1910 & Bibliographie. LC 72-147145. (Research & Source Works Ser.: No. 665). 1971. Repr. of 1910 ed. lib. bdg. 14.00 (ISBN 0-8337-0360-9). B Franklin.
Brebner, Daphne B., ed. see Wallower, Lucille.
Brebner, J. Environmental Psychology in Building Design. (Architectural Science Ser.). (Illus.). x, 213p. 1982. 37.00 (ISBN 0-85334-969-X, Pub. by Elsevier Applied Sci England). Elsevier.
Brebner, John B. The Explorers of North America, Fourteen Ninety-Two to Eighteen Hundred Six. LC 83-45719. Repr. of 1933 ed. 67.50 (ISBN 0-404-20043-5). AMS Pr.
--New England's Outpost: Acadia Before the Conquest of Canada. LC 72-81954. (Columbia University. Faculty of Political Science. Studies in History, Economics, & Public Law: No. 293). 1974. lib. bdg. 21.00 (ISBN 0-8337-5107-7). B Franklin.
--North Atlantic Triangle: The Interplay of Canada, the United States, & Great Britain. enl. ed. LC 77-110676. (Relations of Canada & the U. S. Ser). (Illus.). 385p. 1970. Repr. of 1966 ed. 25.00x (ISBN 0-8462-1195-5). Russell.
Brebner, John B., tr. see Hansen, Marcus L.
Breccia, A. & Cavalleri, B., eds. Nitroimidazoles: Chemistry, Pharmacology & Clinical Application. (NATO ASI Series A, Life Science: Vol. 42). 225p. 1982. 37.50 (ISBN 0-306-40916-X, Plenum Pr). Plenum Pub.
Breccia, A., et al, eds. Advanced Topics on Radiosensitizers of Hypoxic Cells. LC 82-427. (NATO ASI Series A, Life Sciences: Vol. 43). 296p. 1982. 45.00 (ISBN 0-306-40915-1, Plenum Pr). Plenum Pub.
Breccia, E., ed. Inscriptiones Graecae Aegypti, No. 2: Alexandria. 1978. 30.00 (ISBN 0-89005-242-5). Ares.
Brech, Michael & Sharp, Margaret. Inward Investment: Policy Options for the United Kingdom. (Chatham House Papers: No. 21). 128p. (Orig.). 1984. pap. 10.95x (ISBN 0-7102-0256-3). Routledge & Kegan.
Brecheen, Carl & Faulkner, Paul. What Every Family Needs or Whatever Happened to Mom, Dad, & the Kids. LC 78-68726. (Journey Bks.). 1979. pap. 2.95 (ISBN 0-8344-0104-5). Sweet.

Brecheen, Joel. Tennis Made Easy. 1971. pap. 4.00 (ISBN 0-87980-160-3). Wilshire.

Brecher. The Rays: A History of Radiology in the United States & Canada. LC 69-19071. 522p. 1977. 32.50 (ISBN 0-88275-926-4). Krieger.

Brecher, Amy, jt. auth. see Miniutti, Denise.

Brecher, Arline, jt. auth. see Cranton, Elmer.

Brecher, Charles. Upgrading Blue Collar & Service Workers. LC 79-186512. (Policy Studies in Employment & Welfare Ser.: No. 12). pap. 31.80 (ISBN 0-317-09670-2, 2020494). Bks Demand UMI.

Brecher, Charles, jt. auth. see Eichner, Alfred S.

Brecher, Charles & Horton, Raymond D., eds. Setting Municipal Priorities: American Cities & the New York Experience. 560p. 1985. 40.00x (ISBN 0-8147-1066-2); pap. text ed. 20.00x (ISBN 0-8147-1067-0). NYU Pr.

--Setting Municipal Priorities, 1968. 540p. 1985. text ed. 50.00x (ISBN 0-8147-1081-6); pap. text ed. 20.00x (ISBN 0-8147-1082-4). NYU Pr.

--Setting Municipal Priorities, 1981. LC 80-67392. 212p. 1981. text ed. 25.00x (ISBN 0-86598-010-1). Allanheld.

--Setting Municipal Priorities, 1982. LC 81-66978. 464p. 1981. text ed. 29.95x (ISBN 0-87154-137-8). Russell Sage.

--Setting Municipal Priorities, 1984. 250p. (Orig.). 1984. pap. 40.00x (ISBN 0-8147-1054-9). NYU Pr.

Brecher, Charles, jt. ed. see Horton, Raymond D.

Brecher, Deborah L. The Women's Computer Literacy Handbook. (Illus.). 1985. pap. 9.95 (ISBN 0-452-25565-1, Plume). NAL.

Brecher, Edward. The Sex Researchers. 410p. 1979. 9.50 (ISBN 0-317-34150-2). Specific Pr.

Brecher, Edward M., jt. auth. see Consumer Reports Books Editors.

Brecher, Edward M., jt. auth. see Consumer Reports Editors.

Brecher, G. see Vyas, G., et al.

Brecher, G., jt. ed. see Bessis, M.

Brecher, Irving. Capital Flows Between Canada & the United States. (Illus.). 141p. 1965. 2.00 (ISBN 0-88806-080-7). Inst C D Howe.

Brecher, Irving & Abbas, S. A. Foreign Aid & Industrial Development in Pakistan. (Perspectives on Development Ser.: No. 1). 1971. 44.50 (ISBN 0-521-08339-7). Cambridge U Pr.

Brecher, J. & Cherry, G. Macintosh Pascal. 1985. 17.95 (ISBN 0-8359-4174-4). Reston.

Brecher, Jeremy. Strike! LC 77-82654. (Illus.). 327p. 1977. pap. 9.00 (ISBN 0-8467-0364-5). South End Pr.

Brecher, Jeremy & Costello, Tim. Common Sense for Hard Times. LC 76-7270. (Institute for Policy Studies). 277p. 1979. pap. 7.00 (ISBN 0-89608-109-5). South End Pr.

Brecher, Jeremy & Costello, Tom. Common Sense for Hard Times. 277p. 1979. pap. 7.50 (ISBN 0-89758-026-5). Inst Policy Stud.

Brecher, Jeremy, et al, eds. Brass Valley: The Story of Working People's Lives & Struggles in an American Industrial Region. 304p. 1982. 29.95 (ISBN 0-87722-271-1); pap. 14.95 (ISBN 0-87722-272-X). Temple U Pr.

Brecher, Jerry & Cherry, George. Macintosh Pascal. (Illus.). 360p. 17.95 (ISBN 0-317-13084-6). P-H.

Brecher, Kenneth & Feirtag, Michael, eds. Astronomy of the Ancients. (Illus.). 1979. pap. 8.95 (ISBN 0-262-52070-2). MIT Pr.

Brecher, Kenneth & Setti, Ginancarlo, eds. High Energy Astrophysics & Its Relation to Elementary Particle Physics. LC 74-19794. 1974. 45.00x. MIT Pr.

Brecher, Michael. Decisions in Crisis: Israel 1967 & 1973 (International Crisis Behavior Project) LC 78-62850. 1980. 30.00 (ISBN 0-520-03766-9). U of Cal Pr.

--Decisions in Israel's Foreign Policy. LC 73-77143. 675p. 1975. 52.00x (ISBN 0-300-01660-3). Yale U Pr.

--The Foreign Policy System of Israel: Setting, Images, Process. LC 73-179469. (Illus.). 692p. 1972. 52.00x (ISBN 0-300-01549-6). Yale U Pr.

--Nehru's Mantle: The Politics of Succession in India. LC 75-32653. 1976. Repr. of 1966 ed. lib. bdg. 19.75x (ISBN 0-8371-8553-X, BRNW). Greenwood.

Brecher, Michael, ed. Studies in Crisis Behavior. 384p. 1979. text ed. 19.95 (ISBN 0-87855-292-8). Transaction Bks.

Brecher, Robert. Anselm's Argument: The Logic of Divine Existence. 144p. 1985. text ed. 31.00x (ISBN 0-86127-105-X, Pub. by Avebury England). Humanities.

--Anselm's Argument: The Logic of Divine Existence. 200p. 1985. write for info. (ISBN 0-566-05022-6). Gower Pub Co.

Brecher, S. M. & Moore, D. W. The Economic Impact of the Introduction of VAT. LC 82-71513. 1982. lib. bdg. 5.00 (ISBN 0-910586-48-9). Finan Exec.

Brecher, Steven L. Beating the Races with a Computer. LC 80-11311. 105p. (Orig.). 1980. pap. 14.95 (ISBN 0-9603792-0-7). Software Supply.

Brechling, Frank. Taxes on Capital as a Means of Stimulating Employment: A Review & Evaluation of the Literature. 67p. 4.70 (ISBN 0-318-16305-5, G-9). Public Int Econ.

Brechna, H. Superconducting Magnet Systems. LC 72-96051. (Technische Physik in Einveldarstellungen: Vol. 18). (Illus.). 480p. 1973. 110.00 (ISBN 0-387-06103-7). Springer-Verlag.

Brechner, Irv. Getting into Computers: A Career Guide to Today's Hottest New Field. 224p. (Orig.). 1983. pap. 4.95 (ISBN 0-345-30172-2). Ballantine.

Brechner, Irv, jt. auth. see Schwartz, Lester.

Brechner, Verne L., et al. Practical Electroencephalography for the Anesthesiologist. (Illus.). 120p. 1962. 14.75x (ISBN 0-398-00217-7). C C Thomas.

Brecht, Arnold. The Art & Technique of Administration in German Ministries. LC 70-138205. (Illus.). 191p. 1972. Repr. of 1940 ed. lib. bdg. 22.50x (ISBN 0-8371-5557-6, BRGM). Greenwood.

--Political Education of Arnold Brecht - An Autobiography: 1884-1970. LC 77-100994. 1970. 44.00 (ISBN 0-691-07527-1). Princeton U Pr.

--Political Theory: The Foundations of Twentieth Century Political Thought. LC 59-5591. pap. 115.40 (ISBN 0-317-09452-1, 2015011). Bks Demand UMI.

Brecht, Bertold. Short Stories: Nineteen Twenty-One to Nineteen Forty-Six. 1983. 19.95 (ISBN 0-413-37050-X, NO. 3765). Methuen Inc.

Brecht, Bertolt. Bertolt Brecht: Diaries Nineteen Twenty to Twenty-Two. 169p. 1980. pap. 5.95 (ISBN 0-312-07704-1). St Martin.

--Bertolt Brecht, Poems, 1913-1956. 2nd ed. Willett, John & Manheim, Ralph, eds. LC 79-17139. 1980. 29.95 (ISBN 0-416-00081-9, NO.0126); pap. 13.95 (ISBN 0-416-00091-6, NO.0127). Methuen Inc.

--Bertolt Brecht Short Stories. Willett, John & Manheim, Ralph, eds. 256p. (Orig.). 1985. pap. 9.95 (ISBN 0-413-52890-1, NO. 9311). Methuen Inc.

--Brecht on Theatre. Willett, John, tr. from Ger. (Illus.). 294p. 1964. pap. 6.95 (ISBN 0-8090-0542-5). Hill & Wang.

--Caucasian Chalk Circle. Bentley, Eric & Apelman, Maja, trs. from German. (YA) (gr. 9 up). 1971. pap. 2.95 (ISBN 0-394-17258-2, B312, BC). Grove.

--Collected Plays, Vols. 1-2, 5, 6-7 & 9. Manheim, Ralph & Willett, John, eds. Incl. Vol. 1. pap. 5.95 (ISBN 0-394-71670-1, V-670); Vol. 2. pap. 6.95 (ISBN 0-394-72085-7, V-85); Vol. 5. pap. 7.95 (ISBN 0-394-71759-7, V-759); Vol. 6. pap. 6.95 (ISBN 0-394-71350-8, V-350); Vol. 7. pap. 4.95 (ISBN 0-394-71216-1, V216); Vol. 9. pap. 3.95 (ISBN 0-394-71819-4, V-819). 1971-73. pap. (Vin). Random.

--Edward Second: A Chronicle Play. Bentley, Eric, tr. from German. & intro. by. (Orig.). 1970. pap. 1.95 (ISBN 0-394-17111-X, B119, BC). Grove.

--Galileo. Bentley, Eric, ed. Laughton, Charles, tr. from German. (Orig.). (YA) (gr. 9 up). 1966. pap. 3.50 (ISBN 0-394-17112-8, B120, BC). Grove.

--Good Woman of Setzuan. Bentley, Eric, tr. from German. & intro. by. 1966. pap. 2.95 (ISBN 0-394-17109-8, B117, BC). Grove.

--The Jewish Wife & Other Short Plays. Bentley, Eric, tr. from Ger. Incl. In Search of Justice; The Informer; The Elephant Calf; The Measures Taken; The Exception & the Rule; Salzburg Dance of Death. 1965. pap. 2.95 (ISBN 0-394-17100-4, B80, BC). Grove.

--Jungle of Cities & Other Plays. Hollo, Anselm, et al, trs. Incl. Drums in the Night; Roundheads & Peakheads. 1966. pap. 3.95 (ISBN 0-394-17428-3, B89, BC). Grove.

--Kalendergeschichten. Hoffman, Charles W., ed. (Ger). 1960. pap. 4.95x (ISBN 0-393-09552-5, NortonC). Norton.

--Leben Des Galilei. 2nd ed. Brookes, H. F. & Fraenkel, C. E., eds. (Orig., Ger.). 1981. pap. text ed. 7.00x (ISBN 0-435-38123-7). Heinemann Ed.

--The Mother. LC 78-10764. 1978. pap. 2.95 (ISBN 0-394-17065-2, B414, BC). Grove.

--Mother Courage & Her Children. Bentley, Eric, tr. from Ger. (Orig.). (YA) 1963. pap. 2.45 (ISBN 0-394-17106-3, B108, BC). Grove.

--Mutter Courage und Ihre Kinder. Brookes, H. F. & Fraenkel, C. E., eds. 1960. pap. text ed. 5.50x (ISBN 0-435-38112-1). Heinemann Ed.

--Parables for the Theatre: Two Plays by Bertolt Brecht. Bentley, Eric, tr. (Illus.). 1965. 10.95x (ISBN 0-8166-0358-8). U of Minn Pr.

--The Rise & Fall of the City of Mahagonny. Auden, W. H. & Kallman, Chester, trs. LC 75-11466. 112p. 1976. 12.95 (ISBN 0-87923-149-1). Godine.

--Saint Joan of the Stockyards. Jones, Frank, tr. LC 69-16006. (Midland Bks.: No. 127). 128p. 1970. 15.00 (ISBN 0-253-17671-9); pap. 3.95x (ISBN 0-253-20127-6). Ind U Pr.

--Threepenny Opera. Bentley, Eric & Vesey, Desmond, trs. from Ger. (Orig.). 1964. pap. 2.45 (ISBN 0-394-17472-0, B333, BC). Grove.

--Threepenny Opera. (English Book by Vesey; Lyrics by Bentley). 12.25 (ISBN 0-8446-1734-2). Peter Smith.

Brecht, Bertolt & Lane, Dorothy. Happy End. 70p. 1983. 12.95 (ISBN 0-413-50950-8, NO. 3762); pap. 3.00 (ISBN 0-413-51020-4, NO. 3763). Methuen Inc.

Brecht, Bertolt see Weiss, Samuel A.

Brecht, George & Filliou, Robert. Games at the Cedilla. LC 68-13352. (Illus.). 1967. 22.50 (ISBN 0-89366-048-5). Ultramarine Pub.

Brecht, George, jt. auth. see Hughes, Patrick.

Brecht, Martin. Martin Luther: His Road to Reformation, 1483-1521. Schaaf, James L., tr. LC 84-47911. 592p. 1985. 36.95 (ISBN 0-8006-0738-4, 1-738). Fortress.

Brecht, Martin, ed. see Hahn, Philip Matthaus.

Brecht, Richard, jt. ed. see Flier, Michael S.

Brecht, Richard D. & Chvany, Catherine V. Slavic Transformational Syntax. (Michigan Slavic Materials: No. 10). 1974. pap. 5.00 (ISBN 0-930042-03-4). Mich Slavic Pubns.

Brecht, Richard D., jt. ed. see Chvany, Catherine V.

Brecht, Stefan. Poems. LC 78-2411. (Pocket Poets Ser.: No. 36). 1978. pap. 3.00 (ISBN 0-87286-099-X). City Lights.

--The Theatre of Visions: Robert Wilson. 440p. (Orig.). 1985. pap. 13.00 (ISBN 3-518-02488-4, 9413). Methuen Inc.

Brecht, Stephan. Queer Theatre. 178p. (Orig.). 1985. pap. 9.00 (ISBN 3-518-02489-2, 9412). Methuen Inc.

Brecht, Ursula. Precious Dolls: A Treasury of Bisque Dolls. (Illus.). 128p. 1984. 19.95 (ISBN 0-89586-330-8). H P Bks.

Breck & Brown. Chemistry for Science & Engineering. 450p. 1982. 29.95 (ISBN 0-07-092372-8). McGraw.

Breck, A. D. & Yourgrau, W., eds. Biology, History, & Natural Philosophy. LC 70-186262. 370p. 1972. 45.00x (ISBN 0-306-30573-9, Plenum Pr). Plenum Pub.

Breck, Allan D. & Yourgrau, Wolfgang, eds. Biology, History & Natural Philosophy. LC 74-774. 370p. 1974. pap. 6.95x (ISBN 0-306-20009-0, Rosetta). Plenum Pub.

Breck, Allen D., jt. ed. see Yourgrau, Wolfgang.

Breck, Donald W. Zeolite Molecular Sieves: Structure, Chemistry & Use. LC 83-26809. 784p. 1984. Repr. of 1974 ed. lib. bdg. 72.50 (ISBN 0-89874-648-5). Krieger.

Breck, Evelyn, ed. see Parker, Elizabeth.

Breck, H. Jean, ed. Magic Ring. 1985. 13.95 (ISBN 0-87603-082-7). Am Camping.

Breck, Louis W. An Atlas of the Osteochondroses. (Illus.). 192p. 1971. photocopy ed. 16.00x (ISBN 0-398-00218-5). C C Thomas.

Breckenridge, A., ed. Drugs in the Management of Heart Disease. 1985. lib. bdg. 43.50 (ISBN 0-85200-724-8, Pub. by MTP Pr England). Kluwer-Academic.

Breckenridge, A. M. Advanced Medicine: Topics in Therapeutics, No. 1. (Pitman Medical Conference Reports Ser.). (Illus.). 200p. 1975. pap. 22.00x (ISBN 0-8464-0114-2). Beekman Pubs.

--Advanced Medicine: Topics in Therapeutics, No. 3. (Pitman Medical Conference Reports Ser.). (Illus.). 1976. pap. 24.95x (ISBN 0-8464-0115-0). Beekman Pubs.

--Advanced Medicine: Topics in Therapeutics, No. 4. (Pitman Medical Conference Reports Ser.). (Illus.). 1977. pap. 24.95x (ISBN 0-8464-0116-9). Beekman Pubs.

Breckenridge, A. M., ed. see Royal College of Physicians.

Breckenridge, Adam C. Congress Against the Court. LC 79-113168. x, 160p. 1970. 13.95x (ISBN 0-8032-0751-4). U of Nebr Pr.

--Electing the President. LC 81-43597. 164p. (Orig.). 1982. lib. bdg. 23.50 (ISBN 0-8191-2287-4); pap. text ed. 11.00 (ISBN 0-8191-2288-2). U Pr of Amer.

--The Right to Privacy. LC 73-88084. viii, 155p. 1970. 13.50x (ISBN 0-8032-0702-6). U of Nebr Pr.

Breckenridge, Kati, jt. auth. see DelliQuadri, Lyn.

Breckenridge, Marilyn, jt. auth. see Lee, Harris.

Breckenridge, Marilyn S. Jesse Tree Devotions: A Family Activity for Lent. 40p. (Orig.). 1985. pap. 4.95 (ISBN 0-8066-2154-0, 10-3475). Augsburg.

Breckenridge, Mary B. Age, Time & Fertility: Applications of Exploratory Data Analysis. (Studies in Population Ser.). 1983. 39.50 (ISBN 0-12-128750-5). Acad Pr.

Breckenridge, Muriel. Lap Quilting: How to Make Beautiful Quilted Projects - Large & Small. LC 81-50545. (Illus.). 96p. 1981. 14.95 (ISBN 0-8069-5446-9); pap. 6.95 (ISBN 0-8069-7522-9). Sterling.

Breckenridge, Robert G. Access to English As a Second Language, Bk. 1. (Illus.). 192p. 1973. text ed. 2.50 (ISBN 0-07-007395-3). McGraw.

Breckenridge, Roger A., ed. Remote Sensing of Earth from Space: Role of "Smart Sensors". LC 79-18200. (Illus.). 505p. 1979. 55.00 (ISBN 0-915928-33-7, PAAS67); members 29.00 (ISBN 0-317-32186-2). AIAA.

Breckenridge, Walter J. Reptiles & Amphibians of Minnesota. (Illus.). 1944. 7.50x (ISBN 0-8166-0573-4). U of Minn Pr.

Breckinridge, Elizabeth L. Effective Use of Older Workers. Stein, Leon, ed. LC 79-8661. (Growing Old Ser.). (Illus.). 1980. Repr. of 1953 ed. lib. bdg. 21.00x (ISBN 0-405-12777-4). Ayer Co Pubs.

Breckinridge, John, jt. auth. see Hughes, John.

Breckinridge, Mary. Wide Neighborhoods: A Story of the Frontier Nursing Service. LC 81-50181. (Illus.). 400p. 1981. 28.00 (ISBN 0-8131-1453-5); pap. 10.00 (ISBN 0-8131-0149-2). U Pr of Ky.

Breckinridge, S. P; see Bernard, William S.

Breckinridge, S. P., jt. auth. see Abbott, Edith.

Breckinridge, Sophonisba P. The Family & the State: Select Documents. LC 76-169375. (Family in America Ser). 584p. 1972. Repr. of 1934 ed. 35.50 (ISBN 0-405-03851-8). Ayer Co Pubs.

--Women in the Twentieth Century: A Study of Their Political, Social, & Economic Activities. LC 72-2593. (American Women Ser.: Images & Realities). 380p. 1972. Repr. of 1933 ed. 24.50 (ISBN 0-405-04450-X). Ayer Co Pubs.

Breckinridge, Sophonisba P. & Abbott, Edith. Delinquent Child & the Home. LC 70-112525. (Rise of Urban America). 1970. Repr. of 1912 ed. 21.00 (ISBN 0-405-02438-X). Ayer Co Pubs.

Breckinridge, Sophonisba P., jt. auth. see Abbott, Edith.

Breckinridge, Sophonisba P., ed. Child in the City: A Series of Papers Presented at the Conference Held During the Chicago Child Welfare Exhibit. LC 70-112541. (Rise of Urban America). (Illus.). 1970. Repr. of 1912 ed. 26.50 (ISBN 0-405-02437-1). Ayer Co Pubs.

--Public Welfare Administration in the United States: Selected Documents. Repr. of 1927 ed. 40.00 (ISBN 0-384-05590-7). Johnson Repr.

Breckle, S. W., jt. auth. see Walter, H.

Breckler, Rosemary. Where Are the Twins? LC 79-10390. (A Hiway Bk.: A High Interest-Low Reading Level Book). 96p. (gr. 7 up). 1979. hardcover 8.95 (ISBN 0-664-32651-X). Westminster.

Breckner, Fred. Upper Iowa University: Doc Dorman's Peacocks. LC 81-52627. (College Sports Ser.). 1981. 9.95 (ISBN 0-87397-195-7). Strode.

Breckon, Don. The Railway Paintings of Don Breckon. LC 81-67015. (Illus.). 200p. 1982. 39.00 (ISBN 0-7153-8206-3). David & Charles.

Breckon, Donald J. Hospital Health Education: A Guide to Program Development. LC 82-1664. 274p. 1982. text ed. 29.95 (ISBN 0-89443-681-3). Aspen Systems.

Breckon, Donald J., et al. Community Health Education: Settings, Roles & Skills. 336p. 1984. 33.95 (ISBN 0-89443-555-8). Aspen Systems.

Breckon, Garry L., tr. see De Muralt, Andre.

Breda, A. Van see Van Breda, A.

Breda, Michael F. van see Van Breda, Michael F.

Bredahl, A. Carl, Jr. Melville's Angles of Vision. LC 73-185795. (University of Florida Humanities Monographs: No. 37). 1972. pap. 3.50 (ISBN 0-8130-0351-2). U Presses Fla.

Bredehoeft, John & Bachmat, Y. Groundwater Management: The Use of Numerical Models. (Water Resources Monograph: Vol. 5). (Illus.). 127p. 1980. pap. 10.00 (ISBN 0-87590-306-1, WR0500). Am Geophysical.

Bredemeier, Harry C. The Federal Public Housing Movement: A Case Study of Social Change. Zuckerman, Harriet & Merton, Robert K., eds. LC 79-8978. (Dissertations in Sociology Ser.). 1980. lib. bdg. 16.00x (ISBN 0-405-12954-8). Ayer Co Pubs.

Bredemeier, Juergen, jt. auth. see Petofi, Janos S.

Bredenforder, Elisabeth. Die Texte der Handel-Oratorien. pap. 9.00 (ISBN 0-384-05595-8). Johnson Repr.

Brederlow, G., et al. The High-Power Iodine Laser. (Springer Ser. in Optical Sciences: Vol. 34). (Illus.). 182p. 1983. 38.00 (ISBN 0-387-11792-X). Springer-Verlag.

Bredero, G. A. The Spanish Brabanter: A Seventeenth-Century Dutch Social Satire in Five Acts. Brumble, H. David, III, tr. from Dutch. & intro. by. LC 81-19004. (Medieval & Renaissance Texts & Studies: Vol. 11). (Illus.). 150p. 1982. 13.00 (ISBN 0-86698-018-0). Medieval & Renaissance NY.

Brederoo, P. & Boom, G., eds. Electron Microscopy 1980, Vol. 1: Physics. xxxii, 584p. 1981. 115.00 (ISBN 0-444-86179-3, North-Holland). Elsevier.

Brederoo, P. & Cosslett, V. E., eds. Electron Microscopy, 1980 Vol. 3 Analysis: Proceedings of the 7th European Congress. xxiv, 272p. 1981. 91.50 (ISBN 0-444-86181-5, North-Holland). Elsevier.

Brederoo, P. & De Priester, W., eds. Electron Microscopy, 1980 Volume 2 Biology: Proceedings of the 7th European Congress, the Hauge, the Netherlands, August 24-29, 1980. xl, 856p. 1981. 159.75 (ISBN 0-444-86180-7, North-Holland). Elsevier.

Bredes, Don. Muldoon. 1982. 15.50 (ISBN 0-03-058281-4). HR&W.

Bredesen, Harald. Yes, Lord. rev. ed. LC 72-91776. 199p. 1982. pap. 4.95 (ISBN 0-910311-00-5). Huntington Hse Inc.

Bredesen, Harold, intro. by. The Eternal Church. 398p. (Orig.). 1981. 12.95 (ISBN 0-939868-01-6); pap. 8.95 (ISBN 0-939868-00-8). Chr Intl Pubs.

Bredigkeit, H. B., tr. see Berendt, Joachim.

Bredimas, A. E. Methods of Interpretation & Community Law. (European Studies in Law: Vol. 6). 220p. 1978. 51.00 (ISBN 0-444-85081-3, North-Holland). Elsevier.

Bredin, Jean-Denis. The Affair: The Case of Alfred Dreyfus. Mehlman, Jeffrey, tr. from Fr. (Illus.). 550p. 1986. 30.00 (ISBN 0-8076-1109-3). Braziller.

Bredo, Eric & Feinberg, Walter, eds. Knowledge & Values in Social & Educational Research. LC 82-10371. 456p. 1982. 34.95 (ISBN 0-87722-242-8); pap. 12.95 (ISBN 0-87722-245-2). Temple U Pr.

Bredon, Glen E. Introduction to Compact Transformation Groups. (Pure & Applied Mathematics Ser). 1972. 77.00 (ISBN 0-12-128850-1). Acad Pr.

Bredow, Miriam. Handbook for the Medical Secretary. 4th ed. (Illus.). 1959. pap. 4.50 (ISBN 0-07-007413-5). McGraw.

Bredow, Miriam, jt. auth. see Cooper, Marian.

Bredow, Miriam, et al. Medical Office Procedures. 2nd ed. (Illus.). 480p. 1981. pap. text ed. 23.60 (ISBN 0-07-007441-0). McGraw.

Bredsdorff, Elias. Danish: An Elementary Grammar & Reader. 1959. 19.95 (ISBN 0-521-09821-1). Cambridge U Pr.

--Danish Literature in English Translation. LC 73-5203. 198p. 1973. Repr. of 1950 ed. lib. bdg. 18.75x (ISBN 0-8371-6867-8, BRDL). Greenwood.

Bredsdorff, Elias, pref. by see Schroeder, Carol L.

Bredsdorff, Elias, tr. Contemporary Danish Prose. LC 74-41. 375p. 1974. Repr. of 1958 ed. lib. bdg. 22.50x (ISBN 0-8371-7358-2, BRDP). Greenwood.

Bredsdorff, Elias, et al. Introduction to Scandinavian Literature. LC 78-98748. Repr. of 1951 ed. lib. bdg. 24.75x (ISBN 0-8371-2849-8, BRSL). Greenwood.

Bredt, J., jt. auth. see Sanger, E.

Bredvold, Louis I. The Brave New World of the Enlightenment. LC 61-10987. pap. 43.00 (ISBN 0-317-08088-1, 2051585). Bks Demand UMI.

--The Natural History of Sensibility. LC 62-10322. (Waynebooks Ser: No. 9). 112p. (Orig.). 1962. 3.95x (ISBN 0-8143-1205-5). Wayne St U Pr.

Bredvold, Louis I., ed. see Burke, Edmund.

Bree, G. & Kroff, A. Y. Twentieth Century French Drama. 1969. text ed. write for info. (ISBN 0-02-313820-3). Macmillan.

Bree, G., ed. see Camus, A.

Bree, G., tr. see Romains, Jules.

Bree, Germaine. Gide. LC 84-27916. ix, 302p. 1985. Repr. of 1963 ed. lib. bdg. 49.75x (ISBN 0-313-24797-8, BRGE). Greenwood.

--Marcel Proust & Deliverance from Time. Richards, R. J. & Truitt, A. D., trs. from Fr. LC 81-13256. vii, 252p. 1982. Repr. of 1969 ed. lib. bdg. 27.50x (ISBN 0-313-23184-2, BRPT). Greenwood.

Bree, Germaine & Guiton, Margaret. The French Novel from Gide to Camus. LC 62-21467. 241p. 1962. pap. 2.25 (ISBN 0-15-633480-1, Harv). HarBraceJ.

Bree, Germaine & Markow-Totevy, G. Contes et Nouvelles, 1950-1970. rev. ed. LC 72-106166. (gr. 10-12). 1970. pap. text ed. 16.95 (ISBN 0-03-081344-1, HoltC). HR&W.

Bree, Germaine, ed. Culture, Literature, & Articulation. Incl. Classical & Modern Foreign Languages: Common Areas & Problems. McCarthy, Barbara P; Foreign Language Instruction in Elementary Schools. Thompson, Mary P; Foreign Language Instruction in the Secondary School. Mead, Robert G., Jr; The Place of Culture & Civilization in Foreign Language Teaching. Wylie, Laurence; The Preparation of Foreign Language Teachers. Grace, Alonzo G; The Role of Foreign Languages in American Life. Starr, Wilmarth H; The Role of Literature in Language Teaching. MacAllister, Archibald T; Teaching Aids & Techniques: Principle Demonstrations. Pleasants, Jeanne V; Tests: All Skills, Speaking Test. Brooks, Nelson. 188p. 1955. pap. 7.95x (ISBN 0-915432-55-2). NE Conf Teach Foreign.

Bree, Germaine, ed. see Beckett, Samuel.

Bree, Germaine, ed. see Flaubert, Gustave.

Bree, Germaine, ed. see Proust, Marcel.

Bree, Germaine, ed. see Robbe-Grillet, Alain.

Bree, Germine. Twentieth-Century French Literature, 1920-1970. Guiney, Louise, tr. LC 82-15980. (Illus.). 352p. 1983. lib. bdg. 30.00x (ISBN 0-226-07195-2). U of Chicago Pr.

--Twentieth-Century French Literature, 1920-1970. Guiney, Louise, tr. from Fr. LC 82-15980. (Illus.). viii, 390p. 1984. pap. 11.95 (ISBN 0-226-07196-0). U of Chicago Pr.

Bree, Josephine P; see Eddy, Frederick D.

Bree, Loris, jt. auth. see Bree, Marlin.

Bree, Loris, ed. State By State Guide to Budget Motels: 1985-1986 Edition. (A MarLor Press Bk.). 264p. 6.95 (ISBN 0-943400-05-8). Contemp Bks.

Bree, Loris, jt. ed. see Bree, Marlin.

Bree, Loris G., ed. State by State Guide to Budget Motels, 1985-1986. (Affordable Travel Ser.). 264p. 1985. pap. text ed. 6.95 (ISBN 0-943400-06-6). Mar Lor Pr.

Bree, M. Groundwork of the Leschetizky Method. LC 68-25284. (Studies in Music, No. 42). (Illus.). 1969. Repr. of 1902 ed. lib. bdg. 49.95x (ISBN 0-8383-0290-4). Haskell.

Bree, Malwine. The Groundwork of the Leschetizky Method. Baker, Th., tr. from Ger. LC 74-144898. (Illus.). 1972. Repr. of 1920 ed. 39.00x (ISBN 0-403-00837-9). Scholarly.

Bree, Marlin & Bree, Loris. Affordable Travel. 1983. pap. 5.95 (ISBN 0-943400-02-3). Mar Lor Pr.

--Affordable Travel. (A MarLor Press Bks.). 160p. 5.95 (ISBN 0-943400-02-3). Contemp Bks.

Bree, Marlin & Bree, Loris, eds. My Trip Book. (Affordable Travel Ser.). 68p. 1984. pap. 3.95 (ISBN 0-943400-07-4). Mar Lor Pr.

--My Trip Book. (A MarLor Press Bk.). 56p. 3.95 (ISBN 0-943400-07-4). Contemp Bks.

Breech, James. The Silence of Jesus: The Authentic Voice of the Historical Man. LC 82-71825. 192p. 1983. 14.95 (ISBN 0-8006-0691-4, 1-691). Fortress.

Breed, Alice G. The Change in Social Welfare from Deregulation: The Case of the Natural Gas Industry. LC 78-22683. (Energy in the American Economy Ser.). (Illus.). 1979. lib. bdg. 16.00x (ISBN 0-405-11986-0). Ayer Co Pubs.

Breed, Bryan. I Know a Rotten Place. 1984. 20.00x (ISBN 0-906549-16-7, Pub. by J Clare Bks Uk). State Mutual Bk.

--White Collar Bird: The White Collar Offenders in Prison & His Problems. 1981. 29.00x (ISBN 0-906549-02-7, Pub. by J Clare Bks England). State Mutual Bk.

Breed, Bryan, jt. auth. see St. George, Mary.

Breed, C. B. Surveying. 3rd ed. 495p. 1971. 43.45x (ISBN 0-471-10070-6). Wiley.

Breed, C. B. & Hosmer, G. L. Principles & Practice of Surveying, 2 vols. Incl. Vol. 1. Elementary Surveying. 11th ed. 728p. 1977. 45.45x (ISBN 0-471-02979-3); Vol. 2. Higher Surveying. 8th ed. 543p. 1962. 44.45X (ISBN 0-471-10164-8). Wiley.

Breed, David K. The Trial of Christ: From a Legal & Scriptural Viewpoint. (Pocket Pulpit Library). 96p. 1982. pap. 2.95 (ISBN 0-8010-0829-8). Baker Bk.

Breed, David R. The History & Use of Hymns & Hymn Tunes. LC 76-39525. Repr. of 1903 ed. 20.00 (ISBN 0-404-09906-8). AMS Pr.

--The History & Use of Hymns & Hymn Tunes. 59.95 (ISBN 0-8490-0313-X). Gordon Pr.

Breed, Michael D., ed. The Biology of Social Insects: Proceedings. 425p. 1982. softcover 30.00x (ISBN 0-86531-291-5). Westview.

Breed, Paul, jt. auth. see De Charms, Desiree.

Breed, Paul F. & Sniderman, Florence M. Dramatic Criticism Index: Bibliography of Commentaries on Playwrights from Ibsen to the Avant-Garde. LC 79-127598. 1972. 60.00x (ISBN 0-8103-1090-2). Gale.

Breed, Warren. The Newspaperman, News & Society. Zuckerman, Harriet & Merton, Robert K., eds. LC 79-8979. (Dissertations on Sociology Ser.). 1980. lib. bdg. 40.00x (ISBN 0-405-12955-6). Ayer Co Pubs.

--Self-Guiding Society. LC 75-128472. 1971. pap. text ed. 6.95 (ISBN 0-02-904650-5). Free Pr.

Breeden, Brooks J. Micro Survey. 128p. 1985. pap. text ed. 20.75 (ISBN 0-534-05400-5, 21R4350, Pub. by PWS Engineering); 1 disk incl. PWS Pubs.

Breeden, David. Picnics. Strahan, Bradley R., ed. (Illustrated Poetry Chapbooks). (Illus.). 24p. (Orig.). 1985. pap. 3.50 (ISBN 0-938872-08-7). Black Buzzard.

Breeden, James O. Joseph Jones, M.D. Scientist of the Old South. LC 73-80462. (Illus.). 320p. 1975. 28.00x (ISBN 0-8131-1296-6). U Pr of Ky.

Breeden, James O., ed. Advice Among Masters: The Ideal in Slave Management in the Old South. LC 79-54054. (Contributions in Afro-American & African Studies: No. 51). (Illus.). xxvi, 350p. 1980. lib. bdg. 29.95 (ISBN 0-313-20658-9, BRS/). Greenwood.

--Medicine in the West. (Illus.). 84p. 1982. pap. text ed. 9.95x (ISBN 0-89745-025-6). Sunflower U Pr.

Breeden, Kay, jt. auth. see Breeden, Stanley.

Breeden, Maurice J. The Intimate Love Story of Antony & Cleopatra. (Great Love Stories of History Library). (Illus.). 83p. 1983. 56.75 (ISBN 0-86650-056-1). Gloucester Art.

Breeden, Stanley & Breeden, Kay. Australia's North. (A Natural History of Australia Ser.: No. 3). 208p. 1980. 34.95 (ISBN 0-00-211441-0, Pub. by W Collins Australia). Intl Spec Bk.

--Tropical Queensland: A Natural History of Australia, No. 1. (Illus.). 262p. 1982. Repr. of 1970 ed. 25.00x (ISBN 0-00-216574-0, Pub. by W Collins Australia). Intl Spec Bk.

--Wildlife of Eastern Australia. (Illus.). 260p. 1974. 12.95 (ISBN 0-8008-8332-2). Taplinger.

Breeding, Julia G., jt. ed. see Le Blanc, Rufus J.

Breedlove, Byron, ed. Successful Managements of Ambulatory Surgery Programs, Vol. II. 600p. 1985. text ed. 127.00 (ISBN 0-9603332-4-X). Am Health Consults.

Breedlove, Byron & Schwartz, David, eds. Clinical Lasers: Expert Strategies for Practical & Profitable Management. 356p. 1981. text ed. 128.00 (ISBN 0-9603332-3-1). Am Health Consults.

Breedlove, Byron, et al, eds. Hospital Employee Health: Practical Solutions to Current & Potential Problems. 502p. 1982. text ed. 89.00 (ISBN 0-9603332-2-3). Am Health Consults.

Breedlove, Dennis E. Introduction to the Flora of Chiapas, Pt. 1. (Flora of Chiapas Ser.). (Illus., Orig.). 1981. pap. 2.50 (ISBN 0-940228-00-9). Calif Acad Sci.

Breedlove, Dennis E., ed. see Smith, Allan R.

Breedlove, Michael A., ed. Journal of Historical Studies. 75p. write for info. Dept Hist Org.

Breemen, Peter G. van. Como el Pan Que Se Comparte. 5.95 (ISBN 0-87193-171-0). Dimension Bks.

Breemen, Peter G. van see Van Breemen, Peter G.

Breemer, Jan S. U. S. Naval Developments. LC 83-13289. 1983. 19.95 (ISBN 0-933852-36-3). Nautical & Aviation.

Breen, Dan. My Fight for Irish Freedom. 218p. 1981. 16.95 (ISBN 0-900068-56-6, Pub. by Anvil Pr Ireland); pap. 4.95 (ISBN 0-900068-34-5, Pub. by Anvil Pr IReland). Irish Bks Media.

Breen, Dana. The Birth of a First Child: Towards an Understanding of Femininity. (Illus.). 1975. pap. 11.95x (ISBN 0-422-74340-2, NO.2770, Pub. by Tavistock England). Methuen Inc.

--Talking with Mothers. 232p. 1981. 30.00x (ISBN 0-906908-35-3, Pub. by Norman England). State Mutual Bk.

Breen, David H. The Canadian Prairie West & the Ranching Frontier. 312p. 1983. 30.00x (ISBN 0-8020-5548-6). U of Toronto Pr.

Breen, G. & Blankenship, A. Do-It-Yourself Marketing Research. 2nd ed. 1982. 29.95 (ISBN 0-07-007446-1). McGraw.

Breen, Gavan. The Mayi Languages of the Queensland Gulf Country. 238p. 1981. pap. text ed. 14.00x (ISBN 0-391-02269-5, Pub. by Australian Inst Australia). Humanities.

Breen, Gertrude. Indian Captive: The Story of Mary Jemison. (Children's Theatre Playscript Ser.). 1961. pap. 2.25x (ISBN 0-88020-030-8). Coach Hse.

Breen, Henry H. St. Lucia: Historical, Statistical & Descriptive. 423p. 1970. Repr. of 1844 ed. 30.00x (ISBN 0-7146-1930-2, F Cass Co). Biblio Dist.

Breen, James & Sanderson, William. How to Start a Successful Restaurant. 1981. 19.95 (ISBN 0-86730-242-9). Lebhar Friedman.

Breen, James L. & Jaffurs, William. Atlas of Gynecologic-Obstetric Pathology. (Complete print edition available). 1973. Set. 90.00x (ISBN 0-8036-1136-6). Davis Co.

Breen, James L. & Paup, Donald C. Winning Badminton: A Coaching & Playing Guide. 138p. 1983. pap. text ed. 6.95 (ISBN 0-87670-067-9). Athletic Inst.

Breen, John F. Encyclopedia of Reptiles & Amphibians. (Illus.). 576p. 1974. text ed. 24.95 (ISBN 0-87666-220-3, H-935). TFH Pubns.

Breen, John J., jt. auth. see Hill, Evan.

Breen, Jon. The Gathering Place. LC 83-42914. (Mysteries Ser.). 192p. 1984. 12.95 (ISBN 0-8027-5575-5). Walker & Co.

Breen, Jon L. Hair of the Sleuthhound: Parodies of Mystery Fiction. LC 81-21276. 218p. 1982. 15.00 (ISBN 0-8108-1505-2). Scarecrow.

--Listen for the Click. 192p. 1983. 12.95 (ISBN 0-8027-5492-9). Walker & Co.

--Novel Verdicts: A Guide to Courtroom Fiction. LC 84-14110. 280p. 1984. 18.50 (ISBN 0-8108-1741-1). Scarecrow.

--What About Murder? A Guide to Books About Mystery Detective Fiction. LC 81-645. 175p. 1981. 15.00 (ISBN 0-8108-1413-7). Scarecrow.

Breen, Matthew P. Thirty Years of New York Politics, Up-to-Date. LC 73-19132. (Politics & People Ser.). (Illus.). 918p. 1974. Repr. 64.00x (ISBN 0-405-05857-8). Ayer Co Pubs.

Breen, Patrick. Diary of Patrick Breen--One of the Donner Party. Teggart, Frederick J., ed. (Illus.). 16p. 1978. pap. 2.00 (ISBN 0-89646-048-7). Outbooks.

Breen, Quirinus see Brauer, Jerald C.

Breen, Richard. Made for TV. LC 82-4325. 224p. 1982. 12.95 (ISBN 0-8253-0103-3). Beaufort Bks NY.

Breen, T. H. Puritans & Adventurers: Change & Persistence in Early America. 1980. 22.50x (ISBN 0-19-502728-0); pap. 8.95x (ISBN 0-19-503207-1). Oxford U Pr.

--Tobacco Culture: The Mentality of the Great Tidewater Planters on the Eve of Revolution. (Illus.). 176p. 1985. 19.95 (ISBN 0-691-04729-4). Princeton U Pr.

Breen, T. H. & Innes, Stephen. Myne Owne Ground: Race & Freedom on Virginia's Eastern Shore, 1640-1676. (Illus.). 1980. 19.95x (ISBN 0-19-502727-2); pap. 7.95x (ISBN 0-19-503206-3). Oxford U Pr.

Breen, T. H., ed. Shaping Southern Society: The Colonial Experience. 1976. pap. text ed. 8.95x (ISBN 0-19-502078-2). Oxford U Pr.

Breen, T. H., jt. auth. see Divine, Robert A.

Breen, W. Proof Coins Struck at the U.S. Mints: Updated. 1983. Repr. of 1953 ed. softcover 10.00 (ISBN 0-915262-94-0). S J Durst.

Breen, Walter. The Darkover Concordance. LC 79-84472. 1979. 17.95 (ISBN 0-930800-10-9); pap. 8.95 (ISBN 0-930800-07-9). Pennyfarthing.

Breen, Walter, jt. auth. see Swiatek, Anthony.

Breen, William J. Uncle Sam at Home: Civilian Mobilization, Wartime Federalism, & the Council of National Defense, 1917-1919. LC 83-12576. (Contributions in American Studies: No. 70). 240p. 1984. lib. bdg. 29.95 (ISBN 0-313-24112-0, BRU/). Greenwood.

Breen-Bond, Patricia. The President's Grass Is Missing. (Orig.). 1980. pap. text ed. 1.75 (ISBN 0-505-51546-6, Pub. by Tower Bks). Dorchester Pub Co.

Breene, R. G., Jr. Theories of Spectral Line Shape. LC 80-20664. 344p. 1981. 50.95x (ISBN 0-471-08361-5, Pub. by Wiley-Interscience). Wiley.

Breer, H., ed. Neurochemical Techniques in Insect Research. (Springer Series in Experimental Entomolgoy). (Illus.). 310p. 1985. 59.50 (ISBN 0-387-13813-7). Springer-Verlag.

Breese, Andrea. Setting Out. 1984. 20.00x (ISBN 0-906549-21-3, Pub. by J Clare Bks UK). State Mutual Bk.

Breese, Andreas. A Loving Imprint. 1984. 20.00x (ISBN 0-906549-30-2, Pub. by J Clare Bks UK). State Mutual Bk.

Breese, B. B. On Inhibition. Bd. with On After-Images. Franz, Shepherd I. Repr. of 1899 ed; Accuracy of Voluntary Movement. Woodworth, R. S. Repr. of 1899 ed; Study of Lapses. Bawden, H. Heath. Repr. of 1900 ed; Mental Life of the Monkeys. Thorndike, Edward L. Repr. of 1901 ed; Correlation of Mental & Physical Tests. Wissler, Clark. Repr. of 1901 ed. (Psychology Monographs General & Applied: Vol. 3). pap. 36.00 (ISBN 0-317-16766-9). Kraus Repr.

Breese, Burtis B. & Hall, Caroline. Beta Hemolytic Streptococcal Diseases. (Illus.). 287p. 1978. 65.00 (ISBN 0-471-09476-5, Pub. by Wiley Med). Wiley.

Breese, Dave. Know the Marks of Cults. LC 74-21907. 128p. 1975. pap. 3.95 (ISBN 0-88207-704-X). Victor Bks.

Breese, Gerald. Urban & Regional Planning for the Delhi-New Delhi Area: Capital for Conquerors & Country. 55p. 1974. pap. 3.50 (ISBN 0-686-09286-4). G Breese.

Breese, Gerald W. & Whiteman, Dorothy E. Approach to Urban Planning. LC 73-90474. Repr. of 1953 ed. lib. bdg. 15.00x (ISBN 0-8371-2284-8, BRUP). Greenwood.

Breese, Mary E. Longsworth Family History: Descendants of Solomon Longsworth, Sr., of Maryland. LC 52-23969. (Illus.). pap. 70.30 (ISBN 0-317-09098-4, 2051676). Bks Demand UMI.

Breese, S., Jr., jt. ed. see Zacharia, Theodore P.

Breeskin, Adelyn D. Mary Cassatt: A Catalogue Raisonne of the Graphic Work. rev ed. LC 78-22472. (Illus.). 189p. 1980. 42.50 (ISBN 0-87474-284-6); deluxe ed. 125.00 (ISBN 0-87474-110-6). Smithsonian.

Breeskin, Adelyn D., jt. auth. see Brooks, Romaine.

Breeze, Carla, jt. auth. see Whiffen, Marcus.

Breeze, D. J. & Reynolds, N. Studies in Scottish Antiquity. (Illus.). 1984. text ed. 57.50x (ISBN 0-85976-075-8, Pub. by John Donald Scotland). Humanities.

Breeze, David. The Northern Frontiers of Roman Britain. LC 81-18401. 1982. 27.50 (ISBN 0-312-57897-0). St Martin.

Breeze, David J. Roman Forts in Britain. (Shire Archaeology Ser.: No. 37). 1983. pap. 5.95 (ISBN 0-85263-654-7, Pub. by Shire Pubns England). Seven Hills Bks.

Breeze, Hector. Cartoon Library, No. 2: Hector Breeze. (Illus.). 96p. 1973. pap. 1.95 (ISBN 0-233-96448-7, Pub. by Private Eye UK). David & Charles.

Breeze, Katie. Nekkid Cowboy. LC 82-73110. 216p. 1982. 11.95 (ISBN 0-931722-17-9). Corona Pub.

Breeze, Paul. While My Guitar Gently Weeps: A Novel. LC 80-22065. 222p. 1981. 9.95 (ISBN 0-8008-8247-4). Taplinger.

Breffny, Brian De see De Breffny, Brian.

Breffny, Brian de see De Breffny, Brian.

Breffny, Brian De see De Breffny, Brian.

Breffny, Brian de see De Breffny, Brian & Ffolliott, Rosemary.

Breffny, Brian de see De Breffny, Brian & Mott, George.

Breffny, Brian De see De Breffny, Brian.

Breffny, Brian de see De Breffny, Brian.

Bregach, Walt. Electronic Projects for Photographers. (Illus.). 304p. (Orig.). 1983. 21.95 (ISBN 0-8306-0144-9, 1544); pap. 15.50 (ISBN 0-8306-1544-X). TAB Bks.

Bregenzer, John. Tryin' to Make It: Adapting to the Bahamas. (Illus.). 96p. (Orig.). 1982. lib. bdg. 20.50 (ISBN 0-8191-2621-7); pap. text ed. 8.00 (ISBN 0-8191-2622-5). U Pr of Amer.

Breger, Louis. From Instinct to Identity: The Development of Personality. LC 73-5766. (P-H Personality Ser). (Illus.). 400p. 1974. ref. ed. 28.95 (ISBN 0-13-331637-8). P-H.

Breger, Louis, ed. Clinical Cognitive Psychology. LC 70-85956. 1969. 29.50x (ISBN 0-13-137620-9). Irvington.

Breger, Louis, et al. The Effect of Stress on Dreams. LC 74-160287. (Psychological Issues Monograph: No. 27, Vol. 7, No. 3). 214p. 1971. text ed. 22.50 (ISBN 0-8236-1536-7); pap. text ed. 17.50 (ISBN 0-8236-1535-9). Intl Univs Pr.

Breggin, Peter R. Electroshock: Its Brain Disabling Effects. LC 79-15223. 1979. text ed. 19.95 (ISBN 0-8261-2710-X). Springer Pub.

--Psychiatric Drugs: Hazards to the Brain. 336p. 1983. text ed. 29.95 (ISBN 0-8261-2930-7). Springer Pub.

--The Psychology of Freedom: Liberty & Love As a Way of Life. LC 80-7459. 242p. 1980. 15.95 (ISBN 0-87975-132-0). Prometheus Bks.

Bregman. Laboratory Investigations in Cell Biology. 2nd ed. 1985. pap. price not set (ISBN 0-471-82569-7). Wiley.

Bregman, Adolph, jt. ed. see Coleman, Satis N.

Bregman, Allyn A. Laboratory Investigations in Cell Biology. 253p. 1983. pap. text ed. 19.45 (ISBN 0-471-86241-X). Wiley.

Bregman, Douglas M. & Everngam, Gary G. Maryland Landlord-Tenant Law: Practice & Procedure. 313p. 1983. 30.00 (ISBN 0-87215-504-8). Michie Co.

Bregman, Douglas M., jt. auth. see Miller, Peter G.

Bregman, Douglas M. & Miller, Peter G., eds. Model Contingencies for Real Estate Sales. 7.50 (ISBN 0-943954-00-2). Tremont Pr.

Bregman, Jay. Synesius of Cyrene: Philosopher-Bishop. LC 81-10293. (The Transformation of the Classical Heritage Ser.: Vol. II). 1982. 30.00 (ISBN 0-520-04192-5). U of Cal Pr.

Bregman, Lucy. The Rediscovery of Inner Experience. LC 81-22600. 200p. 1982. text ed. 18.95x (ISBN 0-88229-686-8). Nelson-Hall.

Bregman, Sue. Sexuality & the Spinal Cord Injured Woman. 24p. 1975. 6.00 (ISBN 0-88440-022-0). Sis Kenny Inst.

Bregy, Katherine. Poets Chantry. LC 70-105766. 1970. Repr. of 1912 ed. 19.50x (ISBN 0-8046-1043-6, Pub. by Kennikat). Assoc Faculty Pr.

--Queen of Paradox: A Stuart Tragedy (Mary Stuart, Queen of Scots) 221p. 1982. Repr. of 1950 ed. lib. bdg. 35.00 (ISBN 0-8495-0612-3). Arden Lib.

--The Story of Saint Francis de Sales: Patron of Catholic Writers. 108p. 1982. Repr. of 1958 ed. lib. bdg. 35.00 (ISBN 0-89984-015-9). Century Bookbindery.

Bregy, Katherine M. From Dante to Jeanne D'Arc: Adventures in Medieval Life & Letters. LC 78-774. (Science & Culture Ser.). 1978. Repr. of 1933 ed. lib. bdg. 19.75x (ISBN 0-313-20290-7, BRFD). Greenwood.

Brehan, Delle. Kicks Is Kicks. (Orig.). 1977. pap. 1.95 (ISBN 0-87067-630-X, BH630). Holloway.

Brehaut, Ernest. Encyclopedist of the Dark Ages, Isidore of Seville. (Columbia University. Studies in History, Economics, & Public Law: Vol. 48, No. 1). 1967. Repr. of 1912 ed. 21.50 (ISBN 0-8337-0361-7). B Franklin.

Brehaut, Ernest, ed. see Gregory Bishop of Tours.

Brehaut, Ernest, tr. see Cato The Censor.

Brehaut, Ernest, tr. see Gregory - Bishop of Tours.

Brehaut, Roger N. Ecology of Rocky Shores. (Studies in Biology: No. 139). 64p. 1982. pap. text ed. 8.95 (ISBN 0-7131-2839-9). E Arnold.

Breheny, M. & Hooper, A., eds. Rationality in Planning: Critical Essays on the Role of Rationality in Urban & Regional Planning. 252p. 1985. 25.95x (ISBN 0-85086-112-8, 9130, Pub. by Pion England). Methuen Inc.

Breheny, Michael see Diamond, Donald R. & McLoughlin, J. B.

Brehier, E. Chrysippe et L'ancien Stoicisme. 300p. (Fr.). 1971. pap. 45.25 (ISBN 0-677-50605-8). Gordon.

Brehier, Emile. History of Philosophy, 5 vols. Incl. Vol. 1. The Hellenic Age. Thomas, Joseph, tr. LC 63-20912. 1963; Vol. 2. The Hellenistic & Roman Age. Baskin, Wade, tr. LC 63-20913. 1965. pap. text ed. 7.00x (ISBN 0-226-07221-5, P199); Vol. 3. The Middle Ages & the Renaissance. Baskin, Wade, tr. LC 63-20912. 1965. pap. text ed. 5.00x (ISBN 0-226-07219-3); Vol. 4. The Seventeenth Century. Baskin, Wade, tr. LC 63-20912. 1966. pap. text ed. 5.00x (ISBN 0-226-07225-8); Vol. 5. The Eighteenth Century. Baskin, Wade, tr. LC 63-20912. 1971; Vol. 6. The Nineteenth Century: Period of Systems 1800-1850. Baskin, Wade, tr. LC 63-20912. 1973. pap. text ed. 5.00x (ISBN 0-226-07229-0); Vol. 7. Contemporary Philosophy - Since 1850. Baskin, Wade, tr. LC 63-20912. 1973. pap. text ed. 5.00x (ISBN 0-226-07231-2, P538). pap. (Phoen). U of Chicago Pr.

--The History of Philosophy, Vol. 7. Beskin, Wade, tr. LC 63-20912. pap. 71.00 (ISBN 0-317-08077-6, 2020037). Bks Demand UMI.

Brehier, L. L' Art Chretien, Son Developement Iconographique des Origines a nos Jours. 2nd ed. (Illus.). 480p. (Fr.). Repr. of 1928 ed. lib. bdg. 125.00 (ISBN 0-89241-138-4). Caratzas.

--The Life & Death of Byzantium. (Europe in the Middle Ages Selected Studies: Vol. 5). 410p. 1978. 57.50 (ISBN 0-444-11128-X, North-Holland). Elsevier.

Brehier, Louis. L' Eglise et l'Orient au moyen age: Les croisades. 2nd ed. LC 76-29834. (Fr.). Repr. of 1907 ed. 31.50 (ISBN 0-404-15413-1). AMS Pr.

--La Querelle des Images Huitieme-Neuvieme Siecle. 1969. 14.00 (ISBN 0-8337-0362-5). B Franklin.

--Schisme orientale du onzieme siecle. 1969. Repr. of 1899 ed. 25.50 (ISBN 0-8337-0363-3). B Franklin.

--La Sculpture et les Arts Mineurs Byzantins. 310p. 1973. 50.00x (ISBN 0-902089-45-5, Pub. by Variorum). State Mutual Bk.

Brehm, Henry P. & Coe, Rodney M. Medical Care for the Aged. LC 80-210261. 160p. 1980. 32.95 (ISBN 0-03-046306-8). Praeger.

Brehm, Henry P., jt. auth. see Coe, Rodney M.

Brehm, Henry P., ed. Widowhood. LC 78-19789. 200p. Date not set. 18.95 (ISBN 0-03-046301-7). Praeger.

Brehm, J. W., jt. auth. see Wicklund, R. A.

Brehm, Jack, jt. auth. see Brehm, Sharon.

Brehm, Madeleine & Tindell, Nancy. Movement with a Purpose: Perceptual Motor-Lesson Plans for Young Children. LC 83-8023. 204p. 1983. 16.95 (ISBN 0-13-604629-0). P-H.

Brehm, Sharon & Brehm, Jack. Psychological Reactance: A Theory of Freedom & Control. 2nd. ed. LC 81-12796. 1981. 47.50 (ISBN 0-12-129840-X). Acad Pr.

Brehm, Sharon S. Intimate Relationships. 450p. 1985. pap. text ed. 17.95 (ISBN 0-394-33588-0, RanC). Random.

Brehm, Sharon S., et al, eds. Developmental Social Psychology: Theory & Research. (Illus.). 384p. 1981. text ed. 27.95x (ISBN 0-19-502840-6); pap. text ed. 15.95x (ISBN 0-19-502841-4). Oxford U Pr.

Breide, Ole. Three Weeks On - Three Weeks Off. LC 80-52960. 1982. 9.95 (ISBN 0-533-04801-X). Vantage.

Breidenbach, Monica E., jt. auth. see Hover, Margot K.

Breidger, J. Henry. How to Harmonize Melodies. 1976. lib. bdg. 29.0u (ISBN 0-403-03607-0). Scholarly.

Breier, Paul V., jt. ed. see Edwards, G. F.

Breihan, Carl & Montgomery, Wayne. The Crimson Trail of Frank & Jesse James. (Illus.). 196p. (Orig.). 1985. pap. 8.95 (ISBN 0-89769-087-7, Dist. by Caroline Hse). Pine Mntn.

Breihan, Carl W. Great Gunfighters of the West. (Illus.). 1981. pap. 2.25 (ISBN 0-451-11120-6, AE1120, Sig). NAL.

--Gunslingers. (Illus.). 300p. 1984. pap. 8.95 (ISBN 0-89769-048-6, Dist. by Caroline Hse.). Pine Mntn.

--Sam Hildebrand, Guerilla. (Illus.). 200p. (Orig.). 1984. pap. 8.95 (ISBN 0-89769-076-1, Dist. by Caroline Hse). Pine Mntn.

--Wild Women of the West. 1982. pap. 2.50 (ISBN 0-451-11951-7, AE1951, Sig). NAL.

Breihan, Carl W. & Montgomery, Wayne. Forty Years on the Wild Frontier. (Illus.). 320p. 1985. 17.50 (ISBN 0-8159-5518-9). Devin.

Breiman, Leo, et al. Classification & Regression Trees. LC 83-19708. (Statistics-Probability Ser.). 358p. 1983. write for info (ISBN 0-534-98053-8); pap. write for info (ISBN 0-534-98054-6). Wadsworth Pub.

Breimer, D. D., ed. Towards Better Safety of Drugs & Pharmaceutical Products: Proceedings of the 39th International Congress of Pharamaceutical Sciences, Brighton, September, 1979. 1980. 59.75 (ISBN 0-444-80216-9). Elsevier.

Breimer, D. D. & Speiser, P., eds. Topics in Pharmaceutical Sciences II: Proceedings of the 43rd International Congress of the F.I.P., Montreux, Switzerland September 5-9,1983. 1984. 69.25 (ISBN 0-444-80549-4, I-009-84, Biomedical Pr). Elsevier.

--Topics in Pharmaceutical Sciences: Proceedings of the 41st International Congress, Brighton, 1979. 536p. 1982. 64.00 (ISBN 0-444-80403-X, Biomedical Pr). Elsevier.

Breimer, T. Environmental Factors & Cultural Measures Affecting the Nitrate of Spinach. 1982. pap. text ed. 22.00 (ISBN 90-247-3053-8, Pub. by Martinus Nijhoff Netherlands). Kluwer Academic.

Breimer, T., jt. auth. see Corre, W. J.

Breimyer, Harold F. Economics of the Product Markets of Agriculture. (Illus.). 208p. 1976. text ed. 12.95x (ISBN 0-8138-1840-0). Iowa St U Pr.

--Farm Policy: Thirteen Essays. 1977. text ed. 7.50x (ISBN 0-8138-0645-3). Iowa St U Pr.

Breinburg, Petronella. Doctor Shawn. LC 74-15265. (Illus.). 32p. (gr. k-2). 1975. 11.49i (ISBN 0-690-00721-3); PLB 11.89 (ISBN 0-690-00722-1). Crowell Jr Bks.

--Shawn Goes to School. LC 73-8003. (Illus.). 32p. (ps-2). 1974. PLB 11.89 (ISBN 0-690-00277-7). Crowell Jr Bks.

Breines, Estelle. Functional Assessment Scale. 1983. manual 21.00 (ISBN 0-318-00569-7). Geri Rehab.

--Perception: Its Development & Recapitulation. LC 81-81244. (Illus.). 304p. 1981. text ed. 17.50 (ISBN 0-941930-01-7). Geri-Rehab.

Breines, Wini. Community & Organization in the New Left: The Great Refusal. 208p. 1983. text ed. 25.95 (ISBN 0-89789-033-7); pap. 12.95. Bergin & Garvey.

--Community & Organization in the New Left 1962-1968: The Great Refusal. 224p. 1982. 31.95x (ISBN 0-03-060099-5). Praeger.

Breinholst, Willy. Hello, Here I Am. 128p. (Orig.). 1984. pap. 3.95 (ISBN 0-671-47867-2). PB.

--Hello Mama, Hello Papa. 112p. (Orig.). 1984. pap. 3.95 (ISBN 0-671-47924-5). PB.

Breinhost, Willy. Cheer up! Things Might Get Worse. 8.50 (ISBN 0-392-08393-0, SpS). Sportshelf.

Breinin, C. M. & Siegel, I. M., eds. Advances in Diagnostic Visual Optics. (Springer Series in Optical Sciences: Vol. 41). (Illus.). 280p. 1983. 29.00 (ISBN 0-387-13079-9). Springer Verlag.

Breining, Greg. Boundary Waters. (Illus.). 96p. 1983. 19.95 (ISBN 0-931714-20-6). Nodin Pr.

Breipohl, Arthur M. Probabilistic System Analysis: An Introduction to Probabilistic Models, Decisions & Applications of Random Processes. LC 77-94920. 352p. 1970. 43.50 (ISBN 0-471-10181-8). Wiley.

Breipohl, W., ed. Olfaction & Endocrine Regulation: Proceedings of the Fourth European Chemoreception Research Organization Mini-Symposium & the Second International Laboratory Workshop on Olfaction, Essen FRG, 1981. 426p. 1982. pap. 35.00 (ISBN 0-904147-35-5). IRL Pr.

Breisach, Ernst. Historiography: Ancient, Medieval, & Modern. LC 82-20246. 475p. 1983. 35.00X (ISBN 0-226-07274-6); pap. 13.50x (ISBN 0-226-07275-4). U of Chicago Pr.

Breisach, Ernst, ed. Classical Rhetoric & Medical Historiography. LC 85-3055. (Studies in Medieval Culture: No. XIX). vi, 237p. 1985. 17.95x (ISBN 0-918720-56-7); pap. 10.95x (ISBN 0-918720-57-5). Medieval Inst.

Breisacher, E. H. & Lorentzen, Sandra, eds. Last Resting Places, Being a Compendium of Fact Pertaining to the Mortal Remains of the Famous & Infamous. LC 79-52704. (Illus.). 320p. 1986. 24.95 (ISBN 0-87850-032-4). Darwin Pr.

Breisch, Linda L. & Wright, David A. Chlorine & the Chesapeake Bay: A Review of Research Literature. 6.00 (ISBN 0-943676-17-7). MD Sea Grant Col.

Breisch, Linda L., jt. auth. see Kennedy, Victor S.

Breise, Frederic H. Fifty Years of Aviation Knowledge. 108p. 1981. 12.00 (ISBN 0-938576-00-3). F H Breise.

Breit, Luke. Words the Air Speaks. 1980. pap. 3.95 (ISBN 0-686-45291-7). Way Up Firm.

Breit, Luke, ed. see Neruda, Pablo.

Breit, R., jt. ed. see Bandmann, H. J.

Breit, William & Elzinga, Kenneth G. The Antitrust Casebook. 400p. 1982. pap. 13.95 (ISBN 0-03-060147-9). Dryden Pr.

Breit, William & Ransom, Roger L. The Academic Scribblers: Economists in Collision. 2nd ed. 288p. 1982. pap. text ed. 12.95x (ISBN 0-03-051236-0). Dryden Pr.

Breit, William, jt. auth. see Elzinga, Kenneth G.

Breit, William & Culbertson, William P., Jr., eds. Science & Ceremony: The Institutional Economics of C. E. Ayres. LC 76-8238. 228p. 1976. text ed. 14.95x (ISBN 0-292-77523-7). U of Tex Pr.

Breit, William, ed. see Hemenway, David.

Breitbart, M., jt. auth. see Kasperson, R. E.

Breitenbach, Edgar. American Poster: Graphic Communications in the Twentieth Century. Cogswell, Margaret, ed. LC 66-18340. (Illus.). 1968. 15.00 (ISBN 0-8079-0002-8); pap. 7.95 (ISBN 0-8079-0003-6). October.

Breitenbach, J. & Franzlin, F., eds. Champignons de Suisse: Tome 1, Les Ascomycetas. (Illus.). 313p. (Fr.). 1981. text ed. 59.50x (ISBN 0-916422-35-6). Mad River.

Breitenbach, J. & Kranzlin, F., eds. Fungi of Switzerland: Ascomycetes, Vol. 1. (Illus.). 313p. (Fr. & Ger.). 1984. 59.50x (ISBN 0-916422-47-X). Mad River.

Breitenkamp, Edward C. & Dabbs, Jack A., trs. from Ger. Church Records of the Pioneer German Families of Berlin, Texas. LC 82-71839. 292p. 1985. lib. bdg. 35.00 (ISBN 0-943162-04-1). Family History.

Breitenkamp, Edward C., tr. see Seele, Hermann.

Breitenlohner, Peter & Duerr, Hans-Peter. Unified Theories of Elementary Particles: Proceedings. (Lecture Notes in Physics: Vol. 160). 217p. 1982. pap. 15.00 (ISBN 0-387-11560-9). Springer-Verlag.

Breitenstein, Detlev Von see Delvolve, Jean-Louis & Von Breitenstein, Detlev.

Breiter, Herta S. Fuel & Energy. LC 77-18560. (Read About Science). (Illus.). (gr. k-3). 1978. PLB 14.25 (ISBN 0-8393-0083-2). Raintree Pubs.

--Fuel & Energy. LC 77-18560. (Read about Science Ser.). (Illus.). 48p. (gr. 2-5). 1983. pap. 9.27g (ISBN 0-8393-0295-9). Raintree Pubs.

--Pollution. LC 77-26886. (Read About Science). (Illus.). (gr. k-3). 1978. PLB 14.25 (ISBN 0-8393-0081-6). Raintree Pubs.

--Pollution. LC 77-26886. (Read about Science Ser.). (Illus.). 48p. (gr. 2-5). 1983. pap. 9.27g (ISBN 0-8393-0299-1). Raintree Pubs.

--Time & Clocks. LC 77-19007. (Read About Science). (Illus.). (gr. k-3). 1978. PLB 14.25 (ISBN 0-8393-0088-3). Raintree Pubs.

--Time & Clocks. LC 77-19007. (Read about Science Ser.). (Illus.). 48p. (gr. 2-5). 1983. pap. 9.27g (ISBN 0-8393-0302-5). Raintree Pubs.

--Weather. LC 77-27239. (Read About Science). (Illus.). (gr. k-3). 1978. PLB 14.25 (ISBN 0-8393-0079-4). Raintree Pubs.

--Weather. LC 77-27239. (Read about Science Ser.). (Illus.). 48p. (gr. 2-5). 1983. pap. 9.27g (ISBN 0-8393-0305-X). Raintree Pubs.

Breiter, M. W. Electrochemical Processes in Fuel Cells. LC 69-17789. (Illus.). 1969. 34.00 (ISBN 0-387-04418-3). Springer-Verlag.

Breiter, Manfred, ed. see Symposium on Electrocatalysis of Fuel Cell Reactions (1978: Brookhaven National Laboratory).

Breiter, Paul, jt. auth. see Kornfield, Jack.

Breithardt, Gunter & Loogen, Franz, eds. New Aspects in the Medical Treatment of Tachyarrhythmias: Role of Amiodarone. Orig. Title: Neue Aspekte Der Medikamentosen Behandlung Von Tachyarrhythmien. (Illus.). 283p. 1983. text ed. 29.50 (ISBN 0-8067-1121-3). Urban & S.

Breithaupt, S. & Agnew, H. W. The Dallas Doctors' Diet. 208p. 1983. 12.95 (ISBN 0-07-007447-X). McGraw.

Breithaupt, Sandra & Agnew, H. Wayne. The Dallas Doctors' Diet: A Revolutionary Way to Eat Yourself Thin. 240p. 1984. pap. 6.95 (ISBN 0-07-007448-8). McGraw.

Breitinger, Eckhard. The Presidential Campaign Nineteen Seventy-Six: A Selection of Campaign Speeches. 183p. 1978. 24.65 (ISBN 3-261-02605-7). P Lang Pubs.

Breitkopf, Herman L. & New Jersey Institute for Continuing Legal Education. Seminar Material for Settlement Techniques. LC 83-187456. (Illus.). 128p. Date not set. price not set. NJ Inst CLE.

Breitmaier, E. & Voelter, W. Thirteen-C NMR Spectroscopy: Methods & Applications. 2nd ed. (Monographs in Modern Chemistry: Vol. 5). (Illus.). 344p. 1978. 57.70x (ISBN 0-89573-004-9). VCH Pubs.

Breitmaier, E., et al. Atlas of Carbon-13 NMR Data, Vol. 1: Compounds 1-1003. LC 76-2126. pap. 59.00 (ISBN 0-317-26279-3, 2055699). Bks Demand UMI.

Breitmaier, Eberhard & Bauer, Gerhard. Thirteen C-NMR Spectroscopy: A Working Manual with Exercises. Cassels, Bruce K., tr. from Ger. (MMI Press Polymer Monographs). 431p. 1984. 108.00 (ISBN 3-7186-0022-6). Harwood Academic.

Breitman, George. Fighting Racism in World War II. 1980. 25.00 (ISBN 0-913460-81-8); pap. 7.95 (ISBN 0-913460-82-6). Monad Pr.

--How a Minority Can Change Society: The Real Potential of the Afro-American Struggle. pap. 0.75 (ISBN 0-87348-050-3). Path Pr NY.

--The Last Year of Malcolm X: The Evolution of a Revolutionary. LC 67-20467. 1970. 16.00 (ISBN 0-87348-003-1); pap. 4.95 (ISBN 0-87348-004-X). Path Pr NY.

--Race Prejudice: How It Began, When Will It End. pap. 0.35 (ISBN 0-87348-256-5). Path Pr NY.

Breitman, George, ed. The Founding of the Socialist Workers Party: Minutes & Resolutions 1938-39. 400p. 1982. lib. bdg. 30.00 (ISBN 0-913460-90-7); pap. 8.95 (ISBN 0-913460-91-5). Monad Pr.

--Malcolm X Speaks: Selected Speeches & Statements. 1969. pap. 5.95 (ISBN 0-394-17114-4, B351, BC). Grove.

Breitman, George, ed. see Cannon, James P.

Breitman, George, ed. see Malcolm X.

Breitman, George, ed. see Trotsky, Leon.

Breitman, George, et al. Marxism & the Negro Struggle. 2nd ed. 1968. pap. 0.75 (ISBN 0-87348-072-4). Path Pr. NY.

--The Assassination of Malcolm X. Miah, Malik, ed. (Illus.). 1977. cloth 10.00 (ISBN 0-87348-472-X); pap. 2.95 (ISBN 0-87348-473-8). Path Pr NY.

Breitman, George, et al, eds. see Trotsky, Leon.

Breitman, George, et al, eds. see Trotsky, Leon, et al.

Breitman, Richard. German Socialism & Weimar Democracy. LC 80-21412. xii, 283p. 1981. 22.00x (ISBN 0-8078-1462-8). U of NC Pr.

Breitmeier, E., et al. Thirteen NMR Spectroscopy. (MMI Press Polymer Monograph). 431p. 1984. text ed. 108.00 (ISBN 3-7186-0022-6). Harwood Academic.

Breitmeyer, Bruno G. Visual Masking: An Integrative Approach. (Oxford Psychology Ser.). (Illus.). 1984. 34.95x (ISBN 0-19-852105-7). Oxford U Pr.

Breitner, Bina, jt. auth. see Perry, Henry B.

Breitner, I. E. The Life of the Victim: A Psychodrama in Three Phases. LC 76-62736. 1977. 12.50 (ISBN 0-918066-07-7); pap. 7.50 (ISBN 0-918066-08-5). Imibooks Pubns.

Breitner, I. Emery. Philotherapy: A New Approach to Psychotherapy. LC 73-90494. 1978. 12.50 (ISBN 0-914252-00-3). Imibooks Pubns.

Breitsameter. Lexikon der Schulphysik: Elektrizitaet und Magnetismus A-K, Vol. 3A. (Ger.). 42.50 (ISBN 3-7614-0168-X, M-7224). French & Eur.

--Lexikon der Schulphysik: Elektrizitaet und Magnetismus L-Z, Vol. 3B. (Ger.). 42.50 (ISBN 3-7614-0169-8, M-7225). French & Eur.

Breitschuh, K. Triangular Plates & Slabs. (Illus.). 199p. (Eng. & Ger.). 1974. 31.25x (ISBN 3-4330-0647-4). Adlers Foreign Bks.

Breitweiser, Mitchell R. Cotton Mather & Benjamin Franklin: The Price of Representative Personality. (Studies in American Literature & Culture). (Illus.). 320p. 1985. 27.95 (ISBN 0-521-26768-4). Cambridge U Pr.

Breivik, Patricia S. Open Admissions & the Academic Library. LC 77-5816. 142p. 1977. pap. 10.00x (ISBN 0-8389-3195-2). ALA.

--Planning the Library Instruction Program. LC 82-8827. 156p. (Orig.). 1982. pap. text ed. 10.00x (ISBN 0-8389-0358-4). ALA.

Breivik, Patricia S. & Gibson, E. Burr. Funding Alternatives for Libraries. LC 78-27865. 182p. 1979. pap. 10.00 (ISBN 0-8389-0273-1). ALA.

Brejcha, M. F. & Samuels, C. L. Automotive Chassis & Accessory Circuits. LC 76-14835. (Illus.). 1977. 24.95 (ISBN 0-13-055475-8). P-H.

Brejcha, Mathias F. Automotive Transmissions--Automotive. LC 72-186233. pap. 87.00 (ISBN 0-317-10791-7, 2014472). Bks Demand UMI.

Brekhman, I. I. Man & Biologically Active Substances: Introduction to the Pharmacology of Health. 2nd ed. 90p. 1980. pap. 5.95 (ISBN 0-08-025524-8). Pergamon.

Brendel, Otto J. Etruscan Art. (Pelican History of Art Ser.). 1979. pap. 18.95 (ISBN 0-14-056143-9, Pelican). Penguin.
--Etruscan Art. (Pelican History of Art Ser.: No. 43). 1979. 35.00 (ISBN 0-670-29880-8). Viking.
--Prolegomena to the Study of Roman Art. LC 78-24455. 1979. pap. 7.95x (ISBN 0-300-02372-3). Yale U Pr.
--Symbolism of the Sphere: A Contribution to the History of Earlier Greek Philosophy. (Etudes Preliminaires Aux Religions Orientales Dans l'empire Romain: No. 67). (Illus.). 1977. text ed. 44.00x (ISBN 90-04052-66-6). Humanities.
--The Visible Idea. (Art History Ser.: No. 2). (Illus.). 1980. 40.00 (ISBN 0-916276-07-4). Decatur Hse.
Brendel, W. & Zink, R. A., eds. High Altitude Physiology & Medicine I: Physiology of Adaptation. (Topics in Environmental Physiology & Medicine Ser.). (Illus.). 190p. 1982. 73.00 (ISBN 0-387-90482-4). Springer-Verlag.
Brendell, Theresa. Willows of the British Isles. (Shire Natural History Ser.: No. 8). (Orig.). 1985. pap. 3.95 (ISBN 0-85263-765-9, Pub. by Shire Pubns England). Seven Hills Bks.
Brenden, B. B., jt. auth. see Hildebrand, B. P.
Brenden, Byron B., jt. auth. see Hildebrand, B. Percy.
Brendon, John A. The Age of Chaucer. LC 72-179301. (Illus.). Repr. of 1924 ed. 16.50 (ISBN 0-404-01070-9). AMS Pr.
--Great Navigators & Discoverers. facs. ed. LC 67-26720. (Essay Index Reprint Ser). 1930. 18.25 (ISBN 0-8369-0248-3). Ayer Co Pubs.
Brendon, Piers. Hawker of Morwenstow. 274p. 1983. pap. 7.50 (ISBN 0-907746-26-8, Pub. by A Mott Ltd). Longwood Pub Group.
--The Life & Death of the Press Barons. LC 82-73017. (Illus.). 288p. 1983. 14.95 (ISBN 0-689-11341-2). Atheneum.
--Winston Churchill: A Bibliography. LC 83-48784. (Illus.). 256p. 1984. 16.30 (ISBN 0-06-015286-9, HarpT). Har-Row.
Brendtio, Larry K., jt. auth. see Vorrath, Harry H.
Brendtro, Larry K. & Ness, Arlin E. Re-Educating Troubled Youth: Environments for Teaching & Treatment. LC 83-11787. (Modern Application of Social Work Ser.). 1983. lib. bdg. 29.95x (ISBN 0-202-36033-4); pap. text ed. 16.95x (ISBN 0-202-36034-2). Aldine Pub.
Breneman, Bren, jt. auth. see Breneman, Lucille N.
Breneman, David & Nelson, Susan C. Financing Community Colleges: An Economic Perspective. LC 81-17042. (Studies in Higher Education Policy). 222p. 1981. 26.95 (ISBN 0-8157-1064-X); pap. 9.95 (ISBN 0-8157-1063-1). Brookings.
Breneman, David W. & Finn, Chester E., eds. Public Policy & Private Higher Education. (Studies in Higher Education Policy). 1978. 29.95 (ISBN 0-8157-1066-6); pap. 11.95 (ISBN 0-8157-1065-8). Brookings.
Breneman, James C. Basics of Food Allergy. 2nd ed. (Illus.). 470p. 1984. 49.75x (ISBN 0-398-04888-6). C C Thomas.
Breneman, John W. Mechanics. 3rd ed. (Illus.). 1960. 28.40 (ISBN 0-07-007538-7). McGraw.
--Strength of Materials. 3rd ed. 1965. 29.40 (ISBN 0-07-007536-0). McGraw.
Breneman, Lucille N. & Breneman, Bren. Once upon a Time: A Storytelling Handbook. LC 83-10990. (Illus.). 208p. 1983. lib. bdg. 18.95x (ISBN 0-8304-1007-4). Nelson-Hall.
Breneman, Mervin, ed. Biblia Con Notas. 1696p. (Span.). 1981. black imit. lea. 19.95 (ISBN 0-89922-365-6); red. imit. lea. 19.95 (ISBN 0-89922-465-2); black imit. lea. with thumb index 23.95 (ISBN 0-89922-366-4); red imit. lea. with thumb index 23.95 (ISBN 0-89922-466-0). Edit Caribe.
--Biblia con Notas. 1696p. (Span.). 1981. black imitation leather 15.95 (ISBN 0-89922-164-5); black imitation leather 19.95 (ISBN 0-89922-364-8); red imitation leather 15.95 (ISBN 0-89922-264-1); red imitation leather 19.95 (ISBN 0-89922-464-4). Edit Caribe.
Breneman, Steven B. Fly Away Home. LC 84-6252. 74p. (Orig.). (gr. 2-6). 1984. pap. 6.95 (ISBN 0-87743-183-3, Pub. by Bellwood Pr). Baha'i.
Brener, David A. The Jews of Lancaster, Pennsylvania: A Story with Two Beginnings. LC 79-21690. (Illus.). 188p. (Orig.). 1979. pap. 12.00x (ISBN 0-9605482-0-3). Cong Shaarai.
Brener, Robert. Apple II, IIe Troubleshooting & Ripais Manual. LC 84-71058. 19.95 (ISBN 0-672-22353-8). Sams.
Brenes, Edin & Patterson, D. H. Conversemos: First Book for Spanish Conversation. (Illus., Span.). 1942. text ed. 12.00x (ISBN 0-89197-112-2); pap. text ed. 4.95x (ISBN 0-89197-714-7). Irvington.
Brenet, Michel, pseud. Bibliographie des Bibliographies Musicales. LC 73-125065. (Music Ser.). 1971. Repr. of 1913 ed. lib. bdg. 25.00 (ISBN 0-306-70002-6). Da Capo.
Brenet, Michel. Les Concerts en France Sous l'Ancien Regime. LC 68-16224. (Music Ser). 1970. Repr. of 1900 ed. lib. bdg. 49.50 (ISBN 0-306-71061-7). Da Capo.
--Diccionario De la Musica: Historico y Tecnico. 3rd ed. 566p. (Span.). 1976. 50.00 (ISBN 84-7082-139-3, S-16685). French & Eur.
--Haydn. LC 72-80497. Repr. of 1926 ed. 20.00 (ISBN 0-405-08304-1, Blom Pubns). Ayer Co Pubs.
Brengelman, Fred. Shaping Sentences & Paragraphs: A Systematic Approach to Sentence & Paragraph Construction. 96p. 1980. pap. 8.95 (ISBN 0-8403-2292-5). Kendall-Hunt.
--Understanding Words: Systematic Spelling & Vocabulary Building. 112p. 1980. pap. 8.95 (ISBN 0-8403-2252-6). Kendall-Hunt.
Brengle. Heart Talks on Holiness. pap. 3.95 (ISBN 0-686-12873-7). Schmul Pub Co.
--Helps to Holiness. pap. 2.95 (ISBN 0-686-12874-5). Schmul Pub Co.
--Resurrection Life. pap. 2.95 (ISBN 0-686-12905-9). Schmul Pub Co.
--Soul Winner's Secret. pap. 2.95 (ISBN 0-686-12909-1). Schmul Pub Co.
--The Way of Holiness. pap. 2.25 (ISBN 0-686-12920-2). Schmul Pub Co.
Brengle, Kenneth G. Principles & Practices of Dryland Farming. 1982. 15.00x (ISBN 0-87081-095-2). Colo Assoc.
Brengle, Richard L., ed. Arthur, King of Britain: History, Romance, Chronicle & Criticism. (Orig.). 1964. pap. 13.95 (ISBN 0-13-049270-1). P-H.
Brengle, Richard L., jt. ed. see Bicknell, David L.
Brengle, Samuel. God As Strategist. (Illus.). 64p. 1978. pap. 1.50 (ISBN 0-89216-017-9). Salvation Army.
Brengle, Samuel L. Ancient Prophets & Modern Problems. 1978. pap. 3.25 (ISBN 0-86544-000-X). Salvation Army.
--Guest of the Soul. 1978. pap. 3.25 (ISBN 0-86544-001-8). Salvation Army.
--Heart Talks on Holiness. 1978. pap. 3.25 (ISBN 0-86544-002-6). Salvation Army.
--Helps to Holiness. 1978. pap. 3.25 (ISBN 0-86544-003-4). Salvation Army.
--Love Slaves. 1960. Repr. of 1923 ed. 3.25 (ISBN 0-86544-004-2). Salvation Army.
--Resurrection Life & Power. 1978. Repr. of 1925 ed. 3.25 (ISBN 0-86544-005-0). Salvation Army.
--Soul Winner's Secret. 1978. pap. 3.25 (ISBN 0-86544-007-7). Salvation Army.
--Way of Holiness. 1966. Repr. of 1902 ed. 3.25 (ISBN 0-86544-008-5). Salvation Army.
--When the Holy Ghost Is Come. 1980. pap. 3.25 (ISBN 0-86544-009-3). Salvation Army.
Brenig, W. & Manzel, D., eds. Desorption Induced by Electronic Transitions: Diet II. (Surface Sciences Ser.: Vol. 4). (Illus.). ix, 291p. 1985. 32.00 (ISBN 0-387-15593-7). Springer Verlag.
Brenig, W., jt. ed. see Stuke, J.
Brenikov, Paul, et al, eds. Land Use in an Urban Environment. 264p. 1961. 39.00x (ISBN 0-85323-002-1, Pub. by Liverpool Univ England). State Mutual Bk.
Brenizer, Sherman. Hydro-Story, Hydroponic Gardening at Home. 1977. pap. 4.95 (ISBN 0-917316-13-4). Nolo Pr.
Brenkert, George G. Marx's Ethics of Freedom. 360p. 1983. 29.95x (ISBN 0-7100-9461-2). Routledge & Kegan.
Brenman, Margaret & Gill, Merton M. Hypnotherapy: A Survey of the Literature. (Menninger Foundation Monograph Ser.: No. 5). 303p. (Orig.). 1971. text ed. 27.50 (ISBN 0-8236-2420-X); pap. text ed. 9.95 (ISBN 0-8236-8073-8, 022420). Intl Univs Pr.
Brenman, Margaret, jt. auth. see Gill, Merton M.
Brennan & Grant. Act of Providence. 10.00 (ISBN 0-937986-00-3); deluxe ed. 20.00x (ISBN 0-937986-01-1). D M Grant.
Brennan, jt. auth. see Banaszak.
Brennan, Alice. Castle Mirage. 1976. pap. 1.25 (ISBN 0-685-72570-7, LB392, Leisure Bks). Dorchester Pub Co.
--Sleep Well, Christine. 1973. pap. 0.75 (ISBN 0-380-01554-4, 17491). Avon.
Brennan, Andrew, ed. Worksite Health Promotion. 96p. 1982. pap. text ed. 9.95 (ISBN 0-89885-142-4). Human Sci Pr.
Brennan, Andrew, ed. see Elder, Crawford.
Brennan, Andrew, ed. see Tiles, J. E.
Brennan, Anne & Janice, Brewi. Mid-Life Directions, Praying & Playing Sources of New Dynamism. 192p. (Orig.). 1985. pap. 7.95 (ISBN 0-8091-2681-8). Paulist Pr.
Brennan, Anne, jt. ed. see Brewi, Janice.
Brennan, Barbara & Heilman, Joan R. The Complete Book of Midwifery. 1977. pap. 4.95 (ISBN 0-525-03180-4). Dutton.
Brennan, Bernard P. William James. (Twayne's United States Authors Ser.). 1968. pap. 5.95x (ISBN 0-8084-0005-3, T131, Twayne). New Coll U Pr.
Brennan, Beth. Who's Who & Why of Successful Florida Women. (Premier Edition Ser.). 512p. 1985. 85.00 (ISBN 0-930507-00-2). Currier-Davis.
Brennan, C. J. Poems: 1913. (Australian Literary Reprints Ser.). 22.00x (ISBN 0-424-06470-7, Pub. by Sydney U Pr); pap. 16.00x (ISBN 0-424-06480-4, Pub. by Sydney U Pr). Intl Spec Bk.
Brennan, Christopher. Christopher Brennan. Sturm, Terry, ed. (Portable Australian Authors Ser.). 512p. 1985. text ed. 25.00 (ISBN 0-7022-1735-2); pap. 14.95 (ISBN 0-7022-1736-0). U of Queensland Pr.
Brennan, Dan. Blood in the Sky. 1977. pap. 1.50 (ISBN 0-8439-0464-X, Leisure Bks). Dorchester Pub Co.
--Double Fault. 1979. pap. 2.25 (ISBN 0-8439-0654-5, Leisure Bks). Dorchester Pub Co.
--One of Our Bombers Is Missing. 1977. pap. 1.50 (ISBN 0-505-51140-1, Pub. by Tower Bks). Dorchester Pub Co.
--The Sky Remembers. 1977. pap. 1.50 (ISBN 0-8439-0484-4, Leisure Bks). Dorchester Pub Co.
--Suicide Squadron. 1978. pap. 1.75 (ISBN 0-505-51282-3, Pub. by Tower Bks). Dorchester Pub Co.
--They Can Only Kill You Once. 1977. pap. 1.50 (ISBN 0-8439-0455-0, Leisure Bks). Dorchester Pub Co.
--Winged Victory. 1978. pap. 1.50 (ISBN 0-505-51254-8, Pub. by Tower Bks). Dorchester Pub Co.
Brennan, Dick, jt. auth. see Brennan, Ella.
Brennan, E. J., ed. Education for National Efficiency: The Contribution of Sidney & Beatrice Webb. 208p. 1975. 39.50 (ISBN 0-485-11151-9, Pub. by Athlone Pr Ltd). Longwood Pub Group.
Brennan, Elaine, jt. auth. see Etsell, Karen.
Brennan, Elizabeth M., ed. see Webster, John.
Brennan, Ella & Brennan, Dick. The Commander's Palace New Orleans Cookbook. (Illus.). 1984. 17.95 (ISBN 0-517-55049-0, C N Potter Bks). Crown.
Brennan, Ellen R., ed. Mortality Patterns in Anthropological Populations. LC 83-6982. 160p. 1983. 13.95 (ISBN 0-8143-1756-1). Wayne St U Pr.
Brennan, Fanny, tr. see Guerard, Micahel.
Brennan, Frank. Too Much Order with Too Little Law. LC 82-19956. (Illus.). 303p. 1983. text ed. 27.95 (ISBN 0-7022-1842-1). U of Queensland Pr.
Brennan, Frank E. Personal Selling: A Professional Approach. 448p. 1983. text ed. 23.95 (ISBN 0-574-20685-X, 13-3685); instr's. guide avail. (ISBN 0-574-20686-8, 13-3686). SRA.
Brennan, G. & Buchanan, J. The Power to Tax. LC 79-56862. (Illus.). 300p. 1980. 32.50 (ISBN 0-521-23329-1). Cambridge U Pr.
Brennan, Gale. Earl the Squirrel. 16p. (Orig.). (gr. k-6). 1981. pap. 1.25. Brennan Bks.
--Toulouse the Mouse. 16p. (Orig.). (gr. k-6). 1981. pap. 1.25. Brennan Bks.
Brennan, Gale, jt. auth. see LaFleur, Tom.
Brennan, Geoffrey & Buchanan, James. The Reason of Rules: Constitutional Political Economy. 176p. Date not set. price not set. (ISBN 0-521-25655-0). Cambridge U Pr.
Brennan, Georgeanne, et al. The American Vegetable Cookbook. 325p. (Orig.). 1985. 21.95 (ISBN 0-943186-24-2, 0-671-60653-0); pap. 14.95 (ISBN 0-943186-25-0, 0-671-60654-9). Aris Bks Harris.
Brennan, Gerry. Classical Records: Starting Your Collection. LC 83-70327. 112p. (Orig.). 1983. pap. 6.95 (ISBN 0-89708-116-1). And Bks.
Brennan, H. Geoffrey & Buchanan, James M. Monopoly in Money & Inflation. (Institute of Economic Affairs, Hobart Papers Ser.: No. 88). pap. 5.95 technical (ISBN 0-255-36138-6). Transatlantic.
Brennan, Irene J., ed. Fort Mojave, Eighteen Fifty-Nine to Eighteen Ninety: Letter of the Commanding Officers. (Illus.). 222p. 1980. pap. 26.00x (ISBN 0-89126-083-8). MA-AH Pub.
Brennan, J. G., et al. Food Engineering Operations. 2ND ed. (Illus.). 532p. 1976. 44.50 (ISBN 0-85334-694-1, Pub. by Elsevier Applied Sci England). Elsevier.
Brennan, J. H. Astral Doorways. 1972. 6.95 (ISBN 0-85030-242-0). Weiser.
--The Castle of Darkness. (Grailquest Ser.: No. 1). 192p. (gr. 5up). pap. 2.25 (ISBN 0-440-91120-6, LFL). Dell.
--Dark Moon. LC 80-20034. 264p. 1981. 13.95 (ISBN 0-03-058013-7). HR&W.
--The Den of Dragons. (Grailquest Ser.: No. 2). 192p. (gr. 5up). pap. 2.25 (ISBN 0-440-91873-1, LFL). Dell.
--Experimental Magic. 1972. pap. 5.95 (ISBN 0-87728-164-5). Weiser.
--Getting What You Want. 176p. 1984. 8.95 (ISBN 0-8128-2175-0); pap. 3.25 (ISBN 0-8128-8049-8). Stein & Day.
--Mindreach: How to Develop Personal PK (Psycho-Kinesis) Power. 128p. (Orig.). 1985. pap. 6.95 (ISBN 0-85030-386-9, Pub. by Aquarian Pr England). Sterling.
--Reincarnation Five Keys to Past Lives. (Paths to Inner Power Ser.). 1981. pap. 2.50 (ISBN 0-85030-275-7). Weiser.
Brennan, J. P. Chronicles of Lucius Leffing. 7.00 (ISBN 0-937986-07-0). D M Grant.
Brennan, James F. Enlightened Despotism in Russia: The Reign of Elisabeth, 1741-1762. (American University Studies IX (History): Vol. 14). 281p. 1986. text ed. price not set (ISBN 0-8204-0262-1). P Lang Pubs.
--History & Systems of Psychology. (Illus.). 1982. ref. ed. 28.95 (ISBN 0-13-392209-X). P-H.
--History & Systems of Psychology. 2nd ed. (Illus.). 384p. 1986. text ed. 29.95 (ISBN 0-13-392218-9). P-H.
Brennan, James R. Patterns of Human Heredity: An Introduction to Human Genetics. (Illus.). 400p. 1985. text ed. 26.95 (ISBN 0-13-654245-X). P-H.
Brennan, Jennifer. The Cuisines of Asia: Nine Great Oriental Cuisines by Cooking Technique. (Illus.). 512p. 1984. 19.95 (ISBN 0-312-17841-7, Pub. by Marek). St Martin.
--One-Dish Meals of Asia. LC 84-40429. (Illus.). 432p. 1985. 17.95 (ISBN 0-8129-1144-X). Times Bks.
--The Original Thai Cookbook. (Illus.). 276p. 1981. 14.95 (ISBN 0-399-90110-8, Perigee); pap. 7.95 (ISBN 0-399-51033-8). Putnam Pub Group.
Brennan, Joe. Duke Kahanamoku - Hawaii's Golden Man. O'Connell, Pat, ed. (Hawaii Cultural Heritage Ser.: Vol. 3). (Illus.). 64p. (gr. 4 up). 1974. pap. 3.50x (ISBN 0-911776-26-5). Hogarth.
Brennan, John. Silver & the First New Deal. LC 68-56289. (Illus.). 187p. 1969. 5.50 (ISBN 0-87417-023-0). U of Nev Pr.
Brennan, John M. The Open Texture of Moral Concepts. LC 74-31826. 171p. 1977. text ed. 26.50x (ISBN 0-06-490656-6, 06364). B&N Imports.
Brennan, John M., ed. Buying Guide to California Wines. 3rd ed. (Illus.). 1985. 30.00 (ISBN 0-916040-53-4). Wine Consul Calif.
Brennan, Joseph. Paniolo. 1978. pap. 4.50 (ISBN 0-914916-39-4). Topgallant.
--The Parker Ranch. pap. 3.95 (ISBN 0-686-79501-6, PBN 5102, BN). B&N NY.
--Social Conditions in Industrial Rhode Island Eighteen Twenty to Eighteen Sixty. LC 78-14597. (Perspectives in American History Ser.: No. 41). 181p. 1979. Repr. of 1940 ed. lib. bdg. 19.50x (ISBN 0-87991-365-7). Porcupine Pr.
Brennan, Joseph K. Gobo & the River. LC 84-22369. (Illus.). 48p. 1985. 6.95 (ISBN 0-03-004552-5). HR&W.
Brennan, Joseph P. Evil Always Ends. (Illus.). 128p. 1983. 15.00 (ISBN 0-937986-53-4). D M Grant.
--Sixty Selected Poems. LC 84-62734. (Illus.). 80p. 1985. 15.00 (ISBN 0-932445-11-X); pap. 5.00 (ISBN 0-932445-10-1). Ganley Pub.
--Stories of Darkness & Dread. 1973. 6.00 (ISBN 0-87054-064-5). Arkham.
Brennan, Leslie, jt. auth. see Galen, Robert.
Brennan, Sr. M. Rose. Intellectual Virtues According to the Philosophy of St. Thomas. (Orig.). 1957. pap. text ed. 4.95x (ISBN 0-87015-075-8). Pacific Bks.
Brennan, Martin. The Stars & the Stones: Ancient Art & Astronomy in Ireland. LC 82-50742. (Illus.). 208p. 1984. 19.95f (ISBN 0-500-01295-4). Thames Hudson.
Brennan, Mary. Show Me How: A Manual for Parents of Preschool Visually Impaired Children. 47p. 1982. 4.00 (ISBN 0-89128-113-4). Am Foun Blind.
Brennan, Mary A., ed. Research on Dance, Vol. III. 176p. 1982. 9.95 (ISBN 0-88314-153-1, 00004427). AAHPERD.
Brennan, Mary E. Managing Corporate Benefit Plans 1983. 121p. 1983. pap. text ed. 15.00 (ISBN 0-89154-221-3). Intl Found Employ.
Brennan, Mary E., ed. Benefits Processing Institute Proceedings. December 8-11, 1982, Orlando, Florida. 61p. (Orig.). 1983. pap. text ed. 10.00 (ISBN 0-89154-203-5). Intl Found Employ.
--Canadian Conference: Proceedings 13th Annual, Oct. 4-8, 1980. 145p. (Orig.). 1981. pap. 11.00 (ISBN 0-89154-145-4). Intl Found Employ.
--Canadian Conference: Proceedings, 15th Annual, 1982. 318p. 1983. pap. text ed. 15.00 (ISBN 0-89154-204-3). Intl Found Employ.
--Canadian Conference, 14th Annual Nov. 23-27, 1981 Proceedings. 280p. (Orig.). 1982. pap. 14.00 (ISBN 0-89154-177-2). Intl Found Employ.
--Canadian Employee Benefit Plans, 1983. LC 77-151688. 302p. (Orig.). 1984. pap. text ed. 15.00 (ISBN 0-89154-217-5). Intl Found Employ.
--Claims Processing for Benefit Plans, 1983. LC 84-80454. 82p. (Orig.). 1984. pap. 10.00 (ISBN 0-89154-220-5). Intl Found Employ.
--Claims Processing for Benefit Plans, 1984. 99p. (Orig.). 1985. pap. 12.00 (ISBN 0-89154-271-X). Intl Found Employ.
--Containing Corporate Health Care Costs, 1983. 47p. (Orig.). 1983. pap. 10.00 (ISBN 0-89154-234-5). Intl Found Employ.
--E D P Institute, Las Vegas, Oct. 12-15, 1980: Proceedings. 63p. (Orig.). 1981. pap. 8.00 (ISBN 0-89154-144-6). Intl Found Employ.
--International Benefits Seminar Proceedings, Oct. 21-24, 1981, Montreal. 115p. (Orig.). 1982. pap. 10.00 (ISBN 0-89154-174-8). Intl Found Employ.
--Public Employee Benefit Plans, 1983. 94p. (Orig.). 1983. pap. text ed. 10.00 (ISBN 0-89154-215-9). Intl Found Employ.
--Public Employees Conference, Dec. 7-10, 1980, Monterey, CA: Proceedings. Incl. Public Employees Conference Proceedings, December 5-8, 1982, Orlando, Florida. Brennan, Mary E., ed. 110p. (Orig.). 1983. pap. 10.00 (ISBN 0-89154-207-8); Public Employees Conference Proceedings, Nov. 11-14, 1981, Williamsburg. Brennan, Mary E., ed. 119p. (Orig.). 1982. pap. 10.00 (ISBN 0-89154-173-X). 114p. (Orig.). 1981. pap. 10.00 (ISBN 0-89154-151-9). Intl Found Employ.
Brennan, Mary E., ed. see Cooper, Robert D.
Brennan, Matthew. Brennan's War: Vietnam Ninteen Sixty-Five to Ninteen Sixty-Nine. (Illus.). 272p. 1985. 17.95 (ISBN 0-89141-236-0). Presidio Pr.

Brennan, Matthew J. The Resource Guide to Chiropractic: A Bibliography of Chiropractic & Related Areas, 1895-1981. 1981. pap. text ed. 19.95 (ISBN 0-9606618-0-8). Am Chiro Assn.

Brennan, Maynard J. Compact Handbook of Composition. 3rd ed. 1978. pap. text ed. 4.95 (ISBN 0-669-00578-9). Heath.

Brennan, Michael. The War in Clare Nineteen Eleven-Nineteen Twenty-One: Personal Memoirs of the Irish War of Independence. 112p. 1980. 12.50x (ISBN 0-906127-26-2, Pub. by Irish Academic Pr Ireland). Biblio Dist.

Brennan, Michael J. Economics of Age. Stein, Leon, ed. LC 79-8693. (Growing Old Ser.). (Illus.). 1980. Repr. of 1967 ed. lib. bdg. 23.00x (ISBN 0-405-12778-2). Ayer Co Pubs.

Brennan, Michael J. & Schwartz, Eduardo S. Pricing & Investment Strategies for Guaranteed Equity-Linked Life Insurance. LC 78-62409. (S. S. Huebner Foundation Monographs: No. 7). (Illus.). 123p. 1979. pap. 12.00 (ISBN 0-918930-07-3). Huebner Foun Insur.

Brennan, Michael J., ed. Patterns of Market Behavior: Essays in Honor of Philip Taft. LC 65-12932. (Illus.). 266p. 1965. 20.00x (ISBN 0-87057-087-0). U Pr of New Eng.

Brennan, Michael J., et al, eds. Breast Cancer: New Concepts in Etiology & Control. 1980. 52.50 (ISBN 0-12-131150-3). Acad Pr.

Brennan, Patricia D. Hitchety Hatchety Up I Go! LC 85-4124. (Illus.). 32p. (gr. k-3). 1985. PLB 12.95 (ISBN 0-02-712300-6). Macmillan.

Brennan, Patrick. Spirituality for an Anxious Age: "Into Your Hands". 151p. 1985. 9.95 (ISBN 0-88347-178-7). Thomas More.

Brennan, Peter. Razorback. 384p. (Orig.). 1981. pap. 2.95 (ISBN 0-515-05392-9). Jove Pubns.

Brennan, R. O. Best Blood Sugar Book. Goodman, Frances B., ed. 256p. 1983. 9.95 (ISBN 0-89896-051-7). Larksdale.

Brennan, R. O. & Mulligan, William C. Nutrigenetics: New Concepts for Relieving Hypoglycemia: Case Studies. LC 75-23063. (Illus.). 264p. 1976. 8.95 (ISBN 0-87131-187-9). M Evans.

Brennan, R. O., ed. see Addanki, Sam & Kindrick, Shirley A.

Brennan, Richard O. Dr. Brennan's Best Blood Sugar Book. LC 83-81263. 256p. (Orig.). 1983. spiral bdg. 9.95 (ISBN 0-933092-06-7). Educ Editions.

--Dr. Brennan's Treasury of Diet Menus. LC 78-74136. (Illus.). 1979. pap. 6.95 (ISBN 0-933092-01-6). Educ Editions.

--Incredible Edibles: The Complete Cottage Cheese Cook Book. 180p. (Orig.). 1981. pap. 9.95 (ISBN 0-933092-02-4). Educ Editions.

Brennan, Robert E., ed. Essays in Thomism. LC 72-1149. (Essay Index Reprint Ser.). Repr. of 1942 ed. 27.50 (ISBN 0-8369-2834-2). Ayer Co Pubs.

Brennan, Robert L. Elements of Generalizability Theory. (Illus.). 162p. (Orig.). 1983. pap. text ed. 10.00 (ISBN 0-937734-05-5). Am Coll Testing.

Brennan, Rory. The Sea on Fire. (Orig.). 1980. pap. text ed. 8.50x (ISBN 0-85105-308-4, Dolmen Pr). Humanities.

Brennan, Steve, ed. Photo Lab Index: Compact Three. 3rd, rev. ed. 700p. (Orig.). 1982. pap. text ed. 13.95 (ISBN 0-87100-185-3, 2185). Morgan.

Brennan, Tim, et al. The Social Psychology of Runaways. LC 75-42947. 1978. 29.00x (ISBN 0-669-00565-7). Lexington Bks.

Brennan, Tom. Politics & Government in Britain. 2nd ed. LC 82-4145. (Illus.). 352p. 1982. pap. 16.95 (ISBN 0-521-28600-X). Cambridge U Pr.

Brennan, Wilfred K. Changing Special Education. 128p. 1982. 32.00x (ISBN 0-335-10046-5, Pub. by Open Univ Pr); pap. 13.00x (ISBN 0-335-10045-7). Taylor & Francis.

--Curriculum for Special Needs. 192p. 1984. 32.00x (ISBN 0-335-10575-0, Pub. by Open Univ Pr); pap. 13.00x (ISBN 0-335-10421-5, Pub. by Open Univ Pr). Taylor & Francis.

Brennan, William. The Abortion Holocaust: Today's Final Solution. LC 82-83960. (Illus.). 230p. (Orig.). 1983. pap. 6.95 (ISBN 0-911439-01-3). Landmark Pr.

Brennan, William J., Jr., frwd. by see Karlen, Delmar.

Brennan, William T. & Crowe, James W. Guide to Problems & Practices in First Aid & Emergency Care. 4th ed. 208p. 1981. write for info. wire coil (ISBN 0-697-07390-4); instr's manual avail. (ISBN 0-697-07396-3). Wm C Brown.

Brennan-Nichols, Patricia. Getting to Know Jesus. (Illus.). 68p. (Orig.). 1984. pap. 3.95 (ISBN 0-89505-130-3). Argus Comm.

--Liturgies & Lessons: Childrens Homilies. 1984. pap. 9.95 (ISBN 0-941850-13-7). Sunday Pubns.

Brennecke, E. The Life of Thomas Hardy. LC 72-8648. (Studies in Thomas Hardy, No. 14). 1973. Repr. of 1925 ed. lib. bdg. 49.95x (ISBN 0-8383-1672-7). Haskell.

--Thomas Hardy's Universe: A Study of a Poet's Mind. LC 68-689. (Studies in Thomas Hardy, No. 14). 1969. Repr. of 1924 ed. lib. bdg. 75.00x (ISBN 0-8383-0651-9). Haskell.

Brennecke, E., ed. see Hardy, Thomas.

Brennecke, Ernest. John Milton the Elder & His Music. LC 73-1770. 224p. 1973. Repr. lib. bdg. 19.00x (ISBN 0-374-90980-6). Octagon.

--Thomas Hardy's Universe. LC 73-15715. 1974. Repr. of 1924 ed. lib. bdg. 15.00 (ISBN 0-8414-3318-6). Folcroft.

Brennecke, Fritz, compiled by. The Nazi Primer: Offical Handbook for Schooling the Hitler Youth. Childs, Harwood L., tr. from Ger. LC 71-180391. Repr. of 1938 ed. 27.50 (ISBN 0-404-56107-1). AMS Pr.

Brenneis, Donald L. & Myers, Fred R. Dangerous Words: Language & Politics in the Pacific. LC 83-23845. 1984. 40.00x (ISBN 0-8147-1051-4); pap. 18.50x (ISBN 0-8147-1052-2). NYU Pr.

Brenneke, Judith S. & Hammil, Mary Lou. Decisions: Making Personal Economic Choices. 368p. (gr. 11-12). 1984. text ed. 14.95 (ISBN 0-8219-0027-7, 30450); tchr's guide 7.50 (ISBN 0-8219-0028-5, 30807); wkbk. 4.95 (ISBN 0-8219-0029-3, 30661). EMC.

Brenneman, Al. Al Brenneman Trains Bird Dogs. (Illus.). 80p. 1983. 16.45 (ISBN 0-87397-258-9). Strode.

Brenneman, H. G. Meditaciones para la Nueva Madre. 80p. 1982. Repr. of 1978 ed. 2.85 (ISBN 0-311-40032-9). Casa Bautista.

Brenneman, Helen G. But Not Forsaken. 1983. 3.25 (ISBN 0-87813-954-0). Christian Light.

--Learning to Cope. LC 75-32724. 88p. 1976. pap. 1.65 (ISBN 0-8361-1782-4). Herald Pr.

--Meditaciones para la Nueva Madre. La Valle, Maria T., tr. 80p. (Span.). 1978. pap. 1.95 (ISBN 0-8361-1212-1). Herald Pr.

--Meditations for the Expectant Mother. LC 68-12025. 80p. (Orig.). 1968. 5.95 (ISBN 0-8361-1639-9); pap. 3.50 (ISBN 0-8361-1567-8). Herald Pr.

--Meditations for the New Mother. LC 53-7585. (Illus.). 78p. (Orig.). 1953. 5.95 (ISBN 0-8361-1640-2); pap. 3.50 (ISBN 0-8361-1391-8). Herald Pr.

--Morning Joy. LC 80-26449. 80p. 1981. pap. 3.95 (ISBN 0-8361-1942-8). Herald Pr.

--My Comforters. LC 66-13156. 80p. (Orig.). 1966. deluxe ed. 3.95 (ISBN 0-8361-1751-4); pap. 2.50 (ISBN 0-8361-1529-5). Herald Pr.

--Para la Futura Mama. 80p. (Span.). 1979. pap. 2.50 (ISBN 0-317-31436-X). Herald Pr.

Brenneman, Richard J., ed. see Fuller, R. Buckminster.

Brenneman, Russell L. & Bates, Sarah M., eds. Land-Saving Action. LC 83-22803. (Illus.). 300p. 1984. 64.95 (ISBN 0-933280-23-8); pap. 34.95 (ISBN 0-933280-22-X). Island CA.

Brenneman, Walter L., Jr., et al. The Seeing Eye: Hermeneutical Phenomenology in the Study of Religion. LC 81-47174. 168p. 1982. 22.50x (ISBN 0-271-00291-3). Pa St U Pr.

Brennen, R. O. Coronary? Cancer? God's Answer: Prevent It! 3.95x (ISBN 0-89081-181-4). Cancer Control Soc.

--Nutrigenetics: Relieving Hypoglycemia. 8.95x (ISBN 0-87131-187-9). Cancer Control Soc.

Brennenstuhl, W., jt. auth. see Ballmer, T.

Brennenstuhl, Waltraud. Control & Ability: Towards a Biocybernetics of Language. (Pragmatics & Beyond Ser.: III: 4). 122p. (Orig.). 1982. pap. 18.00x (ISBN 90-272-2522-2). Benjamins North Am.

Brenner, A. Your Mexican Holiday. 1976. lib. bdg. 59.95 (ISBN 0-8490-2853-1). Gordon Pr.

Brenner, Alfred. The TV Scriptwriter's Handbook. LC 80-23700. 322p. (Orig.). 1985. pap. 9.95 (ISBN 0-89879-178-2). Writers Digest.

Brenner, Anita. Influence of Technique on the Decorative Style in the Domestic Pottery of Culhuacan. LC 78-82356. (Columbia Univ. Contributions to Anthropology Ser.: Vol. 13). Repr. of 1931 ed. 22.50 (ISBN 0-404-50563-5). AMS Pr.

Brenner, Anita & Leighton, George R. The Wind That Swept Mexico: The History of the Mexican Revolution of 1910-1942. LC 77-149021. (Texas Pan American Ser.). (Illus.). 320p. 1984. pap. 12.95 (ISBN 0-292-79024-4). U of Tex Pr.

Brenner, Anita, tr. see Frank, Waldo.

Brenner, Anita, tr. see Frank, Waldo D.

Brenner, Anita, tr. see Lopez y Fuentes, Gregorio.

Brenner, Anita, tr. see Magdaleno, Mauricio.

Brenner, Athalya. Colour Terms in the Old Testament. (Journal for the Study of the Old Testament, Supplement Ser.: No. 21). 296p. 1983. text ed. 29.95x (ISBN 0-905774-42-6, Pub. by JSOT Pr England); pap. text ed. 14.95x (ISBN 0-905774-43-4, Pub. by JSOT Pr England). Eisenbrauns.

Brenner, Avis. Helping Children Cope with Stress. LC 83-47502. 208p. 1984. 22.00x (ISBN 0-669-06678-8); pap. 10.95x (ISBN 0-669-08995-8). Lexington Bks.

Brenner, B. & Stein, J., eds. Chronic Renal Failure. (Contemporary Issues in Nephrology: Vol. 6). 1981. text ed. 40.00 (ISBN 0-686-34352-2). Churchill.

Brenner, Barbara. Baltimore Orioles. LC 73-14327. (Science I Can Read Bk.). (Illus.). 64p. (gr. k-3). 1974. PLB 9.89 (ISBN 0-06-020665-9). HarpJ.

--Bodies. (Illus.). 48p. (ps-3). 1973. 12.95 (ISBN 0-525-26770-0, 01258-370). Dutton.

--A Dog I Know. LC 82-47572. (Illus.). 32p. (gr. k-4). 1983. 9.57i (ISBN 0-06-020684-5); PLB 10.89g (ISBN 0-06-020685-3). HarpJ.

--Faces. (Illus.). (ps-1). 1970. 11.95 (ISBN 0-525-29518-6, 01160-350). Dutton.

--The Gorilla Signs Love. LC 84-841. 160p. (gr. 9 up). 1984. 11.00 (ISBN 0-688-00995-6). Lothrop.

--Have You Ever Heard of a Kangaroo Bird? (Illus.). 48p. (gr. 3-5). 1980. 7.95 (ISBN 0-698-20446-8, Coward). Putnam Pub Group.

--Hemi: A Mule. (Harper Trophy Ser.). (Illus.). 128p. (gr. 3-7). 1975. pap. 1.25 (ISBN 0-06-440063-8, Trophy). HarpJ.

--The Killing Season. 192p. (gr. 7 up). 1985. pap. 2.50 (ISBN 0-440-94463-5, LFL). Dell.

--Mystery of the Disappearing Dogs. LC 82-186. (Capers Ser.). (Illus.). 128p. (gr. 3-6). 1982. 1.95 (ISBN 0-394-85162-5); PLB 4.99 (ISBN 0-394-95162-X). Knopf.

--Mystery of the Plumed Serpent. LC 80-17316. (Capers Ser.). (Illus.). 128p. (gr. 3-6). 1981. PLB 4.99 (ISBN 0-394-94531-X); pap. 1.95 (ISBN 0-394-84531-5). Knopf.

--On the Frontier with Mr. Audubon. (Illus.). (gr. 3-6). 1977. 8.95 (ISBN 0-698-20385-2, Coward). Putnam Pub Group.

--The Snow Parade. LC 83-18999. (Illus.). 32p. (ps-1). 1984. 8.95 (ISBN 0-517-55210-8). Crown.

--Wagon Wheels. LC 76-21391. (I Can Read History Bk.). (Illus.). 64p. (gr. k-3). 1978. 8.61i (ISBN 0-06-020668-3); PLB 9.89 (ISBN 0-06-020669-1). HarpJ.

--Wagon Wheels. LC 76-21391. (Trophy I Can Read Bk.). (Illus.). 64p. (ps-3). 1984. pap. 2.84i (ISBN 0-06-444052-4, Trophy). HarpJ.

--Walt Disney's The Penguin That Hated the Cold. (Disney's Wonderful World of Reading Ser.: No. 7). (Illus.). (ps-3). 1973. (BYR); PLB 4.99 (ISBN 0-394-92628-5). Random.

--Walt Disney's The Three Little Pigs. (Disney's Wonderful World of Reading Ser.: No. 6). (Illus.). (ps-3). 1974. 5.95 (ISBN 0-394-82522-5, BYR); PLB 4.99 (ISBN 0-394-92522-X). Random.

--A Year in the Life of Rosie Bernard. rev. ed. (Illus.). 184p. (gr. 3-7). 1983. pap. 1.50 (ISBN 0-380-01630-3, 43380-X, Camelot). Avon.

--Year in the Life of Rosie Bernard. LC 70-157902. (Illus.). 170p. (gr. 3-7). 1971. PLB 11.89 (ISBN 0-06-020657-8). HarpJ.

Brenner, Barbara & Bank Street College of Education. Love & Discipline. LC 82-90851. 224p. (Orig.). 1983. pap. 5.95 (ISBN 0-345-30520-5). Ballantine.

Brenner, Barbara & Endreweit, Marie. Bank Street's Family Computer Book. 224p. (Orig.). 1984. pap. 6.95 (ISBN 0-345-31367-4). Ballantine.

Brenner, Barry E., jt. auth. see Simon, Robert.

Brenner, Barry E., ed. Comprehensive Management of Respiratory Emergencies. (Illus.). 450p. 1985. 61.50 (ISBN 0-87189-117-4). Aspen Systems.

Brenner, Barry M. & Lazarus, J. Michael. Acute Renal Failure. (Illus.). 837p. 1983. 89.00 (ISBN 0-7216-1964-9). Saunders.

Brenner, Barry M. & Stein, Jay H. Acute Renal Failure. (Contemporary Issues in Nephrology: Vol. 6). (Illus.). 320p. 1980. text ed. 40.00 (ISBN 0-443-08116-6). Churchill.

--Nephrotic Syndrome. (Contemporary Issues in Nephrology Ser.: Vol. 9). (Illus.). 1982. 45.00 (ISBN 0-443-08175-1). Churchill.

Brenner, Barry M. & Rector, Floyd C., eds. The Kidney, 2 vols. 2nd ed. LC 74-25474. (Illus.). 2708p. 1981. Set. text ed. 173.00 (ISBN 0-7216-1969-X); Vol. 1. text ed. 89.00 (ISBN 0-7216-1967-3); Vol. 2. text ed. 89.00 (ISBN 0-7216-1968-1). Saunders.

Brenner, Barry M. & Stein, Jay H., eds. Hormonal Function & the Kidney. (Contemporary Issues in Nephrology: Vol. 4). (Illus.). 1979. text ed. 40.00 (ISBN 0-443-08039-9). Churchill.

--Hypertension. (Contemporary Issues in Nephrolog Ser.: Vol. 8). (Illus.). 383p. 1982. text ed. 42.00 (ISBN 0-443-08145-X). Churchill.

Brenner, Barry M., et al. Principles of Renal Medicine. (Illus.). 352p. Date not set. price not set (ISBN 0-7216-1973-8). Saunders.

Brenner, Benjamin. Effect of Immediate & Delayed Praise & Blame Upon Learning & Recall. LC 70-176588. (Columbia University. Teachers College. Contributions to Education: No. 620). Repr. of 1934 ed. 22.50 (ISBN 0-404-55620-5). AMS Pr.

Brenner, Charles. An Elementary Textbook of Psychoanalysis. rev. ed. 280p. 1974. pap. 4.95 (ISBN 0-385-09884-7, Anch). Doubleday.

--An Elementary Textbook of Psychoanalysis. enl. & rev. ed. LC 72-86658. x, 280p. (Orig.). 1973. text ed. 27.50 (ISBN 0-8236-1620-7). Intl Univs Pr.

--Mind in Conflict. LC 82-21391. v, 266p. (Orig.). 1982. text ed. 26.50 (ISBN 0-8236-3365-9). Intl Univs Pr.

--Psychoanalytic Technique & Psychic Conflict. LC 76-15047. 126p. (Orig.). 1976. text ed. 22.50 (ISBN 0-8236-5054-5). Intl Univs Pr.

Brenner, Charles, jt. auth. see Arlow, Jacob A.

Brenner, Clarence D. Bibliographical List of Plays in the French Language, Seventeen Hundred to Seventeen Eighty-Nine. LC 76-43909. (Music & Theatre in France in the 17th & 18th Centuries). Repr. of 1947 ed. 31.50 (ISBN 0-404-60152-9). AMS Pr.

Brenner, Daniel, jt. auth. see Price, Monroe E.

Brenner, Daniel & Rivers, William, eds. Free but Regulated: Conflicting Traditions in Media Law. 284p. 1982. text ed. 24.95x (ISBN 0-8138-0756-5). Iowa St U Pr.

Brenner, David. The Effective Psychotherapist: Conclusions from Practice & Research. (Pergamon General Psychology Ser.: No. 105). 160p. 1982. 19.25 (ISBN 0-08-028056-0); pap. 8.95 (ISBN 0-08-028055-2). Pergamon.

--Nobody Ever See you Eat Tuna Fish. (Illus.). 320p. 1986. pap. 15.95 (ISBN 0-87795-730-4). Arbor Hse.

--Nobody Ever Sees You Eat Tuna Fish. (Illus.). Date not set. 15.95 (ISBN 0-87795-730-4). Arbor Hse.

--Revenge Is the Best Exercise. (Illus.). 192p. (Orig.). 1984. pap. 9.95 (ISBN 0-87795-655-3). Arbor Hse.

--Soft Pretzels with Mustard. (Illus.). 324p. 1983. 14.95 (ISBN 0-87795-442-9). Arbor Hse.

--Soft Pretzels with Mustard. 336p. 1984. pap. 3.50 (ISBN 0-425-06593-6). Berkley Pub.

Brenner, Egon, jt. auth. see Javid, Mansour.

Brenner, Eleanor P. Gourmet Cooking Without Salt. LC 79-6856. (Illus.). 432p. 1981. 15.95 (ISBN 0-385-14821-6). Doubleday.

Brenner, Elizabeth. The Hand Book. LC 79-54863. (Illus.). 1980. pap. 7.95 (ISBN 0-89087-259-7). Celestial Arts.

--Winning by Letting Go: Control Without Compulsion, Surrender Without Defeat. 240p. 1985. 14.95 (ISBN 0-15-197130-7). HarBraceJ.

Brenner, Erma. When Baby Comes Home. (Illus.). 128p. 1984. pap. text ed. 5.95 (ISBN 0-88102-038-9); tchr's guide 6.95 (ISBN 0-88102-039-7). Janus Bks.

Brenner, Gerry. Concealments in Hemingway's Works. LC 83-6283. 300p. 1983. 22.50 (ISBN 0-8142-0338-8). Ohio St U Pr.

Brenner, H. Transport Processes in Porous Media. 1986. write for info. (ISBN 0-07-007645-6). McGraw.

Brenner, H., jt. ed. see Happel, J.

Brenner, Harold J. Therapeutic Exercises for the Treatment of the Neurologically Disabled: A Text for Corrective Therapists & Corrective Physical Educators. (Illus.). 84p. 1957. 9.75x (ISBN 0-398-00219-3). C C Thomas.

Brenner, Howard, jt. auth. see Happel, John.

Brenner, J. L., tr. see Krasovskii, Nikolai N.

Brenner, Jacques, ed. see Voltaire.

Brenner, Jo Ann F. Articulation Handbook: Creative Remedial Techniques for Any Sound. LC 83-83337. (Illus.). 58p. 1984. 3.95 (ISBN 0-8134-2397-X). Interstate.

Brenner, Joel F. & Franklin, Herbert M. Rent Control in North America & Four European Countries. 78p. 1977. pap. 4.75 (ISBN 0-87855-733-4). Transaction Bks.

--Rent Control in North America & Four European Countries. (International Urban Reports Ser.). 78p. 1977. 4.75 (ISBN 0-318-13838-7). Coun Intl Urb.

Brenner, Joel L., tr. see Faddeev, D. K. & Sominskii, I. S.

Brenner, Jules. The Brenner Restaurant Index: A Computerized Guide to Choice Restaurants in the Greater Los Angeles Area. 290p. (Orig.). 1984. pap. 12.95 Ref. manual (ISBN 0-930437-00-4). NewTek Indust.

Brenner, Lenni. The Iron Wall: Zionist Revisionism from Jabotinsky to Shamir. 230p. 1984. 26.25x (ISBN 0-86232-216-2, Pub. by Zed Pr England); pap. text ed. 9.25 (ISBN 0-86232-217-0, Pub. by Zed Pr England). Biblio Dist.

--Zionism in the Age of the Dictators. 256p. 1983. 16.95 (ISBN 0-88208-163-2); pap. 8.95 (ISBN 0-88208-164-0). Lawrence Hill.

Brenner, Louis. West African Sufi: The Religious Heritage & Spiritual Quest of Cerno Bokar Saalif Taal. LC 83-4803. 215p. 1984. lib. bdg. 22.50x (ISBN 0-520-05008-8). U of Cal Pr.

Brenner, M. Harvey. Mental Illness & the Economy. LC 72-85144. 320p. 1973. 20.00x (ISBN 0-674-56875-3). Harvard U Pr.

Brenner, Marcella B. & Lieberman, E. James. Interview Art & Skill. 192p. 1980. pap. text ed. 8.95x (ISBN 0-937286-00-1). Irvington.

Brenner, Marie. Intimate Distance: Portraits of Famous People by One of New York Magazine's Leading Journalist. LC 83-61856. 284p. 1983. 10.95 (ISBN 0-688-02137-9). Morrow.

Brenner, Martha. Fireworks Tonight. (Illus.). 128p. (gr. 4 up). 1984. PLB 10.95 (ISBN 0-8038-2400-9). Hastings.

Brenner, Menachem. Option Pricing: Theory & Applications. (Salomon Brothers Center Bks.). 256p. 1983. 27.50x (ISBN 0-669-05714-2). Lexington Bks.

Brenner, Michael. Nuclear Power & Non-Proliferation: The Remaking of US Policy. LC 80-28561. 320p. 1981. 28.00 (ISBN 0-521-23517-0). Cambridge U Pr.

--The Structure of Action. LC 80-16125. 1980. 27.50 (ISBN 0-312-76710-2). St Martin.

Brenner, Michael, ed. Social Method & Social Life. 1981. 37.00 (ISBN 0-12-131550-9). Acad Pr.

Brenner, Michael, et al, eds. The Research Interview: Uses & Approaches. Date not set. 49.00 (ISBN 0-12-131580-0). Acad Pr.

Brenner, N., ed. International Gas Chromatography Symposium, Third. 1962. 109.00 (ISBN 0-12-131650-5). Acad Pr.

Brenner, P., et al. Besov Spaces & Applications to Difference Methods for Initial Value Problems. (Lecture Notes in Mathematics Ser.: Vol. 434). ii, 154p. 1975. pap. 13.00 (ISBN 0-387-07130-X). Springer-Verlag.

Brenner, Paul. Health Is a Question of Balance. 143p. 1980. pap. 5.95 (ISBN 0-87516-415-3). De Vorss.

--Life Is a Shared Creation. 176p. (Orig.). 1981. pap. 6.95 (ISBN 0-87516-454-4). De Vorss.

--Mi. (Orig.). 1983. pap. 5.00 (ISBN 0-914135-00-7). Rainbow Med Clinic.

Brenner, Paul F., jt. ed. see Mishell, Daniel R.

Brenner, Peter. King for One Day. LC 74-151271. (Illus.). 36p. (ps-3). 7.95 (ISBN 0-87592-027-6). Scroll Pr.

Brenner, Phillip. The Limits & Possibilities of Congress. LC 82-60469. 225p. 1983. text ed. 16.95 (ISBN 0-312-48682-0); pap. text ed. 10.95 (ISBN 0-312-48683-9). St Martin.

Brenner, R. P., jt. ed. see Brand, E. W.

Brenner, Reeve R. The Faith & Doubt of Holocaust Survivors. LC 79-6764. 1980. 12.95 (ISBN 0-02-904420-0). Free Pr.

Brenner, Reuven. History-The Human Gamble. LC 83-5780. xiv, 248p. 1983. 17.50x (ISBN 0-226-07402-1). U of Chicago Pr.

Brenner, Rica. Ten Modern Poets. facs. ed. LC 68-22091. (Essay Index Reprint Ser). 1930. 18.00 (ISBN 0-8369-0249-1). Ayer Co Pubs.

--Twelve American Poets Before Nineteen Hundred. facs. ed. LC 68-22092. (Essay Index Reprint Ser). 1933. 18.00 (ISBN 0-8369-0250-5). Ayer Co Pubs.

Brenner, Richard. All That Evolve. Brenner, Sherry, ed. (Illus., Orig.). 1984. pap. 4.95. Applause Pub.

Brenner, Robert. Christmas Past. (Illus.). 256p. 1985. 24.98 (ISBN 0-88740-051-5). Schiffer.

--Commodore 64 Troubleshooting & Repair Guide. LC 84-51406. 18.95 (ISBN 0-672-22363-5). Sams.

--IBM PC Troubleshooting & Repair Guide. LC 84-52214. 18.95 (ISBN 0-672-22358-9). Sams.

Brenner, Robert L. Petroleum Stratigraphy: A Guide for Nongeologists. 193p. 1984. 27.00 (ISBN 0-934634-38-6). Intl Human Res.

Brenner, S. The Brenner Chart. LC 72-84833. 30p. 1972. 36.00 (ISBN 0-913314-02-1). Am Classical Coll Pr.

Brenner, S. & Murray, J. D., eds. Theories of Biological Pattern Formation: Proceedings. (Royal Society of London). (Illus.). 191p. 1982. Repr. text ed. 62.00x (ISBN 0-85403-176-6, Pub. by Royal Soc London). Scholium Intl.

Brenner, S., et al, eds. New Horizons in Industrial Microbiology: Philosophical Transactions of the Royal Society, 1980. rev. ed. (Ser. B: Vol. 290). (Illus.). 152p. text ed. 47.50x (ISBN 0-85403-146-4, Pub. by Dechema Germany). Scholium Intl.

Brenner, Samuel. The Brenner Chart, the Economic Future of the United States & Stock Market Prognostications. (The New Stock Market Library). (Illus.). 1978. deluxe ed. 49.75x (ISBN 0-918968-14-3). Inst Econ Finan.

Brenner, Saul, ed. American Judicial Behavior. LC 73-10235. 250p. 1974. text ed. 28.50x (ISBN 0-8422-5116-2); pap. text ed. 12.50x (ISBN 0-8422-0307-9). Irvington.

Brenner, Shauna C. & Smoot, Deborah. The Vegetable Lover's Cookbook. (Illus.). 192p. (Orig.). 1983. pap. 9.95 (ISBN 0-8092-5642-8). Contemp Bks.

Brenner, Sherry, ed. see Brenner, Richard.

Brenner, Summer. Everyone Came Dressed As Water. 1973. pap. 2.50 (ISBN 0-685-40900-7, Pub. by Grasshopper Pr). Small Pr Dist.

--From the Heart to the Center. 1976. signed ed. 10.00 (ISBN 0-685-79215-3); pap. 3.00 (ISBN 0-685-79216-1). Figures.

--The Soft Room. 1978. signed 10.00 (ISBN 0-685-63387-X); pap. 4.00 wrappers (ISBN 0-685-63388-8). Figures.

Brenner, Teddy & Nagler, Barney. Only the Ring Was Square. LC 81-5940. 164p. 1981. 10.95. P-H.

Brenner, Thomas E. Five Years of Foundation Building: The University of Puerto Rico, 1924-1929. 3.10 (ISBN 0-8477-0819-5). U of PR Pr.

Brenner, Vincent C. & Davies, Jonathan. West's Intermediate Accounting. (Illus.). 1100p. 1983. text ed. 35.95 (ISBN 0-314-63307-3); instrs.' manual avail. (ISBN 0-314-75991-3); Working Papers, Pt. I avail. (ISBN 0-314-72286-6); Working Papers, Pt. II avail. (ISBN 0-314-72287-4); student guide 9.95 (ISBN 0-314-63308-1); solutions manual avail. (ISBN 0-314-63309-X); key figures avail. (ISBN 0-314-80324-6). West Pub.

Brenner, Vladimir. Count Witte: Scenes from His Life & Times, 1902-1915. LC 78-74647. 186p. 1979. 7.50 (ISBN 0-682-49293-0). Exposition Pr FL.

Brenner, W., jt. ed. see Berger, G.

Brenner, Y. S. Agriculture & the Economic Development of Low Income Countries. LC 77-146701. (Publications of the Institute of Social Studies Paperbacks: No. 2). 254p. 1972. pap. text ed. 8.40x (ISBN 90-2791-713-2). Mouton.

--Looking into the Seeds of Time: Social Mechanisms in Economic Development. 1979. pap. text ed. 29.50x (ISBN 90-232-1691-1). Humanities.

--Short History of Economic Progress. LC 68-21447. (Illus.). 1969. 27.50x (ISBN 0-678-05014-7). Kelley.

--Short History of Economic Progress: Course in Economic History. 304p. 1969. 30.00x (ISBN 0-7146-1277-4, F Cass Co); pap. 12.50x (ISBN 0-7146-4016-6, F Cass Co). Biblio Dist.

Brennert, Alan. Kindred Spirits. 320p. (Orig.). 1984. pap. 3.50 (ISBN 0-8125-8103-2). Tor Bks.

Brennglass, Alan C. The Overseas Private Investment Corporation: A Study in Political Risk. 304p. 1983. 37.95x (ISBN 0-03-062472-X). Praeger.

Brenni, Vito J. The Bibliographic Control of American Literature: Nineteen Twenty to Nineteen Seventy-Five. LC 79-12542. 217p. 1979. 16.00 (ISBN 0-8108-1221-5). Scarecrow.

--Edith Wharton: A Bibliography. 1966. 5.00 (ISBN 0-685-30816-2). McClain.

--Essays on Bibliography. LC 75-14082. 1975. 22.50 (ISBN 0-8108-0826-9). Scarecrow.

Brenni, Vito J., compiled by. American English: A Bibliography. LC 81-13412. 221p. 1982. Repr. of 1964 ed. lib. bdg. 24.75x (ISBN 0-313-23344-6, BRAE). Greenwood.

--The Art & History of Book Printing: A Topical Bibliography. LC 83-20696. v, 147p. 1984. lib. bdg. 35.00 (ISBN 0-313-24306-9, BHI). Greenwood.

--Book Illustration & Decoration: A Guide to Research. LC 80-1701. (Art Reference Collection Ser.: No. 1). viii, 191p. 1980. lib. bdg. 35.00 (ISBN 0-313-22340-8, BBI/). Greenwood.

--Book Printing in Britain & America: A Guide to the Literature & a Directory of Printers. LC 83-12656. xiii, 158p. 1983. lib. bdg. 35.00 (ISBN 0-313-23988-6, BBO/). Greenwood.

--Bookbinding: A Guide to the Literature. LC 82-15810. viii, 199p. 1983. lib. bdg. 35.00 (ISBN 0-313-23718-2, BBB/). Greenwood.

Brenot, John W. The Substitute's Handbook: A Survivor's Guide. LC 84-60972. 150p. (Orig.). 1985. pap. text ed. 9.95 (ISBN 0-88247-729-3). R & E Pubs.

Brenson, Ian, jt. ed. see Lane, Eric.

Brent, Allen. Philosophy & Educational Foundations. (Unwin Education Bks). 1983. text ed. 28.50x (ISBN 0-04-370143-4); pap. text ed. 12.50x (ISBN 0-04-370144-2). Allen Unwin.

Brent, Carol D. Barbecue: The Fine Art of Charcoal & Gas Outdoor Cooking. LC 77-152731. 1971. 5.95 (ISBN 0-88351-005-7). Test Recipe.

--Crepes: The Fine Art of Crepe & Blintz Cooking. LC 76-25350. 1976. 5.95. Test Recipe.

--Eggs: The Fine Art of Egg, Omelet & Souffle Cooking. LC 73-122450. 1970. 5.95 (ISBN 0-88351-006-5). Test Recipe.

--Fondue: The Fine Art of Fondue, Chinese Wok & Chaffing Dish Cooking. LC 79-95289. 1969. 5.95 (ISBN 0-88351-000-6). Test Recipe.

--Pancakes-Waffles: The Fine Art of Pancake, Waffle, Crepe & Blintz Cooking. LC 73-122449. 1970. 5.95 (ISBN 0-88351-007-3). Test Recipe.

Brent, Carol D. & Hughes, Betty A. Barbecuing the Weber Covered Way. LC 72-85084. 1980. 7.95 (ISBN 0-88351-002-2). Test Recipe.

Brent, Charles H. Inspiration of Responsibility, & Other Papers. facs. ed. LC 67-22081. (Essay Index Reprint Ser). 1915. 13.00 (ISBN 0-8369-0251-3). Ayer Co Pubs.

Brent, Daniel & Jurkowitz, Carolyn. School Board Study Programs: Board Members Manual. (Series I). 1983. 5.00 (ISBN 0-318-00790-8). Natl Cath Educ.

Brent, Daniel, jt. auth. see Jurkowitz, Carolyn.

Brent, Edward, jt. auth. see Sykes, Richard.

Brent, Gerry. The Pigman's Handbook. (Illus.). 240p. pap. 16.95 (ISBN 0-85236-126-2, Pub. by Farming Pr UK). Diamond Farm Bk.

Brent, Harry & Lutz, William. Rhetorical Considerations. 4th ed. 1983. 11.95 (ISBN 0-316-10783-2); write for info. tchr's ed. (ISBN 0-316-10784-0). Little.

Brent, Harry, jt. auth. see Lutz, William.

Brent, Jonathan, ed. The Best of Triquarterly. (Orig.). 1982. pap. 4.95 (ISBN 0-671-43419-5). WSP.

Brent, L. & Holbrow, J., eds. Progress in Immunology II, 5 Vols. 1975. Set. 134.25 (ISBN 0-7204-7033-1, North Holland); Vol. 1. 26.00 (ISBN 0-444-10753-3); Vol. 2. 33.75 (ISBN 0-444-10754-1); Vol. 3. 29.50 (ISBN 0-444-10755-X); Vol. 4. 27.25 (ISBN 0-444-10756-8); Vol. 5. 31.75 (ISBN 0-444-10757-6). Elsevier.

Brent, Leslie, et al, eds. Transplantation Today, Vol. VII. (Transplantation Proceedings Reprint Ser.). 1983. 98.50 (ISBN 0-8089-1603-3, 790659). Grune.

Brent, Linda, pseud. Incidents in the Life of a Slave Girl. Child, L. Maria, ed. LC 72-90506. (Illus.). 210p. 1973. pap. 4.95 (ISBN 0-15-644350-3, Harv). HarBraceJ.

Brent, Madeleine. A Heritage of Shadows. 352p. 1985. pap. 3.50 (ISBN 0-449-20643-2, Crest). Fawcett.

--The Long Masquerade. LC 81-43048. 360p. 1982. 14.95 (ISBN 0-385-14597-7). Doubleday.

--Moonraker's Bride. 1978. pap. 1.95 (ISBN 0-449-23594-7, Crest). Fawcett.

--Stormswift. LC 84-8128. 336p. 1985. 15.95 (ISBN 0-385-19047-6). Doubleday.

--Tregaron's Daughter. 320p. 1981. pap. 2.50 (ISBN 0-449-24391-5, Crest). Fawcett.

Brent, Madeline. A Heritage of Shadows. LC 83-45164. 312p. 1984. 15.95 (ISBN 0-385-19041-7). Doubleday.

Brent, Paul, illus. Beyond the Bay. (Illus.). 352p. 1985. 13.95x (ISBN 0-9615014-1-3). Jr Serv Panama City.

Brent, Peter. Charles Darwin: A Man of Enlarged Curiosity. (Illus.). 560p. 1983. pap. 9.50 (ISBN 0-393-30109-5). Norton.

--Darwin. LC 80-7889. 512p. 1981. 23.99i (ISBN 0-06-014880-2, HarpT). Har-Row.

Brent, Ruth H. Earthquake!!! Home Preparedness. 1976. pap. 2.00 (ISBN 0-87516-223-1). De Vorss.

Brent, Sandor B. Psychological & Social Structures: Their Organization, Activity & Development. 328p. 1984. text ed. 36.00 (ISBN 0-89859-414-6). L Erlbaum Assocs.

Brent, Stephen M. & Stiller, Sharon P. Handling Drunk Driving Cases. LC 84-52337. 1985. 66.50 (ISBN 0-318-04534-6). Lawyers Co-Op.

Brentano, Clemens. The Legend of Rose Petal. Bell, Anthea, tr. from Ger. LC 84-27386. (Illus.). 32p. (gr. 2-6). 1985. 13.95 (ISBN 0-907234-71-2, Pub. by Picture Bk Studio USA). Neugebauer Pr.

Brentano, Clemens see Scher, Helene, et al.

Brentano, Franz. Aristotle & His World View. George, Rolf & Chisholm, Roderick, trs. from Ger. LC 76-50245. 1978. 25.00 (ISBN 0-520-03390-6). U of Cal Pr.

--The Foundation & Construction of Ethics, Compiled from His Lectures on Practical Philosophy by Franziska Mayer-Hillebrand. Schneewind, Elizabeth H., tr. from Ger. (International Library of Philosophy & Scientific Method). 381p. (Orig.). 1973. text ed. 26.75x (ISBN 0-391-00254-6). Humanities.

--On the Several Senses of Being in Aristotle. George, Rolf, tr. LC 72-89796. 213p. 1981. Repr. of 1975 ed. 23.00x (ISBN 0-520-04420-7). U of Cal Pr.

--The Origin of Our Knowledge of Right & Wrong. Chisholm, R. & Schneewind, E., trs. (International Library of Philosophy & Scientific Method). 1976. Repr. of 1969 ed. 15.00x (ISBN 0-391-00980-X). Humanities.

--Psychology from an Empirical Standpoint. Kraus, Oskar & McAlister, Linda L., eds. Rancurello, Antos C., et al, trs. from Ger. (International Library of Philosophy & Scientific Method). 520p. 1973. text ed. 35.00x (ISBN 0-391-00253-8). Humanities.

--The Psychology of Aristotle: In Particular His Doctrine of the Active Intellect with an Appendix Concerning the Activity of Aristotle's God. George, Rolf, tr. LC 75-17303. 1977. 25.00x (ISBN 0-520-03081-8). U of Cal Pr.

--Sensory & Noetic Consciousness: Psychology from an Empirical Standpoint -Three. Kraus, Oskar, ed. McAlister, Linda & Schattle, M., trs. from Ger. 139p. 1981. text ed. 22.75x (ISBN 0-391-01175-8, Pub. by Routledge England). Humanities.

--True & the Evident. Kraus, Oskar, ed. (International Library of Philosophy & Scientific Method). 1971. text ed. 17.50x (ISBN 0-391-00183-3). Humanities.

Brentano, Franz Clemens. The Origin of the Knowledge of Right & Wrong. 1976. lib. bdg. 59.95 (ISBN 0-8490-2387-4). Gordon Pr.

Brentano, L. English Gilds, Their Statutes & Customs, A. D. 1389, with an Essay on Gilds & Trade-Unions. Smith, Toulmin & Smith, LucyT., eds. (EET OS Ser.: Vol. 40). Repr. of 1870 ed. 39.00 (ISBN 0-317-15526-1). Kraus Repr.

Brentano, L., ed. see Heynen, Reinhard.

Brentano, Lujo. Geschichte De Wirtschaftlichen Entwicklung Englands, 3 Vols. in 4. LC 68-56762. (Research & Source Works Ser.: No. 246). (Ger). 1969. Repr. of 1927 ed. Set. 101.00 (ISBN 0-8337-0367-6). B Franklin.

--On the History & Development of Gilds & the Origin of Trade Unions. 1969. Repr. of 1870 ed. 20.00 (ISBN 0-8337-0368-4). B Franklin.

--On the History & Development of Gilds & the Origin of Trade Unions. 59.95 (ISBN 0-8490-0766-6). Gordon Pr.

Brentano, Sr. Mary B. Nature in the Works of Fray Luis De Granada. LC 75-94164. (Catholic University. Studies in Romance Languages & Literatures: No. 15). Repr. of 1936 ed. 21.00 (ISBN 0-404-50315-2). AMS Pr.

Brentano, Robert. Early Middle Ages. LC 64-21204. 1964. pap. text ed. 16.95 (ISBN 0-02-904670-X). Free Pr.

Brentano, Robyn & Savitt, Mark. One Hundred Twelve Workshop: One Hundred & Twelve Greene Street. (Illus.). 400p. 1981. 60.00x (ISBN 0-8147-1037-9). NYU Pr.

Brentano, Ron, pref. by. Ballou-Wright Automobile Accessories Catalog, 1906. LC 74-635336. (Illus.). 80p. 1971. pap. 2.95 (ISBN 0-87595-028-0). Oreg Hist Soc.

Brentano, Ron B. Historic Vehicles in Miniature: The Genius of Ivan Collins. (Illus.). 112p. (Orig.). 1983. 11.95 (ISBN 0-87595-072-8, Western Imprints). Oreg Hist Soc.

Brentar, Joseph C. The Social & Economic Adjustment of the Croatian Displaced Persons in Cleveland Compared with That of the Earlier Croatian Immigrants. LC 77-155331. 1971. softcover 8.00 (ISBN 0-88247-099-X). Ragusan Pr.

Brentlinger, John A., ed. see Plato.

Brenton, H. & Hare, D. Pravda. (Modern Plays Ser.). 96p. (Orig.). 1985. pap. 6.95 (ISBN 0-413-58480-1, 9481). Methuen Inc.

Brenton, Howard. Bloody Poetry. (Modern Plays Ser.). 96p. 1985. pap. 6.95 (ISBN 0-413-58350-3, 9648). Methuen Inc.

--The Churchill Play. 90p. 1974. pap. 6.95 (ISBN 0-413-33390-6, NO.2994). Methuen Inc.

--Epsom Downs. (Illus.). 85p. 1977. pap. 6.95 (ISBN 0-413-38930-8, NO. 2997). Methuen Inc.

--The Genius. 56p. 1984. pap. 4.95 (ISBN 0-413-54650-0, NO. 4098). Methuen Inc.

--Hitler Dances. 1982. pap. 6.95 (ISBN 0-413-50060-8, NO. 3640). Methuen Inc.

--Magnificence: A Play. 80p. 1980. pap. 6.95 (ISBN 0-413-46750-3, NO. 2105). Methuen Inc.

--Plays for the Poor Theatre: Five Short Plays (the Saliva Milkshake, Christie in Love, Heads, Skinny Spew, Gum & Goo) 104p. 1980. pap. 7.95 (ISBN 0-413-47080-6, NO. 2115). Methuen Inc.

--Revenge. 2nd ed. 1982. 6.95 (ISBN 0-413-50010-1, NO. 3652). Methuen Inc.

--The Romans in Britain: A Play. 3rd ed. 112p. 1982. pap. 3.95 (ISBN 0-413-49930-8, NO. 3654). Methuen Inc.

--Sore Throats & Sonnets of Love & Opposition. 47p. 1979. pap. 4.95 (ISBN 0-413-46580-2, 3012). Methuen Inc.

--Thirteenth Night & A Short Sharp Shock. Incl. (New Theatrescripts Ser.). 76p. 1981. pap. 4.95 (ISBN 0-413-48500-5, O. 3500). Methuen Inc.

--Weapons of Happiness. 79p. 1976. pap. 6.95 (ISBN 0-413-36650-2, NO. 2995). Methuen Inc.

Brenton, Howard & Hare, David. Brassneck. 102p. 1974. pap. 6.95 (ISBN 0-413-31760-9, NO.2998). Methuen Inc.

Brenton, Howard, tr. see Buchner, George.

Brenton, Howard, et al. Layby. 1981. pap. 4.95 (ISBN 0-7145-0929-9). Riverrun NY.

Brenton, Maria & Jones, Catherine, eds. The Year Book of Social Policy in Britain, 1984-1985. 256p. 1985. 42.50x (ISBN 0-7102-0603-8). Routledge & Kegan.

Brenton, Myron. Emotional Health. Prevention Magazine Staff & Keough, Carol, eds. (Prevention Total Health System Ser.). (Illus.). 176p. 1985. 14.95 (ISBN 0-87857-551-0). Rodale Pr Inc.

Brenton, Myron & Prevention Magazine Editors. Aging Slowly. (The Prevention Total Health System Ser.). (Illus.). 176p. 1984. 14.95 (ISBN 0-87857-465-4, 05-129-0). Rodale Pr Inc.

Brenton, Thaddeus R. Bahia: Ensenada & It's Bay; Farce, Fiesta & Frustration in a Small Mexican City. LC 77-26758. (Illus.). 1978. Repr. of 1961 ed. lib. bdg. 16.00x (ISBN 0-313-20173-0, BRBA). Greenwood.

Brenton, Willis C. According to White Eyes. 1985. 15.95 (ISBN 0-87949-256-2). Ashley Bks.

Brenzel, Barbara M. Daughters of the State: A Social Portrait of the First Reform School for Girls in North America 1856-1905. (Joint Center for Urban Studies Ser.). (Illus.). 272p. 1985. 22.50x (ISBN 0-262-02194-3); pap. 8.95x (ISBN 0-262-52104-0). MIT Pr.

Breo, Dennis L., jt. auth. see Eliot, Robert S.

Breo, Dennis L., jt. auth. see Keane, Noel P.

Breon, Etta B. Off We Go to Mexico. (Illus.). 48p. (gr. 4 up). 1985. 7.95 (ISBN 0-89962-433-2). Todd & Honeywell.

Brereton, Austin. Henry Irving. 75p. 1981. Repr. of 1905 ed. lib. bdg. 30.00 (ISBN 0-89984-065-5). Century Bookbindery.

--Life of Henry Irving, 2 Vols. in 1. LC 74-88604. (Illus.). 1908. 25.00 (ISBN 0-405-08305-X, Blom Pubns). Ayer Co Pubs.

Brereton, Bridget. A History of Modern Trinidad Seventeen Eighty-Three to Nineteen Sixty-Two. x, 262p. (Orig.). 1982. pap. text ed. 15.00x (ISBN 0-435-98116-1). Heinemann Ed.

--Race Relations in Colonial Trinidad 1870-1900. LC 78-72081. (Illus.). 1980. 52.50 (ISBN 0-521-22428-4). Cambridge U Pr.

Brereton, Bridget & Dookeran, Winston, eds. East Indians in the Caribbean: Colonialism & the Struggle for Identity. LC 81-13656. (Orig.). 1981. lib. bdg. 35.00 (ISBN 0-527-10848-0). Kraus Intl.

Brereton, Cloudesley, tr. see Bergson, Henri.

Brereton, Geoffrey. French Comic Drama from the Sixteenth to the Eighteenth Century. 1977. 15.95x (ISBN 0-416-78220-5, NO. 2109). Methuen Inc.

--French Tragic Drama in the Sixteenth & Seventeenth Centuries. (Illus.). 320p. 1973. 12.95x (ISBN 0-416-07630-0, NO. 2107). Methuen Inc.

--Introduction to French Poets. 2nd ed. 1973. pap. 11.95x (ISBN 0-416-76630-7, NO.2106). Methuen Inc.

--Principles of Tragedy: A Rational Examination of the Tragic Concept in Life & Literature. LC 69-12459. 1968. 14.95x (ISBN 0-87024-104-4). U of Miami Pr.

Brereton, Geoffrey, tr. see Froissart.

Brereton, Georgine E. & Ferrier, Janet M., eds. Le Menagier de Paris: A Critical Edition. 1981. 95.00x (ISBN 0-19-815748-7). Oxford U Pr.

--Handbook of Reactive Chemical Hazards. CRC. 996p. 1975. 49.95 (ISBN 0-685-69893-9). CRC Pr.
Bretherick, Leslie. Handbook of Reactive Chemical Hazards. 3rd ed. 1280p. 1985. text ed. 139.95 (ISBN 0-408-01388-5). Butterworth.
Bretherton, C. H. Midas, or the United States & the Future. LC 73-13123. (Foreign Travelers in America 1810-1935 Ser.). 100p. 1974. Repr. 13.00 (ISBN 0-405-05445-9). Ayer Co Pubs.
Bretherton, Inge, ed. Symbolic Play: The Developmental Psychology of Social Cognition. LC 83-11958. 1984. 44.50 (ISBN 0-12-132680-2). Acad Pr.
Brethower, Dale M. Behavioral Analysis in Business & Industry: A Total Performance System. (Illus.). 130p. (Orig.). 1972. pap. 10.00 (ISBN 0-914474-06-5); instr's. manual avail. F Fournies.
Brethren, Hutterian, ed. see Arnold, Annemarie.
Bretnor, Helen H., tr. see Perlot, Jean N.
Bretnor, Reginald. Decisive Warfare: A Study in Military Theory. rev. ed. LC 84-315. (Stokvis Studies in Historical Chronology & Thought: No. 5). 192p. 1985. lib. bdg. 19.95x (ISBN 0-89370-320-6); pap. text ed. 9.95x (ISBN 0-89370-420-2). Borgo Pr.
--Of Force & Violence & Other Imponderables: Essays on War, Politics, & Government. LC 84-306. (Stokvis Studies in Historical Chronology & Thought: No. 6). 160p. (Orig.). 1985. lib. bdg. 14.95x (ISBN 0-89370-321-4); pap. 6.95x (ISBN 0-89370-421-0). Borgo Pr.
Bretnor, Reginald see Briarton, Grendel, pseud.
Bretnor, Reginald, ed. The Craft of Science Fiction: A Symposium on Writing Science Fiction & Science Fantasy. LC 75-23872. 288p. (YA) 1976. 12.45i (ISBN 0-06-010461-9, HarpT). Har-Row.
--The Future at War: The Spear of Mars, Vol. II. 1980. pap. 2.25 (ISBN 0-441-25971-5). Ace Bks.
--Modern Science Fiction: Its Meaning & Its Future. new ed. LC 78-71414. 1979. 10.00 (ISBN 0-911682-23-6). Advent.
Breton, Albert. Discriminatory Government Policies in Federal Countries. (Illus.). 80p. 1967. 2.00 (ISBN 0-88806-081-5). Inst C D Howe.
--The Economic Constitution of Federal States. LC 77-18526. pap. 44.00 (ISBN 0-317-26937-2, 2023597). Bks Demand UMI.
Breton, Albert & Breton, Raymond. Why Disunity? 83p. 1980. pap. text ed. 6.95x (ISBN 0-920380-70-0, Inst Res Pub Canada). Brookfield Pub Co.
Breton, Albert & Scott, Anthony. The Design of Federations. 60p. 1980. pap. text ed. 6.95x (ISBN 0-920380-43-3, Pub. by Inst Res Pub Canada). Brookfield Pub Co.
Breton, Albert & Wintrobe, Ronald. The Logic of Bureaucratic Conduct. LC 81-21722. (Illus.). 208p. 1982. 34.50 (ISBN 0-521-24589-3). Cambridge U Pr.
Breton, Andre. L' Amour Fou: Essai. (Coll. Soleil). 12.95 (ISBN 0-685-37227-8); pap. 3.95 (ISBN 0-686-66852-9). French & Eur.
--Anthologie de l'Humour Noir. 15.95 (ISBN 0-685-23924-1); pap. 3.95 (ISBN 0-686-66638-0). French & Eur.
--Arcane Seventeen. 9.95 (ISBN 0-685-37228-6); pap. 3.95 (ISBN 0-686-57668-3). French & Eur.
--Les Champs Magnetiques. 1968. 9.95 (ISBN 0-686-51933-7); pap. 3.95 (ISBN 0-686-51934-5). French & Eur.
--Clair de Terre. pap. 3.95 (ISBN 0-686-51935-3). French & Eur.
--La Cle des Champs. 15.95 (ISBN 0-685-37229-4). French & Eur.
--Entretiens avec Andre Parinaud (1913-1952) (Coll. Le Point du Jour). 9.95 (ISBN 0-685-37230-8); pap. 3.95 (ISBN 0-686-66853-7). French & Eur.
--Farouche a Quatre Feuilles. 1955. 9.95 (ISBN 0-686-50133-0). French & Eur.
--Fata Morgana. Mills, Clark, tr. (Illus.). 36p. (Fr.). 1982. pap. 3.95 (ISBN 0-941194-01-9). Black Swan Pr.
--Flagrant Delit. (Coll. Libertes). pap. 2.95 (ISBN 0-685-37231-6). French & Eur.
--L' Imaculee Conception. 1961. pap. 3.95 (ISBN 0-686-50134-9). French & Eur.
--Lexico Sucinto del Erotismo. 110p. (Span.). 1974. pap. 6.75 (ISBN 84-339-0419-1, S-50153). French & Eur.
--Magritte. (Illus.). 1964. pap. 3.50 (ISBN 0-914412-24-8). Inst for the Arts.
--Les Malformations Congenitales du Poumon. 1957. pap. 9.95 (ISBN 0-686-51936-1). French & Eur.
--Les Manifestes du Surrealisme. 16.95 (ISBN 0-685-37232-4); pap. 3.95 (ISBN 0-686-66854-5). French & Eur.
--Manifestoes of Surrealism. Seaver, Richard & Lane, Helen R., trs. from Fr. 1972. pap. 8.95 (ISBN 0-472-06182-8, 182, AA). U of Mich Pr.
--Martinique, Charmeuse des Serpents. 1972. 9.95 (ISBN 0-686-51937-X). French & Eur.
--Nadja. Howard, Richard, tr. (Orig.). 1960. pap. 5.95 (ISBN 0-394-17393-7, E580, Ever). Grove.
--Nadja: Roman. (Coll. Soleil). 15.95 (ISBN 0-685-23916-0); pap. 3.95 (ISBN 0-686-66637-2). French & Eur.
--Ode a Charles Fourier. Gaulmier, ed. 12.95 (ISBN 0-685-37233-2). French & Eur.
--Les Pas Perdus: Essai. (Coll. Soleil). 11.50 (ISBN 0-685-37234-0); pap. 3.95 (ISBN 0-686-66855-3). French & Eur.
--Perspectives Cavaliere. Bonnet, ed. 14.50 (ISBN 0-685-37235-9). French & Eur.
--Poemes. (Coll. Soleil). 12.50 (ISBN 0-685-37236-7). French & Eur.
--Poems of Andre Breton: A Bilingual Anthology. Cauvin, Jean-Pierre & Caws, Mary A., trs. 298p. 1982. text ed. 27.50x (ISBN 0-292-76476-6); pap. 12.95 (ISBN 0-292-76477-4). U of Tex Pr.
--Point du Jour. (Coll. Soleil). 16.50 (ISBN 0-685-37237-5); pap. 3.95 (ISBN 0-686-66856-1). French & Eur.
--Position Politique Du Surrealisme. (La Bibliotheque Volante). pap. 9.95 (ISBN 0-685-37238-3). French & Eur.
--Signe Ascendant. Bd. with Fata Morgana; Les Etats-generaux; Des epingles tremblantes; Xenophile; Ode a Charles Fourier; Constellation; Le la. (Coll. Poesie). pap. 4.50 (ISBN 0-685-37239-1). French & Eur.
--Le Surrealisme au Service de la Revolution. 59.95 (ISBN 0-686-51938-8). French & Eur.
--L' Un Dans L'autre. (Coll. Desordee). 8.50 (ISBN 0-685-37240-5). French & Eur.
--Les Vases Communicants: Essai. pap. 3.95 (ISBN 0-685-37241-3). French & Eur.
--What Is Surrealism. LC 74-6446. (Studies in Comparative Literature, No. 35). 1973. Repr. of 1936 ed. lib. bdg. 49.95x (ISBN 0-8383-1709-X). Haskell.
--What Is Surrealism? Selected Writings. Rosemont, Franklin, ed. LC 71-186691. (Illus.). 1978. lib. bdg. 35.00x (ISBN 0-913460-59-1); pap. 14.95 (ISBN 0-913460-60-5). Monad Pr.
Breton, Andre see Apollinaire, Guillaume & Guillaume, Paul.
Breton, Andre, jt. auth. see Eluard, Paul.
Breton, Andre, ed. Surrealisme au Service de la Revolution, Nos. 1-6. LC 68-28661. (Contemporary Art Ser). (Illus., Fr.). 1968. Repr. of 1930 ed. 66.00 (ISBN 0-405-00707-8). Ayer Co Pubs.
Breton, Andre, et al. The Surrealists Look at Art. Hulten, Pontus, ed. (Illus.). 96p. (Orig.). 1985. 15.00 (ISBN 0-932499-08-2); pap. 8.00 (ISBN 0-932499-09-0). Lapis Pr.
Breton, Anna L. Le see Le Breton, Anna L.
Breton, Denise. This Lie Called Evil. LC 82-80906. 130p. (Orig.). 1983. pap. 8.50 (ISBN 0-942958-02-0). Kappeler Inst Pub.
Breton, Nicholas. The Good & the Badde. LC 77-6859. (English Experience Ser.: No. 853). 1977. Repr. of 1616 ed. lib. bdg. 6.00 (ISBN 90-221-0853-8). Walter J Johnson.
--Mad World, My Masters & Other Prose Works, 2 vols. Kentish-Wright, Ursula, ed. LC 30-11771. 1968. Repr. of 1929 ed. Set. 49.00x (ISBN 0-403-00108-0). Scholarly.
--Pasquils Mad-Cap & Mad-Cappes Message. LC 79-25850. (English Experience Ser.: No. 200). 88p. 1969. Repr. of 1600 ed. 13.00 (ISBN 90-221-0200-9). Walter J Johnson.
--Poems by Nicholas Breton. LC 72-161960. 229p. 1952. Repr. 39.00x (ISBN 0-403-01335-6). Scholarly.
--Two Pamphlets. Morice, E. G., ed. 1936. lib. bdg. 15.00 (ISBN 0-8414-6097-3). Folcroft.
--Works in Verse & Prose, 2 Vols. 1967. Repr. of 1879 ed. Set. 67.75x (ISBN 3-4870-2378-4). Adlers Foreign Bks.
--Works in Verse & Prose of Nicholas Breton, 2 Vols. Grosart, Alexander B., ed. LC 75-181917. (BCL Ser. II). Repr. of 1879 ed. Set. 57.50 (ISBN 0-404-50294-6). Vol. 1 (ISBN 0-404-50383-7). Vol. 2 (ISBN 0-404-50384-5). AMS Pr.
Breton, Preston P. Le see Le Breton, Preston P.
Breton, Raymond. The Canadian Condition: A Guide to Research in Public Policy. 65p. 1977. pap. text ed. 2.95x (ISBN 0-920380-00-X, Pub. by Inst Res Pub Canada). Brookfield Pub Co.
Breton, Raymond & Akian, Gail G. Urban Institutions & People of Indian Ancestry. 52p. 1978. pap. text ed. 3.00x (ISBN 0-920380-14-X, Pub. by Inst Res Pub Canada). Brookfield Pub Co.
Breton, Raymond, jt. auth. see Breton, Albert.
Breton, Raymond, et al. Cultural Boundaries & the Cohesion of Canada. (Illus.). 422p. 1980. pap. text ed. 18.95x (ISBN 0-920380-37-9, Pub. by Inst Res Pub Canada). Brookfield Pub Co.
Breton, Thierry & Beneich, Denis. Softwar: A Novel. Howson, Mark, tr. 256p. 1985. 15.95 (ISBN 0-03-004998-9). HR&W.
Breton, Valentine. Life & Prayer. 189p. 1960. 5.95 (ISBN 0-933932-21-9). Scepter Pubs.
Breton, William H. Excursions in New South Wales, Western Australia & Van Diemen's Land During the Years 1830, 1831, 1832 & 1833. 2nd rev. ed. LC 4-24180. Repr. of 1834 ed. lib. bdg. 34.00 (ISBN 0-384-05680-6). Johnson Repr.
Bretscher, J., jt. auth. see Schams, H.
Bretscher, Paul G. Cain, Come Home! LC 76-1810. (Illus.). 144p. 1976. pap. text ed. 4.25 (ISBN 0-915644-05-3). Clayton Pub Hse.
Bretschi, Jurgen. Automated Inspection Systems for Industry: Scope for Intelligent Measuring. (Illus.). 190p. (Eng.). 1982. Repr. of 1979 ed. text ed. 52.00x softbound (ISBN 0-903608-20-0, IFSPUBS). Scholium Intl.
Bretschneider, Ann, jt. auth. see Burns, Willard A.
Bretschneider, Charles L. Topics in Ocean Engineering, 3 vols. Incl. Vol. 1. 428p. 1969 (ISBN 0-87201-598-X); Vol. 2. (Illus.). 229p. 1970 (ISBN 0-87201-599-8); Vol. 3. 328p. 1976 (ISBN 0-87201-600-5). LC 78-87230. 29.50x ea. Gulf Pub.
Bretschneider, Diana. Bible Puzzle Time, Friends of God. 16p. (gr. 2-7). 1983. pap. 0.60 (ISBN 0-87239-655-X, 2303). Standard Pub.
Brett, Arlene, jt. auth. see Provenzo, Eugene F., Jr.
Brett, Barbara. Between Two Eternities. 1978. pap. 1.95 (ISBN 0-380-39925-3, 39925). Avon.
--Love after Hours. 352p. 1981. pap. 2.50 (ISBN 0-380-76257-9, 76257). Avon.
Brett, Barbara, jt. auth. see Brett, Hy.
Brett, Bernard. Ghosts. LC 82-13373. (Chiller Ser.). (Illus.). 128p. (gr. 8-12). 1983. PLB 9.29 (ISBN 0-671-46746-8). Messner.
--Monsters. Barish, Wendy, ed. (Chiller Ser.). (Illus.). 128p. (gr. 3-7). 1983. pap. 3.95 (ISBN 0-671-46160-5). Wanderer Bks.
--Monsters. LC 82-13452. (Chiller Ser.: Vol. 127). (Illus.). 128p. (gr. 4-8). 1983. PLB 9.29 (ISBN 0-671-46745-X); pap. 3.95 (ISBN 0-671-46160-5). Messner.
Brett, Bernard see Allen, W. S.
Brett, Bernard, jt. auth. see Arneson, D. J.
Brett, Bill. The Stolen Steers: A Tale of the Big Thicket. LC 76-51651. (Illus.). 116p. 1977. 11.95 (ISBN 0-89096-026-7). Tex A&M Univ Pr.
--There Ain't No Such Animal & Other East Texas Tales. LC 78-21777. (Illus.). 128p. 1979. 11.95 (ISBN 0-89096-068-2). Tex A&M Univ Pr.
--This Here's a Good'un. LC 83-45094. (Illus.). 112p. 1983. 11.95 (ISBN 0-89096-162-X). Tex A&M Univ Pr.
Brett, C. T. & Hillman, J. R., eds. Biochemistry of Plant Cell Walls. (Society for Experimental Biology Seminar Ser.: Vol. 28). 250p. 1985. 34.50 (ISBN 0-521-30487-3). Cambridge U Pr.
Brett, David. High Level: The Alps From End to End. (Illus.). 206p. 1983. 23.50 (ISBN 0-575-03202-2, Pub by Gollancz England). David & Charles.
Brett, E. International Money & Capitalist Crisis: The Anatomy of Global Disintegration. LC 82-51289. 271p. 1983. 26.50x (ISBN 0-86531-575-2). Westview.
Brett, E. A. Colonialism & Underdevelopment in East Africa. LC 72-97704. 330p. 1973. text ed. 18.95 (ISBN 0-88357-000-9); pap. 7.95 (ISBN 0-88357-001-7). Nok Pubs.
--Colonialism & Underdevelopment In East Africa: The Politics of Economic Change, 1919-1939. 336p. 1973. pap. text ed. 17.00x (ISBN 0-435-94510-6). Heinemann Ed.
--The World Economy Since the War: The Politics of Uneven Development. 1985. 29.95 (ISBN 0-03-005724-8); pap. 14.95 (ISBN 0-03-005727-2). Praeger.
Brett, George. Psychology, Ancient & Modern. LC 63-10293. (Our Debt to Greece & Rome Ser). Repr. of 1930 ed. 18.50 (ISBN 0-8154-0031-4). Cooper Sq.
Brett, Gerard. Dinner Is Served: A Study in Manners. (Illus.). 144p. 1968. 17.50 (ISBN 0-208-00704-0, Archon). Shoe String.
--English Furniture & Its Setting from the Later Sixteenth to the Early Century. pap. 31.80 (ISBN 0-317-28480-0, 2019175). Bks Demand UMI.
Brett, Hugh, jt. ed. see Perry, Lawrence.
Brett, Hy & Brett, Barbara. Promises to Keep. LC 81-47247. 224p. 1981. 12.45i (ISBN 0-06-014881-0, HarpT). Har-Row.
Brett, James. The Kitchen. (Illus.). 1977. 25.00 (ISBN 0-8230-7320-3, Whitney Lib). Watson-Guptill.
--The Kitchen: One Hundred Solutions to Design Problems. 2nd ed. (Illus.). 208p. 1983. 32.50 (ISBN 0-8230-7327-0, Whitney Lib). Watson-Guptill.
--Looking into Houses. (Illus.). 192p. (Orig.). 1976. (Whitney); pap. 11.95 (ISBN 0-8230-7359-9). Watson-Guptill.
Brett, Jan. Annie & the Wild Animals. LC 84-19818. (Illus.). 32p. (gr. k-3). 1985. 12.95 (ISBN 0-395-37800-1). HM.
--Fritz & the Beautiful Horses. (Illus.). 32p. (gr. k-3). 1981. 10.95 (ISBN 0-395-30850-X). HM.
Brett, Jan, illus. Favorite Fairy Tales to Color. (Color-&-Keep Bks.). (Illus.). 64p. (ps-3). 1985. pap. 2.95 (ISBN 0-394-87276-2, BYR). Random.
--The Night Before Christmas & Other Christmas Poems to Color. (Color-&-Keep Bks.). (Illus.). 64p. (ps-3). 1985. pap. 2.95 (ISBN 0-394-87461-7, BYR). Random.
Brett, Jennifer, ed. see Dilendik, John R.
Brett, Lawrence. Redeemed Creation: The Sacramentals Today. (Message of the Sacraments Ser.: Vol. 8). 10.95 (ISBN 0-89453-398-3); pap. 6.95 (ISBN 0-89453-234-0). M Glazier.
Brett, Lionel. Our Selves Unknown: An Autobiography. (Illus.). 194p. 1985. 24.95 (ISBN 0-575-03552-8, Pub. by Gollancz England). David & Charles.
Brett, Martin, jt. auth. see Whitlock, Dorothy.
Brett, Michael & Forman, Werner. The Moors: Islam in the West. (The Echoes of the Ancient World Ser.). (Illus.). 128p. 1984. 20.00 (ISBN 0-85613-279-9, Pub. by Salem Hse Ltd). Merrimack Pub Cir.
Brett, Michael, ed. Northern Africa: Islam & Modernization. 156p. 1973. 28.50x (ISBN 0-7146-2972-3, F Cass Co). Biblio Dist.
Brett, Oliver. A Defense of Liberty. 225p. 1984. lib. bdg. 28.95 (ISBN 0-930439-03-1); pap. 16.95 (ISBN 0-930439-04-X). Cobden Pr.
Brett, Patricia, jt. auth. see Brett, Robert.
Brett, Philip, ed. Benjamin Britten: Peter Grimes. LC 82-14627. (Cambridge Opera Handbooks). (Illus.). 180p. 1983. 32.50 (ISBN 0-521-22916-2); pap. 9.95 (ISBN 0-521-29716-8). Cambridge U Pr.
Brett, R. I. & Grant, G. F., eds. Andrew Marvell: Essays on the Tercentenary of His Death. 1979. 19.95x (ISBN 0-19-713435-1). Oxford U Pr.
Brett, R. L., ed. Barclay Fox's Journal. (Illus.). 426p. 1979. 23.50x (ISBN 0-8476-6187-3). Rowman.
--Poems of Faith & Doubt: The Victorian Age. LC 70-116469. (English Library). (Orig.). 1970. pap. text ed. 4.95x (ISBN 0-87249-153-6). U of SC Pr.
--Writers & Their Background: Samuel Taylor Coleridge. LC 72-85533. (Writers & Their Background Ser.). xvii, 296p. 1972. 20.00x (ISBN 0-8214-0109-2, 82-81123); pap. 10.00x (ISBN 0-8214-0110-6, 82-81131). Ohio U Pr.
Brett, R. L. & Jones, A. R., eds. Lyrical Ballads: Wordsworth & Coleridge, 1798-1805. 2nd ed. 1968. pap. 12.95x (ISBN 0-416-29720-X, NO. 2112). Methuen Inc.
Brett, Richard M. The Country Journal Woodlot Primer: The Right Way to Manage Your Woodland. (Illus.). 144p. (Orig.). 1983. pap. 9.95 (ISBN 0-918678-04-8). Historical Times.
Brett, Robert & Brett, Patricia. Hispanoamerica One: Al Sur Del Ecuador. LC 78-15378. 1978. pap. 5.95 (ISBN 0-88436-496-8, 70252). EMC.
Brett, Simon. Bad Form: Etiquette of Bad Taste. (Illus.). 160p. 1984. 12.95 (ISBN 0-241-11324-5, Pub. by Hamish Hamilton England). David & Charles.
--Cast in Order of Disappearance. 1986. pap. 3.50 (ISBN 0-440-11123-4). Dell.
--Dead Giveaway. (Charles Paris Mystery Ser.). 160p. 1986. 13.95 (ISBN 0-317-19459-3, ScribT). Scribner.
--The Faber Book of Useful Verse. 254p. 1982. pap. 7.95 (ISBN 0-571-11782-1). Faber & Faber.
--Murder in the Title. (Murder Ink Ser.: No. 73). 192p. 1984. pap. 2.95 (ISBN 0-440-16016-2). Dell.
--Murder in the Title: A Charles Paris Mystery. 192p. 1983. 11.95 (ISBN 0-684-17898-2, ScribT). Scribner.
--Murder Unprompted. (Nightingale Ser.). 290p. 1983. pap. 9.95 (ISBN 0-8161-3540-1, Large Print Bks). G K Hall.
--Murder Unprompted. (Murder Ink Ser.: No. 69). 1984. pap. 2.95 (ISBN 0-440-16145-2). Dell.
--Murder Unprompted: A Charles Paris Mystery. 160p. 1982. 10.95 (ISBN 0-684-17659-9, ScribT). Scribner.
--Not Dead, Only Resting. (Nightingale-Lythway Ser.). 1985. pap. 10.95 (ISBN 0-8161-3831-1, Large Print Bks). G K Hall.
--Not Dead, Only Resting. 1986. pap. 3.50 (ISBN 0-440-16442-7). Dell.
--Not Dead, Only Resting: A Charles Paris Mystery. 176p. 1984. 11.95 (ISBN 0-684-18193-2, ScribT). Scribner.
--A Shock to the System. 256p. 1985. 13.95 (ISBN 0-684-18351-X, ScribT). Scribner.
--Situation Tragedy. 192p. 1981. 9.95 (ISBN 0-684-17268-2, ScribT). Scribner.
--Situation Tragedy. 1983. pap. 2.50 (ISBN 0-440-18792-3). Dell.
--Tickled to Death. 1985. 13.95 (ISBN 0-684-18486-9). Scribner.
--Tickled to Death & Other Stories of Crime & Suspense. 232p. 1985. 13.95 (ISBN 0-317-31593-5, ScribT). Scribner.
Brett, Simon, ed. The Faber Book of Parodies. LC 83-25296. 256p. 1984. 21.95 (ISBN 0-571-13125-5); pap. 9.95 (ISBN 0-571-13254-5). Faber & Faber.
--Take a Spare Truss: Tips for 19th Century Travellers. (Illus.). 128p. 1984. 14.95 (ISBN 0-241-11068-8, Pub. by Hamish Hamilton England). David & Charles.
Brett, Stephen. Some Die Hard. (Orig.). 1979. pap. 1.75 (ISBN 0-532-17221-3). Woodhill.
--The Vampire Chase. (Orig.). 1979. pap. 1.75 (ISBN 0-532-17217-5). Woodhill.
Brett, Vanessa. Phaidon Guide to Pewter. (Illus.). 256p. 1983. 12.95 (ISBN 0-13-662049-3); pap. 6.95 (ISBN 0-13-662031-0). P-H.
--The Sotheby's Directory of Silver 1600-1940. LC 85-50360. (Illus.). 432p. 1985. 39.95 (ISBN 0-85667-193-2, Pub. by P Wilson Pubs). Sotheby Pubns.
Brett, Virginia, tr. see Steffen, Albert.
Brett, William. Biological Explorations I: Laboratory Manual. 1978. pap. text ed. 10.95 (ISBN 0-8403-1925-8). Kendall-Hunt.
Brett, William & Sentlowitz, Michael. Elementary Algebra by Example. LC 76-11979. (Illus.). 1977. pap. text ed. 24.95 (ISBN 0-395-24425-0); instr's. manual 1.90. HM.
Brett, William F., et al. An Introduction to the History of Mathematics, Number Theory, & Operations Research. 1974. pap. text ed. 16.50x (ISBN 0-8422-0379-6). Irvington.
--Contemporary College Mathematics. 320p. 1975. text ed. 22.95 (ISBN 0-8299-0038-1). West Pub.

Brett, William H. Legends & Myths of the Aboriginal Indians of British Guiana. LC 78-67691. (The Folktale). Repr. of 1880 ed. 22.00 (ISBN 0-404-16059-X). AMS Pr.

Brett, William J. Biological Explorations II: Laboratory Manual. 1979. 12.95 (ISBN 0-8403-1938-X, 40193801). Kendall-Hunt.

Brettel, Caroline B. We Have Already Cried Many Tears: The Stories of Three Portuguese Migrant Women. (Illus.). 170p. 1982. pap. 9.95 (ISBN 0-87073-233-1). Schenkman Bks Inc.

Brettell, Caroline, jt. auth. see Brettell, Richard R.

Brettell, Caroline B., jt. ed. see Simon, Rita J.

Brettell, Richard & Flukinger, Roy. Paper & Light: The Calotype in France & Great Britain, 1839-1870. (Illus.). 192p. 1983. 30.00 (ISBN 0-86559-053-2); pap. 18.95 (ISBN 0-686-44391-8). Art Inst Chi.

Brettell, Richard & Lloyd, Christopher, eds. Catalogue of Drawings by Camille Pissarro in the Ashmolean Museum, Oxford. (Illus.). 1980. 115.00x (ISBN 0-19-817357-1). Oxford U Pr.

Brettell, Richard, et al. A Day in the Country: Impressionism & the French Landscape. (Illus.). 376p. 1984. (Co-Pub. by Abrams); pap. 19.95 (ISBN 0-87587-118-6). LA Co Art Mus.

Brettell, Richard R. Historic Denver: The Architects & the Architecture, 1858-1893. 1979. pap. 14.95 (ISBN 0-914248-00-6). Hist Denver.

Brettell, Richard R. & Brettell, Caroline. Painters & Peasants in the Nineteenth Century. LC 83-9699. (Illus.). 160p. 1983. 35.00 (ISBN 0-8478-0502-6). Rizzoli Intl.

Brettell, Richard R. & McCullagh, Suzanne F. Degas: In the Art Institute of Chicago. (Illus.). 200p. 1984. 37.50 (ISBN 0-8109-0804-2). Abrams.

Brettell, Richard R., et al. A Day in the Country: Impressionism & the French Landscape. (Illus.). 376p. 1984. 40.00 (ISBN 0-8109-0827-1). Abrams.

Bretteville, Sheila L. de see Nodal, Al & De Bretteville, Sheila L.

Brett-James, Anthony. The Triple Stream: Four Centuries of English, French & German Literature 1531-1930. LC 74-13161. 1973. lib. bdg. 25.00 (ISBN 0-8414-5306-3). Folcroft.

Brett-James, Anthony, ed. see Hewson.

Brett-James, Antony. The Triple Stream. 1978. Repr. of 1954 ed. lib. bdg. 27.50 (ISBN 0-8495-0351-5). Arden Lib.

Brettle, R. Infection & Communicable Diseases. 288p. 1984. pap. 12.00 (ISBN 0-433-04040-8, 991430085, Pub. by Heinemann Medical). Heyden.

Bretton, Barbara. Love Changes. (American Romance Ser.). 192p. 1983. pap. 2.25 (ISBN 0-373-16003-8). Harlequin Bks.

Bretton, Dalton G. The Three Great Choices: Money, Women & God: A Guide to the Perplexed. (Illus.). 98p. 1984. 49.75 (ISBN 0-89266-458-4); pap. 19.75 (ISBN 0-89266-459-2). Am Classical Coll Pr.

Bretton, Henry L. The Power of Money. LC 79-23484. 1980. 43.50x (ISBN 0-87395-425-4); pap. 17.95x (ISBN 0-87395-426-2). State U NY Pr.

--Stresemann & the Revision of Versailles. 1953. 17.50x (ISBN 0-8047-0444-9). Stanford U Pr.

Brettschneider, Bertram D. Philosophy of Samuel Alexander: Idealism in Space, Time & Deity. 1964. text ed. 10.50x (ISBN 0-391-00440-9). Humanities.

Brettschneider, Gunter & Lehmann, Christian, eds. Wege zur Universalienforschung: Sprachwissenschaftliche Beitraege zum 60, Geburtstag von Hansjakob Seiler. (Tuebinger Beitraege zur Linguistik Ser.: No. 145). 598p. (Ger.). 1980. 74.00 (ISBN 3-87808-145-6). Benjamins North Am.

Brett-Smith. Peacock's Four Ages of Poetry. LC 77-27644. 1921. 25.00 (ISBN 0-8414-0697-9). Folcroft.

Brett-Smith, H. B., ed. see Peacock, Thomas L.

Brett-Smith, H. F. Peacock's Four Ages of Poetry: Shelley's Defence of Poetry. (Illus.). 112p. 1981. Repr. of 1921 ed. lib. bdg. 30.00 (ISBN 0-8495-0474-0). Arden Lib.

--Peacock's Four Ages of Poetry-Shelley's Defence of Poetry: Browning's Essay on Shelley. 1973. Repr. of 1937 ed. 20.00 (ISBN 0-8274-1461-7). R West.

Brett-Smith, H. F., ed. see Etherege, George.

Bretz, Jeff & Craig, John C. One Hundred & One Ready-to-Run Programs & Subroutines for the IBM PCjr. (Illus.). 320p. (Orig.). 1984. 18.95 (ISBN 0-8306-0940-7); pap. 12.95 (ISBN 0-8306-1940-2, 1940). TAB Bks.

--One Hundred Ready-to-Run Programs & Subroutines for the IBM PC. (Illus.). 320p. (Orig.). 1983. 22.95 (ISBN 0-8306-0540-1); pap. 16.50 (ISBN 0-8306-1540-7, 1540). TAB Bks.

Bretz, Jeff, jt. auth. see Craig, John C.

Bretz, Mary L. Concha Espina. (World Authors Ser.). 1980. lib. bdg. 16.95 (ISBN 0-8057-6401-1, Twayne). G K Hall.

Bretz, Mary L. & Dvorak, Patrisha. Pasajes: Gramatica. 1983. 352 pp. 17.00, (ISBN 0-394-32875-2, RanC); activities manual, 192 pp. 8.95 (ISBN 0-394-32876-0); cultural reader, 256 pp. 9.95 (ISBN 0-394-32877-9); literary reader 9.95 (ISBN 0-394-32878-7); wkbk. lab. manual, 256 pp. 9.00 (ISBN 0-394-33114-1); tape program 100.00 (ISBN 0-394-33113-3). Random.

Bretz, Rudy. Handbook for Producing Educational & Public-Access Programs for Cable Television. LC 75-44365. 160p. 1976. pap. 24.95 (ISBN 0-87778-089-7). Educ Tech Pubns.

--Media for Interactive Communication. 264p. 1983. 25.00 (ISBN 0-8039-1986-7). Sage.

--Taxonomy of Communication Media. LC 72-125874. (Illus.). 192p. 1971. 24.95 (ISBN 0-87778-012-9). Educ Tech Pubns.

Breucker, H. Seasonal Spermatogenesis in the Mute Swan (Cygnus Olor) (Advances in Anatomy, Embryology, & Cell Biology Ser.: Vol. 72). (Illus.). 104p. 1982. pap. 27.00 (ISBN 0-387-11326-6). Springer-Verlag.

Breuel, A., ed. How to Dispose of Oil & Hazardous Chemical Spill Debris. LC 81-14235. (Pollution Technical Review: No. 87). (Illus.). 420p. 1982. 48.00 (ISBN 0-8155-0876-X). Noyes.

--Oil Spill Cleanup & Protection Techniques for Shorelines & Marshlands. LC 81-2461. (Pollution Technology Review: No. 78). (Illus.). 404p. 1981. 42.00 (ISBN 0-8155-0848-4). Noyes.

Breuer. Crawford Co. & Cuba, Mo. 10.00 (ISBN 0-911208-23-2). Ramfre.

Breuer, Gail. Pregnant Vegetarian. 1985. 7.95 (ISBN 0-14-008150-X). Penguin.

Breuer, Georg. Air in Danger: Ecological Perspectives of the Atmosphere. Fabian, P., tr. from Ger. LC 79-18820. (Illus.). 180p. 1980. 32.50 (ISBN 0-521-22417-9); pap. 11.95 (ISBN 0-521-29483-5). Cambridge U Pr.

--Sociobiology & the Human Dimension. LC 82-1293. 235p. 1983. 39.50 (ISBN 0-521-24544-3); pap. 16.95 (ISBN 0-521-28778-2). Cambridge U Pr.

--Weather Modification, Prospect & Problems. Morth, H. T., tr. from Ger. LC 79-73236. (Illus.). 1980. 34.50 (ISBN 0-521-22453-5); pap. 12.95 (ISBN 0-521-29577-7). Cambridge U Pr.

Breuer, H., jt. ed. see Von Kleist, Sabine.

Breuer, Hans-Peter, ed. The Note-Books of Samuel Butler, 1874-1883, Vol. I. (The Complete Note-Books of Samuel Butler Ser.). 402p. 1984. lib. bdg. 24.50 (ISBN 0-8191-4193-3). U Pr of Amer.

Breuer, Hans-Peter & Howard, Daniel F., eds. Erewhon; Or, Over the Range, by Samuel Butler. 2nd ed. LC 77-92568. 280p. 1981. Repr. of 1872 ed. 29.50 (ISBN 0-87413-142-1). U Delaware Pr.

Breuer, Harry, jt. auth. see Hassibi, Mahin.

Breuer, Isaac. Concepts of Judaism. Levinger, Jacob S., tr. 1974. 10.00 (ISBN 0-87306-058-X). Feldheim.

Breuer, Jacob. Fundamentals of Judaism. 1969. 8.95 (ISBN 0-87306-041-5); pap. 4.95 (ISBN 0-87306-208-6). Feldheim.

Breuer, Jacob, ed. see Hirsch, Samson R.

Breuer, Jacob, tr. see Breuer, Salomon.

Breuer, Joseph. The Freud's Theory of Hysteria in Both the Male & the Female. (Illus.). 131p. 1982. 63.55 (ISBN 0-89920-037-0). Am Inst Psych.

Breuer, Joseph M. A Handbook of Assistive Devices for the Handicapped Elderly: New Help for Independent Living. LC 81-20270. (Physical & Occupational Therapy in Geriatrics: Vol. 1, No. 2). (Illus.). 77p. 1982. text ed. 22.95 (ISBN 0-86656-152-8, B152). Haworth Pr.

Breuer, K. German-English, English-German Technical Pocket Dictionary. 6th. ed. (Ger. & Eng.). 322p. pap. 22.50 (ISBN 0-685-25495-X). Heinman.

Breuer, Lee. Animations: A Trilogy for Mabou Mines. Marranca, Bonnie & Dasgupta, Gautam, eds. LC 79-84185. 1979. 16.95 (ISBN 0-933826-01-X); signed ltd. ed. 25.00 (ISBN 0-933826-01-X); pap. 8.95 (ISBN 0-933826-03-6). Performing Arts.

Breuer, Lee, et al. New Plays U. S. A, No. 1. Leverett, James, ed. 396p. (Orig.). 1982. 17.95 (ISBN 0-930452-23-2). Theatre Comm.

Breuer, M., ed. Cosmetic Science. Vol. 1, 1978. 61.50 (ISBN 0-12-133001-X); Vol. 2, 1981. 56.00 (ISBN 0-12-133002-8). Acad Pr.

Breuer, M. & Hartenstein, R., eds. Computer Hardware Description Languages & Their Applications. 350p. 1982. 36.25 (ISBN 0-444-86279-X, North-Holland). Elsevier.

Breuer, Melvin A. & Friedman, Arthur D. Diagnosis & Reliable Design of Digital Systems. LC 76-19081. 308p. 1976. 33.95 (ISBN 0-914894-57-9). Computer Sci.

Breuer, Melvin A., ed. Digital System Design Automation: Languages, Simulation & Data Base. LC 75-11751. (Digital System Design Ser.). (Illus.). 417p. 1975. 37.95 (ISBN 0-914894-53-6). Computer Sci.

Breuer, Michael, photos by. San Juan Islands. (Illus.). 1985. 16.95 (ISBN 0-318-12038-0). Skyline Press.

Breuer, Michael & Jensen, Peter, photos by. Coast of Oregon. (Illus.). 1985. 16.95 (ISBN 0-318-12037-2). Skyline Press.

Breuer, Miklos M., ed. Milton Harris: Chemist, Innovator, & Entrepreneur. LC 82-13926. 170p. 1982. pap. text ed. 18.95x (ISBN 0-8412-0740-2). Am Chemical.

Breuer, N., jt. auth. see Liebfried, G.

Breuer, R. A. Gravitational Perturbation Theory & Synchrotron Radiation. (Lecture Notes in Physics: Vol. 44). 210p. 1975. pap. 14.00 (ISBN 0-387-07530-5). Springer-Verlag.

Breuer, Reinhard. Contact with the Stars: The Search for Extraterrestrial Life. LC 81-9908. (Illus.). 292p. 1982. text ed. 31.95 (ISBN 0-7167-1355-1). W H Freeman.

Breuer, Rosemarie, jt. auth. see Steffny, Manfred.

Breuer, Salomon. Chochmah U'Mussar, Vol. 2. Breuer, Jacob, tr. 1976. 6.00 (ISBN 0-87306-035-0). Feldheim.

--Chochmo U'Mussar, 3 vols. 1972. Set. 24.00 (ISBN 0-87306-205-1). Feldheim.

--Chochmo U'Mussar: Bereshith-Shemoth, Vol.1. Breuer, Jacob, tr. 1972. 8.50 (ISBN 0-87306-034-2). Feldheim.

--Chochmo U'Mussar, Vol. 3: Bamidbar-Devarim. Breuer, Jacob, tr. from Ger. Orig. Title: Belehre und Mahnung. 1977. 9.75 (ISBN 0-87306-036-9). Feldheim.

--The Torah-im-Derekh-Eretz of Samson Raphael Hirsch. 2.50 (ISBN 0-87306-047-4). Feldheim.

Breuer, William B. Agony at Anzio. 288p. 1984. write for info. (ISBN 0-931743-25-7). Zeus Pubs.

--Death of Nazi Army: The Falaise Pocket. LC 84-40736. 272p. 1985. 19.95 (ISBN 0-8128-3024-5). Stein & Day.

--Drop Zone Sicily. 288p. 1985. pap. 3.50 (ISBN 0-515-08395-X). Jove Pubns.

--Drop Zone Sicily: Allied Airborne Strike, July 1943. (Illus.). 256p. 1984. 15.95 (ISBN 0-89141-196-8). Presidio Pr.

--Hitler's Fortress Cherbourg: The Conquest of a Bastion. LC 83-40364. (Illus.). 256p. 1984. 19.95 (ISBN 0-8128-2952-2). Stein & Day.

--Operation Dragoon: The Allied Invasion of the South of France. LC 85-45006. (Illus.). 272p. 1986. 18.95 (ISBN 0-8128-3067-9). Stein & Day.

--Storming Hitler's Rhine: The Allied Assault, February-March 1945. (Illus.). 336p. 1985. 18.95 (ISBN 0-312-76250-X). St Martin.

Breugger, Walter. Diccionario de Filosofia. 9th ed. 684p. (Span.). 1978. 29.95 (ISBN 84-254-0722-2, S-12715, French & Eur); pap. 23.95 (ISBN 84-254-0146-1, S-50197). French & Eur.

Breuil, Alice Du see Du Breuil, Alice.

Breuil, Henri. Beyond the Bounds of History: Scenes from the Old Stone Age. Boyle, Mary E., tr. LC 76-44694. (Illus.). Repr. of 1949 ed. 29.50 (ISBN 0-404-15934-6). AMS Pr.

--Four Hundred Centuries of Cave Art. Boyle, Mary E., tr. from Fr. LC 79-83858. (Illus.). 1979. Repr. of 1952 ed. lib. bdg. 90.00 (ISBN 0-87817-247-5). Hacker.

Breuil, Henri & Burkitt, M. C. Rock Paintings of Southern Andalusia: A Description of a Neolithic & Copper Age Art Group. LC 76-44695. Repr. of 1929 ed. 30.00 (ISBN 0-404-15935-4). AMS Pr.

Breuil, Henri & Lantier, Raymond. The Men of the Old Stone Age: Palaeolithic & Mesolithic. Rafter, B. B., tr. LC 79-16777. (Illus.). 1980. Repr. of 1965 ed. lib. bdg. 32.50x (ISBN 0-313-21289-9, BRMO). Greenwood.

Breuilly, John. Nationalism & the State. 366p. 1982. 25.00x (ISBN 0-312-56005-2). St Martin.

--Nationalism & the State. x, 412p. 1985. pap. 13.95 (ISBN 0-226-07412-9). U of Chicago Pr.

Breukelman, John & Smith, Hobart M. Selected Records of Reptiles & Amphibians from Kansas. (Museum Ser.: Vol. 1, No. 5). 12p. 1946. 1.25 (ISBN 0-317-04837-6). U of KS Mus Nat Hist.

Breul, Frank R. & Diner, Steven J., eds. Compassion & Responsibility: Readings in the History of Social Welfare Policy in the United States. LC 79-56040. 1980. pap. text ed. 11.95x (ISBN 0-226-07413-7). U of Chicago Pr.

Breul, Karl, ed. see Cambridge Songs.

Breunig, Charles. Age of Revolution & Reaction, 1789-1850. 2nd ed. (Illus.). 1977. 12.95 (ISBN 0-393-05612-0); pap. 7.95x (ISBN 0-393-09143-0). Norton.

Breunig, Charles see Gilbert, Felix.

Breunig, Jerome. Have You Had Your Rice Today? LC 64-4839. pap. 48.00 (ISBN 0-317-08503-4, 2001372). Bks Demand UMI.

Breunig, L. C., et al. Forme et Fond. 1964. text ed. 10.95 (ISBN 0-02-314210-3). Macmillan.

Breunig, LeRoy C. Guillaume Apollinaire. LC 79-92030. (Columbia Essays on Modern Writers Ser.: No. 46). 48p. 1969. pap. 2.50 (ISBN 0-231-02995-0). Columbia U Pr.

Breuning, S., et al. Advances in Mental Retardation & Developmental Disabilities, Vol. 2. 1985. 47.50 (ISBN 0-89232-287-X). Jai Pr.

Breuning, Stephen, jt. ed. see Matson, Johnny.

Breuning, Stephen E. & Poling, Alan D. Drugs & Mental Retardation. (Illus.). 450p. 1982. 44.75x (ISBN 0-398-04599-2). C C Thomas.

Breuning, Stephen E., jt. ed. see Hersen, Michel.

Breuning, Stephen E., et al, eds. Applied Psychopharmacology: Methods for Assessing Medication. 384p. 1985. 34.50 (ISBN 0-8089-1698-X, 790661). Grune.

Breur, Joseph. The Jewish Marriage. 3.00 (ISBN 0-87306-097-0). Feldheim.

Breur, K. see Barendsen, G. W. & Broerse, J.

Breurr, D. F., ed. Progress in Low Temperature Physics, Vol. 9. Date not set. price not set (North-Holland). Elsevier.

Breva-Claramonte, Manuel. Sanctius' Theory of Language: A Contribution to the History of Renaissance Linguistics. (Studies in the History of Linguistics Ser.: 27). 294p. 1983. 36.00x (ISBN 90-272-4505-3). Benjamins North Am.

Brevard, C. & Granger, P. Handbook of High Resolution Multinuclear NMR. LC 81-8603. 229p. 1981. 30.95 (ISBN 0-471-06323-1, Pub. by Wiley-Interscience). Wiley.

Brevard, Joseph. Capital Facilities Planning: A Tactical Approach. LC 85-70761. (Illus.). 400p. 1985. pap. 37.95 (ISBN 0-918286-40-9). Planners Pr.

Brew, J. O. Archaeology of Alkali Ridge, Southeastern Utah. (MU.PMP). 1946. 72.00 (ISBN 0-685-13693-0). Kraus Repr.

Brew, J. O., ed. One Hundred Years of Anthropology. (Illus.). 276p. 1968. text ed. 22.00x (ISBN 0-674-63900-6); pap. 5.95x o. p. (ISBN 0-674-63901-4). Harvard U Pr.

Brew, Kwesi. African Panorama. LC 80-66985. 64p. (Orig.). 1981. pap. 3.00. Greenfld Rev Pr.

Breward, Ian. William Perkins. 661p. 1981. 90.00x (ISBN 0-686-79496-6, Pub. by Sutton Courtenay). State Mutual Bk.

Brewer & Smith. Emmy Noether. (Pure & Applied Mathematics Ser.: Vol. 69). 216p. 1981. 25.00 (ISBN 0-8247-1550-0). Dekker.

Brewer, jt. auth. see Pitzer.

Brewer, Allen A. & Morrow, Robert M. Overdentures. 2nd ed. LC 80-19356. (Illus.). 426p. 1980. text ed. 64.95 (ISBN 0-8016-0785-X). Mosby.

Brewer, Amanda M. I Sing of Appalachia. (Illus.). 1967. Repr. of 1972 ed. 5.00 (ISBN 0-87012-118-9). McClain.

Brewer, Annie, ed. Abbreviations, Acronyms, Ciphers & Signs: A Reference Source for Identifying Books in Many Languages Which Concern Themselves with Short Forms of Communications. 315p. 1981. 90.00x (ISBN 0-8103-0529-1). Gale.

Brewer, Annie M. Indexes, Abstracts & Digests. 801p. 1982. 210.00x (ISBN 0-8103-1686-2). Gale.

Brewer, Annie M., ed. Dictionaries, Encyclopedias, & Other Word-Related Books, 3 vols. 3rd ed. LC 81-20247. 1982. Vol. 1: English. 130.00x (ISBN 0-8103-1191-7); Vol. 2: Polyglot. 185.00x (ISBN 0-8103-1192-5); Vol. 3: Foreign. 185.00x (ISBN 0-8103-1193-3). Gale.

--Youth-Serving Organizations Directory. 2nd ed. 1980. 72.00x (ISBN 0-8103-0238-1). Gale.

Brewer, Anthony. A Guide to Marx's Capital. LC 83-14329. 220p. 1984. 29.95 (ISBN 0-521-25730-1); pap. 8.95 (ISBN 0-521-27676-4). Cambridge U Pr.

--The Love-Sick King, 1655. Swaen, A. E., ed. (Material for the Study of the Old English Drama Ser.: No. 1, Vol. 18). pap. 11.00 (ISBN 0-317-16736-7). Kraus Repr.

--Marxist Theories of Imperialism. 304p. 1980. 35.00 (ISBN 0-7100-0531-8); pap. 14.95x (ISBN 0-7100-0621-7). Routledge & Kegan.

Brewer, Bartholomew F. & Furrell, Alfred W. Pilgrimage from Rome. (Illus.). 169p. (Orig.). 1982. pap. 4.95 (ISBN 0-89084-175-6). Bob Jones Univ Pr.

Brewer, Bill & Willis, Jerry. How to Use the TI 99-4A. 124p. 1983. pap. 3.95 (ISBN 0-88056-135-1). Dilithium Pr.

--How to Use the TRS-80 Color Computer. (How to Use Ser.). (Illus.). 128p. 1984. pap. 5.95 (ISBN 0-88056-342-7). Dilithium Pr.

Brewer, Bryan. Eclipse. LC 78-73047. (Illus., Orig.). 1978. pap. 5.95 (ISBN 0-932898-26-2). Earth View.

Brewer, Bryan, jt. auth. see Hester, Debbie.

Brewer, Clifton H. A History of Religious Education in the Episcopal Church to Eighteen Thirty-Five. 1924. 14.50x (ISBN 0-686-51401-7). Elliots Bks.

--History of Religious Education in the Episcopal Church to 1835. LC 73-89152. (American Education Its Men, Institutions & Ideas, Ser. 1). 1969. Repr. of 1924 ed. 16.00 (ISBN 0-405-01390-6). Ayer Co Pubs.

Brewer, Colin & Lait, June. Can Social Work Survive? 1981. 29.00x (ISBN 0-85117-217-2, Pub. by M Temple Smith). State Mutual Bk.

Brewer, D. Chaucer: The Poet As Storyteller. 192p. 1984. text ed. 36.50x (ISBN 0-333-28428-3, Pub. by Macmillan England). Humanities.

--Tradition & Innovation in Chaucer. 256p. 1982. text ed. 37.50x (ISBN 0-333-28427-5, 50794, Pub. by Macmillan England). Humanities.

Brewer, D. F., ed. Progress in Low Temperature Physics, 2 vols, Vol. 7. 1979. Set. o.p 114.75 (ISBN 0-444-85210-7, North Holland); Vol. 7b. 85.00 (ISBN 0-444-85209-3). Elsevier.

--Progress in Low Temperature Physics, Vol. 8. 298p. 1983. 68.00 (ISBN 0-444-86228-5, North-Holland). Elsevier.

Brewer, D. S. Proteus: Chaucer, Shakespeare, Wordsworth, E. M. Forster. 1958. lib. bdg. 20.00 (ISBN 0-8414-2540-X). Folcroft.

Brewer, D. S., ed. see Chaucer, Geoffrey.

Brewer, D. S., ed. see Malory, Thomas.

Brewer, David J., ed. The World's Best Essays From the Earliest Period to the Present Time, 10 vols. 1982. Repr. of 1900 ed. lib. bdg. 500.00 (ISBN 0-8495-0230-6, SET). Arden Lib.

--World's Best Orations, 2 Vols. LC 75-15323. 1970. Repr. of 1901 ed. Set. 150.00 (ISBN 0-8108-0341-0). Scarecrow.

Brewer, Deborah J. ARBA Guide to Education. 250p. 1985. lib. bdg. 23.50 (ISBN 0-87287-490-7). Libs Unl.

Brewer, Derek. Chaucer in His Time. LC 77-77517. 1977. Repr. lib. bdg. 27.50x (ISBN 0-8371-9649-3, BRCI). Greenwood.

--Chaucer's Mentality. LC 83-12290. (Chaucer Studies: XI). 224p. 1985. 43.50x (ISBN 0-389-20429-3, 07315). B&N Imports.

--Childe Roland to the Dark Tower: An Approach to English Studies. 32p. Date not set. pap. price not set (ISBN 0-521-31868-8). Cambridge U Pr.

--Symbolic Stories: Traditional Narratives of the Family Drama in English Literature. 190p. 1980. 31.50x (ISBN 0-8476-6900-9). Rowman.

Brewer, Derek, ed. Chaucer-the Critical Heritage, 2 vols. Incl. Vol. 1. 1385-1837; Vol. 2. 1837-1933. 30.00 (ISBN 0-7100-0224-6). (Critical Heritage Ser). 1978. Set. 50.00x (ISBN 0-7100-8497-8). Routledge & Kegan.

Brewer, Derek & Jeffares, A. Norman, eds. English Gothic Literature. (History of Literature Ser.). (Illus.). 328p. 1983. 28.50 (ISBN 0-8052-3861-1). Schocken.

Brewer, Derek, intro. by see Malory, Thomas.

Brewer, Derek, jt. ed. see Takamiya, Toshiyuki.

Brewer, Derek S., ed. Chaucer & Chaucerians. LC 66-17566. 278p. 1966. pap. 8.50 (ISBN 0-8173-7352-7). U of Ala Pr.

--Writers & Their Background: Geoffrey Chaucer. LC 74-84295. (Writers & Their Background Ser.). xiv, 401p. 1975. pap. 10.00x (ISBN 0-8214-0184-X, 82-81842). Ohio U Pr.

Brewer, Donald D., jt. auth. see Truitt, John O.

Brewer, Donald J. Hans Hofmann Paintings. (Illus.). 16p. 1968. 6.00x (ISBN 0-686-99836-7). La Jolla Mus Contemp Art.

Brewer, Donald J. & Reich, Sheldon. Marsden Hartley-John Marin. (Illus.). 48p. 1966. 4.00x (ISBN 0-686-99839-1). La Jolla Mus Contemp Art.

Brewer, Donald R. The Jesse Tree. 1979. spiral bdg. 4.00 (ISBN 0-89536-407-7). CSS of Ohio.

Brewer, E. The Historic Notebook. 59.95 (ISBN 0-8490-0307-5). Gordon Pr.

--The Reader's Handbook of Famous Names in Fiction. 69.95 (ISBN 0-8490-0928-6). Gordon Pr.

Brewer, E. C. The Dictionary of Phrase & Fable. 1978. 7.98 (ISBN 0-517-25921-4, Avenel). Outlet Bk Co.

Brewer, E. Cobban. Character Sketches of Romance, Fiction & the Drama: A Revised American Edition of the Reader's Handbook, 4 vols. Harland, Marion, ed. Repr. of 1892 ed. Set. lib. bdg. 600.00 (ISBN 0-89987-951-9). Darby Bks.

Brewer, E. Cobham. Authors & Their Works. 59.95 (ISBN 0-87968-679-0). Gordon Pr.

--Authors & Their Works, with Dates. LC 71-134907. (Readers Handbook Ser.: Vol. 3). 1970. Repr. of 1898 ed. 47.00x (ISBN 0-8103-3025-3). Gale.

--Brewer's Dictionary of Phrase & Fable: Centenary Edition. rev. ed. Evans, Ivor, pref. by. LC 81-47407. 1248p. 1981. 25.91i (ISBN 0-06-014903-5, HarpT). Har-Row.

--A Dictionary of Miracles, Imitative, Realistic, & Dogmatic. LC 66-29783. 1966. Repr. of 1885 ed. 48.00x (ISBN 0-8103-3000-8). Gale.

--Historical Note-Book. LC 66-23191. 1966. Repr. of 1891 ed. 70.00x (ISBN 0-8103-0152-0). Gale.

--Reader's Handbook: Famous Names in Fiction, Allusions, References, Proverbs, Plots, Stories, & Poems, 3 vols. LC 71-134907. 1966. Repr. of 1899 ed. Set. 105.00x (ISBN 0-8103-0153-9). Gale.

Brewer, Earl D. Continuation or Transformation? The Involvement of United Methodism in Social Movements & Issues. (Into our Third Century Ser.). 128p. (Orig.). 1982. pap. 4.95 (ISBN 0-687-09623-5). Abingdon.

Brewer, Earl J. Juvenile Rheumatoid Arthritis. 2nd ed. LC 78-64701. (Major Problems in Clinical Pediatrics Ser.: Vol. 6). 1982. text ed. 50.00 (ISBN 0-7216-1986-X). Saunders.

Brewer, Ebenezer. A Dictionary of Miracles. 75.00 (ISBN 0-8490-0040-8). Gordon Pr.

Brewer, Edward S. & Betts, Jim. Understanding Boat Design. 3rd ed. LC 70-147872. (Illus.). 1980. pap. 9.95 (ISBN 0-87742-015-7). Intl Marine.

Brewer, Elisabeth, jt. auth. see Taylor, Beverly.

Brewer, Elizabeth. The Novel of Entertainment During the Gallant Era: A Study of the Novels of August Bohse, Vol. 13. (Arbeiten zur Mittleren Deutschen Literatur und Sprache). 145p. 1983. 16.85 (ISBN 3-261-03241-3). P Lang Pubs.

Brewer, Forrest & Brewer, Jean. Vocabulario Mexicano de Tetelcingo. (Vocabularios Indigenas Ser.: No. 8). 274p. (Span.). 1962. pap. 4.00x (ISBN 0-88312-658-3); microfiche 3.00x (ISBN 0-88312-363-0). Summer Inst Ling.

Brewer, G. J. Introduction to Isozyme Techniques. 1970. 50.00 (ISBN 0-12-133250-0). Acad Pr.

Brewer, G. R. Ion Propulsion, Technology & Applications. 550p. 1970. 145.75 (ISBN 0-677-02600-5). Gordon.

Brewer, Gail S. An Italian Family Reunion Cookbook. LC 81-16621. (Illus.). 288p. 1982. 12.95 (ISBN 0-312-43922-9). St Martin.

--Nine Months, Nine Lessons. (Orig.). 1983. pap. 9.95 (ISBN 0-671-45788-8, Fireside). S&S.

Brewer, Gail S. & Brewer, Thomas H. The Brewer Medical Diet for Normal & High-Risk Pregnancy: A Leading Obstetrician's Guide to Every Stage of Pregnancy. 1983. 8.95 (ISBN 0-686-44924-X, Fireside). S&S.

Brewer, Gail S. & Brewer, Tom. What Every Pregnant Woman Should Know: The Truth about Diets & Drugs in Pregnancy. 256p. 1985. pap. 6.95 (ISBN 0-14-007974-2). Penguin.

--What Every Pregnant Woman Should Know: The Truth About Diet & Drugs in Pregnancy. 1977. 9.95 (ISBN 0-394-41117-X). Random.

Brewer, Gail S. & Greene, Janice P. Right from the Start: Meeting the Challenges of Mothering Your Unborn & Newborn Baby. Gerras, Charlie, ed. (Illus.). 224p. (Orig.). 1981. pap. 11.95 (ISBN 0-87857-273-2). Rodale Pr Inc.

Brewer, Gail S., jt. auth. see Presser, Janice.

Brewer, Gail S., ed. Pregnancy After Thirty Workbook. 1978. pap. 11.95 (ISBN 0-87857-215-5). Rodale Pr Inc.

Brewer, Garry & Shubik, Martin. The War Game: A Critique of Military Problem Solving. (Illus.). 404p. 1979. text ed. 27.50x (ISBN 0-674-94600-6). Harvard U Pr.

Brewer, Garry D. & DeLeon, Peter. Foundation of Policy Analysis. 492p. 1983. 28.00x (ISBN 0-256-02323-9). Dorsey.

Brewer, Garry D. & Brunner, Ronald D., eds. Political Development & Change. LC 74-482. (Illus.). 1975. 28.00 (ISBN 0-02-904710-2). Free Pr.

Brewer, George, ed. see International Conference on Red Cell Metabolism & Function, 3rd, Ann Arbor, Michigan, Oct., 1974.

Brewer, George D. The Fighting Editor: Or Warren & the Appeal. (Amer. Newspapermen Ser.: 1790-1933). 1975. Repr. of 1910 ed. 14.50x (ISBN 0-8464-0030-8). Beekman Pubs.

Brewer, George J. Orphan Drugs & Orphan Diseases: Clinical Realities & Public Policy. LC 83-9865. (Progress in Clinical & Biological Research Ser.: Vol. 127). 298p. 1983. 38.00 (ISBN 0-8451-0127-7). A R Liss.

--The Red Cell: Sixth Ann Arbor Conference. (Progress in Clinical & Biological Research Ser.: Vol. 165). 608p. 1984. 86.00 (ISBN 0-8451-5015-4). A R Liss.

Brewer, George J. & Sing, Charles F. Introductory Genetics. (Biology Ser.). (Illus.). 784p. 1983. text ed. 38.95 (ISBN 0-201-10138-6); Courseware avail.; Solutions Manual 2.00 (ISBN 0-201-10139-4); text ed. 2.00. Addison-Wesley.

Brewer, George J., jt. auth. see Eaton, John W.

Brewer, George J., ed. Hemoglobin & Red Cell Structure & Function. LC 72-86140. (Advances in Experimental Medicine & Biology Ser.: Vol. 28). 558p. 1972. 65.00x (ISBN 0-306-39028-0, Plenum Pr). Plenum Pub.

--The Red Cell. LC 78-71. (Progress in Clinical & Biological Research Ser.: Vol. 21). 782p. 1978. 74.00 (ISBN 0-8451-0021-1). A R Liss.

--The Red Cell: Fifth Ann Arbor Conference. LC 81-2653. (Progress in Clinical & Biological Research Ser.: Vol. 55). 840p. 1981. 78.00 (ISBN 0-8451-0055-6). A R Liss.

--Red Cell Metabolism & Function. LC 77-110798. (Advances in Experimental Medicine & Biology Ser.: Vol. 6). 407p. 1970. 52.50x (ISBN 0-306-39006-X, Plenum Pr). Plenum Pub.

Brewer, George J. & Prasad, Ananda S., eds. Zinc Metabolism: Current Aspects in Health & Disease. LC 77-3584. (Progress in Clinical & Biological Research: Vol. 14). 376p. 1977. 40.00x (ISBN 0-8451-0014-9). A R Liss.

Brewer, George J., jt. ed. see Hanash, Samir M.

Brewer, George R., jt. auth. see Wilson, Robert. G.

Brewer, George R., ed. Electron Beam Technology in Microelectric Fabrication. LC 79-8856. 1980. 49.50 (ISBN 0-12-133550-X). Acad Pr.

Brewer, H. W. Old London Illustrated. (Illus.). 1962. deluxe ed. 27.50x (ISBN 0-89563-012-5). Intl Ideas.

Brewer, Henry & Clark, Chloe. The Journal of Henry Bridgman Brewer. Date not set. price not set (ISBN 0-87770-332-9). Ye Galleon.

Brewer, Ilma M. Learning More & Teaching Less: A Decade of Innovation in Self-Instruction & Small Group Learning. 176p. 1985. 26.00 (ISBN 1-85059-003-6). Taylor & Francis.

Brewer, J. The Common People & Politics Seventeen Fifty to Seventeen Nineties. LC 85-6632. (English Satirical Print Ser.). 174p. 1985. lib. bdg. 50.00 (ISBN 0-85964-174-0). Chadwyck-Healey.

Brewer, J. E. Distance: A New, Yet Old Approach to Art. Barrett, Benjamin & Young, Madilyn, eds. (Illus.). 142p. 1983. 15.95 (ISBN 0-939502-05-4); pap. 6.95 (ISBN 0-939502-03-8). St Luke Pub.

--Handbook of Style for Art History. Barrett, Benjamin & Schaefer, V. A., eds. (Illus.). 127p. (Orig.). 1983. 15.95 (ISBN 0-939502-04-6); pap. 6.95. St Luke Pub.

Brewer, J. Gordon. The Literature of Geography: A Guide to Its Organisation & Use. 2nd ed. (Guide to Subject Literature Ser.). (Illus.). 264p. 1978. 25.00 (ISBN 0-208-01683-X, Linnet). Shoe String.

Brewer, J. S. & Wace, Henry. English Studies, or Essays in English History & Literature. 448p. 1982. Repr. of 1881 ed. lib. bdg. 75.00 (ISBN 0-8495-0611-5). Arden Lib.

Brewer, J. S., ed. Fr. Rogeri Bacon Opera Quaedam Hactenus Inedita: Opus Tertium, Opus Minus - Compendium Philosophiae. (Rolls Ser.: No. 15). Repr. of 1859 ed. 60.00 (ISBN 0-317-16662-X). Kraus Repr.

Brewer, J. S. & Howlett, Richard, eds. Monumenta Franciscana, 2 vols. (Rolls Ser.: No. 4). Repr. of 1882 ed. Set. 95.00 (ISBN 0-317-16651-4). Kraus Repr.

Brewer, J. S. & Martin, Charles T., eds. Registrum Malmesburiense: The Register of Malmesbury Abbey, 2 vols. (Rolls Ser.: No. 72). Repr. of 1880 ed. 88.00 (ISBN 0-317-16795-2). Kraus Repr.

Brewer, J. S., et al, eds. Giraldi Cambrensis Opera, 8 vols. Incl. Vol. 1. Invectionum Libellus; Vol. 2. Gemma Ecclesiastica; Vol. 3. De Invectionibus; Vol. 4. Speculum Ecclesiae; Vol. 5. Topographia Hibernica; Vol. 6. Itinerarium Kambriae; Vol. 7. Vita S. Remigii; Vol. 8. De Principis Instructione. (Rolls Ser.: No. 21). Repr. of 1891 ed. Set. 352.00 (ISBN 0-317-16667-0). Kraus Repr.

Brewer, J. W., ed. see Conference on Commutative Algebra.

Brewer, J. W., et al. Readings in Insect-Plant Disease Relationships. new ed. LC 72-10029. (Illus.). 1973. pap. text ed. 13.25x (ISBN 0-8422-0264-1). Irvington.

Brewer, James, et al. Power Selling. 200p. 1985. 15.95 (ISBN 0-13-688425-3); pap. 8.95 (ISBN 0-13-688417-2). P H.

Brewer, James H., et al. Power Management: A Three Step Program for Successful Leadership. (Illus.). 166p. 1984. 15.95 (ISBN 0-13-687682-X); pap. 8.95 (ISBN 0-13-687674-9). P-H.

Brewer, James K. Everything You Always Wanted to Know About Statistics but Didn't Know How to Ask. 2nd ed. 1978. pap. text ed. 7.95 (ISBN 0-8403-1868-5). Kendall-Hunt.

Brewer, James W., Jr. Jerome. 15th ed. (Illus.). 1976. pap. 0.25 (ISBN 0-911408-16-9). SW Pks Mnmts.

Brewer, Jean, jt. auth. see Brewer, Forrest.

Brewer, Jeutonne. Anthony Burgess: A Bibiliography. LC 80-413. (Scarecrow Author Bibiliographies Ser.: No. 47). 193p. 1980. lib. bdg. 16.50 (ISBN 0-8108-1286-X). Scarecrow.

Brewer, Jo. Butterflies. LC 74-23357. (Illus.). 1976. pap. 12.95 (ISBN 0-8109-2064-6). Abrams.

Brewer, Joan S. & Davidman, Lyn. Sex & the Modern Jewish Woman: Bibliography-Guide, Annotated. 100p. Date not set. pap. price not set (ISBN 0-930395-01-8). Biblio NY.

Brewer, Joan S., jt. ed. see Institute for Sex Research.

Brewer, John. Party Ideology & Popular Politics at the Accession of George Third. (Illus.). 400p. pap. 19.95 (ISBN 0-521-28701-4). Cambridge U Pr.

Brewer, John & Styles, John, eds. An Ungovernable People: The English & Their Law in the Seventeenth & Eighteenth Centuries. 1980. 30.00x (ISBN 0-8135-0891-6); pap. 9.95 (ISBN 0-8135-0976-9). Rutgers U Pr.

Brewer, John, jt. auth. see McKendrick, Neil.

Brewer, John D. Mosley's Men: The British Union of Fascists in the West Midlands. LC 84-1549. 159p. 1984. text ed. 30.95x (ISBN 0-566-00696-0). Gower Pub Co.

Brewer, John E., ed. see Salinger, John P.

Brewer, John E., ed. see Salinger, John. P.

Brewer, John M. Negrito: Negro Dialect Poems of the Southwest. facsimile ed. LC 78-37585. (Black Heritage Library Collection Ser.). Repr. of 1933 ed. 12.25 (ISBN 0-8369-8961-9). Ayer Co Pubs.

Brewer, John M., et al. The Vocational-Guidance Movement. (Educational Ser.). 1926. Repr. 40.00 (ISBN 0-8482-7420-2). Norwood Edns.

Brewer, John S. Reign of Henry Eighth from His Accession to the Death of Wolsey, 2 Vols. Gairdner, James, ed. LC 70-52901. Repr. of 1884 ed. Set. 65.00 (ISBN 0-404-01072-5). AMS Pr.

Brewer, K. R. & Hanif, M. Sampling with Unequal Probabilities. (Lecture Notes in Statistics Ser.: Vol. 15). (Illus.). 164p. 1982. pap. 15.00 (ISBN 0-387-90807-2). Springer-Verlag.

Brewer, Kenneth W. To Remember What is Lost. 59p. 1982. 9.95x (ISBN 0-87421-114-X). Utah St U Pr.

Brewer, L. Leigh Hunt & Charles Dickens: The Skimpole Caricature. LC 72-160466. (English Literature Ser., No. 33). 1971. Repr. of 1930 ed. lib. bdg. 54.95x (ISBN 0-8383-1301-9). Haskell.

Brewer, L. E., ed. see Chaucer, Geoffrey.

Brewer, Lewis, jt. auth. see United States Tennis Association.

Brewer, Lucy. The Female Marine: Adventures of Miss Lucy Brewer. 2nd ed. LC 65-23390. 1966. Repr. of 1817 ed. 19.50 (ISBN 0-306-70913-9). Da Capo.

Brewer, Luther A. Leaves from a Leigh Hunt Note-Book. LC 74-7183. 1932. lib. bdg. 10.00 (ISBN 0-8414-3171-X). Folcroft.

--Leigh Hunt & Charles Dickens: The Skimpole Caricature. LC 74-7385. 1930. lib. bdg. 10.00 (ISBN 0-8414-3169-8). Folcroft.

--Some Lamb & Browning Letters to Leigh Hunt. LC 72-196923. 1924. lib. bdg. 8.50 (ISBN 0-8414-2541-8). Folcroft.

Brewer, Luther A. & Iowa University Library, eds. My Leigh Hunt Library, Vol. 1: The First Editions. 1970. Repr. of 1932 ed. 25.50 (ISBN 0-8337-0369-2). B Franklin.

--My Leigh Hunt Library, Vol. 2: The Holograph Letters. 1967. Repr. of 1938 ed. 29.50 (ISBN 0-8337-0370-6). B Franklin.

Brewer, Lyman A., jt. auth. see Beijing Symposium on Cardiothoracic Surgery.

Brewer, Marilyn B., et al. Ethnocentrism & Intergroup Attitudes: East African Evidence. LC 75-26930. (Cross-Cultural Research & Methodology Ser.). pap. 56.00 (ISBN 0-317-09960-4, 2021874). Bks Demand UMI.

Brewer, Marilynn B., jt. auth. see Miller, Norman.

Brewer, Marilynn B. & Collins, Barry E., eds. Scientific Inquiry & the Social Sciences: A Volume in Honor of Donald T. Campbell. LC 81-6023. (Social & Behavioral Science Ser.). 1981. text ed. 35.00x (ISBN 0-87589-496-8). Jossey-Bass.

Brewer, Marilynn B., jt. ed. see Struening, Elmer L.

Brewer, Mary. What Floats? LC 75-34107. (Illus.). (ps-3). 1976. PLB 6.95 (ISBN 0-913778-25-7); pap. 2.75 (ISBN 0-89565-065-7). Childs World.

--Which Is Biggest? LC 75-35970. (Illus.). (ps-3). 1976. PLB 6.95 (ISBN 0-913778-26-5); pap. 2.75 (ISBN 0-89565-067-3). Childs World.

--Wind Is Air. LC 75-34141. (Illus.). (ps-3). 1976. PLB 6.95 (ISBN 0-913778-27-3); pap. 2.75 (ISBN 0-89565-068-1). Childs World.

Brewer, Mary, jt. ed. see Scott, Thomas.

Brewer, Nancy, jt. auth. see Brock, Nancy.

Brewer, P. G. Oceanography: The Present & the Future. (Illus.). 392p. 1983. 42.00 (ISBN 0-387-90720-3). Springer-Verlag.

Brewer, R. G., et al, eds. NC-CNC Machining II. (E.I.T.B. Training Manuals Ser.). (Illus.). 230p. 1982. 42.50x (ISBN 0-85083-539-9). Intl Ideas.

Brewer, Ralph J. Journey Through the Bible. 167p. (Orig.). 1983. pap. text ed. 5.95 (ISBN 0-87148-450-1); instrs. guide 2.50 (ISBN 0-87148-451-X). Pathway Pr.

Brewer, Richard. Principles of Ecology. LC 77-84666. (Illus.). 1979. pap. text ed. 18.95 (ISBN 0-7216-1988-6). HR&W.

Brewer, Richard & McCann, Margaret. Laboratory & Field Manual of Ecology. 1982. pap. text ed. 18.95 (ISBN 0-03-057879-5, CBS C). SCP.

Brewer, Richard, ed. Proceedings of the Eighth North American Prairie Conference. 200p. 1983. pap. text ed. 25.00 (ISBN 0-912244-16-X). Western Michigan.

Brewer, Richard G. & Mooradian, Aram, eds. Laser Spectroscopy. LC 74-12090. 671p. 1974. 69.50x (ISBN 0-306-30802-9, Plenum Pr). Plenum Pub.

Brewer, Robert N., et al. Solar Applications in Agriculture. 143p. 1981. 12.95 (ISBN 0-89168-034-9). L Erlbaum Assocs.

Brewer, Robert S. & Curtis, Don B. Winning FFA Speeches. LC 76-8592. 1976. pap. 8.50x (ISBN 0-8134-1806-2, 1806). Interstate.

Brewer, Robert S., jt. auth. see Curtis, Dan B.

Brewer, Roy. Eric Gill: The Man Who Loved Letters. (Illus.). 86p. 1973. 16.50x (ISBN 0-87471-148-7). Rowman.

--Fabric & Mineral Analysis of Soils. LC 75-17850. 498p. 1976. Repr. of 1964 ed. 27.50 (ISBN 0-88275-314-2). Krieger.

Brewer, Stephen. Solving Problems in Analytical Chemistry. LC 79-17164. 528p. 1980. pap. text ed. 20.95x (ISBN 0-471-04098-3). Wiley.

Brewer, Ted. Ted Brewer Explains Sailboat Design. LC 84-48686. (Illus.). 240p. 1985. 17.95 (ISBN 0-87742-193-5). Intl Marine.

Brewer, Terry, jt. auth. see Lahue, Kalton C.

Brewer, Thomas H. Metabolic Toxemia of Late Pregnancy. Rev. ed. 1982. pap. 7.95 (ISBN 0-87983-308-4). Keats.

Brewer, Thomas H., jt. auth. see Brewer, Gail S.

Brewer, Thomas L. American Foreign Policy: A Contemporary Introduction. (Illus.). 1980. pap. text ed. 18.95 (ISBN 0-13-026740-6). P-H.

--American Foreign Policy: A Contemporary Introduction. 2nd ed. (Illus.). 320p. 1986. text ed. 18.95 (ISBN 0-13-026733-3). P-H.

Brewer, Thomas L., ed. Political Risks in International Business: New Directions for Research, Management & Public Policy. 384p. 1985. 36.95 (ISBN 0-03-063758-9). Praeger.

Brewer, Tom, jt. auth. see Brewer, Gail S.

Brewer, W. D., tr. see Haken, H. & Wolf, H. C.

Brewer, Waldo L. Factors Affecting Student Achievement & Change in a Physical Science Survey Course. LC 70-176691. (Columbia University. Teachers College. Contributions to Education Ser.: No. 868). Repr. of 1943 ed. 22.50 (ISBN 0-404-55868-2). AMS Pr.

Brewer, Warren A., jt. auth. see Anttila, Raimo.

Brewer, William H. Up & Down California in Eighteen Sixty to Eighteen Sixty-Four: The Journal of William H. Brewer. Farquhar, Francis P., ed. LC 66-26246. (California Library Reprint Ser: No. 59). (Illus.). 1974. pap. 10.95 (ISBN 0-520-02762-0, CAL 294). U of Cal Pr.

Brewer, Wilmon. About Poetry & Other Matters. 2.00 (ISBN 0-8338-0004-3). M Jones.

--Adventures Further. (Illus.). 1958. 2.00 (ISBN 0-8338-0006-X). M Jones.

--Adventures in Verse. rev. ed. 1963. 2.00 (ISBN 0-8338-0005-1). M Jones.

--Concerning the Art of Poetry. LC 79-50684. (Illus.). 1979. 3.00 (ISBN 0-8338-0184-8). M Jones.
--Latest Adventures. (Illus.). 1981. 3.00. M Jones.
--Life & Poems of Brookes More. (Illus.). 1980. 3.00. M Jones.
--Life of Maurice Parker. 2.00 (ISBN 0-8338-0009-4). M Jones.
--New Adventures. (Illus.). 2.00 (ISBN 0-8338-0010-8). M Jones.
--Ovid's Metamorphoses in European Culture, 2 vols. (Illus.). 1978. Set. 10.00. M Jones.
--Shakespeare's Influence on Sir Walter Scott. Repr. of 1925 ed. 18.50 (ISBN 0-404-01075-X). AMS Pr.
--Sonnets & Sestinas. 1983. write for info. (ISBN 0-8338-0189-9). M Jones.
--Still More Adventures. (Illus.). 1965. 3.00 (ISBN 0-8338-0011-6). M Jones.
--Talks About Poetry. (Illus.). 2.00 (ISBN 0-8338-0016-7). M Jones.

Brewer, Wilmon, tr. Dante Eclogues. 2.00 (ISBN 0-8338-0007-8). M Jones.

Brewerton, G. Douglas. The War in Kansas. facsimile ed. LC 74-164381. (Black Heritage Library Collection). Repr. of 1856 ed. 17.00 (ISBN 0-8369-8840-X). Ayer Co Pubs.

Brewi, Janice & Brennan, Anne, eds. Mid life: Psychological & Spiritual Perspectives. 224p. 1982. 12.95 (ISBN 0-8245-0417-8). Crossroad NY.

Brewin, Bob & Shaw, Sydney. Vietnam on Trial: Westmoreland vs. CBS. LC 85-47595. 288p. 1985. 17.95 (ISBN 0-689-11610-1). Atheneum.

Brewin, Bob, jt. auth. see Hughes, Richard.

Brewin, Chris, jt. ed. see Antaki, Charles.

Brewin, Robert, jt. auth. see Hughes, Richard.

Brewington, Dorothy. Dictionary of Marine Artists. (Illus.). 450p. 40.00 (ISBN 0-686-47022-2). Apollo.

Brewington, Dorothy, jt. auth. see Brewington, M. V.

Brewington, Dorothy, jt. auth. see Brewington, Marion V.

Brewington, Dorothy E. Dictionary of Marine Artists. (Illus.). 431p. 1982. 35.00 (ISBN 0-913372-24-2). Mystic Seaport.
--Marine Paintings & Drawings in Mystic Seaport Museum. (Illus.). 219p. 1982. 45.00 (ISBN 0-913372-25-0). Mystic Seaport.

Brewington, Doyle W. The Parables of the Kingdom. 64p. 1981. 4.95 (ISBN 0-8059-2774-3). Dorrance.

Brewington, M. V. Check List of the Paintings, Drawings & Prints at the Kendall Whaling Museum. (Illus.). 74p. 1957. pap. 2.00 (ISBN 0-937854-02-6). Kendall Whaling.
--Chesapeake Bay Log Canoes & Bugeyes. LC 62-18218. (Illus.). 182p. 1963. 22.50 (ISBN 0-87033-011-X). Tidewater.
--Shipcarvers of North America. LC 79-187020. (Illus.). 190p. 1972. pap. 4.95 (ISBN 0-486-22168-7). Dover.
--Special Exhibition of the Irving S. Olds Collection of American Naval Prints & Paintings. 1959. pap. 1.00 (ISBN 0-87577-024-X). Peabody Mus Salem.

Brewington, M. V. & Brewington, Dorothy. Kendall Whaling Museum Paintings. LC 65-28071. (Illus.). 137p. 1965. 30.00 (ISBN 0-937854-03-4). Kendall Whaling.
--Kendall Whaling Museum Prints. LC 70-107611. (Illus.). 209p. 1969. 40.00 (ISBN 0-937854-04-2). Kendall Whaling.

Brewington, Marion V. & Brewington, Dorothy. Marine Paintings & Drawings in the Peabody Museum of Salem. rev. ed. (Illus.). xvii, 530p. 1981. 125.00 (ISBN 0-87577-066-5). Peabody Mus Salem.

Brewis, Henry. Funny Way t'mekalivin' (Illus.). 128p. (Orig.). pap. 6.95 (ISBN 0-85236-142-4, Pub. by Farming Pr UK). Diamond Farm Bk.

Brewitt-Taylor, C. H., tr. see Lo, Kuan-Chung.

Brews, J. R., jt. auth. see Nicollian, E. H.

Brewster, Adolph B. Hill Tribes of Fiji. (Illus.). Repr. of 1922 ed. 27.00 (ISBN 0-384-05690-3). Johnson Repr.

Brewster, Albert H., Jr. How to Convert Gasoline Lawn Mowers for Cordless Electric Mowing. 3rd ed. LC 76-48500. (Illus.). 1981. pap. 10.00x (ISBN 0-918166-03-9). Amonics.
--How to Convert Salvage Auto Starter to Powerful DC Motor. 2nd ed. (Illus.). 1981. pap. 6.00x (ISBN 0-918166-04-7). Amonics.

Brewster, Barney. Antarctica: Wilderness at Risk. LC 82-70159. (Illus.). 125p. 1982. pap. 14.95 (ISBN 0-913890-51-0). Brick Hse Pub.

Brewster, Ben, tr. see Althusser, Louis.

Brewster, Ben, tr. see Richter, Hans.

Brewster, Benjamin. First Book of Baseball. rev. ed. LC 78-24230. (First Bks). (Illus.). (gr. 4-6). 1979. PLB 8.90 (ISBN 0-531-02932-8). Watts.

Brewster, C. Ray. The Cluster of Jesse Mercer. Volkoff, Vladimir, ed. LC 83-62474. (Illus.). 240p. 1983. 12.00 (ISBN 0-914707-01-9). Renaissance Pr.

Brewster, Charles. Rambles about Portsmouth, 2 vols. LC 70-181350. 1972. Repr. 55.00x set; Vol. 1, 1971. 0.00 (ISBN 0-912274-12-3); Vol. 2, 1972. 0.00 (ISBN 0-912274-21-2). NH Pub Co.

Brewster, David. The Best Places. (Illus.). 450p. (Orig.). 1985. pap. 12.95 (ISBN 0-912365-06-4). Sasquatch Pub.
--The Best Places, Nineteen Eighty-Four. 5th ed. (Illus.). 506p. 1983. pap. 11.95 (ISBN 0-912365-26-9). Sasquatch Pub.
--The Best Places: Restaurants, Lodging, & Tourism in Washington, Oregon, & British Columbia. 5th ed. LC 83-5184. (Illus.). 507p. (Orig.). 1983. pap. 11.95 (ISBN 0-912365-01-3). Sasquatch Pub.
--British Columbia Best Places. (The Best Places Ser.). (Illus.). 200p. 1985. pap. 7.95 (ISBN 0-912365-07-2). Sasquatch Pub.
--Memoirs of the Life, Writings & Discoveries of Sir Isaac Newton, 2 Vols. Repr. of 1855 ed. Set. 60.00 (ISBN 0-384-05703-9). Johnson Repr.
--Seattle Best Places. 2nd ed. (Illus.). 295p. 1984. pap. 8.95 (ISBN 0-912365-02-1). Sasquatch Pub.
--The Stereoscope, Its History, Theory & Construction. LC 77-167716. (Illus.). 235p. 1971. Repr. of 1856 ed. 14.95 (ISBN 0-87100-017-2, 2017). Morgan.

Brewster, David, ed. see Chasan, Daniel J.

Brewster, David C., jt. auth. see Hallett, John W., Jr.

Brewster, David E., et al, eds. Farms in Transition: Interdisciplinary Perspective on Farm Structure. (Illus.). 170p. 1983. pap. 9.75x (ISBN 0-8138-0636-4). Iowa St U Pr.

Brewster, Dorothy. Aaron Hill: Poet, Dramatist, Projector. LC 13-21690. Repr. of 1913 ed. 9.00 (ISBN 0-404-01076-8). AMS Pr.
--Virginia Woolf. LC 62-19050. (Gotham Library). 184p. (Orig.). 1962. pap. 13.50x (ISBN 0-8147-0057-8). NYU Pr.
--Virginia Woolf's London. LC 78-26590. 1979. Repr. of 1960 ed. lib. bdg. 22.50x (ISBN 0-313-20788-7, BRVW). Greenwood.

Brewster, Dorothy & Burrell, Angus. Adventure or Experience: Four Essays on Certain Writers & Readers of Novels. facs. ed. LC 67-23185. (Essay Index Reprint Ser). 1967. Repr. of 1930 ed. 17.00 (ISBN 0-8369-0252-1). Ayer Co Pubs.
--Dead Reckonings in Fiction. facsimile ed. LC 76-90614. (Essay Index Reprint Ser). 1924. 19.00 (ISBN 0-8369-1248-9). Ayer Co Pubs.
--Modern Fiction. facs. ed. LC 75-86732. (Essay Index Reprint Ser). 1934. 23.75 (ISBN 0-8369-1123-7). Ayer Co Pubs.

Brewster, Dorothy & Burrell, John A. Modern World Fiction. (Quality Paperback: No. 18). 220p. (Orig.). 1963. pap. 3.95 (ISBN 0-8226-0018-8). Littlefield.

Brewster, Earl H., compiled by. The Life of Gotama Buddha (Compiled Exclusively from the Pali Canon) LC 78-72380. Repr. of 1926 ed. 27.50 (ISBN 0-404-17229-6). AMS Pr.

Brewster, Ellis. The Bank Holiday of Nineteen Thirty-Three & Plymouth Payroll Scrip. (Pilgrim Society Notes Ser.: No. 21). 1.00 (ISBN 0-940628-09-0). Pilgrim Hall.

Brewster, Ellis, jt. auth. see Burgess, Edward.

Brewster, Ellis W. Funeral Bills. (Pilgrim Society Notes Ser.: No. 4). 1955. 1.00 (ISBN 0-940628-19-8). Pilgrim Hall.
--Thrasherville: An Old Plymouth Settlement. (Pilgrim Society Notes Ser.: No. 10). 1960. 1.00 (ISBN 0-940628-40-6). Pilgrim Hall.

Brewster, Ethel H. Roman Craftsmen & Tradesmen of the Early Empire. LC 72-81956. 101p. 1972. Repr. of 1917 ed. lib. bdg. 20.00 (ISBN 0-8337-4822-X). B Franklin.

Brewster, Harold P. Saints & Festivals of the Christian Church. LC 73-159869. (Illus.). xiv, 558p. 1975. Repr. of 1904 ed. 48.00x (ISBN 0-8103-3992-7). Gale.

Brewster, J. H., ed. Aspects of Mechanism & Organometallic Chemistry. LC 78-21684. 361p. 1979. 59.50x (ISBN 0-306-40071-5, Plenum Pr). Plenum Pub.

Brewster, James. Sketches of Southern Mystery, Treason, & Murder. LC 70-39529. Repr. of 1903 ed. 18.50 (ISBN 0-404-00006-1). AMS Pr.

Brewster, Jennifer, jt. ed. see Reid, Anthony.

Brewster, Jennifer, tr. see Fujiwara no Nagako.

Brewster, John W. & Gentry, Deborah. Index to Book Reviews in Historical Periodicals, 1977. LC 75-18992. 411p. 1979. 24.00 (ISBN 0-8108-1192-8). Scarecrow.

Brewster, Kingman, et al. The Tanner Lectures on Human Values, Vol. IV: 1983. 300p. 1983. 20.00x (ISBN 0-87480-216-4). U of Utah Pr.

Brewster, Kingman, Jr. Antitrust & American Business Abroad. Bruchey, Stuart & Bruchey, Eleanor, eds. LC 76-4768. (American Business Abroad Ser.). 1976. Repr. of 1958 ed. 43.00x (ISBN 0-405-09266-0). Ayer Co Pubs.

Brewster, Lawrence. The Public Agenda: Issues in American Politics. LC 83-61615. 307p. 1984. pap. text ed. 10.95 (ISBN 0-312-65393-X). St Martin.

Brewster, Lawrence F. Summer Migrations & Resorts of South Carolina Low-Country Planters. LC 76-115992. (Trinity College Historical Papers Ser.: No. 26). Repr. of 1947 ed. 24.50 (ISBN 0-404-51776-5). AMS Pr.

Brewster, Marge A. Clinical Chemistry Self-Assessment: Five Hundred Multiple-Choice Questions with Answers Explained. 155p. 1982. pap. 15.00 (ISBN 0-915274-18-3, 306); pap. 12.00 member. Am Assn Clinical Chem.
--Self-Assessment of Current Knowledge in Clinical Biochemistry. 2nd ed. 1976. 13.00 (ISBN 0-87488-266-4). Med Exam.

Brewster, Marge A. & Naito, Herbert K., eds. Nutritional Elements & Clinical Biochemistry. LC 80-21136. 478p. 1980. 65.00x (ISBN 0-306-40569-5, Plenum Pr). Plenum Pub.

Brewster, Maryjane. Verses in the Wind. LC 84-50316. 36p. 1985. pap. 8.00 (ISBN 0-934172-10-2). Wim Pubns.

Brewster, Mela S. A Practical Study of the Use of the Natural Vegetable Dyes in New Mexico. LC 38-28365. 1982. lib. bdg. 19.95x (ISBN 0-89370-726-0). Borgo Pr.

Brewster, Melvin & Hoyem, George A. Remington Bullet Knives. (Illus.). 60p. (Orig.). 1985. pap. write for info (ISBN 0-9604982-5-7). Armory Pubns.

Brewster, Patience. Ellsworth & the Cats from Mars. LC 80-16298. (Illus.). 32p. (gr. 1-5). 1981. 9.95 (ISBN 0-395-29612-9, Clarion). HM.
--Nobody. (Illus.). 32p. (ps-3). 1982. 9.95 (ISBN 0-89919-110-X, Clarion). HM.

Brewster, Patience, jt. auth. see Brightbill, Steven.

Brewster, Patricia L. Credit & Collections Manual. Medical Group Management Association, ed. Date not set. price not set (ISBN 0-933948-11-5). Med Group Mgmt.

Brewster, Paul G. Ballads & Songs of Indiana. Goldstein, Kenneth S., ed. LC 81-68632. (Publications in Folksong & Balladry Ser.). 376p. 1982. pap. 15.95 (ISBN 0-939544-03-2). Folklorica Pr.

Brewster, Paul G., ed. Ballads & Songs of Indiana. LC 81-68632. (Folksong & Balladry Ser.: No. 4). vi, 376p. pap. 15.95 (ISBN 0-939544-03-2). Wildman Pr.
--Children's Games & Rhymes. LC 75-35063. (Studies in Play & Games: Vol. 1). 1976. Repr. 16.00x (ISBN 0-405-07914-1). Ayer Co Pubs.

Brewster, Townsend T., tr. see Dadie, Bernard.

Brewton, J. L., jt. auth. see McGowen, J. H.

Brewton, John E. & Brewton, Sara W. Index to Children's Poetry. 966p. 1942. 30.00 (ISBN 0-8242-0021-7); first suppl. 1954, 405 p. 18.00 (ISBN 0-8242-0022-5); second suppl. 1965, 453 p. 18.00 (ISBN 0-8242-0023-3). Wilson.

Brewton, John E., ed. Index to Poetry for Children & Young People: 1964-1969. Brewton, Sara W. & Blackburn, G. M., III. LC 71-161574. 574p. 1972. 28.00 (ISBN 0-8242-0435-2). Wilson.
--Index to Poetry for Children & Young People: 1970-1975. Blackburn, G. M, III & Blackburn, Lorraine. 471p. 1978. 26.00 (ISBN 0-8242-0618-5). Wilson.

Brewton, John E. & Blackburn, Lorraine A., eds. They've Discovered a Head in the Box for the Bread & Other Laughable Limericks. LC 77-26598. (Illus.). (gr. 3-7). 1978. PLB 11.89 (ISBN 0-690-03883-6). Crowell Jr Bks.

Brewton, John E., jt. ed. see Brewton, Sara.

Brewton, John E., et al. In the Witch's Kitchen: Poems for Halloween. LC 79-7822. (Illus.). 96p. (gr. 2-5). 1980. PLB 11.89 (ISBN 0-690-04062-8). Crowell Jr Bks.

Brewton, John E., et al, eds. Index to Poetry for Children & Young People: 1976-1981. 350p. 1983. 35.00 (ISBN 0-8242-0681-9). Wilson.

Brewton, Sara & Brewton, John E., eds. America Forever New: A Book of Poems. LC 67-23663. (Illus.). (gr. 4 up). 1968. 11.95i (ISBN 0-690-06988-X). Crowell Jr Bks.
--Laughable Limericks. LC 65-16179. (Illus.). (gr. 2 up). 1965. 11.95i (ISBN 0-690-48667-7). Crowell Jr Bks.
--Shrieks at Midnight: Macabre Poems, Eerie & Humorous. LC 69-11824. (Illus.). (gr. 4 up). 1969. 11.95i (ISBN 0-690-73518-9). Crowell Jr Bks.

Brewton, Sara, et al. Of Quarks, Quasars & Other Quirks: Quizzical Poems for the Supersonic Age. LC 76-54747. (Illus.). (gr. 4 up). 1977. 11.95i (ISBN 0-690-01286-1). Crowell Jr Bks.

Brewton, Sara, et al, eds. My Tang's Tungled & Other Ridiculous Situations. LC 73-254. (Illus.). (gr. 4 up). 1973. 11.95i (ISBN 0-690-57223-9). Crowell Jr Bks.

Brewton, Sara W., jt. auth. see Brewton, John E.

Brewton, Sara W. see Brewton, John E.

Brewyn, William. A Fifteenth Century Guidebook to the Principal Churches of Rome. Woodruff, C. Eveleigh, tr. LC 78-63451. (The Crusades & Military Orders: Second Ser.). Repr. of 1933 ed. 17.00 (ISBN 0-404-16374-2). AMS Pr.

Brey, Barry. The Microprocessor 8085A: Software, Programming & Architecture. (Illus.). 484p. 1986. text ed. 29.95 (ISBN 0-13-246711-9). P-H.

Brey, Barry B. Microprocessor-Hardware Interfacing & Applications. 448p. 1984. Additional supplements may be obtained from publisher. text ed. 29.95 (ISBN 0-675-20158-6). Merrill.

Brey, Barry B., jt. auth. see Forbes, Mark M.

Brey, Catherine F., et al. The Complete Bloodhound. LC 77-81706. (The Complete Breed Bk.). (Illus.). 304p. 1984. 15.95 (ISBN 0-87605-052-6). Howell Bk.

Brey, Rita J. Du see DuBrey, Rita J.

Brey, Ron & Grigsby, Charles. Telecourse Student Survey, 1984. 60p. (Orig.). 1985. pap. 5.00 (ISBN 0-87117-153-8). Am Assn Comm Jr Coll.

Breyer, Betty J., ed. see Trollope, Anthony.

Breyer, Donald E. & Ank, John A. Design of Wood Structures. (Illus.). 1980. 47.95 (ISBN 0-07-007671-5). McGraw.

Breyer, Pamela. GrammarWork Four. (Illus.). 128p. 1983. pap. text ed. 5.25 (ISBN 0-88345-448-3, 20610). Regents Pub.
--Grammarwork One. (The Grammerwork Ser.). (gr. 7-12). 1982. pap. text ed. 5.25 (ISBN 0-88345-445-9, 20583). Regents Pub.
--Grammarwork Three. (Grammarwork Ser.). (gr. 7-12). 1982. pap. text ed. 5.25 (ISBN 0-88345-447-5, 20608). Regents Pub.
--Grammarwork Two. (The Grammarguide Ser.). (gr. 7-12). 1982. pap. text ed. 5.25 (ISBN 0-88345-446-7, 20596). Regents Pub.

Breyer, Ralph F. The Marketing Institution. Assael, Henry, ed. LC 78-245. (Century of Marketing Ser.). 1978. Repr. of 1934 ed. lib. bdg. 29.00x (ISBN 0-405-11160-6). Ayer Co Pubs.
--Quantitative Systemic Analysis & Control. Assael, Henry, ed. LC 78-250. (Century of Marketing Ser.). 1978. Repr. of 1949 ed. lib. bdg. 30.00x (ISBN 0-405-11164-9). Ayer Co Pubs.

Breyer, Richard & Moller, Peter. Making Television Programs: A Professional Approach. LC 83-19941. (Communication & Careers Ser.). 208p. 1984. pap. text ed. 15.95 (ISBN 0-582-28464-3). Longman.

Breyer, Siegfried. Battleships of the World. (Illus.). 570p. 1980. 50.00 (ISBN 0-686-65674-1, Mayflower Bks). Smith Pubs.

Breyer, Stephen. Regulation & Its Reform. LC 81-6753. (Illus.). 480p. 1982. text ed. 25.00 (ISBN 0-674-75375-5). Harvard U Pr.
--Regulation & Its Reform. 488p. 1984. pap. text ed. 8.95x (ISBN 0-674-75376-3). Harvard U Pr.

Breyer, Stephen & Stewart, Richard. Administrative Law & Regulatory Policy. 1979. text ed. 30.95 (ISBN 0-316-10796-4). Little.
--Administrative Law & Regulatory Policy, 1982 Supplement. 1982. pap. 7.95 (ISBN 0-316-10802-2). Little.

Breyer, Stephen G. & MacAvoy, Paul W. Energy Regulation by the Federal Power Commission. LC 74-273. (Studies in the Regulation of Economic Activity). 163p. 1974. 16.95 (ISBN 0-8157-1076-3). Brookings.

Breyer, Stephen G. & Stewart, Richard B. Administrative Law & Regulatory Policy. 2nd ed. LC 84-81768. 1985. text ed. 33.00 (ISBN 0-316-10805-7). Little.

Breyer, Stephen G., jt. auth. see Goldenberg, Norman S.

Breyer-Brandwijk, Maria G., jt. auth. see Watt, John M.

Breyfogle, Newell D. The Common Sense Medical Guide & Outdoor Reference. McGraw, Robert P., ed. (Illus.). 416p. 1981. text ed. 16.00 (ISBN 0-07-007672-3); pap. text ed. 9.95 (ISBN 0-07-007673-1). McGraw.

Breyfogle, Valorie, et al. Fourfront. 80p. 1983. pap. 5.95 (ISBN 0-941152-05-7). Bearstone Shepherd Pub.

Breymayer, Reinhard, jt. ed. see Haeusermann, Friederich.

Breymeyer, A. I., ed. see Van Dyne, G. M.

Breytenbach, Breyten. Mouroir: Mirrornotes of a Novel. LC 84-5981. 240p. 1984. 15.95 (ISBN 0-374-21391-7). FS&G.
--A Season in Paradise. Vaughan, Rike, tr. from Afrikaans. LC 79-91172. 300p. 1981. pap. 7.95 (ISBN 0-89255-052-X). Persea Bks.
--The True Confessions of an Albino Terrorist. LC 84-25966. 396p. 1985. 18.95 (ISBN 0-374-27935-7). FS&G.

Breytenbach, Bryten. In Africa Even the Flies Are Happy. Hirson, Denis, tr. from Afrikaans. 148p. 1982. 11.95 (ISBN 0-7145-3696-2); pap. 7.95 (ISBN 0-7145-3871-X). Riverrun NY.

Breytenbach, V. Death White as Words. Rex Collings Ltd., ed. 29.00x (ISBN 0-317-20259-6, Pub. by R Collings UK). State Mutual Bk.

Breytspraak, Linda M. The Development of Self in Later Life. (Gerontology Ser.). 1984. text ed. 6.95 (ISBN 0-316-10803-0); pap. text ed. 8.95 (ISBN 0-316-10804-9). Little.

Brez, E. M. Those Dark Eyes. 224p. 1984. 12.95 (ISBN 0-312-80195-5, J Kahn). St Martin.

Brezhnev, L. Memorias. 79p. (Span.). 1982. pap. 1.00 (ISBN 0-8285-2233-2, Pub. by Progress Pubs USSR). Imported Pubns.

Brezhnev, L. I. & Tikhonov, A. N. Reports of the Central Committee of the USSR Communist Party to the 26th CPSU Congress. Karsavina, Jean, ed. Novosti Press, tr. (Reprints from the Soviet Press Ser.: Vol. XXXII, No. 5-6-7). 1981. pap. 6.00 (ISBN 0-9606282-3-1). Compass Pubns NY.

Brezhnev, Lenoid I. Peace, Detente, Cooperation. LC 80-25943. 210p. 1981. 17.50x (ISBN 0-306-10971-9, Consultants). Plenum Pub.

Brezhnev, Leonid, et al. The Lie of a Soviet War Threat. 103p. 1980. pap. 3.45 (ISBN 0-8285-1823-8, Pub. by Progress Pubs USSR). Imported Pubns.

Brezhnev, Leonid I. How It Was: The War & Post-War Reconstruction in the Soviet Union. LC 78-41080. (Illus.). 1979. 14.25 (ISBN 0-08-023579-4); pap. 6.00 (ISBN 0-08-023578-6). Pergamon.
--Memoirs. (Illus.). 54p. 1982. pap. 9.50 (ISBN 0-08-028164-8). Pergamon.
--Selected Speeches & Writings on Foreign Affairs. LC 78-40614. 1979. text ed. 48.00 (ISBN 0-08-023569-7). Pergamon.
--A Short Biography. LC 77-30493. 1978. text ed. 16.25 (ISBN 0-08-022266-8). Pergamon.

--Socialism Democracy & Human Rights. LC 79-42659. 256p. 1981. 22.50 (ISBN 0-08-023605-7). Pergamon.

--Trilogy: Little Land, Rebirth; the Virgin Lands. 400p. (Orig.). 1980. 3.50 (ISBN 0-7178-0576-X). Intl Pubs Co.

--Virgin Lands: Two Years in Kazakhstan Nineteen Fifty-Four to Nineteen Fifty-Five. LC 79-42773. (Illus.). viii, 100p. 1979. 17.75 (ISBN 0-08-023584-0); pap. 7.25 (ISBN 0-08-023583-2). Pergamon.

Brezhnev, Leonid I., ed. Leonid I. Brezhnev: His Life & Work. (Illus.). 224p. 1984. 17.95 (ISBN 0-8236-8653-1). Sphinx Pr.

Brezik, Victor B. About Living. 156p. 1980. 4.95 (ISBN 0-912414-29-4). Lumen Christi.

--One Hundred Years of Thomism. 210p. 1981. 9.95 (ISBN 0-9605456-0-3). Lumen Christi.

Brezik, Victor B., ed. One Hundred Years of Thomism: Aeterni Patris & Afterwards - A Symposium. LC 85-14986. 210p. pap. text ed. 9.95 (ISBN 0-9605456-0-3). U of Notre Dame Pr.

--Thomistic Papers, No. I. LC 85-18508. 176p. 1983. text ed. 20.95 (ISBN 0-268-01850-2); pap. text ed. 10.95 (ISBN 0-268-01851-0). U of Notre Dame Pr.

Brezin, J. P. Harmonic Analysis on Compact Solvmanifolds. LC 77-22142. (Lecture Notes in Mathematics: Vol. 602). 1977. pap. text ed. 14.00 (ISBN 0-387-08354-5). Springer-Verlag.

Brezin, Jonathan. Unitary Representation Theory for Solvable Lie Groups. LC 52-42839. (Memoirs: No. 79). 122p. 1968. pap. 9.00 (ISBN 0-8218-1279-3, MEMO-79). Am Math.

Brezina, Dennis W. & Overmyer, Allen. Congress in Action: The Environmental Education Act. LC 73-6492. 1974. 12.95 (ISBN 0-02-904900-8). Free Pr.

Brezinski, C. Pade-Typed Approximation & General Orthogonal Polynomials. (International Series of Numerical Mathematics: No. 50). 250p. 1979. pap. 59.95 (ISBN 0-8176-1100-2). Birkhauser.

Brezis, H. & Lions, J. L. Nonlinear Partial Differential Equations & Their Applications: College de France Seminar Vol. 1. (Research Notes in Mathematics Ser.: No. 53). 350p. 1981. pap. text ed. 27.50 (ISBN 0-273-08491-7). Pitman Pub MA.

--Nonlinear Partial Differential Equations & Their Applications: College de France Seminar, Vol. 6. (Research Notes in Mathematics Ser.: No. 109). 336p. 1984. pap. text ed. 27.50 (ISBN 0-273-08646-4). Pitman Pub MA.

Brezis, H., jt. auth. see Berestyci, H.

Brezis, H. & Lions, J., eds. Nonlinear Partial Differential Equations & Their Applications: College de France Seminar, Vol. 4. (Research Notes in Mathematics: No. 84). 312p. 1983. pap. text ed. 27.50 (ISBN 0-273-08592-1). Pitman Pub MA.

Brezis, H. & Lions, J. L., eds. Nonlinear Partial Differential Equations & Their Applications, Vol. 3. (Research Notes in Mathematics: No. 70). 350p. 1982. pap. text ed. 27.50 (ISBN 0-273-08568-9). Pitman Pub MA.

--Nonlinear Partial Differential Equations & Their Applications, Vol. 7. (Research Notes in Mathematics Ser.: No. 122). 300p. 1985. pap. text ed. 21.50 (ISBN 0-273-08679-0). Pitman Pub MA.

--Nonlinear Partial Differential Equations & Their Applications: College de France Seminar, Vol. 2. (Research Notes in Mathematics Ser.: No. 60). 250p. 1982. pap. text ed. 27.50 (ISBN 0-273-08541-7). Pitman Pub MA.

--Nonlinear Partial Differential Equations & their Applications: College de France Seminar, Vol. 5. (Research Notes in Mathematics: No. 93). 384p. 1983. pap. text ed. 27.50 (ISBN 0-273-08620-0). Pitman Pub MA.

Breznau. The Real Happily Ever after Book. LC 80-80256. (Illus.). (gr. k-3). 1980. pap. 6.95 (ISBN 0-913916-66-8, IP 66-8). Incentive Pubns.

Breznitz, Shlomo. Cry Wolf: The Psychology of False Alarms. 280p. 1984. text ed. 29.95x (ISBN 0-89859-296-8). L Erlbaum Assocs.

--The Denial of Stress. LC 82-13044. xiv, 316p. 1983. text ed. 30.00 (ISBN 0-8236-1185-X). Intl Univs Pr.

--Stress in Israel. 304p. 1982. 19.95 (ISBN 0-442-24422-3). Van Nos Reinhold.

Breznitz, Shlomo, jt. ed. see Goldberger, Leo.

Brezsny, Rob. Images Are Dangerous. 88p. (Orig.). 1985. pap. 5.95 (ISBN 0-937310-22-0). Jazz Pr.

Brezzi, F., ed. Numerical Methods in Fluid Dynamics. (Lecture Notes in Mathematics: Vol. 1127). vii, 333p. 1985. pap. 20.50 (ISBN 0-387-15225-3). Springer-Verlag.

Brezzi, P. & Lee, E., eds. Source of Social History: Private Acts of the Late Middle Ages. (Papers in Mediaeval Studies: No. 5). (Illus.). 328p. 1984. pap. text ed. 32.75x (ISBN 0-88844-805-8). Humanities.

Brian, Breffny De see De Breffny, Brian.

Brian, Denis. The Enchanted Voyager: The Life of J. B. Rhine, an Authorized Biography. LC 81-12029. 367p. 1982. 16.95 (ISBN 0-13-275107-0). P-H.

Brian, George C. & Smith, Bessie G. Makeup for the Dark Complexioned Actor. LC 82-62535. (Illus.). 100p. (Orig.). 1983. pap. 13.50 (ISBN 0-88127-012-1). Oracle Pr LA.

Brian L. Famous Couples of the Bible. LC 78-60053. 1979. pap. 4.95 (ISBN 0-8054-5630-9). Broadman.

Brian, M. V. Social Insects: Ecology & Behavioral Biology. 1983. 49.95 (ISBN 0-412-22920-X, NO. 6820, Pub. by Chapman & Hall); pap. 25.00 (ISBN 0-412-22930-7, NO. 6821). Methuen Inc.

Brian, M. V., ed. Production Ecology of Ants & Termites. LC 76-54061. (International Biological Programme Ser.: No. 13). (Illus.). 1977. 95.00 (ISBN 0-521-21519-6). Cambridge U Pr.

Brian, Marilyn. Passion's Glow. (To Have & to Hold Ser.: No. 19). 1984. pap. 1.95 (ISBN 0-515-06946-9). Jove Pubns.

Brian, P. L. Staged Cascades in Chemical Processing. (International Series in the Physical & Chemical Engineering Sciences). (Illus.). 272p. 1972. ref. ed. 38.95 (ISBN 0-13-840280-9). P-H.

Brian, St. Pierre. John Steinbeck: The California Years. LC 83-17186. 1984. pap. 7.95 (ISBN 0-87701-281-4). Chronicle Bks.

Brian, William L., II. Moongate: Suppressed Findings of the U. S. Space Program. LC 81-69211. (Illus.). 231p. (Orig.). 1982. pap. 11.95 (ISBN 0-941292-00-2). Future Sci Res.

Brianchaninov, Ignatius. Fasting. pap. 0.25 (ISBN 0-686-05642-6). Eastern Orthodox.

--Three Essays: On Reading the Gospel, on Reading the Holy Fathers, on Shunning Reading of Books Containing False Teachings. pap. 0.25 (ISBN 0-686-16365-6). Eastern Orthodox.

Briandet, Philippe A., jt. auth. see Goris, Michael L.

Briani, Vittorio. Italian Immigrants Abroad: A Bibliography on the Italian Experience Outside Italy in Europe, the Americas, Australia, & Africa. LC 79-11239. 1979. 25.00 (ISBN 0-87917-069-7). Ethridge.

Brians, Bert. Leoni Meadows Experiences. large print ed. 62p. 1984. pap. 9.00 (ISBN 0-914009-07-9). Chr Overeaters Bks.

--My Wife the Prophetess. large print ed. (Illus.). 55p. 1982. pap. 9.50 (ISBN 0-9608650-7-1). Chr Overeaters Bks.

Brians, Charlene. How I Use Herbs. large print ed. 37p. 1985. pap. 5.50 (ISBN 0-914009-43-5). Chr Overeaters Bks.

--Light after Ellen White. large print ed. 1984. pap. 5.00 (ISBN 0-914009-06-0). Chr Overeaters Bks.

Brians, Charlene, jt. auth. see Moss, Michele.

Brians, Charline. Ellen White & Charline. large type ed. 35p. 1984. pap. 6.00x (ISBN 0-914009-21-4). Chr Overeaters Bks.

--My Diary on Appetite. large print ed. 32p. 1984. pap. 5.00 (ISBN 0-914009-08-7). Chr Overeaters Bks.

--My Friends the Adventists. large print ed. (Illus.). 57p. 1982. pap. 9.50 (ISBN 0-9608650-6-3). Chr Overeaters Bks.

--My Hope Psalms: Nineteen Eighty-Two Diary. large type ed. 38p. 1984. pap. 6.00 (ISBN 0-914009-13-3). Chr Overeaters Bks.

--Sunday Sister. large print ed. 24p. 1985. pap. 4.00 (ISBN 0-914009-53-2). Chr Overeaters Bks.

--Testing Myself As a Prophet. large print ed. 1985. pap. 5.00 (ISBN 0-914009-10-9). Chr Overeaters Bks.

Brians, Charline & Moss, Michele. Eye Book. 23p. 1983. pap. 5.00 (ISBN 0-9608650-8-X). Chr Overeaters Bks.

Brians, Charline, ed. Spirit of Prophecy, Vol. I & II. large print ed. 27p. 1984. pap. 5.00 (ISBN 0-9608650-3-9). Chr Overeaters Bks.

Brians, Pearl. Adventist Evangelist's Diary. large print ed. 1985. pap. 4.00 (ISBN 0-914009-25-7). Chr Overeaters Bks.

--Appetite Control for Christians. large print ed. 28p. 1985. pap. 4.50 (ISBN 0-914009-30-3). Chr Overeaters Bks.

--Carelessness & Indifference. large print ed. 25p. 1985. pap. 5.00 (ISBN 0-914009-39-7). Chr Overeaters Bks.

--Compulsive Overeaters Guide, Vol. I: Compulsiveness. large type ed. 45p. 1984. pap. 8.00x (ISBN 0-914009-04-4). Chr Overeaters Bks.

--Compulsive Overeaters Guide, Vol. II: Understanding Yourself. large type ed. 52p. 1984. pap. 8.00x (ISBN 0-914009-17-6). Chr Overeaters Bks.

--Compulsive Overeaters Guide, Vol. III: Overweight Teenagers. large type ed. 52p. 1984. pap. 8.00x (ISBN 0-914009-18-4). Chr Overeaters Bks.

--Compulsive Overeaters Guide, Vol. IV: Being Honest With Yourself. large type ed. 89p. 1984. pap. 9.00 (ISBN 0-914009-19-2). Chr Overeaters Bks.

--Defending the Blind Man. large print ed. 1985. pap. 4.00 (ISBN 0-914009-28-1). Chr Overeaters Bks.

--During My Conversion. large print ed. 44p. 1984. pap. 8.00 (ISBN 0-914009-11-7). Chr Overeaters Bks.

--Indecision about Baptism. large print ed. 34p. 1985. pap. 5.00 (ISBN 0-914009-41-9). Chr Overeaters Bks.

--Ingathering Experience, Vol. 1. large print ed. 33p. 1985. pap. 5.00 (ISBN 0-914009-32-X). Chr Overeaters Bks.

--Kind SDA's. large print ed. 30p. 1985. pap. 5.00 (ISBN 0-914009-49-4). Chr Overeaters Bks.

--Mama's Life on a Missouri Farm. large print ed. 86p. pap. 8.00 (ISBN 0-914009-26-5). Chr Overeaters Bks.

--My Appetite Control. large print ed. 1985. pap. 6.00 (ISBN 0-914009-40-0). Chr Overeaters Bks.

--My First SDA Camp Meeting. large print ed. 44p. 1985. pap. 6.00 (ISBN 0-914009-27-3). Chr Overeaters Bks.

--Out of Confusion-into the Light. large print ed. 58p. 1984. pap. 9.50 (ISBN 0-914009-12-5). Chr Overeaters Bks.

--Overeaters Feelings & Faith. large print ed. 40p. 1985. pap. 5.50 (ISBN 0-914009-31-1). Chr Overeaters Bks.

--Overeaters Sex Life. large type ed. 35p. 1984. pap. 6.00x (ISBN 0-914009-24-9). Chr Overeaters Bks.

--Overweight Ladies. large type ed. 37p. 1984. pap. 6.00x (ISBN 0-914009-23-0). Chr Overeaters Bks.

--Pearl's Prophetic Poetry. large print ed. 25p. 1985. pap. 4.00 (ISBN 0-914009-01-X). Chr Overeaters Bks.

--Personal Psalms. large type ed. 17p. 1984. pap. 4.50 (ISBN 0-914009-14-1). Chr Overeaters Bks.

--Pleading with the Father. large print ed. 27p. 1985. pap. 4.50 (ISBN 0-914009-36-2). Chr Overeaters Bks.

--Prayer Changes My Life. large print ed. 23p. 1985. pap. 4.00 (ISBN 0-914009-35-4). Chr Overeaters Bks.

--Prayer Meeting at Our House. large print ed. 25p. 1985. pap. 4.00 (ISBN 0-914009-33-8). Chr Overeaters Bks.

--Recovery from Compulsive Overeating. large print ed. 31p. 1985. pap. 5.00 (ISBN 0-914009-29-X). Chr Overeaters Bks.

Brians, Pearl, ed. Hangups, Health & Heaven. large print ed. 50p. pap. 9.95 (ISBN 0-9608650-0-4). Chr Overeaters Bks.

--Overeating, Its Cause & Cure. large print ed. 30p. 1983. pap. 6.00 (ISBN 0-9608650-4-7). Chr Overeaters Bks.

Briansky, Oleg, tr. see Kostrovitskaya, Vera.

Briant, C. L. Metallurgical Aspects of Environmental Failures. (Materials Science Monographs: No. 12). 248p. 1985. 65.00 (ISBN 0-444-42491-1). Elsevier.

--Metallurgy of Environmental Fracture. (Materials Science Monographs: No. 12). 300p. 1984. write for info. Elsevier.

Briar, Katharine H. The Effect of Long-Term Unemployment on Workers & Their Families. LC 77-94280. 1978. soft cover 10.00 (ISBN 0-88247-533-9). R & E Pubs.

Briar, Scott & Miller, Henry. Problems & Issues in Social Casework. LC 79-170924. 274p. 1971. 22.00x (ISBN 0-231-02771-0). Columbia U Pr.

Briarpatch Community. The Briarpatch Book: Experiences in Right Livelihood & Simple Living. LC 78-5990. (Illus.). 313p. 1978. 15.00 (ISBN 0-912078-63-4); pap. 8.00 (ISBN 0-912078-60-X). Volcano Pr.

Briarton, Grendel, pseud. Compleat Feghoot: The Lives & Times of History's Greatest Traveler. (Illus.). 1974. pap. 5.00 (ISBN 0-88358-019-5). Mirage Pr.

Briault, Eric & Smith, Frances. Falling Rolls in Secondary Schools, Pt. I. 269p. 1980. 15.00x (ISBN 0-85633-207-0, Pub. by NFER Nelson UK). Taylor & Francis.

--Falling Rolls in Secondary Schools, Pt. II. 404p. 1980. 20.00x (ISBN 0-85633-208-9, Pub. by NFER Nelson UK). Taylor & Francis.

Briaune, Michel. Des crises commerciales, de leurs causes et de leurs remedes. LC 76-147146. (Research & Source Works Ser.: No. 824). 1971. Repr. of 1840 ed. lib. bdg. 16.00 (ISBN 0-8337-0371-4). B Franklin.

Briazack, Norman J. & Mennick, Simon. The UFO Guidebook. 1978. 10.00 (ISBN 0-8065-0636-9). Citadel Pr.

Bricas, E., ed. see European Peptide Symposium, 9th, France, 1968.

Bricault, G. C., ed. Credit Control Letters in Fifteen Languages. 110p. 1984. spiral bdg. 42.50 (ISBN 0-89397-203-7). Nichols Pub.

--Major Companies of the Arab World 1985. 675p. 1980. 250.00x (ISBN 0-86010-205-X, Pub. by Graham & Trotman England); soft cover 99.00x (ISBN 0-86010-226-2). State Mutual Bk.

--Major Companies of the Arab World: 1985. 850p. 1982. 300.00x (ISBN 0-86010-330-7, Pub. by Graham & Trotman England); soft cover 232.00x (ISBN 0-86010-329-3). State Mutual Bk.

Bricca, John, tr. see Del Bo, Dino.

Brice, David K. Ion Implantation Range & Energy Deposition Distributions, Vol. 1: High Incident Ion Energies. LC 74-34119. 602p. 1975. 95.00x (ISBN 0-306-67401-7, IFI Plenum). Plenum Pub.

Brice, David K. see Chernow, Fred, et al.

Brice, Donaly. Eighteen Seventy Census: Caldwell Co., Texas. LC 84-81335. 200p. 1984. pap. 15.00 (ISBN 0-911317-35-X). Ericson Bks.

Brice, Donna. Step-By-Step Guide For Making Busts & Masks (Cold-Cast Bronze or Plaster-Hydrocal) LC 82-15703. (Illus.). 52p. 1983. 18.95 (ISBN 0-910733-00-7); pap. 10.95 (ISBN 0-910733-01-5). ICTL Pubns.

Brice, Eugene W. Books That Bring Life. 112p. 1983. pap. 7.95 (ISBN 0-937462-00-4). Net Pr.

Brice, J C. Crystal Growth. 288p. 1985. 43.00 (ISBN 0-317-14037-X, Pub by Blackie & Son UK). Heyden.

Brice, James C. & Levin, Harold L. Laboratory Studies in Earth History. 3rd ed. 224p. 1982. wire coil write for info. (ISBN 0-697-05057-2); instrs.' manual (ISBN 0-697-05058-0). Wm C Brown.

Brice, James C., et al. Laboratory Studies in Geology, 25 studies. 1962-66. looseleaf 0.75 ea. W H Freeman.

Brice, Joseph. Pentecost. 6.95 (ISBN 0-686-12901-6). Schmul Pub Co.

Brice, M. Axis Blockade Runners of World War II. (Illus.). 300p. 1981. 18.95 (ISBN 0-87021-908-1); bulk rates avail. Naval Inst Pr.

Brice, Martin. Axis Blockade Runners of World War II. LC 81-80883. 300p. 1981. 18.95 (ISBN 0-87021-908-1). Naval Inst Pr.

--Stronghold: A History of Military Architecture. (Illus.). 192p. 1984. 24.50x (ISBN 0-8052-3938-3). Schocken.

Brice, Pat, ed. see Hubbard, L. Ron.

Brice, William C., ed. The Environmental History of the Near & Middle East Since the Last Ice Age. 1978. 60.00 (ISBN 0-12-133850-9). Acad Pr.

--Europa: Studien zur Geschichte und Epigraphik der fruehen Aegaeis Festschrift fuer Ernst Grumach. (Illus., Ger.). 1967. 59.20x (ISBN 3-11-005182-6). De Gruyter.

Brichant, Colette D. Premier Guide de France: The First Year Reader. (Illus.). 1978. pap. text ed. 17.95 (ISBN 0-13-695460-X). P-H.

Brichant, Collette. French Grammar: The Key to Reading. (Orig.). 1968. pap. text ed. 15.95 (ISBN 0-13-331264-X). P-H.

Brichant, Collette, ed. French for the Humanities. 1968. pap. text ed. 13.95 (ISBN 0-13-331199-6). P-H.

Brichant, Francis. Force-Commutated Inverters: Design & Industrial Applications. Griffin, E., tr. from Fr. (Illus.). 200p. 1984. 34.95x (ISBN 0-02-948680-7). Macmillan.

Brichard, Pierre. Fishes of Lake Tanganyika. (Illus.). 1978. 29.95 (ISBN 0-87666-464-8, H-972). TFH Pubns.

Brichford, Maynard J. Archives & Manuscripts: Appraisal & Accessioning. rev. ed. LC 77-14523. (SAA Basic Manual Ser.). 24p. 1977. pap. 5.00 (ISBN 0-931828-01-5). Soc Am Archivists.

Brichford, Maynard J., et al. Manuscripts Guide to Collections at the University of Illinois at Urbana-Champaign. LC 75-38797. 384p. 1976. 17.50x (ISBN 0-252-00599-6). U of Ill Pr.

Brichta, A. & Sharp, P. E. From Project to Production. LC 79-97830. 1970. pap. 14.50 (ISBN 0-08-006639-9). Pergamon.

Bricianer, Serge. Pannekoek & the Workers' Councils. Carroll, Malachy, tr. from Fr. LC 78-50978. 1978. 16.00 (ISBN 0-914386-17-4); pap. 6.50 (ISBN 0-914386-18-2). Telos Pr.

Brick, J., jt. ed. see Pohorecky, L. A.

Brick, James, jt. auth. see Mick, John.

Brick, John R. Bank Management: Concepts & Issues. 1983. pap. 24.95 (ISBN 0-8359-0379-6). Reston.

--Commercial Banking: Text & Readings. 500p. 1984. pap. text ed. 19.95x (ISBN 0-912503-02-5). Systems Pubns.

--Financial Markets: Instruments & Concepts. 1983. pap. text ed. 24.95 (ISBN 0-8359-2030-5). Reston.

Brick, John R., ed. Bank Management: Concepts & Issues. LC 80-68804. (Banking Ser.). 551p. (Orig.). 1980. pap. 24.95 (ISBN 0-936328-00-2); pap. text ed. 16.95 (ISBN 0-686-94976-5). Dame Inc.

--Financial Markets: Instruments & Concepts. LC 81-66816. (Finance Ser.). 500p. (Orig.). 1981. pap. 22.95 (ISBN 0-936328-08-8); pap. text ed. 17.50 (ISBN 0-686-94978-1). Dame Inc.

Brick, R. M., et al. Structure & Properties of Engineering Materials. 4th ed. (McGraw-Hill Ser. in Materials Science & Engineering). (Illus.). 1977. text ed. 44.00 (ISBN 0-07-007721-5). McGraw.

Brickbauer, Elwood A. & Mortenson, William P. Approved Practices in Crop Production. 2nd ed. LC 77-89853. (Illus.). 396p. (gr. 9-12). 1978. 18.60 (ISBN 0-8134-1975-1, 1975); text ed. 13.95x. Interstate.

Bricke, John. Hume's Philosophy of Mind. LC 79-48025. 200p. 1980. 22.00 (ISBN 0-691-07255-8). Princeton U Pr.

Brickel Assoc., Inc. & Green. The Wood Chair in America. LC 82-90454. (Illus.). 120p. 1982. pap. 19.95 (ISBN 0-9609844-0-2). E & S Brickel.

Brickell, Alfred. Few, but Roses: Poems from the French. 1977. Repr. of 1924 ed. 15.00 (ISBN 0-89984-242-9). Century Bookbindery.

Brickell, C., et al. Petaloid Monocotyledons: Horticultural & Botanical Research. (Linnean Society Symposium Ser.: No.8). 1980. 75.00 (ISBN 0-12-133950-5). Acad Pr.

Brickell, Christopher. Step-by-Step Guide to Pruning. 1979. pap. 7.95 (ISBN 0-671-24831-6, Fireside). S&S.

Brickell, Henry & Paul, Regina. Minimum Competency Testing & Transferable Skills: What Can Be Learned from the Two Movements. 66p. 1978. 5.10 (ISBN 0-318-15514-1, IN 142). Natl Ctr Res Voc Ed.

Brickell, Henry M., jt. auth. see Aslanian, Carol B.

Brickell, Herschel, et al, trs. see Rojas, Ricardo.

Brickell, John. The Natural History of North Carolina. (American Studies). (Illus.). Repr. of 1737 ed. lib. bdg. 36.00 (ISBN 0-384-05740-3). Johnson Repr.

Brickell, Sean & Rothschild, Rich. The Pages of Rock History. LC 83-1957. (Illus.). 1983. pap. 6.95 (ISBN 0-89865-304-5). Donning Co.

Brickenden, Jack. We Live in Canada. (Living Here Ser.). (Illus.). 64p. 1984. PLB 10.90 (ISBN 0-531-03818-1). Watts.

Bricker, Diane D., ed. Intervention with At-Risk & Handicapped Infants. LC 82-7018. (Illus.). 296p. 1982. 22.00 (ISBN 0-936104-65-1). Pro Ed.

Bricker, Dianne D., jt. ed. see Schiefelbusch, Richard L.

Bricker, Florence M. Church & Pastoral Records in the Archives of the United Church of Christ. 1982. pap. 6.00 (ISBN 0-910564-01-9). Evang & Ref.

Bricker, George H., ed. see Schaff, Philip.

Bricker, George H., jt. ed. see Yrigoyen, Charles, Jr.

Bricker, George H, jt. ed. see Yrigoyen, Charles, Jr.

Bricker, Harvey, jt. ed. see David, Nicholas.

Bricker, Harvey M. & David, Nicholas. Excavation of the Abri Pataud, Les Eyzies (Dordogne) The Perigordian VI (Level 3) Assemblage. Movius, Hallam L., Jr., et al, eds. (American School of Prehistoric Research Bulletin Ser.: No. 34). (Illus.). 130p. (Orig.). 1984. pap. 30.00x (ISBN 0-87365-537-0). Peabody Harvard.

Bricker, Herschel L., ed. Our Theatre Today. facs. ed. LC 79-128213. (Essay Index Reprint Ser). 1936. 32.00 (ISBN 0-8369-1823-1). Ayer Co Pubs.

Bricker, J. Douglas, jt. auth. see Gossel, Thomas A.

Bricker, Neal S. & Kirschenbaum, Michael A. The Kidney: Diagnosis & Management. LC 82-24753. 540p. 1984. 37.50x (ISBN 0-471-09572-9, Pub. by Wiley Med). Wiley.

Bricker, Owen P. & Teasley, John I., eds. Geological Effects of Acid Deposition. (Acid Percipitation Ser.: Vol. 7). 160p. 1984. text ed. 32.50 (ISBN 0-250-40572-5). Butterworth.

Bricker, Owen P., et al. Seminar on Organism-Sediment Interrelationships, 1971. (Bermuda Biological Station Special Pubn.: No. 9). (Illus.). ii, 171p. 1971. pap. 9.00 (ISBN 0-917642-09-0). Bermuda Bio.

Bricker, Victoria R. The Indian Christ, the Indian King: The Historical Substrate of Maya Myth & Ritual. (Illus.). 382p. 1981. text ed. 45.00x (ISBN 0-292-73824-2). U of Tex Pr.

--Ritual Humor in Highland Chiapas. LC 73-6501. (Texas Pan American Ser). (Illus.). 293p. 1973. 20.00x (ISBN 0-292-77004-9). U of Tex Pr.

--Ritual Humor in Highland Chiapas. (Texas Pan American Series & Texas Press Sourcebooks in Anthropology: No. 12). (Illus.). 278p. 1983. pap. 8.95 (ISBN 0-292-77029-4). U of Tex Pr.

Bricker, Victoria R. & Edmonson, Munro S., eds. Supplement to the Handbook of Middle American Indians, Vol. 2: Linguistics. 156p. 1984. text ed. 35.00x (ISBN 0-292-77577-6). U of Tex Pr.

--Supplement to the Handbook of Middle American Indians, Vol. 3: Literatures. 224p. 1985. text ed. 35.00x (ISBN 0-292-77593-8). U of Tex Pr.

Bricker, Victoria R. & Sabloff, Jeremy A., eds. Supplement to the Handbook of Middle American Indians: Vol. 1, Archaeology. (Illus.). 475p. 1981. text ed. 55.00x (ISBN 0-292-77556-3). U of Tex Pr.

Bricker-Jenkins, Mary & Hoojman, Nancy, eds. Not for Women Only: Social Work Practice in a Feminist Future. 1985. 6.95 (ISBN 0-87101-131-X). Natl Assn Soc Wkrs.

Brickey, Homer, Jr. Master Manipulator. LC 85-47675. 192p. 1985. 15.95 (ISBN 0-8144-5818-1). Amacom.

Brickey, Kathy. Corporate Criminal Liability, 3 vols. LC 84-9465. 1984. 190.00. Callaghan.

Brickham, Jack M. The Regensburg Legacy. 288p. 1983. pap. 2.95 (ISBN 0-523-48062-8, Pinnacle Bks). Tor Bks.

Brickhill, Paul. The Great Escape. 1978. pap. 2.50 (ISBN 0-449-23717-6, Crest). Fawcett.

Brickley, James E. The Dear Old Book of Hattie Thomas. 247p. 1983. write for info. J E Brickley.

Bricklin, Alice G. Motherlove: Natural Mothering, Birth to Three Years. Williams, Betsy, ed. LC 79-9724. 1979. lib. bdg. 12.90 (ISBN 0-89471-070-2); pap. 4.95 (ISBN 0-89471-069-9). Running Pr.

Bricklin, Barry, et al. Hand Test: A New Projective Test with Special Reference to the Prediction of Overt Aggressive Behavior. 112p. 1981. 14.75x (ISBN 0-398-00223-1). C C Thomas.

Bricklin, Mark. Lose Weight Naturally: The No-Diet, No Willpower Plan from Prevention Magazine. 1979. 14.95 (ISBN 0-87857-252-X). Rodale Pr Inc.

--The Practical Encyclopedia of Natural Healing. LC 76-26864. 1976. 19.95 (ISBN 0-87857-136-1). Rodale Pr Inc.

--The Practical Encyclopedia of Natural Healing. rev. ed. (Illus.). 592p. 1983. 21.95 (ISBN 0-87857-480-8). Rodale Pr Inc.

--Rodale's Encyclopedia of Natural Home Remedies. (Illus.). 528p. 1982. 19.95 (ISBN 0-87857-396-8). Rodale Pr Inc.

Bricklin, Mark & Claessens, Charon. Natural Healing Cookbook: Over Four Hundred Fifty Delicious Ways to Get Better & Stay Healthy. (Illus.). 496p. 1981. 24.95 (ISBN 0-87857-338-0); deluxe 27.95 (ISBN 0-87857-358-5). Rodale Pr Inc.

Bricklin, Mark, ed. see Padus, Emrika.

Brickman, Bruce. Legal Aspects of Acquiring & Protecting Software. 343p. 1984. looseleaf 59.95 (ISBN 0-935506-26-8). Carnegie Pr.

Brickman, Bruce K. Solving the Computer Contract Dilemma: A How-To Book for Decision Makers. 176p. pap. 21.95 (6259). Hayden.

Brickman, Richard, jt. auth. see Irwin, Robert.

Brickman, Ronald, et al. Controlling Chemicals: The Politics of Regulation in Europe & the United States. LC 84-29340. 336p. 1985. 34.95x (ISBN 0-8014-1677-9). Cornell U Pr.

Brickman, W. W. Research in Educational History. 1985. 62.50 (ISBN 0-317-19974-9). Porter.

Brickman, William E., ed. & compiled by. The Jewish Community in America: An Annotated & Classified Bibliographical Guide. (Ethnic Bibliographical Ser: No. 2). 1977. PLB 19.95 (ISBN 0-89102-057-8). B Franklin.

Brickman, William W. Bibliographical Essays on Comparative & International Education. LC 76-28420. 1976. Repr. of 1975 ed. lib. bdg. 25.00 (ISBN 0-8414-1783-0). Folcroft.

--Bibliographical Essays on Curriculum & Instruction. LC 76-45180. 1976. lib. bdg. 25.00 (ISBN 0-8414-1778-4). Folcroft.

--Bibliographical Essays on Educational Reference Works. 1978. Repr. of 1975 ed. lib. bdg. 25.00 (ISBN 0-8414-1735-0). Folcroft.

--Bibliographical Essays on the History & Philosophy of Education. LC 76-25428. 1976. Repr. of 1975 ed. lib. bdg. 25.00 (ISBN 0-8414-3244-9). Folcroft.

--Comparative Education: Concepts, Research & Application. LC 73-16718. (Educational Ser). Repr. of 1949 ed. 35.00 (ISBN 0-88305-091-9). Norwood Edns.

--Education in Russia from the Middle Ages to the Present. LC 83-48214. (Education Ser.). 330p. 1985. lib. bdg. 45.00 (ISBN 0-8240-9052-7). Garland Pub.

--Educational Roots & Routes in Western Europe. LC 85-70176. viii, 404p. (Orig.). 1985. pap. 19.00 (ISBN 0-943694-01-9). Emeritus Inc.

--Ideas & Issues in Educational Thought, Past & Recent. 1978. lib. bdg. 35.00 (ISBN 0-8482-7368-0). Norwood Edns.

--Research in Educational History. LC 73-17650. 1973. Repr. 37.50 (ISBN 0-88305-097-8). Norwood Edns.

--The Thomas Woody Collection. LC 73-18795. 1973. Repr. 27.50 (ISBN 0-88305-093-5). Norwood Edns.

--Two Millenia of International Relations in Higher Education. 263p. 1980. Repr. of 1976 ed. lib. bdg. 30.00 (ISBN 0-8414-1660-5). Folcroft.

Brickman, William W. & Lehrer, Stanley. A Century of Higher Education: Classical Citadel to Collegiate Colossus. LC 73-17857. 293p. 1974. Repr. of 1962 ed. lib. bdg. 17.25x (ISBN 0-8371-7267-5, BCHE). Greenwood.

Brickman, William W. & Lehrer, Stanley, eds. John Dewey. LC 73-17858. (Illus.). 172p. 1975. Repr. of 1965 ed. lib. bdg. 15.00x (ISBN 0-8371-7268-3, BRJD). Greenwood.

--Religion, Government & Education. LC 77-24684. 1977. Repr. of 1961 ed. lib. bdg. 20.00x (ISBN 0-8371-9749-X, BRRG). Greenwood.

Brickman, William W., jt. ed. see Cordasco, Francesco.

Brickman, William W., ed. see De Garmo, Charles.

Brickman, William W., ed. see Hazelton, M. W.

Brickman, William W., ed. see Payne, W. H.

Brickman, William W., ed. see Shuttleworth, James K.

Bricknell, Rodger H., ed. see Fifth International Symposium on Superalloys, Champion, Pennsylvania, Oct. 7-11, 1984, et al.

Brickner, Balfour & Vorspan, Albert. Searching the Prophets for Values. 1981. 6.95 (ISBN 0-8074-0047-5). UAHC.

Brickner, Dave, et al. Annotated BASIC: A New Technique for Neophytes, Vol. 2. McCarthy, Nan & Crocker, Chris, eds. (Illus.). 125p. 1982. pap. 10.95 (ISBN 0-88006-037-9, BK 7385). Green Pub Inc.

Brickner, Philip, et al. Health Care of Homeless People. 368p. 1985. 29.95 (ISBN 0-8261-4990-1). Springer Pub.

Brickner, Richard. Tickets. 256p. 1982. pap. 3.25 (ISBN 0-441-80701-1). Ace Bks.

Brickner, Richard P. Bringing down the House. 1977. pap. 1.75 (ISBN 0-505-51139-8, Pub. by Tower Bks). Dorchester Pub Co.

Bricktop & Haskins, James. Bricktop. LC 82-73006. 320p. 1983. 15.95 (ISBN 0-689-11349-8). Atheneum.

Briconnet, Guillaume, et al, eds. see Marguerite D'Angouleme, Reine de Navarre.

Bricose, Jill. Here Am I; Send Aaron! 1984. pap. 2.95 (ISBN 0-89693-712-7). Victor Bks.

Bricq, Ron S. Technically Write! Communicating in a Technological Era. 2nd ed. (Illus.). 448p. 1981. pap. text ed. 20.95 (ISBN 0-13-898700-9). P-H.

Bridbury, A. R. Economic Growth: England in the Later Middle Ages. LC 83-8540. xxiv, 115p. 1983. Repr. of 1975 ed. lib. bdg. 25.00 (ISBN 0-313-24066-3, BREG). Greenwood.

--England & the Salt Trade in the Later Middle Ages. LC 73-9261. (Illus.). 198p. 1973. Repr. of 1955 ed. lib. bdg. 15.00x (ISBN 0-8371-7001-X, BRES). Greenwood.

--Medieval English Clothmaking: An Economic Survey. (Pasold Studies in Textile History). 160p. 1982. 27.50x (ISBN 0-435-32138-2). Gower Pub Co.

Bridel, ed. see Bernanos, Georges.

Bridenbaugh, Carl. Cities in Revolt: Urban Life in America, 1743-1776. (Illus.). 1971. pap. 9.95 (ISBN 0-19-501362-X, GB). Oxford U Pr.

--Early Americans. (Illus.). 1981. 22.50x (ISBN 0-19-502788-4). Oxford U Pr.

--Jamestown, Fifteen Forty-Four to Sixteen Ninity-Nine. (Illus.). 1980. 25.00x (ISBN 0-19-502650-0). Oxford U Pr.

--Myths & Realities: Societies of the Colonial South. LC 52-13024. 1963. pap. text ed. 2.95x (ISBN 0-689-70023-7, 17). Atheneum.

--Myths & Realities: Societies of the Colonial South. LC 80-25280. (The Walter Lynwood Fleming Lectures in Southern History Ser., Louisiana State University). x, 208p. 1981. Repr. of 1952 ed. lib. bdg. 19.75x (ISBN 0-313-22770-5, BRMR). Greenwood.

--Silas Downer - Forgotten Patriot: His Life & Writings. LC 74-83462. (Rhode Island Revolutionary Heritage Ser.: Vol. 1). (Illus.). 1974. 3.75 (ISBN 0-917012-01-1). Ri Pubns Soc.

--Spirit of Seventy-Six: The Growth of American Patriotism Before Independence. 1975. 16.95x (ISBN 0-19-501931-8). Oxford U Pr.

--Spirit of Seventy-Six: The Growth of American Patriotism Before Independence, 1607-1776. LC 75-4323. 1975. pap. 5.95 (ISBN 0-19-502179-7, 488, GB). Oxford U Pr.

--Vexed & Troubled Englishmen, 1590-1642. 1968. 25.00x (ISBN 0-19-500493-0). Oxford U Pr.

Bridenbaugh, Carl & Bridenbaugh, Jessica. Rebels & Gentlemen: Philadelphia in the Age of Franklin. LC 78-657. (Illus.). 1978. Repr. of 1942 ed. lib. bdg. 31.25x (ISBN 0-313-20300-8, BRRE). Greenwood.

Bridenbaugh, Carl & Tomlinson, Juliette, eds. The Pynchon Papers: Selections from the Account Books of John Pynchon, Vol. II. 500p. 1985. 30.00x (ISBN 0-8139-1074-9, Colonial Soc MA). U Pr of Va.

Bridenbaugh, Carl, ed. & intro. by see Hamilton, Alexander.

Bridenbaugh, Jessica, jt. auth. see Bridenbaugh, Carl.

Bridenbaugh, Phillip O., jt. auth. see Cousins, Michael J.

Bridenbecker, Henry. A Scratch Modeler's Log. Gentle, Ernest J., ed. (Illus.). 112p. (Orig.). 1985. pap. 17.95 (ISBN 0-317-07652-3). Aero.

--A Scratch Modelers Log. (Moonraker Ser.). 112p. 1985. 17.95 (ISBN 0-8168-0014-6). Aero.

Bridenhagen, Keith. Decoy Pattern Book. LC 84-16242. (Illus.). 128p. (Orig.). 1985. pap. 9.95 (ISBN 0-8069-7898-8). Sterling.

--Realistic Decoys. 224p. 1985. pap. 14.95 (ISBN 0-88317-129-5). Stoeger Pub Co.

Bridenhagen, Keith & Spielman, Patrick. Realistic Decoys: Carving, Texturing, Painting & Finishing. LC 84-8608. (Illus.). 232p. (Orig.). 1985. pap. 14.95 (ISBN 0-8069-7908-9). Sterling.

Bridenthal, Renate & Koonz, Claudia. Becoming Visible: Women in European History. LC 76-11978. 1977. pap. text ed. 15.95 (ISBN 0-395-24477-3). HM.

Bridenthal, Renate, et al. When Biology Became Destiny: Women in Weimar & Nazi Germany. (New Feminist Library). 416p. 1984. 27.50 (ISBN 0-85345-642-9); pap. 12.00 (ISBN 0-85345-643-7). Monthly Rev.

Bride's Magazine. Bride's Lifetime Guide to Good Food & Entertaining. (Illus.). 320p. 1984. 25.00 (ISBN 0-312-92067-9). Congdon & Weed.

Bride's Magazine Editors. Bride's Book of Etiquette: Golden Anniversary Edition. (Illus.). 240p. 1985. 16.95 (ISBN 0-399-51096-6, Perigee); pap. 6.95 (ISBN 0-399-51084-2). Putnam Pub Group.

--The Bride's Wedding Planner. 1982. pap. 6.95 (ISBN 0-449-90005-3, Columbine). Fawcett.

--The New Bride's Book of Etiquette. rev. ed. Conde Nast, ed. LC 80-84126. (Illus.). 1981. pap. 5.95 (ISBN 0-399-50775-2, Perigee). Putnam Pub Group.

--Questions & Answers about Love & Sex. LC 78-21401. 1979. 8.95 (ISBN 0-312-66041-3). St Martin.

Bride's Magazine Editors & Calderone, Mary. Questions & Answers about Love & Sex. 144p. 1980. pap. 2.95 (ISBN 0-380-52977-7, 65615-9). Avon.

Bridge, Anthony. Suleiman the Magnificent. (Illus.). 256p. 1983. 18.95 (ISBN 0-531-09897-4). Watts.

--Theodora: Portrait in a Byzantine Landscape. (Illus.). 194p. 1984. Repr. of 1978 ed. 13.95 (ISBN 0-89733-102-8). Academy Chi Pubs.

Bridge, Antony. The Crusades. (Illus.). 320p. 1982. 17.95 (ISBN 0-531-09872-9). Watts.

Bridge, Brian. Employment Services for the Disadvantaged: Research Paper. 1977. 20.00x (ISBN 0-317-05805-3, Pub. by Natl Inst Social Work). State Mutual Bk.

Bridge, C. R., jt. ed. see Close, D. H.

Bridge, Carl J. Alcoholism & Driving. (Illus.). 96p. 1972. 13.75x (ISBN 0-398-02243-7). C C Thomas.

Bridge, Darlene. The I in You. 1973. pap. 4.95 (ISBN 0-915358-01-8). Bridgeberg.

Bridge, Donald & Phypers, David. Communion: The Meal That Unites? LC 82-62820. 192p. 1983. pap. 5.95 (ISBN 0-87788-160-X). Shaw Pubs.

--Growing in God's Family. 160p. pap. 3.50 (ISBN 0-87788-330-0). Shaw Pubs.

Bridge, Frederick. The Old Cryes of London. LC 74-24050. 1976. Repr. of 1921 ed. 17.50 (ISBN 0-404-12872-6). AMS Pr.

--Old Cryes of London. LC 77-75209. 1977. Repr. of 1921 ed. lib. bdg. 12.50 (ISBN 0-89341-109-4). Longwood Pub Group.

--Shakespearean Music in the Plays & Early Operas. LC 68-358. (Studies in Shakespeare, No. 24). 1969. Repr. of 1923 ed. lib. bdg. 39.95x (ISBN 0-8383-0513-X). Haskell.

--Twelve Good Musicians: From John Bull to Henry Purcell. LC 77-75210. 1977. Repr. of 1920 ed. lib. bdg. 17.50 (ISBN 0-89341-110-8). Longwood Pub Group.

--Twelve Good Musicians: From John Bull to Henry Purcell. 152p. 1984. pap. 6.50 cancelled (ISBN 0-89341-527-8). Longwood Pub Group.

Bridge, Horatio. Journal of an African Cruiser. LC 78-92421. 1853. 19.00x (ISBN 0-403-00154-4). Scholarly.

--Personal Recollections of Nathaniel Hawthorne. LC 68-24931. (Studies in Hawthorne, No. 15). 1969. Repr. of 1893 ed. lib. bdg. 75.00 (ISBN 0-8383-0916-X). Haskell.

Bridge, J. Bai & Sapirie, S. Health Project Management: A Manual of Procedures for Formulating & Implementing Health Projects. (Offset Pub.: No. 12). (Also avail. in French). 1974. pap. 15.20 (ISBN 92-4-170012-2). World Health.

Bridge, James H. The Inside History of the Carnegie Steel Company. LC 73-38274. (The Evolution of Capitalism Ser.). 390p. 1972. Repr. of 1903 ed. 34.50 (ISBN 0-405-04112-8). Ayer Co Pubs.

--Millionaires & Grub Street: Comrades - Contacts in the Last Half Century. facs. ed. LC 68-8441. (Essay Index Reprint Ser). (Illus.). 1968. Repr. of 1931 ed. 20.00 (ISBN 0-8369-0253-X). Ayer Co Pubs.

--Uncle Sam at Home. LC 73-13153. (Foreign Travelers in America, 1810-1935 Ser.). (Illus.). 248p. 1974. Repr. 18.00x (ISBN 0-405-05446-7). Ayer Co Pubs.

Bridge, James H., ed. The Trust: Its Book. LC 73-1995. (Big Business; Economic Power in a Free Society Ser.). Repr. of 1902 ed. 18.00 (ISBN 0-405-05077-1). Ayer Co Pubs.

Bridge, Jane. Beginning Model Theory: The Completeness Theorem & Some Consequences. (Oxford Logic Guides Ser.). 1977. 17.95x (ISBN 0-19-853157-5). Oxford U Pr.

Bridge, John & Dodds, J. C. Planning & the Growth of the Firm. 211p. 1978. 28.00 (ISBN 0-85664-362-9, Pub. by Croom Helm Ltd). Longwood Pub Group.

Bridge, John F. Shakespearean Music in the Plays & Early Operas. LC 75-153307. Repr. of 1923 ed. 16.50 (ISBN 0-404-07808-7). AMS Pr.

Bridge, John S. A History of France from the Death of Louis Sixteenth, 5 vols. 1972. lib. bdg. 112.00 (ISBN 0-374-90984-9). Octagon.

Bridge, R. Gary, et al. The Determinants of Educational Outcomes: Impact of Families, Peers, Teachers & Schools. LC 78-26467. 384p. 1979. prof. ref. 29.95 (ISBN 0-88410-182-7). Ballinger Pub.

Bridge, Raymond. America's Backpacking Book. rev. ed. 1981. Encore Ed. 6.95 (ISBN 0-684-16872-3, ScribT). Scribner.

--Bike Touring: The Sierra Club Guide to Outings on Wheels. LC 79-474. (Outdoor Activities Guide Ser.). (Illus.). 464p. 1979. pap. 8.95 (ISBN 0-87156-250-2). Sierra.

--New Complete Snow Camper's Guide. (Illus.). 416p. 1981. encore ed. 7.95 (ISBN 0-684-16842-1, ScribT). Scribner.

--Running Without Pain: Avoiding & Treating Injury. 1980. pap. 6.95 (ISBN 0-385-27105-0, Dial). Doubleday.

--Tour Guide to the Rocky Mountain Wilderness. LC 80-10598. (Illus.). 1980. pap. 5.95 (ISBN 0-87108-557-7). Pruett.

Bridge, Roy, jt. auth. see Bullen, Roger.

Bridge, Ruth E. Challenge of Change: Three Centuries of Enfield, Connecticut History. LC 77-7148. (Illus.). 1977. 6.50x (ISBN 0-914016-43-1). Phoenix Pub.

Bridge, Ursula, ed. see Yeats, William B.

Bridge, W. & MacLeod, C. J. Communication in Nursing Care. 176p. 1981. 10.95 (ISBN 0-471-25604-8, Pub. by Wiley Heyden). Wiley.

Bridge, William. A Lifting up for the Downcast. 1979. pap. 4.45 (ISBN 0-85151-298-4). Banner of Truth.

Bridgeforth, Med. Another Chance. LC 73-18569. Repr. of 1951 ed. 12.50 (ISBN 0-404-11379-6). AMS Pr.

Bridgeland, Michael, tr. see Kaup, Ludger & Kaup, Burchard.

Bridgeland, William M. & Duane, Edward A., eds. Young Children & Social Policy. (The Annals of the American Academy of Political & Social Science Ser.: Vol. 461). (Illus.). 224p. 1982. 15.00 (ISBN 0-8039-1831-3); pap. 7.95 (ISBN 0-8039-1832-1). Sage.

Bridgeman, jt. auth. see Drury, Elizabeth.

Bridgeman, Bruce & Bridgeman, Dinae, eds. Readings on Fundamental Issues on Learning & Memory. 343p. 1977. pap. text ed. 14.95x (ISBN 0-8422-0548-9). Irvington.

Bridgeman, Cunningham, jt. auth. see Cellier, Francois.

Bridgeman, Diane L., ed. The Nature of Prosocial Development: Interdisciplinary Theories & Strategies. (Developmental Psychology Ser.). 1983. 39.00 (ISBN 0-12-133980-7). Acad Pr.

Bridgeman, Dinae, jt. ed. see Bridgeman, Bruce.

Bridgeman, George B. Bridgman's Life Drawing. 15.50 (ISBN 0-8446-0038-5). Peter Smith.

--Heads, Features & Faces. LC 74-78681. 1974. lib. bdg. 10.50x (ISBN 0-88307-602-0). Gannon.

Bridgeman, J. C., jt. auth. see Davis, H. C.

Bridgeman, Peter. Trees for Town & Country. LC 79-52380. (Illus.). 1979. 18.95 (ISBN 0-7153-7841-4). David & Charles.

Bridgeman, T., jt. auth. see Baldock, G. R.

Bridgeman, William & Hazard, Jacqueline. The Lonely Sky. Gilbert, James, ed. LC 79-7232. (Flight: Its First Seventy-Five Years Ser.). (Illus.). 1979. Repr. of 1955 ed. lib. bdg. 27.50x (ISBN 0-405-12148-2). Ayer Co Pubs.

Bridger & Wolk. The New Jewish Encyclopedia. rev. ed. LC 76-15251. (Illus.). 542p. 1976. 14.95 (ISBN 0-87441-120-3). Behrman.

Bridger, David. Hebrew & Heritage, 4 vols. LC 75-1812. (Illus.). 1976. Vol. I. pap. 3.95x (ISBN 0-87441-254-4); Vol. II. pap. 3.95x (ISBN 0-87441-252-8); Vol. III. pap. 3.95x (ISBN 0-87441-259-5); Vol. IV. pap. 3.95x (ISBN 0-87441-274-9). Behrman.

--Programmed Hebrew Series, 2 vols. Incl. Vol. 1. 1971. pap. text ed. 3.50x (ISBN 0-87441-079-7); Vol. 2. 1971. pap. text ed. 3.50x (ISBN 0-87441-080-0). (Reshit Tefillah V'lashon). 62p. (Prog. Bk.). (YA) pap. Behrman.

Bridger, J. P. & Foster, J. J. Glossary of United Kingdom Fishing Gear Terms. 128p. 1981. 47.25 (ISBN 0-85238-119-0, FN95, FNB). Unipub.

Bridger, M., jt. auth. see Auslander, M.

Bridger, William A. & Hendessen, J. Frank. Cell ATP. LC 82-24797. (Transport in Life Science Ser.). 170p. 1983. 59.95 (ISBN 0-471-08507-3, Pub. by Wiley-Interscience). Wiley.

Bridgers, Sue E. All Together Now. (YA) 1979. PLB 8.99 (ISBN 0-394-94098-9). Knopf.

--Home Before Dark. (gr. 6 up). 1985. pap. 2.25 (ISBN 0-553-24354-3). Bantam.

--Home Before Dark. LC 76-8661. (gr. 6 up). 1976. 10.95 (ISBN 0-394-83299-X). Knopf.

--Notes for Another Life. LC 81-1673. 256p. (YA) 1981. 9.95 (ISBN 0-394-84889-6); PLB 10.99 (ISBN 0-394-94889-0). Knopf.

--Sara Will. LC 84-48139. 288p. 1985. 15.34i (ISBN 0-06-015385-7, HarpT). Har-Row.

Bridges, jt. auth. see Brambilla, F.

Bridges, Amy. A City in the Republic: Antebellum New York & the Origins of Machine Politics. (Illus.). 208p. 1984. 29.95 (ISBN 0-521-24721-7). Cambridge U Pr.

Bridges, B. A. Bacterial Reaction to Radiation. 78p. 1976. 39.00x (ISBN 0-904095-21-5, Pub. by Meadowfield Pr England). State Mutual Bk.

Bridges, B. A. & Harnden, D. G. Ataxia Telangiectasia: A Cellular & Molecular Link Between Cancer, Neuropathology & Immune Deficiency. LC 81-13146. 424p. 1982. 50.00x (ISBN 0-471-10055-2, Pub. by Wiley Med). Wiley.

Bridges, Brian, ed. see Harris, Stuart.

Bridges, Bryn A., jt. auth. see Friedberg, Errol G.

Bridges, Bryn A., et al, eds. Banbury Report 13: Indicators of Genotoxic Exposure. LC 82-12972. (Banbury Report Ser.: Vol. 13). 580p. 1982. 62.50X (ISBN 0-87969-212-X). Cold Spring Harbor.

Bridges, Charles. The Christian Ministry. 1980. 13.95 (ISBN 0-85151-087-6). Banner of Truth.

--Ecclesiastes. 319p. 1981. Repr. 10.95 (ISBN 0-85151-322-0). Banner of Truth.

--Proverbs. (Geneva Commentaries Ser.). 1979. 15.95 (ISBN 0-85151-088-4). Banner of Truth.

--Psalm One Hundred Nineteen. 1977. 12.95 (ISBN 0-85151-176-7). Banner of Truth.

Bridges, Charles W. & Lunsford, Ronald F. Writing: Discovering Form & Meaning. 399p. 1984. text ed. write for info. (ISBN 0-534-02998-1). Wadsworth Pub.

Bridges, Christina. The Hero. (Illus.). 29p. (gr. k-6). 1981. pap. text ed. 8.95 (ISBN 0-917002-39-3). Joyce Media.

Bridges, D., jt. auth. see Bishop, E.

Bridges, David. Education, Democracy & Discussion. 184p. 1979. 16.00x (ISBN 0-85633-176-7, Pub. by NFER Nelson UK). Taylor & Francis.

Bridges, David & Bailey, Charles. Mixed Ability Grouping: A Philosophical Perspective. (Introductory Studies in Philosophy of Education). 96p. 1983. text ed. 19.95x (ISBN 0-04-370134-5); pap. text ed. 7.50x (ISBN 0-04-370135-3). Allen Unwin.

Bridges, David & Naylor, Helen. The Commodore Disk & Printer Handbook. (Illus.). 192p. 1984. pap. 14.95 (ISBN 0-946576-23-8, Pub. by Phoenix Pub). David & Charles.

Bridges, Derek, jt. auth. see Tovey, John.

Bridges, Douglas S. Constructive Functional Analysis. (Research Notes in Mathematics Ser.: No. 28). 203p. (Orig.). 1979. pap. text ed. 23.95 (ISBN 0-273-08418-6). Pitman Pub MA.

Bridges, E. M. World Soils. 2nd ed. LC 77-90204. (Illus.). 1979. 32.50 (ISBN 0-521-21956-6); pap. 11.95 (ISBN 0-521-29339-1). Cambridge U Pr.

Bridges, E. M. & Davidson, D. A., eds. Principles & Applications of Soil Geography. LC 80-41509. (Illus.). 320p. 1982. text ed. 15.95x (ISBN 0-582-30014-2). Longman.

Bridges, Edwin M. Managing the Incompetent Teacher. rev. ed. LC 84-80939. x, 81p. 1984. pap. 4.25 (ISBN 0-86552-086-0). U of Oreg ERIC.

Bridges, G. Wilson. Annals of Jamaica, 2 vols. 1968. Repr. of 1828 ed. Set. 95.00x (ISBN 0-7146-1931-0, F Cass Co). Biblio Dist.

Bridges, Geoffrey G. Identity & Distinction in Petrus Thomae. (Philosophy Ser). 1959. 10.00 (ISBN 0-686-11544-9). Franciscan Inst.

Bridges, George. Forty IBM PCjr Programs for Home, School & Office. 96p. 1984. 7.95 (ISBN 0-86668-037-3). ARCsoft.

--IBM PCjr Charts & Graphs. 96p. 1984. 7.95 (ISBN 0-86668-042-X). ARCsoft.

--IBM PCjr Games Programs. 96p. 1984. 7.95 (ISBN 0-86668-036-5). ARCsoft.

--IBM PCjr Personal Finance Programs. 96p. 1984. 7.95 (ISBN 0-86668-043-8). ARCsoft.

--The IBM PCjr Songbook. 96p. 1984. 7.95 (ISBN 0-86668-041-1). ARCsoft.

--IBM Personal Computer Program Writing Workbook. 96p. 1983. 4.95 (ISBN 0-86668-818-8). ARCsoft.

--One Hundred One Programming Tips & Tricks for IBM PCjr. 136p. 1984. 8.95 (ISBN 0-86668-038-1). ARCsoft.

Bridges, George W. Annals of Jamaica, 2 Vols. LC 76-106830. Repr. of 1827 ed. 38.00x set (ISBN 0-8371-3452-8, BJA&, Pub. by Negro U Pr). Greenwood.

Bridges, Herb. The Filming of Gone with the Wind: A Photographic Essay. LC 83-23624. (Illus.). 291p. 1983. 27.95 (ISBN 0-86554-073-X, MUP/H43). Mercer Univ Pr.

Bridges, Horace J. As I Was Saying. facs. ed. LC 70-121451. (Essay Index Reprint Ser). 1923. 19.00 (ISBN 0-8369-1698-0). Ayer Co Pubs.

--Criticisms of Life. facsimile ed. LC 75-99684. (Essay Index Reprint Ser). 1915. 20.00 (ISBN 0-8369-1342-6). Ayer Co Pubs.

--God of Fundamentalism & Others Studies. facs. ed. LC 79-86733. (Essay Index Reprint Ser). 1925. 19.00 (ISBN 0-8369-1249-7). Ayer Co Pubs.

--Humanity on Trial. facs. ed. LC 74-142609. (Essay Index Reprint Ser). 1941. 20.00 (ISBN 0-8369-2039-2). Ayer Co Pubs.

--Our Fellow Shakespeare. LC 73-494. 1974. lib. bdg. 30.00 (ISBN 0-8414-1500-5). Folcroft.

--Taking the Name of Science in Vain. facs. ed. LC 72-86734. (Essay Index Reprint Ser). 1928. 18.00 (ISBN 0-8369-1168-7). Ayer Co Pubs.

Bridges, Horace J., ed. Aspects of Ethical Religion: Essays in Honor of Felix Adler on the Fiftieth Anniversary of His Founding of the Ethical Movement. facs. ed. LC 68-29190. (Essay Index Reprint Ser). 1968. Repr. of 1926 ed. 20.00 (ISBN 0-8369-0161-4). Ayer Co Pubs.

--Aspects of Ethical Religion: Essays in Honor of Felix Adler. 1977. lib. bdg. 59.95 (ISBN 0-8490-1459-X). Gordon Pr.

Bridges, J. F. Double Counterpoint & Canon. 59.95 (ISBN 0-8490-0059-9). Gordon Pr.

Bridges, J. W. & Chasseaud, L. F. Progress in Drug Metabolism, Vol. 5. LC 80-40128. (Progress in Drug Metabolism Ser.). 362p. 1980. 104.00 (ISBN 0-471-27776-2, Pub. by Wiley-Interscience). Wiley.

--Progress in Drug Metabolism, Vol. 6. LC 80-42314. (Progress in Drug Metabolism Ser.). 320p. 1981. 79.95x (ISBN 0-471-28023-2, Pub. by Wiley Interscience). Wiley.

--Progress in Drug Metabolism, Vol. 7. (Drug Metabolism Ser.). 446p. 1983. 96.95 (ISBN 0-471-10487-6). Wiley.

Bridges, J. W. & Chasseaud, L. F., eds. Progress in Drug Metabolism, Vols. 1-4. Incl. Vol. 1. 286p. 1976. 68.95x (ISBN 0-471-10370-5); Vol. 2. 350p. 1977. 79.95 (ISBN 0-471-99442-1); Vol. 3. LC 75-19446. 372p. 1979. 84.95x (ISBN 0-471-99711-0); Vol. 4. LC 79-42723. 335p. 1980. 89.95x (ISBN 0-471-27702-9). Pub. by Wiley-Interscience). Wiley.

--Progress in Drug Metabolism, Vol. 8. 407p. 1984. 77.00x (ISBN 0-85066-269-9). Taylor & Francis.

Bridges, J. W. & Gorrod, J. W., eds. Biological Oxidation of Nitrogen in Organic Molecules. 282p. 1972. cancelled (ISBN 0-85066-058-0). Taylor & Francis.

Bridges, James W. An Experimental Study of Decision Types & Their Mental Correlates. Bd. with Genetic Aspect of Consonance & Dissonance. Moore, H. T. Repr. of 1914 ed; Influence of Distractions. Mitchell, D. Repr. of 1914 ed; Yale Psychological Studies. Angier, R. P., ed. (New Ser.: Vol. 2, No. 1). Repr. of 1914 ed; Measurement of Attention. Woodrow, H. Repr. of 1914 ed. (Psychology Monographs General & Applied: Vol. 17). pap. 29.00 (ISBN 0-317-16767-7). Kraus Repr.

Bridges, Jerry. The Practice of Godliness. LC 83-61499. 272p. 1983. pap. 3.95 (ISBN 0-89109-497-0). NavPress.

--The Practice of Godliness. 272p. 1985. 8.95 (ISBN 0-89109-466-0). NavPress.

--The Pursuit of Holiness. LC 78-18109. 158p. 1978. pap. 3.50 (ISBN 0-89109-430-X, 14308). NavPress.

--The Pursuit of Holiness. 160p. 1985. 8.95 (ISBN 0-89109-467-9). NavPress.

Bridges, John H. Illustrations of Positivism. Jones, H. Gordon, ed. LC 77-170184. 1974. Repr. of 1915 ed. lib. bdg. 32.00 (ISBN 0-8337-4003-2). B Franklin.

--The Life & Work of Roger Bacon. Jones, H. Gordon, ed. LC 79-8597. Repr. of 1914 ed. 21.50 (ISBN 0-404-18450-2). AMS Pr.

--The Life & Work of Roger Bacon: An Introduction to the Opus Majus. Jones, H. Gordon, ed. LC 76-1120. 1977. Repr. of 1914 ed. lib. bdg. 15.00x (ISBN 0-915172-14-3). Richwood Pub.

Bridges, Julian C. & Estudio, Guias de. Guia De Estudios Sobre Bases Biblicas De la Etica. 96p. 1982. Repr. of 1973 ed. 4.50 (ISBN 0-311-43505-X). Casa Bautista.

Bridges, Julian C., ed. Sociology: A Pragmatic Approach. 2nd ed. (Illus.). 379p. 1982. pap. text ed. 21.95x (ISBN 0-89459-169-X). Hunter Textbks.

Bridges, Kent W. see Mueller-Dombois, Dieter.

Bridges, L. T. Flags of Louisiana. (ps-8). 1971. 3.95 (ISBN 0-87511-010-X). Claitors.

Bridges, Laurie. The Ashton Horror. (Dark Forces Ser.: No. 12). 160p. (gr. 7 up). 1984. pap. 2.25 (ISBN 0-553-25104-X). Bantam.

Bridges, Laurie & Alexander, Paul. Devil Wind. 1983. pap. 2.25 (ISBN 0-553-25210-0). Bantam.

Bridges, Laurie, jt. auth. see Alexander, Paul.

Bridges, Marjorie. Eastern Indian Basketry. (Illus.). 96p. Date not set. pap. 7.95 (ISBN 0-88839-169-2). Hancock House.

Bridges, Martin F. This Time & Place. 1979. 10.95 (ISBN 0-87881-077-3). Mojave Bks.

Bridges, P. K. Psychiatric Emergencies: Diagnosis & Management. (Illus.). 208p. 1971. 15.50x (ISBN 0-398-00224-X). C C Thomas.

Bridges, Pat. Where is the Wilderness? (Illus.). 28p. (Orig.). 1984. pap. 4.00 (ISBN 0-916897-00-1); ltd. ed. 10.00 (ISBN 0-916897-01-X). Andrew Mtn Pr.

Bridges, Robert. Bibliographies of Modern Authors, No. 1. LC 74-7014. 1921. lib. bdg. 8.50 (ISBN 0-8414-3163-9). Folcroft.

--Collected Essays, Papers, Etc. Vols. 1-10. LC 74-8430. 1927-36. lib. bdg. 15.00 ea. Folcroft.

--Collected Essays, Papers, Etc. 30 Parts in 1. Repr. of 1927 ed. 80.00x (ISBN 3-4870-4382-3). Adlers Foreign Bks.

--A Critical Introduction to Keats. 1929. Repr. 10.00 (ISBN 0-8274-2119-2). R West.

--Influence of the Audience on Shakespeare's Drama. LC 74-8430. 1973. lib. bdg. 15.00 (ISBN 0-8414-9851-2). Folcroft.

--John Keats. LC 72-1976. (Studies in Keats, No. 19). 1972. Repr. of 1895 ed. lib. bdg. 29.95x (ISBN 0-8383-1453-8). Haskell.

--Necessity of Poetry. LC 77-657. 1918. lib. bdg. 12.50 (ISBN 0-8414-9949-7). Folcroft.

--The Spirit of Man: An Anthology in English & French. 1983. Repr. of 1934 ed. lib. bdg. 40.00 (ISBN 0-89984-128-7). Century Bookbindery.

--Twenty-One Letters: Robert Bridges & R. C. Trevelyan. 1955. lib. bdg. 12.50 (ISBN 0-8414-2897-2). Folcroft.

--Wordsworth & Kipling in Collected Essays, Papers, Etc, Vol. 11. Repr. 10.00 (ISBN 0-8274-3750-1). R West.

Bridges, Robert, ed. The Chilswell Book of English Poetry. facsimile ed. LC 74-168774. (Granger Index Reprint Ser.). Repr. of 1924 ed. 18.00 (ISBN 0-8369-6294-X). Ayer Co Pubs.

Bridges, Robert, ed. see Dixon, Richard W.

Bridges, Robert, ed. & memoir by see Dolben, Digby M.

Bridges, Robert, et al. Preliminary Announcement. Commager, Steele, ed. Incl. On English Homophones; A Few Practical Suggestions; The Pronunciation of English Words; The Englishing of French Words; On Hyphens & Shall & Will, Should & Would; English Influence on the French Vocabulary; What Is Pure French; The Language of Anatomy; On Grammatical Inversion. (Society for Pure English Ser.: Vol. 1). 1979. lib. bdg. 46.00 (ISBN 0-8240-3665-4). Garland Pub.

--The Society's Work. Commager, Steele, ed. Incl. The Nature of Human Speech; English Handwriting; Notes on Relative Clauses; On Some Disputed Points in English Grammar; English Vowel Sounds; The Study of American English; English Handwriting; Shakespeare's English; American Pronunciation. (Society for Pure English: Vol. 3). 1979. lib. bdg. 50.00 (ISBN 0-8240-3667-0). Garland Pub.

Bridges, Robert S. Poetical Works of Robert Bridges, Excluding the Eight Dramas. 2nd ed. LC 75-41036. (BCL Ser. II). Repr. of 1936 ed. 28.00 (ISBN 0-404-14511-6). AMS Pr.

--The Shorter Poems of Robert Bridges. LC 78-59008. (Illus.). 1979. Repr. of 1931 ed. 21.00 (ISBN 0-88355-683-9). Hyperion Conn.

--Three Friends. LC 75-3863. (Illus.). 243p. Repr. of 1932 ed. lib. bdg. 19.75x (ISBN 0-8371-8094-5, BRTFR). Greenwood.

Bridges, Roger D., ed. see Grant, Ulysses S.

Bridges, Ronald A. Industrial Systems Desk Book. 256p. 1982. 40.00x (ISBN 0-13-463604-X). P-H.

Bridges, Thomas, ed. see Waters, Somerset R.

Bridges, Thomas C. & Tiltman, Hubert H. Heroes of Modern Adventure. facsimile ed. LC 76-152160. (Essay Index Reprint Ser.). Repr. of 1927 ed. 22.00 (ISBN 0-8369-2216-6). Ayer Co Pubs.

--Kings of Commerce. facs. ed. LC 68-8442. (Essay Index Reprint Ser). 1928. 18.00 (ISBN 0-8369-0102-9). Ayer Co Pubs.

--Master Minds of Modern Science. facs. ed. LC 68-57307. (Essay Index Reprint Ser.). 1931. 18.00 (ISBN 0-8369-0064-2). Ayer Co Pubs.

--More Heroes of Modern Adventure. facsimile ed. LC 76-86735. (Essay Index Reprint Ser). 1930. 21.50 (ISBN 0-8369-1343-4). Ayer Co Pubs.

Bridges, Toby. Advanced Muzzle Loader's Guide. 256p. 1985. pap. 11.95 (ISBN 0-88317-126-0). Stoeger Pub Co.

Bridges, Wake. Hickory: It's One Hell of a Town. 156p. 1982. 8.95 (ISBN 0-932298-25-7). Copple Hse.

Bridges, William. Transitions: Making Sense of Life's Changes. 160p. 1980. o. p. 10.95 (ISBN 0-201-00081-4); pap. 6.95 (ISBN 0-201-00082-2). Addison-Wesley.

Bridges, William B., jt. auth. see Birdsall, Charles K.

Bridges-Adam, W. The British Theatre. 1944. 15.00 (ISBN 0-8482-0146-9). Norwood Edns.

Bridget. The Magnificent Prayers of Saint Bridget of Sweden. (Illus.). 19p. 1983. pap. 1.00 (ISBN 0-89555-220-5). TAN Bks Pubs.

Bridgewater, A. & Lidgren, H. Household Waste Management in Europe. 1981. 32.00 (ISBN 0-442-30464-1). Van Nos Reinhold.

Bridgewater, Alan & Bridgewater, Gill. Printing with Wood Blocks, Stencils & Engravings. LC 82-74506. (Illus.). 160p. 1983. 19.95 (ISBN 0-668-05839-0, 5839). Arco.

Bridgewater, Gill, jt. auth. see Bridgewater, Alan.

Bridgewater, Patrick. Nietzsche in Anglosaxony: A Study of Nietzsche's Impact on English & American Literature. 250p. 1972. text ed. 15.00x (ISBN 0-7185-1104-2, Leicester). Humanities.

Bridgid, Herridge. Every Bear's Life Guide. (Illus.). 80p. 1984. pap. 5.95 (ISBN 0-943392-66-7). Tribeca Comm.

Bridgman, George B. Book of One-Hundred Hands. (Illus.). 1972. pap. 4.50 (ISBN 0-486-22709-X). Dover.

--Bridgman's Life Drawing. (Illus.). 1971. pap. 4.50 (ISBN 0-486-22710-3). Dover.

--Constructive Anatomy. (Illus.). 160p. 1973. pap. 3.95 (ISBN 0-486-21104-5). Dover.

--Heads, Features, & Faces. LC 74-78681. (Illus.). 64p. 1974. pap. 2.75 (ISBN 0-486-22708-1). Dover.

--The Human Machine: The Anatomical Structure & Mechanism of the Human Body. LC 70-187018. (Illus.). 160p. 1972. pap. 3.95 (ISBN 0-486-22707-3). Dover.

Bridgman, J. The Christmas Book: Christmas in the Olden Time: Its Customs & Their Origin. 1978. Repr. of 1859 ed. lib. bdg. 15.00 (ISBN 0-8492-3711-4). R West.

Bridgman, Jon & Clarke, David E. German Africa: A Select Annotated Bibliography. LC 64-7917. (Bibliographical Ser.: No. 19). 120p. 1965. pap. 6.95x (ISBN 0-8179-2192-3). Hoover Inst Pr.

Bridgman, Jon M. The Revolt of the Hereros. LC 80-13965. (Perspectives on Southern Africa Ser.: Vol. 30). 200p. 1980. 17.95 (ISBN 0-520-04113-5). U of Cal Pr.

Bridgman, P. W. A Sophisticates Primer of Relativity. 2nd ed. 1982. 20.00x (ISBN 0-8195-5077-9); pap. 9.95 (ISBN 0-8195-6078-2). Wesleyan U Pr.

--The Thermodynamics of Electrical Phenomena in Metals & a Condensed Collection of Thermodynamic Formulas. (Illus.). 12.00 (ISBN 0-8446-1737-7). Peter Smith.

Bridgman, Percy W. Collected Experimental Papers, 7 Vols. LC 64-16060. (Illus.). 1964. Set. 250.00x (ISBN 0-674-13750-7). Harvard U Pr.

--Dimensional Analysis. rev. ed. LC 75-41035. Repr. of 1931 ed. 11.50 (ISBN 0-404-14774-7). AMS Pr.

--The Logic of Modern Physics. Cohen, I. Bernard, ed. LC 79-3117. (Three Centuries of Science in America Ser.). 1980. Repr. of 1927 ed. lib. bdg. 21.00x (ISBN 0-405-12594-1). Ayer Co Pubs.

--Philosophical Writings of Percy William Bridgman: An Original Anthology, 2 vols. in 1. Cohen, I. Bernard, ed. LC 79-7952. (Three Centuries of Science in America Ser.). 1980. lib. bdg. 19.00x (ISBN 0-405-12532-1). Ayer Co Pubs.

--Reflections of a Physicist. 2nd ed. Cohen, I. Bernard, ed. LC 79-3118. (Three Centuries of Science in America Ser.). 1980. Repr. of 1955 ed. lib. bdg. 48.50x (ISBN 0-405-12595-X). Ayer Co Pubs.

Bridgman, Peter. Tree Surgery: The Complete Guide. LC 75-31320. (Illus.). 160p. 1976. 18.95 (ISBN 0-7153-7050-2). David & Charles.

Bridgman, R. F. Rural Hospital: Its Structure & Organization. (Monograph Ser: No. 21). (Illus.). 162p. (Eng. & Fr.). 1970. 8.00 (ISBN 92-4-140021-8). World Health.

Bridgman, R. F. & Roemer, M. I. Hospital Legislation & Hospital Systems. (Public Health Paper: No. 50). (Also avail. French & Spanish). 1973. pap. 4.80 (ISBN 92-4-130050-7). World Health.

Bridgman, Raymond. First Book of World Law. LC 79-147597. (Library of War & Peace; International Law). lib. bdg. 46.00 (ISBN 0-8240-0358-6). Garland Pub.

--World Organization. LC 77-147575. (Library of War & Peace; Int'l. Organization, Arbitration & Law). 1972. 46.00 (ISBN 0-8240-0341-1). Garland Pub.

Bridgman, Raymond L., ed. see Alcott, A. Bronson.

Bridgman, Richard. Dark Thoreau. LC 81-4788. xvi, 306p. 1982. 23.50x (ISBN 0-8032-1167-8). U of Nebr Pr.

--Gertrude Stein in Pieces. 1970. 27.50x (ISBN 0-19-501280-1). Oxford U Pr.

Bridgman, Richard W. A Short View of Legal Bibliography: Bridgman's Legal Bibliography. xviii, 430p. 1958. Repr. of 1807 ed. lib. bdg. 40.00 (ISBN 0-89941-353-6). W S Hein.

Bridgwater, A. V. & Lidgren, K. Energy in Packaging & Waste. 1983. 64.50 (ISBN 0-442-30570-2). Van Nos Reinhold.

Bridgwater, Anthony V., ed. Thermochemical Processing of Biomass. (Illus.). 340p. 1984. text ed. 49.95 (ISBN 0-408-01469-5). Butterworth.

Bridgwater, J., ed. Developments in Chemical Engineering: A Festschrift for P. V. Danckwerts. (Illus.). 190p. 1983. pap. 35.00 (ISBN 0-08-030251-3). Pergamon.

Bridgwater, W. P. The German Poets of the First World War. LC 85-40075. 208p. 1985. 27.50 (ISBN 0-312-32604-1). St Martin.

Bridie, James. George Bernard Shaw in Great Contemporaries. Repr. of 1935 ed. 30.00 (ISBN 0-8274-3851-6). R West.

Bridinger, Don. Waiting in Hope. 1973. 4.75 (ISBN 0-89536-253-8). CSS of Ohio.

Bridle, Martin & Eaton, Su. Punch & Judy in the Rain. (Illus.). 32p. (gr. 3-7). 1985. 8.95 (ISBN 0-241-11222-2, Pub. by Hamish Hamilton England). David & Charles.

Bridner, E. L., Jr., jt. auth. see Wilson, Richard.

Brids, John, jt. ed. see Walmsley, Keith.

Bridson, Gavin & Wakeman, Geoffrey. Printmaking & Picture Printing: A Bibliographical Guide to Artistic & Industrial Techniques in Britain, 1750-1900. 1984. 55.00 (ISBN 0-317-13575-9). BkPr Ltd.

Bridson, Gavin D., et al, eds. Natural History Manuscript Resources in the British Isles. LC 79-92886. 6000p. 1980. 245.00 (ISBN 0-8352-1281-5). Bowker.

Bridwell, E. Nelson, intro. by. Superman: From the Thirties to the Eighties. 1983. 15.95 (ISBN 0-517-55100-4). Crown.

Bridwell, J., jt. auth. see Kazeck, M.

Bridwell, Lillian, jt. ed. see Beach, Richard.

Bridwell, Norman. Clifford & the Grouchy Neighbors. (Illus.). 32p. (Orig.). (gr. k-3). 1985. pap. 1.95 (ISBN 0-590-33461-1). Scholastic Inc.

--Clifford at the Circus. (Illus.). 32p. (gr. k-3). 1985. pap. 1.95 (ISBN 0-590-33588-X). Scholastic Inc.

--Clifford Gets a Job. (Illus.). 32p. (gr. k-3). 1985. pap. 1.50 (ISBN 0-590-33727-0). Scholastic Inc.

--Clifford Goes to Hollywood. (Orig.). (ps-3). 1981. pap. 1.25 (ISBN 0-590-31607-9). Scholastic Inc.

--Clifford Takes a Trip. (Illus.). 32p. (gr. k-3). 1985. pap. 1.95 (ISBN 0-590-33554-5). Scholastic Inc.

--Clifford, the Big Red Dog. (Illus.). 32p. (Orig.). (gr. k-3). 1985. pap. 1.95 (ISBN 0-590-33470-0). Scholastic Inc.

--Clifford, the Small Red Puppy. (Illus.). 32p. (gr. k-3). 1973. pap. 1.50 (ISBN 0-590-33726-2). Scholastic Inc.

--Clifford, the Small Red Puppy. (Illus.). 32p. (gr. k-3). 1985. pap. 1.95 (ISBN 0-590-33583-9). Scholastic Inc.

--Clifford Va de Viaje. Palacios, Argentina, tr. from Span. (gr. k-3). 1979. pap. 1.95 (ISBN 0-590-09417-3). Scholastic Inc.

--Clifford's ABC. (Illus.). 32p. (ps-2). 1984. board bk. 5.95 (ISBN 0-590-33154-X). Scholastic Inc.

--Clifford's Christmas. (Illus.). 32p. (Orig.). (ps-3). 1984. pap. 1.50 (ISBN 0-590-33277-5). Scholastic Inc.

--Clifford's Family. (Illus.). 32p. (Orig.). (ps-3). 1984. pap. 1.50 (ISBN 0-590-33275-9). Scholastic Inc.

--Clifford's Good Deeds. (Illus.). (ps-3). 1985. pap. 1.95 (ISBN 0-590-33589-8). Scholastic Inc.

--Clifford's Halloween. (Illus.). (gr. k-3). 1970. pap. 1.25 (ISBN 0-590-01466-8). Scholastic Inc.

--Clifford's Kitten. (Illus.). 32p. (Orig.). (ps-3). 1984. pap. 1.50 (ISBN 0-590-33276-7). Scholastic Inc.

--Clifford's Pals. (Illus.). 32p. (gr. k-3). 1985. pap. 1.95 (ISBN 0-590-33582-0). Scholastic Inc.

--Clifford's Riddles. (Illus.). 32p. (Orig.). (ps-3). 1984. pap. 1.50 (ISBN 0-590-33361-5). Scholastic Inc.

--Clifford's Sticker Book. (Illus.). 24p. (ps-3). 1984. pap. 2.95 (ISBN 0-590-33309-7). Scholastic Inc.

--Clifford's Tricks. (Illus.). (gr. k-3). 1971. pap. 1.50 (ISBN 0-590-33820-X). Scholastic Inc.

--Clifford's Tricks. (Illus.). 32p. (gr. k-3). 1986. pap. 1.95 (ISBN 0-590-33612-6). Scholastic Inc.

--Count on Clifford. (Illus.). 32p. (gr. k-3). 1985. 5.95 (ISBN 0-590-33614-2). Scholastic Inc.

--How to Care for Your Monster. (Illus.). (gr. 4-6). 1972. pap. 1.50 (ISBN 0-590-09177-8). Scholastic Inc.

--Kangaroo Stew. (gr. k-3). 1979. pap. 1.50 (ISBN 0-590-12099-9). Scholastic Inc.

--Monster Holidays. (Illus.). (gr. 4-6). 1975. pap. 1.75 (ISBN 0-590-09930-2). Scholastic Inc.

--A Tiny Family. (Illus.). (gr. k-3). 1972. pap. 1.50 (ISBN 0-590-02539-2). Scholastic Inc.

--The Witch's Christmas. (Illus.). (gr. k-3). 1972. pap. 1.50 (ISBN 0-590-09216-2); pap. 4.50 Witch's Christmas & Clifford the Big Red Dog (2 bks.) & 1 record (ISBN 0-590-04385-4). Scholastic Inc.

Bridwell, Randall & Whitten, Ralph U. The Constitution & the Common Law. LC 77-5281. 1977. 27.00x (ISBN 0-669-01601-2). Lexington Bks.

Bridwell, Raymond. Hydroponic Gardening: The Magic of Hydroponics for the Home Gardener. LC 72-86151. (Illus.). 224p. 1972. pap. 7.95 (ISBN 0-912800-09-7). Woodbridge Pr.

Bridwell, Rodger W. High Tech Investing: How to Profit from the Explosive New Growth in Companies in the 80's. LC 82-40358. 83p. 1983. 19.75 (ISBN 0-8129-1033-8). Times Bks.

Bridwell, Tom. Anacoluthon. (Orig.). 1980. limited signed ed. o.p. 30.00 (ISBN 0-915316-79-X); pap. 6.00 (ISBN 0-915316-78-1). Pentagram.

Brie, F., ed. The Brut, or the Chronicle of England, Pt. 1. (EETS OS Ser.: Vol. 131). Repr. of 1906 ed. 22.00 (ISBN 0-317-16536-4). Kraus Repr.

Brie, Henry G. La see La Brie, Henry G., III.

Brie, Vicki G. La see La Brie, Vicki G.

Brief, et al. Managing Job Stress. (Orig.). 1981. pap. text ed. 10.95 (ISBN 0-316-10799-9). Little.

Brief, Arthur, jt. auth. see Aldag, Ramon.

Brief, Arthur P. Managing Human Resources in Retail Organizations. LC 83-49496. (The Advances in Retailing Ser.). 192p. 1984. 23.00x (ISBN 0-669-08149-3). Lexington Bks.

Brief, Arthur P., jt. auth. see Aldag, Ramon J.

Brief, Arthur P., ed. Productivity Research in the Behavioral & Social Sciences. LC 84-5877. 316p. 1984. 24.95 (ISBN 0-03-060568-7). Praeger.

Brief, Jean-Claude. Beyond Piaget: A Philosophical Psychology. 1983. text ed. 16.95x (ISBN 0-8077-2739-3). Tchrs Coll.

Brief, Richard P. Fourth International Congress on Accounting, 1933. (Accountancy in Transition Ser.). 88.00 (ISBN 0-317-20382-7). Garland Pub.

--Nineteenth Century Capital Accounting & Business Investment. LC 75-18459. (History of Accounting Ser.). 1976. 15.00x (ISBN 0-405-07543-X). Ayer Co Pubs.

Brief, Richard P., ed. Depreciation & Capital Maintenance. LC 83-49437. (Accounting History & the Development of a Profession Ser.). 127p. 1984. lib. bdg. 20.00 (ISBN 0-317-14001-9). Garland Pub.

--The Development of Contemporary Accounting Thought Series, 57 bks. (Illus.). 1978. lib. bdg. 1701.00x set (ISBN 0-405-10891-5). Ayer Co Pubs.

--Dicksee's Contribution to Accounting Theory & Practice. original anthology ed. LC 80-1454. (Dimensions of Accounting Theory & Practice Ser.). 1981. lib. bdg. 40.00x (ISBN 0-405-13476-2). Ayer Co Pubs.

--Dimensions of Accounting Theory & Practice Ser, 70 vols. 1981. Set. lib. bdg. 2079.50x (ISBN 0-405-13475-4). Ayer Co Pubs.

--The Etiquette of the Accountancy Profession & the Ethical Problems of Modern Accountancy: Lectures Delivered in 1932 on the William Vawter Foundation on Business Ethics, 2 vols. in one. LC 80-1491. (Dimensions of Accounting Theory & Practice Ser.). 1981. Repr. of 1933 ed. lib. bdg. 25.50x (ISBN 0-405-13521-1). Ayer Co Pubs.

--Four Classics on the Theory of Double Entry Bookkeeping. LC 82-82949. (Accountancy in Transition Ser.). 90p. 1982. lib. bdg. 22.00 (ISBN 0-8240-5333-8). Garland Pub.

--The Herwood Library of Accountancy: A Catalogue of Books Printed Between 1494 to 1900. LC 80-1495. (Dimensions of Accounting Theory & Practice Ser.). 1981. Repr. of 1938 ed. lib. bdg. 25.50x (ISBN 0-405-13525-4). Ayer Co Pubs.

--The Institute of Chartered Accountants in England & Wales Library Catalogue, 1913, 2 vols. LC 80-1501. (Dimensions of Accounting Theory & Practice Ser.). 1981. Repr. of 1913 ed. Set. lib. bdg. 92.00x (ISBN 0-405-13526-2). Ayer Co Pubs.

--The Institute of Chartered Accountants in England & Wales Library Catalogue, 1937, 2 vols. in one. LC 80-1502. (Dimensions of Accounting Theory & Practice Ser.). 1981. Repr. of 1937 ed. lib. bdg. 51.50x (ISBN 0-405-13527-0). Ayer Co Pubs.

Brief, Richard P. & Previts, Gary J., eds. Early Twentieth Century Developments in American Accounting Thought: A Pre-Classical School. new ed. LC 77-87316. (Development of Contemporary Accounting Thought Ser.). 1978. lib. bdg. 27.50x (ISBN 0-405-10929-6). Ayer Co Pubs.

Brief, Richard P., ed. see American Association of University Instructors in Accounting.

Brief, Richard P., ed. see Baily, Francis.

Brief, Richard P., ed. see Baldwin, Harry G. & Holz, William B.

Brief, Richard P., ed. see Baxter, William T.

Brief, Richard P., ed. see Beckett, Thomas.

Brief, Richard P., ed. see Blough, Carman G.

Brief, Richard P., ed. see Bray, Frank S.

Brief, Richard P., ed. see Brinton, Willard C.

Brief, Richard P., ed. see Broaker, Frank & Chapman, Richard M.

Brief, Richard P., jt. ed. see Brooks, Collin.

Brief, Richard P., ed. see Burns, Thomas J. & Coffman, Edward N.

Brief, Richard P., ed. see Canning, John B.

Brief, Richard P., ed. see Carey, John L.

Brief, Richard P., ed. see Cerboni, Giuseppe.

Brief, Richard P., jt. ed. see Chatfield, Michael.

Brief, Richard P., ed. see Cleveland, Frederick A.

Brief, Richard P., ed. see Cocke, Hugh.

Brief, Richard P., ed. see Cole, William M. & Geddes, Anne E.

Brief, Richard P., ed. see Congress of Accountants,World Fair,St Louis, September 26-28th, 1904.

Brief, Richard P., ed. see Cotter, Arundel.

Brief, Richard P., ed. see Courcelle-Seneuil, J. G.

Brief, Richard P., ed. see Cronhelm, Frederick W.

Brief, Richard P., ed. see Daniels, Mortimer B.

Brief, Richard P., ed. see Davidson, Sydney.

Brief, Richard P., ed. see DeMond, C. W.

Brief, Richard P., ed. see De Motte Green, Catherine.

Brief, Richard P., ed. see De Paula, Frederic & Zeff, Stephen A.

Brief, Richard P., ed. see Devine, Carl T.

Brief, Richard P., ed. see Dicksee, Lawrence R.

Brief, Richard P., ed. see Edwards, J. R.

Brief, Richard P., ed. see Epstein, Marc J.

Brief, Richard P., ed. see Esquerre, Paul-Joseph.

Brief, Richard P., ed. see Ficker, Nicholas T.

Brief, Richard P., ed. see Fitzgerald, Adolf A.

Brief, Richard P., ed. see Goldberg, Louis.

Brief, Richard P., ed. see Green, David, Jr.

Brief, Richard P., ed. see Hain, Hans P.

Brief, Richard P., ed. see Haskins, Charles W.

Brief, Richard P., ed. see Hawawini, Gabriel A. & Vora, Ashok.

Brief, Richard P., ed. see Hein, Leonard W.

Brief, Richard P., ed. see Hendriksen, Eldon S.

Brief, Richard P., ed. see Hepworth, Samuel R.

Brief, Richard P., ed. see Holmes, William & Kistler, Linda H.

Brief, Richard P., ed. see Horngen, Charles T.

Brief, Richard P., jt. ed. see Horrigan, James O.

Brief, Richard P., ed. see Johnson, Thomas H.

Brief, Richard P., ed. see Jones, Edward T.

Brief, Richard P., ed. see King, George.

Brief, Richard P., ed. see Lamden, Charles W.

Brief, Richard P., ed. see Langenderfer, Harold Q.

Brief, Richard P., ed. see Langer, Russell D.

Brief, Richard P., ed. see Leake, P. D.

Brief, Richard P., ed. see Leautey, Eugene & Guilbaut, Adolfe.

Brief, Richard P., ed. see Levy, Saul.

Brief, Richard P., ed. see Lewis, J. Slater.

Brief, Richard P., jt. ed. see Lisle, George.

Brief, Richard P., ed. see Lubell, Myron S.

Brief, Richard P., ed. see Mair, John.

Brief, Richard P., ed. see Mann, Helen S.

Brief, Richard P., ed. see Marchi, Francesco.

Brief, Richard P., ed. see Marsh, Christopher C.

Brief, Richard P., ed. see Merino, Barbara.

Brief, Richard P., ed. see Mitchell, William.

Brief, Richard P., ed. see Montgomery, Robert H.

Brief, Richard P., ed. see Moonitz, Maurice.

Brief, Richard P., jt. ed. see Moonitz, Maurice.

Brief, Richard P., ed. see Murray, David.

Brief, Richard P., ed. see Nicholson, Jerome L.

Brief, Richard P., ed. see Norris, Harry.

Brief, Richard P., ed. see O'Neill, Michael T.

Brief, Richard P., ed. see Parker, R. H.

Brief, Richard P., ed. see Paton, William A. & Stevenson, Russell A.

Brief, Richard P., ed. see Perera, M. H.

Brief, Richard P., ed. see Pixley, Francis W.

Brief, Richard P., ed. see Preinreich, Gabriel A.

Brief, Richard P., ed. see Previts, Gary J.

Brief, Richard P., ed. see Rich, Wiley D.

Brief, Richard P., jt. ed. see Richardson, Alphyon P.

Brief, Richard P., ed. see Roberts, Alfred R.

Brief, Richard P., ed. see Ronen, Joshua & Sorter, George H.

Brief, Richard P., ed. see Saliers, Earl A.

Brief, Richard P., ed. see Schiff, Michael.

Brief, Richard P., ed. see Schmalenbach, Eugen.

Brief, Richard P., ed. see Scovell, Clinton H.

Brief, Richard P., ed. see Second International Accountants Congress, Amsterdam, 1926.

Brief, Richard P., ed. see Simpson, Kemper.

Brief, Richard P., ed. see Sneed, Florence R.

Brief, Richard P., ed. see Sorter, George H.

Brief, Richard P., ed. see Sprague, Thomas B.

Brief, Richard P., ed. see Stacey, Nicholas A.

Brief, Richard P., ed. see Stamp, Edward, et al.

Brief, Richard P., ed. see Staubus, George J.

Brief, Richard P., ed. see Sweeney, Henry W.

Brief, Richard P., ed. see Taylor, R. Emmett.

Brief, Richard P., ed. see Todhunter, Ralph.

Brief, Richard P., ed. see Van De Linde, Gerald.

Brief, Richard P., ed. see Vatter, William J.

Brief, Richard P., ed. see Walker, R. G.

Brief, Richard P., jt. ed. see Webster, Norman E.

Brief, Richard P., jt. ed. see Wells, M. C.

Brief, Richard P., ed. see Wells, Murry C.

Brief, Richard P., ed. see Wildman, John R. & Powell, Weldon.

Brief, Richard P., ed. see Worthington, Beresford.

Brief, Richard P., ed. see Yamey, Basil S.

Brief, Richard P., jt. ed. see Yamey, Basil S.

Brief, Richard P., ed. see Yang, Ju Mei.

Brief, Richard P., ed. see Zeff, Stephen A.

Brief, Richard S. Basic Industrial Hygiene Manual. 1975p. 1975. 12.00 (ISBN 0-932627-01-3); members 9.75 (ISBN 0-317-32855-7). Am Indus Hygiene.

Briefs, Goetz A. The Proletariat: A Challenge to Western Civilization. LC 74-25742. (European Sociology Ser.). 320p. 1975. Repr. 24.50x (ISBN 0-405-06498-5). Ayer Co Pubs.

Briefs, U. & Tagg, E. D., eds. Education for System Designer-User Cooperation. 1985. 28.00 (ISBN 0-444-87716-9). Elsevier.

Briefs, U., et al, eds. Systems Design for, with, & by the Users. 424p. 1983. 55.50 (ISBN 0-444-86613-2, I-174-83, North Holland). Elsevier.

--Computerization & Work. viii, 180p. 1985. pap. 22.00 (ISBN 0-387-15367-5). Springer-Verlag.

Brieger, E. M. Structure & Ultrastructure of Microorganisms. 1963. 60.00 (ISBN 0-12-134350-2). Acad Pr.

Brieger, Gert H., ed. Medical America in the Nineteenth Century: Readings from the Literature. LC 76-165053. 348p. 1972. 30.00x (ISBN 0-8018-1237-2). Johns Hopkins.

Brieger, N. Business Issues: Materials for Developing Reading & Speaking Skills for Students of Business English. LC 83-23609. (Materials for Language Practice). (Illus.). 128p. 1984. pap. 5.95 (ISBN 0-08-030472-9). Pergamon.

Brieger, Peter & Verdier, Philippe. Art & the Courts: France & England from 1259 to 1328. (Illus.). 350p. 1972. 20.00 (ISBN 0-88884-233-3, 56270-0, Pub. by Natl Mus Canada). U of Chicago Pr.

Brieger, Robert. The Joy of Mate. 40p. (Orig.). 1985. pap. 2.00 (ISBN 0-931462-36-3). Chess Ent Inc.

Brieland, D. & Costin, L. B. Contemporary Social Work: An Introduction to Social Work & Social Welfare. 3rd ed. 448p. 1985. 28.95 (ISBN 0-07-007769-X). McGraw.

Brieland, Donald & Lemmon, John. Social Work & the Law. 2nd ed. (Illus.). 800p. 1985. 26.95 (ISBN 0-314-77848-9). West Pub.

Brien, Sidney. Artists-in-Residence: A Sponsors Planning Guide. (Illus., Orig.). 1983. pap. 4.00 (ISBN 0-932246-03-6). Artists Found.

Brien, Terence J. John Crow. 288p. 1971. 5.95 (ISBN 0-87482-025-1). Wake Brook.

Brieno, Linda. Brain Dead. 384p. (Orig.). 1985. pap. 3.75 (ISBN 0-8439-2248-6, Leisure Bks). Dorchester Pub Co.

Brier, Alan, et al. Computers & the Social Sciences. LC 74-12052. 285p. 1974. 30.00x (ISBN 0-231-03914-X); pap. 15.00x (ISBN 0-231-03915-8). Columbia U Pr.

Brier, Bob. Ancient Egyptian Magic. LC 80-15608. (Illus.). 322p. 1981. pap. 8.95. Morrow.

--Ancient Egyptian Magic. LC 81-11224. (Illus.). 1981. pap. 7.95 (ISBN 0-688-00796-1, Quill). Morrow.

Brier, Bob & Digby, Joan. Permutations: Reading in Science & Literature. 1985. pap. 12.95 (ISBN 0-688-01945-5, Quill). Morrow.

--Permutations: Readings in Science & Literature. LC 85-546. 1985. 19.95 (ISBN 0-688-01944-7). Morrow.

Brier, Herbert S. & Orr, William I. VHF Handbook for Radio Amateurs. 3rd ed. LC 74-75450. (Illus.). 336p. 1974. 11.95 (ISBN 0-933616-00-7). Radio Pubns.

Brier, Peter A. & Arthur, Anthony, eds. American Prose & Criticism, Nineteen Hundred to Nineteen Fifty: A Guide to Information Sources. (American Literature, English Literature & World Literatures in English Information Guide Ser.: Vol. 35). 260p. 1981. 60.00x (ISBN 0-8103-1214-X). Gale.

Brier, Warren J. & Blumberg, Nathan B., eds. A Century of Montana Journalism. LC 78-169031. 352p. 1971. 7.50 (ISBN 0-87842-023-1). Mountain Pr.

Briere, Elizabeth, tr. see Vasileios of Stavronikita.

Briere, Elizabeth, tr. see Yannaras, Christos.

Briere, Eloise A., et al. Rendez-Vous: La France et la Francophonie. 250p. 1982. pap. text ed. 8.95 (ISBN 0-394-32883-3, RanC). Random.

Briere, Eugene J. Psycholinguistic Study of Phonological Interference. LC 68-13339. (Janua Linguarum, Ser. Minor: No. 66). 1968. pap. text ed. 9.60x (ISBN 90-2790-594-0). Mouton.

Briere, Eugene J. & Hinofotis, Frances Butler, eds. Concepts in Language Testing: Some Recent Studies. 100p. 1979. 5.00 (ISBN 0-318-16637-2). Tchrs Eng Spkrs.

Briere, Gaston, jt. ed. see Vitry, Paul.

Briere, O. Fifty Years of Chinese Philosophy: Eighteen Ninety-Eight to Nineteen Fifty. Thompson, Laurence G., tr. LC 78-31391. 1979. Repr. of 1956 ed. lib. bdg. 19.75x (ISBN 0-313-20650-3, BRFY). Greenwood.

Briere, Russell O., jt. auth. see Batsakis, John G.

Brierley, Alec. An Illustrated History of the Kelly Gang. 1978. pap. 6.00x (ISBN 0-522-84168-6, Pub. by Melbourne U Pr). Intl Spec Bk.

Brierley, Corale L., jt. ed. see Caldwell, Douglas E.

Brierley, David. Blood Group O. 208p. 1984. 9.95 (ISBN 0-671-47754-4). Summit Bks.

--Cold War. 224p. 1985. pap. 2.95 (ISBN 0-523-42561-9). Pinnacle Bks.

--Shooting Star. 224p. 1983. 12.95 (ISBN 0-684-17899-0, ScribT). Scribner.

Brierley, J. K. Biology & the Social Crisis. LC 71-120071. (Illus.). 260p. 1970. 18.00 (ISBN 0-8386-7719-3). Fairleigh Dickinson.

Brierley, John. Children's Well-Being. 172p. 1980. 15.00x (ISBN 0-85633-218-6, Pub. by NFER Nelson UK). Taylor & Francis.

--A Natural History of Man. 184p. 1970. 15.00 (ISBN 0-8386-7819-X). Fairleigh Dickinson.

Brierly, David. Cold War. 192p. 1984. 9.95 (ISBN 0-671-47753-6). Summit Bks.

Brierly, J. Parking of Motors Vehicles. 2nd ed. (Illus.). 347p. 1979. 39.00 (ISBN 0-85334-528-7, Pub. by Elsevier Applied Sci England). Elsevier.

Brierly, James L. Law of Nations: An Introduction to the International Law of Peace. new ed. Waldock, Humphrey, ed. 1963. 15.95x (ISBN 0-19-825105-X). Oxford U Pr.

Brierly, John. The Thinking Machine. LC 72-14220. 195p. 1973. 18.50 (ISBN 0-8386-1364-0). Fairleigh Dickinson.

Brierly, John E., jt. auth. see David, Rene.

Brierly, Marjorie, ed. see Sharpe, Ella Freeman.

Brierre De Boismont, Alexandre-Jacques-Francois. Hallucinations. LC 75-16689. (Classics in Psychiatry Ser.). 1976. Repr. of 1853 ed. 42.00x (ISBN 0-405-07419-0). Ayer Co Pubs.

Briers, Audrey. True Stories of Coins & Kings. 46p. 20.00x (ISBN 0-900090-90-1, Pub. by Ashmolean Mus UK). State Mutual Bk.

Briese, Garry L. & Schottke, David. Your First Response in the Streets. 1984. pap. text ed. 14.95 (ISBN 0-316-10810-3). Little.

Briese, K. English-German Dictionary. 624p. (Eng. & Ger.). 1980. 20.00x (ISBN 0-569-06892-4, Pub. by Collet's). State Mutual Bk.

Brieskorn, E. & Knorrer, H. Ebene Algebraische Kurven. 928p. (Ger.). 1981. text ed. 29.95x (ISBN 0-8176-3030-9). Birkhauser.

Briessen, Fritz Van see Van Briessen, Fritz.

Briet, E., ed. Festschrift for Emil Alfred Loeliger. (Journal: Haemostasis: Vol. 15, No. 4, 1985). (Illus.). 68p. 1985. pap. 23.00 (ISBN 3-8055-4146-5). S Karger.

Briet, William & Elzinga, Kenneth G., eds. Political Economy & Public Policy: Contemporary Economists in Perspective, 2 vols, Vol. 1. 1983. 40.00 (ISBN 0-89232-347-7). Jai Pr.

--Political Economy & Public Policy: Methodological Controversy in Economics. 1983. 40.00 (ISBN 0-89232-395-7). Jai Pr.

Brietzke, Paul H. Law, Development, & the Ethiopian Revolution. LC 80-65574. 600p. 1981. 39.50 (ISBN 0-8387-5008-7). Bucknell U Pr.

Brietzmann, Franz. Die Boese Frau in der Deutschen Literatur Des Mittelalters. 27.00 (ISBN 0-384-05766-7); pap. 22.00 (ISBN 0-384-05765-9). Johnson Repr.

Briffault, Herma, tr. see Colette.

Briffault, Herma, tr. see De Broucker, Jose.

Briffault, Herma, tr. see Duras, Marguerite.

Briffault, Herma, tr. see Mallet, Francoise.

Briffault, Herma, tr. see Moliere, Jean B.

Briffault, Herma, tr. see Racine, Jean B.

Briffault, R. Sin & Sex. LC 72-6300. (Studies in Philosophy, No. 40). 228p. 1972. Repr. of 1931 ed. lib. bdg. 49.95x (ISBN 0-8383-1631-X). Haskell.

Briffault, Robert. The Mothers: A Study of the Origins of Sentiments & Institutions, 3 vols. (Anthropology Ser). Repr. of 1927 ed. Set. 150.00 (ISBN 0-384-05800-0). Johnson Repr.

--Reasons for Anger. facs. ed. LC 68-58774. (Essay Index Reprint Ser). 1936. 17.75 (ISBN 0-8369-1024-9). Ayer Co Pubs.

--Sin & Sex. LC 72-9623. (Human Sexual Behavior Ser.). Repr. of 1931 ed. 12.50 (ISBN 0-404-57418-1). AMS Pr.

Briffault, Robert & Malinowski, Bronislaw. Marriage-Past & Present. (Extending Horizons Ser). 1956. 3.95 (ISBN 0-87558-027-0); pap. 2.45 (ISBN 0-87558-028-9). Porter Sargent.

Brigadere, Anna. Spriditis: A Children's Musical Play. Baumanis, Vilnis, tr. from Latvia. 60p. (Orig.). 1984. pap. 3.50x (ISBN 0-88020-109-6); pap. text ed. 25.00x piano score. Coach Hse.

Brigadoon Editors. Bountiful: A Poetry Digest. (Second Annual Anthology Ser.). 113p. 1981. pap. 4.95 (ISBN 0-938512-02-1). Brigadoon.

Brigance, William N. Jeremiah Sullivan Black, a Defender of the Constitution & the Ten Commandments. LC 72-139196. (American Scene Ser). (Illus.). 1971. Repr. of 1934 ed. lib. bdg. 39.50 (ISBN 0-306-70078-6). Da Capo.

Brigance, William N., ed. see Speech Association Of America.

Brigandi, Pat. Ghostbusters Haunted House Activity Book. 24p. (gr. 5-8). 1985. 1.50 (ISBN 0-590-33791-2). Scholastic Inc.

Brigandi, Pat & Lovitt, Chip. Ghostbusters: Coloring Book. (Illus.). 64p. (gr. k-3). 1985. pap. 1.50 (ISBN 0-590-33792-0). Scholastic Inc.

Briganti, Giuliano, ed. see Bologna, Ferdinando, 1st.

Brigard, Raul De see DeBrigard, Raul & Helmer, Olaf.

Brigden, C. A., jt. auth. see John, M.

Brigden, Raymond J. Operating Theatre Technique. 4th ed. (Illus.). 840p. 1980. text ed. 97.50 (ISBN 0-443-01999-1). Churchill.

Brigden, Roy. Agricultural Hand Tools. (Album Ser.: No. 100). (Illus.). 32p. 1985. pap. 3.50 (ISBN 0-85263-630-X, Pub. by Shire Pubns England). Seven Hills Bks.

--Ploughs & Ploughing. (Shire 'Album' Ser.: No. 125). (Orig.). 1985. pap. 2.95 (ISBN 0-85263-695-4, Pub. by Shire Pubns England). Seven Hills Bks.

Brigermann, Chuck. Record Collector's Fact Book, Vol. I. LC 82-73474. (Illus.). 96p. 1983. pap. 7.95 (ISBN 0-89709-037-3). Liberty Pub.

Brigg, Peter. J. G. Ballard. (Starmont Reader's Guides Ser.: No. 26). 96p. 1985. lib. bdg. 14.95x (ISBN 0-89370-953-0). Borgo Pr.

--J. G. Ballard. (Reader's Guides to Contemporary Science Fiction & Fantasy Authors: No. 26). (Illus., Orig.). 1985. 14.95 (ISBN 0-916732-84-3); pap. 6.95x (ISBN 0-916732-83-5). Starmont Hse.

Briggaman, Joan. Practical Problems in Mathematics for Office Workers. LC 76-54051. 1977. pap. text ed. 7.40 (ISBN 0-8273-1612-7); instr.'s guide o.p. 4.25 (ISBN 0-8273-1613-5). Delmar.

Briggs. Sources & Methods in Geography: Sediments. 1977. 13.50 (ISBN 0-408-70815-8). Butterworth.

Briggs, A. D. Alexander Pushkin: A Critical Study. LC 82-16242. 258p. 1983. text ed. 28.50x (ISBN 0-389-20340-8, 07184). B&N Imports.

Briggs, A. D., tr. see Medvedev, Roi.

Briggs, A. D., tr. see Medvevdev, Roy A.

Briggs Amasco Ltd. Flat Roofing: A Guide to Good Practice. (Illus.). 216p. 1982. pap. 33.95x (ISBN 0-9507919-0-3, Pub. by RIBA). Intl Spec Bk.

Briggs, Andrew, jt. auth. see Ridgway, John.

Briggs, Andrew J. Warehouse Operations Planning & Management. LC 78-15299. 320p. 1979. Repr. of 1960 ed. 22.50 (ISBN 0-88275-715-6). Krieger.

Briggs, Anna & Oliver, Judith, eds. Caring: Experiences of Looking after Severely Disabled Relatives. 160p. (Orig.). 1985. pap. 9.95x (ISBN 0-7102-0332-2). Routledge & Kegan.

Briggs, Anna M., tr. see Werner, David & Bower, Bill.

Briggs, Anne K. & Agrin, Alice R., eds. Crossroads: A Reader for Psychosocial Occupational Therapy. 2nd ed. 215p. 1982. pap. text ed. 15.00 (ISBN 0-910317-04-6). Am Occup Therapy.

Briggs, Anne K., et al. Case Simulations in Psychosocial Occupational Therapy. LC 79-4674. 235p. 1979. pap. 16.95x (ISBN 0-8036-1201-X). Davis Co.

Briggs, Arthur E. Walt Whitman: Thinker & Artist. LC 68-8052. 1968. Repr. of 1952 ed. lib. bdg. 24.75x (ISBN 0-8371-0028-3, BRWW). Greenwood.

Briggs, Asa. Age of Improvement, 1783 to 1867. (A History of England Ser.). (Illus.). 1959. pap. text ed. 13.95x (ISBN 0-582-49100-2). Longman.

--The BBC: The First Fifty Years. (Illus.). 310p. 1985. 24.95x (ISBN 0-19-212971-6). Oxford U Pr.

--Collected Essays of Asa Briggs, Volume II: Images, Problems, Standpoint, Forecasts. LC 84-24484. 352p. 1985. 37.50x (ISBN 0-252-01217-8). U of Ill Pr.

--Collected Essays of Asa Briggs, Volume I: Words, Numbers, Places, People. LC 84-24484. 268p. 1985. 32.50x (ISBN 0-252-01216-X). U of Ill Pr.

--The History of Broadcasting in the United Kingdom: Sound Vision, Vol. IV. (Illus.). 1979. 69.00x (ISBN 0-19-212967-8). Oxford U Pr.

--Iron Bridge to Crystal Palace: Impact & Images of the Industrial Revolution. (Illus., Orig.). 1979. 19.95 (ISBN 0-500-01222-9). Thames Hudson.

--The Power of Steam: An Illustrated History of the World's Steam Age. LC 82-40321. (Illus.). 208p. 1983. 22.50x (ISBN 0-226-07495-1); pap. 10.00 (ISBN 0-226-07497-8). U of Chicago Pr.

--Social History & Human Experience. (Grace A. Tanner Lecture in Human Values Ser.). 22p. 1984. pap. text ed. 9.00 (ISBN 0-910153-02-7). Woolf UT Sys.

--A Social History of England. (Illus.). 320p. 1984. 25.00 (ISBN 0-670-65549-X). Viking.

--Social History of England. 320p. 1986. pap. 9.95 (ISBN 0-14-007492-9). Penguin.

--Social Thought & Social Action. LC 73-17859. (Illus.). 371p. 1974. Repr. of 1961 ed. lib. bdg. 19.00x (ISBN 0-8371-7269-1, BSOT). Greenwood.

--Victorian People: A Reassessment of Persons & Themes, 1851-67. rev. ed. LC 55-7479. (Illus.). 1973. 25.00x (ISBN 0-226-07487-0). U of Chicago Pr.

--Victorian People: A Reassessment of Persons & Themes, 1851-67. new rev. ed. LC 55-5118. (Chicago Collectors Editions Ser.). (Illus.). x, 314p. 1975. pap. 10.95 (ISBN 0-226-07488-9, P365, Phoen). U of Chicago Pr.

Briggs, Asa & Dekker, John. Marx in London. 96p. 1982. 25.00x (ISBN 0-563-20076-6, Pub. by BBC Pubns). State Mutual Bk.

Briggs, Asa & Macartney, Anne. Toynbee Hall: The First Hundred Years. (Illus.). 256p. 1984. 35.00x (ISBN 0-7102-0283-0). Routledge & Kegan.

Briggs, Asa & Saville, John, eds. Essays in Labour History, 1886-1923. vii, 360p. 1971. 27.50 (ISBN 0-208-01239-7, Archon). Shoe String.

--Essays in Labour History: 1918-1939. 292p. 1977. 25.00 (ISBN 0-208-01641-4, Archon). Shoe String.

Briggs, Asa, ed. see Morris, William.

Briggs, Carl & Trudell, Clyde F. Quarterdeck & Saddlehorn: The Story of Edward F. Beale, 1822-1893. (Western Frontiersmen Ser.: Vol. xx). (Illus.). 300p. 1983. 29.50 (ISBN 0-87062-148-3). A H Clark.

Briggs, Carole S. Ballooning. (Superwheels & Thrill Sports Bks.). (Illus.). 48p. (gr. 4 up). 1985. PLB 8.95 (ISBN 0-8225-0441-3). Lerner Pubns.

--Diving is for Me. LC 82-17242. (Sports for Me Bks.). (Illus.). 48p. (gr. 2-5). 1983. PLB 7.95 (ISBN 0-8225-1135-5). Lerner Pubns.

--Skin Diving is for Me. LC 80-27409. (Sports for Me Bks.). (Illus.). (gr. 2-5). 1981. PLB 7.95 (ISBN 0-8225-1132-0, AACR1). Lerner Pubns.

--Sport Diving. LC 82-35. (Superwheels & Thrill Sports Bks.). (Illus.). (gr. 4 up). 1982. PLB 7.95 (ISBN 0-8225-0503-7). Lerner Pubns.

--Water Skiing Is for Me. 1986. 7.95 (ISBN 0-8225-1140-1). Lerner Pubns.

Briggs, Charles A. Inaugural Address & Defense, Eighteen Ninety-One to Eighteen Ninety-Three. LC 70-38442. (Religion in America, Ser. 2). 336p. 1972. Repr. of 1972 ed. 22.00 (ISBN 0-405-04062-8). Ayer Co Pubs.

Briggs, Charles F. The Adventures of Harry Franco: A Tale of the Great Panic. 1972. Repr. of 1839 ed. 26.50 (ISBN 0-8422-8010-3). Irvington.

--The Trippings of Tom Pepper; or the Results of Romancing: An Autobiography, 2 vols. LC 78-64066. (Harry Franco, pseud.). Repr. of 1847 ed. 75.00 set (ISBN 0-404-17170-2). AMS Pr.

--Working a Passage: Or, Life in a Liner. 1972. Repr. of 1845 ed. lib. bdg. 23.00 (ISBN 0-8422-8009-X). Irvington.

Briggs, Charles L. The Wood Carvers of Cordova, New Mexico: Social Dimensions of an Artistic "Revival". LC 79-20883. 272p. 1980. 24.95x (ISBN 0-87049-275-6). U of Tenn Pr.

Briggs Company Ltd. Designs & Patterns for Embroiderers & Craftsmen: Five Hundred & Twelve Motifs from "Album of Transfer Patterns". Nichols, Marion, ed. LC 73-93081. (Illus.). 160p. 1974. pap. 5.95 (ISBN 0-486-23030-9). Dover.

Briggs, D. & Seah, M. P. Practical Surface Analysis by Auger & Photo-Electron Spectoscopy. 533p. 1983. 83.95x (ISBN 0-471-26279-X, Pub. by Wiley-Interscience). Wiley.

Briggs, D. E. Barley. 1978. 85.00 (ISBN 0-412-11870-X, NO.6043, Pub. by Chapman & Hall). Methuen Inc.

Briggs, D. N. Distribution of Groceries. 1968. 14.00x (ISBN 0-85564-003-0, Pub by U of W Austral Pr). Intl Spec Bk.

Briggs, David & Smithson, Peter. Fundamentals of Physical Geography. LC 85-2495. (Illus.). 576p. 1985. pap. 15.95 (ISBN 0-09-160951-8, Pub. by Hutchinson Educ). Longwood Pub Group.

Briggs, David & Walters, S. M. Plant Variation & Evolution. 2nd ed. LC 83-14310. (Illus.). 350p. 1984. 59.50 (ISBN 0-521-25706-9); pap. 17.95 (ISBN 0-521-27665-9). Cambridge U Pr.

Briggs, Desmond. The Partners. 336p. 1983. 14.95 (ISBN 0-436-06855-9, Pub. by Secker & Warburg UK). David & Charles.

Briggs, Dinus M., jt. auth. see Briggs, Hilton M.

Briggs, Donald C. & Alisky, Marvin. Historical Dictionary of Mexico. LC 80-27320. (Latin American Historical Dictionaries Ser.: No. 21). 275p. 1981. lib. bdg. 20.00 (ISBN 0-8108-1391-2). Scarecrow.

Briggs, Dorothy C. Celebrate Your Self. LC 76-58099. 1977. 14.95 (ISBN 0-385-13104-6). Doubleday.

--Embracing Life: Growing Through Love & Loss. LC 84-25946. 144p. 1985. 11.95 (ISBN 0-385-23000-1). Doubleday.

--Your Child's Self-Esteem: The Key to His Life. LC 70-121948. 360p. 1970. pap. 8.95 (ISBN 0-385-04020-2, Dolp). Doubleday.

Briggs, Enang, jt. auth. see Ojo, O. A.

Briggs, Eric. Supplementary Benefits & the Consumer. 172p. 1980. pap. text ed. 14.75x (ISBN 0-7199-1042-0, Pub. by Bedford England). Brookfield Pub Co.

Briggs, Faye A., jt. auth. see Hwang, Kai.

Briggs, Freda I. Mom, Can We Still Keep Roger? 1985. text ed. 4.95 (ISBN 0-8010-0888-3). Baker Bk.

Briggs, G. A. Plume Rise. LC 77-603261. (AEC Critical Review Ser.). 81p. 1969. pap. 10.00 (ISBN 0-87079-304-7, TID-25075); microfiche 4.50 (ISBN 0-87079-305-5, TID-25075). DOE.

Briggs, Gary O. Move Over Jet--Here Comes the Zep. (Orig.). 1977. pap. text ed. 4.25 (ISBN 0-87881-059-5). Mojave Bks.

Briggs, Geoffrey, ed. Civic & Corporate Heraldry: A Dictionary of Impersonal Arms of England, Wales, & Northern Ireland. (Illus.). 432p. 1971. 32.00x (ISBN 0-685-29194-4). Gale.

Briggs, Geoffrey A. & Taylor, Frederick W. The Cambridge Photographic Atlas of the Planets. LC 81-38529. (Illus.). 224p. 1982. 27.95 (ISBN 0-521-23976-1). Cambridge U Pr.

Briggs, George. The Cognizance. 48p. 1984. 7.95 (ISBN 0-533-06100-8). Vantage.

Briggs, George M. & Calloway, Doris H. Bogert's Nutrition & Physical Fitness. 11th ed. 1984. pap. text ed. 30.95 (ISBN 0-03-058587-2). HR&W.

Briggs, George M., jt. auth. see Weininger, Jean.

Briggs, George W. Gorakhnath & the Kanphata Yogis. 1973. 18.50 (ISBN 0-89684-479-X). Orient Bk Dist.

Briggs, Gerald G. Drugs In Pregnancy & Lactation: A Reference Guide To Fetal & Neonatal Risk. 400p. 1983. 45.50 (ISBN 0-683-01057-3). Williams & Wilkins.

Briggs, Hazel F. I'll Tell You Tomorrow. 98p. 1983. pap. 5.95 (ISBN 0-942802-01-2). Northword.

--Mary Carter: On Behalf of the Aunts. 52p. (Orig.). 1979. pap. 4.95 (ISBN 0-942802-08-X). Northword.

Briggs, Herbert W. The Doctrine of Continuous Voyage. LC 78-64120. (Johns Hopkins University. Studies in the Social Sciences. Forty-Fourth Ser. 1926: 2). Repr. of 1926 ed. 21.50 (ISBN 0-404-61234-2). AMS Pr.

Briggs, Hilton M. & Briggs, Dinus M. Modern Breeds of Livestock. 4th ed. (Illus.). 1980. text ed. write for info. (ISBN 0-02-314730-X). Macmillan.

Briggs, J. Alden, Jr. The Official Football Fundraiser's Guide. Maradie, F. R., ed. LC 84-71836. 128p. (Orig.). 1984. pap. write for info. Athletic Inst.

Briggs, J. Robert & Kosy, Eugene J. Electronic Calculators. 1984. text ed. 8.95 (ISBN 0-538-13600-6, M60). SW Pub.

--Electronic Calculators & Office Machines. (gr. 9-12). 1984. text ed. 8.55 (ISBN 0-538-13690-1, M69). SW Pub.

Briggs, James I. & Nelson, Robert B., eds. The Berkeley Guide to Employment for New College Graduates. LC 84-51136. 256p. (Orig.). 1984. pap. 7.95 (ISBN 0-89815-136-8). Ten Speed Pr.

Briggs, Jean L. Never in Anger: Portrait of an Eskimo Family. LC 75-105368. (Illus.). 1970. 25.50x (ISBN 0-674-60825-9); pap. 8.95x (ISBN 0-674-60828-3). Harvard U Pr.

Briggs, Jeanine & Crean, John E. Alles Gute! Basic German for Communication. LC 81-23417. 350p. 1983. text ed. 23.00 (ISBN 0-394-32872-8, RanC); wkbk. 9.00 (ISBN 0-394-32873-6); lab manual 9.00 (ISBN 0-394-33028-5); Cultural Reader by Lalande 7.95 (ISBN 0-394-33013-7). Random.

--Alles Gute! Basic German for Communication. 2nd ed. 1986. text ed. 23.00 (ISBN 0-394-34260-7); 9.00 (ISBN 0-394-34259-3); 9.00 (ISBN 0-394-34258-5). Random.

Briggs, Joe B. Joe Bob Briggs Goes to the Drive-in. (Orig.). 1985. pap. 5.95 (ISBN 0-440-54368-1, Pub. by Dell Trade Pbks). Dell.

--Joe Bob Goes to the Drive-in. 1986. pap. 6.95 (ISBN 0-318-11916-1). Delacorte.

Briggs, John. The Collector's Beethoven. LC 77-28258. (Keystone Books in English Ser.). 1978. Repr. of 1962 ed. lib. bdg. 15.50x (ISBN 0-313-20243-5, BRBE). Greenwood.

Briggs, John & Peat, F. David. The Looking Glass Universe. (Orig.). 1983. pap. 9.95 (ISBN 0-346-12594-4, Cornerstone). S&S.

Briggs, John, tr. see Firishtah, Muhammed Kasim.

Briggs, John W. An Italian Passage: Immigrants to Three American Cities, 1890-1930. LC 77-22006. (Illus.). 1978. 33.00x (ISBN 0-300-02095-3). Yale U Pr.

Briggs, Julia. This Stage Play World: English Literature & Its Background, 1580-1625. LC 82-22473. 1983. pap. 7.95 (ISBN 0-19-289134-0). Oxford U Pr.

Briggs, K. M. Hobberdy Dick. LC 76-39896. (gr. 5-9). 1977. PLB 11.88 (ISBN 0-688-84079-5). Greenwillow.

--Kate Crackernuts. LC 79-9229. (Illus.). 224p. (gr. 7 up). 1980. 14.00 (ISBN 0-688-80240-0). Greenwillow.

Briggs, Katharine M. An Encyclopedia of Fairies: Hobgoblins, Brownies, Bogies, & Other Supernatural Creatures. LC 76-12939. (Illus.). (gr. 4 up). 1978. pap. 8.95 (ISBN 0-394-73467-X). Pantheon.

--Fairies in Tradition & Literature. 1977. pap. 8.95 (ISBN 0-7100-8687-3). Routledge & Kegan.

--Personnel of Fairyland: A Short Account of the Fairy People of Great Britain for Those Who Tell Stories to Children. LC 70-147084. (Illus.). 1971. Repr. of 1953 ed. 35.00x (ISBN 0-8103-3372-4). Gale.

--The Vanishing People: Fairy Lore & Legends. LC 78-53523. (Illus.). (YA) 1978. 8.95 (ISBN 0-394-50248-5). Pantheon.

Briggs, Katherine M. The Anatomy of Puck: An Examination of Fairy Beliefs among Shakespeare's Contemporaries & Successors. Dorson, Richard M., ed. LC 77-70581. (International Folklore Ser.). 1977. Repr. of 1959 ed. lib. bdg. 22.00x (ISBN 0-405-10082-5). Ayer Co Pubs.

--British Folktales. (Fairy Tale & Folklore Library). 1980. pap. 7.95 (ISBN 0-394-73993-0). Pantheon.

--Pale Hecates Team: Examination of the Beliefs on Witchcraft & Magic Among Shakespeare's Contemporaries & His Immediate Succesors. Dorson, Richard M., ed. LC 77-70582. (International Folklore Ser.). (Illus.). 1977. lib. bdg. 24.50x (ISBN 0-405-10083-3). Ayer Co Pubs.

Briggs, Katherine M. & Tongue, Ruth L., eds. Folktales of England. LC 65-18341. (Folktales of the World Ser). 1965. 14.00x (ISBN 0-226-07493-5); pap. 6.95x (ISBN 0-226-07494-3, FW3). U of Chicago Pr.

Brigham, Judith. A Historical Study of the Educational Agencies of the Southern Baptist Convention, 1845-1945. LC 77-177047. (Columbia University. Teachers College. Contributions to Education Ser.: No. 974). Repr. of 1951 ed. 17.50 (ISBN 0-404-55974-3). AMS Pr.

Brigham, Nancy. How to Do Leaflets, Newsletters & Newspapers. (Illus.). 144p. (Orig.). 1982. pap. 7.95 (ISBN 0-8038-3062-9). Hastings.

Brigham, Steven, jt. auth. see Swihart, Judson J.

Brigham, T. A., jt. ed. see Catania, A. Charles.

Brigham, Thomas A., jt. ed. see Catania, A. Charles.

Brigham, Thomas A., jt. ed. see Catania, Charles A.

Brigham, W. Guatemala. 1976. lib. bdg. 59.95 (ISBN 0-8490-1909-5). Gordon Pr.

Brigham, William T. Guatemala, Land of the Quetzal: A Sketch. Popenoe, Wilson, ed. LC 65-14894. (Latin American Gateway Ser). 1965. Repr. of 1887 ed. 12.50 (ISBN 0-8130-0028-9). U Presses Fla.

--Guatemala: The Land of the Quetzal. 1976. lib. bdg. 59.95 (ISBN 0-8490-1916-8). Gordon Pr.

Brigham, William T., tr. see Remy, M. Jules.

Brigham Young Univ., Provo, Utah Law Library. Legal Research Manual for Law Students, 1980. LC 80-137925. 1980. write for info. BYU Law Lib.

Brigham Young University Microbiology Faculty. Introductory Laboratory Manual of Microbiology for Health Related Professions. 2nd ed. 1977. spiral bdg. 8.95x (ISBN 0-8087-4538-7). Burgess.

Brigham Young University Press, ed. How to Involve Parents in Early Childhood Education. 200p. (Orig.). 1982. pap. text ed. 9.95x (ISBN 0-8425-2089-9). Brigham.

Brighouse, Harold, et al. Granada's Manchester Plays. 310p. 1962. 19.00 (ISBN 0-7190-1228-7, Pub. by Manchester Univ Pr). Longwood Pub Group.

Bright, Alfred L., et al. An Interdisciplinary Introduction to Black Studies. LC 77-15285. (Illus.). 1977. pap. text ed. 9.95 (ISBN 0-8403-1789-1). Kendall-Hunt.

Bright, Allan H. New Lights on Piers Plowman. 1984. Repr. of 1950 ed. deluxe ed. 19.00x (ISBN 0-403-01320-8). Scholarly.

Bright, Arthur A., Jr. The Electric-Lamp Industry: Technological Change & Economic Development from 1800 to 1947. LC 72-5037. (Technology & Society Ser.). 554p. 1972. Repr. of 1949 ed. 41.00 (ISBN 0-405-04690-1). Ayer Co Pubs.

Bright, Bill. Believing God for the Impossible. LC 78-73565. 1979. 8.95 (ISBN 0-918956-55-2). Campus Crusade.

--Come Help Change Our World. LC 79-53543. 1979. 8.95 (ISBN 0-918956-01-3). Campus Crusade.

--Handbook for Christian Maturity. 360p. (Orig.). 1981. pap. 7.95 (ISBN 0-86605-010-8). Campus Crusade.

--Handbook of Concepts for Living. 545p. (Orig.). 1981. pap. 7.95 (ISBN 0-86605-011-6). Campus Crusade.

--How to Be Filled with the Spirit. (Transferable Concepts Ser.). 58p. 1981. pap. 1.25 (ISBN 0-918956-90-0). Campus Crusade.

--How to Be Sure You Are a Christian. (Transferable Concepts Ser.). 63p. 1981. pap. 1.25 (ISBN 0-918956-88-9). Campus Crusade.

--How to Experience God's Love & Forgiveness. (Transferable Concepts Ser.). 63p. 1981. pap. 1.25 (ISBN 0-918956-89-7). Campus Crusade.

--How to Help Fulfill the Great Commission. (Transferable Concepts Ser.). 64p. 1981. pap. 1.25 (ISBN 0-918956-94-3). Campus Crusade.

--How to Introduce Others to Christ. (Transferable Concepts Ser.). 64p. 1981. pap. 1.25 (ISBN 0-918956-93-5). Campus Crusade.

--How to Love by Faith. (Transferable Concepts Ser.). 64p. 1981. pap. 1.25 (ISBN 0-918956-95-1). Campus Crusade.

--How to Pray. (Transferable Concepts Ser.). 63p. 1981. pap. 1.25 (ISBN 0-918956-96-X). Campus Crusade.

--How to Walk in the Spirit. (Transferable Concepts Ser.). 64p. 1981. pap. 1.25 (ISBN 0-918956-91-9). Campus Crusade.

--How to Witness in the Spirit. (Transferable Concepts Ser.). 64p. 1981. pap. 1.25 (ISBN 0-918956-92-7). Campus Crusade.

--Promises: A Daily Guide to Supernatural Living. LC 82-72302. 365p. 1983. 9.95 (ISBN 0-317-00638-X). Campus Crusade.

--Ten Basic Steps Teachers Manual. 2nd ed. 512p. 1983. pap. 8.95 (ISBN 0-918956-97-8). Campus Crusade.

Bright, Bill & Bright, Vonette. Love's Not Enough. 192p. 1985. 10.95 (ISBN 0-8407-5474-4). Nelson.

Bright, Bob. Pocket Guide: Assembly Language for the 6502. (Pitman Programming Pocket Guides Ser.). 64p. (Orig.). 1984. pap. 6.95 (ISBN 0-273-01990-2). Pitman Pub MA.

Bright, Charles. Submarine Telegraphs: Their History, Construction & Working. LC 74-4669. (Telecommunications Ser). (Illus.). 744p. 1974. Repr. of 1898 ed. 57.50x (ISBN 0-405-06035-1). Ayer Co Pubs.

Bright, Charles C. & Harding, Susan F., eds. Statemaking & Social Movements: Essays in History & Theory. LC 84-7430. 404p. 1984. text ed. 19.95 (ISBN 0-472-10050-5). U of Mich Pr.

Bright, Charles D. The Jet Makers: The Aerospace Industry from 1945 to 1972. LC 78-2377. (Illus.). 1978. 22.50x (ISBN 0-7006-0172-4). U Pr of KS.

Bright, Chuck. University of Iowa Football: The Hawkeyes. LC 82-50031. (College Sports Ser.). 1982. 10.95 (ISBN 0-87397-233-3). Strode.

Bright, David F. & Ramage, Edwin T., eds. Classical Texts & Their Traditions: Studies in Honor of C. R. Trahman. LC 84-1326. (Scholars Press Homage Ser.). 270p. 1984. text ed. 19.50 (ISBN 0-89130-729-X, 00 16 06). Scholars Pr GA.

Bright, Elizabeth. Destiny's Thunder. 320p. (Orig.). 1983. pap. 2.95 (ISBN 0-440-01897-8, Emerald). Dell.

--The Virginians. 256p. 1984. pap. 2.95 (ISBN 0-441-86482-1). Ace Bks.

Bright, F. T., et al, eds. Jig Boring. (Engineering Craftsmen: No. H27). (Illus.). 1969. spiral bdg. 39.95x (ISBN 0-85083-043-5). Intl Ideas.

Bright, FR. Barron's How to Prepare for the Professional & Administrative Career Examination: PACE. LC 76-30580. 1977. pap. 6.50 (ISBN 0-8120-0579-1). Barron.

Bright, Freda. Decisions. 416p. 1984. 16.95 (ISBN 0-312-19016-6). St Martin.

--Decisions. 384p. 1985. pap. 3.95 (ISBN 0-312-90169-0). St Martin.

--Futures. 1984. pap. 3.95 (ISBN 0-671-46183-4). PB.

Bright, George M., ed. Medical & Sociological Principles of Adolescent Care. 126p. 1980. 9.95 (ISBN 0-87762-295-7). Technomic.

Bright, Greg. The Great Maze Book: Extraordinary Puzzles for Extraordinary People. LC 74-26198. (Illus.). 1975. pap. 4.95 (ISBN 0-394-73054-2). Pantheon.

Bright, Harry. I Lived on Air for Forty Years. 1981. 8.00 (ISBN 0-87012-424-2). McClain.

Bright, Hazel M. Out in the Back Forty: A Voice from the Field. (Illus.). 1983. pap. 20.00 (ISBN 0-686-26607-2). Redwood Pub Co.

--Some Remediation Suggestions for Concepts of Boehm Test of Basic Concepts, Bk. 1, Form A Or B. rev. ed. (Illus.). (gr. k-3). 1979. pap. 7.00 (ISBN 0-686-26609-9). Redwood Pub Co.

--Some Remediation Suggestions for Concepts of Boehm Test of Basic Concepts, Bk. 2, Form A Or B. (Illus.). (gr. k-3). 1979. pap. 8.00 (ISBN 0-686-26608-0). Redwood Pub Co.

Bright, Henry A. Happy Country, This America: The Travel Diary of Henry Arthur Bright. Ehrenpreis, Anne H., ed. LC 77-11167. (Illus.). 496p. 1978. 19.50 (ISBN 0-8142-0271-3). Ohio St U Pr.

Bright, Henry A., ed. see Coleridge, Samuel T.

Bright, J. Diaries of John Bright. Walling, R., ed. Repr. of 1931 ed. 24.00 (ISBN 0-527-10900-2). Kraus Repr.

--Speeches on Questions of Public Policy, 2 Vols. 2nd ed. Rogers, J., ed. Repr. of 1868 ed. Set. 48.00 (ISBN 0-527-10920-7). Kraus Repr.

--Speeches on the American Question. 1865. 17.00 (ISBN 0-527-10930-4). Kraus Repr.

Bright, J. Franck. Joseph, Second. LC 78-112795. 1970. Repr. of 1897 ed. 20.00x (ISBN 0-8046-1062-2, Pub. by Kennikat). Assoc Faculty Pr.

Bright, James F. Maria Theresa. facsimile ed. LC 71-154145. (Select Bibliographies Reprint Ser.). Repr. of 1897 ed. 18.00 (ISBN 0-8369-5761-X). Ayer Co Pubs.

Bright, James L. Home Repair. 378p. 1983. write for info. (ISBN 0-89434-030-1). Ferguson.

Bright, James R. A Brief Introduction to Technology Forecasting: Concepts & Exercises. 2nd ed. pap. 66.50 (ISBN 0-317-10863-8, 2007106). Bks Demand UMI.

Bright, James W., ed. Evangelium Secundum Iohannem: The Gospel of Saint John in West-Saxon. LC 71-144447. (Belle Lettres Ser, Section 1: No. 4). Repr. of 1904 ed. 17.50 (ISBN 0-404-53605-0). AMS Pr.

--Evangelium Secundum Lucam: The Gospel of Saint Luke in West-Saxon. LC 75-144448. (Belle Lettres Ser, Section 1: No. 3). Repr. of 1906 ed. 12.50 (ISBN 0-404-53602-6). AMS Pr.

--Evangelium Secundum Marcum: The Gospel of Saint Mark in West-Saxon. LC 74-144445. (Belle Lettres, Ser. Section 1: No. 2). Repr. of 1905 ed. 12.50 (ISBN 0-404-53603-4). AMS Pr.

--Evangelium Secundum Mattheum: The Gospel of Saint Matthew in West Saxon. LC 78-144446. (Belle Lettres Ser, Section 1: No. 1). Repr. of 1904 ed. 12.50 (ISBN 0-404-53604-2). AMS Pr.

Bright, Joan M., jt. ed. see Turner, Darwin T.

Bright, John. The Authority of the Old Testament. (Twin Brooks Ser.). 272p. 1975. pap. 6.95 (ISBN 0-8010-0637-6). Baker Bk.

--Covenant & Promise: The Prophetic Understanding of the Future in Pre-Exilic Israel. LC 76-13546. 208p. 1976. 10.00 (ISBN 0-664-20752-9). Westminster.

--A History of Israel. 3rd ed. LC 80-22774. (Illus.). 528p. 1981. 18.95 (ISBN 0-664-21381-2). Westminster.

--Hizzoner Big Bill Thompson. 1930. 25.00 (ISBN 0-932062-19-9). Sharon Hill.

--Kingdom of God. rev. ed. (Series A). 1957. pap. 6.95 (ISBN 0-687-20908-0, Apex). Abingdon.

--Public Letters. 2nd ed. Leech, H. J., ed. 1969. Repr. of 1895 ed. 16.00 (ISBN 0-527-10910-X). Kraus Repr.

--Speeches on Questions of Public Policy. 2 vols. Rogers, James E., ed. 1868. Set. 65.00 (ISBN 0-8482-7409-1). Norwood Edns.

Bright, John & McGregor, Gordon. Teaching English As a Second Language. (English As a Second Language Bk.). 1975. text ed. 12.75x (ISBN 0-582-54003-8). Longman.

Bright, John, tr. Jeremiah. LC 65-13603. (Anchor Bible Ser.: Vol. 21). 1965. 18.00 (ISBN 0-385-00823-6, Anchor Pr). Doubleday.

Bright, John W. & Miller, Raymond D. The Elements of English Versification. LC 73-16287. 1973. Repr. of 1910 ed. lib. bdg. 15.00 (ISBN 0-8414-9889-X). Folcroft.

Bright, Joyce. The Passion Season. LC 78-31894. 1981. 15.95 (ISBN 0-87949-144-2). Ashley Bks.

Bright, Laren. Laughter Is the Best Meditation: The Best of the Inner Jester. LC 78-4491. 1979. pap. 5.00 (ISBN 0-686-10176-6). Baraka Bk.

Bright, Laurence, jt. auth. see Swanston, Hamish.

Bright, Laurence & Clements, Simon, eds. The Committed Church. 1966. 39.50x (ISBN 0-317-27423-6). Elliots Bks.

Bright, Laurence, ed. see Blenkinsopp, Joseph & Challenor, John.

Bright, Laurence, ed. see Freyne, Sean & Wansbrough, Henry.

Bright, Laurence, ed. see Johnston, Leonard & Smith, Michael.

Bright, Laurence, ed. see Macpherson, Ann, et al.

Bright, Laurence, ed. see Macpherson, Duncan, et al.

Bright, Laurence, ed. see Swanston, Hamish.

Bright, Laurence, et al. Paul Two. LC 71-173033. (Scripture Discussion Commentary Ser.: Pt. 11). 224p. 1971. pap. text ed. 4.50 (ISBN 0-87946-010-5). ACTA Found.

Bright, Laurey. Sweet Vengeance. (Nightingale Ser.). 1982. pap. 6.95 (ISBN 0-8161-3417-0, Large Print Bks). G K Hall.

Bright, Leonard D., pseud. The Gifted Kids Guide to Puzzles & Mind Games. (THe Gifted Kids Guides Ser.). 144p. (Orig.). (gr. 6-12). 1985. pap. 7.95 (ISBN 0-936750-15-4). Wetherall.

Bright, Marjorie B. Nellie's Boardinghouse: A Dual Biography of Nellie Coffman & Palm Springs. 1981. 12.95 (ISBN 0-88280-068-X). ETC Pubns.

Bright, Michael. Animal Language. (Illus.). 247p. (Orig.). 1985. text ed. 24.95x (ISBN 0-8014-1837-2); pap. 12.95 (ISBN 0-8014-9340-4). Cornell U Pr.

--Cities Built to Music: Aesthetic Theories of the Victorian Gothic Revival. LC 83-23651. (Illus.). 320p. 1984. 20.00 (ISBN 0-8142-0355-8). Ohio St U Pr.

--Living with Your Allergy. 156p. 1983. 11.95 (ISBN 0-13-538736-1); pap. 5.95 (ISBN 0-13-538728-0). P-H.

Bright, Mynors, tr. see Pepys, Samuel.

Bright, Pamela. Dr. Richard Bright Seventeen Eighty-Nine to Eighteen Fifty-Eight. 312p. 1984. 22.95 (ISBN 0-370-30474-8, Pub. by the Bodley Head). Merrimack Pub Cir.

Bright, Robert. Georgie. 44p. (gr. k-1). 1959. 8.95 (ISBN 0-385-07307-0); PLB 7.95 (ISBN 0-385-07612-6). Doubleday.

--Georgie & the Baby Birds. LC 82-45865. (Balloon Bks.). (Illus.). 32p. (ps-2). 1983. 3.95 (ISBN 0-385-17246-X). Doubleday.

--Georgie & the Ball of Yarn. LC 82-45864. (Balloon Bks.). (Illus.). 32p. (ps-2). 1983. 3.95 (ISBN 0-385-17244-3). Doubleday.

--Georgie & the Buried Treasure. LC 78-22305. (Illus.). 40p. 1979. 7.95 (ISBN 0-385-14626-4); PLB (ISBN 0-385-14627-2). Doubleday.

--Georgie & the Little Dog. LC 82-45863. (Balloon Bks.). (Illus.). 32p. (ps-2). 1983. 3.95 (ISBN 0-385-17247-8). Doubleday.

--Georgie & the Magician. LC 66-10822. 45p. (ps-1). 1966. (Zephyr); pap. 2.50 (ISBN 0-385-01021-4). Doubleday.

--Georgie & the Robbers. LC 63-11384. (Illus.). 28p. (ps-1). 1963. 7.95a (ISBN 0-385-01470-8); PLB (ISBN 0-385-04483-6); pap. 2.50 (ISBN 0-385-13341-3). Doubleday.

--Georgie & the Runaway Balloon. LC 82-45862. (Balloon Bks.). (Illus.). 32p. (ps-2). 1983. 3.95 (ISBN 0-385-17245-1). Doubleday.

--Georgie Goes West. LC 73-79650. 48p. (gr. k-3). 1973. 7.95a; PLB (ISBN 0-385-05277-4). Doubleday.

--Georgie's Christmas Carol. LC 74-4832. 48p. (ps-k). 1975. 9.95 (ISBN 0-385-02344-8). Doubleday.

--Georgie's Halloween. 28p. (ps-3). 1971. 7.95a (ISBN 0-385-07773-4, 58-7154, Zephyr); pap. 2.50 (ISBN 0-385-01017-6, Zephyr); PLB 7.95 (ISBN 0-385-07778-5). Doubleday.

--Jorgito Y los Ladrones. Palacios, Argentina, tr. from Span. (gr. k-3). 1979. pap. 1.95 (ISBN 0-590-12098-0). Scholastic Inc.

--Me & the Bears. (Illus.). (ps-k). 1951. pap. 1.95 (ISBN 0-385-00969-0, Zephyr). Doubleday.

--My Red Umbrella. (Illus.). (ps-1). 1959. PLB 10.88 (ISBN 0-688-31619-0). Morrow.

--My Red Umbrella. (Illus.). 32p. (ps-1). 1985. 7.00 (ISBN 0-688-05249-5, Morrow Junior Books); pap. 3.95. Morrow.

Bright, Ruth. Music in Geriatric Care. 128p. 1981. pap. text ed. 12.95 (ISBN 0-941814-01-7). Musicgraphics.

--Practical Planning in Music Therapy for the Aged. (Illus.). 64p. (Orig.). 1981. pap. text ed. 8.95 (ISBN 0-941814-00-9). Musicgraphics.

Bright, Sarah. Hello Kitty's Early Day. LC 83-63390. (Hello Kitty Mini-Storybooks Ser.). (Illus.). 32p. (ps). 1984. pap. 1.25 (ISBN 0-394-86759-9, BYR). Random.

--Hello Kitty's Happy Christmas. LC 84-60295. (Chunky Bks.). (Illus.). 28p. (ps-k). 1984. bds. 2.95 (ISBN 0-394-86800-5, BYR). Random.

--Hello Kitty's Paper Kiss. LC 82-3734. (Illus.). 24p. (ps). 1982. bds. 3.50 (ISBN 0-394-85398-9). Random.

--Hello Kitty's Special Present. LC 83-63389. (Hello Kitty Mini Storybooks Ser.). 32p. (ps). 1984. pap. 1.25 (ISBN 0-394-86758-0, BYR). Random.

Bright, Sigrid. Hardanger Embroidery: A Complete & Practical Course. LC 77-87845. (Needlework Ser.). (Illus.). 1978. pap. 1.75 (ISBN 0-486-23592-0). Dover.

Bright, Stephen, ed. see McCarty, Dwight.

Bright, Susan. Altar. 24p. 1984. chapbook 6.00 (ISBN 0-911051-10-4). Plain View.

--Eulogy for the ERA. 1983. 3.00 (ISBN 0-911051-06-6). Plain View.

--Imago. 24p. 1983. 3.00 (ISBN 0-911051-05-8). Plain View.

--Julia. Lomax, Joseph F. & Whitebird, J., eds. (Illus.). 1977. pap. 3.00 (ISBN 0-930324-01-3). Wings Pr.

--Pewter Wheel. 1982. 3.00 (ISBN 0-911051-04-X); chapbook & VHS video. Plain View.

--Swimming the English Channel. (Fastbook 1985 Ser.). 20p. 1985. 6.00 (ISBN 0-911051-19-8). Plain View.

Bright, Thomas & Pequegnat, Linda, eds. Biota of the West Flower Garden Bank. LC 74-10372. 436p. 1974. 19.95x (ISBN 0-87201-058-9). Gulf Pub.

Bright, Timothy. A Treatise of Melancholie, Containing the Causes Thereof. LC 72-176. (English Experience Ser.: No. 212). 1969. Repr. of 1586 ed. 35.00 (ISBN 90-221-0212-2). Walter J Johnson.

--A Treatise Wherein Is Declared the Sufficiencie of English Medicines, for Cure of All Diseases, Cured with Medicine. LC 77-6860. (English Experience Ser.: No. 854). 1977. Repr. of 1580 ed. lib. bdg. 6.00 (ISBN 90-221-0854-6). Walter J Johnson.

Bright, Velma. The Story of the Little Round Barn. LC 81-65540. (Illus.). 48p. (Orig.). (gr. 2-3). 1981. 9.95x (ISBN 0-9605968-2-8); pap. 3.95 (ISBN 0-9605968-3-6). Bright Bks.

--What Would You Like to Be? (Illus.). 32p. (ps-1). PLB 7.95x (ISBN 0-9605968-0-1); pap. 2.95 (ISBN 0-9605968-1-X). Bright Bks.

Bright, Verne. Mountain Man. 190p. 1948. 9.95 (ISBN 0-87595-091-4, Western Imprints). Oreg Hist Soc.

Bright, Vonette, jt. auth. see Bright, Bill.

Bright, William. Age of the Fathers, 2 Vols. LC 77-113564. Repr. of 1903 ed. Set. 85.00 (ISBN 0-404-01077-6). Vol. 1 (ISBN 0-404-01078-4). Vol. 2 (ISBN 0-404-01079-2). AMS Pr.

--American Indian Linguistics & Literature. LC 83-24949. 159p. (Orig.). 1984. 24.50x (ISBN 3-11-009846-6); pap. 9.50x (ISBN 3-11-010241-2). Mouton.

--Bibliography of the Languages of Native California: Including Closely Related Languages of Adjacent Areas. LC 82-3331. (Native American Bibliography Ser.: No. 3). 234p. 1982. 16.50 (ISBN 0-8108-1547-8). Scarecrow.

--Chapters in Early English Church History. 3rd ed. 1897. 25.00 (ISBN 0-8337-4005-9). B Franklin.

--Variation & Change in Language: Essays by William Bright. Dil, Anwar S., ed. LC 76-23370. (Language Science & National Development Ser.). 304p. 1976. 25.00x (ISBN 0-8047-0926-2). Stanford U Pr.

Bright, William & Kahn, Saeed A. The Urdu Writing System. LC 76-40672. 48p. 1976. pap. 3.00x (ISBN 0-87950-256-8). Spoken Lang Serv.

Bright, William E. Avocations. 100p. 1984. pap. 10.00 (ISBN 0-911051-12-0). Plain View.

Brightbill, Charles K. Man & Leisure: A Philosophy of Recreation. LC 73-3009. 292p. 1973. Repr. of 1961 ed. lib. bdg. 22.50x (ISBN 0-8371-6836-8, BRML). Greenwood.

Brightbill, Steven & Brewster, Patience. Children's Storybook: Spencer's a Little Worried. incl. disk 39.95 (ISBN 0-8359-0754-6). Reston.

Brightfield. Your Amazing Adventures: Island of Fear, No. 2. 1.95 (ISBN 0-317-31918-3). Tor Bks.

--Your Amazing Adventures: Terror under the Earth, No. 3. 1.95 (ISBN 0-317-31919-1). Tor Bks.

--Your Amazing Adventures: The Castle of Doom, No. 1. 1.95 (ISBN 0-317-31917-5). Tor Bks.

--Your Amazing Adventures: The Dragonmonster, No. 4. 1.95 (ISBN 0-317-31920-5). Tor Bks.

Brightfield, Myron F. Issue in Literary Criticism. LC 68-23278. 1968. Repr. of 1932 ed. lib. bdg. 22.50x (ISBN 0-8371-0029-1, BRLC). Greenwood.

--Scott, Hazlitt, & Napoleon. LC 74-7037. 1973. lib. bdg. 10.00 (ISBN 0-8414-3173-6). Folcroft.

Brightfield, Richard. Battle of the Dragons: Your Amazing Adventure, No. 6. 128p. (Orig.). 1986. pap. 1.95 (ISBN 0-8125-6046-9, Dist. by Warner Pub Services & St. Martin). TOR Bks.

--The Castle of Doom. (What-Do-I-Do-Now-Bks.: No. 1). 128p. 1984. pap. 1.95 (ISBN 0-8125-6036-1). Tor Bks.
--The Curse of Batterstea Hall, No. 30. (Choose Your Own Adventure Ser.). 128p. 1984. pap. 1.95 (ISBN 0-553-23937-6). Bantam.
--The Dragonmaster. (What-Do-I-Do-Now-Bks.: No. 4). 129p. 1985. pap. 1.95 (ISBN 0-8125-6042-6). Tor Bks.
--The Dragon's Den. (Choose Your Own Adventure Ser.: No. 33). (Illus.). 128p. (gr. 5-9). 1984. pap. 1.95 (ISBN 0-553-24249-0). Bantam.
--Island of Fear. (What-Do-I-Do-Now-Bks.: No. 2). 128p. 1984. pap. 1.95 (56038-8). Tor Bks.
--The Phantom Submarine. (Choose Your Own Adventure Ser.: No. 26). 111p. (gr. 3-6). 1983. pap. 1.95 (ISBN 0-553-23635-0). Bantam.
--Revenge of the Dragonmaster. (Your Maze Adventures Ser.: No. 5). 128p. (Orig.). 1985. pap. 1.95 (ISBN 0-8125-6044-2, Dist. by Warner Pub Services & St. Martin). Tor Bks.
--The Secret Treasure of Tibet. (Choose Your Own Adventure Ser.: No. 36). 128p. (Orig.). 1984. pap. 1.95 (ISBN 0-553-24522-8). Bantam.
--Terror under the Earth. (What-Do-I-Do-Now-Bks.: No. 3). 128p. 1984. pap. 1.95 (ISBN 0-8125-6040-X). Tor Bks.
Brightfield, Rick, jt. auth. see Orser, Mary.
Bright-Holmes, John. The Joy of Cricket. (Illus.). 1984. 27.00 (ISBN 0-436-06857-5, Pub. by Secker & Warburg UK). David & Charles.
Bright-Holmes, John, ed. see Muggeridge, Malcolm.
Brightly, Charles. The Method of Founding Stereotype as Practised by Charles Brightly. Bidwell, John, ed. (Nineteenth Century Book Arts & Printing History Ser.). 36.00 (ISBN 0-8240-3883-5). Garland Pub.
Brightly, S. G. Setting Out: A Guide for Site Engineers. 262p. 1975. pap. text ed. 17.50x (ISBN 0-258-96929-6, Pub. by Granada England). Brookfield Pub Co.
Brightman. Statistics in Plain English. 1986. pap. text ed. price not set (ISBN 0-538-13210-8, M21). SW Pub.
Brightman, Alan. Like Me. (Illus.). 48p. (gr. k-3). 1976. PLB 12.45 (ISBN 0-316-10808-1); pap. 6.95 (ISBN 0-316-10807-3). Little.
Brightman, Edgar S. Moral Laws. LC 33-4178. 1968. Repr. of 1933 ed. 17.00 (ISBN 0-527-11000-0). Kraus Repr.
--Personality & Religion. LC 75-3084. (Philosophy in America Ser.). Repr. of 1934 ed. 14.50 (ISBN 0-404-59083-7). AMS Pr.
--Philosophy of Religion. LC 72-95112. Repr. of 1940 ed. lib. bdg. 29.75x (ISBN 0-8371-2468-9, BRPR). Greenwood.
--The Problem of God. LC 75-3085. (Philosophy in America Ser.). Repr. of 1930 ed. 21.50 (ISBN 0-404-59084-5). AMS Pr.
--Religious Values. Repr. of 1925 ed. 22.00 (ISBN 0-527-11010-8). Kraus Repr.
--The Spiritual Life. LC 75-3086. (Philosophy in America Ser.). Repr. of 1942 ed. 22.00 (ISBN 0-404-59085-3). AMS Pr.
--Studies in Personalism. Steinkraus, Warren & Beck, Robert, eds. (Signature Series of Philosophy & Religion). Date not set. 16.00 (ISBN 0-86610-067-9). Meridian Pub.
Brightman, Edgar S., ed. Personalism in Theology. LC 75-3088. (Philosophy in America Ser.). Repr. of 1943 ed. 18.00 (ISBN 0-404-59086-1). AMS Pr.
Brightman, Edgare S. The Problem of God. 1979. Repr. of 1930 ed. lib. bdg. 30.00 (ISBN 0-8482-7365-6). Norwood Edns.
Brightman, F. E., tr. & intro. by see Andrewes, Lancelot.
Brightman, Frank. Barbara Nicholson's Plants of the British Isles. 80p. 1982. 45.00x (ISBN 0-00-410416-1, Pub. by Brit Mus England). State Mutual Bk.
Brightman, Frank, ed. Natural History Book Reviews: An International Biography. 1981. 35.00x (ISBN 0-686-72935-8, Pub by A B Academic England). State Mutual Bk.
Brightman, Harvey J. Problem-Solving: A Logical & Creative Approach. LC 80-25078. 1980. 18.95 (ISBN 0-88406-131-0). Ga St U Busn Pub.
Brightman, Robert. Bernzomatic Torch Tips. LC 77-71478. (Illus.). 1977. 6.95 (ISBN 0-916752-16-X). Dorison Hse.
--One-Hundred One Practical Uses for Propane Torches. (Illus.). 1978. pap. 5.95 (ISBN 0-8306-1030-8, 1030). TAB Bks.
--Torch Tips: Hundreds of Hot Jobs for the Job. rev. ed. LC 77-771478. (Illus.). 144p. 1985. 10.95 (ISBN 0-916752-16-X). Dorison Hse.
Brighton, C. A., jt. auth. see Dubois, P.
Brighton, C. A., et al. Styrene Polymers: Technology & Environmental Aspects. (Illus.). 284p. 1979. 44.50 (ISBN 0-85334-810-3, Pub. by Elsevier Applied Sci England). Elsevier.
Brighton, Carl T., et al. Electical Properties of Bone & Cartilage: Experimental Effects & Clinical Applications. 686p. 1979. 65.00 (ISBN 0-8089-1228-3, 790663). Grune.
Brighton, Catherine. My Hands, My World. LC 84-9670. (Illus.). 32p. (gr. k-3). 1984. 11.95 (ISBN 0-02-712900-4). Macmillan.
--The Picture. (Illus.). 28p. 1986. price not set (ISBN 0-571-13641-9). Faber & Faber.
Brighton, Howard. Handbook for Teacher Aides. LC 71-168583. 126p. 1972. 9.90 (ISBN 0-87812-017-3). Pendell Pub.
--Utilizing Teacher Aides in Differentiated Staffing. LC 75-168584. 244p. 1972. 14.00 (ISBN 0-87812-016-5). Pendell Pub.
Brighton, J. A., jt. auth. see Hughes, W. F.
Brighton, Ray. The Checkered Career of Tobias Lear. (Illus.). 320p. 1984. 30.00 (ISBN 0-915819-03-1). Portsmouth Marine Soc.
--Clipper Ships from the Port of Portsmouth & the Men Who Built Them. (Illus.). 175p. 1985. 25.00 (ISBN 0-915819-05-8). Portsmouth Marine Soc.
--The Prescott Story. (Illus.). 119p. 1982. 15.00 (ISBN 0-915819-01-5). Portsmouth Marine Soc.
Brighton Women & Science Group. Alice Through the Microscope: The Power of Science Over Women's Lives. 310p. 19.95 (ISBN 0-86068-078-9, Virago Pr); pap. 9.95 (ISBN 0-86068-079-7). Merrimack Pub Cir.
Brightwell, D. B. Concordance to Tennyson. LC 72-124396. (Studies in Tennyson, No. 27). 1970. Repr. of 1869 ed. lib. bdg. 46.95x (ISBN 0-8383-1099-0). Haskell.
Brightwell, Robin, jt. auth. see Gilling, Dick.
Brighty, S. Setting Out: A Guide for Site Engineers. (Illus.). 264p. 1975. text ed. 18.95x. Beekman Pubs.
Brighty, S. G. Setting Out: Guide for Site Engineers. 272p. 1975. 14.00x (ISBN 0-246-11485-1, Pub. by Granada England). Sheridan.
Brigley, Catherine M. Pediatrics for the Practical Nurse. LC 72-9384. (Illus.). 224p. 1973. pap. 12.00 (ISBN 0-8273-0332-7); instructor's guide 3.80 (ISBN 0-8273-0333-5). Delmar.
Brignac, Margie. Southern Spice a la Microwave. LC 81-19241. (Illus.). 240p. (Orig.). 1982. spiral 8.95 (ISBN 0-88289-318-1). Pelican.
Brignal, T. J., jt. auth. see Bryer, R. A.
Brignano, Russell. Black Americans in Autobiography: An Annotated Bibliography of Autobiographies & Autobiographical Books Written since the Civil War. Revised & Expanded Edition ed. LC 83-20505. 193p. 1984. text ed. 27.50 (ISBN 0-8223-0559-3). Duke.
--Black Americans in Autobiography: An Annotated Bibliography of Autobiographies & Autobiographical Books Written Since the Civil War. LC 73-92535. pap. 31.50 (ISBN 0-317-20093-3, 2023373). Bks Demand UMI.
Brignano, Russell C. Richard Wright: An Introduction to the Man & His Works. LC 72-81667. (Critical Essays in Modern Literature Ser). 1970. pap. 7.95x (ISBN 0-8229-5211-4). U of Pittsburgh Pr.
Brignoli, Paolo M. A Catalogue of the Araneae Described Between 1940 & 1981. LC 83-7937. 784p. 1983. 90.00 (ISBN 0-7190-0856-5, Pub. by Manchester Univ Pr). Longwood Pub Group.
Brigstocke, T. D., jt. auth. see Wilson, P. N.
Brihaye, J., ed. Proceedings of the Sixth European Congress of Neurosurgery: Organized by the European Association of Neurosurgical Societies of Paris, July 15-20, 1979. (Act Neurochirurgica Supplements: Vol. 28). (Illus.). 1979. pap. 115.10 (ISBN 0-387-81534-1). Springer-Verlag.
Brihaye, J., jt. ed. see Samii, M.
Brijbhushan, Jamila. Masterpieces of Indian Jewelry. (Illus.). viii, 53p. 1981. text ed. 35.00x (ISBN 0-86590-051-5, Pub. by Taraporevala India). Apt Bks.
--Muslim Women: In Purdah & Out of It. 150p. 1980. text ed. 15.00x (ISBN 0-7069-1074-5, Pub. by Vikas India). Advent NY.
Brik, Lily, jt. auth. see Mayakovsky, Vladimir.
Briles, Judith. Money Phases. 1985. pap. 7.95 (ISBN 0-671-55451-4, Fireside). S&S.
--Money Phases: The Six Financial Stages of a Woman's Life. 224p. 1984. 14.95 (ISBN 0-671-45609-1). S&S.
--The Woman's Guide to Financial Savvy. Rev. ed. 240p. 1982. pap. 6.95 (ISBN 0-312-88651-9). St Martin.
Briley, Alice, ed. Encore, Encore. LC 75-30253. (Poetry Ser.: No. 5). (Illus.). 1976. 8.00x (ISBN 0-910042-25-X); pap. 3.00x (ISBN 0-910042-26-8). Allegheny.
Briley, Bruce E. Introduction to Telephone Switching. LC 83-8835. 251p. 1983. 26.95 (ISBN 0-201-11246-9). Addison-Wesley.
Briley, J. M., Jr. Pediatric Ward. LC 82-39991. 1985. 16.95 (ISBN 0-87949-229-5). Ashley Bks.
Briley, John. Gandhi: Screenplay for the Film by Richard Attenborough. LC 83-80383. 192p. 1983. 6.95 (ISBN 0-394-62471-8, E856, Ever). Grove.
Brilhart, John K. Effective Group Discussion. 4th ed. 352p. 1982. pap. text ed. write for info. (ISBN 0-697-04194-8); instr's. manual avail. (ISBN 0-697-04204-9). Wm C Brown.
Brilhart, John K., jt. auth. see Edwards, Barba J.
Brill. Damages, Brill's Ark Law. 532p. 1984. 69.95 (ISBN 0-317-18674-4). Harrison Co GA.
Brill, A. Right to Financial Privacy Act: A Compliance Guide for Financial Institutions. 1979. 45.00 (ISBN 0-13-781161-6). P-H.
Brill, A. A. Basic Principles of Psychoanalysis. 316p. 1985. pap. text ed. 10.75 (ISBN 0-8191-4665-X). U Pr of Amer.
--Fundamental Conceptions of Psychoanalysis. LC 73-2390. (Mental Illness & Social Policy; the American Experience Ser.). Repr. of 1921 ed. 22.00 (ISBN 0-405-05198-0). Ayer Co Pubs.
--Psychoanalysis, Its Theories & Practical Application. LC 78-180559. (Medicine & Society in America Ser). 346p. 1972. Repr. of 1913 ed. 20.00 (ISBN 0-405-03939-5). Ayer Co Pubs.
Brill, A. A., ed. & intro. by see Freud, Sigmund.
Brill, A. A., tr. see Freud, Sigmund.
Brill, A. B., et al. Low-Level Radiation Effects: A Fact Book. 2nd ed. Bigler, Rodney E., ed. LC 82-16937. 156p. 1982. looseleaf incl. 1985 updates 32.00 (ISBN 0-932004-23-7); Updates 1985; 80p. Insert Package 10.00 (ISBN 0-317-19594-8). Soc Nuclear Med.
Brill, A. Bertrand. Low Level Radiation Fact Book. Adelstein, James, et al, eds. LC 82-16939. 156p. 1982. 27.50 (ISBN 0-932004-14-8). Soc Nuclear Med.
Brill, A. S. Transition Metals in Biochemistry. (Molecular Biology, Biochemistry & Biophysics: Vol. 26). 1977. 34.00 (ISBN 0-387-08291-3). Springer-Verlag.
Brill, Abraham A. Basic Principles of Psychoanalysis. LC 75-31431. 298p. 1976. Repr. of 1949 ed. lib. bdg. 24.75x (ISBN 0-8371-8500-9, BRBP). Greenwood.
--Basic Principles of Psychoanalysis. (Problems of American Society). 1968. pap. 0.75 (ISBN 0-671-47147-3). WSP.
--Freud's Contribution to Psychiatry. 11.25 (ISBN 0-8446-1738-5). Peter Smith.
Brill, Abraham A., tr. see Freud, Sigmund.
Brill, Alan E. Building Controls into Structured Systems. LC 82-70209. (Illus.). 168p. (Orig.). 1983. 29.00 (ISBN 0-917072-38-3); pap. 22.00 (ISBN 0-917072-27-8). Yourdon.
Brill, Alan E., ed. Techniques of EDP Project Management: A Book of Readings. (Illus.). 296p. (Orig.). 1984. pap. 29.00 (ISBN 0-917072-42-1). Yourdon.
Brill, Alida, jt. auth. see McClosky, Herbert.
Brill, Charles. Indian & Free: A Contemporary Portrait of Life on a Chippewa Reservation. LC 73-91450. (Illus.). vi, 138p. 1974. 12.95 (ISBN 0-8166-0710-9). U of Minn Pr.
Brill, Chip, ed. New York Casting-Survival Guide & Datebook 1985. 200p. 1984. pap. 13.85 (ISBN 0-87314-040-0). Peter Glenn.
--New York Casting-Survival Guide & Datebook 1984: 1984. 200p. 1983. pap. 12.95 (ISBN 0-87314-039-7). Peter Glenn.
Brill, Chip, jt. ed. see Glenn, Peter.
Brill, Chip, jt. ed. see Vando, David.
Brill, Earl H. The Christian Moral Vision. (Church's Teaching Ser.: Vol. 6). 254p. 1979. 5.95 (ISBN 0-8164-0423-2, Pub. by Seabury); pap. 4.95 (ISBN 0-8164-2219-2). Winston Pr.
Brill, Ernie. I Looked Over Jordan & Other Stories. LC 80-51042. 291p. 1980. 15.00 (ISBN 0-89608-118-4); pap. 6.00 (ISBN 0-89608-117-6). South End Pr.
Brill, Ester & Kilts, Dawn. Foundations for Nursing. (Illus.). 813p. 1980. 37.50 (ISBN 0-8385-2687-X). ACC.
Brill, Harry. Why Organizers Fail: The Story of a Rent Strike. LC 76-104103. (California Studies in Urbanization & Environmental Design). 1971. 26.00 (ISBN 0-520-01672-6). U of Cal Pr.
Brill, Henry, jt. auth. see Mule, S. J.
Brill, James E. & Woodall, Linda D., eds. Texas Probate System, 2 Vols. rev. ed. LC 83-50453. 1281p. 1983. Set. loose-leaf 135.00 (ISBN 0-938160-34-6, 6263). State Bar TX.
Brill, Laura. Business Writing Quick & Easy. 192p. (Orig.). 1982. 13.95 (ISBN 0-8144-5625-1); pap. 5.95 (ISBN 0-8144-7598-1). AMACOM.
Brill, Leon. The Clinical Treatment of Substance Abusers. 1981. 21.95x (ISBN 0-317-30547-6). Free Pr.
--The De-Addiction Process: Studies in the De-Addiction of Confirmed Heroin Addicts. 180p. 1972. 19.75x (ISBN 0-398-02532-0). C C Thomas.
Brill, Leon & Winick, Charles. The Yearbook of Substance Use & Abuse, Vol. II. LC 70-174271. 360p. 1980. 34.95 (ISBN 0-87705-487-8). Human Sci Pr.
Brill, Leon & Harms, Ernest, eds. The Yearbook of Drug Abuse, Vol. I. LC 70-174271. (Illus.). 386p. 1973. text ed. 34.95 (ISBN 0-87705-060-0). Human Sci Pr.
Brill, Leon, jt. ed. see Chambers, Carl D.
Brill, Leon, et al. The Treatment of Substance Abusers. Turner, Francis J. & Strean, Herbert S., eds. LC 81-66433. (Fields of Practice Ser.). 256p. 1981. 21.95 (ISBN 0-02-905160-6). Free Pr.
Brill, Michael E. Bamboozled. (Orig.). 1985. pap. 3.00 (ISBN 0-87602-240-9). Anchorage.
Brill, Mordecai, et al. Write Your Own Wedding: A Personal Guide for Couples of All Faiths. rev. ed. LC 85-7156. 120p. 1985. pap. 5.95 (ISBN 0-317-14437-5). New Century.
Brill, Naomi I. Working with People: The Helping Process. 3rd ed. LC 84-941. (Orig.). 1984. pap. 13.95x (ISBN 0-582-28460-0). Longman.
Brill, Richard. Schule Neidharts. 36.00 (ISBN 0-384-05840-X); pap. 31.00 (ISBN 0-685-02227-7). Johnson Repr.
Brill, Richard G. The Education of the Deaf: Administrative & Professional Developments. 301p. 1974. pap. 2.75 (ISBN 0-913580-03-1). Gallaudet Coll.
--International Congresses on Education of the Deaf: An Analytical History, 1878-1980. LC 83-16578. x, 470p. 1984. 24.95 (ISBN 0-913580-87-2). Gallaudet Coll.
--Mainstreaming the Prelingually Deaf Child. LC 78-64566. 196p. 1978. pap. 2.75 (ISBN 0-913580-60-0). Gallaudet Coll.
Brill, Steven. The American Lawyer Guide to Leading Law Firms, 1983-1984, 2 vols. Kenyon, Joan, ed. 1000p. 1983. 475.00 set. Vol. 1 (ISBN 0-9606682-2-5). Vol. 2 (ISBN 0-9606682-3-3). Set. write for info. (ISBN 0-9606682-1-7). Am Law Pub.
--The Teamsters. 1979. pap. 2.75 (ISBN 0-671-82905-X). PB.
Brill, Thomas B. Light: Its Interaction with Art & Antiquities. LC 80-16975. (Illus.). 300p. 1980. 32.50x (ISBN 0-306-40416-8, Plenum Pr). Plenum Pub.
Brill, Thomas M. & Kitchens, John G., eds. Gator Country Cooks. 5th ed. LC 75-12456. (Illus.). 1981. pap. 9.95 (ISBN 0-9606616-0-3); pap. 5.97. Jr League Gainesville.
Brilla, J., ed. Trends in Applications of Pure Mathematics to Mechanics, Vol. 4. (Monographs & Studies: No. 20). 288p. 1984. text ed. 39.95 (ISBN 0-273-08606-5). Pitman Pub MA.
Brillant, R. The Arch of Septimius Severus in the Roman Forum. (Memoirs: No. 29). (Illus.). 270p. 1967. 37.00 (ISBN 0-318-12316-9). Am Acad Rome.
Brillat-Savarin. The Physiology of Taste. Fisher, M. F., tr. LC 78-7199. 1978. pap. 9.95 (ISBN 0-15-671770-0, Harv). HarBraceJ.
Brillat-Savarin, Anselme. The Physiology of Taste. Orig. Title: La Physiologie du Gout. (Illus.). 350p. 1982. pap. 9.95 (ISBN 0-918172-11-X). Leetes Isl.
Brillat-Savarin, Jean. The Philosopher in the Kitchen. (Handbook Ser.). 384p. 1981. pap. 5.95 (ISBN 0-14-046157-4). Penguin.
Briller, Bert R., ed. see Knight, Pamela.
Briller, Bert R., jt. ed. see Television Information Office Staff.
Brilliant, Alan. Journeyman. pap. 3.50 (ISBN 0-87775-014-9). Unicorn Pr.
Brilliant, Alan, tr. see Garcia Lorca, Federico.
Brilliant, Ashleigh. All I Want Is a Warm Bed & a Kind Word & Unlimited Power. (Illus.). 168p. 1985. 12.95 (ISBN 0-88007-155-9); pap. 5.95 (ISBN 0-88007-156-7). Woodbridge Pr.
--Appreciate Me Now & Avoid the Rush. LC 81-11582. (Illus.). 160p. (Orig.). 1981. 12.95 (ISBN 0-912800-97-6); pap. 4.95 (ISBN 0-912800-94-1). Woodbridge Pr.
--I Feel Much Better, Now That I've Given up Hope. LC 84-2284. (Illus.). 168p. 1984. 12.95 (ISBN 0-88007-145-1); pap. 5.95 (ISBN 0-88007-147-8). Woodbridge Pr.
--I Have Abandoned My Search for Truth, & Am Now Looking for a Good Fantasy. LC 80-22852. (Illus.). 160p. (Orig.). 1981. 12.95 (ISBN 0-912800-66-6); pap. 5.95 (ISBN 0-912800-90-9). Woodbridge Pr.
--I May Not Be Totally Perfect, but Parts of Me Are Excellent. LC 79-10052. (Illus.). 1979. 12.95 (ISBN 0-912800-66-6); pap. 5.95 (ISBN 0-912800-67-4). Woodbridge Pr.
Brilliant, Lawrence B. The Management of Smallpox Eradication in India. (Illus.). 200p. 1985. text ed. 18.50x (ISBN 0-472-10059-9). U of Mich Pr.
Brilliant, Livia see Rothschild, Eric.
Brilliant, Richard. Gesture & Rank in Roman Art. (Connecticut Academy of Arts & Sciences Memoirs: No. 14). 238p. 1963. pap. 35.00 (ISBN 0-208-00639-7). Shoe String.
--Visual Narratives: Storytelling in Etruscan & Roman Art. LC 83-18869. (Illus.). 208p. 1984. 37.50s (ISBN 0-8014-1558-6). Cornell U Pr.
Brilliantov, A. I. Ioann Skot Erigena. LC 80-2358. Repr. of 1898 ed. 64.50 (ISBN 0-404-18904-0). AMS Pr.
Brillinger, D. R. & Krishnaiah, P. R. Handbook of Statistics: Time Series in the Frequency Domain. (Handbook of Statistics: Vol. 3). 1984. 88.50 (I-461-83). Elsevier.
Brillinger, David R. Time Series: Data Analysis & Theory. enl. ed. LC 80-84117. (Illus.). 552p. 1980. text ed. 44.00x (ISBN 0-8162-1150-7). Holden-Day.
Brillinger, David R., ed. see Tukey, John W.
Brillinger, Peter C., jt. auth. see Cohen, Doron J.
Brill Koln, E. J. Alo Raun Bibliography. (Arcadia Bibliographica Virorum Eruditorum Ser.: Fasc. 2). 29p. 1980. 18.00 (ISBN 0-931922-02-X). Eurolingua.
--Erich Kunze Bibliographie: Mit Unterstutzung der Friedrich-Ebert-Stiftung. (Arcadia Bibliographica Virorum Eruditorum Ser.: Fasc. 3). 33p. 1980. 18.00 (ISBN 0-931922-07-0). Eurolingua.
--Felix Johannes Oinas Bibliography. Feldstein, R. F., compiled by. (Arcadia Bibliographica Virorum Eruditorum Ser.: Fasc. 4). 51p. 1981. 18.00 (ISBN 0-931922-03-8). Eurolingua.
Brillouin, Leon. Relativity Reexamined. 1970. 30.50 (ISBN 0-12-134945-4). Acad Pr.

--Wave Propagation & Group Velocity. (Pure & Applied Physics Ser.: Vol. 8). 1960. 33.50 (ISBN 0-12-134968-3). Acad Pr.

Briloff, Abraham J. More Debits Than Credits: The Burnt Investor's Guide to Financial Statements. LC 74-15812. (Illus.). 448p. 1976. 16.30i (ISBN 0-06-010476-7, HarpT). Har-Row.

--Unaccountable Accounting. LC 71-156509. 1972. 16.30i (ISBN 0-06-010471-6, HarpT). Har-Row.

Brim, Frank M. Satan's Secret Revealed: From the Files of a Christian Exorcist. 176p. 1983. pap. 5.00 (ISBN 0-9612676-0-7). World Wide Mini.

Brim, John A. & Spain, David H. Research Design in Anthropology: Paradigms & Pragmatics in the Testing of Hypotheses. 123p. 1982. pap. text ed. 6.95x (ISBN 0-8290-0583-8). Irvington.

Brim, O. C., Jr., jt. ed. see Baltes, P. B.

Brim, Orville G., jt. ed. see Baltes, Paul B.

Brim, Orville G., Jr. & Wheeler, Stanton. Socialization after Childhood: Two Essays. 116p. 1966. pap. text ed. 19.00 (ISBN 0-471-10418-3). Wiley.

Brim, Orville G., Jr. & Kagan, Jerome, eds. Constancy & Change in Human Development. (Illus.). 760p. 1980. 35.00x (ISBN 0-674-16625-6). Harvard U Pr.

Brim, Orville G., Jr., jt. ed. see Baltes, Paul.

Brim, Orville G., Jr., jt. ed. see Baltes, Paul B.

Brim, Orville G., Jr., et al. The Dying Patient. LC 80-20141. 390p. 1981. pap. 9.95x (ISBN 0-87855-684-2). Transaction Bks.

--American Beliefs & Attitudes about Intelligence. LC 75-76746. 292p. 1969. 9.95x (ISBN 0-87154-152-1). Russell Sage.

--Personality & Decision Processes: Studies in the Social Psychology of Thinking. LC 62-8659. 1962. 27.50x (ISBN 0-8047-0047-8). Stanford U Pr.

Brim, Orville G., Jr., et al, eds. The Dying Patient. Freeman, Howard E. LC 77-104181. 1970. 12.95x (ISBN 0-87154-155-6). Russell Sage.

Brimacombe, J. K., et al. Continious Casting, Vol. II. LC 83-81654. 244p. 1984. 50.00 (ISBN 0-89520-160-7). Iron & Steel.

Brimacombe, J. S., ed. Carbohydrate Chemistry, Vols. 1-11. Incl. Vol. 1. 1967 Literature. 1968. 31.00 (ISBN 0-85186-002-8); Vol. 2. 1968 Literature. 1969. 31.00 (ISBN 0-85186-012-5); Vol. 3. 1969 Literature. 1970. 34.00 (ISBN 0-85186-022-2); Vol. 4. 1970 Literature. 1971. 34.00 (ISBN 0-85186-032-X); Vol. 5. 1971 Literature. 1972. 36.00 (ISBN 0-85186-042-7); Vol. 6. 1972 Literature. 1973. 38.00 (ISBN 0-85186-052-4); Vol. 7. 1973 Literature. 1975. 56.00 (ISBN 0-85186-062-1); Vol. 8. 1974 Literature. 1976. 61.00 (ISBN 0-85186-072-9); Vol. 9. 1975-76 Literature. 1977. 82.00 (ISBN 0-85186-082-6); Vol. 10. 1976-77 Literature. 1978. 82.00 (ISBN 0-85186-092-3); Vol. 11. LC 79-67610. 1979. 97.00 (ISBN 0-85186-102-4). LC 79-67610 (Pub. by Royal Soc Chem London). Am Chemical.

Brimah, Farouk K. Black Voter Registration in the South: 1940-1982. 1983. pap. 1.00 (ISBN 0-318-00992-7). Voter Ed Proj.

--Statistical Profile of Arkansas. 1983. pap. 1.00 (ISBN 0-318-00982-X). Voter Ed Proj.

--Statistical Profile of Congressional Districts in the South. 1983. pap. 1.00 (ISBN 0-318-00981-1). Voter Ed Proj.

--Statistical Profile of Congressional Districts of North Carolina. 1983. pap. 1.00 (ISBN 0-318-00980-3). Voter Ed Proj.

Brimah, Farouk K., jt. auth. see Hudlin, Richard A.

Brimah, K. Farouk. Black Representation at the Federal & State Legislative Levels in the South. 1983. pap. 1.00 (ISBN 0-318-00965-X). Voter Ed Proj.

--Black Voter Participation in the General Elections in the South: 1982. 1983. pap. 1.00 (ISBN 0-318-00967-6). Voter Ed Proj.

--The General Election of 1982: Fulton County. 1983. pap. 1.00 (ISBN 0-318-00964-1). Voter Ed Proj.

--Number of Electoral Votes for Each of the Eleven Southern States. 1983. write for info. Voter Ed Proj.

--Number of Electoral Votes for the Fifty States. 1983. write for info. Voter Ed Proj.

--Representation of Blacks in Elective Offices in Majority Black Southern Counties. 1983. write for info. Voter Ed Proj.

--Statistical Profile of Majority Black Counties in the South. 1983. write for info. Voter Ed Proj.

--Whither the Future of Blacks in the Republican Party? Reprint from Political Science Quarterly (Summer 1982, 207-23) pap. 1.00 (ISBN 0-318-00968-4). Voter Ed Proj.

Brimah, K. Farouk, jt. auth. see Hudlin, Richard.

Brimah, K. Farouk, jt. auth. see Hudlin, Richard A.

Brimblecombe, F. S., et al, eds. Separation & Special Care Units. (Clinics in Developmental Medicine Ser.: Vol. 68). 120p. 1978. text ed. 19.75 (ISBN 0-433-30423-5, Pub. by Spastics Intl England). Lippincott.

Brimblecombe, Frederic & Barltrop, Donald. Children in Health & Disease. (Illus.). 1978. text ed. 45.00 (ISBN 0-7216-0707-1, Pub. by Bailliere-Tindall). Saunders.

Brimblecombe, R. W., jt. auth. see Bradley, P. B.

Brimer, A., et al. Sources of Difference in School Achievement. 228p. 1978. 17.00x (ISBN 0-85633-155-4, Pub. by NFER Nelson UK). Taylor & Francis.

Brimer, John. Growing Herbs in Pots. 1978. pap. 6.95 (ISBN 0-671-24207-5, Fireside). S&S.

Brimer, John B. The Homeowner's Complete Outdoor Building Book (Wood & Masonry Construction) (Popular Science Ser.). (Illus.). 512p. 1985. 29.95 (ISBN 0-943822-47-5). Rodale Pr Inc.

Brimley, Herbert H. North Carolina Naturalist, H. H. Brimley. facs. ed. Odum, Eugene P., ed. LC 78-134058. (Essay Index Reprint Ser). 1949. 18.00 (ISBN 0-8369-2145-3). Ayer Co Pubs.

Brimley, Johnson R., ed. see Marryat, Frederick.

Brimley, Vern, jt. auth. see Burrup, Percy.

Brimlow, George F. Harney County Oregon & Its Rangeland. rev. ed. (Illus.). 360p. 1980. pap. 12.00 (ISBN 0-89288-039-2). Maverick.

Brimmer, Andrew F. Central Banking & Credit Allocation. (W. H. Irons Memorial Lecture Ser.: No. 2). 14p. 1975. pap. 1.00 (ISBN 0-87755-217-7). Bureau Busn UT.

Brimmer, Andrew F. & Hawkins, Robert G. The World Banking System: Outlook in a Context of Crisis. (Joseph I. Lubin Memorial Lecture Ser.). 100p. 1985. 15.00x (ISBN 0-8147-1068-9). NYU Pr.

Brin, Andre. Energy & the Oceans. 164p. 1981. 40.00x (ISBN 0-86103-024-9, Pub. by Westbury House). State Mutual Bk.

Brin, David. The Postman. LC 85-47647. 256p. 1985. 15.95 (ISBN 0-553-05107-5). Bantam.

--The Practice Effect. 288p. (Orig.). 1984. pap. text ed. 2.95 (ISBN 0-553-25215-1). Bantam.

--Startide Rising. 352p. 1983. pap. 3.50 (ISBN 0-553-23495-1). Bantam.

--Sundiver. 1980. pap. 2.95 (ISBN 0-553-25216-X). Bantam.

--The Uplift War. 1985. pap. cancelled (ISBN 0-317-17807-5). Bantam.

Brin, Herb. ICH Bin Ein Jude. LC 81-15256. 146p. 1983. 9.95 (ISBN 0-8246-0275-7). Jonathan David.

Brin, Ruth. Butterflies Are Beautiful. LC 73-21359. (Nature Books for Young Readers). 32p. (gr. 4-8). 1974. PLB 5.95 (ISBN 0-8225-0290-9). Lerner Pubns.

--The Shabbat Catalogue. 1971. 5.00x (ISBN 0-87068-636-4). Ktav.

Brin, Ruth F. Contributions of Women: Social Reform. LC 77-9585. (Contributions of Women Ser.). (Illus.). (gr. 6 up). 1977. PLB 8.95 (ISBN 0-87518-145-7). Dillon.

--David & Goliath. (Foreign Lands Bks). (Illus.). 32p. (gr. k-5). 1977. PLB 5.95 (ISBN 0-8225-0365-4). Lerner Pubns.

--A Rag of Love. 1969. pap. text ed. 3.95 (ISBN 0-934682-00-3). Emmett.

--The Story of Esther. LC 75-743. (Outstanding Books from Foreign Lands Ser.). 32p. (gr. 1-4). 1976. PLB 5.95 (ISBN 0-8225-0364-6). Lerner Pubns.

Brin, Ruth F. & Stalland, Mary K. Wildflowers to Color. (Illus.). 36p. 1982. pap. 1.00 (ISBN 0-686-83871-8). Nodin Pr.

Brinberg, David & McGrath, Joseph E. Validity & the Research Process. 1985. 19.95 (ISBN 0-8039-2303-1). Sage.

Brinberg, David & Kidder, Louise H., eds. Forms of Validity in Research. LC 81-48577. (Methodology of Social & Behavioral Science Ser.: No. 12). 1982. 9.95x (ISBN 0-87589-912-9). Jossey-Bass.

Brincard, Marie-Therese, ed. The Art of Metal in Africa. LC 82-72765. (Illus.). 148p. 1982. pap. 18.00 (ISBN 0-89192-347-0, Pub. by African Am Inst). Interbk Inc.

Brincat, Matthew De. Salt & Light. 56p. (gr. 6up). 1983. pap. 3.00 (ISBN 0-911423-00-1). Bible-Speak.

Brinch-Hanson, P. Architecture of Concurrent Programs. 1977. 36.95 (ISBN 0-13-044628-9). P-H.

Brinckle, Gertrude, jt. auth. see Morse, Willard S.

Brinckloe, Julie. Fireflies! LC 84-20158. (Illus.). 32p. (gr. k-3). 1985. PLB 11.95 (ISBN 0-02-713310-9). Macmillan.

--A Stitch in Time for the Brothers Rhyme. LC 84-17721. (Imagination Clippers Ser.). (Illus.). 32p. (ps-3). 1985. PLB 27.97 (ISBN 0-8172-2284-7); cassette only 14.00. Raintree Pubs.

Brinckloe, William D. & Coughlin, Mary T. Managing Organizations. 1977. text ed. write for info. (ISBN 0-02-471200-0). Macmillan.

Brinckman, F. E. & Bellama, J. M., eds. Organometals & Organometalloids: Occurrence & Fate in the Environment. LC 78-24316. (ACS Symposium Ser.: No. 82). 1978. 44.95 (ISBN 0-8412-0461-6). Am Chemical.

Brinckmeyer, Edward, ed. Mitternachzeitung Fuer Gebildete Stand, Vol 11, Nos 1-212. 1973. Repr. of 1836 ed. 155.00 (ISBN 0-384-39224-5). Johnson Repr.

Brindamour, Jean-Louis, ed. see Vogt, Douglas & Sultan, Gary.

Brindel, June. Nobody is Ever Missing. LC 83-18087. (Illinois Writers Ser.: No. 3). (Illus.). 160p. 1984. 11.95 (ISBN 0-931704-15-4); pap. 3.95 (ISBN 0-931704-14-6). Story Pr.

Brindel, June R. Ariadne. 246p. 1981. pap. 6.95 (ISBN 0-312-04912-9). St Martin.

--Ariadne. 272p. 1980. 10.95 (ISBN 0-312-04911-0). St Martin.

--Phaedra: A Novel of Ancient Athens. 256p. 1985. 14.95 (ISBN 0-312-60399-1). St Martin.

Brindle, J. V. & White, J. J. Reflections from the Third Day: Photographic Revelations of Plant Design. (Illus., Orig.). 1978. pap. 6.00x (ISBN 0-913196-20-7). Hunt Inst Botanical.

Brindle, J. V. & White, J. J., eds. A Northeast Folio. (Illus.). 1979. soft cover, 750 ltd. ed. hand-numbered copies 10.00x (ISBN 0-913196-22-3). Hunt Inst Botanical.

Brindle, J. V., et al, eds. Flora Portrayed: Classics of Botanical Art from the Hunt Institute Collection. (Illus.). 92p. 1983. pap. text ed. 18.00 (ISBN 0-317-19691-X). Hunt Inst Botanical.

Brindle, John. Shotgun Shooting. 263p. 1984. 22.50 (ISBN 0-904558-91-6, Pub. by Saiga-Triplegate). Longwood Pub Group.

Brindle, John V. & White, James J., eds. Talking in Flowers: Japanese Botanical Art. (Illus.). 96p. 1982. pap. 15.00x (ISBN 0-913196-40-1). Hunt Inst Botanical.

Brindle, Reginald S. Contemporary Percussion. 1970. 47.50x (ISBN 0-19-318802-3). Oxford U Pr.

--The New Music. (Illus.). 1975. pap. 11.75x (ISBN 0-19-315424-2). Oxford U Pr.

--Serial Composition. (YA) (gr. 9 up). 1966. 14.50x (ISBN 0-19-311906-4). Oxford U Pr.

Brindle, Reginald S., ed. see Bartolozzi, Bruno.

Brindley, G. W. & Brown, G., eds. Crystal Structures of Clay Minerals & Their X-Ray Identification. 495p. 1982. text ed. 70.00x (ISBN 0-903056-08-9, Mineralogical). Brookfield Pub Co.

Brindley, Louise. In the Shadow of the Brontes. 272p. 1983. 11.95 (ISBN 0-312-41167-7). St Martin.

Brindley, Marianne. Western Coloured Township: Problems of an Urban Slum. (Illus.). 110p. 1976. pap. text ed. 9.95x (ISBN 0-86975-049-6, Pub. by Ravan Pr). Ohio U Pr.

Brindy, James. Shoplifting: A Manual for Store Detectives. rev. ed. LC 79-92049. (Illus.). 1975. pap. 8.00 (ISBN 0-910338-01-9). Cavalier.

Brindze, Ruth. Charting the Oceans. LC 77-134674. (Illus.). 128p. (gr. 6-12). 1972. 9.95 (ISBN 0-8149-0002-X). Vanguard.

--Gulf Stream. (Illus.). (gr. 4-7). 1945. 9.95 (ISBN 0-8149-0279-0). Vanguard.

--Not to Be Broadcast: The Truth About the Radio. LC 73-19802. (Civil Liberties in American History Ser.). 310p. 1974. Repr. of 1937 ed. lib. bdg. 37.50 (ISBN 0-306-70598-2). Da Capo.

--Story of Gold. LC 55-11840. (Illus.). (gr. 4-8). 1954. 9.95 (ISBN 0-8149-0276-6). Vanguard.

--Story of Our Calendar. (Illus.). (gr. 4-8). 1949. 9.95 (ISBN 0-8149-0278-2). Vanguard.

--Story of the Totem Pole. (Illus.). (gr. 4-8). 1951. 9.95 (ISBN 0-8149-0277-4). Vanguard.

Brine, Jenny, et al, eds. Home School & Leisure in the Soviet Union. (Illus.). 304p. 1980. text ed. 28.50x (ISBN 0-04-335040-2). Allen Unwin.

Brinegar, Bonnie, jt. auth. see Kay, Linda.

Brinegar, Bonnie C. & Skates, Craig B. Technical Writing: A Guide with Models. 1983. pap. 15.15x (ISBN 0-673-15410-6). Scott F.

Briner, Andreas. Paul Hindemith. Bradley, F., tr. 352p. 1984. 29.95 (ISBN 0-7145-3821-3). Riverrun NY.

Briner, Merlin G., et al. Smith's Review of Federal Income Taxation. 2nd ed. (Smith's Review Ser.). 350p. 1985. pap. text ed. write for info. (ISBN 0-314-88580-3). West Pub.

Brines, Steven F., ed. see Willcutt, J. Robert & Ball, Kenneth R.

Briney, Doug. The Home Machinist's Handbook. (Illus.). 228p. (Orig.). 1983. 21.95o.p (ISBN 0-8306-0573-8, 1573); pap. 15.50 (ISBN 0-8306-1573-3). TAB Bks.

Bring, Mitchell & Wayembergh, Josse. Design & Meaning in Japanese Gardens. (Illus.). 1981. 36.50 (ISBN 0-07-007825-4). McGraw.

Bringas, Ernie. The Malignant Majority. Horwege, Richard A., ed. LC 82-9758. 164p. (Orig.). 1984. pap. 6.95 cancelled (ISBN 0-89865-143-3). Donning Co.

Bringezu, Volker, jt. auth. see Ruster, Bernd.

Bringgold, Diane. Life Instead. 1979. pap. 4.95 (ISBN 0-8499-3910-0). Word Bks.

--Life Instead. 128p. 1984. pap. 4.95 (ISBN 0-9614225-0-5). Howard Pub.

Bringgold, Diane A. Life Instead. 1979. 6.95 (ISBN 0-318-03630-4); 4.95 (ISBN 0-318-03631-2). Phoenix Soc.

Bringhurst, Bruce. Antitrust & Oil Monopoly: The Standard Oil Cases, 1890-1911. LC 78-67908. (Contributions in Legal Studies Ser.: No. 8). (Illus.). x, 296p. 1979. lib. bdg. 29.95 (ISBN 0-313-20642-2, BRA/). Greenwood.

Bringhurst, Newell G. Saints, Slaves, & Blacks: The Changing Place of Black People Within Mormonism. LC 81-1093. (Contributions to the Study of Religion Ser.: No. 4). (Illus.). 256p. 1981. lib. bdg. 29.95 (ISBN 0-313-22752-7, BSB/). Greenwood.

Bringhurst, Robert. The Beauty of the Weapons: Selected Poems 1972-82. 160p. 1985. pap. 10.00 (ISBN 0-914742-90-6). Copper Canyon.

Bringhurst, Robert, et al, eds. Visions: Contemporary Art in Canada. (Illus.). 238p. 1984. 30.00 (ISBN 0-88894-392-X, Pub. by Salem Hse Ltd). Merrimack Pub Cir.

Bringle, Jerald, ed. see Shaw, George B.

Bringle, Mary. Fortunes. LC 82-81379. 384p. 1982. pap. 3.50 (ISBN 0-86721-183-0). Jove Pubns.

--Hacks at Lunch: A Novel of the Literary Life. 176p. 1985. 11.95 (ISBN 0-312-35637-4). St Martin.

Bringmann, Wolfgang G. & Tweney, Ryan D., eds. Wundt Studies. 445p. (Orig.). 1980. pap. text ed. 28.00 (ISBN 0-88937-001-X). Hogrefe Intl.

Brings, Allen, et al. A New Approach to Keyboard Harmony. (Illus.). 1979. pap. text ed. 9.95x (ISBN 0-393-95001-8). Norton.

Bringsvaard, T. Phantoms & Fairies. (Tanum of Norway Tokens Ser). (Illus.). 1979. pap. 13.50x (ISBN 82-518-0853-7, N498). Vanous.

Bringuier, Jean-Claude. Conversations with Jean Piaget. Gulati, Basia, tr. LC 79-15669. 1982. pap. 6.95 (ISBN 0-226-07504-4). U of Chicago Pr.

Brinig, Myron. Singermann. facsimile ed. LC 74-27968. (Modern Jewish Experience Ser.). 1975. Repr. of 1929 ed. 36.50x (ISBN 0-405-06698-8). Ayer Co Pubs.

--This Man Is My Brother. LC 78-63980. (The Gay Experience). Repr. of 1932 ed. 28.00 (ISBN 0-404-61501-5). AMS Pr.

Brinig, Robert, jt. auth. see Reese, Terence.

Brininstool, E. A. Fighting Red Cloud's Warriors: True Tales of Indian Days When the West Was Young. LC 74-12557. (Illus.). 241p. 1974. Repr. of 1926 ed. lib. bdg. 20.00 (ISBN 0-8154-0499-9). Cooper Sq.

--A Trooper with Custer & Other Historic Incidents of the Battle of the Little Big Horn. LC 74-12558. (Illus.). 214p. 1975. Repr. of 1926 ed. lib. bdg. 20.00 (ISBN 0-8154-0500-6). Cooper Sq.

Brininstool, E. A., ed. see Standing Bear, Luther.

Brininstool, Earl A., jt. auth. see Hebard, Grace R.

Brink, A. B. & Partridge, T. C. Soil Survey for Engineering. (Monographs on Soil Survey). (Illus.). 1982. text ed. 74.00x (ISBN 0-19-854537-1); pap. text ed. 21.95x (ISBN 0-19-854583-5). Oxford U Pr.

Brink, A. W., ed. see Trosse, George.

Brink, Andre. A Chain of Voices. LC 82-80315. 352p. 1982. 15.50 (ISBN 0-688-01131-4). Morrow.

--A Chain of Voices. 526p. 1983. pap. 5.95 (ISBN 0-14-006538-5). Penguin.

--A Dry White Season. 320p. 1984. pap. 6.95 (ISBN 0-14-006890-2). Penguin.

--An Instant in the Wind. (Fiction Ser.). 256p. 1985. pap. 6.95 (ISBN 0-14-008014-7). Penguin.

--Rumors of Rain. 448p. 1984. pap. 6.95 (ISBN 0-14-006891-0). Penguin.

--The Wall of the Plague. LC 84-16325. 447p. 1985. 17.95 (ISBN 0-671-54189-7). Summit Bks.

--Writing in a State of Seige: Essays on Politics & Literature. 256p. 1984. 15.95 (ISBN 0-671-47751-X). Summit Bks.

Brink, B. Language of Metre of Chaucer. LC 68-24899. (Studies in Chaucer, No. 6). 1969. Repr. of 1901 ed. lib. bdg. 49.95x (ISBN 0-8383-0917-8). Haskell.

Brink, Bernhard. Language & Metre of Chaucer. Smith, M. Bentinck, tr. LC 69-13838. Repr. of 1901 ed. lib. bdg. 18.75x (ISBN 0-8371-1927-8, BRLM). Greenwood.

Brink, Bernhard A. Ten. Five Lectures on Shakespeare. Franklin, Julia, tr. Repr. of 1895 ed. 10.00 (ISBN 0-404-01080-6). AMS Pr.

--History of English Literature, 3 Vols. LC 73-154132. Repr. of 1893 ed. Set. 95.00 (ISBN 0-404-09210-1). AMS Pr.

Brink, Bernhard A. Ten see Brink, Bernhard A. Ten.

Brink, Beverly E. Wyoming, Land of Echoing Canyons. LC 85-80478. (Old West Region Ser.). (Illus.). 180p. 1986. 21.95x (ISBN 0-918532-15-9). Flying Diamond Bks.

Brink, Carol. Harps in the Wind: The Story of The Singing Hutchinsons. (Illus.). v, 312p. 1980. Repr. of 1947 ed. lib. bdg. 35.00 (ISBN 0-306-76024-X). Da Capo.

Brink, Carol R. All Over Town. LC 39-22450. (Illus.). (gr. 4-6). 1968. Repr. of 1939 ed. 4.95 (ISBN 0-686-66478-7). Macmillan.

--Baby Island. 1973. pap. 0.95x (ISBN 0-02-041890-6, Collier). Macmillan.

--The Bad Times of Irma Baumlein. LC 76-182018. (Illus.). 144p. (gr. 4-6). 1972. 11.95 (ISBN 0-02-714220-5); pap. 3.95x (ISBN 0-02-041900-7). Macmillan.

--Caddie Woodlawn. rev. ed. LC 73-588. 288p. (gr. 4-6). 1970. 10.95x (ISBN 0-02-713670-1); pap. 2.95x (ISBN 0-02-041880-9). Macmillan.

--Magical Melons. LC 44-9999. (Illus.). 206p. (gr. 4-6). 1967. 9.95 (ISBN 0-02-714210-8); pap. 3.95x (ISBN 0-02-041960-0). Macmillan.

--Magical Melons. LC 44-9999. (gr. 4-6). 1972. pap. 4.95 (ISBN 0-02-041960-0, Collier). Macmillan.

--Pink Motel. LC 59-12838. 224p. (gr. 4-6). 1972. pap. 1.95 (ISBN 0-02-041940-6, Collier). Macmillan.

--Winter Cottage. LC 68-12086. (Illus.). 192p. (gr. 3-6). 1974. pap. 0.95 (ISBN 0-02-041970-8, 04197, Collier). Macmillan.

Brinton, Clarence C. A Decade of Revolution, 1789-1799. LC 83-10715. (The Rise of Modern Europe Ser.). (Illus.). x, 330p. 1983. Repr. of 1934 ed. lib. bdg. 45.00x (ISBN 0-313-24077-9, BRDE). Greenwood.
--From Many, One: The Process of Political Integration. LC 70-143309. 1971. Repr. of 1948 ed. lib. bdg. 15.00x (ISBN 0-8371-5964-4, BRFO). Greenwood.
--Temper of Western Europe. LC 70-97339. Repr. of 1953 ed. lib. bdg. 15.00x (ISBN 0-8371-2799-8, BRWE). Greenwood.
--United States & Britain. LC 75-97340. Repr. of 1948 ed. lib. bdg. 15.00x (ISBN 0-8371-2964-8, BRUS). Greenwood.
Brinton, Crane. Anatomy of Revolution. 13.50 (ISBN 0-8446-1740-7). Peter Smith.
--Anatomy of Revolution. rev. ed. 1965. pap. 4.95 (ISBN 0-394-70044-9, V44, Vin). Random.
--Decade of Revolution, 1789-1799. (Rise of Modern Europe Ser). pap. 7.95xi (ISBN 0-06-133018-3, TB3018, Torch). Har-Row.
--Ideas & Men: The Story of Western Thought. 2nd ed. 1963. ref. ed. 27.95 (ISBN 0-13-449249-8). P-H.
--The Jacobins: An Essay in the New History. LC 61-13765. 1961. Repr. of 1930 ed. 19.00x (ISBN 0-8462-0137-2). Russell.
Brinton, Crane & Christopher, John B. A History of Civilization: 1648 to the Present, Vol. II. 6th ed. (Illus.). 608p. 1984. pap. 20.95 (ISBN 0-13-389874-1). P-H.
Brinton, Crane, et al. A History of Civilization: Prehistory to 1715, Vol. I. 6th ed. (Illus.). 608p. 1984. pap. 20.95 (ISBN 0-13-389866-0). P-H.
Brinton, D. Rig Veda Americanus: Sacred Songs of the Ancient Mexicans. 1976. lib. bdg. 59.95 (ISBN 0-8490-2524-9). Gordon Pr.
Brinton, D. G. Aboriginal American Authors & Their Productions. 59.95 (ISBN 0-87968-574-3). Gordon Pr.
--American Hero Myths. 59.95 (ISBN 0-87968-602-2). Gordon Pr.
--Myths of the New World: A Treatise on the Symbolism & Mythology of the Red Race of America. LC 68-24972. (American History & Americana Ser., No. 47). 1969. Repr. of 1876 ed. lib. bdg. 49.95x (ISBN 0-8383-0918-6). Haskell.
Brinton, Daniel G. American Hero-Myths: A Study in the Native Religions of the Western Continent. LC 15-7574. (American Studies Ser). Repr. of 1882 ed. 18.00 (ISBN 0-384-05860-4). Johnson Repr.
--The American Race: A Linguistic Classification & Ethnographic Description of the Native Tribes of North & South America. LC 4-12237. (American Studies). Repr. of 1901 ed. lib. bdg. 25.00 (ISBN 0-384-05870-1, D025). Johnson Repr.
--Essays of an Americanist. LC 12-30954. (Series in American Studies). Repr. of 1890 ed. 23.00 (ISBN 0-384-05880-9). Johnson Repr.
--A Guidebook of Florida & the South, for Tourists, Invalids & Emigrants, with a Map of the St Johns River. Goza, William M., ed. LC 77-28658. (Floridiana Facsimile & Reprint Ser.). 1978. Repr. of 1869 ed. 9.00 (ISBN 0-8130-0415-2). U Presses Fla.
--The Myths of the New World. LC 71-144901. 331p. 1972. Repr. of 1876 ed. 10.00 (ISBN 0-403-00839-5). Scholarly.
--The Myths of the New World: A Treatise on the Symbolism & Mythology of the Red Race in America. LC 74-1038. 360p. 1974. Repr. of 1896 ed. 30.00x (ISBN 0-8103-3959-5). Gale.
--Myths of the New World: A Treatise on the Symbolism & Mythology of the Red Race of America. 2nd ed. LC 69-13839. 1969. Repr. of 1876 ed. lib. bdg. 15.00x (ISBN 0-8371-2040-3, BRMN). Greenwood.
--Myths of the New World: A Treatise on the Symbolism & Mythology of the Red Race of America. LC 78-31682. 1979. Repr. of 1868 ed. lib. bdg. 30.00 (ISBN 0-89341-326-7). Longwood Pub Group.
--Myths of the New World: The Symbolism & Mythology of the Indians of the Americas. LC 72-81594. (Illus.). 348p. 1976. pap. 8.50 (ISBN 0-89345-207-6, Steinerbks). Garber Comm.
--Notes on the Floridian Penninsula. LC 69-19548. Repr. of 1859 ed. 15.00 (ISBN 0-404-01084-9). AMS Pr.
--Religions of Primitive Peoples. LC 79-88423. Repr. of 1897 ed. 13.25x (ISBN 0-8371-1763-1, BRR&). Greenwood.
Brinton, Daniel G., ed. Ancient Nahuatl Poetry. LC 70-83462. (Library of Aboriginal American Literature Ser.: No. 7). Repr. of 1890 ed. 30.00 (ISBN 0-404-52187-8). AMS Pr.
--Gueguence: A Comedy Ballet in the Nahutl-Spanish Dialect of Nicaragua. LC 78-83459. (Library of Aboriginal American Literature: No. 3). Repr. of 1883 ed. 30.00 (ISBN 0-404-52183-5). AMS Pr.
--The Lenape & Their Legends. LC 77-102641. (Library of Aboriginal American Literature Ser.: No. 5). Repr. of 1884 ed. 30.00 (ISBN 0-404-52185-1). AMS Pr.
--Library of Aboriginal American Literature, 8 vols. 1977. Repr. of 1890 ed. Set. 240.00 (ISBN 0-404-52180-0); 30.00 ea. AMS Pr.
--The Maya Chronicles. LC 70-83457. (Library of Aboriginal American Literature Ser.: No. 1). Repr. of 1882 ed. 30.00 (ISBN 0-404-52181-9). AMS Pr.
--Rig Veda Americanus. LC 73-83463. (Library of Aboriginal American Literature Ser.: No. 8). Repr. of 1890 ed. 30.00 (ISBN 0-404-52188-6). AMS Pr.
Brinton, Daniel G. & Anthony, Albert S., eds. A Lenape-English Dictionary. LC 76-43670. (Eng. & Lenape.). Repr. of 1888 ed. 22.50 (ISBN 0-404-15764-5). AMS Pr.
Brinton, Daniel G., tr. see Olum, Walam.
Brinton, Donna & Neuman, Regina. Getting Along: English Grammar & Writing Book I & II. 1982. pap. text ed. 13.50 (ISBN 0-13-354456-7); pap. text ed. 13.50 (ISBN 0-13-354464-8). P-H.
Brinton, Ethel, tr. see Yanez, Agustin.
Brinton, Ethel, tr. see Yanez, Augustin.
Brinton, Howard. Ethical Mysticism in the Society of Friends. LC 67-31429. (Orig.). 1983. pap. 5.00x (ISBN 0-87574-156-8). Pendle Hill.
--Light & Life in the Fourth Gospel. LC 76-128679. (Orig.). 1971. pap. 2.30x (ISBN 0-87574-179-7). Pendle Hill.
--The Pendle Hill Idea. LC 50-11234. (Orig.). 1950. pap. 5.00x (ISBN 0-87574-055-3). Pendle Hill.
Brinton, Howard H. Evolution & the Inward Light. LC 77-137101. (Orig.). 1970. pap. 2.30x (ISBN 0-87574-173-8). Pendle Hill.
--Friends for Three Hundred Years. LC 52-5424. (Orig.). 1965. pap. 4.00 (ISBN 0-87574-903-8). Pendle Hill.
--Guide to Quaker Practice. LC 43-11899. (Orig.). 1943. pap. 2.55x (ISBN 0-87574-020-0). Pendle Hill.
--How They Became Friends. LC 61-12670. (Orig.). 1961. pap. 5.00x (ISBN 0-87574-114-2, 114). Pendle Hill.
--Meeting House & Farm House. LC 72-80096. (Orig.). 1972. pap. 2.30x (ISBN 0-87574-185-1). Pendle Hill.
--The Nature of Quakerism. 1983. pap. 5.00x (ISBN 0-87574-047-2, 047). Pendle Hill.
--Prophetic Ministry. 1983. pap. 5.00x (ISBN 0-87574-054-5, 054). Pendle Hill.
--Quaker Doctrine of Inward Peace. LC 64-23230. (Orig.). 1948. pap. 5.00x (ISBN 0-87574-044-8). Pendle Hill.
--Quaker Education in Theory & Practice. rev. ed. LC 58-12843. (Orig.). 1940. pap. 10.00x (ISBN 0-87574-009-X). Pendle Hill.
--Quaker Journals: Varieties of Religious Experience among Friends. LC 78-188399. (Illus., Orig.). 1983. 5.75 (ISBN 0-87574-952-6). Pendle Hill.
--Quakerism & Other Religions. 1983. pap. 5.00x (ISBN 0-87574-093-6, 093). Pendle Hill.
--Reaching Decisions. 1983. pap. 5.00x (ISBN 0-87574-065-0, 065). Pendle Hill.
--Religion of George Fox: As Revealed in His Epistles. LC 68-57978. (Orig.). 1968. pap. 5.00x (ISBN 0-87574-161-4). Pendle Hill.
--The Religious Philosophy of Quakerism. LC 73-80041. 1979. pap. 2.75 (ISBN 0-87574-953-4, 953). Pendle Hill.
--A Religious Solution to the Social Problem. 1983. pap. 5.00x (ISBN 0-87574-002-2, 002). Pendle Hill.
--The Society of Friends. 1983. pap. 5.00x (ISBN 0-87574-048-0, 048). Pendle Hill.
--Sources of the Quaker Peace Testimony. 1983. pap. 5.00x (ISBN 0-87574-027-8, 027). Pendle Hill.
Brinton, J. W. Wheat & Politics. facsimile ed. McCurry, Dan C. & Rubenstein, Richard E., eds. LC 74-30621. (American Farmers & the Rise of Agribusiness Ser.). 1975. Repr. of 1931 ed. 24.50x (ISBN 0-405-06768-2). Ayer Co Pubs.
Brinton, Maurice. The Bolsheviks & Worker's Control. 1975. pap. 1.50x (ISBN 0-934868-05-0). Black & Red.
--The Irrational in Politics. 1975. pap. 1.10x (ISBN 0-934868-11-5). Black & Red.
Brinton, Sybil G. Old Friends & New Fancies (Jane Austen) 25.00 (ISBN 0-8274-3058-2). R West.
Brinton, Willard C. Grapic Methods for Presenting Facts. Brief, Richard P., ed. LC 80-1474. (Dimensions of Accounting Theory & Practice Ser.). 1981. Repr. of 1914 ed. lib. bdg. 37.00x (ISBN 0-405-13504-1). Ayer Co Pubs.
Brinton, William F., Jr., ed. Effects of Organic & Inorganic Fertilizers on Soils & Crops. LC 79-55519. (Illus., Orig.). 1979. pap. 6.50 (ISBN 0-9603554-0-5). W F Brinton.
Brinton, William, Jr., ed. see Schmid, Otto & Klay, Ruedi.
Brinton, William M. The Alaska Deception. 260p. 1984. 15.95 (ISBN 0-916515-00-1). Mercury Hse Inc.
Brion, John M. Corporate Marketing Planning. LC 67-19446. (Wiley Marketing Ser.). Repr. of 1967 ed. 147.80 (ISBN 0-8357-9867-4, 2017001). Bks Demand UMI.
Brion, M. Bartolome de las Casas. 1976. lib. bdg. 59.95 (ISBN 0-8490-1476-X). Gordon Pr.
Brioschi, Francesco, jt. auth. see Bertele, Umberto.
Briquet, Charles M. Filigranes, 8 vols. in 4. 2nd ed. LC 66-8252. 1985. Set. 250.00 (ISBN 0-87817-004-9). Hacker.
Briquet de Leomos, Antonio A. Descriptions of Interlibrary Lending in various countries & a Bibliography of Interlibrary Lending. 136p. 1980. 50.00x (ISBN 0-85350-175-0, Pub. by Pubns Sec Brit Lib England). State Mutual Bk.
Brisac, Catherine, jt. auth. see Grodecki, Louis.
Brisbane. Developing Child. rev. ed. (gr. 9-12). 1980. text ed. 18.64 (ISBN 0-02-663230-6); tchr's guide 11.20 (ISBN 0-02-663240-3); student guide 6.64 (ISBN 0-02-663260-8). Bennett IL.
Brisbane, Albert. Association: Or, a Concise Exposition of the Practical Part of Fourier's Social Science. LC 72-2947. (Communal Societies in America Ser). Repr. of 1843 ed. 11.50 (ISBN 0-404-10713-3). AMS Pr.
--General Introduction to the Social Sciences. LC 75-303. (The Radical Tradition in America Ser.). 276p. 1975. Repr. of 1876 ed. 23.65 (ISBN 0-88355-208-6). Hyperion Conn.
--Social Destiny of Man. LC 68-18217. Repr. of 1840 ed. 35.00x (ISBN 0-678-00471-4). Kelley.
--Social Destiny of Man: Or Association & Reorganization of Industry. LC 68-56752. 1967. Repr. of 1840 ed. 15.00 (ISBN 0-8337-0376-5). B Franklin.
--The Social Destiny of Mankind. 100.00 (ISBN 0-87968-025-3). Gordon Pr.
--Theory of the Functions of the Human Passions. LC 75-304. (The Radical Tradition in America Ser). (Illus.). 166p. 1975. Repr. of 1856 ed. 17.00 (ISBN 0-88355-209-4). Hyperion Conn.
Brisbane, Frances L. & Womble, Maxine, eds. Treatment of Black Alcoholics. LC 85-13975. (Alcoholism Treatment Quarterly: Vol. 2, No. 3-4). 240p. 1985. text ed. 22.95 (ISBN 0-86656-403-9, B403); pap. text ed. 16.95 (ISBN 0-86656-419-5, B419). Haworth Pr.
Brisbane, Holly E. Developing Child. rev. ed. (Illus.). (gr. 9-12). 1971. text ed. 18.64 (ISBN 0-02-663220-9). Bennett IL.
Brisbane, Redelia. Albert Brisbane: A Biography. 59.95 (ISBN 0-87968-588-3). Gordon Pr.
--Albert Brisbane: A Mental Biography with a Character Study. LC 68-56790. (Research & Source Works Ser.: No. 280). 1969. Repr. of 1893 ed. 23.50 (ISBN 0-8337-0375-7). B Franklin.
Brisbane, Robert H. Black Activism. LC 74-2892. 336p. 1974. 10.00 (ISBN 0-8170-0619-2); pap. 9.50 (ISBN 0-8170-0674-5). Judson.
--The Black Vanguard: Origins of the Negro Social Revolution, 1900-1960. LC 69-18900. Repr. of 1970 ed. 54.20 (ISBN 0-8357-9356-7, 2014868). Bks Demand UMI.
Brisbin, I. Lehr, jt. ed. see Adriano, Domy C.
Brisbin, James S., ed. Belden, the White Chief: Or, Twelve Years among the Wild Indians of the Plains from the Diaries & Manuscripts of George P. Belden. facsimile ed. LC 73-92900. (Illus.). xxvi, 513p. 1974. Repr. of 1870 ed. 10.95 (ISBN 0-8214-0150-5, 82-81537). Ohio U Pr.
Brisbin, Richard A., Jr., jt. auth. see Buell, Emmett H., Jr.
Brisby, Liliana, tr. see Markov, Georgi.
Briscall, C. M. & Farrell, Gordon H. Canadian Hardware Supplied Ltd: Four Parts. (Illus.). 1982. pap. text ed. 15.95 (ISBN 0-8403-2613-0). Kendall-Hunt.
Brisch, Hans, jt. ed. see Volgyes, Ivan.
Brisco. Too Much in Love. (gr. 7 up). 1980. pap. 1.95 (ISBN 0-590-32199-4, Wishing Star Bks). Scholastic Inc.
Brisco, Norris A. Economic Policy of Robert Walpole. LC 7-36150. (Columbia University Studies in the Social Sciences: No. 72). Repr. of 1907 ed. 18.50 (ISBN 0-404-51072-8). AMS Pr.
Brisco, Patty. House of Candles. 192p. (Orig.). 1976. pap. 1.25 (ISBN 0-532-12434-0). Woodhill.
--Mist of Evil. 1976. pap. 1.25 (ISBN 0-532-12417-0). Woodhill.
--Raging Rapids. (Challenge Bks). (Illus.). (gr. 4-8). 1979. PLB 7.95 (ISBN 0-87191-683-5). Creative Ed.
Briscoe, A. O. Size of the Local Unit for Administration & Supervision of Public Schools. LC 78-176590. (Columbia University. Teachers College. Contributions to Education: No. 649). Repr. of 1935 ed. 22.50 (ISBN 0-404-55649-3). AMS Pr.
Briscoe, Alan. Cooking with Wild Plants: How to Recognize & Prepare Edible Wilderness Plants of the Rocky Mountains. LC 78-52405. (Illus.). 1979. pap. 2.95 (ISBN 0-88290-091-9). Horizon Utah.
--Home Garden Hints. 1975. pap. 1.95 (ISBN 0-88290-049-8). Horizon Utah.
--Soybean Granule Recipes. 1974. pap. 1.95 (ISBN 0-88290-040-4). Horizon Utah.
--Your Guide to Home Storage. 1974. pap. 1.95 (ISBN 0-88290-041-2). Horizon Utah.
Briscoe, Alan K. Timely Tips on Quantity Food Buying. 1974. pap. 1.95 (ISBN 0-88290-044-7). Horizon Utah.
Briscoe, Anne & Pfafflin, Sheila M., eds. Expanding the Role of Women in the Sciences. (Annals of the New York Academy of Sciences Ser.: Vol. 323). 344p. (Orig.). 1979. 47.00x (ISBN 0-89766-014-5); pap. 47.00x. NY Acad Sci.
Briscoe, Clarence C. Abortion: The Emotional Issue. 112p. 1984. pap. 6.95 (ISBN 0-8059-2927-4). Dorrance.
Briscoe, D. Stuart. Discovering God: A Personal Bible Story. 1977. Zondervan.
--Getting into God. 128p. 1975. pap. 2.95 (ISBN 0-310-21722-9). Zondervan.
--A Heart for God. 160p. 1984. 9.95 (ISBN 0-8407-5401-9). Nelson.
--Let's Get Moving. LC 77-91773. 160p. 1978. pap. 3.50 (ISBN 0-8307-0538-4, S322102). Regal.
--Patterns for Power. LC 78-68850. (Bible Commentary for Laymen Ser.). 160p. 1979. pap. 3.50 (ISBN 0-8307-0701-8, S331101). Regal.
--Spirit Life. 160p. 1983. 8.95 (ISBN 0-8007-1352-4). Revell.
--When the Going Gets Tough. LC 82-11205. 1982. 5.95 (ISBN 0-8307-0802-2, 5417507). Regal.
Briscoe, Eugenia R. City by the Sea: A History of Corpus Christi, Texas, 1519-1875. 1985. 15.95 (ISBN 0-533-06440-6). Vantage.
Briscoe, J. P. Nottinghamshire Folk-Lore. (Folklore Ser). 20.00 (ISBN 0-8482-3423-5). Norwood Edns.
Briscoe, Jill. Fight for the Family. 192p. (Orig.). 1981. pap. 5.95 (ISBN 0-310-21841-1). Zondervan.
--Harrow Sparrow. (Illus.). 144p. 1985. 5.95 (ISBN 0-8407-5428-0). Nelson.
--How to Follow the Shepherd When You're Being Pushed Around by the Sheep. 192p. 1984. pap. 5.95 (ISBN 0-8007-5166-3, Power Bks). Revell.
--Hush, Hush. 1978. pap. 4.95 (ISBN 0-310-21831-4). Zondervan.
--The Innkeeper's Daughter. (Illus.). 48p. (gr. k-6). 1984. 5.95 (ISBN 0-8249-8073-5). Ideals.
--The Innkeeper's Daughter. (gr. k-3). 1984. 5.95 (ISBN 0-516-09484-X). Childrens.
--Jonah & the Worm. LC 83-6323. 120p. 1983. 5.95 (ISBN 0-8407-5289-X). Nelson.
--Prime Rib & Apple. 1976. pap. 4.95 (ISBN 0-310-21811-X). Zondervan.
--Queen of Hearts: The Role of Today's Woman Based on Proverbs 31. 192p. 1984. 9.95 (ISBN 0-8007-1387-7). Revell.
--Thank You for Being a Friend. 192p. (Orig.). 1981. pap. 5.95 (ISBN 0-310-21851-9). Zondervan.
--There's a Snake in My Garden. 1977. pap. 4.95 (ISBN 0-310-21821-7, 9256P). Zondervan.
--Wings. 384p. 1984. 11.95 (ISBN 0-8407-5328-4). Nelson.
Briscoe, Jill & Briscoe, Stuart. Desert Songs. 80p. 1985. 10.95 (ISBN 0-8407-4152-9). Nelson.
--Mountain Songs. 76p. 1982. 10.95 (ISBN 0-8407-4100-6). Nelson.
--River Songs. (Illus.). 80p. 1984. 10.95 (ISBN 0-8407-5366-7). Nelson.
--Songs from Deep Waters. (Illus.). 80p. 1984. 10.95 (ISBN 0-8407-5368-3). Nelson.
--Songs from Green Pastures. 76p. 1982. 10.95 (ISBN 0-8407-4101-4). Nelson.
--Songs from Heaven & Earth. (Briscoe Gift Bks.). 80p. 1985. 10.95 (ISBN 0-8407-4151-0). Nelson.
--Songs of Light. 80p. 1985. 10.95 (ISBN 0-8407-4153-7). Nelson.
Briscoe, Jill & Golz, Judy. Space to Breathe, Room to Grow. 176p. 1985. pap. 6.95 (ISBN 0-8407-9528-9). Nelson.
Briscoe, John. A Commentary on Livy, Bks, 31-33. 1973. 49.00x (ISBN 0-19-814442-3). Oxford U Pr.
--A Commentary on Livy, Books Thirty-Four to Thirty-Seven. (Illus.). 1981. 74.00x (ISBN 0-19-814455-5). Oxford U Pr.
--Surveying the Courtroom: A Land Expert's Guide to Evidence & Civil Procedure. 199p. 1985. 42.00 (ISBN 0-910845-21-2, 958). Landmark Ent.
Briscoe, Laurel. Lectura y Lengua: Curso Intermedio. LC 77-83324. (Illus.). 1978. text ed. 25.95 (ISBN 0-395-25545-7); instr's annotated ed. 26.95 (ISBN 0-395-25539-2). HM.
Briscoe, Mary L., et al. A Bibliography of American Autobiography, 1945-1980. LC 82-70547. 384p. 1982. text ed. 30.00x (ISBN 0-299-09090-6). U of Wis Pr.
Briscoe, Stuart. Bound for Joy. LC 84-17778. (Bible Commentary for Laymen Ser.). 192p. 1984. pap. 3.95 (ISBN 0-8307-1004-3, S383107). Regal.
--Dry Bones. 168p. 1985. pap. 4.95 (ISBN 0-89693-522-1). Victor Bks.
--Tough Truths for Today's Living. 178p. 1984. pap. text ed. 5.95 (ISBN 0-8499-2999-7, 2999-7). Word Bks.
--What Works When Life Doesn't. rev. ed. 176p. 1984. pap. 2.95 (ISBN 0-89693-709-7). Victor Bks.
Briscoe, Stuart, jt. auth. see Briscoe, Jill.
Briscoe, Walter A. Byron the Poet: A Collection of Essays & Addresses by Contemporary Critics. LC 67-30803. (Studies in Byron, No. 5). (Illus.). 1969. Repr. of 1924 ed. lib. bdg. 49.95x (ISBN 0-8383-0694-2). Haskell.
Brisette, Claire M. Reflective Living: A Spiritual Approach to Everyday Life. LC 83-21369. (Illus.). 136p. (Orig.). 1983. pap. 8.00 (ISBN 0-89571-019-6). Affirmation.
Brish, Linda K. CK & LD Isoenzymes: A Self-Instructional Text. LC 84-9239. 146p. 1984. 15.00 (ISBN 0-89189-174-9, 45-2-039- 00). Am Soc Clinical.
Brisk, William J., tr. see Campos, German J. B.
Briskey, Ernest J., jt. ed. see Manassah, Jamal.
Briskey, Ernest J., et al, eds. Physiology & Biochemistry of Muscle As a Food: Proceedings, 1965, 2 vols. (Illus.). 1966. Vol. 1. 50.00x (ISBN 0-299-04110-7); Vol. 2. 50.00x (ISBN 0-299-05680-5). U of Wis Pr.

Briskin, Jacqueline. Everything & More. 496p. 1984. pap. 3.95 (ISBN 0-425-07052-2). Berkley Pub.
--Everything & More. (General Ser.). 1984. lib. bdg. 16.95 (ISBN 0-8161-3747-1, Large Print Bks). G K Hall.
--The Onyx. 448p. 1982. 15.95 (ISBN 0-385-28762-3). Delacorte.
--The Onyx. 512p. 1983. pap. 3.95 (ISBN 0-440-16667-5). Dell.
--Paloverde. 1978. 10.95 (ISBN 0-07-007915-3). McGraw.
--Rich Friends. 1983. pap. 3.95 (ISBN 0-440-17380-9). Dell.
--Too Much Too Soon. LC 84-26363. 480p. 1985. 16.95 (ISBN 0-399-13071-3). Putnam Pub Group.
Briskin, Jaqueline. Everything & More. 480p. 1983. 15.95 (ISBN 0-399-12874-3, Putnam). Putnam Pub Group.
Brisley, Chester L., ed. Fixed Interval Work Sampling. (Reprinted from the Journal of Industrial Engineering). 1969. pap. text ed. 13.00 (ISBN 0-89806-025-7, 115); pap. text ed. 8.00 members. Inst Indus Eng.
Brislin, jt. auth. see Triandis.
Brislin, Richard W. Crosscultural Encounters: Face-to-Face Interaction. LC 80-20202. (Pergamon General Psychology Ser.: No. 94). 350p. 1981. 42.00 (ISBN 0-08-026313-5); pap. 15.25 (ISBN 0-08-026312-7). Pergamon.
Brislin, Richard W. & Segall, Marshall H. Cross-Cultural Research: The Role of Culture in Understanding Human Behavior. (CISE Learning Package Ser.: No.16). 95p. (Orig.). 1975. pap. text ed. 4.00x (ISBN 0-936876-29-8). Learn Res Intl Stud.
Brislin, Richard W. see Hamnett, Michael P.
Brislin, Richard W., jt. ed. see Landis, Dan.
Brislin, Richard W., et al. Cross-Cultural Research Methods. LC 73-772. (Comparative Studies in Behavioral Sciences). 1973. 45.95 (ISBN 0-471-10470-1, Pub. by Wiley-Interscience). Wiley.
--Cross-Cultural Research Methods. LC 85-5624. 368p. 1985. Repr. of 1973 ed. lib. bdg. price not set (ISBN 0-89874-860-7). Krieger.
Brislin, Richard W., et al, eds. Cross-Cultural Perspectives on Learning. LC 73-91353. (Cross-Culutral Research & Methodology Ser.). pap. 86.50 (ISBN 0-317-09954-X, 2021875). Bks Demand UMI.
Brisman, S. A History & Guide to Judaic Bibliography. (Bibliographica Judaica Ser.: No. 7). 35.00x (ISBN 0-87820-900-X, HUC Pr). Ktav.
Brisolara, Ashton. The Alcoholic Employee: A Handbook of Helpful Guidelines. LC 78-15763. 168p. 1979. text ed. 24.95 (ISBN 0-87705-327-8). Human Sci Pr.
Brison, Fred R., jt. auth. see Adriance, Guy W.
Brissaud, J. B. History of French Private Law. (Continental Legal History Ser.: Vol. 3). (Illus.). xlvii, 922p. 1969. Repr. of 1912 ed. 37.50x (ISBN 0-8377-1931-3). Rothman.
--History of French Public Law. Garner, James W., tr. (Continental Legal History Ser.: Vol. 9). lviii, 581p. 1969. Repr. of 1915 ed. 37.50x (ISBN 0-8377-1932-1). Rothman.
Brissenden. Shakespeare & the Dance. 1979. text ed. 31.75x (ISBN 0-391-01810-8). Humanities.
Brissenden, Alan, ed. Portable Rolf Boldrewood. (Portable Australian Authors Ser.). 1979. 30.00x (ISBN 0-7022-1288-1); pap. 12.95x (ISBN 0-7022-1277-6). U of Queensland Pr.
Brissenden, Alan, ed. see Middleton, Thomas.
Brissenden, Paul F. Earnings of Factory Workers, 1899 to 1927. LC 79-158773. (Research & Source Works Ser.: No. 732). 1971. Repr. of 1929 ed. lib. bdg. 29.50 (ISBN 0-8337-4636-7). B Franklin.
--Launching of the I. W. W. LC 78-169188. (American History & Americana Ser., No. 47). 1971. Repr. of 1913 ed. lib. bdg. 31.95x (ISBN 0-8383-1275-6). Haskell.
--The Settlement of Labor Disputes on Rights in Australia. (Monograph & Research Ser.: No.13). 131p. 1966. 5.00 (ISBN 0-89215-014-9). U Cal LA Indus Rel.
Brissenden, R. F. The Whale in Darkness. LC 79-56757. 71p. 1980. 9.95 (ISBN 0-7081-1083-5, 0576). Australia N U P.
Brissenden, R. F. & Eade, J. C. Studies in the Eighteenth Century-IV. LC 78-67481. 1980. text ed. 15.50 (ISBN 0-7081-1066-5, 0199, Pub. by ANUP Australia). Australia N U P.
Brissenden, R. F., ed. see Fielding, Henry.
Brissenden, Rosemary. Asia's Undiscovered Cuisine: Recipes from Thailand, Indonesia & Malaysia. 1982. pap. 5.95 (ISBN 0-394-71002-9). Pantheon.
Brissenden, T. H. F. Mathematics Teaching. 1980. text ed. 21.00 (ISBN 0-06-318159-2, IntlDept); pap. text ed. 11.90 (ISBN 0-06-318160-6). Har-Row.
Brissett, Dennis & Edgley, Charles. Life As Theater: A Dramaturgical Sourcebook. LC 74-82604. 1975. text ed. 29.95x (ISBN 0-202-30277-6). Aldine Pub.
Brissie, Eugene, ed. Astroscope Profile. 352p. 1981. pap. 8.95 (ISBN 0-671-43511-6, Wallaby). S&S.
Brissie, Eugene, ed. see Browne, Dik.
Brissie, Sam C. One Man in His Time. 1984. 10.95 (ISBN 0-8062-2162-3). Carlton.
Brissiere, P. De see De Brissiere, P.
Brisson, David W. Hypergraphics: Visualizing Complex Relationships in Art, Science & Technology. (Illus.). 1979. 28.50x (ISBN 0-89158-292-4). Westview.
Brisson, Germain J. Lipids in Human Nutrition. LC 81-17013. (Illus.). 200p. 1981. text ed. 22.50 (ISBN 0-937218-12-X). J K Burgess.
Brisson, Jean P. Problemes de la Guerre a Rome. (Civilisations et Societes: No. 12). 1969. pap. 14.00x (ISBN 0-686-20921-4). Mouton.
Brisson, Jean Paul. Autonomisme et Christianisme dans l'Afrique Romaine de Septime Severe a L'invasion Vandale. LC 82-45808. 1983. Repr. of 1958 ed. 49.50 (ISBN 0-404-62377-8). AMS Pr.
Brisson, Pierre R. De see Saugnier & De Brisson, Pierre R.
Brissot De Warville, Jean P. Commerce of America with Europe. LC 74-11218. Repr. of 1794 ed. lib. bdg. 37.50x (ISBN 0-678-04029-X). Kelley.
--New Travels in the United States. LC 74-11214. Repr. of 1792 ed. lib. bdg. 37.50x (ISBN 0-678-04028-1). Kelley.
Brister, Bob. Shotgunning: The Art & the Science. LC 82-62603. 1976. 15.95 (ISBN 0-8329-1840-7, Pub. by Winchester Pr). New Century.
Brister, C. W. Becoming You. rev. ed. LC 79-57361. (gr. 9-12). 1980. pap. 4.95 (ISBN 0-8054-5332-6). Broadman.
--Caring for the Caregivers. 1985. pap. 8.95 (ISBN 0-8054-5537-X). Broadman.
--El Cuidado Pastoral De la Iglesia. Tinao, D., et al, trs. Orig. Title: Pastoral Care in the Church. 226p. (Span.). 1980. pap. 5.50 (ISBN 0-311-42040-0). Casa Bautista.
--Pastoral Care in the Church. LC 64-19497. 1977. pap. 7.64i (ISBN 0-06-061051-4, RD 222, HarpR). Har-Row.
--Take Care. LC 76-51022. 1979. pap. 3.95 (ISBN 0-8054-5578-7). Broadman.
Brister, C. W., et al. Beginning Your Ministry. LC 80-25763. 160p. (Orig.). 1981. pap. 7.75 (ISBN 0-687-02780-2). Abingdon.
Brister, Elaine H. Once upon a River: His, Pineville, Louisiana. 1968. 12.50 (ISBN 0-87511-578-0). Claitors.
Brister, Judith, tr. see Galeano, Eduardo.
Bristol, C. & Sherman, H. TNT: The Power Within You. 1954. pap. 2.95 (ISBN 0-13-922674-5). P-H.
Bristol, Claude. The Magic of Believing. 245p. 1982. pap. 4.95 (ISBN 0-13-543884-5). P-H.
--The Magic of Believing. 1983. pap. 2.95 (ISBN 0-671-47095-7). PB.
Bristol, Claude M. Magic of Believing. 1967. pap. 3.95 (ISBN 0-346-12293-7). Cornerstone.
--The Magic of Believing: Setting Your Goal & Reaching It. 244p. 1985. pap. 6.95 (ISBN 0-13-543927-2). P H.
Bristol, David. Paradise & Cash. LC 80-50064. (Ser. Five). 50p. 1980. pap. 2.50 (ISBN 0-931846-14-5). Wash Writers Pub.
Bristol (England) Women's Studies Group. Half the Sky: Introduction to Women's Studies. 306p. 1983. pap. 9.95 (ISBN 0-86068-086-X, Pub. by Virago Pr). Merrimack Pub Cir.
Bristol, Evelyn, ed. & intro. by. East European Literature: Papers from the Second World Congress for Soviet & East European Studies. 106p. 1982. pap. 8.00 (ISBN 0-933884-26-5). Berkeley Slavic.
Bristol, Evelyn, ed. Russian Literature & Criticism: Selected Papers from the Second World Congress for Soviet & East European Studies. 254p. 1983. pap. 17.00 (ISBN 0-933884-27-3). Berkeley Slavic.
Bristol, Evelyn, ed. see Sologub, Fedor.
Bristol, Frank M. Shakespeare & America. LC 70-113565. Repr. of 1898 ed. 14.50 (ISBN 0-404-01085-7). AMS Pr.
Bristol, Goldie & McGinnis, Carol. When It's Hard to Forgive. 168p. 1982. pap. 4.95 (ISBN 0-88207-311-7). Victor Bks.
Bristol, James. Nonviolence: Not First for Export. 1972. pap. 0.30 (ISBN 0-686-95383-5). Am Fr Serv Comm.
Bristol, James E. McCarthyism: The Seed Is in Us. 1983. pap. 5.00x (ISBN 0-87574-076-6, 076). Pendle Hill.
--Stand Fast in Liberty. 1983. pap. 5.00x (ISBN 0-87574-119-3, 119). Pendle Hill.
Bristol, Marc. Homegrown Music. LC 82-17217. (Illus.). 144p. (Orig.). 1983. pap. 8.95 (ISBN 0-914842-91-9). Madrona Pubs.
Bristol, Michael D. Carnival & Theatre: Plebian Culture & the Structure of Authority in Renaissance England. 350p. 1985. text ed. 25.00 (ISBN 0-416-35070-4, 9448). Methuen Inc.
Bristol, Roger P. Index to Supplement to Charles Evans' American Bibliography. LC 73-94761. (Bibliographical Society). 191p. 1971. 20.00x (ISBN 0-8139-0337-8). U Pr of Va.
--Supplement to Charles Evans' American Bibliography. LC 73-94761. (Bibliographical Society Ser). 640p. 1970. 40.00x (ISBN 0-8139-0287-8). U Pr of Va.
Bristol, Thomas. DMSO: The Responsible User's Guide. (Illus.). 128p. (Orig.). 1982. pap. 5.95 (ISBN 0-940530-00-7). DMSO News Serv.
Briston, J. H. & Gosselin, C. C. Introduction to Plastics. 7.50 (ISBN 0-685-28367-4). Philos Lib.
Briston, Richard J. & Liversidge, Jack. A Practical Approach to Business Investment Decisions. (Illus.). 1981. 15.95 (ISBN 0-13-689232-9, Spec); pap. 6.95 (ISBN 0-13-689224-8, Spec). P-H.
Bristor, Kirk, et al. What Do You Do When the Fad Fades? You Make Cole Slaw! (Illus.). 64p. (Orig.). 1984. pap. 2.95 (ISBN 0-910937-50-8). Laranmark.
Bristow & Dalton. Federal Tax Planning for Vacation Homes & Condominiums. 2nd ed. 1983. 39.95 (ISBN 0-686-90781-7). Harrison Co GA.
Bristow, jt. auth. see Connor.
Bristow, Alec. The Easy Garden. LC 78-65630. (Illus.). 1979. pap. 5.95i (ISBN 0-690-01822-3, TYC-T). T Y Crowell.
--Grow Your Own. LC 78-65629. (Illus.). 1979. pap. 5.95 (ISBN 0-690-01821-5, TYC-T). T Y Crowell.
--The Practical Guide to Successful Gardening in Colloboration with the Royal Horticultural Society. (Illus.). 256p. 1985. 17.95 (ISBN 0-88162-078-5, Pub. by Salem Hse Ltd). Merrimack Pub Cir.
Bristow, Allen P. Effective Police Manpower Utilization. (Illus.). 128p. 1969. 14.75x (ISBN 0-398-00225-8). C C Thomas.
--Field Interrogation. 2nd ed. (Illus.). 168p. 1980. photocopy ed. 17.75x (ISBN 0-398-00226-6). C C Thomas.
--Police Disaster Operations. (Illus.). 240p. 1972. photocopy ed. spiral 19.50x (ISBN 0-398-02244-5). C C Thomas.
--Police Supervision Readings. 488p. 1971. 29.75x (ISBN 0-398-00227-4). C C Thomas.
--Rural Law Enforcement. 200p. 1982. pap. 18.95 (ISBN 0-205-07366-2, 827366). Allyn.
--The Search for an Effective Police Handgun. (Illus.). 256p. 1973. 26.75x (ISBN 0-398-02554-1). C C Thomas.
Bristow, Allen P. & Gabard, E. C. Decision-Making in Police Administration. (Illus.). 128p. 1961. 14.75x (ISBN 0-398-04221-7). C C Thomas.
Bristow, Ann, jt. auth. see Calvocoressi, Peter.
Bristow, Benny. From Kneepants to Romance. pap. 1.75 (ISBN 0-89137-810-3). Quality Pubns.
--Ten Commandments for Wives. pap. 4.95 (ISBN 0-89137-430-2). Quality Pubns.
Bristow, Camille & Cohn, Marian R. Services for Sexually Active, Pregnant, & Parenting Adolescents in New York City: Planning for the Future, Vol. 1. LC 82-71262. (Illus.). 140p. (Orig.). 1982. pap. write for info. (ISBN 0-943138-01-9). Ctr Pub.
Bristow, Edward J. Prostitution & Prejudice: The Jewish Fight Against White Slavery 1870-1939. 368p. 1983. 21.95 (ISBN 0-8052-3866-2). Schocken.
Bristow, Eugene K., ed. see Chekhov, Anton.
Bristow, Geoff, ed. Electronic Speech Synthesis. 256p. 1984. 35.00 (ISBN 0-07-007912-9). McGraw.
Bristow, George. Rip Van Winkle. (Earlier American Music Ser.: No. 25). 297p. 1983. 39.50 (ISBN 0-306-76124-6). Da Capo.
Bristow, Gwen. Calico Palace. 1979. pap. 2.50 (ISBN 0-671-82471-6). PB.
--Calico Palace. LC 72-106584. 1970. 12.45i (ISBN 0-690-16608-7). T Y Crowell.
--Celia Garth. LC 59-10435. 1959. 10.95i (ISBN 0-690-18348-8). T Y Crowell.
--Deep Summer. 310p. 1979. Repr. lib. bdg. 15.95x (ISBN 0-89966-025-8). Buccaneer Bks.
--Deep Summer. LC 37-1118. 1964. 12.45 (ISBN 0-690-23318-3). T Y Crowell.
--From Pigtails to Wedding Bells. pap. 1.75 (ISBN 0-89137-811-1). Quality Pubns.
--Golden Dreams. (Illus.). 1980. 12.45i (ISBN 0-690-01678-6). T Y Crowell.
--Handsome Road. 320p. 1979. Repr. lib. bdg. 17.95 (ISBN 0-89966-028-2). Buccaneer Bks.
--This Side of Glory. 278p. 1979. Repr. lib. bdg. 16.95x (ISBN 0-89966-026-6). Buccaneer Bks.
--Tomorrow Is Forever. 320p. 1976. lib. bdg. 15.95x (ISBN 0-89966-027-4). Buccaneer Bks.
Bristow, Hennie. Something to Think About. pap. 2.50 (ISBN 0-89315-292-7). Lambert Bk.
Bristow, Linda K. Bed & Breakfast: California. 2nd ed. 256p. 1985. pap. 8.95 (ISBN 0-87701-332-2). Chronicle Bks.
--Bread & Breakfast. LC 85-11416. (Illus.). 192p. (Orig.). 1985. pap. 7.95 (ISBN 0-89286-246-7). One Hund One Prods.
Bristow, M. J., jt. ed. see Reed, W. L.
Bristow, M. R., ed. Drug Induced Heart Disease. (Drug Induced Diseases Ser.: Vol. 5). 476p. 1981. 101.50 (ISBN 0-444-80206-1, Biomedical Pr). Elsevier.
Bristow, M. R., jt. ed. see Cross, D. T.
Bristow, M. Roger. Land-Use Planning in Hong Kong: History, Policies & Processes. (Illus.). 1984. 32.95x (ISBN 0-19-581496-7). Oxford U Pr.
Bristow, P. A. Liquid Chromatography in Practice. 28.00 (ISBN 0-9504833-1-1); pap. 20.00 (ISBN 0-9504833-0-3); microfiche 10.00 (ISBN 0-9504833-2-X). Lab Data Control.
Bristow, Page S. & Farstrup, Alan E. Reading in Health, Physical Education, Recreation Classes. 72p. 1981. 6.95 (ISBN 0-8106-3206-3). NEA.
Bristow, Philip. Down the Spanish Coast. 196p. 1980. 25.00x (ISBN 0-245-52935-7, Pub. by Nautical England). State Mutual Bk.
--Round the Italian Coast. 256p. 1980. 15.00x (ISBN 0-245-52648-X, Pub. by Nautical England). State Mutual Bk.
--Through the Belgian Canals. 160p. 1980. 9.00x (ISBN 0-245-50975-5, Pub. by Nautical England). State Mutual Bk.
--Through the Dutch Canals. 250p. 1980. 15.00x (ISBN 0-686-69886-X, Pub. by Nautical England). State Mutual Bk.
--Through the French Canals. 200p. 1980. 18.00 (ISBN 0-245-53403-2, Pub. by Nautical England). State Mutual Bk.
--Through the German Waterways. 168p. 1980. 15.00x (ISBN 0-245-51000-1, Pub. by Nautical England). State Mutual Bk.
Bristow, Thelma. Library Learning: The Way to Self-Help in Education. 1977. 30.00x (ISBN 0-900008-21-0, Pub. by U of London England). State Mutual Bk.
Bristowe, W. S. The Comity of Spiders, 2 Vols. Repr. of 1941 ed. Set. 34.00 (ISBN 0-384-05895-7). Johnson Repr.
Britain, Ian. Fabianism & Culture: A Study in British Socialism & the Arts, c. 1884-1918. LC 81-12273. 358p. 1982. 39.50 (ISBN 0-521-23563-4). Cambridge U Pr.
Britan, Gerald M. Bureaucracy & Innovation: An Ethnography of Policy Change. LC 80-26464. (Sage Library of Social Research: Vol. 115). 170p. 1981. 24.00 (ISBN 0-8039-1506-3); pap. 12.00 (ISBN 0-8039-1507-1). Sage.
Britan, Gerald M. & Cohen, Ronald, eds. Hierarchy & Society: Anthropological Perspectives on Bureaucracy. LC 80-10835. 192p. 1980. text ed. 17.50 (ISBN 0-89727-009-6); pap. text ed. 7.95 (ISBN 0-89727-010-X). ISHI PA.
Britan, Halbert H. The Affective Consciousness. Repr. of 1931 ed. 15.00 (ISBN 0-89987-043-0). Darby Bks.
Britan, Halbert H., tr. see De Spinoza, Benedictus.
Britch, Carroll, et al. Speech Acts: Hints & Samples. 112p. (Orig.). 1983. pap. text ed. 7.50x (ISBN 0-88133-016-7). Waveland Pr.
Britchky, Seymour. The Restaurants of New York: 1985 Edition. 352p. 1984. pap. 9.95 (ISBN 0-671-46375-6). S&S.
Brite, Robert L. Business Statistics. LC 79-25657. 1980. text ed. 24.95 (ISBN 0-201-00561-1); solutions manual 2.95 (ISBN 0-201-00562-X). Addison-Wesley.
--Introduction to Business Statistics. LC 76-17717. (Illus.). 1977. text ed. 23.95 (ISBN 0-201-00593-X). Addison-Wesley.
British Academy, 1979. Proceedings, Vol. LXV. (Illus.). 1981. 175.00x (ISBN 0-19-725998-7). Oxford U Pr.
British Air Ministry. The Rise & Fall of the German Air Force. (Illus.). 422p. 1983. 22.50 (ISBN 0-312-68369-3). St Martin.
British Assn of Illustrators Staff, ed. Images Ten. (Illus.). 240p. (Eng. Fr. & Ger.). 1985. 41.95 (ISBN 2-88046-053-0, Pub. by Rotovision). R Silver.
British Assoc. for Comm. & Ind. Educ., ed. Vocational Education & Training in the Soviet Union, 1963. 60p. 1963. 25.00x (ISBN 0-686-79051-0, Pub. by Brit Assn Comm England). State Mutual Bk.
British Association for Commercial & Industrial Education, ed. Vocational Training in the European Economic Community. 124p. 1972. 35.00x (ISBN 0-85171-051-4, Pub. by Brit Assn Comm England). State Mutual Bk.
British Association for the Advancement of Science. Conflicts in Policy Objects. Kaldor, Nicholas, ed. LC 70-166516. 189p. 1971. lib. bdg. 25.00x (ISBN 0-678-06276-5). Kelley.
British Association for the Advancement of Science (Section F Economics) Economics & Technical Change. Hugh-Jones, E. M., ed. LC 71-93848. 1969. lib. bdg. 25.00x (ISBN 0-678-06265-X). Kelley.
British Association For The Advancement Of Science. March of Science: A First Quinquennial Review 1931-1935. facs. ed. LC 68-55841. (Essay Index Reprint Ser). 1937. 17.00 (ISBN 0-8369-0254-8). Ayer Co Pubs.
British Association for the Advancement of Science, Section F, Economics. Public Sector Economics. Prest, A. R., ed. LC 68-6526. 1968. 25.00x (ISBN 0-678-06765-1). Kelley.
British Association of Illustrators, ed. Images Nine. (Illus.). 240p. (Fr. & Ger.). 1984. 39.50 (ISBN 0-317-13733-6, Pub. by Rotovision). R Silver.
British Astronomical Association. Guide to Observing the Moon. LC 83-1610. (Illus.). 128p. 1985. pap. text ed. 11.95x (ISBN 0-89490-085-4). Enslow Pubs.
British Automobile Association. Camping & Caravanning in Britain. (British Automobile Association Accomodation Guides). 288p. (Orig.). 1984. pap. 10.95 (ISBN 0-86145-188-0, Pub. by Auto Assn-British Tourist Authority England). Merrimack Pub Cir.
--Eat Out in Britain for Around Five Pounds. (British Automobile Association Accommodation Guides). 224p. (Orig.). 1984. pap. 10.95 (ISBN 0-86145-190-2, Pub. by Auto Assn-British Tourist Authority England). Merrimack Pub Cir.
--Guesthouses, Farmhouses & Inns in Britain. (British Automobile Association Accommodation Guides Ser.). 368p. (Orig.). 1984. pap. 9.95 (ISBN 0-86145-186-4, Pub. by Auto Assn-British Tourist Authority England). Merrimack Pub Cir.

--Guide to National Trust Properties in Britain. 192p. (Orig.). 1984. pap. 14.95 (ISBN 0-86145-194-5, Pub. by Auto Assn-British Tourist Authority England). Merrimack Pub Cir.
--Illustrated Touring Atlas of Britain: British Automobile Association Maps & Atlases. 192p. (Orig.). 1984. pap. 16.95 (ISBN 0-86145-203-8, Pub. by Auto Assn-British Tourist Authority England). Merrimack Pub Cir.
--Lake District: Ordnance Survey Leisure Guide. (British Automobile Association Ordance Survey Leisure Guides). 120p. (Orig.). 1984. pap. 15.95 (ISBN 0-86145-192-9, Pub. by Auto Assn-British Tourist Authority England). Merrimack Pub Cir.
--Self Catering in Britain. (British Automobile Association Accomodation Guides). 304p. (Orig.). 1984. pap. 10.95 (ISBN 0-86145-189-9, Pub. by Auto Assn-British Tourist Authority England). Merrimack Pub Cir.
--Stately Homes, Museums, Castles & Gardens in Britain. (British Automobile Association Accommodation Guides). 304p. (Orig.). 1984. pap. 10.95 (ISBN 0-86145-191-0, Pub. by Auto Assn-British Tourist Authority England). Merrimack Pub Cir.
--The Touring Book of Britain. 320p. (Orig.). 1984. pap. 19.95 (ISBN 0-86145-193-7, Pub. by Auto Assn-British Tourist Authority England). Merrimack Pub Cir.
--Town Walks in Britain. 136p. (Orig.). 1984. 19.95 (ISBN 0-86145-195-3, Pub. by Auto Assn-British Tourist Authority England). Merrimack Pub Cir.
British Automobile Association in Association with Baedeker. Baedeker's Copenhagen. (Baedeker City Guides). 102p. (Orig.). 1984. pap. 11.95 (ISBN 0-86145-214-3, Pub. by Auto Assn-British Tourist Authority England). Merrimack Pub Cir.
--Baedeker's Florence. (Baedeker City Guides). 148p. (Orig.). 1984. pap. 11.95 (ISBN 0-86145-183-X, Pub. by Auto Assn-British Tourist Authority, England). Merrimack Pub Cir.
--Baedeker's Hong Kong. (Baedeker City Guides). 108p. (Orig.). 1984. pap. 11.95 (ISBN 0-86145-213-5, Pub. by Auto Assn-British Tourist Authority England). Merrimack Pub Cir.
--Baedeker's Jerusalem. (Baedeker City Guides). 168p. (Orig.). 1984. pap. 11.95 (ISBN 0-86145-207-0, Pub. by Auto Assn-British Tourist Authority England). Merrimack Pub Cir.
--Baedeker's Madrid. (Baedeker City Guides). 124p. (Orig.). 1984. pap. 11.95 (ISBN 0-86145-212-7, Pub. by Auto Assn-British Tourist Authority England). Merrimack Pub Cir.
--Baedeker's San Francisco. (Baedeker City Guides). 154p. (Orig.). 1984. pap. 11.95 (ISBN 0-86145-184-8, Pub. by Auto Assn-British Tourist Authority England). Merrimack Pub Cir.
--Baedeker's Tokyo. (Baedeker City Guides). 138p. (Orig.). 1984. pap. 11.95 (ISBN 0-86145-206-2, Pub. by Auto Assn-British Tourist Authority England). Merrimack Pub Cir.
--Baedeker's Venice. (Baedeker City Guides). 108p. (Orig.). 1984. pap. 11.95 (ISBN 0-86145-205-4, Pub. by Auto Assn-British Tourist Authority England). Merrimack Pub Cir.
--Baedeker's Vienna. (Baedeker City Guides). 172p. (Orig.). 1984. pap. 11.95 (ISBN 0-86145-204-6, Pub. by Auto Assn-British Tourist Authority England). Merrimack Pub Cir.
British Automobile Association Staff & Baedeker Staff. Baedeker's Berlin. (Baedeker City Guides Ser.). 172p. (Orig.). 1984. pap. 11.95 (ISBN 0-86145-211-9, Pub. by Auto Assn-British Tourist Authority England). Merrimack Pub Cir.
British Automobile Association Staff. Discover France: A Travellers' Guide. 144p. (Orig.). 1984. pap. 13.95 (ISBN 0-86145-176-7, Pub. by Auto Assn-British Tourist Authority England). Merrimack Pub Cir.
British Broadcasting Company, jt. auth. see Automobile Association of Great Britain.
British Broadcasting Company (BBC), ed. BBC Annual Report & Handbook, 1982. 55th ed. LC 49-35358. (Illus.). 228p. (Orig.). 1981. pap. 12.50x (ISBN 0-563-20049-9). Intl Pubns Serv.
British Cast Iron Research Association. Effects of Copper on Iron. 65p. 1965. 9.75 (ISBN 0-317-34518-4, 82). Intl Copper.
British Cast Iron Research Association, Conference, Great Britain. Foundry Technology of the Eighties: Papers. 365p. 67.00 (ISBN 0-317-32628-7, OS7905). Am Foundrymen.
British Ceramic Research Association Symposium. Special Ceramics: Proceedings, 3 vols. Popper, P., ed. Incl. Vol. 1. 1961. 55.00 (ISBN 0-12-561650-3); Vol. 2. 1963; Vol. 3. 1966. Acad Pr.
British Ceramic Society, ed. Load-Bearing Brickwork. 60.00x (ISBN 0-686-78853-2, Pub. by Brit Ceramic Soc England). State Mutual Bk.
--Load-Bearing Brickwork, No. 6. 1982. 77.00x (ISBN 0-686-44604-6, Pub. by Brit Ceramic Soc England). State Mutual Bk.
--The Mechanical Engineering Properties & Applications of Ceramics. 50.00x (ISBN 0-686-78852-4, Pub. by Brit Ceramic Soc England). State Mutual Bk.
--Mechanical Properties of Ceramics. 1981. 50.00x (ISBN 0-686-78729-3, Pub. by Brit Ceramic Soc England). State Mutual Bk.
--Mineralogy of Ceramics. 60.00x (ISBN 0-686-78854-0, Pub. by Brit Ceramic Soc England). State Mutual Bk.
British Columbia Institute of Technology, jt. auth. see Currie, John M.
British Combinatorial Conference, Sixth. Combinatorial Surveys: Proceedings. Cameron, Peter, ed. 1977. 47.00 (ISBN 0-12-157150-5). Acad Pr.
British Computer Society. Banking & Finance: An Annotated Bibliography. 48p. 1981. pap. 18.95 (ISBN 0-471-26202-1). Wiley.
--Britain & the Information Society. (British Computer Society Ser.). 1985. pap. write for info. (ISBN 0-471-26235-8). Wiley.
--Buying Financial Accounting Software. (Software Package Buyer's Guides Ser.). 48p. 1985. pap. 8.95 (ISBN 0-521-31781-9). Cambridge U Pr.
--Buying Payroll Software. (Software Package Buyer's Guides Ser.). 48p. 1985. pap. 8.95 (ISBN 0-521-31783-5). Cambridge U Pr.
--Buying Purchases Software. (Software Package Buyer's Guides Ser.). 48p. Date not set. pap. 8.95 (ISBN 0-521-31782-7). Cambridge U Pr.
--Buying Sales Software. (Software Package Buyer's Guides Ser.). 48p. Date not set. pap. 8.95 (ISBN 0-521-31784-3). Cambridge U Pr.
--A Glossary of Computing Terms: An Introduction. 4th ed. LC 84-45366. 64p. 1985. pap. 3.95 (ISBN 0-521-31777-0). Cambridge U Pr.
--Transportation: An Annotated Bibliography. 48p. 1981. pap. 21.95 (ISBN 0-471-26203-X). Wiley.
British Computer Society (BCS) Agriculture: An Annotated Bibliography. (British Computer Society Ser.). 48p. 1981. pap. 21.95 (ISBN 0-471-26201-3). Wiley.
British Computer Society (BCS), jt. auth. see Schofield, J.
British Council. Higher Education in the U. K. 1984-1986. (Illus.). 368p. (Orig.). 1982. pap. text ed. 15.95x (ISBN 0-582-49718-3). Longman.
British Council, ed. English As an International Language. (English Lanuage Teaching Documents Ser.: Vol. 102). 72p. 1983. pap. 5.75 (ISBN 0-08-029480-4). Pergamon.
--The Foreign Language Learning Process. (English Language Teaching Documents Ser.). 182p. 1983. pap. 9.00 (ISBN 0-08-030304-8). Pergamon.
--Games, Simulation & Role-Playing. (English Language Teaching Documents Ser.: Vol. 77/1). 48p. 1983. pap. 2.50 (ISBN 0-08-029478-2). Pergamon.
--Humanistic Approaches - an Empirical View. (English Language Teaching Documents Ser.: Vol. 113). 136p. 1983. pap. 7.50 (ISBN 0-08-030303-X). Pergamon.
--Issues in Language Testing. (English Language Teaching Documents: Vol. 111). 210p. 1983. pap. 9.00 (ISBN 0-08-030301-3). Pergamon.
--The Management & Diseases of Sheep. 600p. 1979. 95.00x (ISBN 0-85198-451-7, Pub. by CAB Bks England). State Mutual Bk.
--National Syllabuses. (English Language Teaching Documents Ser.: Vol. 108). 104p. 1983. pap. 6.50 (ISBN 0-08-030298-X). Pergamon.
--The Teaching of Comprehension. (English Language Teaching Documents Ser.). 112p. 1983. pap. 7.50 (ISBN 0-08-030306-4). Pergamon.
--The Teaching of Listening Comprehension. (English Language Teaching Documents Ser.). 150p. 1983. pap. 8.25 (ISBN 0-08-030308-0). Pergamon.
--Team Teaching in English for Specific Purposes. (English Language Teaching Documents Ser.: Vol. 106). 128p. 1983. pap. 7.50 (ISBN 0-08-030296-3). Pergamon.
--The Use of the Media in English Language Teaching. (English Language Teaching Documents Ser.: Vol. 105). 112p. 1983. pap. 7.50 (ISBN 0-08-030295-5). Pergamon.
British Council & Scott-Kilvert, Ian, eds. British Writers, Vol. II. LC 78-23483. (British Council Pamphlet Ser.). 1979. lib. bdg. 65.00 (ISBN 0-684-16407-8, ScribR). Scribner.
British Electrical & Allied Manufacturers' Association. Combines & Trusts in the Electrical Industry: The Position in Europe in 1927. Wilkins, Mira, ed. LC 76-29775. (European Business Ser.). (Illus.). 1977. Repr. of 1927 ed. lib. bdg. 23.50x (ISBN 0-405-09787-5). Ayer Co Pubs.
British Family Research Committee. Families in Britain. 350p. 1983. pap. 25.00x (ISBN 0-7100-9236-9). Routledge & Kegan.
British Feminism & Nonviolence Study Group. Piecing It Together: Feminism & Nonviolence. (Illus.). 60p. 1983. 3.00 (ISBN 0-9508602-0-4). J Tiffany.
British Film Inst. First Supplement of the Catalogue of the Book Library of the British Film Institute. 1983. lib. bdg. 240.00 (ISBN 0-8161-0388-7, Hall Library). G K Hall.
British Film Institute, London. Catalogue of the Book Library of the British Film Institute, 3 vols. 1975. Set. lib. bdg. 297.00 (ISBN 0-8161-0004-7, Hall Library). G K Hall.
British Foreign Office. British Foreign Office: Russia Correspondence, 1914 - 1918: Indexes & Guides to the Microfilm Collection. LC 76-44647. 1976. 20.00 (ISBN 0-8420-2107-8). Scholarly Res Inc.
British Horse Society & Pony Club & Cubitt. Aids & Their Application. 1977. pap. 3.95 (ISBN 0-8120-0760-3). Barron.
British Horse Society & Pony Club. Bits & Bitting. LC 76-55354. 1976. pap. 1.95 (ISBN 0-8120-0759-X). Barron.
--The Foot & Shoeing. LC 76-55015. 1976. pap. 3.95 (ISBN 0-8120-0758-1). Barron.
--A Guide to the Purchase of Children's Ponies. 1977. pap. 3.95 (ISBN 0-8120-0786-7). Barron.
--The Instructors' Handbook. LC 76-55317. 1977. 8.95 (ISBN 0-8120-5125-4). Barron.
British Horse Society & Pony Club & Fandel. Keeping a Pony at Grass. LC 76-54872. 1977. Barron.
British Horse Society & Pony Club. The Manual of Horsemanship. (Illus.). Repr. of 1950 ed. Barron.
--Mounted Games & Gymkhanas. LC 76-56448. 1977. 7.95 (ISBN 0-8120-5124-6). Barron.
--Polo for the Pony Club. LC 76-54905. 1977. pap. 3.95 (ISBN 0-8120-0785-9). Barron.
British Hotels, Restaurants, & Caterers Association. Hotels & Restaurants in Britain: The Official Guide, 1984. (Illus.). 616p. 1984. pap. 12.95 (ISBN 0-13-394925-7). P-H.
British Hotels, Restaurants, & Caterers Associations Staff. Hotels & Restaurants in Britain: The Offical Guide, 1985. price not set. P-H.
British Hotels, Restaurants & Caterers Association. Hotels & Restaurants in Britain 1983. (Illus.). 550p. 1983. pap. 12.95 (ISBN 0-13-394916-8). P-H.
British Institute of Human Rights. Detention: Minimum Standards of Treatment. 97p. 1975. 30.00x (ISBN 0-85992-018-6, Pub. by B Rose Pub). State Mutual Bk.
British Institute of International & Comparative Law. Selected Documents on International Environmental Law. LC 75-15273. 197p. 1977. 15.00 (ISBN 0-379-00348-1). Oceana.
British Institute of Management Foundation, ed. Job Evaluation: Theory & Practice. 1979. 50.00x (ISBN 0-85946-096-7, Pub. by Brit Inst Mgmt England). State Mutual Bk.
British Leather Manufacturers Research Association Staff. The Conservation of Bookbinding Leather. (Illus.). 96p. (Orig.). 1984. pap. 37.50 (ISBN 0-7123-0034-1, Pub. by British Lib). Longwood Pub Group.
British Leyland Motors. Complete Official Austin-Healey 100-Six & 3000, 1956-1968. LC 77-72588. (Illus.). 416p. 1977. pap. 25.00 (ISBN 0-8376-0133-9). Bentley.
--The Complete Official Jaguar 'E' Comprising the Official Driver's Handbook, Workshop Manual, Special Tuning Manual. 2nd, rev. ed. LC 73-94377. (Orig.). 1974. pap. 40.00 (ISBN 0-8376-0136-3). Bentley.
--The Complete Official MG Midget 1500, Model Years 1975-1979, Comprising the Official Driver's Handbook & Workshop Manual. LC 79-53185. (Illus.). 1980. pap. 35.00 (ISBN 0-8376-0131-2). Bentley.
--The Complete Official MGB Model Years 1962-1974: Comprising the Official Driver's Handbook, Workshop Manual, Special Tuning Manual. 4th rev. ed. LC 75-7766. (Illus.). 480p. 1975. pap. 25.00 (ISBN 0-8376-0115-0). Bentley.
--Complete Official MGB, Model Years 1975-1980: Comprising the Official Driver's Handbook & Workshop Manual. LC 80-65229. (Illus.). 304p. 1980. pap. 29.95 (ISBN 0-8376-0112-6). Bentley.
--Complete Official Sprite-Midget 948cc & 1098cc: Comprising the Official Driver's Handbook, Workshop Manual, Special Tuning Manual. LC 67-28432. (Illus.). 384p. (Orig.). 1968. pap. 25.00 (ISBN 0-8376-0023-5). Bentley.
--Complete Official Triumph GT6, GT6 Plus & GT6 MD III 1967-1973: Official Driver's Handbook & Official Workshop Manual. LC 74-21353. (Illus.). 480p. 1975. pap. 25.00 (ISBN 0-8376-0120-7). Bentley.
--The Complete Official Triumph Spitfire MK III, MK IV & 1500, Model Years 1968-1974: Comprising the Official Driver's Handbook & Workshop Manual. LC 74-20004. (Illus.). 480p. 1975. pap. 35.00 (ISBN 0-8376-0123-1). Bentley.
--The Complete Official Triumph Spitfire 1500, Model Years 1975-1980: Comprising the Official Driver's Handbook & Workshop Manual. LC 79-53184. (Illus.). 1980. pap. 25.00 (ISBN 0-8376-0122-3). Bentley.
--The Complete Official Triumph TR2 & TR3: Comprising the Official Driver's Instruction Book & Service Instruction Manual, Model Years 1953-1961. LC 75-42893. (Illus.). 464p. (Orig.). 1976. pap. 40.00 (ISBN 0-8376-0125-8). Bentley.
--Complete Official Triumph TR4 & TR4A 1961-1968: Official Driver's Handbook, Workshop Manual, Competition Preparation Manual. LC 74-21354. (Illus.). 400p. 1975. pap. 35.00 (ISBN 0-8376-0121-5). Bentley.
--The Complete Official Triumph TR6 & TR250, 1967-1976: Comprising the Official Driver's Handbook & Workshop Manual. LC 77-91592. (Illus.). 608p. 1978. pap. 35.00 (ISBN 0-8376-0108-8). Bentley.
--Complete Official Triumph TR7, 1975-1981: Comprising the Official Driver's Handbook & Repair Operation Manual. LC 78-73515. (Illus.). 464p. 1979. pap. 35.00 (ISBN 0-8376-0116-9). Bentley.
--The Complete Official 1275 cc Sprite-Midget 1967-1974: Comprising the Official Driver's Handbook, Workshop Manual, Emission Control Supplement. LC 75-37232. (Illus.). 400p. 1975. pap. 35.00 (ISBN 0-8376-0127-4). Bentley.
British Library. The British Library General Catalogue of Printed Books 1976-1982, 50 Vols. 1983. lib. bdg. 4650.00 (ISBN 0-86291-485-X). K G Saur.
British Library, ed. Checklist of British Official Serial Publications. 1980. 40.00x (ISBN 0-686-78918-0, Pub. by Brit Lib England). State Mutual Bk.
--The Gladstone Papers. 408p. 1953. 35.00x (ISBN 0-7141-0418-3, Pub. by Brit Lib England). State Mutual Bk.
--Research in British Universities Polytechnics & Colleges: Biological Sciences, Vol. 2. 1982. 150.00x (ISBN 0-7123-2004-0, Pub. by Pubns Sec Brit Lib England). State Mutual Bk.
--Research in British Universities Polytechnics & Colleges: Physical Sciences, Vol. 1. 1982. 150.00x (ISBN 0-7123-2003-2, Pub. by Pubns Sec Brit Lib England). State Mutual Bk.
--Research in British Unviersities Polytechnics & Colleges: Social Sciences, Vol. 3. 1982. 130.00x (ISBN 0-7123-2005-9, Pub. by Pubns Sec Brit Lib England). State Mutual Bk.
--Short-Title Catalogue of Books Printed in Italy & of Italian Books Printed in Other Countries from 1465-1600 Now in the British Museum. 1000p. 1958. 60.00x (ISBN 0-7141-0269-5, Pub. by Brit Lib England). State Mutual Bk.
--Short-Title Catalogue of Books Printed in the Netherlands & Belgium & of Dutch & Flemish Books Printed in Other Countries from 1470 to 1600 Now in the British Museum. 284p. 1965. 40.00x (ISBN 0-7141-0270-9, Pub. by Brit Lib England). State Mutual Bk.
British Library Dept. of Manuscripts Staff, ed. Index of Manuscripts in the British Library, 11 Vols. 6000p. 1984. Set. lib. bdg. 1800.00 (ISBN 0-85964-140-6). Chadwyck-Healey.
British Library Science Reference Library Staff. A Who's Who of Invention, 1617-1980. 1985. diazo microfiche 450.00 (ISBN 0-317-26889-9, Pub. by British Lib). Longwood Pub Group.
British Library Staff. Abstracting & Indexing Periodicals in the Science Reference Library. 3rd ed. (Orig.). 1985. pap. 7.50 (ISBN 0-7123-0716-8, Pub. by British Lib). Longwood Pub Group.
--Access to Local Government Documentattion. (R&D Report: No. 5619). (Illus.). 88p. (Orig.). 1981. pap. 12.00 (ISBN 0-905984-68-4, Pub. by British Lib). Longwood Pub Group.
--The American War of Independence Seventeen Seventy-Five to Seventeen Eighty-Five. (Illus.). 168p. 1975. 11.25 (ISBN 0-7141-0377-2, Pub. by British Lib); pap. 7.50 (ISBN 0-7141-0378-0). Longwood Pub Group.
--Bibliography of British Newspapers: Durham & Northumberland, Vol. 3. 152p. 1982. 15.00 (ISBN 0-7123-0008-2, Pub. by British Lib). Longwood Pub Group.
--Bibliography of British Newspapers: Kent, Vol. 2. 208p. 1982. 22.50 (ISBN 0-7123-0007-4, Pub. by British Lib). Longwood Pub Group.
--Bibliography of British Newspapers: Wiltshire, Vol. 1. 28p. (Orig.). 1982. pap. 2.25 (ISBN 0-85365-038-1, Pub. by British Lib). Longwood Pub Group.
--British Library Occasional Papers, No. 2: Library Publishing. 80p. (Orig.). 1985. pap. 5.95 (ISBN 0-7123-0040-6, Pub. by British Lib). Longwood Pub Group.
--British Library Occasional Papers, No. 4: Australian & New Zealand Studies. 208p. (Orig.). 1985. pap. 14.25 (ISBN 0-7123-0048-1, Pub. by British Lib). Longwood Pub Group.
--British Library Occasional Papers, No. 6: African Studies. 208p. (Orig.). 1985. pap. 15.75 (ISBN 0-7123-0050-3, Pub. by British Lib). Longwood Pub Group.
--Catalogue of Additions to the Manuscripts in the British Library, Index 1854-1875. 792p. 1968. Repr. of 1810 ed. Vol. 1: A-Israelites. 2vol. set 45.00 (ISBN 0-7141-0409-4, Pub. by British Lib). Vol. 2: Issac-Z (ISBN 0-7141-0410-8). Longwood Pub Group.
--Catalogue of Additions to the Manuscripts in the British Library: The Blenheim Papers, 3 vols, Vols. 1-3. 964p. 1985. Set. 3 vol. set 172.50 (ISBN 0-7123-0019-8, Pub. by British Lib). Vol. 1 Descriptions. Vol. 2 Index A-La. Vol. 3 Index La-Z. Longwood Pub Group.
--Catalogue of Additions to the Manuscripts in the British Museum, 1756-1782. 716p. 1977. 67.50 (ISBN 0-7141-0490-6, Pub. by British Lib). Longwood Pub Group.
--Catalogue of Additions to the Manuscripts in the British Museum, Index 1783-1835. 522p. 1967. Repr. of 1849 ed. 22.50 (ISBN 0-7141-0402-7, Pub. by British Lib). Longwood Pub Group.
--Catalogue of Additions to the Manuscripts in the British Museum, 1836-1840. 307p. 1964. Repr. of 1843 ed. 18.75 (ISBN 0-7141-0403-5, Pub. by British Lib). Longwood Pub Group.

--Catalogue of Additions to the Manuscripts in the British Museum, 1841-1845. 870p. 1964. Repr. of 1850 ed. 26.25 (ISBN 0-7141-0404-3, Pub. by British Lib). Longwood Pub Group.
--Catalogue of Additions to the Manuscripts in the British Museum, 1846-1847. 529p. 1964. Repr. of 1864 ed. 22.50 (ISBN 0-7141-0405-1, Pub. by British Lib). Longwood Pub Group.
--Catalogue of Additions to the Manuscripts in the British Museum, 1848-1853. 578p. 1965. Repr. of 1868 ed. 22.50 (ISBN 0-7141-0406-X, Pub. by British Lib). Longwood Pub Group.
--Catalogue of Additions to the Manuscripts in the British Museum, 1854-1860. 947p. 1966. Repr. of 1875 ed. 26.25 (ISBN 0-7141-0407-8, Pub. by British Lib). Longwood Pub Group.
--Catalogue of Additions to the Manuscripts in the British Museum, 1861-1875. 1065p. 1967. Repr. of 1877 ed. 26.25 (ISBN 0-7141-0408-6, Pub. by British Lib). Longwood Pub Group.
--Catalogue of Additions to the Manuscripts in the British Museum, 1876-1881. 628p. 1967. Repr. of 1882 ed. 22.50 (ISBN 0-7141-0452-3, Pub. by British Lib). Longwood Pub Group.
--Catalogue of Additions to the Manuscripts in the British Museum, 1882-1887. 1160p. 1968. Repr. of 1889 ed. 30.00 (ISBN 0-7141-0453-1, Pub. by British Lib). Longwood Pub Group.
--Catalogue of Additions to the Manuscripts in the British Museum, 1880-1893. 944p. 1969. Repr. of 1894 ed. 26.25 (ISBN 0-7141-0456-6, Pub. by British Lib). Longwood Pub Group.
--Catalogue of Additions to the Manuscripts in the British Museum, 1894-1899, 2 Vols. 1969. Repr. of 1903 ed. Vol. 1: Descriptions, 582p. 45.00 set (ISBN 0-7141-0457-4, Pub. by British Lib). Vol. 2: Index, 936p (ISBN 0-7141-0459-0). Longwood Pub Group.
--Catalogue of Additions to the Manuscripts in the British Museum, 1900-1905. 940p. 1969. Repr. of 1907 ed. 26.25 (ISBN 0-7141-0461-2, Pub. by British Lib). Longwood Pub Group.
--Catalogue of Additions to the Manuscripts in the British Museum, 1906-1910. 812p. 1969. Repr. of 1912 ed. 26.25 (ISBN 0-7141-0462-0, Pub. by British Lib). Longwood Pub Group.
--Catalogue of Additions to the Manuscripts in the British Museum, 1911-1915, 2 Vols. 1969. Repr. of 1925 ed. Vol. 1: Descriptions, 988p. 45.00 set (ISBN 0-7141-0458-2, Pub. by British Lib). Vol. 2: Index, 516p (ISBN 0-7141-0460-4). Longwood Pub Group.
--Catalogue of Additions to the Manuscripts in the British Museum, 1926-1930. 622p. 1959. 22.50 (ISBN 0-7141-0414-0, Pub. by British Lib). Longwood Pub Group.
--Catalogue of Additions to the Manuscripts in the British Museum, 1931-1935. 898p. 1967. 30.00 (ISBN 0-7141-0415-9, Pub. by British Lib). Longwood Pub Group.
--Catalogue of Additions to the Manuscripts in the British Museum, 1936-1945, 2 Vols. 1970. Vol. 1: Descriptions 488p. 52.50 set (ISBN 0-7141-0416-7, Pub. by British Lib). Vol. 2: Index 452p. Longwood Pub Group.
--Catalogue of Additions to the Manuscripts in the British Museum, 1946-1950, 3 Vols. 1980. Vol. 1: Descriptions, 432p. 142.50 set (ISBN 0-904654-41-9, Pub. by British Lib). Vol. 2: Index, A-K, 556p. Vol. 3: Index L-Z, 544p. Longwood Pub Group.
--Catalogue of Additions to the Manuscripts in the British Museum, 1951-1955, 2 Vols. 1982. Vol. 1: Descriptions, 296p. 135.00 set (ISBN 0-904654-69-9, Pub. by British Lib). Vol. 2: Index, 424p. Longwood Pub Group.
--Catalogue of Books Printed in the Fifteenth Century Now in the British Library: Italy (Supplement, Part XII. (Illus.). 108p. 1985. 90.00 (ISBN 0-7123-0022-8, Pub. by British Lib). Longwood Pub Group.
--Catalogue of Books Printed in the Fifteenth Century Now in the British Library: Holland & Belgium. (Pt. IX). 312p. 1967. Repr. of 1962 ed. 52.50 (ISBN 0-7141-0113-3, Pub. by British Lib). Longwood Pub Group.
--Catalogue of Books Printed in the Fifteenth Century Now in the British Library: Spain & Portugal. (Pt. X). (Illus.). 148p. 1971. 52.50 (ISBN 0-7141-0114-1, Pub. by British Lib). Longwood Pub Group.
--Catalogue of Printed Maps, Charts & Plans, 16 Vols. 1967. 600.00 (ISBN 0-7141-0324-1, Pub. by British Lib). Longwood Pub Group.
--Catalogue of Printed Maps, Charts & Plans: Ten-Year Supplement 1965-1974. 696p. 1978. 67.50 (ISBN 0-7141-0366-7, Pub. by British Lib). Longwood Pub Group.
--Catalogue of Printed Music in the British Museum: Music in the Hirsch Library. Pt. 53. 444p. 1951. 37.50 (ISBN 0-7141-0116-8, Pub. by British Lib). Longwood Pub Group.
--Catalogue of the Manuscript Maps, Charts, & Plans of the Topographical Drawings, Vol. 1. 486p. 1962. Repr. of 1844 ed. 30.00 (ISBN 0-7141-0422-1, Pub. by British Lib). Longwood Pub Group.
--Checklist of British Official Serial Publications. 12th ed. (Orig.). 1985. pap. 13.50 (ISBN 0-7123-0017-1, Pub. by British Lib). Longwood Pub Group.
--The Christian Orient. (Illus.). 112p. (Orig.). 1978. pap. 7.50 (ISBN 0-7141-0666-6, Pub. by British Lib). Longwood Pub Group.
--European Biotechnology Information Project (EBIP) Biotechnology Information Seminar Course Book. 1984. 30.00 (Pub. by British Lib). Longwood Pub Group.
--European Biotechnology Information Project (EBIP) Business Information Sources in Biotechnology. 1984. 15.00 (ISBN 0-317-26872-4, Pub. by British Lib). Longwood Pub Group.
--European Biotechnology Information Project (EBIP) Culture Collections. 1984. 7.50 (ISBN 0-317-26875-9, Pub. by British Lib). Longwood Pub Group.
--European Biotechnology Information Project (EBIP) Forthcoming Conferences. 1984. 7.50 (ISBN 0-317-26881-3, Pub. by British Lib). Longwood Pub Group.
--European Biotechnology Information Project (EBIP) Market Research Reports. 2nd ed. 1984. 7.50 (ISBN 0-317-26879-1, Pub. by British Lib). Longwood Pub Group.
--Guide to Government Department & Other Libraries. 26th ed. 100p. (Orig.). 1984. pap. 15.00 (ISBN 0-7123-0709-5, Pub. by British Lib). Longwood Pub Group.
British Library's Science Reference Library Staff. A Who's Who of Invention, 1617-1980: Nineteen Hundred to Nineteen Hundred-Eighty. 1985. microfiche 360.00 (ISBN 0-317-26888-0, Pub. by British Lib). Longwood Pub Group.
British Mechanical Engineering Confederation in Association with 'Engineering' The European Economic Community & United Kingdom Engineering Companies. 57p. 1980. 78.75x (ISBN 0-89771-002-9). State Mutual Bk.
British Medical Assocaition. The Handbook of Medical Ethics. 104p. 1984. 10.50x (ISBN 0-7279-0077-3, Pub. by British Med Assoc UK). Taylor & Francis.
British Medical Association, jt. auth. see Times Books.
British Medical Association Staff. How to Do It. 2nd ed. 156p. 1985. pap. 14.50 (ISBN 0-7279-0056-0, Pub. by British Med Assoc UK). Taylor & Francis.
--Procedures in Practice. 74p. 1981. 13.00x (ISBN 0-7279-0075-7, Pub. by British Med Assoc UK). Taylor & Francis.
British Medical Journal. Emergencies in the Home. 112p. 1982. 13.00x (ISBN 0-7279-0088-9, Pub. by British Med Assoc UK). Taylor & Francis.
British Medical Journal, ed. Britsh National Formulary. 1981. 30.00x (ISBN 0-686-87357-2, Pub. by British Medical). State Mutual Bk.
British Medical Journal Editors, ed. ABC of Hypertension, 1981. 1981. 50.00x (ISBN 0-686-87351-3, Pub. by British Medical). State Mutual Bk.
--ABC of Ophthalmology. 1979. 30.00x (ISBN 0-686-87352-1, Pub. by British Medical). State Mutual Bk.
--Becoming a Doctor. 1980. 25.00x (ISBN 0-686-87354-8, Pub. by British Medical). State Mutual Bk.
--Bone & Joint Diseases. 1977. 40.00x (ISBN 0-686-87355-6, Pub. by Britsh Medical). State Mutual Bk.
--Epidemiology for the Uninitiated. 1979. 30.00x (ISBN 0-686-87358-0, Pub. by British Medical). State Mutual Bk.
--The First Year of Life. 1980. 39.00x (ISBN 0-686-87360-2, Pub. by British Medical). State Mutual Bk.
--The Handbook of Medical Ethics. 1980. 35.00x (ISBN 0-686-87362-9, Pub. by British Medical). State Mutual Bk.
--How to Do It. 1979. 30.00x (ISBN 0-686-87363-7, Pub. by British Medical). State Mutual Bk.
--Marital Pathology. 1980. 15.00x (ISBN 0-686-87365-3, Pub. by British Medical). State Mutual Bk.
--Our Children's Health. 1979. 20.00x (ISBN 0-686-87368-8, Pub. by British Medical). State Mutual Bk.
--Personal View: An Anthology. 1975. 37.00x (ISBN 0-686-87374-2, Pub. by Medical Journal). State Mutual Bk.
--Procedures in Practice. 1981. 60.00x (ISBN 0-686-87377-7, Pub. by British Medical). State Mutual Bk.
--Statistics at Square One. 1980. 30.00x (ISBN 0-686-87379-3, Pub. by British Medical). State Mutual Bk.
--Today's Treatment, No. 1. 1976. 30.00x (ISBN 0-686-87381-5, Pub. by British Medical). State Mutual Bk.
--Today's Treatment, No. 2. 1977. 30.00x (ISBN 0-686-87382-3, Pub. by British Medical). State Mutual Bk.
--Today's Treatment, No. 3. 1979. 39.00x (ISBN 0-686-87383-1, Pub. by British Journal). State Mutual Bk.
--Uniform Requirements for Manuscripts: Submitted to Biomedical Journal. 1979. 20.00x (ISBN 0-686-87385-8, Pub. by British Medical). State Mutual Bk.
British Medical Journal Staff. New Drugs. 215p. 1983. 13.00x (ISBN 0-7279-0190-7, Pub. by British Med Assoc UK). Taylor & Francis.
--Organizing a Practice. 1983. 13.00x (ISBN 0-7279-0185-0, Pub. by British Med Assoc UK). Taylor & Francis.
--Practising Prevention. 112p. 1983. 13.00x (ISBN 0-7279-0155-9, Pub. by British Med Assoc UK). Taylor & Francis.
British Museum. Dinosaurs & Their Living Relatives. LC 79-14504. (Natural History Ser.). 1980. 24.95 (ISBN 0-521-22887-5); pap. 8.95 (ISBN 0-521-29698-6). Cambridge U Pr.
--Human Biology: An Exhibition of Ourselves. 2nd ed. LC 81-7641. (Natural History Ser.). 124p. 1982. 29.95 (ISBN 0-521-23832-3); pap. 9.95 (ISBN 0-521-28247-0). Cambridge U Pr.
--Life Before Birth. LC 78-60029. (Natural History Ser.). (Illus.). 1979. 8.95 (ISBN 0-521-22382-2); pap. 4.95 (ISBN 0-521-29464-9). Cambridge U Pr.
--Man's Place in Evolution. (Natural History Ser.). (Illus.). 120p. 1981. 24.95 (ISBN 0-521-23177-9); pap. 9.95 (ISBN 0-521-29849-0). Cambridge U Pr.
--Medallic Illustrations of the History of Great Britain & Ireland. (Illus.). 1980. 115.00x (ISBN 0-88000-001-5). Quarterman.
--Nature at Work. LC 78-66795. (Natural History Ser.). (Illus.). 1978. 18.95 (ISBN 0-521-22390-3); pap. 8.95 (ISBN 0-521-29469-X). Cambridge U Pr.
--Origin of Species. LC 80-42170. (Natural History Ser.). 120p. 1981. 27.95 (ISBN 0-521-23878-1); pap. 9.95 (ISBN 0-521-28276-4). Cambridge U Pr.
British Museum, et al. Rhodesian Man & Associated Remains. LC 77-86422. (Illus.). Repr. of 1928 ed. 17.00 (ISBN 0-404-16624-5). AMS Pr.
British Museum. Department of Egyptian & Assyrian Antiquities. Babylonian Boundary-Stones & Memorial Tablets in the British Museum, 2 vols. King, L. W., ed. LC 78-72731. (Ancient Mesopotamian Texts & Studies). Repr. of 1912 ed. Set. 65.00 (ISBN 0-404-18166-X). AMS Pr.
British Museum, Department of Paleontology Staff. Prehistoric Age. (Orig.). (gr. 8 up). 1984. pap. 3.98 (ISBN 0-85112-632-4, Pub. by Guinness Superlatives England). Sterling.
British Museum. Dept. of Egyptian & Assyrian Antiquities. Annals of the Kings of Assyria. LC 78-72730. (Ancient Mesopotamian Texts & Studies). Repr. of 1902 ed. 75.00 (ISBN 0-404-18165-1). AMS Pr.
British Museum (Natural History) British Mesozoic Fossils. 6th. rev. ed. (Illus.). 209p. 1983. pap. 10.50x (ISBN 0-565-00872-2, Pub by Brit Mus Nat Hist England). Sabbot-Natural Hist Bks.
--Nature Stored, Nature Studied: Collections, Conservation & Allied Research at the British Museum (Natural History) (Illus.). 64p. 1981. pap. 6.50x (ISBN 0-565-00835-8, Pub. by Brit Mus Nat Hist England). Sabbot-Natural Hist Bks.
British Museum (Natural History), ed. Conspectus Florae Angolensis, 6 vols. Set. 500.00x (ISBN 0-686-78653-X, Pub. by Brit Mus Pubns England). State Mutual Bk.
--Flora de Mocambique. 1981. 500.00x (ISBN 0-686-78654-8, Pub. by Brit Mus Pubns England). State Mutual Bk.
British Non-Ferrous Metals Research Association. Clear Lacquers for Copper & Copper Alloys. 75p. 1965. 11.25 (ISBN 0-317-34498-6, 5). Intl Copper.
--Energy Requirements in the Electrode-Position of Copper, including a Summary of Work on the Deposition of Copper for Direct Working to Wire. 54p. 1965. 8.10 (ISBN 0-317-34521-4, 42). Intl Copper.
--Physical Studies of Water-Formed Corrosion Products on Copper & Proposals for an Alternative Mechanism of Pitting Corrosion. 73p. 10.95 (ISBN 0-317-34539-7, 34). Intl Copper.
British-North American Committee. Higher Oil Prices: Worldwide Financial Implications. LC 75-29675. 64p. 1975. 3.00 (ISBN 0-902594-27-3). Natl Planning.
--Mineral Development in the Eighties: Prospects & Problems. LC 76-53628. 64p. 1977. 3.00 (ISBN 0-902594-29-X). Natl Planning.
British Nuclear Energy Society, ed. Active Working on Reactors. 84p. 1971. 40.00x (ISBN 0-901948-86-1, Pub. by Brit Nuclear England). State Mutual Bk.
--The Applications of Ionizing Radiation in the Chemical & Allied Industries. 74p. 1968. 40.00x (ISBN 0-901948-95-0, Pub. by Brit Nuclear England). State Mutual Bk.
--Boiler Dynamics & Control in Nuclear Power Stations, No. 1. 215p. 1973. 90.00x (ISBN 0-901948-73-X, Pub. by Brit Nuclear England). State Mutual Bk.
--Boiler Dynamics & Control in Nuclear Power Stations, No. 2. 436p. 1980. 100.00x (ISBN 0-7277-0095-2, Pub. by Brit Nuclear England). State Mutual Bk.
--Chemical Nuclear Data-Measurements & Applications. 296p. 1971. 90.00x (ISBN 0-901948-89-6, Pub. by Brit Nuclear England). State Mutual Bk.
--Effects of Environment on Material Properties in Nuclear Energy Systems. 242p. 1971. 60.00x (ISBN 0-7277-0028-6, Pub. by Brit Nuclear England). State Mutual Bk.
--Ferritic Steels for Fast Reactor Steam Generators, 2 vols. 510p. 1978. 150.00x (ISBN 0-686-79377-3, Pub. by Brit Nuclear England). State Mutual Bk.
--The High Temperature Reactor & Process Applications. 430p. 1975. 125.00x (ISBN 0-7277-0004-9, Pub. by Brit Nuclear England). State Mutual Bk.
--Liquid Alkali Metals. 315p. 1973. 70.00x (ISBN 0-901948-77-2, Pub. by Brit Nuclear England). State Mutual Bk.
--Nuclear Desalination. 64p. 1968. 60.00x (ISBN 0-901948-94-2, Pub. by Brit Nuclear England). State Mutual Bk.
--Optimisation of Sodium-Cooled Fast Reactors. 470p. 1978. 125.00x (ISBN 0-7277-0054-5, Pub. by Brit Nuclear England). State Mutual Bk.
--The Physics of Fast Reactor Operation & Design. 470p. 1978. 125.00x (ISBN 0-7277-0054-5, Pub. by Brit Nuclear England). State Mutual Bk.
--The Physics Problems in Thermal Reactor Design. 336p. 1967. 90.00x (ISBN 0-901948-88-8, Pub. by Brit Nuclear England). State Mutual Bk.
--Post-Irradiation Examination. 366p. 1981. 100.00x (ISBN 0-7277-0111-8, Pub. by Brit Nuclear England). State Mutual Bk.
--Post-Irradiation Examination Techniques. 250p. 1972. 75.00x (ISBN 0-901948-78-0, Pub. by Brit Nuclear England). State Mutual Bk.
--Probabilistic & Extreme Load Design of Nuclear Plant Facilities. 1979. 60.00x (ISBN 0-87262-146-4, Pub. by Brit Nuclear England). State Mutual Bk.
--Radiation Protection in Nuclear Power Plants & the Fuel Cycle, 2 vols. 498p. 1979. 125.00x (ISBN 0-7277-0072-3, Pub. by Brit Nuclear England). State Mutual Bk.
--Radiography with Neutrons. 167p. 1975. 80.00x (ISBN 0-7277-0019-7, Pub. by Brit Nuclear England). State Mutual Bk.
--Reactor Inspection Technology. 192p. 1975. 80.00x (ISBN 0-7277-0011-1, Pub. by Brit Nuclear England). State Mutual Bk.
--Safety & Siting. 136p. 1972. 59.00x (ISBN 0-901948-93-4, Pub. by Brit Nuclear England). State Mutual Bk.
--A Status Review of Alloy Eight Hundred. 389p. 1975. 70.00x (ISBN 0-7277-0021-9, Pub. by Brit Nuclear England). State Mutual Bk.
--Steam Generating & Other Heavy Water Reactors. 336p. 1968. 59.00x (ISBN 0-901948-84-5, Pub. by Brit Nuclear England). State Mutual Bk.
--Structural Analysis & Design of Nuclear Plant Facilities. 553p. 1980. 45.00x (ISBN 0-87262-238-X, Pub. by Brit Nuclear England). State Mutual Bk.
--Structural Design of Nuclear Plant Facilities, 3 vols. 448p. 1973. 150.00x (ISBN 0-87262-155-3, Pub. by Brit Nuclear England). State Mutual Bk.
--Uranium Isotope Separation. 260p. 1975. 70.00x (ISBN 0-7277-0022-7, Pub. by Brit Nuclear England). State Mutual Bk.
--Vibration in Nuclear Plant, 2 vols. 1008p. 1979. 125.00x (ISBN 0-7277-0062-6, Pub. by Brit Nuclear England). State Mutual Bk.
--Voids Formed by Irradiation of Reaction Materials. 376p. 1971. 60.00x (ISBN 0-901948-85-3, Pub. by Brit Nuclear England). State Mutual Bk.
--Water Chemistry of Nuclear Reactor Systems. 534p. 1978. 125.00x (ISBN 0-7277-0053-7, Pub. by Brit Nuclear England). State Mutual Bk.
--Water Chemistry of Nuclear Reactor Systems, No. 2. 430p. 1981. 135.00x (ISBN 0-7277-0126-6, Pub. by Brit Nuclear England). State Mutual Bk.
--Welding & Fabrication in the Nuclear Industry. 416p. 1979. 125.00x (ISBN 0-7277-0083-9, Pub. by Brit Nuclear England). State Mutual Bk.
British Occupational Hygiene Society, International Symposium. Inhaled Particles III: Proceedings, 2 vols. Walton, W. H., ed. 1977. 90.00 set (ISBN 0-9502121-0-5, Pub. by Gresham England). State Mutual Bk.
British People's Party. Failure at Nuremberg. (Illus.). 42p. 1983. pap. 2.50 (ISBN 0-939484-04-8). Inst Hist Rev.
British Pumps Manufacturers Association, 6th Technical Conference. Proceedings. 270p. 1979. pap. 54.00x (ISBN 0-906085-27-6, Dist. by Air Science Co.). BHRA Fluid.
British Record Society. Abstracts of Inquisitiones Post Mortem for Gloucestershire, Pt. VI: 33 Edward 33 to 14 Henry IV, 1359-1413. Stokes, Ethel, compiled by. (Index Library: Vol. 47). pap. 19.00 (ISBN 0-317-15676-4). Kraus Repr.
--Abstracts of Wiltshire Inquisitiones Post Mortem Returned into the Court of Chancery in the Reign of King Edward III, A. D. 1327-1377. Stokes, Ethel, compiled by. (Index Library: Vol. 48). pap. 30.00 (ISBN 0-317-15679-9). Kraus Repr.
--Index of Wills Proved in the Prerogative Court of Canterbury, Vol. 2: 1383-1558, & Now Preserved in the Principal Probate Registry, Somerset House, London. Smith, Challenor C., compiled by. (Index Library Ser.: Vol. 11). pap. 30.00 (ISBN 0-317-15659-4). Kraus Repr.
--Index of Wills Proved in the Prerogative Court of Canterbury, Vol. 4: 1584-1604. Fry, E. A. & Smith, S. A., eds. (Index Library Ser.: Vol. 25). pap. 44.00 (ISBN 0-317-15665-9). Kraus Repr.
--Index of Wills Proved in the Prerogative Court of Canterbury, Vol. 5: 1605-19. Stokes, Ethel, compiled by. (Index Library Ser.: Vol. 43). pap. 44.00 (ISBN 0-317-15672-1). Kraus Repr.

British Records Society. Index to Administrations in the Prerogative Court of Canterbury, Vol. 1: 1649-1654. (Index Library Ser.: Vols. 67-68). write for info. Kraus Repr.
British Robot Association Annual Conference, 6th, Birmingham, UK, May 1983. Proceedings. Brock, T. E., ed. iv, 256p. 1983. 53.25 (ISBN 0-444-86685-X, North-Holland). Elsevier.
British Sports Association for the Disabled. Water Sports for the Disabled. (Illus.). 256p. 1983. 16.95 (ISBN 0-7158-0864-8, Pub by EP Publishing England). Sterling.
British Sulfur Corporation. Mineral Resources of the Arab Countries. 100p. 1983. 130.00 (ISBN 0-902777-54-8, NO. 5055). Methuen Inc.
British Sulphur Corporation Ltd, ed. World Directory of Fertilizer Manufacturers. 5th ed. 288p. 1981. 275.00x (ISBN 0-902777-52-1). Intl Pubns Serv.
--World Directory of Fertilizer Products. 5th ed. 126p. 1981. 165.00x (ISBN 0-902777-46-7). Intl Pubns Serv.
British Sulphur Corporation Ltd., ed. World Fertilizer Atlas. 6th ed. (Illus.). 112p. 1979. 200.00x (ISBN 0-902777-47-5). Intl Pubns Serv.
British Sulphur Corporation Ltd, ed. World Guide to Fertilizer Plant Equipment. 2nd ed. 197p. 1977. 80.00x (ISBN 0-8002-2964-9). Intl Pubns Serv.
--World Guide to Fertilizer Processes & Constructors. 6th ed. 174p. 1979. 145.00x (ISBN 0-902777-36-X). Intl Pubns Serv.
--World Sulphuric Acid Atlas. 3rd ed. (Illus.). 90p. 1980. 210.00x (ISBN 0-902777-44-0). Intl Pubns Serv.
--World Survey of Potash Resources. 3rd ed. (Illus.). 290p. 1979. 312.50x (ISBN 0-902777-42-4). Intl Pubns Serv.
British Tourist Authority. AA Alternative Routes in Britain. 288p. 1982. 27.95 (ISBN 0-86145-063-9, Pub. by B T A). Merrimack Pub Cir.
--AA Big Road Atlas of Britain. 94p. 1982. 9.95 (ISBN 0-86145-122-8, Pub. by B T A). Merrimack Pub Cir.
--AA-BTA: The Second Touring Guide to Britain. 192p. 1982. 14.95 (ISBN 0-86145-080-9, Pub. by B T A). Merrimack Pub Cir.
--AA Touring Guide to England. (Illus.). 414p. 1979. 24.95 (ISBN 0-86145-054-X, Pub. by B T A). Merrimack Pub Cir.
--AA Touring Guide to Ireland. (Illus.). 336p. 1979. 24.95 (ISBN 0-09-127020-0, Pub. by B T A). Merrimack Pub Cir.
--AA Touring Guide to Scotland. (Illus.). 263p. 1979. 24.95 (ISBN 0-86145-093-0, Pub. by B T A). Merrimack Pub Cir.
--Country Life Living History of Britain. 1982. 39.95 (ISBN 0-600-36783-5, Pub. by B T A). Merrimack Pub Cir.
--Discover America. 192p. 1982. 19.95 (ISBN 0-86145-081-7, Pub. by B T A). Merrimack Pub Cir.
--Hotels & Restaurants in Britain, 1982-3. LC 52-21171. (Illus.). 600p. 1982. pap. 10.00x (ISBN 0-7095-0897-2). Intl Pubns Serv.
--London & the Famous. 160p. 1982. 8.95 (ISBN 0-7095-0938-3, Pub. by B T A). Merrimack Pub Cir.
--Museums & Galleries in Scotland. 96p. 1982. 5.50 (ISBN 0-85419-196-8, Pub. by B T A). Merrimack Pub Cir.
--Shell Book of the Islands of Britain. 198p. 1982. 19.95 (ISBN 0-7112-0087-4, Pub. by B T A). Merrimack Pub Cir.
British Tourist Authority, jt. auth. see Automobile Association.
British Tourist Authority Staff. London Hotels & Inexpensive Accommodation, 1984. 150p. (Orig.). 1984. pap. 4.95 (ISBN 0-946837-00-7, Pub. by Auto Assn-British Tourist Authority England). Merrimack Pub Cir.
British Welding Research Association. The Welding of Sand Cast Incramet 800. 75p. 1965. 11.25 (ISBN 0-317-34556-7, 57). Intl Copper.
Britnell, George E. & Fowke, V. C. Canadian Agriculture in War & Peace, 1935-1950. (Illus.). 518p. 1962. 35.00x (ISBN 0-8047-0089-3). Stanford U Pr.
Britnieva, Mary, tr. see Benois, Alexandre.
Brito, Dagobert & Intriligator, Michael D., eds. Strategies for Managing Nuclear Proliferation: Economic & Political Issues. LC 82-49525. 336p. 1983. 33.00x (ISBN 0-669-06442-4). Lexington Bks.
Britsch, R. Lanier & Olson, Terrance. Counseling: A Guide to Helping Others. LC 83-72396. 238p. 1983. 8.95 (ISBN 0-87747-960-7). Deseret BK.
Britsch, Ralph A. & Britsch, Todd A. The Arts in Western Culture. (Illus.). 450p. 1985. pap. text ed. 20.95 (ISBN 0-13-047812-1). P-H.
Britsch, Todd A., jt. auth. see Britsch, Ralph A.
Britt, jt. auth. see Jenkins.
Britt, Albert. Great Biographers. facs. ed. LC 71-84300. (Essay Index Reprint Ser). 1936. 17.50 (ISBN 0-8369-1077-X). Ayer Co Pubs.
--Great Indian Chiefs. facs. ed. LC 76-76895. (Essay Index Reprint Ser). 1938. 21.50 (ISBN 0-8369-0006-5). Ayer Co Pubs.
--Great Indian Chiefs. (Essay Index Reprint Ser.). 280p. 1982. Repr. of 1938 ed. lib. bdg. 19.50 (ISBN 0-8290-0792-X). Irvington.
Britt, Albert, jt. auth. see Richberg, Donald R.
Britt, Beverly A., jt. ed. see Aldrete, J. Antonio.
Britt, David. All American Cocaine Story. LC 84-70083. 1984. pap. 10.95 (ISBN 0-89638-073-4). CompCare.
Britt, George, jt. auth. see Broun, Heywood.
Britt, George L. When Dust Shall Sing. 1958. 5.25 (ISBN 0-87148-922-8). Pathway Pr.
Britt, Judith S. Nothing More Agreeable: Music in George Washington's Family. (Illus.). 120p. 1984. pap. 6.95. Mt Vernon Ladies.
Britt, Katrina. Hotel Jacarandas. (Romances Ser.). 192p. 1982. pap. 1.50 (ISBN 0-373-02449-5). Harlequin Bks.
Britt, Kenneth W., ed. Retention of Fine Solids During Paper Manufacture. 114p. 1975. 29.95 (ISBN 0-317-36045-0, 01-01-R057). TAPPI.
Britt, Lora S. My Gold Coast: South Florida in Earlier Years. (Illus.). 245p. 1985. 14.95 (ISBN 0-9613982-0-5). Brittany Hse.
Britt, N. Wilson. Biology of Two Species of Lake Erie Mayflies. 1962. 2.50 (ISBN 0-86727-047-0). Ohio Bio Survey.
Britt, N. Wilson, et al. Limmological Studies of the Island Area of Western Lake Erie. 1973. 3.00 (ISBN 0-86727-062-4). Ohio Bio Survey.
Britt, Stan. The Jazz Guitarists. (Illus.). 128p. (Orig.). 1985. pap. 7.95 (ISBN 0-7137-1511-1, Pub. by Blandford Pr England). Sterling.
Britt, Steuart, ed. Consumer Behavior & the Behavioral Sciences: Theories & Applications. LC 78-9748. 624p. 1979. Repr. of 1966 ed. lib. bdg. 34.50 (ISBN 0-88275-704-0). Krieger.
Britt, Steuart H. Marketing Manager's Handbook. 1983. 60.50 (ISBN 0-85013-135-9). Dartnell Corp.
Britt, Steuart H. & Boyd, Harper W. Marketing Management & Administrative Action. 5th ed. (Illus.). 480p. 1983. text ed. 22.95 (ISBN 0-07-006949-2). McGraw.
Britt, Steuart H., jt. auth. see Graeber, Isacque.
Britt, Steuart H., jt. auth. see Lucas, Darrell B.
Britt, Stewart H. Psychological Principles of Marketing & Consumer Behavior. LC 77-75658. 1978. 35.00x (ISBN 0-669-01513-X). Lexington Bks.
Brittain & Kinmonth. English Elegance. LC 85-8448. (Illus.). 160p. 1985. 19.95 (ISBN 0-03-005854-6). HR&W.
Brittain, Bill. All the Money in the World. LC 77-25635. (Illus.). 160p. (gr. 3-7). 1979. 10.53i (ISBN 0-06-020675-6); PLB 10.89 (ISBN 0-06-020676-4). HarpJ.
--All the Money in the World. LC 77-25635. (A Trophy Bk.). (Illus.). 160p. (gr. 3-7). 1982. pap. 2.84i (ISBN 0-06-440128-6, Trophy). HarpJ.
--Devil's Donkey. LC 80-7907. (Illus.). 128p. (gr. 3-7). 1981. 10.53i (ISBN 0-06-020682-9); PLB 10.89 (ISBN 0-06-020683-7). HarpJ.
--Devil's Donkey. LC 80-7907. (A Trophy Bk.). (Illus.). 128p. (gr. 3-7). 1982. pap. 2.84i (ISBN 0-06-440129-4, Trophy). HarpJ.
--Who Knew There'd Be Ghosts? LC 84-48496. (Illus.). 128p. (gr. 4-7). 1985. 11.06i (ISBN 0-06-020699-3); PLB 10.89g (ISBN 0-06-020700-0). HarpJ.
--The Wish Giver: Three Tales of Coven Tree. LC 82-48264. (Illus.). 192p. (gr. 3-7). 1983. 10.53i (ISBN 0-06-020686-1); PLB 10.89g (ISBN 0-06-020687-X). HarpJ.
Brittain, Fred. Medieval Latin & Romance Lyric to A. D. 1300. 2nd ed. LC 38-9391. 1969. Repr. of 1951 ed. 17.00 (ISBN 0-527-11300-X). Kraus Repr.
Brittain, Frederick. Arthur Quiller-Couch: A Biographical Study of Q. LC 83-45720. Repr. of 1947 ed. 27.50 (ISBN 0-404-20044-3). AMS Pr.
Brittain, Grady B. Platy: The Child in Us. LC 81-6503. (Illus.). 53p. (Orig.). (ps-8). 1981. pap. 1.95 (ISBN 0-86663-761-3). Ide Hse.
Brittain, James E., ed. Turning Points in American Electrical History. LC 76-18433. (Illus.). 1977. 42.60 (ISBN 0-87942-081-2, PC00828). Inst Electrical.
Brittain, Jan, jt. auth. see Keith, Louis.
Brittain, John A. Inheritance & the Inequality of Material Wealth. LC 77-91814. (Brookings Institution Studies in Social Economics Ser.). pap. 27.80 (ISBN 0-317-30183-7, 2025365). Bks Demand UMI.
--The Inheritance of Economic Status. LC 76-56369. (Brookings Institution Studies in Social Economics). pap. 49.80 (ISBN 0-317-20776-8, 2025366). Bks Demand UMI.
Brittain, Mary A., jt. auth. see Williams, Mel.
Brittain, Robert. The Booklover's Almanac. LC 84-73257. 416p. 24.95 (ISBN 0-913720-59-3). Beil.
--A Pocket Guide to Correct Punctuation. 96p. 1982. pap. 2.95 (ISBN 0-8120-2599-7). Barron.
--Punctuation the Easy Way. 225p. (gr. 10-12). Date not set. pap. text ed. 1.95 (ISBN 0-8120-2426-5). Barron.
Brittain, Vera. Born Nineteen Twenty-Five. 384p. 1983. pap. 7.95 (ISBN 0-86068-270-6, Pub. by Virago Pr). Merrimack Pub Cir.
--Chronicle of Youth: The War Diary 1913-1917. Bishop, Alan, ed. LC 82-6340. 1982. 15.50 (ISBN 0-688-01523-9). Morrow.
--In the Steps of John Bunyan. (Illus.). 1973. 30.00 (ISBN 0-8274-1456-0). R West.
--Massacre by Bombing. 1981. lib. bdg. 59.95 (ISBN 0-686-72723-1). Revisionist Pr.
--Testament of Experience. 480p. 1985. pap. 7.95 (ISBN 0-86068-110-6, Pub. by Virago Pr). Merrimack Pub Cir.
--Testament of Friendship. 480p. 1985. pap. 7.95 (ISBN 0-86068-150-5, Pub. by Virago Pr). Merrimack Pub Cir.
--Valiant Pilgrim: The Story of John Bunyan & Puritan England. 1950. 30.00 (ISBN 0-8274-3665-3). R West.
Brittain, Virginia T. The Berryhill Family History. (Illus.). 338p. 1982. Repr. of 1962 ed. 25.00 (ISBN 0-89308-293-7, FH 16). Southern Hist Pr.
Brittain, W. Bruce, jt. auth. see Cleveland, Harold Van B.
Brittain, W. Lambert. Creativity, Art, & the Young Child. (Illus.). 1979. text ed. 17.95 (ISBN 0-02-314990-6). Macmillan.
Brittain, W. Lambert, jt. auth. see Lowenfeld, Viktor.
Brittan, Arthur. Meanings & Situations. (International Library of Sociology). 222p. 1973. 19.95x (ISBN 0-7100-7509-X). Routledge & Kegan.
--The Privatised World. (International Library of Sociology Ser.). 1978. 22.95x (ISBN 0-7100-8769-1). Routledge & Kegan.
Brittan, Arthur & Maynard, Mary. Sexism, Racism & Oppression. 220p. 1984. 29.95x (ISBN 0-85520-674-8); pap. 10.95x (ISBN 0-85520-675-6). Basil Blackwell.
Brittan, E. M., jt. auth. see Townsend, H. E.
Brittan, Gordon G., Jr. Kant's Theory of Science. LC 77-85531. 1978. 25.00 (ISBN 0-691-07221-3). Princeton U Pr.
Brittan, Gordon G., Jr., jt. auth. see Lambert, Karel.
Brittan, Harriett G. Scenes & Incidents of Everyday Life in Africa. LC 70-75541. Repr. of 1860 ed. 22.50x (ISBN 0-8371-0981-7, BRL&). Greenwood.
Brittan, Martin. Rasbora. (Illus.). 1972. 19.95 (ISBN 0-87666-136-3, PS-681). TFH Pubns.
Brittan, Samuel. Capitalism & the Permissive Society. 1973. text ed. 18.75x (ISBN 0-333-12464-2). Humanities.
--Government & the Market Economy. (Hobart Paperbacks: Ser. No. 2). 1972. pap. 4.25 technical (ISBN 0-255-36018-5). Transatlantic.
--How to End the Monetarist Controversy. 2nd ed. (Institute of Economic Affairs, Hobart Papers Ser.: No. 90). pap. 10.95 technical (ISBN 0-255-36144-0). Transatlantic.
--Is There an Economic Consensus? An Attitude Survey. 1973. text ed. 7.50x (ISBN 0-333-14410-4). Humanities.
--Participation Without Politics. (Institute of Economic Affairs, Hobart Papers Ser.: No. 62). pap. 5.95 technical (ISBN 0-255-36123-8). Transatlantic.
--Steering the Economy: The British Experiment. LC 71-152814. 505p. 1971. 22.95 (ISBN 0-912050-05-5, Library Pr). Open Court.
Brittan, Samuel & Lilley, Peter. Delusion of Incomes Policy. 254p. 1977. pap. 13.50x (ISBN 0-8419-6900-0). Holmes & Meier.
Brittan, Samuel, ed. The Role & Limits of Government: Essays in Political Economy. 288p. 1984. 37.50x (ISBN 0-8166-1278-1); pap. 14.95 (ISBN 0-8166-1276-5). U of Minn Pr.
Britten, Anthony F., jt. ed. see Kolins, Jerry.
Britten, Benjamin. On Receiving the First Aspen Award. 23p. 1982. pap. 1.95 (ISBN 0-571-10023-6). Faber & Faber.
--Peter Grimes & Gloriana. (English National Opera Guide: No.24). 128p. (Orig.). 1984. pap. 5.95 (ISBN 0-7145-4016-1). Riverrun NY.
Britten, Benjamin, jt. auth. see Kendall, Alan.
Britten, Emma. Nineteenth Century Miracles. 1977. lib. bdg. 59.95 (ISBN 0-8490-2348-3). Gordon Pr.
Britten, Emma H. Nineteenth Century Miracles: Or, Spirits & Their Work in Every Country of the Earth. LC 75-36831. (Occult Ser.). (Illus.). 1976. Repr. of 1884 ed. 43.00x (ISBN 0-405-07943-5). Ayer Co Pubs.
Britten, F. J. Old Clocks & Watches. 1932. 70.00x (ISBN 0-686-45467-7, Pub. by EP Pub England). State Mutual Bk.
--Old Clocks & Watches & Their Makers. (Illus.). 1976. Repr. 48.00x (ISBN 0-85409-703-1). Charles River Bks.
--Watch & Clockmakers' Handbook. (Illus.). 1976. 29.50 (ISBN 0-902028-46-4). Apollo.
--Watch & Clockmakers' Handbook, Dictionary & Guide. (Illus.). 499p. 1976. Repr. of 1907 ed. 29.50 (ISBN 0-902028-46-4). Antique Collect.
Britten, F. J., intro. by. Old English Clocks - The Wetherfield Collection. (Illus.). 114p. 1981. 62.50 (ISBN 0-907462-00-6). Antique Collect.
Britten, F. W. Britten's Old Clocks & Watches & Their Makers. 3rd ed. (Illus.). 1980. 49.50. Apollo.
--Horological Helps & Hints. (Illus.). 375p. 1977. Repr. of 1929 ed. 29.50 (ISBN 0-902028-64-2). Antique Collect.
--Horological Hints & Helps. (Illus.). 1977. 21.50 (ISBN 0-902028-64-2). Apollo.
Britten, James. Old Country & Farming Words: Gleaned from Agricultural Books. (English Dialect Society Publications Ser.: No. 30). pap. 20.00 (ISBN 0-317-15841-4). Kraus Repr.
Britten, James & Holland, Robert. A Dictionary of English Plant-Names. (English Dialect Society Publications Ser.: No's. 22, 26, 45). pap. 62.00 (ISBN 0-317-15774-4). Kraus Repr.
Britten, James, ed. & intro. by. The Names of Herbes: A. D. 1548. (English Dialect Society Publications: No. 34). pap. 16.00 (ISBN 0-317-15877-5). Kraus Repr.
Britten, James, ed. see Aubrey, John.
Britten, James, et al, eds. William Turner, Libellus de re Herbaria 1538, the Names of Herbes 1548. ix, 275p. 1965. Repr. of 1548 ed. 22.50x (ISBN 0-318-02524-8, Pub by Brit Mus Nat Hist England). Sabbot-Natural Hist Bks.
Britten, Paul, tr. see Goran, Ulf.
Britter, R. E. & Griffiths, R. F. Dense Gas Dispersion. (Chemical Engineering Monographs Ser.: Vol. 16). 248p. 1982. Repr. 68.00 (ISBN 0-444-42095-9). Elsevier.
Brittin, Burdick H. International Law for Seagoing Officers. 4th ed. LC 80-81095. (Illus.). 624p. 1981. 21.95x (ISBN 0-87021-304-0). Naval Inst Pr.
--International Law for Seagoing Officers. 5th ed. 480p. 1986. 24.95 (ISBN 0-87021-305-9). Naval Inst Pr.
--International Law for Seagoing Officers. 4th ed. (Illus.). 624p. 1981. 21.95 (ISBN 0-87021-304-0); bulk rates avail. Naval Inst Pr.
Brittin, Norman & Brittin, Ruth. A Writing Apprenticeship. 5th ed. LC 80-23807. 305p. 1981. pap. text ed. 14.95 (ISBN 0-03-055421-7, HoltC). HR&W.
Brittin, Norman A. Edna St. Vincent Millay. (Twayne's United States Authors Ser.). 1967. pap. 5.95x (ISBN 0-8084-0114-9, T116, Twayne). New Coll U Pr.
--Edna St. Vincent Millay. rev. ed. (United States Authors Ser.). 1982. lib. bdg. 13.50 (ISBN 0-8057-7362-2, Twayne). G K Hall.
--Thomas Middleton. (English Authors Ser.). lib. bdg. 15.95 (ISBN 0-8057-1388-3, Twayne). G K Hall.
Brittin, Ruth, jt. auth. see Brittin, Norman.
Brittin, W., ed. Lectures in Theoretical Physics, Vol. 14 B: Mathematical Methods in Theoretical Physics. LC 59-13034. (Illus.). 520p. 1973. 22.50x (ISBN 0-87081-047-2). Colo Assoc.
Brittin, Wesley E. & Barut, A. O., eds. Boulder Lecture Notes in Theoretical Physics, 1967: Vol. 10-B, High Energy Physics & Fundamental Particles. 722p. 1968. 169.95 (ISBN 0-677-12900-9). Gordon.
--Boulder Lecture Notes in Theoretical Physics, 1967: Vol. 10A Quantum Theory & Statistical Theory. 584p. 1968. 132.95 (ISBN 0-677-12890-8). Gordon.
Brittin, Wesley E. & Odabasi, Halis, eds. Topics in Modern Physics: Tribute to E. U. Condon. LC 70-135286. 1971. 19.50x (ISBN 0-87081-010-3). Colo Assoc.
Brittin, Wesley E., jt. ed. see Barut, A. O.
Brittin, Wesley E., jt. ed. see Barut, Asim O.
Brittin, Wesley E., jt. ed. see Mahanthappa, K. T.
Brittin, Wesley E., et al. Air & Water Pollution. LC 72-165367. 1971. 19.50x (ISBN 0-87081-024-3); pap. 7.95x (ISBN 0-87081-040-5). Colo Assoc.
Brittin, Wesley E., et al, eds. Boulder Lecture Notes in Theoretical Physics, 1963, Vol. 6. 526p. 1964. 132.95 (ISBN 0-677-13030-9). Gordon.
--Boulder Lecture Notes in Theoretical Physics, 1968: Vol. 11-C, Atomic Collision Processes. 352p. 1969. 93.75 (ISBN 0-677-13130-5). Gordon.
--Boulder Lecture Notes in Theoretical Physics, 1968: Vol. 11-D, Mathematical Methods. 664p. 1969. 142.50 (ISBN 0-677-13140-2). Gordon.
--Boulder Lecture Notes in Theoretical Physics, 1968: Vol. 11-B, Quantum Fluids & Nuclear Matter. 444p. 1969. 119.25 (ISBN 0-677-13120-8). Gordon.
--Boulder Lecture Notes in Theoretical Physics, 1968: Vol. 11-A, Elementary Particle Physics, Pts. 1 & 2. 1969. Pt. 1, 650p. 142.50 (ISBN 0-677-13110-0); Pt. 2, 380p. 101.25 (ISBN 0-677-13400-2). Gordon.
--Boulder Lecture Notes in Theoretical Physics, 1964: Vol. 7-A, Lorentz Group. 394p. 1968. 106.50 (ISBN 0-677-13040-6). Gordon.
--Boulder Lecture Notes in Theoretical Physics, 1964: Vol. 7-B, Elementary Particles. 480p. 1968. 129.50 (ISBN 0-677-13050-3). Gordon.
--Boulder Lecture Notes in Theoretical Physics, 1964: Vol. 7-C, Statistical Phases, Weak Interactions, Field Theory. 496p. 1968. 132.95 (ISBN 0-677-13060-0). Gordon.
--Boulder Lecture Notes in Theoretical Physics, 1965: Vol. 8-C, Nuclear Structure Physics. 698p. 1966. 169.95 (ISBN 0-677-13090-2). Gordon.
--Boulder Lecture Notes in Theoretical Physics, 1965: Vol. 8-B, Fundamental Particles & High Energy Physics. 436p. 1966. 119.25 (ISBN 0-677-13080-5). Gordon.
--Boulder Lecture Notes in Theoretical Physics, 1965: Vol. 8-A, Statistical Physics & Solid State Physics. 364p. 1966. 93.75 (ISBN 0-677-13070-8). Gordon.
--Boulder Lecture Notes in Theoretical Physics, 1966: Vol. 9-A, Mathematical Methods of Theoretical Physics. 448p. 1967. 102.95 (ISBN 0-677-11600-4). Gordon.
--Boulder Lecture Notes in Theoretical Physics, 1966: Vol. 9-B, High Energy & Particle Physics. 448p. 1967. 119.25 (ISBN 0-677-11610-1). Gordon.

--Boulder Lecture Notes in Theoretical Physics, 1966: Vol. 9-C, Kinetic Theory. 804p. (Orig.). 1967. 187.25 (ISBN 0-677-11620-9). Gordon.

Britting, Kenneth R. Inertial Navigation Systems Analysis. LC 70-168635. 249p. 1971. 42.95 (ISBN 0-471-10485-X, Pub. by Wiley-Interscience). Wiley.

Brittingham, Janet R. Census Index of Bucks County, PA, 1910. LC 84-60426. 266p. 1984. spiral bdg. 18.00 (ISBN 0-9613351-0-6). J R Brittingham.

--Eighteen Eighty Census Index of Bucks County, PA. LC 85-70527. (Illus.). 182p. 1985. pap. 14.00 spiral (ISBN 0-9613351-1-4). J R Brittingham.

Brittker, Boris, et al. Supplement to Federal Income Taxation, 1985. 1985. pap. text ed. write for info. Little.

Brittle, Gerald. The Demonologist: The Extraordinary Career of Ed & Lorraine Warren. LC 80-21065. (Illus.). 216p. 1981. 9.95 (ISBN 0-13-198333-4). P-H.

Britton. Nazi Daggers. 1984. 14.95 (ISBN 0-912958-49-9); spiral bound 7.95 (ISBN 0-912958-24-3). MCN Pr.

Britton, Andrew. Once upon a Line, Vol. 1. 160p. 40.00x (ISBN 0-86093-277-X, Pub. by ORPC Ltd UK). State Mutual Bk.

Britton, Andrew, ed. Employment, Output & Inflation: The National Institute Model of the British Economy. x, 196p. 1983. text ed. 48.50 (ISBN 0-435-84089-4). Gower Pub Co.

Britton, Anne. Blackie: The Biography of Blackbird. 9.50 (ISBN 0-392-07664-0, SpS). Sportshelf.

Britton, Bruce K. & Black, John B., eds. Understanding Expository Text: A Theoretical & Practical Handbook for Analizing Explanatory Text. 424p. 1984. text ed. 39.95 (ISBN 0-89859-412-X). L Erlbaum Assocs.

Britton, Bryce. The Love Muscle. 1983. pap. 3.50 (ISBN 0-451-12668-8, Sig). NAL.

Britton, Burt. Self Portrait: Book People Picture Themselves. 1976. pap. 6.95 (ISBN 0-394-73104-2). Random.

Britton, Celia, et al, trs. see Metz, Christian.

Britton, Christopher. Paybacks. LC 84-73449. 304p. 1985. 16.95 (ISBN 0-917657-20-9). D I Fine.

Britton, Coburn. Second Seasons. LC 82-48443. (Illus.). 80p. (Orig.). 1982. pap. 6.95 (ISBN 0-8180-1584-5). Horizon.

Britton, Colleen. Celebrate Communion. 79p. (gr. 1-8). 1984. pap. 9.95 (ISBN 0-940754-26-6). Ed Ministries.

Britton, Denis K., et al. Statistical Handbook of U. K. Agriculture. 20.00x (ISBN 0-686-79165-7, Pub. by Dominican Ireland). State Mutual Bk.

Britton, Dorothy. The Japanese Crane. LC 81-82027. (Illus.). 60p. 1982. 15.50 (ISBN 0-87011-484-0). Kodansha.

Britton, Dorothy, jt. auth. see Sutherland, Mary.

Britton, Dorothy, ed. see Japanese Language Teaching Association.

Britton, Dorothy, tr. see Basho.

Britton, Dorothy, et al, trs. see Kuroyanagi, Tetsuko.

Britton, Edward C. & Winans, J. Merritt. Growing from Infancy to Adulthood: A Summary of the Changing Characteristics of Children & Youth. LC 58-7149. (Illus., Orig.). 1958. pap. text ed. 3.95x (ISBN 0-89197-193-9). Irvington.

Britton, F. J. The Escapements: Their Action Contruction & Proportion. LC 84-16875. (Illus.). 66p. 1985. pap. 6.95 (ISBN 0-930163-22-2). Arlington Bk.

Britton, F. L. Behind Communism: The Jewish Background of Communism. 1982. lib. bdg. 59.95 (ISBN 0-87700-425-0). Revisionist Pr.

Britton, Frances. Basic Nursing Skills. (Illus.). 272p. 1981. pap. text ed. 7.95 (ISBN 0-87619-921-X). Brady Comm.

Britton, Frank. English Delftware in the Bristol Collection. (Illus.). 336p. 1983. 105.00x (ISBN 0-85667-152-5, Pub. by Sotheby Pubns England). Biblio Dist.

Britton, Frank L. Behind Communism. 97p. (Orig.). 1979. pap. 1.75x (ISBN 0-911038-82-5). Noontide.

Britton, G. The Biochemistry of Natural Pigments. LC 82-9512. (Cambridge Texts in Chemistry & Biochemistry). (Illus.). 275p. 1983. 62.50 (ISBN 0-521-24892-2). Cambridge U Pr.

Britton, G., ed. see International Symposium on Carotenoids, 6th, Liverpool, U. K., July 26-31, 1981.

Britton, Jack. German Medals & Decorations of World War II. LC 79-112464. (Illus.). 1976. pap. 2.95 (ISBN 0-912958-01-4). MCN Pr.

--United States Military Medals & Decorations. LC 79-112479. (Illus.). 1978. 11.95 (ISBN 0-912958-15-4); pap. 6.95 (ISBN 0-912958-03-0). MCN Pr.

Britton, Jack, jt. auth. see Bello, Ignacio.

Britton, Jack L. Nazi Belt Buckles. (Illus.). 1984. 14.95 (ISBN 0-912958-48-0); spiral bound 7.95 (ISBN 0-912958-23-5). MCN Pr.

--Nazi Dagger I.D. (Illus.). 1983. pap. 7.95 (ISBN 0-912958-08-1). MCN Pr.

--Uniform Insignia of the United States Military Forces. LC 80-83871. (Illus.). 1980. 13.95 (ISBN 0-912958-14-6); pap. 7.95 (ISBN 0-912958-06-5). MCN Pr.

Britton, Jack L. & Washington, George, Jr. Military Shoulder Patches of the United States Armed Forces. 3rd ed. LC 81-80699. (Illus.). 1981. 21.95 (ISBN 0-912958-13-8); pap. 14.95 (ISBN 0-912958-12-X). MCN Pr.

Britton, Jack L., jt. auth. see Borthick, David.

Britton, Jack R. Matematicas Contemporaneas. 2nd ed. Bello, Ignacio, ed. 704p. 1982. pap. text ed. write for info (ISBN 0-06-310069-X, Pub. by HarLA Mexico). Har-Row.

Britton, Jack R. & Bello, Ignacio. Contemporary College Algebra & Trigonometry. 581p. 1982. text ed. 23.50 scp (ISBN 0-06-040989-4, HarpC); instr. manual avail. (ISBN 0-06-360922-3); chapter test avail. (ISBN 0-06-360923-1). Har-Row.

--Topics in Contemporary Mathematics. 3rd ed. 720p. 1984. text ed. 23.95 scp (ISBN 0-06-040992-4, HarpC); inst. manual avail. (ISBN 0-06-360924-X). Har-Row.

Britton, James. Language & Learning. LC 74-137564. 1971. pap. 15.95x (ISBN 0-87024-307-1). U of Miami Pr.

--Language & Learning. 304p. (Orig.). 1972. pap. text ed. 7.50x (ISBN 0-14-021456-9). Boynton Cook Pubs.

--Prospect & Retrospect: Selected Essays of James Britton. Pradl, Gordon M., ed. LC 82-14608. 224p. 1982. pap. text ed. 9.75x (ISBN 0-686-38081-9). Boynton Cook Pubs.

Britton, James, ed. English Teaching: An International Exchange. LC 84-15820. viii, 199p. (Orig.). 1984. pap. text ed. 14.00x (ISBN 0-435-10116-1). Heinemann Ed.

Britton, James, et al. The Development of Writing Abilities (11-18) 226p. 1975. 10.00 (ISBN 0-8141-1100-9); members 7.50. NCTE.

Britton, James, jt. auth. see Barnes, Douglas.

Britton, Janet. To Live Each Moment. LC 83-26532. 192p. 1984. pap. 5.95 (ISBN 0-87784-282-5). Inter-Varsity.

Britton, Jean O., jt. auth. see Britton, Joseph H.

Britton, John. Remarks on the Life & Writings of William Shakespeare. LC 79-39531. Repr. of 1818 ed. 19.00 (ISBN 0-404-01086-5). AMS Pr.

Britton, John, jt. auth. see Shepherd, Thomas H.

Britton, Joseph H. & Britton, Jean O. Personality Changes in Aging. LC 72-81165. 1972. text ed. 13.50 (ISBN 0-8261-1310-9). Springer Pub.

Britton, Kate. Nightmare at Lilybrook. (YA) 1979. 8.95 (ISBN 0-685-90724-4, Avalon). Bouregy.

Britton, L., tr. see Yan, Vasilii G.

Britton, L., tr. see Yan, Vasilli G.

Britton, Lewis W. Spectacles for Specialists. 1985. 10.95 (ISBN 0-533-06416-3). Vantage.

Britton, Mariah, ed. Long Journey Home. 230p. (Orig.). 1984. write for info. Meta Pr.

Britton, Nan. The President's Daughter. 27.50 (ISBN 0-8369-7132-9, 7966). Ayer Co Pubs.

Britton, Nathaniel L. & Brown, Addison. Illustrated Flora of the Northern United States & Canada, 3 Vols. (Illus.). 1970. pap. 12.95 ea.; Vol. 1. pap. (ISBN 0-486-22642-5); Vol. 2. pap. (ISBN 0-486-22643-3); Vol. 3. pap. (ISBN 0-486-22644-1). Dover.

--Illustrated Flora of the Northern United States & Canada, 3 Vols. 2nd rev & enl. ed. (Illus.). Set. 49.50 (ISBN 0-8446-0514-X); 16.50 ea. Peter Smith.

Britton, Nathaniel L. & Rose, J. N. Cactaceae: Descriptions & Illustrations of Plants of the Cactus Family, 4 Vols in 2. 2nd ed. (Illus.). 1937. 25.00 ea.; Vol. 1. (ISBN 0-486-21191-6); Vol. 2. (ISBN 0-486-21192-4). Dover.

Britton, Phil, jt. auth. see Daniel, Joe.

Britton, Raymond L. The Arbitration Guide. (Illus.). 304p. 1982. three-ring binder 49.00 (ISBN 0-13-043984-3). P-H.

Britton, Scott G. Construction Engineering in Underground Coal Mines. LC 82-71994. (Illus.). 312p. 1983. 48.00x (ISBN 0-89520-403-7). Soc Mining Eng.

--Practical Coal Mine Management. LC 81-11426. 233p. 1981. 37.50 (ISBN 0-471-09035-2, Pub. by Wiley-Interscience). Wiley.

Britton, Vickie. Legend of the Sea Wolf. 358p. 1984. 12.97 (ISBN 0-89697-193-7). Intl Univ Pr.

Britton, W. Conjugate Duality & the Exponential Fourier Spectrum. (Lecture Notes in Statistics: Vol. 18). (Illus.). 226p. 1983. pap. 18.00 (ISBN 0-387-90826-9). Springer-Verlag.

Britts, Maurice. I Will Survive. LC 82-90701. 54p. (Orig.). 1982. pap. 3.50 (ISBN 0-940248-09-3). Guild Pr.

Britts, Maurice W. Billy Williams: Minnesota's Assistant Governor. (Illus.). 176p. 1976. 7.95 (ISBN 0-87839-025-1); pap. 5.95 (ISBN 0-87839-026-X). North Star.

Britts, Maurice W., ed. see Bogar, Rosa.

Britvec, S. J. The Stability of Elastic Systems. 480p. 1973. text ed. 45.00 (ISBN 0-08-016859-0). Pergamon.

Britz, B. Digital Simulation in Electrochemistry. (Lecture Notes in Chemistry Ser.: Vol. 23). 120p. 1981. pap. 16.50 (ISBN 0-387-10564-6). Springer-Verlag.

Britz, Billie Sherrill see Sherrill Britz, Billie.

Britz, Richard, et al. The Edible City Resource Manual. LC 81-8187. (Illus.). 360p. (Orig.). 1981. pap. 14.95 (ISBN 0-913232-97-1). W Kaufmann.

Briusov, Valerii. The Fiery Angel: A Sixteenth Century Romance. Montagu, Ivor & Nalbandov, Sergei, trs. from Rus. LC 76-23872. (Classics of Russian Literature). 1977. 15.00 (ISBN 0-88355-475-5); pap. 4.95 (ISBN 0-88355-476-3). Hyperion Conn.

Briusov, Valerii I. The Republic of the Southern Cross & Other Stories. LC 76-23873. (Classics of Russian Literature). 1977. 15.00 (ISBN 0-88355-477-1); pap. 10.00 (ISBN 0-88355-478-X). Hyperion Conn.

Briusov, Valery. Complete Short Stories. Gilbert, Gail & Hart, Pierre, trs. from Rus. 250p. 1985. 20.00 (ISBN 0-88233-790-4); pap. 5.00 (ISBN 0-88233-791-2). Ardis Pubs.

Brivic, Sheldon. Joyce the Creator. LC 84-40492. 224p. 1985. text ed. 21.50x (ISBN 0-299-10080-4). U of Wis Pr.

Brivic, Sheldon R. Joyce Between Freud & Jung. (National University Publications, Literary Criticism Ser.). 1980. 20.00x (ISBN 0-8046-9249-1). Assoc Faculty Pr.

Brivois, Jules J. Essai de bibliographie des oeuvres de M. Alphonse Daudet avec fragments inedits. LC 79-126401. (Bibliography & Reference Ser.: No. 370). (Fr). 1970. Repr. of 1895 ed. lib. bdg. 21.00 (ISBN 0-8337-0378-1). B Franklin.

Brix, Dale, jt. auth. see Wimer, Arthur.

Brix, Dale, jt. auth. see Wimer, Arthur C.

Brix, V. H. You Are a Computer: Cybernetics in Everyday Life. (gr. 9 up). 1970. 9.95 (ISBN 0-87523-169-1). Emerson.

Brizan, George. Grenada: Island of Conflict: From Amerindians to People's Revolution, 1498-1979. (Latin America Ser.). (Illus.). 399p. 1985. 35.50x (ISBN 0-86232-230-8, Pub. by Zed Pr England); pap. 13.95 (ISBN 0-86232-231-6, Pub. by Zed Pr England). Biblio Dist.

Brizee, Sandra L., tr. see Mayer, Karl H.

Brizendine, Nancy. The Braless Express. (Masterworks Ser.: No. 12). (Illus.). 1977. pap. 1.95 (ISBN 0-916982-14-9). Realities.

Brizendine, Nancy H. & Thomas, James L. Learning Through Dramatics: Ideas for Teachers & Librarians. 232p. 1982. pap. text ed. 22.50x (ISBN 0-89774-005-X). Oryx Pr.

Brizova, Joza, et al. Czechoslovak Cookbook. Adams, C., ed. Vahalla, A., tr. (International Cookbook Ser.). 1965. 8.95 (ISBN 0-517-50547-9). Crown.

Brizzee, K. R., jt. ed. see Ordy, J. M.

Brizzee, Kenneth, jt. ed. see Ordy, J. Mark.

Brizzi, Mary T. Anne McCaffrey. (Starmont Reader's Guide: No. 30). 96p. 1985. Repr. lib. bdg. 15.95x (ISBN 0-89370-957-3). Borgo Pr.

--Anne McCaffrey. (Reader's Guides to Contemporary Science Fiction & Fantasy Authors Ser.: No. 30). (Illus., Orig.). 1985. 15.95x (ISBN 0-930261-30-5); pap. 7.95x (ISBN 0-930261-29-1). Starmont Hse.

--Philip Jose Farmer. LC 80-19171. (Starmont Reader's Guide Ser.: No. 3). 80p. 1980. Repr. of 1980 ed. lib. bdg. 13.95x (ISBN 0-89370-034-7). Borgo Pr.

--Reader's Guide to Philip Jose Farmer. Schlobin, Roger C., ed. LC 79-17691. (Starmont Reader's Guides to Contemporary Science Fiction & Fantasy Authors Ser.: Vol. 3). (Illus., Orig.). 1980. 13.95x (ISBN 0-916732-14-2); pap. text ed. 5.95x (ISBN 0-916732-05-3). Starmont Hse.

Brizzolara, Andrew, compiled by. A Directory of Italian & Italian American Organizations & Community Services in the Metropolitan Area of Greater New York, Vols. I & II. rev. ed. LC 80-69277. Vol. I, 241p, 1980, LC#80-69277. pap. 9.95x (ISBN 0-913256-44-7); Vol. II, 1976. pap. 5.00x (ISBN 0-913256-20-X). Ctr Migration.

Brjuno, A. D., et al. Transactions of the Moscow Mathematical Society, Vol. 25. LC 65-7413. 1971. text ed. 62.00 (ISBN 0-8218-1625-X, MOSCOW-25). Am Math.

--Transactions of the Moscow Mathematical Society, Vol. 26 (1972) LC 65-4713. 239p. 1974. 71.00 (ISBN 0-8218-1626-8, MOSCOW-26). Am Math.

Brkic, Jovan. Legal Reasoning: Semantic & Logical Analysis. LC 84-47744. (American University Studies V (Philosophy): Vol. 7). 335p. 1985. text ed. 35.75 (ISBN 0-8204-0134-X). P Lang Pubs.

Brkic, S. Serbocroatian-English Dictionary. 416p. (Serbocroatian & Eng.). 1980. pap. 14.95 (ISBN 0-686-97436-0, M-9631). French & Eur.

Bro, Harmon H. Edgar Cayce on Dreams. 224p. 1968. pap. 3.50 (ISBN 0-446-32519-8). Warner Bks.

--Edgar Cayce on Religion & Psychic Experience. Cayce, Hugh L., ed. (Orig.). 1970. pap. 3.50 (ISBN 0-446-32791-3). Warner Bks.

Bro, Lu. Drawing: A Studio Guide. (Illus.). 1979. pap. price not set. Norton.

--Drawing: A Studio Guide. (Illus.). 1978. pap. text ed. 14.95x (ISBN 0-393-95018-2). Norton.

Broad, C. D. Berkeley's Argument. LC 75-1069. (Studies in Philosophy: No. 40). 1975. lib. bdg. 22.95x (ISBN 0-8383-0113-4). Haskell.

--Ethics. Lewyt, C., ed. 1985. lib. bdg. 49.00 (ISBN 90-247-3088-0, Pub. by Martinus Nijhoff Netherlands). Kluwer Academic.

--Examination of McTaggart's Philosophy, 3 vols. 1972. lib. bdg. 92.00x (ISBN 0-374-90994-6). Octagon.

--Five Types of Ethical Theory. 8th ed. (International Library of Philosophy & Scientific Method). 1930. text ed. 28.00x (ISBN 0-7100-3080-0). Humanities.

--Induction Probability & Causation: Selected Papers. (Synthese Library). 296p. 1968. lib. bdg. 34.00 (ISBN 90-277-0012-5, Pub. by Reidel Holland). Kluwer Academic.

--Lectures on Psychical Research. (International Library of Philosophy & Scientific Method). 1962. text ed. 33.00x (ISBN 0-7100-3611-6). Humanities.

--The Mind & Its Place in Nature. (International Library of Philosophy, Psychology & Scientific Method). 1976. Repr. of 1925 ed. text ed. 55.50x (ISBN 0-7100-3034-7). Humanities.

--Religion, Philosophy & Psychical Research. (International Library of Psychology, Philosophy & Scientific Method). 1969. Repr. of 1953 ed. text ed. 15.50x (ISBN 0-391-00441-7). Humanities.

Broad, C. D. & Lewy, C. Leibniz: An Introduction. LC 74-31784. 192p. 1975. 32.50 (ISBN 0-521-20691-X); pap. 10.95 (ISBN 0-521-09925-0). Cambridge U Pr.

Broad, C. L. & Broad, V. M. Dictionary to Plays & Novels of Shaw. 69.95 (ISBN 0-87968-016-4). Gordon Pr.

Broad, C. Lewis & Broad, Violet M. Dictionary to the Plays & Novels of Bernard Shaw: With Bibliography of His Works & of the Literature Concerning Him with the Record of the Principle Shawian Play Production. LC 76-131645. (Illus.). 1972. Repr. of 1929 ed. 29.00x (ISBN 0-403-00532-9). Scholarly.

Broad, Charles D. Ethics & the History of Philosophy: Selected Essays. LC 78-14104. 1979. Repr. of 1952 ed. 22.50 (ISBN 0-88355-777-0). Hyperion Conn.

--Scientific Thought. (Quality Paperback: No. 208). 555p. 1959. pap. 4.95 (ISBN 0-8226-0208-3). Littlefield.

Broad, Ian, jt. auth. see Rosney, Bride.

Broad, Laura, jt. auth. see Butterworth, Nancy.

Broad, Laura P. & Butterworth, Nancy T. The Playgroup Handbook. LC 73-87399. (Griffin Ser.). (Illus.). 1974. pap. 7.95 (ISBN 0-312-61600-7). St Martin.

Broad, Lewis. The Friendships & Follies of Oscar Wilde. LC 79-8056. Repr. of 1954 ed. 29.50 (ISBN 0-404-18367-0). AMS Pr.

--Winston Churchill: A Biography, 2 vols. LC 74-138206. (Illus.). 1972. Repr. of 1963 ed. lib. bdg. 47.00x (ISBN 0-8371-5558-4, BRWC). Greenwood.

Broad, Lewis & Broad, V. M. Dictionary to Plays & Novels of Shaw. LC 75-92947. (Studies in Irish Literature, No. 16). 1969. Repr. of 1929 ed. lib. bdg. 49.95x (ISBN 0-8383-0961-5). Haskell.

Broad, Lewis & Russell, Leonard. Way of the Dictators. LC 71-112796. (Illus.). 1970. Repr. of 1935 ed. 22.50x (ISBN 0-8046-1063-0, Pub. by Kennikat). Assoc Faculty Pr.

Broad, Lewis C. & Broad, Violet M. Dictionary to the Plays & Novels of Bernard Shaw. LC 72-191671. 1929. lib. bdg. 30.00 (ISBN 0-8414-2543-4). Folcroft.

Broad, O. D. Kant: An Introduction. Lewy, C., ed. LC 77-80829. 1978. 52.50 (ISBN 0-521-21755-5); pap. 14.95 (ISBN 0-521-29265-4). Cambridge U Pr.

Broad, Richard & Fleming, Suzie, eds. Nella Last's War: A Mother's Diary 1939-45. 320p. 1981. 19.95 (ISBN 0-905046-15-3). Falling Wall.

Broad, V. M., jt. auth. see Broad, C. L.

Broad, V. M., jt. auth. see Broad, Lewis.

Broad, Violet M., jt. auth. see Broad, C. Lewis.

Broad, Violet M., jt. auth. see Broad, Lewis C.

Broad, William & Wade, Nicholas. Betrayers of the Truth: Fraud & Deceit in the Halls of Science. 256p. 1983. pap. 6.95 (ISBN 0-671-49549-6, Touchstone). S&S.

Broad, William J. Star Warriors. 1985. 17.95 (ISBN 0-671-54566-3). S&S.

Broadbelt, Eileen C. Shooting Stars. (Contemporary Poets of Dorrance Ser.). 84p. 1983. 8.95 (ISBN 0-8059-2876-6). Dorrance.

Broadbent, Belle B. Where Flowers Grow. 16p. 1982. pap. 2.95 (ISBN 0-939298-04-X). J M Prods.

Broadbent, D. Contingency Planning. (Illus.). 1979. pap. 34.00x (ISBN 0-85012-192-2). Intl Pubns Serv.

--Contingency Planning. 195p. 1979. pap. 30.60 (ISBN 0-471-89438-9). Wiley.

Broadbent, D. E. Decision & Stress. 1971. 59.50 (ISBN 0-12-135550-0). Acad Pr.

Broadbent, D. E., ed. Functional Aspects of Human Memory. (Philosophical Transactions of the Royal Society: Series B, Vol. 302). (Illus.). 198p. 1984. Repr. lib. bdg. 62.00x (ISBN 0-85403-213-4, Pub. by Royal Soc London). Scholium Intl.

Broadbent, D. E. & Weiskrantz, L., eds. The Neuropsychology of Cognitive Function: Proceedings of a Royal Society Discussion Meeting, November 18-19, 1981. (RSL Philosophical Transcriptions of the Royal Society of London, Ser. B: Vol. 298, No. 1089). (Illus.). 230p. 1982. text ed. 68.00x (ISBN 0-85403-190-1, Pub. by Royal Soc London). Scholium Intl.

Broadbent, D. T. & Masubuchi, M., eds. Multilingual Glossary of Automatic Control Technology: English, French, German, Russian, Italian, Spanish, Russian, Japanese. 250p. (Polyglot.). 1981. 50.00 (ISBN 0-08-027607-5). Pergamon.

Broadbent, Geoffrey. Design in Architecture & the Human Sciences. LC 71-39233. 504p. 1973. pap. 32.95x (ISBN 0-471-99527-4). Wiley.

Broadbent, Geoffrey, et al. Signs, Symbols & Architecture. LC 78-13557. 446p. 1980. 72.95x (ISBN 0-471-99718-8, Pub. by Wiley-Interscience). Wiley.

Broadbent, Geoffrey, et al, eds. Meaning & Behaviour in the Built Environment. LC 79-41490. 372p. 1980. 74.95x (ISBN 0-471-27708-8, Pub. by Wiley-Interscience). Wiley.

Broadbent, J., ed. see Milton, John.

Broadbent, John. Introduction to Paradise Lost. (Milton for Schools & Colleges Ser.). (Illus.). 1971. 34.50 (ISBN 0-521-08068-1); pap. 11.95 (ISBN 0-521-09639-1). Cambridge U Pr.

Broadbent, John, ed. John Milton: Introductions. LC 72-93144. (Milton for Schools & Colleges Ser.). (Illus.). 350p. 1973. 45.00 (ISBN 0-521-20172-1); pap. 12.95 (ISBN 0-521-09799-1). Cambridge U Pr.

Broadbent, John, ed. see Milton, John.

Broadbent, John, et al, eds. see Milton, John.

Broadbent, K. Dictionary of China's Rural Economy. 406p. (Chinese & Eng.). 1978. 125.00 (ISBN 0-85198-381-2, M-9712). French & Eur.

Broadbent, K. P. Dissemination of Scientific Information in the People's Republic of China. (Illus.). 60p. 1980. pap. 8.00 (ISBN 0-88936-238-6, IDRC148, IDRC). Unipub.

Broadbent, Michael. The Great Vintage Wine Book. LC 80-7622. (Illus.). 432p. 1980. 27.50 (ISBN 0-394-51099-2). Knopf.

--Michael Broadbent's Complete Guide to Wine Tasting & Wine Cellars. 272p. 1984. 12.95 (ISBN 0-671-50889-X). S&S.

--Michael Broadbent's Pocket Guide to Wine Tasting. (Illus.). 1982. 6.95 (ISBN 0-671-45235-5). S&S.

Broadbent, R. J. Annals of the Liverpool Stage. LC 70-83872. (Illus.). 1908. 27.50 (ISBN 0-405-08306-8, Blom Pubns). Ayer Co Pubs.

--History of Pantomime. LC 64-14694. 1901. 20.00 (ISBN 0-405-08307-6, Blom Pubns). Ayer Co Pubs.

Broadbent, Simon. Spending Advertising Money. 2nd ed. 1976. 30.00x (ISBN 0-8464-0880-5); pap. 18.95x (ISBN 0-686-77120-6). Beekman Pubs.

--Spending Advertising Money. 3rd ed. 381p. 1979. 36.75x (ISBN 0-220-67020-X, Pub. by Busn Bks England). Brookfield Pub Co.

Broadbent, Simon & Jacobs, Brian. Spending Advertising Money. 4th ed. 424p. 1984. pap. text ed. 26.95x (ISBN 0-09-155971-5, Pub. by Busn Bks England). Brookfield Pub Co.

Broadbent, T. A. Planning & Profit in the Urban Economy. 1977. 13.95x (ISBN 0-416-56320-1, NO. 2768). Methuen Inc.

Broadbridge, Seymour. Industrial Dualism in Japan: A Problem of Economic Growth & Structural Change. 105p. 1966. 29.50x (ISBN 0-7146-1208-1, F Cass Co). Biblio Dist.

--Studies in Railway Expansion & the Capital Market in England: 1825-73. 216p. 1970. 35.00x (ISBN 0-7146-1287-1, F Cass Co). Biblio Dist.

Broadcast Information Bureau, The Radio Programs Source Book. Doris, Liz, ed. 100p. (Orig.). 1983. pap. 62.95 (ISBN 0-317-00692-4). Broadcast Info.

Broadcast Information Bureau. The Radio Programs Source Book. 3rd ed. Doris, Liz, ed. 150p. (Orig.). 1984. pap. 64.95 (ISBN 0-943174-05-8). Broadcast Info.

Broadcast Information Bureau, Inc. Radio Programs Source Book. 2nd ed. Fliegelman, Avra & Doris, Liz, eds. 240p. 1983. pap. write for info. (ISBN 0-943174-02-3). Broadcast Info.

--The Radio Programs Source Book Supplement. Doris, Liz, ed. 100p. (Orig.). 1982. pap. 62.95 (ISBN 0-943174-01-5). Broadcast Info.

Broadcast Information Bureau Staff. The Radio Programs Source Book. Doris, Liz, ed. (Illus., Orig.). 1982. pap. 62.95 (ISBN 0-943174-00-7). Broadcast Info.

--The Radio Programs Source Book. 3rd, Rev. Suppl. ed. Doris, Liz, ed. LC 82-654122. 300p. (Orig.). 1984. pap. 64.95 (ISBN 0-943174-04-X). Broadcast Info.

Broadfoot, Barry. My Own Years: People, Places & Peregrinations. LC 78-68345. 288p. 1984. 21.95 (ISBN 0-385-14319-2). Doubleday.

Broadfoot, Patricia. Assessment, Schools & Society. 1979. 19.95x (ISBN 0-416-71570-2, NO.2854). Methuen Inc.

Broadfoot, Patricia, jt. auth. see Black, Harry.

Broadfoot, Patricia, ed. Selection, Certification & Control: Social Issues in Educational Assessment. (Politics & Education Monograph). 270p. 1984. 29.00x (ISBN 0-905273-78-8, Pub. by Falmer Pr); pap. 17.00x (ISBN 0-905273-77-X). Taylor & Francis.

Broadfoot, Tom, et al. Civil War Books: A Priced Checklist. rev. ed. 250p. 1983. 30.00x (ISBN 0-916107-08-6). Broadfoot.

Broadhead, Edward. Ceran St. Vrain. (Illus.). 40p. 1982. pap. 2.50x (ISBN 0-915617-03-X). Pueblo Co Hist Soc.

--Fort Pueblo. (Illus.). 32p. 1981. pap. 2.50x (ISBN 0-915617-01-3). Pueblo Co Hist Soc.

--John Simpson Smith, Eighteen Ten to Eighteen Seventy-One. (Illus.). 30p. (Orig.). 1985. pap. 3.50 (ISBN 0-915617-10-2). Pueblo Co Hist Soc.

Broadhead, G. F. Orchestral & Band Instruments. 1976. lib. bdg. 29.00 (ISBN 0-403-03788-3). Scholarly.

Broadhead, Philip, ed. see Cargill-Thompson, W. D.

Broadhead, Robert S. The Private Lives & Professional Identity of Medical Students. LC 82-19502. 140p. 1983. 24.95 (ISBN 0-87855-478-5). Transaction Bks.

Broadhead, T. W., ed. Foraminifera: Notes for a Short Course Organized by M. A. Buzas & B. K. Sen Gupta. (University of Tennessee Studies in Geology). (Illus.). iv, 219p. 1982. pap. 6.00 (ISBN 0-910249-05-9). U of Tenn Geo.

--Lophophorates: Notes for A Short Course Organized by J. T. Dutro. Jr. & R. S. Boardman. (University of Tennessee Studies in Geology). (Illus.). iv, 251p. 1981. pap. 6.00 (ISBN 0-910249-03-2). U of Tenn Geo.

--Mammals: Notes for a Short Course Organized by P. D. Gingerich & C. E. Badgley. (Studies in Geology). (Illus.). 234p. 1984. pap. 9.00 (ISBN 0-910249-07-5). U Of Tenn Geo.

--Sponges & Spongiomorphs: Notes for a Short Course Organized by J. K. Rigby & C. W. Stearn. (University of Tennessee Studies in Geology). (Illus.). 220p. 1983. pap. 7.50 (ISBN 0-910249-06-7). U of Tenn Geo.

Broadhead, T. W. & Waters, J. A., eds. Echinoderms: Notes for a Short Course. (University of Tennessee Studies in Geology). (Illus.). iv, 235p. 1980. pap. 6.00 (ISBN 0-910249-01-6). U of Tenn Geo.

Broadhead, T. W., jt. auth. see McSween, H. Y., Jr.

Broadhouse, John. How to Make a Violin. Repr. lib. bdg. 29.00 (ISBN 0-403-03872-3). Scholarly.

--Musical Acoustics: Or the Phenomena of Sound As Connected with Music. LC 72-181115. 425p. 1926. Repr. 35.00x (ISBN 0-403-01630-4). Scholarly.

--Musical Acoustics: Student's Helmholtz. LC 77-81653. 1977. Repr. of 1926 ed. lib. bdg. 20.00 (ISBN 0-89341-073-X). Longwood Pub Group.

--The Violin, Its History & Construction. Repr. lib. bdg. 24.00 (ISBN 0-403-03867-7). Scholarly.

--Violin: It's History & Construction. 172p. 1984. pap. cancelled (ISBN 0-89341-528-6). Longwood Pub Group.

Broadhouse, John, tr. see Abele, Hyacinth & Niederheitman, Friedrich.

Broadhurst, Anne, jt. ed. see Feldman, M. Philip.

Broadhurst, Arlene I., ed. The Future of European Alliance Systems: NATO & the Warsaw Pact. LC 82-50954. (International Relations Ser.). (Illus.). 316p. 1982. softcover 26.00x (ISBN 0-86531-413-6). Westview.

Broadhurst, Henry. The Story of His Life from a Stonemason's Bench to the Treasury Bench, Told by Himself. LC 83-48475. (World of Labour: English Workers, 1850-1890 Ser.). 316p. 1984. lib. bdg. 40.00 (ISBN 0-8240-5703-1). Garland Pub.

Broadhurst, P. L. Science of Animal Behaviour. 1963. lib. bdg. 13.50x (ISBN 0-88307-035-9). Gannon.

Broadhurst, P. L., ed. Drugs & the Inheritance of Behavior. LC 78-3617. (Illus.). 214p. 1978. 25.00x (ISBN 0-306-31105-4, Plenum Pr). Plenum Pub.

Broadhurst, V. A. The Health & Safety at Work Act in Practice. 256p. 1978. 33.95 (ISBN 0-471-25614-5, Pub. by Wiley Heyden). Wiley.

Broadie, Alexander. The Circle of John Mair: Logic & Logicians in Pre-Reformation Scotland. 320p. 1985. 34.50x (ISBN 0-19-824735-4). Oxford U Pr.

--George Lokert: Late-Scholastic Logician. 252p. 1984. 27.50x (ISBN 0-85224-469-X, Pub. by Edinburgh U Pr Scotland). Columbia U Pr.

Broadley, Mae. Children's Bedtime Book. (Illus.). 160p. 1982. 5.98 (ISBN 0-89673-156-1). Bookthrift.

Broadley, Margaret E. Your Natural Gifts: How to Recognize & Develop Them for Success & Self-Fulfillment. LC 77-23379. (Illus.). 1977. pap. 6.95 (ISBN 0-914440-19-5). EPM Pubns.

Broadman, Henry G. & Montgomery, W. David. Natural Gas Markets after Deregulation. LC 83-42907. (Resources for the Future Ser.). 112p. (Orig.). 1983. pap. text ed. 18.00x (ISBN 0-8018-3125-3). Johns Hopkins.

Broadribb, Violet. Introductory Pediatric Nursing. 3rd ed. (Illus.). 392p. 1982. pap. text ed. 16.75 (ISBN 0-397-54330-1, 64-02739, Lippincott Nursing). Lippincott.

Broadston, Donald A., jt. auth. see Broadston, James A.

Broadston, James A. & Broadston, Donald A. Control of Surface Quality. 11th ed. LC 77-73765. (Illus.). 1977. pap. 24.00 (ISBN 0-911464-02-6). Surf-Chek.

Broadus, Boyce. History of First Baptist Church Russellville. 1967. 10.00 (ISBN 0-317-13830-8); pap. 7.00. Banner Pr AL.

Broadus, E. K. Thomas Fuller, Selections: With Essays by Charles Lamb, Leslie Stephen & Co. 1979. Repr. of 1928 ed. lib. bdg. 20.00 (ISBN 0-8492-3742-4). R West.

Broadus, Edmund K. Laureateship. facs. ed. LC 67-22082. (Essay Index Reprint Ser.). 1921. 19.00 (ISBN 0-8369-1326-4). Ayer Co Pubs.

--Saturday & Sunday. facs. ed. LC 67-23186. (Essay Index Reprint Ser). 1935. 17.00 (ISBN 0-8369-0255-6). Ayer Co Pubs.

--The Story of English Literature. 1933. Repr. 35.00 (ISBN 0-8274-3515-0). R West.

Broadus, Edmund K., ed. A Book of Canadian Prose & Verse. Repr. of 1923 ed. lib. bdg. 30.00 (ISBN 0-8482-3430-8). Norwood Edns.

Broadus, J. A. Tratado Sobre la Predicacion. Barocio, Ernesto, tr. Orig. Title: On the Preparation & Delivery of Sermons. 336p. 1981. pap. 5.25 (ISBN 0-311-42034-6). Casa Bautista.

Broadus, John A. On the Preparation & Delivery of Sermons. 4th ed. Stanfield, Vernon L., rev. by. LC 78-20602. 1979. 12.45 (ISBN 0-06-061112-X, HarpR). Har-Row.

Broadus, John A. see Hovey, Alvah.

Broadus, Loren. How to Stop Procrastinating & Start Living. LC 82-72641. 128p. 1983. pap. 5.50 (ISBN 0-8066-1947-3, 10-3178). Augsburg.

Broadus, Robert, ed. The Role of the Humanities in the Public Library. LC 79-24117. 213p. 1980. 20.00x (ISBN 0-8389-0297-9). ALA.

Broadus, Robert N. Selecting Materials for Libraries. 2nd ed. LC 81-6506. xiv, 464p. 1981. 20.00 (ISBN 0-8242-0659-2). Wilson.

Broadwater, Elaine. Woodburning: Art & Craft. (Illus.). 160p. 1980. 14.95 (ISBN 0-517-53587-4); pap. 6.95 (ISBN 0-517-53588-2). Crown.

Broadway, tr. see Caxton, William.

Broadway, Beth, ed. see Chicago Metropolitan Board YMCA.

Broadway, Frank. State Intervention in British Industry, 1964-68. LC 79-115974. 191p. 1970. 16.50 (ISBN 0-8386-7690-1). Fairleigh Dickinson.

Broadwell, Bruce, jt. auth. see Edwards, Perry.

Broadwell, Debra C. & Jackson, Bettie S. Principles of Ostomy Care. LC 81-14073. (Illus.). 815p. 1981. pap. text ed. 42.95 (ISBN 0-8016-2378-2). Mosby.

Broadwell, Martin & House, Ruth S. Supervising Technical & Professional People. 48.50 (ISBN 0-471-81785-6). Wiley.

Broadwell, Martin M. The Lecture Method of Instruction. Langdon, Danny G., ed. LC 79-23528. (Instructional Design Library). 116p. 1980. 19.95 (ISBN 0-87778-147-8). Educ Tech Pubns.

--Supervisor & on the Job Training. 2nd ed. LC 74-30695. (Illus.). 176p. 1975. text ed. 12.95 (ISBN 0-201-00754-1). Addison-Wesley.

Broadwell, Martin M., jt. auth. see Diekelmann, Nancy.

Broadwell, Martin M., ed. Supervisory Handbook: A Management Guide to Principles & Applications. 536p. 39.95 (ISBN 0-471-88783-8). Wiley.

Broadwin, Judith & Lenchner, George. Solution, A.P. Calculus Problems: Part II AB & BC, 1970-1984. 168p. (Orig.). 1984. pap. text ed. 6.50 (ISBN 0-9612940-2-7). Nassau Co Assn Mathematics Supv.

Broadwood, Lucy E. & Fuller-Maitland, J. A., eds. English County Songs: Words & Music. 1984. Repr. of 1893 ed. lib. bdg. 35.00 (ISBN 0-89341-430-1). Longwood Pub Group.

Broady, K. O. School Provision for Individual Differences. LC 71-176591. (Columbia University. Teachers College. Contributions to Education: No. 395). Repr. of 1930 ed. 22.50 (ISBN 0-404-55395-8). AMS Pr.

Broaker, Frank & Chapman, Richard M. The American Accountants' Manual: Examinations Questions Together with Answers, Vol. 1. Brief, Richard P., ed. LC 77-87264. (Development of Contemporary Accounting Thought Ser.). 1978. Repr. of 1897 ed. lib. bdg. 20.00x (ISBN 0-405-10893-1). Ayer Co Pubs.

Broassard, E. B. Petroleum: Politics & Power. 272p. 1983. 37.50 (ISBN 0-318-17607-6, O-5); 33.50 (ISBN 0-318-17608-4). Petro MkTg Ed Found.

Brobeck, Steven & Averyt, Anne C. The Product Safety Book. LC 83-71915. 441p. 1983. pap. 9.95 (ISBN 0-525-48087-0, 0966-290). Dutton.

Broberg, Gunnar, ed. Linnaeus: Progress & Prospects in Linnaean Research. (Illus.). 318p. 1980. 49.50x (ISBN 0-913196-31-2). Hunt Inst Botanical.

Broberg, Rose F. Stories & Games for Easy Lipreading Practice. rev. ed. LC 77-70167. 1963. softcover 7.95 (ISBN 0-88200-080-2, B0664). Alexander Graham.

Brobst, Bob & Bush, Ronald F. Marketing Simulation: Analysis for Decision Making. 2nd ed. 152p. 1983. pap. text ed. 10.95 scp (ISBN 0-06-041104-X, HarpC); instr's. manual avail. (ISBN 0-06-361069-8); computer deck or tape avail. Har-Row.

Brobst, Harry M. Understanding Personal Computers: A Home Study Course. (Home Study Ser.). 25p. 1982. 24.00 (ISBN 0-939926-17-2); write for info. audio tape (ISBN 0-939926-16-4). Fruition Pubns.

Brobst, William A. Directory of Clock & Watch Collections. LC 82-99818. 1986. price not set (ISBN 0-9608112-1-4). Transport Env.

--Pulling Your Tail: A Primer on the Art of Motorcycle Trailering. LC 82-90072. (Illus.). 64p. 1982. pap. 5.65 (ISBN 0-9608112-0-6). Transport Env.

Broca, Paul, et al. Early Homo Sapiens in France. LC 78-72694. Repr. of 1912 ed. 32.50 (ISBN 0-404-18265-8). AMS Pr.

Brocard, Lucien. Doctrines economiques et sociales du Marquis de Mirabeau dans "L'Ami des hommes". LC 79-121220. (Research & Source Ser.: No. 500). (Fr). 1970. Repr. of 1902 ed. 23.50 (ISBN 0-8337-0379-X). B Franklin.

Brocardo, G. Minerals & Gemstones: An Identification Guide. (Illus.). 220p. (gr. 6 up). 1983. 12.95 (ISBN 0-88254-756-9). Hippocrene Bks.

Brocas, J. & Gielen, M. Permutational Approach to Dynamic Stereochemistry. 720p. 1983. 87.95 (ISBN 0-07-007971-4). McGraw.

Brocchi, Paul. Mission Scientifique Au Mexique et Dans L'amerique Centrale....Recherches Zoologiques: Etude Des Batraciens De l' Amerque Centrale. Sterling, Keir B., ed. LC 77-81099. (Biologists & Their World Ser.). (Illus.). 1978. Repr. of 1882 ed. lib. bdg. 17.00x (ISBN 0-405-10681-5). Ayer Co Pubs.

Broccoletti, Pete. Building Up: The Young Athlete's Guide to Weight Training. (Illus.). 192p. 1981. 14.95 (ISBN 0-89651-053-0); wire bound 9.95 (ISBN 0-89651-054-9). Icarus.

--Prime Cut: Total Fitness for Men Eighteen to Thirty-Four. (Illus.). 200p. 1984. 16.95 (ISBN 0-89651-604-0); wire bdg. 10.95 (ISBN 0-89651-605-9). Icarus.

--Thirty-Five & Holding: Complete Conditioning for the Adult Male. (Illus.). 192p. 1982. wire bdg. 10.95 (ISBN 0-89651-779-9). Icarus.

Broccoletti, Pete & Hunter, Rich. Shape up for Soccer. (Illus.). 232p. 1981. 14.95 (ISBN 0-89651-750-0); wirebd. 9.95 (ISBN 0-89651-751-9). Icarus.

Broccoletti, Peter P. & Scanlon, Pat. The Notre Dame Weight-Training Program for Baseball, Hockey, Wrestling, & Your Body. (Illus.). 216p. 1980. 14.95 (ISBN 0-89651-505-2); wire bdg. 9.95 (ISBN 0-89651-506-0). Icarus.

--The Notre Dame Weight Training Program for Football. LC 78-20947. (Illus.). 1979. pap. 9.95 spiral bdg. (ISBN 0-89651-503-6). Icarus.

Broccolo, Gerald T., jt. ed. see Larkin, Ernest.

Broccolo, Gerald T., jt. ed. see Larkin, Ernest E.

Broce, Gerald. History of Anthropology. LC 72-97620. (Basic Concepts in Anthropology Ser.). pap. 15.00 (ISBN 0-8357-9051-7, 2015878). Bks Demand UMI.

Broce, Thomas E. Fund Raising: The Guide to Raising Money from Private Sources. LC 78-21388. (Illus.). 1979. 17.50 (ISBN 0-8061-1531-9). U of Okla Pr.

Broce, Thomas E. & Junkin, Daniel P. Directory of Oklahoma Foundations. Rev., 2nd ed. LC 82-6984. 304p. 1982. 22.50x (ISBN 0-8061-1827-X). U of Okla Pr.

Broch, Hermann. Death of Virgil. 15.75 (ISBN 0-8446-1742-3). Peter Smith.

--The Death of Virgil. Untermeyer, Jean S., tr. LC 82-73718. 496p. 1983. pap. 15.50 (ISBN 0-86547-115-0). N Point Pr.

--Hugo Von Hofmannsthal & His Time: The European Imagination, 1860-1920. Steinberg, Michael P., ed. LC 84-76. 208p. 1984. 28.00x (ISBN 0-226-07514-1); pap. 13.95x (ISBN 0-226-07516-8). U of Chicago Pr.

--The Sleepwalkers: A Trilogy by Hermann Broch. Muir, Wilma & Muir, Edwin, trs. from Ger. 648p. 1985. pap. 16.50 (ISBN 0-86547-200-9). N Point Pr.

Broch, Yitzhak I. The Book of Ruth. 1975. 6.00 (ISBN 0-87306-012-1). Feldheim.

Brocher, Maggi. American Beauty. 352p. 1984. pap. 3.50 (ISBN 0-8439-2143-9, Leisure Bks). Dorchester Pub Co.

--The Cheerleaders. 352p. 1984. pap. 3.50 (ISBN 0-8439-2132-3, Leisure Bks). Dorchester Pub Co.

--Partings. 336p. (Orig.). 1985. pap. 3.50 (ISBN 0-8439-2207-9, Leisure Bks). Dorchester Pub Co.

Brocher, Tobias. Lexikon der Sozialerziehung. (Ger.). 1972. 15.95 (ISBN 3-7831-0378-9, M-7221). French & Eur.

Broches, Charles F. & Spranger, Michael S., eds. The Politics & Economics of Columbia River Water. LC 85-11506. (Orig.). 1985. pap. 10.00 (ISBN 0-934539-02-2). Wash Sea Grant.

Brochier, Jean Jacques, ed. see Sade, Donatien Alphonse Francois de.

Brochmann, Elizabeth. What's the Matter, Girl? LC 79-2022. 128p. (gr. 7 up). 1980. PLB 10.89 (ISBN 0-06-020678-0). HarpJ.

Brochmann-Hanssen, Einar, jt. ed. see Higuchi, Takeru.

Brochner, Jessie, tr. see Lagerlof, Selma O.

Brock, ed. Robot Vision & Sensory Control: Proceedings of the Second International Conference, Stuttgart, BRD, Nov. 1982. iv, 388p. 1983. 85.00 (ISBN 0-444-86548-9, North-Holland). Elsevier.

Brock, A. A. & Chambliss, W. J. Organizing Crime. 1981. 26.50 (ISBN 0-444-99079-8). Elsevier.

Brock, Alice M. My Life As a Restaurant. LC 75-4378. (Illus.). 144p. 1975. 15.95 (ISBN 0-87951-032-3). Overlook Pr.

Brock, Ann. Riding & Stable Safety. (Illus.). 192p. 1983. 12.95 (ISBN 0-7153-7951-8). David & Charles.

Brock, Arthur J., ed. Greek Medicine, Being Extracts Illustrative of Medical Writing from Hippocrates to Galen. LC 76-179302. (Library of Greek Thought: No. 8). Repr. of 1929 ed. 16.00 (ISBN 0-404-07806-0). AMS Pr.

Brock, Bernard L. & Scott, Robert L., eds. Methods of Rhetorical Criticism: A Twentieth-Century Perspective. 2nd rev. ed. LC 80-11922. 503p. 1980. 16.95 (ISBN 0-8143-1648-4). Wayne St U Pr.

Brock, Betty. No Flying in the House. LC 79-104755. (Illus.). 144p. (gr. 3-7). 1970. PLB 10.89 (ISBN 0-06-020643-8). HarpJ.

--No Flying in the House. LC 79-104755. (A Trophy Bk.). (Illus.). 144p. (gr. 3-6). 1982. pap. 2.84i (ISBN 0-06-440130-8, Trophy). HarpJ.

Brock, C. E. The Humour of America. 1893. 30.00 (ISBN 0-932062-11-3). Sharon Hill.

Brock, Charles. The Principles & Practice of Indigenous Church Planting. 1981. pap. 3.95 (ISBN 0-8054-6328-3). Broadman.

Brock, Clifton. Americans for Democratic Action: Its Role in National Politics. LC 85-7976. 240p. 1985. Repr. of 1982 ed. lib. bdg. 39.75x (ISBN 0-313-24284-4, BRAD). Greenwood.

--The Literature of Political Science: A Guide for Students, Librarians, & Teachers. LC 79-79426. pap. 46.40 (ISBN 0-317-10354-7, 2017586). Bks Demand UMI.

Brock, Colin & Lawlor, Hugh, eds. Education in Latin America. LC 84-3750. 208p. 1985. 31.00 (ISBN 0-7099-3273-1, Pub. by Croom Helm Ltd). Longwood Pub Group.

Brock, Colin & Tulasiewicz, Witold, eds. Cultural Identity & Educational Policy. 368p. 1985. 35.00 (ISBN 0-312-17849-2). St Martin.

Brock, D. Heyward. A Ben Jonson Companion. LC 81-48383. 320p. 1983. 25.00x (ISBN 0-253-31159-4). Ind U Pr.

Brock, D. Heyward & Welsh, James M. Ben Jonson: A Quadricentennial Bibliography, 1947-1972. LC 74-2424. (Author Bibliography Ser.: No. 16). 166p. 1974. 16.50 (ISBN 0-8108-0710-6). Scarecrow.

Brock, D. Heyward, ed. The Culture of Biomedicine. LC 82-40438. (Studies in Science & Culture: Vol. 1). 200p. 1983. 24.50 (ISBN 0-87413-229-0). U Delaware Pr.

Brock, D. J. & Mayo, O., eds. The Biochemical Genetics of Man. 2nd ed. 1979. 87.50 (ISBN 0-12-134760-5). Acad Pr.

Brock, D. J. H. Early Diagnosis of Fetal Defects. LC 82-4135. (Current Reviews in Obstetrics & Gynaecology Ser.: No. 2). (Illus.). 165p. (Orig.). 1983. pap. text ed. 16.00 (ISBN 0-443-02302-6). Churchill.

Brock, Dee & Howard, C. Jeriel. Writing for a Reason. LC 77-12617. 1978. pap. text ed. 14.70x (ISBN 0-673-15657-5). Scott F.

Brock, E., jt. ed. see Cockayne, O.

Brock, Earl E. Devotional Interpretation of Familiar Hymns. facsimile ed. LC 72-93319. (Essay Index Reprint Ser.). 1947. 14.00 (ISBN 0-8369-1395-7). Ayer Co Pubs.

Brock, Edith. The Brighter Side. new ed. LC 77-92340. 1978. pap. 3.25 (ISBN 0-87148-109-X). Pathway Pr.

Brock, Edwin. The Blocked Heart. LC 75-6528. 64p. 1976. 7.25 (ISBN 0-8112-0577-0); pap. 2.45 (ISBN 0-8112-0578-9, NDP399). New Directions.

--Here. Now. Always. LC 76-54314. 1977. 8.50 (ISBN 0-8112-0638-6); pap. 2.95 (ISBN 0-8112-0639-4, NDP429). New Directions.

--Invisibility is the Art of Survival. LC 72-80979. 96p. 1972. 7.50 (ISBN 0-8112-0450-2); pap. 1.95 (ISBN 0-8112-0451-0, NDP342). New Directions.

--Paroxisms: A Guide to the Isms. LC 74-8647. (Illus.). 96p. 1974. 5.95 (ISBN 0-8112-0549-5); pap. 2.25 (ISBN 0-8112-0554-1, NDP385). New Directions.

--The Portraits & the Poses. LC 73-78783. 64p. 1973. 6.95 (ISBN 0-8112-0486-3); pap. 1.95 (ISBN 0-8112-0487-1, NDP360). New Directions.

--The River & the Train. LC 78-27463. 1979. 7.95 (ISBN 0-8112-0722-6); pap. 3.75 (ISBN 0-8112-0723-4, NDP478). New Directions.

Brock, Eleanor, jt. ed. see Brock, Michael.

Brock, G. C. Physical Aspects of Aerial Photography. (Illus.). 11.25 (ISBN 0-8446-1743-1). Peter Smith.

Brock, Geoffrey E., ed. Metallurgy of Advanced Electronic Materials: Proceedings of a Technical Conference. Philadelphia, Pennsylvania, August 27-29, 1962. LC 63-13589. (Metallurgical Society Conferences Ser.: Vol. 19). pap. 91.30 (ISBN 0-317-08053-9, 2001507). Bks Demand UMI.

Brock, Gerald W. The Telecommunications Industry: The Dynamics of Market Structure. LC 80-25299. (Harvard Economic Studies: No. 151). (Illus.). 384p. 1981. text ed. 25.00x (ISBN 0-674-87285-1). Harvard U Pr.

--The Telecommunications Industry: The Dynamics of Market Structure. 336p. 1981. 25.00 (ISBN 0-686-98080-8). Telecom Lib.

Brock, Greg, ed. How Road Racers Train. LC 77-94968. (Illus., Orig.). 1980. pap. 6.00 (ISBN 0-911520-84-8). Tafnews.

Brock, H. I., ed. Little Book of Limericks. facsimile ed. LC 71-84351. (Granger Index Reprint Ser). 1947. 17.00 (ISBN 0-8369-6053-X). Ayer Co Pubs.

Brock, H. R. & Palmer, C. E. Accounting: Basic Principles. 5th ed. 432p. 1985. 16.25 (ISBN 0-07-008262-6). McGraw.

--Accounting: Principles & Applications. 5th ed. 1024p. 1985. 28.00 (ISBN 0-07-008260-X). McGraw.

--Financial Accounting: Principles & Applications. 5th ed. 784p. 1985. 21.60 (ISBN 0-07-008261-8). McGraw.

Brock, Henry C. Parent Volunteer Programs in Early Childhood Education: A Practical Approach. pap. 5.95 (ISBN 0-915794-08-X). Gaylord Prof Pubns.

Brock, Henry C., 3rd. Parent Volunteer Programs in Early Childhood Education: A Practical Guide. 114p. 1976. 15.00 (ISBN 0-208-01566-3, Linnet). Shoe String.

Brock, Horace, ed. Game Theory, Social Choice, & Ethics. 1979. lib. bdg. 31.50 (ISBN 0-686-26826-1, Pub. by Reidel Holland). Kluwer Academic.

Brock, Horace R. & Palmer, Charles E. Cost Accounting: Principles & Applications. 4th ed. (Illus.). 512p. 1984. text ed. 18.75 (ISBN 0-07-008045-3); study guide 10.65 (ISBN 0-07-008046-1). McGraw.

--Individualized Performance Guide for Accounting: Principles & Applications, Fourth Edition, Part I. (College Accounting Instructional System). (Illus.). 160p. wkbk. 9.65 (ISBN 0-07-008095-X). McGraw.

--Sole Proprietorship Merchandising Business Practice Set: Schier Furniture Company. 2nd ed. (College Accounting Instructional System Ser.). (Illus.). 120p. 1981. 12.15 (ISBN 0-07-008106-9). McGraw.

--Sole Proprietorship Service Business Practice Set: Garden Real Estate. (College Accounting Instructional System Ser.). (Illus.). 232p. 1981. 10.90 (ISBN 0-07-008104-2). McGraw.

Brock, Horace R., jt. auth. see Klingstedt, John P.

Brock, Horace R., et al. Petroleum Accounting: Principles, Procedures & Issues. LC 85-60604. 600p. 1985. 49.95x (ISBN 0-940966-09-3). N Texas St U Pro Devel Inst.

--Accounting, Principles & Applications. 3rd ed. 320p. 1974. text ed. 24.45 (ISBN 0-07-008021-6). McGraw.

Brock, J., jt. ed. see Hidy, G. M.

Brock, J. H. Dramatic Purpose of Hamlet. LC 74-7117. 1935. lib. bdg. 10.00 (ISBN 0-8414-3180-9). Folcroft.

--Iago & Some Shakespearean Villains. LC 73-15996. 1937. lib. bdg. 10.00 (ISBN 0-8414-9854-7). Folcroft.

--Iago & Some Shakespearean Villains. 70p. 1983. Repr. of 1937 ed. lib. bdg. 10.00 (ISBN 0-8492-3778-5). R West.

Brock, James G. & Brock, Jannye D. Analyzing Your Logs: Fundamentals of Open Hole Log Interpretation, Vol. I. (Illus.). 260p. 1984. 45.00 (ISBN 0-916647-01-3); pap. 30.00 (ISBN 0-916647-00-5). Petro-Media.

Brock, James H. Dramatic Purpose of Hamlet. LC 79-153308. Repr. of 1935 ed. 5.00 (ISBN 0-404-01087-3). AMS Pr.

--Iago & Some Shakespearean Villains. LC 72-153309. Repr. of 1937 ed. 5.00 (ISBN 0-404-01088-1). AMS Pr.

Brock, James L. A Forecast for the Grocery Retailing Industry in the 1980's. Dufey, Gunter, ed. LC 81-16498. (Research for Business Decisions Ser.: No. 45). 172p. 1981. 39.95 (ISBN 0-8357-1259-1). UMI Res Pr.

Brock, Jannye, ed. see Brock, Jim.

Brock, Jannye D., jt. auth. see Brock, James G.

Brock, Jim. Analyzing Your Logs Vol. II: Advanced Open Hole Interpretation. Brock, Jannye, ed. (Illus.). 160p. (Orig.). 1984. pap. 30.00 (ISBN 0-916647-02-1). Petro-Media.

Brock, John M. An Illustrated History of Kern County. (Illus.). 83p. (gr. 3-8). 1976. pap. 5.00 (ISBN 0-943500-05-2). Kern Historical.

Brock, Jonathan. Bargaining Beyond Impasse: Joint Resolution of Public Sector Labor Disputes. LC 81-20652. 279p. 1982. 24.95 (ISBN 0-86569-110-X). Auburn Hse.

--Managing People in Public Agencies: Personnel & Labor Relations. 1984. 20.95 (ISBN 0-316-10889-8); tchr's manual avail. (ISBN 0-316-10890-1). Little.

Brock, Karen, tr. see Shin'ichi, Miyajima & Yasuhiro, Sato.

Brock, Karen L. Autumn Grasses & Water: Motifs in Japanese Art. 1983. pap. 15.00 (ISBN 0-317-06768-0); 25.00 (ISBN 0-317-06769-9). Japan Soc.

Brock, Katherine M., jt. auth. see Brock, Thomas D.

Brock, Leslie V. The Currency of the American Colonies, Seventeen Hundred to Seventeen Sixty-Four: A Study in Colonial Finance & Imperial Relations. LC 75-2576. (Dissertations in American Economic History). (Illus.). 1975. 57.50x (ISBN 0-405-07257-0). Ayer Co Pubs.

Brock, Luther A. How to Build Goodwill Through Credit Correspondence. 115p. 1976. pap. 8.50 (ISBN 0-934914-19-2). NACM.

--How to Communicate by Letter & Memo. (Illus.). 304p. 1974. text ed. 23.00 (ISBN 0-07-008043-7). McGraw.

Brock, M., ed. Modern Neurosurgery, Vol. I. (Illus.). 400p. 1982. pap. 50.00 (ISBN 0-387-10972-2). Springer-Verlag.

Brock, M. & Dietz, H., eds. Intracranial Pressure: Experimental & Clinical Aspects. LC 72-91885. (Illus.). 383p. 1972. 53.00 (ISBN 0-387-06039-1). Springer-Verlag.

Brock, M., ed. see Annual Meeting of the Deutsche Gesellschaft Fuer Neurochirurgie, Heidelberg, May 1-3, 1975, et al.

Brock, M., jt. ed. see Hartmann, A.

Brock, M., ed. see Piotrowski, W., et al.

Brock, Michael. The Great Reform Act. Hurstfield, Joel, ed. (Illus.). 411p. 1974. (Hutchinson U Lib); pap. text ed. 15.75x (ISBN 0-09-115911-3, Hutchinson U Lib). Humanities.

Brock, Michael & Brock, Eleanor, eds. H. H. Asquith: Letters to Venetia Stanley. (Illus.). 1982. 35.00x (ISBN 0-19-212200-2). Oxford U Pr.

Brock, Nancy & Brewer, Nancy. Traipsin' North Mississippi Roads. (Illus.). 88p. 1984. pap. 4.95 (ISBN 0-88107-016-5). Natl ShareGraphics.

Brock, Neely W. & Gary, Blau, eds. Environmental Exposure From Chemicals, Vol. 2. 192p. 1985. 60.00 (ISBN 0-8493-6166-4). CRC Pr.

Brock, Para L. Sahani. LC 81-10611. (Illus.). (gr. 6-8). 1981. 8.95 (ISBN 0-931948-19-3). Peachtree Pubs.

Brock, Peter. The Mahatma & Mother India. 231p. 1984. 13.00 (ISBN 0-934676-71-2). Greenlf Bks.

--Pacifism in Europe to 1914. LC 75-166362. 544p. 1972. 53.00x (ISBN 0-691-04608-5); pap. 21.00x LPE (ISBN 0-691-10006-3, LPE). Princeton U Pr.

--Pioneers of the Peaceable Kingdom: The Quaker Peace Testimony from the Colonial Era to the First World War. 1970. pap. 11.95 (ISBN 0-691-00573-7). Princeton U Pr.

--The Slovak National Awakening: An Essay in the Intellectual History of Central Europe. LC 75-42013. 1976. 17.50x (ISBN 0-8020-5337-8). U of Toronto Pr.

Brock, Peter & Skilling, H. Gordon, eds. The Czech Renascence of the Nineteenth Century: Essays Presented to Otakar Odlozilik in Honour of His Seventieth Birthday. LC 76-18281. pap. 89.80 (ISBN 0-317-29883-6, 2019447). Bks Demand UMI.

Brock, R. A., ed. see Grigsby, Hugh B.

Brock, R. A., ed. see Spotswood, Alexander.

Brock, R. A., ed. see Virginia Company of London, 1619-1624.

Brock, R. A., ed. see Virginia Historical Society Annual Meeting, Dec 21-22, 1891.

Brock, Ray. Go Fly a Kite. (Illus.). 1976. pap. 2.95 (ISBN 0-912846-17-8). Bookstore Pr.

Brock, Raymond, jt. auth. see Schmidt, Jerry.

Brock, Raymond T. The Christ-Centered Family. LC 76-46036. (Radiant Life Ser.). 128p. 1977. pap. 2.50 (ISBN 0-88243-903-0, 02-0903); teacher's ed 3.95 (ISBN 0-88243-173-0, 32-0173). Gospel Pub.

--Dating & Waiting for Marriage. LC 81-84763. 128p. 1982. pap. 2.50 (ISBN 0-88243-881-6, 02-0881); teacher's ed. 3.95 (ISBN 0-88243-192-7, 32-0192). Gospel Pub.

--Into the Highways & Hedges. LC 61-18608. 1961. 1.25 (ISBN 0-88243-533-7, 02-0533). Gospel Pub.

Brock, Richards, et al. Ready or Not. 1977. 6.95 (ISBN 0-8027-0586-3); pap. 3.95 (ISBN 0-8027-7121-1). Walker & Co.

Brock, Robert A. Huguenot Emigration to Virginia. LC 63-526. (Collections of the Virginia Historical Society, New Ser: Vol. 5). 1979. Repr. of 1886 ed. with suppl. 17.50 (ISBN 0-8063-0050-7). Genealog Pub.

Brock, Robert A., jt. auth. see Robertson, Wyndham.

Brock, Robert A., compiled by. Documents, Chiefly Unpublished, Relating to the Huguenot Emigration to Virginia & the Settlement at Manakin-Town. LC 72-14424. (Virginia Historical Society. Collections, New Ser.: No. 5). Repr. of 1886 ed. 38.50 (ISBN 0-404-57655-9). AMS Pr.

Brock, Robert A., ed. Miscellaneous Papers, 1672-1865: Now First Printed from the Manuscript in the Collections of the Virginia Historical Society. LC 72-14425. (Virginia Historical Society. Collections, New Ser.: No. 6). Repr. of 1887 ed. 27.50 (ISBN 0-404-57656-7). AMS Pr.

Brock, Sebastian. Syriac Version of the Ps. Nonnos Mythological Scholia. LC 79-139712. (Oriental Publications: No. 20). 1971. 62.50 (ISBN 0-521-07990-X). Cambridge U Pr.

Brock, Sebastian, tr. see Saint Ephrem.

Brock, Stanley E. Jungle Cowboy. LC 79-163885. (Illus.). 1972. 8.95 (ISBN 0-8008-4444-0). Taplinger.

--More About Leemo. (Illus.). 1968. 7.95 (ISBN 0-8008-5350-4). Taplinger.

Brock, Susan & Pringle, Marian J. The Shakespeare Memorial Theatre, Nineteen Nineteen to Nineteen Forty-Five. (Theatre in Focus Ser.). (Illus.). 120p. 1984. pap. 55.00 incl. 50 slides (ISBN 0-85964-157-0). Chadwyck Healey.

Brock, T. E. Sixth British Robot Association Annual Conference. 1984. 48.00 (ISBN 0-444-86685-X, I-506-83). Elsevier.

Brock, T. E., ed. British Robot Association Annual Conference, 7th: Proceedings of the Conference, Cambridge, UK, 14-16 May, 1984. 300p. 1984. 53.75 (ISBN 0-444-87532-8, Pub. by North Holland). Elsevier.

--Fluidics Applications Bibliography. 1968. text ed. 23.00x (ISBN 0-900983-00-0, Dist. by Air Science Co.). BHRA Fluid.

Brock, T. E., ed. see British Robot Association Annual Conference, 6th, Birmingham, UK, May 1983.

Brock, T. E., ed. see International Conference on Industrial Robot Technology, 3rd, Univ. Nottingham, Eng., Mar. 1976 & International Symposium on Industrial Robots, 6th, Univ. Nottingham, Eng., Mar. 1976.

Brock, Ted & Campbell, Jim. First Official NFL Trivia Book. 1980. pap. 1.95 (ISBN 0-451-09541-3, J9541, Sig). NAL.

--The Super Official NFL Trivia Book. 1985. pap. 3.95 (ISBN 0-451-13822-8, Sig). NAL.

Brock, Ted & Eldridge, Larry, Jr. Twenty Five Years: The NFL Since 1960. 1985. 22.95 (ISBN 0-671-60441-4, Fireside); pap. 14.95 (ISBN 0-671-60440-6, Fireside). S&S.

Brock, Thomas D. Membrane Filtration: A User's Guide & Reference Manual. (Illus.). 1983. 35.00x (ISBN 0-910239-00-2). Sci Tech Inc.

--The Successful Textbook Publishing: The Author's Guide. 1985. 28.50 (ISBN 0-910239-01-0). Sci Tech Inc.

--Thermophilic Microorganisms & Life at High Temperatures. LC 78-6110. (Springer Ser. in Microbiology). (Illus.). 1978. 39.00 (ISBN 0-387-90309-7). Springer-Verlag.

Brock, Thomas D. & Brock, Katherine M. Basic Microbiology with Applications. 2nd ed. (Illus.). 1978. 33.95 (ISBN 0-13-065284-9). P-H.

Brock, Thomas D., jt. auth. see Phillips, Jane A.

Brock, Thomas D., ed. Milestones in Microbiology. 272p. 1979. 8.00 (ISBN 0-914826-06-9). Am Soc Microbio.

Brock, Thomas D., et al. Biology of Microorganisms. 4th ed. (Illus.). 868p. 1984. text ed. 39.95 (ISBN 0-13-078113-4). P-H.

Brock, Van K. The Hard Essential Landscape. LC 79-21071. (University of Central Florida Contemporary Poetry Ser.). 93p. 1979. 8.95 (ISBN 0-8130-0659-7). U Presses Fla.

--Spelunking. 1978. 1.50 (ISBN 0-936814-04-7). New Collage.

Brock, Van K. & Jordan, David, eds. Cafe at St. Marks. pap. 3.50 (ISBN 0-938078-03-8). Anhinga Pr.

Brock, Van K. & Poole, Francis, eds. Lime Tree Prison. pap. 3.00 (ISBN 0-938078-00-3). Anhinga Pr.

--A Spot of Purple Is Deaf. pap. 3.50 (ISBN 0-686-81801-6). Anhinga Pr.

Brock, W. H. & Meadows, A. J. The Lamp of Learning: Taylor & Francis & the Development of Science Publishing. 256p. 1984. 30.00x (ISBN 0-85066-253-2, Pub. by Falmer Pr). Taylor & Francis.

--The Lamps of Learning: Taylor & Francis & the Development of Science Publishing. 256p. 1984. 30.00 (ISBN 0-85066-253-2). Taylor & Francis.

Brock, W. R. Character of American History. 1960. lib. bdg. 17.50x (ISBN 0-88307-036-7). Gannon.

--Character of American History. 2nd ed. (Illus.). 1969. 25.00 (ISBN 0-312-12985-8). St Martin.

--The United States 1789-1890. (Sources of History Ser.). 352p. 1975. 27.50x (ISBN 0-8014-0723-0). Cornell U Pr.

Brock, William R. Investigation & Responsibility: Public Responsibility in the United States, 1865-1900. LC 83-26205. 296p. 1984. 39.50 (ISBN 0-521-25897-9). Cambridge U Pr.

--Lord Liverpool & Liberal Toryism: 1820-1827. 2nd ed. (Illus.). 300p. 1967. 29.00x (ISBN 0-7146-1457-2, F Cass Co). Biblio Dist.

--Lord Liverpool & Liberal Toryism 1820-1827. ix, 300p. 1967. Repr. of 1941 ed. 23.00 (ISBN 0-208-00428-9, Archon). Shoe String.

--Scotus Americanus: A Study of 18th Century Sources. 293p. 1982. 22.50x (ISBN 0-85224-420-7, Pub. by Edinburgh U Pr Scotland). Columbia U Pr.

Brockbank, Bernard P. Commandments & Promises of God. LC 82-23629. 667p. 1983. 15.95 (ISBN 0-87747-889-9). Deseret Bk.

Brockbank, Philip, ed. Players of Shakespeare: Essays in Shakespeare: A Performance by Twelve Players with the Royal Shakespeare Company. 200p. 1985. 22.95 (ISBN 0-521-24428-5). Cambridge U Pr.

Brockbank, Philip, ed. see Jonson, Ben.

Brockbank, Phillip, ed. see Shakespeare, William.

Brockbank, Reed & Westby-Gibson, D., eds. Mental Health in a Changing Community. LC 66-22942. 176p. 1966. 33.00 (ISBN 0-8089-0073-0, 790665). Grune.

Brockdorff, E. Von see Prinzhorn, H.

Brockelman, Paul T. Existential Phenomenology & the World of Ordinary Experience: An Introduction. LC 80-67208. 83p. 1980. lib. bdg. 19.00 (ISBN 0-8191-1191-0); pap. text ed. 8.25 (ISBN 0-8191-1192-9). U Pr of Amer.

Brockelman, Paul T., tr. see Gusdorf, Georges.

Brockelmann, C. History of the Islamic Peoples. 1980. 26.95X (ISBN 0-7100-1118-0); pap. 15.00 (ISBN 0-7100-0521-0). Routledge & Kegan.

Brocker, T. & Dieck, Tom T. Representations of Compact Lie Groups. (Graduate Texts in Mathematics Ser.: Vol. 98). (Illus.). x, 313p. 1985. 39.00 (ISBN 0-387-13678-9). Springer-Verlag.

Brocker, T. H. Differentiable Germs & Catastrophes. Lander, L., tr. from Ger. LC 74-17000. (London Mathematical Society Lecture Note Ser.: No. 17). 160p. (Eng.). 1975. pap. text ed. 22.95 (ISBN 0-521-20681-2). Cambridge U Pr.

Brocker, Theodor & Janich, Klaus. Introduction to Differential Topology. LC 81-21591. (Illus.). 150p. 1982. 32.50 (ISBN 0-521-24135-9); pap. 13.95 (ISBN 0-521-28470-8). Cambridge U Pr.

Brockerhoff, Hans & Jensen, Robert G. Lipolytic Enzymes. 1974. 70.00 (ISBN 0-12-134550-5). Acad Pr.

Brockes, Barthold H. Herrn B. H. Brockes... Aus Dem Englischen Ubersetzte Jahreszeiten Des Herrn Thomson. 640p. 1972. Repr. of 1745 ed. 55.00 (ISBN 0-384-05910-4). Johnson Repr.

Brockes, Jeremy, ed. Neuroimmunology. LC 82-3679. (Current Topics in Neurobiology Ser.). 272p. 1982. 29.50x (ISBN 0-306-40955-0, Plenum Pr). Plenum Pub.

Brockett, C. W. Antiphons, Responsories & other Chants from the Mozarabic Rite. (Wissenschaftliche Abhandlungen - Musicological Studies Ser.: No. 15). 300p. 1968. lib. bdg. 60.00 (ISBN 0-912024-85-2). Inst Mediaeval Mus.

Brockett, Joseph R. Myths of Wyoming: Jackson Hole, Vol. 1. (Myths of Wyoming Ser.). (Illus.). 32p. 1985. pap. 2.25 (ISBN 0-318-04804-3). Dovehaven Pr Ltd.

Brockett, L. P. Woman: Her Rights, Wrongs, Privileges, & Responsibilities. facs. ed. LC 70-114869. (Select Bibliographies Reprint Ser.). 1869. 32.00 (ISBN 0-8369-5274-X). Ayer Co Pubs.

Brockett, Lenyth, jt. auth. see Brockett, Oscar G.

Brockett, O. & Findlay, R. Century of Innovation: A History of European & American Theatre & Drama, 1870-1970. (Theater & Drama Ser.). 1973. 38.95 (ISBN 0-13-122747-5). P-H.

Brockett, Oscar, ed. see Frick, John W.

Brockett, Oscar, ed. see Manifold, Gay.

Brockett, Oscar, ed. see Mittman, Barbara G.

Brockett, Oscar G. The Essential Theatre. 3rd ed. 402p. 1984. pap. text ed. 20.95 (ISBN 0-03-063553-5, HoltC). HR&W.

--Historical Edition: The Theatre: an Introduction. LC 78-10000. 1979. pap. text ed. 22.95 (ISBN 0-03-043116-6, HoltC). HR&W.

--History of the Theatre. 4th ed. 768p. 1981. text ed. 37.14 (ISBN 0-205-07661-0, 487661X). Allyn.

--Modern Theater: Realism & Naturalism to the Present. 200p. 1982. 21.95x (ISBN 0-205-07760-9, EDP 487760, Pub. by Longwood Div). Allyn.

--Perspectives on Contemporary Theatre. LC 75-154268. viii, 158p. 1971. 17.50x (ISBN 0-8071-0939-8). La State U Pr.

--The Theatre: An Introduction. 4th ed. LC 78-11850. 1979. text ed. 28.95 (ISBN 0-03-021676-1, HoltC). HR&W.

Brockett, Oscar G. & Brockett, Lenyth. Plays for the Theatre: An Anthology of World Drama. 4th ed. LC 78-12119. 652p. 1984. pap. text ed. 17.95 (ISBN 0-03-063697-3, HoltC). HR&W.

Brockett, Oscar G. & Pape, Mark. World Drama. 1984. pap. text ed. 18.95 (ISBN 0-03-057668-7). HR&W.

Brockett, Oscar G., ed. & frwd. by. Studies in Theatre & Drama. (De Proprietatibus Litterarum, Ser. Major: No. 23). 217p. 1972. text ed. 29.60 (ISBN 90-2792-112-1). Mouton.

Brockett, Paul. Bibliography of Aeronautics. LC 66-25692. 1966. Repr. of 1910 ed. 85.00x (ISBN 0-8103-3320-1). Gale.

Brockett, R. W., ed. see NATO Advanced Study Institute, 1973.

Brockett, Roger & Millman, Richard, eds. Differential Geometric Control Theory. (Progress in Mathematics: Vol. 27). 340p. 1983. 25.00x (ISBN 0-8176-3091-0). Birkhauser.

Brockett, W. A., et al. Elements of Applied Thermodynamics. 4th ed. LC 77-73341. (Illus.). 552p. 1978. text ed. 23.95x (ISBN 0-87021-169-2). Naval Inst Pr.

Brockhaus, Peter & Stanciu, Ulrich. Sailboarding: Basic & Advanced Techniques. 2nd ed. (Illus.). 144p. 1980. 14.50 (ISBN 0-229-11651-5). Sheridan.

Brockhous, Albert. Netsukes. LC 71-78364. (Illus.). 1969. Repr. of 1924 ed. 25.00 (ISBN 0-87817-025-1). Hacker.

Brockhuizen, S., jt. ed. see Thran, P.

Brockhurst, Robert J., et al, eds. Controversy in Ophthalmology. LC 75-40634. (Illus.). 1977. text ed. 30.95 (ISBN 0-7216-1989-4). Saunders.

Brockie, Keith. One Man's Island: A Naturalist's View. LC 84-47708. (Illus.). 192p. 1984. 19.18i (ISBN 0-06-015360-1, HarpT). Har-Row.

Brockie, William. Legends & Superstitions of the County of Durham. LC 76-49066. 1976. Repr. of 1886 ed. lib. bdg. 29.50 (ISBN 0-8414-1761-X). Folcroft.

Brockington, A. Allen. Browning & the Twentieth Century. LC 74-7259. Repr. of 1932 ed. lib. bdg. 9.50 (ISBN 0-8414-3165-5). Folcroft.

Brockington, Dave, jt. auth. see White, Roger.

Brockington, I. F. & Kumar, R., eds. Motherhood & Mental Illness. 288p. 1982. 35.00 (ISBN 0-8089-1481-2, 790666). Grune.

Brockington, J. L. Righteous Rama: The Evolution of an Epic. 373p. 1985. 32.50x (ISBN 0-317-19694-4). Oxford U Pr.

--The Sacred Thread: Hinduism in Continuity & Diversity. 222p. 1981. pap. 12.00x (ISBN 0-85224-393-6, Pub. by Edinburgh U Pr Scotland). Columbia U Pr.

Brockington, L. H. Ezra, Nehemiah & Esther. (New Century Bible Ser). 262p. 1969. text ed. 12.95 (ISBN 0-551-00530-0). Attic Pr.

Brockington, L. H., ed. see Robinson, H. Wheeler.

Brockington, L. H., jt. ed. see Robinson, T. H.

Brockington, N. R. Computer Modeling in Agriculture. (Illus.). 1979. 35.00x (ISBN 0-19-854523-1). Oxford U Pr.

Brockington, R. Financial Accounting. (Higher Business Education Ser.). (Illus.). 240p. 1983. text ed. 28.50x (ISBN 0-7121-0644-8); pap. 24.95x (ISBN 0-7121-0639-1). Trans-Atlantic.

Brockington, R. B. Financial Management. 1980. 20.00x (ISBN 0-905435-07-9, Pub. by DP Pubns). State Mutual Bk.

--Financial Management: An Instructional Manual. 2nd ed. 304p. 1981. 25.00x (ISBN 0-686-81215-8, Pub by DP Pubns). State Mutual Bk.

Brocklehurst, Gordon, ed. Spina Bifida for the Clinician. (Clinics in Developmental Medicine Ser.: Vol. 57). 300p. 1976. text ed. 27.50 (ISBN 0-433-04410-1, Pub. by Spastics Intl England). Lippincott.

Brocklehurst, J. C. & Tucker, J. S. Progress in Geriatric Day Care. 204p. 1980. 40.00x (ISBN 0-900889-79-9, Pub. by Kings Fund). State Mutual Bk.

Brocklehurst, J. C., jt. auth. see Kamal, Asif.

Brocklehurst, J. C., ed. Textbook of Geriatric Medicine & Gerontology. 3rd ed. (Illus.). 1985. text ed. 98.00 (ISBN 0-443-02696-3). Churchill.

Brocklehurst, John C. & Hanley, Thomas. Geriatric Medicine for Students. 2nd ed. (Livingstone Medical Texts Ser.). (Illus.). 1981. pap. text ed. 12.50 (ISBN 0-686-34354-9). Churchill.

Brocklehurst, Thomas U. Mexico Today. 1976. lib. bdg. 59.95 (ISBN 0-8490-0632-5). Gordon Pr.

Brockley, M. Elissa. Arts & Crafts Lessons Anyone Can Teach. 237p. 1982. 16.50 (ISBN 0-13-047043-0, Parker). P-H.

Brockman, Bennett see Butler, Francelia, et al.

Brockman, C. Frank. Trees of North America. Zim, Herbert S. & Fichter, George S., eds. (Golden Field Guide Ser.). (Illus.). (gr. 9 up). 1968. pap. 7.95 (ISBN 0-307-13658-2, Golden Pr). Western Pub.

Brockman, C. Frank & Merriam, Lawrence C., Jr. Recreational Use of Wild Lands. 3rd ed. (M-H Series in Forest Resources). (Illus.). 1979. text ed. 35.95 (ISBN 0-07-007982-X). McGraw.

Brockman, Chris. What about Gods? (Skeptic's Bookshelf Ser.). (Illus.). 1978. pap. 5.95 (ISBN 0-87975-106-1). Prometheus Bks.

Brockman, David D. Late Adolescence: Psychoanalytic Studies. LC 84-25181. 400p. 1985. text ed. 37.50 (ISBN 0-8236-2948-1, 02948). Intl Univs Pr.

Brockman, Dorothy. Exploring Careers in Computer Software. (Careers in Depth Ser.). (Illus.). 140p. 1985. lib. bdg. 8.97 (ISBN 0-8239-0653-1). Rosen Group.

Brockman, Ellen M. Handicapped Students Mathematics: Teaching. 64p. 1981. 7.96 (ISBN 0-8106-3177-6). NEA.

Brockman, Ellis. Laboratory Manual for Microbiology. new ed. LC 74-28777. 121p. 1980. pap. 15.00 (ISBN 0-87812-085-8). Pendell Pub.

Brockman, Ellis R. & Lampky, James R. Laboratory Textbook & Exercises for General Bacteriology. 1971. text ed. 13.00 (ISBN 0-87812-038-6). Pendell Pub.

Brockman, Eric. The Two Sieges of Rhodes. LC 71-436060. 1969. text ed. 10.00x (ISBN 0-8401-0241-0). A R Allenson.

Brockman, H. A. The Caliph of Fonthill: William Beckford. LC 73-14570. 1956. lib. bdg. 25.00 (ISBN 0-8414-3258-9). Folcroft.

Brockman, H. L., jt. auth. see Borgstrom, B.

Brockman, Harold. The British Architect in Industry, 1841-1940. LC 74-189063. pap. 46.50 (ISBN 0-317-20039-9, 2023261). Bks Demand UMI.

Brockman, James R. The Word Remains: A Life of Oscar Romero. LC 82-3607. (Illus.). 256p. (Orig.). 1982. pap. 12.95 (ISBN 0-88344-364-3). Orbis Bks.

Brockman, James R., ed. The Church Is All of You: Thoughts of Archbishop Oscar A. Romero. 150p. 1984. pap. 6.95 (ISBN 0-86683-838-4). Winston Pr.

Brockman, Jennifer D., jt. ed. see Rudram, Alan.

Brockman, John. Science Universe. 1985. 14.95 (ISBN 0-670-80480-0). Viking.

Brockman, John, jt. auth. see Schlossberg, Edwin.

Brockman, Norbert. Ordained to Service: A Theology of the Permanent Diaconate. 1976. 7.50 (ISBN 0-682-48561-6, University). Exposition Pr FL.

Brockman, Norbert C. & Piediscalzi, Nicholas, eds. Contemporary Religion & Social Responsibility. new ed. LC 72-11982. 366p. (Orig.). 1973. pap. 4.95 (ISBN 0-8189-0257-4). Alba.

Brockmann, Ellen-Mary. Teaching Handicapped Students in the Mathematics Classroom. 64p. 1981. 7.95 (ISBN 0-8106-3177-6). NEA.

Brockmann, J. R. Writing Better Software Computer Documentation. 500p. 1985. 30.00 (ISBN 0-471-88472-3). Wiley.

Brockmann, John, jt. ed. see Anderson, Paul.

Brockmann, Karen & Kagen, Annalee. Coping in English: Beyond the Basics. (Illus.). 288p. 1985. pap. text ed. 13.95 (ISBN 0-13-172487-8). P-H.

Brockmann, L. O., jt. auth. see Aronson, J. Hugo.

Brockmeyer, Lloyd & Collison, Kathleen. New Beginnings: A Confirmation Resource. 58p. (Orig.). (gr. 7-8). pap. text ed. 4.50 (ISBN 0-941988-00-7); tchr's ed. 3.50 (ISBN 0-941988-01-5). K Q Assocs.

Brockner, J. & Rubin, J. Z. Entrapment in Escalating Conflicts. (Springer Series in Social Psychology). (Illus.). 335p. 1985. 37.00 (ISBN 0-387-96089-9). Springer-Verlag.

Brockopp, Gene W., jt. auth. see Lester, David.

Brockriede, Wayne, jt. auth. see Ehninger, Douglas.

Brockriede, Wayne, jt. ed. see Scott, Robert L.

Brockton Art Museum & Baldaia, Peter J. Marion Huse: An Artist's Evolution. Haff, Elizabeth, ed. LC 85-47809. (Illus.). 94p. (Orig.). 1985. pap. 10.00 Museum Exhibition Catalogue (ISBN 0-934358-15-X). Brockton Art-Fuller.

Brock-Utne, Birgit. Educating for Peace: A Feminist Perspective on Peace Research & Action. (Athene Ser.). 180p. 1985. 21.50 (ISBN 0-08-032370-7); pap. 10.95 (ISBN 0-08-032369-3). Pergamon.

Brockway, A. Fenner, jt. ed. see Hobhouse, Stephen.

Brockway, Archibald F. Will Roosevelt Succeed? A Study of Fascist Tendencies in America. LC 75-180392. Repr. of 1934 ed. 25.00 (ISBN 0-404-56108-X). AMS Pr.

Brockway, David & Fuller, James P. Tax Reform Act of 1984. (Tax Law & Practice Course Handbook Ser.: No. 213). (Illus.). write for info. Amer Bar Assn.

Brockway, Fenner. Britain's First Socialists. 11.95 (ISBN 0-7043-2207-2, Pub. by Quartet England). Charles River Bks.

Brockway, George P. Economics: What Went Wrong & Why & Some Things to Do about It. LC 84-47559. 224p. 1985. 17.79 (ISBN 0-06-039037-9, C&M Bessie Bk). Har-Row.

--What Went Wrong & Why & Some Things to Do about It. 1985. 18.50 (ISBN 0-317-18504-7, C&M Bessie Bk). Har-Row.

Brockway, L. O., ed. Fifty Years of Electron Diffraction. (Transactions of the American Crystallographic Association Ser.: Vol. 13). 126p. 1977. pap. 15.00 (ISBN 0-686-60383-4). Polycrystal Bk Serv.

Brockway, Lucile H. Science & Colonial Expansion: The Role of the British Royal Botanic Gardens. LC 79-51669. (Studies in Social Discontinuity). 1979. 29.50 (ISBN 0-12-134150-X). Acad Pr.

Brockway, Michael. Charles Knight. 116p. 1981. 37.00x (ISBN 0-85317-300-1, Pub. by Lewis Pubs). State Mutual Bk.

Brockway, Thomas. Basic Documents in United States Foreign Policy. 192p. (Orig.). pap. 6.95 (ISBN 0-686-47369-8). Krieger.

Brockway, Thomas P. Bennington College: In the Beginning. (Illus.). 280p. 1981. 12.95 (ISBN 0-914378-78-3); pap. 10.00 (ISBN 0-914378-77-5). Countryman.

Brockway, William R. Recreating the Double Barrell Muzzle-Loading Shotgun. (Illus.). 1985. 27.50 (ISBN 0-87387-090-5); pap. 20.00 (ISBN 0-87387-089-1). Shumway.

Brockway, Zebulon R. Fifty Years of Prison Service: An Autobiography. LC 69-14914. (Criminology, Law Enforcement, & Social Problems Ser.: No. 61). (Illus.). 1969. Repr. of 1912 ed. 17.00x (ISBN 0-87585-061-8). Patterson Smith.

Brockwell, C. J. Aborigines & the Law: A Bibliography. 71p. (Orig.). 1980. pap. text ed. 5.95 (ISBN 0-909596-33-6, 0582, Pub. by ANUP Australia). Australia N U P.

Brockwell, Maurice W. Erasmus: Humanist & Painter a Study of a Triptych in a Private Collection. LC 79-14635. 1979. Repr. of 1918 ed. lib. bdg. 17.50 (ISBN 0-8414-9830-X). Folcroft.

--Van Eyck Problem. LC 78-138101. (Illus.). 1971. Repr. of 1954 ed. lib. bdg. 22.50x (ISBN 0-8371-5677-7, BRVE). Greenwood.

Brocquy, Sybil Le see Le Brocquy, Sybil.

Brod, Alice F. Estate Planning: Complete Guide & Workbook. rev. ed. 1984. 125.00 (ISBN 0-916592-49-9). Panel Pubs.

Brod, Craig & St. John, Wes. Technostress: The Human Cost of the Computer Revolution. 288p. 16.95 (ISBN 0-201-11211-6). Addison-Wesley.

Brod, J. & Knell, A. J. Diagnose in der Inneren Medizin. (Illus.). xiv, 362p. 1982. pap. 17.25 (ISBN 3-8055-3483-3). S Karger.

--Diagnose in der Inneren Medizin. 2nd ed. (Illus.). xiv, 362p. 1985. pap. 12.00 (ISBN 3-8055-4148-1). S Karger.

Brod, J., jt. ed. see Bahlmann, J.

Brod, J., jt. ed. see Eisenbach, G. M.

Brod, J., et al, eds. Proteinuria. (Contributions to Nephrology: Vol. 1). (Illus.). 250p. 1975. 25.25 (ISBN 3-8055-2183-9). S Karger.

Brod, Jack & Tuleja, Thaddeus F. Consumer's Guide to Buying & Selling Gold, Silver & Diamonds. LC 84-5918. (Illus.). 264p. 1985. 15.95 (ISBN 0-385-27848-9, Dial). Doubleday.

Brod, Jan, jt. ed. see Eisenbach, G. M.

Brod, Max. Franz Kafka: A Biography. 2nd ed. LC 60-14601. (gr. 7-12). 1963. pap. 5.95 (ISBN 0-8052-0047-9). Schocken.

--Heinrich Heine: The Artist in Revolt. Witriol, Joseph, tr. from Ger. LC 76-21292. (Illus.). 355p. 1976. Repr. of 1957 ed. lib. bdg. 24.75x (ISBN 0-8371-8992-6, BRHA). Greenwood.

--Paganism - Christianity - Judaism: A Confession of Faith. Wolf, William, tr. LC 78-104937. 231p. 1970. 15.50 (ISBN 0-8173-6700-4). U of Ala Pr.

Brod, Max, ed. see Kafka, Franz.

Brod, Richard I. & Franklin, Phyllis. Profession '83. 60p. (Orig.). 1983. pap. 4.00x (ISBN 0-87352-318-0). Modern Lang.

Brod, Richard I., ed. Language Study for the Nineteen Eighties: Reports of the MLA-ACLS Language Task Forces. LC 79-87582. 106p. 1980. pap. 14.50x (ISBN 0-87352-088-2, A325). Modern Lang.

Brod, Richard I. & Fisher, Dexter, eds. Profession '80. 60p. (Orig.). 1980. pap. 4.00x (ISBN 0-87352-315-6). Modern Lang.

--Profession '81. 60p. (Orig.). 1981. pap. 4.00x (ISBN 0-87352-316-4). Modern Lang.

Brod, Richard I. & Franklin, Phyllis, eds. Profession Eighty-Four. 60p. 1984. 4.00 (ISBN 0-87352-319-9). Modern Lang.

--Profession '82. (Illus.). 60p. 1982. pap. 4.00x (ISBN 0-686-46774-4). Modern Lang.

Brod, Richard I. & Neel, Jasper P., eds. Profession '77. 60p. 1977. pap. 4.00x (ISBN 0-87352-312-1). Modern Lang.

--Profession '78. 60p. 1978. pap. 4.00x (ISBN 0-87352-313-X). Modern Lang.

--Profession '79. 60p. 1979. pap. 4.00x (ISBN 0-87352-314-8). Modern Lang.

Brod, Richard I., et al, eds. English & Foreign Languages: Employment & the Profession. v, 77p. 1976. pap. 6.00x (ISBN 0-87352-311-3, W360). Modern Lang.

Brod, Ruth H., jt. auth. see Reilly, Harold J.

Brod, William F. You Have a Great Idea, Now What? LC 83-90898. 73p. 1984. 6.95 (ISBN 0-533-05919-4). Vantage.

Broda, E. Evolution of Bioenergetic Processes. LC 75-6847. 220p. 1978. text ed. 50.00 (ISBN 0-08-024397-5); pap. text ed. 18.00 (ISBN 0-08-022651-5). Pergamon.

Broda, Engelbert. Ludwig Boltzmann: Man, Physicist, Philosopher. LC 82-80707. (Illus.). 179p. 1983. 22.50 (ISBN 0-918024-24-2). Ox Bow.

Broda, Paul. Plasmids. LC 79-10665. (Illus.). 197p. 1979. text ed. 25.95 (ISBN 0-7167-1111-7). W H Freeman.

Brodal, A. Neurological Anatomy in Relation to Clinical Medicine. 3rd ed. (Illus.). 1981. text ed. 47.50x (ISBN 0-19-502694-2). Oxford U Pr.

Brodal, A. & Kawamura, K. The Olivocerebellar Projection: A Review. (Advances in Anatomy, Embryology & Cell Biology Ser.: Vol. 64). (Illus.). 144p. 1980. pap. 46.10 (ISBN 0-387-10305-8). Springer-Verlag.

Brodatz, Phil. Land, Sea & Sky: A Photographic Album for Artists & Designers. (Illus.). 1976. pap. 6.95 (ISBN 0-486-23249-2). Dover.

--Land, Sea & Sky: A Photographic Album for Artists & Designers. 11.25 (ISBN 0-8446-5453-1). Peter Smith.

--Photographics: A Workshop in High-Contrast Techniques. (Illus.). 96p. 1981. 10.95 (ISBN 0-8174-5417-9, Amphoto). Watson-Guptill.

--Textures: A Photographic Album for Artists & Designers. (Illus., Orig.). 1966. pap. 6.00 (ISBN 0-486-21669-1). Dover.

--Wood & Wood Grains: A Photographic Album for Artists & Designers. 1972. 6.95 (ISBN 0-486-22424-4). Dover.

--Wood & Wood Grains: A Photographic Album for Artists & Designers. (Illus.). 15.50 (ISBN 0-8446-0040-7). Peter Smith.

Brodbeck, Arthur J, jt. ed. see Burdick, Eugene.

Brodbeck, U. Enzyme Inhibitors. (Illus.). 282p. (Orig.). 1980. pap. 42.50x (ISBN 0-89573-037-5). VCH Pubs.

Brode, Douglas. The Films of Dustin Hoffman. (Illus.). 256p. 1983. 18.95 (ISBN 0-8065-0869-8). Citadel Pr.

--The Films of the Fifties. (Illus.). 288p. 1976. 14.00 (ISBN 0-8065-0510-9). Citadel Pr.

--The Films of the Fifties. (Illus.). 1978. pap. 8.95 (ISBN 0-8065-0621-0). Citadel Pr.

--The Films of the Sixties. (Illus.). 288p. 1982. pap. 8.95 (ISBN 0-8065-0798-5). Citadel Pr.

--The Films of the Sixties. (Illus.). 1980. 16.95 (ISBN 0-8065-0694-6). Citadel Pr.

--The Films of Woody Allen. (Illus.). 256p. 1985. 19.95 (ISBN 0-8065-0959-7). Citadel Pr.

Brode, Heinrich. British & German East Africa: Their Economic & Commercial Relations. Wilkins, Mira, ed. LC 76-29766. (European Business Ser.). (Illus.). 1977. Repr. of 1911 ed. lib. bdg. 18.00x (ISBN 0-405-09780-8). Ayer Co Pubs.

--Tippoo Tib, the Story of His Career in Central Africa. Havelock, H., tr. LC 78-99351. 1969. Repr. of 1907 ed. lib. bdg. 13.75 (ISBN 0-8411-0022-5). Metro Bks.

Brode, Patrick. Sir John Beverley Robinson: Bone & Sinew of the Compact. (Publications of the Osgoode Society). 344p. 1984. 45.00x (ISBN 0-8020-3406-3); pap. 14.95 (ISBN 0-8020-3419-5). U of Toronto Pr.

Brode, Robyn, ed. see McLaughlin, Jim.

Brode, Wallace R., ed. Science in Progress, Fourteenth Series. LC 78-37534. (Essay Index Reprint Ser.). 1972. Repr. of 1964 ed. 21.00 (ISBN 0-8369-7274-0). Ayer Co Pubs.

--Science in Progress, Twelfth Series. LC 78-37534. (Essay Index Reprint Ser). 1972. Repr. of 1962 ed. 23.00 (ISBN 0-8369-7275-9). Ayer Co Pubs.

Brode, Wallace R., ed. see Waterman, Alan T., et al.

Brodehl, J. & Ehrich, J. H. Paediatric Nephrology: Proceedings of the Sixth International Symposium of Paediatric Nephrology, Hannover, Federal Republic of Germany, 29. August to 2. September 1983. (Illus.). 410p. 1984. pap. 43.00 (ISBN 0-387-13598-7). Springer-Verlag.

Brodell, James J. How to Purchase a Newspaper & Succeed. (Illus.). 118p. (Orig.). 1983. pap. 22.50 (ISBN 0-9610968-0-2). Mountain West.

Broder, Aaron J. Trial Handbook for New York Lawyers. LC 73-83028. 384p. 69.50; Suppl. 1984. 21.50; Suppl. 1983. 19.50. Lawyers Co-Op.

Broder, Aaron J., jt. auth. see Baer, Harold.

Broder, Bill. The Sacred Hoop: A Cycle of Earth Tales. LC 79-13286. (Illus.). 256p. 1979. 12.95 (ISBN 0-87156-260-X). Sierra.

Broder, Bill, jt. auth. see Broder, Gloria K.

Broder, David. Changing of the Guard: Power & Leadership in America. 512p. 1981. pap. 7.95 (ISBN 0-14-005940-7). Penguin.

Broder, David, et al. The Pursuit of the Presidency, 1980. Harwood, Richard, ed. (Orig.). 1980. pap. 3.95 (ISBN 0-425-04703-2). Berkley Pub.

Broder, Gloria K. & Broder, Bill. Remember This Time. LC 83-4249. 336p. 1983. 14.95 (ISBN 0-937858-23-4). Newmarket.

Broder, James F. Risk Analysis & the Security Survey. 320p. 1984. text ed. 22.95 (ISBN 0-409-95085-8). Butterworth.

Broder, Lawrence E. & Carter, Stephen K. Meningeal Leukemia. LC 74-190394. pap. 35.00 (ISBN 0-317-07814-3, 2020706). Bks Demand UMI.

Broder, Nathan. The Collector's Bach. LC 77-28265. (Keystone Books in English Ser.). 1978. Repr. of 1958 ed. lib. bdg. 18.25x (ISBN 0-313-20240-0, BRBAC). Greenwood.

--Great Operas of Mozart. 1962. 9.95 (ISBN 0-02-870440-1). Schirmer Bks.

Broder, Nathan, ed. see Mozart, Wolfgang A.

Broder, Patricia J. The American West: The Modern Vision. (Illus.). 360p. 75.00 (ISBN 0-8212-1578-7, 037931); deluxe ed. 500.00 leather bd. (ISBN 0-8212-1579-5, 037923). NYGS.

--Taos: A Painter's Dream. 368p. 1980. 59.00 (ISBN 0-8212-1103-X, 831670). NYGS.

Broderick, Albert, ed. French Institutionalists: Maurice Hauriou, Georges Renard, Joseph T. Delos. Welling, Mary, tr. from Fr. (Twentieth Century Legal Philosophy Ser: No. 8). 1970. 25.00x (ISBN 0-674-32125-1). Harvard U Pr.

--Law & the Liberal Arts. LC 67-20497. pap. 65.30 (ISBN 0-317-09575-7, 2005218). Bks Demand UMI.

Broderick, Carlfred. Couples. 1981. pap. 6.95 (ISBN 0-671-43827-1, Touchstone Bks). S&S.

Broderick, Carlfred B. Marriage & the Family. (Illus.). 1979. text ed. 24.95 O.P. (ISBN 0-13-559112-0). P-H.

--Marriage & the Family. 2nd ed. (Illus.). 448p. 1984. 26.95 (ISBN 0-13-559138-4). P-H.

--The Theraputic Triangle: A Sourcebook on Marital Therapy. (Illus.). 200p. 1983. 20.00 (ISBN 0-8039-1943-3). Sage.

Broderick, Damien. The Judas Mandala. (Orig.). 1982. pap. 2.50 (ISBN 0-671-45032-8, Timescape). PB.

Broderick, Damien, jt. auth. see Barnes, Rory.

Broderick, Damon. The Dreaming Dragons. (Orig.). 1980. pap. 2.25 (ISBN 0-671-83150-X, Timescape). PB.

Broderick, Dorothy, jt. auth. see Curley, Arthur.

Broderick, Dorothy M., ed. Library Work with Children. 197p. 1977. 14.00 (ISBN 0-8242-0620-7). Wilson.

Broderick, Francis, et al, eds. Black Protest Thought in the Twentieth Century. 2nd ed. LC 79-119007. (American Heritage Ser.). 1971. pap. write for info. (ISBN 0-02-380120-4, AHS-56R). Macmillan.

Broderick, Francis L. W. E. B. DuBois: Negro Leader in a Time of Crisis. 1959. 20.00x (ISBN 0-8047-0558-5). Stanford U Pr.

Broderick, J. P. Modern English Linguistics: A Structural & Transformational Grammar. 1975. text ed. 19.50 scp (ISBN 0-690-00067-7, HarpC). Har-Row.

Broderick, James. The Economic Morals of the Jesuits. LC 76-38248. (The Evolution of Capitalism Ser.). 168p. 1972. Repr. of 1934 ed. 12.00 (ISBN 0-405-04113-6). Ayer Co Pubs.

Broderick, Janice K. Charles M. Russell: American Artist. (Illus.). 103p. (Orig.). 1983. pap. 14.95 (ISBN 0-295-96023-X, Pub. by Jefferson Natl). U of Wash Pr.

Broderick, John. Chameleons. 1961. 7.95 (ISBN 0-8392-1010-8). Astor-Honor.

--Don Juaneen. 1965. 7.95 (ISBN 0-8392-1156-2). Astor-Honor.

--Fugitives. 1962. 7.95 (ISBN 0-8392-1036-1). Astor-Honor.

--A Prayer for Fair Weather. LC 83-6341. 192p. 1984. 13.95 (ISBN 0-7145-2796-3, Dist. by Scribner). M Boyars.

--The Rose Tree. (Fiction Ser.). 192p. 1985. 14.95 (ISBN 0-7145-2824-2, Dist. by Scribner). M Boyars.

--The Trial of Father Dillingham. 224p. 1981. 14.95 (ISBN 0-7145-2747-5, Dist by Scribner). M Boyars.

Broderick, John C. see Thoreau, Henry D.

Broderick, John P. The Able Writer: A Rhetoric & Handbook. 350p. 1982. pap. text ed. 12.50 scp (ISBN 0-690-00891-0, HarpC); instr. manual avail. (ISBN 0-06-360950-9). Har-Row.

Broderick, M. & Morton, A. A. Concise Dictionary of Egyptian Archaeology. 1985. pap. 7.50 (ISBN 0-89005-303-0). Ares.

Broderick, Mary E., jt. auth. see Peterson, Carol J.

Broderick, Richard. Night Sale. LC 82-61652. (Minnesota Voices Project Ser.: No. 8). (Illus.). 135p. 1982. pap. 5.00 (ISBN 0-89823-040-3). New Rivers Pr.

Broderick, Robert, ed. The Catholic Encyclopedia. LC 76-10976. 1981. pap. 10.95 (ISBN 0-8407-5787-5). Nelson.

Broderick, Robert C. Days of Praise. 1977. 5.50 (ISBN 0-8199-0653-0). Franciscan Herald.

--Parish Council Handbook. 1968. pap. 2.25 (ISBN 0-8199-0083-4, L38623). Franciscan Herald.

--Your Parish - Where the Action Is. 1974. pap. 2.25 (ISBN 0-8199-0486-4). Franciscan Herald.

Broderick, Warren F., ed. Brunswick: A Pictorial History. (Illus., Orig.). 1978. pap. 9.95 (ISBN 0-686-26173-9). Brunswick Hist Soc.

Brodersen, Robert W., ed. see Gray, Paul, et al.

Brodetsky, S. Sir Isaac Newton. 1927. Repr. 20.00 (ISBN 0-8274-3425-1). R West.

Brodeur, A. G., tr. see Sturluson, S.

Brodeur, Armand E. & Silberstein, Michael J. Fundamentals of Radiologic Pathology. (Illus.). Date not set. 27.00 (ISBN 0-8391-1803-1, 15636). Univ Park.

Brodeur, Arthur G. Arthur Dux Bellorum. LC 73-16320. 1939. lib. bdg. 15.00 (ISBN 0-8414-9864-4). Folcroft.

--Climax of the Finn Episode. LC 74-17118. 1943. lib. bdg. 15.00 (ISBN 0-8414-3167-1). Folcroft.

--Riddle of the Runes. 1932. lib. bdg. 15.00 (ISBN 0-8414-3210-4). Folcroft.

Brodeur, Paul. An Industry on Trial. LC 85-655802. 351p. 1985. 19.95 (ISBN 0-394-53320-8). Pantheon.

--Restitution: The Land Claim Cases of the Mashpee, Passamaquoddy, & Penobscot Indians of New England. (Illus.). 160p. 1985. 18.95x (ISBN 0-939359-69-3). NE U Pr.

Brodey, Jean L. Mid-Life Careers. LC 82-24478. 248p. 1983. 12.95 (ISBN 0-664-27003-4, A Bridgebooks Publication). Westminster.

Brodey, Warren. Earthchild: Glories of the Asphyxiated Spectrum. (Social Change Ser.). 166p. 1974. 37.25 (ISBN 0-677-04300-7). Gordon.

Brodhead, Frank, jt. auth. see Herman, Edward S.

Brodhead, John R., et al, eds. Documents Relative to the Colonial History of the State of New York, 15 Vols. Repr. of 1887 ed. Set. 1275.00 (ISBN 0-404-19516-4); 85.00 ea. AMS Pr.

Brodhead, Michael J. Persevering Populist: The Life of Frank Doster. LC 69-20037. xi, 196p. 1969. 5.00 (ISBN 0-87417-024-9). U of Nev Pr.

Brodhead, Michael J., jt. auth. see Cutright, Paul R.

Brodhead, Richard. Faulkner: A Collection of Critical Essays. 218p. 1983. 12.95 (ISBN 0-13-308288-1); pap. 5.95 (ISBN 0-13-308270-9). P-H.

Brodhead, Richard H. Hawthorne, Melville & the Novel. LC 75-5071. (Midway Reprint Ser.). 1982. 8.00X (ISBN 0-226-07524-9). U of Chicago Pr.

Brodie, B. B., ed. see Conference on Bioavailability of Drugs, Washington, D.C., Nov. 1971.

Brodie, B. B., et al, eds. see International Workshop on Ergot Alkaloids, Rome, Dec. 6-7, 1976.

Brodie, Benjamin. Psychological Inquiries: A Series of Essays Intended to Illustrate the Mutual Relations of the Physical Organization & the Mental Faculties. Bd. with On Animal Electricity. DuBois-Reymond, E. (Contributions to the History of Psychology Ser., Vol. VI, Pt. E). 1983. Repr. of 1854 ed. 30.00 (ISBN 0-89093-325-1). U Pubns Amer.

Brodie, Bernard. Escalation & the Nuclear Option. LC 66-23765. pap. 39.80 (ISBN 0-317-08162-4, 2000886). Bks Demand UMI.

--A Guide to Naval Strategy. LC 77-22392. (Illus.). 1977. Repr. of 1958 ed. lib. bdg. 24.75x (ISBN 0-8371-9735-X, BRGN). Greenwood.

--Sea Power in the Machine Age. LC 69-13840. Repr. of 1943 ed. lib. bdg. 24.75x (ISBN 0-8371-1445-4, BRSP). Greenwood.

--Strategy in the Missile Age. (Rand Corporation Research Studies). 1959. pap. 12.95 (ISBN 0-691-01852-9). Princeton U Pr.

--War & Politics. 514p. 1974. write for info. (ISBN 0-02-315020-3); pap. 7.75 (ISBN 0-685-28575-8). Macmillan.

Brodie, Bernard & Brodie, Fawn M. From Crossbow to H-Bomb. rev. enl. ed. LC 72-90408. (Midland Bks.: No. 161). (Illus.). 320p. 1973. 20.00 (ISBN 0-253-32490-4); pap. 8.95 (ISBN 0-253-20161-6). Ind U Pr.

Brodie, Bernard, ed. Absolute Weapon: Atomic Power & World Order. LC 77-167314. (Essay Index Reprint Ser.). Repr. of 1946 ed. 16.00 (ISBN 0-8369-2754-0). Ayer Co Pubs.

Brodie, Bernard & Intriligator, Michael D., eds. National Security & International Stability. LC 82-18913. 432p. 1983. text ed. 35.00 (ISBN 0-89946-172-7). Oelgeschlager.

Brodie, David A. & Thornhill, John J. Microcomputing in Sport & Physical Education. (Illus.). 160p. 1984. 16.95 (ISBN 0-86019-106-0, Pub. by Lepus England). Sterling.

Brodie, Donald W. & Williams, Peg A. School Contract Language. 412p. 1983. 35.00 (ISBN 0-409-24962-9). Butterworth Legal Pubs.

--School Grievance Arbitration: What the Arbitrators Are Doing. 317p. 1982. Incl. pocket supplement. 35.00 (ISBN 0-409-24955-6). Butterworth Legal Pubs.

Brodie, Earl D. When Your Name Is on the Door: The Independent Businessowner's Guide to Survival, Profits & Happiness. LC 80-66756. 225p. 1981. 24.95 (ISBN 0-916728-45-5). Bks in Focus.

Brodie, Edmund, jt. auth. see Smith, Hobart M.

Brodie, Edmund D., Jr., jt. auth. see Nussbaum, Ronald A.

Brodie, Fawn. Thaddeus Stevens, Scourge of the South. (Illus.). 1966. pap. 7.95x (ISBN 0-393-00331-0, Norton Lib). Norton.

Brodie, Fawn M. The Devil Drives: A Life of Sir Richard Burton. (Illus.). 408p. 1984. pap. 9.95 (ISBN 0-393-30166-4). Norton.

--No Man Knows My History: The Life of Joseph Smith. (Illus.). 1971. 19.95 (ISBN 0-394-46967-4). Knopf.

--Richard Nixon: The Shaping of His Character. (Illus.). 1981. 18.95 (ISBN 0-393-01467-3). Norton.

--Richard Nixon: The Shaping of His Character. 576p. 1983. pap. 8.95 (ISBN 0-674-76880-9). Harvard U Pr.

--Thaddeus Stevens, Scourge of the South. (Illus.). 17.25 (ISBN 0-8446-0329-5). Peter Smith.

--Thomas Jefferson: An Intimate History. (Illus.). 800p. 1974. 24.95 (ISBN 0-393-07480-3). Norton.

Brodie, Fawn M., jt. auth. see Brodie, Bernard.

Brodie, H. J. The Bird's Nest Fungi. LC 75-18476. 1975. 25.00x (ISBN 0-8020-5307-6). U of Toronto Pr.

Brodie, H. Keith, jt. auth. see Kolb, Lawrence C.

Brodie, H. Keith, jt. ed. see Hamburg, David A.

Brodie, Henry, et al. South Asia in the World Today. Talbot, Phillips, ed. LC 78-161774. (BCL Ser. I). Repr. of 1950 ed. 16.00 (ISBN 0-404-09042-7). AMS Pr.

Brodie, Ivor & Muray, Julius J. The Physics of Microfabrication. LC 82-3835. 522p. 1982. text ed. 55.00x (ISBN 0-306-40863-5, Plenum Pr). Plenum Pub.

Brodie, Jim, jt. auth. see Plum, Thomas.

Brodie, John & Houston, James D. Open Field. (A San Francisco Ser.). 1974. 7.95 (ISBN 0-395-19882-8). HM.

Brodie, Juliet. Grassland Studies. (Practical Ecology Ser.). (Illus.). 88p. 1985. pap. text ed. 9.95x (ISBN 0-04-574020-8). Allen Unwin.

Brodie, K. Mathematical Methods in Computer Graphics & Design. LC 79-50302. 1980. 33.00 (ISBN 0-12-134880-6). Acad Pr.

Brodie, Keith H., jt. ed. see Arieti, Silvano H.

Brodie, Keith H., jt. ed. see Cavenar, Jesse O.

Brodie, Keith H., jt. ed. see Cavenar, Jesse O., Jr.

Brodie, L. Starting FORTH. 1984. 17.95 (ISBN 0-317-06051-1). Micro Works.

Brodie, Leo. Thinking FORTH: A Language & Philosophy for Solving Problems. (Illus.). 224p. 1984. 22.95 (ISBN 0-13-917576-8); pap. 15.95 (ISBN 0-13-917568-7). P-H.

Brodie, Leo, jt. auth. see Forth, Inc. Staff.

Brodie, M. L., jt. ed. see Schmidt, J. W.

Brodie, M. L., et al, eds. On Conceptual Modelling: Perspectives from Artificial Intelligence, Databases & Programming Languages. LC 83-10552. (Topics in Information Sciences Ser.). (Illus.). 510p. 1984. 29.50 (ISBN 0-387-90842-0). Springer-Verlag.

Brodie, Marilyn. An Essential Love Affair. 160p. 1983. pap. 5.95 (ISBN 0-914187-00-7). Bodhi.

Brodie, Peter R. Dictionary of Shipping & Shipbroking Terms: French-English, English-French. 1980. 38.00 (ISBN 0-904093-82-4). Lloyds London Pr.

Brodie, Regis. The Energy-Efficient Potter: How to Save Money for Building Your Own Fuel-Efficient Kiln & Firing It Economically. (Illus.). 208p. (Orig.). 1982. pap. 12.95 (ISBN 0-8230-1614-5). Watson-Guptill.

Brodie, Thomas G. Bombs & Bombings: A Handbook to Detection, Disposal & Investigation for Police & Fire Departments. (Illus.). 200p. 1980. photycopy ed. 24.75x (ISBN 0-398-02245-3). C C Thomas.

Brodie, Walter. Pitcairn's Island, & the Islanders, in 1850. 3rd ed. LC 75-3441. Repr. of 1851 ed. 21.50 (ISBN 0-404-14445-4). AMS Pr.

Brodin. Presences Contemporaines: Auteurs Francais du XXe Siecle. 9.95 (ISBN 0-685-37147-6). French & Eur.

Brodin, Dorothy. Marcel Ayme. LC 68-54455. (Columbia Essays on Modern Writers Ser.: No. 38). 48p. (Orig.). 1968. pap. 2.50 (ISBN 0-231-03128-9). Columbia U Pr.

Brodin, Dorothy, jt. auth. see Brodin, Pierre.

Brodin, Dorothy see Levy, Harold L.

Brodin, Pierre & Brodin, Dorothy. Presence Contemporaines: Auteurs Franeais du Vingtieme Siecle. 376p. (Fr.). 1972. pap. 12.95 (ISBN 0-686-46611-X). French & Eur.

Brodine, Karen. Illegal Assembly. 1980. pap. 3.00 (ISBN 0-914610-17-1). Hanging Loose.

--Slow Juggling. 48p. (Orig.). 1975. pap. 3.00 (ISBN 0-917658-02-7). BPW & P.

Broding, G. Agnus Castus: A Middle English Herbal Reconstructed from Various Manuscripts. (Essays & Studies on English Language & Literature: Vol. 6). pap. 28.00 (ISBN 0-317-16716-2). Kraus Repr.

Brodinsky, Ben. Defining the Basics of American Education. LC 77-84044. (Fastback Ser.: No. 95). 1977. pap. 0.75 (ISBN 0-87367-095-7). Phi Delta Kappa.

--How a School Board Operates. LC 76-57301. (Fastback Ser.: No. 88). 1977. pap. 0.75 (ISBN 0-87367-088-4). Phi Delta Kappa.

Brodinsky, Ben, ed. see Pine, Patricia.

Brodish, H., ed. see International Symposium on Brain-Pituitary-Adrenal Interrelationships, Cincinnati, Ohio, June 1973.

Brodkey, Harold. Women & Angels. (The Author's Workshop Ser.). 157p. 1985. boxed 30.00 (ISBN 0-8276-0251-0). Jewish Pubns.

Brodkey, Robert S., ed. see Symposium at Pittsburgh, Penn., June, 1974.

Brodkin, Sylvia Z. & Pearson, Elizabeth J., eds. Science Fiction. rev. ed. (Special Literature Ser.). 1979. pap. text ed. 6.78 (ISBN 0-88343-164-5); tchrs'. manual 2.84 (ISBN 0-88343-165-3). McDougal-Littell.

Brodman, Estelle. The Development of Medical Bibliography. 226p. 1981. Repr. of 1954 ed. 8.25 (ISBN 0-912176-00-8). Med Lib Assn.

Brodnick, Max. Fun & Games. (Illus.). 1976. pap. 1.25 (LB394, Leisure Bks). Dorchester Pub Co.

--Indoor Sports. 1976. pap. 1.25 (ISBN 0-685-73455-2, LB396, Leisure Bks). Dorchester Pub Co.

--The International Joke Book, No. 2. 1976. pap. 1.25 (ISBN 0-685-69150-0, LB349ZK, Leisure Bks). Dorchester Pub Co.

--International Joke Book, No. 4. 1980. pap. 1.75 (ISBN 0-8439-0794-0, Leisure Bks). Dorchester Pub Co.

--The Sex Joke Book. (Illus., Orig.). 1975. pap. 1.25 (ISBN 0-685-52937-1, LB264ZK, Leisure Bks). Dorchester Pub Co.

Brodoff, Bernard N. & Bleicher, Sheldon. Diabetes Mellitus & Obesity. (Illus.). 876p. 1982. lib. bdg. 69.00 (ISBN 0-683-01071-9). Williams & Wilkins.

Brodoff, Maureen, jt. ed. see Patterson, Andrew M.

Brodribb, C. W. Pope: His Friends & His Poetry. LC 73-4440. 1973. lib. bdg. 10.00 (ISBN 0-8414-1555-2). Folcroft.

Brodrick, Alan H. Early Man: A Survey of Human Origins. 1976. lib. bdg. 59.95 (ISBN 0-8490-1741-6). Gordon Pr.

--Father of Prehistory: The Abbe Henri Breuil. LC 73-2342. (Illus.). 306p. 1973. Repr. of 1963 ed. lib. bdg. 17.75x (ISBN 0-8371-6840-6, BRFP). Greenwood.

--Little China: The Annamese Lands. LC 74-179173. (South & Southeast Asia Studies Ser.). Repr. of 1942 ed. 17.50 (ISBN 0-404-54803-2). AMS Pr.

--Mirage of Africa. LC 78-139. (Illus.). 1979. Repr. of 1953 ed. lib. bdg. 23.25x (ISBN 0-8371-5186-4, BMA&, Pub. by Negro U Pr). Greenwood.

Brodrick, G. C. History of England from Addington's Administration to the Close of William Fourth's Reign, 1801-1837: Political History of England. Repr. of 1906 ed. 35.00 (ISBN 0-527-00856-7). Kraus Repr.

Brodrick, George C. English Land & English Landlords. LC 67-29495. Repr. of 1881 ed. 37.50x (ISBN 0-678-00360-2). Kelley.

Brodrick, George C. & Fotheringham, John K. History of England from Addington's Administration to the Close of William Fourth's Reign. LC 71-5624. (Political History of England Ser.). Repr. of 1906 ed. 22.50 (ISBN 0-404-50781-6). AMS Pr.

Brodrick, James. Origin of the Jesuits. LC 70-138604. 1971. Repr. of 1940 ed. lib. bdg. 19.75x (ISBN 0-8371-5523-1, BROJ). Greenwood.

--The Origin of the Jesuits. LC 83-45590. Date not set. Repr. of 1940 ed. 33.50 (ISBN 0-404-19883-X). AMS Pr.

--Procession of Saints. LC 72-5436. (Biography Index Reprint Ser). 1972. Repr. of 1949 ed. 20.50 (ISBN 0-8369-8134-0). Ayer Co Pubs.

--Saint Peter Canisius. (Request Reprint). (Illus.). 1962. 19.95 (ISBN 0-8294-0008-7). Loyola.

--Saint Peter Canisius, S. J., 1521-1597. LC 83-45589. Date not set. Repr. of 1935 ed. 65.00 (ISBN 0-404-19882-1). AMS Pr.

Brodrogligeti, A. J., jt. ed. see Decsy, Gyula.

Brodshaug, Melvin. Buildings & Equipment for Home Economics in Secondary Schools. LC 75-176592. (Columbia University. Teachers College. Contributions to Education: No. 502). Repr. of 1932 ed. 22.50 (ISBN 0-404-55502-0). AMS Pr.

Brodskaya, Minna, tr. see Kamshilov, M. M.

Brodskaya, N. Henri Rousseau. 1983. pap. 7.95 (ISBN 0-8285-2637-0, Pub. by Aurora Pubs USSR). Imported Pubns.

Brodskii, Iosif. Uraniia. 150p. (Rus.). 1985. 19.50 (ISBN 0-88233-840-4). Ardis Pubs.

Brodskii, M. S. Triangular & Jordan Representations of Linear Operators. LC 74-162998. (Translations of Mathematical Monographs: Vol. 32). 1972. 34.00 (ISBN 0-8218-1582-2, MMONO-32). Am Math.

Brodskii, M. S., et al. Nine Papers on Number Theory & Operator Theory. LC 51-5559. (Translations Ser.: No. 2, Vol. 13). 346p. 1980. pap. 46.00 (ISBN 0-8218-1713-2, TRANS 2-13). Am Math.

--Nine Papers on Partial Differential Equations & Functional Analysis. LC 51-5559. (Translations Ser.: No. 2, Vol. 65). 1967. 37.00 (ISBN 0-8218-1765-5, TRANS 2-65). Am Math.

--Thirteen Papers on Functional Analysis & Partial Differential Equations. LC 51-5559. (Translations Ser.: No. 2, Vol. 47). 1965. 25.00 (ISBN 0-8218-1747-7, TRANS 2-47). Am Math.

Brodsky & Rothblatt. The Holistic Diet & Cookbook. 1979. 4.95x (ISBN 0-686-40231-6). Cancer Control Soc.

Brodsky, Allen. Handbook of Radiation Measurement & Protection, CRC: Selection A-General Scientific & Engineering Information, 2 vols. Vol. 1, 1979 720 Pgs. 86.50 (ISBN 0-8493-3756-9); Vol. 2, Oct 1982, 736 Pgs. 94.00 (ISBN 0-8493-3757-7). CRC Pr.

Brodsky, Allen & Klement, eds. Handbook of Radiation Measurement & Protection: Section B, Vol. III. 496p. 1982. 74.50 (ISBN 0-8493-3768-2). CRC Pr.

Brodsky, Allyn, ed. see Shapiro, Bob & Mabe, Edouard.

Brodsky, Anna, tr. see Dolson, Gina.

Brodsky, Annette M., ed. The Female Offender. LC 75-27014. (Sage Contemporary Social Science Issues Ser.: No. 19). pap. 27.00 (ISBN 0-317-08974-9, 2021876). Bks Demand UMI.

Brodsky, Annette M. & Hare-Mustin, Rachel, eds. Women & Psychotherapy. LC 80-14842. 428p. 1980. 25.00 (ISBN 0-89862-605-6, 2605). Guilford Pr.

Brodsky, Archie, jt. auth. see Edelwich, Jerry.

Brodsky, Archie, jt. auth. see Peele, Stanton.

Brodsky, B. The Treasures from Moscow Museums. 374p. 1980. 85.00x (ISBN 0-686-97673-8, Pub. by Collet's). State Mutual Bk.

Brodsky, Bernard. Anti-Haiku. 48p. 1985. pap. 4.95 (ISBN 0-931896-05-3). Cove View.

--The Will to Go on. 64p. (Orig.). 1981. pap. 3.75 (ISBN 0-931896-01-0). Cove View.

Brodsky, Beverley. Secret Places. LC 77-16391. (Illus.). (gr. 1-3). 1979. lib. bdg. 9.89 (ISBN 0-397-31811-1). Lipp Jr Bks.

Brodsky, Bob & Treadway, Toni. Super Eight in the Video Age. 2nd ed. (Illus.). 124p. (Orig.). 1983. pap. text ed. 14.95 (ISBN 0-9610914-2-8). B&T.

--El Super 8 en La Era del Video. (Illus.). 100p. (Span.). 1983. pap. text ed. 10.00 (ISBN 0-9610914-1-X). B&T.

--Super 8 in the Video Age. 2nd ed. (Illus.). 123p. 1983. pap. text ed. 14.95 (ISBN 0-9610914-2-8). B&T.

Brodsky, Edward & Adamski, M. Patricia. Law of Corporate Officers & Directors: Rights, Duties, & Liabilities. LC 84-14310. 738p. 1984. 85.00. Callaghan.

Brodsky, Garry, et al, eds. Contemporary Readings in Social & Political Ethics. LC 84-42957. 450p. (Orig.). 1984. pap. text ed. 15.95 (ISBN 0-87975-265-3). Prometheus Bks.

Brodsky, Isadore, et al, eds. Cancer Chemotherapy III: Forty-Sixth Hahnemann Symposium. 496p. 1978. 72.50 (ISBN 0-8089-1086-8, 790673). Grune.

Brodsky, Jay B., jt. ed. see Baden, Jeffrey M.

Brodsky, Jean, ed. see Pilon, Daniel H. & Bergquist, William H.

Brodsky, Joseph. Less Than One. 280p. 1984. 18.95 (ISBN 0-374-18503-4). FS&G.

--Mramor. 62p. (Rus.). 1984. 14.00 (ISBN 0-88233-901-X). Ardis Pubs.

--A Part of Speech. Hecht, Anthony, et al, trs. from Rus. LC 80-613. 160p. 1980. 12.95 (ISBN 0-374-22987-2); pap. 7.95 (ISBN 0-374-51633-2). FS&G.

--Rimskie Elegii. LC 82-60519. 20p. (Rus.). 1982. pap. 5.00 (ISBN 0-89830-062-2). Russica Pubs.

--Roman Elegies. bilingual ed. 32p. pap. 9.95 (ISBN 0-374-25149-5). FS&G.

Brodsky, Joseph & Karpowicz, Tymoteusz. Three Slavic Poets. pap. 3.00 (ISBN 0-318-01988-4). Elpenor.

Brodsky, K. A. Mountain Torrent of the Tien Shan: An Ecology-Faunistic Essay. (Monographiae Biologicae: No. 39). (Illus.). 311p. 1980. lib. bdg. 79.00 (ISBN 90-6193-091-X, Pub. by Junk Pubs Netherlands). Kluwer Academic.

Brodsky, Louis D., jt. auth. see Hamblin, Robert W.

Brodsky, Louis D. & Hamblin, Robert W., eds. Faulkner: A Comprehensive Guide to the Brodsky Collection, Vol. 1: The Bibliography. LC 82-6966. 1983. 35.00x (ISBN 0-87805-240-2). U Pr of Miss.

--Faulkner: A Comprehensive Guide to the Brodsky Collection, Vol. 2: The Letters. LC 82-6966. (Center for the Study of Southern Culture Ser.). (Illus.). 334p. 1984. 35.00x (ISBN 0-87805-189-9); pap. 14.95 (ISBN 0-87805-215-1). U Pr of Miss.

Brodsky, Louis D., ed. see Faulkner, William.

Brodsky, M., et al, eds. see AIP Conference Proceedings, No. 20 Yorktown Heights.

Brodsky, M. H., ed. Amorphous Semiconductors. LC 79-16148. (Topics in Applied Physics: Vol. 36). (Illus.). 1979. 59.00 (ISBN 0-387-09496-2). Springer-Verlag.

Brodsky, M. S., et al. Nine Papers in Analysis. LC 51-5559. (Translations Ser.: No. 2, Vol. 103). 208p. 1974. 39.00 (TRANS 2-103). Am Math.

Brodsky, Michael. Circuits. 128p. 1983. 8.95 (ISBN 0-941062-13-9); pap. 5.95 (ISBN 0-941062-12-0); Edition) 85.00(Ltd. (ISBN 0-941062-14-7). Guignol Bks.

--Detour. 360p. 1984. pap. 8.95 (ISBN 0-941062-18-X). Guignol Bks.

--Project & Other Short Pieces by Michael Brodsky. (Illus.). 224p. 1982. 11.95 (ISBN 0-941062-02-3); pap. 7.95 (ISBN 0-941062-03-1); signed ed. 85.00 (ISBN 0-941062-04-X). Guignol Bks.

--Wedding Feast. (Orig.). 1984. 14.95 (ISBN 0-941062-20-1); pap. 8.95 (ISBN 0-941062-19-8). Guignol Bks.

Brodsky, Michael, et al. The Holistic Diet & Cookbook. LC 79-9113. 135p. 1979. pap. 5.70 (ISBN 0-318-14468-9). Inst Rheumatic.

Brodsky, Patricia P. Russia in the Works of Rainer Maria Rilke. LC 84-75570. 264p. 1984. 26.00 (ISBN 0-8143-1757-X). Wayne St U Pr.

Brodsky, Stanley L. Psychologists in the Criminal Justice System. LC 72-87472. 189p. 1973. pap. 7.95x (ISBN 0-252-00432-9). U of Ill Pr.

Brodsky, Stanley L. & Smitherman, O'Neal. Handbook of Scales for Research in Crime & Delinquency. (Perspectives in Law & Psychology Ser.: Vol. 5). 600p. 1982. text ed. 42.50x (ISBN 0-306-40792-2, Plenum Pr). Plenum Pub.

Brodsky, Stanley L., jt. ed. see Fischer, Constance T.

Brodsky, V. Y. & Uryvaeva, I. V. Genome Multiplication in Growth & Development: Biology of Polyploid & Polytene Cells. (Developmental & Cell Biology Ser.: No. 15). (Illus.). 312p. 1985. 79.50 (ISBN 0-521-25323-3). Cambridge U Pr.

Brodsky, William A., ed. Anion & Proton Transport, Vol. 341. LC 80-15917. (Annals of the New York Academy of Sciences). 570p. 1980. 109.00x (ISBN 0-89766-070-6); pap. 107.00x (ISBN 0-89766-071-4). NY Acad Sci.

Brodsly, David. L. A. Freeway: An Appreciative Essay. LC 80-29620. (Illus.). 224p. 1981. 19.95 (ISBN 0-520-04068-6). U of Cal Pr.

--L. A. Freeway: An Appreciative Essay. (Illus.). 188p. 1983. pap. 10.95 (ISBN 0-520-04546-7, CAL 535). U of Cal Pr.

Brodwer. Andre Breton, Arbiter of Surrealism. 21.50 (ISBN 0-685-37242-1). French & Eur.

Brody, A., jt. ed. see Carter, A.

Brody, Alvan & Brody, Betty. The Legal Rights of Nonsmokers. pap. 1.75 (ISBN 0-380-01771-7, 35048). Avon.

Brody, Andrew. Slowdown: Global Economic Maladies. 1985. 17.95 (ISBN 0-8039-2352-X). Sage.

Brody, Arnold G., jt. auth. see Stuhlman, Daniel D.

Brody, Baruch, ed. Readings in the Philosophy of Religion: An Analytic Approach. LC 73-20485. 608p. 1974. text ed. 33.95 (ISBN 0-13-759340-6). P-H.

Brody, Baruch A. Beginning Philosophy. 1977. pap. text ed. 18.95 (ISBN 0-13-073882-4). P-H.

--Ethics & Its Applications. 200p. 1983. pap. text ed. 10.95 (ISBN 0-15-524510-4, HC). HarBraceJ.

--Identity & Essence. LC 80-7511. 1980. 22.00 (ISBN 0-691-07256-6); pap. 6.95 (ISBN 0-691-02013-2). Princeton U Pr.

Brody, Baruch A. & Englehardt, H. Tristram. Mental Illness: Law & Public Policy. (Philosophy & Medicine Ser.: No. 5). 276p. 1980. lib. bdg. 29.00 (ISBN 0-686-27528-4, Pub. by Reidel Holland). Kluwer Academic.

Brody, Betty, jt. auth. see Brody, Alvan.

Brody, Boruch. Readings in the Philosophy of Science. LC 71-98091. (Philosophy Ser). 1970. text ed. 33.95 (ISBN 0-13-760702-4). P-H.

Brody, Claire, ed. Women Therapists Working with Women: New Theory & Process of Feminist Therapy. (Focus on Women: Vol. 7). 192p. 1984. text ed. 20.95 (ISBN 0-8261-4550-7). Springer Pub.

Brody, David. The American Labor Movement. 168p. 1985. pap. 6.75 (ISBN 0-8191-4667-6). U Pr of Amer.

--Bluegrass Masters: Kenny Baker Fiddle. 1979. pap. 6.95 (ISBN 0-8256-0224-6, Oak). Music Sales.

--Butcher Workmen: A Study of Unionization. LC 64-21240. (Wertheim Publications in Industrial Relations Ser). 1964. 25.00x (ISBN 0-674-08925-1). Harvard U Pr.

--Fiddler's Fake Book. 1983. pap. 16.95 (ISBN 0-8256-0238-6, Pub. by Oak). Music Sales.

--Labor in Crisis: The Steel Strike of 1919. LC 82-11746. (Critical Periods of History Ser.). 208p. 1982. Repr. lib. bdg. 25.00x (ISBN 0-313-23499-X, BROL). Greenwood.

--Mandolin Picker's Fake Book. 1984. 16.95 (ISBN 0-8256-0239-4, Oak). Music Sales.

--Steelworkers in America: The Non-Union Era. 1970. pap. 6.50xi (ISBN 0-06-131485-4, TB1485, Torch). Har-Row.

--Steelworkers in America: The Non-Union Era. LC 76-83855. (Illus.). 1970. Repr. of 1960 ed. 13.00x (ISBN 0-8462-1406-7). Russell.

--Workers in Industrial America: Essays on the 20th Century Struggle. 1980. pap. text ed. 7.95x (ISBN 0-19-502491-5). Oxford U Pr.

Brody, David E. The American Legal System. 1978. text ed. 24.95 (ISBN 0-669-01439-7); instr's manual 1.95 (ISBN 0-669-01840-6). Heath.

Brody, Elaine. Long-Term Care of Older People: A Practical Guide. LC 77-5944. 402p. 1977. text ed. 34.95 (ISBN 0-87705-274-3). Human Sci Pr.

--Mental & Physical Health Practices of Older People: A Guide for Health Professionals. 288p. 1985. text ed. 25.95 (ISBN 0-8261-4870-0). Springer Pub.

Brody, Elaine & Fowkes, Robert A. The German Lied & Its Poetry. LC 76-124520. 1971. 35.00x (ISBN 0-8147-0958-3). NYU Pr.

Brody, Elizabeth G. Genetic Basis at Spontaneous Activity in the Albino Rat. (Comparative Psychology Monographs). 1942. pap. 5.00 (ISBN 0-527-24924-6). Kraus Repr.

Brody, Erness B. & Brody, Nathan, eds. Intelligence: Nature, Determinants, & Consequences. 1976. 35.00 (ISBN 0-12-134250-6). Acad Pr.

Brody, Ervin C. Demetrius Legend & Its Literary Treatment in the Age of the Baroque. LC 73-141869. 323p. 1972. 28.50 (ISBN 0-8386-7969-2). Fairleigh Dickinson.

Brody, Eugene B. The Lost Ones: Social Forces & Mental Illness in Rio de Janeiro. LC 72-8794. 808p. 1973. text ed. 40.00 (ISBN 0-8236-3050-1). Intl Univs Pr.

--Sex, Contraception, & Motherhood in Jamaica. LC 81-4133. (Commonwealth Fund Ser.). (Illus.). 232p. 1981. text ed. 20.00x (ISBN 0-674-80277-2). Harvard U Pr.

Brody, Eugene B. & Redlich, Fredrick C., eds. Psychotherapy with Schizophrenics. (Monograph Series on Schizophrenia: No. 3). 246p. (Orig.). 1964. text ed. 25.00 (ISBN 0-8236-5420-6). Intl Univs Pr.

Brody, H., jt. ed. see Apelian, D.

Brody, Harry. As Once to Birth I Went, Now I Am Taken Back. 1981. 2.00 (ISBN 0-936814-07-1). New Collage.

Brody, Harvey. The Book of Low Fire Ceramics. LC 79-944. (Illus.). 176p. (Orig.). 1980. 18.95 (ISBN 0-03-042116-0); pap. 11.95 (ISBN 0-03-042111-X). HR&W.

Brody, Howard. Ethical Decisions in Medicine. 2nd ed. 1981. pap. text ed. 19.95 (ISBN 0-316-10899-5). Little.

--Placebos & the Philosophy of Medicine: Clinical, Conceptual, & Ethical Issues. LC 79-18481. 1980. lib. bdg. 15.00x (ISBN 0-226-07531-1). U of Chicago Pr.

Brody, Hugh. Maps & Dreams. (Pantheon Village Ser.). (Illus.). 1982. 16.00 (ISBN 0-394-52104-8); pap. 7.95 (ISBN 0-394-74871-9). Pantheon.

Brody, Hugh & Ignatieff, Michael. Nineteen Nineteen. LC 85-10232. 96p. (Orig.). 1985. pap. 7.95 (ISBN 0-571-13714-8). Faber & Faber.

Brody, Ilene, jt. ed. see Vardin, Patricia.

Brody, Irwin A., jt. auth. see Wilkins, Robert H.

Brody, J. A., et al see Arber, W., et al.

Brody, J. J. Mimbres Painted Pottery. LC 76-57542. (Southwest Indian Arts Ser). (Illus.). 253p. 1977. 40.00x (ISBN 0-8263-0452-4). U of NM Pr.

Brody, J. J. & Scott, Catherine J. Mimbres Pottery: Ancient Art of the American Southwest. LC 83-10812. (Illus.). 132p. 1983. 35.00 (ISBN 0-933920-46-6); pap. 15.00 for museum distribution only (ISBN 0-933920-47-4). Hudson Hills.

Brody, J. J., jt. auth. see Wagner, Sallie.

Brody, Jane. Jane Brody's Nutrition Book. 1982. pap. 9.95 (ISBN 0-553-34121-9). Bantam.

--Jane Brody's Nutrition Book: A Lifetime Guide to Good Eating for Better Health & Weight Control by the Personal Health Columnist for the New York Times. LC 80-25117. (Illus.). 576p. 1981. 12.98 (ISBN 0-393-01429-0). Norton.

--Jane Brody's The New York Times Guide to Personal Health. 736p. 1982. 19.95 (ISBN 0-686-95972-8). Times Bks.

--Jane Brody's the New York Times Guide to Personal Health. 752p. 1983. pap. 12.95 (ISBN 0-380-64121-6, 64121). Avon.

Brody, Jane, jt. auth. see Adams, W. Royce.

Brody, Jane E. Jane Brody's Good Food Book: Living the High Carbohydrate Way. 1985. 19.95 (ISBN 0-393-02210-2). Norton.

Brody, Jean. Gideon's House. 208p. 1984. 13.95 (ISBN 0-399-12937-5, Putnam). Putnam Pub Group.

Brody, Jean P. Braille Me. 64p. (Orig.). 1984. pap. 5.95 (ISBN 0-941374-02-5). Grapetree Prods.

Brody, Jerome. The Grand Central Oyster Bar & Restaurant Seafood Cookbook: Compiled & Edited from 64 Years of Recipes & Recollections. 1977. 12.95 (ISBN 0-517-52829-0). Crown.

Brody, Jerome, illus. Grand Central Oyster Bar & Restaurant Seafood Cookbook. 1983. pap. 7.95 (ISBN 0-517-54907-7). Crown.

Brody, Jerome S. & Snider, Gordon, eds. Current Topics in the Management of Respiratory Diseases, Vol. 1. (Illus.). 182p. 1981. pap. text ed. 22.00 (ISBN 0-443-08104-2). Churchill.

--Current Topics in the Management of Respiratory Diseases, Vol. 2. (Illus.). 294p. 1985. pap. text ed. 27.00 (ISBN 0-443-08103-4). Churchill.

Brody, Joel, tr. see Lubich, Gino & Lazzarin, Piero.

Brody, Jules. Du Style a la Pensee: Trois Etudes Sur les Caracteres de la Bruyere. LC 80-66328. (French Forum Monographs: No. 20). 88p. (Orig., Fr.). 1980. pap. 9.50x (ISBN 0-917058-19-4). French Forum.

--Lectures de Montaigne. LC 82-82428. (French Forum Monographs: No. 39). 181p. (Orig.). 1982. pap. 15.00x (ISBN 0-917058-38-0). French Forum.

Brody, Jules, jt. auth. see Spitzer, Leo.

Brody, Jules, jt. ed. see Cabeen, David C.

Brody, Lawrence & Mulligan, Michael D. Practical Probate in Missouri. LC 85-127702. (Illus.). Date not set. price not set. Natl Busn Inst.

Brody, Linda, ed. see Hyman Blumberg Symposium on Research in Early Childhood Education, 1976.

Brody, Lora A. Growing Up on the Chocolate Diet: A Memoir with Recipes. 320p. 1985. 16.45i (ISBN 0-316-10897-9). Little.

Brody, Marcia, et al. Bioenergetics & Metabolism of Green Algae, 2 vols. LC 74-515. 1974. Vol. 1. text ed. 21.50x (ISBN 0-8422-7200-3); Vol. 2. text ed. 21.50x (ISBN 0-8422-7201-1). Irvington.

Brody, Nathan. Personality: Research & Theory. 1972. 41.50 (ISBN 0-12-134850-4). Acad Pr.

Brody, Nathan, ed. Motivation. LC 82-22654. 1983. 27.50 (ISBN 0-12-134840-7). Acad Pr.

Brody, Nathan, jt. ed. see Brody, Erness B.

Brody, Ralph. Problem Solving: Concepts & Methods for Community Organizations. LC 81-7221. 240p. 1982. 29.95x (ISBN 0-89885-078-9); pap. 14.95x (ISBN 0-89885-079-7). Human Sci Pr.

Brody, Robert & Rossman, Charles, eds. Carlos Fuentes: A Critical View. (Texas Pan American Ser.). 229p. 1982. text ed. 22.50x (ISBN 0-292-71077-1). U of Tex Pr.

Brody, Saul N. & Schechter, Harold, eds. City University of New York, CUNY English Forum, Vol. 1. LC 83-45285. 1984. 37.50 (ISBN 0-404-62451-0). AMS Pr.

Brody, Stanley J. & Persily, Nancy, eds. Hospitals & the Aged: The New Old Market. LC 83-19754. 277p. 1983. 29.95 (ISBN 0-89443-898-0). Aspen Systems.

Brody, Stephen. Crime, Science & Morals. 300p. (Orig.). 1984. pap. 11.95x cancelled (ISBN 0-7102-0062-5). Routledge & Kegan.

Brody, Steve. How to Break Ninety Before You Reach It. 3rd ed. LC 80-10704. 1980. pap. 6.95 (ISBN 0-88427-040-8). North River.

Brody, Sylvia. Passivity: A Study of Its Development & Expression in Boys. LC 64-18623. 184p. 1964. text ed. 20.00 (ISBN 0-8236-4020-5). Intl Univs Pr.

--Patterns of Mothering: A Study of Maternal Influence During Infancy. LC 56-8839. 446p. (Orig.). 1970. text ed. 30.00 (ISBN 0-8236-4040-X). Intl Univs Pr.

Brody, Sylvia & Axelrad, Sidney. Anxiety & Ego Formation in Infancy. LC 74-141660. 1971. text ed. 22.50 (ISBN 0-8236-0390-3). Intl Univs Pr.

--Mothers, Fathers & Children. LC 77-14711. (Illus.). 669p. (Orig.). 1978. text ed. 45.00 (ISBN 0-8236-3462-0). Intl Univs Pr.

Brody, T. A. Symbol Manipulation Techniques for Physics. (Documents on Modern Physics Ser.). 104p. 1968. 44.25 (ISBN 0-677-01820-7). Gordon.

Brody, T. A. & Moshinsky, M. Tables of Transformation Brackets for Nuclear Shell-Model Calculations. 2nd ed. 250p. 1967. 69.50 (ISBN 0-677-01320-5). Gordon.

Brody, William R. Digital Radiography. (Illus.). 240p. 1984. text ed. 40.50 (ISBN 0-89004-242-X). Raven.

Brodzinski, Ignatius, jt. auth. see Greenwood, Richard.

Brodzinski, Konrad, tr. see Glowacki, Janusz.

Brodzinsky, David M., jt. auth. see Ambron, Sueann R.

Brodzinsky, David M., jt. ed. see Ashmore, Richard D.

Broe, Bert. Theatrical Makeup. (Illus.). 96p. 1985. 13.95 (ISBN 0-8253-0295-1). Beaufort Bks NY.

Broe, Mary L. Protean Poetic: The Poetry of Sylvia Plath. LC 79-3334. 256p. 1980. text ed. 20.00x (ISBN 0-8262-0291-8). U of Mo Pr.

Broecker, W. S. & Peng, T. H. Tracers in the Sea. (Illus.). 690p. 1982. text ed. 40.00 (ISBN 0-86542-310-5). Blackwell Sci.

Broecker, Wallace S. & Peng, Tsung-Hung. Tracers in the Sea. (Illus.). 690p. 1982. 35.00 (ISBN 0-686-40838-1). Lamont-Doherty.

Broeckhover, Egide van. A Friend to All Men. 5.95 (ISBN 0-317-06463-0). Dimension Bks.

Broeg, Bob. Bob Broeg's Redbirds. LC 81-50102. 224p. 1981. 16.95 (ISBN 0-933150-21-0). River City MO.

--Ol' Mizzou: A Story of Missouri Football. LC 74-82943. (College Sports Ser.). Orig. Title: Missouri Football. 1974. 9.95 (ISBN 0-87397-051-9). Strode.

Broeg, Bob, ed. Front Page: A Century of News & Sports. LC 82-8099. 320p. 1982. 24.95 (ISBN 0-933150-99-7). River City MO.

Broeg, Bob, ed. see Baker, William J. & Carroll, John M.

Broeg, R. & Ewbank, Weeb. Football Greats. (Illus.). 1977. pap. 4.95 (ISBN 0-8272-1007-8). CBP.

Broeg, Robert. The Pilot Light & the Gas House Gang. (Illus.). 176p. 1980. 6.95 (ISBN 0-8272-2927-5). CBP.

Broehl, Wayne G. John Deere's Company. LC 84-6023. (Illus.). 936p. 1984. 24.95 (ISBN 0-385-19664-4). Doubleday.

Broehl, Wayne G., Jr. Precision Valley: The Machine Tool Companies of Springfield, Vermont. LC 75-41748. (Companies & Men: Business Enterprises in America). (Illus.). 1976. Repr. of 1959 ed. 29.00x (ISBN 0-405-08065-4). Ayer Co Pubs.

--Trucks, Trouble & Triumph: The Norwalk Truck Line Company. LC 75-41749. (Companies & Men: Business Enterprises in America). (Illus.). 1976. Repr. of 1954 ed. 29.00x (ISBN 0-405-08066-2). Ayer Co Pubs.

--The Village Entrepreneur: Change Agents in India's Rural Development. LC 77-18880. 1978. 18.50x (ISBN 0-674-93915-8). Harvard U Pr.

Broehl, Wayne G., Jr. see Friedman, Leon.

Broek, C. M. & Webb, John W. A Geography of Mankind. 3rd ed. (Illus.). 1978. text ed. 40.95 (ISBN 0-07-008012-7). McGraw.

Broek, D. Elementary Engineering Fracture Mechanics. rev. ed. 450p. 1978. 60.00x (ISBN 90-286-0208-9); pap. 20.00x (ISBN 90-286-0218-6). Sijthoff & Noordhoff.

Broek, David. Elementary Engineering Fracture Mechanics. 1982. lib. bdg. 69.00 (ISBN 90-247-2580-1, Pub. by Martinus Nijhoff Netherlands); pap. 29.50 (ISBN 90-247-2656-5, Pub. by Martinus Nijhoff Netherlands). Kluwer Academic.

Broek, Jacobus ten see Ten Broek, Jacobus.

Broek, Jan O. Economic Development of the Netherlands Indies. LC 75-143554. (Illus.). 1971. Repr. of 1942 ed. 11.00x (ISBN 0-8462-1573-X). Russell.

Broek, P. Van den see Van den Broek, P., et al.

Broek, Silvere van den see Van den Broek, Silvere.

Broekel. Chocolate Chronicles. LC 84-51257. 168p. 1985. 13.95 (ISBN 0-87069-431-6). Wallace Homestead.

Broekel, Ray. Aquariums & Terrariums. LC 82-4428. (New True Bks.). (gr. k-4). 1982. 10.60 (ISBN 0-516-01660-1). Childrens.

--Baseball. LC 81-38480. (New True Bks.). (Illus.). 48p. (gr. k-4). 1982. PLB 10.60 (ISBN 0-516-01616-4); pap. 3.95 (ISBN 0-516-41616-2). Childrens.

--Dangerous Fish. LC 82-4464. (New True Bks.). (gr. k-4). 1982. 10.60 (ISBN 0-516-01635-0). Childrens.

--Fire Fighters. (The New True Books). (Illus.). 48p. (gr. k-4). 1981. PLB 10.60 (ISBN 0-516-01620-2); pap. 3.95 (ISBN 0-516-41620-0). Childrens.

--Football. LC 81-15484. (New True Bks.). (Illus.). 48p. (gr. k-4). 1982. PLB 10.60 (ISBN 0-516-01629-6); pap. 3.95 (ISBN 0-516-41629-4). Childrens.

--Gerbil Pets & Other Small Rodents. LC 82-23501. (New True Bks.). (Illus.). 48p. (gr. k-4). 1983. PLB 10.60 (ISBN 0-516-01679-2); pap. 3.95 (ISBN 0-516-41679-0). Childrens.

--Maps & Globes. LC 83-7509. (New True Bks.). (Illus.). 48p. (gr. k-4). 1983. PLB 10.60 (ISBN 0-516-01695-4); pap. 3.95 (ISBN 0-516-41695-2). Childrens.

--The Moustache Pickpocket. LC 79-52410. (Carolrhoda Mini-Mysteries Ser.). (Illus.). (gr. 1-4). 1980. PLB 4.95g (ISBN 0-87614-116-5). Carolrhoda Bks.

--The Mystery of the Funny Money. LC 79-52408. (Carolrhoda Mini-Mysteries Ser.). (Illus.). (gr. 1-4). 1980. PLB 4.95g (ISBN 0-87614-114-9). Carolrhoda Bks.

--The Mystery of the Stolen Base. LC 79-52405. (Carolrhoda Mini-Mysteries Ser.). (Illus.). (gr. 1-4). 1980. PLB 4.95g (ISBN 0-87614-111-4). Carolrhoda Bks.

--Police. LC 81-7693. (The New True Books). (Illus.). 48p. (gr. k-4). 1981. PLB 10.60 (ISBN 0-516-01643-1); pap. 3.95 (ISBN 0-516-41643-X). Childrens.

--The President Jackson Case. LC 79-52406. (Carolrhoda Mini-Mysteries Ser.). (Illus.). (gr. 1-4). 1980. PLB 4.95g (ISBN 0-87614-112-2). Carolrhoda Bks.

--The Shoelace Solution. LC 79-52409. (Carolrhoda Mini-Mysteries Ser.). (Illus.). (gr. 1-4). 1980. PLB 4.95g (ISBN 0-87614-115-7). Carolrhoda Bks.

--Snakes. LC 81-38487. (New True Bks.). (Illus.). 48p. (gr. k-4). 1982. PLB 10.60 (ISBN 0-516-01649-0); pap. 3.95 (ISBN 0-516-41649-9). Childrens.

--Sound Experiments. LC 82-17869. (New True Bks.). (Illus.). 48p. (gr. k-4). 1983. PLB 10.60 (ISBN 0-516-01686-5); pap. 3.95 (ISBN 0-516-41686-3). Childrens.

--Storms. LC 81-15455. (New True Bks.). (Illus.). 48p. 1982. PLB 10.60 (ISBN 0-516-01654-7). Childrens.

--Trains. (The New True Books). (Illus.). 48p. (gr. k-4). 1981. PLB 10.60 (ISBN 0-516-01652-0); pap. 3.95 (ISBN 0-516-41652-9). Childrens.

--Tropical Fish. LC 82-19738. (New True Bks.). (Illus.). 48p. (gr. k-4). 1983. PLB 10.60 (ISBN 0-516-01687-3). Childrens.

--Trucks. LC 82-17907. (New True Bks.). (Illus.). 48p. (gr. k-4). 1983. PLB 10.60 (ISBN 0-516-01688-1); pap. 3.95 (ISBN 0-516-41688-X). Childrens.

--The Twist Tie Riddle. LC 79-52407. (Carolrhoda Mini-Mysteries Ser.). (Illus.). (gr. 1-4). 1980. PLB 4.95g (ISBN 0-87614-113-0). Carolrhoda Bks.

--Word Problems: Grades 5-6 Math. Hoffman, Joan, ed. (An I Know It! Bk.). (Illus.). 32p. (gr. 5-6). 1981. pap. text ed. 1.95 (ISBN 0-938256-42-4). Sch Zone Pub Co.

--Your Five Senses. LC 84-7603. (New True Bks.). (Illus.). 48p. (gr. k-4). 1984. lib. bdg. 10.60 (ISBN 0-516-01932-5); pap. 3.95 (ISBN 0-516-41932-3). Childrens.

--Your Skeleton & Skin. LC 84-7746. (New True Bks.). (Illus.). 48p. (gr. k-4). 1984. lib. bdg. 10.60 (ISBN 0-516-01934-1); pap. 3.95 (ISBN 0-516-41934-X). Childrens.

Broekel, Ray & White, Laurence. Now You See It: Easy Magic for Beginners. (Illus.). (gr. 1-3). 1979. 8.70 (ISBN 0-316-93595-6). Little.

Broekel, Ray & White, Laurence B., Jr. Abra-Ca-Dazzle: Easy Magic Tricks. Fay, Ann, ed. LC 81-11578. (Idea Bks.). (Illus.). 48p. (gr. 2 up). 1982. PLB 10.25 (ISBN 0-8075-0121-2). A Whitman.

--Hocus Pocus: Magic You Can Do. Fay, Anne, ed. LC 83-26096. (Illus.). 48p. (gr. 3 up). 1984. PLB 10.25 (ISBN 0-8075-3350-5). A Whitman.

Broekel, Ray, jt. auth. see White, Lawrence B., Jr.

Broekhuizen, Richard. Graphic Communications. 380p. 1979. text ed. 17.28 (ISBN 0-87345-246-1); study guide 6.00 (ISBN 0-87345-247-X); ans. key free (ISBN 0-87345-248-8). McKnight.

Broekhuizen, S. & Thran, P., eds. Atlas of Cereal Growing in Europe. (Agro-Ecological Atlas Ser.: Vol. 2). 156p. 1970. 159.50 (ISBN 0-444-40819-3). Elsevier.

Broekman. Phanomenologie und Egologie. (Phaenomenologica Ser: No. 12). 1963. lib. bdg. 26.00 (ISBN 90-247-0245-3, Pub. by Martinus Nijhoff Netherlands). Kluwer Academic.

Broekman, J. M. Structuralism, Moscow, Prague, Paris. Beekman, J. F. & Helm, B., trs. from Ger. LC 74-79570. (Synthese Library: No. 67). Orig. Title: Strukturalismus. 175p. 1974. lib. bdg. 26.00 (ISBN 90-277-0478-3, Pub. by Reidel Holland). Kluwer Academic.

Broekmeyer, M. J., ed. see Symposium, Amsterdam, 1970.

Broemel, Percy R. The Languages of Britain: A Philological Study. Repr. of 1933 ed. 25.00 (ISBN 0-686-19891-3). Ridgeway Bks.

Broemeling. Bayesian Analysis of Linear Models. (Monographs & Textbooks in Statistics). 384p. 1984. 59.75 (ISBN 0-8247-7230-X); text ed. 35.00 (ISBN 0-317-13011-0). Dekker.

Broemser, Bernd. Funktionale Satzperspektive Im Englishchen. (Tuebinger Beitraege zur Linguistik Ser.: No. 171). 205p. (Orig.). 1982. pap. 22.00x (ISBN 3-87808-171-5, Pub. by G N Verlag Germany). Benjamins North Am.

Broening, Angela M., ed. English Language Arts in the Secondary School. LC 56-10731. (Illus.). 1956. 20.00x (ISBN 0-89197-142-4). Irvington.

Broenner, Herbert. Berlin Promotion Law in Its Version of Februrary 18, 1976 Including a Brief Commentary. 2nd ed. pap. 7.20x (ISBN 3-11-007037-5). De Gruyter.

Broennimann, P. Auca on the Cononaco: Indians of the Ecuadorian Rain Forest. 184p. 1981. 29.95x (ISBN 0-8176-1259-9). Birkhauser.

Broennimann, Rolf. Villen Des Historismus in Basel. 132p. (Ger.). 1983. pap. 26.95 (ISBN 0-8176-1367-6). Birkhauser.

Broer, Jill S., et al. Governors of Tennessee, Seventeen Ninety to Eighteen Thirty-Five: No. I. Crawford, Charles W., ed. LC 79-129790. (The Tennessee Ser.: Vol. 3). (Illus.). 1979. 12.95 (ISBN 0-87870-075-7). Memphis St Univ.

Broer, Marion & Wilson, Ruth M. Fundamentals of Marching. LC 65-21807. 132p. (Orig.). pap. 13.50 (ISBN 0-471-07068-8). Krieger.

Broer, Marion R. & Houtz, Sara J. Patterns of Muscular Activity in Selected Sport Skills: An Electromyographic Study. (Illus.). 96p. 1967. photocopy ed. 13.75x (ISBN 0-398-00229-0). C C Thomas.

Broer, Marion R. & Zernicke, Ronald F. Efficiency of Human Movement. 4th ed. (Illus.). 453p. 1973. 28.95 (ISBN 0-7216-2088-4). HR&W.

Broers, A. & Smit, J. English-Dutch Dictionary. Born, R., ed. 674p. (Eng. & Dutch.). 1980. pap. 24.95 (ISBN 90-01-81264-3, M-9748). French & Eur.

Broers, B. C. Mysticism in the Neo-Romanticists. LC 68-767. (Studies in Comparative Literature, No. 35). 1969. Repr. of 1923 ed. lib. bdg. 75.00 (ISBN 0-8383-0514-8). Haskell.

Broerse, J., jt. ed. see Barendsen, G. W.

Broerse, J. J., ed. Ion Chambers for Neutron Dosimetry. (European Applied Research Reports Special Topics). 351p. 1980. 79.75 (ISBN 3-7186-0048-X). Harwood Academic.

Broerse, J. J. & MacVittie, T. J., eds. Response of Different Species to Total Body Irradiation. (Radiology Ser.). 1985. lib. bdg. 40.25 (ISBN 0-89838-678-0, Pub. by Martinus Nijhoff Netherlands). Kluwer Academic.

Broersma, G. Applied Mechanics of Machine Elements in Advanced Use. 182p. 1967. 50.00x (ISBN 0-85950-040-3, Pub. by Stam Pr England). State Mutual Bk.

--Behavior of Granular Materials. 266p. 1972. 50.00x (ISBN 0-85950-045-4, Pub. by Stam Pr England). State Mutual Bk.

--Couplings & Bearings. 122p. 1968. 50.00x (ISBN 0-85950-050-0, Pub. by Stam Pr England). State Mutual Bk.

--Design of Gears. 194p. 1967. 50.00x (ISBN 0-85950-055-1, Pub. by Stam Pr England). State Mutual Bk.

--Manufacture & Testing of Gears. 192p. 1969. 50.00x (ISBN 0-85950-060-8, Pub. by Stam Pr England). State Mutual Bk.

Broertjes, C. Induced Variability in Plant Breeding: Proceedings of the International Symposium of the Section Mutation & Polyploidy of the European Association for Research on Plant Breeding EUCARPIA, Wageningen, The Netherlands, Aug. 31-Sept. 4, 1981. 149p. (25 papers, 12 posters). 1982. pap. 22.25 (ISBN 90-220-0796-0, PDC236, Pudoc). Unipub.

Broertjes, C. & Van Harten, A. M. The Application of Mutation Breeding Methods in the Improvement of Vegetatively Propagated Crops. (Developments in Crop Science Ser.: Vol. 2). 316p. 1978. 76.75 (ISBN 0-444-41618-8). Elsevier.

Broes, Arthur T. Lectures on Modern Novelists. Carnegie Institute of Technology, Department of English, ed. LC 72-1312. (Essay Index Reprint Ser.). Repr. of 1963 ed. 15.00 (ISBN 0-8369-2835-0). Ayer Co Pubs.

Broesamle, John J. William Gibbs McAdoo: A Passion for Change, 1863-1917. LC 73-83261. 320p. 1974. 24.50x (ISBN 0-8046-9043-X, Pub. by Kennikat). Assoc Faculty Pr.

Broeshart, Hans, jt. auth. see Fried, Maurice.

Broeze, J. J. Combustion in Piston Engines. 216p. 1963. 50.00x (ISBN 0-85950-036-5, Pub. by Stam Pr England). State Mutual Bk.

Brof, Janet, tr. see Slote, Alfred.

Brofenbrenner, Urie. Two Worlds of Childhood: U.S. & U.S.S.R. (Illus.). (gr. 10 up). 1979. pap. 2.50 (ISBN 0-671-83404-5). PB.

Broff, Sidney du see Du Broff, Sidney.

Brofoss, Karl E., jt. auth. see Cowart, Andrew T.

Brofoss, Karl Erik, jt. auth. see Cowart, Andrew T.

Brofsky, Howard, jt. auth. see Bamberger, Jeanne S.

Brofsky, Howard, et al, eds. see Martini, Padre G. & Lampugnani, Giovanni B.

Brog, Molly J., jt. auth. see Hafen, Brent Q.

Brogan, D. W. Abraham Lincoln. rev. ed. 145p. 1974. 16.00x (ISBN 0-7156-0865-7, BPA-03320, Pub. by Duckworth England). Biblio Dist.

--American Character. 11.75 (ISBN 0-8446-1746-6). Peter Smith.

--Development of Modern France 1870-1939, 2 vols. rev. ed. 16.50 ea. (ISBN 0-8446-0515-8). Peter Smith.

--France under the Republic. LC 74-11934. 744p. 1974. Repr. of 1940 ed. lib. bdg. 45.50x (ISBN 0-8371-7718-9, BRFU). Greenwood.

Brogan, Denis W. America in the Modern World. LC 79-25851. 117p. 1980. Repr. of 1960 ed. lib. bdg. 19.75x (ISBN 0-313-22254-1, BRAW). Greenwood.

--American Themes. LC 79-85996. (Essay & General Literature Index Reprint Ser). 1969. Repr. of 1949 ed. 22.50x (ISBN 0-8046-0545-9, Pub by Kennikat). Assoc Faculty Pr.

Brogan, Denis W see Johnson, Allen & Nevins, Allan.

Brogan, Frankie. The Snare of the Fowler. 208p. 1983. 9.95 (ISBN 0-310-60280-7, Pub by Chosen Bks). Zondervan.

Brogan, Hugh, ed. see Ransome, Arthur.

Brogan, J. C. Nitrogen Losses & Surface Run-off from Landspreading of Manures: Proceedings of a Workshop in the EEC Programme of Co-Ordination & Research on Effluents from Livestock. 487p. 1981. 49.50 (ISBN 90-247-2471-6, Pub. by Martinus Nijhoff Netherlands). Kluwer Academic.

Brogan, John. The Official Travis McGee Quiz Book. 128p. (Orig.). 1984. pap. 2.25 (ISBN 0-449-12709-5, GM). Fawcett.

Brogan, John A. Clear Technical Writing. 1973. 20.30 (ISBN 0-07-007974-9). McGraw.

Brogan, Patrick & Zarca, Albert. Deadly Business: Sam Cummings, Interarms, & the Arms Trade. LC 83-4044. 384p. 1983. 17.95 (ISBN 0-393-01766-4). Norton.

Brogan, Peggy, jt. auth. see Martin, Bill, Jr.

Brogan, Peggy, ed. see Domjan, Evelyn A.

Brogan, Phil F. East of the Cascades. LC 63-23702. (Illus.). 1976. 9.95 (ISBN 0-8323-0005-5); pap. 7.95 (ISBN 0-8323-0277-5). Binford.

Brogan, T. V., ed. English Versification: 1570-1980: a Reference Guide with a Global Appendix. LC 80-8861. 832p. 1981. text ed. 49.50x (ISBN 0-8018-2541-5). Johns Hopkins.

Brogan, Whit. The Work of Placement Officers in Teacher Training Institutions. LC 79-176593. (Columbia University. Teachers College. Contributions to Education Ser.: No. 434). Repr. of 1930 ed. 22.50 (ISBN 0-404-55434-2). AMS Pr.

Brogan, William L. Modern Control Theory. (Illus.). 404p. 1982. pap. 14.95 (ISBN 0-13-590307-6). P-H.

--Modern Control Theory. 2nd ed. (Illus.). 496p. 1985. text ed. 29.95 (ISBN 0-13-590316-5); pap. text ed. 11.95 (ISBN 0-317-13636-4). P-H.

Brogden, Michael. The Police: Autonomy & Consent. (Law, State & Society Ser.). 1983. 41.50 (ISBN 0-12-135180-7). Acad Pr.

Brogden, Stanley. Sky Diggers: Aces of the R.A.A.F. 1944. 7.50 (ISBN 0-913076-02-3). Beachcomber Bks.

Brogdon, Byron G. Opinions, Comments & Reflections on Radiology. LC 82-82972. (Illus.). 249p. 1982. 14.95 (ISBN 0-939442-01-9). Brentwood Pub.

Broger, Achim. Bruno. Van Stockum, Hilda, tr. from Ger. LC 75-15800. (Illus.). 160p. (gr. 3-6). 1975. 10.00 (ISBN 0-688-22051-7); PLB 10.88 (ISBN 0-688-32051-1). Morrow.

--Francie's Paper Puppy. LC 83-24987. Orig. Title: Wollen Wir Freunde Sein? (Illus.). 28p. (gr. 1 up). 1984. 10.95 (ISBN 0-907234-56-9, Pub. by Picture Bk Studio USA). Neugebauer Pr.

Brogger, A. W. & Shetelig, H. Viking Ships. (Illus.). 190p. 1971. 37.50x (ISBN 82-09-00030-6, N-515). Vanous.

Brogger, Jan. Montevarese: A Study of Peasant Society & Culture in Southern Italy. 160p. 1971. 19.50x (ISBN 8-200-06143-4, Dist. by Columbia U Pr). Universitet.

Broglia, R. A. & Ricci, R. A. Nuclear Structure & Heavy Ion Collisions. (Enrico Fermi Summer School Ser.: Vol. 77). 724p. 1982. 153.25 (ISBN 0-444-85462-2, North-Holland). Elsevier.

Broglia, R. A. & Winther, Aage. Heavy Ion Reactions: Elastic & Inelastic Reactions, Vol. 1. 1980. 46.95 (ISBN 0-8053-1302-8). Benjamin-Cummings.

Broglie, Louis De see De Broglie, Louis.

Broglie, Marie-Blanche de see De Broglie, Marie-Blanche & Zukas, Harriet.

Broglio, John, tr. see Paque, Boris.

Broglio, John, tr. see Volguine, Alexander.

Broglio, John, tr. see Volguine, Alexandre.

Brogyanyi, Bela, ed. Studies in Diachronic, Synchronic & Typological Linguistics: Festschrift for Oswald Szemerenyi on the Occasion of His 65th Birthday, 2 vols. (Current Issues in Linguistic Theory: No. 11). 1980. Set. 100.00 (ISBN 90-272-3504-X). Benjamins North Am.

Brogyanyi, Bela, jt. ed. see Untermann, Juergen.

Broh, Robert A. Managing Quality for Higher Profits: A Guide for Corporate Executives & Quality Managers. LC 81-19292. 224p. 1982. 18.50 (ISBN 0-07-007975-7). McGraw.

Brohi, A. K. Iqbal & the Concept of Islamic Socialism. pap. 1.00 (ISBN 0-686-18447-5). Kazi Pubns.

Brohl, Noreen, jt. auth. see Fischhoff, Joseph.

Brohm, Jean-Marie. Sport: A Prison of Measured Time. Fraser, Ian, tr. from Fr. 185p. 1981. (Pub. by Ink Links Ltd.); pap. 6.95 (ISBN 0-906133-03-3). Longwood Pub Group.

Brohn, David. Understanding Structural Analysis. (Illus.). 224p. 1984. pap. text ed. 23.50x (ISBN 0-246-12238-2, Pub. by Granada England). Sheridan.

Broicher, D. German Lyrics & Ballads Done into English Verse. 59.95 (ISBN 0-8490-0229-X). Gordon Pr.

Broida, H. P., jt. ed. see Badash, Lawrence.

Broida, H. P., jt. ed. see Bass, Arnold M.

Broida, Helen. Coping with Stroke. LC 79-220. 152p. 1979. text ed. 15.00 (ISBN 0-933014-50-3). College-Hill.

Broida, Patricia, jt. ed. see Colgate, Craig, Jr.

Broida, V., ed. Automatic Control. 1058p. 1964. 243.95 (ISBN 0-677-00090-1). Gordon.

Broido, Lucy. French Opera Posters, 1868-1930. LC 75-32586. (Illus.). 80p. (Orig.). 1976. pap. 6.95 (ISBN 0-486-23306-5). Dover.

Broido, Lucy, jt. auth. see Cheret, Jules.

Broinowski, Alison, ed. Understanding ASEAN. LC 81-9036. 320p. 1982. 29.95x (ISBN 0-312-83076-9). St Martin.

Brokamp, Sr. Marilyn, jt. auth. see Brokamp, Sr. Marlene.

Brokamp, Sr. Marlene & Brokamp, Sr. Marilyn. Eucharist: God's Gift of Love. (Illus.). 28p. (Orig.). 1976. pap. 1.95 (ISBN 0-912228-25-3). St Anthony Mess Pr.

Brokaw, Charles J., ed. see International Meeting of the Mechanism & Control of Ciliary Movement, Friday Harbor, Washington, September 9-12, 1981.

Brokaw, David. Howl-O-Ween Activity Book. (Stick-Out-Your-Neck Ser.). (Illus.). 32p. (gr. 3-6). 1982. pap. 1.79 (ISBN 0-88724-039-9, CD-8015). Carson-Dellos.

Brokaw, David, jt. auth. see Dietz, Sarah S.

Brokaw, Tom, pref. by. The Gang of Eight: America's Best Political Cartoonists Pick Their Best Work. LC 84-28699. (Illus.). 182p. (Orig.). 1985. pap. 14.95 (ISBN 0-571-12531-X). Faber & Faber.

Broke, Arthur. Brooke's Romeus & Juliet, Being the Original of Shakespeare's Romeo & Juliet. Munro, J. J., ed. LC 74-134609. Repr. of 1908 ed. 14.00 (ISBN 0-404-04539-1). AMS Pr.

--The Tragicall Historye of Romeus & Juliet. LC 78-26035. (English Experience Ser.: No. 134). 168p. 1969. Repr. of 1562 ed. 21.00 (ISBN 90-221-0134-7). Walter J Johnson.

Brokensha, David, et al, eds. Indigenous Knowledge Systems & Development. LC 80-5481. 474p. 1980. lib. bdg. 32.25 (ISBN 0-8191-1102-3); pap. text ed. 19.25 (ISBN 0-8191-1103-1). U Pr of Amer.

Broker, Ignatia. Night Flying Woman: An Ojibway Narrative. 135p. 1983. 12.95 (ISBN 0-87351-164-6); pap. 7.50 (ISBN 0-87351-167-0). Minn Hist.

Brokering, Herb. The Luther Journey. (Illus.). 96p. (Orig.). 1983. pap. 6.95 (ISBN 0-942562-02-X). Brokering Pr.
--Wholly Holy. 96p. (Orig.). 1981. pap. 3.95 (ISBN 0-942562-00-3). Brokering Pr.
Brokering, Herb & Bainton, Roland. A Pilgrimage to Luther's Germany. 80p. 1983. 14.95 (ISBN 0-86683-629-2). Winston Pr.
Brokering, Herb & Brokering, Lois. Love Songs: Musical Activities for Christian Celebration. 36p. (Orig.). 1981. pap. 3.95 (ISBN 0-942562-01-1). Brokering Pr.
Brokering, Herb, jt. auth. see Bimler, Rich.
Brokering, Herbert. I Opener. LC 74-4912. (YA) 1974. pap. 2.50 (ISBN 0-570-06472-4, 12-2584). Concordia.
--Lord, If. 1977. pap. 2.95 (ISBN 0-570-03046-3, 6-1171). Concordia.
--The Night Before Jesus. (Continued Applied Christianity Ser.). 1983. 5.95 (ISBN 0-570-04084-1, 56-1439). Concordia.
Brokering, Herbert F. Pilgrimage to Renewal. 96p. (Orig.). 1979. pap. 1.95 (ISBN 0-03-053791-6). Winston Pr.
--Surprise Me, Jesus. LC 73-83785. 96p. (YA) 1973. pap. 5.50 (ISBN 0-8066-1338-6, 10-6150). Augsburg.
Brokering, Herbert F., ed. Luthers Prayers. Kistler, Charles E., tr. LC 67-25366. 1967. lea. bdg. 6.50 (ISBN 0-8066-0721-1, 10-4231). Augsburg.
Brokering, L. Thirty Six Creative Ideas for Children in the Church School. LC 12-2958. 1982. pap. 4.95 (ISBN 0-570-03865-0). Concordia.
Brokering, Lois, jt. auth. see Brokering, Herb.
Brokering, Mark, jt. auth. see Jackson, Marcy.
Brokhoff, Barbara. Bitter-Sweet Recollections. 1983. 6.50 (ISBN 0-89536-638-X). CSS of Ohio.
--For Losers & Cowards. 1977. pap. 4.75 (ISBN 0-89536-272-4). CSS of Ohio.
--Making Angels Sing. 1982. 5.50 (ISBN 0-89536-569-3). CSS of Ohio.
Brokhoff, Barbara & Brokhoff, John. Faith Alive! 1978. 5.00 (ISBN 0-89536-342-9). CSS of Ohio.
Brokhoff, Barbara, jt. auth. see Brokhoff, John.
Brokhoff, John. Advent & Event. 88p. (Orig.). 1980. pap. text ed. 3.25 (ISBN 0-89536-453-0). CSS of Ohio.
--The Case of the Missing Body. 1982. 5.00 (ISBN 0-89536-556-1). CSS of Ohio.
--Lectionary Preaching Workbook B: (Con. Rev.) (Incl. Lutheran Lectionary). 1984. 23.75 (ISBN 0-89536-645-2, 4864). CSS of Ohio.
--Lectionary Preaching Workbook C. rev. ed. 1985. 23.75 (ISBN 0-89536-756-4, 5862). CSS of Ohio.
Brokhoff, John & Brokhoff, Barbara. There's Always Hope! Advent Christmas Sermons, Ser. A. 1980. pap. text ed. 4.50 (ISBN 0-89536-452-2). CSS of Ohio.
Brokhoff, John, jt. auth. see Brokhoff, Barbara.
Brokhoff, John R. Cross Purposes. 1976. pap. 4.50 (ISBN 0-89536-044-6). CSS of Ohio.
--If Your Dearest Should Die. 1975. 2.50 (ISBN 0-89536-107-8). CSS of Ohio.
--Jesus...Who? 1977. pap. 6.75 (ISBN 0-89536-116-7). CSS of Ohio.
--Lectionary Preaching Workbook: Pentacost Edition. (Ser. B). 1982. 11.50 (ISBN 0-89536-566-9). CSS of Ohio.
--Lectionary Preaching Workbook: Series A. 300p. (Orig.). 1980. pap. text ed. 20.00 (ISBN 0-89536-442-5). CSS of Ohio.
--Lectionary Preaching Workbook: Series C. 1979. pap. 6.30 (ISBN 0-89536-390-9). CSS of Ohio.
--Lent: A Time of Tears. 1984. 3.50 (ISBN 0-89536-649-5). CSS of Ohio.
--Luther Lives! 1983. 4.75 (ISBN 0-89536-571-5). CSS of Ohio.
--Old Truths for New Times. 1983. 8.50 (ISBN 0-89536-637-1). CSS of Ohio.
--Table for Lovers. 1973. pap. 4.50 (ISBN 0-89536-235-X). CSS of Ohio.
--Wrinkled Wrappings. 80p. (Orig.). 1975. pap. 5.00 (ISBN 0-89536-251-1). CSS of Ohio.
Brokke, Harold J. A Guide to Understanding Romans. LC 80-67446. 211p. 1980. pap. 3.95 (ISBN 0-87123-193-X, 210193). Bethany Hse.
--Salvados por Su Vida. 224p. 1978. 2.50 (ISBN 0-88113-317-5). Edit Betania.
--Ten Steps to the Good Life. LC 75-44926. 160p. 1976. pap. 1.95 (ISBN 0-87123-332-0, 200332). Bethany Hse.
Brokmeyer, Henry C. A Mechanics Diary. LC 75-3090. Repr. of 1910 ed. 18.00 (ISBN 0-404-59088-8). AMS Pr.
Brokmeyer, Ron, jt. auth. see Moon, Terry.
Brokoph-Mauch, Gudrun. Robert Musil's "Nachlass zu Lebzeiten". (New Yorker Studien zur Neueren Deutschen Literaturgeschichte: Band 4). 228p. (Orig.). 1984. pap. text ed. 24.35 (ISBN 0-8204-0174-9). P Lang Pubs.
Brolewicz, Walter. My Brother, Lech Walesa. 160p. 1983. 8.98 (ISBN 0-943392-52-7). Tribeca Comm.
Brolin, Brent C. Flight of Fancy: The Banishment & Return of Ornament. (Illus.). 416p. 1985. 30.00 (ISBN 0-312-29613-4). St Martin.
Brolin, Brent C. & Richards, Jean. Sourcebook of Architectural Ornament. 1983. pap. 19.95 (ISBN 0-442-21178-3). Van Nos Reinhold.
Brolin, Don E. Vocational Preparation of Retarded Citizens. (Illus.). 320p. 1976. text ed. 19.95 (ISBN 0-675-08667-1). Merrill.
Brolin, Don E. & Brolin, James C. Vocational Preparation of Handicapped Individuals. 2nd ed. 368p. 1982. pap. text ed. 23.95 (ISBN 0-675-09878-5). Merrill.
Brolin, Donn E. & Kolstoe, Oliver P. The Career & Vocational Development of Handicapped Learners. 72p. 1978. 5.10 (ISBN 0-318-15402-1, IN135). Natl Ctr Res Voc Ed.
Brolin, Donn E., jt. auth. see Kokaska, Charles J.
Brolin, Donn E., ed. Life Centered Career Education: A Competency Based Approach. rev. ed. LC 78-67417. 160p. 1983. pap. text ed. 15.25 (ISBN 0-86586-049-1). Coun Exc Child.
Brolin, Donn E., et al. Trainer's Guide to Life Centered Career Education. LC 78-73703. 1979. text ed. 30.00 (ISBN 0-86586-088-2). Coun Exc Child.
Brolin, James C., jt. auth. see Brolin, Don E.
Brom, Elgar. Sagasha: Mysterious Dust from Space. (Illus.). 72p. 1981. pap. 7.95 (ISBN 0-938294-00-8). Global Comm.
Brom, Libor. Between the Currents. (Czech.). 1985. price not set. Comenius World.
--For the Re-Establishment of the Moral Order. (Illus.). 212p. 1980. lib. bdg. write for info. (ISBN 0-916824-07-1); pap. write for info. (ISBN 0-916824-08-X). Comenius World.
--In the Storm Winds of Anger. 148p. 1976. lib. bdg. write for info. (ISBN 0-916824-01-2); pap. write for info. (ISBN 0-916824-02-0). Comenius World.
--On Restoring the Moral Order. (Czech.). Date not set. pap. price not set. (ISBN 0-916824-08-X). Comenius World.
--On the Attack. (Czech.). Date not set. price not set. (ISBN 0-916824-06-3). Comenius World.
--Our Epoch & Obligation. 244p. 1981. lib. bdg. write for info. (ISBN 0-916824-09-8); pap. write for info. (ISBN 0-916824-10-1). Comenius World.
--The Teacher of Nations & Our Era. (Czech.). Date not set. pap. price not set. (ISBN 0-916824-03-9). Comenius World.
--Time & Duty. (Czech.). Date not set. pap. price not set. (ISBN 0-916824-10-1). Comenius World.
--The Way of Light. (Czech.). Date not set. pap. price not set. (ISBN 0-916824-05-5). Comenius World.
Bromage, Arthur W. A Councilman Speaks. 1951. 1.25x (ISBN 0-685-21778-7). Wahr.
--Councilmen at Work. 1954. 1.75x (ISBN 0-685-21779-5). Wahr.
--Introduction to Municipal Government & Administration. 2nd ed. LC 57-7072. (Illus.). 1957. 29.50x (ISBN 0-89197-243-9). Irvington.
Bromage, Arthur W., ed. Political Representation in Metropolitan Agencies. LC 74-4656. (University of Michigan, Michigan Governmental Studies: No. 42). 102p. 1974. Repr. of 1962 ed. lib. bdg. 15.00x (ISBN 0-8371-7475-9, BRAG). Greenwood.
Bromage, M. C. Writing Audit Reports. 2nd ed. 32.50 (ISBN 0-07-008064-X). McGraw.
Bromage, Mary C. Writing for Business. 2nd ed. LC 79-25634. 192p. 1980. pap. text ed. 6.95x (ISBN 0-472-06317-0). U of Mich Pr.
Bromage, Philip R. Epidural Analgesia. LC 79-9389. (Illus.). 1978. text ed. 49.95 (ISBN 0-7216-2005-1). Saunders.
Broman, Betty. The Early Years in Childhood Education. 2nd ed. LC 81-82557. 1982. 26.50 (ISBN 0-395-31803-3); instr's manual 1.00 (ISBN 0-395-31804-1). HM.
Broman, Betty, jt. auth. see Burns, Paul C.
Broman, Sarah H., et al, eds. Low Achieving Children: The First Seven Years. 184p. 1985. text ed. 19.95 (ISBN 0-89859-637-8). L Erlbaum Assocs.
Bromberg, et al. English Now. Date not set. 5.95 (ISBN 0-8120-2407-9). Barron.
Bromberg, Alan R. & Lowenfels, Lewis D. Securities Fraud & Commodities Fraud, 5 vols. (Securities Law Publications). 1750p. 1980. write for info. (Pub. By Shepards-McGraw). McGraw.
Bromberg, Andrew. Computer Overbyte & Other Stories. LC 82-81248. (Illus.). 48p. (gr. 2-6). 1982. pap. 4.95 (ISBN 0-688-00943-3). Greenwillow.
--Flute Revenge. LC 82-81246. (Hidden Clue Mystery Ser.). (Illus.). 48p. (gr. 2-6). 1982. pap. 4.95 (ISBN 0-688-00942-5). Greenwillow.
--The House on Blackthorn Hill: A Hidden Clue Mystery. LC 82-81245. 48p. (gr. 2-6). 1982. pap. 4.95 (ISBN 0-688-00941-7). Greenwillow.
--Rubik's Ruse & Other Stories. LC 82-81247. (Hidden Clue Codebreaker Ser.). (Illus.). 48p. (gr. 2-6). 1982. pap. 4.95 (ISBN 0-688-00944-1). Greenwillow.
Bromberg, Anna B., jt. auth. see Felder, Mira B.
Bromberg, Anne R. Dallas Museum of Art: Selected Works. LC 83-71457. (Illus.). 223p. 1984. 24.50 (ISBN 0-9609622-2-0); pap. 17.50 (ISBN 0-9609622-3-9). Dallas Mus.
--Dallas Museum of Art: Selected Works. (Illus.). 154p. 24.50 (ISBN 0-9609622-2-0); pap. 17.50 (ISBN 0-9609622-3-9). U of Tex Pr.
Bromberg, Charles M. The Meeting Will Come to Order. LC 81-43862. 74p. (Orig.). 1982. pap. text ed. 5.25 (ISBN 0-8191-2328-5). U Pr of Amer.
Bromberg, Eleanor M., jt. ed. see Arnonowitz, Eugene.
Bromberg, J. Philip. Clean Air Act Handbook: "How to Comply with the Clean Air Act". LC 83-82074. 275p. 1983. pap. 48.00 (ISBN 0-86587-059-4). Gov Insts.
--Physical Chemistry. 2nd ed. 1983. text ed. 10.00 (ISBN 0-205-08020-0, 688020); 42.50 (ISBN 0-205-08020-0, 688019). Allyn.
Bromberg, Joan L. Fusion: Science, Politics & the Invention of a New Energy Source. (Illus.). 376p. 1985. 40.00x (ISBN 0-262-02180-3); pap. 9.95 (ISBN 0-262-52106-7). MIT Pr.
Bromberg, Karen G. Sarah Faulkner's Planning a Home: A Projects Manual. LC 78-22021. 1980. projects manual 12.95 (ISBN 0-03-045476-X). HR&W.
Bromberg, Liebb. Six Hundred & One Words You Need to Know for the SAT. 1981. pap. text ed. 5.50 (ISBN 0-8120-2409-5). Barron.
Bromberg, Murray & Gordon, Melvin. Eleven Hundred Words You Need to Know. LC 70-12919. 1971. pap. 5.95 (ISBN 0-8120-0405-1). Barron.
--Readings in Sports. LC 77-29059. (gr. 9-12). 1978. pap. 3.95 (ISBN 0-8120-0975-4). Barron.
Bromberg, Murray & Katz, Milton. Getting Your Words Across. 256p. (gr. 7-12). 1984. pap. text ed. 5.95 (ISBN 0-8120-2082-0). Barron.
Bromberg, Murray & Liebb, Julius. Words with a Flair. LC 78-17661. 1979. pap. 6.95 (ISBN 0-8120-0979-7). Barron.
--You Can Succeed in Reading & Writing: 30 Steps in Mastering English. LC 80-16743. (gr. 8-12). 1981. pap. text ed. 6.95 (ISBN 0-8120-2081-2). Barron.
Bromberg, Murray, ed. see Drabkin, Marjorie.
Bromberg, Murray, et al. Five Hundred Four Absolutely Essential Words. 2nd ed. 139p. 1984. pap. 5.95 (ISBN 0-8120-2338-2). Barron.
Bromberg, Norbert & Volz Small, Verna. Hitler's Psychopathology, Vol.2. LC 83-261. xi, 335p. 1984. 30.00 (ISBN 0-8236-2345-9). Intl Univs Pr.
Bromberg, Ruth. Canaletto's Etchings. (Illus.). 208p. 1974. 90.00x (ISBN 0-85667-007-3, Pub. by Sotheby Pubns England). Biblio Dist.
Bromberg, Sarah. Abortion, Morality & Science: Feminine Perspectives of Authority. Murry, Ron, ed. 56p. (Orig.). 1984. pap. 3.80 (ISBN 0-9610450-4-3). Dianic Pubns.
Bromberg, Walter. The Mold of Murder: A Psychiatric Study of Homicide. LC 61-14610. 230p. Repr. of 1961 ed. lib. bdg. 22.50x (ISBN 0-8371-8070-8, BRMM). Greenwood.
--Psychiatry Between the Wars, Nineteen Eighteen to Nineteen Forty-Five: A Recollection. LC 82-6153. (Contributions in Medical History Ser.: No. 10). xxix, 184p. 1982. 35.00 (ISBN 0-313-23460-4, BWN/). Greenwood.
--The Uses of Psychiatry in the Law: A Clinical View of Forensic Psychiatry. LC 78-22724. (Illus.). x, 442p. 1979. lib. bdg. 35.00 (ISBN 0-89930-000-6, BRP, Quorum). Greenwood.
Bromberg, Walter, jt. auth. see Halleck, Seymour.
Brombert, Beth A. A Concert of Hells. 205p. 1980. 17.95 (ISBN 0-241-10303-7, Pub. by Hamish Hamilton England). David & Charles.
--Cristina: Portraits of a Princess. (Illus.). xii, 402p. 1977. pap. 10.95 (ISBN 0-226-07551-6). U of Chicago Pr.
Brombert, Victor. Novels of Flaubert: A Study of Themes & Techniques. 1967. 32.00x (ISBN 0-691-06085-1); pap. 11.95x (ISBN 0-691-01290-3). Princeton U Pr.
--The Romantic Prison: The French Tradition. LC 77-85532. 1978. 26.00x (ISBN 0-691-06352-4). Princeton U Pr.
--Victor Hugo & the Visionary Novel. (Illus.). 304p. 1984. text ed. 20.00x (ISBN 0-674-93550-0). Harvard U Pr.
Brombert, Victor H., ed. Stendhal: A Collection of Critical Essays. 1962. 12.95 (ISBN 0-13-846535-5, Spec). P-H.
Brome, tr. see Horace.
Brome, Alexander. Poems, 2 Vols. Dubinski, Roman R., ed. 560p. 1982. 75.00x set (ISBN 0-8020-5535-4). U of Toronto Pr.
Brome, Richard. The Antipodes. Haaker, Ann, ed. LC 66-13403. (Regents Renaissance Drama Ser.). xxii, 138p. 1966. 13.95x (ISBN 0-8032-0253-9); pap. 3.25x (ISBN 0-8032-5254-4, BB 219, Bison). U of Nebr Pr.
--Dramatic Works of Richard Brome, 3 Vols. Shepherd, R. H., ed. Repr. of 1873 ed. Set. 55.00 (ISBN 0-404-01110-1); 19.00 ea. Vol. 1 (ISBN 0-404-01111-X). Vol. 2 (ISBN 0-404-01112-8). Vol. 3 (ISBN 0-404-01113-6). AMS Pr.
--A Jovial Crew. Haaker, Ann, ed. LC 68-10433. (Regents Renaissance Drama Ser). xxii, 144p. 1968. 14.50x (ISBN 0-8032-0254-7); pap. 3.95x (ISBN 0-8032-5255-2, BB 228, Bison). U of Nebr Pr.
--A Mad Couple Well Match'd. Spove, Steen H. & Orgel, Stephen, eds. LC 78-13873. (Renaissance Drama Ser.). 1979. lib. bdg. 37.00 (ISBN 0-8240-9730-0). Garland Pub.
--The Weeding of Covent Garden & the Sparagus Garden. McClure, Donald S. & Orgel, Stephen, eds. LC 79-54351. (Renaissance Drama Second Ser.). 438p. 1980. lib. bdg. 61.00 (ISBN 0-8240-4468-1). Garland Pub.
Brome, Vincent. Aneurin Bevan: A Biography. (Illus.). 1953. 10.00 (ISBN 0-686-00952-5). Wellington.
--Ernest Jones: A Biography. (Illus.). 1983. 20.00 (ISBN 0-393-01594-7). Norton.
--Frank Harris. LC 79-8057. Repr. of 1959 ed. 20.00 (ISBN 0-404-18368-9). AMS Pr.
--Freud & His Disciples: The Struggle for Supremacy. LC 84-29215. 236p. 1984. pap. 5.95 (ISBN 0-904573-92-3, Pub. by Caliban Bks). Longwood Pub Group.
--H. G. Wells: A Biography. LC 78-133515. (Select Bibliographies Reprint Ser.). 1972. Repr. of 1951 ed. 16.00 (ISBN 0-8369-5547-1). Ayer Co Pubs.
--H. G. Wells, a Biography. LC 70-109284. Repr. of 1951 ed. lib. bdg. 24.75x (ISBN 0-8371-3827-2, BRHW). Greenwood.
--H. G. Wells: A Biography. 1979. Repr. of 1952 ed. lib. bdg. 20.00 (ISBN 0-8492-3743-2). R West.
--Jung: Man & Myth. LC 77-14736. 1978. pap. 6.95 (ISBN 0-689-70588-3, 262). Atheneum.
--Six Studies in Quarrelling. LC 72-6176. 197p. 1973. Repr. of 1958 ed. lib. bdg. 24.75x (ISBN 0-8371-6484-2, BRSQ). Greenwood.
Bromell, Henry. The Follower. LC 83-10930. 228p. 1983. 15.95 (ISBN 0-399-12863-8, Putnam). Putnam Pub Group.
Bromfield, Avery P. OLIO Large Print Crossword Puzzle Book. 64p. 1984. spiral bdg. 4.00 (ISBN 0-934381-00-3). Olio Pubs.
Bromfield, K. R., ed. Soybean Rust. (Monograph Ser.: No. 11). 65p. 1984. 10.50 (ISBN 0-89054-062-4). Am Phytopathol Soc.
Bromfield, Louis. Colorado. 15.95 (ISBN 0-88411-509-7, Pub by Aeonian Pr). Amereon Ltd.
--Early Autumn. 264p. Repr. of 1926 ed. lib. bdg. 15.95 (ISBN 0-88411-508-9, Pub. by Aeonian Pr). Amereon Ltd.
--The Farm. 1976. Repr. of 1943 ed. lib. bdg. 18.95 (ISBN 0-88411-501-1, Pub. by Aeonian Pr). Amereon Ltd.
--From My Experience. 355p. Repr. of 1955 ed. lib. bdg. 18.95 (ISBN 0-88411-540-2, Pub. by Aeonian Pr). Amereon Ltd.
--Malabar Farm. 1976. Repr. of 1948 ed. lib. bdg. 20.95 (ISBN 0-88411-506-2, Pub. by Aeonian Pr). Amereon Ltd.
--The Man Who Had Everything. 278p. Repr. of 1935 ed. lib. bdg. 15.95 (ISBN 0-88411-390-6, Pub. by Aeonian Pr). Amereon Ltd.
--Mrs. Parkington. 1976. Repr. of 1943 ed. lib. bdg. 18.95 (ISBN 0-88411-502-X, Pub. by Aeonian Pr). Amereon Ltd.
--Mrs. Parkington. 320p. 1974. pap. 1.95 (ISBN 0-532-19101-3). Woodhill.
--New Pattern for a Tired World. LC 72-174234. (Right Wing Individualist Tradition in America Ser). 1972. Repr. of 1954 ed. 23.50 (ISBN 0-405-00416-8). Ayer Co Pubs.
--Night in Bombay. 1976. Repr. of 1940 ed. lib. bdg. 18.95x (ISBN 0-88411-503-8, Pub. by Aeonian Pr). Amereon Ltd.
--Out of the Earth. 305p. Repr. of 1950 ed. lib. bdg. 17.95x (ISBN 0-88411-541-0, Pub. by Aeonian Pr). Amereon Ltd.
--Pleasant Valley. 1976. Repr. of 1945 ed. lib. bdg. 19.95x (ISBN 0-88411-504-6, Pub. by Aeonian Pr). Amereon Ltd.
--The Rains Came. 1976. Repr. of 1937 ed. lib. bdg. 27.95x (ISBN 0-88411-505-4, Pub. by Aeonian Pr). Amereon Ltd.
--The Rains Came. 528p. 1974. pap. 1.75 (ISBN 0-532-17101-2). Woodhill.
--Wild Country. 274p. Repr. of 1948 ed. lib. bdg. 16.95x (ISBN 0-88411-542-9, Pub. by Aeonian Pr). Amereon Ltd.
--Wild Is the River. 332p. Repr. of 1941 ed. lib. bdg. 18.95x (ISBN 0-88411-507-0, Pub. by Aeonian Pr). Amereon Ltd.
Bromhall, A. J. Hudson Taylor & China's Open Century: Bk. II, Over the Treaty Wall. 1981. pap. 9.95 (ISBN 0-340-27561-8). OMF Bks.
Bromhead, E. N. The Stability of Slopes. 352p. 1985. text ed. 49.95 (ISBN 0-412-01061-5, 9358, Pub. by Chapman & Hall). Methuen Inc.
--The Stability of Slopes. (Illus.). 352p. 1985. 49.95 (ISBN 0-412-01061-5, 9358). Methuen Inc.
Bromhead, P. A. The House of Lords & Contemporary Politics: 1911-1957. LC 75-27676. 283p. 1976. Repr. of 1958 ed. lib. bdg. 18.50x (ISBN 0-8371-8458-4, BRHL). Greenwood.
--Private Members' Bills in the British Parliament. LC 75-27677. 216p. 1976. Repr. of 1956 ed. lib. bdg. 14.00x (ISBN 0-8371-8462-2, BRPM). Greenwood.
Bromige, David. Threads. Orig. Title: Fascination of What's Difficult. 101p. (Orig.). 1971. pap. 4.00 (ISBN 0-87685-020-4). Black Sparrow.
--Tight Corners & What's Around Them. 100p. (Orig.). 1974. pap. 4.00 (ISBN 0-87685-193-6). Black Sparrow.
Bromige, Iris. A Distant Song. DeRoin, Gene, ed. (Aston Hall Presents Ser.). (Orig.). pap. 1.50 (ISBN 0-89936-009-2). Aston Hall.
--Rough Weather. DeRoin, Gene, ed. (Aston Hall Presents Ser.). (Orig.). 1980. pap. 1.50 (ISBN 0-89936-016-5). Aston Hall.
--A Slender Thread. 192p. 1985. 15.95 (ISBN 0-340-36628-1, Pub. by Hodder & Stoughton UK). David & Charles.

Bromiley, G. W., ed. Zwingli & Bullinger. LC 53-1533. (Library of Christian Classics). 360p. 1979. softcover 8.95 (ISBN 0-664-24159-X). Westminster.

Bromiley, Geoffrey, tr. see Kittel, Gerhard & Friedrich, Gerhard.

Bromiley, Geoffrey W. Children of Promise: The Case for Baptizing Infants. LC 79-10346. 1979. pap. 3.95 (ISBN 0-8028-1797-1). Eerdmans.

--God & Marriage. 96p. (Orig.). 1980. pap. 4.95 (ISBN 0-8028-1851-X). Eerdmans.

--Historical Theology: An Introduction. LC 77-17030. 1978. 14.95 (ISBN 0-8028-3509-0). Eerdmans.

--An Introduction to the Theology of Karl Barth. LC 79-15397. (Orig.). pap. 8.95 (ISBN 0-8028-1804-8). Eerdmans.

Bromiley, Geoffrey W., ed. International Standard Bible Encyclopedia, Vol. 1, A-D. rev. ed. LC 79-12280. (Illus.). 1979. 32.50 (ISBN 0-8028-8161-0). Eerdmans.

--The International Standard Bible Encyclopedia, Vol. 2: E-J. rev. ed. 1132p. 1981. 35.00 (ISBN 0-8028-8162-9). Eerdmans.

Bromiley, Geoffrey W., ed. see Barth, Karl.

Bromiley, Geoffrey W., ed. see Thielicke, Helmut.

Bromiley, Geoffrey W., tr. see Barth, Karl.

Bromiley, Geoffrey W., tr. see Barth, Karl & Bultmann, Rudolf.

Bromiley, Geoffrey W., tr. see Barth, Karl & Zuckmayer, Carl.

Bromiley, Geoffrey W., tr. see Kasemann, Ernst.

Bromilow, F. J. Cost Escalation of Building Contracts. (Illus.). 1977. pap. 3.50x (ISBN 0-643-01152-8, Pub. by CSIRO). Intl Spec Bk.

Bromilow, William E. Twenty Years Among Primitive Papuans. LC 75-32800. Repr. of 1929 ed. 26.00 (ISBN 0-404-14103-X). AMS Pr.

Bromke, Adam. Poland's Politics: Idealism vs. Realism. LC 66-21331. (Harvard University, Russian Research Center Studies: Vol. 51). pap. 82.50 (ISBN 0-317-08918-8, 2017754). Bks Demand UMI.

Bromley, Alistair. Playing with Panthers. LC 80-52191. 134p. 1982. 8.95 (ISBN 0-533-04749-8). Vantage.

Bromley, Anne. Midwinter Transport. LC 85-70429. (Poetry Ser.). 80p. 1985. 14.95 (ISBN 0-88748-041-1); pap. 6.95 (ISBN 0-88748-042-X). Carnegie Mellon.

Bromley, D. A., ed. see International Conference on Nuclear Structure.

Bromley, D. Allan. Treatise on Heavy-Ion Science, Vol. 4: Extreme Nuclear States. 722p. 1985. 92.50x (ISBN 0-306-41574-7, Plenum Pr). Plenum Pub.

Bromley, D. Allan, ed. Treatise on Heavy-Ion Science: Vol. 1, Elastic & Quasi-Elastic Phenomena. LC 84-8384. 750p. 1984. 95.00x (ISBN 0-306-41571-2, Plenum Pr). Plenum Pub.

--Treatise on Heavy-Ion Science, Vol. 2: Fusion & Quasi-Fusion Phenomena. 752p. 1985. 95.00x (ISBN 0-306-41572-0, Plenum Pr). Plenum Pub.

--Treatise on Heavy-Ion Science, Vol. 3: Compound Systems Phenomena. 610p. 1985. 89.50x (ISBN 0-306-41573-9, Plenum Pr). Plenum Pub.

--Treatise on Heavy-Ion Science, Vol. 5: High-Energy Atomic Physics. 518p. 1985. 79.50x (ISBN 0-306-41575-5, Plenum Pr). Plenum Pub.

--Treatise on Heavy Ion Science, Vol. 6: Astrophysics, Chemistry, & Condensed Matter, Volume 6. 452p. 1985. 69.50x (ISBN 0-306-41786-3, Plenum Pr). Plenum Pub.

--Treatise on Heavy Ion Science, Vol. 7: Instrumentation & Techniques. 494p. 1985. 79.50x (ISBN 0-306-41787-1, Plenum Pr). Plenum Pub.

Bromley, D. Allan & Hughes, V. W., eds. Facets of Physics. 1970. 50.50 (ISBN 0-12-135350-8). Acad Pr.

Bromley, D. B., jt. auth. see Livesley, W. J.

Bromley, D. B., ed. Gerontology: Social & Behavioural Perspectives. LC 84-17490. 254p. 1984. 27.00 (ISBN 0-7099-3283-9, Pub. by Croom Helm Ltd). Longwood Pub Group.

Bromley, Daniel W. Improving Irrigated Agriculture: Institutional Reform & the Small Farmer. (Working Paper: No. 531). 96p. 1982. pap. 3.00 (ISBN 0-8213-0064-4). World Bank.

Bromley, Daniel W., jt. auth. see Buse, Rueben C.

Bromley, David & Shupe, Anson. A Documentary History of the Anti-Cult Movement. LC 84-25560. (Studies in American Religion: Vol. 13). 420p. 1985. 69.95x (ISBN 0-88946-656-4). E Mellen.

--Strange Gods: The Great American Cult Scare. LC 81-65763. 192p. 1982. 18.95x (ISBN 0-8070-3256-5); pap. 8.95 (ISBN 0-8070-1109-6, BP641). Beacon Pr.

Bromley, David G. & Shupe, Anson D., Jr. Moonies in America: Cult, Church, & Crusade. LC 79-16456. (Sage Library of Social Research: Vol. 92). 269p. 1979. 28.00 (ISBN 0-8039-1060-6). Sage.

--New Christian Politics. LC 84-6598. 300p. 1984. 23.95x (ISBN 0-86554-115-9, MUP/H108). Mercer Univ Pr.

Bromley, David G. & Richardson, James T., eds. The Brainwashing-Deprogramming Controversy: Sociological, Psychological, Legal & Historical Perspectives. LC 83-4346. (Studies in Religion & Society: Vol. 5). 376p. 1984. 59.95x (ISBN 0-88946-868-0). E Mellen.

Bromley, Dudley. Bedford Fever. LC 81-82039. (Doomsday Journals). 80p. (gr. 6-12). 1982. lib. bdg. 9.25 (ISBN 0-516-02241-5). Childrens.

--Comet! LC 81-82040. (Doomsday Journals). (gr. 6-12). 1982. 9.25 (ISBN 0-516-02242-3). Childrens.

--Final Warning. LC 81-82037. (Doomsday Journals). 80p. (gr. 6-12). 1982. lib. bdg. 9.25 (ISBN 0-516-02243-1). Childrens.

--Fireball. LC 81-82035. (Doomsday Journals). 80p. (gr. 6-12). 1982. lib. bdg. 9.25 (ISBN 0-516-02244-X). Childrens.

--Guide to Kaypro Computers. 1984. 13.95 (ISBN 0-317-05698-0). S&S.

--Lost Valley. LC 81-82036. (Doomsday Journals). 80p. (gr. 6-12). 1982. lib. bdg. 9.25 (ISBN 0-516-02245-8). Childrens.

--The Seep. LC 81-82038. (Doomsday Journals). 80p. (gr. 6-12). 1982. lib. bdg. 9.25 (ISBN 0-516-02246-6). Childrens.

Bromley, Ida. Tetraplegia & Paraplegia. 2nd ed. (Illus.). 264p. 1981. pap. text ed. 16.25 (ISBN 0-443-01992-4). Churchill.

Bromley, J. S. & Kossma, E. H., eds. Britain & the Netherlands in Europe & Asia. LC 68-17096. (Illus.). 1969. text ed. 27.50x (ISBN 0-312-10395-6). St Martin.

Bromley, J. V., et al. Present Day Ethnic Processes in the USSR. 277p. 1982. 7.95 (ISBN 0-8285-2327-4, Pub. by Progress Pubs USSR). Imported Pubns.

Bromley, James F., jt. ed. see Henderson, James M.

Bromley, James F., et al, eds. Abstracts of Supreme Court Decisions Interpreting the Interstate Commerce Act, Vol. III. 104p. 1972. 12.50 (ISBN 0-318-14382-8). Assn ICC Practitioners.

Bromley, John, ed. The Clockmakers' Library: The Catalogue of the Books & Manuscripts in the Library of the Worshipful Company of Clockmakers. (Illus.). 136p. 1977. 52.50x (ISBN 0-85667-033-2, Pub. by Sotheby Pubns England). Biblio Dist.

Bromley, K., ed. Real Time Signal Processing, Vol. 431. 37p. 48.00 (ISBN 0-89252-466-9). Photo-Optical.

Bromley, Lynn. Monkeys, Apes & Other Primates. (Illus.). 64p. 1981. pap. 3.95 (ISBN 0-686-80426-0). Bellerophon Bks.

Bromley, R., ed. Planning for Small Enterprises in Third World Cities. (Urban & Regional Planning Ser.: Vol. 34). 360p. 1984. 50.00 (ISBN 0-08-025236-2); pap. 29.50 (ISBN 0-08-031333-7). Pergamon.

Bromley, Ray. The Urban Informal Sector: Critical Perspectives. (Illus.). 1979. 44.00 (ISBN 0-08-024270-7). Pergamon.

Bromley, Ray, jt. auth. see Bromley, Rosemary.

Bromley, Ray & Gerry, Chris, eds. Casual Work & Poverty in Third World Cities. LC 78-11329. 323p. 1979. 63.95 (ISBN 0-471-99731-5, Pub. by Wiley-Interscience). Wiley.

Bromley, Rosemary & Bromley, Ray. South American Development: A Geographical Introduction. 2nd ed. LC 82-1171. (Cambridge Topics in Geography Ser.: No. 2). (Illus.). 112p. 1982. 14.95 (ISBN 0-521-23496-4); pap. 7.95 (ISBN 0-521-28008-7). Cambridge U Pr.

Bromley, S. C., jt. ed. see Thornton, C. S.

Bromley, Willard S., ed. Pulpwood Productions. 3rd ed. LC 75-14771. (Illus.). 1976. text ed. 15.95 (ISBN 0-8134-1738-4, 1738); text ed. 11.95x. Interstate.

Bromley, Yu, ed. Soviet Ethnology & Anthropology Today. (Studies in Anthropology Ser.: No. 1). 401p. 1974. pap. text ed. 44.00x (ISBN 90-2792-725-1). Mouton.

Bromm, B. Pain Measurement in Man: Neurophysiological Correlates of Pain. 1984. 94.50 (ISBN 0-444-80571-0, I-389-84). Elsevier.

Brommel, Bernard J. Eugene V. Debs, Spokesman for Labor & Socialism. LC 75-23910. (Illus.). 265p. 1978. 15.00 (ISBN 0-88286-006-2); pap. 6.95 (ISBN 0-88286-024-0). C H Kerr.

--Eugene V. Debs: Spokesman for Labor & Socialism. 265p. 5.95 (ISBN 0-317-06697-8). Indus Workers World.

Brommel, Bernard J., jt. auth. see Galvin, Kathleen M.

Brommer, ed. Lexique Anglais-Francais des Termes Appartenant Aux Techniques En Usage a I.G.N, Pt.2. 122p. (Fr. & Eng., English-French Lexicon of Terms Pertaining to Techniques Used at I.G.N). 1958. pap. 7.95 (ISBN 0-686-56778-1, M-6356). French & Eur.

Brommer, Frank. Heracles: The Twelve Labors of the Hero in Ancient Art & Literature. Schwarz, Shirley J., tr. (Illus.). 128p. 1985. lib. bdg. 20.00 (ISBN 0-89241-375-1). Caratzas.

Brommer, Gerald. Drawing: Ideas, Materials, Techniques. rev. ed. Horn, George F., ed. LC 78-59861. (Illus.). 1978. text ed. 14.95 (ISBN 0-87192-099-9). Davis Mass.

Brommer, Gerald & Gatto, Joseph. Careers in Art. (Illus.). 256p. 1984. 18.95 (ISBN 0-87192-149-9, Pub. by Davis Mass). Sterling.

Brommer, Gerald F. The Art of Collage. Horn, George F. & Rainey, Sarita, eds. LC 77-92192. (Illus.). 1978. 18.95 (ISBN 0-87192-096-4, 96-4). Davis Mass.

--Discovering Art History. LC 79-57018. (Illus.). 384p. 1981. 26.95 (ISBN 0-87192-121-9); teachers guide 8.95 (ISBN 0-87192-137-5). Davis Mass.

--Landscapes. Horn, George F., ed. LC 76-50508. (Insights to Art Ser.). (Illus.). 1977. 10.95 (ISBN 0-87192-086-7). Davis Mass.

--Movement & Rhythm: A Design Principle. LC 75-21111. (Concepts of Design Ser.). (Illus.). 80p. (gr. 7-12). 1975. 9.95 (ISBN 0-87192-076-X). Davis Mass.

--Relief Printmaking. LC 77-113860. (Illus.). (gr. 7-12). 12.95 (ISBN 0-87192-034-4). Davis Mass.

--Space: A Design Element. LC 74-82680. (Concepts of Design Ser). (Illus.). 80p. (gr. 7up). 1974. ref. ed. 9.95 (ISBN 0-87192-062-X). Davis Mass.

--Transparent Watercolor: Ideas & Techniques. LC 72-97154. 1973. 14.95 (ISBN 0-87192-052-2). Davis Mass.

--Wire Sculpture & Other Three Dimensional Construction. LC 68-19999. (Illus.). (gr. 5-12). 1968. 12.95 (ISBN 0-87192-025-5). Davis Mass.

Brommer, Gerald F. & Gatto, Joseph A. Careers in Art: An Illustrated Guide. LC 83-73179. (Illus.). 256p. 1984. 18.95 (ISBN 0-87192-149-9). Davis Mass.

Brommer, Gerald F. & Horn, George F. Art in Your World. LC 76-4384. (Books in Art Education). (Illus.). 1977. text ed. 18.95 (ISBN 0-87192-083-2). Davis Mass.

--Art: Your Visual Environment. LC 76-40856. (Illus.). 1977. text ed. 18.95 (ISBN 0-87192-084-0). Davis Mass.

Brommer, Gerald F., ed. see Gatto, Joseph, et al.

Brommer, Gerald F., ed. see Gatto, Joseph A.

Brommer, Gerald F., ed. see Porter, Albert W.

Brommer, Gerald F., ed. see Selleck, Jack.

Brompton, Sally. Chameleon: The Boy George Story. (Illus.). 155p. pap. 9.95 (ISBN 0-946771-91-X, Pub. by Spellmont Ltd England). Hippocrene Bks.

Bromwell, C. David, jt. auth. see Warshaw, Steven.

Bromwell, William J. History of Immigration to the United States. LC 69-18760. (American Immigration Collection Ser., No. 1). 1969. Repr. of 1856 ed. 12.00 (ISBN 0-405-00508-3). Ayer Co Pubs.

--History of Immigration to the United States. LC 68-27676. Repr. of 1856 ed. 25.00x (ISBN 0-678-00533-8). Kelley.

Bromwich, David. Hazlitt: The Mind of a Critic. 1983. 35.00x (ISBN 0-19-503343-4). Oxford U Pr.

--Hazlitt: The Mind of a Critic. 416p. 1985. pap. 12.95 (ISBN 0-19-503687-5). Oxford U Pr.

Bromwich, Geoffrey. Insuring Business Risks in Canada: How to Get the Most for Your Money. 1st ed. 103p. 1978. 3.50 (ISBN 0-88908-037-2). Self Counsel Pr.

Bromwich, Michael & Hopwood, Anthony, eds. Essays in British Accounting Research. (Finance & Accounting Ser.). 350p. text ed. 79.95 (ISBN 0-273-01596-6). Pitman Pub MA.

Bromwich, P. D. & Parsons, A. D. Contraception. (The Facts Ser.). 1984. 11.95x (ISBN 0-19-261410-X). Oxford U Pr.

Bromwich, Rose. Working with Parents & Infants. LC 80-16141. 384p. 1978. pap. text ed. 18.00 (ISBN 0-936104-41-4). Pro Ed.

Bronarski, L., ed. see Chopin, Frederic.

Bronaugh, Richard, ed. Philosophical Law: Authority, Equality, Adjudication, Privacy. (Contributions in Legal Studies Ser.: No. 2). x, 208p. 1978. lib. bdg. 29.95 (ISBN 0-8371-9809-7, BPL/). Greenwood.

Bronaugh, Richard, et al. Readings in the Philosophy of Constitutional Law. LC 82-83807. 320p. 1983. pap. text ed. 19.50 (ISBN 0-8403-2887-7). Kendall-Hunt.

Bronaugh, Robert, compiled by. The Celebrity Birthday Book. LC 80-14221. 492p. 1981. 19.95 (ISBN 0-8246-0253-6); pap. 9.95 (ISBN 0-8246-0272-2). Jonathan David.

Bronckers, M. C. Selective Safeguard Measures in Multilateral Trade Relations: Issues of Protectionism in GATT, European Community, & United StatesLaw. LC 85-5587. Date not set. price not set (ISBN 9-06-544222-7). Kluwer Academic.

Brondal, Viggo, jt. ed. see Jeppesen, Knud.

Bronder, Saul E. Social Justice & Church Authority: The Public Life of Archbishop Robert E. Lucey. 215p. 1982. 29.95 (ISBN 0-87722-239-8). Temple U Pr.

Brondfield, Jerry. The Great NFL Funbook II. (Illus.). (gr. 3-7). pap. 1.95 (ISBN 0-590-31628-1). Scholastic Inc.

--Roberto Clemente: Pride of the Pirates. LC 75-22145. (Sports Library Ser.). (Illus.). 96p. (gr. 3-6). 1976. PLB 7.98 (ISBN 0-8116-6675-1). Garrard.

--Rockne: Football's Greatest Coach. 1976. 8.95 (ISBN 0-394-40145-X). Random.

Brondoli, Michael. The Love Letter Hack. 2nd ed. LC 81-85610. (Illus.). 70p. 1982. pap. 3.00 (ISBN 0-9602424-7-3). Paycock Pr.

--Showdown & Other Stories. LC 83-63129. 240p. 1984. pap. 12.50 (ISBN 0-86547-152-5). N Point Pr.

--Smithsburg. (The Treacle Story Ser.: No. 2). (Illus.). 48p. 1976. signed ed. 8.00 (ISBN 0-914232-09-6); pap. 2.50 (ISBN 0-914232-08-8). McPherson & Co.

Brondolo, Barbara. Small Patchwork Projects. (Illus.). 64p. (Orig.). 1981. pap. 3.95 (ISBN 0-486-24030-4). Dover.

--Small Patchwork Projects. 56p. 5.25 (ISBN 0-318-14900-1, W107). Midwest Old Settlers.

Brondsted, Johannes. The Vikings. rev. ed. 1960. pap. 5.95 (ISBN 0-14-020459-8, Pelican). Penguin.

Brondum, Jack, tr. see Ditlevsen, Tove.

Broneer, Oscar. The South Stoa & Its Roman Successors. LC 75-25700. (Corinth Ser: Vol. 1, Pt. 4). (Illus.). 1971. Repr. of 1954 ed. 25.00x (ISBN 0-87661-014-9). Am Sch Athens.

--Temple of Poseidon. LC 73-61010. (Isthmia Ser: Vol. 1). (Illus.). 1971. 25.00x (ISBN 0-87661-931-6). Am Sch Athens.

--Terracotta Lamps. LC 76-362971. (Isthmia Ser: Vol. 3). 1977. 25.00x (ISBN 0-87661-933-2). Am Sch Athens.

--Topography & Architecture. LC 75-27618. (Isthmia Ser: Vol. 2). (Illus.). 1973. 30.00x (ISBN 0-87661-932-4). Am Sch Athens.

Bronemann, LeRoy B. Once upon a Tide: Tales from a Foxhole in the South Pacific. 208p. 1982. 10.95 (ISBN 0-8059-2818-9). Dorrance.

Broner, E. M. Her Mothers. LC 84-48447. 264p. pap. 8.95 (ISBN 0-253-20353-8). Ind U Pr.

--A Weave of Women. LC 84-48548. 320p. 1985. pap. 8.95. Ind U Pr.

Broner, E. M., jt. ed. see Davidson, Cathy N.

Bronetsky, I., ed. Stories & Poems for Children. 143p. 1982. 7.95 (ISBN 0-8285-2361-4, Pub. by Raduga Pubs USSR). Imported Pubns.

Bronfeld, Stewart. How to Produce a Film. (Illus.). 176p. 1984. 16.95 (ISBN 0-13-429432-7); pap. 8.95 (ISBN 0-13-429424-6). P-H.

--Writing for Film & Television. 160p. 1980. 11.95 (ISBN 0-13-970608-9, Spec); pap. 4.95 (ISBN 0-13-970590-2). P-H.

Bronfen, Nan. Nutrition for a Better Life: A Sourcebook for the 80's. LC 80-17326. (Illus.). 240p. (Orig.). 1980. pap. 8.95 (ISBN 0-88496-152-4). Capra Pr.

Bronfenbrenner, Martin. Income Distribution Theory. LC 77-131045. 496p. 1971. text ed. 44.95x (ISBN 0-202-06037-3). Aldine Pub.

--Macroeconomic Alternatives. LC 79-50880. (Illus.). 1979. text ed. 25.95x (ISBN 0-88295-404-0). Harlan Davidson.

Bronfenbrenner, Martin, et al. Economics. Incl. Macroeconomics. LC 83-82353. 400p. pap. text ed. 17.95 (ISBN 0-395-34228-7); Microeconomics. LC 83-82354. 496p. pap. text ed. 17.95 (ISBN 0-395-34229-5). LC 83-82341. 848p. 1983. pap. text ed. 28.95 (ISBN 0-395-34227-9); transparencies 125.00 (ISBN 0-395-34233-3); study guide 10.95 (ISBN 0-395-34231-7); test items 5.00 (ISBN 0-395-34232-5). HM.

Bronfenbrenner, Urie. The Ecology of Human Development: Experiments by Nature & Design. LC 78-27232. 352p. 1981. pap. 9.95x (ISBN 0-674-22457-4). Harvard U Pr.

--The Ecology of Human Development: Experiments by Nature & Design. LC 78-27232. 1979. text ed. 25.00x (ISBN 0-674-22456-6). Harvard U Pr.

--Reality & Research in the Ecology of Human Development. (Master Lectures on Developmental Psychology: Manuscript No. 1333). 9.50x (ISBN 0-912704-30-6). Am Psychol.

--Two Worlds of Childhood. 1972. pap. 9.95 (ISBN 0-671-21238-9, Touchstone Bks). S&S.

Bronikowski, R. J. Managing the Engineering Design Function. (Illus.). 416p. 1985. 42.95 (ISBN 0-442-21440-5). Van Nos Reinhold.

Bronin, Andrew. Gus & Buster Work Things out. (Illus.). 64p. (gr. k-4). 1976. pap. 0.95 (ISBN 0-440-43318-5, YB). Dell.

Bronk, Detev W., ed. see Rockefeller University & State University of New York, Nov. 26-27, 1965.

Bronk, William. Empty Hands. 1969. 6.00 (ISBN 0-685-00986-6). Elizabeth Pr.

--Finding Losses. (Illus.). 1976. pap. 8.00 (ISBN 0-685-79195-5). Elizabeth Pr.

--The Force of Desire. (Illus.). 1979. 100.00x (ISBN 0-686-59672-2); pap. 14.00 (ISBN 0-686-59673-0). Elizabeth Pr.

--Life Supports: New & Collected Poems. LC 81-2068. 256p. 1981. 20.00 (ISBN 0-86547-039-1). N Point Pr.

--Life Supports: New & Collected Poems. LC 81-2068. 256p. 1982. pap. 10.50 (ISBN 0-86547-040-5). N Point Pr.

--Light & Dark. 1975. 16.00 (ISBN 0-685-56228-X). Elizabeth Pr.

--The Meantime. 1976. 10.00 (ISBN 0-685-79191-2); pap. 5.00 (ISBN 0-685-79192-0). Elizabeth Pr.

--My Father Photographed with Friends. 1976. pap. 8.00 (ISBN 0-685-79193-9). Elizabeth Pr.

--The New World. 1974. pap. 8.00 (ISBN 0-685-40883-3). Elizabeth Pr.

--A Partial Glossary. 1974. pap. 6.00 (ISBN 0-685-40885-X). Elizabeth Pr.

--Silence & Metaphor. 1975. 16.00 (ISBN 0-685-56226-3); pap. 8.00 (ISBN 0-685-56227-1). Elizabeth Pr.

--That Tantalus. 1971. pap. 8.00 (ISBN 0-685-00987-4). Elizabeth Pr.

--To Praise the Music. 1972. 16.00 (ISBN 0-685-27707-0); pap. 8.00 (ISBN 0-686-66726-3). Elizabeth Pr.

--Vectors & Smoothable Curves: Collected Essays of William Bronk. 240p. 1983. 20.00 (ISBN 0-86547-125-8); pap. 12.50 (ISBN 0-86547-126-6). N Point Pr.

--The World, the Worldless. LC 64-16822. 1964. 6.00 (ISBN 0-685-79023-1); sewn in wrappers 1.50. Small Pr Dist.

Bronkhorst, H. J., jt. auth. see Gijlstra, D. J.

Bronkowska, Krystyna, tr. see Nowakowski, Marek.

Bronner, Augusta F. A Comparative Study of the Intelligence of Delinquent Girls. LC 72-176594. (Columbia University. Teachers College. Contributions to Education: No. 68). Repr. of 1914 ed. 22.50 (ISBN 0-404-55068-1). AMS Pr.

Bronner, Augusta F., jt. auth. see Healy, William.

Bronner, E. & Kleinzeller, A., eds. Current Topics in Membranes & Transport, Vol. 12. (Serial Publication). 1979. 61.50 (ISBN 0-12-153312-3). Acad Pr.

Bronner, Edwin. The Encyclopedia of the American Theatre. LC 75-2439. (Illus.). 1980. 30.00 (ISBN 0-498-01219-0). A S Barnes.

Bronner, Edwin & Fraser, David, eds. The Papers of William Penn: Vol. V, Bibliography of the Publications of William Penn. Date not set. price not set. U of Pa Pr.

Bronner, Edwin B. Quakerism & Christianity. LC 67-18689. (Orig.). 1967. pap. 5.00x (ISBN 0-87574-152-5, 152). Pendle Hill.

--William Penn: 17th Century Founding Father. LC 75-32728. (Illus.). 36p. (Orig.). 1975. pap. 2.30x (ISBN 0-87574-204-1). Pendle Hill.

--William Penn's Holy Experiment; the Founding of Pennsylvania Sixteen Eighty-One to Seventeen Hundred & One. LC 78-5882. (Illus.). 306p. 1978. Repr. of 1963 ed. lib. bdg. 22.50x (ISBN 0-313-20432-2, BRWP). Greenwood.

Bronner, Edwin B., ed. see Robson, Walter.

Bronner, Felix & Peterlik, Meinrad. Epithelial Calcium & Phosphate Transport: Molecular & Cellular Aspects. LC 84-17149. (Progress in Clinical & Biological Research Ser.: Vol. 168). 416p. 1984. 68.00 (ISBN 0-8451-5018-9). A R Liss.

Bronner, Felix, ed. Current Topics in Membranes & Transport: Membrane Receptors 2, Vol. 19. (Serial Publication). 1983.. 95.00 (ISBN 0-12-153319-0). Acad Pr.

Bronner, Felix & Coburn, Jack, eds. Disorders of Mineral Metabolism, Vol. I. LC 80-2761. 1981. 69.50 (ISBN 0-12-135301-X). Acad Pr.

--Disorders of Mineral Metabolism: Pathophysiology of Calcium, Phosphorus & Magnesium, Vol. 3. LC 81-12713. 1981. 73.50 (ISBN 0-12-135303-6). Acad Pr.

Bronner, Felix & Coburn, Jack W., eds. Disorders of Mineral Metabolism, Vol. 2. LC 81-20522. 1982. 75.00 (ISBN 0-12-135302-8). Acad Pr.

Bronner, Felix & Kleinzeller, Annost, eds. Current Topics in Membranes & Transport, Vols. 1-9, 11. Incl. Vol. 1. 1970. 47.50 (ISBN 0-12-153301-8); Vol. 2. 1971. 47.50 (ISBN 0-12-153302-6); Vol. 3. 1972. 69.00 (ISBN 0-12-153303-4); Vol. 4. 1974. 69.00 (ISBN 0-12-153304-2); Vol. 5. 1974. 69.00 (ISBN 0-12-153305-0); Vol. 6. 1975. 65.00 (ISBN 0-12-153306-9); Vol. 7. 1975. 65.00 (ISBN 0-12-153307-7); Vol. 8. 1976. 65.00 (ISBN 0-12-153308-5); Vol. 9. 1977. 69.50 (ISBN 0-12-153309-3); Vol. 11. 1978. 70.00 (ISBN 0-12-153311-5). Acad Pr.

Bronner, Felix & Kleinzeller, Arnost, eds. Current Topics in Membranes & Transport, Vol. 18. (Serial Publication). 1983. 59.00 (ISBN 0-12-153318-2). Acad Pr.

--Current Topics in Membranes & Transport, Vol. 21. 1984. 79.00 (ISBN 0-12-153321-2). Acad Pr.

Bronner, Felix & Miller, William, eds. Current Topics in Membranes & Tranport: Vol. 15, Molecular Mechanisms of Photo-Receptor Transduction. LC 70-117091. 1981. 67.50 (ISBN 0-12-153315-8). Acad Pr.

Bronner, Felix & Peterlik, Meindrad, eds. Calcium & Phosphate Transport Across Biomembranes. LC 81-17617. 1981. 40.00 (ISBN 0-12-135280-3). Acad Pr.

Bronner, Felix & Razin, Shmuel, eds. Current Topics in Membranes & Transport: Vol. 17: Membrane Lipids of Prokaryotes. (Serial Publication). 1982. 55.00 (ISBN 0-12-153317-4). Acad Pr.

Bronner, Felix & Slayman, Clifford, eds. Current Topics in Memebranes & Transport: Vol. 16: Electrogenic Ion Pumps. (Serial Publication). 1982. 69.50 (ISBN 0-12-153316-6). Acad Pr.

Bronner, Felix, jt. ed. see Comar, C. L.

Bronner, Felix, et al, eds. Current Topics in Membranes & Transport, Vol. 14. 1980. 65.00 (ISBN 0-12-153314-X). Acad Pr.

Bronner, Hedin. Three Faroese Novelists: An Appreciation of Jorgen-Frantz Jacobsen, William Heinesen & Heolin Bru. LC 73-8069. (Library of Scandinavian Literature). 1973. 19.50x (ISBN 0-8057-3374-4). Irvington.

Bronner, Hedin, ed. see Heinesen, William.

Bronner, Hedin, tr. Faroese Short Stories. (Library of Scandinavian Literature). 1972. lib. bdg. 18.50x (ISBN 0-8057-3308-6). Irvington.

Bronner, Hedin, tr. see Heinesen, William.

Bronner, Leah. Biblical Personalities & Archaeology. (Illus.). 216p. 1975. 7.95x (ISBN 0-685-58308-2). Bloch.

Bronner, Rolf. Decision Making under Time Pressure: An Experimental Study of Stress Behavior in Business Management. LC 81-47626. 208p. 1982. 0.25.00x (ISBN 0-669-04696-5). Lexington Bks.

Bronner, Simon. American Material Culture & Folklife: A Prologue & Dialogue. LC 84-23755. (American Material Culture & Folklife Ser.). 270p. 1984. 24.95 (ISBN 0-8357-1622-8). UMI Res Pr.

Bronner, Simon J. American Folk Art: A Guide to Sources. LC 83-49308. (Reference Library of the Humanities). 300p. 1984. lib. bdg. 35.00 (ISBN 0-8240-9006-3). Garland Pub.

--Chain Carvers: Old Men Crafting Meaning. LC 84-11930. 224p. 1985. 21.00x (ISBN 0-8131-1523-X). U Pr of Ky.

Bronner, Stephen & Kellner, Douglas, eds. Passion & Rebellion: The Expressionist Heritage. 480p. 1983. 29.95x (ISBN 0-686-86220-1); pap. 16.95 (ISBN 0-89789-017-5). Bergin & Garvey.

--Passion & Rebellion: The Expressionist Heritage. LC 81-40492. (Illus.). 468p. 1983. text ed. 35.00x (ISBN 0-87663-356-4). Universe.

Bronner, Stephen E. A Revolutionary for Our Times: Rosa Luxemburg. 128p. 1981. pap. 5.95 (ISBN 0-86104-348-0). Pluto Pr.

Bronner, Stephen E., ed. see Pachter, Henry.

Bronner, Steven, ed. see Pachter, Henry.

Bronosted, A. An Introduction to Convex Polytopes. (Graduate Texts in Mathematics: Vol. 90), (Illus.). 160p. 1983. 33.00 (ISBN 0-387-90722-X). Springer-Verlag.

Bronowski, J. The Common Sense of Science. LC 53-9924. 1978. pap. 4.95 (ISBN 0-674-14651-4). Harvard U Pr.

--Identity of Man. rev. ed. LC 71-188042. 1971 (AMS). pap. 3.50 (ISBN 0-385-00171-1, AMS). Natural Hist.

--William Blake: A Man Without a Mask. LC 67-30809. (Studies in Blake, No. 3). 1969. Repr. of 1947 ed. lib. bdg. 49.95x (ISBN 0-8383-0709-4). Haskell.

Bronowski, J., ed. see Blake, William.

Bronowski, Jacob. The Ascent of Man. LC 73-20446. (Illus.). 448p. 1974. 34.00 (ISBN 0-316-10930-4); pap. 19.45i (ISBN 0-316-10933-9). Little.

--Magic, Science, & Civilization. LC 78-1660. (Bampton Lectures in America Ser.: No. 20). 88p. 1978. 15.00x (ISBN 0-231-04484-4); pap. 8.00 (ISBN 0-231-04485-2). Columbia U Pr.

--On Being an Intellectual. LC 70-570. 1968. pap. 1.25 (ISBN 0-87391-013-3). Smith Coll.

--The Origins of Knowledge & Imagination. LC 77-13209. (Silliman Lectures Ser.). 1978. 17.50x (ISBN 0-300-02192-5); pap. 5.95x (ISBN 0-300-02409-6). Yale U Pr.

--Poet's Defense. LC 78-14105. 1979. Repr. of 1939 ed. 21.00 (ISBN 0-88355-778-9). Hyperion Conn.

--Science & Human Values. pap. 4.95xi (ISBN 0-06-130505-7, TB505, Torch). Har-Row.

--Science & Human Values. rev. & enl. ed. Bd. with The Abacus & the Rose. (Illus.). 142p. 1972. pap. 3.37i (ISBN 0-06-080269-3, P269, PL). Har-Row.

--A Sense of the Future: Essays in Natural Philosophy. Ariotti, Piero & Bronowski, Rita, eds. LC 77-9292. 1977. pap. 6.95 (ISBN 0-262-52050-8). MIT Pr.

--The Visionary Eye: Essays in the Arts, Literature, & Science. Ariotti, Piero & Bronowski, Rita, eds. 1978. 22.50x (ISBN 0-262-02129-3); pap. 5.95 (ISBN 0-262-52068-0). MIT Pr.

--William Blake: A Man Without a Mask. 1976. lib. bdg. 59.95 (ISBN 0-8490-1300-3). Gordon Pr.

Bronowski, Jacob & Mazlish, Bruce. The Western Intellectual Tradition: From Leonardo to Hegel. facsimile ed. LC 70-167315. (Essay Index Reprint Ser.). Repr. of 1960 ed. 37.00 (ISBN 0-8369-2448-7). Ayer Co Pubs.

--Western Intellectual Tradition: From Leonardo to Hegel. pap. 7.95xi (ISBN 0-06-133001-9, TB 3001, Torch). Har-Row.

Bronowski, Jacob & Selsam, Millicent E. Biography of an Atom. LC 64-19708. (Illus.). 48p. (gr. 4-7). 1965. PLB 10.89 (ISBN 0-06-020641-1). HarpJ.

Bronowski, Rita, ed. see Bronowski, Jacob.

Bronsen, Hugo H. Sports & Athletic Injuries: Medical Subject Analysis & Research Index with Bibliography. LC 83-71667. 120p. 1985. 29.95 (ISBN 0-88164-052-2); pap. 21.95 (ISBN 0-88164-053-0). ABBE Pubs Assn.

--Sports Medicine: International Survey with Research Subject Index & Bibliography. LC 82-72013. 158p. 1983. 29.95 (ISBN 0-941864-42-1); pap. 21.95 (ISBN 0-941864-43-X). ABBE Pubs Assn.

Bronshtein, I. N. & Semendyayev, K. A. Handbook of Mathematics. 1100p. 1985. flexible plastic cover 37.95 (ISBN 0-442-21171-6). Van Nos Reinhold.

Bronski, Michael. Culture Clash: The Making of Gay Sensibility. 220p. (Orig.). 1984. 20.00 (ISBN 0-89608-218-0); pap. 9.00 (ISBN 0-89608-217-2). South End Pr.

Bronson, B. H., et al. Studies in the Comic. LC 76-29415. Repr. of 1941 ed. 23.50 (ISBN 0-404-15324-0). AMS Pr.

Bronson, Bertrand H. The Ballad As Song. LC 74-84045. (Illus.). 1969. 38.50x (ISBN 0-520-01399-9). U of Cal Pr.

--Chaucer's House of Fame. LC 73-3434. 1934. lib. bdg. 10.00 (ISBN 0-8414-1768-7). Folcroft.

--Facets of the Enlightenment: Studies in English Literature & Its Contexts. LC 68-56074. 1968. 35.00x (ISBN 0-520-00176-1). U of Cal Pr.

--Five Studies in Literature. LC 72-194755. 1940. lib. bdg. 17.50 (ISBN 0-8414-2502-7). Folcroft.

--In Appreciation of Chaucer's Parlement of Foules. LC 77-13748. 1935. lib. bdg. 10.00 (ISBN 0-8414-1717-2). Folcroft.

--Johnson Agonistes & Other Essays. Orig. Title: Johnson & Boswell: Three Essays. 1965. pap. 2.50x (ISBN 0-520-00175-3, CAL114). U of Cal Pr.

--Johnson & Boswell. 475p. 1980. Repr. of 1944 ed. lib. bdg. 30.00 (ISBN 0-8495-0397-3). Arden Lib.

--Johnson & Boswell. LC 76-23460. 1944. lib. bdg. 15.00 (ISBN 0-8414-3242-2). Folcroft.

--Traditional Tunes of the Child Ballads, 4 vols. Incl. Vol. 1. 1959; Vol. 2. 1962 (ISBN 0-691-09105-6). 82.50x (ISBN 0-686-66603-8); Vol. 3. 1966 (ISBN 0-691-09106-4); Vol. 4. 1972 (ISBN 0-691-09115-3). 82.50x (ISBN 0-686-66605-4). o.p. 210.00 set (ISBN 0-685-23096-1). Princeton U Pr.

Bronson, Bertrand H., ed. The Singing Tradition of Child's Popular Ballads. abr. ed. LC 75-2980. 488p. 1976. 55.00 (ISBN 0-691-09119-6); pap. 19.95 (ISBN 0-691-02704-8). Princeton U Pr.

Bronson, Bertrand H., ed. see Johnson, Samuel.

Bronson, Bertrand H., et al. Five Studies in Literature. LC 78-58253. (Essay Index in Reprint Ser.). 1978. Repr. 18.50x (ISBN 0-8486-3015-7). Core Collection.

--Studies in the Comic. LC 74-3333. lib. bdg. 22.50 (ISBN 0-8414-3128-0). Folcroft.

Bronson, Dorrance C. Concepts of Actuarial Soundness in Pension Plans. 1957. 10.00 (ISBN 0-256-00641-5). Irwin.

Bronson, Edgar B. Reminiscences of a Ranchman. LC 62-8407. xvi, 370p. 1962. 25.50x (ISBN 0-8032-0886-3); pap. 6.95 (ISBN 0-8032-5023-1, BB 127, Bison). U of Nebr Pr.

Bronson, Fred. The Billboard Book of Number One Hits. (Illus.). 624p. 1985. 14.95 (ISBN 0-8230-7522-2, Billboard Bks). Watson-Guptill.

Bronson, Gary J. & Bronson, R. Mathemathics for Management. 1977. text ed. 28.50 scp (ISBN 0-7002-2503-X, HarpC); scp solutions manual 9.50 (ISBN 0-7002-2505-6). Har-Row.

Bronson, Gordon. The Scanning Patterns of Human Infants: Implications for Visual Learning. LC 81-20543. (Monographs on Infancy: Vol. 2). 1982. 24.50 (ISBN 0-89391-114-3). Ablex Pub.

Bronson, Harold. Rock Explosion. Ochs, Michael, ed. (Illus.). 128p. 1984. pap. 10.95 (ISBN 0-930589-00-9). Rhino Books.

Bronson, Harriet. Do I Have a House for You? 1980. 1.50 (ISBN 0-8431-0155-5). Price Stern.

Bronson, J. & Bronson, R. Early American Weaving & Dyeing: The Domestic Manufacturer's Assistant, & Family Directory in the Arts of Weaving & Dyeing. (Illus.). 224p. 1977. pap. 4.50 (ISBN 0-486-23440-1). Dover.

--Early American Weaving & Dyeing: The Domestic Manufacturer's Assistant & Family Directory in the Arts of Weaving & Dyeing. 14.00 (ISBN 0-8446-5560-0). Peter Smith.

Bronson, Judith Gunn, jt. ed. see Dreesman, Gordon R.

Bronson, Julien L. Parrots. Orig. Title: Parrot Family: Their Training, Care, & Breeding. (Illus.). 80p. 1985. pap. text ed. 3.95 (ISBN 0-86622-232-4, PB-120). TFH Pubns.

Bronson, Marion B. Pea River Reflections: History & Legends of Coffee County, Alabama. 3rd ed. (Illus.). 1984. 7.95 (ISBN 0-916620-76-X). Portals Pr.

Bronson, R. Matrix Methods: An Introduction. 1970. text ed. 21.75i (ISBN 0-12-135250-1). Acad Pr.

--Schaum's Outline of Operations Research. (Schaum Paperback Ser.). 1982. pap. 9.95 (ISBN 0-07-007977-3). McGraw.

Bronson, R., jt. auth. see Bronson, Gary J.

Bronson, R., jt. auth. see Bronson, J.

Bronson, Richard. Modern Introductory Differential Equations. (Schaum Outline Ser.). 1973. pap. text ed. 8.95 (ISBN 0-07-008009-7). McGraw.

Bronson, Richard A., frwd. by see Barker, Graham H.

Bronson, Walter C. American Poems: Sixteen Twenty-Five to Eighteen Ninety-Two. 1977. Repr. of 1912 ed. 30.00 (ISBN 0-89984-141-4). Century Bookbindery.

--American Poems: Sixteen Twenty-Five to Eighteen Ninety-Two. Repr. of 1925 ed. 25.00 (ISBN 0-686-18748-2). Scholars Ref Lib.

--English Poems. 1979. Repr. of 1907 ed. lib. bdg. 30.00 (ISBN 0-8495-0539-9). Arden Lib.

--English Poems. LC 70-109135. (Granger Index Reprint Ser.). 424p. 1982. Repr. of 1910 ed. lib. bdg. 17.00 (ISBN 0-8290-0527-7). Irvington.

--English Poems: Old English & Middle English Periods 450-1550. 1978. Repr. of 1910 ed. lib. bdg. 35.00 (ISBN 0-8492-3560-X). R West.

--English Poems: The Elizabethan Age & the Puritan Period,1550-1660. 1977. Repr. of 1909 ed. 25.00 (ISBN 0-89984-139-2). Century Bookbindery.

--English Poems: The Nineteenth Century. 1977. Repr. of 1907 ed. 25.00 (ISBN 0-89984-140-6). Century Bookbindery.

--History of Brown University, 1764-1914. LC 75-165708. (American Education Ser, No. 2). 1972. Repr. of 1914 ed. 25.00 (ISBN 0-405-03697-3). Ayer Co Pubs.

--A Short History of American Literature. 1900. Repr. 30.00 (ISBN 0-8274-3398-0). R West.

Bronson, Walter C., ed. American Prose. facs. ed. LC 71-121525. (Short Story Index Reprint Ser). 1916. 32.00 (ISBN 0-8369-3481-4). Ayer Co Pubs.

--English Essays. facs. ed. LC 74-111817. (Essay Index Reprint Ser.). 1905. 24.50 (ISBN 0-8369-1595-X). Ayer Co Pubs.

--English Poems. 424p. 1982. Repr. of 1910 ed. lib. bdg. 35.00 (ISBN 0-89760-086-X). Telegraph Bks.

--English Poems: Four Fifty to Fifteen Fifty. facsimile ed. LC 70-109135. (Granger Index Reprint Ser). 1910. 18.00 (ISBN 0-8369-6119-6). Ayer Co Pubs.

--English Poems: Sixteen Sixty to Eighteen Hundred. facs. ed. LC 70-109135. (Granger Index Reprint Ser). 1908. 24.00 (ISBN 0-8369-6195-1). Ayer Co Pubs.

--English Poems: The Elizabethan Age & the Puritan Period (1550-1660, Vol. 2. LC 7-29843. (Granger Poetry Library). 1979. Repr. of 1909 ed. 36.50x (ISBN 0-89609-154-6). Granger Bk.

--English Poems: The Nineteenth Century. facsimile ed. LC 76-38595. (Granger Index Reprint Ser). Repr. of 1907 ed. 29.00 (ISBN 0-8369-6327-X). Ayer Co Pubs.

--English Poems: The Nineteenth Century, Vol. 4. LC 7-29843. (Granger Poetry Library). 1979. Repr. of 1907 ed. 32.50x (ISBN 0-89609-155-4). Granger Bk.

--English Poems: The Restoration & the Eighteenth Century 1660-1800. 1978. Repr. of 1908 ed. lib. bdg. 25.00 (ISBN 0-8414-1658-3). Folcroft.

--English Poems: Vol. 3-Restoration & Eighteenth Century. LC 7-29843. (Granger Poetry Library). 552p. 1982. Repr. of 1908 ed. 36.50x (ISBN 0-89609-227-5). Granger Bk.

--English Poems: Volume 1, Old English & Middle Periods, 450-1550. LC 7-29843. (Granger Poetry Library). 1979. Repr. of 1910 ed. 29.75x (ISBN 0-89609-153-8). Granger Bk.

Bronson, Walter C., ed. see Collins, W.

Bronson, Walter L. American Prose: Sixteen Seven to Eighteen Sixty-Five. 1916. Repr. 35.00 (ISBN 0-8274-3917-2). R West.

Bronson, Wanda C. Toddler's Behaviors with Age Mates: Issues of Interaction, Cognition & Affect. LC 81-12896. (Monographs on Infancy: Vol. 1). 144p. 1981. text ed. 24.50 (ISBN 0-89391-080-5). Ablex Pub.

Bronstein. Chess Struggle & Practice. 1980. 17.95 (ISBN 0-679-13064-0); pap. 9.95 (ISBN 0-679-14152-9). McKay.

Bronstein, Alvin J. Representing Prisoners: A Course Handbook. (Litigation & Adminstrative Practice Ser.). 973p. 1981. softcover 35.00 (ISBN 0-686-79681-0, C4-4154). PLI.

Bronstein, Alvin J. & Hirschkop, Philip J. Prisoner's Rights Nineteen Seventy-Nine, 2 vols. (Litigation & Administrative Practice Course Handbook Ser. 1978-79: Vols. 105 & 106). 1979. pap. 35.00 (ISBN 0-685-94312-7, C6-4133). PLI.

Bronstein, Arthur J. Pronunciation of American English. (Illus.). 1960. 22.95 (ISBN 0-13-730887-6). P-H.

Bronstein, Audrey. The Triple Struggle: Latin American Peasant Women. 268p. 1983. 20.00 (ISBN 0-89608-180-X); pap. 7.50 (ISBN 0-89608-179-6). South End Pr.

Bronstein, Daniel J. & Schulweis, Harold M., eds. Approaches to the Philosophy of Religion. facsimile ed. LC 77-93320. (Essay Index Reprint Ser). 1954. 33.00 (ISBN 0-8369-1344-2). Ayer Co Pubs.

Bronstein, Daniel J., et al. Basic Problems of Philosophy. 4th ed. LC 79-179449. 656p. 1972. text ed. 30.95 (ISBN 0-13-067637-3). P-H.

Bronstein, David. Zurich International Chess Tournament, Nineteen Fifty-Three. Marfia, Jim, tr. from Rus. LC 78-74881. (Illus.). 1979. pap. 6.95 (ISBN 0-486-23800-8). Dover.

Bronstein, David & Smolyan, Georgy. Chess in the Eighties. Neat, Kenneth P., tr. (Pergamon Russian Chess Ser.). 112p. 1982. 14.95 (ISBN 0-08-024126-3). Pergamon.

Bronstein, Eugene, jt. auth. see Hisrich, Bob.

Bronstein, Harry. Siddur Shomrei Emunah. vi, 618p. 1982. 5.50 (ISBN 0-914787-01-2). Mutzal Me'esh Inst.

Bronstein, Harry, ed. see Friedman, Avraham A.

Bronstein, Herbert, ed. A Passover Haggadah. (Illus.). 1974. 79.00 set (ISBN 0-916694-66-6); 8.50 (ISBN 0-916694-71-2); lib. bdg. 27.50 (ISBN 0-916694-06-2); pap. 7.50 (ISBN 0-916694-05-4). Central Conf.

Bronstein, Herbert & Friedlander, Albert, eds. The Five Scrolls. 324p. 1984. 12.00 (ISBN 0-916694-80-1); deluxe ed. 60.00 (ISBN 0-916694-81-X); special ltd. ed., leatherbound 675.00 (ISBN 0-916694-82-8). Central Conf.

Bronstein, Herbert, ed. see Central Conference of American Rabbis.

Bronstein, I. U. Extensions of Minimal Transformation Groups. 327p. 1979. 47.50x (ISBN 90-286-0368-9). Sijthoff & Noordhoff.

Bronstein, I. U., et al. Eleven Papers on Logic, Algebra, Analysis & Topology. LC 51-5559. (Translations, Ser.: No. 2, Vol. 97). 1970. 33.00 (ISBN 0-8218-1797-3, TRANS 2-97). Am Math.

Bronstein, Leo. El Greco. (Library of Great Painters Ser). (Illus.). 1950. 40.00 (ISBN 0-8109-0155-2). Abrams.

--Five Variations on the Theme of Japanese Painting. LC 65-27614. (Illus.). 1969. 25.00 (ISBN 0-87027-105-9). Cumberland Pr.

--Kabbalah & Art. LC 78-63585. (Illus.). 146p. 1980. 25.00x (ISBN 0-87451-163-1). U Pr of New Eng.

Bronstein, Raphael. Science of Violin Playing. 2nd ed. 288p. 1981. 25.00 (ISBN 0-87666-638-1, Z-10). Paganiniana Pubns.

Bronstein, Ricki A., et al. Teleconferencing: A Practical Guide to Teaching by Telephone. LC 82-11534. (Illus.). 115p. 1982. pap. text ed. 7.50 (ISBN 0-89189-150-1, 45-9-014-00). Am Soc Clinical.

Bronte, Anne. Agnes Grey. 256p. 1985. pap. 3.95x (ISBN 0-460-02509-0, Evman). Biblio Dist.

--The Brontes: Selected Poems. Barker, Juliet R., ed. 160p. 1985. pap. 3.95x (ISBN 0-460-01496-X, Pub. by Evman England). Biblio Dist.

--Complete Poems. 1971. Repr. of 1924 ed. 39.00x (ISBN 0-403-01758-0). Scholarly.

--The Tenant of Wildfell Hall. 339p. 1979. pap. 5.95 (ISBN 0-586-02657-6, Pub. by Granada England). Academy Chi Pubs.

--The Tenant of Wildfell Hall. Bd. with Agnes Grey. 1979. 14.95x (ISBN 0-460-00685-1, Evman). Biblio Dist.

--The Tenant of Wildfell Hall. 1982. pap. 4.75x (ISBN 0-460-11685-1, Evman). Biblio Dist.

--The Tenant of Wildfell Hall. (The Zodiac Press Ser.). 416p. 1978. 10.95 (ISBN 0-7011-1238-7, Pub. by Chatto & Windus). Merrimack Pub Cir.

--The Tenant of Wildfell Hall. Hargreaves, G. D., ed. (Penguin English Library). 1980. pap. 4.95 (ISBN 0-14-043137-3). Penguin.

--The Tenant of Wildfell Hall. LC 79-4122. (Banquo Bks). 1979. pap. 4.95 (ISBN 0-912800-70-4). Woodbridge Pr.

Bronte, Anne, jt. auth. see Charlotte, Emily.

Bronte, Charlotte. Complete Poems of Charlotte Bronte. LC 73-131647. (Literature Ser). 266p. 1972. Repr. of 1924 ed. 39.00x (ISBN 0-403-00534-5). Scholarly.

--An Hour with Charlotte Bronte. LC 76-24882. 1976. Repr. of 1883 ed. lib. bdg. 20.00 (ISBN 0-8414-4839-6). Folcroft.

--Jane Eyre. (Classics Ser.). (gr. 9 up). 1964. pap. 2.50 (ISBN 0-8049-0017-5, CL-17). Airmont.

--Jane Eyre. (Literature Ser.). (gr. 7-12). 1969. pap. text ed. 5.17 (ISBN 0-87720-706-2). AMSCO Sch.

--Jane Eyre. (Bantam Classics Ser.). 433p. (gr. 7-12). 1981. pap. 1.95 (ISBN 0-553-21140-4). Bantam.

--Jane Eyre. Kendrick, Walter, ed. (Macdonald Classics Ser.). 508p. 1980. deluxe ed. 14.95 (ISBN 0-8464-1070-2). Beekman Pubs.

--Jane Eyre. 1977. (Evman); pap. 3.50x (ISBN 0-460-01287-8, DEL-04530, Evman). Biblio Dist.

--Jane Eyre. (Great Illlustrated Classics Ser.). (Illus.). (gr. 9 up). 1979. 13.95 (ISBN 0-396-08259-9). Dodd.

--Jane Eyre. (The Zodiac Press Ser.). 464p. 1978. 9.95 (ISBN 0-7011-1239-5, Pub. by Chatto & Windus). Merrimack Pub Cir.

--Jane Eyre. (RL 7). 1971. pap. 1.95 (ISBN 0-451-51884-5, Sig Classics). NAL.

--Jane Eyre. Dunn, Richard J., ed. (Critical Editions Ser). 1971. pap. text ed. 8.95x (ISBN 0-393-09966-0). Norton.

--Jane Eyre. Jack, Jane & Smith, Margaret, eds. (Clarendon Editions of the Novels of the Brontes Ser.). 1969. 52.00x (ISBN 0-19-811490-7). Oxford U Pr.

--Jane Eyre. Smith, Margaret, ed. (World's Classics Ser.). 1980. pap. 2.25 (ISBN 0-19-281513-X). Oxford U Pr.

--Jane Eyre. Shefter, Harry, et al, eds. (Enriched Classic Ser.). (YA) 1982. pap. 3.95 (ISBN 0-671-45996-1, RE). PB.

--Jane Eyre. Farr, Naunerle, ed. (Now Age Illustrated III Ser.). (Illus.). (gr. 4-12). 1977. text ed. 5.00 (ISBN 0-88301-278-2); pap. text ed. 1.95 (ISBN 0-88301-266-9). Pendulum Pr.

--Jane Eyre. Leavis, Q. D., ed. (English Library Ser.). pap. 2.25 (ISBN 0-14-043011-3). Penguin.

--Jane Eyre. LC 80-14426. (Raintree Short Classics). (Illus.). 48p. (gr. 4 up). 1981. PLB 15.15 (ISBN 0-8172-1661-8). Raintree Pubs.

--Jane Eyre. 560p. 1982. pap. 3.95 (ISBN 0-671-45996-1). WSP.

--Jane Eyre. Stewart, Diana, adapted by. LC 80-14426. (Raintree Short Classics Ser.). (Illus.). 48p. (gr. 4-8). 1983. pap. 9.27 (ISBN 0-8172-2012-7). Raintree Pubs.

--Jane Eyre. (Illustrated Junior Library). (Illus.). 1983. deluxe ed. 10.95 (ISBN 0-448-06031-0, G&D). Putnam Pub Group.

--Jane Eyre. 599p. 1984. Repr. lib. bdg. 21.95x (ISBN 0-89966-493-8). Buccaneer Bks.

--Jane Eyre. LC 84-61675. (Illus.). 480p. 1984. 12.95 (ISBN 0-89577-200-0). RD Assn.

--Jane Eyre. Date not set. price not set. S&S.

--Life & Works of the Sisters Bronte, 7 Vols. LC 77-148757. Repr. of 1903 ed. Set. 315.00 (ISBN 0-404-08830-9); 45.00 ea. AMS Pr.

--Professor & Emma. (A Fragment Ser.). 1975. Repr. 9.95x (ISBN 0-460-00417-4, Evman). Biblio Dist.

--The Professor & Emma. 1985. pap. 5.50 (ISBN 0-460-02508-2, Evman). Biblio Dist.

--The Secret & Lily Hart: Two Tales. Holtz, William, ed. LC 78-19645. 96p. 1979. pap. 5.95 (ISBN 0-8262-0268-3). U of Mo Pr.

--Shirley. 1975. Repr. of 1908 ed. 9.95x (ISBN 0-460-00288-0, Evman). Biblio Dist.

--Shirley. (Clarendon Edition of the Novels of Brontes). (Illus.). 1981. text ed. 85.00x (ISBN 0-19-812565-8). Oxford U Pr.

--Shirley. Hook, Andrew & Hook, Judith, eds. (English Library Ser.). (Orig.). 1974. pap. 4.95 (ISBN 0-14-043095-4). Penguin.

--Shirley. Smith, Margaret & Rosengarten, Herbert, eds. (The World's Classics-Paperback Ser.). 1981. pap. 3.95 (ISBN 0-19-281562-8). Oxford U Pr.

--Something About Arthur. Alexander, Christine, ed. 1981. 12.95 (ISBN 0-87959-095-5). U of Tex H Ransom Ctr.

--The Spell: An Extraveganza. 1979. Repr. of 1931 ed. lib. bdg. 27.00 (ISBN 0-8495-0511-9). Arden Lib.

--Spell: Extravanganza. Maclean, George E, ed. LC 72-191958. 1931. lib. bdg. 25.00 (ISBN 0-8414-0804-1). Folcroft.

--Villette. 1974. 9.95x (ISBN 0-460-00351-8, Evman); pap. 2.75x (ISBN 0-460-01351-3, Evman). Biblio Dist.

--Villette. (The Zodiac Press Ser.). 488p. 1978. 10.95 (ISBN 0-7011-1240-9, Pub. by Chatto & Windus). Merrimack Pub Cir.

--Villette. Lilly, Mark, ed. Tanner, Tony, tr. (English Library). 1980. pap. 5.95 (ISBN 0-14-043118-7). Penguin.

--Villette. 1983. pap. text ed. 3.95x (ISBN 0-460-11351-8, Pub. by Evman England). Biblio Dist.

--Villette. Rosengarten, Herbert & Smith, Margaret, eds. (Illus.). 1984. 69.00 (ISBN 0-19-812597-6). Oxford U Pr.

Bronte, Charlotte see Eyre, A. G.

Bronte, Charlotte see Swan, D. K.

Bronte, Emily. Wuthering Heights. (Classics Ser). (gr. 9 up). 1964. pap. 2.95 (ISBN 0-8049-0011-6, CL-11). Airmont.

--Wuthering Heights. (Literature Ser.). (gr. 9-12). 1969. pap. text ed. 5.33 (ISBN 0-87720-720-8). AMSCO Sch.

--Wuthering Heights. (Bantam Classics Ser.). 320p. (gr. 7-12). 1981. pap. 1.95 (ISBN 0-553-21141-2). Bantam.

--Wuthering Heights. Kendrick, Walter, ed. (Classics Ser.). 400p. 1980. deluxe ed. 14.95 (ISBN 0-8464-1072-9). Beekman Pubs.

--Wuthering Heights. 1961. pap. 2.75 (ISBN 0-440-39728-6, LE). Dell.

--Wuthering Heights. (Reader's Request Ser.). 1980. lib. bdg. 13.95 (ISBN 0-8161-3074-4, Large Print Bks). G K Hall.

--Wuthering Heights. Clay, N. L., ed. (Guide Novel Ser.). pap. text ed. 4.50x (ISBN 0-435-16100-8). Heinemann Ed.

--Wuthering Heights. Pritchett, V. S., ed. LC 56-14017. (YA) (gr. 9 up). 1956. pap. 5.50 (ISBN 0-395-05102-9, RivEd). HM.

--Wuthering Heights. (The Zodiac Press Ser.). 320p. 1978. 9.95 (ISBN 0-7011-1241-7, Pub. by Chatto & Windus). Merrimack Pub Cir.

--Wuthering Heights. (Modern Library College Editions). 1950. pap. text ed. 5.00 (ISBN 0-394-30904-9, T4, RanC). Random.

--Wuthering Heights. 320p. (RL 10). 1973. pap. 1.95 (ISBN 0-451-51958-2, CE1650, Sig Classics). NAL.

--Wuthering Heights. rev. ed. Sale, William M., Jr., ed. (Critical Editions Ser.). (Annotated). (gr. 9-12). 1972. pap. text ed. 5.95x (ISBN 0-393-09400-6, 9601). Norton.

--Wuthering Heights. Marsden, Hilda & Jack, Ion, eds. (Clarendon Edition of the Novels of the Brontes Ser.). 1976. 49.00x (ISBN 0-19-812511-9). Oxford U Pr.

--Wuthering Heights. Jack, Ian, ed. (World's Classics Ser.). 1981. pap. 2.95 (ISBN 0-19-281543-1). Oxford U Pr.

--Wuthering Heights. Shefter, Harry, et al, eds. (Enriched Classic Ser.). (YA) 1983. pap. 3.50 (ISBN 0-671-47718-8, RE). PB.

--Wuthering Heights. new & abr. ed. Farr, Naunerle, ed. (Now Age Illustrated III Ser.). (Illus.). (gr. 4-12). 1977. text ed. 5.00 (ISBN 0-88301-284-7); pap. text ed. 1.95 (ISBN 0-88301-272-3). Pendulum Pr.

--Wuthering Heights. Daiches, David, ed. (English Library Ser.). 1965. pap. 2.50 (ISBN 0-14-043001-6). Penguin.

--Wuthering Heights. Wright, Betty R., adapted by. LC 81-15786. (Raintree Short Classics). (Illus.). 48p. (gr. 4 up). 1982. PLB 15.15 (ISBN 0-8172-1682-0). Raintree Pubs.

--Wuthering Heights. 360p. 35.00 (ISBN 0-913720-31-3, Sandstone). Beil.

--Wuthering Heights. Shefter, Harry, ed. (Enriched Classics Edition Ser.). 460p. pap. 2.95 (ISBN 0-671-42465-3). WSP.

--Wuthering Heights. LC 25-26570. (Illus.). 1950. 8.95 (ISBN 0-394-60458-X). Modern Lib.

--Wuthering Heights. Wright, Betty R., adapted by. LC 81-15786. (Raintree Short Classics Ser.). (Illus.). 48p. (gr. 4-12). 1983. pap. 9.27 (ISBN 0-8172-2029-1). Raintree Pubs.

--Wuthering Heights. LC 82-62131. (Illus.). 303p. 1982. 12.95 (ISBN 0-89577-159-4). RD Assn.

--Wuthering Heights. (Madhuban Abridged Classics Ser.). 96p. 1983. pap. 3.95x (ISBN 0-7069-2528-9, Pub by Vikas India). Advent NY.

--Wuthering Heights. (Illus.). 384p. 1985. 11.95 (ISBN 0-396-08533-4). Dodd.

--Wuthering Heights & Poems. 1978. 12.95x (ISBN 0-460-00243-0, Evman); pap. 3.95x (ISBN 0-460-01243-6, Evman). Biblio Dist.

--Wuthering Heights with Reader's Guide. (AMSCO Literature Program Ser.). (gr. 10-12). 1970. pap. text ed. 6.08 (ISBN 0-87720-809-3); with model ans. 3.85 (ISBN 0-87720-909-X). AMSCO Sch.

Bronte, Emily see Eyre, A. G.

Bronte, Emily J. The Complete Poems of Emily J. Bronte. Hatfield, C. W., ed. LC 41-21750. 262p. 1941. 24.00x (ISBN 0-231-01222-5). Columbia U Pr.

--Five Essays Written in French. 1978. Repr. of 1948 ed. lib. bdg. 10.00 (ISBN 0-8495-0433-3). Arden Lib.

Bronte, Louisa. The Vallette Heritage. 1978. pap. 2.25 (ISBN 0-515-04309-5). Jove Pubns.

--The Van Rhyne Heritage. (Orig.). 1979. pap. 2.25 (ISBN 0-515-04310-9). Jove Pubns.

Bronte, Louisa & Roberts, Janet L. This Shining Splendor. 320p. 1984. pap. 3.50 (ISBN 0-515-07610-4). Jove Pubns.

Bronte, Patrick. Bronteana. 304p. 1980. Repr. of 1898 ed. lib. bdg. 35.00 (ISBN 0-8495-5156-0). Arden Lib.

--Bronteana: The Rev. Patrick Bronte, His Collected Works & Life. LC 77-148320. Repr. of 1898 ed. 16.00 (ISBN 0-404-08920-8). AMS Pr.

--Complete Transcript of the Leyland Manuscripts. Symington, J. Alex, ed. LC 72-193739. 1925. lib. bdg. 10.00 (ISBN 0-8414-2503-5). Folcroft.

Bronte, Patrick B. The Poems of Patrick Branwell Bronte. Winnifrith, Tom, ed. 384p. 1983. 40.00x (ISBN 0-8147-9198-0). NYU Pr.

Bronte Society. Catalogue of the Museum & the Library of the Bronte Society. 1927. 21.00 (ISBN 0-8337-3464-4). B Franklin.

Bronte, Stephen. Japanese Finance. 258p. 1982. 88.00 (ISBN 0-8002-3404-9). Intl Pubns Serv.

Bronwell, Arthur B. Science & Technology in the World of the Future. LC 74-114914. 1970. 22.50 (ISBN 0-471-10594-5, Pub. by Wiley). Krieger.

Bronwell, Nancy. Lubbock: A Pictorial History. Friedman, Donna R., ed. LC 80-22748. (Illus.). 208p. 1980. pap. 12.95 (ISBN 0-89865-076-3). Donning Co.

Bronwen, Meredith. Young Beauty. (Illus.). 208p. 1984. pap. 13.95 cancelled (ISBN 0-317-01519-2). Macmillan.

Bronx County Historical Society, jt. auth. see Ultan, Lloyd.

Bronz, S. The Challenge of America: From Reconstruction to the Present. text ed. 23.52 (ISBN 0-03-002866-3, HoltE); pap. 6.72 studybk. (ISBN 0-03-008301-X); T.E. of studybk. paper 6.44 (ISBN 0-03-008306-0); key to tests paper 2.92 (ISBN 0-03-008316-8). HR&W.

--The Challenge of America: From the Early Beginnings to Reconstruction. text ed. 23.52 (ISBN 0-03-002861-2); pap. 6.72 studybk. (ISBN 0-03-008286-2); T.E. of studybk. paper 6.44 (ISBN 0-03-008291-9); tests paper 3.08 (ISBN 0-03-008296-X) (ISBN 0-03-008316-8). HR&W.

Bronz, Stephen H. Roots of Negro Racial Consciousness. 1964. 5.00 (ISBN 0-87212-019-8). Libra.

Bronzino, Joseph D. Computer Applications for Patient Care. 1982. o. p. 24.95 (ISBN 0-201-10156-4, 10156, Pub. by Med-Nurse); pap. 21.95 (ISBN 0-201-10157-2, Pub. by Med-Nurse). Addison-Wesley.

Bronznick, jt. auth. see Uveeler.

Bronzo, Mary L., et al. An Introduction to Black Nonstandard English for Teachers. Smith, Donald E., ed. (Michigan Learning Modules Ser.: No. 30). 56p. (Orig.). 1979. pap. text ed. 3.25x (ISBN 0-914004-33-6). Ulrich.

Broods, Anne T. Evergreen Girl. (Sharon Romance Ser.). 224p. (Orig.). 1981. pap. 2.25 (ISBN 0-89531-125-9, 0198-96). Sharon Pubns.

Brook. Applied Regression Analysis & Experimental Design. (Statistics: Monographs & Textbooks). 264p. 1985. 39.75 (ISBN 0-8247-7252-0). Dekker.

--Introduction to the Symphony. (Symphony Ser.). 1985. lib. bdg. 90.00 (ISBN 0-8240-3860-6). Garland Pub.

Brook, Alan J. The Biology of Desmids. LC 80-26374. (Botanical Monographs.: Vol. 16). (Illus.). 275p. 1981. 60.00x (ISBN 0-520-04281-6). U of Cal Pr.

Brook, Alan J., jt. auth. see Lind, Edna M.

Brook, Andrew T., tr. see Gindely, Anton.

Brook, Barry S. Thematic Catalogues in Music: An Annotated Bibliography. (RILM Retrospectives Ser.: No. 1). 1972. lib. bdg. 32.00 (ISBN 0-918728-02-9). Pendragon NY.

Brook, Barry S., ed. see Conti, Francesco B., et al.

Brook, Barry S., ed. see D'Ordonez, Carlo.

Brook, Barry S., ed. see Gossec, Francois-Joseph.

Brook, Barry S., ed. see Holzbauer, Ignaz.

Brook, Barry S., jt. ed. see Jenkins, Newell.

Brook, Barry S., ed. see Le Duc, Simon & Saint-Georges, Le Chevalier de.

Brook, Barry S., ed. see Tritto, Domenico, et al.

Brook, Barry S., et al, eds. The Overture in France Seventeen Ninety to Eighteen Ten. (The Symphony Ser.). 328p. 1983. lib. bdg. 90.00 (ISBN 0-8240-3836-3). Garland Pub.

--Perspectives in Musicology. 2nd ed. LC 78-103964. (Illus.). 382p. 1985. Repr. of 1972 ed. lib. bdg. 24.00 (ISBN 0-918728-50-9). Pendragon NY.

--Antecedents of the Symphony: The Ripieno Concerto & the 18th Century Overture in Naples. LC 83-8936. (The Symphony Ser.). 324p. 1983. lib. bdg. 90.00 (ISBN 0-8240-3828-2). Garland Pub.

Brook, Barry S., et al, eds. see Abel, Carl F. & Bach, Johan C.

Brook, Barry S., et al, eds. see Croubelis, Simoni dall, et al.

Brook, Barry S., et al, eds. see Davaux, Jean-Baptiste, et al.

Brook, Barry S., et al, eds. see Gyrowit, Adalbert & Dussek, Jan L.

Brook, Barry S., et al, eds. see Herschel, William, et al.

Brook, Barry S., et al, eds. see Hoffmeister, Franz A., et al.

Brook, Barry S., et al, eds. see Vogler, Georg J., et al.

Brook, Barry S., et al, eds. see Witt, Friedrich, et al.

Brook, C. G. Practical Paediatric Endocrinology. 152p. 1978. 24.50 (ISBN 0-8089-1084-1, 790683). Grune.

Brook, Charles G. Clinical Pediatric Endocrinology. (Illus.). 704p. 1981. text ed. 108.00 (ISBN 0-632-00698-6, B 0888-0). Mosby.

Brook, Claire, jt. ed. see Clinkscale, Edward.

Brook, David, ed. see Society for Academic Gaming & Simulation in Education & Training.

Brook, Donald. Composer's Gallery: Biographical Sketches of Contemporary Composers. facs. ed. LC 76-136641. (Biography Index Reprint Ser). 1946. 18.00 (ISBN 0-8369-8036-0). Ayer Co Pubs.

--Conductors' Gallery. facs. ed. LC 70-136642. (Biography Index Reprint Ser). 1947. 24.50 (ISBN 0-8369-8037-9). Ayer Co Pubs.

--Five Great French Composers: Berlioz, Cesar Franck, Saint-Saens, Debussy, Ravel; Their Lives & Works. LC 77-160916. (Biography Index Reprint Ser). Repr. of 1946 ed. 21.00 (ISBN 0-8369-8079-4). Ayer Co Pubs.

--International Gallery of Conductors. LC 71-114478. (Illus.). 232p. 1973. Repr. of 1951 ed. lib. bdg. 15.00x (ISBN 0-8371-4767-0, BRIG). Greenwood.

--Masters of the Keyboard. facsimile 2nd ed. LC 76-148206. (Biography Index Reprint Ser.). 1947. 19.00 (ISBN 0-8369-8053-0). Ayer Co Pubs.

--Masters of the Keyboard. LC 75-114479. 1971. Repr. of 1946 ed. lib. bdg. 22.50x (ISBN 0-8371-4768-9, BRMK). Greenwood.

--Pageant of English Actors. LC 71-38315. (Biography Index Reprint Ser). Repr. of 1950 ed. 18.25 (ISBN 0-8369-8116-2). Ayer Co Pubs.

--The Pageant of English Actors. 1950. 20.00 (ISBN 0-8482-3422-7). Norwood Edns.

--The Romance of the English Theatre. 1945. 25.00 (ISBN 0-8482-7403-2). Norwood Edns.

--Singers of Today. LC 70-160917. (Biography Index Reprint Ser). Repr. of 1949 ed. 19.75 (ISBN 0-8369-8080-8). Ayer Co Pubs.

--Six Great Russian Composers. facs. ed. LC 73-136643. (Biography Index Reprint Ser). Repr. of 1946 ed. 25.00 (ISBN 0-8369-8038-7). Ayer Co Pubs.

--Violinists of To-Day. LC 74-38313. (Biography Index Reprint Ser). Repr. of 1948 ed. 16.00 (ISBN 0-8369-8117-0). Ayer Co Pubs.

--Writers' Gallery. LC 78-105768. (Illus.). 1970. Repr. of 1944 ed. 19.50x (ISBN 0-8046-0942-X, Pub. by Kennikat). Assoc Faculty Pr.

--Writer's Gallery. 1944. Repr. 25.00 (ISBN 0-8482-7423-7). Norwood Edns.

Brook, Donald E. Elementary Algebra for Today. rev. ed. (Illus.). 352p. 1985. text ed. 25.95 (ISBN 0-13-252842-8). P-H.

Brook, Donna. Notes on Space-Time. 1977. 2.00 (ISBN 0-914610-11-2). Hanging Loose.

Brook, Eve & Davis, Ann, eds. Women, the Family & Social Work. (Tavistock Library of Social Work Practice Ser.). 192p. (Orig.). Date not set. 27.50 (ISBN 0-422-77940-7, 9485, Pub. by Tavistock England); pap. text ed. 12.95 (ISBN 0-422-77950-4, 9475, Pub. by Tavistock England). Methuen Inc.

Brook, G. L. Books & Book-Collecting. 176p. 1980. 17.00 (ISBN 0-233-97154-8, 05772-X, Pub. by Gower Pub Co England). Lexington Bks.

--English Dialects. 3rd ed. Crystal, David, ed. (Language Library). 232p. 1978. 21.95x (ISBN 0-233-95641-7). Basil Blackwell.

--English Sound Changes. 1957. lib. bdg. 8.00 (ISBN 0-8414-3199-X). Folcroft.

--English Sound Changes. 1935. pap. 3.00 (ISBN 0-7190-0111-0, Pub. by Manchester Univ Pr). Longwood Pub Group.

--An Introduction to Old English. 1955. pap. 5.50 (ISBN 0-7190-0569-8, Pub. by Manchester Univ Pr). Longwood Pub Group.

--The Language of Shakespeare. Crystal, David, ed. (Language Library). 231p. 1976. 14.95x (ISBN 0-233-96762-1). Basil Blackwell.

--Words in Everyday Life. 207p. 1981. 28.50x (ISBN 0-389-20218-5, 07000). B&N Imports.

Brook, George, jt. auth. see Heyl, James.

Brook, George, et al. Exercises in Physical Geography. (Illus.). 350p. 1984. 14.95 (ISBN 0-89892-054-X). Contemp Pub Co of Raleigh.

Brook, George L., ed. The Harley Lyrics: The Middle English Lyrics of Ms. Harley, 2253. 3rd ed. (Old & Middle English Texts). 131p. 1968. 9.50x (ISBN 0-06-490680-9, 06365). B&N Imports.

Brook, George L., ed. see Layamon.

Brook, Itzhak. A Medical Update on Lincomycin: The Management of Infectious Disease. (Illus.). 70p. (Orig.). 1983. pap. 13.95 (ISBN 0-88678-000-4). Omega Comms.

Brook, Judith S., et al, eds. Alcohol & Substance Abuse in Adolescence. LC 84-29004. (Advances in Alcohol & Substance Abuse Ser.: Vol. 4, Nos. 3 & 4). 216p. 1985. text ed. 19.95 (ISBN 0-86656-333-4). Haworth Pr.

Brook, Judy. Hector & Harriet The Night Hamsters. (Illus.). (gr. k-2). 1985. 10.95 (ISBN 0-233-97625-6). Andre Deutsch.

Brook, Judy, illus. The Wind in the Willows Activity Book. 1985. pap. 3.95 (ISBN 0-14-031871-2, Puffin). Penguin.

Brook, K. M., jt. auth. see Murdock, L. J.

Brook, Michael & Rubinstein, Sarah P. Reference Guide to Minnesota History Supplement: A Subject to Bibliography, 1970-80. LC 83-5438. 69p. pap. 6.95 (ISBN 0-87351-160-3). Minn Hist.

--Supplement to Reference Guide to Minnesota History: A Subject Bibliography 1970-80. LC 83-5438. 69p. 1983. pap. 6.95 (ISBN 0-87351-160-3). Minn Hist.

Brook, Michael, compiled by. Reference Guide to Minnesota History: A Subject Bibliography of Books, Pamphlets & Articles in English. LC 74-4222. 132p. 1974. pap. 8.95 (ISBN 0-87351-082-8). Minn Hist.

Brook, Paula. Vancouver Rainy Day Guide. (Rainy Day Guides Ser.). (Orig.). 1984. pap. 6.95 (ISBN 0-87701-315-2). Chronicle Bks.

Brook, Peter. The Empty Space. LC 68-12531. 1978. pap. text ed. 4.95x (ISBN 0-689-70558-1, 237). Atheneum.

Brook, Robert & Whitehead, Paul. Drug-Free Therapeutic Community: An Evaluation. LC 79-20477. 158p. 1980. 19.95 (ISBN 0-87705-383-9). Human Sci Pr.

Brook, Robert C. & Whitehead, Paul C., eds. Drug-Free Therapeutic Community. 158p. 9.98x (ISBN 0-317-29643-4). Human Sci Pr.

Brook, Roger. And After That Nurse? 1977. 3.50 (ISBN 0-285-50192-5, Pub. by Souvenir Pr). Intl Spec Bk.

--Really Nurse. 1977. 2.95 (ISBN 0-285-50091-0, Pub. by Souvenir Pr). Intl Spec Bk.

Brook, Stephen. A Bibliography of the Gehenna Press, 1942-1975. 2nd ed. 1976. 40.00 (ISBN 0-686-18219-7). J P Dwyer.

--Honkytonk Gelato: Travels through Texas. LC 85-47593. 288p. 1985. 15.95 (ISBN 0-689-11639-X). Atheneum.

--New York Days, New York Nights. LC 84-14575. 304p. 1985. 14.95 (ISBN 0-689-11511-3). Atheneum.

--The Oxford Book of Dreams. 1983. 16.95 (ISBN 0-19-214130-9). Oxford U Pr.

Brook, Tania. Cinquain. 1980. 5.95 (ISBN 0-686-27976-X). Wagon & Star.

Brook, Wallace. Growing & Showing Chrysanthemums. (Growing & Showing Ser.). (Illus.). 68p. 1984. 9.95 (ISBN 0-7153-8574-7). David & Charles.

Brookbank, John W., ed. Improving the Quality of Health Care for the Elderly. LC 78-4081. (Center for Gerontological Studies & Programs Ser.: No. 25). 1978. pap. 7.50 (ISBN 0-8130-0595-7). U Presses Fla.

Brookby, Peter, ed. Virgin Wholly Marvelous. LC 81-13928. (Illus.). 204p. 1981. 10.95 (ISBN 0-911218-18-1); pap. 6.95 (ISBN 0-911218-17-3). Ravengate Pr.

Brooke, A. Method for Flute. Pappoutsakis, James, ed. 211p. 1962. pap. 14.00 (ISBN 0-8258-0145-1, CU-20). Fischer Inc NY.

Brooke, A. E., ed. The Fragments of Heracleon. (Texts & Studies Ser.: No. 1, Vol. 1, Pt. 4). pap. 13.00 (ISBN 0-317-16747-2). Kraus Repr.

Brooke, Amos. Black in a White Paradise. rev. ed. (Orig.). 1985. pap. 2.50 (ISBN 0-87067-255-X, BH255). Holloway.

--Doing Time. rev. ed. (Orig.). 1985. pap. 2.25 (ISBN 0-87067-261-4, BH261). Holloway.

--The Last Toke. rev. ed. (Orig.). 1985. pap. 2.50 (ISBN 0-87067-256-8, BH256). Holloway.

Brooke, Anabel. Natalya. 352p. (Orig.). 1981. pap. 2.75 (ISBN 0-345-29254-5). Ballantine.

Brooke, Anthony. Towards Human Unity. 133p. 1976. pap. 4.50 (ISBN 0-7051-0234-3). Attic Pr.

Brooke, Arthur. Brooke's "Romeus & Juliet". 1908. lib. bdg. 15.00 (ISBN 0-8414-2504-3). Folcroft.

--Romeus & Iuliet. Daniel, P. A., ed. Bd. with Rhomeo & Julietta. Painter, William. (New Shakespeare Society London Ser.: Vol. 1, No. 3). pap. 23.00 (ISBN 0-317-16742-1). Kraus Repr.

Brooke, Avery. Doorway to Meditation. 1976. pap. 6.95 (ISBN 0-8164-0903-X, Pub. by Seabury). Winston Pr.

--How to Meditate Without Leaving the World. 96p. 1976. pap. 3.00 (ISBN 0-8164-0906-4, Pub. by Seabury). Winston Pr.

--Plain Prayers for a Complicated World. 124p. 1983. 5.95 (ISBN 0-8164-0501-8, Pub. by Seabury); pap. 2.95 (ISBN 0-8164-2428-4). Winston Pr.

Brooke, Bryan N. Inflammatory Disease of the Bowel. 300p. 1980. 100.00x (ISBN 0-272-79556-9, Pub. by Pitman Bks England). State Mutual Bk.

Brooke, C. Europe in the Central Middle Ages 962-1154. 2nd ed. LC 75-308112. (General History of Europe Ser.). 404p. 1975. pap. text ed. 14.95x (ISBN 0-582-48476-6). Longman.

Brooke, C., et al, eds. Church & Government in the Middle Ages. LC 75-41614. (Illus.). 1977. 59.50 (ISBN 0-521-21172-7). Cambridge U Pr.

Brooke, C. F. Tudor Drama: A History of English National Drama to the Retirement of Shakespeare. xiii, 461p. 1970. Repr. of 1939 ed. 25.00 (ISBN 0-208-00578-1, Archon). Shoe String.

Brooke, C. F., ed. see Marlowe, Christopher.

Brooke, C. F. Tucker see Marlowe, Christopher.

Brooke, C. F. Tucker, ed. see Shakespeare, William.

Brooke, C. H. & Ryder, M. L. Declining Breeds of Mediterranean Sheep. (Animal Production & Health Papers: No. 8). (Illus.). 68p. (Eng. & Fr.). 1978. pap. 7.50 (ISBN 92-5-100507-9, F1596, FAO). Unipub.

Brooke, C. N. & Postan, M. M. Carte Nativorum: A Peterborough Cartulary of the 14th Century. 1960. 48.00x (ISBN 0-686-87138-3, Pub. by Northamptonshire). State Mutual Bk.

Brooke, C. N., ed. see Foliot, G.

Brooke, C. N., ed. see John Of Salisbury.

Brooke, C. N., et al, eds. Studies in Numismatic Method. LC 81-15524. (Illus.). 368p. 1983. 94.50 (ISBN 0-521-22503-5). Cambridge U Pr.

Brooke, Charles F. The Tudor Drama. LC 75-144902. 1911. Repr. 69.00 (ISBN 0-403-00840-9). Scholarly.

Brooke, Charles F. & Paradise, Nathaniel B. English Drama, 1580-1642. 1933. text ed. 24.95x (ISBN 0-669-06144-1). Heath.

Brooke, Charlotte, ed. Reliques of Irish Poetry, 1789. Bd. with A Memoir of Miss Brooke, 1816. Seymour, A. C. LC 76-133327. 544p. 1970. 75.00x (ISBN 0-8201-1082-5). Schol Facsimiles.

Brooke, Christopher. From Alfred to Henry the Third, Eight Hundred Seventy-One to Twelve Seventy-Two. (Illus.). 1966. pap. 7.95 (ISBN 0-393-00362-0, Norton Lib). Norton.

--London, Eight Hundred to Twelve Sixteen: The Shaping of a City. LC 73-92620. (The History of London Ser). (Illus.). 1975. 44.50x (ISBN 0-520-02686-1). U of Cal Pr.

--The Twelfth Century Renaissance. (History of European Civilization Library). (Illus.). 216p. 1969. pap. text ed. 11.95 (ISBN 0-15-592385-4, HC). HarBraceJ.

Brooke, Christopher & Brooke, Rosalind. Popular Religion in the Middle Ages: Western Europe 1000-1300. LC 83-50769. (Illus.). 176p. 1984. 19.95f (ISBN 0-500-25087-1). Thames Hudson.

Brooke, Christopher, jt. auth. see Brooke, Rosalind.

Brooke, E. M., ed. Suicide & Attempted Suicide. (Public Health Paper: No. 58). (Also avail. in French, Russian & Spanish). 1974. pap. 3.20 (ISBN 92-4-130058-2). World Health.

Brooke, Eileen M. Current & Future Use of Registers in Health Information Systems. (Offset Pub.: No. 8). (Also avail. in French). 1974. pap. 5.60 (ISBN 92-4-170008-4). World Health.

Brooke, Francis J. A Family Narrative: Being the Reminiscences of a Revolutionary Officer, Afterwards Judge of the Court Appeals. LC 74-140856. (Eyewitness Accounts of the American Revolution Ser., No. 3). 1970. Repr. of 1921 ed. 11.50 (ISBN 0-405-01196-2). Ayer Co Pubs.

Brooke, Fulke G. Poems & Dramas of Fulke Greville First Lord Brooke, 2 vols. Repr. of 1939 ed. 49.00 (ISBN 0-403-04210-0). Somerset Pub.

--The Works in Verse & Prose Complete of the Right Honourable Fulke Greville, 4 vols. Grosart, Alexander B., ed. LC 79-181918. (Fuller Worthies Library). Repr. of 1870 ed. Set. 200.00 (ISBN 0-404-02940-X). AMS Pr.

Brooke, G. C. English Coins. 1977. 20.00 (ISBN 0-685-51518-4, Pub by Spink & Son England). S J Durst.

Brooke, Geoffrey. Training Your Horses to Jump. 1978. Repr. of 1913 ed. 35.00 (ISBN 0-8492-3566-9). R West.

Brooke, George J. Exegesis at Qumran: Four Q Florilegium in Its Jewish Context. (JSOT Supplement Ser.: No. 29). 370p. 1984. text ed. 28.50x (ISBN 0-905774-76-0, Pub. by JSOT Pr England); pap. text ed. 13.50x (ISBN 0-905774-77-9, Pub. by JSOT Pr England). Eisenbrauns.

Brooke, George M., Jr. John M. Brooke, Naval Scientist & Educator. LC 79-18559. (Illus.). xiii, 372p. 1980. 24.95x (ISBN 0-8139-0809-4). U Pr of Va.

Brooke, Henry. The Fool of Quality, 5 vols. Paulson, Ronald, ed. LC 78-60842. (Novel 1720-1805 Ser.: Vol. 6). 1979. Set. lib. bdg. 181.00 (ISBN 0-8240-3655-7). Garland Pub.

--Leslie Brooke & Johnny Crow. (Illus.). 152p. 1982. 21.95 (ISBN 0-7232-2878-7). Warne.

Brooke, I. English Children's Costume Since 1775. (English Costume Ser.). (Illus.). 1965. Repr. of 1930 ed. text ed. 9.50x (ISBN 0-7136-0160-4). Humanities.

--English Costume in the Age of Elizabeth. 2nd ed. (English Costume Ser.). (Illus.). 1977. Repr. of 1950 ed. text ed. 10.75x (ISBN 0-7136-0156-6). Humanities.

--English Costume of the Early Middle Ages. (English Costume Ser.). 1977. Repr. of 1936 ed. text ed. 10.75x (ISBN 0-7136-0154-X). Humanities.

--English Costume of the Later Middle Ages. (English Costume Ser.). (Illus.). 1977. text ed. 11.50x (ISBN 0-7136-0155-8). Humanities.

--English Costume of the Nineteenth Century. (English Costume Ser.). (Illus.). 1977. text ed. 10.75x (ISBN 0-7136-0159-0). Humanities.

--English Costume of the Seventeenth Century. 2nd ed. (English Costume Ser.). (Illus.). 1977. Repr. of 1950 ed. text ed. 8.25x (ISBN 0-7136-0157-4). Humanities.

Brooke, Iris. Costume in Greek Classic Drama. LC 73-3010. (Illus.). 112p. 1973. Repr. of 1962 ed. lib. bdg. 24.75x (ISBN 0-8371-6828-7, BRGC). Greenwood.

--Dress & Undress, the Restoration & Eighteenth Century. LC 73-3011. (Illus.). 161p. 1973. Repr. of 1958 ed. lib. bdg. 19.75x (ISBN 0-8371-6829-5, BRDU). Greenwood.

--Footwear. LC 79-109116. (Illus.). 1971. 9.95 (ISBN 0-87830-047-3). Theatre Arts.

--History of English Costume. LC 72-85476. (Illus.). 1973. pap. 10.95 (ISBN 0-87830-569-6). Theatre Arts.

--Medieval Theatre Costume. LC 67-25699. (Illus.). 1967. 10.95 (ISBN 0-87830-081-3). Theatre Arts.

--Western European Costume & Its Relation to the Theatre. Incl. Vol. 1. 13th to 17th Centuries (ISBN 0-87830-511-4); Vol. 2. 17th Through 19th Centuries. 1963 (ISBN 0-87830-514-9). LC 63-18334. (Illus., Orig.). pap. 7.95 ea. Theatre Arts.

Brooke, James W. Disability Reporting. 1985. 27.50 (ISBN 0-87527-262-2). Green.

Brooke, Jocelyn. Image of a Drawn Sword. 192p. 1983. 14.95 (ISBN 0-436-06951-2, Pub. by Secker & Warburg UK). David & Charles.

Brooke, John. The Chatham Administration Seventeen Sixty-Five to Seventeen Sixty-Eight. LC 76-6170. 1976. Repr. of 1956 ed. lib. bdg. 24.00x (ISBN 0-8371-8869-5, BRCAD). Greenwood.

--King George III. (Illus.). 640p. 1974. pap. 5.95 (ISBN 0-586-03944-9, Pub. by Granada England). Academy Chi Pubs.

Brooke, John, jt. ed. see Namier, Lewis.

Brooke, John, ed. see Walpole, Horace.

Brooke, John, et al. Decision Making in General Practice. 1985. 50.00x (ISBN 0-943818-11-7). Stockton Pr.

Brooke, L. T., et al, eds. Acute Toxicities of Organic Chemicals to Fathead Minnows (Pimephales Promelas, Vol. 1. (Toxicity of Organic Chemicals Ser.). (Illus.). 414p. (Orig.). 1984. pap. 62.95 (ISBN 0-9614968-0-0). U of WI-Superior.

Brooke, Leslie, illus. The Golden Goose Book. new ed. LC 76-2919. (Illus.). (ps-3). 1977. 8.95 (ISBN 0-7232-1979-6). Warne.

--Ring o' Roses. new ed. LC 76-2920. (Illus.). (ps-3). 1977. 8.95 (ISBN 0-7232-1980-X). Warne.

Brooke, Leslie L. Johnny Crow's Party. (Illus.). (ps-2). 1907. 6.95 (ISBN 0-7232-0566-3). Warne.

Brooke, Marcus. Singapore. LC 73-89702. (This Beautiful World Ser.: No. 64). (Illus.). 1980. pap. 4.95 (ISBN 0-87011-225-2). Kodansha.

Brooke, Margaret. Good Morning & Good Night. (Century Travellers). 320p. 1984. pap. 9.95 (ISBN 0-7126-0348-4). Hippocrene Bks.

Brooke, Margaret L. Lace in the Making. 1975. Repr. of 1923 ed. 11.95 (ISBN 0-686-11142-7). Robin & Russ.

Brooke, Maxey. Coin Games & Puzzles. Orig. Title: Fun for the Money. 96p. 1973. pap. 3.50 (ISBN 0-486-22893-2). Dover.

--One Hundred & Fifty Puzzles in Crypt-Arithmetic. 1972. pap. 2.95 (ISBN 0-486-21039-1). Dover.

--Tricks, Games & Puzzles with Matches. (Illus.). 64p. 1973. pap. 1.50 (ISBN 0-486-20178-3). Dover.

Brooke, Meridith & Rodrick, Leigh. Twenty Unique Ways to Tie the Knot. Calder, Raven, ed. (Illus.). 64p. (Orig.). 1981. pap. 3.95 (ISBN 0-942408-00-4). Harvard Group.

Brooke, Michael Z. Autonomy & Centralisation: A Study in Organisation Behaviour. LC 84-60042. 404p. 1984. 39.95x (ISBN 0-03-068674-1). Praeger.

Brooke, Michael Z. & Remers, H. Lee. The Strategy of Multinational Enterprise. 277p. 1979. text ed. 31.50 (ISBN 0-273-01178-2). Pitman Pub MA.

Brooke, Michael Z. & Van Beusedom, Mark. International Corporate Planning. LC 79-4356. 323p. text ed. 32.95 (ISBN 0-273-01130-8). Pitman Pub MA.

Brooke, Nicholas. Horid Laughter in Jacobean Tragedy. 136p. 1979. 30.00x (ISBN 0-7291-0101-0, Pub. by Open Bks England). State Mutual Bk.

--Horrid Laughter in Jacobean Tragedy. LC 79-53305. 135p. 1979. text ed. 27.50x (ISBN 0-06-490701-5, 06367). B&N Imports.

--Shakespeare's Early Tragedies. 214p. 1973. pap. 10.95x (ISBN 0-416-77560-8, NO. 2114). Methuen Inc.

Brooke, Nicholas, ed. see Chapman, George.

Brooke, Odo. Studies in Monastic Theology. (Cistercian Studies Ser.: No. 37). 1980. 8.95 (ISBN 0-87907-837-5). Cistercian Pubns.

Brooke, R. N. & Wilkinson, Andrew. Inflammatory Disease of the Bowel. 300p. text ed. cancelled (ISBN 0-272-79556-9, Pub. by Pitman Bks Ltd UK). Pitman Pub MA.

Brooke, Richard. Visits to Fields of Battle in England of the 15th Century. (Illus.). 342p. 1975. Repr. of 1857 ed. 19.75x (ISBN 0-87471-746-9). Rowman.

Brooke, Roger. Santa's Christmas Journey. LC 84-9796. (Raintree Stories Clippers Ser.). (Illus.). 32p. (gr. k-4). 1984. lib. bdg. 14.25 (ISBN 0-8172-2116-6); pap. 9.27 (ISBN 0-8172-2259-6); incl. cassette 27.99 (ISBN 0-8172-2244-8); incl. cassette 23.95 (ISBN 0-8172-2269-3); cassette 14.00. Raintree Pubs.

--Santa's Christmas Journey. (Illus.). 32p. (ps-3). 1985. 5.95 (ISBN 0-528-82688-3). Rand.

Brooke, Rosalind. Information & Advice Services. 181p. 1972. pap. text ed. 5.65x (ISBN 0-7135-1709-3, Pub. by Bedford England). Brookfield Pub Co.

--Law, Justice & Social Policy. 136p. 1979. 20.00 (ISBN 0-85664-636-9, Pub. by Croom Helm Ltd). Longwood Pub Group.

Brooke, Rosalind & Brooke, Christopher. Popular Religion in the Middle Ages. (Illus.). 1985. pap. 10.95 (ISBN 0-500-27381-2). Thames Hudson.

Brooke, Rosalind, jt. auth. see Brooke, Christopher.

Brooke, Rupert. The Collected Poems of Rupert Brooke. LC 80-16869. 1980. pap. 4.95 (ISBN 0-396-07894-X). Dodd.

--The Complete Poems of Rupert Brooke. 2nd ed. LC 75-41038. (BCL Ser. II). Repr. of 1942 ed. 17.50 (ISBN 0-404-14647-3). AMS Pr.

--Letters from America. 180p. Repr. of 1916 ed. lib. bdg. 40.00 (ISBN 0-8482-3299-2). Norwood Edns.

--Letters from Rupert Brooke to His Publisher, 1911-1914. LC 75-4445. 1975. lib. bdg. 29.00x (ISBN 0-374-90997-0). Octagon.

--Rupert Brooke. (Pocket Poet Ser.). 1968. pap. 2.00 (ISBN 0-8023-9042-0). Dufour.

Brooke, Stopford. English Literature. 1882. Repr. 10.00 (ISBN 0-8274-3830-3). R West.

--Naturalism in English Poetry. 1920. Repr. 25.00 (ISBN 0-8274-3012-4). R West.

--Theology in the English Poets: Blake, Scott, Shelley & Keats. 1973. Repr. of 1907 ed. 15.00 (ISBN 0-8274-0525-1). R West.

Brooke, Stopford & Green, John R. English Literature. 226p. Date not set. Repr. of 1879 ed. lib. bdg. 15.00 (ISBN 0-8482-3298-4). Norwood Edns.

Brooke, Stopford & Rolleston, T. W., eds. A Treasury of Irish Poetry. LC 78-74812. (Granger Poetry Library). 1979. Repr. of 1900 ed. 34.50x (ISBN 0-89609-130-9). Granger Bk.

Brooke, Stopford A. English Literature. 283p. 1984. Repr. of 1897 ed. lib. bdg. 25.00 (ISBN 0-918377-05-6). Russell Pr.

--English Literature from the Beginning of the Norman Conquest. 1973. Repr. of 1898 ed. 17.50 (ISBN 0-8274-1290-8). R West.

--English Literature: With Chapters on English Literature (1832-1892) & on American Literature by George R. Carpenter. 358p. 1982. Repr. of 1896 ed. lib. bdg. 40.00 (ISBN 0-89984-082-5). Century Bookbindery.

--History of Early English Literature, Being the History of English Poetry from Its Beginnings to the Accession of King Aelfred. facsimile ed. LC 70-114905. (Select Bibliographies Reprint Ser). 1892. 32.00 (ISBN 0-8369-5309-6). Ayer Co Pubs.

--History of Early English Literature: Being the History of English Poetry from It Beginnings to the Accession of King Alfred. 1892. 27.50 (ISBN 0-8274-2503-1). R West.

--Milton. LC 70-39534. Repr. of 1879 ed. 9.00 (ISBN 0-404-01108-X). AMS Pr.

--Milton. LC 72-189881. 1973. lib. bdg. 10.00 (ISBN 0-8414-1118-2). Folcroft.

--Naturalism in English Poetry. 289p. Repr. of 1920 ed. 29.00 (ISBN 0-403-03079-X). Somerset Pub.

--On Ten Plays of Shakespeare. LC 72-149655. Repr. of 1905 ed. 12.50 (ISBN 0-404-01109-8). AMS Pr.

--Poetry of Robert Browning. LC 2-24748. Repr. of 1902 ed. 17.50 (ISBN 0-404-01114-4). AMS Pr.

--Poetry of Robert Browning. 1973. Repr. of 1902 ed. 17.45 (ISBN 0-8274-1714-4). R West.

--The Poetry of Robert Browning. 461p. 1982. Repr. 40.00 (ISBN 0-8495-0633-6). Arden Lib.

--Some Philosophical Aspects of Poetry. LC 74-8074. 1872. lib. bdg. 8.50 (ISBN 0-8414-3188-4). Folcroft.

--Tennyson: His Art & Relation to Modern Life. LC 74-123761. Repr. of 1894 ed. 15.00 (ISBN 0-404-01115-2). AMS Pr.

--Tennyson: His Art & Relation to Modern Life. 1973. Repr. of 1894 ed. 14.95 (ISBN 0-8274-1454-4). R West.

--Theology in the English Poets. 59.95 (ISBN 0-8490-1189-2). Gordon Pr.

--Theology in the English Poets: Cowper, Coleridge, Wordsworth & Burns. 6th ed. LC 79-129367. Repr. of 1880 ed. 10.00 (ISBN 0-404-01116-0). AMS Pr.

Brooke, Stopford A. & Rolleston, T. W., eds. Treasury of Irish Poetry in the English Tongue. 1971. Repr. of 1932 ed. 79.00 (ISBN 0-403-00841-7). Scholarly.

Brooke, Tal. Avatar of Night: The Hidden Side of Sai Baba. 392p. 1982. pap. text ed. 6.95x (ISBN 0-686-91763-4, Pub. by Vikas India). Advent NY.

Brooks, Alan & Nielsen, Nancy L. Living on Salt & Stone: Poems from Straight Bay. (Illus., Orig.). 1984. pap. 3.50 (ISBN 0-914473-00-X). Stone Man Pr.

Brooks, Alden. Will Shakespeare: A Factotum & Agent. LC 77-39536. Repr. of 1937 ed. 25.00 (ISBN 0-404-01117-9). AMS Pr.

Brooks, Alexander D. Law, Psychiatry & the Mental Health System. 1974. 33.00 (ISBN 0-316-10970-3); Suppl., 1980. pap. 8.95 (ISBN 0-316-10971-1). Little.

Brooks, Alfred. From Holbein to Whistler: Notes on Drawing & Engraving. (Illus.). 1920. 95.00x (ISBN 0-685-69792-4). Elliots Bks.

Brooks, Alfred H. Blazing Alaska's Trails. LC 73-88211. (Illus.). 567p. 1973. 12.50 (ISBN 0-912006-01-3). U of Alaska Pr.

Brooks, Alfred M. Architecture. LC 63-10303. (Our Debt to Greece & Rome Ser). Repr. of 1930 ed. 18.50 (ISBN 0-8154-0032-2). Cooper Sq.

--Dante: How to Know Him. 1916. lib. bdg. 30.00 (ISBN 0-8414-2506-X). Folcroft.

--Gloucester Recollected: A Familiar History. Garland, Joseph E., ed. (Illus.). 11.00 (ISBN 0-8446-5012-9). Peter Smith.

Brooks, Allen H., ed. Projects pour un Stade Olympique Bagdad & Other Buildings & Projects. (Le Corbusier Ser.). 1984. lib. bdg. 200.00 (ISBN 0-8240-5076-2). Garland Pub.

Brooks, Andreas, illus. The Pudgy Book of Make-Believe. (Pudgy Bks.). (Illus.). 16p. (gr. k). 1984. 2.95 (ISBN 0-448-10209-9, G&D). Putnam Pub Group.

Brooks, Anna M., jt. auth. see Worth, Cecilia.

Brooks, Anne. Grieving Time: A Year's Account of Recovery from Loss. (Illus.). 64p. 1985. 12.95 (ISBN 0-385-19801-9, Dial). Doubleday.

Brooks, Anne M. The Grieving Time: A Month by Month Account of Recovery from Loss. LC 82-17955. (Illus.). 36p. 1982. 8.95 (ISBN 0-911293-00-0). Delapeake Pub Co.

Brooks, Anne T. Point Virtue. 1979. pap. 2.25 (ISBN 0-505-51370-6, Pub. by Tower Bks). Dorchester Pub Co.

Brooks, Arle see Hassler, Alfred.

Brooks, Aubrey J., ed. see Clark, Walter.

Brooks, Aubrey L. Selected Addresses of a Southern Lawyer. ix, 165p. 1954. 15.00 (ISBN 0-8078-0657-9). U of NC Pr.

Brooks, B. A. & Bajandas, F. J., eds. Eye Movements: ARVO Symposium, 1976. 232p. 1977. 35.00x (ISBN 0-306-31082-1, Plenum Pr). Plenum Pub.

Brooks, B. David, jt. auth. see Goble, Frank.

Brooks, B. David, jt. auth. see Goble, Frank G.

Brooks, Barbara. Teaching Mentally Handicapped Children: A Handbook of Practical Activities. 238p. 25.00x (ISBN 0-7062-3634-3, Pub. by Ward Lock Ed England). State Mutual Bk.

Brooks, Barbara, ed. see Reynolds, Lloyd G.

Brooks, Barry S., et al, eds. see Moreira, Antonio L., et al.

Brooks, Bearl. Alphabet. (Early Education Ser.). 26p. (ps-1). 1979. wkbk. 5.00 (ISBN 0-8209-0199-7, K-1). ESP.

--American Indians. (Social Studies). 24p. (gr. 4-6). 1977. wkbk. 5.00 (ISBN 0-8209-0239-X, SS-6). ESP.

--Basic Cursive Handwriting. (Handwriting Ser.). 24p. (gr. 2-3). 1979. wkbk. 5.00 (ISBN 0-8209-0270-5, W-2). ESP.

--Basic Manuscript Handwriting. (Handwriting Ser.). 24p. (gr. 1-2). 1978. wkbk. 5.00 (ISBN 0-8209-0269-1, W-1). ESP.

--Basic Reading Comprehension: Grade Eight. (Reading Ser.). 24p. 1979. wkbk. 5.00 (ISBN 0-8209-0194-6, R-8). ESP.

--Basic Reading Comprehension: Grade Five. (Reading Ser.). 24p. 1977. wkbk. 5.00 (ISBN 0-8209-0191-1, R-5). ESP.

--Basic Reading Comprehension: Grade Four. (Reading Ser.). 24p. 1980. wkbk. 5.00 (ISBN 0-8209-0190-3, R-4). ESP.

--Basic Reading Comprehension: Grade One. (Reading Ser.). 24p. 1980. wkbk. 5.00 (ISBN 0-8209-0187-3, R-1). ESP.

--Basic Reading Comprehension: Grade Seven. (Reading Ser.). 24p. 1977. wkbk. 5.00 (ISBN 0-8209-0193-8, R-7). ESP.

--Basic Reading Comprehension: Grade Six. (Reading Ser.). 24p. 1979. wkbk. 5.00 (ISBN 0-8209-0192-X, R-6). ESP.

--Basic Reading Comprehension: Grade Three. (Reading Ser.). 24p. 1976. wkbk. 5.00 (ISBN 0-8209-0189-X, R-3). ESP.

--Basic Reading Comprehension: Grade Two. (Reading Ser.). 24p. 1977. wkbk. 5.00 (ISBN 0-8209-0188-1, R-2). ESP.

--Basic Skills Beginning Sounds Workbook. (Basic Skills Workbooks). 32p. (gr. k-1). 1983. 0.99 (ISBN 0-8209-0562-3, EEW-3). ESP.

--Basic Skills Following Directions Workbook. (Basic Skills Workbooks). 32p. (ps-1). 1983. 0.99 (ISBN 0-8209-0586-0, EEW-9). ESP.

--Basic Skills Handwriting Workbook: Grade 1. (Basic Skills Workbooks). 32p. 1982. tchrs' ed. 0.99 (ISBN 0-8209-0370-1, CHW-1). ESP.

--Basic Skills Handwriting Workbook: Grade 2. (Basic Skills Workbooks). 32p. 1982. tchr's ed. 0.99 (ISBN 0-8209-0371-X, CHW-2). ESP.

--Basic Skills Handwriting Workbook: Grade 3. (Basic Skills Workbooks). 32p. 1982. tchr's ed. 0.99 (ISBN 0-8209-0372-8, CHW-3). ESP.

--Basic Skills Healthy Body Workbook. (Basic Skills Workbooks). 32p. (gr. 6-7). 1983. 0.99 (ISBN 0-8209-0575-5, HW-2). ESP.

--Basic Skills Learning to Think Workbook. (Basic Skills Workbooks). 32p. (ps-1). 1983. 0.99 (ISBN 0-8209-0587-9, EEW-10). ESP.

--Basic Skills Listening for Sounds Workbook. (Basic Skills Workbooks). 32p. (gr. 2-3). 1983. 0.99 (ISBN 0-8209-0546-1, PW-6). ESP.

--Basic Skills Phonics Workbook: Part I. (Basic Skills Workbooks). 32p. (gr. 1-3). 1982. tchrs' ed. 0.99 (ISBN 0-8209-0385-X, PW-1). ESP.

--Basic Skills Phonics Workbook: Part II. (Basic Skills Workbooks). 32p. (gr. 1-3). 1982. tchrs' ed. 0.99 (ISBN 0-8209-0386-8, PW-2). ESP.

--Basic Skills Phonics Workbook: Part III. (Basic Skills Workbooks). 32p. (gr. 1-3). 1982. tchrs' ed. 0.99 (ISBN 0-8209-0387-6, PW-3). ESP.

--Basic Skills Punctuation Workbook. (Basic Skills Workbooks). 32p. (gr. 4-7). 1983. 0.99 (ISBN 0-8209-0548-8, EW-4). ESP.

--Basic Skills Reading Comprehension Workbook. (Basic Skills Workbooks). 32p. (gr. 1-2). 1982. 0.99 (ISBN 0-8209-0554-2, RCW-1). ESP.

--Basic Skills Reading Comprehension Workbooks. (Basic Skills Workbooks). 32p. (gr. 3-4). 1983. 0.99 (ISBN 0-8209-0555-0, RCW-2). ESP.

--Basic Skills Reading Comprehension Workbook. (Basic Skills Workbooks). 32p. (gr. 5-6). 1983. 0.99 (ISBN 0-8209-0556-9, RCW-3). ESP.

--Basic Skills Reading Comprehension Workbook. (Basic Skills Workbooks). 32p. (gr. 7-8). 1983. 0.99 (ISBN 0-8209-0557-7, RCW-4). ESP.

--Basic Skills Reading Workbook: Grade 8. (Basic Skills Workbooks). 32p. (gr. 8). 1982. wkbk. 0.99 (ISBN 0-8209-0362-0, RW-A). ESP.

--Basic Skills Telling Time Workbook. (Basic Skills Workbooks). 32p. (gr. 2-3). 1983. 0.99 (ISBN 0-8209-0552-6, EEW-13). ESP.

--Basic Skills World Neighbors Workbook. (Basic Skills Workbooks). 32p. (gr. 4-7). 1983. 0.99 (ISBN 0-8209-0558-5, SSW-6). ESP.

--Basic Spelling: Grade One. (Spelling Ser.). 24p. 1979. wkbk. 5.00 (ISBN 0-8209-0165-2, SP-1). ESP.

--Basic Spelling: Grade Three. (Spelling Ser.). 24p. 1977. wkbk. 5.00 (ISBN 0-8209-0167-9, SP-3). ESP.

--Basic Spelling: Grade Two. (Spelling Ser.). 24p. 1979. wkbk. 5.00 (ISBN 0-8209-0166-0, SP-2). ESP.

--Beginning Phonics. (Phonics Ser.). 24p. (gr. 1). 1979. 5.00 (ISBN 0-8209-0329-9, P-1). ESP.

--Beginning Science. (Science Ser.). 24p. (gr. 1). 1979. 5.00 (ISBN 0-8209-0139-3, S-1). ESP.

--Beginning Sounds. (Early Education Ser.). 24p. (ps-1). 1978. 5.00 (ISBN 0-8209-0204-7, K-6). ESP.

--Bilingual Mathematics: Grade 2. (Math Ser.). 24p. 1977. wkbk. 5.00 (ISBN 0-8209-0135-0, BLM-1). ESP.

--Bilingual Mathematics: Grade 3. (Math Ser.). 24p. 1977. wkbk. 5.00 (ISBN 0-8209-0136-9, BLM-2). ESP.

--Bilingual Mathematics: Grade 4. (Math Ser.). 24p. 1977. wkbk. 5.00 (ISBN 0-8209-0137-7, BLM-3). ESP.

--Bilingual Reading: Level One. (Reading Ser.). 24p. 1979. wkbk. 5.00 (ISBN 0-8209-0196-2, BLR-1). ESP.

--Bilingual Reading: Level Three. (Reading Ser.). 24p. 1981. wkbk. 5.00 (ISBN 0-8209-0198-9, BLR-3). ESP.

--Bilingual Reading: Level Two. (Reading Ser.). 24p. 1981. wkbk. 5.00 (ISBN 0-8209-0197-0, BLR-2). ESP.

--Cursive Practice. (Handwriting Ser.). 24p. (gr. 2-3). 1979. wkbk. 5.00 (ISBN 0-8209-0271-3, W-3). ESP.

--Famous American Indian Leaders. (Social Studies). 24p. (gr. 4-6). 1979. wkbk. 5.00 (ISBN 0-8209-0243-8, SS-10). ESP.

--Following Directions. (Early Education Ser.). 24p. (ps-3). 1980. wkbk. 5.00 (ISBN 0-8209-0208-X, K-10). ESP.

--Health & Fun. (Health Ser.). 24p. (gr. 2-4). 1979. wkbk. 5.00 (ISBN 0-8209-0343-4, H-4). ESP.

--Health & Good Manners. (Health Ser.). 24p. (gr. 2-3). 1979. wkbk. 5.00 (ISBN 0-8209-0342-6, H-3). ESP.

--Health & Safety. (Health Ser.). 24p. (gr. 1-2). 1979. wkbk. 5.00 (ISBN 0-8209-0341-8, H-2). ESP.

--Health Habits. (Health Ser.). 24p. (gr. 1-2). 1980. wkbk. 5.00 (ISBN 0-8209-0340-X, H-1). ESP.

--The Healthy Body. (Health Ser.). 24p. (gr. 4-6). 1977. wkbk. 5.00 (ISBN 0-8209-0345-0, H-6). ESP.

--Home School Workbook: Fifth. 64p. (gr. 5). 1983. wkbk. 2.39 (ISBN 0-8209-0595-X, HOSW-5). ESP.

--Home School Workbook: First. 64p. (gr. 1). 1983. wkbk. 2.39 (ISBN 0-8209-0591-7, HOSW-1). ESP.

--Home School Workbook: Fourth. 64p. (gr. 4). 1983. wkbk. 2.39 (ISBN 0-8209-0594-1, HOSW-4). ESP.

--Home School Workbook: Kindergarten. 64p. (gr. k). 1983. wkbk. 2.39 (ISBN 0-8209-0590-9, HOSW-K). ESP.

--Home School Workbook: Second. 64p. (gr. 2). 1983. wkbk. 2.39 (ISBN 0-8209-0592-5, HOSW-2). ESP.

--Home School Workbook: Sixth. 64p. (gr. 6). 1983. 2.39 (ISBN 0-8209-0596-8, HOSW-6). ESP.

--Home School Workbook: Third. 64p. (gr. 3). 1983. wkbk. 2.39 (ISBN 0-8209-0593-3, HOSW-3). ESP.

--Jumbo Cursive Handwriting Yearbook. (Jumbo Handwriting Ser.). 96p. (gr. 3). 1978. wkbk. 14.00 (ISBN 0-8209-0019-2, JHWY-3). ESP.

--Jumbo Phonics Yearbook. (Jumbo Phonics Ser.). 96p. (gr. 1-3). 1977. 14.00 (ISBN 0-8209-0049-4, JPY 1). ESP.

--Jumbo Reading Yearbook: Kindergarten. (Jumbo Reading Ser.). 96p. (gr. k). 1980. 14.00 (ISBN 0-8209-0011-7, JRY R). ESP.

--Learning Phonics: Grade 1. (Phonics Ser.). 24p. 1979. wkbk. 5.00 (ISBN 0-8209-0330-2, P-2). ESP.

--Learning Phonics: Grade 3. (Phonics Ser.). 24p. 1977. wkbk. 5.00 (ISBN 0-8209-0333-7, P-5). ESP.

--Learning to Tell Time. (Early Education Ser.). 24p. (ps-2). 1979. wkbk. 5.00 (ISBN 0-8209-0207-1, K-9). ESP.

--Learning to Think. (Early Education Ser.). 24p. (gr. k). 1979. wkbk. 5.00 (ISBN 0-8209-0205-5, K-7). ESP.

--Listening for Sounds. (Phonics Ser.). 24p. (gr. 2). 1977. wkbk. 5.00 (ISBN 0-8209-0332-9, P-4). ESP.

--My Fifth Grade Yearbook. (My Yearbook Ser.). 832p. (gr. 5). 1981. 14.00 (ISBN 0-8209-0085-0, MFG-5). ESP.

--My First Grade Yearbook. (My Yearbook Ser.). 544p. (gr. 1). 1979. 14.00 (ISBN 0-8209-0081-8, MFG-1). ESP.

--My Kindergarten Yearbook. (My Yearbook Ser.). 544p. (gr. k). 1980. 14.00 (ISBN 0-8209-0080-X, MKY_K). ESP.

--My Second Grade Yearbook. (My Yearbook Ser.). 640p. (gr. 2). 1979. 14.00 (ISBN 0-8209-0082-6, MSG-2). ESP.

--My Sixth Grade Yearbook. (My Yearbook Ser.). 832p. 1981. 14.00 (ISBN 0-8209-0086-9, MSG-6). ESP.

--My Third Grade Yearbook. (My Yearbook Ser.). 768p. (gr. 3). 1979. 14.00 (ISBN 0-8209-0083-4, MTG-3). ESP.

--Nonreading Exercises. (Early Education Ser.). 24p. (ps-1). 1975. wkbk. 5.00 (ISBN 0-8209-0202-0, K-4). ESP.

--Our Community. (Social Studies). 24p. (gr. 2-3). 1979. wkbk. 5.00 (ISBN 0-8209-0236-5, SS-3). ESP.

--Our Home. (Social Studies). 24p. (gr. 1). 1979. wkbk. 5.00 (ISBN 0-8209-0234-9, SS-1). ESP.

--Our Neighborhood. (Social Studies). 24p. (gr. 2). 1979. wkbk. 5.00 (ISBN 0-8209-0235-7, SS-2). ESP.

--Our World Neighbors. (Social Studies). 24p. (gr. 5-6). 1979. wkbk. 5.00 (ISBN 0-8209-0242-X, SS-9). ESP.

--Phonetic Sounds. (Phonics Ser.). 24p. (gr. 2). 1979. wkbk. 5.00 (ISBN 0-8209-0331-0, P-3). ESP.

--Phonetic Sounds & Symbols: Part 1. (Phonics Ser.). 24p. (gr. 1). 1978. wkbk. 5.00 (ISBN 0-8209-0335-3, P-7). ESP.

--Phonetic Sounds & Symbols: Part 2. (Phonics Ser.). 24p. (gr. 1). 1978. wkbk. 5.00 (ISBN 0-8209-0336-1, P-8). ESP.

--Phonics for Reading & Spelling: Grade 2. (Phonics Ser.). 24p. 1978. wkbk. 5.00 (ISBN 0-8209-0337-X, P-9). ESP.

--Phonics for Reading & Spelling: Grade 3. (Phonics Ser.). 24p. 1978. wkbk. 5.00 (ISBN 0-8209-0338-8, P-10). ESP.

--Phonics for Reading & Spelling: Grade 4. (Phonics Ser.). 24p. 1978. wkbk. 5.00 (ISBN 0-8209-0339-6, P-11). ESP.

--Shelter & the Family. (Social Studies). 24p. (gr. 4-6). 1976. wkbk. 5.00 (ISBN 0-8209-0249-7, SS-16). ESP.

--Understanding Punctuation: Grades 4-7. (English Ser.). 24p. (gr. 4-7). 1979. wkbk. 5.00 (ISBN 0-8209-0186-5, E-15). ESP.

--Using Phonics. (Phonics Ser.). 24p. (gr. 1-4). 1978. wkbk. 5.00 (ISBN 0-8209-0334-5, P-6). ESP.

--Writing Letters & Words. (Handwriting Ser.). 24p. (gr. k-1). 1980. wkbk. 5.00 (ISBN 0-8209-0268-3, W-0). ESP.

Brooks, Bearl, jt. auth. see Taylor, Ralph.

Brooks, Bearl, et al. Jumbo Word Games Yearbook. (Jumbo Vocabulary Ser.). 96p. (gr. 3). 1980. 14.00 (ISBN 0-8209-0059-1, JWG 1). ESP.

Brooks, Benjamin T. Peace, Plenty, & Petroleum. LC 75-6463. (The History & Politics of Oil Ser). 197p. 1976. Repr. of 1944 ed. 17.50 (ISBN 0-88355-283-3). Hyperion Conn.

Brooks, Benjy F. Malignant Tumors of Childhood. (The Robert E. Gross Lectureship Ser.). (Illus.). 248p. 1986. text ed. 35.00x (ISBN 0-292-75082-X). U of Tex Pr.

Brooks, Benjy F., ed. Controversies in Pediatric Surgery. (Robert E. Gross Lectureship Ser.). (Illus.). 256p. 1984. text ed. 35.00x (ISBN 0-292-71084-4). U of Tex Pr.

--The Injured Child. (Robert E. Gross Lectureship Ser.). (Illus.). 240p. 1985. text ed. 35.00X (ISBN 0-292-73835-8). U of Tex Pr.

Brooks, Brian S. Student's Workbook for the Art of Editing. viii, 247p. 1986. pap. price not set (ISBN 0-02-315140-4). Macmillan.

Brooks, Brian S., et al. News Reporting & Writing. 2nd ed. LC 83-61604. 575p. 1985. pap. text ed. 18.95 (ISBN 0-312-57205-0); instr's. manual avail.; Student wkbk. 10.95 (ISBN 0-312-57209-3). St Martin.

Brooks Bright Foundation. Aspects of Anglo-American Relations. 1928. 34.50x (ISBN 0-685-69830-0). Elliots Bks.

Brooks, Bruce. The Moves Make the Man. LC 83-49476. 288p. (YA) (gr. 7-10). 1984. 13.50i (ISBN 0-06-020679-9); PLB 12.89g (ISBN 0-06-020698-5). HarpJ.

Brooks, C. E. Climate Through the Ages. 1970. pap. 6.95 (ISBN 0-486-22245-4). Dover.

--Climate Through the Ages: A Study of the Climatic Factors & Their Variations. 2nd ed. 13.25 (ISBN 0-8446-0516-6). Peter Smith.

Brooks, C. H., jt. auth. see Coue, Emile.

Brooks, C. Harry. The Practice of Autosuggestion by the Method of Emile Coue. 120p. 1981. pap. 6.00 (ISBN 0-89540-076-6, SB-076). Sun Pub.

Brooks, C. M., et al, eds. Integrative Functions of the Autonomic Nervous System. 508p. 1979. 104.75 (ISBN 0-444-80140-5, Biomedical Pr). Elsevier.

Brooks, C. T., tr. see Busch, Wilhelm.

Brooks, Carl N., jt. auth. see Silvern, Leonard C.

Brooks, Caroline. An Old Scandal. 1985. pap. 2.50 (ISBN 0-451-13404-4, Sig). NAL.

Brooks, Chandler M., et al. Humors, Hormones, & Neurosecretions: The Origins & Development of Man's Present Knowledge of the Humoral Control of Body Functions. LC 61-14336. 1962. 39.00x (ISBN 0-87395-006-2). State U NY Pr.

Brooks, Chandler McC., et al, eds. The Life & Contributions of Walter Bradford Cannon, 1871-1945. LC 74-20825. 1975. 39.50x (ISBN 0-87395-261-8). State U NY Pr.

Brooks, Charles, ed. Best Editorial Cartoons of the Year: 1972 Edition. (Best Editorial Cartoon Ser.). (Illus.). 143p. 1973. 13.95 (ISBN 0-911116-95-8). Pelican.

--Best Editorial Cartoons of the Year: 1974 Edition. LC 74-3807. (Best Editorial Cartoon Ser.). (Illus.). 160p. 1974. 13.95 (ISBN 0-88289-027-1). Pelican.

--Best Editorial Cartoons of the Year: 1975 Edition. LC 74-29707. (Best Editorial Cartoon Ser.). (Illus.). 160p. 1975. 13.95 (ISBN 0-88289-077-8). Pelican.

--Best Editorial Cartoons of the Year: 1976 Edition. LC 74-29707. (Best Editorial Cartoon Ser.). (Illus.). 160p. 1976. 13.95 (ISBN 0-88289-122-7). Pelican.

--Best Editorial Cartoons of the Year: 1977 Edition. LC 74-29707. (Best Editorial Cartoon Ser.). (Illus.). 1977. 13.95 (ISBN 0-88289-170-7); pap. 9.95 (ISBN 0-88289-171-5). Pelican.

--Best Editorial Cartoons of the Year: 1978 Edition. LC 73-643645. (Best Editorial Cartoon Ser.). (Illus.). 1978. pap. 9.95 (ISBN 0-88289-193-6). Pelican.

--Best Editorial Cartoons of the Year: 1979 Edition. (Best Editorial Cartoon Ser.). (Illus.). 1979. 13.95 (ISBN 0-88289-229-0). Pelican.

--Best Editorial Cartoons of the Year: 1980 Edition. LC 73-643645. (Illus.). 160p. (Orig.). 1980. 13.95 (ISBN 0-88289-264-9); pap. 9.95 (ISBN 0-88289-265-7). Pelican.

--Best Editorial Cartoons of the Year: 1981 Edition. LC 73-643645. (Best Editorial Cartoons of the Year Ser.: Vol. 9). (Illus.). 160p. 1981. pap. 9.95 (ISBN 0-88289-281-9). Pelican.

--Best Editorial Cartoons of the Year: 1982 Edition. LC 73-643645. (Illus.). 160p. (Orig.). 1982. pap. 9.95 (ISBN 0-88289-319-X). Pelican.

--Best Editorial Cartoons of the Year: 1984. 12th ed. 1984. pap. 9.95 (ISBN 0-88289-445-5). Pelican.

--Best Editorial Cartoons of the Year 1985. (Best Editorial Cartoons of the Year Ser.). (Illus.). 160p. 1985. pap. 9.95 (ISBN 0-88289-478-1). Pelican.

Brooks, Charles E. Climate in Everyday Life. LC 75-36507. (Illus.). 314p. 1976. Repr. of 1950 ed. lib. bdg. 19.25x (ISBN 0-8371-8647-1, BRCEL). Greenwood.

--The Evolution of Climate. LC 77-10221. Repr. of 1922 ed. 18.00 (ISBN 0-404-16201-0). AMS Pr.

--Fishing Yellowstone Waters. LC 83-23765. (Illus.). 120p. 1984. pap. 12.95 (ISBN 0-8329-0324-8, Pub. by Winchester Press); 19.95 (ISBN 0-8329-0353-1). New Century.

--Larger Trout for the Western Fly Fisherman. (Illus.). 224p. 1983. pap. 10.95 (ISBN 0-8329-0329-9, Pub. by Winchester Pr). New Century.

--The Living River. LC 84-62782. 208p. 1985. 19.95 (ISBN 0-8329-0395-7, Pub. by Winchester Pr); pap. 14.95 (ISBN 0-8329-0381-7, Pub. by Winchester Pr). New Century.

--Nymph Fishing for Larger Trout. LC 83-5832. (Illus.). 224p. 1983. pap. 8.95 (ISBN 0-8329-0330-2, Pub. by Winchester Pr). New Century.

--The Trout & the Stream. (Illus.). 224p. 1984. pap. 10.95 (ISBN 0-8329-0348-5, Pub. by Winchester Pr). New Century.

Brooks, Charles E. & Carruthers, N. Handbook of Statistical Methods in Meteorology. LC 77-10222. Repr. of 1953 ed. 30.50 (ISBN 0-404-16202-9). AMS Pr.

Brooks, Charles H. Official History & Manual of the Grand United Order of Odd Fellows in America. facs. ed. LC 74-157362. (Black Heritage Library Collection). 1902. 20.75 (ISBN 0-8369-8800-0). Ayer Co Pubs.

Brooks, Charles L., ed. see Habenicht, Donna & Bell, Anne.

Brooks, Charles M., Jr., jt. auth. see Barr, Alfred H., Jr.

Brooks, Charles T. Poems, Original & Translated. Andrews, W. P., ed. LC 72-4952. (The Romantic Tradition in American Literature Ser.). 256p. 1972. Repr. of 1885 ed. 19.00 (ISBN 0-405-04624-3). Ayer Co Pubs.

Brooks, Charles V. Sensory Awareness: The Rediscovery of Experiencing. 2nd ed. (Illus.). 256p. 1982. pap. 8.95 (ISBN 0-915520-56-7). Ross Erikson.

Brooks, Charlie R. Heat Treatment of Ferrous Alloys. LC 78-16513. (Illus.). 1979. text ed. 45.00x (ISBN 0-07-008076-3). McGraw.

Brooks, Charlie R., ed. Heat Treatment, Structure, & Properties of Nonferrous Alloys. 1982. 85.00 (ISBN 0-87170-138-3). ASM.

Brooks, Cheryl. Unusual Soups: Hot & Cold Soups for All Occasions. 176p. 1981. 13.95 (ISBN 0-13-937821-9); pap. 6.95 (ISBN 0-13-937813-8). P-H.

Brooks, Christine. Women's Hurdling. LC 81-82408. (Illus.). 160p. (Orig.). 1982. pap. 9.95 (ISBN 0-918438-85-3). Leisure Pr.

Brooks, Christopher L. Signs for the Times: Symbolic Realism in the Mid-Victorian World. 224p. 1984. text ed. 29.95 (ISBN 0-04-800030-2). Allen Unwin.

Brooks, Cleaneth, ed. see Percy, Thomas.

Brooks, Cleanth. Hidden God: Studies in Hemingway, Faulkner, Yeats, Eliot & Warren. (Orig.). 1963. 24.00x (ISBN 0-300-00327-7). Yale U Pr.

--The Language of the American South. LC 84-28065. (Mercer University Lamar Memorial Lectures). 88p. 1985. 9.95 (ISBN 0-8203-0782-3). U of Ga Pr.

--The Well Wrought Urn: Studies in the Structure of Poetry. LC 47-3143. (Orig.). (YA) 1956. pap. 5.95 (ISBN 0-15-695705-1, Harv). HarBraceJ.

--William Faulkner: First Encounters. LC 83-3634. 224p. 1983. 25.00x (ISBN 0-300-02995-0). Yale U Pr.

--William Faulkner: First Encounters. LC 83-3634. 224p. 1985. pap. 7.95 (ISBN 0-300-03399-0, Y-523). Yale U Pr.

--William Faulkner: The Yoknapatawpha Country. LC 63-17023. (Illus.). 1963. 42.00x (ISBN 0-300-00329-3); pap. 14.95x (ISBN 0-300-00028-6, Y170). Yale U Pr.

--William Faulkner: Toward Yoknapatawpha & Beyond. LC 77-10898. 1978. 36.00x (ISBN 0-300-02204-2); pap. 14.95 (ISBN 0-300-02493-2). Yale U Pr.

Brooks, Cleanth & Warren, Robert Penn. Modern Rhetoric. 4th ed. 401p. 1979. pap. text ed. 14.95 (ISBN 0-15-562815-1, HC). HarBraceJ.

--Scope of Fiction. 1960. text ed. 17.95 (ISBN 0-13-796656-3). P-H.

--Understanding Poetry. 4th ed. LC 75-25539. 1976. pap. text ed. 18.95 (ISBN 0-03-076980-9, HoltC); instrs' manual 1.00 (ISBN 0-03-016701-9). HR&W.

Brooks, Cleanth see Milton, John.

Brooks, Cleanth, jt. auth. see Warren, Robert Penn.

Brooks, Cleanth, jt. auth. see Wimsatt, William K.

Brooks, Cleanth, jt. ed. see Wood, Harriet H.

Brooks, Cleanth, et al. American Literature: The Makers & the Making, 2 vols. 1200p. 1973. Vol. 1. pap. text ed. 18.95 (ISBN 0-312-02590-4); Vol. 2. pap. text ed. 18.95 (ISBN 0-312-02660-9). St Martin.

--American Literature: The Makers & the Making, 4 vols. Incl. Bk. A. The Beginnings to 1826. 364p. 1974. pap. text ed. 11.95 (ISBN 0-312-02765-6); Bk. B. 1826 to 1861. 920p. 1974. pap. text ed. 13.95 (ISBN 0-312-02800-8); Bk. C. 1861 to 1914. 656p. pap. text ed. 12.95 (ISBN 0-312-02835-0); Bk. D. 1914 to the Present. 1216p. pap. text ed. 14.95 (ISBN 0-312-02870-9). 1974. pap. St Martin.

--American Literature: The Makers & the Making. 1856p. (Shorter edition). 1974. text ed. 20.95 (ISBN 0-312-02730-3). St Martin.

--An Approach to Literature. 5th ed. 832p. 1975. ref. ed. 26.95 (ISBN 0-13-043802-2). P-H.

Brooks, Clifford F. Essentials for Ophthalmic Lens Work. 1985. 50.00 (ISBN 0-87873-049-4). Prof Press.

Brooks, Clifford F. & Borish, Irving. System for Ophthalmic Dispensing. LC 76-5734. 1979. 60.00 (ISBN 0-87873-025-7). Prof Press.

Brooks, Collin & Brief, Richard P., eds. The Royal Mail Case: Rex V. Lord Kylsant, & Another. LC 80-1475. (Dimensions of Accounting Theory & Practice Ser.). 1981. Repr. of 1933 ed. lib. bdg. write for info. Ayer Co Pubs.

Brooks, Courtaney. The Case of the Stolen Dinosaur: A Play in Two Versions: Stage & Radio. (Illus.). 26p. (Orig.). (gr. 4 up). 1983. pap. text ed. 4.00x (ISBN 0-941274-02-0). Belnice Bks.

--Eight Steps to Choral Reading. (Orig.). (gr. 1 up). 1983. pap. text ed. 3.00x (ISBN 0-941274-01-2). Belnice Bks.

--Little Red & the Wolf: A Puppet Play. (gr. k up). 1983. pap. text ed. 2.00x (ISBN 0-941274-04-7). Belnice Bks.

--Pardner & Freddie: A Puppet Play. (Illus.). (gr. k up). 1983. pap. text ed. 2.00x (ISBN 0-941274-03-9). Belnice Bks.

--Plays & Puppets et Cetera. LC 81-68933. (Illus.). 100p. (Orig.). (gr. k up). 1981. pap. 9.00x (ISBN 0-941274-00-4). Belnice Bks.

--Plays & Puppets Etcetera. rev., 2nd ed. (Illus.). 150p. Date not set. pap. 14.00 (ISBN 0-941274-05-5). Belnice Bks.

Brooks, Cyril. Grace Triumphant: Autobiography. (Orig.). 1985. pap. price not set (ISBN 0-937396-66-4). Walterick Pubs.

Brooks, D. P. Bible: How to Understand & Teach It. LC 68-14365. 1969. pap. 3.95 (ISBN 0-8054-1118-6). Broadman.

--Dealing with Death: A Christian Perspective. LC 73-85697. cancelled (ISBN 0-8054-8229-6). Broadman.

Brooks, D. R., ed. see Willi Henning Society, 1st Meeting.

Brooks, Dale, ed. Who's Who in Karate: 1982-83. (Illus.). 112p. 1983. pap. 17.95 (ISBN 0-931981-00-X). Am Martial Arts Pub.

--Who's Who in the Martial Arts. (Illus.). 180p. (Orig.). 1985. pap. 12.95 (ISBN 0-931981-04-2). Am Martial Arts Pub.

Brooks, Daniel R., et al. Principles & Methods of Phylogenetic Systematics: A Cladistics Workbook. (Special Publication Ser.: No. 12). (Illus.). v, 92p. (Orig.). 1984. pap. 6.50 (ISBN 0-89338-022-9). U of KS Mus Nat Hist.

Brooks, Daniel T. Computer Law Institute. rev. ed. (Commercial Law & Practices Course Handbook 1983-84). 775p. 1983. pap. text ed. 35.00 (ISBN 0-317-02424-8, G4-3736). PLI.

Brooks, David. How to Control & Use Photographic Lighting. LC 80-82382. (Orig.). 1980. pap. 10.95 (ISBN 0-89586-059-7). H P Bks.

--How to Photograph Landscapes & Scenic Views. (Illus.). 144p. (Orig.). 1983. pap. 11.95 (ISBN 0-89586-208-5). H P Bks.

--Lenses & Lens Accessories. (Illus.). 128p. 1982. pap. 14.95 (ISBN 0-930764-34-X). Curtin & London.

--Narcissism on Rye. 12p. 1984. pap. 1.00 (ISBN 0-317-13316-0). Samisdat.

--The Railway Navvy. (Illus.). 216p. 1983. 21.00 (ISBN 0-7153-8449-X). David & Charles.

Brooks, David & Mallick, Netar. Renal Medicine & Urology: Library of General Practice, Vol. 4. (Illus.). 294p. 1982. pap. 21.00 (ISBN 0-443-01718-2). Churchill.

Brooks, David B. Low-grade & Nonconventional Sources of Manganese. LC 66-24411. pap. 33.80 (ISBN 0-317-26034-0, 2023787). Bks Demand UMI.

Brooks, David B. & Krutilla, John V. Peaceful Use of Nuclear Explosives: Some Economic Aspects. LC 69-15904. pap. 20.00 (ISBN 0-317-26030-8, 2023788). Bks Demand UMI.

Brooks, David B., ed. Resource Economics: Selected Works of Orris C. Herfindahl. LC 74-6814. (Resources for the Future Research Report Ser). (Illus.). 346p. 1974. 27.50x (ISBN 0-8018-1645-9). Johns Hopkins.

Brooks, David B, ed. Resource Economics: Selected Works of Orris C. Herfindahl. 348p. 1974. 27.50 (ISBN 0-8018-1645-9). Resources Future.

Brooks, David K. & Harrold, A. J. Modern Emergency Department Practice. 1983. text ed. 98.50 (ISBN 0-7131-4423-8). E Arnold.

Brooks, David K., Jr., jt. ed. see McFadden, John.

Brooks, Dennis L. & Henley, Arthur. Don't Be Afraid of Cataracts. (Illus.). 1978. 8.95 (ISBN 0-8184-0272-5). Lyle Stuart.

--Don't Be Afraid of Cataracts. 128p. 1983. pap. 5.95 (ISBN 0-8065-0823-X). Citadel Pr.

Brooks, Don. Washington Rock: A Climbing Guide. (Illus., Orig.). 1982. pap. 7.95 (ISBN 0-89886-046-6). Mountaineers.

Brooks, Douglas L. America Looks to the Sea: Ocean Use & the National Interest. 266p. 1984. write for info. (ISBN 0-86720-250-5). Jones & Bartlett.

Brooks, Douglas M. Common Sense in Teaching & Supervising. 1977. pap. text ed. 8.00 (ISBN 0-8191-0271-7). U Pr of Amer.

Brooks, Douglas M. & Van Cleaf, David W. Pupil Evaluation in the Classroom: An All Level Guide to Practice. LC 82-13650. (Illus.). 170p. 1983. lib. bdg. 25.00 (ISBN 0-8191-2736-1); pap. text ed. 11.25 (ISBN 0-8191-2737-X). U Pr of Amer.

Brooks, E. S., tr. see Duhamel, Georges.

Brooks, Earl & Odiorne, George S. Managing by Negotiations. 1981. 26.95 (ISBN 0-442-20962-2). Van Nos Reinhold.

Brooks, Edward. The Bessie Smith Companion. (Roots of Jazz Ser.). x, 250p. 1983. lib. bdg. 22.50 (ISBN 0-306-76202-1). Da Capo.

Brooks, Edward, jt. ed. see Ross, Thomas W.

Brooks, Edward F. & Wade, Torlen L. Planning & Managing Rural Health Centers. LC 78-27667. (Rural Health Center Ser.). (Illus.). 192p. 1979. prof ref 20.00x (ISBN 0-88410-536-9); pap. 12.95 (ISBN 0-88410-542-3). Ballinger Pub.

Brooks, Ellen J. Language Development, Aesthetic Development, & Literacy: A Resource Book. LC 84-48392. 175p. 1985. lib. bdg. 24.00 (ISBN 0-8240-8800-X). Garland Pub.

Brooks, Elston. I've Heard Those Songs Before: The Weekly Top Ten Tunes for the Past Fifty Years. LC 80-39725. 444p. 1981. pap. 12.95 (ISBN 0-688-00379-6, Quill). Morrow.

Brooks, Emile J. An Historical & Political Assessment of Woodrow Wilson as President of the United States, 2 vols. (Illus.). 374p. 1986. Set. 187.45 (ISBN 0-89266-537-8). Am Classical Coll Pr.

Brooks, Eric. Setting Up the IBM PCjr: An Introduction to Using the System. 224p. (Orig.). pap. cancelled (ISBN 0-916688-72-0, 72-0). Creative Comp.

Brooks, Fowler D. Change in Mental Traits with Age Determined by Annual Re-Tests. LC 76-176595. (Columbia University. Teachers College. Contributions to Education: No. 116). Repr. of 1921 ed. 22.50 (ISBN 0-404-55116-5). AMS Pr.

Brooks, Frank. Diseases of the Exocrine Pancreas. LC 79-67788. (Major Problems in Internal Medicine Ser.: Vol. 20). (Illus.). 139p. 1980. text ed. 23.00 (ISBN 0-7216-2077-9). Saunders.

Brooks, Frank, ed. Peptic Ulcer Disease. (Contemporary Issues in Gastroenterology Ser.: Vol. 3). (Illus.). 344p. 1985. text ed. 48.50 (ISBN 0-443-08368-1). Churchill.

Brooks, Frank P., ed. Gastrointestinal Pathophysiology. 2nd ed. (Pathophysiology Ser.). 1978. pap. text ed. 17.95x (ISBN 0-19-502331-5). Oxford U Pr.

Brooks, Frederick P., et al. Automatic Data Processing: System-360 Edition. LC 68-31293. pap. 122.50 (ISBN 0-317-09380-0, 2055097). Bks Demand UMI.

Brooks, Frederick P., Jr. The Mythical Man-Month: Essays on Software Engineering. (Illus.). 200p. 1974. pap. text ed. 15.95 (ISBN 0-201-00650-2). Addison-Wesley.

Brooks, G. T. Chlorinated Insecticides, 2 vols. Incl. Vol. 1. Technology & Applications. 249p (ISBN 0-8493-5062-X); Vol. 2. Biological & Environmental Aspects (ISBN 0-8493-5063-8). LC 73-90535. (Uniscience Ser.). 1974. 56.00 ea. CRC Pr.

--Chlorinated Insecticides, Vol. I. LC 83-13605. 260p. 1983. Repr. of 1974 ed. lib. bdg. 56.00 (ISBN 0-89874-664-7). Krieger.

--Chlorinated Insecticides, Vol. II. LC 83-13605. 208p. 1985. Repr. of 1974 ed. lib. bdg. 56.00 (ISBN 0-89874-663-9). Krieger.

Brooks, G. T., jt. ed. see Pratt, G. E.

Brooks, Gary D., jt. ed. see Burns, Richard W.

Brooks, George, jt. auth. see Orloff, Neil.

Brooks, George A. & Fahey, Thomas D. Exercise Physiology: Human Bioenergetics &Its Applications. LC 3-14582. 810p. 1984. text ed. 30.45 (ISBN 0-471-88827-3). Wiley.

Brooks, George A., ed. Perspectives on the Academic Discipline of Physical Education. LC 80-85203. (Illus.). 1981. text ed. 19.95x (ISBN 0-931250-18-8, BBRO0018). Human Kinetics.

Brooks, George E. Yankee Traders, Old Coasters, & African Middlemen: A History of American Legitimate Trade with West Africa in the Nineteenth Century. LC 79-129253. (Pub. by Boston U Pr). 1970. 20.00x (ISBN 0-8419-8707-6, Africana). Holmes & Meier.

Brooks, George E., jt. ed. see Bennett, Norman R.

Brooks, George E., Jr. Themes in African & World History: A Schema for Integrating Africa into World History; Tropical Africa: The Colonial Heritage; The African Heritage & the Slave Trade. rev. ed. (African Humanities Ser.). 59p. 1983. pap. text ed. 4.00 (ISBN 0-941934-06-3). Indiana Africa.

Brooks, George, Jr The Kru Mariner in the Nineteenth Century: An Historical Compendium. (Liberian Studies Monograph Ser.: No. 1). 1972. 5.50 (ISBN 0-916712-05-2). Liberian Studies.

Brooks, George R., ed. see Flint, Timothy.

Brooks, Geraldine. Dames & Daughters of Colonial Days. LC 74-3979. (Women in America Ser). (Illus.). 308p. 1974. Repr. of 1900 ed. 26.50x (ISBN 0-405-06080-7). Ayer Co Pubs.

--Dames & Daughters of Colonial Days. 284p. 1982. Repr. of 1900 ed. 16.95 (ISBN 0-87928-109-X). Corner Hse.

--Dames & Daughters of the French Court. facs. ed. LC 68-8443. (Essay Index Reprint Ser). 1904. 19.00 (ISBN 0-8369-0256-4). Ayer Co Pubs.

--Romances of Colonial Days. 1978. Repr. of 1903 ed. lib. bdg. 25.00 (ISBN 0-8495-0336-1). Arden Lib.

Brooks, Glenn E., jt. auth. see Rourke, Francis E.

Brooks, Glenwood C., Jr., jt. auth. see Sedlacek, William E.

Brooks, Gregory. Monroe's Island. LC 79-1568. (Illus.). (ps-1). 1979. 7.95 (ISBN 0-02-714810-6). Bradbury Pr.

Brooks, Gwendolyn. Aloneness. 1971. 3.00 (ISBN 0-910296-75-8); pap. 2.00 (ISBN 0-910296-55-3). Broadside.

--Annie Allen. LC 78-138207. 60p. 1972. Repr. of 1949 ed. lib. bdg. 18.75x (ISBN 0-8371-5561-4, BRAA). Greenwood.

--Beckonings. 1975. pap. 2.00 (ISBN 0-685-51286-X). Broadside.

--Bronzeville Boys & Girls. LC 56-8152. (Illus.). 48p. (gr. 3-6). 1956. PLB 10.89 (ISBN 0-06-020651-9). HarpJ.

--Family Pictures. 5.00 (ISBN 0-910296-43-X); pap. 1.00 (ISBN 0-910296-67-7); tape 5.00 (ISBN 0-685-24799-6). Broadside.

--In the Mecca. LC 68-26544. 1968. 11.49i (ISBN 0-06-010537-2, HarpT). Har-Row.

--Maud Martha: A Novel. LC 73-18553. (BCL Ser. II). Repr. of 1953 ed. 18.00 (ISBN 0-404-11368-0). AMS Pr.

--Report from Part One: An Autobiography. new ed. LC 72-77308. 192p. 1972. 5.95 (ISBN 0-910296-82-0). Broadside.

--Selected Poems. 1963. 11.49i (ISBN 0-06-010535-6, HarpT); (HarpT). Har-Row.

--To Disembark. 63p. 1981. 8.95 (ISBN 0-88378-101-8); pap. 4.25 (ISBN 0-88378-102-6). Third World.

--World of Gwendolyn Brooks. LC 74-160646. 1971. 15.00i (ISBN 0-06-010538-0, HarpT). Har-Row.

Brooks, Gwendolyn, ed. The Black Position. No. 1, 1971. 1.00 (ISBN 0-685-42543-6); No. 2, 1972. 2.00 (ISBN 0-685-42544-4); No. 3, 1973. 3.00 (ISBN 0-685-42545-2); No. 4. 2.50 (ISBN 0-685-42546-0). Broadside.

--A Broadside Treasury, 1965-1970. 6.00 (ISBN 0-910296-53-7); pap. 4.00 (ISBN 0-910296-51-0). Broadside.

--Jump Bad: A New Chicago Anthology 1971. 1971. 6.00 (ISBN 0-685-07547-8); pap. 4.00 (ISBN 0-685-07548-6). Broadside.

Brooks, Gwendolyn, et al. A Capsule Course in Black Poetry Writing. 64p. 1975. pap. 6.00 (ISBN 0-685-57551-9). Broadside.

Brooks, H. Allen. Frank Lloyd Wright & the Prairie School. LC 83-15621. (Illus.). 120p. (Orig.). 1984. pap. 11.95 (ISBN 0-8076-1084-4). Braziller.

--The Prairie School: Frank Lloyd Wright & His Midwest Contemporaries. (Illus.). 400p. 1976. pap. 12.95 (ISBN 0-393-00811-8, N811). Norton.

Brooks, H. Allen, ed. Cite Frages & Other Buildings & Projects 1923-1927. Tzonis, Alexander. LC 83-1584. (Le Corbusier Archive Ser.). 1983. lib. bdg. 200.00 (ISBN 0-8240-5051-7). Garland Pub.

--Musee D'Art Occidental, Tokio, & other Buildings & Projects. (The Le Corbusier Archive Ser.). 200.00 (ISBN 0-8240-5079-7). Garland Pub.

--Prairie School Architecture: Studies from the Western Architect. 352p. 1983. pap. 19.95 (ISBN 0-442-21309-3). Van Nos Reinhold.

--La Tourette & Other Buildings. (Le Corbusier Ser.). 1985. lib. bdg. 200.00 (ISBN 0-8240-5077-0). Garland Pub.

--Writings on Wright: Selected Comment on Frank Lloyd Wright. (Illus.). 160p. 1981. 25.00 (ISBN 0-262-02161-7); pap. 8.95 (ISBN 0-262-52086-9). MIT Pr.

Brooks, H. Allen & Ttonis, Alexander, eds. Buildings & Projects: Nineteen Twenty-Eight to Nineteen Twenty-Nine. LC 83-1581. (Le Corbusier Archive Ser.). 1983. lib. bdg. 200.00 (ISBN 0-8240-5054-1). Garland Pub.

Brooks, H. Allen & Tzonis, Alexander, eds. Ahmedabad, 1953-1960. LC 83-11617. (Le Corbusier Archive Ser.). 1983. lib. bdg. 200.00 (ISBN 0-8240-5075-4). Garland Pub.

--Chandigarh: Capitole: Assemblec & Other Buildings & Projects, Vol. I. LC 83-11607. 1985. lib. bdg. 200.00 (ISBN 0-8240-5071-1). Garland Pub.

--Chandigarh: Capitole: Palais du Gouverneur & Other Buildings & Projects, Vol. III. LC 83-11607. (Le Corbusier Archive Ser.). 1983. lib. bdg. 200.00 (ISBN 0-8240-5073-8). Garland Pub.

--Chandigarh: City & Musee. LC 83-11607. (Le Corbusier Archive Ser.). 1983. lib. bdg. 200.00 (ISBN 0-8240-5074-6). Garland Pub.

--Palais des Nations Unies & Other Buildings & Projects, 1946-1948. LC 83-1578. (Le Corbusier Archive Ser.). 1983. lib. bdg. 200.00 (ISBN 0-8240-5067-3). Garland Pub.

--Projet Roq et Rog, Roquebrane - Cap Martin & Other Building Projects, 1948-1950. LC 83-5567. (Le Corbusier Archive Ser.). 1983. lib. bdg. 200.00 (ISBN 0-8240-5068-1). Garland Pub.

--Ronchamp, Maisons Jaoul, & Other Buildings & Projects, 1951-1952. LC 83-5566. (Le Corbusier Archive Ser.). 1983. lib. bdg. 200.00 (ISBN 0-8240-5069-X). Garland Pub.

--Unite d'Habitation, Reze-les-Nantes. LC 83-9074. (Le Corbusier Archive Ser.). 1983. lib. bdg. 200.00 (ISBN 0-8240-5070-3). Garland Pub.

--Urbanisme, Algiers & Other Buildings & Projects. LC 83-5568. (Le Corbusier Archive Ser.). 1983. lib. bdg. 200.00 (ISBN 0-8240-5059-2). Garland Pub.

Brooks, H. Allen, ed. see Le Corbusier.

Brooks, H. F. A Bibliography of John Oldham (1653-1683) The Restoration Satirist. rev. ed. (Oxford Bible Society Ser.: Vol. 5, Pt. 1). pap. 13.00 (ISBN 0-317-16743-X). Kraus Repr.

Brooks, H. F. see Pennar, Davis W.

Brooks, Harold A., ed. Prairie School Architecture: Studies from "The Western Architect". LC 73-91567. pap. 87.80 (ISBN 0-317-28690-0, 2020459). Bks Demand UMI.

Brooks, Harold F., ed. A Midsummer Night's Dream. 3rd ed. (The Arden Shakespeare Ser.). 1979. 32.00x (ISBN 0-416-17930-4, NO. 2629); pap. 6.95 (ISBN 0-416-17940-1, NO. 2628). Methuen Inc.

Brooks, Harold F. & Seldon, Raman, eds. The Poems of John Oldham. (Illus.). 760p. 1985. 95.00x (ISBN 0-19-812456-2). Oxford U Pr.

Brooks, Harold L., jt. auth. see Bonchek, Lawrence I.
Brooks, Harold L., jt. auth. see Soin, Jagneet S.
Brooks, Harry F. & Malecki, Donald S. Insuring the Lease Exposure. LC 81-83114. 1982. pap. text ed. 17.75 (ISBN 0-87218-313-0). Natl Underwriter.
Brooks, Harvey, jt. ed. see Hollander, Jack M.
Brooks, Harvey, et al, eds. Public & Private Partnership: New Opportunities for Meeting Social Needs. (American Academy of Arts & Sciences Ser.). 392p. 1984. professional reference 25.00x (ISBN 0-88410-482-6). Ballinger Pub.
Brooks, Harvey, et al, eds. see Barbour, Ian.
Brooks, Helen M. A Slat of Wood & Other Poems. 46p. 1976. 5.00 (ISBN 0-686-34466-9). Whimsie Pr.
Brooks, Henry, jt. auth. see Dame, Lorin L.
Brooks, Henry M. Olden-Time Music. LC 70-39537. Repr. of 1888 ed. 21.00 (ISBN 0-404-09919-X). AMS Pr.
Brooks, Herb. Investing with a Computer: A Time-Series Analysis Approach. 1984. 19.95 (ISBN 0-89433-194-9). Petrocelli.
--Investing with a Computer: A Time-Series Analysis Approach. (A Petrocelli Bk.). 1984. 19.95. Van Nos Reinhold.
Brooks, Hindi. Making It! 60p. 1984. pap. 2.75 (ISBN 0-88680-216-4). I E Clark.
Brooks, Hugh. Encyclopedia of Building & Construction Terms. LC 82-21565. 416p. 1983. 50.00 (ISBN 0-13-275511-4). P-H.
Brooks, Hugh, ed. Illustrated Encyclopedic Dictionary of Building & Construction Terms. (Illus.). 320p. 1975. 29.95 (ISBN 0-13-451013-5, Busn). P-H.
Brooks, Hugh C. & El-Ayouty, Yassin, eds. Refugees South of the Sahara: An African Dilemma. LC 71-105994. (Contributions in Afro-American & African Studies: No. 14). 1970. 35.00 (ISBN 0-8371-3324-6, BSS&). Greenwood.
Brooks, J. & Shaw, G. Origin & Development of Living Systems. 1973. 61.00 (ISBN 0-12-135740-6). Acad Pr.
Brooks, J., ed. Organic Maturation Studies & Fossil Fuel Exploration. LC 80-41958. 1981. 60.00 (ISBN 0-12-135760-0). Acad Pr.
--Petroleum Geochemistry & Exploration of Europe. (Illus.). 396p. 1983. text ed. 60.00x (ISBN 0-632-01076-2). Blackwell Pubns.
Brooks, J. L., ed. Benito Perez Galdos: Torquemada en la Hoguera. 100p. 1973. text ed. 6.30 (ISBN 0-08-016917-1); pap. text ed. 5.25 (ISBN 0-08-016918-X). Pergamon.
Brooks, Jack. Front Row Center: A Guide to Northern California Theaters. LC 81-14069. (Illus., Orig.). 1981. pap. 6.95 (ISBN 0-89286-193-2). One Hund One Prods.
--Front Row Center: Southern California. (Illus.). 252p. (Orig.). 1984. pap. 10.95 (ISBN 0-89286-205-X). One Hund One Prods.
Brooks, James & Draper, James. Interior Design for Libraries. 164p. (Orig.). 1979. 10.00x (ISBN 0-8389-0282-0). ALA.
Brooks, James A. & Winbery, Carlton L. Syntax of New Testament Greek. LC 78-51150. 1978. pap. text ed. 8.00 (ISBN 0-8191-0473-6). U Pr of Amer.
Brooks, James W., ed. History of the Court of Common Pleas of the City & County of New York, with Full Reports of All Important Proceedings. 253p. 1979. Repr. of 1896 ed. lib. bdg. 35.00x (ISBN 0-8377-0308-5). Rothman.
Brooks, Jane B. The Process of Parenting. LC 80-84014. (Illus.). 353p. 1981. 14.95 (ISBN 0-87484-474-6); instructors manual avail. Mayfield Pub.
Brooks, Janice Y. Glory. 1985. pap. 3.50 (ISBN 0-440-12921-4). Dell.
--Our Lives, Our Fortunes. 384p. (Orig.). 1984. pap. 3.50 (ISBN 0-440-16817-1). Dell.
--Still the Mighty Waters. (Orig.). 1983. pap. 3.95 (ISBN 0-440-17630-1). Dell.
Brooks, Jean S. & Reich, David L. The Public Library in Non-Traditional Education. LC 73-21903. (Illus.). 256p. 1974. 12.95 (ISBN 0-88280-008-6). ETC Pubns.
Brooks, Jeffrey. When Russia Learned to Read: Literacy & Popular Literature, 1861-1917. LC 85-42677. (Illus.). 475p. 1985. text ed. 39.50x (ISBN 0-691-05450-9). Princeton U Pr.
Brooks, Jeremy, tr. see Gorky, Maxim.
Brooks, Jerome. The Big Dipper Marathon. (gr. 7-9). 1982. pap. 1.75 (ISBN 0-671-43918-9). Archway.
--Testing of Charlie Hammelman. (gr. 7-9). 1979. pap. 1.75 (ISBN 0-671-29916-6). Archway.
Brooks, Jim & Welte, Dietrich H. Advances in Petroleum Geochemistry, Vol. 1. (Serial Publication Ser.). 1984. 49.50 (ISBN 0-12-032001-0). Acad Pr.
Brooks, Joae G. No More Diapers! 1982. pap. 6.95 (ISBN 0-385-29308-9, Delta). Dell.
Brooks, Joe. Trout Fishing. LC 70-178838. (Outdoor Life Bk.). (Illus.). 320p. 1972. 15.00i (ISBN 0-06-010532-1, HarpT). Har-Row.
Brooks, JoeAnn, jt. auth. see Clay, Susan.
Brooks, John. Go-Go Years. (Truman Talley Bk.). 375p. 1984. pap. 10.95 (ISBN 0-525-48096-X, 01063-320, Obelisk). Dutton.
--Once in Golconda: A True Drama of Wall Street 1920-38. (Truman Talley Bk.). 320p. 1985. pap. 11.95 (ISBN 0-525-48166-4, 01160-350). Dutton.
--Once in Golconda: A True Dream of Wall Street, 1920-1938. 1981. 15.95 (ISBN 0-393-01375-8). Norton.
--Telephone: The First Hundred Years. LC 75-23874. (Illus.). (YA) 1976. 13.95i (ISBN 0-06-010540-2, HarpT). Har-Row.
Brooks, John, ed. South American Handbook. 1985. 24.95 (ISBN 0-528-84970-0). Rand.
--South American Handbook, 1982. 58th ed. LC 25-514. (Illus.). 1341p. 1981. 25.00 (ISBN 0-900751-18-5). Intl Pubns Serv.
--South American Handbook: 1983. 59th ed. LC 25-514. (Illus.). 1394p. 1982. 25.00x (ISBN 0-900751-19-3). Intl Pubns Serv.
--The South American Handbook 1986. rev. ed. (Illus.). 1472p. 1985. 24.95 (ISBN 0-528-84009-6). Rand.
Brooks, John G. An American Citizen: The Life of William Henry Baldwin Jr. Bruchey, Stuart, ed. LC 80-1295. (Railroads Ser.). 1981. Repr. of 1910 ed. lib. bdg. 30.00x (ISBN 0-405-13765-6). Ayer Co Pubs.
--American Syndicalism. LC 78-86170. Repr. of 1913 ed. 10.00 (ISBN 0-404-01118-7). AMS Pr.
--American Syndicalism. LC 70-89722. (American Labor, from Conspiracy to Collective Bargaining Ser. 1). 264p. 1969. Repr. of 1913 ed. 14.00 (ISBN 0-405-02107-0). Ayer Co Pubs.
--American Syndicalism: The I.W.W. LC 78-107407. (Civil Liberties in American History Ser). 1970. Repr. of 1913 ed. lib. bdg. 32.50 (ISBN 0-306-71887-1). Da Capo.
--Labor's Challenge to the Social Order. LC 74-137931. (Economic Thought, History & Challenge Ser). 1971. Repr. of 1920 ed. 32.50x (ISBN 0-8046-1437-7, Pub. by Kennikat). Assoc Faculty Pr.
Brooks, John H. Highlights of the Sterling & Francine Clark Art Institute. 2nd ed. LC 81-80217. (Illus.). 98p. 1985. cloth 14.95 (ISBN 0-931102-16-2); pap. 9.95 (ISBN 0-931102-17-0). S & F Clark Art.
Brooks, John L. Just Before the Origin: Alfred Russel Wallace's Theory of Evolution. LC 83-7710. (Illus.). 284p. 1983. 31.50x (ISBN 0-231-05676-1). Columbia U Pr.
--The Systematics of North American Daphnia. (Memoirs of the Connecticut Academy of Arts & Sciences Ser.: Vol. 13). 180p. 1963. 22.50 (ISBN 0-317-03797-8). Shoe String.
Brooks, John L., jt. ed. see Bowyer, John W.
Brooks, John P. The Divine Church. Dayton, Donald W., ed. (The Higher Christian Life Ser.). 283p. 1985. 35.00 (ISBN 0-8240-6408-9). Garland Pub.
Brooks, John R. Surgery of the Pancreas. (Illus.). 528p. 1983. 58.00 (ISBN 0-7216-2082-5). Saunders.
Brooks, Juani ta. Emma Lee. rev., 2nd ed. (Illus.). 108p. 1984. pap. 7.95 (ISBN 0-87421-121-2). Utah St U Pr.
Brooks, Juanita. The History of the Jews in Utah & Idaho, 1853-1950. 252p. 1973. 7.95 (ISBN 0-914740-12-1). Western Epics.
--Jacob Hamblin: Mormon Apostle to the Indians. LC 80-80395. (Illus.). 160p. 1980. pap. 6.95 (ISBN 0-935704-03-5). Howe Brothers.
--John Doyle Lee: Zealot, Pioneer Builder, Scapegoat. LC 84-12849. 406p. 1984. pap. 12.50 (ISBN 0-935704-21-3). Howe Brothers.
--Mountain Meadows Massacre. (Illus.). 342p. 1979. Repr. of 1963 ed. 18.95 (ISBN 0-8061-0549-6). U of Okla Pr.
--Quicksand & Cactus: A Memoir of the Southern Mormon Frontier. LC 82-11698. (Illus.). 400p. 1982. 19.95 (ISBN 0-935704-11-6). Howe Brothers.
Brooks, Juanita, ed. Not by Bread Alone: The Journal of Martha Spence Heywood, 1850-56. LC 78-50411. (Illus.). 1978. 10.95 (ISBN 0-913738-27-1). Utah St Hist Soc.
--On the Mormon Frontier: The Diary of Hosea Stout, 2 Vols. 832p. 1982. Repr. of 1964 ed. 39.95 (ISBN 0-87480-214-8, SET). U of Utah Pr.
Brooks, Juanita, jt. ed. see Cleland, Robert G.
Brooks, Judith K., jt. auth. see Chriss, Michael.
Brooks, Karen. The Complete Vegetarian Cookbook. 240p. 1984. pap. 3.95 (ISBN 0-671-52642-1). PB.
Brooks, Karen M., jt. auth. see Johnson, D. Gale.
Brooks, Kate. The Immaculate Murders. (Orig.). 1979. pap. 1.95 (ISBN 0-532-23268-2). Woodhill.
--Murder in the Laboratory. (Orig.). 1979. pap. 1.75 (ISBN 0-532-17212-4). Woodhill.
--The Secret of Killer Mountain Inn. 1978. pap. 1.50 (ISBN 0-532-15375-8). Woodhill.
Brooks, Keith L. Acts, Adventures of the Early Church. (Teach Yourself the Bible Ser). 1961. pap. 2.25 (ISBN 0-8024-0125-2). Moody.
--Basic Bible Study for New Christians. (Teach Yourself the Bible Ser). 1961. pap. 2.25 (ISBN 0-8024-0478-2). Moody.
--Christian Character Course. (Teach Yourself the Bible Ser). 1961. pap. 2.25 (ISBN 0-8024-1301-3). Moody.
--Colossians & Philemon. (Teach Yourself the Bible Ser). 81p. (Orig.). 1961. pap. 2.25 (ISBN 0-8024-1525-3). Moody.
--Ephesians, the Epistle of Christian Maturity. (Teach Yourself the Bible Ser.). 1944. pap. 2.25 (ISBN 0-8024-2333-7). Moody.
--First & Second Thessalonians. (Teach Yourself the Bible Ser). 1961. pap. 2.25 (ISBN 0-8024-2645-X). Moody.
--First Corinthians. (Teach Yourself the Bible Ser). 1964. pap. 2.25 (ISBN 0-8024-2649-2). Moody.
--Galatians, the Epistle of Christian Maturity. (Teach Yourself the Bible Ser.). 1963. pap. 2.25 (ISBN 0-8024-2925-4). Moody.
--Great Prophetic Themes. (Teach Yourself the Bible Ser). 1962. pap. 2.25 (ISBN 0-8024-3320-0). Moody.
--Hebrews: The Beauty of Christ Unveiled. (Teach Yourself the Bible Ser). 1961. pap. 2.25 (ISBN 0-8024-3507-6). Moody.
--How to Pray. (Teach Yourself the Bible Ser). 1961. pap. 2.25 (ISBN 0-8024-3708-7). Moody.
--James: Belief in Action. (Teach Yourself the Bible Ser). 1961. pap. 2.25 (ISBN 0-8024-4227-7). Moody.
--Luke, the Gospel of God's Man. (Teach Yourself the Bible Ser). 1964. pap. 2.25 (ISBN 0-8024-5047-4). Moody.
--Mark: Gospel of God's Servant. (Teach Yourself the Bible Ser). 64p. 1961. pap. 2.25 (ISBN 0-8024-5183-7). Moody.
--Matthew, the Gospel of God's King. (Teach Yourself the Bible Ser.). 1963. pap. 2.25 (ISBN 0-8024-5212-4). Moody.
--Philippians, The Epistle of Christian Joy. (Teach Yourself the Bible Ser). 1964. pap. 2.25 (ISBN 0-8024-6506-4). Moody.
--Practical Bible Doctrine. (Teach Yourself the Bible Ser). 1962. pap. 2.25 (ISBN 0-8024-6733-4). Moody.
--Revelation, the Future Foretold. (Teach Yourself the Bible Ser). 1962. pap. 2.25 (ISBN 0-8024-7308-3). Moody.
--Romans: The Gospel for All. (Teach Yourself the Bible Ser). 1962. pap. 2.25 (ISBN 0-8024-7372-5). Moody.
Brooks, Kenneth A. The Software Primer: Lotus 1-2-3 Level 1. Harper, Larry D., ed. LC 83-82215. (Software Primer Ser.). 191p. 1984. binder 24.95 (ISBN 0-913871-02-8). JNZ.
--The Software Primer: Multiplan. Harper, Larry D., ed. LC 83-82213. (The Software Primer Ser.). 150p. 1984. binder cancelled 24.95 (ISBN 0-913871-03-6). JNZ.
Brooks, Larimore S. Vision of Creation. LC 83-82426. (Illus.). 72p. (Orig.). 1984. pap. 2.25 (ISBN 0-9612682-0-4). Galilee Pr.
Brooks, Lee. First Ladies of the White House: Washington Thru Nixon. LC 76-86857. (Illus.). 156p. 1969. 9.95 (ISBN 0-87319-022-X). C Hallberg.
Brooks, Leroy D. Financial Management Decision Game (Fingame) rev. ed. 1982. pap. 15.25x (ISBN 0-256-02622-X). Irwin.
Brooks, Lester, jt. auth. see Brooks, Pat.
Brooks, Lisa. Thomas B. Turtle. (Illus.). (ps-3). 1978. 10.00 (ISBN 0-682-49034-2). Exposition Pr FL.
Brooks, Lloyd & Dickerson, Susan. Brookson House Inns: A Typing Practice Set. 208p. (Orig.). 1984. pap. text ed. 11.95 (ISBN 0-574-20730-9, 13-3730); Personnel Services module. 4.95 (ISBN 0-574-20732-5, 13-3732); Conventions Services module. 4.95 (ISBN 0-574-20733-3, 13-3733); Medical Services module. 4.95 (ISBN 0-574-20734-1, 13-3734); Financial Services module. 4.95 (ISBN 0-574-20738-4, 13-3738); Legal Services module. 4.95 (ISBN 0-574-20739-2, 13-3739); instr's guide avail. 0.00 (13-3731). SRA.
Brooks, Lloyd D. Consultamation, Inc. Word Processing Practice & Applications. 192p. 1982. 13.15 (ISBN 0-07-008081-X). McGraw.
--Practical Business Mathematics. 464p. 1984. text ed. 19.95 (ISBN 0-574-20725-2, 13-3725); write for info. tchr's ed. (ISBN 0-574-20728-7, 13-3728); write for info. wkbk. resource manual (ISBN 0-574-20729-5, 13-3729). SRA.
Brooks, Louise. Early History of Divine Science. 1963. 5.95 (ISBN 0-686-24363-3). Divine Sci Fed.
--Lulu in Hollywood. LC 81-48108. 1982. 15.00 (ISBN 0-394-52071-8); pap. 7.95 (ISBN 0-394-72179-9). Knopf.
Brooks, Lucy. The Nurse Assistant. LC 77-73939. 1978. pap. text ed. 12.80 (ISBN 0-8273-1620-8); instr.'s guide 3.00 (ISBN 0-8273-1621-6). Delmar.
--The Nurse Assistant. 1978. 12.95 (ISBN 0-442-20943-6). Van Nos Reinhold.
Brooks, Lyman B. Upward: A History of Norfolk State University. LC 83-4328. 272p. 1983. 19.95 (ISBN 0-88258-084-1). Howard U Pr.
Brooks, M., jt. auth. see Kearey, P.
Brooks, M., ed. see Meeting of European Geological Societies.
Brooks, Maggie. Loose Connections. 1984. 11.95 (ISBN 0-312-49827-6). St Martin.
Brooks, Margaret & Knight, Charles. Complete Guide to British Butterflies. (Illus.). 168p. 1982. 24.95 (ISBN 0-224-01958-9, Pub. by Jonathan Cape). Merrimack Pub Cir.
Brooks, Margeret M. & Knight, Charles. A Complete Pocket Guide to British Butterflies. (Illus.). 165p. 1985. 9.95 (ISBN 0-224-02225-3, Pub. by Jonathan Cape). Merrimack Pub Cir.
Brooks, Maria Z. Polish Reference Grammar. LC 74-78500. (Slavistic Printings & Reprintings Textbook Ser.: No. 2). 580p. 1976. text ed. 64.00x (ISBN 90-2793-313-8). Mouton.
Brooks, Marvin & Brooks, Sally W. Lifelong Lover. LC 84-25926. 240p. 1985. pap. 8.95 (ISBN 0-385-17713-5). Doubleday.
Brooks, Marvin B. & Brooks, Sally W. Lifelong Sexual Vigor: How to Avoid & Overcome Impotence. LC 81-43115. 264p. 1981. 12.95 (ISBN 0-385-17712-7). Doubleday.
Brooks, Mary E. Bonus Provision in Central City Areas. (PAS Reports). 52p. 1970. 5.00 (ISBN 0-318-13113-7); subscribers 3.00 (ISBN 0-318-13114-5). Am Plan Assn.
--Housing Equity & Environmental Protection: The Needless Conflict. 136p. 1976. pap. 10.00 (ISBN 0-318-13003-3); pap. 8.00 members (ISBN 0-318-13004-1). Am Plan Assn.
--Lower Income Housing: The Planner's Response. (PAS Reports: No. 282). 69p. 1972. 6.00 (ISBN 0-318-13024-6). Am Plan Assn.
Brooks, Maurice. The Appalachians. LC 75-3897. (Illus.). 1975. 8.50 (ISBN 0-89092-005-2). Seneca Bks.
Brooks, Maurice G. Appalachians. (Illus.). 1965. 11.95 (ISBN 0-395-07458-4). HM.
Brooks, Michael P. Social Planning & City Planning. (PAS Reports: No. 261). 61p. 1970. 6.00 (ISBN 0-318-13082-3). Am Plan Assn.
Brooks, N. R. & Frost, W. A. Safety & Security Handbook: A Modern Investigative Approach. 100p. 1985. pap. 19.95 (ISBN 0-932041-00-0). Creative Alter Pr.
Brooks, Nancy A., jt. auth. see Deegan, Mary Jo.
Brooks, Nancy A., jt. auth. see Riemer, Jeffrey W.
Brooks, Nancy C., jt. tr. see Spindler, Frank M.
Brooks, Nancy C., et al. Ocho Siglos de Cuentos y Narraciones de Espana. (gr. 12 up). 1976. pap. text ed. 5.95 (ISBN 0-88345-280-4, 18465). Regents Pub.
Brooks, Nancy J. The Golden Leprechaun. 128p. (gr. 3-6). 1980. 5.95 (ISBN 0-8059-2767-0). Dorrance.
Brooks, Natalie A., jt. auth. see Brooks, Stewart M.
Brooks, Neal A., et al. A History of Baltimore County. LC 78-31598. (Illus.). 1979. 15.95 (ISBN 0-9602326-1-3). Friends Towson Lib.
Brooks, Neil, ed. Closed Head Injury: Psychological, Social, & Family Consequences. (Illus.). 1984. 39.95x (ISBN 0-19-261252-2). Oxford U Pr.
Brooks, Neil C. The Sepulchre of Christ in Art & Liturgy. pap. 9.00 (ISBN 0-384-05925-2). Johnson Repr.
Brooks, Nelson see Bottiglia, William F.
Brooks, Nelson see Bree, Germaine.
Brooks, Nelson see Eddy, Frederick D.
Brooks, Nicholas. The Early History of the Church at Canterbury. (Studies in the Early History of Britain). 237p. 1983. text ed. 45.50x (ISBN 0-7185-1182-4, Leicester). Humanities.
Brooks, Nicholas, ed. Latin & the Vernacular Languages in Early Medieval Britain. (Studies in the Early History of Britain: Vol. 1). 200p. 1982. text ed. 45.50x (ISBN 0-7185-1209-X, Leicester). Humanities.
Brooks, Noah. Abraham Lincoln & the Downfall of American Slavery. LC 73-14436. (Heroes of the Nation Ser.). Repr. of 1894 ed. 30.00 (ISBN 0-404-58254-0). AMS Pr.
--Henry Knox, a Soldier of the Revolution. LC 74-8496. (Era of the American Revolution Ser.). (Illus.). xiv, 286p. 1974. Repr. of 1900 ed. lib. bdg. 32.50 (ISBN 0-306-70617-2). Da Capo.
--Tales of the Maine Coast. 1980. 8.50 (ISBN 0-686-64301-1). Bookfinger.
Brooks, Noel. Ephesians. pap. 5.95 (ISBN 0-911866-02-7). Advocate.
--Let There Be Life. pap. 3.95 (ISBN 0-911866-88-4). Advocate.
--Scriptural Holiness. 3.95 (ISBN 0-911866-53-1); pap. 2.95 (ISBN 0-911866-54-X). Advocate.
Brooks, Nona L. Mysteries. 1977. 6.95 (ISBN 0-686-24364-1); pap. 4.50 (ISBN 0-686-24365-X). Divine Sci Fed.
--Short Lessons in Divine Science. 1973. pap. 4.95 (ISBN 0-686-24348-X). Divine Sci Fed.
Brooks, Olive. Panama Quadrant. 1962. 11.95x (ISBN 0-8084-0234-X). New Coll U Pr.
Brooks, Oscar S. The Sermon on the Mount: Authentic Human Values. 124p. (Orig.). 1985. lib. bdg. 19.75 (ISBN 0-8191-4740-0); pap. text ed. 8.50 (ISBN 0-8191-4741-9). U Pr of Amer.
Brooks, Pat. A Call to War with Prayer Power. LC 84-61052. 1985. pap. text ed. 7.00 (ISBN 0-932050-26-3). New Puritan.
--Healing of the Mind. 4th. ed. Orig. Title: Using Your Spiritual Authority. 1983. pap. text ed. 2.50 (ISBN 0-932050-00-X). New Puritan.
--Out!, in the Name of Jesus. 3rd ed. 1985. pap. text ed. 5.00 (ISBN 0-932050-27-1). New Puritan.
--The Return of the Puritans. 4th ed. LC 83-62390. 1983. pap. 5.00 (ISBN 0-932050-23-9). New Puritan.
Brooks, Pat & Brooks, Lester. Spain 1985. Fisher, Robert C., ed. (Fisher Annotated Travel Guides Ser.). 384p. 1984. 12.95 (ISBN 0-8116-0063-7). NAL.
Brooks, Pat & Garvan, Fran J. Country Inns of New England. (Country Inns Ser.). (Illus.). 200p. 1984. pap. 7.95 (ISBN 0-89286-229-7). One Hund One Prods.
Brooks, Patricia. Best Restaurants Southern New England. LC 83-61463. (Best Restaurants Ser.). (Illus.). 200p. 1983. pap. 4.95 (ISBN 0-89286-214-9). One Hund One Prods.

Brooks, Paul. The House of Life: Rachel Carson at Work. (Nonfiction Ser.). 1985. pap. 9.95 (ISBN 0-8398-2866-7). G K Hall.

--Speaking for Nature. LC 82-16997. (The Sierra Club Paperback Library Bks.). (Illus.). 320p. 1983. pap. 8.95 (ISBN 0-87156-332-0). Sierra.

--Speaking for Nature: How Our Literary Naturalists Have Shaped America. (Illus.). 288p. 1980. 12.95 (ISBN 0-395-29610-2). HM.

Brooks, Paynton & Brooks. The Human Body: Structure & Function in Health & Disease. 2nd ed. LC 79-24085. (Illus.). 1980. pap. text ed. 25.95 (ISBN 0-8016-0808-2). Mosby.

Brooks, Peggy, ed. see Travis, Carole A.

Brooks, Penelope, et al, eds. Learning & Cognition in the Mentally Retarded: Proceedings of a Conference held at the John F. Kennedy Center for Research on Education & Human Development. LC 84-10289. 576p. 1984. text ed. 49.50 (ISBN 0-89859-374-3). L Erlbaum Assocs.

Brooks, Peter. The Melodramatic Imagination: Balzac, Henry James, Melodrama, & the Mode of Excess. (A Morningside Book). 235p. 1984. 30.00x (ISBN 0-231-06006-8); pap. 12.50x (ISBN 0-231-06007-6). Columbia U Pr.

--Novels of Worldliness, Crebillon, Marivaux, Laclos, Stendhal. LC 68-56303. 1969. 32.00x (ISBN 0-691-06154-8). Princeton U Pr.

--Reading for the Plot. LC 83-48929. 1984. 17.95 (ISBN 0-394-50597-2). Knopf.

Brooks, Peter see Giamatti, A. Bartlett.

Brooks, Peter, ed. see James, Henry.

Brooks, Peter, et al, eds. Yale French Studies, No. 69: The Lesson of Paul de Man. 288p. (Orig.). 1985. pap. 11.95x (ISBN 0-300-03409-1). Yale U Pr.

Brooks, Peter N., ed. Reformation Principles & Practice: Essays in Honour of A. G. Dickens. 1980. 40.00 (ISBN 0-85967-579-3). Scolar.

--Seven-Headed Luther: Essays in Commemoration of Quincentenary, 1483-1983. (Illus.). 1983. 47.50x (ISBN 0-19-826648-0). Oxford U Pr.

Brooks, Philip C. Research in Archives: The Use of Unpublished Primary Sources. LC 69-19273. (Midway Reprint Ser.). xii, 128p. 1982. pap. text ed. 8.00x (ISBN 0-226-07576-1). U of Chicago Pr.

Brooks, Philip R. & Hayes, Edward F., eds. State-to-State Chemistry. LC 77-14164. (ACS Symposium Ser.: No. 56). 1977. 31.95 (ISBN 0-8412-0386-5). Am Chemical.

Brooks, Phillips. Selected Sermons. facs. ed. Scarlett, William, ed. LC 79-142610. (Essay Index Reprint Ser). 1949. 19.50 (ISBN 0-8369-2146-1). Ayer Co Pubs.

Brooks, Phillips V. A Bibliography of & about the Works of Anthony Edward Montagu Compton Mackenzie (Sir Compton Mackenzie) 1893-1972. 274p. 1984. lib. bdg. 32.50 (ISBN 0-8482-7451-2). Norwood Edns.

Brooks, Pierre R. Officer Down Code Three. LC 75-23841. 1975. 8.95 (ISBN 0-916070-01-8). MTI Tele.

Brooks, Polly S. Queen Eleanor: Independent Spirit of the Medieval World: a Biography of Eleanor of Aquitaine. LC 82-48776. (Illus.). 160p. (gr. 6 up). 1983. 9.57i (ISBN 0-397-31994-0); PLB 9.89g (ISBN 0-397-31995-9). Lipp Jr Bks.

Brooks, R. A., ed. see Floy, Michael.

Brooks, R. M., ed. see Symposium On Several Complex Variables, Park City, Utah, 1970.

Brooks, R. R. Biological Methods of Prospecting for Minerals. LC 82-21819. 322p. 1983. 48.50 (ISBN 0-471-87400-0, Pub. by Wiley-Interscience). Wiley.

Brooks, R. R., jt. auth. see Reeves, R. D.

Brooks, R. T. A Place to Start: The Bible As a Guide for Today. 120p. 1983. pap. 4.95 (ISBN 0-86683-708-6). Winston Pr.

Brooks, R. T., ed. Ask the Bible. LC 83-3841. 400p. 1983. 19.95 (ISBN 0-672-52765-0). Bobbs.

Brooks, Randy. Barbwire Holds Its's Ground. 32p. 1981. 10.00 (ISBN 0-913719-17-X); pap. 3.50 (ISBN 0-913719-16-1). High-Coo Pr.

--The Rosebud Bursts. 40p. 1979. 25.00 (ISBN 0-913719-68-4); pap. 10.00 (ISBN 0-913719-67-6). High-Coo Pr.

Brooks, Randy & Brooks, Shirley, eds. Haiku Review '84. 76p. (Orig.). 1984. pap. 5.00 (ISBN 0-913719-71-4). High Coo Pr.

Brooks, Reid M. & Olmo, Harold P. Register of New Fruit & Nut Varieties. 2nd rev. & enl. ed. LC 76-100017. 512p. 1972. 37.50x (ISBN 0-520-01638-6). U of Cal Pr.

Brooks, Richard A., ed. Critical Bibliography of French Literature, Vol. 4a: The Eighteenth Century-Supplement. LC 47-3282. 1968. 34.95x (ISBN 0-8156-2009-8). Syracuse U Pr.

Brooks, Richard A., jt. ed. see Alden, Douglas W.

Brooks, Richard A., jt. ed. see Hall, H. Gaston.

Brooks, Richard A., jt. ed. see LaCharite, Raymond C.

Brooks, Robert. So That's How I Was Born! (Illus.). 48p. (ps-3). 1983. 6.95 (ISBN 0-671-44501-4, Little Simon). S&S.

Brooks, Robert & Gray, Alfred, eds. Differential Geometry: Proceedings, Special Year, Maryland 1981-1982. (Progress in Mathematics). 263p. 1983. 18.95 (ISBN 0-8176-3134-8). Birkhauser.

Brooks, Robert, tr. see Euripides.

Brooks, Robert A. Ennis & Roman Tragedy. Connor, W. R., ed. LC 81-2642. (Monographs in Classical Studies). 1981. Repr. of 1949 ed. lib. bdg. 35.00 (ISBN 0-405-14030-4). Ayer Co Pubs.

--Roman Epistle. LC 83-21044. 72p. (Orig.). 1984. pap. 6.95 (ISBN 0-87233-072-9). Bauhan.

Brooks, Robert C. Bibliography of Municipal Problems & City Conditions. LC 78-112527. (Rise of Urban America). 1970. Repr. of 1901 ed. 23.50 (ISBN 0-405-02439-8). Ayer Co Pubs.

--Corruption in American Politics & Life. LC 73-19133. (Politics & People Ser.). 326p. 1974. Repr. 22.00x (ISBN 0-405-05858-6). Ayer Co Pubs.

--Deliver Us from Dictators. 14.25 (ISBN 0-8369-7154-X, 7986). Ayer Co Pubs.

Brooks, Robert E. Utopian Universe. LC 73-89334. 1973. 7.95 (ISBN 0-686-11431-0). Utopian Universe.

Brooks, Robert F. Childrens Stories for Teenage Adults. rev. ed. (Illus.). 32p. (Orig.). (gr. 5-9). pap. 3.00 (ISBN 0-936868-05-8). Freeland Pubns.

--Do You Play the Drum, or Does the Drum Play You? Matunde, Nwandu S., ed. (Illus.). 20p. (Orig.). 1981. pap. 3.00 (ISBN 0-936868-03-1). Freeland Pubns.

--Nwandu's Child of Life Reader. (Illus.). 20p. (Orig.). (gr. k-4). pap. 2.00 (ISBN 0-936868-00-7). Freeland Pubns.

Brooks, Robert P. The Agrarian Revolution in Georgia, 1865-1912. LC 72-181919. Repr. of 1914 ed. 15.00 (ISBN 0-404-00007-X). AMS Pr.

--Agrarian Revolution in Georgia, 1865-1912. LC 73-129939. Repr. of 1914 ed. 15.00x (ISBN 0-8371-1603-1, BRG&, Pub. by Negro U Pr). Greenwood.

--Georgia Studies, Selected Writings of Robert Preston Brooks. facs. ed. LC 69-17565. (Essay Index Reprint Ser). 1952. 18.50 (ISBN 0-8369-1025-7). Ayer Co Pubs.

Brooks, Robert R. As Steel Goes: Unionism in a Basic Industry. LC 40-27479. (History of American Economy Ser). 1970. Repr. of 1940 ed. 17.00 (ISBN 0-384-05935-X). Johnson Repr.

--When Labor Organizes. LC 76-156407. (American Labor Ser., No. 2). (Illus.). 1971. Repr. of 1937 ed. 23.00 (ISBN 0-405-02916-0). Ayer Co Pubs.

Brooks, Robert W. Systematics & Bionomics of Anthophora: The Bomboides Group & Species Groups of the New World (Hymenoptera: Apoidea, Anthophoridae) LC 82-40445. (Publications in Entomology: Vol. 98). 96p. pap. text ed. 10.50x (ISBN 0-520-09658-4). U of Cal Pr.

Brooks, Rodney A. Model-Based Computer Vision. Stone, Harold, ed. LC 84-2416. (Computer Science Series: Artificial Intelligence: No. 14). 162p. 1984. 39.95 (ISBN 0-8357-1526-4). UMI Res Pr.

Brooks, Roger. Support for the Poor in the Mishnaic Law of Agriculture: Tractate Peah. LC 83-8719. (Brown Judaic Studies: No. 43). 220p. 1983. pap. 21.00 (ISBN 0-89130-632-3, 14 00 43). Scholars Pr GA.

Brooks, Romaine. Portraits, Tableaux, Dessins. LC 75-12306. (Homosexuality Ser.). (Illus.). 1975. Repr. of 1952 ed. 11.00x (ISBN 0-405-07396-8). Ayer Co Pubs.

Brooks, Romaine & Breeskin, Adelyn D. Romaine Brooks, "Thief of Souls". LC 79-150515. (Illus.). pap. 36.00 (ISBN 0-317-10220-6, 2051197). Bks Demand UMI.

Brooks, Ron. Timothy & Gramps. LC 78-17389. (Illus.). (ps-2). 1979. 7.95 (ISBN 0-02-714790-8). Bradbury Pr.

Brooks, Sally W., jt. auth. see Brooks, Marvin.

Brooks, Sally W., jt. auth. see Brooks, Marvin B.

Brooks, Sandra. I Can Pray to God. LC 82-80031. (Happy Day Bks.). (Illus.). 24p. (Orig.). (ps-3). 1982. pap. 1.39 (ISBN 0-87239-540-5, 3586). Standard Pub.

--What Happens in Autumn? LC 81-86708. (Primary Picture Storybooks). (Illus.). 32p. (Orig.). (ps-3). 1982. pap. 1.95 (ISBN 0-87239-548-0, 2880). Standard Pub.

--What Happens in Spring? LC 81-86710. (Primary Picture Storybooks). (Illus.). 32p. (Orig.). (ps-3). 1982. pap. 1.95 (ISBN 0-87239-546-4, 2878). Standard Pub.

--What Happens in Summer? LC 81-86709. (Primary Picture Storybooks). (Illus.). 32p. (Orig.). (ps-3). 1982. pap. 1.95 (ISBN 0-87239-547-2, 2879). Standard Pub.

--What Happens in Winter? LC 81-86707. (Primary Picture Storybooks). (Illus.). 32p. (Orig.). (ps-3). 1982. pap. 1.95 (ISBN 0-87239-549-9, 2881). Standard Pub.

Brooks, Sara. Fun for Girls. pap. 1.00 (ISBN 0-87497-055-5). Assoc Bk.

Brooks, Sarah W. English Poetry & Poets. facsimile ed. LC 72-37511. (Essay Index Reprint Ser.). Repr. of 1890 ed. 24.00 (ISBN 0-8369-2537-8). Ayer Co Pubs.

Brooks, Shirley, jt. ed. see Brooks, Randy.

Brooks, Shirley M. Fundamentals of Operating Room Nursing. 2nd ed. LC 79-500. (Illus.). 198p. 1979. pap. 15.95 (ISBN 0-8016-0814-7). Mosby.

--Instrumentation for the Operating Room: A Photographic Manual. 2nd ed. LC 82-2225. (Illus.). 476p. 1982. pap. text ed. 23.95 (ISBN 0-8016-0817-1). Mosby.

Brooks, Stanley J. Brooks Standard Rate Book 1985-86. 256p. 1985. 22.00x (ISBN 0-941806-00-6). S J Brooks.

Brooks, Stanley J., ed. see Chamness, Danford.

Brooks, Steve. Phillip Blanc in San Francisco. (Illus.). 20p. 1972. pap. 3.00 (ISBN 0-915572-12-5). Panjandrum.

Brooks, Stewart M. The Cancer Story. (Quality Paperback: No. 265). 207p. 1973. pap. 2.50 (ISBN 0-8226-0265-2). Littlefield.

--Nurse's Drug Reference. 1978. pap. text ed. 16.95 (ISBN 0-316-10975-4). Little.

--Review of Nursing: Essentials for the State Boards. 1978. text ed. 15.95 (ISBN 0-316-10974-6). Little.

--The VD Story: Medicine's Battle Against the Scourge of Venereal Disease. (Quality Paperback Ser.: No. 252). (Illus.). 162p. 1973. pap. 3.50 (ISBN 0-8226-0252-0). Littlefield.

Brooks, Stewart M. & Brooks, Natalie A. Turner's Personal & Community Health. 16th ed. LC 82-7948. (Illus.). 511p. 1983. pap. text ed. 22.95 (ISBN 0-8016-5128-X). Mosby.

Brooks, Stewart M., et al. Handbook of Infectious Diseases. 1980. 12.95 (ISBN 0-316-10968-1). Little.

Brooks, Susan, ed. see Chamness, Danford.

Brooks, Svevo & Burkhart, John. A Guide to Political Fasting. LC 82-13008. 56p. 1982. pap. 3.95 (ISBN 0-943726-01-8). Langdon Pubns.

Brooks, Sydna. Prose Poetry. 14p. 1983. 2.00x (ISBN 0-86516-025-2). Bolchazy-Carducci.

Brooks, Terrance see Rosenbaum, Judith.

Brooks, Terrance V. see Rosenbaum, Judith.

Brooks, Terry. The Elfstones of Shannara. 1982. 15.95 (ISBN 0-345-30253-2, Del Rey); pap. 7.95 (ISBN 0-345-28555-7, Del Rey). Ballantine.

--The Sword of Shannara. 1983. pap. 3.95 (ISBN 0-345-31425-5, Del Rey). Ballantine.

--The Wishsong of Shannara. LC 84-24185. 544p. 1985. 18.95 (ISBN 0-345-31823-4, Del Rey); pap. 8.95 (ISBN 0-345-30833-6, Del Rey). Ballantine.

Brooks, Thomas. Complete Works of Thomas Brooks, 6 Vols. Grosart, Alexander B., ed. LC 74-39538. Repr. of 1866 ed. Set. lib. bdg. 240.00 (ISBN 0-404-01120-9); lib. bdg. 40.00 ea. Vol. 1 (ISBN 0-404-01121-7). Vol. 2 (ISBN 0-404-01122-5). Vol. 3 (ISBN 0-404-01123-3). Vol. 4 (ISBN 0-404-01124-1). Vol. 5 (ISBN 0-404-01125-X). Vol. 6 (ISBN 0-404-01126-8). AMS Pr.

--Heaven on Earth. 320p. 1983. pap. 5.45 (ISBN 0-85151-356-5). Banner of Truth.

--Precious Remedies Against Satan's Devices. 253p. 1984. pap. 5.45x (ISBN 0-85151-002-7). Banner of Truth.

--Works of Brooks, 6 vols. 1980. Set. 99.95 (ISBN 0-85151-302-6). Banner of Truth.

Brooks, Thomas B. The Augusta Tract: Map & Manual, 1858. LC 72-78924. (Illus.). 100p. 1972. 12.95 (ISBN 0-912526-03-3). Lib Res.

Brooks, Thomas R. Toil & Trouble: A History of American Labor. rev ed. 402p. 1972. pap. 9.95 (ISBN 0-385-29071-3, Delta). Dell.

Brooks, Tilford. America's Black Musical Heritage. (Illus.). 384p. 1984. 23.95 (ISBN 0-13-024315-9); pap. 16.95 (ISBN 0-13-024307-8). P-H.

Brooks, Tim & Marsh, Earl. The Complete Directory of Prime Time Network Television, 1946-Present. (Illus.). 1979. 19.95 (ISBN 0-345-28248-5). Ballantine.

Brooks, Tim & Marsh, Earle. Complete Directory of Prime Time Network Television Shows 1946 to the Present. 1981. pap. 14.95 (ISBN 0-345-31864-1). Ballantine.

--TV in the Sixties. 288p. (Orig.). 1985. pap. 3.50 (ISBN 0-345-31866-8). Ballantine.

--TV's Greatest Hits. (Orig.). 1985. pap. 3.50 (ISBN 0-345-31865-X). Ballantine.

Brooks, Tom, ed. see BIS Applied Systems & MacKintosh International.

Brooks, Tommy C. The Flip-Flop Spy. 1983. 10.95 (ISBN 0-533-05251-3). Vantage.

Brooks, Valerie, jt. auth. see Maiorano, Robert.

Brooks, Van W. John Addington Symonds: A Biographical Study. LC 77-121648. 1971. Repr. of 1971 ed. 21.00 (ISBN 0-403-00535-3). Scholarly.

Brooks, Van W., tr. Philine from the Unpublished Journals of Henri-Frederic Amiel. 401p. 1981. Repr. of 1930 ed. lib. bdg. 40.00 (ISBN 0-8495-0071-0). Arden Lib.

Brooks, Van W., tr. see Gauguin, Paul.

Brooks, Van Wyck. A Chilmark Miscellany: Essays Old & New. LC 73-3227. 315p. 1973. Repr. of 1948 ed. lib. bdg. 21.50x (ISBN 0-374-90999-7). Octagon.

--Emerson & Others. LC 73-3132. 250p. 1973. Repr. lib. bdg. 20.50x (ISBN 0-374-90998-9). Octagon.

--The Flowering of New England, Eighteen Fifteen to Eighteen Sixty-Five. LC 80-2898. Repr. of 1936 ed. 45.00 (ISBN 0-404-18007-8). AMS Pr.

--The Flowering of New England, 1815-1865. 1981. pap. 7.95 (ISBN 0-395-30522-5). HM.

--The Life of Emerson. LC 80-2528. Repr. of 1932 ed. 37.00 (ISBN 0-404-19252-1). AMS Pr.

--The Malady of the Ideal. 1979. Repr. of 1913 ed. lib. bdg. 15.00 (ISBN 0-8495-0533-X). Arden Lib.

--New England: Indian Summer, 1865-1915. LC 84-8545. xii, 558p. 1984. pap. text ed. 14.95x (ISBN 0-226-07578-8). U of Chicago Pr.

--The Ordeal of Mark Twain. LC 75-41039. (BCL Ser. II). Repr. of 1933 ed. 18.00 (ISBN 0-404-14512-4). AMS Pr.

--The Pilgrimage of Henry James. LC 75-159169. vii, 170p. 1972. Repr. of 1925 ed. lib. bdg. 18.50x (ISBN 0-374-91004-9). Octagon.

--The Wine of the Puritans: A Study of Present Day America. 1978. Repr. of 1908 ed. lib. bdg. 22.50 (ISBN 0-8495-0446-5). Arden Lib.

Brooks, Van-Wyck. The World of H. G. Wells. 190p. 1973. Repr. of 1915 ed. lib. bdg. 59.95 (ISBN 0-8490-1334-8). Gordon Pr.

--The World of H. G. Wells. LC 72-92949. (English Literature Ser., No. 33). Repr. of 1915 ed. lib. bdg. 39.95x (ISBN 0-8383-0962-3). Haskell.

--World of H. G. Wells. LC 70-131649. 1970. Repr. of 1915 ed. 15.00 (ISBN 0-403-00536-1). Scholarly.

Brooks, Van Wyck & Mumford, Lewis, eds. The American Caravan: A Yearbook of American Literature. 843p. Date not set. Repr. of 1927 ed. lib. bdg. 85.00 (ISBN 0-89984-027-2). Century Bookbindery.

Brooks, Van Wyck, pref. by see Rourke, Constance M.

Brooks, Van Wyck, tr. see Amiel, Henri-Frederic.

Brooks, Virginia R. Minority Stress & Lesbian Women. LC 80-8116. 240p. 1981. 28.00x (ISBN 0-669-03953-5). Lexington Bks.

Brooks, Vivia. Heritage of the Lord. (Illus.). 96p. 1985. 10.00 (ISBN 0-87770-314-0). Ye Galleon.

Brooks, W. D. & Vogel, R. A., eds. Interpersonal Communication. LC 76-44141. (Ser. in Speech Communication). 1977. pap. text ed. 13.95 (ISBN 0-8465-7603-1); instr's. guide o.p. 4.95 (ISBN 0-8465-7607-4). Benjamin-Cummings.

Brooks, W. D., ed. see Kelley, Robert.

Brooks, W. D., ed. see Leth, Pamela C. & Leth, Steven A.

Brooks, Walter R. Freddie Goes to Florida. (Illus.). 224p. (gr. 3-7). 1980. pap. 1.75 (ISBN 0-440-42577-8, YB). Dell.

--Freddy & the Baseball Team From Mars. (Illus.). 256p. (gr. 3-7). pap. 2.95 (ISBN 0-440-42724-X, YB). Dell.

--Freddy the Detective. (gr. 3 up). 1979. pap. 1.75 (ISBN 0-440-42739-8, YB). Dell.

--Jimmy Takes Vanishing Lessons. (Illus.). 32p. (gr. 3-6). pap. 1.50 (ISBN 0-440-44165-X, YB). Dell.

Brooks, William. Fun for Boys. pap. 1.00 (ISBN 0-87497-054-7). Assoc Bk.

Brooks, William A. A B C Shorthand. pap. 1.50 (ISBN 0-87497-049-0). Assoc Bk.

Brooks, William D., et al. Speech Communication. 5th ed. 368p. 1985. pap. text ed. price not set (ISBN 0-697-00461-9); instr's. manual avail. (ISBN 0-697-00520-8); student wkbk. avail. (ISBN 0-697-00521-6). Wm C Brown.

--Verbal Language & Communication. (Comm Comp Ser.). (Illus.). 32p. 1980. pap. text ed. 2.95x (ISBN 0-89787-306-8). Gorsuch Scarisbrick.

Brooks, William E. Grant of Appomattox, a Study of the Man. LC 73-138577. (Illus.). 1971. Repr. of 1942 ed. lib. bdg. 14.75x (ISBN 0-8371-5776-5, BRGR). Greenwood.

--Lee of Virginia: A Biography. LC 75-16842. (Illus.). 361p. 1975. Repr. of 1932 ed. lib. bdg. 20.00x (ISBN 0-8371-8270-0, BRLV). Greenwood.

Brooks, Wyck Van, tr. see Bazalgette, Leon.

Brooks, Yvonne C., ed. see Grant, Steven C.

Brooksby, J. B., ed. The Aerial Transmission of Disease. (Philosophical Transactions of the Royal Society: Ser. B, Vol. 302). (Illus.). 166p. 1984. Repr. text ed. 54.00x (ISBN 0-85403-214-2, Pub. by Royal Soc London). Scholium Intl.

Brooks-Davies, Douglas. The Mercurian Monarch: Magical Politics from Spenser to Pope. LC 83-12043. (Illus.). 228p. 1983. 26.00 (ISBN 0-7190-0954-5, Pub. by Manchester Univ Pr). Longwood Pub Group.

--Pope's Dunciad & the Queen of Night: A Study in Emotional Jacobitism. LC 84-17135. 300p. 1985. 29.00 (ISBN 0-7190-1735-1, Pub. by Manchester Univ Pr). Longwood Pub Group.

Brooks-Gunn, Jeanne, jt. auth. see Lewis, Michael.

Brooks-Gunn, Jeanne & Petersen, Anne C., eds. Girls at Puberty: Biological & Psychosocial Perspectives. 350p. 1983. 32.50x (ISBN 0-306-41144-X, Plenum Pr). Plenum Pub.

Brooks-Gunn, Jeanne, jt. ed. see Baruch, Grace.

Brookshear. Computer Science: An Overview. 1984. 23.95 (ISBN 0-8053-0900-4); instr's. manual 5.95 (ISBN 0-8053-0901-2); Pascal Programming Supplement, by Mark A. Barnard. pap. 7.95 (ISBN 0-8053-0902-0). Benjamin-Cummings.

Brook-Shephard, Gordon. Archduke of Sarajevo: The Romance & Tragedy of Franz Ferdinand of Austria. (Illus.). 320p. 1984. 19.45i (ISBN 0-316-10951-7). Little.

Brook-Shepherd, G. The Storm Petrels. (Ballantine Espionage-Intelligence Library: No. 11). 224p. 1982. pap. 2.75 (ISBN 0-345-30125-0). Ballantine.

Brook-Shepherd, Gordon. Anschluss: The Rape of Austria. LC 76-890. (Illus.). 222p. 1976. Repr. of 1963 ed. lib. bdg. 19.75x (ISBN 0-8371-8754-0, BSAN). Greenwood.

--Dollfuss. LC 78-17396. 1978. Repr. of 1961 ed. lib. bdg. 25.50x (ISBN 0-313-20527-2, SHDO). Greenwood.

Brookshire, Paul. Bluegrass Boy in Florida. LC 73-89072. 118p. 1974. 5.95 (ISBN 0-912458-10-0). E A Seemann.

Brooks-Rose, Christine. A Rhetoric of the Unreal: Studies in Narrative & Structure, Especially of the Fantastic. LC 80-41720. 446p. 1983. pap. 17.95 (ISBN 0-521-27656-X). Cambridge U Pr.

Brookstone, Jeffrey M. The Multinational Businessman & Foreign Policy: Entrepreneurial Politics in East-West Trade & Investment. LC 76-12845. (Illus.). 204p. 1976. text ed. 36.95 (ISBN 0-275-23360-X). Praeger.

Brooks Van, Wyck see Brooks, Van Wyck.

Broom, D. M. Biology of Behaviour: An Introductory Book for Students of Zoology, Psychology & Agriculture. (Illus.). 350p. 1981. 44.50 (ISBN 0-521-23316-X); pap. 16.95 (ISBN 0-521-29906-3). Cambridge U Pr.

Broom, Dorothy, ed. Unfinished Business: Social Justice for Women in Australia. 240p. (Orig.). 1984. text ed. 29.95x (ISBN 0-86861-577-3); pap. text ed. 12.95x (ISBN 0-86861-585-4). Allen Unwin.

Broom, H. N., et al. Small Business Management. 1983. text ed. 21.35 (ISBN 0-538-07250-4, G25). SW Pub.

Broom, Herbert. The Philosophy of Law: Being Notes of Lectures Delivered During Twenty-Three Years (1852 to 1875) in the Inner Temple Hall Adapted for Students & the Public. xi, 338p. 1980. Repr. of 1878 ed. lib. bdg. 27.50x (ISBN 0-8377-0310-7). Rothman.

Broom, Iris, jt. auth. see Shaw, Josephine.

Broom, L., et al. Investigating Social Mobility. (ANU Department of Sociology Monograph: No. 1). (Illus.). 220p. (Orig.). 1980. pap. text ed. 8.00 (ISBN 0-909851-32-8, 1561). Australia N U P.

Broom, Leonard & Jones, F. Lancaster. Opportunity & Attainment in Australia. LC 76-14271. 1977. 15.00x (ISBN 0-8047-0927-0). Stanford U Pr.

Broom, Leonard & Kitsuse, John, I. The Managed Casualty: The Japanese American Family in World War II. LC 57-9006. (University of California Publications in Culture & Society: Vol. 6). pap. 58.00 (ISBN 0-317-29099-1, 2021394). Bks Demand UMI.

Broom, Leonard & Kitsuse, John I. The Managed Casualty: The Japanese-American Family in World War II. (Library Reprint Ser.: No. 40). 1974. Repr. 25.00x (ISBN 0-520-02523-7). U of Cal Pr.

Broom, Leonard & Riemer, Ruth. Removal & Return: The Socio-Economic Effects of the War on Japanese Americans. (California Library Reprint: No. 39). 1974. 32.50x (ISBN 0-520-02522-9). U of Cal Pr.

Broom, Leonard & Selznick, Philip. Essentials of Sociology: From "Sociology: A Text with Adapted Readings". 6th ed. 324p. 1979. pap. text ed. 18.50 scp (ISBN 0-06-040976-2, HarpC); instructor's manual avail. (ISBN 0-06-361496-0). Har-Row.

Broom, Leonard, jt. auth. see Speck, Frank G.

Broom, Leonard, et al. Essentials of Sociology. 3rd ed. LC 83-61555. 263p. 1984. pap. text ed. 14.95 (ISBN 0-87581-295-3). Peacock Pubs.

--Sociology: A Text with Adapted Readings. 7th ed. 608p. 1981. text ed. 22.50 scp (ISBN 0-06-040991-6, HarpC); instructors manual avail. (ISBN 0-06-360955-X); scp study guide 10.50 (ISBN 0-06-040967-3). Har-Row.

Broom, Robert. Finding the Missing Link. LC 75-11916. 104p. 1975. Repr. of 1951 ed. lib. bdg. 22.50x (ISBN 0-8371-8141-0, BRFM). Greenwood.

Broom, Robert & Robinson, J. T. Swartkranz Ape-Man: Paranthropus Crassidens. LC 76-44697. Repr. of 1952 ed. 24.50 (ISBN 0-404-15911-7). AMS Pr.

Broom, Robert & Schepers, G. W. The South African Fossil Ape-Man: The "Australopithecinae". LC 76-44698. Repr. of 1946 ed. 40.00 (ISBN 0-404-15910-9). AMS Pr.

Broom, Robert, et al. Sterkfontein Ape-Man Plesianthropus. LC 76-44699. Repr. of 1949 ed. 24.50 (ISBN 0-404-15909-5). AMS Pr.

Broomall, Robert W. The Bank Robber. 160p. 1985. pap. 2.50 (ISBN 0-449-12827-X, GM). Fawcett.

Broome, Annabel & Wallace, Louise. Psychology & Gynaecological Problems. 320p. (Orig.). 1985. pap. 35.00x (ISBN 0-422-79460-0, 9250, Pub. by Tavistock England); pap. 13.95x (ISBN 0-422-78590-3, 9251). Methuen Inc.

Broome, C. E., jt. auth. see Berkeley, M. J.

Broome, Connie. Vessels Unto Honor. LC 76-22242. 1977. pap. 3.50 (ISBN 0-87148-879-5). Pathway Pr.

Broome, H. B. The Meanest Man in West Texas. LC 85-1524. (Double D Western Ser.). 192p. 1985. 12.95 (ISBN 0-385-23102-4). Doubleday.

Broome, Harvey. Faces of the Wilderness. LC 72-78038. (Illus.). 271p. 1972. 7.95 (ISBN 0-87842-027-4). Mountain Pr.

Broome, J. H. A Student's Guide to Corneille. 1971. pap. text ed. 5.00x (ISBN 0-435-37575-X). Heinemann Ed.

Broome, Mary A. Life in South Africa. LC 70-97379. Repr. of 1877 ed. 15.00x (ISBN 0-8371-2441-7, BLS&, Pub. by Negro U Pr). Greenwood.

Broome, P. & Chesters, G. The Appreciation of Modern French Poetry: 1850 to 1950. LC 75-40768. 176p. 1976. 29.95 (ISBN 0-521-20792-4); pap. 10.95 (ISBN 0-521-20930-7). Cambridge U Pr.

Broome, Peter. Henri Michaux. (French Poets Ser.). 154p. 1977. 32.50 (ISBN 0-485-14605-3, Pub. by Athlone Pr Ltd); pap. 18.95 (ISBN 0-485-12205-7). Longwood Pub Group.

Broome, Peter, ed. see Michaux, Henri.

Broome, Richard. Aboriginal Australians: Black Response to White Dominance 1788-1980. (The Australian Experience Ser.). 1982. text ed. 25.00x; pap. 12.50x. Allen Unwin.

--Treasure in Earthen Vessels: Protestant Christianity in New South Wales Society 1900-1914. 216p. 1981. text ed. 36.25x (ISBN 0-7022-1525-2). U of Queensland Pr.

Broome, Susannah. The Pearl Pagoda. 320p. 1982. pap. 2.95 (ISBN 0-449-24469-5, Crest). Fawcett.

Broomell, Anna P. Friendly Story Caravan. LC 49-11035. (gr. 3-7). 1962. pap. 6.75 (ISBN 0-87574-901-1). Pendle Hill.

--Poets Walk In. 1983. pap. 5.00x (ISBN 0-87574-077-4, 077). Pendle Hill.

Broomfield, John. Mostly About Bengal. 1983. 16.50x (ISBN 0-8364-0985-X, Pub. by Manohar india). South Asia Bks.

Broomfield, Olga R. Arnold Bennett. LC 83-18391. (English Authors Ser.: No. 390). 163p. 1984. lib. bdg. 19.95 (ISBN 0-8057-6876-9, Twayne). G K Hall.

Broomfield, Robert. Baby Animal ABC. (Picture Ser.). (Orig.). 1968. pap. 2.95 (ISBN 0-14-050006-5, Puffin). Penguin.

Broomhall, A. J. Hudson Taylor & China's Open Century: Bk. I, Barbarians at the Gates. 1981. pap. 7.95 (ISBN 0-340-26210-9). OMF Bks.

--Hudson Taylor & China's Open Century: If I Had a Thousand Lives, Bk. III. 1983. pap. 9.955 (ISBN 0-340-32392-2). OMF Bks.

--Hudson Taylor & China's Open Century: Refiner's Fire, Bk. V. 1985. pap. 9.95 (ISBN 0-340-36866-7). OMF Bks.

Broomhall, Fra. J. Hudson Taylor & China's Open Century: Survivors' Pact, Bk. IV. 1984. pap. 9.95 (ISBN 0-340-34922-0). OMF Bks.

Broomhall, Marshall. Islam in China: A Neglected Problem. 1980. lib. bdg. 75.00 (ISBN 0-8490-3137-0). Gordon Pr.

Broomhill, Ray. Unemployed Workers: A Social History of the Great Depression in Adelaide. (Illus.). 1979. 24.95x (ISBN 0-7022-1235-0). U of Queensland Pr.

Broon, M. J. Synopsis of Biological Data on Scallops: Chlamys (Aequipecten) Opercularis (Linaeus) Argopecten Irradians (Lamarck) Argopecten Gibbus (Linnaeus) (Fisheries Synopses: No. 114). (Illus.). 44p. 1976. pap. 7.50 (ISBN 92-5-100213-4, F846, FAO). Unipub.

Brooner, E. G. BASIC Business Software. LC 80-52232. 144p. 1981. pap. 11.95 (ISBN 0-672-21751-1, 21751). Sams.

--The Local Area Network Book. LC 83-51227. 128p. 1984. pap. 7.95 (ISBN 0-672-22254-X, 22254). Sams.

Brooner, E. G. & Wells, Phil. Computer Communication Techniques. LC 83-60166. 144p. 1983. pap. text ed. 15.95 (ISBN 0-672-21998-0). Sams.

Brooner, Ernie. Microcomputer Data-Base Management. LC 81-86552. 144p. 1983. pap. 12.95 (ISBN 0-672-21875-5, 21875). Sams.

Brooten. Managerial Leadership in Nursing. 1984. 13.95 (ISBN 0-397-54320-4, Lippincott Medical). Lippincott.

Brooten, Bernadette J. Women Leaders in the Ancient Synagogue: Inscriptional Evidence & Background Issues. LC 82-10658. (Brown Judaic Studies). 292p. 1982. pap. 20.00 (ISBN 0-89130-587-4, 14 00 36). Scholars Pr GA.

Brooten, Dorothy, jt. auth. see Downs, Florence.

Brooten, Dorothy A., jt. auth. see Miller, Mary A.

Brophy, A. Blake. Foundlings on the Frontier: Racial & Religious Conflict in Arizona Territory, 1904-1905. LC 79-187824. (Southwest Chronicles). 129p. 1972. pap. 3.95 (ISBN 0-8165-0319-2). U of Ariz Pr.

Brophy, Ann. Flash & the Swan. 224p. 1982. pap. 2.25 (ISBN 0-448-16931-2). Ace Bks.

Brophy, Beth. Everything College Didn't Teach You about Money: Money Management for the Young Professional. 224p. 1985. 13.95 (ISBN 0-312-27234-0). St Martin.

Brophy, Brigid. Black & White: A Portrait of Aubrey Beardsley. LC 69-15906. 1970. pap. 1.95 (ISBN 0-8128-1295-6). Stein & Day.

--Flesh. 144p. 1980. 12.95 (ISBN 0-8052-8005-7, Pub. by Allison & Busby England); pap. 4.95 (ISBN 0-8052-8004-9, Pub. by Allison & Busby England). Schocken.

--Guide to Public Lending Right. 178p. 1983. text ed. 21.50x (ISBN 0-566-03485-9). Gower Pub Co.

--Hackenfeller's Ape. 128p. 1980. 12.95 (ISBN 0-8052-8009-X, Pub. by Allison & Busby England); pap. 4.95 (ISBN 0-8052-8008-1, Pub. by Allison & Busby England). Schocken.

--The Snow Ball. 144p. 1980. 12.95 (Pub. by Allison & Busby England); pap. 4.95 (ISBN 0-8052-8006-5, Pub. by Allison & Busby England). Schocken.

Brophy, Brigid, et al. Fifty Works of English & American Literature We Could Do Without. LC 68-13491. 1968. pap. 1.95 (ISBN 0-8128-1230-1). Stein & Day.

Brophy, Catherine. The Liberation of Margaret McCabe. 176p. 1985. 13.95 (ISBN 0-86327-068-9, Pub. by Wolfhound Pr Ireland); pap. 5.95 (ISBN 0-86327-067-0, Pub. by Wolfhound Pr Ireland). Irish Bks Media.

Brophy, Elizabeth B. Samuel Richardson: The Triumph of Craft. LC 74-3248. 152p. 1974. 11.50x (ISBN 0-87049-153-9). U of Tenn Pr.

Brophy, James & Paolucci, Henry, eds. The Achievement of Galileo. 1962. pap. 7.95x (ISBN 0-8084-0389-3). New Coll U Pr.

Brophy, James D. Edith Sitwell: The Symbolist Order. LC 68-10118. (Crosscurrents-Modern Critiques Ser.). 188p. 1968. 7.95 (ISBN 0-8093-0289-6). S Ill U Pr.

Brophy, James D. & Porter, Raymond J., eds. Contemporary Irish Writing. 1983. lib. bdg. 18.95 (ISBN 0-8057-9016-0, Twayne). G K Hall.

--Modern Irish Literature: Essays in Honor of William York Tyndall. lib. bdg. 10.50 (ISBN 0-8057-5717-1, Twayne). G K Hall.

Brophy, James J. Basic Electronics for Scientists. 4th ed. (Illus.). 464p. 1982. text ed. 43.95 (ISBN 0-07-008133-6). McGraw.

Brophy, Jere, et al. Student Characteristics & Teaching. LC 80-32741. (Professional Ser.). 224p. 1981. text ed. 25.00x (ISBN 0-582-28152-0). Longman.

--Structure & Properties of Materials, Vol. 2: Thermodynamics of Structure. pap. 57.00 (ISBN 0-317-28066-X, 2055769). Bks Demand UMI.

Brophy, Jere E. & Good, Thomas L. Teacher-Student Relationship: Causes & Consequences. LC 73-14740. 1974. pap. text ed. 12.95 (ISBN 0-03-085749-X, HoltC). HR&W.

Brophy, Jere E. & Willis, Sherry L. Human Development & Behavior. LC 79-20848. 434p. 1982. text ed. 22.95 (ISBN 0-312-39885-9); Instr's. manual avail. St Martin.

Brophy, Jere E., jt. auth. see Good, Thomas L.

Brophy, John & Partridge, Eric. The Long Trail: Soldiers Songs & Slang, 1914-18. LC 72-8462. (Select Bibliographies Reprint Ser.). 1972. Repr. of 1965 ed. 18.00 (ISBN 0-8369-6966-9). Ayer Co Pubs.

Brophy, Julia & Smart, Carol, eds. Women in Law: Explorations in Law, Family & Sexuality. 192p. 1985. 26.95x (ISBN 0-7102-0607-0); pap. 12.95 (ISBN 0-7102-0259-8). Routledge & Kegan.

Brophy, Loire. There's Plenty of Room at the Top: A Practical Guide to Success in Business. 1946. 12.50 (ISBN 0-932062-18-0). Sharon Hill.

Brophy, P. Computers Can Read. 1985. text ed. write for info. (ISBN 0-566-00805-X). Gower Pub Co.

Brophy, Paul C., jt. auth. see Nenno, Mary K.

Brophy, Peter. Management Information Systems in Libraries. 200p. 1985. text ed. price not set (ISBN 0-566-03551-0). Gower Pub Co.

Brophy, Robert J. Robinson Jeffers. LC 75-29982. (Western Writers Ser.: No. 19). (Illus., Orig.). 1975. pap. 2.00x (ISBN 0-88430-018-8). Boise St Univ.

--Robinson Jeffers: Myth, Ritual & Symbol in His Narrative Poems. (Illus.). xxii, 321p. 1976. Repr. of 1973 ed. 23.00 (ISBN 0-208-01574-4, Archon). Shoe String.

Brophy, William S. The Krag Rifle. 29.95 (ISBN 0-686-43084-0). Gun Room.

--L. C. Smith Shotguns. 29.95 (ISBN 0-88227-046-X). Gun Room.

--The Springfield Nineteen Hundred & Three Rifles: The Illustrated, Documented Story of the Design, Development, & Production of All the Models, Appendages, & Accessories. Schnell, Judith, ed. (Illus.). 608p. 1985. 49.95 (ISBN 0-8117-0872-1). Stackpole.

Broquard, Victor & Westley, John W. Structured Problem Analysis & Logic Design. (Illus.). 304p. 1985. pap. text ed. 20.95 (ISBN 0-13-854712-2). P-H.

Brosch, Dieter. Der Hafturlaub von Strafgefangenen unter Beruecksichtigung des Strafvollzugszieles. (European University Studies Ser.: No. 2, Vol. 332). 206p. (Ger.). 1983. 26.85 (ISBN 3-8204-7687-3). P Lang Pubs.

Brosche, F. & Suendermann, J., eds. Tidal Friction & the Earth's Rotation, Bielefeld, FRG, 1981: Proceedings. (Illus.). 345p. 1983. pap. 30.00 (ISBN 0-387-12011-4). Springer-Verlag.

Broschek, Anja. Michel Erhart: Ein Beitrag zur schwaebischen Plastik der Spaetgotik. LC 72-81548. (Beitraege Zur Kunstgeschichte: Vol. 8). 1973. 74.00x (ISBN 3-11-001765-2). De Gruyter.

Brose, David S. The Archaeology of Summer Island: Changing Settlement Systems in Northern Lake Michigan. (Anthropological Papers: No. 41). (Illus.). 1970. pap. 3.00x (ISBN 0-932206-39-5). U Mich Mus Anthro.

Brose, David S. & Greber, N'omi, eds. Hopewell Archaeology: The Chillicothe Conference. LC 79-88607. (MCJA Special Paper: No. 3). (Illus.). 309p. 1980. 16.00x (ISBN 0-87338-235-8). Kent St U Pr.

Brose, David S., et al. Ancient Art of the American Woodland Indians. (Illus.). 240p. 1985. 35.00 (ISBN 0-8109-1827-7). Abrams.

Brose, E. F. Twenty New Ways to Get the Minister Out of Moneyraising. 1976. 2.50 (ISBN 0-941500-18-7). Sharing Co.

Brose, Eric D. Christian Labor & the Politics of Frustration in Imperial Germany. LC 83-25172. 410p. 1985. 34.95x (ISBN 0-8132-0589-1). Cath U Pr.

Brose, Margaret, jt. ed. see White, Hayden.

Brose, Olive J. Church & Parliament: The Reshaping of the Church of England, 1828-1860. 1959. write for info. Univ. Microfilm (ISBN 0-8047-0572-0). Stanford U Pr.

--Frederick Denison Maurice: Rebellious Conformist, 1805-1872. LC 74-141380. xxiii, 308p. 1971. 16.00x (ISBN 0-8214-0092-4, 82-80976). Ohio U Pr.

Brosens, Fons, jt. ed. see Devreese, Jozef T.

Brosens, I. & Winston, R., eds. Reversability of Female Sterilization. 204p. 1979. 27.50 (ISBN 0-8089-1150-3, 790685). Grune.

Brosh, Israel. Quantitative Techniques in Management. 1983. text ed. 29.95 (ISBN 0-8359-6113-3); instr's. manual avail. (ISBN 0-8359-6114-1). Reston.

Brosh, John, ed. Guitar Gear: The Definitive Guide to Equipment for Today's Guitar Player. LC 84-62774. (Illus.). 256p. (Orig.). 1985. 12.95 (ISBN 0-688-03108-0, Quill). Morrow.

Broshears, Robert, jt. auth. see Barth, Robert H.

Brosheer, J. C., ed. see Munson, Robert D.

Broskii, Iosif. Novye Stansy K. Avguste: Stikhotvoreniia K. M. B. 144p. (Russian.). 1983. 18.95 (ISBN 0-686-79333-1). Ardis Pubs.

Broskowski, Anthony, et al, eds. Linking Health & Mental Health. LC 81-8875. (Sage Annual Reviews in Community Health Ser.: Vol. 5). (Illus.). 320p. 1981. pap. 14.00 (ISBN 0-8039-1601-9). Sage.

--Linking Health & Mental Health Ser. Coordinating Care in the Community. LC 81-8875. (Sage Annual Reviews of Community Mental Health: Vol. 5). 320p. 1981. 28.00 (ISBN 0-8039-1600-0). Sage.

Brosman, Catharine S., et al. Studies in French in Honor of Andre Bourgeois. (Rice University Studies: Vol. 59, No. 3). 100p. 1973. pap. 10.00x (ISBN 0-89263-217-8). Rice Univ.

Brosman, Catherine S. Abiding Winter. 12p. (Orig.). 1984. pap. 4.00 (ISBN 0-941150-19-4). Barth.

--Jean-Paul Sartre. (World Authors Ser.). 1983. lib. bdg. 13.50 (ISBN 0-8057-6544-1, Twayne). G K Hall.

--Jean-Paul Sartre. (World Authors Ser.). 168p. 1984. pap. 5.95 (ISBN 0-8057-6590-5, Twayne). G K Hall.

Brosnac, Donald. The Electric Guitar: Its History & Constuction. (Illus.). 96p. 1975. pap. 6.95 (ISBN 0-915572-00-1). Panjandrum.

--Guitar Electronics. (Illus.). 150p. 1984. pap. 13.95 (ISBN 0-933224-07-9). Bold Strummer Ltd.

--An Introduction to Scientific Guitar Design. Clarke, Nicholas, ed. LC 79-50925. (Illus.). 1979. pap. text ed. 8.95 (ISBN 0-933224-01-X). Bold Strummer Ltd.

--The Steel String Guitar: Its History & Construction. 2nd rev ed. (Illus.). 112p. 1976. pap. 6.95 (ISBN 0-915572-26-5). Panjandrum.

Brosnahan, Carol S. Debt Collection Tort Practice. LC 78-634774. 242p. 1971. 30.00 (ISBN 0-88124-020-6, TO-30100). Cal Cont Ed Bar.

Brosnahan, Carol S., et al. California Civil Discovery Practice. LC 73-620207. (California Practice Bk.: No. 67). (Illus.). xii, 557p. 1975. 65.00 (ISBN 0-88124-037-0). Cal Cont Ed Bar.

Brosnahan, James J. Trial Handbook for California Lawyers. LC 76-13583. 543p. 52.50; Suppl. 1984. 18.00; Suppl. 1983. 15.75. Lawyers Co-Op.

Brosnahan, Jo A. & Milne, Barbara. A Calendar of Home-School Activities. 1979. 14.95 (ISBN 0-673-16345-8); pap. 12.95 (ISBN 0-673-16346-6). Scott F.

Brosnahan, L. F. & Malmberg, B. Introduction to Phonetics. LC 75-26277. (Illus.). 243p. 1975. 34.50 (ISBN 0-521-21100-X); pap. 10.95 (ISBN 0-521-29042-2). Cambridge U Pr.

Brosnahan, Leonard F. The Sounds of Language: An Inquiry into the Role of Genetic Factors in the Development of Sound Systems. LC 82-975. 250p. 1982. Repr. of 1961 ed. lib. bdg. 27.50x (ISBN 0-313-23353-5, BRSOL). Greenwood.

Brosnahan, Tom. Mexico on Twenty-Five Dollars a Day. 484p. 1985. pap. 9.95 (ISBN 0-671-52474-7). Frommer-Pasmantier.

Brosnan, Barbara. Yoga for Handicapped People. (Human Horizon Ser.). (Illus.). 208p. 1982. pap. 15.95 (ISBN 0-285-64952-3, Pub. by Souvenir Pr England). Brookline Book.

Brosnan, Cornelius J. Jason Lee: Prophet of the New Oregon. LC 84-71620. (Illus.). 376p. 1985. pap. text ed. 9.95 (ISBN 0-914960-52-0). Academy Bks.

Brosnan, James. The Long Season. 1981. Repr. of 1960 ed. 17.95 (ISBN 0-941372-01-4). Holtzman Pr.

Brosnan, Jim. Great Baseball Pitchers. (Major League Baseball Library: No. 6). (Illus.). (gr. 4-7). 1965. 2.50 (ISBN 0-394-90183-5, BYR). Random.

--The Long Season. (Penguin Sports Library). 272p. 1983. pap. 5.95 (ISBN 0-14-006754-X). Penguin.

--Pennant Race. (Penguin Sports Library). 252p. 1983. pap. 5.95 (ISBN 0-14-006755-8). Penguin.

Brosnan, John. Movie Magic: The Story of Special Effects in the Cinema. 304p. 1976. pap. 6.95 (ISBN 0-452-25355-1, Z5355, Plume). NAL.

Brosnan, Kat. A Cry in the Night. 1978. pap. 1.50 (ISBN 0-8439-0518-2, Leisure Bks). Dorchester Pub Co.

Brosnan, Rosemary, ed. see D'Ignazio, Fred.

Brosnan, Rosemary, ed. see Gondosch, Linda.

Brosnan, Rosemary, ed. see Wisler, G. Clifton.

Brosnan, Thomas J. Emergency Rescue Techniques. (Illus.). 1976. pap. 8.50x (ISBN 0-89368-302-7). Davis Pub Co.

Brosowski, B. Parametric Optimization & Approximation. (North-Holland Mathematics Studies). 350p. 1984. write for info. (North-Holland). Elsevier.

Brosowski, B. & Martensen, E., eds. Methods & Techniques of Mathematical Physics: Proceedings of Conferences held at Oberwolfach, December 4-10, 1977, Vol. 17. 172p. 1978. pap. 24.20. P Lang Pubs.

--Methods & Techniques of Mathematical Physics: Proceedings of Conferences held in Oberwolfach, Feb. 3-9, 1980-Methods & Techniques of Mathematical Physics, Vol. 21. 202p. 1981. pap. write for info. P Lang Pubs.

Brosowski, Bruno. Parametric Semi-Infinite Optimization, Vol. 22. (Methoden und Verfaliren der Mathematischen Physik). 260p. 1981. pap. 32.95. P Lang Pubs.

Brosowski, Bruno & Martensen, Erich, eds. Approximation & Optimization in Mathematical Physics. 205p. 1983. pap. 25.80 (ISBN 3-8204-7631-8). P Lang Pubs.

--Dynamical Problems in Mathematical Physics. (Methoden v. Verfahren d. Math. Physik Ser.: Vol. 26). 229p. 1983. pap. 31.60 (ISBN 3-8204-7628-8). P Lang Pubs.

--Methods & Techniques of Mathematical Physics: Proceedings of a Conference Held in Oberwolfach, February 3-9, 1980. (Methoden und Verfahren der mathematischen Physik: Vol. 21). 201p. 1981. pap. 24.20 (ISBN 3-8204-5850-6). P Lang Pubs.

--Proceedings of the Conference Oberwolfach: December 4-10, 1977. (Methoden und Verfahren der Mathematischen Physik Ser.: Vol. 17). 172p. 1978. pap. write for info. P Lang Pubs.

Brosowski, F. & Deutsch, F., eds. Parametric Optimization & Approximation. (ISNM Ser.: No. 72). 264p. 1985. text ed. 29.95x (ISBN 3-764316-71-3). Birkhauser.

Bross. Scientific Strategies. (Statistics: Textbooks & Monographs: Vol. 35). 1981. 29.75 (ISBN 0-8247-1273-0). Dekker.

Bross, Allon. Family Therapy. LC 82-15555. (Family Therapy Ser.). 253p. 1983. 22.50 (ISBN 0-89862-045-7, 2045). Guilford Pr.

Bross, Irwin D. Design for Decision. 1965. pap. text ed. 6.95 (ISBN 0-02-904740-4). Free Pr.

Bross, Olive J. Church & Parliament: The Reshaping of the Church of England, 1828-1860. LC 59-7423. pap. 30.00 (ISBN 0-317-26542-3, 2023992). Bks Demand UMI.

Bross, Theodore D. Anton. LC 82-91118. 106p. 1983. 8.95 (ISBN 0-533-05669-1). Vantage.

Brossard. Dictionary of Music. Gruber, Albion, ed. (Musical Theorists in Translation Ser.: No. 12). 280p. lib. bdg. 55.00 (ISBN 0-931902-15-0). Inst Mediaeval Mus.

Brossard, Chandler. Raging Joys Sublime Violations. LC 80-25617. 160p. 1981. signed & lettered ed. 25.00x (ISBN 0-916156-59-1). Cherry Valley.

Brossard, Chandler, ed. see Poe, Edgar Allan.

Brossard, E. B. Petroleum Politics & Power. LC 82-24638. 272p. 1983. 41.95 (ISBN 0-87814-224-X, P-4320). Pennwell Bks.

Brosse, La. Diccionario del Cristianismo. 1104p. (Span.). 1976. 53.95 (ISBN 84-254-0777-X, S-50202). French & Eur.

Brosselin, Arlette. Les Forets De la Cote D'or Au XIX Siecle, et L'utilisation De Leurs Produits. Bruchey, Stuart, ed. LC 77-81822. (Dissertations in European Economic History Ser.). (Illus., Fr.). 1977. lib. bdg. 28.00x (ISBN 0-405-10775-7). Ayer Co Pubs.

Brosset, Raymond & Fondaneche, Pierre. Dictionnaire Memento D'electronique. 3rd ed. 512p. (Fr.). 1969. 39.95 (ISBN 0-686-56929-6, M-6047). French & Eur.

Brossi. The Alkaloids, Vol. 23. 1984. 85.00 (ISBN 0-12-469523-X). Acad Pr.

Brossi, Arnold. The Alkaloids, Vol. 27. (Serial Publication). Date not set. price not set (ISBN 0-12-469527-2). Acad Pr.

Brossi, Arnold, ed. The Alkaloids: Chemistry & Pharmacology, Vol. 24. 1985. 85.00 (ISBN 0-12-469524-8). Acad Pr.

Brossi, Arnold & Benson, Richard E., eds. Organic Syntheses: An Annual Publication of Satisfactory Methods for the Preparation of Organic Chemicals, Vol. 53. LC 21-17747. pap. 51.80 (ISBN 0-317-28689-7, 2055283). Bks Demand UMI.

Brossman, Mark E., jt. auth. see Levin, Noel A.

Brost, Fred B. & Coale, Robert D. Guide to Shell Collecting in the Kwajalein Atoll. LC 78-130418. (Illus.). 1971. pap. 11.00 (ISBN 0-8048-0942-9). C E Tuttle.

Brosten, Olga. The Mystic Eye-Manifestations of Psychic Phenomenon. Ashton, Sylvia, ed. LC 78-54162. 1981. 14.95 (ISBN 0-87949-122-1). Ashley Bks.

Broster, E. J. Glossary of Applied Management & Financial Statistics. 243p. 1974. 29.50x (ISBN 0-8448-0608-0). Crane-Russak Co.

Brosterman, Robert. The Complete Estate Planning Guide. rev. ed. 1981. pap. 4.95 (ISBN 0-451-62334-7, ME2334, Ment). NAL.

Brostoff, Laya. Double Weave: Theory & Practice. LC 79-91202. (Illus.). 45p. 1979. 5.00 (ISBN 0-934026-01-7). Interweave.

--Weaving a Tapestry. LC 82-82243. (Illus.). 162p. 1982. pap. text ed. 17.50 (ISBN 0-934026-10-6). Interweave.

Brostow, Witold. Science of Materials. LC 84-15484. 460p. 1985. Repr. of 1979 ed. lib. bdg. 49.50 (ISBN 0-89874-780-5). Krieger.

Brostrom, Anders, jt. auth. see Abrahamsson, Bengt.

Brostrom, Kenneth, ed. Russian Literature & American Critics. (Papers in Slavic Philology Ser.: No. 4). 1985. 15.00 (ISBN 0-930042-58-1). Mich Slavic Pubns.

Brosz, Allyn & Morgan, David R. Improving Municipal Productivity: A Handbook for Local Officials. 1978. 3.50 (ISBN 0-686-22969-X). Univ OK Gov Res.

Broszat, Martin. The Hitler State: The Foundation & Development of the Internal Structure of the Third Reich. Hiden, John, tr. from Ger. (Illus.). 400p. 1981. pap. text ed. 15.95x (ISBN 0-582-48997-0). Longman.

Broszat, Martin, jt. auth. see Krausnick, Helmut.

Brotanek, R. Untersuchungen Ueber Das Leben Und Die Dichtungen Alexander Montgomeries. 1896. pap. 25.00 (ISBN 0-384-05955-4). Johnson Repr.

Brotanek, R., jt. ed. see Bang, W.

Brotanek, Rudolf. Die Englischen Maskenspiele. 1902. pap. 25.00 (ISBN 0-384-05945-7). Johnson Repr.

Brotby, W. Krag. From Taxes to Riches. LC 81-71934. 190p. (Orig.). 1981. pap. 7.95 (ISBN 0-941204-01-4). Amen Pub.

Brotchie, J. F., et al. TOPAZ - General Planning Technique & Its Applications at the Regional, Urban, & Facility Planning Levels. (Lecture Notes in Economics & Mathematical Systems: Vol. 180). (Illus.). 356p. 1980. pap. 33.00 (ISBN 0-387-10020-2). Springer-Verlag.

Brotchie, John, ed. The Future of Urban Form: The Impact of New Technology. 250p. 1985. 43.50 (ISBN 0-89397-213-4). Nichols Pub.

Brotemarkle, Robert A., ed. Clinical Psychology. 1978. Repr. of 1931 ed. lib. bdg. 65.00 (ISBN 0-8492-3721-1). R West.

Brother Aloysius. Comfort to the Sick: A Recipe Book of Medicinal Herbs. LC 82-60161. 416p. pap. price not set (ISBN 0-87728-525-X). Weiser.

Brother Andrew, et al. God's Smuggler. (Illus.). 224p. 1968. pap. 2.75 (ISBN 0-8007-8016-7, Spire Bks); pap. 0.79 (ISBN 0-8007-8501-0, Spire Comics). Revell.

Brother Anthony. The Revelation of Bethlehem. 1985. pap. price not set (ISBN 0-932506-41-0). St Bedes Pubns.

Brotherhead, William. Forty Years Among the Old Booksellers of Philadelphia: With Bibliographical Remarks. LC 72-5538. (Select Bibliographies Reprint Ser). 1972. Repr. of 1891 ed. 15.00 (ISBN 0-8369-6900-6). Ayer Co Pubs.

Brotherhood Of Liberty. Justice & Jurisprudence: An Inquiry Concerning the Constitutional Limitations of the Thirteenth, Fourteenth & Fifteenth Amendments. LC 75-77191. Repr. of 1889 ed. 26.00x (ISBN 0-8371-1301-6, JUJ&, Pub. by Negro U Pr). Greenwood.

Brotherhood of St. Herman of Alaska. St. Herman Calendar of Orthodox Saints. pap. 5.00 (ISBN 0-686-05410-5). Eastern Orthodox.

Brother John of Taize. The Pilgrim God: A Biblical Journey. (Orig.). 1985. pap. write for info (ISBN 0-912405-18-X). Pastoral Pr.

Brother Lawrence. God-Illuminated Cook: The Practice of the Presence of God. 2nd ed. Dawes, Robin, ed. (Illus.). 144p. 1979. pap. 3.95 (ISBN 0-914896-00-8). East Ridge Pr.

--God-Illuminated Cook: The Practice of the Presence of God. (East Ridge Press Ser.). (Illus.). 144p. 1980. pap. 4.00 (ISBN 0-89345-217-3). Garber Comm.

Brother Lawrence & Laubach, Frank. Practicing His Presence. 3rd ed. Edwards, Gene, ed. 1973. pap. 4.95 (ISBN 0-940232-01-4). Christian Bks.

Brother Lawrence, jt. ed. see Demaray, Donald E.

Brother Lawrence Of The Resurrection, see Delaney, John J.

Brother Leonard of Taize. Belonging. 172p. 1985. pap. 7.95 (ISBN 0-8298-0569-9). Pilgrim NY.

Brother Nectario M. Juan Colon Alias Christopher Columbus. Josephson, Emanuel M., ed. LC 72-166573. (Blacked-Out History Ser.). 1971. pap. 5.00 (ISBN 0-686-29300-2, Pub. by Chedney). A-albionic Res.

Brothers. Church & School. 196p. 1982. 39.00x (ISBN 0-85323-021-8, Pub. by Liverpool Univ England). State Mutual Bk.

Brothers, Betty. Triggerfish: Tales of the Florida Keys. (Illus.). 1965. 5.95 (ISBN 0-87482-012-X). Wake-Brook.

Brothers, Connie, ed. The Iowa Writer's Workshop Cookbook. (Illus.). 224p. 1985. 14.95 (ISBN 0-8119-0690-6). Fell.

Brothers, Dwight S. & Solis, M. Leopoldo. Mexican Financial Development. 252p. 1965. 12.95x (ISBN 0-292-73304-6). U of Tex Pr.

Brothers Grimm. The Best of Grimm's Fairy Tales. LC 79-63439. (Illus.). (gr. k-3). 1980. PLB 10.95 (ISBN 0-88332-122-X). Larousse.

--Brave Little Tailor. LC 78-18075. (Illus.). 32p. (gr. k-4). 1979. PLB 7.89 (ISBN 0-89375-137-5); pap. 1.95 (ISBN 0-89375-115-4). Troll Assocs.

--The Bremen Town Musicians. LC 79-16944. (Illus.). 32p. (gr. k-3). 1980. 11.75 (ISBN 0-688-80233-8); PLB 11.88 (ISBN 0-688-84233-X). Greenwillow.

--Bremen Town Musicians. new ed. LC 78-18064. (Illus.). 32p. (gr. k-4). 1979. PLB 7.89 (ISBN 0-89375-133-2); pap. 1.95 (ISBN 0-89375-111-1). Troll Assocs.

--Cinderella. LC 80-15394. (Illus.). 32p. (gr. k-3). 1981. 10.25 (ISBN 0-688-80299-0); PLB 10.88 (ISBN 0-688-84299-2). Greenwillow.

--The Complete Grimm's Fairy Tales. Stern, James, ed. LC 44-40373. (gr. 6 up). 1976. pap. 6.95 (ISBN 0-394-70930-6). Pantheon.

--The Devil with the Three Golden Hairs. LC 82-12735. (Illus.). 40p. (gr. k-3). 1983. 10.95 (ISBN 0-394-85560-4); lib. bdg. 10.99 (ISBN 0-394-95560-9). Knopf.

--The Elves & the Shoemaker. LC 80-27634. (Illus.). 32p. (gr. k-4). 1981. PLB 7.89 (ISBN 0-89375-472-2); pap. text ed. 1.95 (ISBN 0-89375-473-0). Troll Assocs.

--Fairy Tales. LC 81-16646. (Classics Ser.). (Illus.). 304p. (gr. 3 up). 1982. lib. bdg. 14.79 (ISBN 0-671-45648-2). Messner.

--The Fisherman & His Wife. (Collection of Fairy Tales Ser.). (Illus.). 32p. 1983. 7.95 (ISBN 0-87191-937-0). Creative Ed.

--Fitcher's Bird. (Collection of Fairy Tales Ser.). 32p. 1983. 7.95 (ISBN 0-87191-942-7). Creative Ed.

--Frog Prince. LC 78-18073. (Illus.). 32p. (gr. k-4). 1979. PLB 7.89 (ISBN 0-89375-126-X); pap. 1.95 (ISBN 0-89375-104-9). Troll Assocs.

--The Golden Goose. LC 80-29207. (Illus.). 32p. (gr. k-4). 1981. PLB 7.89 (ISBN 0-89375-476-5); pap. 1.95 (ISBN 0-89375-477-3). Troll Assocs.

--The Goose Girl. (Collection of Fairy Tales Ser.). (Illus.). 32p. 1984. 7.95 (ISBN 0-87191-934-6). Creative Ed.

--Grimms' Fairy Tales. (Classics Ser). (gr. 3 up). pap. 1.25 (ISBN 0-8049-0168-6, CL-168). Airmont.

--Grimm's Fairy Tales. (Span. & Fr.). Span. ed. 3.95 (ISBN 0-685-23350-2); fr. ed 5.50 (ISBN 0-685-23351-0). French & Eur.

--Grimms' Fairy Tales. (Nancy Drew's Favorite Classics). (Illus.). (gr. 6-9). 1981. 5.95 (ISBN 0-448-11009-1, G&D). Putnam Pub Group.

--Grimms' Fairy Tales. (Illus.). (gr. 4-9). deluxe ed. 10.95 (ISBN 0-448-06009-4, G&D); (G&D). Putnam Pub Group.

--Grimm's Fairy Tales. Dobbs, Rose, ed. (Illus.). (gr. k-3). 1955. (BYR). Random.

--Grimm's Fairy Tales. Barish, Wendy, ed. (Illus.). 304p. 1982. 15.95 (ISBN 0-671-43792-5). Wanderer Bks.

--Hansel & Gretel. LC 80-15079. (Illus.). 32p. (gr. k up). 1980. 12.95 (ISBN 0-8037-3492-1, 01258-370); PLB 12.89 (ISBN 0-8037-3491-3). Dial Bks Young.

--Hansel & Gretel. Crawford, Elizabeth D., tr. from Ger. LC 79-989. (Illus.). 25p. (gr. k-3). 1980. PLB 11.88 (ISBN 0-688-32198-4). Morrow.

--Hansel & Gretel. (Illus.). 32p. (gr. k-3). 1982. PLB 8.95 (ISBN 0-531-04503-X, MacRae). Watts.

--Hansel & Gretel. Crawford, Elizabeth D., tr. from Ger. (Illus.). 22p. (gr. 1 up). 1983. pap. 5.95 (ISBN 0-907234-46-1, Pub. by Picture Bk Studio USA). Neugebauer Pr.

--Hansel & Gretel, the Seven Ravens, & the Little Red Cap. Crawford, Elisabeth D., tr. from Ger. (Illus.). 66p. (gr. 1 up). 1983. pap. 14.95 slipcased set (ISBN 0-907234-49-6, Pub. by Picture Bk Studio USA). Neugebauer Pr.

--Hansel & Grettel. (Collection of Fairy Tales Ser.). (Illus.). 32p. 1983. 7.95 (ISBN 0-87191-935-4). Creative Ed.

--Household Stories by the Brothers Grimm. (Illus.). 14.25 (ISBN 0-8446-2167-6). Peter Smith.

--Household Stories from the Collection of the Brothers Grimm. 16.95 (ISBN 0-88411-663-8, Pub. by Aeonian Pr). Amereon Ltd.

--Household Tales. LC 79-64122. (gr. 3-9). 1979. lib. bdg. 9.95x (ISBN 0-8052-3721-6); pap. 4.95 (ISBN 0-8052-0633-7). Schocken.

--How Six Men Got on in the World. Alderson, Brian, tr. LC 81-40418. (Moonlight Editions Ser.). (Illus.). 28p. 1981. 5.95 (ISBN 0-8052-3781-X, Moonlight Edns). Schocken.

--Little Red Cap. Crawford, Elizabeth d., tr. from Ger. Orig. Title: Rottkapchen. (Illus.). 24p. 1983. 10.25 (ISBN 0-688-01715-0); PLB 10.88 (ISBN 0-688-01716-9). Morrow.

--The Little Red Cap. Crawford, Elizabeth D., tr. from Ger. (Illus.). 22p. (gr. 1 up). 1983. pap. 5.95 (ISBN 0-907234-48-8, Pub. by Picture Bk Studio USA). Neugebauer Pr.

--Little Red Riding Hood. LC 80-27684. (Illus.). 32p. (gr. k-4). 1981. PLB 7.89 (ISBN 0-89375-488-9); pap. 1.95 (ISBN 0-89375-489-7). Troll Assocs.

--Little Red Riding Hood. Hyman, Trina S., retold by. & illus. LC 82-7700. (Illus.). 32p. (ps-3). 1982. reinforced binding 14.95 (ISBN 0-8234-0470-6). Holiday.

--The Musicians of Bremen. LC 74-78599. (Illus.). 6.95 (ISBN 0-88332-060-6, 8027). Larousse.

--The Queen Bee. (Collection of Fairy Tales Ser.). (Illus.). 32p. 1984. 7.95 (ISBN 0-87191-939-7). Creative Ed.

--Rapunzel. LC 75-8847. 32p. (ps-3). 1975. PLB 9.89 (ISBN 0-690-00980-1). Crowell Jr Bks.

--Rapunzel. LC 78-18066. (Illus.). 32p. (gr. k-4). 1979. PLB 7.89 (ISBN 0-89375-135-9); pap. 1.95 (ISBN 0-89375-113-8). Troll Assocs.

--Rapunzel. Rogasky, Barbara, retold by. LC 81-6419. (Illus.). 32p. (ps-3). 1982. Reinforced bdg. 14.95 (ISBN 0-8234-0454-4). Holiday.

--Rapunzel. (Collection of Fairy Tales Ser.). (Illus.). 32p. 1984. 7.95 (ISBN 0-87191-936-2). Creative Ed.

--Rumpelstiltskin. LC 78-18079. (Illus.). 32p. (gr. k-4). 1979. PLB 7.89 (ISBN 0-89375-140-5); pap. 1.95 (ISBN 0-89375-118-9). Troll Assocs.

--Rumpelstiltskin. LC 83-90. (Illus.). 32p. (gr. k-3). 1983. reinforced bdg. 9.95 (ISBN 0-8234-0488-9). Holiday.

--The Seven Ravens. Crawford, Elizabeth D., tr. from Ger. (Illus.). 22p. (gr. 1 up). 1983. pap. 7.50 (ISBN 0-907234-47-X, Pub. by Picture Bk Studio USA). Neugebauer Pr.

--The Sleeping Beauty. LC 78-64772. (Illus.). 32p. (ps up). 1979. 9.95 (ISBN 0-689-50131-5, McElderry Bk). Atheneum.

--Snow White & Rose Red. LC 78-18074. (Illus.). 32p. (gr. k-4). 1979. PLB 7.89 (ISBN 0-89375-136-7); pap. 1.95 (ISBN 0-89375-114-6). Troll Assocs.

--Snow White & Rose Red. (Blackbird Bks.). (Illus.). 48p. 1984. 5.95 (ISBN 0-531-03756-8, Macrae). Watts.

--Snow White & Rose Red. LC 84-4910. (Illus.). 32p. (gr. k-3). 1984. PLB 10.95 (ISBN 0-13-815234-9). P-H.

--Snow White & the Seven Dwarfs. (Illus., Fr.). (gr. 3-8). 5.95 (ISBN 0-685-11566-6). French & Eur.

--Thorn Rose. LC 75-16835. (Illus.). 32p. (ps-2). 1977. 8.95 (ISBN 0-02-737270-7). Bradbury Pr.

--Three Feathers. (Collection of Fairy Tales Ser.). (Illus.). 32p. 1984. 7.95 (ISBN 0-87191-941-9). Creative Ed.

--Three Languages. (Collection of Fairy Tales Ser.). (Illus.). 32p. 1984. 7.95 (ISBN 0-87191-940-0). Creative Ed.

--Twelve Dancing Princesses. new ed. LC 78-18077. (Illus.). 32p. (gr. k-4). 1979. PLB 7.89 (ISBN 0-89375-139-1); pap. 1.95 (ISBN 0-89375-117-0). Troll Assocs.

--Wolf & the Seven Kids. new ed. LC 78-18076. (Illus.). 32p. (gr. k-4). 1979. PLB 7.89 (ISBN 0-89375-138-3); pap. 1.95 (ISBN 0-89375-116-2). Troll Assocs.

Brothers Grimm & Pincus, Harriet. Little Red Riding Hood. LC 68-11505. (Illus.). 32p. (ps-3). 1973. pap. 1.25 (ISBN 0-15-652850-9, AVB75, VoyB). HarBraceJ.

Brothers, Joan. Church & School: A Study of the Impact of Education on Religion. 188p. 1964. 35.00x (ISBN 0-85323-012-9, Pub. by Liverpool Univ England). State Mutual Bk.

--Religious Institutions. (Aspects of Modern Sociology Ser.). 1971. pap. text ed. 3.25x (ISBN 0-582-48120-1). Humanities.

Brothers, Joyce. The Brothers System for Liberated Love & Marriage. 1973. pap. 1.50 (ISBN 0-380-01073-9, 15834). Avon.

--What Every Woman Ought to Know about Love & Marriage. 335p. 1984. 15.95 (ISBN 0-671-44159-0). S&S.

--What Every Woman Ought to Know about Love & Marriage. Date not set. pap. 3.95 (ISBN 0-317-20401-7). Ballantine.

--What Every Woman Should Know about Men. 288p. 1985. pap. 3.50 (ISBN 0-345-32594-X). Ballantine.

--What Every Women Wants to Know about Love & Marriage. 384p. 1985. pap. 3.95 (ISBN 0-345-32113-8). Ballantine.

Brothers Grimm, jt. auth. see Adams, Adrienne.

Brother Stanley. Pure Grace. 96p. 1984. 6.95 (ISBN 0-89962-414-6). Todd & Honeywell.

Brotherston, G. & Llosa, M. V., eds. Seven Stories from Spanish America. 1968. pap. 4.60 (ISBN 0-08-012675-8). Pergamon.

Brotherston, Gordon. The Emergence of the Latin American Novel. LC 76-40834. 1977. pap. text ed. 10.95 (ISBN 0-521-29565-3). Cambridge U Pr.

--Image of the New World: The American Continent Portrayed in Native Texts. (Illus.). 1979. 19.95 (ISBN 0-500-01206-7). Thames Hudson.

--Image of the New World: The American Continent Portrayed in Native Texts. (Illus., Orig.). 1982. pap. 10.95 (ISBN 0-500-27232-8). Thames Hudson.

Brotherston, Gordon, tr. see Arenas, Reinaldo.

Brotherton, Blanche. The Vocabulary of Intrigue in Roman Comedy. Steele, Commager, ed. (Latin Poetry Ser.). 34.00 (ISBN 0-8240-2983-6). Garland Pub.

Brotherton, Christopher J., jt. auth. see Stephenson, Geoffrey M.
Brotherton, Jack. The Annals of Stanislaus County California. (Illus.). 260p. 1982. 22.95 (ISBN 0-934136-29-7). Western Tanager.
Brotherton, Miner. Twelve-Volt Bible. (Illus.). 1985. 12.95 (ISBN 0-915160-81-1). Seven Seas.
Brotherus, V. F. Hawaiian Mosses. (BMB Ser.: No. 40). pap. 10.00 (ISBN 0-527-02143-1). Kraus Repr.
--Die Laubmoose Fennoskandias. (Flora Fennica Ser.: Vol. 1). (Illus.). 635p. (Ger.). 1974. Repr. of 1923 ed. lib. bdg. 69.30x (ISBN 3-87429-078-6). Lubrecht & Cramer.
Brotherwood, Clive. Honda Owner's Workshop Manual: One Hundred & One Twenty-Five Singles Roads & Trails '70-75. (Owners Workshop Manuals Ser.: No. 188). 1979. 10.50 (ISBN 0-85696-188-4, Pub. by J H Haynes England). Haynes Pubns.
--Triumph 350 & 500 Unit Twins '57 - '73. new ed. (Owners Workshop Manuals Ser.: No. 137). 1979. 10.50 (ISBN 0-85696-137-X, Pub. by J H Haynes England). Haynes Pubns.
Brothwell, C., et al, eds. Maintenance of Numerically Controlled Machine Tools, 2 vols. 2nd ed. (Engineering Craftsmen Ser.: No. J27). (Illus.). 1973. Set. sprial bdg. 75.00x (ISBN 0-85083-155-5). Intl Ideas.
Brothwell, D. R. Digging up Bones. 3rd rev. ed. LC 80-66914. (Illus.). 196p. 1981. pap. 17.95x (ISBN 0-8014-9875-9). Cornell U Pr.
Brothwell, D. R., jt. auth. see Baker, J. R.
Brothwell, Don & Sandison, A. T. Diseases in Antiquity: A Survey of the Diseases, Injuries & Surgery of Early Populations. (Illus.). 792p. 1967. photocopy ed. 80.25x (ISBN 0-398-00233-9). C C Thomas.
Brott, Thomas & Kelley, Philip, eds. Richard Barrett's Journal New York & Canada 1816: Critique of the Young Nation by an Englishman Abroad. LC 83-50936. (Illus.). 144p. (Orig.). 1983. pap. 18.50x (ISBN 0-911459-07-3). Wedgestone Pr.
Brotz, Howard. The Politics of South Africa. LC 76-49406. (Illus.). 1977. 19.95x (ISBN 0-19-215671-3). Oxford U Pr.
Brouard, F., et al. Notes on Observations of Daily Rings on Otoliths of Deepwater Snappers. (ICLARM Translations Ser.: No. 3). Orig. Title: Note sur les lectures de stries journalieres observees sur les otolithes de poissons. (Illus.). 8p. (Orig.). 1984. pap. 2.00x (ISBN 0-317-17297-2, Pub. by ICLARM Philippines). Intl Spec Bk.
Brouchey, Stuart, ed. see Ibrahim A. Al-Moneef.
Brouchey, Stuart, ed. see U. S. Senate.
Broucker, Jose De see De Broucker, Jose.
Broude, Henry W. Steel Decisions & the National Economy. LC 63-13958. (Yale Studies in Economics Ser.: No. 16). pap. 86.80 (ISBN 0-317-29591-8, 2021983). Bks Demand UMI.
Broude, Norma, ed. Seurat in Perspective. LC 78-1600. (Artists in Perspective Ser.). (Illus.). 1979. 12.95 (ISBN 0-13-807115-2, Spec); pap. 5.95 (ISBN 0-13-807107-1). P-H.
Broude, Norma & Garrard, Mary D., eds. Feminism & Art History: Questioning the Litany. LC 81-48062. (Icon Editions). (Illus.). 336p. 1982. 28.80i (ISBN 0-06-430525-2, HarpT); pap. 15.95xi (ISBN 0-06-430117-6, IN117, HarpT). Har-Row.
Broude, V. L., et al. Spectroscopy of Molecular Excitons. (Springer Series in Chemical Physics: Vol. 16). (Illus.). 290p. 1985. 48.00 (ISBN 0-387-12409-8). Springer-Verlag.
Broudy, C., jt. auth. see Barr, V.
Broudy, Harry. General Education: The Search for a Rationale. LC 73-90400. (Fastback Ser.: No. 37). (Illus., Orig.). 1974. pap. 0.75 (ISBN 0-87367-037-X). Phi Delta Kappa.
Broudy, Harry S. Paradox & Promise. 1961. pap. text ed. 1.95x (ISBN 0-8134-0960-8, 960). Interstate.
--Truth & Credibility: A Citizen's Dilemma. LC 80-28305. (Longman Professional Ser.). 1981. text ed. 19.95x (ISBN 0-582-28208-X). Longman.
Broudy, Harry S., et al. Philosophy of Education: An Organization of Topics & Selected Sources. LC 67-27774. Repr. of 1967 ed. 56.90 (ISBN 0-8357-9693-0, 2019050). Bks Demand UMI.
Broudy, Harry S., et al, eds. Philosophy of Educational Research. LC 72-2332. (Readings in Educational Research Ser.). 1973. 32.50x (ISBN 0-471-10625-9); text ed. 29.50x 10 or more copies. McCutchan.
Brouers, M., jt. ed. see Sironval, C.
Brough, Bruce A. Publicity & Public Relations Guide for Business. (Successful Business Library). 200p. 1984. 3-ring binder 33.95 (ISBN 0-916378-41-1, Oasis Pr). PSI Res.
Brough, Charles H. Irrigation in Utah. LC 78-64265. (Johns Hopkins University. Studies in the Social Sciences, Extra Volumes: 19). Repr. of 1898 ed. 21.50 (ISBN 0-404-61367-5). AMS Pr.
Brough, D. K. The Passing of Marine Griffiths. 1981. 15.00x (ISBN 0-7223-1413-2, Pub. by Stockwell). State Mutual Bk.
Brough, James. Margaret: The Tragic Princess. 1979. pap. 2.25 (ISBN 0-380-44206-X, 44206). Avon.
Brough, James, jt. auth. see Stephens, Woodford C.
Brough, John. Selections from Classical Sanskrit Literature. 2nd, rev ed. 1978. pap. 9.00x (ISBN 0-8364-0259-6). South Asia Bks.
Brough, John, tr. Poems from the Sanskrit. 1977. pap. 4.95 (ISBN 0-14-044198-0). Penguin.
Brough, John B., ed. Philosophical Knowledge. LC 80-69505. (Proceedings: Vol. 54). 250p. (Orig.). 1980. pap. 15.00 (ISBN 0-918090-14-8). Am Cath Philo.
Brough, Michael. Development Ordinance Guidebook. LC 85-70182. (Illus.). 215p. (Orig.). 1985. pap. write for info. (ISBN 0-918286-39-5). Planners Pr.
Brough, Michael B., et al. The Zoning Board of Adjustment in North Carolina. 128p. 1984. 7.50 (ISBN 0-686-39447-X). U of NC Inst Gov.
Brough, R. Clayton. His Servants Speak: Statements by Latter-day Saint Leaders on Contemporary Topics. LC 75-17101. 298p. 1975. 9.95 (ISBN 0-88290-054-4). Horizon Utah.
--The Lost Tribes: History Doctrine, Prophecies & Theories About Israel's Lost Ten Tribes. LC 79-89351. 1979. 7.95 (ISBN 0-88290-123-0). Horizon Utah.
--Our First Estate: The Doctrine of Man's Pre-Mortal Existence. LC 77-79753. 1977. 7.95 (ISBN 0-88290-084-6). Horizon Utah.
--They Who Tarry: The Doctrine of Translated Beings. LC 76-29255. (Orig.). 1976. 6.95 (ISBN 0-88290-069-2). Horizon Utah.
Brough, Walter & Sutton, Michael. Explosion: The Day Texas City Died. 1980. pap. 2.75 (ISBN 0-380-75838-5, 75838-5). Avon.
Brougham, Eleanor M. Corn from Olde Fieldes: An Anthology of English Poems from the 14th to the 17th Century with Biographical Notes. 294p. 1982. Repr. of 1918 ed. lib. bdg. 40.00 (ISBN 0-89760-095-9). Telegraph Bks.
--A Miscellany of Verse & Prose, Ancient & Modern: Varia. 1925. 17.50 (ISBN 0-89984-033-7). Century Bookbindery.
Brougham, Eleanor M., ed. Corn from Olde Fields: Anthology of English Poems from the XIVth to the XVIIth Century. 1981. Repr. of 1918 ed. lib. bdg. 25.00 (ISBN 0-8495-0490-2). Arden Lib.
Brougham, Henry. Inquiry into the Colonial Policy of the European Powers, 2 Vols. LC 75-118017. Repr. of 1803 ed. Set. 87.50x (ISBN 0-678-00658-X). Kelley.
Brougham, Henry & Routh, E. J. Analytical View of Sir Isaac Newton's Principia. 1972. Repr. of 1855 ed. 35.00 (ISBN 0-384-05960-0). Johnson Repr.
Broughel, Barbara, jt. auth. see Conrad, Tony.
Brougher, Kerry, jt. auth. see Colpitt, Frances.
Brougher, Toni. A Way with Words: How to Improve Your Relationships Through Better Communications. LC 81-18841. 352p. 1982. text ed. 23.95x (ISBN 0-88229-645-0); pap. text ed. 12.95x (ISBN 0-88229-810-0). Nelson-Hall.
Broughtn, Geoffrey, et al, eds. Teaching English As a Foreign Language. 2nd ed. (Routledge Education Bks.). 256p. 1980. 21.95x (ISBN 0-7100-0642-X); pap. 9.95x (ISBN 0-7100-8951-1). Routledge & Kegan.
Broughton, Carrie L. Marriage & Death Notices from the Raleigh Register & North Carolina State Gazette: 1799-1825. LC 66-26935. 178p. 1975. Repr. of 1945 ed. 14.00 (ISBN 0-8063-0052-3). Genealog Pub.
--Marriage & Death Notices in the Raleigh Register & North Carolina State Gazette 1846-1867, 2 vols. in 1. LC 75-7876. 206p. 1975. Repr. of 1949 ed. 15.00 (ISBN 0-8063-0677-7). Genealog Pub.
Broughton, Hugh. An Epistle to the Learned Nobility of England: Touching Translating the Bible. LC 77-6862. (English Experience Ser.: No. 855). 1977. Repr. of 1597 ed. lib. bdg. 7.00 (ISBN 90-221-0855-4). Walter J Johnson.
Broughton, Irv. The Art of Interviewing for Television, Radio & Film. LC 79-9399. (Illus.). 1981. 18.95 (ISBN 0-8306-9743-8, 1125). TAB Bks.
--The Blessing of the Fleet. LC 77-8971. (Lost Roads Poetry Ser.: No. 6). 1978. 6.00 (ISBN 0-918786-10-X); pap. 3.00 (ISBN 0-918786-11-8). Lost Roads.
Broughton, Jacqueline. A Sketchbook of Santa Barbara's Native Wildflowers. LC 76-42943. (The Santa Barbara Bicentinnial Historical Series). 1976. 10.00 (ISBN 0-916436-02-0). Santa Barb Botanic.
Broughton, Jacqueline P. Garden Flowers to Color. (Illus.). 32p. (ps-2). 1972. pap. 1.25 (ISBN 0-913456-51-9). Interbk Inc.
Broughton, James. Ecstasies. 128p. 1983. 20.00 (ISBN 0-9608372-3-X); pap. 7.00 (ISBN 0-9608372-2-1). Syzygy Pr.
--Erogeny. 1976. 1.00 (ISBN 0-686-18844-6); signed ed. o.p. 5.00 (ISBN 0-686-18845-4). Man-Root.
--Graffiti for the Johns of Heaven. LC 82-60091. (Illus.). 80p. 1982. pap. 6.00 (ISBN 0-9608372-1-3). Syzygy Pr.
--High Kukus. LC 68-58535. 1968. 4.95 (ISBN 0-912330-09-0, Dist. by Inland Bk). Jargon Soc.
--Hymns to Hermes. 1979. pap. 20.00 signed ed. (ISBN 0-686-26037-6). Man-Root.
--Long Undressing: Collected Poems 1949-69. LC 74-137209. 1971. 10.00 (ISBN 0-912330-10-4, Dist. by Inland Bk); ltd. ed. o.p. 25.00x (ISBN 0-912330-11-2); pap. 7.50 (ISBN 0-912330-24-4). Jargon Soc.
--Odes for Odd Occasions. 1977. 6.00 (ISBN 0-686-19030-0). Man-Root.
--The Playground. (Illus.). 1949. 7.50 (ISBN 0-685-79022-3). Small Pr Dist.
--Seeing the Light. LC 76-30681. 1977. pap. 3.00 (ISBN 0-87286-090-6). City Lights.
--Shaman Psalm. 1981. 3.00 (ISBN 0-9608372-0-5). Syzygy Pr.
--Song of the God Body. 1978. pap. 20.00 signed (ISBN 0-686-23064-7). Man-Root.
Broughton, John. The Wild Man of the Four Winds. (Illus.). 32p. (gr. 1-3). 1983. 10.95 (ISBN 0-241-10816-0, Pub. by Hamish Hamilton England). David & Charles.
Broughton, John, et al, eds. see Basseches, Michael.
Broughton, John C. Recollections of a Long Life: With Additional Extracts from His Private Diaries, 6 vols. Lady Dorchester, ed. LC 9-25987. Repr. of 1911 ed. Set. 240.00 (ISBN 0-404-03320-2); 40.00 ea. AMS Pr.
Broughton, John M. & Freeman-Moir, John D. The Cognitive Developmental Psychology of James Mark Baldwin: Current Theory & Research in Genetic Epistemology. LC 81-7885. (Publications for the Advancement of Theory & History in Psychology (PATH) Ser.). 480p. 1982. 42.50x (ISBN 0-89391-043-0). Ablex Pub.
Broughton, L. N. Robert Browning: A Bibliography, 1830-1950. LC 72-115427. (Cornell Studies in English: Vol. 39). 1970. Repr. of 1953 ed. text ed. 29.50 (ISBN 0-8337-0381-1). B Franklin.
Broughton, L. N. & Baldwin, D. C. Concordance to Poems of John Keats. 59.95 (ISBN 0-87968-922-6). Gordon Pr.
Broughton, L. N., jt. auth. see Baldwin, Dane L.
Broughton, Leslie. Theocritan Element in the Works of William Wordsworth. LC 74-8708. 1920. lib. bdg. 20.00 (ISBN 0-8414-3198-1). Folcroft.
Broughton, Leslie N. & Stelter, Benjamin F. Concordance to the Poems of Robert Browning 1924-1925, 4 Vols. LC 77-92950. (Studies in Browning, No. 4). 1970. Repr. of 1924 ed. lib. bdg. 325.00x (ISBN 0-8383-1101-6). Haskell.
Broughton, Pamela. The Creation. (Golden Bible Stories Ser.). (Illus.). 32p. (ps-2). 1985. 3.95 (ISBN 0-307-11620-4, 11620, Pub. by Golden Bks). Western Pub.
--Noah's Ark. (Golden Bible Stories Ser.). (Illus.). 32p. (ps-2). 1985. 3.95 (ISBN 0-307-11621-2, 11621, Pub. by Golden Bks). Western Pub.
Broughton, Panthea, ed. The Art of Walker Percy: Stratagems for Being. LC 78-27494. (Southern Literary Studies). xxii, 312p. 1979. text ed. 27.50x (ISBN 0-8071-0560-0). La State U Pr.
Broughton, Panthea R. William Faulkner: The Abstract & the Actual. LC 74-77324. xviii, 222p. 1974. 22.50x (ISBN 0-8071-0083-8). La State U Pr.
Broughton, R. J., ed. Henri Gastaut & the Marseilles School's Contribution to the Neurosciences: Proceedings of the 25th & Final Colloque de Marseille. (Electroencephalography & Clinical Neurophysiology Ser.: Suppl. No. 35). 448p. 1982. 119.25 (ISBN 0-444-80363-7, Biomedical Pr). Elsevier.
Broughton, Rhoda. Belinda: A Novel. LC 78-108463. 460p. 1884. 39.00x (ISBN 0-403-00448-9). Scholarly.
--Cometh up As a Flower: An Autobiography, 2 vols. in 1. LC 79-8240. Repr. of 1867 ed. 44.50 (ISBN 0-404-61794-8). AMS Pr.
--Not Wisely, but Too Well. Van Thal, Herbert, ed. 1967. 7.95 (ISBN 0-8023-9053-6); pap. 4.95 (ISBN 0-304-92524-1). Dufour.
Broughton, Richard. English Protestants Plea. LC 76-57380. (English Experience Ser.: No. 798). 1977. Repr. of 1621 ed. lib. bdg. 9.50 (ISBN 90-221-0798-1). Walter J Johnson.
Broughton, Richard S., jt. auth. see White, Rhea A.
Broughton, Roger, jt. auth. see Gastaut, Henri.
Broughton, Roger, ed. see Roth, B.
Broughton, T. Alan. Adam's Dream. (Juniper Bk.: No. 15). 1974. 4.00 (ISBN 0-686-61871-8). Juniper Pr WI.
--Far from Home. LC 78-74989. (Poetry Ser.). 1979. pap. 4.50 (ISBN 0-915604-26-4). Carnegie-Mellon.
--Hob's Daughter. LC 84-3840. 288p. 1984. 15.95 (ISBN 0-688-03911-1). Morrow.
--The Man on the Moon. LC 78-71899. 1979. 12.95 (ISBN 0-87929-052-8). Barlenmir.
--The Others We Are. (Juniper Bks: No. 29). 1979. pap. 4.00 (ISBN 0-686-61798-3). Juniper Pr WI.
--Winter Journey. 320p. 1981. pap. 2.95 (ISBN 0-449-24369-9, Crest). Fawcett.
Broughton, T. Allan. Dreams Before Sleep. LC 81-71589. 1982. 14.95 (ISBN 0-915604-68-X); pap. 6.95 (ISBN 0-915604-69-8). Carnegie-Mellon.
Broughton, T. Robert. The Magistrates of the Roman Republic. (American Philological Association Philological Monographs). 588p. 1968. Vol. I: 509 B. C. - 100 B.C. 48.00 (ISBN 0-89130-706-0, 40 00 15); Vol. II: 99 B. C. - 31 B.C. 59.95 (ISBN 0-89130-812-1). Scholars Pr GA.
Broughton, T. Robert, ed. see Mommsen, Theodor.
Broughton, Thomas R. The Romanization of Africa Proconsularis. LC 78-64276. (Johns Hopkins University. Studies in the Social Sciences. Extra Volumes-New Ser.: 5). Repr. of 1929 ed. 11.50 (ISBN 0-404-61377-2). AMS Pr.
--Romanization of Africa Proconsularis. LC 68-23279. 1968. Repr. of 1929 ed. lib. bdg. 19.00x (ISBN 0-8371-0030-5, BRAP). Greenwood.
Broughton, W. J. Nitrogen Fixation, Vol. 1: Ecology. (Illus.). 1981. 59.00x (ISBN 0-19-854540-1). Oxford U Pr.
Broughton, W. J., ed. Nitrogen Fixation: Rhizobium, Vols. 2 & 3. (Illus.). 1983. Vol. 2. 59.00x (ISBN 0-19-854552-5); Vol. 3, 339. 59.00x (ISBN 0-19-854555-X). Oxford U Pr.
Broughton, W. J. & Puhler, S., eds. Nitrogen Fixation: Molecular Biology, Vol. IV. (Illus.). 300p. 1985. 49.95 (ISBN 0-19-854575-4). Oxford U Pr.
Broughton, Wynne. Crochet by Design. (Illus.). 176p. 1975. 18.95x (ISBN 0-8464-0304-8). Beekman Pubs.
Brouillard, F., ed. Physics of Ion-Ion & Electron-Ion Collisions. (NATO ASI Series B, Physics: Vol. 83). 550p. 1983. 79.50 (ISBN 0-306-41105-9, Plenum Pr). Plenum Pub.
Brouillet, George A. Voice Manual. LC 74-14145. 1974. pap. 2.00 (ISBN 0-8008-8024-2, Crescendo). Taplinger.
Brouk, B. Plants Consumed by Man. 1975. 73.50 (ISBN 0-12-136450-X). Acad Pr.
Brouker, Jose de see Camara, Dom H.
Broul, M. & Hyvit, J. Solubility in Inorganic Two-Component Systems. (Physical Sciences Data Ser.: Vol. 6). 574p. 1981. 85.00 (ISBN 0-444-99763-6). Elsevier.
Broumas, Olga. Beginning with O. LC 76-49697. (Younger Poets Ser.). 1977. 13.95x (ISBN 0-300-02106-2); pap. 5.95 (ISBN 0-300-02111-9). Yale U Pr.
--Pastoral Jazz. 80p. (Orig.). 1983. pap. 7.00 (ISBN 0-914742-70-1). Copper Canyon.
--Soie Sauvage. 1979. 22.00 (ISBN 0-914742-46-9); pap. 5.00 (ISBN 0-685-96732-8). Copper Canyon.
Broun, Elizabeth. Form, Illusion, Myth: Prints & Drawings of Pat Steir. LC 83-60278. (Illus.). 128p. (Orig.). 1983. pap. 12.00 (ISBN 0-913689-05-X). Spencer Muse Art.
Broun, Elizabeth, jt. auth. see Shoemaker, Innis H.
Broun, Elizabeth, et al. Benton's Bentons. LC 80-52316. (Illus.). 72p. (Orig.). 1980. pap. 6.00 (ISBN 0-913689-03-3). Spencer Muse Art.
Broun, G. B., et al, eds. Enzyme Engineering, Vol. 4. LC 74-13768. 512p. 1978. 65.00x (ISBN 0-306-40021-9, Plenum Pr). Plenum Pub.
Broun, H. H., ed. see Broun, Heywood C.
Broun, Heywood. The Fifty-First Dragon. Redpath, Ann, ed. (Classic Short Stories Ser.). (Illus.). 32p. (gr. 5 up). 1985. PLB 8.95 (ISBN 0-88682-005-7). Creative Ed.
Broun, Heywood & Britt, George. Christians Only: A Study in Prejudice. LC 73-19688. (Civil Liberties in American History Ser). 333p. 1974. Repr. of 1931 ed. lib. bdg. 39.50 (ISBN 0-306-70599-0). Da Capo.
Broun, Heywood C. Collected Edition of Heywood Broun. facsimile ed. Broun, H. H., ed. LC 70-90615. (Essay Index Reprint Ser). 1941. 35.50 (ISBN 0-8369-1345-0). Ayer Co Pubs.
Broun, Heywood H. A Studied Madness. LC 79-84436. 1979. 15.95 (ISBN 0-933256-00-0); pap. 7.95 (ISBN 0-933256-03-5). Second Chance.
--A Studied Madness. LC 79-84436. 298p. 1983. pap. 5.95 (ISBN 0-933256-40-X). Second Chance.
--Whose Little Boy Are You? A Memoir of the Broun Family. (Illus.). 224p. 1983. 14.95 (ISBN 0-312-87765-X, Pub. by Marek). St Martin.
--Whose Little Boy Are You? A Memoir of the Broun Family. 1984. pap. 6.95 (ISBN 0-312-87766-8). St Martin.
Broun, Hob. Inner Tube. Lish, Gordon, ed. LC 85-40227. 224p. 1985. 14.95 (ISBN 0-394-54201-0). Knopf.
--Odditorium. LC 82-48101. 228p. 1983. 14.37i (ISBN 0-06-015027-0, HarpT). Har-Row.
Broun, Kenneth S. & Blakey, Walker J. Evidence. LC 84-15302. (Black Letter Ser.). 269p. 1984. pap. text ed. 13.95 (ISBN 0-314-84448-1). West Pub.
Broun, Kenneth S. & Meisenholder, Robert. Evidence Problems. 2nd ed. LC 80-28083. (American Casebook Ser.). 304p. 1981. pap. text ed. 8.95 (ISBN 0-8299-2125-7); tchr's manual avail. (ISBN 0-314-60971-7). West Pub.
Broun, May H., tr. see Del Valle-Inclan, Ramon.
Broussais, Francois J. On Irritation & Insanity. Cooper, Thomas, tr. LC 75-3091. Repr. of 1831 ed. 31.50 (ISBN 0-404-59089-6). AMS Pr.
Broussard, E. Joseph & Holgate, Jack F. Writing & Reporting Broadcast News. 1982. text ed. write for info. (ISBN 0-02-315270-2). Macmillan.
Broussard, James H. Southern Federalists, 1800-1816. LC 78-2374. 488p. 1978. 37.50x (ISBN 0-8071-0288-1). La State U Pr.
Broussard, Neonetta, jt. auth. see Iwataki, Sadae.
Broussard, Sharon, jt. auth. see Alexander, Stan.
Brousse, P., ed. Structural Optimization. (CISM-International Center for Mechanical Sciences: Vol. 237). 1976. pap. 23.10 (ISBN 0-387-81376-4). Springer-Verlag.
Broussine, Michael & Guerrier, Yvonne. Surviving As a Middle Manager. (Illus.). 224p. 1983. 27.25 (ISBN 0-7099-1137-8, Pub. by Croom Helm Ltd). Longwood Pub Group.
Brousson, Jean J. Anatole France Himself. Pollock, John, tr. 1973. 20.00 (ISBN 0-8274-0075-6). R West.
Brout, R. & Carruthers, P. Lectures on the Many-Electron Problem. 214p. 1969. 57.75 (ISBN 0-677-02470-3). Gordon.

Broutman, L. J., jt. auth. see Agarwal, B. D.

Broutman, L. J., et al, eds. Composite Materials, 8 vols. Incl. Vol. 1. Interfaces in Metal Matrix Composites. 1974. 79.50 (ISBN 0-12-136501-8); Vol. 2. Mechanics of Composite Materials. Sendeckyj, G. P., ed. 1974. 79.50 (ISBN 0-12-136502-6); Vol. 3. Engineering Applications of Composites. Noton, Bryan R., ed. 1974. 79.50 (ISBN 0-12-136503-4); Vol. 4. Metallic Matrix Composites. Kreider, Kenneth G., ed. 1974. 77.00 (ISBN 0-12-136504-2); Vol. 5. Fracture & Fatigue. 1974. 77.00 (ISBN 0-12-136505-0); Vol. 6. Interfaces in Polymer Matrix Composites. Plueddeman, E. P., ed. 1974. 70.50 (ISBN 0-12-136506-9); Vol. 7. Structural Design & Analysis - Part 1. Chamis, C. C., ed. 1975. 79.50 (ISBN 0-12-136507-7); Vol. 8. 1975. 77.50 (ISBN 0-12-136508-5). 512.00 set (ISBN 0-685-48720-2). Acad Pr.

Broutman, Lawrence J., jt. auth. see Agarwal, Bhagwan D.

Brouwer, A. General Palaeontology. Kaye, R. H., tr. LC 67-18435. (Illus.). 1968. pap. 2.45x (ISBN 0-226-07602-4). U of Chicago Pr.

Brouwer, Arie R. Reformed Church Roots. write for info. (ISBN 0-685-62275-4). Reformed Church.

Brouwer, Jasp W., et al. Anthon Van Rappard: Companion & Correspondent of Vincent Van Gogh; His Life & All His Works. (Illus.). 160p. 1975. 27.50 (ISBN 0-8390-0150-9). Abner Schram Ltd.

Brouwer, L. E. L. E. J. Brouwer, Collected Works: Philosophy & Foundations of Mathematics, Vol. 1. Heyting, A., ed. LC 73-75529. 628p. 1976. 127.75 (ISBN 0-444-10643-X, North-Holland). Elsevier.

Brouwer, L. E. & Freudenthal, H. L. E. J. Brouwer, Collected Works, Vol. 2: Geometry, Analysis, Topology & Mechanics. 706p. 1976. 127.75 (ISBN 0-7204-2805-X, North-Holland). Elsevier.

Brouwer, R., et al, eds. see Second International Symposium Bratislava, September, 1980.

Brouzas, C. G. Byron's Maid of Athens, Her Family & Surroundings. LC 74-4346. 1949. lib. bdg. 10.00 (ISBN 0-8414-3101-9). Folcroft.

Brovald, Ken C. Alaska's Wilderness Rails: From the Taiga to the Tundra. LC 82-80963. (Illus.). 104p. 1982. pap. text ed. 8.95 (ISBN 0-933126-21-2). Pictorial Hist.

Broven, John. Rhythm & Blues in New Orleans. LC 77-13351. Orig. Title: Walking To New Orleans. (Illus.). 250p. 1983. pap. 9.95 (ISBN 0-88289-433-1). Pelican.

--South To Louisiana: The Music of the Cajun Bayous. LC 82-11247. (Illus.). 416p. 1983. 19.95 (ISBN 0-88289-300-9). Pelican.

Brow, Dix. Sea of Cortez Guide: For Fishermen, Cruisers, Trailerboaters & Cartoppers in Mexico's Gulf of California. New ed. LC 82-15877. (Illus.). 272p. (Orig.). 1982. pap. 19.95 (ISBN 0-930030-26-5). Western Marine Ent.

Brow, Edward M., jt. ed. see Brown, Edward M.

Brow, James. Vedda Villages of Anuradhapura: The Historical Anthropology of a Community in Sri Lanka. LC 77-16663. (Publications of the School of International Studies: No. 33). (Illus.). 288p. 1978. 25.00x (ISBN 0-295-95585-6). U of Wash Pr.

Brow, Thea J. The Secret Cross of Lorraine. (gr. 5-8). 1981. 8.95 (ISBN 0-395-30344-3). HM.

Broward, Robert C. The Architecture of Henry John Klutho: The Prairie School in Jacksonville. LC 83-6460. (Illus.). 379p. 1984. 45.00 (ISBN 0-8130-0731-3). U Presses Fla.

Browder, Earl. Marx & America. LC 73-16734. 146p. 1974. Repr. of 1958 ed. lib. bdg. 15.00x (ISBN 0-8371-7218-7, BRMA). Greenwood.

Browder, Earl, jt. auth. see Bowers, Claude G.

Browder, F., ed. Nonlinear Functional Analysis, Pts. 1 & 2. LC 73-91392. (Proceedings of Symposia in Pure Mathematics Ser.: Vol. 18). 1970. Set. 81.00 (ISBN 0-8218-0243-7); Pt. 1 36.00 (ISBN 0-8218-0244-5); Pt. 2 55.00. Am Math.

Browder, F E, jt. tr. see Sobolev, Sergei L.

Browder, Felix see Siu, Yum-Tong.

Browder, Felix, ed. Mathematical Heritage of Henri Poincare: Proceedings of Symposia in Pure Mathematics, No. 39. LC 83-2774. 905p. 1984. pap. 79.00 (ISBN 0-8218-1442-7); pap. 42.00 Pt. 1 (ISBN 0-8218-1448-6); pap. 42.00 Pt. 2 (ISBN 0-8218-1449-4). Am Math.

Browder, Felix E., ed. see Conference on Functional Analysis & Related Fields, University of Chicago, 1968.

Browder, Jefferson & Kaplan, Harry A. Cerebral Dural Sinuses & Their Tributaries. (Illus.). 140p. 1976. photocopy ed. 19.75x (ISBN 0-398-03556-3). C C Thomas.

Browder, Leon W. Developmental Biology. 2nd ed. 1984. text ed. 37.95 (ISBN 0-03-063506-3, CBS C). SCP.

Browder, Leon W., ed. Developmental Biology: A Comprehensive Synthesis. (Oogenesis Ser.: Vol. 1). 646p. 1985. 75.00x (ISBN 0-306-41866-5, Plenum Pr). Plenum Pub.

Browder, Olin L., et al. Basic Property Law. 4th ed. LC 84-5223. (American Casebook Ser.). 1431p. 1984. text ed. 30.95 (ISBN 0-314-80501-X). West Pub.

Browder, Robert P. The Origins of Soviet-American Diplomacy. LC 84-19123. xi, 256p. 1984. Repr. of 1953 ed. lib. bdg. 35.00x (ISBN 0-313-24616-5, BROS). Greenwood.

Browder, Robert P. & Kerensky, Alexander F., eds. The Russian Provisional Government, 1917: Documents, 3 Vols. 1961. 100.00x set (ISBN 0-8047-0023-0). Stanford U Pr.

Browder, Robyn, jt. auth. see Barrow, Mary R.

Browder, Robyn, ed. see Barrow, Mary R.

Browder, Robyn, ed. see Carlton, Jan.

Browder, Robyn, ed. see DeBolt, Margaret W.

Browder, Robyn, ed. see DuSablon, Mary Anna.

Browder, Robyn, ed. see Weiner, Melissa R. & Ruffner, Budge.

Browder, Sue. The American Biking Atlas & Touring Guide. LC 75-8816. (Illus.). 320p. 1974. pap. 7.95 (ISBN 0-911104-36-4, 048). Workman Pub.

--The New Age Baby Name Book. 272p. 1974. pap. 3.50 (ISBN 0-446-30824-2). Warner Bks.

--The New Age Baby Name Book. LC 77-18435. 270p. 1978. pap. 4.95 (ISBN 0-89480-029-9, 179). Workman Pub.

Browder, W. Surgery on Simply-Connected Manifolds. LC 70-175907. (Ergebnisse der Mathematik und Ihrer Grenzgebiete: Vol. 65). 140p. 1972. 21.00 (ISBN 0-387-05629-7). Springer-Verlag.

Browdy, Jerad D. Health Care Executive Compensation: Principles & Strategies. LC 82-11384. 214p. 1982. 34.50 (ISBN 0-89443-827-1). Aspen Systems.

Brower, A. E., ed. see Holland, W. J.

Brower, Carol, jt. auth. see Wilhelm, Henry.

Brower, Charles D. Fifty Years Below Zero. LC 42-22432. (Illus.). 1942. 12.95 (ISBN 0-396-02379-7). Dodd.

Brower, Charles N. A Lawyer's Guide to International Business Transactions: International Legal Protection of United States Investment Abroad (Second Ed., Pt. III, Folio 6) - No. B406. 92p. 1981. pap. 14.00 (ISBN 0-317-30777-0). Am Law Inst.

Brower, Charles N. & Marks, Lee R. International Commercial Arbitration. LC 83-159741. vi, 362p. Date not set. price not set (Law & Business). HarBraceJ.

Brower, Daniel, ed. The Russian Revolution. LC 78-67917. (Problems in Civilization Ser.). (Orig.). 1979. pap. text ed. 5.95x (ISBN 0-88273-406-7). Forum Pr IL.

Brower, David. Only a Little Planet. 1975. pap. 6.95 (ISBN 0-345-24469-9). Ballantine.

Brower, David, ed. see Jeffers, Robinson.

Brower, David, et al. Managing Development in Small Towns. LC 84-61635. 176p. 1984. 19.95 (ISBN 0-918286-34-4). Planners Pr.

Brower, David J., jt. auth. see Godschalk, David R.

Brower, David J, jt. auth. see Godschalk, David R.

Brower, Harriette M. Modern Masters of the Keyboard. facs. ed. LC 70-86736. (Essay Index Reprint Ser). 1926. 18.75 (ISBN 0-8369-1124-5). Ayer Co Pubs.

--Story-Lives of Master Musicians. facsimile ed. LC 74-167316. (Essay Index Reprint Ser). Repr. of 1922 ed. 24.00 (ISBN 0-8369-2338-3). Ayer Co Pubs.

Brower, James E. & Zar, Jerrold H. Field & Laboratory Methods of General Ecology. 2nd ed. 240p. 1984. write for info. wire coil. (ISBN 0-697-04657-5). Wm C Brown.

Brower, Kenneth. Micronesia: The Land, the People & the Sea. 128p. 1982. 22.50 (ISBN 0-8071-0992-4). La State U Pr.

--A Song for Satawal. 224p. 1984. pap. 6.95 (ISBN 0-14-007041-9). Penguin.

--A Song For Satawal: A Magical Passage to a Faraway Eden. LC 82-48110. 224p. 1983. 13.41i (ISBN 0-06-015093-9, HarpT). Har-Row.

--The Starship & the Canoe. LC 82-48519. 256p. 1983. pap. 5.72i (ISBN 0-06-091030-5, CN 1030, CN). Har-Row.

--With Their Islands Around Them. LC 74-4455. (Illus.). 1974. 8.95 (ISBN 0-03-013121-9). Friends of Earth.

Brower, Margaret & Brower, Scott. How You Can Go from Broke to Broker in Real Estate. 256p. 1981. 10.00 (ISBN 0-682-49744-4, Banner). Exposition Pr FL.

Brower, Millicent. Young Performers: On the Stage, In Film, & on TV. (Illus.). 128p. (gr. 7 up). 1985. PLB 8.79 (ISBN 0-671-50229-8). Messner.

Brower, Millicent & Koshkin, Naomi. One Hundred Luscious Diet Drinks. 112p. 1983. 4.80 (ISBN 0-671-46019-6, Fireside). S&S.

Brower, Pauline, jt. auth. see Behrens, June.

Brower, R. H., tr. see Teika, Fujiwara.

Brower, Reuben. Mirror on Mirror: Translation, Imitation, Parody. LC 74-80442. (Studies in Comparative Literature: Vol. 34). 224p. 1974. 15.00x (ISBN 0-674-57645-4). Harvard U Pr.

Brower, Reuben, ed. Twentieth Century Literature in Retrospect. LC 76-168430. (English Studies: No. 2). viii, 363p. 1971. pap. 7.95x (ISBN 0-674-91424-4). Harvard U Pr.

Brower, Reuben, ed. & frwd. by see Columbia University. English Institute. Annual Publications.

Brower, Reuben, ed. see Shakespeare, William.

Brower, Reuben, et al, eds. I. A. Richards: Essays in His Honor. 1973. 22.50x (ISBN 0-19-501709-9). Oxford U Pr.

Brower, Reuben A. The Fields of Light: An Experiment in Critical Reading. LC 80-19289. xii, 218p. 1980. Repr. of 1951 ed. lib. bdg. 27.50x (ISBN 0-313-22653-9, BRFI). Greenwood.

Brower, Reuben A., ed. Forms of Lyric: Essays of the English Institute. LC 78-121567. 187p. 1970. 21.00x (ISBN 0-231-03413-X). Columbia U Pr.

Brower, Reuben A., jt. auth. see Kalstone, David.

Brower, Reuben A., et al, eds. Beginning with Poems. (Orig.). 1966. 17.95x (ISBN 0-393-09685-8); pap. 10.95x (ISBN 0-393-09509-6). Norton.

Brower, Robert H. & Miner, Earl. Japanese Court Poetry. (Illus.). 1961. 35.00x (ISBN 0-8047-0536-4). Stanford U Pr.

Brower, Scott, jt. auth. see Brower, Margaret.

Brower, Soloff S. The Faithful Jew, Bk. I. (The Faithful Jew Ser.). (gr. 4-9). 1984. pap. text ed. write for info (ISBN 0-86628-047-2). Ridgefield Pub.

--The Faithful Jew Series. 1984. pap. write for info (ISBN 0-86628-046-4). Ridgefield Pub.

Brower, Walter A., jt. auth. see Lee, Dorothy E.

Browing, Ellen. Teaching Students with Severe Emotional & Learning Impairments. 331p. 1983. 32.95x (ISBN 0-205-07677-7, Pub. by Longwood Div). Allyn.

Browining & Skinner. Tidy's Physiotherapy. 1986. price not set. PSG Pub Co.

Browining, Don S., ed. see Anderson, Herbert.

Browm, Alfred E., jt. auth. see Atlas, Ronald M.

Browm, Edmund R. The Twenty Seventh Indiana Volunteer Infantry in the War of the Rebellion 1861-65: First Division 12th & 20th Corps. 640p. 1984. Repr. of 1899 ed. 40.00x (ISBN 0-913419-16-8). Butternut Pr.

Browman, D. L., ed. Early Native Americans. (World Anthropology Ser.). 1979. text ed. 37.20x (ISBN 90-279-7940-5). Mouton.

Browman, David L., ed. Spirits, Shamans, & Stars: Perspectives from South America. Scwartz, Ronald A. (World Anthropology Ser.). 1979. text ed. 21.60x (ISBN 90-279-7890-5). Mouton.

Browman, David L. & Schwartz, Ronald A., eds. Peasants, Primitives, & Proletariats: The Struggle for Identity in South America. (World Anthropology Ser.). 1979. text ed. 32.80x (ISBN 90-279-7880-8). Mouton.

Browman, Ethel, jt. auth. see Palmer, Margaret.

Brown. Barron's How to Prepare for the New Medical College Admission Test (MCAT) 4th ed. 1983. pap. 7.95 (ISBN 0-8120-2608-X). Barron.

--Georgia Pleading, Practice & Legal Forms Annotated, 11 vols. incl. latest pocket part supplements 395.95 (ISBN 0-686-90332-3); separate pocket part supplements,1984, set 100.95; write for info. separate pocket part supplements, individual 1984; Volumes, individual, incl. latest pocket part suppl. 69.95; Volumes, individual revised 69.95; separate supplements, 1984 100.95; volumes, individual & revised 69.95. Harrison Co GA.

--Hagar the Horrible: Face-Stuffer's Anonymous, No. 9. pap. 1.95 (ISBN 0-317-31779-2). Tor Bks.

--Hazardous Waste Land Treatment. 49.95 (ISBN 0-250-40636-5). Butterworth.

--Mission. 1978. 5.20 (ISBN 0-8298-0397-1). Pilgrim NY.

--Personal Exposure. 1984. 6.50 (ISBN 0-8233-0379-9). Golden Quill.

--Skillbooster Series, Level D. Incl. Building Word Power. pap. text ed. 1.92 (ISBN 0-87895-411-2); Increasing Comprehension. pap. text ed. 1.92 (ISBN 0-87895-412-0); Organizing Information. pap. text ed. 1.92 (ISBN 0-87895-414-7); Using References. pap. text ed. 1.92 (ISBN 0-87895-415-5); Working with Facts & Details. pap. text ed. 1.92 (ISBN 0-87895-413-9). (gr. 4). 1976. pap. Modern Curr.

--Skillbooster Series, Level E. Incl. Building Word Power. pap. text ed. 1.92 (ISBN 0-87895-511-9); Increasing Comprehension. pap. text ed. 1.92 (ISBN 0-87895-512-7); Organizing Information. pap. text ed. 1.92 (ISBN 0-87895-514-3); Using References. pap. text ed. 1.92 (ISBN 0-87895-515-1); Working with Facts & Details. pap. text ed. 1.92 (ISBN 0-87895-513-5). (gr. 5). 1976. pap. Modern Curr.

--Skillbooster Series, Level F. Incl. Building Word Power. pap. text ed. 1.92 (ISBN 0-87895-611-5); Increasing Comprehension. pap. text ed. 1.92 (ISBN 0-87895-612-3); Organizing Information. pap. text ed. 1.92 (ISBN 0-87895-614-X); Using References. pap. text ed. 1.92 (ISBN 0-87895-615-8); Working with Facts & Details. pap. text ed. 1.92 (ISBN 0-87895-613-1). (gr. 6). 1976. pap. Modern Curr.

--Spelling: A Mnemonics Approach. 1986. pap. text ed. 5.10 (ISBN 0-538-14190-5, N19). SW Pub.

--Student Manual of Physical Examination. 2nd ed. 1983. 12.50 (ISBN 0-397-54431-6, 64-03729, Lippincott Nursing). Lippincott.

Brown & Connell. Dirty Bits. Date not set. price not set (ISBN 0-670-27336-8). Viking.

Brown & MacDonald. Creative Art for Home & School. (Illus.). pap. 3.95 (ISBN 0-87505-060-3). Borden.

Brown & Reese. Correlated Dictation & Transcription. 3rd ed. 1983. 352 pp 12.36x, (ISBN 0-912036-06-0); study guide, 260 pp 5.47x, (ISBN 0-912036-08-7); 48 pp 6.84x, (ISBN 0-912036-09-5). Forkner.

Brown & Sampson. Program Debugging. LC 72-12417. (Computer Monograph Ser.: Vol. 18). 1973. 32.50 (ISBN 0-444-19565-3). Elsevier.

Brown & Smith. Handbook of Institutional Pharmacy Practice. (Illus.). 700p. 1985. pap. text ed. 34.00 (ISBN 0-683-01090-5). Williams & Wilkins.

Brown & Tawes. Review Questions in General Vascular Surgery, Vol. I. (Illus.). 226p. (Orig.). 1984. pap. 45.00x (ISBN 0-930328-05-1). Travel Pr.

Brown, jt. auth. see Grill.

Brown, jt. auth. see Nishiyama, H.

Brown, ed. see Aubrey, John.

Brown, et al. Rip, Strip & Row: A Builder's Guide to the Cosine Wherry. LC 85-51141. 1985. pap. 19.95 (ISBN 0-917436-02-4). Tamal Vista.

--Prerequisites for Community Wellbeing. 1972. pap. 1.50 (ISBN 0-910420-20-3). Comm Serv.

Brown, jt. auth. see Breck.

Brown, jt. auth. see Cargill.

Brown, et al, eds. Lichenology: Progress & Problems. 634p. 1976. 90.00 (ISBN 0-12-136750-9). Acad Pr.

Brown, A. The Christian World. LC 83-50692. (Religions of the World Ser.). 1984. PLB 15.00 (ISBN 0-382-06721-5); 10.75 (ISBN 0-382-06929-3). Silver.

Brown, A. & Draper, R. A to Z of Disco & Fever Dancing. (Ballroom Dance Ser.). 1985. lib. bdg. 71.00 (ISBN 0-87700-857-4). Revisionist Pr.

Brown, A. & Pearcy, C. Introduction to Operator Theory, Vol. 1: Elements of Functional Analysis. LC 77-23438. (Graduate Texts in Mathematics: Vol. 55). (Illus.). 1977. 36.00 (ISBN 0-387-90257-0). Springer-Verlag.

Brown, A. & Weiner, E. Super Managing: How to Harness Change for Personal & Organizational Success. 1985. pap. 4.95 (ISBN 0-451-62382-7, Sig). NAL.

Brown, A., jt. auth. see McAfee, A.

Brown, A., tr. see Tynianov, Iurri N.

Brown, A. A. & Davis, Kenneth P. Forest Fire: Control & Use. 2nd ed. (Forest Resources Ser.). (Illus.). 544p. 1973. text ed. 42.95 (ISBN 0-07-008205-7). McGraw.

Brown, A. A., tr. see Botvinnik, M. M.

Brown, A. A., tr. see Palamodov, V. P.

Brown, A. A., tr. see Petrov, V. V.

Brown, A. Barratt. Great Democrats: Carlyle, Cobbett, Godwin, J. S. Mill, William Morris, Rousseau, Ruskin, Whitman, Mary Wollstonecraft. Repr. of 1934 ed. 35.00 (ISBN 0-686-19847-6). Ridgeway Bks.

Brown, A. C. Knosso: Sir Arthur Evans's Excavations at Knossos. 1982. 30.00x (ISBN 0-900090-92-8, Pub. by Ashmolean Mus UK). State Mutual Bk.

Brown, A. C. & Crounse, Robert G., eds. Hair: Trace Elements & Human Illness. LC 80-10280. 376p. 1980. 61.95 (ISBN 0-03-055441-1). Praeger.

Brown, A. E. & Jeffcott, H. A., Jr. Absolutely Mad Inventions. Orig. Title: Beware of Imitations. (Illus.). 1970. pap. 2.50 (ISBN 0-486-22596-8). Dover.

Brown, A. F. The Incubation Book. 256p. 1979. 14.95 (ISBN 0-85115-418-2, Pub. by Boydell & Brewer). Longwood Pub Group.

Brown, A. F., jt. auth. see Isham, N. M.

Brown, A. G. Organization in the Spinal Cord. (Illus.). 260p. 1981. 89.00 (ISBN 0-387-10549-2). Springer-Verlag.

--X-Rays & Their Applications. LC 75-34146. 258p. 1975. pap. 8.95x (ISBN 0-306-20021-X, Rosetta). Plenum Pub.

Brown, A. G., jt. auth. see Willis, W. E.

Brown, A. G., ed. Spinal Cord Sensation: Sensory Processing in the Dorsal Horn. 357p. 1981. 32.50x (ISBN 0-7073-0295-1, Pub. by Scottish Academic Pr Scotland). Columbia U Pr.

Brown, A. G. & Roberts, S. M., eds. Recent Advances in the Chemistry of B-Lactum Antibiotics: Third International Symposium, 1984. 398p. 1985. pap. 48.00 (ISBN 0-85186-955-6, 996104712, Pub. by Royal Soc Chem UK). Heyden.

Brown, A. G., jt. ed. see Hillis, W. E.

Brown, A. H. Soviet Politics & Political Science. LC 75-29858. 128p. 1976. 20.00 (ISBN 0-312-74865-5). St Martin.

Brown, A. J. The Framework of Regional Economics in the United Kingdom. LC 72-83665. (Publications of the National Institute of Economic & Social Studies: No. 27). (Illus.). 384p. 1972. 44.50 (ISBN 0-521-08743-0). Cambridge U Pr.

--The Great Inflation Nineteen Thirty-Nine to Nineteen Fifty-One. LC 82-48175. (Gold, Money, Inflation & Deflation Ser.). 1983. lib. bdg. 44.00 (ISBN 0-8240-5226-9). Garland Pub.

--World Inflation Since Nineteen Fifty: An International Comparative Study. (National Institute of Economic & Social Research Economic & Social Studies: No. XXXIV). 350p. Date not set. price not set. (ISBN 0-521-30351-6). Cambridge U Pr.

Brown, A. L., ed. see Loyn, H. R.

Brown, A. L., ed. see Sophocles.

Brown, A. L., ed. see Warren, W. L.

Brown, A. Lee. Rules & Conflicts: An Introduction to Political Life & Its Study. (Illus.). 384p. 1981. pap. text ed. 19.95 (ISBN 0-13-783738-0). P-H.

Brown, A. Peter. Performing Haydn's "The Creation". Reconstructing the Earliest Renditions. LC 84-43053. (Music: Scholarship & Performance Ser.). (Illus.). 160p. 1985. 29.95 (ISBN 0-253-38820-1). Ind U Pr.
Brown, A. S. Fuel Resources. (Natural Resources Ser.: Bk. 1). (Illus.). 72p. (gr. 4 up). 1985. lib. bdg. 9.40 (ISBN 0-531-04911-6). Watts.
Brown, A. Theodore, jt. auth. see Glaab, Charles N.
Brown, A. Theodore & Dorsett, Lyle W. K.C. A History of Kansas City, Missouri. LC 78-14514. (Western Urban History Ser.). (Illus.). 1978. 14.95 (ISBN 0-87108-526-7); pap. 8.50 (ISBN 0-87108-563-1). Pruett.
Brown, A. W. & Pal, R. Insecticide Resistance in Arthropods. 2nd ed. (Monograph Ser: No. 38). (Illus.). 491p. 1971. pap. 16.40 (ISBN 92-4-140038-2, 943). World Health.
Brown, A. W., jt. ed. see Watson, David L.
Brown, A. Winnifred, jt. auth. see Howells, John G.
Brown, Abbie F. The Lantern & Other Plays for Children. LC 77-94333. (One-Act Plays in Reprint Ser.). (Illus.). 1978. Repr. of 1928 ed. 18.50x (ISBN 0-8486-2033-X). Core Collection.
Brown, Abe A. Medical Crossword Puzzles & Other Literary Diversions. 96p. 1982. pap. 3.95 (ISBN 0-668-05423-9). Arco.
Brown, Addison, jt. auth. see Britton, Nathaniel L.
Brown, Aggrey. Color, Class & Politics in Jamaica. LC 76-58231. 250p. 1980. text ed. 14.95 (ISBN 0-87855-099-2). Transaction Bks.
Brown, Alan. Invitation to Sailing. 1968. pap. 7.95 (ISBN 0-671-21134-X, Fireside). S&S.
--Skoolplay. 1980. pap. 3.95 (ISBN 0-7145-3672-5). Riverrun NY.
--Wheelchair Willie & Other Plays. 1980. pap. 4.95 (ISBN 0-7145-3655-5). Riverrun NY.
--Wind up the Willow. 1981. 9.95 (ISBN 0-7145-3808-6); pap. 4.95 (ISBN 0-7145-3734-9). Riverrun NY.
Brown, Alan, jt. auth. see Brown, Leslie.
Brown, Alan, et al. An Introduction to Subject Indexing: A Programmed Text. 2nd ed. 256p. 1982. 19.50 (ISBN 0-85157-331-2, Pub. by Bingley England). Shoe String.
Brown, Alan A. & Neuberger, Egon. Internal Migration: A Comparative Perspective. 1977. 60.00 (ISBN 0-12-137350-9). Acad Pr.
Brown, Alan A. & Neuberger, Egon, eds. International Trade & Central Planning: An Analysis of Economic Interactions. LC 68-13821. 1968. 44.50x (ISBN 0-520-00187-7). U of Cal Pr.
Brown, Alan C. & Fyffe, E. W. Intracellular Staining of Mammalian Neurones. (Biological Techniques Ser.). 1984. for info. 23.00 (ISBN 0-12-137220-0). Acad Pr.
Brown, Alan C. D. Computer Management of Operating Room Services. 250p. 86. 31.50tx (ISBN 0-03-059696-3). Praeger.
Brown, Alan G., jt. ed. see Hillis, W. Edward.
Brown, Alan R., ed. Prejudice in Children. 224p. 1972. 17.50x (ISBN 0-398-02247-X). C C Thomas.
Brown, Alan R. & Avery, Connie, eds. Modifying Children's Behavior. (Illus.). 296p. 1974. 17.00x (ISBN 0-398-02953-9). C C Thomas.
Brown, Alan W. The Metaphysical Society: Victorian Minds in Crisis, 1869-1880. LC 73-8422. xiv, 372p. 1973. Repr. of 1947 ed. lib. bdg. 27.50x (ISBN 0-374-91008-1). Octagon.
Brown, Albert, jt. auth. see Berner, Loretta.
Brown, Albert F., jt. auth. see Isham, Norman M.
Brown, Albert J., Jr. The Effective Branch Manager: Ways to Develop Management Skills. 2nd ed. LC 79-28337. 127p. 1983. text ed. 26.50 (ISBN 0-87267-035-X). Bankers.
Brown, Alec, tr. see Cocteau, Jean.
Brown, Alec, tr. see Leonov, Leonid M.
Brown, Alec, tr. see Remizov, Aleksel M.
Brown, Alec, tr. see Sukhotina, Tat'Iana L.
Brown, Alex. Making Books Work. 13.50x (ISBN 0-392-16526-0, ABC). Sportshelf.
Brown, Alex & Draper, Raymond. A to Z of Disco & Fever Dancing. 2nd ed. pap. text ed. 6.50x (ISBN 0-392-05722-0, SpS). Sportshelf.
Brown, Alexander. Juniper Waterway: A History of the Albemarle & Chesapeake Canal. LC 80-14093. (Illus.). xiii, 255p. 1981. 22.50x (ISBN 0-917376-35-8). U Pr of Va.
Brown, Alexander C. The Good Ships of Newport News. LC 76-12100. (Illus.). 254p. 1976. 12.75 (ISBN 0-87033-220-1). Tidewater.
--Life with Grover. LC 62-18217. (Illus.). 80p. 1962. pap. 4.00 (ISBN 0-87033-271-6). Tidewater.
--Longboat to Hawaii. LC 74-22317. (Illus.). 254p. 1974. 12.50 (ISBN 0-87033-201-5). Cornell Maritime.
--Steam Packets on the Chesapeake. LC 61-12580. (Illus.). 207p. 1961. 12.95 (ISBN 0-87033-111-6). Tidewater.
Brown, Alexis, tr. see Keller, Horst.
Brown, Alfred B., ed. Great Democrats. facs. ed. LC 70-128216. (Essay Index Reprint Ser). 1934. 35.50 (ISBN 0-8369-1942-4). Ayer Co Pubs.
--Great Democrats. (Essay Index Reprint Ser.). 704p. Repr. of 1934 ed. lib. bdg. 31.00 (ISBN 0-8290-0791-1). Irvington.
Brown, Alice. The County Road. LC 68-23713. (Americans in Fiction Ser.). lib. bdg. 16.50 (ISBN 0-8398-0172-6); pap. text ed. 4.50x (ISBN 0-89197-715-5). Irvington.
--High Noon. facs. ed. LC 75-121526. (Short Story Index Reprint Ser.). 1904. 19.00 (ISBN 0-8369-3482-2). Ayer Co Pubs.
--Meadow-Grass: Tales of New England Life. 1972. Repr. of 1885 ed. lib. bdg. 18.00 (ISBN 0-8422-8011-1). Irvington.
--Meadow-Grass: Tales of New England Life, Vol. 1. LC 72-4456. (Short Story Index Reprint Ser.). Repr. of 1895 ed. 21.00 (ISBN 0-8369-4172-1). Ayer Co Pubs.
--Mercy Warren. LC 67-30159. (Illus.). 319p. 1968. Repr. of 1896 ed. 11.50 (ISBN 0-87152-042-7). Reprint.
--Tiverton Tales. LC 67-29259. (Americans in Fiction Ser.). 1968. Repr. of 1899 ed. lib. bdg. 14.50 (ISBN 0-8398-0173-4). Irvington.
--Vanishing Points. facsimile ed. LC 71-106250. (Short Story Index Reprint Ser). 1913. 19.00 (ISBN 0-8369-3287-0). Ayer Co Pubs.
Brown, Alice H. Tom Dooley, Jungle Doctor. (Stories About Christian Heroes Ser.). (Illus.). (gr. 1-3). 1979. pap. 1.95 (ISBN 0-03-049441-9). Winston Pr.
Brown, Alison. Bartolomeo Scala, Fourteen Thirty to Fourteen Ninety-Seven, Chancellor of Florence: The Humanist As Bureacrat. LC 78-70280. 1979. 40.00x (ISBN 0-691-05270-0). Princeton U Pr.
Brown, Allan. Consultation: An Aid to Successful Social Work. (Community Care Practice Handbook Ser.). xiv, 104p. 1984. pap. text ed. 9.00x (ISBN 0-435-82092-3). Gower Pub Co.
--Groupwork. Davies, Martin, ed. LC 80-670034. (Community Care Practice Handbook Ser.). (Orig.). 1980. pap. text ed. 8.50x (ISBN 0-435-82091-5). Gower Pub Co.
Brown, Allan E. The History of the American Speedway. LC 84-51373. 352p. (Orig.). 1984. 14.95 (ISBN 0-931105-03-X); pap. 8.95 (ISBN 0-931105-04-8). Slideways Pubns.
Brown, Allen, jt. auth. see Teller, Edward.
Brown, Allen D. The Great Lobster Chase: The Real Story of Maine Lobsters & the Men Who Catch Them. LC 84-47847. (Illus.). 210p. 1985. pap. 22.95 (ISBN 0-87742-174-9). Intl Marine.
Brown, Allen W. The Inner Fire. rev. ed. 1984. pap. 1.95 (ISBN 0-88028-033-6). Forward Movement.
Brown, Allison L. Ecology of Soil Organisms. LC 78-313368. 1978. pap. text ed. 9.95x (ISBN 0-435-60621-2). Heinemann Ed.
Brown, Alpha. One Hundred & One Practical Activities for Use in Classes of Pupils Who Are Retarded. 1970. pap. 3.25x (ISBN 0-88323-058-5, 156). Richards Pub.
Brown, Andreas, jt. auth. see Morgan, Hal.
Brown, Andreas, ed. A Creative Century: Selections from the Twentieth-Century Collections. (Illus.). 1970. pap. 4.00 (ISBN 0-87959-004-1). U of Tex H Ransom Ctr.
Brown, Andreas, jt. ed. see Morgan, Hal.
Brown, Andrew. A New Companion to Greek Tragedy. LC 83-3842. (Illus.). 210p. 1983. text ed. 25.75x (ISBN 0-389-20389-0, 07267); pap. text ed. 10.50x (ISBN 0-389-20396-3, 07274). B&N Imports.
Brown, Andrew W. The Unevenness of the Abilities of Dull & of Bright Children. LC 70-176596. (Columbia University. Teachers College. Contributions to Education: No. 220). Repr. of 1926 ed. 22.50 (ISBN 0-404-55220-X). AMS Pr.
Brown, Angela. Prayers That Avail Much for Children. (Illus.). 32p. (Orig.). (gr. 1-3). 1983. pap. 3.50 (ISBN 0-89274-296-8). Harrison Hse.
Brown, Anita D., et al. My Grandmother's Cookbook. 4th ed. (Illus.). 1982. pap. 2.25 (ISBN 0-685-93631-7). The Little Brown House.
--Little Brown Cookbook. 7th rev. ed. (Illus.). 1982. pap. 2.25 (ISBN 0-915782-01-4). The Little Brown House.
Brown, Ann. Arthur Evans & the Palace of Minos. 110p. 1983. 30.00x (ISBN 0-900090-92-8, Pub. by Ashmolean Mus UK). State Mutual Bk.
Brown, Ann A., jt. auth. see Towle, Laird.
Brown, Ann B., jt. auth. see Brown, Stuart E.
Brown, Ann K. & Parker, Monica. Dance Notation for Beginners: Labanotation & Benesh Movement Notation. (Illus.). 1984. 12.95 (ISBN 0-903102-71-4, Pub. by Dance Bks England). Princeton Bk Co.
Brown, Ann L., jt. auth. see Salzman, Ed.
Brown, Ann L., jt. ed. see Lamb, Michael E.
Brown, Ann M., ed. see Brown, Michael E.
Brown, Anne B., as told to see Hemlin, Mary Buffum.
Brown, Anne E. Monarchs of the Forest: The Story of the Redwoods. (Illus.). 96p. (gr. 5 up). 1984. PLB 9.95 (ISBN 0-396-08322-6). Dodd.
--Wonders of Sea Horses. LC 78-22439. (Wonder Ser.). (Illus.). (gr. 5 up). 1979. 9.95 (ISBN 0-396-07664-5). Dodd.
Brown, Anne S., jt. ed. see Rice, Howard C.
Brown, Anthony C. Bodyguard of Lies. (Illus.). 1976. pap. 12.95 (ISBN 0-553-34016-6). Bantam.
--The Last Hero: Wild Bill Donovan. 768p. 1982. 24.95 (ISBN 0-686-95975-2). Times Bks.
--The Last Hero: Wild Bill Donovan: The Biography & Political Experience of Major General William J. Donovan, Founder of the OSS & "Father" of the CIA (from His Personal & Secret Papers & the Diaries of Ruth Donovan) LC 83-19811. 1984. 9.95 (ISBN 0-394-72305-8, Vin). Random.
Brown, Anthony C. & McDonald, Charles. The Secret History of the Atomic Bomb. (Illus.). 1977. 16.95 (ISBN 0-385-27363-0, J Wade). Dial.
Brown, Anthony C. & MacDonald, Charles. Secret History of the Atomic Bomb. 16.95 (ISBN 0-385-27363-0, Dial). Doubleday.
Brown, Anthony E. Boswellian Studies: A Bibliography. 2nd ed. LC 75-155892. xii, 134p. 1972. 16.50 (ISBN 0-208-01214-1, Archon). Shoe String.
Brown, Anthony E., jt. auth. see Welborn, David M.
Brown, Anthony M. Discipline Concepts in Education. (Orig.). 1964. pap. 4.00 (ISBN 0-8198-0037-6). Dghtrs St Paul.
Brown, Antoinette B., jt. auth. see Wing, Elizabeth S.
Brown, Arch. News Boy. LC 80-84131. (Illus.). 88p. (Orig.). 1980. pap. 3.95 (ISBN 0-935672-02-8). JH Pr.
Brown, Archie, ed. Political Culture & Communist Studies. LC 84-20314. 256p. (Orig.). 1984. 35.00 (ISBN 0-87332-309-2); pap. 14.95 (ISBN 0-87332-310-6). M E Sharpe.
Brown, Archie & Gray, Jack, eds. Political Culture & Political Change in Communist States. 2nd, rev. ed. LC 76-41832. 375p. 1979. text ed. 34.50x (ISBN 0-8419-0508-8); pap. text ed. 16.50x (ISBN 0-8419-0509-6). Holmes & Meier.
Brown, Archie & Kaser, Michael, eds. Soviet Policy for the 1980s. LC 82-48593. 296p. 1983. 22.50x (ISBN 0-253-35412-9). Ind U Pr.
--The Soviet Union Since the Fall of Khrushchev. LC 75-39856. 1976. 17.95 (ISBN 0-02-904870-2). Free Pr.
Brown, Archie, et al, eds. The Cambridge Encylopedia of Russia & the Soviet Union. (Cambridge Regional Encyclopedias). (Illus.). 1982. 39.50 (ISBN 0-521-23169-8). Cambridge U Pr.
Brown, Arlen D. & Strickland, R. Mack. Tractor & Small Engine Maintenance. 5th ed. 350p. 1983. 17.00 (ISBN 0-8134-2258-2); text ed. 12.75x. Interstate.
Brown, Arlett, ed. see Choi, Jai.
Brown, Arlett, ed. see Taffel, Selma.
Brown, Arlin J. March of Truth on Cancer. 7th & rev. ed. 1968. pap. 6.95 (ISBN 0-686-02389-7). Arlin J Brown.
Brown, Arnold. Physiological & Psychological Considerations in the Management of Stroke. LC 72-7682. 160p. 1976. 12.50 (ISBN 0-87527-094-8). Green.
Brown, Arnold & Weiner, Edith. Supermanaging: How to Harness Change for Personal & Organizational Success. 288p. 17.95 (ISBN 0-07-008201-4). McGraw.
Brown, Arthur, ed. The Marriage of Wit & Science. LC 82-45713. (Malone Society Reprint Ser.: No. 113). Repr. of 1960 ed. 40.00 (ISBN 0-404-63113-4). AMS Pr.
Brown, Arthur, jt. ed. see Davison, Peter H.
Brown, Arthur C. Iwain: Study of the Origin of the Arthurian Romance. LC 68-8365. (Arthurian Legend & Literature Ser., No. 1). 1969. Repr. of 1903 ed. lib. bdg. 39.95x (ISBN 0-8383-0515-6). Haskell.
Brown, Arthur E. Canopy of Ice. (Illus.). 238p. (Orig.). 1985. pap. 3.95 (ISBN 0-9614302-5-7). E D M Digest.
Brown, Arthur E. & Armstrong, Donald, eds. Infectious Complications of Neoplastic Disease: Controversies in Management. (Illus.). 350p. 1985. text ed. 40.00 (ISBN 0-914316-43-5). Yorke Med.
Brown, Arthur M. & Stubbs, Donald W., eds. Medical Physiology. LC 82-8585. (Illus.). 904p. 1983. 35.95 (ISBN 0-471-05207-8). Wiley.
Brown, Arthur W. Always Young for Liberty: Biography of William Ellery Channing. 1956. 17.95x (ISBN 0-8156-0004-6). Syracuse U Pr.
--Margaret Fuller. (Twayne's United States Authors Ser.). 1964. pap. 5.95x (ISBN 0-8084-0209-9, T48, Twayne). New Coll U Pr.
--Sexual Analysis of Dickens' Props. Orig. Title: Freudian Symbolism in Dickens. 1971. 9.95 (ISBN 0-87523-176-4). Emerson.
--William Ellery Channing. (Twayne's United States Authors Ser). 1961. pap. 5.95x (ISBN 0-8084-0325-7, T7, Twayne). New Coll U Pr.
Brown, Arthur W., ed. see Brown, Stuart G.
Brown, Ashley & Kimmey, John L. Comedy. LC 69-10745. 1968. pap. text ed. 3.95 (ISBN 0-675-09591-3). Merrill.
Brown, Ashley & Dartford, Mark, eds. War in Peace: The Marshall Cavendish Illustrated Encyclopedia of Postwar Conflict, 12 vols, Vols. 1-12. (Illus.). 3000p. 1984. Set. lib. bdg. 501.95 (ISBN 0-86307-293-3). M Cavendish Corp.
Brown, Ashley & Haller, Robert S., eds. The Achievement of Wallace Stevens. LC 73-189246. 287p. 1973. Repr. of 1962 ed. 12.00x (ISBN 0-87752-161-1). Gordian.
Brown, Ashley & Kimmey, John L., eds. Satire: An Anthology. 1978. pap. text ed. 11.50 scp (ISBN 0-690-01524-0, HarpC). Har-Row.
Brown, Ashley, ed. see Tate, Allen.
Brown, Austin R., Jr. & Harris, Mark. Arbplot: A Computer Graphics Utility for Calculus. (A Software Microcomputer Program Ser.). 1982. scp Users guide manual 14.95 (ISBN 0-06-041027-2, HarpC); scp computer package 125.00 (ISBN 0-06-041026-4). Har-Row.
Brown, B. Images of Family Life in Magazine Advertising: 1920-1978. 156p. 1981. 31.95 (ISBN 0-03-059697-1). HR&W.
--Talking Pictures. 1976. lib. bdg. 69.95 (ISBN 0-8490-2730-6). Gordon Pr.
Brown, B. Baldwin, ed. see Vasari, Giorgio.
Brown, B. F., ed. Stress Corrosion Cracking Control Measures. (Illus.). 71p. 25.00 (ISBN 0-317-35124-9, 52137); members 20.00 (ISBN 0-317-35125-7). Natl Corrosion Eng.
Brown, B. Frank. Crisis in Secondary Education: Rebuilding America's High Schools. LC 84-6923. 163p. 1984. 16.50 (ISBN 0-13-193517-8, Busn). P-H.
Brown, B. H. & Smallwood, R. H. Medical Physics & Physiological Measurement. (Illus.). 544p. 1982. text ed. 31.95 (ISBN 0-632-00704-4, B 0893-7). Mosby.
Brown, Barbara. Between Health & Illness: New Notions on Stress & the Nature of Well Being. 256p. 1984. 14.95 (ISBN 0-395-34634-7). HM.
--Disaster Preparedness & the United Nations: Advance Planning for Disaster Relief. LC 79-179. (Pergamon Policy Studies). 120p. 1979. 21.00 (ISBN 0-08-022486-5). Pergamon.
--Stress & the Art of Biofeedback. 1978. pap. 4.95 (ISBN 0-553-25223-2). Bantam.
--Stress & the Art of Biofeedback. LC 76-5115. (Illus.). 1977. 14.37i (ISBN 0-06-010544-5, HarpT). Har-Row.
--Supermind: The Ultimate Energy. 304p. pap. 4.95 (ISBN 0-553-25344-1). Bantam.
Brown, Barbara, jt. auth. see Hawkins, David.
Brown, Barbara, jt. ed. see Rose, James M.
Brown, Barbara A. Hematology: Principles & Procedures. 4th ed. LC 83-24849. (Illus.). 405p. 1984. text ed. 26.50 (ISBN 0-8121-0927-9). Lea & Febiger.
Brown, Barbara A., et al. Women's Rights & the Law: The Impact of the ERA on State Laws. LC 77-9961. 448p. 1977. text ed. 48.95 (ISBN 0-03-022316-4); pap. 18.95 (ISBN 0-03-022311-3). Praeger.
Brown, Barbara B. Between Health & Illness: New Notions on Stress & the Nature of Well Being. 304p. 1985. pap. 3.95 (ISBN 0-553-24798-0). Bantam.
--The Biofeedback Syllabus: A Handbook for the Psychophysiologic Study of Biofeedback. 516p. 1975. 45.50x (ISBN 0-398-03268-8). C C Thomas.
--Infinite Well-Being. 400p. 1985. 16.95 (ISBN 0-8290-1158-7). Irvington.
--New Mind, New Body. 523p. 1985. 34.50 (ISBN 0-8290-1002-5); pap. 12.95 (ISBN 0-8290-0996-5). Irvington.
--New Mind, New Body: Bio-Feedback; New Directions for the Mind. LC 73-14249. (Illus.). 416p. 1974. 16.50i (ISBN 0-06-010549-6, HarpT). Har-Row.
--Supermind: The Ultimate Energy. LC 79-2614. (Illus.). 1980. 12.45i (ISBN 0-06-010518-6, HarpT). Har-Row.
Brown, Barbara B. & Klug, Jay, eds. The Alpha Syllabus: A Handbook of Human EEG Alpha Activity. 368p. 1974. pap. 37.75x spiral (ISBN 0-398-03020-0). C C Thomas.
Brown, Barbara J. Nurse Staffing: A Practical Guide. LC 80-12353. 188p. 1980. 31.95 (ISBN 0-89443-291-5). Aspen Systems.
--Perspectives in Primary Nursing: Professional Practice Environments. LC 81-20579. 366p. 1982. text ed. 31.95 (ISBN 0-89443-683-X). Aspen Systems.
Brown, Barbara J. & Chinn, Peggy L., eds. Nursing Education: Practical Methods & Models. LC 82-11370. 297p. 1982. 30.95 (ISBN 0-89443-807-7). Aspen Systems.
Brown, Barbara W., jt. auth. see Rose, James M.
Brown, Barrie J. & Christie, Maralyn. Social Learning Practice in Residential Child Care. 150p. 1981. 29.00 (ISBN 0-08-026779-3); pap. 14.25 (ISBN 0-08-026778-5). Pergamon.
Brown, Barron. Comanche. Bd. with Marching with Custer. Nye, Elwood L. (Illus.). 1941. 12.50 (ISBN 0-914074-02-4, Pub. by J M C & Co). Amereon Ltd.
Brown, Barry S., ed. Addicts & Aftercare: Community Integration of the Former Drug User. (Sage Annual Reviews of Drug & Alcohol Abuse: Vol. 3). (Illus.). 294p. 1979. 28.00 (ISBN 0-8039-1148-3); pap. 14.00 (ISBN 0-8039-1149-1). Sage.
Brown, Beatrice. The Southern Passion. LC 74-10772. 1927. 20.00 (ISBN 0-8414-3122-1). Folcroft.
Brown, Beatrice C. Anthony Trollope. 1950. Repr. 10.00 (ISBN 0-8274-3794-3). R West.
--Jonathan Bing. (gr. 4 up). 1976. pap. 0.95 (ISBN 0-440-44253-2, YB). Dell.
Brown, Benjamin H. Tariff Reform Movement in Great Britain, 1881-1895. Repr. of 1943 ed. 8.00 (ISBN 0-404-01119-5). AMS Pr.
Brown, Bernard, jt. auth. see Macridis, Roy.
Brown, Bernard E. American Conservatives: The Political Thought of Francis Lieber & John W. Burgess. LC 78-181923. (Columbia University Studies in the Social Sciences: No. 565). Repr. of 1951 ed. 17.50 (ISBN 0-404-51565-7). AMS Pr.
--Intellectuals & Other Traitors. 196p. 1980. 12.95 (ISBN 0-935764-01-1). Irvington.

--Socialism of a Different Kind: Reshaping the Left in France. LC 82-6125. (Contributions in Political Science Ser.: No. 85). xiv, 201p. 1982. lib. bdg. 29.95 (ISBN 0-313-23377-2, BFL/). Greenwood.

Brown, Bernard E., ed. Eurocommunism & Eurosocialism: The Left Confronts Modernity. LC 78-71538. 400p. text ed. 37.50x (ISBN 0-8290-0394-0); pap. text ed. 16.95x (ISBN 0-8290-0395-9). Irvington.

--Great American Political Thinkers: Vol. II, Modern America since Civil War & Industrialization. 432p. 1983. pap. 4.95 (ISBN 0-380-83923-7, 83923-7, Discus). Avon.

--Great American Political Thinkers, Vol. 1: Creating America: From Settlement to Mass Democracy. 464p. 1983. pap. 4.95 (ISBN 0-380-83915-6, 83915-6, Discus). Avon.

Brown, Bernard L. Risk Management for Hospitals: A Practical Approach. LC 78-31925. 216p. 1979. text ed. 35.00 (ISBN 0-89443-090-4). Aspen Systems.

Brown, Bernard O. Ideology & Community Action: The West Side Organization of Chicago, 1964-1967. LC 77-91842. (Studies in Religion & Society). 1978. 16.95x (ISBN 0-913348-16-3); pap. 8.95x (ISBN 0-913348-17-1). Ctr Sci Study.

Brown, Bernice. Men of Earth. facs. ed. LC 70-122692. (Short Story Index Reprint Ser). 1924. 18.00 (ISBN 0-8369-3525-X). Ayer Co Pubs.

Brown, Beth. Dogs. rev. ed. LC 68-9405. (Illus.). (gr. 3 up). 1981. PLB 7.95 (ISBN 0-87460-095-2). Lion Bks.

--House Without a Home. LC 70-112367. (Illus.). 48p. (gr. k-3). 1971. PLB 8.95 (ISBN 0-87460-221-1). Lion Bks.

--Lightyears. LC 81-82663. 70p. 1982. pap. 4.50x perfect bdg. (ISBN 0-916418-36-7). Lotus.

Brown, Beth, compiled by. Fairy Tales of Birds & Beasts, Vol. 1. (Illus.). 128p. (gr. 3-7). 1985. PLB 8.95 (ISBN 0-87460-375-7). Lion Bks.

Brown, Beth, jt. auth. see Thackeray, Helen.

Brown, Bette. The Runaway. 7.95 (ISBN 0-8062-2424-X). Carlton.

Brown, Beverly S. Erica the Ecologist. LC 81-71554. (Illus.). 20p. (Orig.). (gr. 3-5). 1982. 3.50x (ISBN 0-943864-13-5). Davenport.

--Erica the Ecologist. (Illus.). 60p. 1982. 2.50 (ISBN 0-943864-01-1). MD Bks.

Brown, Beverly S., illus. Key Soup. LC 78-73538. (Illus.). (gr. 1-5). Date not set. price not set (ISBN 0-89799-155-9); pap. price not set (ISBN 0-89799-073-0). Dandelion Pr.

Brown, Bill, jt. auth. see Brown, Joan W.

Brown, Bill, jt. auth. see Elser, Smoke.

Brown, Bill, jt. auth. see Rimmer, C. Brandon.

Brown, Bill, jt. auth. see Sullivan, William C.

Brown, Bill W. A Casebook on Administration & Supervision in Industrial-Technical Education. LC 76-127888. (Illus.). pap. 29.80 (ISBN 0-317-10631-7, 2011580). Bks Demand UMI.

Brown, Bob. Science Circus, No. 1. LC 60-8779. (Illus.). (gr. 7-12). 1960. 9.95 (ISBN 0-8303-0050-3). Fleet.

--Science Treasures: Let's Repeat the Great Experiments. LC 68-23980. (Illus.). (gr. 7-12). 1968. 9.95 (ISBN 0-8303-0052-X). Fleet.

--The Turtle's Darshan for All the Animals. (Illus.). 32p. (gr. 2 up). 1973. pap. 2.00 (ISBN 0-913078-17-4). Sheriar Pr.

Brown, Bob, et al. South American Cook Book; Including Central America, Mexico & the West Indies. LC 72-166427. 1971. pap. 4.95 (ISBN 0-486-20190-2). Dover.

Brown, Bob W. It's Been One of Those Days, Lord. 144p. (Orig.). 1985. pap. 2.95 (ISBN 0-310-28912-2, Pub. by Daybreak). Zondervan.

Brown, Bonaventure A. The Numerical Distinction of Sins According to the Franciscan School of the Seventeenth & Eighteenth Centuries. 1948. 3.50 (ISBN 0-686-11581-3). Franciscan Inst.

Brown, Bonnie. Sunbeam Portable Electric Cookery. LC 74-121732. 6.95 (ISBN 0-87502-008-9); pap. 1.95 (ISBN 0-685-30861-8). Benjamin Co.

Brown, Bonnie M., et al, eds. Kentucky Appellate Handbook. 1985. 32.50 (ISBN 0-317-29548-9). Baldner J V.

Brown, Brendan. The Dollar-Mark Axis: On Currency Power. LC 79-5354. 1980. 11.95 (ISBN 0-312-21623-8). St Martin.

--The Forward Market in Foreign Exchange: A Study in Market-Making Arbitrage & Speculation. LC 82-42562. 176p. 1983. 25.00x (ISBN 0-312-29985-0). St Martin.

Brown, Brendan & Geisst, Charles. Financial Futures Markets. LC 83-11001. 192p. 1983. 25.00 (ISBN 0-312-28955-3). St Martin.

Brown, Brendon. A Theory of Hedge Investment. LC 82-5651. 240p. 1982. 25.00 (ISBN 0-312-79783-4). St Martin.

Brown, Brian. Chinese Nights Entertainment: Stories of Old China. lib. bdg. 79.95 (ISBN 0-87968-491-7). Krishna Pr.

--The Wisdom of the Chinese: Their Philosophy in Sayings & Proverbs. lib. bdg. 79.95 (ISBN 0-87968-138-1). Krishna Pr.

--The Wisdom of the Hindus. 320p. 1981. pap. 14.00 (ISBN 0-89540-093-6, SB-093). Sun Pub.

Brown, Brian, ed. The Wisdom of the Chinese: Their Philosophy in Saying & Proverbs. 207p. 1983. 40.00 (ISBN 0-89984-129-5). Century Bookbindery.

Brown, Brisbane & Powers, Susan, eds. Practical Accounting Cost-Keeping for Contractors. 9th. ed. (Illus.). 250p. 1982. 21.95 (ISBN 0-911592-09-1). F R Walker.

Brown, Bruce. The Cheap Date Handbook: The Complete How-to Guide to Successful Inexpensive Dating. (Illus.). 176p. 1982. pap. 12.95 (ISBN 0-941256-00-6). New Lifestyle.

--The Complete Roommate Handbook: How to Sucessfully Find, Live with & Lose a Roommate. (Illus.). 32p. (Orig.). 1982. pap. 5.00 (ISBN 0-941256-01-4). New Lifestyle.

--The Complete Roommate Handbook: How to Successfully Find, Live with, or Lose a Roommate. LC 83-40144. (Illus.). 192p. 1984. pap. 4.50 (ISBN 0-385-19289-4, Dolp). Doubleday.

--Marx, Freud, & the Critique of Everyday Life: Toward a Permanent Cultural Revolution. LC 72-93460. 192p. 1973. pap. 4.95 (ISBN 0-85345-306-3). Monthly Rev.

--Mountain in the Clouds: A Search for the Wild Salmon. 249p. 1983. pap. 6.95 (ISBN 0-671-49264-0, Touchstone). S&S.

Brown, Bruce, jt. auth. see Nelson, Tom.

Brown, Bruce L., jt. auth. see Fallik, Fred.

Brown, Bruce R. Everything You Always Wanted to Know about Personal Computers but Didn't Know How to Ask. 172p. (Orig.). 1984. pap. cancelled (ISBN 0-8159-5409-3). Devin.

Brown, Bruce W., jt. auth. see Straus, Murray A.

Brown, Burnell R. & Blitt, Casey D. Clinical Anesthesiology: A Text for Medical Students & Practitoners. 1984. 29.95 (ISBN 0-8016-0858-9). Mosby.

Brown, Burnell R., Jr. Fluid & Blood Therapy in Anesthesia. LC 82-10075. (Contemporary Anesthesia Practice Ser.: Vol. 6). 189p. 1983. 26.00 (ISBN 0-8036-1273-7). Davis Co.

--Outpatient Anesthesia. LC 78-14424. (Contemporary Anesthesia Practice Ser.: Vol. 1). 1978. 14.00x (ISBN 0-8036-1256-7). Davis Co.

Brown, Burnell R., Jr., ed. Anesthesia & the Obese Patient. LC 81-12463. (Contemporary Anesthesia Practice Ser.: Vol. 5). (Illus.). 139p. 1981. 22.00x (ISBN 0-8036-1271-0). Davis Co.

--Anesthesia & the Patient with Endocrine Disease. LC 80-13067. (Contemporary Anesthesia Practice Ser.: Vol. 3). (Illus.). 210p. 1980. text ed. 24.00x (ISBN 0-8036-1264-8). Davis Co.

--Anesthesia & the Patient with Heart Disease. LC 79-17989. (Contemporary Anesthesia Practice Ser.: Vol. 2). (Illus.). 193p. 1980. text ed. 26.00x (ISBN 0-8036-1260-5). Davis Co.

--Anesthesia & the Patient with Liver Disease. LC 80-22088. (Contemporary Anesthesia Practice Ser.: Vol. 4). 190p. 1981. 24.00x (ISBN 0-8036-1268-0). Davis Co.

--Future Anesthesia Delivery Systems. LC 83-7844. (Contemporary Anesthesia Practice Ser.: Vol. 8). 254p. 1983. 32.00x (ISBN 0-8036-1277-X). Davis Co.

--New Pharmacologic Vistas in Anesthesia. LC 83-1846. (Contemporary Anesthesia Practice Ser.: Vol. 7). 199p. 1983. 26.00 (ISBN 0-8036-1275-3). Davis Co.

Brown, Byron W., Jr. & Hollander, Myles. Statistics: A Biomedical Introduction. LC 77-396. (Probability & Mathematical Statistics Ser). 456p. 1977. 34.95 (ISBN 0-471-11240-2, Pub. by Wiley-Interscience). Wiley.

Brown, Byrson A. The Essential Problems of Philosophy. (Illus.). 143p. 1983. 47.50 (ISBN 0-89266-455-X). Am Classical Coll Pr.

Brown, C. A. Shakespeare's Autobiographical Poems. 59.95 (ISBN 0-8490-1038-1). Gordon Pr.

Brown, C. A., jt. auth. see Blackler, F. H.

Brown, C. B., tr. see Volney, C. F.

Brown, C. C. High & Low from Life (Poems & Verse) 1975. pap. 2.00 (ISBN 0-9600378-0-2). C C Brown Pub.

--A New Look at Psychic Power. (Illus.). 1975. 6.00 (ISBN 0-9600378-1-0). C C Brown Pub.

--One Hundred & One Frauds to Avoid & More. 1980. pap. 2.00 (ISBN 0-9600378-2-9). C C Brown Pub.

--Philosophy of Hope. 1972. 2.95 (ISBN 0-9600378-0-2); pap. 2.00 (ISBN 0-9600378-3-7). C C Brown Pub.

--Revelations from the Half-Seer. 1977. pap. 3.00 (ISBN 0-9600378-4-5). C C Brown Pub.

Brown, C. C. & Saucer, Rayford T. Electronic Instrumentation for the Behavioral Sciences. (Illus.). 176p. 1958. 18.75x (ISBN 0-398-04222-5). C C Thomas.

Brown, C. C., tr. Sejarah Melayu or Malay Annals. (Oxford in Asia Historical Reprints). 1970. 10.50x (ISBN 0-19-638106-1). Oxford U Pr.

Brown, C. Caldwell, et al. The Many Facets of Touch. (PRT Ser.: No. 10). 1984. 7.50 (ISBN 0-931562-12-0). J & J Child Develop.

Brown, C. Christopher. Introduction to Maryland Civil Litigation. 258p. 1982. 30.00 (ISBN 0-87215-528-5). Michie Co.

Brown, C. H., ed. see Ameer, B., et al.

Brown, C. Harmon, jt. auth. see Puhl, Jacqueline L.

Brown, C. L., jt. auth. see Zimmermann, M. H.

Brown, C. M., jt. ed. see Nedwell, D. B.

Brown, C. N. Modern English-Greek Dictionary. 420p. (Gr. & Eng.). 1976. 12.50 (ISBN 0-686-92187-9, M-9592). French & Eur.

Brown, C. R. Joseph Rusling Meeker: Images of the Mississippi. LC 81-83078. (Delta Ser.). (Illus.). 40p. (Orig.). pap. 7.00 (ISBN 0-89280-018-6). Montgomery Mus.

Brown, C. Reynolds. American Paintings from the Collection of Mr. & Mrs. Charles H. Wampold, Jr. (Illus.). 20p. (Orig.). 1984. pap. 5.00 (ISBN 0-89280-023-2). Montgomery Mus.

--Clara Weaver Parrish. LC 80-82147. (Illus.). 1980. pap. 3.00 (ISBN 0-89280-016-X). Montgomery Mus.

--Montgomery Museum of Fine Arts: A Handbook to the Collection. LC 80-80053. (Illus.). 68p. 1980. pap. 3.00 (ISBN 0-89280-014-3). Montgomery Mus.

Brown, C. V. Taxation & the Incentive to Work. 2nd ed. (Illus.). 1983. 29.95 (ISBN 0-19-877213-0); pap. 13.50 (ISBN 0-19-877212-2). Oxford U Pr.

Brown, C. V., ed. Taxation & Labour Supply. (Illus.). 304p. 1981. text ed. 49.95x (ISBN 0-04-336073-4). Allen Unwin.

Brown, Calvin, et al, eds. Masterworks of World Literature, 2 vols. 3rd ed. Incl. Vol. 1. Homer to Cervantes. text ed. 24.50x (ISBN 0-8290-0130-1); Vol. II. Shakespeare to Sartre. text ed. 24.50x (ISBN 0-8290-0131-X). LC 75-92884. 1970. Irvington.

Brown, Calvin S. Archaeology of Mississippi. LC 72-5011. (Antiquities of the New World Ser.: Vol. 16). (Illus.). Repr. of 1926 ed. 49.50 (ISBN 0-404-57316-9). AMS Pr.

--A Glossary of Faulkner's South. LC 75-43308. (Illus.). 1976. 26.00x (ISBN 0-300-01944-0); pap. 6.95x (ISBN 0-300-02240-9). Yale U Pr.

--The Later English Drama. 1978. Repr. of 1898 ed. lib. bdg. 40.00 (ISBN 0-8492-3722-X). R West.

Brown, Carl. American Law & the Trained Fighter. (Series 431). (Orig.). 1984. pap. 5.95 (ISBN 0-89750-091-1). Ohara Pubns.

--Essential dBASE II. write for info. Wadsworth Pub.

--Essential dBASE II. (Computer Science Ser.). 128p. 1985. pap. text ed. 12.95 (ISBN 0-534-05070-0). Brooks-Cole.

--Essential dBASE III. write for info. Wadsworth Pub.

--Essential WordStar. LC 84-23891. (Computer Science Ser.). 128p. 1985. pap. 9.95 (ISBN 0-534-04950-8). Brooks-Cole.

--Essential WordStar: With MailMerge & SpellStar. write for info. Wadsworth Pub.

Brown, Carl & Henschell, Todd. American Law & the Trained Fighter. (Orig.). 1983. pap. 5.95 (ISBN 0-317-01215-0). Ohara Pubns.

Brown, Carl F. & Brown, Mac H. Handbook of Reading Activities: From Teacher to Parent to Child. 162p. (Orig.). 1982. pap. 12.95 (ISBN 0-89334-036-7). Humanics Ltd.

Brown, Carleton. Religious Lyrics of the Thirteenth, Fourteenth, & Fifteenth Centuries, 3 vols. 300.00 (ISBN 0-8490-0942-1). Gordon Pr.

Brown, Carleton & Robbins, Rossell H. Index of Middle English Verse. xix, 785p. 1943. 40.00x (ISBN 0-87352-017-3, Z2). Modern Lang.

Brown, Carleton F. A Register of Middle English Religious & Didactic Verse. 52.00 (ISBN 0-8369-7155-8, 7987). Ayer Co Pubs.

Brown, Carol & Glascock, Scot. Eating is Believing: An Eater's Guide to Seattle's Great Inexpensive Restaurants. rev., 2nd ed. (Illus.). 144p. (Orig.). 1985. pap. 6.95 (ISBN 0-913481-01-7). Small Pleasures.

Brown, Carol & Glascock, Scott. Eating is Believing: An Eater's Guide to Seattle's Great Inexpensive Restaurants. (Illus.). 144p. (Orig.). 1983. pap. 5.95 (ISBN 0-913481-00-9). Small Pleasures.

Brown, Carol W. The Minicomputer Simplified: An Executive's Guide to the Basics. LC 80-1031. (Illus.). 1980. 14.95 (ISBN 0-02-905130-4). Free Pr.

Brown, Carolyn, jt. auth. see Brown, Stephen.

Brown, Carolyn C. Developing Christian Education in a Smaller Church. LC 81-17563. (Griggs Educational Resources Ser.). 96p. (Orig.). 1982. pap. 7.75 (ISBN 0-687-10508-0). Abingdon.

--Youth Ministries: Thinking Big With Small Groups. 96p. 1984. pap. 7.50 (ISBN 0-687-47203-2). Abingdon.

Brown, Carolyn S. & Brown, Joseph H. Counseling Children for Social Competence: A Manual for Teachers & Counselors. 126p. 1982. spiral bdg. 15.75x (ISBN 0-398-04512-7). C C Thomas.

Brown, Carolyn S., jt. auth. see Brown, Joseph H.

Brown, Carroll N., tr. see Andreades, A. M. & Finley, Moses.

Brown, Carter. Busted Wheeler. 1979. pap. 1.50 (ISBN 0-505-51414-1, Pub. by Tower Bks). Dorchester Pub Co.

--Death to a Downbeat. (Orig.). 1980. pap. 1.75 (ISBN 0-505-51572-5, Pub. by Tower Bks). Dorchester Pub Co.

--Donavan's Delight. 1979. pap. 1.50 (ISBN 0-505-51382-X, Pub. by Tower Bks). Dorchester Pub Co.

--Kiss Michelle Goodbye. 176p. (Orig.). 1981. pap. 1.95 (ISBN 0-505-51756-6, Pub. by Tower Bks). Dorchester Pub Co.

--Model for Murder. (Orig.). 1980. pap. 1.50 (ISBN 0-505-51527-X, Pub. by Tower Bks). Dorchester Pub Co.

--The Phantom Lady. (Orig.). 1980. pap. 1.50 (ISBN 0-505-51516-4, Pub. by Tower Bks). Dorchester Pub Co.

--The Rip-Off. 1979. pap. 1.50 (ISBN 0-505-51425-7, Pub. by Tower Bks). Dorchester Pub Co.

--See It Again, Sam. 1979. pap. 1.50 (ISBN 0-505-51415-X, Pub. by Tower Bks). Dorchester Pub Co.

--The Spanking Girls. 1979. pap. 1.50 (ISBN 0-505-51383-8, Pub. by Tower Bks). Dorchester Pub Co.

--The Strawberry-Blonde Jungle. 1979. pap. 1.50 (ISBN 0-505-51405-2, Pub. by Tower Bks). Dorchester Pub Co.

--The Swingers. (Orig.). 1980. pap. 1.75 (ISBN 0-505-51583-0, Pub. by Tower Bks). Dorchester Pub Co.

--The Wicked Widow. (Orig.). 1981. pap. 1.75 (ISBN 0-505-51610-1, Pub. by Tower Bks). Dorchester Pub Co.

Brown, Cassie. Standing into Danger. LC 85-4473. (Illus.). 375p. 1985. pap. 9.95 (ISBN 0-385-23144-X). Doubleday.

Brown, Catherine. Scottish Regional Recipes. 1984. 35.00x (ISBN 0-904002-37-3, Pub. by R Drew Scotland). State Mutual Bk.

Brown, Catherine, ed. see Damon, S. Foster.

Brown, Catherine C., ed. Childhood Learning Disabilities & Prenatal Risk. (PRT Ser.: No. 9). 1983. 6.00 (ISBN 0-931562-11-2). J & J Child Develop.

--Infants at Risk: Assessment & Intervention. (Pediatric Round Table Ser.: No. 5). 130p. (Orig.). 1981. pap. text ed. 6.00 (ISBN 0-931562-06-6). J & J Child Develop.

Brown, Catherine C. & Gottfried, Allen, eds. Play Interactions: The Role of Toys & Parental Involvement in Children's Development. (Pediatric Round Table Ser.: No. 11). 150p. (Orig.). 1985. pap. text ed. write for info. (ISBN 0-931562-13-9). J & J Child Develop.

Brown, Catherine R., et al. Building for the Arts: A Guidebook for the Planning & Design of Cultural Facilities. LC 83-27339. (Illus.). 272p. 1984. pap. 21.95x (ISBN 0-9611710-1-4). Western States.

Brown, Cathy J. & Paterson, Debi. Bouncy Bunny's Birthday: A Family Story About Bravery. (Illus.). 32p. (Orig.). (gr. 1-3). 1985. pap. 8.75 (ISBN 0-9614796-0-4). C J Brown.

Brown, Cecil. Days Without Weather. 250p. 1982. 12.95 (ISBN 0-374-13530-4). FS&G.

Brown, Cecil H. Language & Living Things: Uniformities in Folk Classification & Naming. 300p. 1984. text ed. 35.00 (ISBN 0-8135-1008-2). Rutgers U Pr.

Brown, Cedric C. John Milton's Aristocratic Entertainments. (Illus.). 220p. Date not set. price not set (ISBN 0-521-30440-7). Cambridge U Pr.

Brown, Charlene, jt. auth. see Chamberlin, Bill F.

Brown, Charlene, et al. The Media & the People. LC 78-8375. 480p. 1978. lib. bdg. 23.50 (ISBN 0-88275-689-3). Krieger.

Brown, Charlene J., et al. The Media & the People. LC 77-27977. 1978. pap. 20.95 (ISBN 0-03-019056-8, HoltC). HR&W.

Brown, Charles. The Art of Rock & Roll. (Illus.). 208p. 1983. pap. 18.95 (ISBN 0-13-047076-7). P-H.

--The Divine Glory of Christ. 96p. 1983. pap. 2.65 (ISBN 0-85151-342-5). Banner of Truth.

Brown, Charles & Kreta, Eleanor. Introduction to Data Entry Devices with a Subset of BASIC. 1979. pap. text ed. 6.95 (ISBN 0-8403-1952-5, 40195201). Kendall-Hunt.

Brown, Charles, ed. Russell Kirk: A Bibliography. (Illus.). 172p. 1981. 7.50 (ISBN 0-916699-05-6). Clarke His.

Brown, Charles A. Life of John Keats. LC 74-3172. 1937. lib. bdg. 17.50 (ISBN 0-8414-3116-7). Folcroft.

--Shakespeare's Autobiographical Poems. LC 76-39541. Repr. of 1838 ed. 21.50 (ISBN 0-404-01127-6). AMS Pr.

Brown, Charles B. Arthur Mervyn, or Memoirs of the Year Seventeen Ninety-Three. Krause, Sydney J. & Reid, S. W., eds. LC 79-92808. (The Novels & Related Works of Charles Brockden Brown Ser.: Vol. 3). 590p. 1980. 35.00x (ISBN 0-87338-241-2). Kent St U Pr.

--Edgar Huntly. Stineback, David, ed. (Masterworks of Literature Ser). 1973. pap. 6.95x (ISBN 0-8084-0360-5). New Coll U Pr.

--Edgar Huntly: Memories of a Sleep Walker. Krause, Sydney & Reid, S. W., eds. LC 84-4376. (The Novels & Related Works of Charles Brockden Brown, C.E.A.A. Edition Ser.: No. 4). 590p. 1985. 35.00x (ISBN 0-87338-305-2). Kent St U Pr.

--Edgar Huntly: Or, Memoirs of a Sleepwalker, 3 vols. LC 79-144587. Repr. of 1799 ed. 75.00 (ISBN 0-404-01130-6). AMS Pr.

--Jane Talbot. 237p. 1980. Repr. of 1857 ed. lib. bdg. 40.00 (ISBN 0-89987-062-7). Century Bookbindery.

--Jane Talbot. 12.50x (ISBN 0-87556-042-3). Saifer.

--Novels of Charles Brockden Brown, 6 Vols. 1968. Repr. of 1887 ed. Set. 114.00 (ISBN 0-8337-0398-6). B Franklin.

--Ormond. Marchand, Ernest, ed. (Library of Classics Ser: No. 24). (Illus.). 1962. pap. text ed. 6.50 (ISBN 0-02-842080-2). Hafner.

--Ormond, or the Secret Witness. Krause, Sydney & Reid, S. W., eds. LC 82-14904. (The Novels & Related Works of Charles Brockden Brown: Vol. 2). 478p. 1983. 35.00X (ISBN 0-87338-277-3). Kent St U Pr.

--The Rhapsodist & Other Uncollected Writings. LC 43-9591. 1977. Repr. of 1943 ed. 35.00x (ISBN 0-8201-1203-8). Schol Facsimiles.

--Wieland & "Memoirs of Carwin". Krause, Sydney J. & Reid, S. W., eds. LC 78-15330. 310p. 1978. pap. text ed. 6.25x (ISBN 0-87338-220-X). Kent St U Pr.

--Wieland: Or, the Transformation. pap. 4.95 (ISBN 0-385-03100-9, Anch). Doubleday.

--Wieland: Or, the Transformation. Pattee, F. L., ed. LC 58-13328. 1969. pap. 6.95 (ISBN 0-15-696680-8, Harv). HarBraceJ.

--Wieland: Or, the Transformation. Bd. with Memoirs of the Carwin Biloquist: A Fragment. 351p. Date not set. Repr. of 1926 ed. lib. bdg. 40.00 (ISBN 0-89760-195-5). Telegraph Bks.

--Wieland or the Transformation Together with Memoirs of Carwin the Biloquist: A Fragment. 351p. Date not set. Repr. of 1926 ed. lib. bdg. 40.00 (ISBN 0-89760-195-5). Telegraph Bks.

Brown, Charles Brockden. The Novels & Related Works of Charles Brockden Brown: Wieland and Memoirs of Carwin, Vol. 1. Kraus, Sydney J. & Reid, S. W., eds. LC 74-79474. (Illus.). 456p. 1977. 35.00x (ISBN 0-87338-160-2). Kent St U Pr.

Brown, Charles C. Perak Malay: Papers on Malay Subjects. LC 77-87481. 128p. Repr. of 1921 ed. 24.50 (ISBN 0-404-16797-7). AMS Pr.

Brown, Charles F. Letters of Artemus Ward to Charles E. Wilson, 1858-1861. 59.95 (ISBN 0-8490-0511-6). Gordon Pr.

Brown, Charles H. Agents of Manifest Destiny: The Lives & Times of the Filibusters. LC 79-383. xi, 525p. 1980. 31.50 (ISBN 0-8078-1361-3). U of NC Pr.

--News Editing & Display. LC 74-109285. (Illus.). 457p. Repr. of 1952 ed. lib. bdg. 24.75x (ISBN 0-8371-3828-0, BRNE). Greenwood.

Brown, Charles H., jt. ed. see Rubin, Joseph J.

Brown, Charles M., jt. auth. see Liljeblad, Sue E.

Brown, Charles P. Dictionary of Telugu & English: Explaining English Idioms & Phrases in Telugu, 2 vols. (Eng. & Telugu.). 1976. Repr. of 1958 ed. 195.00 (ISBN 0-518-19008-0). Ayer Co Pubs.

Brown, Charles R. They Were Giants. facs. ed. LC 68-54332. (Essay Index Reprint Ser). 1934. 18.00 (ISBN 0-8369-0257-2). Ayer Co Pubs.

--They Were Giants. (Essay Index Reprint Ser.). 285p. 1982. Repr. of 1934 ed. lib. bdg. 15.00 (ISBN 0-8290-0835-7). Irvington.

--Yale Talks. 1919. 24.50x (ISBN 0-686-51327-4). Elliots Bks.

Brown, Charles R. & Yale Divinity School Faculty Members. Education for Christian Service: A Volume in Commemoration of the 100th Anniversary of the Divinity School of Yale University. 1922. 49.50x (ISBN 0-685-89749-4). Elliots Bks.

Brown, Charles R., jt. auth. see Gabriel, Ralph H.

Brown, Charles T. Country & Western Music. (Illus.). 250p. 1985. text ed. 22.95 (ISBN 0-13-184284-6); pap. 12.95 (ISBN 0-13-184276-5). P-H.

--The Rock & Roll Story. (Illus.). 128p. 1984. pap. 12.95 (ISBN 0-13-782227-8). P-H.

Brown, Charles T. & Keller, Paul T. Monologue to Dialogue: An Exploration of Interpersonal Communication. 2nd ed. LC 78-16541. (Special Communication Ser.). 1979. pap. 21.95 (ISBN 0-13-600825-9). P-H.

Brown, Charles V. The Nigerian Banking System. LC 66-19192. pap. 53.00 (ISBN 0-317-27799-5, 2015289). Bks Demand UMI.

Brown, Charles W. American Star Speaker. facs. ed. LC 79-139755. (Granger Index Reprint Ser). 1902. 35.50 (ISBN 0-8369-6209-5). Ayer Co Pubs.

Brown, Charles W., ed. Comic Recitations & Readings. facs. ed. LC 72-139756. (Granger Index Reprint Ser). 1902. 15.00 (ISBN 0-8369-6210-9). Ayer Co Pubs.

Brown, Charline H. Brief Lightning. LC 79-50433. 1979. 9.95 (ISBN 0-9602570-0-4). Bayou Pub Co.

Brown, Charlotte & Hyman, Paula. The Jewish Woman in America. 1977. pap. 6.95 (ISBN 0-452-25479-5, Z5282, Plume). NAL.

Brown, Chas. William Cullen Bryant. LC 79-143949. (Illus.). 1971. 12.50 (ISBN 0-684-12370-3, ScribT). Scribner.

Brown, Cherie. The Art of Coalition Building: A Guide for Community Leaders. LC 84-70911. 56p. 1984. pap. 3.50 (ISBN 0-87495-053-8). Am Jewish Comm.

Brown, Cheryl L. & Olson, Karen, eds. Feminist Criticism: Essays on Theory, Poetry & Prose. LC 78-8473. 383p. 1978. 21.00 (ISBN 0-8108-1143-X). Scarecrow.

Brown, Chris, intro. by. World Repeater Atlas. 274p. 1980. pap. 2.00 (ISBN 0-88006-005-0, BK 7315). Green Pub Inc.

Brown, Christopher. Dutch Paintings. (The National Gallery Schools of Painting Ser.). (Illus.). 116p. 1984. 21.95 (ISBN 0-00-217145-7, Pub. by Salem Hse Ltd); pap. 14.95 (ISBN 0-00-217146-5). Merrimack Pub Cir.

--Ghostbusters Training Manual. 24p. (gr. 3-7). 1985. pap. 1.95 (ISBN 0-89954-358-8). Antioch Pub Co.

--Images of a Golden Past: Dutch Genre Painting of the 17th Century. LC 84-6257. (Illus.). 240p. 1984. 49.95 (ISBN 0-89659-439-4). Abbeville Pr.

--Misty the Mermaid. (Illus.). 24p. (gr. 3-7). 1985. pap. 1.95 (ISBN 0-89954-293-X). Antioch Pub Co.

--Misty the Mermaid in Song of the Whales. (Illus.). 24p. (gr. 3-7). 1984. pap. 1.95 (ISBN 0-89954-293-X). Antioch Pub Co.

--The Paintings of Carel Fabritius: Complete Edition with a Catalogue Raisonne. LC 80-69741. (Illus.). 1981. 85.00x (ISBN 0-8014-1394-X, Cornell Phaidon Books). Cornell U Pr.

--Van Dyck. LC 82-72566. (Illus.). 240p. 1983. 50.00x (ISBN 0-8014-1537-3). Cornell U Pr.

--Whisper & the Secret of Dark Hollow. (Whisper the Winged Unicorn Ser.). (Illus.). 24p. (gr. 3-7). 1985. pap. 1.95 (ISBN 0-89954-289-1). Antioch Pub Co.

--Whisper the Winged Unicorn in Flying Is Fun. (Whisper the Winged Unicorn Ser.). (Illus.). 22p. (ps-2). 1985. 2.95 (ISBN 0-89954-327-8). Antioch Pub Co.

--A Wish for Whisper. (Whisper the Winged Unicorn Ser.). (Illus.). 24p. (gr. 2-6). 1984. pap. 1.95 (ISBN 0-89954-278-6). Antioch Pub Co.

Brown, Christopher & Dunham, Judith. New Bay Area Painting & Sculpture. LC 82-80488. 1982. pap. 7.50 (ISBN 0-9608270-0-5). Squeezer.

Brown, Christopher, adapted by. Ghostbusters. 1984. 1.95 (ISBN 0-89954-296-4). Antioch Pub Co.

Brown, Christopher, ed. Noah's Ark. (Illus.). 24p. (gr. 2-6). 1984. pap. 1.95 (ISBN 0-89954-287-5). Antioch Pub Co.

--Wild & Wonderful Horses. (Illus.). 24p. (gr. 3-7). 1985. pap. 1.95 (ISBN 0-89954-295-6). Antioch Pub Co.

Brown, Christopher C. & Thosing, William B., eds. English Prose & Criticism, Nineteen Hundred to Nineteen-Fifty: A Guide to Information Sources. LC 83-11581. (American Literature, English Literature, & World Literatures in English Information Guide Ser.: Vol. 42). 553p. 1983. 60.00x (ISBN 0-8103-1236-0). Gale.

Brown, Christopher K., jt. auth. see Gruner, Mark.

Brown, Christopher M., jt. auth. see Ballard, Dana H.

Brown, Christopher P. The Political & Social Economy of Commodity Control. LC 79-88568. 394p. 1980. 49.95 (ISBN 0-03-053351-1). Praeger.

Brown, Christopher W. Life Songs. (Illus.). 102p. 1984. 6.95 (ISBN 0-916193-01-2); pap. 4.95 (ISBN 0-317-03705-6). Heartwind Pubns.

--Song Poems. (Illus.). 130p. (gr. 1-12). 1984. pap. 9.50 (ISBN 0-916193-02-0). Heartwind Pubns.

Brown, Christy. Collected Poems. 216p. 1983. 16.95 (ISBN 0-436-07089-8, Pub. by Secker & Warburg UK). David & Charles.

--Down All the Days. 1970. 14.95 (ISBN 0-436-07090-1, Pub. by Secker & Warburg UK). David & Charles.

--A Promising Career. 248p. 1983. 13.95 (ISBN 0-436-07097-9, Pub. by Secker & Warburg UK). David & Charles.

Brown, Clair. Louisiana Trees & Shrubs. 1965. 7.50 (ISBN 0-87511-012-6). Claitors.

Brown, Clair A. Wildflowers of Louisiana & Its Adjoining States. LC 72-79327. (Illus.). xi, 248p. 1972. 20.00 (ISBN 0-8071-0232-6); pap. 8.95 (ISBN 0-8071-0780-8). La State U Pr.

Brown, Clara D. & Smith, Lynn S. Serials: Past, Present & Future. LC 80-81267. 1980. 19.50x (ISBN 0-913956-05-8). EBSCO Ind.

Brown, Clare. Austrian Country Inns & Castles. (Karen Brown's Travel Press: European Country Inns Ser.). (Illus.). 288p. (Orig.). 1986. pap. 10.95 (ISBN 0-930328-13-2). Travel Pr.

--Italian Country Inns & Villas. 2nd ed. (European Country Inns Ser.). (Illus.). 224p. 1986. pap. 10.95 (ISBN 0-930328-16-7). Travel Pr.

Brown, Clare, jt. auth. see Brown, Karen.

Brown, Clarence. Mandelstam. LC 72-90491. (Illus.). 400p. 1973. 42.50 (ISBN 0-521-20142-X); pap. 14.95 (ISBN 0-521-29347-2). Cambridge U Pr.

Brown, Clarence, ed. The Portable Twentieth Century Russian Reader. (Portable Library). 624p. (Orig.). 1985. pap. 7.95 (ISBN 0-14-015100-1). Penguin.

Brown, Clarence, ed. see Robertson, R. Hope.

Brown, Clarence, et al, trs. see Mandelstam, Osip.

Brown, Clarence A. & Zoellner, Ronald. The Strategy of Composition: A Rhetoric with Readings. LC 68-13470. pap. 160.00 (ISBN 0-317-09507-2, 2012470). Bks Demand UMI.

Brown, Clarence W. & Ghiselli, Edwin E. Scientific Method in Psychology. LC 55-6150. (McGraw-Hill Series in Psychology). pap. 95.50 (ISBN 0-317-08270-1, 2003752). Bks Demand UMI.

Brown, Clarence W., jt. auth. see Ghiselli, Edwin E.

Brown, Claude. Manchild in the Promised Land. (gr. 8 up). 1965. 15.95 (ISBN 0-02-517320-0). Macmillan.

--Manchild in the Promised Land. (YA) (RL 7). 1971. pap. 3.95 (ISBN 0-451-13445-1, Sig). NAL.

Brown, Claudia. Chinese Ceramics: The Wong Collection. LC 82-80346. (Illus.). 100p. (Orig.). 1982. pap. 10.00 (ISBN 0-910407-06-1). Phoenix Art.

--Chinese Cloisonne: The Clague Collection. LC 80-80709. (Illus.). 181p. (Orig.). 1980. 30.00 (ISBN 0-910407-05-3); pap. 20.00 (ISBN 0-910407-04-5). Phoenix Art.

Brown, Claudine K. Something Old, Something Nubian. (Illus.). 20p. (gr. 3-7). pap. 1.25 (ISBN 0-686-74788-7). Bklyn Mus.

Brown, Cliff. George Brown: Sprint Superstar. 141p. 15.95 (ISBN 0-85429-295-0, F295). Haynes Pubns.

Brown, Clifford A. Jung's Hermeneutic of Doctrine. LC 80-20795. (American Academy of Religion Dissertation Ser.). 1981. pap. 12.50 (ISBN 0-89130-437-1, 01-01-32). Scholars Pr GA.

Brown, Clifford D. Emergence of Income Reporting: An Historical Study. LC 71-634897. 1971. pap. 4.25 (ISBN 0-87744-106-5). Mich St U Pr.

Brown, Clifford W., Jr. & Walker, Robert J., eds. A Campaign of Ideas: The Nineteen Eighty Anderson-Lucey Platform. LC 84-6564. (Contributions in American Studies Ser.: No. 76). lxxii, 486p. 1984. lib. bdg. 35.00 (ISBN 0-313-24535-5, BCA/). Greenwood.

Brown, Clifton F., jt. auth. see Williams, Ethel L.

Brown, Clifton F., compiled by. Ethiopian Perspectives: A Bibliographical Guide to the History of Ethiopia. LC 77-89111. (African Bibliographic Center, Special Bibliographic Series, New Ser.: No. 5). lib. bdg. 39.95 (ISBN 0-8371-9850-X, BET/). Greenwood.

Brown, Clive. Louis Spohr: A Critical Biography. 376p. 1984. 49.50 (ISBN 0-521-23990-7). Cambridge U Pr.

Brown, Colin. Black & White Britain: The Third P. S. I. Survey. xvii, 420p. (Orig.). pap. 17.50x (ISBN 0-435-83125-9); 34.00x (ISBN 0-435-83124-0). Gower Pub Co.

--Jesus in European Protestant Thought, 1778-1860. (Studies in Historical Theology: Vol. 1). 380p. 1985. lib. bdg. 35.00x (ISBN 0-939464-18-7). Labyrinth Pr.

--Miracles & the Critical Mind. LC 83-16600. 432p. 1984. 19.95 (ISBN 0-8028-3590-2). Eerdmans.

--The New International Dictionary of New Testament Theology, 3 vols. Set. 100.00 (ISBN 0-310-21928-0). Zondervan.

Brown, Colin & Edwards, Tony. Revolution in China, 1911-1949. 1974. pap. text ed. 8.50x (ISBN 0-435-31090-9). Heinemann Ed.

Brown, Colin, jt. auth. see Chadwich-Jones, J. K.

Brown, Colin, ed. The New International Dictionary of New Testament Theology, Vol. 1,a-f. 1976. 29.95 (ISBN 0-310-21890-X). Zondervan.

--The New International Dictionary of New Testament Theology, Vol. 2. 1977. 31.95 (ISBN 0-310-21900-0). Zondervan.

--The New International Dictionary of New Testament Theology, Vol. 3 (Pri-Z) 1978. 44.95 (ISBN 0-310-21910-8). Zondervan.

Brown, Conrad & Gavett, Bruce. Skiing for Beginners. (Illus.). (gr. 6 up). 1971. 5.95 (ISBN 0-684-12510-2, ScribJ). Scribner.

Brown, Constance C., et al. Preparing Documents with UNIX. (Illus.). 240p. 1986. text ed. 21.95 (ISBN 0-13-699976-X). P-H.

Brown, Cora, et al. The South American Cookbook: Including Central America, Mexico, & the West Indies. 13.50 (ISBN 0-8446-0041-5). Peter Smith.

Brown, Cornelius. An Appreciative Life of the Right Honorable the Earl of Beacons Field, 2 vols. 1882. 100.00 (ISBN 0-8274-1874-4). R West.

Brown, Courtney C. Beyond the Bottom Line. LC 79-1954. (Studies of the Modern Corporation Ser.). 1979. 13.95 (ISBN 0-02-904660-2). Free Pr.

--The Dean Meant Business. LC 83-20625. 288p. (Orig.). 1985. 17.50 (ISBN 0-9612584-0-3). Grad Sch Bus NY.

--Putting the Corporate Board to Work. LC 75-14918. (Studies of the Modern Corporation). 1976. 14.95 (ISBN 0-02-904760-9). Free Pr.

Brown, Courtney C. & Smith, E. Everett, eds. The Director Looks at His Job. LC 57-13485. 150p. 1958. 19.00x (ISBN 0-231-02228-X). Columbia U Pr.

Brown, Craig. The Marsh Marlowe Letters. 152p. 1985. 11.95 (ISBN 0-434-08885-4, Pub. by W Heinemann Ltd). David & Charles.

Brown, Craig & Cunliffe, Lesley. The Book of Royal Lists. 292p. (Orig.). 1983. 15.95 (ISBN 0-671-46507-4); pap. 7.95 (ISBN 0-671-47282-8). Summit Bks.

Brown, Curtis M. Boundary Control & Legal Principles. 2nd ed. LC 68-8712. 371p. 1969. 42.95 (ISBN 0-471-10660-7, Pub. by Wiley-Interscience). Wiley.

Brown, Curtis M., et al. Evidence & Procedures for Boundary Location. 2nd ed. LC 81-11440. 450p. 1981. 47.50x (ISBN 0-471-08382-8, Pub. by Wiley-Interscience). Wiley.

Brown, Cynthia & Kohl, Herb. Spelling for Fun, Bk. 2. (Illus.). 48p. (gr. 4-9). wkbk. 3.00 (ISBN 0-939408-01-5). Continuity Pr.

--Spelling for Fun Book 1. (Illus.). 48p. (gr. 5-9). wkbk 3.00 (ISBN 0-939408-00-7). Continuity Pr.

Brown, Cynthia, ed. With Friends Like These: The Americas Watch Report on Human Rights & U. S. Policy in Latin America. LC 84-26410. 241p. 1985. pap. 8.95 (ISBN 0-394-72949-8). Pantheon.

Brown, Cynthia J. The Shaping of History & Poetry in Late Medieval France. LC 85-61597. 1985. 18.95 (ISBN 0-917786-10-6). Summa Pubns.

Brown, Cynthia S. Alexander Meiklejohn: Teacher of Freedom. Ginger, Ann F., ed. LC 81-81355. (Studies in Law & Social Change: No. 2). (Illus.). 304p. 1981. 13.95 (ISBN 0-913876-16-X, 176); pap. 7.95 (ISBN 0-913876-17-8, 177). Meiklejohn Civ Lib.

Brown, Cyril, jt. auth. see Brown, Emmett E.

Brown, D. Price Guide to Antiques. 11th ed. 1985. cancelled 9.95 (ISBN 0-87069-392-1). Wallace-Homestead.

--Systems Analysis & Design for Safety. 399p. 1976. text ed. 31.95 (ISBN 0-13-881177-6). P-H.

Brown, D. A., tr. see Fedorov, K. N.

Brown, D. B. English Drawings from the Ashmolean Museum (16th-18th Century) 45p. 1983. 30.00x (ISBN 0-907849-03-2, Pub. by Ashmolean Mus UK). State Mutual Bk.

Brown, D. C. High Peak Power Nd: Class Laser Systems. (Springer Series in Optical Sciences: Vol. 25). (Illus.). 276p. 1981. 47.00 (ISBN 0-387-10516-6). Springer-Verlag.

Brown, D. Clayton. Electricity for Rural America: The Fight for the REA. LC 79-8287. (Contributions in Economics & Economic History Ser.: No. 29). (Illus.). 1980. lib. bdg. 29.95 (ISBN 0-313-21478-6, BEF/). Greenwood.

Brown, D. F. A Monographic Study of the Fern Genus Woodsia. (Illus.). 1964. 21.00 (ISBN 3-7682-5416-X). Lubrecht & Cramer.

Brown, D. G., jt. auth. see Warne, A. E.

Brown, D. J. The Pyrimidines: Supplement 2. (Chemistry of Hetercyclic Compounds Monographs). 1184p. 1985. 225.00 (ISBN 0-471-02745-6). Wiley.

Brown, D. J., jt. ed. see Lister, J. H.

Brown, D. K. An Introduction to the Finite Element Method Using BASIC Programs. 196p. 1984. pap. 16.95 (ISBN 0-412-00581-6, NO. 9021, Pub. by Chapman & Hall); 34.00 (ISBN 0-412-00571-9, NO. 9020). Methuen Inc.

Brown, D. S. Freshwater Snails of Africa & Their Medical Importance. 488p. 1980. cancelled (ISBN 0-85066-145-5). Taylor & Francis.

Brown, D. S. W., et al. The Geological Evolution of Australia & New Zealand. 1968. pap. 17.00 (ISBN 0-08-012277-9). Pergamon.

Brown, Dakota B. Data on Some Virginia Families. (Illus.). 282p. 1979. 25.00 (ISBN 0-686-63646-5). Va Bk.

Brown, Dale. Cooking of Scandinavia. LC 68-21587. (Foods of the World Ser.). (Illus.). (gr. 7 up). 1968. lib. bdg. 19.94 (ISBN 0-8094-0058-8, Pub. by Time-Life). Silver.

--Simulations on Brethren History. pap. 6.95 (ISBN 0-87178-794-6). Brethren.

--World of Velazquez. LC 77-84575. (Library of Art Ser.). (Illus.). (gr. 6 up). 1969. 19.94 (ISBN 0-8094-0281-5, Pub. by Time-Life). Silver.

Brown, Dale, et al. American Cooking: The Melting Pot. LC 76-173191. (Foods of the World Ser.). (Illus.). (gr. 7 up). 1971. lib. bdg. 19.94 (ISBN 0-8094-0082-0, Pub. by Time-Life). Silver.

Brown, Dale W. Biblical Pacifism: A Peace Church Perspective. 176p. 1985. pap. 8.95 (ISBN 0-87178-108-5). Brethren.

--Brethren & Pacifism. 1970. pap. 4.95 (ISBN 0-87178-107-7). Brethren.

--Brethren & Pacifism. rev. ed. 1985. pap. write for info. Brethren.

--Flamed by the Spirit. 1978. pap. 2.95 (ISBN 0-87178-277-4). Brethren.

Brown, Dale W., ed. see Hatfield, Mark, et al.

Brown, Daniel, jt. auth. see Cannon, Tom.

Brown, Daniel J. Assessing Retail Trade: A Review of the Consumer Behaviour Literature. 1978. 90.00x (ISBN 0-905440-77-3, Pub. by MCB Pubns). State Mutual Bk.

Brown, Daniel J. & Burnette, William E. Connections: A Rhetoric-Short Prose Reader. LC 83-82434. 400p. 1983. pap. text ed. 15.95 (ISBN 0-395-34101-9); instr's manual 2.00 (ISBN 0-395-34102-7). HM.

Brown, Daniel P. Giovanni's Europe. LC 83-81929. (Illus.). 50p. (Orig.). 1983. pap. 6.95x (ISBN 0-9612528-0-4). Giovanni's Tour.

--The Protectorate & The Northumberland Conspiracy: Political Intrigue in the Reign of Edward VI. LC 80-65156. (European History: Ser. I-1001). (Illus.). 74p. (Orig.). 1982. pap. 3.15x (ISBN 0-930860-02-0). Golden West Hist.

--The Tragedy of Libby & Andersonville Prison Camps. LC 79-54263. (U. S. History Civil War Ser. Ii: No. 1102). (Illus.). 1980. pap. 2.95x (ISBN 0-930860-01-2). Golden West Hist.

Brown, Daphne M. Mother Tongue in English. LC 77-83987. 1979. 27.95 (ISBN 0-521-21873-X); pap. 11.95 (ISBN 0-521-29299-9). Cambridge U Pr.

Brown, David. AIGA Graphic Design U. S. A, No. 3. (The Annual of the American Institute of Graphic Arts). (Illus.). 432p. 1982. 45.00 (ISBN 0-8230-2143-2). Watson-Guptill.

--Anglo-Saxon England. (Illus.). 110p. 1978. 18.50x (ISBN 0-8476-6045-1). Rowman.

--Chad Can Not Be Rotten. (Illus.). 1984. pap. cancelled (ISBN 0-318-01383-5). CLCB Pr.

--Choices: Ethics & the Christian. (Faith & the Future Ser.). 176p. 1984. pap. 24.95x (ISBN 0-631-13182-5); pap. 6.95 (ISBN 0-631-13222-8). Basil Blackwell.

--The Divine Trinity. LC 85-18941. 328p. 1985. 24.95 (ISBN 0-87548-439-5). Open Court.
--Draw Birds. LC 79-64251. (Learn to Draw Ser.). (Illus.). 1980. pap. 2.25 (ISBN 0-8008-2276-5, Pentalic). Taplinger.
--Draw Cats. LC 78-14061. (Learn to Draw Ser.). (Illus.). 1980. pap. 2.25 (ISBN 0-8008-4579-X, Pentalic). Taplinger.
--Draw Horses. LC 79-87588. (Learn to Draw Ser.). (Illus.). 48p. (Orig.). 1981. pap. 2.25 (ISBN 0-8008-2280-3, Pentalic). Taplinger.
--Draw Wild Animals. LC 78-14064. (Learn to Draw Ser.). (Illus.). 1980. pap. 2.25 (ISBN 0-8008-4589-7, Pentalic). Taplinger.
--Electromechanical Energy Conversion. (Illus.). 624p. 1984. text ed. write for info. (ISBN 0-02-315590-6). Macmillan.
--Fight Your Ticket. 2nd ed. LC 81-86158. (Illus.). 300p. 1984. pap. 12.95 (ISBN 0-917316-90-8). Nolo Pr.
--The Four Gospels. 18.95 (ISBN 0-85151-016-7). Banner of Truth.
--Guide to Model Railways. (Hobby Guides Ser.). (gr. 4-9). 1980. 7.95 (ISBN 0-86020-504-5, Usborne-Hayes); PLB 12.95 (ISBN 0-88110-023-4); pap. 4.95 (ISBN 0-86020-503-7). EDC.
--Mikhail Glinka. (Music Reprint Ser.). (Illus.). 342p. 1985. Repr. of 1974 ed. lib. bdg. 37.50 (ISBN 0-306-76247-1). Da Capo.
--Planter; or, Thirteen Years in the South. LC 71-100281. Repr. of 1902 ed. 12.75x (ISBN 0-8371-2910-9, BTP&). Greenwood.
--The Planter: Or, Thirteen Years in the South. LC 75-104423. 276p. lib. bdg. 11.25 (ISBN 0-8398-0174-2); pap. text ed. 6.95x (ISBN 0-89197-888-7). Irvington.
--Tchaikovsky: The Crisis Years (1874-1878) (Illus.). 1983. 25.00 (ISBN 0-393-01707-9). Norton.
--Tchaikovsky: The Early Years, 1840-1874. (Illus.). 1979. 24.95 (ISBN 0-393-07535-4). Norton.
--Thomas Weelkes. 1979. Repr. of 1969 ed. lib. bdg. 27.50 (ISBN 0-306-79523-X). Da Capo.
Brown, David & Warner, Ralph. Landlord's Law Book: Rights & Responsibilities. LC 85-61224. (Illus.). 260p. (Orig.). 1985. 19.95 (ISBN 0-87337-003-1). Nolo Pr.
Brown, David, jt. ed. see Strong, Donald.
Brown, David, tr. see Jentschura, Hansgeorg & Jung, Dieter.
Brown, David A. Raphael & America. LC 82-22405. (Illus.). pap. 5.00 (ISBN 0-89468-064-1). Natl Gallery Art.
--The Tertiary Cheilostomatous Polyzoa of New Zealand. (Illus.). 406p. 1952. 42.00x (ISBN 0-565-00064-0, Pub. by Brit Mus Nat Hist England). Sabbot-Natural Hist Bks.
--The Young Correggio & His Leonardesque Sources. LC 79-57510. (Outstanding Dissertations in the Fine Arts Ser.: No. 5). 390p. 1985. lib. bdg. 53.00 (ISBN 0-8240-3928-9). Garland Pub.
Brown, David A., tr. see Sobolev, N. V.
Brown, David B. Augustus Wall Callcott. (Illus.). 96p. pap. 9.95 (ISBN 0-905005-87-2, Pub. by Salem Hse Ltd). Merrimack Pub Cir.
Brown, David B. & Herbanek, Jeffrey A. Systems Analysis for Applications: Software Design. (Illus.). 466p. 1984. text ed. 37.95x (ISBN 0-8162-1160-4). Holden-Day.
Brown, David B., ed. Catalogue of the Collection of Drawings in the Ashmolean Museum: Earlier British Drawings, Vol. IV. (Illus.). 1982. 110.00x (ISBN 0-19-817375-X). Oxford U Pr.
--Mixed-Valence Compounds: Theory & Applications in Chemistry, Physics, Geology & Biology. (NATO Advanced Study Institute, C. Mathematical & Physical Sciences Ser.: No. 58). 525p. 1980. lib. bdg. 60.50 (ISBN 90-277-1152-6, Pub. by Reidel Holland). Kluwer Academic.
--Samuel Palmer. 74p. 1983. 30.00x (ISBN 0-900090-95-2, Pub. by Ashmolean Mus UK). State Mutual Bk.
Brown, David C. A Guide to the Salem Witchcraft Hysteria of 1692. LC 84-164658. (Illus.). 130p. (Orig.). 1984. pap. 5.95 (ISBN 0-9613415-0-5). D C Brown.
Brown, David E. Arizona Wetlands & Waterfowl. (Illus.). 180p. 1985. 24.95 (ISBN 0-8165-0904-2). U of Ariz Pr.
--The Grizzly in the Southwest: Documentary of an Extinction. LC 80-40684. (Illus.). 280p. 1985. 19.95 (ISBN 0-8061-1930-6). U of Okla Pr.
--Made in North Carolina: An Illustrated History of Tal Heel Business & Industry. 248p. 1985. 24.95 (ISBN 0-89781-157-7). Windsor Pubns Inc.
Brown, David E., ed. The Wolf in the Southwest: The Making of an Endangered Species. LC 82-17399. 195p. 1983. pap. 9.95 (ISBN 0-8165-0796-1). U of Ariz Pr.
Brown, David E., jt. ed. see Carmony, Neil B.
Brown, David G. Leadership Vitality: A Workbook for Academic Administrators. 10.00 (ISBN 0-02-904280-1). ACE.
--Partnership with China: Sino-Foreign Joint Ventures in Historical Perspective. (Replica Edition). 130p. 1985. pap. 15.00x (ISBN 0-86531-891-3). Westview.
Brown, David L. Three Years in the Rocky Mountains. 28p. 1975. pap. 4.95 (ISBN 0-87770-151-2). Ye Galleon.
Brown, David L. & Wardwell, John M., eds. New Directions in Urban-Rural Migration: The Population Turnaround in Rural America. (Studies in Population). 1980. 37.50 (ISBN 0-12-136380-5). Acad Pr.
Brown, David M. Dramatic Narrative in Preaching. 96p. 1981. pap. 4.95 (ISBN 0-8170-0911-6). Judson.
Brown, David R. AIGA Graphic Design U. S. A, No. 2. (The Annual of the American Institute of Graphic Arts). (Illus.). 432p. 1981. 45.00 (ISBN 0-8230-2144-0). Watson-Guptill.
Brown, David S. Freshwater Snails of Africa & Their Medical Importance. LC 81-670043. (Illus.). 450p. 1980. 27.50x (ISBN 0-85066-145-5). Am Malacologists.
--Managing the Large Organization: Issues, Ideas, Precepts, Innovations. 307p. 1982. 27.50x (ISBN 0-912338-31-8). Lomond.
Brown, David W., jt. auth. see Loeb, David V.
Brown, De Soto. Aloha Waikiki. (Illus.). 98p. (Orig.). 1985. pap. 7.95 (ISBN 0-9607938-9-5). Editions Ltd.
Brown, Deaver. The Entrepreneur's Guide. 1981. pap. 2.75 (ISBN 0-345-29634-6). Ballantine.
Brown, Deborah, jt. auth. see Gust, Katharine.
Brown, Dee. American Spa: Hot Springs, Arkansas. (Illus.). 96p. 1982. 14.95 (ISBN 0-914546-41-4). Rose Pub.
--Bury My Heart at Wounded Knee. (Illus.). 480p. 1984. pap. 4.95 (ISBN 0-671-49412-0). WSP.
--Bury My Heart at Wounded Knee: An Indian History of the American West. LC 70-121633. (Illus.). 1971. 16.95 (ISBN 0-03-085322-2). HR&W.
--Creek Mary's Blood. 496p. 1983. pap. 4.95 (ISBN 0-671-50709-5). PB.
--The Fetterman Massacre: An American Saga. LC 83-19805. (Illus.). 259p. 1971. pap. 7.50 (ISBN 0-8032-5730-9, BB 523, Bison). U of Nebr Pr.
--The Gentle Tamers: Women of the Old Wild West. LC 81-3428. (Illus.). 335p. 1981. pap. 6.50 (ISBN 0-8032-5025-8, BB 370, Bison). U of Nebr Pr.
--Hear That Lonesome Whistle Blow: Railroads in the West. LC 76-25046. (Illus.). 1977. 13.95 (ISBN 0-03-016936-4). HR&W.
--Killdeer Mountain. LC 82-15460. 256p. 1983. 14.95 (ISBN 0-03-040691-9). HR&W.
--Killdeer Mountain. 256p. 1984. pap. 3.95 (ISBN 0-671-46996-7). WSP.
--Lonesome Whistle. LC 79-18990. (Illus.). 160p. (gr. 4-8). 1980. 8.95 (ISBN 0-03-050666-2). HR&W.
--Pardon My Pandemonium. LC 83-45294. (Illus.). 219p. 1984. 14.95 (ISBN 0-935304-64-9). August Hse.
--Wounded Knee: An Indian History of the American West. 192p. (gr. 7 up). 1975. pap. 1.75 (ISBN 0-440-95768-0, LFL). Dell.
--Wounded Knee: An Indian History of the American West. Ehrlich, Amy, ed. LC 73-21821. (Illus.). 224p. (gr. 6 up). 1974. reinforced bdg. 6.95 (ISBN 0-03-091559-7). HR&W.
Brown, Dee A. Grierson's Raid. 261p. 1981. Repr. 17.50 (ISBN 0-89029-061-X). Pr of Morningside.
Brown, Deena, ed. American Yoga. LC 79-6156. (Illus.). 144p. (Orig.). 1981. pap. 9.95 (ISBN 0-394-17649-X, E751, Ever). Grove.
Brown, Delmer M. Nationalism in Japan: An Introductory Historical Analysis. LC 79-143555. 1971. Repr. of 1955 ed. 28.00x (ISBN 0-8462-1574-8). Russell.
Brown, Delmer M. & Ishida, Ichiro, eds. The Future & the Past: A Translation & Study of the Gukansho, an Interpretive History of Japan Written in 1219. LC 77-73493. 1979. 42.50x (ISBN 0-520-03460-0). U of Cal Pr.
Brown, Delwin. To Set at Liberty: Christian Faith & Human Freedom. LC 80-21783. 144p. (Orig.). 1981. pap. 6.95 (ISBN 0-88344-501-8). Orbis Bks.
Brown, Delwin, et al. Process Philosophy & Christian Thought. LC 74-127586. 1971. 59.50x (ISBN 0-672-51529-6). Irvington.
Brown, Demetra V. Haremlik: Some Page from the Life of Turkish Women. LC 77-87626. Repr. of 1910 ed. 22.50 (ISBN 0-404-16451-X). AMS Pr.
Brown, Demetra V. & Phoutrides, Aristides, trs. Modern Greek Stories. LC 79-136414. Repr. of 1920 ed. 21.00 (ISBN 0-404-01134-9). AMS Pr.
Brown, Deming. Soviet Russian Literature Since Stalin. LC 77-73275. 1978. 44.50 (ISBN 0-521-21694-X); pap. 11.95 (ISBN 0-521-29649-8). Cambridge U Pr.
Brown, Denise S., jt. auth. see Venturi, Robert.
Brown, Dennis, ed. The Complete Indoor Gardener. rev. ed. LC 79-4799. (Illus.). 1979. pap. 15.95 (ISBN 0-394-73813-6). Random.
Brown, Dennis G. & Pedder, Jonathan R. Introduction to Psychotherapy: An Outline to Psychodynamic Principles & Practice. 1979. 10.95x (ISBN 0-422-76670-4, NO.2049, Pub. by Tavistock England). Methuen Inc.
Brown, Dennis P. Foxglove Hollow. 192p. (Orig.). 1982. pap. 2.50 (ISBN 0-449-14484-4, GM). Fawcett.
Brown, Derek. Guinness Book of Darts. rev. ed. (Guinness Superlatives Ser.). (Illus.). 168p. 1982. pap. 10.95 (ISBN 0-85112-254-X, Pub. by Guinness Superlatives England). Sterling.
Brown, Diana. Come Be My Love. 378p. 1981. 13.95 (ISBN 0-312-15090-3). St Martin.
--A Debt of Honor. 1982. pap. 2.25 (ISBN 0-451-11417-5, AE1417, Sig). NAL.
--The Hand of a Woman. 528p. 1984. 16.95 (ISBN 0-312-36107-6). St Martin.
--The Hand of a Woman. 1985. pap. 3.95 (ISBN 0-451-13907-0, Sig). NAL.
--St. Martin's Summer. 1982. pap. 2.25 (ISBN 0-451-11624-0, AE1624, Sig). NAL.
--The Sandalwood Fan. LC 83-2894. 272p. 1983. 13.95 (ISBN 0-312-69909-3). St Martin.
--Sandalwood Fan. 1984. pap. 2.50 (ISBN 0-451-13052-9, Sig). NAL.
Brown, Diana D. Umbanda: Religion & Politics in Urban Brazil. Kottak, Conrad, ed. (Studies in Cultural Anthropology: No. 7). 1985. price not set (ISBN 0-8357-1556-6). UMI Res Pr.
Brown, Diana L. Developmental Handicaps in Babies & Young Children: A Guide for Parents. 100p. 1972. 12.75x (ISBN 0-398-02534-7). C C Thomas.
Brown, Diane. Notemaking. 245p. 1977. text ed. 10.88 (ISBN 0-7715-0858-1); tchr's. manual 13.64x (ISBN 0-7715-0859-X). Forkner.
Brown, Dolores. Amphoto Guide to SLR Photography. (Illus.). 168p. 1981. (Amphoto); pap. 7.95 (ISBN 0-8174-2178-5). Watson-Guptill.
Brown, Dolores C. Yukon Trophy Trails. 204p. 1971. 9.95 (ISBN 0-88826-031-8). Superior Pub.
Brown, Dolores L. My Little Friends. 1983. 5.75 (ISBN 0-8062-2180-1). Carlton.
Brown, Don A. Reading Diagnosis & Remediation. (Illus.). 384p. 1982. 29.95 (ISBN 0-13-754952-0). P-H.
Brown, Don W., jt. ed. see Brigham, John.
Brown, Donald. Basic Metallurgy. LC 80-68584. (Mechanical Ser.). (Illus.). 323p. (Orig.). 1981. pap. text ed. 13.80 (ISBN 0-8273-1769-7); instr's. guide 3.60 (ISBN 0-8273-1770-0). Delmar.
Brown, Donald, et al. Molecular Biology of Amphibian Development. 261p. 1972. text ed. 39.50x (ISBN 0-8422-7002-7). Irvington.
Brown, Donald A. & Clary, Chanda. Sexuality in America: Contemporary Perspectives on Sexual Identity, Dysfunction & Treatment. LC 81-81824. 1981. 24.50 (ISBN 0-87650-132-3). Pierian.
Brown, Donald D. Developmental Biology Using Purified Genes. LC 81-17554. (ICN-UCLA Symposia on Molecular & Cellular Biology Ser.: Vol. 23). 1981. 65.00 (ISBN 0-12-137420-3). Acad Pr.
Brown, Donald F., tr. see Monge, Carlos.
Brown, Donald G. Action. LC 68-132946. pap. 41.00 (ISBN 0-317-07999-9, 2014146). Bks Demand UMI.
Brown, Donald M. The White Umbrella: Indian Political Thought from Manu to Ghandi. LC 81-13391. (Illus.). xii, 204p. 1982. Repr. of 1953 ed. lib. bdg. 19.75x (ISBN 0-313-23210-5, BRWU). Greenwood.
Brown, Donald R. Neurosciences for Allied Health Therapies. LC 79-19685. (Illus.). 368p. 1980. PLB 23.95 (ISBN 0-8016-0827-9). Mosby.
Brown, Donald R. & Mathews, Wendell G. Real Estate Advertising Handbook. Berlin, Helene, ed. LC 81-51380. (Illus.). 96p. 1981. Repr. of 1980 ed. 9.95 (ISBN 0-686-73397-5, 340). Realtors Natl.
Brown, Donald R., jt. auth. see Harvey, Donald F.
Brown, Donald V. Metallurgy Basics. 240p. 1983. 15.95 (ISBN 0-442-21434-0). Van Nos Reinhold.
Brown, Donaldson. Some Reminiscences of an Industrialist. LC 74-34383. (Management History Ser.: No. 73). (Illus.). 185p. 1975. Repr. of 1958 ed. 20.00 (ISBN 0-87960-109-4). Hive Pub.
Brown, Dorothy H. God & the Tree & Me. LC 79-66196. 1979. pap. 4.25x (ISBN 0-8358-0386-4). Upper Room.
Brown, Dorothy M. Mabel Walker Willebrandt: A Study of Power, Loyalty, & Law. LC 83-6651. (Illus.). 348p. 1984. 29.95x (ISBN 0-87049-402-3); pap. 14.95x (ISBN 0-87049-403-1). U of Tenn Pr.
Brown, Dorothy S. Handle with Care: A Question of Alzheimer's. LC 84-61253. 120p. 1985. 14.95 (ISBN 0-87975-271-8); pap. 8.95 (ISBN 0-87975-272-6). Prometheus Bks.
--Handle with Care: A Question of Alzheimer's. 120p. 1984. pap. 8.95 (ISBN 0-932910-47-5). Potentials Development.
Brown, Dorris D. Agricultural Development in India's Districts. LC 71-131467. (Center for International Affairs Ser). 1971. 14.00x (ISBN 0-674-01230-5). Harvard U Pr.
Brown, Dort F. Souvenir Buildings: A Collection of Identified Miniatures, 2 vols. (Illus.). 203p. (Orig., Vol. 1, 1977, Vol. 2, 1979). pap. 6.95 set (ISBN 0-9603420-0-1). D E Brown.
Brown, Douglas. Flyers. LC 82-50397. (History Eye Witness Ser.). PLB 15.96 (ISBN 0-382-06667-7). Silver.
--From Pascal to C: An Introduction to the C Programming Language. 176p. 1985. write for info. (ISBN 0-534-04602-9). Wadsworth Pub.
--Thomas Hardy. LC 79-19057. (Illus.). 1980. Repr. of 1954 ed. lib. bdg. 27.50x (ISBN 0-313-22105-7, BRTH). Greenwood.
Brown, Douglas, ed. see Jonson, Ben.
Brown, Douglas R. The Restaurant Managers Handbook: How to Set up, Operate, & Manage a Financially Successful Resturant. Montgomery, Robert, ed. LC 82-72992. (Illus.). 326p. 1983. text ed. 49.95 (ISBN 0-910627-00-2). Atlantic FL.
Brown, Douglas T., jt. auth. see Prout, H. Thompson.
Brown, Douglas V., et al. The Economics of the Recovery Program. LC 70-163644. (FDR & the Era of the New Deal Ser). 1971. Repr. of 1934 ed. lib. bdg. 27.50 (ISBN 0-306-70197-9). Da Capo.
Brown, Drollene. Sybil Rides for Independence. Levine, Abby, ed. (Illus.). 48p. (gr. 2-5). 1985. 9.25 (ISBN 0-8075-7684-0). A Whitman.
Brown, Duane, et al. Career Choice & Developement: Applying Contemporary Theory to Pratice. LC 83-49258. (Management Ser.). 1984. text ed. 25.00x (ISBN 0-87589-593-X). Jossey-Bass.
--Consultation: Strategy for Improving Education. 305p. 1979. 27.95x (ISBN 0-205-06554-6, 246554, Pub. by Longwood Div). Allyn.
Brown, E. Carey & Solow, Robert, eds. Paul Samuelson & Modern Economic Theory. 350p. 1983. 32.95 (ISBN 0-07-059667-0). McGraw.
Brown, E. D., jt. auth. see Schwarzenberger, Georg.
Brown, E. E. Life of Oliver Wendell Holmes. 1903. lib. bdg. 27.50 (ISBN 0-8482-9995-7). Norwood Edns.
Brown, E. Evan. World Fish Farming: Cultivation & Economics. 2nd ed. (Illus.). 1983. text ed. 47.50 (ISBN 0-87055-427-1). AVI.
Brown, E. Evan & Gratzek, J. B. Fish Farming Handbook. (Illus.). 1980. 29.50 (ISBN 0-87055-341-0). AVI.
Brown, E. Evan, jt. auth. see Huner, Jay V.
Brown, E. Francis. Joseph Hawley: Colonial Radical. LC 31-29646. Repr. of 1931 ed. 15.00 (ISBN 0-404-01128-4). AMS Pr.
Brown, E. H., ed. Geography Yesterday & Tomorrow. 1980. 32.50x (ISBN 0-19-874096-4). Oxford U Pr.
Brown, E. H. & Waters, R. S., eds. Progress in Geomorphology: Papers in Honour of David L. Linton. (Special Publication of the Institute of British Geographers: No. 7). 1980. 27.50 (ISBN 0-12-137780-6). Acad Pr.
Brown, E. K. Rhythm in the Novel. LC 77-14165. xvi, 118p. 1978. 11.95x (ISBN 0-8032-1150-3); pap. 3.25x (ISBN 0-8032-6050-4, BB 667, Bison). U of Nebr Pr.
Brown, E. K. & Edel, Leon. Willa Cather: A Critical Biography. 304p. (YA) (gr. 8 up). 1980. pap. 2.95 (ISBN 0-380-49676-3, Discus). Avon.
Brown, E. K. & Miller, J. E. Syntax: A Linguistic Introduction to Sentence Structure. 394p. 1981. text ed. 29.00x (ISBN 0-09-138620-9, Hutchinson U Lib); pap. text ed. 16.00x (ISBN 0-09-138621-7). Humanities.
--Syntax: Generative Grammar. 240p. 1982. text ed. 32.00x (ISBN 0-09-144110-2, Hutchinson U Lib); pap. text ed. 17.50x (ISBN 0-09-144111-0). Humanities.
Brown, E. K., ed. see Arnold, Matthew.
Brown, E. K., tr. see Cazamian, Louis F.
Brown, E. Richard. Rockefeller Medicine Men: Medicine & Capitalism in America. LC 78-65461. (Illus.). 295p. 1979. 18.50x (ISBN 0-520-03817-7); pap. 5.95 (ISBN 0-520-04269-7, CAL 467). U of Cal Pr.
Brown, E. T., jt. auth. see Brady, B. H.
Brown, E. T., jt. auth. see Hoek, E.
Brown, E. T., ed. Rock Characterization, Testing & Monitoring: ISRM Suggested Methods. LC 80-49711. 200p. 1981. pap. 22.00 (ISBN 0-08-027309-2). Pergamon.
Brown, E. T., jt. ed. see Jenkins, J. P.
Brown, Earl K. Women of Mr. Wesley's Methodism. LC 83-22010. (Studies in Women & Religion: Vol. 11). 273p. 1984. 49.95x (ISBN 0-88946-538-X). E Mellen.
Brown, Earl L. Why Race Riots? LC 74-22734. (The Labor Movement in Fiction & Non-Fiction). Repr. of 1944 ed. 11.50 (ISBN 0-404-58486-1). AMS Pr.
Brown, Earl L. & Leighton, George R. Negro & the War. LC 75-172045. Repr. of 1942 ed. 11.50 (ISBN 0-404-00194-7). AMS Pr.
Brown, Earle B. Modern Optics. LC 73-92134. 656p. 1974. Repr. of 1965 ed. 36.50 (ISBN 0-88275-149-2). Krieger.
Brown, Ed. A History of Voter Education Project. 1979. 2.00 (ISBN 0-686-36622-0). Voter Ed Proj.
--Race & Class in Southern Politics & a History of Voter Education Project. 1979. 2.00 (ISBN 0-686-38003-7). Voter Ed Proj.
Brown, Edgar & Behrens, Kaye. Humanetics Testing Procedure. (Illus.). 12p. (Orig.). 1985. pap. 2.95 (ISBN 0-9613697-2-8). Madison Ave Pub.
--Your Body's Response. LC 82-90165. (Illus.). 192p. (Orig.). 1985. 19.95 (ISBN 0-9613697-1-X); pap. 14.95 (ISBN 0-9613697-0-1). Madison Ave Pub.
Brown, Edgar P., jt. auth. see Clark, Anthony M.
Brown, Edmund R. & Very, Alice. How to Use Peat Moss. (Orig.). 1953. pap. 2.00 (ISBN 0-8283-1162-5). Branden Pub Co.
Brown, Edmund R., ed. Five Modern Plays. Incl. Dreamy Kig. O'Neill, Eugene; Farewell Supper. Schnitzler, Arthur; Lost Silk Hat. Dunsany, Edward; Sisters Tragedy. Hughes, Richard; Intruder. Maeterlinck, Maurice. pap. 4.00 (ISBN 0-8283-1435-7). Branden Pub Co.
--Modern Essays. Incl. Civil Disobedience. Thoreau, Henry D; Religion of the Future. Eliot, Charles; On Going to Church. Shaw, George B. pap. 3.00 (ISBN 0-8283-1449-7). Branden Pub Co.
Brown, Edmund R., ed. see Dunsany, Lord.
Brown, Edmund R., ed. see Eliot, Charles W.
Brown, Edmund R., ed. see Hughes, Richard.
Brown, Edmund R., ed. see Maeterlinck, Maurice.

Brown, Edmund R., ed. see O'Neill, Eugene.

Brown, Edmund R., ed. see Schnitzler, Arthur.

Brown, Edmund R., ed. see Shaw, George B.

Brown, Edmund R., ed. see Thoreau, Henry D.

Brown, Edward, jt. auth. see Duckworth, William.

Brown, Edward E. Tassajara Bread Book. LC 75-143877. 145p. (Orig.). 1970. pap. 5.95 (ISBN 0-87773-025-3, 73003-8). Shambhala Pubns.

--The Tassajara Bread Book. rev. & updated ed. LC 85-2462. (Illus.). 146p. 1985. pap. 8.95 (ISBN 0-87773-343-0, 74196-X). Shambhala Pubns.

--Tassajara Cooking. LC 85-8185. (Illus.). 252p. 1985. pap. 9.95 (ISBN 0-87773-344-9, 74193-5). Shambhala Pubns.

--Tassajara Cooking: A Vegetarian Cooking Book. LC 73-86144. (Illus.). 256p. 1973. pap. 8.95 (ISBN 0-87773-047-4, 70949-7). Shambhala Pubns.

--The Tassajara Recipe Book: Favorites of the Guest Season. LC 84-23576. (Illus.). 160p. (Orig.). 1985. pap. 8.95 (ISBN 0-87773-308-2, 73520-X). Shambhala Pubns.

Brown, Edward G. A Year among the Persians. (Century Travel Classics Ser.). 319p. 1985. pap. 11.95 (ISBN 0-7126-0453-7, Pub. by Century Pubs UK). Hippocrene Bks.

Brown, Edward J. Mayakovsky: A Poet in Revolution. LC 72-14022. (Studies of the Russian Institute, Columbia University). 475p. 1973. 40.00 (ISBN 0-691-06255-2). Princeton U Pr.

--Proletarian Episode in Russian Literature, 1928-1932. LC 77-120236. 1971. Repr. lib. bdg. 23.00x (ISBN 0-374-91020-0). Octagon.

--Russian Literature since the Revolution. Rev. & Enl. ed. (Illus.). 400p. 1982. text ed. 27.50x (ISBN 0-674-78203-8); pap. text ed. 9.95x (ISBN 0-674-78204-6). Harvard U Pr.

--Stankevich & His Moscow Circle, 1830-1840. 1966. 12.50x (ISBN 0-8047-0295-0). Stanford U Pr.

Brown, Edward J., ed. Major Soviet Writers: Essays in Criticism. new ed. 1973. pap. 8.95 (ISBN 0-19-501684-X, GB371, GB). Oxford U Pr.

Brown, Edward K. Edith Wharton: Etude Critique. LC 76-40303. 1935. lib. bdg. 39.50 (ISBN 0-8414-1792-X). Folcroft.

--Studies in the Text of Matthew Arnold's Prose Works. 59.95 (ISBN 0-8490-1151-5). Gordon Pr.

Brown, Edward M., ed. English Literature from Its Beginning to 1100, 9 vols. (Belles Lettres Ser.: Sec. 1). Repr. of 1912 ed. Set. write for info. (ISBN 0-404-53600-X). AMS Pr.

Brown, Edward M. & Brow, Edward M., eds. The Battle of Maldon & Short Poems from the Saxon Chronicle. 96p. 1981. Repr. of 1904 ed. lib. bdg. 25.00 (ISBN 0-8495-4958-2). Arden Lib.

Brown, Edwin & Sweet, Avron Y., eds. Neonatal Necrotizing Enterocolitis. (Monographs in Neonatology). 224p. 1980. 29.00 (ISBN 0-8089-1244-5, 790686). Grune.

Brown, Edwin G., jt. auth. see Feinstein, Barbara.

Brown, Edwin J., et al. Managing the Classroom: The Teacher's Part in School Administration. 2nd ed. LC 61-7744. (Douglass Series in Education). pap. 108.80 (ISBN 0-317-07746-5, 2012469). Bks Demand UMI.

Brown, Elaine K. Mobile Intensive Care Manual. 176p. 1982. pap. text ed. 11.50 (ISBN 0-397-54379-4, 64-01632, Lippincott Nursing). Lippincott.

Brown, Eleanor. The Forest Preserve of New York State. LC 85-3936. (Illus.). 240p. 1985. pap. 2.50 (ISBN 0-935272-27-5). ADK Mtn Club.

--Milton's Blindness. 1968. lib. bdg. 18.50x (ISBN 0-374-91007-3). Octagon.

Brown, Eleanor D., ed. see De Schauensee, Rodolphe M.

Brown, Eleanor F. Bibliotherapy & Its Widening Applications. LC 74-28187. 414p. 1975. 21.00 (ISBN 0-8108-0782-3). Scarecrow.

--Cutting Library Costs: Increasing Productivity & Raising Revenues. LC 79-19448. 274p. 1979. 16.00 (ISBN 0-8108-1250-9). Scarecrow.

--Modern Branch Libraries & Libraries in Systems. LC 77-12808. (Illus.). 747p. 1970. 22.50 (ISBN 0-8108-0276-7). Scarecrow.

Brown, Elijah. The Real America. LC 73-13124. (Foreign Travelers in America, 1810-1935 Ser.). 308p. 1974. Repr. 24.50x (ISBN 0-405-05447-5). Ayer Co Pubs.

Brown, Elizabeth B. Vegetables: An Illustrated History with Recipes. (Illus.). (gr. 5-9). 1981. 9.95 (ISBN 0-13-941351-0). P-H.

Brown, Elizabeth G. British Statutes in American Law. LC 73-21605. (American Constitutional & Legal History Ser). 1974. Repr. of 1964 ed. lib. bdg. 42.50 (ISBN 0-306-70610-5). Da Capo.

Brown, Elizabeth Gasper. British Statutes in American Law: 1776-1836. LC 64-64845. (Michigan Legal Publications). xii, 377p. 1984. Repr. of 1964 ed. lib. bdg. 35.00 (ISBN 0-89941-321-8). W S Hein.

Brown, Elizabeth M. New Haven: A Guide to Architecture & Urban Design. LC 75-18166. (Illus.). 1976. pap. 8.95 (ISBN 0-300-01993-9). Yale U Pr.

Brown, Elizabeth M., et al, eds. Pilgrims & Their Times. rev. ed. (Illus.). 32p. (gr. 2-6). 1973. pap. 2.50 (ISBN 0-87534-121-7). Highlights.

Brown, Ellen. Cooking with the New American Chefs. LC 84-48141. (Illus.). 320p. 1985. pap. 12.45i (ISBN 0-06-091237-5, CN). Har-Row.

--Cooking with the New American Chefs. LC 84-48141. (Illus.). 320p. 1985. 22.07i (ISBN 0-06-015373-3, HarpT). Har-Row.

Brown, Elmer B. Progress in Hematology, Vol. 13. 368p. 1983. 47.50 (ISBN 0-8089-1615-7, 790703). Grune.

Brown, Elmer B., ed. Progress in Hematology, Vol. XIV. LC 79-704. 1985. price not set (ISBN 0-8089-1769-2). Grune.

--Progress in Hematology, Vol. 9. (Illus.). 352p. 1975. 85.50 (ISBN 0-8089-0912-6, 790699). Grune.

--Progress in Hematology, Vol. 11. 335p. 1979. 51.50 (ISBN 0-8089-1223-2, 790701). Grune.

--Progress in Hematology, Vol. 12. 1981. 42.50 (ISBN 0-8089-1410-3, 790702). Grune.

Brown, Elmer B. & Moore, Carl V., eds. Progress in Hematology, Vols. 4-7. LC 56-58463. 384p. 1964-71. Vol. IV, 309pps. 78.00 (ISBN 0-8089-0332-2, 790694); Vol. V, 408pps. 87.50 (ISBN 0-8089-0079-X, 790695); Vol. VI, 400pps. 87.50 (ISBN 0-8089-0080-3, 790696); Vol. VII, 448pps. 87.50 (ISBN 0-8089-0722-0, 790697). Grune.

Brown, Elmer B., et al, eds. Proteins of Iron Metabolism. 480p. 1977. 75.00 (ISBN 0-8089-1050-7, 790687). Grune.

Brown, Elmer E. Making of Our Middle Schools. LC 77-89153. (American Education: Its Men, Institutions & Ideas Ser.: No. 1). 1969. Repr. of 1905 ed. 32.00 (ISBN 0-405-01391-4). Ayer Co Pubs.

--The Making of Our Middle Schools. (Quality Paperback Ser.: No. 243). 547p. 1970. pap. 4.95 (ISBN 0-8226-0243-1). Littlefield.

Brown, Elsa. Creative Quilting. (Illus.). 144p. 1975. 13.50 (ISBN 0-8230-1105-4). Watson-Guptill.

Brown, Elsa L., jt. auth. see Lyons, John M.

Brown, Emily C. Har Dayal: Hindu Revolutionary & Rationalist. LC 74-16895. 321p. 1975. 14.50x (ISBN 0-8165-0422-9); pap. 7.95x (ISBN 0-8165-0512-8). U of Ariz Pr.

--Soviet Trade Unions & Labor Relations. LC 66-21332. pap. 101.50 (ISBN 0-317-29769-4, 2017260). Bks Demand UMI.

Brown, Emily C., jt. auth. see Millis, Harry A.

Brown, Emily I. The Roots of Ticasuk: An Eskimo Woman's Family Story. LC 81-3458. 120p. (Orig.). 1981. pap. 4.95 (ISBN 0-88240-117-3). Alaska Northwest.

Brown, Emmett E. & Brown, Cyril. Polychromatic Assembly for Woodturning. rev. ed. Sorsky, R., ed. LC 82-80340. (Illus.). 120p. 1982. pap. 15.95 spiral bound (ISBN 0-941936-00-7). Linden Pub Fresno.

Brown, Eric. Knave of Clubs. (Illus.). 14.50x (ISBN 0-392-03582-0, SpS). Sportshelf.

--Throw Away Your Pencil: Writing More Effectively with a Word Processor. 1984. pap. 14.95 (ISBN 0-8359-7689-0). Reston.

Brown, Eric D. Writing with a Word Processor: Communication in the Computer Age. 1984. pap. text ed. 15.95 (ISBN 0-8359-8857-0). Reston.

Brown, Eric W. Wings on My Sleeve. 200p. 1981. 30.00x (ISBN 0-9504543-6-2, Pub. by Airlife England). State Mutual Bk.

Brown, Erica. Interior Views: Design at Its Best. LC 80-5356. 176p. 1980. 30.00 (ISBN 0-670-39978-7, Studio). Viking.

--Sixty Years of Interior Design: The World of McMillen. LC 82-70185. (Illus.). 320p. 1982. 50.00 (ISBN 0-670-64775-6, Studio). Viking.

Brown, Erik. Seat in a Wild Place. LC 81-15017. (Illus.). 128p. 1983. 8.95 (ISBN 0-87233-059-1). Bauhan.

Brown, Ernest & Hedrick, Henry B. Tables of the Motion of the Moon, 3 vols. 1920. pap. 300.00x set (ISBN 0-685-89789-3). Elliots Bks.

Brown, Ernest H. The Growth of British Industrial Relations. LC 74-14024. (Illus.). 414p. 1975. Repr. of 1959 ed. lib. bdg. 26.00x (ISBN 0-8371-7781-2, BRBI). Greenwood.

--Pay & Profits. LC 68-56546. (Illus.). 1968. 10.00x (ISBN 0-678-06753-8). Kelley.

Brown, Estelle P. Twice Fifteen. 300p. 1970. pap. text ed. price not set (ISBN 0-02-315320-2, Pub. by Scribner). Macmillan.

Brown, Esther E. The French Revolution & the American Man of Letters. 1951. Repr. lib. bdg. 10.00 (ISBN 0-8274-2374-8). R West.

Brown, Esther L. Lawyers & the Promotion of Justice. (Russell Sage Foundation Reprint Ser). Repr. of 1938 ed. lib. bdg. 29.00x (ISBN 0-697-00201-2). Irvington.

--Lawyers, Law Schools & the Public Service. (Russell Sage Foundation Reprint Ser). Repr. of 1948 ed. lib. bdg. 27.50x (ISBN 0-697-00200-4). Irvington.

--Newer Dimensions of Patient Care, 3 pts. Incl. Pt. 1. The Use of the Physical & Social Environment of the General Hospital for Therapeutic Purposes. LC 61-13217. 160p. 1961. pap. 4.95x (ISBN 0-87154-183-1); Pt. 2. Improving Staff Motivation & Competence in the General Hospital. LC 62-18147. 194p. 1962. pap. 4.95x (ISBN 0-87154-184-X); Pt. 3. Patients As People. LC 64-17897. 164p. 1964. pap. 4.95x (ISBN 0-87154-185-8). 160p. pap. 4.95x ea.; Three Vol. Set. (ISBN 0-87154-182-3). Russell Sage.

--Social Work as a Profession. 4th ed. LC 75-17207. (Social Problems & Social Policy Ser.). 1976. Repr. of 1942 ed. 18.00x (ISBN 0-405-07479-4). Ayer Co Pubs.

Brown, Esther M., jt. ed. see Dellmann, Horst-Dieter.

Brown, Eugene. J. William Fulbright: Advice & Dissent. LC 84-16134. 183p. 1985. 22.50 (ISBN 0-87745-130-3). U of Iowa Pr.

Brown, Eugene & Tarratt, Sara L. Small Bytes: An Irreverent Computer Dictionary. 96p. 1983. pap. 4.95 (ISBN 0-02-003920-4). Macmillan.

Brown, Eva M. By the Big Shiny Blue Waters. LC 81-90378. 89p. 1983. 7.95 (ISBN 0-533-05147-9). Vantage.

--Prairie Children. 1983. 8.95 (ISBN 0-533-05952-6). Vantage.

Brown, Evan L. & Deffenbacher, Kenneth A. Perception & the Senses. (Illus.). 1979. 23.95x (ISBN 0-19-502504-0). Oxford U Pr.

Brown, Everett S. Constitutional History of the Louisiana Purchase, 1803-1812. LC 68-55492. Repr. of 1920 ed. 27.50x (ISBN 0-678-00742-X). Kelley.

--Ratification of the Twenty-First Amendment to the Constitution of the United States. LC 78-114757. (American Constitutional & Legal History Ser). 1970. Repr. of 1938 ed. 85.00 (ISBN 0-306-71928-2). Da Capo.

Brown, Everett S., ed. William Plumer's Memorandum of Proceedings in the United States Senate 1803-1807. LC 74-94626. (Law, Politics & History Ser). 1969. Repr. of 1923 ed. 85.00 (ISBN 0-306-71823-5). Da Capo.

Brown, Everett S., ed. see Plumer, William, Jr.

Brown, F. Topley & Wilson's Principles of Bacteriology, Virology & Immunity, Vol. 4. 7th ed. 704p. 1984. 90.00 (ISBN 0-683-09067-4). Williams & Wilkins.

Brown, F., et al, eds. Vehicle Painting, Pt. 1. (Engineering Craftsmen: No. E1). (Illus.). 1968. spiral bdg. 45.00x (ISBN 0-85083-032-X). Intl Ideas.

--Vehicle Painting, Pt. 2. (Engineering Craftsmen: No. E21). 1970. spiral bdg. 45.00x (ISBN 0-85083-116-4). Intl Ideas.

Brown, F. B. Cornaceae & Allies in the Marquesas & Neighboring Islands. (BMB). pap. 8.00 (ISBN 0-527-02158-X). Kraus Repr.

--Flora of Southeastern Polynesia: Bayard Dominick Expedition Publication Nos. 20, 21, & 22, 3 vols. (BMB). Repr. of 1931 ed. Vol. 1. 21.00 (ISBN 0-527-02190-3); Vol. 2. 19.00 (ISBN 0-527-02195-4); Vol. 3. 45.00 (ISBN 0-527-02236-5). Kraus Repr.

Brown, F. C. & Noriaki Itoh, eds. Recombination-Induced Defect Formation in Crystals. (Special Topics Issue of Semiconductors & Insulators Ser.). 484p. 1983. 88.75 (ISBN 0-677-40365-8). Gordon.

Brown, F. Christine. Hallucinogenic Drugs. (Illus.). 164p. 1972. 22.75x (ISBN 0-398-02249-6). C C Thomas.

Brown, F. E. Marketing Research: A Structure for Decision Making. LC 79-25541. 1980. text ed. 36.95 (ISBN 0-201-00205-1); instr's. manual 3.95 (ISBN 0-201-00206-X). Addison-Wesley.

Brown, F. E. & Oxenfeldt, A. R. Misperceptions of Economic Phenomena. LC 72-79606. 1977. 18.95x (ISBN 0-89197-851-8); pap. text ed. 7.95x (ISBN 0-89197-852-6). Irvington.

Brown, F. K., jt. auth. see Frazier, Claude A.

Brown, F. Lee & Lebeck, A. O. Cars, Cans, & Dumps: Solutions for Rural Residuals. (Resources for the Future Ser). 222p. 1976. 17.50x (ISBN 0-8018-1797-8). Johns Hopkins.

--Cars, Cans & Dumps: Solutions for Rural Residuals. 222p. 1976. 17.50 (ISBN 0-8018-1797-8). Resources Future.

Brown, F. Lee, jt. auth. see Kneese, Allen V.

Brown, F. Martin & Bailey, Wayne. Earth Science. 1978. text ed. 23.80x (ISBN 0-673-15311-8). Scott F.

Brown, F. Martin & Heinemann, Bernard. Jamaica & Its Butterflies. 492p. 1972. 99.00x (ISBN 0-317-07104-1, Pub. by EW Classey UK). State Mutual Bk.

Brown, F. Martin, jt. ed. see Ferris, Clifford D.

Brown, F. Yeats. Bengal Lancer. 224p. Date not set. pap. 7.50 (ISBN 0-907746-35-7, Pub. by A Mott Ltd). Longwood Pub Group.

Brown, Fern. Behind the Scenes at the Horse Hospital. Tucker, Kathleen, ed. LC 81-94. (Behind the Scenes Ser.). (Illus.). 48p. (gr. 3-9). 1981. PLB 11.25 (ISBN 0-8075-0610-9). A Whitman.

--Racing Against the Odds: Robyn C. Smith. LC 75-42320. (Sports Profiles). (Illus.). 48p. (gr. 4-11). 1976. PLB 13.31 (ISBN 0-8172-0118-1). Raintree Pubs.

Brown, Fern G. Amelia Earhart Takes Off. Tucker, Kathleen, ed. (Biography Ser.). (Illus.). 64p. (gr. 3-7). 1985. PLB 9.75 (ISBN 0-8075-0309-6). A Whitman.

--Etiquette. LC 84-20935. (First Book Ser.). (Illus.). 84p. (gr. 4-7). 1985. PLB 9.40 (ISBN 0-531-04908-6). Watts.

--Valentine's Day. (First Bks.). (Illus.). 72p. (gr. 4 up). 1983. PLB 8.90 (ISBN 0-531-04533-1). Watts.

--You're Somebody Special on a Horse. LC 77-7506. (Pilotbooks). (Illus.). (gr. 4-8). 1977. PLB 8.50 (ISBN 0-8075-9447-4). A Whitman.

Brown, Fletch. Street Boy. LC 82-8221. 152p. (gr. 6-9). 1980. pap. 2.95 (ISBN 0-8024-8365-8). Moody.

--Street Boy Returns. pap. 2.95 (ISBN 0-8024-8366-6). Moody.

Brown, Florence, jt. ed. see Beil, Preston J.

Brown, Forbes T., ed. see Fluidics Symposium, Chicago, 1967.

Brown, Forbes T., ed. see Symposium on Fluid Jet Control Devices, New York, 1962.

Brown, Ford K. The Life of William Godwin. LC 72-10170. 1974. Repr. of 1926 ed. lib. bdg. 42.50 (ISBN 0-8414-0641-3). Folcroft.

Brown, Forman. Small Wonder: The Story of the Yale Puppeteers & the Turnabout Theatre. LC 80-17815. 288p. 1980. 16.00 (ISBN 0-8108-1334-3). Scarecrow.

Brown, Foster F., et al. Statistical Concepts: A Basic Program. 2nd ed. 160p. 1975. pap. text ed. 11.50 scp (ISBN 0-06-040988-6, HarpC). Har-Row.

Brown, Frances. My First Book of Words. LC 78-58344. 144p. (gr. k-6). 1979. pap. text ed. 4.50 (ISBN 0-8027-7134-3). Walker Educ.

Brown, Frances A. Comprehensive Forkner Shorthand Dictionary. rev. ed. LC 81-66122. 297p. 1982. text ed. 12.78x (ISBN 0-912036-37-0). Forkner.

Brown, Frances A., jt. auth. see Forkner, Hamden L., Jr.

Brown, Francis, ed. A Dartmouth Reader. LC 79-108876. 339p. 1969. 20.00x (ISBN 0-87451-045-7). U Pr of New Eng.

Brown, Francis, et al, eds. see Gesenius, William.

Brown, Francis A. & Forkner, Hamden L. Correlated Dictation & Transcription. 2nd. ed. (Forkner Shorthand). 1974. 12.36x (ISBN 0-912036-15-X); pap. 8.88x (ISBN 0-912036-16-8); tape library (18 cassettes) 240.00x (ISBN 0-912036-42-7). Forkner.

Brown, Francis J. Educational Sociology. LC 73-94579. Repr. of 1954 ed. lib. bdg. 23.00x (ISBN 0-8371-2581-2, BREP). Greenwood.

--One America: The History, Contributions, & Present Problems of Our Racial & National Minorities. LC 72-111566. Repr. of 1952 ed. 34.00x (ISBN 0-8371-4587-2, BMR&). Greenwood.

Brown, Frank B. Transfiguration: Poetic Metaphor & the Languages of Religious Belief. LC 82-24714. (Studies in Religion). x, 230p. 1983. 24.00x (ISBN 0-8078-1560-8). U of NC Pr.

--The Transition of Youth to Adulthood: A Bridge Too Long. 1980. pap. text ed. 12.95x (ISBN 0-89158-756-X). Westview.

Brown, Frank C. The Frank C. Brown Collection of North Carolina Folklore, 7 vols. White, Newman I., ed. Incl. Vol. 1. Games & Rhymes, Beliefs & Customs, Riddles, Proverbs, Speech, Tales & Legends (ISBN 0-8223-0027-3); Vol. 2. Folk Ballads from North Carolina (ISBN 0-8223-0254-3); Vol. 3. Folk Songs from North Carolina (ISBN 0-8223-0255-1); Vol. 4. Music of the Ballads (ISBN 0-8223-0256-X); Vol. 5. Music of the Folk Songs (ISBN 0-8223-0257-8); Vol. 6. Popular Beliefs & Superstitions from North Carolina, Pt. 1 (ISBN 0-8223-0258-6); Vol. 7. Popular Beliefs & Superstitions from North Carolina, Pt. 2 (ISBN 0-8223-0284-5). LC 58-10967. (Illus.). 1952-64. 25.00 ea.; 150.00 set (ISBN 0-685-22682-4, 58-10967). Duke.

Brown, Frank E. Cosa: The Making of a Roman Town. (Illus.). 150p. 1980. 20.00x (ISBN 0-472-04100-2). U of Mich Pr.

--The House in Block E4, Block F3, the Roman Baths, Discoveries in the Temple of Artemis-Manaia, Arms & Armor, New & Revised Material from the Temple of Azzanathkona. (Illus.). 1936. pap. 59.50x (ISBN 0-686-52157-9). Elliots Bks.

--Roman Architecture. LC 61-13688. (Great Ages of World Architecture Ser). (Illus.). 1961. pap. 7.95 (ISBN 0-8076-0331-7). Braziller.

Brown, Frank L. How to Play Cribbage--Well. LC 85-12065. (Parks & Recreation Ser.). (Illus.). 72p. (Orig.). 1985. pap. 9.95 (ISBN 0-942280-12-1). Pub Horizons.

Brown, Fred, jt. ed. see Finn, Michael H.

Brown, Fred R., ed. Management: Concepts & Practice. LC 77-84858. 1977. 8.95 (ISBN 0-912338-15-6); microfiche 7.95 (ISBN 0-912338-16-4). Lomond.

Brown, Frederic. Night of the Jabberwock. Penzler, Otto, ed. LC 84-60106. (Quill Mysterious Classics Ser.). 246p. 1984. pap. 3.95 (ISBN 0-688-03150-1). Morrow.

Brown, Frederic J. Chemical Warfare: A Study in Restraints. LC 80-27993. xix, 355p. 1981. Repr. of 1968 ed. lib. bdg. 37.50x (ISBN 0-313-22823-X, BRCHW). Greenwood.

Brown, Frederic J., jt. auth. see Bradford, Zeb B., Jr.

Brown, Frederick. From Tientsin to Peking with the Allied Forces. LC 73-111735. (American Imperialism: Viewpoints of United States Foreign Policy, 1898-1941). 1970. Repr. of 1902 ed. 11.00 (ISBN 0-405-02004-X). Ayer Co Pubs.

--Principles of Educational & Psychological Testing. 3rd ed. 1983. text ed. 32.95 (ISBN 0-03-060103-7). HR&W.

--Rogue in Space. 1976. Repr. of 1957 ed. lib. bdg. 6.95 (ISBN 0-88411-891-6, Pub. by Aeonian Pr). Amereon Ltd.

--Theater & Revolution. 512p. 1980. 20.00 (ISBN 0-670-69802-4). Viking.

--What Mad Universe. 1976. Repr. of 1949 ed. lib. bdg. 6.95 (ISBN 0-88411-892-4, Pub. by Aeonian Pr). Amereon Ltd.

Brown, Frederick G. Measuring Classroom Achievement. LC 80-24807. 224p. 1981. pap. text ed. 19.95 (ISBN 0-03-052421-0, HoltC). HR&W.

Brown, Frederick M. & Graeber, R. Curtis, eds. Rhythmic Aspects of Behavior. (Illus.). 512p. 1982. text ed. 49.95x (ISBN 0-89859-168-6). L Erlbaum Assocs.

Brown, Fredric. The Deep End. Barzun, J. & Taylor, W. H., eds. LC 81-47340. (Crime Fiction 1950-1975 Ser.). 220p. 1983. lib. bdg. 18.00 (ISBN 0-8240-4990-X). Garland Pub.

--The Deep End. LC 84-60846. (Quill Mysterious Classic Ser.). 256p. 1984. pap. 3.50 (ISBN 0-688-03919-7, Quill). Morrow.

--The Fabulous Clipjoint. 1979. lib. bdg. 10.50 (ISBN 0-8398-2541-2, Gregg). G K Hall.

--Homicide Sanitarium. 200p. (Orig.). 1985. pap. 5.95 (ISBN 0-9609986-2-4). D McMillan.

Brown, Fredric, Jr. Carnival of Crime: The Best Mystery Stories of Fredric Brown. Nevins, Francis M., Jr. & Greenberg, Martin H., eds. 332p. 1985. 19.95 (ISBN 0-8093-1192-5). S Ill U Pr.

Brown, Friedl, tr. see Van Der Meer, Frederik.

Brown, G., jt. ed. see Brindley, G. W.

Brown, G. B. The Unknown Indian. 1977. lib. bdg. 59.95 (ISBN 0-8490-2789-6). Gordon Pr.

Brown, G. Baldwin, ed. see Vasari, Giorgio.

Brown, G. C. & Mussett, A. E. The Inaccessible Earth. (Illus.). 272p. 1981. pap. text ed. 22.50x (ISBN 0-04-550028-2). Allen Unwin.

Brown, G. E. & Jackson, A. D. The Nucleon-Nucleon Interaction. LC 75-37972. 242p. 1976. 34.00 (ISBN 0-444-10894-7, North-Holland); pap. 46.50 (ISBN 0-444-11064-X). Elsevier.

Brown, G. F. Population Policy & National Development. 12p. 1972. pap. 5.00 (ISBN 0-88936-008-1, IDRC7, IDRC). Unipub.

Brown, G. H., jt. auth. see Thompson, T. E.

Brown, G. M., jt. auth. see Wager, L. R.

Brown, G. M., ed. Six Lives of Fankle the Cat. 122p. 12.95 (ISBN 0-7011-2534-9, Pub. by Chatto & Windus). Merrimack Pub Cir.

Brown, G. M., jt. ed. see Kisliuk, R. L.

Brown, G. R. Drug Consultant: 1984-85 A Current Guide to Clinical Drug Treatments & Their Usefulness. Michaels, Rhoda M., ed. 383p. 1984. pap. text ed. 18.95 (ISBN 0-471-80894-6, Pub. by Wiley Med). Wiley.

Brown, G. R., jt. auth. see Stpierre, L. E.

Brown, G. Thompson. Christianity in the People's Republic of China. LC 82-49018. 240p. 1983. pap. 7.25 (ISBN 0-8042-1484-0). John Knox.

Brown, G. W. Desert Biology, 2 vols. Set. 152.50; Vol. 1, 1968. 92.50 (ISBN 0-12-135901-8); Vol. 2. 92.50 (ISBN 0-12-135902-6). Acad Pr.

--Forestry & Water Quality. 1983. pap. text ed. 8.65x (ISBN 0-88246-007-2). Oreg St U Bkstrs.

--Understanding Business & Personal Law. 7th ed. 576p. 1983. 17.00 (ISBN 0-07-053635-X). McGraw.

Brown, G. W., jt. auth. see Wing, J. K.

Brown, G. W. see Halpenny, Francess.

Brown, G. Z. Sun, Wind & Light: Architectural Design Strategies. 192p. 1985. 32.95 (ISBN 0-471-89506-7); pap. text ed. 15.95 (ISBN 0-471-82063-6). Wiley.

Brown, Gabrielle. The New Celibacy. 224p. 1981. pap. 2.75 (ISBN 0-345-29803-9). Ballantine.

--The New Celibacy: Why More Men & Women Are Abstaining from Sex & Enjoying It. 300p. 1980. 10.95 (ISBN 0-07-008430-0). McGraw.

Brown, Gail. Sensational Silk. LC 82-80827. (Orig.). 1982. pap. 6.95 (ISBN 0-935278-07-9). Palmer-Pletsch.

Brown, Gail & Palmer, Pati. Sewing with Sergers: The Complete Handbook for Overlock Sewing. LC 85-60347. (Illus.). 200p. (Orig.). 1985. pap. 6.95 (ISBN 0-935278-11-7). Palmer-Pletsch.

Brown, Gail, jt. auth. see Dillon, Karen.

Brown, Gar, jt. auth. see Spence, Jim.

Brown, Gardner M., Jr., jt. auth. see Hammack, Judd.

Brown, Gardner M., Jr. & Crutchfield, James, eds. Economics of Ocean Resources: A Research Agenda. LC 82-17471. 242p. (Orig.). 1983. pap. 12.00 (ISBN 0-295-95982-7, Pub. by Wash Sea Grant). U of Wash Pr.

Brown, Gardner Mallard, Jr., jt. auth. see Hammack, Judd.

Brown, Gary & Tasman, William, eds. Congenital Anomalies of the Optic Disc. 304p. 1982. 52.00 (ISBN 0-8089-1515-0, 790688). Grune.

Brown, Gary D. Advanced ANS COBOL: With Structured Programming. LC 76-55706. 497p. 1977. 37.50X (ISBN 0-471-10642-9, Pub. by Wiley-Interscience). Wiley.

--Beyond COBOL: Survival in Business Applications Programming. LC 80-28650. 200p. 1981. 21.95 (ISBN 0-471-09030-1, Pub. by Wiley-Interscience); pap. 18.50 (ISBN 0-471-09949-X). Wiley.

--FORTRAN to PL-I Dictionary: PL-I to FORTRAN Dictionary. LC 82-21283. 218p. 1984. Repr. of 1975 ed. lib. bdg. 19.50 (ISBN 0-89874-587-X). Krieger.

--System-360 Job-Control Language. 292p. 1970. pap. 23.50 (ISBN 0-471-10870-7, Pub. by Wiley-Interscience). Wiley.

--System-370 Job Control Language. LC 77-24901. 297p. 1977. pap. 23.50x (ISBN 0-471-03155-0, Pub. by Wiley-Interscience). Wiley.

Brown, Gary D. & Sefton, Donald. Surviving with Financial Application Packages for the Computer. 233p. 1983. 24.50 (ISBN 0-471-87065-X, Pub. by Wiley-Interscience). Wiley.

Brown, Gary E. How to Improve Your Grades & Live Happily Ever After: A Brief Guide to Academic Survival. 1973. pap. 2.75 (ISBN 0-87212-034-1). Libra.

Brown, Gaye L., ed. The Dial: Arts & Letters in the 1920s. LC 80-54667. (Illus.). 160p. (Orig.). 1983. pap. 14.95 (ISBN 0-87023-407-2). U of Mass Pr.

Brown, Gene. Lower Your Cholesterol: A Guide to a Healthier & Longer Life. LC 84-2550. (Illus.). 112p. (Orig.). 1984. pap. 4.95 (ISBN 0-943392-53-5). Tribeca Comm.

--Sports of the Times: Great Moments in Sports History. Keylin, Arleen & Lundy, Daniel, eds. 14.98 (ISBN 0-405-14225-0, 19816). Ayer Co Pubs.

Brown, Gene, jt. auth. see Hechinger, Fred M.

Brown, Gene, jt. auth. see Hovey, Graham.

Brown, Gene, jt. auth. see Kalinsky, George.

Brown, Gene, jt. auth. see Lipsyte, Robert.

Brown, Gene, jt. auth. see Middleton, Drew.

Brown, Gene, ed. Central America & the Caribbean. LC 79-26120. (Great Contemporary Issues Ser.). (Illus.). 1980. lib. bdg. 35.00x (ISBN 0-686-63415-2). Ayer Co Pubs.

--The Kennedys: A New York Times Profile. LC 80-10744. (Illus.). 256p. 1980. lib. bdg. 12.98 (ISBN 0-405-13142-9). Ayer Co Pubs.

--The New York Times Encyclopedia of Film, 1896-1979, 13 vols. LC 81-3607. (Illus.). 6000p. 1984. Set. lib. bdg. 2000.00 (ISBN 0-8129-1059-1). Times Bks.

Brown, Gene & Keylin, Arleen, eds. Sports: As Reported by the New York Times. new ed. LC 76-2450. (Illus.). 1976. 12.98 (ISBN 0-405-06689-9). Ayer Co Pubs.

Brown, Gene, jt. ed. see Keylin, Arleen.

Brown, Gene, ed. see New York Times.

Brown, Gene, jt. ed. see Shenton, James P.

Brown, Gene, jt. ed. see Teifer, Leonore.

Brown, Geoff. Diana Ross. (Illus.). 144p. 1983. pap. 9.95 (ISBN 0-312-19932-5). St Martin.

--Michael Jackson-Body & Soul: An Illustrated Biography. (Illus.). 120p. 1984. pap. 9.95 (ISBN 0-8253-0213-7). Beaufort Bks NY.

Brown, Geoffrey & Desforges, Charles. Piaget's Theory: A Psychological Critique. (Illus.). 1979. 22.95x (ISBN 0-7100-0392-7); pap. 9.95 (ISBN 0-7100-0393-5). Routledge & Kegan.

Brown, Geoffrey, jt. auth. see Thorpe, Richard.

Brown, Geoffrey, et al. Experiments in Social Sciences. 1975. 7.80x (ISBN 0-06-318014-6, IntlDept). Har-Row.

Brown, Geoffrey G. An Introduction to Histotechnology: A Manual for the Student, Practicing Technologist, & Resident in Pathology. 2nd ed. (Illus.). 480p. 1978. 29.95 (ISBN 0-8385-4340-5). ACC.

Brown, George. George Brown, D.D. Pioneer-Missionary & Explorer, an Autobiography. LC 75-32802. (Illus.). 1976. Repr. of 1908 ed. 51.00 (ISBN 0-404-14104-8). AMS Pr.

--Lecturing & Explaining. 1978. pap. 12.95 (ISBN 0-416-70920-6, NO. 2009). Methuen Inc.

--Melanesians & Polynesians. LC 71-174440. (Illus.). Repr. of 1910 ed. 17.00 (ISBN 0-405-08308-4, Blom Pubns). Ayer Co Pubs.

--Microteaching. 1975. pap. 19.95x (ISBN 0-416-83020-X, NO. 2117). Methuen Inc.

Brown, George, jt. auth. see Flanders, Helen H.

Brown, George A, ed. see American Society of Mechanical Engineers.

Brown, George D. House with the Green Shutters. 1901. 29.00 (ISBN 0-403-00447-0). Scholarly.

--Syllabification & Accent in the Paradise Lost. LC 73-39543. Repr. of 1901 ed. 12.00 (ISBN 0-404-01129-2). AMS Pr.

Brown, George E. Shade Plants for Garden & Woodland. (Illus.). 240p. 1980. 24.95 (ISBN 0-571-10377-4). Faber & Faber.

Brown, George H. And Part of Which I Was - Recollections of a Research Engineer. LC 82-72256. (Illus.). 342p. 1982. 20.00 (ISBN 0-9612524-0-5). Angus Cupar.

--Doodles, Diddles, Puzzles, Quizzes & Fun Stuff for the Sports Fan, Vol. 3. Donaldson, Judith E., ed. (Illus.). 144p. (Orig.). 1982. pap. 2.50 (ISBN 0-939942-02-X). Larkspur.

--Travel Games: Vol. 3, Sports. Donaldson, Judith E., ed. (Illus.). 36p. pap. text ed. 1.50 (ISBN 0-939942-07-0). Larkspur.

Brown, George H., jt. auth. see Donaldson, Judith E.

Brown, George H., ed. see Donaldson, Judith E.

Brown, George I., jt. auth. see Shiflett, John M.

Brown, George M. Andrina & Other Stories. 160p. 1984. 14.95 (ISBN 0-7012-0546-6, Pub. by Chatto & Windus). Merrimack Pub Cir.

--Pictures in the Cave. (Illus.). 136p. (gr. 4-7). 1980. 9.95 (ISBN 0-7011-5081-5, Pub. by Chatto & Windus). Merrimack Pub Cir.

--Portrait of Orkney. 128p. 1981. 40.00x (ISBN 0-7012-0513-X, Pub. by Chatto Bodley Head England). State Mutual Bk.

--Three Plays: The Loom of Light, the Well, & the Voyage of Saint Brandon. 160p. 1984. 15.95 (ISBN 0-7011-2742-2, Pub. by Chatto & Windus-Hogarth Pr). Merrimack Pub Cir.

--Time in a Red Coat: A Haunting Parable of War that Echoes Long in the Memory. 256p. 1985. 14.95 (ISBN 0-8149-0898-5). Vanguard.

--Under Brinkie's Brae. 152p. 1981. 25.00x (ISBN 0-903065-29-0, Pub. by Wright Pub Scotland). State Mutual Bk.

--Voyages. 48p. (Orig.). 1984. pap. 6.95 (ISBN 0-7011-2736-8, Pub. by Chatto & Windus-Hogarth Pr). Merrimack Pub Cir.

Brown, George M., intro. by. Orkney Short Stories. 145p. 29.00x (ISBN 0-907618-05-7, Pub. by Orkney Pr Uk). State Mutual Bk.

Brown, George R. The Leadership of Congress. LC 73-19135. (Politics & People Ser.). 318p. 1974. Repr. 21.00x (ISBN 0-405-05859-4). Ayer Co Pubs.

Brown, George T. The Gas Light Company of Baltimore: A Study of Natural Monopoly. LC 78-64162. (Johns Hopkins University. Studies in the Social Sciences. Fifty-Fourth Ser. 1936: 2). Repr. of 1936 ed. 15.00 (ISBN 0-404-61272-5). AMS Pr.

Brown, George W. Baltimore & the Nineteenth of April, 1861. LC 81-85924. (Illus.). 186p. 1982. pap. 4.95 (ISBN 0-940776-02-2). Maclay Assoc.

--Baltimore & the Nineteenth of April 1861: A Study of the War. LC 78-64247. (Johns Hopkins University. Studies in the Social Sciences. Extra Volumes: 3). Repr. of 1887 ed. 18.00 (ISBN 0-404-61352-7). AMS Pr.

--Canada in the Making. LC 72-100217. Repr. of 1953 ed. lib. bdg. 15.00x (ISBN 0-8371-3032-8, BRCA). Greenwood.

--Reminiscences of Gov. R. J. Walker: With the True Story of the Rescue of Kansas from Slavery. facsimile ed. LC 79-38010. (Black Heritage Library Collection). Repr. of 1902 ed. 17.50 (ISBN 0-8369-8978-3). Ayer Co Pubs.

--Reminiscences of Gov. R. J. Walker: With the True Story of the Rescue of Kansas from Slavery. LC 73-137230. Repr. of 1902 ed. 17.50x (ISBN 0-8371-1605-8, BRW&). Greenwood.

Brown, George W. & Harris, Tirril. Social Origins of Depression: A Study of Psychiatric Disorder in Women. LC 78-3209. 1978. 24.95 (ISBN 0-02-904890-7). Free Pr.

Brown, George W., ed. Canada. facs. ed. LC 71-134059. (Essay Index Reprint Ser). 1950. 40.10 (ISBN 0-8369-2147-X). Ayer Co Pubs.

Brown, Gerald R. How to Read & Interpret Automotive Oscilloscope Patterns. LC 84-17900. 1984. text ed. 24.95 (ISBN 0-8359-2930-2); pap. text ed. 17.95 (ISBN 0-8359-2929-9). Reston.

Brown, Gerald S., jt. auth. see Fine, Sidney.

Brown, Gerda. Carismas de Dios. 589p. (Orig., Span.). 1983. pap. 8.95 (ISBN 0-939868-98-9). Chr Intl Pubs.

Brown, Gilbert, jt. auth. see Gotsch, Carl.

Brown, Gilbert T. Korean Pricing Policies & Economic Development in the 1960s. LC 73-8121. pap. 84.00 (ISBN 0-317-19886-6, 2023086). Bks Demand UMI.

Brown, Gillian & Yule, George. Discourse Analysis. LC 82-23571. (Cambridge Textbooks in Linguistics Ser.). 300p. 1983. 42.50 (ISBN 0-521-24144-8); pap. 13.95 (ISBN 0-521-28475-9). Cambridge U Pr.

Brown, Gillian, et al. Teaching Talk: Strategies for Production & Assessment. (Illus.). 192p. 1985. 18.95 (ISBN 0-521-26528-2); pap. 8.95 (ISBN 0-521-31942-0). Cambridge U Pr.

Brown, Gilmor & Garwood, Alice. General Principles of Play Direction. 1936. 5.75 (ISBN 0-573-69010-3). French.

Brown, Glen H. & Labes, M. M., eds. Liquid Crystals Three: Proceedings, 2 pts. 1198p. 1972. Set. 321.25 (ISBN 0-677-15010-5). Gordon.

Brown, Glen H., et al, eds. Liquid Crystals One: Proceedings. 494p. 1967. 132.95 (ISBN 0-677-11840-6). Gordon.

--Liquid Crystals Two: Proceedings, 2 pts. 910p. 1969. Pt. 1, 252p. 69.50 (ISBN 0-677-13830-X); Pt. 2, 910p. 236.95x (ISBN 0-677-13840-7). Gordon.

Brown, Glenn. History of the United States Capitol, 2 Vols. in 1. LC 71-77734. (Architecture & Decorative Art Ser.: Vol. 34). (Illus.). 1970. Repr. of 1903 ed. lib. bdg. 85.00 (ISBN 0-306-71372-1). Da Capo.

Brown, Glenn H. & Wolken, Jerome J. Liquid Crystals & Biological Structures. LC 78-67873. 1979. 37.50 (ISBN 0-12-136850-5). Acad Pr.

Brown, Glenn H., ed. Advances in Liquid Crystals, 3 vols. Incl. Vol. 1. 1975. 85.00 (ISBN 0-12-025001-2); Vol. 2. 1976. 90.00 (ISBN 0-12-025002-0); Vol. 3. 1978. 70.00 (ISBN 0-12-025003-9). LC 74-17973. Acad Pr.

--Advances in Liquid Crystals, Vol. 4. (Serial Publication Ser.). 1979. 50.00 (ISBN 0-12-025004-7). Acad Pr.

--Advances in Liquid Crystals, Vol. 5. 1983. 50.00 (ISBN 0-12-025005-5). Acad Pr.

--Advances in Liquid Crystals, Vol. 6. (Serial Publication Ser.). 1983. 80.00 (ISBN 0-12-025006-3). Acad Pr.

Brown, Godfrey, jt. ed. see Anene, Joseph C.

Brown, Godfrey N. Apartheid: A Teacher's Guide. (Illus.). 104p. 1981. pap. 9.50 (ISBN 92-3-101896-5, U1163, UNESCO). Unipub.

Brown, Godfrey N. & Hiskett, Mervyn. Conflict & Harmony in Education in Tropical Africa. 496p. 28.50 (ISBN 0-8386-1938-X). Fairleigh Dickinson.

Brown, Goold. The Institutes of English Grammar. LC 81-18517. 1982. Repr. of 1853 ed. 50.00x (ISBN 0-8201-1372-7). Schol Facsimiles.

Brown, Gordon, jt. auth. see Drucker, Henry M.

Brown, Gordon & Cook, Robin, eds. Scotland: The Real Divide (Poverty & Deprivation in Scotland) 272p. 1983. text ed. 19.50x (ISBN 0-906391-18-0, Pub. by Mainstream Scotland). Humanities.

Brown, Gordon H. & Hamish, Keith. An Introduction to New Zealand Painting, 1839-1930. (Illus.). 256p. 1982. 29.95 (ISBN 0-00-216989-4, Pub. by W Collins New Zealand). Intl Spec Bk.

Brown, Gordon W. & Rosenberg, R. Robert. Understanding Business & Personal Law: Performance Guide. 7th ed. (Illus.). 144p. 1983. pap. text ed. 6.56 (ISBN 0-07-053636-8). McGraw.

Brown, Grady, jt. auth. see Pleasants, Larry C.

Brown, Grafton T. Pollen-Slide Studies. (Illus.). 142p. 1949. photocopy ed. 19.50x (ISBN 0-398-00235-5). C C Thomas.

Brown, Graham. My First Pop-Up Book of Opposites. (Golden Pop-Up Bks). (Illus.). 12p. (ps-2). 1985. 5.95 (ISBN 0-307-15200-6, Pub. by Golden Bks). Western Pub.

--My First Pop-Up Book of Togethers. (Golden Pop-Up Bks.). (Illus.). 12p. (ps-2). 1985. 5.95 (ISBN 0-307-15201-4, Pub. by Golden Bks). Western Pub.

Brown, Gregory M., et al, eds. Neuroendocrinology & Psychiatric Disorder. 448p. 1984. text ed. 68.50 (ISBN 0-89004-742-1). Raven.

Brown, Gregory N., jt. ed. see Duryea, Mary L.

Brown, Gwen, et al. Educating Adolescents with Behavior Disorders. (Special Education Ser.). 448p. 1981. text ed. 24.95 (ISBN 0-675-08056-8). Merrill.

Brown, H. Rabelais in English Literature. 59.95 (ISBN 0-8490-0923-5). Gordon Pr.

Brown, H. & Berry, M., eds. Speak to the Hills: An Anthology of Twentieth Century British & Irish Mountain Poetry. (Illus.). 550p. 1985. 21.50 (ISBN 0-08-030406-0, Pub. by AUP). Pergamon.

Brown, H. C. The Story of Old New York. 1977. lib. bdg. 59.95 (ISBN 0-8490-2683-0). Gordon Pr.

Brown, H. C., ed. The Nonclassical Ion Problem. LC 76-45175. (Illus.). 301p. 1977. 39.50x (ISBN 0-306-30950-5, Plenum Pr). Plenum Pub.

Brown, H. D. Biochemical Microcalorimetry. 1969. 70.50 (ISBN 0-12-136150-0). Acad Pr.

Brown, H. Douglas. Principles of Language Learning & Teaching. (Illus.). 1980. pap. text ed. 15.95 (ISBN 0-13-709295-4). P-H.

Brown, H. Douglas, jt. ed. see Wardhaugh, Ronald.

Brown, H. G., jt. auth. see Wilson, J. I.

Brown, H. H., rev. by. Brown's Rules of the Road Manual. 17th ed. 165p. 1981. pap. 14.50x (ISBN 0-85174-405-2). Sheridan.

Brown, H. Jackson, Jr., ed. see Kosser, Michael.

Brown, H. James, jt. ed. see Roberts, Neal A.

Brown, H. K., ed. see Conference on the HP-1000 International Users Group, 1st.

Brown, H. Miles. Cornish Clocks & Clockmakers. (Illus.). 102p. 1980. Repr. 14.95 (ISBN 0-7153-4999-6). David & Charles.

Brown, H. T. Five Hundred Seven Mechanical Movements. 1984. pap. 7.95 (ISBN 0-917914-25-2). Lindsay Pubns.

Brown, H. U. Telecommunications for Health Care. 112p. 1982. 42.50 (ISBN 0-8493-5588-5). CRC Pr.

Brown, H. W., tr. see Preyer, William.

Brown, Hallie Q., ed. Homespun Heroines. facs. ed. LC 70-152917. (Black Heritage Library Collection Ser). 1926. 21.00 (ISBN 0-8369-8761-6). Ayer Co Pubs.

Brown, Hamish. The Great Walking Adventure. (Great Adventure Ser.). (Illus.). 256p. 1986. 12.95 (ISBN 0-946609-12-8, Pub. by Oxford Ill Pr). Interbook.

--Hamish's Groats End Walk: One Man & His Dog on a Hill Route Through Britain & Ireland. (Illus.). 1981. 22.50 (ISBN 0-575-03029-1, Pub. by Gollancz England). David & Charles.

--Hamish's Mountain Walk. 1978. 24.95 (ISBN 0-575-02362-7, Pub. by Gollancz England). David & Charles.

--Hamish's Mountain Walk. (Illus.). 359p. 1982. pap. 8.95 (ISBN 0-586-08332-4, Pub. by Granada England). Academy Chi Pubs.

Brown, Hamish, selected by. Poems of the Scottish Hills: An Anthology. 216p. 1982. 19.00 (ISBN 0-08-028476-0); pap. 10.35 (ISBN 0-08-028477-9). Pergamon.

Brown, Hanbury. Man & the Stars. (Illus.). 1978. 22.50x (ISBN 0-19-851001-2). Oxford U Pr.

Brown, Handy N. Necromancer, Or, Voo-Doo Doctor. LC 77-39544. Repr. of 1904 ed. 13.50 (ISBN 0-404-00008-8). AMS Pr.

Brown, Harcourt. Scientific Organizations in Seventeenth Century France, 1620-1680. LC 66-27046. 1967. Repr. of 1934 ed. 8.50x (ISBN 0-8462-0974-8). Russell.

Brown, Harold. Thinking about National Security: Defense & Foreign Policy in a Dangerous World. LC 82-23859. 278p. 1983. 16.95 (ISBN 0-86531-548-5); pap. text ed. 11.95x (ISBN 0-86531-702-X). Westview.

Brown, Harold & Davis, Lynn E. Nuclear Arms Control: Where Do We Stand, No. 5. (A Westview Foreign Policy Inst. Ser.). 64p. 1984. pap. 8.95x (ISBN 0-86531-888-3). Westview.

Brown, Harold, et al. Crystallographic Groups of Four-Dimensional Space. (Wiley Monographs in Crystallography). 1978. 110.00 (ISBN 0-471-03095-3, Pub. by Wiley-Interscience). Wiley.

--Security in the 1980's. write for info. Trilateral Comm.

Brown, Harold I. Perception, Theory & Commitment: A New Philosophy of Science. LC 76-22991. 1979. pap. 7.50x (ISBN 0-226-07618-0, P812, Phoen). U of Chicago Pr.

--Perception, Theory & Commitment: The New Philosophy of Science. LC 76-22991. (Illus.). 1977. 19.95 (ISBN 0-913750-13-1). Precedent Pub.

--Perception, Theory, & Commitment: The New Philosophy of Science. 203p. 1977. 19.95. Transaction Bks.

Brown, Harold J. The Reconstruction of the Republic. 1981. pap. 5.95 (ISBN 0-915134-86-1). Mott Media.

Brown, Harold N. Pilot's Aeromedical Guide. (Modern Aviation Ser.). (Illus.). 64p. (Orig.). 1980. pap. 3.95 (ISBN 0-8306-2287-X, 2287). TAB Bks.

Brown, Harold O. Heresies: The Image of Christ in the Mirror of Heresy & Orthodoxy from the Apostles to the Present. LC 80-2558. (Illus.). 504p. 1984. 17.95 (ISBN 0-385-15338-4). Doubleday.

Brown, Harold W. & Neva, F. A. Basic Clinical Parasitology. 5th ed. (Illus.). 350p. 1983. 29.50 (ISBN 0-8385-0551-1). ACC.

Brown, Harriet C. Grandmother Brown's Hundred Years: 1827-1927. Baxter, Annette K., ed. LC 79-8778. (Signal Lives Ser.). (Illus.). 1980. Repr. of 1929 ed. lib. bdg. 42.00x (ISBN 0-405-12827-4). Ayer Co Pubs.

Brown, Harrison. The Challenge of Man's Future. (Encore Editions Ser.). 290p. 1984. Repr. of 1954 ed. 28.00x (ISBN 0-8133-0033-9). Westview.

--The Human Future Revisited. (Illus.). 1978. 4.95x (ISBN 0-393-95122-7). Norton.

Brown, Harrison, ed. China among the Nations of the Pacific. LC 81-14828. (Special Study on China & East Asia). 136p. (Orig.). 1982. pap. 9.50x (ISBN 0-86531-279-6). Westview.

Brown, Harry. Economic Science & the Common Welfare. 6th ed. LC 36-8877. 1936. 4.00x (ISBN 0-911090-04-5). Pacific Bk Supply.

--A Walk in the Sun. 192p. Repr. of 1970 ed. lib. bdg. 13.95x (ISBN 0-88411-075-3, Pub. by Aeonian Bks). Amereon Ltd.

--A Walk in the Sun. 187p. 1985. pap. 3.95 (ISBN 0-88184-117-X). Carroll & Graf.

Brown, Harry A. Certain Basic Teacher-Education Policies & Their Development & Significance in a Selected State. LC 73-176597. (Columbia University. Teachers College. Contributions to Education: No. 714). Repr. of 1937 ed. 22.50 (ISBN 0-404-55714-7). AMS Pr.

Brown, Harry D. Chemistry of the Cell Interface, 2 vols. 1971. Vol. 1. 72.00 (ISBN 0-12-136101-2); Vol. 2. 72.00 (ISBN 0-12-136102-0). Acad Pr.

Brown, Harry G. The Economics of Taxation. LC 79-10160. (Midway Reprint). 1979. pap. text ed. 15.00x (ISBN 0-226-07620-2). U of Chicago Pr.

--Selected Articles by Harry Gunnison Brown: The Case for Land Value Taxation. 245p. 1980. 12.50 (ISBN 0-911312-50-1). Schalkenbach.

Brown, Harry H. Stories of Yesterday: Horse & Buggy Days. LC 82-90882. (Illus.). 74p. 1982. 6.95 (ISBN 0-9610806-0-4). Kemah Pr.

Brown, Harry J. & Williams, Frederick D., eds. Diary of James A. Garfield: Vol. I, 1848-1871, Vol. II, 1872-1874, 2 vols. 1967. Set. 30.00x (ISBN 0-87013-111-7). Mich St U Pr.

--The Diary of James A. Garfield, Vol. IV: 1878-1881. 1982. 40.00 (ISBN 0-87013-221-0). Mich St U Pr.

Brown, Harry J., ed. see Kendall, George W.

Brown, Harry J., jt. ed. see Williams, Frederick D.

Brown, Harry L., ed. Energy Analysis of One Hundred Eight Industrial Processes. LC 84-48572. (Illus.). 313p. 1985. 39.00 (ISBN 0-915586-93-2). Fairmont Pr.

Brown, Harry M. How to Write: A Practical Rhetoric. LC 77-21524. 1978. 15.95 (ISBN 0-03-020881-5, HoltC); instructor's manual 19.95 (ISBN 0-03-022996-0). HR&W.

Brown, Harry W., tr. see Azevedo, Aluizio.

Brown, Harvey E., ed. see U. S. Surgeon-General's Office.

Brown, Hazel. Speechphone Spoken Word List. (Speechphone Ser.). 125p. 1980. Repr. of 1959 ed. incl. 3 tapes 39.50x (ISBN 0-88432-064-2, S23713, Speechphone). J Norton Pubs.

Brown, Hazel P. American Speech Sounds & Rhythm: Advanced. 2nd ed. (Speechphone Ser.). 64p. (Orig.). 1981. pap. text ed. 39.50x 3 cassettes incl. (ISBN 0-88432-063-4, S23709, Speechphone). J Norton Pubs.

--American Speech Sounds & Rhythm: Elementary. 2nd ed. (Speechphone Ser.). 64p. (Orig.). 1981. pap. text ed. 39.50x 3 cassettes incl. (ISBN 0-88432-061-8, S23701, Speechphone). J Norton Pubs.

--American Speech Sounds & Rhythm: Intermediate. 3rd ed. (Speechphone Ser.). 64p. 1981. pap. text ed. 39.50x 3 cassettes incl. (ISBN 0-88432-062-6, S23705, Speechphone). J Norton Pubs.

Brown, Helen G. Cosmopolitan's Love Book: A Guide to Ecstasy in Bed. 1978. pap. 5.00 (ISBN 0-87980-355-X). Wilshire.

--Having It All. 400p. 1983. pap. 3.95 (ISBN 0-671-47629-7). PB.

--Helen Gurley Brown's Outrageous Opinions. 1982. pap. 2.95 (ISBN 0-380-63289-6, 63289-6). Avon.

--Sex & the Office. 1983. pap. 2.95 (ISBN 0-380-64048-1, 64048-1). Avon.

--Sex & the Single Girl. 1983. pap. 2.95 (ISBN 0-380-64030-9, 64030-9). Avon.

Brown, Helen Gurley. Cosmopolitan's New Etiquette Guide. pap. 4.00 (ISBN 0-87980-337-1). Borden.

Brown, Helen W. Index of Marriage Licenses, Prince George's County, Maryland 1777-1886. LC 73-12384. 249p. 1973. Repr. of 1971 ed. 17.50 (ISBN 0-8063-0579-7). Genealog Pub.

Brown, Henry. Sonnets of Shakespeare Solved. LC 70-39545. Repr. of 1870 ed. 20.00 (ISBN 0-404-01135-7). AMS Pr.

Brown, Henry & Hardwick, David F., eds. Intermediary Metabolism of the Liver. (Illus.). 204p. 1973. 19.75x (ISBN 0-398-02248-8). C C Thomas.

Brown, Henry, tr. see Johnson, Broderick H.

Brown, Henry C. In the Golden Nineties. facs. ed. LC 71-133516. (Select Bibliographies Reprint Ser). 1927. 32.00 (ISBN 0-8369-5548-X). Ayer Co Pubs.

Brown, Henry C., Jr., et al. Steps to the Sermon. LC 63-19068. 1963. 11.95 (ISBN 0-8054-2103-3). Broadman.

Brown, Henry L. EDP for Auditors. LC 68-22301. pap. 51.80 (ISBN 0-317-09784-9, 2007369). Bks Demand UMI.

Brown, Henry P. & Hopkins, Sheila V. Perspectives of Wages & Prices. 256p. 1981. 28.00x (ISBN 0-416-31950-5, NO. 3478). Methuen Inc.

Brown, Henry Phelps. The Origins of Trade Union Power. LC 83-1920. 1983. 32.00x (ISBN 0-19-877115-0). Oxford U Pr.

Brown, Henry T. Five Hundred Seven Mechanical Movements. LC 81-50440. (Illus.). 102p. Repr. of 1896 ed. 12.50x (ISBN 0-935164-06-5). N T Smith.

Brown, Herbert C. Boranes in Organic Chemistry. LC 79-165516. (Baker Lecture Ser.). (Illus.). 464p. 1972. 52.50x (ISBN 0-8014-0681-1). Cornell U Pr.

Brown, Herbert C., et al. Organic Syntheses Via Boranes. LC 74-20520. 283p. 1975. 45.50 (ISBN 0-471-11280-1, Pub. by Wiley-Interscience). Wiley.

Brown, Herbert P. & Schanzer, Stephan N. Female Sterilization. 126p. 1982. text ed. 19.50 (ISBN 0-88416-356-3). PSG Pub Co.

Brown, Herbert R. Sentimental Novel in America, 1789-1860. facsimile ed. LC 75-107685. (Essay Index Reprint Ser). Repr. of 1940 ed. 22.00 (ISBN 0-8369-1490-2). Ayer Co Pubs.

Brown, Herbert Ross. The Sentimental Novel in America, 1789-1860. 1972. lib. bdg. 29.00x (ISBN 0-374-91032-4). Octagon.

Brown, Hilda M. Kleist & the Tragic Ideal: A Study of "Penthesilea" & Its Relationship to Kleist's Personal & Literary Development, 1806-1808. (European University Studies: Series 1, German Language & Literature: Vol. 203). 149p. 1977. pap. 21.55 (ISBN 3-261-02969-2). P Lang Pubs.

Brown, Hilton. Rudyard Kipling. LC 74-7017. (English Literature Ser., No. 33). 1974. lib. bdg. 49.95x (ISBN 0-8383-1853-3). Haskell.

--Rudyard Kipling. 1945. Repr. 25.00 (ISBN 0-8482-7404-0). Norwood Edns.

--Rudyard Kipling. 237p. Repr. of 1945 ed. lib. bdg. 45.00 (ISBN 0-89984-040-X). Century Bookbindery.

--Twice Told Tales. 1946. 15.00 (ISBN 0-686-18177-8). Havertown Bks.

--Twice Told Tales: Short Stories Broadcast by the B. C. 64p. 1982. Repr. of 1946 ed. lib. bdg. 20.00 (ISBN 0-8495-0080-X). Arden Lib.

Brown, Homer E. Solution of Large Networks by Matrix Methods. LC 74-34159. 256p. 1975. 40.50X (ISBN 0-471-11045-0, Pub. by Wiley-Interscience). Wiley.

Brown, Horatio F. Letters & Papers of John Addington Symonds. 1923. Repr. 25.00 (ISBN 0-8274-2852-9). R West.

--Studies in the History of Venice, 2 vols. LC 72-81957. 1973. Repr. of 1907 ed. Set. lib. bdg. 46.50 (ISBN 0-8337-4007-5). B Franklin.

Brown, Howard. Familiar Faces, Hidden Lives: The Story of Homosexual Men in America Today. LC 77-3423. 1977. pap. 2.95 (ISBN 0-15-630120-2, Harv). HarBraceJ.

--Modern Bank Accounting & Auditing Forms: Annual Supplement. 2nd ed. LC 79-63337. 300p. 1979. 68.00 (ISBN 0-88262-266-8). Warren.

Brown, Howard, jt. auth. see Keim, Curtis A.

Brown, Howard, ed. see Cesti.

Brown, Howard, ed. see Cocchi.

Brown, Howard, ed. see Freschi.

Brown, Howard, ed. see Gasparini, Francesco.

Brown, Howard, ed. see Traetta, Tommaso.

Brown, Howard J. & Strumolo, Tom R., eds. Decentralizing Electricity Production. LC 83-3677. 288p. 1983. 31.00x (ISBN 0-300-02569-6). Yale U Pr.

Brown, Howard M. Embellishing Sixteenth-Century Music. (Early Music Ser.). 1976. pap. 10.95x (ISBN 0-19-323175-1). Oxford U Pr.

--Instrumental Music Printed Before 1600: A Bibliography. LC 65-12783. (Illus.). 1965. 37.50x (ISBN 0-674-45610-6). Harvard U Pr.

--Italian Opera Librettos: 1640-1770, Vol. 6. LC 76-20993. 1979. lib. bdg. 77.00 (ISBN 0-8240-2655-1). Garland Pub.

--Music in the Renaissance. (History of Music Ser.). (Illus.). 368p. 1976. pap. text ed. 16.95 (ISBN 0-13-608497-4). P-H.

Brown, Howard M. & Lascelle, Joan. Musical Iconography: A Manual for Cataloguing Musical Subjects in Western Art Before 1800. LC 76-180151. (Illus.). 224p. 1972. 15.00x (ISBN 0-674-59220-4). Harvard U Pr.

Brown, Howard M., jt. auth. see Handel, George F.

Brown, Howard M., jt. auth. see Hasse, Johann A.

Brown, Howard M., ed. A Florentine Chansonnier from the Time of Lorenzo the Magnificent: Monuments of Renaissance Music Ser, Vol. VII. LC 81-16515. 1983. Vol. 1 (Text), 322 p. lib. bdg. 150.00x 2 vol. set (ISBN 0-226-07623-7). Vol. 2 (Music), 656 p. U of Chicago Pr.

--Italian Opera Librettos. LC 76-20993. (Italian Opera 1640-1770 Ser.: Vol. 52). 1979. lib. bdg. 77.00 (ISBN 0-8240-2651-9). Garland Pub.

--Italian Opera Librettos. LC 76-20993. (Italian Opera Ser. 1640 to 1770: Vol. 60). 1979. lib. bdg. 77.00 (ISBN 0-8240-2659-4). Garland Pub.

--Italian Opera Librettos: 1640-1770. Incl. Arsace (Sarri) Salvi, Antonio; Artaserse (Graun) Metastasio, Pietro; Il Bajazet (Gasparini) Piovene, Agostino; Catone in Utica (Piccinni) Metastasio, Pietro. LC 76-20993. (Italian Opera 1640-1770 Ser.: Vol. 53). 1978. lib. bdg. 77.00 (ISBN 0-8240-2652-7). Garland Pub.

--Italian Opera Librettos: 1640-1770. Incl. Demofoonte (Jommelli) Metastasio, Pietro; La Diavolessa (Galuppi) Goldoni, Carlo; Didone Abbandonata (Vinci) Metastasio, Pietro. LC 76-20993. (Italian Opera 1640-1770 Ser: Vol. 54). 1978. lib. bdg. 77.00 (ISBN 0-8240-2653-5). Garland Pub.

--Italian Opera Librettos: 1640-1770. Incl. L'Adelaide (Sartario) Dolfino, Pietro; Adriano in Siria (Maio) Metastasio, Pietro; Alessandro Severo (Lotti) Zeno, Apostolo; Gli Amanti Generosi (Mancini) Candi, Giovanni P; L' Amazore Corsara Overo L'alvilda Regina De Goti (Pallavicino) Corradi, Giulio C. LC 76-20993. (Italian Opera 1640-1770 Ser.: Vol. 51). 1978. lib. bdg. 77.00 (ISBN 0-8240-2650-0). Garland Pub.

Brown, Howard M., ed. see Albinoni, Tomaso.

Brown, Howard M., ed. see Ariosti, Attilio.

Brown, Howard M., ed. see Aureli.

Brown, Howard M., ed. see Bononcini, Antonio M.

Brown, Howard M., ed. see Bononcini, Giovanni.

Brown, Howard M., ed. see Boretti, Giovanni A.

Brown, Howard M., ed. see Caldara, Antonio.

Brown, Howard M., ed. see Cavalli, Francesco.

Brown, Howard M., ed. see Conti, Francesco.

Brown, Howard M., ed. see DiCapua, Rinaldo.

Brown, Howard M., ed. see Di Maio, Gian F.

Brown, Howard M., ed. see Fischietti, Domenico.

Brown, Howard M., ed. see Fux, Johann J.

Brown, Howard M., ed. see Galuppi, Baldassare.

Brown, Howard M., ed. see Gassmann, Florian L.

Brown, Howard M., ed. see Hasse.

Brown, Howard M., ed. see Hasse, Johann A.

Brown, Howard M., ed. see Jommelli, Niccolo.

Brown, Howard M., ed. see Latilla, Gaetano.

Brown, Howard M., ed. see Legrenzi, Giovanni.

Brown, Howard M., ed. see Leo, et al.

Brown, Howard M., ed. see Leo, Francesco.

Brown, Howard M., ed. see Leo, Leonardo.

Brown, Howard M., ed. see Logroscino, Nicola.

Brown, Howard M., ed. see Mancini, Francesco.

Brown, Howard M., ed. see Melani, Jacopo.

Brown, Howard M., ed. see Metastasio.

Brown, Howard M., ed. see Orlandini, Guiseppe M.

Brown, Howard M., ed. see Pasquini, Bernardo.

Brown, Howard M., ed. see Perez, David.

Brown, Howard M., ed. see Piccinni, Niccolo.

Brown, Howard M., ed. see Pollarolo, Carlo F.

Brown, Howard M., ed. see Porsile, Giuseppe.

Brown, Howard M., ed. see Provenzale, Francesco.

Brown, Howard M., ed. see Rospigliosi.

Brown, Howard M., ed. see Rossi, Luigi.

Brown, Howard M., ed. see Sarri, Domenico.

Brown, Howard M., ed. see Sarti.

Brown, Howard M., ed. see Sartorio, Antonio.

Brown, Howard M., ed. see Scarlatti, Alessandro.

Brown, Howard M., ed. see Stradella, Alessandro.

Brown, Howard M., ed. see Traetta, Tommaso.

Brown, Howard M., ed. see Vinci, et al.

Brown, Howard M., ed. see Vinci, Leonardo.

Brown, Howard M., ed. see Vivaldi, Antonio.

Brown, Howard M., ed. see Zeno, et al.

Brown, Howard M., ed. see Ziani, Pietro A.

Brown, Hubert L. Black & Mennonite. LC 76-44043. 112p. 1976. pap. 3.95 (ISBN 0-8361-1801-4). Herald Pr.

Brown, Hudson. The First Official Gay Handbook. LC 83-152145. (Illus.). 160p. (Orig.). 1983. pap. 5.95 (ISBN 0-943084-03-2). Turnbull & Willoughby.

Brown, Hugh. Brain & Behavior: A Textbook of Physiological Psychology. (Illus.). 1976. text ed. 17.95x (ISBN 0-19-501945-8). Oxford U Pr.

Brown, Hugh A. Cataclysms of the Earth. (Illus.). 288p. cancelled (ISBN 0-89345-005-7, Freedeeds Bks). Garber Comm.

Brown, Huntington. Rabelais in English Literature. 254p. 1967. Repr. of 1933 ed. 29.50x (ISBN 0-7146-2051-3, F Cass Co). Biblio Dist.

--Rabelais in English Literature. 1967. Repr. lib. bdg. 23.00x (ISBN 0-374-91027-8). Octagon.

Brown, I. H. G. Wells. LC 75-30878. (H. G. Wells Ser, No. 78). 1975. lib. bdg. 39.95x (ISBN 0-8383-2108-9). Haskell.

Brown, I. D. & Dolley, M. Bibliography of Coin Hoards of Great Britain & Ireland, Fifteen Hundred to Nineteen Sixty-Seven. 1977. 20.00 (ISBN 0-685-51521-4, Pub by Spink & Son England). S J Durst.

Brown, I. D., et al, eds. Bond Index to the Determinations of Inorganic Crystal Structures: BIDICS-1981. 132p. 1982. pap. 40.00 (ISBN 0-686-45046-9, 0318-126X). Polycrystal Bk Serv.

Brown, I. J. Mines of Shropshire. 1977. 15.00 (ISBN 0-903485-32-X). State Mutual Bk.

Brown, I. L. Multiple Choice Questions in Pathology. 64p. 1983. pap. text ed. 6.95 (ISBN 0-7131-4436-X). E Arnold.

Brown, Ian, ed. Molecular Approaches to Neurobiology. LC 81-17593. (Cell Biology Ser.). 1982. 65.00 (ISBN 0-12-137020-8). Acad Pr.

Brown, Ian W. Natchez Indian Archaeology: Culture Change & Stability in the Lower Mississippi Valley. (Mississippi Department of Archives & History Archaeological Report Ser.: No. 15). (Illus.). xiv, 304p. (Orig.). 1984. pap. write for info (ISBN 0-938896-42-3). Mississippi De.

--The Southeastern Check Stamped Pottery Tradition: A View from Louisiana. LC 82-10101. (MCJA Special Papers Ser.: Vol. 4). (Illus.). 112p. 1982. pap. text ed. 6.25x (ISBN 0-87338-272-2). Kent St U Pr.

Brown, Imogene E. American Aristides: A Biography of George Wythe. LC 77-89776. 324p. 1980. 32.50 (ISBN 0-8386-2142-2). Fairleigh Dickinson.

Brown, Ina C. Understanding Other Cultures. (Orig.). 1963. pap. 3.95x (ISBN 0-13-936161-8, Spec). P-H.

Brown, Ina L. A Breath of Beauty. 1982. 6.50 (ISBN 0-8233-0355-1). Golden Quill.

--Homespun. 1959. 3.00 (ISBN 0-8233-0010-2). Golden Quill.

--One Star. LC 84-90443. 96p. 1984. 7.00 (ISBN 0-8233-0397-7). Golden Quill.

Brown, Irene B. Answer Me, Answer Me. LC 85-7452. 192p. (gr. 7 up). 1985. 13.95 (ISBN 0-689-31114-1). Atheneum.

--Before the Lark. LC 82-1729. 204p. (gr. 4-7). 1982. 12.95 (ISBN 0-689-30920-1). Atheneum.

--Just Another Gorgeous Guy. LC 83-17914. 240p. (gr. 7 up). 1984. 14.95 (ISBN 0-689-31011-0). Atheneum.

--Just Another Gorgeous Guy. 192p. 1985. pap. 2.25 (ISBN 0-449-70121-2, Juniper). Fawcett.

--Morning Glory Afternoon. LC 80-18495. 224p. (gr. 5-9). 1981. PLB 9.95 (ISBN 0-689-30802-7). Atheneum.

Brown, Irving, jt. auth. see Dunlop, John T.

Brown, Irving H. Gypsy Fires in America. LC 74-1035. Repr. of 1924 ed. 40.00x (ISBN 0-8103-3942-0). Gale.

--Leconte De Lisle: A Study of the Man & His Poetry. LC 24-19430. (Columbia University. Studies in Romance Philology & Literature: No. 37). Repr. of 1924 ed. 22.50 (ISBN 0-404-50637-2). AMS Pr.

--Nights & Days on the Gypsy Trail: Through Andalusia & Other Mediterranean Shores. LC 75-3452. (Illus.). Repr. of 1922 ed. 23.50 (ISBN 0-404-16885-X). AMS Pr.

Brown, Isaac V. Biography of the Reverend Robert Finley. LC 73-82178. (Anti-Slavery Crusade in America Ser). 1969. Repr. of 1857 ed. 18.00 (ISBN 0-405-00617-9). Ayer Co Pubs.

Brown, Isabel M. The Magic Whimseys. (Illus.). 30p. (Orig.). (gr. k-3). 1985. pap. 3.95 (ISBN 0-9613804-0-3). Green Crown Pr.

Brown, Ivan W., ed. see International Conference on Hyperbaric Medicine - 3rd - Durham - N. C. - 1965.

Brown, Ivor. Chosen Words. LC 78-26764. 1979. Repr. of 1955 ed. lib. bdg. 24.75x (ISBN 0-313-20895-6, BRCW). Greenwood.

--H. G. Wells. LC 72-8641. 1972. Repr. of 1923 ed. lib. bdg. 15.00 (ISBN 0-8414-0396-1). Folcroft.

--I Give You My Word, & Say the Word. LC 77-11628. 1977. Repr. of 1948 ed. lib. bdg. 24.75x (ISBN 0-8371-9801-1, BRGY). Greenwood.

--No Idle Words, & Having the Last Word. LC 77-11610. 1977. Repr. of 1951 ed. lib. bdg. 22.50x (ISBN 0-8371-9800-3, BRNO). Greenwood.

--Shakespeare in His Time. 238p. 1982. Repr. of 1960 ed. lib. bdg. 40.00 (ISBN 0-89984-090-6). Century Bookbindery.

--Words in Our Time. LC 74-4840. 127p. 1974. Repr. of 1958 ed. lib. bdg. 18.75x (ISBN 0-8371-7488-0, BRWT). Greenwood.

--Words in Season. LC 74-4839. 159p. 1974. Repr. of 1961 ed. lib. bdg. 24.75x (ISBN 0-8371-7489-9, BRWS). Greenwood.

Brown, Ivor & Fearon, George. Amazing Monument. LC 73-113362. 1970. Repr. of 1939 ed. 23.75x (ISBN 0-8046-1009-6, Pub. by Kennikat). Assoc Faculty Pr.

--Amazing Monument. 1939. Repr. 12.50 (ISBN 0-8274-1846-9). R West.

--This Shakespeare Industry. LC 70-92951. (Studies in Shakespeare, No. 24). 1970. Repr. of 1939 ed. lib. bdg. 52.95x (ISBN 0-8383-1063-X). Haskell.

Brown, Ivor, ed. see Observer.

Brown, Ivor J. Ivor Brown's Books of Word, Comprising a Word in Your Ear & Just Another Word. LC 78-5328. 264p. 1978. Repr. of 1944 ed. lib. bdg. 24.75x (ISBN 0-313-20393-8, BRWY). Greenwood.

--Shakespeare. 1973. Repr. of 1949 ed. 17.50 (ISBN 0-8274-1450-1). R West.

--Shakespeare in His Time. LC 76-3664. (Illus.). 238p. 1976. Repr. of 1960 ed. lib. bdg. 39.75x (ISBN 0-8371-8782-6, BRSH). Greenwood.

--Shaw in His Time. LC 79-17319. (Illus.). 1979. Repr. of 1965 ed. lib. bdg. 27.50x (ISBN 0-313-21999-0, BRSW). Greenwood.

Brown, Ivor J. & Fearon, George. This Shakespeare Industry: Amazing Monument. LC 77-98824. Repr. of 1939 ed. lib. bdg. 19.75x (ISBN 0-8371-2850-1, BRSI). Greenwood.

Brown, J. Pilgrim Fathers of New England & Their Puritan Successors. 4th ed. (Illus.). Repr. of 1920 ed. 29.00 (ISBN 0-527-12050-2). Kraus Repr.

Brown, J. & MIT Writing Program Members. Free Writing: A Group Approach. (gr. 10 up). 1977. text ed. 7.20 (ISBN 0-8104-5982-5); pap. text ed. 7.20x (ISBN 0-8104-5981-7). Boynton Cook Pubs.

Brown, J., ed. Modern British Dramatists: A Collection of Critical Essays. 1968. 12.95t (ISBN 0-13-588053-X, S-TC-74, Spec). P-H.

Brown, J., ed. see Cheldelin, Larry V.

Brown, J., et al, eds. An Arctic Ecosystem: The Coastal Tundra at Barrow, Alaska. LC 78-22901. (US-IBP Synthesis Ser.: Vol. 12). 571p. 1981. 38.50 (ISBN 0-87933-370-7). Van Nos Reinhold.

Brown, J. A., jt. auth. see Aitchison, J.

Brown, J. B. Three P's in Recovery. 2nd ed. 24p. 1984. pap. write for info. H-&-H Pubs.

Brown, J. C. Gastric Inhibitory Polypeptide. (Monographs on Endocrinology: Vol. 24). (Illus.). 200p. 1982. 34.00 (ISBN 0-387-11271-5). Springer-Verlag.

Brown, J. Carter, ed. Early Italian Engravings from the National Gallery of Art. LC 73-79624. (Illus.). pap. 19.95 (ISBN 0-89468-008-0). Natl Gallery Art.

Brown, J. Douglas. An American Philosophy of Social Security. LC 71-39781. 212p. 1972. 26.00x (ISBN 0-691-03092-8). Princeton U Pr.

--The Human Nature of Organizations. LC 73-85862. 180p. 1979. pap. 3.95 (ISBN 0-8144-7514-0). Am Mgmt Assns.

Brown, J. Edward. New Neighbours: Short Stories. 65p. (Orig.). 1983. pap. 3.45x (ISBN 0-86863-688-6, Pub. by Heinemann Pub New Zealand). Intl Spec Bk.

Brown, J. H. Advances in Biomedical Engineering, Vol. 5. (Serial Publication Ser.). 1975. 85.00 (ISBN 0-12-004905-8). Acad Pr.

--The High Cost of Healing: Physicians & the Health Care System. 224p. 1985. 26.95 (ISBN 0-89885-222-6). Human Sci Pr.

--Lamb's Biographical Dictionary of the United States, 7 vols. 700.00 (ISBN 0-8490-0481-0). Gordon Pr.

--Management in Health Care Systems. 152p. 1984. 49.50 (ISBN 0-8493-5572-9). CRC Pr.

Brown, J. H., ed. Advances in Biomedical Engineering, Vol. VII. LC 71-141733. 1979. 60.00 (ISBN 0-12-004907-4). Acad Pr.

--Advances in Biomedical Engineering, Vol. 4. (Serial Publication Ser.). 1974. 85.00 (ISBN 0-12-004904-X). Acad Pr.

Brown, J. H. & Dickson, James F., eds. Advances in Biomedical Engineering, Vol. 6. 1976. 85.00 (ISBN 0-12-004906-6). Acad Pr.

Brown, J. H., jt. ed. see Dickson, J. F., 3rd.

Brown, J. H. see Kenedi, R. M.

Brown, J. H., et al. Laboratory Manual in Animal Physiology. 225p. 1983. pap. text ed. 14.95x (ISBN 0-89787-115-4). Gorsuch Scarisbrick.

Brown, J. H. U. The Health Care Dilemma. LC 78-3891. 183p. 1978. 19.95 (ISBN 0-87705-360-X). Human Sci Pr.

Brown, J. H. U. & Gann, Donald, eds. Engineering Principles in Physiology, 2 vols. Vol. 1, 1973. 65.00 (ISBN 0-12-136201-9); Vol. 2, 1973. 76.50 (ISBN 0-12-136202-7). Acad Pr.

Brown, J. L., jt. auth. see Owler, L. W.

Brown, J. L., jt. ed. see Bailes, N. J.

Brown, J. Lewis & Howard, Leslie R. Managerial Accounting & Finance. 4th ed. 896p. 1982. pap. text ed. 32.50x (ISBN 0-7121-1751-2). Trans-Atlantic.

Brown, J. Marvin. A. U. A. Language Center Thai Course, 3 Bks. Bks. 1-3. 4.50 ea.; Bks. 1-3. tape suppl. 2.00 ea. Cornell SE Asia.

Brown, J. Marvin, jt. auth. see Hsu Ying.

Brown, J. Newton. Baptist Church Manual. pap. 0.95 (ISBN 0-8170-0015-1). Judson.

Brown, J. P. The Economic Effects of Floods. LC 72-86100. (Lecture Notes in Economics & Mathematical Systems: Vol. 70). v, 87p. 1972. pap. 9.00 (ISBN 0-387-05925-3). Springer-Verlag.

Brown, J. Quantin. The Consultant of Finance. (Illus.). 101p. 1984. pap. 35.00 (ISBN 0-931067-00-6). Maximum Mktg.

Brown, J. R. & Finkel, L. IBM PC: Data File Programming. 367p. 1983. pap. 14.95 (ISBN 0-471-89717-5). Wiley.

Brown, J. S., jt. ed. see Sleeman, D.

Brown, Jack H., jt. auth. see Stratton, John M.

Brown, Jack H., ed. Physiology of Man in Space: Proceedings. 1963. 71.00 (ISBN 0-12-136350-3). Acad Pr.

Brown, James. History of the Origin & Progress of the Sikhs, ISPP Vol. II, No. 4. 74p. 1975. Repr. 2.00 (ISBN 0-88065-068-0, Pub. by Messers Today & Tommorrows Printers & Publishers India). Scholarly Pubns.

--Hot Wire. 237p. 1985. 15.95 (ISBN 0-87795-630-8). Arbor Hse.

--Introductory Solid Mechanics. LC 74-156805. pap. 112.00 (ISBN 0-317-07989-1, 2051225). Bks Demand UMI.

Brown, James, jt. auth. see Margiotta, Franklin D.

Brown, James & Snyder, William P., eds. THe Regionalization of Warfare: The Falkland Islands, Lebanon & the Iran-Iraq Conflict. (Illus.). 266p. 1984. 34.95 (ISBN 0-88738-022-0); pap. 14.95 (ISBN 0-87855-985-X). Transaction Bks.

Brown, James, et al. AV Instruction: Technology, Media & Methods. 6th ed. (Illus.). 512p. 1983. text ed. 30.95 (ISBN 0-07-008176-X). McGraw.

--The Relationship of the Library to Instructional Systems. Corrigan, John T., ed. (Catholic Library Association Studies in Librarianship: No. 2). 1978. pap. 3.00 (ISBN 0-87507-006-X). Cath Lib Assn.

Brown, James A. The Gentleman Farm Site, La Salle County, Illinois. (Reports of Investigation Ser.: No. 12). (Illus.). 48p. 1967. pap. 2.00 (ISBN 0-89792-032-5). Ill St Museum.

--Prehistoric Southern Ozark Marginality: A Myth Exposed. Wood, W. Raymond, ed. LC 83-63187. (Special Publications Ser.: No. 6). (Illus.). 85p. (Orig.). 1984. pap. 5.00 (ISBN 0-943414-18-0). MO Arch Soc.

--The Word & the World: God's Priorities for Today. 64p. 1984. 7.95 (ISBN 0-89962-419-7). Todd & Honeywell.

Brown, James A. see Phillips, James L.

Brown, James A., jt. auth. see Phillips, Philip.

Brown, James A., jt. auth. see Quaal, Ward L.

Brown, James A., ed. see Orr, Kenneth G., et al.

Brown, James A., jt. ed. see Price, T. Douglas.

Brown, James A., jt. ed. see Whallon, Robert.

Brown, James B., jt. auth. see Zaydon, Thomas J.

Brown, James Baldwin. Memoirs of Howard, Compiled from His Diary. LC 73-156007. Repr. of 1831 ed. 18.50 (ISBN 0-404-09107-5). AMS Pr.

Brown, James Buchan. Bible Truths with Shakespearian Parallels. 6th ed. LC 74-19106. Repr. of 1886 ed. 15.00 (ISBN 0-404-01136-5). AMS Pr.

Brown, James C. The Origin & Early History of the Office of Notary. 1976. lib. bdg. 59.95 (ISBN 0-8490-2383-1). Gordon Pr.

--Paper Menagerie. (Illus.). (gr. k-3). 1984. pap. 3.95 (ISBN 0-8224-5191-3). Pitman Learning.

--Papercrafts for All Seasons. (Illus.). (gr. k-3). 1984. pap. 3.95 (ISBN 0-8224-5189-1). Pitman Learning.

Brown, James C. & Blakeman, John D. Managing Patients & Stress Effectively: A Skills Manual for the Health Professional. 116p. 1983. spiral bdg. 12.75x (ISBN 0-398-04864-9). C C Thomas.

Brown, James D. Subject Classification for the Arrangement of Libraries & the Organization of Information with Tables, Indexes, Etc. For the Subdivision of Subjects. 1976. lib. bdg. 59.95 (ISBN 0-8490-2715-2). Gordon Pr.

Brown, James D. & Stratton, Stephen S. British Musical Biography: A Dictionary of Musical Artists, Authors & Composers, Born in Britain & Its Colonies. LC 76-139197. (Music Ser.). 1971. Repr. of 1897 ed. lib. bdg. 49.50 (ISBN 0-306-70076-X). Da Capo.

Brown, James F. Affectivity: Its Language & Meaning. 280p. (Orig.). 1982. lib. bdg. 27.25 (ISBN 0-8191-2613-6); pap. text ed. 13.25 (ISBN 0-8191-2614-4). U Pr of Amer.

Brown, James H. & Gibson, Arthur C. Biogeography. LC 82-14124. (Illus.). 653p. 1983. text ed. 32.95 (ISBN 0-8016-0824-4). Mosby.

Brown, James I. Efficient Reading, Form B. 6th ed. 320p. 1976. pap. text ed. 13.95x (ISBN 0-669-94466-1). Heath.

--Efficient Reading Instructors Manual. 5th ed ed. 75p. 1982. pap. text ed. 19.95 (ISBN 0-943000-07-6). Telstar Inc.

--Efficient Reading Revised, Form A. pap. text ed. 13.95x 1971 ed. (ISBN 0-669-61036-4); pap. text ed. 13.95x 1962 ed. (ISBN 0-669-20370-X). Heath.

--Guide to Effective Reading. 1966. pap. text ed. 7.95x (ISBN 0-669-20412-9). Heath.

--Programmed Vocabulary. 3rd ed. (The CPD Approach). 1980. pap. text ed. 15.95 (ISBN 0-13-729707-6). P-H.

--Reading Power. alternate ed. 1978. pap. text ed. 12.95 (ISBN 0-669-00774-9). Heath.

--Reading Power. 2nd ed. 400p. 1982. pap. text ed. 12.95 (ISBN 0-669-05318-X); answer key 1.95 (ISBN 0-669-07498-5). Heath.

--Word Power Study Guide. (Illus.). 50p. 1982. pap. text ed. 4.95 (ISBN 0-943000-04-1). Telstar Inc.

Brown, James I. & Pearsall, Thomas E. Better Spelling. 2nd ed. 1978. pap. text ed. 7.95x (ISBN 0-669-01904-6). Heath.

Brown, James I. & Prois, Karyn. A Study Guide for Efficient Reading: Form B. 52p. 1982. pap. text ed. 4.95 (ISBN 0-943000-06-8). Telstar Inc.

Brown, James I. & Prois, Karyn S. A Study Guide for Efficient Reading: Alternate Edition. Kemmerer, W. W., ed. 52p. pap. text ed. 4.95 (ISBN 0-943000-05-X). Telstar Inc.

Brown, James J., ed. State & Local Government Finance: A Selectively Annotated Bibliography, No. 783. 1975. 5.50 (ISBN 0-686-20351-8). CPL Biblios.

Brown, James K. This Business of Issues: Coping with the Company's Environments. LC 79-87756. (Report Ser.: No. 758). (Illus.). 74p. 1979. pap. 30.00 (ISBN 0-8237-0194-8); pap. 10.00 member. Conference Bd.

Brown, James K. & Kay, Lillian W. Corporate R&D Strategy: Innovation & Funding Issues. (Report Ser.: No. 863). 64p. 1985. 100.00 (ISBN 0-8237-0304-5); 20.00 (ISBN 0-317-36910-5). Conference Bd.

Brown, James K. & O'Connor, Rochelle. Planning & the Corporate Planning Director. (Report Ser.: No. 627). 94p. 1974. pap. 22.50 (ISBN 0-8237-0045-3); pap. 7.50 member. Conference Bd.

Brown, James K. & Stothoff, George S. The Defense Industry: Some Perspectives from the Financial Community. LC 76-22015. (Report Ser.: No. 693). 38p. 1976. pap. 30.00 (ISBN 0-8237-0127-1); pap. 10.00 member. Conference Bd.

Brown, James K., jt. auth. see Bacon, Jeremy.

Brown, James K. & Elvers, Lita M., eds. Research & Development: Key Issues for Management. (Report Ser.: No. 842). (Illus.). x, 102p. (Orig.). 1983. pap. 125.00 (ISBN 0-8237-0283-9); pap. 25.00 member. Conference Bd.

Brown, James L. Beowulf. (Illus.). 1974. 11.75 (ISBN 0-912314-06-0). Academy Santa Clara.

--Dissension in Arcady: Bear Flag Revolution. 1978. 14.50 (ISBN 0-912314-15-X). Academy Santa Clara.

--The Mussel Slough Tragedy. (Illus.). 153p. 1980. pap. 6.00 (ISBN 0-686-31567-7). J L Brown.

--Treasures on Earth. 1979. pap. 7.50 (ISBN 0-912314-19-2). Academy Santa Clara.

--Treasures on Earth. LC 79-54075. 282p. 1979. pap. 7.50 (ISBN 0-912314-19-2). J L Brown.

Brown, James L., tr. see Valery, Paul.

Brown, James M. Dickens: Novelist in the Market-Place. LC 81-8077. 188p. 1982. 28.50x (ISBN 0-389-20219-3, 07001). B&N Imports.

Brown, James R. Ergodic Theory & Topological Dynamics. (Pure & Applied Math Ser.). 1976. 42.50 (ISBN 0-12-137150-6). Acad Pr.

Brown, James R. & Butwill, N. Religion, Society, & the Homosexual. LC 73-10095. 44p. 1973. pap. 2.95 (ISBN 0-8422-0343-5). Irvington.

Brown, James R. & Wardell, David B. Teaching & Coaching Gymnastics for Men & Women. 441p. 1980. text ed. 32.00 (ISBN 0-471-10798-0). Wiley.

Brown, James R., jt. auth. see Ryser, Otto E.

Brown, James R. & Woodruff, A. M., eds. Land for the Cities of Asia. LC 77-161842. 416p. 1971. pap. 3.00 (ISBN 0-686-01012-4). Lincoln Inst Land.

Brown, James S. Life of a Pioneer. LC 77-17574. Repr. of 1900 ed. 25.00 (ISBN 0-404-08432-X). AMS Pr.

Brown, James S., Jr., ed. Up Before Daylight: Life Histories from the Alabama Writers' Project, 1938-1939. LC 81-21988. 261p. 1982. pap. 9.95 (ISBN 0-8173-0099-6). U of Ala Pr.

Brown, James T. Harvest of the Sun: An Illustrated History of Riverside County. 256p. 1985. 24.95 (ISBN 0-89781-145-3). Windsor Pubns Inc.

Brown, James V., et al. AV Instructional Technology Manual for Independent Study. 6th ed. (Illus.). 208p. 1983. pap. text ed. 13.95 (ISBN 0-07-008179-4). McGraw.

Brown, James W. California Style, Level 2. McConochie, Jean, ed. (Regents Readers Ser.). (Illus.). 64p. 1983. pap. text ed. 1.95 (ISBN 0-88345-525-0, 20824). Regents Pub.

--Fictional Meals & Their Function in the French Novel 1789-1848. (University of Toronto Romance Ser.: No. 48). 232p. 1984. 25.00x (ISBN 0-8020-5605-9). U of Toronto Pr.

--Modos de Ser: Modos de Ver. LC 84-10375. 167p. 1985. pap. text ed. 13.95 (ISBN 0-471-88643-2). Wiley.

--New Media in Public Libraries: A Survey of Current Practices. LC 76-5463. 1976. pap. 12.50x (ISBN 0-88432-003-0, Dist. by Gaylord Bros). J Norton Pubs.

Brown, James W., jt. auth. see Churchill, Ruel V.

Brown, James W. & Brown, Shirley N., eds. Educational Media Yearbook, 1980. 6th ed. LC 73-4891. 445p. 1980. lib. bdg. 42.50 (ISBN 0-87287-223-8). Libs Unl.

--Educational Media Yearbook, 1981. LC 73-4891. 451p. 1981. lib. bdg. 42.50x (ISBN 0-87287-259-9). Libs Unl.

--Educational Media Yearbook, 1982. LC 73-4891. 450p. 1982. lib. bdg. 42.50x (ISBN 0-87287-290-4). Libs Unl.

--Educational Media Yearbook, 1983. 586p. 1983. lib. bdg. 47.50 (ISBN 0-87287-384-6). Libs Unl.

--Educational Media Yearbook, 1984. 580p. 1984. lib. bdg. 47.50 (ISBN 0-87287-423-0). Libs Unl.

Brown, Jan. Buy It Right. LC 73-81039. pap. 3.45 (ISBN 0-911744-14-2). Career Pub IL.

Brown, Jan & Kmetz, Yoko Sakakibara. Exploring Tohoku: A Guide to Japan's Back Country. LC 82-17467. (Illus.). 312p. (Orig.). 1983. pap. 11.95 (ISBN 0-8348-0177-9). Weatherhill.

Brown, Jane. Gardens of a Golden Afternoon. (Penguin Nonfiction Ser.). 224p. 1985. pap. 12.95 (ISBN 0-14-007231-4). Penguin.

Brown, Jane D., jt. auth. see Rubenstein, Eli A.

Brown, Jane K. Goethe's Cyclical Narratives: Die Unterhaltungen Deutscher Ausgewanderten & Wilhelm Meisters Wanderjahre. (Studies in the Germanic Languages & Literatures: No. 82). 154p. 1975. 13.00 (ISBN 0-8078-8082-5). U of NC Pr.

Brown, Janet. Feminist Drama: Definition & Critical Analysis. LC 79-22382. 167p. 1979. 16.00 (ISBN 0-8108-1267-3). Scarecrow.

Brown, Janet F., ed. Administering Programs for Young Children. LC 84-61999. 224p. 1984. 7.00 (ISBN 0-912674-90-3, NAEYC 307). Natl Assn Child Ed.

--Curriculum Planning for Young Children. LC 82-61723. 276p. 1982. pap. text ed. 6.50 (ISBN 0-912674-83-0, NAEYC 113). Natl Assn Child Ed.

--Curriculum Planning for Young Children. LC 82-61723. 276p. 1982. 6.50 (ISBN 0-912674-83-0, NAEYC 113). Natl Assn Child Ed.

Brown, Jason. Mind, Brain, & Conciousness: The Neuropsychology of Cognition. (Perspectives in Neurolinguistics & Psycholinguistics Ser.). 1977. 29.50 (ISBN 0-12-137550-1). Acad Pr.

Brown, Jason W. Aphasia, Apraxia & Agnosia: Clinical & Theoretical Aspects. (Illus.). 320p. 1979. 34.50x (ISBN 0-398-02211-9). C C Thomas.

Brown, Jason W., ed. Jargonaphasia. LC 80-2328. (Perspectives in Neurolinguistics & Psycholinguistics Ser.). 1981. 37.50 (ISBN 0-12-137580-3). Acad Pr.

Brown, Jay C., jt. auth. see Flickinger, Charles J.

Brown, Jean. Keeping Your Kids Safe. 1985. pap. 6.95 (ISBN 0-671-55621-5, Pub. by Monarch Pr). S&S.

Brown, Jean, jt. ed. see Hartigan, Evelyn G.

Brown, Jean M., ed. The Vision of Modern Dance. LC 79-88382. (Illus.). 206p. 1979. pap. text ed. 7.95 (ISBN 0-916622-12-6). Princeton Bk Co.

Brown, Jeannette A. & Pate, Robert H., Jr. Being a Counselor: Directions & Challenges. LC 82-20764. (Psychology Ser.). 450p. 1983. text ed. 20.50 pub net (ISBN 0-534-01261-2). Brooks-Cole.

Brown, Jeff. Flat Stanley. LC 63-17525. (Illus.). 64p. (gr. 1-5). 1964. PLB 11.89 (ISBN 0-06-020681-0). HarpJ.

--A Lamp for the Lambchops. LC 82-48628. (Illus.). 96p. (gr. 2-6). 1983. 9.57i (ISBN 0-06-020693-4); PLB 9.89g (ISBN 0-06-020694-2). HarpJ.

Brown, Jeff & Fete, Ray. Meyers Lake Revisited. (Illus.). 192p. 1984. 24.95 (ISBN 0-938936-27-1). Daring Bks.

Brown, Jeffrey. Secret Ingredients: Inactive Ingredients in Drugs. 1985. 15.95 (ISBN 0-8016-0865-1). Mosby.

Brown, Jeffrey D. The Tower Site & Ohio Monongahela. LC 81-17171. (Research Papers in Archaeology Ser.: No. 3). (Illus.). 96p. 1982. pap. 7.00x (ISBN 0-87338-263-3). Kent St U Pr.

Brown, Jeffrey L. The Complete Parents' Guide to Telephone Medicine: How, When & Why to Call Your Child's Doctor. 224p. 1982. pap. 6.95 (ISBN 0-399-50582-2, Perigee). Putnam Pub Group.

--The Complete Parent's Guide to Telephone Medicine: How, When & Why to Call Your Child's Doctor. 304p. 1983. pap. 3.50 (ISBN 0-425-05496-9). Berkley Pub.

--Telephone Medicine: A Practical Guide to Pediatric Telephone Advice. LC 80-16674. (Illus.). 154p. 1980. pap. text ed. 16.95 (ISBN 0-8016-0856-2). Mosby.

Brown, Jennifer. Scottish Society in the Fifteenth Century. LC 77-81309. 1978. 27.50 (ISBN 0-312-70539-5). St Martin.

Brown, Jennifer S., jt. ed. see Peterson, Jacqueline.

Brown, Jerald & Finkel, LeRoy. PCjr Data File Programming: A Self-Teaching Guide. 320p. 1984. pap. 15.95 (ISBN 0-471-81580-2, Pub. by Wiley Pr). Wiley.

Brown, Jerald R. Instant BASIC: Third Edition. (Illus.). 224p. 1984. pap. 12.95 (ISBN 0-88056-344-3). Dilithium Pr.

Brown, Jerald R. & Finkel, LeRoy. IBM PC, Data File Programming: IBM Data File Set. LC 82-24849. (IBM Personal Computing Ser.). 320p. 1983. pap. 39.90 (ISBN 0-471-88904-0, Pub by Wiley Pr); programming disk incl. Wiley.

Brown, Jerald R., jt. auth. see Finkel, Leroy.

Brown, Jerald R., jt. auth. see Finkel, LeRoy.

Brown, Jerald R., et al. BASIC for the Apple II. LC 82-10962. (Self-Teaching Guide Ser.: No. 1-581). 410p. 1982. pap. 12.95 (ISBN 0-471-86596-6, Pub. by Wiley Pr); pap. tchr's guide avail. Wiley.

Brown, Jeremy & Powell-Smith, Vincent. Horse & Stable Management. 256p. 1984. 19.50 (ISBN 0-246-11217-4, Pub. by Granada England). Sheridan.

Brown, Jeri W. Space Safety & Rescue: 1979-1981, Vol. 54. (Science & Technology Ser.). (Illus.). 456p. 1983. lib. bdg. 45.00x (ISBN 0-87703-177-0, Pub. by Am Astronaut); pap. text ed. 35.00x (ISBN 0-87703-178-9). Univelt Inc.

Brown, Jerome C. Cartoon Bulletin Boards. 1971. pap. 4.95 (ISBN 0-8224-1265-9). Pitman Learning.

--Christmas in the Classroom. 1969. pap. 4.95 (ISBN 0-8224-1365-5). Pitman Learning.

--Classroom Cartoons for All Occasions. 1966. pap. 4.95 (ISBN 0-8224-1380-9). Pitman Learning.

--Holiday Art Projects. (gr. k-3). 1984. pap. 3.95 (ISBN 0-8224-3821-6). Pitman Learning.

--Holiday Crafts & Greeting Cards: Paper Crafts Ser. (gr. 1-6). 1982. pap. 5.95 (ISBN 0-8224-5194-8). Pitman Learning.

--Paper Designs. (Paper Crafts Ser.). (gr. 1-6). 1982. pap. 5.95 (ISBN 0-8224-5193-X). Pitman Learning.

--Puppets & Mobiles. (Paper Crafts Ser.). (gr. 1-6). 1982. pap. 5.95 (ISBN 0-8224-5195-6). Pitman Learning.

Brown, Jerram. The Evolution of Behavior. 900p. 1975. text ed. 22.95x (ISBN 0-393-09295-X). Norton.

Brown, Jerry E. Darkhold. 352p. 1985. pap. 2.95 (ISBN 0-441-13784-9). Ace Bks.

Brown, Jerry E., ed. Clearings in the Thicket: An Alabama Humanities Reader. LC 84-25589. xix, 188p. 1985. 16.50 (ISBN 0-86554-144-2, MUP/H134). Mercer Univ Pr.

Brown, Jesse & Willard, A. M. The Black Hills Trails: A History of the Struggles of the Pioneers... facsimile ed. LC 75-83. (Mid-American Frontier Ser.). (Illus.). 1975. Repr. of 1924 ed. 44.00x (ISBN 0-405-06852-2). Ayer Co Pubs.

Brown, Jim. The Case for the Cruising Trimaran. LC 78-64789. (Illus.). 1979. 15.95 (ISBN 0-87742-100-5). Intl Marine.

--Fishing Reel Patents of the United States, 1838-1940. (Illus.). 50p. (Orig.). 1985. pap. write for info. (ISBN 0-916751-00-7). Trico Pr.

--Tennis: Strokes, Strategy, & Programs. (Illus.). 1980. text ed. 21.95 (ISBN 0-13-903351-3). P-H.

--Tennis: Teaching, Coaching, & Directing Programs. (Illus.). 256p. 1976. 19.95 (ISBN 0-13-903344-0). P-H.

Brown, Joan C., jt. auth. see Berthoud, Richard.

Brown, Joan W. Another Love. LC 83-81269. (Rhapsody Romance Ser.). 192p. (Orig.). 1983. pap. 2.95 (ISBN 0-89081-390-6). Harvest Hse.

--Best of Christmas Joys. LC 83-45165. 64p. (Orig.). 1983. pap. 2.95 (ISBN 0-385-19039-5, Galilee). Doubleday.

--Every Knee Shall Bow. 194p. 1984. pap. 5.95 (ISBN 0-89066-054-9). World Wide Pubs.

--If Love Be Ours. 192p. 1983. pap. 2.95 (ISBN 0-89081-413-9). Harvest Hse.

--Let Me Love Again. 1984. pap. 2.95 (ISBN 0-89081-439-2). Harvest Hse.

--Love's Tender Voyage. (Rhapsody Romance Ser.). 192p. (Orig.). 1983. pap. 2.95 (ISBN 0-89081-395-7). Harvest Hse.

--Wings of Joy. 192p. 1977. 12.95 (ISBN 0-8007-0877-6). Revell.

Brown, Joan W. & Brown, Bill. Together Each Day. 256p. 1980. 12.95 (ISBN 0-8007-1127-0). Revell.

Brown, Joan W., compiled by. Dia-Tras-Dia Con Billy Graham. Orig. Title: Day by Day with Billy Graham. 192p. 1982. Repr. of 1978 ed. 3.95 (ISBN 0-311-40039-6, Edit Mundo). Casa Bautista.

Brown, Joan W., ed. see Bonhoeffer, Dietrich.

Brown, Joan W., compiled by. Day-by-Day with Billy Graham. 1976. pap. 5.95 (ISBN 0-89066-000-X). World Wide Pubs.

Brown, Joanna C. Figures in a Wessex Landscape: Thomas Hardy's Pictures of English Country Life. (Illus.). 352p. 1985. 25.00 (ISBN 0-8052-8218-1, Pub. by Allison & Busby England). Schocken.

Brown, Jody. The Best Little Rivalry in Town: A Game by Game History of the USC-UCLA Football Rivalry 1929 to 1981. LC 82-81806. (Great Rivalry Ser.). (Illus.). 400p. 1982. pap. 10.95 (ISBN 0-88011-069-4). Leisure Pr.

--Don Shula: Countdown to Supremacy. LC 83-80710. (Illus.). 320p. (Orig.). 1983. pap. 12.95 (ISBN 0-88011-160-7). Leisure Pr.

Brown, Joe D. Paper Moon. (YA) (RL 9). 1972. pap. 2.50 (ISBN 0-451-09940-0, Sig). NAL.

Brown, John. Analytical Exposition of the Epistle of Paul to the Romans. (Religious Heritage Reprint Library). 644p. 1981. Repr. of 1857 ed. 14.95 (ISBN 0-8010-0805-0). Baker Bk.

--Arthur H. Hallam. LC 73-1672. 1973. Repr. of 1862 ed. lib. bdg. 7.50 (ISBN 0-8414-1796-2). Folcroft.

--Brief Sketch of the First Settlement of the County of Schoharie by the Germans. 1981. pap. 2.00 (ISBN 0-686-97285-6). Hope Farm.

--The English Puritans. 1978. Repr. of 1910 ed. lib. bdg. 15.00 (ISBN 0-8495-0434-1). Arden Lib.

--The English Puritans. LC 73-12821. 1910. lib. bdg. 22.50 (ISBN 0-8414-3235-X). Folcroft.

--Essays on the Characteristics of the Earl of Shaftesbury. 1969. Repr. of 1751 ed. 47.00x (ISBN 3-4870-2035-1). Adlers Foreign Bks.

--An Estimate of the Manners & Principles of the Times. LC 75-31085. Repr. of 1758 ed. 21.50 (ISBN 0-404-13504-8). AMS Pr.

--First Peter, 2 vols. 1980. 29.95 (ISBN 0-85151-204-6); Vol. 1, 577 Pp. (ISBN 0-85151-205-4); Vol. 2, 640 Pp. (ISBN 0-85151-206-2). Banner of Truth.

--Galatians. 1982. lib. bdg. 16.00 (ISBN 0-86524-083-3, 4802). Klock & Klock.

--Hebrews. (Geneva Ser.). 329p. 1983. Repr. of 1862 ed. text ed. 14.95 (ISBN 0-85151-099-X). Banner of Truth.

--The History of the English Bible. LC 77-13187. 1977. Repr. lib. bdg. 15.00 (ISBN 0-8414-9929-2). Folcroft.

--The Intercessory Prayer of Our Lord Jesus Christ. 1978. 11.50 (ISBN 0-86524-104-X, 4301). Klock & Klock.

--I've Got Mixed-Up Feelings, God. 64p. 1984. pap. 4.95 (ISBN 0-8170-1035-1). Judson.

--John Bunyan, 1628-1688: His Life, Times & Work. Harrison, Frank M., ed. (Illus.). xxiv, 515p. 1969. Repr. of 1928 ed. 28.50 (ISBN 0-208-00726-1, Archon). Shoe String.

--Letters Upon the Poetry & Music of the Italian Opera: Addressed to a Friend. LC 80-2261. 1981. Repr. of 1789 ed. 22.50 (ISBN 0-404-18814-1). AMS Pr.

--Life, Trial & Execution of Captain John Brown, Known As "Old Brown of Ossawatomie". LC 69-18827. (Law, Politics & History Ser). 1969. Repr. of 1859 ed. lib. bdg. 22.50 (ISBN 0-306-71250-4). Da Capo.

--A Memoir of Robert Blincoe. 100p. 1977. 12.75 (ISBN 0-904573-05-2). Caliban Bks.

--No Drums, No Bugles. 1985. 18.95 (ISBN 0-89526-589-3). Regnery-Gateway.

--Parting Counsels: Exposition of II Peter 1. (Banner of Truth Geneva Series Commentaries). 1980. 12.95 (ISBN 0-85151-301-8). Banner of Truth.

--The Pilgrim Fathers of New England. 352p. 4.95 (ISBN 0-686-09112-4). Pilgrim Pubns.

--Provisional Constitution & Ordinances for the People of the United States. 32p. 1969. 10.00x (ISBN 0-87730-001-1). M&S Pr.

--Rab & His Friends. LC 72-5910. (Short Story Index Reprint Ser.). 1972. Repr. of 1906 ed. 19.00 (ISBN 0-8369-4193-4). Ayer Co Pubs.

--Rab & His Friends & Other Papers. 1970. 12.95x (ISBN 0-460-00116-7, Evman); pap. 2.95x (ISBN 0-460-01116-2, Evman). Biblio Dist.

--The Resurrection of Life. 1978. 15.50 (ISBN 0-86524-962-8, 4601). Klock & Klock.

--Slave Life in Georgia. facsimile ed. Chamerovzow, L. A., ed. LC 77-168512. (Black Heritage Library Collection). Repr. of 1855 ed. 18.75 (ISBN 0-8369-8865-5). Ayer Co Pubs.

--The Sufferings & the Glories of the Messiah. (Giant Summit Bks.). 352p. 1981. pap. 5.95 (ISBN 0-8010-0792-5). Baker Bk.

--Thackeray's Death (Spare Hours) 1978. Repr. of 1866 ed. lib. bdg. 25.00 (ISBN 0-8482-3403-0). Norwood Edns.

--War & after War: American Traditions under Fire. (Illus.). 275p. 1985. 18.95 (ISBN 0-89526-589-3). Regnery-Gateway.

--Worship Celebrations for Youth. 1980. pap. 7.95 (ISBN 0-8170-0866-7). Judson.

--Zaibatsu. 320p. 1985. pap. 3.50 (ISBN 0-380-89516-1). Avon.

Brown, John, jt. auth. see Clarke, R. H.

Brown, John, jt. auth. see Moore, Colin.

Brown, John, ed. Recall & Recognition. LC 75-8770. 1976. 64.95 (ISBN 0-471-11229-1, Pub. by Wiley-Interscience). Wiley.

Brown, John, et al. Hemingway: A New Critical & Personal Assessment. Wiener, Amy D., tr. from Fr. LC 79-88630. (Illus.). Date not set. 12.95 (ISBN 0-85690-080-X). Peebles Pr.

Brown, John, jt. auth. see Jones, Kathleen.

Brown, John A. Computers & Automation. rev. ed. LC 73-76928. (Illus.). 248p. 1974. 7.50 (ISBN 0-668-01623-X); pap. 5.95 (ISBN 0-668-01745-7). Arco.

Brown, John A., jt. auth. see Ruby, Robert H.

Brown, John Brewer. Sword & Firearm Collection of the Society of the Cincinnati in the Anderson House Museum. LC 65-25758. (Illus.). 120p. 1965. 10.00 (ISBN 0-318-16567-8). Anderson Hse Mus.

Brown, John C. A Hundred Years of Merchant Banking. Wilkins, Mira, ed. LC 78-3900. (International Finance Ser.). (Illus.). 1978. Repr. of 1909 ed. lib. bdg. 38.50x (ISBN 0-405-11205-X). Ayer Co Pubs.

Brown, John D. Two Kids & the Three Bears. LC 75-40538. (Lucky Heart Bks.). 40p. 1975. pap. 3.00 (ISBN 0-913198-10-2). Salt Lick.

Brown, John E. & Brown, Margaret H. The Crossworder's List Book. LC 77-14662. 1978. pap. 4.95 (ISBN 0-312-17690-2). St Martin.

Brown, John F. Engineering Report Writing. 2nd ed. 171p. 1985. 11.95 (ISBN 0-9612488-2-3). J F Brown.

Brown, John H. Elizabethan Schooldays. 1976. lib. bdg. 59.95 (ISBN 0-8490-1759-9). Gordon Pr.

--Toxicology & Pharmacology of Venoms from Poisonous Snakes. (Illus.). 208p. 1973. pap. 12.75x (ISBN 0-398-03018-9). C C Thomas.

Brown, John H. & Grant, Steven A. The Russian Empire & Soviet Union: A Guide to Manuscripts & Archival Materials in the United States. 1981. lib. bdg. 100.00 (ISBN 0-8161-1300-9, Hall Library). G K Hall.

Brown, John H. & Speer, William S. Encyclopedia of the New West. (Illus.). 1180p. 1978. Repr. of 1881 ed. 50.00 (ISBN 0-89308-121-3). Southern Hist Pr.

Brown, John L. Methodus Ad Facilem Historiarum Cognitionem of Jean Bodin: A Critical Study. LC 76-94167. (Catholic University of America Studies in Romance Languages & Literatures Ser: No. 18). Repr. of 1939 ed. 24.00 (ISBN 0-404-50318-7). AMS Pr.

--Valery Larbaud. (World Authors Ser.). 15.95 (ISBN 0-8057-6439-9, Twayne). G K Hall.

Brown, John M. As They Appear. LC 71-138208. 258p. 1972. Repr. of 1952 ed. lib. bdg. 18.75x (ISBN 0-8371-5563-0, BRAT). Greenwood.

--Letters from Greenroom Ghosts. facs. ed. LC 67-23187. (Essay Index Reprint Ser). 1967. Repr. of 1934 ed. 18.00 (ISBN 0-8369-0258-0). Ayer Co Pubs.

--Maori & Polynesian, Their Origin, History & Culture. LC 75-35240. Repr. of 1907 ed. 26.50 (ISBN 0-404-14415-2). AMS Pr.

--Morning Faces: A Book of Children & Parents. LC 78-167317. (Essay Index Reprint Ser.). (Illus.). Repr. of 1949 ed. 18.00 (ISBN 0-8369-2755-9). Ayer Co Pubs.

--Peoples & Problems of the Pacific, 2 vols. LC 75-35176. Repr. of 1927 ed. Set. 70.00 (ISBN 0-404-14250-8). AMS Pr.

--The Portable Charles Lamb. LC 75-11488. 594p. 1975. Repr. of 1949 ed. lib. bdg. 32.50x (ISBN 0-8371-8202-6, LAPCL). Greenwood.

--The Riddle of the Pacific. LC 75-35177. Repr. of 1924 ed. 38.00 (ISBN 0-404-14205-2). AMS Pr.

--Seeing Things. LC 75-138209. viii, 341p. Repr. of 1946 ed. lib. bdg. 19.75x (ISBN 0-8371-5564-9, BRST). Greenwood.

--Still Seeing Things. LC 79-156176. 1971. Repr. of 1950 ed. lib. bdg. 19.75x (ISBN 0-8371-6119-3, BRSS). Greenwood.

--Through These Men: Some Aspects of Our Passing History. LC 71-167318. (Essay Index Reprint Ser.). Repr. of 1956 ed. 20.00 (ISBN 0-8369-2756-7). Ayer Co Pubs.

--The Worlds of Robert E. Sherwood: Mirror to His Times, Eighteen Ninety-Six to Nineteen Thirty-Nine. LC 78-27835. (Illus.). 1979. Repr. of 1962 ed. lib. bdg. 37.50x (ISBN 0-313-20937-5, BRWO). Greenwood.

Brown, John M., jt. auth. see Carr, Joseph J.

Brown, John M; see Youtz, Phillip N.

Brown, John M. & Moses, Montrose J., eds. American Theatre As Seen by Its Critics, 1752-1934. LC 66-30782. Repr. of 1934 ed. 22.50x (ISBN 0-8154-0033-0). Cooper Sq.

Brown, John M., ed. see Lamb, Charles.

Brown, John P. Dervishes: Or Oriental Spiritualism. Rose, Horace A., ed. (Illus.). 496p. 1968. 32.50x (ISBN 0-7146-1980-9, F Cass Co). Biblio Dist.

--Lebanon & Phoenicia: Ancient Texts Illustrating Their Physical Geography & Native Industries, Vol. 1. The Physical Setting & The Forest. 1969. 20.00x (ISBN 0-8156-6014-6, Am U Beirut). Syracuse U Pr.

--Old Frontiers: The Story of the Cherokee Indians from the Earliest Times to the Date of Their Removal to the West, 1838. LC 74-146379. (First American Frontier Ser). (Illus.). 1971. Repr. of 1938 ed. 38.50 (ISBN 0-405-02830-X). Ayer Co Pubs.

Brown, John R. Discovering Shakespeare: A New Guide to the Plays. 192p. 1981. 26.00x (ISBN 0-231-05358-4). Columbia U Pr.

--Effective Theatre. 1969. pap. text ed. 8.50x (ISBN 0-435-18080-0). Heinemann Ed.

--How to Play Saxophone. (Illus.). 128p. 1984. 18.95 (ISBN 0-241-11081-5, Pub. by Hamish Hamilton England); pap. 9.95 (ISBN 0-241-11082-3, Pub. by Hamish Hamilton England). David & Charles.

--Modern British Dramatists: New Perspectives. 168p. 1984. 12.95 (ISBN 0-13-588021-1); pap. 5.95 (ISBN 0-13-588013-0). P-H.

--Shakespeare & His Theatre. LC 81-8441. (Illus.). 64p. (gr. 6 up). 1982. 12.50 (ISBN 0-688-00850-X). Lothrop.

--Shakespeare & His Theatre. (gr. 7 up). 1982. 12.50 (ISBN 0-688-00850-X). Morrow.

--Shakespeare's Dramatic Style. 1970. pap. text ed. 8.50x (ISBN 0-435-18082-7). Heinemann Ed.

--Shakespeare's Othello: The Harbrace Theater Edition. (Illus.). 108p. 1973. pap. text ed. 8.95 (ISBN 0-15-567678-4, HC). HarBraceJ.

--A Short Guide to Modern British Drama. LC 82-22699. 110p. 1983. pap. text ed. 9.95x (ISBN 0-389-20353-X, 07213). B&N Imports.

Brown, John R., ed. Focus on Macbeth. (Critical Essays Ser.). 224p. 1982. 22.95x (ISBN 0-7100-9015-3). Routledge & Kegan.

Brown, John R. & Harris, Bernard, eds. American Poetry. (Stratford-Upon-Avon Studies: No. 7). 244p. 1973. pap. text ed. 27.50x (ISBN 0-8419-5814-9). Holmes & Meier.

--Hamlet. (Stratford-Upon-Avon Studies: No. 5). 212p. 1979. pap. text ed. 10.75x (ISBN 0-8419-5812-2). Holmes & Meier.

--Later Shakespeare. (Stratford-Upon-Avon Studies: No. 8). 264p. 1966. pap. text ed. 27.50 (ISBN 0-8419-5815-7). Holmes & Meier.

Brown, John R., ed. see Master, Wakefield.

Brown, John R., ed. see Shakespeare, William.

Brown, John R., ed. see Webster, John.

Brown, John S., ed. Genesis of Stratiform Lead, Zinc, Barite, Fluorite Deposits in Carbonate Rocks (The So-called Missisipi Valley Type Deposits) A Symposium. (Economic Geology, Monograph Ser.: No. 3). pap. 113.30 (ISBN 0-317-27600-X, 2014765). Bks Demand UMI.

Brown, John T. Among the Bantu Nomads. LC 77-79270. (Illus.). Repr. of 1926 ed. 22.50x (ISBN 0-8371-1466-7, BRB&, Pub. by Negro U Pr). Greenwood.

Brown, Jonathan. History & Present Condition of St. Domingo, 2 vols. 1972. Repr. of 1837 ed. 75.00x (ISBN 0-7146-2704-6, F Cass Co). Biblio Dist.

--Murillo's Drawings. LC 76-9395. (Publications of the Art Museum, Princeton University). (Illus.). 1977. text ed. 42.00 (ISBN 0-691-03916-X). Princeton U Pr.

--A Socioeconomic History of Argentina: Seventeen Seventy-Six to Eighteen Sixty. LC 78-6800. (Latin American Studies: No. 35). (Illus.). 1979. 44.50 (ISBN 0-521-22219-2). Cambridge U Pr.

Brown, Jonathan & Elliott, John H. A Palace for a King: The Buen Retiro & the Court of Philip IV. LC 80-13659. (Illus.). 320p. 1980. 42.00x (ISBN 0-300-02507-6). Yale U Pr.

Brown, Jonathan & Ward, Sadie. Village Life in England Eighteen Sixty to Ninteen Forty: A Photographic Record. (Illus.). 144p. 1985. 18.95 (ISBN 0-7134-4765-6, Pub. by Batsford England). David & Charles.

Brown, Jonathan, jt. auth. see Brown, Sanborn C.

Brown, Jonathan, jt. auth. see Enggass, Robert.

Brown, Jonathan, ed. see National Gallery of Art.

Brown, Jonathan, et al. Studies in the History of Art 1982, Vol. 11. (Illus.). 112p. (Orig.). 1983. pap. text ed. 8.95 (ISBN 0-89468-058-7, Dist. by U of New England Pr). Natl Gallery Art.

Brown, Joseph E. The Mormon Trek West. LC 77-16900. (Illus.). 1980. 35.00 (ISBN 0-385-13030-9). Doubleday.

--Oil Spills: Danger in the Sea. LC 78-7743. (Illus.). (gr. 5 up). 1978. 6.95 (ISBN 0-396-07607-6). Dodd.

--Rescue from Extinction. (Illus.). 128p. (gr. 5 up). 1981. PLB 8.95 (ISBN 0-396-07979-2). Dodd.

--The Return of the Brown Pelican. LC 83-901. (Illus.). 128p. 1983. 24.95 (ISBN 0-8071-1114-7). La State U Pr.

--Spiritual Legacy of American Indian. 160p. 1984. pap. 8.95 (ISBN 0-8245-0618-9). Crossroad NY.

--Spiritual Legacy of the American Indian. LC 64-17425. (Illus., Orig.). 1964. pap. 2.30x (ISBN 0-87574-135-5). Pendle Hill.

--Wonders of Seals & Sea Lions. (Wonders Ser.). (gr. 4 up). 1976. 9.95 (ISBN 0-396-07344-1). Dodd.

Brown, Joseph E., jt. auth. see Drysdale, Vera L.

Brown, Joseph E., ed. The Sacred Pipe: Black Elk's Account of the Seven Rites of Oglala Sioux. LC 53-8810. (Civilization of the American Indian Ser.: No. 36). (Illus.). 1953. 15.95 (ISBN 0-8061-0272-1). U of Okla Pr.

--Sacred Pipe: Black Elk's Account of the Seven Rites of the Oglala Sioux. (Metaphysical Library Ser.). 1971. pap. 3.95 (ISBN 0-14-003346-7). Penguin.

Brown, Joseph F. Diabetes Dictionary & Guide. LC 77-92938. (Illus.). 1978. 16.95 (ISBN 0-9601484-1-8). Press West.

Brown, Joseph H. & Brown, Carolyn S. Consulting with Parents & Teachers. LC 81-10100. 1982. 21.00x (ISBN 0-910328-35-8); pap. 16.00x (ISBN 0-910328-36-6). Carroll Pr.

Brown, Joseph H., jt. auth. see Brown, Carolyn S.

Brown, Josephine C. Public Relief, 1929-1939. LC 77-173841. xx, 524p. 1972. Repr. of 1940 ed. lib. bdg. 43.00x (ISBN 0-374-91022-7). Octagon.

Brown, Joshua & Ment, David. Factories, Foundries, & Refineries: A History of Five Brooklyn Industries. LC 80-66220. (Brooklyn Rediscovery Booklet Ser.). (Illus.). 75p. 1980. pap. 3.50 (ISBN 0-933250-06-1). Bklyn Educ.

Brown, Judith C. Immodest Acts: The Life of a Lesbian Nun in Renaissance Italy. 192p. 1985. 14.95 (ISBN 0-19-503675-1). Oxford U Pr.

--In the Shadow of Florence: Provencial Society in Renaissance Pescia. (Illus.). 1982. 32.50 (ISBN 0-19-502993-3). Oxford U Pr.

Brown, Judith E. Nutrition for Your Pregnancy: The University of Minnesota Guide. LC 82-21852. (Illus.). 140p. 1983. 12.95 (ISBN 0-8166-1151-3). U of Minn Pr.

--Nutrition for Your Pregnancy: The University of Minnesota Guide. LC 83-22012. 160p. 1984. pap. 7.95 (ISBN 0-452-25534-1, Plume). NAL.

--Nutrition for Your Pregnancy: The University of Minnesota Guide. Brown, Judith E., ed. 1985. pap. 3.95 (ISBN 0-451-13808-2, Sig). NAL.

Brown, Judith G. I Sing a Song of the Saints of God. (Illus.). 32p. (Orig.). 1981. pap. 5.95 (ISBN 0-8164-2339-3, Pub. by Seabury). Winston Pr.

Brown, Judith K. & Kerns, Virginia, eds. In Her Prime: A New View of Middle-Aged Women. (Illus.). 240p. 1985. 27.95 (ISBN 0-89789-056-6); pap. 14.95 (ISBN 0-89789-059-0). Bergin & Garvey.

Brown, Judith M. Modern India: The Origins of an Asian Democracy. (Short Oxford History of the Modern World Ser.). (Illus.). 500p. 1984. 29.95x (ISBN 0-19-913124-4); pap. 12.95x (ISBN 0-19-822859-7). Oxford U Pr.

Brown, Judith R. Back to the Beanstalk: Enchantment & Reality for Couples. LC 79-89476. 1980. 8.95 (ISBN 0-930626-03-6); pap. 4.95 (ISBN 0-930626-04-4). Psych & Consul Assocs.

Brown, Judson S., ed. Nebraska Symposium on Motivation, 1953. LC 53-11655. (Nebraska Symposia on Motivation Ser: Vol. 1). vi, 194p. 1953. pap. 4.50x (ISBN 0-8032-5600-0). U of Nebr Pr.

Brown, Julia. Robert Therrien. LC 83-62370. (Illus.). 68p. (Orig.). 1984. pap. 15.00 (ISBN 0-295-96243-7). U of Wash Pr.

Brown, Julia & Johnson, Bridget. The First Show: Painting & Sculpture from Eight Collections 1940-1980. LC 83-62369. (Illus.). 1983p. (Orig.). pap. 25.00 (ISBN 0-295-96240-2). U of Wash Pr.

Brown, Julia, et al. Occluded Front: James Turrell. (Illus.). 320p. (Orig.). 1985. 35.00 (ISBN 0-932499-10-4); pap. 19.50 (ISBN 0-932499-11-2). Lapis Pr.

Brown, Julia P. Jane Austen: Social Change & Literary Form. LC 78-16879. 1979. 14.00x (ISBN 0-674-47172-5). Harvard U Pr.

--A Reader's Guide to the Nineteenth Century-English Novel. 160p. 1985. 15.95 (ISBN 0-02-517370-7). MacMillan.

Brown, Julian & Gibbs, Joan, eds. The Collected Writings of Francis Wormwald: Studies in Medieval Art from the Sixth to the Twelfth Century. (Illus.). 253p. 1984. 59.00x (ISBN 0-19-921042-X). Oxford U Pr.

Brown, June, jt. auth. see Brown, Karen.

Brown, June H., et al. Child, Family, Neighborhood: A Master Plan for Social Service Delivery. 1982. 6.75 (ISBN 0-87868-209-0, CW-34). Child Welfare.

Brown, K. Blood Feuds in Scotlands: Fifteen Seventy-Three to Sixteen Twenty-Five. (Illus.). 224p. 1986. text ed. 38.00x (ISBN 0-85976-134-7, Pub. by Donald Scotland). Humanities.

Brown, K. & Cooper, S. J., eds. Chemical Influence on Behavior. 1979. 95.00 (ISBN 0-12-136780-0). Acad Pr.

Brown, K. D. John Burns. (Royal Historical Society-Studies in History Ser.: Vol. 3). 217p. 1977. text ed. 24.00x (ISBN 0-901050-34-2, Pub. by Swiftbks England). Humanities.

--John Burns. 1982. 45.00 (ISBN 0-901050-34-2, 07550418, Royal Hist Soc England). State Mutual Bk.

Brown, K. D., ed. Essays in Anti-Labour History: Responses to the Rise of Labour in Britain. viii, 409p. (Orig.). 1974. 27.50 (ISBN 0-208-01335-0, Archon). Shoe String.

--The First Labour Party Nineteen Six to Nineteen Fourteen. LC 85-4190. 297p. 1985. 31.00 (ISBN 0-7099-3209-X, Pub. by Croom Helm Ltd). Longwood Pub Group.

Brown, K. R., ed. The Challenge of Information Technology: Proceedings of the 41st FID Congress, Hong-Kong, September 13-16, 1982. xii, 356p. 1983. 51.00 (ISBN 0-444-86646-9, North-Holland). Elsevier.

Brown, K. S. Cohomology of Groups. (Graduate Text in Mathematics Ser.: Vol. 87). (Illus.). 336p. 1982. 33.00 (ISBN 0-387-90688-6). Springer-Verlag.

Brown, K. W. & Warner, A. R. Economics of Our Free Enterprise System. 1981. 19.16 (ISBN 0-07-067501-5). McGraw.

Brown, Karen. French Country Inns & Chateau. rev. 4th ed. (European Country Inns Ser.). Orig. Title: French Country Inns & Chateau Hotels. 288p. 1986. pap. 10.95 (ISBN 0-930328-15-9). Travel Pr.

--French Country Inns & Chateau Hotels. 3rd rev. ed. (Karen Brown's Country Inns Travel Guide Ser.). (Illus.). 288p. (Orig.). 1985. pap. 9.95 (ISBN 0-930328-09-4). Travel Pr.

Brown, Karen & Brown, Clare. Italian Country Inns & Villas. (Karen Brown's European Country Inns Ser.). (Illus.). 224p. (Orig.). 1985. pap. text ed. 9.95 (ISBN 0-930328-07-8). Travel Pr.

--Swiss Country Inns & Chalets. 2nd ed. (Karen Brown's European Country Inn Ser.). (Illus.). 256p. (Orig.). 1985. pap. 9.95 (ISBN 0-930328-11-6). Travel Pr.

Brown, Karen & Brown, June. English, Welsh & Scottish Country Inns. 2nd rev. ed. (Karen Brown's European Country Inns Ser.). (Illus.). 286p. 1985. pap. 9.95 (ISBN 0-930328-10-8). Travel Pr.

--German Country Inns & Castles. (Karen Brown's Travel Press: European Country Inn Ser.). (Illus.). 288p. 1986. pap. 10.95 (ISBN 0-930328-12-4). Travel Pr.

Brown, Karl. Adventures with D. W. Griffith. Brownlow, Kevin, ed. LC 75-31755. 1976. pap. 6.95 (ISBN 0-306-80032-2). Da Capo.

Brown, Karl & Haskell, Daniel C., eds. Shorthand Collection in the New York Public Library: A Catalogue of Books, Periodicals & Manuscripts. LC 77-137704. (New York Public Library Publications in Reprint Ser). 1971. Repr. of 1935 ed. 46.50 (ISBN 0-405-01746-4). Ayer Co Pubs.

Brown, Katherine. Commentary: Nineteen Forty to Nineteen Eighty. 1983. 5.95 (ISBN 0-533-05473-7). Vantage.

Brown, Kathleen R., jt. ed. see Lecker, Robert A.

Brown, Kathryn M., pseud. Blossom Hollow. (ps-5). Date not set. 5.95 (ISBN 0-8062-2511-4). Carlton.

Brown, Kathy, ed. see Haynes, Elmer E.

Brown, Katy. Spellcaster. (Twistaplot Ser.: No. 15). (Illus.). 96p. (Orig.). (gr. 4 up). 1985. pap. 1.95 (ISBN 0-317-17160-7). Scholastic Inc.

Brown, Keith C. Bidding for Offshore Oil: Toward an Optimal Strategy. LC 74-97802. 1969. pap. 9.95 (ISBN 0-87074-026-1). SMU Press.

--Regulation of the Natural Gas Producing Industry. 272p. 1972. pap. 10.00 (ISBN 0-8018-1383-2). Resources Future.

Brown, Keith C., ed. Regulation of the Natural Gas Producing Industry. LC 71-186502. (Resources for the Future Ser.). (Illus.). 271p. 1972. pap. 10.00x (ISBN 0-8018-1383-2). Johns Hopkins.

Brown, Ken. Notes from the Nervous Breakdown Lane. LC 85-42733. (Illus.). 96p. (Orig.). 1985. pap. 7.95 (ISBN 0-06-096014-0, PL 6014, PL). Har-Row.

Brown, Kenneth D. The English Labour Movement, Seventeen to Nineteen Fifty-one. LC 81-48397. 366p. 1982. 27.50x (ISBN 0-312-25432-6). St Martin.

--Labour & Unemployment, 1900-1914. 219p. 1971. 15.00x (ISBN 0-87471-039-1). Rowman.

Brown, Kenneth E. General Mathematics in American Colleges. LC 73-176692. (Columbia University. Teachers College. Contributions to Education: No. 893). Repr. of 1943 ed. 22.50 (ISBN 0-404-55893-3). AMS Pr.

Brown, Kenneth I., ed. see Gray, Harold S.

Brown, Kenneth J. Covert Facts & Acts: Crossword Puzzles. LC 84-90891. 65p. 1985. pap. 7.50x (ISBN 0-9613137-0-6). K J Brown.

Brown, Kenneth L. People of Sale. 1976. text ed. 18.00x (ISBN 0-674-66155-9). Harvard U Pr.

Brown, Kenneth S. & ReVelle, Jack B. Quantitative Methods for Managerial Decisions. LC 76-10408. (Illus.). 1978. text ed. 36.95 (ISBN 0-201-06448-0). Addison-Wesley.

Brown, Kenneth S., et al. Craniofacial Mesenchyme in Morphogenesis & Malformation. (Birth Defects: Original Article Ser.: Vol. 20, No. 3). 162p. 1984. 44.00 (ISBN 0-8451-1058-6). A R Liss.

Brown, Kenneth W., ed. R & D Tax Credit: Issues in Tax Policy & Industrail Innovation. 1984. pap. 4.95 (ISBN 0-8447-2250-2). Am Enterprise.

Brown, Kenny L. The Italians in Oklahoma. LC 79-23342. (Newcomers to a New Land Ser.: Vol. 4). (Illus.). 96p. (Orig.). 1980. pap. 3.95 (ISBN 0-8061-1624-2). U of Okla Pr.

Brown, Kent R. The Screenwriter As Collaborator. Jowett, Garth S., ed. LC 79-6669. (Dissertations on Film, 1980 Ser.). 1980. lib. bdg. 26.50x (ISBN 0-405-12903-3). Ayer Co Pubs.

Brown, Kermit E. The Technology of Artificial Lift Methods, 6 Vol. Set. Incl. Vol. 1. Beggs, Dale H. 487p. 1977. 89.95 (ISBN 0-87814-031-X, P-4105); Vol. 2A. 720p. 1980. 89.95 (ISBN 0-87814-119-7, P-4205); Vol. 2B. 596p. 1980. 89.95 (P-4206); Vol. 3A. 596p. 1980. 89.95 (ISBN 0-87814-133-2, P-4244); Vol. 3B. 1125p. 1980. 89.95 (P-4245); Vol. 4. 464p. 1984. 89.95 (ISBN 0-87814-252-5). (Illus.). price (w. slipcase) 484.95 set (ISBN 0-87814-138-3). Pennwell Bks.

Brown, Keven, ed. see Moffet, Ruth.

Brown, Kirsten, jt. auth. see Evans, Susan.

Brown, Kitt. Alyssa Deane. 304p. (Orig.). 1985. pap. 3.50 (ISBN 0-449-12478-9, GM). Fawcett.

--Caitlyn McGregor. (Frontier Women Ser.: No. 1). 352p. (Orig.). 1981. pap. 2.95 (ISBN 0-449-14413-5, GM). Fawcett.

--Kentucky Spitfire: Caitlyn McGregor. (Frontier Woman Saga Ser.: No. 1). 1982. pap. 2.95 (ISBN 0-686-87390-4, GM). Fawcett.

--Laurian Kane. 320p. 1982. pap. 3.50 (ISBN 0-449-14466-6, GM). Fawcett.

--Texas Wildflower: Laurian Kane. (Frontier Woman Saga Ser.: No. 3). 1982. pap. 2.95 (ISBN 0-686-87387-4, GM). Fawcett.

Brown, L. A Rusty Person is Worse than Rusty Iron: Adult Education & the Development of Africa. (Tolley Medal Ser). 1975. pap. text ed. 1.50 (ISBN 0-685-76692-6, WPT 6). Syracuse U Cont Ed.

Brown, L., ed. see Kiefer, J. C., et al.

Brown, L., et al, eds. Reviews of Physiology & Biochemistry. Incl. Vol. 57. 1966. 64.90 (ISBN 0-387-03499-4); Vol. 59. 1967. 73.80 (ISBN 0-387-03783-7); Vol. 60. 1968. 79.70 (ISBN 0-387-04103-6); Vol. 61. 1969; Vol. 62. 1970. o.p. (ISBN 0-387-04811-1); Vol. 63. 1971; Vol. 64. 1972. o.p.; Vol. 65. 1972; Vol. 66. 1972; Vol. 67. 1972; Vol. 68. 1973. Springer-Verlag.

--The Birds of Africa. LC 81-69594. 1982. Vol. 1. 90.00 (ISBN 0-12-137301-0). Acad Pr.

Brown, L. B. Advances in the Psychology of Religion. (International Series in Experimental Social Psychology: Vol. 11). (Illus.). 236p. 1985. 27.50 (ISBN 0-08-027948-1, Pub by PPL). Pergamon.

--Psychology in Contemporary China. 320p. 1981. 41.00 (ISBN 0-08-026063-2). Pergamon.

Brown, L. Carl. International Politics & the Middle East: Old Rules, Dangerous Game. (Illus.). 356p. 1984. 37.00 (ISBN 0-691-05410-X); pap. 15.00x (ISBN 0-691-10159-0). Princeton U Pr.

--The Tunisia of Ahmad Bey: 1837-1855. LC 73-16770. (Studies on the Near East). 408p. 1974. 46.00x (ISBN 0-691-03100-2). Princeton U Pr.

Brown, L. Carl, ed. From Madina to Metropolis: Heritage & Change in the Near Eastern City. LC 76-161054. (Illus.). 343p. 1973. pap. text ed. 17.95x (ISBN 0-87850-007-3). Darwin Pr.

--State & Society in Independent North Africa. LC 66-20316. (James Terry Duce Ser.: Vol. 1). 1966. 7.50 (ISBN 0-916808-09-2). Mid East Inst.

Brown, L. Carl & Itzkowitz, Norman, eds. Psychological Dimensions of Near Eastern Studies. LC 75-43499. 382p. 1977. 9.95x (ISBN 0-87850-028-6). Darwin Pr.

Brown, L. Dave. Managing Conflict at Organizational Interfaces. LC 82-6762. (Managing Human Resources Ser.). 250p. 1983. pap. text ed. 10.95 (ISBN 0-201-00884-X). Addison-Wesley.

Brown, L. David. Take Care: A Guide for Responsible Living. LC 78-52200. 1978. pap. 5.50 (ISBN 0-8066-1665-2, 10-6190). Augsburg.

Brown, L. Dean. The Land of Palestine: West Bank Not East Bank. LC 83-107611. (Middle East Problem Paper Ser.: No. 23). pap. 20.00 (ISBN 0-317-20639-7, 2024130). Bks Demand UMI.

Brown, L. F., et al. Pennsylvanian Depositional Systems in North-Central Texas: A Guide for Interpreting Terrigenous Clastic Facies in a Cratonic Basin. (Guidebook Ser.: GB 14). (Illus.). 122p. 1973. Repr. 4.00 (ISBN 0-686-29322-3). Bur Econ Geology.

Brown, L. F., Jr., jt. auth. see Fisher, W. L.

Brown, L. F., Jr., jt. auth. see Galloway, W. E.

Brown, L. M. Aims of Education. LC 76-120600. 1970. pap. text ed. 8.95x (ISBN 0-8077-1129-2). Tchrs Coll.

Brown, L. M., jt. ed. see Ashby, M. F.

Brown, L. M., tr. see Yukawa, Hideki.

Brown, L. P., Jr., ed. Geology of Industrial Minerals: Proceedings, 4th Forum, Austin TX, 14-15 March 1968. (Illus.). 174p. 1969. 2.00 (ISBN 0-318-03314-3). Bur Econ Geology.

Brown, Lance J. Design Arts: Grants Recognition Program. The National Endowment for the Arts, Vol. 1. (Illus.). 160p. 1980. pap. 7.00 (ISBN 0-89062-171-3). Pub Ctr Cult Res.

Brown, Lance J., ed. Design Arts Two: Places & Spaces for the Arts. LC 81-643399. (Illus.). 112p. 1981. pap. 7.00 (ISBN 0-89062-172-1). Pub Ctr Cult Res.

Brown, LaRita. Ginalyn's Surprise. LC 83-61847. (Illus.). 55p. 1982. PLB write for info (ISBN 0-914967-00-2). N & Out.

Brown, Larry. Sailing on a Micro-Budget. LC 84-13951. (Illus.). 176p. 1985. pap. 14.95 oversized (ISBN 0-915160-80-3). Seven Seas.

Brown, Larry, jt. auth. see Bing, Stephen.

Brown, Larry T. & Weiner, Elliot A. Introduction to Psychology. 1979. text ed. 20.95 (ISBN 0-316-11222-4); tchr's ed. free (ISBN 0-316-11226-7); study guide 6.95 (ISBN 0-316-11224-0). Little.

Brown, Laura. Alexander Pope. Eagleton, Terry, ed. (Re-Reading Literature Ser.). 190p. 1985. 24.95x (ISBN 0-631-13502-2); pap. 6.95x (ISBN 0-631-13503-0). Basil Blackwell.

--English Dramatic Form, Sixteen Sixty to Seventeen Sixty: An Essay in Generic History. LC 80-25702. 264p. 1981. 27.00x (ISBN 0-300-02585-8). Yale U Pr.

Brown, Laura E. & Moll, Don. The Status of the Nearly Extinct Illinois Mud Turtle (Kinosternon Flavescens Spooneri Smith 1951) with Recommendations for its Conservation. 49p. 1979. 2.25 (ISBN 0-89326-042-8). Milwaukee Pub Mus.

Brown, Lauren. Grasses: An Identification Guide. (Peterson Native Library). 1979. 9.95 (ISBN 0-395-27624-1). HM.

--Grasslands. Elliott, Charles, ed. LC 84-48675. (The Audubon Society Nature Guides Ser.). (Illus.). 606p. 1985. pap. 14.95 (ISBN 0-394-73121-2). Knopf.

Brown, Laurie M. & Hoddeson, Lillian, eds. The Birth of Particle Physics: Proceedings of the International Symposium on the History of Particle Physics, May, 1980. LC 82-1162. (Illus.). 500p. 1983. 47.50 (ISBN 0-521-24005-0). Cambridge U Pr.

Brown, Laverne K. The Year of Birth: A Guide for Expectant Parents. (Illus.). 215p. (Orig.). 1982. pap. 5.95 (ISBN 0-9608446-0-0). Lake Pr.

Brown, LaVyrne H. I Am Glad I Have Had My Flight. (Illus.). 80p. (Orig.). 1983. pap. text ed. 7.75 (ISBN 0-930982-04-5). U of Evansville Pr.

Brown, Lawerance D., ed. Accounting Research Directory: A Bibliography of Accounting Literature. Vasarhelyi, Miklos A. LC 85-40013. 360p. 1985. text ed. 39.00 (ISBN 0-910129-26-6). Wiener Pub Inc.

Brown, Lawrence. Diffusion Processes & Location. (Bibliography Ser.: No. 4). 177p. 1968. 4.00 (ISBN 0-686-32163-4). Regional Sci Res Inst.

--Might of the West. 1962. 19.95 (ISBN 0-8392-1069-8). Astor-Honor.

Brown, Lawrence A. Innovation Diffusion: A New Perspective. LC 80-49706. 375p. 1981. 22.00 (ISBN 0-416-74270-X, NO. 3469). Methuen Inc.

Brown, Lawrence D. New Policies, New Politics: Government's Response to Government's Growth. LC 82-45979. 100p. 1983. pap. 6.95 (ISBN 0-8157-1165-4, 82-45979). Brookings.

--The Political Structure of the Federal Health Planning Program. LC 81-70468. 70p. 1982. pap. 6.95 (ISBN 0-8157-1159-X). Brookings.

--Politics & Health Care Organization: HMO's as Federal Policy. LC 81-70466. 600p. 1983. 33.95 (ISBN 0-8157-1158-1); pap. 16.95 (ISBN 0-8157-1157-3). Brookings.

Brown, Lawrence D. & Vasarhelyi, Miklos A. Accounting Research Directory: Database of Accounting Literature. LC 85-40013. (Reference Ser.). 360p. 1985. pap. 29.00x (ISBN 0-910129-35-5). Wiener Pub Inc.

Brown, Lawrence D., et al. The Changing Politics of Federal Grants. LC 84-45275. 200p. 1984. 28.95 (ISBN 0-8157-1168-9); pap. 9.95 (ISBN 0-8157-1167-0). Brookings.

Brown, Lawrence G. Immigration: Cultural Conflicts & Social Adjustments. LC 69-18761. (American Immigration Collection Ser., No. 1). 1969. Repr. of 1933 ed. 23.50 (ISBN 0-405-00509-1). Ayer Co Pubs.

Brown, Lawrence K. A Thesaurus of Spanish Idioms & Everyday Language. 165p. (Span.). 1975. pap. 4.95 (ISBN 0-8044-6059-0). Ungar.

Brown, Lawrence R. The Might of the West. LC 79-52119. 1979. 20.00 (ISBN 0-89674-006-4, Dist. by The National Alliance). J J Binns.

Brown, Lee, jt. ed. see Weatherford, Gary.

Brown, Lee F., jt. auth. see Folger, H. Scott.

Brown, Lela K. see Brown, Kathryn M., pseud.

Brown, Leland. Communicating Facts & Ideas in Business. 3rd ed. (Illus.). 496p. 1982. reference 25.95 (ISBN 0-13-153403-3). P-H.

--Effective Business Report Writing. 3rd ed. (Illus.). 448p. (Reference ed.). 1973. 24.95 (ISBN 0-13-241653-0). P-H.

--Effective Business Report Writing. 4th ed. (Illus.). 480p. 1985. text ed. 24.95 (ISBN 0-13-241456-2). P-H.

Brown, Len & Gelman, Woody, eds. Those Great Old Bubble Gum Cards. LC 77-88498. (Illus.). 1978. pap. 6.95 (ISBN 0-87897-033-9). Nostalgia Pr.

Brown, Lena M., ed. see Brown, Lewis S.

Brown, Lennox see Harrison, Paul C.

Brown, Leo & Mamorsky, Jeffrey D. Rules Against Discrimination: No. B445. (Requirements for Qualification of Plans Ser.). 17p. 1983. pap. 6.00 (ISBN 0-317-31140-9). Am Law Inst.

Brown, Leo, jt. auth. see Mamorsky, Jeffrey.

Brown, Leon C., tr. see Al Tunisi, Khayr.

Brown, Leonard. Genesis, Growth & Meaning of Endymion. LC 74-3369. 1933. lib. bdg. 10.00 (ISBN 0-8414-3107-8). Folcroft.

--Modern Short Stories. 676p. 1982. Repr. of 1929 ed. lib. bdg. 25.00 (ISBN 0-8495-0632-8). Arden Lib.

Brown, Leonard, ed. see Falk, Lee.

Brown, Leonard, jt. ed. see Kartman, Ben.

Brown, Leonard, ed. see Raymond, Alex.

Brown, Leroy, jt. auth. see Marcus, Michael.

Brown, Les. Justice, Morality & Education: A New Focus in Ethics in Education. 384p. 1985. 35.00 (ISBN 0-317-20001-1). St Martin.

--Keeping Your Eye on Television. LC 79-15828. (Orig.). 1979. pap. 4.95 (ISBN 0-8298-0376-9). Pilgrim NY.

--Les Brown's Encyclopedia of Televsion. LC 82-7867. (Illus.). 496p. 1982. 29.95 (ISBN 0-918432-28-6); pap. 16.95 (ISBN 0-918432-29-4). NY Zoetrope.

--Television: The Business Behind the Box. LC 77-153684. 347p. 1973. pap. 4.95 (ISBN 0-15-688440-2, Harv). HarBraceJ.

Brown, Les & Channels Magazine Editors. Fast Forward: The New Television & American Society. 264p. 1983. pap. 9.95 (ISBN 0-8362-6208-5). Andrews McMeel Parker.

Brown, Leslie. The African Fish Eagle. 160p. 1980. 40.00x (ISBN 0-561-00304-1, Pub. by Bailey & Swinfen South Africa). State Mutual Bk.

--The Indian Christians of St. Thomas: An Account of the Ancient Syrian Church of Malabar. LC 81-21766. (Illus.). 330p. 1982. 39.50 (ISBN 0-521-21258-8). Cambridge U Pr.

--Three Worlds: One Word; Account of a Mission. 278p. 1981. text ed. 22.50x (ISBN 0-8476-4740-4). Rowman.

Brown, Leslie & Brown, Alan. Transitional Light: Facing Death with Dignity. LC 83-61016. (Illus.). 60p. 1983. pap. 7.95 (ISBN 0-934306-04-4). Springfield.

Brown, Leslie, jt. auth. see Weick, Friedhelm.

Brown, Leslie H., ed. Birds of Africa, Vol. 1. 1983. leatherbound 275.00 (ISBN 0-12-137321-5). Acad Pr.

Brown, Leslie P. Some Romance Words of Arabic or Germanic Origin. LC 38-33359. 68p. 1982. lib. bdg. 22.95x (ISBN 0-89370-735-X). Borgo Pr.

Brown, Lester. Soil Erosion: Quiet Crisis in the World Economy. (Worldwatch Papers Ser.). 1984. pap. 4.00 (ISBN 0-916468-60-7). Worldwatch Inst.

--The Twenty-Ninth Day. 1978. 11.95 (ISBN 0-393-05664-3); pap. 7.95 (ISBN 0-393-05673-2). Norton.
--U. S. & Soviet Agriculture: The Shifting Balance of Power. LC 82-61876. (Worldwatch Papers). 1982. pap. 2.00 (ISBN 0-916468-51-8). Worldwatch Inst.
Brown, Lester, et al. Running on Empty: The Future of the Automobile in An Oil-Short World. 1979. 9.95 (ISBN 0-393-01334-0). Norton.
Brown, Lester R. Building a Sustainable Society. 1981. 14.95 (ISBN 0-393-01482-7); pap. 6.95 (ISBN 0-393-30027-7). Norton.
--Food or Fuel: New Competition for the World's Cropland. LC 80-50216. (Worldwatch Papers). 1980. pap. 2.00 (ISBN 0-916468-34-8). Worldwatch Inst.
--The Global Economic Prospect: New Sources of Economic Stress. LC 78-55351. (Worldwatch Papers). 1978. pap. 2.00 (ISBN 0-916468-19-4). Worldwatch Inst.
--Human Needs & the Security of Nations. LC 78-51516. (Headline Ser.: 238). (Illus.). 1978. pap. 3.00 (ISBN 0-87124-045-9). Foreign Policy.
--In the Human Interest: A Strategy to Stabilize World Population. LC 74-6339. 190p. 1974. 6.95 (ISBN 0-393-05526-4); cloth 3.95x (ISBN 0-393-09288-7). Norton.
--In the Human Interest: A Strategy to Stabilize World Population. 190p. 1974. pap. 2.95 (ISBN 0-318-16152-4). Overseas Dev Council.
--Increasing World Food Output. LC 75-26298. (World Food Supply Ser). (Illus.). 1976. Repr. of 1965 ed. 14.00x (ISBN 0-405-07770-X). Ayer Co Pubs.
--The Interdependence of Nations. LC 72-90074. (Headline Ser.: No. 212). (Illus., Orig.). 1972. pap. 3.00 (ISBN 0-87124-018-1). Foreign Policy.
--The Interdependence of Nations. (Development Papers: No. 10). 70p. 1972. pap. 1.00 (ISBN 0-686-28679-0). Overseas Dev Council.
--Man, Land & Food. LC 75-26299. (World Food Supply Ser.). (Illus.). 1976. Repr. of 1963 ed. 14.00x (ISBN 0-405-07771-8). Ayer Co Pubs.
--Our Daily Bread. LC 75-851. (Headline Ser.: No. 225). (Illus.). 1975. pap. 3.00 (ISBN 0-87124-030-0). Foreign Policy.
--The Politics & Responsibility of the North American Breadbasket. (Worldwatch Papers). 1975. pap. 2.00 (ISBN 0-916468-01-1). Worldwatch Inst.
--Population Policies for a New Economic Era. LC 83-60702. (Worldwatch Papers). 1983. pap. text ed. 2.00 (ISBN 0-916468-52-6). Worldwatch Inst.
--Population Policies for a New Economic Era. (Worldwatch Institute Papers: No. 53). 45p. 1983. pap. 2.95 (ISBN 0-916468-52-6, WW53, WW). Unipub.
--Redefining National Security. LC 77-86155. (Worldwatch Papers). 1977. pap. 2.00 (ISBN 0-916468-13-5). Worldwatch Inst.
--Resource Trends & Population Policy: A Time for Reassessment. LC 79-64839. (Worldwatch Papers). 1979. pap. 2.00 (ISBN 0-916468-28-3). Worldwatch Inst.
--U.S. & Soviet Agriculture: The Shifting Balance. (Worldwatch Institute Papers: No. 51). 48p. 1982. pap. 2.95 (ISBN 0-916468-51-8, WW51, WMO). Unipub.
--World Population Trends: Signs of Hope, Signs of Stress. LC 76-39757. (Worldwatch Papers). 1976. pap. 2.00 (ISBN 0-916468-07-0). Worldwatch Inst.
--World Without Borders. 1973. pap. 4.95 (ISBN 0-394-71929-8, V929, Vin). Random.
--The Worldwide Loss of Cropland. LC 78-64454. (Worldwatch Papers). 1978. pap. 2.00 (ISBN 0-916468-23-2). Worldwatch Inst.
Brown, Lester R. & Eckholm, Erik P. By Bread Alone. 272p. 1974. pap. 3.95 (ISBN 0-318-16145-1). Overseas Dev Council.
Brown, Lester R. & Shaw, Pamela. Six Steps to a Sustainable Society. LC 81-51798. (Worldwatch Papers). 1982. pap. 2.00 (ISBN 0-916468-47-X). Worldwatch Inst.
Brown, Lester R. & Wolf, Edward C. Reversing Africa's Decline. (Worldwatch Papers). 1985. pap. 4.00 (ISBN 0-916468-65-8). Worldwatch Inst.
Brown, Lester R., jt. auth. see Eckholm, Erik.
Brown, Lester R., et al. State of The World, 1984. LC 83-25123. (Worldwatch Bk.). 1984. 15.95 (ISBN 0-393-01835-0). Worldwatch Inst.
--State of the World, 1985: A Worldwatch Institute Report on Progress Toward a Sustainable Society. (Illus.). 301p. 1985. 18.95 (ISBN 0-393-01930-6); pap. 8.95 (ISBN 0-393-30218-0). Norton.
--Twenty-Two Dimensions of the Population Problem. LC 76-5963. (Worldwatch Papers). 1976. pap. 2.00 (ISBN 0-916468-04-6). Worldwatch Inst.
--The Future of the Automobile in an Oil-Short World. LC 79-67316. (Worldwatch Papers). 1979. pap. 2.00 (ISBN 0-916468-31-3). Worldwatch Inst.
Brown, Lewis S. Yes, Helen, There Were Dinosaurs. Brown, Lena M., ed. (Illus.). 152p. (Orig.). 1982. pap. 7.95 (ISBN 0-9608542-0-7). L S Brown Pub.
Brown, Lewis S., ed. see Ellenberger, W., et al.
Brown, Lewis S., ed. see Muybridge, Eadweard.
Brown, Lin, jt. ed. see Protopappas, John J.
Brown, Linda. An Annotated Bibliography of the Literature on Livability: With an Introduction & an Analysis of the Literature, No. 853. 1975. 6.00 (ISBN 0-686-20366-6). CPL Biblios.
--Problems in Implementing Statutory Requirements for Title One ESEA Parent Advisory Councils. (IRE Reports: No. 2). 1981. pap. 2.50 (ISBN 0-317-00495-6). Inst Responsive.
Brown, Linda K. & Mussell, Kay, eds. Ethnic & Regional Foodways in the United States: The Performance of Group Identity. LC 83-16715. (Illus.). 284p. 1984. text ed. 24.95x (ISBN 0-87049-418-X); pap. text ed. 12.95x (ISBN 0-87049-419-8). U of Tenn Pr.
Brown, Lionel A. A Slice of Life: Readings in General Anthropology. LC 73-18243. 1974. pap. text ed. 13.95 (ISBN 0-03-002886-8, HoltC). HR&W.
Brown, Lionel H. Victor Trumper & the 1922 Australians. 1981. 24.95 (ISBN 0-436-07107-X, Pub. by Secker & Warburg UK). David & Charles.
Brown, Lisa & Panter, Gideon. The Pregnancy Diary. (Orig.). 1985. pap. 3.95 (ISBN 0-440-57127-8, Dell Trade Pbks). Dell.
Brown, Lisa M. Pregnancy Datebook. (Illus.). 1983. 9.95 (ISBN 0-911491-04-X). Nassau Pr.
Brown, Lloyd. The Story of Maps. (Illus.). 1979. pap. 7.95 (ISBN 0-486-23873-3). Dover.
Brown, Lloyd A. The Story of Maps. (Illus.). 16.00 (ISBN 0-8446-5739-5). Peter Smith.
--The Story of Maps. LC 79-52395. (Illus.). 417p. 1980. Repr. of 1949 ed. 11.95 (ISBN 0-938164-00-7). Vintage Bk Co.
Brown, Lloyd A. & Peckham, Howard H., eds. Revolutionary War Journals of Henry Dearborn, 1775-1783. LC 74-146143. (Era of the American Revolution Ser). 1971. Repr. of 1939 ed. lib. bdg. 37.50 (ISBN 0-306-70107-3). Da Capo.
Brown, Lloyd A., ed. see Dearborn, Henry.
Brown, Lloyd W. Amiri Baraka (LeRoi Jones) (United States Authors Ser.). 1980. lib. bdg. 13.50 (ISBN 0-8057-7317-7, Twayne). G K Hall.
--West Indian Poetry. 2nd. Ed. ed. (Studies in Caribbean Literature). 202p. (Orig.). 1984. pap. text ed. 15.00x (ISBN 0-435-91830-3). Heinemann Ed.
--Women Writers in Black Africa. LC 80-1710. (Contributions in Women's Studies: No. 21). vii, 204p. 1981. lib. bdg. 27.50 (ISBN 0-313-22540-0, BRW/). Greenwood.
Brown, Lloyd W., ed. Black Writer in Africa & the Americas. LC 70-188989. (University of Southern California Studies in Comparative Literature Ser: No. 6). 1973. pap. 7.95x (ISBN 0-912158-51-4). Hennessey.
Brown, Loren R. Point Loma Theosophical Society: A List of Publications, 1898 - 1942. LC 81-187499. (Illus.). 136p. 1977. pap. 10.00 (ISBN 0-913510-46-7). Wizards.
Brown, Lorna, ed. Sex Education in the Eighties: The Challenge of Healthy Sexual Evolution. LC 81-15738. (Perspectives in Sexuality Ser.). 278p. 1981. 27.50 (ISBN 0-306-40762-0, Plenum Pr). Plenum Pub.
Brown, Lou B. My Country Roads. Buck, Janie B., ed. LC 79-89004. (Illus.). 1979. 12.98 (ISBN 0-934530-01-7). Buck Pub.
Brown, Louis J., jt. ed. see Haring, Norris G.
Brown, Louis M. Preventive Law. LC 72-97326. xix, 346p. Repr. of 1950 ed. lib. bdg. 17.50x (ISBN 0-8371-3077-8, BRPL). Greenwood.
Brown, Louisa. What's a Girl to Do? pap. 1.50x (ISBN 0-914053-05-1). Liberty Bell Pr.
Brown, Louise C. Elephant Seals. LC 78-25623. (Skylight Bks.). (Illus.). (gr. 2-5). 1979. 7.95 (ISBN 0-396-07665-3). Dodd.
--Giraffes. LC 79-52037. (A Skylight Bk.). (Illus.). (gr. 2-5). 1980. 7.95 (ISBN 0-396-07730-7). Dodd.
Brown, Louise F. Political Activities of the Baptists & the Fifth Monarchy Men in England During the Interregnum. 1964. Repr. of 1911 ed. 20.50 (ISBN 0-8337-0399-4). B Franklin.
Brown, Louise F. & Carson, George B. Men & Centuries of European Civilization. facs. ed. LC 76-134060. (Essay Index Reprint Ser). 1948. 46.50 (ISBN 0-8369-2100-3). Ayer Co Pubs.
Brown, Louise K. A Revolutionary Town. LC 74-30897. (Illus.). 336p. 1975. 15.00 (ISBN 0-914016-14-8). Phoenix Pub.
Brown, Lowell & Haystead, Wes. The Church Computer Manual. 160p. (Orig.). 1985. pap. 12.95 (ISBN 0-8423-0271-9). Tyndale.
Brown, Lucy G. Core Media Collection for Secondary Schools. 2nd ed. LC 79-6969. 1979. 18.95 (ISBN 0-8352-1162-2). Bowker.
Brown, Lucy G. & McDavid, Betty. Core Media Collection for Elementary Schools. 2nd ed. LC 78-11674. 1978. 18.95 (ISBN 0-8352-1096-0). Bowker.
Brown, Lucy M. & Christie, Ian R. Bibliography of British History Seventeen Eighty-Nine to Eighteen Fifty-One. 1977. 110.00x (ISBN 0-19-822390-0). Oxford U Pr.
Brown, Lyle C., jt. auth. see Jones, Eugene W.
Brown, Lynn. Fire & Firecrackers. 3rd ed. Walker, Granville, Jr., ed. (Fun & Safety Ser.). (Illus.). 14p. (Orig.). (ps-6). 1982. pap. 2.97x (ISBN 0-9608466-1-1). Fun Reading.
--Ms. Worm. 3rd ed. Walker, Granville, Jr., ed. (Fun & Safety Ser.). (Illus., Orig.). (ps-6). 1982. pap. 2.95x (ISBN 0-9608466-0-3). Fun Reading.
Brown, M., et al. American Art: Painting, Sculpture, Architecture, Decorative Arts, Photography. 1979. 33.95 (ISBN 0-13-024653-0). P-H.
--Essays in Modern Capital Theory. (Contributions to Economic Analysis: Vol. 95). 276p. 1976. 57.50 (ISBN 0-444-10896-3, North-Holland). Elsevier.
Brown, M. B., jt. ed. see Dixon, W. J.
Brown, M. C., jt. auth. see Hopkins, W. G.
Brown, M. H., ed. Meat Microbiology. (Illus.). 528p. 1982. 89.00 (ISBN 0-85334-138-9, I-305-82, Pub. by Elsevier Applied Sci England). Elsevier.
Brown, M. J. Advance Medicine Twenty-One. 400p. 1985. text ed. 52.00 (ISBN 0-272-79831-2, Pub. by Pitman Med UK). Urban & S.
Brown, M. L. Firearms in Colonial America: The Impact on History & Technology 1492-1792. LC 80-27221. (Illus.). 448p. 1980. 55.00 (ISBN 0-87474-290-0). Smithsonian.
Brown, M. Ralph. Legal Psychology. (Historical Foundations of Forensic Psychiatry & Psychology Ser.). (Illus.). 346p. 1980. Repr. of 1926 ed. lib. bdg. 39.50 (ISBN 0-306-76065-7). Da Capo.
Brown, M. T. Making Money with the Telephone: The Complete Handbook of Telephone Marketing. LC 77-89655. 1977. 12.95 (ISBN 0-930490-01-0). Future Shop.
Brown, M. W., jt. ed. see Miller, K. J.
Brown, Mac H., jt. auth. see Brown, Carl F.
Brown, MacAlister & Zasloff, Joseph J. Apprentice Revolutionaries: The Communist Movement in Laos, 1930-1985. (Histories of Ruling Communist Parties Publication Ser.: No. 312). (Illus.). 350p. 1986. pap. 13.95x. Hoover Inst Pr.
Brown, MacAlister, jt. auth. see Zasloff, Joseph J.
Brown, MacKenzie, jt. auth. see Easton, Robert.
Brown, Malcolm. The Politics of Irish Literature: From Thomas Davis to W. B. Yeats. LC 72-152328. (Washington Paperback Ser.: No. 67). 443p. 1972. 20.00x (ISBN 0-295-95170-2); pap. 7.95x (ISBN 0-295-95280-6). U of Wash Pr.
--Tommy Goes to War. (Illus.). 272p. 1978. 17.95x (ISBN 0-460-04327-7, Pub by J M Dent England). Biblio Dist.
Brown, Malcolm & Seaton, Shirley. Christmas Truce (The Western Front December 1914) (Illus.). 228p. 1985. 22.50 (ISBN 0-87052-015-6). Hippocrene Bks.
Brown, Malcolm & Webb, John N. Seven Stranded Coal Towns: A Study of an American Depressed Area. LC 76-165680. (Research Monograph: Vol. 23). 1971. Repr. of 1941 ed. lib. bdg. 25.00 (ISBN 0-306-70355-6). Da Capo.
Brown, Malcolm, jt. auth. see Webb, John N.
Brown, Malcolm, ed. see Asafiev.
Brown, Malcolm, ed. see Orlova, Alexandra.
Brown, Malcolm, ed. see Ridenour, Robert C.
Brown, Malcolm, ed. see Taruskin, Richard.
Brown, Malcolm H., ed. Musorgsky: In Memoriam, 1881-1981. LC 82-1861. (Russian Music Studies: No. 3). 344p. 1982. 44.95 (ISBN 0-8357-1295-8). UMI Res Pr.
--Papers of the Yugoslav-American Seminar on Music. 1970. 7.95 (ISBN 0-89357-007-9); pap. 4.95 (ISBN 0-89357-006-0). Slavica.
--Russian & Soviet Music: Essays for Boris Schwarz. LC 84-50049. (Russian Music Studies: No. 11). 336p. 1984. 49.95 (ISBN 0-8357-1545-0). UMI Res Pr.
Brown, Malcolm H. & Wiley, Roland J., eds. Slavonic & Western Music: Essays for Gerald Abraham. LC 84-2625. (Russian Music Studies: No. 12). 322p. 1984. 39.95 (ISBN 0-8357-1594-9). UMI Res Pr.
Brown, Malcolm H., ed. see Joseph, Charles M.
Brown, Malcolm H., ed. see Mischakoff, Anne.
Brown, Malcolm H., ed. see Olkhovsky, Yuri.
Brown, Malcolm H., ed. see Vershinina, Irina.
Brown, Malcolm M., jt. auth. see McGovern, Vincent.
Brown, Malcom. Sir Samuel Ferguson. (Irish Writers Ser.). 101p. 1973. 4.50 (ISBN 0-8387-1083-2); pap. 1.95 (ISBN 0-8387-1208-8). Bucknell U Pr.
Brown, Marc. Arthur Goes to Camp. LC 81-15588. (Illus.). 32p. (gr. 1 up). 1982. 13.45i (ISBN 0-316-11218-6, Pub. by Atlantic-Little Brown). Little.
--Arthur Goes to Camp. (Illus.). (gr. 1-3). 1984. pap. 3.70i (ISBN 0-316-11058-2, An Atlantic-Little, Brown Book). Little.
--Arthur's April Fool. LC 82-20368. (Illus.). 32p. (gr. 1-3). 1983. 13.45i (ISBN 0-316-11196-1, Pub. by Atlantic Little, Brown); pap. 3.70i (ISBN 0-316-11234-8). Little.
--Arthur's Christmas. LC 84-4373. (Illus.). (gr. 1-3). 13.45i (ISBN 0-316-11180-5). Little.
--Arthur's Christmas. (Illus.). 32p. (gr. 1-3). 1985. pap. 3.95 (ISBN 0-316-10993-2, Pub. by Atlantic Monthly Pr). Little.
--Arthur's Eyes. (Illus.). 32p. (gr. 1-3). 1981. pap. 2.50 (ISBN 0-380-53389-8, 70000-X, Camelot). Avon.
--Arthur's Eyes. LC 79-11734. (Illus.). (gr. k-3). 1979. 13.45i (ISBN 0-316-11063-9, Pub. by Atlantic-Little Brown). Little.
--Arthur's Halloween. (Illus.). 32p. (gr. 1-3). 1982. PLB 12.45i (ISBN 0-316-11116-3, Pub. by Atlantic Pr). Little.
--Arthur's Halloween. LC 82-14286. (Illus.). 32p. (gr. 1-3). 1983. pap. 3.70i (ISBN 0-316-11059-0, Pub. by Atlantic Monthly Pr). Little.
--Arthur's Nose. (Illus.). 32p. (gr. 1-3). 1981. pap. 2.25 (ISBN 0-380-53397-9, 68940-5, Camelot). Avon.
--Arthur's Nose. (Illus.). 32p. (gr. k-3). 1976. 13.45i (ISBN 0-316-11193-7, Pub. by Atlantic Monthly Pr). Little.
--Arthur's Thanksgiving. LC 83-798. (Illus.). 32p. (gr. 1-3). 1983. PLB 12.45i (ISBN 0-316-11060-4, Pub. by Atlantic Monthly Pr). Little.
--Arthur's Thanksgiving. (Illus.). 1984. pap. 3.70i (ISBN 0-316-11232-1, Pub. by Atlantic Monthly Pr). Little.
--Arthur's Tooth: An Arthur Adventure. Kroupa, Melanie, ed. LC 85-72092. (Arthur Adventure Ser.). (Illus.). 32p. (gr. 1-3). 1985. reinforced bdg. 13.95 (ISBN 0-87113-006-8, 112453). Atlantic Monthly.
--Arthur's Valentine. (Snuggle & Read Ser.). (Illus.). 32p. (Orig.). (ps-3). 1982. pap. 1.95 (ISBN 0-380-57075-0, 57075-0, Camelot). Avon.
--Arthur's Valentine. (Illus.). (gr. 1-3). 1980. 12.45i (ISBN 0-316-11062-0, Pub. by Atlantic-Little Brown). Little.
--The Bionic Bunny Show. (Reading Rainbow Ser.). (Illus.). 32p. (ps up). 1985. pap. 5.95 (ISBN 0-316-10992-4, Pub. by Atlantic Monthly Pr). Little.
--Finger Rhymes. LC 80-10173. (Illus.). 32p. (ps-2). 1980. 10.95 (ISBN 0-525-29732-4, 01063-320, Unicorn Bk). Dutton.
--Hand Rhymes. Durell, Ann, ed. LC 84-25918. (Illus.). 32p. (ps-1). 1985. 11.95 (ISBN 0-525-44201-4). Dutton.
--One Two Three: An Animal Counting Book. 32p. (gr. k-3). 1976. PLB 10.45i (ISBN 0-316-11064-7, Pub. by Atlantic Monthly Pr). Little.
--Pickle Things. LC 80-10540. (Illus.). 48p. (ps-3). 1980. 5.95 (ISBN 0-686-86566-9); PLB 5.95 (ISBN 0-686-91532-1). Parents.
--The Silly Tail Book. LC 83-2250. (Illus.). 48p. (ps-2). 1983. 5.95 (ISBN 0-8193-1109-X). Parents.
--Spooky Riddles. (Beginner Bks.: No.69). (Illus.). 48p. (gr. k-3). 1983. cancelled 4.95 (ISBN 0-394-86093-4). Random.
--There's No Place Like Home. LC 84-4229. (Illus.). 48p. (ps-3). 1984. 5.95 (ISBN 0-8193-1125-1). Parents.
--The True Francine. (Snuggle & Read Ser.). (Illus.). 32p. (ps-3). 1982. pap. 1.95 (ISBN 0-380-57083-1, 57083-1, Camelot). Avon.
--The True Francine. (Illus.). 32p. (gr. 1-3). 1981. 12.45i (ISBN 0-316-11212-7, Atlantic). Little.
--What Do You Call a Dumb Bunny? & Other Rabbit Riddles, Games, Jokes & Cartoons. (Illus.). 32p. (gr. 1-3). 1983. PLB 9.70i (ISBN 0-316-11117-1, Pub. by Atlantic Monthly Pr); pap. 3.70i (ISBN 0-316-11119-8, Pub. by Atlantic Monthly Pr); 10-copy counter display 37.00i (ISBN 0-316-11192-9). Little.
--Wings & Things. LC 81-12095. (Bright & Early Ser.: No. 26). 36p. (ps-1). 1982. 4.95 (ISBN 0-394-85130-7); PLB 5.99 (ISBN 0-394-95130-1). Random.
--Witches Four. LC 79-5263. (Illus.). 48p. (ps-3). 1980. 5.95 (ISBN 0-686-86576-6); PLB 5.95 (ISBN 0-686-91536-4). Parents.
--Your First Garden Book. (Illus.). (gr. 1 up). 1981. 9.95 (ISBN 0-316-11217-8, Pub. by Atlantic Pr); pap. 4.95 (ISBN 0-316-11215-1). Little.
Brown, Marc & Krasny, Lauren K. The Bionic Bunny Show. (Illus.). 32p. (ps-3). 1984. 13.95 (ISBN 0-316-11120-1, Pub. by Atlantic Monthly Pr). Little.
Brown, Marc & Krensky, Stephen. Dinosaurs, Beware! A Safety Guide. LC 82-15207. (Illus.). 32p. (gr. k-3). 1982. 13.45i (ISBN 0-316-11228-3, Pub. by Atlantic Pr). Little.
--Dinosaurs Beware! A Safety Guide. (Illus.). (ps-3). 1984. pap. 5.70i (ISBN 0-316-11219-4, Pub. by Atlantic Monthly Pr). Little.
--Perfect Pigs: An Introduction to Manners. LC 83-746. (Illus.). 32p. (gr. k-3). 1983. PLB 13.45i (ISBN 0-316-11079-5, Pub. by Atlantic Monthly Pr); pap. 5.70i (ISBN 0-316-11080-9). Little.
Brown, Marc, ed. Voices for Deep Ecology. 300p. Date not set. pap. cancelled (ISBN 0-942688-07-4). Dream Garden.
Brown, Marc, ed. see Coello, Dennis.
Brown, Marc, ed. see Thompson, George A.
Brown, Marcia. All Butterflies. (Illus.). 32p. (ps-2). pap. 2.95 (ISBN 0-689-70483-6, A-110, Aladdin). Atheneum.
--All Butterflies: An ABC. LC 73-19364. (Illus.). 32p. (ps-1). 1974. reinforced bdg. o.s.i. 9.95 (ISBN 0-684-13771-2, ScribJ); pap. 2.95 (ISBN 0-689-70483-6). Scribner.
--Backbone of the King. (Illus.). 180p. (gr. 4-8). 1984. Repr. of 1966 ed. 12.95 (ISBN 0-8248-0963-7). UH Pr.
--Listen to a Shape. (Marcia Brown Concept Library). (gr. 1-4). 1979. PLB 8.90 s&l (ISBN 0-531-02930-1). Watts.
--Lotus Seeds: Children, Pictures & Books. LC 85-40288. (Illus.). 192p. 1985. 13.95 (ISBN 0-684-18490-7). Scribner.
--Once a Mouse. LC 61-14769. (Illus.). (ps-5). 1961. reinforced bdg. 12.95 (ISBN 0-684-12662-1, ScribJ); pap. 2.95 (ISBN 0-689-70751-7). Scribner.
--Once a Mouse. LC 61-14769. (Illus.). 32p. (gr. k-3). 1982. pap. 2.95 (ISBN 0-689-70751-7, A127, Aladdin). Atheneum.
--Stone Soup. (Illus.). (gr. k-3). 1947. reinforced bdg. 12.95 (ISBN 0-684-92296-7, ScribJ); pap. 5.95 (ISBN 0-684-16217-2, SBF1, ScribJ). Scribner.

--Touch Will Tell. (Marcia Brown Concept Library Ser.). (Illus.). (gr. 1-4). 1979. PLB 8.90 s&l (ISBN 0-531-02931-X). Watts.

--Walk with Your Eyes. (Marcia Brown Concept Library). (Illus.). (gr. 1-4). 1979. PLB 8.90 s&l (ISBN 0-531-02925-5). Watts.

Brown, Marcia & Andersen, Hans Christian. The Snow Queen. LC 72-168499. (Illus.). 96p. (gr. 1-5). 1972. 6.95 (ISBN 0-684-12611-7, ScribJ). Scribner.

Brown, Marcia & Perrault, Charles. Cinderella. (Illus.). 32p. (gr. k-3). pap. 2.95 (ISBN 0-689-70484-4, A-111, Aladdin). Atheneum.

--Cinderella. (Illus.). (gr. k-5). 1954. reinforced bdg. 12.95 (ISBN 0-684-12676-1, ScribJ); pap. 2.95 (ScribJ). Scribner.

Brown, Marcia, ed. & illus. Three Billy Goats Gruff. LC 57-5265. (Illus.). (gr. k-3). 1957. 10.95 (ISBN 0-15-286399-0, HJ). HarBraceJ.

Brown, Marel. Three Wise Women of the East. pap. 1.75x (ISBN 0-8358-0245-0). Upper Room.

Brown, Margaret D. Shepherdess of Elk River Valley. 2nd ed. (Illus.). 1967. 5.50x (ISBN 0-87315-037-6). Golden Bell.

Brown, Margaret H., jt. auth. see Brown, John E.

Brown, Margaret K. The Zimmerman Site: Further Excavations at the Grand Village of Kaskaskia. (Reports of Investigations Ser.: No. 32). (Illus.). 124p. 1975. pap. 3.00 (ISBN 0-89792-058-9). Ill St Museum.

Brown, Margaret K. & Dean, Lawrie, eds. The Village of Chartres in Colonial Illinois: 1720-1765. 1977. 30.00x (ISBN 0-686-09340-2). Polyanthos.

Brown, Margaret R. & Etherington, Don. Boxes for the Protection of Rare Books: Their Design & Construction. LC 81-607965. (Illus.). 293p. 1982. pap. 18.00 (ISBN 0-8444-0365-2). Lib Congress.

Brown, Margaret W. Christmas in the Barn. LC 52-7858. (Illus.). (gr. k-3). 1949. 10.10i (ISBN 0-690-19272-X); PLB 10.89 plb. Crowell Jr Bks.

--Christmas in the Barn. LC 85-42738. (A Trophy Picture Bk.). (Illus.). 40p. (gr. k-3). 1985. pap. 2.95i (ISBN 0-06-443082-0, Trophy). HarpJ.

--Country Noisy Book. LC 40-32066. (Illus.). 42p. (ps-1). 1940. PLB 10.89 (ISBN 0-06-020811-2). HarpJ.

--Good Night, Moon. 1977. pap. 2.95 (ISBN 0-06-443017-0). Har-Row.

--Goodnight, Moon. LC 47-30762. (Illus.). 30p. (ps-1). 1947. 6.61i (ISBN 0-06-020705-1); PLB 8.89 (ISBN 0-06-020706-X). HarpJ.

--Goodnight, Moon. (Picture Bk.). (Illus.). (ps-2). 1977. pap. 2.95 (ISBN 0-06-443017-0, Trophy). HarpJ.

--Goodnight, Moon. (gr. k-3). 1984. incl. cassette 19.95 (ISBN 0-941078-30-2); pap. 12.95 incl. cassette (ISBN 0-941078-28-0); incl. 4 bks., cassette, & guide 27.95 (ISBN 0-317-07120-3). Live Oak Media.

--The Goodnight Moon Room: A Pop-Up Book. LC 83-48169. (Illus.). 10p. (ps-1). 1984. 8.61i (ISBN 0-694-00003-5). HarpJ.

--Home for a Bunny. (Big Golden Story Bks.). (Illus.). 24p. (ps-2). 1983. 3.50 (ISBN 0-307-10446-X, 10388, Golden Bks.). Western Pub.

--Important Book. LC 49-9133. (Illus.). 22p. (ps-1). 1949. 9.57 (ISBN 0-06-020720-5); PLB 10.89 (ISBN 0-06-020721-3). HarpJ.

--Indoor Noisy Book. LC 42-23589. (Illus.). 42p. (ps-1). 1942. PLB 11.89 (ISBN 0-06-020821-X). HarpJ.

--Little Chicken. LC 43-16942. (Illus.). 32p. (gr. k-3). 1982. 8.64i (ISBN 0-06-020739-6); PLB 8.89g (ISBN 0-06-020740-X). HarpJ.

--The Little Fir Tree. LC 85-42743. (A Trophy Picture Bk.). (Illus.). 40p. (gr. k-3). 1985. pap. 2.84i (ISBN 0-06-443083-9, Trophy). HarpJ.

--The Little Fir Tree. LC 54-5534. 1985. PLB 11.89 (ISBN 0-690-04016-4). Crowell Jr Bks.

--Little Fur Family. LC 51-11657. (Illus.). 32p. (ps-2). 1984. fur covered boards 3.95 (ISBN 0-06-020745-0). HarpJ.

--Noisy Book (City) LC 39-31264. Orig. Title: City Noisy Book. (Illus.). 42p. (ps-1). 1939. PLB 11.89 (ISBN 0-06-020831-7). HarpJ.

--Quiet Noisy Book. LC 50-9797. (Illus.). 32p. (ps-1). 1950. HarpJ.

--The Runaway Bunny. LC 71-183168. (Illus.). 40p. (ps-2). 1972. 8.89i (ISBN 0-06-020765-5); PLB 7.89 (ISBN 0-06-020766-3). HarpJ.

--The Runaway Bunny. (Picture Bk.). (Illus.). (ps-2). 1977. pap. 2.95 (ISBN 0-06-443018-9, Trophy). HarpJ.

--The Runaway Bunny. (Illus.). (gr. k-3). 1985. incl. cassette 19.95 (ISBN 0-941078-78-7); pap. 12.95 incl. cassette (ISBN 0-941078-76-0); cassette, 4 paperbacks & guide 27.95 (ISBN 0-941078-77-9). Live Oak Media.

--Sleepy Little Lion. LC 47-11482. (Illus.). 24p. (gr. k-3). 1947. PLB 11.89 (ISBN 0-06-020771-X). HarpJ.

--The Sleepy Little Lion. (Illus.). (ps-3). 1976. pap. 1.95 (ISBN 0-06-443015-4, Trophy). HarpJ.

--Wait Till the Moon Is Full. LC 48-9278. (Illus.). 32p. (ps-1). 1948. 10.53 (ISBN 0-06-020800-7). HarpJ.

--Wheel on the Chimney. LC 84-48379. (Illus.). 32p. (ps-3). 1985. 11.49i (ISBN 0-397-30288-6); PLB 11.89g (ISBN 0-397-30296-7). Lipp Jr Bks.

--When the Wind Blew. LC 76-58734. (Illus.). 32p. (ps-3). 1977. 9.53i (ISBN 0-06-020867-8); PLB 8.89 (ISBN 0-06-020868-6). HarpJ.

--The Winter Noisy Book. LC 47-30809. (Illus.). (ps-1). 1976. pap. 1.95 (ISBN 0-06-443004-9, Trophy). HarpJ.

Brown, Margery. Cane & Rush Seating. (Craft Ser). (Illus.). (gr. 7). 1977. 10.95 (ISBN 0-88332-049-5); pap. 8.95 (ISBN 0-88332-075-4, 8096). Larousse.

--The Complete Book of Rush & Basketry Techniques. LC 82-83971. (Illus.). 144p. 1983. pap. 16.95 (ISBN 0-88332-292-7, 8108). Larousse.

Brown, Margie. The Stick Stories. (Illus., Orig.). 1982. pap. 5.56 (ISBN 0-89390-035-4); pap. text ed. 6.95 o.p. (ISBN 0-686-83133-0). Resource Pubns.

Brown, Marguerite. Magnificent Muslims. LC 81-80056. 98p. 1981. 8.00 (ISBN 0-911026-10-X). New World Press NY.

Brown, Marguerite D. Women of Calvary. 1982. pap. 4.50 ea. (ISBN 0-89536-526-X). CSS of Ohio.

Brown, Marice C. Amen, Brother Ben: A Mississippi Collection of Children's Rhymes. LC 78-32017. 1979. pap. text ed. 5.00 (ISBN 0-87805-094-9). U Pr of Miss.

Brown, Marie & Murphy, Mary A. Ambulatory Pediatrics for Nurses. 2nd ed. LC 80-12462. (Illus.). 624p. 1980. text ed. 28.00 (ISBN 0-07-008291-X). McGraw.

Brown, Marie S., jt. auth. see Alexander, Mary M.

Brown, Marie Scott see Bower, Fay L. & Scott Brown, Marie.

Brown, Marilyn R. Gypsies & Other Bohemians: The Myth of the Artists in Nineteenth-Century France. (Studies in the Fine Arts; The Avant-Garde: No. 51). 230p. 1985. 44.95 (ISBN 0-8357-1704-6). UMI Res Pr.

Brown, Marion. Leadership Among High School Pupils. LC 77-176598. (Columbia University. Teachers College. Contributions to Education: No. 559). Repr. of 1933 ed. 22.50 (ISBN 0-404-55559-4). AMS Pr.

--Marion Brown's Southern Cook Book. rev. ed. ix, 489p. 1968. 12.95 (ISBN 0-8078-1065-7); pap. 8.95 (ISBN 0-8078-4078-5). U of NC Pr.

Brown, Marion E. & Prentice, Marjorie G. Christian Education in the Year Two Thousand. 160p. 1984. pap. 8.95 (ISBN 0-8170-1055-6). Judson.

Brown, Marion M. Homeward the Arrow's Flight. LC 80-11957. (Illus.). 176p. (gr. 7 up). 1980. 8.75g (ISBN 0-687-17300-0). Abingdon.

Brown, Marion M. & Crone, Ruth. Only One Point of the Compass: Willa Cather in the Northeast. LC 80-11384. 136p. 1980. 12.50 (ISBN 0-89097-017-3). Archer Edns.

Brown, Marion M. & Leech, Jane K. Dreamcatcher: The Life of John Neihardt. 144p. (Orig.). 1983. pap. 6.95 (ISBN 0-687-11174-9). Abingdon.

Brown, Marion M., et al. The Silent Storm. 1985. Repr. of 1963 ed. 6.95 (ISBN 0-8010-0884-0). Baker Bk.

Brown, Marjorie J., jt. ed. see Hall, James L.

Brown, Mark. Memory Matters. LC 77-71252. (Illus.). 160p. 1977. 14.50x (ISBN 0-8448-1091-6). Crane-Russak Co.

Brown, Mark D. Intradiscal Therapy: Chymopapain or Collagenase. 1983. 49.95 (ISBN 0-8151-6637-0). Year Bk Med.

Brown, Mark H. The Flight of the Nez Perce. LC 82-2717. (Illus.). 480p. 1982. pap. 9.95 (ISBN 0-8032-6069-5, BB 808, Bison). U of Nebr Pr.

--The Plainsmen of the Yellowstone: A History of the Yellowstone Basin. LC 60-5262. (Illus.). 480p. 1969. pap. 10.95 (ISBN 0-8032-5026-6, BB 397, Bison). U of Nebr Pr.

Brown, Marsha H., jt. auth. see Mason, Bethny H.

Brown, Marshall. The Shape of German Romanticism. LC 79-14313. 256p. 1979. 24.95x (ISBN 0-8014-1228-5). Cornell U Pr.

Brown, Marshall G. & Stein, Gordon. Freethought in the United States: A Descriptive Bibliography. LC 77-91103. 1978. lib. bdg. 35.00 (ISBN 0-313-20036-X, BFT/). Greenwood.

Brown, Martha C. Schoolwise: A Parents Guide to Getting the Best Education for Your Child. 252p. 1985. pap. 9.95 (ISBN 0-87477-364-4). J P Tarcher.

Brown, Martin. A Maine Deeper In. LC 81-66264. (Illus.). 128p. 1982. pap. 10.95 (ISBN 0-89272-127-8). Down East.

Brown, Martin, ed. Social Responsibility of the Scientist. LC 75-143503. 1971. pap. text ed. 11.95 (ISBN 0-02-904730-7). Free Pr.

Brown, Martin B. Compendium & Communication & Broadcast Satellites 1958-1981. LC 81-81858. 375p. 1981. 38.95x (ISBN 0-471-86198-7, Pub. by Wiley Interscience). Wiley.

Brown, Martin P. Jr., ed. Compendium of Communication & Broadcast Satellites. LC 81-81858. 1981. 40.50 (ISBN 0-87942-153-3, PC01461). Inst Electrical.

Brown, Martyn. Somerset. (Shire Country Guides: No. 1). (Illus., Orig.). 1982. pap. 4.95 (ISBN 0-85263-618-0, Pub. by Shire Pubns England). Seven Hills Bks.

Brown, Marvin L., Jr. Heinrich Von Haymerle: Austro-Hungarian Career Diplomat 1828-81. LC 79-183904. (Illus.). xii, 238p. 1973. 14.95x (ISBN 0-87249-243-5). U of SC Pr.

--The Wisdom of Christendom. 131p. 1982. pap. 5.95. Edenwood Hse.

Brown, Mary. Playing the Jack. 584p. 1985. 16.95 (ISBN 0-671-54252-4). S&S.

Brown, Mary, et al. Agricultural Education in a Technical Society: An Annotated Bibliography of Resources. LC 72-7501. pap. 60.00 (ISBN 0-317-26603-9, 2024189). Bks Demand UMI.

Brown, Sr. Mary A., ed. Paul of Pergula: Logica & Tractatus De Sensu Composito et Diviso. (Text Ser). 1961. 11.00 (ISBN 0-686-11558-9). Franciscan Inst.

Brown, Mary E. Burns & Tradition. LC 83-10311. 192p. 1984. 19.95x (ISBN 0-252-01102-3). U of Ill Pr.

--Dedications: An Anthology of the Forms Used from the Earliest Days of Bookmaking to the Present Time. 1964. Repr. of 1913 ed. 23.50 (ISBN 0-8337-3383-8). B Franklin.

Brown, Mary G., jt. auth. see Brown, William F.

Brown, Mary H. Exercises in Communication. 144p. 1984. pap. 11.95 (ISBN 0-8403-3364-1). Kendall-Hunt.

--Memories of Concord. LC 72-10118. 1974. Repr. of 1926 ed. lib. bdg. 16.50 (ISBN 0-8414-0633-2). Folcroft.

Brown, Mary K. Aunt Mary's Kitchen Cookbook. (Illus.). 224p. 1983. pap. 7.95 (ISBN 0-02-009320-9, Collier). Macmillan.

Brown, Mary L. Occupational Health Nursing. LC 80-21024. 352p. 1981. text ed. 24.50 (ISBN 0-8261-2250-7). Springer Pub.

Brown, Mason L., ed. Respond, Vol. 3. LC 77-159050. (Illus.). 144p. (Orig.). 1973. pap. 5.95 (ISBN 0-8170-0600-1). Judson.

Brown, Maurice F. Estranging Dawn: The Life & Works of William Vaughn Moody. LC 73-252. (Illus.). 320p. 1973. 12.50x (ISBN 0-8093-0618-2). S Ill U Pr.

Brown, Maurice J. Essays on Schubert. LC 77-22216. (Music Reprint Ser.). (Illus.). 1978. Repr. of 1966 ed. lib. bdg. 35.00 (ISBN 0-306-77439-9). Da Capo.

--Schubert: A Critical Biography. LC 77-4160. (Music Reprint Ser.). (Illus.). 1977. Repr. of 1958 ed. lib. bdg. 39.50 (ISBN 0-306-77409-7). Da Capo.

--Schubert Songs. LC 76-80514. 62p. 1969. pap. 4.95 (ISBN 0-295-95023-4). U of Wash Pr.

--Schubert Symphonies. LC 70-127653. (BBC Music Guides Ser.). (Illus.). 64p. 1971. pap. 4.95 (ISBN 0-295-95106-0). U of Wash Pr.

Brown, Maurice J. E. Chopin: An Index of His Works in Chronological Order. 2nd ed. LC 70-39498. (Music Ser.). 1972. 27.50 (ISBN 0-306-70500-1). Da Capo.

Brown, Maurice J. E. & Sams, Eric. The New Grove Schubert. (The New Grove Composer Biography Ser.). (Illus.). 1983. 16.50 (ISBN 0-393-01683-8); pap. 7.95 (ISBN 0-393-30087-0). Norton.

Brown, Maxwell L. Farm Budgets: From Farm Income Analysis to Agricultural Project Analysis. LC 79-3704. (World Bank Ser.). 160p. 1980. text ed. 15.00x (ISBN 0-8018-2386-2); pap. text ed. 6.50x (ISBN 0-8018-2387-0). Johns Hopkins.

Brown, Meg. Exhibition & Pet Rabbits. 1981. 14.00 (ISBN 0-904558-24-X). Saiga.

--Exhibition & Pet Rabbits. 2nd ed. (Illus.). 240p. 1982. 15.50 (ISBN 0-86230-050-9). Triplegate.

Brown, Merle E. The Double Lyric: Divisiveness & Communal Creativity in Recent English Poetry. LC 80-11578. 256p. 1980. 26.00x (ISBN 0-231-05032-1). Columbia U Pr.

--Kenneth Burke. (Pamphlets on American Writers Ser: No. 75). (Orig.). 1969. pap. 1.25x (ISBN 0-8166-0525-4, MPAW75). U of Minn Pr.

--Wallace Stevens: The Poem As Act. LC 72-111042. 220p. 1971. 9.50x (ISBN 0-8143-1427-9). Wayne St U Pr.

Brown, Merrill. Teaching the Successful High School Brass Section. LC 80-19128. 238p. 1981. 17.95x (ISBN 0-13-895805-X, Parker). P-H.

Brown, Mervyn. Madagascar Rediscovered: A History from Early Times to Independence. (Illus.). x, 310p. 1979. 25.00 (ISBN 0-208-01828-X, Archon). Shoe String.

Brown, Michael. Baby's Santa Mouse. (Baby's Board Bks.). (Illus.). (ps). 1983. 3.95 (ISBN 0-448-03091-8, G&D). Putnam Pub Group.

--Laying Waste: The Poisoning of America by Toxic Chemicals. 384p. 1981. pap. 3.95 (ISBN 0-671-45359-9). WSP.

--Marked to Die. (Illus.). 352p. 1984. 16.95 (ISBN 0-671-45090-5). S&S.

--Marked to Die. 1985. pap. 3.95 (ISBN 0-671-54106-4). PB.

--Santa Mouse. (Illus.). (gr. k-3). 1966. 2.95 (ISBN 0-448-04213-4, G&D); PLB 3.09 (ISBN 0-448-13914-6). Putnam Pub Group.

--Santa Mouse. (Pudgy Pals Ser.). (Illus.). 16p. (ps). 1984. 3.50 (ISBN 0-448-10215-3, G&D). Putnam Pub Group.

--Santa Mouse Meets Marmaduke. LC 74-92384. (Elephant Books Ser.). (Illus.). (gr. k-7). 1978. pap. 2.50 (ISBN 0-448-14749-1, G&D). Putnam Pub Group.

Brown, Michael & Woolams, Stan. TA: The Total Handbook of Transcendental Analysis. (Illus.). 1979. 15.95 (ISBN 0-13-881920-3, Spec); pap. 6.95 (ISBN 0-13-881912-2). P-H.

Brown, Michael A., jt. auth. see Ross, Kenneth.

Brown, Michael B. Essays on Imperialism. (Illus.). 1972. pap. text ed. 5.75x (ISBN 0-85124-110-7). Humanities.

--Models in Political Economy: A Guide to the Arguments. LC 85-14258. 282p. 1985. lib. bdg. 27.50 (ISBN 0-931477-54-9); pap. text ed. 13.50 (ISBN 0-931477-55-7). Lynne Rienner.

Brown, Michael D. Resource Recovery Project Studies. (Illus.). 169p. 1983. 39.95 (ISBN 0-250-40611-X). Butterworth.

Brown, Michael E. Ink Bottle Dreams. Brown, Ann M., ed. (Illus.). (gr. 10up). 1984. pap. 5.95 (ISBN 0-915701-00-6). Expressive Images Studio.

Brown, Michael F. Tsewa'a Gift: Magic & Meaning in an Amazonian Society. LC 85-40401. (Ethnographic Inquiry Ser.). (Illus.). 192p. 1985. 19.95x (ISBN 0-87474-294-3, BRTG). Smithsonian.

Brown, Michael H. PK: A Report on the Power of Psychokinesis, the Mental Energy to Move Matter. LC 76-21121. (Rudolf Steiner Publications). (Illus.). 320p. 1976. 12.00 (ISBN 0-89345-013-8); pap. 6.00 (ISBN 0-89345-200-9). Garber Comm.

Brown, Michael J. Itinerant Ambassador: The Life of Sir Thomas Roe. LC 77-94064. (Illus.). 324p. 1970. 28.00x (ISBN 0-8131-1192-7). U Pr of Ky.

Brown, Michael K. Working the Street: Police Discretion & the Dilemmas of Reform. LC 80-69175. 365p. 1981. 18.00 (ISBN 0-87154-190-4). Russell Sage.

Brown, Michael R., ed. Resistance of Pseudomonas Aeruginosa. LC 74-30224. pap. 65.00 (ISBN 0-317-07742-2, 2016181). Bks Demand UMI.

Brown, Michael S., jt. auth. see Nelkin, Dorothy.

Brown, Michele. The Little Royal Book. 1977. 2.50 (ISBN 0-7153-7490-7). David & Charles.

--Ritual of Royalty: The Ceremony & Pageantry of Britain's Monarchy. (Illus.). 178p. 1983. 19.95 (ISBN 0-13-781047-4); pap. 12.95 (ISBN 0-13-781039-3). P-H.

Brown, Michelle. Prince Charles. (Illus.). 192p. 1980. 12.95 (ISBN 0-517-54019-3). Crown.

Brown, Mik & Offerman, Lynn. Little Simon Jokes & Riddles. (Animal Fun Jokes & Riddles Ser.). (Illus.). 40p. (gr. k-3). 1984. 5.95 (ISBN 0-671-52814-9, Little Simon). S&S.

Brown, Mike. Computers from First Principles. (Hatfield Polytechnic Computer Science Series). 126p. (Orig.). 1982. pap. text ed. 11.95x (ISBN 0-86238-027-8, Pub. by Chartwell-Bratt England). Brookfield Pub Co.

Brown, Mildred W. The Three Secrets. 24p. (Orig.). 1984. pap. 6.50 (ISBN 0-939296-12-8). Bond Pub Co.

Brown, Millie. Low-Stress Fitness: The-Low Stress Way to Get in Shape. (Illus.). 160p. 1985. pap. 8.95 (ISBN 0-89586-355-3). H P Bks.

Brown, Milton P., Jr. Authentic Writings of Ignatius: A Study of Linguistic Criteria. LC 63-19458. pap. 33.30 (ISBN 0-8357-9096-7, 2017888). Bks Demand UMI.

Brown, Milton W. American Painting from the Armory Show to the Depression. 1970. 47.00x (ISBN 0-691-03868-6); pap. 15.95x (ISBN 0-691-00301-7). Princeton U Pr.

--One Hundred Masterpieces of American Painting. LC 83-600104. (Illus.). 250p. 1983. 45.00 (ISBN 0-87474-291-9); pap. 24.95. Smithsonian.

Brown, Milton W., et al. American Art: Painting, Sculpture, Architecture, Decorative Arts, Photography. (Illus.). 616p. 45.00 (ISBN 0-8109-0658-9). Abrams.

Brown, Montague & Lewis, Howard L. Hospital Management Systems: Multi-Unit Organization & Delivery of Health Care. LC 76-15769. 305p. 1976. 39.00 (ISBN 0-912862-22-X). Aspen Systems.

Brown, Montague & McCool, Barbara P. Multihospital Systems: Strategies for Organization & Management. LC 79-23439. 564p. 1980. text ed. 52.00 (ISBN 0-89443-169-2). Aspen Systems.

Brown, Montague, ed. Health Care Management Review. LC 75-45767. annual subscription 66.00 (ISBN 0-912862-50-5). Aspen Systems.

Brown, Montague, jt. ed. see Shortell, Stephen M.

Brown, Muriel. Introduction to Social Administration in Britain. 6th ed. LC 84-25942. 304p. (Orig.). 1985. pap. 10.95 (ISBN 0-09-159971-7, Pub. by Hutchinson Educ). Longwood Pub Group.

Brown, Muriel & Madge, Nicola. Despite the Welfare State. (SSRC-DHSS Studies in Deprivation & Disadvantage). xii, 388p. 1982. text ed. 29.00x (ISBN 0-435-82095-8). Gower Pub Co.

Brown, Muriel, ed. The Structure of Disadvantage. (SSRC-DHSS Studies in Deprivation & Disadvantages: No. 12). viii, 210p. 1983. pap. text ed. 17.50x (ISBN 0-435-82093-1). Gower Pub Co.

Brown, Muriel J., jt. auth. see Farmer, Geraldine M.

Brown, Murray, et al, eds. Regional National Econometric Modeling with an Application to the Italian Economy. 204p. 1978. 23.00x (ISBN 0-85086-064-4, NO. 2932, Pub. by Pion England). Methuen Inc.

Brown, Myrtle L., jt. auth. see Pike, Ruth L.

Brown, N. O., et al. Facing the Apocalypse. 200p. (Orig.). 1986. pap. price not set (ISBN 0-88214-329-8). Spring Pubns.

Brown, Nacio J. Rag Theater: The Twenty-Four Hundred Block of Telegraph Avenue 1969-1973. LC 75-15320. (Illus.). 74p. 1979. pap. 10.95 (ISBN 0-915572-42-7). Panjandrum.

Brown, Nancy A. The Milanese Architecture of Galeazzo Alessi, 2 vols. LC 79-57506. (Outstanding Dissertations in the Fine Arts Ser.: No. 5). 871p. 1982. lib. bdg. 107.00 (ISBN 0-8240-3933-5). Garland Pub.

Brown, Nancy P., ed. see Southwell, Robert.

Brown, Nathalie B. Hugo & Dostoevsky. 1978. 15.00x (ISBN 0-88233-268-6); pap. 5.00 (ISBN 0-88233-273-2). Ardis Pubs.

Brown, Nathaniel. Sexuality & Feminism in Shelley. LC 79-4634. 1979. text ed. 17.50x (ISBN 0-674-80285-3). Harvard U Pr.

Brown, Nettie. Albert C-One-Thirty & the Blue Angels' A-4 Skyhawk Jets. (Illus.). 64p. 1981. pap. 4.00 (ISBN 0-682-49802-5). Exposition Pr FL.

Brown, Neville. The Future Global Challenge: A Predictive Study of World Security, 1977-1990. LC 77-82865. 410p. 1977. 26.50x (ISBN 0-8448-1256-0). Crane-Russak Co.

Brown, Nina W., jt. ed. see Grob, Paul.

Brown, Norma, ed. see Douglass, Frederick.

Brown, Norman D. Hood, Bonnet, & Little Brown Jug: Texas Politics, 1921-1928. LC 83-45099. (Texas A&M Southwestern Studies: No. 1). (Illus.). 568p. 1983. 29.50x (ISBN 0-89096-157-3). Tex A&M Univ Pr.

Brown, Norman D., ed. Journey to Pleasant Hill: The Civil War Letters of Captain Elijah P. Petty, Walker's Texas Division, C.S.A. (Illus.). 504p. 1982. 35.00 (ISBN 0-933164-94-7); Two Vols. Set. deluxe ed. 75.00 ltd ed (ISBN 0-933164-95-5). U of Tex Inst Tex Culture.

Brown, Norman H., jt. auth. see Whitman, Robert.

Brown, Norman O. Life Against Death: The Psychoanalytical Meaning of History. LC 59-5369. 1959. 20.00x (ISBN 0-8195-3005-0); pap. 9.95 (ISBN 0-8195-6010-3). Wesleyan U Pr.

--Love's Body. 1968. pap. 3.95 (ISBN 0-394-70419-3, V419, Vin). Random.

--Theogony Hesiod. 1953. pap. text ed. write for info. (ISBN 0-02-315310-5). Macmillan.

Brown, Norman O., tr. see Hesiod.

Brown, O., jt. auth. see Hendrick, W.

Brown, O. Phelps. The Complete Herbalist or the People Their Own Physicians. 504p. Date not set. pap. 25.00 (ISBN 0-89540-118-5, SB-118). Sun Pub.

Brown, Oliver M. Gabriel Denver. LC 72-129368. Repr. of 1873 ed. 22.00 (ISBN 0-404-01137-3). AMS Pr.

Brown, Olympia. Suffrage & Religious Principle: Speeches & Writings of Olympia Brown. Greene, Dana, ed. LC 83-20129. 192p. 1983. 15.00 (ISBN 0-8108-1665-2). Scarecrow.

Brown, Osa. The Metropolitan Museum of Art Activity Book. (Illus.). 96p. (gr. 5-9). 1983. 6.95 (ISBN 0-394-85241-9). Random.

Brown, Oscar C., Sr. By a Thread. 1983. 8.95 (ISBN 0-533-05464-8). Vantage.

Brown, Otis S. One Day Celestial Navigation. 132p. 1984. 10.00 (ISBN 0-686-94857-2). Maryland Hist Pr.

--One Day Celestial Navigation. LC 79-67243. (Illus.). 133p. 1984. pap. 6.95 (ISBN 0-89709-132-9). Liberty Pub.

Brown, P. Chathamites. (Illus.). 1969. 26.00 (ISBN 0-312-13160-7). St Martin.

Brown, P. A. London Publishers & Printers, 1800-1870. 144p. 1982. lib. bdg. 34.00 (ISBN 0-7123-0012-0, Pub. by British Lib). Longwood Pub Group.

--Modern British & American Private Presses (1850-1965) 216p. 1980. 60.00x (ISBN 0-7141-0367-5, Pub. by Brit Lib England). State Mutual Bk.

Brown, P. A. H. London Publishers & Printers: 1800-1870. 144p. 1982. 60.00x (ISBN 0-7123-0012-0, Pub. by Brit LIb England). State Mutual Bk.

Brown, P. Charles, jt. auth. see Mullen, Norma D.

Brown, P. H. The Youth of Goethe. LC 77-133283. (Studies in German Literature, No. 13). Repr. of 1913 ed. lib. bdg. 54.95x (ISBN 0-8383-1182-2). Haskell.

Brown, P. Hume. Life of Goethe, 2 Vols. LC 77-163114. (Studies in German Literature, No. 13). 1971. Repr. of 1920 ed. Set. lib. bdg. 79.95x (ISBN 0-8383-1307-8). Haskell.

Brown, P. J. Macroprocessors & Techniques for Portable Software. LC 3-17597. (Computing Ser.). 244p. 1974. 53.95 (ISBN 0-471-11005-1, Pub. by Wiley-Interscience). Wiley.

--Starting with UNIX. pap. 12.95 (ISBN 0-201-10924-7). Addison-Wesley.

--Writing Interactive Compilers & Interpreters. LC 79-40513. (Computing Ser.). 265p. 1981. pap. 17.95x (ISBN 0-471-10072-2, Pub. by Wiley-Interscience). Wiley.

--Writing Interactive Compilers & Interpreters. LC 79-40513. (Wiley Series in Computing). 265p. 1979. 44.95 (ISBN 0-471-27609-X, Pub. by Wiley-Interscience). Wiley.

Brown, P. J. see Halpern, M., et al.

Brown, P. J. B., jt. auth. see Masser, I.

Brown, P. Jane & Forsyth, J. B. The Crystal Structure of Solids. (Structures & Properties of Solids Ser.). 184p. 1973. pap. text ed. 17.50 (ISBN 0-7131-2388-5). E Arnold.

Brown, P. R. Dictionary of Electrical, Electronic & Computer Abbreviations. 232p. 1985. text ed. 34.95 (ISBN 0-408-01210-2). Butterworth.

--User's Guide to COBOL 85. 700p. 1985. 90.00 (ISBN 0-470-20170-3). Halsted Pr.

Brown, Palmer. Beyond the Paw-Paw Trees. (gr. 3-5). 1973. pap. 0.95 (ISBN 0-380-01055-0, 14605, Camelot). Avon.

--Hickory. LC 77-11849. (Illus.). 48p. (ps-3). 1978. PLB 9.57i (ISBN 0-06-020887-2); PLB 9.89 (ISBN 0-06-020888-0). HarpJ.

Brown, Pamela A., jt. auth. see Brown, Peter H.

Brown, Pat. Locating & Preserving Your Church's Records. Deweese, Charles W., ed. (Resource Kit for Your Church's History Ser.). 8p. 1984. 0.50 (ISBN 0-939804-15-8). Hist Comm S Baptist.

Brown, Pat R. T. E. Rhine, M.D. Recollections of an Arkansas Country Doctor. (Illus.). 368p. 1985. 14.95 (ISBN 0-935304-94-0). August Hse.

Brown, Patricia. Humanism in Education. 70p. 1981. pap. 2.00 (ISBN 0-913098-39-6). Myrin Institute.

--The Mountain Dulcimer. LC 85-71923. (Illus.). 130p. 1985. pap. 12.95 (ISBN 0-9614939-3-3). Backyard Music.

Brown, Patricia L., et al, eds. To Gwen with Love: A Tribute to Gwendolyn Brooks. LC 76-128546. (Illus., Orig.). 1971. pap. 1.95 (ISBN 0-87485-044-4). Johnson Chi.

Brown, Patrick & Muster, John. UNIX for People. 1984. text ed. 24.95 (ISBN 0-13-937459-0); pap. text ed. 21.95 (ISBN 0-13-937442-6). P-H.

Brown, Patrika, jt. auth. see Dwyer, Karen.

Brown, Patty & Sequoia, Anna. Chunks: An Intimate Look at Some Very Available Men. LC 84-1544. (Illus.). 64p. (Orig.). 1984. pap. 4.95 (ISBN 0-87131-430-4). M Evans.

Brown, Patty, jt. auth. see Boswell, John.

Brown, Paul. An Enquiry Concerning the Nature, End, & Practicability of a Course of Philosophical Education. LC 75-305. (The Radical Tradition in America Ser.). 394p. 1975. Repr. of 1822 ed. 25.50 (ISBN 0-88355-210-8). Hyperion Conn.

--The Radical: And Advocate of Equality. LC 75-307. (The Radical Tradition in America Ser). 170p. 1975. Repr. of 1834 ed. 18.70 (ISBN 0-88355-211-6). Hyperion Conn.

--Twelve Months in New Harmony. LC 78-187439. (The American Utopian Adventure Ser.). 128p. 1973. Repr. of 1827 ed. lib. bdg. 17.50x (ISBN 0-87991-000-3). Porcupine Pr.

Brown, Paul & Faulder, Carolyn. Learning to Love: How to Make Bad Sex Good & Good Sex Better. LC 78-52202. 188p. (Orig.). 1981. 10.00x (ISBN 0-87663-319-X); pap. 4.95 (ISBN 0-87663-559-1). Universe.

Brown, Paul L. The Magic & Fun of Inventing. 125p. 4.95 (ISBN 0-318-14605-3). Inventor Work.

--The Magic & Fun of Inventing. 91p. 4.95 (ISBN 0-318-14608-8). Inventors Licensing.

--Managing Behavior on the Job. LC 81-23063. (Self-Teaching Guide Ser.). 190p. 1982. pap. text ed. 10.95 (ISBN 0-471-86516-8, Pub. by Wiley Pr); pap. text ed. 11.50 members. Assn Inform & Image Mgmt.

Brown, Paul L., jt. auth. see Presbie, Robert J.

Brown, Paula. The Chimbu: A Study of Change in the New Guinea Highlands. (Illus.). 192p. 1972. pap. 9.95 (ISBN 0-87073-757-0). Schenkman Bks Inc.

--Highland Peoples of New Guinea. LC 77-80830. (Illus.). 1978. pap. 11.95 (ISBN 0-521-29249-2). Cambridge U Pr.

Brown, Paula S. The Incredible Body Machine. (Three-Two-One Contact Bks.). (Illus.). 48p. (gr. 4-7). 1981. pap. 3.95 (ISBN 0-394-84773-3). Random.

Brown, Pauline. Embroidery Backgrounds. (Illus.). 1984. 22.50 (ISBN 0-7134-3660-3). Branford.

Brown, Pean. Gifts of Silence. 84p. 1983. pap. 6.95 (ISBN 0-942494-79-2). Coleman Pub.

Brown, Percey, jt. auth. see Watts, George.

Brown, Percy. American Martyrs to Science Through the Roentgen Rays. (Illus.). 276p. 1936. photocopy ed. 27.50x (ISBN 0-398-04223-3). C C Thomas.

--Indian Architecture (Buddhist & Hindu) 7th ed. (Illus.). 216p. 1981. Repr. 45.00x (ISBN 0-86590-035-3, Pub. by Taraporevala India). Apt Bks.

--Indian Architecture: Islamic Period. (Illus.). xv, 134p. 1981. text ed. 50.00x (ISBN 0-86590-061-2, Pub. by Taraporevala India). Apt Bks.

--Indian Painting Under the Mughals, A. D. 1550-1750. LC 73-86328. (Illus.). 1974. Repr. of 1924 ed. lib. bdg. 50.00 (ISBN 0-87817-147-9). Hacker.

--Picturesque Nepal. (Illus.). 206p. 1972. Repr. 15.00 (ISBN 0-88065-069-9, Pub. by Messers Today & Tomorrows Printers & Publishers India). Scholarly Pubns.

Brown, Peter. Augustine of Hippo: A Biography. 1967. pap. 8.95 (ISBN 0-520-01411-1, CAL179). U of Cal Pr.

--The Book of Kells. abr. ed. (Illus.). 1981. 22.50 (ISBN 0-500-23326-8). Thames Hudson.

--The Book of Kells: A Selection from the Irish Medieval Manuscripts. LC 80-7973. (Illus.). 96p. 1980. pap. 10.95 (ISBN 0-394-73960-4). Knopf.

--The Cult of the Saints: Its Rise & Function in Latin Christianity. LC 80-11210. xvi, 188p. 1982. pap. 6.95 (ISBN 0-226-07622-9, Phoen). U of Chicago Pr.

--Into Music, 3 bks. (Illus.). 64p. 1984. Bk. 1. pap. 8.95 (ISBN 0-7175-1097-2); Bk. 2. pap. 8.95 (ISBN 0-7175-1098-0); Bk. 3. pap. 8.95 (ISBN 0-7175-1099-9); write for info. tchr's ed. (ISBN 0-7175-1155-3). Dufour.

--The Making of Late Antiquity. LC 78-6844. (Carl Newell Jackson Lectures Ser.). 1978. 12.50x (ISBN 0-674-54320-3). Harvard U Pr.

--Pascal from BASIC. 1982. pap. 12.95 (ISBN 0-201-10158-0). Addison-Wesley.

--Society & the Holy in Late Antiquity. LC 80-39862. 350p. 1982. 27.50x (ISBN 0-520-04305-7). U of Cal Pr.

Brown, Peter & Gaines, Steven. The Love You Make. 1984. pap. 4.50 (ISBN 0-451-12797-8, Sig). NAL.

--The Love You Make: An Insider's Story of the Beatles. 1983. 14.95 (ISBN 0-07-008159-X). McGraw.

Brown, Peter, jt. auth. see Raysman, Richard.

Brown, Peter, ed. see D'Ordonez, Carlo.

Brown, Peter, tr. see Van Der Meer, Frederik.

Brown, Peter A. Carlos d'Ordonez (1754-1786) LC 78-61024. (Detroit Studies in Music Bibliography Ser.: No.39). 1978. pap. 15.50 (ISBN 0-911772-89-8). Info Coord.

Brown, Peter B. Ordering & Claiming Music Materials: Tips from a Dealer. LC 81-159838. (Front Music Publications: No. 4). 26p. (Orig.). 1981. pap. 5.00 (ISBN 0-934082-04-9). Theodore Front.

Brown, Peter D. Oskar Panizza: His Life & Works. LC 83-48749. (American University Studies V: Vol. 27). 228p. 1983. pap. text ed. 24.65 (ISBN 0-8204-0038-6). P Lang Pubs.

--William Pitt, Earl of Chatham. 1978. text ed. 32.50x (ISBN 0-04-942145-X). Allen Unwin.

Brown, Peter G. & MacLean, Douglas, eds. Human Rights & U. S. Foreign Policy: Principles & Applications. 1979. 11.00x (ISBN 0-669-02807-X); pap. 11.00 (ISBN 0-669-04326-5). Lexington Bks.

Brown, Peter G. & Shue, Henry, eds. The Border That Joins: Mexican Migrants & U. S. Responsibility. LC 82-7526. (Maryland Studies in Public Philosophy). 264p. 1983. text ed. 33.95x (ISBN 0-8476-7072-4); pap. text ed. 20.50x (ISBN 0-8476-7206-9). Rowman.

--Boundaries: National Autonomy & Its Limits. LC 81-5896. (Maryland Studies in Public Philosophy). 234p. 1981. 27.50x (ISBN 0-8476-7011-2); pap. 9.95x (ISBN 0-8476-7048-1). Rowman.

--Food Policy: The Responsibility of the United States in the Life & Death Choices. LC 76-57803. (Illus.). 1979. pap. text ed. 14.95 (ISBN 0-02-905170-3). Free Pr.

--Food Policy: The Responsibility of the United States in the Life & Death Choices. LC 76-57803. 1977. 16.95 (ISBN 0-02-904980-6). Free Pr.

Brown, Peter G., jt. ed. see MacLean, Douglas.

Brown, Peter G., et al, eds. Income Support: Conceptual & Policy Issues. LC 80-26540. (Maryland Studies in Public Philosophy). 392p. 1981. 32.50x (ISBN 0-8476-6969-6). Rowman.

Brown, Peter H. History of Scotland, 3 Vols. LC 74-181922. (BCL Ser. I). Repr. of 1909 ed. Set. 55.00 (ISBN 0-404-09940-8); 19.00 ea. Vol. 1 (ISBN 0-404-09941-6). Vol. 2 (ISBN 0-404-09942-4). Vol. 3 (ISBN 0-404-09943-2). AMS Pr.

--Such Devoted Sisters: Those Fabulous Gabors. (Illus.). 320p. 1984. 17.95 (ISBN 0-312-77498-2). St Martin.

Brown, Peter H. & Brown, Pamela A. MGM Girls: Behind the Velvet Curtain. 256p. 1983. 13.95 (ISBN 0-312-50161-7). St Martin.

Brown, Peter H., ed. Early Travellers in Scotland. LC 73-147148. (Research & Source Works Ser.: No. 650). (Geography & discovery, No. 10). 1971. Repr. of 1891 ed. 23.50 (ISBN 0-8337-0384-6). B Franklin.

--Scotland Before 1700: From Contemporary Documents. LC 77-87675. Repr. of 1893 ed. 27.50 (ISBN 0-404-16467-6). AMS Pr.

Brown, Peter L. Astronomy. LC 84-1654. (The Junior World of Science Ser.). (gr. 7 up). 9.95 (ISBN 0-87196-985-8). Facts on File.

--Astronomy in Color. (Illus.). 264p. 1982. 9.95 (ISBN 0-7137-0729-1, Pub. by Blandford Pr England). Sterling.

--Megaliths, Myths & Men: An Introduction to Astro-Archaeology. LC 76-15090. (Illus.). 324p. (YA) (gr. 10 up). 1976. 13.95 (ISBN 0-8008-5187-0). Taplinger.

--Star & Planet Spotting: A Field Guide to the Night Sky. rev. ed. (Illus.). 176p. 1981. 9.95 (ISBN 0-7137-0655-4, Pub. by Blandford Pr England); pap. 6.95 (ISBN 0-7137-1265-1). Sterling.

Brown, Phil. The Transfer of Care: Psychiatric Deinstitutionalization & Its Aftermath. 280p. 1984. 22.50x (ISBN 0-7100-9900-2). Routledge & Kegan.

Brown, Phil, ed. Mental Health Care & Social Policy. 256p. 1985. 42.00x (ISBN 0-7100-9899-5); pap. 19.95x (ISBN 0-7102-0472-8). Routledge & Kegan.

Brown, Philip. Uncle Whiskers. 1976. pap. 2.95 (ISBN 0-446-87108-7). Warner Bks.

Brown, Philip A. French Revolution in English History. 234p. 1965. Repr. 28.50x (ISBN 0-7146-1458-0, F Cass Co). Biblio Dist.

--The French Revolution in English History. 1918. 10.00 (ISBN 0-8482-7376-1). Norwood Edns.

Brown, Philomena. A Basic Dictionary of Home Economics. 64p. 1982. 25.00x (ISBN 0-7135-1317-9, Pub. by Bell & Hyman England). State Mutual Bk.

Brown, Phyllis R. High Pressure Liquid Chromatography: Biochemical & Biomedical Applications. 1973. 33.00 (ISBN 0-12-136950-1). Acad Pr.

Brown, Phyllis R., jt. auth. see Krstulovic, Ante M.

Brown, Pia T., compiled by. O. S. U. Theses & Dissertations, Nineteen Seventy-One to Nineteen Seventy-Seven. (Bibliographic Ser.: No. 17). 128p. 1980. pap. 5.95x (ISBN 0-87071-137-7). Oreg St U Pr.

Brown, R. Prodromus Flora Novae-Hollandiae et Insulae Van Dieman (Now Australia & Tasmania) 1960. Repr. of 1830 ed. 49.00 (ISBN 3-7682-0033-7). Lubrecht & Cramer.

--Semitic Influence in Hellenic Mythology. xvi, 228p. Repr. of 1898 ed. lib. bdg. 35.00x (ISBN 0-89241-206-2). Caratzas.

Brown, R., jt. auth. see Laumer, K.

Brown, R., ed. The Memoranda Roll for the 10th Year of the Reign of King John, 1207-1208. Bd. with Curia Regis Rolls of Hilary 7, Richard I, & Easter 9 Richard I, 1198; Roll of Plate Held by Hugh de Neville, 9 John, 1207-1208; Fragments of the Close Rolls of 16 & 17 John, 1215-1216. (Pipe Roll Society, London, Ser.: No. 2, Vol. 31). Repr. of 1956 ed. 36.00 (ISBN 0-317-15927-5). Kraus Repr.

Brown, R. & Thickstun, T. L., eds. Low-Dimensional Topology: Proceedings of the Conference on Topology in Low Dimension, Bangor, 1979. LC 81-2664. (London Mathematical Society Lecture Notes Ser.: No. 48). 300p. 1982. pap. 32.50 (ISBN 0-521-28146-6). Cambridge U Pr.

Brown, R., et al, eds. Tradition & Transformation: Essays on Migration & the India Diaspora. 400p. 1984. pap. 18.25x (ISBN 0-391-03159-7, Pub. by Radiant Pub India). Humanities.

Brown, R. A., ed. see Geoscience Information Society Staff.

Brown, R. Allen. Castles. 10/1985 ed. (Shire Archaeology Ser.: No. 36). (Orig.). pap. 6.95 (ISBN 0-85263-653-9, Pub. by Shire Pubns England). Seven Hills Bks.

--The Origins of Modern Europe: The Medieval Heritage of Western Civilization. LC 72-11597. 1973. pap. 6.95x (ISBN 0-88295-705-8). Harlan Davidson.

Brown, R. Allen, ed. Anglo-Norman Studies II: Proceedings 1979. (Illus.). 210p. 1980. 35.00 (ISBN 0-85115-126-4, Pub. by Boydell & Brewer). Longwood Pub Group.

--Anglo-Norman Studies: Proceedings of the Battle Conference 1982, No. 5. (Illus.). 243p. 1983. 35.00 (ISBN 0-85115-178-7, BAB-04925, Pub. by Boydell & Brewer). Longwood Pub Group.

--Anglo-Norman Studies: Proceedings 1980, Vol. III. (Illus.). 254p. 1981. 35.00 (ISBN 0-85115-141-8, Pub. by Boydell & Brewer). Longwood Pub Group.

--Anglo-Norman Studies: Proceedings 1981, Vol. IV. (Illus.). 237p. 1982. 35.00 (ISBN 0-85115-161-2, Pub. by Boydell & Brewer). Longwood Pub Group.

--Anglo-Norman Studies: Proceedings 1982, Vol. V. (Illus.). 243p. 1983. 35.00 (ISBN 0-85115-178-7, Pub. by Boydell & Brewer). Longwood Pub Group.

--Anglo-Norman Studies VI: Proceedings of the Battle Conference 1983. (Anglo-Norman Studies: No. VI). (Illus.). 246p. 1984. 41.25 (ISBN 0-85115-197-3, Pub. by Boydell & Brewer). Longwood Pub Group.

--Anglo-Norman Studies VI: Proceedings of the Battle Conference 1983. (Anglo-Norman Studies). (Illus.). 246p. 41.25 (ISBN 0-85115-197-3, Pub. by Boydell & Brewer). Longwood Pub Group.

--Anglo-Norman Studies VII: Proceedings of the Battle Conference, 1984. (Anglo-Norman Studies: No. VII). (Illus.). 224p. 1985. 39.50 (ISBN 0-85115-416-6, Pub. by Boydell & Brewer). Longwood Pub Group.

--Battle Conference on Anglo-Norman Studies IV: Proceedings 1981. (Illus.). 237p. 1982. text ed. 35.00 (ISBN 0-85115-161-2, BAB-04692, Pub. by Boydell & Brewer). Longwood Pub Group.

--Battle Conference on Anglo-Norman Studies, 1st, 1978: Proceedings. (Illus.). 247p. 1979. 36.50x (ISBN 0-8476-6184-9). Rowman.

--Proceedings of the Battle Conference on Anglo-Norman Studies III, 1980. (Illus.). 254p. 1981. 35.00 (ISBN 0-85115-141-8, BAB-01025, Pub. by Boydell & Brewer). Longwood Pub Group.

--Proceedings of the Battle Conference on Anglo-Norman Studies II: 1979. (Illus.). 210p. 1979. 49.50x (ISBN 0-8476-3455-8). Rowman.

Brown, R. B. Clinical Urology Illustrated. (Illus.). 400p. 1982. 54.00 (ISBN 0-683-11035-7). Williams & Wilkins.

Brown, R. C., et al. The Invitro Effects of Mineral Dusts. 1980. 55.00 (ISBN 0-12-137240-5). Acad Pr.

Brown, R. Craig, ed. Minorities, Schools & Politics. LC 23-16213. (Canadian Historical Readings Ser.: No. 7). 1969. pap. 4.00x (ISBN 0-8020-1617-0). U of Toronto Pr.

--Upper Canadian Politics in the 1850's. LC 23-16213. (Canadian Historical Readings Ser.: No. 2). (Orig.). 1967. pap. 4.00x (ISBN 0-8020-1458-5). U of Toronto Pr.

Brown, R. D. Prime Suspect. (Orig.). 1981. pap. 1.95 (ISBN 0-505-51685-3, Pub. by Tower Bks). Dorchester Pub Co.

Brown, R. D. & O'Donnell, T. A. Manual of Elementary Practical Chemistry. 3rd ed. 1965. 11.00x (ISBN 0-522-83545-7, Pub. by Melbourne U Pr). Intl Spec Bk.

Brown, R. Don & Daigneault, Ernest A. Pharmacology of Hearing: Experimental & Clinical Bases. LC 81-437. 364p. 1981. 64.95 (ISBN 0-471-05074-1). Krieger.

Brown, R. Douglas. East Anglia Nineteen Forty. 176p. 1982. 49.00x (ISBN 0-86138-008-8, Pub. by Terence Dalton England). State Mutual Bk.

--East Anglia Nineteen Thirty-Nine. 216p. 1981. 30.00x (ISBN 0-86138-000-2, Pub. by Terence Dalton England). State Mutual Bk.

--The Port of London. (Illus.). 1979. 20.00x (ISBN 0-900963-87-5, Pub. by Terence Dalton England). State Mutual Bk.

Brown, R. F. Compartmental Systems Analysis. (Cybernetics & Systems Ser.). 1984. 58.00 (ISBN 0-9901003-8-3, Pub. by Abacus England). Heyden.

--English-Spanish Dictionary. (Eng. & Span.). 18.50 (ISBN 0-87559-172-8). Shalom.

Brown, R. F., ed. Spanish-English Dictionary. (Span. & Eng.). 18.50 (ISBN 0-87559-033-0). Shalom.

Brown, R. G. Electronics for the Modern Scientist. 496p. 1982. 33.50 (ISBN 0-444-00660-5, Biomedical Pr). Elsevier.

--The Male Nurse. 139p. 1973. pap. text ed. 5.00x (ISBN 0-7135-1879-0, Pub. by Bedford England). Brookfield Pub Co.

--The Management of Welfare: A Study of British Social Service Administration. 317p. 1975. 16.50x (ISBN 0-87471-769-8). Rowman.

--Schaum's Outline of Contemporary Mathematics of Finance. (Schaum Outline Ser.). 192p. 1983. 8.95 (ISBN 0-07-008146-8). McGraw.

Brown, R. G., et al. Lines, Waves & Antennas: The Transmission of Electric Energy. 2nd ed. (Illus.). 471p. 1973. text ed. 41.50 (ISBN 0-471-06677-X). Wiley.

--Report Upon the Illegal Practices of the United States Department of Justice. LC 73-90206. (Mass Violence in America Ser). Repr. of 1920 ed. 14.00 (ISBN 0-405-01301-9). Ayer Co Pubs.

Brown, R. Gene & Johnston, Kenneth S. Paciolo on Accounting. LC 83-49104. (Accounting History & the Development of a Profession Ser.). 144p. 1984. lib. bdg. 22.00 (ISBN 0-8240-6318-X). Garland Pub.

Brown, R. H. A Poetics for Sociology. LC 75-35454. (Illus.). 1977. 39.50 (ISBN 0-521-21121-2); pap. 11.95 (ISBN 0-521-29391-X). Cambridge U Pr.

Brown, R. H. & Lyman, S. M., eds. Structure, Consciousness, & History. LC 77-90212. (Illus.). 1978. 39.50 (ISBN 0-521-22047-5); pap. 12.95 (ISBN 0-521-29340-5). Cambridge U Pr.

Brown, R. H., et al, eds. Ground Water Studies: An International Guide for Research, Suppl. 4. pap. price not set (ISBN 92-3-101471-4, U271, UNESCO). Unipub.

Brown, R. I. & Hughson, E. A. Training of the Developmentally Handicapped Adult. (Illus.). 214p. 1980. 20.75x (ISBN 0-398-03993-3). C C Thomas.

Brown, R. K., jt. auth. see Parker, S. R.

Brown, R. L. Design & Manufacture of Plastic Parts. (Illus.). 204p. 1980. 58.00 (ISBN 0-686-48177-1, 0802). T-C Pubns CA.

Brown, R. L., jt. auth. see Zima, P.

Brown, R. L. E. Design & Manufacture of Plastic Parts. 204p. 1980. 57.95 (ISBN 0-471-05324-4). Wiley.

Brown, R. Malcolm, jt. auth. see Parker, Bruce C.

Brown, R. Malcolm, Jr., ed. Cellulose & Other Natural Polymer Systems: Biogenesis, Structure, & Degradation. LC 82-3796. 540p. 1982. text ed. 59.50 (ISBN 0-306-40856-2, Plenum Pr). Plenum Pub.

Brown, R. P. Physical Testing of Rubbers. (Illus.). 327p. 1979. 44.50 (ISBN 0-85334-788-3, Pub. by Elsevier Applied Sci England). Elsevier.

Brown, R. P. & Reed, B. E., eds. Measurement Techniques for Polymeric Solids. 236p. 1984. 78.00 (ISBN 0-85334-274-1, I-257-84, Pub. by Elsevier Applied Sci England). Elsevier.

Brown, R. S., Jr., ed. see Walpole, Horace.

Brown, R. W., et al. The Larousse Guide to Animal Tracks, Trails & Signs. LC 84-47822. (Illus.). 320p. 1984. 12.95 (ISBN 0-88332-366-4). Larousse.

Brown, Rachel. The Weaving, Spinning, & Dyeing Book. LC 77-1653. (Illus.). 1978. 25.00 (ISBN 0-394-49801-1). Knopf.

--The Weaving, Spinning & Dyeing Book. 2nd ed. (Illus.). 1984. 18.95 (ISBN 0-394-71595-0). Knopf.

Brown, Rachel, ed. see Davis, Steve.

Brown, Rachel, ed. see Galipault, Joanne & Kinsman, Barbara.

Brown, Rachel, ed. see Henley, Daniel & Henley, Jane.

Brown, Rachel, ed. see Masalski, William.

Brown, Rae L. Music, Printed & Manuscript, in the James Weldon Johnson Memorial Collection of Negro Arts & Letters, Yale University: An Annotated Catalog. 1982. lib. bdg. 61.00 (ISBN 0-8240-9319-4). Garland Pub.

Brown, Ralph. Mathematical Difficulties of Students of Educational Statistics. LC 70-176599. (Columbia University. Teachers College. Contributions to Education Ser.: No. 569). Repr. of 1933 ed. 22.50 (ISBN 0-404-55569-1). AMS Pr.

Brown, Ralph A. The Presidency of John Adams. LC 75-5526. (American Presidency Ser). (Illus.). 256p. 1975. 19.95x (ISBN 0-7006-0134-1). U Pr of Ks.

Brown, Ralph H. Historical Geography of the United States. (Illus.). 596p. 1948. text ed. 26.95 (ISBN 0-15-539194-1, HC). HarBraceJ.

--Mirror for Americans: Likeness of the Eastern Seaboard, 1810. LC 67-27449. (American Scene Ser). 1968. Repr. of 1943 ed. 45.00 (ISBN 0-306-70974-0). Da Capo.

Brown, Ralph H., tr. see Diderot, Denis.

Brown, Ralph S. & Denicola, Robert C. Copyright, Unfair Competition, & Other Topics Bearing on the Protection of Literary, Musical, & Other Artistic Works: Cases. 4th ed. LC 85-6902. 648p. 1985. write for info. (ISBN 0-88277-239-2); write for info. 1985 statutory suppl. (ISBN 0-88277-246-5). Foundation Pr.

Brown, Ralph S., Jr. Loyalty & Security: Employment Tests in the United States. LC 79-151417. (Civil Liberties in American History Ser). 522p. 1972. Repr. of 1958 ed. lib. bdg. 59.50 (ISBN 0-306-70218-5). Da Capo.

Brown, Ralph S., Jr., jt. auth. see Dahl, Robert A.

Brown, Ramona A. Memories of Abdu'l-Baha: Recollections of the Early Days of the Baha'i Faith in California. LC 79-16412. (Illus.). 1980. 16.95 (ISBN 0-87743-128-0, 332-010); pap. 9.95 (ISBN 0-87743-139-6, 332-011). Baha'i.

Brown, Ranell B., ed. Superlatives. LC 84-80833. 288p. 1984. 14.95 (ISBN 0-9613374-0-0). Jr League OK.

Brown, Raphael. The Roots of St. Francis. 9.50 (ISBN 0-686-45828-1). Franciscan Herald.

--True Joy from Assisi. 1978. 8.95 (ISBN 0-8199-0688-3). Franciscan Herald.

Brown, Raphael, tr. Little Flowers of St. Francis. 1971. pap. 5.50 (ISBN 0-385-07544-8, Im). Doubleday.

Brown, Raphael, tr. see Habig, Marion A.

Brown, Rawdon, tr. see Giustiniani, Sebastiano.

Brown, Ray. The Brown Book: The Complete Guide to Buying & Selling H-O Brass Locomotives. 2nd ed. (Illus.). 192p. 1982. pap. 13.95 (ISBN 0-933506-10-4). Darwin Pubns.

--Characteristics of Local Media Audiences. 144p. 1978. text ed. 37.95x (ISBN 0-566-00218-3). Gower Pub Co.

Brown, Ray & Ward, Scott. Children & Commercial Television. 300p. 1985. text ed. price not set (ISBN 0-566-05073-0). Gower Pub Co.

Brown, Ray, ed. Children & Television. LC 76-50500. (Illus.). 368p. 1976. 29.95 (ISBN 0-8039-0821-0); pap. 14.95 (ISBN 0-8039-0822-9). Sage.

--Children Australia. 320p. 1981. text ed. 22.50x (ISBN 0-86861-186-7); pap. text ed. 12.50x (ISBN 0-86861-194-8). Allen Unwin.

Brown, Ray E. Judgment in Administration. LC 82-82148. 248p. 1982. Repr. of 1966 ed. 25.00 (ISBN 0-931028-31-0). Pluribus Pr.

Brown, Ray H. Robert Stewart Hyer, the Man I Knew. (Illus.). 1957. 10.00 (ISBN 0-685-05005-X). A Jones.

Brown, Raymond. Let's Read the Old Testament. 1972. pap. 2.95 (ISBN 0-87508-034-0). Chr Lit.

--The Message of Hebrews. Motyer, J. A. & Stott, John R., eds. LC 82-15321. (The Bible Speaks Today Ser.). 272p. (Orig.). 1982. pap. 6.95 (ISBN 0-87784-289-2). Inter-Varsity.

--Timothy-James. 1983. pap. 4.50 (ISBN 0-87508-174-6). Chr Lit.

--Waterfront Organization in Hull, 1870-1900. (Occasional Papers in Economic & Social History: No. 5). 130p. 1972. pap. text ed. 4.75x (ISBN 0-900480-17-3). Humanities.

Brown, Raymond B. Marcos Presenta Al Salvador. Lerin, Olivia Y Alfredo, tr. Orig. Title: Mark - the Saviour for Sinners. 160p. 1982. pap. 4.25 (ISBN 0-311-04346-1). Casa Bautista.

Brown, Raymond D. How to Do Your Own Professional Picture Framing. (Illus.). 160p. 1981. pap. 8.25 (ISBN 0-8306-1238-6). TAB Bks.

Brown, Raymond E. Biblical Exegesis & Church Doctrine. 176p. (Orig.). 1986. pap. 4.95 (ISBN 0-8091-2750-4). Paulist Pr.

--Biblical Reflections on Crises Facing the Church. LC 75-19861. 132p. 1975. pap. 3.95 (ISBN 0-8091-1891-2). Paulist Pr.

--The Birth of the Messiah: A Commentary on the Infancy Narratives in Matthew & Luke. LC 76-56271. 1977. pap. 8.95 (ISBN 0-385-05405-X, Im). Doubleday.

--The Churches the Apostles Left Behind. 160p. (Orig.). 1984. pap. 4.95 (ISBN 0-8091-2611-7). Paulist Pr.

--The Community of the Beloved Disciple. LC 78-65894. 204p. 1979. 6.95 (ISBN 0-8091-0274-9); pap. 4.95 (ISBN 0-8091-2174-3). Paulist Pr.

--The Critical Meaning of the Bible. LC 81-82333. 160p. (Orig.). 1981. pap. 4.95 (ISBN 0-8091-2406-8). Paulist Pr.

--Daniel. (Bible Ser.). pap. 1.00 (ISBN 0-8091-5024-7). Paulist Pr.

--The Epistles of John. LC 81-43380. (Anchor Bible Ser.: Vol. 30). 840p. 1982. 18.00 (ISBN 0-385-05686-9). Doubleday.

--Jesus, God & Man. LC 67-29587. (Impact Books). 1967. pap. 3.95 (ISBN 0-02-084000-4). Macmillan.

--New Testament Essays. 1968. pap. 1.95 (ISBN 0-385-05276-6, Im). Doubleday.

--New Testament Essays. pap. 4.95 (ISBN 0-8091-2470-X). Paulist Pr.

--Priest & Bishop. LC 78-139594. 96p. 1970. pap. 3.95 (ISBN 0-8091-1661-8). Paulist Pr.

--Recent Discoveries & the Biblical World. 4.95 (ISBN 0-89453-363-0). M Glazier.

--The Virginal Conception & Bodily Resurrection of Jesus. LC 72-97399. 1973. pap. 3.95 (ISBN 0-8091-1768-1). Paulist Pr.

Brown, Raymond E. & Meier, John. Antioch & Rome: New Testament Cradles of Catholic Christianity. 256p. 1983. o. p. 9.95 (ISBN 0-8091-0339-7); pap. 4.95 (ISBN 0-8091-2532-3). Paulist Pr.

Brown, Raymond E., tr. Gospel According to John One - Twelve. LC 66-12209. (Anchor Bible Ser.: Vol. 29). 1966. 18.00 (ISBN 0-385-01517-8, Anchor Pr). Doubleday.

--Gospel According to John Thirteen - Twenty-One. LC 66-12209. (Anchor Bible Ser.: Vol. 29A). 1970. 18.00 (ISBN 0-385-03761-9, Anchor Pr). Doubleday.

Brown, Raymond E., et al. Peter in the New Testament. LC 73-83787. 1973. 5.95 (ISBN 0-8066-1401-3, 10-4930). Augsburg.

--Peter in the New Testament. LC 73-84424. (Orig.). 1973. pap. 4.95 (ISBN 0-8091-1790-8). Paulist Pr.

Brown, Raymond E., et al, eds. Jerome Biblical Commentary. 1969. 57.95 (ISBN 0-13-509612-X). P-H.

--Mary in the New Testament. LC 78-8797. 336p. 1978. pap. 5.95 (ISBN 0-8091-2168-9). Paulist Pr.

--Mary in the New Testament: A Collaborative Assessment by Protestant & Roman Catholic Scholars. LC 78-8797. 336p. 1978. pap. 5.95 (ISBN 0-8006-1345-7, 1-1345). Fortress.

Brown, Raymond K. Reach Out to Singles: A Challenge to Ministry. LC 79-15495. 192p. 1979. pap. 7.95 (ISBN 0-664-24270-7). Westminster.

Brown, Raymond L. Robert Burns's Tour of the Borders: 5 May-1 June, 1787. (Illus.). 74p. 1972. 8.50x (ISBN 0-87471-123-1). Rowman.

--Robert Burns's Tour of the Highlands & Stirlingshire 1787. (Illus.). 82p. 1973. 8.50x (ISBN 0-87471-439-7). Rowman.

Brown, Rebecca. Three-Way Split. LC 77-8993. (Illus.). 1978. pap. 2.00 (ISBN 0-916382-14-1). Telephone Bks.

Brown, Reeve L. Moving to the Country. LC 82-45963. (Illus.). 288p. 1983. 14.95 (ISBN 0-385-12279-9). Doubleday.

Brown, Regina. Little Brother. (Illus.). (gr. 3-7). 1962. 5.95 (ISBN 0-8392-3019-2). Astor-Honor.

--Play at Your House. (Illus.). (gr. 3-7). 1962. 6.95 (ISBN 0-8392-3027-3). Astor-Honor.

Brown, Rex V., et al. Decision Analysis: An Overview. LC 74-1212. 1974. pap. text ed. 14.95 (ISBN 0-03-088408-X, HoltC). HR&W.

Brown, Richard. James Joyce & Sexuality. 224p. 1985. 29.95 (ISBN 0-521-24811-6). Cambridge U Pr.

--Voyage of the Iceberg: The Story of the Iceberg That Sank the Titanic. (Illus.). 1984. 13.95 (ISBN 0-8253-0187-4). Beaufort Bks NY.

Brown, Richard & Cook, Melva. Special Occasion Cookbook. LC 82-73491. 1983. 10.95 (ISBN 0-8054-7001-8). Broadman.

Brown, Richard & Lewinsohn, Peter. Participant Workbook for the Coping with Depression Course. 54p. 1984. Set of 10 wkbks. 24.95 (ISBN 0-916154-14-9). Castalia Pub.

Brown, Richard & Robbins, David. Advanced Mathematics: An Introductory Course. (gr. 11-12). 1981. text ed. 21.76 (ISBN 0-395-29335-9); instrs.' guide & solns. 13.00 (ISBN 0-395-29336-7). HM.

Brown, Richard & Watson, Bob. Buffalo: Lake City in Niagaraland. 336p. 1981. 24.95 (ISBN 0-89781-036-8). Windsor Pubns Inc.

Brown, Richard, jt. auth. see Lieff, Jonathan D.

Brown, Richard, ed. History of Accounting & Accountants. (Illus.). 460p. 1968. Repr. of 1905 ed. 35.00x (ISBN 0-7146-1279-0, F Cass Co). Biblio Dist.

Brown, Richard C. Social Attitudes of American Generals, Eighteen Ninety-Eight to Nineteen Forty. Kohn, Richard H., ed. LC 78-22413. (American Military Experience Ser.). 1979. lib. bdg. 28.50x (ISBN 0-405-11887-2). Ayer Co Pubs.

Brown, Richard C., jt. auth. see Nishiyama, Hidetaka.

Brown, Richard D. Massachusetts. (States & the Nations Ser.). (Illus.). 1978. 14.95 (ISBN 0-393-05666-X). Norton.

--Modernization: The Transformation of American Life, 1600-1865. (American Century Ser.). 229p. 1976. o. p. 10.00; pap. 6.95 (ISBN 0-8090-0125-X). Hill & Wang.

--National Environmental Policiea & Research Programs. LC 83-50572. 165p. 1983. pap. 25.00 (ISBN 0-87762-330-9). Technomic.

--Revolutionary Politics in Massachusetts: The Boston Committee of Correspondence & the Towns, 1772-1774. LC 71-119072. (Illus.). 1970. 17.50x (ISBN 0-674-76781-0). Harvard U Pr.

--Revolutionary Politics in Massachusetts: The Boston Committee of Correspondence & the Towns, 1772-1774. (Illus.). 304p. 1976. pap. 4.95x (ISBN 0-393-00810-X, Norton Lib). Norton.

Brown, Richard D. & Ouellette, Robert P. Pollution Control at Electric Power Stations: Comparisons for U. S. & Europe. 113p. 1983. 39.95 (ISBN 0-250-40618-7). Butterworth.

Brown, Richard D. & Petrello, George J. Introduction to Business. 2nd ed. 622p. 1979. text ed. write for info. (ISBN 0-02-471310-4). Macmillan.

Brown, Richard D. & Rabe, Steven G., eds. Slavery in American Society. 2nd ed. (Problems in American Civilization Ser.). 1976. pap. text ed. 5.95 (ISBN 0-669-00073-6). Heath.

Brown, Richard E. The GAD: Untapped Source of Congressional Power. LC 78-111049. pap. 35.00 (ISBN 0-317-29911-5, 2021773). Bks Demand UMI.

--The Planning Process on the Pine Ridge & Rosebud Indian Reservations. 1969. write for info. U of SD Gov Res Bur.

Brown, Richard E. & MacDonald, David W. Social Odours in Mammals, 2 vols. (Illus.). 1983. Vol. 1. 89.00x (ISBN 0-19-857546-7); Vol. 2. 59.00x (ISBN 0-19-857617-X). Oxford U Pr.

Brown, Richard E., ed. The Effectiveness of Legislative Program Review. LC 78-66237. 150p. 1979. pap. text ed. 9.95 (ISBN 0-87855-712-1). Transaction Bks.

Brown, Richard E. & Fehrenbacher, Don E., eds. Tradition, Conflict & Change: Perspectives on the American Revolution. (Studies in Social Discontinuity Ser.). 1977. 29.00 (ISBN 0-12-137650-8). Acad Pr.

Brown, Richard E., et al. Auditing Performance in Government: Concepts & Cases. 298p. 1982. 42.95 (ISBN 0-471-08188-4, Pub. by Ronald Pr). Wiley.

Brown, Richard H., jt. ed. see Winston, Patrik H.

Brown, Richard M. Strain of Violence: Historical Studies of American Violence & Vigilantism. LC 75-7351. 1975. pap. 9.95 (ISBN 0-19-502247-5, GB513, GB). Oxford U Pr.

Brown, Richard M., jt. ed. see Olson, Alison G.

Brown, Rita M. A Plain Brown Rapper. (Illus.). 1976. pap. 6.95 (ISBN 0-88447-011-3). Diana Pr.

--Rubyfruit Jungle. 1977. pap. 3.95 (ISBN 0-553-23813-2). Bantam.

--Southern Discomfort. LC 81-47683. 224p. 1982. 14.37i (ISBN 0-06-014928-0, HarpT). Har-Row.

--Sudden Death. 256p. 1984. pap. text ed. 3.95 (ISBN 0-553-24030-7). Bantam.

Brown, Rita Mae. The Hand That Cradles the Rock. (Illus.). 1974. pap. 4.50 (ISBN 0-685-77036-2). Diana Pr.

--Six of One. 1979. pap. 3.95 (ISBN 0-553-23768-3). Bantam.

--Southern Discomfort. 1983. pap. 3.95 (ISBN 0-553-23108-1). Bantam.

Brown, Robert. Luke: Doctor-Writer. (BibLearn Ser.). (Illus.). (gr. 1-6). 1977. bds. 5.95 (ISBN 0-8054-4233-2, 4242-33). Broadman.

--The Nature of Social Laws: Machaivelli to Mill. LC 83-15194. 275p. 1984. 39.50 (ISBN 0-521-25782-4). Cambridge U Pr.

--The Rights of Older Persons. 1979. pap. 2.50 (ISBN 0-380-44362-7, 44362-7, Discus). Avon.

--Semetic Influence in Hellenic Mythology. LC 65-27053. (Library of Religious & Philosophical Thought). Repr. of 1898 ed. lib. bdg. 25.00x (ISBN 0-678-09952-9, Reference Bk Pubs). Kelley.

--Student Developement in Tomorrow's Higher Education: A Return to the Academy. 56p. 1974. pap. text ed. 4.00 (ISBN 0-911547-72-X, 72157W34). Am Assn Coun Dev.

--Three Hundred Thirty-Three More Science Tricks & Experiments. (Illus.). 208p. 1984. 15.95 (ISBN 0-8306-0835-4); pap. 10.95 (ISBN 0-8306-1835-X, 1835). TAB Bks.

--Three Hundred Thirty-Three Science Tricks & Experiments. (Illus.). 208p. (Orig.). 1984. 15.95 (ISBN 0-8306-0825-7); pap. 9.95 (ISBN 0-8306-1825-2, 1825). TAB Bks.

Brown, Robert & Ballard, Lou. Beginnings: From Sentences to Paragraphs. 360p. 1983. pap. text ed. 12.95 (ISBN 0-89892-002-7). Contemp Pub Co Raleigh.

Brown, Robert & Reed, Peter. Marine Reinsurance. 335p. 1981. 90.00x (ISBN 0-900886-61-7, Pub. by Witherby & Co England). State Mutual Bk.

Brown, Robert, ed. Boater's Safety Handbook. (Illus.). 52p. (Orig.). 1982. pap. 2.95 (ISBN 0-89886-072-5). Mountaineers.

Brown, Robert B. Guide to Life Insurance. 1981. 15.00 (ISBN 0-686-31055-1, 29121). Rough Notes.

Brown, Robert B., jt. auth. see Bell, Irene W.

Brown, Robert C. Canada's National Policy, Eighteen Eighty-Three to Nineteen Hundred: A Study in Canadian-American Relations. LC 77-25010. (Illus.). 1978. Repr. of 1964 ed. lib. bdg. 28.00x (ISBN 0-313-20121-8, BRCN). Greenwood.

--Perchance to Dream: The Patient's Guide to Anesthesia. LC 80-25690. 96p. 1981. 14.95 (ISBN 0-88229-622-1). Nelson-Hall.

Brown, Robert D. Student Development in Tomorrow's Higher Education: A Return to the Academy. (ACPA Student Personnel Monograph: No. 16). 56p. 1972. pap. text ed. 4.00 nonmembers (ISBN 0-686-04998-5, 72157W34); pap. text ed. 3.00 (ISBN 0-686-34305-0). Am Assn Coun Dev.

Brown, Robert D., ed. Antler Development in Cervidae. (Illus.). 400p. 1983. 15.00 (ISBN 0-912229-04-7); pap. 10.00 (ISBN 0-912229-05-5). CK Wildlife Res.

Brown, Robert D. & DeCoster, David A., eds. Mentoring-Transcript Systems for Promoting Student Growth. LC 81-48581. (Student Services Ser.: No. 19). 1982. 8.95x (ISBN 0-87589-921-8). Jossey-Bass.

Brown, Robert D., jt. ed. see Canon, Harry J.

Brown, Robert D., et al, eds. Oregon Signatures. (Illus.). 128p. 1959. 7.95x (ISBN 0-87071-303-5). Oreg St U Pr.

Brown, Robert E. Charles Beard & the Constitution. A Critical Analysis of "An Economic Interpretation of the Constitution". LC 78-14426. 1979. Repr. of 1956 ed. lib. bdg. 22.50x (ISBN 0-313-21048-9, BRBC). Greenwood.

--Gathering the Light. 1976. pap. 2.50 (ISBN 0-88031-026-X). Invisible-Red Hill.

--Middle-Class Democracy & the Revolution in Massachusetts, 1691-1780. LC 68-10906. (Illus.). 1968. Repr. of 1955 ed. 28.00x (ISBN 0-8462-1073-8). Russell.

Brown, Robert E. & Mouser, G. W. Techniques for Teaching Conservation Education. LC 64-24115. Repr. of 1964 ed. 30.00 (ISBN 0-8357-9054-1, 2013323). Bks Demand UMI.

Brown, Robert F. The Later Philosophy of Schelling: The Influence of Boehme on the Works of 1809-1815. LC 75-10138. 295p. 1976. 25.00 (ISBN 0-8387-1755-1). Bucknell U Pr.

--Schelling's Treatise on "the Deities of Samothrace". A Translation & an Interpretation. LC 76-42239. (American Academy of Religion. Studies in Religion). 1977. pap. 9.95 (ISBN 0-89130-087-2, 010012). Scholars Pr GA.

Brown, Robert G. Introduction to Random Signal Analysis & Kalman Filtering. 416p. 1983. text ed. 36.00 (ISBN 0-471-08732-7). Wiley.

--Materials Management Systems. LC 83-19978. 448p. 1984. Repr. of 1977 ed. lib. bdg. 42.50 (ISBN 0-89874-707-4). Krieger.

--Materials Management Systems: A Modular Library. LC 77-8281. 436p. 1977. 45.95x (ISBN 0-471-11182-1, Pub. by Ronald Pr). Wiley.

Brown, Robert G., et al. Experience with a Patient Planning Organization: An Interim Analysis. 34p. 1961. pap. text ed. 1.50 (ISBN 0-89143-054-7). U NC Inst Res Soc Sci.

Brown, Robert H. Farm Electrification. (Agricultural Engineering Ser). 1956. 39.95 (ISBN 0-07-008462-9). McGraw.

--Wyoming: A Geography. (Geographies of the United States Ser.). (Illus.). 375p. 1980. lib. bdg. 38.50x (ISBN 0-89158-560-5); text ed. 20.00 (ISBN 0-686-96923-5). Westview.

Brown, Robert H. & Wishard, Roy H. Biology Lab Text. 2nd ed. 1978. pap. text ed. 13.95 (ISBN 0-8403-0366-1). Kendall-Hunt.

Brown, Robert H., ed. Perspectives on Liberian Literature. 250p. (Orig.). 1985. 20.00 (ISBN 0-913491-09-8); pap. 12.00 (ISBN 0-913491-08-X). Strug Comm Pr.

Brown, Robert J. & Yanuck, Rudolph R. Introduction to Life Cycle Costing. LC 84-48108. 300p. 1984. text ed. 29.95 (ISBN 0-915586-97-5). Fairmont Pr.

--Introduction to Life Cycle Costing. 336p. 1985. 29.95 (ISBN 0-13-485905-7). P-H.

--Life Cycle Costing. 299p. 32.00 (ISBN 0-915586-17-7). Fairmont Pr.

Brown, Robert K., jt. auth. see Mallin, Jay.

Brown, Robert K., ed. see Bayo, Alberto.

Brown, Robert L. Colorado Ghost Towns, Past & Present. LC 77-140121. (Illus.). 1972. 10.95 (ISBN 0-87004-218-1). Caxton.

--Ghost Towns of the Colorado Rockies. LC 68-10099. 1968. 12.95 (ISBN 0-87004-020-0). Caxton.

--The Great Pikes Peak Gold Rush. LC 85-5767. (Illus.). 1985. 12.95 (ISBN 0-87004-311-0); pap. 7.95 (ISBN 0-87004-323-4). Caxton.

--Holy Cross, Mountain & City. LC 73-109538. (Orig.). 1970. pap. 2.95 (ISBN 0-87004-198-3). Caxton.

--Jeep Trails to Colorado Ghost Towns. LC 63-7443. (Illus.). 1963. pap. 9.95 (ISBN 0-87004-021-9). Caxton.

--Uphill Both Ways: Hiking Colorado's High Country. LC 73-83111. (Illus.). 1976. pap. 5.95 (ISBN 0-87004-249-1). Caxton.

Brown, Robert L. & Collman, Ed. Saloons of the American West: An Illustrated Chronicle. (Illus.). 144p. 1978. 16.50 (ISBN 0-913582-24-7). Sundance.

Brown, Robert M. The Bible Speaks to You. LC 55-7089. 320p. 1978. pap. 5.95 (ISBN 0-664-24193-X). Westminster.

--The Bible Speaks to You. LC 84-19578. 324p. 1985. pap. 8.95 (ISBN 0-664-24597-8). Westminster.

--Creative Dislocation: The Movement of Grace. LC 80-16433. (Journey in Faith Ser.). 144p. 1980. 7.95 (ISBN 0-687-09826-2). Abingdon.

--The Electronic Invasion. rev. 2nd ed. (Illus.). 192p. 1975. pap. 7.15 (ISBN 0-8104-0825-2). Hayden.

--Elie Wiesel: Messenger to All Humanity. LC 82-40383. 244p. 1983. 16.95 (ISBN 0-268-00908-2). U of Notre Dame Pr.

--Elie Wiesel: Messenger to All Humanity. LC 82-40383. 249p. 1984. pap. text ed. 7.95 (ISBN 0-317-03878-8, 85-09135). U of Notre Dame Pr.

--Gustavo Gutierrez. LC 80-82185. (Makers of Contemporary Theology Ser.). 89p. 1981. pap. 3.95 (ISBN 0-8042-0651-1). John Knox.

--Is Faith Obsolete? LC 74-13420. 160p. 1979. pap. 3.95 (ISBN 0-664-24230-8). Westminster.

--Making Peace in the Global Village. LC 80-27213. 118p. 1981. pap. 5.95 (ISBN 0-664-24343-6). Westminster.

--Religion & Violence: A Primer for White Americans. LC 73-14710. (Illus.). 128p. 1973. Westminster.

--Significance of the Church. LC 56-6172. (Layman's Theological Library). 96p. 1956. pap. 2.45 (ISBN 0-664-24001-1). Westminster.

--Spirit of Protestantism. (YA) (gr. 9 up). 1961. pap. 8.95 (ISBN 0-19-500724-7, GB). Oxford U Pr.

--Theology in a New Key: Responding to Liberation Themes. LC 78-6494. 212p. 1978. pap. 7.95 (ISBN 0-664-24204-9). Westminster.

--Unexpected News: Reading the Bible with Third World Eyes. LC 84-2380. 166p. 1984. pap. 7.95 (ISBN 0-664-24552-8). Westminster.

Brown, Robert M. & Lawrence, Paul. How to Read Electronic Circuit Diagrams. LC 72-105970. 1970. 13.95 (ISBN 0-8306-0510-X); pap. 7.95 (ISBN 0-8306-9510-9, 510). TAB Bks.

Brown, Robert M., tr. see Casalis, George.

Brown, Robert M., tr. see De Dietrich, Suzanne.

Brown, Robert T., jt. ed. see Reynolds, Cecil R.

Brown, Robert W. Residential Foundations: Design, Behavior & Repair. 2nd ed. 128p. 1984. 19.95 (ISBN 0-442-21302-6). Van Nos Reinhold.

Brown, Robert W., jt. auth. see Kottler, Jeffrey.

Brown, Robert W., ed. New Directions in Utility Marketing. (Michigan Business Papers: No. 53). 1970. pap. 2.00 (ISBN 0-87712-102-8). U Mich Busn Div Res.

Brown, Robert W., et al. Africa & International Crises. LC 77-17820. (Foreign & Comparative Studies Program, Eastern Africa Ser.: No. 22). 106p. 1976. pap. text ed. 5.50x (ISBN 0-915984-19-9). Syracuse U Foreign Comp.

Brown, Robin. The Lure of the Dolphin. (YA) 1979. pap. 3.95 (ISBN 0-380-43158-0, 43158). Avon.

--Megalodon. LC 82-81995. 224p. 1982. pap. 2.75 (ISBN 0-86721-225-X). Jove Pubns.

Brown, Rodney H. American Polearms, Fifteen Twenty-Six to Eighteen Sixty-Five. LC 67-19981. (Illus.). 1968. 14.50 (ISBN 0-910598-08-8). Flayderman.

Brown, Roger. A First Language: The Early Stages. LC 72-95455. (Illus.). 1973. 22.50x (ISBN 0-674-30325-3); pap. 8.95x (ISBN 0-674-30326-1). Harvard U Pr.

--Social Psychology. 2nd ed. 704p. text ed. 27.95x (ISBN 0-317-20721-0). Free Pr.

--Social Psychology. 2nd. ed. 720p. 1985. 27.95x (ISBN 0-317-30504-2). Free Pr.

--Words & Things. LC 58-9395. 1968. 18.95 (ISBN 0-02-904800-1); pap. text ed. 8.95 (ISBN 0-02-904810-9). Free Pr.

Brown, Roger, jt. auth. see Bellugi, Ursula.

Brown, Roger, jt. auth. see Mason, Linda.

Brown, Roger, ed. Psycholinguistics: Selected Papers. LC 73-95296. 1972. pap. text ed. 13.95 (ISBN 0-02-904840-0). Free Pr.

Brown, Roger F. Pyrolytic Methods in Organic Chemistry: Applications of Flow & Flash Vacuum Pyrolytic Techniques. LC 79-52787. (Organic Chemistry Ser.). 1980. 55.00 (ISBN 0-12-138050-5). Acad Pr.

Brown, Roger H. Republic in Peril: 1812. 1971. pap. 5.95 (ISBN 0-393-00578-X, Norton Lib). Norton.

Brown, Roger J. Permafrost in Canada: Its Influence on Northern Development. LC 70-464841. (Illus.). 1970. 27.50x (ISBN 0-8020-1602-2). U of Toronto Pr.

Brown, Roger L. Wilhelm Von Humboldt's Conception of Linguistic Relativity. LC 67-30542. (Janua Linguarum, Ser. Minor: No. 65). (Orig.). 1967. pap. text ed. 13.60x (ISBN 90-2790-593-2). Mouton.

Brown, Roland W. Composition of Scientific Words. 882p. 1979. Repr. of 1956 ed. lib. bdg. 65.00 (ISBN 0-89987-050-3). Darby Bks.

--Composition of Scientific Words. LC 78-14717. 882p. 1978. Repr. of 1956 ed. 19.95x (ISBN 0-87474-286-2). Smithsonian.

Brown, Rollo W. Creative Spirit: An Inquiry into American Life. LC 70-85999. 1970. Repr. of 1925 ed. 21.00x (ISBN 0-8046-0604-8, Pub.by Kennikat). Assoc Faculty Pr.

--The Creative Spirit: An Inquiry into American Life. 1925. Repr. 12.00 (ISBN 0-8274-2113-3). R West.

--The Firemakers: A Novel of Environment. LC 74-22770. Repr. of 1931 ed. 24.00 (ISBN 0-404-58409-8). AMS Pr.

--Lonely Americans. facs. ed. LC 74-121452. (Essay Index Reprint Ser). 1929. 21.00 (ISBN 0-8369-1699-9). Ayer Co Pubs.

--Lonely Americans: Whistler, Emily Dickinson, Lincoln. 1929. Repr. 15.00 (ISBN 0-8274-2980-0). R West.

--The Writer's Art by Those Who Have Practiced It: Hazlitt, Emerson, Poe, Stevenson. 1921. Repr. 30.00 (ISBN 0-8274-3773-0). R West.

Brown, Rollo W. & Barnes, Nathaniel W. The Art of Writing English. 1913. Repr. 10.00 (ISBN 0-8274-1891-4). R West.

Brown, Ron. Beekeeping: A Seasonal Guide. (Illus.). 192p. 1985. 26.00 (ISBN 0-7134-4489-4, Pub. by Batsford England). David & Charles.

Brown, Ronald. From Selling to Managing. LC 70-114204. 1968. 11.95 (ISBN 0-8144-2116-4); pap. 5.95 (ISBN 0-8144-7500-0). AMACOM.

--Lasers: Tools of Modern Technology. LC 68-18081. (Doubleday Science Ser.). (Illus.). pap. 48.00 (ISBN 0-317-08831-9, 2011716). Bks Demand UMI.

--The Practical Manager's Guide to Excellence in Management. LC 79-11883. pap. 32.00 (ISBN 0-317-26946-1, 2023587). Bks Demand UMI.

Brown, Ronald & Oren, John W. Physical Distribution in Agribusiness: Activity Guide. Lee, Jasper S., ed. (Career Preparation for Agriculture-Agribusiness). 1980. pap. text ed. 12.56 (ISBN 0-07-008181-6). McGraw.

Brown, Ronald B. Fundamentals of Real Property Law: A Programmed Introduction. LC 81-86561. 215p. (Orig.). 1982. pap. 14.50 (ISBN 0-86733-019-8, 5019). Assoc Faculty Pr.

Brown, Ronald C. Hard-Rock Miners: The Intermountain West, 1860-1920. LC 78-21778. (Illus.). 336p. 1979. 18.50 (ISBN 0-89096-066-6). Tex A&M Univ Pr.

Brown, Ronald L., jt. auth. see Foster, Henry Hubbard.

Brown, Rose. The Land & People of Brazil. rev. ed. Warren, Leslie F., rev. by. LC 79-38952. (Portraits of the Nations Ser.). (Illus.). (gr. 6 up). 1972. lib. bdg. 9.89 (ISBN 0-397-31342-X). Lipp Jr Bks.

Brown, Rosel G., jt. auth. see Laumer, Keith.

Brown, Rosellen. The Autobiography of My Mother. 272p. 1981. pap. 2.95 (ISBN 0-345-28738-X). Ballantine.

--Civil Wars. LC 83-48866. 512p. 1984. 16.95 (ISBN 0-394-53478-6). Knopf.

--Civil Wars. (Contemporary American Fiction Ser.). 432p. 1985. pap. 6.95 (ISBN 0-14-007783-9). Penguin.

--Some Deaths in the Delta & Other Poems. LC 70-123540. 76p. 1970. 7.50x (ISBN 0-87023-064-6); pap. 4.50 (ISBN 0-87023-070-0). U of Mass Pr.

--Street Games. 224p. 1983. pap. 2.75 (ISBN 0-345-28739-8). Ballantine.

--Tender Mercies. LC 78-1315. 1978. 10.00 (ISBN 0-394-42741-6). Knopf.

Brown, Rosellen, et al. Banquet: Five Short Stories. LC 78-56621. (Illus.). 1978. 12.00x (ISBN 0-915778-24-6); pap. 5.00 (ISBN 0-915778-25-4); deluxe ed. 175.00x (ISBN 0-915778-23-8). Penmaen Pr.

Brown, Rosellen, et al, eds. The Whole Word Catalogue 1: Creative Writing Ideas for Elementary & Secondary Schools. rev. ed. 72p. (Orig.). 1975. pap. 6.95 (ISBN 0-915924-02-1). Tchrs & Writers Coll.

Brown, Rosemary S., jt. auth. see Savicki, Victor.

Brown, Ross & Jurasek, Lubo, eds. Hydrolysis of Cellulose: Mechanisms of Enzymatic & Acid Catalysis. LC 79-20842. (Advances in Chemistry Ser.: No. 181). 1979. 59.95 (ISBN 0-8412-0460-8). Am Chemical.

Brown, Ross E. Ultrasonography: Basic Principles & Clinical Applications. LC 72-13842. (Illus.). 320p. 1975. 28.50 (ISBN 0-87527-095-6). Green.

Brown, Ross F. Basic Arithmetic. 1979. pap. 16.25x (ISBN 0-673-15106-9). Scott F.

--Basic Arithmetic. 2nd ed. 1985. pap. text ed. 18.95x (ISBN 0-673-18017-4). Scott F.

Brown, Roxanna M. Legend & Reality: Early Ceramics from South-East Asia. (Oxford in Asia Studies in Ceramics). (Illus.). 1977. 45.00x (ISBN 0-19-580383-3). Oxford U Pr.

Brown, Roy. Find Debbie! LC 75-25511. 160p. (gr. 6 up). 1976. 7.95 (ISBN 0-395-28894-0, Clarion). HM.

Brown, Roy I., jt. auth. see Gibson, David.

Brown, Roy I., ed. Integrated Programs for Handicapped Adolescents & Adults. 250p. 1984. 25.00 (ISBN 0-89397-199-5). Nichols Pub.

Brown, Roy M. Public Poor Relief in North Carolina. LC 75-17208. (Social Problems & Social Policy Ser.). (Illus.). 1976. Repr. of 1928 ed. 17.00x (ISBN 0-405-07480-8). Ayer Co Pubs.

Brown, Roy M., jt. auth. see Steiner, Jesse F.

Brown, Royston. Public Library Administration. (Outline of Modern Librarianship Ser.). 1979. 12.00 (ISBN 0-85157-276-6, Pub. by Bingley England). Shoe String.

Brown, Ruben S. Hydro for the Eighties: Bringing Hydroelectric Power to Poor People. (Orig.). 1980. 15.00 (ISBN 0-936130-01-6). Intl Sci Tech.

Brown, Russ see White, Denis, et al.

Brown, Rustie. The Titanic, the Psychic & the Sea. LC 80-70551. (Illus.). 176p. 1981. 12.95 (ISBN 0-9605278-0-X). Blue Harbor.

Brown, Rusty. Women As We See Ourselves. LC 84-60583. 128p. (Orig.). 1984. pap. 5.95 (ISBN 0-89730-145-5). News Bks Intl.

Brown, Ruth. The Big Sneeze. LC 84-23385. (Illus.). 32p. (ps-1). 1985. 11.75 (ISBN 0-688-04665-7); lib. bdg. 11.88 (ISBN 0-688-04666-5). Lothrop.

--A Dark Dark Tale. LC 81-66798. (Illus.). 32p. (ps-3). 1981. 10.95 (ISBN 0-8037-1672-9, 01063-320); PLB 10.89 (ISBN 0-8037-1673-7). Dial Bks Young.

--A Dark Dark Tale. LC 81-66798. (Pied Piper Book). (Illus.). 32p. (ps-3). 1984. pap. 3.95 (ISBN 0-8037-0093-8, 0383-120). Dial Bks Young.

--If at First You Do Not See. LC 82-15527. (Illus.). 24p. 1983. 11.95 (ISBN 0-03-063521-7). HR&W.

Brown, Ruth A. S. Aureli Augustini: De Beata Vita: A Translation with an Introduction & Commentary, Vol. 72. (Patristic Studies). 211p. 1984. Repr. of 1944 ed. 30.00x (ISBN 0-939738-30-9). Zubal Inc.

Brown, Ruthanne, jt. auth. see Clark, Raymond C.

Brown, S. A., ed. Cell-Culture Test Methods. LC 83-70421. (Special Technical Publications: No. 810). 157p. 1983. text ed. 30.00 (ISBN 0-8031-0249-6, 04-810000-54). ASTM.

Brown, S. B. An Introduction to Spectroscopy for Biochemists. LC 79-41632. 1980. 49.50 (ISBN 0-12-137080-1). Acad Pr.

Brown, S. C. Electron-Molecule Scattering. 196p. 1979. 34.95 (ISBN 0-471-05205-1). Krieger.

Brown, S. C., ed. Philosophers Discuss Education. 260p. 1975. 21.00x (ISBN 0-87471-774-4). Rowman.

--Philosophers of the Enlightenment. (Royal Institute of Philosophy Lecture Ser.: No. 12). 1979. text ed. 37.00x (ISBN 0-391-01638-5). Humanities.

Brown, S. C. & Mays, Wolfe, eds. Linguistic Analysis & Phenomenology. LC 70-165551. 307p. 1972. 26.50 (ISBN 0-8387-1025-5). Bucknell U Pr.

Brown, S. E. & Parker, C. A. Thru the Knothole: A Touch of Len Eckman. 96p. 1983. write for info (ISBN 0-943432-11-1). Slack Inc.

Brown, S. G. The Song of Narwa. 1984. 5.75 (ISBN 0-8062-2272-7). Carlton.

Brown, S. J., Jr., jt. ed. see Au-Yang, M. K.

Brown, S. J., Jr., jt. ed. see Gangadharan, A. C.

Brown, S. S. Topics in Child Psychology. 1970. pap. text ed. 7.25x (ISBN 0-8290-1198-6). Irvington.

Brown, S. S. & Davies, D. S. Organ-Directed Toxicity: Symposium on Chemical Indices & Mechanisms of Organ-Directed Toxicity, Barcelona, Spain, 4-7 March 1981. (IUPAC Symposium Ser.). (Illus.). 400p. 1981. 99.00 (ISBN 0-08-026197-3). Pergamon.

Brown, S. S., ed. Clinical Chemistry & Chemical Toxicology. 1977. 47.00 (ISBN 0-444-41601-3). Elsevier.

Brown, S. S., et al, eds. Chemical Diagnosis of Disease. 1374p. 1979. 78.50 (ISBN 0-444-80089-1, North Holland). Elsevier.

Brown, S. W. Secularization of American Education As Shown by State Legislation, State Constitutional Provisions & State Supreme Court Decisions. LC 70-176600. (Columbia University. Teachers College. Contributions to Education: No. 49). Repr. of 1912 ed. 22.50 (ISBN 0-404-55049-5). AMS Pr.

Brown, Sam. All about Telescopes. 3rd ed. LC 67-31540. (Illus.). 1976. 19.95x (ISBN 0-933346-20-4). Sky Pub.

Brown, Sam E. Activities for Teaching Metrics in Kindergarden. LC 77-95155. 1978. pap. text ed. 8.25 (ISBN 0-8191-0462-0). U Pr of Amer.

--Bubbles, Rainbows & Worms: Science Experiments for Pre-School Children. LC 80-84598. (Illus.). 105p. 1981. pap. 6.95 (ISBN 0-87659-100-4). Gryphon Hse.

--One, Two, Buckle My Shoe: Math Activities for Young Children. (Illus., Orig.). 1982. pap. 6.95 (ISBN 0-87659-103-9). Gryphon Hse.

Brown, Samuel A., et al. FSI German Basic Course, Units 1-12. 1976. pap. text ed. 11.25x (ISBN 0-686-10722-5); 25 cassettes 150.00x (ISBN 0-686-10723-3). Intl Learn Syst.

--FSI German Basic Course, Units 13-24. 1975. pap. text ed. 15.00X (ISBN 0-686-10724-1); 25 cassettes 150.00x (ISBN 0-686-10725-X). Intl Learn Syst.

Brown, Samuel G., ed. see Choate, Rufus.

Brown, Samuel R. Western Gazetteer: Or Emigrant's Directory. LC 79-146380. (First American Frontier Ser). (Illus.). 1971. Repr. of 1817 ed. 23.00 (ISBN 0-405-02831-8). Ayer Co Pubs.

Brown, Sanborn C. Benjamin Thompson, Count Rumford. (Illus.). 1979. 32.50x (ISBN 0-262-02138-2); pap. 9.95x (ISBN 0-262-52069-9). MIT Pr.

--Count Rumford, Physicist Extraordinary. LC 78-25712. (Illus.). 1979. Repr. of 1962 ed. lib. bdg. 27.50x (ISBN 0-313-20772-0, BRCR). Greenwood.

Brown, Sanborn C. & Brown, Jonathan. Wines & Beers of Old New England: A How-to-Do-It History. LC 77-72519. (Illus.). 187p. 1978. 12.50x (ISBN 0-87451-144-5); pap. 6.95 (ISBN 0-87451-148-8). U Pr of New Eng.

Brown, Sanborn C., jt. ed. see Oleson, Alexandra.

Brown, Sanborn C., ed. see Rumford, Benjamin T.

Brown, Sandi, jt. auth. see LaFray-Young, Joyce.

Brown, Sandra. Another Dawn. 1985. pap. price not set. Bantam.

--Heaven's Price. (Loveswept Ser.: No. 1). 1983. pap. 2.25 (ISBN 0-553-21720-8). Bantam.

--In a Class by Itself. 208p. (Orig.). 1984. pap. 2.25 (ISBN 0-553-21672-4). Bantam.

--Relentless Desire. (Second Chance at Love Ser.: No. 106). 192p. 1983. pap. 1.75 (ISBN 0-515-06870-5). Jove Pubns.

--Send No Flowers. (Loveswept Ser.: No. 51). 192p. (Orig.). 1984. pap. 2.25 (ISBN 0-553-21659-7). Bantam.
--Sunset Embrace. 1985. pap. 3.50 (ISBN 0-553-24658-5). Bantam.
--Tempest in Eden. 192p. 1983. pap. 1.95 (ISBN 0-515-07579-5). Jove Pubns.
--Temptation's Kiss. (Second Chance at Love Ser.: No. 137). 192p. 1983. pap. 1.95 (ISBN 0-515-07225-7). Jove Pubns.
--Thursday's Child. (Loveswept Ser.: No. 79). 208p. 1985. pap. 2.25 (ISBN 0-553-21686-4). Bantam.
--Tomorrow's Promise. (American Romance Ser.). 192p. 1983. pap. 2.25 (ISBN 0-373-16001-1). Harlequin Bks.

Brown, Sandy. Isn't There Anybody Out There Who Can Help Me? 1984. pap. 4.95 (ISBN 0-917726-61-8). Hunter Bks.

Brown, Sanford J. Getting into Medical School. 6th ed. 256p. 1983. 5.95 (ISBN 0-8120-2542-3). Barron.

Brown, Sanford M. & Clark, Wayne N. Environmental Health Field Practice. 302p. 1983. 18.95 (ISBN 0-03-062528-9). Praeger.

Brown, Sanger. Sex Worship & Symbolism: An Interpretation. LC 72-9624. Repr. of 1922 ed. 14.00 (ISBN 0-404-57419-X). AMS Pr.

Brown, Sara L. & Moersch, Martha S., eds. Parents on the Team. LC 78-18517. (Illus.). 1978. lib. bdg. 13.95x (ISBN 0-472-09302-9); pap. 8.50 (ISBN 0-472-06302-2). U of Mich Pr.

Brown, Schuyler. The Origins of Christianity: A Historical Introduction to the New Testament. (Oxford Bible Ser.). (Orig.). 1984. pap. 8.95 (ISBN 0-19-826202-7). Oxford U Pr.

Brown, Schuyler & Saliers, Don E. Pentecost Three. Actemeier, Elizabeth, et al, eds. LC 79-7377. (Proclamation Ser.: No. 2). 64p. 1982. pap. 3.50 (ISBN 0-8006-4099-3, 1-4099). Fortress.

Brown, Scott S. Bounds on Transfer Principles for Algebraically Closed & Complete Discretely Valued Fields. LC 78-9121. 92p. 1978. pap. 12.00 (ISBN 0-8218-2204-7, MEMO-204). Am Math.

Brown, Seyom. The Crisis of Power: Foreign Policy in the Kissinger Years. LC 79-15796. 1979. 17.00x (ISBN 0-231-04264-7). Columbia U Pr.
--The Faces of Power: Constancy & Change in United States Foreign Policy from Truman to Reagan. 2nd ed. LC 83-1861. 656p. 1983. 37.00x (ISBN 0-231-04736-3); pap. 13.00x (ISBN 0-231-04737-1). Columbia U Pr.
--New Forces in World Politics. LC 74-912. 200p. 1974. 22.95 (ISBN 0-8157-1118-2); pap. 8.95 (ISBN 0-8157-1117-4). Brookings.
--On the Front Burner: Issues In U.S. Foreign Policy. 1984. pap. text ed. 10.94 (ISBN 0-316-11061-2). Little.

Brown, Seyom, et al. Regimes for the Ocean, Outer Space, & Weather. 1977. 22.95 (ISBN 0-8157-1156-5); pap. 8.95 (ISBN 0-8157-1155-7). Brookings.

Brown, Sharon, ed. Poetry of Our Times. LC 79-51956. (Granger Poetry Library). 1980. Repr. of 1928 ed. 34.75x (ISBN 0-89609-179-1). Granger Bk.

Brown, Shelagh. Someone There. 96p. (Orig.). 1982. pap. 1.90 (ISBN 0-88028-019-0). Forward Movement.

Brown, Sheldon S. A Guide to Study Children & Adolescents. 2nd ed. 1978. pap. text ed. 9.95 (ISBN 0-8403-1304-7). Kendall-Hunt.
--Learning Psychology by Doing. 1978. pap. text ed. 12.95 (ISBN 0-8403-3363-3). Kendall-Hunt.

Brown, Sheri, jt. ed. see Witt, Loretta.

Brown, Sherry. Ernest Leonard Blumenschein Catalogue-Raisonne. (Illus.). 1985. write for info. (ISBN 0-937634-04-2). Fenn Pub Co.

Brown, Shirley N., jt. ed. see Brown, James W.

Brown, Shiron L. Expressions from the Heart. Cherry, Annie, ed. 44p. (Orig.). 1982. pap. 4.95 (ISBN 0-910515-00-X). Brown Cherry Pub.

Brown, Sidney D., ed. see Takayoshi, Kido.

Brown, Skip & Graham, John. Target Twenty-Six, Revised for the Eighties: A Practical Guide to Running the Marathon. Rev. ed. (Illus.). 288p. 1983. pap. 7.95 (ISBN 0-02-028100-5). Macmillan.

Brown, Sonia & Wilkening, Howard. Bufano, an Intimate Biography. LC 72-79789. (Illus.). 233p. 1972. 12.95 (ISBN 0-8310-7089-7). Howell-North.

Brown, Spencer. Child's Game, on a Journey. 1979. 22.00 (ISBN 0-686-59668-4); pap. 10.00 (ISBN 0-686-59669-2). Elizabeth Pr.
--Looking into the Fire. 1967. pap. 4.00 (ISBN 0-685-00988-2). Elizabeth Pr.

Brown, Stanford H. & Forrest, Theodore R., Jr. Environmental Health Law. LC 84-9850. 144p. 1984. 22.95 (ISBN 0-03-064066-0). Praeger.

Brown, Stanley. Men from under the Sky: The Arrival of Westerners in Fiji. LC 72-96774. (Illus.). 1973. 10.00 (ISBN 0-8048-1103-2). C E Tuttle.

Brown, Stanley E. The Directory of Office Information Systems. 3rd ed. 336p. 1984. pap. 49.95 (ISBN 0-935220-12-7). Knowledge Indus.

Brown, Stanley H., jt. auth. see Girard, Joe.

Brown, Stanley S. & Savory, John, eds. Chemical Toxicology & Clinical Chemistry of Metals. 1984. 38.50 (ISBN 0-12-137520-X). Acad Pr.

Brown, Stanley S. & Sunderman, F. William, Jr., eds. Nickel Toxicology. 1981. 40.00 (ISBN 0-12-137680-X). Acad Pr.

Brown, Stephanie. Religious Painting. LC 78-24454. (Mayflower Gallery). (Illus.). 1979. 12.50 (ISBN 0-8317-7370-7, Mayflower Bks); pap. 6.95 (ISBN 0-8317-7371-5). Smith Pubs.
--Treating the Alcoholic: A Developmental Model of Recovery. Mellick, Jill, ed. (Personality Processes Ser.). 400p. 1985. 30.00 (ISBN 0-471-81736-8). Wiley.

Brown, Stephen. Heirs with the Prince. 176p. 1985. 10.95 (ISBN 0-8407-5939-8). Nelson.
--If God Is In Charge. LC 83-2240. 180p. 1983. pap. 4.95 (ISBN 0-8407-5844-8). Nelson.
--The Pike: Past Its Peak. LC 81-51941. (Illus.). 64p. (Orig.). 1981. pap. 14.00 (ISBN 0-940468-01-8); signed, ltd. ed. 19.00 (ISBN 0-940468-00-X). SCB Photos.

Brown, Stephen & Brown, Carolyn. Do-It-Yourself Curriculum. (Sunday School Curriculum Ser.). 274p. 1980. pap. 7.50x (ISBN 0-940644-02-9). River Hse.

Brown, Stephen & Sibley, David. The Theory of Public Utility Pricing. 216p. Date not set. price not set. (ISBN 0-521-30626-4); pap. price not set. (ISBN 0-521-31400-3). Cambridge U Pr.

Brown, Stephen, jt. ed. see Boehner, Philotheus.

Brown, Stephen D. Harpers Ferry. 5th ed. LC 75-15007. (Illus.). 40p. 1982. pap. 2.25 (ISBN 0-685-93080-7). The Little Brown House.
--Haunted Houses of Harpers Ferry: Regional Ghost Stories. 6th ed. LC 76-398. (Illus.). 72p. (Orig.). 1982. pap. 2.95 (ISBN 0-915782-04-9). The Little Brown House.

Brown, Stephen F., ed. Guillelmi de Ockham: Scriptum in Librum Primum Sententiarum, Ordinatio, Opera Theologica, Vol. 2, Distinctiones Secunda et Tertia. 1970. 37.00 (ISBN 0-686-11529-5). Franciscan Inst.

Brown, Stephen G. & DiSaisa, Philip J. Cancer of the Cervix. (Oncologic Ser.: Vol. 14). (Illus.). 308p. 1981. pap. 110.00 (ISBN 0-08-027465-X). Pergamon.

Brown, Stephen I. Some "Prime" Comparisons. LC 78-12339. (Illus.). 106p. 1979. pap. 6.00 (ISBN 0-87353-131-0). NCTM.

Brown, Stephen I., jt. auth. see Walter, Marion I.

Brown, Stephen J. The Realm of Poetry. 1973. Repr. of 1921 ed. 20.00 (ISBN 0-8274-1449-8). R West.

Brown, Stephen J., ed. Ireland in Fiction: A Guide to Irish Novels, Tales, Romances, & Folk-Lore. LC 76-113998. (Bibliography & Reference Ser.: No. 311). 1970. Repr. of 1919 ed. text ed. 18.50 (ISBN 0-8337-0388-9). B Franklin.

Brown, Stephen W. Voice of the New West: John G. Jackson, His Life & Times. xxvi, 262p. 1985. 22.95x (ISBN 0-86554-162-0, MUP/H152). Mercer Univ Pr.

Brown, Stephen W. & Fisk, Raymond P. Marketing Theory: Distinguished Contributions. LC 83-23452. 375p. 1984. text ed. 39.95 (ISBN 0-471-89085-5, Pub by Wiley). Wiley.

Brown, Stephen W., jt. auth. see Morley, Andrew.

Brown, Sterling. Negro in American Fiction. 1969. Repr. of 1937 ed. 12.50 (ISBN 0-87266-002-8). Argosy.
--Negro in American Fiction. Bd. with Negro Poetry & Drama. LC 69-18582. (American Negro-His History & Literature Ser., No.2). 372p. Repr. of 1937 ed. 15.00 (ISBN 0-405-01851-7). Ayer Co Pubs.
--Negro Poetry & Drama & the Negro in American Fiction. LC 69-15521. (Studies in American Negro Life Ser). 1969. pap. text ed. 3.45x (ISBN 0-689-70024-5, NL12). Atheneum.

Brown, Sterling, jt. auth. see Haynes, George E.

Brown, Sterling, et al, eds. Negro Caravan. LC 69-18584. (American Negro: His History & Literature Ser., No. 2). 1969. 39.00 (ISBN 0-405-01852-5); pap. 4.95 (ISBN 0-685-06513-8, Dist, by Random Hse). Ayer Co Pubs.

Brown, Sterling A. The Collected Poems of Sterling A. Brown. LC 79-5221. (National Poetry Ser.). 1980. 14.37i (ISBN 0-06-010517-8, HarpT). Har-Row.
--The Collected Poems of Sterling A. Brown. Harper, Michael S., selected by. LC 82-48230. 270p. 1983. pap. 7.21i (ISBN 0-06-091016-X, CN 1016, CN). Har-Row.
--The Last Ride of Wild Bill & Eleven Narrative Poems. 70p. 1975. 6.00 (ISBN 0-910296-01-4); pap. 3.00 (ISBN 0-910296-02-2). Broadside.

Brown, Steven D. & Lent, Robert W., eds. Handbook of Counseling Psychology. LC 84-7395. 982p. 1984. 60.00x (ISBN 0-471-09905-8). Wiley.

Brown, Steven F. Contemporary Literature in Birmingham: An Anthology. LC 82-60123. (Anthology Ser.). (Illus.). 240p. (Orig.). 12.00 (ISBN 0-918644-28-3); pap. 7.00 (ISBN 0-918644-27-5). Thunder City.
--Erotic Mask. LC 83-903. (Contemporary Poetry Ser.: No. 2). 48p. (Orig.). 1984. signed limited ed. 10.00 (ISBN 0-938136-02-X); pap. 5.00 (ISBN 0-938136-01-1). Lunchroom Pr.

Brown, Steven F., ed. see Imbert, Enrique A.

Brown, Steven R. Political Subjectivity: Applications of Q Methodology in Political Science. LC 79-24393. 376p. 1980. text ed. 48.00x (ISBN 0-300-02363-4); pap. 14.95x (ISBN 0-300-02579-3). Yale U Pr.

Brown, Stewart J. Thomas Chalmers & Godly Commonwealth in Scotland. (Illus.). 1982. 55.00x (ISBN 0-19-213114-1). Oxford U Pr.

Brown, Stuart. Leibniz. 1985. 35.00 (ISBN 0-8166-1390-7); pap. 12.95 (ISBN 0-8166-1391-5). U of Minn Pr.

Brown, Stuart, ed. Philosophical Disputes in the Social Sciences. 1979. text ed. 28.00x (ISBN 0-391-00933-8). Humanities.
--Reason & Religion. LC 77-3115. 336p. 1977. 29.95x (ISBN 0-8014-1025-8); pap. 9.95x (ISBN 0-8014-9166-5). Cornell U Pr.

Brown, Stuart E. Virginia Baron: The Story of Thomas, Sixth Lord of Fairfax. LC 65-19262. (Illus.). 245p. 1965. 15.00 (ISBN 0-685-65062-6). Va Bk.

Brown, Stuart E. & Brown, Ann B. Carter Hall & Some Genealogical Notes on the Burwell Family of Virginia. (Illus.). 1978. 25.00x (ISBN 0-685-89823-7). Va Bk.

Brown, Stuart E., et al. Virginia Genealogies, Vol. 2. 351p. 1980. 28.50 (ISBN 0-686-64384-4). Va Bk.

Brown, Stuart E., Jr. Annals of Blackwater & the Land of Canaan, 1746-1880. LC 59-10184. (Illus.). 42p. 1959. pap. 1.75 (ISBN 0-685-65060-X). Va Bk.
--Annals of Clarke County, Virginia: Old Homes, Families, Etcetera of the Southern (South of U.S Route 50) Section, Vol. 1. (Illus.). 425p. 1983. 42.50x (ISBN 0-317-05706-5). VA Bk.
--Virginia Genealogies: A Trial List of Printed Books & Pamphlets. LC 67-7956. 310p. 1967. 27.50 (ISBN 0-685-65061-8). Va Bk.

Brown, Stuart E., Jr., compiled by. Scrip. Trade Tokens Issued by United States Coal Mining Companies & Company Store. (Illus.). 1978. 22.50 (ISBN 0-686-50094-6). Va Bk.

Brown, Stuart E., Jr., ed. see Pollock, George F.

Brown, Stuart G. Alexander Hamilton. Brown, Arthur W. & Knight, Thomas S., eds. (Great American Thinkers Ser). (Orig.). pap. 0.60 (ISBN 0-686-00967-3, W875). WSP.
--Conscience in Politics: Adlai E. Stevenson in the 1950's. 1961. 16.95x (ISBN 0-8156-0022-4). Syracuse U Pr.
--The First Republicans: Political Philosophy & Public Policy in the Party of Jefferson & Madison. LC 76-48247. 1977. Repr. of 1954 ed. lib. bdg. 16.00x (ISBN 0-8371-9339-7, BRFR). Greenwood.
--Presidency on Trial: Robert Kennedy's 1968 Campaign & Afterwards. 1972. 10.00x (ISBN 0-8248-0202-0). UH Pr.

Brown, Stuart G., ed. Great Issues. facs. ed. LC 70-134061. (Essay Index Reprint Ser). 1951. 31.00 (ISBN 0-8369-2148-8). Ayer Co Pubs.
--Revolution, Confederation & Constitution. LC 78-151607. (Literature of History Ser.). 1971. 24.50x (ISBN 0-89197-384-2); pap. text ed. 6.95x (ISBN 0-89197-385-0). Irvington.

Brown, Stuart G., ed. see Royce, Josiah.

Brown, Susan, tr. see Pessoa, Fernando.

Brown, Susan A., jt. ed. see Bancroft, T. A.

Brown, Susan E. & Vasquez, Hector G. Pluralism in the Legal Profession: Models for Minority Access. LC 83-116891. (Illus.). Date not set. price not set. Mex Am Legal.

Brown, Susan J. Robber Rocks: Letters & Memories of Hart Crane, 1923-1932. LC 73-82537. (Illus.). 1969. 16.00x (ISBN 0-8195-4007-2). Wesleyan U Pr.

Brown, Susan T., jt. auth. see Strecicfus, Charles F.

Brown, Suzanne, ed. see Korenblit, Joan & Janger, Kathie.

Brown, Suzanne S., jt. auth. see Neal, James M.

Brown, T. Freeze Branding. (Orig.). 1982. pap. 5.00 (ISBN 0-911217-00-2). SW Amer Pub Co.
--Three Worlds: One Word. Rex Collings Ltd., ed. 50.00x (ISBN 0-86036-146-2, Pub. by R Collings Ltd.). State Mutual Bk.

Brown, T. & Alanzel, W. Scientometric Indicators: A Thirty-Two Country Comparative Evaluation of Publishing Performance & Citation Impact. 250p. 1984. 33.00x (ISBN 9971-966-69-7, Pub. by World Sci Singapore). Taylor & Francis.

Brown, T. A. A History of the New York Stage. 59.95 (ISBN 0-8490-0358-X). Gordon Pr.

Brown, T. A., tr. see Rosenzweig, Mark R.

Brown, T. D., ed. Wool in Double Jersey. 122p. 1973. 45.00x (ISBN 0-900541-79-2, Pub. by Meadowfield Pr England). State Mutual Bk.

Brown, T. I., ed. Economic Co-Operation among the Negroes of Georgia. (Atlanta Univ. Publ. Ser.: No. 19). (Orig.). pap. 14.00 (ISBN 0-527-03120-8). Kraus Repr.

Brown, T. J. see Malone, Kemp & Schibsbye, Knud.

Brown, T. Merritt. Specification & Uses of Econometric Models. LC 70-88172. 1970. 27.50 (ISBN 0-312-75110-9). St Martin.

Brown, T. Nigel, ed. Brown's Nautical Almanac. 1982. 105th ed. LC 32-280. (Illus.). 967p. 1981. 37.50x (ISBN 0-8002-2868-5). Intl Pubns Serv.
--Brown's Nautical Almanac, 1983. 106th ed. LC 32-280. (Illus.). 946p. 1982. 47.00x (ISBN 0-8002-3066-3). Intl Pubns Serv.

Brown, T. S. Onesicritus: A Study in Hellenistic Historiography. 196p. 12.50 (ISBN 0-89005-384-7). Ares.

Brown, Tasman. Morphology of the Australian Skull: Studies by Multivariate Analysis. (AIAS Human Biology Ser.: No. 4). (Illus.). 1973. pap. text ed. 14.00x (ISBN 0-85575-027-8). Humanities.

Brown, Terence. Ireland: A Social & Cultural History, 1922 to the Present. LC 85-47695. 296p. (Orig.). 1985. text ed. 39.50x (ISBN 0-8014-1731-7); pap. text ed. 12.95x (ISBN 0-8014-9349-8). Cornell U Pr.
--Northern Voices: Poets from Ulster. 248p. 1975. 19.50x (ISBN 0-87471-627-6). Rowman.

Brown, Terence D. Quality Control in Lumber Manufacturing. LC 82-80244. (A Forest Industries Bk.). (Illus.). 288p. 1982. 55.00 (ISBN 0-87930-138-4, 463); pap. 44.50 (ISBN 0-87930-142-2). Miller Freeman.

Brown, Terrance, tr. see Piaget, Jean.

Brown, Terry & Hunter, Rob. The Book of Sailing. (Illus.). 1977. pap. 2.95 (ISBN 0-7715-9375-9). Vanguard.
--The Concise Book of Orienteering. 1979. pap. 2.95 (ISBN 0-686-70999-3). Vanguard.
--The Concise Book of Outdoor First Aid. (Illus.). 1978. pap. 2.95 (ISBN 0-7715-9433-X, Pub. by Gage). Vanguard.
--The Concise Book of Winter Camping. (Concise Ser.). (Illus.). 1978. pap. 2.95 (ISBN 0-7715-9441-0). Vanguard.

Brown, Theo. The Fate of the Dead: A Study in Folk-Eschatology in the West Country After the Reformation. (Folklore Society Mistletoe Ser.). 118p. 1979. 24.50x (ISBN 0-8476-6214-4). Rowman.

Brown, Theo W. Sharks: The Silent Savages. (Illus.). 200p. pap. 5.95 (ISBN 0-88317-085-X). Stoeger Pub Co.

Brown, Theodore & LeMay, Eugene. Chemistry: The Central Science, Qualitative Inorganic Analysis. 3rd ed. (Illus.). 160p. 1985. pap. text ed. 7.95 (ISBN 0-13-127549-6). P-H.

Brown, Theodore & Le May, Eugene. Qualitative Inorganic Analysis. (Illus.). 160p. 1983. pap. 7.95 (ISBN 0-13-744946-1). P H.

Brown, Theodore & Cohen, I. Bernard, eds. The Mechanical Philosophy & the "Animal Oeconomy". LC 80-2085. (Development of Science Ser.). (Illus.). 1981. lib. bdg. 35.00x (ISBN 0-405-13851-2). Ayer Co Pubs.

Brown, Theodore L. & Le May, H. Eugene, Jr. Chemistry: The Central Science. 3rd ed. (Illus.). 896p. 1985. text ed. 37.95 (ISBN 0-13-128950-0); solutions manual, 536 pp. 8.95. P-H.

Brown, Thomas. Account of the People Called Shakers. LC 77-17584. Repr. of 1812 ed. 27.00 (ISBN 0-404-08459-1). AMS Pr.
--Inquiry into the Relation of Cause & Effect. 4th ed. LC 77-16224. 1977. Repr. of 1835 ed. lib. bdg. 75.00x (ISBN 0-8201-1301-8). Schol Facsimiles.
--Langue et Litterature. 3rd ed. 416p. 1984. text ed. 20.95 (ISBN 0-669-06682-6). Heath.
--Observations on the Nature & Tendency of the Doctrine of Mr. Hume Concerning the Relation of Cause & Effect. LC 82-48341. (The Philosophy of David Hume Ser.). 221p. 1983. lib. bdg. 33.00 (ISBN 0-8240-5401-6). Garland Pub.
--Politics & Statesmanship: Essays on the American Whig Party. 328p. 1985. 27.50x (ISBN 0-231-05602-8). Columbia U Pr.
--Sketch of a System of the Philosophy of the Human Mind. Bd. with Logic of Condillac. (Contributions to the History of Psychology Ser., Pt. A: Orientations). 1978. Repr. of 1820 ed. 30.00 (ISBN 0-89093-150-X). U Pubns Amer.

Brown, Thomas, jt. auth. see Holladay, Sylvia.

Brown, Thomas A. The Aesthetics of Robert Schumann. LC 73-16607. (Illus.). 207p. 1975. Repr. of 1968 ed. lib. bdg. 15.00x (ISBN 0-8371-7184-9, BRAS). Greenwood.
--History of the American Stage. LC 72-81206. (Illus.). 1968. Repr. of 1870 ed. 29.00 (ISBN 0-405-08309-2, Blom Pubns). Ayer Co Pubs.
--History of the American Stage. 1969. Repr. of 1870 ed. lib. bdg. 26.50 (ISBN 0-8337-0387-0). B Franklin.
--History of the New York Stage, 3 vols. LC 64-14704. Repr. of 1903 ed. Set. 132.00 (ISBN 0-405-08310-6, Blom Pubns); 44.00 ea. Vol. 1 (ISBN 0-405-08311-4). Vol. 2 (ISBN 0-405-08312-2). Vol. 3 (ISBN 0-405-08313-0). Ayer Co Pubs.

Brown, Thomas E. & Miller, Scott. Layman's Guide to Oil & Gas Investments & Royalty Income. 2nd, rev. ed. LC 84-28994. (Illus.). 182p. (Orig.). 1985. pap. 9.95x (ISBN 0-87201-341-3). Gulf Pub.

Brown, Thomas H. French: Listening, Speaking, Reading, Writing. 4th ed. (Illus.). 512p. 1983. text ed. 33.95 (ISBN 0-07-008411-4). McGraw.
--Themes et Discussions. 240p. 1982. pap. text ed. 10.95 (ISBN 0-669-02844-4). Heath.

Brown, Thomas H. & Gross, Jeffrey T. Dimensions: Essays for Composition. (Orig.). 1980. pap. text ed. 12.95 (ISBN 0-316-11220-8); tchrs' manual avail. (ISBN 0-316-11221-6). Little.

Brown, Thomas I., ed. Economic Co-operation among the Negroes of Georgia. LC 17-28675. (Atlanta University Publications Ser.: No. 19). (Orig.). 1917. pap. 14.00 (ISBN 0-317-17939-X). Kraus Repr.

Brown, Thomas K., tr. see Jorns, Auguste.

Brown, Thomas N. Irish-American Nationalism, Eighteen Seventy to Eighteen Ninety. LC 80-11094. (Critical Periods of History Ser.). xvii, 206p. 1980. Repr. of 1966 ed. lib. bdg. 24.75x (ISBN 0-313-22204-5, BRIA). Greenwood.
--Life & Times of Hugh Miller. (Folklore Ser.). Repr. 25.00 (ISBN 0-8482-7394-X). Norwood Edns.
Brown, Thomas R., jt. ed. see Smith, Mickey C.
Brown, Thomas S. The Personal Relevance of Truth. 1983. pap. 5.00x (ISBN 0-87574-081-2, 081). Pendle Hill.
Brown, Thomas S. & Wallace, Patricia. Physiological Psychology. 1980. tchrs' ed. 21.75i (ISBN 0-12-136660-X); study guide 8.00i (ISBN 0-12-136663-4). Acad Pr.
Brown, Tim. Shaken & Stirred: The Seducer's Guide to Cocktails. (Illus.). 80p. 1984. pap. 11.95 (ISBN 0-88715-003-9). Delilah Comm.
Brown, Timothy G. see Media Institute.
Brown, Tina. Life As a Party. (Illus.). 168p. 1984. pap. 13.95 (ISBN 0-233-97600-0, Pub. by A Deutsch England). David & Charles.
Brown, Tom & Watkins, William J. The Tracker. 1984. pap. 3.50 (ISBN 0-425-07759-4). Berkley Pub.
Brown, Tom, tr. see Scarron, Paul.
Brown, Tom, Jr. Tom Brown's Guide to Wild Edible & Medicinal Plants. 288p. 1985. pap. 7.95 (ISBN 0-425-08452-3). Berkley Pub.
--The Tracker. 1982. pap. 5.95 (ISBN 0-425-05347-4). Berkley Pub.
--The Tracker: The Story of Tom Brown, Jr. LC 78-17981. 1978. 9.95 (ISBN 0-13-925917-1). P-H.
Brown, Tom, Jr. & Morgan, Brandt. Tom Brown's Field Guide to City & Suburban Survival, Vol. 3. 288p. (Orig.). 1984. pap. 6.95 (ISBN 0-425-06815-3). Berkley Pub.
--Tom Brown's Field Guide to Living with the Earth. 288p. 1984. pap. 6.95 (ISBN 0-425-07213-4). Berkley Pub.
--Tom Brown's Field Guide to Nature Observation & Tracking. 256p. 1983. pap. 6.95 (ISBN 0-425-06177-9). Berkley Pub.
--Tom Brown's Guide to Wilderness Survival. (Illus.). 240p. (Orig.). 1984. pap. 7.95 (ISBN 0-425-07702-0). Berkley Pub.
Brown, Tom, Jr. & Owen, William. The Search. 1982. pap. 5.95 (ISBN 0-425-05346-6). Berkley Pub.
Brown, Toni S. & Flint, Joe. The D. J.'s Almanac of Country Music. 394p. (Orig.). 1983. pap. 14.95 (ISBN 0-936860-11-1). Liberty Pr.
Brown, Tony, jt. auth. see Charlesworth, John.
Brown, Tricia. Someone Special, Just Like You. (Illus.). (gr. 5-9). 11.95 (ISBN 0-03-069706-9). HR&W.
Brown, Truesdell S. The Greek Historians. (Civilization & Society Ser.). 1973. pap. text ed. 5.95x (ISBN 0-669-83881-0). Heath.
Brown University. Dictionary Catalog of the Harris Collection of American Poetry & Plays, Brown University, 13 vols. 1972. Set. lib. bdg. 1690.00 (ISBN 0-8161-0974-5, Hall Library). G K Hall.
Brown University, Department of Art. Caricature & Its Role in Graphic Satire. (Illus.). 1971. pap. 4.50 (ISBN 0-686-10419-6). Mus of Art RI.
--Portrait Bust, Renaissance to Enlightenment. (Illus.). 1969. 1.00 (ISBN 0-686-00763-8). Mus of Art RI.
--Transformation of the Court Style Gothic Art in Europe 1270-1330. LC 77-70260. (Illus.). 1977. pap. 7.50 (ISBN 0-686-10417-X). Mus of Art RI.
Brown University - John Carter Brown Library. Bibliotheca Americana, Books to Sixteen Seventy Four, 3 Vols. 3rd ed. 1919-1931. Set. 150.00 (ISBN 0-527-46200-4). Kraus Repr.
Brown University Library. A Contribution to a Union Catalog of Sixteenth Century Imprints in Certain New England Libraries. LC 54-1641. 474p. 1953. 40.00x (ISBN 0-87057-032-3). U Pr of New Eng.
--The Life & Works of John Hay, 1838-1905: A Commemorative Catalogue of the Exhibition Shown at the John Hay Library of Brown University in Honor of the Centennial of His Graduation at the Commencement of 1858. LC 61-3289. (Illus.). 63p. 1961. 8.00x (ISBN 0-87057-063-3). U Pr of New Eng.
Brown, V. K. Acute Toxicity in Theory & Practice: With Special Reference to the Toxicoloty of Pesticides. LC 79-42905. (Monographs in Toxicology; Environmental & Safety Aspects). 159p. 1980. 41.95 (ISBN 0-471-27690-1, Pub. by Wiley-Interscience). Wiley.
--Grasshoppers. LC 81-17091. (Cambridge Naturalists' Handbooks: No. 2). (Illus.). 68p. 1983. pap. 17.95 (ISBN 0-521-23903-6). Cambridge U Pr.
Brown, Velma D. After Weeping, a Song. LC 79-53321. 1980. 7.50 (ISBN 0-8054-5425-X). Broadman.
Brown, Vera & Culligan, Pat. Vera Brown's Natural Beauty Book. 220p. 1983. 15.95 (ISBN 0-89037-265-9). Anderson World.
Brown, Vernon K. A Cathedral of Healing. (Illus.). 264p. 1981. 12.50 (ISBN 0-9605996-1-4). Northwest Memorial.
Brown, Vinson. The Amateur Naturalist's Diary. (Illus.). 184p. 1983. 16.95 (ISBN 0-13-023689-6); pap. 9.95 (ISBN 0-13-023671-3). P-H.
--The Amateur Naturalists's Handbook. (Illus.). 448p. 1980. 15.95 (ISBN 0-13-023739-6, Spec); pap. 7.95 (ISBN 0-13-023721-3). P-H.
--Building Your Own Nature Museum for Study & Pleasure. (Illus.). 160p. (Orig.). 1984. lib. bdg. 12.95 (ISBN 0-668-06057-3); pap. 7.95 (ISBN 0-668-06061-1). Arco.
--Investigating Nature Through Outdoor Projects. 256p. 1983. pap. 12.95 (ISBN 0-8117-2213-9). Stackpole.
--It All Happened in Santa Clara County. LC 67-2821. (Illus.). (gr. 3-6). Date not set. price not set (ISBN 0-685-52884-7). Pacific Bks.
--Native Americans of the Pacific Coast. (Illus.). 272p. 1985. 14.95 (ISBN 0-87961-134-0); pap. 8.95 (ISBN 0-87961-135-9). Naturegraph.
--Pomo Indians of California & Their Neighbors. Elsasser, Albert B., ed. LC 78-13946. (American Indian Map Bk.: Vol. 1). (Illus.). 64p. (Orig.). (gr. 4 up). 1969. 10.95 (ISBN 0-911010-31-9); pap. 4.95 (ISBN 0-911010-30-0). Naturegraph.
--Reading the Outdoors at Night. LC 82-1949. (Illus.). 192p. 1982. pap. 9.95 (ISBN 0-8117-2187-6). Stackpole.
--Reading the Woods: Seeing More in Nature's Familiar Faces. LC 70-85652. (Illus.). 160p. 1973. pap. 7.95 (ISBN 0-02-062270-8, Collier). Macmillan.
--Reptiles & Amphibians of the West. LC 74-3204. (Illus.). 80p. 1974. text ed. 11.95 (ISBN 0-87961-029-8); pap. text ed. 5.95 (ISBN 0-87961-028-X). Naturegraph.
--Return of the Indian Spirit. LC 81-65887. 64p. 1982. pap. 5.95 (ISBN 0-89087-401-8). Celestial Arts.
--Voices of Earth & Sky. LC 76-41761. (Illus.). 177p. 1976. pap. 5.95 (ISBN 0-87961-060-3). Naturegraph.
Brown, Vinson & Lawrence, George. The Californian Wildlife Region. (American Wildlife Region Ser.: Vol. 1). (Illus.). 128p. (gr. 4 up). 1965. 10.95 (ISBN 0-911010-01-7); pap. 4.95 (ISBN 0-911010-00-9). Naturegraph.
Brown, Vinson & Livezey, Robert. The Sierra Nevadan Wildlife Region. 2nd rev. ed. (American Wildlife Region Ser.: Vol. 2). (Illus.). 96p. (gr. 4 up). 1962. 10.95 (ISBN 0-911010-03-3); pap. 4.95 (ISBN 0-911010-02-5). Naturegraph.
Brown, Vinson & Yocom, Charles. Wildlife & Plants of the Cascades. LC 75-29118. (American Wildlife Region Ser.: Vol. 8). (Illus.). 296p. 1971. 13.95 (ISBN 0-911010-81-5); pap. 7.95 (ISBN 0-911010-80-7). Naturegraph.
Brown, Vinson, jt. auth. see Allan, David.
Brown, Vinson, jt. auth. see Braun, Earnest.
Brown, Vinson, jt. auth. see Willoya, William.
Brown, Vinson, ed. see Allen, Elsie.
Brown, Vinson, et al. Handbook of California Birds. 3rd rev. ed. LC 73-6826. (Illus.). 223p. 1979. 14.95 (ISBN 0-911010-17-3); pap. 8.95 (ISBN 0-911010-16-5). Naturegraph.
--Prevent Doomsday! An Anti Nuclear Anthology. new ed. (Illus.). 96p. 1983. pap. 4.00 (ISBN 0-8283-1875-1). Branden Pub Co.
--Rocks & Minerals of California. 3rd. rev. ed. LC 72-13423. (Illus.). 200p. (gr. 4 up). 1972. 11.95 (ISBN 0-911010-59-9); pap. 5.95 (ISBN 0-911010-58-0). Naturegraph.
--Wildlife of the Intermountain West. (American Wildlife Region Ser.: Vol. 4). (Illus.). 144p. (gr. 4 up). 1968. 10.95 (ISBN 0-911010-15-7); pap. 4.95 (ISBN 0-911010-14-9). Naturegraph.
Brown, Virginia. Defy the Thunder. (Avon Romance Ser.). 416p. 1984. pap. 2.95 (ISBN 0-380-89537-4). Avon.
Brown, Virginia & Stayman, Susan. Macrobiotic Miracle: A Woman Cures Herself of Cancer. (Illus.). 240p. 1983. pap. 14.95 (ISBN 0-87040-573-X). Japan Pubns USA.
Brown, Virginia P. The Gold Disc of Coosa. LC 75-24616. 5.95 (ISBN 0-87397-085-3). Strode.
--Grand Old Days of Birmingham Golf. Owens, Laurella, ed. (Illus.). 64p. (Orig.). 1984. pap. 12.95 (ISBN 0-912221-01-1). Beechwood.
Brown, Virginia P. & Akens, Helen M. Alabama Heritage. LC 67-28403. (Illus.). 1967. 15.95 (ISBN 0-87397-001-2). Strode.
--Alabama Mounds to Missiles. LC 66-23127. (Illus.). 1966. pap. 5.95 (ISBN 0-87397-002-0). Strode.
Brown, Virginia P. & Owens, Laurella. Toting the Lead Row: Ruby Pickens Tartt, Alabama Folklorist. 208p. 1981. 19.95 (ISBN 0-8173-0074-0). U of Ala Pr.
--World of the Southern Indians. (Illus.). 176p. (gr. 6-9). 1983. 15.95 (ISBN 0-912221-00-3). Beechwood.
Brown, Virginia P. & Nabers, Jane P., eds. Mary Gordon Duffee's Sketches of Alabama. LC 74-139830. 96p. 1970. 9.95 (ISBN 0-8173-5311-9). U of Ala Pr.
Brown, Virginia P. & Owens, Laurella, eds. Southern Indian Myths & Legends. (Illus.). 160p. 1985. 15.95 (ISBN 0-912221-02-X). Beechwood.
Brown, W. Psychological Care During Pregnancy & the Postpartum Period. 171p. 1979. 26.50 (ISBN 0-89004-371-X); pap. 16.00 (ISBN 0-686-66187-7). Raven.
Brown, W. C. Sheepeater Campaign, Idaho 1879. (Shorey Lost Arts Ser.). (Illus.). 29p. pap. 3.95 (ISBN 0-8466-0251-2, S251). Shorey.
Brown, W. C., et al. Bosporus Bridge. 96p. 1976. pap. 7.25x (ISBN 0-7277-0039-1). Am Soc Civil Eng.
Brown, W. D. Welcome Stress, It Can Help You Be Your Best. 150p. 1983. pap. 8.95 (ISBN 0-89638-067-X). CompCare.
Brown, W. Elgar. Hydraulics for Operators. rev. ed. 145p. 1985. pap. text ed. 19.95 (ISBN 0-250-40650-0). Butterworth.
Brown, W. G. Lower South in American History. LC 68-24973. (American History & Americana Ser.: No. 47). 1969. Repr. of 1902 ed. lib. bdg. 49.95x (ISBN 0-8383-0919-4). Haskell.
Brown, W. Henry. Charles Kingsley. LC 73-12770. 1924. lib. bdg. 17.50 (ISBN 0-8414-3231-7). Folcroft.
Brown, W. J. Tax Strategies for Separation & Divorce. (Family Law Publications). 526p. 1984. 75.00 (ISBN 0-07-043038-1, Shepards-McGraw). McGraw.
Brown, W. Jann & Voge, Marietta. Neuropathology of Parasitic Infections. (Illus.). 1982. text ed. 35.00x (ISBN 0-19-261246-8). Oxford U Pr.
Brown, W. Jethro, jt. auth. see Austin, John.
Brown, W. L., et al, eds. International Symposium on the Conservation of Crop Germplasm. 67p. 1983. 11.00 (ISBN 0-89118-518-6). Crop Sci Soc Am.
Brown, W. L., jt. ed. see Narayan, J.
Brown, W. Norman. India & Indology. Rocher, Rosane, ed. (Illus.). 1978. 52.50 (ISBN 0-89684-066-2). Orient Bk Dist.
--India & Indology. Rocher, Rosane, ed. 1979. 52.00x (ISBN 0-8364-0362-2). South Asia Bks.
--The Mahimnastava or Mahimna Stotra. 1983. Repr. of 1955 ed. 34.00x (ISBN 0-8364-1001-7, Pub. by Motilal Banasidas). South Asia Bks.
--Man in the Universe: Some Cultural Continuities in Indian Thought. LC 66-12648. (Rabindranath Tagore Memorial Lectures). 1966. 22.00x (ISBN 0-520-00185-0). U of Cal Pr.
--Manuscript Illustrations of the Uttaradhyayana Sutra. (American Oriental Ser.: Vol. 21). (Illus.). 1941. 10.00 (ISBN 0-940490-21-8). Kraus Repr.
--The United States & India, Pakistan, Bangladesh. 3rd ed. LC 72-81270. (American Foreign Policy Library). Orig. Title: The United States & India & Pakistan. (Illus.). 396p. 1972. 27.50x (ISBN 0-674-92446-0); pap. 8.95x (ISBN 0-674-92447-9, HP31). Harvard U Pr.
Brown, W. Norman, jt. auth. see Mayeda, Noriko.
Brown, W. Norman, ed. The Vasanta Vilasa. (American Oriental Ser.: Vol. 46). (Illus.). 1962. 20.00x (ISBN 0-940490-46-3). Am Orient Soc.
Brown, W. R., jt. auth. see Bowen, B. A.
Brown, W. S., jt. auth. see Priest, Josiah.
Brown, W. Steven. Thirteen Fatal Errors Managers Make: And How to Avoid Them. 192p. 1985. 15.95 (ISBN 0-8007-1423-7). Revell.
Brown, W. W. Black Man, His Antecedents, His Genius and His Achievements. 1865. 17.00 (ISBN 0-527-12100-2). Kraus Repr.
--Negro in the American Rebellion, His Heroism & His Fidelity. 1867. 31.00 (ISBN 0-527-12150-9). Kraus Repr.
Brown, Wallace. The King's Friends: The Composition & Motives of the American Loyalist Claimants. LC 66-10179. (Illus.). 425p. 1965. 35.00x (ISBN 0-87057-092-7, Pub. by Brown U Pr). U Pr of New Eng.
Brown, Wallace C. The Triumph of Form. LC 73-13452. 212p. 1973. Repr. of 1948 ed. lib. bdg. 22.50x (ISBN 0-8371-7135-0, BRTF). Greenwood.
Brown, Waln. The Other Side of Delinquency. (Crime, Law & Deviance Ser.). 155p. 1983. 17.95 (ISBN 0-8135-0993-9); pap. 10.00 (ISBN 0-8135-0994-7). Rutgers U Pr.
Brown, Walt, Jr., ed. An American for Lafayette: The Diaries of E. C. C. Genet, Lafayette Escadrille. LC 81-10383. (Illus.). xxvii, 224p. 1981. 16.95x (ISBN 0-8139-0893-0). U Pr of Va.
Brown, Walter. Two Thousand Eight Hundred Ninety-Four, or, the Fossil Man: A Mid-Winter Night's Dream. LC 76-42720. (Communal Societies in America Ser.). Repr. of 1894 ed. 23.50 (ISBN 0-404-60055-7). AMS Pr.
Brown, Walter, jt. auth. see Anderson, Norman.
Brown, Walter C. Basic Mathematics. 128p. 1981. pap. text ed. 5.60 (ISBN 0-87006-315-4). Goodheart.
--Basic Mathematics Test Sheets. 1981. 0.60 (ISBN 0-87006-317-0). Goodheart.
--Blueprint Reading for Construction. LC 79-23958. 336p. 1980. pap. text ed. 16.80 spiral bdg. (ISBN 0-87006-286-7). Goodheart.
--Blueprint Reading for Industry. Rev. ed. LC 82-20949. 345p. 1983. spiral bdg. 15.00 (ISBN 0-87006-429-0). Goodheart.
--Drafting. LC 81-20004. (Illus.). 128p. 1982. text ed. 6.40 (ISBN 0-87006-508-4). Goodheart.
--Drafting for Industry. rev. ed. (Illus.). 616p. 1984. text ed. 21.00 (ISBN 0-87006-463-0); workbook 6.00 (ISBN 0-87006-464-9). Goodheart.
Brown, Walter C., et al. Modern General Shop. LC 81-13274. (Illus.). 488p. 1982. text ed. 19.00 (ISBN 0-87006-407-X). Goodheart.
Brown, Walter L. Up Front with U. S. Day by Day in the Life of a Combat Infantryman in General Patton's Third Army. LC 79-54035. (Illus.). 744p. 1979. 14.95x (ISBN 0-9604822-0-2); lib. bdg. write for info. Brown's Studio.
Brown, Walter R. & Anderson, Norman D. Earth Science: A Search for Understanding. rev. ed. 1977. text ed. 18.60i (ISBN 0-397-43747-1); tchr's. ed. 20.80i (ISBN 0-397-43748-X). Har-Row.
Brown, Walter R., jt. auth. see Anderson, Norman D.
Brown, Walter T. & Leder, Robert. The Council for Intercultural Studies & Programs International Studies Funding Book. 3rd rev ed. 295p. 1983. 50.00 (ISBN 0-939288-01-X); members 30.00 (ISBN 0-317-34808-6). Learn Res Intl Stud.
Brown, Walton J. Home at Last. (Discovery Ser.). 96p. pap. 5.95 (ISBN 0-317-01321-1). Review & Herald.
Brown, Warren B. & Moberg, Dennis G. Organization Theory & Management: A Macro Approach. LC 79-18709. (Wiley Series in Management). 685p. 1980. 38.45 (ISBN 0-471-02023-0). Wiley.
Brown, Warren J. A Doctor's Advice to Folks Over Fifty. 23p. 1976. pap. 1.00x (ISBN 0-912522-60-7). Aero-Medical.
--Florida's Aviation History. 1980. pap. 6.95 (ISBN 0-912522-70-4). Aero-Medical.
Brown, Warren J., ed. Patients' Guide to Medicine: From the Drugstore Through the Hospital. 9th ed. 1981. pap. 7.95 (ISBN 0-912522-71-2). Aero-Medical.
Brown, Wayne S., et al, eds. Monograph on Rock Mechanics Applications in Mining. LC 76-45924. 1977. pap. text ed. 18.00x (ISBN 0-89520-046-5). Soc Mining Eng.
Brown, Weldon A. The Last Chopper: The Denouement of the American Role in Vietnam, 1964-1975. 1976. 27.50x (ISBN 0-8046-9121-5, Pub. by Kennikat). Assoc Faculty Pr.
Brown, Wilburt S. Amphibious Campaign for West Florida & Louisiana, 1814-1815: A Critical Review of Strategy & Tactics at New Orleans. LC 68-10992. (Illus.). Repr. of 1969 ed. 61.30 (ISBN 0-8357-9615-9, 2050448). Bks Demand UMI.
Brown, Wilford. Piecework Abandoned: The Effect of Wage Incentive Systems on Managerial Authority. (Glacier Project Ser.). 127p. 1962. 5.95x (ISBN 0-8093-0371-X). S Ill U Pr.
Brown, Wilfred. Organization. 1971. text ed. 26.00x (ISBN 0-435-85103-9). Gower Pub Co.
--Participation. 1975. 90.00x (ISBN 0-903763-19-2, Pub. by MCB Pubns). State Mutual Bk.
Brown, Wilfred & Jaques, Elliot. Glacier Project Papers: Some Essays on Organization & Management from the Glacier Project Research. (Glacier Project Ser.). 285p. 1965. 7.95x (ISBN 0-8093-0373-6). S Ill U Pr.
--Product Analysis Pricing. (Glacier Project Ser). 160p. 1964. 5.95x (ISBN 0-8093-0372-8). S Ill U Pr.
Brown, Wilkes. Images of Family Life in Magazine Advertising: Nineteen Twenty-Nineteen Seventy Eight. LC 81-14366. 156p. 1981. 31.95 (ISBN 0-03-059697-1). Praeger.
Brown, Will C. The Nameless Breed. 192p. 1985. pap. 2.50 (ISBN 0-441-56450-X, Pub. by Charter Bks). Ace Bks.
Brown, Willard J. The Signal Corps, U. S. A. in the War of the Rebellion. LC 74-4670. (Telecommunications Ser). (Illus.). 916p. 1974. Repr. of 1896 ed. 57.50x (ISBN 0-405-06036-X). Ayer Co Pubs.
Brown, William. Cosmetic Surgery. 1979. pap. 4.95 (ISBN 0-8128-6002-0). Stein & Day.
Brown, William & Payne, Tyrone. Strategies for Learning. 1979. pap. text ed. 9.00x (ISBN 0-87879-219-8). Acad Therapy.
Brown, William A. Christian Theology in Outline. LC 75-41044. (BCL Ser. II). Repr. of 1906 ed. 28.00 (ISBN 0-404-14648-1). AMS Pr.
Brown, William A., Jr. England & the New Gold Standard: 1919-1926. Wilkins, Mira, ed. LC 78-3901. (International Finance Ser.). (Illus.). 1978. Repr. of 1929 ed. lib. bdg. 29.00x (ISBN 0-405-11206-8). Ayer Co Pubs.
--International Gold Standard Reinterpreted, 1914-1934, 2 Vols. Repr. of 1940 ed. 95.00 (ISBN 0-404-04645-2). AMS Pr.
Brown, William D. The Way to the Uncle Sam Hotel. (Orig.). 1966. pap. 2.75 (ISBN 0-940556-00-6). Coyote.
Brown, William E. Alaska National Parklands: This Last Treasure. LC 82-71677. (Illus.). 128p. (Orig.). 1982. 25.00; pap. 10.95 (ISBN 0-9602876-5-5). Alaska Natural.
--A History of Eighteenth Century Russian Literature. 1980. 29.50 (ISBN 0-88233-341-0). Ardis Pubs.
--A History of Russian Literature of the Romantic Period, 4 vols. 1700p. 1985. Set. 150.00 (ISBN 0-88233-938-9). Vol. I (ISBN 0-88233-939-7). Vol. II (ISBN 0-88233-940-0). Vol. III (ISBN 0-88233-941-9). Vol. IV (ISBN 0-88233-942-7). Ardis Pubs.
--History of Seventeenth Century Russian Literature. 1980. 20.00 (ISBN 0-88233-343-7). Ardis Pubs.
--Hydraulics Manual for Operators. LC 81-68896. (Illus.). 145p. 1981. pap. text ed. 19.95 (ISBN 0-250-40503-2). Butterworth.
Brown, William E. & Lamperti, Giovanni B. Vocal Wisdom. Strongin, Lillian, ed. 1957. (Crescendo); pap. 4.95 (ISBN 0-8008-8023-4, Crescendo). Taplinger.

Brown, William E. & Sacks, Richard S. Review Manual for Operators. LC 81-68888. (Illus.). 182p. 1981. pap. text ed. 19.95 (ISBN 0-250-40501-6). Butterworth.

Brown, William F. Physiological & Technical Basis of EMG. (Illus.). 448p. 1984. text ed. 59.95 (ISBN 0-409-95042-4). Butterworth.

--Student-to-Student Counseling: An Approach to Motivating Academic Achievement. rev. ed. (Hogg Foundation Research Ser). (Illus.). 370p. 1977. 14.95x (ISBN 0-292-77542-3). U of Tex Pr.

Brown, William F. & Brown, Mary G. Wood Works: Experiments with Common Wood & Tools. LC 83-15905. (Illus.). 128p. (gr. 3 up). 1984. 11.95 (ISBN 0-689-31033-1). Atheneum.

Brown, William F., Jr. Magnetoelastic Interactions. (Springer Tracts in Natural Philosophy: Vol. 9). (Illus.). 1966. 39.00 (ISBN 0-387-03674-1). Springer-Verlag.

--Micromagnetics. LC 78-2342. 152p. 1978. Repr. of 1963 ed. lib. bdg. 13.50 (ISBN 0-88275-665-6). Krieger.

Brown, William G. Life of Oliver Ellsworth. LC 76-118028. (American Constitutional & Legal History Ser). 1970. Repr. of 1905 ed. lib. bdg. 45.00 (ISBN 0-306-71940-1). Da Capo.

--Lower South in American History. LC 69-13843. Repr. of 1902 ed. lib. bdg. 17.50x (ISBN 0-8371-0925-6, BRO&). Greenwood.

--Lower South in American History. LC 71-108464. 1970. Repr. of 1902 ed. 15.00x (ISBN 0-403-00446-2). Scholarly.

Brown, William G., ed. Reviews in Graph Theory, 4 vols. LC 80-17817. 1980. Set. 300.00 (ISBN 0-8218-0214-3); Vol. 1. 100.00 (ISBN 0-8218-0210-0); Vol. 2. 100.00 (ISBN 0-8218-0211-9); Vol. 3. 100.00 (ISBN 0-8218-0212-7); Vol. 4. 60.00 (ISBN 0-8218-0213-5). Am Math.

Brown, William H. Brother Sunshine-Father Rain. 64p. 1981. 6.95 (ISBN 0-682-49816-5). Exposition Pr FL.

--Concepts & Inquiries in Biology, Vols. 1 & 2. 1978. pap. text ed. 9.95 ea. (Ed Methods); Vol. 1, 3rd Ed. pap. text ed. (ISBN 0-88462-048-4, Ed Methods); Vol. 2, 2nd Ed. pap. text ed. (ISBN 0-88462-049-2). Longman USA.

--How to Stop the Corporate Polluters. (Illus.). 1972. pap. 1.50 (ISBN 0-88388-020-2). Bellerophon Bks.

--Ira & Isabella; or the Natural Children. LC 78-64067. Repr. of 1807 ed. 37.50 (ISBN 0-404-17393-4). AMS Pr.

--On the South African Frontier. LC 71-100257. Repr. of 1899 ed. 23.50x (ISBN 0-8371-2863-3, BSF&, Pub. by Negro U Pr). Greenwood.

--On the Southern African Frontier. LC 70-116276. xxii, 428p. 1972. Repr. of 1899 ed. 18.00x (ISBN 0-403-00445-4). Scholarly.

--The Power of Sympathy. Bd. with The Coquette. Foster, Hannah. Osborne, William S., ed. (Masterworks of Literature Ser.). 1970. 9.95x (ISBN 0-8084-0345-1); pap. 6.95x (ISBN 0-8084-0346-X). New Coll U Pr.

--The Power of Sympathy. Kable, William S., ed. LC 72-76389. (Illus.). 242p. 1970. 7.50 (ISBN 0-8142-0007-9). Ohio St U Pr.

--Selected Poems & Verse Fables, Seventeen Eighty-Four to Seventeen Ninety-Two. Walser, Richard, ed. LC 82-2660. 94p. 1982. 20.00 (ISBN 0-87413-223-1). U Delaware Pr.

Brown, William H. & Tawes, Roy L. Review Questions in General Vascular Surgery, Vol. II. 2nd ed. (Illus.). 288p. (Orig.). 1984. pap. 45.00x (ISBN 0-930328-08-6). Travel Pr.

Brown, William J. The Life of William J. Brown, of Providence, R. I. With Personal Recollections of Incidents in Rhode Island. facsimile ed. LC 78-164382. (Black Heritage Library Collection). Repr. of 1883 ed. 17.50 (ISBN 0-8369-8841-8). Ayer Co Pubs.

Brown, William J., et al. Syphilis & Other Venereal Diseases. LC 77-88803. (Vital & Health Statistics Monographs, American Public Health Association). 1970. 16.50x (ISBN 0-674-86122-1). Harvard U Pr.

Brown, William L., jt. auth. see Hilty, Steven L.

Brown, William L., ed. Feldspars & Feldspathoids: Structures, Properties & Occurances. lib. bdg. 74.00 (ISBN 90-277-1826-1, Pub. by Reidel Holland). Kluwer Academic.

Brown, William M. Communism & Christianism. 252p. lib. bdg. 14.95 (ISBN 0-88286-046-1); pap. 4.00 (ISBN 0-88286-045-3). C H Kerr.

--The Future Role of Geopressured Resources in U.S. Energy Policy: A Scenario Approach & Analysis. 58p. 1979. 15.00 (ISBN 0-318-14341-0, HI2991RR). Hudson Inst.

--Personal Computers: A Complete Handbook for Beginners. (Illus.). 250p. 1984. pap. 9.95 (ISBN 0-914091-49-2). Chicago Review.

Brown, William M. & Yokelson, Doris. Postattack Recovery Strategies. 178p. 1980. 20.00 (ISBN 0-318-14352-6, HI3100RR). Hudson Inst.

Brown, William N. The Indian & Christian Miracles of Walking on the Water. LC 78-72381. Repr. of 1928 ed. 16.50 (ISBN 0-404-17243-1). AMS Pr.

Brown, William N., ed. Resources for South Asian Language Studies in the United States: Report of a Conference Convened by the University of Pennsylvania for the United States Office of Education, January 15-16, 1960. LC 60-15611. pap. 25.80 (ISBN 0-317-11022-5, 2002898). Bks Demand UMI.

Brown, William N., ed. see Sankaracarya.

Brown, William R. Academic Politics. LC 81-23100. 202p. 1982. text ed. 17.50 (ISBN 0-8173-0116-X). U of Ala Pr.

--The Last Crusade: A Negotiator's Middle East Handbook. LC 79-18462. 416p. 1980. text ed. 26.95x (ISBN 0-88229-554-3). Nelson-Hall.

Brown, William R., jt. auth. see Bowen, B. A.

Brown, William S., jt. auth. see Parker, William S.

Brown, William W. American Fugitive in Europe, Sketches of Places & People Abroad. LC 72-88424. Repr. of 1855 ed. 19.75x (ISBN 0-8371-1906-5, BRF&, Pub. by Negro U Pr). Greenwood.

--Black Man, His Antecedents, His Genius, & His Achievements. LC 77-82179. (Anti-Slavery Crusade in America Ser). 1969. Repr. of 1863 ed. 16.00 (ISBN 0-405-00618-7). Ayer Co Pubs.

--The Black Man: His Antecedents, His Genius & His Achievements. 2nd ed. (Basic Afro-American Reprint Library Ser). 1969. Repr. of 1863 ed. 16.00 (ISBN 0-384-05975-9). Johnson Repr.

--Black Man, His Antecedents, His Genius, & His Achievements. pap. 2.95 (ISBN 0-685-16779-8, N189P). Mnemosyne.

--Clotel, or the President's Daughter. LC 75-75852. (American Negro: His History & Literature, Ser. No. 2). 1969. Repr. of 1853 ed. 21.00 (ISBN 0-405-01853-3). Ayer Co Pubs.

--Clotelle: Or, the Colored Heroine. facs. ed. LC 71-81108. (Black Heritage Library Collection Ser). 1867. 8.75 (ISBN 0-8369-8517-6). Ayer Co Pubs.

--Clotelle: Or, the Colored Heroine. pap. 1.95 (ISBN 0-685-16780-1, N247P). Mnemosyne.

--My Southern Home: The South & Its People. LC 79-90107. Repr. of 1880 ed. 19.75x (ISBN 0-8371-2012-8, BSH&, Pub. by Negro U Pr). Greenwood.

--My Southern Home: The South & Its People. LC 70-78570. (The Muckrakers Ser.). (Illus.). lib. bdg. 17.75 (ISBN 0-8398-0177-7). Irvington.

--Narrative of William W. Brown a Fugitive Slave. 1970. Repr. of 1847 ed. 14.00 (ISBN 0-384-05976-7). Johnson Repr.

--Negro in the American Rebellion, His Heroism & Fidelity. pap. 3.50 (ISBN 0-685-16792-5, N190P). Mnemosyne.

--Negro in the American Rebellion: His Heroism & His Fidelity. facs. ed. LC 78-79021. (Black Heritage Library Collection Ser). 1880. 17.00 (ISBN 0-8369-8518-4). Ayer Co Pubs.

--Negro in the American Rebellion: His Heroism & His Fidelity. 1971. 7.95 (ISBN 0-685-03374-0); pap. 3.95 (ISBN 0-8065-0238-X). Citadel Pr.

--The Negro in the American Rebellion: His Heroism & His Fidelity. (Basic Afro-American Reprint Library). 1969. Repr. of 1867 ed. 20.00 (ISBN 0-384-05985-6). Johnson Repr.

--Rising Son, Or, the Antecedents & Advancement of the Colored Race. LC 75-100258. Repr. of 1874 ed. 25.00x (ISBN 0-8371-2856-0, BSU&). Greenwood.

--Rising Son: The Antecedents & Advancement of the Colored Race. facs. ed. LC 79-79008. (Black Heritage Library Collection Ser). 1874. 22.50 (ISBN 0-8369-8519-2). Ayer Co Pubs.

--The Rising Sun or the Antecedents & Advancement of the Colored Race. (Basic Afro-American Reprint Library). 1970. Repr. of 1874 ed. lib. bdg. 26.00 (ISBN 0-384-05995-3). Johnson Repr.

--Sketches of Places & People Abroad. facs. ed. LC 71-133149. (Black Heritage Library Collection Ser). 1854. 17.00 (ISBN 0-8369-8705-5). Ayer Co Pubs.

Brown, Willie & Peterson, James A. Defensive Halfback Fundamentals & Techniques. (Illus.). 208p. (Orig.). (gr. 6 up). 1985. pap. 14.95 (ISBN 0-88011-250-6). Leisure Pr.

Brown, Willis M. How I Got Faith. 199p. 2.00 (ISBN 0-686-29117-4). Faith Pub Hse.

Brown, Wilmore, ed. Legal Architect. 1959. 14.50 (ISBN 0-87215-015-1). Michie Co.

Brown, Wilmore, ed. see Musmanno, Michael A.

Brown, Wilson H., jt. auth. see Hogendorn, Jan S.

Brown, Wm. A., Jr. Groping Giant: Russia. 1920. 29.50x (ISBN 0-685-69793-2). Elliots Bks.

Brown, Zenia H., jt. auth. see Glickman, Albert S.

Brown-Azarowicz, Marjory F. Individual & Group Procedures in Reading: For the Classroom Teacher in Grades 4-7. LC 81-40095. (Illus.). 310p. (Orig.). 1982. pap. text ed. 14.25 (ISBN 0-8191-2264-5). U Pr of Amer.

Brownback, Glenda. Mata Hari. (Orig.). 1981. pap. cancelled (ISBN 0-914476-92-0). Thorp Springs.

Brownback, Paul. Danger of Self-Love. LC 82-12543. 1982. pap. 5.95 (ISBN 0-8024-2068-0). Moody.

Browndorf, Eric & Reimer, Scott. Bibliography of Multinational Corporations & Foreign & Direct Investment. Simmonds, Kenneth R., ed. LC 78-24051. (Multinational Corporations Law). 1980. binders 200.00 (ISBN 0-379-20372-3). Oceana.

Browne. Hagar: Room for One More, No. 6. pap. 1.95 (ISBN 0-317-31775-X). Tor Bks.

--Hagar the Horrible: All the World Loves A Lover, No. 8. pap. 1.95 (ISBN 0-317-31777-6). Tor Bks.

--Hagar the Horrible: Golden Maiden. pap. 1.95 (ISBN 0-317-31772-5). Tor Bks.

--Hagar the Horrible: Hear No Evil. pap. 1.95 (ISBN 0-317-31774-1). Tor Bks.

--Hagar the Horrible: Sacking Paris On A Budget. pap. 1.95 (ISBN 0-317-31771-7). Tor Bks.

--Hagar the Horrible: Tall Tails. pap. 1.95 (ISBN 0-317-31773-3). Tor Bks.

--Hagar the Horrible: Vikings Are Fun, No. 1. pap. 1.75 (ISBN 0-317-31770-9). Tor Bks.

--Icons of America. LC 77-84917. 1978. 14.95 (ISBN 0-87972-090-5); pap. 6.95 (ISBN 0-87972-091-3). Bowling Green Univ.

--Look What I've Got. (gr. k-3). 1980. PLB 8.90 (ISBN 0-531-04118-2). Watts.

Browne, jt. auth. see Walker.

Browne, A. L. The General Problem of Rolling Contact. Tsai, N. T., ed. (AMD: Vol. 40). 170p. 1980. 28.00 (ISBN 0-686-69852-5, G00173). ASME.

Browne, Aaron V. Oregon Territory. 24p. 1968. Repr. pap. 2.50 (ISBN 0-87770-034-6, A825). Ye Galleon.

Browne, Alan L., jt. ed. see Hays, Donald F.

Browne, Allan & Califonia Continuing Education of the Bar. Attorney's Guide to the Law of Competitive Business Practices. LC 80-68324. xvi, 571p. 1981. 65.00 (ISBN 0-88124-079-6). Cal Cont Ed Bar.

Browne, Anita. The One Hundred Best Books by American Women, 1833-1933. 59.95 (ISBN 0-8490-0767-4). Gordon Pr.

Browne, Anita, ed. Homespun. LC 78-73481. (Granger Poetry Library). 1979. Repr. of 1936 ed. 32.50x (ISBN 0-89609-108-2). Granger Bk.

Browne, Anthony. Bear Hunt. LC 79-21964. (Illus.). 24p. (ps-2). 1980. 8.95 (ISBN 0-689-30733-0). Atheneum.

--Gorrilla. LC 85-13. (Illus.). (gr. 4-8). 1985. PLB 8.99 (ISBN 0-394-87525-7); pap. 7.95 (ISBN 0-317-18909-3). Knopf.

--Willy the Wimp. LC 84-14320. (Illus.). 32p. (ps-3). 1985. PLB 8.99 (ISBN 0-394-97061-6); pap. 7.95 (ISBN 0-394-87061-1). Knopf.

Browne, Antony. Gorilla. (Julia Macrae Bks). (Illus.). 32p. (gr. 4-8). PLB 8.95 (ISBN 0-531-04609-5). Watts.

Browne, Arthur, et al. I, Koch: A Decidedly Unauthorized Biography of the Mayor of New York City. 384p. 1985. 18.95 (ISBN 0-396-08647-0). Dodd.

Browne, Bellmore H. Guns & Gunning. (Shorey Lost Arts Ser.). (Illus.). 122p. pap. 4.95 (ISBN 0-8466-6014-8, U14). Shorey.

Browne, Benjamin P. Illustrations for Preaching. LC 76-39713. 1977. 9.50 (ISBN 0-8054-2228-5). Broadman.

Browne, Benjamin P., jt. auth. see Hoadley, Frank T.

Browne, Bernadine, ed. see Bikram, Mahendra, et al.

Browne, C. A. Story of Our National Ballads. rev. ed. Heaps, Willard A., ed. LC 60-15255. (gr. 5 up). 1960. 13.41i (ISBN 0-690-77707-8). Crowell Jr Bks.

Browne, Chalres F. see Ward, Artemus, pseud.

Browne, Charles A. A Source Book of Agricultural Chemistry. Egerton, Frank N., 3rd, ed. LC 77-74205. (History of Ecology Ser.). 1978. Repr. of 1944 ed. lib. bdg. 23.50x (ISBN 0-405-10375-1). Ayer Co Pubs.

Browne, Charles F. Artemus Ward Among the Fenians. 59.95 (ISBN 0-87968-662-6). Gordon Pr.

--The Complete Works of Artemus Ward (Charles Farrar Browne) with a Biographical Sketch. LC 78-143666. Repr. of 1889 ed. 25.50 (ISBN 0-8337-3684-1). B Franklin.

Browne, Charles F. & Ward, Artemus. Artemus Ward: His Book. 1981. Repr. of 1862 ed. 11.95 (ISBN 0-686-79335-8). B of A.

Browne, Charles F. see Ward, Artemus, pseud.

Browne, Charles F., jt. auth. see Ward, Artemus.

Browne, Collette & Onzuka-Anderson, Roberta. Our Aging Parents: A Practical Guide to Eldercare. (Illus.). 304p. 1985. pap. 12.95 (ISBN 0-8248-0997-1). UH Pr.

Browne, Corinne, jt. auth. see Bodie, Scott.

Browne, Cynthia, compiled by. State Constitutional Conventions Bibliography. LC 73-9327. xi, 250p. 1973. lib. bdg. 45.00 (ISBN 0-8371-7005-2, SCB/). Greenwood.

Browne, D. J. Economics for 'A' Level. (Illus.). 328p. 1983. pap. text ed. 17.95x (ISBN 0-7131-0866-5). Intl Ideas.

Browne, Dan. Alternative Home Heating. LC 79-3445. (Illus.). 208p. (Orig.). 1980. (Owl Bks.); pap. 6.95 (ISBN 0-03-041536-5). HR&W.

Browne, David D. The Wind & the Book: Memoirs of a Country Doctor. 1976. 18.00x (ISBN 0-522-84099-X, Pub. by Melbourne U Pr). Intl Spec Bk.

Browne, David M. Roman Cambridgeshire. (Cambridge Town, Gown & County Ser.: Vol. 13). (Illus.). 1977. pap. 4.25 (ISBN 0-900891-09-2). Oleander Pr.

Browne, Dik. All the World Loves a Lover. (Hagar the Horrible Ser.: No. 8). 128p. 1985. pap. 1.95 (ISBN 0-8125-6780-3). Tor Bks.

--Best of Hagar. (Illus.). 240p. 1985. pap. 10.95 (ISBN 0-317-20764-4). Comicana.

--The Best of Hagar the Horrible. Brissie, Eugene, ed. 96p. 1981. pap. 4.95 (ISBN 0-671-42485-8, Wallaby). S&S.

--The Best of Hagar the Horrible. 240p. 1985. pap. 10.95 (ISBN 0-03-005599-7). HR&W.

--Brung 'Em Back Alive. 128p. 1983. pap. 1.95 (ISBN 0-441-31448-1). Ace Bks.

--Face Stuffer's Anonymous. (Hagar the Horrible Ser.: No. 9). 128p. 1985. pap. 1.95 (ISBN 0-8125-6784-6). Tor Bks.

--Hagar, No. 4. (Illus.). 128p. (Orig.). 1983. pap. 1.95 (ISBN 0-8125-6734-X, Pinnacle Bks). Tor Bks.

--Hagar at Work, No. 7. (Hagar Ser.: No. 7). 128p. (Orig.). 1985. pap. 1.95 (ISBN 0-8125-6749-8). Tor Bks.

--Hagar the Horrible, No. 1. 128p. 1983. pap. 1.75 (ISBN 0-448-16883-9, Pub. by Tempo). Ace Bks.

--Hagar the Horrible & the Golden Maiden. 128p. (Orig.). 1983. pap. 1.95 (ISBN 0-523-49046-1, Pinnacle Bks). Tor Bks.

--Hagar the Horrible: Animal Haus. 128p. 1983. pap. 1.75 (ISBN 0-686-87719-5). Ace Bks.

--Hagar the Horrible: Born Leader. 128p. (gr. 3 up). 1983. pap. 1.75 (ISBN 0-441-31446-5, Tempo). Ace Bks.

--Hagar the Horrible: Hagar's Knight Out. 128p. 1984. pap. 1.75 (ISBN 0-441-31455-4). Ace Bks.

--Hagar the Horrible: Hagar's Knight Out. 128p. 1985. pap. 1.95 (ISBN 0-441-31462-7); pap. text ed. 2.25 (ISBN 0-317-31754-7). Ace Bks.

--Hagar the Horrible: Helga's Revenge, No. 14. 128p. 1983. pap. 1.95 (ISBN 0-441-31453-8). Ace Bks.

--Hagar the Horrible: Horns of Plenty. 128p. (Orig.). 1985. pap. 1.95 (ISBN 0-8125-6786-2, Dist. by Warner Pub Services & St. Martin). Tor Bks.

--Hagar the Horrible: My Feet Are Really Drunk. (Hagar the Horrible Ser.: No. 10). 128p. (gr. 3 up). 1983. pap. 1.75 (ISBN 0-448-17009-4). Ace Bks.

--Hagar the Horrible, No. 12: Midnight Munchies. (Illus.). 128p. 1983. pap. 1.75 (Pub. by Tempo). Ace Bks.

--Hagar the Horrible, No. 13: Happy Hour, No. 13. 128p. 1984. pap. 1.95 (ISBN 0-441-31456-2). Ace Bks.

--Hagar the Horrible, No. 16: Excuse Me. 128p. 1984. pap. 1.95 (ISBN 0-441-31457-0, Pub. by Charter Bks). Ace Bks.

--Hagar the Horrible, No. 17: Have You Been Uptight Lately? 128p. 1985. pap. 1.95 (ISBN 0-441-31458-9, Pub. by Charter Bks). Ace Bks.

--Hagar the Horrible, No. 2. 1983. pap. 1.75 (ISBN 0-441-31550-X, Tempo). Ace Bks.

--Hagar the Horrible, No. 3: On the Loose. (Illus.). 128p. (Orig.). 1983. pap. 1.75 (ISBN 0-448-16885-5, Tempo). Ace Bks.

--Hagar the Horrible Puzzlers. 128p. (gr. 5 up). 1982. pap. 1.75 (ISBN 0-448-15531-1, Pub. by Tempo). Ace Bks.

--Hagar the Horrible: Sacking Paris on a Budget. (Tor Bks.). (Orig.). 1983. pap. 1.95 (ISBN 0-523-49045-3, Hagar II). Pinnacle Bks.

--Hagar the Horrible: The Brutish Are Coming. (Hagar the Horrible Cartoons Ser.: No. 4). 128p. (gr. 5 up). 1983. pap. 1.75 (ISBN 0-448-16886-3, Tempo). Ace Bks.

--Hagar the Horrible: The Simple Life, No. 13. 128p. 1984. pap. 1.95 (ISBN 0-441-31454-6). Ace Bks.

--Hear No Evil. (Hagar Ser.: No. 5). 128p. (Orig.). 1984. pap. 1.95 (ISBN 0-8125-6739-0, Pinnacle Bks). Tor Bks.

--Horns of Plenty. (Hagar the Horrible: No. 18). 128p. 1985. pap. 1.95 (ISBN 0-441-31463-5). Ace Bks.

--Room for One More. (Hagar Ser.: No. 6). 128p. 1984. pap. 1.95 (ISBN 0-8125-6744-7). Tor Bks.

--The Very Best of Hagar the Horrible. 128p. 1982. pap. 4.95 (ISBN 0-671-44732-7, Wallaby). S&S.

--Vikings Are Fun. (Hagar the Horrible Ser.: No. 1). 128p. 1985. pap. 1.95 (ISBN 0-523-49039-9). Tor Bks.

Browne, Dik & Walker, Mort. Hi & Lois Family Ties. 256p. 1982. pap. 2.25 (ISBN 0-448-16973-8, Pub. by Tempo). Ace Bks.

--Hi & Lois in Darkest Suburbia. (Illus.). 1978. pap. 1.25 (ISBN 0-448-17113-9, Pub. by Tempo). Ace Bks.

--Mom, Where's My Homework? (Hi & Lois Ser.: No. 5). 288p. (Orig.). 1984. pap. 2.50 (ISBN 0-8125-6919-9). Tor Bks.

Browne, Dik, jt. auth. see Walker, Mort.

Browne, Dik B. Hagar the Horrible: On the Rack, No. 5. (Hagar the Horrible Cartoons Ser.). 128p. (gr. 8-12). 1983. pap. 1.75 (ISBN 0-448-16887-1, Tempo). Ace Bks.

Browne, Donald R. International Radio Broadcasting: The Limits of the Limitless Medium. LC 81-22707. 384p. 1982. 34.95 (ISBN 0-03-059619-X). Praeger.

Browne, Douglas & Tullet, Tom. Bernard Spilsbury: Famous Murder Cases of the Great Pathologist. 2nd ed. (Illus.). 442p. 1983. pap. 5.95 (ISBN 0-586-05574-6, Pub. by Granada England). Academy Chi Pubs.

Browne, Douglas G. The Rise of Scotland Yard, a History of the Metropolitan Police. LC 73-6257. (Illus.). 392p. 1973. Repr. of 1956 ed. lib. bdg. 22.50x (ISBN 0-8371-6898-8, BRSY). Greenwood.

--Too Many Cousins. (Detective Stories Ser.). 192p. 1985. pap. 3.95 (ISBN 0-486-24774-0). Dover.

Browne, E. E. Life of Lowell. Repr. 20.00 (ISBN 0-8274-2934-7). R West.

Browne, E. G. Letters from Tabriz. (Illus.). 1985. text ed. 55.00 (ISBN 0-933770-41-3). Kalimat.

Browne, E. Martin. Making of T. S. Eliot's Plays. 1969. 52.50 (ISBN 0-521-07372-3). Cambridge U Pr.

Browne, E. Martin & Browne, Henzie. Two in One. (Illus.). 250p. 1981. 44.50 (ISBN 0-521-23254-6). Cambridge U Pr.

Browne, E. Martin, ed. Religious Drama, Vol. 2: 21 Medieval Mystery & Morality Plays. 11.25 (ISBN 0-8446-2793-3). Peter Smith.

Browne, Edgar. Phiz & Dickens. LC 72-39035. (Studies in Dickens, No. 52). 320p. 1972. Repr. of 1914 ed. lib. bdg. 49.95x (ISBN 0-8383-1391-4). Haskell.

Browne, Edmond C. The Coming of the Great Queen: A Narrative of the Acquisition of Burma. LC 77-87009. Repr. of 1888 ed. 38.50 (ISBN 0-404-16798-5). AMS Pr.

Browne, Edward G. Arabian Medicine. LC 79-2852. (Illus.). 138p. 1981. Repr. of 1962 ed. 17.50 (ISBN 0-8305-0028-6). Hyperion Conn.

--Literary History of Persia, 4 Vols. 1928. 75.00 ea. Vol. 1 (ISBN 0-521-04344-1). Vol. 2 (ISBN 0-521-04345-X). Vol. 3 (ISBN 0-521-04346-8). Vol. 4. Cambridge U Pr.

--Persian Revolution of 1905-09. 1966. Repr. 35.00x (ISBN 0-7146-1968-X, F Cass Co). Biblio Dist.

--The Press & Poetry of Modern Persia. (Illus.). xi, 357p. 1983. Repr. of 1914 ed. 35.00 (ISBN 0-933770-39-1). Kalimat.

--A Year Amongst the Persians: Impressions As to the Life, Character, & Thought of the People of Persia. 3rd ed. LC 83-45722. Repr. of 1950 ed. 61.50 (ISBN 0-404-20046-X). AMS Pr.

Browne, Edward G., tr. see Abdu'l-Baha.

Browne, Elizabeth W. The Right to Treatment Under Civil Commitment. 160p. 1975. 7.50 (ISBN 0-318-15773-X, T350). Natl Juv & Family Ct Judges.

Browne, Elizabeth W. & Penny, Lee. The Non-Delinquent Child in Juvenile Court: A Digest of Case Law. 100p. 1974. 4.00 (ISBN 0-318-15772-1, T301). Natl Juv & Family Ct Judges.

Browne, Ellen V. & Beck, Edward N., eds. Miss Aunt Nellie: The Autobiography of Nellie C. Cornish. LC 64-25730. (Illus.). 303p. 1965. 20.00x (ISBN 0-295-73848-0). U of Wash Pr.

Browne, Frances. Granny's Wonderful Chair. (gr. 4-6). 1985. pap. 2.25 (ISBN 0-14-035036-5, Puffin). Penguin.

--An Irish Granny's Magical Chair. (Illus.). 109p. (Orig.). (gr. 4 up). 1984. pap. 7.95 (ISBN 0-85342-719-4, Pub. by Mercir Pr Ireland). Irish Bks Media.

Browne, Frances G. Pests & Diseases of Forest Plantation Trees: An Annotated List of the Principle Species Occurring in the British Commonwealth. 1968. 98.00x (ISBN 0-19-854367-0). Oxford U Pr.

Browne, Francis F., ed. Bugle Echoes. facsimile ed. LC 75-116394. (Granger Index Reprint Ser). 1916. 18.00 (ISBN 0-8369-6135-8). Ayer Co Pubs.

--Golden Poems: By British & American Authors. facsimile ed. LC 73-152146. (Granger Index Reprint Ser). Repr. of 1881 ed. 26.50 (ISBN 0-8369-6249-4). Ayer Co Pubs.

Browne, G. F. The Venerable Bede: His Life & Writings. LC 76-52505. 1972. Repr. of 1919 ed. lib. bdg. 32.50 (ISBN 0-8414-1652-4). Folcroft.

Browne, Gary F., jt. auth. see Bee, Roger.

Browne, Gary L. Baltimore in the Nation, Seventeen Eighty-Nine to Eighteen Sixty-One. LC 79-13180. xiii, 349p. 1980. 29.00 (ISBN 0-8078-1397-4). U of NC Pr.

Browne, George E. A Book of R.L.S. 1919. Repr. 15.00 (ISBN 0-8274-1956-2). R West.

Browne, George H. Notes on Shakespeare's Versification. 4th ed. LC 78-39547. Repr. of 1901 ed. 11.50 (ISBN 0-404-01138-1). AMS Pr.

Browne, Gerald. Green Ice. pap. 2.95 (ISBN 0-440-13224-X). Dell.

Browne, Gerald A. Eleven Harrowhouse. LC 70-183382. 1972. 15.95 (ISBN 0-87795-024-5). Arbor Hse.

--Green Ice. 368p. 1984. pap. 3.95 (ISBN 0-425-07261-4). Berkley Pub.

--Hazard. LC 72-82171. 1973. 7.95 (ISBN 0-87795-040-7). Arbor Hse.

--Hazard. 320p. 1983. pap. 3.50 (ISBN 0-425-06279-1). Berkley Pub.

--Nineteen Purchase Street. 480p. 1983. pap. 3.95 (ISBN 0-425-07171-5). Berkley Pub.

--Slide. LC 75-40510. 1976. 8.95 (ISBN 0-87795-099-7). Arbor Hse.

--Slide. 224p. 1983. pap. 2.95 (ISBN 0-425-06294-5). Berkley Pub.

--Stone Five Eighty-Eight. 1985. 16.95 (ISBN 0-87795-539-5). Arbor Hse.

Browne, Gerald M. Michigan Papyri, Vol. XII. 125p. 1975. 24.00 (ISBN 0-88866-014-6, 31-00-14); members 16.00 (ISBN 0-317-35702-6). Scholars Pr GA.

--Michigan Papyri: P Mich. XII. (American Society of Papyrology Ser.). 24.00 (ISBN 0-89130-701-X, 31-00-14). Scholars Pr GA.

Browne, Geraldine A. Eleven Harrowhouse. 320p. 1985. pap. 3.95 (ISBN 0-425-07649-0). Berkley Pub.

Browne, H. Joseph Chamberlain. (Seminar Studies in History Ser.). 164p. 1974. pap. text ed. 6.25x (ISBN 0-582-35214-2). Longman.

Browne, Hablot K., tr. see Miller, Thomas.

Browne, Harold see Evans, John, pseud.

Browne, Harry. How I Found Freedom in an Unfree World. 1974. pap. 3.95 (ISBN 0-380-00423-2, 60119-2). Avon.

--New Profits from the Monetary Crisis. 1979. pap. 3.50 (ISBN 0-446-36021-X). Warner Bks.

--Suez & Sinai. LC 72-101536. (Flashpoints Ser.). pap. 34.00 (ISBN 0-317-09516-1, 2004920). Bks Demand UMI.

Browne, Henry J. The Catholic Church & the Knights of Labor. LC 76-6326. (Irish Americans Ser). (Illus.). 1976. Repr. of 1949 ed. 32.00 (ISBN 0-405-09323-3). Ayer Co Pubs.

Browne, Henzie, jt. auth. see Browne, E. Martin.

Browne, Howard. Thin Air. 192p. 1983. pap. 3.25 (ISBN 0-88184-058-0, Publishers Group West). Carroll & Graf.

Browne, Howard see Evans, John, pseud.

Browne, Irving. Elements of the Law of Domestic Relations & of Employer & Employed. xxi, 162p. 1981. Repr. of 1883 ed. lib. bdg. 22.50x. Rothman.

--Humorous Phases of the Law. (Legal Recreations Ser.: Vol. 1). vii, 190p. 1982. Repr. of 1876 ed. lib. bdg. 20.00x (ISBN 0-8377-0323-9). Rothman.

--The Judicial Interpretation of Common Words & Phrases. vii, 538p. 1983. Repr. of 1883 ed. lib. bdg. 35.00x (ISBN 0-8377-0337-9). Rothman.

--Law & Lawyers in Literature. xv, 413p. 1982. Repr. of 1883 ed. lib. bdg. 30.00x (ISBN 0-8377-0329-8). Rothman.

--Law & Lawyers in Literature. LC 82-82459. 413p. 1982. Repr. of 1883 ed. lib. bdg. 45.00x (ISBN 0-912004-22-3). W W Gaunt.

--Short Studies of Great Lawyers. iv, 382p. 1982. Repr. of 1878 ed. lib. bdg. 30.00x (ISBN 0-8377-0330-1). Rothman.

--A Treatise on the Admissibility of Parol Evidence in Respect to Written Instruments. xlviii, 510p. 1982. Repr. of 1893 ed. lib. bdg. 38.50x (ISBN 0-8377-0325-5). Rothman.

Browne, J. C., et al. Antenatal Care. 11th ed. LC 77-1557. (Illus.). 1978. 35.00 (ISBN 0-443-01476-0). Churchill.

Browne, J. H. Essays, Critical & Political, 2 vols. 1907. Repr. Set. 65.00 (ISBN 0-8274-2292-X). R West.

--Recollections: Literary & Political. 1917. Repr. 20.00 (ISBN 0-8274-3252-6). R West.

Browne, J. J. Management Analysis of Service Systems Operations. 432p. 1984. 34.00 (ISBN 0-444-00789-X, North-Holland). Elsevier.

Browne, J. Ross. The Coast Rangers. (Illus.). Repr. of 1862 ed. 7.50 (ISBN 0-686-73991-4). Acoma Bks.

--A Peep at Washoe & Washoe Revisited. (Illus.). Repr. of 1959 ed. 7.50 (ISBN 0-685-59750-4). Acoma Bks.

--A Trip to Bodie Bluff & the Dead Sea of the West-in 1863. Jones, William R., pref. by. (Illus.). 1978. pap. 2.95 (ISBN 0-89646-076-2). Outbooks.

Browne, James. The Letter Book of James Browne: Of Providence, Merchant, 1735-1738. facsimile ed. LC 75-164613. (Select Bibliographies Reprint Ser.). Repr. of 1929 ed. 12.00 (ISBN 0-8369-5897-7). Ayer Co Pubs.

Browne, Janet. Growing from Cuttings. (Concorde Gardening Bks.). (Illus.). 115p. 1981. pap. 7.95x (ISBN 0-8464-1213-6). Beekman Pubs.

--Growing from Cuttings. 108p. 1981. 25.00x (ISBN 0-7063-5993-3, Pub. by Ward Lock Ed England). State Mutual Bk.

--The Secular Ark: Studies in the History of Biogeography. LC 82-17497. (Illus.). 273p. 1983. text ed. 31.00x (ISBN 0-300-02460-6). Yale U Pr.

Browne, John. The Marchants Aviso, 1589. McGrath, Patrick, ed. (Kress Library Publications: No. 11). 1957. pap. 8.95x (ISBN 0-678-09906-5, Baker Lib). Kelley.

Browne, John H. South Africa: A Glance at Current Conditions. LC 70-76494. Repr. 19.25x (ISBN 0-8371-1091-2, BRS&). Greenwood.

Browne, John R. Adventures in the Apache Country: A Tour Through Arizona & Sonora, with Notes on the Silver Regions of Nevada. LC 72-9430. (The Far Western Frontier Ser.). (Illus.). 540p. 1973. Repr. of 1871 ed. 35.50 (ISBN 0-405-04961-7). Ayer Co Pubs.

--Adventures in the Apache Country: A Tour through Arizona & Sonora, 1864. LC 74-83332. pap. 78.30 (ISBN 0-317-28056-2, 2025551). Bks Demand UMI.

--Report of the Debates in the Convention of California on the Formation of the State Constitution, in Sept. & Oct., 1849. LC 72-9431. (The Far Western Frontier Ser.). 532p. 1973. Repr. of 1850 ed. 36.50 (ISBN 0-405-04962-5). Ayer Co Pubs.

--Yusef: The Journey of the Frangi; a Crusade in the East. Davis, Moshe, ed. LC 77-70686. (America & the Holy Land Ser.). (Illus.). 1977. Repr. of 1853 ed. lib. bdg. 24.00x (ISBN 0-405-10232-1). Ayer Co Pubs.

Browne, Joseph W. Personal Dignity. LC 82-18944. 1983. 15.00 (ISBN 0-8022-2409-1). Philos Lib.

Browne, Jr. Circuit Interruption: Theory & Techniques. 672p. 1984. 79.50 (ISBN 0-8247-7177-X). Dekker.

Browne, Juanita K. Nuggets of Nevada County History. LC 83-23781. (Illus.). xii, 143p. (Orig.). 1983. pap. 9.00 (ISBN 0-915641-00-3). Nevada County Hist Society.

Browne, Junius H. Four Years in Secessia. LC 72-125681. (American Journalists Ser). 1970. Repr. of 1865 ed. 22.00 (ISBN 0-405-01656-5). Ayer Co Pubs.

--The Great Metropolis: A Mirror of New York... facsimile ed. LC 75-1833. (Leisure Class in America Ser.). (Illus.). 1975. Repr. of 1869 ed. 46.50x (ISBN 0-405-06902-2). Ayer Co Pubs.

Browne, Kathryn W., jt. auth. see Gordon, Ann.

Browne, Kevin, et al, eds. Doctor-Patient Relationship. 3rd ed. 145p. 1983. pap. text ed. 11.50 (ISBN 0-443-02375-1). Churchill.

Browne, Kingsbury. Federal Tax Aspects of Open-Space Preservation. LC 80-8637. Date not set. price not set (ISBN 0-669-04336-2). Lexington Bks.

Browne, L. In the Track of the Bookworm. 1976. lib. bdg. 59.95 (ISBN 0-8490-2046-8). Gordon Pr.

Browne, Lewis. That Man Heine: A Biography. 420p. 1984. Repr. of 1927 ed. lib. bdg. 25.00 (ISBN 0-89760-199-8). Telegraph Bks.

Browne, Lewis & Weihl, Elsa. That Man Heine: A Biography. 420p. Date not set. Repr. of 1927 ed. lib. bdg. 30.00 (ISBN 0-8492-3601-0). R West.

Browne, Louis & Romero, Adrian. Manual de Investigaciones Biologicas. (Span.). 1979. pap. text ed. 6.95 (ISBN 0-8403-1949-5, 40194901). Kendall-Hunt.

Browne, M., ed. Ferment in the Ukraine. 267p. 1973. write for info. Ukrainian Pol.

Browne, M. Neil & Hoag, John. Understanding Economic Analysis. 164p. 1983. 11.43scp (ISBN 0-205-07795-1, 097795). Allyn.

Browne, M. Neil & Keeley, Stuart M. Asking the Right Questions: A Guide to Critical Thinking. 2nd ed. 256p. 1986. pap. text ed. 12.95 (ISBN 0-13-049438-0). P-H.

Browne, M. Neil & Keely, Stuart M. Asking the Right Questions. 224p. 1981. pap. text ed. 11.95 (ISBN 0-13-049395-3). P-H.

Browne, Marmaduke E., tr. see Mozart, Wolfgang & Nicholas, John.

Browne, Martha G. Autobiography of a Female Slave. LC 71-92745. Repr. 25.00x (ISBN 0-8371-2194-9, GRS&, Pub. by Negro U Pr). Greenwood.

Browne, Matthew, pseud. Chaucer's England, 2 Vols. LC 74-113566. Repr. of 1869 ed. Set. 55.00 (ISBN 0-404-01139-X). AMS Pr.

Browne, Matthew. Chaucer's England, 2 Vols. 1984. Repr. of 1869 ed. Vol. 1, 317 pp. lib. bdg. 150.00 set (ISBN 0-89987-965-9). Vol. 2, 331 pp. Darby Books.

Browne, Merle L. Arousers. LC 74-80702. 1974. 6.95 (ISBN 0-87795-064-4). Arbor Hse.

Browne, Michael D. Smoke from the Fires. LC 84-72533. (Poetry Ser.). 80p. 1985. 14.95 (ISBN 0-88748-006-3); pap. 6.95 (ISBN 0-88748-007-1). Carnegie-Mellon.

--Sun Exercises. LC 76-288. (Illus.). 1976. pap. 4.95 (ISBN 0-916320-02-2). Red Studio.

--The Sun Fetcher. LC 76-55070. (Poetry Ser). 1978. 8.95 (ISBN 0-915604-17-5); pap. 4.50 (ISBN 0-915604-10-8). Carnegie-Mellon.

Browne, Muriel. Exalt His Name: A Christmas Program. 1984. pap. 0.95 (ISBN 0-8024-3551-3). Moody.

Browne, Nick. The Rhetoric of Filmic Narration. Kirkpatrick, Diane, ed. LC 82-1905. (Studies in Cinema: No. 12). 120p. 1982. 39.95 (ISBN 0-8357-1296-6). UMI Res Pr.

Browne, Nina E. Bibliography of Nathaniel Hawthorne. 1967. Repr. of 1908 ed. 16.50 (ISBN 0-8337-0400-1). B Franklin.

--Bibliography of Nathaniel Hawthorne. 1905. 14.00 (ISBN 0-384-06005-6). Johnson Repr.

Browne, Pat, jt. ed. see Landrum, Larry.

Browne, Patrick. Civil & Natural History of Jamaica. LC 71-141130. (Research Library of Colonial Americana). (Illus.). 1972. Repr. of 1756 ed. 66.00 (ISBN 0-405-03276-5). Ayer Co Pubs.

Browne, Patrick S. Basic Facts in Orthopaedics. (Illus.). 352p. 1981. pap. text ed. 15.95 (ISBN 0-632-00718-4, B 0877-5). Mosby.

Browne, Peter. The Procedure, Extent & Limits of Human Understanding, 1728. Wellek, Rene, ed. LC 75-11201. (British Philosophers & Theologians of the 17th & 18th Centuriy Ser.: Vol. 8). 487p. 1976. Repr. of 1728 ed. lib. bdg. 51.00 (ISBN 0-8240-1757-9). Garland Pub.

--Things Divine & Supernatural Conceived by Analogy with Things Natural & Human. Wellek, Rene, ed. LC 75-11203. (British Philosophers & Theologians of the 17th & 18th Centuries: Vol. 9). 1976. Repr. of 1733 ed. lib. bdg. 51.00 (ISBN 0-8240-1758-7). Garland Pub.

Browne, Peter S. Security: Checklist for Computer Center Self-Audits. LC 79-56012. (Illus.). 189p. 1979. pap. 29.95. AFIPS Pr.

Browne, R. C. The Chemistry & Therapy of Industrial Pulmonary Diseases. 144p. 1966. 14.75x (ISBN 0-398-00242-8). C C Thomas.

Browne, R. D. & Larsen, B. A. Poking Fun at the G-Spot. (Illus.). 72p. (Orig.). 1984. pap. 3.95 (ISBN 0-915653-00-1). Art in Motion.

Browne, R. M., jt. auth. see Marsland, E. A.

Browne, R. M., et al. A Radiological Atlas of Diseases of the Teeth & Jaws. (Illus.). 262p. 1983. 56.00 (ISBN 0-471-25616-1, 991600010, Pub. by John Wiley & Sons England). Heyden.

Browne, Ray, ed. A Night with the Hants & Other Alabama Experiences. LC 76-43449. 1976. 12.95 (ISBN 0-87972-075-1); pap. 6.95 (ISBN 0-87972-167-7). Bowling Green Univ.

Browne, Ray B. Forbidden Fruits: Taboos & Tabooism in Culture. LC 84-71938. 192p. 1984. 21.95 (ISBN 0-317-14769-2); pap. 9.95 (ISBN 0-87972-256-8). Bowling Green Univ.

--Objects of Special Devotion: Fetishes & Fetishism in Popular Culture. LC 81-85521. 1982. 21.95 (ISBN 0-87972-191-X); pap. 11.95 (ISBN 0-87972-192-8). Bowling Green Univ.

--Popular Abstracts. 1978. 12.95 (ISBN 0-87972-166-9); pap. 6.95 (ISBN 0-87972-165-0). Bowling Green Univ.

--Rituals & Ceremonies in Popular Culture. LC 80-83188. 1981. 21.95 (ISBN 0-87972-160-X); pap. 10.95 (ISBN 0-87972-161-8). Bowling Green Univ.

Browne, Ray B. & Fishwick, Marshall W. The Hero in Transition. LC 83-71003. 1983. 22.95 (ISBN 0-87972-237-1); pap. 10.95 (ISBN 0-87972-238-X). Bowling Green Univ.

Browne, Ray B., jt. auth. see Hoppenstand, Gary.

Browne, Ray B., ed. The Alabama Folk Lyric: A Study in Origins & Media of Dissemination. LC 78-61076. 1979. 25.00 (ISBN 0-87972-129-4). Bowling Green Univ.

--Popular Culture & Curricula. rev. ed. 101p. pap. 5.95 (ISBN 0-87972-002-6). Bowling Green Univ.

Browne, Ray B., ed. see Twain, Mark.

Browne, Ray B., et al, eds. Celtic Cross. facs. ed. LC 78-121453. (Essay Index Reprint Ser). 1964. 21.00 (ISBN 0-8369-1744-8). Ayer Co Pubs.

--New Voices in American Studies. LC 66-63485. (Illus.). 166p. 1966. 4.75 (ISBN 0-911198-10-5). Purdue U Pr.

--Heroes of Popular Culture. LC 72-88413. 1972. casebound o.p. 12.95 (ISBN 0-87972-044-1); pap. 5.95 (ISBN 0-87972-045-X). Bowling Green Univ.

Browne, Richmond, ed. Music Theory: Special Topics. LC 80-70592. 1981. 29.50 (ISBN 0-12-138080-7). Acad Pr.

Browne, Robert S. & Cummings, Robert J. The Lagos Plan of Action versus the Berg Report. 2nd. ed. LC 85-71413. (Monographs in African Studies). 216p. 1985. 20.00 (ISBN 0-931494-72-9); pap. 10.50 (ISBN 0-931494-74-5). Brunswick Pub.

--The Lagos Plan of Action Versus the Berg Report: Contemporary Issues in African Economic Development. LC 83-72686. (Monographs in African Studies). 210p. 1983. 19.95 (ISBN 0-931494-44-3); pap. 13.50. Brunswick Pub.

Browne, Roland A. The Rose-Lover's Guide: A Practical Handbook for Rose Gardening. LC 73-92067. (Illus.). 256p. 1983. pap. 9.95 (ISBN 0-689-70642-1, 291). Atheneum.

Browne, Roland A., tr. see Ogier VIII.

Browne, Rollo. An Aboriginal Family. LC 84-19447. (Families the World Over Ser.). (Illus.). 32p. (gr. 2-5). 1985. PLB 8.95 (ISBN 0-8225-1655-1). Lerner Pubns.

Browne, Sarah. The Best of Vegetarian Cuisine. 1985. 19.95 (ISBN 0-394-54374-2). Random.

Browne, Scribner. Tidal Swings of the Stock Market. (Illus.). 131p. 1980. 69.85x (ISBN 0-918968-75-5). Inst Econ Finan.

Browne, Steven E. Getting That Job in the Motion Picture, Cable & Television Industry & What the Jobs Are. (Illus.). 201p. 1983. comb bdg. 10.00 (ISBN 0-914499-01-7). Wilton Place.

--The Video Tape Post-Production Primer. (Illus.). 218p. 1983. 25.00 (ISBN 0-914499-00-9). Wilton Place.

--The Video Tape Post Production Primer. (Illus.). 216p. 1984. 25.00 (ISBN 0-914499-02-5). Wilton Place.

Browne, T. & Johnson, Samuel. Christian Morals. 2nd ed. Roberts, S. C., ed. 1927. 15.00 (ISBN 0-527-12200-9). Kraus Repr.

Browne, Terry. Playwrights' Theatre: The English Stage Company at the Royal Court. 112p. 1975. 15.00x (ISBN 0-273-00757-2); pap. 7.00x (ISBN 0-273-00758-0). Wesleyan U Pr.

--Playwright's Theatre: The English Stage Company of the Royal Court. 160p. 1975. 12.00x (ISBN 0-8464-1119-9). Beekman Pubs.

Browne, Thomas. Hydriotaphia (Urn Burial) Huntley, Frank L., ed. Bd. with The Garden of Cyrus. LC 66-16496. (Crofts Classics Ser.). 1966. pap. text ed. 3.50x (ISBN 0-88295-017-7). Harlan Davidson.

--Hydriotaphia, Urne-Buriall, or, a Discourse of the Sepulchrall Urnes Lately Found in Norfolk. Together with the Garden of Cyrus, or the Quincunciall Lozenge, or Network Plantations of the Ancients, Artificially, Naturally Mystically Considered. Kastenbaum, Robert, ed. LC 76-19562. (Death & Dying Ser.). 1977. Repr. of 1927 ed. lib. bdg. 17.00x (ISBN 0-405-09558-9). Ayer Co Pubs.

--Religio Medici, Hydriotaphia & the Garden of Cyrus. Robbins, R. H., ed. 1972. pap. 7.95x (ISBN 0-19-871064-X). Oxford U Pr.

--Selected Writings of Sir Thomas Browne. Keynes, Geoffrey, ed. LC 68-55536. (Illus.). 1970. pap. 3.25 (ISBN 0-226-07636-9, P347, Phoen). U of Chicago Pr.

--Sir Thomas Browne's Pseudodoxia Epidemica, 2 vols. Robbins, R. H., ed. (Oxford English Texts Ser.). (Illus.). 1981. 174.00x (ISBN 0-19-812706-5). Oxford U Pr.

--Works & Life of Thomas Browne, 4 Vols. Wilkin, Simon, ed. LC 68-57225. Repr. of 1836 ed. Set. 190.00 (ISBN 0-404-01150-0); 47.50 ea. Vol. 1 (ISBN 0-404-01151-9). Vol. 2 (ISBN 0-404-01152-7). Vol. 3 (ISBN 0-404-01153-5). Vol. 4 (ISBN 0-404-01154-3). AMS Pr.

Browne, Thomas R. & Feldman, Robert G., eds. Epilepsy: Diagnosis & Management. 376p. 1983. text ed. 39.50 (ISBN 0-316-11114-7). Little.

Browne, Tom. Rivers & People. LC 82-50394. (Nature's Landscape Ser.). 91p. PLB 15.96 (ISBN 0-382-06671-5). Silver.

Browne, Turner & Partnow, Elaine. Macmillan Biographical Encyclopedia of Photographic Artists & Innovators. LC 82-4664. (Illus.). 872p. 1983. 45.00 (ISBN 0-02-517500-9). Macmillan.

Browne, Turner, photos by. Louisiana Cajuns. LC 77-24171. (Illus.). 1977. 16.95 (ISBN 0-8071-0363-2); pap. 6.95 (ISBN 0-8071-0853-7). La State U Pr.

Browne, W. A. What Asylums Were, Are, & Ought to Be: Being the Substance of Five Lectures Delivered Before the Managers of the Montrose Royal Lunatic Asylum. LC 75-16691. (Classics in Psychiatry Ser.). 1976. Repr. 19.00x (ISBN 0-405-07421-2). Ayer Co Pubs.

Browne, Waldo R. Books & the Quiet Life. 59.95 (ISBN 0-87968-776-2). Gordon Pr.

Browne, Waldo R., ed. Joys of the Road. facsimile ed. LC 79-107686. (Essay Index Reprint Ser.). 1911. 14.00 (ISBN 0-8369-1491-0). Ayer Co Pubs.

Browne, Waldo R., ed. see Barnum, Phineas T.

Browne, Walter L., ed. Documents on Politics & Political Parties Under the French Mandate, 1920-1936. (The Political History of Lebanon: Vol. 1). 1976. 27.95x (ISBN 0-89712-022-1). Documentary Pubns.

--Documents on the French Mandate & World War II, 1936-1943. (The Political History of Lebanon, 1920-1950: Vol. 2). 1977. lib. bdg. 27.95x (ISBN 0-89712-023-X). Documentary Pubns.

--Lebanon's Struggle for Independence, 2 vols. 1980. Set. 55.90x (ISBN 0-89712-025-6). Documentary Pubns.

Browne, William. Whole Works, 2 vols. in 1. Hazlitt, W. Carew, ed. 1868-69. Repr. 54.00 (ISBN 3-4870-2767-4). Adlers Foreign Bks.

--The Whole Works: 2 Vols. in 1. Hazlitt, W. C., ed. (English Literary Reference Ser.). 1969. Repr. of 1869 ed. 35.00 (ISBN 0-384-06015-3). Johnson Repr.

Browne, William & Hadwiger, Don, eds. Rural Policy. (Orig.). 1982. pap. 8.00 (ISBN 0-918592-55-0). Policy Studies.

Browne, William, jt. ed. see Hadwiger, Don.

Browne, William H. Maryland, the History of a Palatinate. rev. & enl. ed. LC 72-3758. (American Commonwealths: No. 3). Repr. of 1904 ed. 35.00 (ISBN 0-404-57203-0). AMS Pr.

--Witty Sayings. 304p. 1981. Repr. of 1878 ed. lib. bdg. 50.00 (ISBN 0-89984-073-6). Century Bookbindery.

--Witty Sayings by Witty People. LC 74-15727. (Popular Culture in America Ser.). 304p. 1975. Repr. 25.50x (ISBN 0-405-06363-6). Ayer Co Pubs.

--Witty Sayings by Witty People. Repr. of 1878 ed. 17.50 (ISBN 0-8274-4148-7). R West.

Browne, William H., jt. auth. see Johnston, Richard M.

Browne, William P. Politics, Programs, & Bureaucrats. (National University Publications, Political Science Ser.). 184p. 1980. 18.95x (ISBN 0-8046-9263-7, Pub. by Kennikat). Assoc Faculty Pr.

Browne, William P. & Hadwiger, Don F., eds. Rural Policy Problems: Changing Dimensions. LC 81-48069. (A Policy Studies Organization Book). (Illus.). 272p. 1982. 32.50x (ISBN 0-669-05242-6). Lexington Bks.

Browne, William P. & Olson, Laura K., eds. Aging & Public Policy: The Politics of Growing Old in America. LC 82-6138. (Contributions in Political Science Ser.: No. 83). (Illus.). 304p. 1983. lib. bdg. 35.00 (ISBN 0-313-22855-8, BAG/). Greenwood.

Browne, William T. Poems, 2 Vols. 1971. Repr. of 1894 ed. Set. 69.00x (ISBN 0-403-00846-8). Scholarly.

Brownell, Ada N. Confessions of a Pentecostal. LC 77-92887. 112p. 1978. pap. 1.25 (ISBN 0-88243-476-4, 02-0476). Gospel Pub.

Brownell, Baker. Art is Action. facsimile ed. LC 73-90616. (Essay Index Reprint Ser.). 1939. 17.00 (ISBN 0-8369-1250-0). Ayer Co Pubs.

--Art Is Action. LC 72-183136. (Essay & General Literature Index Reprint Ser). 232p. 1971. Repr. of 1939 ed. 21.00x (ISBN 0-8046-1690-6, Pub by Kennikat). Assoc Faculty Pr.

--College & the Community: A Critical Study of Higher Education. LC 70-98214. Repr. of 1952 ed. lib. bdg. 15.00x (ISBN 0-8371-2879-X, BRCD). Greenwood.

Brownell, Baker, ed. see Slosson, Edwin E.

Brownell, Blaine A. The Urban Ethos in the South, 1920-1930. LC 74-82003. pap. 64.80 (ISBN 0-317-28674-9, 2055299). Bks Demand UMI.

--Using Microcomputers. 1985. 16.95 (ISBN 0-8039-2291-4). Sage.

Brownell, Blaine A., jt. auth. see Goldfield, David R.

Brownell, Blaine A., jt. auth. see Mowry, George E.

Brownell, Blaine A. & Goldfield, David R., eds. The City in Southern History: The Growth of Urban Civilization in the South. (Interdisciplinary Urban Ser.). 1976. pap. 14.00x (ISBN 0-8046-9160-6, Pub. by Kennikat). Assoc Faculty Pr.

Brownell, C. L. Scale for Measuring the Antero-Posterior Posture of Ninth Grade Boys. LC 74-176601. (Columbia University. Teachers College. Contributions to Education: No. 325). Repr. of 1928 ed. 22.50 (ISBN 0-404-55325-7). AMS Pr.

Brownell, David. A Book of Great Composers: Book 1, Bk. 1. (Illus.). 1978. pap. 2.95 (ISBN 0-88388-058-X). Bellerophon Bks.

--Hemmings' Vintage Auto Almanac. 6th ed. LC 76-649715. 320p. 1984. pap. 9.95 (ISBN 0-917808-07-X). Hemmings.

--Ludwig van Beethoven. (Illus.). 64p. 1980. pap. 3.50 (ISBN 0-88388-057-1). Bellerophon Bks.

Brownell, David & Knill, Harry, eds. Kings & Queens of England. 1978. pap. 3.50 (ISBN 0-88388-053-9). Bellerophon Bks.

Brownell, Emery A. Legal Aid in the United States: A Study of the Availability of Lawyers Services for Persons Unable to Pay Fees. LC 77-141417. (Illus.). xxiv, 333p. 1971. Repr. of 1951 ed. lib. bdg. 26.50x (ISBN 0-8371-4689-5, BRLE). Greenwood.

Brownell, George A. The Origin & Development of the National Security Agency. 98p. 1981. pap. text ed. 16.80 (ISBN 0-89412-054-9). Aegean Park Pr.

Brownell, George B. Reincarnation. 153p. 1981. pap. 7.00 (ISBN 0-89540-107-X, SB-107). Sun Pub.

Brownell, George G. Travel Agency Management. LC 75-15476. 1975. pap. 12.50x (ISBN 0-87651-206-6). Southern U Pr.

Brownell, Gertrude, ed. see Brownell, William C.

Brownell, Gertrude H. William Cary Brownell: An Anthology of His Writings. 1933. Repr. 30.00 (ISBN 0-8274-3703-X). R West.

Brownell, Henry H. War-Lyrics & Other Poems. LC 72-4953. (The Romantic Tradition in American Literature Ser.). 256p. 1972. 19.00 (ISBN 0-405-04625-1). Ayer Co Pubs.

Brownell, John A. A Directory of Selected Resources for the Study of English in Japan. LC 76-10955. 1976. pap. text ed. 3.95x (ISBN 0-8248-0463-5). UH Pr.

Brownell, Jospeh W. Outline Maps for World Regional Geography. 1981. pap. 1.50 (ISBN 0-910042-40-3). Allegheny.

Brownell, Judith L. Building Active Listening Skills. (Illus.). 224p. 1986. pap. text ed. 16.95 (ISBN 0-13-085960-5). P-H.

Brownell, Lloyd E. & Young, Edwin H. Process Equipment Design: Vessel Design. LC 59-5882. 408p. 1959. 74.95 (ISBN 0-471-11319-0, Pub by Wiley-Interscience). Wiley.

Brownell, Morris R. Alexander Pope & the Arts of Georgian England. (Illus.). 1978. text ed. 64.00x (ISBN 0-19-817338-5). Oxford U Pr.

Brownell, Salomon. Critical Analyses in English Renaissance Drama: A Bibliographic Guide. 2nd ed. LC 84-48867. (Humanities Ser.). 200p. 1985. lib. bdg. 27.00 (ISBN 0-8240-8739-9). Garland Pub.

Brownell, Tom. How to Restore Your Collector Car. (Illus.). 320p. 1984. pap. 18.95 (ISBN 0-87938-174-4). Motorbooks Intl.

Brownell, W. C. Democratic Distinction in America. 1927. Repr. 10.00 (ISBN 0-8274-2162-1). R West.

Brownell, W. E. Structural Clay Products. LC 76-40216. (Applied Mineralogy Ser: Vol. 9). 1976. 61.00 (ISBN 0-387-81382-9). Springer-Verlag.

Brownell, William A. Arithmetical Abstractions: The Movement Toward Conceptual Maturity under Differing Systems of Instructions. LC 67-65751. (University of California Publications in Education Ser.: Vol. 17). pap. 58.00 (ISBN 0-317-11014-4, 2021359). Bks Demand UMI.

Brownell, William C. Criticism: An Essay on Form, Function & Method. LC 67-27579. 1914. Repr. 12.00x (ISBN 0-8046-0051-1, Pub. by Kennikat). Assoc Faculty Pr.

--Genius of Style. LC 76-153204. 1971. Repr. of 1924 ed. 19.50x (ISBN 0-8046-1514-4, Pub. by Kennikat). Assoc Faculty Pr.

--Victorian Prose Masters. 59.95 (ISBN 0-8490-1260-0). Gordon Pr.

--Victorian Prose Masters. LC 79-86000. 1969. Repr. of 1901 ed. 19.50x (ISBN 0-8046-0548-3, Pub by Kennikat). Assoc Faculty Pr.

--Victorian Prose Masters: Thackeray-Carlyle-George Eliot-Matthew Arnold-Ruskin-George Meredith. LC 72-108771. (BCL Ser. I). Repr. of 1901 ed. 21.00 (ISBN 0-404-01142-X). AMS Pr.

--William Crary Brownell, an Anthology of His Writings. Brownell, Gertrude, ed. LC 70-144909. 1971. Repr. of 1933 ed. 16.00 (ISBN 0-403-00847-6). Scholarly.

Browneye, Ray. Through African Skies. 136p. 1983. pap. 5.95 (ISBN 0-8010-0853-0). Baker Bk.

Brownfield, Janice. Reporter vs Publisher: What Journalism Professors Don't Tell You. LC 85-70671. 240p. (Orig.). 1985. pap. 14.95 (ISBN 0-9614521-7-X). Alpenstock.

Brownhill, R. J. Education & the Nature of Knowledge. (New Patterns of Learning Ser.). 135p. 1983. 27.25 (ISBN 0-7099-0654-4, Pub. by Croom Helm Ltd). Longwood Pub Group.

Browning. The Loss Rate Concept in Safety Engineering. (Occupational Safety & Health Ser.: Vol. 6). 176p. 1980. 29.75 (ISBN 0-8247-1249-8). Dekker.

Browning, A. W. Early Quarter Dollars. LC 77-74032. (Illus.). 1977. Repr. of 1925 ed. lib. bdg. 15.00 (ISBN 0-915262-15-0). S J Durst.

Browning, Al. Bowl, Bama, Bowl. LC 77-91209. (College Sports Ser.). 1981. 10.95 (ISBN 0-87397-138-8). Strode.

Browning, Anne. Anne's Back Door Cookbook: With Helpful Hints for the Hypersensitive. (Illus.). vii, 70p. (Orig.). 1985. pap. 6.99 (ISBN 0-933145-00-4). StoneGround Pub.

Browning, B. L. Analysis of Paper, No. 2. rev. ed. (Illus.). 1977. 65.00 (ISBN 0-8247-6408-0). Dekker.

Browning, B. L., ed. The Chemistry of Wood. LC 74-23593. 700p. 1975. Repr. of 1963 ed. 46.50 (ISBN 0-88275-245-6). Krieger.

Browning, Bertie L. Methods of Wood Chemistry, 2 vols. LC 66-28537. (Illus.). Vol. 1. pap. 101.50 (ISBN 0-317-10830-1, 2006346); Vol. 2. pap. 130.30 (ISBN 0-317-10831-X). Bks Demand UMI.

Browning, C. E., ed. Composite Materials: Quality Assurance & Processing. LC 82-72889. (Special Technical Publications Ser.: No. 797). 173p. 1983. 19.95 (ISBN 0-8031-0234-8, 04-797000-30). ASTM.

Browning, Carl H. Bacteriology. 1920. 10.00 (ISBN 0-8274-4188-6). R West.

Browning, Charles H. How to Build a Practice Clientele Using Key Referral Sources: A Sourcebook. 76p. 1983. pap. 12.95 (ISBN 0-911663-03-7). Duncliffs Intl.

--How to Turn the Tables on Bill Collectors, Quickly & Easily. 31p. 1984. pap. 7.00 (ISBN 0-317-06831-8). Duncliffs Intl.

--Private Practice Handbook: The Tools, Tactics & Techniques for Successful Practice Development. 2nd ed. 238p. 1982. 24.95 (ISBN 0-911663-02-9); pap. 21.95 (ISBN 0-911663-01-0). Duncliffs Intl.

--Some Colonial Dames of Royal Descent: Pedigrees Showing Lineal Descent from Kings of Some Members of the National Society of the Colonial Dames of America, & of the Order of the Crown. LC 76-81187. 360p. 1969. Repr. of 1900 ed. 20.00 (ISBN 0-8063-0057-4). Genealog Pub.

Browning, Christine. Guide to Effective Software Technical Writing. (Illus.). 140p. 1984. 23.95 (ISBN 0-13-369463-1); pap. text ed. 16.95 (ISBN 0-13-369455-0). P-H.

Browning, Christopher R. Fateful Months: Essays on the Emergence of the Final Solution, 1941-1942. LC 84-9089. (Illus.). 100p. 1985. text ed. 29.50x (ISBN 0-8419-0967-9). Holmes & Meier.

--The Final Solution & the German Foreign Office. LC 78-8996. 276p. 1978. text ed. 35.00x (ISBN 0-8419-0403-0). Holmes & Meier.

Browning, David R. Physical Sciences: Level I. LC 77-27083. (Longman Technician Ser.). pap. 62.30 (ISBN 0-317-10981-2, 2019607). Bks Demand UMI.

Browning, David R. & McKenzie-Smith, I. Engineering Science for Techniques, Level I. LC 77-30749. (Longman Tehnician Ser. in Mathematics & Sciences). pap. 46.30 (ISBN 0-317-27765-0, 2023236). Bks Demand UMI.

Browning, Dixie. Island on the Hill. (Nightingale Ser.). 229p. 1983. pap. 9.95 (ISBN 0-8161-3542-8, Large Print Bks). G K Hall.

Browning, Don S. The Moral Context of Pastoral Care. LC 76-5858. 144p. 1983. pap. 8.95 (ISBN 0-664-24483-1). Westminster.

--Pluralism & Personality: William James & Some Contemporary Cultures of Psychology. LC 78-75196. 280p. 26.50 (ISBN 0-8387-2265-2). Bucknell U Pr.

--Religious Ethics & Pastoral Care. LC 83-5589. (Theology & Pastoral Care Ser.). 128p. 1983. pap. 6.95 (ISBN 0-8006-1725-8, 1-1725). Fortress.

Browning, Don S., ed. Practical Theology: The Emerging Field in Theology, Chruch & World. LC 82-47739. 128p. (Orig.). 1982. pap. 7.64i (ISBN 0-06-061153-7, RD-410, HarpR). Har-Row.

Browning, Edgar K. Redistribution & the Welfare System. LC 75-15155. (Orig.). 1975. pap. 5.25 (ISBN 0-8447-3170-6). Am Enterprise.

Browning, Edgar K. & Browning, Jacquelene M. Microeconomic Theory & Application. 1982. text ed. 27.95 (ISBN 0-316-11223-2); teacher's manual avail. (ISBN 0-316-11227-5); study guide 8.95 (ISBN 0-316-11229-1). Little.

Browning, Edgar K. & Browning, Jacqueline M. Public Finance & the Price System. 2nd ed. 500p. 1983. text ed. write for info. (ISBN 0-02-315660-0). Macmillan.

Browning, Edgar K. & Johnson, William R. Distribution of the Tax Burden. 1979. pap. 4.25 (ISBN 0-8447-3349-0). Am Enterprise.

Browning, Elizabeth B. Aurora Leigh. 400p. 1979. lib. bdg. 14.95 (ISBN 0-915864-86-X); pap. 5.95 (ISBN 0-915864-85-1). Academy Chi Pubs.

--Sonnets from the Portuguese. (Classics Ser.). (gr. 9 up). slip case 4.95 (ISBN 0-442-82509-9). Peter Pauper.

Browning, Elizabeth Barrett. The Complete Poetical Works. LC 75-14491. (Illus.). xviii, 548p. 1972. Repr. of 1900 ed. 69.00x (ISBN 0-403-00848-4). Scholarly.

--Complete Works of Elizabeth Barrett Browning, 6 Vols. Porter, Charlotte & Clarke, Helen A., eds. LC 74-148759. Repr. of 1900 ed. Set. 240.00 (ISBN 0-404-08840-6). AMS Pr.

--The Earlier Poems of Elizabeth Barrett Browning: 1826-1833. 1978. Repr. of 1878 ed. lib. bdg. 30.00 (ISBN 0-8495-0332-9). Arden Lib.

--Essays on the Greek Christian Poets & the English Poets. LC 72-7041. (Essay Index Reprint Ser.). 1972. Repr. of 1863 ed. 19.00 (ISBN 0-8369-7273-2). Ayer Co Pubs.

--The Letters of Elizabeth Barrett Browning, 2 vols. Kenyon, Frederic G., ed. 942p. 1981. Repr. of 1897 ed. Set. lib. bdg. 75.00 (ISBN 0-89760-078-9). Telegraph Bks.

--The Letters of Elizabeth Barrett Browning to Mary Russell Mitford, 1836-1854, 3 vols. Raymond, Meredith B. & Sullivan, Mary R., eds. LC 82-51316. (Illus.). 1983. Set. 160.00x (ISBN 0-911459-00-6). Vol. 1, i-xliv, 432pp (ISBN 0-911459-01-4). Vol. 2, i-xii, 464 (ISBN 0-911459-02-2). Vol. 3, i-xii, 496 (ISBN 0-911459-03-0). Wedgestone Pr.

--Poetical Works of Elizabeth Barrett Browning. (Cambridge Editions Ser.). 1974. 22.95 (ISBN 0-395-18012-0). HM.

--Sonnets from the Portuguese. 1932. 10.53i (ISBN 0-06-010555-0, HarpT). Har-Row.

--Sonnets from the Portuguese. 4.95 (ISBN 0-88088-060-0). Peter Pauper.

--Sonnets from the Portuguese & Other Love Poems. LC 54-10779. (Illus.). 9.95 (ISBN 0-385-01463-5). Doubleday.

--Twenty-Two Unpublished Letters of Elizabeth Browning & Robert Browning: Addresssed to Henrietta & Arabella Mouton-Barrett. 1978. Repr. of 1935 ed. lib. bdg. 20.00 (ISBN 0-8495-0357-4). Arden Lib.

--Twenty-Two Unpublished Letters of Elizabeth Barrett Browning & Robert Browning. LC 75-163206. (Studies in Browning, No. 4). 1971. Repr. of 1935 ed. lib. bdg. 39.95x (ISBN 0-8383-1313-2). Haskell.

Browning, Elizabeth Barrett & Browning, Robert. Twenty-Two Unpublished Letters of Elizabeth Barrett Browning & Robert Browning Addressed to Henrietta & Arabella Moulton-Barrett. LC 75-44045. 1973. Repr. of 1935 ed. lib. bdg. 17.50 (ISBN 0-8414-3236-8). Folcroft.

Browning, Elizabeth Barrett, jt. auth. see Browning, Robert.

Browning, Ellen. Teaching Students with Severe Emotional & Learning Impairments. 1985. 30.00 (ISBN 0-205-07677-7, 247677). Allyn.

Browning, Frank. Steam Plant Errors. (Shorey Lost Arts Ser.). 90p. pap. 4.00 (ISBN 0-8466-6010-5, U10). Shorey.

--The Vanishing Land: The Corporate Theft of America. 12.00 (ISBN 0-8446-5166-4). Peter Smith.

Browning, Freddie Melton, jt. auth. see Byrd, Ronald James.

Browning, Gary. Boris Pilnyak: Scythian at a Typewriter. 200p. 1985. 22.50 (ISBN 0-88233-888-9). Ardis Pubs.

Browning, George L. The Early Landscape Masters of Italian Art. (Illus.). 166p. 1985. 89.50 (ISBN 0-86650-140-1). Gloucester Art.

Browning, Grace. Rural Public Welfare: Selected Records. LC 75-17209. (Social Problems & Social Policy Ser.). 1976. Repr. of 1941 ed. 43.00x (ISBN 0-405-07481-6). Ayer Co Pubs.

Browning, Harley L., jt. ed. see Portes, Alejandro.

Browning, Iain. Jerash & the Decapolis. (Illus.). 224p. 1983. 22.95 (ISBN 0-7011-2591-8, Pub by Chatto & Windus). Merrimack Pub Cir.

--Palmyra. LC 79-16591. (Illus.). 223p. 1980. 18.00 (ISBN 0-8155-5054-5, Np). Noyes.

--Petra. (Illus.). 256p. 1982. 27.50 (ISBN 0-7011-2622-1, Pub. by Chatto & Windus). Merrimack Pub Cir.

Browning, Iben & Garriss, Evelyn M. Past & Future History: A Planner's Guide. 1981. 16.00 (ISBN 0-87034-063-8). Fraser Pub Co.

Browning, Iben, jt. auth. see Winkless, Nels, III.

Browning, J. D. Biography in the Eighteenth Century: Publications of the McMaster University Association for 18th Century Studies. LC 80-14652. (Vol. 8). 207p. 1980. 31.00 (ISBN 0-8240-4007-4). Garland Pub.

Browning, Jacquelene M., jt. auth. see Browning, Edgar K.

Browning, Jacqueline M., jt. auth. see Browning, Edgar K.

Browning, Jeffrey, ed. see Register, John.

Browning, John. Tarantulas. (Illus.). 96p. 1981. 4.95 (ISBN 0-87666-931-3, KW-075). TFH Pubns.

Browning, John & Morton, Richard. Religion in the Eighteenth Century. LC 79-17715. (McMaster University Eighteenth Century Studies). 145p. 1979. lib. bdg. 22.00 (ISBN 0-8240-4005-8). Garland Pub.

Browning, John, ed. Education in the Eighteenth Century. LC 79-18182. (The McMaster Eighteenth Century Studies). 145p. 1979. lib. bdg. 31.00 (ISBN 0-8240-4006-6). Garland Pub.

Browning, John D. Satire in the Eighteenth Century. LC 82-49148. (McMaster Studies in the 18th Century). 231p. 1983. lib. bdg. 36.00 (ISBN 0-8240-4009-0). Garland Pub.

Browning, K. A., ed. Nowcasting. LC 82-45030. 1982. 50.00 (ISBN 0-12-137760-1). Acad Pr.
Browning, M. E., jt. ed. see Rice, R. G.
Browning, Mac, ed. see Kemper, Donald W., et al.
Browning, Martha, ed. see Mayfield, Peggy, et al.
Browning, Myron E., jt. ed. see Rice, Rip G.
Browning, N. & Ogg, R. He Saw a Hummingbird. 143p. 1984. Repr. of 1978 ed. 9.95 (ISBN 0-87359-043-0). Northwood Inst Pr.
Browning, Norma L., jt. auth. see Lowell, Florence.
Browning, O., ed. see Leeds, Francis O.
Browning, Oscar. Dante: His Life & Writings. LC 72-3093. (Studies in Dante, No. 9). 1972. Repr. of 1891 ed. lib. bdg. 46.95x (ISBN 0-8383-1520-8). Haskell.
--Dante: His Life & Writings. 1891. 7.75 (ISBN 0-8274-2135-4). R West.
--Goethe: His Life & Writings. LC 72-2126. (Studies in German Literature, No. 13). 1972. Repr. of 1892 ed. lib. bdg. 39.95x (ISBN 0-8383-1493-7). Haskell.
--Life of George Eliot. 1977. Repr. of 1890 ed. lib. bdg. 15.00 (ISBN 0-8414-0877-7). Folcroft.
--Life of George Eliot. Robertson, Eric S., ed. 174p. 1982. Repr. of 1892 ed. lib. bdg. 20.00 (ISBN 0-89984-087-6). Century Bookbindery.
--Memories of Sixty Years. 1973. Repr. of 1910 ed. 20.00 (ISBN 0-8274-1451-X). R West.
Browning, Peter. Fell's International Directory of Stamp-Auction Houses. LC 82-71749. 336p. 1982. 24.95 (ISBN 0-8119-0452-0). Fell.
--Sierra Nevada Place Names. LC 84-52655. 352p. (Orig.). 1985. pap. 11.95 (ISBN 0-89997-047-8). Wilderness Pr.
--The Works Minis. (Illus.). 206p. pap. 6.95 (ISBN 0-85429-278-0, F278). Haynes Pubns.
Browning, Peter R. Economic Images. LC 82-13086. (Illus.). 1983. pap. text ed. 7.95x (ISBN 0-582-29630-7). Longman.
Browning, Philip L. Mental Retardation: Rehabilitation & Counseling. (Illus.). 464p. 1974. 46.50x (ISBN 0-398-03006-5). C C Thomas.
--Rehabilitation & the Retarded Offender. (Illus.). 360p. 1976. 45.50x (ISBN 0-398-03481-8). C C Thomas.
Browning, Reed. Political & Constitutional Ideas of the Court Whigs. LC 81-19372. 290p. 1982. text ed. 27.50x (ISBN 0-8071-0980-0). La State U Pr.
Browning, Robert. Browning: Plain Texts of the Poets. 1968. pap. 2.50x (ISBN 0-7022-0630-X). U of Queensland Pr.
--Browning: Selected Poems. DeVane, William C., ed. LC 49-11359. (Crofts Classics Ser.). 1949. pap. text ed. 3.75x (ISBN 0-88295-019-3). Harlan Davidson.
--Browning's Essay on Chatterton. Smalley, Donald, ed. LC 79-100145. Repr. of 1948 ed. lib. bdg. 18.75x (ISBN 0-8371-3257-6, BRCH). Greenwood.
--The Complete Works of Robert Browning, with Variant Readings & Annotations, 4 vols. King, Roma A., Jr., et al, eds. Incl. Vol. 1. xx, 306p. 1969 (ISBN 0-8214-0049-5, 82-80547); Vol. 2. xx, 422p. 1970 (ISBN 0-8214-0074-6, 82-80794); Vol. 3. xxviii, 397p. 1971 (ISBN 0-8214-0084-3, 82-80885); Vol. 4. xxviii, 404p. 1973 (ISBN 0-8214-0115-7, 82-81180). LC 68-18389. 30.00x ea. Ohio U Pr.
--The Complete Works of Robert Browning: With Variant Readings & Annotations, Vol. V. King, Roma A., Jr., et al, eds. LC 68-18389. (Illus.). xxiv, 395p. 1981. 40.00x (ISBN 0-8214-0220-X, 82-82261). Ohio U Pr.
--Dearest Isa: Robert Browning's Letters to Isabella Blagden. McAleer, Edward C., ed. (Illus.). 1977. pap. text ed. 17.50x (ISBN 0-292-71513-7). U of Tex Pr.
--Dramatic Idyls. (Illus.). 101p. 1981. Repr. of 1879 ed. 59.25 (ISBN 0-89901-037-7). Found Class Reprints.
--The Emperor Julian. LC 75-13159. 1976. pap. 4.95 (ISBN 0-520-03731-6). U of Cal Pr.
--An Essay on Percy Bysshe Shelley. Harden, W. Tyas, ed. LC 74-30276. (Shelley Society, Fourth Ser.: No. 8). Repr. of 1888 ed. 20.00 (ISBN 0-404-11518-7). AMS Pr.
--An Essay on Percy Bysshe Shelley. 1973. Repr. of 1888 ed. 10.00 (ISBN 0-8274-0079-9). R West.
--Intimate Glimpses from Browning's Letter File. LC 76-28548. 1976. Repr. of 1934 ed. lib. bdg. 20.00 (ISBN 0-8414-2886-7). Folcroft.
--Learned Lady: Letters from Robert Browning to Mrs. Thomas Fitzgerald, 1876-1889. McAleer, E. C., ed. LC 66-11358. (Illus.). 1966. 15.00x (ISBN 0-674-51900-0, Belknap Pr). Harvard U Pr.
--The Letters of Robert Browning & Elizabeth Barrett Browning: 1845-1846, 2 vols. 1899. 85.00 set (ISBN 0-8495-6288-0). Arden Lib.
--Medieval & Modern Greek. LC 82-19771. 176p. 1983. 32.50 (ISBN 0-521-23488-3); pap. 13.95 (ISBN 0-521-29978-0). Cambridge U Pr.
--Men & Women. Turner, Paul, ed. 1972. pap. 10.95x (ISBN 0-19-911019-0). Oxford U Pr.
--Men & Women & Other Poems: And Other Poems. Harper, J. W., ed. 264p. 1984. pap. 5.95x (ISBN 0-460-11427-1, Evman). Biblio Dist.
--Pauline. LC 76-30813. 1977. Repr. of 1931 ed. lib. bdg. 25.00 (ISBN 0-8414-1772-5). Folcroft.
--Pied Piper of Hamelin. (gr. 2-5). 1889. 10.95 (ISBN 0-7232-0586-8). Warne.
--Poems, Eighteen Thirty-Five to Eighteen Eighty-Nine. Milford, Humphrey, ed. (World's Classics Ser.). 1954. 12.95 (ISBN 0-19-250513-0). Oxford U Pr.
--Poems of Robert Browning. Smalley, Donald, ed. LC 56-3004. (YA) (gr. 9 up). 1956. pap. 6.50 (ISBN 0-395-05103-7, RivEd). HM.
--Poetical Works Eighteen Thirty-Three to Eighteen Sixty-Four. Jack, Ian, ed. (Oxford Standard Authors Ser.). 1970. 29.95 (ISBN 0-19-254165-X); pap. 9.95x (ISBN 0-19-281185-1, OPB 355). Oxford U Pr.
--The Poetical Works of Robert Browning. (Cambridge Editions Ser.). 1974. 27.50 (ISBN 0-395-18485-1). HM.
--The Ring & the Book. 1968. Repr. of 1911 ed. 8.95x (ISBN 0-460-00502-2, Evman). Biblio Dist.
--Ring & the Book. 1967. pap. 8.95x (ISBN 0-393-00433-3, Norton Lib). Norton.
--The Ring & the Book. Altick, Richard D., ed. LC 80-53977. 707p. 1981. text ed. 42.00x (ISBN 0-300-02677-3); pap. 11.95x (ISBN 0-300-02685-4, YEP-3). Yale U Pr.
--Robert Browning: Men & Women & Other Poems. Harper, J. W., ed. (Rowman & Littlefield University Library). 244p. 1975. 9.50x (ISBN 0-87471-648-9); pap. 5.00x (ISBN 0-87471-649-7). Rowman.
--Robert Browning, Poetry & Prose. Nowell-Smith, Simon, ed. LC 66-11358. (The Reynard Library). (Orig.). 1967. pap. 7.95x (ISBN 0-674-67876-1). Harvard U Pr.
--Robert Browning: The Poems, Vol. I. Pettigrew, John, ed. LC 80-53976. 1218p. 1981. text ed. 52.00x (ISBN 0-300-02675-7); pap. 14.95x (ISBN 0-300-02683-8, YEP 1). Yale U Pr.
--Robert Browning: The Poems, Vol. II. Pettigrew, John, ed. LC 80-53976. 1156p. 1981. text ed. 52.00x (ISBN 0-300-02676-5); pap. 14.95x (ISBN 0-300-02684-6, YEP 3). Yale U Pr.
--Robert Browning's Poetry. Loucks, James M., ed. (Critical Editions). 1979. pap. 10.95x (ISBN 0-393-09092-2). Norton.
--Selected Poetry of Browning. Ridenour, George, ed. pap. 2.95 (ISBN 0-451-51599-4, CE1599, Sig Classics). NAL.
--Shelley, the Man & the Poet. LC 75-26948. 1975. Repr. of 1908 ed. lib. bdg. 9.50 (ISBN 0-8414-3248-1). Folcroft.
--Shorter Poems of Robert Browning. DeVane, William C., ed. 1934. 47.50x (ISBN 0-89197-405-9). Irvington.
--Studies on Byzantine History, Literature & Education. 390p. 1980. 60.00x (ISBN 0-86078-003-1, Pub. by Variorum England). State Mutual Bk.
--Works, 10 vols. Kenyon, F. G., ed. LC 73-10024. Repr. of 1912 ed. Set. 250.00 (ISBN 0-404-01160-8). AMS Pr.
Browning, Robert & Browning, Elizabeth Barrett. The Letters of Robert Browning & Elizabeth Barrett Browning, 1845-1846, 2 vols. Kinter, Elvan, ed. 1173p. 1969. Set. 55.00x (ISBN 0-674-52605-8); Vol 1 January 1845-March 1846. Vol. 2 March 1846-September 1846. Harvard U Pr.
--New Poems. 1971. Repr. of 1915 ed. 29.00 (ISBN 0-403-00849-2). Scholarly.
Browning, Robert & Holleuffer, Carol. Roaming the Back Roads. rev. ed. LC 78-27569. (Illus.). 175p. (Orig.). 1981. pap. 6.95 (ISBN 0-87701-235-0). Chronicle Bks.
Browning, Robert, jt. auth. see Browning, Elizabeth Barrett.
Browning, Robert, ed. The Greek World: Classical, Byzantine & Modern. LC 84-52748. (Illus.). 1985. 60.00 (ISBN 0-500-25092-8, Dist. by Norton). Thames Hudson.
Browning, Robert, jt. ed. see Ryder, Frank G.
Browning, Robert J. Fisheries of the North Pacific: History, Species, Gear & Processes. rev. ed. LC 80-17194. (Illus.). 432p. 1980. pap. 24.95 (ISBN 0-88240-128-9). Alaska Northwest.
Browning, Robert L. & Reed, Roy A. The Sacraments in Religious Education & Liturgy: An Ecumenical Model. LC 84-27536. 313p. (Orig.). 1985. pap. 14.95 (ISBN 0-89135-044-6). Religious Educ.
Browning, Robert M. German Baroque Poetry, Sixteen Eighteen to Seventeen Twenty-Three. LC 77-136959. 1971. 24.50x (ISBN 0-271-01146-7). Pa St U Pr.
--German Poetry in the Age of the Enlightenment: From Brockes to Klopstock. LC 77-26832. (Series in German Literature). 1978. text ed. 24.50x (ISBN 0-271-00541-6). Pa St U Pr.
--Teaching the Severely Handicapped Child: Basic Skills for the Developmentally Disabled. 292p. 1980. 28.95x (ISBN 0-205-06877-4, 246877, Pub. by Longwood Div). Allyn.
Browning, Robert M., ed. Freude am Lesen: A German Reader. (Orig., Ger.). 1964. pap. text ed. 7.95x (ISBN 0-89197-180-7). Irvington.
Browning, Robert M., ed. see Von Kleist, Heinrich & Paul, Jean.
Browning, Robert M., tr. see Goethe, et al.
Browning, Robert S., III. Two If by Sea: The Development of American Coastal Defense Policy. LC 83-1638. (Contributions in Military History Ser.: No. 33). (Illus.). xii, 210p. 1983. lib. bdg. 29.95 (ISBN 0-313-23688-7, BRT/). Greenwood.
Browning, Rufus P., et al. Protest Is Not Enough: The Struggle of Blacks & Hispanics for Equality in Urban Politics. LC 83-15552. (Illus.). x, 311p. 1985. 27.50 (ISBN 0-520-05033-9). U of Cal Pr.
Browning, Ruth & Durbin, Sandra. Computers in the Home Economics Classroom. 1985. 6.00 (ISBN 0-318-04256-8). Home Econ Educ.
Browning, Sinclair. Enju. LC 82-81689. 154p. 1983. pap. 9.95 (ISBN 0-87358-312-4). Northland.
Browning Society. Browning Studies: Being Selected Papers by Members of the Browning Society. 1895. 45.00 (ISBN 0-8274-1981-3). R West.
Browning, Stella. Butter in the Buttercups. (Illus.). 62p. 1980. 5.50 (ISBN 0-682-49528-X). Exposition Pr FL.
Browning, Tatiana, jt. auth. see Fitzlyon, Kyril.
Browning, Vivienne. My Browning Family Album. Coley, Betty A., ed. (Illus.). 128p. 1979. 10.50x (ISBN 0-905947-22-3). Wedgestone Pr.
Browning, William G. Memory Power for Exams. (Cliffs Test Preparation Ser.). (Illus.). 113p. 1983. pap. text ed. 3.95 (ISBN 0-8220-2020-3). Cliffs.
Browning, William S. The History of the Huguenots During the Sixteenth Century, 2 vols. LC 83-45604. Date not set. Repr. of 1829 ed. Set. 59.50 (ISBN 0-404-19871-6). AMS Pr.
Brownjohn, Alan. Collected Poems, 1952-83. 256p. 1983. 18.95 (ISBN 0-436-07115-0, Pub. by Secker & Warburg UK). David & Charles.
--Lions' Mouths. LC 67-28704. 1967. 9.95 (ISBN 0-8023-1132-6). Dufour.
--Sandgrains on a Tray: Poems. LC 69-19125. 1969. 9.95 (ISBN 0-8023-1212-8). Dufour.
Brownjohn, J. Maxwell, tr. see Gregor-Dellin, Martin.
Brownjohn, J. Maxwell, tr. see Herlin, Hans.
Brownjohn, J. Maxwell, tr. see Riefenstahl, Leni.
Brownjohn, Maxwell, tr. see Hecht, Ingeborg.
Brownlee, jt. auth. see Coleman.
Brownlee, David B. The Law Courts: The Architecture of George Edmund Street. LC 83-25625. (The Architectural History Foundation-MIT Press Ser.: Vol. 8). 432p. 1984. 45.00x (ISBN 0-262-02199-4). MIT Pr.
Brownlee, Frank, ed. Transkeian Native Territories: Historical Records. LC 75-129942. Repr. of 1923 ed. 19.75x (ISBN 0-8371-1611-2, BTN&). Greenwood.
Brownlee, G. G. Determination of Sequences in RNA. (Laboratory Techniques in Biochemistry & Molecular Biology Ser.: Vol. 3, No. 1). 1973. Repr. 21.75 (ISBN 0-444-10102-0, North-Hollnd). Elsevier.
Brownlee, Gardner E. Trial Judge's Guide: Objections to Evidence. (Ser. 550). 1974. 15.00 (ISBN 0-686-00407-8). Natl Judicial Coll.
Brownlee, Juanita. Tangram Geometry in Metric. (Illus., Orig.). (gr. 5-10). 1976. pap. 6.50 (ISBN 0-918932-43-2, 0140701407). Activity Resources.
Brownlee, K. A. Statistical Theory & Methodology: In Science & Engineering. LC 84-3941. 608p. 1984. Repr. of 1965 ed. lib. bdg. 47.00 (ISBN 0-89874-748-1). Krieger.
Brownlee, Kevin. Poetic Identity in Guillaume de Machaut. LC 83-14498. 262p. 1984. text ed. 30.00x (ISBN 0-299-09200-3). U of Wis Pr.
Brownlee, Kevin & Brownlee, Marina S., eds. Romance: Generic Transformation from Chretien de Troyes to Cervantes. LC 84-40581. 320p. 1985. text ed. 35.00x (ISBN 0-87451-338-3). U Pr of New Eng.
Brownlee, Marina S., jt. ed. see Brownlee, Kevin.
Brownlee, Mary H., jt. auth. see Brownlee, W. Elliot.
Brownlee, Oswald H. Taxing the Income from U. S. Corporate Investment Abroad. 1980. pap. 3.25 (ISBN 0-8447-3367-9). Am Enterprise.
Brownlee, Richard S. Gray Ghosts of the Confederacy: Guerilla Warfare in the West, 1861-1865. LC 83-19634. (Illus.). 296p. 1984. pap. 8.95 (ISBN 0-8071-1162-7). La State U Pr.
Brownlee, W. D. The First Ships Around the World. LC 76-22430. (Cambridge Topic Bks). (Illus.). (gr. 5-10). 1977. PLB 7.95 (ISBN 0-8225-1204-1). Lerner Pubns.
Brownlee, W. Elliot. Dynamics of Ascent: A History of the American Economy. 2nd ed. 1978. text ed. 25.00x (ISBN 0-394-32154-5, KnopfC). Knopf.
Brownlee, W. Elliot & Brownlee, Mary H. Women in the American Economy: A Documentary History, 1675-1927. LC 75-18168. 360p. 1976. pap. 9.95x (ISBN 0-300-01994-7). Yale U Pr.
Brownlee, W. Elliot, Jr. Progressivism & Economic Growth: The Wisconsin Income Tax, 1911-1929. LC 74-80065. 1974. 15.95x (ISBN 0-8046-9091-X, Pub. by Kennikat). Assoc Faculty Pr.
Brownlee, Walter. The First Ships Round the World. LC 73-91815. (Cambridge Introduction to the History of Mankind Ser.). (Illus.). 48p. 1974. 4.95 (ISBN 0-521-20438-0). Cambridge U Pr.
--The Navy That Beat Napoleon. LC 78-18091. (Cambridge Introduction to the History of Mankind Ser.). 1981. 4.50 (ISBN 0-521-22145-5). Cambridge U Pr.
--The Navy That Beat Napoleon. LC 81-13733. (Cambridge Topic Bks.). (Illus.). 52p. (gr. 6 up). 1982. PLB 7.95 (ISBN 0-8225-1226-2). Lerner Pubns.
--Warrior: The First Modern Battleship. (Cambridge Introduction to the History of Mankind Ser.). 48p. Date not set. pap. price not set. (ISBN 0-521-27579-2). Cambridge U Pr.
Brownlee, William H. The Midrash Pesher of Habakkuk. LC 76-30560. (Society of Biblical Literature Monograph). 220p. 1979. pap. 9.95 (ISBN 0-89130-147-X, 06 00 24). Scholars Pr GA.
Brownleigh, Eleanora. Heirloom. 1983. pap. 3.95 (ISBN 0-8217-1200-4). Zebra.
--Keepsake. 1984. pap. 3.95 (ISBN 0-8217-1414-7). Zebra.
--A Woman of the Century. (Orig.). 1981. pap. 3.50 (ISBN 0-8217-1409-0). Zebra.
Brownley, Martine W. Clarendon & the Rhetoric of Historical Form. LC 85-1197. (Illus.). 296p. 1985. text ed. 24.95 (ISBN 0-8122-7988-3). U of Pa Pr.
Brownley, Martine W., jt. ed. see Perry, Ruth.
Brownley, Nancie, jt. ed. see McGiffin, Heather.
Brownlie, G. The Pteridophyte Flora of Fiji. (Beihefte Zur Nova Hedwigia 55). 1977. lib. bdg. 70.00x (ISBN 3-7682-5455-0). Lubrecht & Cramer.
Brownlie, I., jt. auth. see Vitta, E.
Brownlie, Ian. African Boundaries: A Legal & Diplomatic Encyclopedia. 1979. 185.00x (ISBN 0-520-03795-2). U of Cal Pr.
--International Law & the Use of Force by States. 1963. 84.00x (ISBN 0-19-825158-0). Oxford U Pr.
--Principles of Public International Law. 3rd ed. 1979. 64.00x (ISBN 0-19-876066-3); pap. 29.95x (ISBN 0-19-876067-1). Oxford U Pr.
--System of the Law of Nations: State Responsibility, Pt. 1. 318p. 1983. 47.50 (ISBN 0-19-825452-0). Oxford U Pr.
Brownlie, Ian & Bowett, D. W. The British Year Book of International Law, Vol. 53. 590p. 1985. 105.00 (ISBN 0-19-825491-1). Oxford U Pr.
Brownlie, Ian, jt. auth. see Jennings, R. Y.
Brownlie, Ian, ed. Basic Documents in International Law. 3rd ed. 1983. 32.50x (ISBN 0-19-876158-9); pap. 15.95x (ISBN 0-19-876159-7). Oxford U Pr.
--Basic Documents of Human Rights. 2nd ed. 1981. pap. 28.95x (ISBN 0-19-876125-2). Oxford U Pr.
--Basic Documents on African Affairs. 1971. 19.25x (ISBN 0-19-876020-5). Oxford U Pr.
Brownlie, Ian, jt. ed. see Jennings, R. Y.
Brownlie, William D. Life Insurance: Its Rate of Return. LC 83-61584. (Illus.). 201p. (Orig.). 1983. pap. 13.75 (ISBN 0-87218-033-6). Natl Underwriter.
Brownlow, Arthur, jt. ed. see Lyons, Paul C.
Brownlow, Arthur H. Geochemistry. (Illus.). 1979. text ed. 38.95 (ISBN 0-13-351064-6). P-H.
Brownlow, Donald G. Checkmate at Ruweisat: Auchinleck's Finest Hour. (Illus.). 1977. 12.95 (ISBN 0-8158-0356-7). Chris Mass.
--Panzer Baron: The Military Exploits of General Hasso Von Manteuffel. LC 75-10245. (Illus.). 176p. 1975. 9.75 (ISBN 0-8158-0325-7); French Ed. 12.95. Chris Mass.
Brownlow, Donald G. & Du Pont, John E. Hell Was My Home. (Illus.). 154p. 1983. 12.95 (ISBN 0-8158-0416-4). Chris Mass.
Brownlow, Jack. Melton Mowbray, Queen of the Shires. 1982. 60.00x (ISBN 0-905837-08-8, Pub. by Sycamore Pr England). State Mutual Bk.
Brownlow, Kevin. Hollywood: The Pioneers. LC 79-1197. (Illus.). 1980. 20.00 (ISBN 0-394-50851-3). Knopf.
--Napoleon: Abel Gance's Silent Classic. LC 83-48098. (Illus.). 304p. 1983. 25.00 (ISBN 0-394-53394-1); pap. 14.95 (ISBN 0-394-72116-0). Knopf.
--The Parade's Gone by. LC 75-17302. 1976. pap. 9.95 (ISBN 0-520-03068-0, CAL 330). U of Cal Pr.
--The War, The West, & The Wilderness. LC 78-54934. 1979. 27.50 (ISBN 0-394-48921-7). Knopf.
Brownlow, Kevin, ed. see Brown, Karl.
Brownlow, Leroy. Better Than Medicine. 1967. gift ed. 6.95 (ISBN 0-915720-07-8); pap. 2.25 class ed. (ISBN 0-915720-35-3). Brownlow Pub Co.
--Christian's Everyday Problems. 1966. pap. 2.25 (ISBN 0-915720-39-6). Brownlow Pub Co.
--A Father's World. 1965. gift ed. 6.95 (ISBN 0-915720-46-9). Brownlow Pub Co.
--Flowers for Mother. 1964. gift ed. 6.95 (ISBN 0-915720-02-7). Brownlow Pub Co.
--Flowers for You. 1963. gift ed. 6.95 (ISBN 0-915720-01-9). Brownlow Pub Co.
--Flowers of Friendship. 1974. gift ed. 6.95 (ISBN 0-915720-04-3). Brownlow Pub Co.
--Flowers That Never Fade. 1959. gift ed. 6.95 (ISBN 0-915720-00-0); leather ed. 10.95 (ISBN 0-915720-69-8). Brownlow Pub Co.
--For Love's Sake. 1975. gift ed. 6.95 (ISBN 0-915720-15-9). Brownlow Pub Co.
--The Fruit of the Spirit. 1982. gift ed. 6.95 (ISBN 0-915720-59-0). Brownlow Pub Co.
--God, the Bible & Common Sense. 1978. pap. 2.25 (ISBN 0-915720-48-5). Brownlow Pub Co.
--Living with the Psalms. 386p. 1976. 7.95 (ISBN 0-915720-17-5). Brownlow Pub Co.
--Making the Most of Life - from A to Z. 1968. gift ed. 6.95 (ISBN 0-915720-09-4); pap. 2.25 class ed. (ISBN 0-915720-36-1). Brownlow Pub Co.
--Thoughts of Gold in Words of Silver. 1974. gift ed. 6.95 (ISBN 0-915720-13-2). Brownlow Pub Co.

--A Time to Laugh - or Grandpa Was a Preacher. 1973. gift ed. 6.95 (ISBN 0-915720-11-6). Brownlow Pub Co.

--Today Is Mine. 1972. gift ed 7.95 (ISBN 0-915720-14-0); leather ed. 12.95 (ISBN 0-915720-57-4). Brownlow Pub Co.

--With the Good Shepherd. 1969. gift ed. 6.95 (ISBN 0-915720-12-4). Brownlow Pub Co.

Brownlow, North. El Rico y Lazaro. (Span.). pap. 2.95 (ISBN 0-317-14915-6). Banner of Truth.

Brownlow, Paul C., jt. auth. see Baw, Cindy.

Brownlow, Paul C., ed. Daybreak. (Illus.). 1978. 7.95 (ISBN 0-915720-43-4). Brownlow Pub Co.

Brownlow, Timothy. John Clare & Picturesque Landscape. (Illus.). 1983. 33.00x (ISBN 0-19-812808-8). Oxford U Pr.

Brownlow, William G. A Political Register, Setting Forth the Principles of the Whig & Locofoco Parties in the United States, with the Life & Public Services of Henry Clay. LC 73-23063. 348p. 1974. Repr. of 1844 ed. 20.00 (ISBN 0-87152-153-9). Reprint.

--Sketches of the Rise, Progress, & Decline of Secession. 2nd ed. LC 68-23813. (American Scene Ser). 1968. Repr. of 1862 ed. 55.00 (ISBN 0-306-71137-0). Da Capo.

Brownlow, William G. & Pryne, Abram. Ought American Slavery to Be Perpetuated. facs. ed. LC 79-83959. (Black Heritage Library Collection Ser). 1858. 15.75 (ISBN 0-8369-8520-6). Ayer Co Pubs.

Brownlow, William R. Lectures on Slavery & Serfdom in Europe. LC 71-75547. Repr. 19.75x (ISBN 0-8371-1013-0, BLE&, Pub. by Negro U Pr). Greenwood.

Brownmiller, Susan. Against Our Will. 544p. 1976. pap. 4.95 (ISBN 0-553-20338-X). Bantam.

--Femininity. 288p. 1984. 16.95 (ISBN 0-671-24692-5, Linden Pr). S&S.

--Femininity. 1985. pap. 7.95 (ISBN 0-449-90142-4, Columbine). Fawcett.

Brownridge, I. C. Lithium-Drifted Germanium Detectors: Their Fabrication & Use. LC 73-183565. 216p. 1972. 65.00x (ISBN 0-306-65180-7, IFI Plenum). Plenum Pub.

Brownrigg, W. Grant. Effective Corporate Fundraising. LC 82-3887. (Illus.). 162p. (Orig.). 1982. pap. 12.95 (ISBN 0-915400-38-3). Am Council Arts.

Browns, Freda, jt. auth. see Arnell, Diane.

Brownsberger, Susan, tr. see Iskander, Fazil.

Brownsberger, Susan, tr. see Saltykov-Shchedrin, Mikhail.

Brownson, Ann. Election Index to Redistricted States, 1972. 4th ed. LC 59-13987. 284p. pap. 5.00 (ISBN 0-87289-026-0). Congr Staff.

Brownson, Anna L. Advance Locator for Capitol Hill, 1984: With Biographical Material on Members. 22nd ed. 440p. 1984. pap. 10.00 (ISBN 0-87289-057-0). Congr Staff.

--Election Index to Redistricted States, 1976. 6th ed. LC 59-13987. 276p. pap. 7.00 (ISBN 0-87289-036-8). Congr Staff.

Brownson, Anna L., jt. auth. see Brownson, Charles.

Brownson, Anna L., jt. auth. see Brownson, Charles B.

Brownson, Anna L., ed. Africa since Independence, N-Z. 4th ed. (Stanley Gibbons Stamp Catalogues Ser.: Part 14). 1981. 28.50 (ISBN 0-85259-181-0). StanGib.

--Election Index to Redistricted States, 1980. LC 59-13987. 1980. pap. 8.00 (ISBN 0-87289-046-5, 87289). Congr Staff.

--Election Index to Redistricted States, 1978. 7th ed. LC 59-13987. 1980. pap. 8.00 (ISBN 0-87289-041-4, 87289). Congr Staff.

--Election Index to Redistricted States, 1982. 20th ed. LC 59-13987. 560p. 1986. pap. 10.00 (ISBN 0-87289-052-X). Congr Staff.

--Election Index to Redistricted States, 1966. LC 59-13987. 250p. pap. 5.00 (ISBN 0-87289-011-2). Congr Staff.

--Election Index to Redistricted States, 1968. 2nd ed. LC 59-13987. 256p. pap. 5.00 (ISBN 0-87289-016-3). Congr Staff.

--Election Index to Redistricted States, 1970. 3rd ed. LC 59-13987. 276p. pap. 5.00 (ISBN 0-87289-021-X). Congr Staff.

--Election Index to Redistricted States, 1974. 5th ed. LC 59-13987. 272p. pap. 5.00 (ISBN 0-87289-031-7). Congr Staff.

Brownson, Anna L., jt. ed. see Brownson, C. B.

Brownson, Anna L., jt. ed. see Brownson, Charles B.

Brownson, C. B. Advance Locator for Capitol Hill, 1965: With Biographical Material on Members. 3rd ed. LC 59-13987. 196p. pap. 1.50 (ISBN 0-87289-007-4). Congr Staff.

--Advance Locator for Capitol Hill, 1966: With Biographical Material on Members. 4th ed. LC 59-13987. 196p. pap. 1.50 (ISBN 0-87289-009-0). Congr Staff.

--Advance Locator for Capitol Hill, 1967: With Biographical Material on Members. 5th ed. LC 59-13987. 196p. pap. 2.00 (ISBN 0-87289-012-0). Congr Staff.

--Advance Locator for Capitol Hill, 1968: With Biographical Material on Members. 6th ed. LC 59-13987. 196p. pap. 2.50 (ISBN 0-87289-014-7). Congr Staff.

--Advance Locator for Capitol Hill, 1969. 7th ed. LC 59-13987. 196p. pap. 2.50 (ISBN 0-87289-017-1). Congr Staff.

--Advance Locator for Capitol Hill, 1970. 8th ed. LC 59-13987. 193p. pap. 2.50 (ISBN 0-87289-019-8). Congr Staff.

--Advance Locator for Capitol Hill, 1971. 9th ed. LC 59-13987. 196p. pap. 3.50 (ISBN 0-87289-022-8). Congr Staff.

--Advance Locator for Capitol Hill, 1972. 10th ed. LC 59-13987. 196p. pap. 3.50 (ISBN 0-87289-024-4). Congr Staff.

--Advance Locator for Capitol Hill, 1973. 11th ed. LC 59-13987. 200p. pap. 3.50 (ISBN 0-87289-027-9). Congr Staff.

--Advance Locator for Capitol Hill, 1975. 13th ed. LC 59-13987. 240p. pap. 5.00 (ISBN 0-87289-032-5). Congr Staff.

--Advance Locator for Capitol Hill, 1976. 14th ed. LC 59-13987. 276p. pap. 5.00 (ISBN 0-87289-034-1). Congr Staff.

--Advance Locator for Capitol Hill, 1977. 15th ed. LC 59-13987. 300p. pap. 5.50 (ISBN 0-87289-037-6). Congr Staff.

--Advance Locator for Capitol Hill, 1979. 17th ed. LC 59-13987. 500p. pap. 9.00 (ISBN 0-87289-042-2). Congr Staff.

--Advance Locator for Capitol Hill, 1980. 18th ed. LC 59-13987. 520p. pap. 8.00 (ISBN 0-87289-044-9). Congr Staff.

--Advance Locator for Capitol Hill, 1982. 20th ed. LC 59-13987. 520p. pap. 10.00 (ISBN 0-87289-050-3). Congr Staff.

Brownson, C. B., ed. Congressional Staff Directory, 1959: With Biographical Material on Members & Congressional Staff. 1st ed. LC 59-13987. 464p. 7.50 (ISBN 0-87289-000-7). Congr Staff.

--Congressional Staff Directory, 1960: With Biographical Material on Members & Key Congressional Staff. 2nd ed. LC 59-13987. 512p. 7.50 (ISBN 0-87289-001-5). Congr Staff.

--Congressional Staff Directory, 1961. 3rd ed. LC 59-13987. 512p. 7.95 (ISBN 0-87289-002-3). Congr Staff.

--Congressional Staff Directory, 1962. 4th ed. LC 59-13987. 528p. 7.95 (ISBN 0-87289-003-1). Congr Staff.

--Congressional Staff Directory, 1963. 5th ed. LC 59-13987. 560p. 7.95 (ISBN 0-87289-004-X). Congr Staff.

--Congressional Staff Directory, 1964. 6th ed. LC 59-13987. 560p. 8.95 (ISBN 0-87289-006-6). Congr Staff.

--Congressional Staff Directory, 1965. 7th ed. LC 59-13987. 566p. 10.00 (ISBN 0-87289-008-2). Congr Staff.

--Congressional Staff Directory, 1966. 8th ed. LC 59-13987. 566p. 10.00 (ISBN 0-87289-010-4). Congr Staff.

--Congressional Staff Directory, 1967: With Biographical Material on Members & Key Congressional Staff. 9th ed. LC 59-13987. 644p. 10.00 (ISBN 0-87289-013-9). Congr Staff.

--Congressional Staff Directory, 1968: With Biographical Material on Member & Key Congressional Staff. 10th ed. LC 59-13987. 672p. 10.00 (ISBN 0-87289-015-5). Congr Staff.

--Congressional Staff Directory, 1969: With Biographical Material on Members & Key Congressional Staff. 11th ed. LC 59-13987. 672p. 12.50 (ISBN 0-87289-018-X). Congr Staff.

--Congressional Staff Directory, 1970: With Biographical Material on Members & Key Congressional Staff. 12th ed. LC 59-13987. 710p. 12.50 (ISBN 0-87289-020-1). Congr Staff.

--Congressional Staff Directory, 1971: With Biographical Materials on Members & Key Congressional Staff. 13th ed. LC 59-13987. 780p. 13.50 (ISBN 0-87289-023-6). Congr Staff.

--Congressional Staff Directory, 1972: With Biographical Materials on Members & Key Congressional Staff. 14th ed. LC 59-13987. 800p. 13.50 (ISBN 0-87289-025-2). Congr Staff.

--Congressional Staff Directory, 1973: With Biographical Material on Members & Key Congressional Staff. 15th ed. 820p. 15.00 (ISBN 0-87289-028-7). Congr Staff.

--Congressional Staff Directory, 1974: With Biographical Materials on Members & Key Congressional Staff. 16th ed. LC 59-13987. 850p. 15.00 (ISBN 0-87289-030-9). Congr Staff.

--Congressional Staff Directory, 1975: With Biographical Material on Members & Key Congressional Staff. 17th ed. LC 59-13987. 850p. 18.00 (ISBN 0-87289-033-3). Congr Staff.

--Congressional Staff Directory, 1976: With Biographical Materials on Members & Key Congressional Staff. 18th ed. LC 59-13987. 850p. 18.00 (ISBN 0-87289-035-X). Congr Staff.

--Congressional Staff Directory, 1977: With Biographical Materials on Members & Key Congressional Staff. 19th ed. LC 59-13987. 870p. 19.50 (ISBN 0-87289-038-4). Congr Staff.

--Congressional Staff Directory, 1979: With Biographical Material on Members & Key Congressional Staff. 21st ed. LC 59-13987. 1000p. 22.00 (ISBN 0-87289-043-0). Congr Staff.

Brownson, C. B. & Brownson, Anna L., eds. Federal Staff Directory, 1982: With Biographical Material on Executive Staff Personel. 2nd ed. LC 59-13987. 1160p. 30.00 (ISBN 0-87289-049-X). Congr Staff.

Brownson, Charles & Brownson, Anna L. Advance Locator for Capitol Hill, 1983. 21st ed. LC 59-13987. 520p. 1983. 10.00 (ISBN 0-87289-054-6). Congr Staff.

Brownson, Charles B. Congressional Staff Directory, 1982: With Biographical Material. 24th ed. LC 59-13987. 1198p. 1982. 30.00 (ISBN 0-87289-051-1). Congr Staff.

Brownson, Charles B. & Brownson, Anna L. Advance Locator for Capitol Hill, 1964: With Biographical Material on Members. 2nd ed. LC 59-13987. 196p. pap. 1.50 (ISBN 0-87289-006-6). Congr Staff.

--Congressional Staff Directory: 1983, With Biographical Material. 25th ed. LC 59-13987. 1176p. 1983. 30.00 (ISBN 0-87289-055-4). Congr Staff.

--Federal Staff Directory, 1984. 3rd ed. LC 82-647381. 1330p. 1984. 35.00 (ISBN 0-87289-053-8). Congr Staff.

Brownson, Charles B., ed. Advance Locator for Capitol Hill, 1978. 16th ed. LC 59-13987. (Congressional Staff Directory Ser.). 1980. pap. 8.00 (ISBN 0-87289-039-2). Congr Staff.

--Advance Locator for Capitol Hill, 1981: With Biographical Material on Members. 19th ed. LC 59-13987. 520p. pap. 9.00 (ISBN 0-87289-047-3). Congr Staff.

--American Congress Biographical Directory, 1774-1984. LC 59-13987. 1200p. 1985. 95.00 (ISBN 0-686-47642-5). Congr Staff.

--Congressional Staff Directory, 1978: With Biographical Materials on Members & Key Congressional Staff. 20th ed LC 59-13987. 1980. 24.00 (ISBN 0-87289-048-1). Congr Staff.

--Congressional Staff Directory, 1980: With Biographical Material on Members & Key Congressional Staff. 22nd ed. LC 59-13987. 1096p. 1980. 24.00 (ISBN 0-87289-045-7). Congr Staff.

--Congressional Staff Directory, 1981: With Biographical Material on Members & Key Congressional Staff. 23rd ed. LC 59-13987. 1096p. 1981. pap. 25.00 (ISBN 0-87289-048-1). Congr Staff.

Brownson, Charles B. & Brownson, Anna L., eds. Advance Locator for Capitol Hill, 1985: With Biographical Material on Members. 23rd ed. LC 59-13987. 464p. 1985. write for info. Congr Staff.

--Congressional Staff Directory, 1985. 27th ed. LC 59-13987. 1232p. 1985. 40.00 (ISBN 0-87289-061-9). Congr Staff.

--Federal Staff Directory, 1981: With Biographical Material on Executive Staff Personel. LC 59-13987. 960p. 1982. casebound 25.00 (ISBN 0-87289-049-X). Congr Staff.

--Federal Staff Directory, 1985. 4th ed. LC 59-13987. 1344p. 1985. 40.00 (ISBN 0-87289-059-7). Congr Staff.

Brownson, Henry F., ed. see Brownson, Orestes A.

Brownson, Howard G. History of the Illinois Central Railroad to 1870. 1915. 15.00 (ISBN 0-384-06025-0). Johnson Repr.

Brownson, Orestes A. The American Republic. Lapati, Americo D., ed. (Masterworks of Literature Ser). 1972. 8.95x (ISBN 0-8084-0012-6); pap. 5.95x (ISBN 0-8084-0013-4). New Coll U Pr.

--American Republic: Its Constitution, Tendencies, & Destiny. rev. ed. LC 68-55493. Repr. of 1865 ed. lib. bdg. 37.50x (ISBN 0-678-00785-3). Kelley.

--Essays & Reviews Chiefly on Theology, Politics & Socialism. LC 72-4954. (The Romantic Tradition in American Literature Ser.). 538p. 1972. Repr. of 1852 ed. 46.50 (ISBN 0-405-04626-X). Ayer Co Pubs.

--The Laboring Classes. LC 78-17952. 1978. Repr. of 1840 ed. 35.00x (ISBN 0-8201-1314-X). Schol Facsimiles.

--Works of Orestes A. Brownson, 20 Vols. Brownson, Henry F., ed. LC 12-30124. Repr. of 1907 ed. Set. 750.00 (ISBN 0-404-01180-2); 37.50 ea. AMS Pr.

Brownstein & Weiner. Barron's Basic Word List. 1977. pap. 3.50 (ISBN 0-8120-0709-3). Barron.

--Barron's How to Prepare for the Graduate Record Examination (GRE) 6th ed. LC 78-15175. 544p. 1982. pap. text ed. 7.95 (ISBN 0-8120-2506-7). Barron.

--Barron's How to Prepare for the Preliminary Scholastic Aptitude Test - National Merit Scholarship Q Test (PSAT - NMSQT) 5th ed. 336p. 1982. pap. 6.95 (ISBN 0-8120-2336-6). Barron.

--Basic Word List. 1977. pap. 3.50 (ISBN 0-8120-0709-3). Barron.

--How to Prepare for the Graduate Record Examination (GRE) 7th ed. 1985. pap. 8.95 (ISBN 0-8120-2927-5). Barron.

--Pocket Guide to Vocabulary. 1984. pap. 2.95 (ISBN 0-8120-2814-7). Barron.

Brownstein, Irv & Lerner, Nancy. Guidelines for Evaluating Software Packages. 200p. 1982. 110.00 (ISBN 0-444-00767-9). Elsevier.

Brownstein, Karen. In a Cerain Light. 276p. 1985. 17.95 (ISBN 0-399-13084-5). Putnam Pub Group.

--In a Certain Light. 240p. 1985. 17.95 (ISBN 0-399-13084-5). Putnam Pub Group.

--Memorial Day. LC 82-45594. 240p. 1983. 14.95 (ISBN 0-385-18427-1). Doubleday.

Brownstein, Karen O. Brainstorm. 208p. 1981. pap. 2.50 (ISBN 0-380-54833-X, 54833-X). Avon.

Brownstein, Larry. Talcott Parsons' General Action Scheme. 310p. 1982. text ed. 22.50x (ISBN 0-87073-097-5). Schenkman Bks Inc.

Brownstein, Michael. Country Cousins. LC 74-79059. 256p. 1974. 7.95 (ISBN 0-8076-0749-5, Venture Bks.). Braziller.

--Highway to the Sky: "The Frank O'Hara Award Series". LC 79-93499. (A Full Court Rebound Bk.). 1978. pap. 6.00 (ISBN 0-916190-27-7). Full Court NY.

--Oracle Night, a Love Poem. LC 82-80711. (Contemporary Literature Ser.: No. 13). (Orig.). 1982. pap. 6.00 (ISBN 0-940650-13-4). Sun & Moon MD.

--Strange Days Ahead. LC 75-26450. (Illus.). 98p. (Orig.). 1976. pap. 5.00 (ISBN 0-915990-01-6). Z Pr.

Brownstein, Michael, ed. see Jacob, Max.

Brownstein, Oscar L. & Daubert, Darlene M. Analytical Sourcebook of Concepts in Dramatic Theory. LC 80-1200. 560p. 1981. lib. bdg. 49.95 (ISBN 0-313-21309-7, BRN/). Greenwood.

Brownstein, R., jt. auth. see Moos, R. H.

Brownstein, Rachel M. Becoming A Heroine: Reading about Women in Novels. LC 81-24021. 320p. 1982. 17.95 (ISBN 0-670-15443-1). Viking.

--Becoming a Heroine: Reading about Women in Novels. 368p. 1984. pap. 7.95 (ISBN 0-14-006787-6). Penguin.

Brownstein, Robert, jt. auth. see Moos, Rudolf.

Brownstein, Ronald. Reagan's Ruling Class: Portraits of the President's Top 100 Officials. Easton, Nina, ed. LC 82-60917. (Illus.). 759p. 1983. 24.50 (ISBN 0-936486-03-1). Presidential Acct.

Brownstein, Ronald & Easton, Nina. Reagan's Ruling Class: Portraits of the President's Top 100 Officials. 1983. pap. 9.95 (ISBN 0-394-71495-4). Pantheon.

Brownstein, Ronald, ed. see Easton, Nina.

Brownstein, Samuel & Weiner, Mitchell. Basic Tips on the Graduate Record Examination (GRE) 1982. pap. text ed. 3.50 (ISBN 0-8120-2414-1). Barron.

Brownstein, Samuel C. & Weiner, Mitchel. Barron's Vocabulary Builder: A Systematic Plan for Building a Vocabulary, Testing Progress & Applying Knowledge. 9th, rev. ed. LC 75-14340. (Orig.). (gr. 9-12). 1982. pap. 5.50 (ISBN 0-8120-2449-4). Barron.

--Basic Tips on the Preliminary Scholastic Aptitude Test - National Merit Scholarship Qualifying Test (PSAT - NMSQT) LC 81-12700. (gr. 9-12). 1981. pap. text ed. 3.50 (ISBN 0-8120-2416-8). Barron.

--Basic Tips on the SAT. 3rd ed. 1984. 3.95 (ISBN 0-8120-2463-X). Barron.

--Compact Guide to Colleges. 4th ed. 1984. pap. 3.95 (ISBN 0-8120-2826-0). Barron.

--How to Prepare for the SAT (College Entrance Exams) 12th ed. 8.95 (ISBN 0-8120-2773-6). Barron.

Brownstone, D. M. Successful Selling Skills for Small Business. 112p. 1978. 5.95 (ISBN 0-471-04029-0, Pub. by Wiley Pr). Wiley.

Brownstone, David. The Saver's Guide to Sound Investments. 204p. 1985. 15.95 (ISBN 0-531-09589-4). Watts.

Brownstone, David M. Moneywise! Financial Survival on the Road to Riches. 224p. 1985. 15.95 (ISBN 0-531-09593-2). Watts.

--Sell Your Way to Success. LC 80-29110. 212p. 1981. (Pub. by Wiley Pr); pap. 8.95 (ISBN 0-471-09242-8). Wiley.

--Successful Selling Skills for Small Business. 120p. 1978. 8.00 (ISBN 0-686-48199-2, 0812). T-C Pubns CA.

Brownstone, David M. & Carruth, Gorton. Where to Find Business Information: A Worldwide Guide for Everyone Who Needs the Answers to Business Questions. 2nd ed. LC 81-16439. 632p. 1982. Set. 70.00 (ISBN 0-471-08736-X, Pub. by Wiley-Interscience). Wiley.

Brownstone, David M. & Franck, Irene M. Dictionary of Publishing. 304p. 1982. 18.95 (ISBN 0-442-25874-7). Van Nos Reinhold.

--The Manager's Advisor: A Personal & Practical Handbook. LC 83-3520. 584p. 1983. 34.95x (ISBN 0-471-86346-7, Pub. by Wiley-Interscience). Wiley.

--The Sales Professional's Advisor. LC 83-6532. 562p. 1983. 39.95 (ISBN 0-471-86352-1, Pub. by Wiley-Interscience). Wiley.

--The Self-Publishing Handbook. 224p. 1985. pap. 7.95 (ISBN 0-452-25685-2, Plume). NAL.

--The VNR Investor's Dictionary. 320p. 1980. 16.95 (ISBN 0-442-21578-9). Van Nos Reinhold.

--The VNR Real Estate Dictionary. 352p. 1981. 18.95 (ISBN 0-442-25856-9). Van Nos Reinhold.

Brownstone, David M. & Hawes, Gene R. The College Money Book: How to Get A High-Quality Education at the Lowest Possible Cost. LC 83-15582. 256p. 1984. pap. 12.95 (ISBN 0-672-52772-3). Bobbs.

Brownstone, David M., et al. Island of Hope, Island of Tears: Through Ellis Island to the New World. (Paperback Ser.). (Illus.). 320p. 1984. 15.95 (ISBN 0-8149-0882-9); pap. 10.95. Vanguard.

--The VNR Concise Dictionary of Business & Finance. 320p. 1980. text ed. 18.95 (ISBN 0-442-20949-5). Van Nos Reinhold.

Brownstone, Douglass. A Field Guide to America's History. (Illus.). 320p. 1984. 15.95 (ISBN 0-87196-622-0). Facts on File.

Brownstone, Jane E. & Dye, Carol J. Communication Workshop for Parents of Adolescents: Leader's Guide. (Orig.). 1973. pap. text ed. 8.95 (ISBN 0-87822-081-X, 0810); Parent's Review. 2.50 (ISBN 0-87822-082-8, 0828). Res Press.

Brownstone, Meyer & Plunkett, T. J. Metropolitan Winnepeg: Politics & the Reform of Local Government. LC 81-19658. (Lane Series in Regional Government). 240p. 1983. 37.50x (ISBN 0-520-04197-6). U of Cal Pr.

Brownw, Dik. Hagar the Horrible, No. 2. 128p. 1985. pap. 1.95 (ISBN 0-441-31460-0). Ace Bks.

--Hagar the Horrible: On the Loose. 128p. 1985. pap. 1.95 (ISBN 0-441-31461-9). Ace Bks.

Brownwell, Carlton. Criminal Procedure in New York, Part One, 1971-1982: Practice & Forms, 2 vols. rev. ed. LC 82-9425. 1982. 160.00 (ISBN 0-317-12189-8); Suppl., 1982. 110.00; Suppl., 1983. 30.00. Callaghan.

--Criminal Procedure in New York, Part Two, 1971-1982: Criminal Evidence. rev. ed. LC 82-9425. 85.00 (ISBN 0-317-12199-5); Suppl., 1982. 62.50; Suppl., 1983. 20.00. Callaghan.

Browse, Norman L. Physiology & Pathology of Bed Rest. (Illus.). 240p. 1965. photocopy ed. 32.50x (ISBN 0-398-00243-6). C C Thomas.

Browse, Philip M. Hardy Woody Plants from Seed. 165p. 1981. 30.00x (ISBN 0-686-75417-4, Pub. by Grower Bks). State Mutual Bk.

Browse, Phillip M. Step-by-Step Guide to Plant Propagation. 1979. pap. 9.95 (ISBN 0-671-24832-4, Fireside). S&S.

Browston, Lee, et al. Programming Expert Systems in OPS5: An Introduction to Rule-Based Programming. (Artificial Intellegence Ser.). 1985. text ed. 35.95 (ISBN 0-201-10647-7). Addison-Wesley.

Brox, Norbert. Understanding the Message of Paul. Blenkinsopp, Joseph, tr. (Orig.). 1968. pap. 1.45x (ISBN 0-268-00286-X). U of Notre Dame Pr.

Broxap, E. The Great Civil War in Lancashire: 1642-51. (Illus.). xv, 226p. Repr. of 1910 ed. lib. bdg. 25.00x (ISBN 0-678-06792-9). Kelley.

Broxis, Peter F. Organizing the Arts. 132p. 1968. 15.00 (ISBN 0-208-00855-1, Archon). Shoe String.

Broxon, Mildred D. Too Long a Sacrifice. LC 84-424. (Illus.). 226p. 1984. pap. 7.95 (ISBN 0-312-94432-2); ltd., signed collector's ed. 35.00 (ISBN 0-312-94433-0). Bluejay Bks.

Broxon, Mildred D., jt. auth. see Anderson, Poul.

Broxup, Marie, jt. auth. see Bennigsen, Alexandre.

Broy, M., ed. Control Flow & Data Flow: Concepts of Distributed Programming. (NATO ASI Ser.: Series F, Vol. 14). viii, 525p. 1985. 59.00 (ISBN 0-387-13919-2). Springer-Verlag.

Broy, M. & Schmidt, G., eds. Theoretical Foundations of Programming Methodology. 1982. lib. bdg. 78.50 (ISBN 90-277-1460-6, Pub. by Reidel Holland); pap. 39.50 (ISBN 90-277-1462-2). Kluwer Academic.

Broy, M., jt. ed. see Bauer, F. L.

Broyard, Anatole. Men, Women & Other Anticlimaxes. LC 79-20710. 1980. 9.95 (ISBN 0-416-00531-4, NO. 0169). Methuen Inc.

Broyde, Steven. Osip Mandelstam & His Age. LC 74-16801. (Slavic Monographs: No. 1). 264p. 1975. text ed. 16.50x (ISBN 0-674-64492-1). Harvard U Pr.

Broyelle, C., et al. China: A Second Look. (Marxist Theory & Contemporary Capitalism Ser.: No. 16). 1979. text ed. 29.00x (ISBN 0-391-00953-2). Humanities.

Broyelle, Claudie. Women's Liberation in China. Cohen, Michele & Herman, Gary, trs. from Fr. LC 76-4524. (Marxist Theory & Contemporary Capitalism Ser.). 1977. text ed. 23.00x (ISBN 0-391-00587-1). Humanities.

Broyer, John A & Minor, William S., eds. Creative Interchange. LC 81-18538. 566p. 1982. 27.50x (ISBN 0-8093-1032-5). S Ill U Pr.

Broyles, Frank & Bailey, James. Hog Wild: The Autobiography of Frank Broyles. (Illus.). 1979. 13.95 (ISBN 0-87870-065-X). Memphis St Univ.

Broyles, J. E., jt. auth. see Franks, J. R.

Broyles, J. Frank & Hay, Robert D. Administration of Athletic Programs: A Managerial Approach. (Illus.). 1979. ref. ed. 28.95 (ISBN 0-13-005249-3). P-H.

Broyles, Jack, et al, eds. Financial Management Handbook. 2nd ed. 456p. 1983. text ed. 47.50x (ISBN 0-566-02175-7). Gower Pub Co.

Broyles, R. L. The Man Who Could Read Cards. (Orig.). 1980. pap. 1.95 (ISBN 0-532-23310-7). Woodhill.

Broyles, Robert. The Management of Working Capital in Hospitals. LC 80-26802. 499p. 1981. text ed. 52.50 (ISBN 0-89443-335-0). Aspen Systems.

Broyles, Robert & Lay, Colin. Mathematics in Health Administration. LC 80-19451. 542p. 1981. text ed. 54.00 (ISBN 0-89443-297-4). Aspen Systems.

--Statistics in Health Administration. Incl. Vol. 1. Basic Concepts & Applications. 1980. 570 pgs. 59.95, (ISBN 0-89443-153-6); Vol. II. Advanced Concepts & Applications. 1980. 557 pgs. 59.50, (ISBN 0-89443-166-8). LC 79-23280. 62.95; 62.50. Aspen Systems.

Broyles, Robert W. Hospital Accounting Practice: Managerial Accounting, Vol. 2. LC 81-12784. 409p. 1982. text ed. 48.95 (ISBN 0-89443-376-8). Aspen Systems.

--Hospital Accounting Practice: Vol. 1 Financial Accounting. LC 81-12784. 359p. 1982. text ed. 44.95 (ISBN 0-89443-340-7). Aspen Systems.

Broyn, Severyn. Quaker Testimonies & Economic Alternatives. LC 80-80915. 35p. pap. 2.10x (ISBN 0-87574-231-9). Pendle Hill.

Brozaitis, Helene M. The Legacy. 1984. 6.50 (ISBN 0-8062-2271-9). Carlton.

Brozec, Josef, ed. see Watson, Robert.

Brozek, Josef, ed. Malnutrition & Human Behavior. (Illus.). 432p. 1985. 46.50 (ISBN 0-442-21108-2). Van Nos Reinhold.

Brozek, Josef & Pongratz, Ludwig J., eds. Historiography of Modern Psychology. 336p. (Orig.). 1980. pap. text ed. 28.00 (ISBN 0-88937-002-8). Hogrefe Intl.

Brozek, Josef & Slobin, Dan I., eds. Psychology in the U. S. S. R. An Historical Perspective. LC 72-112930. 1972. Repr. 78.00 (ISBN 0-317-08146-2, 2021853). Bks Demand UMI.

Brozek, Josef, tr. see Naumenko, A. I. & Benua, N. N.

Brozek, Josef M., ed. Explorations in the History of Psychology. LC 81-72024. (Illus.). 336p. 1983. 39.50 (ISBN 0-8387-5039-7). Bucknell U Pr.

Brozen, Yale. Concentration, Mergers & Public Policy. (Illus.). 496p. 1982. text ed. 29.95 (ISBN 0-02-904270-4). Free Pr.

--Is Government the Source of Monopoly? & Other Essays. LC 80-14176. (Cato Paper Ser.: No. 9). 87p. 1979. pap. 4.00x (ISBN 0-932790-09-7). Cato Inst.

--Mergers in Perspective. 1982. 14.95 (ISBN 0-8447-3489-6); pap. 6.95 (ISBN 0-8447-3483-7). Am Enterprise.

Brozo, William & Schmelzer, Ron. Setting the Pace: A Speed, Comprehension & Study Skills Program. (No. 174). 208p. 1984. pap. text ed. 11.95 (ISBN 0-675-20152-7); audio cassettes 125.00 (ISBN 0-675-20179-9). Merrill.

Brozovic & Geran, O. Pocket Dictionary: English-Serbo Croatian-English. 322p. 1982. pap. 9.50x (ISBN 0-89918-788-9, Y-788). Vanous.

Brozovic, Blanka & Gercan, Oktavija. English-Serbocroatian & Serbocroatian-English Dictionary. 7th ed. (Eng. & Serbocroatian.). 1980. pap. 4.50x (ISBN 0-686-31617-5). Intl Learn Syst.

Bru, Heoin. Old Man & His Sons. West, John F., tr. from Faroese. (Illus.). 1970. 5.95 (ISBN 0-8397-8412-0). Eriksson.

Brualdi, R. A. Introductory Combinatorics. 374p. 1977. text ed. 30.50 (ISBN 0-7204-8610-6, North-Holland). Elsevier.

--Introductory Combinatorics. 374p. 1984. Repr. of 1977 ed. 30.50 (ISBN 0-317-30900-5, North-Holland). Elsevier.

Bruandet, Pierre. Painting on Silk. LC 84-3026. (Hobbycraft Bks.). (Illus.). 64p. 1984. pap. 4.95 (ISBN 0-668-06239-8, 6239-8). Arco.

Brubacher, D., et al, eds. Methods for the Determination of Vitamins in Foods. 152p. 1985. 30.00 (ISBN 0-85334-339-X, Pub. by Elsevier Applied Sci England). Elsevier.

Brubacher, John. The Law & Higher Education: A Casebook, 2 Vols. LC 70-150238. 701p. 1971. Set. 60.00 (ISBN 0-685-02293-5). Vol. 1 (ISBN 0-8386-7897-1). Vol. 2 (ISBN 0-8386-7947-1). Fairleigh Dickinson.

Brubacher, John S. The Courts & Higher Education. LC 74-138458. (Jossey-Bass Series in Higher Education). pap. 41.50 (ISBN 0-317-08571-9, 2013944). Bks Demand UMI.

--The Judicial Power of the New York State Commissioner of Education. LC 78-176602. (Columbia University. Teachers College. Contributions to Education: No. 295). Repr. of 1927 ed. 22.50 (ISBN 0-404-55295-1). AMS Pr.

--On the Philosophy of Higher Education. LC 82-48076. (Higher Education Ser.). 1982. Repr. of 1977 ed. text ed. 17.95x (ISBN 0-87589-536-0). Jossey-Bass.

--Philosophies of Education. (National Society for the Study of Education Yearbooks Ser.: No. 41, Pt. 1). 1942. pap. 4.50x (ISBN 0-226-59975-2). U of Chicago Pr.

Brubacher, John S. & Rudy, Willis. Higher Education in Transition: A History of American Colleges & Universities, 1636-1976. 3rd, rev. ed. LC 75-6331. 546p. 1976. 28.80xi (ISBN 0-06-010548-8, HarpT). Har-Row.

Brubacher, John S., ed. see Barnard, Henry.

Brubacher, Lewis J., jt. auth. see Bender, Myron L.

Brubaker, Dale. Who's Teaching? Who's Learning? Active Learning in Elementary Schools. LC 77-20894. 1979. pap. 12.95 (ISBN 0-673-16152-8). Scott F.

Brubaker, Dale L. Curriculum Planning: The Dynamics of Theory & Practice. 1982. text ed. 15.45x (ISBN 0-673-16031-9). Scott F.

Brubaker, Dale L. & Sloan, Molly J. So You Want to Join the Team: A Handbook for Teacher Aides, Volunteers, & Cooperating Teachers & Administrators. 64p. 1981. pap. text ed. 9.95 (ISBN 0-8403-2338-7). Kendall-Hunt.

Brubaker, Darrel J., jt. ed. see Sider, Ronald J.

Brubaker, David. The Theatre Student-Court & Commedia: Medieval & Renaissance Theatre. (Theatre Student Ser.). (Illus.). (gr. 7-12). 1975. PLB 15.00 (ISBN 0-8239-0317-6). Rosen Group.

Brubaker, Edward & Brubaker, Mary. Golden Fire: The Anniversary Book of the Oregon Shakespearean Festival. LC 85-2905. (Illus.). 141p. 1985. 22.95 (ISBN 0-9614515-0-5). Or Shakespearean.

Brubaker, Edward S. Shakespeare Aloud: A Guide to His Verse on Stage. LC 76-52176. 1977. pap. 3.75 (ISBN 0-9613496-0-3). Brubaker.

Brubaker, George R. & Phipps, P. Beverley, eds. Corrosion Chemistry. LC 78-25554. (ACS Symposium Ser.: No. 89). 1979. 29.95 (ISBN 0-8412-0471-3). Am Chemical.

Brubaker, J. Lester. Personnel Administration in the Christian School. 168p. (Orig.). 1980. pap. 6.95 (ISBN 0-88469-130-6). BMH Bks.

Brubaker, J. Omar & Clark, Robert E. Understanding People: Children, Youth, Adults. LC 75-172116. 96p. 1981. pap. text ed. 4.95 (ISBN 0-910566-15-1); Perfect bdg. instr's. guide 4.95 (ISBN 0-910566-25-9). Evang Tchr.

Brubaker, Lloyd W., et al. Guide to the Pioneer Cemetery. Rev. ed. (Illus.). 13p. (Orig.). 1972. pap. 0.50 (ISBN 0-939666-06-5). Yosemite Natl Hist.

Brubaker, Mary, jt. auth. see Brubaker, Edward.

Brubaker, Pamela. She Hath Done What She Could. 224p. (Orig.). 1985. pap. 7.95 (ISBN 0-87178-942-6). Brethren.

Brubaker, Robert, ed. Contemporary Film Criticism. (Contemporary Film Criticism Ser.: Vol. 1). 450p. Date not set. 75.00x (ISBN 0-8103-1595-5). Gale.

--Contemporary Issues Criticism, Vol. 2. (Contemporary Issues Criticism Ser.). 600p. 1983. 85.00x (ISBN 0-8103-1588-2). Gale.

--Contemporary Issues Criticism: Excerpts from Criticism of Contemporary Writings in Sociology, Politics, Psychology, Anthropology, Education, History, Law, Biography, & Related Fields, Vol. 1. 600p. 1982. 85.00x (ISBN 0-8103-1550-5). Gale.

Brubaker, Rogers. The Limits of Rationality: An Essay on the Social & Moral Thought of Max Weber. LC 83-15152. (Controversies in Sociology Ser.: No. 16). 119p. 1984. text ed. 22.50x (ISBN 0-04-301172-1); pap. text ed. 8.95x (ISBN 0-04-301173-X). Allen Unwin.

Brubaker, Sterling. In Command of Tomorrow: Resource and Environment Strategies for Americans. 192p. 1975. pap. 5.95 (ISBN 0-8018-1957-1). Resources Future.

--In Command of Tomorrow: Resources & Environmental Strategies for Americans. (Resources for the Future Ser.). 192p. 1975. pap. 5.95x (ISBN 0-8018-1957-1). Johns Hopkins.

--In Commnand of Tomorrow: Resources & Environmental Strategies. LC 74-24401. (Resources for the Future Study Ser.). pap. 48.00 (ISBN 0-317-26027-8, 2023789). Bks Demand UMI.

--To Live on Earth: Man & His Environment in Perspective. LC 75-185514. (Resources for the Future Ser.). 218p. 1972. 16.50x (ISBN 0-8018-1378-6). Johns Hopkins.

--To Live on Earth: Man & His Environment in Perspective. 218p. 1972. 16.50 (ISBN 0-8018-1378-6); pap. 1.50 (ISBN 0-317-35677-1). Resources Future.

--Trends in the World Aluminum Industry. LC 67-16035. pap. 68.50 (ISBN 0-317-26024-3, 2023790). Bks Demand UMI.

Brubaker, Sterling, jt. auth. see Crosson, Pierre R.

Brubaker, Sterling, ed. Rethinking the Federal Lands. LC 83-43261. 322p. 1984. lib. bdg. 39.00x (ISBN 0-915707-00-4); pap. 11.95X (ISBN 0-915707-01-2). Resources Future.

Brubaker, Susan H. Sourcebook for Aphasia: A Guide to Family Activities & Community Resources. 206p. 1982. pap. 12.00 (ISBN 0-8143-1697-2). Wayne St U Pr.

--Workbook for Aphasia: Exercises for the Redevelopment of Higher Level Language Functioning. LC 78-5305. 404p. 1978. 10.95 (ISBN 0-8143-1595-X). Wayne St U Pr.

--Workbook for Language Skills: Exercises for Written & Verbal Expression. LC 84-11893. 228p. 1985. spiral bound 25.00 (ISBN 0-8143-1778-2). Wayne St U Pr.

--Workbook for Reasoning Skills: Exercises for Cognitive Facilitation. LC 83-50961. 300p. 1983. spiral bound 25.00 (ISBN 0-8143-1760-X). Wayne St U Pr.

Brubaker, Timothy, jt. auth. see Springer, Dianne.

Brubaker, Timothy H. Later Life Families. 1985. 15.95 (ISBN 0-8039-2402-X); pap. 7.95 (ISBN 0-8039-2403-8). Sage.

Brubaker, Timothy H., ed. Family Relationships in Later Life. (Sage Focus Editions: Vol. 64). 272p. 1983. 25.00 (ISBN 0-8039-2104-7); pap. 12.50 (ISBN 0-8039-2105-5). Sage.

Brubaker, Timothy H. & Ade-Ridder, Linda, eds. Long-Term Marriages: A Special Isssue of Lifestyles. 64p. 1984. 9.95 (ISBN 0-89885-248-X). Human Sci Pr.

Brubakken, David M., et al. Treatment of Psychotic & Neurologically Impaired Children: A Systems Approach. 288p. 1980. 22.50 (ISBN 0-442-26647-2). Van Nos Reinhold.

Brubeck, William H. The American National Interest & Middle East Peace. (Seven Springs Studies). 48p. 1981. pap. 3.00 (ISBN 0-943006-03-1). Seven Springs.

--Reflections on the Path to Middle East Peace. (Seven Springs Studies). 31p. 1982. pap. 3.00 (ISBN 0-943006-00-7). Seven Springs.

Brubidge, R. Brinsley. A Dictionary of British Flower, Fruit & Still Life Painters, Vol. 2. 1981. 40.00x (ISBN 0-85317-024-X, Pub. by Lewis Pubs). State Mutual Bk.

Brucan, Silviu. The Dialectic of World Politics. LC 77-85349. 1978. 22.50 (ISBN 0-02-904680-7). Free Pr.

--The Post-Brezhnev Era. LC 83-16158. 144p. 1983. 24.95 (ISBN 0-03-069409-4). Praeger.

Brucar, Wayne E., jt. auth. see Rich, Malcolm C.

Bruccoli. Some Sort of Epic Grandeur. 640p. 1983. 12.95 (ISBN 0-15-683803-6, Harv). HarBraceJ.

Bruccoli, M. J., ed. see James, Henry.

Bruccoli, Mary. Dictionary of Literary Biography. (DLB Documentary Series: An Illustrated Chronicle: Vol. 2). (Illus.). 400p. 1982. 90.00x (ISBN 0-8103-1114-3). Gale.

Bruccoli, Mary, ed. Dictionary of Literary Biography Documentary Series: An Illustrated Chronicle, Vol. 3. 450p. 1983. 90.00x (ISBN 0-8103-1115-1). Gale.

Bruccoli, Mary & Ross, Jean W., eds. Dictionary of Literary Biography Yearbook: 1983. (Dictionary of Literary Biography). 355p. 1985. 92.00x (ISBN 0-8103-1627-7, Pub by Bruccoli). Gale.

Bruccoli, Mathew J. F. Scott Fitzgerald: A Descriptive Bibliography. LC 77-181395. (Pittsburg Series in Bibliography). pap. 98.30 (ISBN 0-317-10320-2, 2020618). Bks Demand UMI.

--Ross MacDonald. pap. 7.95 (ISBN 0-15-679082-3, Harv). HarBraceJ.

Bruccoli, Matt, ed. see O'Hara, John.

Bruccoli, Matthew. Conversations with Ernest Hemingway. (Literary Conversations Ser.). 1987. 17.95 (ISBN 0-87805-272-0); pap. 9.95 (ISBN 0-87805-273-9). U Pr of Miss.

--Reconquest of Mexico: An Amiable Journey in Persuit of Cortes. LC 74-76440. 1974. 8.95 (ISBN 0-8149-0742-3). Vanguard.

--Scott & Ernest: The Authority of Failure & the Authority of Success. LC 79-26848. 186p. 1980. pap. 7.95 (ISBN 0-8093-0977-7). S Ill U Pr.

Bruccoli, Matthew, ed. see Bryer, Jackson.

Bruccoli, Matthew, ed. & intro. by see Cozzens, James G.

Bruccoli, Matthew J. James Gould Cozzens: A Descriptive Bibliography. LC 80-53553. (Pittsburgh Ser. in Bibliography). (Illus.). 206p. 1981. 32.95x (ISBN 0-8229-3435-3). U of Pittsburgh Pr.

--James Gould Cozzens: A Life Apart. 384p. 1983. 15.95 (ISBN 0-15-146048-5). HarBraceJ.

--James Gould Cozzens: A Life Apart. 384p. 1984. pap. 9.95 (ISBN 0-15-645952-3, Harv). HarBraceJ.

--John O'Hara: A Descriptive Bibliography. LC 77-15737. (Pittsburgh Ser. in Bibliography). (Illus.). 1978. 42.00x (ISBN 0-8229-3349-7). U of Pittsburgh Pr.

--The Last of the Novelists: F. Scott Fitzgerald & "The Last Tycoon". LC 77-4381. (Illus.). 173p. 1977. 9.95 (ISBN 0-8093-0820-7). S Ill U Pr.

--The O'Hara Concern: A Biography of John O'Hara. LC 75-9736. (Illus.). 416p. 1975. 15.00 (ISBN 0-394-48446-0). Random.

--The Price Was High: The Last Uncollected Stories of F. Scott Fitzgerald. LC 78-14074. 832p. 1981. 19.95 (ISBN 0-15-174020-8). HarBraceJ.

--Profile of F. Scott Fitzgerald. LC 75-139588. 1971. pap. text ed. 6.95x (ISBN 0-675-09263-9). Merrill.

--Raymond Chandler: A Checklist. LC 68-16892. (Serif Ser.: No. 2). pap. 15.00 (ISBN 0-8357-9373-7, 2015383). Bks Demand UMI.

--Raymond Chandler: A Descriptive Bibliography. LC 78-4280. (Pittsburgh Series in Bibliography). 1979. 23.00x (ISBN 0-8229-3382-9). U of Pittsburgh Pr.

--Ross MacDonald-Kenneth Millar: A Descriptive Bibliography. LC 83-1398. (Pittsburgh Ser. in Bibliography). (Illus.). 278p. 1983. 40.00x (ISBN 0-8229-3482-5). U of Pittsburgh Pr.

--Some Sort of Epic Grandeur: The Life of F. Scott Fitzgerald. LC 80-8740. 640p. 1981. 25.00 (ISBN 0-15-183242-0). HarBraceJ.

--Supplement to F. Scott Fitzgerald: A Descriptive Bibliography. LC 79-21728. (Pittsburgh Ser. in Bibliography). 235p. 1980. 30.00x (ISBN 0-8229-3409-4). U of Pittsburgh Pr.

Bruccoli, Matthew J. & Layman, Richard. Ring W. Lardner: A Descriptive Bibliography. LC 75-9126. (Pittsburgh Ser. in Bibliography). 1976. 52.00x (ISBN 0-8229-3306-3). U of Pittsburgh Pr.

Bruccoli, Matthew J., ed. The Chief Glory of Every People: Essays on Classic American Writers. LC 73-1783. 310p. 1973. 14.95x (ISBN 0-8093-0615-8). S Ill U Pr.

--The Correspondence of F. Scott Fitzgerald. LC 79-4765. 1980. 25.00 (ISBN 0-394-41773-9). Random.

--F. Scott Fitzgerald: Poems 1911 to 1940. 1981. 11.95 (ISBN 0-89723-026-4); signed numbered copies 25.00 (ISBN 0-686-85738-0). Bruccoli.

--Fitzgerald-Hemingway Annual 1969. 25.00 (ISBN 0-685-77405-8). Bruccoli.

--Fitzgerald-Hemingway Annual 1976. 1978. 25.00 (ISBN 0-910972-62-1). Bruccoli.
--The Great Gatsby a Facsimile of the Manuscript. 1973. deluxe ed. 100.00 boxed (ISBN 0-89723-032-9). Bruccoli.
--James Gould Cozzens: New Acquist of True Experience. LC 79-14581. (Crosscurrents-Modern Critiques-New Ser.). 158p. 1979. 17.95 (ISBN 0-8093-0930-0). S Ill U Pr.
--Just Representations: A James Gould Cozzens Reader. LC 78-9357. 601p. 1978. 14.95 (ISBN 0-8093-0886-X). S Ill U Pr.
--Kenneth Millar-Ross Macdonald: A Checklist. LC 77-39690. (Modern Authors Checklist Ser.). (Illus.). 86p. 1971. 30.00x (ISBN 0-8103-0901-7, Bruccoli Clark Book). Gale.
--New Essays on "The Great Gatsby". (The American Novel Ser.). 144p. Date not set. price not set (ISBN 0-521-26589-4); pap. price not set (ISBN 0-521-31963-3). Cambridge U Pr.
Bruccoli, Matthew J. & Clark, C. E., eds. Fitzgerald-Hemingway Annual 1970. 1970. 25.00 (ISBN 0-910972-03-6). Bruccoli.
Bruccoli, Matthew J. & Clark, C. E. Frazer, Jr., eds. First Printings of American Authors. Layman, Richard. per vol 45.00 (ISBN 0-685-88842-8); 4 vol. set 272.00 (ISBN 0-685-88843-6). Bruccoli.
Bruccoli, Matthew J. & Clark, C. E., Jr., eds. First Printings of American Authors, 4 vols. LC 74-11756. (Illus.). 1978. Set. 400.00x (ISBN 0-8103-0933-5); per vol. 100.00x. Gale.
--First Printings of American Authors: Supplement, Vol. 5. (Illus.). Date not set. 100.00x (ISBN 0-8103-0934-3, Bruccoli Clark Bk). Gale.
--Fitzgerald-Hemingway Annual 1972. 1973. 25.00 (ISBN 0-910972-12-5). Bruccoli.
--Fitzgerald-Hemingway Annual 1973. 1969. 25.00 (ISBN 0-89723-045-0). Bruccoli.
Bruccoli, Matthew J. & Layman, Richard, eds. Fitzgerald-Hemingway Annual, 3 vols. Incl. 1977 Annual. 1978 (ISBN 0-8103-0909-2); 1978 Annual. 1979 (ISBN 0-8103-0910-6); 1979 Annual. 1980 (ISBN 0-8103-0911-4). LC 75-83781. (Illus.). 64.00x ea. (Bruccoli Clark). Gale.
Bruccoli, Matthew J., ed. see Chandler, Raymond.
Bruccoli, Matthew J., ed. see Charvat, William.
Bruccoli, Matthew J., jt. ed. see Clark, C. E., Jr.
Bruccoli, Matthew J., ed. see Cozzens, James G.
Bruccoli, Matthew J., ed. see Fitzgerald, F. Scott.
Bruccoli, Matthew J., ed. see Lardner, Ring.
Bruccoli, Matthew J., jt. ed. see Layman, Richard.
Bruccoli, Matthew J., ed. see Maddow, Ben & Huston, John.
Bruccoli, Matthew J., ed. see Minelli, Vincente.
Bruccoli, Matthew J., intro. by see O'Hara, John.
Bruccoli, Matthew J., ed. see Sayre, Joel & Faulkner, William.
Bruccoli, Matthew J. & Frazer Clark, C. E., Jr.compiled by. Hemingway at Auction. (Illus.). 25.00 (ISBN 0-89723-002-7). Bruccoli.
Bruccoli, Matthew J. & Millar, Kenneth. Kenneth Millar - Ross Macdonald: A Checklist. (Illus.). 18.00 (ISBN 0-685-77422-8). Gale.
Bruccoli, Matthew J., et al, eds. Conversations with Jazz Musicians. LC 77-9143. (Conversations Ser.: Vol. 2). 1977. 46.00x (ISBN 0-8103-0944-0, A Bruccoli Clark Book). Gale.
--Conversations with Writers. LC 77-9142. (Conversations Ser.: Vol. 1). 1977. 46.00x (ISBN 0-8103-0943-2, Bruccoli Clark Book). Gale.
--Conversations with Writers II. LC 77-27992. (Conversations Ser.: Vol. 3). 1978. 46.00x (ISBN 0-8103-0945-9, Bruccoli Clark Book). Gale.
--The Romantic Egoist. Repr. of 1984 ed. 19.95 (ISBN 0-89723-049-3). Bruccoli.
Bruce, jt. auth. see Rajki.
Bruce, A. American Mineralogical Journal to Elucidate the Mineralogy & Geology of the U. S, Vol. 1. LC 84-62807. 1968. 24.75x (ISBN 0-02-846280-7). Hafner.
Bruce, A. B. The Epistle to the Hebrews. 1980. 17.25 (ISBN 0-86524-028-0, 5802). Klock & Klock.
--The Miracles of Christ. 1980. 20.00 (ISBN 0-86524-060-4, 9504). Klock & Klock.
--The Parables of Christ. 1980. 15.50 (ISBN 0-86524-059-0, 9503). Klock & Klock.
Bruce, A. B., jt. auth. see Moulton, Richard G.
Bruce, A. D. & Cowley, R. A. Structural Phase Transitions. 325p. 1981. 35.00x (ISBN 0-85066-206-0, NO.6589, Pub by Pion England). Methuen Inc.
Bruce, A. D., et al. Structural Phase Transitions. 326p. 1981. 33.00x (ISBN 0-85066-206-0). Taylor & Francis.
Bruce, A. M. Sewage Sludge Stabilisation & Disinfection. (Water & Waste Water Technology Ser.: No. 1-714). 624p. 1984. text ed. 69.95x (ISBN 0-470-20080-4). Halsted Pr.
Bruce, A. M. & Connor, E. S., eds. Stabilisation, Disinfection & Odour Control in Sewage Sludge Treatment. 200p. 1984. text ed. 59.95x (ISBN 0-470-20033-2). Halsted Pr.
Bruce, A. M. & Havelaar, A. H., eds. Disinfection of Sewage Sludge: Technical, Economic & Microbiological Aspects. 1982. lib. bdg. 34.95 (ISBN 90-277-1502-5, Pub. by Reidel Holland). Kluwer Academic.
Bruce, A. Ninian, ed. see Wilson, S. Kinnier.
Bruce, A. P. Annotated Bibliography of the British Army, Sixteen Sixty to Nineteen Fourteen. LC 75-23072. (Reference Library of Social Science: Vol. 14). 255p. 1975. lib. bdg. 34.00 (ISBN 0-8240-9988-5). Garland Pub.
--The Purchase System in the British Army, 1660-1871. (Royal Historical Society Studies in History: Vol. 20). 190p. 1980. text ed. 35.50x (ISBN 0-901050-57-1, Pub. by Swiftbks England). Humanities.
Bruce, A. Wayne. Basic Quality Assurance & Quality Control in the Clinical Laboratory. 179p. 1984. pap. text ed. 13.95 (ISBN 0-316-11252-6). Little.
Bruce, Alexander B. The Moral Order of the World in Ancient & Modern Thought. LC 77-527224. (Gifford Lectures: 1898). Repr. of 1899 ed. 32.00 (ISBN 0-404-60456-0). AMS Pr.
--The Providential Order of the World. LC 77-27225. (Gifford Lectures: 1897). 1978. Repr. of 1897 ed. 30.00 (ISBN 0-404-60455-2). AMS Pr.
--The Training of the Twelve. LC 79-88121. (Shepherd Illustrated Classics). 1979. pap. 6.95 (ISBN 0-87983-206-1). Keats.
--Training of the Twelve. LC 73-129738. 1979. 12.95 (ISBN 0-8254-2212-4); pap. 8.95 (ISBN 0-8254-2236-1). Kregel.
Bruce, Alfred & Sandbank, Harold. The History of Prefabrication. LC 72-5038. (Technology & Society Ser.). (Illus.). 80p. 1972. Repr. of 1944 ed. 20.00 (ISBN 0-405-04691-X). Ayer Co Pubs.
Bruce, Andasia K. Uncle Tom's Cabin of To-Day. LC 72-6488. (Black Heritage Library Collection Ser). 1972. Repr. of 1906 ed. 14.50 (ISBN 0-8369-9161-3). Ayer Co Pubs.
Bruce, Andrew A., et al. Workings of the Indeterminate-Sentence Law & the Parole System in Illinois. LC 68-19466. (Criminology, Law Enforcement, & Social Problems Ser.: No. 5). 1968. Repr. of 1928 ed. 15.00x (ISBN 0-87585-005-7). Patterson Smith.
Bruce, Anthony. Bibliography of the British Army, 1660-1914. 280p. 1985. lib. bdg. 28.00 (ISBN 3-598-10574-6). K G Saur.
Bruce, C., ed. see Armistead, Lew.
Bruce, C., ed. see Reum, Earl.
Bruce, Calvin E. & Jones, William R., eds. Black Theology II: Essays on the Formation & Outreach of Contemporary Black Theology. LC 75-39113. 285p. 1978. 25.00 (ISBN 0-8387-1893-0). Bucknell U Pr.
Bruce, Carrol. The Commitment Factor. LC 84-5005. 1984. pap. 3.95 (ISBN 0-8054-5541-8). Broadman.
Bruce, Charles. The Broad Stone of Empire: Problems of Crown Colony Administration, 2 vols. facsimile ed. LC 70-179507. (Select Bibliographies Reprint Ser.). Repr. of 1910 ed. Set. 68.50 (ISBN 0-8369-6636-8). Ayer Co Pubs.
Bruce, Chris, jt. auth. see West, Harvey.
Bruce, Colin. Social Cost-Benefit Analysis: A Guide for Country & Project Economists to the Derivation & Application of Economic & Social Accounting Prices. (Working Paper: No. 239). iii, 143p. 1976. 5.00 (ISBN 0-686-36092-3, WP-0239). World Bank.
--Social Cost-Benefit Analysis: A Guide for Country & Project Economists to the Derivation & Application of Economic & Social Accounting Prices. (Working Paper: No. 239). 143p. 1976. pap 5.00 (ISBN 0-686-39655-3, WP-0239). World Bank.
Bruce, Colin, jt. auth. see Scanduzzo, Pasquale L.
Bruce, Colin, ed. see Galloway, Albert.
Bruce, Colin, II, ed. see Mishler, Clifford & Krause, Chester.
Bruce, Colin, II, ed. see Mishler, Clifford L. & Krause, Chester.
Bruce, Colin R., II & Rhodes, Nicholas. The Standard Guide to South Asian Coins & Paper Money Since 1556, A. D. LC 82-81657. 1982. 42.50. Krause Pubns.
Bruce, Colin R., II, ed. see DeClermont, Andre R. & Wheeler, John.
Bruce, Colin R., 2nd. Standard Catalog of Mexican Coins, Paper Money, Bonds & Medals. rev. ed. LC 81-80932. (Illus.). 352p. (Eng. & Span.). 1981. pap. 14.50 (ISBN 0-87341-060-2). Krause Pubns.
Bruce, Curt. The Great Houses of New Orleans. 1977. 16.95 (ISBN 0-394-40716-4). Knopf.
Bruce, Curt & Aidala, Thomas. The Great Houses of San Francisco. LC 73-7287. (Illus.). 192p. 1981. pap. 10.95 (ISBN 0-394-70773-7). Knopf.
Bruce, David. Electronics: Basics, Device & Applications. 1984. text ed. 49.95 (ISBN 0-8359-1585-9); solutions manual avail. (ISBN 0-8359-4547-2). Reston.
--Modern Electronics: Basics, Devices & Applications. 1984. text ed. 31.95 (ISBN 0-8359-4546-4). Reston.
--Vest Pocket Electronics Handbook. 1984. pap. 9.95 (ISBN 0-8359-8311-0). Reston.
Bruce, David L. Functional Toxicity of Anesthesia. LC 80-82766. (The Scientific Basis of Clinical Anesthesia Ser.). (Illus.). 144p. 1980. 24.00 (ISBN 0-8089-1276-3, 790710). Grune.
Bruce, David L., jt. auth. see Applebaum, Edward L.
Bruce, Debra. Dissolves. (Burning Deck Poetry Ser.). 1977. pap. 15.00 signed handmade. Burning Deck.
--Pure Daughter. LC 83-80588. 80p. 1983. 9.95 (ISBN 0-938626-21-3); pap. 5.95 (ISBN 0-938626-22-1). U of Ark Pr.
Bruce, Debra F., jt. auth. see Bruce, Robert G.
Bruce, Derek A., jt. auth. see Ivan, Leslie P.
Bruce, Dickson D., Jr. And They All Sang Hallelujah: Plain-Folk Camp-Meeting Religion, 1800-1845. LC 74-11344. (Illus.). 1974. 13.50x (ISBN 0-87049-157-1); pap. 5.95x (ISBN 0-87049-310-8). U of Tenn Pr.
--The Rhetoric of Conservatism: The Virginia Convention of 1829-30 & the Conservative Tradition in the South. LC 82-9224. 218p. 1982. 18.00 (ISBN 0-87328-121-7). Huntington Lib.
Bruce, Donald. Topics of Restoration Comedy. LC 74-80652. 224p. 1974. 25.00 (ISBN 0-312-80920-4). St Martin.
Bruce, Erica. The Great Cat Game Book. LC 85-42556. (Illus.). 56p. 1985. 13.41 (ISBN 0-06-015462-4, HarpT). Har-Row.
Bruce, Errol. This Is Rough Weather Cruising. (Illus.). 136p. 1980. 19.95 (ISBN 0-914814-23-0). Sail Bks.
Bruce, Erroll. This Is Rough Weather Cruising. 136p. 1982. 35.00x (ISBN 0-333-32090-5, Pub. by Nautical England). State Mutual Bk.
Bruce, F. F. Abraham & David: Places They Knew. (Illus.). 128p. 1984. 12.95 (ISBN 0-8407-5402-7). Nelson.
--Acts. 1983. pap. 4.50 (ISBN 0-87508-170-3). Chr Lit.
--Commentary on First & Second Corinthians. Black, Matthew, ed. (New Century Bible Commentary Ser.). 224p. 1980. pap. 6.95 (ISBN 0-8028-1839-0). Eerdmans.
--The Defence of the Gospel in the New Testament. rev. ed. LC 77-2282. 1977. pap. 4.95 (ISBN 0-8028-1024-1). Eerdmans.
--Epistle to the Ephesians. 144p. 1962. 10.95 (ISBN 0-8007-0083-X). Revell.
--The Epistles of John. LC 78-22069. 1978. pap. 4.95 (ISBN 0-8028-1783-1). Eerdmans.
--The Epistles to the Colossians, to Philemon, & to the Ephesians. (New International Commentary on the New Testament Ser.). 464p. 1984. 18.95 (ISBN 0-8028-2401-3). Eerdmans.
--The Gospel of John. 440p. 1984. 13.95 (ISBN 0-8028-3407-8). Eerdmans.
--The Hard Sayings of Jesus. LC 83-10793. (The Jesus Library). 216p. 1983. pap. 6.95 (ISBN 0-87784-927-7). Inter-Varsity.
--History of the Bible in English. 3rd ed. 1978. pap. 8.95 (ISBN 0-19-520088-8, GB542, GB). Oxford U Pr.
--In Retrospect: Remembrance of Things Past. 292p. 35.00x (ISBN 0-7208-0471-X, Pub. by Pickering & Inglis Scotland). State Mutual Bk.
--Israel y las Naciones. Orig. Title: Israel & the Nations. 298p. (Span.). 1979. 7.75 (ISBN 0-8254-1076-2). Kregel.
--Jesus & Christian Origins Outside the New Testament. 1974. pap. 5.95 (ISBN 0-8028-1575-8). Eerdmans.
--Jesus & Paul: Places They Knew. 128p. 1983. Repr. of 1981 ed. 12.95 (ISBN 0-8407-5281-4). Nelson.
--New Testament History. LC 78-144253. 462p. 1972. pap. 8.95 (ISBN 0-385-02533-5, Anch). Doubleday.
--Paul & His Converts. rev. ed. 155p. 1985. pap. 5.95 (ISBN 0-87784-593-X). Inter-Varsity.
--Paul: Apostle of the Heart Set Free. LC 77-26127. 1978. 16.95 (ISBN 0-8028-3501-5). Eerdmans.
--The Pauline Circle. 112p. (Orig.). 1985. pap. 4.95 (ISBN 0-8028-0066-1). Eerdmans.
--Peter, Stephen, James & John: Studies in Non-Pauline Christianity. (Orig.). 1980. 8.95 (ISBN 0-8028-3532-5). Eerdmans.
--Philippians: A Good News Commentary. LC 82-48919. 176p. (Orig.). 1983. pap. 7.64i (ISBN 0-06-061138-3, RD/446, HarpR). Har-Row.
--Places They Knew - Jesus & Paul. 128p. 1981. 30.00x (ISBN 0-686-75528-6, Pub. by Ark Pub England). State Mutual Bk.
--Romans. Tasker, R. V., ed. (Tyndale New Testament Commentaries Ser.). 288p. (Orig.). 1986. pap. 6.95 (ISBN 0-8028-0062-9). Eerdmans.
--The Spreading Flame: The Rise & Progress of Christianity from Its Beginnings to the Conversion of the English. 432p. 1980. pap. 7.95 (ISBN 0-8028-1805-6). Eerdmans.
--The Time Is Fulfilled. LC 78-7373. 1978. pap. text ed. 3.95 (ISBN 0-8028-1756-4). Eerdmans.
--Understanding the New Testament: Matthew. LC 78-9115. 1982. pap. 3.95 (ISBN 0-8054-1327-8). Broadman.
--What the Bible Teaches about What Jesus Did. 1979. pap. 3.95 (ISBN 0-8423-7885-5). Tyndale.
Bruce, F. F., ed. see Howley, G. C. D.
Bruce, F. F., ed. see Van Elderen, Bastiaan.
Bruce, F. F., ed. see Vine, W. E.
Bruce, F. F., et al, eds. Nelson's Bible Encyclopedia for the Family. LC 81-22560. 300p. 1982. 19.95 (ISBN 0-8407-5258-X). Nelson.
Bruce, Frederick F. The Message of the New Testament. 120p. 1973. pap. 4.95 (ISBN 0-8028-1525-1). Eerdmans.
--New Testament Documents: Are They Reliable. pap. 2.95 (ISBN 0-87784-691-X). Inter-Varsity.
Bruce, Frederick F., ed. Acts of the Apostles. (Greek text). 1953. 15.95 (ISBN 0-8028-3056-0). Eerdmans.
--The Book of the Acts. (New International Commentary on the New Testament). 1954. 16.95 (ISBN 0-8028-2182-0). Eerdmans.
--Epistle of Paul to the Romans. (Tyndale Bible Commentaries). 1963. pap. 5.95 (ISBN 0-8028-1405-0). Eerdmans.
--The Epistle to the Hebrews. (New International Commentary on the New Testament Ser.). 1964. 15.95 (ISBN 0-8028-2183-9). Eerdmans.
--Israel & the Nations. LC 63-22838. 1963. pap. 5.95 (ISBN 0-8028-1450-6). Eerdmans.
--New Testament Development of Old Testament Themes. 1969. pap. 3.95 (ISBN 0-8028-1729-7). Eerdmans.
--New Testament Documents: Are They Reliable? (Orig.). 1959. pap. 2.95 (ISBN 0-8028-1025-X). Eerdmans.
Bruce, G. Brazil & the Brazilians. 1976. lib. bdg. 59.95 (ISBN 0-8490-1543-X). Gordon Pr.
Bruce, G. L. Flightdeck. (Illus.). 10.00 (ISBN 0-392-03002-0, SpS). Sportshelf.
Bruce, Gail C., jt. auth. see Harper, Frederick D.
Bruce, Gustav M. Luther As an Educator. LC 77-114482. (Illus.). 318p. Repr. of 1928 ed. lib. bdg. 35.00x (ISBN 0-8371-4771-9, BRLD). Greenwood.
Bruce, H. William Blake in This World. LC 73-18085. (Studies in Blake, No. 3). 1974. Repr. of 1925 ed. lib. bdg. 49.95x (ISBN 0-8383-1732-4). Haskell.
Bruce, H. A. Adventurings in the Physical. 59.95 (ISBN 0-87968-581-6). Gordon Pr.
Bruce, Harold. William Blake in This World. LC 73-3184. Repr. of 1925 ed. lib. bdg. 30.00 (ISBN 0-8414-1779-2). Folcroft.
Bruce, Harold L. William Blake in This World. 1978. Repr. of 1925 ed. lib. bdg. 30.00 (ISBN 0-8495-0440-6). Arden Lib.
--William Blake in This World. 15.75 (ISBN 0-8369-6924-3, 7805). Ayer co Pubs.
Bruce, Harry J. Distribution & Transportation Handbook. LC 76-132669. (Illus.). 416p. 1971. 18.95 (ISBN 0-8436-1400-5). Van Nos Reinhold.
Bruce, Helen F. Your Guide to Photography. 2nd ed. LC 73-19475. (Illus.). 323p. 1974. 16.50x (ISBN 0-06-480103-9, 06368). B&N Imports.
--Your Guide to Photography. 2nd ed. (Orig.). 1974. pap. 5.29i (ISBN 0-06-463342-X, EH 342, EH). B&N NY.
Bruce, Henry C. New Man: Twenty-Nine Years a Slave. LC 77-94474. Repr. of 1874 ed. 15.00x (ISBN 0-8371-2367-4, BNM&, Pub. by Negro U Pr). Greenwood.
--New Man, Twenty-Nine Years a Slave: Twenty-Nine Years a Free Man. facs. ed. LC 72-89421. (Black Heritage Library Collection Ser). 1845. 14.25 (ISBN 0-8369-8526-5). Ayer Co Pubs.
Bruce, Herbert A. Our Heritage, & Other Addresses. facs. ed. LC 68-54334. (Essay Index Reprint Ser). 1968. Repr. of 1934 ed. 20.00 (ISBN 0-8369-0259-9). Ayer Co Pubs.
Bruce, I. A. Historical Commentary on the Hellenica Oxyrhynchia. (Cambridge Classical Studies). 1967. 22.95 (ISBN 0-521-04352-2). Cambridge U Pr.
Bruce, I. M., jt. auth. see Landon, H. C.
Bruce, Isabel & Eickhoff, Edith. The Michigan Poor Law: Its Development & Administration with Special Reference to State Provision for Medical Care of the Indigent. LC 75-17210. (Social Problems & Social Policy). 1976. Repr. of 1936 ed. 23.50x (ISBN 0-405-07482-4). Ayer Co Pubs.
Bruce, J. Douglas, ed. Mort Artu: An Old French Prose Romance of the Thirteenth Century. LC 75-178546. Repr. of 1910 ed. 32.00 (ISBN 0-404-56649-9). AMS Pr.
--Le Morte Arthur, a Romance in Stanzas of Eight Lines. LC 75-41201. Repr. of 1903 ed. 14.50 (ISBN 0-404-14793-3). AMS Pr.
--Le Morte D'Arthur. (EETS, ES Ser.: No. 88). Repr. of 1903 ed. 38.00 (ISBN 0-527-00293-3). Kraus Repr.
Bruce, J. L. Black & White. LC 83-61303. 52p. (Orig.). 1983. pap. 1.25 (ISBN 0-940776-07-3). Maclay Assoc.
--Eureka. LC 83-61302. 52p. (Orig.). 1983. pap. 1.25 (ISBN 0-940776-08-1). Maclay Assoc.
Bruce, J. M. Aeroplanes of the Royal Flying Corps (Military Wing) (Putnam Aeronautical Bks.). (Illus.). 1982. 39.95 (ISBN 0-370-30084-X, Pub. by the Bodley Head). Merrimack Pub Cir.
--The Bristol Fighter. (Vintage Warbirds Ser.). (Illus.). 64p. (Orig.). 1985. pap. 5.95 (ISBN 0-85368-704-8, Pub. by Arms & Armour). Sterling.
Bruce, J. P. & Clark, R. H. Introduction to Hydrometeorology. 1966. pap. 13.25 (ISBN 0-08-011714-7). Pergamon.
--Introduction to Hydrometeorology. 1986. price not set (ISBN 0-08-023852-1); 30.00 (ISBN 0-08-023851-3). Pergamon.
Bruce, J. Percy, tr. see Chu Hsi.
Bruce, J. T., Jr., jt. auth. see Reid, Catha W.
Bruce, J. T., Jr. & Reid, Catha W., eds. Sandlapper Cookbook. 3rd ed. 1979. 6.95 (ISBN 0-87844-020-8). Sandlapper Pub Co.
Bruce, James, tr. see Bloch, Iwan.
Bruce, James B. The Politics of Soviet Policy Formation: Khrushchev's Innovative Policies in Education & Agriculture. (Monograph Series in World Affairs: Vol. 13, 1975-76, Bk. 4). 138p. (Orig.). 1976. pap. 5.95 (ISBN 0-87940-048-X). Monograph Series.
Bruce, Janet. The Kansas City Monarchs: Champions of Black Baseball. LC 85-8535. (Illus.). 224p. 1985. 19.95X (ISBN 0-7006-0273-9). U Pr of KS.

Bruce, Jeannette. Judo: A Gentle Beginning. LC 74-26503. (Illus.). 160p. (gr. 3 up). 1975. 11.06i (ISBN 0-690-00557-1). Crowell Jr Bks.

Bruce, Jeffrey & Cohen, Sherry S. About Face: An Hour a Week to Radiant Skin & Flawless Make-Up. 1984. 18.95 (ISBN 0-399-12916-2, Putnam). Putnam Pub Group.

--About Face: An Hour a Week to Radiant Skin & Flawless Make-Up. (Illus.). 160p. 1985. pap. 8.95 (ISBN 0-399-51112-1, Perigee). Putnam Pub Group.

Bruce, Jerome. Studies in Black & White. 18.75 (ISBN 0-8369-9160-5, 9035). Ayer Co Pubs.

Bruce, Jo Anne C. Privacy & Confidentiality of Health Care Information. LC 84-9231. (Illus.). 168p. (Orig.). 1984. 27.50 (ISBN 0-939450-06-2, 148171). AHPI.

Bruce, John. Breathing Space. LC 74-76302. (Anansi Fiction Ser.: No. 31). 120p. 1974. 10.95 (ISBN 0-88784-432-4, Pub. by Hse Anansi Pr Canada); pap. 5.95 (ISBN 0-88784-330-1). U of Toronto Pr.

Bruce, John, ed. Historie of the Arrivall of Edward Fourth in England & the Finall Recoverye of His Kingdomes from Henry Sixth, A. D. 1471. LC 77-164757. (Camden Society, London. Publications. First Ser.: No. 1). Repr. of 1838 ed. 10.00 (ISBN 0-404-50101-X). AMS Pr.

--Historie of the Arrivall of Edward Fourth in England & the Finall Recouerye of His Kingdomes from Henry Sixth. 1838. 10.00 (ISBN 0-384-06035-8). Johnson Repr.

Bruce, John, ed. see Borough, John.

Bruce, John, ed. see Charles First, King of Great Britain.

Bruce, John, jt. ed. see Crosby, Allan J.

Bruce, John, ed. see Elizabeth First, Queen Of England.

Bruce, John, ed. see Hayward, John.

Bruce, John, ed. see James First-King Of England.

Bruce, John, ed. see Leicester, Robert D.

Bruce, John, ed. see Manningham, John.

Bruce, John, jt. ed. see Nichols, John G.

Bruce, John, ed. see Verney Family.

Bruce, John, ed. see Verney, Ralph.

Bruce, John, ed. see Whitelocke, James.

Bruce, John E. The Awakening of Hezekiah Jones. LC 73-18567. Repr. of 1916 ed. 16.50 (ISBN 0-404-11381-8). AMS Pr.

Bruce, John W. Real Estate Finance in a Nutshell. 2nd ed. (Nutshell Ser.). 300p. 1985. pap. text ed. 8.95 (ISBN 0-314-85866-0). West Pub.

Bruce, Jon W. Real Estate Finance in a Nutshell. LC 79-289. (Nutshell Ser.). 292p. 1979. pap. text ed. 7.95 (ISBN 0-8299-2031-5). West Pub.

Bruce, Jon W., et al. Modern Property Law Cases & Materials. LC 84-2317. (American Casebook Ser.). 1004p. 1984. text ed. 28.95 (ISBN 0-314-80459-5); pap. text ed. write for info. (ISBN 0-314-83524-5). West Pub.

Bruce, Joseph P. Chu Hsi & His Masters, An Introduction to Chu Hsi & the Sung School of Chinese Philosophy. LC 78-38050. Repr. of 1923 ed. 21.50 (ISBN 0-404-56904-8). AMS Pr.

--Chu Hsi & His Masters: An Introduction to Chu Hsi & the Sung School of Chinese Philosophy. lib. bdg. 79.95 (ISBN 0-87968-078-4). Krishna Pr.

Bruce, Kathleen. Virginia Iron Manufacture in the Slave Era. LC 67-30856. Repr. of 1930 ed. 37.50x (ISBN 0-678-00414-5). Kelley.

Bruce, Kenneth R. Yowsah! Yowsah! Yowsah! The Roaring Twenties. (Illus.). 160p. 1981. pap. 8.95 (ISBN 0-686-73518-8). Star Pub CA.

Bruce, Lennart. The Broker. 80p. 1984. pap. 4.50 (ISBN 0-915572-75-3). Panjandrum.

--Exposure. 1975. perfect bound in wrappers 2.50 (ISBN 0-685-78907-1, Pub. by Cloud Marauder). Small Pr Dist.

--Letter of Credit. (Illus.). 1973. pap. 1.50 (ISBN 0-87711-051-4). Kayak.

--Subpoemas. 68p. 1974. pap. 4.50 (ISBN 0-915572-06-0). Panjandrum.

Bruce, Lennart, tr. see Ekeland, Vilhelm.

Bruce, Lenny. The Unpublished Lenny Bruce. LC 84-2034. pap. 8.95 (ISBN 0-89471-259-4); 19.80 (ISBN 0-89471-260-8). Running Pr.

Bruce, Leo. A Bone & a Hank of Hair. (Carolous Deeme Mystery Ser.). 192p. 1985. 14.95 (ISBN 0-89733-176-1); pap. 4.95 (ISBN 0-89733-175-3). Academy Chi Pubs.

--Case with No Conclusion. 288p. 14.95 (ISBN 0-89733-117-6); pap. 4.95 (ISBN 0-89733-118-4). Academy Chi Pubs.

--Case with Ropes & Rings. 192p. 1980. 14.95 (ISBN 0-89733-034-X); pap. 4.50 (ISBN 0-89733-035-8). Academy Chi Pubs.

--Case Without a Corpse. (Sgt. Beef Mystery ser.). 284p. 1982. 14.95 (ISBN 0-89733-052-8); pap. 4.50 (ISBN 0-89733-051-X). Academy Chi Pubs.

--Cold Blood. (Sgt. Beef Mystery Ser.). 205p. 1980. 14.95 (ISBN 0-89733-039-0); pap. 4.50 (ISBN 0-89733-038-2). Academy Chi Pubs.

--Death at St. Asprey's School. 221p. 1984. 14.95 (ISBN 0-89733-095-1); pap. 4.95 (ISBN 0-89733-094-3). Academy Chi Pubs.

--Death in Albert Park. (Carolus Deene Mystery Ser.). 239p. 1983. pap. 4.95 (ISBN 0-89733-073-0). Academy Chi Pubs.

--Furious Old Women. Barzun, J. & Taylor, W. H., eds. LC 81-47375. (Crime Fiction 1950-1975 Ser.). 191p. 1983. lib. bdg. 18.00 (ISBN 0-8240-4976-4). Garland Pub.

--Furious Old Women. (A Carolus Deene Mystery Ser.). 191p. 1983. pap. 4.95 (ISBN 0-89733-084-6). Academy Chi Pubs.

--Jack on the Gallows Tree. (Carolus Deene Mystery Ser.). 189p. 1983. 14.95 (ISBN 0-89733-072-2); pap. 4.95 (ISBN 0-89733-071-4). Academy Chi Pubs.

--Neck & Neck. (Sgt. Beef Mystery Ser.). 224p. 1980. 14.95 (ISBN 0-89733-041-2); pap. 4.50 (ISBN 0-89733-040-4). Academy Chi Pubs.

--Nothing Like Blood. 192p. 1985. 14.95 (ISBN 0-89733-128-1); pap. 4.95 (ISBN 0-89733-127-3). Academy Chi Pubs.

Bruce, Leo, pseud. Such Is Death. (Academy Mystery Ser.: No. 6). 1985. 14.95 (ISBN 0-89733-159-1); pap. 4.95 (ISBN 0-89733-160-5). Academy Chi Pubs.

Bruce, Linda. Al Phillip Bettle. (Illus.). (gr. k-3). 1965. 6.95 (ISBN 0-8392-3050-8). Astor-Honor.

Bruce, Marjory. The Book of Craftsmen: The Story of Man's Handiwork Through the Ages. LC 70-185352. (Illus.). 283p. 1974. Repr. of 1937 ed. 40.00x (ISBN 0-8103-3960-9). Gale.

Bruce, Martin M. A Guide to Human Relations in Business & Industry. LC 73-6907. 1969. pap. 12.50 (ISBN 0-935198-00-8). M M Bruce.

Bruce, Maurice. The Coming of the Welfare State. 1974. 31.50 (ISBN 0-7134-1351-4, Pub. by Batsford England); pap. 14.95 (ISBN 0-7134-1359-X). David & Charles.

Bruce, Muriel. Mukara: A Novel. Reginald, R. & Melville, Douglas, eds. LC 77-84204. (Lost Race & Adult Fantasy Ser.). 1978. Repr. of 1930 ed. lib. bdg. 24.50x (ISBN 0-405-10960-1). Ayer Co Pubs.

Bruce, Neil. Three Essays on Taxation in Simple General Equilibrium Models. LC 79-53822. (Outstanding Dissertations in Economics Ser.). 125p. 1984. lib. bdg. 22.00 (ISBN 0-8240-4170-4). Garland Pub.

Bruce, Neil, jt. auth. see Boadway, Robin.

Bruce, Nigel. Teamwork for Preventive Care, Vol. 1. LC 80-41095. (Social Policy Research Monographs). 241p. 1980. 68.95 (ISBN 0-471-27883-1, Pub. by Res Stud Pr). Wiley.

Bruce, P. A. Institutional History of Virginia in the Seventeenth Century, 2 vols. 1964. 16.00 ea. (ISBN 0-8446-1090-9). Peter Smith.

Bruce, Peter H. Memoirs of Peter Henry Bruce: A Military Officer in the Services of Prussia, Russia, & Great Britian. (Russia Through European Eyes Ser). 1970. Repr. of 1782 ed. 59.50 (ISBN 0-306-77029-6). Da Capo.

Bruce, Philip A. Economic History of Virginia in the Seventeenth Century, 2 Vols. 1896. Set. 75.00 (ISBN 0-384-06080-3). Johnson Repr.

--Economic History of Virginia in the Seventeenth Century, 2 Vols. Set. 32.00 (ISBN 0-8446-1091-7). Peter Smith.

--Plantation Negro As a Freeman. 262p. 1970. Repr. of 1889 ed. 15.00 (ISBN 0-87928-010-7). Corner Hse.

--The Plantation Negro As a Freeman: Observations on His Character, Condition & Prospects in Virginia. LC 79-99354. ix, 262p. 1972. Repr. of 1889 ed. lib. bdg. 14.75 (ISBN 0-8411-0025-X). Metro Bks.

--Social Life of Virginia in the Seventeenth-Century. 268p. 1968. Repr. of 1907 ed. 16.00 (ISBN 0-87928-002-6). Corner Hse.

Bruce, Phillip & Pederson, Sam. The Software Development Project: Planning & Management. LC 81-10457. 210p. 1982. 28.50x (ISBN 0-471-06269-3, Pub. by Wiley-Interscience). Wiley.

Bruce, Preston & Johnson, Katharine. From the Door of the White House. LC 81-23672. (Illus.). 160p. (gr. 6 up). 1984. 11.50 (ISBN 0-688-00883-6). Lothrop.

Bruce, R. Teach Yourself Cantonese. (Teach Yourself Ser). 1971. pap. 5.95 (ISBN 0-679-10208-6). McKay.

Bruce, R. D. Lacandon Dream Symbolism: Dream Symbolism & Interpretation among the Lacandon Maya. (Illus.). 1979. 25.00 (ISBN 968-414-000-2). Heinman.

Bruce, R. R., et al, eds. Field Soil Water Regime. (Illus.). 212p. 1973. pap. 5.00 (ISBN 0-89118-760-X). Soil Sci Soc Am.

Bruce, Richard L. Physiological Psychology. LC 76-25484. 1977. text ed. 19.95 (ISBN 0-03-002841-8, HoltC); tchr's manual 25.00 (ISBN 0-03-018276-X). HR&W.

Bruce, Robert. Early Marine Navigation. (Illus.). 30p. 1976. pap. 1.00 (ISBN 0-913346-05-5). Phila Maritime Mus.

Bruce, Robert & Keller, Bruce P. Worldwide Restrictions on Advertising: An Outline of Principles, Problems & Solutions. 75p. 1985. avail. Intl Advertising Assn.

Bruce, Robert D., jt. auth. see Perera, Victor.

Bruce, Robert G. The Influence of Community Characteristics on the Relationship of Unemployment Changes to Employment Changes in Major Labor Market Areas. (Criteria for Water Resources Investment Ser.: CWR 12). 122p. 1967. pap. 5.00 (ISBN 0-318-00013-X). Inst for Urban & Regional.

Bruce, Robert G. & Bruce, Debra F. C.A.R.E.S. 1984. 4.25 (ISBN 0-89536-672-X). CSS of Ohio.

Bruce, Robert V. Lincoln & the Tools of War. LC 73-15241. (Illus.). 368p. 1974. Repr. of 1956 ed. lib. bdg. 19.00x (ISBN 0-8371-7167-9, BRLS). Greenwood.

Bruce, Sheilah. The Radish Day Jubilee. (Fraggle Rock Bk.). (Illus.). 48p. (gr. 1-4). 1983. 6.95 (ISBN 0-03-068678-4). HR&W.

Bruce, Sheilah B. Gonzo & the Giant Chicken. LC 82-3862. (Muppet Press Bks.). (Illus.). 32p. (gr. 1-4). 1982. pap. 1.95 (ISBN 0-394-85411-X). Random.

Bruce, Shelley. Tomorrow Is Today. LC 83-3797. (Illus.). 224p. 1983. 15.95 (ISBN 0-672-52756-1). Bobbs.

Bruce, Stephen R. Pension Claims Handbook. 1985. price not set. BNA.

Bruce, Steve. Firm in the Faith. LC 84-5964. 227p. 1984. text ed. 32.95x (ISBN 0-566-00705-3). Gower Pub Co.

Bruce, T., jt. auth. see Collins, T.

Bruce, Thomas A. & Norton, Richard W. Improving Rural Health: Initiatives of an Academic Medical Center. (Illus.). 188p. 1984. 14.95 (ISBN 0-914546-53-8). Rose Pub.

Bruce, Vicki & Green, Patrick. Visual Perception: Psychology & Ecology. 384p. 1985. text ed. 39.95 (ISBN 0-86377-012-6); pap. 19.95 (ISBN 0-86377-013-4). L Erlbaum Assocs.

Bruce, W. R. & Johns, H. E. The Spectra of X Rays Scattered in Low Atomic Number Materials. 1980. 10.00x (ISBN 0-686-69958-0, Pub. by Brit Inst Radiology). State Mutual Bk.

Bruce, W. Robert, et al, eds. Banbury Report 7: Gastrointestinal Cancer: Endogenous Factors. LC 80-28016. (Banbury Report Ser.: Vol. 7). (Illus.). 410p. 1981. 75.00x (ISBN 0-87969-206-5). Cold Spring Harbor.

Bruce, Wallace. Along the Hudson with Washington Irving. LC 77-776. 1913. lib. bdg. 22.00 (ISBN 0-8414-9880-6). Folcroft.

--The Hudson. Centennial Edition ed. 280p. (4 foldout maps). 1982. pap. 9.95 (ISBN 0-915850-04-4). Walking News Inc.

--Robert Burns: Poet-Laureate. LC 73-18124. 1893. lib. bdg. 10.00 (ISBN 0-8414-9895-4). Folcroft.

--Robert Burns: Poet-Laurete of Lodge Canongate Kilwinning. 1978. Repr. of 1893 ed. lib. bdg. 10.00 (ISBN 0-8495-0436-8). Arden Lib.

Bruce, William C. John Randolph of Roanoke, 1773-1833, 2 Vols. LC 68-23979. 1969. Repr. of 1922 ed. lib. bdg. 75.00x (ISBN 0-374-91045-6). Octagon.

Bruce-Briggs, B. The War Against the Autombile. LC 77-3909. 1977. 10.95 (ISBN 0-525-23008-4). Dutton.

Bruce-Briggs, B., ed. The New Class? LC 78-62999. (McGraw-Hill Paperbacks Ser.). 252p. 1981. pap. 5.95 (ISBN 0-07-008573-0). McGraw.

--The New Class? LC 78-62999. 225p. 1979. 16.95 (ISBN 0-87855-306-1). Transaction Bks.

Bruce-Chwatt, L. J. Essentials of Mariology. 2nd ed. Date not set. 40.00 (ISBN 0-471-82831-9). Wiley.

Bruce-Chwatt, L. J. & DeZulueta, Julian. The Rise & Fall of Malaria in Europe: A Historico-Epidemiological Study. (Illus.). 1980. text ed. 33.00x (ISBN 0-19-858168-8). Oxford U Pr.

Bruce-Gardyne, Jock. Mrs. Thatcher's First Administration: The Prophets Confounded. LC 84-11528. 256p. 1984. 27.50 (ISBN 0-312-55140-1). St Martin.

Bruce-Gardyne, Jock & Lawson, Nigel. The Power Game: An Examination of Decision-Making in Government. (Illus.). 204p. 1976. 22.50 (ISBN 0-208-01598-1, Archon). Shoe String.

Bruce-Lockhart. Scotch: The Whiskey of Scotland in Fact & Story. 5th ed. 184p. 12.95 (ISBN 0-370-30910-3, Pub. by the Bodley Head). Merrimack Pub Cir.

Bruce-Mitford, R. L., tr. see Glob, P. V.

Bruce-Novoa. Chicano Authors: Inquiry by Interview. (Illus.). 306p. 1980. text ed. 20.00x (ISBN 0-292-71059-3); pap. text ed. 8.95 (ISBN 0-292-71062-3). U of Tex Pr.

--Chicano Poetry: A Response to Chaos. LC 81-23129. 246p. 1984. pap. 8.95 (ISBN 0-292-71092-5). U of Tex Pr.

Brucer, Marshall, ed. A History of Airborne Command & Airborne Center. LC 78-71270. (Illus.). 1978. Repr. of 1946 ed. 13.95x (ISBN 0-932572-04-9). Phillips Pubns.

Bruce's Son & Company. Victorian Frames, Borders & Cuts. LC 76-3052. (Pictorial Archive Ser.). (Illus.). 128p. (Orig.). 1976. pap. 4.50 (ISBN 0-486-23320-0). Dover.

--Victorian Frames, Borders & Cuts from the 1882 Type Catalog of George Bruce's Son & Co. 13.25 (ISBN 0-8446-5468-X). Peter Smith.

Bruch, Catherine B., et al. The Faces & Forms of Creativity: Presentations from the Conference on Creativity & the Gifted-Talented Held March 21-22, 1980, Houston, Texas. 212p. 14.95 (ISBN 0-318-02146-3). NSLTIGT.

Bruch, Catherine B., jt. auth. see Conference on Creativity & the Gifted-Talented.

Bruch, Charles D. Strength of Materials for Technology. LC 77-27629. 376p. 1978. text ed. 29.95x (ISBN 0-471-11372-7); solutions manual avail. (ISBN 0-471-04513-6). Wiley.

Bruch, Hans A. & Caviers, Luis M. Vital Statistics Systems in Five Developing Countries. Shipp, Audrey, ed. (Ser. 2: No. 79). 1979. pap. text ed. 1.95 (ISBN 0-8406-0169-7). Natl Ctr Health Stats.

Bruch, Hilde. Eating Disorders: Obesity, Anorexia Nervosa, & the Person Within. LC 72-89189. 1979. pap. 8.95x (ISBN 0-686-52338-5, TB-5052). Basic.

--The Golden Cage: The Enigma of Anexoria Nervosa. LC 78-11185. 1979. pap. 3.95 (ISBN 0-394-72688-X, Vin). Random.

--The Golden Cage: The Enigma of Anorexia Nervosa. 1978. 10.00x (ISBN 0-674-35650-0). Harvard U Pr.

--Learning Psychotherapy: Rationale & Ground Rules. LC 74-83848. 200p. 1974. text ed. 10.00x (ISBN 0-674-52025-4); pap. text ed. 6.95x (ISBN 0-674-52026-2). Harvard U Pr.

Bruch, Marilyn. Phonics Art Projects. 1985. pap. 5.95 (ISBN 0-8224-5541-2). Pitman Learning.

Bruch, Mathias & Hiemenz, Ulrich. Small & Medium Scale Industries in the ASEAN Countries: Agents or Victims of Economic Development? (Replica Edition Ser.). 130p. 1984. pap. 15.00x (ISBN 0-86531-848-4). Westview.

Bruch, P., et al. Brvologie Europaea, Seu Genera Muscorum Europaeorum Monographice Illustrated: Collarium, Index & Supplement. Incl. Music Europaei Novi Vel Bryologiae Supplementum. Florschuetz, P. A., pref. by.. (Illus.). Repr. of 1866 ed. 502.00 (ISBN 90-6123-220-1). Lubrecht & Cramer.

Bruchac, Joseph. Ancestry. 4.00 (ISBN 0-318-11912-9). Great Raven Pr.

--The Good Message of Handsome Lake. LC 79-973335. (Keepsake Ser.: Vol. 9). 1979. 15.00 (ISBN 0-87775-112-9); pap. 6.00 (ISBN 0-87775-113-7). Unicorn Pr.

--Iroquois Stories: Heroes & Heroines, Monsters & Magic. (Illus.). 208p. (gr. 3-7). 1985. 16.95 (ISBN 0-89594-167-8). Crossing Pr.

--The Road to Black Mountain. LC 76-28248. (Orig.). 1976. pap. 4.00x (ISBN 0-914476-45-9). Thorp Springs.

--Stone Giants & Flying Heads, Adventure Stories from the Iroguois. LC 78-15556. (Children's Stories Ser.). (Illus.). (gr. 5-12). 1979. 10.95 (ISBN 0-89594-006-X); pap. 4.95 (ISBN 0-89594-007-8). Crossing Pr.

--There Are No Trees in the Prison. 1978. pap. 2.50 (ISBN 0-942396-24-3). Blackberry ME.

--Translator's Son. Barkan, Stanley H., ed. (Cross-Cultural Review Chapbook 10: Native American Abenaki Poetry 1). 40p. 1980. pap. 3.50 (ISBN 0-89304-809-7). Cross Cult.

--The Wind Eagle & Other Abenaki Folk Stories. (Bowman Books). (Illus.). 48p. (Orig.). 1985. pap. 5.00 (ISBN 0-912678-64-X). Greenfld Rev Pr.

Bruchac, Joseph, intro. by. Breaking Silence: An Anthology of Contemporary Asian American Poets. LC 83-80759. 300p. (Orig.). 1984. pap. 9.95 (ISBN 0-912678-59-3). Greenfld Rev Pr.

Bruchac, Joseph, ed. The Last Stop. perfect bdg. 3.00 (ISBN 0-912678-10-0). Greenfld Rev Pr.

--The Light from Another Country: Poetry from American Prisons. LC 83-788. 350p. (Orig.). 1984. pap. 9.95 (ISBN 0-912678-60-7). Greenfld Rev Pr.

Bruchac, Joseph, intro. by. Songs from This Earth on Turtle's Back: An Anthology of Poetry by American Indian Writers. LC 82-82420. 300p. (Orig.). 1983. pap. 9.95 (ISBN 0-912678-58-5). Greenfld Rev Pr.

Bruche, Gert, jt. auth. see Casey, Bernard.

Bruchey, Eleanor, ed. see Abrahams, Paul P.

Bruchey, Eleanor, ed. see Adams, Frederick U.

Bruchey, Eleanor, ed. see Arnold, Dean A.

Bruchey, Eleanor, ed. see Bain, Foster H. & Read, Thomas T.

Bruchey, Eleanor, ed. see Brewster, Kingman, Jr.

Bruchey, Eleanor, jt. ed. see Bruchey, Stuart.

Bruchey, Eleanor, ed. see Callis, Helmut G.

Bruchey, Eleanor, ed. see Crowther, Samuel.

Bruchey, Eleanor, ed. see David, Jules.

Bruchey, Eleanor, ed. see Davies, Robert B.

Bruchey, Eleanor, ed. see De La Torre, Jose, Jr.

Bruchey, Eleanor, ed. see Dunning, John H.

Bruchey, Eleanor, ed. see Edelberg, Guillermo S.

Bruchey, Eleanor, ed. see Edwards, Corwin & Bruchey, Stuart.

Bruchey, Eleanor, ed. see Elliott, William Y., et al.

Bruchey, Eleanor, ed. see Eysenbach, Mary L.

Bruchey, Eleanor, ed. see Gates, Theodore R. & Linden, Fabian.

Bruchey, Eleanor, ed. see Gordon, Wendell C.

Bruchey, Eleanor, ed. see Hufbauer, G. & Adler, F. W.

Bruchey, Eleanor, ed. see Lewis, Cleona & Schlotterbeck, Karl T.

Bruchey, Eleanor, ed. see McKenzie, Fred A.

Bruchey, Eleanor, ed. see Moore, John R.

Bruchey, Eleanor, ed. see National Planning Association.

Bruchey, Eleanor, ed. see Nordyke, James W.

Bruchey, Eleanor, ed. see O'Connor, Harvey.

Bruchey, Eleanor, ed. see Overlach, Theodore W.

Bruchey, Eleanor, ed. see Phelps, William C.

Bruchey, Eleanor, ed. see Porter, Robert P.

Bruchey, Eleanor, ed. see Queen, George S.

Bruchey, Eleanor, ed. see Rippy, Fred J.

Bruchey, Eleanor, ed. see Southard, Frank A., Jr.

Bruchey, Stuart, ed. see Prosper, Peter A., Jr.
Bruchey, Stuart, ed. see Proxmire, William.
Bruchey, Stuart, ed. see Przeworski, Joanne F.
Bruchey, Stuart, ed. see Queen, George S.
Bruchey, Stuart, ed. see Rakestraw, Lawrence.
Bruchey, Stuart, ed. see Raveed, Sion.
Bruchey, Stuart, ed. see Reed, Clyde G.
Bruchey, Stuart, ed. see Reed, S. G.
Bruchey, Stuart, ed. see Reeder, Clarence A., Jr.
Bruchey, Stuart, ed. see Renforth, William & Raveed, Sion.
Bruchey, Stuart, ed. see Rettig, Rudi.
Bruchey, Stuart, ed. see Richards, Max D.
Bruchey, Stuart, ed. see Ripley, William Z.
Bruchey, Stuart, ed. see Rippy, Fred J.
Bruchey, Stuart, ed. see Robinson, John R.
Bruchey, Stuart, ed. see Robinson, William W.
Bruchey, Stuart, ed. see Rollins, George W.
Bruchey, Stuart, ed. see Rostow, Walt W.
Bruchey, Stuart, ed. see Russell, Robert R.
Bruchey, Stuart, ed. see Sacks, David H.
Bruchey, Stuart, ed. see Saly, Pierre.
Bruchey, Stuart, ed. see Sanborn, John B.
Bruchey, Stuart, ed. see Schachter, Joseph.
Bruchey, Stuart, ed. see Schaefer, Donald F.
Bruchey, Stuart, ed. see Schmitz, Mark.
Bruchey, Stuart, ed. see Schor, Stanley S.
Bruchey, Stuart, ed. see Schramm, Gunter.
Bruchey, Stuart, ed. see Scott, William A.
Bruchey, Stuart, ed. see Secretan, J. H.
Bruchey, Stuart, ed. see Shambaugh, Benjamin F.
Bruchey, Stuart, ed. see Sharpless, John B.
Bruchey, Stuart, ed. see Shepherd, James F.
Bruchey, Stuart, ed. see Sheridan, George J., Jr.
Bruchey, Stuart, ed. see Shields, Roger E.
Bruchey, Stuart, ed. see Shrimpton, Colin.
Bruchey, Stuart, ed. see Siddiqi, Shahid.
Bruchey, Stuart, ed. see Simon, Simon M.
Bruchey, Stuart, ed. see Smathers, George H.
Bruchey, Stuart, ed. see Smith, David B.
Bruchey, Stuart, ed. see Smith, Philip R.
Bruchey, Stuart, ed. see Sorey, Gordon K.
Bruchey, Stuart, ed. see Southard, Frank A., Jr.
Bruchey, Stuart, ed. see Spann, Robert M.
Bruchey, Stuart, ed. see Spooner, Robert D.
Bruchey, Stuart, ed. see Stafford, Marshall P.
Bruchey, Stuart, ed. see Staley, Eugene.
Bruchey, Stuart, ed. see Stanford Research Institute.
Bruchey, Stuart, ed. see Starr, John W., Jr.
Bruchey, Stuart, ed. see Steckel, Richard H.
Bruchey, Stuart, ed. see Steele, Henry B.
Bruchey, Stuart, ed. see Stern, Siegfried.
Bruchey, Stuart, ed. see Stettler, Henry L.
Bruchey, Stuart, ed. see Stewart, Lowell O.
Bruchey, Stuart, ed. see Stigum, Marcia L.
Bruchey, Stuart, ed. see Still, Jack W.
Bruchey, Stuart, ed. see Stopford, John M.
Bruchey, Stuart, ed. see Strausberg, Stephen.
Bruchey, Stuart, ed. see Striner, Herbert E.
Bruchey, Stuart, ed. see Strout, Alan M.
Bruchey, Stuart, ed. see Sturm, James L.
Bruchey, Stuart, ed. see Sutton, Robert M.
Bruchey, Stuart, ed. see Talbot, Frederick A.
Bruchey, Stuart, ed. see Tatter, Henry W.
Bruchey, Stuart, ed. see Taylor, George & Neu, Irene D.
Bruchey, Stuart, ed. see Taylor, Paul S.
Bruchey, Stuart, ed. see Tedesco, Paul H.
Bruchey, Stuart, ed. see Teele, Ray P.
Bruchey, Stuart, ed. see Tenebaum, Marcel.
Bruchey, Stuart, ed. see Thbaut, Louis.
Bruchey, Stuart, ed. see Thomas, Robert P.
Bruchey, Stuart, ed. see Thomas, Rollin G.
Bruchey, Stuart, ed. see Thompson, G. Richard.
Bruchey, Stuart, ed. see Thorp, Rosemary & Bertram, Geoffrey.
Bruchey, Stuart, ed. see Thwaite, et al.
Bruchey, Stuart, ed. see Tortella, Gabriel C.
Bruchey, Stuart, ed. see Tosiello, Rosario J.
Bruchey, Stuart, ed. see Toyne, Brian.
Bruchey, Stuart, ed. see Trent, Logan D.
Bruchey, Stuart, ed. see Tsurumi, Yoshihiro.
Bruchey, Stuart, ed. see U. S. Comptroller of the Currency.
Bruchey, Stuart, ed. see U. S. Congress, House of Representatives.
Bruchey, Stuart, ed. see U. S. Congress, Senate.
Bruchey, Stuart, ed. see U. S. Department of Commerce.
Bruchey, Stuart, ed. see U. S. Department of Commerce & Labor.
Bruchey, Stuart, ed. see U. S. Federal Trade Commission.
Bruchey, Stuart, ed. see U. S. House of Representatives.
Bruchey, Stuart, ed. see U. S. House of Representatives, Committee No. 1 of the Select Committee on Small Business.
Bruchey, Stuart, ed. see United States House of Representatives, Select Committee on Small Business.
Bruchey, Stuart, ed. see U. S. House of Representatives, Select Committee on Small Business.
Bruchey, Stuart, ed. see U. S. House of Representatives, Subcommittee No. 1 of the Select Committee on Small Business.
Bruchey, Stuart, ed. see United States House of Representatives, Subcommittee No. 2 of the Select Committee on Small Business.
Bruchey, Stuart, ed. see U. S. House of Representatives, Subcommittee No. 4 on Distribution Problems Affecting Small Business.
Bruchey, Stuart, ed. see U. S. Senate.
Bruchey, Stuart, ed. see U. S. Senate Subcommittee of the Committee on Banking & Currency.
Bruchey, Stuart, ed. see U. S. Senate, Subcommittee on Monopoly of the Select Committee on Small Business.
Bruchey, Stuart, ed. see University of Pittsburgh, Bureau of Business Research.
Bruchey, Stuart, ed. see Vanderlip, Frank A.
Bruchey, Stuart, ed. see Van Name, Willard G.
Bruchey, Stuart, ed. see Van Young, James.
Bruchey, Stuart, ed. see Vatter, Barbara A.
Bruchey, Stuart, ed. see Vatter, Harold G.
Bruchey, Stuart, ed. see Vatter, Paul A.
Bruchey, Stuart, ed. see Viallon, Jean-Baptiste.
Bruchey, Stuart, ed. see Vickery, William E.
Bruchey, Stuart, ed. see Villard, Henry.
Bruchey, Stuart, ed. see Villiers, Patrick.
Bruchey, Stuart, ed. see Von Laer, Hermann.
Bruchey, Stuart, ed. see Wade, William W.
Bruchey, Stuart, ed. see Walters, R. H.
Bruchey, Stuart, ed. see Waltrip, John R.
Bruchey, Stuart, ed. see Waters, Joseph P.
Bruchey, Stuart, ed. see Watkins, Leonard L.
Bruchey, Stuart, ed. see Wedemeyer, Karl E.
Bruchey, Stuart, ed. see Weissman, Rudolph L.
Bruchey, Stuart, ed. see Wells, Louis T., Jr.
Bruchey, Stuart, ed. see Wendt, Lloyd & Kogan, Herman.
Bruchey, Stuart, ed. see Westerfield, Ray B.
Bruchey, Stuart, ed. see Wettereau, James O.
Bruchey, Stuart, ed. see Wheelwright, William B.
Bruchey, Stuart, ed. see Whillier, Austin.
Bruchey, Stuart, jt. ed. see Whyman, John.
Bruchey, Stuart, ed. see Wiel, Samuel C.
Bruchey, Stuart, ed. see Wilkinson, Norman R.
Bruchey, Stuart, ed. see Willis, H. Parker.
Bruchey, Stuart, ed. see Winkler, Donald R.
Bruchey, Stuart, ed. see Winkler, Max.
Bruchey, Stuart, ed. see Winter, Charles E.
Bruchey, Stuart, ed. see Wirth, Fremont P.
Bruchey, Stuart, ed. see Wright, Benjamin C.
Bruchey, Stuart, ed. see Wright, Ivan.
Bruchey, Stuart, ed. see Yeoman, Wayne A.
Bruchey, Stuart, ed. see Yudin, Elinor B.
Bruchey, Stuart, ed. see Zeigler, Harmon.

Bruchey, Stuart W. Robert Oliver & Mercantile Bookkeeping in the Early Nineteenth Century. LC 75-18460. (History of Accounting Ser.). 1976. 14.00x (ISBN 0-405-07544-8). Ayer Co Pubs.

--Robert Oliver: Merchant of Baltimore, 1783-1819. LC 78-64225. (Johns Hopkins University. Studies in the Social Sciences. Seventy-Fourth Ser. 1956: 1). Repr. of 1956 ed. 31.00 (ISBN 0-404-61327-6). AMS Pr.

--Robert Oliver, Merchant of Baltimore, 1783-1819. Carosso, Vincent P., ed. LC 78-18954. (Small Business Enterprise in America Ser.). 1979. Repr. of 1956 ed. lib. bdg. 32.50x (ISBN 0-405-11458-3). Ayer Co Pubs.

Bruchez, Dardo. Mensaje a la Conciencia. 128p. (Orig., Span.). 1979. pap. 3.50 (ISBN 0-89922-143-2). Edit Caribe.

Bruchez, Dardo, tr. see Tozer, A. W.

Bruchis, Michael. Nations, Nationalities Peoples: A Study of the Nationality Policies of the Communist Party in Soviet Moldavia. 293p. 1984. 25.00x (ISBN 0-88033-057-0). East Eur Quarterly.

--One Step Back, Two Steps Forward: On the Language Policy of the Communist Party of the Soviet Union in the National Republics. (East European Monographs: No. 109). 371p. 1982. 30.00x (ISBN 0-88033-002-3). East Eur Quarterly.

Bruchley, Stuart, ed. see Ankli, Robert E.
Bruchley, Stuart, ed. see Ayarslan, Solmaz D.
Bruchley, Stuart, jt. ed. see Chandler, Alfred D., Jr.
Bruchley, Stuart, jt. ed. see Daniel, James.
Bruchley, Stuart, ed. see Whartenby, Franklee G.

Bruchovsky, Nicholas & Goldie, James H., eds. Drug & Hormone Resistance in Neoplasia: Basic Concepts, Vol. I. 208p. 1983. 62.50 (ISBN 0-8493-6516-3). CRC Pr.

Bruchovsky, Nicholas & Goldine, James H., eds. Drug & Hormone Resistance in Neoplasia: Clinical Concepts, Vol. II. 184p. 1983. 62.50 (ISBN 0-8493-6517-1). CRC Pr.

Bruchy, Stuart, ed. see Hamburg, James F.

Brucie, Thomas. Residential Construction Costs, 1985. 4th ed. Felber, Paul, ed. (Illus.). 280p. (Orig.). 1985. pap. 31.95 (ISBN 0-931708-12-5). Saylor.

Bruck, Axel. Close-up Photography in Practice. (Illus.). 144p. 1984. 22.00 (ISBN 0-7153-8403-1). David & Charles.

--Landscape Photography in Practice. (Photography in Practice Ser.). (Illus.). 160p. 1985. Repr. of 1983 ed. 22.00 (ISBN 0-7153-8405-8). David & Charles.

--Practical Composition in Photography. LC 80-40759. (Practical Photography Ser.). (Illus.). 192p. 1981. 24.95 (ISBN 0-240-51060-7). Focal Pr.

Bruck, H. A. The Story of Astronomy in Education: From Its Beginnings until 1975. 151p. 1984. 18.50 (ISBN 0-85224-480-0, Pub. by Edinburgh Pr Scotland). Columbia U Pr.

Bruck, Maria, ed. More Children's Liturgies. LC 81-80877. 256p. (Orig.). 1981. pap. 9.95 (ISBN 0-8091-2362-2). Paulist Pr.

Bruck, Mary T. Night Sky. (Illus.). (gr. 5 up). 2.50 (ISBN 0-7214-0104-X). Merry Thoughts.

Bruck, Nicholas, ed. Capital Markets under Inflation. LC 82-16623. 456p. 1982. 35.95x (ISBN 0-03-063249-8). Praeger.

--Mercados de Capitales Bajo Inflacion. (Illus.). 496p. 1982. 24.95 (ISBN 0-910365-00-8). Decade Media.

Bruck, P. & Karrer, W., eds. The Afro-American Novel since Nineteen Sixty. 325p. 1982. pap. text ed. 28.25x (ISBN 90-6032-219-3, Pub. by B R Gruner Netherlands). Humanities.

Bruck, Peter. Von der "Store Front Church" Zum "American Dream". James Baldwin und der Amerikanische Rassenkonflikt. (Bochum Studies in English: No. 2). (Illus.). viii, 147p. (Orig., Ger.). 1975. pap. 16.00x (ISBN 90-6032-056-5). Benjamins North Am.

Bruck, Peter, ed. The Black American Short Story in the 20th Century: A Collection of Critical Essays. (Illus.). viii, 209p. (Orig.). 1977. pap. 20.00x (ISBN 90-6032-085-9). Benjamins North Am.

--The Black American Short Story in the 20th Century: A Collection of Critical Essays. 1977. pap. text ed. 25.75x (ISBN 90-6032-085-9). Humanities.

Bruck, Peter & Karrer, Wolfgang, eds. The Afro-American Novel since Nineteen-Sixty: A Collection of Critical Essays. 280p. 1982. pap. 26.00x (ISBN 9-06032-219-3). Benjamins North Am.

Bruck, R. H. Survey of Binary Systems. 3rd ed. LC 79-143906. (Ergebnisse der Mathematik und Ihrer Grenzebiete: Vol. 20). 1971. 22.00 (ISBN 0-387-03497-8). Springer-Verlag.

Bruck, Stephen D. Blood Compatible Synthetic Polymers: An Introduction. (Illus.). 144p. 1974. 16.75x (ISBN 0-398-02931-8). C C Thomas.

--Properties of Biomaterials in the Physiological Environment. 160p. 1980. 62.00 (ISBN 0-8493-5685-7). CRC Pr.

Bruck, Stephen D., ed. Controlled Drug Delivery, 2 vols. 528p. 1983. Vol. I: Basic Concepts. 62.00 (ISBN 0-8493-5181-2); Vol. II: Clinical Applications. 85.50 (ISBN 0-8493-5182-0). CRC Pr.

Bruckberger, R. L. God & Politics. LC 78-190754. (Howard Greenfield Bk.). 1971. 9.95 (ISBN 0-87955-302-2). O'Hara.

Brucker, Betty, jt. auth. see Brucker, Jeff.

Brucker, Gene. The Civic World of Early Renaissance Florence. LC 76-45891. 1977. text ed. 50.00x (ISBN 0-691-05244-1). Princeton U Pr.

Brucker, Gene, ed. Society of Renaissance Florence. 1972. pap. 6.95xi (ISBN 0-06-131607-5, TB1607, Torch). Har-Row.

Brucker, Gene A. Florence: The Golden Age, 1138-1737. LC 84-441. (Illus.). 280p. 1984. 55.00 (ISBN 0-89659-457-2). Abbeville Pr.

--Jean-Sylvain Bailly: Revolutionary Mayor of Paris. LC 84-702. vii, 134p. 1984. Repr. lib. bdg. 25.00x (ISBN 0-313-24457-X, BJSB). Greenwood.

--Renaissance Florence. LC 74-10921. 320p. 1975. Repr. of 1969 ed. lib. bdg. 12.50 (ISBN 0-88275-184-0). Krieger.

--Renaissance Florence. rev. ed. LC 82-40097. (Illus.). 320p. 1983. text ed. 33.00x (ISBN 0-520-04919-5, CAL 616); pap. 9.95 (ISBN 0-520-04695-1). U of Cal Pr.

Brucker, Herbert. Communication Is Power: Unchanging Values in a Changing Journalism. 1973. 19.95x (ISBN 0-19-501599-1). Oxford U Pr.

--Freedom of Information. LC 81-1711. 307p. 1981. Repr. of 1951 ed. lib. bdg. 32.50x (ISBN 0-313-22956-2, BRFRI). Greenwood.

Brucker, Jeff & Brucker, Betty. Preparation & Presentation of the Show Dog. 2nd, rev. ed. LC 82-7427. (Illus.). 96p. 1982. 14.95 (ISBN 0-87714-099-5); pap. 9.95 (ISBN 0-87714-105-3). Denlingers.

Brucker, Jerry. Horsethief Canyon. 1981. pap. 1.95 (ISBN 0-8439-0911-0, Leisure Bks). Dorchester Pub Co.

Brucker, Meredith. On the Monitor. 1978. pap. 1.95 (ISBN 0-532-19189-7). Woodhill.

Brucker, Roger W. & Watson, Richard A. The Longest Cave. 1976. 13.95 (ISBN 0-394-48793-1). Knopf.

Brucker, Roger W., jt. auth. see Lawrence, Joe, Jr.
Brucker, Roger W., jt. auth. see Murray, Robert K.
Brucker, Roger W., ed. see Crowther, Patricia P., et al.
Bruckheim, Allan H., jt. ed. see Bollet, Alfred J.

Bruck-Kan, Roberta. Introduction to Human Anatomy. (Illus.). 1979. text ed. 26.75 scp (ISBN 0-06-041015-9, HarpC). Har-Row.

Bruckl, Renate. Structural & Thematic Analysis of George Meredith's Novel "Diana of the Crossways". (Salzburg Studies in English Literature: Romantic Reassessment Ser.: No. 73). 1978. 25.50x (ISBN 0-391-01332-7). Humanities.

Bruckmann, G. SARUM & MRI: Description & Comparison of a World Model & a National Model. 97.00 (ISBN 0-08-023423-2). Pergamon.

Bruckmann, G., ed. Contributions to the Von Neumann Growth Model. LC 71-155280. (Illus.). xv, 116p. 1971. 55.00 (ISBN 0-387-81011-0). Springer-Verlag.

--Input-Output Approaches in Global Modeling: Proceedings of the Fifth IIASA Symposium on Global Modeling, Sept. 26-29,1977. (IIASA Proceedings: Vol. 9). (Illus.). 518p. 1980. 140.00 (ISBN 0-08-025663-5). Pergamon.

Bruckner, A. M. Differentiation of Real Functions. (Lecture Notes in Mathematics: Vol. 659). 1978. pap. 17.00 (ISBN 0-387-08910-1). Springer-Verlag.

Bruckner, Christine. Flight of Cranes. Hein, Ruth, tr. from Ger. LC 81-22176. Orig. Title: Nirgendwo ist Poenichen. 384p. 1982. 14.95 (ISBN 0-88064-001-4). Fromm Intl Pub.

--Gillyflower Kid. Hein, Ruth, tr. from Ger. LC 82-13531. Orig. Title: Jauche und Levkojen. 368p. 1982. 14.95 (ISBN 0-88064-006-5). Fromm Intl Pub.

--The Time of the Leonids. Comjean, Marlies I., tr. from Ger. Orig. Title: Die Zeit Von Den Leoniden. 160p. 13.95 (ISBN 0-89182-040-X). Charles River Bks.

Bruckner, D. J., ed. Politics & Language: Spanish & English in the United States. (Orig.). 1980. pap. 4.00x (ISBN 0-686-28732-0). U Chi Ctr Policy.

Bruckner, D. J., jt. ed. see Murphy, William M.
Bruckner, D. J. R., jt. auth. see Van der Steen, Germain.

Bruckner, Dwight. From Hell to Texas. 192p. 1981. pap. 1.95 (ISBN 0-505-51762-0, Pub. by Tower Bks). Dorchester Pub Co.

--Hot Lead. 1977. pap. 1.25 (ISBN 0-505-51217-3, Pub. by Tower Bks). Dorchester Pub Co.

--The Vengeance Trail. 128p. 1982. pap. 1.75 (ISBN 0-505-51764-7, Pub. by Tower Bks). Dorchester Pub Co.

Bruckner, J. A Bibliographical Catalogue of Seventeenth-Century German Books Published in Holland. (Anglica Germanica: No. 13). 1971. text ed. 64.80x (ISBN 0-686-20922-2). Mouton.

Bruckner, J. R. & Chwast, Seymour. Art Against War: Four Centuries of Antiwar Art. LC 83-6342. (Illus.). 128p. 1984. pap. 16.95 (ISBN 0-89659-389-4). Abbeville Pr.

Bruckner, Matilda T. Narrative Invention in Twelfth-Century French Romance: The Convention of Hospitality (1160-1200) LC 79-53400. (French Forum Monographs: No. 17). 230p. 1980. pap. 12.50x (ISBN 0-917058-16-X). French Forum.

Bruckner, R., jt. ed. see Gloor, B.
Bruckner, Steven, jt. auth. see Bergman, Samuel.

Brudenell-Bruce, P. G. Birds of the Bahamas. LC 74-7342. (Illus.). 160p. 1975. 10.95 (ISBN 0-8008-0780-4). Taplinger.

Bruder, Karl. Theatre Student: Properties & Dressing the Stage. Kozelka, Paul, ed. LC 68-21661. (Theatre Student Ser). (Illus.). (gr. 9 up). 1969. PLB 15.00 (ISBN 0-8239-0150-5). Rosen Group.

Bruder, Mary N. MMC: Developing Communicative Competence in English As a Second Language. (Pitt Series in English as a Second Language). 1974. pap. text ed. 11.95x (ISBN 0-8229-8203-X); audiotapes & teacher's manual avail. U of Pittsburgh Pr.

Bruder, Mary N. & Esarey, Gary. MMC: Developing Communicative Competence in ESL, 2 pts. rev. ed. LC 84-21975. (Pitt Series in English as a Second Language). 1985. Pt. 1, 240 p. pap. 9.95x (ISBN 0-8229-8213-7); Pt.2, 240 p. pap. 9.95x (ISBN 0-8229-8214-5). U of Pittsburgh Pr.

Bruder, Mary N., jt. auth. see Paulson, Christina B.
Bruder, Mary N., jt. ed. see Tillitt, Bruce.

Bruder, Reinhold. Die Germanische Frau im Lichte der Runeninschriften und der antiken Historiographie. LC 73-75482. (Quellen und Forschungen Zur Sprach - und Kulturgeschichte der Germanischen Voelker N. F. 57 181). 192p. 1974. 43.20x (ISBN 3-11-004152-9). De Gruyter.

Bruder, Roy. Discovering Natural Foods. LC 82-2705. (Illus.). 288p. (Orig.). 1982. pap. 7.95 (ISBN 0-912800-86-0). Woodbridge Pr.

Bruderhof, Woodcrest, ed. see Arnold, Annemarie.

Brudidge, Brinsley R. A Dictionary of British Flower, Fruit & Still Life Painters, Vol. 1. 1981. 40.00x (ISBN 0-85317-016-9, Pub. by Lewis Pubs). State Mutual Bk.

Brudigan, Nancy A. Training of Caged Birds. (Illus.). 96p. 1982. 8.95 (ISBN 0-87666-827-9, PS-788). TFH Pubns.

Brudney, jt. auth. see Meier.

Brudney, Jeffrey L. & England, Robert E. Citizen-Based Indicators of Community Service Performance: The Case of Norman, Oklahoma. 50p. 1980. 3.50 (ISBN 0-686-32060-3). Univ OK Gov Res.

Brudney, Jeffrey L. & McDonald, Jean G. The Nineteen Eighty Oklahoma State Party Conventions: A Survey of Delegates. 100p. 1981. 5.50 (ISBN 0-318-01376-2). Univ OK Gov Res.

Brudney, Victor & Chirelstein, Marvin A. Corporate Finance, Cases & Materials: 1984 Supplement. 2nd ed. (University Casebook Ser.). 235p. 1984. pap. text ed. 5.95 (ISBN 0-88277-202-3). Foundation Pr.

Brudno, A. L., et al. Eighteen Papers on Algebra. LC 51-5559. (Translations, Ser.: No. 2, Vol. 27). 1963. 25.00 (ISBN 0-8218-1727-2, TRANS 2-27). Am Math.

Brudno, Barbara E. Income Redistribution Theories & Programs: Cases, Commentary & Analyses. 481p. 1976. write for info. West Pub.

--Poverty, Inequality & the Law: Cases, Commentary & Analyses. 934p. 1976. write for info. West Pub.

Brudon-Jakubowicz, Pascale, tr. see Management Sciences for Health Staff.

Brue, S. L., jt. auth. see McConnell, C. R.

Brue, Stanley L. & Wentworth, Donald R. Economic Scenes: Theory in Today's World. 3rd ed. (Illus.). 368p. 1984. pap. text ed. 20.95 (ISBN 0-13-233536-0). P-H.

Brueckman, Henry & Moreau, Jeffrey. Forty Four Forty Nine: The Queen of Steam. LC 83-72151. 64p. 1984. 23.00 (ISBN 0-934406-01-4). Carbarn Press.

Brueckner, Hannes. Geographic Survey of Norway, No. 332, Bulletin 41. 1977. pap. 12.00x (ISBN 82-00-31366-2). Universitet.

Brueckner, Hans-Dieter, ed. Fabeln, Marchen, Anekdoten und Anderes: Geschichten aus zwei Jahrhunderten. LC 83-6538. (Illus.). 328p. (Orig., Ger. & Eng.). 1983. lib. bdg. 29.00 (ISBN 0-8191-3232-2); pap. text ed. 13.25 (ISBN 0-8191-3233-0). U Pr of Amer.

--Fabeln, Marchen, Anekdoten und Anders: Geschichten Aus zwei Jahrhunderten. 66p. (Orig., Ger. & Eng.). 1983. pap. text ed. 5.00 instr's. manual (ISBN 0-8191-3234-9). U Pr of Amer.

Brueckner, Keith A., jt. auth. see Sinanogly, Oktay.

Brueckner, Keith A., ed. Advances in Theoretical Physics, 2 Vols. Vol. 1 1965. 68.50 (ISBN 0-12-038501-5); Vol. 2 1968. 60.00 (ISBN 0-12-038502-3). Acad Pr.

Brueckner, Leo J. Educational Diagnosis: Nat'l Society for the Study of Education 34th Yearbook. 1935. 4.50x (ISBN 0-226-59964-7). U of Chicago Pr.

Brueesch, P. Phonons: Theory & Experiments I. Lattice Dynamics & Models of Interatomic Forces. (Springer Series in Solid-State Sciences: Vol. 34). (Illus.). 261p. 1982. 33.00 (ISBN 0-387-11306-1). Springer-Verlag.

Bruegel, Peter. Graphic Worlds. Klein, ed. (Illus.). 15.25 (ISBN 0-8446-1755-5). Peter Smith.

--Graphic Worlds of Peter Bruegel the Elder: Reproducing Sixty-Four Engravings & a Woodcut After Designs by Peter Bruegel the Elder. Klein, H. Arthur, ed. (Illus., Orig.). pap. 7.95 (ISBN 0-486-21132-0). Dover.

Brueggeman, Walter, ed. see Westermann, Claus.

Brueggemann, Ludwig W. View of English Editions, Translations & Illustrations of the Ancient Greek & Latin Authors, 2 Vols. Repr. of 1797 ed. Set. 61.50 (ISBN 0-8337-0403-6). B Franklin.

Brueggemann, Walter. Advent-Christmas: Series B. LC 84-6020. (Proclamation 3: Aids for Interpreting the Lessons of the Church Year Ser.). 64p. 1984. pap. 3.50 (ISBN 0-8006-4101-9). Fortress.

--The Bible Makes Sense. LC 76-29883. (Biblical Foundation Ser.). 1977. pap. 7.95 (ISBN 0-8042-0063-7). John Knox.

--The Bible Makes Sense. LC 76-29883. 1977. pap. 6.95 (ISBN 0-88489-087-2). St Mary's.

--The Creative Word: Canon as a Model for Biblical Education. LC 81-71387. 176p. 1982. pap. 9.95 (ISBN 0-8006-1626-X, 1-1626). Fortress.

--David's Truth: In Israel's Imagination & Memory. LC 85-47717. 128p. 1985. pap. 5.95 (ISBN 0-8006-1865-3). Fortress.

--Genesis. LC 81-82355. (Interpretation: the Bible Commentary for Teaching & Preaching). 432p. 1982. 23.95 (ISBN 0-8042-3101-X). John Knox.

--In Man We Trust: The Neglected Side of Biblical Faith. LC 72-1761. 144p. 1972. 7.95 (ISBN 0-8042-0199-4). John Knox.

--In Man We Trust: The Neglected Side of Biblical Faith. LC 72-1761. 144p. 1984. pap. 7.95 (ISBN 0-8042-0198-6). John Knox.

--Kings I. (Knox Preaching Guide Ser.). 132p. 1983. pap. 4.95 (ISBN 0-8042-3212-1). John Knox.

--Kings II. Hayes, John, ed. LC 82-48094. (Knox Preaching Guide Ser.). 120p. 1983. pap. 4.95 (ISBN 0-8042-3214-8). John Knox.

--The Land: Place As Gift, Promise & Challenge in Biblical Faith, No. 1. Donahue, John R., ed. LC 76-15883. (Overtures to Biblical Theology Ser.). 228p. 1977. pap. 7.95 (ISBN 0-8006-1526-3, 1-1526). Fortress.

--Living Toward a Vision: Biblical Reflections on Shalom. rev. ed. LC 76-22172. (Shalom Resource Ser.). 1982. pap. 6.95 (ISBN 0-8298-0613-X). Pilgrim NY.

--The Message of the Psalms: A Theological Commentary. (Augsburg Old Testament Studies). 224p. (Orig.). 1984. pap. 10.95 (ISBN 0-8066-2120-6, 10-4370). Augsburg.

--Praying the Psalms. LC 81-86045. (Illus.). 90p. (Orig.). 1982. pap. 6.95 (ISBN 0-88489-143-7). St Mary's.

--The Prophetic Imagination. LC 78-54546. 128p. 1978. pap. 5.95 (ISBN 0-8006-1337-6, 1-1337). Fortress.

--Tradition for Crisis: A Study in Hosea. LC 68-21008. 164p. 1981. pap. 7.95 (ISBN 0-8042-0181-1). John Knox.

Brueggemann, Walter & Wolff, Hans W. The Vitality Old Testament Traditions. 2nd ed. LC 82-7141. pap. 7.95 (ISBN 0-8042-0112-9). John Knox.

Brueggemann, Walter, ed. see Bailey, Lloyd R., Sr.

Brueggemann, Walter, ed. see Fretheim, Terence E.

Brueggemann, Walter, ed. see Hamerton-Kelly, Robert.

Brueggemann, Walter, ed. see Harrelson, Walter.

Brueggemann, Walter, ed. see Harrington, Daniel J.

Brueggemann, Walter, ed. see Johnson, Luke T.

Brueggemann, Walter, ed. see Patrick, Dale.

Brueggemann, Walter, ed. see Zimmerli, Walther.

Brueggemann, Walter, tr. see Klein, Ralph W.

Brueggman, William B. & Stone, Leo D. Real Estate Finance. 7th ed. 1981. 27.95x (ISBN 0-256-02444-8). Irwin.

Bruehl, Charles P. The Pope's Plan for Social Reconstruction. 10.00 (ISBN 0-8159-6507-9). Devin.

Bruehl, Margaret, jt. auth. see Pneuman, Roy.

Brueke, Franz Von see Von Bruecke, Franz, et al.

Bruell, S. C. & Balbo, G., eds. Computational Algorithms for Closed Queuing Networks. (Operating & Programming Systems Ser.: Vol. 7). 190p. 1980. 29.95 (ISBN 0-444-00421-1, North-Holland). Elsevier.

Bruell, Steven C., jt. auth. see Schneider, G. Michael.

Bruemmer, Alice. Library Management in Review. LC 81-13562. 112p. 1981. pap. 13.75 (ISBN 0-87111-294-9). SLA.

Bruemmer, Fred. The Arctic World. Taylor, William E., ed. LC 85-2051. (Illus.). 256p. 1985. 39.95 (ISBN 0-87156-842-X). Sierra.

Bruemmer, S. Suzanne, jt. auth. see Tiedt, Iris M.

Bruen, Alexander J. & Taylor, Willard B. Federal Income Taxation of Oil & Gas Investments: Annual Cumulative Supplementation. 1980. 96.00 (ISBN 0-88262-339-7). Warren.

Bruening, Andrew C. Journal of Voyage to Australia. 62p. 1984. 5.50x (ISBN 0-86516-034-1). Bolchazy-Carducci.

Bruening, William H. Introduction to the Philosophy of Law. LC 78-62249. 1978. pap. text ed. 11.00 (ISBN 0-8191-0570-8). U Pr of Amer.

--The Is-Ought Problem: Its History, Analysis, & Dissolution. LC 77-18569. 1978. pap. text ed. 10.50 (ISBN 0-8191-0364-0). U Pr of Amer.

--Wittgenstein. 1977. pap. text ed. 11.00 (ISBN 0-8191-0289-X). U Pr of Amer.

Bruere, Martha B. & Beard, Mary R. Laughing Their Way: Women's Humor in America. Repr. of 1934 ed. lib. bdg. 35.00 (ISBN 0-8495-0310-8). Arden Lib.

Bruerton, C., jt. auth. see Morley, S. G.

Brues, Alice M. People & Races. 1977. write for info. (ISBN 0-02-315670-8, 31567). Macmillan.

Brues, Austin M. & Sacher, George A., eds. Aging & Levels of Biological Organization. LC 65-17281. pap. write for info. (2019957). Bks Demand UMI.

Brues, Charles T. Insects, Food & Ecology. Orig. Title: Insect Dietary. (Illus.). 466p. 1972. pap. 7.95 (ISBN 0-486-21070-7). Dover.

--Insects' Food & Ecology. Orig. Title: Insect Dietary. (Illus.). 10.25 (ISBN 0-8446-4521-4). Peter Smith.

Bruess, et al. Decisions for Health. 1984. write for info. (ISBN 0-534-01257-4). Wadsworth Pub.

Bruetsch, Walter L. Syphilitic Optic Atrophy. (Illus.). 150p. 1954. photocopy ed. 16.00x (ISBN 0-398-04224-1). C C Thomas.

Bruette, William A. & Donnelly, Kerry V. The Complete Dog Buyer's Guide. rev. updated ed. (Illus.). 608p. (Orig.). 1983. 8.95 (ISBN 0-86622-026-7, H-1061). TFH Pubns.

Bruey, Alfred J. From BASIC to FORTRAN. (Illus.). 144p. (Orig.). 1984. 17.95 (ISBN 0-8306-0753-6); pap. 9.95 (ISBN 0-8306-1753-1, 1753). TAB Bks.

Brueziere, jt. auth. see Mauger.

Bruff, Nancy. Cider from Eden. 320p. (Orig.). 1982. pap. 2.95 (ISBN 0-505-51770-1, Pub. by Tower Bks). Dorchester Pub Co.

--The Country Club. 400p. 1986. pap. 3.95 (ISBN 0-8439-2320-2, Leisure Bks). Dorchester Pub Co.

--Desire on the Dunes. 352p. 1984. pap. 3.50 (ISBN 0-8439-2094-7). Dorchester Pub Co.

Bruffee, Kenneth A. Elegiac Romance: Cultural Change & Loss of the Hero in Modern Fiction. LC 83-45140. 248p. 1983. 19.95x (ISBN 0-8014-1579-9). Cornell U Pr.

--A Short Course in Writing. 3rd ed. 1985. pap. text ed. 13.95 (ISBN 0-316-11242-9). Little.

Bruford, A., ed. The Green Man of Knowledge: And Other Scots Traditional Tales. (Illus.). 128p. 1982. 17.00 (ISBN 0-08-025757-7); pap. 9.00 (ISBN 0-08-025758-5). Pergamon.

Bruford, Walter H. The German Tradition of Self-Cultivation: Bildung from Humboldt to Thomas Mann. LC 74-79143. pap. 75.00 (ISBN 0-317-27992-0, 2025578). Bks Demand UMI.

--Theatre, Drama, & Audience in Goethe's Germany. LC 73-10579. 388p. 1974. Repr. of 1950 ed. lib. bdg. 32.50x (ISBN 0-8371-7016-8, BRTD). Greenwood.

Brugel, W., ed. Handbook of NMR Spectral Parameters, 3 vols. 990p. casebound set 625.00 (ISBN 0-471-25617-X, Pub. by Wiley Heyden). Wiley.

Brugel, Werner. Nuclear Magnetic Resonance Spectra & Chemical Structure. 1968. 58.50 (ISBN 0-12-137450-5). Acad Pr.

Brugge, David M. Navajos in the Catholic Church Records of New Mexico 1694-1875. LC 84-60510. 1985. 10.99x (ISBN 0-912586-59-1). Navajo Coll Pr.

Bruggeling, Ir A. Prestressed Concrete for the Storage of Liquefied Gas. Van Amerongen, C., tr. from Dutch. (Viewpoint Ser.). (Illus.). 111p. 1981. pap. text ed. 49.50x (ISBN 0-7210-1187-X, Pub. by C&CA London). Scholium Intl.

Bruggeman, Gordon & Weiss, Volker, eds. Innovations in Materials Processing. (Sagamore Army Materials Research Conference Proceedings Ser.: Vol. 30). 494p. 1985. 79.50x (ISBN 0-306-41839-8, Plenum Pr). Plenum Pub.

Bruggemann, Diethelm. Drei Mystifikationen Heinrich von Kleists: Kleists Wurzburger Reise-Kleists Lust-Spiel mit Goethe-Aloysius, Marquis von Montferrat. (Germanic Studies in America: Vol. 51). 220p. (Ger.). 1985. text ed. 20.00 (ISBN 0-8204-0228-1). P Lang Pubs.

Bruggen, Carol. Crumbs Under the Skin. 176p. 1985. 13.95 (ISBN 0-233-97658-2, Pub. by A Deutsch England). David & Charles.

Bruggen, Coosje van see Van Bruggen, Coosje.

Bruggen, Jakob Van see Van Bruggen, Jakob.

Bruggen, Theodore Van. The Vascular Plants of South Dakota. 2nd ed. 476p. 1985. pap. text ed. 24.95x (ISBN 0-8138-0650-X). Iowa St U Pr.

Bruggen, Theodore Van see Van Bruggen, Theodore.

Bruggencate, K. T. Dutch-English Dictionary. Gerritsen, J., et al, eds. 1048p. (Dutch & Eng.). 1980. 24.95 (ISBN 90-01-96819-8, M-9746). French & Eur.

--English-Dutch Dictionary. Gerritsen, J., et al, eds. 898p. (Eng. & Dutch.). 1980. 24.95 (ISBN 90-01-96818-X, M-9747). French & Eur.

Bruggencate, K. Ten. Dutch-English, English-Dutch Dictionary, 2 vols. (Dutch & Eng.). Set. 50.00 (ISBN 9-0019-6819-8). Dutch-Eng. Eng.-Dutch (ISBN 90-01-96818-X). Heinman.

Bruggenwert, M. G., jt. auth. see Bolt, G. H.

Brugger, Bill. Chinese Marxism in Flux. LC 84-26880. 215p. 1985. 30.00 (ISBN 0-87332-322-X); pap. 14.95 (ISBN 0-87332-323-8). M E Sharpe.

Brugger, Bill & Hannan, Kate. Modernisation & Revolution. 64p. 1983. pap. 11.50 (ISBN 0-7099-0695-1, Pub. by Croom Helm Ltd). Longwood Pub Group.

Brugger, Bill, ed. China since the Gang of Four. LC 80-10251. 288p. 1980. 30.00 (ISBN 0-312-13323-5). St Martin.

--China: The Impact of the Cultural Revolution. LC 77-28197. 300p. 1978. text ed. 28.50x (ISBN 0-06-490760-0, 06370). B&N Imports.

--Chinese Periodicals in British Libraries: Handlist, No. 4. 204p. (Orig.). 1972. pap. 15.00 (ISBN 0-7141-0647-X, Pub. by British Lib). Longwood Pub Group.

Brugger, E. & Stuckey, B. Self Reliant Development in Europe. 300p. 1986. text ed. price not set (ISBN 0-566-05095-1). Gower Pub Co.

Brugger, Robert J., ed. Our Selves-Our Past: Psychological Approaches to American History. LC 80-81425. 448p. 1981. pap. text ed. 11.95x (ISBN 0-8018-2382-X). Johns Hopkins.

Brugger, Suzanne. Australians & Egypt, Nineteen Fourteen to Nineteen Nineteen. 188p. 1980. 27.00x (ISBN 0-522-84175-9, Pub. by Melbourne U Pr Australia). Intl Spec Bk.

Brugger, W. Philosophisches Woerterbuch. 14th ed. 592p. 1976. pap. 55.00 (ISBN 0-686-56637-8, M-7587, Pub. by Herder). French & Eur.

Brugmann, Karl. Kurze Vergleichende Grammatik der Indogermanischen Sprachen. (Ger). 1969. Repr. of 1904 ed. 80.00x (ISBN 3-11-000179-9). De Gruyter.

Brugmann, Karl & Delbrueck, Berthold. Grundriss der Vergleichenden Grammatik der Indogermanischen Sprachen, 5 vols. (Ger). 1967. Repr. of 1893 ed. 462.00x (ISBN 3-11-000180-2). De Gruyter.

Brugmans, Linette F., ed. see Gide, Andre & Gosse, Edmund.

Brugnola, Orlanda. King of Thornbushes. 1972. pap. 2.00 (ISBN 0-685-36813-0). Oyez.

Bruguera Grane, Francisco. Diccionario Ingles-Espanol, Espanol-Ingles. 3rd ed. 680p. (Eng. & Span.). 1979. pap. 4.95 (ISBN 84-02-00835-6, S-50345). French & Eur.

Bruhn, E. F. Analysis & Design of Flight Vehicle Structures. (Illus.). 1973. write for info. Jacobs Pub.

Bruhn, Erik. Beyond Technique. 1973. pap. 8.00 (ISBN 0-384-06086-2). Johnson Repr.

Bruhn, John G. & Wolf, Stewart. The Roseto Story: An Anatomy of Health. LC 78-21364. (Illus.). 1979. 13.50 (ISBN 0-8061-1491-6). U of Okla Pr.

Bruhn, John G., et al. Medical Sociology: An Annotated Bibliography, 1972-82. (Bibliographies in Sociology; Reference Library of Social Science). 801p. 1985. lib. bdg. 100.00 (ISBN 0-8240-8938-3). Garland Pub.

Bruhn, Wolfgang, jt. auth. see Tilke, Max.

Bruhns. New Manual of Logarithms. 634p. 1941. 25.00 (ISBN 0-442-01145-8, Pub. by Van Nos Reinhold). Krieger.

Bruhns, Karen O. Cihuatan: An Early Postclassic Town of El Salvador: the 1977-78 Excavations. Feldman, Lawrence, ed. (Monographs in Anthropology: No. 5). (Illus.). vii, 171p. 1980. pap. 9.00 (ISBN 0-913134-82-1). Mus Anthro MO.

Bruicker, S. De see Ward, S. & De Bruicker, S.

Bruijn, N. G. de see De Bruijn, N. G.

Bruin, A. De see De Bruin, A.

Bruin, Frans & Vonjidis, Alexander, trs. from Greek. The Books of Autolykos: On a Moving Sphere & on Risings & Settings. (Illus.). 83p. 1971. text ed. 12.00x (ISBN 0-8156-6034-0, Am U Beirut). Syracuse U Pr.

Bruin, M. G. de see De Bruin, M. G. & Van Rossum, H.

Bruington, Patricia. Get It In Writing. (No. 174). 320p. 1984. Additional supplements may be obtained from publisher. pap. text ed. 15.95 (ISBN 0-675-20149-7). Merrill.

Bruininks, Robert H. & Lakin, K. Charlie, eds. Living & Learning in the Least Restrictive Environment. LC 84-12142. (Illus.). 304p. (Orig.). 1985. pap. text ed. 22.95 (ISBN 0-933716-42-7, 427). P H Brookes.

Bruininks, Robert H., jt. ed. see Lakin, K. Charlie.

Bruininks, Robert H., et al, eds. Deinstitutionalization & Community Adjustment of Mentally Retarded People. LC 80-70191. (Monographs of the American Association on Mental Deficiency: No. 4). 412p. 1981. text ed. 24.75x (ISBN 0-317-17827-X). Am Assn Mental.

Bruins, C., tr. see Van Mierop, L. H. & Opperheimer-Dekker, A.

Bruins, Elton J. Americanization of a Congregation. LC 63-11498. pap. 3.95 (ISBN 0-8028-1330-5). Eerdmans.

Bruins, Paul. Basic Principles of Rotational Molding. 294p. 1971. 55.75 (ISBN 0-677-14980-8). Gordon.

Bruins, Paul, ed. Basic Principles of Thermoforming. LC 75-188122. 294p. 1973. 56.75x (ISBN 0-677-14990-5). Gordon.

Bruins, Paul F. Unsaturated Polyester Technology. new ed. LC 74-12774. 448p. 1976. 69.50 (ISBN 0-677-21160-0). Gordon.

Bruins, Paul F., ed. Packaging with Plastics. LC 72-78922. 220p. 1974. 48.75 (ISBN 0-677-12200-4). Gordon.

--Polyurethane Technology. LC 68-545498. (Polymar Engineering & Technology Ser.). pap. 74.80 (ISBN 0-317-28160-7, 2055763). Bks Demand UMI.

Bruinsma, Domien H., et al. Selection of Technology for Food Processing in Developing Countries. 199p. 1984. pap. text ed. 7.50 (ISBN 90-220-0837-1, PDC264, Pudoc). Unipub.

Bruinsma, Sheryl. Easy-to-Use Object Lessons. (Object Lesson Ser.). 96p. (Orig.). 1983. pap. 3.95 (ISBN 0-8010-0832-8). Baker Bk.

--New Object Lessons for Children of All Ages. (Object Lesson Ser.). 1980. pap. 3.95 (ISBN 0-8010-0775-5). Baker Bk.

Bruinvels, J., jt. auth. see Parnham, M. J.

Bruinvels, J., jt. ed. see Parnham, M. J.

Brukner, Fritz Von see Nestroy, Johann N.

Brukner, Ira. Hardon. LC 80-18377. (Illus.). 1980. cloth 16.00 (ISBN 0-916906-30-2); pap. 9.00 (ISBN 0-916906-31-0). Konglomerati.

--Hubba Hubba. 240p. 1980. pap. 5.00 (ISBN 0-9604364-3-X). Duck Pr.

Brul, E. Lloyd Du see DuBrul, E. Lloyd & Sicher, Harry.

Bruland, Esther B. & Mott, Stephen C. A Passion for Jesus: A Passion for Justice. 176p. 1983. pap. 9.95 (ISBN 0-8170-0994-9). Judson.

Brule, G., et al. Drug Therapy of Cancer. (Also avail. in French & Russian). 1973. 8.00 (ISBN 0-686-16780-5). World Health.

Brule, Marcel, tr. see Fisher, David & Bragonier, Reginald, Jr.

Bruley, Duane, et al, eds. Oxygen Transport to Tissue VI. (Advances in Experimental Medicine & Biology Ser.: Vol. 180). 924p. 1985. 125.00x (ISBN 0-306-41887-8, Plenum Pr). Plenum Pub.

Bruley, Duane F., jt. ed. see Bicher, Haim I.

Brulin, O. & Hsieh, R. K., eds. Continuum Models of Discrete Systems. 520p. 1981. 72.50 (ISBN 0-444-86309-5, North-Holland). Elsevier.

--Mechanics of Micropolar Media. vi, 478p. 1982. 41.00x (ISBN 9971-950-02-2, Pub. by World Sci Singapore). Taylor & Francis.

Brull, Ignaz, ed. see Schubert, Franz.

Brull, Sheila, jt. auth. see May, Rosalind G.

Bruller, Jean see Vercors, pseud.

Brum, Gilbert D., et al. Biology & Man. 3rd ed. 1978. pap. text ed. 15.95 (ISBN 0-8403-1018-8). Kendall-Hunt.

Brum, L. J. How to Beat the Car Dealer at His Own Game: Buying a New or Used Car. LC 82-70174. (Illus.). 134p. 1982. pap. 5.95 (ISBN 0-942662-00-8). BM Consumer Pubns.

Brumat, jt. ed. see Aykac, A.

Brumback, Carl. God in Three Persons. 192p. 1959. pap. 4.95 (ISBN 0-87148-354-8). Pathway Pr.

--Like a River. LC 76-58782. (Illus.). 176p. 1977. pap. 2.95 (ISBN 0-88243-564-7, 02-0564). Gospel Pub.

--What Meaneth This? a Pentecostal Answer to a Pentecostal Question. 352p. 1947. pap. 4.95 (ISBN 0-88243-626-0, 02-0624). Gospel Pub.

Brumbaugh, J. Frank. How to Write How-To Books. Goodman, James, ed. (Orig.). 1984. pap. 7.95 (ISBN 0-89896-178-5). Larksdale.

--Mail Order Made Easy. 1982. pap. 10.00 (ISBN 0-87980-394-0). Wilshire.

--Mail Order... Starting up, Making It Pay. LC 78-14623. 1979. pap. 9.95 (ISBN 0-8019-6805-4). Chilton.

Brumbaugh, James. Heating, Ventilating, & Air Conditioning Library, 3 vols. 2nd ed. LC 83-7064. (Illus.). 1983. 14.95 ea. Vol. 1 (ISBN 0-672-23389-4, 23248). Vol. 2 (ISBN 0-672-23390-8, 23249). Vol. 3 (ISBN 0-672-23391-6, 23250). 41.95, set of 3 vols. (ISBN 0-672-23227-8). Audel.

--Upholstering. 2nd ed. LC 82-17781. (Illus.). 394p. 1983. 12.95 (ISBN 0-672-23372-X). Audel.

--Welders Guide. 3rd ed. LC 82-17797. 940p. 1983. 19.95 (ISBN 0-672-23374-6). Audel.

Brumbaugh, James E. Heating, Ventilating & Air Conditions Library. (Audel). (Illus.). Set. 41.95 (ISBN 0-672-23388-6); Vol. 1. 14.95 (ISBN 0-672-23389-4); Vol. 2. 14.95 (ISBN 0-672-23390-8); Vol. 3. 14.95 (ISBN 0-672-23391-6); 41.95. G K Hall.

--Truck Guide, Vols. 1-2. Incl. Vol. 1. Engines & Auxiliary Systems. (Audel). 370p. 16.95 (ISBN 0-672-23356-8); Vol. 2. Transmissions, Steering & Brakes. 304p. 16.95 (ISBN 0-672-23357-6); Vol. 3. 16.95 (ISBN 0-672-23406-8). (Audel Ser.). 47.85 set (ISBN 0-672-23392-4). G K Hall.

--Upholstering. updated ed. LC 82-17781. (Audel Ser.). (Illus.). 400p. 1983. 12.95 (ISBN 0-672-23372-X). G K Hall.

--Wood Furniture: Finishing, Refinishing, Repairing. LC 73-91640. (Illus.). 352p. 1974. 9.95 (ISBN 0-672-23216-2). Audel.

Brumbaugh, Judy & Mowat, Jean. His & Hers Tailoring: A Self-Instructional Guide. rev. ed. LC 76-23687. 1977. pap. 14.95 (ISBN 0-89305-003-2). Anna Pub.

Brumbaugh, Martin G. A History of the German Baptist Brethren in Europe & America. LC 73-134377. (Communal Societies in America Ser.). (Illus.). Repr. of 1899 ed. 37.50 (ISBN 0-404-08425-7). AMS Pr.

--Life & Works of Christoper Dock. LC 70-89154. (American Education: Its Men, Institutions & Ideas, Ser. 1). 1969. Repr. of 1908 ed. 20.00 (ISBN 0-405-01392-2). Ayer Co Pubs.

Brumbaugh, Robert S. Ancient Greek Gadgets & Machines. LC 75-3983. (Illus.). 152p. 1975. Repr. of 1966 ed. lib. bdg. 18.75x (ISBN 0-8371-7427-9, BRGG). Greenwood.

--The Philosophers of Greece. LC 81-9120. (Illus.). 274p. 1981. 32.50x (ISBN 0-87395-550-1); pap. 8.95x (ISBN 0-87395-551-X). State U NY Pr.

--Plato for the Modern Age. LC 78-13271. (Illus.). 1979. Repr. of 1962 ed. lib. bdg. 27.25x (ISBN 0-313-20630-9, BRPF). Greenwood.

--Plato's Mathematical Imagination: The Mathematical Passages in the Dialogues & Their Interpretation. LC 55-62013. (Illus.). 1954. 20.00 (ISBN 0-527-12900-3). Kraus Repr.

--Unreality & Time. (Philosophy Ser.). 242p. 1984. 29.50x (ISBN 0-87395-799-7); pap. 12.95x (ISBN 0-87395-798-9). State U NY Pr.

--Whitehead, Process Philosophy, & Education. LC 81-14329. 144p. 1982. 38.50x (ISBN 0-87395-574-9); pap. 13.95x (ISBN 0-87395-575-7). State U NY Pr.

Brumbaugh, Robert S. & Lawrence, Nathaniel M. Philosophical Themes in Modern Education. (Illus.). 304p. 1985. pap. text ed. 12.75 (ISBN 0-8191-4718-4). U Pr of Amer.

Brumbaugh, Robert S., jt. auth. see Stallknecht, Newton P.

Brumbaugh, Robert S., ed. The Most Mysterious Manuscript: The Voynich "Roger Bacon" Cipher Manuscript. LC 77-15024. (Illus.). 189p. 1978. 12.50x (ISBN 0-8093-0808-8). S Ill U Pr.

Brumbaugh, Sara B. Democratic Experience & Education in the National League of Women Voters. LC 71-176603. (Columbia University. Teachers College. Contributions to Education: No. 916). Repr. of 1946 ed. 22.50 (ISBN 0-404-55916-6). AMS Pr.

Brumbaugh, Thoburn T. My Marks & Scars I Carry: The Story of Ernst Kisch. (Bold Believers Ser.). 1969. pap. 0.95 (ISBN 0-377-84151-X). Friend Pr.

Brumbaugh, Thomas B., et al, eds. Architecture of Middle Tennessee. LC 72-2879. (Historic American Building Survey Ser.). (Illus.). 184p. 1974. 17.95 (ISBN 0-8265-1184-8). Vanderbilt U Pr.

Brumberg, Abraham, ed. Poland: Genesis of a Revolution. LC 82-40137. 367p. 1983. 19.95 (ISBN 0-394-52323-7, Vin); pap. 7.95 (ISBN 0-394-71025-8). Random.

Brumberg, Esther & Rubin, Sy, eds. The Lower East Side: Contemporary Photographs. (Illus.). 106p. 1984. pap. 14.95 (ISBN 0-89255-088-0). Persea Bks.

Brumberg, Joan J. Mission for Life: The Judson Family & American Evangelical Culture. (Illus.). 320p. 1984. pap. 15.00x (ISBN 0-8147-1053-0). NYU Pr.

--Mission for Life: The Story of the Family of Adoniram Judson. LC 79-54667. (Illus.). 1980. 12.95 (ISBN 0-02-905100-2). Free Pr.

Brumberger, H., ed. Small-Angle X-Ray Scattering. 518p. 1967. 116.95 (ISBN 0-677-11190-8). Gordon.

Brumberger, Tom. Monster Maker. 1984. pap. 4.95 (ISBN 0-451-82094-0, Sig). NAL.

Brumblay, Ray U. Qualitative Analysis. (Illus., Orig). 1964. pap. 5.95 (ISBN 0-06-460116-1, CO 116, COS). B&N NY.

--Quantitative Analysis. 2nd ed. (Orig.). 1972. pap. 4.95 (ISBN 0-06-460050-5, CO 50, COS). B&N NY.

Brumble, H. David, III. An Annotated Bibliography of American Indian & Eskimo Autobiographies. LC 80-23449. xii, 170p. 1981. 15.50x (ISBN 0-8032-1175-9). U of Nebr Pr.

Brumble, H. David, III, tr. from Dutch. see Bredero, G. A.

Brumel, Antoine see Expert, Henry.

Brumell, G. British Post Office Numbers. 138p. 1982. 37.00x (ISBN 0-686-45769-2, Pub. by R C Alcock Ltd Scotland). State Mutual Bk.

--The Local Posts of London, 1680-1840. 2nd ed. 91p. 1982. 20.00x (ISBN 0-686-45772-2, Pub. by R C Alcock Ltd Scotland). State Mutual Bk.

Brumer, Andy. Turtle (Poems: Book) LC 79-67479. 1977. pap. 4.95 (ISBN 0-917986-14-8). NFS Pr.

Brumfield, Allaire C. The Attic Festivals of Demeter & Their Relation to the Agricultural Year. Connor, W. R., ed. LC 80-2643. (Monographs in Classical Studies). 1981. lib. bdg. 29.00 (ISBN 0-405-14031-2). Ayer Co Pubs.

Brumfield, Charles, jt. auth. see Bairstow, Jeffrey.

Brumfield, Gregory W. Partially Ordered Rings & Semi-Algebraic Geometry. (London Mathematical Society Lecture Note Ser.: No. 37). 1980. pap. 29.95 (ISBN 0-521-22845-X). Cambridge U Pr.

Brumfield, J. C. Comfort for Troubled Christians. (Moody Acorn Ser.). 1975. pap. 7.50 package of 10 (ISBN 0-8024-1400-1). Moody.

Brumfield, William C. Gold in Azure: One Thousand Years of Russian Architecture. LC 81-47320. (Illus.). 448p. 1983. 60.00 (ISBN 0-87923-436-9). Godine.

Brumfit, C. J. & Roberts, J. T. An Introduction to Language & Language Teaching. 224p. (Orig.). 1983. pap. 15.95 (ISBN 0-7134-1599-1, Pub. by Batsford England). David & Charles.

Brumfit, C. J., ed. English for International Communication. LC 81-21071. (Language Teaching Methodology Ser.). (Illus.). 128p. 1982. pap. 11.95 (ISBN 0-08-028613-5). Pergamon.

--Language Teaching Projects for the Third World. (English Language Teaching Documents Ser.: Vol. 116). 160p. 1983. pap. 7.50 (ISBN 0-08-030342-0, 667). Pergamon.

--Teaching Literature Overseas: Language-Based Approaches. (English Language Teaching Documents Ser.: Vol. 115). 128p. 1983. pap. 7.50 (ISBN 0-08-030341-2, 67). Pergamon.

--Video Applications in ELT. (English Language Teaching Documents Ser.: Vol. 114). 128p. 1983. pap. 7.50 (ISBN 0-08-029476-6). Pergamon.

Brumfit, C. J. & Johnson, K., eds. The Communicative Approach to Language Teaching. (Illus.). 1979. pap. text ed. 10.95x (ISBN 0-19-437078-X). Oxford U Pr.

Brumfit, Christopher. Communicative Methodology in Language Teaching: The Roles of Fluency & Accuracy. LC 83-26239. (Language Teaching Library). 180p. 1984. pap. 8.95 (ISBN 0-521-26968-7). Cambridge U Pr.

Brumfit, Christopher, jt. auth. see Finocchiaro, Mary.

Brumfit, W., ed. see Symposium on Urinary Tract Infection, London, England, Sept. 23-24, 1974.

Brumfitt, J. H. Voltaire, Historian. LC 84-29037. 178p. 1985. Repr. of 1958 ed. lib. bdg. 35.00x (ISBN 0-313-24734-X, BRVO). Greenwood.

Brumfitt, J. H., ed. see De Voltaire, Francois M.

Brumfitt, W., ed. New Perspectives in Clinical Microbiology. 1978. lib. bdg. 31.50 (ISBN 90-247-2074-5, Pub. by Martinus Nijhoff Netherlands). Kluwer Academic.

Brumfitt, W. & Hamilton-Miller, J. M., eds. A Clinical Approach to Progress in Infectious Diseases. (Illus.). 1983. 26.95x (ISBN 0-19-261460-6). Oxford U Pr.

Brumfitt, W., et al, eds. Combined Antimicrobial Therapy. (New Perspectives in Clinical Microbiology Ser.: No. 3). 1980. lib. bdg. 47.00 (ISBN 90-247-2280-2, Pub. by Martinus Nijhoff Netherlands). Kluwer Academic.

Brumfitt, William, ed. see Kass, Edward H.

Brumgardt, John R. & Bowles, Larry L. People of the Magic Waters: The Cahuilla Indians of Palm Springs. (Illus.). 1981. 9.95 (ISBN 0-88280-060-4). ETC Pubns.

Brumgardt, John R., ed. Civil War Nurse: The Diary & Letters of Hannah Ropes. LC 79-28372. 164p. 1980. 14.50x (ISBN 0-87049-280-2). U of Tenn Pr.

Brumlik, Joel & Chong-Bun Yap. Normal Tremor: A Comparative Study. (Illus.). 112p. 1970. 14.50x (ISBN 0-398-00244-4). C C Thomas.

Brumm, Barbara. Marxismus und Realismus Am Beispiel Balzac. (European University Studies: No. 20, Vol. 91). 153p. (Ger.). 1982. 18.95 (ISBN 3-8204-5784-4). P Lang Pubs.

Brummel, George H. Bible Medicine with Healing Verses. LC 83-91263. 172p. (Orig.). 1984. pap. 9.95 (ISBN 0-9613041-0-3). G Brummel Pub.

Brummell, George B. Male & Female Costume. Parker, Eleanor, ed. LC 71-177521. (Illus.). Repr. of 1932 ed. 30.00 (ISBN 0-405-08314-9, Blom Pubns). Ayer Co Pubs.

Brummer, Sidney D. Political History of New York State During the Period of the Civil War. LC 11-19977. (Columbia University Studies in the Social Sciences: No. 103). Repr. of 1911 ed. 23.50 (ISBN 0-404-51103-1). AMS Pr.

Brummer, Vincent. Theology & Philosophical Inquiry: An Introduction. LC 81-11557. 320p. (Orig.). 1982. pap. 16.95 (ISBN 0-664-24398-3). Westminster.

Brummund, Peter & Institut fur Zeitungsforschung. Struktur und Organisation des Pressevertriebs, Vol. 1: Der Deutsche Zeitungs-und ZeitschriftengroBhandel. (Dortmunder Beitrage: Vol. 40). 502p. 1985. pap. 17.50 (ISBN 3-598-21297-6). K G Saur.

Brumont, Francis. La Burebs L'Epoque De Philippe II. Bruchey, Stuart, ed. LC 77-81824. (Dissertations in European Economic History). (Illus., Fr.). 1977. lib. bdg. 26.50x (ISBN 0-405-10776-5). Ayer Co Pubs.

Brumpton, Karen B. Freeman Earns a Bike. LC 84-60947. (Illus.). 32p. (ps-4). 1984. 10.95 (ISBN 0-917487-00-1). McVie Pub.

Brun & Olsen. Atlas of Renal Biopsy. (Illus.). 266p. 1981. text ed. 40.00 (ISBN 0-7216-2164-3). Saunders.

Brun, Christian F., jt. auth. see Wheat, James C.

Brun, Ellen & Hersh, Jacques. Socialist Korea: A Case Study in the Strategy of Economic Development. LC 76-1651. (Illus.). 432p. 1977. 16.50 (ISBN 0-85345-386-1). Monthly Rev.

Brun, Geoffrey. Europe & the French Imperium, 1799-1814. LC 83-10737. (The Rise of Modern Europe Ser.). (Illus.). xiv, 280p. 1983. Repr. of 1938 ed. lib. bdg. 45.00x (ISBN 0-313-24078-7, BREU). Greenwood.

Brun, Henry J. The Social Scientist Investigates Women of the Ancient World. (Illus.). (gr. 7-12). 1976. PLB 8.97 (ISBN 0-8239-0361-3). Rosen Group.

--Social Studies Student Investigates the Retreat from Imperialism. (YA) 1978. PLB 8.97 (ISBN 0-8239-0414-8). Rosen Group.

Brun, Herbert & Gaburo, Kenneth. Collaboration One. 24p. 1976. soft cover saddle-stitched 15.00 (ISBN 0-939044-10-2). Lingua Pr.

Brun, J. Diatomees des Alpes et du Jura et de la region suisse et francaise de Environs de Geneve. (Illus.). 1965. 12.40 (ISBN 90-6123-028-4). Lubrecht & Cramer.

Brun, Kim, ed. see Federico, Pat A., et al.

Brun, L., jt. ed. see Mandel, J.

Brun, Padraig De see De Brun, Padraig & Herbert, Marie.

Brun, Roger Le see Le Brun, Roger.

Bruna, Dick. Animals. (Dick Bruna Bks.). 1984. 2.95 (ISBN 0-8431-1575-0). Price Stern.

--Another Story to Tell. (Dick Bruna Bks). (Illus.). 28p. (ps-k). cancelled (ISBN 0-8431-1586-6). Price Stern.

--The Apple. (Dick Bruna Bks.). 1984. 2.95 (ISBN 0-8431-1540-8). Price Stern.

--B Is for Bear. (Dick Bruna Bks.). (Illus.). 28p. (ps-k). cancelled (ISBN 0-8431-1585-8). Price Stern.

--Christmas Crib Punch-Outs. (Bruna Books). (Illus.). 1974. 2.50 (ISBN 0-416-78170-5, NO.0012). Methuen Inc.

--Farmer John. (Dick Bruna Bks.). 1984. 2.95 (ISBN 0-8431-1526-2). Price Stern.

--The Fish. (Dick Bruna Bks.). 1984. 2.95 (ISBN 0-8431-1538-6). Price Stern.

--I Can Count. (Dick Bruna Bks.). 1984. 2.95 (ISBN 0-8431-1577-7). Price Stern.

--I Can Count More. (Dick Bruna Bks.). 1984. 2.95 (ISBN 0-8431-1578-5). Price Stern.

--I Can Dress Myself. (Dick Bruna Bks.). (Illus.). 28p. (ps-k). cancelled (ISBN 0-8431-1581-5). Price Stern.

--I Can Read. (Dick Bruna Bks.). 1984. 2.95 (ISBN 0-8431-1542-4). Price Stern.

--I Can Read Difficult Words. (Dick Bruna Bks.). (Illus.). 28p. (ps-k). cancelled (ISBN 0-8431-1584-X). Price Stern.

--I Can Read More. (Dick Bruna Bks.). 1984. 2.95 (ISBN 0-8431-1539-4). Price Stern.

--I Know about Numbers. (Dick Bruna Bks.). 1984. 2.95 (ISBN 0-8431-1547-5). Price Stern.

--I Know about Shapes. (Dick Bruna Bks.). 1984. 2.95. Price Stern.

--The Little Bird. (Dick Bruna Bks.). 1984. 2.95 (ISBN 0-8431-1541-6). Price Stern.

--Lynn & Lisa. (Dick Bruna Bks.). 1984. 2.95 (ISBN 0-8431-1537-8). Price Stern.

--Miffy. (Dick Bruna Bks.). 32p. 1984. 2.95 (ISBN 0-8431-1531-9). Price Stern.

--Miffy at the Playground. (Dick Bruna Bks.). 1984. 2.95 (ISBN 0-8431-1543-2). Price Stern.

--Miffy at the Seaside. (Dick Bruna Bks.). 32p. 1984. 2.95 (ISBN 0-8431-1533-5). Price Stern.

--Miffy at the Zoo. (Dick Bruna Bks.). 32p. 1984. 2.95 (ISBN 0-8431-1532-7). Price Stern.

--Miffy Goes Flying. (Dick Bruna Bks.). 32p. 1984. 2.95 (ISBN 0-8431-1535-1). Price Stern.

--Miffy Goes to School. (Dick Bruna Bks.). 32p. 1984. 2.95 (ISBN 0-8431-1530-0). Price Stern.

--Miffy in the Hospital. (Dick Bruna Bks.). 32p. 1984. 2.95 (ISBN 0-8431-1544-0). Price Stern.

--Miffy in the Snow. (Dick Bruna Bks.). 32p. 1984. 2.95 (ISBN 0-8431-1534-3). Price Stern.

--Miffy's Bicycle. (Dick Bruna Bks.). 32p. 1984. 2.95 (ISBN 0-8431-1527-0). Price Stern.

--Miffy's Birthday. (Dick Bruna Bks.). 32p. 1984. 2.95 (ISBN 0-8431-1536-X). Price Stern.

--Miffy's Dream. (Dick Bruna Bks.). 1984. 2.95 (ISBN 0-8431-1545-9). Price Stern.

--My Shirt Is White. (Dick Bruna Bks.). (Illus.). 28p. (ps-k). Date not set. cancelled (ISBN 0-8431-1583-1). Price Stern.

--One-Two-Three Frieze. (Bruna Books). (Illus.). 24p. (Orig.). (ps-2). 1976. pap. 5.95 four foldout paper panels (ISBN 0-416-80350-4, NO. 0011). Methuen Inc.

--The Orchestra. (Dick Bruna Bks.). 1984. 2.95 (ISBN 0-8431-1529-7). Price Stern.

--Poppy Pig. (Dick Bruna Bks.). (Illus.). 28p. (ps-k). Date not set. cancelled (ISBN 0-8431-1582-3). Price Stern.

--The Rescue. (Dick Bruna Bks.). 1984. 2.95 (ISBN 0-8431-1528-9). Price Stern.

--Snuffy. (Dick Bruna Bks.). 1984. 2.95. Price Stern.

--Snuffy & the Fire. (Dick Bruna Bks.). 1984. 2.95 (ISBN 0-8431-1549-1). Price Stern.

--A Story to Tell. (Dick Bruna Bks.). 1984. 2.95 (ISBN 0-8431-1576-9). Price Stern.

--When I'm Big. (Dick Bruna Bks.). 1984. 2.95 (ISBN 0-8431-1546-7). Price Stern.

Brunacci, G., jt. auth. see Cusatelli, G.

Brunanburh. The Battle of Brunanburh. Campbell, Alistair, ed. 184p. Repr. of 1938 ed. lib. bdg. 29.00x (ISBN 0-403-03315-2). Scholarly.

Bruncken, Ernest & Register, Layton B., trs. Science of Legal Method: Select Essays. (Modern Legal Philosophy Ser: Vol. 9). lxxxvi, 593p. 1969. Repr. of 1917 ed. 37.50x (ISBN 0-8377-2600-X). Rothman.

Brundage, Anthony. The Making of the New Poor Law: The Politics of Inquiry, Enactment, & Implementation, 1832-1839. 1978. 22.50x (ISBN 0-8135-0855-X). Rutgers U Pr.

Brundage, Barbara, jt. auth. see Sax, Alan.

Brundage, Burr C. Empire of the Inca. LC 63-18070. (Civilization of the American Indian Ser.: No. 69). (Illus.). 1974. Repr. of 1963 ed. 24.95 (ISBN 0-8061-0573-9). U of Okla Pr.

--The Fifth Sun: Aztec Gods, Aztec World. (Texas Pan American Ser.). (Illus.). 283p. 1983. pap. 8.95 (ISBN 0-292-72438-1). U of Tex Pr.

--Gian Carlo. (Illus.). 64p. 1975. pap. 3.00 (ISBN 0-912760-04-4). Valkyrie Pub Hse.

--The Jade Steps: A Ritual Life of the Aztecs. (Illus.). 256p. 1985. 22.50 (ISBN 0-87480-247-4). U of Utah Pr.

--The Juniper Palace. LC 76-573. (Illus.). 1976. 6.95 (ISBN 0-912760-26-5). Valkyrie Pub Hse.

--Lords of Cuzco: A History & Description of the Inca People in Their Final Days. 1967. 11.95 (ISBN 0-8061-0749-9). U of Okla Pr.

--Lords of Cuzco: A History & Description of the Inca People in Their Final Days. LC 67-15576. (The Civilization of the American Indian Ser.: Vol. 88). (Illus.). 472p. (Orig.). 1985. pap. text ed. 12.95 (ISBN 0-8061-1955-1). U of Okla Pr.

--The Phoenix of the Western World: Quetzalcoatl & the Sky Religion. LC 81-40278. (The Civilization of the American Indian Ser.: Vol. 160). (Illus.). 320p. 1982. 22.50 (ISBN 0-8061-1773-7). U of Okla Pr.

--A Rain of Darts: The Mexica Aztecs. LC 72-680. (Texas Pan American Ser.). 372p. 1972. 20.00x (ISBN 0-292-77002-2). U of Tex Pr.

Brundage, Burr Cartwright. Empire of the Inca. LC 63-18070. (Civilization of the American Indian Ser.: Vol. 69). 414p. (Orig.). 1985. pap. 10.95 (ISBN 0-8061-1924-1). U of Okla Pr.

Brundage, Dorothy J. Nursing Management of Renal Problems. 2nd ed. LC 80-11720. (Illus.). 1980. pap. text ed. 15.95 (ISBN 0-8016-0849-X). Mosby.

Brundage, James, jt. ed. see Bullough, Vern.

Brundage, James A. Crusades: A Documentary Survey. 1962. 14.95 (ISBN 0-87462-423-1). Marquette.

Brundage, Paul D., jt. auth. see Starchild, Adam.

Brundage, Percival F. Changing Concepts of Business Income. LC 75-21163. 1975. Repr. of 1952 ed. text ed. 13.00 (ISBN 0-914348-18-3). Scholars Bk.

Brundenius, Claes. Revolutionary Cuba: The Challenge: Economic Growth, with Equity. (WVSS on Latin America & the Caribbean). 160p. 1984. lib. bdg. 22.00x (ISBN 0-86531-355-5). Westview.

Brundenius, Claes & Lundal, Mats, eds. Development Strategies in Latin America. 200p. 1982. 21.50x (ISBN 0-86531-261-3). Westview.

Brundidge, Glenna M., et al, eds. Brazos County History: Rich Past-Bright Future. 800p. 1985. lib. bdg. 50.00 (ISBN 0-943162-08-4). Family History.

--Bibliography of Brazos County History. 160p. 1985. lib. bdg. 30.00 (ISBN 0-943162-09-2). Family History.

Brundidge, Harry. Twinkle Twinkle Movie Star. Kupelnick, Bruce S., ed. LC 76-52094. (Classics of Film Literature Ser.). 1978. lib. bdg. 22.00 (ISBN 0-8240-2868-6). Garland Pub.

Brundin, C. L. see Von Mises, Richard & Von Karman, Theodore.

Brundle, C. R. & Baker, A. D. Electron Spectroscopy, Vol. 5. 1984. 75.00 (ISBN 0-12-137805-5). Acad Pr.

Brundle, C. R. & Baker, A. D., eds. Electron Spectroscopy: Theory, Techniques, & Applications. Vol. 1, 1977. 79.00 (ISBN 0-12-137801-2); Vol. 2, 1979. 60.00 (ISBN 0-12-137802-0); Vol. 3, 1979. 63.00 (ISBN 0-12-137803-9). Acad Pr.

--Electron Spectroscopy: Theory, Techniques & Applications, Vol. 4. LC 76-1691. 1981. 77.00 (ISBN 0-12-137804-7). Acad Pr.

Brundle, C. R. & Morawitz, H., eds. Vibrations at Surfaces. 734p. 1983. 147.00 (ISBN 0-444-42166-1). Elsevier.
Brundle, C. R., ed. see Interdisciplinary Surface Science Conference, 2nd, England, 1975.
Brundritt, Alan. Elementary ALGOL. (Illus.). 80p. 1976. pap. text ed. 16.50x (ISBN 0-7121-0549-2, Pub. by Macdonald & Evans Engalnd). Trans-Atlantic.
Brundy, Clyde M. Call Up the Morning. 544p. 1983. pap. 3.50 (ISBN 0-380-82339-X, 82339-X). Avon.
--Grasslands. 496p. 1980. pap. 2.50 (ISBN 0-380-75499-1, 75499-1). Avon.
--High Empire. 432p. 1980. pap. 3.50 (ISBN 0-380-00040-7, 85290-X). Avon.
Brune, D., et al. Nuclear Analytical Chemistry. 557p. 1984. pap. text ed. 49.50x (ISBN 0-86238-047-2, Pub. by Chartwell-Bratt England). Brookfield Pub Co.
Brune, Genevieve A., ed. see Caldwell, John.
Brune, Gunnar. Springs of Texas, Vol. 1. LC 80-71016. (Illus.). 584p. 1981. 35.00 (ISBN 0-9604766-0-1). G Brune.
Brune, J. A., ed. see Wood, Manfri F.
Brune, John. Resonant Rubbish. 3.50 (ISBN 0-913714-66-6). Legacy Bks.
Brune, K. see Rainsford, K. D., et al.
Brune, K. & Baggiolini, M., eds. Arachidonic Acid Metabolism in Inflammation & Thrombosis: Proceedings of the First European Workshop on Inflammation, Basel, 1979. (Agents & Actions Supplements: No. 4). (Illus.). 300p. 1979. text ed. 43.95x (ISBN 0-8176-1095-2). Birkhauser.
Brune, K., jt. ed. see Rainsford, K. D.
Brune, Lester H. Chronological History of United States Foreign Relations, 1766 to Present. LC 83-48210. 1985. 100.00 (ISBN 0-8240-9056-X). Garland Pub.
--The Missile Crisis of October Nineteen Sixty-Two: A Review of Issues & References. (Guides to Historical Issues Ser.: No. 2). (Illus.). 165p. 1985. lib. bdg. 18.95 (ISBN 0-941690-16-4); pap. 10.95 (ISBN 0-941690-17-2); pap. text ed. 7.45x. Regina Bks.
--Origins of American National Security Policy: Sea Power, Air Power & Foreign Policy, 1980-194. 348p. 1981. pap. text ed. 26.00x (ISBN 0-89126-075-7). MA-AH Pub.
Bruneau see Brunot.
Bruneau, T. C. The Political Transformation of the Brazilian Catholic Church. LC 73-79318. (Perspectives on Development Ser.: No. 2). 302p. 1974. 49.50 (ISBN 0-521-20256-6). Cambridge U Pr.
Bruneau, Thomas C. The Church in Brazil: The Politics of Religion. (Latin American Monograph: No. 56). 253p. 1982. text ed. 27.00x (ISBN 0-292-71071-2). U of Tex Pr.
--The Political Transformation of the Brazilian Catholic Church. LC 73-79318. (Perspective on Development Ser.: Vol. 2). pap. 71.00 (ISBN 0-317-28009-0, 2025579). Bks Demand UMI.
--Politics & Nationhood: Post Revolutionary Portugal. LC 83-17784. 192p. 1984. 29.95 (ISBN 0-03-069464-7). Praeger.
Brunel, Francis. Splendour of Indian Miniatures, Fr. 160p. 1981. 35.00 (ISBN 0-86710-005-2). Edns Vilo.
Brunel, Gaston. A Guide to the Vineyards of the Cotes du Rhone. (Illus.). 254p. 30.00 (ISBN 0-312-92274-4). St Martin.
Brunel, Isambard. The Life of Isambard Kingdom Brunel: Civil Engineer (1870) LC 72-850. (Illus.). 568p. 1972. 50.00 (ISBN 0-8386-1201-6). Fairleigh Dickinson.
Brunell, Lillian F. & Young, Wayne T., eds. Multimodal Handbook for a Mental Hospital: Designing Specific Treatments for Specific Problems. (Springer Series on Behavior Therapy & Behavioral Medicine: Vol. 7). 367p. 1982. text ed. 34.95 (ISBN 0-8261-3700-8). Springer Pub.
Brunell, Richard, jt. auth. see Vazsonyi, Andrew.
Brunell, Shirl. I Hear Bluebirds. (Illus.). 120p. 1983. 13.95 (ISBN 0-317-12801-9). Coltrane & Beach.
--I Hear Bluebirds. 152p. 1984. 15.95 (ISBN 0-913425-16-8). Coltrane & Beach.
Brunelle, Jacques M. Nidus. (Psychic Phenomenon Ser.). (Illus.). 224p. (Orig.). 1985. 18.00 (ISBN 0-943920-41-8); pap. 10.00 (ISBN 0-943920-42-6). Metamorphous Pr.
Brunelle, Jim. Maine Geographic Book of Lists: Interesting & Unusual Facts about Maine. (Maine Geographic Ser.). 48p. 1983. pap. 2.95 (ISBN 0-89933-065-7). DeLorme Pub.
Brunelle, Jim, ed. Over to Home & from Away. (Illus.). 340p. (Orig.). 1980. pap. 8.95 (ISBN 0-930096-11-8). G Gannett.
Brunelle, Jim, ed. see Clark, William.
Brunelle, Richard L. & Reed, Robert W. Forensic Examination of Ink & Paper. LC 83-18039. (Illus.). 302p. 1984. 49.50x (ISBN 0-398-04935-1). C C Thomas.
Brunelle, Wallace & O'Neill, Robert. Constructional Geometry: Student Syllabus. 2nd ed. Gray, Allan W., ed. 1972. pap. text ed. 8.35 (ISBN 0-89420-229-4, 350299); cassette recordings 108.05 (ISBN 0-89420-201-4, 350300). Natl Book.
Brunelli, B. Driven Magnetic Fusion Reactors: Proceedings. (Commission of the European Communities Ser.: EUR 6146). (Illus.). 1979. pap. 97.00 (ISBN 0-08-024459-9). Pergamon.
Brunelli, B. & Leotta, G. G., eds. Unconventional Approaches to Fusion. LC 82-3836. (Ettore Majorana International Science Series, Physical Sciences: Vol. 13). 544p. 1982. 85.00x (ISBN 0-306-41002-8, Plenum Pr). Plenum Pub.
Brunenghi, jt. auth. see Benedetti.
Bruner, Charlotte H., intro. by. Unwinding Threads: Writing by Women in Africa. LC 83-17175. (African Writers Ser.: No. 256). xvi, 208p. 1983. pap. text ed. 6.00x (ISBN 0-435-90256-3). Heinemann Ed.
Bruner, Elaine, ed. see Engelmann, Siegfried.
Bruner, F., ed. The Science of Chromatography: Lectures Presented at the A. J. P. Martin Honorary Symposium Urbino, Italy May 27-31, 1985. (Journal of Chromatography Library: No. 32). 476p. 1985. 92.75 (ISBN 0-444-42443-1). Elsevier.
Bruner, Frederick D. Theology of the Holy Spirit. LC 76-103445. 1970. pap. 7.95 (ISBN 0-8028-1547-2). Eerdmans.
Bruner, Frederick D. & Hordern, William E. The Holy Spirit-Shy Member of the Trinity. LC 83-72124. 112p. (Orig.). 1984. pap. 5.50 (ISBN 0-8066-2068-4, 10-3070). Augsburg.
Bruner, Herbert B. The Junior High School at Work. LC 72-176606. (Columbia University. Teachers College. Contributions to Education: No. 177). Repr. of 1925 ed. 22.50 (ISBN 0-404-55177-7). AMS Pr.
Bruner, Jerome. Child's Talk: Learning to Use Language. LC 83-42676. (Illus.). 1983. 13.95 (ISBN 0-393-01753-2). Norton.
--Under Five in Britain. LC 80-24693. (Oxford Preschool Research Project Ser.: Vol. 1). 228p. 1980. pap. 9.50 (ISBN 0-931114-09-8). High-Scope.
Bruner, Jerome, intro. by see Gay, John.
Bruner, Jerome, et al, eds. see Bower, T. G.
Bruner, Jerome, et al, eds. see Goodnow, Jacqueline.
Bruner, Jerome, et al, eds. see Stern, Daniel.
Bruner, Jerome S. Beyond the Information Given: Studies in the Psychology of Knowing. Anglin, Jeremey M., ed. (Illus.). 1973. pap. text ed. 10.95x (ISBN 0-393-09363-8). Norton.
--Contemporary Approaches to Cognition. LC 57-12963. (Illus.). 1957. pap. 55.00 (ISBN 0-317-08054-7, 2016734). Bks Demand UMI.
--In Search of Mind: Essays in Autobiography. LC 83-47526. 320p. 1984. pap. 6.68 (ISBN 0-06-091168-9, CN). Har-Row.
--On Knowing: Essays for the Left Hand. expanded ed. LC 62-13264. (Illus.). 1979. 10.00x (ISBN 0-674-63475-6, Belknap Pr); pap. 4.95 (ISBN 0-674-63525-6, Belknap Pr). Harvard U Pr.
--Process of Education. LC 60-15235. 1960. 5.95x (ISBN 0-674-71000-2); pap. 3.50 (ISBN 0-674-71001-0). Harvard U Pr.
--Processes of Cognitive Growth: Infancy. LC 68-27831. (Heinz Werner Lec. Ser.: No. 3). 1968. 3.00x (ISBN 0-8271-6810-1). Clark U Pr.
--The Relevance of Education. LC 74-139376. 192p. 1971. 5.95x (ISBN 0-393-04334-7, Norton Lib.); pap. 4.95x (ISBN 0-393-00690-5, Norton Lib). Norton.
--Toward a Theory of Instruction. LC 66-13179. (Illus.). 1966. 8.95x (ISBN 0-674-89700-5, Belknap Pr); pap. 4.95 (ISBN 0-674-89701-3). Harvard U Pr.
Bruner, Jerome S. & Krech, David, eds. Perception & Personality: A Symposium. LC 68-21325. (Illus.). 1968. Repr. of 1950 ed. lib. bdg. 19.75x (ISBN 0-8371-0031-3, BRPP). Greenwood.
Bruner, Jerome S., et al. Contemporary Approaches to Cognition: A Symposium Held at the University of Colorado. LC 57-12963. (Illus.). 1957. 12.50x (ISBN 0-674-16650-7). Harvard U Pr.
Bruner, Katherine, ed. see Wolff, Robert Lee.
Bruner, Katherine F., ed. see Hart, Robert.
Bruner, William T. The Sex Problem: Its Cause, Its Curse & Its Cure. 1977. 3.00 (ISBN 0-9606566-0-X). Bruner.
--The Truth about Sin: What Does the Bible Say? 1977. 2.00 (ISBN 0-9606566-1-8). Bruner.
Brunes, Tons. The Secrets of Ancient Geometry, 2 vols. 1967. Set. text ed. 75.50x (ISBN 0-391-01117-0). Humanities.
Brunet. Manuel Du Libraire et De l'Amateur Des Livres, 7 tomes. Set. 525.00 (ISBN 0-685-11350-7). French & Eur.
--Supplement aux supercheries litteraires. 43.75 (ISBN 0-685-35982-4). French & Eur.
Brunet, Charles. Table des pieces de theatre decrites dans le catalogue de la bibliotheque de M. de Soleinne. 491p. 1914. Repr. 34.00 (ISBN 0-8337-3312-5). B Franklin.
Brunet, David P. Fumbling for Words. LC 83-21378. (Orig.). 1984. pap. 2.25 (ISBN 0-9603840-6-5). Andrew Mtn Pr.
Brunet, G. Dictionnaire des Apocryphes, 2 vols. Migne, J. P., ed. (Troisieme et Derniere Encyclopedie Theologique Ser.: Vols. 23-24). 1310p. (Fr.). Repr. of 1858 ed. lib. bdg. 167.50x (ISBN 0-89241-305-0). Caratzas.
Brunet, Gustave. Imprimeurs imaginaires et libraires supposes. 1962. Repr. of 1866 ed. 23.50 (ISBN 0-8337-0404-4). B Franklin.
Brunet, Jacques, ed. Oriental Music: A Selected Discography. (Occasional Publication). 104p. 1971. pap. 3.00 (ISBN 0-89192-148-6). Interbk Inc.
Brunet, M., ed. see Frick.
Brunet, Mario. All about Sailing: A Handbook for Juniors. 1976. pap. 8.95 (ISBN 0-8120-0699-2). Barron.
Brunet, Roger, intro. by. Bibliographie Geographique Internationale-International Geographical Bibliography, 1983, 2 vols, Vol. 83. LC 25-1167. (Orig., Fr. & Eng.). 1981. Set. pap. 67.50 (ISBN 0-8002-2999-1). Intl Pubns Serv.
Brunet, Roger, ed. The Churches & Abbeys of France. Date not set. price not set. Larousse.
Brunetiere, F. Honore De Balzac. 59.95 (ISBN 0-8490-0373-3). Gordon Pr.
--Manual of French Literature. LC 71-127998. (Studies in French Literature, No. 45). 1970. Repr. of 1898 ed. lib. bdg. 59.95x (ISBN 0-8383-1149-0). Haskell.
Brunetieve, F. Essays in French Literature. 59.95 (ISBN 0-8490-0127-7). Gordon Pr.
Brunetti, Argentina, jt. auth. see Reynolds, Althea C.
Brunetti, E. Diptera: Brachycera, Vol. II. (Fauna of British India Ser.). (Illus.). x, 410p. 1977. Repr. of 1920 ed. 30.00 (ISBN 0-88065-071-0, Pub. by Messers Today & Tomorrows Printers & Publishers India). Scholarly Pubns.
--Diptera: Nematocera (Excluding Chironomidae & Culcidae, Vol. 1. (Fauna of British India Ser.). (Illus.). xxviii, 610p. 1977. Repr. of 1912 ed. 30.00 (Pub. by Messers Today & Tomorrows Printers & Publishers India). Scholarly Pubns.
--Diptera: Pipunculidae, Syrphidae, Conopidae, Ostridae, Vol. III. (Fauna of British India Ser.). (Illus.). xii, 436p. 1977. Repr. of 1923 ed. 30.00 (ISBN 0-88065-072-9, Pub. by Messers Today & Tomorrows Printers & Publishers India). Scholarly Pubns.
Brunetti, Mendor T., tr. see Verne, Jules.
Brunetti, Paolo, et al, eds. Artificial Systems for Insulin Delivery. (Serono Symposia Publications: Vol. 6). 640p. 1983. text ed. 96.00 (ISBN 0-89004-875-4). Raven.
Brungardt, Helen. Beyond Liberation. LC 84-23407. 64p. (Orig.). 1984. pap. 5.00 (ISBN 0-941992-04-7). Los Arboles Pub.
--The Mystical Meaning of Jesus the Christ: Significant Episodes in the Life of the Master. 2nd ed. (Illus.). 64p. 1983. pap. 5.00 (ISBN 0-941992-03-9). Los Arboles Pub.
Brungardt, Terrence, jt. auth. see Arnold, William.
Brungraber, Robert L. Timber Design for the Civil Professional Engineering Exam. 175p. 1984. pap. 15.95 (ISBN 0-932276-38-5). Prof Engine.
Brunhammer, Yvonne. Art Deco Style. 176p. 1984. pap. 14.95 (ISBN 0-312-05224-3). St Martin.
Brunhammer, Yvonne, et al. Art Nouveau Belgium-France. LC 76-1649. 1976. 20.00 (ISBN 0-914412-11-6). Inst for the Arts.
Brunhes, Jean. Human Geography, an Attempt at a Positive Classification: Principles & Examples. LC 75-41040. (Illus.). Repr. of 1920 ed. 44.50 (ISBN 0-404-14724-0). AMS Pr.
Brunhes Delamarre, Mariel J., et al. Geographie Regionale, 2 vols. (Methodique Ser.). Vol. 1. 69.95 (ISBN 0-686-56439-1); Vol. 2. write for info. French & Eur.
Brunhoff, Jean de. A. B. C. de Babar. new ed. 46p. 1978. 7.95 (ISBN 0-686-54120-0). French & Eur.
--Babar en Famille. 26p. 1975. 7.95 (ISBN 0-686-54122-7). French & Eur.
--Babar et le Crocodile. 16p. 1975. 1.95 (ISBN 0-686-54123-5). French & Eur.
--Babar et le Pere Noel. 29p. 1975. 7.95 (ISBN 0-686-54124-3). French & Eur.
--Barbar au Cirque. (Illus.). 16p. 1974. 1.95 (ISBN 0-686-54121-9). French & Eur.
--Le Couronnement de Babar. 16p. 1975. 1.95 (ISBN 0-686-54126-X). French & Eur.
--L' Enfance de Babar. 16p. 1975. 1.95 (ISBN 0-686-54127-8). French & Eur.
--Histoire de Babar, le Petite Elephant. (Illus.). 16p. 25.00 (ISBN 0-686-54129-4). French & Eur.
--Vive le Roi Babar. 20p. 1976. 3.95 (ISBN 0-686-54131-6). French & Eur.
--Le Voyage de Babar. 27p. 1975. 7.95 (ISBN 0-686-54132-4). French & Eur.
Brunhoff, Jean De see De Brunhoff, Jean.
Brunhoff, Jean de see De Brunhoff, Jean.
Brunhoff, Jean de see De Brunhoff, Jean & De Brunhoff, Laurent.
Brunhoff, L. De see De Brunhoff, L.
Brunhoff, Laurent de. L' Anniversaire de Babar. 28p. 1975. 7.95 (ISBN 0-686-54133-2). French & Eur.
--Les Aventures de Babar. 18p. 1977. 3.95 (ISBN 0-686-54134-0). French & Eur.
--Babar a Celesteville. 16p. 1974. 1.95 (ISBN 0-686-54135-9). French & Eur.
--Babar aux Sports d'Hiver. (Illus.). 20p. 1976. 3.95 (ISBN 0-686-54136-7). French & Eur.
--Babar Aviateur. 16p. 1974. 1.95 (ISBN 0-686-54137-5). French & Eur.
--Babar Campeur. 16p. 1974. 1.95 (ISBN 0-686-54138-3). French & Eur.
--Babar dans l'Ile aux Oiseaux. 29p. 7.95 (ISBN 0-686-54139-1). French & Eur.
--Babar en Amerique. 23p. 1975. 7.95 (ISBN 0-686-54140-5). French & Eur.
--Babar et le Docteur. 16p. 1975. 1.95 (ISBN 0-686-54141-3). French & Eur.
--Babar et le Wouly-Wouly. 26p. 7.95 (ISBN 0-686-54142-1). French & Eur.
--Babar et Sa Famille. 26p. 1976. 3.95 (ISBN 0-686-54143-X). French & Eur.
--Babar Patissier. 16p. 1975. 1.95 (ISBN 0-686-54144-8). French & Eur.
--Bonhomme et la Grosse Bete qui avait des Escailles sur le Dos. (Illus.). 1975. 12.95 (ISBN 0-686-54145-6). French & Eur.
Brunhoff, Laurent De see De Brunhoff, Jean & De Brunhoff, Laurent.
Brunhoff, Laurent De see De Brunhoff, Laurent.
Brunhoff, Laurent de see De Brunhoff, Laurent.
Brunhoff, Laurent De see De Brunhoff, Laurent.
Brunhoff, Laurent de see De Brunhoff, Laurent.
Brunhouse, Robert L. Counter-Revolution in Pennsylvania: 1776-1790. LC 70-120237. 1971. Repr. lib. bdg. 20.00x (ISBN 0-374-91050-2). Octagon.
--The Counter-Revolution in Pennsylvania: 1776-1790. LC 42-5025. (Illus.). 368p. 1971. 6.95 (ISBN 0-911124-65-9). Pa Hist & Mus.
Brunhuber, E. Giesserei - Fachwoerterbuch. 802p. (Ger., Eng., Fr. & Ital., Dictionary of Foundry). 1977. 120.00 (ISBN 3-7949-0283-1, M-7424, Pub. by Fachverlag, Schiele & Schon). French & Eur.
--Giesserei - Lexikon 1978. 960p. (Ger.). 1977. 62.50 (ISBN 3-7949-0282-3, M-7425, Pub. by Fachverlag, Schiele & Schon). French & Eur.
Brunhubner. Pluto. 5.50 (ISBN 0-86690-062-4). Am Fed Astrologers.
Bruni, C., ed. Systems Theory in Immunology. (Lecture Notes in Biomathematics: Vol. 32). 273p. 1979. pap. 19.00 (ISBN 0-387-09728-7). Springer-Verlag.
Bruni, J. Edward, jt. auth. see Montemurro, Donald G.
Bruni, Joseph, jt. auth. see Wilder, B. Joseph.
Bruni, V., et al, eds. Pediatric & Adolescent Gynecology. 1983. 75.00 (ISBN 0-12-137880-2). Acad Pr.
Bruning, James L. & Kintz, B. L. Computational Handbook of Statistics. 2nd ed. 1977. pap. 17.95x (ISBN 0-673-15014-3). Scott F.
Bruning, Nancy. Coping with Chemotherapy. LC 84-9612. 336p. 1985. 15.95 (ISBN 0-385-27907-8, Dial). Doubleday.
Bruning, Nancy P., jt. auth. see Katz, Jane.
Bruning, Roger H., jt. auth. see Glover, John A.
Bruning, Ted & Paulin, Keith. The David & Charles Book of Historic English Inns. (Illus.). 256p. 1982. 23.95 (ISBN 0-7153-8178-4). David & Charles.
Brunini, John G., ed. From One Word: Selected Poems. 1950. 3.50 (ISBN 0-8159-5511-1). Devin.
Brunk, George R., ed. Encounter with the Holy Spirit. LC 72-2053. 240p. 1972. pap. 4.95 (ISBN 0-8361-1693-3). Herald Pr.
Brunk, Gregory. Countermarked Coins of the United States & Canada. 500p. 35.00 (ISBN 0-912317-07-8). World Exo.
Brunk, Gregory G., ed. World Countermarks on Medieval & Modern Coins. LC 75-39496. (Gleanings from the Numismatist Ser.: Vol. 8). (Illus.). 1976. 30.00x (ISBN 0-88000-074-0). Quarterman.
Brunk, H. D. Introduction to Mathematical Statistics. 3rd ed. LC 74-82348. 400p. 1975. text ed. 38.50 (ISBN 0-471-00834-6). Wiley.
Brunk, J. D. & Wayland, J. W. His Name Is Wonderful. Hochstetler, Walter, ed. 1967. pap. 1.50x (ISBN 0-87813-103-5). Park View.
Brunk, J. D., ed. Church & Sunday School Hymnal with Supplement. LC 72-2053. 384p. (532 hymns & songs, & 50 german songs, words only, 1902; supplement 1911). 1902. 6.95x (ISBN 0-8361-1110-9). Herald Pr.
Brunk, Jason W. Child & Adolescent Development. LC 74-16258. Repr. of 1975 ed. 120.00 (ISBN 0-8357-9856-9, 2012612). Bks Demand UMI.
Brunk, M. J. Fulfilled Prophecies. 160p. 5.80 (ISBN 0-686-05601-9). Rod & Staff.
Brunke. Star Point Series & Ceremonies. rev. & enl. ed. 96p. 1984. pap. 6.50 (ISBN 0-88053-362-5). Macoy Pub.
Brunke, Ottilie. O.E.S. Floor Work. 18p. 1977. pap. 1.25 (ISBN 0-88053-331-5, S-241). Macoy Pub.
Brunke, Ottilie S. Chapter Ceremonies & Poems. pap. text ed. 2.50 (ISBN 0-88053-305-6, S-192). Macoy Pub.
Brunkhorst, Martin. Shakespeares Coriolanus in deutscher Bearbeitung: Sieben Beispiele zum literaturaesthetischen Problem der Umsetzung und Vermittlung Shakespeares. (Komparatistische Studien: Vol. 3). 1973. 31.60x (ISBN 3-11-003997-4). De Gruyter.
Brunkow, Robert de V., ed. Religion & Society in North America: An Annotated Bibliography. LC 82-24304. (Clio Bibliography Ser.: No. 12). 515p. 1983. lib. bdg. 68.25 (ISBN 0-87436-042-0). ABC-Clio.
Brunn, Emilie Z. Augustine. Date not set. price not set. Paragon Hse.

--Le Dilemme de L'etre et du Neant Chez Saint Augustin: Des Premiers Dialogues aux "Confessions". (Bochumer Studien Zur Philosophie Band 4). 102p. (French.). 1984. 18.00x (ISBN 90-6032-234-7, Pub. by B R Gruener Netherlands). Benjamins North Am.

Brunn, Fritz. Memoirs of a Doctor of the Old & New Worlds. Bernays, Hella F., ed. 9.95 (ISBN 0-686-74609-0); deluxe ed. 25.00 (ISBN 0-686-74610-4). Crambruck.

Brunn, H. O. The Story of the Original Dixieland Jazz Band. LC 77-3791. (Roots of Jazz Ser.). (Illus.). 1977. Repr. of 1960 ed. lib. bdg. 27.50 (ISBN 0-306-70892-2). Da Capo.

Brunn, Robert. The Initiation. (Twilight Ser.: No. 3). (gr. 5 up). 1982. pap. 1.95 (ISBN 0-440-94047-8, LFL). Dell.

Brunn, Stanley & Williams, Jack. Cities of the World: World Regional Urban Development. 506p. 1983. pap. text ed. 19.50 scp (ISBN 0-06-381225-8, HarpC). Har-Row.

Brunnarius, Martin. The Windmills of Sussex. 1979. 39.00x (ISBN 0-85033-345-8, Pub. by Phillimore England). State Mutual Bk.

Brunner & Gravas. Clinical Hypertension & Hypotension. (Vol. 2). 498p. 1982. 67.50 (ISBN 0-8247-1279-X). Dekker.

Brunner & Suddarth. Lippincott Manual of Medical Surgical Nursing, Vol. 1. 512p. 1982. pap. text ed. 15.50 (ISBN 0-06-318207-6, Pub. by Har-Row Ltd England). Har-Row.

--Lippincott Manual of Medical Surgical Nursing, Vol. 2. 512p. 1982. pap. text ed. 18.50 (ISBN 0-06-318208-4, Pub. by Har-Row Ltd England). Har-Row.

--Lippincott Manual of Medical Surgical Nursing, Vol. 3. 512p. 1982. pap. text ed. 15.50 (ISBN 0-06-318209-2, Pub. by Har-Row Ltd England). Har-Row.

Brunner, Andre, jt. auth. see Luine, Mario.

Brunner, August. New Creation: Towards a Theology of the Christian Life. 1956. 10.00 (ISBN 0-8022-0189-X). Philos Lib.

Brunner, C. F. & Waber, B. G. Special Techniques in Internal Fixation. (Illus.). 198p. 1981. 79.00 (ISBN 0-387-11056-9). Springer-Verlag.

Brunner, Calvin R. Design of Sewage Sludge Incineration Systems. LC 80-21916. (Pollution Technology Review Ser.: No. 71). (Illus.). 380p. 1981. 48.00 (ISBN 0-8155-0825-5). Noyes.

--Hazardous Air Emissions from Incineration. 250p. 1985. text ed. 35.00 (ISBN 0-412-00721-5, NO. 9093, Pub. by Chapman & Hall England). Methuen Inc.

--Incineration Systems: Selection & Design. LC 83-26124. (Illus.). 417p. 1984. 52.50 (ISBN 0-442-21192-9). Van Nos Reinhold.

--Incineration Systems Seminar Notebook. 477p. 1982. Wkbk. 95.00 (ISBN 0-86587-111-6). Gov Insts.

Brunner, Calvin R., jt. auth. see Schwarz, Stephen C.

Brunner, Christopher J. A Syntax of Western Middle Iranian. LC 75-17528. (Persian Studies Ser.). 311p. 1977. text ed. 35.00x (ISBN 0-88206-005-8). Caravan Bks.

Brunner, D., jt. ed. see Jokl, E.

Brunner, Edmund & Kolb, John H. Rural Social Trends. LC 70-98825. Repr. of 1933 ed. lib. bdg. 20.75x (ISBN 0-8371-2889-7, BRRS). Greenwood.

Brunner, Edmund D. Church Life in the Rural South. LC 70-90129. (Illus.). Repr. of 1949 ed. 19.75x (ISBN 0-8371-1994-4, BRC&, Pub. by Negro U Pr). Greenwood.

--Rural Australia & New Zealand: Some Observations of Current Trends. LC 75-30123. (Institute of Pacific Relations). Repr. of 1938 ed. 11.50 (ISBN 0-404-59513-8). AMS Pr.

--Working with Rural Youth. facsimile ed. LC 74-1669. (Children & Youth Ser.). 132p. 1974. Repr. of 1942 ed. 14.00 (ISBN 0-405-05949-3). Ayer Co Pubs.

Brunner, Edmund D. & Lorge, Irving. Rural Trends in Depression Years: A Survey of Village-Centered Agricultural Communities, 1930-1936. LC 75-137157. (Poverty U.S.A. Historical Record Ser). 1971. Repr. of 1937 ed. 26.50 (ISBN 0-405-03095-9). Ayer Co Pubs.

Brunner, Edmund D., jt. auth. see Wayland, Sloan.

Brunner, Edmund D., et al, eds. Farmers of the World. facs. ed. LC 73-134062. (Essay Index Reprint Ser). 1945. 16.00 (ISBN 0-8369-2182-8). Ayer Co Pubs.

Brunner, Edmund de S., jt. auth. see Chase, Stuart.

Brunner, Edward. Splendid Failure: Hart Crane & the Making of The Bridge. LC 84-2690. 296p. 1985. 22.95x (ISBN 0-252-01094-9). U of Ill Pr.

Brunner, Emil. The Christian Doctrine of Creation & Redemption. Wyon, Olive, tr. LC 50-6821. (Dogmatic Ser.: Vol. 2). 396p. 1979. pap. 10.95 (ISBN 0-664-24248-0). Westminster.

--The Christian Doctrine of God. Wyon, Olive, tr. LC 50-6821. (Dogmatics Ser.: Vol. 1). 376p. 1980. pap. 11.95 (ISBN 0-664-24304-5). Westminster.

--The Christian Doctrine of the Church, Faith, & the Consummation. LC 50-6821. (Dogmatic Ser., Vol. 3). 472p. 1978. softcover o.s.i. 9.95 (ISBN 0-664-24218-9). Westminster.

--The Divine-Human Encounter. Loos, Amandus W., tr. from Ger. 207p. 1980. Repr. of 1943 ed. lib. bdg. 24.75x (ISBN 0-313-22398-X, BRDH). Greenwood.

--The Divine Imperative. LC 47-2443. 728p. 1979. softcover 9.95 (ISBN 0-664-24246-4). Westminster.

--Man in Revolt: A Christian Anthropology. Wyon, Olive, tr. LC 47-2442. 564p. 1979. softcover 9.95 (ISBN 0-664-24245-6). Westminster.

--Our Faith. 1936. pap. text ed. 7.95 (ISBN 0-684-16856-1, SL87, ScribT). Scribner.

--Our Faith. 153p. 1980. pap. text ed. price not set (ISBN 0-02-315940-5, Pub. by Scribner). Macmillan.

--Revelation & Reason. 448p. 1984. pap. 12.95 (ISBN 0-913029-01-7). Chanticleer Pub.

--Scandal of Christianity: The Gospel as Stumbling Block to Modern Man. LC 65-12729. 1965. pap. 5.95 (ISBN 0-8042-0708-9). John Knox.

Brunner, Emma B. Bits of Background in One-Act Plays. LC 77-94334. (One-Act Plays in Reprint Ser.). 1978. Repr. of 1919 ed. 17.50x (ISBN 0-8486-2034-8). Core Collection.

Brunner, F. K., ed. Geodetic Refraction. (Illus.). 230p. 1984. pap. 17.00 (ISBN 0-387-13830-7). Springer-Verlag.

Brunner, Felix. Handbook of Graphic Reproduction Processes: Technical Guide for Art Collectors, Artists, & Print Makers. (Illus.). 1984. 67.50 (ISBN 0-8038-3066-1). Hastings.

Brunner, Francis A., tr. see Fellerer, Karl G.

Brunner, Francis A., tr. see Jungmann, Josef A.

Brunner, Frank. Seven Samuroid. Jones, Bruce & Campbell, April, eds. (Pacific Comics Graphic Novel Ser.: No. 1). (Illus.). 60p. (Orig.). 1984. pap. 6.95 (ISBN 0-943128-06-4). Blue Dolphin.

Brunner, G., ed. Artificial Liver Support: Proceedings. Schmidt, F. W. (Illus.). 332p. 1981. 60.00 (ISBN 0-387-10591-3). Springer-Verlag.

Brunner, Gerhard. Aquarium Plants. Vevers, Gwynne, tr. from Ger. 1973. 19.95 (ISBN 0-87666-455-9, H-966). TFH Pubns.

Brunner, Harald & Thaler, Heribert, eds. Hepatology: Festschrift for Hans Popper. (Illus.). 408p. 1985. text ed. 93.50 (ISBN 0-88167-037-5). Raven.

Brunner, Harold J. I Am. 1984. 6.95 (ISBN 0-533-05320-X). Vantage.

Brunner, Heinrich E. Christianity & Civilisation, 2 vols. in one. LC 77-27182. (Gifford Lectures: 1947-48). Repr. of 1949 ed. 35.00 (ISBN 0-404-60530-3). AMS Pr.

--Eternal Hope. Knight, Harold, tr. LC 72-6930. 232p. 1973. Repr. of 1954 ed. lib. bdg. 20.50x (ISBN 0-8371-6508-3, BREH). Greenwood.

--The Philosophy of Religion from the Standpoint of Protestant Theology. LC 78-14106. 1979. Repr. of 1937 ed. 18.50 (ISBN 0-88355-779-7). Hyperion Conn.

Brunner, Herb. Introduction to Microprocessors. 1982. text ed. 28.95 (ISBN 0-8359-3247-8); instr's. manual avail. (ISBN 0-8359-3248-6). Reston.

Brunner, Ingrid & Mathes, J. C. The Technician As Writer: Preparing Technical Reports. 240p. 1980. pap. text ed. write for info. (ISBN 0-02-315950-2). Macmillan.

Brunner, Ingrid, et al. The Technician As Writer: Preparing Technical Reports. 1980. pap. 18.76 scp (ISBN 0-672-61523-1); scp tchrs manual 3.67 (ISBN 0-672-61524-X). Bobbs.

Brunner, Jerome S. In Search of Mind: Essays in Autobiography. LC 83-47526. (Sloan Foundation Ser.). 256p. 1983. 19.23i (ISBN 0-06-015191-9, HarpT). Har-Row.

Brunner, John. Age of Miracles. 240p. 1985. pap. 2.95 (ISBN 0-88677-024-6). DAW Bks.

--Bedlam Planet. 1982. pap. 2.25 (ISBN 0-345-30678-3, Del Rey). Ballantine.

--Catch a Falling Star. 224p. 1982. pap. 2.75 (ISBN 0-345-30681-3, Del Rey). Ballantine.

--The Crucible of Time. 304p. 1983. 12.95 (ISBN 0-345-31224-4, Del Rey). Ballantine.

--The Crucible of Time. 432p. 1984. pap. 3.50 (ISBN 0-345-30235-4, Del Rey). Ballantine.

--The Dramaturges of Yan. 208p. 1982. pap. 2.50 (ISBN 0-345-30677-5, Del Rey). Ballantine.

--The Great Steamboat Race. LC 82-90222. (Illus.). 592p. 1983. pap. 7.95 (ISBN 0-345-25853-3). Ballantine.

--The Long Result. 192p. (Orig.). 1981. pap. 2.25 (ISBN 0-345-29639-7, Del Rey). Ballantine.

--National Plan: A Preliminary Assessment. 2nd ed. (Institute of Economic Affairs, Eaton Papers: No. 4). (Illus.). 1968. pap. 2.50 technical (ISBN 0-255-69552-7). Transatlantic.

--A New Settlement of Old Scores. LC 83-62071. (Illus.). 68p. 1983. pap. 8.00 (ISBN 0-915368-22-6); lib. bdg. 8.00 GBC Bound Ed. (ISBN 0-915368-26-9). New Eng SF Assoc.

--Players at the Game of People. 224p. 1980. pap. 2.25 (ISBN 0-345-29235-9). Ballantine.

--The Sheep Look up. 192p. 1981. pap. 2.95 (ISBN 0-345-27503-9, Del Rey). Ballantine.

--The Shockwave Rider. (A Del Rey Bk.). 1978. pap. 1.50 (ISBN 0-345-24853-8). Ballantine.

--Stand on Zanzibar. 1976. pap. 2.50 (ISBN 0-345-28845-9). Ballantine.

--Stand on Zanzibar. LC 79-19062. 1979. Repr. of 1968 ed. lib. bdg. 16.50x (ISBN 0-8376-0438-9). Bentley.

--The Tides of Time. 240p. 1984. pap. 2.95 (ISBN 0-345-31838-2, Del Rey). Ballantine.

--Times Without Number. 224p. 1983. pap. 2.50 (ISBN 0-345-30679-1, Del Rey). Ballantine.

--Timescoop. 239p. 1984. pap. 2.50 (ISBN 0-87997-966-6). DAW Bks.

--Total Eclipse. (Science Fiction Ser.). 1984. pap. 2.50 (ISBN 0-87997-911-9). DAW Bks.

--The Webs of Everywhere. 192p. 1983. pap. 2.25 (ISBN 0-345-30680-5, Del Rey). Ballantine.

--The Whole Man. (Del Rey Bks). 1977. pap. 1.50 (ISBN 0-345-27088-6). Ballantine.

Brunner, Joseph F. & Campbell, John J. Participating in Secondary Reading: A Practical Approach. (Illus.). 1978. ref. 25.95 (ISBN 0-13-651323-9). P-H.

Brunner, K. & Meltzer, A., eds. The Economics of Price & Wage Controls. (Carnegie-Rochester Conference Series on Public Policy: Vol. 2). 305p. 1976. pap. 25.75 (ISBN 0-444-11099-2, North-Holland). Elsevier.

--Optimal Policies, Control Theory & Technology Exports. (Carnegie-Rochester Conference Series on Public Policy: Vol. 7). 238p. 1977. 21.50 (ISBN 0-444-85027-9, North-Holland). Elsevier.

Brunner, K. & Meltzer, A. H., eds. The Problem of Inflation. (Carnegie-Rochester Conference Series on Public Policy: Vol. 8). 372p. 1978. pap. 32.00 (ISBN 0-444-85147-X, North-Holland). Elsevier.

Brunner, K & Meltzer, A. H., eds. Theory, Policy, Institutions: Papers from the Carnegie-Rochester Conference on Public Policy. 446p. 1983. 19.50 (ISBN 0-444-86809-7, I-415-83, North-Holland). Elsevier.

Brunner, K. & Metlyer, A. H., eds. Policies for Employment, Prices, & Exchange Rates. (Carnegie-Rochester Conference Series on Public Policy: Vol. 11). 252p. 1979. 19.75 (ISBN 0-444-85392-8, North-Holland). Elsevier.

Brunner, Karl. An Outline of Middle English Grammar. LC 72-14364. 1974. Repr. of 1963 ed. lib. bdg. 10.00 (ISBN 0-8414-1371-1). Folcroft.

Brunner, Karl, ed. Economics & Social Institutions. (Rochester Studies in Economics & Policy Issues). 1979. lib. bdg. 17.95 (ISBN 0-89838-019-7, Pub. by Martinus Nijhoff Netherlands). Kluwer Academic.

--The First World & the Third World: Essays on the New International Economic Order. LC 78-62660. 1978. 9.95 (ISBN 0-932468-00-4); pap. 3.95 (ISBN 0-932468-01-2). U Rochester Policy.

--The Great Depression Revisited. (Rochester Studies in Economics & Policy Issues: Vol. 2). 368p. 1980. lib. bdg. 20.00 (ISBN 0-89838-051-0, Pub. by Martinus Nijhoff Netherlands). Kluwer Academic.

Brunner, Karl & Meltzer, A. H., eds. Institutional Policies & Economic Performance. (Carnegie-Rochester Conference Series on Public Policy: Vol. 4). 254p. 1976. pap. 23.50 (ISBN 0-7204-0564-5, North-Holland). Elsevier.

Brunner, Karl & Meltzer, Allan M., eds. Institutional Arrangements & the Inflation Problem. (Carnegie-Rochester Conference Series on Public Policy: Vol. 3). 248p. 1976. pap. 25.75 (ISBN 0-7204-0525-4, North-Holland). Elsevier.

Brunner, Karl, ed. see Econometrics Conferences, Ohio State U., 1967 & 1968.

Brunner, L. & Suddarth, D. Pediatric Nursing. 1981. pap. text ed. 22.50 (ISBN 0-06-318183-5, Pub. by Har-Row Ltd England). Har-Row.

Brunner, Lawrence P. U. S. Productivity Growth: Who Benefited? Bateman, Fred, ed. LC 83-9108. (Research in Business Economics & Public Policy Ser.: No. 3). 160p. 1983. 39.95 (ISBN 0-8357-1442-X). UMI Res Pr.

Brunner, Lillian & Suddarth, Doris. The Lippincott Manual of Nursing Practice. 3rd ed. (Illus.). 1531p. 1982. text ed. 45.00 (ISBN 0-397-54352-2, 64-02945, Lippincott Nursing). Lippincott.

--Textbook of Medical-Surgical Nursing. 5th ed. (Illus.). 1536p. 1984. text ed. 46.50 (ISBN 0-397-54419-7, 64-03604, Lippincott Nursing); study guide 9.50 (ISBN 0-397-54477-4, 64-04180). Lippincott.

Brunner, Marguerite. Gold Mine of Money-Making Ideas. 1977. 7.95 (ISBN 0-89328-015-1); pap. 4.95 (ISBN 0-89328-017-8). Lorenz Pr.

Brunner, Nancy A. Orthopedic Nursing: A Programmed Approach. 4th ed. LC 82-14346. (Illus.). 301p. 1983. spiral 15.95 (ISBN 0-8016-0839-2). Mosby.

Brunner, Ronald D. & Sandenburgh, Robin. Community Energy Options: Getting Started in Ann Arbor. (Illus.). 296p. 1982. text ed. 14.50x (ISBN 0-472-08025-3). U of Mich Pr.

Brunner, Ronald D., jt. ed. see Brewer, Garry D.

Brunner, S., ed. Radiology in Oto-Rhino-Laryngology. (Advances in Oto-Reino-Laryngology: Vol. 21). (Illus.). 162p. 1974. 39.25 (ISBN 3-8055-1632-0). S Karger.

Brunner, S., et al, eds. Early Detection of Breast Cancer. (Recent Results in Cancer Research Ser.: Vol. 90). (Illus.). 240p. 1984. 46.00 (ISBN 0-387-12348-2). Springer-Verlag.

Brunner, S. I., ed. see International Congress of Radiology in Oto-Rhine-Larymgology, 5th, Copenhagen, June 1976.

Brunner, T. & Kundert, M. Geruestprethetik: Planungsrichtlinien und Konstruktionsvorschlaege. (Illus.). 1979. pap. 8.75 (ISBN 3-8055-3040-4). S Karger.

Brunner, Theodore F. & Berkowitz, Luci. The Elements of Scientific & Specialized Terminology. 1967. spiral bdg. 12.95x (ISBN 0-8087-0235-1). Burgess.

Brunner, Thomas W., et al. Legal Assistant's Handbook. 225p. 1982. pap. 17.50 (ISBN 0-87179-369-5). BNA.

--Mergers in the New Antitrust Era. 325p. 1985. text ed. 40.00 (ISBN 0-87179-472-1). BNA.

Brunner-Traut, Emma, ed. see Schafer, Heinrich.

Brunngraber, Eric G. Neurochemistry of Aminosugars: Neurochemistry & Neuropathology of the Complex Carbohydrates. (Illus.). 720p. 1979. 34.75x (ISBN 0-398-03843-0). C C Thomas.

Brunnings, Florence E. Folk Song Index. LC 80-8522. 700p. 1981. lib. bdg. 91.00 (ISBN 0-8240-9462-X). Garland Pub.

Brunnstrom, Signe. Movement Therapy in Hemiplegia. (Illus.). 1970. 35.75x (ISBN 0-06-140547-7, 14-05471, Harper Medical). Lippincott.

Brunnstrom, Signe, jt. auth. see Kerr, Donald.

Bruno. Haircutting the Professional Way. (Everyday Handbook Ser.). pap. 2.95 (ISBN 0-06-463459-0, EH 459, EH). B&N NY.

Bruno, Agnes M. Toward a Quantitative Methodology for Stylistic Analyses. LC 73-80835. (University of California Publications in Modern Philology Ser.: Vol. 109). pap. 22.50 (ISBN 0-317-29556-X, 2021259). Bks Demand UMI.

Bruno, Angela & Jessie, Karen. Hands-On Activities for Children's Writing. (Illus.). 256p. 1983. pap. 7.95 (ISBN 0-13-383596-0). P-H.

Bruno, Carole. Paralegal's Litigation Handbook. LC 79-19960. 544p. 1980. 49.50 (ISBN 0-87624-425-8). Inst Busn Plan.

Bruno, Clarke, jt. auth. see White, James J.

Bruno, Clarke, tr. see White, James J. & Bruno, Clarke.

Bruno, E. J., ed. Adhesives in Modern Manufacturing. LC 79-93212. (Manufacturing Data Ser). (Illus., Orig.). 1970. pap. 11.50x (ISBN 0-87263-017-X). SME.

--High-Velocity Forming of Metals. rev. ed. LC 68-23027. (Manufacturing Data Ser.). 1968. pap. 10.75 (ISBN 0-87263-009-9). SME.

--High-Velocity Forming of Metals. LC 68-23024. (American Society of Tool & Manufacturing Engineers. Manufacturing Data Ser.). (Illus.). pap. 59.80 (ISBN 0-317-11079-9, 2016004). Bks Demand UMI.

Bruno, E. J., ed. see Weyher, Douglas F.

Bruno, Frank J. Adjustment & Personal Growth: Seven Pathways. 2nd ed. LC 82-8520. 466p. 1983. text ed. 29.50 (ISBN 0-471-09296-7); tchr's manual 20.00 (ISBN 0-471-87195-8). Wiley.

--Behavior & Life: An Introduction to Psychology. 660p. 1980. text ed. 30.95 (ISBN 0-471-02191-1); study guide 13.95 (ISBN 0-471-06340-1). Wiley.

--Think Yourself Thin. 272p. 1975. pap. 5.72i (ISBN 0-06-463348-9, EH 348). B&N NY.

--Trends in Social Work, Eighteen Seventy-Four to Nineteen Fifty-Six: A History Based on the Proceedings of the National Conference of Social Work. 2nd ed. LC 80-19210. xviii, 462p. 1980. Repr. of 1957 ed. lib. bdg. 42.50x (ISBN 0-313-22665-2, BRTI). Greenwood.

Bruno, Giordano. The Ash Wednesday Supper. Jaki, Stanley L., tr. (Illus.). 174p. 1975. text ed. 19.60x (ISBN 90-2797-581-7). Mouton.

--Cause, Principle & Unity: Five Dialogues. Lindsay, Jack, tr. LC 76-28448. 1976. Repr. of 1962 ed. lib. bdg. 22.50x (ISBN 0-8371-9040-1, BRCP). Greenwood.

--The Heroic Enthusiasts. 1976. lib. bdg. 59.95 (ISBN 0-8490-1947-8). Gordon Pr.

--Selected Works. 75.00 (ISBN 0-8490-1021-7). Gordon Pr.

Bruno, Guido. Moore Versus Harris. LC 77-16706. 1977. Repr. of 1925 ed. lib. bdg. 10.00 (ISBN 0-8414-6222-4). Folcroft.

Bruno, Harry. Wings Over America: The Inside Story of American Aviation. 1942. 30.00 (ISBN 0-932062-21-0). Sharon Hill.

Bruno, James E. Designing Education Information Systems Using 2BaseII & the Apple II: A Systems Guide to the Apple & dBase II. 250p. 1985. pap. text ed. 29.95 (ISBN 0-86542-314-8). Blackwell Pubns.

--Educational Policy Analysis: A Quantitative Approach. LC 74-24987. 295p. 1976. 24.50x (ISBN 0-8448-0623-4). Crane-Russak Co.

Bruno, Janet & Dakan, Peggy. Cooking in the Classroom. 1974. pap. 5.25 (ISBN 0-8224-1610-7). Pitman Learning.

Bruno, Leone, ed. The Middle East: Opposing Views. LC 85-8151. (Opposing Views Ser.). 1982. lib. bdg. 11.95 (ISBN 0-89908-340-4); pap. 6.95 (ISBN 0-89908-315-3). Greenhaven.

Bruno, Michael. Venus in Hollywood: The Continental Enchantress from Garbo to Loren. LC 71-90838. (Illus.). 1970. 6.95 (ISBN 0-8184-0091-9). Lyle Stuart.

Bruno, Michael & Sachs, Jeffrey. Economics of Worldwide Stagflation. (Illus.). 336p. 1985. text ed. 25.00x (ISBN 0-674-23475-8). Harvard U Pr.

Bruno, Michael S., jt. auth. see DePasquale, Nicholas P.

Bruno, Michael S., jt. ed. see DePasquale, Nicholas P.

Bruno, Pasquale, Jr. The Official Gourmet Handbook. (Illus.). 192p. (Orig.). 1984. pap. 5.95 (ISBN 0-8092-5475-1). Contemp Bks.

--Pasta Tecnica. (Illus.). 128p. 1982. 13.95 (ISBN 0-8092-5895-1); pap. 8.95 (ISBN 0-8092-5894-3). Contemp Bks.

Bruno, Sam, ed. Proceedings: ABCA Nineteen Eighty-Two International Convention. 1983. pap. 8.60 (ISBN 0-931874-13-0). Assn Busn Comm.

Bruno, Susan & Quaresima, Donna. Insiders' Guide to Williamsburg, Virginia. LC 83-51606. (Insiders' Guides Ser.). (Illus.). 250p. 1984. pap. 4.95 (ISBN 0-912367-06-7). Storie McOwen.

Bruno, Thomas A. Take Your Dream & Run. LC 84-70051. 1984. pap. 2.95 (ISBN 0-88270-568-7, Haven Bks). Bridge Pub.

Bruno, Vincent J. Form & Color in Greek Painting. (Illus.). 1977. 15.00x (ISBN 0-393-04445-9). Norton.

Bruno, William & Boslund, Lois. CICS: Mastering Command Level Coding Using COBOL Programming. 208p. 1984. 24.95 (ISBN 0-13-134040-9). P-H.

Brunoff, Laurent De see De Brunoff, Laurent.

Brunold, Paul, ed. see Chambonnieres, Jacques C.

Bruno Natlis, Elena. Estudio Comparativo de Vocabularios Tobas y Pilagas. 107p. (Span.). 1965. pap. 49.95 (ISBN 0-686-56659-9, S-33083). French & Eur.

Brunor, Martin A. Arts & Crafts of the Austral Islands: A Special Exhibition, 17 December 1968 to 30 April 1969. 1969. pap. 2.00 (ISBN 0-87577-018-5). Peabody Mus Salem.

Bruno Schuller, S. J. Wholly Human: Essays on the Theory & Language of Morality. Heinegg, Peter, tr. from Ger. Orig. Title: Der Manschliche Mensch. 256p. (Orig.). 1985. 17.95 (ISBN 0-87840-427-9); pap. 9.95 (ISBN 0-87840-422-8). Georgetown U Pr.

Brunot. Histoire de la Langue Francaise des Origines a nos Jours, 13 tomes. Incl. Tome I. De L'epoque Latine a la Renaissance. 29.95 (ISBN 0-685-36636-7); Tome II. Le XVIe Siecle. 25.50 (ISBN 0-685-36637-5); Tome III. La Formation de la langue classique, 2 pts. Set. 59.95 (ISBN 0-685-36638-3); Tome IV. La Langue Classique (1660-1715, 2 pts. Set. 59.95 (ISBN 0-685-36639-1); Tome V. Le Francais en France et hors De France au XVIIe Siecle. 29.95 (ISBN 0-685-36640-5); Tome VI. Le XVIIIe Siecle, 4 pts. Set. 118.95 (ISBN 0-685-36641-3); Tome VII. La Propagation du Francais en France jusqu'a la Fin de L'ancien Regime. 29.95 (ISBN 0-685-36642-1); Tome VIII. Le Francais hors de France au XVIIIe Siecle, 3 pts. en 2 pts. Set. 59.95 (ISBN 0-685-36643-X); Tome IX. La Revolution et l'Empire, 2 pts. Set. 59.95 (ISBN 0-685-36644-8); Tome X. La Langue Classique dans la Tourmente, 2 pts. Set. 59.95 (ISBN 0-685-36645-6); Tome XI. Le Francais au-dehors sous la Revolution, le Consulat et l'Empire. 29.95 (ISBN 0-685-36646-4); Tome XII. L'Epoque Romantique. Bruneau. 29.95 (ISBN 0-685-36647-2); Tome XIII. L'Epoque Realiste. Bruneau. 59.95 (ISBN 0-685-36648-0). French & Eur.

Brunot, Ferdinand. Doctrine de Malherbe d'apres son commentaire sur Desportes. 1971. Repr. of 1891 ed. lib. bdg. 34.50 (ISBN 0-8337-0405-2). B Franklin.

--Histoire de la Langue Francaise des Origines a Nos Jours, 13 vols. in 22 pts. Repr. of 1972 ed. Set. per pt. 35.50x (ISBN 0-686-57670-5). Adlers Foreign Bks.

Brunovskii, Vladimir K. The Methods of the Ogpu. LC 75-39047. (Russian Studies: Perspectives on the Revolution Ser). (Illus.). xvii, 255p. 1977. Repr. of 1931 ed. 25.85 (ISBN 0-88355-426-7). Hyperion Conn.

Bruns, Bill. A World of Animals: The San Diego Zoo & the Wild Animal Park. LC 83-7289. 288p. 1983. 35.00 (ISBN 0-8109-1601-0). Abrams.

Bruns, Bill, jt. auth. see Braden, Vic.

Bruns, Bill, jt. auth. see Nosler, Cary.

Bruns, Bill, jt. auth. see Sorensen, Jacki.

Bruns, Bill, jt. auth. see Sorenson, Jacki.

Bruns, Bill, jt. auth. see Strandemo, Steve.

Bruns, Friedrich. Modern Thought in the German Lyric Poets from Goethe to Dehmel. 59.95 (ISBN 0-8490-0654-6). Gordon Pr.

Bruns, Friedrich, ed. Lese der Deutschen Lyrik: Von Klopstock bis Rilke. (Orig., Ger.,). 1961. pap. text ed. 14.95x (ISBN 0-89197-274-9). Irvington.

Bruns, G. R., jt. auth. see Shaw, Alan.

Bruns, Gerald L. Inventions: Writing, Textuality, & Understanding in Literary History. LC 82-1992. 216p. 1982. 21.00x (ISBN 0-300-02786-9). Yale U Pr.

Bruns, James H. Philatelic Truck. (Illus., Orig.). 1982. pap. 8.00 (ISBN 0-930412-11-7). Bureau Issues.

Bruns, Roger. Jefferson. (World Leaders: Past & Present Ser.). (Illus.). 112p. 1985. lib. bdg. 15.95x (ISBN 0-87754-583-9). Chelsea Hse.

Bruns, Roger, jt. ed. see Schlesinger, Arthur M., Jr.

Bruns, Roger A. Knights of the Road: A Hobo History. (Illus.). 224p. 1980. 10.95 (ISBN 0-416-00721-X, NO. 0147). Methuen Inc.

Bruns, W., et al. Monte Carlo Applications in Polymer Science. (Lecture Notes in Chemistry Ser.: Vol. 27). 179p. 1981. pap. 16.20 (ISBN 0-387-11165-4). Springer-Verlag.

Bruns, W. J. Introduction to Accounting: Economic Measurement for Decisions. 1971. 28.50 (ISBN 0-201-00676-6); instructor's manual 2.95 (ISBN 0-201-00677-4). Addison-Wesley.

Bruns, William J., jt. auth. see Barrett, M. Edgar.

Brunschvicg, Leon, jt. auth. see Pascal, Blaise.

Brunschwig, C., et al. Cent Ans of Chansons Francaise. 447p. (Fr.). 1981. pap. 12.95 (ISBN 2-02-006000-0, M-12411). French & Eur.

Brunschwig, Henri. Enlightenment & Romanticism in Eighteenth-Century Prussia. Jellinek, Frank, tr. from Fr. LC 73-87299. 1977. 11.00x (ISBN 0-226-07769-1). U of Chicago Pr.

Brunschwig, Henri, et al. Brazza Explorateur: Les Traites Makoko, 1880-1882. (Documents Pour Servir a L'histoire De L'afrique-Equatoriale Francaise: Brazza et la Fondation Du Congo Francais: No. 2). 1972. pap. 21.20x (ISBN 0-686-20923-0). Mouton.

Brunschwig, Hieronymus. Book of Distillation. facsimile ed. (Illus.). 274p. 1971. Repr. of 1530 ed. 58.00 (ISBN 0-384-06099-4). Johnson Repr.

Brunschwig, L. Study of Some Personality Aspects of Deaf Children. LC 70-176608. (Columbia University. Teachers College. Contributions to Education: No. 687). Repr. of 1936 ed. 22.50 (ISBN 0-404-55687-6). AMS Pr.

Brunsdale, Mitzi M. The German Effect on D. H. Lawrence & His Works 1885-1912. (Utah Studies in Literature & Linguistics: Vol. 13). 310p. 1978. pap. 31.60 (ISBN 3-261-03191-3). P Lang Pubs.

Brunsden, D. Slopes: Form & Process. (The Special Publication of the Institute of British Geographers Ser.: No. 3). 1980. 27.50 (ISBN 0-12-137980-9). Acad Pr.

Brunsden, D. & Prior, D. B., eds. Slope Instability: Landscape Systems. (Geomorphology Ser.). 608p. 1984. text ed. 39.95x (ISBN 0-471-90348-5). Wiley.

Brunsden, D., jt. auth. see Cooke, R. U.

Brunsden, Denys, jt. auth. see Thornes, John.

Brunsden, Denys, et al, eds. The Unquiet Landscape. LC 77-15583. (The Geographical Magazine Ser.). 168p. 1975. Repr. of 1972 ed. 29.95x (ISBN 0-470-99345-6). Halsted Pr.

Brunsken, E. & Register, L. B., eds. The Science of Legal Method. 1977. lib. bdg. 59.95 (ISBN 0-8490-2571-0). Gordon Pr.

Brunskill, R. W. Houses. (Collins Archaeology Ser.). 224p. 1982. text ed. 30.00x (ISBN 0-00-216243-1, Pub. by Collins Sons England). Humanities.

--Illustrated Handbook of Vernacular Architecture. new ed. (Illus.). 232p. 1979. pap. 8.95 (ISBN 0-571-11244-7). Faber & Faber.

--Timber Building in Britain. (Illus.). 256p. 1985. 28.00 (ISBN 0-575-03379-7, Pub. by Gollancz England). David & Charles.

--Traditional Buildings of Britain. (Illus.). 160p. 1985. pap. 12.95 (ISBN 0-575-03616-8, Pub. by Gollancz England). David & Charles.

--Traditional Buildings of Britain: An Introduction to Vernacular Architecture. (Illus.). 160p. 1981. 22.50 (ISBN 0-575-02887-4, Pub. by Gollancz England). David & Charles.

--Traditional Buildings of Britain: An Introduction to Vernacular Architecture. (Illus.). 160p. 1985. pap. 9.95 (ISBN 0-575-03616-8, Pub. by Gollancz England). David & Charles.

--Traditional Farm Buildings of Britain. (Illus.). 160p. 1982. 27.50 (ISBN 0-575-03117-4, Pub. by Gollancz England). David & Charles.

Brunskill, Ronald & Clifton-Taylor, Alec. English Brickwork. (Illus.). 160p. 1977. 21.50x (ISBN 0-8476-1474-3). Rowman.

Brunsman, Barry. New Hope for Divorced Catholics: A Concerned Pastor Offers Alternatives to Annulment. LC 85-42770. 128p. 1985. 12.95 (ISBN 0-06-061147-2, HarpR). Har-Row.

Brunson, Alfred. A Western Pioneer: Or, Incidents of the Life & Times of Rev. Alfred Brunson.., 2 vols. in 1. facsimile ed. LC 75-89. (Mid-American Frontier Ser.). 1975. Repr. of 1872 ed. 60.50x (ISBN 0-405-06856-5). Ayer Co Pubs.

Brunson, Doyle. According to Doyle. (Illus., Orig.). 1984. pap. text ed. 6.95 (ISBN 0-89746-003-0). Gambling Times.

Brunson, E., jt. auth. see Gearing, P.

Brunson, Madelon. Dying, Death & Grief. 1978. pap. 4.50 (ISBN 0-8309-0223-6). Herald Hse.

Brunson, Madelon & Goodyear, Imogene. No Graven Images. LC 77-24081. 1977. 4.00 (ISBN 0-8309-0189-2). Herald Hse.

Brunstein, Karl. Beyond the Four Dimensions: Reconciling Physics, Parapsychology & UFO's. LC 78-58870. 1979. pap. 7.95 (ISBN 0-8027-7154-8). Walker & Co.

Brunstetter, Max R. Business Management in School Systems of Different Sizes. LC 76-176607. (Columbia University. Teachers College. Contributions to Education: No. 455). Repr. of 1931 ed. 17.50 (ISBN 0-404-55455-5). AMS Pr.

Brunsvold, Brian G., jt. auth. see Mayers, Harry R.

Brunsvold, Brian G., ed. Licensing Law Handbook, 1984. (Orig.). 1984. pap. 42.50 (ISBN 0-87632-329-8). Boardman.

Brunswick, Ann F. Evaluation of College of the Air Course, "the American Economy," on the Basis of a National Survey of High School Social Studies Teachers. (Report Ser: No. 100). 1964. 1.50x (ISBN 0-932132-01-4). NORC.

Brunswick Schneply, Mary see Schneply, Mary Brunswick.

Brunswig, Heinrich. Explosives: A Synoptic & Critical Treatment of the Literature of the Subject As Gathered from Various Sources. Monroe, Charles E. & Kibler, Alton L., trs. 1980. lib. bdg. 69.95 (ISBN 0-8490-3153-2). Gordon Pr.

Brunt. Physiology For Nurses. 256p. 1982. pap. text ed. 17.00 (ISBN 0-06-318227-0, Pub. by Har-Row Ltd England). Har-Row.

Brunt, Andrew. Phaidon Guide to Furniture. (Phaidon Guide Ser.). (Illus.). 256p. 1984. 12.95 (ISBN 0-13-661967-3); pap. 6.95 (ISBN 0-13-661959-2). P-H.

Brunt, H. L. Van see Van Brunt, H. L.

Brunt, Henry Van see Van Brunt, Henry.

Brunt, John. Decisions. LC 79-16158. (Horizon Ser.). 1979. pap. 5.95 (ISBN 0-8127-0235-2). Review & Herald.

Brunt, Leroy B. Van see Van Brunt, Leroy B.

Brunt, P., et al, eds. The Liver & Biliary System. (Aids to Higher Medical Training Ser.). 256p. 1984. pap. text ed. 15.00 (ISBN 0-433-04560-4, 991430042, Pub. by Heinemann Medical). Heyden.

Brunt, P. A. Social Conflicts in the Roman Republic. (Illus.). 176p. 1972 o.p. 6.00 (ISBN 0-393-04335-5, Norton Lib); pap. 5.95x 1974 (ISBN 0-393-00586-0). Norton.

Brunt, P. A., ed. see Augustus.

Brunt, Samuel see Clarke, John.

Bruntjen, Carol R., jt. auth. see Bruntjen, Scott.

Bruntjen, Carol R., jt. ed. see Bruntjen, Scott.

Bruntjen, Scott & Bruntjen, Carol R. A Checklist of American Imprints for 1833: Items 17208-22795. LC 64-11784. (Checklist of American Imprints Ser.: Vol. 1833). 482p. 1979. lib. bdg. 32.50 (ISBN 0-8108-1191-X). Scarecrow.

--Checklist of American Imprints for 1831. LC 64-11784. (Checklist of American Imprints Ser.: Vol. 1831). 433p. 1975. 25.00 (ISBN 0-8108-0828-5). Scarecrow.

Bruntjen, Scott & Young, Melissa L. Douglas C. McMurtrie: Bibliographer & Historian of Printing. LC 78-25682. (The Great Bibliographers Ser.: No. 4). 220p. 1979. lib. bdg. 16.00 (ISBN 0-8108-1188-X). Scarecrow.

Bruntjen, Scott, jt. auth. see Carter, Ruth C.

Bruntjen, Scott, jt. auth. see Rinderknecht, Carol.

Bruntjen, Scott & Bruntjen, Carol R., eds. A Checklist of American Imprints for 1832. LC 64-11784. (Checklist of American Imprints Ser.: Vol. 1832). 527p. 1977. 27.50 (ISBN 0-8108-1019-0). Scarecrow.

Bruntjen, Sven H. John Boydell (Seventeen Nineteen to Eighteen Four) A Study of Art Patronage & Publishing In Georgian London. Freedberg, S. J., ed. (Outstanding Dissertations in Fine Arts Ser.). (Illus.). 302p. 1985. Repr. of 1974 ed. 50.00 (ISBN 0-8240-6880-7). Garland Pub.

Brunton, Anatol. Tomorrow Knocks. (Inner Visions Ser.: No. 1). 176p. (Orig.). 1982. pap. 9.95 (ISBN 0-917086-39-2). A C S Pubns Inc.

Brunton, David W., ed. Index to the Contemporary Scene, Vol. 1. LC 73-645955. 122p. 1973. 46.00x (ISBN 0-8103-1056-2). Gale.

--Index to the Contemporary Scene, Vol. 2. xvi, 120p. 1975. 46.00x (ISBN 0-8103-1057-0). Gale.

Brunton, Douglas & Pennington, D. H. Members of the Long Parliament. xxi, 256p. 1968. Repr. of 1954 ed. 22.50 (ISBN 0-208-00686-9, Archon). Shoe String.

Brunton, Guy. British Museum Expedition to Middle Egypt. LC 77-86429. Repr. of 1937 ed. 45.00 (ISBN 0-404-16626-1). AMS Pr.

Brunton, Guy & Caton-Thompson, Gertrude. The Badarian Civilisation & Predynastic Remains Near Badari. LC 77-86424. (British School of Archaeology in Egypt & Egyptian Research Account. 30th Yr., 1924. Publication Ser.: No. 46). Repr. of 1928 ed. 42.50 (ISBN 0-404-16625-3). AMS Pr.

Brunton, John, jt. auth. see Elson, Howard.

Brunton, Mary. Discipline: A Novel, 3 vols. in 1. LC 79-8241. Repr. of 1814 ed. 44.50 (ISBN 0-404-61797-2). AMS Pr.

Brunton, Paul. Discover Yourself. rev ed. LC 83-60832. 1983. pap. 7.95 (ISBN 0-87728-592-6). Weiser.

--Essays on the Quest. LC 85-50520. 224p. 1985. pap. 8.95 (ISBN 0-87728-645-0). Weiser.

--A Hermit in the Himalayas. rev. ed. LC 84-50367. 188p. (Orig.). 1984. pap. 7.95 (ISBN 0-87728-601-9). Weiser.

--Hidden Teaching Beyond Yoga. LC 83-60830. (Orig.). 1984. pap. 8.95 (ISBN 0-87728-590-X). Weiser.

--The Notebooks of Paul Brunton: Perspectives (Posthumous) Cash, Paul, et al, eds. LC 84-47752. 408p. 1984. smyth-sewn 21.95 (ISBN 0-943914-09-4, Dist. by Kampmann & Co); deluxe, limited, numbered, (500 copies) 50.00x (ISBN 0-943914-10-8). Larson Pubns Inc.

--The Notebooks of Paul Brunton: Perspectives (Posthumous) Cash, Paul, et al, eds. 408p. 21.95 (ISBN 0-943914-09-4). Larson Pubns Inc.

--The Notebooks of Paul Brunton: The Quest, Volume 2. Cash, Paul & Smith, Timothy, eds. 400p. 1985. smyth-sewn, acid free 21.95 (ISBN 0-943914-13-2). Larson Pubns Inc.

--The Quest of the Overself. rev. ed. LC 83-159508. 234p. (Orig.). 1970. pap. 7.95 (ISBN 0-87728-594-2). Weiser.

--Search in Secret Egypt. LC 83-50399. (Orig.). 1984. pap. 8.95 (ISBN 0-87728-603-5). Weiser.

--Search in Secret India. LC 83-160558. (Illus., Orig.). 1985. pap. 8.95 (ISBN 0-87728-602-7). Weiser.

--The Secret Path. LC 85-50917. 128p. Date not set. pap. 4.95 (ISBN 0-87728-652-3). Weiser.

--Spiritual Crisis of Man. rev ed. LC 83-60829. 1984. pap. 7.95 (ISBN 0-87728-593-4). Weiser.

--Wisdom of the Overself. rev ed. LC 83-60833. (Orig.). 1984. pap. 8.95 (ISBN 0-87728-591-8). Weiser.

Brunton, Virginia H. A Brevity, a Brilliance & Other Poems. 1979. 5.00 (ISBN 0-682-49493-3). Exposition Pr FL.

Bruntz, George G. Allied Propaganda & the Collapse of the German Empire in 1918. LC 72-4658. (International Propaganda & Communications Ser.). (Illus.). 246p. 1972. Repr. of 1938 ed. 17.00 (ISBN 0-405-04741-X). Ayer Co Pubs.

Bruntz, Nelle L. Contemporary Psalms. (Illus.). 64p. 1984. 4.50 (ISBN 0-938462-13-X). Green Leaf Ca.

Brunvand, Jan H. The Choking Doberman: And Other "New" Urban Legends. LC 83-22031. (Illus.). 1984. 13.95 (ISBN 0-393-01844-X). Norton.

--Folklore: A Handbook for Study & Research. LC 75-38016. 178p. 1976. pap. text ed. 7.95 (ISBN 0-312-29750-5). St Martin.

--Readings in American Folklore. (Illus.). 1979. pap. text ed. 9.95x (ISBN 0-393-95029-8). Norton.

--Study of American Folklore: An Introduction. 2nd ed. 1978. 16.95x (ISBN 0-393-09048-5, NortonC). Norton.

--The Vanishing Hitchhiker: American Urban Legends & Their Meanings. (Orig.). 1981. 14.95 (ISBN 0-393-01473-8); pap. text ed. 6.95x 1982 (ISBN 0-393-95169-3). Norton.

Brus, W. & Kaser, M. C., eds. The Economic History of Eastern Europe: Institutional Change Within a Planned Economy, Vol. 3. (Illus.). 1984. 36.00x (ISBN 0-19-828446-2). Oxford U Pr.

Brus, Wlodzimierz. Socialist Ownership & Political Systems under Socialism. 256p. 1975. 26.95x (ISBN 0-7100-8247-9). Routledge & Kegan.

Brusa, Betty W. Salinan Indians of California & Their Neighbors. LC 74-13249. (American Indian Map Bk. Ser., Vol. 2). (Illus.). 96p. 1975. 10.95 (ISBN 0-87961-023-9); pap. 4.95 (ISBN 0-87961-022-0). Naturegraph.

Brusatti, Otto, jt. ed. see Hilmar, Ernst.

Brusaw, Charles, et al. The Business Writer's Handbook. 2nd ed. LC 81-51835. 650p. 1982. 19.95 (ISBN 0-312-10994-6); pap. 13.95 (ISBN 0-312-10993-8). St Martin.

Brusaw, Charles T. & Alred, Gerald J. Handbook of Technical Writing. 2nd ed. LC 81-51836. 695p. 1982. pap. text ed. 13.95 (ISBN 0-312-35808-3). St Martin.

Brusca, Gary J. & Brusca, Richard C. A Naturalist's Seashore Guide: Common Marine Life Along the Northern California Coast & Adjacent Shores. 215p. 1978. pap. 8.95x (ISBN 0-916422-12-7). Mad River.

Brusca, Richard C. Common Intertidal Invertebrates of the Gulf of California. rev. ed. LC 79-19894. (Illus.). 513p. 1980. pap. 26.95x (ISBN 0-8165-0682-5). U of Ariz Pr.

Brusca, Richard C., jt. auth. see Brusca, Gary J.

Bruscemi, John N., jt. auth. see Funkhouser, Charles W.

Bruscia, Kenneth, jt. auth. see Levinson, Sandra.

Bruseth, Nels. Indian Stories & Legends. 1977. pap. 3.95 (ISBN 0-87770-078-8). Ye Galleon.

Brusewitz, Gunnar. Wings & Seasons. Wheeler, Walston, tr. from Swedish. (Illus.). 119p. 1983. 20.00 (ISBN 0-88072-029-8, Pub. by Tanager). Longwood Pub Group.

Brush, Alan H. & Clark, George A., Jr., eds. Perspectives in Ornithology: Essays Presented for the Centennial of the American Ornithologists' Union. LC 83-3931. 544p. 1983. 32.50 (ISBN 0-521-24857-4). Cambridge U Pr.

Brush, Candida G., jt. auth. see Hisrich, Robert D.

Brush, Christine. Colonel's Opera Cloak. facs. ed. LC 78-137723. (American Fiction Reprint Ser). Repr. of 1879 ed. 17.00 (ISBN 0-8369-7022-5). Ayer Co Pubs.

Brush, Craig B., tr. see Gassendi, Pierre.

Brush, Edward H. Iroquois Past & Present. LC 74-7944. Repr. of 1901 ed. 16.00 (ISBN 0-404-11831-3). AMS Pr.

Brush, F. Robert, ed. Aversive Conditioning & Learning. LC 70-127680. 1971. 78.00 (ISBN 0-12-137950-7). Acad Pr.

Brush, John E. & Gautier, Howard L., Jr. Service Centers & Consumer Trips: Studies on the Philadelphia Metropolitan Fringe. LC 67-25274. (Research Papers: No. 113). 182p. 1968. pap. 10.00 (ISBN 0-89065-021-7). U Chicago Dept Geog.

Brush, Lorelei R. Encouraging Girls in Mathematics: The Problems & the Solution. LC 79-55774. (Illus.). 1980. text ed. 16.00 (ISBN 0-89011-542-7). Abt Bks.

Brush, Lorelei R., et al. Encouraging Girls in Mathematics: The Problem & the Solution. (Illus.). 180p. 1984. Repr. of 1980 ed. lib. bdg. 18.50 (ISBN 0-8191-4109-7). U Pr of Amer.

Brush, M., et al, eds. Endometrial Cancer. (Illus.). 1979. text ed. 49.50 (ISBN 0-7216-0708-X, Pub. by Bailliere-Tindall). Saunders.

Brush, M. G., jt. auth. see Taylor, R. W.

Brush, Michael G., jt. auth. see Lever, Judy.

Brush, Robert & Overmier, Bruce J. Affect, Conditioning & Cognition: Essays on the Determinants of Behavior. 420p. 1985. text ed. 39.95 (ISBN 0-317-29110-6). L Erlbaum Assocs.

Brush, S. G. The Kind of Motion We Call Heat: A History of the Kinetic Theory of Gases in the Nineteenth Century, 2 bks. (Studies in Statistical Mechanics: Vol. 6). 1976. Bk. 1. 53.25 (ISBN 0-7204-0370-7, North-Holland); Bk. 2. 93.75 (ISBN 0-7204-0482-7); Set. 121.25 (ISBN 0-686-67836-2). Elsevier.

--Kinetic Theory, 3 vols. Incl. Vol. 1. The Nature of Gases & of Heat. 1965. 12.00 (ISBN 0-08-010867-9); pap. 5.00 (ISBN 0-08-010866-0); Vol. 2. Irreversible Processes. 1966; Vol. 3. The Chapman-Enskog Solution of the Transport Equation for Moderately Dense Gases. 1972. 59.00 (ISBN 0-08-016714-4). Pergamon.

Brush, Stephanie. Men: An Owner's Manual. 1984. 11.95 (ISBN 0-671-49459-7, Linden Pr). S&S.

Brush, Stephen B. Mountain, Field, & Family: The Economy & Human Ecology of an Andean Valley. LC 77-24364. 1977. 20.00x (ISBN 0-8122-7728-7). U of Pa Pr.

Brush, Stephen G. Statistical Physics & the Atomic Theory of Matter, from Boyle & Newton to Landau & Onsager. LC 82-61357. (Princeton Series in Physics). (Illus.). 324p. 1983. 45.00x (ISBN 0-691-08325-8); pap. 14.50x (ISBN 0-691-08320-7). Princeton U Pr.

--The Temperature of History, Phases of Science & Culture in the Nineteeth Century. LC 77-11999. (Studies in the History of Science). (Illus.). 1978. lib. bdg. 18.95 (ISBN 0-89102-073-X). B Franklin.

Brush, Stephen G. & Belloni, Lanfranoo. The History of Modern Physics: An International Bibliography. LC 82-49291. (The History of Science & Technology Ser.: Vol. 4). 400p. 1983. lib. bdg. 42.00 (ISBN 0-8240-9117-5). Garland Pub.

Brush, Stephen G., jt. auth. see Holton, Gerald.

Brush, Stephen G., ed. Maxwell on Saturn's Rings: James Clerk Maxwell's Unpublished Manuscripts & Letters on the Stability of Saturn's Rings. Everitt, C. W., et al. 240p. 1983. text ed. 27.50x (ISBN 0-262-13190-0). MIT Pr.

--Resources for the History of Physics: Guide to Books & Audiovisual Materials, Guide to Original Works of Historical Importance & Their Translations into Other Languages. LC 70-186306. pap. 48.00 (ISBN 0-317-10599-X, 2022324). Bks Demand UMI.

Brush, Stephen G., rev. by see Holton, Gerald.

Brush, Stephen G., ed. see International Working Seminar on the Role of the History of Physics in Physics Education.

Brush, Stephen G., et al. The History of Geophysics & Meteorology: An Annotated Bibliography. Collins, Martin & Mutthauf, Robert, eds. LC 82-49292. (History of Science & Technology Ser.). 600p. 1984. lib. bdg. 70.00 (ISBN 0-8240-9116-7). Garland Pub.

Brush, W., jt. auth. see Collingwood, G.

Brushfield, J. Broadside Ballads of Devonshire & Cornwall. (Folklore Ser). 15.00 (ISBN 0-8482-0147-7). Norwood Edns.

Brushfield, T. N. The Bibliography of the History of the World & of the Remains of Sir Walter Raleigh. LC 72-10381. 1972. Repr. of 1886 ed. lib. bdg. 8.50 (ISBN 0-8414-0454-2). Folcroft.

Brushfield, Thomas N. Bibliography of Sir Walter Raleigh. 2nd ed. 1967. Repr. of 1908 ed. 15.00 (ISBN 0-8337-0406-0). B Franklin.

Brushhausen, F. V., ed. see Altszuler, N., et al.

Brushwell, William, ed. Painting & Decorating Encyclopedia. LC 81-13513. (Illus.). 272p. 1982. text ed. 16.00 (ISBN 0-87006-404-5). Goodheart.

Brushwood, Carolyn, tr. see Aguilera-Malta, Demetrio.

Brushwood, Carolyn, tr. see Galindo, Sergio.

Brushwood, John, tr. see Aguilera-Malta, Demetrio.

Brushwood, John, tr. see Galindo, Sergio.

Brushwood, John S. Enrique Gonzalez Martinez. LC 71-75878. (World Authors Ser.). 1969. lib. bdg. 15.95 (ISBN 0-8057-2592-X). Irvington.

--Genteel Barbarism: Experiments in Analysis of Nineteenth-Century Spanish-American Novels. LC 80-27722. xiv, 241p. 1981. 19.95x (ISBN 0-8032-1165-1). U of Nebr Pr.

--Mexico in Its Novel: A Nation's Search for Identity. LC 65-27534. (Texas Pan American Ser.). 306p. 1966. 17.50x (ISBN 0-292-73608-8); pap. 8.95x (ISBN 0-292-70070-9). U of Tex Pr.

Brusick, David. Principles of Genetic Toxicology. LC 80-16514. 300p. 1980. 29.50x (ISBN 0-306-40414-1, Plenum Pr). Plenum Pub.

Brusiloff, Phyllis & Witenberg, Mary J. The Emerging Child. 208p. 1983. 15.00 (ISBN 0-87668-680-3). Aronson.

Brusilov, Aleksiei A. Soldiers Note-Book, 1914-1918. LC 75-84265. Repr. of 1930 ed. lib. bdg. 35.00x (ISBN 0-8371-5003-5, BRSN). Greenwood.

Brusius, Ron & Noettl, Margaret. Family Evening Activity Devotions. (gr. k-7). pap. 4.95 (ISBN 0-570-03803-0, 12-2912). Concordia.

Bruso, Dick. Bible Promises, Help & Hope for Your Finances. 156p. (Orig.). 1985. pap. 2.95 (ISBN 0-89840-075-9). Heres Life.

Brusone, Pablo Le Riverend see Le Riverend Brusone, Pablo.

Bruss, Elizabeth W. Autobiographical Acts: The Changing Situation of a Literary Genre. LC 76-13460. 192p. 1977. 16.50x (ISBN 0-8018-1821-4). Johns Hopkins.

--Beautiful Theories: The Spectacle of Discourse in Contemporary Criticism. LC 81-48178. 528p. 1982. text ed. 35.00x (ISBN 0-8018-2670-5). Johns Hopkins.

Bruss, Michael, jt. ed. see Woodard, James C.

Bruss, Paul. Conrad's Early Sea Fiction: The Novelist As Navigator. LC 77-74402. 185p. 1979. 18.50 (ISBN 0-8387-2133-8). Bucknell U Pr.

--Victims: Textual Strategies in Recent American Fiction. LC 80-67319. 256p. 1981. 25.00 (ISBN 0-8387-5006-0). Bucknell U Pr.

Bruss, Robert J. Effective Real Estate Investing. 280p. 1984. 16.95 (ISBN 0-910019-22-3). Invest Tax Pubn.

Brussard, Peter F., ed. Ecological Genetics: The Interface. LC 78-27196. (Proceedings in Life Sciences). (Illus.). 1979. 30.50 (ISBN 0-387-90378-X). Springer-Verlag.

Brussel, E. W. Van see Van Brussel, E. W.

Brussel, Isidore R. Bibliography of the Writings of James Branch Cabell. 1978. Repr. of 1932 ed. lib. bdg. 12.00 (ISBN 0-8495-0435-X). Arden Lib.

Brussel, James A. & Cantzlaar, George L. Diccionario de Psiquiatria. 306p. (Span.). pap. 25.50 (ISBN 0-686-57366-8, S-50209). French & Eur.

Brussel, Morton K., jt. auth. see Nayfeh, Munir H.

Brussel, Nicolas. Nouvel Examen de l'usage General des Fiefs en France Pendant le XIe, le XIIe, le XIIIe & XIVe Siecle, 2 vols. LC 79-8359. Repr. of 1750 ed. Set. 175.00 (ISBN 0-404-18337-9). AMS Pr.

Brussell, Eugene E. Dictionary of Quotable Definitions. 640p. 1984. pap. 14.95 (ISBN 0-13-210626-4). P-H.

Brussell, Isidore. Bibliography of the Writings of James Branch Cabell. LC 74-8034. 1932. lib. bdg. 15.00 (ISBN 0-8414-3184-1). Folcroft.

Brusselle, Michael. The Photographer's Question & Answer Book: Your Picture Taking Problems Solved. (Illus.). 224p. 1983. 17.95 (ISBN 0-8174-5411-X, Amphoto); pap. 12.95 (ISBN 0-8174-5412-8). Watson-Guptill.

Brusselmans, C., ed. Jesus Loves Children. 5.95 (ISBN 0-8215-9889-9). Sadlier.

Brusselmans, Christiane & Wakin, Edward. Religion for Little Children: A Parent's Guide. LC 76-140110. 1977. pap. 6.95 (ISBN 0-87973-825-1). Our Sunday Visitor.

Brussel-Smith, B., jt. auth. see Weart, Edith.

Brust, Steven. Jhereg. 256p. 1985. pap. 2.95 (ISBN 0-441-38553-2, Pub. by Ace Science Fiction). Ace Bks.

--To Reign in Hell. LC 84-50225. (Illus.). 258p. 1984. 17.00 (ISBN 0-916595-00-5). SteelDragon Pr.

--To Reign in Hell. 304p. 1985. pap. 2.95 (ISBN 0-441-81496-4, Pub. by Ace Science Fiction). Ace Bks.

--Yendi: Jhereg, No. 2. 224p. 1985. pap. 2.95 (ISBN 0-441-94457-4, Pub. by Ace Science Fiction). Ace Bks.

Brustein, Michael, et al. Manual on Civil Rights in Vocational Education. LC 83-621186. 1984. write for info. U St NY Zd.

Brustein, Robert. Critical Moments: Reflecting on Theater & Society. 1980. 9.95 (ISBN 0-394-51093-3). Random.

--Making Scenes: A Personal History of the Turbulent Years at Yale, 1966-1979. 1981. 15.00 (ISBN 0-394-51094-1). Random.

--Making Scenes: A Personal History of the Turbulent Years at Yale, 1968-1979. (Illus.). 352p. 1984. pap. 9.95 (ISBN 0-87910-002-8). Limelight Edns.

--Revolution As Theatre: Essays on Radical Style. 1970. pap. 1.95 (ISBN 0-87140-238-6). Liveright.

--The Theatre of Revolt: An Approach to the Modern Drama. 1964. pap. 8.95 (ISBN 0-316-11287-9, Pub. by Atlantic Monthly Pr). Little.

Bruster, Bill G. & Dale, Robert D. How to Encourage Others. LC 82-70868. (Orig.). 1983. pap. 6.95 (ISBN 0-8054-2247-1). Broadman.

Brustman, Barbara & Kastenbaum, Roberts. Condemned to Life. (Cushing Hospital Series on Aging & Terminal Care). cancelled prof. ref. (ISBN 0-88410-715-9). Ballinger Pub.

Bruteau, Beatrice. Evolution Toward Divinity. LC 73-16198. 260p. 1974. 10.00 (ISBN 0-8356-0216-8). Theos Pub Hse.

--The Psychic Grid. LC 79-64096. 1979. pap. 6.50 (ISBN 0-8356-0531-0, Quest). Theos Pub Hse.

--Worthy Is the World: The Hindu Philosophy of Sri Aurobindo. LC 73-144091. (Illus.). 288p. 1972. 18.00 (ISBN 0-8386-7872-6). Fairleigh Dickinson.

Brutents, K. National Liberation Revolutions Today, 2 vols. 555p. 1977. Set. 7.95 (ISBN 0-8285-3218-4, Pub. by Progress Pubs USSR). Imported Pubns.

--Newly-Free Countries in the Seventies. 280p. 1984. 6.95 (ISBN 0-8285-2655-9, Pub. by Progress Pubs USSR). Imported Pubns.

Brutents, Karen. The Newly Free Countries in the Seventies. Burova, Nadezhda, tr. 280p. 1983. 5.95 (Pub. by Progress Pubs USSR). Imported Pubns.

Bruter, C. P., et al, eds. Bifurcation Theory, Mechanics & Physics. 1983. lib. bdg. 58.00 (ISBN 90-2771-631-5, Pub. by Reidel Holland). Kluwer Academic.

Bruton, David. Baird T. Spalding As I Knew Him. 122p. 1980. pap. 5.95 (ISBN 0-87516-392-0). De Vorss.

Bruton, David L., ed. Aspects of the Ordovician System. (Illus.). 275p. 1984. pap. 19.00x (ISBN 82-00-06319-4). Universitet.

Bruton, Eric. The Longcase Clock. (Illus.). 1977. 29.95x (ISBN 0-8464-0578-4). Beekman Pubs.

Bruton, Eric & Scribner Press. The Longcase Clock. 2nd ed. (Illus.). 1979. 22.95 (ISBN 0-684-16247-4, ScribT). Scribner.

Bruton, J. W., jt. auth. see Smith, Arthur.

Bruton, Len T. RC-Active Networks: Theory & Design. (Series in Electrical & Computer Engineering). (Illus.). 1980. text ed. 45.95 (ISBN 0-13-753467-1). P-H.

Bruton, M. J., ed. The Spirit & Purpose of Planning. 2nd ed. (The Built Envionment Ser.). (Illus.). 208p. 1984. pap. 14.95 (ISBN 0-09-153401-1, Pub. by Hutchinson Educ). Longwood Pub Group.

Bruton, Mary, ed. Focus: A Design Arts Film & Video Guide. 80p. (Orig.). 1981. pap. 5.00 (ISBN 0-941182-11-8). Partners Livable.

Bruton, Ronald W. An Ounce of Prevention Plus a Pound of Cure: Tests & Techniques for Aiding Individual Readers. LC 76-20600. (Illus.). 1977. text ed. 11.95 (ISBN 0-673-16412-8). Scott F.

Bruton, Sheila, ed. Indaba: Let's Talk. Bassingthwaighte, Brian & Hooper, Janet. 1976. pap. 1.95 (ISBN 0-377-00052-3). Friend Pr.

Bruton, William. Grover. 32p. (Orig.). 1985. pap. 4.95 (ISBN 0-317-19201-9). Quality Ohio.

Brutsaert, Wilfrid H. Evaporation into the Atmosphere: Theory, History & Applications. 308p. 1982. 34.95 (ISBN 90-277-1247-6, Pub. by Reidel Holland). Kluwer Academic.

Brutsaert, Wilfried & Jirka, Gerhard H., eds. Gas Transfer at Water Surfaces. 1984. lib. bdg. 78.00 (ISBN 0-318-00439-9, Pub. by Reidel Holland). Kluwer Academic.

Brutten, et al. Something's Wrong with My Child: A Parent's Handbook About Children with Learning Disabilities. LC 79-10285. 1979. pap. 6.95 (ISBN 0-15-683805-2, Harv). HarBraceJ.

Brutus, Dennis. Letters to Martha. (African Writers Ser.). 1968. pap. text ed. 4.50x (ISBN 0-435-90046-3). Heinemann Ed.

--A Simple Lust. (African Writers Ser.). 1973. pap. text ed. 6.00x (ISBN 0-435-90115-X). Heinemann Ed.

--Stubborn Hope: Poems. LC 77-90993. (Orig.). 1978. 14.00 (ISBN 0-914478-25-7); pap. 7.00 (ISBN 0-89410-430-6). Three Continents.

Brutvan, Cheryl A. Milton Rogovin: The Forgotten Ones. LC 84-13187. (Illus.). 184p. 1985. text ed. 35.00x (ISBN 0-295-96196-1); pap. 19.95 (ISBN 0-295-96213-5). U of Wash Pr.

Brutvan, Cheryl A., jt. auth. see Cathcart, Linda.

Brutzkus, Boris. Economic Planning in Soviet Russia. Gardner, Gilbert, tr. from Ger. LC 79-51857. 1981. Repr. of 1935 ed. 24.50 (ISBN 0-88355-950-1). Hyperion Conn.

Bruum, Kettil. Controlling Psychotropic Drugs: The Nordic Experience. LC 83-2970. 305p. 1983. 35.00x (ISBN 0-312-16926-4). St Martin.

Bruun, Bertel. The Larouse Guide to Birds of Britain & Europe. rev. ed. 1984. pap. 12.95 (ISBN 0-88332-092-4). Larousse.

Bruun, Bertel, jt. auth. see Bruun, Ruth D.

Bruun, Geoffrey. Clemenceau. (Illus.). x, 225p. 1968. Repr. of 1943 ed. 19.50 (ISBN 0-208-00152-2, Archon). Shoe String.

--Saint-Just: Apostle of the Terror. viii, 168p. 1966. Repr. of 1932 ed. 17.50 (ISBN 0-208-00531-5, Archon). Shoe String.

Bruun, Geoffrey, jt. auth. see Ferguson, Wallace K.

Bruun, K., et al. Alcohol Control Policies in Public Health Perspective. (The Finnish Foundation for Alcohol Studies: Vol. 25). (Illus.). 1975. 8.00 (ISBN 951-9191-29-1). Rutgers Ctr Alcohol.

Bruun, Kettil & Hauge, Ragnar. Drinking Habits Among Northern Youth: A Cross-National Study in the Scandinavian Capitals. (The Finnish Foundation for Alcohol Studies: Vol. 12). 1963. 4.00 (ISBN 951-9192-04-2). Rutgers Ctr Alcohol.

Bruun, Kettil, et al. The Gentlemen's Club: International Control of Drugs & Alcohol. LC 74-21343. (Studies in Crime & Justice Ser). xiv, 338p. 1975. 20.00x (ISBN 0-226-07777-2, Phoen); pap. 5.95x (ISBN 0-226-07778-0). U of Chicago Pr.

Bruun, P. Design & Construction of Mounds for Breakwater & Coastal Protection. (Developments in Geotechnical Engineering Ser.: Vol. 37). 1985. 92.75 (ISBN 0-444-42391-5). Elsevier.

Bruun, P. & Mehta, A. J. Stability of Tidal Inlets: Theory & Engineering. (Developments in Geotechnical Engineering Ser.: Vol. 23). 510p. 1978. 76.75 (ISBN 0-444-41728-1). Elsevier.

Bruun, Per. Port Engineering. 3rd ed. LC 81-603. 800p. 1981. 79.95x (ISBN 0-87201-739-7). Gulf Pub.

Bruun, Ruth D. & Bruun, Bertel. The Human Body. LC 82-5210. (The Random House Library of Knowledge). (Illus.). 96p. (gr. 5 up). 1982. PLB 9.99 (ISBN 0-394-94424-0); pap. 8.95 smythe-sewn (ISBN 0-394-84424-6). Random.

Bruun-Rasmussen, Ole & Petersen, Grete. Make-Up, Costumes & Masks for the Stage. LC 76-19803. (Illus.). 96p. (gr. 4-12). 1981. pap. 7.95 (ISBN 0-8069-8992-0). Sterling.

Bruwer, Andre J. Classic Descriptions in Diagnostic Roentgenology, 2 vols. (Illus.). 2094p. 1964. photocopy ed 240.00x (ISBN 0-398-00245-2). C C Thomas.

Brux, J. de see De Brux, J., et al.

Bruyas, Jacques. Radical Words of the Mohawk Language, with Their Derivatives. LC 10-30198. (Library of American Linguistics Ser.: Vol. 10). Repr. of 1862 ed. 28.50 (ISBN 0-404-50990-8). AMS Pr.

Bruyer, Raymond. The Neuropsychology of Face Perception & Facial Expression. 350p. 1985. text ed. 36.00 (ISBN 0-89859-602-5). L Erlbaum Assocs.

Bruyere, Christian, jt. auth. see Inwood, Robert.

Bruyere, Jean De La see De La Bruyere, Jean.

Bruyere, Toni M. & Robey, Sidney J. For Gourmets with Ulcers. 224p. 1981. pap. 4.95 (ISBN 0-393-00984-X). Norton.

Bruyn, C. S. van see Van Dobben de Bruyn, C. S.

Bruyn, C. V., tr. see Carling, Finn & Haecker, Theodor.

Bruyn, Chris de see De Bruyn, Chris, et al.

Bruyn, Chris H. de see De Bruyn, Chris H., et al.

Bruyn, G. W. A Centennial Bibliography of Huntington's Chorea: 1872-1972. 1974. lib. bdg. 30.00 (ISBN 90-6186-011-3). Kluwer Academic.

Bruyn, G. W., jt. ed. see Vinken, P. J.

Bruyn, J. A Corpus of Rembrandt Paintings, Vol. 1. 1983. lib. bdg. 325.00 (ISBN 90-247-2614-X, Pub. by Martinus Nijhoff Netherlands). Kluwer Academic.

Bruyn, Severyn T. Human Perspective in Sociology: The Methodology of Participant Observation. 302p. 1985. text ed. 29.00x (ISBN 0-8290-0731-8); pap. text ed. 14.95x (ISBN 0-8290-0734-2). Irvington.

Bruyn, Severyn T., ed. Field Research in Sociology: An Annotated Bibliography. 1985. text ed. 29.50x (ISBN 0-8290-1058-0). Irvington.

Bruyn, Severyn T. & Rayman, Paula, eds. Nonviolent Action & Social Change. LC 79-11618. 316p. 1979. 18.75x (ISBN 0-470-26738-0). Halsted Pr.

--Nonviolent Action & Social Change. 320p. 1980. pap. text ed. 9.95x (ISBN 0-8290-0271-5). Irvington.

--Nonviolent Action & Social Change. 320p. 1979. text ed. 18.75x (ISBN 0-8290-0854-3). Irvington.

Bruyn, Severyn T., Jr. Communities in Action: A Comparative Study. 1963. 9.95x (ISBN 0-8084-0085-1); pap. 6.95x (ISBN 0-8084-0086-X). New Coll U Pr.

Bruyne, K. I. De see De Bruyne, K. I., et al.

Bruyninckx, Jozef. Phototypography & Graphic Arts Dimension Control Photography. LC 74-115394. (Illus.). 150p. 1976. 18.25 (ISBN 0-911126-03-1). Perfect Graphic.

Bruyns, M. F. & Wolff, W. J., eds. Nature Conservation, Management & Physical Planning in the Wadden Sea Area: Final Report of the Section "Physical Planning & Nature Management" of the Wadden Sea Working Group, Report 11. 164p. 1983. lib. bdg. 8.00 (ISBN 90-6191-061-7, Pub. by Balkema RSA). IPS.

Bruz, J. de see De Bruz, J. & Gautrey, J. P.

Bruzek, Anton & Durrant, Christopher J., eds. Illustrated Glossary for Solar & Solar-Terrestrial Physics. (Astrophysics & Space Science Library: No. 69). 1977. lib. bdg. 34.00 (ISBN 90-277-0825-8, Pub. by Reidel Holland). Kluwer Academic.

Bruzelius, Anders & Thelin, Krister, eds. The Swedish Code of Judicial Procedure. rev ed. (The American Ser. of Foreign Penal Codes: No. 24). xvii, 253p. 1979. 28.50x (ISBN 0-8377-0044-2). Rothman.

Bruzelius, Andre, et al, eds. Concise English-Swedish Dictionary of Legal Terms. 175p. (Eng. & Swedish.). 39.95 (ISBN 0-686-80959-9). French & Eur.

Bruzina, Ronald. Logos & Eidos: The Concept in Phenomenology. LC 70-129299. (Janua Linguarum, Ser. Minor: No. 93). (Orig.). 1971. pap. text ed. 13.60x (ISBN 90-2791-542-3). Mouton.

Bruzina, Ronald & Wilshire, Bruce, eds. Phenomenology: Dialogues & Bridges. LC 82-10593. (Selected Studies in Phenomenology & Existential Philosophy: No. 8). 376p. 1982. 44.50x (ISBN 0-87395-690-7); pap. 24.50x (ISBN 0-87395-691-5). State U NY Pr.

Bruzina, Ronald & Wilshire, Bruce W., eds. Crosscurrents in Phenomenology. (Selected Studies in Phenomenology & Existential Philosophy: No. 7). 1978. pap. 39.50 (ISBN 90-247-2044-3, Pub. by Martinus Nijhoff Netherlands). Kluwer Academic.

Bruzonsky, Mark A., jt. ed. see Wells, Samuel F., Jr.

Bry, Adelaide. EST. 1976. pap. 3.95 (ISBN 0-380-00697-9, 69823-X). Avon.

--The T. A. Primer: Transactional Analysis in Everyday Life. LC 73-3833. (Illus., Orig.). 1973. pap. 1.95i (ISBN 0-06-080297-9, P297, PL). Har-Row.

Bry, Adelaide & Bair, Marjorie. Directing the Movies of Your Mind: Visualization for Health & Insight. LC 77-3741. 1978. 12.45i (ISBN 0-06-010528-3, HarpT). Har-Row.

--Visualization: Directing the Movies of Your Mind. LC 77-3741. (Illus.). 192p. 1979. pap. 5.72 (ISBN 0-06-464033-7, BN4033, BN). B&N NY.

Bry, Gerhard. The Average Workweek as an Economic Indicator. 6.00 (ISBN 0-405-18756-4, 16470). Ayer Co Pubs.

Bry, Gerhard & Boschan, Charlotte. Cyclical Anaylsis of Time Series: Selected Procedures & Computer Programs. (Technical Paper Ser.: No. 20). (Illus.). 230p. 1971. text ed. 14.00x (ISBN 0-87014-223-2, Dist. by Columbia U Pr). Natl Bur Econ Res.

Bryan see Sohn, David A.

Bryan & Potter, eds. Effect of Load Variables on Fatigue Crack Initiation & Propagation - STP 714. 242p. 1980. 27.00 (ISBN 0-8031-0720-X, 04-714000-30). ASTM.

Bryan, et al, eds. The English Familiar Essay: Representative Texts. 1978. Repr. of 1916 ed. lib. bdg. 40.00 (ISBN 0-8495-0400-7). Arden Lib.

Bryan, Alfred C. History of State Banking in Maryland. LC 78-63868. (Johns Hopkins University. Studies in the Social Sciences. Seventeenth Ser. 1899: 1-3). Repr. of 1899 ed. 11.50 (ISBN 0-404-61124-9). AMS Pr.

--History of State Banking in Maryland. 1973. pap. 14.00 (ISBN 0-384-06115-X). Johnson Repr.

Bryan, Anne M. & Hull, Alexander. Situations: Une Grammaire Pour Aujourd'hui. 288p. 1973. pap. text ed. 17.95 (ISBN 0-13-810697-5); tapes 100.00 (ISBN 0-13-810705-X). P-H.

Bryan, Anne-Marie & Duche, Jean. Pour Parler: Manual De Conversation Francaise. 2nd ed. (Illus.). 1977. text ed. 21.95 (ISBN 0-13-686386-8); tapes 125.00 (ISBN 0-13-686378-7). P-H.

Bryan, Arthur H., et al. Bacteriology: Principles & Practice. 6th rev ed. (Orig.). 1962. pap. 5.95 (ISBN 0-06-460003-3, CO 3, COS). B&N NY.

Bryan, Ashley. The Adventures of Aku. LC 75-44245. (Illus.). 80p. (gr. 4-6). 1976. 7.95 (ISBN 0-689-30519-2). Atheneum.

--Beat the Story-Drum, Pum-Pum. LC 80-12045. (Illus.). 80p. (gr. 4-6). 1980. 10.95 (ISBN 0-689-30769-1). Atheneum.

--The Cat's Purr. LC 84-21534. (Illus.). 48p. (gr. 3-7). 1985. 9.95 (ISBN 0-689-31086-2). Atheneum.

--The Dancing Granny. LC 76-25847. (Illus.). 64p. (gr. k-3). 1977. 8.95 (ISBN 0-689-30548-6). Atheneum.

--I'm Going to Sing: Black American Spirituals, Vol. II. (Illus.). 64p. (ps up). 1982. 10.95 (ISBN 0-689-30915-5). Atheneum.

--Ox of the Wonderful Horns & Other African Folktales. LC 75-154749. (Illus.). 48p. (gr. 1-5). 1971. PLB 8.95 (ISBN 0-689-20690-9). Atheneum.

--Walk Together Children. LC 73-84821. (Illus.). 64p. (gr. 2 up). 1974. 7.95 (ISBN 0-689-30131-6). Atheneum.

--Walk Together Children. (gr. 2 up). pap. 2.95 (ISBN 0-689-70485-2, A-112, Aladdin). Atheneum.

Bryan, Bruce. Archeological Explorations on San Nicolas Island. (Illus.). 160p. 1970. 12.50 (ISBN 0-916561-07-0). Southwest Mus.

Bryan, C. D. Beautiful Women, Ugly Scenes. LC 82-4609. (Illus.). 384p. 1983. 16.95 (ISBN 0-385-17143-9). Doubleday.

--Beautiful Women, Ugly Scenes. 1985. pap. 4.95 (ISBN 0-440-30536-5, LE). Dell.

--National Air & Space Museum. (Illus.). 1979. 60.00 (ISBN 0-8109-0666-X). Abrams.

--National Air & Space Museum. 160p. 1982. 12.95 ea. Vol. I (ISBN 0-553-01384-X). Vol. II (ISBN 0-553-01385-8). Bantam.

Bryan, Charles V. The Child That Nobody Wanted. LC 57-12228. 284p. 1957. 4.00 (ISBN 0-87004-022-7). Caxton.

Bryan County Heritage Association, Inc., compiled by. History of Bryan County, Oklahoma. 596p. 1983. 65.00 (ISBN 0-88107-007-6). Natl ShareGraphics.

Bryan, Cyril. Ancient Egyptian Medicine: The Papyrus Ebers. 224p. 1974. 20.00 (ISBN 0-89005-004-X). Ares.

Bryan, E. H., Jr., et al. Insects of Hawaii, Johnston Island, & Wake Island. (BMB: No. 31). Repr. of 1926 ed. 12.00 (ISBN 0-527-02134-2). Kraus Repr.

Bryan, E. Lewis. A Financial Reporting Model for Not For Profit Associations. Dufey, Gunter, ed. LC 81-7398. (Research for Business Decisions: No. 41). 190p. 1981. 39.95 (ISBN 0-8357-1195-1). UMI Res Pr.

Bryan, E. R. & Davies, J. M. Steel Diaphragm Roof Decks: A Design Guide with Tables for Engineers & Architects. 92p. 1981. pap. 23.95x (ISBN 0-470-27158-2). Halsted Pr.

Bryan, Edwin H., Jr. Stars Over Hawaii. (Illus.). 1977. pap. 4.50 (ISBN 0-912180-30-7). Petroglyph.

Bryan, Eileen. Against All Odds. (Candlelight Ecstasy Supreme Ser.: No. 25). (Orig.). 1984. pap. 2.50 (ISBN 0-440-10069-0). Dell.

--Crossfire. (Candlelight Ecstasy Supreme Ser.: No. 14). 288p. (Orig.). 1984. pap. 2.50 (ISBN 0-440-11599-X). Dell.

--Loving Adversaries. (Candlelight Ecstasy Ser.: No. 155). (Orig.). 1983. pap. 1.95 (ISBN 0-440-14885-5). Dell.

--Memory & Desire. (Candlelight Ecstasy Romance Ser.: No. 193). (Orig.). 1983. pap. 1.95 (ISBN 0-440-15608-4). Dell.

--Run for the Roses. (Candlelight Ecstasy Ser.: No. 48). 288p. 1984. pap. 2.50 (ISBN 0-440-17517-8). Dell.

Bryan, Felicity. Town Gardener's Companion. (Illus.). 192p. 1981. 14.95 (ISBN 0-233-97351-6, Pub. by A Deutsch England). David & Charles.

--Town Gardner's Companion. (Illus.). 192p. 1981. 14.95 (ISBN 0-233-97351-6). Andre Deutsch.

Bryan, Frank & Mares, Bill. Real Vermonters Don't Milk Goats. LC 83-61500. (Illus.). 96p. (Orig.). 1983. pap. 4.95 (ISBN 0-933050-16-X). New Eng Pr VT.

Bryan, Frank L., jt. ed. see Riemann, Hans.

Bryan, Frank M. Politics in Rural America: People, Parties, & Policy. (Special Study Ser.). 320p. (Orig.). pap. text ed. 12.95x (ISBN 0-89158-984-8). Westview.

--Yankee Politics in Rural Vermont. LC 73-78913. (Illus.). 334p. 1974. 25.00x (ISBN 0-87451-082-1). U Pr of New Eng.

Bryan, G. McLeod. Dissenter in the Baptist Southland: Fifty Years in the Career of William Wallace Finlator. (Illus.). xi, 198p. 1985. 17.95 (ISBN 0-86554-176-0, MUP-H166). Mercer Univ Pr.

Bryan, G. McLeod, et al. Documents Concerning Baptism & Church Membership: A Controversy Among North Carolina Baptists. LC 76-45687. (Special Studies Ser.: No. 1). 1977. pap. 2.00 (ISBN 0-932180-00-0). NABPR.

Bryan, George. The Law of Petroleum & Natural Gas, with Forms. xvi, 522p. 1983. Repr. of 1898 ed. lib. bdg. 42.50x (ISBN 0-8377-0335-2). Rothman.

Bryan, George B. Ethelwold & Medieval Music-Drama at Winchester: The Easter Play, Its Author, & Its Milieu. (European University Studies, Theatre, Film & Television: Ser. 30, Vol. 10). 150p. 1981. pap. 17.05 (ISBN 3-261-04841-7). P Lang Pubs.

--An Ibsen Companion: A Dictionary-Guide to the Life, Works & Critical Reception of Henrik Ibsen. LC 83-18551. xxix, 437p. 1984. lib. bdg. 49.95 (ISBN 0-313-23506-6, BIB/). Greenwood.

--Stage Lives: A Bibliography & an Index to Theatrical Biographies in English. LC 84-19833. (Bibliographies & Indexes in the Performing Arts Ser.: No. 2). xvi, 368p. 1985. lib. bdg. 45.00 (ISBN 0-313-24577-0, BSV/). Greenwood.

Bryan, George M. & Heirtzler, James R. Ocean Margin Drilling Program Atlases, Vol. 5. (Regional Atlas Ser.). 1984. write for info. spiral bdg (ISBN 0-86720-255-6, Marine Sci Intl). Jones & Bartlett.

Bryan, George T., ed. Nitrofurans. LC 77-72824. (Carcinogenesis-A Comprehensive Survey Ser.: Vol. 4). 243p. 1978. 36.00 (ISBN 0-89004-250-0). Raven.

Bryan, George T. & Cohen, Samuel M., eds. The Pathology of Bladder Cancer, 2 Vols. 1983. Vol. I, 148p. 67.00 (ISBN 0-8493-6225-3); Vol. II, 256p. 75.00 (ISBN 0-8493-6226-1). CRC Pr.

Bryan, Glenda J. Johnson & Kennedy Radiographic Skeletal Anatomy. LC 82-12971. (Illus.). 288p. 1983. pap. 30.00 (ISBN 0-443-01627-5). Churchill.

Bryan, Gordon, compiled by. Scottish Nationalism & Cultural Identity in the Twentieth Century: An Annotated Bibliography of Secondary Sources. LC 84-4667. (Bibliographies & Indexes in Law & Political Science Ser.: No. 1). (Illus.). xii, 180p. 1984. lib. bdg. 35.00 (ISBN 0-313-23998-3, BNA/). Greenwood.

Bryan, Harrison & Greenwood, Gordon, eds. Design for Diversity: Library Services for Higher Education & Research in Australia. (Illus.). 1977. 39.95x (ISBN 0-7022-1314-4). U of Queensland Pr.

Bryan, Harrison & Horacek, John, eds. Australian Academic Libraries in the Seventies: Essays in Honour of Dietrich Borchardt. LC 83-3557. (Scholars' Library). (Illus.). 331p. 1984. text ed. 37.50x (ISBN 0-7022-1883-9). U of Queensland Pr.

Bryan, J., jt. auth. see Halsey, William.

Bryan, J., III. Merry Gentlemen (& One Lady) LC 84-45610. 256p. 1985. 14.95 (ISBN 0-689-11533-4). Atheneum.

Bryan, J. Thomas. Literature of Japan. LC 79-103218. 1970. Repr. of 1929 ed. 18.50x (ISBN 0-8046-0855-5, Pub. by Kennikat). Assoc Faculty Pr.

Bryan, J. W. Development of the English Law of Conspiracy. LC 72-77737. (Law, Politics, & History Ser). 1970. Repr. of 1909 ed. lib. bdg. 25.00 (ISBN 0-306-71375-6). Da Capo.

Bryan, James & Murphy, Charles. The Windsor Story. 1981. pap. 3.95 (ISBN 0-440-19346-X). Dell.

Bryan, James H. see Hetherington, E. Mavis.

Bryan, James W. The Development of the English Law of Conspiracy. LC 78-63932. (Johns Hopkins University. Studies in the Social Sciences. Twenty-Seventh Ser. 1909: 3-5). Repr. of 1909 ed. 14.50 (ISBN 0-404-61181-8). AMS Pr.

Bryan, John E. Small World Vegetable Gardening. LC 76-58364. (Illus.). 144p. 1977. 4.95 (ISBN 0-912238-79-8); pap. 4.95 (ISBN 0-912238-78-X). One Hund One Prods.

Bryan, John L. Fire Suppression & Detections Systems. 2nd ed. 464p. 1982. text ed. write for info. (ISBN 0-02-471300-7). Macmillan.

Bryan, John L. & Picard, Raymond C., eds. Managing Fire Services. LC 79-10067. (Municipal Management Ser.). (Illus.). 574p. 1979. text ed. 37.50 (ISBN 0-87326-018-X). Intl City Mgt.

Bryan, John M. An Architectural History of the South Carolina College, 1801-1855. LC 76-54242. xxxii, 134p. 1976. pap. 12.95 (ISBN 0-87249-353-9). U of SC Pr.

Bryan, John R. Managing Restaurant Personnel: A Handbook for Food Service Operators. LC 73-94217. (Illus.). 192p. 1974. 15.95 (ISBN 0-86730-217-8). Lebhar Friedman.

Bryan, John T. A History of Japan. LC 78-7683. 1978. Repr. of 1928 ed. lib. bdg. 15.00 (ISBN 0-8414-0264-7). Folcroft.

Bryan, Joseph, jt. auth. see Halsey, William F.

Bryan, Joseph, III. Aircraft Carrier. 1982. pap. 2.75 (ISBN 0-345-30486-1). Ballantine.

Bryan, Kay. Look! I Can Cook! A Simplified Guide to Cooking & Household Skills. LC 79-89358. 1979. pap. 9.95 (ISBN 0-88290-130-3). Horizon Utah.

Bryan, L. E. Antimicrobial Drug Resistance. LC 83-22377. 1984. 79.00 (ISBN 0-12-138120-X). Acad Pr.

--Bacterial Resistance & Susceptibility to Chemotherapeutic Agents. LC 81-7724. (Illus.). 225p. 1982. 39.50 (ISBN 0-521-23039-X); pap. 16.95 (ISBN 0-521-29785-0). Cambridge U Pr.

Bryan, Lee. The Searching Years. 1981. pap. 2.25 (ISBN 0-8439-0871-8, Leisure Bks). Dorchester Pub Co.

Bryan, Liz. British Columbia: This Favoured Land. (Illus.). 160p. 1982. 29.95 (ISBN 0-295-95952-5, Pub. by Douglas & McIntyre Canada). U of Wash Pr.

Bryan, Lydia, ed. see Sandifer, Kevin, et al.

Bryan, M. B., jt. auth. see Bryan, William J.

Bryan, M. Leonard, ed. Remote Sensing of Earth Resources: A Guide to Information Sources. LC 79-22792. (Geography & Travel Information Guide Ser.: Vol. 1). (Illus.). 188p. 1979. 60.00x (ISBN 0-8103-1413-4). Gale.

Bryan, Mary, jt. auth. see Dumont, William.

Bryan, Miriam, jt. auth. see Findley, Warren.

Bryan, Nancy. Thin Is a State of Mind. LC 81-22168. 208p. 1982. 12.95 (ISBN 0-89638-055-6); pap. 8.95 (ISBN 0-89638-056-4). CompCare.

Bryan, Nonobah G. & Young, Stella. Navajo Native Dyes. (Wild & Woolly West Ser: No. 34). (Illus.). 1978. 8.00 (ISBN 0-910584-49-4); pap. 2.50 (ISBN 0-910584-57-5). Filter.

Bryan, Paul. Programming Your Apple II Computer. (Illus.). 294p. 1982. 15.95o.p (ISBN 0-8306-0081-7); pap. 10.25 (ISBN 0-8306-1394-3, 1394). TAB Bks.

Bryan, Ray. Four Historic Walking Tours of Pueblo, Colorado. (Illus.). 32p. 1983. pap. 2.00x (ISBN 0-915617-06-4). Pueblo Co Hist Soc.

Bryan, Robert, jt. auth. see Dodge, Marshall.

Bryan, Robert A., et al, eds. All These to Teach: Essays in Honor of C. A. Robertson. LC 65-23168. 1965. 6.50 (ISBN 0-8130-0030-0). U Presses Fla.

Bryan, Roy C. Pupil Rating of Secondary School Teachers. LC 73-176609. (Columbia University. Teachers College. Contributions to Education: No. 708). Repr. of 1937 ed. 22.50 (ISBN 0-404-55708-2). AMS Pr.

Bryan, Sharon. Salt Air. (New Poets Ser.). 64p. 1983. 15.00x (ISBN 0-8195-2112-4); pap. 6.95 (ISBN 0-8195-1112-9). Wesleyan U Pr.

Bryan, Stuart W. Barchives Revue. Pride, Suzanne, ed. 172p. (Orig.). 1983. pap. 6.95 (ISBN 0-915055-00-7). Enchanted Knolls.

--Barchives Revue: Marin County Edition, 1985. Pride, Suzanne, ed. (Illus.). 210p. Date not set. pap. price not set (ISBN 0-915055-01-5). Enchanted Knolls.

Bryan, Stuart W. & Pride, Suzanne. Barchives Revue: South Bay Edition, 1985. (Illus., Orig.). Date not set. pap. price not set (ISBN 0-915055-02-3). Enchanted Knolls.

Bryan, T. Avril. Censorship & Social Conflict in the Spanish Theatre: The Case of Alfonso Sastre. LC 82-17445. 156p. (Orig.). 1983. lib. bdg. 22.00 (ISBN 0-8191-2829-5); pap. text ed. 9.75 (ISBN 0-8191-2830-9). U Pr of Amer.

Bryan, T. Scott. The Geysers of Yellowstone. LC 78-73980. 1979. 15.00 (ISBN 0-87081-078-2); pap. 6.95 (ISBN 0-87081-079-0). Colo Assoc.

Bryan, Thalia T. Poems of Inspiration, Vol. 2. LC 84-90111. 101p. 1984. 7.95 (ISBN 0-533-06191-1). Vantage.

--Poems of Inspiration, Vol. 1. 1981. 5.95 (ISBN 0-533-04682-3). Vantage.

Bryan, W. W., jt. auth. see Shaw, N. H.

Bryan, William A. Administrative Psychiatry. LC 58-14143. 1958. Repr. of 1936 ed. 20.00 (ISBN 0-8154-0034-9). Cooper Sq.

--George Washington in American Literature, 1775-1865. LC 72-100146. Repr. of 1952 ed. lib. bdg. 18.75x (ISBN 0-8371-3258-4, BRGW). Greenwood.

--Key to the Birds of the Hawaiian Group. (BMM). 1901. Repr. of 1901 ed. 24.00 (ISBN 0-527-01628-4). Kraus Repr.

Bryan, William B, et al. Software Configuration Management. (Tutorial Texts Ser.). 452p. 1980. 25.00 (ISBN 0-8186-0309-7, Q309). IEEE Comp Soc.

Bryan, William F. Your Future in Credit Management. rev. ed. (Careers in Depth Ser.). 1984. lib. bdg. 8.97 (ISBN 0-8239-0514-4). Rosen Group.

Bryan, William F. & Crane, Ronald S. The English Familar Essay. 1916. 25.00 (ISBN 0-8482-7361-3). Norwood Edns.

--The English Familiar Essay: Representative Texts. 1979. Repr. of 1916 ed. lib. bdg. 35.00 (ISBN 0-8492-3744-0). R West.

Bryan, William H. The Computer Book for Managing Credit. Andover, James J., ed. LC 85-4808. 136p. 1985. pap. 17.95 (ISBN 0-934914-61-3). NACM.

--Credit Management for the Office Manager. (New Horizons Ser.: No. 5). 39p. 1976. pap. 3.25 (ISBN 0-934914-27-3). NACM.

--Credit Sleuth. (New Horizons Ser.: No. 4). 39p. 1975. 3.25 (ISBN 0-934914-26-5). NACM.

Bryan, William J. Bryan on Imperialism. LC 71-111701. (American Imperialism: Viewpoints of United States Foreign Policy, 1898-1941). 1970. Repr. of 1900 ed. 16.00 (ISBN 0-405-02005-8). Ayer Co Pubs.

--The Chosen Ones: The Art of Jury Selection. 2nd ed. (Illus.). 438p. 1985. 27.50 (ISBN 0-930298-24-1). Westwood Pub Co.

--First Battle, 2 Vols. LC 70-137903. (American History & Culture in the Nineteenth Century Ser). 1971. Repr. of 1896 ed. Set. 45.00x (ISBN 0-8046-1471-7, Pub.by Kennikat). Assoc Faculty Pr.

--In His Image. facsimile ed. LC 73-156618. (Essay Index Reprint Ser). Repr. of 1922 ed. 18.00 (ISBN 0-8369-2270-0). Ayer Co Pubs.

Bryan, William J. & Bryan, M. B. Memoirs of William Jennings Bryan. LC 72-130261. (American Biography Ser., No. 32). 1970. Repr. of 1925 ed. lib. bdg. 49.95x (ISBN 0-8383-1165-2). Haskell.

Bryan, William J., jt. auth. see Taft, William H.

Bryan, William L. Wars of Families of Minds. 1940. 29.50x (ISBN 0-686-51324-X). Elliots Bks.

Bryan, William S. & Rose, Robert. A History of Pioneer Families of Missouri. LC 76-55479. (Illus.). 569p. 1984. Repr. of 1935 ed. 25.00 (ISBN 0-8063-0753-6). Genealog Pub.

Bryans, C. & Hendy, F. J. The History of the Roman Republic. 1889. 30.00 (ISBN 0-8274-3935-0). R West.

Bryans, J. Lonsdale. The Curve of Fate: From Man-Ape to the Man-God. 1977. lib. bdg. 59.95 (ISBN 0-8490-1696-7). Gordon Pr.

Bryans, J. T., ed. see International Conference on Equine Infectious Diseases, 2nd, Paris, 1969.

Bryans, J. T., ed. see International Conference on Equine Infectious Diseases, 3rd.

Bryant. Day by Day with C. H. Spurgeon. 1985. Repr. 7.95 (ISBN 0-317-27135-0). Word Bks.

--Keep in Touch. 1985. Repr. 7.95 (ISBN 0-317-27133-4). Word Bks.

--Laboratory Control of Antibacterial Chemotherapy. 150p. 1981. pap. 16.00 (ISBN 0-7236-0594-7). PSG Pub Co.

--Love Songs. 1985. Repr. pap. 7.95 (ISBN 0-317-27132-6). Word Bks.

Bryant, Al. Keep in Touch. 1981. 8.95 (ISBN 0-8499-3037-5). Word Bks.

--Love Songs: Daily Meditations for Married Couples. 1985. 7.95 (ISBN 0-8499-3036-7). Word Bks.

--New Compact Bible Dictionary. 1967. 9.95 (ISBN 0-310-22080-7); pap. 4.95 (ISBN 0-310-22082-3). Zondervan.

--New Every Morning: Three Hundred Sixty-Six Daily Meditations from Your Favorite Christian Writers. 224p. 1985. 9.95 (ISBN 0-8499-0507-9, 0507-9). Word Bks.

--A Pocket Treasury of Daily Devotions. LC 77-82183. 112p. 1978. pap. 2.95 (ISBN 0-87123-464-5, 200464). Bethany Hse.

--Religious Plays That Click. 1954. pap. 3.95 (ISBN 0-310-22101-3). Zondervan.

Bryant, Al, compiled by. A Pocket Treasury of Devotional Verse. 160p. (Orig.). 1980. pap. 2.95 (ISBN 0-87123-466-1, 200466). Bethany Hse.

Bryant, Alan. Second Chance: The Story of the New Quay Hospital. (Illus.). 208p. 1982. 11.95 (ISBN 0-312-70828-9). St Martin.

Bryant, Alfred T. Zulu People As They Were Before the White Man Came. LC 75-100282. Repr. of 1949 ed. 31.00x (ISBN 0-8371-2933-8). Greenwood.

Bryant, Alice. Gifts of the Crystal Skull: The Dorland Discoveries. (Illus.). 1980. cancelled (ISBN 0-914350-38-2). Vulcan Bks.

Bryant, Andrew. The Italians: How They Live & Work. 3rd ed. LC 75-27493. 164p. 1976. text ed. 9.95 (ISBN 0-275-22680-8, HoltC). HR&W.

Bryant, Anita & Green, Bob. Running the Good Race. (General Ser.). 1977. lib. bdg. 10.95- (ISBN 0-8161-6521-1, Large Print Bks). G K Hall.

Bryant, Anthony. Hijack. 2nd ed. LC 83-83333. 1984. 14.95 (ISBN 0-915031-03-5). Freedom Intl.

Bryant, Arthur. American Ideal. facs. ed. LC 77-90617. (Essay Index Reprint Ser). 1936. 19.00 (ISBN 0-8369-1251-9). Ayer Co Pubs.

--The England of Charles Two. facsimile ed. LC 78-37873. (Select Bibliographies Reprint Ser). Repr. of 1934 ed. 16.00 (ISBN 0-8369-6710-0). Ayer Co Pubs.

--Macaulay. 2nd rev. ed. LC 78-27536. (Illus.). 145p. 1979. Repr. of 1932 ed. text ed. 26.50x (ISBN 0-06-490761-9, 06371). B&N Imports.

--Macaulay. 1933. Repr. 20.00 (ISBN 0-8274-2655-0). R West.

--Pepys. Incl. The Man in the Making 1633-1669. 352p (ISBN 0-586-06470-2); The Years of Peril 1669-1683. 384p (ISBN 0-586-06471-0); The Savior of the Navy 1683-1689. 352p (ISBN 0-586-06472-9). pap. 8.95 ea. Academy Chi Pubs.

--Postman's Horn. facs. ed. LC 77-119927. (Select Bibliographies Reprint Ser). 1936. 22.00 (ISBN 0-8369-5370-3). Ayer Co Pubs.

--Spirit of England. 236p. Date not set. 14.95 (ISBN 0-88186-379-3). Parkwest Pubns.

--Triumph in the West. LC 73-22634. (Illus.). 438p. 1974. Repr. of 1959 ed. lib. bdg. 65.00x (ISBN 0-8371-7344-2, BRTR). Greenwood.

Bryant, B. & Bryant, R. Change & Conflict: A Study of Community Work in Glasgow. 250p. 1983. 20.00 (ISBN 0-08-028475-2); pap. 10.80 (ISBN 0-08-028480-9). Pergamon.

Bryant, Betty, jt. auth. see Taylor, Louise.

Bryant, Beverley & Williams, Jean. Portraits in Roses: One Hundred Nine Years of Kentucky Derby Winners. LC 83-23872. (Illus.). 160p. 1984. 49.95 (ISBN 0-07-008602-8). McGraw.

Bryant, Bill. The Armadillo Book. LC 82-18938. (Illus.). 128p. 1983. pap. 3.95 (ISBN 0-88289-383-1). Pelican.

Bryant, Brad. Special Foster Care: A History & Rationale. 50p. 1980. 4.85 (ISBN 0-9604068-0-8, KGH-150). Child Welfare.

Bryant, Bradford A. Special Foster Care: A History & Rationale. (Orig.). 1980. pap. text ed. 4.50 (ISBN 0-9604068-0-8). People Places.

Bryant, Bridget, et al. Children & Minders. LC 80-24692. (Oxford Preschool Research Project: Vol. 3). 244p. 1980. pap. 9.50 (ISBN 0-931114-11-X). High-Scope.

Bryant, Carl. Modern Ballroom Dancing for Amateur Tests. (Illus.). 228p. 1985. lib. bdg. 79.95 (ISBN 0-8490-3247-4). Gordon Pr.

Bryant, Carol A., et al. The Cultural Feast: An Introduction to Food Society & Change. (Illus.). 450p. 1985. pap. text ed. 20.95 (ISBN 0-314-85222-0). West Pub.

Bryant, Charles J. The Art & Drawings of Francesco Guardi. (Illus.). 148p. 1985. 87.85 (ISBN 0-86650-138-X). Gloucester Art.

Bryant, Christopher. The Heart in Pilgrimage: Christian Guidelines for the Human Journey. 208p. 1980. 9.95 (ISBN 0-8164-0457-7, Pub. by Seabury). Winston Pr.

--Jung & the Christian Way. 144p. (Orig.). 1984. pap. 7.95 (ISBN 0-86683-872-4, 7917, Pub. by Seabury). Winston Pr.

--The River Within: The Search for God in Depth. 160p. 1983. pap. 5.50 (ISBN 0-8358-0468-2). Upper Room.

Bryant, Christopher G. Positivism in Social Theory & Research. LC 84-17719. (Theoretical Traditions in the Social Sciences Ser.). 224p. 1985. 29.95 (ISBN 0-312-63189-8); pap. 11.95 (ISBN 0-312-63190-1). St Martin.

Bryant, Christopher R. The City's Countryside. 1983. pap. 16.95x (ISBN 0-582-30045-2). Longman.

Bryant, Claire. Candlewicking: Twenty-Four Iron-on Transfer Patterns & Complete Instructions. (Crafts Ser.). 56p. (Orig.). 1983. pap. 2.50 (ISBN 0-486-24572-1). Dover.

Bryant, Clifton. The Rural Workforce: Non-Agricultural Occupations in America. 304p. 1985. text ed. 27.95 (ISBN 0-89789-076-0). Bergin & Garvey.

--Sexual Deviancy & Social Proscription. LC 81-6216. 432p. 1982. text ed. 34.95x (ISBN 0-89885-024-X); pap. text ed. 16.95x (ISBN 0-89885-094-0). Human Sci Pr.

Bryant, Clifton D. Deviancy & the Family. LC 72-77588. pap. 12.95x (ISBN 0-88295-201-3). Harlan Davidson.

--Khaki-Collar Crime: Deviant Behavior in the Military Context. LC 79-7105. 1979. 14.95 (ISBN 0-02-904930-X). Free Pr.

Bryant College Staff, jt. auth. see Guay, E. Joseph.

Bryant, Coralie & White, Louise G. Managing Development in the Third World. LC 81-16494. 324p. (Orig.). 1982. lib. bdg. 34.00x (ISBN 0-89158-927-9); pap. 13.95x (ISBN 0-89158-928-7). Westview.

--Managing Rural Development with Small Farmer Participation. LC 84-4445. (KP Monographs). xii, 79p. (Orig.). 1984. pap. text ed. 6.95x (ISBN 0-931816-52-1). Kumarian Pr.

Bryant, D. Physics. (Teach Yourself Ser.). 1974. pap. 6.95 (ISBN 0-679-10406-2). McKay.

Bryant, D. & Niehaus, R., eds. Manpower Planning & Organization Design. LC 78-4623. (NATO Conference Series II, Systems Science: Vol. 7). 803p. 1978. 105.00x (ISBN 0-306-40006-5, Plenum Pr). Plenum Pub.

Bryant, D. C., et al. An Historical Anthology of Select British Speeches. LC 67-21676. Repr. of 1967 ed. 106.10 (ISBN 0-8357-9904-2, 2012471). Bks Demand UMI.

Bryant, Darrol, ed. Proceedings of the Virgin Islands' Seminar on Unification Theology. LC 80-52594. (Conference Ser.: No. 6). (Illus.). xv, 323p. (Orig.). 1980. pap. text ed. 9.95 (ISBN 0-932894-06-2). Unif Theol Sem.

--Unification Theology Seminar, Virgin Islands: Proceedings. LC 80-52594. 323p. 1980. pap. 9.95 (ISBN 0-932894-06-2). Rose Sharon Pr.

Bryant, Darrol & Foster, Durwood, eds. Hermeneutics & Unification Theology. LC 80-66201. (Conference Ser.: No. 5). (Illus.). 154p. (Orig.). 1980. pap. 7.95 (ISBN 0-932894-05-4, Pub. by New Era Bks). Paragon Hse.

--Hermeneutics & Unification Theology. LC 80-66201. 154p. (Orig.). 1980. pap. 7.95 (ISBN 0-932894-05-4). Rose Sharon Pr.

Bryant, Darrol & Hodges, Susan, eds. Exploring Unification Theology. LC 78-63274. 168p. (Orig.). 1978. pap. 7.95 (ISBN 0-932894-00-3). Rose Sharon Pr.

Bryant, Darrol, jt. ed. see Sontag, Frederick.

Bryant, David. In the Gap: What It Means to Be a World Christian. LC 84-4880. 280p. 1984. pap. 7.95 (ISBN 0-8307-0952-5, 5418217). Regal.

--With Concerts of Prayer. LC 84-17916. 1985. pap. 6.95 (ISBN 0-8307-0975-4, 5418295). Regal.

Bryant, Donald C. Edmund Burke & His Literary Friends. LC 78-7990. 1939. 25.00 (ISBN 0-8414-0168-3). Folcroft.

--Edmund Burke & His Literary Friends. 323p. 1980. Repr. of 1939 ed. lib. bdg. 37.50 (ISBN 0-8482-0133-7). Norwood Edns.

--Rhetorical Dimensions in Criticism. LC 72-94149. x, 146p. 1973. 17.50x (ISBN 0-8071-0214-8). La State U Pr.

Bryant, Donald C. & Wallace, Karl R. Fundamentals of Public Speaking. 5th ed. (Illus.). 640p. 1976. pap. 23.95 (ISBN 0-13-342725-0). P-H.

Bryant, Donald C., ed. Rhetoric & Poetic. 96p. 1965. pap. 4.50x (ISBN 0-87745-007-2). U of Iowa Pr.

Bryant, Donald C., et al. Oral Communication: A Short Course in Speaking. 5th ed. (Illus.). 288p. 1982. 18.95 (ISBN 0-13-638437-4). P-H.

Bryant, Dorothy. Day in San Francisco. LC 82-73209. 144p. 1983. 12.00 (ISBN 0-931688-09-4); pap. 6.00 (ISBN 0-931688-10-8). Ata Bks.

--Ella Price's Journal. LC 75-39758. 227p. 1982. pap. text ed. 6.00 (ISBN 0-931688-08-6). Ata Bks.

--The Garden of Eros. LC 78-73215. 1979. pap. 6.00 (ISBN 0-931688-03-5). Ata Bks.

--Killing Wonder. LC 81-66995. 180p. 1981. 10.00 (ISBN 0-931688-06-X); pap. 6.00 (ISBN 0-931688-07-8). Ata Bks.

--Killing Wonder. 1985. pap. 2.95 (ISBN 0-445-20127-4, Pub. by Popular Lib). Warner Bks.

--The Kin of Ata Are Waiting for You. 1976. pap. 5.95 (ISBN 0-394-73292-8). Random.

--Miss Giardino. LC 78-54280. 1978. pap. 6.00 (ISBN 0-931688-01-9). Ata Bks.

--Myths to Lie By. LC 83-51600. 192p. 1984. 13.00 (ISBN 0-931688-11-6); pap. 7.00 (ISBN 0-931688-12-4). ATA Bks.

--Prisoners. LC 79-55170. (Orig.). 1980. 10.00 (ISBN 0-931688-04-3); pap. 6.00 (ISBN 0-931688-05-1). Ata Bks.

--Writing a Novel. LC 78-69766. 1978. pap. 5.00 (ISBN 0-931688-02-7). Ata Bks.

Bryant, E. H., jt. auth. see Atchley, W. R.

Bryant, E. T. Music. 1965. 4.95 (ISBN 0-8022-0190-3). Philos Lib.

Bryant, Edward. Models & Moments: Paintings & Drawings by John Koch. (Illus.). 52p. 1977. pap. 5.00 exhibition catalogue (ISBN 0-911209-11-5). Penn St Art.

--Particle Theory. (Orig.). 1981. pap. 2.95 (ISBN 0-671-43107-2, Timescape). PB.

--Wyoming Sun. (Illus.). 132p. 1980. pap. 6.00 (ISBN 0-936204-12-5). Jelm Mtn.

Bryant, Edward, jt. auth. see Pennell, Joseph.

Bryant, Edward A., ed. The Best English & Scottish Ballads. LC 81-84877. (Granger Poetry Library). 390p. 1982. Repr. of 1911 ed. 29.75x (ISBN 0-89609-228-3). Granger Bk.

Bryant, Edward C., jt. auth. see King, Donald W.

Bryant, Edwin. What I Saw in California. 1967. Repr. 12.50 (ISBN 0-87018-004-5). Ross.

--What I Saw in California. LC 84-28003. xxii, 455p. 1985. pap. 9.95 (ISBN 0-8032-6070-9, BB 887, Bison). U of Nebr Pr.

Bryant, Eric T. Collecting Gramophone Records. LC 77-28263. (Illus.). 1978. Repr. of 1962 ed. lib. bdg. 22.50x (ISBN 0-313-20258-3, BRCGR). Greenwood.

Bryant, Estrella S., et al, eds. Bibliography of Asian Studies, Nineteen Seventy-seven. pap. 160.00 (ISBN 0-317-27590-9, 2014786). Bks Demand UMI.

Bryant, F. Carlene. We're All Kin: A Cultural Study of a Mountain Neighborhood. LC 81-473. 164p. 1981. 12.95x (ISBN 0-87049-312-4). U of Tenn Pr.

Bryant, Frank E. A History of English Balladry, & Other Studies. 1979. Repr. of 1913 ed. lib. bdg. 35.00 (ISBN 0-8492-3576-6). R West.

--History of English Balladry & Other Studies. LC 66-53186. 443p. 1913. write for info. (ISBN 0-8414-1754-7). Folcroft.

--A History of English Balladry Through the Reign of Elizabeth. LC 77-18205. 1977. Repr. of 1913 ed. lib. bdg. 25.00 (ISBN 0-8414-1372-X). Folcroft.

--On the Limits of Descriptive Writings Apropos of Lessings Laocoon. LC 76-58443. Repr. of 1906 ed. 8.50 (ISBN 0-8414-1654-0). Folcroft.

Bryant, Franklin H. Black Smiles: Or, the Sunny Side of Sable Life. facsimile ed. LC 72-178469. (Black Heritage Library Collection). Repr. of 1903 ed. 12.00 (ISBN 0-8369-8917-1). Ayer Co Pubs.

Bryant, Gay, jt. auth. see Working Woman Editors.

Bryant, Gordon, jt. ed. see Taylor, Raymond G.

Bryant, Gordon E., jt. auth. see Taylor, Raymond G.

Bryant, Hannah, tr. see Brahms, Johannes.

Bryant, Harold, jt. auth. see Wampler, Joseph.

Bryant, Harold S. History of Coos Turnpike (New Hampshire) (Orig.). 1985. pap. 4.00 (ISBN 0-9607906-6-7). ACETO Bookmen.

Bryant, Henry A., ed. Black Politics & Race: A Contemporary Reader of Racism & Black Politics. 1976. pap. text ed. 7.50 (ISBN 0-8191-0003-X). U Pr of Amer.

Bryant, Henry E. Tar Heel Tales. LC 72-6511. (Black Heritage Library Collection Ser). 1972. Repr. of 1909 ed. 20.00 (ISBN 0-8369-9162-1). Ayer Co Pubs.

Bryant, J. A. & Francis, D., eds. The Cell Division Cycle in Plants. (Illus.). 240p. 1985. 34.50 (ISBN 0-521-30046-0). Cambridge U Pr.

Bryant, J. A., Jr. Hippolyta's View: Some Christian Aspects of Shakespeare's Plays. LC 61-6555. 256p. 1961. 24.00x (ISBN 0-8131-1057-2). U Pr of Ky.

Bryant, J. H. Open Decision. LC 79-129473. 1970. 12.95 (ISBN 0-02-904860-5). Free Pr.

Bryant, Jacob. A New System, or, an Analysis of Ancient Mythology, 3 vols. Feldman, Burton & Richardson, Robert, eds. LC 78-60881. (Myth & Romanticism Ser.: Vol. 5). (Illus.). 1980. Set. lib. bdg. 240.00 (ISBN 0-8240-3554-2). Garland Pub.

Bryant, James C., Jr. Tudor Drama & Religious Controversy. (Mercer Sesquicentennial Ser.). 178p. 1984. 14.50x (ISBN 0-86554-129-9, MUP-H120). Mercer Univ Pr.

Bryant, James E. Tennis: A Guide for the Developing Tennis Player. (Illus.). 208p. 1984. pap. 6.95x (ISBN 0-89582-101-X). Morton Pub.

Bryant, James E., jt. auth. see Norton, Cheryl.

Bryant, James M. The Conquest. 1972. pap. 5.50 (ISBN 0-686-27963-8). J M Bryant.

--The Fulfillment. 1976. pap. 6.50 (ISBN 0-686-27964-6). J M Bryant.

--Loves & Tragedies. (Illus.). 1968. 22.00 (ISBN 0-686-27960-3). J M Bryant.

--One More Time. (Illus.). 1980. 22.00 (ISBN 0-686-27966-2). J M Bryant.

--Out of Darkness. 1971. pap. 6.50 (ISBN 0-686-27962-X). J M Bryant.

--Poems & Lyrics of Life. LC 74-77292. 1974. pap. 5.50 (ISBN 0-686-18745-8). J M Bryant.

--The Reckless Era. 1968. pap. 5.50 (ISBN 0-686-27961-1). J M Bryant.

--The Three Billionaires. 1977. pap. 7.00 (ISBN 0-686-19545-0). J M Bryant.

--The Timetable. (Illus.). 1981. 20.00 (ISBN 0-686-28942-0). J M Bryant.

--The Two Brothers. LC 69-17331. 1974. pap. 6.50 (ISBN 0-686-09047-0). J M Bryant.

Bryant, James McKinley. Tomorrow Tomorrow. 1976. pap. 7.00 (ISBN 0-686-15543-2). J M Bryant.

Bryant, James W. Financial Modelling in Corporate Management. 448p. 1983. 46.00x (ISBN 0-471-10021-8, Pub. by Wiley-Interscience). Wiley.

Bryant, Jane C. Why Art, How Art: A Comprehensive Curriculum Guide. (Illus.). 304p. (Orig.). 1983. pap. text ed. 49.50 Smyth-sewn Perfect binding (ISBN 0-87562-078-7). Spec Child.

Bryant, Jean. Anybody Can Write-A Playful Approach: Ideas for the Unwriter, Beginner & Would-be Writer. 156p. 1985. 6.95 (ISBN 0-931432-21-9). Whatever Pub.

Bryant, Jeannette, ed. Conservation Directory. 27th ed. LC 70-10646. 297p. 1982. 6.00 (ISBN 0-912186-42-9). Natl Wildlife.

--Conservation Directory 1980. 25th rev. ed. LC 70-10646. 290p. 1980. 4.00 (ISBN 0-912186-34-8). Natl Wildlife.

--Conservation Directory, 1984. 29th ed. LC 70-10646. 297p. 1984. 9.00 (ISBN 0-912186-51-8). Natl Wildlife.

--Conservation Directory, 1985. LC 70-10646. 1985. 15.00 (ISBN 0-912186-56-9). Natl Wildlife.

Bryant, Jennings & Anderson, Daniel, eds. Understanding TV: Research in Children's Attention & Comprehension. LC 82-16280. 320p. 1983. 33.50 (ISBN 0-12-138160-9). Acad Pr.

Bryant, Jennings & Zillman, Dolf, eds. Perspectives on Media Effects. (Communication Ser.). 435p. 1985. text ed. 44.00 (ISBN 0-89859-641-6). L Erlbaum Assocs.

Bryant, Jennings, jt. ed. see Zillmann, Dolf.

Bryant, Jim. The Wild Game & Fish Cookbook. (Illus.). 224p. 1984. 15.45i (ISBN 0-316-11327-1, 113271). Little.

Bryant, John. Health & the Developing World. LC 75-87015. (Illus.). 362p. 1972. pap. 8.95x (ISBN 0-8014-9129-0). Cornell U Pr.

--Melville Dissertations, 1924-1980: An Annotated Bibliography & Subject Index. LC 83-5683. xxi, 166p. 1983. lib. bdg. 39.95 (ISBN 0-313-23811-1, BMD/). Greenwood.

Bryant, Joseph, ed. see Shakespeare, William.

Bryant, Joseph A., Jr. Eudora Welty. (Pamphlets on American Writers Ser: No. 66). (Orig.). 1968. pap. 1.25x (ISBN 0-8166-0470-3, MPAW66). U of Minn Pr.

Bryant, Katherine, et al. Basic English for Business Communication. 1984. pap. 11.20 (ISBN 0-02-831360-7); tchrs. manual, key & tests 5.60 (ISBN 0-02-831370-4). Glencoe.

Bryant, Keith L., Jr. Arthur E. Stilwell: Promoter with a Hunch. LC 78-170282. (Illus.). 1971. 12.95x (ISBN 0-8265-1173-2). Vanderbilt U Pr.

--History of the Atchison, Topeka & Santa Fe Railway. LC 81-16024. (Illus.). xxii, 398p. 1982. pap. 10.95 (ISBN 0-8032-6066-0, BB 796, Bison). U of Nebr Pr.

Bryant, Keith L., Jr. & Dethloff, Henry C. A History of American Business. (Illus.). 368p. 1983. pap. 19.95 (ISBN 0-13-389247-6). P-H.

Bryant, Keith L., Jr., jt. auth. see Dethloff, Henry C.

Bryant, Kenneth E. Poems to the God-Child: Structures & Strategies in the Poetry of Surdas. LC 77-80467. (Center for South & Southeast Asian Studies). 1978. 30.00x (ISBN 0-520-03540-2). U of Cal Pr.

Bryant, Kim & Meloan, Becky. Prematurely Yours. Quaintance, Cheryl, ed. (Illus.). 40p. 1985. 20.00 (ISBN 0-9614786-0-8). Sunrise Publ.

Bryant, Laurie J. see Gregory, Joseph T.

Bryant, Lawrence C. Autobiography of Lawrence C. Bryant. 230p. 1971. 15.00 (ISBN 0-686-01113-9); pap. 10.00 (ISBN 0-686-01114-7). L C Bryant.

--Bills & Resolutions Proposed by Negro Legislators in South Carolina. 1967. pap. 5.00 (ISBN 0-686-05557-8). L C Bryant.

--A Guidance Handbook of Junior & Senior Colleges in Mississippi. 1957. pap. 5.00 (ISBN 0-686-05555-1). L C Bryant.

--A Historical & Genealogical Record of Fanny Sills & Related Lines of Nash County, North Carolina. 1968. pap. 10.00 (ISBN 0-686-05560-8). L C Bryant.

--A Historical & Genealogical Record of Lawrence Bryant & Pattie Sessoms' Five Other Sons. 1968. 15.00 (ISBN 0-686-05561-6); pap. 10.00 (ISBN 0-686-05562-4). L C Bryant.

--A Historical & Genealogical Record of Lee Clay & Related Families. 1972. 15.00 (ISBN 0-686-05820-8); pap. 10.00 (ISBN 0-686-05821-6). L C Bryant.

--Negro Lawmakers in the South Carolina Legislature, 1868-1902. 1968. pap. 10.00 (ISBN 0-686-05563-2). L C Bryant.

--Negro Legislators in South Carolina, 1865-1894. 1966. 15.00 (ISBN 0-686-05568-3); pap. 10.00 (ISBN 0-686-05569-1). L C Bryant.

--Negro Legislators in South Carolina, 1868-1902. 1967. 15.00 (ISBN 0-686-05564-0); pap. 10.00 (ISBN 0-686-05565-9). L C Bryant.

--Negro Senators & Representatives in the South Carolina Legislature. 1968. 15.00 (ISBN 0-686-05566-7); pap. 10.00 (ISBN 0-686-05567-5). L C Bryant.

--Record of Achievement of Dr. Lawrence C. Bryant. 1966. 5.00 (ISBN 0-686-05556-X). L C Bryant.

--South Carolina Negro Legislators: A Glorious Success. 1974. 15.00 (ISBN 0-686-05553-5); pap. 10.00 (ISBN 0-686-05554-3). L C Bryant.

Bryant, Lawrence E. & McIntire, Paul, eds. Radiography & Radiation Testing. 2nd ed. (Nondestructive Testing Handbook). (Illus.). 925p. 1984. 99.95 (ISBN 0-931403-00-6, 128). Am Soc Nondestructive.

Bryant Library & Pribek, Glenn M. Pathways to the Past. Houk, Patricia, et al, eds. (gr. 6 up). 1983. 3 by 4" VHS Format 85.00 (ISBN 0-9602242-2-X); 1 by 2" VHS Format 75.00 (ISBN 0-9602242-3-8); tchr's. manual, 20 pp; videotape 15 min. Bryant Library.

Bryant, Lorinda M. Pictures & Their Painters: The History of Paintings. Repr. of 1907 ed. 20.00 (ISBN 0-8482-3444-8). Norwood Edns.

Bryant, Louise. Mirrors of Moscow. LC 73-834. (Russian Studies: Perspectives on the Revolution). xv, 209p. 1973. Repr. of 1923 ed. 20.50 (ISBN 0-88355-030-X). Hyperion Conn.

--Six Red Months in Russia: An Observer's Account of Russia Before & During the Proletarian Dictatorship. LC 70-115578. (Russia Observed, Series 1). 1970. Repr. of 1918 ed. 23.50 (ISBN 0-405-03006-1). Ayer Co Pubs.

Bryant, M., tr. see Goncharov, Ivan A.

Bryant, M. D., ed. The Future of Anglican Theology. LC 84-8983. (Toronto Studies in Theology: Vol. 17). 208p. 1984. 49.95x (ISBN 0-88946-763-3). E Mellen.

Bryant, M. Darrol & Richardson, Herbert W. A Time for Consideration: A Scholarly Appraisal of the Unification Church. 2nd ed. LC 78-61364. (Symposium Ser.: Vol. 3). xi, 332p. 1978. 19.95x (ISBN 0-88946-954-7). E Mellen.

Bryant, M. Darrol & Dayton, Donald W., eds. Coming Kingdom: Essays in American Millennialism & Eschatology. LC 83-82211. (New Era Bks.). xii, 246p. 1984. text ed. 15.95 (ISBN 0-913757-01-2, Pub. by New Era Bks); pap. text ed. 11.95 (ISBN 0-913757-00-4, Pub. by New Era Bks). Paragon Hse.

Bryant, M. Darrol & Hodges, Susan, eds. Exploring Unification Theology. 2nd ed. LC 78-63274. (Conference Ser.: No. 1). 168p. 1978. pap. text ed. 7.95x (ISBN 0-932894-00-3, Pub. by New Era Bks). Paragon Hse.

Bryant, M. Darrol & Mataragnon, Rita H., eds. The Many Faces of Religion & Society. LC 84-26539. (God Ser.). 208p. (Orig.). 1985. 17.95 (ISBN 0-913757-20-9, Pub. by New Era Bks.); pap. 12.95 (ISBN 0-913757-21-7, Pub. by New Era Bks). Paragon Hse.

Bryant, M. Darrol, jt. ed. see Sontag, Frederick.

Bryant, Marcus D. The Art of Christian Caring. 1979. 8.50 (ISBN 0-8272-0015-3). CBP.

Bryant, Margaret M. Maple Sugar Language in Vermont. (Publications of the American Dialect Society Ser.: No. 8). 41p. 1947. pap. 3.85 (ISBN 0-8173-0608-0). U of Ala Pr.

--Proverbs & How to Collect Them. (Publications of the American Dialect Society: No. 4). 25p. 1945. pap. 2.35 (ISBN 0-8173-0604-8). U of Ala Pr.

--A Selected List of Compounds from Present-Day Reading. Bd. with On the Interpretation of Occasional Spellings. Stephenson, Edward A; The Stressed Vowels of Yiddish-American English. Davis, Lawrence M. (Publications of the American Dialect Society: No. 48). 61p. 1967. pap. 5.50 (ISBN 0-8173-0648-X). U of Ala Pr.

Bryant, Margaret M; see Malmstrom, Jean.

Bryant, Margaret M., ed. Current American Usage: How Americans Say It & Write It. LC 62-9735. (Funk & W Bk.). 1965. 11.49 (ISBN 0-308-40056-9). T Y Crowell.

Bryant, Marija & Bryant, Tod. The Working Photographer: The Complete Manual for the Money-Making Professional. 128p. 1985. pap. 7.95 (ISBN 0-380-89526-9). Avon.

Bryant, Marjorie. Recall the Poppies. 1985. pap. 6.00 (ISBN 0-941150-35-6). Barth.

Bryant, Mark. Riddles: Ancient & Modern. LC 83-73464. 208p. 1984. pap. 6.95 (ISBN 0-911745-50-5). P Bedrick Bks.

Bryant, Nellie L. Shades of Blue. 1984. 4.50 (ISBN 0-8062-1705-7). Carlton.

Bryant, Neville J. Examination Review for Medical Technology. 352p. 1983. pap. 15.95 (ISBN 0-7216-2165-1). Saunders.

--An Introduction to Immunohematology. 2nd ed. (Illus.). 448p. 1982. text ed. 27.95 (ISBN 0-7216-2167-8). Saunders.

--Laboratory Immunology & Serology. LC 77-88302. (Illus.). 1979. text ed. 17.95 (ISBN 0-7216-2171-6). Saunders.

--Review Manual for Immunohematology. 352p. 1982. 16.95 (ISBN 0-7216-2166-X). Saunders.

Bryant, Nigel, tr. The High Book of the Grail: A Translation of the 13th Century Romance of "Perlesvaus". 265p. 1978. 26.75x (ISBN 0-8476-6042-7). Rowman.

Bryant, Nigel, tr. see De Troyes, Chretien.

Bryant, Page. Crystals & Thier Use. 64p. 1984. pap. 4.50 (ISBN 0-89540-151-7, SB-151). Sun Pub.

--Earth Changes Survival Handbook. (Illus.). 440p. 1983. pap. 15.00 (ISBN 0-89540-150-9, SB-150). Sun Pub.

Bryant, Pat, ed. Mark of the Beast. (Southern Exposure Ser.). (Illus.). 112p. (Orig.). 1980. pap. 3.00 (ISBN 0-943810-09-4). Inst Southern Studies.

Bryant, Pat, ed. & intro. by. Mark of the Beast. (Southern Exposure Ser.). (Illus.). 112p. (Orig.). 1980. pap. 3.00 (ISBN 0-943810-09-4). Inst Southern Studies.

Bryant, Pat, ed. Stayed on Freedom. (Southern Exposure Ser.). (Illus.). 128p. (Orig.). 1981. pap. 4.50 (ISBN 0-943810-10-8). Inst Southern Studies.

Bryant, Patricia S., jt. ed. see Cohen, Lois K.

Bryant, Paul. Bear Bryant on Winning Football. 240p. 1983. 16.95 (ISBN 0-13-071274-4); pap. 7.95 (ISBN 0-13-071266-3, Reward). P-H.

Bryant, Paula, tr. see Tersac, Helene.

Bryant, Peter & Bradley, Lynette. Children's Reading Problems. 256p. 1985. 24.95x (ISBN 0-631-13682-7); pap. 9.95 (ISBN 0-631-13683-5). Basil Blackwell.

Bryant, Peter, jt. auth. see Bradley, Lynette.

Bryant, Peter, ed. Piaget: Issues & Experiments. 144p. 1982. 35.00x (ISBN 0-901715-16-6, Pub. by Brit Psych Soc England). State Mutual Bk.

Bryant, Peter S. & Johnson, Jane A., eds. Advancing the Two-Year College. LC 81-48480. (Institutional Advancement Ser.: No. 15). 1982. 9.95x (ISBN 0-87589-899-8). Jossey-Bass.

Bryant, Philip, jt. auth. see Seal, Alan.

Bryant, R., jt. auth. see Bryant, B.

Bryant, Ralph C. Controlling Money: The Federal Reserve & Its Critics. LC 82-45983. 150p. 1983. 18.95 (ISBN 0-8157-1136-0); pap. 7.95 (ISBN 0-8157-1135-2). Brookings.

--Financial Interdependence & Variability in Exchange Rates. 1980. pap. 4.95 (ISBN 0-8157-1127-1). Brookings.

--Money & Monetary Policy in Interdependent Nations. LC 80-19225. 584p. 1980. 32.95 (ISBN 0-8157-1130-1); pap. 15.95 (ISBN 0-8157-1129-8). Brookings.

--Notes on the Analysis of Capital Flows to Developing Nations & the "Recycling" Problem. (Working Paper: No. 476). 67p. 1981. 5.00 (ISBN 0-686-36165-2, WP-0476). World Bank.

Bryant, Ramona L. de see De Bryant, Ramona L.

Bryant, Raymond C. & McGorray, J. J. Managing Energy for Buildings. LC 82-84596. 407p. 1983. text ed. 38.00 (ISBN 0-86587-109-4). Gov Insts.

Bryant, Raymond C. & McGorray, J. J., eds. Managing Energy for Industry. (Illus.). 277p. 1983. 38.00 (ISBN 0-86587-108-6). Gov Insts.

Bryant, Rhys. The Pharmaceutical Quality Control Handbook. (Illus.). 220p. 1984. 45.00 (ISBN 0-943330-04-1); pap. 38.00. Aster Pub Corp.

Bryant, Robert D. A World Rule of Law, a Way to Peace. LC 76-24727. 1977. soft bdg. 13.00 (ISBN 0-88247-412-X). R & E Pubs.

Bryant, Rosalie & Oliver, Eloise M. Complete Elementary Physical Education Guide. 1974. 16.95 (ISBN 0-13-159939-9, Parker). P-H.

Bryant, Ry & Vaget, Brian W., eds. Simulation in Strongly Typed Languages: Ada, Pascal, Simula... (SCS Simulation Ser.: Vol. 13, No. 2). 1984. 30.00 (ISBN 0-317-05019-2). Soc Computer Sim.

Bryant, Sandra, jt. auth. see Tucker, Susan M.

Bryant, Sara C. Epaminondas & His Auntie. (Illus.). 16p. 1984. Repr. of 1907 ed. 7.95 (ISBN 0-910220-03-4). Berg.

--How to Tell Stories to Children. LC 72-12693. 1973. Repr. of 1924 ed. 34.00x (ISBN 0-8103-3740-1). Gale.

--How to Tell Stories to Children. 1980. lib. bdg. 59.95 (ISBN 0-8490-3176-1). Gordon Pr.

--How to Tell Stories to Children. (Educational Ser.). 1905. Repr. 27.50 (ISBN 0-8482-7384-2). Norwood Edns.

--Stories to Tell Children. (Educational Ser.). 1911. Repr. 27.50 (ISBN 0-8482-7410-5). Norwood Edns.

Bryant, Shasta M. A Selective Bibliography of Bibliographies of Hispanic American Literature. 2nd ed. (Ilas Guides & Bibliographies Ser.: No. 8). 110p. 1976. pap. 4.95x (ISBN 0-292-77522-9). U of Tex Pr.

--The Spanish Ballad in English. LC 72-81314. (Studies in Romance Languages: No. 8). 264p. 1973. 24.00x (ISBN 0-8131-1280-X). U Pr of Ky.

Bryant, Solena V. Brazil. (World Bibliographical Ser.: No. 57). 246p. 1985. 37.50 (ISBN 1-85109-000-2, Pub. by ABC-Clio Pr England). ABC-Clio.

Bryant, Spurgeon Q., Sr. Ole Nell, Mama, & Me. LC 78-55926. 1978. 4.95 (ISBN 0-87397-137-X). Strode.

Bryant, Steve J., et al. College Algebra. LC 73-81071. 1980. 25.55x (ISBN 0-673-16228-1). Scott F.

Bryant, Steven & Saltz, Daniel. Precalculus & Mathematics: Algebra & Trigonometry. (Illus.). 1980. text ed. 25.55x (ISBN 0-673-16242-7). Scott F.

Bryant, Steven, jt ed. see Chapman, Gary.

Bryant, Susan V., jt. ed. see Malacinski, George M.

Bryant, T. A., compiled by. Today's Dictionary of the Bible. LC 82-12980. 678p. (Orig.). 1982. 15.95 (ISBN 0-87123-569-2, 230569). Bethany Hse.

Bryant, T. H. E. & Lovell, J. MCQs in Radiological Physics. LC 82-4478. 135p. 1983. pap. text ed. 11.00 (ISBN 0-443-02225-9). Churchill.

Bryant, Ted, ed. see Askins, Charles.

Bryant, Tod, jt. auth. see Bryant, Marija.

Bryant, V. W. Metric Spaces: Interation & Application. (Illus.). 120p. 1985. 29.95 (ISBN 0-521-26857-5); pap. 9.95 (ISBN 0-521-31897-1). Cambridge U Pr.

Bryant, Vaughn M. & Holloway, Richard G., eds. Pollen Records of Late Quaternary North American Sediments. (Illus.). 350p. 1985. 35.00 (ISBN 0-931871-01-8). Am Assn Strat.

Bryant, Victor & Postill, Ronald. The Sunday Times Book of Brain Teasers. LC 81-21429. (Illus.). 160p. 1982. pap. 5.95 (ISBN 0-312-77565-2). St Martin.

--The Sunday Times Book of Brain Teasers, Bk. 2. 156p. 1983. 11.95 (ISBN 0-13-875872-7); pap. 4.95 (ISBN 0-13-875864-6). P-H.

Bryant, William C. Poetical Works of William Cullen Bryant. LC 79-85192. 1969. Repr. of 1903 ed. 42.50 (ISBN 0-404-01143-8). AMS Pr.

Bryant, William C., ed. The Letters of William Cullen Bryant: Eighteen Fifty-Eight to Eighteen Sixty-Four, Vol. IV. LC 74-27169. (Illus.). viii, 450p. 1984. 45.00 (ISBN 0-8232-0994-6). Fordham.

--The Letters of William Cullen Bryant, Vol. III: 1849-1857. LC 74-27169. (Illus.). viii, 564p. 1981. 40.00 (ISBN 0-8232-0993-8). Fordham.

--The Library of Poetry & Song: Revised & Enlarged with Recent Authors & Dictionary of Poetical Quotations, 3 vols. LC 72-3178. (Granger Reprint Ser.). Repr. of 1925 ed. Set. 75.00 (ISBN 0-8369-8238-X). Ayer Co Pubs.

--Picturesque America: Or the Land We Live in, 2 vols. 1975. Set. 59.95 (ISBN 0-8184-0212-1). Lyle Stuart.

--Tales of Glauber-Spa, 2 vols. 1972. Repr. of 1832 ed. Vol. 1. lib. bdg. 22.00 (ISBN 0-8422-8012-X); Vol. 2. lib. bdg. 22.00 (ISBN 0-8422-8013-8). Irvington.

Bryant, William C., II & Voss, Thomas G., eds. The Letters of William Cullen Bryant, Vol. 1: 1809-1836. LC 74-27169. (Illus.). viii, 501p. 1975. 40.00 (ISBN 0-8232-0991-1). Fordham.

Bryant, William Cullen, II & Voss, Thomas, eds. The Letters of William Cullen Bryant, Vol. II: 1836-1849. LC 74-27169. (Illus.). viii, 567p. 1977. 40.00 (ISBN 0-8232-0992-X). Fordham.

Bryant, William M. Hegel's Educational Ideas. LC 72-136415. Repr. of 1896 ed. 14.00 (ISBN 0-404-01144-6). AMS Pr.

Bryant, William M., tr. see Hegel, Georg W.

Bryant, Willis R. Mortgage Lending: Fundamentals & Practices. 2nd ed. 1962. text ed. 35.95 (ISBN 0-07-008609-5). McGraw.

Bryant-Greenwood, G. D., et al, eds. Relaxin. 402p. 1982. 81.00 (ISBN 0-444-00643-5, Biomedical Pr). Elsevier.

Bryce, Alexandre. Teacher. 288p. (Orig.). 1981. pap. 2.50 (ISBN 0-523-41012-3). Pinnacle Bks.

Bryce, Charles F., ed. Biochemical Education. (Illus.). 220p. 1981. 33.00 (ISBN 0-7099-0600-5, Pub. by Croom Helm Ltd). Longwood Pub Group.

Bryce, D. & Hobart, A. The Biology & Identification of the Larvae of the Chironomidae. 43p. 1979. Repr. of 1972 ed. 25.00x (ISBN 0-317-07036-3, Pub. by EW Classey UK). State Mutual Bk.

Bryce, D. P. Differential Diagnosis & Treatment of Hoarseness. (Illus.). 88p. 1974. photocopy ed. 19.75x (ISBN 0-398-03166-5). C C Thomas.

Bryce, George. The Hudson's Bay Company, 2 vols. 1910. Set. 65.00 (ISBN 0-8482-7385-0). Norwood Edns.

--Remarkable History of the Hudson's Bay Company: Induding That of the French Traders of Northwestern Canada, & of the Astor Fur Companies. (Research & Source Works Ser.: No. 171). (Illus.). 1968. 29.50 (ISBN 0-8337-0407-9). B Franklin.

Bryce, Glendon E. A Legacy of Wisdom: The Egyptian Contribution to the Wisdom of Israel. LC 74-4984. 336p. 1979. 24.50 (ISBN 0-8387-1576-1). Bucknell U Pr.

Bryce, Herrington J., ed. Cities & Firms. LC 80-8367. (The Urban Roundtable Ser.). 272p. 1980. 25.00x (ISBN 0-669-04042-8). Lexington Bks.

--Revitalizing Cities. (Urban Round Table Ser.: No. 2). (Illus.). 320p. 1979. 29.50x (ISBN 0-669-02846-0). Lexington Bks.

Bryce, Iris. Canals Are My Home. (Illus.). 144p. 1979. 13.50 (ISBN 0-85937-171-9). Sheridan.

--Canals Are My Life. (Illus.). 104p. 1982. 14.50 (ISBN 0-85937-277-4). Sheridan.

Bryce, Ivar. You Only Live Once: Memories of Ian Fleming. rev. ed. (Illus.). 152p. 1985. 14.95x (ISBN 0-297-77022-5, GWN 05235, Pub. by Weidenfeld & Nicolson England). Biblio Dist.

--You Only Live Once: Memories of Ian Fleming. (Foreign Intelligence Bk.). 152p. 1984. Repr. 12.00 (ISBN 0-89093-486-X). U Pubns Amer.

Bryce, J. C., ed. see Smith, Adam.

Bryce, James. The American Commonwealth, 2 vols. 1978. Repr. of 1891 ed. Set. lib. bdg. 87.00 (ISBN 0-8414-0197-7). Folcroft.

--The Hindrances to Good Citizenship. 1909. 29.50x (ISBN 0-686-51399-1). Elliots Bks.

--The Holy Roman Empire. 1978. Repr. of 1911 ed. lib. bdg. 65.00 (ISBN 0-8495-0333-7). Arden Lib.

--The Holy Roman Empire. 1911. 47.50 (ISBN 0-8482-7383-4). Norwood Edns.

--International Relations. LC 66-21391. Repr. of 1922 ed. 20.50x (ISBN 0-8046-0053-8, Pub. by Kennikat). Assoc Faculty Pr.

--Modern Democracies, 2 Vols. 682p. 1983. Repr. of 1924 ed. Set. lib. bdg. 85.00 (ISBN 0-8495-0637-9). Arden Lib.

--Reflections on the American Institutions: Selections from the American Commonwealth. 12.00 (ISBN 0-8446-0517-4). Peter Smith.

--South America: Observations & Impressions. (Latin America in the 20th Century Ser.). 1977. Repr. of 1912 ed. lib. bdg. 69.50 (ISBN 0-306-70835-3). Da Capo.

--South America: Observations & Impressions. 1977. Repr. of 1912 ed. lib. bdg. 45.00 (ISBN 0-8482-3380-8). Norwood Edns.

--Study of American History. LC 72-136056. 1971. Repr. of 1922 ed. lib. bdg. 22.50x (ISBN 0-8371-5206-2, BRAH). Greenwood.

--The Theory of the Holy Roman Empire. (Illus.). 157p. 1984. Repr. of 1866 ed. 77.85 (ISBN 0-89901-145-4). Found Class Reprints.

--Transcaucasia & Ararat Being Notes of a Vacation Tour in the Autumn of 1876. LC 73-115509. (Russia Observed, Series 1). 1970. Repr. of 1896 ed. 26.50 (ISBN 0-405-03007-X). Ayer Co Pubs.

Bryce, James & Polick, Bill. Power Basics of Basketball. LC 84-18342. (Power Basics of Sports Ser.). 112p. 1985. pap. 5.95 (ISBN 0-13-688300-1, Busn). P-H.

--The Power Basics of Football. LC 84-22838. (Power Basics of Sports Ser.). 112p. 1985. pap. 5.95 (ISBN 0-13-688318-4, Busn). P-H.

Bryce, James, et al. Power Basics of Soccer. LC 84-22839. (Power Basics of Sports Ser.). 112p. 1985. pap. 5.95 (ISBN 0-13-688326-5, Busn). P-H.

--The Power Basics of Baseball. LC 84-22839. 109p. 1985. pap. 5.95 (ISBN 0-13-688292-7, Busn). P-H.

Bryce, James B. American Commonwealth, 3 vols. LC 73-39551. Repr. of 1888 ed. Set. 150.00 (ISBN 0-404-03770-4). Vol. 1 (ISBN 0-404-03771-2). Vol. 2 (ISBN 0-404-03772-0). Vol. 3 (ISBN 0-404-03773-9). AMS Pr.

--Essays & Addresses in War Time. facs. ed. LC 68-16914. (Essay Index Reprint Ser). 1918. 20.00 (ISBN 0-8369-0260-2). Ayer Co Pubs.

--The Holy Roman Empire. new enl. rev. ed. LC 75-41045. (BCL Ser. II). Repr. of 1913 ed. 28.50 (ISBN 0-404-14516-7). AMS Pr.

--Impressions of South Africa. LC 73-76495. (Illus.). Repr. of 1897 ed. 24.75x (ISBN 0-8371-1315-6, BSA&, Pub. by Negro U Pr). Greenwood.

--Predictions of Hamilton & De Tocqueville. LC 78-63775. (Johns Hopkins University. Studies in the Social Sciences. Fifth Ser. 1887: 9). Repr. of 1887 ed. 11.50 (ISBN 0-404-61041-2). AMS Pr.

--The Predictions of Hamilton & De Tocqueville. 1973. pap. 9.00 (ISBN 0-384-06100-1). Johnson Repr.

--Studies in Contemporary Biography. facsimile ed. LC 77-156619. (Essay Index Reprint Ser). Repr. of 1903 ed. 25.50 (ISBN 0-8369-2271-9). Ayer Co Pubs.

--Studies in History & Jurisprudence, 2 Vols. facs. ed. LC 68-8444. (Essay Index Reprint Ser). 1968. Repr. of 1901 ed. Set. 44.00 (ISBN 0-8369-0261-0). Ayer Co Pubs.

--University & Historical Addresses. facs. ed. LC 68-55842. (Essay Index Reprint Ser). 1913. 20.00 (ISBN 0-8369-0262-9). Ayer Co Pubs.

Bryce, James R. Basic Finance: An Introduction to Financial Theory, Practices & Institutions. 158p. 1980. pap. text ed. 6.95x (ISBN 0-89641-038-2). American Pr.

--First Principles of Accounting. (Illus.). 197p. (Orig.). 1983. pap. text ed. 9.95x (ISBN 0-89641-115-X). American pr.

Bryce, Lawrence. To Love a Nun. (Illus.). 1978. 49.75 (ISBN 0-89266-114-3). Am Classical Coll Pr.

Bryce, Margaret. Physical Therapy After Amputation: The Treatment of the Unilateral Lower-Extremity Amputee. (Illus.). 104p. 1954. pap. 4.25x (ISBN 0-299-01153-4). U of Wis Pr.

Bryce, Marvin & Lloyd, June C. Treating Families in the Home: An Alternative to Placement. (Illus.). 352p. 1981. 35.50x (ISBN 0-398-04085-0). C C Thomas.

Bryce, Marvin, jt. auth. see Maybanks, Sheila.

Bryce, Mary C. Place of Pride: The Role of the Bishops in the Development of Catechesis in the United States. LC 84-17065. 227p. 1985. 25.95x (ISBN 0-8132-0595-6). Cath U Pr.

Bryce, R. A., et al. Group Theory. (Lectures Notes in Mathematics: Vol. 573). 1977. pap. 13.00 (ISBN 0-387-08131-3). Springer-Verlag.

Bryce, Smith, ed. Photo Chemistry, Vol. 15. 576p. 1985. 197.00 (ISBN 0-85186-135-0, Pub. by Royal Soc Chem UK). Heyden.

Bryce, W. A., tr. see Jelinek, Z. K.

Bryce-Laporte, Roy S., ed. Sourcebook on New Immigration, Vol. II. 302p. 1980. pap. text ed. 6.95x (ISBN 0-87855-796-2). Transaction Bks.

--Sourcebook on New Immigration. LC 78-64477. 511p. 1979. 29.95 (ISBN 0-87855-305-3). Transaction Bks.

Bryce-Smith, D. Photochemistry, Vols. 1-10. Incl. Vol. 1. 1968-69 Literature. 1970. 30.00 (ISBN 0-85186-005-2); Vol. 2. 1969-70 Literature. 1971. 47.00 (ISBN 0-85186-015-X); Vol. 3. 1970-71 Literature. 1972. 47.00 (ISBN 0-85186-025-7); Vol. 4. 1971-72 Literature. 1973. 50.00 (ISBN 0-85186-035-4); Vol. 5. 1972-73 Literature. 1974. 56.00 (ISBN 0-85186-045-1); Vol. 6. 1973-74 Literature. 1975. 70.00 (ISBN 0-85186-055-9); Vol. 7. 1974-75 Literature. 1976. 82.00 (ISBN 0-85186-065-6); Vol. 8. 1975-76 Literature. 1977. 95.00 (ISBN 0-85186-075-3); Vol. 9. 1976-77 Literature. 1978. 97.00 (ISBN 0-85186-085-0); Vol. 10. 1979. 102.00 (ISBN 0-85186-590-9). LC 73-17909. Am Chemical.

Bryce-Smith, D. & Dickerson, J. W. Environmental Influences on Pre & Postnatal Development. 104p. 1981. Write for Info. (ISBN 0-677-05990-6). Gordon.

Bryce-Smith, D. & Gilbert, A. The Organic Photochemistry of Benzene-I. 18p. 1976. pap. text ed. 14.00 (ISBN 0-08-020464-3). Pergamon.

Bryce-Smith, R., jt. ed. see Lee, J. A.

Bryce-Smith, Roger, jt. auth. see Ostlere, Gordon.

Bryceson & Pfaltzgraff. Leprosy. 2nd ed. (Medicine in the Tropics Ser.). (Illus.). 208p. 1978. pap. text ed. 12.00 (ISBN 0-443-01588-0). Churchill.

Brycha, M. Automatic Transmissions. 2nd ed. 1982. 26.95 (ISBN 0-13-054577-5). P-H.

Brychta, Alex. Wishwhat. (Illus.). 32p. (ps-1). 1984. bds. 9.95 laminated (ISBN 0-19-279786-7, Pub. by Oxford U Pr Childrens). Merrimack Pub Cir.

Bryde, Konrad & Gyllstoem, Walter, eds. Norwegian Directory of Commerce, 1979, 2 vols. 54th ed. LC 66-4838. Orig. Title: Norges Handels-Kalendar. 1979. Set. 80.00x (ISBN 82-7030-054-3). Intl Pubns Serv.

Bryden, Bill see Goldoni, Carolo.

Bryden, David P. A Phantom Doctrine: The Origins & Effects of Just vs. Marinette County. 117p. (Reprinted from 1978 ABF Research Journal No. 3). 1978. 3.25 (ISBN 0-317-33350-X). Am Bar Foun.

Bryden, James D. Your Child's Experience in Speech Correction. (Illus.). 1966. pap. text ed. 0.40x (ISBN 0-8134-0851-2, 851). Interstate.

Bryden, John M. Tourism & Development: A Case Study of the Commonwealth Caribbean. LC 73-77260. pap. 62.00 (ISBN 0-317-26084-7, 2024415). Bks Demand UMI.

Bryden, John R. & Hughes, David G., eds. An Index of Gregorian Chant. Incl. Vol. 1. Alphabetical Index; Vol. 2. Thematic Index. LC 71-91626. 1969. Set. 55.00x (ISBN 0-674-44875-8). Harvard U Pr.

Bryden, Kenneth. Old Age Pensions & Policy Making in Canada. (Canadian Public Administration Ser.). 288p. 1974. 17.50x (ISBN 0-7735-0206-8); pap. 7.50 (ISBN 0-7735-0221-1). McGill-Queens U Pr.

Bryden, M. P. Laterality, Functional Asymetry in the Intact Brain. (Perspectives in Neurolinguistics, Neuropsychology & Psycholingusitcs Ser.). 315p. 1982. 35.00 (ISBN 0-12-138180-3). Acad Pr.

Bryden, Ronald. Old Movies. (National Theatre Plays Ser.). 1977. pap. text ed. 7.50x (ISBN 0-435-23141-3). Heinemann Ed.

Bryden, W. W. The Christian's Knowledge of God. 278p. 1960. 8.50 (ISBN 0-227-67434-0). Attic Pr.

Brydensholt, Hans H., jt. auth. see European Committee on Crime Problems.

Brydges, Egerton, ed. see Milton, John.

Brydges, Grey. Horae Subsecivae: Observations & Discourses. LC 70-26258. (English Experience Ser.: No. 232). 542p. 1970. Repr. of 1620 ed. 67.00 (ISBN 90-221-0232-7). Walter J Johnson.

Brydges, Harford J. The Dynasty of the Kajars. LC 73-6272. (The Middle East Ser.). Repr. of 1833 ed. 46.00 (ISBN 0-405-05327-4). Ayer Co Pubs.

Brydges, Samuel E. British Bibliographer, 4 Vols. LC 3-25390. Repr. of 1814 ed. Set. 185.00 (ISBN 0-404-01200-0). AMS Pr.

--Censura Literaria, 10 Vols. in 5. LC 3-25387. Repr. of 1809 ed. 250.00 (ISBN 0-404-01210-8). AMS Pr.

Brydon, Norman F. The Passaic River: Past, Present, Future. (Illus.). 400p. 1974. 30.00x (ISBN 0-8135-0770-7). Rutgers U Pr.

Brydson, J. Rubber Chemistry. (Illus.). 458p. 1978. 89.00 (ISBN 0-85334-779-4, Pub. by Elsevier Applied Sci England). Elsevier.

Brydson, J. & Peacock, D. G., eds. Principles of Plastics Extrusion: A Teaching Programmer. (Illus.). 108p. 1973. 9.25 (ISBN 0-85334-563-5, Pub. by Elsevier Applied Sci England). Elsevier.

Brydson, J. A., ed. Developments with Natural Rubber. (Illus.). 148p. 1967. 16.75 (ISBN 0-85334-062-5, Pub. by Elsevier Applied Sci England). Elsevier.

Brydson, J. A., jt. ed. see Whelan, A.

Brye, David L. Wisconsin Voting Patterns in the Twentieth Century, 1900 to 1950. Freidel, Frank, ed. LC 78-62376. (Modern American History Ser.: Vol. 3). 1979. lib. bdg. 43.00 (ISBN 0-8240-3627-1). Garland Pub.

Brye, David L., ed. European Immigration & Ethnicity in the United States & Canada: A Historical Bibliography. LC 82-24306. (Clio Bibliography Ser.: No. 7). 458p. 1982. 64.00 (ISBN 0-87436-258-X). ABC Clio.

Brye, Joseph. Basic Principles of Music Theory. (Illus.). 278p. 1965. 31.95 (ISBN 0-394-34410-3). Knopf.

Bryen, Diane N. Inquiries into Child Language. 400p. 1982. text ed. 31.43 (ISBN 0-205-07642-4, 2476428). Allyn.

Bryen, Diane N., jt. auth. see Gerber, Adele.

Bryer, Anthony. The Empire of Trebizond & the Pontos. 366p. 1980. 65.00x (ISBN 0-86078-062-7, Pub. by Variorum). State Mutual Bk.

Bryer, Anthony & Winfield, David. The Byzantine Monuments & Topography of the Pontos, 2 vols, Vol. 20. LC 84-1661. (Dumbarton Oaks Studies). (Illus.). 752p. 1985. Set. 80.00x (ISBN 0-88402-122-X). Dumbarton Oaks.

Bryer, J. R. & Rees, R. A., eds. Emerson Bibliographies. LC 80-2526. (AMS Anthology Ser.). 34.50 (ISBN 0-404-19255-6). AMS Pr.

Bryer, Jackson. Conversations with Lillian Hellman. (Literary Conversations Ser.). 1986. 17.95 (ISBN 0-87805-270-4); pap. 9.95 (ISBN 0-87805-271-2). U Pr of Miss.

--Critical Reputation of F. Scott Fitzgerald: A Bibliographical Study. xviii, 434p. 1967. 30.00 (ISBN 0-208-00412-2, Archon). Shoe String.

--F. Scott Fitzgerald in His Own Time: A Miscellany. Bruccoli, Matthew, ed. LC 76-126919. 95.60 (ISBN 0-8357-9365-6, 2003018). Bks Demand UMI.

Bryer, Jackson, ed. F. Scott Fitzgerald: The Critical Reception. (American Critical Tradition Ser). (Illus.). 1978. lib. bdg. 22.50 (ISBN 0-89102-111-6). B Franklin.

Bryer, Jackson, et al. Hamlin Garland & the Critics: An Annotated Bibliography. LC 75-183300. v, 280p. 1973. 12.50x (ISBN 0-87875-020-7). Whitston Pub.

Bryer, Jackson R. The Critical Reputation of F. Scott Fitzgerald: A Bibliographical Study Supplement I Through 1981. 542p. 1984. 45.00 (ISBN 0-208-01489-6, Archon Bks). Shoe String.

Bryer, Jackson R., ed. The Short Stories of F. Scott Fitzgerald: New Approaches in Criticism. 416p. 1982. pap. 8.95x (ISBN 0-299-09084-1). U of Wis Pr.

--Sixteen Modern American Authors: A Survey of Research & Criticism. LC 73-97454. 672p. 1973. 25.00 (ISBN 0-8223-0297-7). Duke.

Bryer, Jackson R., ed. see Fitzgerald, F. Scott.

Bryer, Jackson R., ed. see O'Neill, Eugene.

Bryer, R. A. & Brignal, T. J. Accounting for British Steel: A Financial Analysis of the Failure of BSC. 320p. 1982. text ed. 37.50x (ISBN 0-566-00531-X). Gower Pub Co.

Bryer, Robin. Jolie Brise: A Tall Ship's Tale. (Illus.). 256p. 1983. 21.00 (ISBN 0-436-07181-9, Pub. by Secker & Warburg UK). David & Charles.

Bryers, R. W., ed. see Ash Deposit & Corrosion from Impurities in Combustion Gases Symposium, June 26-July 1, 1977, New England College, Henniker, New Hampshire.

Bryers, Richard W., ed. Fouling & Slagging Resulting from Impurities in Combustion Gases. LC 83-80600. 550p. 1983. text ed. 45.00 (ISBN 0-939204-18-5, 81-18). Eng Found.

Bryfogle, R. Charles. City in Print: An Urban Studies Bibliography. Incl. City in Print Supplement One. 1975. (ISBN 0-88874-046-8). 1974. 35.00 set (ISBN 0-88874-003-4). City in Print-Bibl Proj.

--City in Print: An Urban Studies Bibliography, Supplement Three. 1979. pap. 15.00 (ISBN 0-918010-01-2). City in Print-Bibl Proj.

--City in Print: An Urban Studies Bibliography, Supplement Two. 1977. pap. 12.00 (ISBN 0-918010-00-4). City in Print-Bibl Proj.

Bryfonski, Dedria, ed. Contemporary Authors Autobiography Series, Vol. 1. 500p. 1984. 72.00x (ISBN 0-8103-4500-5). Gale.

Bryher. The Coin of Carthage. LC 63-13687. 1965. pap. 4.95 (ISBN 0-15-618407-9, Harv). HarBraceJ.

Bryher, Winifred. The Days of Mars: A Memoir, Nineteen Forty to Nineteen Forty-Six. 160p. 1981. pap. 7.95 (ISBN 0-7145-2745-9, Dist by Scribner). M Boyars.

Bryher, Winifred, jt. ed. see MacPherson, Kenneth.

Bryjak, George J., jt. auth. see Soroka, Michael A.

Bryk, Felix. Circumcision in Man & Woman: Its History, Psychology & Ethnology. LC 72-9625. Repr. of 1934 ed. 27.50 (ISBN 0-404-57420-3). AMS Pr.

--Dark Rapture: The Sex Life of the African Negro. Norton, Arthur J., tr. LC 72-9712. Repr. of 1939 ed. 14.50 (ISBN 0-404-57421-1). AMS Pr.

Brykowski, F. J., ed. Ammonia & Synthesis Gas: Recent & Energy-Saving Processes. LC 81-11033. (Chem. Tech. Rev. 193; Energy Tech. Rev. 68). (Illus.). 354p. 1982. 48.00 (ISBN 0-8155-0859-X). Noyes.

Bryl, Y. First Snow. 288p. 1982. 9.45 (ISBN 0-8285-2489-0, Pub. by Progress Pubs USSR). Imported Pubns.

Brylawski, E. Fulton & Goldman, Abe, eds. Legislative History of the 1909 Copyright Act, 6 vols. 1976. Set. text ed. 225.00x (ISBN 0-8377-0806-0). Rothman.

Bryld, Claus, et al. Fremad og Aldrig Glemme: Ti Aars Forskning i Arbejderbevaegelsens Historie. Callesen, Gerd, et al, eds. (Illus.). 328p. (Orig., Danish.). 1981. pap. 19.50 (ISBN 87-87739-14-3). Kent Popular.

Brym, Robert J. Intellectuals & Politics. (Controversies in Sociology Ser.: No. 9). (Orig.). 1980. text ed. 19.95x (ISBN 0-04-322005-3). Allen Unwin.

--The Jewish Intelligentsia & Russian Marxism: A Sociological Study of Intellectual Radicalism & Ideological Divergence. LC 77-14724. 1978. 16.95x (ISBN 0-8052-3685-6). Schocken.

Brym, Robert J., jt. auth. see Zaslavsky, Victor.

Brymer, Harvey P. The Most Memorable Passages of the New Testament Fully & Dramatically Illustrated. (Promotion of the Arts Library). (Illus.). 141p. 1982. 69.85 (ISBN 0-86650-039-1). Gloucester Art.

Brymer, Jack. Clarinet. LC 77-275. (The Yehudi Menuhin Music Guides Ser.). (Illus.). 1977. 14.95 (ISBN 0-02-871430-X); pap. 9.95 (ISBN 0-02-871440-7). Schirmer Bks.

Brymer, Robert A. Introduction to Hotel & Restaurant Management: A Book of Readings. 3rd ed. 1984. pap. text ed. 14.95 (ISBN 0-8403-3283-1, 40328301). Kendall-Hunt.

Bryna, J. A Crow for Courage. 1979. 3.95 (ISBN 0-937540-01-3, HPP-12). Human Policy Pr.

Bryna, Stevens. Deborah Sampson Goes to War. LC 83-20950. (Carolrhoda On My Own Bks.). (Illus.). 48p. (gr. k-4). 1984. PLB 8.95 (ISBN 0-87614-254-4). Carolrhoda Bks.

Bryne, James, jt. auth. see Anderson, Scott.

Bryne, P. & Cadman, B. D. Risk: Uncertainty & Decision Making in Property Management. 130p. 1984. 30.00 (ISBN 0-419-11950-7, 6673, Pub. by E & FN Spon England). Methuen Inc.

Bryne, Renee. Let's Talk about Stammering: Information & Practical Help for All Ages. (Illus.). 127p. 1983. text ed. 16.95x (ISBN 0-04-616024-8); pap. 7.95 (ISBN 0-04-616025-6). Allen Unwin.

Bryne, Richard. The Complete Art of Breaking. Lee, Mike, ed. (Ser. 434). 128p. 1984. pap. 7.95 (ISBN 0-89750-099-7). Ohara Pubns.

Bryne, Robert. Skycsraper. 1985. pap. 3.95 (ISBN 0-451-13557-1, Sig). NAL.

Brynger, Hans. Clinical Kidney Transplant. (Transplantation Proceedings Reprint). 240p. 1982. 52.00 (ISBN 0-8089-1523-1, 790713). Grune.

Brynn, Edward. The Church of Ireland in the Age of Catholic Emancipation. Stansky, Peter & Hume, Leslie, eds. LC 81-48356. (Modern British History Ser.). 360p. 1982. lib. bdg. 85.00 (ISBN 0-8240-5151-3). Garland Pub.

--Crown & Castle. (Illus.). 176p. 1982. 12.95 (ISBN 0-905140-11-7, Pub. by O'Brien Pr Ireland). Irish Bks Media.

--Crown & Castle: British Rule in Ireland, 1800-1830. (Illus.). 176p. (Orig.). 1985. pap. 9.95 (ISBN 0-86278-089-6, Pub. by O'Brien Pr Ireland). Irish Bks Media.

Brynner, Joseph F., jt. ed. see Schantz, Maria E.

Brynner, Yul & Reed, Susan. The Yul Brynner Cookbook: Foods Fit for the King & You. LC 82-40005. 252p. 1982. 16.95 (ISBN 0-8128-2882-8). Stein & Day.

Brynteson, Donna, jt. auth. see Brynteson, Paul.

Brynteson, Paul & Brynteson, Donna. Fitness & Faith. 224p. 1985. pap. 7.95 (ISBN 0-8407-5920-7). Nelson.

Brynteson, Paul, jt. auth. see Cundiff, David E.

Brysch, O. P. & Ball, W. E. Expansion Behavior of Coal During Carbonization: A Literature Study. (Research Bulletin Ser.: No. 11). iv, 60p. 1951. write for info. Inst Gas Tech.

Bryskett, Lodowick. A Discourse of Civil Life: Containing the Ethike Part of Morall Philosophie. LC 70-38162. (English Experience Ser.: No. 358). 288p. 1971. Repr. of 1606 ed. 40.00 (ISBN 90-221-0358-7). Walter J Johnson.

Bryson & Bentley. Ability Grouping of Public School Students: Legal Aspects of Tracking Methods. 190p. 1980. 15.00 (ISBN 0-87215-332-0). Michie Co.

Bryson, A. E. & Ho, Y. C. Applied Optimal Control: Optimization, Estimation, & Control. rev. ed. LC 75-16114. (Illus.). 481p. 1981. pap. text ed. 27.95 (ISBN 0-89116-228-3). Hemisphere Pub.

Bryson, Bill. Blook of Bunders. (Orig.). 1982. pap. 3.95 (ISBN 0-440-50645-X, Dell Trade Pbks). Dell.

--The Facts on File Dictionary of Troublesome Words. 176p. 1984. 15.95x (ISBN 0-87196-889-4). Facts on File.

--The Penguin Dictionary of Troublesome Words. (Reference Ser.). 264p. 1984. pap. 5.95 (ISBN 0-14-051130-X). Penguin.

Bryson, Carlton W. & Gray, Allan W. Numerical Trigonometry: Syllabus. 1973. pap. text ed. 7.55 (ISBN 0-89420-050-X, 355110); cassette recordings 70.70 (ISBN 0-89420-164-6, 355000). Natl Book.

Bryson, Conrey. Down Went McGinty: El Paso in the Wonderful Nineties. LC 76-52178. 1977. 10.00 (ISBN 0-87404-056-6). Tex Western.

Bryson, Gladys. Man & Society: The Scottish Inquiry of the Eighteenth Century. LC 66-21657. Repr. of 1945 ed. 29.50x (ISBN 0-678-00373-4). Kelley.

Bryson, Harold, jt. auth. see Leavell, Landrum P.

Bryson, Harold T. How Faith Works. LC 84-17601. 1985. pap. 5.95 (ISBN 0-8054-1394-4). Broadman.

--Increasing the Joy: Studies in I John. LC 81-67200. 1982. pap. 5.95 (ISBN 0-8054-1390-1). Broadman.

--The Reality of Hell & the Goodness of God. LC 83-51674. 192p. 1984. pap. 4.95 (ISBN 0-8423-5279-1); leader's guide 2.95 (ISBN 0-8423-5280-5). Tyndale.

Bryson, Harold T. & Taylor, James C. Building Sermons to Meet People's Needs. LC 78-74962. 1980. 7.95 (ISBN 0-8054-2109-2). Broadman.

Bryson, Jeff B. & Bryson, Rebecca B., eds. Dual-Career Couples. LC 77-89983. (A Special Issue of Psychology of Women Quaterly). 120p. 1978. pap. 9.95x (ISBN 0-87705-371-5). Human Sci Pr.

Bryson, John, ed. The World of Armand Hammer. (Illus.). 1985. write for info. Abrams.

Bryson, Joseph E. & Detty, Elizabeth W. The Legal Aspects of Censorship of Public School Library & Instructional Materials. 248p. 1982. 20.00 (ISBN 0-87215-556-0). Michie Co.

Bryson, Judy, ed. Baptist Dishes Worth Blessing. LC 78-631. (Illus.). 300p. 1978. 6.95 (ISBN 0-88289-188-X). Pelican.

Bryson, L., et al, eds. see Conference on Science-Philosophy & Religion-13th Symposium.

Bryson, L., et al, eds. see Conference on Science - Philosophy & Religion - 6th Symposium.

Bryson, L., et al, eds. see Conference On Science - Philosophy And Religion - 7th Symposium.

Bryson, Linda R. Are You Ready to Quit Smoking? 80p. 1983. pap. text ed. 7.95 (ISBN 0-8403-2988-1). Kendall-Hunt.

Bryson, Lyman, ed. Science & Freedom. facsimile ed. LC 71-156620. (Essay Index Reprint Ser). Repr. of 1947 ed. 18.00 (ISBN 0-8369-2385-5). Ayer Co Pubs.

Bryson, Lyman, ed. see Institute for Religious & Social Studies.

Bryson, Norman. Vision & Painting: The Logic of the Gaze. LC 82-10901. (Illus.). 208p. 1983. Repr. 18.95x (ISBN 0-300-02855-5). Yale U Pr.

--Word & Image: French Painting of the Ancient Regime. LC 81-10124. 304p. 1983. pap. 17.95 (ISBN 0-521-27654-3). Cambridge U Pr.

Bryson, Norman, jt. ed. see Kappeler, Susanne.

Bryson, Peter. Comprehensive Review in Clinical Toxicology. 1985. text ed. 30.00 (ISBN 0-8391-2084-2, 22128). Univ Park.

Bryson, Phillip J. The Consumer Under Socialist Planning: The East German Case. LC 84-8270. 219p. 1984. 26.95x (ISBN 0-03-071464-8). Praeger.

Bryson, R. A. & Hare, F., eds. Climates of North America. LC 74-477739. (World Survey of Climatology Ser.: Vol. 11). 420p. 1974. 113.00 (ISBN 0-444-41062-7). Elsevier.

Bryson, R. E. & Kutzbach, J. E., eds. Air Pollution. LC 68-54859. (CCG Resource Papers Ser.: No. 2). (Illus.). 1968. pap. text ed. 4.00 (ISBN 0-89291-049-6). Assn Am Geographers.

Bryson, R. Eugene, Jr. Robert M. Trueblood, CPA: The Consummate Professional. LC 76-48284. (Research Monograph: No. 75). 302p. 1977. spiral bdg. 35.00 (ISBN 0-88406-112-4). Ga St U Busn Pub.

Bryson, Rebecca B., jt. ed. see Bryson, Jeff B.

Bryson, Reid A. & Murray, Thomas J. Climates of Hunger: Mankind & the World's Changing Weather. LC 76-53649. (Illus.). 190p. 1977. 27.50x (ISBN 0-299-07370-X); pap. 10.00x (ISBN 0-299-07374-2). U of Wis Pr.

Bryson, Sandy. Search Dog Training. (Illus.). 359p. (Orig.). 1984. pap. 12.50 (ISBN 0-910286-94-9). Boxwood.

Bryson, Susan M. Understanding APL. LC 82-18462. (An Alfred Handy Guide Ser.). 45p. 1982. pap. 3.50 (ISBN 0-88284-220-X). Alfred Pub.

Bryson, Thomas A. An American Consular Officer in the Middle East in the Jacksonian Era: A Biography of William Brown Hodgson, 1801-1871. LC 79-44344. 1979. 9.95 (ISBN 0-89583-010-8). Resurgens Pubns.

--Seeds of Mideast Crisis: The United States Diplomatic Role in the Middle East During World War II. LC 80-15896. 224p. 1981. lib. bdg. 18.95 (ISBN 0-89950-019-6). McFarland & Co.

--Tars, Turks & Tankers: The Role of the United States Navy in the Middle East, Eighteen Hundred to Nineteen Seventy-Nine. LC 80-12281. 283p. 1980. lib. bdg. 20.00 (ISBN 0-8108-1306-8). Scarecrow.

--United States-Middle East Diplomatic Relations 1784-1978: An Annotated Bibliography. LC 78-26754. 219p. 1979. lib. bdg. 17.50 (ISBN 0-8108-1197-9). Scarecrow.

--Walter George Smith. 225p. 1978. 19.95x (ISBN 0-8132-0539-5). Cath U Pr.

Bryson, Vernon & Vogel, Henry J., eds. Evolving Genes & Proteins: A Symposium. 1965. 83.50 (ISBN 0-12-138250-8). Acad Pr.

Bryson, W. H. The Equity Side of the Exchequer. LC 73-93394. (Cambridge Studies in English Legal History). 280p. 1975. 42.50 (ISBN 0-521-20406-2). Cambridge U Pr.

Bryson, William. The Palace Under the Alps & Over Two Hundred Other Unusual, Unspoiled & Infrequently Visited Spots in Sixteen European Countries. (Illus.). 250p. 1985. 16.95 (ISBN 0-312-92635-9). Congdon & Weed.

Bryson, William H. Bibliography of Virginia Legal History Before Nineteen Hundred. LC 78-26684. x, 133p. 1979. 14.95x (ISBN 0-8139-0773-X). U Pr of Va.

--Census of Law Books in Colonial Virginia. LC 77-22067. xxvii, 90p. 1978. 12.00x (ISBN 0-8139-0746-2). U Pr of Va.

--A Dictionary of Sigla & Abbreviations to & in Law Books Before 1607. LC 75-5675. (Virginia Legal Studies). 224p. 1975. 20.00x (ISBN 0-8139-0615-6). U Pr of Va.

--Handbook of Virginia Civil Procedure. 451p. 1983. 35.00 (ISBN 0-87215-638-9). Michie Co.

--Legal Education in Virginia, Seventeen Seventy-Nine to Nineteen Seventy-Nine. LC 81-7462. (Illus.). 600p. 1982. 47.50x (ISBN 0-8139-0901-5). U Pr of Va.

Bryson, William H., ed. The Virginia Law Reporters Before 1880. LC 77-21451. 130p. 1977. 9.75x (ISBN 0-8139-0747-0). U Pr of Va.

Brzezinski, J., ed. Consciousness: Methodological & Psychological Approaches. (Poznan Studies Ser.: Vol. 8). 206p. 1985. pap. text ed. 21.25x (ISBN 90-6203-537-X, Pub. by Rodopi Holland). Humanities.

Brzezinski, Z. Dilemmas of Change in Soviet Politics. 163p. 1969. write for info. Ukrainian Pol.

Brzezinski, Zbigniew. Between Two Ages: America's Role in the Technetronic Era. 1976. pap. 4.95 (ISBN 0-14-004314-4). Penguin.

--Between Two Ages: America's Role in the Technetronic Era. LC 82-15867. xvii, 334p. 1982. Repr. of 1970 ed. lib. bdg. 35.00x (ISBN 0-313-23498-1, BRZB). Greenwood.

--Power & Principle: Memoirs of the National Security Advisor 1977-1981. 1983. 22.50 (ISBN 0-374-23663-1); pap. 11.95 (ISBN 0-374-51877-7). FS&G.

Brzezinski, Zbigniew & Huntington, Samuel P. Political Power: U. S. A., U. S. S. R. LC 82-9178. xiv, 461p. 1982. Repr. lib. bdg. 35.00x (ISBN 0-313-23497-3, BRZP). Greenwood.

Brzezinski, Zbigniew & Kupperman, Robert H. The International Implications of the Papal Assassination Attempt: A Case of State-Sponsored Terrorism, Vol. VI. (Significant Issues Ser.: No. 20). 23p. 1984. 12.95 (ISBN 0-89206-073-5). CSI Studies.

Brzezinski, Zbigniew, ed. Africa & the Communist World. 1963. 28.50x (ISBN 0-8047-0179-2). Stanford U Pr.

Brzezinski, Zbigniew K. Ideology & Power in Soviet Politics. LC 76-6571. 1976. Repr. of 1962 ed. lib. bdg. 22.50x (ISBN 0-8371-8880-6, BRIP). Greenwood.

--Soviet Bloc: Unity & Conflict. rev. & enl. ed. LC 67-12531. (Russian Research Center Studies: No. 37). 1967. 32.50x (ISBN 0-674-82545-4); pap. 11.00x (ISBN 0-674-82548-9). Harvard U Pr.

Brzin, M., et al, eds. Cholinesterases: Fundamental & Applied Aspects. LC 84-12062. xiv, 527p. 1984. 90.00x (ISBN 3-11-009873-3). De Gruyter.

--Synaptic Constituents in Health & Disease: Proceedings of the Third Meeting of the European Society for Neurochemistry, Bled, August 31st-Sept, 5th, 1980. (Illus.). 760p. 1980. 150.00 (ISBN 0-08-025921-9). Pergamon.

Btesh, S., ed. Drug Abuse: Nonmedical Use of Dependence-Producing Drugs. LC 76-190227. (Advances in Experimental Medicine & Biology Ser.: Vol. 20). 289p. 1972. 37.50x (ISBN 0-306-39020-5, Plenum Pr). Plenum Pub.

Bua & Barnes, eds. Actors Almanac: Original Scene Book. LC 83-18995. (Actors Almanac Ser.: Vol. 1). 1984. pap. 4.95 (ISBN 0-913290-54-8). Camaro Pub.

Buachalla, Seamus O., ed. A Significant Irish Educationalist: The Educational Writings of Patrick Pearse. 415p. 1980. 13.95 (ISBN 0-85342-569-8, XPub. by Mercier Pr Ireland). Irish Bk Ctr.

Buah, F. A., ed. see Davidson, Basil.

Bub, J. The Interpretation of Quantum Mechanics. (Western Ontario Ser: No. 3). ix, 155p. 1974. lib. bdg. 26.00 (ISBN 90-277-0465-1, Pub. by Reidel Holland); pap. text ed. 16.00 (ISBN 90-277-0466-X, Pub. by Reidel Holland). Kluwer Academic.

Buback, Kenneth A. & Grant, Mary K., eds. Quality of Work Life: Health Care Applications. LC 82-12766. 300p. 1985. pap. 24.00 (ISBN 0-87125-074-8). Cath Health.

Bubacz, Bruce. St. Augustine's Theory of Knowledge: A Contemporary Analysis. LC 81-18754. (Texts & Studies in Religion: Vol. 11). 248p. 1982. 49.95x (ISBN 0-88946-959-8). E Mellen.

Buban, P., et al. Understanding Electricity & Electronics. 4th ed. 1981. text ed. 22.64 (ISBN 0-07-008678-8). McGraw.

Buban, Peter & Schmitt, Marshall L. Technical Electricity & Electronics. 2nd ed. (Illus.). (gr. 11-12). 1976. text ed. 25.92 (ISBN 0-07-008643-5). McGraw.

Bubani, Pietro. Flora Virgiliana. 134p. 1974. Repr. of 1869 ed. lib. bdg. 17.50x (ISBN 3-87429-075-1). Lubrecht & Cramer.

Bubb, Diana I. Neurologic Problems, Vol. 3. (RN Nursing Assessment Ser.). 160p. 1984. pap. 12.95 (ISBN 0-87489-287-2). Med Economics.

Bubber, Purobi. The Joys of Chinese Cooking. (Illus.). 1978. text ed. 10.00x (ISBN 0-7069-0553-9, Pub. by Vikas India). Advent NY.

Bube, Richard, jt. auth. see Fahrenbruch, Alan.

Bube, Richard H. Electronic Properties of Crystalline Solids: An Introduction to Fundamentals. 1974. 59.00 (ISBN 0-12-138550-7). Acad Pr.

--Electrons in Solids: An Introductory Survey. LC 80-1689. 229p. 1980. 27.50 (ISBN 0-12-138650-3). Acad Pr.

--Photoconductivity of Solids. LC 78-1084. 484p. 1978. Repr. of 1960 ed. 28.50 (ISBN 0-88275-660-5). Krieger.

Bubeck, Mark I. The Adversary. 1975. pap. 5.95 (ISBN 0-8024-0143-0). Moody.

--Overcoming the Adversary. 1984. pap. 5.95 (ISBN 0-8024-0333-6). Moody.

Bubeck, Marne F. H., jt. auth. see Arons, Harry.

Bubel, Mike & Bubel, Nancy. Root Cellaring the Simple no-Processing Way to Store Fruits & Vegetables. (Illus.). 320p. 1979. 12.95 (ISBN 0-87857-277-5). Rodale Pr Inc.

Bubel, Nancy. The Adventurous Gardener. LC 78-74251. (Illus.). 224p. 1979. 17.95 (ISBN 0-87923-275-7); pap. 7.95 (ISBN 0-87923-276-5). Godine.

--The Country Journal Book of Vegetable Gardening. (Illus.). 256p. (Orig.). 1983. pap. 10.00 (ISBN 0-918678-03-X). Historical Times.

--The Seed Starter's Handbook. LC 77-25332. 1978. 14.95 (ISBN 0-87857-209-0). Rodale Pr Inc.

Bubel, Nancy, jt. auth. see Bubel, Mike.

Bubel, Nancy W. Vegetables Money Can't Buy but You Can Grow. LC 76-57875. 144p. 1977. 15.00 (ISBN 0-87923-202-1); pap. 6.95 (ISBN 0-87923-203-X). Godine.

Bubenick, David V. Acid Rain Information Book. 2nd ed. LC 83-21986. (Illus.). 397p. 1984. 39.00 (ISBN 0-8155-0967-7). Noyes.

Bubenik, Vit. The Phonological Interpretation of Ancient Greek: A Pandialectal Analysis. (Phoenix Supplementary Ser.: Vol. 19). 352p. 1983. 37.50x (ISBN 0-8020-5476-5). U of Toronto Pr.

Bubenko, Janis. Conceptual Information Modelling: Papers from the Nordic Research Course on "Conceptual Information Modelling for Data Bases", August 1979 in Ystad, Sweden. 687p. (Orig.). 1983. 36.95 (ISBN 0-86238-006-5, Pub. by Chartwell-Bratt England). Brookfield Pub Co.

Bubenzer, Rainer. Grundlagen fuer Staatspflichten auf dem Gebiet der Weiterbildung. (European University Studies Ser.: No. 11, Vol 157). 511p. (Ger.). 1983. 39.45 (ISBN 3-8204-7621-0). P Lang Pubs.

Buber, Edward J., jt. auth. see Karch, Robert R.

Buber, Martin. Between Man & Man. Smith, Ronald G., tr. 256p. 1985. pap. 6.95 (ISBN 0-02-084210-4). MacMillan.

--Eclipse of God: Studies in the Relation Between Religion & Philosophy. 1979. pap. text ed. 6.45x (ISBN 0-391-00902-8). Humanities.

--Ecstatic Confessions: The Heart of Mysticism. Mendes-Flor, Paul, ed. LC 84-48212. 224p. 1985. 16.30 (ISBN 0-06-061154-5, HarpR). Har-Row.

--For the Sake of Heaven. Lewisohn, Ludwig, tr. LC 77-97311. Repr. of 1953 ed. lib. bdg. 60.50x (ISBN 0-8371-2592-8, BUSH). Greenwood.

--For the Sake of Heaven: A Chronicle. Lewisohn, Ludwig, tr. LC 58-8531. (Temple Bks.). 1969. pap. 7.95 (ISBN 0-689-70026-1, T2). Atheneum.

--Good & Evil. 185p. pap. text ed. 7.95 (ISBN 0-684-16990-8). Scribner.

--Good & Evil. 1984. 15.00 (ISBN 0-8446-6121-X). Peter Smith.

--Good & Evil. 143p. 1980. pap. text ed. price not set (ISBN 0-02-316280-5, Pub. by Scribner). Macmillan.

--Hasidism & Modern Man. LC 58-10225. 256p. 1972. pap. 5.95 (ISBN 0-8180-1326-5). Horizon.

--Israel & the World: Essays in a Time of Crisis. LC 48-9322. 1963. pap. 6.50 (ISBN 0-8052-0066-5). Schocken.

--Knowledge of Man: Selected Essays. Friedman, Maurice, ed. Smith, Ronald, tr. (Orig.). pap. 5.95xi (ISBN 0-06-130135-3, TB135, Torch). Har-Row.

--The Legend of the Baal-Shem. LC 76-86849. 1969. pap. 7.95 (ISBN 0-8052-0233-1). Schocken.

--Mamre, Essays in Religion. Hort, Greta, tr. LC 72-97271. Repr. of 1946 ed. lib. bdg. 15.00x (ISBN 0-8371-2591-X, BUMA). Greenwood.

--Meetings. Friedman, Maurice, ed. & tr. from Ger. LC 73-82780. 123p. 1973. 9.95 (ISBN 0-87548-085-3). Open Court.

--On Judaism. Glatzer, Nahum, ed. LC 67-28091. 256p. 1972. pap. 7.50 (ISBN 0-8052-0343-5). Schocken.

--On the Bible: Eighteen Studies. Glatzer, Nahum N., ed. LC 81-16555. 288p. 1982. 17.95x (ISBN 0-8052-3796-8); pap. 7.95 (ISBN 0-8052-0691-4). Schocken.

--The Origin & Meaning of Hasidism. LC 60-8161. 256p. 1972. pap. 5.95 (ISBN 0-8180-1315-X). Horizon.

--Paths in Utopia. 1958. pap. 7.95x (ISBN 0-8070-1577-6, BP64). Beacon Pr.

--Pointing the Way. facs. ed. LC 77-134063. (Essay Index Reprint Ser). 1957. 16.00 (ISBN 0-8369-2149-6). Ayer Co Pubs.

--The Tales of Rabbi Nachman. LC 56-12330. 214p. 1972. 5.95 (ISBN 0-8180-1325-7). Horizon.

--Tales of the Hasidim, 2 vols. Incl. The Early Masters. pap. 6.95 (ISBN 0-8052-0001-0); The Later Masters. pap. 5.95 (ISBN 0-8052-0002-9). LC 47-2952. 1961. pap. Schocken.

--Ten Rungs: Hasidic Sayings. LC 62-13135. 1962. pap. 3.95 (ISBN 0-8052-0018-5). Schocken.

--To Hallow This Life: An Anthology. Trapp, Jacob, ed. LC 73-11862. 174p. 1974. Repr. of 1958 ed. lib. bdg. 15.00x (ISBN 0-8371-7096-6, BUHL). Greenwood.

--Way of Man. 1966. pap. 2.95 (ISBN 0-87574-106-1, 106). Citadel Pr.

--The Way of Man. 44p. 1985. pap. 3.50 (ISBN 0-8065-0024-7). Citadel Pr.

--The Way of Response: Selections from His Writings. Glatzer, Nahum N., ed. LC 66-26977. 1971. pap. 5.95 (ISBN 0-8052-0292-7). Schocken.

--Writings of Martin Buber. Herberg, Will, ed. (Orig.). pap. 8.95 (ISBN 0-452-00616-3, F616, Mer). NAL.

Buber, Martin, jt. auth. see Magnes, Judah L.

Buber, Martin & Magnes, J. L., eds. Towards Union in Palestine: Essays on Zionism & Jewish-Arab Cooperation. LC 76-97272. (Judaica Ser.). 124p. 1972. Repr. of 1947 ed. lib. bdg. 15.00x (ISBN 0-8371-2564-2, BUUP). Greenwood.

Buber, Martin, et al. I & Thou. Kaufman, Walter & Smith, G. S., trs. LC 72-123845. (Hudson River Edition). 1970. 20.00 (ISBN 0-684-15575-3, ScribT); pap. 6.95 (ISBN 0-684-71725-5, ScribT). Scribner.

Bubic, S. Dictionary of Economic Terms. 1040p. (Eng. & Serbocroation.). 1975. 95.00 (ISBN 0-686-92261-1, M-9699). French & Eur.

Bubin, Barry, jt. ed. see Laqueur, Walter.

Bubis, G. B., ed. Serving the Jewish Family. 25.00x (ISBN 0-87068-439-6). Ktav.

Bubis, Gerald B. & Wasserman, Harry. Synagogue Havurot: A Comparative Study. LC 82-23912. 160p. (Orig.). 1983. lib. bdg. 24.25 (ISBN 0-8191-2969-0, Co-pub. by Ctr Jewish Comm Studies); pap. text ed. 10.75 (ISBN 0-8191-2970-4). U Pr of Amer.

Bubley, Esther. Esther Bubley's World of Children in Photographs. (Illus.). 106p. (Orig.). 1981. pap. 6.95 (ISBN 0-486-24168-8). Dover.

--Esther Bubley's World of Children in Photographs. (Illus.). 1982. 14.50 (ISBN 0-8446-5880-4). Peter Smith.

Bubley, Esther & Knauth, Percy. A Mysterious Presence: The Inner Life of Plants. LC 77-79683. (Illus.). 192p. 1976. pap. 5.95 (ISBN 0-911104-99-2). Workman Pub.

Bublitz, Ruth M. ONE-drous Light. 128p. (Orig.). 1985. pap. 5.95 (ISBN 0-87516-556-7). De Vorss.

Bubna, Donald. Como Edificar Otros. 160p. 1981. 2.75 (ISBN 0-88113-038-9). Edit Betania.

Bubna, Donald & Ricketts, Sarah. Building People Through a Caring, Sharing Fellowship. 1982. pap. 4.95 (ISBN 0-8423-0185-2); leader's guide 2.95 (ISBN 0-8423-0188-7). Tyndale.

Bubna, Paul, frwd. by see Schroeder, David.

Bubner, R. Modern German Philosophy. Matthews, Eric, tr. LC 81-3901. 240p. 1981. 39.50 (ISBN 0-521-22908-1); pap. 13.95 (ISBN 0-521-29711-7). Cambridge U Pr.

Bubnicki, Z. Identification of Control Plants. (Studies in Automation & Control: Vol. 3). 312p. 1980. 64.00 (ISBN 0-444-99767-9). Elsevier.

Bubnov, A. D., jt. auth. see Golovin, Nikolai N.

Bubnov, Yu N., jt. auth. see Mikhailov, B. M.

BuBnova, E. Old Russian Faience. 186p. 1973. 33.00x (ISBN 0-317-14267-4, Pub. by Collet's). State Mutual Bk.

Bubnys, V. Under Summer Skies. 249p. 1979. pap. 5.45 (ISBN 0-686-91847-9, Pub. by Progress Pubs USSR). Imported Pubns.

Bubolz, George C. Father Julius & Mother Emilie: A Personal Biography of Midwestern Pioneers. LC 75-329401. (An Exposition-Lochinvar Bk.). (Illus.). pap. 49.00 (ISBN 0-317-09521-8, 2010735). Bks Demand UMI.

Bubser, R. K. & Koepke, W. Deutsch Im sprachgebrauch. LC 82-20290. 338p. 1983. 22.95 (ISBN 0-471-08794-7). Wiley.

--Workbook to Accompany Deutsch im Sprachebrauch. 281p. 1983. pap. 11.95 (ISBN 0-471-08795-5). Wiley.

Bucaille, Maurice. The Bible, the Quran & Science. Beg, Anwer, ed. Bucaille, Maurice & Pannell, Alastair D., trs. from Fr. LC 77-90336. 253p. 1978. 11.95 (ISBN 0-89259-010-6); pap. 8.50. Am Trust Pubns.

Bucaille, Maurice, tr. see Bucaille, Maurice.

Buccellati, G. & Rouault, O. Tergra Preliminary Report, No. 12: Digital Plotting of Archaeological Floor Plans. (Computer Aided Research in Near Eastern Studies: Vol. 1, Issue 1). 40p. 1983. pap. text ed. 6.50x (ISBN 0-89003-146-0). Undena Pubns.

Buccellati, G., et al. Terqa Data Bases, I: Old Babylonian & Khana Texts Through the Fourth Season of Excavation. (Cybernetica Mesopotamica, Graphemic Categorization Ser.: Vol. I). 1984. write for info. (ISBN 0-89003-119-3). Undena Pubns.

Buccellati, Giorgio. Terqa Preliminary Reports, No. 10: The Fourth Season, Introduction & the Stratigraphic Record. (Bibliotheca Mesopotamica Ser.: Vol. 10). (Illus.). 150p. 1979. 34.50x (ISBN 0-89003-042-1); pap. 24.50x (ISBN 0-89003-043-X). Undena Pubns.

Buccellati, Giorgio & Speroni, Charles, eds. The Shape of the Past: Studies in Honor of Franklin D. Murphy. (Illus.). xi, 320p. 1981. 30.00x (ISBN 0-917956-31-1). UCLA Arch.

Buccheri, R., jt. ed. see Morfill, G. E.

Bucchioni, Eugene, jt. auth. see Cordasco, Francesco.

Bucci, jt. ed. see Hudak, Jr.

Bucci, G. & Valle, G., eds. Computing '85: A Broad Perspective of Current Developments: Proceedings of the Computing Symposium, 8th, Florence, Italy, 27-29 March, 1985. 263p. 1985. 74.00 (ISBN 0-444-87738-X, North-Holland). Elsevier.

Buccianti, G., ed. Risk Profiles in Clinical Nephrology. (Contributions to Nephrology: Vol. 37). (Illus.). x, 202p. 1984. pap. 38.50 (ISBN 3-8055-3739-5). S Karger.

Bucco, Martin. An American Tragedy Notes. 75p. (Orig.). 1974. pap. text ed. 3.25 (ISBN 0-8220-0169-1). Cliffs.

--E. W. Howe. LC 77-76322. (Western Writers Ser.: No. 26). 1977. pap. 2.00x (ISBN 0-88430-050-1). Boise St Univ.

--Rene Wellek. (United States Authors Ser.). 1981. lib. bdg. 14.50 (ISBN 0-8057-7339-8, Twayne). G K Hall.

--Western American Literary Criticism. LC 84-70250. (Western Writers Ser.: No. 62). (Orig.). 1984. pap. 2.00x (ISBN 0-88430-036-6). Boise St Univ.

Bucer, Martin. A Briefe Treatise Concerning the Burnynge of Bucer & Phagius at Cambridge. LC 76-57362. (English Experience Ser.: No. 780). 1977. Repr. of 1562 ed. lib. bdg. 14.00 (ISBN 90-221-0780-9). Walter J Johnson.

--Instruction in Christian Love. write for info. John Knox.

--A Treatise How by the Worde of God, Christian Mens Almose Oght to Be Distributed. LC 76-57360. (English Experience Ser.). 1977. Repr. of 1557 ed. lib. bdg. 3.50 (ISBN 90-221-0779-5). Walter J Johnson.

Buch, Jane. Conditioning & Nutrition for the Athlete: The Winning Combination. Cooper, William H., ed. LC 84-51951. (Illus.). 88p. (Orig.). (gr. 7-12). 1985. pap. text ed. 10.60 (ISBN 0-914127-18-7); wkbk. 5.27 (ISBN 0-914127-19-5). Univ Class.

Buchachenko, Anatoli L. Stable Radicals. LC 65-11336. 180p. 1965. 32.50x (ISBN 0-306-10729-5, Consultants). Plenum Pub.

Buchachenko, Anatolii L. Stable Radicals. Turton, C. Nigel & Turton, Tatiana I., trs. from Rus. LC 65-900. (Illus.). pap. 47.00 (ISBN 0-317-09364-9, 2020670). Bks Demand UMI.

Buchan, Alastair. Change Without War: The Shifting Structure of World Power. LC 74-19962. 112p. 1975. 22.50 (ISBN 0-312-12880-0). St Martin.

--Spare Chancellor: The Life of Walter Bagehot. 1960. 5.00 (ISBN 0-87013-051-X). Mich St U Pr.

Buchan, David. Scottish Tradition: A Collection of Scottish Folklore. 288p. 1984. 25.00 (ISBN 0-7100-9531-7). Routledge & Kegan.

Buchan, David, ed. A Book of Scottish Ballads. 232p. 1985. pap. 8.95 (ISBN 0-7102-0539-2). Routledge & Kegan.

Buchan, J. Foreign Birds: Exhibition & Management. 1981. 15.75 (ISBN 0-86230-039-8). Saiga.

Buchan, James. Jeddah Old & New. 144p. 1984. 79.00 (ISBN 0-905743-22-9, Pub. by Stacey Intl Pubs UK). State Mutual Bk.

--A Parish of Rich Women. LC 84-45611. 256p. 1985. 14.95 (ISBN 0-689-11534-2). Atheneum.

--Thatched Village. (Illus.). 240p. 1984. 18.95 (ISBN 0-340-32666-2, Pub. by Hodder & Stoughton UK). David & Charles.

Buchan, John. A Book of Escapes & Hurried Journeys. 208p. 1983. Repr. of 1925 ed. lib. bdg. 30.00 (ISBN 0-89984-095-7). Century Bookbindery.

--Canadian Occasions. facs. ed. LC 70-90618. (Essay Index Reprint Ser). 1940. 19.00 (ISBN 0-8369-1275-6). Ayer Co Pubs.

--Comments & Characters. facsimile ed. LC 79-104999. (Essay Index Reprint Ser.). 1940. 27.50 (ISBN 0-8369-1453-8). Ayer Co Pubs.

--The History of the Great War. LC 79-90170. (Great War Stories). 2400p. 1980. Repr. of 1922 ed. 120.00 (ISBN 0-933852-10-X). Nautical & Aviation.

--A History of the Great War, 4 Vols. 160.00 (ISBN 0-405-13279-4). Ayer Co Pubs.

--Homilies & Recreations. facs. ed. LC 73-86737. (Essay Index Reprint Ser). 1926. 19.00 (ISBN 0-8369-1172-5). Ayer Co Pubs.

--Huntingtower. 316p. Repr. of 1922 ed. lib. bdg. 17.95 (ISBN 0-89190-244-9, Pub. by River City Pr). Amereon Ltd.

--John Burnet of Barns. 317p. 1982. 9.95 (ISBN 0-903937-51-4). Pelican.

--John Burnet of Barns: A Romance. 1971. Repr. of 1924 ed. 29.00 (ISBN 0-403-00877-8). Scholarly.

--John MacNab. 1983. 30.00x (ISBN 0-904265-34-X, Pub. by Macdonald Pub UK). State Mutual Bk.

--Men & Deeds. facs. ed. LC 69-17567. (Essay Index Reprint Ser). 1935. 18.00 (ISBN 0-8369-0065-0). Ayer Co Pubs.

--Midwinter. 1971. Repr. of 1923 ed. 39.00x (ISBN 0-403-00878-6). Scholarly.

--Mister Standfast. LC 77-144916. 374p. 1928. Repr. 39.00x (ISBN 0-403-00879-4). Scholarly.

--Montrose: A History. LC 74-14349. (Illus.). 385p. 1975. Repr. of 1928 ed. lib. bdg. 22.75x (ISBN 0-8371-7795-2, BUMO). Greenwood.

--The Northern Muse: An Anthology of Scots Vernacular Poetry. 547p. 1983. Repr. of 1924 ed. lib. bdg. 35.00 (ISBN 0-89984-096-5). Century Bookbindery.

--The Novel & the Fairy Tale. LC 77-28042. 1931. 10.00 (ISBN 0-8414-0055-5). Folcroft.

--Oliver Cromwell. 1957. 25.00 (ISBN 0-8274-3062-0). R West.

--Pilgrim's Way. 352p. 1984. pap. 10.95 (ISBN 0-88184-107-2). Carroll & Graf.

--Pilgrim's Way: An Essay in Recollection. LC 76-6591. (BCL Ser. II). Repr. of 1940 ed. 32.50 (ISBN 0-404-15278-3). AMS Pr.

--Pilgrim's Way: An Essay in Recollection. 336p. 1983. Repr. of 1940 ed. lib. bdg. 45.00 (ISBN 0-89760-974-3). Telegraph Bks.

--Poems: Scots & English. 105p. 1981. Repr. lib. bdg. 20.00 (ISBN 0-89987-069-4). Darby Bks.

--Prester John. LC 75-131650. (Illus.). 1970. 49.00x (ISBN 0-403-00537-X). Scholarly.

--Sir Walter Raleigh. 232p. 1983. lib. bdg. 35.00 (ISBN 0-89984-132-5). Century Bookbindery.

--Sir Walter Scott. 1932. lib. bdg. 20.00 (ISBN 0-8414-2515-9). Folcroft.

--Sir Walter Scott. LC 67-27580. Repr. of 1932 ed. 19.50x (ISBN 0-8046-0054-6, Pub. by Kennikat). Assoc Faculty Pr.

--Sir Walter Scott. 384p. Repr. of 1932 ed. lib. bdg. 40.00 (ISBN 0-89984-135-X). Century Bookbindery.

--Some Eighteenth Century Byways. LC 72-13299. 1972. Repr. of 1908 ed. lib. bdg. 40.00 (ISBN 0-8414-1178-6). Folcroft.

--Some Notes on Sir Walter Scott. 1924. Repr. 8.50 (ISBN 0-8274-3460-X). R West.

--The Thirty-Nine Steps. 1976. Repr. of 1915 ed. lib. bdg. 15.95x (ISBN 0-89190-243-0, Pub. by River City Pr). Amereon Ltd.

--The Thirty-Nine Steps. (Children's Illustrated Classics). (Illus.). 151p. 1975. Repr. of 1964 ed. 11.00x (ISBN 0-460-05064-8, BKA 01577, Pub by J M Dent England). Biblio Dist.

--The Thirty-Nine Steps & the Power House. 213p. 1981. 15.00x (ISBN 0-85158-049-1, Pub. by Blackwood & Sons England). State Mutual Bk.

--The Three Hostages. 284p. Repr. of 1924 ed. lib. bdg. 16.95x (ISBN 0-89190-245-7, Pub. by River City Pr). Amereon Ltd.

--Watcher by the Threshold. 1971. Repr. of 1918 ed. 39.00x (ISBN 0-403-00880-8). Scholarly.

Buchan, John see Eyre, A. G.

Buchan, John, ed. A History of English Literature. (Illus.). 675p. 1985. Repr. of 1925 ed. lib. bdg. 50.00 (ISBN 0-89987-971-3). Darby Bks.

--A History of English Literature: From Chaucer to the End of the 19th Century. 675p. 1982. Repr. of 1923 ed. lib. bdg. 45.00 (ISBN 0-89987-088-0). Darby Bks.

Buchan, Peter. Ancient Ballads & Songs of the North of Scotland, 2 vols. LC 73-10190. (Folklore Ser.). Set. 49.50 (ISBN 0-88305-081-1). Norwood Edns.

--Ancient Scottish Tales. LC 72-7082. 1972. lib. bdg. 15.00 (ISBN 0-88305-054-4). Norwood Edns.

--Gleanings of Scarce Old Ballads. LC 74-7269. (Folklore Ser.). 1891. 17.50 (ISBN 0-88305-087-0). Norwood Edns.

Buchan, Robert J. & Johnston, C. Christopher. Telecommunications Regulation & the Constitution. 276p. (Orig.). 1982. pap. text ed. 18.95x (ISBN 0-920380-69-7, Pub. by Inst Res Pub Canada). Brookfield Pub Co.

Buchan, Roy M., jt. auth. see Beaulieu, Harry J.

Buchan, Ruth, jt. auth. see Anderson, Jean.

Buchan, Stuart. Bitter Promises. (The Roots of Love Ser.: No. 40). (Orig.). (gr. k-12). Date not set. pap. text ed. 2.50 (ISBN 0-440-90621-0, LFL). Dell.

--Flames from the Ashes. (Roots of Love Ser.: No. 5). (Orig.). (gr. k-12). 1986. pap. 2.50 (ISBN 0-440-92602-5, LFL). Dell.

--Forbidden Longings. (Roots of Love Ser.: No. 3). (Orig.). (gr. 7-12). 1985. pap. 2.50 (ISBN 0-440-92675-0, LFL). Dell.

--Restless Nights. (The Roots of Love Ser.: No. 2). (Orig.). (gr. k-12). 1985. pap. 2.50 (ISBN 0-440-97414-3, LFL). Dell.

--The Ripening Years. 192p. (gr. 5-9). Date not set. price not set (YB). Dell.

--The Roots of Love. (The Roots of Love Ser.: No. 1). 224p. (Orig.). (gr. k-12). 1985. pap. 2.25 (ISBN 0-440-97484-4, LFL). Dell.

--A Space of His Own. LC 79-15745. (Encore Edition Ser.). (gr. 7 up). 1979. 1.49 (ISBN 0-684-17358-1, ScribJ). Scribner.

--Tender Beginnings. (Roots of Love Ser.). 192p. (Orig.). (gr. 9 up). 1985. pap. 2.50 (ISBN 0-440-98602-8, LFL). Dell.

Buchan, Vivian. Cat Sun Signs. LC 79-65117. (Illus.). 156p. 1982. pap. 5.95 (ISBN 0-8128-6097-7). Stein & Day.

--Cat Sun Signs. LC 79-65117. 1979. 8.95 (ISBN 0-8128-2686-8). Stein & Day.

Buchan, William. Domestic Medicine. LC 83-48605. (Marriage, Sex & the Family in England Ser.). 795p. 1985. lib. bdg. 80.00 (ISBN 0-8240-5931-X). Garland Pub.

--John Masefield: Letters to Reyna. 508p. 1985. 22.00 (ISBN 0-907675-14-X, Pub. by Salem Acad). Merrimack Pub Cir.

--Observations Concerning the Prevention & Cure of the Venereal Disease. LC 83-48591. (Marriage, Sex & the Family in England Ser.). 248p. 1985. lib. bdg. 35.00 (ISBN 0-8240-5915-8). Garland Pub.

Buchanan. The Secret of the Unknown Powers. 1985. 7.95 (ISBN 0-317-28941-1). Vantage.

Buchanan, ed. see Aubrey, John.

Buchanan, et al. Multiple Choice Questions in Rheumatology. (Illus.). 160p. (Orig.). 1984. pap. text ed. 13.95 (ISBN 0-407-00239-1). Butterworth.

Buchanan, A. Russell. United States & World War Two, Vol. 2. (New American Nation Ser.). (Illus.). (YA) 1964. 17.50xi (ISBN 0-06-010571-2, HarpT). Har-Row.

--The United States in World War II, Vol. I. LC 63-20287. (Illus.). 1964. 19.18xi (ISBN 0-06-010570-4, HarpT). Har-Row.

Buchanan, Allen. Ethics, Efficiency & the Market. LC 84-27525. 148p. 1985. 24.50x (ISBN 0-8476-7395-2); Texts in Philosophy Ser., delayed. pap. 10.95x (ISBN 0-8476-7396-0). Rowman & Allanheld.

--Marx & Justice: The Radical Critique of Liberalism. 220p. 1982. 25.50 (ISBN 0-318-02977-4). Biblio Dist.

Buchanan, Allen E. Marx & Justice: The Radical Critique of Liberalism. LC 81-23436. 220p. 1982. 25.50 (ISBN 0-8476-7039-2). Rowman.

--Marx & Justice: The Radical Critique of Liberalism. LC 81-23436. (Philosophy & Society Ser.). 220p. 1982. pap. 9.50x (ISBN 0-8476-7356-1). Rowman & Allanheld.

Buchanan, Angus. Three Years of War in East Africa. LC 72-90108. Repr. of 1919 ed. 22.50 (ISBN 0-8371-2026-8, BUY&). Greenwood.

Buchanan, Annette, jt. auth. see Weaver, Peter.

Buchanan, Annette M. & Martin, Kay A. The Twelve Months of Christmas. Bolt, John, ed. 192p. 1980. pap. 7.95 (ISBN 0-939114-01-1). Partridge Pair.

Buchanan, Brian. Theory of Library Classification. (Outlines of Modern Librarianship Ser.). 141p. 1980. text ed. 12.00 (ISBN 0-85157-270-7, Pub. by Bingley England). Shoe String.

Buchanan, Briggs. Catalogue of Ancient Near Eastern Seals in the Ashmolean Museum, Vol. II: The Prehistoric Stamp Seals. Moorey, P. R., ed. 42p. 1984. 90.00x (ISBN 0-317-20320-7, Pub. by Ashmolean Mus UK). State Mutual Bk.

--Catalogue of Ancient Near Eastern Seals in the Ashmolean Museum, Vol. 2. Moorey, Roger, ed. (Illus.). 1984. 36.00x (ISBN 0-19-813403-7). Oxford U Pr.

--Early Near Eastern Seals in the Yale Babylonian Collection. Kasten, Ulla, ed. LC 75-43309. (Illus.). 520p. 1981. text ed. 82.00x (ISBN 0-300-01852-5). Yale U Pr.

Buchanan, Bruce. The Presidential Experience: What the Office Does to the Man. LC 78-16770. (Illus.). 1978. (Spec); pap. 3.95 (ISBN 0-13-697482-1). P-H.

Buchanan, C. D. Substantivized Adjectives in Old Norse. (LD). pap. 16.00 (ISBN 0-527-00761-7). Kraus Repr.

Buchanan, C. R. & Eng, C. Control of Manufacture: An Introduction to Engineering Management. 160p. 1983. pap. text ed. 11.95 (ISBN 0-7131-3462-3). E Arnold.

Buchanan, Cynthia D. Programed Introduction to Linguistics: Phonetics & Phonemics. 1963. pap. text ed. 18.95x (ISBN 0-669-20453-6). Heath.

Buchanan, D. L. Nickel: A Commodity Review, Paper #1. (Occasional Papers of the Institution of Mining & Metallurgy Ser.). (Orig.). 1984. pap. text ed. 12.00x (ISBN 0-318-02037-8). IMM North Am.

Buchanan, D. L. & Jones, M. J., eds. Sulphide Deposits in Mafic & Ultramafic Rocks: Proceedings of Nickel Sulphide Field Conference III, Western Australia, 1982. (Orig.). 1984. pap. text ed. 69.95x (ISBN 0-900488-71-9). Imm North Am.

Buchanan, Daniel H. Development of Capitalistic Enterprise in India. 489p. 1966. Repr. 35.00x (ISBN 0-7146-1998-1, F Cass Co). Biblio Dist.

Buchanan, David. Davidis Buchanani De Scriptoribus Scotis. Irving, David, ed. LC 74-39554. (Bannatyne Club, Edinburgh. Publications Ser.: No. 55). Repr. of 1837 ed. 20.00 (ISBN 0-404-52765-5). AMS Pr.

--Greek Athletics. McLeish, Kenneth & McLeish, Valerie, eds. (Aspects of Greek Life Ser.). (Illus.). 48p. (YA) (gr. 7-12). 1976. pap. text ed. 3.95 (ISBN 0-582-20059-8). Longman.

--Observations on the Subjects Treated of in Dr. Smith's Inquiry into the Nature & Causes of the Wealth of Nations. 2nd ed. LC 65-26360. Repr. of 1817 ed. 39.50x (ISBN 0-678-00191-X). Kelley.

--Observations on the Subjects Treated of in Dr. Smith's Inquiry into the Wealth of Nations: 1817 Edition. 1981. write for info. (ISBN 0-08-027635-0, HE 018); microfiche 26.50 (ISBN 0-686-79354-4). Pergamon.

--Roman Sport & Entertainment. Hodge, Peter, ed. (Aspects of Roman Life Ser.). (Illus.). 64p. (Orig.). (gr. 7-12). 1976. pap. text ed. 3.95 (ISBN 0-582-31415-1). Longman.

Buchanan, David A. The Development of Job Design Theories & Techniques. LC 79-83808. 180p. 1979. 38.95x (ISBN 0-03-052376-1). Praeger.

Buchanan, David A. & Boddy, David. Organizations in the Computer Age. 279p. 1983. text ed. 45.00 (ISBN 0-566-00488-7). Gower Pub Co.

Buchanan, Diane E., jt. auth. see Clements, Imelda W.

Buchanan, Duncan. The Counselling of Jesus. Green, Michael, ed. (The Jesus Library). 160p. 1985. pap. 6.95 (ISBN 0-87784-931-5). Inter-Varsity.

Buchanan, Edward A. Broken Jars & Empty Cisterns: Studies in Jeremiah. 32p. 1982. pap. 3.50 (ISBN 0-939298-09-0). J M Prods.

Buchanan, Emerson, tr. see Ricoeur, Paul.

Buchanan, Forest W. The Breeding Birds of Carroll & Northern Jefferson Counties, Ohio, with Notes on Selected Vascular Plant Species. 1980. 6.00 (ISBN 0-86727-086-1). Ohio Bio Survey.

Buchanan, G. Sidney. Morality, Sex & the Constitution: A Christian Perspective on the Power of Government to Regulate Private Sexual Conduct Between Consenting Adults. LC 85-3249. 242p. (Orig.). 1985. lib. bdg. 23.75 (ISBN 0-8191-4602-1); pap. text ed. 11.50 (ISBN 0-8191-4603-X). U Pr of Amer.

Buchanan, George. The Boat Repair Manual. Boyd, Alan, ed. (Illus.). 304p. 1985. 29.95 (ISBN 0-668-06167-7, 6167). Arco.

--Jephthah & the Baptist. Sutherland, Robert G., tr. 1979. Repr. of 1959 ed. lib. bdg. 20.00 (ISBN 0-8495-0549-6). Arden Lib.

--The Politics of Culture. 1977. 4.00 (ISBN 0-685-04167-0, Pub. by Menard Pr). Small Pr Dist.

--The Tragedy of Mesopotamia. LC 71-180324. (Mid-East Studies Ser.). Repr. of 1938 ed. 14.00 (ISBN 0-404-56218-3). AMS Pr.

--The Tyrannous Reign of Mary Stewart. Gatherer, W. A., tr. from Latin. LC 78-3556. (Edinburgh University Publication: History, Philosophy, & Economics: No. 10). 1978. Repr. of 1958 ed. lib. bdg. 24.00x (ISBN 0-313-20343-1, BUTR). Greenwood.

Buchanan, George W. The Prophet's Mantle in the Nation's Capital. LC 78-59167. 1978. pap. text ed. 7.50 (ISBN 0-8191-0545-7). U Pr of Amer.

--Revelation & Redemption. 1978. text ed. 29.50 (ISBN 0-915948-04-4). Western NC Pr.

Buchanan, George W., tr. To the Hebrews. LC 72-76127. (Anchor Bible Ser.: Vol. 36). 1972. 14.00 (ISBN 0-385-02995-0, Anchor Pr). Doubleday.

Buchanan, George Wesley. Jesus: The King & His Kingdom. LC 83-24939. 366p. 1984. 21.95x (ISBN 0-86554-072-1, H66). Mercer Univ Pr.

Buchanan, George 1506-1582. Deiure Regni Apud Scotos Dialogus. LC 73-6075. (English Experience Ser.: No. 80). 106p. 1969. Repr. of 1579 ed. 14.00 (ISBN 90-221-0080-4). Walter J Johnson.

Buchanan, George, 1854-1924. My Mission to Russia & Other Diplomatic Memories. LC 78-115510. (Russia Observed, Series 1). 1970. Repr. of 1923 ed. 30.00 (ISBN 0-405-03008-8). Ayer Co Pubs.

Buchanan, George, 1904- Green Seacoast. LC 68-24548. 108p. 1969. 4.95 (ISBN 0-87376-008-5); pap. 3.00 (ISBN 0-87376-009-3). Red Dust.

Buchanan, Georges. Marguerite de Valois & the War of the Huguenots, 2 vols. (Illus.). 317p. 1986. Repr. of 1896 ed. Set. 187.75 (ISBN 0-89901-245-0). Found Class Reprints.

Buchanan, Handasyde. Nature into Art: A Treasury of Great Natural History Books. LC 79-12481. (Illus.). 1980. 25.00 (ISBN 0-8317-6337-X, Mayflower Bks). Smith Pubs.

Buchanan, Heather S. Emily Mouse Saves the Day. (Illus.). 1985. 3.95 (ISBN 0-318-11869-6). Dial Bks Young.

--George Mouse Learns to Fly. (Illus.). 1985. 3.95 (ISBN 0-318-11868-8). Dial Bks Young.

--George Mouse Learns to Fly. LC 84-1721. (George & Emily Mouse Bks.). (Illus.). 32p. (ps-1). 1985. 3.95 (ISBN 0-8037-0172-1). Dial Bks Young.

--George Mouse's First Summer. LC 84-15584. (George & Emily Mouse Bks.). (Illus.). 32p. (ps-1). 1985. 3.95 (ISBN 0-8037-0173-X). Dial Bks Young.

Buchanan, Ian. Encyclopedia of British Athletics Records. 10.00 (ISBN 0-392-08930-0, SpS). Sportshelf.

Buchanan, Ian, jt. auth. see Mallon, Bill.

Buchanan, J. Consumers Guide to Mobile Home Living. 1982. pap. 3.50 (ISBN 0-918734-32-0). Reymont.

Buchanan, J., jt. auth. see Brennan, G.

Buchanan, J. E. Houston: A Chronological & Documentary History 1519-1970. LC 74-30380. (American Cities Chronology Ser.). 153p. 1975. 8.50 (ISBN 0-379-00615-4). Oceana.

--Phoenix: A Chronological & Documentary History, 1865-1976. LC 77-26763. (American Cities Chronology Ser.). 149p. 1978. 8.50 (ISBN 0-379-00617-0). Oceana.

Buchanan, J. M., et al. The Consequences of Mr. Keynes: An Analysis of the Misuse of Economic Theory for Political Profiteering, with Proposals for Constitutional Disciplines. (Hobart Papers Ser.: No. 78). 1978. pap. 5.95 technical (ISBN 0-255-36110-6). Transatlantic.

Buchanan, J. T. Discrete & Dynamic Decision Analysis. 260p. 1982. 42.95 (ISBN 0-471-10130-3); pap. 24.95 (ISBN 0-471-10131-1). Wiley.

Buchanan, Jack. Hanoi Deathgrip. (M.I.A. Ser.: No. 3). 208p. 1985. pap. 2.75 (ISBN 0-515-08228-7). Jove Pubns.

--M.I.A. Hunter: Mountain Massacre. 208p. 1985. pap. 2.75 (ISBN 0-515-08363-1). Jove Pubns.

Buchanan, James. The Doctrine of Justification. 514p. 1985. Repr. of 1867 ed. 14.95 (ISBN 0-85151-440-5). Banner of Truth.

--James Buchanan's Mission to Russia: 1831-1833, His Speeches, State Papers & Private Correspondence. Moore, John B., ed. LC 71-115511. (Russia Observed, Ser., No. 1). 1970. Repr. of 1908 ed. 14.00 (ISBN 0-405-03009-6). Ayer Co Pubs.

--Miami: A Chronological & Documentary History, 1513-1977. LC 77-27462. (American Cities Chronology Ser.). 155p. 1978. 8.50 (ISBN 0-379-00616-2). Oceana.

--Mister Buchanan's Administration on the Eve of the Rebellion. facsimile ed. LC 70-107795. (Select Bibliographies Reprint Ser). 1865. 22.00 (ISBN 0-8369-5212-X). Ayer Co Pubs.

--What Should Economists Do? LC 79-19511. 1979. 8.00 (ISBN 0-913966-64-9, Liberty Pr); pap. 3.50 (ISBN 0-913966-65-7). Liberty Fund.

Buchanan, James, jt. auth. see Brennan, Geoffrey.

Buchanan, James, jt. auth. see Gilbert, Robert P.

Buchanan, James M. Cost & Choice: An Inquiry in Economic Theory. LC 78-70150. (Midway Reprints Ser.). 1979. pap. text ed. 6.00x (ISBN 0-226-07818-3). U of Chicago Pr.

--The Economics of Politics. (Institute of Economic Affairs: Readings 18). 1979. pap. 10.95 technical (ISBN 0-255-36114-9). Transatlantic.

--Freedom in Constitutional Contract: Perspectives of a Political Economist. LC 77-89513. (Texas A&M Univ. Economics Ser.: No. 2). 328p. 1977. 24.50x (ISBN 0-89096-038-0). Tex A&M Univ Pr.

--The Limits of Liberty: Between Anarchy & Leviathan. LC 74-11616. 1977. pap. 4.95x (ISBN 0-226-07820-5, P714, Phoen). U of Chicago Pr.

--Public Finance in the Democratic Process. x, 307p. 1967. 25.00 (ISBN 0-8078-1014-2). U of NC Pr.

Buchanan, James M. & Flowers, Marilyn R. The Public Finances: An Introductory Textbook. 5th ed. 1980. 28.50x (ISBN 0-256-02333-6). Irwin.

Buchanan, James M. & Tollison, Robert D. The Theory of Public Choice, II. 512p. 1984. text ed. 30.00x (ISBN 0-472-10040-8); pap. text ed. 14.95x (ISBN 0-472-08041-5). U of Mich Pr.

Buchanan, James M. & Tullock, Gordon. Calculus of Consent: Logical Foundations of Constitutional Democracy. 1962. pap. 9.95 (ISBN 0-472-06100-3, 100, AA). U of Mich Pr.

Buchanan, James M. & Wagner, Richard E. Democracy in Deficit: The Political Legacy of Lord Keynes. 1977. 24.50 (ISBN 0-12-138850-6). Acad Pr.

--Fiscal Responsibility in Constitutional Democracy. (Studies in Public Choice: Vol. 1). 1978. lib. bdg. 22.50 (ISBN 90-207-0743-4, Pub. by Martinus Nijhoff Netherlands). Kluwer Academic.

--Public Debt in a Democratic Society. 1967. pap. 4.25 (ISBN 0-8447-3055-6). Am Enterprise.

Buchanan, James M., jt. auth. see Brennan, H. Geoffrey.

Buchanan, James M. & Thirlby, G. F., eds. L.S.E Essays on Cost. (The Institute for Humane Studies Ser. in Economic Theory). 1981. 27.00x (ISBN 0-8147-1034-4); pap. 12.00x (ISBN 0-8147-1035-2). NYU Pr.

Buchanan, James M., et al, eds. Toward a Theory of the Rent-Seeking Society. LC 79-5276. (Texas A&M University Economics Ser.: No. 4). 384p. 1981. 28.50x (ISBN 0-89096-090-9). Tex A&M Univ Pr.

Buchanan, James W. Minnesota Walk Book, Vol. 2. (Illus.). 1977. pap. 4.50 (ISBN 0-685-88677-8). Nodin Pr.

--Minnesota Walk Book, Vol. 3. (Illus.). 1978. pap. 4.50 (ISBN 0-931714-00-1). Nodin Pr.

--Minnesota Walk Book: A Guide to Hiking & Cross-Country Skiing in the Pioneer Region. (Minnesota Walk Book Ser.: Vol. 5). (Illus.). 59p. (Orig.). 1979. pap. 4.50 (ISBN 0-931714-07-9). Nodin Pr.

--Minnesota Walk Book: A Guide to Hiking & Cross-Country Skiing in the Viking-Land Region, Vol. VI. (Walk Book Ser.). (Illus.). 64p. 1982. pap. 4.50 (ISBN 0-931714-19-2). Nodin Pr.

--Minnesota Walk Book: A Guide to Hiking & Cross-Country Skiing in the Metroland Region, Vol. 4. (The Minnesota Walk Books). (Illus.). 1979. pap. 4.50 (ISBN 0-931714-03-6). Nodin Pr.

Buchanan, James W., et al. Dogs & Other Large Mammals in Aging Research, Vol. 2. LC 74-8039. 194p. 1974. text ed. 29.50x (ISBN 0-8422-7227-5). Irvington.

Buchanan, Jami L. Letters to My Little Sisters. (Orig.). 1985. pap. 3.95 (ISBN 0-8307-0999-1, S185100). Regal.

Buchanan, Jerry. Twenty-Two Mistakes the Beginner Always Makes in Mail Order. 32p. (Orig.). 1984. pap. 6.95x (ISBN 0-930668-01-4). Towers Club.

--Writer's Utopia Formula Report. 10.00 (ISBN 0-930668-00-6). Towers Club.

Buchanan, Jim. A Guide to Materials about Public Aid to Religious Schools. (Public Administration Ser.: Bibliography P 1621). 1985. pap. 3.75 (ISBN 0-89028-291-9). Vance Biblios.

Buchanan, John C. & Bos, Carole D. How to Use Video in Litigation: A Guide to Technology, Strategies, & Techniques. LC 85-9461. Date not set. 75.00 (ISBN 0-13-437070-8). P-H.

Buchanan, John G. Thomas Paine: American Revolutionary Writer. Rahmas, D. Steve, ed. (Outstanding Personalities Ser.: No. 85). (YA) (gr. 7-12). 1976. lib. bdg. 3.50 incl. catalog cards (ISBN 0-87157-585-X); pap. 1.95 vinyl laminated covers (ISBN 0-87157-085-8). SamHar Pr.

Buchanan, Joseph. The Philosophy of Human Nature. Adams, James F., ed. 368p. 1971. 20.00x (ISBN 0-87730-005-4). M&S Pr.

--Philosophy of Human Nature. LC 71-90941. (History of Psychology Ser.). (Illus.). 1969. Repr. of 1812 ed. 50.00x (ISBN 0-8201-1064-7). Schol Facsimiles.

Buchanan, Joseph R. The Story of a Labor Agitator. facsimile ed. LC 75-148873. (Select Bibliographies Reprint Ser.). 1972. Repr. of 1903 ed. 26.50 (ISBN 0-8369-5644-3). Ayer Co Pubs.

Buchanan, Julia W., jt. auth. see Wagner, Henry N., Jr.

Buchanan, Keith & Pough, J. C. Land & People in Nigeria. 1976. lib. bdg. 60.00 (ISBN 0-8490-2122-7). Gordon Pr.

Buchanan, Laurie. Pages To Go!! How to Start & Maintain a Successful Freelance Typing Service. 80p. (Orig.). 1982. pap. 14.95 (ISBN 0-943102-00-6). Pages to Go.

--Pages to Go!!! How to Start & Maintain a Successful Freelance Typing Service. write for info. (ISBN 0-943102-00-6). Buchanan L.

Buchanan, Malcolm, et al. Transport Planning for Greater London. 328p. 1980. text ed. 42.75x (ISBN 0-566-00314-7). Gower Pub Co.

Buchanan, Marcellus, jt. auth. see Terrell, Bob.

Buchanan, Meriel. Dissolution of an Empire. LC 75-115512. (Russia Observed Ser). (Illus.). 1971. Repr. of 1932 ed. 17.00 (ISBN 0-405-03078-9). Ayer Co Pubs.

Buchanan, Neal C. & Chamberlain, Eugene. Helping Children of Divorce. LC 81-67994. 1982. 8.50 (ISBN 0-8054-4926-4). Broadman.

Buchsbaum, John, jt. auth. see Buchsbaum, Mildred.
Buchsbaum, Mildred & Buchsbaum, John. Living Invertebrates. (Illus.). 800p. 1985. text ed. 35.00 (ISBN 0-86542-312-1). Blackwell Pubns.
Buchsbaum, Mildred, jt. auth. see Buchsbaum, Ralph.
Buchsbaum, Ralph. Animals Without Backbones. rev., 2nd ed. LC 48-9508. (Illus.). 405p. 1975. pap. 14.00x (ISBN 0-226-07870-1). U of Chicago Pr.
--Animals Without Backbones: An Introduction to the Invertebrates. rev. ed. LC 48-9508. (Illus.). (gr. 9 up). 1948. text ed. 20.00x (ISBN 0-226-07869-8). U of Chicago Pr.
Buchsbaum, Ralph & Buchsbaum, Mildred. Basic Ecology. (Illus., Orig.). (gr. 9-12). 1957. pap. text ed. 5.95x (ISBN 0-910286-05-1). Boxwood.
Buchsbaum, Steven, jt. auth. see Council on Economic Priorities.
Buchsbaum, W. H. & Mauro, R. Microprocessor-Based Electronic Games. 350p. 1983. pap. 9.95 (ISBN 0-07-008722-9, BYTE Bks). McGraw.
Buchsbaum, Walter. Microprocessor & Microcomputer Data Digest. 1983. text ed. 29.95 (ISBN 0-8359-4381-X). Reston.
Buchsbaum, Walter H. Buchsbaum's Complete Handbook of Practical Electronics Reference Data. 2nd ed. 672p. 1978. 29.95 (ISBN 0-13-084624-4, Busn). P-H.
--Complete Guide to Digital Test Equipment. 240p. 1977. 14.95 (ISBN 0-686-92199-2). P-H.
--Complete TV Servicing Handbook. 256p. 1982. 21.95 (ISBN 0-13-164459-9). P-H.
--Digital IC. (Vestpocket Handbook). (Illus.). 1984. pap. 8.95 (ISBN 0-13-212316-9, Busn). P-H.
--Digital IC Vestpocket Handbook. Date not set. price not set. P-H.
--Encyclopedia of Integrated Circuits: A Handbook of Essential Reference Data. LC 80-21596. 384p. 1981. 24.95 (ISBN 0-13-275875-X). P-H.
--Interface IC. (Vestpocket Handbook). (Illus.). 1984. pap. 8.95 (ISBN 0-13-469205-5, Busn). P-H.
--Interface IC Vestpocket Handbook. price not set. P-H.
--Personal Computers Handbook. 2nd ed. LC 83-50591. 320p. 1984. pap. 14.95 (ISBN 0-672-22094-6, 22094). Sams.
--Tested Electronic Troubleshooting Methods. 2nd ed. LC 82-13167. 272p. 1982. 19.95 (ISBN 0-13-906966-6). P-H.
Buchsenschutz, B. & Blumner, Hugo. Die Hauptstatten des Gewerbfleisses im Klassischen Alterthume & die Gewerbliche Thatigkeit der Volker des Klassischen Alterthums, 2 vols. in 1. Finley, Moses, ed. LC 79-4964. (Ancient Economic History Ser.). (Ger.). 1980. Repr. of 1869 ed. lib. bdg. 23.00x (ISBN 0-405-12353-1). Ayer Co Pubs.
Buchtal, Hugo. Historia Troiana: Studies in the History of Mediaeval Secular Illustration. (Warburg Institute Studies: Vol. 32). pap. 33.00 (ISBN 0-317-16765-0). Kraus Repr.
--The Miniatures of the Paris Psalter: A Study in Middle Byzantine Painting. (Warburg Institute Studies: Vol. 2). Repr. of 1938 ed. 88.00 (ISBN 0-317-16761-8). Kraus Repr.
Buchtal, Hugo & Kurz, Otto. Hand List of Illuminated Oriental Christian Manuscripts. (Warburg Institute Studies: Vol. 12). Repr. of 1942 ed. 20.00 (ISBN 0-317-16762-6). Kraus Repr.
Buchtel, Henry A. The Conceptual Nervous System. LC 82-16509. (Foundations & Philosophy of Science & Technology Ser.). (Illus.). 196p. 1982. 33.00 (ISBN 0-08-027418-8). Pergamon.
Buchter, H. H. Industrial Sealing Technology. 441p. 1979. 64.50 (ISBN 0-471-03184-4, EM20, Pub. by Wiley-Interscience). Wiley.
Buchthal, Hugo. Art of the Mediterranean World: 100-1400 A. D. Folda, Jaroslav, et al, eds. (Art History Ser.: No. V.). (Illus.). 207p. 1983. 75.00 (ISBN 0-916276-11-2). Decatur Hse.
Buchthal, Hugo & Belting, Hans. Patronage in Thirteenth-Century Constantinople. An Atelier of Late Byzantine Book Illumination & Calligraphy. LC 77-99269. (Dumbarton Oaks Studies: Vol. 16). (Illus.). 124p. 1978. 35.00x (ISBN 0-88402-076-2). Dumbarton Oaks.
Buchwald, Ann. Seems Like Yesterday. large print ed. LC 81-8845. 1981. Repr. of 1980 ed. 11.95 (ISBN 0-89621-294-7). Thorndike Pr.
Buchwald, Ann & Buchwald, Art. Seems Like Yesterday. 1981. pap. 2.75 (ISBN 0-425-04833-0). Berkley Pub.
Buchwald, Ann, jt. auth. see Stewart, Marjabelle Y.
Buchwald, Ann, jt. auth. see Young, Marjabelle.
Buchwald, Art. The Bollo Caper: A Furry Tail for All Ages. (Illus.). (gr. 3 up). 1983. pap. 4.95 (ISBN 0-399-21003-2, Putnam). Putnam Pub Group.
--Down the Seine & up the Potomac with Art Buchwald. 1980. pap. 2.75 (ISBN 0-449-23689-7, Crest). Fawcett.
--The Establishment Is Alive & Well in Washington. 256p. 1981. pap. 2.50 (ISBN 0-449-23290-5, Crest). Fawcett.
--I Am Not a Crook. 1977. pap. 2.50 (ISBN 0-449-23404-5, Crest). Fawcett.
--Irving's Delight. 1976. pap. 1.50 (ISBN 0-380-00678-2, 29660). Avon.
--Laid Back in Washington. 384p. 1984. pap. 3.50 (ISBN 0-425-07577-X). Berkley Pub.
--Washington Is Leaking. 1977. pap. 2.50 (ISBN 0-449-23294-8, Crest). Fawcett.
--While Reagan Slept. LC 83-10900. (Illus.). 336p. 1983. 14.95 (ISBN 0-399-12841-7, Putnam). Putnam Pub Group.
--While Reagan Slept. (General Ser.). 1984. lib. bdg. 15.95 (ISBN 0-8161-3664-5, Large Print Bks). G K Hall.
--While Reagan Slept. 1984. pap. 3.95 (ISBN 0-449-12762-1, GM). Fawcett.
--You Can Fool All of the People All of the Time. 1985. 16.95 (ISBN 0-399-13104-3). Putnam Pub Group.
--You Can Fool All of the People All the Time. 336p. 1985. 16.95 (ISBN 0-399-13104-3). Putnam Pub Group.
Buchwald, Art, jt. auth. see Buchwald, Ann.
Buchwald, Emilie. Floramel & Esteban. LC 81-7135. (Illus.). 72p. 1982. 9.95 (ISBN 0-15-228678-0, HJ). HarBraceJ.
Buchwald, Emilie, ed. One-of-a-Kind Monoprints: A Creative Process. 40p. 1984. pap. write for info. (ISBN 0-9613083-0-3). Forecast PAP.
Buchwald, Emilie & Roston, Ruth, eds. The Poet Dreaming in the Artist's House. LC 83-73502. (Illus.). 144p. 1984. 13.95 (ISBN 0-915943-00-X); pap. 7.95 (ISBN 0-915943-01-8). Milkweed Ed.
Buchwald, Emilie, ed. see Burns, Ralph & Pfingston, Roger.
Buchwald, Emilie, ed. see Paddock, Joe.
Buchwald, Emily, ed. see Keenan, Deborah & Moore, Jim.
Buchwald, Henry, et al, eds. Metabolic Surgery. (Modern Surgical Monographs). 336p. 1978. 64.50 (ISBN 0-8089-1077-9, 790720). Grune.
Buchwald, Jed Z. From Maxwell to Microphysics: Aspects of Electromagnetic Theory in the Last Quarter of the Nineteenth-Century. LC 85-1191. (Illus.). 384p. 1985. lib. bdg. 70.00x (ISBN 0-226-07882-5). U of Chicago Pr.
Buchwald, Nathaniel A. & Brazier, Mary A., eds. Brain Mechanisms in Mental Retardation: Based upon a Symposium. (UCLA Forum in Medical Sciences Ser.: No. 18). 1975. 33.50 (ISBN 0-12-139050-0). Acad Pr.
Buchwald, Vagn F. Handbook of Iron Meteorites: Their History, Distribution, Composition & Structure, 3 vols. LC 74-27286. 1976. boxed set 250.00x (ISBN 0-520-02934-8). U of Cal Pr.
Buchwalter, Andrew, tr. see Habermas, Jurgen.
Buci, Moreno. Drawings for the Stage: Italian Set Designs 1790-1850. 1984. pap. write for info (ISBN 0-917105-01-X). W Whitney.
Buci-Glucksmann, Christine. Gramsci & the State. Fernbach, David, tr. from Fr. 485p. 1980. text ed. 37.00x (ISBN 0-85315-483-X). Humanities.
Bucior, Carolyn. Professional Dieters Don't Lose Weight. 57p. 1984. 3.95 (ISBN 0-89697-185-6). Intl Univ Pr.
Buck, jt. auth. see Fuhrman.
Buck, A. A., ed. Onchocerciasis: Symptomatology, Pathology, Diagnosis. (Also avail. in French). 1974. 4.80 (ISBN 92-4-156041-X). World Health.
Buck, Albert H. The Dawn of Modern Medicine. LC 75-23687. Repr. of 1920 ed. 28.50 (ISBN 0-404-13240-5). AMS Pr.
--The Growth of Medicine from the Earliest Times to About 1800. LC 75-23688. Repr. of 1917 ed. 52.50 (ISBN 0-404-13241-3). AMS Pr.
--A Treatise on Hygiene & Public Health, 2 vols. Rosenkrantz, Barbara G., ed. LC 76-25654. (Public Health in America Ser.). 1977. Repr. of 1879 ed. Set. lib. bdg. 106.00x (ISBN 0-405-09810-3); lib. bdg. 53.00x ea. Vol. 1 (ISBN 0-405-09811-1). Vol. 2 (ISBN 0-405-09812-X). Ayer Co Pubs.
Buck, Alfred A. & Sasaki, TOm T. Health & Disease in Four Peruvian Villages: Contrasts in Epidemiology. LC 68-15455. (The John Hopkins Monograph in International Health Ser.). pap. 40.00 (ISBN 0-317-28473-8, 2020739). Bks Demand UMI.
Buck, Alfred A., et al. Health & Disease in Rural Afghanistan. LC 77-186935. (The Johns Hopkins Monographs in International Health). (Illus.). 270p. 1972. 12.00x (ISBN 0-912752-00-9). York Pr.
Buck, Anne. Dress in Eighteenth Century England. LC 79-14489. (Illus.). 240p. 1979. text ed. 34.50 (ISBN 0-8419-0517-7). Holmes & Meier.
--Thomas Lester: His Lace & the East Midlands Industry. 29.95 (ISBN 0-903585-09-X). Robin & Russ.
Buck, Arthur C. Jean Giraudoux & Oriental Thought: A Study of Affinities. LC 83-48764. (American University Studies III (Comparative Literature): Vol. 6). (Orig.). 1984. pap. text ed. 22.00 (ISBN 0-8204-0057-2). P Lang Pubs.
Buck, Barbara D. The Enchanted Heart. 416p. (Orig.). 1980. pap. 2.50 (ISBN 0-523-40520-0). Pinnacle Bks.
Buck, Bruce. Monopoly on Terror. 1978. pap. 1.95 (ISBN 0-89083-431-8). Zebra.
Buck, Carl D. Comparative Grammar of Greek & Latin. LC 33-11254. 1933. 31.00x (ISBN 0-226-07931-7). U of Chicago Pr.
--Dictionary of Selected Synonyms in the Principal Indo-European Languages. LC 49-11769. 1949. 100.00x (ISBN 0-226-07932-5). U of Chicago Pr.
--Greek Dialects. 3rd ed. LC 55-5115. (Midway Reprint Ser). 1973. 20.00x (ISBN 0-226-07934-1). U of Chicago Pr.
Buck, Carl D., jt. auth. see Hale, William G.
Buck, Carlton C. Communion Thoughts & Prayers. new ed. 1977. 5.95 (ISBN 0-8272-0440-X). CBP.
Buck, Carole. At Long Last Love. (Second Chance at Love Ser.: No. 261). 192p. 1985. pap. 1.95 (ISBN 0-425-08019-6). Berkley Pub.
--Encore. (Second Chance at Love Ser.: No. 219). 192p. 1984. pap. 1.95 (ISBN 0-515-08075-6). Jove Pubns.
--Fallen Angel. (Second Chance At Love Ser.: No. 289). 192p. 1985. pap. 2.25 (ISBN 0-425-08511-2). Berkley Pub.
--Intruder's Kiss. (Second Chance at Love Ser.: No. 246). 192p. 1985. pap. 1.95 (ISBN 0-317-13682-8). Jove Pubns.
--Love Play. (Second Chance at Love Ser.: No. 269). 192p. 1985. pap. 2.25 (ISBN 0-425-08200-8). Berkley Pub.
Buck, Craig, jt. auth. see Forward, Susan.
Buck, Craig, jt. auth. see Foward, Susan.
Buck, Daniel. Indian Outbreaks. 1965. Repr. 10.00 (ISBN 0-87018-005-3). Ross.
Buck, David C., tr. see Pampatti.
Buck, David D. Urban Change in China: Politics & Development in Tsinan, Shantung, 1890-1949. (Illus.). 314p. 1978. 29.50x (ISBN 0-299-07110-3). U of Wis Pr.
Buck, Dudley. Illustrations in Choir Accompaniment. LC 79-137316. Repr. of 1892 ed. 18.00 (ISBN 0-404-01145-4). AMS Pr.
--Musical Pronouncing Dictionary. Repr. lib. bdg. 19.00x (ISBN 0-403-03787-5). Scholarly.
--Pronouncing Musical Dictionary. 1976. lib. bdg. 19.00x (ISBN 0-403-03787-5). Scholarly.
--Prouncing Musical Art. lib. bdg. 19.00 (ISBN 0-685-95460-9). Scholarly.
Buck, Edith V. Treasure in Golden Canyon. 120p. (gr. 2-6). 1983. pap. 2.95 (ISBN 0-88207-494-6). Victor Bks.
Buck, Edward R. Introduction to Data Security & Controls. LC 82-62128. (Illus.). 247p. (Orig.). 1982. pap. 19.50 (ISBN 0-89435-062-5). QED Info Sci.
Buck, Elizabeth H., jt. auth. see Buck, Solon J.
Buck, Fraser, jt. auth. see Thompson, George A.
Buck, Frederick H. Glossary of Mongolian Technical Terms. LC 58-59834. (American Council of Learned Societies Publications). 79p. (Orig., Mongolian.). 1958. pap. 3.00x (ISBN 0-87950-257-6). Spoken Lang Serv.
Buck, George. The History of King Richard the Third (1619) Kincaid, A. N., ed. 512p. 1982. text ed. 61.00x (ISBN 0-904387-26-7); pap. text ed. 34.50x (ISBN 0-86299-008-4). Humanities.
Buck, George C., tr. see Von Humboldt, Wilhelm.
Buck, Gertrude. The Metaphor. 1978. Repr. of 1899 ed. lib. bdg. 10.00 (ISBN 0-8495-0439-2). Arden Lib.
--The Metaphor: A Study in the Psychology of Rhetoric. LC 74-847. Repr. of 1899 ed. lib. bdg. 16.50 (ISBN 0-8414-3108-6). Folcroft.
--The Social Criticism of Literature. LC 73-472. 1974. Repr. of 1916 ed. lib. bdg. 10.00 (ISBN 0-8414-1496-3). Folcroft.
Buck, Gordon S. Machinery Alignment Tables: Face-OD & Reverse Indicator Methods. LC 83-22692. 320p. (Orig.). 1984. pap. 18.95x spiral bound (ISBN 0-87201-015-5). Gulf Pub.
Buck, Harry M. Spiritual Discipline in Hinduism, Buddhism, & the West. LC 81-12812. (Focus on Hinduism & Buddhism Ser.). 64p. 1981. pap. 3.95x (ISBN 0-89012-022-6). Anima Pubns.
Buck, Harry M. & Yocum, Glenn A., eds. Structural Approaches to South India Studies. LC 74-77412. 1974. pap. 5.95 (ISBN 0-89012-000-5). Anima Pubns.
Buck, Howard S. Smollett As Poet. 1927. 9.50x (ISBN 0-686-51313-4). Elliots Bks.
--Smollett As Poet. LC 74-3310. 1971. Repr. of 1927 ed. lib. bdg. 10.00 (ISBN 0-8414-3120-5). Folcroft.
--A Study in Smollett Chiefly "Peregrine Pickle". 228p. Repr. of 1925 ed. 10.00x (ISBN 0-911858-09-1). Appel.
--Tempering. LC 70-144708. (Yale Ser. of Younger Poets: No. 1). Repr. of 1919 ed. 18.00 (ISBN 0-404-53801-0). AMS Pr.
Buck, Jack, jt. auth. see Musial, Stan.
Buck, James. Economic Risk Decisions in Engineering & Management. 400p. 1986. text ed. 27.00x (ISBN 0-8138-0544-9). Iowa St U Pr.
Buck, James H., ed. The Modern Japanese Military System, Vol. V. (Armed Forces & Society Ser.). 256p. 1975. 28.00 (ISBN 0-8039-0513-0); pap. 14.00 (ISBN 0-8039-0514-9). Seven Locks Pr.
Buck, James H. & Korb, Lawrence J., eds. Military Leadership, Vol. X. (War, Revolution & Peacekeeping Ser.). 270p. 1981. 28.00; pap. 14.00. Seven Locks Pr.
Buck, James R. & Park, Chan S., eds. Inflation & Its Impact on Investment Decisions. 1984. pap. text ed. 34.95 (ISBN 0-89806-048-6). Inst Indus Eng.
Buck, Jane B. Keeping Cool in Life's Fires. LC 82-6164. 1982. pap. 8.95 (ISBN 0-87397-236-8). Strode.
Buck, Janie B., ed. see Brown, Lou B.
Buck, Jirah D. Symbolism of Freemasonry. 12.00 (ISBN 0-685-19503-1). Powner.
Buck, Joan. Petroleum Lands & Leasing. 184p. 1983. 39.95 (ISBN 0-87814-239-8). PennWell Bks.
Buck, Johanna, jt. auth. see Shelly, Maynard.
Buck, John L. Chinese Farm Economy. Myers, Ramon H., ed. LC 80-8828. (Chinese During the Interregnum 1911-1949, The Economy & Society Ser.). 476p. 1982. lib. bdg. 61.00 (ISBN 0-8240-4683-8). Garland Pub.
--Land Utilization in China, Statistics. Myers, Ramon H., ed. LC 80-8829. (China During the Interregnum 1911-1949, the Economy & Society). 473p. 1981. lib. bdg. 182.00 (ISBN 0-8240-4684-6). Garland Pub.
--Three Essays on Chinese Farm Economy. LC 78-74308. (Modern Chinese Economy Ser.: Vol. 10). 155p. 1980. lib. bdg. 24.00 (ISBN 0-8240-4259-X). Garland Pub.
Buck, John N. House-Tree-Person Technique: Manual. rev. ed. LC 65-28468. (Illus.). 350p. 1970. 39.50x (ISBN 0-87424-301-7). Western Psych.
Buck, L. E. & Goodwin, L. M. Alternative Energy: The Federal Role. 700p. 1982. 80.00 (ISBN 0-07-008730-X). Mcgraw.
Buck, Lee & Schneider, Richard. Tapping Your Secret Source of Power. 14.95 (ISBN 0-8007-1422-9). Revell.
Buck, Linda E. & Goodwin, Lee M. Alternative Energy: The Federal Role. (Federal Regulatory Publications). 600p. 1982. write for info. (Pub. By Shepards-McGraw). McGraw.
Buck, Lucien A. Autonomy Psychotherapy: Authoritarian Control versus Individual Choice. 1979. text ed. 9.95 (ISBN 0-8158-0379-6). Chris Mass.
--Psychological Research & Human Values. LC 76-4267. 80p. 1976. 8.95 (ISBN 0-8158-0340-0). Chris Mass.
Buck, Marcia C. & Smith, Patricia C. Gold Rush Nuggets: A Gold Mine of Information About Ten Counties in California's Mother Lode. (Illus., Orig.). 1984. pap. 9.95 (ISBN 0-930211-00-6). Castle Vent.
Buck, Margaret W. The Face: What It Means. LC 78-56844. 1980. 7.95 (ISBN 0-87212-138-0); pap. 4.95 (ISBN 0-87212-106-2). Libra.
Buck, Mark. Politics, Finance & the Church in the Reign of Edward II: Walter Stapeldon, Treasurer of England. LC 82-17695. (Cambridge Studies in Medieval Life & Thought 19). 248p. 1983. 49.50 (ISBN 0-521-25025-0). Cambridge U Pr.
Buck, Mitchell. The Life of Casanova. LC 76-51406. (Studies in Italian Literature, No. 46). 1977. lib. bdg. 35.95x (ISBN 0-8383-2120-8). Haskell.
Buck, Neal A., jt. auth. see Quick, Allen N.
Buck, Norman S. Development of the Organisation of Anglo-American Trade, 1800-1850. xii, 190p. 1969. Repr. of 1925 ed. 17.50 (ISBN 0-208-00746-6, Archon). Shoe String.
Buck, Otto & Wolf, Stanley M., eds. Nondestructive Evaluation: Microstructural Characterization & Reliability Strategies Proceedings. Fall Meeting, Pittsburgh, 1980. (Illus.). 410p. 32.00 (ISBN 0-89520-375-8); members 20.00 (ISBN 0-317-36255-0); student members 12.00 (ISBN 0-317-36256-9). ASM.
Buck, Otto, et al, eds. Electron & Positron Spectroscopies in Material Science & Engineering. (Materials Science Ser.). 1979. 67.50 (ISBN 0-12-139150-7). Acad Pr.
Buck, Otto, jt. ed. see Wells, Joseph M.
Buck, P. American Science & Modern China, 1876-1936. LC 79-19190. (Illus.). 1980. 34.50 (ISBN 0-521-22744-5). Cambridge U Pr.
Buck, P. see Hadow, William H.
Buck, P. C., ed. John Taverner: Part 1. (Tudor Church Music Ser.: Vol. 1). 1963. Repr. of 1923 ed. write for info. (ISBN 0-8450-1851-5). Broude.
--John Taverner: Part 2. (Tudor Church Music Ser.: Vol. 3). 1963. Repr. of 1924 ed. 85.00x (ISBN 0-8450-1853-1). Broude.
--Orlando Gibbons. (Tudor Church Music Ser.: Vol. 4). 1963. Repr. of 1925 ed. 85.00x (ISBN 0-8450-1854-X). Broude.
Buck, P. C. & Fellowes, E. H., eds. Tudor Church Music. Incl. Vol. 1. John Taverner - Part One (ISBN 0-8450-1851-5); Vol. 2. William Byrd - English Church Music, Part One (ISBN 0-8450-1852-3); Vol. 3. John Tavernen - Part Two (ISBN 0-8450-1853-1); Vol. 4. Orlando Gibbons (ISBN 0-8450-1854-X); Vol. 5. Robert White (ISBN 0-8450-1855-8); Vol. 6. Tallis, Thomas (ISBN 0-8450-1856-6); Vol. 7. Byrd, William (ISBN 0-8450-1857-4); Vol. 8. Thomas Tomkins (ISBN 0-8450-1858-2); Vol. 9 (ISBN 0-8450-1859-0); Vol. 10. Aston, Hugh & Marbeck, John. (ISBN 0-8450-1860-4). 1963. Repr. of 1922 ed. 750.00x set (ISBN 0-8450-1850-7); 85.00x ea.; appendix 50.00x (ISBN 0-8450-1861-2). Broude.
Buck, P. C., ed. see Byrd, William, et al.
Buck, P. C., ed. see Tallis, Thomas, et al.
Buck, P. C., ed. see Tomkins, Thomas.
Buck, P. C., et al, eds. Robert White. (Tudor Church Music Ser.: Vol. 5). 1963. Repr. of 1926 ed. 85.00x (ISBN 0-8450-1855-8). Broude.
Buck, P. H., jt. auth. see Shapiro, H. L.
Buck, P. M., Jr., jt. auth. see Schuyler, W.
Buck, P. S. The Chinese Novel. LC 73-20425. (Studies in Asiatic Literature, No. 57). 1974. lib. bdg. 39.95x (ISBN 0-8383-1766-9). Haskell.
Buck, Paul. Libraries & Universities: Addresses & Reports. Williams, E. E., ed. LC 64-25053. 1964. 12.50x (ISBN 0-674-53050-0, Belknap Pr). Harvard U Pr.

Buck, Paul H., ed. Social Sciences at Harvard, Eighteen Sixty to Nineteen Twenty: From Inculcation to the Open Mind. LC 65-22059. 1965. 22.50x (ISBN 0-674-81420-7). Harvard U Pr.

Buck, Pearl. The Good Earth. 421p. 1981. Repr. lib. bdg. 16.95x (ISBN 0-89966-299-4). Buccaneer Bks.

--The Good Earth. (Arabic.). pap. 8.95x (ISBN 0-86685-137-2). Intl Bk Ctr.

Buck, Pearl S. American Unity & Asia. facsimile ed. LC 72-107687. (Essay Index Reprint Ser.). 1942. 17.00 (ISBN 0-8369-1550-X). Ayer Co Pubs.

--Come, My Beloved. 1975. pap. 1.75 (ISBN 0-671-80084-1). PB.

--East Wind, West Wind. (John Day Bk.). 1973. 14.37i (ISBN 0-381-98026-X, A21660). T Y Crowell.

--God's Men. 1978. pap. 2.25 (ISBN 0-671-82278-0). PB.

--The Good Earth. (gr. 8-12). 1983. pap. 3.95 (ISBN 0-671-50437-1); 2.95 (ISBN 0-671-50086-4). PB.

--Good Earth. (John Day Bk.). 1965. 16.30i (ISBN 0-381-98033-2, A30860). T Y Crowell.

--The Good Earth. Shefter, Harry, ed. (Enriched Classics Edition Ser.). 320p. 1983. pap. 3.95 (ISBN 0-671-50437-1). WSP.

--The Good Earth. 1983. pap. 2.95 (ISBN 0-671-50086-4, RE). WSP.

--The Joy of Children. new ed. LC 74-84887. 1974. 10.00 (ISBN 0-914242-01-6); pap. 7.95 (ISBN 0-686-96679-1). Bookworld Comm.

--The Lovers & Other Stories. LC 76-56819. (John Day Bk.). 1977. 14.37 (ISBN 0-381-97109-0). T Y Crowell.

--The Old Demon. (Classic Short Stories Ser.). (Illus.). 40p. (gr. 6-12). 1982. PLB 8.95 (ISBN 0-87191-828-5). Creative Ed.

--Other Gods: An American Legend. (John Day Bk.). 1940. 8.95i (ISBN 0-381-98047-2, A58200). T Y Crowell.

--Patriot. (John Day Bk.). 1963. 8.95i (ISBN 0-381-98048-0, A60200). T Y Crowell.

--The Rainbow. 1976. pap. 1.75 (ISBN 0-671-80319-0). PB.

--Secrets of the Heart. LC 76-6550. (John Day Bk.). 1965. 14.37i (ISBN 0-381-98287-4). T Y Crowell.

--Sons. 467p. 1985. Repr. of 1932 ed. lib. bdg. 30.00 (ISBN 0-8482-7459-8). Norwood Edns.

--The Story Bible. 1984. lib. bdg. 17.95 (ISBN 0-8161-3661-0, Large Print Bks). G K Hall.

--The Story Bible: New Testament, Vol. 2. 1972. pap. 2.95 (ISBN 0-451-12694-7, AE2694, Sig). NAL.

--The Story Bible: Old Testament, Vol. 1. 1972. pap. 3.95 (ISBN 0-451-13458-3, Sig). NAL.

--Tell the People: Talks with James Yen About the Mass Education Movement. 141p. 1959. 5.00 (ISBN 0-318-14581-2); pap. 4.00 (ISBN 0-318-14582-0). Intl Inst Rural.

--Three Daughters of Madame Liang. (John Day Bk.). 1969. 9.95i (ISBN 0-381-98055-3, A79000). T Y Crowell.

--What America Means to Me. facsimile ed. LC 79-156622. (Essay Index Reprint Ser). Repr. of 1943 ed. 16.00 (ISBN 0-8369-2387-1). Ayer Co Pubs.

--The Woman Who Was Changed & Other Stories. LC 78-69522. 1979. 11.49 (ISBN 0-690-01789-8). T Y Crowell.

Buck, Pearl S. & Reader's Digest Editors. A Pearl Buck Reader, 2 vols. LC 84-6784. (Illus.). 1008p. 1985. Set. 17.97 (ISBN 0-89577-196-9). RD Assn.

Buck, Pearl S. see Howe, D. H.

Buck, Pearl S., tr. All Men Are Brothers - Shui Huchuan, Vol. I. (John Day Bk.). 1968. Repr. of 1933 ed. 10.00i (ISBN 0-381-98017-0, A2000). T Y Crowell.

Buck, Peggy J. Tommy Learns About Time & Eternity. (Illus.). 68p. (Orig.). (gr. 1-3). 1980. pap. 2.50 (ISBN 0-89323-006-5, 023). Bible Memory.

Buck, Peggy S. I'm Divorced - Are You Listening Lord? 1976. pap. 1.25 (ISBN 0-8170-0711-3). Judson.

Buck, Percy C. Psychology for Musicians. 1944. pap. 11.75x (ISBN 0-19-311914-5). Oxford U Pr.

--Scope of Music. facsimile ed. LC 70-93321. (Essay Index Reprint Ser). 1924. 14.00 (ISBN 0-8369-1276-4). Ayer Co Pubs.

Buck, Peter & Hiroa, Te Rangi. Arts & Crafts of Hawaii: Canoes. (Special Pulbication Ser.: No. 45 (6)). (Illus.). 41p. 1957. pap. 3.00 (ISBN 0-910240-39-6). Bishop Mus.

--Arts & Crafts of Hawaii: Clothing. (Special Publication Ser.: No. 45 (5)). (Illus.). 97p. 1957. pap. 4.50 (ISBN 0-910240-38-8). Bishop Mus.

--Arts & Crafts of Hawaii: Death & Burial. (Special Publication Ser.: No. 45 (13)). (Illus.). 26p. 1957. pap. 2.00 (ISBN 0-910240-46-9). Bishop Mus.

--Arts & Crafts of Hawaii: Fishing. (Special Publication Ser.: No. 45 (7)). (Illus.). 78p. 1957. pap. 4.50 (ISBN 0-910240-40-X). Bishop Mus.

--Arts & Crafts of Hawaii: Food. (Special Publication Ser.: No. 45 (1)). (Illus.). 83p. 1957. pap. 4.50 (ISBN 0-910240-34-5). Bishop Mus.

--Arts & Crafts of Hawaii: Games & Recreation. (Special Publication Ser.: No. 45 (8)). (Illus.). 32p. 1957. pap. 3.00 (ISBN 0-910240-41-8). Bishop Mus.

--Arts & Crafts of Hawaii: Houses. (Special Publication Ser.: No. 45 (2)). (Illus.). 52p. 1957. pap. 3.00 (ISBN 0-910240-35-3). Bishop Mus.

--Arts & Crafts of Hawaii: Index. (Special Publication Ser.: No. 45 (14)). 19p. 1957. pap. 1.50 (ISBN 0-910240-47-7). Bishop Mus.

--Arts & Crafts of Hawaii: Musical Instruments. (Special Publication Ser.: No. 45 (9)). 39p. 1957. pap. 3.00 (ISBN 0-910240-42-6). Bishop Mus.

--Arts & Crafts of Hawaii: Ornaments & Personal Adornment. (Special Publication Ser.: No. 45 (12)). (Illus.). 40p. 1957. pap. 3.50 (ISBN 0-910240-45-0). Bishop Mus.

--Arts & Crafts of Hawaii: Plaiting. (Special Publication Ser.: No. 45 (3)). (Illus.). 39p. 1957. pap. 3.00 (ISBN 0-910240-36-1). Bishop Mus.

--Arts & Crafts of Hawaii: Religion. (Special Publication Ser.: No. 45 (11)). (Illus.). 77p. 1957. pap. 3.00 (ISBN 0-910240-44-2). Bishop Mus.

--Arts & Crafts of Hawaii: Twined Baskets. (Special Publication Ser.: No. 45 (4)). (Illus.). 33p. 1957. pap. 3.00 (ISBN 0-910240-37-X). Bishop Mus.

--Arts & Crafts of Hawaii: War & Weapons. (Special Publication Ser.: No. 45 (10)). (Illus.). 57p. 1957. pap. 3.00 (ISBN 0-910240-43-4). Bishop Mus.

Buck, Peter H. Anthropology & Religion. LC 72-121753. viii, 96p. 1970. Repr. of 1939 ed. 12.50 (ISBN 0-208-00950-7, Archon). Shoe String.

--Anthropology & Religion. 1939. 11.50x (ISBN 0-686-83471-2). Elliots Bks.

--Arts & Crafts of the Cook Islands. (BMB). Repr. of 1941 ed. 66.00 (ISBN 0-527-02287-X). Kraus Repr.

--Ethnology of Mangareva. (BMB). Repr. of 1938 ed. 60.00 (ISBN 0-527-02265-9). Kraus Repr.

--Ethnology of Manihiki & Rakahanga. (BMB). Repr. of 1932 ed. 42.00 (ISBN 0-527-02205-5). Kraus Repr.

--Ethnology of Tongareva. (BMB). Repr. of 1932 ed. 37.00 (ISBN 0-527-02198-9). Kraus Repr.

--Introduction to Polynesian Anthropology. (BMB). Repr. of 1945 ed. 21.00 (ISBN 0-527-02295-0). Kraus Repr.

--Mangaian Society. (BMB). Repr. of 1934 ed. 25.00 (ISBN 0-527-02228-4). Kraus Repr.

--Material Culture of Kapingamarangi: Coordinated Investigation of Micronesian Anthropology. (BMB). Repr. of 1950 ed. 37.00 (ISBN 0-527-02308-6). Kraus Repr.

--The Material Culture of the Cook Islands (Aitutaki) LC 75-35178. Repr. of 1927 ed. 36.00 (ISBN 0-404-14206-0). AMS Pr.

--Samoan Material Culture. (BMB). Repr. of 1930 ed. 90.00 (ISBN 0-527-02181-4). Kraus Repr.

--Vikings of the Sunrise. LC 84-22482. (Illus.). xiv, 339p. 1985. Repr. of 1954 ed. lib. bdg. 49.75x (ISBN 0-313-24522-3, BUVS). Greenwood.

Buck, Peter H. see Hiroa, Te Rangi, pseud.

Buck, Philip W. Amateurs & Professionals in British Politics, 1918-59. LC 63-13073. pap. 29.50 (ISBN 0-317-08623-5, 2015751). Bks Demand UMI.

--Politics of Mercantilism. 1964. lib. bdg. 20.00x (ISBN 0-374-91083-9). Octagon.

Buck, Philo M. Directions in Contemporary Literature. LC 75-58254. (Essay Index in Reprint Ser.). 1978. Repr. 26.75x (ISBN 0-8486-3016-5). Core Collection.

--Social Forces in Modern Literature. 1979. Repr. of 1913 ed. lib. bdg. 25.00 (ISBN 0-8495-0393-0). Arden Lib.

--Social Forces in Modern Literature. LC 76-58444. 1913. lib. bdg. 12.50 (ISBN 0-8414-1651-6). Folcroft.

Buck, Philo M., Jr. Directions in Contemporary Literature. 353p. 1983. Repr. of 1942 ed. lib. bdg. 45.00 (ISBN 0-89760-063-0). Telegraph Bks.

--Literary Criticism: A Study of Values in Literature. 432p. Repr. of 1930 ed. lib. bdg. 50.00 (ISBN 0-89760-064-9). Telegraph Bks.

--Milton on Liberty. 1925. lib. bdg. 8.50 (ISBN 0-8414-2517-5). Folcroft.

--The World's Great Age: The Story of a Century's Search for a Philosophy of Life. 382p. 1983. Repr. of 1936 ed. lib. bdg. 45.00 (ISBN 0-89987-959-4). Darby Bks.

Buck, Polly S. Adopted Son of Salem. 1971. 7.95 (ISBN 0-87233-020-6). Bauhan.

Buck, R. C., jt. auth. see Boas, R. P., Jr.

Buck, R. C., ed. Studies in Modern Analysis. LC 62-11884. (MAA Studies: No. 1). 182p. 1962. 16.50 (ISBN 0-88385-101-6). Math Assn.

Buck, R. C., ed. see Philosophy of Science Association, Biennial Meeting, 1970.

Buck, R. Creighton. Advanced Calculus. 3rd ed. LC 77-2859. (McGraw-Hill Intl. Series in Pure & Applied Mathematics). (Illus.). 1978. text ed. 38.95 (ISBN 0-07-008728-8). McGraw.

Buck, Ray. Carlton Fisk: The Catcher who Changed "Sox". LC 81-18090. (Sports Stars Ser.). (Illus.). 48p. (gr. 2-8). PLB 9.25 (ISBN 0-516-04319-6); pap. 2.95 (ISBN 0-516-44319-4). Childrens.

--Danny White: The Kicking Quarterback. (Sports Stars Ser.). (Illus.). 48p. (gr. 2-8). 1983. PLB 9.25 (ISBN 0-516-04335-8); pap. 2.95 (ISBN 0-516-44335-6). Childrens.

--Gary Carter; The Kid. LC 83-21084. (Sports Stars Ser.). (Illus.). 48p. (gr. 2-8). 1984. lib. bdg. 9.25 (ISBN 0-516-04337-4); pap. 2.95 (ISBN 0-516-44337-2). Childrens.

--Jim Plunkett: The Comeback Kid. LC 84-7711. (Sports Stars Ser.). 48p. (gr. 2-8). 1984. lib. bdg. 9.25 (ISBN 0-516-04340-4); pap. 2.95 (ISBN 0-516-44340-2). Childrens.

--Pete Rose: "Charlie Hustle". LC 82-23482. (Sports Stars Ser.). (Illus.). 48p. (gr. 2-8). 1983. PLB 9.25 (ISBN 0-516-04329-3); pap. 2.95 (ISBN 0-516-44329-1). Childrens.

Buck, Ray, jt. auth. see Phillips, O. A.

Buck, Ray, jt. auth. see Phillips, O. Bum.

Buck, Robert N. The Art of Flying: An Eleanor Friede Book. (Illus.). 208p. 1984. 17.95 (ISBN 0-02-518220-X). Macmillan.

--Flying Know-How. 1982. 12.95 (ISBN 0-02-518210-2). Macmillan.

--Weather Flying. rev. ed. (Illus.). 1978. 16.95 (ISBN 0-02-518020-7). Macmillan.

Buck, Robert T., et al. Fernand Leger. LC 81-12869. (Illus.). 160p. 1982. 29.95 (ISBN 0-89659-256-1); pap. 19.95 (ISBN 0-89659-254-5). Abbeville Pr.

Buck, Robert T., et al, eds. Sonia Delaunay: A Retrospective. LC 79-57450. (Illus.). 236p. 1980. pap. 27.50 (ISBN 0-914782-32-0). Buffalo Acad.

Buck, Robert T., Jr., pref. by. The Armand Hammer Collection: Four Centuries of Masterpieces. 1978. 10.00 (ISBN 0-685-46368-0). Buffalo Acad.

Buck, Ross. The Communication of Emotion. (Social Psychology Ser.). 373p. 1984. 27.50 (ISBN 0-89862-110-0). Guilford Pr.

Buck, Ross W. Human Motivation & Emotion. LC 75-37893. 529p. 1976. text ed. 35.45x (ISBN 0-471-11570-3). Wiley.

Buck, Roy C. & Jones, Richard. Heritage Sampler: An Introduction to the Domestic Arts & Crafts of Central Pennsylvania, 1750-1900. (Illus.). 36p. 1979. pap. 5.00 exhibition catalogue (ISBN 0-911209-18-2). Penn St Art.

Buck, Samuel D. With the Old Confeds. 155p. 1984. Repr. of 1925 ed. 16.50 (ISBN 0-913419-01-X). Butternut Pr.

Buck, Solon J. Agrarian Crusade. 1920. 8.50x (ISBN 0-686-83457-7). Elliots Bks.

--The Granger Movement: A Study of Agricultural Organization & Its Political, Economic, & Social Manifestations, 1870-1880. LC 63-9713. (Illus.). xii, 384p. 1963. pap. 6.50x (ISBN 0-8032-5027-4, BB 166, Bison). U of Nebr Pr.

--Illinois in Eighteen Eighteen. LC 67-14657. (Illus.). 369p. 1967. Repr. of 1918 ed. 19.95x (ISBN 0-252-72508-5). U of Ill Pr.

--Travel & Description, 1765-1865. LC 71-147150. (Research & Source Works Ser.: No. 827). 1971. Repr. of 1914 ed. lib. bdg. 29.50 (ISBN 0-8337-0411-7). B Franklin.

Buck, Solon J. & Buck, Elizabeth H. Planting of Civilization in Western Pennsylvania. LC 39-25307. (Illus.). 1939. 20.00 (ISBN 0-910294-28-3). Brown Bk.

--The Planting of Civilization in Western Pennsylvania. LC 39-25307. (Illus.). 1969. pap. 9.95 (ISBN 0-8229-5202-5). U of Pittsburgh Pr.

Buck, Solon J see Johnson, Allen & Nevins, Allan.

Buck, Stratton. Gustave Flaubert. (World Authors Ser.). 1966. pap. 15.95 (ISBN 0-8057-2312-9, Twayne). G K Hall.

Buck, Stuart H., ed. Tibetan-English Dictionary with Supplement. LC 69-16882. (Publications in the Languages of Asia: No. 1). 833p. (Tibetan & Eng.). 1969. 36.95 (ISBN 0-8132-0269-8). Cath U Pr.

Buck, Trevor W. Comparative Industrial Systems. LC 81-9433. 1982. 22.50 (ISBN 0-312-15341-4). St Martin.

Buck, Vernon E. Working Under Pressure. 95.00x (ISBN 0-286-11011-3, Pub. by MCB Pubns). State Mutual Bk.

Buck, William. Mahabarata. 1979. pap. 3.95 (ISBN 0-451-62347-9, ME1783, Ment). NAL.

--Mahabharata. (Illus.). 1974. pap. 7.95 (ISBN 0-520-04393-6). U of Cal Pr.

--Ramayana. 1978. pap. 3.50 (ISBN 0-451-62346-0, Ment). NAL.

--Ramayana. LC 78-153549. (Illus.). 1976. 19.95 (ISBN 0-520-02016-2, CAL 492); pap. 7.95 (ISBN 0-520-04394-4). U of Cal Pr.

Buck, William Pettus. Taming the Buck. 1979. 1.98 (ISBN 0-934530-02-5). Buck Pub.

Buck, Wolfgang. Lenkungsstrategien fuer die Optimale Allokation von Umweltgutern. (European University Studies: No. 5, Vol. 454). 346p. (Ger.). 1983. 38.95 (ISBN 3-8204-7879-5). P Lang Pubs.

Buckalew, J. W. Incidents in the Life of J. W. Buckalew. 1981. pap. 3.25 (ISBN 0-87148-433-1). Pathway Pr.

Buckalew, Jean, ed. see Lurie, H. R.

Buckalew, M. W., Jr. Learning to Control Stress. (Coping with Ser.). (Illus.). (gr. 7-12). 1979. PLB 8.97 (ISBN 0-8239-0496-2). Rosen Group.

Buckalew, Marshall, ed. see Coffey, William E., et al.

Buckalew, Marshall, ed. see Doherty, William T.

Buckalew, Marshall, et al. Teacher's Guide to West Virginia Studies, Our Heritage. 74p. (Orig.). 1984. pap. 10.00 tchr's guide (ISBN 0-914498-06-1). Educ Found.

Buckalew, Vardaman M. & Moore, Michael A. Renal Tubular Dysfunction. LC 79-92915. (Contemporary Patient Management Ser.). 1980. pap. 20.50 (ISBN 0-87488-889-1). Med Exam.

Buck-Alterbaum. Listen Speak: Pathways to Better Speech. 504p. 1983. pap. 19.95 (ISBN 0-8403-3128-2). Kendall-Hunt.

Buckberrough, Sherry A. Robert Delaunay: The Discovery of Simultaneity. Foster, Stephen, ed. LC 82-1869. (Studies in the Fine Arts: The Avant-Garde: No. 21). 416p. 1982. 49.95 (ISBN 0-8357-1297-4). UMI Res Pr.

--Sonia Delaunay: A Retrospective. LC 79-57450. (Illus.). 236p. 1979. pap. 27.50 (ISBN 0-295-96113-9). U of Wash Pr.

Buckby, M. see Allen, W. S.

Buckby, R. J., jt. auth. see Johnson, R. P.

Bucke, Richard. Notes & Fragments: Left by Walt Whitman. 1973. lib. bdg. 35.00 (ISBN 0-8414-0016-4). Folcroft.

Bucke, Richard M. Cosmic Consciousness. rev. ed. 1969. pap. 8.95 (ISBN 0-525-47245-2, 0869-260). Dutton.

--Cosmic Consciousness. 1961. 7.95 (ISBN 0-8216-0000-1). Univ Bks.

--Cosmic Consciousness. 326p. 1984. 6.95 (ISBN 0-8065-0211-8). Citadel Pr.

--Cosmic Consciousness & the Evolution of the Human Mind, 3 vols. (Illus.). 317p. 1984. Set. 317.85 (ISBN 0-317-04417-6). Am Inst Psych.

--Manuscripts, Autograph Letters, First Editions & Portraits of Walter Whitman. LC 72-12956. 1974. Repr. of 1936 ed. lib. bdg. 35.00 (ISBN 0-8414-0987-0). Folcroft.

--Richard Maurice Bucke, Medical Mystic: Letters of Dr. Bucke to Walt Whitman & His Friends. Lozynsky, Artem, ed. LC 77-6818. 172p. 1977. 12.95 (ISBN 0-8143-1576-3). Wayne St U Pr.

--Walt Whitman. 59.95 (ISBN 0-8490-1272-4). Gordon Pr.

--Walt Whitman. LC 30-28216. 1970. Repr. of 1883 ed. 23.00 (ISBN 0-384-06190-7, F401). Johnson Repr.

Buckelew, Alvin H. Terrorism & the American Response. LC 84-61050. 161p. (Orig.). 1984. 12.95 (ISBN 0-917919-00-9). Mira.

Buckenham, June & McGarth, Gerry, eds. The Social Reality of Nursing. 110p. 1983. pap. 11.00 (ISBN 0-683-10017-3). Williams & Wilkins.

Bucker, Bradley, jt. auth. see Lovaas, Ivar.

Bucker, R. C., jt. ed. see Bush, L. P.

Buckeridge, Justin P. A Bolt from the Blue: Five Hundred Fiftieth Airborne Infantry Battalion, 1941-1945. (Airborne Ser.: No. 6). (Illus.). 1978. pap. 10.00 (ISBN 0-89839-006-0). Battery Pr.

Buckett, M. Introduction to Farm Organization & Managements. (Illus.). 280p. 1981. 53.00 (ISBN 0-08-024433-5); pap. 18.00 (ISBN 0-08-024432-7). Pergamon.

--Introduction to Livestock Husbandry. 2nd ed. 1977. 28.00 (ISBN 0-08-021180-1); pap. 10.25 (ISBN 0-08-021179-8). Pergamon.

Buckeye, Nancy M. International Subscription Agents: An Annotated Directory. 4th ed. LC 77-2667. 124p. 1978. pap. 6.00x (ISBN 0-8389-0259-6). ALA.

Buckham, J. W., ed. see Howison, George H.

Buckhingham, James S. Slave States of America, 2 Vols. LC 68-55873. (Illus.). Repr. of 1842 ed. 45.00x (ISBN 0-8371-0330-4, BUS&). Greenwood.

Buckholdt, David, jt. auth. see Gubrium, Jaber F.

Buckholdt, David R. & Gubrium, Jaber F. Caretakers: Treating Emotionally Disturbed Children. 268p. 1985. pap. text ed. 12.50 (ISBN 0-8191-4265-4). U Pr of Amer.

Buckholdt, David R., jt. auth. see Gubrium, Jaber F.

Buckholtz, Eileen & Buckholtz, Howard. ABPC: A Kid's Guide to the IBM Personal Computer. LC 84-50175. (Illus.). 165p. (Orig.). 1984. pap. 10.95 (ISBN 0-672-22227-2, 22227). Sams.

Buckholtz, Eileen & Glick, Ruth. Captain Kid & the Pirates. (Magic Micro Ser.: No. 1). (Illus.). 80p. (Orig.). (gr. 2-5). 1985. pap. 2.25 (ISBN 0-590-33476-X). Scholastic Inc.

--The Cats of Castle Mountain. (Magic Micro Ser.: No. 4). 80p. (Orig.). (gr. 2-5). 1986. pap. 1.95 (ISBN 0-590-33479-4). Scholastic Inc.

--Space Attack. (Micro Adventure Ser.: No. 1). 128p. (gr. 4-7). pap. 1.95 (ISBN 0-590-33165-5). Scholastic Inc.

Buckholtz, Eileen & Settel, Joanne. Kids' Computer IQ Book. LC 83-50176. (Illus.). 152p. (Orig.). (gr. 4-6). 1983. pap. 5.95 (ISBN 0-672-22082-2, 22082). Sams.

Buckholtz, Eileen, jt. auth. see Glick, Ruth.

Buckholtz, Howard, jt. auth. see Buckholtz, Eileen.

Buckholtz, J. D., ed. Complex Analysis, Kentuckt 1976. (Lecture Notes in Mathematics: Vol. 599). 1977. 14.00 (ISBN 0-387-08343-X). Springer-Verlag.

Buckhory, Somduth. The Call of the Ganges: Recollections of a Magical Journey Through India. 1979. 18.00x (ISBN 0-7069-0724-8, Pub. by Vikas India). Advent NY.

Buckhout, Robert, jt. auth. see Ellison, Katherine W.

Buckhout, Robert, jt. auth. see Miller, George A.

Buckingham, A. D., et al. Organic Liquids: Structure, Dynamics & Chemical Properties. LC 78-8462. 352p. 1978. 87.95 (ISBN 0-471-99673-4, Pub. by Wiley-Interscience). Wiley.

--Light Scattering in Physics, Chemistry & Biology. (Royal Society Ser.). (Illus.). 261p. 1980. Repr. of 1979 ed. text ed. 71.00x (ISBN 0-85403-127-8, Pub. by Royal Society London). Scholium Intl.

Buckingham, B. R. Spelling Ability: Its Measurement & Distribution. LC 78-176610. (Columbia University. Teachers College. Contributions to Education: No. 59). Repr. of 1913 ed. 22.50 (ISBN 0-404-55059-2). AMS Pr.

Buckingham, Callie. Nurse at Orchard Hill. (YA) 1978. 8.95 (ISBN 0-685-87346-3, Avalon). Bouregy.

Buckingham, G. L. What to Do about Equal Pay for Women in the United Kingdom. 144p. 1973. 14.95x (ISBN 0-8464-0968-2). Beekman Pubs.

Buckingham, Hugh W. & Kertesz, Andrew. Neologistic Jargon Aphasia. (Neurolinguistics Ser.: Vol. 3). 100p. 1976. text ed. 16.50 (ISBN 90-265-0227-3, Pub. by Swets & Zeitlinger Netherlands). Hogrefe Intl.

Buckingham, J. Dictionary of Organometallic Compounds. (Chemistry Sourcebooks Ser.). 600p. 1985. 230.00 (ISBN 0-412-26320-3, 9076, Pub. by Chapman & Hall). Methuen Inc.

--Heilbron's Dictionary of Organic Compounds: Second Supplement. 5th ed. 700p. 1984. 199.00 (ISBN 0-412-17020-5, NO. 6800, Pub. by Chapman & Hall). Methuen Inc.

Buckingham, J., jt. auth. see Klyne.

Buckingham, J., ed. Dictionary of Organic Compounds: Third Supplement. 5th ed. 800p. 1985. 230.00 (ISBN 0-412-17030-2, 9553, Pub. by Chapman & Hall England). Methuen Inc.

Buckingham, J., et al, eds. Dictionary of Organic Compounds, 7 Vols. 5th ed. 1982. Set. 1950.00x (ISBN 0-412-17000-0, NO.6611, Pub. by Chapman & Hall). Methuen Inc.

Buckingham, J. B., ed. Heilbron's Dictionary of Organic Compounds, 7 vols. 5th ed. 7848p. 1982. 2150.00 (ISBN 0-412-17000-0, NO. 6611). Methuen Inc.

Buckingham, J. B., et al, eds. Dictionary of Organic Compounds: First Supplement. 1983. 175.00 (ISBN 0-412-17010-8, NO. 6798, Pub. by Chapman & Hall). Methuen Inc.

Buckingham, J. E., Sr. Reminiscences & Souvenirs of the Assassination of Abraham Lincoln. LC 80-128964. (Illus.). 89p. 22.50 (ISBN 0-939128-01-2); pap. 17.50 (ISBN 0-939128-02-0). J L Barbour.

Buckingham, Jack. The Accompaniment Guitar: A Beginner's Guide to Song Accompaniment for Individual or Classroom Use. (Illus.). 80p. 1979. pap. 5.95 (ISBN 0-8258-0003-X, 05065). Fischer Inc NY.

Buckingham, James S. National Evils & Practical Remedies, with the Plan of a Model Town. LC 73-21. (Illus.). Repr. of 1849 ed. lib. bdg. 45.00x (ISBN 0-678-00786-1). Kelley.

Buckingham, Jamie. Coping with Criticism. LC 78-60994. 1978. 2.95 (ISBN 0-88270-502-4, Pub. by Logos). Bridge Pub.

--Daughter of Destiny. LC 76-12034. 1976. (Pub. by Logos); pap. 2.95 pocket ed. (ISBN 0-88270-318-8). Bridge Pub.

--Hija del Destino. 288p. 1980. 3.95 (ISBN 0-88113-098-2). Edit Betania.

--Jesus World. 144p. 1981. pap. 4.95 (ISBN 0-310-60021-9, Pub by Chosen Bks). Zondervan.

--The Last Word. LC 78-56932. 1978. pap. 4.95 (ISBN 0-88270-303-X, Pub. by Logos). Bridge Pub.

--Risky Living: The Key to Inner Healing. LC 76-12033. 1976. (Pub. by Logos); pap. 4.95 (ISBN 0-88270-177-0). Bridge Pub.

--A Way Through the Wilderness. (Illus.). 224p. 1983. 10.95 (ISBN 0-310-60550-4, Pub by Chosen Bks). Zondervan.

--Where Eagles Soar. 208p. 1980. pap. 5.95 (ISBN 0-310-60330-7, Pub by Chosen Bks). Zondervan.

Buckingham, Jamie, jt. auth. see Cruz, Nicky.

Buckingham, Jamie, jt. auth. see Ford, Frank.

Buckingham, Jamie, jt. auth. see Katz, Arthur.

Buckingham, Jamie, jt. auth. see Ortiz, Juan Carlos.

Buckingham, Jamie, jt. auth. see Riley, Jeannie C.

Buckingham, Jamie, jt. auth. see Robertson, Pat.

Buckingham, Jamie, jt. auth. see Ten Boom, Corrie.

Buckingham, Jamie, compiled by see Kuhlman, Kathryn.

Buckingham, John, et al, eds. Dictionary of Organometallic Compounds, 3 vols. 3000p. 1984. Set. 990.00 (ISBN 0-412-24710-0, NO. 9075, Pub. by Chapman & Hall). Methuen Inc.

--Dictionary of Organometallic Compounds: Supplement. 400p. 1985. 130.00 (ISBN 0-412-26320-3, NO. 9076). Methuen Inc.

Buckingham, Joseph T. Personal Memoirs & Recollections of Editorial Life. LC 76-125682. (American Journalists Ser). 1970. Repr. of 1852 ed. 24.00 (ISBN 0-405-01657-3). Ayer Co Pubs.

Buckingham, M. J. Noise in Electronic Devices & Systems. (Electrical & Electronic Engineering Ser.). 1985. pap. 34.95 (ISBN 0-470-20164-9). Halsted Pr.

Buckingham, Margaret E. Development & Differentiation, Vol. III. (Biochemistry of Cellular Regulation Ser.). 272p. 1981. 79.50 (ISBN 0-8493-5456-0). CRC Pr.

Buckingham, Melissa F., compiled by. New Reader Development. 3rd ed. 86p. 1982. pap. 15.95 (ISBN 0-88336-577-4, New Readers' Press). Bowker.

Buckingham, Michael J. Noise in Electronic Devices & Systems. (Electrical & Electronic Engineering Ser.). 368p. 1983. 89.95x (ISBN 0-470-27467-0). Halsted Pr.

Buckingham, Nancy. Call of Glengarron. 1980. pap. 1.95 (ISBN 0-441-09102-4). Ace Bks.

--The Jade Dragon. 1976. pap. 1.25 (ISBN 0-532-12444-8). Woodhill.

Buckingham, Nash. The Best of Nash Buckingham. Evans, George B., ed. LC 82-73793. 1973. 17.95 (ISBN 0-8329-1033-3, Pub. by Winchester Pr). New Century.

Buckingham, Peter H. International Normalcy: The Open Door Peace with the Former Central Powers, 1921-29. LC 83-18935. 206p. 1983. lib. bdg. 28.00 (ISBN 0-8420-2215-5). Scholarly Res Inc.

Buckingham, Richard A., jt. auth. see Valvassori, Galdino F.

Buckingham, Richard A., ed. Education & Large Information Systems: Proceedings of the IFIP TC3-TC8 Working Conference, The Hague, The Netherlands, April 1977. 198p. 1978. 42.75 (ISBN 0-444-85047-3, North-Holland). Elsevier.

Buckingham, Robert W. Complete Book of Home Health Care. LC 84-12706. 256p. 1984. 19.50 (ISBN 0-8264-0350-6); pap. 9.95 (ISBN 0-8264-0352-2). Continuum.

--The Complete Hospice Guide. LC 83-47527. 192p. 1983. 13.41i (ISBN 0-06-015192-7, HarpT). Har-Row.

--The Complete Hospice Guide. 180p. 1983. pap. 6.68i (ISBN 0-06-091084-4, CN 1084, CN). Har-Row.

--A Special Kind of Love: Care for the Dying Child. LC 82-22073. 192p. 1983. 12.95 (ISBN 0-8264-0229-1). Continuum.

Buckingham, Thomas. Needs Assessment in ESL. LC 81-38534. (Language in Education Ser.: No. 41). 46p. 1981. pap. 5.95x (ISBN 0-15-599019-5). Ctr Appl Ling.

--Three...Two...One Lift Off. (Readers Ser.). 1984. pap. text ed. 2.50 (ISBN 0-88345-528-5). Regents Pub.

Buckingham, Thomas & Yorkey, Richard. Cloze Encounters: ESL Exercises in a Cultural Context. 160p. 1984. pap. text ed. 9.95 (ISBN 0-13-138875-4). P-H.

Buckingham, W. & Ross, G. W. Honorable Alexander Mackenzie, His Life & Times. LC 68-25225. (English Biography Ser., No. 31). 1969. Repr. of 1892 ed. lib. bdg. 59.95x (ISBN 0-8383-0920-8). Haskell.

Buckingham, Walter S. Automation: Its Impact on Business & People. LC 81-20228. ix, 196p. 1982. Repr. of 1961 ed. lib. bdg. 19.75x (ISBN 0-313-23339-X, BUAU). Greenwood.

Buckingham, Willis J., ed. Emily Dickinson, An Annotated Bibliography: Writings, Scholarship, Criticism & Ana 1850-1968. LC 75-108205. pap. 84.00 (ISBN 0-317-10802-6, 2050039). Bks Demand UMI.

Buckland, Augustus R. John Bunyan: The Man & His Work. LC 76-16025. 1976. Repr. of 1928 ed. lib. bdg. 20.00 (ISBN 0-8414-3319-4). Folcroft.

Buckland, C. E. Dictionary of Indian Biography. LC 68-26350. (Reference Ser. No. 44). 1969. Repr. of 1906 ed. lib. bdg. 59.95x (ISBN 0-8383-0277-7). Haskell.

Buckland, Charles E. Dictionary of Indian Biography. LC 68-23140. 512p. 1968. Repr. of 1906 ed. 65.00x (ISBN 0-8103-3156-X). Gale.

Buckland, D. G. Gymnastics in the Primary School. 1969. pap. text ed. 4.50x (ISBN 0-435-80601-7). Heinemann Ed.

Buckland, Elfreda. The World of Donald McGill. (Illus.). 128p. 1985. 16.95 (ISBN 0-7137-1400-X, Pub. by Blandford England). Sterling.

Buckland, Francis T. Curiosities of Natural History. (Illus.). 318p. Repr. of 1858 ed. 16.95x (ISBN 0-8464-0307-2). Beekman Pubs.

Buckland, Gail. Fox Talbot & the Invention of Photography. LC 79-90358. (Illus.). 216p. 1980. 50.00 (ISBN 0-87923-307-9). Godine.

--Fox Talbot & the Invention of Photography. 216p. 1981. 60.00x (ISBN 0-85967-599-8, Pub. by Scolar England). State Mutual Bk.

Buckland, Gail, jt. auth. see Vaczek, Louis.

Buckland, Michael K. Book Availability & the Library User. LC 74-8682. 220p. 1975. pap. text ed. 12.75 (ISBN 0-08-018160-0). Pergamon.

--Library Services in Theory & Context. 250p. 1983. 25.00 (ISBN 0-08-030134-7); pap. 9.95 (ISBN 0-08-030133-9). Pergamon.

Buckland, P. C. The Environmental Evidence from the Church Street Roman Sewer System. (Archaeology of York-the Past Environment of York Ser.: Vol. 14, Fas. 1). 44p. pap. text ed. 6.45x (ISBN 0-900312-41-6, Pub. by Coun Brit Archaeology). Humanities.

Buckland, Patricia B. Advent to Pentecost-A History of the Church Year. 1979. pap. 4.95 (ISBN 0-8192-1251-2). Morehouse.

Buckland, Patrick. The Factory of Grievances: Devolved Government in Northern Ireland, 1921-1939. LC 79-52164. 364p. 1979. text ed. 28.50x (ISBN 0-06-490752-X, 06372). B&N Imports.

--A History of Northern Ireland. LC 81-909. 220p. 1981. text ed. 22.50x (ISBN 0-8419-0700-5). Holmes & Meier.

--James Craig. (Gill's Irish Lives Ser.). 143p. 1980. 15.95 (ISBN 0-7171-1078-8, Pub. by Gill & Macmillan Ireland); pap. 5.95 (ISBN 0-7171-0984-4). Irish Bk Ctr.

Buckland, R. A. Broadcasting by Satellite. 220p. 1985. pap. text ed. 400.00x (ISBN 0-86353-028-1, Pub. by Online). Brookfield Pub Co.

Buckland, Raymond. Practical Candle-Burning Rituals. (Illus.). 189p. 1984. pap. 5.95 (ISBN 0-87542-048-6). Llewellyn Pubns.

--Ray Buckland's Complete Witchcraft Workbook. Weschcke, Carl L., ed. (Sourcebook Ser.). (Illus.). 320p. (Orig.). 1985. wkbk. 19.95 (ISBN 0-87542-050-8, L-050). Llewellyn Pubns.

--The Tree: The Complete Book of Saxon Witchcraft. LC 74-79397. (Illus.). 158p. 1974. pap. 5.95 (ISBN 0-87728-258-7). Weiser.

--Witchcraft from the Inside. 2nd ed. (Illus.). 145p. 1975. pap. 3.95 (ISBN 0-87542-085-0). Llewellyn Pubns.

Buckland, Raymond & Carrington, Hereward. Amazing Secrets of the Psychic World. 1976. 4.95 (ISBN 0-13-024059-1, Reward). P-H.

Buckland, Raymond, ed. see Schueler, Gerald J.

Buckland, W. R., jt. auth. see Kendall, M. G.

Buckland, W. W. Equity in Roman Law: Lectures Delivered in the University of London, at the Request of the Faculty of Laws. vii, 136p. 1983. Repr. of 1911 ed. lib. bdg. 22.50x (ISBN 0-8377-0339-5). Rothman.

--Some Reflections on Jurisprudence. viii, 118p. 1974. Repr. of 1945 ed. 13.50 (ISBN 0-208-01407-1, Archon). Shoe String.

Buckland, William. Geology & Mineralogy Considered with Reference to Natural Theology, 2 vols. Gould, Stephen J., ed. LC 79-8326. (The History of Paleontology Ser.). (Illus.). 1980. Repr. of 1836 ed. Set. lib. bdg. 69.00x (ISBN 0-405-12706-5); lib. bdg. 34.50x ea. Vol. 1 (ISBN 0-405-12707-3). Vol. 2 (ISBN 0-405-12708-1). Ayer Co Pubs.

--Reliquiae Diluvianae: Observations on the Organic Remains Contained in Caves Fissures, & Diluvial Gravel. Albritton, Claude C., Jr., ed. LC 77-6510. (History of Geology Ser.). (Illus.). 1978. Repr. of 1823 ed. lib. bdg. 30.00x (ISBN 0-405-10433-2). Ayer Co Pubs.

Buckland, William W. Roman Law of Slavery. LC 70-94318. (BCL Ser. I). Repr. of 1908 ed. 41.50 (ISBN 0-404-00140-8). AMS Pr.

--The Roman Law of Slavery: The Condition of the Slave in Private Law from Augustus to Justinian. pap. 160.00 (ISBN 0-317-26066-9, 2024426). Bks Demand UMI.

Buckland-Wright, John. Etching & Engraving. (Illus.). 251p. 1973. pap. 5.95 (ISBN 0-486-22888-6). Dover.

--Etching & Engraving Techniques & the Modern Trend. (Illus.). 14.00 (ISBN 0-8446-4714-4). Peter Smith.

Buckle, D. & Lebovici, S. Child Guidance Centres. (Monograph: No. 40). 133p. (Eng, Fr, Span.). 1960. 5.60 (ISBN 92-4-140040-4). World Health.

Buckle, D. R. & Smith, H., eds. Development of Anti-Asthma Drugs. 420p. 1984. text ed. 89.95 (ISBN 0-408-11576-9). Butterworth.

Buckle, E., ed. Dams of National Hunt Winners, 1955-60. pap. 2.50 (ISBN 0-85131-076-1, NL51, Dist. by Miller). J A Allen.

Buckle, E., compiled by. Dams of National Hunt Winners, 1963-64. pap. 2.95 (ISBN 0-85131-077-X, NL51, Dist. by Miller). J A Allen.

--Dams of National Hunt Winners, 1966-73. (Illus.). pap. 11.50 (ISBN 0-85131-237-3, NL51, Dist. by Miller). J A Allen.

Buckle, Esme. Dams of National Hunt Winners: 1973-1975. 11.95 (ISBN 0-85131-340-X, NL51). J A Allen.

Buckle, Gerard F. Mind & the Film: A Treatise on the Psychological Factors in the Film. LC 70-112573. (Literature of Cinema, Ser. 1). Repr. of 1926 ed. 13.50 (ISBN 0-405-01604-2). Ayer Co Pubs.

Buckle, Henry T. History of Civilization in England. abr ed. Wood, Clement, ed. LC 64-15688. (Milestones of Thought Ser.). 12.00 (ISBN 0-8044-1125-5); pap. 4.95 (ISBN 0-8044-6062-0). Ungar.

--On Scotland - the Scotch Intellect. Hanham, H. J. & Clive, John, eds. LC 78-114958. (Classics of British Historical Literature Ser). 1970. 22.50x (ISBN 0-226-07976-7). U of Chicago Pr.

--On Scotland & the Scotch Intellect. Hanham, H. J., ed. LC 78-114958. (Classics of British Historical Literature Ser). 1972. pap. 3.45x (ISBN 0-226-07977-5, P383, Phoen). U of Chicago Pr.

Buckle, I., ed. see Morgan, William.

Buckle, Ian. W. Morgan's the Elements of Structures. 2nd ed. 252p. 1977. pap. text ed. 24.95 (ISBN 0-273-01079-4). Pitman Pub MA.

Buckle, J. K. Managing Software Projects. LC 84-796. 124p. 1984. Repr. of 1977 ed. lib. bdg. 29.75 (ISBN 0-89874-743-0). Krieger.

--Software Configuration Management. (Computer Science Ser.). (Illus.). 168p. 1983. 35.00x (ISBN 0-333-30719-4); pap. 19.95x (ISBN 0-333-33228-8). Scholium Intl.

Buckle, John W. Animal Hormones. (Studies in Biology: No. 158). 80p. 1983. pap. text ed. 8.95 (ISBN 0-7131-2874-7). E Arnold.

Buckle, Leonard & Buckle, Suzann. Standards Relating to Planning for Juvenile Justice. LC 77-3938. (IJA-ABA Juvenile Justice Standards Project Ser.). 132p. 1980. prof ref 22.50 (ISBN 0-88410-754-X); pap. 12.50 (ISBN 0-88410-807-4). Ballinger Pub.

Buckle, Mary, jt. auth. see Day, Lewis F.

Buckle, Richard. Diaghilev. LC 83-15707. (Illus.). 672p. 1984. pap. 14.95 (ISBN 0-689-70664-2, 306). Atheneum.

--In the Wake of Diaghilev. LC 82-12096. (Illus.). 367p. 1983. 19.95 (ISBN 0-03-062493-2). HR&W.

Buckle, Suzann, jt. auth. see Buckle, Leonard.

Buckleitner, Warren. Survey of Early Childhood Software. 100p. (Orig.). 1985. pap. 19.95 (ISBN 0-931114-32-2). High-Scope.

--Survey of Early Childhood Software. 100p. 1985. 19.95 (ISBN 0-931114-32-2). High-Scope.

Buckler, Francis W. Harunu'l-Rashid & Charles the Great. LC 75-41041. (BCL Ser. II). Repr. of 1931 ed. 11.50 (ISBN 0-404-14761-5). AMS Pr.

Buckler, John. The Theban Hegemony, 371 - 362 B. C. (Harvard Historical Studies: No. 98). (Illus.). 355p. 1980. text ed. 25.00x (ISBN 0-674-87645-8). Harvard U Pr.

Buckler, Robert. Poetry & Truth in Robert Brownings' The Ring & the Book. 352p. 1985. 42.50x (ISBN 0-8147-1072-7). NYU Pr.

Buckler, W. H. The Origin & History of Contract in Roman Law Down to the End of the Republican Period: Being the Yorke Prize Essay for the Year 1893. xi, 228p. 1983. Repr. of 1895 ed. lib. bdg. 24.00x (ISBN 0-8377-0341-7). Rothman.

Buckler, William E. Man & His Myths: Tennyson's "Idylls of the King" in Critical Context. 352p. 1984. 45.00x (ISBN 0-8147-1059-X). NYU Pr.

--Matthew Arnold's Prose: Three Essays in Literary Enlargement. LC 83-45276. (Studies In the 19th Century: No. 3). 116p. 1984. 22.50 (ISBN 0-404-61481-7). AMS Pr.

--On the Poetry of Matthew Arnold. (The Gotham Library). 228p. 1982. 35.00x (ISBN 0-8147-1039-5). NYU Pr.

--The Poetry of Thomas Hardy. (Illus.). 296p. 1983. 37.50x (ISBN 0-8147-1046-8). NYU Pr.

--The Victorian Imagination: Essays in Aesthetic Exploration. (The Gotham Library). 384p. 1980. 40.00x (ISBN 0-8147-1032-8); pap. 20.00x (ISBN 0-8147-1033-6). NYU Pr.

Buckler, William E., jt. auth. see Anderson, George K.

Buckler, William E., ed. The Major Victorian Poets. LC 72-5645. 650p. (Orig.). 1973. pap. 6.50 (ISBN 0-395-14024-2, RivEd). HM.

--Passages from the Prose Writings of Matthew Arnold. 235p. 1983. Repr. of 1963 ed. lib. bdg. 35.00 (ISBN 0-89984-131-7). Century Bookbindery.

--Passages from the Prose Writings of Matthew Arnold: Selected by the Author. LC 63-11302. (Gotham Library). 235p. (Orig.). 1963. 27.00x (ISBN 0-8147-0013-6). NYU Pr.

--Prose of the Victorian Period. (YA) (gr. 9 up). 1958. pap. 6.50 (ISBN 0-395-05128-2, RivEd). HM.

Buckler, William E., ed. see Hardy, Thomas.

Buckles, Mary P. The Flowers Around Us: A Photographic Essay on Their Reproductive Structures. LC 82-24815. 128p. 1985. 29.95 (ISBN 0-8262-0402-3). U of Mo Pr.

Buckles, Patricia, jt. auth. see Elmendorf, Mary.

Buckley. Practical Chess Analysis. Date not set. pap. price not set (ISBN 0-938650-35-1). Thinkers Pr.

Buckley, jt. auth. see Fox.

Buckley, jt. auth. see Goldstein.

Buckley, jt. auth. see Molluzzo.

Buckley, jt. auth. see Pike.

Buckley, A. & Swain, C. Retail Trade Developments in Great Britain. 4th ed. 208p. 1980. text ed. 99.95x (ISBN 0-566-02152-8). Gower Pub Co.

Buckley, A., ed. UK Commodities Yearbook. 1977. 14.00 (ISBN 0-85941-050-1). State Mutual Bk.

Buckley, A., jt. ed. see Hartley, Michael G.

Buckley, A. G. & Goffin, J. L. Algorithms for Constrained Minimization of Smooth Nonlinear Functions. (Mathematical Programming Studies: Vol. 16). 190p. 1982. Repr. 25.75 (ISBN 0-444-86390-7, North-Holland). Elsevier.

Buckley, Amelia K. The Keeneland Association Library: A Guide to the Collection. LC 58-12481. 240p. 1958. 20.00x (ISBN 0-8131-1040-8). U Pr of KY.

Buckley, Ann, tr. see Baker, Theodore.

Buckley, Anne, jt. ed. see Hartley, Michael G.

Buckley, Anthony D. Yoruba Medicine. 320p. 1985. 32.50 (ISBN 0-19-823254-3). Oxford U Pr.

Buckley, Arthur H. & Cook, John B. Gems of Mental Magic. 132p. 1973. pap. 4.00 (ISBN 0-911996-39-7). Gamblers.

Buckley, Barbara E., jt. auth. see Abel, Ernest L.

Buckley, C. H., jt. auth. see Fox, H.

Buckley, Charles. Going to Yukon & Other Things. 5.75 (ISBN 0-8062-2248-4). Carlton.

Buckley, Charles B. An Anecdotal History of Old Times in Singapore, 1819 to 1867. (Illus.). 1984. Repr. of 1902 ed. 69.00x (ISBN 0-19-582602-7). Oxford U Pr.

Buckley, Christopher. Blue Hooks in Weather. 56p. (Orig.). 1983. pap. 15.00 (ISBN 0-939952-03-3). Moving Parts.

--Five Small Meditations on Summer & Birds. 1984. pap. 15.00 (ISBN 0-931460-25-5). Bieler.

--Last Rites. LC 80-12937. 92p. 1980. 4.50 (ISBN 0-87886-109-2). Ithaca Hse.

--Other Lives. LC 85-5545. 75p. (Orig.). 1985. pap. 6.00 (ISBN 0-87886-125-4). Ithaca Hse.

--Steaming to Bamboola: The World of a Tramp Freighter. LC 81-17291. 222p. 1982. 14.95 (ISBN 0-312-92792-4). Congdon & Weed.

--Steaming to Bamboola: The World of a Tramp Freighter. 224p. 1983. pap. 7.95 (ISBN 0-312-92793-2). Congdon & Weed.

Buckley, Cornelius M., tr. see Gache, Louis-Hippolyte.

Buckley, D. H. Surface Effects in Adhesion, Friction, Wear & Lubrication. (Tribiology Ser.: Vol. 5). 632p. 1981. 106.50 (ISBN 0-444-41966-7). Elsevier.

Buckley, David G., ed. Archaeology in Sussex to AD 1500. (CBA Research Report: No. 34). 101p. 1980. pap. text ed. 28.45x (ISBN 0-900312-83-1, Pub. by Coun Brit Archaeology). Humanities.

Buckley, E. F., tr. see Recouly, Raymond.

Buckley, Earle A. How to Write Better Business Letters. 4th ed. (Illus.). 1957. pap. 4.95 (ISBN 0-07-008779-2). McGraw.

Buckley, Edmund H. & Solkov, Arnold. A Conceptual Approach to College Writing. 2nd ed. 112p. 1980. pap. text ed. 7.95 (ISBN 0-8403-2308-5). Kendall-Hunt.

Buckley, Francis J. Reconciling. LC 81-68699. 96p. (Orig.). 1981. pap. 2.95 (ISBN 0-87793-237-9). Ave Maria.

Buckley, Francis J., jt. auth. see De la Cruz Aymes, Maria.

Buckley, Francis J., jt. auth. see Hofinger, Johannes.

Buckley, Gary J., jt. auth. see Mansfield, Don L.

Buckley, H. A., et al. Catalogue of the Ocean Deposits Collection in the British Museum (Natural History), Pt. 2: Indian & Pacific Oceans. (Illus.). 1984. 32.00x (ISBN 0-565-00863-3, Pub. by Brit Mus Nat Hist England); microfiche incl. Sabbot-Natural Hist Bks.

Buckley, Harold. Squadron Ninety-Five. LC 78-169409. (Literature & History of Aviation Ser). 1971. Repr. of 1933 ed. 19.00 (ISBN 0-405-03754-6). Ayer Co Pubs.

Buckley, Harry E. Guillaume Apollinaire as an Art Critic. Kuspit, Donald, ed. LC 80-28095. (Studies in the Fine Arts. Criticism: No. 11). 354p. 1981. 49.95 (ISBN 0-8357-1164-1). UMI Res Pr.

Buckley, Hattie & Kroger, Kenneth. The Mysterious Beau Yeux. 180p. 1982. 10.95 (ISBN 0-89962-266-6). Todd & Honeywell.

Buckley, Helen E. Grandmother & I. LC 60-12031. (Illus.). (gr. k-3). 1961. PLB 11.88 (ISBN 0-688-51204-6). Lothrop.

--Someday with My Father. LC 85-42637. (Illus.). 32p. (ps-3). 1985. 11.06i (ISBN 0-06-020877-5); PLB 11.89g (ISBN 0-06-020878-3). HarpJ.

Buckley, J. H., ed. see Tennyson, Alfred L.

Buckley, J. M. Two Weeks in the Yosemite & Vicinity. facs. ed. (Illus.). 36p. pap. 3.95 (ISBN 0-8466-0153-2, S153). Shorey.

Buckley, James. Street Railways of St. Petersburg, Florida. (Illus.). 48p. (Orig.). 1983. pap. 7.00 (ISBN 0-911940-37-5). Cox.

Buckley, James M. Travels in Three Continents, Europe, Africa, Asia. LC 72-5586. (Black Heritage Library Collection). 1972. Repr. of 1894 ed. 55.00 (ISBN 0-8369-9136-2). Ayer Co Pubs.

Buckley, Jerome H. Season of Youth: The Bildungsroman from Dickens to Golding. LC 73-85887. 352p. 1974. 22.50x (ISBN 0-674-79640-3). Harvard U Pr.

--Tennyson: The Growth of a Poet. LC 60-13298. 298p. 1974. pap. 7.95x (ISBN 0-674-87408-0). Harvard U Pr.

--Triumph of Time: A Study of the Victorian Concepts of Time, History, Progress & Decadence. LC 66-21333. 1966. 12.50x (ISBN 0-674-90960-7, Belknap Pr). Harvard U Pr.

--The Turning Key: Autobiography & the Subjective Impulse Since 1800. 208p. 1984. text ed. 15.00x (ISBN 0-674-91330-2). Harvard U Pr.

--Victorian Poets & Prose Writers. 2nd ed. LC 76-5212. (Goldentree Bibliographies in Language & Literature Ser.). 1977. pap. text ed. 14.95x (ISBN 0-88295-560-8). Harlan Davidson.

--Victorian Temper: A Study in Literary Culture. new ed. (Illus.). 282p. 1966. 27.50x (ISBN 0-7146-2052-1, F Cass Co). Biblio Dist.

--The Victorian Temper: A Study in Literary Culture. LC 81-6142. (Illus.). 282p. 1981. pap. 12.95 (ISBN 0-521-28448-1). Cambridge U Pr.

--Victorian Temper: A Study in Literary Culture. LC 74-89967. (Illus.). 1969. 15.00x (ISBN 0-674-93680-9). Harvard U Pr.

--William Ernest Henley: A Study in the Counter-Decadence of the Nineties. LC 74-120238. 1971. Repr. lib. bdg. 18.50x (ISBN 0-374-91087-1). Octagon.

Buckley, Jerome H. & Woods, George B. Poetry of the Victorian Period. 3rd ed. 1965. text ed. 23.80x (ISBN 0-673-05630-9). Scott F.

Buckley, Jerome H., ed. The Worlds of Victorian Fiction. LC 75-5549. (English Studies: No. 6). 432p. 1975. text ed. 27.50x (ISBN 0-674-96205-2); pap. text ed. 7.95x (ISBN 0-674-96207-9). Harvard U Pr.

Buckley, Jerome H., ed. see Dickens, Charles.

Buckley, John. Course Manual for Public Speaking. 6th ed. 100p. 1984. pap. text ed. 4.95 (ISBN 0-89892-013-2). Contemp Pub Co of Raleigh.

--The Training of Secondary School Heads in Western Europe. 192p. 1985. 20.00 (ISBN 0-7005-0691-8). Taylor & Francis.

Buckley, John D., ed. Advanced Materials: Composites & Carbons. LC 72-181591. (Illus.). pap. text ed. 13.00 (ISBN 0-916094-20-0); pap. text ed. 11.00 members (ISBN 0-686-85593-0); pap. text ed. 9.00 students (ISBN 0-686-91498-8). Am Ceramic.

Buckley, John J., jt. auth. see Mulliken, Ruth K.

Buckley, John J. see Roosevelt, Theodore, et al.

Buckley, John P. The New York Irish: Their View of American Foreign Policy, 1914-1921. LC 76-6327. (Irish Americans Ser). 1976. 31.00 (ISBN 0-405-09324-1). Ayer Co Pubs.

Buckley, John W. Executives Digest of Financial Research-1975. LC 77-91131. 1977. 8.00 (ISBN 0-910586-18-7). Finan Exec.

--Income Tax Allocation: An Inquiry into Problems of Methodology & Estimation. LC 72-87212. 1972. 12.00 (ISBN 0-910586-04-7). Finan Exec.

Buckley, John W. & Buckley, Marlene H. The Accounting Profession. LC 74-8880. (Melville Series on Management, Accounting, & Information Systems). (Illus.). pap. 43.90 (ISBN 0-317-09576-5, 2015174). Bks Demand UMI.

Buckley, John W., ed. see UCLA Extension.

Buckley, John W., et al. Research Methodology & Business Decisions. 89p. 9.95 (ISBN 0-86641-039-2, 7581). Natl Assn Accts.

Buckley, Joseph C. The Retirement Handbook: A Complete Guide to Planning Your Future. 6th ed. Schmidt, Henry, ed. LC 78-138712. (Illus.). 1977. 12.45i (ISBN 0-06-010568-2, HarpT). Har-Row.

Buckley, Joseph P. & Ferrario, Carlos, eds. Central Nervous System Mechanisms in Hypertension. (Perspectives in Cardiovascular Research Ser.: Vol. 6). 434p. 1981. 57.50 (ISBN 0-89004-545-3). Raven.

Buckley, Julian G. & Loll, Leo M. The Over-the-Counter Securities Markets. (Illus.). 480p. 1981. text ed. 27.95 (ISBN 0-13-647172-2). P-H.

Buckley, Kathleen & Kulb, Nancy. Handbook of Maternal-Newborn Nursing. LC 82-20048. (Red Book Ser.). 654p. 1983. pap. 18.50 (ISBN 0-471-86984-8, Pub. by Wiley Med). Wiley.

Buckley, Larry. Easy-to-Make Slotted Furniture. (Illus.). 52p. (Orig.). 1980. pap. 2.25 (ISBN 0-486-23983-7). Dover.

Buckley, Lord. Hiparama of the Classics. 1980. pap. 3.00 (ISBN 0-87286-120-1). City Lights.

Buckley, Marie. Breaking into Prison: A Citizen Guide to Volunteer Action. LC 74-206. 192p. 1974. 10.95x (ISBN 0-8070-0876-1). Beacon Pr.

Buckley, Marlene H., jt. auth. see Buckley, John W.

Buckley, Mary & Keep, Deborah. Colorado Corporation Formation Package & Minute Book. (Successful Business Library). 1985. 3-ring binder 33.95 (ISBN 0-916378-53-5). PSI Res.

Buckley, Mary & Baum, David, eds. Color Theory: A Guide to Information Sources. LC 73-17517. (Art & Architecture Information Guide Ser.: Vol. 2). x, 173p. 1975. 60.00x (ISBN 0-8103-1275-1). Gale.

Buckley, Mary I., jt. ed. see Klaven, Janet.

Buckley, Michael. Why Are You Afraid. pap. 5.95 (ISBN 0-87061-060-0). Chr Classics.

Buckley, Michael, jt. auth. see Samagalski, Alan.

Buckley, Michael J. Motion & Motion's God: Thematic Variations in Aristotle, Cicero, Newton, & Hegel. LC 73-132234. 1971. 29.00 (ISBN 0-691-07124-1). Princeton U Pr.

Buckley, Mort. Single's Pocket Guide to Survival: Single's Survival. DeMente, Boye, ed. LC 83-90907. (Illus.). 304p. (Orig.). 1983. pap. 9.95 (ISBN 0-914067-00-1). Single Graph.

Buckley, Mortimer J., ed. Cardiovascular Surgery, 1975. LC 66-9486. (AHA Monograph: Vol. 50). cancelled 5.00 (ISBN 0-87493-051-0, 73-036-A). Am Heart.

--Cardiovascular Surgery, 1977. (AHA Monograph: No. 59). 1979. cancelled 5.00 (ISBN 0-685-49694-5, 73-045-A). Am Heart.

Buckley, Nancy K. & Walker, Hill M. Modifying Classroom Behavior: A Manual of Procedure for Classroom Teachers. rev. ed. LC 78-61156. (Illus.). 142p. 1978. pap. text ed. 8.95 (ISBN 0-87822-189-1, 0089). Res Press.

Buckley, P. M., jt. auth. see Hoskyns, A. H.

Buckley, Page S. Techniques of Process Control. LC 78-10782. 316p. 1979. Repr. of 1964 ed. lib. bdg. 27.50 (ISBN 0-88275-777-6). Krieger.

Buckley, Page S., et al. Design of Distillation Column Control Systems. LC 84-27813. (Illus.). 576p. 1985. 49.95 (ISBN 0-87664-812-X). Instru Soc.

Buckley, Patricia, jt. auth. see Maffei, Anthony C.

Buckley, Paul & Peat, F. David. A Question of Physics: Conversations in Physics & Bio. LC 78-8096. 1978. 20.00x (ISBN 0-8020-2295-2). U of Toronto Pr.

Buckley, Peter, ed. Essential Papers on Object Relations. 384p. 1985. text ed. 40.00x (ISBN 0-8147-1079-4); pap. text ed. 20.00x (ISBN 0-8147-1080-8). NYU Pr.

Buckley, Peter J. & Casson, Mark. The Economic Theory of the Multinational Enterprise: Selected Papers. LC 84-18198. 208p. 1985. 27.50 (ISBN 0-312-23636-0). St Martin.

--The Future of the Multinational Enterprise. LC 76-6058. 120p. 1976. text ed. 24.50x (ISBN 0-8419-0272-0). Holmes & Meier.

Buckley, Peter J. & Enderwick, Peter. The Industrial Relations Practices of Foreign-Owned Firms in Britain. 160p. 1985. 29.50x (ISBN 0-8448-1478-4). Crane-Russak Co.

Buckley, Peter J. & Roberts, Brian R. European Direct Investment in the U. S. A. Before World War I. 1981. 27.50 (ISBN 0-312-26940-4). St Martin.

Buckley, Peter J., et al. Direct Investment in the United Kingdom by Smaller European Firms. 251p. 1984. 29.50x (ISBN 0-8448-1457-1). Crane Russak Co.

Buckley Press Ltd., ed. The Insurance Directory & Year Book 1985. (Post Magazine Almanack Ser.). 700p. 210.00 (ISBN 0-686-45448-0, Pub. by Buckley Pr England). State Mutual Bk.

Buckley, R. Ant-Plant Interactions in Australia. 1982. text ed. 54.50 (ISBN 90-6193-684-5, Pub. by Junk Pubs Netherlands). Kluwer Academic.

--Oscillations & Waves. (Student Monographs in Physics). 64p. 1985. pap. write for info. (Pub. by Adam Hilger Techo Hse UK). Heyden.

Buckley, Raymond, jt. auth. see Haw, Frank.

Buckley, Raymond M., jt. auth. see Haw, Frank.

Buckley, Reginald R. The Shakespeare Revival & the Stratford-Upon Avon Movement. 223p. 1981. Repr. of 1911 ed. lib. bdg. 35.00 (ISBN 0-89984-068-X). Century Bookbindery.

--The Shakespeare Revival & the Stratford-Upon-Avon Movement. 1977. Repr. of 1911 ed. lib. bdg. 30.00 (ISBN 0-8492-0349-X). R West.

Buckley, Richard. The Foolish Tortoise. Saunders, Robert, ed. (Illus.). 20p. (ps up). 1985. pap. 3.95 (ISBN 0-88708-002-2, Pub. by Picture Bk Studio USA). Neugebauer Pr.

--The Greedy Python. Saunders, Robert, ed. (Illus.). 20p. (ps up). 1985. pap. 3.95 (ISBN 0-88708-001-4, Pub. by Picture Bk Studio USA). Neugebauer Pr.

Buckley, Rober N. Slaves in Red Coats: The British West India Regiments, 1795-1815. LC 78-16830. (Illus.). 1979. 27.00x (ISBN 0-300-02216-6). Yale U Pr.

Buckley, Robert H., et al, eds. Capital Markets & the Housing Sector: Perspectives on Financial Reform. LC 77-5117. 416p. 1977. prof ref 22.50x (ISBN 0-88410-658-6). Ballinger Pub.

Buckley, Roger. Japan Today. (Illus.). 168p. 1985. 24.95 (ISBN 0-521-26089-2); pap. 7.95 (ISBN 0-521-27832-5). Cambridge U Pr.

--Occupation Diplomacy: Britain, the United States & Japan, 1945-1952. LC 82-4147. (International Studies). (Illus.). 296p. 1982. 44.50 (ISBN 0-521-23567-7). Cambridge U Pr.

Buckley, Shawn. Sun Up to Sun Down: Understanding Solar Energy. (Illus.). 1979. pap. 6.95 (ISBN 0-07-008790-3). McGraw.

Buckley, Steve, jt. auth. see Favazza, Auggie.

Buckley, Theodore A. The Dawnings of Genius. 1973. Repr. of 1853 ed. 50.00 (ISBN 0-8274-1447-1). R West.

Buckley, Thomas C. & Green, Ellen, eds. Rendezvous: Selected Papers of the Fourth North American Fur Trade Conference, 1981. LC 84-5985. (Illus.). 231p. (Orig.). 1984. pap. write for info. (ISBN 0-9613451-0-1). Fourth NA Am Fur.

Buckley, Thomas E. Church & State in Revolutionary Virginia, 1776-1787. LC 77-4283. xii, 217p. 1977. 14.95x (ISBN 0-8139-0692-X). U Pr of Va.

Buckley, Thomas H. The United States & the Washington Conference, 1921-1922. LC 79-100409. pap. 59.00 (ISBN 0-317-20137-9, 2023166). Bks Demand UMI.

Buckley, Tom. Violent Neighbors: El Salvador, Central America, & the United States. LC 82-40366. 358p. 1984. 17.95 (ISBN 0-8129-1035-4). Times Bks.

Buckley, Vincent. Essays in Poetry. facs. ed. LC 77-86738. (Essay Index Reprint Ser). 1957. 18.00 (ISBN 0-8369-1174-1). Ayer Co Pubs.

--Henry Handel Richardson. LC 73-4429. 1973. lib. bdg. 7.50 (ISBN 0-8414-1759-8). Folcroft.

--Memory Ireland: Nonfiction Ser. 272p. 1985. pap. 6.95 (ISBN 0-317-19374-0). Penguin.

Buckley, Virgina, jt. auth. see Seide, Diame.

Buckley, Virginia, ed. see Hopper, Nancy J.

Buckley, Virginia, ed. see Kidd, Ronald.

Buckley, Virginia, ed. see Levinson, Nancy S.

Buckley, Walter, ed. Modern Systems Research for the Behavioral Scientist: A Sourcebook. LC 66-19888. (Illus.). 1968. 45.00 (ISBN 0-202-30011-0). Aldine Pub.

Buckley, William F. Who's on First. LC 79-55374. 1980. 13.95 (ISBN 0-385-14681-7). Doubleday.

Buckley, William F. & Little, Stuart, eds. The Buckley-Little Catalogue, 1985. Bio. 185p. 1985. pap. 8.50 (ISBN 0-317-30251-5). NY Zoetrope.

Buckley, William F., Jr. Airborne: A Sentimental Journey. 1984. 19.45i (ISBN 0-316-11438-3); pap. 9.70i (ISBN 0-316-11439-1). Little.

--Atlantic High. (Illus.). 280p. 1983. pap. 9.70i (ISBN 0-316-11440-5). Little.

--Atlantic High: A Celebration. LC 81-43455. (Illus.). 280p. 1982. 22.50 (ISBN 0-385-15233-7). Doubleday.

--The Buckley-Little Catalogue, 1985. 1985. pap. 8.50 (ISBN 0-916667-02-2). Buckley Little.

--Buckley-Little Catalogue, 1986. 1986. pap. 8.50 (ISBN 0-916667-03-0). Buckley Little.

--God & Man at Yale: The Superstitions of "Academic Freedom". 304p. 1977. pap. 6.95 (ISBN 0-89526-692-X). Regnery-Gateway.

--A Hymnal. 320p. 1981. pap. 3.50 (ISBN 0-425-04583-8). Berkley Pub.

--Marco Polo, If You Can. 1983. pap. 3.95 (ISBN 0-380-61424-3, 61804-4). Avon.

--Overdrive: A Personal Documentary. LC 82-45349. (Illus.). 272p. 1983. 16.95 (ISBN 0-385-18269-4). Doubleday.

--Overdrive: A Personal Documentary. (Illus.). 272p. 1984. pap. 8.70i (ISBN 0-316-11449-9). Little.

--Right Reason. LC 85-4475. 456p. 1985. 19.95 (ISBN 0-385-15235-3). Doubleday.

--Saving the Queen. 288p. 1981. pap. 3.50 (ISBN 0-380-55111-X, 69393). Avon.

--Saving the Queen. LC 75-17405. 1976. 13.95 (ISBN 0-385-03800-3). Doubleday.

--See You Later, Alligator. LC 84-18813. 312p. 1985. 16.95 (ISBN 0-385-19442-0). Doubleday.

--Stained Glass. 352p. 1981. pap. 3.50 (ISBN 0-380-54791-0, 69443). Avon.

--Stained Glass. LC 77-91557. 1978. 13.95 (ISBN 0-385-12542-9). Doubleday.

--The Story of Henri Tod. LC 83-45201. 264p. 1984. 14.95 (ISBN 0-385-15234-5). Doubleday.

--The Story of Henri Tod. large print ed. LC 84-5973. 397p. 1984. Repr. of 1984 ed. 14.95 (ISBN 0-89621-537-7). Thorndike Pr.

--The Story of Henri Tod. 272p. 1985. pap. 3.95 (ISBN 0-440-18327-8). Dell.

--The Temptation of Wilfred Malachey. (Goblin Tales Ser.). 1985. 10.95 (ISBN 0-317-30493-3). Workman Pub.

--Up from Liberalism. 304p. 1985. 16.95 (ISBN 0-8128-2969-7); pap. 3.95 (ISBN 0-8128-8130-3). Stein & Day.

Buckley, William F., Jr. & Little, Stuart W. The Buckley-Little Catalogue, 1984. 152p. 1984. pap. 7.50 (ISBN 0-916667-01-4). Buckley-Little.

Buckley, William F., Jr., ed. Committee & Its Critics. LC 62-7342. 1963. pap. 1.95 (ISBN 0-911956-06-9). Constructive Action.

Buckley, William, Jr. Who's on First. 288p. 1981. pap. 2.95 (ISBN 0-380-52555-0, 52555-0). Avon.

Buckley, William K., jt. auth. see Luce, Stanford L.

Bucklin, Louis. Studies in Distribution Systems, Vol. 1. Date not set. 40.00 (ISBN 0-89232-274-8). Jai Pr.

Bucklin, Louis P. Productivity in Marketing. LC 78-24445. pap. 32.50 (ISBN 0-317-29936-0, 2021521). Bks Demand UMI.

Buckman, David. James Bolivar Manson: An English Impressionist. 56p. 1981. 25.00x (ISBN 0-686-97684-3, Pub. by Redcliffe England). State Mutual Bk.

Buckman, Joseph. Immigrants & the Class Struggle: The Jewish Immigrant in Leeds, 1880-1914. LC 83-822. 208p. 1983. 21.00 (ISBN 0-7190-0908-1, Pub. by Manchester Univ Pr). Longwood Pub Group.

Buckman, P. Let's Dance: Social & Ballroom Dancing. (Ballrom Dance Ser.). 1985. lib. bdg. 79.50 (ISBN 0-87700-856-6). Revisionist Pr.

Buckman, Peter. All for Love: A Study in Soap Opera. 1985. 15.95 (ISBN 0-88162-083-1, Pub. by Salem Hse Ltd). Merrimack Pub Cir.

Buckman, Thomas R., tr. see Lagerkvist, Par.

Buckmann, Carol I., jt. auth. see Siegel, Mayer.

Buckmaster, Henrietta. Flight to Freedom: The Story of the Underground Railroad. LC 58-9731. (gr. 7 up). 1958. Crowell Jr Bks.

Buckmaster, J. D. & Ludford, G. S. S. Lectures on Mathematical Combustion. LC 83-61375. (CBMS-NSF Regional Conference Ser.: No. 43). viii, 126p. 1983. pap. text ed. 14.50 (ISBN 0-89871-186-X). Soc Indus-Appl Math.

--Theory of Laminar Flames. LC 81-21573. (Cambridge Monographs on Mechanics & Applied Mathematics Ser.). (Illus.). 250p. 1982. 54.50 (ISBN 0-521-23929-X). Cambridge U Pr.

Buckmaster, J. D., ed. Fluid Mechanics in Energy Conversion. LC 80-65817. (SIAM-SIMS Conference Ser.: No. 7). ix, 315p. 1980. pap. 31.00 (ISBN 0-89871-165-7). Soc Indus-Appl Math.

Buckmaster, John. A Village Politician. 340p. 1982. 19.75 (ISBN 0-904573-37-0); pap. 9.75 (ISBN 0-904573-76-1). Caliban Bks.

Buckmaster, John D., ed. The Mathematics of Combustion. LC 85-50339. (Frontiers in Applied Mathematics: No. 2). xii, 288p. 1985. 32.50 (ISBN 0-89871-053-7). Soc Indus-Appl Math.

Buckmill, John C. The Mad Folk of Shakespeare. 59.95 (ISBN 0-8490-0574-4). Gordon Pr.

Buckminster Staff. Synergetic Stew: Explorations in Dymaxion Dining. 120p. (Orig.). 1982. 6.95 (ISBN 0-911573-00-3). Buckminster Fuller.

Buck-Morss, Susan. The Origin of Negative Dialectics: Theodor W. Adorno, Walter Benjamin, & the Frankfurt Institute. LC 76-55103. 1979. pap. text ed. 14.95 (ISBN 0-02-905150-9). Free Pr.

Bucknall, Barbara J. Religion of Art in Proust. LC 78-83546. (Studies in Language & Literature, Vol. 60). 222p. 1970. 19.95x (ISBN 0-252-00022-6). U of Ill Pr.

--Ursula K. LeGuin. LC 81-10371. (Recognitions). 186p. 1981. 11.95 (ISBN 0-8044-2085-8); pap. 5.95 (ISBN 0-8044-6063-9). Ungar.

Bucknall, Benjamin, tr. see Viollet-Le-Duc, Eugene E.

Bucknall, Caroline. One Bear All Alone. (Illus.). 32p. (ps-2). 1985. 9.95 (ISBN 0-8037-0238-8). Dial Bks Young.

Bucknell, Arthur, jt. auth. see Dentinger, Jane.

Bucknell, Howard, III. Energy & the National Defense. Davis, Vincent, ed. LC 79-57566. (Essays for the Third Century). 256p. (General editor, Vincent Davis). 1981. 22.00x (ISBN 0-8131-0402-5). U Pr of Ky.

Bucknell, P. Controlled Drugs & the Law. (Library of Criminal Law Ser.). 352p. 1985. 40.00 (ISBN 0-08-039203-2). Pergamon.

Bucknell, Peter A. Entertainment & Ritual, Six Hundred to Sixteen Hundred. (Illus.). 223p. 1979. 29.50x (ISBN 0-8476-6239-X). Rowman.

Bucknell, Peter A., jt. auth. see Hill, Margot H.

Buckner, Chester A. Educational Diagnosis of Individual Pupils. LC 71-176611. (Columbia University. Teachers College. Contributions to Education: No. 98). Repr. of 1919 ed. 22.50 (ISBN 0-404-55098-3). AMS Pr.

Buckner, Donald N. & McGrath, James J., eds. Vigilance: A Symposium. LC 75-31356. 1976. Repr. of 1963 ed. lib. bdg. 22.50x (ISBN 0-8371-8528-9, BUVI). Greenwood.

Buckner, Hugh, ed. Business Planning for the Board. (Director's Bookshelf Ser). 256p. 1971. 27.95x (ISBN 0-8464-0227-0). Beekman Pubs.

Buckner, John E. Son of Man. 1981. 4.95 (ISBN 0-8062-1796-0). Carlton.

Buckner, John W. Cap Gate's Tent City: A History of Crossett, Arkansas. (Illus.). 206p. 1983. 12.50 (ISBN 0-914546-48-1). Rose Pub.

Buckner, Kathryn D. Littleton's Contribution to the Theory of Accountancy. LC 75-12596. (Research Monograph: No. 62). 1975. spiral bdg. 35.00 (ISBN 0-88406-094-2). Ga St U Busn Pub.

Buckner, Leroy M. Customer Services. (Occupational Manuals & Projects in Marketing). (Illus.). 1978. pap. text ed. 8.68 text-wkbk. (ISBN 0-07-008823-3). McGraw.

Buckner, Michael D., jt. auth. see Abrams, Natalie.

Buckner, Nancy, jt. auth. see Isbit, Arthur.

Buckner, Phillip A. The Transition to Responsible Government: British Policy in British North America 1815-1850. LC 84-12811. (Contributions in Comparative Colonial Studies: No. 17). xi, 358p. 1985. lib. bdg. 35.00 (ISBN 0-313-24630-0, BTV/). Greenwood.

Buckner, Phillip A., jt. ed. see Bercuson, David J.

Buckner, R. B. A Manual on Astronomic & Grid Azimuth. (Illus.). 255p. 1984. pap. text ed. 17.50 (ISBN 0-910845-22-0, 955). Landmark Ent.

--Surveying Measurements & Their Analysis. (Illus.). 274p. 1983. 28.50x (480). Landmark Ent.

--Surveying Measurements & Their Analysis. (Illus.). 288p. 1983. text ed. 28.50 (ISBN 0-910845-11-5, 480). Landmark Ent.

Bucknill, John C. Mad Folk of Shakespeare: Psychological Essays. 2nd ed. LC 71-103835. (Research & Source Works Ser.: No. 394). 1970. Repr. of 1867 ed. 20.50 (ISBN 0-8337-0412-5). B Franklin.

--Medical Knowledge of Shakespeare. LC 72-155634. Repr. of 1860 ed. 12.50 (ISBN 0-404-01146-2). AMS Pr.

--Notes on Asylums for the Insane in America. LC 73-2391. (Mental Illness & Social Policy; the American Experience Ser.). Repr. of 1876 ed. 11.50 (ISBN 0-405-05199-9). Ayer Co Pubs.

--Psychology of Shakespeare. LC 72-131514. Repr. of 1859 ed. 21.00 (ISBN 0-404-01147-0). AMS Pr.

--Unsoundness of Mind in Relation to Criminal Acts. Bd. with Care of the Insane & Their Legal Control; Factors of the Unsound Mind. Guy, W. A. (Contributions to the History of Psychology Ser., Vol. IV Pt. F: Insanity & Jurisprudence). 1983. Repr. of 1854 ed. 30.00 (ISBN 0-89093-329-4). U Pubns Amer.

Bucknill, John C. & Hammond, William. Insanity & the Law: Two Nineteenth Century Classics. LC 81-916. (The Historical Foundations of Forensic Psychiatry & Psychology Ser.). 145p. 1981. Repr. of 1856 ed. lib. bdg. 29.50 (ISBN 0-306-76066-5). Da Capo.

Buckroyd, Julia. Church & State in Scotland: Sixteen Sixty to Sixteen Eighty-One. 1980. text ed. 33.00x (ISBN 0-85976-042-1). Humanities.

Bucks County Community College, jt. auth. see Carter, James J.

Bucksbaum, Philip H., jt. auth. see Commins, Eugene D.

Bucksch. Diccionario Para Obras Publica, Edificacion y Maquinaria En Obra. 1116p. (Ger. & Span.). 1976. 60.00 (ISBN 84-254-0105-4, S-50187). French & Eur.

Bucksch, H. Dictionary of Mechanisms. (Ger. & Eng.). 1976. leatherette 133.00 (ISBN 3-7625-0707-4, M-7111). French & Eur.

--Woerterbuch fuer Bautechnik und Baumaschinen. 4th ed. (Ger. & Fr.). 1976. pap. 112.00 (ISBN 0-686-56607-6, M-6922). French & Eur.

Bucksch, H. & Altemeyer, A. Dictionnaire des Canalisations a Grande Distance: Anglais-Francais-Allemand. 288p. (Eng., Fr. & Ger.). 1969. 120.00 (ISBN 0-686-56931-8, M-6052). French & Eur.

Bucksch, H. & Altmeyer, A. P. Pipeline Dictionary. 288p. (Eng., Ger. & Fr.). 1969. 99.50 (ISBN 3-7625-1166-7, M-7588, Pub. by Bauverlag). French & Eur.

Bucksch, Hector. Dictionnaire pour les Travaux Publics, le Batiment et l'Equipement des Chantiers de Construction. 7th ed. 420p. (Eng. & Fr.). 1979. 42.50 (ISBN 0-686-56930-X, M-6051). French & Eur.

Bucksch, Herbert. Dictionary of Architecture, Building Construction & Materials, Vol. II. 1137p. (Eng. & Ger.). 1976. 175.00 (ISBN 3-7625-0714-7, M-7130). French & Eur.

--Dictionary of Architecture, Building Construction & Materials, Vol. I. 942p. (Eng. & Ger.). 1974. 175.00 (ISBN 3-7625-0357-5, M-7131). French & Eur.

--Dictionary of Architecture, Building Construction & Materials, 2 vols. 1974-76. plastic bdg.cancelled 120.00x ea. Vol. 1, Ger.-Eng (ISBN 3-7625-0357-5). Vol. 2, Eng.-Ger (ISBN 3-7625-0714-7). Intl Pubns Serv.

--Dictionary of Civil Engineering & Construction Machinery & Equipment, Vol. 1. 5th ed. 420p. (Fr. & Eng.). 1976. 30.00 (ISBN 3-7625-0533-0, M-7120). French & Eur.

--Dictionary of Civil Engineering & Construction Machinery & Equipment, Vol. 1. 7th ed. (Eng. & Ger.). 1978. leatherette 135.00 (ISBN 3-7625-0950-6, M-7122). French & Eur.

--Dictionary of Civil Engineering & Construction Machinery & Equipment, Vol. 2. 5th ed. 548p. (Fr. & Eng.). 1976. 40.00 (ISBN 3-7625-0534-9, M-7119). French & Eur.

--Dictionary of Civil Engineering & Construction Machinery & Equipment, Vol. 2. 7th ed. (Eng. & Ger.). 1978. leatherette 135.00 (ISBN 3-7625-0951-4, M-7121). French & Eur.

--Getriebe-Worterbuch. (Ger. & Eng., Dictionary of Transmissions). 1976. 132.00 (ISBN 0-686-56477-4, M-7423, Pub. by Bauverlag). French & Eur.

--Holz Woerterbuch, Vol. 1. (Ger. & Eng., Dictionary of wood & woodworking practice). 1966. 59.95 (ISBN 3-7625-1168-3, M-7465, Pub. by Bauverlag). French & Eur.

--Holz Woerterbuch, Vol. 2. (Ger. & Eng., Dictionary of wood & woodworking practice). 1966. 67.50 (ISBN 3-7625-1170-5, M-7466, Pub. by Bauverlag). French & Eur.

Bucksch, Herbert & Galan e Hildalgo, Arturo. Diccionario Frances-Espanol de la Construccion y Obras Publicas. 564p. (Fr. & Span.). 1975. 35.95 (ISBN 84-7146-047-5, S-50133). French & Eur.

Bucksch, Herbert, ed. Dictionary of Architecture, Building Constrution & Materials-Worterbuch Fur Architektur, Hochbau Und Baustoffe, 2 vols. 2nd ed. Incl. Vol. 1. 942p. 1980. English-German. plastic cover 180.00x (ISBN 3-7625-1399-6); Vol. 2. 1137p. 1983. English-German. plastic cover 180.00x (ISBN 3-7625-2075-5). Intl Pubns Serv.

Buckton, David, ed. The Treasures of San Marco. 1985. 75.00 (ISBN 0-317-31359-2). Metro Mus Art.

Buckton, K. E. & Evans, H. J. Methods for the Analysis of Human Chromosome Aberrations. (Also avail. in French & Russian). 1973. 4.80 (ISBN 92-4-154031-1). World Health.

Buckton, La Verne. College & University Bands, Their Organization & Administration. LC 75-176612. (Columbia University. Teachers College. Contributions to Education: No. 374). Repr. of 1929 ed. 22.50 (ISBN 0-404-55374-5). AMS Pr.

Buckvar, Felice. All the Way. (Orig.). 1980. pap. 2.25 (ISBN 0-89083-571-3). Zebra.

--Happily Ever After. 192p. (Orig.). 1980. pap. 2.25 (ISBN 0-89083-595-0). Zebra.

--Ten Miles High. LC 81-2509. 160p. (gr. 7-9). 1981. 11.25 (ISBN 0-688-00698-1); PLB 11.88 (ISBN 0-688-00699-X). Morrow.

Buckwalter, Art. Interviews & Interrogations. (Library of Investigation). 1983. text ed. 19.95 (ISBN 0-409-95096-3). Butterworth.

--Investigative Methods. LC 83-13509. (Library of Investigation Ser.). 1983. text ed. 19.95 (ISBN 0-409-95078-5). Butterworth.

--Search for Evidence. LC 83-15424. (Library of Investigation). 1983. text ed. 19.95 (ISBN 0-409-95097-1). Butterworth.

--Surveillance & Undercover Investigation. LC 83-15425. (Library of Investigation Ser.). 208p. 1983. 19.95 (ISBN 0-409-95098-X). Butterworth.

Buckwalter, Harold R. Susquehanna River Decoys. LC 78-66823. (Illus.). 162p. 1978. 12.95 (ISBN 0-916838-47-1). Schiffer.

Buckwalter, Len. One Hundred Ways to Use Your Pocket Calculator. 128p. 1978. pap. 1.95 (ISBN 0-449-13356-7, GM). Fawcett.

--The Pilot's Night Flying Handbook. LC 73-9143. (Illus.). 192p. 1976. 9.95 (ISBN 0-385-05460-2). Doubleday.

Buckwalter, Robert. Law Books Published: Supplement to Law Books in Print. 1984. 100.00 (ISBN 0-317-30228-0). Glanville.

Buckwalter, Robert L., ed. Law Books in Print Through December 1981, 5 vols. 4th ed. LC 82-62461. 1982. 500.00 set (ISBN 0-87802-015-2). Glanville.

Buckwell, Allan, et al. The Costs of the Common Agricultural Policy. 208p. 1982. 28.50 (ISBN 0-7099-0671-4, Pub. by Croom Helm Ltd). Longwood Pub Group.

Bucovetsky, Meyer W. Studies on Public Employment & Compensation in Canada. 177p. 1979. pap. text ed. 14.95x (ISBN 0-409-88601-7, Pub. by Inst Res Pub Canada). Brookfield Pub Co.

Bucur, Ionel. Selected Topics in Algebra. LC 83-24609. 1984. lib. bdg. 79.00 (ISBN 90-277-1671-4, Pub. by Reidel Holland). Kluwer Academic.

Bucurescu, D., et al, eds. Nuclear Collective Dynamics: Proceedings of the 1982 International Summer School of Nuclear Physics, Poiana Brasov, Romania, Aug. 26-Sept. 7, 1982. 522p. 1983. 58.00x (ISBN 9971-950-69-3, Pub. by World Sci Singapore); pap. 26.00x (ISBN 9971-950-73-1, Pub. by World Sci Singapore). Taylor & Francis.

Bucuvalas, E. Treasured Greek Proverbs. (Gr. & Eng.). 1980. 5.95 (ISBN 0-686-64282-1). Divry.

Bucuvalas, Michael J., jt. auth. see Weiss, Carol H.

Bucy, P. C., ed. Neurosurgical Giants: Feet of Clay & Iron. 459p. 1985. 65.00 (ISBN 0-444-00939-6). Elsevier.

Bucy, R. S., et al. Stochastic Differential Equations. McKean, H. P. & Keller, J. B., eds. LC 72-13266. (SIAM-AMS Proceedings: No. 6). 1973. 39.00 (ISBN 0-8218-1325-0, SIAMS-6). Am Math.

Bucy, Richard S. & Moura, Jose M., eds. Nonlinear Stochastic Problems. 1983. PLB 79.50 (ISBN 90-277-1590-4, Pub. by Reidel Holland). Kluwer Academic.

Buczacki, S. T. Zoosporic Plant Pathogens: A Modern Perspective. 1983. 60.00 (ISBN 0-12-139180-9). Acad Pr.

Buczek, Arora P. Maria. 176p. 1986. 10.50 (ISBN 0-89962-491-X). Todd & Honeywell.

Buczkowska. Coping with Stress. 100p. 1986. pap. 12.00 (ISBN 0-683-12111-1). Williams & Wilkins.

Buczyski, Edmund M. Witchcraft Fact Book. (Illus.). 24p. 1984. pap. 4.00 (ISBN 0-939708-04-3). Magickal Childe.

Bud, Porter-Roth. Proposal Development: A Winning Approach. (Successful Business Library). 200p. 1985. 3-ring binder 33.95 (ISBN 0-916378-67-5, Oasis). PSI Res.

Bud, Robert F. & Roberts, Gerrylynn K. Science Versus Practice: Chemistry in Victorian Britain. LC 84-853. 256p. 1984. 35.00 (ISBN 0-7190-1070-5, Pub. by Manchester Univ Pr). Longwood Pub Group.

Bud, Robert F., et al. Chemistry in America, 1876-1976. 1984. lib. bdg. 79.50 (ISBN 90-277-1720-6, Pub. by Reidel Holland). Kluwer Academic.

Buda, Andrew J. & Delp, Edward J., eds. Digital Cardiac Imaging. 1985. lib. bdg. 60.00 (ISBN 0-89838-697-7, Pub. by Martinus Nijhoff Netherlands). Kluwer Academic.

Buda, Francis B. The Neurology of Developmental Disabilities. (Illus.). 280p. 1981. 27.50x (ISBN 0-398-04373-6). C C Thomas.

Budai, Joan. What's in an Egg? LC 80-80559. 1980. pap. 4.95 (ISBN 0-89051-061-X). Master Bks.

Budak, Aram. Circuit Theory Fundamentals & Applications. LC 77-22344. (Illus.). 1978. 40.95 (ISBN 0-13-133975-3). P-H.

--Passive & Active Network Analysis & Synthesis. 600p. 1974. text ed. 39.95 (ISBN 0-395-17203-9). HM.

Budak, B. M. & Fomin, S. V. Multiple Integrals, Field Theory & Series. 640p. 1978. 18.00 (ISBN 0-8285-2096-8, Pub. by Mir Pubs USSR). Imported Pubns.

Budak, Edward. Budak's Modern Organon of Medicine. LC 83-9111. 115p. (Orig.). 1984. pap. 4.95 (ISBN 0-9612386-0-7). Ultra-Nutri.

--Budak's Standard Ultra-Nutrimol Medical Repertory. 1st. ed. (Illus.). 200p. (Orig.). 1986. pap. price not set (ISBN 0-9612386-1-5). Ultra-Nutri.

Budapest, Z. Selene: The Most Famous Bull-Leaper on Earth. (Illus.). 1976. pap. 3.75 (ISBN 0-88447-010-5). Diana Pr.

Budassi, Susan, jt. ed. see Auerbach, Paul.

Budassi, Susan A. & Barber, Janet. Emergency Nursing: Principles & Practice. LC 80-21629. (Illus.). 775p. 1981. pap. text ed. 29.95 (ISBN 0-8016-0451-6). Mosby.

--Mosby's Manual of Emergency Care: Practices & Procedures. 2nd ed. (Illus.). 704p. 1984. text ed. 25.95 (ISBN 0-8016-0453-2). Mosby.

Budassi, Susan A., jt. auth. see Barber, Janet M.

Buday, George. The History of the Christmas Card. LC 74-174012. (Tower Bks.). (Illus.). xxiii, 304p. 1972. Repr. of 1954 ed. 48.00x (ISBN 0-8103-3931-5). Gale.

Budberg, Marie, tr. see Sergieev-Tsensky, Sergiei N.

Budberg, Moura, tr. see Hertzen, Aleksandr I.

Budberg, Moura, tr. see Herzen, Alexander.

Budberg, Moura, tr. see Kagarlitski, J.

Budberg, Moura, tr. see Panova, Vera F.

Budbill, David. The Chain Saw Dance. 64p. 1983. pap. 4.95 (ISBN 0-88150-012-7). Countryman.

--Pulp Cutter' Nativity. 64p. 1981. 11.95 (ISBN 0-914378-79-1); pap. 6.95 (ISBN 0-914378-80-5). Countryman.

--Snowshoe Trek to Otter River. (Skylark Bks.). (Illus.). 96p. (gr. 4-6). 1984. pap. text ed. 1.95 (ISBN 0-553-15252-1, Skylark). Bantam.

--Snowshoe Trek to Otter River. LC 75-27603. (Illus.). 96p. (gr. 4-7). 1976. PLB 5.47 (ISBN 0-8037-8056-7). Dial Bks Young.

Budd, Anne Dallas, compiled by. Richland County, Ohio, Abstracts of Wills: 1813-1873. 1983. 19.50 (ISBN 0-318-02073-4). OH Genealogical.

Budd, Art. The Kook Book. 72p. 1979. pap. 3.95 (ISBN 0-939116-05-7). Creative Comm.

Budd, Brian & Glery, Val. Executive Guide to Fitness. 224p. 1982. 16.95 (ISBN 0-442-29670-3). Van Nos Reinhold.

Budd, Charles. A Few Famous Chinese Poems. 1911. 20.00 (ISBN 0-89984-034-5). Century Bookbindery.

Budd, D. A. & Loucks, R. G. Smackover & Lower Buckner Formations, Jurassic, South Texas: Depositional Systems on a Carbonate Ramp. (Report of Investigations Ser.: No. 112). (Illus.). 38p. 1981. 2.25 (ISBN 0-686-36593-3). Bur Econ Geology.

Budd, Edward C., ed. Inequality & Poverty. (Problems of the Modern Economy Ser.). 217p. 1967. pap. text ed. 4.95x (ISBN 0-393-09502-9, NortonC). Norton.

Budd, Elaine. Thirteen Mistresses of Murder. (Recognitions Ser.). 180p. 1985. 13.95 (ISBN 0-8044-2086-6); pap. 8.95 (ISBN 0-8044-6054-X). Ungar.

--You & Your Hair. (Illus.). 144p. (gr. 7 up). 1984. pap. 1.95 (ISBN 0-590-03861-3, Wildfire Bks). Scholastic Inc.

Budd, Frederick E. A Book of Lullabies. 1978. Repr. of 1930 ed. lib. bdg. 17.50 (ISBN 0-8495-0438-4). Arden Lib.

Budd, John, compiled by. Eight Scandanavian Novelists: Criticism & Reviews in English. LC 80-24895. viii, 180p. 1981. lib. bdg. 35.00 (ISBN 0-313-22869-8, BSN/). Greenwood.

--Henry James: A Bibliography of Criticism, 1975-1981. LC 82-21463. 216p. 1983. lib. bdg. 35.00 (ISBN 0-313-23515-5, BHJ/). Greenwood.

Budd, John F., Jr. Corporate Video in Focus: A Management Guide to Private TV. (Illus.). 210p. 1983. 21.95 (ISBN 0-13-176206-0); pap. 10.95 (ISBN 0-13-176198-6). P-H.

Budd, Leonard H. Days Multiplied. 1984. 4.00 (ISBN 0-89536-666-5, 0424). CSS of Ohio.

--Stories of an Ancient Present. 1978. pap. 3.50 (ISBN 0-89536-298-8). CSS of Ohio.

Budd, Lillian. April Harvest. 304p. 1980. pap. 2.25 (ISBN 0-380-49593-7, 49593). Avon.

--Land of Strangers. 1979. pap. 2.25 (ISBN 0-380-48314-9, 48314). Avon.

Budd, Louis J. Critical Essays on Mark Twain, 1867-1910. (Critical Essays on American Literature Ser.). 1982. lib. bdg. 33.50 (ISBN 0-8161-8619-7, Twayne). G K Hall.

--Critical Essays on Mark Twain, 1910-1980. (Critical Essays in American Literature Ser.). 1983. lib. bdg. 34.50 (ISBN 0-8161-8652-9). G K Hall.

--Our Mark Twain: The Making of a Public Personality. LC 82-23758. (Illus.). 264p. 1983. 13.95x (ISBN 0-8122-1204-5). U of Pa Pr.

Budd, Louis J., ed. New Essays on Adventures on Huckleberry Finn. (The American Novel Ser.). 160p. Date not set. price not set (ISBN 0-521-26729-3); pap. price not set (ISBN 0-521-31836-X). Cambridge U Pr.

Budd, Louis J., et al, eds. Toward a New American Literary History: Essays in Honor of Arlin Turner. LC 79-51499. (Illus.). viii, 279p. 1980. 21.00 (ISBN 0-8223-0430-9). Duke.

Budd, Malcolm. Music & the Emotions: The Philosophical Theories. (International Library of Philosophy). 224p. 1985. 24.95x (ISBN 0-7102-0520-1). Routledge & Kegan.

Budd, Martin. Diets to Help Diabetics. 1981. pap. 4.95x (ISBN 0-317-07292-7, Regent House). B of A.

Budd, Martin L. Low Blood Sugar (Hypoglycaemia) The Twentieth Century Epidemic? LC 83-5053. 128p. (Orig.). 1983. pap. 5.95 (ISBN 0-8069-7792-2). Sterling.

Budd, Martin L. & Wolfson, Nicholas. Securities Regulation: Cases & Materials. (Contemporary Legal Education Ser.). xvii, 970p. 1984. 32.00 (ISBN 0-87215-778-4). Michie Co.

Budd, Mavis. So Beautiful: My Grandmother's Natural Beauty Creams, Lotions, & Remedies. (Illus.). 64p. 1982. 7.95 (ISBN 0-7188-2511-X, Pub. by Salem House). Merrimack Pub Cir.

Budd, Richard W., jt. auth. see Ruben, Brent D.

Budd, S. A., jt. auth. see Bowker, R. M.

Budd, Susan. Sociologists & Religion. 1971. pap. text ed. 2.45x (ISBN 0-02-972450-3). Macmillan.

Budd, Thomas. Good Order Established in Pennsylvania & New Jersey. LC 68-56749. (Research & Source Works Ser.: No. 232). 1971. Repr. of 1685 ed. lib. bdg. 21.00 (ISBN 0-8337-0413-3). B Franklin.

Budd, William. On the Causes of Fever (Eighteen Thirty-Nine) On the Causes & Mode of Propagation of the Common Continued Fevers of Great Britain & Ireland. Smith, Dale C., ed. LC 83-23875. 176p. 1984. pap. text ed. 9.95x (ISBN 0-8018-3166-0). Johns Hopkins.

--Typhoid Fever: Its Nature, Mode of Spreading & Prevention. Rosenkrantz, Barbara G., ed. LC 76-25656. (Public Health in America Ser.). (Illus.). 1977. Repr. of 1931 ed. lib. bdg. 19.00x (ISBN 0-405-09809-X). Ayer Co Pubs.

Budd, William C. Behavior Modification: The Scientific Way to Self Control. LC 73-79774. 1973. 5.95 (ISBN 0-87212-027-9). Libra.

Budd, William C., jt. auth. see Blood, Donald F.

Budde, Bernhard. Ueber Die Wahrheit und ueber die Luege des Radikalen, Antibuergerlichen Individualismus. (European University Studies: No. 1, Vol. 679). 215p. (Ger.). 1983. 28.95 (ISBN 3-8204-7581-8). P Lang Pubs.

Budde, Fritz. Wieland und Bodmer. 1910. 27.00 (ISBN 0-384-06206-7); pap. 22.00 (ISBN 0-384-06205-9). Johnson Repr.

Budde, James F. Measuring Performance in Human Service Systems: Planning, Organization & Control. (Illus.). 1980. 16.95 (ISBN 0-8144-5551-4). AMACOM.

--Measuring Performance in Human Service Systems: Planning, Organization, & Control. LC 79-19551. pap. 55.30 (ISBN 0-317-26905-4, 2023557). Bks Demand UMI.

Budde, R., et al. Approaches to Prototyping: Proceedings of the Working Conference on Prototyping, Namur, October 1983. Kuhlenkamp, K. & Mathiassen, L., eds. (Illus.). xii, 458p. 1984. pap. 23.00 (ISBN 0-387-13490-5). Springer-Verlag.

Budde, William L. & Eichelberger, James W., eds. Organics Analysis Using Gas Chromatography-Mass Spectrometry: A Techniques & Procedures Manual. LC 79-88484. (Illus.). 1979. 39.95 (ISBN 0-250-40318-8). Butterworth.

Buddecke, Eckhart. Pathobiochemie: Ein Lehrbuch fur Studierende und Arzte. 2nd ed. (Illus.). 477p. 1983. 23.60 (ISBN 3-11-009658-7). De Gruyter.

Budden, Julian. The Operas of Verdi: From Don Carlos to Falstaff, Vol. 3. (Galaxy Bks.). (Illus.). 1981. pap. 15.95 (ISBN 0-19-520451-4, GB767). Oxford U Pr.

--Operas of Verdi: From Il Trovatore to la Forza Del Destino, Vol. 2. (The Operas of Verdi Ser). (Illus.). 1978. 49.95x (ISBN 0-19-520068-3); pap. 15.95 (ISBN 0-19-520450-6, GB766, Galaxy Bks.). Oxford U Pr.

--The Operas of Verdi: From Oberto to Rigoletto, Vol. 1. (Illus.). 1978. 49.95x (ISBN 0-19-520030-6); pap. 15.95 (ISBN 0-19-520449-2, GB765). Oxford U Pr.

--The Operas of Verdi, Vol. 3: From Don Carlos to Falstaff. 1981. 49.95x (ISBN 0-19-520254-6). Oxford U Pr.

--Verdi. (The Master Musicians Ser.). 416p. 1985. 26.95x (ISBN 0-460-03165-1, Pub. by J M Dent England). Biblio Dist.

Budden, K. G. Lectures on Magnetoionic Theory. (Documents on Modern Physics Ser.). 96p. 1964. 30.25 (ISBN 0-677-00100-2). Gordon.

--Radio Waves in the Ionosphere: The Mathematical Theory of the Reflection of Radio Waves from Stratified Ionized Layers. pap. 141.50 (ISBN 0-317-27909-2, 2055781). Bks Demand UMI.

Budden, R., et al, eds. The Rat Electrocardiogram in Acute & Chronic Pharmacology & Toxicology: Proceedings of an International Workshop Held in Hanover, July 1980. (Illus.). 208p. 1981. 66.00 (ISBN 0-08-026867-6). Pergamon.

Buddenhagen, I. W. & Persley, G., eds. Rice in Africa. 1979. 49.50 (ISBN 0-12-139350-X). Acad Pr.

Buddensieg, Rudolf. John Wycliffe: Patriot & Reformer. Life & Writings. 1979. Repr. of 1884 ed. lib. bdg. 40.00 (ISBN 0-8495-0535-6). Arden Lib.

Buddensieg, Rudolf, et al, eds. see Wycliffe, John.

Buddensieg, Tilmann. Industriekulture: Peter Behrens & the AEG, 1907-1914. Whyte, Iain B., tr. LC 83-5375. (Illus.). 536p. 1984. 75.00 (ISBN 0-262-02195-1). MIT Pr.

Buddha, Gautama. Dhammapada. Babbitt, Irving, tr. LC 64-23655. 1965. pap. 4.95 (ISBN 0-8112-0004-3, NDP188). New Directions.

Buddhadatta. Buddhadatta's Manuals, 2 vols. in 1. Buddhadatta, A. P., ed. LC 78-72382. Repr. of 1928 ed. 47.50 (ISBN 0-404-17244-X). AMS Pr.

Buddhadatta, A. P., ed. see Buddhadatta.

Buddhadharma. Upasaka Two & One. 1981. pap. 3.95 (ISBN 0-87881-078-1). Mojave Bks.

Buddhaghosa. The Atthasalini, Buddhaghosa's Commentary on the Dhammasangani. Muller, Edward, ed. LC 78-72383. Repr. of 1897 ed. 39.50 (ISBN 0-404-17245-8). AMS Pr.

--Buddhaghosa's Parables. Rogers, T., tr. from Burmese. LC 78-72384. Repr. of 1870 ed. 37.50 (ISBN 0-404-17246-6). AMS Pr.

--Expositor (Atthasalini, 2 vols. in 1. rev. ed. Maung Tin, tr. Davis, Carolina A., rev. by. LC 78-72385. Repr. of 1920 ed. 49.50 (ISBN 0-404-17247-4). AMS Pr.

--The Padyacudamani of Buddhaghosacarya. LC 78-72387. Repr. of 1921 ed. 32.50 (ISBN 0-404-17248-2). AMS Pr.

--Papancasudani Majjhimanikayatthakatha of Buddhaghosacariya, 5 vols. in 4. LC 78-72388. Repr. of 1938 ed. Set. 165.00 (ISBN 0-404-17560-0). AMS Pr.

--The Path of Purity, 3 vols. Pe Maung Tin, tr. LC 78-72389. Repr. of 1931 ed. Set. 95.00 (ISBN 0-404-17570-8). AMS Pr.

--The Sumangala-Vilasini, 3 vols. LC 78-72390. Repr. of 1886 ed. Set. 110.00 (ISBN 0-404-17580-5). Vol. 1 (ISBN 0-404-17581-3). Vol. 2 (ISBN 0-404-17582-1). Vol. 3 (ISBN 0-404-17583-X). AMS Pr.

--Visuddhimagga of Buddhaghosacariya. rev. ed. Warren, Henry C., ed. LC 50-8905. (Oriental Ser.: No. 41). 1950. 35.00x (ISBN 0-674-94110-1). Harvard U Pr.

Budd Hahotta Mahathera, A. Pali-English Dictionary. (Pali & Eng.). 32.50 (ISBN 0-87557-056-9, 056-9). Saphrograph.

Buddhananda, tr. see Ramprasad.

Buddha Sakyamuni. The Dhammapada. Dharma Publishing Staff, ed. & tr. from Pali. (Tibetan Translation Ser.). (Illus.). 381p. (Orig.). 1985. pap. 12.95 (ISBN 0-913546-98-4). Dharma Pub.

Buddhavamsa. The Buddavamsa & the Carlya-Pitaka, Pt. 1. Morris, Richard, ed. LC 78-72391. Repr. of 1882 ed. 17.00 (ISBN 0-404-17249-0). AMS Pr.

Buddhist Association of the United States, tr. see Chang, Garma C.

Buddhist Books International, tr. see Yamaguchi, Susumu.

Buddhist Text Translation Society. Cherishing Life, Vol. I. (Illus.). 150p. (Orig.). 1983. pap. 7.00 (ISBN 0-88139-004-6). Buddhist Text.

--Cherishing Life, Vol. 2. Bhikshuni Heng Tao & Bhikshuni Heng Ch'ih, trs. from Chinese. (Illus.). 160p. 1983. pap. 7.00 (ISBN 0-88139-015-1). Buddhist Text.

--Filiality, the Human Source, Vol. 1. 132p. 1983. pap. 7.00 (ISBN 0-88139-006-2). Buddhist Text.

--Filiality, the Human Source, Vol. 2. 120p. (Orig.). 1983. pap. 7.00 (ISBN 0-88139-020-8). Buddhist Text.

Buddhist Text Translation Society, tr. from Chinese. Sutra of the Past Vows of Earth Store Bodhisattva. (Illus.). 120p. (Orig.). 1982. pap. 6.00 (ISBN 0-88139-502-1). Buddhist Text.

Buddhist Text Translation Society, tr. see Chr, Great Master Lyan, et al.

Buddhist Text Translation Society, tr. see Hua, Tripitaka M.

Buddhist Text Translation Society, tr. see Master Hua, Tripitaka.

Buddhist Text Translation Society, tr. see Master Hua, Triptaka.

Buddhist Text Translation Society, tr. see Tripitaka Master Hua.

Buddhist Text Translation Society, et al, trs. see Ch'an Master Yung Chia.

Buddhist Text Translation Society, et al, trs. see Master Hua, Tripitaka.

Buddhist Text Translation Society, et al, trs. see Tripitaka Master Hua.

Buddinger, Peyton B., jt. auth. see Chamberlain, V. M.

Buddington, Anita & Vuilleumier, Marion. What's Cooking on Cape Cod. (Illus.). 228p. (Orig.). 1983. pap. 7.95 (ISBN 0-88492-043-7). W S Sullwold.

Buddle, Thomas. The Maori King Movement in New Zealand. LC 75-35241. Repr. of 1860 ed. 12.50 (ISBN 0-404-14416-0). AMS Pr.

Budds, Michael J. Jazz in the Sixties: The Expansion of Musical Resources & Techniques. LC 78-17438. 128p. 1978. 10.00x (ISBN 0-87745-086-2); pap. 5.95x (ISBN 0-87745-087-0). U of Iowa Pr.

Buddy, Cynthia M., et al, eds. see Griggs, John D.

Buddy, Lee. Living Triumphantly: Selected Inspirational Verses. (Illus.). 1982. 5.95 (ISBN 0-533-05240-8). Vantage.

Bude, Guy de, ed. see Doi Chrysostomus.

Budeit, Janice L., jt. ed. see Cox, Susan M.

Budeit, Janice L., ed. see Research Publications.

Budel, Julius. Climatic Geomorphology. Fischer, Lenore & Busche, Detlef, trs. LC 81-47909. (Illus.). 443p. 1982. 55.00x (ISBN 0-691-08294-4); pap. 20.00x (ISBN 0-691-08295-2). Princeton U Pr.

Buden, David, jt. auth. see Angelo, Joseph A., Jr.

Budenz, Jozsef. Comparative Dictionary of the Finno-Ugric Elements in the Hungarian Vocabulary. LC 66-64927. (Uralic & Altaic Ser: Vol. 78). (Finnish & Hungarian., Repr. of 1881 ed). 1966. pap. text ed. 22.50x (ISBN 0-87750-029-0). Res Ctr Lang Semiotic.

Budenz, Julia. From the Gardens of Flora Baum. (Wesleyan New Poets Ser.). 64p. 1984. 15.00x (ISBN 0-8195-2115-9); pap. 6.95. Wesleyan U Pr.

Budenz, Louis F. The Techniques of Communism. LC 76-46068. (Anti-Movements in America). 1977. Repr. of 1954 ed. lib. bdg. 25.00x (ISBN 0-405-09942-8). Ayer Co Pubs.

Buder, Kathryn M. Fruitful Vine. (Illus.). 112p. 1985. 7.95 (ISBN 0-89962-457-X). Todd & Honeywell.

Buder, Stanley. Pullman: An Experiment in Industrial Order & Community Planning, 1880-1930. (Urban Life in America). 1967. pap. 6.95x (ISBN 0-19-500838-3). Oxford U Pr.

Buderi, L. O., jt. ed. see Caron, David D.

Budevsky, Omortag. Foundations of Chemical Analysis. LC 79-40240. (Ellis Horwood Series in Analytical Chemistry). 372p. 1979. 79.95x (ISBN 0-470-26692-9). Halsted Pr.

Budge, A. E., tr. from Syriac. The Paradise of the Fathers, 2 vols. (Illus.). 1984. Set. pap. 25.00 (ISBN 0-913026-56-5). Vol. 1, 386 pp. Vol. 2, 352 pp. St Nectarios.

Budge, D. R. & Sheehan, P. M. The Upper Ordovician Through Middle Silurian of the Eastern Great Basin: Part Two - Lithologic Descriptions. 80p. 1980. 5.50 (ISBN 0-89326-041-X). Milwaukee Pub Mus.

Budge, E. A. Apophthegmata Patrum. 150p. 1975. pap. 5.95 (ISBN 0-686-10938-4). Eastern Orthodox.

--Book of the Dead. (Illus.). 1960. 25.00 (ISBN 0-8216-0021-4). Univ Bks.

--The Book of the Dead. (Illus.). 992p. 1985. pap. 9.95 (ISBN 1-85063-020-8, Ark Paperbacks). Routledge & Kegan.

--The Book of the Dead: An English Translation of the Chapters, Hymns, Etc., of the Theban Recension. 2nd ed. (Illus.). 1969. 35.00 (ISBN 0-7100-1128-8). Routledge & Kegan.

--Book of the Mysteries of the Heavens & the Earth. 75.00 (ISBN 0-87968-772-X). Gordon Pr.

--Egyptian Book of the Dead: The Papyrus of Ani. 16.00 (ISBN 0-8446-1764-4). Peter Smith.

--Egyptian Heaven & Hell. 1980. lib. bdg. 59.95 (ISBN 0-8490-3203-2). Gordon Pr.

--Gods of the Egyptians or Studies in Egyptian Mythology, 2 Vols. (Illus.). Set. 36.00 (ISBN 0-8446-0520-4). Peter Smith.

--The Gods of the Egyptians: Studies in Egyptian Mythology, 2 Vols. LC 67-28633. (Illus.). 1969. pap. 10.00 ea.; Vol. 1. pap. (ISBN 0-486-22055-9); Vol. 2. pap. (ISBN 0-486-22056-7). Dover.

--Mummy. 2nd ed. LC 64-13391. (Illus.). 1894. 18.00x (ISBN 0-8196-0139-X). Biblo.

--Sayings of the Fathers. 1975. pap. 5.95 (ISBN 0-686-10941-4). Eastern Orthodox.

--A Short History of the Egyptian People with Chapters on Their Religion, Daily Life, Etc. LC 78-14274. 1978. Repr. of 1914 ed. lib. bdg. 30.00 (ISBN 0-8414-0390-2). Folcroft.

Budge, E. A., jt. auth. see Prince, J. D.

Budge, E. A., intro. by. The Book of the Dead. 1977. pap. 9.95 (ISBN 0-8065-0591-5). Citadel Pr.

Budge, E. A., tr. The Book of the Dead. (Illus.). 704p. 1984. pap. 12.95. Citadel Pr.

Budge, E. A., tr. see Isho, Anan.

Budge, E. A., tr. see Lefafa Sedek.

Budge, E. A., tr. see Pachomius, Saint.

Budge, E. A. W. Cleopatra's Needles & Other Egyptian Obelisks. 1985. Repr. of 1926 ed. 20.00 (ISBN 0-89005-278-6). Ares.

Budge, E. A. Wallis. Divine Origin of the Craft of the Herbalist. LC 78-174013. (Illus.). 1971. Repr. of 1928 ed. 40.00x (ISBN 0-8103-3794-0). Gale.

--Egyptian Book of the Dead: The Papyrus of Ani in the British Museum. 1967. pap. 8.95 (ISBN 0-486-21866-X). Dover.

--Egyptian Language. 1975. pap. 7.50 (ISBN 0-89005-095-3). Ares.

--Egyptian Language: Easy Lessons in Egyptian Hieroglyphics with Sign List. 8th ed. 5.00 (ISBN 0-486-21394-3). Dover.

--Herb-Doctors & Physicians in the Ancient World: The Divine Origin of the Craft of the Herbalist. 1978. pap. 10.00 (ISBN 0-89005-252-2). Ares.

Budge, E. Wallis. Amulets & Superstitions. LC 77-86708. (Illus.). 1978. pap. 8.95 (ISBN 0-486-23573-4). Dover.

--Amulets & Superstitions. 15.75 (ISBN 0-8446-5676-3). Peter Smith.

--Babylonian Life & History. LC 74-84545. (Illus.). xvi, 296p. 1975. Repr. of 1925 ed. lib. bdg. 26.50 (ISBN 0-8154-0502-2). Cooper Sq.

--The Book of Opening the Mouth: The Egyptian Texts with English Translations, 2 vols. in 1. LC 72-80498. (Illus.). Repr. of 1909 ed. 33.00 (ISBN 0-405-08315-7, Blom Pubns). Ayer Co Pubs.

--The Dwellers on the Nile. LC 72-80141. (Illus.). Repr. of 1926 ed. 17.00 (ISBN 0-405-08316-5, Blom Pubns). Ayer Co Pubs.

--The Dwellers on the Nile: The Life, History, Religion, & Literature of the Ancient Egyptians. (Illus.). 326p. 1977. pap. 5.95 (ISBN 0-486-23501-7). Dover.

--Egyptian Hieroglyphic Dictionary, Vols. 1 & 2. LC 77-86708. 1978. pap. 13.95 ea. Vol. 1 (ISBN 0-486-23615-3). Vol. 2 (ISBN 0-486-23616-1). Dover.

--Egyptian Magic. 1971. pap. 4.00 (ISBN 0-486-22681-6). Dover.

--Egyptian Magic. (Illus.). 14.25 (ISBN 0-8446-0044-X). Peter Smith.

--Egyptian Magic. (Illus.). 1979. pap. 6.95 (ISBN 0-7100-0135-5). Routledge & Kegan.

--Egyptian Religion. (Illus.). 1979. pap. 6.95 (ISBN 0-7100-0134-7). Routledge & Kegan.

--From Fetish to God in Ancient Egypt. LC 72-82206. (Illus.). Repr. of 1934 ed. 33.00 (ISBN 0-405-08317-3, Blom Pubns). Ayer Co Pubs.

--Life & Exploits of Alexander the Great, 2 Vols. LC 68-56521. (Illus.). Repr. of 1896 ed. Set. 50.00 (ISBN 0-405-08318-1, Blom Pubns); 25.00 ea. Vol. 1 (ISBN 0-405-08319-X). Vol. 2 (ISBN 0-405-08320-3). Ayer Co Pubs.

--The Liturgy of Funerary Offerings: The Egyptian Texts with English Translations. LC 72-83744. (Illus.). Repr. of 1909 ed. 22.00 (ISBN 0-405-08322-X, Blom Pubns). Ayer Co Pubs.

--Osiris & the Egyptian Resurrection, 2 vols. LC 72-81534. (Illus.). 906p. 1973. Vol. 1. pap. 7.95 (ISBN 0-486-22780-4); Vol. 2. pap. 7.95 (ISBN 0-486-22781-2). Dover.

--Osiris & the Egyptian Resurrection, 2 vols. (Illus.). 30.50 (ISBN 0-8446-4715-2). Peter Smith.

--Tutankhamen: Amenism, Atenism & Egyptain Monotheism. LC 79-160615. (Illus.). Repr. of 1923 ed. 12.75 (ISBN 0-405-08323-8, Blom Pubns). Ayer Co Pubs.

Budge, E. Wallis, ed. The Laughable Stories Collected by Mar Gregory John Bar-Hebraeus. LC 72-173158. Repr. of 1897 ed. 22.00 (ISBN 0-405-08321-1, Blom Pubns). Ayer Co Pubs.

Budge, E. Wallis, tr. see Pachomius, Saint.

Budge, Ernest A. Alexander Book in Ethiopia. LC 73-18834. (Illus.). Repr. of 1933 ed. 18.50 (ISBN 0-404-11307-9). AMS Pr.

--Babylonian Life & History. LC 73-18836. (Illus.). Repr. of 1925 ed. 22.50 (ISBN 0-404-11308-7). AMS Pr.

--The Book of the Kings of Egypt, 2 vols. LC 73-18837. Repr. of 1908 ed. 34.50 set (ISBN 0-404-11309-5). AMS Pr.

--By Nile & Tigris. LC 75-28120. (Illus.). Repr. of 1920 ed. Set. 75.00 (ISBN 0-404-11312-5). AMS Pr.

--Cleopatra's Needles & Other Egyptian Obelisks. LC 73-18841. (Illus.). Repr. of 1926 ed. 27.50 (ISBN 0-404-11315-X). AMS Pr.

--Coptic Texts Edited with Introductions & English Translations, 5 vols. Repr. of 1915 ed. 345.00 set (ISBN 0-404-11550-0); write for info. AMS Pr.

--The Decrees of Memphis & Canopus, 3 vols. Incl. Vols. 1 & 2. The Rosetta Stone. Vol. 1 (ISBN 0-404-11323-0). Vol. 2 (ISBN 0-404-11324-9); Vol. 3. The Decree of Canopus (ISBN 0-404-11325-7). LC 73-18842. Repr. of 1904 ed. Set. 57.50 (ISBN 0-404-11322-2). AMS Pr.

--The Egyptian Heaven & Hell, 3 vols. LC 73-18844. (Illus.). Repr. of 1906 ed. Set. 57.50 (ISBN 0-404-11326-5). AMS Pr.

--The Egyptian Heaven & Hell. (Illus.). 200p. 1974. lib. bdg. 16.95 (ISBN 0-87548-311-9); pap. 5.95 (ISBN 0-87548-298-8). Open Court.

--Egyptian Ideas of the Future Life. LC 73-18839. Repr. of 1899 ed. 14.00 (ISBN 0-404-11330-3). AMS Pr.

--An Egyptian Reading Book for Beginners. LC 73-18845. Repr. of 1896 ed. 37.50 (ISBN 0-404-11331-1). AMS Pr.

--The Egyptian Sudan: Its History & Monuments, 2 vols. LC 73-18840. (Illus.). Repr. of 1907 ed. 85.00 set (ISBN 0-404-11332-X). AMS Pr.

--A Hieroglyphic Vocabulary to the Theban Recension of the Book of the Dead. LC 73-18846. Repr. of 1911 ed. 26.50 (ISBN 0-404-11335-4). AMS Pr.

--The Histories of Rabban Hormizd the Persian & Rabban Bar-'Idta, 3 pts. in 2 vols. LC 73-18847. (Luzac's Semitic Text & Translation Ser.: Nos. 9, 10, 11). Repr. of 1902 ed. 46.00 set (ISBN 0-404-11336-2). AMS Pr.

--The Monks of Kublai Khan, Emperor of China. LC 71-38051. Repr. of 1928 ed. 20.00 (ISBN 0-404-56905-6). AMS Pr.

--Nile-Notes for Travellers in Egypt & the Egyptian Sudan: Notes for Travellers in Egypt & the Egyptian Sudan. 12th ed. LC 74-106772. (Illus.). Repr. of 1912 ed. 47.00x (ISBN 0-8371-3550-8, BUN&, Pub. by Negro U Pr). Greenwood.

--The Rise & Progress of Assyriology. LC 73-18849. (Illus.). Repr. of 1925 ed. 27.50 (ISBN 0-404-11340-0). AMS Pr.

--The Rosetta Stone in the British Museum. LC 73-16549. (Illus.). Repr. of 1929 ed. 18.50 (ISBN 0-404-11362-1). AMS Pr.

--Short History of the Egyptian People. 280p. 1980. lib. bdg. 37.50 (ISBN 0-8482-0148-5). Norwood Edns.

Budge, Ernest A., ed. Baralam & Yewasef - Baralaam & Joasaph, 3 pts. in 2 vols. LC 73-18832. (Illus.). Repr. of 1923 ed. Set. 67.50 (ISBN 0-404-11300-1). AMS Pr.

--Coptic Apocrypha in the Dialect of Upper Egypt. LC 77-3589. (Coptic Texts: Vol. 3). (Illus.). Repr. of 1913 ed. 55.00 (ISBN 0-404-11553-5). AMS Pr.

--Coptic Biblical Texts in the Dialect of Upper Egypt. LC 77-3590. (Coptic Texts: Vol. 2). (Illus.). 1977. Repr. of 1912 ed. 45.00 (ISBN 0-404-11552-7). AMS Pr.

--Coptic Homilies in the Dialect of Upper Egypt. LC 77-3585. (Coptic Texts: Vol. 1). (Illus.). Repr. of 1910 ed. 50.00 (ISBN 0-404-11551-9). AMS Pr.

--Coptic Martyrdoms, Etc. in the Dialect of Upper Egypt. LC 77-3588. (Coptic Texts: Vol. 4). (Illus.). Repr. of 1914 ed. 60.00 (ISBN 0-404-11554-3). AMS Pr.

--Miscellaneous Coptic Texts in the Dialect of Upper Egypt, 2 vols. LC 77-3587. (Coptic Texts: Vol. 5). (Illus.). Repr. of 1915 ed. 135.00 (ISBN 0-404-11555-1). AMS Pr.

Budge, Ernest A., tr. George of Lydda, the Patron Saint of England. LC 77-87668. (Luzac's Semitic Texts & Translations: No. 20). (Illus., Eng. & Ethiopic.). Repr. of 1930 ed. 55.00 (ISBN 0-404-11348-6). AMS Pr.

--The History of the Blessed Virgin Mary & the History of the Likeness of Christ Which the Jews of Tiberius Made to Mock At, 2 vols. LC 73-18848. (Luzac's Semitic Text & Translation Ser.: Nos. 4-5). Repr. of 1899 ed. 45.00 set (ISBN 0-404-11341-9). AMS Pr.

Budge, Ernest A., tr. see Bar Hebraeus.

Budge, Ernest A., tr. see Dorson, Richard M.

Budge, Ernest A. Wallis see Anan Isho.

Budge, Frances A. Thomas Ellwood & Other Worthies of the Olden Time. 1891. Repr. 20.00 (ISBN 0-8274-3609-2). R West.

Budge, Helen. Study of Chord Frequencies Based on the Music of the Eighteenth & Nineteenth Centuries. LC 75-176604. (Columbia University. Teachers College. Contributions to Education: No. 882). Repr. of 1943 ed. 22.50 (ISBN 0-404-55882-8). AMS Pr.

Budge, Ian. The New British Political System: Government & Society in the 1980's. LC 82-12675. (Illus.). 1983. pap. 10.95 (ISBN 0-582-29553-X). Longman.

Budge, Ian & Farlie, Dennis J. Explaining & Predicting Elections: Issue Effects & Party Strategies in Twenty-Three Democracies. (Illus.). 240p. 1983. text ed. 29.95x (ISBN 0-04-324008-9). Allen Unwin.

Budge, Wallis. Egyptian Magic. 1978. pap. 3.95 (ISBN 0-8065-0629-6). Citadel Pr.

--Egytian Religion. 224p. 12.00 (ISBN 0-89005-263-8). Ares.

--The Rosetta Stone. 27p. pap. 3.00 (ISBN 0-89005-331-6). Ares.

Budge, Wallis E., ed. Book of the Dead: Egyptian Literature. rev. ed. (Illus.). 417p. pap. 14.95 (ISBN 0-88697-013-X). Life Science.

Budgell, Eustace, tr. see Theophrastus.

Budgett, Winifred, tr. see Steiner, Rudolf & Steiner Von Sivers, Marie.

Budhananda. The Saving Challenge of Religion. 272p. (Orig.). 1982. pap. 9.50 (ISBN 0-87481-567-3). Vedanta Pr.

Budhananda, Swami. Can One Be Scientific & Yet Spiritual? 114p. 1973. pap. 2.00 (ISBN 0-87481-145-7). Vedanta Pr.

--The Mind & Its Control. 119p. (Orig.). 1972. pap. 1.75 (ISBN 0-87481-128-7). Vedanta Pr.

Budiansky, B., ed. see Symposium in Cambridge, Mass, June 17-21, 1974.

Budiardjo, Carmel & Liong, Liem S. The War Against East Timor. (Asia Ser.). (Illus.). 272p. 1984. 29.50x (ISBN 0-86232-228-6, Pub. by Zed Pr England); pap. 10.75 (ISBN 0-86232-229-4, Pub. by Zed Pr England). Biblio Dist.

Budick, E. Miller. Emily Dickinson & the Life of Language: A Study in Symbolic Poetics. LC 85-9609. 240p. 1985. text ed. 22.50 (ISBN 0-8071-1239-9). La State U Pr.

Budick, Sanford. The Dividing Muse: Images of Sacred Disjunction in Milton's Poetry. LC 84-17270. 224p. 1985. text ed. 18.00 (ISBN 0-300-03288-9). Yale U Pr.

--Poetry of Civilization: Mythopoeic Displacement in the Verse of Milton, Dryden, Pope, & Johnson. LC 73-86887. pap. 48.80 (ISBN 0-317-29590-X, 2021984). Bks Demand UMI.

Budig, Gene A. Higher Education: Surviving the 1980's. LC 81-50932. 1981. 4.00 (ISBN 0-937058-01-7). West Va U Pr.

Budig, Gene A., ed. Perceptions in Public Higher Education. LC 71-5647. xiv, 163p. 1970. 15.50x (ISBN 0-8032-0749-2). U of Nebr Pr.

Budig, P. K., ed. Dictionary of Electrical Engineering & Electronics: German-English. 690p. 1985. 134.75 (ISBN 0-444-99594-3). Elsevier.

Budig, Peter K. Fachwoerterbuch Elektrotechnik, Elektronik. (Eng. & Ger., Dictionary of Electrical Engineering and Electronics). 1976. 86.50 (ISBN 3-7785-0357-X, M-7394, Pub. by Huethig). French & Eur.

Budig, Peter-Klaus. Dictionary of Electrical Engineering & Electronics: English-German. 1985. 129.75 (ISBN 0-444-99595-1, I-422-84). Elsevier.

Budin, Howard. Speed Walker: Fun to Program Your Apple II Plus or IIe. 96p. (Orig.). 1984. pap. 2.95 (ISBN 0-523-42243-1). Pinnacle Bks.

--Speed Walker: Fun to Program Your Commodore 64. 89p. (Orig.). 1984. pap. 2.95 (ISBN 0-523-42245-8). Pinnacle Bks.

--Speed Walker: Fun to Program Your IBM-PC. 89p. (Orig.). 1984. pap. 2.95 (ISBN 0-523-42246-6). Pinnacle Bks.

--Speed Walker: Fun to Program Your TI 99. 39p. (Orig.). 1984. pap. 2.95 (ISBN 0-523-42247-4). Pinnacle Bks.

--Speed Walker: Fun to Program Your TRS-80. 89p. (Orig.). 1984. pap. 2.95 (ISBN 0-523-42244-X). Pinnacle Bks.

Budin, Howard, et al. Using Computers in the Social Studies. (Computers in the Curriculum Ser.: No. 1). 136p. (Orig.). 1986. pap. text ed. 11.95x (ISBN 0-8077-2781-4). Tchrs Coll.

Budinger, Thomas, jt. ed. see Lawrence, Jon H.

Budinger, Thomas F., et al, eds. Noninvasive Techniques for Assessment of Atherosclerosis in Peripheral, Carotid, & Coronary Arteries. 272p. 1982. text ed. 64.00 (ISBN 0-89004-679-4). Raven.

Budinski, Kenneth. Engineering Materials: Properties & Selection. 2nd ed. 1983. text ed. 30.95 (ISBN 0-8359-1692-8); instr's. manual free (ISBN 0-8359-1695-2). Reston.

Budjanu, M. S., et al. Nine Papers on Analysis. LC 77-11203. (Translation Ser.: No. 2, Vol. 110). 1977. 46.00 (ISBN 0-8218-3060-0, TRANS2-110). Am Math.

--Ten Papers in Analysis. LC 73-16013. (Translations Ser.: No. 2, Vol. 102). 1973. 42.00 (ISBN 0-8218-3052-X, TRANS 2-102). Am Math.

Budke, George H. & Christie, J. Elmer, eds. Old Nyack: The Finest Written Historical Sketch of Old Nyack Village. (Illus.). 1984. pap. 5.00 (ISBN 0-911183-25-6). Rockland County Hist.

Budke, Wesley E. Directory of Vocational Education Personnel 1984-85. 195p. 1984. 12.50 (ISBN 0-318-17784-6, SN43). Natl Ctr Res Voc Ed.

Budker, Paul. The Life of Sharks. LC 71-148462. (Illus.). 222p. 1971. 27.50x (ISBN 0-231-03551-9); pap. 11.00s (ISBN 0-231-08314-9). Columbia U Pr.

Budkin, Alberto, jt. auth. see Lindsay, Alan E.

Budlong, John P. Shoreline & Sextant: Practical Coastline Navigation. 1977. 12.95 (ISBN 0-442-21928-8). Van Nos Reinhold.

Budman, Alan D. Comparative Negligence. LC 84-72422. (Illus.). Date not set. price not set. Bender.

Budman, Simon, ed. Forms of Brief Therapy. LC 81-2779. 482p. 1981. 35.00 (ISBN 0-89862-608-0). Guilford Pr.

Budman, Simon H. & Wertlieb, Donald, eds. Psychologists in Health Care Settings. 248p. (Reprinted from Professional Psychology, Aug, 1979). 13.00 (ISBN 0-317-33163-9); members 10.00 (ISBN 0-317-33164-7). Am Psychol.

Budnick, F. S. Finite Mathematics with Applications in Management & Social Sciences. 512p. 1985. 29.95 (ISBN 0-07-008861-6). McGraw.

Budnick, Frank S. Applied Mathematics for Business, Economics & the Social Sciences. 2nd ed. 832p. 1983. 31.95 (ISBN 0-07-008858-6). McGraw.

Budnick, Frank S., et al. Principles of Operations Research for Management. 1977. 33.50x (ISBN 0-256-01796-4). Irwin.

Budnick, J. I. & Kawatra, M. P. Dynamical Aspects of Critical Phenomena. LC 77-183846. 638p. 1972. 148.00 (ISBN 0-677-12350-7). Gordon.

Budnick, S. D. Handbook of Pediatric Oral Pathology. 1981. 36.50 (ISBN 0-8151-1303-X). Year Bk Med.

Budnikov, P. P. & Ginstling, A. M. Principles of Solid State Chemistry. 468p. 1970. 119.50 (ISBN 0-677-61250-8). Gordon.

--Principles of Solid State Chemistry. Shaw, K., tr. (Illus.). 454p. 1968. 52.00 (ISBN 0-85334-028-5, Pub. by Elsevier Applied Sci England). Elsevier.

Budoff, Milton & Orenstein, Alan. Due Process in Special Education: On Going to a Hearing. 268p. 1983. 19.95x (ISBN 0-938552-51-1). Acad Guild.

--Due Process in Special Education: On Going to a Hearing. LC 84-1787. 352p. 1984. pap. 14.95 (ISBN 0-914797-05-0). Brookline Book.

Budoff, Milton, et al. Due Process in Special Education: On Going to a Hearing. LC 82-21930. 352p. 1982. 19.95 (ISBN 0-938552-51-1). Brookline Book.

--Microcomputers in Special Education: An Introduction to Instructional Applications. LC 84-7596. 237p. 1984. 19.95 (ISBN 0-914797-07-7). Brookline Book.

Budoff, Penny W. No More Hot Flashes & Other Good News. LC 83-3334. (Illus.). 288p. 1983. 14.95 (ISBN 0-399-12793-3, Putnam). Putnam Pub Group.

--No More Hot Flashes & Other Good News. 296p. 1984. pap. 3.95 (ISBN 0-446-32410-8). Warner Bks.

--No More Menstrual Cramps & Other Good News. 1981. pap. 6.95 (ISBN 0-14-005938-5). Penguin.

Budovsky, E. I., jt. ed. see Kochetkov, N. K.

Budreckis, Algirdas, ed. The Lithuanians in America, 1651-1975: A Chronology & Fact Book. LC 76-6680. (Ethnic Chronology Ser: No. 21). 174p. 1976. lib. bdg. 8.50 (ISBN 0-379-00517-4). Oceana.

Budreckis, Algirdas, tr. see Gerutis, Albertas, et al.

Budrow, Nancy, jt. auth. see Hartline, Jane.

Budrys, Algis. Benchmarks: Galaxy Bookshelf. 1985. 16.95 (ISBN 0-8093-1187-9). S Ill U Pr.

--Rogue Moon. 1981. pap. 1.50 (ISBN 0-380-00100-4, 38950-9, Equinox). Avon.

Budson, R. D., jt. ed. see Barofsky, I.

Budson, Richard D. The Psychiatric Halfway House: A Handbook of Theory & Practice. LC 77-74548. (Contemporary Community Health Ser.). 1978. 14.95 (ISBN 0-8229-3350-0). U of Pittsburgh Pr.

Budurowycz, Bohdan B. Polish-Soviet Relations, Nineteen Thirty-Two to Nineteen Thirty-Nine. LC 63-7509. (East-Central Studies of the Russian Institute). 229p. 1963. 25.00x (ISBN 0-231-02593-9). Columbia U Pr.

Budwig, Andrew, jt. auth. see Chase, Gilbert.

Budworth. Public Science Private View. 1981. 24.00 (ISBN 0-9960021-3-8, Pub. by Inst Physics England); pap. 13.00 (ISBN 0-9960021-4-6, Pub. by Inst Physics England). Heyden.

Budworth, Geoffrey. The Knot Book. LC 84-26843. (Illus.). 160p. (gr. 7 up). 1985. 9.95 (ISBN 0-8069-5714-X); lib. bdg. 12.49 (ISBN 0-8069-5715-8); pap. 5.95 (ISBN 0-8069-7944-5). Sterling.

Budy, A. M., jt. auth. see McLean, F. C.

Budy, A. M., ed. see Interdisciplinary Conference, 1st.

Budy, A. M., ed. see Interdisciplinary Conference, 3rd.

Budy, Andrea H. Living on the Cusp. Hettich, M. & Ahern, Colleen, eds. 35p. 1980. 3.00 (ISBN 0-686-38059-2). MoonsQuilt Pr.

Budy, Bertrand. Mary, the Faithful Disciple. 144p. (Orig.). 1985. pap. 6.95 (ISBN 0-8091-2703-2). Paulist Pr.

Budyko, M. I. Climate & Life. Miller, David H., tr. (International Geophysics Ser.: Vol. 18). 1974. 70.00 (ISBN 0-12-139450-6). Acad Pr.

--Climate Changes. Zolina, R., tr. from Rus. (Illus.). 261p. 1977. 24.00 (ISBN 0-87590-206-5). Am Geophysical.

--The Earth's Climate: Past & Future. LC 81-17673. (International Geophysics Ser.). 1982. 43.00 (ISBN 0-12-139460-3). Acad Pr.

--Global Ecology. 1980. 8.95 (ISBN 0-8285-1764-9, Pub. by Progress Pubs USSR). Imported Pubns.

Budyko, M. I., ed. Climatic Changes. 261p. 1977. 24.00 (ISBN 0-87590-206-5). Am Geophysical.

Budynas, Richard G. Advanced Strength & Applied Stress Analysis. (Illus.). 1977. text ed. 45.00 (ISBN 0-07-008828-4). McGraw.

Budzik, Janet, jt. auth. see Budzik, Richard.

Budzik, Janet K., jt. auth. see Budzik, Richard S.

Budzik, Richard. Opportunities in Refrigeration & Air Conditioning. (VGM Career Bks.). (Illus.). 160p. 1983. 7.95 (ISBN 0-8442-6624-8, 6624-8, Passport Bks.); pap. 5.95 (ISBN 0-8442-6626-4, 6626-4). Natl Textbk.

Budzik, Richard & Budzik, Janet. Today's Practical Guide to Increasing Profits for Contractors. 342p. 37.30 (ISBN 0-318-13170-6, PPI2701). Am Soc Conc Constr.

Budzik, Richard S. Fittings Used Today That Require Triangulation Including the Theory of Triangulation. 2nd ed. LC 75-182389. (Illus.). 1982. 19.95 (ISBN 0-912914-21-1). Practical Pubns.

--Practical Sheet Metal Projects-130 Graded Projects with Drawings, Forming Information & Sequences. LC 79-93132. (Illus.). (gr. 7-12). 1979. 24.95 (ISBN 0-912914-06-8). Practical Pubns.

--Precision Sheet Metal Blueprint Reading. LC 75-86373. (Illus.). 127p. 1969. text ed. 17.95 (ISBN 0-912914-11-4); tchr's materials 24.95 (ISBN 0-912914-13-0); wkbk 16.95 (ISBN 0-912914-12-2). Practical Pubns.

--Precision Sheet Metal Mathematics. LC 71-83129. (Illus.). 349p. 1969. text ed. 17.95 (ISBN 0-912914-14-9); instr's guide 24.95 (ISBN 0-912914-16-5); wkbk 19.95 (ISBN 0-912914-15-7). Practical Pubns.

--Precision Sheet Metal Shop Practice. LC 78-97566. (Illus.). 96p. 1969. 13.95 (ISBN 0-912914-17-3); tchrs' materials 24.95 (ISBN 0-912914-19-X); wkbk 17.95 (ISBN 0-912914-18-1). Practical Pubns.

--Precision Sheet Metal Shop Theory. LC 79-77566. (Illus.). 334p. 1969. 17.95 (ISBN 0-912914-08-4); tchrs' materials 24.95 (ISBN 0-912914-10-6); wkbk 19.95 (ISBN 0-912914-09-2). Practical Pubns.

--Round Fittings Used Today Including Methods & Techniques of Fabricating Round Work. 2nd ed. LC 71-182388. (Illus.). 1982. 19.95 (ISBN 0-912914-20-3). Practical Pubns.

--Sheet Metal Shop Fabrication Projects Including Over Three Hundred Fifty Graded Parts. LC 80-84009. (Illus.). (gr. 7-12). 1980. 19.95 (ISBN 0-912914-07-6). Practical Pubns.

--Sheet Metal Technology. 2nd ed. 1981. scp 19.96 (ISBN 0-672-97360-X); scp instr's. guide 3.67 (ISBN 0-672-97361-8); scp students manual 10.28 (ISBN 0-672-97362-6). Bobbs.

--Short Course in Sheet Metal Shop Theory: Including 25 Practical Projects. LC 79-93131. (Illus.). (gr. 7-12). 1979. 17.95 (ISBN 0-912914-05-X). Practical Pubns.

--Specialty Items Used Today (Sheet Metal) Including Methods of Design & Fabrication & Important Trade Topics. LC 74-79537. (Illus.). 1979. 44.95 (ISBN 0-912914-04-1). Practical Pubns.

--Today's Forty Most Frequently-Used Fittings. 2nd ed. LC 73-188876. (Illus.). 184p. 1983. 19.95 (ISBN 0-912914-22-X). Practical Pubns.

Budzik, Richard S. & Budzik, Janet K. Today's Practical Guide to Increasing Profits for Contractors with Easy-to-Use Suggestions & Aids. LC 74-79535. (Illus.). 1974. 39.95 (ISBN 0-912914-03-3). Practical Pubns.

Budzikiewicz, Herbert & Djerassi, Carl. Interpretation of Mass Spectra of Organic Compounds. LC 64-14625. (Holden-Day Series in Physical Techniques in Chemistry). pap. 72.00 (ISBN 0-317-09615-X, 2051040). Bks Demand UMI.

--Mass Spectrometry of Organic Compounds. LC 67-26374. (Holden-Day Series in Physical Techinques in Chemistry). pap. 160.00 (ISBN 0-317-09621-4, 2051041). Bks Demand UMI.

Budzilovich, G. N., tr. see Pashkov, P.

Budzine, Leona. Glances at Life: The Poetry of Leona Budzine. 110p. pap. 5.00 (ISBN 0-942698-12-6). Trends & Events.

Bue, F. Lo see Lo Bue, F.

Bue, Henri, tr. see Carroll, Lewis.

Bue, Marion. Turning Mirrors into Windows: Teaching the Best Short Films. 275p. 1984. lib. bdg. 21.50 (ISBN 0-87287-397-8). Libs Unl.

Bueche, F. Physical Properties of Polymers. LC 78-27015. 364p. 1979. Repr. of 1962 ed. text ed. 27.50 (ISBN 0-88275-833-0). Krieger.

Bueche, F. J. Introduction to Physics for Scientists & Engineers. 4th ed. 1024p. 1986. price not set (ISBN 0-07-008871-3). McGraw.

Bueche, Fred. Physical Science. LC 73-182927. (Illus.). 1972. 21.95x (ISBN 0-87901-019-3). Worth.

Bueche, Frederick. Introduction to Physics for Scientists & Engineers. 3rd ed. LC 79-20613. (Illus.). 1980. text ed. 43.95 (ISBN 0-07-008875-6). McGraw.

--Principles of Physics. 4th ed. (Illus.). 864p. 1982. 36.95x (ISBN 0-07-008867-5). McGraw.

--Schaum's Outline of College Physics. 7th ed. (Schaum's Outline Ser.). (Illus.). 1979. pap. 8.95 (ISBN 0-07-008857-8). McGraw.

--Technical Physics. 3rd ed. 758p. 1984. text ed. 28.95 scp (ISBN 0-06-041036-1, HarpC). Har-Row.

--Understanding the World of Physics. (Illus.). 752p. 1981. text ed. 29.95 (ISBN 0-07-008863-2). McGraw.

Buecher, T., et al, eds. Biological Chemistry of Organelle Formation: Proceedings. (Colloquium Mosbach Ser.: Vol. 31). (Illus.). 254p. 1980. 49.50 (ISBN 0-387-10458-5). Springer-Verlag.

Buecher, W. Grillparzers Verhaeltnis Zur Politik Seiner Zeit. 1913. pap. 9.00 (ISBN 0-384-06220-2). Johnson Repr.

Buecherl, Emil S., ed. see International Symposium, First, Berlin, Nov. 1972.

Buechi, J. R. & Siefkes, D. Decidable Theories Two: The Monadic Second Order Theory of All Countable Ordinals. (Lecture Notes in Mathematics: Vol. 328). 217p. 1973. pap. 16.00 (ISBN 0-387-06345-5). Springer-Verlag.

Buechler, Hans & Buechler, Judith-Maria. Carmen: The Autobiography of a Spanish Galician Peasant Woman. 256p. 1981. text ed. 16.95x (ISBN 0-87073-880-1); pap. text ed. 8.95x (ISBN 0-87073-846-1). Schenkman Bks Inc.

Buechler, Hans C. The Masked Media: Aymara Fiestas & Social Interaction in the Bolivian Highlands. (Approaches to Semiotics Ser.: No. 59). 400p. 1980. 36.00 (ISBN 90-279-7777-1). Mouton.

Buechler, Judith-Maria, jt. auth. see Buechler, Hans.

Buechler, Sandra. Sesquicentennial of Effingham County. (Illus.). 808p. 1982. 75.00 (ISBN 0-9609598-0-7). Banbury Pub Co.

Buechner, Alvin, ed. Cellist's First Concert Album. (Illus.). 1911. pap. 7.50 (ISBN 0-8258-0172-9, 0-107). Fischer Inc NY.

Buechner, Frederick. The Alphabet of Grace. (Orig.). 1977. pap. 4.95 (ISBN 0-8164-2163-3, Pub. by Seabury). Winston Pr.

--The Alphabet of Grace. 228p. 1985. pap. 7.95 (ISBN 0-8027-2480-9). Walker & Co.

--The Alphabet of Grace. LC 84-48765. 128p. 1985. 11.49 (ISBN 0-06-061173-1, HarpR). Har-Row.

--The Book of Bebb. LC 79-63795. 512p. 1979. 19.95 (ISBN 0-689-10986-5). Atheneum.

--The Final Beast. LC 81-47438. 1982. 10.53i (ISBN 0-686-97205-8, HarpR). Har-Row.

--Godric: A Novel. LC 83-47717. 192p. 1983. pap. 6.68 (ISBN 0-06-061162-6, CN 4078, HarpR). Har-Row.

--Hungering Dark. LC 68-29987. 1969. pap. 5.95 (ISBN 0-8164-2314-8, Pub. by Seabury). Winston Pr.

--The Hungering Dark. LC 84-48763. 144p. 1985. pap. 6.68 (ISBN 0-06-061175-8, HarpR). Har-Row.

--Lion Country: A Novel. LC 84-47713. (Books of Bebb). 240p. 1984. pap. 3.80 (ISBN 0-06-061164-2, HarpR). Har-Row.

--Love a Feast. LC 84-47714. (Books of Bebb). 380p. 1984. pap. 3.80 (ISBN 0-06-061167-7, P-5009, HarpR). Har-Row.

--Magnificent Defeat. 1968. pap. 5.95 (ISBN 0-8164-2045-9, SP44, Pub. by Seabury). Winston Pr.

--The Magnificent Defeat. LC 84-48764. 144p. 1985. pap. 6.68 (ISBN 0-06-061174-X, HarpR). Har-Row.

--Now & Then. LC 82-48413. 128p. 1983. 9.57i (ISBN 0-06-061161-8, HarpR). Har-Row.

--Open Heart. LC 84-47715. (Books of Bebb). 1984. pap. 3.80i (ISBN 0-06-061166-9, P-5008, HarpR). Har-Row.

--Peculiar Treasures: A Biblical Who's Who. Buechner, Katherine A., tr. LC 78-20586. 1979. 11.49i (ISBN 0-06-061157-X, HarpR). Har-Row.

--A Room Called Remember: Uncollected Pieces. LC 83-48457. 192p. 1984. 12.45 (ISBN 0-06-061163-4, HarpR). Har-Row.

--The Sacred Journey. LC 81-47843. 128p. 1982. 9.57i (ISBN 0-06-061158-8, HarpR). Har-Row.

--The Sacred Journey. 224p. 1984. pap. 8.95 large print ed. (ISBN 0-8027-2479-5). Walker & Co.

--Telling the Truth: The Gospel As Tragedy, Comedy, & Fairy Tale. LC 77-7839. 1977. 12.45 (ISBN 0-06-061156-1, HarpR). Har-Row.

--Treasure Hunt. LC 84-47716. (Books of Bebb). 1984. pap. 3.80 (ISBN 0-06-061168-5, P-5010, HarpR). Har-Row.

--Wishful Thinking: A Theological ABC. LC 72-9872. 128p. 1973. 10.53 (ISBN 0-06-061155-3, HarpR). Har-Row.

Buechner, Howard A., ed. Management of Fungus Diseases of the Lungs. (Illus.). 248p. 1971. photocopy ed. 29.50x (ISBN 0-398-00247-9). C C Thomas.

Buechner, Katherine A., tr. see Buechner, Frederick.

Buechner, Robert. Prosper Through Tax Planning. (Illus.). 288p. 1983. 17.95 (ISBN 0-698-11196-6, Coward). Putnam Pub Group.

Buechner, Thomas & Warmus, William. Czechoslovakia Diary. 16p. 1980. pap. 0.50 (ISBN 0-87290-102-5). Corning.

Buechner, Thomas S., ed. see Rockwell, Norman.
Buechner, Thomas S., jt. ed. see Von Saldern, Axel.
Buegler, Joseph. God's Love Machine. 160p. 1983. 7.95 (ISBN 0-89962-305-0). Todd & Honeywell.
Buehholz, Ted, jt. auth. see Dusthimer, David.
Buehler, Alfred G. The Property Tax: Problems & Potentials. 1976. Repr. of 1967 ed. 24.00 (ISBN 0-527-89014-6). Kraus Repr.
Buehler, Calvin A. & Pearson, Donald E. Survey of Organic Syntheses, 2 vols. LC 73-112590. Vol. 1, 1970, 1166p. 95.00 (ISBN 0-471-11670-X); Vol. 2, 1977, 1105p. 56.50 (ISBN 0-471-11671-8, Pub. by Wiley-Interscience). Wiley.
Buehler, Dan Y., jt. auth. see Stewart, J. David.
Buehler, Ezra C. & Johannesen, Richard L. Building the Contest Oration. 202p. 1965. 10.00 (ISBN 0-8242-0008-X). Wilson.
Buehler, George. Laws of Manu. LC 73-149682. (BCL Ser. II). Repr. of 1886 ed. 34.50 (ISBN 0-404-01148-9). AMS Pr.
Buehler, Janice A. Nurses & Physicians in Transition. Kalisch, Philip & Kalisch, Beatrice, eds. LC 82-10940. (Studies in Nursing Management: No. 10). 164p. 1982. 39.95 (ISBN 0-8357-1379-2). Univ Microfilms.
Buehler, Philip G. The Middle English Genesis & Exodus: A Running Commentary on the Text of the Poem. LC 73-79277. (De Proprietatibus Litterarum, Ser. Practica: No. 74). 85p. 1974. pap. text ed. 12.00x (ISBN 90-2793-082-1). Mouton.
Buehler, Vernon M. & Shetty, Y. Krishna, eds. Productivity Improvement: Case Studies of Proven Practice. 304p. 1981. 19.95 (ISBN 0-8144-5701-0). AMACOM.
Buehler, Vernon M., jt. ed. see Shetty, Y. K.
Buehler, W. K. Gauss: A Biographical Study. (Illus.). 208p. 1981. 19.80 (ISBN 0-387-10662-6). Springer-Verlag.
Buehlmann, A. A., et al. Pathophysiology. (Illus.). 1979. pap. 31.00 (ISBN 0-387-90370-4). Springer-Verlag.
Buehlmann, Hans. Mathematical Methods in Risk Theory. LC 79-126042. (Grundlehren der Mathematischen Wissenschaften: Vol. 17). (Illus.). 1970. 36.00 (ISBN 0-387-05117-1). Springer-Verlag.
Buehne, Sheema Z., tr. see Emrich, Wilhelm.
Buehne, Sheema Z., tr. see Hartmann Von Aue.
Buehne, Sheema Z., et al, trs. see Kraus, Karl.
Buehner, William J. & Ambrose, John W. Preparatory Latin, 2 bks. (gr. 6-9). 1977-78. pap. text ed. 7.00x ea.; Bk. 1. (ISBN 0-88334-007-0); Bk. 2. (ISBN 0-88334-028-3). Ind Sch Pr.
Buehner, William J. & Colby, John K. Comprehensive Second Year Latin. (Orig.). (gr. 9-10). 1977. pap. text ed. 7.95x. Ind Sch Pr.
Buehrig, Edward. Wilson's Foreign Policy in Perspective. 11.25 (ISBN 0-8446-0521-2). Peter Smith.
Buehrig, Edward H. Woodrow Wilson & the Balance of Power. 13.25 (ISBN 0-8446-0522-0). Peter Smith.
Buehring, Gernot, ed. Vaterunser Polyglott: The Lord's Prayer in 42 Languages. 278p. (Ger.). 1984. 10.00x (ISBN 3-87118-666-X, Pub. by Helmut Buske Verlag Hamburg). Benjamins North AM.
Buehrio, Edward H. The U. N. & the Palestinian Refugees: A Study in Nonterritorial Administration. LC 71-160124. (Indiana University International Development Research Center Studies in Development: No. 3). pap. 57.80 (ISBN 0-317-09059-3, 2055235). Bks Demand UMI.
Buehrle, Marie C. Rafael: Cardinal Merry del Val. 308p. (Orig.). 1980. pap. 6.50 (ISBN 0-912414-28-6). Lumen Christi.
--Who Are You: The Life of St. Cecilia. LC 70-158918. 1971. pap. 3.25 (ISBN 0-317-17657-9, 101-7). Prow Bks-Franciscan.
Buek, H. W. Genera, Species & Synonyma Candolleana Alphabetico Ordine Disposita: Seu Index Generalis & Specialis Ad A. P. De Candolle Prodromum Systematis Naturalis Regni Vegetabilis, 4 vols. in two. 1967. 97.65 (ISBN 90-6123-029-2). Lubrecht & Cramer.
Buel, J. W. Heroes of the Dark Continent. facs. ed. LC 73-138333. (Black Heritage Library Collection). 1889. 32.75 (ISBN 0-8369-8725-X). Ayer Co Pubs.
--The Life & Wonderful Adventures of Wild Bill. Jones, William R., ed. (Illus.). 1977. pap. 2.95 (ISBN 0-89646-013-4). Outbooks.
--Life of Wild Bill Hickok. (Golden West Ser.). 1976. pap. 1.25 (ISBN 0-685-74573-2, LB422ZK, Leisure Bks). Dorchester Pub Co.
Buel, James W. The Magic City. LC 74-15728. (Popular Culture in America Ser.). (Illus.). 294p. 1975. Repr. 79.50x (ISBN 0-405-06364-4). Ayer Co Pubs.
Buel, Jesse. The Farmer's Companion: Or Essays on the Principles & Practice of American Husbandry. LC 72-89092. (Rural America Ser.). 1973. Repr. of 1839 ed. 28.00 (ISBN 0-8420-1478-0). Scholarly Res Inc.
Buel, Joy D. & Buel, Richard, Jr. The Way of Duty: A Woman & Her Family in Revolutionary America. LC 83-42677. (Illus.). 300p. 1984. 19.95 (ISBN 0-393-01767-2). Norton.
--The Way of Duty: A Woman & Her Family in Revolutionary America. (Illus.). 336p. 1985. pap. 6.95 (ISBN 0-393-30225-3). Norton.
Buel, Richard. Securing the Revolution: Ideology in American Politics 1789-1815. LC 74-38120. 403p. 1972. 29.95x (ISBN 0-8014-0705-2). Cornell U Pr.
Buel, Richard, Jr. Dear Liberty: Connecticut's Mobilization for the Revolutionary War. LC 80-14511. 425p. 1980. 25.00x (ISBN 0-8195-5047-7). Wesleyan U Pr.
--Securing the Revolution: Ideology & American Politics, 1789-1815. LC 74-38120. 403p. (Orig.). 1974. pap. 13.50x (ISBN 0-8014-9147-9). Cornell U Pr.
Buel, Richard, Jr., jt. auth. see Buel, Joy D.
Bueler, Gladys. Colorado's Colorful Characters. (Illus.). 115p. 1981. pap. 4.95 (ISBN 0-87108-595-X). Pruett.
Bueler, Lois E. Wild Dogs of the World. LC 72-96435. (Illus.). 274p. (Orig.). 1980. pap. 6.95 (ISBN 0-8128-6075-6). Stein & Day.
Bueler, William M. Chinese Sayings. LC 79-182059. (YA) 1972. pap. 4.50 (ISBN 0-8048-1018-4). C E Tuttle.
--U. S. China Policy & the Problem of Taiwan. LC 79-25371. 143p. 1980. Repr. of 1971 ed. lib. bdg. 19.75x (ISBN 0-313-22153-7, BUUS). Greenwood.
Buell, Augustus C. Paul Jones: Founder of the American Navy, 2 vols. facsimile ed. LC 70-157326. (Select Bibliographies Reprint Ser.). Repr. of 1900 ed. Set. 45.00 (ISBN 0-8369-5786-5). Ayer Co Pubs.
Buell, Bradley. Community Planning for Human Services. LC 72-9588. 464p. 1973. Repr. of 1952 ed. lib. bdg. 25.00x (ISBN 0-8371-6585-7, BUHS). Greenwood.
Buell, Charles E. Physical Education for Blind Children. 2nd ed. (Illus.). 250p. 1983. pap. 16.50x (ISBN 0-398-04816-9). C C Thomas.
Buell, Ellen L., ed. Treasury of Little Golden Books. Rev. ed. 96p. (ps-2). 1982. 6.95 (ISBN 0-307-96540-6, Golden Bks). Western Pub.
Buell, Emmett H., Jr. & Brisbin, Richard A., Jr. School Desegregation & Defended Neighborhoods: The Boston Controversy. LC 78-19598. (Illus.). 208p. 1981. 25.00x (ISBN 0-669-02646-8). Lexington Bks.
Buell, Frederick. Full Summer. LC 78-25914. (The Wesleyan Poetry Program: Vol. 95). 1979. 15.00x (ISBN 0-8195-2095-0); pap. 6.95 (ISBN 0-8195-1095-5). Wesleyan U Pr.
--Theseus & Other Poems. LC 73-24550. 89p. 1971. 2.95 (ISBN 0-87886-003-7). Ithaca Hse.
Buell, John. The Shrewsdale Exit. 279p. 1972. 6.95 (ISBN 0-374-26342-6). FS&G.
--The Shrewsdale Exit. 288p. 1984. pap. 3.50 (ISBN 0-88184-039-4). Carroll & Graf.
Buell, Jon A. & Hyder, O. Quentin. Jesus: God, Ghost or Guru? (Christian Free University Curriculum Ser.). 1978. pap. 4.95 (ISBN 0-310-35761-6). Zondervan.
Buell, Lawrence. Literary Transcendentalism: Style & Vision in the American Renaissance. 347p. 1973. 20.00x (ISBN 0-8014-0787-7). Cornell U Pr.
--Literary Transcendentalism: Style & Vision in the American Rennaisance. LC 73-8409. 336p. (Orig.). 1975. pap. 7.95x (ISBN 0-8014-9152-5). Cornell U Pr.
Buell, Lawrence, ed. see Stoddard, Elizabeth.
Buell, Lawrence, ed. see Whitman, Walt.
Buell, Marray F., jt. auth. see Robichaud, Beryl.
Buell, Raymond L. Liberia: A Century of Survival Eighteen Forty-Seven to Nineteen Forty-Seven. LC 47-1714. 1969. Repr. of 1947 ed. 15.00 (ISBN 0-527-13400-7). Kraus Repr.
--Liberia: A Century of Survival, 1847-1947. (African Handbooks Ser.: Vol. 7). (Illus.). 140p. 1947. 7.50x (ISBN 0-686-24090-1). Univ Mus of U.
--Native Problem in Africa, 2 vols. 1965. Repr. Set. 85.00x (ISBN 0-7146-1639-7, F Cass Co). Biblio Dist.
Buell, Raymond L., ed. see Dean, Vera, et al.
Buell, Thomas J. Master of Sea Power: A Biography of Fleet Admiral Ernest J. King. (Illus.). 543p. 1980. avail. members only 22.50 (ISBN 0-316-11469-3); bulk rates avail. Naval Inst Pr.
Buell, V. P. Handbook of Modern Marketing. 2nd ed. 1312p. 1986. price not set (ISBN 0-07-008854-3). McGraw.
Buell, Victor. Marketing Management: A Strategic Planning Approach. 704p. 1984. text ed. 34.95 (ISBN 0-07-008865-9). McGraw.
Buell, Victor P., et al, eds. Handbook of Modern Marketing. LC 78-96238. (Illus.). 1504p. 1970. 83.95 (ISBN 0-07-008838-1). McGraw.
Buell, William A. Hamlets of the Theater. (Illus.). 1965. 19.95 (ISBN 0-8392-1158-9). Astor-Honor.
Buelow, Bernhard H. Von see Von Buelow, Bernhard H.
Buelow, Bernhard von see Von Buelow, Bernhard.
Buelow, Edeltraud & Schmitter, Peter, eds. Integrale Linguistik. (Illus.). xiv, 817p. 1979. 80.00 (ISBN 90-272-2001-8). Benjamins North Am.
Buelow, George & Marx, Hans J., eds. New Mattheson Studies. LC 83-5157. 400p. 1984. 49.50 (ISBN 0-521-25115-X). Cambridge U Pr.
Buelow, George, ed. see Anderson, Donna K.
Buelow, George, ed. see Archbold, Lawrence.
Buelow, George, ed. see Bailey, Walter B.
Buelow, George, ed. see Berger, Karol.
Buelow, George, ed. see Block, Adrienne F.
Buelow, George, ed. see Bussey, William M.
Buelow, George, ed. see Caluori, Eleanor.
Buelow, George, ed. see Cardamone, Donna G.
Buelow, George, ed. see Cooper, Jeffrey H.
Buelow, George, ed. see Cowart, Georgia.
Buelow, George, ed. see Cunningham, Walker.
Buelow, George, ed. see Cusick, Suzanne G.
Buelow, George, ed. see Daniel, Keith W.
Buelow, George, ed. see Duffy, John.
Buelow, George, ed. see Freeman, Robert.
Buelow, George, ed. see Friedland, Bea.
Buelow, George, ed. see Glass, Frank W.
Buelow, George, ed. see Gustafson, Bruce.
Buelow, George, ed. see Hallmark, Rufus E.
Buelow, George, ed. see Hancock, Virginia.
Buelow, George, ed. see Hanning, Barbara R.
Buelow, George, ed. see Harriss, Ernest C.
Buelow, George, ed. see Herz, Gerhard.
Buelow, George, ed. see Hill, John.
Buelow, George, ed. see Holoman, D. Kern.
Buelow, George, ed. see Hosler, Bellamy.
Buelow, George, ed. see Hyde, Martha M.
Buelow, George, ed. see Johnson, Douglas P.
Buelow, George, ed. see Josephson, David S.
Buelow, George, ed. see Joyce, John J.
Buelow, George, ed. see Kowalke, Kim H.
Buelow, George, ed. see Lessem, Alan P.
Buelow, George, ed. see Lewis, Christopher O.
Buelow, George, ed. see McClymonds, Marita P.
Buelow, George, ed. see McCreless, Patrick P.
Buelow, George, ed. see Mann, Brian.
Buelow, George, ed. see Mead, Rita.
Buelow, George, ed. see Meyer, Kenton T.
Buelow, George, ed. see Milligan, Thomas B.
Buelow, George, ed. see Millner, Fredrick L.
Buelow, George, ed. see Monson, Craig.
Buelow, George, ed. see Moore, James H.
Buelow, George, ed. see Murata, Margaret.
Buelow, George, ed. see Neumann, Frederick.
Buelow, George, ed. see Newman, Joyce.
Buelow, George, ed. see Nicolaisen, Jay.
Buelow, George, ed. see Olmstead, Andrea.
Buelow, George, ed. see Palmer, A. Dean.
Buelow, George, ed. see Pemberton, Carol A.
Buelow, George, ed. see Pendle, Karin.
Buelow, George, ed. see Pennington, Neil D.
Buelow, George, ed. see Petersen, Barbara A.
Buelow, George, ed. see Petty, Fred C.
Buelow, George, ed. see Pinnell, Richard T.
Buelow, George, ed. see Pollack, Howard.
Buelow, George, ed. see Price, Curtis A.
Buelow, George, ed. see Prizer, William F.
Buelow, George, ed. see Rivera, Benito V.
Buelow, George, ed. see Root, Deane L.
Buelow, George, ed. see Sadie, Julie A.
Buelow, George, ed. see Samuel, Harold E.
Buelow, George, ed. see Schmidt, John C.
Buelow, George, ed. see Schulenberg, David.
Buelow, George, ed. see Silbiger, Alexander.
Buelow, George, ed. see Stauffer, George B.
Buelow, George, ed. see Steblin, Rita K.
Buelow, George, ed. see Stein, Deborah J.
Buelow, George, ed. see Tick, Judith.
Buelow, George, ed. see Tomasello, Andrew.
Buelow, George, ed. see Troy, Charles E.
Buelow, George, ed. see Virga, Patricia H.
Buelow, George, ed. see Vollen, Gene E.
Buelow, George, ed. see Wade, Rachel W.
Buelow, George, ed. see Wason, Robert W.
Buelow, George, ed. see Weimer, Eric.
Buelow, George, ed. see White, Pamela C.
Buelow, George, ed. see Whitesitt, Linda.
Buelow, George, ed. see Winklhofer, Sharon.
Buelow, George, ed. see Winter, Robert S., III.
Buelow, George, ed. see Witherell, Anne L.
Buelow, George, ed. see Zuck, Barbara A.
Buelow, George J., jt. ed. see Daviau, Donald G.
Buelow, Hans Von see Von Buelow, Hans.
Buelow, Marie Von see Von Buelow, Hans.
Buenaventura de Oreyegui, P., jt. auth. see Aberlaitz.
Buenger, H. J., jt. ed. see Werner, H.
Buenger, Walter L. Secession & the Union in Texas. 267p. 1984. text ed. 17.50x (ISBN 0-292-77581-4). U of Tex Pr.
Buenger, Walter L., ed. Texas History. (The Texas History Ser.). (Illus.). 546p. 1983. pap. text ed. 19.95x (ISBN 0-89641-138-9). American Pr.
Buening, Charles R. Communicating on the Job: A Practical Guide for Supervisors. 100p. 1974. text ed. 10.95 (ISBN 0-201-00855-6). Addison-Wesley.
Buenker, John, et al, eds. Urban History: a Guide to Information Sources. LC 80-19643. (American Government & History Ser., Part of the Gale Information Guide Library: Vol. 9). 400p. 1981. 60.00x (ISBN 0-8103-1479-7). Gale.
Buenker, John D. The Income Tax & the Progressive Era. Burke, Robert E. & Feidel, Frank, eds. (Modern American History Ser.). 50.00 (ISBN 0-8240-5665-5). Garland Pub.
Buenker, John D. & Burckel, Nicholas C. Immigration & Ethnicity: A Guide to Information Sources. LC 74-11515. (American Government & History Information Guide Ser.: Vol. 1). 1977. 60.00x (ISBN 0-8103-1202-6). Gale.
Buenker, John D. & Burckel, Nicholas C., eds. Progressive Reform: A Guide to Information Sources. (The American Government & History Information Guide Ser.: Vol. 8). 300p. 1981. 60.00x (ISBN 0-8103-1485-1). Gale.
Buenker, John D., et al. Progressivism. 250p. 1977. 11.25x (ISBN 0-87073-687-6); pap. text ed. 7.95x (ISBN 0-87073-688-4). Schenkman Bks Inc.
Bueno, Dorothy Del see Del Bueno, Dorothy.
Bueno, Dorothy Del see Del Bueno, Dorothy J.
Bueno, Julian A. La Sotana De Juan Ruiz -Elementos Eclesiasticos En el Libro De Buen Amor. LC 81-84295. 166p. 1983. 17.00x (ISBN 0-938972-02-2). Spanish Lit Pubns.
Bueno de Mesquita, Bruce. Strategy, Risk, & Personality in Coalition Politics: The Case of India. LC 75-3853. pap. 52.00 (ISBN 0-317-20837-3, 2024439). Bks Demand UMI.
--The War Trap. LC 80-24631. (Illus.). 238p. 1981. 32.00x (ISBN 0-300-02558-0); pap. 8.95x (ISBN 0-300-03091-6, Y-469). Yale U Pr.
Bueno De Mesquita, Bruce & Park, Richard L. India's Political System. 2nd ed. (Illus.). 1979. pap. 15.95 ref. (ISBN 0-13-456921-0). P-H.
Buenos Aires, Universidad Nacional, Facultad de Derecho y Ciencias Sociales Biblioteca. Catalogo Metodico de la Biblioteca de la Facultad de Derecho y Ciencias Sociales de Buenos Aires Seguidode de una Table Alfabetica de Autores. 1976. lib. bdg. 134.95 (ISBN 0-8490-1584-7). Gordon Pr.
Buergenthal, Thomas. Law-Making in the International Civil Aviation Organization, Vol. 7. (Procedural Aspects of International Law Ser.). 247p. 1969. 20.00x (ISBN 0-8156-2139-6). U Pr of Va.
Buergenthal, Thomas & Maier, Harold G. Public International Law in a Nutshell. (Nutshell Ser.). 245p. 1985. pap. text ed. write for info. (ISBN 0-314-93816-8). West Pub.
Buergenthal, Thomas & Norris, Robert. Human Rights: The Inter-American System. LC 82-81889. (Human Rights Ser.). 1982. Set. loose-leaf 255.00 (ISBN 0-379-20723-0). Oceana.
Buergenthal, Thomas, ed. Human Rights, International Law & the Helsinki Accord. LC 77-11762. 216p. 1978. text ed. 25.00x (ISBN 0-916672-91-3). Allanheld.
Buerger, A. & Tobis, Jerome S. Approaches to the Validation of Manipulation Therapy. (Illus.). 352p. 1977. 38.50x (ISBN 0-398-03565-2). C C Thomas.
Buerger, A. A. & Tobis, Jerome S. Neurophysiologic Aspects of Rehabilitation Medicine. (Illus.). 352p. 1976. 40.50x (ISBN 0-398-03405-2). C C Thomas.
Buerger, A. A. & Greenman, Philip E., eds. Empirical Approaches to the Validation of Spinal Manipulation. (Illus.). 308p. 1985. 34.75x (ISBN 0-398-05086-4). C C Thomas.
Buerger, E. Woerterbuch Datenerfassung-Programmierung. (Eng., Ger., Fr. & Rus., Dictionary of Data Processing & Programming). 1976. 56.00 (ISBN 3-87144-265-8, M-6967). French & Eur.
Buerger, Ing E., ed. Data Processing Programming: Datenerfassung Programmiering. (Eng., Ger., Fr., Rus.). 1978. 55.00x (ISBN 3-87144-264-X). Adlers Foreign Bks.
Buerger, Jane. Growing As Jesus Grew. LC 80-17187. (Illus.). 32p. (ps-2). 1980. PLB 5.95 (ISBN 0-89565-173-4). Childs World.
--Growing as Jesus Grew. (Child's World Books of Understanding). (Illus.). 1985. PLB 5.95 (ISBN 0-89565-173-4, R4924). Standard Pub.
--Helping. LC 84-23750. (Values to Live By Ser.). (Illus.). 32p. (gr. k-3). lib. bdg. 9.95 (ISBN 0-516-06519-X). Childrens.
--Obedience. LC 80-39520. (Values to Live by). (Illus.). 32p. (ps-3). 1981. PLB 9.95 (ISBN 0-516-06526-2). Childrens.
--Obedience. LC 80-14590. (What Does the Bible Say? Ser.). (Illus.). 32p. (ps-2). 1980. PLB 5.95 (ISBN 0-89565-164-5). Childs World.
--Obedience. rev. ed. LC 80-39520. (What Is It? Ser.). (Illus.). 32p. (gr. k-3). 1981. PLB 7.45 (ISBN 0-89565-206-4). Childs World.
Buerger, Jane & Davis, Jennie. Helping Is. (ps). 1984. 4.95 (ISBN 0-89693-218-4). Victor Bks.
--Helping Is-- LC 84-7042. (Illus.). 32p. (ps-k). 1984. lib. bdg. 4.95 (ISBN 0-89693-218-4). Dandelion Hse.
Buerger, Jane, ed. see Baker, Eugene.
Buerger, Jane, ed. see Colina, Tessa.
Buerger, Jane, ed. see Moncure, Jane B.
Buerger, Jane, ed. see Odor, Ruth.
Buerger, Jane, ed. see Odor, Ruth S.
Buerger, Jane, ed. see Ziegler, Sandy.
Buerger, Janet E. The Era of the French Calotype. LC 82-82296. (Illus.). 64p. (Orig.). 1982. pap. 15.00 (ISBN 0-935398-07-4). Intl Mus Photo.
--The Last Decade: The Emergence of Art Photography in the 1890s. (Illus.). 40p. (Orig.). 1984. pap. 10.00 (ISBN 0-935398-09-0). Intl Mus Photo.
Buerger, Martin J. Crystal-Structure Analysis. LC 79-1407. 690p. 1979. Repr. of 1960 ed. lib. bdg. 40.50 (ISBN 0-88275-900-0). Krieger.
--Vector Space & Its Application in Crystal-Structure Investigation. LC 59-6760. pap. 91.30 (ISBN 0-317-08653-7, 2011964). Bks Demand UMI.
--X-Ray Crystallography. LC 80-12459. 554p. 1980. Repr. of 1942 ed. lib. bdg. 34.00 (ISBN 0-89874-176-9). Krieger.
Bueringer, Helmut & Schriever, Karl-Heinz. Nonparametric Sequential Selection Procedures. 500p. 1981. pap. 35.00x (ISBN 0-8176-3021-X). Birkhauser.
Buerk, Charles A., jt. auth. see Van Way, Charles W.

Buerkel-Rothfuss, Nancy. Communications: Competencies & Contexts. 432p. 1985. pap. text ed. 17.95 (ISBN 0-394-35035-9, RanC); wkbk. 8.95 (ISBN 0-394-35036-7). Random.

Buerki, F. A. Stagecraft for Nonprofessionals. 3rd ed. (Illus.). 144p. (Orig.). 1972. pap. 9.95 (ISBN 0-299-06234-1). U of Wis Pr.

--Stagecraft for Nonprofessionals. 4th ed. LC 83-1244. 196p. text ed. 25.00x (ISBN 0-299-09350-6); pap. 9.95x (ISBN 0-299-09354-9). U of Wis Pr.

Buerki, K., et al see Huth, F., et al.

Buerki, Robert A. & Veatch, Robert M. The Challenge of Ethics in Pharmacy Practice: A Symposium. 1985. avail. (ISBN 0-931292-15-8). Am Inst Hist Pharm.

Buerkle, Jack V. & Barker, Danny. Bourbon Street Black: The New Orleans Black Jazzman. LC 73-77926. (Illus.). 1973. pap. 6.95 (ISBN 0-19-501832-X, GB415, GB). Oxford U Pr.

Buerlein, Robert A. Allied Military Fighting Knives & the Men Who Made Them Famous. 2nd ed. LC 85-70203. (Illus.). 194p. (Orig.). 1985. 24.95 (ISBN 0-933489-00-5); pap. 17.95 (ISBN 0-933489-01-3); deluxe ed. write for info. ltd. ed. (ISBN 0-933489-02-1). Amer Hist Found.

Buerlen, Wolfgang, tr. see Schubring, Walther.

Buero, Antonio. Historia de una Escalera. Sanchez, Jose, ed. 179p. 1971. pap. text ed. price not set (ISBN 0-02-422380-8, Pub. by Scribner). Macmillan.

Buero, Antonio & Wofsy, Samuel A., eds. En la Ardente Oscuridad. 196p. (Span.). 1950. pap. text ed. 9.95 (ISBN 0-02-422370-0, Pub. by Scribner). Macmillan.

Buero-Vallejo, Antonio. Antonio Buero-Vallejo: Three Plays. Holt, Marion P., tr. from Span. (Illus.). 204p. 1985. pap. text ed. 14.95 (ISBN 0-939980-09-6). Trinity U Pr.

Buesch, Otto, et al. Industrialisierung und "Europaeische Wirtschaft" Im 19. Jahrhundert: Ein Tagungsbericht. (Veroeffentlichungen der Historischen Komimission Zu Berlin: Vol. 46). 1976. 27.20x (ISBN 3-11-006521-5). De Gruyter.

Bueschel, Richard. Japanese Aircraft Code Names of WW-2 Aircraft. 1960. pap. 1.95x (ISBN 0-685-55080-X, Pub. by WW). Aviation.

Buescher, E. Stephen, jt. auth. see Hughes, Walter T.

Buescher, Gabriel. The Eucharistic Teaching of William Ockham. (Theology Ser). 1974. Repr. of 1950 ed. 10.00 (ISBN 0-686-11585-6). Franciscan Inst.

Buescher, Walter M. Instant Meeting Planning. (Illus.). 32p. 1982. pap. text ed. 2.50x (ISBN 0-8134-2223-X). Interstate.

--Walt Buescher's Library of Humor. 200p. 1984. 19.95 (ISBN 0-13-944207-3, Busn); pap. 6.95 (ISBN 0-13-944199-9). P-H.

Bueso, Alberto T., jt. auth. see Conner, Dennis J.

Bueso, Alberto T., jt. auth. see O'Connor, Dennis J.

Buess, Bob. Deliverance from the Bondage of Fear. 1972. pap. 1.50 (ISBN 0-934244-03-0). Sweeter Than Honey.

--Discipleship Pro & Con. 1975. pap. 1.95 (ISBN 0-934244-06-5). Sweeter Than Honey.

--Favor the Road to Success. 1982. pap. 2.25 (ISBN 0-934244-17-0). Sweeter Than Honey.

--High Flight. 143p. 1980. pap. 1.95 (ISBN 0-934244-10-3). Sweeter Than Honey.

--Implanted Word. 1978. pap. 1.95 (ISBN 0-934244-10-3). Sweeter Than Honey.

--King David & I. 1980. pap. 1.95 (ISBN 0-934244-09-X). Sweeter Than Honey.

--The Laws of the Spirit. 1968. pap. 1.50 (ISBN 0-934244-01-4). Sweeter Than Honey.

--The Pendulum Swings. 92p. (Orig.). 1974. pap. 1.95 (ISBN 0-934244-12-X, TX 391-560). Sweeter Than Honey.

--The Race Horse. 1978. pap. 1.25 (ISBN 0-934244-08-1). Sweeter Than Honey.

--Setting the Captives Free. LC 42-1127. 1975. pap. 1.50 (ISBN 0-934244-02-2). Sweeter Than Honey.

--You Can Receive the Holy Ghost Today. 1967. pap. 1.50 (ISBN 0-934244-14-6). Sweeter Than Honey.

Buess, Lynn M. Numerology for the New Age. (Illus.). 1979. pap. 6.95 (ISBN 0-87516-265-7). De Vorss.

--Synergy Session. LC 80-67932. (Illus.). 113p. (Orig.). 1980. pap. 4.95 (ISBN 0-87516-427-7). De Vorss.

--The Tarot & Transformation. LC 73-77608. (Illus.). 1977. pap. 6.95 (ISBN 0-87516-238-X). De Vorss.

Buetow, Dennis, ed. The Biology of Euglena: Vol. 3, Physiology. LC 68-14645. 1982. 60.00 (ISBN 0-12-139903-6). Acad Pr.

Buetow, Dennis E., ed. Biology of Euglena, 2 Vols. 1968. Set. 150.00; Vol. 1. 60.00 (ISBN 0-12-139901-X); Vol. 2. 70.00 (ISBN 0-12-139902-8). Acad Pr.

Buetow, Harold A. The Scabbardless Sword: Criminal Justice & the Quality of Mercy. LC 82-71695. (New Studies on Law & Society). 390p. (Orig.). 1982. 37.50x (ISBN 0-86733-022-8); pap. 17.50x (ISBN 0-86733-048-1). Assoc Faculty Pr.

Buettgenbach, S. Hyperfine Structure in 4d- & 5d-Shell Atoms. (Springer Tracts in Modern Physics Ser.: Vol. 96). (Illus.). 97p. 1982. 23.00 (ISBN 0-387-11740-7). Springer-Verlag.

Buettner, jt. auth. see Fisher.

Buettner, Johann C. Narrative of Johann Carl Buettner in the American Revolution. LC 75-180037. Repr. of 1915 ed. 16.00 (ISBN 0-405-08324-6, Blom Pubns). Ayer Co Pubs.

Buettner, Shirley. Walking Out the Dark. (W. N. J. Ser.: No. 20). Signed Edition. 20.00 (ISBN 0-317-26495-8); pap. 6.00 (ISBN 0-317-26496-6). Juniper Pr WI.

Buettner, Stewart. American Art Theory, 1945-1970. Kuspit, Donald, ed. LC 81-1812. (Studies in Fine Arts: Art Theory, No. 1). 226p. 1981. 39.95 (ISBN 0-8357-1178-1). UMI Res Pr.

Buettner-Janusch, John. Origins of Man: Physical Anthropology. LC 66-14128. pap. 120.00 (ISBN 0-317-28455-X, 2055138). Bks Demand UMI.

Bueva, L. P. Man: His Behavior & Social Relations. 256p. 1981. pap. 4.00 (ISBN 0-8285-2004-6, Pub. by Progress Pubs USSR). Imported Pubns.

Bufe, Charles Q. An Understandable Guide to Music Theory. (Illus.). 71p. (Orig.). 1984. pap. 5.95 (ISBN 0-9613289-0-8). See Sharp Pr.

Buferd, Norma B., jt. auth. see Cooper, Patricia.

Buff, Iva M. A Thematic Catalog of the Sacred Works of Giacomo Carissimi. LC 80-142011. 157p. 1979. 39.00 (ISBN 0-913574-15-5). Eur Am Music.

Buffa & Newman. Production & Operations Management. rev. ed. (Plaid Ser.). 1981. 9.95 (ISBN 0-256-02222-4). Dow Jones-Irwin.

Buffa, A., jt. auth. see Hafemeister, David.

Buffa, Dudley W. Union Power & American Democracy: The UAW & the Democratic Party, 1972-83. 296p. 1984. 27.00 (ISBN 0-472-10053-X). U of Mich Pr.

Buffa, Elwood S. Elements of Production Operations Management. LC 80-26666. 250p. 1981. pap. text ed. 20.95 (ISBN 0-471-08532-4). Wiley.

--Meeting the Competitive Challenge: Manufacturing Strategy for U. S. Companies. LC 83-73706. 250p. 1984. 19.95 (ISBN 0-87094-465-7). Dow Jones-Irwin.

--Meeting the Competitive Challenge: Manufacturing Strategies for U. S. Companies. 1984. 19.95x (ISBN 0-256-03124-X). Irwin.

--Modern Production-Operations Management. 7th ed. LC 82-10860. (Wiley Series in Management). 681p. 1983. text ed. 34.95 (ISBN 0-471-86384-X). Wiley.

Buffa, Elwood S. & Miller, Jeffrey G. Production-Inventory Systems: Planning & Control. 3rd ed. 1979. 28.95x (ISBN 0-256-02041-8). Irwin.

Buffa, Elwood S. & Pletcher, Barbara A. Understanding Business Today. 1980. 25.95x (ISBN 0-256-02257-7). Irwin.

Buffa, Elwood Spencer. Basic Production Management. 2nd ed. LC 74-28396. (Illus.). pap. 120.00 (ISBN 0-317-11135-3, 2017836). Bks Demand UMI.

Buffa, S., ed. The Complete Prints of Cornelis Cort. (Illustrated Bartsch Ser.: Vol. 52). (Illus.). 1985. 120.00 (ISBN 0-89835-151-0). Abaris Bks.

--Vivant Denon. (Illustrated Bartsch Ser.: Vol. 121). (Illus.). 1984. 120.00 (ISBN 0-89835-220-7). Abaris Bks.

Buffa, Sebastian, ed. Italian Artists of the Sixteenth Century, Vols. 34-38. (Illus.). 1983. 120.00 (ISBN 0-89835-034-4). Abaris Bks.

Buffalo Fine Arts Academy. Aristide Maillol. Ritchie, Andrew C., ed. LC 71-184839. (Illus.). 128p. 1972. Repr. of 1945 ed. lib. bdg. 15.00x (ISBN 0-8371-6329-3, BFAM). Greenwood.

Buffalo Fine Arts Academy & Cranbook Academy of Art-Museum. Donald Blumberg. LC 79-50455. (Illus.). 1983. pap. 8.95 (ISBN 0-914782-24-X). Buffalo Acad.

Buffalo Symposium on Modernist Interpretation of Ancient Logic, 21 & 22 April, 1972. Ancient Logic & Its Modern Interpretations: Proceedings. Corcoran, J., ed. LC 73-88589. (Synthese Historical Library: No. 9). 1974. lib. bdg. 42.00 (ISBN 90-277-0395-7, Pub. by Reidel Holland). Kluwer Academic.

Buffalo Bill, pseud. Buffalo Bill's True Tales. (Illus.). 24p. 1977. pap. 2.00 (ISBN 0-89646-022-3). Outbooks.

Buffaloe, Neal D. & Ferguson, Dale V. Microbiology. 2nd ed. LC 80-82842. (Illus.). 752p. 1981. text ed. 32.95 (ISBN 0-395-29649-8); lab manual 12.50 (ISBN 0-395-29652-8); instr's manual 1.50 (ISBN 0-395-29650-1); study guide 10.95 (ISBN 0-395-29651-X). HM.

Buffam, C. John. The Life & Times of an MK. LC 84-27482. (Mission Candidate Aids Ser.). 224p. (Orig.). 1985. pap. 9.95 (ISBN 0-87808-198-4). William Carey Lib.

Buffet, Bernard, jt. auth. see Sagan, Francoise.

Buffet, Guy. Guy Buffet's Hawaii. LC 80-67292. 1981. 9.95 (ISBN 0-918684-11-0). Cameron & Co.

Buffet, Guy, jt. auth. see Buffet, Pam.

Buffet, Pam & Buffet, Guy. Kahala: Where the Rainbow Ends. Tabrah, Ruth, ed. LC 72-76459. (Illus.). (gr. 1-7). 1973. pap. 5.95 (ISBN 0-89610-006-5). Island Herit.

Buffet-Challie, Laurence. Art Nouveau Style. (Illus.). 1982. pap. 19.95 (ISBN 0-8478-0331-7). Rizzoli Intl.

Buffham, B. A., jt. auth. see Nauman, E. B.

Buffinghon, Charles, jt. auth. see Graham, Frank.

Buffington, jt. auth. see Graham, Frank D.

Buffington, Albert F. Pennsylvania German Secular Folk Songs. LC 74-78062. (Penn. German Ser.: Vol. 8). 1974. 15.00 (ISBN 0-911122-30-3). Penn German Soc.

Buffington, Albert F., ed. The Reichard Collection of Early Pennsylvania German Dialogues & Plays. (Penn. German Ser.: Vol. 61). 1962. 20.00 (ISBN 0-911122-15-X). Penn German Soc.

Buffington, Albert F., et al. Something for Everyone, Something for You: Essays in Memoriam Albert Franklin Buffington, Vol. 14. (Illus.). 1980. 25.00 (ISBN 0-911122-41-9). Penn German Soc.

Buffington, Audrey V., jt. auth. see Sohns, Marvin L.

Buffington, C. Your First Personal Computer: How to Buy & Use It. 256p. 1983. pap. 8.95 (ISBN 0-07-008832-2, BYTE Bks). McGraw.

Buffington, Robert. Equilibrist: A Study of John Crowe Ransom's Poems, 1916-1963. LC 67-27555. 1967. 9.95x (ISBN 0-8265-1107-4). Vanderbilt U Pr.

Buffinton, Arthur H. The Second Hundred Years War, 1689-1815. LC 75-14080. 114p. 1975. Repr. of 1929 ed. lib. bdg. 15.00x (ISBN 0-8371-8204-2, BUSYW). Greenwood.

Buffler, Richard T. Ocean Margin Drilling Program Atlases, Vol. 6. (Regional Atlas Ser.). 1985. write for info. spiral bdg (ISBN 0-86720-256-4, Marine Sci Intl). Jones & Bartlett.

Buffler, Richard T., jt. auth. see Ladd, John W.

Buffon, Georges L. The History of Singing Birds Containing an Exact Description of Their Habits & Customs... Sterling, Keir B., ed. LC 77-81118. (Biologists & Their World Ser.). (Illus.). 1978. Repr. of 1791 ed. lib. bdg. 22.00x (ISBN 0-405-10709-9). Ayer Co Pubs.

--The Natural History of Oviparous Quadrupeds & Serpents: Arranged & Published from the Papers & Collections of the Count De Buffon, 4 vols. in one. Sterling, Keir B., ed. Kerr, Robert, tr. LC 77-81119. (Biologists & Their World Ser.). (Illus.). 1978. Repr. of 1802 ed. Set. lib. bdg. 132.00x (ISBN 0-405-10710-2); lib. bdg. 66.00x ea. Vol. 1 (ISBN 0-405-10711-0). Vol. 2 (ISBN 0-405-10712-9). Ayer Co Pubs.

Buffone, Gary W., jt. ed. see Sachs, Michael L.

Buffum, Imbrie. Agrippa d'Aubigne's "Les Tragiques". A Study of the Baroque Style in Poetry. LC 75-41042. Repr. of 1951 ed. 12.50 (ISBN 0-404-14804-2). AMS Pr.

--Studies in the Baroque From Montaigne to Rotrov. 1957. 49.50x (ISBN 0-686-83793-2). Elliots Bks.

Buffum, Marjie, jt. auth. see Hatton, Henry.

Buffum, Richard D. The Brema Brasses. LC 79-52206. (Illus.). 164p. 1981. 34.95x (ISBN 0-934542-00-7). Abracadabra Pr.

Bufhanan, James W. Minnesota Walk Book: A Guide to Backpacking & Hiking in the Arrowhead & Isle Royale, Vol. 1. Reprint ed. 105p. 1982. pap. 4.50 (ISBN 0-931714-02-8). Nodin Pr.

Bufithis, Philip H. Norman Mailer. LC 74-78438. (Literature and Life Ser.). 1978. 12.95 (ISBN 0-8044-2097-1); pap. 6.95 (ISBN 0-8044-6064-7). Ungar.

Bufkin, Don, jt. auth. see Walker, Henry P.

Bufkin, E. C. Foreign Literary Prizes: Romance & Germanic Languages. 1980. 24.95 (ISBN 0-8352-1243-2). Bowker.

--The Twentieth Century Novel in English: A Checklist. write for info. U of Ga Pr.

--The Twentieth-Century Novel in English: A Checklist. 2nd ed. LC 83-6598. 192p. 1983. 20.00x (ISBN 0-8203-0685-1). U of Ga Pr.

Buford, Elizabeth, jt. auth. see Crovitz, Elaine.

Buford, Janine, ed. see DuBose, Sybil.

Buford, Thomas O. Personal Philosophy: The Art of Living. 1984. text ed. 25.95 (ISBN 0-03-059341-7). HR&W.

--Philosophy for Adults. LC 80-5524. 639p. 1980. pap. text ed. 19.50 (ISBN 0-8191-1118-X). U Pr of Amer.

Buford, Thomas O., ed. Essays on Other Minds. LC 73-122911. 434p. 1970. 25.95x (ISBN 0-252-00123-0). U of Ill Pr.

--Essays on Other Minds. LC 73-122911. pap. 108.00 (ISBN 0-317-09330-4, 2019011). Bks Demand UMI.

Bugaev, Boris N. Lug Zelenyi: Kniga Statei. 1967. Repr. of 1910 ed. 30.00 (ISBN 0-384-06245-8). Johnson Repr.

Bugaeva, Klavdiia N. Vospominaniia o Belom. Malmstad, John, ed. (Modern Russian Literature & Culture, Studies & Texts: Vol. 2). 392p. (Orig., Text in russian; introduction & annotations in english). 1981. pap. 19.50 (ISBN 0-933884-15-X). Berkeley Slavic.

Bugat, Paul, jt. auth. see Healy, Bruce.

Bugayev, K., et al. Iron & Steel Production. Savin, Ivan V., tr. from Rus. (Illus.). 246p. 1971. 12.00x (ISBN 0-8464-0533-4). Beekman Pubs.

Bugbee, Edward E. A Textbook of Fire Assaying. 3rd ed. Raese, Jon W., ed. LC 81-17021. (Illus.). 314p. 1981. Repr. of 1940 ed. text ed. 16.80 (ISBN 0-918062-47-0). Colo Sch Mines.

Bugbee, James M. The City Government of Boston. LC 78-63769. (Johns Hopkins University. Studies in the Social Sciences. Fifth Ser. 1887: 3). Repr. of 1887 ed. 11.50 (ISBN 0-404-61036-6). AMS Pr.

--The City Government of Boston. 1973. pap. 9.00 (ISBN 0-384-06250-4). Johnson Repr.

Bugbee, Percy. Men Against Fire. 200p. 1971. 8.00 (ISBN 0-685-46053-3). Natl Fire Prot.

--Principles of Fire Protection. Tower, Keith & Dean, Amy, eds. LC 76-50848. 1978. text ed. 16.50 (ISBN 0-87765-084-5, TXT-4); instr. manual 3.50 (ISBN 0-87765-122-1, TXT-4A). Natl Fire Prot.

Bugday, M. Celalettin. Dizionario Italiano-Turco, Turco-Italiano. 410p. (Ital. & Turkish.). 1979. leatherette 5.95 (ISBN 0-686-97351-8, M-9178). French & Eur.

Bugeja, Pawlu. Maltese-English,English-Maltese Dictionary. 1982. pap. 20.00 (ISBN 0-318-00238-8). Heinman.

Bugelski, B. R. Principles of Learning & Memory. LC 78-19760. 442p. 1979. 31.95 (ISBN 0-03-046596-6). Praeger.

--Some Practical Laws of Learning. LC 77-84042. (Fastback Ser.: No. 96). 1977. pap. 0.75 (ISBN 0-87367-096-5). Phi Delta Kappa.

Bugelski, B. R., ed. Empirical Studies in the Psychology of Learning. LC 74-22867. (Illus.). 276p. 1975. lib. bdg. 17.50x (ISBN 0-915144-01-8); pap. text ed. 4.95 (ISBN 0-915144-02-6). Hackett Pub.

Bugelski, Richard & Graziano, Anthony M. Handbook of Practical Psychology. 320p. 1980. text ed. 13.95 (ISBN 0-13-380600-6, Spec); pap. text ed. 6.95 (ISBN 0-13-380592-1). P-H.

Bugen, Larry A. Death & Dying: Theory, Research & Practice. 400p. 1979. pap. text ed. write for info. (ISBN 0-697-06630-4). Wm C Brown.

Bugental, James F. Challenges of Humanistic Psychology. 1967. pap. 29.00 (ISBN 0-07-008842-X). McGraw.

--Psychotherapy & Process: The Fundamentals of an Existential-Humanistic Approach. 163p. 1978. pap. text ed. 11.95 (ISBN 0-394-34758-7, RanC). Random.

--Search for Authenticity: An Existential-Analytic Approach to Psychotherapy. enl. ed. 477p. 1981. text ed. 27.50x (ISBN 0-8290-0108-5). Irvington.

--The Search for Authenticity: An Existential-Analytic Approach to Psychotheraphy. enl. ed. 477p. 1981. pap. text ed. 12.95x (ISBN 0-8290-1298-2). Irvington.

Bugental, James F. T. The Search for Existential Identity: Patient-Therapist Dialogues in Humanistic Psychotherapy. LC 75-44882. (Social & Behavioral Science Ser.). 1976. 19.95x (ISBN 0-87589-273-6). Jossey-Bass.

Bugg, Charles B. Things My Children Are Teaching Me. LC 81-70409. 1982. pap. 3.95 (ISBN 0-8054-5650-3). Broadman.

Bugg, E. G. see Ruckwick, Christian A.

Bugg, J. L., Jr. & Stewart, P. C. Jacksonian Democracy. 2nd ed. LC 75-36667. 1976. pap. text ed. 7.95 (ISBN 0-03-014151-6, HoltC). HR&W.

Bugg, Phillip W. Microcomputers in the Corporate Environment. (Illus.). 192p. 1986. text ed. 30.00 (ISBN 0-13-580234-2). P-H.

Bugg, Ralph & Whitehead, Geoffrey. Elements of Transportation & Documentation. LC 83-21755. (Elements of Overseas Trade Ser.). 290p. 1984. pap. 11.25 (ISBN 0-85941-229-6, Pub. by Woodhead-Faulkner). Longwood Pub Group.

Bugge, Sophus. Home of the Eddic Poems. Schofield, William H., tr. LC 74-144524. (Grimm Library: No. 11). Repr. of 1899 ed. 21.00 (ISBN 0-404-53554-2). AMS Pr.

Buggenhaut, J. Van see Degreef, E. & Van Buggenhaut, J.

Buggey, J. The Energy Crisis: What Are Our Choices? 1976. pap. text ed. 9.24 (ISBN 0-13-277301-5). P-H.

Buggey, JoAnne & Tyler, June. Perspectives on the Soviet World. (Illus.). (gr. 9-12). 1976. pap. 1.50 (ISBN 0-88436-374-0). EMC.

Buggie, Frederick D. New Product Development Strategies. 192p. 1981. 17.95 (ISBN 0-8144-5626-X). AMACOM.

--New Product Development Strategies. LC 81-66230. 176p. 1983. pap. 8.95 (ISBN 0-8144-7602-3). AMACOM.

Buggs, Clarence S. A Portrait of Diane. 48p. 1985. 7.95 (ISBN 0-89962-492-8). Todd & Honeywell.

Buggs, George. Music from the Middle Passage. pap. 1.50 (ISBN 0-918476-02-X). Cornerstone Pr.

Bugialli, Giuliano. Giuliano Bugialli's Classic Techniques of Italian Cooking. LC 82-10753. 526p. 1982. 19.95 (ISBN 0-671-25218-6). S&S.

--Giuliano Bugialli's Foods of Italy. LC 84-2543. (Illus.). 304p. 1984. 45.00 (ISBN 0-941434-52-4). Stewart Tabori & Chang.

Bugialli, Guiliano. The Fine Art of Italian Cooking. LC 76-9699. (Illus.). 1977. 19.95 (ISBN 0-8129-0640-3). Times Bks.

Buglass, Leslie J. General Average & the York-Antwerp Rules, 1974. 2nd ed. LC 59-12835. 190p. 10.00x (ISBN 0-87033-027-6). Cornell Maritime.

--Marine Insurance & General Average in the United States. 2nd ed. LC 81-746. 640p. 1981. 27.50 (ISBN 0-87033-274-0). Cornell Maritime.

Bugler, Caroline. Dutch Painting in the Seventeenth Century. LC 78-24553. (Mayflower Gallery Ser.). (Illus.). 1979. 12.50 (ISBN 0-8317-2483-8, Mayflower Bks); pap. 6.95 (ISBN 0-8317-2484-6). Smith Pubs.

Bugliarello, George & Doner, Dean B., eds. History & Philosophy of Technology. LC 78-26846. 392p. 1979. 22.50 (ISBN 0-252-00462-0). U of Ill Pr.

Bukharin, Nikolai I., et al. Marxism & Modern Thought. Fox, Ralph, tr. from Rus. LC 73-835. (Russian Studies: Perspectives on the Revolution Ser). 1973. Repr. of 1935 ed. 27.50 (ISBN 0-88355-031-8). Hyperion Conn.

Bukhsh, S. K. Islamic Studies. 9.95 (ISBN 0-686-18357-6). Kazi Pubns.

--The Renaissance of Islam. 1981. 29.00 (ISBN 0-686-97863-3). Kazi Pubns.

Bukhsl, Salahuddin K, tr. see Mez, Adam.

Bukiet, Melvin J. Sandman's Dust. 288p. 1985. 14.95 (ISBN 0-87795-731-2). Arbor Hse.

Bukkila, Laura, jt. auth. see Sandhu, Harpreet.

Bukoba, Bara. Church & Community in Tanzania. 240p. 1981. 50.00x (ISBN 0-317-20349-5, Pub. by C Hurst & Co UK). State Mutual Bk.

Bukofzer, Manfred, et al, eds. The Place of Musicology in American Institutions of Higher Learning, 2 vols. in one. Incl. Some Aspects of Musicology. LC 77-4226. (Music Reprint Ser.). 1977. Repr. of 1957 ed. lib. bdg. 25.00 (ISBN 0-306-77407-0). Da Capo.

Bukofzer, Manfred F. Music in the Baroque Era. (Illus.). 1947. 20.95x (ISBN 0-393-09745-5, NortonC). Norton.

Bukovsky, Vladimir. To Build a Castle: My Life As a Dissenter. Scammell, Michael, tr. 1979. 17.50 (ISBN 0-670-71640-5). Viking.

Bukowski see Stafford, William.

Bukowski, Charles. Bring Me Your Love. (Illus.). 16p. (Orig.). 1983. pap. 4.00 (ISBN 0-87685-606-7); 10.00 (ISBN 0-87685-608-3). Black Sparrow.

--Burning in Water, Drowning in Flame. 236p. (Orig.). 1983. 14.00 (ISBN 0-87685-192-8); pap. 8.00 (ISBN 0-87685-191-X). Black Sparrow.

--Dangling in the Tournefortia. 285p. (Orig.). 1981. 14.00 (ISBN 0-87685-526-5). pap. 9.50 (ISBN 0-87685-525-7). Black Sparrow.

--Days Run Away Like Wild Horses over the Hills. 156p. (Orig.). 1983. 14.00 (ISBN 0-87685-006-9); pap. 6.00 (ISBN 0-87685-005-0). Black Sparrow.

--Factotum. 212p. 1983. 14.00 (ISBN 0-87685-264-9); pap. 8.00 (ISBN 0-87685-263-0). Black Sparrow.

--Ham on Rye. 288p. 1982. 14.00 (ISBN 0-87685-558-3); pap. 9.00 (ISBN 0-87685-557-5). Black Sparrow.

--Horses Don't Bet on People & Neither Do I. 44p. 1984. pap. 2.50 (ISBN 0-935390-09-X). Wormwood Rev.

--Hot Water Music. 226p. 1983. 14.00 (ISBN 0-87685-597-4). pap. 9.00 (ISBN 0-87685-596-6). Black Sparrow.

--Love Is a Dog from Hell: Poems 1974-1977. 312p. (Orig.). 1982. 14.00 (ISBN 0-87685-363-7); pap. 8.00 (ISBN 0-87685-362-9). Black Sparrow.

--Mockingbird Wish Me Luck. 160p. (Orig.). 1982. 14.00 (ISBN 0-87685-139-1); pap. 5.00 (ISBN 0-87685-138-3). Black Sparrow.

--The Most Beautiful Woman in Town. 1983. pap. 6.95 (ISBN 0-87286-156-2). City Lights.

--Notes of a Dirty Old Man. 2nd ed. LC 73-84226. 1973. pap. 5.95 (ISBN 0-87286-074-4). City Lights.

--Play the Piano Drunk Like a Percussion Instrument Until the Fingers Begin to Bleed a Bit. 128p. 1982. 14.00 (ISBN 0-87685-438-2); pap. 5.00 (ISBN 0-87685-437-4). Black Sparrow.

--Post Office. 115p. (Orig.). 1983. 14.00 (ISBN 0-87685-087-5); pap. 6.00 (ISBN 0-87685-086-7). Black Sparrow.

--Shakespeare Never Did This. (Illus.). 1979. 14.95 (ISBN 0-87286-118-X); pap. 6.95 (ISBN 0-87286-117-1). City Lights.

--South of No North. 189p. (Orig.). 1983. 14.00 (ISBN 0-87685-190-1); pap. 7.50 (ISBN 0-87685-189-8). Black Sparrow.

--Tales of Ordinary Madness. 1983. pap. 6.95 (ISBN 0-87286-155-4). City Lights.

--There's No Business. (Illus.). 24p. (Orig.). 1984. 10.00 (ISBN 0-87685-623-7); pap. 4.00 (ISBN 0-87685-622-9). Black Sparrow.

--War All the Time: Poems, 1981-1984. 285p. 1984. 14.00 (ISBN 0-87685-638-5); pap. 9.00 (ISBN 0-87685-637-7). Black Sparrow.

--Women. 296p. 1982. 14.00 (ISBN 0-87685-391-2); pap. 9.50 (ISBN 0-87685-390-4). Black Sparrow.

Bukowski, Charles, et al. Six Poets. 1979. 3.00 (ISBN 0-912824-21-2). Vagabond Pr.

Buksbazen, Lydia. They Looked for a City. 1977. pap. 3.95 (ISBN 0-87508-041-3). Chr Lit.

Buksbazen, Victor. Feasts of Israel. 1976. pap. 2.95 (ISBN 0-87508-043-X). Chr Lit.

Bukstein, Don A. & Strunk, Robert C. Manual of Clinical Problems in Asthma, Allergy, & Related Disorders. (The Spiral Manual Ser.). 293p. 1984. spiral bdg. 18.95 (ISBN 0-316-11473-1). Little.

Bukstein, Edward J. Practice Problems in Number Systems, Logic, & Boolean Algebra. 2nd ed. LC 77-72632. (Illus.). 144p. 1977. pap. 11.95 (ISBN 0-672-21451-2, 21451). Sams.

Bula, G., jt. auth. see Schnetter, R.

Bula, M. Grand Prix Motorcycle Championships of the World 1949-1975. (Illus.). pap. 11.75 (ISBN 0-85429-208-X, F208). Haynes Pubns.

Bulani, W., jt. auth. see Dumas, T.

Bulanowski, Gerard. Resource Recovery Teleconference. 66p. 1982. 5.00 (ISBN 0-317-36334-4). Natl Conf State Legis.

Bulanowski, Gerard A., jt. ed. see Speer, R. D.

Bulanowski, Gerarg. Solid Waste Teleconference-Summary Report. 51p. 1981. 5.00 (ISBN 0-317-36333-6). Natl Conf State Legis.

Bulas, Kazimierz, et al. The Kosciuszko Foundation Dictionary, 2 vols. Incl. Vol. I. English-Polish. (Eng. & Pol.). 1959 (ISBN 90-2790-983-0); Tome II. Polish-English. (Eng. & Pol.). 1961 (ISBN 90-2790-984-9). (Eng. & Pol.). 32.80x. Mouton.

Bulas, Kazimirierz. Kosciusko Foundation English-Polish, Polish-English Dictionary, 2 vols. (Poland's Millennium Ser.). 1983. Repr. text ed. 20.00 english-polish (ISBN 0-317-07550-0); text ed. 20.00 polish-english. Kosciuszko.

Bulatao, Rodolfo A. & Fawcett, James T. Influences on Childbearing Intentions Across the Fertility Career: Demographic & Socioeconomic Factors & the Value of Children. Ward, Sandra E., ed. LC 83-11693. (Papers of the East-West Population Institute). x, 152p. (Orig.). 1983. pap. text ed. 3.00 (ISBN 0-86638-043-4). E W Center HI.

Bulatao, Rodolfo A. & Lee, Ronald D. Determinants of Fertility in Developing Countries. LC 83-17135. (Studies Population Ser.). 1983. Vol. 1: Supply & Demand for Children. 37.00 (ISBN 0-12-140501-X); Vol. 2: Fertility Regulation & Institutional Influences. 45.00 (ISBN 0-12-140502-8). Acad Pr.

Bulatao, Rodolfo A. see Arnold, Fred, et al.

Bulatkin, Eleanor W. Structural Arithmetic Metaphor in the Oxford "Roland.". LC 71-141496. (Illus.). 130p. 1972. 8.00 (ISBN 0-8142-0154-7). Ohio St U Pr.

Bulba-Borovets, Otaman Taras. Armiya Bez Derzhavy. 327p. (Ukrainian.). 1981. write for info. Ukrainian Pol.

Bulbring, E. & Shuba, M. F., eds. Physiology of Smooth Muscle. LC 75-14566. 448p. 1976. 59.50 (ISBN 0-89004-051-6). Raven.

Bulbring, Edith, et al, eds. Smooth Muscle: An Assessment of Current Knowledge. (Illus.). 576p. 1981. text ed. 95.00x (ISBN 0-292-77569-5). U of Tex Pr.

Bulbring, Karl K., ed. see Defoe, Daniel.

Bulbrook, Mary Jo. Development of Theraputic Skills. 1980. text ed. 14.95 (ISBN 0-316-11472-3, Little Med Div). Little.

Bulbrook, R. D. & Taylor, D. Jane. Commentaries on Research in Breast Disease, Vol. 3. 216p. 1983. 42.00 (ISBN 0-8451-1902-8). A R Liss.

Bulbrook, R. D. & Taylor, D. Jane, eds. Commentaries on Research in Breast Disease, Vol. 2. 180p. 1981. 28.00 (ISBN 0-8451-1901-X). A R Liss.

Bulbrook, R. D., jt. ed. see Taylor, D. Jane.

Bulbulian, Arthur H. Facial Prosthetics. (Illus.). 416p. 1973. photocopy ed. 59.75x (ISBN 0-398-02462-6). C C Thomas.

Bulcke, J. A. & Baert, A. L. Clinical & Radiological Aspects of Myopathies: CT Scanning-EMG-Radio-Isotopes. (Illus.). 187p. 1982. 58.00 (ISBN 0-387-11443-2). Springer-Verlag.

Buley, Ernest C. North Brazil: Physical Features, Natural Resources, Means of Communication, Manufactures & Industrial Development. 1976. lib. bdg. 59.95 (ISBN 0-8490-2352-1). Gordon Pr.

Buley, Jerry L. Relationships & Communication: A Book for Friends, Co-Workers & Lovers. 2nd ed. 1979. pap. text ed. 11.95 (ISBN 0-8403-2945-8, 40294501). Kendall-Hunt.

Buley, R. Carlyle. The Old Northwest: Pioneer Period, 1815-1840, 2 vols. LC 83-48117. 1983. 40.00x set (ISBN 0-253-34168-X). Ind U Pr.

Bulfield, Anthony. The Icknield Way. (Illus.). 1979. 24.00x (ISBN 0-900963-43-3, Pub. by Terence Dalton England). State Mutual Bk.

Bulfin, William. Rambles in the West of Ireland. abr. ed. 90p. 1979. pap. 4.50 (ISBN 0-85342-585-X, Co-dist. by Irish Bks Media). Irish Bk Ctr.

Bulfinch, Thomas. Age of Chivalry. (Classics Ser). (gr. 8 up). pap. 1.95 (ISBN 0-8049-0061-2, CL-61). Airmont.

--The Age of Chivalry. 59.95 (ISBN 0-87968-585-9). Gordon Pr.

--Age of Fable. (Classics Ser). (gr. 8 up). pap. 1.95 (ISBN 0-8049-0080-9, CL-80). Airmont.

--Age of Fable. 1973. Repr. of 1908 ed. 12.95x (ISBN 0-460-00472-7, Evman). Biblio Dist.

--Bulfinch's Mythology. abr. ed. Fuller, Edmund, ed. 448p. 1959. pap. 4.50 (ISBN 0-440-30845-3, LE). Dell.

--Bulfinch's Mythology, 3 vols. Incl. Vol. 1. The Age of Fable. pap. 2.95 (ISBN 0-451-62230-8, ME2230); Vols 2 & 3. The Age of Chivalry & Legends of Charlemagne. pap. 3.95 (ISBN 0-451-62252-9, ME2252). (YA) (RL 7). pap. (Ment). NAL.

--Bulfinch's Mythology. 2nd rev. ed. LC 69-11314. (Illus.). 1970. 15.34i (ISBN 0-690-57260-3). T Y Crowell.

--Bulfinch's Mythology. LC 34-27086. 7.95 (ISBN 0-394-60437-7). Modern Lib.

--Legends of Charlemagne. 59.95 (ISBN 0-8490-0505-1). Gordon Pr.

--Poetry of the Age of Fable. 59.95 (ISBN 0-8490-0864-6). Gordon Pr.

Bulfinch, Thomas, jt. auth. see Sewell, H.

Bulgakov, M. Master & Margarita. 1974. pap. 4.95 (ISBN 0-452-00757-7, Sig Classics). NAL.

--Master I Margarita. 400p. 1980. pap. 5.95 (ISBN 0-88233-666-5). Ardis Pubs.

Bulgakov, Mikhail. Flight & Bliss. Ginsburg, Mirra, tr. LC 84-29445. Orig. Title: Rus. 192p. 1985. 17.95 (ISBN 0-8112-0940-7); pap. 9.95 (ISBN 0-8112-0941-5, NDP593). New Directions.

--Heart of a Dog. Ginsburg, Mirra, tr. from Russian. 1968. pap. 2.95 (ISBN 0-394-17442-9, B193, BC). Grove.

--Master & Margarita. Ginsburg, Mirra, tr. from Russian. 1970. pap. 4.95 (ISBN 0-394-17439-9, B147, BC). Grove.

--Sobranie Sochinenii, Vol. 3. 248p. (Rus.). 1983. 25.00 (ISBN 0-88233-698-3). Ardis Pubs.

--Sobranie Sochinenii: Vol. 1. Ranniaia, Tom I., tr. 421p. (Rus.). 1982. 25.00 (ISBN 0-88233-506-5). Ardis Pubs.

Bulgakov, Sergius. A Bulgakov Anthology: From Marxism to Christian Orthodoxy. Zernov, Nicolas & Pain, James, eds. LC 76-23245. 220p. 1976. 12.50 (ISBN 0-664-21338-3). Westminster.

Bulgakow, Mikahail. Moliere. (Royal Shakespeare Company PIT Playtext Ser.). 39p. 1983. pap. 4.95 (ISBN 0-413-52320-9, NO. 3552). Methuen Inc.

Bulgarian Academy of Sciences. International Conference on Chemistry & Biotechnology of Biologically Active Natural Products: First, Varna, Bulgaria, September, 21 to 26, 1981. 1982. pap. 34.50 (ISBN 0-686-37434-7, Pub. by Reidel Holland). Kluwer Academic.

Bulger, A. Explorations: Insights into English Life & Language for Visitors of All Ages. (Pergamon Institute of English Courses Ser.). 48p. 1983. tchr's. guide 3.20 (ISBN 0-08-030345-5). Pergamon.

Bulger, A., ed. Explorations: The English Language Course of the British European Centre. (Pergamon Institute of English Courses). (Illus.). 160p. 1981. pap. 6.35 (ISBN 0-08-025358-X). Pergamon.

Bulger, Dorothy. All about Breeding Cockatiels. (Illus.). 96p. 1983. 4.95 (ISBN 0-87666-942-9, PS-801). TFH Pubns.

Bulger, Ruth E. & Strum, Judy M. The Functioning Cytoplasm. LC 73-7570. 135p. 1974. 32.50x (ISBN 0-306-30807-X, Plenum Pr). Plenum Pub.

Bulgren, William. Discrete System Simulation. (Illus.). 224p. 1982. text ed. 27.95 (ISBN 0-13-215764-0). P-H.

Bulhof. Nijhoff, Van Ostaijen, "De Stijl". 1976. pap. 25.00 (ISBN 90-247-1857-0, Pub. by Martinus Nijhoff Netherlands). Kluwer Academic.

Bulhof, Francis, ed. Nijhoff, Van Ostaijen, "De Stijl": Modernism in the Netherlands & Belgium in the First Quarter of the 20th Century.- Six Essays (1976) (Illus., Orig.). 1976. pap. 27.50 (ISBN 90-247-1857-0). Heinman.

Bulhof, Francis, ed. see Du Perron, E.

Bulhof, Ilse N. Wilhelm Dilthey: A Hermeneutic Approach to the Study of History & Culture. (Martinus Nijhoff Philosophy Library: No. 2). 225p. 1980. lib. bdg. 37.00 (ISBN 90-247-2360-4, Pub. by Martinus Nijhoff). Kluwer Academic.

Bulick, Stephen. Structure & Subject Interaction: Toward a Sociology of Knowledge in the Social Sciences. (Books in Library & Information Science: Vol. 41). (Illus.). 256p. 1982. 35.00 (ISBN 0-8247-1847-X). Dekker.

Bulik, Robert V. The Lacquer Screen. Barzun, J. & Taylor, W. H., eds. LC 81-47391. (Crime Fiction 1950-1975 Ser.). 182p. 1983. lib. bdg. 16.00 (ISBN 0-8240-4951-9). Garland Pub.

Bulin, Rudolf K. Untersuchungen zur Politik und Kriegfuehrung Roms im Osten Von 100-68 V. Chr. (European University Studies: No. 3, Vol. 177). 110p. (Ger.). 1983. 15.25 (ISBN 3-8204-7109-X). P Lang Pubs.

Bulinski, Eugene, et al. Solving Sheet Fed Offset Press Problems. 124p. 1981. 32.00 (ISBN 0-88362-035-9); members 16.00 (ISBN 0-318-17663-7). Graphic Arts Tech Found.

Bulirsch, R., jt. auth. see Stoer, J.

Bulirsch, R., ed. see Conference Held at Oberwolfach, Nov. 17-23, 1974, et al.

Bulirsch, R., et al, eds. see Conference, Oberwolfach, Germany, July 4-10, 1976.

Bulka, Reuven. Jewish Marriage: A Halakhic Ethic. 1985. text ed. 17.50x (ISBN 0-88125-077-5); pap. 9.95x (ISBN 0-317-27896-7). Ktav.

--The Quest for Ultimate Meaning: Applications of Logotherapy. LC 78-61105. 1979. 11.95 (ISBN 0-8022-2232-3). Philos Lib.

Bulka, Reuven P. Torah Therapy: Reflections on the Weekly Sedra & Special Occasions. LC 83-6155. 1983. 15.00x (ISBN 0-88125-033-3). Ktav.

--Wit & Wisdom of the Talmud. 2nd ed. (PPP Gift Editions). (Illus.). 1983. 4.95 (ISBN 0-88088-507-6). Peter Pauper.

Bulka, Reuven P. & Spero, Moshe H. A Psychology-Judaism Reader. 338p. 1982. pap. 24.50x (ISBN 0-398-04582-8). C C Thomas.

Bulka, Reuven P., ed. Holocaust Aftermath: Continuing Impact on the Generations. LC 81-84341. (A Special Issue of Journal of Psychology & Judaism: Vol. 6). 76p. 1982. pap. 9.95 (ISBN 0-89885-127-0). Human Sci Pr.

--Mystics & Medics: A Comparison of Mystical & Psychotherapeutic Encounters. LC 79-87593. 120p. 1979. pap. 9.95 (ISBN 0-87705-377-4). Human Sci Pr.

Bulka, Rueven P., ed. Dimensions of Orthodox Judaism. LC 83-260. 471p. 1983. 25.00x (ISBN 0-87068-894-4). Ktav.

Bulkin, Elly, jt. ed. see Larkin, Joan.

Bulkin, Elly, et al. Yours in Struggle: Three Feminist Perspectives on Anti-Semitism & Racism. LC 84-80956. 233p. 1984. pap. 7.95 (ISBN 0-9602284-3-8). Long Haul.

Bulkin, V. Dionysius. 53p. 1982. pap. 8.45 (ISBN 0-8285-2470-X, Pub. by Aurora Pubs USSR). Imported Pubns.

Bulkley, Ian G. Who Gains from Deep Ocean Mining? Simulating the Impact of Regimes for Regulating Nodule Exploitation. LC 79-87567. (Research Ser.: No. 40). (Illus.). 1979. pap. 3.50x (ISBN 0-87725-140-1). U of Cal Intl St.

Bulkley, Mildred E. Bibliographical Survey of Contemporary Sources for the Economic & Social History of the World War. 1922. 85.00x (ISBN 0-686-83490-9). Elliots Bks.

Bull, A. T. & Slater, J. H. Microbial Interactions & Communities, Vol. 2. write for info. (ISBN 0-12-140302-5). Acad Pr.

Bull, A. T. & Slater, J. H., eds. Microbial Interactions & Communities, Vol. 1. 1982. 63.00 (ISBN 0-12-140301-7). Acad Pr.

Bull, A. T., jt. ed. see Quayle, J. R.

Bull, A. T., et al. Microbial Technology: Society for General Microbiology Symposium 29. LC 78-12206. (Illus.). 1979. 75.00 (ISBN 0-521-22500-0). Cambridge U Pr.

Bull, Alvin & Runkle, Sylvian. Wildflowers of Iowa Woodlands. 262p. pap. 14.95 (ISBN 0-87069-309-3). Wallace-Homestead.

Bull, Angela. The Accidental Twins. (Illus.). 63p. (gr. 2-4). 1983. 8.95 (ISBN 0-571-11761-9). Faber & Faber.

--Anne Frank. (Profiles Ser.). (Illus.). 64p. (gr. 3-6). 1984. 7.95 (ISBN 0-241-11294-X, Pub. by Hamish Hamilton England). David & Charles.

--Florence Nightingale. (Profiles Ser.). (Illus.). 64p. (gr. 4-8). 1985. 7.95 (ISBN 0-241-11477-2, Pub. by Hamish Hamilton England). David & Charles.

Bull, C. Neil, jt. ed. see Johannis, Theodore B.

Bull, David. A Growing Problem: Pesticides & the Third World Poor. pap. 9.95 (ISBN 0-85598-064-8). Inst Food & Develop.

Bull, Donald. Beer Advertising Openers: A Pictorial Guide. LC 77-94261. (Illus.). 1978. pap. 8.95 (ISBN 0-9601190-4-3). Bullworks.

--Beer Trivia: Five Hundred Questions & Answers about the World's Most Popular Drink. 128p. 1985. pap. 4.95 (ISBN 0-8253-0317-6). Beaufort Bks NY.

--A Price Guide to Beer Advertising Openers & Corkscrews. LC 80-70998. (Illus.). 1981. pap. 5.00 (ISBN 0-9601190-5-1). Bullworks.

Bull, Donald, et al. American Breweries. LC 83-73558. 400p. 1984. pap. 17.95 (ISBN 0-9601190-6-X). Bullworks.

Bull, Emma, jt. auth. see Shetterly, Will.

Bull, Emma, jt. ed. see Shetterly, Will.

Bull, Ethel F. The Spirit of the Santee. LC 84-90124. 218p. 1985. 12.95 (ISBN 0-533-06207-1). Vantage.

Bull Family. Fifty Years of the Bull Family Picnic, 1922-1972. 4.95x (ISBN 0-686-14963-7). T E Henderson.

Bull, Francis. Ibsen: The Man & the Dramatist. LC 73-11340. 1973. lib. bdg. 8.50 (ISBN 0-8414-3216-3). Folcroft.

Bull, G. M. Dartmouth Time-Sharing System. LC 80-41327. (Computers & Their Applications Ser.). 240p. 1980. 89.95x (ISBN 0-470-27082-9). Halsted Pr.

Bull, G. M., jt. auth. see Bacon, M. D.

Bull, G. M., ed. Real-Time Programming, 1983: Proceedings of the IFAC-IFIP Workshop, 12th, Hertford, UK, March 1983. 100p. 1983. 26.00 (ISBN 0-08-030568-7). Pergamon.

Bull, Geoffrey. I Am a Donkey. (Tell-Tale Books Ser.). 1975. 1.95 (ISBN 0-87508-875-9). Chr Lit.

--I Am a Fish. (Tell-Tale Books Ser.). 1975. 1.95 (ISBN 0-87508-876-7). Chr Lit.

--I Am a Lamb. (Tell-Tale Books Ser.). 1975. 1.95 (ISBN 0-87508-877-5). Chr Lit.

--I Am a Mouse. (Tell-Tale Books Ser.). 1975. 1.95 (ISBN 0-87508-878-3). Chr Lit.

--I Am a Puppy. (Tell-Tale Books Ser.). 1975. 1.95 (ISBN 0-87508-879-1). Chr Lit.

--I Am a Sparrow. (Tell-Tale Books Ser.). 1975. 1.95 (ISBN 0-87508-880-5). Chr Lit.

--I Hid in a Basket. (Hide & Seek Bks). 1975. 1.95 (ISBN 0-87508-881-3). Chr Lit.

--I Hid in a Boat. (Hide & Seek Books Ser.). 1975. 1.95 (ISBN 0-87508-882-1). Chr Lit.

--I Hid in a House. (Hide & Seek Books Ser.). 1975. 1.95 (ISBN 0-87508-884-8). Chr Lit.

--I Hid in a Tree. (Hide & Seek Books Ser.). 1975. 1.95 (ISBN 0-87508-886-4). Chr Lit.

--I Hid in the Hay. (Hide & Seek Books Ser.). 1975. 1.95 (ISBN 0-87508-883-X). Chr Lit.

--I Hid in the Reeds. (Hide & Seek Books Ser.). 1975. 1.95 (ISBN 0-87508-885-6). Chr Lit.

--I Wish I Lived When Daniel Did. (Far-Away Books Ser.). 1977. 1.95 (ISBN 0-87508-892-9). Chr Lit.

--I Wish I Lived When David Did. (Far-Away Bks). 1975. 1.95 (ISBN 0-87508-890-2). Chr Lit.

--I Wish I Lived When Esther Did. (Far-Away Books Ser.). 1977. 1.95 (ISBN 0-87508-891-0). Chr Lit.

--I Wish I Lived When Gideon Did. (Far-Away Books Ser.). 1977. 1.95 (ISBN 0-87508-889-9). Chr Lit.

--I Wish I Lived When Joseph Did. (Far-Away Books Ser.). 1977. 1.95 (ISBN 0-87508-888-0). Chr Lit.

--I Wish I Lived When Noah Did. (Far-Away Bk. Ser.). (gr. 1-6). 1975. 1.95 (ISBN 0-87508-887-2). Chr Lit.

--Love Song in Harvest. 1977. pap. 3.95 (ISBN 0-87508-042-1). Chr Lit.

Bull, George. Harmony on Justification, Defense of the Nicene Creed, Judgement of the Catholic Church, 5 vols. LC 71-39556. (Library of Anglo-Catholic Theology: No. 4). Repr. of 1855 ed. Set. 150.00 (ISBN 0-404-52070-7). AMS Pr.

--Industrial Relations: The Boardroom Viewpoint. 208p. 1972. 8.75 (ISBN 0-370-01387-5). Transatlantic.

--Inside the Vatican. 294p. 1983. 13.95 (ISBN 0-312-41884-1). St Martin.

--Venice: The Most Triumphant City. (Illus.). 192p. 1982. 16.95 (ISBN 0-312-83864-6). St Martin.

Bull, George, tr. see Castiglione, Baldesar.

Bull, George, tr. see Machiavelli, Niccolo.

Bull, George, tr. see Vasari, Giorgio.

Bull, Hedley. The Anarchical Society: A Study of Order in World Politics. LC 76-21786. 335p. 1977. 29.00x (ISBN 0-231-04132-2); pap. 13.00x (ISBN 0-231-04133-0). Columbia U Pr.

--Intervention in World Politics. 1984. 19.95x (ISBN 0-19-827467-X). Oxford U Pr.

Bull, Hedley & Watson, Adam, eds. The Expansion of International Society. LC 83-23813. 480p. 1984. 39.95x (ISBN 0-19-821942-3). Oxford U Pr.

Bull, Hedley, ed. see Wight, Martin.

Bull, Hedley, intro. by see Wight, Martin.

Bull, Henry, ed. Christian Prayers & Holy Meditations. 1842. 21.00 (ISBN 0-384-06285-7). Johnson Repr.

Bull, Inez. Ole Bull's Activities in the United States Between 1843 & 1880. (Illus.). 144p. 1982. pap. 12.95 (ISBN 0-682-49801-7). Exposition Pr FL.

Bull, James. Evolution of Sex Determining Mechanisms. 1983. 23.95 (ISBN 0-8053-0400-2). Benjamin-Cummings.

Bull, John. Birds of the New York Area. LC 75-16037. (Illus.). 576p. 1975. Repr. of 1964 ed. 7.50 (ISBN 0-486-23222-0). Dover.

--Birds of the New York Area. (Illus.). 11.50 (ISBN 0-8446-5167-2). Peter Smith.

--New British Political Dramatists. (Modern Dramatist Ser.). 272p. 1984. 22.50 (ISBN 0-394-54242-8, GP942). Grove.

--New British Political Dramatists. (Modern Dramatists Ser.). 1984. pap. 7.95 (ISBN 0-394-62309-6, E-958, Ever). Grove.

--S&S Guide to Birds of the World. 1981. (Fireside); pap. 9.95 (ISBN 0-671-42235-9). S&S.

Bull, John, jt. auth. see Audubon Society.

Bull, John, jt. ed. see Barrell, John.

Bull, John, et al. Birds of North America: Eastern Region. (Field Guides Ser.). (Illus.). 160p. 1985. 16.95 (ISBN 0-02-518230-7, Collier); lexotone bdg. 9.95 (ISBN 0-02-079660-9). Macmillan.

Bull, M. J., ed. Progress in Industrial Microbiology, Vol. 14. 294p. 1978. 68.00 (ISBN 0-444-41665-X). Elsevier.

--Progress in Industrial Microbiology, Vol. 15. 1979. 68.00 (ISBN 0-444-41815-6). Elsevier.

--Progress in Industrial Microbiology, Vol. 16. 350p. 1982. 78.75 (ISBN 0-444-42037-1). Elsevier.

Bull, Nina. The Attitude Theory of Emotion. (Nervous & Mental Disease Monographs Ser.). 1969. Repr. of 1951 ed. 14.00 (ISBN 0-384-06295-4). Johnson Repr.

Bull, Norman. One Hundred New Testament Stories. 160p. (Orig.). 1984. pap. 7.95 (ISBN 0-687-29073-2). Abingdon.

--The Story of Jesus. 160p. 1983. 15.35 (ISBN 0-687-39659-X). Abingdon.

Bull, Norman J. One Hundred Great Lives. (Illus.). 352p. (gr. 4-9). 1975. pap. 10.95 (ISBN 0-7175-0582-0). Dufour.

Bull, Norman J., retold by. One Hundred Bible Stories. (Illus.). 175p. (gr. 5 up). 1983. pap. 7.95 (ISBN 0-687-29071-6). Abingdon.

Bull, Peter. Body Movement & Interpersonal Communication. LC 82-23767. 208p. 1983. 32.95x (ISBN 0-471-90069-9, Pub. by Wiley-Interscience). Wiley.

--A Hug of Teddy Bears. (Illus.). 96p. 1984. 14.95 (ISBN 0-525-24273-2, 01451-440). Dutton.

Bull, R. K, jt. auth. see Durrani, S. A.

Bull, Ray, jt. auth. see Clifford, Brian.

Bull, Ray, et al. Psychology for Police Officers. LC 83-6806. 240p. 1984. pap. text ed. 19.95x (ISBN 0-471-90194-6). Wiley.

Bull, Richard H. & Ide, Sachiko. English Made Polite. 2nd ed. (Illus., Orig.). 1981. pap. text ed. 6.50x (ISBN 0-19-581710-9). Oxford U Pr.

Bull, Robert L. Technical Illustration. (Illus.). 350p. Date not set. pap. cancelled (ISBN 0-86576-011-X). W Kaufmann.

Bull, Sara & Crosby, A. B. Ole Bull: A Memoir. LC 77-75211. 1977. Repr. of 1883 ed. 45.00 (ISBN 0-89341-112-4). Longwood Pub Group.

Bull, Sara C. Ole Bull: A Memoir. (Music Ser.). (Illus.). iv, 417p. 1981. Repr. of 1886 ed. lib. bdg. 32.50 (ISBN 0-306-76120-3). Da Capo.

Bull, Sheila. Skeletal Radiography. (Illus.). 224p. 1985. pap. text ed. 27.95 (ISBN 0-407-00278-2). Butterworth.

Bull, Storm. Index to Biographies of Contemporary Composers. LC 64-11781. 405p. 1964. 27.50 (ISBN 0-8108-0065-9). Scarecrow.

--Index to Biographies of Contemporary Composers, Vol. 2. LC 64-11781. 567p. 1974. 30.00 (ISBN 0-8108-0734-3). Scarecrow.

Bull, T. R. Color Atlas of Ear, Nose, & Throat Diagnosis. (Year Book Color Atlas Ser.). (Illus.). 240p. 1974. 42.95 (ISBN 0-8151-1316-1). Year Bk Med.

Bull, T. R. & Cook, Joyce L. Speech Theraphy & ENT Surgery. (Blackwell Scientific Pubns.). (Illus.). 1976. 13.95 (ISBN 0-632-09410-9, B0883X). Mosby.

Bull, T. R. & Ransome, Joselen. Recent Advances in Otolaryngology, No. 5. (Illus.). 1978. text ed. 32.50 (ISBN 0-443-01794-8). Churchill.

Bull, Tony & Myers, Eugene N. Plastic Reconstruction in the Head & Neck: BIMR Otolaryngology, Vol. 2. (Illus.). 320p. 1985. text ed. 39.95 (ISBN 0-407-02328-3). Butterworth.

Bull, Vivian, et al. A Vous de Choisir: Traditional & Self-Paced Learning in French. rev. ed. (Illus.). 384p. (Fr.). 1985. lib. bdg. 27.50 (ISBN 0-8191-4730-3); pap. text ed. 15.50 (ISBN 0-8191-4731-1). U Pr of Amer.

Bull, Webster, et al. Marco the Magi's Production of Le Grand David & His Own Spectacular Magic Company: (A Stage Magic Extravaganza) LC 81-51987. 112p. (Orig.). 1981. pap. 5.00 (ISBN 0-940376-00-8). White Horse.

Bull, William E. Spanish for Teachers: Applied Linguistics. LC 84-12529. 314p. 1984. Repr. of 1965 ed. lib. bdg. 22.95 (ISBN 0-89874-776-7). Krieger.

Bull, William E., et al. Spanish for Communication, Level 1. 1972. Pt. A. text ed. 17.28 (ISBN 0-395-12449-2); Pt. B. text ed. 17.28 (ISBN 0-395-12450-6); Combined Ed. text ed. 21.20 (ISBN 0-395-19942-5); write for info. Additional Ancellaries available. (ISBN 0-395-19944-1). HM.

Bulla & Cheng. Pathobiology of Invertebrate Vectors of Disease, Vol. 266. 1975. 64.00x (ISBN 0-89072-020-7). NY Acad Sci.

Bulla, Clyde. Squanto: Friend of the Pilgrims. (gr. 2-3). 1971. pap. 1.95 (ISBN 0-590-02558-9, Schol Pap). Scholastic Inc.

Bulla, Clyde R. Almost a Hero. LC 81-2060. (Illus.). 48p. (gr. 6-10). 1981. 9.75 (ISBN 0-525-25470-6, 0947-280, Skinny Book). Dutton.

--The Beast of Lor. LC 77-6751. (Illus.). (gr. 3-7). 1977. 10.53i (ISBN 0-690-01377-9). Crowell Jr Bks.

--The Cardboard Crown. LC 83-45049. (Illus.). 96p. (gr. 2-5). 1984. 10.53i (ISBN 0-690-04360-0); PLB 11.89g (ISBN 0-690-04361-9). Crowell Jr Bks.

--Charlie's House. LC 82-45576. (Illus.). 128p. (gr. 2-5). 1983. 10.10i (ISBN 0-690-04259-0); PLB 10.89g (ISBN 0-690-04260-4). Crowell Jr Bks.

--Dandelion Hill. LC 81-15164. (Illus.). 32p. (ps-1). 1982. 9.75 (ISBN 0-525-45101-3, 0947-280). Dutton.

--Daniel's Duck. LC 77-25647. (I Can Read Bk.). (Illus.). 64p. (gr. k-3). 1979. 8.61i (ISBN 0-06-020908-9); PLB 9.89 (ISBN 0-06-020909-7). HarpJ.

--Daniel's Duck. LC 78-22156. (A Trophy I Can Read Bk.). (Illus.). 64p. (gr. k-3). 1982. pap. 2.84i (ISBN 0-06-444031-1, Trophy). HarpJ.

--Dexter. LC 73-5595. (Illus.). (gr. 3-6). 1973. 10.89 (ISBN 0-690-00121-5). Crowell Jr Bks.

--Down the Mississippi. LC 54-5614. (Illus.). (gr. 2-5). 1954. Crowell Jr Bks.

--Ghost of Windy Hill. LC 68-11059. (gr. 3-7). 1968. PLB 11.89 (ISBN 0-690-32764-1). Crowell Jr Bks.

--Ghost Town Treasure. LC 58-5046. (Illus.). (gr. 2-5). 1958. Crowell Jr Bks.

--Grain of Wheat: A Writer Begins. LC 84-48750. 64p. (gr. 3-7). 1985. 10.00 (ISBN 0-87923-568-3). Godine.

--Indian Hill. LC 63-15085. (Illus.). (gr. 2-5). 1963. Crowell Jr Bks.

--Keep Running, Allen! LC 77-23311. (Illus.). (gr. k-2). 1978 (ISBN 0-690-01374-4). PLB 10.89 (ISBN 0-690-01375-2). Crowell Jr Bks.

--Last Look. LC 78-22507. (Illus.). (gr. 3-5). 1979. 11.06i (ISBN 0-690-03965-4); lib. bdg. 10.89 (ISBN 0-690-03966-2). Crowell Jr Bks.

--Lincoln's Birthday. LC 65-27291. (Holiday Ser.). (Illus.). (gr. 1-3). 1966. PLB 10.89 (ISBN 0-690-49450-5). Crowell Jr Bks.

--A Lion to Guard Us. LC 80-2455. (Illus.). 128p. (gr. 2-5). 1981. 11.49i (ISBN 0-690-04096-2); PLB 11.89 (ISBN 0-690-04097-0). Crowell Jr Bks.

--A Lion to Guard Us. (Illus.). 128p. (gr. 3-6). Date not set. pap. 2.25 (ISBN 0-590-33788-2). Scholastic Inc.

--Marco Moonlight. LC 75-33203. (Illus.). (gr. 3-7). 1976. 10.53i (ISBN 0-690-01011-7). Crowell Jr Bks.

--Marco Moonlight. (Illus.). 112p. (gr. 3-7). pap. 1.25 (ISBN 0-440-45848-X, YB). Dell.

--My Friend the Monster. LC 79-7826. (Illus.). 96p. (gr. 2-5). 1980. 11.49i (ISBN 0-690-04031-8); PLB 11.89 (ISBN 0-690-04032-6). Crowell Jr Bks.

--Open the Door & See All the People. LC 73-184980. (Illus.). (gr. 2-5). 1972. PLB 10.89i (ISBN 0-690-60046-1). Crowell Jr Bks.

--Pirate's Promise. LC 58-8209. (Illus.). (gr. 2-5). 1958. Crowell Jr Bks.

--Poor Boy, Rich Boy. LC 79-2685. (I Can Read Bk.: Charlotte Zolotow Bk.). (Illus.). 64p. (gr. k-3). 1982. 8.64i (ISBN 0-06-020896-1); PLB 9.89g (ISBN 0-06-020897-X). HarpJ.

--The Poppy Seeds. LC 55-5835. (Illus.). (gr. k-3). 1955. 11.49i (ISBN 0-690-64856-1). Crowell Jr Bks.

--Saint Valentine's Day. LC 65-11643. (Holiday Ser.). (Illus.). (gr. 1-3). 1965. PLB 10.89 (ISBN 0-690-71744-X). Crowell Jr Bks.

--Shoeshine Girl. LC 75-8516. (Illus.). 80p. (gr. 3 up). 1975. 11.06i (ISBN 0-690-00758-2). Crowell Jr Bks.

--Shoeshine Girl. (gr. 3-5). pap. 1.50 (ISBN 0-590-11897-8). Scholastic Inc.

--Song of Saint Francis. LC 52-6739. (Illus.). (gr. 2-5). 1952. 10.95i (ISBN 0-690-75222-9). Crowell Jr Bks.

--Squanto, Friend of the Pilgrims. LC 54-9145. (Illus.). (gr. 2-5). 1954. 11.49i (ISBN 0-690-76642-4). Crowell Jr Bks.

--The Stubborn Old Woman. LC 78-22506. (Illus.). 48p. (gr. 1-4). 1980. 9.57i (ISBN 0-690-03945-X); PLB 9.89 (ISBN 0-690-03946-8). Crowell Jr Bks.

--Surprise for a Cowboy. LC 50-8508. (Illus.). (gr. 2-5). 1950. 11.49i (ISBN 0-690-79837-7). Crowell Jr Bks.

--Sword in the Tree. LC 56-5699. (Illus.). (gr. 2-5). 1956. 11.49i (ISBN 0-690-79908-X). Crowell Jr Bks.

--A Tree Is a Plant. LC 60-11540. (Crocodile Paperbacks Ser.). (Illus.). (gr. k-3). 1973. pap. 2.95i (ISBN 0-690-00201-7). Crowell Jr Bks.

--Tree Is a Plant. LC 60-11540. (A Let's-Read-&-Find-Out Science Bk). (Illus.). (gr. k-3). 1960. PLB 10.89 (ISBN 0-690-83529-9). Crowell Jr Bks.

--Washington's Birthday. LC 66-10504. (Holiday Ser.). (Illus.). (gr. 1-3). 1967. PLB 10.89 (ISBN 0-690-86796-4). Crowell Jr Bks.

--What Makes a Shadow. LC 62-11001. (A Let's-Read-&-Find-Out Science Bks.). (Illus.). (gr. k-3). 1962. PLB 11.89 (ISBN 0-690-87648-3). Crowell Jr Bks.

--The Wish at the Top. LC 74-5028. (Illus.). 32p. (gr. 1-5). 1974. PLB 10.89 (ISBN 0-690-00527-X). Crowell Jr Bks.

Bulla, Clyde R. & Syson, Michael. Conquista! LC 77-26585. (Illus.). (gr. 2-5). 1978. 11.06i (ISBN 0-690-03870-4); PLB 9.89i (ISBN 0-690-03871-2). Crowell Jr Bks.

Bulla, Clyde R., tr. see Bolliger, Max.

Bulla, L. & Cheng, T., eds. Comparative Pathobiology: Treatise. Incl. Vol. 1. Biology of the Microsporidia. 387p. 1976. 55.00x (ISBN 0-306-38121-4); Vol. 2. Systematics of the Microsporidia. 521p. 1977. 59.50x (ISBN 0-306-38122-2); Vol. 3. Invertebrate Immune Responses. 206p. 1977. 32.50x (ISBN 0-306-38123-0); Vol. 4. Invertebrate Models for Biomedical Research. 179p. 1978. 29.50x (ISBN 0-306-40055-3). LC 76-46633 (Plenum Pr). Plenum Pub.

Bulla, Monika, ed. Renal Insufficiency in Children, Cologne, Germany, 1981: Proceedings. (Illus.). 280p. 1982. pap. 38.40 (ISBN 0-387-10902-1). Springer-Verlag.

Bullard, Arthur. Comrade Yetta. LC 68-57516. (Muckrakers Ser.). Repr. of 1913 ed. lib. bdg. 14.00x (ISBN 0-8398-0178-5). Irvington.

Bullard, C. & Wameldorff, P., eds. Trends in Electric Utility Research: Proceedings of the Electric Utility Research Conference, Chicago, April 1984. 500p. 1984. pap. 75.00 (ISBN 0-08-030982-8); pap. 55.00 (ISBN 0-08-030983-6). Pergamon.

Bullard, David G. & Knight, Susan E. Sexuality & Physical Disability: Personal Perspectives. LC 81-11008. 318p. 1981. pap. text ed. 19.95 (ISBN 0-8016-0861-9). Mosby.

Bullard, Dexter M., ed. see Fromm-Reichmann, Frieda.

Bullard, E. John. Mary Cassatt Oils & Pastels. (Illus.). 1976. pap. 12.95 (ISBN 0-8230-0570-4). Watson-Guptill.

Bullard, E. John, jt. auth. see Laughlin, Clarence J.

Bullard, Ernie & Knuth, Larry. Triple Jump Encyclopedia. LC 77-4265. 1977. pap. 9.95 (ISBN 0-87095-057-6). Athletic.

Bullard, F. M. The Geology of Grayson County, Texas. (Illus.). 72p. 1931. 0.50 (ISBN 0-686-29350-9, BULL 3125). Bur Econ Geology.

Bullard, Fred M. Volcanoes of the Earth. rev. ed. LC 76-2560. (Illus.). 613p. 1976. pap. 19.95 (ISBN 0-292-78705-7). U of Tex Pr.

--Volcanoes of the Earth. 2nd rev. ed. (Illus.). 655p. 1984. 35.00 (ISBN 0-292-78706-5). U of Tex Pr.

Bullard, Frederick L. Famous War Correspondents. (American Newspapermen 1790-1933 Ser.). (Illus.). xii, 437p. 1974. Repr. of 1914 ed. 20.00x (ISBN 0-8464-0029-4). Beekman Pubs.

Bullard, Gary, jt. auth. see Christie, Linda G.

Bullard, Gary J., jt. auth. see Christie, Linda G.

Bullard, Helen. My People in Wood. (Illus.). 88p. 1984. pap. 9.95 (ISBN 0-87588-208-0). Hobby Hse.

Bullard, Jean, ed. see Trimble, Stephen A., et al.

Bullard, John R. & Mether, Calvin E. Audiovisual Fundamentals. 3rd ed. 205p. 1984. pap. write for info (ISBN 0-697-06071-3); write for info instr's. manual (ISBN 0-697-06066-7). Wm C Brown.

Bullard, Laura J. Now-a-Days. 309p. 1980. pap. 4.95 (ISBN 0-89101-042-4). U Maine Orono.

Bullard, Melissa M. Filippo Strozzi & the Medici: Favour & Finance in Sixteenth-Century Florence & Rome. LC 79-51822. (Cambridge Studies in Early Modern History). 216p. 1980. 37.50 (ISBN 0-521-22301-6). Cambridge U Pr.

Bullard, Monte. China's Political-Military Evolution: The Party & the Military in the PRC, 1960-1984. (A Westview Special Study on China & East Asia). 200p. 1985. pap. 18.75x (ISBN 0-8133-7041-8). Westview.

Bullard, Oral. Crisis on the Columbia. LC 68-57012. (Illus.). 160p. 1968. 4.95 (ISBN 0-911518-00-2). Touchstone Pr Ore.

--Konapee's Eden Historic & Scenic Handbook: The Columbia River Gorge. Worcester, Thomas K., ed. (Illus.). 96p. (Orig.). 1985. pap. 6.95 (ISBN 0-911518-69-X). Touchstone Pr Or.

--Lancaster's Road: The Historic Columbia River Scenic Highway. Worcester, Thomas K., ed. (Illus.). 80p. (Orig.). 1982. pap. 6.95 (ISBN 0-911518-64-9). Touchstone Pr Or.

Bullard, Oral, ed. Flight of the Dove: The Story of Jeannette Rankin. (Illus.). 256p. (Orig.). 1980. 13.95 (ISBN 0-918688-02-7); pap. 8.95 (ISBN 0-918688-03-5). Touchstone Pr OR.

Bullard, Oral, ed. see Lowe, Don & Lowe, Roberta.

Bullard, Peter D. Preventing Employee Theft. 90p. (Orig.). 1983. pap. 75.00 (ISBN 0-9604710-1-4). Psychomet Res.

Bullard, Peter D., ed. Coping with Stress: A Psychological Survival Manual. (Illus.). 220p. (Orig.). 1980. pap. 7.95 (ISBN 0-9604710-0-6). Psychomet-Res.

Bullard, R. K. & Dixon-Gough, R. W. Britain from Space: An Atlas of Landsat Images. 120p. 1984. 23.00 (ISBN 0-85066-277-X, Pub. by Falmer Pr). Taylor & Francis.

Bullard, Rayford. Glimpses into Revelation. 5.95 (ISBN 0-911866-74-4). Advocate.

Bullard, Robert L. Personalities & Reminiscences of the War. 16.00 (ISBN 0-8369-6967-7, 7848). Ayer Co Pubs.

Bullard, Roger A., ed. The Hypostasis of the Archons: The Coptic Text with Translation & Commentary. (Patristische Texte und Studien Ser.: Vol. 10). (Coptic & Eng). 1970. 20.80x (ISBN 3-11-006356-5). De Gruyter.

Bullard, Roger W., ed. Flavor Chemistry of Animal Foods. LC 77-27295. (ACS Symposium Ser.: No. 67). 1978. 19.95 (ISBN 0-8412-0404-7). Am Chemical.

Bullard, Scott R. & Collins, Michael. Who's Who in Sherlock Holmes. LC 79-66638. 1980. 14.95 (ISBN 0-8008-8281-4); pap. 7.95 (ISBN 0-8008-8282-2). Taplinger.

Bullard, Scott R., ed. Library Acquisitions Special Reports. 115p. 1981. pap. 28.00 (ISBN 0-08-026112-4). Pergamon.

Bullard, Thomas R. Street, Interurban & Rapid Transit Railways of the United States: A Selective Historical Bibliography. (Illus.). 96p. (Orig.). 1984. pap. 10.00 (ISBN 0-911940-38-3). Cox.

Bullard, William R., Jr., ed. Monographs & Papers in Maya Archaeology. LC 72-105721. (Peabody Museum Papers: Vol. 61). 1970. pap. 20.00x (ISBN 0-87365-175-8). Peabody Harvard.

Bullard-Johnson, Mary, jt. auth. see Johnson, Ben.

Bullaro & Edginton. Commercial Leisure Services. 600p. 1986. text ed. price not set (ISBN 0-02-316600-2). Macmillan.

Bullas, K. & Whitfield, F. J. Dictionary English-Polish, Polish-English, 2 vols. (Eng. & Pol.). 1969. Set. 38.50x (ISBN 0-685-05192-7). Adlers Foreign Bks.

Bullaty, Sonja. Sudek. (Illus.). 1978. 25.00 (ISBN 0-517-53294-8, C N Potter Bks). Crown.

Bullaty, Sonja & Lomeo, Angelo, illus. The Baby Bears. (Golden Look-Look Bks.). (Illus.). 24p. (ps-3). 1983. pap. 1.50 (ISBN 0-307-11884-3, 11892, Golden Bks). Western Pub.

Bullaty, Sonja & Lomeo, Angelo, photos by. Circle of Seasons: Central Park Celebrated. LC 84-71238. (Illus.). 112p. 1984. ltd. ed. 850.00 (ISBN 0-943276-11-X); 40.00 (ISBN 0-943276-07-1). Amaryllis Pr.

Bullchild, Percy. The Sun Came Down: The History of the World as My Blackfeet Elders Told It. LC 85-42771. 384p. 1985. 22.95 (ISBN 0-06-250107-0, HarpR). Har-Row.

Bulle, Florence. God Wants You Rich: And Other Enticing Doctrines. 223p. (Orig.). 1983. pap. 5.95 (ISBN 0-87123-264-2). Bethany Hse.

--Lord of the Valleys: Overcoming Suffering by Faith. LC 72-85630. 240p. 1972. pap. 4.95 (ISBN 0-912106-01-8, Pub. by Logos). Bridge Pub.

Bullein, William. Bulleins Bulwarke of Defence Againste All Sickness, Sorness & Woundes. LC 73-37139. (English Experience Ser.: No. 350). (Illus.). 488p. 1971. Repr. of 1562 ed. 83.00 (ISBN 90-221-0350-1). Walter J Johnson.

Bullen, A. H. Some Longer Elizabethan Poems. LC 64-16751. (Arber's an English Garner Ser.). 1964. Repr. of 1890 ed. 23.50 (ISBN 0-8154-0040-3). Cooper Sq.

--Some Shorter Elizabethan Poems. LC 64-16746. (Arber's an English Garner Ser.). 1964. Repr. of 1890 ed. 23.50 (ISBN 0-8154-0041-1). Cooper Sq.

--Thomas Campion. LC 72-6433. 1972. Repr. of 1903 ed. lib. bdg. 20.00 (ISBN 0-8414-0150-0). Folcroft.

Bullen, A. H. & Nimmo, J. C. Lyrics from the Song-Books of the Elizabethan Age. 59.95 (ISBN 0-8490-0568-X). Gordon Pr.
Bullen, A. H., ed. Lyrics from the Song-Books of the Elizabethan Age. 2143p. 1982. Repr. of 1897 ed. lib. bdg. 40.00 (ISBN 0-8495-0631-X). Arden Lib.
--The Works of Christopher Marlowe, 3 vols. 1979. Repr. of 1885 ed. Set. lib. bdg. 300.00 (ISBN 0-8492-3731-9). R West.
Bullen, A H., ed. The Works of Christopher Marlowe, 3 vols. 1063p. Repr. of 1835 ed. Set. lib. bdg. 400.00 (ISBN 0-8414-2824-7). Folcroft.
Bullen, A. H., ed. The Works of John Marston, 3 vols. 1979. Repr. of 1887 ed. Set. lib. bdg. 400.00 (ISBN 0-8495-0502-X). Arden Lib.
Bullen, A. H., ed. see Beaumont, Francis.
Bullen, A. H., ed. see Bullen, Mark W.
Bullen, A. H., ed. see Campion, Thomas.
Bullen, A. H., ed. see Davenport, Robert.
Bullen, A. H., ed. see Davidson, Francis.
Bullen, A. H., ed. see Day, John.
Bullen, A. H., ed. see Marston, John.
Bullen, A. H., ed. see Middleton, Thomas.
Bullen, A. H., ed. see Nabbes, Thomas.
Bullen, Adelaide. Jim Tall & Count Small. LC 74-29741. (Illus.). 48p. 1975. 3.95 (ISBN 0-935678-02-6); pap. 1.95 (ISBN 0-935678-03-4). Kendall Bks.
Bullen, Adelaide K. New Answers to the Fatigue Problem. LC 56-12857. (Illus.). 191p. 1980. pap. 4.95 (ISBN 0-935678-10-7). Kendall Bks.
Bullen, Anne. Showing Ponies. (Illus.). 48p. pap. write for info. (ISBN 0-85131-106-7, NL51, Dist. by Miller). J A Allen.
Bullen, Arthur, ed. Lyrics from the Dramatists of the Elizabethan Age. racs. ed. LC 72-38342. (Select Bibliographies Reprint Ser.). Repr. of 1891 ed. 20.00 (ISBN 0-8369-6759-3). Ayer Co Pubs.
Bullen, Arthur H. Elizabethans. LC 78-58255. (Essay Index in Reprint Ser.). 1978. Repr. 21.50x (ISBN 0-8486-3017-3). Core Collection.
--Speculum Amantis: Love Poems. 1902. 25.00 (ISBN 0-89984-035-3). Century Bookbindery.
Bullen, Arthur H., ed. Collection of Old English Plays, 7 vols. in 4. LC 64-14699. Repr. of 1882 ed. Set. 765.00 (ISBN 0-405-08325-4, Blom Pubns); 40.00 ea.; Vol. 1. 40.00 (ISBN 0-405-08326-2); Vol. 2. 44.00 (ISBN 0-405-08327-0); Vol. 3. 44.00 (ISBN 0-405-08328-9). Vol. 4 (ISBN 0-405-08329-7). Ayer Co Pubs.
--Collections of Lyrics & Poems: Sixteenth & Seventeenth Centuries, 6 vols. Incl. Lyrics from the Song-Books of the Elizabethan Age. Repr. of 1887 ed (ISBN 0-404-01221-3); More Lyrics from the Song-Books of the Elizabethan Age. Repr. of 1888 ed (ISBN 0-404-01222-1); Lyrics from the Dramatists of the Elizabethan Age. Repr. of 1889 ed (ISBN 0-404-01223-X); Musa Proterva: Love Poems of the Restoration. Repr. of 1889 ed (ISBN 0-404-01224-8); Speculum Amantis: Love Poems from Rare Song-Books & Miscellanies of the Seventeenth Century. Repr. of 1902 ed (ISBN 0-404-01225-6); Poems, Chiefly Lyrical, from Romances & Prose-Tracts of the Elizabethan Age: With Chosen Poems of Nicholas Breton. Repr. of 1890 ed (ISBN 0-404-01226-4). LC 70-164695. 27.50 ea.; Set. 165.00 (ISBN 0-404-01220-5). AMS Pr.
--England's Helicon: A Collection of Lyrical & Pastoral Poems, Published in 1600. facsimile ed. LC 75-119956. (Select Bibliographies Reprint Ser). Repr. of 1899 ed. 21.00 (ISBN 0-8369-5399-1). Ayer Co Pubs.
Bullen, F. T. The Distribution of the Damage Potential of the Desert Locust (Schistocerca Gregaria Forskal) 1969. 35.00x (ISBN 0-85135-045-3, Pub. by Centre Overseas Research). State Mutual Bk.
Bullen, Frank T. Creatures of the Sea: Sea Birds, Beasts, & Fishes. 1977. lib. bdg. 69.95 (ISBN 0-8490-1682-7). Gordon Pr.
--The Cruise of the Cachalot. (Illus.). 1980. pap. 4.95 (ISBN 0-918172-06-3). Leetes Isl.
--The Cruise of the Cachalot. Repr. of 1899 ed. 22.50 (ISBN 0-686-19866-2). Ridgeway Bks.
--Deep-Sea Plunderings. facsimile ed. LC 75-106251. (Short Story Index Reprint Ser). 1901. 21.50 (ISBN 0-8369-3288-9). Ayer Co Pubs.
--Idylls of the Sea. facsimile ed. LC 71-98564. (Short Story Index Reprint Ser). 1899. 18.00 (ISBN 0-8369-3138-6). Ayer Co Pubs.
--The Men of the Merchant Service. (Seafaring Men: Their Ship & Times Ser.). 1980. Repr. of 1900 ed. text ed. 29.50 (ISBN 0-930576-26-8). E M Coleman Ent.
Bullen, G. J. & Greenslade, D. J., eds. Problems in Molecular Structure. (Illus.). 466p. 1983. 32.00 (ISBN 0-85086-083-0, NO. 8007, Pub. by Pion). Methuen Inc.
Bullen, J. B., ed. see Fry, Roger.
Bullen, John S. Time & Space in the Novels of Samuel Richardson. 53p. (Orig.). 1965. pap. 3.50 (ISBN 0-87421-024-0). Utah St U Pr.
Bullen, K. E. The Earth's Density. 1975. 49.95 (ISBN 0-412-10860-7, NO.6045, Pub. by Chapman & Hall). Methuen Inc.
--Introduction to the Theory of Mechanics. 8th ed. 1971. 39.50 (ISBN 0-521-08291-9). Cambridge U Pr.
--An Introduction to the Theory of Seismology. 3rd ed. LC 79-7707. (Illus.). 1979. 52.50 (ISBN 0-521-04367-0); pap. 17.95x (ISBN 0-521-29686-2). Cambridge U Pr.
Bullen, K. E. & Bolt, B. A. An Introduction to the Theory of Seismology. 4th ed. (Illus.). 470p. Date not set. price not set (ISBN 0-521-23980-X); pap. price not set (ISBN 0-521-28389-2). Cambridge U Pr.
Bullen, Keith & Cromer, John, eds. Salamander. facsimile ed. LC 79-103084. (Granger Index Reprint Ser). 1947. 17.00 (ISBN 0-8369-6099-8). Ayer Co Pubs.
Bullen, Mark W. Bullein's Dialogue Against the Fever Pestilence. Bullen, A. H., ed. (EETS, ES Ser.: No. 52). Repr. of 1888 ed. 37.00 (ISBN 0-527-00258-5). Kraus Repr.
Bullen, Mary S. L., ed. see Legare, H. S.
Bullen, R. Excavations in Northeastern Massachusetts, Vol. 1, No. 3. LC 49-48491. 1949. 7.00 (ISBN 0-939312-02-6). Peabody Found.
Bullen, R. J., et al, eds. Ideas into Politics: Aspects of European History 1880-1950. LC 84-2854. 234p. 1984. 27.50x (ISBN 0-389-20484-6, 08046). B&N Imports.
Bullen, Ripley P. A Guide to the Identification of Florida Projectile Points. Rev. ed. LC 75-2972. (Illus.). 64p. 1975. pap. 3.00 (ISBN 0-935678-01-8). Kendall Bks.
--The Terra Ceia Site, Manatee County, Florida. pap. 7.00 (ISBN 0-384-06299-7). Johnson Repr.
Bullen, Ripley P., jt. ed. see Griffin, John W.
Bullen, Roger. The Foreign Office: Seventeen Eighty-Two to Nineteen Eighty-Two. 144p. 1984. 20.00x (ISBN 0-89093-492-4). U Pubns Amer.
--Palmerston, Guizot & the Collapse of the Entente Coriale. 352p. 1974. 54.50 (ISBN 0-485-13136-6, Pub. by Athlone Pr Ltd). Longwood Pub Group.
Bullen, Roger & Bridge, Roy. The Great Powers & the European States System: 1815-1914. LC 79-41567. (Illus.). 208p. (Orig.). 1980. text ed. 23.00x (ISBN 0-582-49134-7); pap. text ed. 11.95x (ISBN 0-582-49135-5). Longman.
Buller, A. J. & Buller, N. P. The Contractile Behavior of Mammalian Skeletal Muscle. rev. ed. Head, J. J., ed. LC 78-52597. (Carolina Biology Readers Ser.). (Illus.). 16p. (gr. 10 up). 1980. pap. 1.60 (ISBN 0-89278-236-6, 45-9636). Carolina Biological.
Buller, Jon. Buller's Professional Course in Bartending for Home Study. LC 82-23309. (Illus.). 160p. 1983. 11.95 (ISBN 0-916782-34-4); pap. 7.95 comb. binding (ISBN 0-916782-33-6). Harvard Common Pr.
--Fanny & May. LC 83-15361. 48p. (ps-2). 1984. lib. bdg. 9.95 (ISBN 0-517-55214-0). Crown.
Buller, N. P., jt. auth. see Buller, A. J.
Buller, Walter L. Buller's Birds of New Zealand: A History of the Birds of New Zealand. Turbott, E. G., ed. LC 67-20253. 1967. 35.00 (ISBN 0-8248-0064-8, Eastwest Ctr). UH Pr.
Bullert, Gary. The Politics of John Dewey. LC 83-62872. 275p. 1983. 24.95 (ISBN 0-87975-208-4). Prometheus Bks.
Bulletin of the Atomic Scientists, ed. The Final Epidemic: Physicians & Scientists on Nuclear War. 252p. 1982. pap. 4.95 (ISBN 0-941682-00-5, 03874-2). U of Chicago Pr.
Bulletin of the Palestine Economic Society, Tel Aviv, Aug. 1921 - Feb. 1934. Palestine Economic Society Bulletin, 6 vols. in 5. Repr. Set. 125.00 (ISBN 0-404-56240-X); 25.00 ea. AMS Pr.
Bullett, Gerald. The English Galaxy of Shorter Poems. 1977. Repr. of 1934 ed. 25.00 (ISBN 0-89984-157-0). Century Bookbindery.
--The English Mystics (William Law, Blake, Wordsworth) LC 79-547. 1973. Repr. of 1950 ed. lib. bdg. 30.00 (ISBN 0-8414-9831-8). Folcroft.
--George Eliot: Her Life & Books. 1978. Repr. of 1947 ed. lib. bdg. 25.00 (ISBN 0-8492-3725-4). R West.
--The Innocence of G. K. Chesterton. 1973. Repr. of 1923 ed. 17.50 (ISBN 0-8274-1799-3). R West.
--The Jury. LC 75-44960. (Fifty Classics of Crime Fiction 1900-1950 Ser.). 1976. Repr. of 1935 ed. lib. bdg. 21.00 (ISBN 0-8240-2356-0). Garland Pub.
--Modern English Fiction. LC 72-194983. 1926. lib. bdg. 10.00 (ISBN 0-8414-2520-5). Folcroft.
--The Pattern of Courtesy: An Anthology. 1977. Repr. of 1934 ed. 20.00 (ISBN 0-89984-159-7). Century Bookbindery.
--Short Stories of Today & Yesterday. 1929. 10.00 (ISBN 0-686-18173-5). Havertown Bks.
--The Story of English Literature. LC 74-9776. 1935. 10.00 (ISBN 0-8414-3207-4). Folcroft.
Bullett, Gerald, ed. The English Galaxy of Shorter Poems. LC 72-3002. (Granger Index Reprint Ser.). Repr. of 1933 ed. 18.75 (ISBN 0-8369-8239-8). Ayer Co Pubs.
--Silver Poets of the Sixteenth Century. 1978. 12.95x (ISBN 0-460-00985-0, Evman); pap. 4.50x (ISBN 0-460-11985-0, Evman). Biblio Dist.
Bullett, Gerald, ed. see Keats, John.
Bullett, Gerald W. Baker's Cart, & Other Tales. facs. ed. LC 77-125208. (Short Story Index Reprint Ser.). 1926. 18.00 (ISBN 0-8369-3575-6). Ayer Co Pubs.
--George Eliot: Her Life & Books. LC 76-156178. 273p. 1972. Repr. of 1948 ed. lib. bdg. 19.75x (ISBN 0-8371-6121-5, BUGE). Greenwood.
--Street of the Eye, & Nine Other Tales. facsimile ed. LC 77-167444. (Short Story Index Reprint Ser). Repr. of 1923 ed. 18.00 (ISBN 0-8369-3970-0). Ayer Co Pubs.
--Sydney Smith: A Biography & a Selection. LC 77-138578. (Illus.). 1971. Repr. of 1951 ed. lib. bdg. 16.25x (ISBN 0-8371-5777-3, BUSS). Greenwood.
Bullett, Gerald W., tr. see Fan, Ch'Eng-ta.
Bullied, George J. People of the Valley. 1976. 4.95 (ISBN 0-686-27654-X). Cole-Outreach.
--Twin Valleys Educational Community. 1976. 2.00 (ISBN 0-686-27658-2). Cole-Outreach.
Bullied, H. A. The Aspinall Era. 25.00x (ISBN 0-392-07597-0, SpS). Sportshelf.
Bullier, C. J. Apples & Madonnas. Repr. of 1927 ed. 25.00 (ISBN 0-8482-0137-X). Norwood Edns.
Bulliet, C. J. The Courtezan Olympia: An Intimate Survey of Artists & Their Mistress Models. 59.95 (ISBN 0-87968-955-2). Gordon Pr.
Bulliet, Richard. The Gulf Scenario. 256p. 1984. 12.95 (ISBN 0-312-35323-5, J Kahn). St Martin.
Bulliet, Richard W. The Camel & the Wheel. LC 75-571. 352p. 1975. text ed. 22.50x (ISBN 0-674-09130-2). Harvard U Pr.
--Conversion to Islam in the Medieval Period: An Essay in Quantitative History. (Illus.). 158p. 1979. text ed. 16.50x (ISBN 0-674-17035-0). Harvard U Pr.
--The Patricians of Nishapur: A Study in Medieval Islamic Social History. LC 70-173413. (Middle Eastern Studies: No. 16). (Illus.). 280p. 1972. 20.00x (ISBN 0-674-65792-6). Harvard U Pr.
Bullinger, E. W. Critical Lexicon & Concordance to the English & Greek New Testament. 1040p. 1975. text ed. 24.95 (ISBN 0-310-20310-4, Pub. by Bagster). Zondervan.
--Figures of Speech Used in the Bible. 24.95 (ISBN 0-8010-0559-0). Baker Bk.
--How to Enjoy the Bible. 436p. 1983. 9.95 (ISBN 0-910068-48-8). Am Christian.
Bullinger, Ethelbert W. Commentary on Revelation. LC 83-24917. 768p. 1984. 19.95 (ISBN 0-8254-2239-6). Kregel.
--Great Cloud of Witnesses in Hebrews Eleven. LC 79-14425. 1979. 11.95 (ISBN 0-8254-2233-7). Kregel.
--Number in Scripture. LC 67-26498. 1980. 11.95 (ISBN 0-8254-2204-3); pap. 7.95 (ISBN 0-8254-2238-8). Kregel.
--Witness of the Stars. LC 68-16762. 1972. 12.95 (ISBN 0-8254-2209-4). Kregel.
--Witness of the Stars. LC 68-16762. 212p. 1984. pap. 9.95 (ISBN 0-8254-2245-0). Kregel.
--Word Studies on the Holy Spirit. LC 85-7631. 232p. 1985. pap. 7.95 (ISBN 0-8254-2246-9). Kregel.
Bullinger, Heinrich. The Christian State of Matrimonye. Coverdale, Myles, tr. LC 74-80167. (English Experience Ser.: No. 646). 168p. 1974. Repr. of 1541 ed. 11.50 (ISBN 90-221-0646-2). Walter J Johnson.
--An Holsom Antidotus or Counter-Poysen Agaynst the Pestylent Heresye & Secte of the Anabaptistes. Veron, J., tr. LC 73-6106. (English Experience Ser.: No. 574). 232p. 1973. Repr. of 1548 ed. 13.00 (ISBN 90-221-0574-1). Walter J Johnson.
Bullinger, Henry. The Decades of Henry Bullinger, Minister of the Church of Zurich, 4 vols. 1849-1851. Set. 144.00 (ISBN 0-384-06315-2). Johnson Repr.
Bullion, John L. A Great & Necessary Measure: George Grenville & the Genesis of the Stamp Act 1763-1765. 360p. 1983. 24.00 (ISBN 0-8262-0375-2). U of MO Pr.
Bullions, Peter. The Principles of English Grammar. LC 82-10418. (American Linguistics Ser.). 1983. 45.00x (ISBN 0-8201-1386-7). Schol Facsimiles.
Bullis, Jerald. Orion. LC 76-40995. (Orig.). 1976. signed numbered ltd. ed. 5.00 (ISBN 0-917492-02-1); pap. 3.00 (ISBN 0-917492-03-X). Jackpine Pr.
--Taking up the Serpent. LC 73-159696. 58p. 1973. 2.95 (ISBN 0-87886-025-8). Ithaca Hse.
Bullis, L. Harold & Mielke, James E. Strategic & Critical Materials. (Special Study Ser.). 245p. 1985. 46.50x (ISBN 0-86531-637-6). Westview.
Bullis, Mary A. Mary, Come Home! LC 82-71445. (Orig.). 1982. pap. 4.95 (ISBN 0-8054-6330-5). Broadman.
Bullit, William C. The Bullitt Mission to Russia: Testimony Before the Committee on Foreign Relations, U. S. Senate. LC 75-39048. (Russia Studies: Perspectives on the Revolution Ser.). 151p. 1977. Repr. of 1919 ed. 18.15 (ISBN 0-88355-427-5). Hyperion-Conn.
Bullitt, Alexander C. Rambles in the Mammoth Cave During the Year 1844 by a Visiter. LC 85-6698. (Illus.). 134p. 1985. pap. 5.00 (ISBN 0-939748-16-9). Cave Bks MO.
Bullitt, Stimson. To Be a Politician. rev. ed. LC 75-43310. 1977. 27.00x (ISBN 0-300-02009-0). Yale U Pr.
Bullivant, Brian. The Pluralist Dilemma in Education: Six Case Studies. 267p. 1983. pap. text ed. 17.50x (ISBN 0-86861-266-9). Allen Unwin.
Bullivant, K., jt. auth. see Hinton-Thomas, R.
Bullmer, Kenneth. The Art of Empathy: A Manual for Improving Accuracy of Interpersonal Perception. LC 74-11280. 140p. 1975. pap. 14.95 (ISBN 0-87705-228-X). Human Sci Pr.
Bulloch, Anthony W., ed. The Fifth Hymn: Callimachus. (Classical Texts & Commentaries Ser.: No. 26). (Illus.). 240p. 1985. 64.50 (ISBN 0-521-26495-2). Cambridge U Pr.
Bulloch, James. Pilate to Constantine. 244p. 1981. 35.00x (ISBN 0-7152-0460-2, Pub. by St Andrew Pr England). State Mutual Bk.
Bulloch, James, et al, eds. Accountant's Cost Handbook: A Guide for Management Accounting. 3rd ed. (Professional Management Accounting Ser.). 792p. 1983. 65.00 (ISBN 0-471-05352-X, Pub. by Ronald Pr). Wiley.
Bulloch, James D. The Secret Service of the Confederate States in Europe: Or How the Confederate Cruisers Were Equipped, 2 vols. 918p. 1972. Repr. of 1883 ed. Set. lib. bdg. 47.50 (ISBN 0-8337-4555-7). B Franklin.
Bulloch, John. The Persian Gulf Unveiled. 240p. 1985. 16.95 (ISBN 0-312-92646-4). Congdon & Weed.
--Studies on the Text of Shakespeare. LC 75-39557. Repr. of 1878 ed. 24.00 (ISBN 0-404-01227-2). AMS Pr.
Bulloch, Linda R. Pogma. LC 76-57104. 1977. pap. 2.25 (ISBN 0-89937-004-7). Ctr Res Soc Chg.
Bulloch, William. The History of Bacteriology. (Illus.). 15.25 (ISBN 0-8446-5740-9). Peter Smith.
Bullock. The Faces of Europe. 448p. 1980. 75.00x (ISBN 0-7148-2094-6, Pub. by Phaidon Pr). State Mutual Bk.
Bullock, ed. see Ginzburg.
Bullock, A. L., ed. see Oxford University, British Commonwealth Group.
Bullock, Alan. Ernest Bevin: Foreign Secretary, 1945-1951. (Illus.). 1984. 37.50 (ISBN 0-393-01825-3). Norton.
--Hitler, a Study in Tyranny. rev. ed. (Illus.). (YA) 1964. 16.95xi (ISBN 0-06-010580-1, HarpT). Har-Row.
--Hitler, a Study in Tyranny. abr. ed. 1971. pap. 4.76i (ISBN 0-06-080216-2, P216, PL). Har-Row.
--Hitler, a Study in Tyranny. rev. ed. (Illus.). pap. 11.95xi (ISBN 0-06-131123-5, TB 1123, Torch). Har-Row.
--The Humanist Tradition in The West. (Illus.). 1985. 24.95 (ISBN 0-393-02237-4). Norton.
Bullock, Alan & Stallybrass, Oliver, eds. The Harper Dictionary of Modern Thought. LC 74-15814. 1977. 25.96i (ISBN 0-06-010578-X, HarpT). Har-Row.
Bullock, Alan & Woodings, R. B., eds. Twentieth Century Culture: A Biographical Companion. LC 83-48331. 867p. 1984. 33.65i (ISBN 0-06-015248-6, HarpT). Har-Row.
Bullock, Alice. Living Legends. LC 72-90383. (Illus.). 1978. pap. 4.25 (ISBN 0-913270-06-7). Sunstone Pr.
--Monumental Ghosts. 48p. (Orig.). 1985. pap. price not set (ISBN 0-86534-029-3). Sunstone Pr.
--Mountain Villages. 2nd ed. LC 81-5687. (Illus.). 1981. pap. 5.95 (ISBN 0-913270-13-X). Sunstone Pr.
--The Squaw Tree: Ghost, Miracles & Mysteries of New Mexico. LC 77-86728. 1978. 12.00 (ISBN 0-89016-041-4); pap. 7.95 (ISBN 0-89016-040-6). Lightning Tree.
Bullock, Alice-May. Lace & Lacemaking. LC 81-81037. (Illus.). 168p. 1981. 19.95 (ISBN 0-88332-261-7, 8193). Larousse.
Bullock, Barbara, et al, eds. Pathophysiology: Adaptations & Alterations in Function. 1984. 35.95 (ISBN 0-316-11479-0) (ISBN 0-316-11481-2). Little.
Bullock, Broderick, tr. see Vivante, Leone.
Bullock, C. Hassell. Introduction to Old Testament Poetic Books. 1979. 11.95 (ISBN 0-8024-4143-2). Moody.
Bullock, C. Hassell, jt. ed. see Inch, Morris A.
Bullock, C. L., jt. auth. see Petrillo, H. V.
Bullock, Caroline C., jt. ed. see Whitney, Annie W.
Bullock, Charles. Mashona. LC 79-107469. Repr. of 1928 ed. cancelled (ISBN 0-8371-3748-9, BUM&, Pub. by Negro U Pr). Greenwood.
--Shakespeare's Debt to the Bible. LC 72-187918. 1870. lib. bdg. 10.00 (ISBN 0-8414-2521-3). Folcroft.
Bullock, Charles, jt. auth. see MacManus, Susan.
Bullock, Charles E., jt. ed. see Grambs, Peter H.
Bullock, Charles J. Economic Essays. facs. ed. LC 68-16915. (Essay Index Reprint Ser). 1936. 24.50 (ISBN 0-8369-0263-7). Ayer Co Pubs.
--Essays on the Monetary History of the United States. LC 69-18301. Repr. of 1900 ed. lib. bdg. 22.50x (ISBN 0-8371-0332-0, BUMH). Greenwood.
--The Finances of the United States from Seventeen Seventy-Five to Seventeen Eighty-Nine: With Special Reference to the Budget. LC 79-12742. (Perspectives in American History: No. 52). (Illus.). 1980. Repr. of 1895 ed. lib. bdg. 19.50x (ISBN 0-87991-821-7). Porcupine Pr.
Bullock, Charles S., jt. auth. see Rodgers, Harrell R.

Bullock, Charles S., III & Lamb, Charles M. Implementation of Civil Rights Policy. LC 83-2668. (Political Science Ser.). 250p. 1983. pap. text ed. 10.50 pub net (ISBN 0-534-01259-0). Brooks-Cole.

Bullock, Chris & Peck, David. Guide to Marxist Literary Criticism. LC 79-3627. 192p. 1980. 17.50x (ISBN 0-253-13144-8). Ind U Pr.

Bullock, Clarence C. Bullock: The Autobiography of an Artist. 1984. 6.95 (ISBN 0-533-06079-6). Vantage.

Bullock, David W., jt. ed. see Glasser, Stanley R.

Bullock, Donald H. Programmed Instruction. Langdon, Danny G., ed. LC 77-25108. (Instructional Design Library). (Illus.). 112p. 1978. 19.95 (ISBN 0-87778-118-4). Educ Tech Pubns.

Bullock, Donald H., jt. auth. see Lineberry, Claude S.

Bullock, Edna, jt. ed. see Bullock-Wilson, Barbara.

Bullock, G. R. & Petrusz, P., eds. Techniques in Immunocytochemistry, Vol. 1. 1982. 55.00 (ISBN 0-12-140401-3). Acad Pr.

--Techniques in Immunocytochemistry, Vol. 2. 1983. 45.00 (ISBN 0-12-140402-1). Acad Pr.

Bullock, G. William, Jr. & Conrad, Clifton F. Management: Perspectives from the Social Sciences. LC 80-6097. 343p. 1981. lib. bdg. 25.25 (ISBN 0-8191-1466-9); pap. text ed. 13.00 (ISBN 0-8191-1467-7). U Pr of Amer.

Bullock, Gillian R. & Petrusz, Peter. Techniques in Immunocytochemistry, Vol. 3. Date not set. 46.00 (ISBN 0-12-140403-X). Acad Pr.

Bullock, H. R. How to Cheat on Your Diet. 48p. (Orig.). 1983. pap. 1.75 (ISBN 0-8431-1032-5). Price Stern.

Bullock, Harry A; see Brandeis, Louis D.

Bullock, Hazel J. Grammaire Francaise: Methode Orale. 1949. 24.00x (ISBN 0-89197-493-8); pap. text ed. 12.50x (ISBN 0-89197-775-9). Irvington.

Bullock, Helen. Williamsburg Art of Cookery. LC 43-6700. (Illus.). 276p. (Orig.). 1938. leather 20.00 (ISBN 0-910412-31-6); hardcover 7.95 (ISBN 0-910412-30-8). Williamsburg.

Bullock, Henry A. History of Negro Education in the South: From 1619 to the Present. LC 67-20873. 1967. 22.50x (ISBN 0-674-39950-1). Harvard U Pr.

Bullock, Hugh. The Story of Investment Companies. LC 59-13778. (Illus.). 305p. 1959. 34.00x (ISBN 0-231-02378-2). Columbia U Pr.

Bullock, J. A., jt. ed. see Harper, D. M.

Bullock, J. Benbow. Art for Instant Printing. (Illus.). 100p. (Orig.). 1982. pap. 8.95 (ISBN 0-937024-03-1). Gourmet Guides.

--Stars for Lincoln, Doctors & Dogs. LC 80-66936. (Illus.). 100p. (Orig.). 1981. pap. 4.95 (ISBN 0-937024-00-7). Gourmet Guides.

Bullock, J. Floyd. The Clingan Clan: Family History 1600-1981 (Clingan Family & Descendants) 1981. pap. 15.00 (ISBN 0-916660-21-4). Hse of York.

Bullock, James B. Ambos Nogales. (Illus.). 100p. (Orig.). 1983. pap. 4.95 (ISBN 0-937024-04-X). Gourmet Guides.

Bullock, James B. & Bullock, Jean F. Artfood. (Illus.). 200p. (Orig.). pap. cancelled (ISBN 0-937024-05-8). Gourmet Guides.

Bullock, James H. Maintenance Planning & Control. 146p. pap. 15.95 (ISBN 0-86641-026-0, 79113). Natl Assn Accts.

Bullock, Jean F., jt. auth. see Bullock, James B.

Bullock, John, jt. auth. see Carotenuto, Rosine.

Bullock, John, jt. auth. see Owen, Robert.

Bullock, Lyndal M. & Blackburn, Gary M. A Modular Learning Approach to Accompany Educational Aspects of Behavioral Problems in Children & Youth. 144p. 1974. pap. 4.75x (ISBN 0-8422-0390-7). Irvington.

Bullock, Lyndal M., et al. Educational Aspects of Behavioral Problems in Children & Youth, Vol. 1. LC 74-1011. 437p. 1974. text ed. 38.50x (ISBN 0-8422-5159-6); pap. text ed. 16.95x (ISBN 0-8422-0388-5). Irvington.

--Educational Aspects of Behavioral Problems in Children & Youth, Vol. 2. LC 74-1011. 225p. 1974. text ed. 29.50x (ISBN 0-8422-5160-X); pap. text ed. 16.95x (ISBN 0-8422-0389-3); avail. modular learning supplement. Irvington.

Bullock, Mary B. An American Transplant: The Rockefeller Foundation & Peking Union Medical College. LC 77-83098. 280p. 1981. 27.50x (ISBN 0-520-03559-3). U of Cal Pr.

Bullock, Michael. Randolph Cranstone & the Glass Thimble. (Illus.). 118p. 1978. 10.95 (ISBN 0-7145-2506-5, Dist by Scribner). M Boyars.

Bullock, Michael, tr. see Fest, Joachim C.

Bullock, Michael, tr. see Frisch, Max.

Bullock, Michael, tr. see Goll, Yvan.

Bullock, Michael, tr. see Hoffmann, E. T.

Bullock, Michael, tr. see Jaspers, Karl.

Bullock, Michael, tr. see Keller, Gottfried.

Bullock, Michael, tr. see Wicki, Peter & Schroeder, Binette.

Bullock, Michael, tr. see Worringer, Wilhelm.

Bullock, Micheal, tr. see Busza, Andrzej.

Bullock, Nadine see Xnadu, pseud.

Bullock, Nicholas & Read, James. The Movement for Housing Reform in Germany & France, 1840-1914. (Cambridge Urban & Architectural Studies: No. 9). (Illus.). 667p. 1985. 79.50 (ISBN 0-521-22537-X). Cambridge U Pr.

Bullock, Orin M., Jr. The Restoration Manual. LC 66-15647. 196p. 1966. 12.95 (ISBN 0-87231-009-4). Silvermine.

--The Restoration Manual: An Illustrated Guide to the Preservation & Restoration of Old Buildings. 192p. 1983. pap. 12.95 (ISBN 0-442-21433-2). Van Nos Reinhold.

Bullock, Paul. Aspiration vs. Opportunity: 'Careers' in the Inner City. LC 73-620101. (Policy Papers in Human Resources & Industrial Relations Ser.: No. 20). 180p. 1973. 8.50x (ISBN 0-87736-122-3); pap. 3.95 (ISBN 0-87736-123-1). U of Mich Inst Labor.

--CETA at the Crossroads: Employment Policy & Politics. (Monograph & Research Ser.: No. 29). 280p. 1981. 8.50 (ISBN 0-89215-113-7). U Cal LA Indus Rel.

--Creative Careers: Minorities in the Arts. 220p. 1977. 5.50 (ISBN 0-89215-063-7). U Cal LA Indus Rel.

--Equal Opportunity in Employment. 1966. 2.00 (ISBN 0-89215-026-2). U Cal LA Indus Rel.

--Standards of Wage Determination. 99p. 1960. 2.00 (ISBN 0-89215-024-6). U Cal LA Indus Rel.

Bullock, Paul & Kautter, William. Executive Wealthbuilding Plans. LC 83-1681. 1983. 24.95 (ISBN 0-910580-35-9). Farnswth Pub.

Bullock, Paul, ed. Directory of Community Services Organizations in Greater Los Angeles. 1979. 5.00 (ISBN 0-89215-106-4). U Cal LA Indus Rel.

--Directory of Community Services Organizations in Greater Los Angeles. 218p. 1985. 10.00 (ISBN 0-89215-128-5). U Cal LA Indus Rel.

--A Full Employment Policy for America: Papers Presented at a UCLA Symposium. 151p. 1974. 3.00 (ISBN 0-89215-044-0). U Cal LA Indus Rel.

--Goals for Full Employment: A Discussion of the Full Employment & Balanced Growth Act of 1976. rev. ed. 113p. 1978. 4.50 (ISBN 0-89215-098-X). U Cal LA Indus Rel.

--Minorities in the Labor Market: American Indians, Asian Americans, Blacks, & Chicanos. 119p. 1978. 5.50 (ISBN 0-89215-095-5). U Cal LA Indus Rel.

Bullock, Penelope L. The Afro-American Periodical Press, 1838-1909. LC 81-1712. (Illus.). xviii, 358p. 1981. 30.00x (ISBN 0-8071-0663-1). La State U Pr.

Bullock, R. J. Improving Job Satisfaction. (Work in America Institute Studies in Productivity Ser.: No. 35). 46p. 1984. pap. 35.00 (ISBN 0-08-030967-4). Pergamon.

Bullock, R. L. & Jacoby, H. J., eds. RETC Proceedings, Nineteen Eighty-One, 2 vols. LC 81-65517. (Illus.). 1759p. Set. 70.00x (ISBN 0-89520-285-9). Soc Mining Eng.

Bullock, Ralph W. In Spite of Handicaps: Brief Biographical Sketches with Discussion Outlines of Outstanding Negroes Now Living Who Are Achieving Distinction in Various Lines of Endeavor. facs. ed. LC 68-25602. (Essay Index Reprint Ser). 1927. 18.00 (ISBN 0-8369-0264-5). Ayer Co Pubs.

Bullock, Robert D. Wilderness Habitat: The Great Plains. (Illus., Orig.). (gr. 2-6). 1984. pap. 2.90 wkbk. (ISBN 0-915881-01-2). Inglewood Dis.

--Wilderness Habitat: The Ozarks. (Illus.). 4p. (Orig.). (gr. 2-6). 1983. pap. 2.90 wkbk. (ISBN 0-915881-00-4). Inglewood Dis.

Bullock, Spencer M. & Hosie, Kenneth. Learning to Care: The Training of Staff for Residential Social Work with Young People. 136p. 1980. text ed. 24.00x (ISBN 0-566-00400-3). Gower Pub Co.

Bullock, Terry L. & Hesse, Karl D. Reading in the Social Studies Classroom. 64p. 1981. 6.95 (ISBN 0-8106-3202-0). NEA.

Bullock, Theodore H. & Horridge, G. Adrian. Structure & Function in the Nervous Systems of Invertebrates, 2 Vols. (Biology Ser.). (Illus.). 1719p. 1965. 175.00x (ISBN 0-7167-0626-1). W H Freeman.

Bullock, Theodore H., ed. Recognition of Complex Acoustic Signals, LSRR 5. (Dahlem Workshop Reports Ser.). 406p. 1977. pap. 37.70x (ISBN 0-89573-089-8). VCH Pubs.

Bullock, Theodore H., et al. Introduction to Nervous Systems. LC 76-3735. (Illus.). 559p. 1977. pap. text ed. 38.95 (ISBN 0-7167-0577-X); pap. text ed. 31.95 (ISBN 0-7167-0030-1). W H Freeman.

Bullock, Theodore L., ed. see Friedheim, Arthur.

Bullock, Waneta B. & Loveless, Ganelle. ABC Mazes. (Educational Ser.). (Illus.). (gr. k-1). 1979. pap. 5.00 (ISBN 0-89039-244-7). Ann Arbor FL.

Bullock, Waneta B. & Meister, Barbara. Ann Arbor Learning Inventory Grades Kindergarten to One Manual. Skill Level A. (Ann Arbor Learning Inventory Ser.). (Illus.). 64p. (gr. k-1). 1978. 4.00 (ISBN 0-89039-246-3); wkbk. 0.50 (ISBN 0-89039-248-X). Ann Arbor FL.

--Ann Arbor Learning Inventory Grades Two to Four Manual: Skill Level B. (Ann Arbor Learning Inventory Ser.). (Illus.). 56p. (gr. 2-4). 1977. 4.00 (ISBN 0-89039-225-0); wkbk. 0.50 (ISBN 0-89039-227-7). Ann Arbor FL.

Bullock, William, jt. auth. see Maidment, Robert.

Bullock, William B. Antiques & the Classics, Bk. 1. LC 79-53073. (Illus.). 1979. spiral 14.95 (ISBN 0-911721-59-2). Aviation.

Bullock, William J. Bach Cantatas Requiring Limited Resources: A Guide to Editions. LC 84-2337. 58p. 1984. lib. bdg. 9.50 (ISBN 0-8191-3863-0). U Pr of Amer.

Bullock, Wynn, et al. Darkroom. Lewis, Eleanor, ed. LC 76-57201. (Illus.). 1977. pap. 17.95 (ISBN 0-912810-19-X). Light Impressions.

Bullock-Davies, C. Menestrellorum Multitudo: Minstrels at a Royal Feast. 188p. 1978. text ed. 19.50x (ISBN 0-7083-0656-X, Pub. by Univ of Wales Pr England). Humanities.

Bullock-Davies, Constance. English Pronunciation from the Fifteenth to the Eighteenth Century: A Handbook to the Study of Historical Grammar. LC 75-109726. Repr. of 1934 ed. lib. bdg. 27.50x (ISBN 0-8371-4216-4, DAEP). Greenwood.

Bullock-Webster, George R., jt. auth. see Groves, James.

Bullock-Wilson, Barbara & Bullock, Edna, eds. Wynn Bullock: Photographing the Nude. (Illus.). 80p. 1984. 27.95 (ISBN 0-87905-170-1, Peregrine Smith). Gibbs M Smith.

Bulloff, J. J., et al, eds. Foundations of Mathematics: Symposium Papers Commemorating the Sixtieth Birthday of Kurt Goedel. LC 68-28757. (Illus.). 1969. 36.00 (ISBN 0-387-04490-6). Springer-Verlag.

Bullogh, V L. Homosexuality: A History. 196p. 1979. 70.00 (ISBN 0-317-14274-7, Pub. by Holdan Bk Ltd UK). State Mutual Bk.

Bullokar, John. English Expositor: Teaching the Interpretation of the Hardest Words Used in Our Language. 1971. Repr. of 1616 ed. 32.00x (ISBN 3-4870-4070-0). Adlers Foreign Bks.

Bullokar, William. Booke at Large (Fifteen Eighty) & Brief Grammar for English (Fifteen Eighty-Six) LC 76-55723. 1977. Repr. of 1580 ed. 30.00x (ISBN 0-8201-1287-9). Schol Facsimiles.

--Bullokars Booke at Large for the Amendment of Orthographie for English Speech. LC 68-54622. (English Experience Ser.: No. 24). 110p. 1968. Repr. of 1580 ed. 9.50 (ISBN 90-221-0024-3). Walter J Johnson.

Bullough, B. & Bullough, V. L. History, Trends & Politics in Nursing. 160p. 1984. pap. 15.95 (ISBN 0-8385-3775-8). ACC.

Bullough, Bonnie & Bullough, Vern. Nursing Issues & Nursing Strategies for the Eighties. 352p. 1983. pap. 17.95 (ISBN 0-8261-4441-1). Springer Pub.

Bullough, Bonnie, jt. auth. see Bullough, Vern.

Bullough, Bonnie, jt. auth. see Bullough, Vern L.

Bullough, Bonnie, et al. Nursing: An Historical Bibliography. LC 80-836. 408p. 1980. lib. bdg. 61.00 (ISBN 0-8240-9511-1). Garland Pub.

Bullough, Bonnie, et al, eds. The Management of Common Human Miseries: A Text for Primary Health Care Practitioners. LC 78-24072. 1979. text ed. 26.50 (ISBN 0-8261-2190-X). Springer Pub.

Bullough, Edward. Aesthetics: Lectures & Essays. Wilkinson, Elizabeth M., ed. LC 77-21814. 1977. Repr. of 1957 ed. lib. bdg. 18.00x (ISBN 0-8371-9789-9, WIAE). Greenwood.

Bullough, Edward, tr. see Gilson, Etienne H.

Bullough, Geoffrey, ed. Narrative & Dramatic Sources of Shakespeare, 7 vols. Incl. Vol. 1. Early Comedies, Poems, Romeo & Juliet. 1957 (ISBN 0-231-08891-4); Vol. 2. The Comedies, 1597-1603. 1958 (ISBN 0-231-08892-2); Vol. 3. Earlier English History Plays: Henry Sixth, Richard Third, Richard Second. 1960 (ISBN 0-231-08893-0); Vol. 4. Later English History Plays: King John, Henry Fourth, Henry Fifth, Henry Eighth. 1962 (ISBN 0-231-08894-9); Vol. 5. The Roman Plays: Julius Caesar, Antony & Cleopatra, Coriolanus. 1964 (ISBN 0-231-08895-7); Vol. 6. Other Classical Plays: Titus Adronicus, Troilus & Cressida, Timon of Athens, Pericles, Prince of Tyre. 1966 (ISBN 0-231-08896-5); Vol. 7. Major Tragedies: Hamlet, Othello, King Lear, Macbeth. 35.00x ea. (ISBN 0-231-08897-3). LC 57-9969. 42.00x ea. Columbia U Pr.

Bullough, Geoffrey, jt. ed. see Grierson, Herbert J.

Bullough, Geoffrey, ed. see Milton, John.

Bullough, Margaret, ed. see Milton, John.

Bullough, Peter G. & Vigorita, Vincent J. Atlas of Orthopaedic Pathology. (Illus.). 324p. 1984. text ed. 85.00 (ISBN 0-8391-1915-1, 20273). Univ Park.

Bullough, Peter G., jt. auth. see Meisel, Allen D.

Bullough, R. K. & Caudrey, P. J., eds. Solitons. (Topics in Current Physics: Vol. 17). (Illus.). 400p. 1980. pap. 51.00 (ISBN 0-387-09962-X). Springer-Verlag.

Bullough, Robert V. Creating Instructional Materials. 2nd ed. (Elementary Education Ser.). 1978. pap. text ed. 16.95x (ISBN 0-675-08361-3). Merrill.

Bullough, Robert V., Jr. Democracy in Education: Boyd H. Bode. LC 80-84621. 258p. 1981. lib. bdg. 25.95x (ISBN 0-930390-37-7); pap. text ed. 11.95x (ISBN 0-930390-35-0). Gen Hall.

Bullough, Robert V., Jr. & Goldstein, Stanley L. Human Interests in the Curriculum: Teaching & Learning in a Technological Society. 1984. pap. text ed. 13.95x (ISBN 0-8077-2745-8). Tchrs Coll.

Bullough, Sr. Robert V. Display Boards. Duane, James E., ed. LC 80-21332. (The Instructional Media Library: Vol. 3). (Illus.). 112p. 1981. 19.95 (ISBN 0-87778-163-X). Educ Tech Pubns.

--Multi-Image Media. Duane, James E., ed. LC 80-21341. (The Instructional Media Library: Vol. 9). (Illus.). 128p. 1981. 19.95 (ISBN 0-87778-169-9). Educ Tech Pubns.

--Photography. Duane, James E., ed. LC 80-21333. (The Instructional Media Library: Vol. 11). (Illus.). 104p. 1981. 19.95 (ISBN 0-87778-171-0). Educ Tech Pubns.

Bullough, V. L., jt. auth. see Bullough, B.

Bullough, Vern. Sex, Society & History. 1976. 15.00 (ISBN 0-88202-154-0); pap. 7.95 o.p (ISBN 0-686-67886-9). Watson Pub Intl.

Bullough, Vern & Bullough, Bonnie. The Care of the Sick: The Emergence of Modern Nursing. LC 78-14238. 1978. 17.50 (ISBN 0-88202-183-4). Watson Pub Intl.

--Health Care for the Other Americans. 2nd ed. 270p. 1982. pap. 17.95 (ISBN 0-8385-3663-8); 19.95 (ISBN 0-8385-3664-6). ACC.

--Sin, Sickness & Sanity: A History of Sexual Attitudes. (Orig.). 1977. pap. 6.95 (ISBN 0-452-00562-0, F562, Mer). NAL.

Bullough, Vern, ed. The Frontiers of Sex Research. LC 79-2462. 190p. 1979. 18.95 (ISBN 0-87975-110-X); pap. 9.95 (ISBN 0-87975-113-4). Prometheus Bks.

Bullough, Vern & Brundage, James, eds. Sexual Practices & the Medieval Church. LC 80-85227. 289p. 1984. pap. 14.95 (ISBN 0-87975-268-8). Prometheus Bks.

Bullough, Vern, jt. auth. see Bullough, Bonnie.

Bullough, Vern L. The Development of Medicine As a Profession. LC 76-56850. 132p. 1966. 20.00 (ISBN 0-686-65683-0). Watson Pub Intl.

--Homosexuality: A History. 1979. pap. 5.95 (ISBN 0-452-00725-9, Mer). NAL.

--Sexual Variance in Society & History. LC 79-26504. 1980. lib. bdg. 40.00x (ISBN 0-226-07995-3, Phoen); pap. 15.00x (ISBN 0-226-07994-5, P861). U of Chicago Pr.

Bullough, Vern L. & Bullough, Bonnie. The Subordinate Sex: A History of Attitudes Towards Women. LC 72-91079. pap. 72.80 (ISBN 0-317-09711-3, 2014930). Bks Demand UMI.

Bullough, Vern L. & Elcano, Barrett W. A Bibliography of Prostitution. LC 75-42891. (Reference Library of Social Science). 430p. lib. bdg. 61.00 (ISBN 0-8240-9947-8). Garland Pub.

Bullough, Vern L., ed. The Scientific Revolution. LC 77-21207. (European Problem Studies). 136p. 1978. pap. text ed. 5.95 (ISBN 0-88275-635-4). Krieger.

Bullough, Vern L., et al. An Annotated Bibliography of Homosexuality, 2 vols. LC 75-24106. (Reference Library of Social Science: Vol. 22). 1000p. 1975. Set. lib. bdg. 107.00 (ISBN 0-8240-9959-1). Garland Pub.

Bullough, Vernl, et al. Issues in Nursing: An Annotated Bibliography. LC 84-48758. 600p. 1985. lib. bdg. 60.00 (ISBN 0-8240-8768-2). Garland Pub.

Bullough, William A. The Blind Boss & His City: Christopher Augustine Buckley & Nineteenth-Century San Francisco. LC 78-64468. 1980. 22.00 (ISBN 0-520-03797-9). U of Cal Pr.

--Cities & Schools in the Gilded Age: The Evolution of an Urban Institution. LC 74-80592. 1974. 18.50x (ISBN 0-8046-9094-4, Pub. by Kennikat). Assoc Faculty Pr.

Bullough, William S. The Dynamic Body Tissues. 1983. 36.95 (ISBN 0-442-21315-8). Van Nos Reinhold.

Bullowa, Margaret, ed. Before Speech. LC 78-51671. (Illus.). 1979. 59.50 (ISBN 0-521-22031-9); pap. 15.95 (ISBN 0-521-29522-X). Cambridge U Pr.

Bullrich, Francisco. New Directions in Latin American Architecture. LC 71-85698. (New Directions in Architecture Ser). (Illus., Orig.). 1969. pap. 3.95 (ISBN 0-8076-0528-X). Braziller.

Bullrich, Kurt. Die Farbigen Dammerungserscheinngen. 100p. 1982. 17.95 (ISBN 0-8176-1355-2). Birkhauser.

Bullus, Gerald E. The Manager's Guide to Sales Incentives. 160p. 1983. text ed. 42.00x (ISBN 0-566-02353-9). Gower Pub Co.

Bullwinkel, Madelaine. Gourmet Preserves Chez Madelaine. (Illus.). 240p. 1984. 14.95 (ISBN 0-8092-5482-4); pap. 7.95 (ISBN 0-8092-5339-9). Contemp Bks.

Bullwinkle, Alice & Galloway, Howard P. Finding Summer Staff. 1979. pap. 6.85 (ISBN 0-87874-016-3). Galloway.

Bulmahn, Heinz. Adolf Glassbrenner: His Development from "Jungdeutscher" to "Vormaerzler". (German Language & Literature Monographs: No. 6). x, 159p. 1978. 21.00x (ISBN 90-272-0966-9, GLLM 6). Benjamins North Am.

Bulman, Alex. Kamloops Cattleman. (Illus.). 184p. 9.95 (ISBN 0-88826-035-0). Superior Pub.

Bulman, J. C. & Nosworthy, J. M., eds. Timon. LC 82-45735. (Malone Society Reprint Ser.: No. 139). 1978. 40.00 (ISBN 0-404-63139-8). AMS Pr.

Bulman, Joan. Strindberg & Shakespeare: Shakespeare's Influence on Strindberg's Historical Drama. LC 73-153482. (Studies in Comparative Literature, No. 35). 1971. Repr. of 1933 ed. lib. bdg. 36.95x (ISBN 0-8383-1239-X). Haskell.

Bulman, Joan, tr. see Glob, P. V.

Bulman, Joan, tr. see Svanstrom, Ragnar & Palmstierna, Carl F.

Bulman, Nachman. Reason, Emotion & Habit in the Training of a Torah Personality. (Annual Fryer Memorial Lecture Ser.). 0.75 (ISBN 0-914131-53-2, I34). Torah Umesorah.

Bulman, Nathan, tr. see Kitov, A. E.
Bulman, Nathan, tr. see Kitov, Eliyahu.
Bulman, O. M. The Caradoc Balclatchie Graptolites from Limestones in Laggan Burn, Ayrshire, Pts. 1-3. (Illus.). 1945-47. Set. pap. 30.00 (ISBN 0-384-06325-X). Johnson Repr.
--The Dendroid Graptolites, Pts. 1-3. 1927-34. Set. pap. 25.00 (ISBN 0-384-06335-7). Johnson Repr.
Bulmer, Charles & Carmichael, John L. Employment & Labor-Relations Policy. LC 79-3145. (Policy Studies Book). 1980. 29.50x (ISBN 0-669-03388-X). Lexington Bks.
Bulmer, Charles, jt. auth. see Carmichael, John, Jr.
Bulmer, David. Functional Anatomy of the Urogenital System. (Illus.). 184p. 1974. pap. text ed. 16.95x (ISBN 0-8464-0444-3). Beekman Pubs.
--The Functional Anatomy of the Urogenital System. 184p. 1974. pap. text ed. 30.00x (ISBN 0-272-00124-4, Pub. by Pitman Bks England). State Mutual Bk.
Bulmer, Glenn S. Introduction to Medical Mycology. (Illus.). 1979. pap. 26.50 (ISBN 0-8151-1320-X); slides 358.50 (ISBN 0-8151-1321-8). Year Bk Med.
Bulmer, James. Your Hyperion Companion. cancelled 15.95 (ISBN 0-318-01429-7). Brady Comm.
Bulmer, Kenneth. The Diamond Contessa. 1983. pap. 2.50 (ISBN 0-87997-853-8). DAW Bks.
Bulmer, M. G. The Biology of Twinning in Man. LC 71-498413. pap. 53.80 (ISBN 0-317-28732-X, 2051313). Bks Demand UMI.
--The Mathematical Theory of Quantitative Genetics. (Illus.). 1980. 74.00x (ISBN 0-19-857530-0). Oxford U Pr.
--Principles of Statistics. LC 78-72991. 1979. pap. 4.95 (ISBN 0-486-63760-3). Dover.
Bulmer, Martin. Censuses, Surveys & Privacy. LC 79-9292. 279p. 1979. text ed. 35.00 (ISBN 0-8419-0536-3). Holmes & Meier.
--The Chicago School of Sociology: Institutionalization, Diversity, & the Rise of Sociological Research. LC 84-8494. (Heritage of Sociology Ser.). (Illus.). 280p. 1985. pap. 29.00x (ISBN 0-226-08004-8). U of Chicago Pr.
--Essays on the History of British Sociological Research. (Illus.). 270p. 1985. 49.50 (ISBN 0-521-25477-9). Cambridge U Pr.
--Social Research & Royal Commissions. 224p. 1980. text ed. 27.50x (ISBN 0-04-351055-8). Allen Unwin.
--The Uses of Social Research: Social Investigation in Public Policy Making. (Contemporary Social Research Ser.: No. 3). (Illus.). 208p. 1982. text ed. 28.50x (ISBN 0-04-312011-3); pap. text ed. 12.50x (ISBN 0-04-312012-1). Allen Unwin.
Bulmer, Martin, ed. Mining & Social Change: Durham County in the Twentieth Century. 320p. 1978. 30.00 (ISBN 0-85664-509-5, Pub. by Croom Helm Ltd). Longwood Pub Group.
--Social Policy Research. 1978. text ed. 31.25x (ISBN 0-333-23142-2); pap. text ed. 13.00x (ISBN 0-333-23143-0). Humanities.
--Social Research Ethics. LC 81-4250. 304p. 1982. text ed. 39.50x (ISBN 0-8419-0713-7); pap. text ed. 14.50x (ISBN 0-8419-0780-3). Holmes & Meier.
--Sociological Research Methods. 2nd ed. 450p. 1984. pap. 12.95 (ISBN 0-333-37346-4). Transaction Bks.
Bulmer, Martin & Warwick, Donald P., eds. Social Research in Developing Countries: Surveys & Censuses in the Third World. (Social Development in the Third World Ser.). 383p. 1983. 39.95 (ISBN 0-471-10352-7). Wiley.
Bulmer, Martin, ed. see Bateson, Nicholas.
Bulmer, Martin, ed. see Hellevik, Ottar.
Bulmer, Ralph, jt. auth. see Majnep, Ian S.
Bulmer, Thomas V. Input-Output Analysis in Developing Countries: Sources, Methods & Applications. (Social Development in the Third World Ser.). 297p. 1982. 52.95 (ISBN 0-471-10149-4). Wiley.
Bulmore, Lawrence, jt. auth. see Lanyen, Milton.
Bulnes, Francisco. The Whole Truth About Mexico: President Wilson's Responsibility. 1976. lib. bdg. 59.95 (ISBN 0-8490-1296-1). Gordon Pr.
Bulnes Aldunate, Jose M., ed. see Universidad De Puerto Rico Centro De Investigaciones Sociales.
Bulnheim, H. P., jt. auth. see Kinne, O.
Bu'Lock, J. D., ed. Biosynthesis, Vols. 1-5. Incl. Vol. 1. 1970-71 Literature. 1972. 36.00 (ISBN 0-85186-503-8); Vol. 2. 1972 Literature. 1973. 38.00 (ISBN 0-85186-513-5); Vol. 3. 1973 Literature. 1975. 38.00 (ISBN 0-85186-523-2); Vol. 4. 1974 Literature. 1976. 43.00 (ISBN 0-85186-533-X); Vol. 5. 1975-76 Literature. 1977. 57.00 (ISBN 0-85186-543-7). LC 72-83455 (Pub. by Royal Soc Chem London). Am Chemical.
Bu'Lock, J. D., jt. ed. see Meyrath, J.
Bu'Lock, J. D., et al. Bioactive Microbial Products: Search & Discovery. (Special Publications of the Society for General Microbiology: No. 6). 1982. 29.00 (ISBN 0-12-140750-0). Acad Pr.
Bulosan, Carlos. America Is in the Heart. LC 73-13007. 352p. 1973. pap. 8.95 (ISBN 0-295-95289-X). U of Wash Pr.
--If You Want To Know What We Are. Juan, E. San, Jr., ed. 80p. (Orig.). 1983. pap. 4.50 (ISBN 0-931122-29-5). West End.
Bulosan, Carlos, Jr. The Philippines Is in the Heart: A Collection of Short Stories. (Illus.). 1979. pap. 5.75x (ISBN 0-686-25219-5, Pub. by New Day Pub). Cellar.
Bulovsky, P. I. & Idelson, E. M. Testing of Aircraft Instruments. LC 75-135081. 312p. 1970. 24.00 (ISBN 0-403-04487-1). Scholarly.
Bulow, B. von Marenholz. Reminiscences of Friedrich Froebel. Mann, Mrs. Horace, tr. 359p. 1980. Repr. of 1877 ed. lib. bdg. 30.00 (ISBN 0-8492-2833-6). R West.
Bulow, Bernhard H. Imperial Germany. Lewenz, Marie A., tr. LC 78-12268. (Illus.). 1979. Repr. of 1914 ed. lib. bdg. 24.75x (ISBN 0-313-21176-0, BUIG). Greenwood.
Bulow, Hans Von see Von Bulow, Hans.
Bulow, Hans Von see Von Bulow, Hans & Strauss, Richard.
Bulow, Henri De see D'Bulow, Henri.
Bulow, Marie von see Von Bulow, Marie.
Bulow, Von Hans see Cramer, J. B.
Bulpett, C. W., ed. King of the Wa-Kikuyu. (Illus.). 320p. 1968. Repr. of 1911 ed. 32.50x (ISBN 0-7146-1638-9, F Cass Co). Biblio Dist.
Bulpitt, C., ed. The Epidemiology of Hypertension. (Handbook of Hypertension: No. 6). 1984. 109.25 (ISBN 0-444-90355-0, Excerpta Medica). Elsevier.
Bulpitt, Christopher J. Randomised Controlled Clinical Trials. 1983. lib. bdg. 52.50 (ISBN 90-247-2749-9, Pub. by Martinus Nijhoff Netherlands). Kluwer Academic.
Bulpitt, Jim. Territory & Power in the United Kingdom: An Interpretation. LC 82-62263. 246p. 1983. 25.00 (ISBN 0-7190-0937-5, Pub. by Manchester Univ Pr). Longwood Pub Group.
Buls, Alfred M. Devotions for New Parents. (Orig.). (YA) 1972. pap. 1.50 (ISBN 0-570-03675-5, 74-1010). Concordia.
Buls, Mark J. Bush Cats. 68p. 1979. 4.50 (ISBN 0-8059-2608-9). Dorrance.
Bulsara, Sohrab J., tr. Aerpatastan & Niragastan: Or, the Code of the Holy Doctorship, etc. LC 74-21249. Repr. of 1915 ed. 47.50 (ISBN 0-404-12800-9). AMS Pr.
Bulson, P. S. Buried Structures: Static & Dynamic Strength. (Illus.). 320p. 1985. 42.50 (ISBN 0-412-21560-8, 6665, Pub. by Chapman & Hall). Methuen Inc.
Bulson, P. S., jt. auth. see Allen, H. G.
Bultema, Harry. Commentary on Isaiah. LC 81-11795. 650p. 1981. 14.95 (ISBN 0-8254-2258-2). Kregel.
--Maranatha. 240p. 1986. 12.95 (ISBN 0-8254-2263-9). Kregel.
Bulter, Anthony R. Problems in Physical Organic Chemistry. LC 72-617. pap. 28.80 (ISBN 0-317-09092-5, 2016972). Bks Demand UMI.
Bulter, J. R. & Doessel, D. P. The Economics of Natural Disaster Relief in Australia. LC 79-50570. (Centre for Research on Federal Financial Relations - Research Monograph: No. 27). 147p. (Orig.). 1980. pap. text ed. 10.00 (ISBN 0-7081-1073-8, 0565). Australia N U P.
Bulter, Linda, jt. auth. see Bahbah, Bishara A.
Bulter, Paul T. Twenty-Six Lessons on Revelation, Pt. 1. LC 82-71688. (Bible Student Study Guide Ser.). 133p. 1982. pap. 2.95 (ISBN 0-89900-173-4). College Pr Pub.
--Twenty-Six Lessons on Revelation, Pt. 2. LC 82-71688. (Bible Student study Guide Ser.). 284p. 1982. pap. 4.95 (ISBN 0-89900-176-9). College Pr Pub.
Bulthaupt, Fritz. Milstater Genesis und Exodus: Eine Grammatisch-Stillistische Ist Untersuchung. (Ger). 21.00 (ISBN 0-384-06341-1); pap. 16.00 (ISBN 0-685-02228-5). Johnson Repr.
Bultitude, John. Apples: A Guide to the Identification of International Varieties. (Illus.). 332p. 1984. 50.00x (ISBN 0-295-96041-8). U of Wash Pr.
Bultmann, Phyllis. Two Burners & an Ice Chest: The Art of Relaxed Cooking in Boats, in Campers, & Under the Stars. (Illus.). 1977. (Spec) pap. 5.95 (ISBN 0-13-935189-2, Spec). P-H.
Bultmann, Rudolf. Gospel of John: A Commentary. LC 70-125197. 758p. 1971. 26.50 (ISBN 0-664-20893-2). Westminster.
--The History of the Synoptic Tradition. 2nd ed. Marsh, John, tr. 1972. Repr. of 1968 ed. 39.95x (ISBN 0-631-11350-9). Basil Blackwell.
--History of the Synoptic Tradition. LC 62-7282. 1963. pap. 8.95x (ISBN 0-06-061172-3, RD 187, HarpR). Har-Row.
--Jesus & the Word. (Hudson River Edition). 20.00 (ISBN 0-684-17596-7, ScribT). Scribner.
--Jesus Christ & Mythology. 94p. 1981. pap. text ed. price not set (ISBN 0-02-305570-7, Pub. by Scribner). Macmillan.
--The Johannine Epistles. Funk, Robert W., ed. O'Hara, R. Philip, et al, trs. from Gr. LC 75-171510. (Hermeneia: a Critical & Historical Commentary on the Bible). 158p. 1973. 15.95 (ISBN 0-8006-6003-X, 20-6003). Fortress.
--The New Testament & Mythology & Other Basic Writings. Ogden, Schubert M., ed. & tr. LC 84-47921. 192p. 1984. 12.95 (ISBN 0-8006-0727-9). Fortress.
--The Presence of Eternity. LC 75-9540. 170p. 1975. Repr. of 1957 ed. lib. bdg. 22.50x (ISBN 0-8371-8123-2, BUPRE). Greenwood.
--Primitive Christianity: In Its Contemporary Setting. Fuller, Reginald H., tr. from Ger. LC 80-8043. 256p. 1980. pap. 8.95 (ISBN 0-8006-1408-9, 1-1408). Fortress.
--The Second Letter to the Corinthians. Linss, Wilhelm C., tr. LC 83-70517. 272p. 1983. pap. 16.50 (ISBN 0-8066-2023-4, 10-5633). Augsburg.
--Theology of the New Testament. (Contemporary Theology Ser.). 278p. 1951. pap. text ed. price not set (ISBN 0-02-305580-4, Pub. by Scribner). Macmillan.
Bultmann, Rudolf, jt. auth. see Barth, Karl.
Bulwa, Lillian, ed. see Ionesco, Eugene.
Bulwer, Edward L. England & the English. Meacham, Standish, ed. LC 71-114959. (Classics of British Historical Literature Ser.). 1972. pap. 3.45x (ISBN 0-226-08015-3, P384, Phoen). U of Chicago Pr.
--England & the English. Meacham, Standish, ed. LC 71-114959. (Classics of British Historical Literature Ser.). 1970. 22.50x (ISBN 0-226-08014-5). U of Chicago Pr.
Bulwer, John. Chirologia, 2 vols. in 1. LC 75-147955. (Language, Man & Society Ser.). Repr. of 1644 ed. 27.00 (ISBN 0-404-08205-X). AMS Pr.
--Chirologia; or the Natural Language of the Hand. Chironomia; or the Art of Manual Rhetoric. Cleary, James W., ed. LC 76-132492. (Landmarks in Rhetoric & Public Address Ser.). 380p. 1974. 19.50x (ISBN 0-8093-0497-X). S Ill U Pr.
Bulwer-Lytton, E. Zanoni: A Rosicrucian Tale, Vol. 4. LC 78-157505. (Spiritual Science Library). 416p. 1971. lib. bdg. 15.00 (ISBN 0-89345-014-6, Spiritual Sci Lib); pap. 11.00 (ISBN 0-89345-015-4, Steinerbks). Garber Comm.
Bulwer-Lytton, E. G. Last Days of Pompeii. 1976. 11.95x (ISBN 0-460-00080-2, Evman). Biblio Dist.
Bulwer-Lytton, Edward. The Coming Race. 186p. 1973. Repr. of 1874 ed. 8.95 (ISBN 0-932785-07-7). Philos Pub.
--The Coming Race. LC 79-4090. (Banquo Bks.). 1979. pap. 3.95 (ISBN 0-912800-68-2). Woodbridge Pr.
--England & the English, 2 vols. (The Development of Industrial Society). 723p. 1971. Repr. of 1833 ed. 45.00x (ISBN 0-7165-1592-X, Pub. by Irish Academic Pr Ireland). Biblio Dist.
--Falkland. Thal, Herbert V., ed. (First Novel Library). 1967. 7.95 (ISBN 0-8023-9054-4); pap. 4.95 (ISBN 0-304-92027-4). Dufour.
--Last Days of Pompeii. 308p. 1983. Repr. lib. bdg. 17.95x (ISBN 0-89966-309-5). Buccaneer Bks.
--Money: Royal Shakespeare Company. (PIT Playtext Ser.). 56p. 1982. pap. 4.95 (ISBN 0-413-51240-1, NO. 3761). Methuen Inc.
--Vril: The Power of the Coming Race. LC 83-83173. (Spiritual Fiction Publications: Vol. 5). 256p. 1985. 15.00 (ISBN 0-8334-0004-5, Spiritual Fiction). Garber Comm.
--Zanoni: A Rosicrucian Tale. 3rd ed. LC 78-157505. (Spiritual Fiction Publications: Vol. 1). 416p. 1985. cloth 16.00 (ISBN 0-8334-0000-2, Spiritual Fiction). Garber Comm.
Bulwer-Lytton, Edward see Lytton, Edward.
Bulwer-Lytton, Edward G. Pelham; or, the Adventures of a Gentleman. McGann, Jerome J., ed. LC 77-88085. xxxvi, 477p. 1972. 31.50x (ISBN 0-8032-0703-4). U of Nebr Pr.
Bulwer-Lytton, Sir Edward. The Last Days of Pompeii. 1979. pap. 11.95 (ISBN 0-933772-00-9). T H Feder Bks.
Bulychev, Kir, et al. Earth & Elsewhere. 320p. 1986. 22.95 (ISBN 0-02-518240-4). MacMillan.
Bulychev, Kirill. Gusliar Wonders. DeGaris, Roger, tr. 320p. 1983. 16.95 (ISBN 0-02-518010-X). Macmillan.
Bulygin, E., jt. auth. see Alchourron, C. E.
Bulygin, Eugenio & Gardies, Jean-Louis, eds. Man, Law, & Modern Forms of Life. International Association for Philosophy of Law & Social Philosophy & World Congress of Philosophy of Law & Social Philosophy. LC 85-11749. (Law & Philosophy Library). 1985. 39.50 (ISBN 9-02-771869-5, Pub. by Reidel Holland). Kluwer Academic.
Bulygin, Paul & Kerensky, Alexander. The Murder of the Romanovs. LC 74-10075. (Russian Studies: Perspectives on the Revolution Ser). (Illus.). 286p. 1974. Repr. of 1935 ed. 30.25 (ISBN 0-88355-183-7). Hyperion Conn.
Bumagin, Victoria E. & Hirn, Kathryn F. Aging Is a Family Affair. LC 78-22459. 1979. 12.45i (ISBN 0-690-01823-1). T Y Crowell.
Bumann, Richard L. Colony Olivenhain. LC 81-90363. (Illus.). 112p. 1981. 15.95 (ISBN 0-9607112-0-1). Bumann Spec Works.
Bumb, Balu. A Survey of the Fertilizer Sector in India. (Working Paper: No. 331). iv, 216p. 1979. 5.00 (ISBN 0-686-36189-X, WP-0331). World Bank.
Bumba, V., jt. auth. see Howard, Robert.
Bumba, Vaclav & Kleczek, Josip, eds. Basic Mechanisms of Solar Activity. (Symposium of the International Astronomical Union Ser.: Vol. 71). 1976. lib. bdg. 74.00 (ISBN 90-277-0680-8, Pub. by Reidel Holland); pap. 39.50 (ISBN 90-277-0681-6). Kluwer Academic.
Bumbalo, Victor. Niagara Falls & Other Plays. write for info. Calamus Bks.
Bumbalough, Marine. A Touch of Fragrance. (Illus.). 32p. 1985. pap. 5.95 (ISBN 0-943574-30-7). That Patchwork.
Bumbarger, W. Bruce. Operation Function Analysis: Do-It-Yourself Productivity Improvement. 288p. 1984. 24.95 (ISBN 0-442-21424-3). Van Nos Reinhold.
Bumby, Fred E., ed. see Thackeray, William.
Bumby, J. R. Superconducting Rotating Electrical Machines. (Monographs in Electrical & Electronic Engineering). (Illus.). 1983. 39.00x (ISBN 0-19-859327-9). Oxford U Pr.
Bumcrot, Robert J., jt. auth. see Althoen, Steven C.
Bumgardner, Georgia B., jt. ed. see Lowance, Mason I.
Bumgarner, Marlene A. Book of Whole Grains. (Illus.). 256p. 1976. pap. 7.95 (ISBN 0-312-09240-7). St Martin.
--Organic Cooking for (Not-So-Organic) Mothers. Olson, Sue, ed. LC 80-23089. (Illus.). 160p. pap. 4.95 lib. lim. (ISBN 0-938006-01-0); spiral bdg. 5.95 (ISBN 0-938006-00-2). Chesbro.
Bumgarner, Norma J. Helping Love Grow. (Illus.). 1983. pap. 1.25 (ISBN 0-912500-17-4). La Leche.
--Mothering Your Nursing Toddler. 2nd ed. LC 82-84383. 210p. 1982. pap. 6.50 (ISBN 0-912500-12-3). La Leche.
Bumgartner, Louis E. Jose del Valle of Central America. LC 63-9007. pap. 78.50 (ISBN 0-8357-9109-2, 2017890). Bks Demand UMI.
Bumke, Joachim. The Concept of Knighthood in the Middle Ages. Jackson, Erika, tr. from Ger. LC 79-8840. (AMS Studies in the Middle Ages Ser.: No. 2). 278p. 1981. 34.50 (ISBN 0-404-18034-5). AMS Pr.
Bumli, George R., ed. Principles of Project Formulation for Irrigation & Drainage Projects. LC 82-73505. 144p. 1982. pap. 15.75x (ISBN 0-87262-345-9). Am Soc Civil Eng.
Bumm, F. Deutschlands Gesundheitsverhaltnisse Unter Dem Einfluss Des Weltkrieges, 2 Vols. (Wirtschafts-Und Sozialgeschichte Des Weltkrieges (Deutsche Serie)). 1928. 150.00x (ISBN 0-317-27441-4). Elliots Bks.
Bump, D. Automorphic Forms on GL (3r R) (Lecture Notes in Mathematics Ser.: Vol. 1083). xi, 184p. 1984. pap. 12.00 (ISBN 0-387-13864-1). Springer-Verlag.
Bump, Jerome. Gerard Manley Hopkins. (English Authors Ser.). 1982. lib. bdg. 13.50 (ISBN 0-8057-6819-X, Twayne). G K Hall.
Bumpass, Donald E. Selected AV Recipes: Materials, Equipment Use & Maintenance. 208p. 1981. pap. text ed. 13.95 (ISBN 0-8403-2518-5). Kendall-Hunt.
Bumpass, Larry I. & Sweet, James A. Patterns of Employment Before & after Childbirth: United States. Shipp, Audrey, ed. (Ser. 23: No. 4). 1979. pap. text ed. 1.75 (ISBN 0-8406-0167-0). Natl Ctr Health Stats.
Bumpass, Larry L., jt. auth. see Westoff, Charles F.
Bumppo, Natalie, jt. auth. see Bumppo, Natty.
Bumppo, Natty. The Columbus Book of Euchre. LC 81-68103. (Illus.). 72p. 1982. pap. 2.75 (ISBN 0-9604894-2-8). Borf Bks.
Bumppo, Natty & Bumppo, Natalie. Ideas for a Better America. LC 80-66966. (Illus.). 80p. 1980. pap. 3.95 (ISBN 0-9604894-0-1). Borf Bks.
Bumpus, F. M., jt. ed. see Page, I. H.
Bumpus, J. A. Dictionary of Ecclesiastical Terms. 75.00 (ISBN 0-8490-0034-3). Gordon Pr.
Bumpus, Jerry. Heroes & Villains. 224p. 1985. 12.95 (ISBN 0-914590-92-8); pap. 6.95 (ISBN 0-914590-93-6). Fiction Coll.
--Special Offer. LC 80-20671. 1981. pap. 5.95x (ISBN 0-914140-08-6). Carpenter Pr.
--Things in Place. LC 75-10744. 141p. 1975. 8.95 (ISBN 0-914590-14-6); pap. 3.95 (ISBN 0-914590-15-4). Fiction Coll.
--The Worms Are Singing. 1979. 1.75 (ISBN 0-912824-22-0). Vagabond Pr.
Bumpus, Jerry, et al. Eight Short Stories. (Illus., Orig.). 1975. pap. 2.50 (ISBN 0-930866-02-9). Helix Hse.
Bumpus, John S. Dictionary of Ecclesiastical Terms: Being a History & Explanation of Certain Terms Used in Architecture, Ecclesiology, Liturgiology, Music, Ritual, Cathedral, Constitution, Etc. LC 68-30653. 1969. Repr. of 1910 ed. 35.00x (ISBN 0-8103-3321-X). Gale.
Bumpus, Judith, tr. see Angulo, Diego & Perez-Sanchez, A. E.
Bumpus, Marguerite J., jt. auth. see McGuire, Marion L.
Bumsted, J. M. Henry Alline, Seventeen Forty-Eight to Seventeen Eighty-Four. LC 73-24664. (Canadian Biographical Studies). pap. 32.00 (ISBN 0-317-26935-6, 2023598). Bks Demand UMI.
Bumsted, J. M., ed. Canadian History Before Confederation: Essays & Interpretations. LC 77-187766. pap. 130.50 (ISBN 0-317-28003-1, 2055804). Bks Demand UMI.
Bumsted, J. M., ed. see Walker, Alexander.
Bunak, Viktor V., et al. Contributions to the Physical Anthropology of the Soviet Union. Howells, William W., tr. LC 60-1045. (Harvard University. Peabody Museum of Archaeology & Ethnology. Russian Translation Ser.: Vol. 1, Pt. 2). Repr. of 1960 ed. lib. bdg. 32.50 (ISBN 0-404-52642-X). AMS Pr.

Bunbury, Charles J. Journal of a Residence at the Cape of Good Hope. LC 71-97358. (Illus.). Repr. of 1848 ed. 19.75x (ISBN 0-8371-2447-6, BUR&, Pub. by Negro U Pr). Greenwood.

Bunbury, E. H. A History of Ancient Geography: Among the Greeks & Romans from the Earliest Ages till the Fall of the Roman Empire, 2 vols. (Illus.). 1979. Repr. of 1879 ed. Set. text ed. 185.75x (ISBN 90-7026-511-7). Humanities.

Bunbury, F. J., tr. see Balbo, Count C.

Bunce, Arthur C. Economic Nationalism & the Farmer. 15.25 (ISBN 0-8369-6968-5, 7849). Ayer Co Pubs.

Bunce, David, tr. see Bharati, Subramania.

Bunce, Donald F., 2nd. Atlas of Arterial Histology. LC 72-13843. (Illus.). 250p. 1975. 37.50 (ISBN 0-87527-096-4). Green.

Bunce, Gerry M., ed. High Energy Spin Physics, 1982: American Institute of Physics Proceedings, No. 95. LC 83-70154. 637p. 1983. lib. bdg. 44.00 (ISBN 0-88318-194-0). Am Inst Physics.

Bunce, J. W. The Integrity of Platform Superstructures: Analysis in Accordance with API RP2A. (Illus.). 200p. 1985. text ed. 40.00x (ISBN 0-00-383162-0, Pub. by Collins England). Sheridan.

Bunce, James E. & Harmond, Richard P., eds. Long Island As America: A Documentary History. (Empire State Historical Publications Ser.). 1977. 17.95x (ISBN 0-8046-9171-1, Pub. by Kennikat). Assoc Faculty Pr.

Bunce, Michael. Rural Settlement in An Urban World. 1981. 25.00x (ISBN 0-312-69605-1). St Martin.

Bunce, Oliver B. see Censor, pseud.

Bunce, Valerie. Do New Leaders Make a Difference? Executive Succession & Public Policy Under Capitalism & Socialism. LC 81-2124. 320p. 1981. 29.00 (ISBN 0-691-07631-6); pap. 9.95 (ISBN 0-691-02205-4). Princeton U Pr.

Bunce, William K., ed. Religions in Japan. LC 59-9234. 216p. 1981. pap. 5.25 (ISBN 0-8048-0500-8). C E Tuttle.

Buncel, E. Carbanions: Mechanistic & Isotopic Aspects. (Reaction Mechanisms in Organic Chemistry Ser.: Vol. 9). 1974. 59.75 (ISBN 0-444-41190-9). Elsevier.

--Tritium in Organic Chemistry. (Isotopes in Organic Chemistry Ser.: Vol. 4). 300p. 1978. 70.25 (ISBN 0-444-41741-9). Elsevier.

Buncel, E. & Durst, T. Comprehensive Carbanion Chemistry: Selectivity in Carbon-Carbon Bond Formation Reactions, Pt. B. (Studies in Organic Chemistry: Vol. 5B). 1984. 75.00 (ISBN 0-444-42267-6). Elsevier.

Buncel, E. & Lee. Isotopes in Cationic Reactions. (Isotopes in Organic Chemistry Ser.: Vol. 5). 234p. 1980. 70.25 (ISBN 0-444-41927-6). Elsevier.

Buncel, E. & Durst, T., eds. Comprehensive Carbanion Chemistry. (Studies in Organic Chemistry: Vol. 5, Pt. A). 400p. 1980. 78.75 (ISBN 0-444-41913-6). Elsevier.

Buncel, E. & Lee, C. C., eds. Carbon-Thirteen in Organic Chemistry. (Isotopes in Organic Chemistry Ser.: Vol. 3). 288p. 1977. 70.25 (ISBN 0-444-41472-X). Elsevier.

--Isotopes in Hydrogen Transfer Processes. (Isotopes in Organic Chemistry: Vol. 2). 318p. 1976. 70.25 (ISBN 0-444-41352-9). Elsevier.

--Isotopes in Molecular Rearrangements. (Isotopes in Organic Chemistry Ser.: Vol. 1). 320p. 1975. 70.25 (ISBN 0-444-41223-9). Elsevier.

--Isotopes in Organic Chemistry: Isotopic Effects - Recent Developments in Theory & Experiment, Vol. 6. 266p. 1984. 85.25 (ISBN 0-444-42368-0, I-236-84). Elsevier.

Buncel, E., et al. Electron Deficient Aromatic & Heteroaromatic-Base Interactions: Chemistry of Anionic Sigma Complexes. (Studies in Organic Chemistry: No. 14). 350p. 1984. 115.50 (ISBN 0-444-42305-2). Elsevier.

Bunch, A. J. Hospital & Medical Libraries in Scotland: An Historical & Sociological Study, 1975. 186p. 1982. 40.00x (ISBN 0-900649-07-0, Pub. by Scot Lib Scotland). State Mutual Bk.

Bunch, Allan. The Basics of Information Work. 159p. 1984. lib. bdg. 17.50 (ISBN 0-85157-376-2, Pub. by Bingley England). Shoe String.

--Community Information Services. 168p. 1982. 17.50 (ISBN 0-85157-318-5, Pub. by Bingley England). Shoe String.

Bunch, Bryan. Mathematical Fallacies & Paradoxes. 1982. 18.95 (ISBN 0-442-24905-5). Van Nos Reinhold.

Bunch, Bryan, ed. The Facts on File Scientific Yearbook 1985. Date not set. price not set. Facts on File.

--The Science Almanac 1985-1986. LC 84-20405. 576p. 1984. 19.95 (ISBN 0-385-19321-1, Anchor Pr); pap. 12.95 (ISBN 0-385-19320-3, Anchor Pr). Doubleday.

Bunch, Bryan H. Practical Herb Gardening: With Recipes. (Illus.). 210p. (Orig.). 1984. 15.95 (ISBN 0-8306-0661-0, 1661); pap. 11.50 (ISBN 0-8306-1661-6). TAB Bks.

Bunch, Charlotte & Myron, Nancy, eds. Class & Feminism. (Illus.). 1974. pap. 3.50 (ISBN 0-88447-004-0). Diana Pr.

Bunch, Charlotte & Pollack, Sandra, eds. Learning Our Way: Essay in Feminist Education. (Crossing Press Feminist Ser.). 334p. (Orig.). 1983. 22.95 (ISBN 0-89594-112-0); pap. 11.95 (ISBN 0-89594-111-2). Crossing Pr.

Bunch, Charlotte, jt. ed. see Myron, Nancy.

Bunch, Chris, jt. auth. see Cole, Allan.

Bunch, Christopher, jt. auth. see Bunch, Michael.

Bunch, Clarence, ed. Art Education: A Guide to Information Sources. LC 73-17518. (Art & Architecture Information Guide Ser.: Vol. 6). 1977. 60.00x (ISBN 0-8103-1272-7). Gale.

Bunch, Gay. Crossword Puzzles for Texas: The Land & Its People. 30p. 1982. pap. 6.95 (ISBN 0-937460-33-8). Hendrick Long.

Bunch, Glynn H. The Chosen. LC 78-51038. 1979. 13.95 (ISBN 0-87949-112-4). Ashley Bks.

Bunch, M. A. Dynamics of the Singing Voice. (Disorders of Human Communications Ser.: Vol. 6). (Illus.). 156p. 1982. 30.00 (ISBN 0-387-81667-4). Springer-Verlag.

Bunch, M. E., jt. ed. see Paillat, P. M.

Bunch, Michael & Bunch, Christopher. I Love the Cubs Coloring Book. (Illus.). 32p. 1984. pap. 3.95 (ISBN 0-912083-03-4). Diamond Communications.

Bunch, Roger, jt. auth. see Bunch, Roland.

Bunch, Roland. Two Ears of Corn: A Guide to People-Centered Agricultural Improvement. (Illus.). 250p. 1982. pap. 7.95 (ISBN 0-942716-03-5). World Neigh.

Bunch, Roland & Bunch, Roger. The Highland Maya: Patterns of Life & Clothing in Indian Guatemala. LC 77-77864. 1977. 7.95 (ISBN 0-930740-01-7). Indigenous Pubns.

Bunch, Wilton H., et al. Modern Management of Myelomeningocele. LC 75-161035. (Illus.). 320p. 1972. 22.50 (ISBN 0-87527-097-2). Green.

Bunche, Ralph J. The Political Status of the Negro in the Age of F. D. R. Grantham, Dewey W., ed. LC 72-96327. (Illus.). xxxiv, 682p. 1975. pap. 10.00x (ISBN 0-226-08029-3). U of Chicago Pr.

Buncher & Tsay. Statistics in the Pharmaceutical Industry. (Statistics; Textbooks & Monographs Ser.: Vol. 36). 544p. 1981. 59.75 (ISBN 0-8247-1163-7). Dekker.

Buncher, Judith, ed. The CIA & the Security Debate, 1971-75, Vol. 1. LC 75-18070. (Editorials on File Ser). 362p. 1976. lib. bdg. 19.95 (ISBN 0-87196-358-2). Facts on File.

--CIA & the Security Debate, 1971-76, Vol. 2. new ed. LC 75-18070. 240p. 1977. lib. bdg. 19.95 (ISBN 0-87196-364-7). Facts on File.

Buncher, Judith F., ed. Crime & Punishment in America. 300p. 1978. lib. bdg. 19.95x. Facts on File.

--Human Rights & American Diplomacy 1975-77. 1977. lib. bdg. 19.95x (ISBN 0-87196-365-5). Facts on File.

Buncke. Microsurgical Transplantation: An Audio-Visual Program. 1983. 500.00 (ISBN 0-8391-1826-0, 19909). Univ Park.

Buncke, Harry, jt. auth. see Serafin, Donald.

Bund, J. W. The Civil War in Worchestershire, 1642-1646. 267p. 1979. Repr. of 1905 ed. text ed. 16.25x (ISBN 0-904387-32-1, Pub. by Alan Sutton England). Humanities.

Bunday, B. D. BASIC Linear Programming. 192p. 1984. pap. 14.95 (ISBN 0-7131-3509-3). E Arnold.

--BASIC Optimization Methods. 192p. 1984. pap. 14.95 (ISBN 0-7131-3506-9). E Arnold.

Bundesen, Lynne. Us: The People of Washington, D.C. LC 76-39648. (Illus.). 193p. 1976. ltd. ed. 35.00 (ISBN 0-87491-176-1). Acropolis.

Bundestag, Deutscher & Datenverarbeitung, Gruppe, eds. Thesaurus fur Parlamentsmaterialien. 180p. 1985. lib. bdg. 36.00 (ISBN 3-598-10584-3). K G Saur.

Bundesverband der Pharmzeutischen Industrie, ed. Rote Liste 1982. 1167p. (Ger.). 1982. 45.00 (ISBN 3-87193-063-6). Intl Pubns Serv.

Bundgaard, Hans, et al. Drug Design & Adverse Reactions. 1977. 75.00 (ISBN 0-12-141150-8). Acad Pr.

Bundgaard, Hans, et al, eds. Optimization of Drug Delivery. (Alfred Benzon Symposium Ser.: Vol. 17). 436p. 1982. text ed. 43.00 (ISBN 87-16-08979-0). Raven.

Bundschuh, Ernest. Physical Education for Handicapped Students: Project Dart. (Illus.). 72p. (Orig.). 1983. pap. text ed. 6.95 (ISBN 0-8331-6690-5, 6690). Hubbard Sci.

Bundschuh, Rick, compiled by. Miles Ahead. LC 84-4799. 154p. 1984. pap. 3.95 (ISBN 0-8307-0950-9, S181102). Regal.

Bundt, Nancy. The Fire Station Book. LC 80-16617. (Illus.). 32p. (ps-3). 1981. PLB 8.95g (ISBN 0-87614-126-2). Carolrhoda Bks.

Bundtzen, Lynda K. Plath's Incarnations: Women & Creative Process. (Women & Culture Ser.). 240p. 1983. text ed. 25.00x (ISBN 0-472-10033-5). U of Mich Pr.

Bundy, et al. Dairy Production. 4th ed. 1977. 31.52 (ISBN 0-13-197079-8). P-H.

Bundy, A., ed. Artificial Intelligence: An Introductory Course. 386p. 1979. 32.50 (ISBN 0-444-19463-0, North Holland). Elsevier.

--Catalogue of Artificial Intelligence Tools. (Symbolic Computation, Artificial Intelligence Ser.). (Illus.). xxv, 150p. 1984. pap. 17.00 (ISBN 0-387-13938-9). Springer-Verlag.

Bundy, Alan. The Computer Modeling of Mathematical Reasoning. 1984. 17.00 (ISBN 0-12-141252-0). Acad Pr.

Bundy, Alan, ed. see International Joint Conference on Artificial Intelligence, 8th, 1983.

Bundy, Alison. A Bad Business: Short Fictions of Alison Bundy. (No. 27). 72p. (Orig.). 1985. pap. 6.95 (ISBN 0-918786-31-2). Lost Roads.

Bundy, Clarence E., et al. Livestock & Poultry Production. 4th ed. 1975. text ed. 31.52 (ISBN 0-13-538579-2). P-H.

--Swine Production. (gr. 10-12). 1976. text ed. 31.50 (ISBN 0-13-879783-8). P-H.

Bundy, Colin. The Rise & Fall of South African Peasantry. LC 79-62841. (Perspectives on Southern Africa Ser.: No. 28). 1979. 34.00x (ISBN 0-520-03754-5). U of Cal Pr.

Bundy, Darcie. The Affordable Baby. LC 84-48581. 224p. 1985. 14.95 (ISBN 0-06-015446-2, HarpT). Har-Row.

--The Affordable Baby. LC 84-48581. 224p. 1985. pap. 6.95 (ISBN 0-06-091263-4, CN). Har-Row.

Bundy, David. One Hundred Acres-More or Less: History of Bow, New Hampshire. LC 75-38922. (Illus.). 576p. 1975. 20.00x (ISBN 0-914016-24-5). Phoenix Pub.

Bundy, David D. Keswick: A Bibliographic Introduction to the Higher Life Movements. LC 76-369083. (Occasional Bibliographic Papers of the B. L. Fisher Library: No. 3). 89p. 1975. 3.00 (ISBN 0-914368-03-6). Asbury Theological.

Bundy, Elroy L. Studia Pindarica. LC 83-40482. (Cal Ser.: No. 696). 150p. 1984. text ed. 18.00x (ISBN 0-520-05098-3); pap. 9.95 (ISBN 0-520-05111-4). U of Cal Pr.

Bundy, McGeorge. Strength of Government. LC 68-54016. (Godkin Lectures: 1968). 1968. 8.95x (ISBN 0-674-84300-2). Harvard U Pr.

Bundy, McGeorge & Muskie, Edmund S. Presidential Promises & Performance. LC 80-1855. (Charles C. Moskowitz Memorial Lectures). 1980. 10.95 (ISBN 0-02-904290-9). Free Pr.

Bundy, McGeorge, jt. auth. see Stimson, Henry L.

Bundy, McGeorge, ed. see Acheson, Dean.

Bundy, Mary L. Metropolitan Public Library Users. 1968. pap. 3.50 (ISBN 0-911808-03-5). U of Md Lib Serv.

Bundy, Mary L. & Goodstein, Sylvia, eds. Library's Public Revisited. (Student Contribution Ser: No. 1). 1967. pap. 3.00 (ISBN 0-911808-01-9). U of Md Lib Serv.

Bundy, Mary L., et al. The National Prison Directory: A Prison Reform Organizational & Resource Directory with a Special Section on Public Library Service to Prisoners. 3rd ed. LC 85-116778. write for info. Urban Info Interp.

Bundy, Mary Lee & Wasserman, Paul, eds. Reader in Research Methods for Librarianship. LC 70-86858. 363p. 1970. 28.50 (ISBN 0-313-24045-0, ZRM/). Greenwood.

Bundy, Mary Lee, jt. ed. see Wasserman, Paul.

Bundy, Robert, ed. Images of the Future: The Twenty-First Century & Beyond. LC 75-32697. 1976. 17.95 (ISBN 0-87975-048-0). Prometheus Bks.

Bundy, Robert E. Just Visiting, & Other Vermont Sketches. 1974. pap. 3.75 (ISBN 0-914378-07-4). Countryman.

Bundy, William, ed. America & the World, 1983. (Pergamon Policy Studies on International Politics). 275p. 1984. pap. 8.95 (ISBN 0-08-031592-5). Pergamon.

Bundy, William P., ed. America & the World, 1978. (Pergamon Policy Studies). 260p. 1979. 36.00 (ISBN 0-08-023896-3); pap. 7.95 (ISBN 0-08-023895-5). Pergamon.

--America & the World, 1979. (Pergamon Policy Studies, Foreign A). 281p. 1980. pap. 7.95 (ISBN 0-08-025951-0). Pergamon.

--America & the World, 1981. (Pergamon Policy Studies on International Politics Ser.). 294p. 1982. 33.00 (ISBN 0-08-028834-0, K125); pap. 7.95 (ISBN 0-08-028827-8). Pergamon.

--The Nuclear Controversy: A Foreign Affairs Reader. 1985. pap. 9.95 (ISBN 0-452-00736-4, Mer). NAL.

Bundy, William P., ed. & intro. by. The World Economic Crisis. 256p. 1975. 8.95x (ISBN 0-393-05545-0). Norton.

Bundy, William P., jt. ed. see Foreign Affairs.

Bung, K. Toward a Theory of Programmed Learning Foreign Language. (Janua Linguarum Ser. Didactica: No. 1). 1973. text ed. 10.80x (ISBN 90-2792-383-3). Mouton.

Bungay, Henry. Advanced Biochemical Engineering. 45.00 (ISBN 0-471-81279-X). Wiley.

Bungay, Henry R. Energy, the Biomass Options. LC 80-19645. 347p. 1981. 46.50x (ISBN 0-471-04386-9, Pub. by Wiley-Interscience). Wiley.

Bungay, Stanley, jt. auth. see Leavell, Stuart.

Bunge, H. J. & Esling, C., eds. Quantitative Texture Analysis. (Illus.). 505p. 1982. lib. bdg. 73.00 (ISBN 3-88355-032-9, Pub. by DGM Metallurgy Germany). IR Pubns.

--Quantitative Texture Analysis. 551p. 1981. 100.00 (ISBN 0-9911001-8-2). Heyden.

Bunge, Hans. Texture Analysis in Materials Science: Mathematical Methods. 2nd ed. Morris, Peter, tr. from Ger. LC 79-40054. 1982. text ed. 99.95 (ISBN 0-408-10642-5). Butterworth.

Bunge, M. Method, Model & Matter. LC 72-86102. (Synthese Library: No. 44). 196p. 1973. lib. bdg. 26.00 (ISBN 90-277-0252-7, Pub. by Reidel Holland). Kluwer Academic.

--Philosophy of Physics. LC 72-86103. (Synthese Library: No. 45). 248p. 1973. lib. bdg. 34.00 (ISBN 90-277-0253-5, Pub. by Reidel Holland). Kluwer Academic.

Bunge, M., ed. & pref. by. The Methodological Unity of Science. LC 73-83554. (Theory & Decision Library Ser: No. 3). 1973. lib. bdg. 39.50 (ISBN 90-277-0354-X, Pub. by Reidel Holland); pap. 24.00 (ISBN 90-277-0404-X, Pub. by Reidel Holland). Kluwer Academic.

Bunge, M., ed. Studies in the Foundations, Methodology & Philosophy of Science, 4 vols. Incl. Vol. 1. Delaware Seminar in the Foundations of Physics. (Illus.); Vol. 2. Quantum Theory & Reality. 1967. 28.00 (ISBN 0-387-03993-7); Vol. 3, Pt. 1. The Search for System. (Illus.). xii, 536p. 1967. 54.50 (ISBN 0-387-03994-5); Vol. 3, Pt. 2. The Search for Truth. (Illus.). viii, 374p. 1967. 47.00 (ISBN 0-387-03995-3); Vol. 4. Problems in the Foundations of Physics. (Illus.). 1971. 28.00 (ISBN 0-387-05490-1). LC 71-163433. Springer-Verlag.

Bunge, M., ed. see Symposium on Exact Philosophy, 1st, Montreal, 1971.

Bunge, M. A., jt. ed. see Shea, William R.

Bunge, Mario. Causality & Modern Science. LC 78-74117. (Illus.). 1979. pap. 8.95 (ISBN 0-486-23728-1). Dover.

--Metascientific Queries. (Illus.). 328p. 1959. 24.50x (ISBN 0-398-00251-7). C C Thomas.

--The Mind-Body Problem: A Psychobiological Approach. (Foundations & Philosophy of Science & Technology: Vol. 1). (Illus.). 245p. 1980. 39.00 (ISBN 0-08-024720-2); pap. 15.00 (ISBN 0-08-024719-9). Pergamon.

--Scientific Materialism. 240p. 1981. 48.00 (ISBN 90-277-1304-9, Pub. by Reidel Holland). Kluwer Academic.

--Treatise on Basic Philosophy: Epistemology & Methodology I. 1983. lib. bdg. 64.00 (ISBN 90-277-1511-4, Pub. by Reidel Holland); pap. text ed. 34.00 (ISBN 90-277-1523-8, Pub. by Reidel Holland). Kluwer Academic.

--Treatise on Basic Philosophy: Epistemology & Methodology II, Vol. 6. 1983. lib. bdg. 50.00 (ISBN 90-277-1634-X, Pub. by Reidel Holland); pap. text ed. 28.00 (ISBN 90-277-1635-8, Pub. by Reidel Holland). Kluwer Academic.

--Treatise on Basic Philosophy: Semantics II, Interpretation & Truth, Vol. 2. LC 74-83872. 1974. lib. bdg. 39.50 (ISBN 90-277-0535-6, Pub. by Reidel Holland); pap. 24.00 (ISBN 90-277-0573-9). Kluwer Academic.

--Treatise on Basic Philosophy: Semantics I, Sense & Reference, Vol. 1. LC 74-83872. 183p. 1974. lib. bdg. 37.00 (ISBN 90-277-0534-8, Pub. by Reidel Holland); pap. 21.000 (ISBN 90-277-0572-0). Kluwer Academic.

--Treatise on Basic Philosophy, Vol. 3: Ontology I--the Furniture of the World. 1977. lib. bdg. 55.00 (ISBN 90-277-0780-4, Pub. by Reidel Holland); pap. 29.00 (ISBN 90-277-0785-5). Kluwer Academic.

--Treatise on Basic Philosophy, Vol. 4, Ontology 11. (Treatise on Basic Philosophy Ser.: No. 4). 1979. lib. bdg. 50.00 (ISBN 90-277-0944-0, Pub. by Reidel Holland); pap. 27.50 (ISBN 90-277-0945-9). Kluwer Academic.

--Treatise on Basic Philosophy, Vol. 7: Epistemology & Methodology III, Philosophy of Science & Technology Pt I: Formal & Physical Science. 1985. lib. bdg. 39.00 (ISBN 90-277-1903-9, Pub. by Reidel Holland); pap. text ed. 22.00 (ISBN 90-277-1904-7). Kluwer Academic.

--Treatise on Basic Philosophy, Vol. 7: Epistemology & Methodology III, Philosophy of Science & Technology Part II: Life Science, Social Science & Technology. 1985. lib. bdg. 49.00 (ISBN 90-277-1913-6, Pub. by Reidel Holland); pap. text ed. 24.50 (ISBN 90-277-1914-4). Kluwer Academic.

Bunge, Nancy. Finding the Words: Interviews with Writers Who Teach. LC 84-8544. xiv, 192p. 1985. 21.95x (ISBN 0-8040-0861-2, Swallow); pap. 9.95 (ISBN 0-8040-0862-0). Ohio U Pr.

Bunge, Nikolai K. Esquisses de litterature politico-economique. LC 68-56719. (Research & Source Works Ser.: No. 697). 1971. Repr. of 1898 ed. lib. bdg. 32.00 (ISBN 0-8337-0418-4). B Franklin.

Bunge, Nikolai K. A Critique of the Russian State. Klimenko, Gennady, ed. 170p. 1982. cancelled (ISBN 0-940670-13-5). Kingston Pr.

Bunge, Robert. An American Urphilosophie: An American Philosophy-BP (Before Pragmatism) LC 83-19782. 218p. (Orig.). 1984. lib. bdg. 22.00 (ISBN 0-8191-3599-2); pap. text ed. 11.50 (ISBN 0-8191-3600-X). U Pr of Amer.

Bunge, William. Fitzgerald: Geography of a Revolution. (Illus.). 256p. 1971. text ed. 24.95 (ISBN 0-87073-084-3). Schenkman Bks Inc.

Bunger, H. J. see Werner, H. & Wuytack, L.

Bunger, James, ed. Chemistry of Asphaltenes. Li, Norman C. LC 81-19053. (Advances in Chemistry Ser.: No. 195). 1981. 49.95 (ISBN 0-8412-0592-2). Am Chemical.

Bunger, Robert L. Islamization among the Upper Pokomo. 2nd ed. LC 80-242. (Foreign & Comparative Studies-African Ser.: No. 33). 128p. (Orig.). 1979. pap. 7.00x (ISBN 0-915984-55-5). Syracuse U Foreign Comp.

Bunger, W. B., jt. auth. see Riddick, J. A.

Bunget, I. & Popescu, M. Physics of Solid Dielectrics. (Materials Science Monographs: No. 19). 446p. 1984. 90.75 (ISBN 0-444-99632-X, I-039-84). Elsevier.

Bungey, J. H., jt. auth. see Mosley, W. H.

Bungey, John H. Testing of Concrete in Structures. 1983. 41.00X (ISBN 0-412-00231-0, NO. 5017, Pub. by Chapman & Hall England). Methuen Inc.

Buni, Andrew. Robert L. Vann of the Pittsburgh Courier: Politics & Black Journalism. LC 73-7700. 1974. 24.95 (ISBN 0-8229-3274-1). U of Pittsburgh Pr.

Buni, Andrew & Rogers, Alan. Boston: City on a Hill. (Illus.). 240p. 1984. 24.95 (ISBN 0-89781-090-2). Windsor Pubns Inc.

Bunich, P. C. & Kharchev, K. Ocean & Its Resources. 149p. 1977. pap. 4.95 (ISBN 0-8285-1513-1, Pub. by Mir Pubs USSR). Imported Pubns.

Bunim. Ethics from Sinai, 3 vols. 1964. Set. 29.50 set (ISBN 0-87306-002-4); Set. pap. 16.95 set (ISBN 0-87306-003-2). Feldheim.

Bunim, Irving M. Ever Since Sinai. Wengrov, Charles, ed. 1978. 12.50 (ISBN 0-87306-138-1). Feldheim.

Bunim, Miriam S. Space in Medieval Painting & the Forerunners of Perspective. (BCL Ser. I). (Illus.). Repr. of 1940 ed. 24.50 (ISBN 0-404-01229-9). AMS Pr.

Bunin, Catherine, jt. auth. see Bunin, Sherry.

Bunin, D. A., et al. Deutsch-Russisches Worterbuch fur Eisenbahnwessen. 531p. (Ger. & Rus.). 1957. 7.95 (ISBN 0-686-92383-9, M-9060). French & Eur.

Bunin, I. Stories & Poems. 515p. 1979. 8.95 (ISBN 0-686-98357-2, Pub. by Progress Pubs USSR). Imported Pubns.

Bunin, Ivan. The Gentleman from San Francisco & Other Stories. 268p. 1979. 6.95 (ISBN 0-7011-1383-9, Pub. by Chatto & Windus). Merrimack Pub Cir.

--The Gentleman from San Francisco & Other Stories. 313p. 1980. Repr. of 1934 ed. lib. bdg. 22.00x (ISBN 0-374-91093-6). Octagon.

--In a Far Distant Land. Bowie, Robert, tr. from Rus. LC 82-21296. 1983. pap. 8.50 (ISBN 0-938920-27-8). Hermitage.

Bunin, Ivan A. Dark Avenues & Other Stories. Hare, R., tr. from Rus. LC 76-23875. (Classics of Russian Literature). 1977. 15.00 (ISBN 0-88355-479-8); pap. 10.00 (ISBN 0-88355-480-1). Hyperion Conn.

--Grammar of Love. Cournos, John, tr. from Rus. LC 76-23876. (Classics of Russian Literature Ser.). 1977. 15.00 (ISBN 0-88355-481-X); pap. 3.50 (ISBN 0-88355-482-8). Hyperion Conn.

--Memories & Portraits. LC 68-8053. (Illus.). 1968. Repr. of 1951 ed. lib. bdg. 27.50x (ISBN 0-8371-0033-X, BUMP). Greenwood.

--The Well of Days. Struve, Gleb & Miles, Hamish, trs. from Rus. LC 76-23877. (Classics of Russian Literature). 1977. 13.50 (ISBN 0-88355-483-6); pap. 4.95 (ISBN 0-88355-484-4). Hyperion Conn.

Bunin, Patricia A. Do You Think We Could Have Made It & Other Love Poems for the Separated & Divorced. LC 77-91010. 1977. pap. 3.95x (ISBN 0-930946-01-4). Newaves Pub.

Bunin, Sherry & Bunin, Catherine. Is That Your Sister? 5.99 (ISBN 0-394-83230-2). NACAC.

Buning, Herbert & Naeve, Peter, eds. Computational Statistics. 348p. 1981. text ed. 39.20 (ISBN 3-11-008419-8). De Gruyter.

Buning, J. E. & Schooneveld, C. H. van. The Sentence Intonation of Contemporary Standard Russian As a Linguistic Structure. (Description & Analysis of Contemporary Standard Russian: No. 3). 1961. 23.20x (ISBN 0-686-20924-9). Mouton.

Buning, Sietze. Purpaleanie & Other Permutations. LC 78-61207. 1978. pap. 5.95 (ISBN 0-931940-00-1). Middleburg Pr.

--Style & Class. LC 82-14541. 1982. pap. 7.95 (ISBN 0-931940-06-0). Middleburg Pr.

Buning, W. De Cock & Alting, J. H. Netherlands & the World War: Studies in the War HIstory of a Neutral: Volume 3-Effect of the War Upon the Colonies. (Economic & Social History of the World War Ser.). 1928. 65.00x (ISBN 0-686-83636-7). Elliots Bks.

Bunis, Al & Williams, Roger. How to Play Winning Tennis in the Prime of Life. LC 82-80145. (Illus.). 161p. 1983. 13.95 (ISBN 0-914178-53-9, A Tennis Mag. Bk). Golf Digest.

Bunis, David M. A Guide to Reading & Writing Judezmo. 49p. 1975. soft cover 5.00 (ISBN 0-917288-01-7). ADELANTRE.

--Sephardic Studies: A Reasearch Bibliography. 1981. lib. bdg. 43.00 (ISBN 0-8240-9759-9). Garland Pub.

--Yiddish Linguistics: A Classified Bilingual Index of Yiddish Serials & Collections, 1913-1958. 1984. lib. bdg. 25.00 (ISBN 0-8240-9758-0). Garland Pub.

Bunjes, jt. auth. see Lejeune.

Bunjes, W E. Medical & Pharmaceutical Dictionary: English-German. 4th ed. 140p. 1981. 25.00 (ISBN 0-317-14286-0, Pub. by Holdan Bk Ltd UK). State Mutual Bk.

Bunjes, W. E., jt. auth. see Lejeune, F.

Bunke, H. & Bunke, O., eds. Statistical Inference in Linear Models, Vol. 1. (Probability & Mathematical Statistics Applied Probability & Statistics Section Ser.: 1-345). 400p. 1985. 54.95x (ISBN 0-471-10334-9, Pub. by Wiley-Interscience). Wiley.

Bunke, O., jt. ed. see Bunke, H.

Bunker, Andrew F. & Chaffee, Margaret. Tropical Indian Ocean Clouds. LC 69-17882. (International Indian Ocean Expedition Meteorological Monographs: No. 4). (Illus.). 1970. 30.00x (ISBN 0-8248-0083-4, Eastwest Ctr). UH Pr.

Bunker, Barbara, et al. Student's Guide to Conducting Social Science Research. LC 74-11814. 120p. 1975. pap. text ed. 7.95 (ISBN 0-87705-238-7). Human Sci Pr.

Bunker, Dusty. Numerology & Your Future. 256p. (Orig.). 1980. pap. 10.95 (ISBN 0-914918-18-4). Para Res.

Bunker, Dusty & Knowles, Victoria. Birthday Numerology. 240p. (Orig.). 1982. pap. 9.95 (ISBN 0-914918-39-7). Para Res.

Bunker, Dusty, jt. auth. see Javane, Faith.

Bunker, Edward. No Beast So Fierce. 192p. 1975. pap. 1.50 (ISBN 0-532-15146-1). Woodhill.

Bunker, Edward & Purim, Flora. Freedom Song: The Story of Flora Purim. (Orig.). 1982. pap. 2.75 (ISBN 0-425-05455-1). Berkley Pub.

Bunker, Emma C., et al. Secret Splendors of the Chinese Court: Qing Dynasty Costume from the Charlotte Hill Grant Collection. LC 81-70586. (Illus.). 80p. (Orig.). 1981. pap. 12.95 (ISBN 0-914738-25-9). Denver Art Mus.

Bunker, Frank F. The Junior High School Movement-Its Beginnings. LC 83-45417. Repr. of 1935 ed. 41.00 (ISBN 0-404-20047-8). AMS Pr.

Bunker, Gary L. & Bitton, Davis. The Mormon Graphic Image, Eighteen Thirty-Four to Nineteen Fourteen: Cartoons, Caricatures, & Illustrations. (Publications in the American West: Vol. 16). (Illus.). 116p. 1983. 19.95 (ISBN 0-87480-218-0). U of Utah Pr.

Bunker, Gerald E. The Peace Conspiracy: Wang Ching-Wei & the China War, 1937-1941. LC 78-180149. (Harvard East Asian Ser.: No. 67). pap. 85.50 (ISBN 0-317-08425-9, 2005486). Bks Demand UMI.

Bunker, Harris F. Principios Fundamentales de Evaluacion para Educadores. 4th ed. 5.00 (ISBN 0-8477-2730-0); pap. 3.75 (ISBN 0-8477-2702-5). U of PR Pr.

Bunker, John G. Liberty Ships. LC 79-6103. (Navies & Men Ser.). (Illus.). 1980. Repr. of 1972 ed. lib. bdg. 28.50x (ISBN 0-405-13032-5). Ayer Co Pubs.

Bunker, John P., et al, eds. Costs, Risks & Benefits of Surgery. (Illus.). 1977. text ed. 37.50x (ISBN 0-19-502118-5). Oxford U Pr.

Bunker, L. K. & Rotella, R. J., eds. Sport Psychology: Psychological Consideration in Maximizing Sport Psychology. 1985. 17.95 (ISBN 0-932392-20-2). Mouvement Pubns.

Bunker, Linda & Owens, De De. Golf: Better Practice for Better Play. LC 83-80712. (Illus.). 192p. (Orig.). 1984. pap. 12.95 (ISBN 0-88011-181-X). Leisure Pr.

Bunker, Linda & Rotella, Robert. Mind, Set & Match: Using Your Head to Play Better Tennis. (Illus.). 173p. 1982. 12.95 (ISBN 0-13-583484-8); pap. 6.95 (ISBN 0-13-583476-7). P-H.

Bunker, Linda, jt. auth. see Rotella, Robert.

Bunker, Linda, et al. Motivating Kids Through Play. LC 81-85625. (Illus.). 192p. (Orig.). 1982. pap. text ed. 7.95 (ISBN 0-918438-22-5). Leisure Pr.

Bunker, M. N. Handwriting Analysis: The Science of Determining Personality by Graphoanalysis. 275p. 15.95 (ISBN 0-911012-68-0). Nelson-Hall.

--What Handwriting Tells You: About Yourself, Your Friends, & Famous People. 1965. 16.95 (ISBN 0-911012-02-8). Nelson-Hall.

Bunker, Philip R. The Molecular Symmetry & Spectroscopy. LC 78-51240. 1979. 55.00 (ISBN 0-12-141350-0). Acad Pr.

Bunker, Raymond. Town & Country, City & Region? (Illus.). 164p. 1971. pap. 14.00x (ISBN 0-522-84012-4, Pub. by Melbourne U Pr). Intl Spec Bk.

Bunker, Robert, jt. auth. see Thorp, Raymond W.

Bunker, Robert M. Other Men's Skies. Repr. of 1956 ed. 26.00 (ISBN 0-527-13500-3). Kraus Repr.

Bunker, Stephen G. Underdeveloping the Amazon: Extraction, Unequal Exchange, & the Failure of the Modern State. LC 83-18197. 296p. 1985. 24.50x (ISBN 0-252-01121-X). U of Ill Pr.

Bunker, Susan M. World Studies for Christian Schools. (Heritage Studies for Christian Schools). (Illus.). (gr. 7). 1985. text ed. 22.60 (ISBN 0-89084-287-6); tchr's ed. 29.50 (ISBN 0-89084-288-4). Bob Jones Univ Pr.

Bunkina, M. Current Problems of Contemporary Capitalism. 206p. 1982. pap. 2.95 (ISBN 0-8285-2508-0, Pub. by Progress Pubs USSR). Imported Pubns.

Bunkina, M. K. U S A vs. Western Europe. 197p. 1979. 6.95 (ISBN 0-8285-1497-6, Pub. by Progress Pubs USSR). Imported Pubns.

Bunkle, Phillida, jt. ed. see Hughes, Beryl.

Bunkley, Allison, ed. see Sarmiento, Domingo F., et al.

Bunkley, Allison W. Life of Sarmiento. LC 77-90475. Repr. of 1952 ed. lib. bdg. 20.00x (ISBN 0-8371-2392-5, BULS). Greenwood.

Bunn. Comparative Models for Electrical Load Forecasting. 1985. 39.95 (ISBN 0-471-90635-2). Wiley.

Bunn, Alfred. Old England & New England, in a Series of Views Taken on the Spot, 2 vols. in 1. LC 68-20213. (Illus.). 1968. Repr. of 1853 ed. 24.50 (ISBN 0-405-08330-0, Blom Pubns). Ayer Co Pubs.

Bunn, D. S. & Warburton, A. B. The Barn Owl. (Illus.). 264p. 1982. 32.50 (ISBN 0-931130-09-3). Buteo.

Bunn, D. S., et al. The Barn Owl. 320p. 1982. 60.00x (ISBN 0-85661-032-1, Pub. by T & AD Boyser England). State Mutual Bk.

Bunn, D. W. Applied Decision & Analysis. 272p. 1984. 28.95 (ISBN 0-07-008292-8). McGraw.

Bunn, Derek W. Analysis for Optimal Decisions. LC 81-19698. 275p. 1982. 44.95 (ISBN 0-471-10132-X, Pub. by Wiley-Interscience); pap. 24.95 (ISBN 0-471-10133-8, Pub. by Wiley-Interscience). Wiley.

Bunn, Frank E., et al. Oceans from Space: Towards the Management of Our Coastal Zone. 82p. (Orig.). 1983. pap. text ed. 5.00x (ISBN 0-920380-96-4, Pub. by Inst Res Pub Canada). Brookfield Pub Co.

Bunn, H. Franklin & Forget, Bernard G. Hemoglobin: Molecular, Genetic & Clinical Aspects. (Illus.). 800p. Date not set. price not set (ISBN 0-7216-2181-3). Saunders.

Bunn, H. Franklin, et al. Hemoglobinopathies. LC 76-14678. (Major Problems in Internal Medicine Ser.: Vol. 12). 1977. text ed. 16.95 (ISBN 0-7216-2179-1). Saunders.

--Human Hemoglobins. LC 76-14677. 1977. text ed. 20.00 (ISBN 0-7216-2178-3). Saunders.

Bunn, H. W., tr. see Agabekov, Grigorii S.

Bunn, James H. The Dimensionality of Signs, Tools & Models: An Introduction. LC 80-8151. (Advances in Semiotics Ser.). (Illus.). 224p. 1981. 17.50x (ISBN 0-253-16916-X). Ind U Pr.

Bunn, John. Scientific Principles of Coaching. 2nd ed. LC 70-159445. (Illus.). 1972. 24.95 (ISBN 0-13-796177-4). P-H.

Bunn, John W. Art of Officiating Sports. 3rd ed. 1967. text ed. 24.95 (ISBN 0-13-047803-2). P-H.

Bunn, Matthew. Journal of the Adventures of Matthew Bunn. facsimile ed. 1962. pap. 1.75 (ISBN 0-911028-15-3). Newberry.

--Narrative of Matthew Bunn. 60p. Date not set. price not set (ISBN 0-685-56551-3). Ye Galleon.

Bunn, Paul. Games for Your Atari Computer: And the All-New 600. (The Dell Computer Games Ser.). 128p. 1983. pap. 5.95 comb-bound (ISBN 0-440-52800-3, Dell Trade Pbks). Dell.

Bunn, Scott. Just Hold On. LC 82-70316. 160p. (gr. 7 up). 1982. 11.95 (ISBN 0-385-28490-X). Delacorte.

--Just Hold On. 160p. (gr. 7 up). 1984. pap. 2.25 (ISBN 0-440-94331-0, LFL). Dell.

Bunn, Verne A. Buying & Selling a Small Business. Bruchey, Stuart & Carosso, Vincent P., eds. LC 78-18955. (Small Business Enterprise in America Ser.). (Illus.). 1979. Repr. of 1969 ed. lib. bdg. 14.00 (ISBN 0-405-11459-1). Ayer Co Pubs.

Bunn, William. Biennial Message of William M. Bunn, Governor of Idaho. (Shorey Historical Ser.). 22p. pap. 3.75 (ISBN 0-8466-0047-1, S47). Shorey.

Bunnag, C., jt. ed. see Prasansuk, S.

Bunnag, Jane. Buddhist Monk, Buddhist Layman: A Study of Urban Monastic Organisation in Central Thailand. LC 72-86420. (Cambridge Studies in Social Anthropology: No. 6). (Illus.). 230p. 1973. 34.50 (ISBN 0-521-08591-8). Cambridge U Pr.

Bunnag, Krachang, tr. see Suriyabongs, Luang.

Bunnell, C. A., jt. auth. see Fuchs, P. L.

Bunnell, Charlene, jt. auth. see Guthrie, Mearl.

Bunnell, David, jt. auth. see Osborne, Adam.

Bunnell, Lafayette H. Discovery of the Yosemite & the Indian War of 1851. facsimile ed. LC 72-146854. (Select Bibliographies Reprint Ser). Repr. of 1880 ed. 21.00 (ISBN 0-8369-5621-4). Ayer Co Pubs.

--Discovery of the Yosemite in 1851. Jones, William R., ed. (Illus.). 1977. pap. 6.95 (ISBN 0-89646-021-5). Outbooks.

Bunnell, Peter, intro. by. Barbara Morgan. LC 72-92282. (Illus.). 160p. pap. 6.95 (ISBN 0-88360-037-4). Amon Carter.

Bunnell, Peter, ed. see Snelling, Henry H. & Anthony, E.

Bunnell, Peter A., ed. see Woodbury, Walter E.

Bunnell, Peter C., ed. The Aesthetics of French Photography Studies. LC 76-24672. (Sources of Modern Photography Ser.). (Illus., Fr.). 1979. lib. bdg. 114.50x (ISBN 0-405-09983-5). Ayer Co Pubs.

--Nonsilver Printing Processes: Four Selections, 1886-1927. LC 72-9221. (The Literature of Photography Ser.). 22.00 (ISBN 0-405-04928-5); pap. 4.50 (ISBN 0-685-32643-8). Ayer Co Pubs.

Bunnell, Peter C. & Sobieszek, Robert A., eds. The Literature of Photography, 62 bks. 1973. Set. 1301.50 (ISBN 0-405-04889-0). Ayer Co Pubs.

--The Sources of Modern Photography Series, 51 bks. (Illus.). 1979. Vols. 1-25. lib. bdg. 559.00x (ISBN 0-405-09597-X); Vols. 26-51. lib. bdg. 1393.00x (ISBN 0-405-18980-X). Ayer Co Pubs.

--The Universal Exposition of Nineteen Hundred: Two Catalogues. LC 76-23041. (Sources of Photography Ser.). (Illus.). 1979. lib. bdg. 25.50x (ISBN 0-405-09603-8). Ayer Co Pubs.

--Willi Warstat on the Aesthetics of Art Photography, Two Selections: Original Anthology. LC 76-24679. (Sources of Modern Photography Ser.). (Illus., Ger.). 1979. lib. bdg. 21.00x (ISBN 0-405-09659-3). Ayer Co Pubs.

Bunnell, Peter C., ed. see Benthe, Arnold.

Bunnell, Peter C., ed. see Chevalier, Charles.

Bunnell, Peter C., ed. see Davanne, A.

Bunnell, Peter C., ed. see Demacy, Robert & Demachy, C. Puyo.

Bunnell, Peter C., ed. see De Saint-Victor, Niepce.

Bunnell, Peter C., ed. see Dillaye, Frederic.

Bunnell, Peter C., ed. see Eder, Josef M.

Bunnell, Peter C., ed. see Eder, Josef-Maria.

Bunnell, Peter C., ed. see Engrand, Bernard.

Bunnell, Peter C., ed. see Evrard-Blanquart, L. D.

Bunnell, Peter C., ed. see Figuier, Louis.

Bunnell, Peter C., ed. see Graff, Werner.

Bunnell, Peter C., ed. see Great Britain, Patent Office.

Bunnell, Peter C., ed. see Guerronnan, Anthony.

Bunnell, Peter C., ed. see Ken, Alexander.

Bunnell, Peter C., ed. see Kodak Limited.

Bunnell, Peter C., ed. see Kuhn, Willy.

Bunnell, Peter C., ed. see Lacan, Ernest.

Bunnell, Peter C., ed. see Lecuyer, Raymond.

Bunnell, Peter C., ed. see Lo Duca, Joseph Marie.

Bunnell, Peter C., ed. see Martin, Anton.

Bunnell, Peter C., ed. see Masuren-Matthies.

Bunnell, Peter C., ed. see Mentienne, A.

Bunnell, Peter C., ed. see Nadar, Gaspard F.

Bunnell, Peter C., ed. see Pierson & Mayer.

Bunnell, Peter C., ed. see Poore, Henry R.

Bunnell, Peter C., jt. ed. see Sobieszek, Robert A.

Bunnell, Peter C., ed. see Stenger, Erich.

Bunnell, Peter C., ed. see Stotz, Gustaf, et al.

Bunnell, Peter C., ed. see Thierry, J.

Bunnell, Peter C., ed. see Van Monckhoven, Desire.

Bunnell, Peter C., ed. see Vogel, Hermann.

Bunnell, Peter C., ed. see Von Rohr, Moritz.

Bunnell, Peter C., ed. see Whiting, John R.

Bunnell, Peter C., et al, eds. Edward Weston on Photography. LC 83-508. (Illus.). 208p. 1983. pap. 14.95 (ISBN 0-87905-147-7, Peregrine Smith). Gibbs M Smith.

Bunnell, Peter C., jt. ed. see Eder, Joseph M.

Bunnell, Robert A., jt. ed. see Campbell, Roald F.

Bunnelle, Hasse. Food for Knapsackers & Other Trail Travellers. LC 74-162395. (Totebooks Ser.). 144p. 1971. pap. 4.95 (ISBN 0-87156-049-6). Sierra.

Bunnelle, Hasse & Sarvis, Shirley. Cooking for Camp & Trail. LC 77-189535. (Totebook Ser.). 194p. 1972. pap. 5.95 (ISBN 0-87156-066-6). Sierra.

Bunnelle, Hasse R. Movable Feasts: The Backpacker Magazine Cookbook. Backpacker Magazine, ed. Date not set. cancelled (ISBN 0-671-25032-9, Fireside); pap. cancelled (ISBN 0-671-25033-7). S&S.

Bunner, Henry C. Airs from Arcadia & Elsewhere. 59.95 (ISBN 0-87968-587-5). Gordon Pr.

--Jersey Street & Jersey Lane. facsimile ed. LC 74-94705. (Short Story Index Reprint Ser.). 1896. 17.00 (ISBN 0-8369-3083-5). Ayer Co Pubs.

--Love in Old Cloathes & Other Stories. facsimile ed. LC 78-94706. (Short Story Index Reprint Ser). 1896. 18.00 (ISBN 0-8369-3084-3). Ayer Co Pubs.

--Made in France. facs. ed. LC 71-94707. (Short Story Index Reprint Ser.). 1893. 14.00 (ISBN 0-8369-3085-1). Ayer Co Pubs.

--More "Short Sixes". 1972. Repr. of 1894 ed. lib. bdg. 18.50 (ISBN 0-8422-8015-4). Irvington.

--Short Sixes: Stories to Be Read While the Candle Burns. 1972. Repr. of 1891 ed. lib. bdg. 18.00 (ISBN 0-8422-8014-6). Irvington.

--Stories: Second Stories, Vol. 1. LC 72-5900. (Short Story Index Reprint Ser). Repr. of 1916 ed. 23.50 (ISBN 0-8369-4194-2). Ayer Co Pubs.

--Suburban Sage. facs. ed. LC 76-90578. (Short Story Index Reprint Ser). 1896. 14.00 (ISBN 0-8369-3061-4). Ayer Co Pubs.

--Zadoc Pine & Other Stories. facsimile ed. LC 70-94704. (Short Story Index Reprint Ser). 1891. 18.00 (ISBN 0-8369-3086-X). Ayer Co Pubs.

Bunnett, Fanny E., tr. see Gervinus, Georg G.

Bunnett, Fanny E., tr. see Grimm, Herman F.

Bunnett, Joseph F., jt. ed. see Simmons, Howard E.

Bunney, Mary H. Viral Warts: Their Biology & Treatment. (Illus.). 1982. text ed. 21.95x (ISBN 0-19-261335-9). Oxford U Pr.

Bunney, William E., Jr. see Usdin, Earl, et al.

Bunney, William, Jr., jt. ed. see Usdin, Earl.

Bunnin, Brad & Beren, Peter. Author Law & Strategies: A Legal Guide for the Working Writer. 1st ed. LC 83-61711. (Illus.). 295p. 1983. pap. 14.95 (ISBN 0-917316-59-2). Nolo Pr.

Bunno, Michiaki, jt. ed. see Sadanaga, Ryoichi.

Bunny. Tigger: Story of a Mayan Ocelot. LC 66-12746. (Illus.). (gr. k-2). 1974. 4.95 (ISBN 0-87208-009-9). Island Pr.

Bunny, Edmund. Of Divorce for Adulterie & Marrying Againe: That There Is No Sufficient Warrant So to Do. (English Experience Ser.: No. 781). 1977. Repr. of 1612 ed. lib. bdg. 20.00 (ISBN 90-221-0781-7). Walter J Johnson.

Bunova, E. Konakovo Faience. 230p. 1978. 32.00x (ISBN 0-317-14244-5, Pub. by Collet's). State Mutual Bk.

Bunsell, A. R., jt. auth. see Harris, Bryan.

Bunsell, A. R., et al, eds. Advances in Composite Materials: Proceedings of the Third International Conference on Composite Materials, Paris, France, 26-29 August, 1980, 2 vols. LC 80-40997. 2000p. 1980. Set. 235.00 (ISBN 0-08-026717-3). Pergamon.

Bunselmeyer, Robert E. The Cost of the War 1914-1919: British Economic War Aims and the Origins of Reparation. 240p. 1975. 21.00 (ISBN 0-208-01551-5, Archon). Shoe String.

Bunshah, R. F., ed. Techniques of Metals Research. 802p. 1968. Vol. 1, Pt. 2. 51.00 (ISBN 0-470-12197-1, Pub. by Wiley). Krieger.

--Techniques of Metals Research: Techniques Involving Extreme Environment, Nondestructive Techniques, Computer Methods in Metals Research, & Data Analysis, Vol. 7, Pt. 2. LC 69-20260. 427p. 1976. 53.50 (ISBN 0-471-12241-6). Krieger.

--Techniques of Metals Research: Techniques of Material Preparation & Handling, Vol. 1, Pt 1. LC 67-20260. 385p. 1968. 28.00 (ISBN 0-470-12195-5). Krieger.

Bunshah, Rointan F., et al. Deposition Technologies for Films & Coatings: Developments & Applications. LC 82-7862. (Illus.). 585p. 1983. 69.00 (ISBN 0-8155-0906-5). Noyes.

Bunson, Maggie. Faith in Paradise. 1977. 8.00 (ISBN 0-8198-0414-2). Dghtrs St Paul.

--Founding of Faith. 1977. 6.00 (ISBN 0-8198-0412-6); pap. 5.00 (ISBN 0-8198-0413-4). Dghtrs St Paul.

Bunster, Ximena & Chaney, Elsa M. Sellers & Servants: Working Women in Lima, Peru. 200p. 1985. 21.95 (ISBN 0-03-060543-1). Praeger.

Bunstock, Richard L. A High Plains Legacy. (Jelm Press Poets Ser.). 1982. pap. 6.95 (ISBN 0-936204-43-5). Jelm Mtn.

Bunt, A. C. Modern Potting Composts. 1976. 23.75x (ISBN 0-271-01221-8, 75-42969). Pa St U Pr.

Bunt, Cyril G. British Potters & Pottery Today. 80p. 1981. 30.00x (ISBN 0-85317-440-7, Pub. by Lewis Pubs). State Mutual Bk.

Bunt, Harry. Mass Terms & Model-Theoretic Semantics. (Cambridge Studies in Linguistics: No. 42). (Illus.). 325p. Date not set. price not set (ISBN 0-521-25681-X). Cambridge U Pr.

Bunt, Richard B., jt. auth. see Tremblay, Jean P.

Bunt, Richard B., jt. auth. see Tremblay, Jean-Paul.

Bunt, Sidney & Gargrave, Ron. The Politics of Youth Clubs. 1982. 30.00x (ISBN 0-86155-034-X, Pub. by Natl Youth Bur England). State Mutual Bk.

Buntain, D. N. The Holy Ghost & Fire. 100p. 1956. 1.25 (ISBN 0-88243-525-6, 02-0525). Gospel Pub.

Buntain, Mark, et al. Miracle in the Mirror. LC 81-70999. (Illus.). 155p. 1982. pap. 3.50 (ISBN 0-87123-352-5, 210352). Bethany Hse.

Buntain, Ruth J. Children in the Shadows. 78p. pap. 4.95 (ISBN 0-686-82632-9). Review & Herald.

--A Cross or a Ladder? (Uplook Ser.). 31p. 1970. pap. 0.75 (ISBN 0-8163-0069-0, 03654-1). Pacific Pr Pub Assn.

Bunte, Hermann & Langhans, Peter, eds. A Century of Ulcer Surgery: Medical & Surgical Therapy Today. (Illus.). 316p. 1984. pap. 44.50 (ISBN 0-8067-2391-2). Urban & S.

Buntebarth, G. Geothermics: An Introduction. Chapman, I. M. & Chapman, D. S., trs. from Ger. (Universitext Ser.). (Illus.). 150p. 1984. pap. 22.50 (ISBN 0-387-12751-8). Springer-Verlag.

Buntenkoetter, S., jt. auth. see Kaemmerer, K.

Buntin, Kathleen R. The Living Half. Knowles, Eleanor, ed. LC 84-71994. 96p. 1984. 5.95 (ISBN 0-87747-812-0). Deseret Bk.

Bunting. Maggie the Freak. (Young Romance Ser.). (Illus.). 32p. (gr. 3-9). 1985. 7.95 (ISBN 0-317-31260-X). Creative Ed.

--Oh, Rick! (Young Romance Ser.). (Illus.). 32p. (gr. 3-9). 1985. 7.95 (ISBN 0-317-31262-6). Creative Ed.

--The Space People. (Science Fiction Ser.). (Illus.). 32p. (gr. 3-9). pap. 3.95 (ISBN 0-317-31268-5); cassette 8.95 (ISBN 0-317-31269-3). Creative Ed.

--Survival Camp. (Young Romance Ser.). (Illus.). 32p. (gr. 3-9). 1985. 7.95 (ISBN 0-317-31264-2). Creative Ed.

--Two Different Girls. (Young Romance Ser.). (Illus.). 32p. (gr. 3-9). 1985. 7.95 (ISBN 0-317-31266-9). Creative Ed.

Bunting, et al. Taos Adobes. 1975. pap. 7.95 (ISBN 0-89013-088-4). Museum NM Pr.

Bunting, A. H., jt. ed. see Summerfield, R. J.

Bunting, Bainbridge. Early Architecture in New Mexico. LC 76-21511. (Illus.). 122p. 1976. pap. 12.95 (ISBN 0-8263-0435-4). U of NM Pr.

--Harvard: An Architectural History. Floyd, Margaret H., ed. (Illus.). 352p. 1985. text ed. 30.00x (ISBN 0-674-37290-5, Belknap Pr). Harvard U Pr.

--Houses of Boston's Back Bay: An Architectural History 1840-1917. LC 66-21334. (Illus.). 1967. 25.00 (ISBN 0-674-40900-0, Belknap Pr); pap. 12.50 (ISBN 0-674-40901-9). Harvard U Pr.

--John Gaw Meem: Southwestern Architect. LC 83-10404. (Illus.). 192p. 1983. 29.95 (ISBN 0-8263-0671-3). U of NM Pr.

Bunting, Basil. Collected Poems. 200p. (Orig.). 1985. 19.95 (ISBN 0-918825-27-X); pap. 12.95 (ISBN 0-918825-16-4). Moyer Bell Ltd.

Bunting, Basil, ed. Joseph Skipsey: Selected Poems. 96p. (Pub. by Ceolfrith Pr England). Intl Spec Bk.

Bunting, Brian. Moses Kotane: South African Revolutionary. (Illus.). 1975. 8.00 (ISBN 0-8285-9082-6, Pub. by Inkululeko). Imported Pubns.

Bunting, Christine, ed. Reference Tools for Fine Arts Visual Resources Collections. (Occasional Papers: 4). 56p. 1984. pap. 12.00 (ISBN 0-942740-02-5). Art Libs Soc.

Bunting, David. Statistical View of the Trusts: A Manual of Large American Industrial & Mining Corporations Active Around 1900. LC 72-9824. (Contributions in Economics & Economic History Ser.: No. 9). 311p. 1974. lib. bdg. 35.00 (ISBN 0-8371-6624-1, BOM/). Greenwood.

Bunting, Diane T., jt. auth. see Dutton, Allen A.

Bunting, E. S. Forage Maize. 346p. 1978. 89.00x (ISBN 0-7084-0082-5, Pub. by CAB Bks England). State Mutual Bk.

Bunting, E. S., ed. Production & Utilisation of Protein in Oilseed Crops. 390p. 1981. 52.00 (ISBN 90-247-2532-1, Pub. by Martinus Nijhoff Netherlands). Kluwer Academic.

Bunting, Ethel-Jane W. Sindhi Tombs & Textiles: The Persistence of Pattern. LC 79-56816. (Illus.). 76p. 1980. 35.00x (ISBN 0-8263-0544-X); pap. 14.95x (ISBN 0-8263-0540-7). U of NM Pr.

Bunting, Eve. The Big Cheese. LC 76-45381. (gr. 2-5). 1977. 8.95 (ISBN 0-02-715370-3, 71537). Macmillan.

--The Big Find. (Challenge Bks). (Illus.). (gr. 4-8). 1979. PLB 7.95 (ISBN 0-87191-681-9). Creative Ed.

--The Big Red Barn. LC 78-12186. (Let Me Read Ser.). (Illus.). (gr. k-3). 1979. pap. 6.95 (ISBN 0-15-611938-2, VoyB). HarBraceJ.

--Blackbird Singing. LC 79-23294. (Illus.). 96p. (gr. 5-9). 1980. 8.95 (ISBN 0-02-715360-6). Macmillan.

--Blackbird Singing. (Illus.). 96p. (gr. 4-6). 1983. pap. 1.95 (ISBN 0-590-32145-5, Apple Paperbacks). Scholastic Inc.

--The Cloverdale Switch. LC 79-2404. (gr. 7 up). 1979. 9.57 (ISBN 0-397-31866-9); PLB 9.89 (ISBN 0-397-31867-7). Lipp Jr Bks.

--The Creature of Cranberry Cove. LC 76-18124. (No Such Things.. Ser.). (Illus.). (gr. 2-6). 1976. PLB 6.95 (ISBN 0-88436-300-7, 35484); pap. 3.95 (ISBN 0-88436-301-5, 35302). EMC.

--The Day of the Dinosaur. LC 75-19023. (The Dinosaur Machine Ser.). (Illus.). 40p. (gr. 7 up). 1975. PLB 6.95 (ISBN 0-88436-193-4, 35476); pap. 3.95 (ISBN 0-88436-194-2, ELA 128055). EMC.

--The Day of the Earthlings. (Science Fiction Ser.). (Illus.). 32p. (gr. 3-9). 1978. pap. 3.95 (ISBN 0-87191-054-3). Creative Ed.

--Death of a Dinosaur. LC 75-17926. (The Dinosaur Machine Ser.). (Illus.). 40p. (gr. 7 up). 1975. PLB 6.95 (ISBN 0-88436-199-3, 35479); pap. 3.95 (ISBN 0-88436-200-0, ELA 128055). EMC.

--Demetrius & the Golden Goblet. LC 79-14865. (Illus.). 48p. (gr. 1-5). 8.95 (ISBN 0-15-223186-2, HJ). HarBraceJ.

--Demetrius & the Golden Goblet. LC 79-14865. (Illus.). (gr. k-4). 1980. pap. 3.95 (ISBN 0-15-625282-1, VoyB). HarBraceJ.

--The Demon. LC 76-18125. (No Such Things Ser.). (Illus.). 1976. 6.95 (ISBN 0-88436-273-6, 35487); pap. 3.95 (ISBN 0-88436-274-4, 35305). EMC.

--The Dinosaur Trap. LC 75-17909. (The Dinosaur Machine Ser.). (Illus.). 40p. (gr. 7 up). 1975. PLB 6.95 (ISBN 0-88436-197-7, 35478); pap. 3.95 (ISBN 0-88436-198-5, ELA 128054). EMC.

--The Empty Window. LC 80-13048. (Illus.). 48p. (gr. 4-9). 1980. 7.95 (ISBN 0-7232-6186-5). Warne.

--Escape from Tyrannosaurus. LC 75-19024. (The Dinosaur Machine Ser.). (Illus.). 40p. (gr. 7 up). 1975. PLB 6.95 (ISBN 0-88436-195-0, 35477); pap. 3.95 (ISBN 0-88436-196-9, ELA 128053). EMC.

--Face at the Edge of the World. LC 85-2684. 192p. (gr. 7 up). 1985. 12.95 (Clarion). HM.

--Fifteen. (Young Romance Ser.). (Illus.). (gr. 3-9). 1978. pap. 3.95 (ISBN 0-87191-064-0). Creative Ed.

--The Followers. (Science Fiction Ser.). (Illus.). (gr. 3-9). 1978. PLB 7.95 (ISBN 0-87191-627-4); pap. 3.95 (ISBN 0-89812-055-1). Creative Ed.

--The Ghost. LC 76-18131. (No Such Things.. Ser.). (Illus.). (gr. 2-6). 1976. PLB 6.95 (ISBN 0-88436-271-X, 35486); pap. 3.95 (ISBN 0-88436-272-8, 35304). EMC.

--Ghost Behind Me. (gr. 7-9). 1984. pap. 2.25 (ISBN 0-671-49865-7). Archway.

--Ghost of Summer. LC 76-45310. (gr. 5 up). 1977. 7.95 (ISBN 0-7232-6141-5). Warne.

--The Ghosts of Departure Point. LC 81-48602. 113p. (gr. 6 up). 1982. 9.57i (ISBN 0-397-31997-5); PLB 9.89g (ISBN 0-397-31998-3). Lipp Jr Bks.

--The Ghosts of Departure Point. 128p. (gr. 7 up). 1984. pap. 2.25 (ISBN 0-590-33116-7, Point). Scholastic Inc.

--The Giant Squid. LC 81-14211. (A Jem Book Ser.). (Illus.). 64p. (Teen reading on a 2-3rd grade level). 1981. lib. bdg. 9.29 (ISBN 0-671-43776-3). Messner.

--Goose Dinner. LC 80-39747. (Let-Me-Read Bk.). (Illus.). 32p. (ps-3). 1981. pap. 2.95 (ISBN 0-15-232225-6, VoyB). HarBraceJ.

--The Great White Shark. LC 82-3415. (Jem High Interest-Low Vocabulary Ser.). 64p. (gr. 4 up). 1982. PLB 9.29 (ISBN 0-671-44004-7); pap. 4.95 (ISBN 0-671-49472-4). Messner.

--The Happy Funeral. LC 81-47719. (Illus.). 48p. (gr. k-4). 1982. 9.57i (ISBN 0-06-020893-7); PLB 9.89g (ISBN 0-06-020894-5). HarpJ.

--The Haunting of Kildoran Abbey. LC 77-84601. (gr. 5 up). 1978. 7.95 (ISBN 0-7232-6152-0). Warne.

--The Haunting of SafeKeep. LC 84-48354. (Lippincott Page-Turner). 160p. (YA) (gr. 7 up). 1985. 11.06i (ISBN 0-397-32112-0); PLB 10.89g (ISBN 0-397-32113-9). Lipp Jr Bks.

--If I Asked You, Would You Stay? LC 82-49052. (A Lippincott Page-Turner Ser.). 160p. (YA) (gr. 7 up). 1984. 9.57i (ISBN 0-397-32065-5); PLB 9.89g (ISBN 0-397-32066-3). Lipp Jr Bks.

--Island of One. (Science Fiction Ser.). (Illus.). (gr. 3-9). 1978. PLB 7.95 (ISBN 0-87191-626-6); pap. 3.95 (ISBN 0-89812-058-6). Creative Ed.

--Jane Martin, Dog Detective. LC 84-4497. (Illus.). 48p. (ps-3). 1984. 13.95 (ISBN 0-15-239586-5, HJ). HarBraceJ.

--Josefina Finds the Prince. LC 76-16063. (For Real Books). (Illus.). 64p. (gr. 2-6). 1976. PLB 7.47 (ISBN 0-8116-4300-X). Garrard.

--Just Like Everyone Else. (Young Romance Ser.). (Illus.). (gr. 3-9). 1978. pap. 3.95 (ISBN 0-89812-062-4). Creative Ed.

--Karen Kepplewhite Is the World's Best Kisser. LC 83-2066. 96p. (gr. 3-6). 1983. 9.95 (ISBN 0-89919-182-7, Clarion). HM.

--Karen Kepplewhite is the World's Best Kisser. (gr. 5-7). 1984. pap. 2.25 (ISBN 0-671-52734-7). Archway.

--The Man Who Could Call Down Owls. LC 83-17568. (Illus.). 32p. (gr. k-3). 1984. SBE 9.95 (ISBN 0-02-715380-0). Macmillan.

--The Mask. (Science Fiction Ser.). (Illus.). (gr. 3-9). 1978. PLB 7.95 (ISBN 0-87191-625-8); pap. 3.95 (ISBN 0-89812-056-X). Creative Ed.

--The Mirror Planet. (Science Fiction Ser.). (Illus.). (gr. 3-9). 1978. PLB 7.95 (ISBN 0-87191-628-2); pap. 3.95 (ISBN 0-89812-057-8). Creative Ed.

--Monkey in the Middle. LC 83-18339. (Illus.). 32p. (ps-2). 1984. PLB 10.95 (ISBN 0-15-255316-9, HJ). HarBraceJ.

--One More Flight. 96p. (gr. 3-7). 1983. pap. 1.25 (ISBN 0-440-46640-7, YB). Dell.

--The Robot Birthday. LC 79-19185. 80p. (gr. 1-3). 1980. 7.95 (ISBN 0-525-38542-8, Smart Cat). Dutton.

--The Robot People. (Science Fiction Ser.). (Illus.). (gr. 3-9). 1978. PLB 7.95 (ISBN 0-87191-622-3); pap. 3.95 (ISBN 0-89812-051-9). Creative Ed.

--St. Patrick's Day in the Morning. LC 79-15934. (Illus.). 32p. (ps-3). 1980. 10.95 (ISBN 0-395-29098-8, Clarion). HM.

--St. Patrick's Day in the Morning. (Illus.). 32p. (ps-3). 1983. pap. 3.95 (ISBN 0-89919-162-2, Clarion). HM.

--The Sea World Book of Sharks. LC 79-63920. (Sea World Press Ser.). (Illus.). 80p. (gr. 4-6). 1980. 12.95 (ISBN 0-15-271947-4, HJ). HarBraceJ.

--The Sea World Book of Sharks. LC 79-639201. (Sea World Press Ser.). (Illus.). 80p. (gr. 4-7). 1984. pap. 6.95 (ISBN 0-15-271952-0, VoyB). HarBraceJ.

--The Sea World Book of Whales. LC 80-51231. (Sea World Press Ser.). (Illus.). 80p. (gr. 4-6). 1980. 9.95 (ISBN 0-15-271948-2, HJ). HarBraceJ.

--The Skate Patrol. Tucker, Kathleen, ed. LC 80-18640. (High-Low Mysteries). (Illus.). 40p. (gr. 2-5). 1980. PLB 7.75 (ISBN 0-8075-7393-0). A Whitman.

--The Skate Patrol & the Mystery Writer. Fay, Ann, ed. LC 82-10843. (Pilot Bks-High-Low Mysteries). (Illus.). 40p. (gr. 2-5). 1982. PLB 7.75 (ISBN 0-8075-7394-9). A Whitman.

--The Skate Patrol Rides Again. LC 81-11504. (Illus.). 48p. (gr. 2-5). 1981. PLB 7.75 (ISBN 0-8075-7395-7). A Whitman.

--Someone Is Hiding on Alcatraz Island. LC 84-5019. 144p. (gr. 5-8). 1984. PLB 10.95 (ISBN 0-89919-219-X, Clarion). HM.

--The Spook Birds. Tucker, Kathleen, ed. LC 81-686. (Illus.). 40p. (gr. 3-7). 1981. PLB 7.50 (ISBN 0-8075-7587-9). A Whitman.

--Strange Things Happen in the Woods. Orig. Title: The Cloverdale Switch. (gr. 7-9). 1984. pap. 1.95 (ISBN 0-671-41098-9). Archway.

--Surrogate Sister. LC 83-49483. 192p. (YA) (gr. 7 up). 1984. 12.02i (ISBN 0-397-32098-1); PLB 11.89g (ISBN 0-397-32099-X). Lipp Jr Bks.

--The Tongue of the Ocean. LC 76-17624. (No Such Things..Ser.). (Illus.). 1976. PLB 6.95 (ISBN 0-88436-302-3, 35485); pap. 3.95 (ISBN 0-88436-303-1, 35303). EMC.

--The Traveling Men of Ballycoo. LC 82-15799. (Illus.). 32p. (ps-3). 1983. 12.95 (ISBN 0-15-289792-5, HJ). HarBraceJ.

--The Undersea People. (Science Fiction Ser.). (Illus.). (gr. 3-9). 1978. pap. 3.95 (ISBN 0-89812-052-7). Creative Ed.

--The Valentine Bears. (Illus.). 32p. (gr. 3). 1983. 10.95 (ISBN 0-89919-138-X, Clarion). HM.

--The Valentine Bears. LC 82-9577. (Illus.). 32p. (ps-3). 1985. pap. 3.95 (ISBN 0-89919-313-7, Clarion). HM.

--The Waiting Game. LC 80-8793. 64p. 1981. 9.57i (ISBN 0-397-31941-X); PLB 9.89 (ISBN 0-397-31942-8). Lipp Jr Bks.

--Winter's Coming. LC 76-28321. (Let Me Read Bk.). (Illus.). 32p. (ps-3). 1977. pap. 1.65 (ISBN 0-15-298037-7, VoyB). HarBraceJ.

Bunting, G. S. A Revision of Spathiphyllum (Araceae, Vol. 10(3) (Memoirs of the New York Botanical Garden Ser.). 54p. 1960. 8.00 (ISBN 0-317-35526-0). NY Botanical.

Bunting, James. Bavaria. (Batsford Countries of Europe Ser). 216p. 1972. 8.95 (ISBN 0-8038-0740-6). Hastings.

--The Lake District. (Batsford Britain Ser). 7.95 (ISBN 0-8038-4287-2). Hastings.

Bunting, John R. The Hidden Face of Free Enterprise: The Strange Economics of the American Businessman. LC 81-13353. vii, 248p. 1982. Repr. of 1964 ed. lib. bdg. 25.00x (ISBN 0-313-23218-0, BUHI). Greenwood.

Bunting, Josiah. The Lionheads. LC 78-188356. 224p. 1972. 12.95 (ISBN 0-8076-0632-4). Braziller.

Bunting, Richard L., jt. auth. see Benton, Allen H.

Bunting, Robert L. Employer Concentration in Local Labor Markets. xiii, 182p. 1982. Repr. of 1962 ed. lib. bdg. 25.00x (ISBN 0-313-23449-3, BUEL). Greenwood.

Bunting, Sharon. Preparing Students for Mainstreaming. 80p. (Orig.). 1982. pap. 8.90 (ISBN 0-936326-02-6). Cedars Pr.

Bunting, William H. Portrait of a Port: Boston, 1852-1914. LC 77-145893. (Illus.). 1971. 25.00 (ISBN 0-674-69075-3, Belknap Pr). Harvard U Pr.

Bunting-Blake, Linda & Parker, Joan. Defibrillation: A Manual for the EMT. (Illus.). 176p. 1985. pap. text ed. 9.50 (ISBN 0-397-54567-3, Lippincott Nursing). Lippincott.

Bunting-Kaye. Breaking Away: An Open Lab Approach to Writing. 352p. 1983. pap. text ed. 18.50 (ISBN 0-8403-3078-2). Kendall-Hunt.

Buntline, Ned. Buffalo Bill: His Adventures in the West. LC 74-15731. (Popular Culture in America Ser.). (Illus.). 320p. 1974. Repr. of 1886 ed. 23.00x (ISBN 0-405-06366-0). Ayer Co Pubs.

Buntman, Peter H. & Saris, E. M. How to Live with Your Teenager: A Survivor's Handbook for Parents. 192p. 1982. pap. 2.50 (ISBN 0-345-30102-1). Ballantine.

Bunton, John, jt. auth. see Hall, James J.

Bunton, Richard, jt. auth. see Mylett, Howard.

Bunuel. Las Tres de la Madrugada. (Easy Reader, A). 1972. pap. 3.25 (ISBN 0-88436-061-X, 70265). EMC.

Bunuel, Luis. L' Age D'Or; Andalusian Dog. (Lorrimer Classic Screenplay Ser.). (Illus.). pap. 7.95 (ISBN 0-8044-6068-X). Ungar.

--Belle De Jour. (Lorrimer Classic Screenplay Ser.). (Illus.). 10.95 (ISBN 0-8044-2090-4); pap. 6.95 (ISBN 0-8044-6071-X). Ungar.

--Exterminating Angel; Nazarin; Olvidados. (Lorrimer Classic Screenplay Ser.). (Illus.). pap. 10.95 (ISBN 0-8044-6072-8). Ungar.

--Luis Bunuel: Three Screenplays. LC 82-49274. (Cinema Classics Ser.). 250p. 1985. lib. bdg. 40.00 (ISBN 0-8240-5753-8). Garland Pub.

--My Last Sigh. LC 83-48105. 1983. 15.95 (ISBN 0-394-52854-9). Knopf.

--My Last Sigh. LC 84-40010. 288p. 1984. pap. 6.95 (ISBN 0-394-72501-8, Vin). Random.

--Tristana. (Lorrimer Classic Screenplay Ser.). (Illus.). 10.95 (ISBN 0-8044-2091-2); pap. 6.95 (ISBN 0-8044-6074-4). Ungar.

Bunyan. Computer Systems Measurement. (Infotech Computer State of the Art Reports). 701p. 1974. 310.00 (ISBN 0-08-028551-1). Pergamon.

--Data Base Systems. (Infotech Computer State of the Art Reports). 722p. 1975. 310.00 (ISBN 0-08-028549-X). Pergamon.

--Virtual Storage. (Infotech Computer State of the Art Reports). 504p. 1976. 85.00 (ISBN 0-08-028516-3). Pergamon.

Bunyan, James. Intervention, Civil War & Communism in Russia, April-December 1918. 1973. lib. bdg. 46.00x (ISBN 0-374-91097-9). Octagon.

Bunyan, James & Fisher, Harold H. Bolshevik Revolution, Nineteen Seventeen to Nineteen Eighteen: Documents & Materials. 1934. 50.00x (ISBN 0-8047-0344-2). Stanford U Pr.

Bunyan, John. The Acceptable Sacrifice. pap. 1.75 (ISBN 0-685-88365-5). Reiner.

--Advice to Sufferers. pap. 3.25 (ISBN 0-685-19821-9). Reiner.

--Barren Fig Tree. pap. 1.25 (ISBN 0-685-19824-3). Reiner.

--Christiana's Journey. Rev. ed. Wright, Christopher, ed. LC 82-70860. 1982. pap. 4.95 (ISBN 0-88270-533-4). Bridge Pub.

--Come & Welcome to Jesus Christ. 1974. pap. 2.50 (ISBN 0-685-52815-4). Reiner.

--The Complete Works, 4 Vols. Stebbing, H., ed. (Illus.). Repr. of 1859 ed. Set. 321.00x (ISBN 3-487-03397-6). Adlers Foreign Bks.

--The Complete Works of John Bunyan, 4 Vols. Stebbing, Henry, ed. (Library of Literature, Drama & Criticism). 1970. Repr. of 1859 ed. Set. 230.00 (ISBN 0-384-06355-1). Johnson Repr.

--Desire of the Righteous Granted. 1974. pap. 1.75 (ISBN 0-685-52816-2). Reiner.

--Doctrine of Law & Grace Unfolded. 1974. pap. 2.95 (ISBN 0-685-52817-0). Reiner.

--Exhortation to Unity & Peace. pap. 0.95 (ISBN 0-685-00744-8). Reiner.

--The Family Pilgrim's Progress. Watson, Jean, retold by. LC 83-50310. 128p. 1983. 9.95 (ISBN 0-8423-0863-6). Tyndale.

--Fear of God. pap. 3.95 (ISBN 0-685-19828-6). Reiner.

--Grace Abounding to the Chief of Sinners & the Life & Death of Mr. Badman. 1979. pap. 3.95x (ISBN 0-460-11815-3, Evman). Biblio Dist.

--Grace Abounding to the Chief of Sinners. (Summit Bks). 1978. pap. 3.50 (ISBN 0-8010-0729-1). Baker Bk.

--Grace Abounding to the Chief of Sinners. Sharrock, Roger, ed. & intro. by. Bd. with The Pilgrim's Progress from This World to That Which Is to Come. (Oxford Standard Authors Ser). 1966. 35.00 (ISBN 0-19-254159-5). Oxford U Pr.

--The Greatness of the Soul. 1975. pap. 1.95 (ISBN 0-685-54807-4). Reiner.

--Groans of a Lost Soul. LC 68-6571. 1967. pap. 3.25 (ISBN 0-685-19830-8). Reiner.

--Heavenly Footman. pap. 1.25 (ISBN 0-685-19831-6). Reiner.

--Holy Life: The Beauty of Christianity. pap. 1.95 (ISBN 0-685-19832-4). Reiner.

--The Holy War. (Summit Bks). 1977. pap. 5.95 (ISBN 0-8010-0714-3). Baker Bk.

--The Holy War. Sharrock, Roger & Forrest, James F., eds. (Oxford English Texts Ser.). 1980. 75.00x (ISBN 0-19-811887-2). Oxford U Pr.

--Holy War. 1975. 12.95 (ISBN 0-685-52819-7). Reiner.

--The Holy War. 250p. 1985. pap. text ed. 3.50 (ISBN 0-88368-165-X). Whitaker Hse.

--House of God. pap. 0.95 (ISBN 0-685-19834-0). Reiner.

--Intercession of Christ. pap. 1.95 (ISBN 0-685-19835-9). Reiner.

--Israel's Hope Encouraged. pap. 1.95 (ISBN 0-685-19836-7). Reiner.

--The Jerusalem Sinner Saved. pap. 3.25 (ISBN 0-685-88378-7). Reiner.

--Justification by an Imputed Righteousness. pap. 2.95 (ISBN 0-685-88380-9). Reiner.

--Light for Them That Sit in Darkness. pap. 3.50 (ISBN 0-685-19838-3). Reiner.

--The Miscellaneous Works of John Bunyan, Vols. 8 & 9. Greaves, Richard L., ed. (Oxford English Texts). 1979. 79.00x (ISBN 0-19-812736-7); Vol. 9, 1981 95.00x, (ISBN 0-19-812737-5). Oxford U Pr.

--The Miscellaneous Works of John Bunyan: Good News for the Vilest of Men; The Advocateship of Jesus Christ, Vol. XI. Greaves, Richard L., ed. (Illus.). 260p. 1985. 36.50 (ISBN 0-19-812739-1). Oxford U Pr.

--The Miscellaneous Works of John Bunyan: The Poems, Vol. VI. Midgley, E. G., ed. (Oxford English Text Ser.). (Illus.). 1980. 79.00x (ISBN 0-19-812734-0). Oxford U Pr.

--Miscellaneous Works: Some Gospel Truths Opened, a Vindication of Some Gospel Truths Opened, & a Few Sighs from Hell, Vol 1. Underwood, T. L. & Sharrock, Roger, eds. (Oxford English Texts Ser.). (Illus.). 1980. 79.00x (ISBN 0-19-812730-8). Oxford U Pr.

--Miscellaneous Works: The Doctrine of the Law & Grace Unfolded & I Will Pray with the Spirit, Vol. 2. Greaves, Richard L., ed. 1975. 59.00x (ISBN 0-19-811871-6). Oxford U Pr.

--My Imprisonment. pap. 1.75 (ISBN 0-686-64391-7). Reiner.

--La Oracion. (Span.). pap. 2.95 (ISBN 0-317-14912-1). Banner of Truth.

--Paul's Departure & Crown. pap. 0.95 (ISBN 0-685-19839-1). Reiner.

--Pharisee & the Publican. pap. 3.95 (ISBN 0-685-19840-5). Reiner.

--Pictorial Pilgrim's Progress. 1960. pap. 3.95 (ISBN 0-8024-0019-1). Moody.

--Pilgrim's Progress. (Classics Ser). (gr. 9 up). 1968. pap. 1.50 (ISBN 0-8049-0183-X, CL-183). Airmont.

--The Pilgrim's Progress. (Giant Summit Bks). pap. 8.95 (ISBN 0-8010-0732-1). Baker Bk.

--The Pilgrim's Progress. 1979. Repr. 18.95 (ISBN 0-85151-259-3). Banner of Truth.

--The Pilgrim's Progress. 1978. 12.95x (ISBN 0-460-00204-X, Evman); pap. 2.95x (ISBN 0-460-01204-5, Evman). Biblio Dist.

--The Pilgrim's Progress. (Illus.). 232p. (gr. 9 up). 1981. pap. text ed. 2.95 (ISBN 0-89323-016-2, 119). Bible Memory.

--The Pilgrim's Progress. Larson, Gladys N., ed. (Illus.). 1978. pap. 6.95 (ISBN 0-910452-36-9). Covenant.

--Pilgrim's Progress. (Great Il. Classics). (Illus.). (gr. 9 up). 1979. 8.95 (ISBN 0-396-07754-4). Dodd.

--The Pilgrim's Progress. (Pivot Family Reader Ser). 352p. 1972. pap. 1.25 (ISBN 0-87983-011-5); 16.95 (ISBN 0-87983-335-1). Keats.

--Pilgrims Progress. 1976. lib. bdg. 18.95 (ISBN 0-89968-156-5). Lightyear.

--Pilgrim's Progress. (Moody Classics Ser.). 1984. pap. 2.95 (ISBN 0-8024-0012-4). Moody.

--Pilgrim's Progress. (YA) (RL 10). pap. 2.75 (ISBN 0-451-51930-2, CE1813, Sig Classics). NAL.

--Pilgrim's Progress. Sharrock, Roger, ed. (English Library Ser.). 1965. pap. 2.50 (ISBN 0-14-043004-0). Penguin.

--Pilgrim's Progress. 1975. 14.95 (ISBN 0-685-52821-9). Reiner.

--Pilgrim's Progress. 288p. 1965. pap. 3.50 (ISBN 0-8007-8032-9, Spire Bks). Revell.

--Pilgrim's Progress. 416p. 1981. pap. 3.95 (ISBN 0-88368-096-3). Whitaker Hse.

--Pilgrim's Progress. 320p. pap. 2.50 (ISBN 0-671-42460-2). WSP.

--Pilgrim's Progress. 256p. 1973. pap. 3.50 (ISBN 0-310-22142-0). Zondervan.

--Pilgrim's Progress. Helms, Hal M., ed. LC 81-85770. (Illus.). 270p. 1982. 5.95 (ISBN 0-941478-02-5). Paraclete Pr.

--Pilgrim's Progress. 1983. Large Print 16.95 (ISBN 0-87983-335-1). Keats.

--The Pilgrim's Progress. (Children's Illustrated Classics). (Illus.). 320p. 1975. Repr. of 1954 ed. 9.95 (ISBN 0-460-05028-1, Pub. by J. M. Dent England). Biblio Dist.

--The Pilgrim's Progress. (World's Classics-Paperback Ser.). 1984. pap. 2.50 (ISBN 0-19-281607-1). Oxford U Pr.

--The Pilgrim's Progress. Helms, Hal M., ed. (Illus.). 268p. pap. 6.95 (ISBN 0-941478-02-5, Pub. by Paraclete Pr). Upper Room.

--Pilgrim's Progress. 1985. pap. 4.95 (ISBN 0-317-18945-X). Barbour & Co.

--Pilgrim's Progress: From This World to That Which Is to Come. 2nd ed. Wharey, James B. & Sharrock, Roger, eds. (Oxford English Texts Ser). 1960. 55.00x (ISBN 0-19-811802-3). Oxford U Pr.

--Pilgrim's Progress in Today's English. LC 64-25255. 1964. pap. 6.95 (ISBN 0-8024-6520-X). Moody.

--Pilgrims Progress, Sixteen Seventy-Eight. 288p. 1984. 30.00x (ISBN 0-905418-29-8, Pub. by Gresham England). State Mutual Bk.

--El Progreso del Peregrino Ilustrado. Orig. Title: Pilgrim's Progress Illustrated. 254p. (Span.). pap. 4.75 (ISBN 0-8254-1096-7). Kregel.

--Reprobation Asserted. pap. 1.25 (ISBN 0-685-19841-3). Reiner.

--Ruin of Antichrist. pap. 1.95 (ISBN 0-685-19842-1). Reiner.

--Saints Knowledge of Christ's Love. pap. 1.50 (ISBN 0-685-19843-X). Reiner.

--Saved by Grace. pap. 2.25 (ISBN 0-685-88393-0). Reiner.

--The Strait Gate. pap. 2.25 (ISBN 0-685-88394-9). Reiner.

--Target Earth. LC 82-61244. 1982. pap. 4.95 (ISBN 0-88270-536-9, Open Scroll). Bridge Pub.

--Treasury of Bunyan. (Giant Summit Ser.). 1016p. (Orig.). 1981. pap. 14.95 (ISBN 0-8010-0809-3). Baker Bk.

--The Water of Life. pap. 1.50 (ISBN 0-685-88397-3). Reiner.

--Work of Jesus Christ As an Advocate. pap. 3.95 (ISBN 0-685-19844-8). Reiner.

--Works of John Bunyan, 3 Vols. Offor, George, ed. LC 78-154136. Repr. of 1856 ed. Set. lib. bdg. 225.00 (ISBN 0-404-09250-0). AMS Pr.

--Young Christian's Pilgrimage. Rev. ed. Wright, Christopher, ed. LC 84-72005. 1982. pap. 4.95 (ISBN 0-88270-523-7). Bridge Pub.

Bunyan, John, et al. How They Found Christ: In Their Own Words. Freeman, Bill, ed. LC 83-62268. 66p. (Orig.). 1983. pap. 1.40 (ISBN 0-914271-00-8). NW Christian Pubns.

Bunyan, John A. More Practical Video. (Video Bookshelf Ser.). (Illus.). 200p. 1985. pap. 24.95 professional (ISBN 0-86729-079-X, 525-BW). Knowledge Indus.

Bunyan, John A., et al. Practical Video: The Manager's Guide to Applications. LC 78-23533. 203p. 1978. pap. 17.95 professional (ISBN 0-914236-20-2, 509-BW). Knowledge Indus.

Bunyan, Juan & Leavell, L. P. El Progreso del Peregrino. Duffer, Hiram F., Jr., tr. from Eng. (Span.). 1980. pap. 2.20 (ISBN 0-311-37006-3). Casa Bautista.

Bunyan, Tony. The History & Practice of the Political Police in Britain. 324p. (Orig.). 1984. pap. 9.95 (ISBN 0-7043-3128-4, Pub. by Quartet Bks). Merrimack Pub Cir.

--The Political Police in Britain. LC 75-45815. (Illus.). 304p. 1976. 22.50 (ISBN 0-312-62405-0). St Martin.

Bunyard, Edward A. Old Garden Roses. LC 78-9609. (Illus.). 1978. Repr. of 1936 ed. text ed. 25.00 (ISBN 0-930576-06-3). E M Coleman Ent.

Bunyard, Peter, jt. auth. see Allaby, Michael.

Bunyard, R. S. Police: Organisation & Command. (Illus.). 400p. 1978. 29.95x (ISBN 0-7121-1671-0, Pub. by Macdonald & Evans England). Trans-Atlantic.

Bunye, Maria V. & Yap, Elsa P. Cebuano Grammar Notes. McKaughan, Howard P., ed. LC 70-152460. (PALI Language Texts: Philippines). (Orig.). 1971. pap. text ed. 7.50x (ISBN 0-87022-092-6). UH Pr.

Bunye, Maria V., jt. auth. see Yap, Elsa P.

Bunzel, John A. The American Small Businessman. Bruchey, Stuart & Carosso, Vincent P., eds. LC 78-18956. (Small Business Enterprise in America Ser.). (Illus.). 1979. Repr. of 1962 ed. lib. bdg. 25.50x (ISBN 0-405-11460-5). Ayer Co Pubs.

Bunzel, John H. Anti-Politics in America: Reflections on the Anti-Political Temper & Its Distortions of the Democratic Process. LC 78-27675. 1979. Repr. of 1967 ed. lib. bdg. 24.75x (ISBN 0-313-20834-4, BUAP). Greenwood.

--New Force on the Left: Tom Hayden & the Campaign Against Corporate America. (Publication Ser.: No. 280). 131p. 1983. pap. 6.95 (ISBN 0-8179-7802-X). Hoover Inst Pr.

Bunzel, John H., ed. Challenge to American Schools: The Case for Standards & Values. 1985. 19.95 (ISBN 0-19-503556-9). Oxford U Pr.

Bunzel, Ruth L. Pueblo Potter: A Study of Creative Imagination in Primitive Art. LC 73-82257. (Columbia Univ. Contributions to Anthropology Ser.: Vol. 8). (Illus.). Repr. of 1929 ed. 55.00 (ISBN 0-404-50558-9). AMS Pr.

--The Pueblo Potter: A Study of Creative Imagination in Primitive Art. (Illus.). 160p. 1973. pap. 5.95 (ISBN 0-486-22875-4). Dover.

--The Pueblo Potter: A Study of Creative Imagination in Primitive Art. (Illus.). 14.00 (ISBN 0-8446-4622-9). Peter Smith.

--Zuni. pap. 5.00 (ISBN 0-685-71705-4). J J Augustin.

--Zuni Katcinas. LC 72-13917. (Beautiful Rio Grande Classics Ser.). (Illus.). 358p. 1984. lib. bdg. 30.00 (ISBN 0-87380-099-0). Rio Grande.

--Zuni Texts. LC 73-3551. (American Ethnological Society. Publications: No. 15). Repr. of 1933 ed. 34.50 (ISBN 0-404-58165-X). AMS Pr.

Bunzel, Ruth L., jt. ed. see Mead, Margaret.

Buol, S. W. Soil Genesis & Classification. 1981. 42.00x (ISBN 0-686-76667-9, Pub. by Oxford & IBH India). State Mutual Bk.

Buol, S. W., et al. Soil Genesis & Classification. 2nd ed. 1980. text ed. 19.50x (ISBN 0-8138-1460-X). Iowa St U Pr.

Buonanno, C. Beyond the Flag. (Orig.). 1981. pap. 1.95 (ISBN 0-505-51616-0, Pub. by Tower Bks). Dorchester Pub Co.

Buonarroti, Michelangelo. Michelangelo: A Record of His Life As Told in His Own Letters & Papers. Carden, Robert W., tr. 1976. lib. bdg. 59.95 (ISBN 0-8490-2256-8). Gordon Pr.

Buonarroti, Michelangelo see Michelangelo.

Buonarroti, Philippe. History of Babeuf's Conspiracy for Equality. O'Brien, Bronterre, tr. LC 64-7661. Repr. of 1836 ed. 45.00x (ISBN 0-678-00087-5). Kelley.

Buonassisi, Vincenzo. Pizza. (Illus.). 183p. 1984. 14.45i (ISBN 0-316-11515-0, 115150). Little.

Buonassisi, Vincenzo & Razzoli, Guido. The Italian Gourmet Diet: A Seven Week Plan for Wine & Pasta Lovers. 224p. 1983. 14.95 (ISBN 0-02-518080-0). Macmillan.

Buoncompagni, Marcellus. Educational Psychology, 2 vols. new ed. (Illus.). 137p. 1984. 147.75x (ISBN 0-89266-434-7). Am Classical Coll Pr.

Buoncristiano, S., et al. A Geometric Approach to Homology Theory. LC 75-22980. (London Mathematical Society Lecture Note Ser.: No. 18). (Illus.). 216p. 1976. pap. text ed. 21.95x (ISBN 0-521-20940-4). Cambridge U Pr.

Buonicore, Anthony & Theodore, Louis. Industrial Control Equipment for Gaseous Pollutants, 2 vols. new ed. LC 74-25260. (Uniscience Ser). 1975. Vol. 1, 209p. 17.47 (ISBN 0-87819-067-8); Vol. 2, 168p. 40.00 (ISBN 0-87819-068-6). CRC Pr.

Buonicore, Anthony, jt. auth. see Theodore, Louis.

Buonicore, Anthony J., jt. ed. see Theodore, Louis.

Buono, Anthon, tr. see Pope John Paul II.

Buono, Anthony. Liturgy: Our School of Faith. 177p. (Orig.). 1982. pap. 6.95 (ISBN 0-8189-0435-6). Alba.

Buono, Anthony, jt. auth. see Bowditch, James.

Buono, Anthony F. & Nichols, Lawrence T. Corporate Policy, Values & Social Responsibility. LC 85-6422. 240p. 1985. 30.95 (ISBN 0-03-063061-4). Praeger.

Buono, Anthony F., jt. auth. see Bowditch, James L.

Buono, Barbara Del see Del Buono, John & Del Buono, Barbara.

Buono, Carmen J. Dello see Dello Buono, Carmen J.

Buono, Dello & Joseph, Carmen. Rare Early Essays on Charles Dickens: Second Series. 207p. lib. bdg. 27.00 (ISBN 0-8482-0644-4). Norwood Edns.

Buono, John Del see Del Buono, John & Del Buono, Barbara.

Buonocore, Michael G. The Use of Adhesives in Dentistry. (Illus.). 472p. 1975. photocopy ed. 54.50x (ISBN 0-398-03367-6). C C Thomas.

Buono Dello, Carmen J. Rare Early Essays on Johnson & Boswell. 212p. 1981. lib. bdg. 25.00 (ISBN 0-8482-3656-4). Norwood Edns.

Burack, A. S., ed. Christmas Plays for Young Actors. rev. ed. (gr. 3 up). 1969. 12.00 (ISBN 0-8238-0221-3). Plays.

--One Hundred Plays for Children. (gr. 1-6). 1970. 15.00 (ISBN 0-8238-0002-4). Plays.

Burack, Benjamin. Ivory & Its Uses. LC 83-51417. (Illus.). 240p. 1984. 19.50 (ISBN 0-8048-1483-X). C E Tuttle.

Burack, E. H. & Mathys, N. J. Introduction to Management: A Career Perspective. (Wiley Series in Management). 594p. 1983. 32.95 (ISBN 0-471-86359-9). Wiley.

Burack, Elmer H. Career Planning & Management: A Managerial Summary. 170p. (Orig.). 1983. pap. 14.95 (ISBN 0-942560-07-8); pap. text ed. 12.50 (ISBN 0-686-38251-X). Brace-Park.

--Personnel Management: Cases & Exercises. (Illus.). 1978. pap. text ed. 19.95 (ISBN 0-8299-0203-1); IM avail. (ISBN 0-8299-0461-1); exam questions avail. (ISBN 0-8299-0463-8). West Pub.

--Planning for Human Resources: A Managerial Summary. 170p. (Orig.). 1983. pap. 14.95 (ISBN 0-942560-09-4); pap. text ed. 12.50 (ISBN 0-686-38254-4). Brace-Park.

Burack, Elmer H. & Mathys, Nicholas J. Career Management in Organizations: A Practical Human Resource Planning Approach. 427p. 1980. 30.95 (ISBN 0-942560-02-7); text ed. 26.00 (ISBN 0-686-33339-X). Brace-Park.

--Human Resource Planning: A Pragmatic Approach to Manpower Staffing & Development. 371p. 1980. 30.95 (ISBN 0-942560-01-9); text ed. 26.00 (ISBN 0-686-33340-3). Brace-Park.

Burack, Elmer H. & Smith, Robert D. Personnel Management: A Human Resource System Approach. (Management Ser.). 609p. 1982. text ed. 35.45 (ISBN 0-471-09283-5); pap. 13.95 (ISBN 0-471-86360-2); tchr's.manual 9.00 (ISBN 0-471-86236-3). Wiley.

Burack, Elmer H. & Torda, Florence. The Manager's Guide to Chance. 226p. 1980. pap. 14.95 (ISBN 0-942560-14-0). Brace Park.

--The Manager's Guide to Change. LC 79-15537. 235p. 1979. 11.95 (ISBN 0-534-97995-5). Lifetime Learn.

Burack, Elmer H. & Negandhi, Anant, eds. Organization Design: Theoretical Perspectives & Empirical Findings. LC 77-24228. 400p. 1977. 17.50x (ISBN 0-87338-206-4, Pub. by Comparative Adm. Research Institute). Kent St U Pr.

Burack, Elmer H., et al. Growing: A Woman's Guide to Career Satisfaction. LC 80-11990. 292p. (Orig.). 1980. pap. 7.95 (ISBN 0-534-97990-4). Lifetime Learn.

Burack, Ethel M., jt. auth. see Miller, Richard A.

Burack, Irving. Etude Critique Des Poemes Inedits de James Russell Lowell. 1939. Repr. 30.00 (ISBN 0-8274-2315-2). R West.

Burack, Richard. The New Handbook of Prescription Drugs. rev. ed. 1975. pap. 2.95 (ISBN 0-345-27162-9). Ballantine.

Burack, Sylvia K. Writing Mystery & Crime Fiction. LC 84-21952. 320p. 1985. pap. 12.95 (ISBN 0-87116-141-9). Writer.

Burack, Sylvia K., ed. The Writer's Handbook, 1985. LC 36-28596. 780p. 1985. 22.95 (ISBN 0-87116-140-0). Writer.

--Writing & Selling Fillers, Light Verse & Short Humor. LC 81-16321. 1982. pap. 8.95 (ISBN 0-87116-127-3). Writer.

--Writing & Selling the Romance Novel. 1983. pap. 9.95 (ISBN 0-87116-134-6). Writer.

Burack-Weiss, Ann, jt. auth. see Silverstone, Barbara.

Buragas, Robert. Decade of Designs, Bk. 2. (Carstens Hobby Bks.: C-19). 1970. pap. 5.00 (ISBN 0-911868-09-7). Carstens Pubns.

Burago, Alla, jt. ed. see Raffel, Burton.

Burago, Iurii D. & Mazya, V. G. A Potential Theory & Function Theory for Irregular Regions. LC 69-15004. (Seminars in Mathematics Ser.: Vol. 3). pap. 20.00 (ISBN 0-317-08891-2, 2020695). Bks Demand UMI.

Burago, Yu. D. Isoperimetric Inequalities in the Theory of Surfaces of Bounded External Curvature. LC 70-122625. (Seminars in Mathematics Ser.: Vol. 10). 99p. 1970. 20.00x (ISBN 0-306-18810-4, Consultants). Plenum Pub.

Burak, John. There Goes My Aching Back. LC 74-21437. 1975. 8.50 (ISBN 0-682-48134-3, Banner). Exposition Pr FL.

Burakoff, Gerald. How to Play the Recorder. 1984. pap. 2.95 (ISBN 0-8256-2320-0, Amsco Music). Music Sales.

Burakovsky, V. I. & Bockeria, L. A. Hyperbaric Oxygenation & Its Value in Cardiovascular Surgery. 343p. 1981. 11.50 (ISBN 0-8285-2282-0, Pub. by Mir Pubs USSR). Imported Pubns.

Buranelli, Nan, jt. auth. see Buranelli, Vincent.

Buranelli, Prosper, et al, eds. The Cross Word Puzzle Book. LC 74-8834. 132p. 1974. Repr. of 1924 ed. 7.50 (ISBN 0-405-06191-9). Ayer Co Pubs.

Buranelli, Vincent. Edgar Allan Poe. 2nd ed. (United States Authors Ser.). 1977. lib. bdg. 13.95 (ISBN 0-8057-7189-1, Twayne). G K Hall.

--Josiah Royce. (Twayne's United States Authors Ser.). 1964. pap. 5.95x (ISBN 0-8084-0194-7, T49, Twayne). New Coll U Pr.

Buranelli, Vincent & Buranelli, Nan. Spy-Counterspy: An Encyclopedia of Espionage. 352p. 1982. 32.95 (ISBN 0-07-008915-9). McGraw.

--Sports Star: Tom Seaver. LC 74-7265. (Sports Star Ser.). (Illus.). (gr. 1-5). 1976. pap. 3.95 (ISBN 0-15-278011-4, VoyB). HarBraceJ.

Burchard, Peter. First Affair. LC 81-15291. 116p. (gr. 7 up). 1981. 9.95 (ISBN 0-374-32336-4). FS&G.

--A Quiet Place. 128p. 1982. pap. 1.75 (ISBN 0-441-17328-4, Pub. by Tempo). Ace Bks.

--Sea Change. LC 84-47524. (Illus.). 116p. (gr. 7 up). 1984. 9.95 (ISBN 0-374-36460-5). FS&G.

Burchard, Rachael C. John Updike: Yea Sayings. LC 78-119501. (Crosscurrents-Modern Critiques Ser.). 185p. 1971. 7.95 (ISBN 0-8093-0477-5). S Ill U Pr.

Burchard, S. H. Sports Star: Bob Griese. LC 75-11779. (Sports Star Ser.). (Illus.). 64p. (gr. 1-5). 1975. 5.25 (ISBN 0-15-277997-3, HJ). HarBraceJ.

--Sports Star: Brad Park. LC 75-11778. (Sports Star Ser.). (Illus.). 64p. (gr. 1-5). 1975. 4.95 (ISBN 0-15-277998-1, HJ). HarBraceJ.

--Sports Star: Carl Lewis. (Sports Star Ser.). (Illus.). (gr. 1-5). 12.95 (ISBN 0-317-13298-9, HJ). HarBraceJ.

--Sports Star: Carl Lewis. (Sports Star Ser.). (Illus.). (gr. 1-5). pap. 5.95 (ISBN 0-317-19775-4, VoyB). HarBraceJ.

--Sports Star: Dorothy Hamill. LC 77-88960. (Sports Star Ser.). (Illus.). 64p. (gr. 1-5). 1978. pap. 4.95 (ISBN 0-15-278014-9, VoyB). HarBraceJ.

--Sports Star: Earl Campbell. LC 80-7979. (Sports Star Ser.). (Illus.). 64p. (gr. 1-5). 1980. 6.95 (ISBN 0-15-278019-X, HJ). HarBraceJ.

--Sports Star: Elvin Hayes. LC 79-24286. (Sports Star Ser.). (Illus.). 64p. (gr. 1-5). 1980. pap. 2.50 (ISBN 0-15-684828-7, VoyB). HarBraceJ.

--Sports Star: Fernando Valenzuela. LC 82-47932. (Sports Star Ser.). (Illus.). 64p. (ps-3). 1982. pap. 2.95 (ISBN 0-15-278045-9, VoyB). HarBraceJ.

--Sports Star: Fernando Valenzuela. LC 82-47932. (Sports Star Ser.). (Illus.). 64p. (ps-3). 1982. 8.95 (ISBN 0-15-278044-0, HJ). HarBraceJ.

--Sports Star: George Brett. LC 81-13293. (Sports Star Ser.). (Illus.). 64p. (gr. 1-5). 1982. pap. 2.95 (ISBN 0-15-278041-6, VoyB). HarBraceJ.

--Sports Star: Herschel Walker. LC 83-22674. (Sports Star Ser.). (Illus.). 64p. (gr. 1-5). 1984. pap. 5.95 (ISBN 0-15-278053-X, VoyB). HarBraceJ.

--Sports Star: Herschel Walker. LC 83-22674. (Sports Star Ser.). (Illus.). 64p. (gr. 1-5). 1984. 11.95 (ISBN 0-15-278052-1, HJ). HarBraceJ.

--Sports Star: John McEnroe. LC 79-87509. (Sports Star Ser.). (Illus.). 64p. (gr. 1-5). 1979. 5.95 (ISBN 0-15-278017-3, HJ). HarBraceJ.

--Sports Star: Larry Bird. LC 83-81264. (Sports Star Ser.). (Illus.). 64p. (ps-3). 1983. pap. 4.95 (ISBN 0-15-278051-3, VoyB). HarBraceJ.

--Sports Star: Mark "The Bird" Fidrych. LC 77-4685. (Sports Star Ser.). (Illus.). 64p. (gr. 1-5). 1977. 4.95 (ISBN 0-15-278012-2, HJ). HarBraceJ.

--Sports Star: Mark "The Bird" Fidrych. LC 77-4685. (Sports Star Ser.). (Illus.). (gr. 1-5). 1977. pap. 2.95 (ISBN 0-15-684826-0, VoyB). HarBraceJ.

--Sports Star: "Mean" Joe Greene. LC 76-18130. (Sports Star Ser.). (Illus.). (gr. 1-5). 1976. pap. 3.95 (ISBN 0-15-278031-9, VoyB). HarBraceJ.

--Sports Star: Nadia Comaneci. LC 77-3967. (Sports Star Ser.). (Illus.). 64p. (gr. 1-5). 1977. 4.95 (ISBN 0-15-278013-0, HJ). HarBraceJ.

--Sports Star: Pele. LC 75-33707. (Sports Star Ser.). (Illus.). 64p. (gr. 1-5). 1976. 4.95 (ISBN 0-15-278001-7, HJ). HarBraceJ.

--Sports Star: Pele. LC 75-33707. (Sports Star Ser.). (Illus.). (gr. 1-5). 1976. pap. 2.95 (ISBN 0-15-278006-8, VoyB). HarBraceJ.

--Sports Star: Reggie Jackson. LC 78-20567. (Sports Star Ser.). (Illus.). 64p. (gr. 1-4). 1979. 6.95 (ISBN 0-15-278016-5, HJ). HarBraceJ.

--Sports Star: Reggie Jackson. LC 78-20567. (Sports Star Ser.). (Illus.). (gr. 1-5). 1979. pap. 2.95 (ISBN 0-15-684791-4, VoyB). HarBraceJ.

--Sports Star: Sugar Ray Leonard. LC 82-48764. (Sports Star Ser.). 64p. (gr. 1-5). 1983. PLB 11.95 (ISBN 0-15-278048-3, HJ). HarBraceJ.

--Sports Star: Sugar Ray Leonard. LC 82-48764. (Sports Star Ser.). (Illus.). 64p. (gr. 1-5). 1983. pap. 4.95 (ISBN 0-15-278049-1, VoyB). HarBraceJ.

--Sports Star: The Book of Baseball Greats. LC 82-48763. (Sports Star Ser.). 64p. (gr. 1-5). 1983. PLB 10.95 (ISBN 0-15-278060-2, HJ). HarBraceJ.

--Sports Star: The Book of Baseball Greats. LC 82-48763. (Sports Star Ser.). (Illus.). 64p. (gr. 1-5). 1983. pap. 4.95 (ISBN 0-15-278061-0, VoyB). HarBraceJ.

--Sports Star: Tony Dorsett. LC 78-52808. (Sports Star Ser.). (Illus.). (gr. 1-5). 1978. pap. 4.95 (ISBN 0-15-684792-2, VoyB). HarBraceJ.

--Sports Star: Tracy Austin. LC 81-84215. (Sports Star Ser.). (Illus.). 64p. (gr. 1-5). 1982. pap. 2.95 (ISBN 0-15-278043-2, VoyB). HarBraceJ.

--Sports Star: Wayne Gretzky. LC 82-47931. (Sports Star Ser.). (Illus.). 64p. (ps-3). 1982. pap. 2.95 (ISBN 0-15-278047-5, VoyB). HarBraceJ.

Burchard, Sue. The Statue of Liberty. LC 85-5525. (Illus.). (gr. 10). 1985. 12.95 (ISBN 0-15-279969-9, HJ). HarBraceJ.

--The Statue of Liberty: Birth to Rebirth. LC 85-5525. (Illus.). 192p. (gr. 5 up). 12.95 (ISBN 0-15-279969-9). HarBraceJ.

Burchard, Sue, jt. auth. see Burchard, Marshall.

Burchardt, Bill. The Lighthorsemen. LC 80-1986. (Double D Western Ser.). 192p. 1981. 10.95 (ISBN 0-385-17148-X). Doubleday.

Burchardt, Carl J. Norwegian Life & Literature. LC 73-136521. 230p. 1974. Repr. of 1920 ed. lib. bdg. 22.50x (ISBN 0-8371-5442-1, BUNL). Greenwood.

Burchardt, F. A., ed. Economics of Full Employment. LC 67-16340. Repr. of 1944 ed. lib. bdg. 19.50x (ISBN 0-678-00212-6). Kelley.

Burche, Jay. How to Create a Tax Shelter for a Travel Agency. 84p. 1979. 50.00 (ISBN 0-933796-00-5). Newport Bch Rent.

Burcheil, Scott W., et al, eds. Tumor Imaging: The Radioimmunochemical Detection of Cancer. (Illus.). 272p. 1981. 43.50x (ISBN 0-89352-156-6). Masson Pub.

Burchell, G., ed. Ideology & Consciousness: Life, Labour & Insecurity, Vol. 9. 122p. 1981. pap. text ed. 4.50x (Pub. by I & C England). Humanities.

Burchell, Lawrence. Victorian Schools Eighteen Thirty-Seven to Nineteen Hundred. (Colonial Government Architecture Ser.). 1980. 44.00x (ISBN 0-522-84160-0, Pub. by Melbourne U Pr Australia). Intl Spec Bk.

Burchell, Mary. Elusive Harmony. (Alpha Books). (Orig.). 1978. pap. text ed. 2.95x (ISBN 0-19-424163-7). Oxford U Pr.

--It's Rumoured in the Village. Bd. with Except My Love; Strangers May Marry. (Harlequin 3-in-1 Romances Ser.). 192p. 1983. pap. 1.75 (ISBN 0-373-20077-3). Harlequin Bks.

--Masquerade with Music. (Harlequin Romances Ser.). 192p. 1983. pap. 1.50 (ISBN 0-373-02528-9). Harlequin Bks.

Burchell, R. A. The San Francisco Irish, Eighteen Forty-Eight to Eighteen Eighty. LC 79-65764. 1980. 18.95 (ISBN 0-520-04003-1). U of Cal Pr.

Burchell, Robert & Hagevik, George. The Environmental Impact Handbook. 96p. 1974. pap. 8.95x (ISBN 0-87855-602-8). Transaction Bks.

Burchell, Robert & Listokin, David, eds. Energy & Land Use. 601p. 1981. 28.95 (ISBN 0-88285-069-5). Transaction Bks.

Burchell, Robert E. & Listokin, David. The Adaptive Reuse Handbook: Procedures to Inventory, Control & Manage Surplus Municipal Properties. 576p. 1981. 28.50 (ISBN 0-318-14936-2, 0310); members 23.00 (ISBN 0-318-14937-0). NAHRO.

Burchell, Robert W. The New Reality of Municipal Finance: The Rise & Fall of the Intergovernmental City. LC 83-7377. 458p. 1984. 20.00 (ISBN 0-88285-091-1). Ctr Urban Pol Res.

--The New Reality of Municipal Finance: The Rise & Fall of the Intergovernmental City. 480p. 1985. pap. 27.50. Transaction Bks.

Burchell, Robert W. & Listokin, David. Cities under Stress. 766p. 1979. 28.50 (ISBN 0-88285-064-4). Transaction Bks.

--Fiscal Impact Handbook: Estimating Local Costs & Revenues of Land Development. LC 78-6216. 1978. text ed. 28.50 (ISBN 0-88285-045-8). Ctr Urban Pol Res.

--The New Practitioner's Guide to Fiscal Impact Analysis. LC 85-5944. Date not set. price not set (ISBN 0-88285-109-8). Ctr Urban Pol Res.

--The New Practitioner's Guide to Fiscal Impact Analysis. 2nd ed. 72p. 1985. pap. 10.00 (ISBN 0-88285-109-8). Transaction Bks.

Burchell, Robert W. & Sternlieb, George, eds. Planning Theory in the Nineteen Eighties: A Search for Future Directions. LC 78-12929. 1978. pap. text ed. 12.95 (ISBN 0-88285-048-2). Ctr Urban Pol Res.

Burchell, Robert W., et al, eds. Mount Laurel II: Challenge & Delivery of Low-Cost Housing. 428p. 1983. text ed. 25.00x (ISBN 0-88285-098-9). Ctr Urban Pol Res.

Burchell, William J. Travels in the Interior of Southern Africa, 2 Vols. (Illus.). 1822-24. Set. 125.00 (ISBN 0-384-06403-5). Johnson Repr.

Burchenal, Joseph, ed. Cancer: Achievements, Challenges, & Prospects for the 1980's, Vol. 2. 944p. 1981. 46.00 (ISBN 0-8089-1357-3, 790735). Grune.

Burchenal, Joseph H. & Oettgn, Herbert, eds. Cancer: Achievements, Challenges, & Prospects for the 1980's, Vol. 1. 685p. 1981. 40.00 (ISBN 0-8089-1351-4, 790734). Grune.

Burchess, D. Specifications & Quantities. 2nd ed. (Illus.). 136p. 1980. pap. text ed. 18.50x (ISBN 0-7114-5640-2). Intl Ideas.

Burchett, Jean. Daze of Our Lives. 1982. pap. 7.95 (ISBN 0-89015-319-1). Eakin Pubns.

Burchett, Wilford & Alley, Rewi. China: The Quality of Life. (Pelican Ser.). 1976. pap. 3.95 (ISBN 0-14-021921-8, Pelican). Penguin.

Burchett, Wilfred. Catapult to Freedom: The Survival of the Vietnamese People. (Illus.). 232p. 1982. pap. 6.95 (ISBN 0-7043-3403-8, Pub. by Quartet Bks). Merrimack Pub Cir.

--The China-Cambodia-Vietnam Triangle. 235p. (Orig.). 1982. pap. 6.95 (ISBN 0-917702-13-1). Vanguard Bks.

--Shadows of Hiroshima. (Illus.). 128p. 1984. 22.00 (ISBN 0-8052-7205-4, Pub. by NLB England); pap. 7.50 (ISBN 0-8052-7206-2). Schocken.

Burchette, Dorothy. More Needlework Blocking & Finishing. (Illus.). 1979. encore ed. 2.95 (ISBN 0-684-16892-8, ScribT). Scribner.

--Needlework Blocking & Finishing. 1981. pap. 2.50 Encore (ISBN 0-684-16939-8, ScribT). Scribner.

--Needlework: Blocking & Finishing. LC 73-1096. (Illus.). 160p. 1974. 7.95 (ISBN 0-684-13867-0, ScribT). Scribner.

Burchfiel, B. C. Geology of Romania. LC 75-32832. (Geological Society of America Ser.: No. 158). pap. 28.00 (ISBN 0-317-28366-9, 2025469). Bks Demand UMI.

Burchfiel, B. Clark, et al. Physical Geology: The Structure & Processes of the Earth. 496p. 1982. text ed. 27.95 (ISBN 0-675-09913-7). Additional Supplement May Be Obtained From Publisher. Merrill.

Burchfield, Jerry. Darkroom Art. (Illus.). 168p. 1981. (Amphoto); pap. 14.95 (ISBN 0-8174-3708-8). Watson-Guptill.

Burchfield, R. W. A Supplement to the Oxford English Dictionary, Volume 2 H-N. 1976. 125.00x (ISBN 0-19-861123-4). Oxford U Pr.

Burchfield, R. W., ed. Supplement to the Oxford English Dictionary Vol. 1: A-G. 1972. 125.00x (ISBN 0-19-861115-3). Oxford U Pr.

Burchfield, Robert. The English Language. LC 84-9677. 194p. 1985. 19.95x (ISBN 0-19-219173-X). Oxford U Pr.

--The Spoken Word: A BBC Guide. 1982. pap. 3.95 (ISBN 0-19-520380-1, GB 693). Oxford U Pr.

Burchfield, Robert W. The Spoken Word. 40p. 1981. 20.00x (ISBN 0-563-17979-1, Pub. by BBC Pubns). State Mutual Bk.

Burchfield, Robert W., ed. A Supplement to the Oxford English Dictionary, Vol. 3. 1982. 125.00x (ISBN 0-19-861124-2). Oxford U Pr.

Burchfield, Susan R., ed. Stress: Psychological & Physiological Interactions. LC 83-12971. (Clinical & Community Psychology Ser.). 399p. 1985. text ed. 44.50 (ISBN 0-89116-267-4). Hemisphere Pub.

Burchhardt, Jacob. Weltgeschichtliche Betrachtungen. Mayer, J. P., ed. LC 78-67340. (European Political Thought Ser.). (Ger.). 1979. Repr. of 1929 ed. lib. bdg. 34.50x (ISBN 0-405-11683-7). Ayer Co Pubs.

Burchiel, S. W. & Rhodes, B. A., eds. Radioimmunoimaging & Radioimmunotherapy. 416p. 1983. 95.00 (ISBN 0-444-00806-3, Biomedical Pr). Elsevier.

Burchill, J. From School to University. pap. 5.50 (ISBN 0-08-028472-8). Pergamon.

Burchill, Julie. Girls on Film. (Illus.). 160p. 1984. 18.95 (ISBN 0-86276-153-0); pap. 11.95 (ISBN 0-86276-152-2). Proteus Pub NY.

Burchill, Julie & Parsons, Tony. The Boy Looked at Johnny: The Obituary of Rock & Roll. (Illus.). 96p. (Orig.). 1978. pap. 3.50 (ISBN 0-86104-030-9). Pluto Pr.

Burchill, Mary D. Index to Law School Alumni Publications. LC 85-10900. 1985. 8.95 (ISBN 0-8377-0345-X). Rothman.

Burchill, R. T. Methods in Plant Pathology. 43p. 1981. 30.00x (ISBN 0-85198-491-6, Pub. by CAB Bks England). State Mutual Bk.

Burchsted, C. A., et al. Nuclear Air Cleaning Handbook. LC 76-52974. (ERDA Technical Information Center). 302p. 1976. pap. 15.50 (ISBN 0-87079-103-6, ERDA-76-21); microfiche 4.50 (ISBN 0-87079-296-2, ERDA-76-21). DOE.

Burcik, Emil J. Properties of Petroleum Reservoir Fluids. LC 57-5906. (Illus.). 190p. 1979. Repr. of 1957 ed. text ed. 29.00 (ISBN 0-934634-00-9). Intl Human Res.

Burck, Frances W. Babysense. LC 79-2476. 1979. pap. 9.95 (ISBN 0-312-06458-6). St Martin.

Burck, Harman D. & Reardon, Robert C. Career Development Interventions. (Illus.). 356p. 1984. pap. 29.75x (ISBN 0-398-04929-7). C C Thomas.

Burck, Harman D., jt. auth. see Reardon, Robert C.

Burck, Joachim von see Von Burck, Joachim.

Burckel, Nicholas C., jt. auth. see Buenker, John D.

Burckel, Nicholas C., jt. ed. see Buenker, John D.

Burckel, R. B. Characterization of C(X) Among Its Subalgebras. (Lecture Notes in Pure & Applied Mathematics Ser: Vol. 6). 176p. 1972. 35.00 (ISBN 0-8247-6038-7). Dekker.

--Weakly Almost Periodic Functions on Semi-Groups. (Notes on Mathematics & Its Applications Ser.). 128p. 1970. 44.25 (ISBN 0-677-02170-4). Gordon.

Burckel, Robert B. An Introduction to Classical Complex Analysis, Vol. 1. LC 78-67403. (Pure and Applied Mathematics Ser.). 1980. 65.00 (ISBN 0-12-141701-8). Acad Pr.

Burckhalter, David. The Seris. LC 75-44915. 80p. 1976. pap. 7.50 (ISBN 0-8165-0517-9). U of Ariz Pr.

Burckhalter, Joseph H., jt. auth. see Korolkovas, Andrejus.

Burckhardt, C. H., et al. Das Gefieder des Huhnes: Abbild des Tieres und seiner Haltung. (Tierhaltung: No. 9). (Illus.). 67p. (Ger.). 1979. pap. 18.95x (ISBN 0-8176-1137-1). Birkhauser.

Burckhardt, J. J. Die Bewegungsgruppen der Kristallographie. rev. 2nd ed. (Mineralogisch-Geotechnische Reihe Ser.: No. 2). 209p. (Ger.). 1966. 44.95x (ISBN 0-8176-0058-2). Birkhauser.

Burckhardt, J. L. Arabic Proverbs: English & Arabic. 1975. 15.00x (ISBN 0-686-47155-5). Intl Bk Ctr.

--Arabic Proverbs: Or the Manners & Customs of the Modern Egyptians, Illustrated from Their Proverbial Sayings Current at Cario, Translated & Explained. 296p. (Orig.). 1984. pap. 8.95x (ISBN 0-7007-0185-0, Pub. by Salem Acad). Merrimack Pub Cir.

Burckhardt, Jacob. The Age of Constantine the Great. Hadas, Moses, tr. 400p. 1982. pap. 7.95 (ISBN 0-520-04680-3, CAL 570). U of Cal Pr.

--The Architecture of the Italian Renaissance. Murray, Peter, ed. LC 83-18113. (Illus.). 320p. 1985. lib. bdg. 50.00x (ISBN 0-226-08047-1). U of Chicago Pr.

--Civilization of the Renaissance in Italy, 2 Vols. Vol. 1. pap. 4.76i (ISBN 0-06-090459-3, CN459, CN); Vol. 2. pap. 4.76i (ISBN 0-06-090460-7, CN460, CN). Har-Row.

--Civilization of the Renaissance in Italy, 2 Vols. (Illus.). Set. 28.00 (ISBN 0-8446-1775-X). Peter Smith.

--The Civilization of the Renaissance in Italy. LC 54-6894. 1954. 6.95 (ISBN 0-394-60497-0). Modern Lib.

--The Civilization of the Renaissance in Italy. Paidon Press, ed. (Illus.). 486p. 1983. 13.95 (ISBN 0-7148-2140-3, Pub. by Salem Hse Ltd). Merrimack Pub Cir.

--Judgements on History & Historians. Winks, Robin W., ed. LC 83-49177. (History & Historiography Ser.). 271p. 1985. lib. bdg. 30.00 (ISBN 0-8240-6351-1). Garland Pub.

--Reflections on History. LC 78-24385. Orig. Title: Force & Freedom. 1979. 9.00 (ISBN 0-913966-37-1, Liberty Clas); pap. 5.00 (ISBN 0-913966-38-X). Liberty Fund.

Burckhardt, Jakob. Letters. Dru, Alexander, tr. from Ger. LC 75-8821. (Illus.). 242p. 1975. Repr. of 1955 ed. lib. bdg. 22.50x (ISBN 0-8371-8114-3, BULE). Greenwood.

Burckhardt, John L. Notes on the Bedouins & Wahabys, 2 Vols. in 1. 1831. 60.00 (ISBN 0-384-06475-2). Johnson Repr.

--Some Account of the Travels in Egypt & Nubia. 2nd ed. 1971. 59.00 (ISBN 0-403-03692-5). Scholarly.

--Travels in Arabia. 478p. 1968. Repr. of 1829 ed. 55.00x (ISBN 0-7146-1982-5, F Cass Co). Biblio Dist.

--Travels in Arabia. (Arab Background Ser.). 25.00x (ISBN 0-86685-007-4). Intl Bk Ctr.

--Travels in Nubia. LC 74-15014. Repr. of 1882 ed. 37.50 (ISBN 0-404-12009-1). AMS Pr.

--Travels in Syria & the Holy Land. LC 77-87614. (Illus.). 720p. 1983. Repr. of 1822 ed. 76.50 (ISBN 0-404-16437-4). AMS Pr.

Burckhardt, Rose E. The Cantatrice, Number II. LC 84-90446. 99p. 1984. 7.50 (ISBN 0-8233-0394-2). Golden Quill.

Burckhardt, Rudy. Mobile Homes. Elmslie, Kenward, ed. LC 79-90670. (Illus.). 1980. 15.00 (ISBN 0-915990-18-0); pap. 7.50 (ISBN 0-915990-19-9). Z Pr.

Burckhardt, Sigurd. The Drama of Language: Essays on Goethe & Kleist. LC 77-97492. 183p. 1970. 17.50x (ISBN 0-8018-1049-3). Johns Hopkins.

Burckhardt, T., jt. auth. see Matheson, D. M.

Burckhardt-Stuker, Ruth. Versuche zur Experimentellen Alalgetika-Abhaengigkeit bei der Ratte. (European University Studies: No. 6, Vol. 107). 284p. (Ger.). 1983. 26.85 (ISBN 3-261-03277-4). P Lang Pubs.

Burckle, L. H., jt. ed. see Saito, T.

Burczynski, J. Introduction to the Use of Sonar Systems for Estimating Fish Biomass. (Fisheries Technical Papers: No. 191, Rev. 1). 109p. (Eng., Fr. & Span.). 1982. pap. 8.00 (ISBN 92-5-101161-3, F2301, FAO). Unipub.

Burd, Gene, jt. auth. see Fontaine, Jacob, III.

Burd, Henry A. Joseph Ritson, a Critical Biography. 1916. 15.00 (ISBN 0-384-06485-X). Johnson Repr.

Burd, James J. & Serfustini, Leonard T. Quest One: Active Living, a Guide to Fitness, Conditioning & Health. 1978. pap. 11.95 (ISBN 0-8403-2520-7). Kendall Hunt.

Burd, Shirley, ed. see Tennessee Nurses' Association.

Burd, Van A., ed. The Ruskin Family Letters: The Correspondence of John James Ruskin, His Wife, & Their Son, John, 1801-1843, 2 vols. Incl. Vol. 1. 1801-1837; Vol. 2. 1837-1843. (Illus.). 792p. 1973. 75.00x (ISBN 0-8014-0725-7). Cornell U Pr.

Burd, Van Akin, ed. see Ruskin, John.

Burda, ed. Flower of the Month. (Burda Bks.). Date not set. 5.95 (ISBN 0-686-64663-0, B804). Toggitt.

--Sampler of the Month. (Burda Bks.). Date not set. 5.95x (ISBN 0-686-64664-9, B805). Toggitt.

--Smocking. Date not set. 3.00x (ISBN 0-686-64665-7, B801). Toggitt.

--Tatting. (Burda Bks.). Date not set. 3.00x (ISBN 0-686-64666-5, B802). Toggitt.

--Whitework & Cutwork. (Burda Bks.). Date not set. 3.00x (ISBN 0-686-64667-3, B803). Toggitt.

Burde & Savino. The Neuro-Ophthalmic Patient. 1985. 59.95 (ISBN 0-8016-0891-0). Mosby.

Burdekin, Katharine. Swastika Night. 216p. (Orig.). pap. 8.95 (ISBN 0-935312-56-0). Feminist Pr.

Burden, Dennis, ed. The Shorter Poems of John Milton. (The Poetry Bookshelf). 1970. pap. text ed. 6.00x (ISBN 0-435-15066-9). Heinemann Ed.

Burden, E. E. Architectural Delineation. 2nd ed. 1982. 41.50 (ISBN 0-07-008925-6). McGraw.

Burden, Ernest. Design Simulation: Use of Photographic & Electronic Media in Design & Presentation. 232p. 1985. text ed. 37.50 (ISBN 0-471-79977-7, Pub. by Wiley-Interscience). Wiley.
--Entourage: A Tracing File for Architecture & Interior Design Drawing. (Illus.). 256p. 1981. pap. 19.95 (ISBN 0-07-008930-2). McGraw.
Burden, Ernest E. Design Presentation: Techniques for Marketing & Project Presentation. (Illus.). 256p. 1983. 42.00 (ISBN 0-07-008931-0). McGraw.
Burden, George & Schurr, Peter. Understanding Epilepsy. (Illus.). 96p. 1976. 10.95x (ISBN 0-8464-0946-1); pap. 7.95x (ISBN 0-686-77142-7). Beekman Pubs.
Burden, Jean. A Celebration of Cats. LC 74-80960. 1977. 10.00 (ISBN 0-8397-1336-3); pap. 5.95 (ISBN 0-8397-1337-1). Eriksson.
--Journey Toward Poetry. (Orig.). 1967. 5.95 (ISBN 0-8079-0145-8); pap. 2.95 (ISBN 0-8079-0146-6). October.
--The Woman's Day Book of Hints for Cat-Owners. 1984. pap. 2.95 (ISBN 0-449-12661-7, Columbine). Fawcett.
Burden, Larry, jt. auth. see Whitt, Robert.
Burden, Richard, et al. Numerical Analysis. 2nd ed. LC 80-29558. 598p. 1981. text ed. write for info. (ISBN 0-87150-314-X, 33L 2511, Prindle). PWS Pubs.
Burden, Richard J., et al. Numerical Analysis. 3rd ed. 1985. pap. text ed. write for info. (ISBN 0-87150-243-7, Prindle). PWS Pubs.
Burden, Richard L. & Faires, J. Douglas. Numerical Analysis. 3rd ed. 1985. text ed. write for info. (ISBN 0-87150-857-5, Prindle). PWS Pubs.
Burden, Robert. John Fowles, John Hawkes, Claude Simon: A Complete Study. (Epistemata: Band V). 367p. 1980. pap. text ed. 20.00x (ISBN 3-88479-027-7, Pub. by Konigshausen Neumann Germany). Humanities.
Burden, Shirley. Chairs. Date not set. price not set. Aperture.
Burden, Shirley, photos by. Presence. (Illus.). 96p. 1981. 20.00 (ISBN 0-89381-075-4); limited ed. 250.00 (ISBN 0-89381-076-2). Aperture.
Burden, Tom & Campbell, Mike. Capitalism & Public Policy in the U. K.: A Marxist Approach. 256p. 1985. 29.00 (ISBN 0-7099-0685-4, Pub. by Croom Helm Ltd); pap. 13.95 (ISBN 0-7099-0686-2, Pub. by Croom Helm Ltd). Longwood Pub Group.
Burden, Vera. Discovering the Ridgeway. (Discovering Ser.: No. 211). (Illus.). 59p. 1985. pap. 3.95 (ISBN 0-85263-725-X, Pub. by Shire Pubns England). Seven Hills Bks.
Burden, Virginia. The Process of Intuition. rev. ed. LC 75-4170. 100p. 1975. pap. 2.50 (ISBN 0-8356-0466-7, Quest). Theos Pub Hse.
Burden, William A. M. The Struggle for Airways in Latin America. Wilkins, Mira, ed. LC 76-29797. (European Business Ser.). (Illus.). 1977. Repr. of 1943 ed. lib. bdg. 32.00x (ISBN 0-405-09716-6). Ayer Co Pubs.
Burder, G., ed. see Watts, Isaac.
Burder, J. Technique of Editing Sixteen Millimeter Films. 4th ed. (Illus.). 152p. 1979. 25.95 (ISBN 0-240-51019-4). Focal Pr.
Burder, John. Sixteen Millimeter Film Cutting. (Media Manual Ser.). (Illus.). 160p. 1975. pap. 14.95 (ISBN 0-240-50857-2). Focal Pr.
--Work of the Industrial Film Maker. (Library of Film & Television Practice). 1974. 16.95 (ISBN 0-8038-8053-7). Hastings.
Burdett, Charles. Chances & Changes. facs. ed. LC 79-76921. (American Fiction Reprint Ser). Repr. of 1846 ed. 13.00 (ISBN 0-8369-7000-4). Ayer Co Pubs.
Burdett, David L. & Seymour, Lawrence. Hix Nix Stix Pix: A Kaleidoscope of Talk & Events. 338p. 1984. 15.95 (ISBN 0-525-24202-3, 01549-460, Seymour Lawrence). Dutton.
Burdett, Eric. The Craft of Bookbinding: A Practical Guide. 1977. 32.00 (ISBN 0-7153-6656-4). David & Charles.
Burdett, Harold N. Yesteryear in Annapolis. LC 74-26773. (Illus.). 102p. 1974. pap. 4.00 (ISBN 0-87033-197-3). Tidewater.
Burdett, Jeremy K. Molecular Shapes: Theoretical Models of Inorganic Stereochemistry. LC 80-15463. 287p. 1980. 42.95 (ISBN 0-471-07860-3, Pub. by Wiley-Interscience). Wiley.
Burdett, O. Two Carlyles. LC 71-130269. (English Biography Ser., No. 31). 1970. Repr. of 1931 ed. lib. bdg. 52.95x (ISBN 0-8383-1176-8). Haskell.
--William Blake. LC 74-1127. (Studies in Blake, No. 3). 1974. lib. bdg. 42.95x (ISBN 0-8383-2021-X). Haskell.
Burdett, Osbert. Beardsley Period. LC 75-79196. 1969. Repr. of 1925 ed. 20.00 (ISBN 0-8154-0297-X). Cooper Sq.
--Beardsley Period: An Essay in Perspective. 1971. Repr. of 1925 ed. 6.00x (ISBN 0-403-00881-6). Scholarly.
--Beardsley Period, Essay in Perspective. LC 72-195439. 1925. lib. bdg. 35.00 (ISBN 0-8414-2524-8). Folcroft.
--The Brownings. LC 78-144919. 345p. 1929. Repr. 59.00 (ISBN 0-403-00882-4). Scholarly.
--Critical Essays. facsimile ed. LC 79-99685. (Essay Index Reprint Ser.). 1925. 18.00 (ISBN 0-8369-1346-9). Ayer Co Pubs.
--The Idea of Coventry Patmore. 1978. Repr. of 1921 ed. lib. bdg. 30.00 (ISBN 0-8495-0423-6). Arden Lib.
--Idea of Coventry Patmore. LC 73-14924. 1921. lib. bdg. 26.50 (ISBN 0-8414-3272-4). Folcroft.
--Memory & Imagination. 1935. Repr. 17.50 (ISBN 0-8274-2721-2). R West.
--The Reverend Smith, Sidney. LC 72-144920. 303p. 1934. Repr. 39.00 (ISBN 0-403-00883-2). Scholarly.
--The Two Carlyles. 1977. Repr. of 1931 ed. lib. bdg. 20.00 (ISBN 0-8495-0319-1). Arden Lib.
--The Two Carlyles. facsimile ed. LC 78-164591. (Select Bibliographies Reprint Ser.). Repr. of 1930 ed. 21.00 (ISBN 0-8369-5875-6). Ayer Co Pubs.
--The Two Carlyles. 319p. 1980. Repr. lib. bdg. 25.00 (ISBN 0-89987-058-9). Darby Bks.
--The Two Carlyles. 1973. lib. bdg. 12.75 (ISBN 0-8414-2545-0). Folcroft.
--The Two Carlyles. 319p. 1983. Repr. of 1930 ed. lib. bdg. 40.00 (ISBN 0-89760-067-3). Telegraph Bks.
--William Blake. LC 74-3371. 1926. lib. bdg. 17.50 (ISBN 0-8414-3132-9). Folcroft.
Burdette, Kay. Fabric Painting in Tole, Vol. 1. (Illus., Orig.). 1982. pap. 7.95 (ISBN 0-941284-16-6). Deco Design Studio.
--Fabric Painting in Tole, Vol. 2. 40p. (Orig.). 1983. pap. 6.95 (ISBN 0-941284-20-4). Deco Design Studio.
Burdette, Marcia. Zambia. (Profiles-Nations of Contemporary Africa Ser.). 135p. 1986. 26.50x (ISBN 0-86531-617-1). Westview.
Burdette, Robert J. Hawk-Eyes. LC 74-166674. (Illus.). 1971. 21.00 (ISBN 0-403-01436-0). Scholarly.
--The Rise & Fall of the Mustache. LC 71-91074. (The American Humorists Ser.). 1878. Repr. of 1878 ed. lib. bdg. 18.50 (ISBN 0-8398-0179-3). Irvington.
--Smiles Yoked with Sighs. facs. ed. LC 76-139757. (Granger Index Reprint Ser). 1900. 17.00 (ISBN 0-8369-6211-7). Ayer Co Pubs.
Burdette, Robert K. The Saga of Prayer: The Poetry of Dylan Thomas. LC 68-23203. (Studies in English Literature: No. 67). 160p. 1973. text ed. 18.40x (ISBN 90-2792-072-9). Mouton.
Burdette, W. J., ed. Invertebrate Endocrinology & Hormonal Heterophylly. (Illus.). 438p. 1974. 39.00 (ISBN 0-387-06594-6). Springer-Verlag.
Burdette, Walter J. & Gehan, Edmund A. Planning & Analysis of Clinical Studies. (Illus.). 116p. 1970. 15.25x (ISBN 0-398-00257-6). C C Thomas.
Burdic, William S. Underwater Acoustic System Analysis. (Illus.). 480p. 1984. 50.95 (ISBN 0-13-936716-0). P-H.
Burdick. Detroit Publishing Company Handbook & Supplement. rev. ed. 96p. Date not set. pap. 4.95 (ISBN 0-686-40532-3). Deltiologists Am.
Burdick, Arthur J. Prospectors' Manual. (Shorey Prospecting Ser.). (Illus.). 160p. pap. 8.95 (ISBN 0-8466-6018-0, U18). Shorey.
Burdick, C. R., jt. ed. see Kruse, E. G.
Burdick, Charles. The Frustrated Raider: The Story of the German Cruiser "Cormoran" in World War I. LC 78-12857. (Illus.). 132p. 1979. 9.95x (ISBN 0-8093-0899-1). S Ill U Pr.
Burdick, Charles & Moessner, Ursula. The German Prisoners-of-War in Japan, 1914-1920. LC 83-23563. (Illus.). 148p. (Orig.). 1984. lib. bdg. 9.255 (ISBN 0-8191-3761-8); pap. text ed. 8.75 (ISBN 0-8191-3762-6). U Pr of Amer.
Burdick, Charles B. Germany's Military Strategy & Spain in World War Two. LC 68-26994. (Illus.). 1968. 16.95x (ISBN 0-8156-2122-1). Syracuse U Pr.
--Ralph Lutz & the Hoover Institution. LC 72-87287. (Publications Ser.: No. 131). 185p. 1974. 11.95x (ISBN 0-8179-6131-3). Hoover Inst Pr.
Burdick, Charles B. & Jacobsen, Hans-Adolf, eds. Contemporary Germany: Politics & Culture. LC 83-5825. 475p. 1984. 37.50x (ISBN 0-86531-443-8, Pub. in cooperation with the U. of Bonn & the National Endowment for the Humanities); pap. text ed. 15.00 (ISBN 0-86531-449-7). Westview.
Burdick, Charles B. & Lutz, Ralph H., eds. The Political Institutions of the German Revolution, 1918-1919. LC 66-13464. (Publications Ser.: No. 40). 305p. 1966. 10.95x (ISBN 0-8179-1401-3). Hoover Inst Pr.
Burdick, Charles B., jt. ed. see Detwiler, Donald S.
Burdick, D., jt. auth. see Ross, M.
Burdick, Donald. Epistles of John. (Everyman's Bible Commentary Ser.). 1970. pap. 5.95 (ISBN 0-8024-2062-1). Moody.
Burdick, Donald L. & Leffler, William L. Petrochemicals for the Nontechnical Person. 238p. 1983. 44.95x (ISBN 0-87814-207-X). Pennwell Bks.
Burdick, Donald W. Letters of John the Apostle. (Orig.). 1985. pap. 12.95 (ISBN 0-8024-2356-6). Moody.
Burdick, E. & Lederer, W. Ugly American. 240p. 1985. pap. 3.50 (ISBN 0-449-20732-3, Crest). Fawcett.
Burdick, Elizabeth B., ed. Contemporary Stage Design - U.S.A. LC 74-26233. (Illus.). 1975. pap. 12.50x (ISBN 0-8195-8023-6). Wesleyan U Pr.
Burdick, Eugene & Wheeler, Harvey. Fail-Safe. 285p. (gr. 9 up). 1978. pap. 3.50 (ISBN 0-440-12459-X). Dell.
Burdick, Eugene, jt. auth. see Lederer, William J.
Burdick, Eugene & Brodbeck, Arthur J, eds. American Voting Behavior. LC 77-7237. (Illus.). 1977. lib. bdg. 27.75x (ISBN 0-8371-9668-X, BUAV). Greenwood.
Burdick, Francis M. The Law of Partnership, Including Limited Partnerships. lii, 422p. 1983. Repr. of 1899 ed. lib. bdg. 37.50x (ISBN 0-8377-0333-6). Rothman.
Burdick, G. R., jt. ed. see Fussell, J. B.
Burdick, G. S. The Accursed. LC 82-81996. 256p. 1982. pap. 2.95 (ISBN 0-86721-218-7). Jove Pubns.
Burdick, Holly, jt. ed. see Carey, Katherine.
Burdick, John & Weiser, Peter B. ProDOS Quick & Simple: For the Apple II Family. 288p. 1985. pap. 19.95 (ISBN 0-673-18077-8). Scott F.
Burdick, Loraine. The Shirley Temple Scrapbook. 1982. pap. 8.95 (ISBN 0-8246-0277-3). Jonathan David.
Burdick, Neal, ed. see Adirondack Mountain Club, Inc.
Burdick, Neal S., ed. A Century Wild: Essays Commemorating the Centennial of the Adirondack Forest Preserve. (Illus.). 170p. 1985. 12.95 (ISBN 0-918517-06-0). Chauncy Pr.
Burdick, Thomas, jt. auth. see Mitchell, Charlene.
Burdick, Usher L. Marquis Demores at War in the Bad Lands. (Shorey Historical Ser.). 29p. pap. 3.95 (ISBN 0-8466-0220-2, S220). Shorey.
Burdick, William L. The Bench & Bar of Other Lands. LC 39-32691. xii, 652p. 1982. Repr. of 1939 ed. lib. bdg. 35.00 (ISBN 0-89941-163-0). W S Hein.
Burdine, Brian, jt. auth. see Hix, Charles.
Burditt, Joyce R. The Craker Factory. 312p. 1977. pap. 3.95 (ISBN 0-318-15304-1). Natl Coun Alcoholism.
Burdman, Geri M. Healthful Aging. (Illus.). 240p. 1986. text ed. 21.95 (ISBN 0-13-385543-0). P-H.
Burdon, J. J., jt. ed. see Groves, R. H.
Burdon, R. H., ed. see Adams, R. L.
Burdon, R. H., jt. ed. see Work, T. S.
Burdon, R. H., jt. auth. see Adams, R. L.
Burdsall, Harold H., Jr. A Contribution to the Taxonomy of the Genus Phanerochaete (Corticiaceae, Aphyllophorales) (Mycologia Memoir Ser.: No. 10). (Illus.). 170p. 1985. lib. bdg. 24.00 (ISBN 3-7682-1392-7). Lubrecht & Cramer.
Burdsall, Richard L. & Emmons, Arthur B., 3rd. Men Against the Clouds. LC 79-25369. (Illus.). 1980. pap. 9.95 (ISBN 0-916890-93-7). Mountaineers.
Bure, Germaine see Born, Warren C.
Bureau European Des Unions De Consommateurs. After Sales Service in the European Economic Community. 271p. 1977. 33.00x (ISBN 0-86010-056-1, Pub. by Graham & Trotman England). State Mutual Bk.
Bureau, Jacques. Dictionnaire de l'Informatique. 250p. (Fr.). 1972. pap. 6.95 (ISBN 0-686-56932-6, M-6053). French & Eur.
Bureau Justice of Statistics, jt. ed. see National Center for State Courts.
Bureau of Adult Occupational Educational, N.Y. State Education Department. Handbook for Teachers of Adult Occupational Education. 96p. 1977. 4.95 (ISBN 0-318-15481-1, SN20). Natl Ctr Res Voc Ed.
Bureau of Applied Social Research, Columbia University. The People Look at Radio. LC 75-22803. (America in Two Centuries Ser). 1976. Repr. of 1946 ed. 16.00x (ISBN 0-405-07675-4). Ayer Co Pubs.
Bureau of Business & Economic Research, Univ. of California, jt. auth. see Weston, John F.
Bureau of Business Practice. Speed Reading: The Computer Course, Apple IIc. Date not set. price not set. P-H.
Bureau of Business Research, ed. Health Care Cost Containment: The Managerial Approach. 1978. 7.50 (ISBN 0-686-28414-3). Bur Busn Res U Nebr.
Bureau of Business Research Staff. Economic Projections, Nineteen Eighty-Four to Nineteen Ninty-Five. 1984. 15.00 (ISBN 0-318-03898-6). Bur Busn Res U Nebr.
Bureau of Census, ed. Congressional District Data Book, 98th Congress. (Congressional District Data Book PHC80-4 Ser.). 1983. three-ring binder 60.00x (ISBN 0-527-67325-0). Kraus Intl.
Bureau of Economic & Business Research Staff, University of Utah, ed. Utah Statistical Abstract 1983. 9th ed. (Illus.). 396p. (Orig.). 1983. 25.00 (ISBN 0-942486-04-8). Univ Utah.
Bureau of Government Research, ed. State Debt & Public Liability in Oklahoma. 22p. 1982. 2.00 (ISBN 0-318-01378-9). Univ OK Gov Res.
Bureau of Governmental Research & Service, University of Oregon, jt. auth. see Westling, A. M.
Bureau of Mining & Reclamation & Bureau of Deep Mine Safety. Nineteen Eighty-Two Annual Report on Mining Activities. Patsie, Nichols & Keffer, Gloria, eds. 485p. 1982. 7.25 (ISBN 0-8182-0028-6). Commonweal PA.
Bureau of Motor Carrier Safety Staff, tr. see U. S. Dept of Transportation Staff.
Bureau of National Affairs. The Consumer Product Safety Act: Texts, Analysis, Legislative History. LC 72-95897. pap. 115.80 (ISBN 0-317-29425-3, 2024303). Bks Demand UMI.
--Highlights of the New Pension Reform Law: Text of Act, Statement of the Managers, Editoral Analysis. LC 74-188898. pap. 92.30 (ISBN 0-317-26776-0, 2024339). Bks Demand UMI.
--The Job Safety & Health Act of 1970: Text, Analysis, Legislative History. LC 78-156236. pap. 87.00 (ISBN 0-317-29419-9, 2024307). Bks Demand UMI.
--Labor Relations Yearbook, Nineteen Seventy-Nine. LC 66-19726. pap. 139.50 (ISBN 0-317-29418-0, 2024308). Bks Demand UMI.
Bureau of National Affairs (Washington D.C.). Research & Special Projects Division. Digest of 1953 Congressional Hearings on Amending the Labor-Management Relations Act, 1947 (Taft-Hartley Act, 1947) LC 84-234114. 411p. Date not set. price not set. BNA.
Bureau of Naval Personnel. Basic Construction Techniques for Houses & Small Buildings Simply Explained. (Illus.). 17.25 (ISBN 0-8446-4506-0). Peter Smith.
--Tools & Their Uses. (Illus.). 12.25 (ISBN 0-8446-4718-7). Peter Smith.
Bureau of Railway Economics. A List of References to Literature: Relating to the Union Pacific System. 299p. 1974. 25.00x (ISBN 0-89020-006-8). Crofton Pub.
Bureau of Social Science Research. International Communication & Political Opinion. Smith, B. L. & Smith, C. M., eds. LC 72-1108. 325p. 1972. Repr. of 1956 ed. lib. bdg. 22.50x (ISBN 0-8371-6007-3, INCO). Greenwood.
Bureau of Statistics, U.S. Dept. of Labor. Labor Unionism in American Agriculture. facsimile ed. McCurry, Dan C. & Rubenstein, Richard E., eds. LC 74-30656. (American Farmers & the Rise of Agribusiness Ser.). (U.S. Dept. of Labor, Bulletin No. 836). 1975. Repr. of 1945 ed. 42.00x (ISBN 0-405-06831-X). Ayer Co Pubs.
Bureau Of The Census, ed. Government Dossier: An Inventory of Government Information About Individuals. LC 69-19367. 1968. Repr. of 1968 ed. 17.00 (ISBN 0-405-00015-4). Ayer Co Pubs.
Bureau of the Census, U.S. Department of Commerce. Housing Construction Statistics, 1889 to 1964. LC 75-22865. (America in Two Centuries Ser). 1976. Repr. of 1966 ed. 67.50x (ISBN 0-405-07731-9). Ayer Co Pubs.
Bureau, Willaim H. What the Printer Should Know About Paper. 320p. 1982. 32.00 (ISBN 0-88362-013-8, 1308); members 16.00 (ISBN 0-318-17922-9). Graphic Arts Tech Found.
Burek, Cynthia V., jt. auth. see Cubitt, John M.
Burek, P. J., tr. see Braitsch, O.
Bureloff, Morris. Brain-Busting Decode Puzzles. Laycock, Mary, ed. (Illus.). 64p. (gr. 7-10). 1985. pap. 6.50 (ISBN 0-918932-86-6). Activity Resources.
--De Code Puzzles - Math. Laycock, Mary, ed. (Illus.). 64p. pap. text ed. 6.50 (ISBN 0-918932-79-3). Activity Resources.
--Horoscore Shade-Ins-Math. Laycock, Mary, ed. (Illus.). (gr. 6-12). 1982. pap. 4.50 (ISBN 0-918932-77-7). Activity Resources.
--Key Word Puzzles. Laycock, Mary, ed. (Illus.). 64p. (gr. 6-10). 1982. pap. 6.50 (ISBN 0-918932-76-9). Activity Resources.
Bureloff, Morris & Johnson, Connie. Calculators, Number Patterns, & Magic. (Illus.). (gr. 4-12). 1977. pap. text ed. 6.50 (ISBN 0-918932-49-1). Activity Resources.
Bureloff, Morris, et al. Number Triangles. Laycock, Mary & Merrick, Paul, eds. (Illus., Orig.). (gr. 5-12). 1977. pap. 6.50 (ISBN 0-918932-36-X). Activity Resources.
Buren, Abigail Van see Van Buren, Abigail.
Buren, Ariane van see Van Buren, Ariane & Pyle, Leo.
Buren, Daniel. The Paris Metro. LC 77-90043. (Illus.). 1978. 75.00 (ISBN 0-902063-11-1). Overlook Pr.
Buren, E. Douglas Van see Van Buren, E. Douglas.
Buren, Elizabeth Van see Van Buren, Elizabeth.
Buren, Elizabeth van see Van Buren, Elizabeth.
Buren, J. M. Van see Van Buren, J. M.
Buren, James Van see Van Buren, James & Dewett, Don.
Buren, Martin Van see Van Buren, Martin.
Buren, Paul M. Van see Van Buren, Paul M.
Burenkov, Sergei. Advances in Soviet Medicine. 1984. text ed. 27.50 (ISBN 0-8236-0111-0). Intl Univs Pr.
Burenkov, Sergei, ed. Medicine & Health Care in the U. S. S. R. 270p. 1985. text ed. 45.00 (ISBN 0-8236-3310-1, 03310). Intl Univs Pr.
Bures, Donald. Abelian Subalgebras of Von Neumann Algebras. LC 52-42839. (Memoirs: No. 110). 127p. 1971. pap. text ed. 9.00 (ISBN 0-8218-1810-4, MEMO-110). Am Math.
Bures, J., et al. Electrophysiological Methods in Biological Research. 3rd ed. 1967. 95.00 (ISBN 0-12-142956-3). Acad Pr.
Bures, Jan & Krekule, Ivan. Practical Guide to Computer Applications in Neurosciences. 398p. 1983. 54.95 (ISBN 0-471-10012-9, Pub. by Wiley-Interscience). Wiley.

Bures, Jan, et al. The Mechanism & Application of Leao's Spreading Depression of Electroencephalographic Activity. 1974. 79.50 (ISBN 0-12-142960-1). Acad Pr.
--Techniques & Basic Experiments for the Study of Brain & Behavior. 1976. 41.50 (ISBN 0-444-41502-5, North Holland). Elsevier.
--Techniques & Basic Experiments for the Study of Brain & Behavior. 2nd, rev. ed. 1983. 80.00 (ISBN 0-444-80448-X, I-351-83); pap. 29.95 (ISBN 0-444-80535-4). Elsevier.
Bures, Ruth A. Here Comes Christmas. 40p. (gr. k-8). 1982. pap. 7.95 (ISBN 0-86704-008-4). Clarus Music.
Buresch, M. Photovoltaic Energy Systems: Design & Installation. 352p. 1983. 27.50 (ISBN 0-07-008952-3). McGraw.
Buresh, Jane G. A Fundamental Goal: Education for the People of Illinois. LC 74-19064. (Studies in Illinois Constitution Making). 152p. 1975. pap. 10.00x (ISBN 0-252-00457-4). U of Ill Pr.
Buret, Frederic. Syphillis Today & Among the Ancients, 3 vols. in 2. LC 72-9627. Repr. of 1895 ed. Set. 42.50 (ISBN 0-404-57422-X). AMS Pr.
Burfeindt-Moral & Zacher, H. H. Satz-Lexikon des Englischen Geschaeftsbriefes. 400p. (Ger.). 1972. 14.50 (ISBN 3-468-39120-X). Langenscheidt.
Burfisher, Mary E. & Horenstein, Nadine R. Sex Roles in the Nigerian Tiv Farm Household. (K. P. Case Studies on Women's Role & Gender Differences in Development). 1985. pap. text ed. 6.75x (ISBN 0-931816-17-3). Kumarian Pr.
Burfoot, J. C. & Taylor, G. W. Polar Dielectrics & Their Applications. LC 78-62835. 1979. 70.00x (ISBN 0-520-03749-9). U of Cal Pr.
Burford. The Greek Temple Builders at Epidauros. 274p. 1982. 50.00x (ISBN 0-85323-080-3, Pub. by Liverpool Univ England). State Mutual Bk.
Burford, jt. auth. see Mathew.
Burford, Anne M. & Greenya, John. Are You Tough Enough? An Insider's View of Washington Power Politics. (Illus.). 1985. 16.95 (ISBN 0-07-008940-X). McGraw.
Burford, E. J. The Orrible Synne. LC 74-172023. (Illus.). 220p. 1979. 15.00 (ISBN 0-7145-0978-7, Dist by Scribner); pap. 7.95 (ISBN 0-7145-1126-9, Dist by Scribner). M Boyars.
Burford, E. J., ed. Bawdy Verse: A Pleasant Collection. 1983. pap. 3.95 (ISBN 0-14-042297-8). Penguin.
Burford, Lolah. Mac Lyon. 1985. pap. 3.95 (ISBN 0-451-13833-3, Sig). NAL.
Burford, Ray, jt. auth. see Matthews, Denis.
Burford, Roger L. A Projections Model for Small Area Economies. LC 67-64023. (Research Monograph: No. 35). 1966. spiral bdg. 7.50 (ISBN 0-88406-049-7). Ga St U Busn Pub.
Burford, William. A Beginning. (Orig.). 1966. 4.50 (ISBN 0-393-04286-3); pap. 1.95x (ISBN 0-393-04279-0, 3). Norton.
--A World. LC 62-19995. (Tower (Poetry) Ser.: No. 3). (Illus.). 1962. 5.95 (ISBN 0-87959-001-7). U of Tex H Ransom Ctr.
Burford Mason, Roger. Up at the Big House. (Illus.). 32p. 1981. 22.00 (ISBN 0-930126-08-4). Typographeum.
Burg, B. R. Richard Mather of Dorchester. LC 75-41987. 224p. 1976. 21.00x (ISBN 0-8131-1343-1). U Pr of Ky.
--Sodomy & the Perception of Evil: English Sea Rovers in the Seventeeth Century Caribbean. 300p. 1983. 25.00x (ISBN 0-8147-1040-9). NYU Pr.
--Sodomy & the Pirate Tradition: English Sea Rovers in the Seventeenth-Century Caribbean. 240p. 1985. pap. 12.50x (ISBN 0-8147-1073-5). NYU Pr.
Burg, B. Richard. Richard Mather. (United States Authors Ser.). 1982. lib. bdg. 16.50 (ISBN 0-8057-7364-9, Twayne). G K Hall.
Burg, Cynthia M., et al. Golda Meir House for the Elderly: An Architectural Evaluation. Moore, Gary T., ed. (Illus.). iv, 125p. 1981. 7.50 (ISBN 0-938744-19-4, R81-6). U of Wis Ctr Arch-Urban.
Burg, David, tr. see Solzhenitsyn, Alexander.
Burg, David F. Chicago's White City of Eighteen Ninety-Three. LC 75-3542. (Illus.). 400p. 1976. 36.00x (ISBN 0-8131-1331-8); pap. 10.00x (ISBN 0-8131-0140-9). U Pr of Ky.
Burg, Frederic & Polin, Richard A. Workbook in Practical Neonatology. (Illus.). 256p. 1983. pap. 20.00 (ISBN 0-7216-2201-1). Saunders.
Burg, G. & Braun-Falco, O. Cutaneous Lymphomas, Pseudolymphomas & Related Disorders. (Illus.). 550p. 1983. 140.00 (ISBN 0-387-10467-4). Springer-Verlag.
Burg, G., jt. ed. see Ring, J.
Burg, H., tr. see Bartknecht, W.
Burg, J. B. The Place of St. Patrick in History & His Life. 59.95 (ISBN 0-8490-0839-5). Gordon Pr.
Burg, Nan C. An Annotated Bibliography of Solar Energy Research & Technology Applicable to Community Buildings & Other Non-Residential Construction. 1977. 3.00 (ISBN 0-686-19118-8, 1263). CPL Biblios.
--Reversing Regional Economic Decline: A Supplement to Exchange Bibliography No. 1193. 1977. 1.50 (ISBN 0-686-19121-8). CPL Biblios.
Burg, Nan C., et al. Home Rule in U. S. Municipalities & Counties & in the Commonwealth of Pennsylvania: A Selected Bibliography, No. 746. rev. ed. 1975. 6.00 (ISBN 0-686-20340-2). CPL Biblios.
Burg, Steven L. Conflict & Cohesion in Socialist Yugoslavia: Political Decision Making since 1966. LC 82-61358. 456p. 1983. 37.50x (ISBN 0-691-07651-0). Princeton U Pr.
Burg, William Van de see Van De Burg, William.
Burgan, Arthur. Basic String Repairs: A Guide for String-Class Teachers. (Illus.). 1974. pap. 10.95x (ISBN 0-19-318509-1). Oxford U Pr.
Burgdorf, Arlene, jt. auth. see Barnes, Donald L.
Burgdorf, Robert L., Jr. & Spicer, Patrick P. The Legal Rights of Handicapped Persons: Cases, Materials & Text; 1983 Supplement. LC 83-2471. 504p. 1983. text ed. 27.95 (ISBN 0-933716-31-1, 311). P H Brookes.
Burgdorf, W. H., et al. Dermatopathology. (Illus.). x, 219p. 1984. 29.50 (ISBN 0-387-96011-2). Springer-Verlag.
Burgdorfer, Willy & Anacker, Robert. Rickettsiae & Rickettsial Diseases. 1981. 70.00 (ISBN 0-12-143150-9). Acad Pr.
Burge, David A. Patent & Trademark Tactics & Practice. 2nd ed. LC 84-2408. 213p. 1984. text ed. 29.95x (ISBN 0-471-80471-1, Pub. by Wiley Interscience). Wiley.
Burge, David L. Color Hearing for Children: A Guide to Perfect Pitch for the Young or Beginning Musician. (Orig.). 1985. pap. 10.00 (ISBN 0-942542-96-7). Am Ed Mus Pubns.
--The Official Transcript of the Perfect Pitch Workshop. (Illus.). 1984. pap. 10.00 (ISBN 0-942542-98-3). Am Ed Mus Pubns.
--The Official Transcript of the Perfect Pitch Master Class. (Orig.). 1984. pap. 10.00 (ISBN 0-942542-99-1). Am Ed Mus Pubns.
--Perfect Pitch: Color Hearing for Expanded Musical Awareness. LC 81-85963. 60p. 1983. pap. 12.50 (ISBN 0-942542-97-5). Am Ed Mus Pubns.
Burge, John H. Occupational Stress in Policing. 232p. 1984. pap. 15.95 (ISBN 0-914330-65-9, Pub. by Pioneer Pub Co). Panorama West.
Burge, William. Commentaries on Colonial & Foreign Laws Generally & in Their Conflict with Each Other & with the Law of England, 4 Vols. in 5 Bks. Renton, Alexander W., et al, eds. LC 80-84956. (Historical Writings in Law & Jurisprudence Ser.: No. 17, Bks. 21-25). 1981. Repr. of 1907 ed. Set. lib. bdg. 265.00set (ISBN 0-89941-186-X). Vol. 1 (ISBN 0-89941-073-1). Vol. 2 (ISBN 0-89941-074-X). Vol. 3 (ISBN 0-89941-075-8). Vol. 4, Pt. 1 (ISBN 0-89941-076-6). Vol. 4, Pt. 2. W S Hein.
--Commentaries on the Law of Suretyship, & the Rights & Obligations of Parties Thereto. Helmholz, R. H. & Reams, Bernard D., Jr., eds. LC 80-84858. (Historical Writings in Law & Jurisprudence Ser.: No. 18, Bk. 26). 616p. 1981. Repr. of 1847 ed. lib. bdg. 42.00 (ISBN 0-89941-078-2). W S HEIN.
Burge, William H. Recursive Programming Techniques. LC 74-28812. (IBM Systems Programming Ser.). (Illus.). 280p. 1975. text ed. 28.95 (ISBN 0-201-14450-6). Addison-Wesley.
Burgee, John, jt. auth. see Johnson, Philip.
Burgelin, Pierre, ed. see Rousseau, Jean-Jacques.
Burgelman, Robert A. & Sayles, Leonard R. Inside Corporate Innovation: Strategy, Structure, & Managerial Skills. 240p. 27.95x (ISBN 0-02-904340-9). Free Pr.
--Inside Corporate Innovation: Strategy, Structure & Managerial Skills. 240p. 1985. 27.95x (ISBN 0-02-904340-9). Free Pr.
Burgen, A. S. & Roberts, G. C. Topics in Molecular Pharmacology, Vol. 2. 1984. 69.25 (ISBN 0-444-80495-1, I-018-84). Elsevier.
Burgen, A. S. & Roberts, G. C., eds. Topics in Molecular Pharmacology, Vol. 1. 250p. 1982. 68.00 (ISBN 0-444-80354-8, Biomedical Pr). Elsevier.
Burgen, A. S., ed. see Gaddum, John.
Burgen, Sir Arnold, et al. Neuroactive Peptides. (Proceedings of the Royal & Society, Series B.: Vol. 210). (Illus.). 192p. 1980. text ed. 35.00x (ISBN 0-85403-149-9, Pub. by Royal Soc London). Scholium Intl.
Burgener, Francis A. & Kormano, Martil. Differential Diagnosis in Conventional Radiology. (Illus.). 748p. 1985. 90.00 (ISBN 0-86577-197-9). Thieme-Stratton.
Burger. Personality: Theory & Research. 1986. text ed. write for info. (ISBN 0-534-06126-5). Wadsworth Pub.
Burger, et al. Marxism, Science & the Movement of History. (Philosophical Currents Ser.: No. 27). 1981. pap. text ed. 34.75x (ISBN 90-6032-186-3). Humanities.
Burger, A. W. Laboratory Exercises in Field Crop Science. 1977. spiral bdg. 8.60x (ISBN 0-87563-031-6). Stipes.
Burger, Alfred. A Guide to the Chemical Basis of Drug Design. LC 83-3575. 300p. 1983. 50.00x (ISBN 0-471-86828-0, Pub. by Wiley-Interscience). Wiley.
Burger, Angela S. Opposition in a Dominant-Party System: A Study of the Jan Sangh, the Praja Socialist & Socialist Parties in Uttar Pradesh, India. LC 77-76540. (Center for South & Southeast Asia Studies, UC Berkeley). 1969. 29.50x (ISBN 0-520-01428-6). U of Cal Pr.
Burger, Chester. The Chief Executive: Realities of Corporate Leadership. LC 77-2844. 224p. 1978. 19.95 (ISBN 0-8436-0747-5). Van Nos Reinhold.
Burger, Chester, jt. auth. see Cantor, Bill.
Burger, Denis R., jt. ed. see Kirkpatrick, Charles H.
Burger, Dionys. Sphereland. Rheinboldt, Cornelie J., tr. from Fr. (Illus.). 224p. 1983. pap. 4.76i (ISBN 0-06-463574-0, EH 574). B&N NY.
Burger, E. Technical Dictionary of Data Processing, Computers & Office Machines, English, German, French, Russian. (Eng., Ger., Fr. & Rus.). 1970. 145.00 (ISBN 0-08-006425-6). Pergamon.
Burger, E., ed. Technical Dictionary of Automatization & Programming: English, French, German, Russian, Slovene. 479p. (Eng., Fr., Ger., Rus. & Slovene.). 1976. 95.00 (ISBN 0-686-92330-8, M-9889). French & Eur.
--Technical Reference Dictionary. 571p. 1979. 95.00 (ISBN 0-686-92324-3, M-9890). French & Eur.
Burger, Edward J. Health Risks: The Challenge of Informing the Public. Media Institute, ed. 81p. (Orig.). 1984. pap. 10.00 (ISBN 0-937790-22-2). Media Inst.
Burger, Edward J., Jr. Science at the White House: A Political Liability. LC 80-81425. 208p. 1981. text ed. 19.00x (ISBN 0-8018-2433-8). Johns Hopkins.
Burger, G., jt. auth. see Dietiker, S.
Burger, G., et al. Radiation Protection Quantities for External Exposure. (Commission of the European Communities Symposium Ser.). 268p. 1981. 61.75 (ISBN 3-7186-0063-3). Harwood Academic.
Burger, Georg. Treatment Planning for External Beam Therapy with Neutrons. (Illus.). 250p. 1982. 52.00 (ISBN 0-8067-0271-0). Urban & S.
Burger, Gottfried A. Lenore. Rosetti, Dante G., tr. from Ger. LC 73-7883. 1900. lib. bdg. 17.50 (ISBN 0-8414-3131-0). Folcroft.
Burger, H. C. Heart & Vector: Physical Basis of Electrocardiography. Julius, H. W., Jr., ed. 156p. 1970. 45.25 (ISBN 0-677-61290-7). Gordon.
Burger, Habil E. Dictionary of Automatic Data Processing. 480p. 1980. 75.00x (Pub. by Collet's). State Mutual Bk.
Burger, Harald. Jakob Bidermanns Belisarius: Edition und Versuch einer Deutung. (Quellen und Forschungen-zur Sprach-und Kulturgeschichte der Germanischen Voelker). (Ger). 1966. 33.60x (ISBN 3-11-000211-6). De Gruyter.
--Zeit und Ewigkeit: Studien zum Wortschatz der Geistlichen Texte des Alt-und Fruehmittelhochdeutschen. LC 74-174177. (Studia Linguistica Germanica: Vol. 6). 1972. 34.00x (ISBN 3-11-003995-8). De Gruyter.
Burger, Henry & Dekretser, David, eds. The Testis. (Comprehensive Endocrinology Ser.). 454p. 1981. text ed. 71.00 (ISBN 0-89004-247-0). Raven.
Burger, Henry G. Wordtree: A Transitive Cladistic for Solving Physical & Social Problems. LC 84-13007. 380p. 1984. 149.00 (ISBN 0-936312-00-9). Wordtree.
Burger, Ing H. Dictionary of Automatic Data Processing. 480p. (Eng., Ger., Fr., Rus. & Slovak.). 1976. 80.00x (ISBN 0-569-08521-7, Pub. by Collets). State Mutual Bk.
Burger, Isabel & DeBear, Constance. Remi's Secret Locket: Nobody's Boy. (Children's Theatre Playscript Ser.). 1957. pap. 2.25x (ISBN 0-88020-049-9). Coach Hse.
Burger, Isabel B. Creative Drama for Senior Adults. LC 80-81101. (Illus.). 144p. (Orig.). 1980. pap. 6.95 (ISBN 0-8192-1269-5). Morehouse.
--Creative Drama in Religious Education. 1977. pap. 6.95 (ISBN 0-8192-1223-7). Morehouse.
Burger, J. & Jarny, Y., eds. Simulation in Engineering Sciences: Applications to the Automatic Control of Mechanical & Energy Systems. 438p. 1984. 52.00 (ISBN 0-444-86795-3, North Holland). Elsevier.
Burger, Jan J., et al, eds. Atmospheric Physics from Spacelab. (Astrophysics & Space Science Library: No. 61). 1976. lib. bdg. 55.00 (ISBN 90-277-0768-5, Pub. by Reidel Holland). Kluwer Academic.
Burger, Joanna. Pattern, Mechanism, & Adaptive Significance of Territoriality in Herring Gulls (Larus argentatus) 92p. 1984. 9.00 (ISBN 0-943610-41-9). Am Ornithologists.
Burger, Joanna & Olla, Bori L., eds. Shorebirds: Breeding Behavior & Populations. (Behavior of Marine Animals Ser.: Vol. 5). 421p. 1984. 59.50x (ISBN 0-306-41590-9, Plenum Pr). Plenum Pub.
--Shorebirds: Migration & Foraging Behavior. (Behavior of Marine Animals Ser.: Vol. 6). 323p. 1984. 49.50x (ISBN 0-306-41591-7, Plenum Pr). Plenum Pub.
Burger, Joanna, et al, eds. Behavior of Marine Animals, Vol. 4: Marine Birds. LC 79-167675. 532p. 1980. 55.00x (ISBN 0-306-37574-5, Plenum Pr). Plenum Pub.
Burger, Joanne. SF Published in Nineteen Seventy-Five. LC 71-10701. 64p. 1980. Repr. of 1976 ed. lib. bdg. 19.95x (ISBN 0-89370-053-3). Borgo Pr.
--SF Published in Nineteen Seventy-Four. LC 71-10701. 64p. 1980. Repr. of 1975 ed. lib. bdg. 19.95x (ISBN 0-89370-052-5). Borgo Pr.
--SF Published in Nineteen Seventy-Seven. LC 71-10701. 64p. 1980. Repr. of 1979 ed. lib. bdg. 19.95x (ISBN 0-89370-055-X). Borgo Pr.
--SF Published in Nineteen Seventy-Seven. (Orig.). 1978. pap. 4.00x (ISBN 0-916188-08-6). J Burger.
--SF Published in Nineteen Seventy-Six. LC 71-10701. 64p. 1980. Repr. of 1977 ed. lib. bdg. 19.95x (ISBN 0-89370-054-1). Borgo Pr.
--SF Published in Nineteen Seventy-Three. LC 71-10701. 64p. 1980. Repr. of 1974 ed. lib. bdg. 19.95x (ISBN 0-89370-051-7). Borgo Pr.
--SF Published in Nineteen Seventy-Two. LC 71-10701. 64p. 1980. Repr. of 1973 ed. lib. bdg. 19.95x (ISBN 0-89370-050-9). Borgo Pr.
Burger, John. The Black Man's Burden. LC 72-89261. 256p. 1973. Repr. of 1943 ed. 24.00x (ISBN 0-8046-1766-X, Pub. by Kennikat). Assoc Faculty Pr.
Burger, K. Solvation: Ionic & Complex Formation in Non-Aqueous Solvents. (Studies in Analytical Chemistry: Vol. 6). 268p. 1983. cloth 61.75 (ISBN 0-444-99697-4). Elsevier.
Burger, Lela. Child of Love. 288p. 1976. 9.95 (ISBN 0-87881-045-5); pap. 3.95 (ISBN 0-87881-046-3). Mojave Bks.
Burger, M. A., jt. auth. see Harmon, R. B.
Burger, M. Leonard, jt. auth. see Prutzman, Priscilla.
Burger, Maria, jt. auth. see Field, Richard J.
Burger, Max M., jt. auth. see Congress of International Society of Development Biologists, Basel, Switzerland, Aug. 28-Sept. 1, 1981.
Burger, Max M., jt. ed. see Lash, James.
Burger, Neal, jt. auth. see Simpson, George.
Burger, Neal R., jt. auth. see Simpson, George.
Burger, Neal R., jt. auth. see Simpson, George E.
Burger, Neal R., jt. auth. see Simpson, George P.
Burger, Peter. Theory of the Avant-Garde. Shaw, Michael, tr. from Ger. (Theory & History of Literature Ser.: Vol. 4). iv, 136p. 1984. 25.00x (ISBN 0-8166-1067-3); pap. 10.95 (ISBN 0-8166-1068-1). U of Minn Pr.
Burger, Peter C. & Vogel, F. Stephen. Surgical Pathology of the Nervous System & Its Coverings. 2nd ed. LC 81-16250. 739p. 1982. 80.00 (ISBN 0-471-05876-9, Pub. by Wiley Med). Wiley.
Burger, Richard L. The Prehistoric Occupation of Chavin de Huantar, Peru. LC 83-1389. (Anthropology Ser.: Vol. 14). 436p. 1984. lib. bdg. 28.00 (ISBN 0-520-09667-3). U of Cal Pr.
Burger, Robert. The Jug Wine Book. LC 79-65110. (Illus.). 1979. 9.95 (ISBN 0-8128-2689-2); pap. 4.95 (ISBN 0-8128-6032-2). Stein & Day.
Burger, Robert, jt. auth. see Morton, Craig.
Burger, Robert E. The Chess of Bobby Fischer. (McGraw-Hill Paperbacks). (Illus.). 1979. pap. 6.95 (ISBN 0-07-008951-5). McGraw.
--The Jogger's Catalog: The Source Book for Runners. LC 78-4271. (Illus.). 192p. 1978. 5.95 (ISBN 0-87131-275-1); pap. 5.95 (ISBN 0-87131-259-X). M Evans.
Burger, Robert E., jt. auth. see Bassler, Thomas J.
Burger, Robert H. Authority Work: The Creation, Use, Maintenance, & Evaluation of Authority Records & Files. 200p. 1985. lib. bdg. 23.50 (ISBN 0-87287-491-5). Libs Unl.
Burger, Robert H., tr. see Mikhailov, A. I., et al.
Burger, Robert J. Siblings. 256p. 1984. 13.00 (ISBN 0-682-40188-9). Exposition Pr FL.
Burger, Robert M., et al. Independence Training, 5 bks. Incl. Bk. 1. Underwear & Footwear. 8.10 (ISBN 0-685-55874-6); Bk. 2. Indoor & Outdoor Clothing. 8.10 (ISBN 0-685-55875-4); Bk. 3. Fastenings. 7.40 (ISBN 0-685-55876-2); Bk. 4. Grooming & Self-Care Skills. 8.90 (ISBN 0-685-55877-0); Bk. 5. Parent's Guide. 7.40 (ISBN 0-685-55878-9). LC 77-85435. 1977. pap. (ISBN 0-685-55873-8). Western Psych.
Burger, Ronna. The Phaedo: A Platonic Labyrinth. LC 84-40191. 288p. 1984. text ed. 25.00x (ISBN 0-300-03163-7). Yale U Pr.
--Plato's "Phaedrus". A Defense of a Philosophic Art of Writing. LC 79-9789. 187p. 1977. 16.75 (ISBN 0-8173-0014-7). U of Ala Pr.
Burger, Sarah G. & D'Erasmo, Martha. Living in a Nursing Home. 1979. pap. 2.50 (ISBN 0-345-28198-5). Ballantine.
--Living in a Nursing Home: A Guide for Residents, Their Families & Friends. LC 76-17890. 1976. 8.95 (ISBN 0-8264-0126-0). Continuum.
Burger, Werner. Ch'ing Cash Until Seventeen Thirty-Five. (Illus.). 126p. 1983. 33.75 (ISBN 0-89955-141-6, Pub. by Mei Ya China). Intl Spec Bk.
Burger, William. Radar Observer's Handbook. 1981. 60.00x (ISBN 0-85174-314-5, Pub. by Nautical England). State Mutual Bk.
--Radar Observer's Handbook. 7th ed. 350p. 1983. pap. 35.00x (ISBN 0-85174-443-5). Sheridan.
Burgers, H. S. Leonardo DaVinci's Psychology of the Twelve Types. Van Rood, A., tr. LC 84-90396. 1984. 10.95 (ISBN 0-87212-184-4). Libra.
Burgers, J. M. Flow Equations for Composite Gases. (Applied Mathematics & Mechanics Ser.: Vol. 11). 1969. 85.00 (ISBN 0-12-143250-5). Acad Pr.
--The Non-Linear Diffusion Equation: Asymtotic Solutions & Statistical Problems. LC 74-81936. 192p. 1975. lib. bdg. 42.00 (ISBN 90-277-0494-5, Pub. by Reidel Holland). Kluwer Academic.
Burgers, Robert L. Powerlines. pap. 4.50 (ISBN 0-89137-317-9). Quality Pubns.

Burgerson, J. J., ed. see AIP Conference, Univ. of British Columbia, Vancouver, 1972.

Burgert, Annette K. Eighteenth Century Emigrants from German Speaking Lands to North America: Northern Kraichgan. (Penn. German Ser.: Vol. 16). (Illus.). 450p. 1983. 40.00 (ISBN 0-911122-46-X). Penn German Soc.

Burges, Bill. Facts & Figures: A Layman's Guide to Conducting Surveys. 125p. (Orig.). 1976. pap. text ed. 4.25 (ISBN 0-917754-02-6). Inst Responsive.

--Facts & Figures: A Layman's Guide to Conducting Surveys. 125p. 1979. 4.25 (ISBN 0-917754-02-6). Inst Responsive.

--Facts for a Change: Citizen Action Research for a Better Schools. 125p. (Orig.). 1976. pap. text ed. 5.00 (ISBN 0-917754-03-4). Inst Responsive.

--Facts for a Change: Citizen Action Research for Better Schools. 125p. 1979. 4.25 (ISBN 0-917754-03-4). Inst Responsive.

Burges, H. D., ed. Microbial Control of Pests & Plant Diseases, 1970 to 1980. LC 80-41480. 960p. 1981. 90.00 (ISBN 0-12-143360-9). Acad Pr.

Burges, James B. James Bland Burges Baronet (1752-1824) Richard the First, a Poem: in Eighteen Books. 1801. Reiman, Donald H., ed. LC 75-31172. (Romantic Context Ser.: Poetry 1789-1830). 1977. lib. bdg. 56.00 (ISBN 0-8240-2125-8). Garland Pub.

Burges, James B. see Reiman, Donald H.

Burgess. Design Assurance: A Guide for Engineers. (Mechanical Engineering Ser.). 352p. 1984. 49.75 (ISBN 0-8247-7258-X). Dekker.

Burgess, et al. International & Comparative Politics: A Handbook. 1985. 25.00 (ISBN 0-205-06009-9, 766009). Allyn.

Burgess, A. Evaluations of Nutrition Interventions: An Annoted Bibliography & Review of Methodologies & Results. 2nd ed. (Food & Nutrition Papers: No. 24). 198p. 1982. pap. 14.50 (ISBN 92-5-101228-8, F2360, FAO). Unipub.

Burgess, A. W. & Nicola, N. A. Growth Factors & Stem Cells. (Molecular Biology Ser.). 1984. 31.00 (ISBN 0-12-143750-7). Acad Pr.

Burgess, Alan. THe Small Woman: The Story of Gladys Aylward of China. 266p. 1985. pap. 5.95 (ISBN 0-89283-232-0). Servant.

Burgess, Alan, jt. auth. see Bergman, Ingrid.

Burgess, Alan, jt. auth. see Sandiford, Kay.

Burgess, Allan. From Twisted Ear to Reverent Tear. (Illus.). 96p. (YA) (gr. 7-12). 1983. 5.98 (ISBN 0-941518-25-6). Perry Enterprises.

Burgess, Allan & Molgard, Max. Zonkers: And Other Games for Home & Classroom. LC 83-72551. 329p. 1983. pap. 4.95 (ISBN 0-87747-958-5). Deseret Bk.

Burgess, Allan, et al. Everest: The Ultimate Challenge. (Illus.). 220p. 1983. 27.95 (ISBN 0-8253-0136-X). Beaufort Bks NY.

Burgess, Allan K. Helping Your Child Stay Morally Clean. Lyon, Jack, ed. LC 84-71705. 100p. 1984. 5.95 (ISBN 0-87747-671-3). Deseret Bk.

Burgess, Andrew J. Passion, Knowing How, & Understanding: An Essay on the Concept of Faith. LC 75-31550. (American Academy of Religion. Dissertation Ser.). 1975. pap. 9.95 (ISBN 0-89130-044-9, 010109). Scholars Pr GA.

Burgess, Ann W. Psychiatric Nursing in the Hospital & the Community. 4th ed. (Illus.). 900p. 1985. pap. text ed. 33.95 (ISBN 0-13-731951-7). P-H.

--Rape & Sexual Assault: A Research Handbook. LC 83-48217. (Reference Library of Social Science). 452p. 1985. lib. bdg. 50.00 (ISBN 0-8240-9049-7). Garland Pub.

Burgess, Ann W. & Baldwin, Bruce. Crisis Intervention Theory & Practice: A Clinical Handbook. (Illus.). 288p. 1981. text ed. 22.95 (ISBN 0-13-193466-X); pap. text ed. 18.95 (ISBN 0-13-193458-9). P-H.

Burgess, Ann W. & Holmstrom, Lynda L. Rape: Crisis & Recovery. LC 79-51507. (Illus.). 350p. 1979. pap. 18.95 (ISBN 0-87619-433-1). Brady Comm.

Burgess, Ann W. & Nichols, Groth A. Sexaul Assault of Children and Adolescents. 245p. 1978. postpaid 12.50 (ISBN 0-318-17072-8). Kemper Nat Ctr.

Burgess, Ann W., jt. auth. see Holmstrom, Lynda L.

Burgess, Ann W., et al. Sexual Assault of Children & Adolescents. LC 77-10217. 1978. 25.00x (ISBN 0-669-01890-2); pap. 11.00x (ISBN 0-669-01892-9). Lexington Bks.

Burgess, Ann W., et al, eds. Child Pornography & Sex Rings. LC 83-47791. 240p. 1984. 18.00x (ISBN 0-669-06741-5). Lexington Bks.

Burgess, Anthony. Beard's Roman Women. 1976. 8.95 (ISBN 0-07-008960-4). McGraw.

--Clockwork Orange. 1963. pap. 3.95 (ISBN 0-393-00224-1). Norton.

--The Clockwork Testament. 1984. pap. 5.95 (ISBN 0-07-008972-8). McGraw.

--The Doctor Is Sick. 272p. 1979. pap. 3.95 (ISBN 0-393-00959-9). Norton.

--Earthly Powers. 720p. 1981. pap. 3.95 (ISBN 0-380-56903-5, 56903-5). Avon.

--The End of the World News. 388p. 1983. 15.95 (ISBN 0-07-008965-5). McGraw.

--The End of the World News: An Entertainment. 388p. 1984. pap. 5.95 (ISBN 0-14-006746-9). Penguin.

--Enderby. LC 68-13483. 1968. 5.95 (ISBN 0-393-08444-2). Norton.

--Enderby Outside. 1984. pap. 5.95 (ISBN 0-07-008971-X). McGraw.

--Enderby's Dark Lady: Or, No End to Enderby. 160p. 1984. 14.95 (ISBN 0-07-008969-8). McGraw.

--Ernest Hemingway & His World. (Illus.). 1978. 10.95 (ISBN 0-684-18504-0, ScribT). Scribner.

--Ernest Hemingway & His World. (Illus.). 128p. 1985. pap. 10.95 (ISBN 0-317-19464-X, ScribT). Scribner.

--The Eve of Saint Venus. 128p. 1979. pap. 1.95 (ISBN 0-393-00915-7). Norton.

--Flame into Being: The Life & Work of D. H. Lawrence. 278p. 1985. 15.00 (ISBN 0-87795-766-5). Arbor Hse.

--Honey for the Bears. 1978. pap. 3.95 (ISBN 0-393-00905-X, N905, Norton Lib). Norton.

--Inside Mr. Enderby. 1984. pap. 5.95 (ISBN 0-07-008970-1). McGraw.

--Joysprick: An Introduction to the Language of James Joyce. LC 74-17009. (Illus.). 187p. 1975. pap. 7.95 (ISBN 0-15-646561-2, Harv). HarBraceJ.

--The Kingdom of the Wicked. 1985. 18.95 (ISBN 0-87795-753-3). Arbor Hse.

--The Long Day Wanes: A Malayan Trilogy. 1977. pap. 4.95 (ISBN 0-393-00864-9, Norton Lib). Norton.

--Man of Nazareth. 1979. 10.95 (ISBN 0-07-008962-0). McGraw.

--Napoleon Symphony. 384p. 1980. pap. 4.95 (ISBN 0-393-00964-5). Norton.

--Nineteen Eighty-Five. LC 78-9583. 1978. 8.95 (ISBN 0-316-11651-3). Little.

--Ninety-Nine Novels. 1985. pap. 4.95 (ISBN 0-671-55485-9). Summit Bks.

--Ninety-Nine Novels: The Best in English Since 1939. 156p. 1984. 10.95 (ISBN 0-671-52407-0). Summit Bks.

--Nothing Like the Sun. 240p. 1975. pap. 5.95 (ISBN 0-393-00795-2, N795, Norton Lib). Norton.

--Re Joyce. 1968. pap. 6.95 (ISBN 0-393-00445-7, Norton Lib). Norton.

--Right to an Answer. 1978. 3.95 (ISBN 0-393-00887-8). Norton.

--This Man & Music. 240p. 1983. 14.95 (ISBN 0-07-008964-7). McGraw.

--This Man & Music. 192p. 1985. pap. 3.95 (ISBN 0-380-69852-8, Discus). Avon.

--Tremor of Intent. 1966. 4.95 (ISBN 0-393-08539-2, Norton Lib); pap. 5.95 1977 (ISBN 0-393-00416-3). Norton.

--The Wanting Seed. 288p. 1976. pap. 6.95 (ISBN 0-393-00808-8, Norton Lib). Norton.

Burgess, Anthony, ed. see DeFoe, Daniel.

Burgess, Anthony, tr. see Rostand, Edmond.

Burgess, Anthony, tr. see Sophocles.

Burgess, Anthony, jt. auth. see Bowen, Elizabeth.

Burgess, Audrey. The Nurse's Guide to Fluid & Electrolyte Balance. 2nd ed. (Illus.). 1979. pap. text ed. 26.95 (ISBN 0-07-008955-8). McGraw.

Burgess, Beverley C. The Biblical Book of ABC's. (Illus.). 32p. Date not set. price not set (ISBN 0-89274-313-1). Harrison Hse.

--I Never Have to Be Afraid. (Illus.). 32p. Date not set. price not set (ISBN 0-89274-311-5). Harrison Hse.

--The Little Red Hen. (Illus.). 32p. (gr. 1-3). 1984. pap. 3.50 (ISBN 0-89274-312-3). Harrison Hse.

Burgess, Beverly. Three Bears in the Ministry. 32p. (Orig.). (ps). 1982. pap. 3.50 (ISBN 0-89274-252-6). Harrison Hse.

--Three Little Pigs: Build Your House Upon the Rock. 32p. (Orig.). (ps). 1983. pap. 3.50 (ISBN 0-89274-283-6). Harrison Hse.

Burgess, Beverly C. Little Red Riding Hood. (Illus.). 32p. (Orig.). (gr. 1-3). 1983. pap. 3.50 (ISBN 0-89274-289-5). Harrison Hse.

Burgess, C. & Knowles, A. Standards in Absorption Spectrometry. (Techniques in Visible & Ultraviolet Spectrometry Ser.). 1981. 22.00x (ISBN 0-412-22470-4, 2230, Pub. by Chapman & Hall). Methuen Inc.

Burgess, C., jt. ed. see Knowles, A.

Burgess, C., jt. ed. see Miket, R.

Burgess, C., jt. ed. see Strickland, C. E.

Burgess, C. F., ed. see Gay, John.

Burgess, C. R. Meteorology for Seamen. metric ed. 1981. 30.00x (ISBN 0-85174-315-3, Pub. by Nautical England). State Mutual Bk.

--Meteorology for Seamen. 4th ed. 251p. 1982. text ed. 25.00x (ISBN 0-85174-315-3). Sheridan.

Burgess, Charles. In Care & into Work. LC 80-42289. (Residential Social Work Ser.). 160p. 1981. 21.00x (ISBN 0-422-77640-8, NO. 3465, Pub by Tavistock England). Methuen Inc.

Burgess, Chester F. The Fellowship of the Craft: Conrad on Ships & Seamen & the Sea. (Literary Criticism Ser.). 1976. 16.00x (ISBN 0-8046-9116-9, Pub. by Kennikat). Assoc Faculty Pr.

Burgess, Colin. The Age of Stonehenge. (History of the Landscape Ser.). (Illus.). 402p. 1980. 25.00x (ISBN 0-460-04254-8, Pub. by J. M. Dent England). Biblio Dist.

Burgess, E. see American Astronautical Society.

Burgess, E. T. Interesting Men of the Bible. 1970. pap. 0.50 (ISBN 0-89114-007-7). Baptist Pub Hse.

--Missions in a Missile Age. 1979. pap. 0.50 (ISBN 0-89114-012-3). Baptist Pub Hse.

Burgess, Ebeneezer, tr. from Sanscrit. Surya Siddhanta. LC 74-78001. (Secret Doctrine Reference Ser.). 368p. 1977. Repr. of 1860 ed. 18.50 (ISBN 0-913510-13-0). Wizards.

Burgess, Edward & Brewster, Ellis. Ancient Names of Localities. (Pilgrim Society Notes Ser.: No. 20). 1.00 (ISBN 0-940628-07-4). Pilgrim Hall.

Burgess, Eric. By Jupiter: Odysseys to a Giant. (Illus.). 192p. 1982. 25.00x (ISBN 0-231-05176-X). Columbia U Pr.

--Celestial BASIC: Astronomy On Your Computer. LC 82-60187. (Illus.). 300p. 1982. pap. 16.95 (ISBN 0-89588-087-3). SYBEX.

--To the Red Planet. LC 78-6911. (Illus.). 181p. 1978. 29.00x (ISBN 0-231-04392-9). Columbia U Pr.

--Venus: An Errant Twin. LC 85-384. (Illus.). 176p. 1985. 29.95 (ISBN 0-231-05856-X). Columbia U Pr.

Burgess, Eric & Burgess, Howard J. More Uses for Your Timex-Sinclair 1000: Astronomy on Your Computer. LC 83-61386. (Illus.). 153p. 1983. pap. 8.95 (ISBN 0-89588-112-8). SYBEX.

Burgess, Eric, jt. auth. see Murray, Bruce C.

Burgess, Ernest W. Ernest W. Burgess on Community, Family & Delinquency. Cottrell, Leonard S., Jr., et al, eds. LC 73-83572. (Illus.). 1977. pap. 4.45x (ISBN 0-226-08058-7, P715, Phoen). U of Chicago Pr.

--On Community, Family & Delinquency. Cottrell, Leonard S., Jr., et al, eds. (Heritage of Sociology Ser). 1974. 22.00x (ISBN 0-226-08057-9). U of Chicago Pr.

Burgess, Ernest W., jt. auth. see Cavan, Ruth S.

Burgess, Ernest W., jt. auth. see Park, Robert E.

Burgess, Ernest W., jt. auth. see Park, Robert W.

Burgess, Ernest W., ed. The Urban Community. LC 71-175038. (BCL Ser. I). Repr. of 1926 ed. 21.50 (ISBN 0-404-01235-3). AMS Pr.

--Urban Community: Selected Papers from the Proceedings of the American Sociological Society, 1925. LC 68-57591. (Illus.). 1969. Repr. of 1926 ed. lib. bdg. 15.00x (ISBN 0-8371-0333-9, BUUC). Greenwood.

Burgess, Ernest W. & Bogue, Donald J., eds. Contributions to Urban Sociology. LC 63-21309. 1964. 30.00x (ISBN 0-226-08055-2). U of Chicago Pr.

--Urban Sociology. abr ed. 1967. pap. 3.95x (ISBN 0-226-08056-0, P253, Phoen). U of Chicago Pr.

Burgess, Eugene W. & Harbison, Frederick H. Casa Grace in Peru: Second Case Study in an NPA Series on United States Business Performance Abroad. Bruchey, Stuart, ed. LC 80-557. (Multinational Corporations Ser.). (Illus.). 1980. Repr. of 1954 ed. lib. bdg. 17.00x (ISBN 0-405-13353-7). Ayer Co Pubs.

Burgess, Francis H. A Dictionary for Yachtsmen. LC 80-85494. (Illus.). 256p. 1981. 11.95 (ISBN 0-7153-6344-1). David & Charles.

Burgess, Frank G. Are You a Bromide? LC 75-96875. Repr. of 1906 ed. lib. bdg. 14.50 (ISBN 0-8398-0180-7). Irvington.

Burgess, G. H., et al. Fish Handling & Processing. (Illus.). 1967. 25.00 (ISBN 0-8206-0045-8). Chem Pub.

Burgess, Galett. Goops & How to Be Them: A Manual of Manners for Polite Infants (Inculcating Many Juvenile Virtues Both by Precept & Example) 88p. 1985. 14.95 (ISBN 0-917320-13-1); pap. 9.95 (ISBN 0-917320-14-X). MHO & MHO.

Burgess, Gelett. Goop Tales. LC 72-93766. (Illus.). 128p. (gr. 1-6). 1973. pap. 3.50 (ISBN 0-486-22914-9). Dover.

--Goop Tales. (Illus.). 14.00 (ISBN 0-8446-4717-9). Peter Smith.

--Goops & How to Be Them: A Manual of Manners for Polite Infants. LC 68-55630. (Illus.). 96p. (ps-4). 1968. pap. 2.95 (ISBN 0-486-22233-0). Dover.

--The Little Father. LC 84-46171. (Illus.). 32p. (ps up). 1984. 10.95 (ISBN 0-374-34596-1). FS&G.

--The Master of Mysteries: Problems Solved by Astro, Seer of Secrets & His Love Affair with Valeska Wynne, His Assistant. LC 75-32736. (Literature of Mystery & Detection Ser.). (Illus.). 1976. Repr. of 1912 ed. 36.50x (ISBN 0-405-07865-X). Ayer Co Pubs.

--More Goops & How Not to Be Them: A Manual of Manners for Impolite Infants. LC 68-55531. (Illus.). 96p. (ps-4). 1968. pap. 3.50 (ISBN 0-486-22234-9). Dover.

--The Purple Cow. 23p. 1966. leatherette 9.00 (ISBN 0-317-11646-0). Dawsons.

--Romance of the Commonplace. facs. ed. LC 68-57308. (Essay Index Reprint Ser). 1916. 19.00 (ISBN 0-8369-0103-7). Ayer Co Pubs.

Burgess, Gelett, ed. My Maiden Effort. being the Personal Confessions of Well-Known American Authors As to Their Literary Beginnings: George Ade, James Lane Allen, Mary Austin, Hamlin Garland, Booth Tarkington. 1921. Repr. 20.00 (ISBN 0-8274-2780-8). R West.

Burgess, Gelett, illus. The Goops Coloring Book. (Coloring Bks.). 48p. 1984. pap. 2.50 (ISBN 0-486-24615-9). Dover.

Burgess, George H. & Kennedy, Miles C. Centennial History of the Pennsylvania Railroad Company, 1846-1946. LC 75-41750. (Companies & Men: Business Enterprises in America). (Illus.). 1976. Repr. of 1949 ed. 67.50x (ISBN 0-405-08067-0). Ayer Co Pubs.

Burgess, Glyn S. & Taylor, Robert A., eds. Spirit of the Court: Selected Proceedings of the Fourth Congress of the International Courtly Literature Society, Toronto 1983. 384p. 1985. 59.25 (ISBN 0-85991-176-4, Pub. by Boydell & Brewer). Longwood Pub Group.

Burgess, Harold D. Sixty Years at the Bar: Anecdotes of a Corporation Lawyer. 167p. 1981. 8.95 (ISBN 0-682-49781-9). Exposition Pr FL.

Burgess, Harold W. An Invitation to Religious Education. LC 75-14980. 173p. 1975. lib. bdg. 12.95 (ISBN 0-89135-004-7); pap. 10.95 (ISBN 0-89135-019-5). Religious Educ.

Burgess, Harold W., ed. see Kelsey, Morton T.

Burgess, Henry J. Enterprise in Education: The Story of the Work of the Established Church in the Education of the People Prior to 1870. LC 59-1586. 1958. text ed. 15.00x (ISBN 0-8401-0289-5). A R Allenson.

Burgess, Hovey. Circus Techniques. LC 76-51205. (Illus.). 162p. pap. 12.00 (ISBN 0-917643-00-3). B Dube.

Burgess, Howard J., jt. auth. see Burgess, Eric.

Burgess, Hugh. Dwell With These Distances, Vol. 10. 50p. 1982. pap. 2.95 (ISBN 0-932616-08-9). New Poets.

Burgess, J. An Introducton to Plant Cell Development. (Illus.). 246p. 1985. 54.50 (ISBN 0-521-30273-0); pap. 19.95 (ISBN 0-521-31611-1). Cambridge U Pr.

Burgess, J. R., ed. see Adair, Frances E.

Burgess, Jacquelin & Gold, John, eds. Geography, the Media & Popular Culture. LC 84-40465. 256p. 1985. 27.50 (ISBN 0-312-32168-6). St Martin.

Burgess, Jacquelin, ed. see Gold, John.

Burgess, James. The Chronology of Modern India For Four Hundred Years From the Close of the Fifteenth Century, A.D. 1494-1894. 490p. 1972. text ed. 35.00x (ISBN 0-7165-2055-9, Pub. by Irish Academic Pr Ireland). Biblio Dist.

--A Guide to Elura Cave Temples. (Illus.). 61p. 1981. text ed. 7.00x (ISBN 0-391-02434-5, Pub. by Concept India). Humanities.

Burgess, James, ed. see Grunwedel, Albert.

Burgess, James A. Burgess, Mullins, Browning, Brown, & Allied Families. LC 78-59336. 262p. 1985. Repr. of 1978 ed. lib. bdg. 19.95x (ISBN 0-89370-870-4). Borgo Pr.

Burgess, James Z. Burgess History: The Tennessee Pioneer. 300p. 1982. lib. bdg. 49.95x (ISBN 0-89370-740-6). Borgo Pr.

Burgess, Jan. The World of Horses. Barish, Wendy, ed. (Illus.). 96p. (gr. 3 up). 1984. 9.95 (ISBN 0-671-52528-X). Wanderer Bks.

Burgess, Jillian. The Coffee Book. (Illus.). 81p. 1985. 4.95 (ISBN 0-9509499-0-6, Pub. by Kato Pr). Interbook.

Burgess, John. Black Gospel, White Church. 128p. 1982. pap. 7.95 (ISBN 0-8164-2380-6, Pub. by Seabury). Winston Pr.

--Designing for Humans: The Human Factor in Engineering. (Illus.). 450p. 1985. text ed. 39.95 (ISBN 0-89433-278-3). Petrocelli.

--Metal Ions in Solutions. (Chemical Science). 481p. 1978. pap. 42.95x (ISBN 0-470-26987-1). Halsted Pr.

Burgess, John A., jt. auth. see Everitt, Arthur V.

Burgess, John H. Christian Pagan: A Naturalistic Survey of Christian History. (Illus.). 1968. 7.00 (ISBN 0-912084-04-9). Mimir.

--Human Factors in Built Environments. LC 81-184028. 137p. 1982. 30.00x (ISBN 0-915250-38-1). Environ Design.

--Human Factors in Forms Design. LC 83-6274. (Illus.). 192p. 1983. lib. bdg. 23.95x (ISBN 0-88229-539-X). Nelson-Hall.

--System Design Approaches to Public Services. LC 76-737. (Illus.). 300p. 1978. 25.00 (ISBN 0-8386-1892-8). Fairleigh Dickinson.

Burgess, John S. Guilds of Peking. LC 77-127446. (Columbia Studies in the Social Sciences Ser.: No. 308). Repr. of 1928 ed. 16.00 (ISBN 0-404-51308-5). AMS Pr.

Burgess, John W. The Middle Period. 1897. 30.00 (ISBN 0-8482-7399-0). Norwood Edns.

--The Middle Period, 1817-1858. facsimile ed. LC 79-37301. (Black Heritage Library Collection). Repr. of 1897 ed. 28.25 (ISBN 0-8369-8938-4). Ayer Co Pubs.

--Recent Changes in American Constitutional Theory. LC 76-172206. (Right Wing Individualist Tradition in America Ser.). 1972. Repr. of 1923 ed. 13.00 (ISBN 0-405-00417-6). Ayer Co Pubs.

--Reconstruction & the Constitution. LC 72-457. Repr. of 1902 ed. 12.50 (ISBN 0-404-00010-X). AMS Pr.

--Reconstruction & the Constitution, 1866-1876. LC 70-99479. (American Constitutional & Legal History Ser.: Americana Ser). 1970. Repr. of 1902 ed. lib. bdg. 42.50 (ISBN 0-306-71849-9). Da Capo.

--Reconstruction & the Constitution, 1866-1876. Repr. of 1902 ed. 22.50x (ISBN 0-8371-1887-5, BRE&). Greenwood.

--Reconstruction & the Constitution 1866-1876. 1902. 15.00 (ISBN 0-8482-3449-9). Norwood Edns.

--Reminiscences of an American Scholar. LC 34-2217. Repr. of 1934 ed. 18.00 (ISBN 0-404-01236-1). AMS Pr.

Burgess, Joseph A. & Winn, Albert C. Epiphany. Achtemeier, Elizabeth, et al, eds. LC 79-7377. (Proclamation 2: Aids for Interpreting the Lessons of the Church Year, Series A). 64p. (Orig.). 1980. pap. 3.50 (ISBN 0-8006-4092-6, 1-4092). Fortress.

Burgess, Joseph A., jt. auth. see Andrews, James E.

Burgess, Joseph A., ed. The Role of the Augsburg Confession: Catholic & Lutheran Views. LC 79-7373. 224p. 1980. 14.95 (ISBN 0-8006-0549-7, 1-549). Fortress.

Burgess, Keith. The Challenge of Labour: Shaping British Society, 1850-1930. LC 80-10251. 224p. 1980. 25.00 (ISBN 0-312-12805-3). St Martin.

--The Origins of British Industrial Relations: The Nineteenth Century Experience. 331p. 1975. 21.50x (ISBN 0-87471-713-2). Rowman.

Burgess, Larry, ed. see Parker-Hinckley, Edith.

Burgess, Leonard. Wage & Salary Administration: Pay & Benefits. 1984. text ed. 27.95 (ISBN 0-675-20080-6); additional supplements avail. Merrill.

Burgess, Leonard R. Top Executive Pay Package. LC 63-8414. 1963. 9.95 (ISBN 0-02-904990-3). Free Pr.

Burgess, Linda C. The Art of Adoption. LC 77-55. 1977. 12.50 (ISBN 0-87491-066-8). Acropolis.

--The Art of Adoption. 176p. 1981. pap. 5.95 (ISBN 0-393-00036-2). Norton.

Burgess, Lorraine M. Garden Art: The Personal Pursuit of Artistic Refinements, Inventive Concepts, Old Follies, & New Conceits for the Home Gardener. (Illus.). 192p. 1981. 25.00 (ISBN 0-8027-0665-7). Walker & Co.

Burgess, Lourdes, jt. auth. see Axelrod, Herbert R.

Burgess, M. Elaine. Negro Leadership in a Southern City. 1962. pap. 7.95x (ISBN 0-8084-0231-5). New Coll U Pr.

Burgess, M. R. The House of the Burgesses. LC 80-10759. (Borgo Family Histories Ser.: No. 1). 168p. 1983. lib. bdg. 16.95x (ISBN 0-89370-801-1); pap. 6.95x (ISBN 0-89370-901-8). Borgo Pr.

Burgess, M. R., jt. ed. see Reginald, Robert.

Burgess, Mallory. Ride the Savage Sea. 448p. (Orig.). 1985. write for info. Pinnacle Bks.

Burgess, Mary A. The Wickizer Annals. LC 80-11075. (Borgo Family Histories Ser.: No. 2). 144p. 1983. lib. bdg. 16.95x (ISBN 0-89370-802-X); pap. 6.95x (ISBN 0-89370-902-6). Borgo Pr.

Burgess, Mary A., jt. auth. see Reginald, R.

Burgess, Mary W., jt. auth. see Burgess, Michael.

Burgess, Mary W., jt. auth. see Clarke, Boden.

Burgess, Mary W., jt. auth. see Reginald, R.

Burgess, Mary W., ed. see Campbell, James B.

Burgess, Mason. Child of Demons. 352p. (Orig.). 1985. pap. 3.75 (ISBN 0-8439-2206-0, Leisure Bks). Dorchester Pub Co.

Burgess, Michael. A Guide to Science Fiction & Fantasy in the Library of Congress Classification Scheme. LC 80-11418. (Borgo Reference Library: Vol. 8). 96p. 1984. lib. bdg. 19.95x (ISBN 0-89370-807-0); pap. 12.95x (ISBN 0-89370-907-7). Borgo Pr.

--Mystery & Detective Fiction in the Library of Congress Classification Scheme. LC 84-12344. (Borgo Reference Library: Vol. 19). 128p. (Orig.). 1985. lib. bdg. 19.95x (ISBN 0-89370-818-6); pap. text ed. 12.95x (ISBN 0-89370-918-2). Borgo Pr.

Burgess, Michael & Burgess, Mary W. The State & Province Vital Records Guide. (Borgo Reference Library: Vol. 16). 100p. 1985. lib. bdg. 19.95x (ISBN 0-89370-815-1); pap. 9.95x (ISBN 0-89370-915-8). Borgo Pr.

--The Work of R. Reginald: An Annotated Bibliography & Guide. LC 84-21672. (Bibliographies of Modern Authors Ser.: No. 5). 64p. 1985. lib. bdg. 19.95x (ISBN 0-89370-384-2); pap. text ed. 9.95x (ISBN 0-89370-484-9). Borgo Pr.

Burgess, Moira & Whyte, Hamish, eds. Streets of Stone: An Anthology of Glasgow Stories. 192p. 1985. pap. 8.95 (ISBN 0-907540-62-7, Pub. by Salamander Pr). Merrimack Pub Cir.

Burgess, N. How to Find Out in Banking & Investment. flexi-cover 10.75 (ISBN 0-08-013045-3). Pergamon.

Burgess, N. G. The Photograph Manual. 8th ed. LC 72-9186. (The Literature of Photography Ser.). Repr. of 1863 ed. 22.00 (ISBN 0-405-04897-1). Ayer Co Pubs.

Burgess, N. T., ed. Quality Assurance of Welded Construction. (Illus.). 193p. 1983. 44.50 (ISBN 0-85334-184-2, Pub. by Elsevier Applied Sci England). Elsevier.

Burgess, P., tr. see Frobel, Folker, et al.

Burgess, Patricia. Erica's School on the Hill: A Child's Journey in Moral Growth. 1978. pap. 4.95 (ISBN 0-03-043911-6). Winston Pr.

Burgess, Pete, tr. see Rosdolsky, Roman.

Burgess, Peter, tr. see Slater, Phil.

Burgess, Peter H., ed. see Gandhi, Mahatma.

Burgess, Philip M. Elite Images & Foreign Policy Outcomes: A Study of Norway. LC 67-24453. 197p. 1968. 6.25 (ISBN 0-8142-0030-3). Ohio St U Pr.

Burgess, Philip M. & Harf, James E. Global Analysis: A Data Scheme & Deck for Univariate & Bivariate Analysis. (CISE Learning Package Ser.: No. 7). (Illus.). 70p. (Orig.). 1975. pap. text ed. 3.50x (ISBN 0-936876-23-9). Learn Res Intl Stud.

Burgess, R. A. The Construction Industry Handbook. 2nd ed. 1973. 31.95 (ISBN 0-8436-0119-1). Van Nos Reinhold.

Burgess, R. E., ed. Fluctuation Phenomena in Solids. (Pure & Applied Physics Ser.: Vol. 19). 1964. 79.50 (ISBN 0-12-143650-0). Acad Pr.

Burgess, R. H. Manufacture & Processing of PVC. 300p. 1982. text ed. 40.00x (ISBN 0-02-949150-9). Macmillan.

Burgess, R. H., ed. Manufacture & Processing of PVC. (Illus.). 276p. 1982. 44.00 (ISBN 0-686-48127-5, 1905). T-C Pubns CA.

Burgess, R. L. & Sharpe, S. M., eds. Forest Island Dynamics in Man-Dominated Landscapes. (Ecological Studies: Vol. 41). (Illus.). 310p. 1981. 37.00 (ISBN 0-387-90584-7). Springer Verlag.

Burgess, R. W. & Clew, J. R. Always in the Picture: A History of the Velocette Motorcycle. 19.95 (ISBN 0-85429-266-7, F266). Haynes Pubns.

Burgess, Robert. Secret Languages of the Sea. LC 81-5544. (Illus.). 320p. 1982. 14.95 (ISBN 0-396-08011-1). Dodd.

Burgess, Robert, jt. ed. see Katz, William A.

Burgess, Robert F. The Cave Divers. LC 75-22130. (Illus.). 1982. 9.95 (ISBN 0-396-07204-6). Florida Classics.

--The Handbook of Trailer Sailing. (Illus.). 266p. 1984. 18.95 (ISBN 0-396-08302-1); pap. 11.95 (ISBN 0-396-08303-X). Dodd.

--Man: Twelve Thousand Years Under the Sea. LC 80-186. (Illus.). 448p. 1980. 12.95 (ISBN 0-396-07801-X). Dodd.

--Man: Twelve Thousand Years Under the Sea. (Illus.). 1980. 12.95 (ISBN 0-396-07801-X). Florida Classics.

--They Found Treasure. (Illus.). 1977. 8.95 (ISBN 0-396-07450-2). Florida Classics.

Burgess, Robert F. & Clausen, Carl J. Florida's Golden Galleons. (Florida Classics Ser.). Orig. Title: Gold, Galleons & Archaeology. (Illus.). 195p. (Orig.). 1982. pap. 10.95 (ISBN 0-912451-07-6). Florida Classics.

Burgess, Robert G. Education, Schools & Schooling. (Issues in Sociology Ser.). 192p. (Orig.). 1985. pap. 12.95x (ISBN 0-333-37421-5, Pub. by Macmillan London). Sheridan.

--Experiencing Comprehensive Education: A Study of Bishop McGregor School. 288p. 1983. 24.00 (ISBN 0-416-35150-6, NO. 4037); pap. 11.95 (ISBN 0-416-35160-3, NO. 4038). Methuen Inc.

--Field Methods in the Study of Education. 1984. 32.00x (ISBN 1-85000-012-3, Pub. by Falmer Pr); pap. 17.00 (ISBN 1-85000-011-5, Pub. by Falmer Pr). Taylor & Francis.

--In the Field: An Introduction to Field Research. (Contemporary Social Research Ser.: No. 8). 180p. 1984. text ed. 24.95x (ISBN 0-04-312017-2); pap. text ed. 9.95x (ISBN 0-04-312018-0). Allen Unwin.

Burgess, Robert G., ed. Field Research: A Source Book & Field Manual. (Contemporary Social Research Ser.: No. 4). 228p. 1982. text ed. 42.00x (ISBN 0-04-312013-X); pap. text ed. 18.50x (ISBN 0-04-312014-8). Allen Unwin.

--The Research Process in Educational Settings: Ten Case Studies. 275p. 1984. 31.00x (ISBN 0-905273-92-3, Pub. by Falmer Pr); pap. 18.00x (ISBN 0-905273-91-5, Pub. by Falmer Pr). Taylor & Francis.

--Strategies of Educational Research: Qualitative Methods. 336p. 1985. text ed. 31.00x (ISBN 1-85000-033-6, Falmer Pr); pap. text ed. 18.00x (ISBN 1-85000-034-4, Falmer Pr). Taylor & Francis.

Burgess, Robert H. Chesapeake Circle. LC 65-20765. (Illus.). 222p. 1965. 15.00 (ISBN 0-87033-013-6). Tidewater.

--Coasting Schooner: The Four-Masted "Albert F. Paul". LC 77-10554. (Mariners Museum Publication: No.35). 1978. 17.50x (ISBN 0-917376-31-5). U Pr of Va.

--Sea, Sails & Shipwreck: The Career of the Purnell T. White. LC 73-124313. (Illus.). 144p. 1970. 6.00 (ISBN 0-87033-147-7). Tidewater.

--This Was Chesapeake Bay. LC 63-20545. (Illus.). 223p. 1963. 20.00 (ISBN 0-87033-125-6). Tidewater.

Burgess, Robert H., ed. see Gregory, Hugh M.

Burgess, Robert L. Behavioral Sociology: The Experimental Analysis of Social Process. Bushell, Don, Jr., ed. LC 79-90821. (Illus.). 1969. 29.50x (ISBN 0-231-03203-X); pap. 15.00x (ISBN 0-231-08673-3). Columbia U Pr.

--Woody Plants of Icelandic Park. LC 68-65253. (Illus.). 64p. 1968. pap. 1.00 (ISBN 0-911042-15-6). N Dak Inst.

Burgess, Robert L. & Huston, Ted L., eds. Social Exchange in Developing Relationships. LC 79-6934. 1979. 39.50 (ISBN 0-12-143550-4). Acad Pr.

Burgess, Roger A., et al, eds. Progress in Construction Science & Technology, 2 vols. Vol. 1. pap. 82.50 (ISBN 0-317-10675-9, 2015502); Vol. 2. pap. 62.80 (ISBN 0-317-10676-7). Bks Demand UMI.

Burgess, Ronald R., ed. see International Symposium on Silicon Materials, Science & Technology (2d: 1973: Chicago).

Burgess, Ross, jt. auth. see St. John Bate, Joseph.

Burgess, Scott A. The Work of Reginald Bretnor: An Annotated Bibliography & Guide. (Bibliographies of Modern Authors: No. 8). 50p. lib. bdg. 19.95x (ISBN 0-89370-387-7); pap. text ed. 9.95x (ISBN 0-89370-487-3). Borgo Pr.

Burgess, Sullivan, jt. auth. see Kelly, Fred C.

Burgess, Thomas. Greeks in America. 1970. Repr. of 1913 ed. 15.00 (ISBN 0-88247-016-7). R & E Pubs.

--Greeks in America: An Account of Their Coming, Progress, Customs, Living & Aspirations. LC 72-129392. (American Immigration Collection, Ser. 2). (Illus.). 1970. Repr. of 1913 ed. 19.00 (ISBN 0-405-00547-4). Ayer Co Pubs.

Burgess, Thonrton W. The Adventures of Johnny Chuck. 13.95 (ISBN 0-88411-787-1, Pub by Aeonian Pr). Amereon Ltd.

Burgess, Thornton. Adventure of Mr. Mocker. 120p. 1977. Repr. of 1914 ed. lib. bdg. 15.95x (ISBN 0-89966-271-4). Buccaneer Bks.

--Billy Mink. 91p. 1981. Repr. PLB 15.95x (ISBN 0-89966-352-4). Buccaneer Bks.

--Billy Mink. 178p. 1981. Repr. PLB 15.95x (ISBN 0-89967-026-1). Harmony Raine.

--Blacky the Crow. 93p. 1981. Repr. PLB 15.95x (ISBN 0-89966-351-6). Buccaneer Bks.

--Blacky the Crow. 198p. 1981. Repr. PLB 11.95x (ISBN 0-89967-025-3). Harmony Raine.

--The Dear Old Briar-Patch. 192p. 1983. pap. 11.95i (ISBN 0-316-11654-8). Little.

--Little Joe Otter. 103p. 1981. Repr. PLB 15.95x (ISBN 0-89966-353-2). Buccaneer Bks.

--Little Joe Otter. 169p. 1981. Repr. PLB 15.95x (ISBN 0-89967-027-X). Harmony Raine.

Burgess, Thornton W. The Adventures of Bob White. 13.95 (ISBN 0-88411-776-6, Pub Aeonian Pr). Amereon Ltd.

--The Adventures of Grandfather Frog. 13.95 (ISBN 0-88411-777-4, Pub by Aeonian Pr). Amereon Ltd.

--The Adventures of Jerry Muskrat. 13.95 (ISBN 0-88411-782-0, Pub by Aeonian Pr). Amereon Ltd.

--The Adventures of Ol' Mistah Buzzard. 13.95 (ISBN 0-88411-784-7, Pub. by Aeonian Pr). Amereon Ltd.

--The Adventures of Old Man Coyote. 13.95 (ISBN 0-88411-781-2, Pub. by Aeonian Pr). Amereon Ltd.

--The Adventures of Old Mr. Toad. 13.95 (ISBN 0-88411-785-5, Pub. by Aeonian Pr). Amereon Ltd.

--The Adventures of Poor Mrs. Quack. 13.95 (ISBN 0-88411-775-8, Pub. by Aeonian Pr). Amereon Ltd.

--The Adventures of Prickly Porky. 13.95 (ISBN 0-88411-783-9, Pub. by Aeonian Pr). Amereon Ltd.

--Adventures of Whitefoot the Woodmouse. (Green Forest Ser.: Vol. 3). (gr. k-3). 1944. (G&D). Putnam Pub Group.

--Mother West Wind's Animal Friends. 14.95 (ISBN 0-88411-779-0, Pub. by Aeonian Pr). Amereon Ltd.

--Mother West Wind's Children. new ed. (Nature Story Bks). (Illus.). (gr. 1-3). 1962. 14.45 (ISBN 0-316-11645-9). Little.

--Mother West Wind's Children. (Illus.). 156p. (ps-3). 1985. pap. 5.95 (ISBN 0-316-11657-2). Little.

--Mother West Wind's How Stories. 14.95 (ISBN 0-88411-780-4, Pub. by Aeonian Pr). Amereon Ltd.

--Mother West Wind's Neighbors. LC 68-21862. (Nature-Story Books). (Illus.). (gr. 1 up). 1968. 14.45i (ISBN 0-316-11650-5). Little.

--Mother West Wind's Neighbors. 14.95 (ISBN 0-88411-786-3, Pub. by Aeonian Pr). Amereon Ltd.

--Mother West Wind's Why Stories. 14.95 (ISBN 0-88411-778-2, Pub. by Aeonian Pr). Amereon Ltd.

--Old Mother West Wind. (Mother West Wind Ser.: Vol. 1). (gr. k-3). 1976. 3.09 (ISBN 0-448-13728-3, G&D). Putnam Pub Group.

--Old Mother West Wind. golden anniversary ed. (Nature-Story Books). (Illus.). (gr. 1 up). 1960. 14.45 (ISBN 0-316-11648-3). Little.

Burgess, Thorton. Favorite Tales by Thorton Burgess. (Platt & Munk Pandabacks Ser.). (Illus.). 24p. (ps-3). 1979. pap. 1.25 (ISBN 0-448-49613-5, G&D). Putnam Pub Group.

Burgess, Tom, jt. ed. see McBee, Robert.

Burgess, Tyrell. Education after School. 1981. 35.00x (ISBN 0-575-02237-X, Pub. by Gollancz). State Mutual Bk.

Burgess, W. J. Brother Burgess. (Illus.). 121p. 1975. 3.50 (ISBN 0-89114-069-7); pap. 1.50 (ISBN 0-89114-068-9). Baptist Pub Hse.

--Glossolalia. 1968. pap. 1.00 (ISBN 0-89114-053-0). Baptist Pub Hse.

--Lord's Table. 1957. pap. 0.75 (ISBN 0-89114-001-8). Baptist Pub Hse.

Burgess, W. Randolph. The Federal Reserve Banks & the Money Markey. LC 82-48176. (Gold, Money, Inflation & Deflation Ser.). 400p. 1982. lib. bdg. 50.00 (ISBN 0-8240-5228-5). Garland Pub.

--Interpretations of Federal Reserve Policy in the Speeches of Benjamin Strong, Governor of the Federal Reserve Bank of New York. LC 82-48177. (Gold, Money, Inflation & Deflation Ser.). 352p. 1983. lib. bdg. 44.00 (ISBN 0-8240-5227-7). Garland Pub.

Burgess, Warren, jt. auth. see Axelrod, Herbert R.

Burgess, Dr. Warren, jt. auth. see Axelrod, Herbert R.

Burgess, Warren E. Butterflyfishes of the World. (Illus.). 1979. 29.95 (ISBN 0-87666-470-2, H-988). TFH Pubns.

--Corals. (Illus.). 1979. 4.95 (ISBN 0-87666-521-0, KW-053). TFH Pubns.

--Marine Aquaria. (Illus.). 96p. text ed. 4.95 (ISBN 0-87666-533-4, KW-088). TFH Pubns.

--The T.F.H. Book of Marine Aquariums. (Illus.). 96p. 1982. 6.95 (ISBN 0-87666-801-5, HP-006). TFH Pubns.

Burgess, Warren E. & Axelrod, Herbert R. Fishes of California & Western Mexico. (Pacific Marine Fishes Ser.: Bk. 8). (Illus.). 267p. 1985. text ed. 29.95 (ISBN 0-86622-012-7, PS-724). TFH Pubns.

--Pacific Marine Fishes, Bk. 3. (Illus.). 272p. 1973. 29.95 (ISBN 0-87666-125-8, PS-719). TFH Pubns.

--Pacific Marine Fishes, Bk. 4. (Illus.). 272p. 1974. 29.95 (ISBN 0-87666-126-6, PS-720). TFH Pubns.

--Pacific Marine Fishes, Bk. 5. (Illus.). 271p. 1975. 29.95 (ISBN 0-87666-127-4, PS-721). TFH Pubns.

Burgess, Warren E., jt. auth. see Axelrod, Herbert R.

Burgess, Wendy. Community Health Nursing Practice: A Workbook of Skill-Building Modules. 172p. 1983. pap. 14.95x (ISBN 0-8385-1182-1). ACC.

Burgess, Wendy & Ragland, Ethel. Community Health Nursing: Philosophy, Process, Practice. 512p. 1983. pap. 24.50 (ISBN 0-8385-1181-3). ACC.

Burgess, William. Bible in Shakespeare. 69.95 (ISBN 0-87968-728-2). Gordon Pr.

--Bible in Shakespeare. LC 68-24900. (Studies in Shakespeare, No. 24). 1969. Repr. of 1903 ed. lib. bdg. 75.00 (ISBN 0-8383-0921-6). Haskell.

Burgess, William A. Recognition of Health Hazards in Industry: A Review of Materials & Processes. LC 81-2132. 275p. 1981. 36.00 (ISBN 0-471-06339-8, Pub. by Wiley-Interscience). Wiley.

Burgess, William C., et al. Financial Decisions. 40p. (Orig.). 1984. pap. 4.95 (ISBN 0-930264-55-X). Century Comm.

Burgess, William E. The Collector's Guide to Antiquarian Bookstores. 480p. 1984. 20.75 (ISBN 0-02-903750-6). Macmillan.

Burgess, Yvonne. Life to Live: A Novel. LC 80-17914. 183p. 1981. 8.95 (ISBN 0-8008-4816-0). Taplinger.

--The Strike. LC 79-23680. 219p. 1980. 9.95 (ISBN 0-8008-7471-4). Taplinger.

Burgess-Kohn, Jane & Kohn, Willard K. The Widower. LC 77-75439. 1979. pap. 4.95x (ISBN 0-8070-2735-9, BP564). Beacon Pr.

Burgess-Wise, David. Ford-U. S. A. Pocket History. (Pocket History Ser.). (Illus.). 66p. (Orig.). pap. 5.95 (ISBN 88-85058-15-9, Pub. by Automobilia Italy). Motorbooks Intl.

Burgest, David R. Social Work Practice with Minorities. LC 81-14461. 322p. 1982. text ed. 18.00 (ISBN 0-8108-1476-5). Scarecrow.

Burgest, Mwalimu D. Social Casework Intervention with People of Color. LC 85-7399. 258p. (Orig.). 1985. lib. bdg. 22.50 (ISBN 0-8191-4691-9); pap. text ed. 13.25 (ISBN 0-8191-4692-7). U Pr of Amer.

Burgett, Gordon. Query Letters-Cover Letters: How to Sell Your Writing. 2nd, rev. ed. 204p. 1986. 12.95 (ISBN 0-9605078-8-4); pap. 9.95 (ISBN 0-9605078-7-6). Write to Sell.

--Ten Sales from One Article Idea: The Process & Correspondence. LC 81-13060. (Illus.). 108p. (Orig.). 1982. pap. 7.95 (ISBN 0-9605078-2-5). Write to Sell.

Burgett, Gordon L. How to Sell Seventy-Five Per Cent of Your Freelance Writing. LC 83-50640. (Illus.). 200p. (Orig.). 1984. 12.95 (ISBN 0-9605078-5-X); pap. 9.95 (ISBN 0-9605078-4-1). Write To Sell.

Burggraaff, Winfield J. The Venezuelan Armed Forces in Politics, 1935-1959. LC 73-185831. 252p. 1972. 20.00x (ISBN 0-8262-0121-0). U of Mo Pr.

Burggraf, Linda. Consuming Passions. 3.50 (ISBN 0-318-04452-8). Pudding.

Burggren, Warren W., jt. ed. see Johansen, Kjell.

Burgh, A. Wallen. Sumida, Edition I. 222p. 1959. write for info. Rural Life.

Burgh, Edward M. Mortgage Investing by Life Insurance Companies. rev. ed. (FLMI Insurance Education Program Ser.). 220p. 1983. pap. text ed. 17.00 (ISBN 0-915322-62-5). LOMA.

Burgh, James. Political Disquisitions, 3 Vols. LC 78-146144. (American Constitutional & Legal History Ser). 1971. Repr. of 1775 ed. Set. lib. bdg. 175.00 (ISBN 0-306-70101-4). Da Capo.

Burghard, jt. auth. see Weidling.

Burghard, August. America's First Family: The Savages of Virginia. LC 74-80943. 60p. 1974. 4.00 (ISBN 0-8059-2038-2). Dorrance.

--Half a Century in Florida. (Illus.). 263p. 1982. 25.00 (ISBN 0-8103-2027-4). Banyan Bks.

Burghardt. Ingenieria Termodinamica. 2nd ed. 600p. (Span.). 1983. pap. text ed. write for info. (ISBN 0-06-310071-1, Pub. by HarLA Mexico). Har-Row.

Burghardt, Andrew F. Borderland, a Historical & Geographical Study of Burgenland, Austria. LC 62-15992. pap. 74.00 (ISBN 0-317-09523-4, 2015356). Bks Demand UMI.

Burghardt, Erich. Early Histological Diagnosis of Cervical Cancer. LC 79-176203. (Major Problem in Obstetrics & Gynecology Ser.: Vol. 6). (Illus.). 1973. text ed. 10.00 (ISBN 0-7216-2175-9). Saunders.

Burghardt, Gordon M., ed. Iguanas of the World: Their Behavior, Ecology & Conservation. Rand, A. Stanley. LC 82-7932. (Animal Behavior, Ecology, Conservation & Management Ser.). (Illus.). 472p. 1983. 55.00 (ISBN 0-8155-0917-0). Noyes.

Burghardt, John A. Major Trends in Population Growth in Texas. (Research Reports Ser.: 1978-3). 1979. pap. 4.00 (ISBN 0-87755-232-0). Bureau Busn UT.

Burghardt, John A. & Geraci, Vincent J. State & Local Annual Population Estimates: Methods, Performance, & Texas Applications. (Research Report Ser: 1978-4). 1979. pap. 4.00 (ISBN 0-87755-230-4). Bureau Busn UT.

Burghardt, M. & Kingsley, G. Marine Diesels. 1981. 19.95 (ISBN 0-13-556985-0). P-H.

Burghardt, M. David. Engineering Thermodynamics with Applications. 2nd. ed. (Illus.). 571p. 1982. text ed. 36.50 scp (ISBN 0-06-041042-6, HarpC); sol. manual avail. (ISBN 0-06-361041-8). Har-Row.

--Know Your Diesel. (Illus.). 160p. 1984. pap. 15.95 (ISBN 0-13-516591-1). P-H.

Burghardt, Steve. The Other Side of Organizing: Personal Dilemmas & Political Demands. 256p. 1982. 18.95 (ISBN 0-87073-482-2); pap. 9.95 (ISBN 0-87073-483-0). Schenkman Bks Inc.

Burghardt, Steven. Organizing for Community Action. (Sage Human Services Guides: Vol. 27). 120p. 1982. pap. 7.95 (ISBN 0-8039-0206-9). Sage.

Burghardt, W. J. & Lawler, T. C., eds. St. Gregory of Nyssa, the Lord's Prayer, the Beatitudes. LC 78-62466. (ACW Ser.: No. 18). 216p. 1954. 14.95 (ISBN 0-8091-0255-2). Paulist Pr.

--St. Irenaeus: Proof of the Apostolic Preaching. LC 78-62503. (ACW Ser.: No. 16). 242p. 1952. 12.95 (ISBN 0-8091-0254-4). Paulist Pr.

Burghardt, W. J., ed. see Augustine, St.

Burghardt, W. J., ed. see St. Augustine.

Burghardt, W. J., et al, eds. St. Augustine, Against the Academics. LC 78-62461. (ACW Ser.: No. 12). 220p. 1950. 9.95 (ISBN 0-8091-0252-8). Paulist Pr.

--St. Maximus the Confessor: The Ascetic Life, the Four Centuries on Charity. LC 55-8642. (ACW Ser.: No. 21). 293p. 1955. 13.95 (ISBN 0-8091-0258-7). Paulist Pr.

--Arnobius of Sicca, the Case Against the Pagans, Vol. 1. (ACW Ser.: No. 7). 372p. 1949. 13.95 (ISBN 0-8091-0248-X). Paulist Pr.

--Arnobius of Sicca, the Case Against the Pagans, Vol. 2. LC 78-62458. (ACW Ser.: No. 8). 659p. 1949. 11.95 (ISBN 0-8091-0249-8). Paulist Pr.

--Athenagoras, Embassy for the Christians, the Resurrection of the Dead. LC 56-11421. (Ancient Christian Writers Ser.: No. 23). 193p. 1956. 9.95 (ISBN 0-8091-0036-3). Paulist Pr.

--The Didache, the Epistle of Barnabas, the Epistle & Martyrdom of St. Polycarp, the Fragments of Papias, the Epistle of Diognetus. LC 78-62453. (ACW Ser.: No. 6). 241p. 1948. 13.95 (ISBN 0-8091-0247-1). Paulist Pr.

--Egeria, Diary of a Pilgrimage. LC 70-119159. (ACW Ser.: No. 38). 292p. 1970. 14.95 (ISBN 0-8091-0029-0). Paulist Pr.

--Firmicus Maternus, the Error of the Pagan Religions. (Ancient Christian Writers Ser.: No. 37). 1970. 11.95 (ISBN 0-8091-0039-8). Paulist Pr.

--Julianus Pomerius, the Contemplative Life. LC 78-62457. (ACW Ser.: No. 4). 220p. 1947. 9.95 (ISBN 0-8091-0245-5). Paulist Pr.

--Origen, Prayer, Exhortation to Martyrdom. LC 78-62467. (ACW Ser.: No. 19). 261p. 1954. 11.95 (ISBN 0-8091-0256-0). Paulist Pr.

--Origen, the Song of Songs: Commentary & Homilies. LC 57-11826. (ACW Ser.: No. 26). 491p. 1957. 14.95 (ISBN 0-8091-0261-7). Paulist Pr.

--Rufinus: A Commentary of the Apostles' Creed. LC 78-62468. (ACW Ser.: No. 20). 167p. 1955. 8.95 (ISBN 0-8091-0257-9). Paulist Pr.

--St. Athanasius: The Life of St. Antony. LC 78-62454. (ACW Ser.: No. 10). 155p. 1950. 12.95 (ISBN 0-8091-0250-1). Paulist Pr.

--St. Augustine, the Lord's Sermon on the Mount. LC 78-62451. (ACW Ser.: No. 5). 227p. 1948. 9.95 (ISBN 0-8091-0246-3). Paulist Pr.

--St. Augustine, the Problem of Free Choice. LC 78-62469. (ACW Ser.: No. 22). 298p. 1955. 11.95 (ISBN 0-8091-0259-5). Paulist Pr.

--St. Cyprian, the Lapsed, the Unity of the Catholic Church. LC 57-7364. (Ancient Christian Writers Ser.: No. 25). 132p. 1957. 8.95 (ISBN 0-8091-0260-9). Paulist Pr.

--St. Gregory the Great: Pastoral Care. (ACW Ser.: No. 11). 282p. 1950. 13.95 (ISBN 0-8091-0251-X). Paulist Pr.

--St. John Chrysostom, Baptismal Instructions. LC 62-21489. (Ancient Christian Writers Ser.: No. 31). 381p. 1963. 14.95 (ISBN 0-8091-0262-5). Paulist Pr.

--St. Methodius, the Symposium: A Treatise on Chastity. (Ancient Christian Writers Ser.: No. 27). 256p. 1958. 11.95 (ISBN 0-8091-0143-2). Paulist Pr.

--St. Prosper of Aquitaine, Defense of St. Augustine. LC 78-62463. (Ancient Christian Writers Ser.: No. 32). 235p. 1963. 10.95 (ISBN 0-8091-0263-3). Paulist Pr.

--St. Prosper of Aquitaine, the Call of All Nations. (Ancient Christian Writers Ser.: No. 14). 250p. 1952. 10.95 (ISBN 0-8091-0253-6). Paulist Pr.

--Tertullian, the Treatise Against Hermogenes. LC 56-13257. (Ancient Christian Writers Ser.: No. 24). 179p. 1956. 8.95 (ISBN 0-8091-0148-3). Paulist Pr.

--Tertullian, Treatise on Marriage & Remarriage: To His Wife, an Exhortation to Chastity Monogamy. LC 78-62462. (Ancient Christian Writers Ser.: No. 13). 103p. 1951. 9.95 (ISBN 0-8091-0149-1). Paulist Pr.

--Tertullian, Treatise on Penance: On Penitence & on Purity. LC 58-10746. (Ancient Christian Writers Ser.: No. 28). 138p. 1959. 12.95 (ISBN 0-8091-0150-5). Paulist Pr.

Burghardt, Walter J. Seasons That Laugh or Weep: Musings on the Human Journey. LC 83-60655. 144p. (Orig.). 1983. 4.95 (ISBN 0-8091-2533-1). Paulist Pr.

--Sir, We Would Like to See Jesus: Homilies from a Hilltop. LC 82-60589. 1983. pap. 8.95 (ISBN 0-8091-2490-4). Paulist Pr.

--Still Proclaiming Your Wonders: Homilies for the Eighties. 256p. (Orig.). 1984. pap. 9.95 (ISBN 0-8091-2632-X). Paulist Pr.

--Tell the Next Generation: Homilies & Near Homilies. LC 79-91895. 240p. 1980. pap. 7.95 (ISBN 0-8091-2252-9). Paulist Pr.

Burghardt, Walter J., ed. Religious Freedom, Nineteen Sixty-Five to Nineteen Seventy-Five: A Symposium on a Historic Document. LC 76-45938. 1977. pap. 2.45 (ISBN 0-8091-1993-5). Paulist Pr.

--Woman: New Dimensions. LC 76-50965. 1977. pap. 5.95 (ISBN 0-8091-2011-9). Paulist Pr.

Burghardt, Wolfgang & Hoelker, Klaus, eds. Text Processing. (Research in Text Theory Ser.). 466p. 1979. text ed. 62.40x (ISBN 3-11-007565-2). De Gruyter.

Burghart, Johannes, jt. ed. see Lawler, Thomas C.

Burghart, Richard & Cantlie, Audrey, eds. Indian Religion. LC 84-15115. 320p. 1985. 27.50 (ISBN 0-312-41400-5). St Martin.

Burghclere, Winifred. George Villiers, Second Duke of Buckingham. LC 74-118511. 1971. Repr. of 1903 ed. 32.50x (ISBN 0-8046-1259-5, Pub. by Kennikat). Assoc Faculty Pr.

Burghelea, D. & Lashof, R. Groups of Automarphisms of Manifolds. (Lecture Notes in Mathematics Ser.: Vol. 473). 156p. 1975. pap. 13.00 (ISBN 0-387-07182-2). Springer-Verlag.

Burgher, Goldene F. Washington County, Tennessee, Wills: 1777-1872. (Illus.). 144p. 1983. pap. 21.50 (ISBN 0-89308-285-6). Southern Hist Pr.

Burgher, Peter H. Changement: Understanding & Managing Business. 1979. 21.50x (ISBN 0-669-02569-0). Lexington Bks.

Burghes, D. N. & Borrie, M. S. Modelling with Differential Equations. (Mathematics & Its Applications Ser.). 172p. 1981. pap. 31.95 (ISBN 0-470-27360-7). Halsted Pr.

Burghes, D. N. & Graham, M. A. Introduction to Control Theory, Including Optimal Control. LC 80-40386. (Mathematics & Its Applications Ser.: I-176). 400p. 1980. 89.95x (ISBN 0-470-26998-7). Halsted Pr.

Burghes, D. N. & Wood, A. D. Mathematical Models in the Social Management & Life Sciences. LC 79-40989. (Mathematics & Its Applications Ser.). 287p. 1980. pap. text ed. 28.95x (ISBN 0-470-27073-X). Halsted Pr.

Burghes, D. N., et al. Applying Mathematics: A Course in Mathematical Modeling. (Mathematics & Its Applications Ser.). 194p. 1982. 48.95X (ISBN 0-470-27523-5). Halsted Pr.

Burgi, Richard T. History of the Russian Hexameter. (Foreign Area Studies: No. 2). ix, 208p. 1954. 16.50 (ISBN 0-208-00047-X, Archon). Shoe String.

Burgin, tr. see Chukovsky, Kornei.

Burgin, Diana, ed. see Chukovsky, Kornei.

Burgin, Hans & Mayer, Hans-Otto. Thomas Mann: A Chronicle of His Life. rev. ed. Dobson, Eugene, tr. LC 68-10989. (Illus.). 320p. 1969. pap. 8.50 (ISBN 0-8173-8064-7). U of Ala Pr.

Burgin, James E. Guide Book for the Family with Alcohol Problems. 64p. 3.95 (ISBN 0-89486-155-7). Hazelden.

--Help for the Marriage Partner of an Alcoholic. 16p. (Orig.). 1976. pap. 0.70 (ISBN 0-89486-059-3). Hazelden.

Burgin, John C. Teaching Singing. LC 72-10594. 290p. 1973. 16.00 (ISBN 0-8108-0565-0). Scarecrow.

Burgin, Miron. Economic Aspects of Argentine Federalism, 1820-1852. LC 70-102473. (Illus.). 1971. Repr. of 1946 ed. 14.00x (ISBN 0-8462-1507-1). Russell.

Burgin, Miron, ed. Handbook of Latin American Studies, Vol. 11: 1945. LC 36-32633. ix, 404p. 1963. 20.00x (ISBN 0-8130-0037-8). U Presses Fla.

--Handbook of Latin American Studies, Vol. 6: 1940. LC 36-32633. xvi, 570p. 1963. 20.00x (ISBN 0-8130-0032-7). U Presses Fla.

--Handbook of Latin American Studies, Vol. 7: 1941. LC 36-32633. xv, 549p. 1963. 20.00x (ISBN 0-8130-0033-5). U Presses Fla.

--Handbook of Latin American Studies, Vol. 8: 1942. LC 36-32633. xv, 521p. 1963. 20.00x (ISBN 0-8130-0034-3). U Presses Fla.

Burgin, Miron, jt. ed. see Hanke, Lewis.

Burgin, Richard, jt. auth. see Singer, Isaac B.

Burgin, Robert, et al, eds. Library Overdues: Analysis, Strategies & Solutions to the Problem. LC 84-19736. (Library & Archival Security Ser.: Vol. 6, Nos. 2 & 3). 144p. 1985. text ed. 19.95 (ISBN 0-86656-376-8). Haworth Pr.

Burgin, Tricia, jt. auth. see Osler, Jack.

Burgin, Victor, ed. Thinking Photography. (Communications & Culture Ser.). 239p. 1982. text ed. 26.50x (ISBN 0-333-27194-7, Pub. by Macmillan England); pap. text ed. 12.50x (ISBN 0-333-27195-5). Humanities.

Burgio, G. R., et al, eds. Triscomy, Twenty-One: An International Symposium. (Human Genetics Supplementa Ser.: Vol. 2). (Illus.). 265p. 1981. pap. 27.00 (ISBN 0-387-10653-7). Springer-Verlag.

Burgis, Mary, jt. auth. see Symoens, J. J.

Burgis, Nina, ed. see Dickens, Charles.

Burglass, Milton E., jt. ed. see Shaffer, Howard.

Burgmann, Verity. In Our Time: Socialism & the Rise of Labor, 1885-1905. 236p. 1985. text ed. 25.00x (ISBN 0-86861-529-3). Allen Unwin.

Burgmeier, James W. & Kost, Larry L. Epic: Exploration Programs in Calculus. (Illus.). 112p. 1985. pap. text ed. 29.95 (ISBN 0-13-283318-2). P-H.

Burgmueller, F. Twenty-Five Easy & Progressive Studies for Piano, Op. 100. Hoffman, Carl, ed. (Carl Fischer Music Library: No. 324). 1909. pap. 3.50 (ISBN 0-8258-0107-9, L324). Fischer Inc NY.

Burgner, Goldene F. Greene County Marriages, 1783 to 1868. 396p. 1981. 25.00 (ISBN 0-89308-202-3). Southern Hist Pr.

--Greene County Wills, 1783-1890. 150p. 1981. 20.00 (ISBN 0-89308-203-1). Southern Hist Pr.

--North Carolina Land Grants in Greene County, Tennessee. 160p. 1981. 20.00 (ISBN 0-89308-204-X). Southern LA.

--North Carolina Land Grants in Tennessee, 1778 to 1791. 214p. 1981. 20.00 (ISBN 0-89308-205-8). Southern Hist Pr.

Burgner, Robert L., ed. Further Studies of Alaska Sockeye Salmon. LC 71-627031. (UWPF, New Ser: Vol. 3). (Illus.). 273p. 1968. pap. 15.00x (ISBN 0-295-95203-2). U of Wash Pr.

Burgo, Joseph. The Lights of Barbrin. 1982. pap. 2.50 (ISBN 0-671-44706-8, Timescape). PB.

Burgoin, Gillian. Guide to the Weimaraner. (Illus.). 198p. 1985. 22.50 (ISBN 0-85115-414-X, Pub. by Boydell & Brewer). Longwood Pub Group.

Burgon, John W. Life & Times of Sir Thomas Gresham, 2 Vols. (Illus.). 1965. Repr. of 1839 ed. Set. 53.00 (ISBN 0-8337-0422-2). B Franklin.

Burgoon, Judee K. & Saine, Thomas. The Unspoken Dialogue: An Introduction to Nonverbal Communication. (Illus., LC 77-078913). 1978. text ed. 22.50 (ISBN 0-395-25792-1); pap. 1.00 instrs.' manual (ISBN 0-395-25793-X). HM.

Burgoon, M. & Ruffner, M. Human Communication. LC 77-17511. 1978. text ed. 19.95 (ISBN 0-03-020416-X, HoltC). HR&W.

Burgoon, M., et al. Small Group Communication. LC 74-686. 1974. pap. text ed. 18.95 (ISBN 0-03-011061-0, HoltC). HR&W.

Burgoon, Michael, jt. auth. see Ruffner, Michael.

Burgoon, Michael, ed. Communication Yearbook, No. 5. 885p. 1982. text ed. 39.95 (ISBN 0-87855-447-5). Transaction Bks.

--Communication Yearbook: An Annual Review Published for the International Commucation Association, No. 6. LC 76-45943. (Communication Yearbook Ser.: Vol. 6). 968p. 1982. 45.00 (ISBN 0-8039-1862-3). Sage.

Burgos, ed. see Apollinaire, Guillaume.

Burgos, David A., et al. Ensayos sobre los Principios y Metodos de la Administracion de Personal Publico. 1974. 3.00 (ISBN 0-87373-356-8). Intl Personnel Mgmt.

Burgos, Elisabeth, ed. I... Rigoberta Menchu: An Indian Woman in Guatemala. 200p. 1984. 19.50 (ISBN 0-8052-7190-2, Pub. by NLB England); pap. 8.50 (ISBN 0-8052-7191-0). Schocken.

Burgos, Julia de. Mar y Tu. LC 81-68710. (Illus.). 1981. pap. 4.95 (ISBN 0-940238-46-2). Ediciones Hura.

Burgos, Julia de see De Burgos, Julia.

Burgos, Julia De see De Burgos, Julia.

Burgos, Luis A. see Berrios Burgos, Luis A., et al.

Burgoyne, Arthur G. Homestead. LC 68-55495. Repr. of 1893 ed. 27.50x (ISBN 0-678-00872-8). Kelley.

--The Homestead Strike of Eighteen Ninety-Two. LC 79-4702. (Illus.). 1979. 24.95x (ISBN 0-8229-3405-1); pap. 6.95 (ISBN 0-8229-5310-2). U of Pittsburgh Pr.

Burgoyne, J. & Stuart, R., eds. Management Development: Context & Strategies. 160p. text ed. 35.50x (ISBN 0-566-02101-3). Gower Pub Co.

Burgoyne, Jacqueline & Clark, David. Making a Go of It: A Study of Stepfamilies in Sheffield. 300p. 1984. 39.95x (ISBN 0-7102-0318-7). Routledge & Kegan.

Burgoyne, John. The Dramatic & Poetical Works of the Late Lieut. Gen. J. Burgoyne. LC 77-2932. 1977. Repr. of 1808 ed. 60.00x (ISBN 0-8201-1285-2). Schol Facsimiles.

--State of the Expedition from Canada, As Laid Before the House of Commons. LC 70-77104. (Eyewitness Accounts of the American Revolution Ser., No. 2). 1969. Repr. of 1780 ed. 21.00 (ISBN 0-405-01146-6). Ayer Co Pubs.

Burgoyne, Thomas H. Light of Egypt, 2 vol. (Illus.). 501p. 1980. pap. 20.00 (ISBN 0-89540-064-2, SB-064). Sun Pub.

Burgreen, David. Design Methods for Power Plant Structures. LC 75-35075. 450p. 1975. text ed. 27.00 (ISBN 0-9600452-1-X). C P Pr.

--Pressure Vessel Analysis. LC 79-51160. 1979. 27.00 (ISBN 0-9600452-3-6). C P Pr.

--Principles of Piping Analysis. LC 77-70079. 1977. text ed. 27.00 (ISBN 0-9600452-2-8). C P Pr.

Burgt, Robert J. Vanden see Vanden Burgt, Robert J.

Burgum, jt. auth. see McCullough, B.

Burgum, Thomas & Anderson, Scott. The Counselor & the Law. 1975. members 14.95 (ISBN 0-686-36428-7, 72005); nonmembers 16.95 (ISBN 0-686-37315-4). Am Assn Coun Dev.

Burgwyn, Diana. Marriage Without Children. LC 80-8197. 256p. 1982. pap. 4.76i (ISBN 0-06-090940-4, CN940, CN). Har-Row.

Burham, I. H., tr. see Dumas, Alexander.

Burhans, Clinton S. The Would-Be Writer. 3rd ed. LC 74-13349. pap. 36.80 (ISBN 0-317-09496-3, 2012513). Bks Demand UMI.

Burhans, Robert D. The First Special Service Force: A War History of the North Americans 1942-1944. (Elite Unit Ser.: No. 1). (Illus.). 376p. 1981. Repr. of 1947 ed. 22.00 (ISBN 0-89839-050-8). Battery Pr.

Burhenne, Diane P., jt. auth. see Berman, Henry S.

Burhenne, H. Joachim & Li, David K. Radiology: Focus on Clinical Diagnosis. 1984. text ed. write for info. (ISBN 0-87488-406-3). Med Exam.

Burhenne, H. Joachim, jt. auth. see Margulis, Alexander R.

Burhop, E. H. see Massey, H. S.

Burhop, E. H., ed. High Energy Physics, 5 vols. (Pure & Applied Physics Ser.: Vol. 25). Vol. 1, 1967. 79.50 (ISBN 0-12-144301-9); Vol. 2, 1967. 79.50 (ISBN 0-12-144302-7); Vol. 3, 1969. 79.50 (ISBN 0-12-144303-5); Vol. 4, 1969. 79.50 (ISBN 0-12-144304-3); Vol. 5, 1972. 79.50 (ISBN 0-12-144305-1). Acad Pr.

Buri, Fritz. Theology of Existence. Oliver, Harold H, tr. 128p. 1965. 6.50 (ISBN 0-87921-001-X). Attic Pr.

Burian, Barbara & Fink, Stuart. Business Data Processing. 2nd ed. LC 81-5207. (Illus.). 544p. 1982. text ed. 25.95 (ISBN 0-13-094045-3); study guide 8.95 (ISBN 0-13-094060-7). P-H.

Burian, Barbara J. A Simplified Approach to S-370 Assembly Language Programming. (Illus.). 1977. 24.95 (ISBN 0-13-810119-1). P-H.

Burian, F. Atlas der Plastischen Chirurgie. Sostmann, H. & Schertel, A., trs. from Eng. Incl. Vol. 1. Allgemeiner Teil und Einfuehrung in den Speziellen Teil; Vol. 2. Der Kopf; Vol. 3. Rumpf und Extremitaeten. (Illus., Ger.). 1977. 231.25 (ISBN 3-8055-1434-4). S Karger.

--Plastic Surgery Atlas, 3 Vols. 1968. write for info. Vol. 1 (ISBN 0-02-317050-6). Vol. 2 (ISBN 0-02-317060-3). Vol. 3 (ISBN 0-02-317070-0). Set. write for info. (ISBN 0-02-317080-8). Macmillan.

Burian, Jarka. The Scenography of Josef Svoboda. LC 77-152101. (Illus.). 197p. 1971. pap. 12.95 (ISBN 0-8195-6032-4). Wesleyan U Pr.

--Svoboda: Wagner: Joseph Svoboda's Scenography for Richard Wagner's Opera. 1983. 35.00 (ISBN 0-8195-5088-4). Wesleyan U Pr.

Burian, Peter, ed. Directions in Euripidean Criticism: A Collection of Essays. 248p. 1985. 27.50 (ISBN 0-8223-0610-7). Duke.

Burian, Peter, tr. see Euripides.

Burian, Richard M., jt. ed. see Brandon, Robert N.

Burich, Nancy J., ed. Alexander the Great: A Bibliography. LC 72-114734. Repr. of 1970 ed. 33.70 (ISBN 0-8357-9358-3, 2011311). Bks Demand UMI.

Buridan, Jean. Iohannis Buridan, Quaestiones Super Libris Quattuor De Caelo et Mundo. Moody, Ernest A., ed. (Mediaeval Academy of America Publications). 1942. 25.00 (ISBN 0-527-01704-3). Kraus Repr.

Buridan, John. John Buridan on Self-Reference: Chapter Eight of Buridan's Sophismata, with a Translation, an Introduction, & a Philosophical Commentary. Hughes, G. E., ed. LC 81-15465. 272p. 1982. 42.50 (ISBN 0-521-24086-7); pap. 12.95 (ISBN 0-521-28864-9). Cambridge U Pr.

--Sophisms on Meaning & Truth. Scott, Theodore K., ed. LC 66-26800. (Orig.). 1966. pap. text ed. 9.95x (ISBN 0-89197-418-0). Irvington.

Burie, Audrey A. & Heltshe, Mary A. Reading with a Smile: Ninety Reading Games That Work. new ed. LC 75-2216. (Illus.). 200p. 1975. pap. 8.95 (ISBN 0-87491-053-6). Acropolis.

Burin, Frederic S., ed. see Kircheimer, Otto.

Buringh, P. Introduction to the Study of Soils in Tropical & Subtropical Regions. 3rd ed. (Illus.). 146p. (16 full colour page photographs of soil profiles). 1979. pap. 14.00 (ISBN 90-220-0691-3, PDC146, Pudoc). Unipub.

Burington, Richard S. Handbook of Mathematical Tables & Formulas. 5th ed. LC 78-39634. (Illus.). 480p. 1973. text ed. 29.95 (ISBN 0-07-009015-7). McGraw.

Burington, Richard S. & May, Donald C., Jr. Handbook of Probability & Statistics with Tables. 2nd ed. 1970. 36.50 (ISBN 0-07-009030-0). McGraw.

Buriot, Henri, tr. see Croce, Benedetto.

Burish, Thomas G. & Bradley, Laurence A. Coping with Chronic Disease: Research & Applications. 1983. 44.00 (ISBN 0-12-144450-3). Acad Pr.

Burish, Thomas G., et al, eds. Cancer, Nutrition & Eating Behavior: A Biobehavioral Perspective. 256p. 1985. text ed. 29.95 (ISBN 0-89859-518-5). L Erlbaum Assocs.

Buritica, P. & Hennen, J. F. Pucciniosireae: Uredinales, Pucciniaceae. LC 79-27151. (Flora Neotropica Monograph: No. 24). (Illus.). 50p. 1980. pap. 7.75x (ISBN 0-89327-219-1). NY Botanical.

Burk, August. Die Padagogik Des Isokrates Als Grundelgung Des Humanistichen Bildungsideals. 1923. pap. 19.00 (ISBN 0-384-06535-X). Johnson Repr.

Burk, Bruce. Game Bird Carving. 2nd ed. LC 82-62347. (Illus.). 304p. 1982. 27.95 (ISBN 0-8329-3591-3, Pub. by Winchester Pr). New Century.

--Waterfowl Studies. LC 82-62596. 1976. 21.95 (ISBN 0-8329-1807-5, Pub. by Winchester Pr). New Century.

--Waterfowl Studies: Dabbling & Whistling Ducks. LC 84-51284. (Waterfowl Studies Ser.: Vol. I). (Illus.). 240p. 1984. 35.00 (ISBN 0-88740-025-6). Schiffer.

--Waterfowl Studies: Diving Ducks. LC 84-51283. (Waterfowl Studies Ser.: Vol. II). (Illus.). 300p. 1984. 39.95 (ISBN 0-88740-026-4). Schiffer.

--Waterfowl Studies: Geese & Swans. LC 84-51260. (Waterfowl Studies Ser.: Vol. III). (Illus.). 200p. 1984. 29.95 (ISBN 0-88740-027-2). Schiffer.

Burk, C. A. & Drake, C. L., eds. The Geology of Continental Margins. LC 74-16250. (Illus.). xiii, 1009p. 1974. 63.00 (ISBN 0-387-06866-X). Springer-Verlag.

Burk, C. John, jt. auth. see Holland, Marjorie.

Burk, Dale, ed. The Black Bear in Modern North America. 299p. 1979. 12.00 (ISBN 0-940864-03-7). Boone & Crockett.

Burk, Dale A. Elmer Sprunger: Wildlife Artist. LC 82-99860. (Illus.). 104p. (Orig.). 1982. 12.95 (ISBN 0-686-46594-6); pap. 8.95 (ISBN 0-912299-06-1). Stoneydale Pr Pub.

--Great Bear, Wild River. LC 77-81463. (Illus.). 160p. 1977. pap. 5.00 (ISBN 0-912299-10-X). Stoneydale Pr Pub.

--Montana Fishing. 2nd. & rev. ed. LC 82-99817. (Illus.). 152p. 1983. pap. 4.95 (ISBN 0-912299-08-8). Stoneydale Pr Pub.

--Montana Hunting Guide. 3rd, rev. & exp. ed. LC 83-60660. (Illus.). 164p. 1985. 13.95 (ISBN 0-912299-19-3); pap. 8.95. Stoneydale Pr Pub.

--New Interpretations. 3rd. ed. LC 82-99859. (Illus.). 204p. 1982. pap. 14.95 (ISBN 0-912299-07-X). Stoneydale Pr Pub.

Burk, Dale A. & Cauble, Chris. Float Fishing in Montana. (Illus.). 152p. (Orig.). 1985. pap. 6.95 (ISBN 0-686-46595-4). Stoneydale Pr Pub.

Burk, Dale A., ed. see Konizeski, Dick.

Burk, Dean. Vitamin B17, B15, Brief Foods-Vitamins. 1.50 (ISBN 0-686-29881-0). Cancer Control Soc.

Burk, Gay. Island Winds Blow Deep. (Orig.). 1979. pap. 1.95 (ISBN 0-532-19233-8). Woodhill.

Burk, Janet L. & Hayes, Stephen. Environmental Concerns: A Bibliography of U.S. Government Publications, 1971-1973. 1975. 4.00 (ISBN 0-932826-06-7). New Issues MI.

Burk, Janet L., jt. ed. see Kiraldi, Louis.

Burk, John D. Bunker-Hill, Or, the Death of General Warren: An Historic Tragedy in Five Acts. LC 78-130091. (Dunlap Society Publications Ser: No. 15). 1970. Repr. of 1891 ed. lib. bdg. 16.50 (ISBN 0-8337-0423-0). B Franklin.

--The History of Virginia, From Its First Settlement to the Commencement of the Revolution, 4 vols. LC 75-31112. Repr. of 1816 ed. 142.00 set (ISBN 0-404-13700-8). AMS Pr.

Burk, John N., ed. see Hale, Philip.

Burk, John N., ed. see Howe, Mark A.

Burk, John N., ed. see Wagner, Richard.

Burk, Kathleen. Britain, America & the Sinews of War, 1914-1918. 224p. 1984. text ed. 29.95x (ISBN 0-04-940076-2). Allen Unwin.

Burk, Kathleen, ed. War & the State: The Transformation of British Government, 1914-1919. 192p. 1982. text ed. 29.50x (ISBN 0-04-940065-7). Allen Unwin.

Burk, Leslie Chamberlin & Esteves, Roberto, eds. Video & Cable Guidelines. 2nd ed. 461p. 1980. 9.75 (ISBN 0-317-32228-1, LITA). ALA.

--Video & Cable Guidelines. 461p. 1980. 9.75 (ISBN 0-318-14752-1). Lib Info Tech.

Burk, M. & Pas, E. Analysis of Food Consumption Survey Data for Developing Countries. (Food & Nutrition Papers: No. 16). 146p. (Eng., Fr., & Span.). 1980. pap. 9.50 (ISBN 92-5-100968-6, F2118, FAO). Unipub.

Burk, Margaret, ed. see Harshfield, Verna.

Burk, Margaret T. Are the Stars Out Tonight? The Story of the Famous Ambassador & Cocoanut Grove... Hollywood's Hotel. (Illus.). 190p. 1980. text ed. 15.00 (ISBN 0-937806-00-5). M Burk.

Burk, Robert F. The Eisenhower Administration & Black Civil Rights. LC 84-2312. (Twentieth-Century America Ser.). 304p. 1984. text ed. 24.95x (ISBN 0-87049-431-7). U of Tenn Pr.

Burk, Tom. How to Photograph Weddings, Groups & Ceremonies. LC 80-83275. (Orig.). 1980. pap. 9.95 (ISBN 0-89586-057-0). H P Bks.

Burk, W. R. A Bibliography of North American Gasteromycetes I: Phalales. 200p. 1981. pap. text ed. 16.00x (ISBN 3-7682-1262-9). Lubrecht & Cramer.

Burka, Jane & Yuen, Lenora. Procrastination: Why You Do It, What To Do About It. (Illus.). 256p. 1984. pap. 8.95 (ISBN 0-201-10191-2). Addison-Wesley.

Burkan, Bruce, jt. auth. see Keyes, Ken.

Burkan, Bruce, jt. auth. see Keyes, Ken, Jr.

Burkan, Peggy D. Guiding Yourself into a Spiritual Reality: A Workbook. LC 83-91310. 96p. (Orig.). 1984. pap. 6.95 (ISBN 0-935616-06-3). Reunion Pr.

Burkan, Peggy D., jt. auth. see Burkan, Tolly.

Burkan, Tolly & Burkan, Peggy D. Firewalking. price not set. Reunion Pr.

--Guiding Yourself into a Spiritual Reality. rev. ed. LC 83-91310. 128p. (Orig.). 1984. pap. 5.95 (ISBN 0-935616-05-5). Reunion Pr.

Burkan, Tolly & Rosin, Mark B. Dying to Live. LC 84-62759. (Illus.). 228p. (Orig.). 1985. pap. 8.95 (ISBN 0-935616-03-9). Reunion Pr.

Burkar, W. & Schmortz, K. Grinding & Polishing. 345p. 1981. 100.00x (ISBN 0-86108-079-3, Pub. by Portcullio Pr). State Mutual Bk.

Burkard, Martha, jt. auth. see Anderson, Pauline.

Burkard, Michael. In a White Light. LC 77-94478. 49p. 1977. perfect bound in wrappers 3.75 (ISBN 0-934332-00-2). L'Epervier Pr.

--None, River. 1979. pap. 3.50 (ISBN 0-686-57434-6, Pub. by Ironwood Pr). Small Pr Dist.

--Ruby for Grief. LC 81-40484. (Pitt Poetry Ser.). 77p. 1981. 12.95 (ISBN 0-8229-3450-7); pap. 5.95 (ISBN 0-8229-5333-1). U of Pittsburgh Pr.

Burkard, R. E., et al. Algebraic & Combinatorial Methods in Operations Research: Proceedings of the Workshop on Algebraic Structures in Operations Research. (Mathematics Studies, Vol. 95; Annals of Discrete Mathematics: No. 19). 382p. 1984. 55.75 (ISBN 0-444-87571-9, North-Holland). Elsevier.

Burkardt, Frederick. A Calendar of the Correspondence of Charles Darwin, 1821-1882. LC 82-14565. (Humanities Ser.). 700p. 1984. lib. bdg. 100.00 (ISBN 0-8240-9224-4). Garland Pub.

Burkart, Adolf, jt. auth. see Helbing, Wolfgang.

Burkart, John & Medlik, S. Management of Tourism. 1981. pap. 16.95 (ISBN 0-434-90196-2, Pub. by W Heinemann Ltd). David & Charles.

Burkart, John, jt. ed. see Chiarenza, Loretta.

Burkart, Rosemarie. Die Kunst des Masses in Mme de Lafayette's "Princesse de Cleves". 1933. pap. 17.00 (ISBN 0-384-06545-7). Johnson Repr.

Burkatt, Leonard, tr. see Munch, Charles.

Burke. Tales from the Beechy Woods. 32p. 1983. 10.95 (ISBN 0-88625-044-7). EDC.

Burke & Kranhold. Big Fearon Bulletin Board Book. 1978. pap. 15.95 (ISBN 0-8224-0702-7). Pitman Learning.

Burke see Sohn, David A.

Burke, A., et al. The Search for a New Europe, 1919-1971. 1971. pap. text ed. 6.95 (ISBN 0-8290-1186-2). Irvington.

Burke, A. M. Microcomputers Can Be Kidstuff: A Friendly Guide to Using a Micro in Your Home or at School. LC 83-181. 173p. (gr. 6-8). 1983. pap. 11.95 (ISBN 0-8104-5202-2). Hayden.

Burke, Abbot G. Magnetic Therapy: Healing in Your Hands. LC 80-22941. (Illus.). 86p. (Orig.). 1980. pap. text ed. 4.95 (ISBN 0-932104-04-5). St George Pr.

Burke, Alan. My Naked Soul. (Illus.). 1968. 3.95 (ISBN 0-87212-021-X). Libra.

Burke, Alan D. The Body Shop Murders. Curtis, C. Michael, ed. 288p. 1985. 15.95 (ISBN 0-87113-033-5, Pub. by Atlantic Monthly Pr). Little.

--Getting Away with Murder. 360p. 1981. 12.95 (ISBN 0-316-11688-2, Pub. by Atlantic Monthly Pr). Little.

Burke, Albert L. He That Hath an Ear. 101p. (Orig.). 1982. pap. 3.50 (ISBN 0-9608662-0-5). Eleventh Hour.

Burke, Anna M. Computer Discovery Workbook, College Version. 144p. 1984. pap. 9.95 wkbk. (ISBN 0-574-21460-7, 13-4460); tchr's ed. 5.95 (ISBN 0-574-21461-5, 13-4461). SRA.

--Microcomputers for Writers. 124p. 1985. 9.95 (ISBN 0-912603-22-4). Micro Info.

--The Plain Brown Wrapper Book of Computers. 184p. (Orig.). 1983. pap. 9.95 (ISBN 0-936602-59-7). Kampmann.

--So You Want a Job in Computers. 150p. 1985. 9.95 (ISBN 0-912603-21-6). Micro Info.

--What Do You Want to Be Now That You're All Grown up? 149p. 1982. 11.95 (ISBN 0-13-952044-9); pap. 5.95 (ISBN 0-13-952036-8). P-H.

Burke, Arnold. Inositol-Nature's Anxiety Fighter. 1981. pap. 4.95x (ISBN 0-317-07300-1, Regent House). B of A.

Burke, Arthur M. Key to the Ancient Parish Registers of England & Wales. LC 62-6577. (Illus.). 163p. 1981. Repr. of 1908 ed. 15.00 (ISBN 0-8063-0445-6). Genealog Pub.

Burke, Arvid J. & Burke, Mary A. Documentation in Education. LC 67-17818. 1967. text ed. 15.95x (ISBN 0-8077-1134-9). Tchrs Coll.

Burke, Barlow. Law of Real Estate Brokers. LC 81-81531. 448p. 1982. 0.59.00 (ISBN 0-316-11689-0). Little.

--Law of Real Estate Brokers: 1984 Supplement. LC 81-81531. 96p. 1984. pap. 22.50 (ISBN 0-316-11678-5). Little.

--Personal Property in a Nutshell. LC 83-6519. (Nutshell Ser.). 322p. 1983. pap. text ed. 7.95 (ISBN 0-314-73427-9). West Pub.

Burke, Barlow, jt. auth. see Ebersole, Joseph L.

Burke, Bill. They Shall Cast Out Demons. 1983. 12.00 (ISBN 0-932526-05-5). Nexus Pr.

Burke, Bobbye, et al. Historic Rittenhouse: A Philadelphia Neighborhood. LC 84-10689. (Illus.). 144p. 1985. 22.50 (ISBN 0-8122-7938-7); pap. 14.95 (ISBN 0-8122-1202-9). U of Pa Pr.

Burke, Carol. Close Quarters. LC 75-319973. 52p. 1975. 3.50 (ISBN 0-87886-066-5). Ithaca Hse.

Burke, Carol, ed. Plain Talk. LC 82-81678. (Illus.). 152p. 1983. pap. 3.50 (ISBN 0-911198-67-9). Purdue U Pr.

Burke, Carol, ed. see Marist Parents' Club.

Burke, Carol S., jt. auth. see Russell, Louise B.

Burke, Carolyn, tr. see Irigaray, Luce.

Burke, Carolyn L., jt. auth. see Goodman, Yetta M.

Burke, Carolyn M. Afraid of the Dark. (Illus.). 22p. (Orig.). 1984. pap. 5.00 (ISBN 0-914925-06-7). Heirloom Bks.

--Cactus in Bloom. 29p. (Orig.). 1984. pap. 5.00 (ISBN 0-914925-00-8). Heirloom Bks.

--Energies-American Folk Poetry. (Illus.). 14p. (Orig.). 1985. pap. 3.00 (ISBN 0-914925-05-9). Heirloom Bks.

--First Heirloom Poetry Sampler. 15p. (Orig.). 1985. pap. 5.00 (ISBN 0-914925-09-1). Heirloom Bks.

--My Own Story: A Children's Book. (Illus.). 14p. (Orig.). (ps). 1985. pap. 3.00 (ISBN 0-914925-08-3). Heirloom Bks.

--The Pride & Beauty Handbook for Black-Skinned Women. (Illus.). 50p. (Orig.). 1985. pap. 7.00 (ISBN 0-914925-07-5). Heirloom Bks.

--Water Color. 16p. (Orig.). 1985. pap. 5.00 (ISBN 0-914925-10-5). Heirloom Bks.

Burke, Catherine G. Innovation & Public Policy: The Case of Personal Rapid Transit. LC 79-2410. (Illus.). 416p. 1979. 28.50x (ISBN 0-669-03167-4). Lexington Bks.

Burke, Charles & Provost, Norman, eds. Loneliness. (Illus.). 101p. (Orig.). 1970. pap. 3.25 (ISBN 0-88489-022-8). St Marys.

Burke, Charles J., jt. auth. see Barnett, Raymond A.

Burke, Clifford. Printing It! (Illus.). 128p. 1974. pap. 4.95 (ISBN 0-914728-03-2). Wingbow Pr.

--Printing Poetry. LC 80-52171. 168p. 1980. 50.00 (ISBN 0-912962-01-1); unbound 37.50 (ISBN 0-912962-02-X). Scarab Pr.

--A Rainy Day Guide to Seattle. LC 83-71602. (Orig.). 1983. pap. 6.95 (ISBN 0-87701-290-3). Chronicle Bks.

Burke, Colin. Kimberley. 480p. 1985. 16.95 (ISBN 0-312-45388-4). St Martin.

Burke, Colin B. American Collegiate Populations. (Education & Socialization in American History Ser.). 384p. 1982. 45.00x (ISBN 0-8147-1038-7). NYU Pr.

Burke, Cormac. Conscience & Freedom. 159p. (Orig.). 1977. pap. 4.95 (ISBN 0-933932-39-1). Scepter Pubs.

Burke, Cornelius G. The Collector's Haydn. LC 77-28259. (Keystone Books in English Ser.: No. KB 7). (Addendum by Arthur Cohn). 1978. Repr. of 1959 ed. lib. bdg. 19.75x (ISBN 0-313-20239-7, BUCH). Greenwood.

Burke, D. Barlow. The Law of Title Insurance. write for info. Little.

Burke, D. C. & Murray, D. D. Handbook of Spinal Cord Medicine. 100p. 1975. pap. 9.00 (ISBN 0-89004-066-4). Raven.

Burke, D. C. & Morris, A. G., eds. Interferons: From Molecular Biology to Clinical Application. LC 83-1938. (Society for General Microbiology Symposia Ser.: No. 35). 350p. 1983. 62.50 (ISBN 0-521-25069-2). Cambridge U Pr.

Burke, Daniel. Notes on Literary Stucture. LC 81-40645. 280p. (Orig.). 1982. lib. bdg. 25.75 (ISBN 0-8191-2119-3); pap. text ed. 13.00 (ISBN 0-8191-2120-7). U Pr of Amer.

Burke, David G., ed. The Poetry of Baruch: A Reconstruction & Analysis of the Original Hebrew Text of Baruch 3: 9-5: 9. LC 80-10271. (Society of Biblical Literature, Septuagint & Cognate Studies: No. 10). pap. 15.95 (ISBN 0-89130-382-0, 06-04-10). Scholars Pr GA.

Burke, DeAnn, jt. auth. see Burke, Todd.

Burke, Dennis. How to Meditate God's Word. 64p. 1982. pap. 2.25 (ISBN 0-89274-241-0, HH-241). Harrison Hse.

--Understanding the Fear of the Lord. 1982. pap. 1.95 (ISBN 0-89274-265-8, HH-265). Harrison Hse.

Burke, Dennis R. Treating Martial Arts Injuries. Griffeth, Bill, ed. LC 81-81332. (Series 412). 1981. pap. 8.95 (ISBN 0-89750-075-X). Ohara Pubns.

Burke, Doreen. J. Alden Weir. (Illus.). 313p. 1983. 50.00 (ISBN 0-87413-220-7). U Delaware Pr.

Burke, Doreen B. American Painting in the Metropolitan Museum of Art: A Catalogue of Works by Artists Born Between 1846 & 1864, Vol. 3. LC 80-81074. 528p. 1980. 85.00x (ISBN 0-691-03961-5). Princeton U Pr.

Burke, E. A., jt. auth. see Uytenbogaardt, E. W.

Burke, Ed, et al. Inside the Cyclist. rev. ed. Velo-News Editors, ed. (Illus.). 160p. 1984. pap. 9.95 (ISBN 0-941950-06-9). Velo-News.

Burke, Edmond & Paine, Thomas. Reflections on the Revolution in France (Burke) Bd. with The Rights of Man (Paine) Doubleday. pap. 7.50 (ISBN 0-385-08190-1, Anch). Doubleday.

Burke, Edmund. Account of the European Settlements in America, 6 pts. in 2 vols. Repr. of 1808 ed. Set. 30.00 (ISBN 0-404-01237-X); 15.50 ea. Vol. 1 (ISBN 0-404-01238-8). Vol. 2 (ISBN 0-404-01239-6). AMS Pr.

--Account of the European Settlements in America, 2 Vols. in 1. LC 77-141082. (Research Library of Colonial Americana). 1972. Repr. of 1777 ed. 53.00 (ISBN 0-405-03277-3). Ayer Co Pubs.

--Correspondence of Edmund Burke, 8 vols. Incl. Vol. 1. Copeland, Thomas W., ed. 1958. 32.00x (ISBN 0-226-11553-4); Vol. 2. Sutherland, Lucy S., ed. 1960; Vol. 3. Guttridge, George H., ed. 1961. (ISBN 0-226-11555-0); Vol. 4. Woods, J. A. 1963. (ISBN 0-226-11556-9); Vol. 5. Furber, Holden, ed. 1965. (ISBN 0-226-11557-7); Vol. 6. Cobban, Alfred & Smith, Robert A., eds. 1967. (ISBN 0-226-11558-5); Vol. 7. Marshall, P. J. & Woods, John A., eds. 1968. (ISBN 0-226-11559-3); Vol. 8. McDowell, R. B., ed. 1970. (ISBN 0-226-11560-7); Vol. 9. McDowell, R. B. & Woods, John A., eds. 1971. (ISBN 0-226-11561-5). LC 58-5615. 32.00x ea. U of Chicago Pr.

--Correspondence of Edmund Burke: Index, Vol. 10. Lowe, Barbara, ed. LC 58-5615. 1978. 40.00x (ISBN 0-226-11562-3). U of Chicago Pr.

--The French Revolution & the Perversions of History, 2 vols. (Illus.). 315p. 1985. Set. 187.50 (ISBN 0-86722-102-X). Inst Econ Pol.

--A Letter to the Sheriffs of Bristol: A Speech at Bristol on Parliamentary Conduct; a Letter to a Noble Lord. Murison, W., ed. LC 76-29423. Repr. of 1920 ed. 34.00 (ISBN 0-404-15344-5). AMS Pr.

--Letters, Speeches & Tracts on Irish Affairs. Arnold, Matthew, ed. LC 75-28809. Repr. of 1881 ed. 36.00 (ISBN 0-404-13802-0). AMS Pr.

--On the American Revolution. 2nd ed. Barkan, E. R., ed. 11.25 (ISBN 0-8446-0045-8). Peter Smith.

--Philosophy of Edmund Burke: A Selection from His Speeches & Writings. Bredvold, Louis I. & Ross, Ralph G., eds. 1961. pap. 7.95 (ISBN 0-472-06121-6, 121, AA). U of Mich Pr.

--Prelude to Protectorate in Morocco: Precolonial Protest & Resistance, 1860-1912. LC 75-43228. (Illus.). 1977. lib. bdg. 25.00x (ISBN 0-226-08075-7). U of Chicago Pr.

--Reflections on the Revolution in France. Mahoney, Thomas H., ed. 1955. pap. 10.28 scp (ISBN 0-672-60213-X, LLA46). Bobbs.

--Selected Letters of Edmund Burke. Mansfield, Harvey C., Jr., ed. LC 83-18138. 1984. lib. bdg. 32.50x (ISBN 0-226-08068-4). U of Chicago Pr.

--Selected Works. Bate, Walter J., ed. LC 75-9946. 536p. 1975. Repr. of 1960 ed. lib. bdg. 25.50x (ISBN 0-8371-8122-4, BUSEW). Greenwood.

--Selected Writings & Speeches. Stanlis, J. P., ed. 12.75 (ISBN 0-8446-1094-1). Peter Smith.

--Speeches. Selby, F. G., ed. LC 73-9127. 328p. 1974. Repr. of 1956 ed. lib. bdg. 22.50x (ISBN 0-8371-6984-4, BUSP). Greenwood.

--Speeches on the American War & Letters to the Sheriffs of Bristol. LC 72-8666. (American Revolutionary Ser.). Repr. of 1891 ed. lib. bdg. 29.50x (ISBN 0-8398-0191-2). Irvington.

--Two Speeches on Conciliation With American & Two Letters on Irish Questions. 284p. 1983. 35.00 (ISBN 0-317-00584-7). Century Bookbindery.

--A Vindication of Natural Society. LC 81-84826. (Illus.). 130p. 1982. 8.50 (ISBN 0-86597-009-2, Liberty Clas); pap. text ed. 4.50 (ISBN 0-86597-010-6). Liberty Fund.

--Works, 12 vols. Repr. of 1899 ed. 695.00x (ISBN 0-403-04342-5). Somerset Pub.

--The Writings & Speeches of Edmund Burke: India, Madras & Bengal, 1774-1785, Vol. 5. Marshall, P. J., ed. 1980. 130.00x (ISBN 0-19-822417-6). Oxford U Pr.

--The Writings & Speeches of Edmund Burke: Party, Parliament & the American Crisis, 1766-1774, Vol. 2. Langford, Paul, ed. 1981. text ed. 120.00x (ISBN 0-19-822416-8). Oxford U Pr.

Burke, Edmund E. Edmund Burke: A Philosophical Inquiry into the Origin of Our Ideas of the Sublime & Beautiful. Boulton, James T., ed. LC 68-27583. 1968. pap. 8.95x (ISBN 0-268-00085-9). U of Notre Dame Pr.

Burke, Edmund H. History of Archery. LC 70-138579. 1971. Repr. of 1957 ed. lib. bdg. 22.50x (ISBN 0-8371-5778-1, BUHA). Greenwood.

Burke, Edmund J. & Humphreys, John H. Fit to Exercise. (Illus.). 192p. 1982. 12.95 (ISBN 0-7207-1224-6, Pub. by Michael Joseph). Merrimack Pub Cir.

Burke, Edmund J., jt. auth. see Scriber, Kent.

Burke, Edmund J., ed. Exercise, Science & Fitness. 1980. text ed. 16.95; pap. 10.95 (ISBN 0-932392-04-0). Mouvement Pubns.

--Toward an Understanding of Human Performance. 2nd ed. 1980. text ed. 17.95 (ISBN 0-932392-01-6); pap. 11.95 (ISBN 0-686-91525-9). Mouvement Pubns.

Burke, Edmund J., tr. see Klausen, Klaus & Hemmingsen, Ib.

Burke, Edmund M. A Participatory Approach to Urban Planning. LC 78-31107. 304p. 1979. text ed. 29.95 (ISBN 0-87705-393-6). Human Sci Pr.

Burke, Edward. Reflections on Revolution in France. 1982. pap. 4.95 (ISBN 0-14-043204-3). Penguin.

Burke, Edward J., ed. Toward an Understanding of Human Performance. 1977. pap. 7.50 (ISBN 0-932392-01-6). Mouvement Pubns.

Burke, Fielding. Call Home the Heart. (Novels of the Thirties Ser.). 462p. 1983. pap. 8.95 (ISBN 0-935312-15-3). Feminist Pr.

Burke, Frank. Federico Fellini: "Variety Lights" to "La Dolce Vita". (Filmmakers Ser.). 1984. lib. bdg. 19.95 (ISBN 0-8057-9300-3, Twayne). G K Hall.

Burke, Frank M., Jr. Valuation & Valuation Planning for Closely-Held Businesses. LC 80-24585. 420p. 1981. 39.50 (ISBN 0-13-940007-9). P-H.

Burke, Fred. Africa's Quest for Order. 11.00 (ISBN 0-8446-0526-3). Peter Smith.

Burke, Fred G. Tanganyika: Preplanning. LC 65-25989. (National Planning Ser.: No. 3). pap. 34.50 (ISBN 0-317-28737-0, 2020396). Bks Demand UMI.

Burke, Harold W. The Dam & the River. (Orig.). 1979. pap. 1.95 (ISBN 0-532-23164-3). Woodhill.

Burke, Harry. Handbook of Magnetic Phenomena for Electronic Engineers. (Illus.). 512p. 1985. 49.50 (ISBN 0-442-21184-8). Van Nos Reinhold.

Burke, Harry E. Handbook of Bar-Coding Systems. (Illus.). 224p. 1984. 42.50 (ISBN 0-442-21430-8). Van Nos Reinhold.

Burke, Helen, et al, eds. Youth & Justice. 1981. 35.00x (ISBN 0-686-78799-4, Pub. by Turoe Pr). State Mutual Bk.

Burke, Helen N. Foods from the Founding Fathers: Recipes from Five Colonial Seaports. 1978. 10.00 (ISBN 0-682-48585-3, Banner). Exposition Pr FL.

Burke, J., et al. The Emergence of the Modern World: 1300-1815. 1971. pap. text ed. 9.50x (ISBN 0-686-80324-8). Irvington.

--The Past in Perspective. 1971. pap. text ed. 3.50x (ISBN 0-8290-1172-2). Irvington.

Burke, J., jt. ed. see Auriche, M.

Burke, J. D. Advertising in the Marketplace. 2nd ed. 1980. text ed. 25.80 (ISBN 0-07-009035-1). McGraw.

Burke, J. E. Progress in Ceramic Science. 1961-1964. Vol. 3. 1964. 68.00 (ISBN 0-08-010026-0); Vol. 4. 1966. 68.00 (ISBN 0-08-011842-9). Pergamon.

Burke, J. J., jt. auth. see Kapany, N. S.

Burke, J. J. & Weiss, V., eds. Advances in Deformation Processing. LC 77-18700. (Sagamore Army Materials Research Conference Ser.: Vol. 21). 606p. 1978. 79.50x (ISBN 0-306-34521-8, Plenum Pr). Plenum Pub.

--Application of Fracture Mechanics to Design. LC 78-14819. (Sagamore Army Materials Research Conference Proceedings Ser.: Vol. 22). 347p. 1978. 55.00x (ISBN 0-306-40040-5, Plenum Pr). Plenum Pub.

--Nondestructive Evaluation of Materials. LC 79-12538. (Sagamore Army Materials Research Conference Proceedings Ser.: Vol. 23). 542p. 1979. 79.50x (ISBN 0-306-40185-1, Plenum Pr). Plenum Pub.

Burke, J. L. & Bensch, D. E. Mount Pleasant & the Early Quakers of Ohio. (Illus.). 45p. 1975. 2.50 (ISBN 0-318-03174-4). Ohio Hist Soc.

Burke, J. Terence, et al. Ohio Supplement for Modern Real Estate Practice. 6th ed. LC 84-2139. 128p. 1984. pap. text ed. 8.95 (ISBN 0-88462-489-7, 1510-04, Real Estate Ed). Longman USA.

Burke, Jack D., et al. Essentials of Histology. LC 75-174346. (Illus.). 176p. (Orig.). 1972. pap. 5.95 (ISBN 0-8120-0439-6). Barron.

Burke, James. Connections. (Illus.). 312p. 1979. pap. 19.45i (ISBN 0-316-11685-8). Little.

--Connections. LC 78-21662. 1979. 24.95 (ISBN 0-316-11681-5). Little.

--A Forgotten Glory. (Illus.). 1979. 11.95 (ISBN 0-87244-049-4). Texian.

--The Life of Thomas Moore. Repr. 25.00 (ISBN 0-8274-2901-0). R West.

Burke, James, jt. auth. see McKenna, Rosalie.

Burke, James D. Jan Both: Paintings, Drawings & Prints. LC 75-23783. (Outstanding Dissertations in the Fine Arts - 17th Century). (Illus.). 1976. lib. bdg. 55.00 (ISBN 0-8240-1980-6). Garland Pub.

Burke, James D. & Whitt, April S., eds. Space Manufacturing 1983. (Advances in the Astronautical Sciences Ser.: Vol. 53). (Illus.). 496p. 1983. lib. bdg. 60.00x (ISBN 0-87703-188-6, Pub. by Am Astronaut); pap. text ed. 50.00x (ISBN 0-87703-189-4). Univelt Inc.

Burke, James H. The Main Street Pocket Guide to Sterling & Silver Plate. rev. ed. LC 84-15498. (Illus.). 256p. 1985. pap. 6.95 (ISBN 0-915590-55-7). Main Street.

--Warner Collector's Guide to Sterling Silver & Silverplated Hollowware. (Illus.). 256p. (Orig.). 1982. pap. 9.95 (ISBN 0-446-97634-2). Warner Bks.

Burke, James L. The Convict. 152p. 1985. text ed. 15.95 (ISBN 0-8071-1273-9); pap. 9.95 (ISBN 0-8071-1275-5). La State U Pr.

--Two for Texas. 167p. (Orig.). 1982. pap. 2.25 (ISBN 0-671-44112-4). PB.

Burke, James L. & Davison, Kenneth E. Ohio's Heritage. LC 83-20091. (Illus.). 340p. (gr. 7). 1984. text ed. 19.50x (ISBN 0-87905-109-4, Peregrine Smith). Gibbs M Smith.

Burke, James W. Crockett, the Man Behind the Myth. LC 83-25326. 1984. 15.95 (ISBN 0-89015-437-6). Eakin Pubns.

Burke, Janet G., jt. auth. see Hales, David A.

Burke, Jerald R. With Liberty & Justice for All: The Political Philosophy of George C. Wallace. LC 75-37228. 1976. 7.76 (ISBN 0-916620-02-6). Portals Pr.

Burke, Jim. The World of Jimmy Connors. (Illus., Orig.). 1976. pap. 1.50 (ISBN 0-685-64019-1, LB330DK, Leisure Bks). Dorchester Pub Co.

Burke, John. Beautiful Britain. 1976. pap. 5.50 (ISBN 0-7134-3200-4, Pub. by Batsford England). David & Charles.

--Beautiful Britain. LC 82-76. (Illus.). 1984. pap. 5.95 (ISBN 0-7134-3200-4, Pub. by Batsford England). Larousse.

--Beginners' Guide to Bible Sharing I. 192p. 1985. pap. 8.95 (ISBN 0-697-02014-2). Wm C Brown.

--Beginners' Guide to Bible Sharing II. 240p. 1984. pap. 9.95 (ISBN 0-697-02015-0). Wm C Brown.

--Bible Sharing: How to Grow in the Mystery of Christ. LC 79-15006. (Orig.). 1979. pap. 5.95 (ISBN 0-8189-0386-4). Alba.

--The Burden of the South, in Verse. facsimile ed. LC 70-170690. (Black Heritage Library Collection Ser.). Repr. of 1864 ed. 14.25 (ISBN 0-8369-8880-9). Ayer Co Pubs.

--Chivalry, Slavery & Young America. facsimile ed. LC 74-170691. (Black Heritage Library Collection). Repr. of 1866 ed. 16.00 (ISBN 0-8369-8881-7). Ayer Co Pubs.

--The English Inn. LC 81-4292. (Illus.). 240p. 1981. 29.50x (ISBN 0-8419-0706-4). Holmes & Meier.

--A Genealogical & Heraldic History of the Commoners of Great Britain & Ireland, 4 vols. LC 76-44267. (Illus.). 3113p. 1977. Repr. of 1834 ed. 115.00 (ISBN 0-8063-0742-0). Genealog Pub.

--Gospel Power: Toward the Revitalization of Preaching. LC 77-14517. 1978. pap. 4.95 (ISBN 0-8189-0359-7). Alba.

--Life in the Castle in Medieval England. (Illus.). 120p. 1978. 12.50x (ISBN 0-8476-6069-9). Rowman.

--Life in the Villa in Roman Britain. 1978. 16.95 (ISBN 0-7134-1013-2, Pub. by Batsford England). David & Charles.

--Look Back on England. (Illus.). 220p. 1983. 16.95 (ISBN 0-85613-065-6, Pub. by Salem Hse Ltd). Merrimack Pub Cir.

--Musical Landscapes. 192p. 1983. 23.95 (ISBN 0-03-063262-5). HR&W.

--Origins of the Science of Crystals. LC 66-13584. 1966. 38.00x (ISBN 0-520-00198-2). U of Cal Pr.

--Pete Culler's Boats: The Complete Design Catalog. LC 82-48429. (Illus.). 296p. 1984. 47.50 (ISBN 0-87742-142-0, P566). Intl Marine.

--Roman England. (Illus.). 152p. 1984. 15.95 (ISBN 0-393-01826-1). Norton.

--Studies in Genesis. pap. 4.95 (ISBN 0-88469-048-2). BMH Bks.

--Suffolk. 1971. 19.95 (ISBN 0-7134-0069-2, Pub. by Batsford England). David & Charles.

Burke, John, ed. A New Look at Preaching. (Good News Studies Ser.: Vol. 7). 1983. pap. 6.95 (ISBN 0-89453-336-3). M Glazier.

Burke, John, jt. ed. see Mathieu, Alix.

Burke, John B. Burke's American Families with British Ancestry. LC 74-32428. (Illus.). 494p. 1983. Repr. of 1939 ed. 30.00 (ISBN 0-8063-0662-9). Genealog Pub.

Burke, John D. & Cruikshank, Warren L. Real Estate Sales & Brokerage. 1975. pap. 21.60 (ISBN 0-07-009040-8). McGraw.

Burke, John E. An Historical-Analytic Study of the Legislative & Political Origins of the Public Broadcasting Act of 1967. Sterling, Christopher H., ed. LC 78-21717. (Dissertations in Broadcasting Ser.). (Illus.). 1979. lib. bdg. 27.50x (ISBN 0-405-11756-6). Ayer Co Pubs.

Burke, John F. Surgical Physiology. (Illus.). 592p. 1983. 56.00 (ISBN 0-7216-2183-X). Saunders.

Burke, John F. & Hildick-Smith, Gavin Y. The Infection-Prone Hospital Patient. 1978. text ed. 22.50 (ISBN 0-316-11680-7). Little.

Burke, John G. The Uses of Science in the Age of Newton. LC 83-1223. (UCLA Clark Library Professorship: No. 8). 226p. 1984. text ed. 22.50x (ISBN 0-520-04970-5). U of Cal Pr.

Burke, John G. & Reddig, Jill S. Guide to Ecology Information & Organizations. LC 75-45400. 292p. 1976. 15.00 (ISBN 0-8242-0567-7). Wilson.

Burke, John J. The Writer in Pennsylvania, 1681-1981. LC 81-85496. 93p. 1982. pap. 5.95 (ISBN 0-686-36440-6). St Joseph.

--The Writer in Philadelphia, 1682-1982. LC 81-51298. 84p. 1981. pap. 5.95 (ISBN 0-686-36439-2). St Joseph.

Burke, John J., ed. Ultrafine-Grain Ceramics. (Sagamore Army Materials Research Conference Ser.: Vol. 15). 416p. 1970. 35.00x (ISBN 0-306-34515-3, Plenum Pr). Plenum Pub.

Burke, John J. & Weiss, Volker, eds. Advances in Metal Processing. LC 81-439. (Sagamore Army Materials Research Conference Ser.: Vol. 25). 398p. 1981. 59.50x (ISBN 0-306-40651-9, Plenum Pr). Plenum Pub.

--Block & Graft Copolymers. LC 73-12903. (Sagamore Army Materials Research Conference Ser.: Vol. 19). 348p. 1973. 35.00x (ISBN 0-306-34519-6, Plenum Pr). Plenum Pub.

--Characterization of Materials in Research: Ceramics & Polymers. LC 75-5272. (Sagamore Army Materials Research Conference Ser.: Vol. 20). 576p. 1975. 45.00x (ISBN 0-306-34520-X, Plenum Pr). Plenum Pub.

--Fatigue: Environment & Temperature Effects. (Sagamore Army Materials Research Conference Proceedings Ser.: Vol. 27). 410p. 1983. 65.00x (ISBN 0-306-41101-6, Plenum Pr). Plenum Pub.

--Powder Metallurgy for High-Performance Applications. LC 72-5215. (Sagamore Army Materials Research Conference Ser.: Vol. 18). 413p. 1972. 35.00x (ISBN 0-306-34518-8, Plenum Pr). Plenum Pub.

--Risk & Failure Analysis for Improved Performance & Reliability. LC 80-12346. (Sagamore Army Materials Research Conference Proceedings Ser.: Vol. 24). 366p. 1980. 55.00x (ISBN 0-306-40446-X, Plenum Pr). Plenum Pub.

--Shock Waves & the Mechanical Properties of Solids. (Sagamore Army Materials Research Conference Ser.: Vol. 17). 427p. 1971. 35.00x (ISBN 0-306-34517-X, Plenum Pr). Plenum Pub.

--Surface Treatment for Improved Performance & Properties. (Sagamore Army Materials Research Conference Proceedings Ser.: Vol. 26). 225p. 1982. text ed. 42.50 (ISBN 0-306-40897-X, Plenum Pr). Plenum Pub.

--Ultrafine-Grain Metals. (Sagamore Army Materials Research Conference Ser.: Vol. 16). 442p. 1970. 35.00x (ISBN 0-306-34516-1, Plenum Pr). Plenum Pub.

Burke, John J., et al, eds. Fatigue: An Interdisciplinary Approach. LC 64-21083. (Sagamore Army Materials Research Conference Ser.: Vol. 10). 414p. 1964. 35.00x (ISBN 0-306-34510-2, Plenum Pr). Plenum Pub.

--Strengthening Mechanisms: Metals & Ceramics. LC 66-22986. (Sagamore Army Materials Research Conference Ser.: Vol. 12). 630p. 1966. 35.00x (ISBN 0-306-34512-9, Plenum Pr). Plenum Pub.

--Surfaces & Interfaces I: Chemical & Physical Characteristics. LC 64-12568. (Sagamore Army Materials Research Conference Ser.: Vol. 13). 488p. 1967. 35.00x (ISBN 0-306-34513-7, Plenum Pr). Plenum Pub.

--Surfaces & Interfaces II: Physical & Mechanical Properties. (Sagamore Army Materials Research Conference Ser.: Vol. 14). 506p. 1968. 35.00x (ISBN 0-306-34514-5, Plenum Pr). Plenum Pub.

Burke, John J., Jr., jt. auth. see Hermann, John P.

Burke, John J., Jr. & Kay, Donald, eds. The Unknown Samuel Johnson. LC 81-70159. (Illus.). 224p. 1983. 32.50x (ISBN 0-299-09150-3). U of Wis Pr.

Burke, John P., et al, eds. Marxism & the Good Society. 224p. 1981. 34.50 (ISBN 0-521-23392-5). Cambridge U Pr.

Burke, Joseph. English Art Seventeen Fourteen to Eighteen Hundred. (Oxford History of English Art Ser.). (Illus.). 1976. 45.00x (ISBN 0-19-817209-5). Oxford U Pr.

--Picture Alaska; an Index. 2nd ed. (The Elmer E. Rasmuson Library Occasional Papers Ser.: No. 1). 206p. 1974. pap. text ed. 5.00x (ISBN 0-937592-01-3). U Alaska Rasmuson Lib.

Burke, Kathy. Handbook for Non-Macho Sailors. LC 85-2097. (Illus.). 208p. 1985. text ed. 16.95 (ISBN 0-915160-76-5). Seven Seas.

Burke, Katy. The Complete Live-Aboard Book. LC 82-16933. (Illus.). 352p. 1982. 39.95 (ISBN 0-915160-50-1). Seven Seas.

--Managing Your Escape: Taking Care of Personal Business So You Can Get Away. LC 83-20258. (Illus.). 192p. 1984. 15.95 (ISBN 0-915160-67-6). Seven Seas.

Burke, Ken & Doty, Walter. All about Vegetables. rev. ed. Ortho Books Editorial Staff, ed. LC 80-66344. (Illus.). 112p. 1981. pap. 5.95 (ISBN 0-917102-90-8). Ortho.

Burke, Ken, ed. see Edwards, David.

Burke, Ken, ed. see McKinley, Michael.

Burke, Ken, ed. see Ortho Books Staff.

Burke, Ken, ed. see Sinnes, A. Cort.

Burke, Ken R., ed. see Ortho Books Staff.

Burke, Kenneth. Collected Poems, 1915-1967. LC 67-29786. 1968. 27.50x (ISBN 0-520-00195-8). U of Cal Pr.

--The Complete White Oxen: Collected Short Fiction. LC 68-17629. 1968. pap. 2.45 (ISBN 0-520-00155-9, CAL 161). U of Cal Pr.

--Counter-Statement. 2nd rev. ed. 1953. 14.95 (ISBN 0-910720-01-0). Archive Pr.

--Counter-Statement. LC 68-20356. 1968. pap. 6.95x (ISBN 0-520-00196-6, CAL 143). U of Cal Pr.

--Dramatism & Development. LC 72-80856. (Heinz Werner Lec. Ser.: No. 6). 1972. 3.00x (ISBN 0-8271-7216-8). Clark U Pr.

--A Grammar of Motives. LC 69-16741. 1969. pap. 10.95x (ISBN 0-520-01544-4). U of Cal Pr.

--Language As Symbolic Action: Essays on Life, Literature, & Method. LC 66-27655. 1966. pap. 10.95x (ISBN 0-520-00192-3, CAMPUS 213). U of Cal Pr.

--The Philosophy of Literary Form. 1974. pap. 10.95x (ISBN 0-520-02483-4, CAL 228). U of Cal Pr.

--A Rhetoric of Motives. LC 69-16742. 1969. pap. 8.95x (ISBN 0-520-01546-0, CAMPUS 111). U of Cal Pr.

--The Rhetoric of Religion: Studies in Logology. 1970. pap. 5.95 (ISBN 0-520-01610-6, CAL188). U of Cal Pr.

--Terms for Order. Hyman, Stanley E. & Karmiller, Barbara, eds. LC 64-18818. (Midland Bks: No. 64). 208p. 1964. pap. 4.95x (ISBN 0-253-20064-4). Ind U Pr.

--Towards a Better Life: Being a Series of Epistles, or Declamations. 1966. 25.00x (ISBN 0-520-00193-1). U of Cal Pr.

--Towards a Better Life: Being a Series of Epistles, or Declamations. LC 66-13268. 244p. 1982. pap. 6.95 (ISBN 0-520-04638-2, CAL 558). U of Cal Pr.

Burke, Kenneth, jt. auth. see Wallace, Emily M.

Burke, Kenneth, tr. see Ludwig, Emil.

Burke, Kenneth, et al. Surrealism Pro & Con. 1973. pap. 2.50 (ISBN 0-910664-27-7). Gotham.

--Rhetoric in Change. Tanner, William E. & Bishop, J. Dean, eds. LC 82-6190. 217p. (Orig.). 1982. 16.95 (ISBN 0-86663-900-4); 10.95 (ISBN 0-86663-901-2). Ide Hse.

Burke, Kenneth B., ed. see Palmer, Derecke.

Burke, Kenneth M. & Durand, Francis. Oil & Gas Limited Partnerships: Accounting, Reporting & Taxation. LC 84-60322. 280p. 1984. pap. 39.95 (ISBN 0-940966-04-2). N Texas St U Pro Devel Inst.

Burke, Lew. Lew Burke's Dog Training. (Illus.). 1976. 12.95 (ISBN 0-87666-656-X, H-962). TFH Pubns.

Burke, Louis & Mathews, Barbara E. Colposcopy in Clinical Practice. LC 77-21063. (Illus.). 1978. text ed. 25.00x (ISBN 0-8036-1425-X). Davis Co.

Burke, Margaret R., ed. Bowdoin College Museum of Art: Art Handbook of the Collections. LC 81-66892. (Illus., Orig.). (YA) 1981. pap. write for info. (ISBN 0-916606-01-5). Bowdoin Coll.

Burke, Marie L. Swami Vivekananda: His Second Visit to the West (New Discoveries) 20.00 (ISBN 0-87481-151-1). Vedanta Pr.

--Swami Vivekananda in the West: New Discoveries: His Prophetic Mission, 2 Vols, Vol. 1. new ed. (Illus.). 515p. text ed. 16.00x (ISBN 0-317-03702-1, Pub. by Advaita Ashrama India). Vedanta Pr.

--Swami Vivekananda in the West: New Discoveries, Vol. II. (Illus.). 457p. 1985. 12.95x (ISBN 0-87481-219-4, Pub. by Advaita Ashrama India). Vedanta Pr.

Burke, Marthy C. Life & Adventures of Calamity Jane: By Herself. (Illus.). 1979. pap. 2.00x (ISBN 0-87770-220-9). Ye Galleon.

Burke, Martyn. The Commissar's Report. 320p. 1984. 14.95 (ISBN 0-395-35490-0). HM.

--The Commissar's Report. 1985. pap. 6.95 (ISBN 0-345-32292-4). Ballantine.

Burke, Mary A., jt. auth. see Burke, Arvid J.

Burke, Mary Alice H. Elizabeth Nourse, Eighteen Hundred Fifty-Nine to Nineteen Hundred Thirty-Eight: A Salon Career. (Illus.). 280p. 1983. text ed. 47.50x (ISBN 0-87474-298-6). Smithsonian.

Burke, Mary J., et al. Sources of Information in Transportation: Part 1, General Transportation. 3rd ed. (Public Administration Ser.: Bibliography P-1599). 71p. 1985. pap. 10.50 (ISBN 0-89028-249-8). Vance Biblios.

Burke, Maurice R. The Evolution of the Human Mind: The Passage from Self to Cosmic Consciousness. (Physic Research Library Bks.). (Illus.). 137p. 1981. Repr. of 1905 ed. 69.85 (ISBN 0-89901-033-4). Found Class Reprints.

Burke, Michael. Outrageous Good Fortune. 480p. 1984. 19.45i (ISBN 0-316-11679-3). Little.

Burke, Michael & Rundberg, William. Arithmetic. 500p. 1984. 23.95 (ISBN 0-02-317320-3). Dellen Pub.

Burke, Michael, jt. auth. see Ruff, Ann.

Burke, Michael E. The Royal College of San Carlos: Surgery & Spanish Medical Reform in the Late Eighteenth Century. LC 76-50237. xv, 215p. 1977. 16.75 (ISBN 0-8223-0382-5). Duke.

Burke, Nancy C., jt. auth. see Page, I. Lee.

Burke, P. G. Potential Scattering in Atomic Physics. LC 76-28965. (Illus.). 138p. 1977. 29.50x (ISBN 0-306-30933-5, Plenum Pr). Plenum Pub.

Burke, P. G. & Eissner, W. B., eds. Atoms in Astrophysics. (Physics of Atoms & Molecules Ser.). 345p. 1983. 52.50x (ISBN 0-306-41097-4, Plenum Pr). Plenum Pub.

Burke, P. G. & Moiseiwitsch, B. L., eds. Atomic Processes & Applications. 1976. 76.75 (ISBN 0-7204-0444-4, North-Holland). Elsevier.

Burke, Patrick. The Fragile Universe: An Essay in the Philosophy of Religions. LC 78-17885. (Library of Philosophy & Religion). 129p. 1979. text ed. 28.50x (ISBN 0-06-490776-7, 06373). B&N Imports.
Burke, Paul J., jt. auth. see Townsend, Edward A.
Burke, Peter. Montaigne. (Past Masters Ser.). 1983. pap. 3.95 (ISBN 0-19-287522-1). Oxford U Pr.
--Popular Culture in Early Modern Europe. 1978. pap. 7.95xi (ISBN 0-06-131928-7, TB 1928, Torch). Har-Row.
--Popular Culture in Early Modern Europe. LC 78-52051. 400p. 1978. 26.00x, UKE (ISBN 0-8147-1011-5). NYU Pr.
--Sociology & History. (Controversies in Sociology Ser.: No. 10). 128p. (Orig.). 1980. pap. text ed. 7.95x (ISBN 0-04-301115-2). Allen Unwin.
Burke, Peter J. & Heideman, Robert G. Career-Long Teacher Education. 272p. 1985. 27.75x (ISBN 0-398-05102-X). C C Thomas.
Burke, Peter J., jt. auth. see Knoke, David.
Burke, Peter J., et al. Teacher Career Stages: Implications for Staff Development. LC 84-61200. (Fastback Ser.: No. 214). 50p. (Orig.). 1984. pap. 0.75 (ISBN 0-87367-214-3). Phi Delta Kappa.
Burke, Pratricia A, et al. Adventures from God's Word. rev. ed. Miller, Marge, ed. (Basic Bible Readers Ser.). (Illus.). 128p. (gr. 3). 1983. text ed. 7.95 (ISBN 0-87239-663-0, 2953). Standard Pub.
Burke, R. S., jt. auth. see Bittel, L. R.
Burke, Richard C., ed. Instructional Television: Bold New Venture. LC 70-143243. pap. 39.50 (ISBN 0-317-27947-5, 2056024). Bks Demand UMI.
Burke, Richard R. Communicating with Students in Schools: A Workbook for Practitioners & Teachers in Training. new, rev. ed. 180p. 1984. wkbk. 9.25 (ISBN 0-8191-3878-9). U Pr of Amer.
Burke, Robert E. Olson's New Deal for California. LC 82-984. (Illus.). 279p. 1982. Repr. of 1953 ed. lib. bdg. 28.75x (ISBN 0-313-23414-0, BUON). Greenwood.
Burke, Robert E. & Lowitt, Richard, eds. The New Era & the New Deal, 1920-1940. (Goldentree Bibliography in American History Ser.). 240p. 1981. text ed. 27.95x (ISBN 0-88295-537-3); pap. text ed. 19.95x (ISBN 0-88295-581-0). Harlan Davidson.
Burke, Robert E., ed. see Buenker, John D.
Burke, Robert E., ed. see Cebula, James E.
Burke, Robert E., ed. see Christie, Jean.
Burke, Robert E., ed. see Dembo, Jonathan.
Burke, Robert E., ed. see Elson, Ruth Miller.
Burke, Robert E., ed. see Harry, Jeffrey.
Burke, Robert E., ed. see Hennings, Robert.
Burke, Robert E., ed. see Johnson, Hiram.
Burke, Robert E., ed. see Keller, Richard C.
Burke, Robert E., ed. see Kurtz, Micheal J.
Burke, Robert E., ed. see McCreesh, Carolyn D.
Burke, Robert E., ed. see Patenaude, Lionel V.
Burke, Robert E., ed. see Prouty, Andrew M.
Burke, Robert E., ed. see Robertson, James O.
Burke, Robert E., ed. see Schonbach, Morris.
Burke, Robert E., ed. see Spritzer, Doanld E.
Burke, Robert E., ed. see Stone, David M.
Burke, Robert E., ed. see Torbjorn, Sirevag.
Burke, Robert E., ed. see Tutle, Dwight W.
Burke, Robert E., ed. see Weisenhunt.
Burke, Robert E., ed. see Wortman, Roy T.
Burke, Robert F., ed. see Acena, Albert.
Burke, Robert L. CAI Sourcebook. (Illus.). 160p. 1982. text ed. 19.95 (ISBN 0-13-110155-2). P-H.
--CAI Sourcebook. (Illus.). 224p. 1982. pap. text ed. 12.95 (ISBN 0-13-110148-X). P-H.
Burke, Roger K., jt. auth. see Rasch, Philip J.
Burke, Ronald & Kramer, Arthur. Microcomputer Courseware for Technical Mathematics (Apple II & TRS-80) User's Manual. 1983. 11.70 (ISBN 0-07-009050-5). McGraw.
Burke, Ronald S. Administrative Skills for the Manager. LC 82-72868. 275p. 1982. ringed binder 29.95x (ISBN 0-87094-348-0). Dow Jones-Irwin.
Burke, Ronald S. & Bittel, Lester R. Introduction to Management Practice. LC 80-19088. (Illus.). 608p. 1981. text ed. 25.90x (ISBN 0-07-009042-4). McGraw.
Burke, S. R. Human Anatomy & Physiology for the Health Sciences. 465p. 1980. 19.95 (ISBN 0-471-05598-0). Wiley.
Burke, Sheila, tr. see Mather, Edith & Chicoine, Rene.
Burke, Shirley R. The Composition & Function of Body Fluids. 3rd ed. LC 80-17952. (Illus.). 208p. 1980. pap. text ed. 12.95 (ISBN 0-8016-0903-8). Mosby.
--Human Anatomy & Physiology for the Health Sciences. 2nd ed. 600p. 1985. 19.95 (ISBN 0-471-80686-2, Pub. by Wiley Med). Wiley.
Burke, Susan. The Island Bike Business. (Illus.). 80p. (gr. 3-7). 1983. 11.95 (ISBN 0-19-554297-5, Pub by Oxford U Pr Childrens). Merrimack Pub Cir.
Burke, Susan, tr. see Vovelle, Michel.
Burke, Suzanne. Ollie Owl. Jordan, Alton, ed. (Elephant Ser.). (Illus.). (gr. k-3). 1975. PLB 3.95 (ISBN 0-89868-015-8, Read Res); text ed. 1.75 softbd. (ISBN 0-89868-048-4). ARO Pub.
--Our Parade. Jordan, Alton, ed. (Elephant Ser.). (Illus.). (gr. k-3). 1975. PLB 3.95 (ISBN 0-89868-017-4, Read Res); pap. text ed. 1.75 (ISBN 0-89868-050-6). ARO Pub.
Burke, T. A., ed. Polly Peablossom's Wedding & Other Tales. 1972. Repr. of 1851 ed. lib. bdg. 26.00 (ISBN 0-8422-8157-6). Irvington.
Burke, T. E. The Philosophy of Popper. LC 83-80361. 200p. 1983. (Pub. by Manchester Univ Pr); pap. 8.00 (ISBN 0-7190-0911-1). Longwood Pub Group.
Burke, T. Patrick, tr. see Schmaus, Michael.
Burke, Theta. And We Have Touched. LC 78-67725. (Orig.). 1978. pap. 3.95 (ISBN 0-916872-05-X). Delafield Pr.
--I've Heard Your Feelings. LC 76-7103. 1976. 7.95 (ISBN 0-916872-01-7); pap. 3.95 (ISBN 0-916872-00-9). Delafield Pr.
--Loving Who You Are Where You Are. LC 82-71079. 80p. 1982. pap. 5.95 (ISBN 0-916872-07-6). Delafield Pr.
--Sounds of Yourself. LC 76-48010. 1977. pap. 3.95 (ISBN 0-916872-02-5). Delafield Pr.
Burke, Thomas. Limehouse Nights. facsimile ed. LC 73-103498. (Short Story Index Reprint Ser). 1917. 19.00 (ISBN 0-8369-3240-4). Ayer Co Pubs.
--Limehouse Nights. 320p. 1973. 6.95 (ISBN 0-8180-0619-6). Horizon.
--Night-Pieces: Eighteen Tales. facsimile ed. LC 78-150539. (Short Story Index Reprint Ser). Repr. of 1936 ed. 18.00 (ISBN 0-8369-3836-4). Ayer Co Pubs.
--Pleasantries of Old Quong, Vol. 1. LC 72-5861. (Short Story Index Reprint Ser). Repr. of 1931 ed. 20.00 (ISBN 0-8369-4195-0). Ayer Co Pubs.
--Tea-Shop in Limehouse. facsimile ed. LC 77-103499. (Short Story Index Reprint Ser). 1931. 18.00 (ISBN 0-8369-3241-2). Ayer Co Pubs.
Burke, Thomas F., ed. Bill Martin, Paintings Nineteen Sixty-Nine to Nineteen Seventy-Nine. LC 79-91015. (Illus.). 1980. pap. cancelled (ISBN 0-517-53896-2). Pomegranate Ca.
--Celestial Visitations: The Art of Gilbert Williams. LC 79-91014. 1979. pap. 8.95 (ISBN 0-517-53900-4). Pomegranate Ca.
--Einstein: A Portrait. (Illus.). 1984. 20.00 (ISBN 0-917556-99-2); pap. 15.00 (ISBN 0-917556-97-6). Pomegranate Calif.
Burke, Thomas F., ed. see Gescheidt, Alfred & Bradley, Josephine.
Burke, Todd & Burke, DeAnn. Anointed for Burial. LC 77-81294. 1977. pap. 2.95 (ISBN 0-88270-485-0, Pub. by Logos). Bridge Pub.
Burke, Tony. Fifty-Five & a Half Running Trails of the San Francisco Bay Area. (Illus.). 144p. (Orig.). 1985. pap. 7.95 (ISBN 0-930588-22-3). Heyday Bks.
Burke, U. R. A History of Spain from the Earliest Times to the Death of Ferdinand the Catholic. 1976. lib. bdg. 125.95 (ISBN 0-685-68719-8). Gordon Pr.
Burke, Ulick R. Spanish Salt: A Collection of All the Proverbs Which Are to Be Found in Don Quixote. LC 73-21636. 1877. lib. bdg. 20.00 (ISBN 0-8414-9902-0). Folcroft.
Burke, Vee, jt. auth. see Burke, Vincent.
Burke, Vernon J. Wisdom from St. Augustine. LC 85-19340. 1984. 21.95 (ISBN 0-268-01934-7, 85-19340); pap. 11.95 (ISBN 0-268-01935-5, 85-19357). U of Notre Dame Pr.
Burke, Vincent & Burke, Vee. Nixon's Good Deed: Welfare Reform. LC 69-16955. 243p. 1974. 25.00x (ISBN 0-231-03850-X); pap. 12.00x (ISBN 0-231-08346-7). Columbia U Pr.
Burke, Virginia M., jt. ed. see Corbett, Edward P.
Burke, W. T. The U. N. Convention on the Law of the Sea: Impacts on Tuna Regulation. (Legislative Studies: No. 26). 19p. (An FAO-EEZ Programme Activity, Norway Funds-in-Trust). 1982. pap. text ed. 7.50 (ISBN 92-5-101292-X, F2398, FAO). Unipub.
Burke, W. Warner. Organization Development: Principles & Practices. 1982. pap. text ed. 23.95 (ISBN 0-316-11686-6). Little.
Burke, W. Warner, ed. Current Issues & Strategies in Organization Development. LC 76-28755. 448p. 1977. 34.95 (ISBN 0-87705-270-0). Human Sci Pr.
Burke, W. Warner, jt. ed. see Eddy, William B.
Burke, Warren. The Killing Touch. 240p. 1983. pap. 2.95 (ISBN 0-441-44410-5). Ace Bks.
Burke, William. Additional Reasons for Our Immediately Emancipating Spanish America. LC 73-128426. Repr. of 1808 ed. 12.50 (ISBN 0-404-01240-X). AMS Pr.
Burke, William, jt. auth. see Kasahara, Hiroshi.
Burke, William J. Literature of Slang. LC 67-982. 1965. Repr. of 1939 ed. 35.00x (ISBN 0-8103-3243-4). Gale.
Burke, William L. Applied Differential Geometry. (Illus.). 400p. 1985. 54.50 (ISBN 0-521-26317-4); pap. 19.95 (ISBN 0-521-26929-6). Cambridge U Pr.
--Spacetime, Geometry, Cosmology. LC 79-57226. 1980. text ed. 26.00x (ISBN 0-935702-01-6). Univ Sci Bks.
Burke, William M. History & Functions of Central Labor Unions. LC 71-7666. (Columbia University, Studies in the Social Sciences: No. 30). Repr. of 1899 ed. 16.50 (ISBN 0-404-51030-2). AMS Pr.
Burke, William P. The Irish Priests in Penal Times. 508p. 1968. Repr. of 1914 ed. 30.00x (ISBN 0-7165-0034-5, Pub. by Irish Academic Pr Ireland). Biblio Dist.
Burke, William T. Fisheries Regulation Under Extended Jurisdiction & International Law. (Fisheries Technical Papers: No. 223). 28p. 1982. pap. 7.50 (ISBN 92-5-101231-8, F2341, FAO). Unipub.
--Ocean Sciences, Technology, & the Future International Law of the Sea. LC 66-63004. 91p. (Orig.). 1966. pap. 1.50 (ISBN 0-8142-0031-1). Ohio St U Pr.
Burke, William T., et al. National & International Law Enforcement in the Ocean. LC 75-38847. 256p. 1976. pap. 10.00x (ISBN 0-295-95489-2, Pub. by Washington Sea Grant). U of Wash Pr.
Burken, Judith L. Introduction to Reporting. 2nd ed. 250p. 1979. pap. text ed. write for info. (ISBN 0-697-04332-0). Wm C Brown.
Burkert, H. & Nagel, G. A., eds. Neue Erfahrungen mit Oxazaphosphorinen unter besonderer Beruecksichtigung des Uroprotektors Uromitexan. (Beitraege zur Onkologie: Band 5). (Illus.). 126p. 1980. pap. 12.50 (ISBN 3-8055-1381-X). S Karger.
Burkert, Ulrich & Allinger, Norman L., eds. Molecular Mechanics. LC 82-11442. (ACS Monographs: No. 177). 339p. 1982. lib. bdg. 64.95 (ISBN 0-8412-0584-1). Am Chemical.
Burkert, Walter. Homo Necans: Interpretationen altgriechischer Opferriten und Mythen. LC 72-83051. (Religionsgeschichtliche Versuche und Vorarbeiten: Vol. 32). 356p. 1972. 43.20x (ISBN 3-11-003875-7). De Gruyter.
--Homo Necans: The Anthropology of Ancient Greek Sacrificial Ritual & Myth. Bing, Peter, ed. LC 77-93473. (Illus.). 360p. 1983. 24.95 (ISBN 0-520-03650-6). U of Cal Pr.
--Lore & Science in Ancient Pythagoreanism. Minar, Edwin L., Jr., tr. from Ger. LC 70-162856. (Illus.). 512p. 1972. 32.50x (ISBN 0-674-53918-4). Harvard U Pr.
--Structure & History in Greek Mythology & Ritual. LC 78-62856. (Sather Classical Lectures Ser.: Vol. 47). 1980. 27.50x (ISBN 0-520-03771-5, CAL 581); pap. 7.95 (ISBN 0-520-04770-2). U of Cal Pr.
Burkert, William. Greek Religion. Raffan, John, tr. from Ger. 512p. 1985. text ed. 30.00x (ISBN 0-674-36280-2). Harvard U Pr.
Burkes, Joyce. Spanish Word Machine Book I & II. Ramirez, Maria, tr. (The Spanish Word Machine Bks.). 26p. 1980. PLB 3.95 ea. (ISBN 0-931218-24-1, 1040). Joybug.
Burkes, Joyce M. Flip & Flashcards & Cassette 1B. (Illus.). 8p. (ps-2). incl. cassette 5.95 (ISBN 0-931218-19-5, 4011). Joybug.
--The Math Machine Book for Addition. LC 81-90590. (The Word Machine & Math Machine Bks.). (Illus.). 48p. (gr. 1-3). 1983. pap. 3.95 (ISBN 0-931218-13-6, 3002). Joybug.
--The Math Machine Book for Multiplication. LC 81-90590. (The Word Machine & Math Machine Bks.). (Illus.). 48p. (gr. 7-9). 1985. 3.95 (ISBN 0-931218-26-8, 3003). Joybug.
--The Math Machine Book for Subtraction. LC 81-90590. (The Word Machine & Math Machine Bks.). (Illus.). 48p. (gr. 1-4). 1983. pap. 3.95 (ISBN 0-931218-14-4, 3022). Joybug.
--The Math Machine Book: Multiplication. LC 79-93267. 64p. (gr. 7-11). 1980. wire-o bdg. 4.95 (ISBN 0-89709-017-9). Liberty Pub.
--The Math Machine Books: Addition, Subtraction & Multiplication. LC 81-90590. (The Word Machine & Math Machine Bks.). (Illus.). 48p. 1984. pap. text ed. 3.95 (ISBN 0-931218-17-9, 2345 MA). Joybug.
--The Spanish Word Machine: Book 1. LC 79-92122. (The Spanish Word Machine Bks.). (Orig.). 1982. pap. 3.95 (ISBN 0-931218-09-8, 1041). Joybug.
--The Spanish Word Machine: Book 2. LC 79-92122. (The Spanish Word Machine Bks.). 26p. (Orig.). 1982. pap. 3.95 (ISBN 0-931218-10-1, 1042). Joybug.
--Witty Ditties & Cassette Tapes 1A through 5. LC 84-52873. (Illus.). 16p. (ps-2). incl. cassette 5.95 ea. (ISBN 0-931218-25-X, 4121). Joybug.
--Witty Ditties with Cassette 1A. LC 84-52873. (Illus.). 16p. (ps-2). 5.95, incl. cassette (ISBN 0-931218-28-4, 4101). Joybug.
--Witty Ditties with Cassette 1B. LC 84-52873. (Illus.). 16p. (ps-2). 5.95, incl. cassette (ISBN 0-931218-29-2, 4111). Joybug.
--Witty Ditties with Cassette 2. LC 84-52873. (Illus.). 16p. (ps-2). 5.95, incl. cassette (ISBN 0-931218-30-6, 4102). Joybug.
--Witty Ditties with Cassette 3. LC 84-52873. (Illus.). 16p. (ps-2). 5.95, incl. cassette (ISBN 0-931218-31-4, 4103). Joybug.
--Witty Ditties with Cassette 4. LC 84-52873. (Illus.). 16p. (gr. 2-4). 5.95, incl. cassette (ISBN 0-931218-32-2, 4104). Joybug.
--The Word Machine, Bk. I. rev. ed. LC 79-67050. (Illus.). (gr. k-1). 1983. pap. 3.95 (ISBN 0-931218-02-0, 1001). Joybug.
--The Word Machine, Bk. II. LC 79-67050. (Illus.). (gr. 2-4). 1979. pap. 3.95 (ISBN 0-931218-03-9, 1002). Joybug.
--The Word Machine, Bk. III. LC 79-67050. (Illus., Orig.). (gr. 2-6). 1979. pap. 3.95 (ISBN 0-931218-04-7, 1003). Joybug.
--The Word Machine Books, Bks. I-III. LC 79-67050. (Illus.). 1984. pap. text ed. 3.95 (ISBN 0-931218-16-0, 2344 WR). Joybug.
Burkes, Joyce M. & Ade, Debi. Witty Ditties with Cassette 5. LC 84-52873. (Illus.). 16p. (ps-2). 5.95, incl. cassette (ISBN 0-931218-33-0, 4105). Joybug.
Burkes, Joyce M. & Daley, Therese. The Music Machine. LC 79-92121. (The Music Machine Bks.). (Orig.). (gr. 1-2). 1981. pap. 7.95 (ISBN 0-931218-07-1, 2022). Joybug.
--The Music Machine: Intermediate. LC 79-92121. (The Music Machine Bks.). (Orig.). 1982. pap. 7.95 (ISBN 0-931218-08-X, 2023). Joybug.
--The Music Machine, Joybug Jazz. LC 79-92121. (The Music Machine Bks.). 20p. (Orig.). 1984. pap. 7.95 (ISBN 0-931218-15-2, 2024). Joybug.
--The Music Machine: Primer. LC 79-92121. (The Music Machine Bks.). 20p. (Orig.). 1981. pap. 6.95 (ISBN 0-931218-06-3, 2021). Joybug.
Burkett, David. Very Good Management: A Guide to Managing-by-Communication. 146p. 1983. 12.95 (ISBN 0-13-941377-4); pap. 6.95 (ISBN 0-13-941369-3). P-H.
Burkett, David & Narcisco, John. Declare Yourself: Discovering the Me in Relationships. LC 75-11802. (Illus.). 1975. 11.95 (ISBN 0-13-197582-X, Spec); pap. 5.95 (ISBN 0-13-197574-9, Spec). P-H.
Burkett, David W. Writing Science News for the Mass Media. 2nd ed. LC 72-84334. 223p. 1973. 12.95x (ISBN 0-87201-924-1). Gulf Pub.
Burkett, Eva M. American Dictionaries of the English Language Before 1861. LC 78-11677. 298p. 1979. lib. bdg. 20.00 (ISBN 0-8108-1179-0). Scarecrow.
--American English Dialects in Literature. LC 78-17742. 222p. 1978. 17.50 (ISBN 0-8108-1151-0). Scarecrow.
--Writing in Subject-Matter Fields: A Bibliographic Guide, with Annotations & Writing Assignments. LC 76-30397. 204p. 1977. 16.00 (ISBN 0-8108-1012-3). Scarecrow.
Burkett, J., ed. Agricultural Research Index: A Guide to Agricultural Research Including Dairy Farming, Fisheries, Food, Forestry, Horticulture, & Veterinary Science, 2vols. 6th ed. LC 78-40700. 1020p. Set. 295.00x (ISBN 0-582-90000-X, Pub. by Longman). Gale.
--Directory of Scientific Directories: A World Guide to Scientific Directories Including Medicine, Agriculture, Engineering, Manufacturing, & Industrial Directories. 3rd ed. LC 79-40288. 649p. 95.00x (ISBN 0-582-90150-2, Pub. by Longman). Gale.
Burkett, Jack, ed. Trends in Special Librarianship. 205p. 1969. 15.00 (ISBN 0-208-00856-X, Archon). Shoe String.
Burkett, John P. The Effects of Economic Reform in Yugoslavia: Investment & Trade Policy, 1959-1976. LC 83-18447. (Research Ser.: No. 55). (Illus.). 189p. 1983. pap. 9.50x (ISBN 0-87725-155-X). U of Cal Intl St.
Burkett, Larry. The Financial Planning Workbook. LC 82-7877. (Christian Financial Concepts Ser.). 1982. pap. 6.95 (ISBN 0-8024-2546-1). Moody.
--How to Manage Your Money. LC 82-7904. (Christian Financial Concepts Ser.). 1982. pap. 7.95 (ISBN 0-8024-2547-X). Moody.
--What Husbands Wish Their Wives Knew about Money. 1977. pap. 3.95 (ISBN 0-88207-758-9). Victor Bks.
--Your Finances in Changing Times. (Christian Financial Concepts Ser.). 1982. pap. 5.95 (ISBN 0-8024-2548-8). Moody.
Burkett, Larry & Proctor, William. How to Prosper in the Underground Economy. LC 81-14172. (Illus.). 288p. 1982. 11.50 (ISBN 0-688-00778-3). Morrow.
Burkett, M. E. The Art of the Felt-Maker. (Illus.). 12.95 (ISBN 0-686-31996-6). Robin & Russ.
Burkett, Prentiss M. The Unofficial History of the 499th Bomb Group (VH) LC 81-82235. (Illus.). 54p. 1981. pap. 6.95 (ISBN 0-911852-91-3). Hist Aviation.
Burkett, Randall K. Garveyism As a Religious Movement: The Institutionalization of a Black Civil Religion. LC 78-15728. (ATLA Monograph Ser.: No. 13). 242p. 1978. 17.50 (ISBN 0-8108-1163-4). Scarecrow.
Burkett, Randall K. & Newman, Richard. Black Apostles: Afro-American Clergy Confront the Twentieth Century. 1978. lib. bdg. 28.50 (ISBN 0-8161-8137-3, Hall Reference). G K Hall.
Burkett, Randall K., ed. Black Redemption: Churchmen Speak for the Garvey Movement. LC 77-81332. 207p. 1978. 27.95 (ISBN 0-87722-116-2). Temple U Pr.
Burkett, Tony. Parties & Elections in West Germany: The Search for Stability. LC 75-6051. 200p. 1975. 22.50 (ISBN 0-312-59745-2). St Martin.
Burkett, Warren. News Reporting: Science, Medicine, & High Technology. 189p. 1985. text ed. 22.50x (ISBN 0-8138-1511-8). Iowa St U Pr.
Burkey, Dave. Rain Lover. 1985. pap. 2.95 (ISBN 0-345-31963-X). Ballantine.
Burkey, F. T., ed. The Brethren: Growth in Life & Thought. 1975. pap. 3.50x (ISBN 0-934970-00-9). Brethren Ohio.
Burkey, Richard M. Ethnic & Racial Groups: The Dynamics of Dominance. LC 77-70556. 1978. text ed. 26.95 (ISBN 0-8465-0742-0). Benjamin-Cummings.
Burkhalter, Mary L. Emperor of Kings. 1980. pap. 10.50 (ISBN 0-934284-01-6). Jolean Pub Co.

--How to Live. (Orig.). 1983. pap. 3.00 (ISBN 0-934284-02-4). Jolean Pub Co.
--Kissed Grass. LC 23-138. (Orig.). 1979. pap. 3.50 (ISBN 0-934284-00-8). Jolean Pub Co.
Burkhalter, Pamela & Donley, Diana, eds. Dynamics of Oncology Nursing. (Illus.). 1977. text ed. 30.00 (ISBN 0-07-009052-1). McGraw.
Burkhalter, Pamela K. Nursing Care of the Alcoholic & Drug Abuser. (Illus.). 384p. 1975. pap. text ed. 22.95 (ISBN 0-07-009051-3). McGraw.
Burkhanov, G. S., jt. auth. see Savitskii, E. M.
Burkhard, Arthur. Franz Grillparzer in England & America. (Illus.). 3.00x (ISBN 0-685-57216-1). M S Rosenberg.
--Grillparzer Im Ausland. (Illus., Ger.). 5.00x (ISBN 0-685-57215-3). M S Rosenberg.
Burkhard, Arthur, tr. see Grillparzer, F.
Burkhard, Arthur, tr. see Grillparzer, Franz.
Burkhard, Barbara, jt. auth. see Domjan, Michael.
Burkhard, Barbara, jt. auth. see Domjan, Micheal P.
Burkhard, Marianne & Waldstein, Edith, eds. Women in German Yearbook 1: Feminist Studies & German Culture. 168p. (Orig.). 1985. lib. bdg. 22.50 (ISBN 0-8191-4600-5); pap. text ed. 10.75 (ISBN 0-8191-4601-3). U Pr of Amer.
Burkhard, R. E. & Derigs, U. Assignment & Matching Problems: Solution Methods with FORTRAN-Programs. (Lecture Notes in Economics & Mathematical Systems Ser.: Vol. 184). 148p. 1980. pap. 18.00 (ISBN 0-387-10267-1). Springer-Verlag.
Burkhard, Ursula. Farbvostellungen blinder Menschen. 56p. (Ger.). 1981. pap. text ed. 6.95x (ISBN 0-8176-1266-1). Birkhauser.
Burkhardt, A. & Maerker, R. Color Atlas of Oral Cancers. (Illus.). 186p. 1981. 69.00 (ISBN 0-8151-1337-4). Year Bk Med.
Burkhardt, A., jt. auth. see Gebbers, J. O.
Burkhardt, Ann. Writing about Food & Families, Fashion & Furnishings. (Illus.). 126p. 1984. 9.25x (ISBN 0-8138-1941-5). Iowa St U Pr.
Burkhardt, Ann M. Town within a City: A History of Five Points South Neighborhood. Bowsher, Alice M., ed. (Illus.). 92p. pap. 9.95 (ISBN 0-943994-13-6). Birmingham Hist Soc.
Burkhardt, Charles H. Domestic & Commercial Oil Burners. 3rd ed. LC 68-31659. (Illus.). 1969. text ed. 30.40 (ISBN 0-07-009039-4). McGraw.
Burkhardt, D. F. & Ittelson, W. H., eds. Environmental Assessment of Socioeconomic Systems. LC 77-23528. (NATO Conference Series II, Systems Science: Vol. 3). 613p. 1978. 85.00x (ISBN 0-306-32843-7, Plenum Pr). Plenum Pub.
Burkhardt, Frederick & Smith, Sydney, eds. The Correspondence of Charles Darwin, 1821-1836, Vol. 1. 672p. 1985. 37.50 (ISBN 0-521-25587-2). Cambridge U Pr.
Burkhardt, Frederick, ed. see James, William.
Burkhardt, Frederick, et al, eds. see James, William.
Burkhardt, Frederick H., ed. Cleavage in Our Culture. facsimile ed. LC 74-90619. (Essay Index Reprint Ser.). 1952. 20.00 (ISBN 0-8369-1396-5). Ayer Co Pubs.
Burkhardt, Gerhard. Klopstock, Friedrich Gottlieb: Werke und Briefe. Historisch-Kritische Ausgabe Section Addenda; Klopstock-Bibliographie, Vol. 1. xii, 340p. 1975. 78.40x (ISBN 3-11-004896-5). De Gruyter.
Burkhardt, Helmut. The Biblical Doctrine of Regeneration. Bockmuehl, Klaus, ed. Johnston, O. R., tr. from Ger. (World Evangelical Fellowship: Outreach & Identify Theological Monograph). 48p. 1978. pap. 1.95 (ISBN 0-87784-322-8). Inter-Varsity.
Burkhardt, Hugh. The Real World & Mathematics. 188p. 1981. pap. text ed. 13.95x (ISBN 0-216-91084-6). Birkhauser.
Burkhardt, John E. Worship. LC 81-23116. 162p. 1982. pap. 8.95 (ISBN 0-664-24409-2). Westminster.
Burkhardt, R. Bone Marrow & Bone Tissue: Color Atlas of Clinical Histopathology. LC 79-126889. (Illus.). xii, 115p. 1971. 125.00 (ISBN 0-387-05059-0). Springer-Verlag.
Burkhardt, Richard W., Jr. The Spirit of System: Lamarck & Evolutionary Biology. 1977. 18.00x (ISBN 0-674-83317-1). Harvard U Pr.
Burkhardt, T. W. & Leeuwen, J. M. Real-Space Renormalization. (Topics in Current Physics Ser.: Vol. 30). (Illus.). 214p. 1982. 30.00 (ISBN 0-387-11459-9). Springer-Verlag.
Burkhart, Charles. Anthology for Musical Analysis. 3rd ed. LC 78-15566. 1979. pap. text ed. 27.95 (ISBN 0-03-018866-0, HoltC). HR&W.
Burkhart, F., ed. Neue Aspekte in der Behandlung der Herzinsuffizienz: Oberrheinisches Kardiologen - Symposium. (Cardiology Ser.: Vol.65, Suppl. 1,1980). (Illus.). 1980. pap. 8.25 (ISBN 3-8055-0652-X). S Karger.
Burkhart, Harold E., jt. auth. see Avery, Thomas E.
Burkhart, John, jt. auth. see Brooks, Svevo.
Burkhart, Judith A., jt. auth. see Gunnar, Peter M.
Burkhart, Lynne C. Old Values in a New Town: The Politics of Race & Class in Columbia, Maryland. LC 80-26556. 188p. 1981. 31.95 (ISBN 0-03-058306-3). Praeger.
Burkhart, Marianne C., jt. ed. see Waife, Ronald S.
Burkhart, Rob. I Hate Witnessing: Leader's Guide. 64p. 1985. pap. 3.95 (ISBN 0-8307-1011-6, 6101987). Regal.
--Yet Will I Trust Him: Leader's Guide. LC 79-91705. (Study & Grow Electives). 64p. 1985. pap. 3.95 (ISBN 0-8307-1016-7, 6102002). Regal.
Burkhart, Robert E. Shakespeare's Bad Quartos: Deliberate Abridgements Designed for Performance by Reduced Cast. (Studies in English Literature: No. 101). (Illus.). 124p. 1975. pap. text ed. 16.80x (ISBN 90-2793-276-X). Mouton.
Burkhart, Susan, jt. auth. see Koski, Barry.
Burkhart, W. Eugene, Jr. Decorating Christmas Trees. (Illus.). 64p. (Orig.). 1985. pap. 8.95 (ISBN 0-9615199-0-8). Burkharts.
Burkhauser, Richard V. & Haveman, Robert. Disability & Work: The Economics of American Policy. LC 82-113. (Policy Studies in Employment & Welfare Ser.: No. 38). 160p. 1982. text ed. 16.50x (ISBN 0-8018-2834-1). Johns Hopkins.
Burkhauser, Richard V., ed. A Challenge to Social Security. LC 82-1596. (Research on Poverty Monograph). 282p. 1982. 37.50 (ISBN 0-12-144680-8). Acad Pr.
Burkhauser, Richard V., ed. see Conference on Income Support Policies for the Aging-University of Chicago.
Burkhead, Jesse. Governmental Budgeting. LC 56-8000. 498p. 1956. 49.45 (ISBN 0-471-12375-7). Wiley.
Burkhead, Jesse, jt. auth. see Premchand, A.
Burkhead, Jesse, jt. ed. see Bahl, Roy W.
Burkhill, H., jt. auth. see Burkhill, John C.
Burkhill, John C. First Course in Mathematical Analysis. 1962. 25.95x (ISBN 0-521-04381-6); pap. 15.95x (ISBN 0-521-29468-1). Cambridge U Pr.
Burkhill, John C. & Burkhill, H. Second Course in Mathematical Analysis. LC 69-16278. (Illus.). 1970. text ed. 47.50 (ISBN 0-521-07519-X); pap. 29.95 (ISBN 0-521-28061-3). Cambridge U Pr.
Burkhill, John Charles. The Theory of Ordinary Differential Equations. LC 76-369325. (Longman Mathematical Ser.). pap. 32.50 (ISBN 0-317-08520-4, 2013563). Bks Demand UMI.
Burkholder, Charles E., jt. auth. see Crilley, Raymond E.
Burkholder, Clyde. The Ox-Bow Incident Notes. 55p. (Orig.). 1974. pap. text ed. 3.25 (ISBN 0-8220-0971-4). Cliffs.
Burkholder, J. Lawrence. To Drink or Not to Drink. 24p. (Orig.). 1981. pap. text ed. 0.75 (ISBN 0-8361-1967-3). Herald Pr.
Burkholder, J. Peter. Charles Ives: The Ideas Behind the Music. LC 85-2469. (Illus.). 192p. 1985. 17.95x (ISBN 0-300-03261-7). Yale U Pr.
Burkholder, J. R. & Redekop, Calvin, eds. Kingdom, Cross, & Community. LC 76-29663. 312p. 1976. 14.95x (ISBN 0-8361-1139-7). Herald Pr.
--Kingdom, Cross, & Community. LC 76-29663. 312p. 1976. 14.95. Herald Pr.
Burkholder, Lawrence J. To Drink or Not to Drink? Towards a Mennonite Consensus on Alcoholic Beverages. 23p. 1981. pap. 0.75 (ISBN 0-8361-1967-3). Herald Hse.
Burkholder, Lloyd K., Sr. Process & Industrial Pipe Estimating. 240p. (Orig.). 1982. pap. 18.25 (ISBN 0-910460-94-9). Craftsman.
Burkholder, Mark A. Politics of a Colonial Career: Jose Baquijano & the Audiencia of Lima. 198p. 1980. 20.00x (ISBN 0-8263-0545-8). U of NM Pr.
Burkholder, Mark A. & Chandler, D. S. Biographical Dictionary of Audiencia Ministers in the Americas, 1687-1821. LC 82-925. 491p. 1982. lib. bdg. 55.00 (ISBN 0-313-22038-7, BBD/). Greenwood.
--From Impotence to Authority: The Spanish Crown & the American Audiencias, 1687-1808. LC 76-45742. 256p. 1977. 18.00x (ISBN 0-8262-0219-5). U of Mo Pr.
Burkholder, Peter M. Atlas of Human Glomerular Pathology: Correlative Light, Immunofluorescence, & Ultrastructural Histology. LC 74-13371. pap. 110.50 (ISBN 0-317-28613-7, 2055406). Bks Demand UMI.
Burkholder, Ralph, jt. auth. see Wingate, Isabel B.
Burkholder, Robert E. & Myerson, Joel. Emerson: An Annotated Secondary Bibliography. LC 84-15352. (Pittsburgh Series in Bibliography). 857p. 1985. 90.00x (ISBN 0-8229-3502-3). U of Pittsburgh Pr.
Burkholder, Robert E. & Myerson, Joel, eds. Critical Essays on Ralph Waldo Emerson. (Critical Essays in American Literature Ser.). 1983. lib. bdg. 62.50 (ISBN 0-8161-8305-8). G K Hall.
Burkholder, Ruth C. Mi Jun's Difficult Decision. LC 83-20494. (Illus.). 14p. (Orig.). (gr. 4-6). 1984. pap. 4.95 (ISBN 0-377-00139-2). Friend Pr.
--Won Gil's Secret Diary. LC 83-16529. (Illus.). 14p. (Orig.). (gr. 1-3). 1984. pap. 4.95 (ISBN 0-377-00138-4). Friend Pr.
Burkholder, Ruth C. & Goddard, Carrie L. Exploring Korea. (Illus.). 17p. (Orig.). 1984. pap. 3.95 (ISBN 0-377-00142-2). Friend Pr.
Burkholz, Herbert. The Snow Gods. LC 84-45612. 512p. 1985. 17.95 (ISBN 0-689-11509-1). Atheneum.
Burkholz, Herbert & Irving, Clifford. The Sleeping Spy. LC 81-69140. 320p. 1983. 14.95 (ISBN 0-689-11252-1). Atheneum.
--The Sleeping Spy. 1984. pap. 2.95 (ISBN 0-345-31465-4). Ballantine.
Burki, N. K. Pulmonary Diseases. (Medical Outline Ser.). 1982. pap. text ed. 26.00 (ISBN 0-87488-583-3). Med Exam.
Burki, Shahid J. Pakistan: A Nation in the Making. (Nations of Contemporary Asia Ser.). 128p. 1985. 28.00x (ISBN 0-86531-353-9). Westview.
--Study of Chinese Communes, 1965. LC 73-82301. (East Asian Monographs Ser: No. 29). 1969. pap. 11.00x (ISBN 0-674-85310-5). Harvard U Pr.
Burki, Shahid J. & LaPorte, Robert, Jr., eds. Pakistan's Development Priorities: Choices for the Future. (Illus.). 398p. 1984. pap. 18.95x (ISBN 0-19-577333-0). Oxford U Pr.
Burki, Shahid Javed, jt. auth. see Haq, Mahbub ul.
Burkig, Valerie C. Photonics: The New Science of Light. (Illus.). 128p. (gr. 5-10). 1985. PLB 11.95 (ISBN 0-89490-107-9). Enslow Pubs.
Burkill, H. M. The Useful Plants of West Tropical Africa, Vol. 1. 900p. 1985. 100.00x (ISBN 0-947643-01-X, Pub. by Prospect England). U Pr of Va.
Burkill, I. H. Notes from a Journey to Nepal. (Records of the Botanical Survey of India Ser.: Vol. 4, No. 4). 1978. Repr. of 1910 ed. 11.50x (ISBN 0-89955-294-3, Pub. by Intl Bk Dist). Intl Spec Bk.
Burkill, John C. Lebesgue Integral. (Cambridge Tracts in Mathematics & Mathematical Physics). 1951. 16.95 (ISBN 0-521-04382-4). Cambridge U Pr.
Burkill, T. A. Evolution of Christian Thought. LC 76-127775. 518p. 1971. 29.50x (ISBN 0-8014-0581-5). Cornell U Pr.
Burkill, T. A., ed. see Winter, Paul.
Burkin, A. R. Topics in Non-Ferrous Extractive Metallurgy. LC 80-17435. (Critical Reports on Applied Chemistry Ser.: Vol. 1). 134p. 1980. 34.95 (ISBN 0-470-27016-0). Halsted Pr.
Burkin, A. R., ed. Leaching & Reduction in Hydrometallurgy. 109p. (Orig.). 1975. pap. text ed. 40.25x (ISBN 0-900488-27-1). IMM North Am.
Burkinshaw, Bill. Introducing Radio Control Model Aircraft. (Illus.). 96p. 1983. pap. 9.95 (ISBN 0-85242-801-4). Aztex.
--Manual of Electric Radio Control Cars. (Illus.). 96p. 1983. pap. 9.95 (ISBN 0-85242-821-9, Pub. by Argus). Aztex.
Burkinshaw, O., jt. auth. see Aliprantis, C. D.
Burkinshaw, Owen, jt. auth. see Aliprantis, Charalambos D.
Burkinshaw, Owen, jt. auth. see Aliprantis, Charalambous D.
Burkitt, B. & Bowers, D. Trade Unions & the Economy. 1979. text ed. 29.50 (ISBN 0-8419-5064-4). Holmes & Meier.
Burkitt, Brian. Radical Political Economy: An Introduction to the Alternative Economics. 208p. 1984. 30.00x (ISBN 0-8147-1057-3); pap. 15.00x (ISBN 0-8147-1058-1). NYU Pr.
--Trade Unions & Wages. 2nd ed. 1981. 36.00x (ISBN 0-901945-39-0, Pub. by Bradford U Pr England). State Mutual Bk.
Burkitt, D. P., jt. auth. see Tromwell, H. C.
Burkitt, D. P. & Trowell, H. C., eds. Refined Carbohydrate Foods & Disease: Some Implications of Dietary Fibre. 1975. 65.00 (ISBN 0-12-144750-2). Acad Pr.
Burkitt, D. P., jt. ed. see Trowell, H. C.
Burkitt, Denis. Don't Forget Fiber in Your Diet. rev. ed. (Positive Health Guides Ser.). (Illus.). 126p. 1984. pap. 7.95 (ISBN 0-668-06021-2). Arco.
--Eat Right--To Keep Healthy & Enjoy Life More. LC 78-24492. (Positive Health Guides). (Illus.). 1979. 8.95 (ISBN 0-668-04676-7); pap. 5.95 (ISBN 0-668-04682-1). Arco.
Burkitt, Dennis. Eat Right to Stay Healthy. 1979. 5.95x (ISBN 0-668-04682-1). Cancer Control Soc.
Burkitt, F. C. Jewish & Christian Apocalypses. (British Academy, London, Schweich Lectures on Biblical Archaeology Series, 1914). pap. 19.00 (ISBN 0-317-15740-X). Kraus Repr.
--The Old Latin & the Itala. (Texts & Studies Ser.: No. 1, Vol. 4, Pt. 3). pap. 13.00 (ISBN 0-317-16751-0). Kraus Repr.
--S. Ephraim's Quotations from the Gospel. (Texts & Studies Ser.: No. 1, Vol. 7, Pt. 2). pap. 13.00 (ISBN 0-317-16759-6). Kraus Repr.
Burkitt, F. C., ed. The Book of Rules of Tyconius. (Texts & Studies Series 1: Vol. 3, Pt. 1). pap. 19.00 (ISBN 0-317-16748-0). Kraus Repr.
Burkitt, F. Crawford. The Earliest Sources for the Life of Jesus. 1977. lib. bdg. 59.95 (ISBN 0-8490-1736-X). Gordon Pr.
Burkitt, Francis C. Church & Gnosis: A Study of Christian Thought & Speculation in the Second Century. LC 77-84696. (The Morse Lectures: 1931). Repr. of 1932 ed. 18.50 (ISBN 0-404-16104-9). AMS Pr.
--Early Christianity Outside the Roman Empire: Two Lectures Delivered at Trinity College, Dublin. LC 82-45806. 1983. Repr. of 1899 ed. 18.00 (ISBN 0-404-62375-1). AMS Pr.
--The Religion of the Manichees: Donnellan Lectures for 1924. LC 77-84698. Repr. of 1925 ed. 18.50 (ISBN 0-404-16105-7). AMS Pr.
Burkitt, George H., jt. auth. see Wheater, Paul R.
Burkitt, Lemuel & Read, Jesse. A Concise History of the Kehukee Bapist Association from Its Original Rise to the Present Time. rev. ed. Gaustad, Edwin S., ed. LC 79-52591. (The Baptist Tradition Ser.). 1980. Repr. of 1850 ed. lib. bdg. 28.50x (ISBN 0-405-12458-9). Ayer Co Pubs.
Burkitt, M. C. Our Early Ancestors: An Introductory Study of Mesolithic, Neolithic, & Copper Age Cultures in Europe & Adjacent Regions. LC 72-80142. (Illus.). Repr. of 1926 ed. 15.00 (ISBN 0-405-08331-9, Blom Pubns). Ayer Co Pubs.
Burkitt, M. C., jt. auth. see Breuil, Henri.
Burkitt, Miles C. Prehistory: Study of Early Cultures in Europe & the Mediterranean Basin. facsimile 2nd ed. LC 73-169752. (Select Bibliographies Reprint Ser). Repr. of 1925 ed. 38.50 (ISBN 0-8369-5972-8). Ayer Co Pubs.
--South Africa's Past in Stone & Paint. LC 76-44700. Repr. of 1928 ed. 23.50 (ISBN 0-404-15912-5). AMS Pr.
Burkle, Fredrick & Sanner, Patricia, eds. Disaster Medicine: Application for the Immediate Management & Triage of Civil & Military Disaster Victims. 1984. pap. text ed. write for info. (ISBN 0-87488-186-2). Med Exam.
Burkle, Howard R. God, Suffering, & Belief. LC 76-26496. Repr. of 1977 ed. 24.40 (ISBN 0-8357-9010-X, 2016364). Bks Demand UMI.
Burklin, Ray. Process Plant Designer's Pocket Handbook of Codes & Standards. LC 79-17599. 172p. (Orig.). 1979. pap. 9.95x (ISBN 0-87201-115-1). Gulf Pub.
Burkman, Katherine H. The Dramatic World of Harold Pinter: Its Basis in Ritual. LC 70-125099. 189p. 1971. 8.00 (ISBN 0-8142-0146-6). Ohio St U Pr.
--Literature Through Performance: "Shakespeare's Mirror" & "A Canterbury Caper". LC 76-25615. (Illus.). xxviii, 104p. 1978. 10.00x (ISBN 0-8214-0365-6, 82-82568); pap. 3.95x (ISBN 0-8214-0384-2, 82-82576). Ohio U Pr.
Burkman, Thomas W., ed. Occupation of Japan: Educational & Social Reform. 529p. 1982. pap. 8.00 (ISBN 0-9606418-3-1). MacArthur Memorial.
--The Occupation of Japan: The International Context. 308p. 1984. pap. 10.00 (ISBN 0-9606418-4-X). MacArthur Memorial.
Burkoff, John M. Criminal Offenses & Defenses in Pennsylvania. 283p. 1984. 49.95 (ISBN 0-317-05563-1). Harrison Co Ga.
Burkom, Selma R. Doris Lessing: A Checklist of Primary & Secondary Sources. LC 72-87109. iv, 88p. 1973. 7.50x (ISBN 0-87875-039-8). Whitston Pub.
Burkowsky, Mitchell R. An Orientation to Learning & Language Disorders in Children. LC 75-176182. 304p. 1973. 16.50 (ISBN 0-87527-098-0). Green.
Burks, jt. auth. see Maloney.
Burks, A. W. see Peirce, Charles S.
Burks, Ardath. The Modernizers: Overseas Students, Foreign Employees, & Meiji Japan. (Replica Edition Ser.). 525p. 1985. softcover 29.85x (ISBN 0-86531-826-3). Westview.
Burks, Ardath W. The Government of Japan. LC 82-6136. (Crowell Comparative Government Ser.). xviii, 284p. 1982. Repr. of 1964 ed. lib. bdg. 35.00x (ISBN 0-313-23575-9, BUGJ). Greenwood.
Burks, Ardath W., jt. auth. see Beck, Clark L.
Burks, Arthur J. En-Don: The Ageless Wisdom. LC 73-80412. 75p. 1973. pap. 3.25 (ISBN 0-913264-10-5). Douglas-West.
Burks, Arthur W. Chance, Cause, Reason: An Inquiry into the Nature of Scientific Evidence. LC 74-11617. (Illus.). 688p. 1977. lib. bdg. 27.50x (ISBN 0-226-08087-0). U of Chicago Pr.
--Chance, Cause, Reason: An Inquiry into the Nature of Scientific Evidence. LC 74-11617. 1979. pap. 12.50x (ISBN 0-226-08088-9, P836, Phoen). U of Chicago Pr.
Burks, B. D. The Mayflies, or Ephemeroptera, of Illinois. LC 75-2296. (Illus.). viii, 216p. 1975. Repr. of 1953 ed. 15.00 (ISBN 0-911836-06-3). Entomological Repr.
Burks, B. S., jt. auth. see Jones, Mary C.
Burks, Barbara S., et al. The Promise of Youth: Follow-up Studies of a Thousand Gifted Children. (Genetic Studies of Genius Ser). 1930. 35.00x (ISBN 0-8047-0011-7). Stanford U Pr.
Burks, Don M., ed. Rhetoric, Philosophy, & Literature: An Exploration. LC 77-92712. 128p. 1978. 7.50 (ISBN 0-911198-52-0). Purdue U Pr.
Burks, James F., jt. ed. see Therio, Adrien.
Burks, James W. Dermabrasion & Chemical Peeling: In the Treatment of Certain Cosmetic Defects & Diseases of the Skin. (Illus.). 256p. 1979. 24.75x (ISBN 0-398-03778-7). C C Thomas.
Burks, John, jt. auth. see Hall, George.
Burks, Julia M., jt. auth. see Wishon, George E.
Burks, Mary P. Requirements for Certification of Teachers, Counselors, Librarians, Administrators: For Elementary Schools, Secondary Schools & Junior Colleges. 49th, 1984-85 ed. LC 43-1905. 240p. 1984. lib. bdg. 24.00x (ISBN 0-226-08103-6). U of Chicago Pr.
--Requirements for Certification of Teachers, Counselors, Librarians, Adminstrators: For Elementary Schools, Secondary Schools & Junior Colleges. 50th ed. 234p. 1985. lib. bdg. 26.00x (ISBN 0-226-08104-4). U of Chicago Pr.

Burks, R. V. East European History: An Ethnic Approach. LC 72-97101. (AHA Pamphlets: No. 425). (Illus.). 1973. pap. text ed. 1.50 (ISBN 0-87229-010-7). Am Hist Assn.

Burks, R. V., ed. The Future of Communism in Europe. LC 68-64186. (Leo M. Franklin Memorial Lectures in Human Relations Ser: Vol. 17). 304p. 1969. 9.95x (ISBN 0-8143-1355-8). Wayne St U Pr.

Burks, Richard V. The Dynamics of Communism in Eastern Europe. LC 73-17027. (Illus.). 1976. Repr. of 1961 ed. lib. bdg. 20.25x (ISBN 0-8371-8961-6, BUDY). Greenwood.

Burks, Rosemary, jt. auth. see Shurley, Kathy.

Burkwalter, Pamela K. Nursing Care of the Alcoholic & Drug Abuser. 297p. 1975. pap. 9.50 (ISBN 0-318-14970-2). Natl Coun Alcoholism.

Burl. Prehistoric Avebury. 1979. 36.00x (ISBN 0-300-02368-5). Yale U Pr.

--The Stone Circles of the British Isles. 1976. 46.00x (ISBN 0-300-01972-6); pap. 16.95x (ISBN 0-300-02398-7, Y-341). Yale U Pr.

Burl, Aubrey. Megalithic Brittany. (Illus.). 1985. 18.95 (ISBN 0-500-01364-0). Thames Hudson.

--Prehistoric Astronomy & Ritual. (Shire Archaeology Ser.: No. 32). (Illus.). 56p. 1983. pap. 5.95 (ISBN 0-85263-621-0, Pub. by Shire Pubns England). Seven Hills Bks.

--Prehistoric Stone Circles. (Shire Archaeology Ser.: No. 9). (Illus.). 1983. pap. 5.95 (ISBN 0-85263-640-7, Pub. by Shire Pubns England). Seven Hills Bks.

--Rites of the Gods. (Illus.). 272p. 1981. text ed. 26.50x (ISBN 0-460-04313-7, BKA 04660, Pub. by J M Dent England). Biblio Dist.

Burlace, C. J. & Whalley, L. Waste Plastics & Their Potential for Recycle, 1977. 1981. 40.00x (ISBN 0-686-97166-3, Pub. by W Spring England). State Mutual Bk.

Burlage, L. Charles & Grunwald, Stefan. How to Think Yourself to Happiness. (Illus.). 140p. 1984. 9.95 (ISBN 0-915133-01-6); deluxe ed. 18.95 (ISBN 0-915133-00-8); pap. 4.95. Grunwald & Radcliff.

Burlamaqui, Jean J. The Principles of Natural & Politic Law. 5th ed. Nugent, Thomas, tr. LC 70-38249. (The Evolution of Capitalism Ser.). 500p. 1972. Repr. of 1807 ed. 35.00 (ISBN 0-405-04114-4). Ayer Co Pubs.

Burland, Cottie. The Incas. LC 78-64225. (Peoples of the Past Ser.). (Illus.). 64p. (gr. 6 up). 1979. lib. bdg. 12.68 (ISBN 0-382-06193-4). Silver.

--The Incas. (Peoples of the Past Ser.). 80p. (gr. 4 up). pap. 5.75 (ISBN 0-382-06919-6). Silver.

--North American Indian Mythology. rev. ed. LC 85-70555. (The Library of the World's Myths & Legends). (Illus.). 144p. 1985. 17.95 (ISBN 0-87226-016-X). P Bedrick Bks.

Burland, Cottie & Forman, Werner. The Aztecs: Gods & Fate in Ancient Mexico. (Illus.). 128p. 1985. 20.00 (ISBN 0-85613-291-8, Pub. by Salem Hse Ltd). Merrimack Pub Cir.

Burland, Cottie A. Ancient China. (Great Civilization Ser.). (Illus.). (gr. 4-8). 1974. Repr. of 1960 ed. 6.50 (ISBN 0-7175-0018-7). Dufour.

--Ancient Egypt. (Great Civilization Ser.). (Illus.). (gr. 4-8). 1974. Repr. of 1957 ed. 6.50 (ISBN 0-7175-0014-4). Dufour.

--Ancient Greece. (Great Civilization Ser.). (Illus.). (gr. 4-8). 1974. Repr. of 1958 ed. 6.50 (ISBN 0-7175-0016-0). Dufour.

--Ancient Rome. (Great Civilization Ser). (Illus.). (gr. 4-8). 1974. Repr. of 1958 ed. 6.50 (ISBN 0-7175-0015-2). Dufour.

--The Arts of the Alchemists. LC 79-8598. Repr. of 1968 ed. 42.50 (ISBN 0-404-18451-0). AMS Pr.

--Inca Peru. (Great Civilization Ser). (Illus.). (gr. 4-8). 1975. Repr. of 1957 ed. 6.50 (ISBN 0-7175-0017-9). Dufour.

Burland, Harris. Dacobra. 1979. 8.50 (ISBN 0-686-65265-7). Bookfinger.

--Dacobra; or, The White Priests of Ahriman. 1979. Repr. of 1903 ed. 8.50 (ISBN 0-686-53053-5). Bookfinger.

Burlatski, F. Materialismo Historico. 366p. (Span.). 1982. pap. 7.95 (ISBN 0-8285-2394-0, Pub. by Progress Pubs USSR). Imported Pubns.

Burlatsky, F. Mao-Tse-Tung: An Ideological & Psychological Portrait. 396p. 1980. 8.95 (ISBN 0-8285-1712-6, Pub. by Progress Pubs USSR). Imported Pubns.

Burleigh, Anne H., ed. Education in a Free Society. LC 73-78807. 188p. 1973. 7.00 (ISBN 0-913966-00-2, Liberty Pr); pap. 3.00 (ISBN 0-913966-45-2). Liberty Fund.

Burleigh, Charles C. Thoughts on the Death Penalty. LC 82-45657. 1983. Repr. of 1845 ed. 37.50 (ISBN 0-404-62404-9). AMS Pr.

Burleigh, Harry T. Negro Spirituals, 2 vols. in 1. LC 74-24262. Repr. of 1922 ed. 45.00 (ISBN 0-404-12874-2). AMS Pr.

Burleigh, John S., ed. Augustine: Earlier Writings. LC 53-13043. (Library of Christian Classics). 410p. 1979. softcover 8.95 (ISBN 0-664-24162-X). Westminster.

Burleigh, Michael. Prussian Society & the German Order: An Aristocratic Corporation in Crisis c. 1410-1466. LC 83-18896. (Cambridge Studies in Early Modern History). 232p. 1984. 39.50 (ISBN 0-521-26104-X). Cambridge U Pr.

Burleigh, R. Carbon-Fourteen Dating. LC 74-183462. (International Monographs on Science in Archaeology). Date not set. price not set (ISBN 0-12-785082-1). Acad Pr.

Burleigh, Robert. Basic Learning Skills: Base Words & Word Parts Learning Module. LC 78-730775. 1978. pap. text ed. 300.00 (ISBN 0-89290-108-X, CM-38D). Soc for Visual.

--Basic Learning Skills: Consonant Sounds Learning Module. (gr. k-2). 1978. pap. text ed. 370.00 (ISBN 0-89290-106-3, CM-38B). Soc for Visual.

--Basic Learning Skills: Vowel Sounds Learning Module. (gr. 1-3). 1978. pap. text ed. 370.00 (ISBN 0-89290-107-1, CM-38C). Soc for Visual.

--Basic Reading Skills: Reading Readiness Learning Module. (gr. k-1). 1977. pap. text ed. 315.00 (ISBN 0-89290-105-5, CM-38A). Soc for Visual.

--A Man Named Thoreau. LC 85-7947. (Illus.). 48p. (gr. 3 up). 1985. 12.95 (ISBN 0-689-31122-2). Atheneum.

Burleigh, Robert & Gray, Mary Jane. Basic Writing Skills. LC 77-730072. (Illus.). (gr. 6-8). 1976. pap. text ed. 325.00 (ISBN 0-89290-115-2, CM-39). Soc for Visual.

Burleigh, Robert & Matlak, Raymond. Percent. LC 79-730248. (Illus.). 1979. pap. 135.00 (ISBN 0-89290-096-2, A512-SATC). Soc for Visual.

Burlend, Edward, jt. auth. see Burlend, Rebecca.

Burlend, Rebecca & Burlend, Edward. A True Picture of Emigration. 180p. 1974. pap. 2.95 (ISBN 0-8065-0457-9). Citadel Pr.

Burleson, Bob. The Shouting Head of Prophet John. new ed. LC 76-27976. (Orig.). 1976. pap. text ed. 3.00x (ISBN 0-914476-60-2). Thorp Springs.

Burleson, Clyde, jt. auth. see McDonald, John.

Burleson, Donald R. Elementary Statistics. 1980. 22.95 (ISBN 0-316-11696-3); teachers manual avail. (ISBN 0-316-11697-1). Little.

--H. P. Lovecraft: A Critical Study. LC 82-24186. (Contributions to the Study of Science Fiction & Fantasy Ser.: No. 5). xi, 243p. 1983. lib. bdg. 29.95 (ISBN 0-313-23255-5, BUL/). Greenwood.

--Topics in Precalculus Mathematics. (Illus.). 544p. 1974. text ed. 27.95 (ISBN 0-13-925461-7); study guide o.p. 1.95 (ISBN 0-13-925214-2). P-H.

Burleson, James J. In the Sandhills. 64p. 1985. 5.95 (ISBN 0-911225-06-4). Clearstream Pr.

Burleson, Joe. Space Colony. (Magic Windows Ser.). (Illus.). 9p. 1984. pap. 4.95 (ISBN 0-399-21058-X, Putnam). Putnam Pub Group.

Burlew, John S., ed. Algal Culture: From Laboratory to Pilot Plant. (Illus.). 366p. 1953. 16.00 (ISBN 0-87279-611-6, 600). Carnegie Inst.

Burley, D. M. & Wink, C. A., eds. Hydralazine in Cardiovascular Medicine. (Royal Society of Medicine International Congress & Symposium Ser.: No. 10). 64p. 1979. 16.00 (ISBN 0-8089-1202-X, 790737). Grune.

Burley, Gertrude S., jt. auth. see Gard, Robert E.

Burley, Gibson J. & Speight, M. R. The Adoption of Agricultural Practices for the Development of Heritable Resistance to Pests & Pathogens in Forest Crops. 1980. 30.00x (ISBN 0-85074-057-6, Pub. by For Lib Comm England). STate Mutual Bk.

Burley, J. & Nikles, D. C. Selection & Breeding to Improve Some Tropical Conifers, 2 Vols, Vol. 1. 1972. Vol. 1. 90.00x (ISBN 0-85074-026-6, Pub. by For Lib Comm England); Vol. 2. 95.00x (ISBN 0-85074-027-4). State Mutual Bk.

Burley, J. & Nikles, G. Tropical Provenance & Progeny Research & International Cooperation. 1973. 100.00x (ISBN 0-85074-022-3, Pub. by For Lib Comm England). State Mutual Bk.

Burley, J. & Palmer, E. R. Pulp & Wood Densitometric Properties of Pinus Caribaea from Fiji. 1979. 30.00x (ISBN 0-85074-046-0, Pub. by For Lib Comm England). State Mutual Bk.

Burley, J. & Wood, P. J. A Manual on Species & Provenance Research with Particular Reference to the Tropics. 1976. 50.00x (ISBN 0-85074-016-9, Pub. by For Lib Comm England). State Mutual Bk.

--A Manual on Species & Provenance Research with Particular Reference to the Tropics. 1977. 30.00x (ISBN 0-85074-024-X, Pub. by For Lib Comm England). State Mutual Bk.

--Manual Sobre Investigaciones de Especies y Procedencias con Referencia Especial a Los Tropicos. 1979. 50.00x (ISBN 0-85074-058-4, Pub. by For Lib Comm England). State Mutual Bk.

Burley, J., jt. auth. see Armitage, F. B.

Burley, J. & Styles, B. T., eds. Tropical Trees: Variation Breeding & Conservation. 1976. 49.50 (ISBN 0-12-145150-X). Acad Pr.

Burley, Jeffrey. Obstacles to Tree Planting in Arid & Semi-Arid Lands: Comparative Case Studies from India & Kenya. 52p. 1983. pap. 11.75 (ISBN 92-808-0391-3, TUNU208, UNU). Unipub.

Burley, Jennifer, jt. auth. see Barron, Pamela.

Burley, Nancy, jt. auth. see Willson, Mary F.

Burley, W. J. Charles & Elizabeth. 1981. 9.95 (ISBN 0-8027-5447-3). Walker & Co.

--Charles & Elizabeth. 176p. 1985. pap. 2.95 (ISBN 0-8027-3106-6). Walker & Co.

--Death in a Salubrious Place. LC 72-95765. (British Mystery Ser.). 175p. 1984. pap. 2.95 (ISBN 0-8027-3069-8). Walker & Co.

--Death in Stanley Street. LC 74-82397. (British Mystery Ser.). 175p. 1984. pap. 2.95 (ISBN 0-8027-3067-1). Walker & Co.

--Death in Willow Pattern. 192p. 1983. pap. 2.95 (ISBN 0-8027-3025-6). Walker & Co.

--The House of Care. 192p. 1982. 10.95 (ISBN 0-8027-5464-3). Walker & Co.

Burley, W J. The House of Care. 184p. 1984. pap. 2.95 (ISBN 0-8027-3083-3). Walker & Co.

Burley, W. J. The Schoolmaster. LC 76-52297. (British Mystery Ser.). 175p. 1984. pap. 2.95 (ISBN 0-8027-3057-4). Walker & Co.

--To Kill a Cat. (British Mysteries Ser.). 1983. pap. 2.95 (ISBN 0-8027-3030-2). Walker & Co.

--Wycliffe & the Beales. LC 83-25364. (Crime Club Ser.). 192p. 1984. 11.95 (ISBN 0-385-19189-8). Doubleday.

--Wycliffe & the Schoolgirls. LC 75-36548. (British Mystery Ser.). 175p. 1984. pap. 2.95 (ISBN 0-8027-3064-7). Walker & Co.

--Wycliffe in Paul's Court. LC 81-5449. (Crime Club Ser.). 192p. 1980. 10.95 (ISBN 0-385-17208-7). Doubleday.

--Wycliffe in Paul's Court. 192p. 1981. pap. 3.95 (ISBN 0-14-005917-2). Penguin.

Burley-Allen, Madelyn. Listening: The Forgotten Skill. LC 81-16219. (Wiley Self-Teaching Guides Ser.). 153p. 1982. pap. 9.95 (ISBN 0-471-08776-9, Pub. by Wiley Pr). Wiley.

--Managing Assertively. (Wiley Self-Teaching Guides Ser.). 174p. 1983. pap. 9.95 (ISBN 0-471-09750-0, Pub. by Wiley Pr). Wiley.

Burlin, Natalie. The Indians Book. 59.95 (ISBN 0-8490-0401-2). Gordon Pr.

Burlin, R. B. Chaucerian Fiction. 1977. 32.00x (ISBN 0-691-06322-2). Princeton U Pr.

Burlina, A. & Galzigna, L., eds. Clinical Enzymology Symposia, Vol. 2. (International Symposia on Clinical Embryology Ser.). (Illus.). 646p. 1980. text ed. 49.50 (ISBN 88-212-0772-2, Pub. by Piccin Italy). J K Burgess.

Burling, Anne. Grazed Knees & Noses. 1984. 15.00x (ISBN 0-906791-29-4, Pub. by Minimax Bks UK). State Mutual Bk.

Burling, R. Man's Many Voices: Language in Its Cultural Context. LC 78-111258. 1970. text ed. 14.95 (ISBN 0-03-081001-9, HoltC). HR&W.

Burling, Robbins. English in Black & White. LC 72-12548. 178p. 1973. (HoltC). HR&W.

--Learning a Field Language. 250p. 1984. pap. text ed. 6.95x (ISBN 0-472-08053-9). U of Mich Pr.

--The Passage of Power: Studies in Political Succession. (Studies in Anthropology Ser.). 1974. 39.50 (ISBN 0-12-785085-6). Acad Pr.

--Proto Lolo-Burmese. LC 66-64406. (General Publications Ser: Vol. 43). (Orig.). 1967. pap. text ed. 5.50x (ISBN 0-87750-131-9). Res Ctr Lang Semiotic.

--Sounding Right. 160p. 1982. pap. text ed. 12.95 (ISBN 0-88377-216-7). Newbury Hse.

Burlingame, et al. Timesharing Two. Bloch, Stuart M. & Ingersoll, William B., eds. LC 82-60331. (Illus.). 223p. (Orig.). 1982. 36.00 (ISBN 0-87420-611-1, TO4); members 27.00. Urban Land.

Burlingame, Anne E. Battle of the Books in Its Historical Setting. LC 68-54230. 1969. Repr. of 1920 ed. 10.00x (ISBN 0-8196-0224-8). Biblo.

Burlingame, Beverley, jt. ed. see Gottesman, Alice J.

Burlingame, Burl & Kasher, Robert K. Da Kine Sound: Conversations with People Who Create Hawaiian Music. Poole-Burlingame, Mary, ed. LC 78-17556. 1978. pap. 5.95 (ISBN 0-916630-08-0). Pr Pacifica.

Burlingame, Carl, jt. auth. see Ragatz, Richard L.

Burlingame, E. W. Buddhist Parables. 59.95 (ISBN 0-87968-803-3). Gordon Pr.

--Buddhist Parables. lib. bdg. 79.95 (ISBN 0-87968-494-1). Krishna Pr.

Burlingame, Eugene W., tr. from Pali. The Grateful Elephant & Other Stories. LC 78-72392. (Illus.). Repr. of 1923 ed. 34.50 (ISBN 0-404-17239-3). AMS Pr.

Burlingame, Eugene W., tr. see Dhammapadatthakatha.

Burlingame, Everett. Consistent Profits in Stock Market Charts. (Illus.). 157p. 1981. 67.85x (ISBN 0-86654-009-1). Inst Econ Finan.

Burlingame, H., tr. see Iskander, Fazil.

Burlingame, Hardin J. Leaves from Conjurors' Scrap Books, Or, Modern Magicians & Their Works. LC 74-148349. 1971. Repr. of 1891 ed. 40.00x (ISBN 0-8103-3371-6). Gale.

Burlingame, Merrill G. & Bell, Edward J., Jr. The Montana Cooperative Extension Service: A History, 1843-1974. 384p. 1985. pap. 11.00 (ISBN 0-934318-45-X). Falcon Pr MT.

Burlingame, Robert. Desert Remains. 1983. pap. 2.00 (ISBN 0-317-13321-7). San Marcos.

Burlingame, Roger. Don't Let Them Scare You. LC 73-21284. (Illus.). 352p. 1974. Repr. of 1961 ed. lib. bdg. 24.75x (ISBN 0-8371-6146-0, BUSY). Greenwood.

--Engines of Democracy: Inventions & Society in Mature America. LC 75-22804. (America in Two Centuries Ser). (Illus.). 1976. Repr. of 1940 ed. 48.50x (ISBN 0-405-07676-2). Ayer Co Pubs.

--General Billy Mitchell: Champion of Air Defense. LC 77-26823. (They Made America Ser.). (Illus.). 1978. Repr. of 1952 ed. lib. bdg. 24.75x (ISBN 0-313-20170-6, BUGM). Greenwood.

--March of the Iron Men: A Social History of Union Through Invention. LC 75-22805. (America in Two Centuries Ser). (Illus.). 1976. Repr. of 1938 ed. 42.00x (ISBN 0-405-07677-0). Ayer Co Pubs.

--Of Making Many Books. 1971. 10.00 (ISBN 0-684-10047-9, ScribT). Scribner.

Burlingham, Dorothy. Psychoanalytic Studies of the Sighted & the Blind. LC 76-184213. 406p. 1972. text ed. 35.00 (ISBN 0-8236-4510-X). Intl Univs Pr.

--Twins: A Study of Three Pairs of Twins (with 30 Charts) LC 53-6599. pap. 57.50 (ISBN 0-317-10374-1, 2010702). Bks Demand UMI.

Burlingham, Dorothy T., jt. auth. see Freud, Anna.

Burlingham, H. H. & Juergenson, Elwood M. Selected Lessons for Teaching Off-Farm Agricultural Occupations. LC 66-19257. (Illus.). 1967. text ed. 7.95x (ISBN 0-8134-0899-7, 899). Interstate.

Burlingham, Russell. Forrest Reid. 1953. Repr. 20.00 (ISBN 0-8274-2355-1). R West.

--Forrest Reid: A Portrait & a Study. 1979. Repr. of 1953 ed. lib. bdg. 27.50 (ISBN 0-8414-9841-5). Folcroft.

Burm, A. C., jt. auth. see Van Kleef, J. W.

Burma, Ian, jt. auth. see Richie, Donald.

Burma, John H. Spanish-Speaking Groups in the United States. LC 73-81471. 214p. (New preface by author). 1974. Repr. of 1954 ed. 15.00 (ISBN 0-87917-024-7). Ethridge.

Burman, Ben L. Blow a Bugle at Catfish Bend. 132p. (gr. 3-5). 1981. pap. 1.95 (ISBN 0-380-53504-1, 53504-1, Camelot). Avon.

--Blow a Wild Bugle for Catfish Bend. LC 67-12429. (Illus.). (gr. 6 up). 3.95 (ISBN 0-8008-0825-8). Taplinger.

--Blow for a Landing. 256p. 1974. pap. 1.50 (ISBN 0-89176-072-5, 6072). Mockingbird Bks.

--Children of Noah. 5.00 (ISBN 0-685-02658-2). Taplinger.

--The Four Lives of Mundy Tolliver. 1974. pap. 1.50 (ISBN 0-89176-806-8, 6806). Mockingbird Bks.

--Four Lives of Mundy Tolliver. LC 53-10498. 3.75 (ISBN 0-685-20503-7). Taplinger.

--Generals Wear Cork Hats: An Amazing Adventure That Made World History. LC 63-18337. (Illus.). 1963. 5.00 (ISBN 0-8008-3150-0). Taplinger.

--High Treason at Catfish Bend. 144p. (gr. 3-5). 1981. pap. 1.95 (ISBN 0-380-53512-2, 53512-2, Camelot). Avon.

--High Treason at Catfish Bend. LC 76-52136. (Illus.). 156p. (gr. 6 up). 1977. 10.95 (ISBN 0-8149-0785-7). Vanguard.

--High Water at Catfish Bend. 132p. (gr. 3-5). 1981. pap. 1.95 (ISBN 0-380-53470-3, 53470-3, Camelot). Avon.

Burman, Ben. L. High Water at Catfish Bend. 2.95 (ISBN 0-685-36539-5). Taplinger.

Burman, Ben L. It's a Big Continent. LC 61-11648. 1961. 4.95 (ISBN 0-685-20504-5). Taplinger.

--Look Down That Winding River: An Informal Profile of the Mississippi. LC 72-6610. (Illus.). 1973. 7.95 (ISBN 0-8008-4960-4). Taplinger.

--The Owl Hoots Twice at Catfish Bend. 132p. (gr. 3-5). 1981. pap. 1.95 (ISBN 0-380-53496-7, 53496-7, Camelot). Avon.

--Seven Stars for Catfish Bend. (Illus.). 88p. (gr. 3-5). 1981. pap. 1.95 (ISBN 0-380-53488-6, 53488-6, Camelot). Avon.

--Sign of the Praying Tiger. 4.95 (ISBN 0-685-02657-4). Taplinger.

--The Strange Invasion of Catfish Bend. 156p. (gr. 3-5). 1981. pap. 1.95 (ISBN 0-380-53520-3, 53520-3, Camelot). Avon.

--The Strange Invasion of Catfish Bend. LC 79-67487. (The Catfish Bend Stories Ser.). (Illus.). 160p. 1980. 10.95 (ISBN 0-8149-0828-4). Vanguard.

--Street of the Laughing Camel. 4.95 (ISBN 0-685-20506-1). Taplinger.

--Three from Catfish Bend. Incl. High Water at Catfish Bend; Seven Stars for Catfish Bend; The Owl Hoots Twice at Catfish Bend. LC 67-12490. (Illus.). (gr. 6 up). 6.95 (ISBN 0-8008-7676-8). Taplinger.

--Thunderbolt at Catfish Bend. (Catfish Bend Ser.). (Illus.). 114p. 1984. 10.95 (ISBN 0-914373-00-5, Dist. by Vanguard); pap. 3.95 (ISBN 0-943436-03-6). Wieser & Wieser.

--Thunderbolt at Catfish Bend. (Illus.). 128p. 1985. 10.95 (ISBN 0-914373-00-5). Vanguard.

Burman, Bina R. Religion & Politics in Tibet. 1979. text ed. 17.50x (ISBN 0-7069-0801-5, Pub. by Vikas India). Advent NY.

--Religion & Politics in Tibet. 180p. 1979. 14.00x (ISBN 0-7069-0801-5, Pub. by Vikas India). Advent NY.

Burman, C. R. How to Find Out in Chemistry. 2nd ed. LC 67-549. 1967. pap. 7.75 (ISBN 0-08-011880-1). Pergamon.

Burman, D., jt. auth. see McLaren, D.

Burman, Ian D. Lobbying at the Illinois Constitutional Convention. LC 72-95000. (Studies in Illinois Constitution Making Ser). 130p. 1973. pap. 10.00x (ISBN 0-252-00336-5). U of Ill Pr.

Burman, Madeleine L. Code of the Prophets. (Illus.). 100p. (Orig.). 1984. 14.95x; pap. 6.95x. M L Burman.

Burman, Margaret. Dream Prom. (Sweet Dreams Ser.: No. 45). 182p. (YA) 1983. pap. 2.25 (ISBN 0-553-24341-1). Bantam.

Burman, Maureen, jt. auth. see Zartman, I. William.

Burman, P. J. Precedence Networks for Project Planning & Control. 1980. 20.00x (ISBN 0-9606344-0-1). Blitz Pub Co.

Burman, S. B., jt. auth. see Bartrip, P. W.

Burman, Sandra. Chiefdom Politics & Alien Law. LC 79-25600. 250p. 1981. text ed. 44.50 (ISBN 0-8419-0591-6, Africana). Holmes & Meier.

Burman, Sandra, ed. Fit Work for Women. LC 78-25895. 1979. 22.50x (ISBN 0-312-29417-4). St Martin.

Burman, Sandra & Genn, Hazel, eds. Accidents in the Home. 140p. 1977. 25.00x (ISBN 0-85664-452-8, Pub. by Croom Helm Ltd). Longwood Pub Group.

Burman, Sandra B. & Harrell-Bond, Barbara E., eds. The Imposition of Law. LC 79-51671. (Studies on Law & Social Control). 1979. 27.50 (ISBN 0-12-145450-9). Acad Pr.

Burmaster, O., ed. see Baker, David.

Burmaster, O., ed. see Davis, H. L.

Burmaster, O., ed. see Deal, Susan S.

Burmaster, O., ed. see Hall, Hazel.

Burmaster, O. C., ed. see Beasley, W. Conger, Jr.

Burmaster, Orvis C., ed. see Ferril, Thomas H.

Burmaster, Orvis C., ed. see Haste, Gwendolen.

Burmaster, Orvis C., ed. see Krieger, Robert.

Burmeister. Foundations & Strategies for Teaching Children to Read. 704p. (Orig.). 1983. text ed. 23.05 (ISBN 0-201-10802-X). Addison-Wesley.

Burmeister, E. Capital Theory & Dynamics. LC 79-28412. (Cambridge Surveys of Economic Literature Ser.). 224p. 1980. 44.50 (ISBN 0-521-22889-1); pap. 17.95 (ISBN 0-521-29703-6). Cambridge U Pr.

Burmeister, Edwin. Nurse Little. (Illus.). 60p. 1984. pap. 4.95 (ISBN 0-8059-2923-1). Dorrance.

Burmeister, Edwin, jt. ed. see Klein, Lawrence R.

Burmeister, Eva, et al. Training for Child Care Staff. LC 63-18016. 1963. pap. 5.15 (ISBN 0-87868-065-9, I-27). Child Welfare.

Burmeister, Eva E. Forty Five in the Family: The Story of a Home for Children. LC 76-100147. Repr. of 1949 ed. lib. bdg. 15.00x (ISBN 0-8371-3259-2, BUFA). Greenwood.

--The Professional Houseparent. LC 60-6548. 244p. 1960. 29.50x (ISBN 0-231-02370-7). Columbia U Pr.

Burmeister, Jill & Hutchinson, Rosemary, eds. Better Homes & Gardens Complete Quick & Easy Cook Book. 1983. 24.95 (ISBN 0-696-00725-8). BH&G.

Burmeister, L. C. Convective Heat Transfer. 790p. 1982. 51.95 (ISBN 0-471-09141-3). Wiley.

Burmeister, Lou E. Reading Strategies for Middle & Secondary School Teaching. 2nd ed. LC 77-88054. (Education Ser.). (Illus.). 1978. text ed. 21.90 (ISBN 0-201-00316-3, Sch Div). Addison-Wesley.

Burmeister, Magdalene. Against the Shifting Sands. 1974. 6.00 (ISBN 0-8233-0203-2). Golden Quill.

Burmeister, Walter F. Appalachian Waters, I: The Delaware River & Its Tributaries. LC 74-80983. 1974. 10.00 (ISBN 0-912660-19-8); pap. 6.95 (ISBN 0-686-96660-0). Appalachian Bks.

--Appalachian Waters 2: The Hudson River & Its Tributaries. LC 74-80983. 1974. pap. 7.50 (ISBN 0-912660-20-1). Appalachian Bks.

--Appalachian Waters 3: The Susquehanna River & Its Tributaries. LC 74-983. 1975. pap. 8.50 (ISBN 0-912660-21-X). Appalachian Bks.

--Appalachian Waters 4: Southeastern U. S. Rivers. LC 74-80983. 1975. pap. 10.00 (ISBN 0-912660-22-8). Appalachian Bks.

--Appalachian Waters 5: The Upper Ohio & Its Tributaries. Mallinoff, Estelle, ed. 600p. 1978. pap. 12.50 (ISBN 0-912660-23-6). Appalachian Bks.

Burmeister, William, jt. auth. see Wright, Joan.

Burmyn, Lynne & Baldwin, Christina. Sun Signs for Kids. 272p. 1985. pap. 6.95 (ISBN 0-312-77562-8). St Martin.

Burn, A. E. The Athanasian Creed & Its Early Commentaries. (Texts & Studies Ser.: No. 1, Vol. 4, Pt. 1). pap. 19.00 (ISBN 0-317-16750-2). Kraus Repr.

Burn, A. R. Persia & the Greeks: The Defense of the West, c. 546-478 B.C. rev. ed. LC 83-40516. (Illus.). 640p. 1984. Repr. of 1962 ed. 39.50x (ISBN 0-8047-1235-2). Stanford U Pr.

Burn, Andrew R. Alexander the Great & the Hellenistic Empire. LC 83-45724. Repr. of 1948 ed. 33.50 (ISBN 0-404-20048-6). AMS Pr.

--Minoans, Philistines & Greeks, B. C. 1400-900. LC 74-14350. (Illus.). 273p. 1975. Repr. of 1930 ed. lib. bdg. 22.50x (ISBN 0-8371-7794-4, BUMI). Greenwood.

--Pelican History of Greece. Orig. Title: Traveller's History of Greece. 1966. pap. 4.95 (ISBN 0-14-020792-9, Pelican). Penguin.

--World of Hesiod. LC 66-29859. 1966. Repr. of 1936 ed. 15.00 (ISBN 0-405-08332-7, Blom Pubns). Ayer Co Pubs.

Burn, Barbara. Metropolitan Children. (Illus.). 112p. 1984. 14.95 (ISBN 0-87099-373-9). Metro Mus Art.

--Metropolitan Children. (Illus.). 112p. 1985. 27.50 (ISBN 0-8109-1321-6). Abrams.

Burn, Barbara, ed. Utamaro: Songs of the Garden. Betchaku, Yasuko & Mirviss, Joan B., trs. from Japanese. LC 84-60004. (Illus.). 48p. 16.95 (ISBN 0-87099-368-2). Metro Mus Art.

--Yves Saint Laurent Exhibition Checklist. 1984. pap. 1.95 (ISBN 0-317-05156-3). Metro Mus Art.

Burn, Barbara B. Expanding the International Dimension of Higher Education. LC 79-24879. (Higher Education Ser.). 1980. text ed. 19.95x (ISBN 0-87589-444-5). Jossey-Bass.

Burn, Barbara B. & Karmal, Peter. Federal-State Responsibilities for Postsecondary Education: Australia & the United States. 1977. pap. 2.00 (ISBN 0-89192-237-7, Pub. by ICED). Interbk Inc.

Burn, Barbara B., ed. Admission to Medical Education in Ten Countries. (Access to Higher Education Ser.). 1978. pap. 6.00 (ISBN 0-89192-214-8, Pub. by ICED). Interbk Inc.

--Higher Education Reform: Implications for Foreign Students. LC 78-58811. 1978. pap. text ed. 11.95 (ISBN 0-87206-089-6). Inst Intl Educ.

Burn, Billie. Stirrin' the Pots on Daufuskie. 212p. (Orig.). 1985. pap. 8.50x (ISBN 0-9614670-0-2). Burn Books.

Burn, Doris. Andrew-Henry's Meadow. (Illus.). (gr. k-3). 1965. PLB 4.99 (ISBN 0-698-30011-4, Coward). Putnam Pub Group.

Burn, Duncan. Nuclear Power & the Energy Crisis: Politics & the Atomic Industry. LC 78-412. 348p. 1978. 32.50x, USA (ISBN 0-8147-0998-2). NYU Pr.

Burn, Duncan, et al. Lessons from Central Forecasting. (Institute of Economic Affairs, Eaton Papers Ser.: No. 6). (Illus., Orig.). 1969. pap. 2.50 technical (ISBN 0-255-69513-6). Transatlantic.

Burn, Edward H., jt. auth. see Maudsley, Ronald H.

Burn, Gordon. Somebody's Husband, Somebody's Son: The Story of the Yorkshire Ripper. 288p. 1985. 16.95 (ISBN 0-670-80328-6). Viking.

Burn, Helen J. Better Than the Birds, Smarter Than the Bees. LC 69-12771. (YA) pap. 21.30 (ISBN 0-8357-9000-2, 2016348). Bks Demand UMI.

Burn, James D. The Autobiography of a Beggar Boy. 1978. cancelled (ISBN 0-905118-26-X). Intl Pubns Serv.

--Three Years among the Working-Classes in the United States During the War. LC 74-22735. 328p. Repr. of 1865 ed. 34.50 (ISBN 0-404-58487-X). AMS Pr.

Burn, L., jt. auth. see Paterson, J. K.

Burn, Lucilla & Glynn, Ruth. Beazley Addenda: Additional References to ABV, ARV2, & Paralipomena. (British Academy Ser.). 1982. 39.95x (ISBN 0-19-726018-7). Oxford U Pr.

Burn, R. P. Groups: A Path to Geometry. (Illus.). 254p. Date not set. 49.50 (ISBN 0-521-30037-1). Cambridge U Pr.

--A Pathway into Number Theory. LC 81-10013. 250p. 1982. 42.50 (ISBN 0-521-24118-9); pap. 16.95 (ISBN 0-521-28534-8). Cambridge U Pr.

Burn, Richard. History of the Poor Laws. LC 72-77052. Repr. of 1764 ed. 37.50x (ISBN 0-678-00928-7). Kelley.

--The History of the Poor Laws: With Observations-1764. 1981. write for info. (ISBN 0-08-027644-X, HE 028); microfiche 25.00 (ISBN 0-686-79344-7). Pergamon.

--The Justice of the Peace & Parish Officer: 1756. 3rd ed. 1981. write for info. (ISBN 0-08-027643-1, HE 072); microfiche 65.00 (ISBN 0-686-79349-8). Pergamon.

Burn, Richard, jt. ed. see Fawcett, Charles.

Burn, Samuel C. Jonah. 1981. lib. bdg. 11.25 (ISBN 0-86524-071-X, 3201). Klock & Klock.

Burn, William L. The British West Indies. LC 73-21259. (Illus.). 196p. 1975. Repr. of 1951 ed. lib. bdg. 22.50x (ISBN 0-8371-6138-X, BUBW). Greenwood.

Burnaby, Andrew. Travels Through the Middle Settlements of North America. 3rd ed. LC 68-55496. Repr. of 1914 ed. 27.50x (ISBN 0-678-00682-2). Kelley.

Burnaby, Fred. Ride to Khiva: Travels & Adventures in Central Asia. LC 79-115513. (Russia Observed, Ser., No. 1). 1970. Repr. of 1877 ed. 20.00 (ISBN 0-405-03010-X). Ayer Co Pubs.

--A Ride to Khiva: Travels & Adventures in Central Asia. 400p. 1983. pap. 11.95 (ISBN 0-7126-0093-0). Hippocrene Bks.

--A Ride to Khiva-Travels & Adventures in Central Asia. (Travel Classics Ser.). 400p. 1985. lib. bdg. 23.95 (ISBN 0-7126-0094-9, Pub. by Century Pubs UK). Hippocrene Bks.

Burnaby, Frederick. On Horseback Through Asia Minor. 324p. 1985. pap. 5.95 (ISBN 0-87052-211-6, Pub. by Settle & Bendall England). Hippocrene Bks.

Burnaby, John, ed. Augustine: Later Works. LC 55-5022. (Library of Christian Classics). 356p. 1980. pap. 11.95 (ISBN 0-664-24165-4). Westminster.

Burnaby, Sherrard B. Elements of the Jewish Muhammadan Calendars. 1976. lib. bdg. 59.95 (ISBN 0-8490-1757-2). Gordon Pr.

Burnacini, Lodovico O. Vestalische Ewige Feuer (Il Fuoco Eterno) LC 68-21208. (Illus., Ger). 1969. Repr. of 1674 ed. 49.50 (ISBN 0-405-08333-5). Ayer Co Pubs.

Burnam, Cissy, ed. see Junior League of Richardson, Inc.

Burnam, Tom. The Dictionary of Misinformation. 1977. pap. 2.50 (ISBN 0-345-29534-X). Ballantine.

--Dictionary of Misinformation. LC 75-15651. 352p. 1975. 18.22i (ISBN 0-690-00147-9). T Y Crowell.

--More Misinformation. 1981. pap. 2.50 (ISBN 0-345-29251-0). Ballantine.

--More Misinformation. 288p. 1980. 16.30i (ISBN 0-690-01685-9). T Y Crowell.

Burnand, F. C; see Gilbert, W. S.

Burnand, Tony. Dictionnaire Chasse. (Dictionnaires de l'homme du vingtieme siecle). (Fr., Fr). 1970. 8.50 (ISBN 0-685-13859-3, 3711). Larousse.

--Dictionnaire de la Chasse. 250p. (Fr.). 1970. pap. 7.50 (ISBN 0-686-56817-6, M-6595, Pub. by Larousse). French & Eur.

Burnap, jt. auth. see Edmundson.

Burnap, Raymond U. Extension of Human Capability & Function Through Reflex Conditioning. pap. 1.00 (ISBN 0-87505-302-5). Borden.

Burnard, Francis C. My Time & What I've Done with It: An Autobiography, Compiled from the Diary, Notes & Personal Recollections of Cecil Colvin, 1874. (Victorian Fiction Ser.). 1976. lib. bdg. 73.00 (ISBN 0-8240-1535-5). Garland Pub.

Burnce, Frances, tr. see Gordon, A. D.

Burnchurch, Richard de. An Outline of Dutch History. (Illus.). 1982. pap. 10.00 (ISBN 90-6432-002-0). Heinman.

Burne, Alfred H. The Agincourt War. LC 75-17190. 1976. Repr. of 1956 ed. lib. bdg. 37.50x (ISBN 0-8371-8300-6, BUAW). Greenwood.

--The Crecy War: A Military History of the Hundred Years War from 1337 to the Peace of Bretigny, 1360. LC 75-17195. (Illus.). 1976. Repr. of 1955 ed. lib. bdg. 29.75 (ISBN 0-8371-8301-4, BUCW). Greenwood.

Burne, Charlotte S., ed. Handbook of Folklore. rev. & enl. ed. (Folk-Lore Society London Monograph: Vol. 73). pap. 29.00 (ISBN 0-317-16726-X). Kraus Repr.

Burne, Glenn S. Remy De Gourmont: His Ideas & Influence in England & America. LC 63-14295. (Crosscurrents-Modern Critiques Ser.). 205p. 1963. 7.95 (ISBN 0-8093-0105-9). S Ill U Pr.

--Richard F. Burton, No. 412. (Twayne English Author Ser.). 192p. 1985. lib. bdg. 21.95 (ISBN 0-8057-6903-X, Twayne). G K Hall.

Burne, Kevin G., et al. Functional English for Writers. 2nd ed. 1978. pap. 14.95x (ISBN 0-673-15105-0). Scott F.

Burne, Neville B. The Restless Ocean. (Illus.). 1979. 20.00 (ISBN 0-900963-45-X, Pub. by Terence Dalton England). State Mutual Bk.

Burne-Jones, Edward. The Pre-Raphaelite Drawings of Edward Burne-Jones. (Dover Art Library). (Illus.). 48p. (Orig.). 1981. pap. 2.50 (ISBN 0-486-24113-0). Dover.

Burne-Jones, Georgiana. Memorials of Edward Burne-Jones, 2 vols. in 1. LC 71-174396. (Illus.). Repr. of 1904 ed. 35.00 (ISBN 0-405-08334-3, Blom Pubns.). Ayer Co Pubs.

--Memorials of Edward Burne-Jones, 2 vols. 1904. Repr. 50.00 set (ISBN 0-8274-2710-7). R West.

Burne-Jones, Georgiana M. Memorials of Edward Burne-Jones, 2 vols. in 1. facsimile ed. LC 74-179508. (Select Bibliographies Reprint Ser). Repr. of 1904 ed. 43.00 (ISBN 0-8369-6637-6). Ayer Co Pubs.

Burnell, Arthur C., ed. see Van Linschoten, Jan H.

Burnell, Genevieve. Golden Thread of Reality. 1967. 6.95 (ISBN 0-8038-2613-3). Hastings.

Burner, David. America: A Portrait in History. 2nd ed. 783p. 1976. pap. text ed. 8.95 (ISBN 0-13-024257-8). Revisionary.

--Herbert Hoover: A Public Life. LC 83-45517. (Illus.). 448p. 1984. pap. 12.95 (ISBN 0-689-70669-3, 311). Atheneum.

--Herbert Hoover: The Public Life. LC 78-54912. (Illus.). 1978. 17.95 (ISBN 0-394-46134-7). Knopf.

--The Politics of Provincialism: The Democratic Party in Transition, 1918 to 1932. LC 81-6542. (Illus.). 1981. Repr. of 1968 ed. lib. bdg. 27.50x (ISBN 0-313-22926-0, BUPP). Greenwood.

Burner, David & Genovese, Eugene D. An American Portrait: A History of the United States, 2 vols. 1983. Vol. I. 14.95 (ISBN 0-686-78514-2); Vol. II. 14.95 (ISBN 0-686-78515-0); combined ed. 19.95 (ISBN 0-686-76463-3). Revisionary.

Burner, David & Marcus, Robert. American Voices: A Historical Reader, 2 vols. 1979. pap. 11.90x ea. Vol. 1 (ISBN 0-673-15172-7). Vol. 2 (ISBN 0-673-15173-5). Scott F.

Burner, David & Marcus, Robert D. America Personified: Portraits from History, 2 vols. LC 74-76210. 224p. (Orig.). 1974. pap. text ed. 10.95 ea. Vol. 1 (ISBN 0-312-03010-X). Vol. 2, o.p (ISBN 0-312-03045-2). St Martin.

Burner, David & West, Thomas. The Torch Is Passed: The Kennedy Brothers & American Liberalism. LC 83-45506. 320p. 1984. 16.95 (ISBN 0-689-11438-9). Atheneum.

Burner, David, jt. ed. see Marcus, Robert D.

Burner, David, et al. An American Portrait, Vol.I. 2nd ed. 416p. 1985. pap. text ed. price not set (ISBN 0-02-371250-3, Pub. by Scribner). Macmillan.

--An American Portrait, Vol. II. 2nd ed. 416p. 1985. pap. text ed. price not set (ISBN 0-02-371270-8, Pub. by Scribner). Macmillan.

--An American Portrait: Combined Edition, Vol. II. 2nd ed. 1985. text ed. price not set (ISBN 0-02-371260-0, Pub. by Scribner). Macmillan.

--The American People, 2 vols. Incl. Vol. I. To Eighteen Seventy-Seven. 342p (ISBN 0-9603726-2-8); Vol. II. From Eighteen Sixty. 440p (ISBN 0-9603726-3-6). (Illus., Orig.). 1980. Combined Edition. pap. text ed. 16.95 (ISBN 0-9603726-0-1); pap. text ed. 11.95 ea. Revisionary.

--America: A Portrait in History. 2nd ed. Incl. Combined Edition. pap. 24.95 (ISBN 0-13-024257-8); Vol. 1. pap. text ed. 16.95 (ISBN 0-13-024232-2); Vol. 2. pap. text ed. 16.95 (ISBN 0-13-024240-3). (Illus.). 1978. P-H.

Burnes, A. Patricia & Steinhoff, Virginia, eds. Connections: Interdisciplinary Approaches to Teaching. LC 83-62569. 171p. (Orig.). 1983. pap. 5.95 (ISBN 0-915032-97-X). Natl Poet Foun.

Burnes, Sir Alexander. Travels into Bokhara, 3 vols. (Oxford in Asia Historical Reprints). 1973. Set. 34.95x (ISBN 0-19-636061-7). Oxford U Pr.

Burnes, Robert I., ed. The Worlds of Alfonso the Learned & James the Conqueror: Intellect & Force in the Middle Ages. LC 85-42678. (Illus.). 276p. 1985. text ed. 27.00x (ISBN 0-691-05451-7). Princeton U Pr.

Burnes, Robert L. Big Red: The Story of the Football Cardinals. new ed. LC 75-11160. (Illus.). 256p. 1975. lib. bdg. 4.95 (ISBN 0-913656-05-4, Piraeus). Forum Pr IL.

Burness, Don, ed. Wanasema: Conversations with African Writers. (CIS Africa Ser.: No. 46). 108p. 1985. pap. text ed. 9.00x (ISBN 0-89680-129-2, Ohio U Ctr Intl). Ohio U Pr.

Burness, Donald. Fire: Six Writers from Angola, Mozambique, & Cape Verde. LC 77-3840. 150p. (Eng. & Port.). 1977. 15.00x (ISBN 0-914478-51-6); pap. 7.00 (ISBN 0-914478-52-4). Three Continents.

--Shaka, King of the Zulus, in African Literature. LC 76-904. 1976. 18.00 (ISBN 0-914478-29-X); pap. 10.00 (ISBN 0-914478-30-3). Three Continents.

Burness, Donald, compiled by. Critical Perspectives on Lusophone Literature from Africa. LC 80-53348. (Illus.). 307p. 1981. 24.00 (ISBN 0-89410-015-7); pap. 14.00 (ISBN 0-89410-016-5). Three Continents.

Burness, Tad. American Car Spotter's Guide 1940-1965. rev. ed. LC 78-14879. (Illus.). 1978. pap. 13.95 (ISBN 0-87938-057-8). Motorbooks Intl.

--American Car Spotter's Guide: 1966-1980. LC 80-26337. (Illus.). 432p. (Orig.). 1981. pap. 18.95 (ISBN 0-87938-102-7). Motorbooks Intl.

--American Truck Spotter's Guide 1920-1970. LC 77-18535. (Illus.). 1978. pap. 16.95 (ISBN 0-87938-040-3). Motorbooks Intl.

--Chevy Spotter's Guide: 1920-1980. 9.95 (ISBN 0-87938-151-5). Motorbooks Intl.

--Imported Car Spotter's Guide. LC 79-24498. (Illus.). 351p. 1980. pap. 15.95 (ISBN 0-87938-067-5). Motorbooks Intl.

Burness, Taqd. Pickup & Van Spotter's Guide, 1945-1982. (Spotter's Guide Ser.). (Illus.). 160p. 1982. pap. 11.95 (ISBN 0-87938-156-6). Motorbooks Intl.

Burnet, Alastair & Landels, Willie. The Time of Our Lives. (Illus.). 208p. 1981. 26.00 (ISBN 0-241-10666-4, Pub. by Hamish Hamilton England). David & Charles.

--The Times of Our Lives: A Pictorial History of Britain since 1945. 208p. 30.00x (ISBN 0-241-10666-4, Pub. by Hamish Hamilton England). State Mutual Bk.

Burnet, Bishop. History of His Own Times. 409p. 1980. Repr. lib. bdg. 12.50 (ISBN 0-89987-056-2). Darby Bks.

Burnet, Charles. Three Centuries to Concorde. 288p. 1979. casebound 22.00 (ISBN 0-85298-412-X, MEP-113, Pub. by Institution of Mechanical Engineers). Soc Auto Engineers.

Burnet, David S. & Davis, Moshe, eds. The Jerusalem Mission: Under the Direction of the American Christian Missionary Society. (America & the Holy Land Ser.). 1977. Repr. of 1853 ed. lib. bdg. 26.50x (ISBN 0-405-10233-X). Ayer Co Pubs.

Burnet, F. M. & Stanley, W. M., eds. The Viruses: Biochemical, Biological & Biophysical Properties. Incl. Vol. 1. General Virology. 1959; Vol. 2. Plant & Bacterial Viruses. 1959. 66.00 (ISBN 0-12-145602-1); Vol. 3. Animal Viruses. 1959. Acad Pr.

Burnet, F. M., intro. by. Immunology: Readings from Scientific American. LC 75-19356. (Illus.). 275p. 1976. pap. text ed. 11.95 (ISBN 0-7167-0524-9). W H Freeman.

Burnet, F. Macfarlane. Endurance of Life. (Illus.). 1980. pap. 11.95 (ISBN 0-521-29783-4). Cambridge U Pr.

--Endurance of Life. LC 78-54323. (Illus.). 1978. 32.50 (ISBN 0-521-22114-5). Cambridge U Pr.

Burnet, F. Macfarlane & White, D. O. Natural History of Infectious Disease. 4th ed. LC 74-174264. (Illus.). 400p. 1972. 47.50 (ISBN 0-521-08389-3); pap. 17.95 (ISBN 0-521-09688-X). Cambridge U Pr.

Burnet, F. Macfarlane, jt. auth. see Mackay, Ian R.

Burnet, Frank M. Integrity of the Body: A Discussion of Modern Immunological Ideas. LC 62-8180. (Books in Biology Ser: No. 3). (Illus.). 1962. 15.00x (ISBN 0-674-45650-5). Harvard U Pr.

Burnet, Gilbert. History of His Own Time. 1979. Repr. of 1906 ed. 12.95x (ISBN 0-460-00085-3, Evman). Biblio Dist.

--The History of the Reformation of the Church of England, 7 vols. rev. ed. LC 83-45575. Date not set. Repr. of 1865 ed. Set. 425.00 (ISBN 0-404-19893-7). Ams Pr.

--Some Passages in the Life & Death of John Earl of Rochester. LC 73-12355. 1787. lib. bdg. 25.00 (ISBN 0-8414-3202-3). Folcroft.

Burnet, Jacob. Notes on the Early Settlement of the North-Western Territory. facsimile ed. LC 75-90. (Mid-American Frontier Ser.). 1975. Repr. of 1847 ed. 37.50x (ISBN 0-405-06857-3). Ayer Co Pubs.

Burnet, Jean. Next-Year Country: A Study of Rural Social Organization in Alberta. LC 52-1704. xii, 188p. 1978. pap. 7.50 (ISBN 0-8020-6340-3). U of Toronto Pr.

Burnet, John. Early Greek Philosophy. 4th ed. 375p. 1963. Repr. of 1930 ed. 23.50x (ISBN 0-06-490783-X, 06374). B&N Imports.

--Essays & Addresses. facs. ed. LC 68-54335. (Essay Index Reprint Ser). 1968. Repr. of 1930 ed. 18.00 (ISBN 0-8369-0265-3). Ayer Co Pubs.

--Platonism. LC 83-1503. (Sather Classical Lectures Ser.: Vol. 5). 130p. 1983. Repr. of 1928 ed. lib. bdg. 27.50x (ISBN 0-313-23699-2, BUPL). Greenwood.

Burnet, John, ed. see Aristotle.

Burnet, John, ed. see Plato.

Burnet, M. The Walter & Eliza Hall Institute, 1915-1965. 1971. 17.50x (ISBN 0-522-84007-8, Pub. by Melbourne U Pr). Intl Spec Bk.

Burnet, Margaret. Letters from Lady Margaret Burnet. LC 74-39562. (Bannatyne Club, Edinburgh. Publications: No. 24). Repr. of 1828 ed. 17.50 (ISBN 0-404-52730-2). AMS Pr.

Burnet, Mary. The Mass Media in a Violent World. (Reports & Papers on Mass Communication: No. 63). 44p. 1971. pap. 5.00 (ISBN 92-3-100904-4, U371, UNESCO). Unipub.

Burnet, Michael & Lawrence, Ian, eds. Music Education Review: A Handbook for Music Teachers, Vol. 2. 228p. 1980. 16.00x (ISBN 0-85633-196-1, Pub. by NFER Nelson UK). Taylor & Francis.

Burnet, Thomas. Remarks upon an Essay Concerning Humane Understanding: In a Letter Address'd to the Author. LC 83-48565. 92p. 1984. lib. bdg. 20.00 (ISBN 0-8240-5600-0). Garland Pub.

--Sacred Theory of the Earth. LC 65-10027. (Centaur Classics Ser.). (Illus.). 414p. 1965. 22.50x (ISBN 0-8093-0186-5). S Ill U Pr.

Burnett & Wiggins. Today's Creative Children: Sing, Play & Move. 320p. 1983. pap. text ed. 17.95 (ISBN 0-8403-2672-6). Kendall-Hunt.

Burnett, Alan, jt. ed. see Burnett, Robin.

Burnett, Alan D. & Taylor, Peter J. Political Studies from Spatial Perspectives: Anglo-American Essays on Political Geography. LC 80-41384. 519p. 1981. 73.95x (ISBN 0-471-27909-9, Pub. by Wiley-Interscience); pap. 34.95 (ISBN 0-471-27910-2). Wiley.

Burnett, Allison L., ed. Biology of Hydra. 1973. 72.00 (ISBN 0-12-145950-0). Acad Pr.

Burnett, Anne P. The Art of Bacchylides. (Martin Classical Lectures Ser.: 29). 224p. 1985. text ed. 22.50x (ISBN 0-674-04666-8). Harvard U Pr.

--Catastrophe Survived: Euripides' Plays of Mixed Reversal. 244p. 1985. pap. 14.95 (ISBN 0-19-814038-X). Oxford U Pr.

--Three Archaic Poets: Archilochus, Alcaeus, Sappho. 336p. 1983. text ed. 25.00x (ISBN 0-674-88820-0). Harvard U Pr.

Burnett, Arthur C. Yankees in the Republic of Texas: Their Origin & Impact. 1952. 7.50 (ISBN 0-685-05007-6). A Jones.

Burnett, Arthur L. A Survey of Significant Court Decisions of the Rights of Federal Employees Since the Civil Reform Act of 1978. 123p. 10.00 (ISBN 0-318-14098-5). Federal Bar.

Burnett, Barbara A. Everywoman's Legal Guide: Protecting Your Rights at Home, in the Workplace, & in the Marketplace. LC 85-10158. 600p. 1983. 19.95 (ISBN 0-385-18523-5). Doubleday.

Burnett, Ben G. Political Groups in Chile: The Dialogue Between Order & Change. (Latin American Monographs Ser.: No. 21). 333p. 1970. 14.95x (ISBN 0-292-70084-9). U of Tex Pr.

Burnett, Ben G. & Troncoso, Moises P. The Rise of the Latin American Labor Movement. 1960. 9.95x (ISBN 0-8084-0405-9); pap. 6.95x (ISBN 0-8084-0406-7). New Coll U Pr.

Burnett, Bernice. Holidays. (First Bks). (Illus.). 96p. (gr. 4up). 8.90 (ISBN 0-531-04646-X). Watts.

Burnett, C. T. see Wang, Tsu Lien.

Burnett, C. W. The Anatomy & Physiology of Obstetrics. 6th ed. Anderson, Mary, ed. (Illus.). 1979. pap. 7.95 (ISBN 0-571-04992-3). Faber & Faber.

Burnett, Collins W., jt. auth. see White, Jane N.

Burnett, Constance B. Captain John Ericsson: Father of the Monitor. LC 60-15070. (gr. 7 up). 6.95 (ISBN 0-8149-0284-7). Vanguard.

--Five for Freedom: Lucretia Mott, Elizabeth Cady Stanton, Lucy Stone, Susan B. Anthony, Carrie Chapman Catt. LC 68-8734. (Illus.). 1968. Repr. of 1953 ed. lib. bdg. 19.25x (ISBN 0-8371-0034-8, BUFF). Greenwood.

Burnett, David & Schiff, Marilyn. Contemporary Canadian Art. (Illus.). 300p. 1984. 27.95x (ISBN 0-295-96116-3, Hurtig Publishers Ltd.); pap. 19.95 (ISBN 0-295-96121-X). U of Wash Pr.

Burnett, David, jt. ed. see Foley, Martha.

Burnett, E. C. Letters of Members of the Continental Congress, 1774-1789, 8 vols. 18.00 ea. (ISBN 0-8446-1095-X); Set. 144.00. Peter Smith.

Burnett, Edmund C. The Continental Congress. LC 75-25252. 757p. 1976. Repr. of 1941 ed. lib. bdg. 43.25x (ISBN 0-8371-8386-3, BUCC). Greenwood.

Burnett, Frances. Jarl's Daughter & Other Novelettes. facsimile ed. LC 75-94708. (Short Story Index Reprint Ser). 1883. 14.00 (ISBN 0-8369-3087-8). Ayer Co Pubs.

--The Secret Garden. 302p. 1981. Repr. PLB 16.95x (ISBN 0-89966-326-5). Buccaneer Bks.

--Secret Garden. 1977. 16.95 (ISBN 0-89967-001-6). Harmony Raine.

--Surly Tim & Other Stories. facsimile ed. LC 77-103500. (Short Story Index Reprint Ser). 1877. 19.00 (ISBN 0-8369-3242-0). Ayer Co Pubs.

Burnett, Frances H. Haworth's. LC 79-3328. Repr. of 1879 ed. 44.50 (ISBN 0-404-61799-9). AMS Pr.

--Little Lord Fauntleroy. (Illus.). 252p. 1981. Repr. PLB 16.95x (ISBN 0-89966-288-9). Buccaneer Bks.

--Little Lord Fauntleroy. 1977. 16.95x (ISBN 0-89967-002-4). Buccaneer Bks.

--Little Lord Fauntleroy. (Puffin Story Bks.). 190p. (gr. 7 up). 1985. pap. 2.25 (ISBN 0-14-035025-X, Puffin). Penguin.

--Little Lord Fauntleroy. (Children's Illustrated Classics). (Illus.). 218p. 1975. Repr. of 1962 ed. 11.00x (ISBN 0-460-05054-0, BKA 01579, Pub. by J. M. Dent England). Biblio Dist.

--Little Lord Fauntleroy. 1986. pap. 4.95 (ISBN 0-317-20483-1, YB). Dell.

--A Little Princess. 232p. 1981. Repr. PLB 15.95 (ISBN 0-89966-327-3). Buccaneer Bks.

--A Little Princess. 240p. (gr. 5-9). 1975. pap. 3.25 (ISBN 0-440-44767-4, YB). Dell.

--Little Princess. LC 63-15435. (Illus.). (gr. 4-6). 1963. 12.45i (ISBN 0-397-30693-8); PLB 12.89 (ISBN 0-397-31339-X). Lipp Jr Bks.

--A Little Princess. 300p. 1977. PLB 12.95x (ISBN 0-89967-005-9). Harmony Raine.

--A Little Princess. (Puffin Classics Ser.). 224p. 1984. pap. 2.25 (ISBN 0-14-035028-4, Puffin). Penguin.

--The One I Know Best of All. LC 79-8779. (Signal Lives Ser.). 1980. Repr. of 1893 ed. lib. bdg. 36.00x (ISBN 0-405-12828-2). Ayer Co Pubs.

--The Racketty-Packetty House. LC 75-8531. (Illus.). 64p. (gr. 2-5). 1975. 9.57i (ISBN 0-397-31642-9). Lipp Jr Bks.

--Secret Garden. 304p. (gr. 4 up). 1971. pap. 3.50 (ISBN 0-440-47706-9, YB). Dell.

--Secret Garden. LC 85-10291. (Illus.). (gr. 5-9). 1985. Repr. of 1962 ed. 8.61i (ISBN 0-397-30632-6); PLB 8.89g (ISBN 0-397-32162-7). Lipp Jr Bks.

--The Secret Garden. (Children's Illustrated Classics). 256p. 1975. 11.00x (ISBN 0-460-05101-6, Pub. by J. M. Dent England). Biblio Dist.

--That Lass O' Lowrie's, 2 vols. in 1. LC 79-3329. Repr. of 1877 ed. 44.50 (ISBN 0-404-61798-0). AMS Pr.

--That Lass O'Lowrie. 224p. 1985. pap. 5.95 (ISBN 0-85115-239-2, Pub. by Boydell England). Academy Chi Pubs.

--Through One Administration. LC 67-29260. lib. bdg. 12.50 (ISBN 0-8398-0181-5); pap. text ed. 6.50x (ISBN 0-89197-965-4). Irvington.

--Through One Administration. (American Studies Ser). 1969. Repr. of 1883 ed. 18.00 (ISBN 0-384-06585-6). Johnson Repr.

Burnett, Frances H; see Avery, Gillian.

Burnett, Frances H see Swan, D. K.

Burnett, Francis, ed. The School Counselor's Involvement in Career Education. 212p. 1980. members 7.50 (ISBN 0-686-36400-7); non-members 9.00 (ISBN 0-911547-65-7, 72142W34). Am Assn Coun Dev.

Burnett, Francis H. Sara Crewe. (Illus.). 96p. (Orig.). (gr. 4-6). 1986. pap. 2.25 (ISBN 0-590-33980-X, Apple Paperbacks). Scholastic Inc.

Burnett, Fred W. The Testament of Jesus-Sophia: A Redaction-Critical Study of the Eschatological Discourse in Matthew. LC 80-67211. 491p. (Orig.). 1981. lib. bdg. 32.25 (ISBN 0-8191-1743-9); pap. text ed. 19.50 (ISBN 0-8191-1744-7). U Pr of Amer.

Burnett, G. F. Field Observations on the Behavior of the Red Locust (Nomadacris Septemfasciata Serville) in the Solitary Phase. 1951. 40.00x (ISBN 0-85135-006-2, Pub. by Centre Overseas Research). State Mutual Bk.

Burnett, Gail, ed. Inner Strings, Poetry. pap. 3.00 (ISBN 0-318-03121-3). Aegis Pub Co.

--Thyrsus-Poems. pap. 6.00 (ISBN 0-318-03122-1). Aegis Pub Co.

Burnett, George, jt. auth. see Woodward, John.

Burnett, Hallie. On Writing the Short Story. LC 82-48111. 192p. 1983. 13.95i (ISBN 0-06-015094-7, HarpT). Har-Row.

Burnett, Hallie & Burnett, Whit. Fiction Writer's Handbook. LC 74-1797. 1979. pap. 5.72i (ISBN 0-06-463492-2, EH 492, EH). B&N NY.

--Fiction Writer's Handbook. LC 74-1797. 224p. 1975. 12.45i (ISBN 0-06-010574-7, HarpT). Har-Row.

Burnett, Hallie & Burnett, Whit, eds. Sextet: Six Story Discoveries in the Novella Form. LC 51-13446. 1968. Repr. of 1951 ed. 15.00 (ISBN 0-527-13700-6). Kraus Repr.

Burnett, J. Dale. LOGO: An Introduction. LC 82-73547. (Illus.). 72p. 1983. pap. 7.95 (ISBN 0-916688-39-9, 12L). Creative Comp.

Burnett, J. H. Mycogenetics: An Introduction to the General Genetics of Fungi. LC 74-13143. 375p. 1975. 79.95 (ISBN 0-471-12445-1, Pub. by Wiley-Interscience); pap. 18.95 o. p. (ISBN 0-471-12446-X). Wiley.

Burnett, J. H. & Trinci, A. P., eds. Fungal Walls & Hyphal Growth. LC 78-72082. (Illus.). 1980. 82.50 (ISBN 0-521-22499-3). Cambridge U Pr.

Burnett, Jacquetta, jt. ed. see Kimball, Solon T.

Burnett, Jacquetta H., et al. Anthropology & Education: An Annotated Bibliographic Guide. LC 73-94324. (Bibliographies Ser.). 168p. 1974. 15.00x (ISBN 0-87536-231-1); pap. 7.50x (ISBN 0-87536-232-X). HRAFP.

Burnett, James. Coleman Hawkins. (Jazz Masters Ser.). (Illus.). 100p. 1985. 6.95 (ISBN 0-87052-009-1). Hippocrene Bks.

--The Music of Gustav Mahler. LC 84-29790. 232p. 1985. 27.50 (ISBN 0-8386-3167-3). Fairleigh Dickinson.

--Of the Origin & Progress of Language, 6 vols. 1975. Repr. 302.00x set (ISBN 3-4870-5432-9). Adlers Foreign Bks.

Burnett, James, jt. auth. see Gammond, Peter.

Burnett, Jane. Crucigramas Para Estudiantes. (Illus.). 64p. (Span.). 1983. pap. 3.95 (ISBN 0-8442-7230-2, 7230-2, Passport Bks). Natl Textbk.

Burnett, John. Plenty & Want. 1979. pap. 7.95 (ISBN 0-85967-462-2). Scolar.

--Plenty & Want: A Social History of Diet in England from 1815 to the Present Day. 388p. (Orig.). 1985. pap. 8.95 (ISBN 0-85967-461-4, NO. 9344). Methuen Inc.

--A Social History of Housing Eighteen Fifteen to Nineteen Seventy. 352p. (Orig.). 1985. pap. 13.95 (ISBN 0-416-73720-X, NO. 9343). Methuen Inc.

Burnett, John, jt. auth. see Putnam, Robert E.

Burnett, John, ed. & intro. by. Destiny Obscure: Autobiographies of Childhood, Education & Family from the 1820s to the 1920s. (Penguin Nonfiction Ser.). 352p. 1985. pap. 10.95 (ISBN 0-14-007345-0). Penguin.

--Useful Toil: Autobiographies of Working People from the 1820s to the 1920s. (Penguin Nonfiction Ser.). 368p. 1985. pap. 10.95 (ISBN 0-14-007346-9). Penguin.

Burnett, John, et al, eds. The Autobiography of the Working Class: An Annotated Critical Bibliography, 1790-1900, Vol. I. 512p. 1985. 85.00x (ISBN 0-8147-1071-9). NYU Pr.

Burnett, John A., jt. auth. see Mayer, Lawrence C.

Burnett, John J. Promotion Management: A Strategic Approach. (Illus.). 500p. 1984. text ed. 28.95 (ISBN 0-314-77851-9); tchrs.' manual avail. (ISBN 0-314-77855-1). West Pub.

Burnett, Joseph A., jt. auth. see Kahn, Sanford R.

Burnett, Joseph D. Capital Funds Campaign Manual for Churches. LC 79-26086. 1980. pap. 5.95 (ISBN 0-8170-0870-5). Judson.

Burnett, Joseph W. & Robinson, Harry M., Jr. Clinical Dermatology for Students & Practitioners. 2nd ed. LC 77-18437. (Illus.). 1978. 55.00 (ISBN 0-914316-12-5). Yorke Med.

Burnett, Joseph W., jt. auth. see Robinson, Harry M., Jr.

Burnett, Keith, ed. Spectral Line Shapes: Proceedings, 6th International Conference, Boulder, CO, July, 1982, Vol. 2. 1057p. 1983. 168.00 (ISBN 3-11-008846-0). De Gruyter.

Burnett, Linda, jt. auth. see Meier, Paul D.

Burnett, M. Delinquent's Challenge: Trust Me If You Dare. 132p. 1978. 25.00x (ISBN 0-85992-106-9, Pub. by B Rose Pub). State Mutual Bk.

Burnett, Mary J. & Dollar, Alta. Business English: A Communications Approach. (gr. 7-12). 1979. pap. text ed. 19.72 (ISBN 0-205-06414-0, 1764144); tchrs'. ed. 6.76 (ISBN 0-205-06415-9, 176415). Allyn.

Burnett, Mary J., jt. auth. see Dollar, Alta.

Burnett, Mary W. Principles of Occult Healing. 135p. 1981. pap. 7.00 (ISBN 0-89540-072-3, SB-072). Sun Pub.

Burnett, Millie & Cummins, Mary Ann. Texas Tales & Tunes: A Suite for Speech, Voices, & Orff Instruments. 1977. pap. 4.00 (ISBN 0-918812-00-3). MMB Music.

Burnett, Neil. Turning Assets into Prosperity: How to Trade Your Way to Financial Success. 206p. 1982. pap. 6.95 (ISBN 0-940986-03-5). ValuWrite.

Burnett, Peter H. Recollections & Opinions of an Old Pioneer. LC 76-87661. (American Scene Ser.). 1969. Repr. of 1880 ed. lib. bdg. 55.00 (ISBN 0-306-71765-4). Da Capo.

Burnett, Philip M. Reparation at the Paris Peace Conference, 2 Vols. 1965. lib. bdg. 86.00x (ISBN 0-374-91102-9). Octagon.

Burnett, Piers, jt. auth. see Aleksander, Igor.

Burnett, Robin & Burnett, Alan, eds. Australia-New Zealand Economic Relations: Issues for the 1980's. 183p. 1981. pap. text ed. 12.00 (ISBN 0-86784-011-0, 0102, Pub. by ANUP Australia). Australia N U P.

Burnett, Ruth. April Games. (YA) 1981. 8.95 (ISBN 0-686-74798-4, Avalon). Bouregy.

--The Beautiful Medic. 1983. 8.95 (ISBN 0-317-17572-6, Avalon). Bouregy.

--The Captain's Nurse. (YA) 1980. 8.95 (ISBN 0-686-73920-5, Avalon). Bouregy.

--Lord of the Island. 1981. 8.95 (ISBN 0-686-84686-9, Avalon). Bouregy.

--Love Star. 1983. 8.95 (ISBN 0-686-84190-5, Avalon). Bouregy.

--Nurse Maggie's Dream. 1982. 8.95 (ISBN 0-686-84156-5, Avalon). Bouregy.

--Racing Hearts. (YA) 1984. 8.95 (ISBN 0-8034-8452-6, Avalon). Bouregy.

--The Sweetest Treasure. (YA) 1981. 8.95 (ISBN 0-686-84691-5, Avalon). Bouregy.

--The Telltale Kiss. (YA) 1984. 8.95 (ISBN 0-8034-8402-X, Avalon). Bouregy.

--To Love a Mermaid. (YA) 1979. 8.95 (ISBN 0-685-65277-7, Avalon). Bouregy.

--The Topaz Promise. 1984. 8.95 (ISBN 0-8034-8423-2, Avalon). Bouregy.

--When Lily Smiles. (YA) 1982. 8.95 (ISBN 0-686-84731-8, Avalon). Bouregy.

Burnett, T. A. The Rise & Fall of a Regency Dandy: The Life & Times of Scrope Berdmore Davies. 1982. 14.95 (ISBN 0-316-11709-9, Pub. by Atlantic Monthly Pr). Little.

Burnett, Thomas & Newkome, George. Lab Course in Organic Chemistry. 1979. wire coil bdg. 11.95 (ISBN 0-88252-099-7). Paladin Hse.

Burnett, V. Compton, tr. see Steiner, Rudolf.

Burnett, V. Compton see Steiner, Rudolf.

Burnett, W. R. The Asphalt Jungle. Penzler, Otto, ed. LC 84-60103. (Quill Mysterious Classics Ser.). 246p. 1984. pap. 3.95 (ISBN 0-688-03126-9). Morrow.

--Captain Lightfoot. 224p. Repr. of 1954 ed. lib. bdg. 14.95x (ISBN 0-89190-495-6, Pub. by River City Pr). Amereon Ltd.

--High Sierra. 1982. Repr. lib. bdg. 16.95x (ISBN 0-89966-422-9). Buccaneer Bks.

--Little Caesar. 308p. Repr. of 1929 ed. lib. bdg. 17.95x (ISBN 0-89190-485-9, Pub. by River City Pr). Amereon Ltd.

Burnett, Whit. Maker of Signs. facsimile ed. LC 79-106252. (Short Story Index Reprint Ser.). 1934. 18.00 (ISBN 0-8369-3289-7). Ayer Co Pubs.

Burnett, Whit, jt. auth. see Burnett, Hallie.

Burnett, Whit, ed. Spirit of Man. facs. ed. LC 68-58775. (Essay Index Reprint Ser). 1958. 22.00 (ISBN 0-8369-0036-7). Ayer Co Pubs.

Burnett, Whit, jt. ed. see Burnett, Hallie.

Burnett, William, ed. Views of Los Angeles. rev. ed. (Illus.). 1979. 24.95 (ISBN 0-9602274-1-5); pap. 14.95 (ISBN 0-9602274-0-7). Portriga Pubns.

Burnett, Yumiko M., tr. see Rodieck, Jorma.

Burnette & Weiss. Colon Cleanse. 2.25 (ISBN 0-89557-057-2). Bi World Indus.

Burnette, William E., jt. auth. see Brown, Daniel J.

Burnett-Hurst, A. R., jt. auth. see Bowley, A. L.

Burney, Anna C. Tempi Moderni. (Ital.). 1982. pap. text ed. 15.95 (ISBN 0-03-059557-6). HR&W.

Burney, C. F. The Book of Judges with Introduction & Notes. 528p. Repr. of 1920 ed. lib. bdg. 100.00 (ISBN 0-8495-0481-3). Arden Lib.

--Israel's Settlement in Canaan: The Biblical Tradition & Its Historical Background. 3rd ed. (British Academy, London, Schweich Lectures on Biblical Archaeology Series, 1917). pap. 19.00 (ISBN 0-317-15757-4). Kraus Repr.

Burney, Charles. An Account of the Musical Performances in Westminster Abbey. (Music Reprint Ser.). 1979. Repr. of 1785 ed. 35.00 (ISBN 0-306-79524-8). Da Capo.

--Dr. Charles Burney's Continental Travels. LC 76-26048. Repr. of 1927 ed. 21.50 (ISBN 0-404-12920-X). AMS Pr.

--Memoirs of the Life & Writings of the Abate Metastasio, 3 Vols. LC 76-162295. (Music Ser). 1971. Repr. of 1796 ed. lib. bdg. 95.00 (ISBN 0-306-71110-9). Da Capo.

--Music, Men & Manners in France & Italy in 1770. Poole, H. Edmund, ed. (Eulenburg Music Ser.). (Illus.). 275p. 1982. pap. text ed. 15.00 (ISBN 0-903873-03-6). Da Capo.

--The Present State of Music in France & Italy. 2nd corr. ed. LC 74-24263. 1976. Repr. of 1773 ed. 27.50 (ISBN 0-404-12875-0). AMS Pr.

Burney, Eugenia. Fort Sumter. LC 74-28435. (Cornerstones of Freedom). (Illus.). 32p. (gr. 3-6). 1975. 9.25 (ISBN 0-516-04611-X). Childrens.

Burney, Fanny. Camilla. Bloom, Edward A. & Bloom, Lillian D., eds. (The World's Classics-Paperback Ser.). 1983. pap. 8.95 (ISBN 0-19-281662-4). Oxford U Pr.

--Evelina. 1965. pap. 6.95 (ISBN 0-393-00294-2, Norton Lib). Norton.

--Evelina. Bloom, Edward A., ed. & intro. by. (World's Classics Ser.). 1982. pap. 6.95 (ISBN 0-19-281596-2). Oxford U Pr.

--The Journals & Letters of Fanny Burney (Madame D'arblay, 2 vols. Derry, Warren, ed. (Illus.). 1982. Set. 174.00x (ISBN 0-19-812508-9). Vol. IX, Bath, 1815-1817. Vol. X, Bath, 1817-18. Oxford U Pr.

--The Journals & Letters of Fanny Burney (Madame D'Arblay), Eighteen Twelve to Eighteen Fourteen: Vol. VII, Letters 632-834. Bloom, Edward A., et al, eds. (Illus.). 1978. 89.00x (ISBN 0-19-812468-6). Oxford U Pr.

--The Journals & Letters of Fanny Burney (Madame D'Arblay) Letters 835-934, Vol. 8 1815. Hughes, Peter, et al, eds. (Illus.). 1980. 94.00x (ISBN 0-19-812507-0). Oxford U Pr.

--Journals of Fanny Burney (Madam D'Arblay, 4 vols. Incl. Vol. 1. Seventeen Ninety-One to Seventeen Ninety-Two, Letters 1-39. Hemlow, Joyce, et al, eds. 1972. 45.00x (ISBN 0-19-811498-2); Vol. 2. Courtship & Marriage Seventeen Ninety-Three, Letters 40-121. Hemlow, Joyce & Douglas, Althea, eds. 1972; Vol. 3. Great Bookham, 1793-1797. Hemlow, Joyce, et al, eds. (Illus., Letters 122-250). 1973. 45.00x (ISBN 0-19-812419-8); Vol. 4. West Humble, 1797-1801. Hemlow, Joyce, ed. (Illus., Letters 251-422). 1973. 59.00x (ISBN 0-19-812432-5); Vol. 5. West Humble & Paris 1801-1803, Letters 423-549. Hemlon, Joyce, ed. 1975. 64.00x (ISBN 0-19-812467-8); Vol. 6. France, 1803-1812, Letters 550-631. Hemlon, Joyce, ed. 1975. 55.00x (ISBN 0-19-812516-X). (Illus.). Oxford U Pr.

Burney, Frances. The Early Diary of Frances Burney, 1768-78, 2 vols. facsimile ed. Ellis, Annie R., ed. LC 70-37331. (Select Bibliographies Reprint Ser). Repr. of 1889 ed. 47.50 (ISBN 0-8369-6678-3). Ayer Co Pubs.

Burney, James. History of the Buccaneers of America. lib. bdg. 59.95 (ISBN 0-8490-1990-7). Gordon Pr.

Burney, Susan L. Prime Time Rhyme Time. (Illus.). 36p. (gr. 2). 1981. spiral binding 4.95 (ISBN 0-89305-039-3). Anna Pub.

Burney, William. Wallace Stevens. (Twayne's United States Authors Ser.). 1968. pap. 5.95x (ISBN 0-8084-0006-1, T127, Twayne). New Coll U Pr.

Burnford, J. F., jt. auth. see Chenault, Joann.

Burnford, Sheila. Bel Ria. 1978. 7.95 (ISBN 0-316-11718-8, Atlantic-Little, Brown). Little.

--The Incredible Journey. 1977. pap. 2.50 (ISBN 0-553-24652-6). Bantam.

--The Incredible Journey. (Illus.). 1961. 12.45 (ISBN 0-316-11714-5, Pub. by Atlantic Monthly Pr). Little.

--The Incredible Journey. 11.95 (ISBN 0-88411-099-0, Pub. by Aeonian Pr). Amereon Ltd.

--Mr. Noah & the Second Flood. 1974. pap. 0.95 (ISBN 0-671-47916-4). WSP.

Burnham. New York City: An Annotated Bibliography. 1985. lib. bdg. 60.00 (ISBN 0-8240-9133-7). Garland Pub.

Burnham, Alan, ed. New York Landmarks: A Study & Index of Architecturally Notable Structures in Greater New York. LC 63-17794. (Illus.). 1963. 40.00x (ISBN 0-8195-3040-9); pap. 16.95 (ISBN 0-8195-6045-6). Wesleyan U Pr.

Burnham, Betsy. When Your Friend Is Dying. 96p. 1983. pap. 4.95 (ISBN 0-310-60341-2, Pub by Chosen Bks). Zondervan.

Burnham, Bonnie. Index of Stolen Art: 1977. (Illus.). 72p. (Orig.). 1978. pap. 25.00 (ISBN 0-89062-082-2, Pub. by Intl Found Art Res). Pub Ctr Cult Res.

Burnham, C. P., jt. auth. see McRae, S. G.

Burnham, Charles R., jt. auth. see Phillips, Ronald L.

Burnham, Clara L. West Point Wooing & Other Stories. facsimile ed. LC 79-94709. (Short Story Index Reprint Ser.). 1899. 18.00 (ISBN 0-8369-3088-6). Ayer Co Pubs.

Burnham, Colin. Customizing Cars. LC 79-24124. (Illus.). 1980. 12.95 (ISBN 0-668-04888-3); pap. 8.95 (ISBN 0-668-04892-1). Arco.

Burnham, Daniel H. & Bennett, Edward H. Plan of Chicago Prepared Under the Direction of the Commercial Club During the Years 1906, 1907, 1908. Moore, Charles, ed. LC 71-75303. (Architecture & Decorative Art Ser.: Vol. 29). (Illus.). 1970. Repr. of 1909 ed. lib. bdg. 95.00 (ISBN 0-306-71261-X). Da Capo.

Burnham, David. The Rise of the Computer State. LC 82-42808. 1983. 17.95 (ISBN 0-394-51437-8). Random.

--The Rise of the Computer State. Date not set. pap. 6.95 (ISBN 0-394-72375-9, Vin). Random.

Burnham, Don, intro. by. Manufacturing Productivity Solutions II. LC 80-54415. (Illus.). 161p. 1980. pap. text ed. 20.00 (ISBN 0-87263-106-0). SME.

Burnham, Donald C. Productivity Improvement. LC 72-97978. (Benjamin Fairless Memorial Lectures Ser). 73p. 1973. 11.00x (ISBN 0-231-03755-4). Columbia U Pr.

Burnham, Donald L., et al. Schizophrenia & the Need-Fear Dilemma. LC 69-17278. (Monograph Ser. on Schizophrenia: No. 8). 1969. text ed. 25.00 (ISBN 0-8236-5980-1). Intl Univs Pr.

Burnham, Dorothy. The Comfortable Arts: Traditional Spinning & Weaving in Canada. (National Gallery of Canada Ser.). (Illus.). 256p. 1982. pap. 24.95 (ISBN 0-88884-474-3, 56315-4, Pub. by Natl Mus Canada). U of Chicago Pr.

Burnham, Dorothy K. Warp & Weft: A Dictionary of Textile Terms. (Illus.). 240p. 1982. 35.00 (ISBN 0-684-17332-8, ScribT). Scribner.

Burnham, Ernest. Two Types of Rural Schools, with Some Facts Showing Economic & Social Conditions. LC 79-176613. (Columbia University. Teachers College. Contributions to Education: No. 51). Repr. of 1912 ed. 22.50 (ISBN 0-404-55051-7). AMS Pr.

Burnham, Forbes. A Destiny to Mould: Selected Speeches by the Prime Minister of Guyana. Nascimento, C. A. & Burrowes, R., eds. LC 70-114298. 275p. 1970. 29.50x (ISBN 0-8419-0042-6, Africana). Holmes & Meier.

Burnham, Frank. Cleared to Land. LC 75-38050. 1977. 11.95 (ISBN 0-8168-4500-X). Aero.

Burnham, Jack. Beyond Modern Sculpture: Effects of Science & Technology on Sculpture of This Century. LC 68-16106. (Illus.). 402p. 1968. 20.00 (ISBN 0-8076-0450-X); pap. 12.95 (ISBN 0-8076-0715-0). Braziller.

--Structure of Art. rev. ed. LC 75-143195. 1970. 12.50 (ISBN 0-8076-0596-4); pap. 8.95 (ISBN 0-8076-0595-6). Braziller.

Burnham, James. Coming Defeat of Communism. LC 68-8735. (Illus.). 1968. Repr. of 1950 ed. lib. bdg. 29.75x (ISBN 0-8371-0035-6, BUDC). Greenwood.

--The Managerial Revolution. LC 60-8308. (Midland Bks.: No. 23). 300p. 1960. pap. 4.95x (ISBN 0-253-20023-7). Ind U Pr.

--The Managerial Revolution: What Is Happening in the World. LC 71-138102. 285p. 1972. Repr. of 1960 ed. lib. bdg. 26.50 (ISBN 0-8371-5678-5, BUMR). Greenwood.

--Suicide of the West: An Essay on the Meaning & Destiny of Liberalism. LC 64-14211. 320p. 1985. 18.95 (ISBN 0-89526-599-0); pap. 8.95 (ISBN 0-89526-822-1). Regnery-Gateway.

Burnham, John C. Jelliffe: American Psychoanalyst & Physician by John C. Burnham, & His Correspondence with Sigmund Freud & C.G. Jung. McGuire, William, ed. LC 83-1076. (Illus.). 344p. 1983. lib. bdg. 25.00x (ISBN 0-226-08114-1). U of Chicago Pr.

--Psychoanalysis & American Medicine, 1894-1918: Medicine, Science, & Culture. LC 67-31293. (Psychological Issues Monograph: No. 20, Vol. 5, No. 4). 249p. (Orig.). 1967. text ed. 17.50 (ISBN 0-8236-5100-2). Intl Univs Pr.

Burnham, John C., jt. ed. see Kempf, Dorothy C.

Burnham, John H. & Davis, George P. School Record of McLean County & Other Papers. (Transactions of the McLean County Historical Society: Vol. II). (Illus.). 695p. 1903. 25.00x (ISBN 0-943788-02-1). McLean County.

Burnham, John M., ed. Japanese Productivity: A Study Mission Report. LC 83-70794. 96p. 1983. pap. 13.50 (ISBN 0-935406-24-7). Am Prod & Inventory.

Burnham, Kenneth E. God Comes to America: Father Divine & the Peace Mission Movement. 167p. 1979. 16.95x (ISBN 0-931186-01-3). Lambeth Pr.

Burnham, Linda F. Bob & Bob: The First Five Years. LC 80-67655. (Illus.). 100p. (Orig.). 1980. pap. 12.00 (ISBN 0-937122-00-9). Astro Artz.

--Heartland Drive in Coke. 100p. (Orig.). 1981. pap. 4.00 (ISBN 0-937122-08-4). Astro Artz.

Burnham, Murry & Tinsley, Russell. Murry Burnham's Hunting Secrets. LC 83-13315. (Illus.). 244p. 1983. 17.95 (ISBN 0-8329-0343-4, Pub. by Winchester Pr). New Century.

Burnham, Nellie. Knitted Toys & Dolls: Complete Instructions for 17 Easy-to-Do Projects. (Illus.). 32p. (Orig.). 1982. pap. 1.95 (ISBN 0-486-24148-3). Dover.

Burnham, P. C. & Allen, R. F., eds. Social & Ecological Systems. (Social Anthropologists Monographs). 1979. 33.00 (ISBN 0-12-146050-9). Acad Pr.

Burnham, Patricia G. Playtraining Your Dog. (Illus.). 256p. 1980. 12.95 (ISBN 0-312-61689-9). St Martin.

Burnham, Patricia M. Painting in Boston: 1670-1970. 3.00 (ISBN 0-685-59554-4). Boston Public Lib.

Burnham, Patricia M. & Price, Martin. John Trumbull: The Hand & Spirit of a Painter. Cooper, Helen, ed. (Illus.). 308p. 1982. 45.00x (ISBN 0-89467-024-7); pap. 19.95x. Yale Art Gallery.

Burnham, Paul S., jt. auth. see Crawford, Albert B.

Burnham, Peter F. The Modular System III for Development Composition. 160p. 1980. pap. text ed. 8.95 (ISBN 0-8403-2212-7). Kendall-Hunt.

Burnham, Philip. Opportunity & Constraint in a Savana Society: The Gbaya of Meiganga Cameroon. LC 80-40926. (AP Studies in Anthropology). 1981. 49.00 (ISBN 0-12-146060-6). Acad Pr.

Burnham, Philip & Lederer, Richard. Basic Verbal Skills. 2nd ed. 243p. (gr. 9-12). 1980. pap. text ed. 5.95x (ISBN 0-88334-134-4); wkbk. 3.25x (ISBN 0-88334-130-1). Ind Sch Pr.

--Basic Verbal Skills for the Middle School. (gr. 6-9). 1976. pap. text ed. 6.95 (ISBN 0-88334-098-4); wkbk. 3.25x (ISBN 0-88334-074-7). Ind Sch Pr.

Burnham, Phillip & Lederer, Richard. Theme & Paragraph. Orig. Title: Basic Composition. (Illus.). 1976. pap. text ed. 4.25x (ISBN 0-88334-078-X). Ind Sch Pr.

Burnham, R. & Hogan, R. The Cork Dramatic Society: Lost Plays of the Irish Renaissance, Vol. III. 1985. pap. 3.95 (ISBN 0-912262-82-6). Proscenium.

Burnham, Robert. The Star Book. LC 83-15603. (Illus.). 20p. 1983. pap. 6.95 (ISBN 0-913135-00-3). AstroMedia Corp.

Burnham, Robert, ed. The Star Book. 1984. spiral bd. 6.95 (ISBN 0-521-25833-2). Cambridge U Pr.

Burnham, Robert E. Who Are the Finns? A Study in Prehistory. LC 76-44701. Repr. of 1946 ed. 14.50 (ISBN 0-404-15913-3). AMS Pr.

Burnham, Robert, Jr. Burnham's Celestial Handbook: An Observer's Guide to the Universe Beyond the Solar System, Vols. 1 & 2. LC 77-82888. (Illus.). 1978. pap. 9.95. Vol. 1 (ISBN 0-486-23567-X). Vol. 2. pap. 10.95 (ISBN 0-486-23568-8). Dover.

--Burnham's Celestial Handbook: An Observer's Guide to the Universe Beyond the Solar System, Vol. 3. (Illus.). 1979. pap. 12.95 (ISBN 0-486-23673-0). Dover.

Burnham, Sue. Dynamics of Christian Living for Women. LC 81-67598. 50p. (Orig.). (YA) 1981. pap. 2.95 (ISBN 0-940386-00-3). Dynamics Chr Liv.

Burnham, W. Dean. Presidential Ballots, 1836-1892. LC 75-22806. (America in Two Centuries Ser.). 1976. Repr. of 1955 ed. 71.50x (ISBN 0-405-07678-9). Ayer Co Pubs.

Burnham, Walter D. Critical Elections & the Mainsprings of American Politics. (Illus.). 1971. pap. 5.95x (ISBN 0-393-09397-2). Norton.

--The Current Crisis in American Politics. (Illus.). 1982. 29.95x (ISBN 0-19-503219-5); pap. 10.95 (ISBN 0-19-503220-9, GB 698). Oxford U Pr.

--Democracy in the Making: American Government & Politics. 640p. 1983. text ed. 26.95 (ISBN 0-13-198366-0); study guide 8.95 (ISBN 0-13-198382-2). P-H.

Burnham, Walter D. & Weinberg, Martha W., eds. American Politics & Public Policy. (MIT Studies in American Politics & Public Policy: 4th). 1978. 32.50x (ISBN 0-262-02132-3); pap. text ed. 12.50x (ISBN 0-262-52061-3). MIT Pr.

Burnham, Walter D., jt. ed. see Chambers, W. N.

Burnham, Walter D., jt. auth. see Kleppner, Paul.

Burnham, William H. Great Teachers & Mental Health: A Study of Seven Educational Hygienists. facsimile ed. LC 72-156623. (Essay Index Reprint Ser). Repr. of 1926 ed. 24.50 (ISBN 0-8369-2273-5). Ayer Co Pubs.

--The Normal Mind: An Introduction to Mental Hygiene & the Hygiene of School Instruction. 1978. Repr. of 1925 ed. lib. bdg. 30.00 (ISBN 0-8492-3539-1). R West.

Burnie, J., jt. auth. see Matthews, R.

Burnim, Kalman, ed. The Plays of George Colman, The Elder, 6 vols. LC 78-66618. (Eighteenth Century English Drama Ser.). 1982. lib. bdg. 436.00 Set (ISBN 0-8240-3584-4). Garland Pub.

Burnim, Kalman A. David Garrick: Director. LC 72-11834. (Arcturus Books Paperbacks). 250p. 1973. pap. 6.95x (ISBN 0-8093-0625-5). S Ill U Pr.

Burnim, Kalmann A., ed. see Hill, Aaron & Popple, William.

Burningham, John. Around the World in Eighty Days. (Illus.). 98p. (ps up). 1979. 14.95 (ISBN 0-224-00659-2, Pub. by Jonathan Cape). Merrimack Pub Cir.

--Avocado Baby. LC 81-43844. (Illus.). 32p. (ps-1). 1982. 9.57i (ISBN 0-690-04243-4); PLB 9.89g (ISBN 0-690-04244-2). Crowell Jr Bks.

--The Baby. LC 75-4564. (Illus.). (ps-1). 1975. 3.95 (ISBN 0-690-00900-3); PLB 7.89 (ISBN 0-690-00901-1). Crowell Jr Bks.

--The Blanket. LC 76-17630. (Illus.). (ps-1). 1976. 3.95 (ISBN 0-690-01269-1); PLB 7.89 (ISBN 0-690-01270-5). Crowell Jr Bks.

--Borka: The Adventures of a Goose with No Feathers. (Illus.). 32p. (ps-2). 1981. 8.95 (ISBN 0-224-60077-X, Pub. by Jonathan Cape). Merrimack Pub Cir.

--Cannonball Simp. LC 66-66489. (Illus.). 30p. (ps-2). 1979. 8.95 (ISBN 0-224-61123-2, Pub. by Jonathan Cape). Merrimack Pub Cir.

--Cluck Baa. LC 83-25979. 24p. 1985. 4.95 (ISBN 0-670-22580-0, Viking Kestrel). Viking.

--Come Away from the Water, Shirley. LC 77-483. (Illus.). (gr. 1-2). 1977. 10.53i (ISBN 0-690-01360-4); PLB 11.89 (ISBN 0-690-01361-2). Crowell Jr Bks.

--Come Away from the Water, Shirley. LC 77-483. (A Trophy Picture Bk.). (Illus.). 32p. (ps-3). 1983. pap. 3.80i (ISBN 0-06-443039-1, Trophy). HarpJ.

--The Cupboard. LC 76-17797. (Illus.). (ps-1). 1976. 3.95i (ISBN 0-690-01300-0); PLB 7.89 (ISBN 0-690-01301-9). Crowell Jr Bks.

--The Dog. LC 76-17626. (Illus.). (ps-1). 1976. 3.95i (ISBN 0-690-01271-3); PLB 7.89 (ISBN 0-690-01272-1). Crowell Jr Bks.

--The Friend. LC 76-16436. (Illus.). (ps-1). 1976. 3.95i (ISBN 0-690-01273-X); PLB 7.89 (ISBN 0-690-01274-8). Crowell Jr Bks.

--Granpa. LC 84-17464. (Illus.). 32p. 1985. 8.95 (ISBN 0-517-55643-X). Crown.

--Harquin. LC 68-90888. (Illus.). 30p. (ps-2). 1979. 8.95 (ISBN 0-224-61213-1, Pub. by Jonathan Cape). Merrimack Pub Cir.

--Jangle Twang. LC 83-25980. 24p. 1985. 4.95 (ISBN 0-670-40570-1, Viking Kestrel). Viking.

--John Burningham's Number Play Series: A Great New Concept in Teaching Math, 6 bks. Incl. Pigs Plus: Learning Addition. LC 82-51283. pap. 4.95 (ISBN 0-670-55508-8); Ride Off: Learning Subtraction. LC 82-51278. 4.95 (ISBN 0-670-59798-8); Read One: Numbers as Words. LC 82-51281. 4.95 (ISBN 0-670-58986-1); Five Down: Numbers as Signs. LC 82-51279. 4.95 (ISBN 0-670-31698-9); Count Up: Learning Sets. LC 82-51282. 4.95 (ISBN 0-670-24410-4); Just Cats: Learning Groups. LC 82-51280. 4.95 (ISBN 0-670-41094-2). (Illus.). (ps-k). 1983 (Viking Kestrel). Viking.

--Jungleland Frieze. (Illus.). (ps-8). 1981. pap. 4.95 (ISBN 0-224-01207-X, Pub. by Jonathan Cape). Merrimack Pub Cir.

--Mr. Gumpy's Motor Car. LC 75-4582. (Illus.). 48p. (gr. k-3). 1976. PLB 11.89 (ISBN 0-690-00799-X). Crowell Jr Bks.

--Mr. Gumpy's Motor Car. (Illus.). (gr. 1-3). 1983. pap. 3.50 (ISBN 0-14-050300-5, Puffin). Penguin.

--Mr. Gumpy's Outing. LC 77-159507. (Illus.). (ps). 1971. reinforced bdg. 10.95 (ISBN 0-03-089733-5). HR&W.

--Mr. Gumpy's Outing. (Picture Puffins Ser.). 32p. (ps-k). 1984. pap. 3.50 (ISBN 0-14-050254-8, Puffin). Penguin.

--The Rabbit. LC 75-4566. (Illus.). (ps-1). 1975. 3.95i (ISBN 0-690-00906-2); PLB 7.89 (ISBN 0-690-00907-0). Crowell Jr Bks.

--The School. LC 75-4611. (Illus.). (ps-1). 1975. 3.95i (ISBN 0-690-00902-X); PLB 7.89 (ISBN 0-690-00903-8). Crowell Jr Bks.

--The Shopping Basket. LC 80-7987. (Illus.). 32p. (ps-2). 1980. 10.53i (ISBN 0-690-04082-2); PLB 10.89 (ISBN 0-690-04083-0). Crowell Jr Bks.

--Skip Trip. LC 83-25981. (Noisy Words Ser.). (Illus.). 24p. (ps). 1984. 4.95 (ISBN 0-670-65016-1, Viking Kestrel). Viking.

--Slam Bang. LC 83-23549. (Noisy World Ser.). 24p. 1985. 4.95 (ISBN 0-670-65076-5, Viking Kestrel). Viking.

--Sniff Shout. LC 83-23551. (Noisy Words Ser.). (Illus.). 24p. (ps). 1984. 4.95 (ISBN 0-670-65349-7, Viking Kestrel). Viking.

--The Snow. LC 75-2492. (Illus.). (ps-1). 1975. 3.95i (ISBN 0-690-00904-6); PLB 7.89 (ISBN 0-690-00905-4). Crowell Jr Bks.

--Time to Get Out of the Bath, Shirley. LC 76-58503. (Illus.). (gr. k-2). 1978. 10.53i (ISBN 0-690-01378-7); PLB 10.89 (ISBN 0-690-01379-5). Crowell Jr Bks.

--Trubloff: The Mouse Who Wanted to Play the Balalaika. (ps). 1965. PLB 5.99 (ISBN 0-394-97316-X, BYR). Random.

--Wobble Pop. LC 83-23533. (Noisy Words Ser.). (Illus.). 24p. (ps). 1984. 4.95 (ISBN 0-670-77713-7, Viking Kestrel). Viking.

--Wonderland Frieze. (Illus.). (ps-3). 1981. 4.95 (ISBN 0-224-61694-3, Pub. by Jonathan Cape). Merrimack Pub Cir.

--Would You Rather... LC 78-7088. (Illus.). (ps-2). 1978. 10.53i (ISBN 0-690-03917-4). Crowell Jr Bks.

Burningham, Robin. Hawaiian Word Book. (Illus.). 104p. (Orig., Hawaiian.). 1982. pap. 6.95 (ISBN 0-935848-12-6). Bess Pr.

Burnip, M. S. & Newton, A. Non-Woven Fabrics. 105p. 1970. 70.00x (ISBN 0-686-63777-1). State Mutual Bk.

Burnip, M. S. & Thomas, J. H. The Production & Properties of Knitted & Woven Fabrics. 139p. 1969. 70.00x (ISBN 0-686-63783-6). State Mutual Bk.

Burnley, David. A Guide to Chaucer's Language. LC 83-10523. (Illus.). 280p. 1984. 22.50x (ISBN 0-8061-1868-7). U of Okla Pr.

Burnley, I. H., et al, eds. Mobility & Community Change in Australia. (Studies in Society & Culture). (Illus.). 286p. 1981. text ed. 30.25x (ISBN 0-7022-1446-9). U of Queensland Pr.

Burnley, Ian & Forrest, James, eds. Living in Cities: Urbanism & Society in Metropolitan Australia. (Illus.). 280p. 1985. text ed. 25.00x (ISBN 0-86861-647-8). Allen Unwin.

Burnley, J. D. Chaucer's Language & the Philosophers' Tradition. (Chaucer Studies: No. 2). 196p. 1979. 33.50x (ISBN 0-8476-6216-0). Rowman.

Burnley, James. History of Wool & Wool-Combing. LC 68-55497. (Illus.). Repr. of 1889 ed. 37.50x (ISBN 0-678-00519-2). Kelley.

Burnley, Judith. Unrepentant Women. 224p. 1984. 14.95 (ISBN 0-8128-2914-X); pap. 3.50 (ISBN 0-8128-8069-2). Stein & Day.

Burns. Polyester Molding Compounds. (Plastics Engineering Ser.: Vol. 2). 304p. 1982. 55.00 (ISBN 0-8247-1280-3). Dekker.

--Use of Discovery Under the North Carolina Rules of Civil Procedure. incl. latest pocket part supplement 49.95 (ISBN 0-686-90887-2); separate pocket part supplement, 1982 32.95 (ISBN 0-686-90888-0). Harrison Co GA.

--VIC-20: Fifty Easy-to-Run Computer Games. 1984. write for info. (ISBN 0-672-22288-4). Sams.

--The Worlds of Alphonso the Learned & James the Conqueror. Joanna, H., ed. 25.00 (ISBN 0-317-14188-0). Princeton U Pr.

Burns & Austin. Management Science Models & the Microcomputer. 400p. 1985. pap. write for info. (ISBN 0-02-317300-9). Macmillan.
Burns & Venit. Practical Finance on the TRS-80 Model 100. 1984. pap. 15.95 (ISBN 0-452-25576-7, Plume). NAL.
Burns, jt. auth. see Bishop.
Burns, et al. The Revival of Religion. 449p. 1984. Repr. of 1840 ed. 12.95 (ISBN 0-85151-435-9). Banner of Truth.
Burns, A. Concurrent Programming in Ada. 250p. Date not set. price not set. Cambridge U Pr.
Burns, A. F. The Management of Prosperity. LC 66-15365. (Benjamin Fairless Memorial Lectures). 69p. 1966. 12.00x (ISBN 0-231-02959-4). Columbia U Pr.
Burns, Aaron, ed. The ITC Typeface Collection. (Illus.). 572p. 1982. 49.95 (ISBN 0-9608034-0-8). Intl Typeface.
Burns, Ada, jt. auth. see Martinez, Julio.
Burns, Adele B., ed. see APLIC International.
Burns, Aidan. Nature & Culture in D. H. Lawrence. 137p. 1980. 27.50x (ISBN 0-389-20091-3, 06864). B&N Imports.
Burns, Ailsa & Bottomley, Gill, eds. The Family in the Modern World. (Studies in Society Ser.: No. 18). 220p. 1983. text ed. 28.50x (ISBN 0-86861-190-5). Allen Unwin.
Burns, Alan. Babel. 1982. pap. 4.95 (ISBN 0-7145-0011-9). Riverrun NY.
--Babel. (Fiction Ser.). 160p. pap. 6.95 (ISBN 0-7145-0011-9, Dist. by Scribner). M Boyars.
--Celebrations. 1980. pap. 4.95 (ISBN 0-7145-0072-0). Riverrun NY.
--Celebrations. (Fiction Ser.). 116p. pap. 6.95 (ISBN 0-7145-0072-0, Dist. by Scribner). M Boyars.
--The Day Daddy Died. (Illus.). 138p. 1982. 13.95 (ISBN 0-8052-8086-3, Pub. by Allison & Busby England); pap. 5.95 (ISBN 0-8052-8085-5). Schocken.
--Dreamerika. (Fiction Ser.). 136p. 12.00 (ISBN 0-7145-0803-9, Dist. by Scribner). M Boyars.
--Europe after the Rain. (Fiction Ser.). 128p. pap. 6.95 (ISBN 0-7145-0222-7, Dist by Scribner). M Boyars.
--Microchip Appropriate or Inappropriate Technology. (Computers & Their Applications Ser.). 180p. 1981. 48.95x (ISBN 0-470-27206-6). Halsted Pr.
--New Information Technology. LC 83-22766. (Computers & Their Applications Ser.: 1-403). 245p. 1984. pap. 26.95x (ISBN 0-470-27494-8, Pub by Halsted Pr). Wiley.
Burns, Alan & Sugnet, Charles. The Imagination on Trial: Conversations with British & American Novelists. 192p. 1981. 17.95x (ISBN 0-8052-8084-7); pap. 7.95 (ISBN 0-8052-8083-9). Schocken.
Burns, Alan, et al. New Writers, No. 1. 1980. pap. 6.00 (ISBN 0-7145-0397-5). Riverrun NY.
--Red Dust Two: New Writing. LC 72-127954. (Orig.). 1972. 5.25 (ISBN 0-87376-019-0); pap. 3.00 (ISBN 0-87376-020-4). Red Dust.
Burns, Alan C. Colour Prejudice. LC 70-155383. 1972. Repr. of 1948 ed. text ed. 17.50x (ISBN 0-8371-6076-6, BCO&, Pub. by Negro U Pr). Greenwood.
--History of Nigeria. 1972. pap. text ed. 17.95x (ISBN 0-04-966014-4). Allen Unwin.
--History of Nigeria. 1976. lib. bdg. 59.95 (ISBN 0-8490-1981-8). Gordon Pr.
--History of the British West Indies. 1976. lib. bdg. 59.95 (ISBN 0-8490-1989-3). Gordon Pr.
Burns, Allan F., tr. An Epoch of Miracles: Oral Literature of the Yucatec Maya. (Texas Pan American Ser.). (Illus.). 282p. 1983. text ed. 24.50x (ISBN 0-292-72037-8). U of Tex Pr.
Burns, Arthur & Williams, Edward. Federal Work, Security, & Relief Programs. LC 71-166956. (Research Monograph: Vol. 24). 1971. Repr. of 1941 ed. lib. bdg. 19.50 (ISBN 0-306-70356-4). Da Capo.
Burns, Arthur E. & Watson, Donald S. Government Spending & Economic Expansion. LC 75-173452. (FDR & the Era of the New Deal Ser). 174p. 1972. Repr. of 1940 ed. lib. bdg. 27.50 (ISBN 0-306-70368-8). Da Capo.
Burns, Arthur F. Business Cycle in a Changing World. LC 69-12462. (Business Cycles Ser.: No. 18). 366p. 1969. 22.00x (ISBN 0-87014-200-3, 67, Dist. by Columbia U Pr). Natl Bur Econ Res.
--The Frontiers of Economic Knowledge: Essays. LC 75-19695. (National Bureau of Economic Research Ser.). (Illus.). 1975. Repr. 29.00x (ISBN 0-405-07576-6). Ayer Co Pubs.
--Production Trends in the United States Since 1870. Repr. of 1934 ed. 35.00x (ISBN 0-678-00024-7). Kelley.
--Reflections of an Economic Policy Maker: Speeches & Congressional Statements, 1969-1978. 1978. 17.25 (ISBN 0-8447-3319-9); pap. 9.25 (ISBN 0-8447-3333-4). Am Enterprise.
Burns, Arthur F. & Mitchell, Wesley C. Measuring Business Cycles. (Business Cycles Ser.: No. 2). 587p. 1946. 35.00x (ISBN 0-87014-085-X, Dist. by Columbia U Pr). Natl Bur Econ Res.
Burns, Arthur F., et al. The Anguish of Central Banking. LC 81-482170. (Per Jacobsson Lectures: 1979). pap. 20.00 (ISBN 0-317-29071-1, 2019262). Bks Demand UMI.
Burns, Arthur L. & Heathcote, Nina. Peace-Keeping by U. N. Forces, from Suez to the Congo. LC 75-27678. (Princeton Studies in World Politics: No. 4). 256p. 1976. Repr. of 1963 ed. lib. bdg. 22.50x (ISBN 0-8371-8452-5, BUPK). Greenwood.
Burns, Arthur R. The Decline of Competition: A Study of the Evolution of American Industry. LC 74-136847. (Illus.). xiv, 619p. Repr. of 1936 ed. lib. bdg. 32.00x (ISBN 0-8371-5281-X, BUCO). Greenwood.
--Money & Monetary Policy in Early Times. 1976. lib. bdg. 59.95 (ISBN 0-8490-2275-4). Gordon Pr.
--Money & Monetary Policy in Early Times. LC 65-19645. Repr. of 1927 ed. 45.00x (ISBN 0-678-00100-6). Kelley.
Burns, Aubrey. Out of a Moving Mist Poems. LC 76-47356. 1977. pap. 6.50 (ISBN 0-912908-05-X). Tamal Land.
Burns, Barbara J., jt. auth. see Cument, Carlos E.
Burns, Beulah M. God Is Living & at Work: A Collection of Inspirational Poems. (Illus.). 50p. 1982. pap. 4.00 (ISBN 0-913491-02-0). Strug Comm Pr.
Burns, Brian. The Science of Table Tennis. (Illus.). 224p. 1984. 14.95 (ISBN 0-7207-1155-X). Merrimack Pub Cir.
Burns, Brian, ed. Footsteps Through History: A Walking Tour of Sturbridge Common & Southbridge. LC 84-60806. (Illus.). 88p. 1984. pap. text ed. 4.95 (ISBN 0-917523-01-6). Worcester County.
Burns, Bryan. The Novels of Thomas Love Peacock. LC 84-19905. 256p. 1985. 27.50x (ISBN 0-389-20532-X, 08094). B&N Imports.
Burns, C. Greek Ideals: A Study in Social Life. 59.95 (ISBN 0-8490-0264-8). Gordon Pr.
Burns, C. D. Greek Ideals. LC 73-20390. (Studies in Classical Literature, No. 60). 1974. lib. bdg. 49.95x (ISBN 0-8383-1767-7). Haskell.
Burns, C. Delisle. Greek Ideals: A Study of Social Life. 1917. 17.50 (ISBN 0-686-20093-4). Quality Lib.
--A Short History of International Intercourse. LC 72-89262. 160p. 1973. Repr. of 1924 ed. 15.00x (ISBN 0-8046-1760-0, Pub. by Kennikat). Assoc Faculty Pr.
Burns, C. L. Elvis Aaron Presley. (Illus.). 112p. 1984. pap. 5.00 (ISBN 0-682-40185-4). Exposition Pr FL.
Burns, C. S. & Parks, T. W. DFT-FFT & Convolution Alogrithms. (Illus.). 232p. 1985. pap. 22.50 (ISBN 0-317-27322-1, LCB8481). Tex Instr Inc.
Burns, Carol, jt. auth. see Miller, Liz.
Burns, Carol, et al. New Writers, No. 6. 1980. pap. 6.00 (ISBN 0-7145-0407-6). Riverrun NY.
Burns, Cherie. Stepmotherhood: How to Survive Without Feeling Frustrated, Left Out, or Wicked. LC 85-40271. 256p. 1985. 14.95 (ISBN 0-8129-1145-8). Times Bks.
Burns, Chester R., ed. Legacies in Ethics & Medicine. LC 76-44908. 1977. 15.00 (ISBN 0-88202-166-4). Watson Pub Intl.
--Legacies in Law & Medicine. LC 76-29641. 1977. 15.00 (ISBN 0-88202-164-8). Watson Pub Intl.
Burns, Constance K., jt. ed. see Formisano, Ronald P.
Burns, D. & Venit, S. Portable Finance: Practical Business Programs for the TRS-80 Model 100. 1984. write for info. NAL.
Burns, D. T. & Townshend, A. Inorganic Reaction Chemistry: Reactions of the Elements & Their Compounds, Vol. 2A. Carter, A. H., ed. (Ser. in Analytical Chemistry). 300p. 1981. 84.95x (ISBN 0-470-27105-1). Halsted Pr.
Burns, D. T., et al. Inorganic Reaction Chemistry: Reactions of the Elements & Their Compounds, Vol. 2B. 410p. 1981. 94.95x (ISBN 0-470-27210-4). Halsted Pr.
--Inorganic Reaction Chemistry: Systematic Chemical Separation, Vol. 1. (Analytical Chemistry Ser.). 248p. 1980. pap. 29.95 (ISBN 0-470-27237-6). Halsted Pr.
Burns, David. Feeling Good: The New Mood Therapy. LC 80-12694. (Illus.). 388p. 1980. 12.95 (ISBN 0-688-03633-3). Morrow.
Burns, David C., jt. auth. see Holmes, Arthur W.
Burns, David D. Feeling Good. 1981. pap. 4.50 (ISBN 0-451-13586-5, Sig). NAL.
--Intimate Connections: How to Get More Love in Your Life. LC 84-61114. 324p. 1984. 15.95 (ISBN 0-688-01746-0). Morrow.
--Intimate Connections: The New Clinically Tested Program for Overcoming Loneliness. 1985. pap. 4.50 (ISBN 0-451-13906-2, Sig). NAL.
Burns, Diane. Portable Tutor: User's Guide to the TRS-80 Model 100. 1984. write for info. NAL.
--Riding the One-Eyed Ford. 2nd ed. (Poetry Ser.). (Illus.). 50p. (Orig.). 1984. pap. 3.50 (ISBN 0-936556-05-6). Contact Two.
Burns, Diane & Venit, Sharyn. Introducing the TRS-80 Model 100. 1984. 15.95 (ISBN 0-452-25574-0, Plume). NAL.
Burns, Diane K. & Venit, Sharyn D. Mac at Work: Macintosh Windows on Business. 224p. 1985. pap. 17.95 (ISBN 0-471-82050-4); Book with program disk. 39.95 (ISBN 0-471-82737-1). Wiley.
Burns, Dolores, ed. The Greatest Health Discovery. (Illus., Orig.). 1972. pap. 2.25 (ISBN 0-914532-05-7). Natural Hygiene.
Burns, Donald H., jt. auth. see Guacho, Juan N.
Burns, Donald J. An Introduction to Karate for Student & Teacher. 1977. pap. text ed. 8.95 (ISBN 0-8403-1692-5). Kendall-Hunt.
Burns, E. Karl Liebknecht. 59.95 (ISBN 0-8490-0469-1). Gordon Pr.
Burns, E. Bradford. A History of Brazil. 2nd ed. 1980. 42.00x (ISBN 0-231-04748-7); pap. 15.00x (ISBN 0-231-04749-5). Columbia U Pr.
--Latin America: A Concise Interpretive History. 3rd ed. (Illus.). 352p. 1982. pap. 17.95 (ISBN 0-13-524322-X). P-H.
--Latin America: A Concise Interpretive History. 4th ed. (Illus.). 336p. 1986. pap. text ed. 18.95 (ISBN 0-13-524356-4). P-H.
--The Poverty of Progress: Latin America in the Nineteenth Century. LC 80-51236. 224p. 1980. 18.95x (ISBN 0-520-04160-7). U of Cal Pr.
--The Poverty of Progress: Latin America in the Nineteenth Century. LC 80-51236. (Illus.). 192p. 1983. pap. 6.95x (ISBN 0-520-05078-9, CAMPUS 312). U of Cal Pr.
--The Unwritten Alliance: Riobanco & Brazilian-American Relations. LC 65-25661. (Institute of Latin American Studies). (Illus.). 305p. 1966. 26.00x (ISBN 0-231-02855-5). Columbia U Pr.
Burns, E. Bradford, ed. Perspectives on Brazilian History. LC 67-13779. (Institute of Latin American Studies). 235p. 1967. 22.00x (ISBN 0-231-02992-6). Columbia U Pr.
Burns, E. Bradford, tr. see Gagini, Carlos.
Burns, E. Jane. Arthurian Fiction: Rereading the Vulgate Cycle. LC 85-7325. 185p. 1985. 22.00x (ISBN 0-8142-0387-6). Ohio St U Pr.
Burns, E. L. Between Arab & Israeli. 336p. 1969. Repr. of 1962 ed. 12.95 (ISBN 0-88728-090-0). Inst Palestine.
Burns, Echo B. Hands that Heal. (Orig.). 1985. pap. 8.95 (ISBN 0-917086-76-7). A C S Pubns Inc.
Burns, Edward. Applied Research & Statistics for Teachers. (Illus.). 264p. 1980. lexotone 12.00x (ISBN 0-398-03984-4). C C Thomas.
--The Development, Use & Abuse of Educational Tests. (Illus.). 180p. 1979. 15.25x (ISBN 0-398-03713-2). C C Thomas.
--TRS-80 Teaching Aid: Ready-to-Run Programs for the Classroom & Home. (Illus.). 1984. pap. 15.95 (ISBN 0-8359-7875-3). Reston.
--VIC-20: Fifty Easy-to-Run Computer Games. LC 83-50375. 128p. 1983. pap. 5.95 (ISBN 0-672-22188-8, 22188); incl. tape 12.95 (ISBN 0-672-26170-7, 26170). Sams.
Burns, Edward, ed. see Toklas, Alice B.
Burns, Edward M. The American Idea of Mission: Concepts of National Purpose & Destiny. LC 72-11302. (Illus.). 385p. 1973. Repr. of 1957 ed. lib. bdg. 23.00x (ISBN 0-8371-6648-9, BUAI). Greenwood.
--Western Civilizations. 8th ed. (Illus.). 990p. 1973. pap. text ed. 9.95x ea. in 2 vols. o.p.; study guide by philip ralph 5.95x (ISBN 0-393-09355-7). Norton.
Burns, Edward M. & Ralph, Philip L. World Civilizations, 2 vols. 5th ed. (Illus.). 1974. Vol. 2. pap. text ed. 13.95x (ISBN 0-393-09272-0); Vol. 1. study guide o.p. 5.95x (ISBN 0-393-09277-1); Vol. 2. study guide 5.95x (ISBN 0-393-09285-2). Norton.
--World Civilizations. 6th ed. (Illus.). 1982. Two Vols. In 1. 26.95x (ISBN 0-393-95077-8); Vol. 1. pap. 18.95x (ISBN 0-393-95083-2); Vol. 2. pap. 18.95x (ISBN 0-393-95095-6); instr's manual avail. (ISBN 0-393-95089-1); Vol. 1. study guide 7.95x (ISBN 0-393-95103-0); Vol. 2. 7.95x (ISBN 0-393-95107-3). Norton.
Burns, Edward M., et al. Western Civilizations, 2 vols. 9th ed. (Illus.). 1980. Vol. 1. pap. text ed. 16.95x (ISBN 0-393-95080-8); instr's manual pap. 2.95x (ISBN 0-393-95099-9); study guide 7.95x (ISBN 0-393-95091-3). Norton.
--Western Civilizations. 10th ed. 1984. Complete ed. 25.95x (ISBN 0-393-95315-7); Vol. I. pap. 18.95x (ISBN 0-393-95319-X); Vol. II. pap. 18.95x (ISBN 0-393-95323-8); tchr's ed 4.95x (ISBN 0-393-95328-9); Vol. I. study guide 6.95x (ISBN 0-393-95433-1); Vol. II. study guide 6.95x (ISBN 0-393-95422-6). Norton.
--World Civilizations, 2 vols. 4th ed. 1968. Vol. 1. pap. 8.95x ea (ISBN 0-393-09828-1, NortonC); Vol. 1. study guide 2.50x (ISBN 0-393-09836-2); Vol. 2. study guide 2.50x (ISBN 0-393-09849-4); instrs'. manual free (ISBN 0-393-09833-8). Norton.
Burns, Edward McNall see McNall Burns, Edward, et al.
Burns, Emile. Introduction to Marxism. LC 57-14973. 124p. 1966. pap. 1.65 (ISBN 0-7178-0101-2). Intl Pubs Co.
Burns, Emile, ed. Handbook of Marxism, 2 Vols. LC 79-119441. (Reference Ser., No. 44). 1970. Repr. of 1935 ed. lib. bdg. 79.95x (ISBN 0-8383-1090-7). Haskell.
Burns, Emile, commentary by. The Marxist Reader. (Illus.). 672p. 1982. 6.98 (ISBN 0-517-38766-2, Avenel). Outlet Bk Co.
Burns, Emile, tr. see Tolstoi, Alexei.
Burns, Eugene. Last King of Paradise. LC 72-10607. (Select Bibliographies Reprint Ser.). 1973. Repr. of 1952 ed. 19.00 (ISBN 0-8369-7102-7). Ayer Co Pubs.
Burns, Eveline M. Social Security & Public Policy. LC 75-17211. (Social Problems & Social Policy Ser.). 1976. Repr. of 1956 ed. 21.00x (ISBN 0-405-07483-2). Ayer Co Pubs.
--Social Welfare in the Nineteen Eighties & Beyond. LC 77-17818. 20p. 1978. pap. 4.00x (ISBN 0-87772-251-X). Inst Gov Stud Berk.
Burns, Eveline M., ed. see Children's Allowance Conference, 1967.
Burns, G. Frank. Wilson County. Corlew, Robert E., ed. (Tennessee County History Ser.: No. 95). (Illus.). 144p. 1984. Repr. of 1983 ed. 12.50x (ISBN 0-87870-190-7). Memphis St Univ.
Burns, G. P. & Otis, C. H. The Handbook of Vermont Trees. LC 78-68710. pap. 5.25 (ISBN 0-8048-1315-9). C E Tuttle.
Burns, Gary, jt. auth. see Sobey, Edwin J.
Burns, George. Dear George: Advice & Answers from America's Leading Expert on Everything from A to B. (Illus.). 1985. 12.95 (ISBN 0-399-13105-1). Putnam Pub Group.
--Dr. Burns' Prescription for Happiness. (Illus.). 192p. 1984. 11.95 (ISBN 0-399-12964-2, Putnam). Putnam Pub Group.
--Dr. Burns' Prescription for Happiness. 192p. 1985. pap. 5.95 (ISBN 0-399-51175-X, Perigee). Putnam Pub Group.
--Dr. Burns' Prescription for Happiness. (Illus.). 1985. pap. 5.95 (ISBN 0-399-51204-7, Perigee). Putnam Pub Group.
--How to Live to Be One Hundred or More. (Illus.). 192p. 1983. 11.95 (ISBN 0-399-12787-9, Putnam). Putnam Pub Group.
Burns, George W. Plant Kingdom. (Illus.). 640p. 1974. text ed. write for info. (ISBN 0-02-317200-2, 31720). Macmillan.
--The Science of Genetics. 5th ed. 624p. 1983. write for info. solns. manual (ISBN 0-02-317130-8). Macmillan.
Burns, George W. & Tullis, James E. Burns: The Science of Genetics- an Introduction to Heredity, Solutions Manual. 4th ed. 1980. write for info. (ISBN 0-02-317150-2). Macmillan.
Burns, Gerald. A Book of Spells First Third. (Lucky Heart Bks.). 1979. pap. 2.00 (ISBN 0-913198-12-9). Salt Lick.
--Introduction to Group Theory with Applications. (Material Science & Technology Ser.). 1977. 29.00 (ISBN 0-12-145750-8). Acad Pr.
--Solid State Physics. Date not set. text ed. price not set (ISBN 0-12-146070-3). Acad Pr.
--Toward a Phenomenology of Written Art. LC 79-15699. 64p. 1979. 12.50 (ISBN 0-914232-36-3); pap. 4.95 (ISBN 0-914232-35-5). McPherson & Co.
Burns, Gerald & Glazer, A. M. Introduction to Space Groups for Solid State Scientists. 1978. 23.00 (ISBN 0-12-145760-5). Acad Pr.
Burns, Gerald, ed. see Lucky Heart Bks.
Burns, Glen. Great Poets Howl: A Study of Allen Ginsberg's Poetry, 1943-1955, Vol. 114. (European University Ser.: No. 14). 540p. 1983. pap. 43.70 (ISBN 3-8204-7761-6). P Lang Pubs.
Burns, Grant. The Atomic Papers: A Citizen's Guide to Selected Books & Articles on the Bomb, the Arms Race, Nuclear Power, the Peace Movement, & Related Issues. LC 84-1390. 323p. 1984. 22.50 (ISBN 0-8108-1692-X). Scarecrow.
Burns, Helen. The American Banking Community & New Deal Banking Reforms: 1933-1935. LC 72-789. (Contributions in Economics & Economic History Ser.: No. 11). 203p. 1974. lib. bdg. 29.95 (ISBN 0-8371-6362-5, BAB). Greenwood.
Burns, Henry. Corrections: Organization & Administration. (Criminal Justice Ser.). 1975. text ed. 23.95 (ISBN 0-8299-0606-1); pap. instrs. manual avail. (ISBN 0-8299-0610-X); instrs. manual avail. West Pub.
Burns, J. A. Growth & Development of the Catholic School System in the United States. LC 78-89156. (American Education: Its Men, Institutions & Ideas, Ser. 1). 1969. Repr. of 1912 ed. 21.00 (ISBN 0-405-01394-9). Ayer Co Pubs.
--The Principles, Origin & Establishment of the Catholic School System in the United States. LC 74-89155. (American Education: Its Men, Institutions & Ideas Ser). 1969. Repr. of 1908 ed. 21.00 (ISBN 0-405-01393-0). Ayer Co Pubs.
Burns, J. H. Scottish Churchmen & the Council of Basle. LC 64-7472. 1962. 15.00 (ISBN 0-8023-9034-X). Dufour.
Burns, J. H., ed. see Bentham, Jeremy.
Burns, J. J., ed. Advances in Reliability & Stress Analysis. 248p. 1979. 30.00 (ISBN 0-317-33402-6, H00119); members 15.00 (ISBN 0-317-33403-4). ASME.
Burns, J. Patout & Fagin, Gerald M. The Holy Spirit. (Message of the Fathers of the Church Ser.: Vol. 3). 15.00 (ISBN 0-89453-343-6); pap. 8.95 (ISBN 0-89453-315-0). M Glazier.
Burns, J. Patout, ed. Theological Anthropology. LC 81-43080. (Sources of Early Christian Thought Ser.). 1981. pap. 6.95 (ISBN 0-8006-1412-7). Fortress.
Burns, J. Patout, ed. see Helgeland, John & Daly, Robert J.
Burns, Jabez. Three Hundred Sermon Sketches on Old & New Testament Texts. LC 61-14902. 1973. 12.95 (ISBN 0-8254-2207-8). Kregel.

--Two Hundred Scriptural Sermon Outlines. LC 75-92502. 424p. 1985. pap. 9.95 (ISBN 0-8254-2264-7). Kregel.

Burns, James. Handling Your Hormones: The "Straight Scoop" on Love & Sexuality. LC 84-60033. 156p. (Orig.). pap. 5.95 (ISBN 0-915929-01-5). Merit Bks.

--New Zealand Novels & Novelists Eighteen Sixty-One to Nineteen Seventy-Nine: A Bibliography. 1981. text ed. 20.00x (ISBN 0-86863-372-0, 00563). Heinemann Ed.

--New Zealand Novels & Novelists, 1861-1979: An Annotated Bibliography. 71p. 1983. lib. bdg. 10.95x (ISBN 0-86863-372-0, Pub. by Heinemann Pub New Zealand). Intl Spec Bk.

Burns, James F., ed. see Andreas, Barbara, et al.

Burns, James J. The Colonial Agents of New England. LC 75-29253. (Perspectives in American History Ser.: No. 26). 156p. 1975. Repr. of 1935 ed. lib. bdg. 19.50x (ISBN 0-87991-350-9). Porcupine Pr.

Burns, James M. Congress on Trial: The Legislative Process & the Administrative State. LC 66-29462. 1966. Repr. of 1949 ed. 10.00x (ISBN 0-87752-013-5). Gordian.

--Leadership. LC 76-5117. 1979. pap. 9.50xi (ISBN 0-06-131975-9, TB 1975, Torch). Har-Row.

--Leadership. LC 76-5117. 1978. 19.95i (ISBN 0-06-010588-7, HarpT). Har-Row.

--The Power to Lead: The Crisis of the American Presidency. 273p. 1984. 16.95 (ISBN 0-671-42731-8). S&S.

--Roosevelt: The Lion & the Fox. LC 56-7920. (Illus.). 1963. pap. 9.95 (ISBN 0-15-678870-5, Harv). HarBraceJ.

--Roosevelt: The Soldier of Freedom. LC 71-95877. (Illus.). 722p. 1973. pap. 10.95 (ISBN 0-15-678875-6, Harv). HarBraceJ.

--The Vineyard of Liberty. LC 83-3506. (Illus.). 768p. 1983. pap. 9.95 (ISBN 0-394-71629-9, Vin). Random.

--The Workshop of Democracy: The American Experiment, Vol. II. LC 85-40231. (Illus.). 704p. 1985. 24.95 (ISBN 0-394-51275-8). Knopf.

Burns, James M., jt. auth. see Mattina, Joseph S.

Burns, James M., et al. Government by the People, 3 pts. 11th ed. Incl. National, State, Local. 800p. text ed. 24.95 (ISBN 0-13-361253-8); wkbk. 8.50 (ISBN 0-13-361295-3); Basic. 480p. text ed. 22.95 (ISBN 0-13-361238-4); National. 640p. text ed. 23.95 (ISBN 0-13-361246-5); study guide 7.95 (ISBN 0-13-361287-2). (Illus.). 1981. study guide 7.95 (ISBN 0-13-361279-1). P-H.

--Government by the People: Basic. 12th ed. (Illus.). 480p. 1984. text ed. 26.95 (ISBN 0-13-361360-7). P-H.

--Government by the People: National. 12th ed. (Illus.). 592p. 1984. text ed. 27.95 (ISBN 0-13-361378-X). P-H.

--Government by the People: National, State & Local. 12th ed. (Illus.). 752p. 1984. text ed. 28.95 (ISBN 0-13-361386-0). P-H.

--Government by the People: State & Local Politics. 4th ed. (Illus.). 304p. 1984. text ed. 14.95 (ISBN 0-13-843524-3). P-H.

--Government by the People: Basic. 12th, alternate ed. (Illus.). 512p. 1985. text ed. 26.95 (ISBN 0-13-361502-2). P-H.

--Government by the People: National. 12th, alternate ed. (Illus.). 640p. 1985. text ed. 27.95 (ISBN 0-317-13557-0). P-H.

--Government by the People: National, State, Local. 12th, alternate ed. (Illus.). 800p. 1985. text ed. 28.95 (ISBN 0-13-361544-8). P-H.

Burns, James MacGregor. The American Experiment I: Vineyard of Liberty. LC 81-47510. 864p. 1982. 22.95 (ISBN 0-394-50546-8). Knopf.

Burns, James R., jt. auth. see Austin, Larry M.

Burns, Jane, jt. auth. see Rice, Martha.

Burns, Jane O., et al. The International Accounting & Tax Researchers' Publication Guide. LC 82-168710. 1982. 7.00 (ISBN 0-86539-039-8). Am Accounting.

Burns, Jerry. Acetylene Flowers. 1968. pap. 2.00 (ISBN 0-686-14903-3). Goliards Pr.

--PM in the AM. 1966. pap. 1.00 (ISBN 0-686-14905-X). Goliards Pr.

--Scherzo for Schizos. 1965. pap. 2.00 (ISBN 0-686-14904-1). Goliards Pr.

--The Way: A Trip in Tao Tarot Time. 1968. pap. 1.50 (ISBN 0-686-14906-8). Goliards Pr.

Burns, Jim. Arthropods: New Design Futures. 168p. 1972. 35.00x (ISBN 0-902620-77-0, Pub. by Academy Editions England). State Mutual Bk.

--Cells. 1967. saddlestitched in wrappers 1.00 (ISBN 0-685-78953-5, Pub. by Grosseteste). Small Pr Dist.

--Connections: Ways to Discover & Realize Community Potentials. 155p. 1979. 28.00 (ISBN 0-318-12949-3); members 26.00 (ISBN 0-318-12950-7). Am Plan Assn.

--Giving Yourself to God: Pursuing Excellence in Your Christian Life. (Orig.). pap. 3.95 wkbk. (ISBN 0-89081-488-0). Harvest Hse.

--Jim Burn's Youth Series--Leaders' Guide. (Orig.). 1985. pap. 4.95 (ISBN 0-89081-495-3). Harvest Hse.

--Living Your Life as God Intended. (Illus., Orig.). 1985. pap. 3.95 (ISBN 0-89081-450-3). Harvest Hse.

--Making Your Life Count. 64p. Wkbk 3.95 (ISBN 0-89081-392-2). Harvest Hse.

--The Ninety Day Experience. 112p. 1984. wkbk. 5.95 (ISBN 0-915929-12-0). Merit Bks.

--Putting God First. (Illus.). 64p. (gr. 7-10). 1983. wkbk. 3.95 (ISBN 0-89081-366-3). Harvest Hse.

Burns, Jim & Bostrom, Carol. Handling Your Hormones. (Illus.). 64p. (Orig.). 1984. involvement guide 4.95 (ISBN 0-915929-10-4); leader's guide 1.95 (ISBN 0-915929-14-7). Merit Bks.

Burns, Jim & Webster, Doug. Commitment to Growth: Experiencing the Fruit of the Spirit. 64p. (Orig.). 1985. wkbk. 3.95 (ISBN 0-89081-480-5). Harvest Hse.

Burns, Jim & McInerney, John, eds. The Food Industry in Britain: Economics & Policies. (Illus.). 320p. 1983. pap. text ed. 23.50 (ISBN 0-434-90191-1, Pub. by W Heinemann Ltd). David & Charles.

Burns, John & Twenty-Four Magazine Editors. Sacred Sex. White, Thomas R., ed. LC 74-84538. (Illus.). 150p. (Orig.). 1975. pap. 1.95 (ISBN 0-914896-01-6, Strength). East Ridge Pr.

Burns, John H. The Gallery. 1985. 6.95 (ISBN 0-87795-709-6). Arbor Hse.

Burns, John H. & Cook, John E. What You Should Know about Reducing Credit Losses. LC 66-25579. (Business Almanac Ser.: No. 10). 96p. 1966. 5.95 (ISBN 0-379-11210-8). Oceana.

Burns, John M. Biograffiti: A Natural Selection. 1981. pap. 3.95 (ISBN 0-393-00031-1). Norton.

--Evolutionary Differentiation: Differentiating Gold-Banded Skippers-Autochton Cellus & More (Lepidoptera: Hesperiidae: Pyrginae. LC 84-600229. (Smithsonian Contributions to Zoology Ser.: No. 405). pap. 20.00 (ISBN 0-317-30477-1, 2024818). Bks Demand UMI.

Burns, John P., jt. ed. see Scott, Ian.

Burns, Joseph A., ed. Planetary Satellites. LC 76-7475. 598p. 1977. text ed. 29.50x (ISBN 0-8165-0552-7). U of Ariz Pr.

Burns, Joseph M. Accounting Standards & International Finance: With Special Reference to Multinationals. LC 76-40618. 1976. pap. 4.25 (ISBN 0-8447-3225-7). Am Enterprise.

--Treatise on Markets: Spot, Futures, & Options. 1979. pap. 5.25 (ISBN 0-8447-3340-7). Am Enterprise.

Burns, Joseph W. A Study of the Antitrust Laws, Their Administration, Interpretation & Effect. LC 75-35360. 574p. 1976. Repr. of 1958 ed. lib. bdg. 29.00x (ISBN 0-8371-8580-7, BUAL). Greenwood.

Burns, Julie & Bialosiewicz, Frank. The Road to Birth Game. (Technical Note Ser.: No. 24). (Illus.). 33p. (Orig.). 1983. pap. text ed. 1.50 (ISBN 0-932288-71-5). Ctr Intl Ed U of Ma.

Burns, Julie & Swan, Dorothy. Reading Without Books. LC 78-72078. 1979. pap. 6.95 (ISBN 0-8224-5830-6). Pitman Learning.

Burns, Julie, jt. auth. see Bialosiewicz, Frank.

Burns, K. M., jt. auth. see Hallenbeck, W. H.

Burns, Karen L., ed. Guiding Catalog Growth: Sucessful Strategies, Management & Techniques. (Illus.). 325p. 1985. pap. text ed. 79.95 (ISBN 0-933641-04-4); pap. text ed. 49.95 members (ISBN 0-317-19314-7). Direct Mktng Assn.

Burns, Kathryn A. Managing the Burn Patient: A Guide for Nurses. LC 82-62402. 1983. 12.00 (ISBN 0-913590-97-5). Slack Inc.

Burns, Ken, tr. see Ohsawa, George.

Burns, Kenneth J., jt. auth. see Miller, Roger L.

Burns, Kenneth R. & Johnson, Patricia J. Health Assessment in Clinical Practice. (Illus.). 1980. text ed. 35.95 (ISBN 0-13-385054-4). P-H.

Burns, Kieran. Life Science & Religions. LC 83-25035. (Illus.). 209p. 1984. 25.00 (ISBN 0-8022-2415-6). Philos Lib.

Burns, Laurence E., jt. auth. see Thorpe, Geoffrey L.

Burns, Leland, jt. auth. see Klaassen, Leo.

Burns, Linda, ed. Ambulatory Surgery: Developing & Managing Successful Programs. LC 83-19732. 216p. 1983. 30.95 (ISBN 0-89443-897-2). Aspen Systems.

Burns, Linda A., jt. ed. see Meshenberg, Kathryn A.

Burns, Linda H., jt. auth. see Ilse, Sherokee.

Burns, Litany. Develop Your Psychic Abilities: And Get Them to Work for You in Your Daily Life. (Illus.). 204p. 1985. 15.95 (ISBN 0-13-205444-2); pap. 6.95 (ISBN 0-13-205436-1). P H.

Burns, Louis F. Osage Indian: Bands & Clans. 196p. 1984. 20.00 (ISBN 0-942574-04-4). Ciga Pr.

--Osage Indian Customs & Myths. (Illus.). 240p. 1984. 20.00x (ISBN 0-942574-06-0). Ciga Pr.

Burns, M. L. & Harding, A. K., eds. Positron-Electron Pairs in Astrophysics: AIP Conference Proceeding Center, Goddard Space Flight Center, 1983, No. 101. LC 83-71926. 447p. 1983. lib. bdg. 38.50 (ISBN 0-88318-200-9). Am Inst Physics.

Burns, Margaret A. & Morrissy, Lois E. Self-Assessment of Current Knowledge for the Operating Room Technician. 2nd ed. 1976. pap. 12.75 (ISBN 0-87488-474-8). Med Exam.

Burns, Margaret D. Pulmonary Care. (Patient Education Ser.). 384p. 1983. pap. 19.95x (ISBN 0-8385-8056-4). ACC.

Burns, Marilyn. The Book of Think: Or How to Solve Problems Twice Your Size. (Brown Paper School Bk.). (Illus.). (gr. 5 up). 1976. 13.45i (ISBN 0-316-11742-0); pap. 6.70i (ISBN 0-316-11743-9). Little.

--Good for Me! All about Food in 32 Bites. LC 78-6727. (Brown Paper School Book). (Illus.). (gr. 5 up). 1978. 11.45i (ISBN 0-316-11749-8); pap. 7.70i (ISBN 0-316-11747-1). Little.

--The Hink Pink Book. (Illus.). (gr. 1 up). 1981. 11.45i (ISBN 0-316-11744-7, Pub. by Atlantic Pr). Little.

--I Am Not a Short Adult: Getting Good at Being a Kid. (A Paper School Bk.). (Illus.). (gr. 5 up). 1977. 11.45 (ISBN 0-316-11745-5); pap. 7.70i (ISBN 0-316-11746-3). Little.

--The I Hate Mathematics! Book. (Brown Paper School Bks.). (Illus.). 128p. (gr. 5 up). 1975. 11.45i (ISBN 0-316-11740-4); pap. 7.70i (ISBN 0-316-11741-2). Little.

--Math for Smarty Pants: Or Who Says Mathematicians Have Little Pig Eyes. (A Paper School Bk.). (Illus.). 140p. (gr. 7 up). 1982. 11.45i (ISBN 0-316-11738-2); pap. 7.70i (ISBN 0-316-11739-0). Little.

--This Book Is about Time. LC 78-6614. (A Brown Paper School Bk.). (Illus.). (gr. 5 up). 1978. 13.45i (ISBN 0-316-11752-8); pap. 7.70 (ISBN 0-316-11750-1). Little.

Burns, Maureen A. Run with Your Dreams. (Illus.). 60p. 1982. pap. 5.00 (ISBN 0-9613084-0-0). Empey Ent.

Burns, Michael. McDonnell Douglas F-4K & F-M Phantom II. (Illus.). 192p. 1984. 19.95 (ISBN 0-85045-564-2, Pub. by Osprey England). Motorbooks Intl.

--Rural Society & French Politics: Boulangism & the Dreyfuss Affair, 1886-1900. LC 84-3253. (Illus.). 264p. 1984. text ed. 26.00x (ISBN 0-691-05423-1). Princeton U Pr.

Burns, Michael & Sanders, Mark, eds. Jumping Pond: Poems & Stories from the Ozarks. 100p. 1983. pap. 5.00 (ISBN 0-913785-00-8). S M S U.

Burns, Morris U. The Dramatic Criticism of Alexander Woollcott. LC 80-12935. 292p. 1980. 17.50 (ISBN 0-8108-1299-1). Scarecrow.

Burns, N. D., jt. auth. see Kochar, A. K.

Burns, Nancy. Nursing & Cancer. (Illus.). 400p. 1982. pap. 21.95 (ISBN 0-7216-2184-8). Saunders.

Burns, Nancy, jt. auth. see Schexnaydre, Linda.

Burns, Ned H., jt. auth. see Lin, T. Y.

Burns, Noel M. Erie: The Lake That Survived. LC 84-29822. (Illus.). 320p. 1985. 34.95x (ISBN 0-8476-7398-7). Rowman & Allanheld.

Burns, Norman. The Tariff of Syria, 1919 to 1932. LC 76-180328. (Mid-East Studies Ser.). Repr. of 1933 ed. 24.00 (ISBN 0-404-56234-5). AMS Pr.

Burns, Norman T. Christian Mortalism from Tyndale to Milton. LC 72-75406. 224p. 1972. 15.00x (ISBN 0-674-12875-3). Harvard U Pr.

Burns, Olive A. Cold Sassy Tree. LC 84-8570. 448p. 1984. 16.95 (ISBN 0-89919-309-9). Ticknor & Fields.

--Cold Sassy Tree. (Large Print Books (General Ser.)). 1985. lib. bdg. 18.95 (ISBN 0-8161-3880-X). G K Hall.

Burns, Patricia. Stacey's Flyer. 256p. 1985. 14.95 (ISBN 0-312-75483-3). St Martin.

Burns, Patricia H. The Book of Revelation Explained, Vol. 1. LC 82-90898. 53p. 1984. pap. 14.95 (ISBN 0-9611368-0-4). B R E Pub.

Burns, Paul, jt. ed. see Cumming, John.

Burns, Paul, jt. ed. see Cummings, John.

Burns, Paul, tr. see Clement, Olivier.

Burns, Paul C. & Bassett, Randall K. Language Arts Activities for Elementary Schools. LC 81-82574. 1982. 14.50 (ISBN 0-395-31688-X). HM.

Burns, Paul C. & Broman, Betty. The Language Arts in Childhood Education. 5th ed. LC 82-83367. 560p. 1982. text ed. 26.95 (ISBN 0-395-32756-3); instr's manual 2.00 (ISBN 0-395-32757-1). HM.

Burns, Paul C. & Roe, Betty D. Informal Reading Assessment. 1980. pap. 10.95 (ISBN 0-395-30574-8). HM.

--Reading Activities for Today's Elementary Schools. 1979. pap. 14.95 (ISBN 0-395-30573-X). HM.

Burns, Paul C. & Singer, Joe. The Portrait Painter's Problem Book. (Illus.). 1979. 21.95 (ISBN 0-8230-4186-7). Watson-Guptill.

Burns, Paul C., et al. Teaching Reading in Today's Elementary Schools. 3rd ed. LC 83-82564. 544p. Date not set. text ed. 24.95 (ISBN 0-395-34234-1); instr's. manual 2.00 (ISBN 0-395-34235-X). HM.

Burns, Peter, jt. auth. see Connelly, Finbarr.

Burns, R., ed. Sociological Backgrounds of Adult Education. (Notes & Essays Ser.: No. 41). 1970. pap. text ed. 2.50 (ISBN 0-685-76690-X, NES 41). Syracuse U Cont Ed.

Burns, R., tr. see Kargapolov, M. I. & Merzljakov, Ju. I.

Burns, R. B. Counseling & Therapy: An Introduction Survey. 1983. text ed. 25.00 (ISBN 0-85200-710-8, Pub. by MTP Pr England). Kluwer Academic.

--Experimental Psychology. (Illus.). 452p. 1981. text ed. 30.00 (ISBN 0-8391-1646-2). Univ Park.

--The Self Concept: Theory, Measurement, Development & Behaviour. (Illus.). 1979. pap. text ed. 13.95x (ISBN 0-582-48951-2). Longman.

Burns, R. B. & Dobson, C. B. Introductory Psychology. 1984. lib. bdg. 20.75 (ISBN 0-85200-491-5, Pub. by MTP Pr England). Kluwer Academic.

Burns, R. C. & Hardy, R. W. Nitrogen Fixation in Bacteria & Higher Plants. LC 75-2164. (Molecular Biology, Biochemistry, & Biophysics Ser.: Vol. 21). (Illus.). 225p. 1975. 38.00 (ISBN 0-387-07192-X). Springer-Verlag.

Burns, R. C. & Kaufman, S. H. Actions Styles & Symbols in Kinetic Family Drawings: An Interpretative Manual. LC 70-186854. 1972. pap. 16.95 (ISBN 0-87630-228-2). Brunner-Mazel.

Burns, R. G. & Slater, J. H. Experimental Microbial Ecology. 696p. 1982. text ed. 110.00x (ISBN 0-632-00765-6). Blackwell Pubns.

Burns, R. G., jt. auth. see Higgins, I. J.

Burns, R. G., ed. Soil Enzymes. 1978. 69.50 (ISBN 0-12-145850-4). Acad Pr.

Burns, R. G., tr. see Dubrovin, B. A., et al.

Burns, R. M. Conflict & Its Resolution in the Administration of Mineral Resources in Canada. 63p. (Orig.). 1976. pap. text ed. 5.00x (ISBN 0-88757-000-3, Pub. by Ctr Resource Stud Canada). Brookfield Pub Co.

--The Great Debate on Miracles: From Joseph Glanvill to David Hume. LC 78-75197. 300p. 1981. 28.50 (ISBN 0-8387-2378-0). Bucknell U Pr.

Burns, Ralph. Any Given Day. LC 84-16230. (The Alabama Poetry Ser.). (Illus.). 64p. 1985. 11.75 (ISBN 0-8173-0259-X); pap. 5.95 (ISBN 0-8173-0260-3). U of Ala Pr.

--Us. (CSU Poetry Ser.: No. 12). 43p. (Orig.). 1983. pap. 4.50 (ISBN 0-914946-38-2). Cleveland St Univ Poetry Ctr.

Burns, Ralph & Pfingston, Roger. Windy Tuesday Nights. Buchwald, Emilie, ed. LC 84-60939. (Mountains in Minnesota Ser.). 48p. 1984. pap. 6.00 (ISBN 0-915943-03-4). Milkweed Ed.

Burns, Ralph O. Basic Bible Truths for New Converts. 30p. 1978. pap. 0.60 (ISBN 0-87227-007-6). Reg Baptist.

Burns, Raymond S. The Ile of Guls. LC 79-54331. (Renaissance Drama Ser.). 302p. 1982. lib. bdg. 40.00 (ISBN 0-8240-4450-9). Garland Pub.

Burns, Rex. The Avenging Angel. (Gabe Wager Mystery Ser.). 240p. 1983. 12.50 (ISBN 0-670-14317-0). Viking.

--The Avenging Angel: A Gabe Wager Mystery. (Crime Monthly Ser.). 240p. 1984. pap. 3.50 (ISBN 0-14-007104-0). Penguin.

--Strip Search. (A Gabe Wager Mystery Ser.). 300p. 1984. 13.95 (ISBN 0-670-67905-4). Viking.

--Strip Search. (Crime Monthly Ser.). 272p. 1985. pap. 3.50 (ISBN 0-14-007747-2). Penguin.

--Success in America: The Yeoman Dream & the Industrial Revolution. LC 75-32482. (Illus.). 224p. 1976. 15.00x (ISBN 0-87023-207-X). U of Mass Pr.

Burns, Richard. Avebury. 1972. signed ltd. ed. 15.00 (ISBN 0-685-36831-9, Pub. by Anvil Pr); 6.95 (ISBN 0-685-36832-7); 4.95. Small Pr Dist.

--Double Flute. 1972. 4.50 (ISBN 0-685-56659-5, Pub. by Enitharmon Pr); signed 13.50 (ISBN 0-685-56660-9); pap. 2.50 (ISBN 0-685-56661-7). Small Pr Dist.

--Roots-Routes. (Illus.). 44p. (Orig.). 1982. pap. 8.00 (ISBN 0-914946-32-3). Cleveland St Univ Poetry Ctr.

--Some Poems. 1977. 9.50 (ISBN 0-685-90001-0, Pub. by Enitharmon Pr). Small Pr Dist.

Burns, Richard, tr. see Vianello, Aldo.

Burns, Richard C., jt. auth. see Cohen, Stephen.

Burns, Richard D. & Leitenberg, Milton. The Wars in Vietnam, Cambodia & Laos, 1945-1982: A Bibliographic Guide. LC 80-13246. (War-Peace Bibliography Ser.: No. 18). 290p. 1984. 58.50 (ISBN 0-87436-310-1). ABC-Clio.

Burns, Richard D., ed. Harry S. Truman: A Bibliography of His Times & Presidency. LC 84-20223. 354p. 1984. 50.00 (ISBN 0-8420-2219-8). Scholarly Res Inc.

Burns, Richard D. & Bennett, Edward M., eds. Diplomats in Crisis: United States-Chinese-Japanese Relations, 1919-1941. 345p. 1974. 16.95x (ISBN 0-686-84012-7). Regina Bks.

Burns, Richard D., ed. see Smith, Myron J., Jr.

Burns, Richard D., et al, eds. Continuing Dialogue: Men & Issues in Early American History. rev. ed. LC 63-23420. (Orig.). 1964. pap. text ed. 3.50x (ISBN 0-87015-141-X). Pacific Bks.

Burns, Richard Dean & Society for Historians of American Foreign Relations. Guide to American Foreign Relations since 1700. LC 82-13905. 1311p. 1982. lib. bdg. 135.00 (ISBN 0-87436-323-3). ABC-Clio.

Burns, Richard W. & Brooks, Gary D., eds. Curriculum Design in a Changing Society. LC 75-122811. 366p. 1970. 26.95 (ISBN 0-87778-003-X). Educ Tech Pubns.

Burns, Richard W. & Klingstedt, Joe L., eds. Competency-Based Education: An Introduction. LC 73-3133. 180p. 1973. pap. 15.95 (ISBN 0-87778-061-7). Educ Tech Pubns.

Burns, Rita. The Books of Ezra & Nehemiah. (Bible Commentary Ser.). 112p. 1985. pap. 2.50 (ISBN 0-8146-1418-3). Liturgical Pr.

--Exodus, Leviticus, Numbers, with Excursus on Feasts, Ritual, Typology. (Old Testament Message Ser.: Vol. 3). 15.95 (ISBN 0-89453-403-3); pap. 9.95 (ISBN 0-89453-238-3). M Glazier.

Burns, Rob. The Quest for Modernity: The Place of Arno Holz in Modern German Literature. (European University Studies, German Language & Literature: Ser. 1, Vol. 431). 278p. 1981. pap. 39.20 (ISBN 3-8204-6225-2). P Lang Pubs.

Burns, Robert. The Caledonian Musical Museum, 3 vols. LC 72-144553. 1976. Repr. of 1811 ed. Set. 92.50 (ISBN 0-404-08520-2). AMS Pr.

--Choice of Burns's Poems & Songs. 156p. 1966. pap. 6.95 (ISBN 0-571-06835-9). Faber & Faber.

--Commonplace Book. 1983. 95.00 (ISBN 0-900000-32-5, Pub. by Centaur Pr England). State Mutual Bk.

--The Glenriddell Manuscripts of Robert Burns: Poems, Vol. I. LC 73-4824. 1914. lib. bdg. 15.00 (ISBN 0-8414-3103-5). Folcroft.

--The Glenriddell Manuscripts of Robert Burns: Letters, Vol. II. LC 73-4824. 1914. lib. bdg. 15.00 (ISBN 0-8414-3100-0). Folcroft.

--Jesuits & the Indian Wars of the Northwest. 550p. (Orig.). 1985. pap. 10.95 (ISBN 0-89301-110-X). U Pr of Idaho.

--The Kilmarnock Poems: (Poems, Chiefly in the Scottish Dialect, 1786) Low, Donald A., ed. 256p. 1985. 22.50x (ISBN 0-460-00343-7, Pub. by Evman England); pap. 6.95x (ISBN 0-460-01343-2). Biblio Dist.

--Letters of Robert Burns, 2 Vols. Lancey furgeson, J. De, ed. LC 76-144921. (Illus.). 1971. Set. 95.00x (ISBN 0-403-00884-0). Scholarly.

--The Letters of Robert Burns. 2 Vols. 2nd ed. Ferguson, De Lancey & Roy, G. Ross, eds. 1985. Vol. 1, 1780-1789, 65.00x (ISBN 0-19-812478-3); Vol. II, 1790-1796, 65.00x (ISBN 0-19-812321-3). Oxford U Pr.

--Poems & Songs. Kinsley, James, ed. (Oxford Standard Authors Ser). 1969. 35.00 (ISBN 0-19-254164-1); pap. 12.95x (ISBN 0-19-281114-2). Oxford U Pr.

--Poems & Songs. 144p. 1981. 20.00x (ISBN 0-903065-20-7, Pub. by Wright Pub Scotland). State Mutual Bk.

--Poems & Songs of Robert Burns, 3 Vols. Kinsley, James, ed. (English Texts Series). 1968. 149.00x (ISBN 0-19-811843-0). Oxford U Pr.

--Poems, Chiefly in the Scottish Dialect. LC 72-153518. Repr. of 1786 ed. 12.50 (ISBN 0-404-08977-1). AMS Pr.

--The Poetical Works of Burns. (Cambridge Editions Ser.). 1974. 25.00 (ISBN 0-395-18486-X). HM.

--Poetry of Robert Burns, 4 Vols. Henley, William E. & Henderson, Thomas F., eds. LC 78-113567. Repr. of 1897 ed. Set. 120.00 (ISBN 0-404-01250-7); 30.00 ea. Vol. 1 (ISBN 0-404-01251-5). Vol. 2 (ISBN 0-404-01252-3). Vol. 3 (ISBN 0-404-01253-1). Vol. 4 (ISBN 0-404-01254-X). AMS Pr.

--The Prose Works of Robert Burns. LC 79-144501. Repr. of 1839 ed. 21.50 (ISBN 0-404-08509-1). AMS Pr.

--Reliques of Robert Burns: Consisting Chiefly of Original Letters, Poems, & Critical Observations on Scottish Songs, Collected & Published by Robert Cromek (1780-1812) LC 78-72777. Repr. of 1808 ed. 44.50 (ISBN 0-404-17628-3). AMS Pr.

--Songs of Robert Burns. Dick, James C., ed. LC 79-144552. Repr. of 1903 ed. 37.50 (ISBN 0-404-08511-3). AMS Pr.

--Twenty Favorite Songs & Poems of Robert Burns. 48p. 1982. 4.95 (ISBN 0-85683-040-2, Pub by Shepheard-Walwyn). Flatiron Book Dist.

Burns, Robert, jt. auth. see Cunningham, Allan.

Burns, Robert, jt. auth. see Kramer-Muirhead, May.

Burns, Robert, et al. The Merry Muses of Caledonia. Barke, James & Smith, Sydney G., eds. 224p. 1983. 35.00x (ISBN 0-904265-71-4, Pub. by Macdonald Pub UK). State Mutual Bk.

Burns, Robert A. Diplomacy, War & Parliamentary Democracy: Further Lessons from the Falklands or Advice from Academe. 62p. (Orig.). 1985. pap. text ed. 7.50 (ISBN 0-8191-4610-2). U Pr of Amer.

Burns, Robert C. Self-Growth in Families: Kinetic Family Drawings (K-F-D Research & Application) LC 81-21659. (Illus.). 220p. 1982. 25.00 (ISBN 0-87630-291-6); pap. 16.95 (ISBN 0-87630-305-X). Brunner-Mazel.

Burns, Robert D. & Stiles, Karl A. Laboratory Explorations in General Zoology. 6th ed. 1977. write for info. (ISBN 0-02-317160-X, 31716). Macmillan.

Burns, Robert E. I Am a Fugitive from a Georgia Chain Gang. LC 76-164143. 257p. 1972. Repr. of 1932 ed. 43.00x (ISBN 0-8103-3016-4). Gale.

--The Shape & Form of Puget Sound. LC 84-15354. (A Pugest Sound Bks.). (Illus.). 114p. (Orig.). 1985. pap. 8.95 (ISBN 0-295-96184-8). U of Wash Pr.

Burns, Robert E., jt. auth. see Farrell, Thomas J.

Burns, Robert E., ed. The Best of U. S. Catholic. 300p. 1984. pap. 15.95 (ISBN 0-88347-198-1). Thomas More.

Burns, Robert I. Diplomatarium of the Crusader Kingdom of Valencia: The Registered Charters of Its Conqueror, Jaume I, 1257-1276. Volume I: Society & Documentation in Crusader Valencia. LC 84-17828. (Illus.). 288p. 1985. text ed. 40.00x (ISBN 0-691-05435-5). Princeton U Pr.

--The Jesuits & the Indian Wars of the Northwest. LC 65-22314. (Yale Western Americana Ser.: No. 11). pap. 139.30 (ISBN 0-317-29588-8, 2021985). Bks Demand UMI.

--Medieval Colonialism: Post-Crusade Exploitation of Islamic Valencia. (Illus.). 432p. 1975. 42.00 (ISBN 0-691-05227-1). Princeton U Pr.

--Muslims, Christians & Jews in the Crusader Kingdom of Valencia: Societies in Symbiosis. LC 83-2007. (Cambridge Iberian & Latin American Studies). 300p. 1984. 62.50 (ISBN 0-521-24374-2). Cambridge U Pr.

Burns, Robert L. Measurement of the Need for Transporting; Basis for State Equalization of Transportation Costs. LC 72-176614. (Columbia University. Teachers College. Contributions to Education Ser.: No. 289). Repr. of 1927 ed. 22.50 (ISBN 0-404-55289-7). AMS Pr.

Burns, Robert M. & Bradley, William W. Protective Coatings for Metals. 3rd ed. LC 67-20826. (ACS Monograph: No. 163). 1967. 53.95 (ISBN 0-8412-0285-0). Am Chemical.

Burns, Robert T. Moors & Crusaders in Mediterranean Spain. 318p. 1978. 60.00x (ISBN 0-86078-018-X, Pub. by Variorum). State Mutual Bk.

Burns, Robert V. & Johnson, Rees C. Sixty Forms for the Entrepreneur: Forms Generator - Apple II, II Plus, IIc & IIe. 192p. 1985. pap. cancelled (ISBN 0-88056-256-0). Dilithium Pr.

--Sixty Forms for the Entrepreneur: Forms Generator - Commodore 64. 192p. 1985. pap. cancelled (ISBN 0-88056-257-9). Dilithium Pr.

--Sixty Forms for the Entrepreneur: Forms Generator - IBM-PC, PCjr & PC XT. 192p. 1985. pap. cancelled (ISBN 0-88056-258-7). Dilithium Pr.

--Sixty Forms for the Landlord: Forms Generator - Apple II, II Plus, IIc & IIe. 192p. 1985. pap. cancelled (ISBN 0-88056-253-6). Dilithium Pr.

--Sixty Forms for the Landlord: Forms Generator - Commodore 64. 192p. 1985. pap. cancelled (ISBN 0-88056-254-4). Dilithium Pr.

--Sixty Forms for the Landlord: Forms Generator - IBM-PC, PCjr & PC XT. 192p. 1985. pap. cancelled (ISBN 0-88056-255-2). Dilithium Pr.

--Sixty Forms for Your Household: Forms Generator for Your Apple II, Apple II Plus, & Apple IIc & IIe. 192p. 1985. pap. 29.95 incl. disk (ISBN 0-88056-250-1). Dilithium Pr.

--Sixty Forms for Your Household: Forms Generator for Your Commodore 64. 192p. 1985. pap. 29.95 incl. disk (ISBN 0-88056-251-X). Dilithium Pr.

--Sixty Forms for Your Household: Forms Generator for Your IBM-PC, IBM-PCjr & IBM-PC XT. 192p. 1985. pap. 29.95 incl. disk (ISBN 0-88056-252-8). Dilithium Pr.

Burns, Roger G., ed. Marine Minerals, Vol. 6. 380p. 1979. 13.00 (ISBN 0-939950-06-5). Mineralogical Soc.

Burns, Ronald M. Intergovernmental Fiscal Transfer: Canadian & Australian Experiences. (Centre for Research on Federal Financial Relations Research Monograph: No. 22). pap. 6.00 (ISBN 0-7081-1056-8, Pub by ANUP Australia). Australia N U P.

--One Country or Two? LC 76-174566. pap. 74.30 (2023836). Bks Demand UMI.

Burns, Ruby. Josephine Clardy Fox. LC 73-83925. 1973. 8.00 (ISBN 0-87404-042-6). Tex Western.

Burns, Samuel T. Harmonic Skills Used by Selected High School Choral Leaders. LC 79-176605. (Columbia University. Teachers College. Contributions to Education: No. 905). Repr. of 1945 ed. 22.50 (ISBN 0-404-55905-0). AMS Pr.

Burns, Shannon, et al. An Annotated Bibliography of Texts on Writing Skills: Grammar, Composition, Rhetoric, Technical Writing. LC 75-24096. (Reference Library of the Humanities: Vol. 38). 250p. 1975. lib. bdg. 34.00 (ISBN 0-8240-9968-0). Garland Pub.

Burns, Sheila, jt. auth. see Walczac, Yvette.

Burns, Sheila L. Cancer: Understanding & Fighting It. Anderson, Madelyn K., ed. LC 82-8151. (Illus.). 64p. (gr. 4 up). 1982. lib. bdg. 9.29 (ISBN 0-671-44250-3). Messner.

--A Christmas Carol. LC 78-72141. (Illus.). (gr. 2-5). Date not set. 6.00 (ISBN 0-89799-093-5); pap. price not set (ISBN 0-89799-064-1). Dandelion Pr.

Burns, Shelia L. Allergies & You. LC 79-26637. (Illus.). 64p. (gr. 4 up). 1980. PLB 9.29 (ISBN 0-671-33044-6). Messner.

Burns, Sherman. From the Heart. 64p. (Orig.). 1981. pap. 3.95 (ISBN 0-686-30386-5). Vistula Pr.

Burns, Steven L. & Nickens, Wayne. Not Guilty, Not Crazy. 150p. (Orig.). (YA) (gr. 11 up). 1985. pap. 6.00 (ISBN 0-933131-00-3). I-Med Pr.

Burns, Stuart L. Whores Before Descartes: Assorted Poetry & Sordid Prose. LC 80-54381. 96p. (Orig.). 1980. pap. 4.50 (ISBN 0-9605326-0-9). Wash Launderan.

Burns, T. & Hendrickson, Harvey. The Accounting Sampler. 3rd ed. 1976. text ed. 24.95 (ISBN 0-07-009202-8). McGraw.

Burns, T. J. & Hendrickson, H. S. Accounting Sampler. 4th, rev. ed. 688p. 1986. 10.95 (ISBN 0-07-009206-0). McGraw.

Burns, Tex, pseud. Hopalong Cassidy & the Riders of High Rock. 320p. 1974. Repr. of 1951 ed. lib. bdg. 15.95 (ISBN 0-88411-207-1, Pub. by Aeonian Pr). Amereon Ltd.

--Hopalong Cassidy & the Rustlers of West Fork. 1976. Repr. of 1950 ed. lib. bdg. 15.95 (ISBN 0-88411-242-X, Pub. by Aeonian Pr). Amereon Ltd.

--Hopalong Cassidy & the Trail to Seven Pines. 1976. Repr. of 1950 ed. lib. bdg. 15.95 (ISBN 0-88411-243-8, Pub. by Aeonian Pr). Amereon Ltd.

--Hopalong Cassidy: Trouble Shooter. 1976. Repr. of 1952 ed. lib. bdg. 15.95 (ISBN 0-88411-241-1, 241, Pub. by Aeonian Pr). Amereon Ltd.

Burns, Thomas A. Doing the Wash. LC 76-25573. 1976. lib. bdg. 30.00 (ISBN 0-8414-3217-1). Folcroft.

Burns, Thomas J. & Coffman, Edward N. Ohio State Institute of Accounting Conference Collected Papers, 1938 to 1963. original anthology ed. Brief, Richard P., ed. LC 80-1455. (Dimensions of Accounting Theory & Practice Ser.). 1981. lib. bdg. 23.00x (ISBN 0-405-13477-0). Ayer Co Pubs.

Burns, Thomas J., ed. Accounting in Transition: Oral Histories of Recent U. S. Experience. 1974. pap. 3.00x (ISBN 0-87776-309-7, AA9). Ohio St U Admin Sci.

Burns, Thomas J., ed. see Accounting Symposium, Ohio State Univ, 1968.

Burns, Thomas J., ed. see Accounting Symposium, Ohio State Univ., 1972.

Burns, Thomas J., jt. ed. see Livingstone, J. Leslie.

Burns, Thomas S. A History of the Ostrogoths. LC 83-49286. (Illus.). 320p. 1984. 29.95x (ISBN 0-253-32831-4). Ind U Pr.

Burns, Tom. The BBC: Public Institution & Private World. 313p. 1977. text ed. 24.50x (ISBN 0-8419-5025-3). Holmes & Meier.

Burns, Tom & Stalker, G. M. Management of Innovation. (Orig.). 1961. pap. 13.95x (ISBN 0-422-72050-X, NO. 2118, Pub. by Tavistock England). Methuen Inc.

Burns, Tom R. Man, Decisions, Society. (Studies In Cybernetics). 356p. 1985. text ed. 52.00 (ISBN 2-88124-004-6); pap. text ed. 22.00 (ISBN 2-88124-026-7). Gordon.

Burns, Tom R., et al. Mans, Decision, Society. (Studies in Cybernetics: Vol. 10). 288p. 1985. text ed. 52.00 (ISBN 2-88124-004-6); pap. 22.00 (ISBN 2-88124-026-7). Gordon.

Burns, Tom R., et al, eds. Work & Power: The Liberation of Work & the Control of Political Power. LC 78-63143. (Sage Studies in International Sociology: Vol. 18). (Illus.). 391p. 1979. 28.00 (ISBN 0-8039-9846-5); pap. 14.00 (ISBN 0-8039-9847-3). Sage.

Burns, Vincent G., ed. The Red Harvest: A Cry for Peace. LC 30-7017. (Granger Poetry Library). 1976. Repr. of 1930 ed. 27.75x (ISBN 0-89609-008-6). Granger Bk.

Burns, Virginia. William Beaumont: Frontier Doctor. LC 78-72566. (Illus.). 1978. lib. bdg. 8.50 (ISBN 0-9604726-0-6). Enterprise Pr.

Burns, Virginia L. Lewis Cass-Frontier Soldier. LC 80-81133. (Illus.). 1980. lib. bdg. 10.50 (ISBN 0-9604726-1-4). Enterprise Pr.

Burns, W. E., jt. auth. see Schaeffer, Glen N.

Burns, Walter N. The Saga of Billy the Kid. Repr. of 1926 ed. 30.00 (ISBN 0-686-19886-7). Ridgeway Bks.

--The Saga of Billy the Kid. 322p. 1984. Repr. of 1925 ed. lib. bdg. 40.00 (ISBN 0-918377-03-X). Russell Pr.

Burns, Wayne. Charles Reade: A Study in Victorian Authorship. LC 61-7182. 360p. 1961. text ed. 28.50x (ISBN 0-8290-0161-1). Irvington.

--Journey Through the Dark Woods. LC 82-15822. 230p. (Orig.). 1982. pap. 6.95 (ISBN 0-9609666-0-9). Howe St Pr.

Burns, Willard A. & Bretschneider, Ann. Thin Is In: Plastic Embedding of Tissue for Light Microscopy. LC 81-10876. (Illus.). 58p. 1981. text ed. 35.00 (ISBN 0-89189-083-1, 16-1-030-00); with slides 75.00 (ISBN 0-89189-145-5, 15-1-030-00). Am Soc Clinical.

Burns, William. Under Pressure. 40p. (Orig.). 1983. pap. 5.00 (ISBN 0-910429-04-9). Stronghold Pr.

--Your Future in Museums. LC 67-15470. (Careers in Depth Ser.). (gr. 8-12). 1974. PLB 8.97 (ISBN 0-8239-0053-3). Rosen Group.

Burns, William A. Enjoying the Arts: Museums. (YA) 1977. PLB 8.97 (ISBN 0-8239-0389-3). Rosen Group.

Burns, William C. Revival Sermons. 205p. 1981. pap. 4.45 (ISBN 0-85151-316-6). Banner of Truth.

Burns, William H. The Voices of Negro Protest in Amercia. LC 80-21197. 88p. 1980. Repr. of 1963 ed. lib. bdg. 22.50x (ISBN 0-313-22219-3, BUVN). Greenwood.

Burns, William J. Economic Aid & American Policy Toward Egypt, 1955-1981. 256p. 1984. 32.50x (ISBN 0-87395-868-3); pap. 10.95x (ISBN 0-87395-869-1). State U NY Pr.

--Masked War: The Story of a Peril That Threatened the United States. LC 76-90168. (Mass Violence in America Ser). Repr. of 1913 ed. 13.50 (ISBN 0-405-01303-5). Ayer Co Pubs.

Burns, William J., jt. auth. see Lavigne, John V.

Burns, William J. & LaVigne, John V., eds. Review of Pediatric Psychology, Vol. 1. 304p. 1984. 44.50 (ISBN 0-8089-1602-5, 790727). Grune.

Burns-Cox, jt. auth. see Read.

Burnshaw, Stanley. In the Terrified Radiance. LC 72-80013. 1972. 6.50 (ISBN 0-8076-0652-9); pap. 2.45 (ISBN 0-8076-0653-7). Braziller.

--My Friend, My Father. 160p. 1985. pap. 7.95 (ISBN 0-19-503723-5). Oxford U Pr.

--The Refusers. 1981. 14.95 (ISBN 0-8180-0630-7). Horizon.

--The Seamless Web. LC 71-97603. 1970. pap. 6.50 (ISBN 0-8076-0535-2). Braziller.

Burnshaw, Stanley, ed. The Poem Itself. 380p. 1980. pap. 7.95 (ISBN 0-8180-1128-9). Horizon.

Burnside, C. D. Electro-Magnetic Distance Measurement. (Illus.). 128p. 1971. pap. text ed. 12.95x (ISBN 0-8464-0363-3). Beekman Pubs.

--Electromagnetic Distance Measurement. 2nd ed. 224p. 1982. pap. 20.00x (ISBN 0-246-11624-2, Pub. by Granada England). Sheridan.

--Electromagnetic Distance Measurement: Aspects of Modern Land Surveying. 117p. 1982. pap. text ed. 24.50x (ISBN 0-258-11624-2, Pub. by Granada England). Brookfield Pub Co.

Burnside, Irene & Ebersole, Priscilla. Psychosocial Caring Throughout the Life Span. (Illus.). 1979. text ed. 32.50 (ISBN 0-07-009213-3). McGraw.

Burnside, Irene M. Nursing & the Aged. 2nd ed. (Illus.). 736p. 1980. text ed. 32.50 (ISBN 0-07-009211-7). McGraw.

--Psychosocial Nursing Care of the Aged. 2nd ed. (Illus.). 1980. text ed. 22.95 (ISBN 0-07-009210-9). McGraw.

--Working with the Elderly: Group Process & Techniques. 2nd ed. LC 83-19774. 700p. 1984. pap. text ed. 17.25x pub net (ISBN 0-534-03022-X). Wadsworth Health.

Burnside, John A. Physical Diagnosis: An Introduction to Clinical Medicine. 16th ed. (Illus.). 260p. 1981. 18.50 (ISBN 0-683-01137-5). Williams & Wilkins.

Burnstein, Chaya. Joseph & Anna's Time Capsule: A Legacy of Old Jewish Prague. (Illus.). 32p. 1984. 8.95 (ISBN 0-318-00228-0). Summit Bks.

Burnstein, M. L. New Directions in Economic Policy. LC 78-3104. (Illus.). 1978. 27.50x (ISBN 0-312-56620-4). St Martin.

Burnstein, Patricia. Family Holiday. LC 81-16865. 320p. 1982. 13.50 (ISBN 0-686-78964-4). Morrow.

Burnstein, Saul, ed. see Jefferson, Roland S.

Burnstock, G., et al, eds. Somatic & Autonomic Nerve-Muscle Interactions: Research Monographs in Cell & Tissue Physiology, Vol. 8. 384p. 1983. 106.50 (ISBN 0-444-80458-7). Elsevier.

Burnyeat, M. F. Conflicting Appearances. 1981. 15.50x (ISBN 0-686-79156-8, Pub. by Brit Acad England). State Mutual Bk.

Burnyeat, Myles, ed. The Skeptical Tradition. LC 78-62833. (Major Thinkers Ser.). 536p. 1983. text ed. 40.00x (ISBN 0-520-03747-2); pap. text ed. 10.95x (ISBN 0-520-04795-8). U of Cal Pr.

Burnyeat, Myles F., ed. see Plato.

Buros, Oscar K., ed. English Tests & Reviews. LC 75-8109. xxiii, 395p. 1975. 30.00x (ISBN 0-910674-15-9). U of Nebr Pr.

--Foreign Language Tests & Reviews. LC 75-8110. xxiii, 312p. 1975. 25.00x (ISBN 0-910674-16-7). U of Nebr Pr.

--Intelligence Tests & Reviews. LC 75-8112. xxvii, 1129p. 1975. 70.00x (ISBN 0-8032-1163-5). U of Nebr Pr.

--Mathematics Tests & Reviews. LC 75-8113. xxv, 435p. 1975. 25.00x (ISBN 0-910674-18-3). U of Nebr Pr.

--Mental Measurements Yearbook. Incl. 1st. xvi, 415p. 1938. 25.00x (ISBN 0-910674-12-4); 3rd. 1949. xvi, 1047p. 35.00x (ISBN 0-910674-03-5); 5th. xxvii, 1292p. 1959. 50.00x (ISBN 0-8032-1164-3); 6th. xxxvi, 1714p. 1965. 65.00x (ISBN 0-910674-06-X); 7th, 2 vols. xl, 1986p. 1972. Set. 100.00x (ISBN 0-8032-1160-0); 8th, 2 vols. xliv, 2182p. 1978. Set. 140.00x (ISBN 0-910674-24-8). LC 39-3422. U of Nebr Pr.

--Mental Measurements Yearbook. 2nd ed. xxi, 674p. 1941. 30.00x (ISBN 0-910674-13-2). U of Nebr Pr.

--Mental Measurements Yearbook. 4th ed. xxvi, 1163p. 1953. 40.00x (ISBN 0-910674-04-3). U of Nebr Pr.

--Personality Tests & Reviews I. xxxi, 1659p. 1970. 50.00x (ISBN 0-910674-10-8). U of Nebr Pr.

--Personality Tests & Reviews II. LC 74-13192. xxxi, 841p. 1975. 55.00x (ISBN 0-910674-19-1). U of Nebr Pr.

--Reading Tests & Reviews I. xxii, 520p. 1968. 20.00x (ISBN 0-910674-09-4). U of Nebr Pr.

--Reading Tests & Reviews II. LC 70-13495. xxvi, 257p. 1975. 20.00x (ISBN 0-910674-20-5). U of Nebr Pr.

--Science Tests & Reviews. LC 75-8114. xxiii, 296p. 1975. 25.00x (ISBN 0-910674-21-3). U of Nebr Pr.

--Social Studies Tests & Reviews. LC 75-8115. xxiii, 227p. 1975. 25.00x (ISBN 0-910674-22-1). U of Nebr Pr.

--Tests in Print I. xxix, 479p. 1961. 25.00x (ISBN 0-910674-08-6). U of Nebr Pr.

--Tests in Print II. LC 74-24605. xxxix, 1107p. 1974. 85.00x (ISBN 0-910674-14-0). U of Nebr Pr.

--Vocational Tests & Reviews. LC 75-8116. xxvi, 1087p. 1975. 65.00x (ISBN 0-8032-4650-1). U of Nebr Pr.

Burov, Michael, tr. see Bogolepov, N. N.

Burov, Micheal, tr. see Volkov, M. V. & Oganesyan, O. V.

Burov, Nadezhda, tr. see Khoros, Vladmir.

Burova, Nadezhda, tr. see Brutents, Karen.

Burow, Daniel R. & Greene, Carol, eds. The Little Christian's Songbook. 64p. 1975. pap. 5.50 (ISBN 0-570-03435-3, 56-1266). Concordia.

Burpee, Lawrence J. Discovery of Canada. LC 74-2412. (Essay Index Reprint Ser.). Repr. of 1944 ed. 20.75 (ISBN 0-518-10161-4). Ayer Co Pubs.

Burpee, Lawrence J., ed. see La Verendrye, Pierre G.

Burpee, Lois. Lois Burpee's Gardener's Companion & Cookbook. LC 82-47736. (Illus.). 256p. 1983. 14.37i (ISBN 0-06-038021-7, HarpT). Har-Row.

Burpee, R. H. Seven Quickly Administered Tests of Physical Capacity & Their Use in Detecting Physical Incapacity for Motor Activity in Men & Boys. LC 76-176615. (Columbia University. Teachers College. Contributions to Education: No. 818). Repr. of 1940 ed. 22.50 (ISBN 0-404-55818-6). AMS Pr.

Burpo, John H. Police Labor Movement: Problems & Perspectives. 224p. 1971. 23.75x (ISBN 0-398-00262-2). C C Thomas.

Burqhardt, ed. see Jerome, Saint.

Burqhardt, ed. see Paulinus of Nola, Saint.

Burquest, D. A. A Preliminary Study of Angas Phonology. (Language Data, African Ser.: No. 1). 52p. 1971. pap. 2.75x (ISBN 0-88312-601-X); microfiche 1.50x (ISBN 0-88312-701-6). Summer Inst Ling.

Burr. Chemi-& Bioluminescence. (Clinical & Biochemical Analysis Ser.). 658p. 1985. 85.00 (ISBN 0-8247-7277-6). Dekker.

--Elementary Statistical Quality Control. (Statistics; Textbooks & Monograph Ser.: Vol. 25). 1978. 29.75 (ISBN 0-8247-6686-5). Dekker.

--Elementary Statistical Quality Control. 432p. 22.50 (ISBN 0-318-13208-7). Am Soc QC.

Burr, A. H. Mechanical Analysis & Design. 640p. 1981. 34.00 (ISBN 0-444-00324-X); instr's. manual avail. Elsevier.

Burr, Aaron. Political Correspondence & Public Papers of Aaron Burr, 2 vols. Kline, Mary-Jo & Ryan, Joanne W., eds. LC 82-61396. (Illus.). 1118p. 125.00 (ISBN 0-691-04685-9). Princeton U Pr.

--The Private Journal of Aaron Burr, 2 vols. LC 75-31113. (Reprinted from orig. MS). Repr. of 1903 ed. 86.50 set (ISBN 0-404-13710-5). AMS Pr.

--Reports of the Trials of Colonel Aaron Burr, 2 Vols. LC 69-11321. (Law, Politics & History Ser). 1969. Repr. of 1808 ed. lib. bdg. 89.50 (ISBN 0-306-71182-6). Da Capo.

Burr, Allston, ed. Sir Walter Scott, an Index, Placing the Short Poems in His Novels & His Long Poems & Dramas. LC 76-148632. vi, 130p. Repr. of 1936 ed. lib. bdg. 18.75 (ISBN 0-8371-5994-6, BUSW). Greenwood.

Burr, Angela. I Am Not My Body: A Study of the International Hare Krishna Sect. 352p. 1984. text ed. 35.00x (ISBN 0-7069-2296-4, Pub by Vikas India). Advent NY.

Burr, Angle, ed. see Thomas, David B.

Burr, Ann M., jt. auth. see Runkel, Philip J.

Burr, Anna R. The Autobiography: A Critical & Comparative Study. LC 73-504. 1972. Repr. of 1909 ed. lib. bdg. 52.50 (ISBN 0-8414-1468-8). Folcroft.

--The Portrait of a Banker: James Stillman Eighteen Fifty - Nineteen Eighteen. 370p. 1980. lib. bdg. 25.00 (ISBN 0-89760-040-1). Telegraph Bks.

--The Portrait of a Banker: James Stillman, 1850-1918. 370p. 1982. Repr. of 1927 ed. lib. bdg. 35.00 (ISBN 0-686-91747-2). Darby Bks.

--Religious Confessions & Confessants. 1977. lib. bdg. 59.95 (ISBN 0-8490-2511-7). Gordon Pr.

--Weir Mitchell: His Life & Works. 1973. Repr. of 1930 ed. 45.00 (ISBN 0-8274-1423-4). R West.

Burr, Anna R., ed. see James, Alice.

Burr, Barbara, jt. auth. see Weisenfeld, Murray F.

Burr, Betty F. Nacogdoches Archives, Eighteen Thirty-Five Entrance Certificates. 1982. 8.95 (ISBN 0-911619-02-X). B F Burr.

Burr, Betty Fagan, produced by. Tyrrell County North Carolina Minutes Court of Pleas & Quarter Sessions, 1735-1754, Bk. 1. 137p. (Orig.). 1981. pap. 14.50 (ISBN 0-911619-01-1). B F Burr.

Burr, Brooks M. & Mayden, Richard L. Life History of the Freckled Madtom, Noturus Nocturnus, in Mill Creek, Illinois: Pisces: Ictaluridae. (Occasional Papers: No. 98). 15p. 1982. 2.25 (ISBN 0-317-04823-6). U of KS Mus Nat Hist.

Burr, Brooks M., jt. auth. see Mayden, Richard L.

Burr, Brooks M., jt. auth. see Page, Lawrence M.

Burr, Clinton S. America's Race Heritage: An Account of the Diffusion of Ancestral Stocks in the United States. LC 76-46069. (Anti-Movements in America). 1977. Repr. of 1922 ed. lib. bdg. 30.00x (ISBN 0-405-09943-6). Ayer Co Pubs.

Burr, David. Eucharistic Presence & Conversion in Late Thirteenth Century Franciscan Thought. LC 83-73283. (Transactions Ser.: Vol. 74 Pt. 3). 113p. 1984. 12.00 (ISBN 0-87169-743-2). Am Philos.

--Persecution of Peter Olivi. LC 76-24254. (Transactions Ser.: Vol. 66, Pt. 5). 1976. pap. 6.00 (ISBN 0-87169-665-7). Am Philos.

Burr, Elisha W. Diseases of Parrots. (Illus.). 318p. 1982. 24.95 (ISBN 0-87666-843-0, H-1037). TFH Pubns.

Burr, Elizabeth, ed. see Khalidi, Walid.

Burr, Esther E. The Journal of Esther Edwards Burr: 1754-1757. Karlsen, Carol F. & Crumpacker, Laurie, eds. LC 83-16958. 320p. 1984. 25.00x (ISBN 0-300-02900-4). Yale U Pr.

Burr, George L. New England's Place in the History of Witchcraft. facsimile ed. LC 71-164592. (Select Bibliographies Reprint Ser). Repr. of 1911 ed. 15.00 (ISBN 0-8369-5876-4). Ayer Co Pubs.

Burr, George L., ed. Narratives of the Witchcraft Cases, Sixteen Forty-Eight to Seventeen Six. (Original Narratives). 465p. 1975. Repr. of 1914 ed. 21.50x (ISBN 0-06-480118-7, 06375). B&N Imports.

Burr, George L., jt. ed. see Lea, Henry C.

Burr, Gillian & Helpful "8" Committee, eds. More Ways to a Man's Heart. (Illus.). 217p. 1976. 12.50x (ISBN 0-85303-190-8, Pub. by Vallentine Mitchell England). Biblio Dist.

Burr, Gray. Choice of Attitudes. LC 69-17790. (Wesleyan Poetry Program: Vol. 44). 1969. 15.00x (ISBN 0-8195-2044-6); pap. 6.95. Wesleyan U Pr.

Burr, Grey. The Moon by Day. 72p. 1983. 7.95 (ISBN 0-931694-25-6). Wampeter Pr.

Burr, H. S. Classics in Neurology. 184p. 1963. 15.50x (ISBN 0-398-00263-0). C C Thomas.

--The Neural Basis of Human Behavior. 272p. 1960. 20.75x (ISBN 0-398-00264-9). C C Thomas.

Burr, Harold S. The Nature of Man & the Meaning of Existence. 108p. 1962. 11.75x (ISBN 0-398-04225-X). C C Thomas.

Burr, Irving. Statistical Quality Control Methods. (Statistics: Textbooks & Monographs: Vol. 16). 1976. 49.75 (ISBN 0-8247-6344-0). Dekker.

Burr, Jeanne. America's Troubled Children. (Editorials on File Ser.). 196p. 1980. lib. bdg. 19.95 (ISBN 0-87196-369-8). Facts on File.

--Sex Roles: Rights & Values in Conflict. (Editorials on File Ser.). 1980. 19.95x (ISBN 0-87196-368-X). Facts on File.

Burr, Jeanne & Maidens, Melinda, eds. America's Troubled Children. LC 80-20541. pap. 48.00 (ISBN 0-317-20507-2, 2022894). Bks Demand UMI.

Burr, John & Goldinger, Milton. Philosophy & Contemporary Issues. 4th ed. (Illus.). 544p. 1984. pap. text ed. write for info. (ISBN 0-02-317250-9). Macmillan.

Burr, John, et al. White-Collar Restiveness: A Growing Challenge. 1963. pap. 2.50 (ISBN 0-87330-009-2). Indus Rel.

Burr, John R., ed. Handbook of World Philosophy: Contemporary Developments Since 1945. LC 80-539. (Illus.). xxii, 639p. 1980. lib. bdg. 65.00 (ISBN 0-313-22381-5, BCD/). Greenwood.

Burr, Keith & Gillis, Joseph. The Screenwriters Guide. LC 82-6451. 160p. (Orig.). 1982. pap. 7.95 (ISBN 0-918432-31-6). NY Zoetrope.

Burr, M. Dermaptera. (Illus.). xviii, 238p. 1973. Repr. of 1910 ed. 12.00 (ISBN 0-88065-074-5, Pub. by Messers Today & Tomorrows Printers & Publishers India). Scholarly Pubns.

Burr, M. Y. Study of Homogeneous Grouping in Terms of Individual Variations & the Teaching Problem. LC 70-176616. (Columbia University. Teachers College. Contributions to Education: No. 457). Repr. of 1931 ed. 22.50 (ISBN 0-404-55457-1). AMS Pr.

Burr, Nelson R., compiled by. Religion in American Life. LC 70-136219. (Goldentree Bibliographies in American History Ser.). (Orig.). 1971. 15.95 (ISBN 0-88295-507-1). Harlan Davidson.

Burr, Norman, jt. auth. see Berger, Alain Y.

Burr, Norman, jt. auth. see Berger, Alan Y.

Burr, Robert N. By Reason or Force: Chile & the Balancing of Power in South America, 1830-1905. LC 66-63190. (California Library Reprint Ser.: No. 54). 1974. 37.50x (ISBN 0-520-02644-6); pap. 9.50x (ISBN 0-520-02629-2). U of Cal Pr.

Burr, Samuel E., Jr. The Aaron Burr Lectures. 2nd, enlarged ed. LC 81-67945. (Illus.). xviii, 447p. 1981. 20.00 (ISBN 0-911994-01-7). Burr Pubns.

--The Burr Hamilton Duel & Related Matters. 2nd ed. (Illus.). 57p. 1983. soft cover 5.00 (ISBN 0-8111-0424-9). Burr Pubns.

--China APO: More than Experience. LC 82-72321. (Illus.). 209p. 1982. soft cover & supplement 5.00 (ISBN 0-911994-07-6). Burr Pubns.

--Colonel Aaron Burr, the American Phoenix. 1963. 10.00 (ISBN 0-682-42019-0). Exposition Pr FL.

--Colonel Aaron Burr: The Misunderstood Man. LC 67-12278. (Illus.). 155p. 1983. 10.00 (ISBN 0-8111-0267-X). Burr Pubns.

--Disaster, Death & Destruction. 2nd ed. (Illus.). 64p. 1983. soft cover 3.50 (ISBN 0-686-45475-8). Burr Pubns.

--Disaster, Death & Destruction, No. 1. (Illus.). 1979. No. 2, 64p, 2nd ed., 1983. 2.85 (ISBN 0-911994-05-X); No. 3, 64p, 2nd ed., 1982. soft cover o.p. 3.50 (ISBN 0-686-45475-8); pap. 5.00 (ISBN 0-911994-00-9). Burr Pubns.

--The Influence of His Wife & His Daughter on the Life & Career of Col. Aaron Burr. LC 75-24506. (Illus.). 1979. pap. 5.00 (ISBN 0-911994-03-3). Burr Pubns.

--Napoleon's Dossier on Aaron Burr: Proposals of Colonel Aaron Burr to the Emperor Napoleon. (Illus.). 65p. 1983. 5.00 (ISBN 0-8111-0267-X). Burr Pubns.

--Thirty-Seven Years of the Aaron Burr Association: 1946-1983, Vol. II. (Illus.). 200p. 1984. pap. 6.35 (ISBN 0-911994-08-4). Burr Pubns.

--Thirty-Seven Years of the Aaron Burr Association: 1946-1983, Vol. 1. (Illus.). 242p. 1983. pap. 7.25. Burr Pubns.

Burr, Samuel Engle, Jr. The Burr Education Foundation: A Statement by the President. 1981. Repr. of 1970 ed. soft cover 1.00 (ISBN 0-911994-04-1). Burr Pubns.

--Disaster, Death & Destruction. 2nd, rev. ed. (Illus.). 64p. 1982. pap. 5.00 (ISBN 0-911994-00-9). Aaron Burr Assn.

Burr, Stefan A., ed. The Mathematics of Networks. LC 82-18469. (Proceedings of Symposia in Applied Mathematics: No. 26). 142p. 1984. pap. 17.00 (ISBN 0-8218-0031-0, PSAPM-26). Am Math.

Burr, Tim. Old Nick. (Illus.). 24p. (Orig.). 1981. pap. 6.95 (ISBN 0-934904-11-1). J & L Lee.

Burr, Wesley R., et al, eds. Contemporary Theories About the Family, Vol. I. LC 77-81430. (Illus.). 1979. 28.50 (ISBN 0-02-904940-7). Free Pr.

--Contemporary Theories About the Family: General Theories & Theoretical Orientations, Vol. II. LC 77-81430. (Illus.). 1979. 18.95 (ISBN 0-02-904950-4). Free Pr.

Burr, William H. Revelations of Antichrist: Concerning Christ & Christianity. LC 79-161340. (Atheist Viewpoint Ser). 448p. 1972. Repr. of 1879 ed. 29.00 (ISBN 0-405-03801-1). Ayer Co Pubs.

Burra, Peter. Baroque & Gothic Sentimentalism. LC 74-3414. 1931. lib. bdg. 10.00 (ISBN 0-8414-3126-4). Folcroft.

--Wordsworth. LC 73-10495. 1974. Repr. of 1936 ed. lib. bdg. 17.50 (ISBN 0-8414-3191-4). Folcroft.

--Wordsworth. LC 72-2096. (Studies in Wordsworth, No. 29). 1972. Repr. of 1935 ed. lib. bdg. 31.95x (ISBN 0-8383-1486-4). Haskell.

Burrage, A. M. Some Ghost Stories. 1981. 8.50 (ISBN 0-686-69311-6). Bookfinger.

Burrage, Alfred M. Someone in the Room. Reginald, R. & Menville, Douglas, eds. LC 75-46259. (Supernatural & Occult Fiction Ser.). 1976. Repr. of 1931 ed. lib. bdg. 21.00x (ISBN 0-405-08118-9). Ayer Co Pubs.

Burrage, Barbara. The Bible Quiz Book. (gr. 5 up). 1979. pap. 2.95 (ISBN 0-8192-1256-3). Morehouse.

--Bible Quizzerama Puzzle Book. 48p. (Orig.). (gr. 6 up). 1981. pap. 1.95 (ISBN 0-87239-446-8, 2836). Standard Pub.

Burrage, Champlin, ed. Answer to John Robinson of Leyden by a Puritan Friend. (Harvard Theological Studies). 1920. pap. 15.00 (ISBN 0-527-01009-X). Kraus Repr.

Burrage, Henry S., ed. Early English & French Voyages, Fifteen Thirty-Four to Sixteen Eight, Chiefly from Hakluyt. (Original Narratives). 453p. 1967. Repr. of 1906 ed. 21.50x (ISBN 0-06-480120-9, 06376). B&N Imports.

Burrage, Walter L., jt. auth. see Kelly, Howard A.

Burr Carter, Jane. Greek Ivory-Caring In the Orientalizing & Archaic Periods. Freedberg, S. J., ed. (Outstanding Dissertations in Fine Arts Ser.). (Illus.). 380p. 1985. Repr. of 1984 ed. 50.00 (ISBN 0-8240-6851-3). Garland Pub.

Burrell, jt. auth. see Feder.

Burrell, jt. auth. see Nebert.

Burrell, Angus, jt. auth. see Brewster, Dorothy.

Burrell, Arthur. A Guide to Story Telling. 1979. Repr. of 1926 ed. lib. bdg. 30.00 (ISBN 0-8495-0548-8). Arden Lib.

--Guide to Story Telling. LC 74-23577. 1971. Repr. of 1926 ed. 37.00x (ISBN 0-8103-3764-9). Gale.

--A Guide to Story Telling. 336p. 1980. Repr. of 1926 ed. lib. bdg. 25.00 (ISBN 0-8492-3795-5). R West.

Burrell, Arthur, ed. A Book of Heroic Verse. (Illus.). 292p. 1981. Repr. of 1912 ed. lib. bdg. 20.00 (ISBN 0-8495-0491-0). Arden Lib.

--A Book of Heroic Verse. facsimile ed. LC 78-168775. (Granger Index Reprint Ser.). Repr. of 1920 ed. 21.00 (ISBN 0-8369-6295-8). Ayer Co Pubs.

Burrell, Bob & Davidson, Paul. Wildwater West Virginia. LC 72-77291. (Illus.). 192p. 1972. pap. cancelled (ISBN 0-89732-009-3). Menasha Ridge.

Burrell, Clarice. Pocketful of Rainbows. 1967. 2.50 (ISBN 0-87511-014-2); pap. 1.50 (ISBN 0-87511-013-4). Claitors.

Burrell, Craig D. & Sheps, Cecil G., eds. Primary Health Care in Industrialized Nations. (Annals of the New York Academy of Sciences: Vol. 310). 274p. 1978. pap. 42.00x professional (ISBN 0-89072-066-5). NY Acad Sci.

Burrell, D. C. Marine Environmental Studies in Boca de Quadra & Smeaton Bay: Chemical & Geochemical. (IMS Report Ser.: No. R82-2). 307p. 1980. pap. 19.25 (ISBN 0-914500-16-3). U of AK Inst Marine.

Burrell, D. C., ed. see International Conference on Port & Ocean Engineering Under Arctic Conditions, Third, Fairbanks, Alaska, 11-15 August 1975.

Burrell, D. C., ed. see International Conference on Port & Ocean Engineering Under Arctic Conditions, Third.

Burrell, D. C., et al. Marine Environmental Studies in Boca de Quadra & Smeaton Bay: Physical & Chemical, Nineteen Seventy-Nine. (Science Technical Report Ser.: No. R80-1). (Illus.). 144p. pap. 10.50 (ISBN 0-914500-10-4). U of AK Inst Marine.

Burrell, David B. Aquinas: God & Action. LC 78-51519. 1979. text ed. 14.95x (ISBN 0-268-00588-5). U of Notre Dame Pr.

--Exercises in Religious Understanding. LC 74-12566. pag. 63.30 (ISBN 0-317-26713-2, 2024366). Bks Demand UMI.

--Knowing the Unknowable God: Ibn-Sina, Maimonides, Aquinas. LC 85-40600. 160p. 1986. text ed. 15.95x (ISBN 0-268-01225-3, 85-12253, Dist. by Har-Row). U of Notre Dame Pr.

Burrell, David B. & Kane, Franzita, eds. Evangelization in the American Context. LC 76-22403. 1976. pap. 2.95x (ISBN 0-268-00902-3). U of Notre Dame Pr.

Burrell, G. & Morgan, G. Sociological Paradigms & Organizational Analysis. 1979. pap. text ed. 16.50x (ISBN 0-435-82131-8). Heinemann Ed.

Burrell, Jill & Burrell, Maurice. Arctic Mission. 1974. 1.60 (ISBN 0-08-017621-6). Pergamon.

Burrell, John A., jt. auth. see Brewster, Dorothy.

Burrell, Lenette O. & Burrell, Zeb L., Jr. Critical Care. 4th ed. LC 81-9544. (Illus.). 622p. 1982. text ed. 27.95 (ISBN 0-8016-0906-2). Mosby.

Burrell, Leon F., jt. auth. see Clements, Zacharie J.

Burrell, Louis V. The Petals of the Rose: Poems & Epigrams. facsimile ed. LC 70-168513. (Black Heritage Library Collection). Repr. of 1917 ed. 11.50 (ISBN 0-8369-8876-0). Ayer Co Pubs.

Burrell, M. C. & Wright, J. S. Todays Sects. 4.50 (ISBN 0-8010-0855-7). Baker Bk.

Burrell, Martin. Betwixt Heaven & Charing Cross. facs. ed. LC 68-16916. (Essay Index Reprint Ser). 1928. 18.00 (ISBN 0-8369-0266-1). Ayer Co Pubs.

--Crumbs Are Also Bread. facs. ed. LC 70-86739. (Essay Index Reprint Ser). 1934. 19.00 (ISBN 0-8369-1173-3). Ayer Co Pubs.

Burrell, Mary W. Catalogue of the Burrell Collection of Wagner Documents, Letters, & Other Biographical Material. Wright, Peter E., compiled by. LC 74-26032. Repr. of 1929 ed. 17.50 (ISBN 0-404-12876-9). AMS Pr.

Burrell, Maurice, jt. auth. see Burrell, Jill.

Burrell, Maurice C. The Challenge of the Cults. (Direction Bks.). 160p. (Orig.). 1982. pap. 3.95 (ISBN 0-8010-0816-6). Baker Bk.

Burrell, O. K. Gold in the Woodpile: An Informal History of Banking in Oregon. LC 68-63377. (Illus.). 1967. 8.50 (ISBN 0-87114-015-2). U of Oreg Bks.

Burrell, Paul B., tr. see Dubois, Jacques, et al.

Burrell, Percival. Suttons Synagogue: Or the English Centurion (A Sermon) LC 74-28822. (English Experience Ser.: No. 647). 1974. Repr. of 1629 ed. 3.50 (ISBN 90-221-0647-0). Walter J Johnson.

Burrell, Randal C., ed. see Capek, Karel.

Burrell, Robert. Experimental Immunology. 5th ed. 1979. spiral bdg. 9.95x (ISBN 0-8087-2876-8). Burgess.

Burrell, Robert G. & Davidson, Paul C. Wildwater West Virginia. 1972. 7.00 (ISBN 0-87012-123-5). McClain.

Burrell, Sidney, jt. auth. see Drake, Peter.

Burrell, T. W., jt. auth. see McGarry, Kevin J.

Burrell, W. Teacher Education at Salve Regina College. 1970. pap. text ed. 3.40x (ISBN 0-8290-1194-3). Irvington.

Burrell, William P. Twenty-Five Years History of the Grand Fountain of the United Order of True Reformers, 1881-1905. LC 72-106848. (Illus.). Repr. of 1909 ed. cancelled (ISBN 0-8371-3470-6). Greenwood.

Burrell, Zeb L., Jr., jt. auth. see Burrell, Lenette O.

Burrello, Leonard C. & Sage, Daniel D. Leadership & Change in Special Education. (P-H Ser. in Special Education). 1979. 26.95 (ISBN 0-13-526921-0). P-H.

Burrello, Leonard C., jt. auth. see Sage, Daniel D.

Burrells, W. Microscope Techniques: A Comprehensive Handbook for General & Applied Microscopy. LC 77-26687. 574p. 1977. 48.95x (ISBN 0-470-99376-6). Halsted Pr.

Burren, Michael, jt. auth. see Martin, George.

Burrett, John. The Bear Who Slept Through Christmas: Book-Cassette. (Illus.). 20p. 1985. pap. 3.95 (ISBN 0-89542-942-X); book-cassette 8.95 (ISBN 0-8249-8119-7). Ideals.

Burri, C. Post-Traumatic Osteomyelitis. 492p. 1975. 195.00 (ISBN 3-456-80122-X, Pub. by Holdan Bk Ltd UK). State Mutual Bk.

Burri, C., ed. The Caval Catheter. LC 77-2784. 1978. pap. 20.00 (ISBN 0-387-08566-1). Springer-Verlag.

Burri, C., et al. Endoprostheses & Alternatives for the Arm-Shoulder Joint. 90p. 1977. 50.00 (ISBN 0-317-14264-X, Pub. by Holdan Bk Ltd UK). State Mutual Bk.

Burri, Caius & Claes, Lutz, eds. Alloplastic Ligament Replacement. (Topical Problems in Surgery & Orthopedics Ser.: No. 26). (Illus.). 151p. (Orig.). 1983. pap. text ed. 47.00 (ISBN 3-456-81281-7, Pub. by Hans Huber Switzerland). J K Burgess.

Burridge, D. M. & Kallen, E., eds. Problems & Prospects in Long & Medium Range Weather Forecasting. (Topics in Atmospheric & Oceanographic Sciences Ser.). (Illus.). 290p. 1984. pap. 19.50 (ISBN 0-387-12827-1). Springer-Verlag.

Burridge, Kenelm. New Heaven, New Earth: A Study of Millenarian Activities. (Pavilion Ser.). 198p. 1969. pap. 9.95x (ISBN 0-631-11950-7). Basil Blackwell.

--Someone, No One: An Essay on Individuality. LC 79-83979. 1979. 28.00x (ISBN 0-691-09384-9). Princeton U Pr.

Burridge, Kenelm O. Encountering Aborigines, a Case Study: Anthropology & the Australian Aboriginal. LC 72-1191. 272p. 1974. 28.00 (ISBN 0-08-017071-4). Pergamon.

Burridge, Kenneth D., et al. Element Masters: Fantasy Role-Playing Game. 2nd, rev. ed. (Illus.). 150p. 1984. pap. 14.95 (ISBN 0-930039-01-7). Escape Ventures.

Burridge, M. J., jt. auth. see Riemann, H. P.

Burridge, R., et al. Macroscopic Properties of Disordered Media: Proceedings 1981, New York. (Lecture Notes in Physics Ser.: Vol. 154). 307p. 1982. pap. 22.00 (ISBN 0-387-11202-2). Springer-Verlag.

Burridge, Robert, ed. Fracture Mechanics. LC 78-24473. (SIAM-AMS Proceedings: Vol. 12). 1979. 20.00 (ISBN 0-8218-1332-3). Am Math.

Burridge, Shirley, ed. Oxford Elementary Learner's Dictionary of English. (Illus., Orig.). 1981. pap. text ed. 9.95x (ISBN 0-19-431253-4). Oxford U Pr.

Burright, Burke K. Cities & Travel. LC 80-8622. (Outstanding Dissertations in Economics Ser.). 350p. 1984. lib. bdg. 36.00 (ISBN 0-8240-4179-8). Garland Pub.

Burright, Orrin U. The Sun Rides High: Pioneering Days in Oklahoma, Kansas & Missouri. 1974. 8.95 (ISBN 0-89015-022-2). Eakin Pubns.

Burrill, Claude & Quinto, Leon. Computer Model of a Growth Company. LC 79-162628. (Illus.). x, 224p. 1972. 46.25 (ISBN 0-677-00410-9). Gordon.

Burrill, Claude W. & Ellsworth, Leon W. Modern Project Management: Foundations for Quality & Productivity. LC 79-24457. (The Data Processing Handbook Ser.). (Illus.). 576p. 1980. text ed. 39.00x (ISBN 0-935310-00-2). Burrill-Ellsworth.

--Quality Data Processing. LC 79-9623. (Data Processing Handbook Ser.). (Illus.). 208p. 1982. text ed. 25.00 (ISBN 0-935310-01-0). Burrill-Ellsworth.

Burrill, Harry & Crist, Raymond F. Report on Trade Conditions in China. LC 78-74353. (The Modern Chinese Economy Ser.). 130p. 1980. lib. bdg. 20.00 (ISBN 0-8240-4265-4). Garland Pub.

Burrill, Kathleen R. The Quatrains of Nesimi Fourteenth-Century Turkic Hurufi. (Publications in Near & Middle East Studies, Ser. A: No. 14). 1972. 72.00x (ISBN 90-2792-328-0). Mouton.

Burrill, Richard. The Human Almanac: People Through Time. (Illus.). 432p. (Orig.). 1983. pap. 14.50 (ISBN 0-943238-00-5). Sierra Pr.

Burrin, Frank K. Edward Charles Elliott, Educator. LC 69-11274. (Illus.). 222p. 1970. 5.50 (ISBN 0-911198-19-9). Purdue U Pr.

Burringh, P. Introduction to the Study of Soils in Tropical & Subtropical Regions. 99p. 1981. 52.00x (ISBN 0-686-76649-0, Pub. by Oxford & IBH India). State Mutual Bk.

Burrington & May. Handbook of Probability & Statistics. 2nd ed. (Illus.). 416p. 31.50 (ISBN 0-318-13216-8, P23). Am Soc QC.

Burrington, Gillian. How to Find Out About the Social Sciences. LC 75-5809. 148p. 1975. text ed. 18.00 (ISBN 0-08-018289-5). Pergamon.

Burris, Beverly. No Room at the Top: Underemployment & Alienation in the Corporation. LC 82-18073. 352p. 1983. 33.95 (ISBN 0-03-061923-8). Praeger.

Burris, Donald. Professional Responsibility. (Primer Ser.). 8.95 (ISBN 0-686-23343-3). Josephson-Kluwer Legal Educ Ctrs.

Burris, J. E., jt. ed. see Ludden, P. W.

Burris, Jim. Spotted Pony & the Manitou. (Illus.). 32p. (gr. 3-6). 1985. 5.95 (ISBN 0-89962-446-4). Todd & Honeywell.

Burris, Joanna. Basic Mathematics: An Individualized Approach, 6, Modules 1-6. 1974. write for info. (ISBN 0-87150-172-4, PWS 1381-6, Prindle). PWS Pubs.

Burris, Quincy G. Richard Doddridge Blackmore: His Life & Novels. LC 70-136909. 219p. Repr. of 1930 ed. lib. bdg. 18.75 (ISBN 0-8371-5356-5, BURB). Greenwood.

Burris, Robert H. & Black, Clayton C., eds. Carbon Dioxide Metabolism & Plant Productivity. (Harry Steenbock Symposia Ser). 446p. 1976. text ed. 64.00 (ISBN 0-8391-0849-4). Univ Park.

Burris, Rod. Velocette: A Development History of the MSS, Venom, Viper, Thruxton, & Scrambler Models. (Illus.). 160p. pap. 10.95 (ISBN 0-85429-283-7, F283). Haynes Pubns.

Burris, Russell. Computer Network Experiments in Teaching Law. 65p. 1980. 10.00 (ISBN 0-318-14010-1); members 5.00 (ISBN 0-318-14011-X). Educom.

Burris, Russell, jt. auth. see Park, Roger.

Burris, S. & Sankappanavar, H. P. A Course in Universal Algebra. (Graduate Texts in Mathematics Ser.: Vol. 78). (Illus.). 320p. 1981. 36.00 (ISBN 0-387-90578-2). Springer-Verlag.

Burris, Stanley & McKenzie, Ralph. Decidability & Boolean Representations. LC 81-7902. (Memoirs of the American Mathematical Society Ser.: No. 246). 108p. 1981. pap. 9.00 (ISBN 0-8218-2246-2). Am Math.

Burris, Thelma. Shut the Door. 256p. 1985. 12.95 (ISBN 0-89962-496-0). Todd & Honeywell.

Burris, Val. The Crisis of the New Middle Class. 270p. 1985. 24.95t (ISBN 0-03-060014-6); text ed. 9.95 (ISBN 0-03-060016-2). Praeger.

Burris, W. Alan. A Liberty Primer. 2nd ed. LC 83-61673. (Illus.). 562p. (Orig.). 1983. pap. 7.95x (ISBN 0-9608490-1-7). Society Indiv Lib.

Burris, W. H. Revelations of Antichrist. 59.95 (ISBN 0-8490-0950-2). Gordon Pr.

Burris-Meyer, Harold & Cole, Edward C. Scenery for the Theatre. 2nd, rev. ed. (Illus.). 1972. 45.00 (ISBN 0-316-11754-4). Little.

Burris-Meyer, Harold & Goodfriend, Lewis S. Acoustics for the Architect. 2nd ed. cancelled (ISBN 0-89874-421-0). Krieger.

Burris-Meyer, Harold, et al. Sound in the Theatre. rev. ed. LC 78-66064. 1979. 14.95 (ISBN 0-87830-157-7). Theatre Arts.

Burrison, John A. Brothers in Clay: The Story of Georgia Folk Pottery. LC 82-14884. (Illus.). 352p. 1983. 35.00 (ISBN 0-8203-0657-6). U of Ga Pr.

Burriss, Eli E. Taboo, Magic, Spirits: A Study of Primitive Elements in Roman Religion. LC 72-114489. x, 250p. Repr. of 1931 ed. lib. bdg. 15.00 (ISBN 0-8371-4724-7, BUTA). Greenwood.

Burriss, Eli E. & Casson, Lionel. Latin & Greek in Current Use. 2nd ed. 1949. text ed. 19.95 (ISBN 0-13-524991-0). P-H.

Burritt, Arthur W., et al. Profit Sharing: Its Principles & Practice. 1978. Repr. of 1918 ed. lib. bdg. 30.00 (ISBN 0-8492-3700-9). R West.

Burritt, Elihu & Curti, Merle E. The Learned Blacksmith: The Letters & Journals of Elihu Burritt. 13.25 (ISBN 0-8369-7133-7). Ayer Co Pubs.

Burritt, Elihu see Curti, Merle E.

Burritt, Mary. The Solera Poems. LC 79-11408. 55p. 1979. pap. 3.75 (ISBN 0-934332-11-8). L'Epervier Pr.

Burro, Marian. Pure & Simple. 1979. pap. 3.50 (ISBN 0-425-04860-8). Berkley Pub.

Burron, Arnold H. Discipline That Can't Fail. 1984. pap. 4.95 (ISBN 0-88062-116-8). Mott Media.

Burros, et al. Freeze with Ease. 248p. 1984. 3.95 (ISBN 0-317-19904-8). Macmillan.

Burros, Marian. Keep It Simple. 400p. 1984. pap. 7.95 (ISBN 0-671-50736-2). PB.

--Keep It Simple: Thirty Minute Meals from Scratch. 416p. 1982. pap. 3.95 (ISBN 0-671-44397-6). PB.

--Pure & Simple: A Cookbook. 1978. 9.95 (ISBN 0-688-03285-0). Morrow.

--Pure & Simple: Delicious Recipes for Additive-Free Cooking. 1982. pap. 5.95 (ISBN 0-425-05643-0). Berkley Pub.

--You've Got It Made: Make-Ahead Meals for the Family & for Cooperative Dinner Parties. LC 84-60444. 352p. 1984. 13.95 (ISBN 0-688-03187-0). Morrow.

Burros, Marian & Levine, Lois. Come for Cocktail, Stay for Supper. 196p. pap. 4.95 (ISBN 0-02-009350-0, Collier). Macmillan.

--Elegant But Easy Cookbook. 214p. pap. 4.95 (ISBN 0-02-009340-3, Collier). Macmillan.

--Freeze with Ease. LC 65-21466. 1968. pap. 3.95 (ISBN 0-02-009280-6, Collier). Macmillan.

--The Summertime Cookbook. LC 79-20799. 1980. pap. 4.50 (ISBN 0-02-011190-8, Collier). Macmillan.

Burros, Marien. You've Got It Made. 1985. pap. 4.95 (ISBN 0-671-55239-2). PB.

Burrough, P. A. & Bie, S. W., eds. Soil Information Systems Technology: Proceedings of the Sixth Meeting of the ISSS Working Group on Soil Information Systems, Bolkesjo, Norway, 28 February - 4 March 1983. (Illus.). 178p. 1985. pap. 16.50 (ISBN 90-220-0854-1, PDC274, Pudoc). Unipub.

Burroughs, Alan. Art Criticism from a Laboratory. LC 70-110267. Repr. lib. bdg. 18.50x (ISBN 0-8371-4493-0, BUAC). Greenwood.

--Limners & Likenesses: Three Centuries of American Painting. LC 65-18793. (Illus.). 1965. Repr. of 1936 ed. 16.50x (ISBN 0-8462-0627-7). Russell.

Burroughs, Barkham. Barkham Burroughs' Encyclopaedia of Astounding Facts & Useful Information 1889. Burroughs, Miggs, ed. (Illus.). 148p. (Orig.). 1983. pap. 8.95 (ISBN 0-9610994-0-2). Brayden.

--Barkham Burroughs' Encyclopaedia of Astounding Facts & Useful Information 1889-1986 Date Book. Burroughs, Miggs, ed. (Illus.). 110p. 1985. pap. 4.95 (ISBN 0-9610994-2-9). Brayden.

Burroughs, Ben. New Sketches. LC 61-11605. 172p. 1982. 8.50 (ISBN 0-8303-0049-X). Fleet.

--Odes to Life. (Sketches Ser.). 144p. (Orig.). 1984. pap. 8.50. Fleet.

--Remembrances. (Sketches Ser.). 144p. (Orig.). 1985. pap. 8.50 (ISBN 0-8303-0168-2). Fleet.

--Sketches. LC 61-11605. 196p. 1981. pap. 8.50 (ISBN 0-8303-0049-X). Fleet.

Burroughs, David & Bezzant, Norman. New Wine Companion. 1979. pap. 14.50 (ISBN 0-434-09867-1, Pub. by W Heinemann Ltd). David & Charles.

--Wine Regions of the World. 1979. pap. 16.50 (ISBN 0-434-09866-3, Pub. by W Heinemann Ltd). David & Charles.

Burroughs, Edgar R. Escape on Venus. 288p. 1984. pap. 2.75 (ISBN 0-441-21567-X, Pub. by Ace Science Fiction). Ace Bks.

--I Am a Barbarian. 288p. 1985. pap. 2.75 (ISBN 0-441-35807-1). Ace Bks.

--Savage Pellucidar. 256p. 1985. pap. 2.75 (ISBN 0-441-75137-7) (ISBN 0-317-31740-7). Ace Bks.

--Tanar of Pellucidar. (Pellucidar Ser.: No. 3). 256p. 1985. pap. 2.75 (ISBN 0-441-79798-9). Ace Bks.

--The Wizard of Venus. pap. 2.75 (ISBN 0-441-90196-4, Pub. by Ace Science Fiction). Ace Bks.

Burroughs, Edgar Rice. Apache Devil. 1976. Repr. of 1933 ed. lib. bdg. 16.20x (ISBN 0-89966-043-6). Buccaneer Bks.

--At the Earth's Core. (Pellucidar Ser.: No. 1). 224p. 1985. pap. 2.75 (ISBN 0-441-03327-X). Ace Bks.

--At the Earth's Core: Pellucidar, Tamar of Pellucidar. (Illus.). 14.00 (ISBN 0-8446-1778-4). Peter Smith.

--Back to the Stone Age. 256p. 1985. pap. 2.75 (ISBN 0-441-04638-X, Pub. by Ace Science Fiction). Ace Bks.

--The Bandit of Hell's Bend. 312p. 1979. pap. 1.95 (ISBN 0-441-04746-7, Pub. by Charter Bks). Ace Bks.

--Beyond the Farthest Star. 1976. pap. 2.25 (ISBN 0-441-05656-3). Ace Bks.

--Carson of Venus. 288p. 1984. pap. 2.75 (ISBN 0-441-09198-9). Ace Bks.

--Cave Girl. 192p. 1975. pap. 1.95 (ISBN 0-441-09285-3). Ace Bks.

--The Cave Girl. LC 62-21541. (Illus.). 12.50 (ISBN 0-940724-01-4). Canaveral.

--Chessman of Mars. 1979. pap. 1.95 (ISBN 0-345-27838-0). Ballantine.

--The Deputy Sheriff of Commanche County. 320p. 1979. pap. 1.95 (ISBN 0-441-14248-6, Charter Bks). Ace Bks.

--Escape on Venus. 282p. 1981. pap. 2.25 (ISBN 0-441-21566-1). Ace Bks.

--Escape on Venus. LC 63-21730. (Illus.). 1975. Repr. 12.50 (ISBN 0-940724-00-6). Canaveral.

--Fighting Man of Mars. 1984. pap. 2.25 (ISBN 0-345-32052-2). Ballantine.

--A Fighting Man of Mars. LC 62-8705. (Illus.). 1975. Repr. 12.50 (ISBN 0-940724-02-2). Canaveral.

--The Girl from Farris's. 144p. 1979. pap. 1.95 (ISBN 0-441-28903-7, Pub. by Charter Bks). Ace Bks.

--Gods of Mars. LC 62-21542. (Illus.). 1975. Repr. 12.50 (ISBN 0-940724-03-0). Canaveral.

--John Carter of Mars. 1985. pap. 2.50 (ISBN 0-345-32955-4). Ballantine.

--John Carter of Mars. LC 64-15790. (Illus.). 12.50 (ISBN 0-940724-04-9). Canaveral.

--Jungle Tales of Tarzan, No. 6. 192p. 1980. pap. 1.95 (ISBN 0-345-29478-5). Ballantine.

--The Lad & the Lion. 192p. 1975. pap. 1.95 (ISBN 0-441-46872-1). Ace Bks.

--Lad & the Lion. LC 64-15791. (Illus.). 12.50 (ISBN 0-940724-05-7). Canaveral.

--The Land of Hidden Men. 1978. pap. 1.95 (ISBN 0-441-47016-5). Ace Bks.

--Land of Terror. 176p. 1985. pap. 2.75 (ISBN 0-441-47002-5). Ace Bks.

--The Land of the Hidden Men. 1982. pap. 2.25. Ace Bks.

--Lost on Venus. 224p. 1984. pap. 2.75 (ISBN 0-441-49509-5). Ace Bks.

--The Martian Tales, 4 vols. 1982. pap. 7.80 (ISBN 0-345-26213-1, Del Rey). Ballantine.

--Monster Men. LC 62-8707. (Illus.). 12.50 (ISBN 0-940724-06-5). Canaveral.

--The Moon Maid. 192p. 1985. pap. 2.75 (ISBN 0-441-53707-3, Pub. by Ace Science Fiction). Ace Bks.

--Moon Men. LC 62-8706. (Illus.). 1975. Repr. 12.50 (ISBN 0-940724-07-3). Canaveral.

--The Moon Men. 256p. 1985. pap. 2.75 (ISBN 0-441-53757-X). Ace Bks.

--The Oakdale Affair. 244p. 1979. pap. 1.95 (ISBN 0-441-60565-6, Pub. by Charter Bks). Ace Bks.

--The Oakdale Affair. 1976. Repr. of 1937 ed. lib. bdg. 15.95 (ISBN 0-89966-041-X). Buccaneer Bks.

--The Outlaw of Torn. 1976. Repr. of 1927 ed. lib. bdg. 10.55x (ISBN 0-89966-042-8). Buccaneer Bks.

--The Outlaw of Torn. 1982. pap. 2.50 (ISBN 0-441-64514-3). Ace Bks.

--Pellucidar. (Pellucidar Ser.). 192p. 1985. pap. 2.75 (ISBN 0-441-65857-1). Ace Bks.

--Pellucidar Novels. Incl. At the Earth's Core. Repr. of 1922 ed; Pellucidar. Repr. of 1923 ed; Tanar of Pellucidar. Repr. of 1929 ed. (Illus.). pap. 5.95 (ISBN 0-486-21051-0). Dover.

--Pirates of Venus. 208p. 1984. pap. 2.75 (ISBN 0-441-66509-8). Ace Bks.

--Pirates of Venus. LC 62-21735. (Illus.). 1975. Repr. 12.50 (ISBN 0-940724-08-1). Canaveral.

--The Return of Tarzan, No. 2. 224p. 1975. pap. 1.95 (ISBN 0-345-28996-X). Ballantine.

--Savage Pellucidar. (Pellucidar Ser.). 256p. 1982. pap. 2.25 (ISBN 0-441-75136-9). Ace Bks.

--The Son of Tarzan, No. 4. 224p. 1975. pap. 1.95 (ISBN 0-345-29415-7). Ballantine.

--Swords of Mars. 1985. pap. 2.50 (ISBN 0-345-32956-2). Ballantine.

--Tales of Three Planets. LC 64-15792. (Illus.). 1975. Repr. 12.50 (ISBN 0-940724-09-X). Canaveral.

--Tarzan & the Ant Men, No. 10. 1985. pap. 2.25 (ISBN 0-345-32393-9). Ballantine.

--Tarzan & the Castaways. 1980. pap. 1.95 (ISBN 0-345-28615-4). Ballantine.

--Tarzan & the Castaways. LC 64-25826. (Illus.). 1975. Repr. 12.50 (ISBN 0-940724-10-3). Canaveral.

--Tarzan & the Forbidden City. 1980. pap. 1.95 (ISBN 0-345-29106-9). Ballantine.

--Tarzan & the Foreign Legion. 1984. pap. 2.25 (ISBN 0-345-32454-4). Ballantine.

--Tarzan & the Golden Lion, No. 9. 1980. pap. 1.95 (ISBN 0-345-28998-6). Ballantine.

--Tarzan & the Jewels of Opar, No. 5. 160p. 1984. pap. 2.25 (ISBN 0-345-32161-8). Ballantine.

--Tarzan & the Leopard Man. 1980. pap. 1.95 (ISBN 0-345-28687-1). Ballantine.

--Tarzan & the Lion Men. 1980. pap. 1.95 (ISBN 0-345-28988-9). Ballantine.

--Tarzan & the Lost Empire, No. 12. 1985. pap. 2.25 (ISBN 0-345-32957-0). Ballantine.

--Tarzan & the Madman. LC 64-15789. (Illus.). 1975. Repr. 12.50 (ISBN 0-940724-11-1). Canaveral.

--Tarzan & the Tarzan Twins. LC 63-10779. (Illus.). 12.50 (ISBN 0-940724-12-X). Canaveral.

--Tarzan at the Earth's Core. (Pellucidar Ser.). 256p. 1985. pap. 2.75 (ISBN 0-441-79858-6, Pub. by Ace Science Fiction). Ace Bks.

--Tarzan at the Earth's Core. 1985. pap. 2.25 (ISBN 0-345-29663-X). Ballantine.

--Tarzan at the Earth's Core. LC 62-21543. (Illus.). 12.50 (ISBN 0-940724-13-8). Canaveral.

--Tarzan Lord of the Jungle, No. 11. 1984. pap. 2.25 (ISBN 0-345-32455-2). Ballantine.

--Tarzan of the Apes. 1976. Repr. of 1906 ed. lib. bdg. 17.95x (ISBN 0-89966-046-0). Buccaneer Bks.

--Tarzan of the Apes, No. 1. 256p. 1984. pap. 2.25 (ISBN 0-345-31977-X). Ballantine.

--Tarzan the Invincible. 1980. pap. 1.95 (ISBN 0-345-28989-7). Ballantine.

--Tarzan the Magnificent. 1980. pap. 1.95 (ISBN 0-345-28980-3). Ballantine.

--Tarzan the Terrible, No. 8. 1985. pap. 2.25 (ISBN 0-345-32392-0). Ballantine.

--Tarzan the Triumphant. 1979. pap. 1.95 (ISBN 0-345-28688-X). Ballantine.

--Tarzan the Untamed, No. 7. 1985. pap. 2.25 (ISBN 0-345-32391-2). Ballantine.

--Three Martian Novels. Incl. Thuvia, Maid of Mars. Repr. of 1920 ed; The Chessmen of Mars. Repr. of 1922 ed; The Master Mind of Mars. Repr. of 1928 ed. vi, 499p. pap. 6.00 (ISBN 0-486-20039-6). Dover.

--Three Martian Novels. Incl. Thuvia, Maid of Mars; The Chessmen of Mars; The Master Mind of Mars. 15.50 (ISBN 0-8446-1779-2). Peter Smith.

--The War Chief. 1976. Repr. of 1927 ed. lib. bdg. 16.95x (ISBN 0-89966-044-4). Buccaneer Bks.

--The Warlord of Mars. 1976. Repr. of 1919 ed. lib. bdg. 15.95x (ISBN 0-89966-045-2). Buccaneer Bks.

--The Wizard of Venus-Pirate Blood. 256p. 1982. pap. 2.50 (ISBN 0-441-90195-6). Ace Bks.

Burroughs, Eliane. French Phonetics. (gr. 8-12). 1972. pap. text ed. 10.00 (ISBN 0-8449-1601-3). Learning Line.

--Modern French A, 2 bks. (gr. 8-12). 1966. pap. text ed. 9.00 each (ISBN 0-686-57756-6); tchr's manual & test avail. Learning Line.

--Modern French B, 3 bks. (gr. 8-12). 1966. pap. text ed. 9.00 each (ISBN 0-686-57757-4); tchr's manual & test avail. Learning Line.

--Programmed French Reading & Writing I. 1971. pap. text ed. 7.00 (ISBN 0-8449-1700-1); tchrs' manual 1.50; test 1.25. Learning Line.

--Programmed French Reading & Writing II. 1964. pap. text ed. 7.00 (ISBN 0-8449-1704-4); tchrs' manual 1.50; test 1.25. Learning Line.

--Programmed French Reading & Writing III. 1972. pap. text ed. 7.00 (ISBN 0-8449-1708-7); tchrs' manual 1.50; test 1.25. Learning Line.

Burroughs, Esther, jt. auth. see Berry, Kathy.

Burroughs, G. E. Education in Venezuela. (World Education Ser.). 121p. 1974. 15.00 (ISBN 0-208-01467-5, Archon). Shoe String.

Burroughs, Jean. On the Trail: The Life & Trail Stories of "Lead Steer" Potter. (Illus.). 1980. 12.95 (ISBN 0-89013-131-7). Museum NM Pr.

Burroughs, Jean M. Bride of the Santa Fe Trail. LC 83-18051. 160p. (Orig.). 1984. pap. 9.95 (ISBN 0-86534-042-0). Sunstone Pr.

--Children of Destiny. (Illus.). 1975. pap. 4.95 (ISBN 0-913270-75-X). Sunstone Pr.

Burroughs, Jeremiah. The Rare Jewel of Christian Contentment. 1979. pap. 4.45 (ISBN 0-85151-091-4). Banner of Truth.

Burroughs, John. Camping & Tramping with Roosevelt. LC 71-125733. (American Environmental Studies). 1970. Repr. of 1906 ed. 13.50 (ISBN 0-405-02658-7). Ayer Co Pubs.

--Literary Values, & Other Papers. facsimile ed. LC 76-156624. (Essay Index Reprint Ser). Repr. of 1902 ed. 19.00 (ISBN 0-8369-2347-2). Ayer Co Pubs.

--Notes on Walt Whitman As Poet & Person. LC 68-24932. (Studies in Whitman, No. 28). 1969. Repr. of 1867 ed. lib. bdg. 29.95x (ISBN 0-8383-0922-4). Haskell.

--A River View & Other Hudson Valley Essays. LC 81-16945. 224p. 1981. 11.95 (ISBN 0-88427-049-1). North River.

--Ways of Nature. facsimile ed. LC 77-157963. (Essay Index Reprint Ser). Repr. of 1905 ed. 19.00 (ISBN 0-8369-2217-4). Ayer Co Pubs.

--Whitman. 1973. Repr. of 1896 ed. 8.45 (ISBN 0-8274-1516-8). R West.

--Whitman: A Study. LC 72-131652. 1979. Repr. of 1896 ed. 29.00x (ISBN 0-403-00539-6). Scholarly.

Burroughs, John, jt. auth. see Immegart, Glenn L.

Burroughs, John, ed. Songs of Nature. facsimile ed. LC 79-98077. (Granger Index Reprint Ser). 1901. 19.00 (ISBN 0-8369-6070-X). Ayer Co Pubs.

--Songs of Nature. 359p. Repr. of 1901 ed. lib. bdg. 50.00 (ISBN 0-8482-7458-X). Norwood Edns.

Burroughs, John R. I Never Look Back. 1967. 3.95 (ISBN 0-933472-45-5). Johnson Bks.

--Steamboat in the Rockies. (Illus.). 1974. 9.95 (ISBN 0-88342-036-8). Old Army.

Burroughs, Margaret G., jt. ed. see Randall, Dudley.

Burroughs, Melba G. The Christian Woman's Resource Book. LC 83-26063. 202p. (Orig.). 1984. pap. 9.95 (ISBN 0-664-26008-X, A Bridgebooks Publication). Westminster.

Burroughs, Miggs, ed. see Burroughs, Barkham.

Burroughs, Polly. Guide to Martha's Vineyard. 3rd, rev. ed. LC 85-9746. (Illus.). 200p. 1985. pap. 8.95 (ISBN 0-87106-870-2). Globe Pequot.

--Guide to Nantucket. 3rd, rev. ed. LC 84-47900. (Illus.). 192p. 1984. pap. 8.95 (ISBN 0-87106-934-2). Globe Pequot.

Burroughs, Roberta. The Fugitive Feet. LC 84-80931. 290p. (Orig.). 1984. pap. 4.95 (ISBN 0-9613554-1-7). Clin Soc Assn.

Burroughs, Stanley. Master Cleanser. 1981. pap. 4.95x (ISBN 0-317-07302-8, Regent House). B of A.

Burroughs, Wayne A., jt. auth. see Jaffee, Cabot L.

Burroughs, William. Cobble Stone Gardens. LC 76-40473. (Illus.). 1976. pap. 3.00x (ISBN 0-916156-14-1). Cherry Valley.

--Lasers. (Understanding Science Ser.). (Illus.). 64p. 1982. lib. bdg. 7.90 (ISBN 0-531-09196-1, Warwick). Watts.

--The Place of Dead Roads. (An Owl Bk.). 1985. pap. 7.95 (ISBN 0-03-003684-4). HR&W.

Burroughs, William & Ginsberg, Allen. The Yage Letters. LC 63-12222. (Orig.). 1963. pap. 3.00 (ISBN 0-87286-004-3). City Lights.

Burroughs, William, et al. New Writing & Writers, No. 16. 1980. pap. 5.95 (ISBN 0-7145-3638-5); 12.95 (ISBN 0-7145-3635-0). Riverrun NY.

Burroughs, William S. Ah Pook Is Here. 1982. pap. 7.95 (ISBN 0-7145-3859-0). Riverrun NY.

--Ah Pook Is Here. 180p. pap. cancelled (ISBN 0-7145-3683-0). Riverrun NY.

--Blade Runner: A Movie. LC 78-21584. 1979. (Dynamite Bks); pap. 6.95 (ISBN 0-912652-46-2); signed ed. o.p. 20.00 (ISBN 0-912652-47-0). Blue Wind.

--Book of Breeething. 2nd ed. LC 75-33858. (Illus.). 1980. 18.95 (ISBN 0-912652-72-1); signed 29.95x (ISBN 0-912652-73-X); pap. 8.95 (ISBN 0-912652-71-3). Blue Wind.

--The Burroughs File. 1984. 19.95 (ISBN 0-87286-158-9); pap. 8.95 (ISBN 0-87286-152-X). City Lights.

--Cities of the Red Night. LC 80-13637. 448p. 1981. 14.95 (ISBN 0-03-053976-5); ltd. ed. 50.00 (ISBN 0-03-058998-3). HR&W.

--Cities of the Red Night. LC 80-13637. 352p. (Orig.). 1982. pap. 7.25 (ISBN 0-03-061521-6, Owl Bks). HR&W.

--The Exterminator. (Fiction Ser.). 1985. pap. 4.95 (ISBN 0-14-005003-5). Penguin.

--The Job: Interviews by Daniel Odier. LC 73-20496. 212p. 1974. pap. 4.95 (ISBN 0-394-17870-X, E642, Ever). Grove.

--Junky. 1985. pap. 3.95 (ISBN 0-14-004351-9). Penguin.

--The Last Words of Dutch Schultz. LC 80-54557. (Illus.). 128p. 1981. pap. 4.95 (ISBN 0-394-17852-1). Seaver Bks.

--Letters to Allen Ginsberg, 1953-1957. 210p. 1982. 17.95 (ISBN 0-916190-16-1); pap. 8.95 (ISBN 0-916190-17-X). Full Court NY.

--Naked Lunch. 1969. pap. 4.95 (ISBN 0-394-17108-X, B115, BC). Grove.

--Naked Lunch: Twenty-Fifth Anniversary Edition. LC 83-83214. 304p. 1984. limited signed ed 60.00 (ISBN 0-394-53883-8, GP 914); 17.95 (ISBN 0-394-53884-6, GP 913). Grove.

--Port of Saints. LC 80-10309. 1980. 24.95 (ISBN 0-912652-64-0); signed, numbered & boxed 49.95x (ISBN 0-912652-66-7); pap. 9.95 (ISBN 0-912652-65-9). Blue Wind.

--Queer. 134p. 1985. 14.95 (ISBN 0-670-80833-4). Viking.

--Roosevelt After Inauguration. LC 79-21111. 1979. pap. 3.00 (ISBN 0-87286-115-5). City Lights.

--The Soft Machine. Bd. with Nova Express; The Wild Boys: Three Novels. LC 80-8062. 544p. (Orig.). 1981. pap. 5.95 (ISBN 0-394-17749-5, B446, BC). Grove.

--Soft Machine. 1966. pap. 2.45 (ISBN 0-394-17115-2, B131, BC). Grove.

--The Third Mind. (Illus.). 194p. 1982. pap. 8.95 (ISBN 0-394-17984-6). Seaver Bks.

--Ticket That Exploded. 1967. pap. 2.95 (ISBN 0-394-17128-4, B164, BC). Grove.

Burroughs, William S. & Leighton, Frances S. The Adding Machine: A Summation of Comments. (Illus.). 1984. 15.95 (Dist. by Arbor Hse). Seaver Bks.

Burroughs, William S., jt. auth. see Walker, Robert.

Burroughs, William S., Jr. Kentucky Ham. LC 83-19447. 176p. 1984. 15.95 (ISBN 0-87951-956-8). Overlook Pr.

--Speed. LC 83-42919. 192p. 1984. 14.95 (ISBN 0-87951-192-3). Overlook Pr.

Burrous, Clifford N., jt. auth. see Deboo, Gordon J.

Burrow, C. Preston. SuperCalc Illustrated: The Complete Guide to Using the SuperCalc Program. LC 84-50173. (Illus.). 133p. (Orig.). 1984. pap. 12.95 (ISBN 0-917065-07-7). Travis Pub Co.

Burrow, Dan. When Jesus Was a Baby. LC 84-70244. (Augsburg Open Window Bks.). (Illus.). 12p. (Orig.). 1984. pap. 4.95 (ISBN 0-8066-2078-1, 10-7082). Augsburg.

Burrow, G. N., jt. ed. see Fisher, D. A.

Burrow, Gerard N. & Ferris, Thomas F. Medical Complications During Pregnancy. 2nd ed. (Illus.). 1982. text ed. 56.00 (ISBN 0-7216-2189-9). Saunders.

Burrow, Gerard N. & Dussault, Jean H., eds. Neonatal Thyroid Screening. 336p. 1980. text ed. 46.00 (ISBN 0-89004-483-X). Raven.

Burrow, Gerard N., jt. ed. see Eggo, Margaret C.

Burrow, J. A. Essays on Medieval Literature. (Illus.). 1984. 29.95x (ISBN 0-19-811187-8). Oxford U Pr.

Burrow, J. A., ed. see Pearl Poet.

Burrow, J. W. Gibbon. (Past Masters Ser.). 112p. 1985. pap. 3.95 (ISBN 0-19-287552-3). Oxford U Pr.

Burrow, Jackie. Four Season Salads. 80p. 1985. pap. 4.95 (ISBN 0-89586-344-8). H P Bks.

Burrow, James L., jt. auth. see Everhard, Kenneth.

Burrow, John A. Medieval Writers & Their Work: Middle English Literature, 1100-1500. 1982. pap. text ed. 6.95x (ISBN 0-19-289122-7). Oxford U Pr.

Burrow, John W. Evolution & Society: A Study in Victorian Social Theory. 1966. 39.50 (ISBN 0-521-04393-X); pap. 12.95 (ISBN 0-521-09600-6). Cambridge U Pr.

--A Liberal Descent: Victorian Historians & the English Past. LC 81-3912. 336p. 1981. 52.50 (ISBN 0-521-24079-4). Cambridge U Pr.

--A Liberal Descent: Victorian Historians & the English Past. LC 81-3912. 318p. 1983. pap. 14.95 (ISBN 0-521-27482-6). Cambridge U Pr.

Burrow, Martha G. Developing Women Managers: What Needs to Be Done? LC 78-10334. 1978. pap. 13.50 (ISBN 0-8144-3135-6). AMACOM.

--Women: A Worldwide View of Their Management Development Needs. LC 76-10796. pap. 20.00 (ISBN 0-317-09919-1, 2051525). Bks Demand UMI.

Burrow, N. Trigant. The Determination of the Position of a Momentary Impression. Colvin, Stephen S., ed. (Illinois University Psychiatry Laboratory Ser.: Vol. 1, No. 1). 1909. write for info. Kraus Repr.

Burrow, Sallie. The Ride Home. 32p. (Orig.). 1982. pap. 3.75 (ISBN 0-9608706-0-1). Waterford Pr.

Burrow, T. The Sanskrit Language. (Great Language Ser.). 1973. text ed. 36.50x (ISBN 0-571-04819-6). Humanities.

Burrow, T., jt. auth. see Emeneau, Murray B.

Burrow, T. & Emeneau, M. B., eds. A Dravidian Etymological Dictionary. 2nd ed. 1984. 74.00x (ISBN 0-19-864326-8). Oxford U Pr.

Burrow, Trigant. The Biology of Human Conflict: An Anatomy of Behavior, Individual & Social. LC 73-14149. (Perspectives in Social Inquiry Ser.). 510p. 1974. Repr. 30.00x (ISBN 0-405-05495-5). Ayer Co Pubs.

--A Search for Man's Sanity. Grob, Gerald N., ed. LC 78-22553. (Historical Issues in Mental Health Ser.). 1979. Repr. of 1958 ed. lib. bdg. 46.00x (ISBN 0-405-11907-0). Ayer Co Pubs.

--Toward Social Sanity & Human Survival. Galt, Alfreda S., ed. 250p. 1984. 15.95 (ISBN 0-8180-1450-4). Horizon.

Burroway, Janet. Material Goods. LC 80-12381. 77p. 1980. 7.95 (ISBN 0-8130-0670-8). U Presses Fla.

--Opening Nights. LC 84-45613. 320p. 1985. 14.95 (ISBN 0-689-11545-8). Atheneum.

--Writing Fiction: A Guide to Narrative Craft. (Orig.). 1982. pap. text ed. 14.95 (ISBN 0-316-11768-4). Little.

Burroway, Janet, jt. auth. see Lord, John V.

Burrowes, George. Song of Solomon. (Geneva Commentaries Ser.). 1977. 12.95 (ISBN 0-85151-157-0). Banner of Truth.

Burrowes, John. Benny: The Life & Times of a Fighting Legend. 208p. 1982. 30.00x (ISBN 0-906391-32-6, Pub. by Mainstream). State Mutual Bk.

--Frontline Report: A Journalist's Notebook. 224p. 1982. 30.00x (ISBN 0-906391-27-X, Pub. by Mainstream). State Mutual Bk.

Burrowes, R., ed. see Burnham, Forbes.

Burrowes, Reynold. The Wild Coast: An Account of Politics in Guyana. 256p. 1984. text ed. 18.95 (ISBN 0-87073-037-1); pap. 11.95 (ISBN 0-87073-127-0). Schenkman Bks Inc.

Burrowes, Wesley. The Becauseway. (The New Abbey Theatre Ser.). Date not set. pap. 2.95x (ISBN 0-912262-74-5). Proscenium.

Burrows & Norman. Psychotropic Drugs. (Experimental & Clinical Psychiatry Ser.: Vol. 4). 528p. 1981. 75.00 (ISBN 0-8247-1009-6). Dekker.

Burrows, Alvina T., et al. They All Want to Write: Written English in the Elementary School. 4th ed. 248p. 1984. lib. bdg. 24.50 (ISBN 0-208-02042-X, Lib Prof Pubns); pap. 16.00x (ISBN 0-208-02043-8). Shoe String.

Burrows, Arthur A. Grammar Exercises: Elementary-Intermediate ESL, Pt. 1. Clark, Raymond C., ed. (Interplay ESL Ser.). (Illus.). 256p. (Orig.). 1985. pap. text ed. 9.95x (ISBN 0-86647-011-5). Pro Lingua.

Burrows, B. Respiratory Disorders. 1983. 19.95 (ISBN 0-8151-1351-X). Year Bk Med.

Burrows, Bernard & Denton, Geoffrey. Revolution or Federalism? Options for a United Kingdom. 94p. 1980. text ed. 26.50x (ISBN 0-333-28176-4, Pub. by Macmillan England). Humanities.

Burrows, Bernard, et al, eds. Federal Solutions to European Issues. LC 78-8066. 1978. 27.50x (ISBN 0-312-28546-9). St Martin.

Burrows, David J., et al. Myths & Motifs in Literature. LC 72-90546. 448p. (Orig.). 1973. pap. text ed. 14.95 (ISBN 0-02-905030-8). Free Pr.

Burrows, David L., ed. see Gasparini, Francesco.

Burrows, Desmond, ed. Chromium: Metabolism & Toxicity. 184p. 1983. 67.00 (ISBN 0-8493-5447-1). CRC Pr.

Burrows, E. G. The Crossings: Poems. 1976. pap. 1.50 (ISBN 0-935858-00-8). Humble Hills.

--Ethnology of Futuna. (BMB). Repr. of 1936 ed. 31.00 (ISBN 0-527-02244-6). Kraus Repr.

--Ethnology of Uvea, Wallis Islands. (BMB). Repr. of 1937 ed. 25.00 (ISBN 0-527-02253-5). Kraus Repr.

--The House of August. LC 85-7586. 67p. (Orig.). 1985. pap. 6.00 (ISBN 0-87886-126-2). Ithaca Hse.

--Kiva. LC 76-150822. 56p. 1976. 3.50 (ISBN 0-87886-077-0). Ithaca Hse.

--Man Fishing. 1969. 7.50 (ISBN 0-912090-05-7); pap. 2.45 (ISBN 0-912090-04-9). Sumac Mich.

--Native Music of the Tuamotus. (BMB). Repr. of 1933 ed. 18.00 (ISBN 0-527-02215-2). Kraus Repr.

--On the Road to Bailey's. 1979. pap. 2.00 (ISBN 0-931598-07-9). Fallen Angel.

--Songs of Urea & Futuna. (BMB). Repr. of 1945 ed. 21.00 (ISBN 0-527-02291-8). Kraus Repr.

Burrows, E. H. & Leeds, Norman E. Neuroradiology, 2 vols. (Illus., Vol. 1, 800 p., vol. 2, 384 p.). 1981. text ed. 175.00x set (ISBN 0-443-08016-X). Churchill.

Burrows, E. H., tr. see Mumenthaler, Mark.

Burrows, E. H., tr. see Suchenwirth, Richard.

Burrows, Edwin G. Atoll Culture: Ethnology of Ifaluk in the Central Carolines. LC 79-11044. Repr. of 1953 ed. lib. bdg. 21.50x (ISBN 0-8371-4426-4, BUAT). Greenwood.

--Hawaiian Americans: An Account of the Mingling of Japanese, Chinese, Polynesian, & American Cultures. 228p. 1970. Repr. of 1947 ed. 17.50 (ISBN 0-208-00949-3, Archon). Shoe String.

Burrows, Fredrika A. The Yankee Scrimshanders. LC 73-80907. (Illus.). 80p. 1973. pap. 2.50 (ISBN 0-88492-000-3). W S Sullwold.

Burrows, Fredrika A., ed. see Rex, Percy F.

Burrows, G. & Dennerstein, L. Handbook of Hypnosis & Psychosomatic Medicine. 554p. 1980. 90.00 (ISBN 0-444-80148-0, Biomedical Pr). Elsevier.

Burrows, G., et al, eds. Anti-Anxiety Agents. (Drugs in Psychiatry Ser.: No. 2). 1984. 45.00 (ISBN 0-444-80555-9, I-271-84, Biomedical Pr). Elsevier.

Burrows, G. D., jt. auth. see Kay, D. W.

Burrows, G. D., ed. Handbook of Studies on Depression. 434p. 1977. 96.50 (ISBN 90-219-2108-1, Biomedical Pr). Elsevier.

Burrows, G. D. & Davies, S. B., eds. Handbook of Studies on Anxiety. 406p. 1981. 85.00 (ISBN 0-444-80224-X, Biomedical Pr). Elsevier.

Burrows, G. D., jt. ed. see Beumont, P. J.

Burrows, G. D., jt. ed. see Dennerstein, L.

Burrows, G. D., et al, eds. Hypnosis Nineteen Hundred Seventy-Nine: Proceedings of the Eighth Int'l Congress, Melbourne. LC 79-16095. 354p. 1979. 73.75 (ISBN 0-444-80142-1, Biomedical Pr). Elsevier.

--Antianxiety Agents. (Drugs in Psychiatry Ser.: Vol. 2). 248p. 1984. 45.00 (ISBN 0-444-80555-9). Elsevier.

--Antidepressants. (Drugs in Psychiatry Ser.: Vol. 1). 350p. 1983. 45.00 (ISBN 0-444-80474-9, I-203-83, Biomedical Pr). Elsevier.

--Antipsychotics: Drugs in Psychiatry, Vol. 3. 288p. 1985. 72.25 (ISBN 0-444-80635-0). Elsevier.

Burrows, George M. Commentaries on the Causes, Forms, Symptoms & Treatment, Moral & Medical, of Insanity. LC 75-16693. (Classics of Psychiatry Ser.). 1976. Repr. of 1828 ed. 54.00x (ISBN 0-405-07422-0). Ayer Co Pubs.

Burrows, Graham D. & Werry, John S., eds. Advances in Human Psychopharmacology, Vol. 2. 375p. 1981. 45.00 (ISBN 0-89232-193-8). Jai Pr.

Burrows, Graham D., jt. ed. see Werry, John S.

Burrows, Hal D. The Value Mandate of Emotional Nature. LC 76-4662. 12.95 (ISBN 0-916886-01-8); pap. 5.95 (ISBN 0-916886-02-6). H D Burrows.

Burrows, J. Jane Austen's Emma. (Sydney Studies in Literature Ser). 1968. 15.00x (ISBN 0-424-05840-5, Pub. by Sydney U Pr). Intl Spec Bk.

Burrows, James C., jt. auth. see Woods, Douglas.

Burrows, L. A Grammar of the Ho Language. 194p. 1980. Repr. of 1915 ed. 20.00 (ISBN 0-89684-258-4, Pub. by Cosmo Pubns India). Orient Bk Dist.

Burrows, L. J. The Middle School: High Road or Dead End. (Woburn Education Ser.). 231p. 1978. 22.50x (ISBN 0-7130-0149-6, Pub. by Woburn Pr England). Biblio Dist.

Burrows, Leonard. Browning: An Introductory Essay. LC 77-791. Repr. of 1952 ed. lib. bdg. 8.50 (ISBN 0-8414-9882-2). Folcroft.

Burrows, Lois M. & Myers, Laura G. Too Many Tomatoes, Squash, Beans, & Other Good Things: A Cookbook for When Your Garden Explodes. LC 75-34581. 288p. 1976. 16.30i (ISBN 0-06-013132-2, HarpT). Har-Row.

--Too Many Tomatoes...Squash, Beans, & Other Good Things: A Cookbook for When Your Garden Explodes. LC 75-34581. 1980. pap. 8.61i (ISBN 0-06-090765-7, CN 765, CN). Har-Row.

Burrows, M., ed. see Oxford University.

Burrows, M. L. E. L. F. Communication Antennas. (IEE Electromagnetic Waves Ser.: No. 5). (Illus.). 343p. 1978. casebound 46.00 (ISBN 0-906048-00-1, EW005, Pub. by Peregrinus England). Inst Elect Eng.

--E.L.F. Communication Antennas, No. 5. (IEE Electromagnetic-Waves). 343p. 1978. 46.00 (ISBN 0-906048-00-1, EW005, Pub. by Peregrinus London). Inst Elect Eng.

Burrows, Margaret, jt. auth. see Kurtz, Harold.

Burrows, Marion. Keep It Simple. LC 81-4398. 256p. 1981. 11.95 (ISBN 0-688-00450-4). Morrow.

Burrows, Marjorie & Ramancese, Avan. The Winter Hearts. (Avon Romance Ser.). 432p. 1985. pap. 3.50 (ISBN 0-380-89513-7). Avon.

Burrows, Millar. Burrows on the Dead Sea Scrolls. 1978. pap. 11.95 (ISBN 0-8010-0752-6). Baker Bk.

Burrows, Millart. Founders of Great Religions: Being Personal Sketches of Famous Leaders. LC 72-13272. (Essay Index Reprint Ser.). Repr. of 1931 ed. 16.75 (ISBN 0-8369-8148-0). Ayer Co Pubs.

Burrows, Paul. Economic Theory of Pollution Control. 240p. 1980. 27.50x (ISBN 0-262-02150-1); pap. text ed. 9.95x (ISBN 0-262-52056-7). MIT Pr.

Burrows, Paul & Hitiris, Theodore. Macroeconomic Theory: A Mathematical Introduction. LC 73-2779. 210p. 1974. text ed. 31.95x (ISBN 0-471-12525-3, Pub. by Wiley-Interscience). Wiley.

Burrows, Ralph. Vital Signs. 256p. 1982. pap. 2.75 (ISBN 0-449-14472-0, GM). Fawcett.

Burrows, Roger. Magnificient Maze Coloring Book, No. 2. 48p. 1984. pap. 2.95 (Orig.). 1984. pap. 2.95 (ISBN 0-8431-1012-0). Price Stern.

Burrows, Ruth. Before the Living God. 6.95 (ISBN 0-87193-155-9). Dimension Bks.

--Guidelines for Mystical Prayer. 5.95 (ISBN 0-87193-134-6). Dimension Bks.

--To Believe in Jesus. 6.95 (ISBN 0-87193-154-0). Dimension Bks.

Burrows, Seymour J. Win - Win Outcomes: A Physician's Negotiating Guide. LC 84-60125. 200p. 1984. text ed. 26.95 (ISBN 0-931028-46-9). Pluribus Pr.

Burrows, Stephen G. God's Daughter in Nassau. 186p. 1980. 8.50 (ISBN 0-682-49497-6). Exposition Pr FL.

--Responsible Parenting Among Men & Nations: A Challenge for Uncle Sam & the World. 96p. 1981. 6.00 (ISBN 0-682-49752-5). Exposition Pr FL.

Burrows, Stephen G. E. That's the Lawyer. 256p. 1980. 10.00 (ISBN 0-682-49594-8). Exposition Pr FL.

Burrows, Susan G. & Gassert, Carole A. Moving Right Along after Open Heart Surgery. Hull, Nancy R., ed. (Illus.). 52p. (Orig.). 1982. pap. text ed. 5.00 (ISBN 0-939838-09-5). Pritchett & Hull.

Burrows, Susan G., jt. auth. see Gassert, Carole A.

Burrows, Thomas D. & Wood, Donald N. Television Production. 2nd ed. 384p. 1982. pap. text ed. write for info. (ISBN 0-697-04349-5). Wm C Brown.

Burrows, William E. On Reporting the News. LC 76-16472. 345p. 1977. 23.50x (ISBN 0-8147-1009-3). NYU Pr.

Burrows, William R. New Ministries: The Global Context. LC 80-17261. 176p. (Orig.). 1980. pap. 7.95 (ISBN 0-88344-329-5). Orbis Bks.

Burrud, Bill & Rich, Allen. Bill Burrud's Animal Quiz. (Illus.). (gr. 4 up). 1979. pap. 1.95 (ISBN 0-448-17079-5, Pub. by Tempo). Ace Bks.

Burrup, Percy & Brimley, Vern. Financing Education in a Climate of Change. 3rd ed. 424p. 30.95x (ISBN 0-205-07748-X, 2377489, Pub. by Longwood Div). Allyn.

Burrus, Bernie R. Administrative Law & Local Government. LC 63-63661. (Michigan Legal Publications Ser.). 139p. 1982. Repr. of 1963 ed. lib. bdg. 27.50 (ISBN 0-89941-170-3). W S Hein.

Burrus, C. S. & Parks, T. W. DFT-FFT & Convolution Algorithms & Implementation. 232p. 1985. 22.50 (ISBN 0-471-81932-8). Wiley.

Burrus, Ernest. Ducrue's Account of Expulsion of the Jesuits from Lower California. 1967. pap. 20.00 (ISBN 88-7041-502-3). Jesuit Hist.

Burrus, Ernest, tr. Wenceslaus Linck's Reports & Letters, 1762-1778. 30.00 (ISBN 0-317-11572-3). Dawsons.

Burrus, Ernest J., ed. Jesuit Relations, Baja California, 1716-1762. (Baja California Travels Ser.: Vol. 47). (Illus.). 280p. 1984. 60.00 (ISBN 0-317-12379-3). Dawsons.

Burrus, Ernest J., tr. see De Salvatierra, Juan M.

Burrus, Ernest S., tr. Wenceslaus Linck's Diary of His 1776 Expedition to Northern Baja California. 50.00 (ISBN 0-317-11551-0). Dawsons.

Burrus, Victoria. A Procedural Manual for Entry Establishment in the Dictionary of the Old Spanish Language. 2nd ed. Moreno, Angel Gomez, tr. from Span. 104p. 1983. 25.00x (ISBN 0-942260-37-6). Hispanic Seminary.
Burry, Anthony, jt. auth. see Kellerman, Henry.
Burry, J. H., jt. ed. see Singh, S. P.
Bursak, Laura Z., jt. auth. see Ives, Josephine.
Bursell, F. Introduction to Insect Physiology. 1971. 55.00 (ISBN 0-12-146650-7). Acad Pr.
Bursell-Hall, G. L., ed. see Hunt, R. W.
Bursian, Konrad. Geschichte der Classischen Philologie in Deutschland Von Den Anfangen Bis Zur Gegenwart. 1965. Repr. of 1883 ed. 65.00 (ISBN 0-384-06603-8). Johnson Repr.
Bursiel, Charles A. The View from Here. 180p. (Orig.). 1984. pap. 8.95 (ISBN 0-912549-05-X). Bread and Butter.
Bursill, Henry. Hand Shadows to Be Thrown upon a Wall. 42p. (gr. 1-6). pap. 1.50 (ISBN 0-486-21779-5). Dover.
--More Hand Shadows to Be Thrown Upon a Wall. (Illus.). 39p. (gr. 1-6). 1971. pap. 1.95 (ISBN 0-486-21384-6). Dover.
Bursill-Hall, G. L. A Check-List of Incipits of Medieval Latin Grammatical Treatises: A-G. 36p. 1978. pap. 5.00 (ISBN 0-8232-0089-2). Fordham.
--Speculative Grammars of the Middle Ages: The Doctrine of Partes Orationis of the Modistae. LC 70-151246. (Approaches to Semiotics Ser: No. 11). 424p. 1971. text ed. 44.80x (ISBN 90-2791-913-5). Mouton.
Bursk, Christopher. Place of Residence. (Sparrow Poverty Pamphlets Ser.: No. 44). 32p. (Orig.). 1983. pap. 2.00x (ISBN 0-935552-16-2). Sparrow Pr.
--Standing Watch. (New Poetry Ser.). 1978. 8.95 (ISBN 0-395-27118-5); pap. 4.50 (ISBN 0-395-27199-1). HM.
Bursk, Edward C. & Grayser, Stephen A. Advanced Cases in Marketing Management. LC 68-24633. (Foundations of Marketing Ser). (Orig.). 1968. pap. 16.95 ref. ed. (ISBN 0-13-011320-4). P-H.
Bursk, Edward C., ed. Human Relations for Management: The Newer Perspective. facsimile ed. LC 70-167320. (Essay Index Reprint Ser). Repr. of 1956 ed. 21.00 (ISBN 0-8369-2582-3). Ayer Co Pubs.
Bursk, Edward C. & Blodgett, Timothy B., eds. Developing Executive Leaders. LC 70-160023. (Illus.). 1971. 15.00x (ISBN 0-674-19975-8). Harvard U Pr.
Bursk, Edward C. & Chapman, John F., eds. New Decision-Making Tools for Managers: Mathematical Programing As an Aid in the Solving of Business Problems. LC 63-11416. (Illus.). Repr. of 1963 ed. 107.80 (ISBN 0-8357-9168-8, 2017752). Bks Demand UMI.
Bursky, Dave. Components for Microcomputer System Design. 272p. 1980. pap. 13.95 (ISBN 0-8104-0975-5). Hayden.
--Memory Systems Design & Applications. 240p. pap. 12.95 (ISBN 0-8104-0980-1). Hayden.
--The S-One Hundred Bus Handbook. 280p. 1980. pap. 17.50 (ISBN 0-8104-0897-X). Hayden.
Bursnall, W., ed. Planning Challenges of the 70's in the Public Domain. (Science & Technology Ser.: Vol. 22). (Illus.). 1969. lib. bdg. 40.00x (ISBN 0-87703-050-2, Pub. by Am Astronaut); microfiche suppl 20.00x (ISBN 0-87703-131-2). Univelt Inc.
Bursnall, W. J., et al, eds. Space Shuttle Missions of the 80's. LC 57-43769. (Advances in the Astronautical Sciences Ser.: Vol. 32, Pts. 1 & 2). (Illus.). 1977. lib. bdg. 95.00x set (ISBN 0-87703-120-7, Pub. by Am Astronaut); Pt. 1. lib. bdg. 40.00x (ISBN 0-87703-078-2); Pt. 2. lib. bdg. 55.00x (ISBN 0-87703-087-1); microfiche suppl. 65.00x (ISBN 0-87703-133-9). Univelt Inc.
Burson, James L. & Williams, Phillip L. Industrial Toxicology: Safety & Health Applications in the Workplace. (Illus.). 400p. 1984. 39.50 (ISBN 0-534-02707-5). Lifetime Learn.
Burssens, Gaston. From the Flemish of Gaston Burssens. Wade, John S., tr. from Flemish. LC 82-8756. 21p. (Orig.). 1982. pap. 2.50 (ISBN 0-933292-10-4). Arts End.
Burst, Jess, jt. auth. see Segal, Hillel.
Burstall, M. L., jt. auth. see Rueben, B. G.
Burstall, Sara A. Education of Girls in the United States. LC 79-165709. (American Education Ser, No. 2). 1972. Repr. of 1894 ed. 15.00 (ISBN 0-405-03698-1). Ayer Co Pubs.
Burstall, Tim. Sebastian & the Sausages. (Illus.). (gr. 4 up). 13.50x (ISBN 0-392-04506-0, ABC). Sportshelf.
Burstein. The Get Well Hotel. 113p. 1980. 4.95 (ISBN 0-07-009244-3). McGraw.
--Management of Hotel & Motel Security. (Occupational Safety & Health Ser.: Vol. 5). 216p. 1980. 29.50 (ISBN 0-8247-1002-9). Dekker.
Burstein, A. Religion, Cults & the Law. 2nd ed. (Legal Almanac Ser.: No. 23). 128p. 1980. 5.95 (ISBN 0-379-11133-0). Oceana.
Burstein, Abraham. Ghetto Messenger: Sixty Tales of a Unique Seventy Year Old Messenger 'Boy' facsimile ed. LC 72-150540. (Short Story Index Reprint Ser). Repr. of 1928 ed. 18.00 (ISBN 0-8369-3837-2). Ayer Co Pubs.
Burstein, Albert H., jt. auth. see Frankel, Victor H.
Burstein, Chaya. Joseph & Anna's Time Capsule: A Legacy of Old Jewish Prague. (Illus.). 40p. 1984. pap. 8.95 (ISBN 0-671-50712-5). Summit Bks.
--What's an Israel? (Illus.). 32p. (ps-4). 1983. pap. 2.95 (ISBN 0-930494-26-1). Kar Ben.
Burstein, Chaya M. A First Jewish Holiday Cookbook. (Activity Book). (Illus.). (gr. 3-8). 1979. (Bonim Bks); pap. 6.95 (ISBN 0-88482-775-5, Bonim Bks). Hebrew Pub.
--The Jewish Kids Catalog. (Illus.). 224p. (gr. 3-7). 1983. pap. 10.95 (ISBN 0-8276-0215-4, 603). Jewish Pubns.
Burstein, David, jt. auth. see Stasiowski, Frank.
Burstein, E., ed. Atomic Structure & Properties of Solid. (Italian Physical Society Ser.: Course 52). 1973. 92.00 (ISBN 0-12-368852-3). Acad Pr.
Burstein, E., ed. see U. S.-Japan Seminar on Inelastic Light Scattering, Santa Monica, California, January 22-25, 1979.
Burstein, Elias, ed. Tunneling Phenomena in Solids. Lindqvist, S. LC 69-12528. (Illus.). 579p. 1969. 79.50x (ISBN 0-306-30362-0, Plenum Pr). Plenum Pub.
Burstein, Elias & De Martini, Francesco, eds. Polaritons: Proceedings, Taormina Research Conference on the Structure of Matter, 1st, Taormina, Italy, Oct, 1972. LC 73-12845. 1975. text ed. 53.00 (ISBN 0-08-017825-1). Pergamon.
Burstein, Harvey. Hotel Security Management. LC 74-14039. 138p. 1975. text ed. 29.95 (ISBN 0-275-09820-6). Praeger.
Burstein, Harvey & Data General Corporation. Hotel Security Management. 2nd ed. LC 84-17717. 188p. 1985. 31.95 (ISBN 0-03-069721-2). Praeger.
Burstein, Joel V. State of New York Law Revision Committee Reports, 1954-1956, 6 vols. LC 79-90809. 1980. Repr. of 1954 ed. Set. lib. bdg. 200.00 (ISBN 0-89941-030-8). W S Hein.
Burstein, John. Slim Goodbody: The Inside Story. (Illus.). (gr. k-6). 1977. pap. 4.95 (ISBN 0-07-009241-9). McGraw.
--Slim Goodbody: What Can Go Wrong & How to Be Strong. (Illus.). (gr. k-6). 1978. 9.95 (ISBN 0-07-009242-7). McGraw.
Burstein, John, jt. auth. see Good Thing Inc.
Burstein, Joseph. Approximation by Exponentials. LC 83-73529. (Illus.). 85p. (Orig.). 1984. pap. 18.50 (ISBN 0-9607126-1-5). Metrics Pr.
--Sequential Optimization. (Illus.). 90p. 1985. pap. 20.00 (ISBN 0-9607126-2-3). Metrics Pr.
Burstein, Leigh, jt. ed. see Roberts, Karlene H.
Burstein, Leigh, et al, eds. Collecting Evaluation Data. 1985. 29.95 (ISBN 0-8039-2449-6). Sage.
Burstein, M. & Legmann, P. Lipoprotein Precipitation. (Monographs on Atherosclerosis: Vol. 11). (Illus.). viii, 132p. 1982. 41.50 (ISBN 3-8055-3512-0). S Karger.
Burstein, M. L. Modern Monetary Theory. 256p. 1985. 27.50 (ISBN 0-312-54108-2). St Martin.
Burstein, Milton B. What You Should Know about Acquisitions & Mergers. LC 72-5483. (Business Almanac Ser: No. 19). 128p. 1973. lib. bdg. 5.95 (ISBN 0-379-11219-1). Oceana.
--What You Should Know about Selling & Salesmanship. LC 69-19798. (Business Almanac Ser.: No. 18). 85p. 1969. 5.95 (ISBN 0-379-11218-3). Oceana.
Burstein, Moshe. Self-Government of the Jews in Palestine Since 1900. LC 75-6426. (The Rise of Jewish Nationalism & the Middle East Ser.). 298p. 1976. Repr. of 1934 ed. 25.00 (ISBN 0-88355-313-9). Hyperion Conn.
Burstein, Nancy. The Executive Body: A Complete Guide to Fitness & Stress Management for the Working Woman. 1984. 16.95 (ISBN 0-671-49437-6). S&S.
--Thirty Days to a Flatter Stomach for Women. 1983. pap. 2.95 (ISBN 0-553-34004-2). Bantam.
Burstein, Nancy, jt. auth. see Matthews, Roy.
Burstein, Paul. Discrimination, Jobs, & Politics: The Struggle for Equal Employment Opportunity in the United States since the New Deal. LC 85-4802. 272p. 1985. 30.00x (ISBN 0-226-08134-6); pap. 12.95x (ISBN 0-226-08135-4). U of Chicago Pr.
Burstein, Paul, jt. auth. see Simon, Julian.
Burstein, Stanley & Okin, Louis, eds. Panhellenica: Essays in Ancient History. 1980. 15.00x (ISBN 0-87291-134-9). Coronado Pr.
Burstein, Stanley M. The Hellenistic Age from the Battle of Ipsos to the Death of Kleopatra VII. (Translated Documents of Greece & Rome: Vol. 3). write for info. (ISBN 0-521-23691-6); pap. write for info. (ISBN 0-521-28158-X). Cambridge U Pr.
--Outpost of Hellenism: The Emergence of Heraclea on the Black Sea. LC 74-620189. (University of California Publications: Classical Studies Ser.: Vol. 14). pap. 41.00 (ISBN 0-317-29519-5, 2021268). Bks Demand UMI.
Burstein, Stanley M. & Pomeroy, Sarah B., eds. Ancient History. LC 83-61356. (Selected Syllabi from American Colleges & Universities Ser.). 1984. pap. text ed. 14.50x (ISBN 0-910129-11-8). Wiener Pub Inc.
Burstein, A. Joseph. Dr. Burstein's Book of Children. (Illus.). 242p. 1983. 12.95 (ISBN 0-7137-1273-2, Pub. by Blandford Pr England). Sterling.
Bursten, Ben. Beyond Psychiatric Expertise. (Illus.). 308p. 1984. 28.50x (ISBN 0-398-04991-2). C C Thomas.
--The Manipulator: A Psychoanalytic View. LC 72-92553. 1973. pap. 71.80 (ISBN 0-317-08049-0, 2017417). Bks Demand UMI.
Bursten, Martin A. Escape from Fear. LC 73-8563. (Illus.). 224p. 1973. Repr. of 1958 ed. lib. bdg. 15.75x (ISBN 0-8371-6961-5, BUEF). Greenwood.
Burstiner, I., jt. auth. see Coventry, W.
Burstinger, Irving. Mail Order Selling: How to Market Almost Anything by Mail. (Illus.). 262p. 1982. 24.95 (ISBN 0-13-545855-2); pap. 12.95 (ISBN 0-13-545848-X). P-H.
--Run Your Own Retail Store: From Raising the Money to Counting the Profits. (Illus.). 304p. 1981. 19.95 (ISBN 0-13-784017-9, Spec); pap. 22.95 (ISBN 0-13-784009-8). P-H.
--Small Business Handbook: Comprehensive Guide to Starting & Running Your Own Business. (Illus.). 1979. (Spec); pap. text ed. 14.95 (ISBN 0-13-814194-0). P-H.
Burstinger, Irving, jt. auth. see Appleby, Robert C.
Burston, W. H., ed. James Mill on Education. LC 69-11268. (Cambridge Texts & Studies in Education: No. 6). 1969. 24.95 (ISBN 0-521-07414-2). Cambridge U Pr.
Burstow, Henry. Reminiscences of Horsham. LC 75-19030. 1975. Repr. of 1911 ed. lib. bdg. 22.50 (ISBN 0-8414-3125-6). Folcroft.
Burstroem, H. see Ruhland, W., et al.
Burstyn, Ellen, intro. by. Reliquaries-Photographs by Steven Arnold. (Illus.). 104p. (Orig.). 1983. pap. 20.00 (ISBN 0-942642-09-0). Twelvetrees Pr.
Burstyn, Joan. Victorian Education & the Ideal of Womanhood. 185p. 1984. pap. text ed. 12.00 (ISBN 0-8135-1031-7). Rutgers U Pr.
Burstyn, Joan N. Song Cycle. LC 76-552177. 1976. 3.75x (ISBN 0-915176-16-5). Job Shop.
--Victorian Education & the Ideal of Womanhood. (Illus.). 185p. 1980. 28.50x (ISBN 0-389-20103-0, 06877). B&N Imports.
Burstyn, Varda, ed. Women Against Censorship. 210p. 1985. pap. 8.95 (ISBN 0-88894-455-1, Pub. by Salem Hse Ltd). Merrimack Pub Cir.
Bursynski, P. R., ed. To Be a Child: A Book of Photographic Essays on the Psychological Rights of the Child. 65p. 1979. 10.00 (ISBN 0-917668-03-0). Intl Schl Psych.
Burszttayn, Harold. Medical Choices, Medical Chances. 480p. 1983. pap. 10.95 (ISBN 0-385-29202-3, Delta). Dell.
Bursztyn, Sylvia & Tunick, Barry. The Los Angeles Times Crossword Puzzle Collection. 1982. 4.95 (ISBN 0-399-50664-0, Perigee). Putnam Pub Group.
Burt, et al. Planning & Building the Minimum Energy Dwelling. LC 77-15078. (Illus.). 1977. pap. 10.00 (ISBN 0-910460-57-4). Craftsman.
Burt, Al. Becalmed in the Mullet Latitudes: Al Burt's Florida. Martin, Val, ed. LC 83-81677. 350p. (Orig.). 1983. 15.95 (ISBN 0-912451-11-4); pap. 10.95 (ISBN 0-912451-10-6). Florida Classics.
Burt, Alvin. Florida a Place in the Sun. (Illus.). 244p. 1974. 8.95 (ISBN 0-685-50329-1). Burda Pubns.
Burt, B. C. A Brief History of Greek Philosophy. Repr. of 1889 ed. 20.00 (ISBN 0-686-20086-1). Quality Lib.
--Stories from the Greek Comedians Aristophanes, Philemon, Diphilus, Menander, Apollodorus. Repr. of 1893 ed. 17.50 (ISBN 0-686-20111-6). Quality Lib.
Burt, Barbara J., jt. ed. see Neiman, Max.
Burt, Brian A., et al. A Study of Relationships Between Diet & Dental Health, United States, 1971-1974. Cox, Klaudia, ed. 60p. 1981. pap. text ed. 1.75 (ISBN 0-8406-0235-9). Natl Ctr Health Stats.
Burt, Bruce C., compiled by. Calculators: Readings from the Arithmetic Teacher & the Mathematics Teacher. LC 79-17365. (Illus.). 231p. 1979. pap. 6.25 (ISBN 0-87353-144-2). NCTM.
Burt, Cyril L., ed. How the Mind Works. facsimile ed. LC 78-105000. (Essay Index Reprint Ser.). 1934. 19.00 (ISBN 0-8369-1454-6). Ayer Co Pubs.
Burt, Sir Cyril. Causes & Treatment of Backwardness. 1954. 5.95 (ISBN 0-8022-0199-7). Philos Lib.
Burt, Daniel S., jt. auth. see Bader, William.
Burt, David N. Proactive Procurement: The Key to Increased Profits, Productivity, & Quality. (Illus.). 288p. 1984. 27.95 (ISBN 0-13-711465-6). P-H.
Burt, Donald X. Colors of My Days. LC 80-23754. 175p. (Orig.). 1980. pap. 3.95 (ISBN 0-8146-1198-2). Liturgical Pr.
--The Inn of the Samaritan. 96p. (Orig.). 1983. pap. 5.95 (ISBN 0-8146-1315-2). Liturgical Pr.
--The Rush to Resurrection. 88p. 1985. pap. 4.95 (ISBN 0-8146-1440-X). Liturgical Pr.
Burt, Edward A. Thelephoraceae of North America. (Illus.). 1966. 45.00x (ISBN 0-02-842320-8). Hafner.
--Thelephoraceae of North America, 15 Pts. (Illus.). 900p. 1966. Repr. of 1926 ed. lib. bdg. 25.00x (ISBN 0-02-842320-8). Lubrecht & Cramer.
Burt, Elinor. Spanish Dishes from the Old Clay Pot. rev. ed. (Cookery Ser.). (Illus.). 280p. 1979. 8.95 (ISBN 0-89496-002-4); pap. 6.95 (ISBN 0-89496-001-6). Ross Bks.
Burt, Elisabeth V., tr. see Palazzoli, Mara S., et al.
Burt, Emma J. The Seen & Unseen in Browning. LC 73-2639. 1973. lib. bdg. 15.00 (ISBN 0-8414-1785-7). Folcroft.
Burt, Eugene C. An Annotated Bibliography of the Visual Arts of East Africa. LC 80-7805. (Traditional Arts of Africa Ser.). 392p. 1980. 25.00x (ISBN 0-253-17225-X). Ind U Pr.
Burt, Forest D. & Want, E. Cleve. Invention & Design: Rhetorical Reader. 3rd ed. 406p. 1981. pap. text ed. 12.00 (ISBN 0-394-32557-5, RanC). Random.
Burt, Forrest D. The Effective Writer. 1978. pap. text ed. 2.95x (ISBN 0-89641-005-6). American Pr.
--W. Somerset Maugham. (English Author Ser.). 1985. lib. bdg. 16.95 (ISBN 0-8057-6885-8, Twayne). G K Hall.
Burt, Forrest D. & Want, Cleve E., eds. Invention & Design. 4th ed. 1985. pap. text ed. 11.95 (ISBN 0-394-33275-X, RanC). Random.
Burt Hill Kosar Rittelmann Associates. Small Office Building Handbook: Design for Reducing First Costs & Utility Costs. (Illus.). 400p. 1984. 40.00 (ISBN 0-442-21126-0). Van Nos Reinhold.
Burt, John J. & Meeks, Linda B. Education for Sexuality: Concepts & Programs for Teaching. 3rd ed. 1985. text ed. 22.95 (ISBN 0-03-063214-5). HR&W.
Burt, John J., et al. Toward a Healthy Lifestyle: Through Elementary Education. 608p. 1980. text ed. write for info. (ISBN 0-534-00776-7). Wadsworth Pub.
Burt, John R. From Phonology to Philology: An Outline of Descriptive & Historical Spanish Linguistics. LC 80-67212. 208p. 1980. lib. bdg. 22.50 (ISBN 0-8191-1310-7); pap. text ed. 11.25 (ISBN 0-8191-1311-5). U Pr of Amer.
Burt, John T. Results of the System of Separate Confinement As Administered at the Pentonville Prison. LC 83-49229. (Crime & Punishment in England 1850-1922 Ser.). 287p. 1984. lib. bdg. 35.00 (ISBN 0-8240-6203-5). Garland Pub.
Burt, Katharine N. Red Lady. Bd. with Hidden Creek. 1979. pap. 2.50 (ISBN 0-451-11596-1, AE1596, Sig). NAL.
Burt, Larry W. Tribalism in Crisis: Federal Indian Policy, 1953-1961. 192p. 1982. 17.50 (ISBN 0-8263-0633-0). U of NM Pr.
Burt, McKinley, Jr. Black Inventors of America. 1969. pap. 7.85 (ISBN 0-89420-095-X, 296959). Natl Book.
Burt, Marina K. & Kiparsky, Carol. The Gooficon: A Repair Manual for English. 1972. pap. 7.95 (ISBN 0-912066-07-5). Newbury Hse.
Burt, Marina K., ed. see Teachers of English to Speakers of Other Languages.
Burt, Martha R., jt. auth. see Moore, Kristin A.
Burt, Marvin R. Policy Analysis: Introduction & Applications to Health Programs. LC 74-81587. (Illus.). xii, 136p. 1974. text ed. 18.00 (ISBN 0-87815-013-7). Info Resources.
Burt, Marvin R., jt. auth. see Sowder, Barbara J.
Burt, Mary E. Browning's Women. 1973. Repr. of 1887 ed. 17.50 (ISBN 0-8274-1510-9). R West.
--Literary Landmarks. 1973. Repr. of 1889 ed. 10.00 (ISBN 0-8274-1509-5). R West.
--Literary Landmarks: A Guide to Good Reading for Young People. 1977. lib. bdg. 59.95 (ISBN 0-8490-2170-7). Gordon Pr.
--Poems That Every Child Should Know: A Selection of the Best Poems of All Times for Young People. 1904. 18.50 (ISBN 0-8274-3160-0). R West.
Burt, Mary E. & Cable, Mary B. Eugene Field Book. facsimile ed. LC 76-86794. (Granger Index Reprint Ser). 1898. 14.00 (ISBN 0-8369-6071-8). Ayer Co Pubs.
Burt, Mary E., ed. Poems That Every Child Should Know: A Selection of the Best Poems of All Times for Young People. facsimile ed. LC 71-168776. (Granger Index Reprint Ser.). Repr. of 1904 ed. 26.50 (ISBN 0-8369-6296-6). Ayer Co Pubs.
Burt, Maxwell S. Delectable Mountains. LC 70-144922. 1971. Repr. of 1927 ed. 29.00x (ISBN 0-403-00885-9). Scholarly.
--Other Side. facsimile ed. LC 70-134064. (Essay Index Reprint Ser). Repr. of 1928 ed. 20.00 (ISBN 0-8369-2218-2). Ayer Co Pubs.
Burt, Nathaniel. Jackson Hole Journal. LC 83-47831. (Illus.). 232p. 1983. 16.95 (ISBN 0-8061-1804-0). U of Okla Pr.
--The Perennial Philadelphians: The Anatomy of an American Aristocracy. facsimile ed. LC 75-1834. (Leisure Class in America Ser.). (Illus.). 1975. Repr. of 1963 ed. 42.00x (ISBN 0-405-06903-0). Ayer Co Pubs.
Burt, Olive W. Horse in America. LC 73-6187. (Illus.). (gr. 7-12). 1940. 12.45i (ISBN 0-381-99630-1, JD-J). Har-Row.
Burt, Philip B. Quantum Mechanics & Nonlinear Waves: Physics. (Monographs & Tracts Ser.). 331p. 1981. 82.50 (ISBN 3-7186-0072-2). Harwood Academic Pubs.
Burt, R. A., jt. auth. see Trotter, W. P.
Burt, R. O. & Mills, C. Gravity Concentration Technology. (Developments in Mineral Processing Ser.: No. 5). 606p. 1984. 120.50 (ISBN 0-444-42411-3). Elsevier.
Burt, Richard, ed. Arms Control & Defense Postures in the Nineteen-Eighties. LC 81-21913. (Special Studies in National Security & Defense Policy Ser.). 230p. 1982. softcover 28.00x (ISBN 0-86531-162-5). Westview.

Burt, Richard & Kemp, Geoffrey, eds. Congressional Hearings on American Defense Policy, Nineteen Forty-Seven to Nineteen Seventy-One: An Annotated Bibliography. LC 73-11321. 360p. (Orig.). 1974. pap. 9.95x (ISBN 0-7006-0109-0). U Pr of KS.

Burt, Rob. The Illustrated Movie Quiz Book. (Illus.). 96p. 1981. 5.95 (ISBN 0-8317-6112-1, Rutledge Pr). Smith Pubs.

--Rockerama: Twenty Five Years of Teen Screen Idols. (Illus.). 208p. (Orig.). 1983. pap. 12.95 (ISBN 0-933328-80-X). Delilah Bks.

Burt, Robert, et al, eds. The Role of Centrosema, Desmodium & Stylosanthes in Improved Tropical Pastures. (Tropical Agriculture Ser.). (Illus.). 315p. 1982. pap. 29.00x (ISBN 0-86531-401-2). Westview.

Burt, Robert A. Taking Care of Strangers: The Rule of Law in Doctor-Patient Relations. LC 79-7364. 1979. 15.95 (ISBN 0-02-905090-1). Free Pr.

Burt, Robert A. & Wald, Michael. Standards Relating to Abuse & Neglect. LC 77-3279. (IJA-ABA Juvenile Justice Standards Project Ser.). 224p. 1982. pref ref 25.00 (ISBN 0-88410-242-4); pap. 12.50 (ISBN 0-88410-830-9). Ballinger Pub.

Burt, Roger, ed. Cornish Mining. LC 70-77258. 1969. 19.95x (ISBN 0-678-05536-X). Kelley.

Burt, Ronald. Toward a Structural Theory of Action: Network Models of Social Structure, Perception & Action. (Quantitative Studies in Social Relations). 1982. 37.50 (ISBN 0-12-147150-0). Acad Pr.

Burt, Ronald S. Corporate Profits & Cooptation: Networks of Market Constraints & Directorate Ties in the American Economy. LC 83-2578. (Quantitative Studies in Social Relations). 1983. 39.00 (ISBN 0-12-147180-2). Acad Pr.

Burt, Ronald S. & Minor, Michael J. Applied Network Analysis: A Methodological Introduction. 352p. 1982. 27.50 (ISBN 0-8039-1906-9); pap. 12.95 (ISBN 0-8039-1907-7). Sage.

Burt, Samuel M. & Lessinger, Leon. Volunteer Industry Involvement in Public Education. LC 73-132557. 1970. 28.50x (ISBN 0-89197-974-3). Irvington.

Burt, Struthers M. Powder River: Let'er Buck. LC 73-144923. (Illus.). 1971. Repr. of 1938 ed. 39.00x (ISBN 0-403-00886-7). Scholarly.

Burt, T. P., jt. auth. see Anderson, M. G.

Burt, Thomas & Watson, Aaron. Thomas Burt, M.P., D.C.L. Pitman & Privy Councillor: An Autobiography, with Supplementary Chapters by Aaron Watson. LC 83-48476. (The World of Labour-English Workers 1850-1890 Ser.). 319p. 1984. lib. bdg. 40.00 (ISBN 0-8240-5704-X). Garland Pub.

Burt, William A. A Key to the Solar Compass. 1978. pap. 8.50 (ISBN 0-686-25540-2, 512). CARBEN Survey.

Burt, William H. A Field Guide to the Mammals. 3rd ed. (Peterson Field Guide Ser.). 1976. 15.95 (ISBN 0-395-24082-4); pap. 10.95 (ISBN 0-395-24084-0). HM.

--Mammals of the Great Lakes Region. (Illus.). (gr. 10-12). 1972. pap. 8.95 (ISBN 0-472-06183-6, 183, AA). U of Mich Pr.

Burt, William H., ed. Antarctic Pinnipedia. LC 76-182566. (Antarctic Research Ser.: Vol. 18). (Illus.). 226p. 1971. 32.00 (ISBN 0-87590-118-2). Am Geophysical.

Burtain, Ruth J. Empties Drifting By. (Friend Ser.). 1985. pap. 3.95 (ISBN 0-8163-0593-5). Pacific Pr Pub Assn.

Burtchaell, James T. For Better, for Worse. 160p. (Orig.). 1985. pap. 5.95 (ISBN 0-8091-2664-8). Paulist Pr.

--Philemon's Problem: The Daily Dilemma of the Christian. LC 73-88935. 1973. pap. 2.95 (ISBN 0-914070-05-3). ACTA Found.

--Rachel Weeping: The Case Against Abortion. LC 83-48986. 400p. 1984. pap. 10.53 (ISBN 0-06-061251-7, RD 517, HarpR). Har-Row.

Burtchaell, James T., ed. Abortion Parley. LC 80-19229. 420p. 1980. 20.00 (ISBN 0-8362-3600-9). Andrews McMeel Parker.

Burtchaell, James T., et al. Marriage Among Christians: A Curious Tradition. LC 77-81396. (Illus.). 192p. 1977. pap. 3.50 (ISBN 0-87793-139-9). Ave Maria.

Burte, H. M. see Jaffee, R. I.

Burtenshaw, D. The City in West Europe. LC 80-41589. 340p. 1981. 51.95 (ISBN 0-471-27929-3, Pub. by Wiley-Interscience). Wiley.

Burthogge, Richard. An Essay upon Reason & the Nature of Spirits. LC 75-11204. (British Philosophers & Theologians of the 17th & 18th Centuries: Vol. 10). 1976. Repr. of 1694 ed. lib. bdg. 51.00 (ISBN 0-8240-1759-5). Garland Pub.

--The Philosophical Writings of Richard Burthogge. Landes, Margaret W., ed. xxi, 266p. 1921. 19.95 (ISBN 0-87548-048-9). Open Court.

Burtis, C. Edward. The Fountain of Youth. 1981. 10.95x (ISBN 0-686-76733-0). B OF A.

--Real American Tragedy. 280p. 1983. 13.95x (ISBN 0-911238-85-9, Regent House). B of A.

Burtis, Warren D. Jesus: The First Human Behaviorist. 128p. 1981. pap. text ed. 5.95 (ISBN 0-939530-00-7). Burtis Ent.

Burtle, James L., jt. auth. see Rolfe, Sidney E.

Burtle, Mary V. see Erulkar, Mary, pseud.

Burtle, Vasanti. Women Who Drink: Alchoholic Experience & Psychotherapy. (Illus.). 304p. 1979. 29.50x (ISBN 0-398-03854-6). C C Thomas.

Burtless, Gary, jt. ed. see Aaron, Henry J.

Burtner, Robert W. & Chiles, Robert E., eds. John Wesley's Theology: A Collection from His Works. 304p. 1982. pap. 7.95 (ISBN 0-687-20529-8). Abingdon.

Burtness, James. Shaping the Future: The Ethics of Dietrich Bonhoeffer. LC 85-47723. 208p. 1985. pap. 16.95 (ISBN 0-8006-1869-6, 1-1869). Fortress.

Burtness, Paul S. & Hulbert, Jack E. Effective Business Communication. 8th ed. (gr. 9-12). 1985. text ed. 12.95 (ISBN 0-317-18601-9, E19). SW Pub.

Burtnett, Francis & McDonough, Patrick. The Political Education Training Program Manual. 300p. 1982. pap. text ed. 400.00 (ISBN 0-911547-60-6, 72144W34). Am Assn Coun Dev.

Burto, William, jt. auth. see Barnet, Sylvan.

Burto, William, ed. see Shakespeare, William.

Burton. All Color World of Farm Animals. (Illus.). 1980. 5.95 (ISBN 0-7064-1008-4, Mayflower Bks). Smith Pubs.

--Elementary Number Theory. rev. ed. 390p. 1980. text ed. 36.07 (ISBN 0-205-06965-7, 5669650). Allyn.

--Modeling & Differential Equations in Biology. (Lecture Notes in Pure & Applied Mathematics Ser.: Vol. 58). 296p. 1980. 49.50 (ISBN 0-8247-1075-4). Dekker.

--Wild Animals I Have Known. Kottmeyer, William A., et al, eds. 1962. pap. 6.92 (ISBN 0-07-009288-5). McGraw.

Burton & Arbuthnot. The Kama Sutra of Vatsyayana. 224p. 1984. pap. 3.95 (ISBN 0-425-07580-X). Berkley Pub.

Burton & Shelton. Business Math Using Calculators. 1986. text ed. price not set (ISBN 0-538-13880-7, M88). SW Pub.

Burton, jt. auth. see Arnold.

Burton, jt. auth. see Clubualt.

Burton & McGee, J. L., eds. Advances in Radiation Chemistry, 2 vols. LC 68-18012. 410p. 1974. Vol. 4. 37.50 (ISBN 0-471-12543-1, Pub. by Wiley); Vol. 5, 352pp., 1976. 45.50 (ISBN 0-471-01669-1). Krieger.

Burton, A. & Henn, Percy U. Wollaston's Albany Journals 1848-1856. 1978. 15.00x (ISBN 0-85564-104-5, U of W Austral Pr). Intl Spec Bk.

--Wollaston's Picton Journal 1841-1844. 1978. 13.50x (ISBN 0-85564-103-7, Pub. by U of W Austral Pr). Intl Spec Bk.

Burton, A. C. Physiology & Biophysics of the Circulation. 1972. pap. 14.95 (ISBN 0-8151-1364-1). Year Bk Med.

Burton, Alan C. Physiology & Biophysics of the Circulation: An Introductory Text. 2nd ed. LC 70-182003. (Physiology Textbook Ser.). pap. 60.00 (ISBN 0-317-28222-0, 2022732). Bks Demand UMI.

Burton, Alex. Just One Kiss Baby. Stowers, Carlton, ed. 240p. 1983. 11.95 (ISBN 0-89015-417-1); pap. 8.95 (ISBN 0-89015-402-3). Eakin Pubns.

Burton, Alfred. Rush-Bearing. LC 77-16804. 1977. Repr. of 1891 ed. lib. bdg. 25.00 (ISBN 0-8414-1723-7). Folcroft.

--Rush-Bearing: An Account of the Old Custom of Strewing Rushes. LC 74-13710. 1974. Repr. of 1891 ed. lib. bdg. 25.00 (ISBN 0-88305-057-9). Norwood Edns.

Burton, Alice E. Miss Carter & the Ifrit. Melville, Douglas & Reginald, R., eds. LC 77-84239. (Lost Race & Adult Fantasy Ser.). 1978. Repr. of 1945 ed. lib. bdg. 17.00x (ISBN 0-405-10987-3). Ayer Co Pubs.

Burton, Alma P. Discourses of the Prophet Joseph Smith. LC 77-23977. 399p. 9.95 (ISBN 0-87747-067-7). Deseret Bk.

Burton, Alma P., jt. auth. see Burton, Clea M.

Burton, Andrew, jt. auth. see Radford, John.

Burton, Andrew, ed. The Pathology & Psychology of Cognition. LC 82-12526. (Psychology in Progress Ser.). 256p. 1982. pap. 12.50 (ISBN 0-416-30820-1, NO. 3793). Methuen Inc.

Burton, Anthony. The Coventry Option. 1977. pap. 1.75 (ISBN 0-380-01659-1, 33274). Avon.

--Embrace of the Butcher. LC 82-5068. 225p. 1982. 12.95 (ISBN 0-396-08059-6). Dodd.

--The National Trust Guide to Our Industrial Past. (Illus.). 240p. 1983. 29.95 (ISBN 0-540-01072-3, Pub. by G Philip). Sheridan.

--The Past Afloat. LC 83-61270. (Illus.). 191p. 1984. 24.95 (ISBN 0-88186-325-4). Parkwest Pubns.

--Revolutionary Violence: The Theories. LC 77-83808. 154p. 1978. 19.50x (ISBN 0-8448-1262-5). Crane-Russak Co.

--The Rise & Fall of King Cotton. (Illus.). 240p. 1985. 19.95 (ISBN 0-233-97148-3, Pub. by A Deutsch England). David & Charles.

--The Shell Book of Curious Britain. LC 81-67007. (Illus.). 304p. 1981. 19.95 (ISBN 0-7153-8083-4). David & Charles.

--Wilderness Britain. (Illus.). 192p. 1985. 28.00 (ISBN 0-233-97640-X, Pub. by A Deutsch England). David & Charles.

Burton, Anthony & Murdoch, John. Byron. (Illus.). 232p. (Orig.). 1984. pap. 7.95 (ISBN 0-901486-76-0, Pub. by Victoria & Albert Mus UK). Faber & Faber.

Burton, Anthony M. Urban Terrorism. LC 75-21937. 1976. 12.95 (ISBN 0-02-905000-6). Free Pr.

Burton, Arthur. Modern Humanistic Psychotherapy. LC 67-27947. (Jossey-Bass Behavioral Science Ser.). Repr. of 1970 ed. 47.00 (ISBN 0-8357-9335-4, 2013915). Bks Demand UMI.

Burton, Arthur, ed. Encounter: Theory & Practice of Encounter Groups. LC 73-92889. (Jossey-Bass Behavioral Science Ser.). Repr. of 1970 ed. 42.60 (ISBN 0-8357-9318-4, 2013911). Bks Demand UMI.

--Psychotherapy of the Psychoses: Perspectives on Current Techiques of Treatment. LC 76-13507. 396p. 1976. Repr. of 1961 ed. 22.50 (ISBN 0-88275-413-0). Krieger.

Burton, Arthur, et al. Twelve Therapists: How They Live & Actualize Themselves. LC 72-83966. (Social & Behavioral Science Ser.). 1972. 27.95x (ISBN 0-87589-139-X). Jossey-Bass.

Burton, Asa. Essays on Some of the First Principles of Metaphysicks, Ethicks, & Theology. LC 73-4839. (History of Psychology Ser.). 432p. 1973. Repr. of 1824 ed. lib. bdg. 60.00x (ISBN 0-8201-1114-7). Schol Facsimiles.

Burton, B. T. Human Nutrition. 3rd ed. (Illus.). 1975. 38.00 (ISBN 0-07-009282-6). McGraw.

Burton, Barry. Let's Weigh the Evidence. 95p. (Orig.). 1983. pap. 2.95 (ISBN 0-937958-17-4). Chick Pubns.

Burton, Belle. A Simple Life. 144p. 1981. 8.95 (ISBN 0-89962-213-5). Todd & Honeywell.

Burton, Bob. THe Bounty Hunter. (Illus.). 136p. (Orig.). 1984. pap. 10.00 (ISBN 0-87364-296-1). Paladin Pr.

Burton, Brenda, ed. see Green, Lewis.

Burton, Bruce A. Hail! Nene Karenna, The Hymn. Butterfield, Stephen, ed. (Illus.). 292p. 1981. 17.75 (ISBN 0-9611422-2-7). Security Dupont.

Burton, Bruce A., ed. see Pohl, Frederick J.

Burton, Charles & Nida, Gail. Be Good to Your Back. Rev. ed. 57p. 1980. 6.00 (ISBN 0-88440-033-6, 738). Sis Kenny Inst.

Burton, Clare. Subordination: Feminism & Social Theory. 146p. (Orig.). 1985. text ed. 18.50x (ISBN 0-86861-718-0); pap. text ed. 10.50x (ISBN 0-86861-710-5). Allen Unwin.

Burton, Clark, ed. The School & the University: An International Perspective. LC 85-1158. 360p. 1985. 32.50x (ISBN 0-520-05423-7). U of Cal Pr.

Burton, Clea M. & Burton, Alma P. For They Shall Be Comforted. 5.95 (ISBN 0-87747-091-X). Deseret Bk.

Burton, D. P. & Dexter, A. L. Microprocessor Systems Handbook. LC 77-88133. (Illus.). 1977. text ed. 9.50 (ISBN 0-916550-04-4). Analog Devices.

Burton, David. Oliver Wendell Holmes, Jr. What Manner of Liberal? LC 78-23645. (American Problem Ser.). 168p. 1979. pap. 6.50 (ISBN 0-88275-793-8). Krieger.

--Theodore Roosevelt: Confident Imperialist. 203p. text ed. 9.00 (ISBN 0-8122-7582-9). Brown Bk.

Burton, David, jt. auth. see Smith, Julius.

Burton, David H. American History-British Historians: A Cross-Cultural Approach to the American Experience. LC 76-8458. 344p. 1976. 24.95x (ISBN 0-88229-280-3); pap. 12.95x (ISBN 0-88229-584-5). Nelson-Hall.

--Oliver Wendell Holmes, Jr. (United States Authors Ser.). 1980. lib. bdg. 13.50 (ISBN 0-8057-7262-6, Twayne). G K Hall.

--Theodore Roosevelt. (World Leaders Ser.). 1973. lib. bdg. 12.50 (ISBN 0-8057-3709-X, Twayne). G K Hall.

--William Howard Taft: In the Public Service. LC 84-27778. 1985. lib. bdg. price not set (ISBN 0-89874-829-1). Krieger.

Burton, David H., ed. Progressive Masks: Letters of Oliver Wendell Holmes, Jr., & Franklin Ford. LC 80-54787. 144p. 1982. 19.50 (ISBN 0-87413-188-X). U Delaware Pr.

Burton, David H., ed. see Holmes, Oliver Wendell.

Burton, David M. A History of Mathematics. 1984. text ed. 40.05 (ISBN 0-205-08095-2, 568095). Allyn.

--History of Mathematics: An Introduction. 1984. text ed. 40.05 (ISBN 0-205-08095-2, 568095). Allyn.

Burton, Dee. I Dream of Woody. LC 83-63297. 192p. 1984. 12.95 (ISBN 0-688-01556-5). Morrow.

Burton, Deirdre. Dialogue & Discourse: A Socio-Linguistic Approach to Modern Drama Dialogue & Naturally-Occurring Conversation. 220p. 1980. 31.95x (ISBN 0-7100-0560-1). Routledge & Kegan.

--Dialogue & Discourse: A Sociolinguistic Approach to Modern Drama, Dialogue, & Naturally Occuring Conversation. 222p. 1984. pap. 13.95x (ISBN 0-7102-0386-1). Routledge & Kegan.

Burton, Dennis A., et al. A Guide to Manuscripts in the Presidential Libraries. 475p. 1985. text ed. write for info. (ISBN 0-934631-00-X). Res Materials.

Burton, Dolores M. Shakespeare's Grammatical Style: A Computer-Assisted Analysis of "Richard II" & "Antony & Cleopatra". LC 73-6795. 382p. 1973. 20.00x (ISBN 0-292-77504-0). U of Tex Pr.

Burton, Dudley J. The Goverance of Energy: Problems, Prospects & Underlying Issues. LC 79-89507. 426p. 1980. 35.95x (ISBN 0-03-055981-2). Praeger.

Burton, E. Milby. Charleston Furniture, Seventeen Hundred to Eighteen Twenty-Five. 2nd ed. LC 73-120917. Orig. Title: Contributions from the Charleston Museum: XII. (Illus.). xii, 200p. 1970. lib. bdg. 19.95 (ISBN 0-87249-198-6). U of SC Pr.

--Siege of Charleston, 1861-1865. LC 70-120584. xxii, 390p. 1970. pap. 7.95 (ISBN 0-87249-345-8). U of SC Pr.

Burton, Earl H., ed. Your Spiritual Deposit. 64p. 1982. pap. 1.50 (ISBN 0-317-17822-9). Am Christian.

Burton, Edward. An Inquiry into the Heresies of the Apostolic Age. LC 78-63166. (Heresies of the Early Christian & Medieval Era: Second Ser.). Repr. of 1829 ed. 43.50 (ISBN 0-404-16179-0). AMS Pr.

Burton, Ella S. God's Word Is Our Only Foundation. 1983. 5.75 (ISBN 0-8062-2164-X). Carlton.

Burton, Elsie, jt. auth. see Werner, Peter H.

Burton, Elsie C. The New Physical Education for Elementary School Children. LC 76-11981. (Illus.). 1977. text ed. 26.95 (ISBN 0-395-20658-8). HM.

--Physical Activities for the Developing Child. (Illus.). 304p. 1980. photocopy ed. 28.75x (ISBN 0-398-03939-9). C C Thomas.

Burton, Elsie C., jt. auth. see Bailey, Rebecca A.

Burton, Eric. Diamonds. 2nd ed. LC 78-66362. (Illus.). 1979. 35.00 (ISBN 0-8019-6789-9). Chilton.

Burton, Ernest D. Syntax of the Moods & Tenses of New Testament Greek. LC 76-25360. 1976. 12.95 (ISBN 0-8254-2256-6). Kregel.

Burton, Ernest D., jt. auth. see Stevens, William A.

Burton, Ernest J. The British Theatre: It's Repertory & Practice, 1100-1900 A.D. LC 77-22954. 1977. Repr. of 1960 ed. lib. bdg. 22.50x (ISBN 0-8371-9739-2, BUBT). Greenwood.

Burton, Eva, et al see Linguistic Circle of Saigon & Summer Institute of Linguistics.

Burton, F. N. Contemporary Trade. (Industrial Studies). 187p. 1984. text ed. 25.75x (ISBN 0-86003-529-8, Pub. by Philip Allan England); pap. text ed. 13.00x (ISBN 0-86003-631-6, Pub. by Philip Allan England). Humanities.

Burton, Frederick R. American Primitive Music, with Special Attention to Songs of the Highways. 1977. lib. bdg. 59.95 (ISBN 0-8490-1416-6). Gordon Pr.

Burton, Gabrielle. I'm Running Away from Home, but I'm Not Allowed to Cross the Street. 1975. pap. 1.65 (ISBN 0-380-01534-X, 21865). Avon.

--I'm Running Away from Home, but I'm Not Allowed to Cross the Street: A Primer on Women's Liberation. 208p. 1972. 5.00 (ISBN 0-912786-00-0). Know Inc.

Burton, Gary. A Musician's Guide to the Road. 164p. 1981. pap. 7.95 (ISBN 0-8230-7583-4, Billboard Bks). Watson-Guptill.

Burton, George G. & Hodgkin, John E., eds. Respiratory Care: A Guide to Clinical Practice. 2nd ed. (Illus.). 1216p. 1984. text ed. 49.50 (ISBN 0-397-50548-5, 65-06992, Lippincott Medical). Lippincott.

Burton, Graeme, jt. auth. see Dimbleby, Richard.

Burton, Gwendolyn. Microbiology for the Health Sciences. 2nd ed. (Illus.). 238p. 1983. text ed. 13.75 (ISBN 0-397-54397-2, 64-03380, Lippincott Nursing); wkbk. 6.50 (ISBN 0-397-54465-0, 64-04065). Lippincott.

Burton, H. Australian Economy Nineteen Twenty-Nine to Nineteen Sixty-Nine. 1969. pap. 3.00x (ISBN 0-85564-038-3, Pub. by U of W Austral Pr). Intl Spec Bk.

Burton, H., et al. Milk Sterilization. (Agricultural Planning Studies: No. 65). (Orig.). 1969. pap. 7.25 (ISBN 0-685-02454-7, F279, FAO). Unipub.

Burton, H. K. The Re-Establishment of the Indians in Their Pueblo Life Through the Revival of Their Traditional Crafts. LC 36-35586. Repr. of 1936 ed. 14.00 (ISBN 0-527-03236-0). Kraus Repr.

Burton, Harry E. Discovery of the Ancient World. facsimile ed. LC 75-102228. (Select Bibliographies Reprint Ser). 1932. 19.00 (ISBN 0-8369-5113-1). Ayer Co Pubs.

Burton, Harry P., ed. Famous Stories by Famous Writers. 14.95 (ISBN 0-89190-126-4, Pub. by Am Repr). Amereon Ltd.

Burton, Henrietta K. The Re-Establishment of the Indians in Their Pueblo Life Through the Revival of Their Traditional Crafts: A Study in Home Extension Education. LC 73-176617. (Columbia University. Teachers College. Contributions to Education: No. 673). Repr. of 1936 ed. 22.50 (ISBN 0-404-55673-6). AMS Pr.

Burton, Henry. An Apology of Appeale: Also, an Epistle to the True Hearted Nobility. LC 76-57364. (English Experience Ser.: No. 782). 1977. Repr. of 1636 ed. lib. bdg. 5.00 (ISBN 90-221-0782-5). Walter J Johnson.

--For God & the King. LC 76-57365. (English Experience Ser.: No. 783). 1977. lib. bdg. 17.50 (ISBN 90-221-0783-3). Walter J Johnson.

--A Tryall of Private Devotions. LC 77-6863. (English Experience Ser.: No. 856). 1977. Repr. of 1628 ed. lib. bdg. 10.50 (ISBN 90-221-0856-2). Walter J Johnson.

Burton, Hester. Five August Days. 176p. 1982. 11.95 (ISBN 0-19-271454-6, Pub. by Oxford U Pr Childrens). Merrimack Pub Cir.
--Kate Ryder. LC 75-8576. (Illus.). 160p. (gr. 7 up). 1975. 10.53i (ISBN 0-690-00978-X). Crowell Jr Bks.
Burton, I., jt. auth. see Brace, Geoffrey.
Burton, Ian & Kates, Robert W. The Environment As Hazard. (Illus.). 1978. pap. text ed. 12.95x (ISBN 0-19-502222-X). Oxford U Pr.
Burton, Ian, jt. auth. see Whyte, Ann V.
Burton, Ian & Kates, Robert W., eds. Readings in Resource Management & Conservation. LC 65-14427. 1965. 15.00x (ISBN 0-226-08237-7). U of Chicago Pr.
Burton, Ian, jt. ed. see White, Rodney.
Burton, Ian, et al. The Human Ecology of Coastal Flood Hazards in Megalopolis. LC 68-57967. (Research Papers Ser.: No. 115). 196p. 1968. pap. 10.00 (ISBN 0-89065-023-3). U Chicago Dept Geog.
Burton, Isabel. The Life of Captain Sir Richard Burton, 2 vols. LC 77-91525. 1977. Repr. of 1898 ed. lib. bdg. 60.00 (ISBN 0-89341-468-9). Longwood Pub Group.
Burton, Isabel, ed. see Burton, Richard F.
Burton, Isabel, tr. see Alencar, Jose M. de.
Burton, Ivor & Drewry, Gavin. Legislation & Public Policy: Public Bills in the 1970-74 Parliament. 300p. 1981. text ed. 47.50x (ISBN 0-8419-5065-2). Holmes & Meier.
Burton, J. A. Effective Warehousing. 3rd ed. (Illus.). 352p. 1981. pap. text ed. 22.50x (ISBN 0-7121-0591-3). Trans-Atlantic.
Burton, J. D. & Liss, P. S., eds. Estuarine Chemistry. 1977. 47.50 (ISBN 0-12-147350-3). Acad Pr.
Burton, J. J., jt. auth. see Nowick, A. S.
Burton, J. L. Aids to Undergraduate Medicine. 4th ed. (Aids to Ser.). (Illus.). 1984. pap. text ed. 7.95 (ISBN 0-443-03154-1). Churchill.
--Essentials of Dermatology. (Churchill Livingstone Medical Text Ser.). 1980. pap. text ed. 12.50 (ISBN 0-443-01646-1). Churchill.
Burton, J. L. & Matthews, R. W. Aids to Medicine for Dental Students. LC 82-23452. (Illus.). 107p. 1983. pap. text ed. 7.95 (ISBN 0-443-02690-4). Churchill.
Burton, J. M. Honore De Balzac & His Figures of Speech. (Elliott Monographs: Vol. 8). 1921. 11.00 (ISBN 0-527-02612-3). Kraus Repr.
Burton, Jack. Blue Book of Broadway Musicals. LC 69-55070. (Burton Blue Book Ser). (Illus.). 344p. 1970. lib. bdg. 21.00 (ISBN 0-87282-012-2). CHB-ALF.
--Blue Book of Hollywood Musicals. (Burton Blue Bk). (Illus.). 1953. lib. bdg. 78.00 (ISBN 0-87282-013-0). CHB-ALF.
--Blue Book of Tin Pan Alley, 2 Vols. LC 62-16426. Set. 25.00 (ISBN 0-686-66390-X); Vol. 1. (ISBN 0-87282-014-9); Vol. 2. (ISBN 0-87282-015-7). CHB-ALF.
Burton, James H. Evolution of the Income Approach. 260p. 1982. 15.00 (ISBN 0-911780-62-9). Am Inst Real Estate Appraisers.
Burton, James J. & Garten, Robert L., eds. Advanced Materials in Catalysis. 1977. 72.00 (ISBN 0-12-147450-X). Acad Pr.
Burton, Jane & Dixon, Dougal. Time Exposure: A Photographic Record of the Dinosaur Age. (Illus.). 96p. 1984. 14.95 (ISBN 0-8253-0217-X). Beaufort Bks NY.
Burton, Jane, jt. auth. see Burton, Maurice.
Burton, Jean. Sir Richard Burton's Wife. 1942. 20.00 (ISBN 0-8274-3429-4). R West.
Burton, Jimalee. Indian Heritage, Indian Pride: Stories That Touched My Life. LC 73-7426. (Illus.). 1981. pap. 14.95 (ISBN 0-8061-1707-9). U of Okla Pr.
--Indian Heritage, Indian Pride: Stories That Touched My Life. LC 73-7426. (Illus.). 160p. 1974. 17.95 (ISBN 0-8061-1124-0). U of Okla Pr.
Burton, John. Accounting for Business Combinations. LC 70-141249. 1970. 8.00 (ISBN 0-910586-00-4). Finan Exec.
--Ascanius; or, the Young Adventurer, 1746. Shugrue, Michael F., ed. (The Flowering of the Novel, 1740-1775 Ser: Vol. 17). 1974. lib. bdg. 61.00 (ISBN 0-8240-1116-3). Garland Pub.
--The Collection of the Qur'an. LC 76-27899. 1977. 49.50 (ISBN 0-521-21439-4); pap. 15.95 (ISBN 0-521-29652-8). Cambridge U Pr.
--Dear Survivors. LC 82-50666. 145p. 1982. 18.50x (ISBN 0-86531-455-1); pap. text ed. 8.95x (ISBN 0-86531-456-X). Westview.
--Deviance, Terrorism & War: The Process of Solving Unsolved Social & Political Problems. LC 79-16484. 1979. 11.95x (ISBN 0-312-19753-5). St Martin.
--Extinct Animals. (How & Why Wonder Books Ser.). (Illus.). (gr. 3-7). 1974. pap. 1.25 (ISBN 0-448-05072-2). Wonder.
--J. S. Tabanini of Thailand above the Isthumus of Kra. LC 76-56190. (Illus.). 165p. (Orig.). 1978. 15.00 (ISBN 0-911836-10-1). Entomological Repr.
--The Naturalist in London. LC 74-78247. (Regional Naturalist). (Illus.). 168p. 5.95 (ISBN 0-7153-6215-1). David & Charles.
--The Oxford Book of Insects: Pocket Edition. (Illus.). 1981. pap. 6.95x (ISBN 0-19-217725-7). Oxford U Pr.
--Picking Losers? The Political Economy of Industrial Policy. (Hobart Papers: No. 99). 79p. 1983. pap. 7.50 technical (ISBN 0-255-36165-3, Pub. by Inst Econ Affairs). Transatlantic.
Burton, John, et al. The Oxford Book of Insects. (Illus.). 1968. 19.95x (ISBN 0-19-910005-5). Oxford U Pr.
--Computers in Teaching Mathematics. (Computers in Education Ser.). 192p. 1983. pap. text ed. 15.95x (ISBN 0-201-10565-9). Addison-Wesley.
--Britain Between East & West: A Concerned Independence. 172p. 1984. text ed. 32.95 (ISBN 0-566-00722-3). Gower Pub Co.
Burton, John A. The National Trust Book of British Wild Animals. (Illus.). 194p. 1985. 17.95 (ISBN 0-224-02104-4, Pub. by Jonathan Cape). Merrimack Pub Cir.
Burton, John A., ed. Owls of the World: Their Evolution, Structure & Ecology. LC 84-16412. (Illus.). 208p. 1985. 29.95 (ISBN 0-88072-060-3, Pub. by Tanager). Longwood Pub Group.
Burton, John C. A Revised Financial Reporting Model for Municipalities, No. 6-7. (Government Auditing Ser.). 1980. pap. 6.00 (ISBN 0-686-70150-X). Coun on Municipal.
Burton, John C. & Palmer, Russell E., eds. Handbook of Accounting & Auditing. LC 80-53166. 1981. 84.00 (ISBN 0-88262-526-8). Warren.
Burton, John F. Interstate Variations in Employers' Cost of Workmen's Compensation: Effect on Plant Location Exemplified in Michigan. 75p. 1966. pap. 0.50 (ISBN 0-911558-57-8). W E Upjohn.
Burton, John F., Jr., jt. auth. see Clabault, James M.
Burton, John H. The Book-Hunter. 1974. Repr. 15.95 (ISBN 0-8274-1958-9). R West.
--Life & Correspondence of David Hume, 2 Vols. 1967. Repr. of 1846 ed. Set. 39.50 (ISBN 0-8337-0433-8). B Franklin.
--The Life & Correspondence of David Hume. LC 82-48342. (The Philosophy of David Hume Ser.). 1038p. 1983. lib. bdg. 110.00 (ISBN 0-8240-5402-4). Garland Pub.
--Narratives from Criminal Trials in Scotland, 2 vols. in 1. LC 71-39564. Repr. of 1852 ed. 45.00 (ISBN 0-404-09925-4). AMS Pr.
--Political & Social Economy. LC 68-55499. Repr. of 1849 ed. 37.50x (ISBN 0-678-00621-0). Kelley.
--Scots Abroad. Repr. 20.00 (ISBN 0-8482-7406-7). Norwood Edns.
Burton, John H., ed. Darien Papers. LC 78-39563. (Bannatyne Club, Edinburgh. Publications: No. 90). Repr. of 1849 ed. 55.00 (ISBN 0-404-52831-7). AMS Pr.
Burton, John H., ed. see Carlyle, Alexander.
Burton, John W. Systems, States, Diplomacy & Rules. 256p. 1968. 34.50 (ISBN 0-521-07316-2). Cambridge U Pr.
--World Society. LC 71-176252. (Illus.). 250p. 1972. pap. 10.95 (ISBN 0-521-09694-4). Cambridge U Pr.
Burton, Jonathan R. & Sordillo, Darlene. How to Ride a Winning Dressage Test: The Judge's Guide to Step-by-Step Improvement. 1985. 17.95; pap. 10.95. HM.
Burton, Julianne, ed. The New Latin American Cinema: An Annotated Bibliography of English-Languages Sources, 1960-1980. LC 83-80377. (Orig.). 1983. pap. 4.00 (ISBN 0-918266-17-3). Smyrna.
Burton, June. Napoleon & Clio: Historical Writing, Teaching, & Thinking During the First Empire. LC 77-88659. 158p. 1979. 14.75 (ISBN 0-89089-077-3). Carolina Acad Pr.
Burton, Katherine K. In No Strange Land. facsimile ed. LC 72-99619. (Essay Index Reprint Ser). 1942. 19.50 (ISBN 0-8369-1551-8). Ayer Co Pubs.
--Paradise Planters, the Story of Brook Farm. LC 72-2949. Repr. of 1939 ed. 25.50 (ISBN 0-404-10714-1). AMS Pr.
Burton, Kathleen, ed. see Milton, John.
Burton, Kevin R. Increasing Productivity with PFS. (Illus.). 128p. (Orig.). 1984. 21.95 (ISBN 0-8306-0789-7, 1789); pap. 14.95 (ISBN 0-8306-1789-2). TAB Bks.
Burton, Linda. Stories from Tennessee. LC 82-16016. 432p. 1983. text ed. 27.95x (ISBN 0-87049-376-0); pap. 12.95 (ISBN 0-87049-377-9). U of Tenn Pr.
Burton, Lindy, ed. Care of the Child Facing Death. 1974. 19.95x (ISBN 0-7100-7863-3). Routledge & Kegan.
Burton, Lloyd E., et al. Public Health & Community Medicine. 3rd ed. (Illus.). 616p. 1980. pap. 33.00 (ISBN 0-683-01236-3). Williams & Wilkins.
Burton, Louise F., jt. ed. see Donlon, Edward T.
Burton, M. E., ed. see McCarty, Raymond.
Burton, Margaret. Bibliography of Librarianship: Classified & Annotated Guide to the Library Literature of the World Excluding Slavonic & Oriental Languages. 1970. 22.50 (ISBN 0-8337-0429-X). B Franklin.
Burton, Margaret & Vosburgh, Marion. A Bibliography of Librarianship. 1976. lib. bdg. 59.95 (ISBN 0-8490-1499-9). Gordon Pr.
Burton, Marilee R. Aaron Awoke. LC 81-48638. (Illus.). 40p. (ps-k). 1982. 9.57i (ISBN 0-06-020891-0); PLB 9.89g (ISBN 0-06-020892-9). HarpJ.
--The Elephant's Nest: Four Wordless Stories. LC 78-20263. (Illus.). (gr. k-3). 1979. HarpJ.
Burton, Mary E. Phases of the Moon. 1976. 8.00x (ISBN 0-89363-009-8); pap. 5.00x (ISBN 0-89363-010-1). Woolf Quarterly.
Burton, Mary E., ed. see Wordsworth, Mary.
Burton, Maurice. Le Dictionnaire En Couleurs Des Animaux. 400p. (Fr.). 1974. 57.00 (ISBN 0-686-56875-3, M-6653). French & Eur.
--Insects & Their Relatives. (The Junior World of Science Ser.). (gr. 7 up). 9.95 (ISBN 0-317-12629-6). Facts on File.
--The Life of Birds. LC 77-88440. (Easy Reading Edition of Introduction to Nature Ser.). (Illus.). 1978. PLB 12.68 (ISBN 0-382-06126-8). Silver.
--The Life of Fishes. LC 77-88434. (Easy Reading Edition of Introduction to Nature Ser.). (Illus.). 1978. PLB 12.68 (ISBN 0-686-51140-9). Silver.
--The Life of Insects. LC 78-56576. (Easy Reading Edition of Introduction to Nature Ser.). (Illus.). 1979. PLB 12.68 (ISBN 0-382-06185-3). Silver.
--The Life of Reptiles & Amphibians. LC 77-88437. (Easy Reading Edition of Introduction to Nature Ser.). (Illus.). 1978. PLB 12.68 (ISBN 0-382-06131-4). Silver.
--Maurice Burton's Daily Telegraph Nature Book. LC 75-10701. (Illus.). 128p. 1975. 5.95 (ISBN 0-7153-7078-2). David & Charles.
--A Revision of the Classification of the Calcarous Sponges: With a Catalogue of the Specimens in the British Museum (Natural History) (Illus.). 693p. 1963. 65.00x (ISBN 0-565-00698-3, Pub. by Brit Mus Nat Hist England). Sabbot-Natural Hist Bks.
--The Sixth Sense of Animals. LC 72-6622. (Illus.). 192p. 1973. 7.95 (ISBN 0-8008-7232-0). Taplinger.
--True Book About Animals. 13.75x (ISBN 0-392-08507-0, SpS). Sportshelf.
--The World of Science: Birds. Date not set. price not set. Facts on File.
--The World of Science: Warm-Blooded Mammals. Date not set. price not set. Facts on file.
Burton, Maurice & Burton, Jane. The Colorful World of Animals. (Illus.). 1979. 10.95 (ISBN 0-8317-1507-3, Mayflower Bks). Smith Pubs.
Burton, Maurice & Burton, Robert. Enciclopedia de la Vida Animal, 6 vols. 2nd ed. 2770p. (Espn.). 1978. Set. leather 264.00 (ISBN 84-02-03435-7, S-50508). French & Eur.
--The Life of Meat Eaters. LC 77-88439. (Easy Reading Edition of Introduction to Nature Ser.). (Illus.). 64p. (gr. 3 up). 1978. PLB 12.68 (ISBN 0-382-06129-2). Silver.
Burton, Miles. The Secret of High Eldersham. LC 75-44961. (Crime Fiction Ser). 1976. Repr. of 1930 ed. lib. bdg. 27.00 (ISBN 0-8240-2357-9). Garland Pub.
Burton, Nathaniel & Lombard, Rudy. Creole Feast: Fifteen Master Chefs of New Orleans Reveal Their Secrets. 1978. 14.95 (ISBN 0-394-41328-8). Random.
Burton, Neil. British Historic Houses Handbook. 672p. 1982. 17.95 (ISBN 0-87196-627-1). Facts on File.
--The English Historic Houses Handbook. (Illus.). 668p. 1981. 17.95 (ISBN 0-87196-538-0). Facts on File.
Burton, Neil, jt. auth. see Bettelheim, Charles.
Burton, O. E. Study in Creative History. LC 71-105821. (Classics Ser). 1971. Repr. of 1932 ed. 26.00x (ISBN 0-8046-1197-1, Pub. by Kennikat). Assoc Faculty Pr.
--A Study in Creative History: The Interaction of the Eastern & Western Peoples to 500 B. C. 1977. lib. bdg. 59.95 (ISBN 0-8490-2708-X). Gordon Pr.
Burton, Orville V. In My Father's House Are Many Mansions. LC 84-25830. (Fred W. Morrison Series in Southern Studies). (Illus.). 500p. 1985. 29.95 (ISBN 0-317-19050-4). U of NC Pr.
Burton, Orville V. & McMath, Robert C., Jr., eds. Class, Conflict, & Consensus: Antebellum Southern Community Studies. LC 81-1071. (Contributions in American History Ser.: No. 96). (Illus.). xxvi, 308p. 1982. lib. bdg. 29.95 (ISBN 0-313-21310-0, BSC/). Greenwood.
Burton, Orville V. & McMath, Robert C, Jr., eds. Toward a New South? Studies in Post-Civil War Southern Communities. LC 81-1666. (Contributions in American History Ser.: No. 97). (Illus.). xx, 319p. 1982. lib. bdg. 29.95 (ISBN 0-313-22996-1, BNC/). Greenwood.
Burton, P. J. Feeding & the Feeding Apparatus in Waders. (Illus.). 1974. text ed. 21.00x (ISBN 0-565-00719-X, Pub. by Brit Mus Nat Hist). Sabbot-Natural Hist Bks.
Burton, Paul. Bibliography of Micros in Libraries. 70p. 1985. text ed. write for info. (ISBN 0-566-03540-5). Gower Pub Co.
--Caught in the Void. 30p. (Orig.). 1982. pap. text ed. 2.25 (ISBN 0-941470-15-6). Hilltop Pr CA.
--The Finnegans Wake Series. 30p. (Orig.). 1982. pap. text ed. 2.25 (ISBN 0-941470-13-X). Hilltop Pr CA.
--Great Are the Myths. 30p. (Orig.). 1982. pap. text ed. 2.25 (ISBN 0-941470-11-3). Hilltop Pr CA.
--The Imitations. 30p. (Orig.). 1982. pap. text ed. 2.25 (ISBN 0-941470-03-2). Hilltop Pr CA.
--Looking for a Chance. 30p. (Orig.). 1982. pap. text ed. 2.25 (ISBN 0-941470-07-5). Hilltop Pr CA.
--Looking for Cinderella. 30p. (Orig.). 1982. pap. text ed. 2.25 (ISBN 0-941470-01-6). Hilltop Pr CA.
--Starry, Starry Night. 30p. (Orig.). 1982. pap. text ed. 2.25 (ISBN 0-941470-09-1). Hilltop Pr CA.
--Stories Your Grandpa Told. 30p. (Orig.). 1982. pap. text ed. 2.25 (ISBN 0-941470-05-9). Hilltop Pr CA.
Burton, Paul F. Microcomputer Applications in Academic Libraries. (LIR Reports Ser.). 133p. (Orig.). 1983. pap. 17.50 (ISBN 0-7123-3021-6, Pub. by British Lib). Longwood Pub Group.
Burton, Peter. Parallel Lives. (Illus.). 128p. (Orig.). 1985. pap. 6.50 (ISBN 0-907040-65-9, Pub. by GMP England). Alyson Pubns.
Burton, Peter, jt. auth. see Crowhurst, Les.
Burton, Peter, ed. see Maugham, Robin.
Burton, Peter A., tr. see Morley, James W.
Burton, Philip. Birds of North America. LC 79-730. (Spotter's Guide Ser.). (Illus.). 1979. 3.95 (ISBN 0-8317-0875-1); pap. 1.95 (ISBN 0-8317-0876-X). Smith Pubs.
--Vanishing Eagles. (Illus.). 140p. 1983. 25.00 (ISBN 0-396-08168-1). Dodd.
Burton, Philip E. A Dictionary of Minicomputing & Microcomputing. 368p. 1985. pap. 20.00 (ISBN 0-8240-7286-3). Garland Pub.
--Dictionary of Minicomputing & Microcomputing. 1984. lib. bdg. 42.50 (ISBN 0-8240-7263-4). Garland Pub.
--A Dictionary of Word Processing. 256p. 1984. pap. 15.95 (ISBN 0-8240-7289-8). Garland Pub.
--A Dictionary of Word Processing & Printers. LC 84-10348. 264p. 1985. 22.95 (ISBN 0-8240-7289-8); pap. 15.95 (ISBN 0-8240-7291-X). Garland Pub.
Burton, Philip W. Advertising Copywriting. 5th ed. LC 82-9319. (Advertising & Journalism Ser.). 384p. 1983. text ed. 32.95 (ISBN 0-471-84152-8, Pub. by Grid). Wiley.
--Which Ad Pulled Best? 4th ed. LC 80-70202. 136p. 1981. pap. text ed. 9.95x (ISBN 0-87251-060-3). Crain Bks.
Burton, Philip W. & Ryan, William. Advertising Fundamentals. 3rd. ed. LC 79-12110. (Advertising & Journal Ser.). 1980. text ed. 34.95 (ISBN 0-471-84153-6, Pub. by Grid). Wiley.
Burton, Philip W. & Sandhusen, Richard. Cases in Advertising. LC 79-21532. (Advertising & Journalism Ser.). 360p. 1981. pap. 18.95 (ISBN 0-471-84154-4, Pub. by Grid). Wiley.
Burton, Phillip E. The Dictionary of Robotics. 1984. write for info. Garland Pub.
Burton, R. Charles Dickens: How to Know Him. 59.95 (ISBN 0-87968-838-6). Gordon Pr.
Burton, R. F., ed. see Staden, Hans.
Burton, R. M. & Obel, B. Designing Efficient Organizations: Modelling & Experimentation. (Advanced Series in Management: Vol. 7). 1984. 42.50 (ISBN 0-444-86859-3, I 086-84, North-Holland). Elsevier.
Burton, R. W. B. The Chorus in Soplocles Tragedies. 1980. 52.00x (ISBN 0-19-814374-5). Oxford U Pr.
Burton, Raffel, ed. Possum & Ole Ez in the Public Eye: Contemporaries & Peers on T. S. Eliot & Ezra Pound. 152p. 1985. lib. bdg. 17.50 (ISBN 0-208-02057-8, Archon Bks). Shoe String.
Burton, Ralph A., ed. Bearing & Seal Design in Nuclear Power Machinery: Proceedings of the Symposium on Lubrication in Nuclear Applications, Miami Beach, Florida, June 5-7, 1967. LC 67-27785. pap. 134.80 (ISBN 0-317-10009-2, 2016809). Bks Demand UMI.
Burton, Rebecca. By Love Divided. 1978. pap. 1.95 (ISBN 0-8439-0558-1, Leisure Bks). Dorchester Pub Co.
--The Loving Season. 1979. pap. 2.25 (ISBN 0-505-51413-3, Pub. by Tower Bk). Dorchester Pub Co.
--The Loving Season. 352p. 1985. pap. 3.50 (ISBN 0-8439-2249-4, Leisure Bks). Dorchester Pub Co.
Burton, Richard. Bernard Shaw: The Man & the Mask. LC 73-683. 1974. Repr. of 1916 ed. lib. bdg. 25.00 (ISBN 0-8414-1615-X). Folcroft.
--Charles Dickens. 1979. Repr. of 1919 ed. lib. bdg. 30.00 (ISBN 0-8482-7366-4). Norwood Edns.
--Charles Dickens: How to Know Him. LC 78-3884. 1919. lib. bdg. 20.00 (ISBN 0-8414-1718-0). Folcroft.
--Forces in Fiction & Other Essays. facs. ed. LC 70-76896. (Essay Index Reprint Ser). 1902. 14.50 (ISBN 0-8369-0008-1). Ayer Co Pubs.
--How to See a Play. 1978. Repr. of 1914 ed. lib. bdg. 20.00 (ISBN 0-8492-3559-6). R West.
--John Greenleaf Whittier. LC 72-193737. 1972. Repr. of 1901 ed. lib. bdg. 10.00 (ISBN 0-8414-1608-7). Folcroft.
--Literary Leaders of America. facsimile ed. LC 71-105001. (Essay Index Reprint Ser). 1904. 19.00 (ISBN 0-8369-1455-4). Ayer Co Pubs.
--Literary Leaders of America. 1973. Repr. of 1903 ed. 18.50 (ISBN 0-8274-1515-X). R West.
--Literary Likings. facsimile ed. LC 79-37510. (Essay Index Reprint Ser). Repr. of 1898 ed. 23.50 (ISBN 0-8369-2538-6). Ayer Co Pubs.
--Little Essays in Literature & Life. facsimile ed. LC 74-93322. (Essay Index Reprint Ser). 1914. 21.50 (ISBN 0-8369-1277-2). Ayer Co Pubs.
--Masters of the English Novel. facs. ed. LC 79-90620. (Essay Index Reprint Ser.). 1909. 21.50 (ISBN 0-8369-1252-7). Ayer Co Pubs.
--The New American Drama. 1979. Repr. of 1913 ed. lib. bdg. 30.00 (ISBN 0-8495-0500-3). Arden Lib.
--The New American Drama. 1978. Repr. of 1913 ed. lib. bdg. 20.00 (ISBN 0-8492-3558-8). R West.

Burwell, Robert L., Jr. Manual of Symbols & Terminology for Physicochemical Quantities & Units: Part 2 - Heterogeneous Catalysis. 1977. pap. text ed. 13.25 (ISBN 0-08-021360-X). Pergamon.

Burwell, Robert L., Jr., jt. ed. see Basolo, Fred.

Burwell, William M. White Acre Vs. Black Acre. facs. ed: LC 72-83941. (Black Heritage Library Collection Ser). 1856. 12.50 (ISBN 0-8369-8514-1). Ayer Co Pubs.

Burwick, Frederick, ed. see De Quincey, Thomas.

Burwick, Ray. Anger: Defusing the Bomb. 128p. 1981. pap. 2.95 (ISBN 0-8423-0053-8). Tyndale.

--Self Esteem: You're Better Than You Think. 1983. pap. 4.95 (ISBN 0-8423-5865-X, 75-5865-X). Tyndale.

Bury. Modern Oratory. 1929. Repr. 10.00 (ISBN 0-8274-2753-0). R West.

Bury, Ange H. Blaze De see Blaze De Bury, Ange H.

Bury, Blaz De see De Bury, Blaz.

Bury, Charles. The One-Minute Business Letter. LC 84-61830. 103p. (Orig.). 1984. pap. 14.95 (ISBN 0-9613854-0-5). Modern Comm Assocs.

--Telephone Techniques That Sell. 148p. 1980. 4.95 (ISBN 0-686-98048-4). Telecom Lib.

Bury, George W. Pan-Islam. LC 80-1938. Repr. of 1919 ed. 30.00 (ISBN 0-404-18956-3). AMS Pr.

Bury, J. B. History of the Later Roman Empire from the Death of Theodosius Eight to the Death of Justinian, 2 vols. Set. 30.50 (ISBN 0-8446-1785-7). Peter Smith.

--Supplement to the History of the Later Roman Empire. 254p. 1974. 15.00. Ares.

Bury, J. B. & Meiggs, Russell. A History of Greece. 4th rev. ed. LC 74-75836. (Illus.). 612p. 1975. 27.95 (ISBN 0-312-37940-4). St Martin.

Bury, J. B., jt. auth. see Freeman, E. A.

Bury, J. B., ed. see Freeman, Edward A.

Bury, J. P. France, Eighteen Fourteen to Nineteen Forty. 5th Ed. ed. 356p. 1985. pap. text ed. 13.95 (ISBN 0-416-37930-3, NO. 9331). Methuen Inc.

Bury, J. P. T. Gambetta's Final Years: The Era of Difficulties, 1877-1882. LC 81-19363. 392p. 1982. 38.00x (ISBN 0-582-50302-7). Longman.

Bury, John B. A History of Freedom of Thought. LC 74-30844. 246p. 1975. Repr. of 1952 ed. lib. bdg. 17.00x (ISBN 0-8371-7935-1, BUHF). Greenwood.

--History of the Later Roman Empire: From the Death of Theodosius I to the Death of Justinian, 2 vols. 1957. pap. 7.95 ea.; Vol. 1. pap. (ISBN 0-486-20398-0); Vol. 2. pap. (ISBN 0-486-20399-9). Dover.

--The Idea of Progress: An Inquiry into Its Origin & Growth. LC 82-6261. xl, 357p. 1982. Repr. of 1932 ed. lib. bdg. 39.75x (ISBN 0-313-23374-8, BUIP). Greenwood.

--Imperial Administrative System of the Ninth Century. (British Academy. Supplemental Papers: No. 1). 1963. Repr. of 1911 ed. 23.50 (ISBN 0-8337-0434-6). B Franklin.

--Invasion of Europe by the Barbarians. 1967. pap. 6.95x (ISBN 0-393-00388-4). Norton.

--The Life of St. Patrick: His Place in History. facsimile ed. LC 79-175691. (Select Bibliographies Reprint Ser). Repr. of 1905 ed. 24.50 (ISBN 0-8369-6606-6). Ayer Co Pubs.

--Selected Essays. facs. ed. Temperley, Harold, ed. LC 68-30177. (Essay Index Reprint Ser). 1930. 18.00 (ISBN 0-8369-0267-X). Ayer Co Pubs.

Bury, John B., ed. Byzantine Texts, 5 vols. Repr. of 1904 ed. Set. 195.00 (ISBN 0-404-60000-X). AMS Pr.

Bury, John B., ed. see Gibbon, Edward.

Bury, John B., ed. see Pindarus.

Bury, John P. Gambetta-the National Defence: A Republican Dictatorship in France. LC 77-114490. (Illus.). 1971. Repr. of 1936 ed. lib. bdg. 17.00x (ISBN 0-8371-4818-9, BUGN). Greenwood.

Bury, Karl V. Statistical Models in Applied Science. LC 84-3934. 648p. 1985. Repr. of 1975 ed. lib. bdg. write for info. (ISBN 0-89874-747-3). Krieger.

Bury, R. G., ed. Plato: The Symposium. 257p. 1973. text ed. 32.50x (ISBN 0-85270-039-3, Pub. by Aris & Philips England). Humanities.

Bury, Richard De see De Bury, Richard.

Bury, Robert G., ed. see Plato.

Bury St. Edmund Commisary Court. Wills & Inventories, from the Register of the Commissary of Bury St. Edmund's & the Archdeacon of Sudbury. Tymms, Samuel, ed. (Camden Society, London. Publications. First Ser.: No. 49). Repr. of 1850 ed. 37.00 (ISBN 0-404-50149-4). AMS Pr.

Bury, Shirley. Jewellery Gallery. (Illus.). 256p. (Orig.). 1984. pap. 12.95 (ISBN 0-317-02549-X, Pub. by Victoria & Albert Mus UK). Faber & Faber.

--Rings. (V & A Introductions to the Decorative Arts Ser.). (Illus.). 48p. 1985. 9.95 (ISBN 0-88045-040-1). Stemmer Hse.

--Wendy Ramshaw. (Illus.). 60p. (Orig.). 1984. pap. 9.95 (ISBN 0-905209-27-3, Pub. by Victoria & Albert Mus UK). Faber & Faber.

Bury, Yetta Blaze De see Blaze De Bury, Yetta.

Buryn, Ed, ed. Vagabonding in the U. S. A. (A Guide to Independent Travel) LC 82-83637. (Illus.). 432p. 1983. pap. 10.95 (ISBN 0-916804-02-X). Ed Buryn Pub.

Burzynski, Michael. A Guide to Fundy National Park. 128p. 1985. pap. 7.95 (ISBN 0-88894-458-6, Pub. by Salem Hse Ltd). Merrimack Pub Cir.

Burzynski, Norbert J. see Melnick, Michael.

Busald, Gerald. An Introduction to Computer Terminals. 64p. 1982. pap. text ed. 4.50 (ISBN 0-8403-3058-8, 40305802). Kendall-Hunt.

Busbee, Jim. Riding Tough. 1981. pap. 1.95 (ISBN 0-8439-0912-9, Leisure Bks). Dorchester Pub Co.

Busbee, Shirlee. Deceive Not My Heart. 496p. (Orig.). 1984. pap. 3.95 (ISBN 0-380-86033-3, 86033). Avon.

--Gyspy Lady. 1977. pap. 3.95 (ISBN 0-380-01824-1, 87601-9). Avon.

--Lady Vixen. 544p. 1980. pap. 3.95 (ISBN 0-380-75382-0, 87593-4). Avon.

--The Tiger Lily. 464p. 1985. pap. 3.95 (ISBN 0-380-89499-8). Avon.

--While Passion Sleeps. 496p. 1983. pap. 3.95 (ISBN 0-380-82297-0, 60132-X). Avon.

Busbey, L. White, ed. see Cannon, Joe.

Busby, D. E. Space Clinical Medicine: A Prospective Look at Medical Problems from Hazards of Space Operations. 276p. 1968. lib. bdg. 34.00 (ISBN 90-277-0110-5, Pub. by Reidel Holland). Kluwer Academic.

Busby, D. E., ed. see International Congress of Aviation and Space Medicine, 18th, Amsterdam, 1969.

Busby, Ellen, jt. auth. see Busby, Floyd.

Busby, Everett, et al. Readings for Social Work Practice, Vol. 2. LC 72-8103. 1973. 26.50x (ISBN 0-8422-5152-9); pap. text ed. 14.95x (ISBN 0-8422-0332-X). Irvington.

--Readings for Social Work Practice, Vol. 1. LC 72-8103. 174p. 1972. pap. text ed. 14.95x (ISBN 0-686-76955-4). Irvington.

Busby, F. M. The Alien Debt. 240p. 1984. pap. 2.75 (ISBN 0-553-24176-1). Bantam.

--The Long View: The Final Volume in the Saga of Rissa. LC 76-28472. 1984. pap. 2.75 (ISBN 0-425-07118-9, Dist. by Putnam); 2.75. Berkley Pub.

--Rebel's Quest. 240p. 1985. pap. 2.75 (ISBN 0-553-24727-1). Bantam.

--Rissa & Tregare. 272p. 1984. pap. 2.75 (ISBN 0-425-07116-2). Berkley Pub.

--The Star Rebel. 208p. (Orig.). 1984. pap. 2.75 (ISBN 0-553-25054-X). Bantam.

--Young Rissa. 192p. 1984. pap. 2.75 (ISBN 0-425-07991-0). Berkley Pub.

Busby, Floyd & Busby, Ellen. Avon-Eight. (Illus.). 336p. 1985. pap. 24.95 (ISBN 0-931864-08-9). Western World.

Busby, H. R., jt. auth. see Rieder, W. G.

Busby, John. The Living Birds of Eric Ennion. (Illus.). 128p. 1983. 21.00 (ISBN 0-575-03157-3, Pub. by Gollancz England). David & Charles.

Busby, John R. & Davies, S. J. Distribution of Birds on the Australian Mainland. 355p. 1982. 39.00x (ISBN 0-643-00280-4, Pub. by CSIRO Australia). State Mutual Bk.

--Distribution of Birds on the Australian Mainland. 355p. 1977. pap. 13.75 (ISBN 0-643-00280-4, C049, CSIRO). Unipub.

Busby, Keith. Gauvain in Old French Literature. (Degre Second Ser.: No. 2). 425p. 1980. pap. text ed. 49.00x (ISBN 90-6203-831-X). Humanities.

Busby, Linda J. & Parker, Donald L. The Art & Science of Radio. 1984. text ed. 21.00 (ISBN 0-205-08049-9, 488049). Allyn.

Busby, Mark. Preston Jones. LC 82-74092. (Western Writers Ser.: No. 58). (Illus., Orig.). 1983. pap. 2.00x (ISBN 0-88430-032-3). Boise St Univ.

Busby, Olive M. Studies in the Development of the Fool in the Elizabethan Drama. LC 72-39567. Repr. of 1923 ed. 5.00 (ISBN 0-404-07849-4). AMS Pr.

--Studies in the Development of the Fool in the Elizabethan Drama. LC 75-17871. 1923. lib. bdg. 16.50 (ISBN 0-8414-3223-6). Folcroft.

Busby, Robert C., jt. auth. see Kolman, Bernard.

Busby, Thomas. General History of Music from the Earliest Times, 2 vols. LC 68-21091. (Music Ser). 1968. Repr. of 1819 ed. Set. 75.00 (ISBN 0-306-71063-3). Da Capo.

--A Grammar of Music. LC 76-20711. (Music Reprint Ser). 1976. Repr. of 1818 ed. lib. bdg. 45.00 (ISBN 0-306-70789-6). Da Capo.

--A Musical Manual, or Technical Directory. LC 76-20708. (Music Reprint Ser). 1976. Repr. of 1828 ed. lib. bdg. 27.50 (ISBN 0-306-70788-8). Da Capo.

Busby, Trent. Be Good to Your Body. 1977. 8.95 (ISBN 0-8065-0558-3). Citadel Pr.

Buscaglia, Leo. The Disabled & Their Parents: A Counseling Challenge. LC 75-13822. 408p. Date not set. 14.00 (ISBN 0-03-063292-7). HR&W.

--The Disabled & Their Parents: A Counseling Challenge. 2nd ed. LC 83-50284. 420p. 1983. 14.95 (ISBN 0-943432-13-8, 285). Slack Inc.

--The Disabled & Their Parents: A Counseling Challenge. rev. ed. 1983. 14.95 (ISBN 0-03-064176-4, Pub by Slack Inc). HR&W.

--The Fall of Freddie the Leaf. LC 81-86645. (Illus.). 34p. 1982. 7.95 (ISBN 0-03-062424-X, Pub by Slack Inc). HR&W.

--Living, Loving, & Learning. LC 81-824284. 300p. 1982. 13.50 (ISBN 0-03-061552-6, Pub by Slack Inc). HR&W.

--Living, Loving & Learning. 288p. 1983. pap. 5.95 (ISBN 0-449-90024-X, Columbine). Fawcett.

--Living, Loving & Learning. LC 81-824284. 264p. 1982. 13.50 (ISBN 0-913590-88-6). Slack Inc.

--Love. 208p. 1986. pap. 2.95 (ISBN 0-449-20024-8, Crest). Fawcett.

--Love. LC 72-92810. 160p. 1982. 9.95 (ISBN 0-03-063201-3, Pub by Slack Inc); Boxed, leather-bnd. gift ed. 15.00 (ISBN 0-03-063293-5). HR&W.

--Loving Each Other. 256p. 1984. 13.95 (ISBN 0-03-000083-1, Pub by Slack Inc); special gift ed. o.p. 24.95 (ISBN 0-03-000757-7). HR&W.

--Personhood. 1982. pap. 5.95 (ISBN 0-449-90000-2, Columbine). Fawcett.

--Personhood. LC 78-66423. 160p. 1982. 9.95 (ISBN 0-03-063202-1, Pub by Slack Inc). HR&W.

Buscaglia, Leo F. Because I Am Human. LC 72-92809. 72p. 1972. 5.95 (ISBN 0-913590-06-1). Slack Inc.

--Because I Am Human. LC 72-92809. 76p. 1982. pap. 5.95 (ISBN 0-03-063039-8, Pub by Slack Inc). HR&W.

--The Disabled & Their Parents: A Counseling Challenge. LC 75-13822. 393p. 1975. 14.00 (ISBN 0-913590-30-4). Slack Inc.

--The Fall of Freddie the Leaf. LC 81-86645. 32p. 1982. 7.95 (ISBN 0-913590-89-4). Slack Inc.

--Love. LC 72-92810. 147p. 1972. 9.95 (ISBN 0-913590-07-X). Slack Inc.

--Personhood. LC 78-66423. 160p. 1978. 9.95 (ISBN 0-913590-63-0). Slack Inc.

--The Way of the Bull. LC 73-83777. 176p. 1974. 9.95 (ISBN 0-913590-08-8). Slack Inc.

--The Way of the Bull. 192p. 1984. pap. 3.50 (ISBN 0-449-20820-6, Crest). Fawcett.

--The Way of the Bull. LC 73-83777. 192p. 1982. 9.95 (ISBN 0-03-062882-2, Pub by Slack Inc). HR&W.

Buscaglia, Leo F. & Williams, Eddie H. Human Advocacy & PL 94-142: The Educator's Roles. LC 79-63974. 117p. 1979. 9.50 (ISBN 0-913590-65-7). Slack Inc.

Buscaino, Dale & Daniel, Scott. IBM BASIC Decoded & Other Mysteries. 29.95 (ISBN 0-317-06580-7). Blue Cat.

--Superzap: IBM-PC Version 1.0. Moore, David & Trapp, Charles, eds. (Illus.). 104p. 1984. text ed. 79.95 (ISBN 0-936200-49-9). Blue Cat.

Buscall, R., et al, eds. Science & Technology of Polymer Colloids. (Illus.). 336p. 1985. 57.00 (ISBN 0-85334-312-8, Pub. by Elsevier Applied Sci England). Elsevier.

Buscema, John, jt. auth. see Lee, Stan.

Busch, Akiko & Industrial Design Magazine Editors, eds. Product Design. LC 84-5915. (Illus.). 256p. 1984. 45.00 (ISBN 0-86636-002-6). PBC Intl Inc.

Busch, Alexander. Die Geschichte des Privatdozenten: Eine Soziologische Studie zur Grossbetrieblichen Entwicklung der Deutschen Universitaten. Metzger, Walter P., ed. LC 76-55208. (The Academic Profession Ser.). (Ger.). 1977. Repr. of 1959 ed. lib. bdg. 14.00x (ISBN 0-405-10036-1). Ayer Co Pubs.

Busch & Wilkie Bros. Foundation. Fundamentals of Dimensional Metrology. LC 64-12593. 428p. 1966. 18.80 (ISBN 0-8273-0193-6); instr.'s guide o.p. 3.60 (ISBN 0-8273-0197-9). Delmar.

Busch, Arthur W. Aerobic Biological Treatment of Waste Waters. LC 70-155639. 418p. 1971. 35.00x (ISBN 0-87201-008-2). Gulf Pub.

Busch, Benjamin, jt. auth. see Sommerich, Otto C.

Busch, Bernd W., jt. auth. see Busch, Eleanore B.

Busch, Brian R. The Complete Choral Conductor: Gesture & Method. (Illus.). 256p. (Orig.). 1984. pap. text ed. 19.95 (ISBN 0-02-870340-5). Schirmer Bks.

Busch, Briton C. Britain & the Persian Gulf, Eighteen Ninety-Four to Nineteen Fourteen. LC 67-24120. 1967. 37.50x (ISBN 0-520-00200-8). U of Cal Pr.

--Britain, India, & the Arabs, Nineteen Fourteen to Nineteen Twenty-One. LC 71-132421. 1971. 42.00x (ISBN 0-520-01821-4). U of Cal Pr.

--Hardinge of Penshurst: A Study in the Old Diplomacy. (Conference on British Studies Biography: Vol. 1). (Illus.). 381p. 1980. 22.50 (ISBN 0-208-01830-1). Shoe String.

--Mudros to Lausanne: Britain's Frontier in West Asia, 1918-1923, Vol. 3. LC 76-21641. 1976. 49.50x (ISBN 0-87395-265-0). State U NY Pr.

Busch, Briton C., ed. Master of Desolation: The Reminiscences of Capt. Joseph J. Fuller. (American Maritime Library: Vol. 9). 349p. 1980. 10.00 (ISBN 0-913372-21-8). Mystic Seaport.

Busch, Briton C, ed. see Phelps, William D.

Busch, C., jt. ed. see Edwards, G.

Busch, Dan & Link, D. A. Exploration Methods for Sandstone Reservoirs. 1985. 49.50 (ISBN 0-930972-07-4). Oil & Gas.

Busch, Daniel A. & Link, David A. Exploration Methods for Sandstone Reservoirs. (Illus.). 300p. 1985. cancelled 49.50x (ISBN 0-87201-237-9). Gulf Pub.

Busch, Daryl H. Reactions of Coordinated Ligands & Homogeneous Catalysis: A Symposium Sponsored by the American Chemical Society, Washington, D.C., March 22-24, 1962. LC 63-13314. (American Chemical Society Advances in Chemistry Ser.: No. 37). pap. 65.80 (ISBN 0-317-09028-3, 2051256). Bks Demand UMI.

Busch, Daryle H. Inorganic Syntheses, Vol. 20. LC 39-23015. (Inorganic Synthesis Ser.). 303p. 1980. 45.50x (ISBN 0-471-07715-1, Pub. by Wiley-Interscience). Wiley.

Busch, David. BASIC Games for Your Commodore 64. cancelled 14.95 (ISBN 0-89303-909-8). Brady Comm.

--BASIC Games for Your IBM Peanut. cancelled 9.95 (ISBN 0-89303-908-X). Brady Comm.

--BASIC Games for Your VIC-20 Computer. 9.95 (ISBN 0-89303-910-1). Brady Comm.

--Commodore 64 Subroutine Cookbook. LC 84-2775. (Illus.). 208p. 1984. pap. 12.95 (ISBN 0-89303-383-9). Brady Comm.

--Expanding Your Commodore 64. (Illus.). 192p. 1984. 11.95 (ISBN 0-13-295205-X). P-H.

--IBM PCjr Subroutine Cookbook. cancelled 12.95 (ISBN 0-89303-541-6). Brady Comm.

--Keyboard Challenge with Commodore 64. (Illus.). 208p. 1984. 12.95 (ISBN 0-89303-601-3). Brady Comm.

--Secrets of MacWrite, MacPaint, & MacDraw. (Microcomputer Bookshelf Ser.). 256p. (Orig.). 1985. pap. 13.95 (ISBN 0-317-18227-7). Little.

--Teach Your TRS-80 to Program Itself. 2nd ed. (Illus.). 238p. 1984. 16.95 (ISBN 0-8306-0798-6); pap. 11.50 (ISBN 0-8306-1798-1, 1798). TAB Bks.

--TRS-80 Model 100 Sub-Routine Cookbook. cancelled 12.95 (ISBN 0-317-05651-4). Brady Comm.

--VIC-20 Games, Graphics, & Applications. LC 83-50374. 136p. 1983. pap. text ed. 8.95 (ISBN 0-672-22189-6, 22189); incl. tape 15.95 (ISBN 0-672-26167-7, 26167). Sams.

--VIC-20 Subroutine Cookbook. (Illus.). 208p. pap. cancelled (ISBN 0-89303-931-4). Brady Comm.

Busch, David D. Apple Soft Subroutine Cookbook. (Illus.). 208p. 1985. pap. 12.95 (ISBN 0-89303-322-7). Brady Comm.

--Blast Off with BASIC Games for Your Commodore 64. LC 83-25682. (Illus.). 1984. pap. 12.95 (ISBN 0-89303-333-2). Brady Comm.

--IBM PC & PCjr Subroutine Cookbook. (Illus.). 224p. 1984. pap. 12.95 (ISBN 0-89303-542-4). Brady Comm.

--IBM PC & PCjr Subroutine Cookbook. (Illus.). 315p. 14.95 (ISBN 0-317-13056-0). P-H.

--Keyboard Challenge with Apple II, IIe & III. (Illus.). 192p. pap. cancelled (ISBN 0-89303-600-5). Brady Comm.

--Keyboard Classroom with Commodore 64: Educational Programs for the Whole Family. (Illus.). 310p. 14.95 (ISBN 0-317-13075-7). P-H.

--Keyboard Classroom with the IBM PCjr: Educational Programs for the Whole Family. (Illus.). 192p. pap. cancelled (ISBN 0-89303-602-1). Brady Comm.

--PC-DOS Customized: Create Your Own DOS Commands for the IBM-PC, XT & AT. 176p. 1985. pap. 14.95 (ISBN 0-89303-753-2). Brady Comm.

--Sorry about the Explosion: A Humorous Guide to Computers. (P-H Personal Computing Ser.). (Illus.). 128p. 1985. pap. text ed. 7.95 (ISBN 0-13-822834-5). P-H.

--TRS-80 Portable Computer Subroutine Cookbook. (Illus.). 192p. 1984. pap. 12.95 (ISBN 0-89303-904-7). Brady Comm.

--Twenty-Five Games for Your TRS-80 Model 100. (Illus.). 160p. (Orig.). 1984. 15.95 (ISBN 0-8306-0698-X, 1698); pap. 10.25 (ISBN 0-8306-1698-5). TAB Bks.

Busch, Duffy, ed. Eighty-Six Twin Cities Gold Book, 1985 to 1986. 576p. (Orig.). 1984. pap. 13.50 (ISBN 0-932053-00-9). Prime Pubns.

Busch, Edna M. I Like Puzzles Games from the Word. (Quiz & Puzzle Bks.). 44p. (YA) 1981. pap. 2.45 (ISBN 0-8010-0810-7). Baker Bk.

Busch, Eleanore B. & Busch, Bernd W. The No-Drugs Guide to Better Health. 223p. 1983. 17.95 (ISBN 0-13-623090-3, Parker); pap. 5.95 (ISBN 0-13-623082-2). P-H.

Busch, Ernestine G., ed. The Avesta: Major Portions from the Holy Book of the Magi. LC 85-90618. 440p. (Orig.). 1985. pap. 17.50 (ISBN 0-9614750-0-5). E G Busch.

Busch, Francis X. Prisoners at the Bar: An Account of the Trials of the William Haywood Case, the Sacco-Vanzetti Case, the Loeb-Leopold Case, the Bruno Hauptmann Case. facs. ed. LC 77-126319. (Biography Index Reprint Ser., Vol. 2). 1952. 18.00 (ISBN 0-8369-8025-5). Ayer Co Pubs.

Busch, Frank J. Power for the People: Montana's Cooperative Utilities. 12.50 (ISBN 0-318-00809-2). U of MT Pubns Hist.

Busch, Frederick. Domestic Particulars: A Family Chronicle. LC 76-8904. 1976. 11.95 (ISBN 0-8112-0605-X); pap. 3.95 (ISBN 0-8112-0611-4, NDP413). New Directions.

--Hawkes: A Guide to His Fictions. LC 72-7765. 210p. 1973. 14.95x (ISBN 0-8156-0089-5). Syracuse U Pr.

--Invisible Mending. 1985. pap. 6.95 (ISBN 0-452-25679-8, Plume). NAL.

--Invisible Mending. Date not set. 9.25 (Plume). NAL.

--Invisible Mending: A Novel. LC 83-48523. 288p. 1984. pap. 14.95 (ISBN 0-87923-493-8). Godine.

--Manual Labor. LC 74-6286. 192p. 1974. 8.50 (ISBN 0-8112-0535-5); pap. 3.95 (ISBN 0-8112-0536-3, NDP376). New Directions.

--Rounds. 176p. 1981. pap. 2.95 (ISBN 0-345-29253-7). Ballantine.

--Rounds. 244p. 1980. 9.95 (ISBN 0-374-25258-0). FS&G.

--Take This Man. 264p. 1981. 11.95 (ISBN 0-374-27246-8). FS&G.

--Take This Man. 224p. 1983. pap. 2.95 (ISBN 0-345-30548-5). Ballantine.

--Too Late American Boyhood Blues. LC 83-48895. 288p. 1984. 15.95 (ISBN 0-87923-511-X). Godine.

Busch, Fredrick. The Mutual Friend. LC 83-47671. (Nonpareil Bk.). 224p. 1983. pap. 8.95 (ISBN 0-87923-482-2, Nonpareil Bks). Godine.

Busch, Fritz. Pages from a Musician's Life. Strachey, Marjorie, tr. LC 71-106715. (Illus.). 223p. Repr. of 1953 ed. lib. bdg. 15.00 (ISBN 0-8371-3445-5, BUML). Greenwood.

Busch, G. K. The Political Role of International Trade Unions. LC 82-16818. 320p. 1983. 30.00 (ISBN 0-312-62447-6). St Martin.

Busch, Gunter, ed. see Modersohn-Becker, Paula.

Busch, H., ed. Mikrofiltration und andere Transfusions-Probleme in der Intensivmedizin. (Beitraege zu Infusionstherapie und klinische Ernaehrung: Band 3). (Illus.). 1979. pap. 7.25 (ISBN 3-8055-3057-9). S Karger.

Busch, H. Ted & Landeck, Terry. The Making of a Television Commercial. LC 80-23192. (Illus.). 228p. 1981. 10.95 (ISBN 0-02-518830-5). Macmillan.

Busch, Hans, tr. from Ital. Verdi's Aida: The History of an Opera in Letters & Documents. LC 76-11495. (Illus.). 1978. 40.00x (ISBN 0-8166-0798-2); pap. 15.00x (ISBN 0-8166-0800-8). U of Minn Pr.

Busch, Harold. U-Boats at War. 1982. pap. 2.50 (ISBN 0-345-30755-0). Ballantine.

Busch, Harris. Histones & Other Nuclear Proteins. 1965. 49.00 (ISBN 0-12-147656-1). Acad Pr.

--The Molecular Biology of Cancer. 1974. 80.00 (ISBN 0-12-147660-X). Acad Pr.

Busch, Harris & Rothblum, Lawrence. The Cell Nucleus: DNA, Vol. 12. 248p. 1982. 50.00 (ISBN 0-12-147612-X). Acad Pr.

Busch, Harris, ed. The Cell Nucleus, 7 vols. Incl. Vol. 1, 1974. 85.00 (ISBN 0-12-147601-4); Vol. 2, 1974. 85.00 (ISBN 0-12-147602-2); Vol. 3, 1974. 85.00 (ISBN 0-12-147603-0); Chromatin, Pt. A. Vol. 4, 1978. 70.00 (ISBN 0-12-147604-9); Chromatin, Pt. B. Vol. 5, 1978. 70.00 (ISBN 0-12-147605-7); Chromatin, Pt. C. Vol. 6, 1978. 70.00 (ISBN 0-12-147606-5); Chromatin, Pt. D. Vol. 7, 1979. 80.00 (ISBN 0-12-147607-3). LC 73-18944. Acad Pr.

--The Cell Nucleus: DNA, Vol. 10. 408p. 1982. 70.00 (ISBN 0-12-147610-3). Acad Pr.

--The Cell Nucleus: Nuclear Particles, Vol. 8. 1981. 60.00 (ISBN 0-12-147608-1). Acad Pr.

--The Cell Nucleus, Vol. 9: Nuclear Particles, Pt.B. LC 81-9447. 1981. 65.00 (ISBN 0-12-147609-X). Acad Pr.

--Methods in Cancer Research, Vol. 20. (Serial Publication Ser.). 1982. 60.00 (ISBN 0-12-147680-4). Acad Pr.

Busch, Harris & Rothblum, Lawrence, eds. The Cell Nucleus, Vol. 11. 310p. 1982. 60.00 (ISBN 0-12-147611-1). Acad Pr.

Busch, Harris & Smetana, Karel, eds. Nucleolus. 1970. 97.50 (ISBN 0-12-147652-9). Acad Pr.

Busch, Harris & Yeoman, Lynn, eds. Methods in Cancer Research: Tumor Markers, Vol. 19. LC 66-29495. 464p. 1982. 70.00 (ISBN 0-12-147679-0). Acad Pr.

Busch, Harris, et al, eds. Effects of Drugs on the Cell Nucleus: Bristol-Meyers Cancer Symposia. LC 79-51690. 1979. 60.00 (ISBN 0-12-147654-5). Acad Pr.

--Methods in Cancer Research. Incl. Vol. 1. 1967. 82.50 (ISBN 0-12-147661-8); Vol. 2. 1967. 87.50 (ISBN 0-12-147662-6); Vol. 3. 1967. 87.50 (ISBN 0-12-147663-4); Vol. 4. 1968. 87.00 (ISBN 0-12-147664-2); Vol. 5. 1970. 69.50 (ISBN 0-12-147665-0); Vol. 6. 1971. 69.50 (ISBN 0-12-147666-9); Vol. 7. 1973. 61.50 (ISBN 0-12-147667-7); Vol. 8. 1973. 61.50 (ISBN 0-12-147668-5); Vol. 9. 1973. 61.50 (ISBN 0-12-147669-3); Vol. 10. 1974. 61.50 (ISBN 0-12-147670-7); Vol. 11. 1975. 61.50 (ISBN 0-12-147671-5); Vol. 12. 1976. 61.50 (ISBN 0-12-147672-3); Vol. 13. 1976. 59.50 (ISBN 0-12-147673-1). Acad Pr.

Busch, Johann G. Kleine Schriften Von der Handlung und Anderem Gemeinnutzigem Inhalte. 1973. Repr. of 1772 ed. 48.00 (ISBN 0-384-06690-9). Johnson Repr.

Busch, John C., pref. by see Goldman, Bert A.

Busch, John C., jt. ed. see Goldman, Bert A.

Busch, Julia. A Decade of Sculpture. (Illus.). 1974. 40.00 (ISBN 0-87982-007-1). Art Alliance.

Busch, Kenneth W., jt. auth. see Kenner, Charles T.

Busch, Lawerence & Lacy, William B. Science, Agriculture, & Government: The Politics of Research. LC 82-15923. (WVSS in Agriculture Aquaculture Science & Policy Ser.). (Illus.). 325p. (Orig.). 1982. lib. bdg. 32.00x (ISBN 0-86531-225-7); pap. text ed. 13.50x (ISBN 0-86531-230-3). Westview.

Busch, Lawrence, ed. Science & Agricultural Development. LC 81-65005. 198p. 1981. text ed. 31.50x (ISBN 0-86598-022-5). Allanheld.

Busch, Lawrence & Lacy, William B., eds. Food Security in the United States. 365p. 1984. softcover 33.00x (ISBN 0-86531-810-7). Westview.

Busch, Marie & Pick, Otto. Selected Czech Tales. 1928. 16.00 (ISBN 0-686-18170-0). Havertown Bks.

Busch, Marie, tr. Selected Austrian Short Stories. facsimile ed. LC 70-37260. (Short Story Index Reprint Ser). Repr. of 1928 ed. 18.00 (ISBN 0-8369-4071-7). Ayer Co Pubs.

Busch, Marie & Pick, Otto, trs. Selected Czech Tales. facsimile ed. LC 73-13412. (Short Story Index Reprint Ser.). Repr. of 1925 ed. 15.00 (ISBN 0-8369-3669-8). Ayer Co Pubs.

Busch, Marie, jt. tr. see Benecke, Else C.

Busch, Marie, tr. see Schumann, Eugenie.

Busch, Marie-Charlotte. La Sociologie du Temps Libre: Problemes et Perspectives. (Interaction, l'Homme et Son Environment Social Ser.: No. 2). 410p. (Fr.). 1975. pap. text ed. 29.60x (ISBN 90-2797-595-7). Mouton.

Busch, Moritz. Bismarck, Some Secret Pages of His History, 2 vols. LC 76-112347. (BCL Ser. I). Repr. of 1898 ed. Set. 42.50 (ISBN 0-404-01242-6). AMS Pr.

--Bismarck: Some Secret Pages of His History. LC 70-144925. (Illus.). 1971. Repr. of 1898 ed. 49.00 (ISBN 0-403-00815-8). Scholarly.

--Our Chancellor: Sketches for a Historical Picture, 2 Vols. facsimile ed. Beatty-Kingston, W., tr. LC 76-109615. (Select Bibliographies Reprint Ser). 1884. Set. 49.50 (ISBN 0-8369-5225-1). Ayer Co Pubs.

--Travels Between the Hudson & the Mississippi, 1851-1852. Binger, Norman H., tr. LC 74-147857. 316p. 1971. 28.00x (ISBN 0-8131-1251-6). U Pr of Ky.

Busch, Niven. Continent's Edge. 1981. pap. 3.95 (ISBN 0-671-81998-4). PB.

--Duel in the Sun. 256p. 1985. pap. 2.95 (ISBN 0-345-32408-0). Ballantine.

--No Place for a Hero. LC 79-53193. (Illus.). 128p. pap. 3.95 (ISBN 0-89395-027-0). Cal Living Bks.

--Twenty-One Americans. facsimile ed. LC 72-99686. (Essay Index Reprint Ser.). 1930. 24.50 (ISBN 0-8369-1552-6). Ayer Co Pubs.

Busch, Noel F. Briton Hadden: A Biography of the Co-Founder of Time. LC 75-25253. 236p. 1975. Repr. of 1949 ed. lib. bdg. 24.75x (ISBN 0-8371-8395-2, BUBH). Greenwood.

Busch, Paul & Houston, Michael J. Marketing: Strategic Foundations. 1985. 30.95x (ISBN 0-256-02843-5). Irwin.

Busch, Phillis S. Wildflowers & the Stories Behind Their Names. LC 73-1351. (Illus.). (gr. 3up). 1977. 10.00 (ISBN 0-684-14820-X, ScribJ). Scribner.

Busch, Phyllis. Cactus in the Desert. LC 78-4771. (A Let's-Read-&-Find-Out Science Bk.). (Illus.). (gr. k-3). 1979 (ISBN 0-690-00292-0). PLB 11.89 (ISBN 0-690-01336-1). Crowell Jr Bks.

Busch, Phyllis S. The Seven Sleepers. LC 84-42984. (Illus.). 64p. (gr. 2-6). 1985. 11.95 (ISBN 0-02-715650-8). Macmillan.

--A Walk in the Snow. (Illus.). 40p. (gr. k-3). 1971. 10.53i (ISBN 0-397-31233-4). Lipp Jr Bks.

Busch, Walter. Caesarismuskritik und Epische Historik. (European University Studies: No. 1, Vol. 522). xv, 415p. (Ger.). 1982. 45.25 (ISBN 3-8204-6266-X). P Lang Pubs.

Busch, Wilhelm. Bushel of Merrythoughts. Rogers, W. Harry, tr. 1971. pap. 1.95 (ISBN 0-486-22426-0). Dover.

--Max & Moritz. Klein, H. Arthur, ed. 216p. (Orig., Bilingual Eng & Ger). (gr. 3-6). 1962. pap. 3.95 (ISBN 0-486-20181-3). Dover.

--Max & Moritz. Brooks, C. T., tr. 1977. lib. bdg. 59.95 (ISBN 0-8490-2215-0). Gordon Pr.

--Max & Moritz. Arndt, Walter, tr. LC 85-1241. (Illus.). 1985. 9.95 (ISBN 0-915361-19-1, Dist. by Watts). Adama Pubs Inc.

--Max und Moritz: Eine Bubengeschichte in Sieben Streichen. In Deutschen Dialekten, Mittelhoch Deutsch und Jiddisch. Gorlach, Manfred, ed. (Illus.). 177p. 1982. Repr. lib. bdg. 16.00x (ISBN 3-87118-522-1, Pub. by Helmut Buske Verlag Hamburg). Benjamins North Am.

Busch, Wilhelm, et al. German Satirical Writings. Lotze, Wilhelm & Sander, Volkmar, trs. from Ger. LC 83-26158. (German Library: Vol. 50). 320p. 1984. 19.50x (ISBN 0-8264-0284-4); pap. 9.95 (ISBN 0-8264-0285-2). Continuum.

Busch, William. The Genius of Wilhelm Busch. Arndt, Walter, ed. LC 79-63545. (Illus.). 450p. 1981. 39.95 (ISBN 0-520-03897-5). U of Cal Pr.

Buschardt, A. Zur Fletchtenflora der Inneralpinen Trockentaeler unter Besonderer Beruecksichtinhung des Vinschgaus. (Bibliotheca Lichenologica 10). 1979. lib. bdg. 28.00x (ISBN 3-7682-1226-2). Lubrecht & Cramer.

Busche, Detlef, tr. see Budel, Julius.

Busche, Don & Locke, Flora. College Mathematics for Business. LC 83-6640. 632p. 1984. text ed. 24.95 (ISBN 0-471-08995-8); wbk., 182 pgs. 9.95 (ISBN 0-471-08997-4). Wiley.

Busche, Suzanne & Schueler, Margo. So a Vegetarian Is Coming to Dinner. (Illus.). 160p. 1979. pap. 7.95 (ISBN 0-934444-00-5). Aazunna.

Busching, Beverly A. & Schwartz, Judith I., eds. Integrating the Language Arts in the Elementary School. (Illus.). x, 228p. 1984. pap. 11.00 (ISBN 0-8141-2351-1). NCTE.

Buschini, Henny & Buschini, Luciano. The Ship in the Field. LC 77-174719. (Illus.). 32p. (gr. k-3). 1973. 6.95 (ISBN 0-87592-045-4). Scroll Pr.

Buschini, Luciano, jt. auth. see Buschini, Henny.

Buschke, Franz, ed. Progress in Radiation Therapy, Vol. 3. (Illus.). 248p. (Vols. 1 & 2 o.p.). 1965. 81.00 (ISBN 0-8089-0088-9, 790730). Grune.

Buschkens, W. & Slikkerveer, L. Health Care in East Africa. (Studies in Developing Countries: No. 28). 144p. 1982. pap. text ed. 13.00x (ISBN 90-232-1866-3, 41379, Pub. by Van Gorcum Holland). Humanities.

Buschkuhl, Matthias. Great Britain & the Holy See 1746-1870. (Illus.). 260p. 1982. text ed. 37.50x (ISBN 0-7165-0290-9, Pub. by Irish Academic Pr Ireland). Biblio Dist.

Buschle, K. B., jt. auth. see Narrow, B. W.

Buschlen, Jack P. Heil Hollywood. Kupelnick, Bruce S., ed. LC 76-52095. (Classics of Film Literature Ser.). 1978. lib. bdg. 22.00 (ISBN 0-8240-2869-4). Garland Pub.

Buschman, Janis & Hunley, Debbie. Strangers Don't Look Like the Big Bad Wolf! Meyer, Linda D. & Lyons, Carole, eds. (Childrens Safety Ser.: Bk. V). (Illus.). 30p. (Orig.). (gr. 2-4). 1985. lib. bdg. 8.00 (ISBN 0-932091-04-0); pap. 3.50 (ISBN 0-932091-05-9). Franklin Pr WA.

Buschman, Penelope, et al, eds. The Pediatric Nurse & the Life-Threatened Child. (Current Thanatology Ser.). 100p. 1985. pap. 13.95 (ISBN 0-930194-39-X). Ctr Thanatology.

Buschman, R. G., jt. auth. see Srivastava, H. M.

Buschman-Gemma, Penelope R., jt. auth. see Arnold, Joan H.

Buschmann, C., ed. Loss Prevention & Safety Promotion in the Process Industries. 1975. pap. 58.75 (ISBN 0-444-41230-1). Elsevier.

Buschor, E. Greek Vase Painting. Richards, G. C., tr. LC 77-94548. 1979. Repr. of 1921 ed. lib. bdg. 30.00 (ISBN 0-89341-231-7). Longwood Pub Group.

Buschor, Ernst. Greek Vase Painting. Richards, G. C., tr. 1978. pap. 15.00 (ISBN 0-89005-267-0). Ares.

--Greek Vase Painting. LC 77-73882. (Illus.). 1978. Repr. of 1921 ed. lib. bdg. 30.00 (ISBN 0-87817-217-3). Hacker.

--On the Meaning of Greek Statues. Benson, J. L., tr. from Ger. LC 79-4697. (Illus.). 112p. 1980. lib. bdg. 14.00x (ISBN 0-87023-279-7). U of Mass Pr.

Busch-Rossnagel, Nancy, jt. ed. see Lerner, Richard.

Buschsbaum, Walter H. Analog IC. (Vestpocket Handbook). (Illus.). 1984. pap. 8.95 (ISBN 0-13-032748-4, Busn). P-H.

Buscombe, Charles. Television: Theory & Servicing. 1983. text ed. 37.95 (ISBN 0-8359-7544-4); student's manual avail. (ISBN 0-8359-7545-2). Reston.

Buscombe, Edward, et al. Film: Historical-Theoretical Speculations. Lawton, Ben & Staiger, Janet, eds. (Film Studies Annual, 1977: Pt. 2). vi, 81p. (Orig.). 1977. pap. 7.50 (ISBN 0-913178-53-5). Redgrave Pub Co.

Buscombe, William. MK Spectral Clasifications-Fifth General Catalogue. LC 81-9555. 250p. (Orig.). 1981. pap. text ed. 10.00x (ISBN 0-939160-03-X). NWU Astro.

--MK Spectral Classification: Fourth General Catalogue. 1980. 10.00x (ISBN 0-939160-02-1). NWU Astro.

--MK Spectral Classifications: Sixth General Catalogue. LC 81-9555. 310p. (Orig.). 1984. pap. 20.00x (ISBN 0-939160-04-8). NWU Astro.

--MK Spectral Classifications: Third General Catalogue. LC 81-9601. 1977. pap. text ed. 10.00x (ISBN 0-939160-01-3). NWU Astro.

Buscombe, William, jt. auth. see Kennedy, Pamela M.

Buse, Dieter K. & Doerr, Juergen C. German Nationalism: A Bibliographic Approach. Spira, Thomas, ed. LC 82-49159. (Canadian Review of Studies in Nationalism). 200p. 1984. lib. bdg. 35.00 (ISBN 0-8240-9160-4). Garland Pub.

Buse, Rueben C. & Bromley, Daniel W. Applied Economics: Resource Allocation in Rural America. 624p. 1975. text ed. 24.50x (ISBN 0-8138-0115-X). Iowa St U Pr.

Buselle, A., Jr., ed. see Caffin, Charles H.

Buseman, Herbert. Geometry of Geodesics. (Pure and Applied Mathematics: Vol. 6). 1955. 69.50 (ISBN 0-12-148350-9). Acad Pr.

Buseman, Herbert & Kelly, Paul J. Projective Geometry & Projective Metrics. (Pure & Applied Mathematics Ser.: Vol. 3). 1953. 65.00 (ISBN 0-12-148356-8). Acad Pr.

Buseman, Herbert H. Metric Methods in Finsler Spaces. (Annals of Mathematics Studies: No. 8). 1942. 18.00 (ISBN 0-527-02724-3). Kraus Repr.

Busemann, H. Recent Synthetic Differential Geometry. LC 13-120381. (Ergebnisse der Mathematik und Ihrer Grenzgebiete: Vol. 54). 1970. 26.00 (ISBN 0-387-04810-3). Springer-Verlag.

Busenbark, R., jt. auth. see Bates, Henry.

Busenbark, Robert, jt. auth. see Bates, Henry.

Busenbark, Robert I., jt. auth. see Bates, Henry J.

Busenberg, Stavros & Cooke, Kenneth. Differential Equations & Applications in Ecology, Epidemics & Population Problems. LC 81-14897. 1981. 47.50 (ISBN 0-12-148360-6). Acad Pr.

Busenkell, Richard L. BMW. (Modern Automobile Ser.). (Illus.). 1981. 12.95 (ISBN 0-393-01342-1). Norton.

--Jaguar: Since 1945. (North Automobile Ser.). (Illus.). 1982. 19.95 (ISBN 0-393-01566-1). Norton.

Buser, P. A. & Cobb, W. A., eds. Kyoto Symposia: Electroencephalography & Clinical Neurophysiology, Supp. No. 36. 770p. 1983. 204.25 (ISBN 0-444-80436-6, Biomedical Pr). Elsevier.

Buser, P. A. & Rougeul-Bueer, A., eds. Cerebral Correlates of Conscious Experience: Proceedings of the International Symposium, Senanque Abbey, France, August 1977. (INSERM Symposium Ser.: Vol. 6). 364p. 1978. 71.00 (ISBN 0-7204-0659-5, Biomedical Pr). Elsevier.

Buser, Robert L., jt. auth. see Gholson, Ronald E.

Busev, A. I., et al. Chemistry: Definitions, Notions, Terminology. 295p. 1984. 7.95 (ISBN 0-8285-2817-9, Pub. by Mir Pubns USSR). Imported Pubns.

Busey, James L. Latin American Political Guide. 18th ed. 208p. 1985. 7.50 (ISBN 0-911312-65-X). Schalkenbach.

--Political Aspects of the Panama Canal: The Problem of Location. LC 73-84606. (Arizona University, Institute of Government Research, Comparative Government Studies: No. 5). pap. 20.00 (ISBN 0-317-28561-0, 2055249). Bks Demand UMI.

Busey, Samuel C. Immigration: Its Evils & Consequences. LC 69-18762. (American Immigration Collection Ser., No. 1). 1969. Repr. of 1856 ed. 9.00 (ISBN 0-405-00510-5). Ayer Co Pubs.

Busfield, Joan & Paddon, M. Thinking about Children. LC 76-22986. (Illus.). 1977. 39.50 (ISBN 0-521-21402-5). Cambridge U Pr.

Busfield, Roger M. Playwright's Art: Stage, Radio, Television, Motion Pictures. LC 78-139125. 1971. Repr. of 1958 ed. lib. bdg. 35.00x (ISBN 0-8371-5741-2, BUPA). Greenwood.

Busfield, Roger M., ed. Theatre Arts Publications in the U. S., 1953-57. 188p. 1964. 5.00x (ISBN 0-940528-15-0). Am Theatre Assoc.

Bush, Alan, ed. see Belza, Igor F.

Bush, Alfred L., ed. American Indian Periodicals in the Princeton University Library: Guide to the Collection. 15.00x (ISBN 0-8287-0902-5). Clearwater Pub.

Bush, Andrew J., jt. auth. see Kennedy, John J.

Bush, Archie C. Studies in Roman Social Structure. LC 81-40816. (Illus.). 266p. (Orig.). 1982. lib. bdg. 26.00 (ISBN 0-8191-2337-4); pap. text ed. 13.00 (ISBN 0-8191-2338-2). U Pr of Amer.

Bush, B. M. & Clarac, F., eds. Co-ordination of Motor Behaviour. (Society for Experimental Biology Seminar Ser.: No. 24). 324p. 1985. 37.50 (ISBN 0-521-26425-1). Cambridge U Pr.

Bush, B. M., jt. ed. see Roberts, A.

Bush, Barbara. Heart Trouble: A Woman's Workshop on Christian Character. Kobobel, Janet, ed. (Woman's Workshop Ser.). (Orig.). 1985. pap. 3.95 (ISBN 0-310-29431-2, Pub. by Lamplight). Zondervan.

--Walking in Wisdom: A Woman's Workshop on Ecclesiastes. (Woman's Workshop Ser.). 128p. (Orig.). 1982. pap. 2.95 (ISBN 0-310-43041-0). Zondervan.

--A Woman's Workshop on Motherhood. (Women's Workshop Ser.). 144p. 1981. pap. 3.95 (ISBN 0-310-43031-3, 12013P). Zondervan.

Bush, Barbara, ed. see Bush, Fred.

Bush, Barney. Inherit the Blood. 110p. (Orig.). 1985. pap. 6.95 (ISBN 0-938410-28-8). Thunder's Mouth.

--Petroglyphs. LC 82-82422. (Illus.). 84p. (Orig.). 1982. pap. 6.00 (ISBN 0-912678-54-2). Greenfld Rev Pr.

Bush, Bernard J. Living in His Love: Essays on Prayer & Christian Living. LC 78-11809. 115p. 1978. pap. 3.95 (ISBN 0-89571-005-6). Affirmation.

Bush, Bernard J., ed. Coping: Issues of Emotional Living in an Age of Stress for Clergy & Religious. LC 76-362761. 83p. 1976. pap. 2.95 (ISBN 0-89571-000-5). Affirmation.

Bush, Carol, jt. auth. see Garland, LaRetta.

Bush, Carol T. Nursing Research. 1985. text ed. 16.95 (ISBN 0-317-06605-6) (ISBN 0-8359-5047-6). Reston.

Bush, Catharine S. Communicards, I. 46p. (Orig.). 1981. pap. text ed. 24.95 (ISBN 0-88450-739-4, 3133-B). Communication Skill.

--Communicards II: Synonyms & Concepts Set. 1983. pap. 24.95 incl. four card decks (ISBN 0-88450-843-9, 4615-B). Communication Skill.

--Language Remediation & Expansion: One Hundred Skill-Building Reference Lists. (Illus.). 216p. 1979. pap. text ed. 16.95 (ISBN 0-88450-797-1, 3052-B). Communication Skill.

--Language Remediation & Expansion: School & Home Program. 1980. pap. 16.95 (ISBN 0-88450-711-4, 3063-B). Communication Skill.

--Language Remediation & Expansion Workshops for Parents & Teachers. 1981. 16.95 (ISBN 0-88450-738-6, 3134-B). Communication Skill.

--Teachers' Treasury of Useful Lists & Facts. 248p. (Orig.). 1984. pap. text ed. 16.95 (ISBN 0-88450-877-3, 4612-B). Communication Skill.

Bush, Catherine. Mahatma Gandhi. (World Leaders: Past & Present Ser.). (Illus.). 112p. 1985. lib. bdg. 15.95x (ISBN 0-87754-555-3). Chelsea Hse.

--Queen Elizabeth I. (World Leaders: Past & Present Ser.). (Illus.). 112p. 1985. lib. bdg. 15.95x (ISBN 0-87754-579-0). Chelsea Hse.

Bush, Chan. Taking the Tiller (A Basic Text of Information for Fledgling Sailors, Vol. 1. LC 81-51368. (Illus.). 80p. 1981. perfect bound 5.95 (ISBN 0-937144-02-9). Triangle Pr.

Bush, Chan, jt. auth. see Olney, Ross R.

Bush, Chan, ed. see Horn, Edythe.

Bush, Charles W. How to Hear God Speak. 128p. (Orig.). 1975. pap. text ed. 1.50 (ISBN 0-89228-028-X). Impact Bks MO.

Bush, Chilton R. Editorial Thinking & Writing: A Textbook with Exercises. LC 74-98826. Repr. of 1932 ed. lib. bdg. 27.50 (ISBN 0-8371-3078-6, BUET). Greenwood.

--Editorial Thinking & Writing: A Textbook with Exercises. LC 74-144926. (Illus.). 1971. Repr. of 1932 ed. 22.00x (ISBN 0-403-00888-3). Scholarly.

Bush, Christine. Nurse at Eagle's Watch. (YA) 1979. 8.95 (ISBN 0-685-95876-0, Avalon). Bouregy.

--Season of Fear. (YA) 1983. 8.95 (ISBN 0-317-17557-2, Avalon). Bouregy.

Bush, Clara N. Phonetic Variation & Acoustic Distinctive Features. (Janua Linguarum, Ser. Practica: No. 12). (Orig.). 1964. pap. text ed. 23.20x (ISBN 90-2790-631-9). Mouton.

Bush, Clifford L. & Andrews, Robert C. Dictionary of Reading & Learning Disabilities. LC 79-57293. 179p. 1978. pap. 17.50x (ISBN 0-87424-153-7). Western Psych.

Bush, D., jt. auth. see Moore, C.

Bush, Danny E. Invitation to the Feast. 1985. pap. 3.25 (ISBN 0-8054-5019-X). Broadman.

Bush, Darrin S. Thoughtful Roads. 1979. 7.95 (ISBN 0-87881-084-6). Mojave Bks.

--Through the Eyes of Man. 76p. 1976. 6.95 (ISBN 0-87881-038-2). Mojave Bks.

Bush, Don. Jack Snake. (Little Brook Bks.). (Illus.). 48p. 1985. 5.50x (ISBN 0-943978-01-7). Rolling Hills Pr.

--Wart Toad. LC 82-60482. (Illus.). 40p. 1982. 4.50x (ISBN 0-943978-00-9). Rolling Hills Pr.

Bush, Donald J. The Streamlined Decade: Design in the Nineteen Thirties. LC 75-10868. (Illus.). 192p. 1975. pap. 14.95 (ISBN 0-8076-0793-2). Braziller.

Bush, Douglas. Engaged & Disengaged. LC 66-23462. 1966. 15.00x (ISBN 0-674-25500-3). Harvard U Pr.

--English Literature in the Earlier Seventeenth Century: 1600-1660. 2nd ed. (Oxford History of English Literature Ser.). 1962. 42.50x (ISBN 0-19-812202-0); pap. 7.95x (ISBN 0-19-881299-X, OPB299). Oxford U Pr.

--Mythology & the Romantic Tradition in English Poetry. rev. ed. LC 72-85071. 1969. 32.50x (ISBN 0-674-59825-3). Harvard U Pr.

--Pagan Myth & Christian Tradition in English Poetry. LC 68-8639. (Memoirs Ser.: Vol. 72). 1968. 5.00 (ISBN 0-87169-072-1). Am Philos.

--Science & English Poetry: A Historical Sketch, 1590-1950. LC 80-18161. (The Patten Lectures Ser., 1949, Indiana Univ.). viii, 166p. 1980. Repr. of 1950 ed. lib. bdg. 27.50x (ISBN 0-313-22654-7, BUSC). Greenwood.

--Themes & Variations in English Poetry of the Renaissance. LC 74-3413. lib. bdg. 10.00 (ISBN 0-8414-3104-3). Folcroft.

Bush, Douglas, ed. see Baptista Mantuanus.

Bush, Douglas, ed. see Keats, John.

Bush, Douglas, ed. see Milton, John.

Bush, Douglas, ed. see Shakespeare, William.

Bush, Douglas, ed. see Tennyson, Alfred.

Bush, Duncan. Aquarium. 60p. 1983. pap. 8.25 (ISBN 0-907476-15-5). Dufour.

Bush, Elsie. The Big Creek Album: Yesterday & Today. LC 82-173212. (Illus.). 132p. 1982. 9.95 (ISBN 0-9609440-0-1). D & E Bush.

Bush, Fred. C. Fred's Story. Bush, Barbara, ed. LC 83-14074. (Illus.). 128p. 1984. 13.95 (ISBN 0-385-18971-0). Doubleday.

Bush, Fred W., ed. The Centennial Atlas of Athens County, Ohio 1905. LC 75-23393. (Illus.). 168p. (Facsimile Ed., reduced). 1975. 20.00 (ISBN 0-8214-0203-X, 82-82105). Ohio U Pr.

Bush, G. P., jt. auth. see Hattery, L. H.

Bush, Geneva L., jt. ed. see Shearer, Barbara S.

Bush, George. Exodus. 1981. 22.50 (ISBN 0-86524-097-3, 0202). Klock & Klock.

--Genesis, 2 vols. 1981. 29.95 (ISBN 0-86524-094-9, 0103). Klock & Klock.

--Joshua & Judges. 1981. 17.95 (ISBN 0-86524-100-7, 0602). Klock & Klock.

--Leviticus. 1981. 10.50 (ISBN 0-86524-098-1, 0302). Klock & Klock.

--Numbers. 1981. 17.95 (ISBN 0-86524-099-X, 0401). Klock & Klock.

Bush, George & Crane, Philip. Great Issues 79-80: A Forum on Important Questions Facing the American Public, Vol. 11. 1980. 11.95x (ISBN 0-916624-32-3). Troy State Univ.

Bush, George, ed. see Fuller, Buckminster, et al.

Bush, George G. Harvard: The First American University. 1978. Repr. of 1886 ed. lib. bdg. 30.00 (ISBN 0-8492-3703-3). R West.

Bush, George P. Bibliography on Research: Annotated. 1954. 4.00 (ISBN 0-87419-005-3). U Pr of Wash.

Bush, George P., jt. auth. see Hatery, Lowell H.

Bush, George P., ed. Technology & Copyright: Annotated Bibliography & Source Materials. LC 72-87129. 454p. 1972. 28.50 (ISBN 0-912338-03-2); microfiche 9.50 (ISBN 0-912338-04-0); pap. 14.50. Lomond.

Bush, George P. & Dreyfuss, Robert, eds. Technology & Copyright: Sources & Materials. 2nd, rev. ed. 552p. 1979. 22.50 (ISBN 0-912338-17-2); microfiche 15.50 (ISBN 0-912338-18-0). Lomond.

Bush, George P. & Hattery, Lowell H., eds. Teamwork in Research. 1953. 4.00 (ISBN 0-87419-007-X). U Pr of Wash.

Bush, George S. An American Harvest: The Story of Weil Brothers-Cotton. LC 82-9797. 495p. 25.00 (ISBN 0-13-027458-5, Busn). P-H.

Bush, Grace A., jt. auth. see Young, John E.

Bush, Graham. Local Government & Politics in New Zealand. 200p. 1980. text ed. 22.95x (ISBN 0-86861-074-7). Allen Unwin.

Bush, Gregory. Campaign Speeches of American Presidential Candidates, 1948-1984. rev. ed. 400p. 1985. 25.00 (ISBN 0-8044-1137-9). Ungar.

Bush, Irving M., jt. auth. see Lanners, Jan.

Bush, John. This Is a Book about Baboons. (This Is a Book about...Ser.). (Illus.). 1983. 1.95 (ISBN 0-531-02193-9). Watts.

--This Is a Book about Giraffes. (This Is a Book about...Ser.). (Illus.). 1983. 1.95 (ISBN 0-531-02194-7). Watts.

--This Is a Book about Hippos. (This Is a Book about...Ser.). (Illus.). 1983. 1.95 (ISBN 0-531-02195-5). Watts.

Bush, John C. Disaster Response: A Handbook for Church Action. LC 79-15090. 160p. 1979. pap. 6.95 (ISBN 0-8361-1893-6). Herald Pr.

Bush, John C., jt. auth. see Tiemann, William H.

Bush, John W. Venetia Redeemed: Franco-Italian Relations, 1864-1866. LC 67-26918. 1967. 12.00x (ISBN 0-8156-2111-6). Syracuse U Pr.

Bush, Julia. Behind the Lines: East London Labour Nineteen Fourteen to Nineteen Nineteen. (Illus.). 254p. 1985. 30.00 (ISBN 0-85036-304-7, Merlin Pr); pap. 12.95 (ISBN 0-85036-306-3, Merlin Pr). Dufour.

Bush, K. J; see Eisen, G.

Bush, Keith, tr. see Wadekin, Karl-Eugen.

Bush, L. P. & Bucker, R. C., eds. Tall Fescue. (Illus.). 1979. 18.75 (ISBN 0-89118-057-5). Am Soc Agron.

Bush, Lee, ed. see Munch, Richard W.

Bush, Lee O. & Chukayne, Edward C. Euclid Beach Park: A Second Look. LC 79-55562. (Illus.). 229p. 1979. 12.95 (ISBN 0-935408-01-0). Amusement Pk Bks.

--Euclid Beach Park is Closed for the Season. LC 77-80228. (Illus.). 331p. 1977. 19.95 (ISBN 0-913228-22-2). Amusement Pk Bks.

Bush, Lester E., Jr. & Mauss, Armand L., eds. Neither White Nor Black. 249p. (Orig.). 1984. pap. 11.95 (ISBN 0-941214-22-2). Signature Bks.

Bush, M. L. The European Nobility: Vol. 1: Noble Privilege, Vol. 1. 294p. 1983. text ed. 35.00x (ISBN 0-8419-0873-7). Holmes & Meier.

--The Government Policy of Protector Somerset. 180p. 1975. text ed. 20.00x (ISBN 0-7735-0260-2). McGill-Queens U Pr.

Bush, Marcella. The Community of God. (Illus.). (gr. 6-7). 1975. pap. 3.75x (ISBN 0-8192-4057-5); tchr's guide 4.95x (ISBN 0-8192-4056-7). Morehouse.

Bush, Martin. Robert Goodnough. LC 81-68051. 260p. 1982. 85.00 (ISBN 0-89659-260-X). Abbeville Pr.

Bush, Martin H. Ben Shahn: The Passion of Sacco & Vanzetti. LC 68-54903. (Illus.). 1969. 11.95x (ISBN 0-8156-8047-3). Syracuse U Pr.

Bush, Max. The Chest of Dreams. rev. ed. (Children's Theatre Playscript Ser.). 44p. 1981. pap. 2.50 (ISBN 0-88020-104-5). Coach Hse.

--The Troll & the Elephant Prince. 1985. pap. 3.00 (ISBN 0-87602-254-9). Anchorage.

Bush, Michael L. The English Aristocracy: A Comparative Synthesis. LC 84-11261. 224p. 1984. 27.00 (ISBN 0-7190-1081-0, Pub. by Manchester Univ Pr). Longwood Pub Group.

Bush, Nancy. Bittersweet Sixteen. (First Love Ser.). 186p. (YA) 1984. pap. 1.95 (ISBN 0-671-53378-9). PB.

Bush, Patricia J., jt. auth. see Wertheimer, Albert I.

Bush, R. The Genesis of Ezra Pound's Cantos. 1976. 35.00 (ISBN 0-691-06308-7). Princeton U Pr.

Bush, R. H., jt. ed. see Sanders, C. L.

Bush, Raymond A. The Gilt Frame. 1984. 8.95 (ISBN 0-8062-2416-9). Carlton.

Bush, Richard. China Briefing, 1982. LC 81-12973. 150p. 1982. lib. bdg. 16.00x (ISBN 0-86531-516-7); pap. text ed. 7.50x (ISBN 0-86531-517-5). Westview.

--When a Child Needs Help: A Parents' Guide to Child Therapy. 1982. pap. 3.95 (ISBN 0-440-39574-7, LE). Dell.

Bush, Richard C. The Politics of Cotton Textiles in Kuomintang China, 1927-1937: China During the Interregnum 1911-1949, the Economy & Society. Myers, Ramon H., ed. LC 80-8836. 360p. 1982. lib. bdg. 36.00 (ISBN 0-8240-4691-9). Garland Pub.

Bush, Richard C., et al. Religious Word. 1982. text ed. write for info. (ISBN 0-02-317480-3). Macmillan.

Bush, Richard J. Reindeer, Dogs, & Snow-Shoes: A Journal of Siberian Travel & Explorations Made in the Years 1865, 1866 & 1867. LC 72-115514. (Russia Observed Ser., No. 1). (Illus.). 1970. Repr. of 1871 ed. 26.50 (ISBN 0-405-03011-8). Ayer Co Pubs.

Bush, Robert. Grace King: A Southern Destiny. LC 83-9849. (Southern Literary Studies). (Illus.). 336p. 1983. text ed. 30.00x (ISBN 0-8071-1111-2). La State U Pr.

Bush, Robert, ed. see King, Grace.

Bush, Robert D., ed. see De Laussat, Pierre C.

Bush, Robert D., ed. see Pitot, James.

Bush, Robert G., jt. auth. see Capp, Robert A.

Bush, Robert R. & Estes, William K., eds. Studies in Mathematical Learning Theory. 1959. 30.00x (ISBN 0-8047-0563-1). Stanford U Pr.

Bush, Robin. The Book of Wellington. 1981. 40.00x (ISBN 0-686-79154-1, Pub. by Barracuda England). State Mutual Bk.

Bush, Rod, ed. The New Black Vote: Politics & Power in Four American Cities. LC 84-8850. 392p. (Orig.). 1984. pap. 9.95 (ISBN 0-89935-038-0). Synthesis Pubns.

Bush, Ronald. T. S. Eliot: A Study in Character & Style. LC 83-4259. (Illus.). 1984. 25.00 (ISBN 0-19-503376-0). Oxford U Pr.

Bush, Ronald F., jt. auth. see Brobst, Bob.

Bush, Ronald F. & Hunt, Shelby D., eds. Marketing Theory: Philosophy of Science Perspectives Proceedings. LC 82-6747. (Illus.). 315p. (Orig.). 1982. pap. text ed. 24.00 (ISBN 0-87757-159-7). Am Mktg.

Bush, Sargent, Jr. The Writings of Thomas Hooker: Spiritual Adventure in Two Worlds. LC 79-5404. 400p. 1980. 27.50x (ISBN 0-299-08070-6). U of Wis Pr.

Bush, Sheila, jt. auth. see McDouall, Robin.

Bush, Susan. Chinese Literati on Painting: Su Shih, 1037-1101 to Tung Ch'i-Ch'ang, 1555-1636. LC 78-152698. (Harvard-Yenching Institute Studies: No. 27). (Illus.). 1971. pap. 8.50x (ISBN 0-674-12425-1). Harvard U Pr.

Bush, Susan & Shih, Hsio-Yen. Early Chinese Texts on Painting. (Harvard Yenching Institute Ser.). (Illus.). 448p. 1985. pap. text ed. 20.00x (ISBN 0-674-22025-0). Harvard U Pr.

Bush, Susan & Murck, Christian, eds. Theories of the Arts in China. LC 83-42551. (Illus.). 544p. 1983. 45.00x (ISBN 0-691-04020-6). Princeton U Pr.

Bush, T., et al. Approaches to School Management. 1980. text ed. 23.65 (ISBN 0-06-318167-3, IntlDept); pap. text ed. 14.00 (ISBN 0-06-318168-1). Har-Row.

Bush, T. L. A Cowboys Cookbook. (Illus.). 224p. 1985. pap. 8.95 (ISBN 0-87719-011-9). Texas Month Pr.

Bush, Tony & Kogan, Maurice. Directors of Education. 208p. 1982. text ed. 28.50x (ISBN 0-04-379001-1). Allen Unwin.

Bush, Vannevar. Endless Horizons. LC 74-26253. (History, Philosophy & Sociology of Science Ser). 1975. Repr. 19.00x (ISBN 0-405-06581-7). Ayer Co Pubs.

--Science the Endless Frontier: A Report to the President. Cohen, I. Bernard, ed. LC 79-7953. (Three Cneturies of Science in America Ser.). 1980. Repr. of 1945 ed. lib. bdg. 16.00x (ISBN 0-405-12534-8). Ayer Co Pubs.

Bush, Virginia. The Colossal Sculpture of the Cinquecento. LC 75-23785. (Outstanding Dissertations in the Fine Arts - 16th Century). (Illus.). 1976. lib. bdg. 58.00 (ISBN 0-8240-1981-4). Garland Pub.

Bush, W. M. Antarctica & International Law, 3 vols. LC 82-12408. 1983. lib. bdg. 50.00 ea. Vol. 1 (ISBN 0-379-20320-0). Vol. 2 (ISBN 0-379-20321-9). Vol. 3 (ISBN 0-379-20323-5). Set. lib. bdg. 150.00. Oceana.

Bush, Wilma J. & Waugh, Kenneth W. Diagnosing Learning Problems. 3rd ed. 480p. 1982. pap. text ed. 24.95 (ISBN 0-675-09822-X). Additional Supplements May Be Obtained From Publisher. Merrill.

Busha, Charles H., ed. A Library Science Research Reader & Bibliographic Guide. LC 80-22507. 201p. 1981. lib. bdg. 25.00 (ISBN 0-87287-237-8). Libs Unl.

Busha, Charles H. & Harter, Stephen P., eds. Research Methods in Librarianship: Techniques & Interpretation. LC 79-8864. (Library & Information Science Ser.). 432p. 1980. tchrs' ed. 21.50 (ISBN 0-12-147550-6). Acad Pr.

Busha, William, ed. see Vermont Castings.

Bush-Brown, Albert & Grube, Oswald W. Skidmore, Owings & Merrill: Architecture & Urbanism 1973-1983. LC 83-16955. (Illus.). 400p. 1984. 50.00 (ISBN 0-442-21169-4). Van Nos Reinhold.

Bush-Brown, James & Bush-Brown, Louise. America's Garden Book. rev. ed. New York Botanical Garden, ed. (Illus.). 1980. 25.00 (ISBN 0-684-16270-9, ScribT). Scribner.

Bush-Brown, Louise, jt. auth. see Bush-Brown, James.

Bush-Cordry, Donald. Costumes & Textiles of the Aztec Indians of the Cuetzalan Region, Puebla, Mexico. 60p. 1964. Repr. of 1940 ed. 5.00 (ISBN 0-916561-15-1). Southwest Mus.

Bushee, Frederick A. Ethnic Factors in the Population of Boston. LC 76-129393. (American Immigration Collection, Ser. 2). 1970. Repr. of 1903 ed. 13.00 (ISBN 0-405-00548-2). Ayer Co Pubs.

Bushe-Fox, Joscelyn P. Fourth Report on the Excavation of the Roman Fort at Richborough, Kent. (Reports of the Research Committe of the Society of Antiquaries of London Ser.: no. 16). pap. 109.80 (ISBN 0-317-28015-5, 2025574). Bks Demand UMI.

Bushell, Chris & Stonham, Peter, eds. Jane's Urban Transport Systems, 1984. 3rd ed. (Jane's Yearbooks). (Illus.). 400p. 1984. 110.00x (ISBN 0-7106-0792-X). Jane's Pub Inc.

--Jane's Urban Transport Systems 1985. 4th ed. (Jane's Yearbooks). (Illus.). 450p. 1985. 110.00 (ISBN 0-7106-0810-1). Jane's Pub Inc.

Bushell, Don, Jr., ed. see Burgess, Robert L.

Bushell, John J. Bermuda Handbook. 1976. lib. bdg. 59.95 (ISBN 0-8490-1492-1). Gordon Pr.

Bushell, Keith. Papuan Epic. LC 75-35276. Repr. of 1936 ed. 26.50 (ISBN 0-404-14106-4). AMS Pr.

Bushell, M. E. Progress in Industrial Microbiology, Vol. 18: Microbial Polysaccharides. 258p. 1983. 68.00 (ISBN 0-444-42246-3). Elsevier.

Bushell, M. E., ed. Modern Applications of Traditional Biotechnologies. (Progress in Industrial Microbiology Ser.: No. 19). 462p. 1984. 85.25 (ISBN 0-444-42364-8, I-226-84). Elsevier.

--Progress in Industrial Microbiology, Vol. 17: Industrial Microbiology, Spectroscopy & Pharmaceuticals. 232p. 1983. 64.00 (ISBN 0-444-42128-9). Elsevier.

Bushell, M. E & Slater, J. H., eds. Mixed Culture Fermentation. LC 81-68019. (Special Publications of the Society for General Microbiology Ser.: No. 5). 1982. 33.00 (ISBN 0-12-147480-1). Acad Pr.

Bushell, Raymond. Collectors' Netsuke: An in Depth Study of Japanese Miniature Sculptures. LC 70-139687. (Illus.). 200p. 1971. 45.00 (ISBN 0-8348-0056-X). Weatherhill.

--The Inro Handbook. LC 78-32054. (Illus.). 263p. 1979. 65.00 (ISBN 0-8348-0135-3). Weatherhill.

--Introduction to Netsuke. LC 78-147176. (Illus.). 1971. 6.50 (ISBN 0-8048-0905-4). C E Tuttle.

--Netsuke Familiar & Unfamiliar. LC 75-22420. (Illus.). 256p. 1976. 75.00 (ISBN 0-8348-0115-9). Weatherhill.

--Netsuke Masks. LC 84-48693. (Illus.). 240p. 1985. 100.00 (ISBN 0-87011-710-6). Kodansha.

--Wonderful World of Netsuke. LC 64-24948. (Illus.). 1964. 8.95 (ISBN 0-8048-0631-4). C E Tuttle.

Bushell, Raymond, tr. see Ueda, Reikichi.

Bushell, S. W. Oriental Ceramic Art. (Illus.). 432p. 1980. 19.95 (ISBN 0-517-52581-X). Crown.

Bushell, S. W., tr. see Tichane, Robert.

Bushell, Stephen W. Chinese Art, 2 vols. LC 77-94549. 1979. Repr. of 1924 ed. lib. bdg. 65.00 (ISBN 0-89341-232-5). Longwood Pub Group.

--Chinese Art, 2 vols. (Illus.). 1977. Set. 47.50 (ISBN 0-89592-030-1). Rare Repr.

--Description of Chinese Pottery & Porcelain. (Oxford in Asia Studies in Ceramics). 1977. 29.95x (ISBN 0-19-580372-8). Oxford U Pr.

Bushell, T. L. Sage of Salisbury: Thomas Chubb, 1679-1747. LC 67-17633. 1968. 6.00 (ISBN 0-8022-0201-2). Philos Lib.

Busher, Jimmie L. Lost Mines & Treasures of the Southwest. (Illus.). 144p. 1975. pap. 5.00 (ISBN 0-686-16911-5). Treasure Guide.

Bushey, Jerry. The Barge Book. LC 83-7746. (Carolrhoda Photo Bks.). (Illus.). 32p. (gr. 1-4). 1984. lib. bdg. 8.95g (ISBN 0-87614-205-6). Carolrhoda Bks.

--Building a Fire Truck. LC 81-6182. (Illus.). 32p. (gr. k-4). 1981. PLB 8.95g (ISBN 0-87614-170-X, AACR2). Carolrhoda Bks.

--Monster Trucks & Other Giant Machines on Wheels. (Carolrhoda Photo Bks.). (Illus.). 32p. (gr. k-4). 1985. PLB 12.95 (ISBN 0-87614-271-4). Carolrhoda Bks.

Bushey, Steve, ed. Vermont Cross-Country Ski Atlas: A Guide to the State's Ski Touring Centers. LC 83-62994. (Illus.). 112p. (Orig.). 1983. pap. 6.95 (ISBN 0-9606738-5-7). NCI.

Bushkin, Frederic L. & Woodward, Edward R. Postgastrectomy Syndromes. LC 76-8569. (Major Problems in Clinical Surgery Ser.: Vol. 20). 1976. text ed. 14.95 (ISBN 0-7216-2208-9). Saunders.

Bushkovitch, Paul. The Merchants of Moscow, Fifteen Eighty to Sixteen Fifty. LC 79-14491. (Illus.). 1980. 34.50 (ISBN 0-521-22589-2). Cambridge U Pr.

Bushkovitch, Paul, jt. ed. see Banac, Ivo.

Bushma, Lizzie E., jt. auth. see St. Clair, Sandy E.

Bushman, Claudia L. A Good Poor Man's Wife: Being a Chronicle of Harriet Hanson Robinson & Her Family in Nineteenth Century New England. LC 80-54470. 292p. 1981. 25.00x (ISBN 0-87451-193-3). U Pr of New Eng.

Bushman, Claudia L., et al. Mormon Sisters: Women in Early Utah. LC 76-53854. (Illus.). 320p. 1980. pap. 9.95 (ISBN 0-913420-95-6). Olympus Pub Co.

Bushman, Dave. Supreme Court Highlights 1982. 83p. 1983. pap. 2.00 (ISBN 0-314-74611-0). West Pub.

--Supreme Court Highlights 1984. (Supreme Court Highlights Ser.). 95p. (gr. 7 up). 1984. pap. text ed. 4.00 (ISBN 0-314-80551-6). West Pub.

Bushman, Dorothy, jt. auth. see Slate, Allen.

Bushman, Eva M. Biology. 205p. (Orig.). 1980. pap. text ed. 8.95 (ISBN 0-89420-110-7, 238040); cassettes 242.20 (ISBN 0-89420-203-0, 238000). Natl Book.

--First Aid: Student Syllabus. (gr. 9-12). 1979. pap. text ed. 5.50 (ISBN 0-89420-075-5, 380020); cassette recordings 84.95 (ISBN 0-89420-207-3, 380000). Natl Book.

--Introductory Chemistry. 130p. pap. text ed. 7.95 (ISBN 0-89420-217-0, 236025); cassettes 165.95 (ISBN 0-89420-216-2, 236000). Natl Book.

Bushman, J. A., jt. ed. see Payne, J. P.

Bushman, John. The Teaching of Writing: A Practical Program to the Composing Process That Works. (Illus.). 186p. 1984. 19.75x (ISBN 0-398-04997-1). C C Thomas.

Bushman, John H. & Jones, Sandra K. Effective Communication: A Handbook of Discussion Skills. (Illus.). 1977. 3.95 (ISBN 0-914634-51-8, 7726). DOK Pubs.

Bushman, John H. & Jones, Sandy. Developing the Art of Discussion. LC 76-48524. 1977. pap. 2.50 (ISBN 0-8170-0741-5). Judson.

Bushman, Richard L. From Puritan to Yankee: Character & the Social Order in Connecticut, 1690-1765. 352p. 1980. pap. 7.95x (ISBN 0-674-32551-6). Harvard U Pr.

--Joseph Smith & the Beginnings of Mormonism. LC 84-2451. 270p. 1984. 17.95 (ISBN 0-252-01143-0). U of Ill Pr.

--King & People in Provincial Massachusetts. LC 84-10383. 290p. 1985. 25.00x (ISBN 0-8078-1624-8). U of NC Pr.

Bushman, Richard L., ed. The Great Awakening: Documents on the Revival of Religion, 1740-1745. (Institute of Early American History & Culture Ser.). xiv, 174p. 1970. 15.00 (ISBN 0-8078-1181-5). U of NC Pr.

Bushnaq, Inea, tr. see Jiryis, Sabri.

Bushnell, Amy. The King's Coffer: The Proprietors of the Spanish Florida Treasury, 1565-1702. LC 81-7403. (Illus.). x, 198p. 1981. 20.00 (ISBN 0-8130-0690-2). U Presses Fla.

Bushnell, C. J. & Froehlich, A. Gauss Sums & -adic Division Algebras. (Lecture Notes in Mathematics: Vol. 987). 187p. 1983. pap. 13.00 (ISBN 0-387-12290-7). Springer-Verlag.

Bushnell, Catharine. Raggedy Ann & Andy in the Tunnel of Lost Toys. LC 79-25675. (Raggedy Ann & Andy Ser.). (Illus.). 32p. (gr. k-3). 1980. 4.95 (ISBN 0-672-52633-6). Bobbs.

Bushnell, Catherine. Raggedy Ann & Andy & the Pirates of Ingo Outlet. LC 80-69646. 1981. 4.95 (ISBN 0-672-52689-1). Bobbs.

Bushnell, D. Computerized Buckling Analysis of Shells. (Mechanics of Elastic Stability Ser.). 1985. lib. bdg. 85.00 (ISBN 0-318-04125-1, Pub. by Martinus Nijhoff Netherlands). Kluwer Academic.

Bushnell, D. I., Jr. Cahokia & Surrounding Mound Groups. (Harvard University Peabody Museum of Archaeology & Ethnology Papers). pap. 14.00 (ISBN 0-527-01192-4). Kraus Repr.

Bushnell, David. Eduardo Santos & the Good Neighbor, 1938-1942. LC 67-65496. (University of Florida Latin American Monographs: No. 4). 1967. pap. 4.50 (ISBN 0-8130-0038-6). U Presses Fla.

--Reform & Reaction in the Platine Provinces, 1810-1852. LC 83-10490. (University of Florida Social Sciences Monographs: No. 69). viii, 182p. (Orig.). 1983. pap. 14.00 (ISBN 0-8130-0757-7). U Presses Fla.

--Santander Regime in Gran Colombia. LC 78-100248. Repr. of 1954 ed. lib. bdg. 18.00x (ISBN 0-8371-2981-8, BUSR). Greenwood.

Bushnell, David I., Jr. Burials of the Algonquian, Siouan & Caddoan Tribes West of the Mississippi. Repr. of 1927 ed. 29.00x (ISBN 0-403-03545-7). Scholarly.

--Native Villages & Village Sites East of the Mississippi. Repr. of 1919 ed. 29.00x (ISBN 0-403-03660-7). Scholarly.

Bushnell, David L., Jr. Native Cemeteries & Forms of Burial East of the Mississippi. Repr. of 1920 ed. 29.00x (ISBN 0-403-03658-5). Scholarly.

--Villages of the Algonquian, Siouan, & Caddoan Tribes West of the Mississippi. Repr. of 1922 ed. 29.00x (ISBN 0-403-03724-7). Scholarly.

Bushnell, David S. Training for New Technology. (Work in America Institute Studoes in Productivity Ser.: No. 27). 50p. 1983. pap. 35.00 (ISBN 0-08-029508-8). Pergamon.

Bushnell, Donald D. The Role of the Computer in Future Instructional Systems. 1963. 12.00 (ISBN 0-384-06720-4). Johnson Repr.

Bushnell, Eleanore & Driggs, Don. The Nevada Constitution: Origin & Growth. 6th ed. LC 80-23682. (History & Political Science Ser.: No. 8). (Illus.). 232p. 1984. pap. text ed. 5.75x (ISBN 0-87417-060-5). U of Nev Pr.

Bushnell, Horace. Christian Nurture. (Twin Brooks Ser.). 1979. pap. 12.95 (ISBN 0-8010-0765-8). Baker Bk.

--God in Christ. LC 76-39568. Repr. of 1849 ed. 25.00 (ISBN 0-404-01245-0). AMS Pr.

--Nature & the Supernatural As Together Constituting the One System of God. LC 70-39569. Repr. of 1858 ed. 29.50 (ISBN 0-404-01246-9). AMS Pr.

--Views of Christian Nurture & Subjects Related Thereto. LC 74-23297. 264p. 1975. Repr. of 1847 ed. lib. bdg. 40.00x (ISBN 0-8201-1147-3). Schol Facsimiles.

--Women's Suffrage: The Reform Against Nature. LC 75-33280. 1976. Repr. of 1869 ed. 10.50 (ISBN 0-89201-000-2). Zenger Pub.

Bushnell, Howard. Maria Malibran: A Biography of the Singer. LC 79-14880. (Illus.). 1979. 24.95 (ISBN 0-271-00222-0). Pa St U Pr.

Bushnell, John. Mutiny Amid Repression: Russian Soldiers in the Revolution of 1905-1906. Rabinowitch, Alexander & Rosenberg, William G., eds. LC 84-48849. (Indiana-Michigan Series in Russian & East European Studies). (Illus.). 320p. 1985. 24.50 (ISBN 0-253-33960-X). Ind U Pr.

Bushnell, Margaret, jt. auth. see Irwin, D. Michelle.

Bushnell, Nelson S. The Historical Background of English Literature. 1930. Repr. 25.00 (ISBN 0-8274-2496-5). R West.

Bushnell, O. A. Ka'a'awa: A Novel About Hawaii in the 1850s. LC 72-83490. (Pacific Classics Ser.: No. 7). 520p. 1980. pap. 10.95 (ISBN 0-8248-0729-4). UH Pr.

--Molokai. LC 74-31402. (Pacific Classics Ser.: No. 4). 539p. 1975. pap. 8.95 (ISBN 0-8248-0287-X). UH Pr.

--Return of Lono. (Pacific Classics Ser.: No. 1). 290p. 1971. pap. 4.95 (ISBN 0-87022-931-1). UH Pr.

--The Stone of Kannon. LC 79-2563. 447p. 1979. 12.95 (ISBN 0-8248-0663-8). UH Pr.

--The Water of Kane. LC 80-5463. 468p. 1980. 12.95 (ISBN 0-8248-0714-6). UH Pr.

Bushnell, O. A., jt. auth. see Daws, Gavan.

Bushnell, Paul E., jt. ed. see Bray, Robert C.

Bushnell, Paul P. An Analytical Contrast of Oral with Written English. LC 77-176618. (Columbia University. Teachers College. Contributions to Education: No. 451). Repr. of 1930 ed. 22.50 (ISBN 0-404-55451-2). AMS Pr.

Bushnell, Rick B. Northwest Waters: Harbors. (Illus.). 122p. pap. write for info. (ISBN 0-941368-01-7). Pub Enterprises.

Bushnell, William R. & Roelfs, Alan P. The Cereal Rusts: Vol. 1: Origins, Specificity, Structure & Physiology. LC 83-15035. 1984. 70.00 (ISBN 0-12-148401-7). Acad Pr.

Bushoff, Hanns-Peter. Underground Press: Die Untergrundpresse der USA als Bestandteil des "New Journalism" Phaenomens. (European University Studies: No. 3, Vol. 203). 388p. (Ger.). 1983. 40.00 (ISBN 3-8204-7848-5). P Lang Pubs.

Bushong, Ann B. A Guide to the Lectionary. 1978. pap. 5.95 (ISBN 0-8164-2156-0, Pub. by Seabury). Winston Pr.

Bushong, Stewart. Radiologic Science Workbook & Laboratory Manual. 2nd ed. (Illus.). 260p. 1981. pap. text ed. 13.95 (ISBN 0-8016-0927-5). Mosby.

Bushong, Stewart C. Radiologic Science for Technologists: Physics, Biology & Protection. 2nd ed. LC 80-19. (Illus.). 504p. 1980. 29.95 (ISBN 0-8016-0928-3). Mosby.

--Radiologic Science for Technologists: Physics, Biology, & Protection. 3rd ed. (Illus.). 560p. 1984. pap. text ed. 31.95 (ISBN 0-8016-0933-X). Mosby.

Bushrui, S., ed. Essays & Studies, 1982. 123p. 1982. text ed. 18.50x (ISBN 0-391-02622-4, 20098). Humanities.

Bushrui, S. B., ed. A Centenary Tribute to John Millington Synge 1871-1909: Sunshine & the Moon's Delight. 1972-1978. pap. text ed. 6.50x (ISBN 0-391-00854-4). Humanities.

Bushrui, S. B. & Munro, J. M., eds. Images & Memories: A Pictorial Record of the Life & Work of W. B. Yeats. (Illus.). 180p. 1970. text ed. 30.00x (ISBN 0-8156-6063-4, Am U Beirut). Syracuse U Pr.

Bushrui, S. B., ed. see Smith, Byron P.

Bushrui, Suheil. Gibran of Lebanon. 12.00x (ISBN 0-86685-008-2). Intl Bk Ctr.

Bushrui, Suheil B. & Benstock, Bernard, eds. James Joyce: An International Perspective. LC 82-6654. (Irish Literary Studies: 10). 316p. 1982. text ed. 28.50x (ISBN 0-389-20290-8, 07114). B&N Imports.

Bushuk, W. Rye: Production, Chemistry, & Technology. LC 76-29382. (AACC Monograph: No. V). 181p. 1976. text ed. 32.00 (ISBN 0-913250-11-2); text ed. 24.00 members. Am Assn Cereal Chem.

Bushwell, John, ed. see Cervantes, Jorge.

Bushwll, Chris, ed. Railway Directory & Year Book, 1982. 87th ed. LC 72-622709. 635p. 1981. Intl Pubns Serv.

Busi, F., jt. auth. see Baxendale, J.

Busi, Frederick. The Transformations of Godot. LC 79-4002. 160p. 1980. 15.00x (ISBN 0-8131-1392-X). U Pr of Ky.

Busia, K. A. Position of the Chief in the Modern Political System of Ashanti. 236p. 1968. 27.50x (ISBN 0-7146-1640-0, F Cass Co). Biblio Dist.

Business & Professional Women's Foundation, jt. auth. see Rubin, Mary.

Business Communications Staff. Advanced Composites. 1985. pap. 1750.00 (ISBN 0-89336-442-8, P-023R). BCC.

--Advanced Composites: Commercial Applications. 1982. text ed. 1250.00 (ISBN 0-89336-160-7, P-023). BCC.

--Agribusiness: What's Ahead? rev. ed. 1985. 1750.00 (ISBN 0-89336-129-1, GA-017N). BCC.

--Amino Acids & Small Polypeptides Business. 1985. pap. 1750.00 (ISBN 0-89336-448-7, CO56). BCC.

--Analytical Instrumentation: Growth Markets. 1980. 750.00 (ISBN 0-89336-218-2, G-052). BCC.

--Antioxidants: Markets, Materials, Trends. 1985. 1750.00 (ISBN 0-89336-367-7, C-020B). BCC.

--Aquaculture: Food from the Sea & Waterways. rev. ed. 192p. 1982. 975.00 (ISBN 0-89336-130-5, GA-014). BCC.

--Artificial Intelligence. 1984. 1750.00 (ISBN 0-89336-392-8, G-086). BCC.

--Aseptic Food Packaging & Processing, GA-050. 1983. 1500.00 (ISBN 0-89336-322-7). BCC.

--Barrier Materials: Markets, Developments, Technologies. 1983. 1500.00 (ISBN 0-89336-364-2, P-071). BCC.

--The Beverage Industry in the U. S. 1985. 1500.00 (ISBN 0-89336-412-6). BCC.

--Biomass: How? What? Where? 1982. 950.00 (ISBN 0-89336-215-8, E-039). BCC.

--Biosensors. 1985. pap. 1750.00 (ISBN 0-317-28148-8, CO53). BCC.

--Biotechnology in Agriculture. 1985. pap. 1750.00 (ISBN 0-89336-440-1, GA-051R). BCC.

--Bulk Vitamins & Their Major Markets. 1980. 975.00 (ISBN 0-89336-235-2, GA-036R). BCC.

--CAD-CAM. 1985. 1750.00 (ISBN 0-89336-323-5, GB-063R). BCC.

--Cancer Treatment Drugs. 1983. 1500.00 (ISBN 0-89336-372-3, C-047). BCC.

--Catalysis, C-023: New Directions. 1981. 950.00 (ISBN 0-89336-271-9). BCC.

--Cellular Mobile Radio. 1985. pap. 1500.00 (ISBN 0-89336-390-1, G-084). BCC.

--The Changing Battery Markets. 1984. 1500.00 (ISBN 0-89336-188-7, E-001N). BCC.

--Changing Film Business. 1985. pap. 1750.00 (ISBN 0-89336-455-X, PO63R). BCC.

--The Changing Gas Industry: Good & Bad. 1982. 950.00 (ISBN 0-89336-018-X, E-019R). BCC.

--Checks & the Future of the Retail Payments System. 1983. 1000.00 (ISBN 0-89336-378-2, G-066-B). BCC.

--Circuit Boards. 1982. 1250.00 (ISBN 0-89336-319-7, G-067). BCC.

--Commercial Opportunities in Electrochemistry. 1985. 1750.00 (ISBN 0-89336-351-0, C-044). BCC.

--Commercial Opportunities in Space, Including Communications Materials, Research. 1984. 1500.00 (ISBN 0-89336-370-7, GB-075). BCC.

--Computer Printers. 1985. pap. 1500.00 (ISBN 0-89336-428-2, G-091). BCC.

--Convenience Foods & Microwave: Directions. 1980. 725.00 (ISBN 0-89336-227-1, GA-044). BCC.

--Corrosion Inhibitors: Market, Material, Trends. 1984. 1750.00 (ISBN 0-89336-366-9, C-020A). BCC.

--Credit Cards & the Future of the Retail Payment System. 1983. 1000.00 (ISBN 0-89336-379-0, G-066-C). BCC.

--Dairy Industry. 1985. 1500.00 (ISBN 0-89336-410-X, GA-048R). BCC.

--Data Transmission Services Industry. 1984. 1750.00 (ISBN 0-89336-417-7, G-080). BCC.

--Debit Cards & the Future of the Retail Payments System. 1984. 1250.00 (ISBN 0-89336-380-4, G-066-D). BCC.

--Developments in Plasma Technology. 1984. 1500.00 (ISBN 0-89336-395-2, GB-078). BCC.

--Distributed Processing. 1980. 700.00 (ISBN 0-89336-217-4, G-051). BCC.

--Drug Delivery Systems. 1984. 1500.00 (ISBN 0-89336-388-X, C-050). BCC.

--Drug Packaging. 1984. 975.00 (ISBN 0-89336-421-5, GB-082). BCC.

--The Dynamic Telephone Related Hardware Business. 172p. 1984. 1250.00 (ISBN 0-89336-338-3, G-071). BCC.

--Dynamics of Cash in the Payments System. 1983. 1550.00 (ISBN 0-89336-316-2, G-066A). BCC.

--Electrically Conductive Plastics, P-067. 1983. 1250.00 (ISBN 0-89336-325-1). BCC.

--Electronic Commercial Publishing. 1984. 1750.00 (ISBN 0-89336-413-4, G-087). BCC.

--Electronic Display Materials & Design: G-072. 1983. 1250.00 (ISBN 0-89336-339-1). BCC.

--Electronic In-House Publishing. 1985. pap. 1750.00 (ISBN 0-89336-427-4, G-090). BCC.

--Electronic Messaging: Mail Revolution. 1985. pap. 1500.00 (ISBN 0-89336-435-5, G-049R). BCC.

--Electronic Sensors. 1983. 1250.00 (ISBN 0-89336-354-5, G-076). BCC.

--Emerging Local Area Network Business. 1985. pap. 1500.00 (ISBN 0-89336-438-X, G-074R). BCC.

--EMI Shielding: Materials, Markets: Update. 1985. cancelled (ISBN 0-89336-341-3, GB-066R). BCC.

--Energy Efficient Reactive CURE Systems. 1982. 950.00 (ISBN 0-89336-213-1, C-026). BCC.

--The Energy Revolution: 1980 Energy Conference Proceedings Fourth Annual International Conference on Energy. 1981. 75.00 (ISBN 0-89336-289-1). BCC.

--Engineering Thermoplastics. 1983. 1500.00 (ISBN 0-89336-342-1, P-015). BCC.

--Existing & New Implants in the Human Body. 1984. 1750.00 (ISBN 0-89336-362-6, GB-072). BCC.

--Fermentation Products & Processes, C-018R. 1984. 1500.00 (ISBN 0-89336-222-0). BCC.

--Fiber Optics: G-044R. 1982. 975.00 (ISBN 0-89336-116-X). BCC.

--Fillers & Extenders for Plastics. 1984. 1500.00 (ISBN 0-89336-407-X, P-031N). BCC.

--Foods under Glass. 1980. 675.00 (ISBN 0-89336-229-8, GA-046). BCC.

--Fuel & Lubricant Additives. 1983. 1250.00 (ISBN 0-89336-239-5, C-027). BCC.

--Future for Coal As a Fuel & Chemical. 1981. 900.00 (ISBN 0-89336-273-5, E-004). BCC.

--Gas Separation. 1985. pap. 1950.00 (ISBN 0-89336-422-3, C-062). BCC.

--Generic Drugs. 1985. pap. 1750.00 (ISBN 0-89336-434-7, C-058). BCC.

--Healthy Foods: Markets, Trends. 1982. 975.00 (ISBN 0-89336-245-X, GA-047). BCC.

--High Tech Filtration. 1984. 1750.00 (ISBN 0-89336-359-6, C-046). BCC.

--High Tech Organic Separation & Extraction. 1985. pap. 1950.00 (ISBN 0-89336-424-X, C-055). BCC.

--High Tech Textiles for Clothing, Insulation, Specialties. 1984. 1500.00 (ISBN 0-89336-358-8, GB-069). BCC.

--High Temperature Thermoplastics. 1983. 1500.00 (ISBN 0-89336-175-5, P-051R). BCC.

--Holography: New Commercial Opportunities. 1985. 1750.00 (ISBN 0-89336-369-3, GB-074). BCC.

--Industrial Coatings: New Trends, Markets. 1982. 950.00 (ISBN 0-89336-221-2, C-017). BCC.

--Industrial Energy Conservation E-033R. 1982. text ed. 950.00 (ISBN 0-89336-167-4). BCC.

--Inks & Printing Chemicals: New Developments. 1982. 975.00 (ISBN 0-89336-212-3, C-025). BCC.

--Insulation: A Resurging Business: E-035. 1981. 750.00 (ISBN 0-89336-293-X). BCC.

--Interpenetrating Networks. 1984. 1500.00 (ISBN 0-89336-375-8, P-075). BCC.

--Large Molded Parts. 1984. 1750.00 (ISBN 0-89336-400-2, P-078). BCC.

--Laser. 1985. pap. 1750.00 (ISBN 0-89336-453-3, GB050N). BCC.

--Livestock & Bio-Technology. 1984. 1750.00 (ISBN 0-89336-361-8, GA-054). BCC.

--Magnetic Recording Equipment-Tapes, 1977-85. 1983. 1250.00 (ISBN 0-89336-377-4, G-073). BCC.

--Mail Delivery: Viable Alternatives, G-015R. 1983. 1250.00 (ISBN 0-89336-328-6). BCC.

--Markets & Materials for High Temp. Wire & Cable: G-070. 1983. 1250.00 (ISBN 0-89336-337-5). BCC.

--Markets for Bugs & Enzymes, C-008: C-008. 1982. 1250.00 (ISBN 0-89336-101-1). BCC.

--Markets for Computer Technology in the Home: G-063. 1982. 950.00 (ISBN 0-89336-300-6). BCC.

--Markets for Desk Top Computers. 1981. 750.00 (ISBN 0-89336-220-4, G-055). BCC.

--Mass Merchandised Healthy Foods. 1985. 1250.00 (ISBN 0-89336-452-5, GA047R). BCC.

--Material Requirements for Fiber Optics. 1985. 1750.00 (ISBN 0-89336-363-4, GB-073). BCC.

--Medical Diagnostic Equipment: New Developments. 1985. pap. 1500.00 (ISBN 0-89336-419-3, GB-084). BCC.

--Medical Diagnostic Kits & Products. 1984. 1500.00 (ISBN 0-89336-403-7, C-045). BCC.

--Membrane & Separation Technology Directory. 1985. 150.00 (ISBN 0-89336-418-5). BCC.

--Membrane & Separation Technology Patents: Patent Printouts for Membrane Market Opportunities. 1984. 150.00 (ISBN 0-89336-247-6). BCC.

--Metals, Materials for Semiconductors: C-028. 1982. 1250.00 (ISBN 0-89336-297-2). BCC.

--Microcomputers: Aftermarkets, Equipment, Supplies, Services & Software. 1984. 1250.00 (ISBN 0-89336-368-5, G-081). BCC.

--Microwave. 1985. pap. 1500.00 (ISBN 0-89336-449-5, GO20N). BCC.

--Microwave Cooking. 1985. pap. 1500.00 (ISBN 0-89336-429-0, GA-055). BCC.

--The Microwave Industry: Trends, Developments. 1981. 875.00 (ISBN 0-89336-275-1, G-020R). BCC.

--Multi-Layer Films: Markets, Technology: P-063. 1982. 1500.00 (ISBN 0-89336-292-1). BCC.

--New Burgeoning Video Industries. 1983. 1250.00 (G-060). BCC.

--New Consumer Product Electronics: Growth Trends, G-040r. 1980. 875.00 (ISBN 0-89336-224-7). BCC.

--New Developments in New Ceramics. 1985. pap. 1500.00 (ISBN 0-89336-441-X, GB-058R). BCC.

--New Diet, Meal Replacement & Substitute Foods. 1985. 1250.00 (ISBN 0-89336-353-7, GA-052). BCC.

--New Directions in Robots for Manufacturing, G-053. 1982. 975.00 (ISBN 0-89336-219-0). BCC.

--New Highway Vehicle Transporation Dynamics, E-046. 1981. 750.00 (ISBN 0-89336-315-4). BCC.

--New Residential, Commercial Hvac & Monitoring Systems E-034. 1981. text ed. 850.00 (ISBN 0-89336-168-2). BCC.
--New Specialty Metals & Metallurgy. 1985. pap. 1750.00 (ISBN 0-89336-454-1, GB085). BCC.
--New Stryenic Materials & Their Markets. 1984. 1750.00 (ISBN 0-89336-385-5, P-076). BCC.
--New Trends in Food Retailing. 1985. 1250.00 (ISBN 0-89336-228-X, GA-045R). BCC.
--Office of the Future, G-057. 1982. 975.00 (ISBN 0-89336-321-9). BCC.
--Oil & Gas Field Chemicals. 1983. 1500.00 (ISBN 0-89336-373-1, C-048). BCC.
--Online Commercial DataBase Industry. 1985. 1500.00 (ISBN 0-89336-320-0, G-068). BCC.
--Opportunities in Specialty Plastics. 1983. 1950.00 (ISBN 0-89336-365-0, P-073). BCC.
--The Pet Industry: Outlook. 1985. cancelled (ISBN 0-89336-164-X, GA-034N). BCC.
--Pet Industry Outlook. 1985. pap. 1500.00 (ISBN 0-89336-439-8, GA-034N). BCC.
--Petrochemicals: Feedstocks-Alternatives, C-003R. 1981. 975.00 (ISBN 0-89336-204-2). BCC.
--Piezo Electricity, GB-064. 1983. 1250.00 (ISBN 0-89336-324-3). BCC.
--Plastic Alternatives to the Metal Can. 1984. 1950.00 (ISBN 0-89336-386-3, P-077). BCC.
--Plastics Compounding. 1985. 1950.00 (ISBN 0-89336-345-6, P-070). BCC.
--Plastics Conference Proceedings, 1982. 1983. 125.00 (ISBN 0-686-84693-1). BCC.
--Plastics Conference Proceedings, 1983. 1984. 125.00 (ISBN 0-89336-376-6). BCC.
--Plastics Conference Proceedings: 7th Annual. 1981. 105.00 (ISBN 0-89336-311-1). BCC.
--Plastics EMI Shielding. 1985. pap. 1950.00 (ISBN 0-89336-409-6, GB-066R). BCC.
--Plastics Forming. 1984. 1500.00 (ISBN 0-89336-401-0, P-079). BCC.
--Plastics in Business Machines. 1985. pap. 1950.00 (ISBN 0-89336-443-6, P-064R). BCC.
--Plastics International Trade: P-058. 1981. 800.00 (ISBN 0-89336-259-X). BCC.
--Plastics Planning Guide: 1980-1981. 6th ed. 1981. 85.00 (ISBN 0-89336-288-3). BCC.
--Plastics UV Stability. 1984. 1750.00 (ISBN 0-89336-402-9, P-080). BCC.
--Plastics vs. Other Pipes, P-043R. 1984. 1500.00 (ISBN 0-89336-270-0). BCC.
--Plastics vs. the Metal Can. 1984. 1950.00 (ISBN 0-89336-386-3, P-077). BCC.
--Polyester Growth Markets. (Illus.). 1983. 1250.00 (ISBN 0-89336-100-3, P-047R). BCC.
--Powder, Metallurgy: Gb-041. 1981. 725.00 (ISBN 0-89336-113-5). BCC.
--Processed Protein. 1985. pap. 1250.00 (ISBN 0-89336-447-9, GA-043R). BCC.
--Rapidly-Solidified Amorphous Materials. 184p. 1984. pap. 1500.00 (ISBN 0-89336-396-0, GB-079). BCC.
--Restaurant & Institutional Food Industry. 1985. 1250.00 (ISBN 0-89336-426-6, GA-039R). BCC.
--Retail Fast Foods: Business Opportunities. 1980. 675.00 (ISBN 0-89336-236-0, GA-038). BCC.
--Rigid & Flexible Printed Circuit Boards. 1985. pap. 1750.00 (ISBN 0-89336-451-7, GO67R). BCC.
--Roadway Maintenance, E-027. 1983. 1000.00 (ISBN 0-89336-224-7). BCC.
--Scaleup in Biotechnology. 1985. pap. 1750.00 (ISBN 0-89336-421-5, C-061). BCC.
--Security Alarm Systems. 1985. pap. 1250.00 (ISBN 0-89336-437-1, G-046N). BCC.
--Sensory Robots. 1985. pap. 1750.00 (ISBN 0-89336-391-X, GO85). BCC.
--Smart Buildings. 1985. pap. 1500.00 (ISBN 0-317-28177-1, GO89). BCC.
--Specialty Agricultural Chemicals. 1982. 950.00 (ISBN 0-89336-225-5, GA-035R). BCC.
--Specialty Foods: New Developments. 1985. text ed. 1250.00 (ISBN 0-89336-357-X, GA-042R). BCC.
--Specialty Water Treatment Chemicals. 1985. pap. 1750.00 (ISBN 0-89336-433-9, C-002N). BCC.
--Speech Synthesis & Recognition Equipment: G-056. 1982. 975.00 (ISBN 0-89336-299-9). BCC.
--Structural & Adhesives Specialty. 1984. 1500.00 (ISBN 0-89336-108-9, C-009N). BCC.
--Substitutes for Asbestos: What-Who-How Much. 1981. 850.00 (ISBN 0-89336-277-8, GB-061). BCC.
--Sugar, Sweeteners & Substitutes. 1983. 1250.00 (ISBN 0-89336-091-0, C-005R). BCC.
--The Superconductivity Industry. 1980. 750.00 (ISBN 0-89336-144-5, E-032R). BCC.
--Synfuels: Equipment, Technology, Supplies, Money, People. 1982. 975.00 (ISBN 0-89336-281-6, E-042). BCC.
--Tamper Resistant Packaging: What's Ahead? 1984. pap. 1500.00 (ISBN 0-89336-394-4, GB-067). BCC.
--Tamperproof Packaging. 1984. 1500.00 (ISBN 0-89336-355-3, GB-067). BCC.
--Tapping Solar Markets in Developing Countries. 1980. 800.00 (ISBN 0-89336-274-3, E-041). BCC.
--Thermoplastics Elastomers: Rubber Substitutes, P-026N. 1985. 1750.00 (ISBN 0-89336-431-2). BCC.
--Thin-Walled Injection, P-065. 1982. 1950.00 (ISBN 0-89336-313-8). BCC.
--Tissue Culture Business. 1985. pap. 1750.00 (ISBN 0-89336-415-0, C-041). BCC.
--Transparent Plastics: Developments Trends, P-053. 1982. 1500.00 (ISBN 0-89336-201-8). BCC.
--Vaccines & Their Alternatives. 1985. pap. 1750.00 (ISBN 0-89336-425-8, C-057). BCC.
--Venereal Disease. 1984. 1500.00 (ISBN 0-89336-374-X, C-049). BCC.
--Vitamins & Food Supplements. 1980. 975.00 (ISBN 0-89336-090-2, GA-036R). BCC.
--Voice Compression Technology. 1985. pap. 1750.00 (ISBN 0-89336-430-4, G-092). BCC.
--Voice Synthesis. 1985. pap. 1750.00 (ISBN 0-89336-450-9, GO56R). BCC.
--Wind Power: Who's Doing What, Why & Where. 1981. 750.00 (ISBN 0-89336-240-9, E-040). BCC.
Business International. Export Financing: A Handbook of Sources & Techniques. 1985. 16.00 (ISBN 0-317-20193-X). Finan Exec.
Business International Corp. Investment Strategies in Mexico: How to Deal with Mexicanization. 280p. 1980. 114.00x (ISBN 0-86010-200-9, Pub. by Graham & Trotman England). State Mutual Bk.
Business International Corporation. International Business Report, 1980-81: Key Developments & Corporate Strategies. LC 81-2491. 352p. 1981. 49.95 (ISBN 0-03-059187-2). Praeger.
--Investing, Licensing & Trading Conditions Abroad. LC 84-102138. 1983. write for info. Busn Intl Corp.
Business Management Clinic for Sawmill Operators, Sawmill & Plywood Clinic, Portland, Oregon, March 1979. Business Management for Sawmill Operators: Proceedings. LC 79-89293. (A Forest Industries Bk.). (Illus.). 1979. pap. 30.00 (ISBN 0-87930-112-0). Miller Freeman.
Business Management Research, ed. see Osborne, Adam & Dvorak, John.
Business Research Division. Incorporating Form Sample Book for the Fifty States. 92p. pap. 19.95 (ISBN 0-318-00823-8). Affinity Pub Serv.
Business Research Division & U. S. Travel Data Center Staff. Tourism's Top Twenty. 109p. 1984. pap. text ed. 25.00 (ISBN 0-89478-108-1). U Co Busn Res Div.
Business Taxation Symposium. Effects of the Corporation Income Tax: Papers Presented at the Symposium on Business Taxation. Krzyzaniak, Marian, ed. LC 65-24513. 268p. 1966. 13.95x (ISBN 0-8143-1277-2). Wayne St U Pr.
Business Traveler's Inc. The Business Traveler's Survival Guide: Chicago. (Business Traveler's Survival Guides Ser.). 288p. 1981. pap. 9.95 (ISBN 0-531-09850-8). Watts.
Business Week Magazine. The Reindustrialization of America. 1982. 19.95 (ISBN 0-07-009324-5). McGraw.
Business Week Team. The Reindustrialization of America. pap. cancelled (ISBN 0-671-45617-2). WSP.
Busing, William R., ed. Intermolecular Forces & Packing in Crystals. (Transactions of the American Crystallographic Association Ser.: Vol. 6). 155p. 1970. pap. 15.00 (ISBN 0-686-60377-X). Polycrystal Bk Serv.
Businger, J. A., ed. Meteorological Studies at Plateau Station, Antarctica. (Antarctic Research Ser.). (Illus.). 155p. 1977. 43.90 (ISBN 0-87590-125-5, AR2500). Am Geophysical.
Businger, Joost A., ed. see Dalrymple, Paul, et al.
Businger, Joost A., ed. see Kuhn, M., et al.
Businger, Joost A., ed. see Lettau, H., et al.
Busino. Good Boy! Animal Cartoons. 1980. pap. 1.25 (ISBN 0-89319-014-4). Andor Pub.
Busino, Orlando. Oh Gus: Dog Cartoons. 1981. pap. 1.25 (ISBN 0-89319-016-0). Andor Pub.
Busk, Fred & Andrews, Peter. Country Inns of America: Pacific Northwest. LC 81-1617. (Illus.). 96p. 1981. pap. 9.95 (ISBN 0-03-059181-3, Owl Bks). HR&W.
Busk, George. Catalogue of the Marine Polyzoa in the British Museum, 1852-75, 3 Pts in One. (Illus.). 1966. Repr. of 1875 ed. 48.00 (ISBN 0-384-06731-X). Johnson Repr.
Busk, Hans. Hand-Book for Hythe. 192p. 1984. Repr. of 1860 ed. 33.00x (ISBN 0-85546-156-X, Pub. by Richmond Pub England). State Mutual Bk.
--The Rifle; & How to Use It. 230p. 1984. Repr. of 1859 ed. 33.00x (ISBN 0-85546-152-7, Pub. by Richmond Pub England). State Mutual Bk.
Busk, Rachel H. The Folk-Songs of Italy: Specimens with Translations & Notes from Each Province & Prefatory Treatise. Dorsen, Richard M., ed. LC 77-70588. (International Folklore Ser.). 1977. Repr. of 1887 ed. lib. bdg. 23.50x (ISBN 0-405-10085-X). Ayer Co Pubs.
--Sagas from the Far East. LC 78-67693. (The Folktale). Repr. of 1873 ed. 33.00 (ISBN 0-404-16064-6). AMS Pr.
--The Valleys of Tirol: Their Traditions & Customs, & How to Visit Them. LC 77-87725. 488p. Repr. of 1874 ed. 43.50 (ISBN 0-404-16513-3). AMS Pr.
Buske, Andreas, jt. ed. see Muench, Ingo V.
Buske, Norm. Physical Reality. (Illus.). 103p. 1985. pap. 9.50 (ISBN 0-932975-00-3). Search Tech Servs.
Buske, Terry, ed. see Cunningham, Scott.
Buske, Terry, ed. see Green, Jeff.
Buske, Terry, ed. see Lewi, Grant.
Buske, Terry, ed. see Llewellyn Publications Staff.
Buske, Terry, ed. see Llewellyn Staff.
Buskin, David. Outdoor Games. (Illus.). (gr. k-4). 1966. PLB 8.95 (ISBN 0-87460-090-1). Lion Bks.
Buskin, John & Gingold, Alfred. Dr. Booboo's Baby & Child Repair. 96p. (Orig.). 1985. pap. 6.95 (ISBN 0-380-89509-9). Avon.
Buskirk, Bruce, jt. auth. see Buskirk, Richard.
Buskirk, Phyllis, jt. auth. see Ford, Katherine.
Buskirk, Richard. Your Career: How to Plan It, How to Manage It, How to Change It. 1977. pap. 3.50 (ISBN 0-451-62244-8, ME2244, Ment). NAL.
Buskirk, Richard & Buskirk, Bruce. Retailing. (Marketing Ser.). (Illus.). 1979. text ed. 32.95 (ISBN 0-07-009318-0). McGraw.
Buskirk, Richard H. Business & Administrative Policy. LC 75-137106. 528p. 1971. 26.00 (ISBN 0-471-12638-1, Pub. by Wiley). Krieger.
--Handbook of Management Tactics: Aggressive Strategies for Getting Things Done Your Way! LC 77-70138. (Orig.). 1978. pap. 5.95 (ISBN 0-8015-3489-5, Hawthorn). Dutton.
Buskirk, Richard H. & Miles, Beverly. Beating Men at Their Own Game: A Woman's Guide to Successful Selling in Industry. (McGraw-Hill Paperbacks Ser.). 288p. 1980. pap. 5.95 (ISBN 0-07-009355-5). McGraw.
Buskirk, Richard H. & Vaughn, Percy J. Managing New Enterprises. LC 75-37999. (Illus.). 400p. 1976. text ed. 19.95 (ISBN 0-8299-0071-3). West Pub.
Buskirk, Richard H., jt. auth. see Stanton, William J.
Buskirk, Robert Van see Van Buskirk, Robert & Bauer, Fred.
Buskirk, Steve. Denali: The Story Behind the Scenery. LC 78-57540. (Illus.). 1978. lib. bdg. 7.95 (ISBN 0-916122-52-2); pap. 3.75 (ISBN 0-916122-23-9). KC Pubns.
Buskirk, W. C. Van see Van Buskirk, W. C.
Buskirk, William R. Van see Frauchiger, Fritz & Van Buskirk, William R.
Buskirk, William R. Van see Van Buskirk, William R.
Buskohl, Esther E. Honey: Mule Sense & Lilac Scents. LC 85-80216. (Illus.). 80p. (Orig.). (gr. 3-5). 1985. 9.95 (ISBN 0-9614991-0-9); pap. 4.95 (ISBN 0-9614991-1-7). EEBrat.
Busman, Gloria. Union Representative's Guide to NLRB RC & CA Cases. (Policy & Practice Publication). 163p. 1977. 7.75 (ISBN 0-89215-089-0). U Cal LA Indus Rel.
--Union Representative's Guide to NLRB RC & CA Cases. 112p. 1984. 9.00 (ISBN 0-89215-127-7). U Cal LA Indus Rel.
Busman, Gloria, jt. auth. see Blackburn, Jack.
Busnar, G., jt. auth. see Namanworth, P.
Busnar, Gene. Careers in Music. LC 82-2290. (Illus.). 256p. (gr. 7 up). 1982. PLB 10.49 (ISBN 0-671-42410-6). Messner.
--It's Rock 'n' Roll. LC 79-10927. (Illus.). 256p. (gr. 7 up). 1979. PLB 9.97 (ISBN 0-671-32977-4). Messner.
--The Rhythm & Blues Story. (Illus.). 224p. (gr. 7 up). 1985. 9.79 (ISBN 0-671-42145-X). Messner.
--Superstars of Country Music. LC 83-2384000002. 256p. (YA) (gr. 7 up). 1984. lib. bdg. 10.79 (ISBN 0-671-45627-X). Messner.
--The Superstars of Rock: Their Lives & Their Music. LC 80-18912. (Illus.). 224p. (gr. 7 up). 1980. PLB 10.79 (ISBN 0-671-32967-7); pap. 4.95. Messner.
--Superstars of Rock Two. (Illus.). 192p. (gr. 7 up). 1985. 9.79 (ISBN 0-671-45626-1). Messner.
Busnel, R. G. & Classe, A. Whistled Languages. (Communication & Cybernetics Ser.: Vol. 13). (Illus.). 1976. 32.00 (ISBN 0-387-07713-8). Springer-Verlag.
Busnel, R. G. & Fish, J. F., eds. Animal Sonar Systems. LC 79-23074. (NATO ASI Series A, Life Sciences: Vol. 28). 1159p. 1980. 95.00x (ISBN 0-306-40327-7, Plenum Pr). Plenum Pub.
Busoni, Ferruccio. Letters to His Wife. Ley, Rosamond, tr. LC 74-34378. (Music Reprint Ser). (Illus.). 319p. 1975. Repr. of 1938 ed. lib. bdg. 32.50 (ISBN 0-306-70732-2). Da Capo.
Busoni, Ferruccio B. The Essence of Music & Other Papers. Ley, Rossmund, tr. LC 78-66899. (Encore Music Editions Ser.). (Illus.). 1979. Repr. of 1957 ed. 21.00 (ISBN 0-88355-728-2). Hyperion Conn.
Busoni, Rafaello. The Man Who Was Don Quixote. (Illus.). 224p. (gr. 5 up). 1982. 9.95 (ISBN 0-13-548107-4, Pub. by Treehouse); pap. 4.95 (ISBN 0-13-548099-X). P-H.
Busool, A. N. Forty Ahadith: Asqalani. 1981. 4.50 (ISBN 0-686-97860-9). Kazi Pubns.
Busrewil, M. T., jt. ed. see Salem, M. J.
Buss, Alan & Poley, Wayne. Individual Differences: Traits & Factors. 1976. text ed. 26.95 (ISBN 0-89876-074-7). Gardner Pr.
Buss, Allan R. A Dialectical Psychology. LC 79-11813. 211p. 1979. 18.50x (ISBN 0-470-26737-2). Halsted Pr.
--A Dialectical Psychology. 222p. 1979. 18.50x (ISBN 0-8290-0856-X). Irvington.
Buss, Allan R., ed. Psychology in Social Context. 421p. 1979. text ed. 24.50x (ISBN 0-8290-0855-1). Irvington.
Buss, Arnold H. Psychology: Behavior in Perspective. 2nd ed. LC 77-11676. 575p. 1978. text ed. 34.50 (ISBN 0-471-12646-2). study guide, 174 p. 15.00x (ISBN 0-471-03060-0). Wiley.
--Psychopathology. 483p. 1966. text ed. 44.00 (ISBN 0-471-12642-X). Wiley.
--Self-Consciousness & Social Anxiety. LC 79-20890. (Psychology Ser.). (Illus.). 270p. 1980. text ed. 20.95 (ISBN 0-7167-1158-3); pap. text ed. 10.95 (ISBN 0-7167-1159-1). W H Freeman.
Buss, Arnold H. & Plomin, Robert. Temperament. 200p. 1984. text ed. 22.50 (ISBN 0-89859-415-4). L Erlbaum Assocs.
Buss, Arnold H. & Buss, Edith H., eds. Theories of Schizophrenia. (Controversy Ser.). 175p. (Orig.). 1969. 11.95x (ISBN 0-88311-400-3). Lieber-Atherton.
Buss, Claude, ed. National Security Interests in the Pacific Basin. (Publication Ser.: 319). 350p. 1985. text ed. 19.95 (ISBN 0-8179-8191-8). Hoover Inst Pr.
Buss, Claude A. The United States & the Philippines: Background for Policy. LC 77-22589. 1977. pap. 6.25 (ISBN 0-8447-3258-3). Am Enterprise.
--The United States & the Republic of Korea: Background for Policy. (Publication Ser.: No. 254). (Illus.). 198p. 1982. pap. 10.95 (ISBN 0-8179-7542-X). Hoover Inst Pr.
Buss, D., jt. auth. see Melen, R.
Buss, David H., et al. Clinical Pathology Continuing Education Review. LC 79-91972. 1980. pap. 22.00 (ISBN 0-87488-320-2). Med Exam.
Buss, Dennis, jt. ed. see Melen, Roger.
Buss, Dietrich G. Henry Villard: A Study of Transatlantic Investment & Interests, 1870-1895. LC 77-14757. (Dissertations in American History Ser.). 1978. 29.00 (ISBN 0-405-11027-8). Ayer Co Pubs.
Buss, Edith H., jt. ed. see Buss, Arnold H.
Buss, Eugen. Lehrbuch der Wirtschaftssoziologie. xii, 272p. (Ger.). 1985. pap. 16.80x (ISBN 3-11-008897-5). De Gruyter.
Buss, Fran L. Dignity: Lower Income Women Tell of Their Lives & Struggles. (Illus.). 312p. 1985. text ed. 22.00x (ISBN 0-472-10061-0); pap. 10.95 (ISBN 0-472-06357-X). U of Mich Pr.
--La Partera: Story of a Midwife. 1980. 10.95x (ISBN 0-472-09322-3); pap. 7.95 (ISBN 0-472-06322-7). U of Mich Pr.
Buss, K. Studies in the Chinese Drama. 1977. lib. bdg. 59.95 (ISBN 0-8490-2704-7). Gordon Pr.
Buss, Martin J. The Prophetic Words of Hosea: A Morphological Study. (Beiheft 111 Zur Zeitschrift Fuer Die alttestamentliche Wissenschaft). 1969. 22.80- (ISBN 3-11-002579-5). De Gruyter.
Buss, Martin J., ed. Encounter with the Text. 224p. 1979. pap. 6.95 (ISBN 0-317-35690-9, 06-06-08). Scholars Pr GA.
Buss, Martin J., et al, eds. Encounter with the Text: Form & History in the Hebrew Bible. LC 78-31182. (Semeia Studies). 240p. (Orig.). 1979. pap. 5.95 (ISBN 0-8006-1508-5, 1-1508). Fortress.
Buss, Nancy. Rose-Petal & the Evil Weeds. (Rose-Petal Place Ser.). 1984. incl. cassette 7.95 (ISBN 0-910313-65-2). Parker Bro.
Buss, Terry, jt. auth. see Redburn, F. Stevens.
Buss, Terry, et al, eds. Symposium on Economic Revitalization of America. 1983. pap. 8.00 (ISBN 0-918592-62-3). Policy Studies.
Buss, Terry F. & Redburn, F. Stevens. Shutdown at Youngstown: Public Policy for Mass Unemployment. (Urban Public Policy Ser.). 176p. 1982. 39.50x (ISBN 0-87395-646-X); pap. 11.95x (ISBN 0-87395-647-8). State U NY Pr.
Buss, Terry F., jt. ed. see Redburn, F. Stevens.
Buss, Terry F., et al. Mass Unemployment: Plant Closings & Community Mental Health. LC 83-4450. (Sage Studies in Community Mental Health Ser.: No. 6). 224p. 1983. 25.00 (ISBN 0-8039-2012-1); pap. 12.50 (ISBN 0-8039-2013-X). Sage.
Buss, William G. & Goldstein, Stephen R. Standards Relating to Schools & Education. LC 77-1741. (IJA-ABA Juvenile Justice Standards Project Ser.). 182p. 1982. prof ref 22.50 (ISBN 0-88410-241-6); pap. 12.50 (ISBN 0-88410-841-4). Ballinger Pub.
Bussabarger, Robert F. & Robins, Betty D. Everyday Art of India. LC 68-20951. (Illus., Orig.). 1968. pap. 7.95 (ISBN 0-486-21988-7). Dover.
--The Everyday Art of India. (Illus.). 11.25 (ISBN 0-8446-1789-X). Peter Smith.
Bussabarger, Robert F. & Stack, Frank, eds. Selection of Etchings by John Sloan. LC 67-22228. (Illus.). 62p. 1967. pap. 12.00x (ISBN 0-8262-0059-1). U of Mo Pr.
Bussagli, Mario, et al. Oriental Architecture. Bussagli, Mario, ed. LC 74-4024. (History of World Architecture Ser.). (Illus.). 436p. 1975. 50.00 (ISBN 0-8109-1016-0). Abrams.
Bussard, Ellen. School Closing & Declining Enrollment. 1981. pap. 3.50 (ISBN 0-934460-12-4). NCCE.
Bussard, Paula. The Glad I Gotcha Day. (Critter County Bks.). (Illus.). 28p. (gr. k-3). 1985. 1.29 (ISBN 0-87239-963-X, 3383). Standard Pub.
--Guess Who's Afraid. (Critter County Bks.). (Illus.). 28p. (gr. k-3). 1985. 1.29 (ISBN 0-87239-966-4, 3386). Standard Pub.
--Rascal's Close Call. (Critter County Bks.). (Illus.). 28p. (gr. k-3). 1985. 1.29 (ISBN 0-87239-962-1, 3382). Standard Pub.
--Sidney Learns to Share. (Critter County Bks.). (Illus.). 28p. (gr. k-3). 1985. 1.29 (ISBN 0-87239-961-3, 3381). Standard Pub.
--Sidney to the Rescue. (Critter County Bks.). (Illus.). 28p. (gr. k-3). 1985. 1.29 (ISBN 0-87239-964-8, 3384). Standard Pub.

--Words Can Hurt. (Critter County Bks.). (Illus.). 28p. (gr. k-3). 1985. 1.29 (ISBN 0-87239-965-6, 3385). Standard Pub.

Bussby, Canon F. Winchester Cathedral, Ten Seventy-Nine to Nineteen Seventy-Nine. 1982. 50.00x (ISBN 0-686-75452-2, Pub. by Cave Pubns England). State Mutual Bk.

Busse, Eberhard K. Ulrich Von Turheim. 18.00 (ISBN 0-384-06735-2); pap. 13.00 (ISBN 0-685-02229-3). Johnson Repr.

Busse, Ewald & Maddox, George. The Duke Longitudinal Studies of Normal Aging 1955-1980: Overview of History, Design & Findings. 1985. text ed. price not set (ISBN 0-8261-4150-1); prepub. 23.95. Springer Pub.

Busse, Ewald W. & Pfeiffer, Eric. Behavior & Adaptation in Late Life. 2nd ed. 1977. 24.50 (ISBN 0-316-11833-8); pap. 16.95 (ISBN 0-316-11834-6). Little.

Busse, Ewald W. & Blazer, Dan G., eds. Handbook of Geriatric Psychiatry. 560p. 1980. 38.50 (ISBN 0-442-20896-0). Van Nos Reinhold.

Busse, Heribert, tr. History of Persia Under Qajar Rule. LC 74-183229. 494p. 1972. 36.00x (ISBN 0-231-03197-1). Columbia U Pr.

Busse, John. Mrs. Montagu, Queen of the Blues. LC 77-16149. 1977. Repr. of 1928 ed. lib. bdg. 10.00 (ISBN 0-8414-9905-5). Folcroft.

--Mrs. Montagu: Queen of the Blues. 1928. Repr. 15.00 (ISBN 0-8274-2774-3). R West.

Busse, R., jt. ed. see Bauer, R. D.

Busse, Thomas V. The Professor's Book of First Names. LC 83-80773. (Illus.). 120p. (Orig.). 1984. 10.95 (ISBN 0-9610950-0-8); pap. 5.95 (ISBN 0-9610950-1-6). Green Ball Pr.

Busse, Thomas V., jt. auth. see Mansfield, Richard S.

Busse, W. & Zelazny, R., eds. Computing in Accelerator Design & Operation. (Lecture Notes in Physics Ser.: Vol. 215). xii, 574p. 1984. pap. 28.00 (ISBN 0-387-13909-5). Springer-Verlag.

Bussell, Frederick W. Marcus Aurelius & the Later Stoics. 1976. lib. bdg. 59.95 (ISBN 0-8490-2207-X). Gordon Pr.

Bussell, Harold. Lord, I Can Resist Anything but Temptation. (Orig.). 1985. pap. 5.95 (ISBN 0-310-37271-2, Pub. by Pyranee). Zondervan.

Bussell, Harold L. Unholy Devotion: Why Cults Lure Christians. 160p. 1983. pap. 4.95 (ISBN 0-310-37251-8). Zondervan.

Busselle. The Encyclopedia of Photography. (Illus.). 208p. 14.98 (ISBN 0-317-18937-9). Smith Pubs.

Busselle, Michael. Complete Guide to Photographing People. (Illus.). 224p. 1983. pap. 14.95 (ISBN 0-89586-292-1). H P Bks.

--The Photographer's Weekend Book: One Hundred One Creative Projects for the Amateur Photographer. (Illus.). 224p. 1982. 14.50 (ISBN 0-8174-5408-X, Amphoto). Watson-Guptill.

--Pocket Guide to Photography. 128p. 1981. 4.95 (ISBN 0-7064-1520-5, Rutledge Pr). Smith Pubs.

Bussey, Charles, et al. America's Heritage in the Twentieth Century. LC 78-52125. (Illus.). 1978. pap. text ed. 6.95x (ISBN 0-88273-275-7). Forum Pr IL.

Bussey, Ellen M., ed. Federal Civil Service Law & Procedures: A Basic Guide. LC 84-9621. 362p. 1984. 25.00 (ISBN 0-87179-448-9). BNA.

Bussey, Gertrude & Tims, Margaret. Pioneers for Peace. 255p. 7.00 (ISBN 0-686-30387-3, Co-Pub. by Addams Peace). WILPF.

Bussey, Henry J. R. Familial Polyposis Coli: Family Studies, Histopathology,Differential Diagnosis, & Results of Treatment. LC 74-24392. 120p. 1975. 30.00x (ISBN 0-8018-1686-6). Johns Hopkins.

Bussey, Kay, jt. auth. see Perry, David G.

Bussey, Lynn E. The Economic Analysis of Industrial Projects. (International Ser. in Industrial & System Engineering). (Illus.). 1978. ref. 33.95 (ISBN 0-13-223388-6). P-H.

Bussey, William M. French & Italian Influence on the Zarzuela: 1700-1770. Buelow, George, ed. LC 81-19759. (Studies in Musicology: No. 53). 312p. 1982. 44.95 (ISBN 0-8357-1285-0). UMI Res Pr.

Busshoff, L., et al, eds. Curricula & Lifelong Education. (Education on the Move Ser.: No. 1). (Illus.). 360p. 1981. pap. 22.50 (ISBN 92-3-101615-6, U1126, UNESCO). Unipub.

Busshoff, Ludger. Das Zehnte Bildungsjahr unter Bildungspolitischem Aspekt. (European University Studies: No. 11, Vol. 135). 234p. (Ger.). 1982. 27.90 (ISBN 3-8204-7044-1). P Lang Pubs.

Bussi, Luciano & Cognazzo, Maria. Nuovo Dizionario Inglese-Italiano Delle Science Mediche. 864p. (Eng. & Ital.). 1980. 78.00x (ISBN 0-913298-55-7). S F Vanni.

Bussing, et al. Laboratory Exercises for Environmental Geography. 144p. 1984. pap. 9.95 (ISBN 0-8403-3413-3). Kendall-Hunt.

Bussing, Irvin. Public Utility Regulation & the So-Called Sliding Scale: A Study of the Sliding Scale As a Means of Encouraging & Rewarding Efficiency in the Management of Regulated Monopolies. LC 68-58552. (Columbia University Studies in the Social Sciences: No. 415). Repr. of 1936 ed. 16.50 (ISBN 0-404-51415-4). AMS Pr.

Bussink, Tine, et al, eds. Sourcebook on Population Nineteen Seventy to Nineteen Seventy-Six. LC 76-27595. 72p. 1976. pap. text ed. 3.95 (ISBN 0-917136-01-2). Population Ref.

Bussink, Willem & Davies, David. Poverty & the Development of Human Resources: Regional Perspective. (Working Paper: No. 406). iii, 193p. 1980. 5.00 (ISBN 0-686-36133-4, WP-0406). World Bank.

Bussino, Giovanni, tr. see Pirandello, Luigi.

Bussino, Giovanni R., tr. see Pirandello, Luigi.

Bussis, A. M., et al. Inquiry into Meaning: An Investigation of Learning to Read. 392p. 1985. text ed. 39.95 (ISBN 0-89859-504-5). L Erlbaum Assocs.

Bussman, John W. & Davidson, Sharon V. P.S.R.O: The Promise, Perspective, & Potential. 1981. 37.50 (ISBN 0-201-00790-8, Med-Nurse). Addison-Wesley.

Bussman, Klaus. DuMont Guide to Paris & the Ile de France. Stockman, Russell, tr. from Ger. LC 83-15546. (DuMont Guides Ser.). (Illus.). 520p. 1984. pap. 14.95 (ISBN 0-941434-39-7). Stewart Tabori & Chang.

Bussmann, Claus. Who Do You Say? Jesus Christ in Latin American Theology. Barr, Robert, tr. from Ger. LC 84-16476. 192p. (Orig.). 1985. pap. 9.95 (ISBN 0-88344-711-8). Orbis Bks.

Bussmann, W. D., et al, eds. Controlled Release Nitroglycerin in Buccal & Oral Form. (Advances in Pharmacotherapy: Vol. 1). (Illus.). xii, 220p. 1982. 49.50 (ISBN 3-8055-3507-4). S Karger.

Busson, Paul, jt. auth. see Meyrink, Gustav.

Busson, Terry & Coulter, Philip, eds. Symposium on Policy Evaluation for Local Government. (Orig.). 1983. pap. 8.00 (ISBN 0-918592-69-0). Policy Studies.

Bussy, Carvel De. Conferences de Litterature Francaise: XVIIIe Siecle. LC 78-66098. (Fr.). 1979. pap. text ed. 15.00 (ISBN 0-9602260-0-1). C de Bussy.

Bussy, Dorothy, tr. see Gide, Andre.

Bussy, Madame Simon, tr. see Breal, Auguste.

Bussy, R. Kenneth. Two Hundred Years of Publishing: A History of the Oldest Publishing Company in the United States, Lea & Febiger, 1785-1985. LC 84-11308. (Illus.). 126p. 1985. text ed. 12.50 (ISBN 0-8121-0947-3). Lea & Febiger.

Bustad, Leo K. Animals, Aging, & the Aged. (Wesley W. Spink Lectures in Comparative Medicine Ser.). (Illus.). 224p. 1981. 19.50x (ISBN 0-8166-0997-7). U of Minn Pr.

Bustad, Leo K., jt. ed. see Goldman, Marvin.

Bustamante, Segura, ed. Problemas de Conducta en los Ninos. 304p. (Orig.). 1983. pap. 6.95 (ISBN 0-89922-222-6). Edit Caribe.

Bustani, Bustros Al. Qutr Al-Muhit: Concise Arabic-Arabic Dictionary, 2 vols. Repr. of 1869 ed. 45.00x (ISBN 0-86685-097-X). Intl Bk Ctr.

Bustanoby, Andre. Being a Single Parent. Ruark, James, ed. 1985. pap. 7.95 (ISBN 0-310-45351-8, Pub. by Pyranee). Zondervan.

--But I Didn't Want a Divorce. 1978. o. p. 6.95 (ISBN 0-310-22170-6); pap. 5.95 (ISBN 0-310-22171-4). Zondervan.

--Just Friends? 160p. (Orig.). 1985. pap. 6.95 (ISBN 0-310-45431-X, 9254P, Pub. by Pyranee). Zondervan.

--The Readymade Family: How to be a Stepparent & Survive. 160p. (Orig.). 1982. pap. 5.95 (ISBN 0-310-45361-5). Zondervan.

Bustanoby, Andre & Bustanoby, Fay. Just Talk to Me. 192p. (Orig.). 1981. pap. text ed. 5.95 (ISBN 0-310-22181-1). Zondervan.

Bustanoby, Fay, jt. auth. see Bustanoby, Andre.

Busteed & Wergin. Phases of the Moon. 224p. 12.50 (ISBN 0-86690-045-4, 2644-01). Am Fed Astrologers.

Busteed, H. E. Echoes from Old Calcutta. (Illus.). 454p. 1972. Repr. of 1908 ed. 35.00x (ISBN 0-7165-2115-6, Pub. by Irish Academic Pr Ireland). Biblio Dist.

Busteed, Mervyn, ed. Developments in Political Geography. 1983. 46.00 (ISBN 0-12-148420-3). Acad Pr.

Bustin, Dillon. If You Don't Outdie Me: The Legacy of Brown County. LC 82-47784. (Midland Bks.: No. 305). 160p. (Orig.). 1983. 20.00x (ISBN 0-253-13916-3); pap. 12.95 (ISBN 0-253-20305-8). Ind U Pr.

Bustin, Edouard. Lunda Under Belgian Rule: The Politics of Ethnicity. (Illus.). 462p. 1975. text ed. 20.00x (ISBN 0-674-53953-2). Harvard U Pr.

Bustin, Francine L. Paroles au Choix. (Fr.). 1980. text ed. 15.95 (ISBN 0-03-046566-4). HR&W.

Bustin, W. & Dukek, W. Electrostatic Hazards in the Petroleum Industry. (Electrostatics & Electrostatic Application Ser.). 100p. 1983. 26.95 (ISBN 0-471-90163-6, Pub. by Res Stud Pr). Wiley.

Busto, M. Pequeno Diccionario Tecnologico: Farmacia, Quimica, Fisica, Medicina y Ciencias Naturales. 226p. (Span.). 1964. 13.50 (ISBN 0-686-57357-9, S-50248). French & Eur.

Bustos-Fernandez, Luis, ed. Colon: Structure & Function. (Topics in Gastroenterology Ser.). 326p. 1983. 39.50x (ISBN 0-306-41056-7, Plenum Pr). Plenum Pub.

Bustow, Sheldon M., jt. auth. see Deutsch, Henri.

Bustros, Gabriel M., ed. Who's Who in Lebanon 1982-83. LC 65-2366. 782p. 1983. text ed. 85.00 (ISBN 2-90-318801-7, PUB10, PUB). Unipub.

Busvine, J. R. Anthropod Vectors of Diseases. (Studies in Biology: No. 55). 72p. 1975. pap. text ed. 8.95 (ISBN 0-7131-2501-2). E Arnold.

--A Critical Review of the Techniques for Testing Insecticides. 2nd ed. 345p. 1971. cloth 49.00x (ISBN 0-85198-030-9, Pub. by CAB Bks England). State Mutual Bk.

--Recommended Methods for Meausurment of Pest Resistance to Pesticides. (Plant Production & Protection Papers: No. 21). 136p. (Eng. & Fr.). 1980. pap. 9.75 (ISBN 92-5-100883-3, F2079, FAO). Unipub.

Busvine, James R. Insects & Hygiene. 3rd ed. 420p. 1980. 58.00x (ISBN 0-412-15910-4, NO. 2881, Pub. by Chapman & Hall England). Methuen Inc.

Buswell, G., tr. see Marxsen, Willi.

Buswell, Guy T. Teaching of Arithmetic. LC 51-9871. (National Society for the Study of Education Yearbooks Ser: No. 50, Pt. 2). 1951. 6.50x (ISBN 0-226-60015-7); pap. 4.50x (ISBN 0-226-60016-5). U of Chicago Pr.

Buswell, James O., Jr. Systematic Theology of the Christian Religion. 24.95 (ISBN 0-310-22190-0). Zondervan.

Buswell, Robert E., Jr., tr. see Chinul.

Busy, F. M. Demu Trilogy. (gr. 10-12). 1980. pap. 3.50 (ISBN 0-671-43288-5, Timescape). PB.

Busza, Andrzej. Astrologer in the Underground. Boraks, Jagna & Bullock, Micheal, trs. from Polish & Eng. LC 70-108331. 61p. 1970. 6.95 (ISBN 0-8214-0073-8, 82-80786). Ohio U Pr.

Busza, Andrzej, tr. see Bialoszewski, Miron.

Butah, Jon, jt. auth. see Grant, Charles W.

Butchart, Harvey. Grand Canyon Treks. rev. ed. (Illus.). 1976. 2.95 (ISBN 0-910856-38-9). La Siesta.

--Grand Canyon Treks II. 1976. 1.95 (ISBN 0-910856-61-3). La Siesta.

--Grand Canyon Treks III. (Illus.). 1984. pap. 3.95 wrappers (ISBN 0-317-14851-6). La Siesta.

Butchart, Ian, jt. auth. see Fothergill, Richard.

Butchart, M. Money in the English Tradition, 1640-1936. 59.95 (ISBN 0-8490-0661-9). Gordon Pr.

Butchart, Ronald E. Northern Schools, Southern Blacks, & Reconstruction: Freedmen's Education, 1862-1875. LC 79-8949. (Contributions in American History: No. 87). (Illus.). xiv, 309p. 1980. lib. bdg. 29.95 (ISBN 0-313-22073-5, BNS/). Greenwood.

Butchbaker, Allen F. Electricity & Electronics for Agriculture. (Illus.). 392p. 1977. text ed. 21.95x (ISBN 0-8138-0525-2). Iowa St U Pr.

Butcher, Alice M. Memories of George Meredith, O. M. LC 72-103172. 1970. Repr. of 1919 ed. 20.00x (ISBN 0-8046-0809-1, Pub. by Kennikat). Assoc Faculty Pr.

Butcher, Bernard L., ed. Genealogical & Personal History of the Upper Monongahela Valley, West Virginia, 2 vols. LC 78-60704. 1036p. 1978. Repr. of 1912 ed. Set. 45.00 (ISBN 0-8063-0821-4). Genealog Pub.

Butcher, D. G. & Parnell, A. C. Smoke Control in Fire Safety Design. 1979. 42.00x (ISBN 0-419-11190-5, Pub. by E & FN Spon, NO. 6558). Methuen Inc.

Butcher, D. W. On-Line Monitoring of Continuous Process Plant. 326p. 1984. 83.95x (ISBN 0-470-27504-9). Halsted Pr.

Butcher, David. Official Publications in Britain. 160p. 1983. 18.50 (ISBN 0-85157-351-7, Pub. by Bingley England). Shoe String.

Butcher, Devereux. Exploring Our National Parks & Monuments. 8th, Rev. ed. (Illus.). 400p. 1985. (Pub. by Gambit); pap. 11.95 (ISBN 0-87645-122-9). Harvard Common Pr.

Butcher, E. G. & Parnell, A. C. Designing for Fire Safety. 372p. 1983. 54.95 (ISBN 0-471-10239-3). Wiley.

Butcher, Edith L. The Story of the Church of Egypt, 2 vols. LC 75-41459. Repr. of 1897 ed. Set. 87.50 (ISBN 0-404-56231-0). AMS Pr.

Butcher, F., et al, eds. Electrical Maintenance & Installation: Part One. 2nd ed. (Engineering Craftsmen: No. J2). (Illus.). 1975. spiral bdg 42.50x (ISBN 0-89563-003-6). Trans-Atlantic.

Butcher, Grace. Before I Go Out on the Road. (Poets Ser.: No. 20). (Orig.). 1979. pap. 3.50 (ISBN 0-914946-15-3). Cleveland St Univ Poetry Ctr.

--Rumors of Ecstasy, Rumors of Death. 64p. (Orig.). 1981. pap. 6.95 (ISBN 0-935306-13-7). Barnwood Pr.

Butcher, H. J., jt. auth. see Cattell, Raymond B.

Butcher, Irene, jt. ed. see Rudkin, Anthony.

Butcher, James & American Legislative Exchange Council. Source Book of American State Legislation, 1985-1986. LC 82-642083. 1985. 10.00 (ISBN 0-317-37050-2). Am Legislative.

Butcher, James, jt. ed. see Spielberger, C. D.

Butcher, James N. & Pancheri, Paolo. A Handbook of Cross-National MMPI Research. LC 75-28919. 1976. 25.00x (ISBN 0-8166-0758-3). U of Minn Pr.

Butcher, James N. & Spielberger, Charles D. Advances in Personality Assessment, Vol. 3. (Advances in Personality Assessment Ser.). 216p. 1983. text ed. 24.95x (ISBN 0-89859-313-1). L Erlbaum Assocs.

Butcher, James N., ed. New Developments in the Use of the MMPI. LC 79-22093. (Illus.). 1979. 29.50 (ISBN 0-8166-0894-6). U of Minn Pr.

--Objective Personality Assessment: Changing Perspectives. (Personality & Psychopathology Ser.). 1972. 39.50 (ISBN 0-12-148450-5). Acad Pr.

Butcher, James N. & Spielberger, Charles D., eds. Advances in Personality Assessment, Vol. 2. 208p. 1983. text ed. 24.95x (ISBN 0-89859-216-X). L Erlbaum Assocs.

--Advances in Personality Assessment, Vol. 4. 288p. 1985. text ed. 29.95 (ISBN 0-89859-341-7). L Erlbaum Assocs.

Butcher, James N., jt. ed. see Kendall, Philip C.

Butcher, James N., jt. ed. see Spielberger, Charles D.

Butcher, James N., jt. auth. see Coleman, James C.

Butcher, John G. The British in Malaya, Eighteen Eighty to Nineteen Forty-One: The Social History of a European Community in Colonial South-East Asia. (Illus.). 1979. 37.50x (ISBN 0-19-580419-8). Oxford U Pr.

Butcher, Julia. The Sheep & the Rowan Tree. LC 83-26423. (Illus.). (gr. k-3). 1984. 12.50 (ISBN 0-03-071602-0). HR&W.

Butcher, Lady. Memories of George Meredith O. M. 1978. Repr. of 1919 ed. lib. bdg. 25.00 (ISBN 0-8495-0334-5). Arden Lib.

Butcher, Larry L., ed. Cholinergic-Monoaminergic Interactions in the Brain. (Behavioral Biology Ser.). 1978. 55.00 (ISBN 0-12-147850-5). Acad Pr.

Butcher, Loretta J. Free & Reduced Tuition Policies for Older Adult Students at Community, Junior, & Technical Colleges. (Orig.). 1980. pap. 3.00 (ISBN 0-87117-100-7). Am Assn Comm Jr Coll.

Butcher, M. V. & Nesbitt, C. J. Mathematics of Compound Interest. LC 70-157152. 1971. 12.00x (ISBN 0-9603000-1-5). Ulrich.

Butcher, Melvyn. Elements of Distribution. 1980. pap. 11.95 (ISBN 0-434-90198-9, Pub. by W Heinemann Ltd). David & Charles.

Butcher, Miriam, jt. auth. see Riddick, Floyd M.

Butcher, Philip. George W. Cable. LC 62-16819. (United States Authors Ser.). 1962. lib. bdg. 15.95 (ISBN 0-89197-769-4); pap. 3.25 (ISBN 0-89197-988-3). Irvington.

--George Washington Cable. (Twayne's United States Authors Ser). 1962. pap. 5.95x (ISBN 0-8084-0143-2, T24, Twayne). New Coll U Pr.

Butcher, Philip, ed. The Ethnic Image in Modern American Literature: 1900-1950, 2 vols. 1984. 19.95 ea.; Set. 35.00 (ISBN 0-88258-110-4). Vol. 1 (ISBN 0-88258-119-8). Vol. 2 (ISBN 0-88258-120-1). Howard U Pr.

--The Minority Presence in American Literature 1600-1900, 2 vols. LC 77-5687. 1977. Vol. 1. 14.95 (ISBN 0-88258-101-5); Vol. 2. 14.95 (ISBN 0-88258-102-3); Vol. 1. pap. 8.95 (ISBN 0-88258-061-2); Vol. 2. pap. 8.95 (ISBN 0-88258-100-7); Set. cloth 25.00 (ISBN 0-88258-103-1); Set. pap. 15.00 (ISBN 0-88258-104-X). Howard U Pr.

Butcher, S. H. Aristotle's Theory of Poetry & Fine Art. 1979. Repr. of 1902 ed. lib. bdg. 50.00 (ISBN 0-8482-3434-0). Norwood Edns.

--Harvard Lectures on Greek Subjects. 1978. Repr. of 1904 ed. lib. bdg. 30.00 (ISBN 0-8495-0386-8). Arden Lib.

--Harvard Lectures on Greek Subjects. 1904. 12.00 (ISBN 0-8274-3936-9). R West.

--On the Art of Poetry: With a Supplement on Music Aristotle. 1956. pap. text ed. write for info. (ISBN 0-02-317580-X). Macmillan.

--Some Aspects of the Greek Genius. 1975. Repr. of 1891 ed. 14.50 (ISBN 0-8274-4044-8). R West.

Butcher, S. H., ed. Demosthenis Orationes: Tomi II, Part 1 Orationes XX-XXVI. (Oxford Classical Texts). 332p. 1985. 13.95 (ISBN 0-19-814519-5). Oxford U Pr.

Butcher, S. H., ed. & tr. The Poetics of Aristotle. 111p. Date not set. Repr. of 1922 ed. lib. bdg. 60.00 (ISBN 0-89760-970-0). Telegraph Bks.

Butcher, S. H. see Demosthenes.

Butcher, S. H., tr. see Aristotle.

Butcher, Samuel H. Aristotle's Theory of Poetry & Fine Art. 4th ed. 1955. pap. 6.95 (ISBN 0-486-20042-6). Dover.

--Harvard Lectures on Greek Subjects. LC 78-101036. 1969. Repr. of 1904 ed. 21.00x (ISBN 0-8046-0703-6, Pub. by Kennikat). Assoc Faculty Pr.

--Some Aspects of the Greek Genius. LC 79-101552. 1969. Repr. of 1891 ed. 26.50x (ISBN 0-8046-0721-4, Pub. by Kennikat). Assoc Faculty Pr.

Butcher, Solomon D. Pioneer History of Custer County. 15.50 (ISBN 0-931068-05-3); pap. 10.00. Purcells.

Butchvarov, Panayot. Being Qua Being: A Theory of Identity, Existence & Predication. LC 78-13812. 288p. 1979. 22.50x (ISBN 0-253-13700-4). Ind U Pr.

--Resemblance & Identity: An Examination of the Problem of Universals. LC 66-22437. Repr. of 1966 ed. 42.20 (ISBN 0-8357-9239-0, 2015811). Bks Demand UMI.

Buteau, June D. Nonprint Materials on Communication: An Annotated Directory of Select Films, Videotapes, Videocassettes, Simulations & Games. LC 76-21857. 454p. 1976. 22.50 (ISBN 0-8108-0973-7). Scarecrow.

Buteaux, Paul. Strategy, Doctrine, & the Politics of Alliance: Theatre Nuclear Force Modernization in NATO. Replica ed. LC 82-20024. 158p. 1982. softcover 18.00x (ISBN 0-86531-940-5). Westview.

Butel, Jane. The Best of Mexican Cooking. (Easy Cooking Ser.). (Illus.). 64p. 1984. pap. 4.95 (ISBN 0-8120-5589-6). Barron.

--Chili Madness. LC 80-51617. (Passionate Cookbook Ser.). 96p. 1980. 7.95 (ISBN 0-89480-135-X, 325); pap. 4.95 (ISBN 0-89480-134-1, 435). Workman Pub.

--Finger Lickin', Rib Stickin', Great Tastin' Hot & Spicy Barbecue. LC 81-43785. (Passionate Cookbook Ser.). (Illus.). 96p. 1982. 8.95 (ISBN 0-89480-207-0, 320); pap. 4.95 (ISBN 0-89480-208-9, 482). Workman Pub.

--Woman's Day Book of New Mexican Cooking. 320p. (Orig.). 1984. pap. 5.95 (ISBN 0-671-44672-X). PB.

Butel-Dumont, Georges M. Histoire et Commerce Des Colonies Angloises, Dans l'Amerique Septentrionale. 1966. Repr. of 1775 ed. 25.00 (ISBN 0-384-06750-6). Johnson Repr.

--Histoire et Commerce Des Colonies Angloises Dans L'amerique Septentrionale, (Londres, 1755) (Canadiana Avant 1867: No. 5). 1966. 24.40x (ISBN 90-2796-325-8). Mouton.

Buten, David & Pelehach, Patricia. Wedgwood & America, Wedgwood Bas-Relief Ware. LC 77-83634. (Monographs in Wedgwood Studies). (Illus.). 1977. pap. text ed. 5.00 (ISBN 0-912014-51-2). Buten Mus.

Buten, Harry M. Fast Figuring for Executives: Present & Future. 4th ed. (Orig.). 1970. pap. 1.00 (ISBN 0-912014-06-7). Buten Mus.

--Wedgwood ABC but Not Middle E. 2nd ed. (Illus.). 112p. 1981. pap. 7.95 (ISBN 0-912014-58-X). Buten Mus.

Buten, Howard. Burt. Marks, Bobbi, ed. LC 80-11196. 168p. 1981. pap. 5.95 (ISBN 0-03-057664-4). HR&W.

Butenandt, O., jt. ed. see Laron, Z.

Butenko, A. P. Consolidation of the Socialist Countries' Unity. 268p. 1981. pap. 3.20 (ISBN 0-8285-2034-8, Pub. by Progress Pubs USSR). Imported Pubns.

Butenschon, Sine & Borchgrevink, Hans. Voice & Song. LC 81-38464. 80p. 1982. pap. 22.95 (ISBN 0-521-28011-7). Cambridge U Pr.

Butera, F. & Thurman, J. E., eds. Automation & Work Design: A Study Prepared by International Labour Office. LC 84-8169. 758p. 1984. 74.00 (ISBN 0-444-87538-7, I-318-84, Pub. by North Holland). Elsevier.

Butera, M. C., et al. College English: Grammar & Style. 1967. text ed. 21.55 (ISBN 0-07-009320-2). McGraw.

Butera, M. Lee, ed. Foreign Banking in America: Fourth Annual Conference. 283p. 1985. pap. 32.50x (ISBN 0-930197-01-1). Focus Pubns.

--Foreign Banking in America: Second Annual Conference 1983. 260p. 1983. pap. 27.50 (ISBN 0-317-11584-7). Focus Pubns.

Buteux, Paul. The Politics of Nuclear Consultation in NATO: 1965-1980. LC 82-22016. (International Studies). 256p. 1983. 42.50 (ISBN 0-521-24798-5). Cambridge U Pr.

Buth, Lenore. Growing Together: Mother & Child. 112p. (Orig.). 1985. pap. 4.95 (ISBN 0-570-03963-0, 12-2998). Concordia.

Butheel, A. & Dewilde, P., eds. Rational Approximation in Systems Engineering. 244p. 1983. 29.95 (ISBN 0-8176-3159-3). Birkhauser.

Buthelezi, Gatsha & Sullivan, Leon. Power Is Ours: Buthelezi Speaks on the Crisis in South Africa. LC 78-74593. (Illus.). 1979. 12.95 (ISBN 0-916728-08-0). Bks in Focus.

Buthlay, Kenneth. Hugh MacDiarmid. (Scottish Writers Ser.). 143p. (Orig.). 1983. pap. 6.50x (ISBN 0-7073-0307-9, Pub. by Scottish Academic Pr Scotland). Columbia U Pr.

Buthman, W. C. The Rise of Integral Nationalism in France with Special Reference to the Ideas & Activities of Charles Maurras. LC 78-120239. 1970. Repr. lib. bdg. 27.50x (ISBN 0-374-91128-2). Octagon.

Butigan, Ken, ed. Dying for Peace: The Current Cost of Nuclear Weapons. 440p. 1986. lib. bdg. 34.95 (ISBN 0-86571-060-0); pap. 12.95 (ISBN 0-86571-059-7). New Soc Pubs.

Butigan, Ken, jt. ed. see Joranson, Philip N.

Butkov, E. Mathematical Physics. 1968. 38.95 (ISBN 0-201-00727-4). Addison-Wesley.

Butkovskiy, A. G. Green's Functions & Transfer Functions Handbook. (Mathematics & Its Applications Ser.). 260p. 1982. 74.95 (ISBN 0-470-27344-5). Halsted Pr.

--Structural Theory of Distributed Systems. LC 83-10727. (Mathematics & Its Applications Ser.). 314p. 1983. 89.95x (ISBN 0-470-27469-7). Halsted Pr.

Butkovsky-Hewitt, Anna. With Gurdjieff in St. Petersburg. 1978. 8.95 (ISBN 0-7100-8527-3). Weiser.

Butland, Gilbert J. Chile: An Outline of Its Geography, Economics & Politics. LC 81-13237. vii, 128p. 1982. Repr. of 1956 ed. lib. bdg. 19.75x (ISBN 0-313-23193-1, BUCL). Greenwood.

Butler. Dynamic Experiments in the Electron Microscope. 458p. 1981. 83.00 (Biomedical Pr); pap. 42.25 (ISBN 0-444-80286-X). Elsevier.

--How to Build & Operate Your Own Small Hydroelectric Plant. (Illus.). 320p. 1982. 17.95 (ISBN 0-8306-0065-5); pap. 11.95 (ISBN 0-8306-1417-6, 1417). TAB Bks.

--Les Parlers Dialectaux et Populaires dans l'Oeuvre de Guy de Maupassant. (Publ. Romanes et Franc.). 15.50 (ISBN 0-685-34943-8). French & Eur.

Butler & Lewis. Aging & Mental Health. 1983. pap. 8.95 (ISBN 0-452-25405-1, Plume). NAL.

Butler & Rosenthal. Behaviour & Rehabilitation. 2nd ed. 1985. price not set (ISBN 0-7236-0824-5). PSG Pub Co.

Butler, jt. auth. see Ottenberite.

Butler, ed. International Conference on Computer Communication, 1974: Computer Communication Today & Up to 1985. 610p. 1974. 42.50 (ISBN 0-444-86194-7, North-Holland). Elsevier.

Butler, A. J. Police Management. LC 84-10343. 224p. (Orig.). 1984. pap. text ed. 21.95x (ISBN 0-566-00646-4). Gower Pub Co.

Butler, A. J., tr. Select Essays of Sainte-Beuve: Chiefley Bearing on English Literature. 1978. lib. bdg. 25.00 (ISBN 0-8495-4830-6). Arden Lib.

Butler, A. R. & Perkins, M. J., eds. Organic Reaction Mechanisms, 1973: An Annual Survey Covering the Literature Dated December 1972 Through November 1973. LC 66-23143. pap. 146.80 (ISBN 0-317-29325-7, 2024016). Bks Demand UMI.

--Organic Reaction Mechanisms, 1974: An Annual Survey Covering the Literature Dated December 2973 Through November 1974. LC 66-23143. pap. 160.00 (ISBN 0-317-29326-5, 2024017). Bks Demand UMI.

--Organic Reaction Mechanisms, 1975: An Annual Survey Covering the Literature Dated December 1974 Through November 1975. LC 66-23143. pap. 157.50 (ISBN 0-317-29327-3, 2024018). Bks Demand UMI.

--Organic Reaction Mechanisms, 1976: An Annual Survey Covering the Literature Dated December 1975 Through November 1976. LC 66-23143. pap. 160.00 (ISBN 0-317-29328-1, 2024019). Bks Demand UMI.

Butler, A. S. The Architecture of Sir Edwin Lutyens, 3 vols. (Illus.). 1984. Repr. of 1950 ed. Set. 350.00 (ISBN 0-907462-72-3). Antique Collect.

Butler, Addie J. The Distinctive Black College: Talladega, Tuskegee, & Morehouse. LC 77-22756. 176p. 1977. 16.00 (ISBN 0-8108-1055-7). Scarecrow.

Butler, Alan, ed. Ageing: Recent Advances & Creative Responses. 320p. 1985. 24.50 (ISBN 0-7099-3927-2, Pub. by Croom Helm Ltd). Longwood Pub-Group.

Butler, Alan, et al. Sheltered Housing for the Elderly: Policy, Practice & the Consumer. (National Institute Social Services Library: No. 44). 1983. text ed. 28.50x (ISBN 0-04-362055-8). Allen Unwin.

Butler, Alban. Lives of the Saints, 4 vols. Attwater, Thurston, ed. 1956. Set. 125.00 (ISBN 0-87061-045-7). Vol. 1. Vol. 2. Vol. 3. Vol. 4. Chr Classics.

Butler, Albert. Get Judge Parker! (Orig.). 1980. pap. 1.75 (ISBN 0-505-51500-8, Pub. by Tower Bks). Dorchester Pub Co.

--Three Rivers to Run. (Orig.). 1981. pap. 1.95 (ISBN 0-505-51672-1, Pub. by Tower Bks). Dorchester Pub Co.

Butler, Albert & Butler, Josephine. Encyclopedia of Social Dance. (Ballroom Dance Ser.). 1985. lib. bdg. 90.00 (ISBN 0-87700-855-8). Revisionist Pr.

Butler, Alfred J. The Arab Conquest of Egypt & the Last Thirty Years of the Roman Dominion. LC 72-180327. Repr. of 1902 ed. 30.00 (ISBN 0-404-56219-1). AMS Pr.

--The Arab Conquest of Egypt & the Last Thirty Years of the Roman Dominion. 2nd ed. Fraser, P. M., ed. 1978. text ed. 64.00x (ISBN 0-19-821678-5). Oxford U Pr.

Butler, Anne. The Arco Encyclopedia of Embroidery Stitches. LC 79-13429. (Illus.). 1979. 22.95 (ISBN 0-668-04799-2). Arco.

--Machine Stitches. 1976. 18.95 (ISBN 0-7134-3150-4, Pub. by Batsford England). David & Charles.

Butler, Anne, jt. auth. see French, Brian.

Butler, Anne M. Daughters of Joy, Sisters of Misery: Prostitutes in the American West, 1865-1890. LC 84-195. (Illus.). 208p. 1985. 16.95x (ISBN 0-252-01139-2). U of Ill Pr.

Butler, Arthur J. Dante His Times & His Work. 201p. 1980. Repr. of 1895 ed. lib. bdg. 40.00 (ISBN 0-8495-0475-9). Arden Lib.

--Dante: His Times & His Work. 1973. Repr. of 1895 ed. 10.50 (ISBN 0-8274-1512-5). R West.

--Dante: His Times & His Work. 12.75 (ISBN 0-8369-7156-6, 7988). Ayer Co Pubs.

Butler, Arthur J., ed. The Forerunners of Dante: A Selection from Italian Poetry Before 1300. 1977. lib. bdg. 59.95 (ISBN 0-8490-1857-9). Gordon Pr.

Butler, B., jt. auth. see Daynes, R.

Butler, B. C. Prayer: An Adventure in Living. (Ways of Prayer Ser.: Vol. 10). 8.95 (ISBN 0-89453-431-9); pap. 4.95 (ISBN 0-89453-302-9). M Glazier.

Butler, B. E. Soil Classification for Soil Survey: Monographs on Soil Survey. (Illus.). 1980. 32.50x (ISBN 0-19-854510-X). Oxford U Pr.

--Soil Survey of the Horticultural Soils in the Murrumbidgee Irrigation Areas, New South Wales. 80p. 1981. 25.00x (ISBN 0-643-02432-8, Pub. by CSIRO Australia). State Mutual Bk.

Butler, B. F. & Marquis Of Lorne. Bering Sea Controversy. facs. ed. (Shorey Historical Ser.). 24p. pap. 2.50 (ISBN 0-8466-0035-8, S35). Shorey.

Butler, B. M., jt. ed. see Jeffries, W. R.

Butler, B. Robert. The Quest for the Historic Fremont & a Guide to the Prehistoric Pottery of Southern Idaho. (Occasional Papers of the Idaho Museum of National History: No. 33). 25p. 1983. pap. 4.00 (ISBN 0-317-11776-9). Idaho Mus Nat Hist.

--When Did the Shoshoni Begin to Occupy Southern Idaho: Essays on Late Prehistoric Cultural Remains from the Upper Snake & Salmon River Countries. (Occasional Papers of the Idaho Museum of Natural History: No. 32). 27p. 1981. pap. 5.00 (ISBN 0-686-30007-6). Idaho Mus Nat Hist.

Butler, Barbara & Elliott, Doreen. Teaching & Learning for Practice. 130p. 1985. pap. text ed. write for info. (ISBN 0-566-00869-6). Gower Pub Co.

Butler, Barbara M. The Evolution of the Black Nurse Midwife. 64p. 1983. 5.50 (ISBN 0-682-49966-8). Exposition Pr FL.

Butler, Benjamin F. Private & Official Correspondence, 5 Vols. LC 74-39570. Repr. of 1917 ed. Set. 125.00 (ISBN 0-404-01310-4). AMS Pr.

Butler, Beverly. Ghost Cat. 192p. (gr. 6 up). 1984. PLB 10.95 (ISBN 0-396-08457-5). Dodd.

--Gift of Gold. (gr. 7-9). 1973. pap. 1.95 (ISBN 0-671-41327-9). Archway.

--Light a Single Candle. (gr. 7-9). 1970. pap. 1.95 (ISBN 0-671-44385-2). Archway.

--Light a Single Candle. LC 62-16326. (gr. 7-9). 1962. 7.95 (ISBN 0-396-04709-2). Dodd.

--Magnolia Plantation. (Orig.). 1982. pap. 3.50 (ISBN 0-89083-914-X). Zebra.

--My Sister's Keeper. LC 79-6637. (gr. 7 up). 1980. 7.95 (ISBN 0-396-07803-6). Dodd.

--My Sister's Keeper. 224p. (gr. 7 up). 1985. pap. 3.95 (ISBN 0-396-08744-2). Dodd.

Butler, Bill. Dictionary of the Tarot. LC 74-9230. (Illus.). 1977. 7.95 (ISBN 0-8052-0559-4); pap. 6.95. Schocken.

--A Long Slow Waltz. 12p. (Orig.). 1968. pap. 5.00 (ISBN 0-932264-08-5). Trask Hse Bks.

Butler, Blaine, jt. auth. see Smith, Ralph J.

Butler, Bonnie. Olympic Hopeful. LC 83-790. 144p. 1983. pap. 1.95 (ISBN 0-449-70055-0). Fawcett.

--Open after School. (gr. 7 up). 1983. pap. 2.25 (ISBN 0-448-15681-4, Pub by Tempo). Ace Bks.

Butler, Brett & Martin, Susan K., eds. Library Automation: The State of the Art II. LC 75-20168. 200p. 1975. pap. text ed. 9.00x (ISBN 0-8389-3152-9). ALA.

Butler, Brett, jt. ed. see Aveney, Brian.

Butler, Brian M. & May, Ernest E., eds. Prehistoric Chert Exploitation: Studies from the Midcontinent. LC 83-71202. (Occasional Papers: No. 2). (Illus.). 340p. (Orig.). 1984. pap. 13.50 (ISBN 0-88104-008-8). Center Archaeo.

Butler, Bryon & Greenwood, Ron. Soccer Choice. (Illus.). 160p. 1980. 13.95 (ISBN 0-7207-1184-3, Pub. by Michael Joseph). Merrimack Pub Cir.

Butler, C. The Lausiac History of Palladius, 2 pts. in 1 vol. Incl. Pt. 1. Critical Discussion Together with Notes on Early Egyptian Monachism; Pt. 2. Greek Text Edition with Introduction & Notes. (Texts & Studies Ser.: No. 1, Vol. 6, Pts. 1 & 2). pap. 54.00 (ISBN 0-317-16755-3). Kraus Repr.

--Western Mysticism: Neglected Chapters in the History of Religion. 69.95 (ISBN 0-87968-244-2). Gordon Pr.

Butler, C. H. Cogeneration: Engineering, Design, Financing & Regulatory Compliance. 448p. 1984. 39.50 (ISBN 0-07-009364-4). McGraw.

Butler, C. S. Poetry & the Computer: Some Quantitative Aspects of the Style of Sylvia Plath. 1981. 15.50 (ISBN 0-85672-202-2, Pub. by Brit Acad England). State Mutual Bk.

Butler, C. V. Domestic Service. LC 79-56953. (The English Working Class Ser.). 1980. lib. bdg. 20.00 (ISBN 0-8240-0107-9). Garland Pub.

Butler, Charles. Principles of Musik, in Singing & Setting. LC 68-13273. (Music Ser.). 1970. Repr. of 1636 ed. lib. bdg. 21.50 (ISBN 0-306-70939-2). Da Capo.

--The Principles of Musik, in Singing & Setting. LC 74-25439. (English Experience Ser.: No. 284). 136p. 1971. Repr. of 1636 ed. 14.00 (ISBN 90-221-0284-X). Walter J Johnson.

Butler, Charles, ed. see Fearne, Charles.

Butler, Charles E. Cut Is the Branch. LC 73-144749. (Yale Ser. of Younger Poets: No. 43). Repr. of 1945 ed. 18.00 (ISBN 0-404-53843-6). AMS Pr.

Butler, Chester. Our Legacy from Ma & Pa. LC 84-91308. 70p. 1985. 7.95 (ISBN 0-533-06392-2). Vantage.

Butler, Chris. Reincarnation Explained. LC 83-61000. 288p. 1984. 12.95 (ISBN 0-88187-000-5). Science Identity.

--Who Are You? Discovering Your Real Identity. LC 83-80825. (Who are You? Ser.: Vol. 1). 489p. 1985. 12.95 (ISBN 0-912093-00-5). Identity Inst.

Butler, Christopher. After the Wake: An Essay on the Contemporary Avant-Garde. (Illus.). 1980. 26.00x (ISBN 0-19-815766-5). Oxford U Pr.

--Interpretation, Deconstruction, & Ideology. LC 84-5526. 1984. 24.95x (ISBN 0-19-815792-4); pap. 10.95x (ISBN 0-19-815791-6). Oxford U Pr.

--Systemic Linguistics: Theory & Applications. (Illus.). 240p. 1985. 42.00 (ISBN 0-7134-3705-7, Pub. by Batsford England). David & Charles.

--The Theology of Vatican II. rev. ed. 238p. 1981. pap. 17.50 (ISBN 0-87061-062-7). Chr Classics.

Butler, Clark, tr. see Hegel, George W. F.

Butler, Cynthia. Michael Hendee. (N. H.-Vermont Historiettes). (Illus.). 56p. (gr. 2-3). 1976. 4.95 (ISBN 0-915892-05-7); pap. text ed. 1.95 (ISBN 0-915892-14-6). Regional Ctr Educ.

Butler, D., et al. Indian Elections: 1952-1984. 200p. 1984. text ed. 15.50x (ISBN 0-391-03200-3, Pub. by Arnold Heinemann India). Humanities.

Butler, David. The Fall of Saigon: Scenes from the Sudden End of a Long War. (Illus.). 493p. 1985. 18.95 (ISBN 0-671-46675-5). S&S.

--Lusitania. 576p. 1982. 17.95 (ISBN 0-394-52809-3). Random.

Butler, David & Jowett, Paul. Party Strategies in Britain: A Study of the 1984 European Elections. LC 84-27605. 172p. 1985. 25.00 (ISBN 0-312-59765-7). St Martin.

Butler, David & Kavanagh, Dennis. The British General Election of Nineteen Eighty-Three. LC 83-26990. 350p. 1984. 27.95 (ISBN 0-312-10256-9). St Martin.

--The British General Election of 1979. 416p. 1980. text ed. 50.00x (ISBN 0-8419-5081-4). Holmes & Meier.

Butler, David & Kitzinger, Uwe. The Nineteen Seventy-Five Referendum. LC 76-16701. 1976. 27.50x (ISBN 0-312-57435-5). St Martin.

Butler, David & Marquand, David. European Elections & British Politics. 208p. 1981. text ed. 25.00x (ISBN 0-582-29528-9); pap. text ed. 10.95x (ISBN 0-582-29529-7). Longman.

Butler, David & Stokes, Donald. Political Change in Britain: The Evolution of Electoral Choice. 2nd ed. LC 75-29935. 300p. 1976. 29.95 (ISBN 0-312-62160-4); pap. 10.95 (ISBN 0-312-62195-7). St Martin.

Butler, David & Stokes, Donald E. Political Change in Britain, Nineteen Sixty-Three to Nineteen Seventy, 2 vols. 1972. write for info., codebk. set (ISBN 0-89138-055-8). Vol. 1 (ISBN 0-89138-056-6). Vol. 2 (ISBN 0-89138-057-4). ICPSR.

Butler, David, jt. auth. see Martin, James.

Butler, David, ed. Coalitions in British Politics. LC 77-17791. 1978. 22.50 (ISBN 0-312-14503-9). St Martin.

Butler, David & Butler, Gareth, eds. British Political Facts, 1900-1985. 6th ed. 512p. 1985. 45.00 (ISBN 0-312-10467-7). St Martin.

Butler, David & Halsey, A. H., eds. Policy & Politics: Essays in Honour of Norman Chester. 1978. text ed. 26.50x (ISBN 0-333-23561-4). Humanities.

Butler, David & Ranney, Austin, eds. Referendums: A Comparative Study of Practice & Theory. 1978. pap. 7.25 (ISBN 0-8447-3318-0). Am Enterprise.

Butler, David, jt. ed. see Bogdanor, Vernon.

Butler, David, et al, eds. Democracy at the Polls: A Comparative Study of Competitive National Elections. 1981. 16.25 (ISBN 0-8447-3405-5); pap. 8.25 (ISBN 0-8447-3403-9). Am Enterprise.

Butler, David E. British General Election of 1955. 236p. 1969. Repr. of 1955 ed. 27.50x (ISBN 0-7146-1549-8, F Cass Co). Biblio Dist.

--British General Election of 1959. Rose, Richard, ed. (Illus.). 293p. 1970. Repr. of 1960 ed. 27.50x (ISBN 0-7156-1549-1, BHA-01550, F Cass Co). Biblio Dist.

--The Canberra Model: Essays on Australian Central Government. LC 73-93820. 200p. 1974. 25.00 (ISBN 0-312-11830-9). St Martin.

Butler, David H. An Income Tax Planning Model for Small Businesses. Dufey, Gunter, ed. LC 81-582. (Research for Business Decisions: No. 36). 332p. 1981. 44.95 (ISBN 0-8357-1131-5); pap. 19.95 (ISBN 0-8357-1156-X). UMI Res Pr.

Butler, David J. The Land Drainage Records of West Sussex. 177p. 1973. 49.00x (ISBN 0-900801-28-X, Pub. by Country Arch). State Mutual Bk.

Butler, Diane. Futurework. 1984. 16.95 (ISBN 0-03-061984-X); pap. 8.95 (ISBN 0-03-064098-9). HR&W.

Butler, Don. The History of Hudson. Dammann, George H., ed. LC 81-121. (Automotive Ser.). (Illus.). 336p. 1982. 29.95 (ISBN 0-912612-19-3). Crestline.

Butler, Don F. The Plymouth-DeSoto Story. 416p. 27.00 (ISBN 0-318-14890-0). Midwest Old Settlers.

Butler, Dorothy. Babies Need Books: How Books Can Help Your Child Become a Happy & Involved Human Being. LC 80-14027. 192p. 1985. pap. 5.95 (ISBN 0-689-70682-0, 322). Atheneum.

--Cushla & Her Books. LC 79-25695. (Illus.). 128p. 1980. 15.00 (ISBN 0-87675-279-2); pap. 12.50 (ISBN 0-87675-283-0). Horn Bk.

--Pre-Reading Kit: The Ideal Way to Introduce Your Child to Reading. (Orig.). 1983. 7.95x (ISBN 0-86863-278-3, Pub. by Heinemann Pub New Zealand). Intl Spec Bk.

Butler, Dorothy & Clay, Marie. Reading Begins at Home: Preparing Children for Reading Before They Go to School. LC 82-6172. (Illus.). 44p. 1982. pap. text ed. 6.00x (ISBN 0-435-08201-9). Heinemann Ed.

Butler, Doug. The Principles of Horseshoeing. LC 73-88039. (Illus.). 428p. 1974. 29.95 (ISBN 0-916992-01-2). Doug Butler.

--Principles of Horseshoeing. 2nd ed. (Illus.). 576p. 1985. 49.95 (ISBN 0-317-20352-5). Doug Butler.

Butler, Dougal, et al. Full Moon: The Amazing Rock & Roll Life of the Late Keith Moon. LC 81-38416. 269p. 1981. 12.95 (ISBN 0-688-00759-7); pap. 6.95 (ISBN 0-688-00757-0). Morrow.

Butler, E. J. Fungi & Disease in Plants. 1978. Repr. of 1918 ed. 37.50x (ISBN 0-89955-282-X, Pub. by Intl Bk Dist). Intl Spec Bk.

Butler, E. M. Byron & Goethe: Analysis of a Passion. 229p. 1980. Repr. lib. bdg. 25.00 (ISBN 0-8495-0626-3). Arden Lib.

--The Fortunes of Faust. 1979. 52.50 (ISBN 0-521-22562-0); pap. 13.95 (ISBN 0-521-29552-1). Cambridge U Pr.

--Goethe & Byron. LC 74-5069. 1949. lib. bdg. 10.00 (ISBN 0-8414-3110-8). Folcroft.

--Heinrich Heine. 291p. 1981. Repr. of 1956 ed. lib. bdg. 30.00 (ISBN 0-89984-070-1). Century Bookbindery.

--The Myth of the Magus. LC 78-73950. 1979. 42.50 (ISBN 0-521-22564-7); pap. 13.95 (ISBN 0-521-29554-8). Cambridge U Pr.

--The Myth of the Magus. 283p. 1982. Repr. of 1948 ed. lib. bdg. 65.00 (ISBN 0-89984-084-1). Century Bookbindery.

--Ritual Magic. LC 80-19324. 329p. 1980. Repr. of 1971 ed. lib. bdg. 15.95x (ISBN 0-89370-601-9). Borgo Pr.

--Ritual Magic. LC 78-73949. 1979. 42.50 (ISBN 0-521-22563-9); pap. 13.95 (ISBN 0-521-29553-X). Cambridge U Pr.

Butler, E. W. Urban Sociology. (Selected Readings Ser.). 1970. pap. text ed. 8.50x (ISBN 0-8290-1200-1). Irvington.

Butler, Eamonn. Hayek: His Contribution to the Political & Economic Thought of Our Time. LC 84-28037. 176p. 1985. 15.00x (ISBN 0-87663-475-7); pap. 7.95 (ISBN 0-87663-877-9). Universe.

--Milton Friedman. LC 85-9020. (Institute for Humane Studies Political Economics Ser.). 256p. (Orig.). 1985. text ed. 16.50x (ISBN 0-87663-476-5); pap. 8.95x (ISBN 0-87663-878-7). Universe.

Butler, Eamonn & Pirie, Madsen. Economy & Local Government. 1981. 19.00x (ISBN 0-686-78993-8, Pub. by Smith Inst England). State Mutual Bk.

Butler, Eamonn, jt. auth. see Schuettinger, Robert.

Butler, Eamonn F., jt. auth. see Schuettinger, Robert L.

Butler, Edgar W. Traditional Marriage & Emerging Alternatives. LC 78-26026. 1979. text ed. 23.50 scp (ISBN 0-06-041114-7, HarpC). Har-Row.

Butler, Edgar W. & Pick, James B. Geothermal Energy Development: Problems & Prospects in the Imperial Valley of California. LC 81-23402. 382p. 1982. text ed. 45.00x (ISBN 0-306-40772-8, Plenum Pr). Plenum Pub.

Butler, Edgar W., jt. ed. see Gutknecht, Douglas B.

Butler, Eliot A., jt. auth. see Swift, Ernest H.

Butler, Eliza M. The Fortunes of Faust. LC 78-14109. (Illus.). 1979. Repr. of 1952 ed. 26.50 (ISBN 0-88355-780-0). Hyperion Conn.

--Heinrich Heine: A Biography. LC 70-106684. Repr. of 1956 ed. lib. bdg. 19.75x (ISBN 0-8371-3607-5, BUHH). Greenwood.

--The Myth of the Magus. LC 78-14108. (Illus.). 1979. Repr. of 1948 ed. 25.85 (ISBN 0-88355-781-9). Hyperion Conn.

--Rainer Maria Rilke. 437p. 1973. Repr. of 1941 ed. lib. bdg. 29.00x (ISBN 0-374-91129-0). Octagon.

Butler, Elizabeth B. Women & the Trades. LC 70-89757. (American Labor, from Conspiracy to Collective Bargaining Ser., No. 1). 440p. 1969. Repr. of 1909 ed. 24.50 (ISBN 0-405-02108-9). Ayer Co Pubs.

--Women & the Trades. LC 84-5175. (Pittsburgh Series in Labor History). (Illus.). 568p. 1984. pap. 14.95x (ISBN 0-8229-5901-1). U of Pittsburgh Pr.

Butler, Ellis P. Pigs Is Pigs. 1907. 27.00 (ISBN 0-932062-20-2). Sharon Hill.

--Pigs Is Pigs & Other Favorites. (Illus.). 109p. pap. 2.50 (ISBN 0-486-21532-6). Dover.

--That Pup. 1909. 15.00 (ISBN 0-932062-24-5). Sharon Hill.

Butler, Eugenia, et al. An Auto-Instructional Text in Correct Writing, Form B. 2nd ed. 1980. pap. text ed. 13.95 (ISBN 0-669-02484-8); answer key 1.95 (ISBN 0-669-02486-4); supp. test to accompany any ed. 1.95 (ISBN 0-669-04324-9); key for supp. test 1.95 (ISBN 0-669-04404-0). Heath.

--Correct Writing, Form Three. 3rd ed. 1983. pap. text ed. 12.95 (ISBN 0-669-02487-2); answer key 1.95 (ISBN 0-669-02488-0). Heath.

--Correct Writing, Form Two. 2nd ed. 1978. pap. text ed. 13.95 (ISBN 0-669-01627-6); answer key 1.95 (ISBN 0-669-01629-2). Heath.

--An Auto-Instructional Text in Correct Writing, Form A. 2nd ed. 416p. 1976. pap. text ed. 13.95 (ISBN 0-669-95844-1); answer key 1.95 (ISBN 0-669-96511-1). Heath.

--Correct Writing Form. 2nd ed. 384p. 1976. pap. text ed. 13.95 (ISBN 0-669-99655-6); answers 1.95 (ISBN 0-669-99663-7). Heath.

Butler, Eugenia W. & Hickman, Mary A. Correct Writing. 3rd ed. 384p. 1983. pap. 13.95 (ISBN 0-669-05437-2); answer key 1.95 (ISBN 0-669-05438-0). Heath.

Butler, Ewan & Young, Gordon. Marshall Without Glory. LC 78-63656. (Studies in Fascism: Ideology & Practice). Repr. of 1951 ed. 31.00 (ISBN 0-404-16915-5). AMS Pr.

Butler, F. Coit. Instructional Systems Development for Vocational & Technical Training. LC 70-168490. 384p. 1972. 28.95 (ISBN 0-87778-027-7). Educ Tech Pubns.

Butler, F. Don. The Plymouth & Desoto Story. (Illus.). 416p. 32.95 (ISBN 0-317-11552-9). Diamond Farm Bk.

Butler, F. Donald. The Plymouth & De Soto Story. Dammann, George H., ed. LC 77-93182. (Automotive Ser.). (Illus.). 1979. 29.95 (ISBN 0-912612-14-2). Crestline.

Butler, Francelia. The Lucky Piece. LC 84-2340. 259p. 1984. 14.95 (ISBN 0-941324-06-0). Van Vactor & Goodheart.

--The Lucky Piece. (The Avon Romance Ser.). 384p. 1985. pap. 3.50 (ISBN 0-380-69818-8). Avon.

Butler, Francelia & Bakker, Jan. Marxism, Feminism & Free Love: The Story of the Ruskin Commonwealth. (Illus.). 140p. 1981. Repr. lib. bdg. 12.95x cancelled (ISBN 0-87991-034-8). Porcupine Pr.

Butler, Francelia & Rees, Compton. Children's Literature, Vol. 12. LC 79-66588. (Illus.). 264p. 1984. pap. text ed. 30.00x (ISBN 0-300-03144-0); pap. 9.95x (ISBN 0-300-03179-3). Yale U Pr.

Butler, Francelia & Rees, Compton, Jr. Children's Literature: Annual of the Modern Language Association Division on Children's Literature & the Children's Literature Association, No. 11. LC 79-66588. (Illus.). 224p. 1983. text ed. 30.00 (ISBN 0-300-02991-8); pap. text ed. 9.95x (ISBN 0-300-02992-6). Yale U Pr.

Butler, Francelia, ed. Sharing Literature with Children: A Thematic Anthology. (English & Humanities Ser.). 1977. text ed. 24.50x (ISBN 0-679-30328-6); pap. text ed. 16.95x (ISBN 0-582-28114-8); instr's manual free. Longman.

Butler, Francelia & Rotert, Richard W., eds. Reflections on Literature for Children: Selected from the Annual, Children's Literature. 296p. 1984. lib. bdg. 27.50 (ISBN 0-208-02054-3, Lib Prof Pubns); pap. text ed. 17.50 (ISBN 0-208-02075-6). Shoe String.

Butler, Francelia, ed. see Silvette, Herbert.

Butler, Francelia, et al, eds. Children's Literature, 6 vols. Brockman, Bennett & Sheidley, William E. Incl. Vol. 1. 1972. (ISBN 0-87722-082-4); pap. (ISBN 0-87722-081-6); Vol. 2. 1973. (ISBN 0-87722-080-8); pap. (ISBN 0-87722-079-4); Vol. 3. 1974. (ISBN 0-87722-078-6); pap. (ISBN 0-87722-077-8); Vol. 4. 1975. (ISBN 0-87722-042-5); pap. (ISBN 0-87722-076-X); Vol. 5. 1976. (ISBN 0-87722-069-7); pap. (ISBN 0-87722-070-0); Vol. 6. 1978. (ISBN 0-87722-104-9); pap. (ISBN 0-87722-105-7). LC 75-21550. 17.95 ea.; pap. 10.95 ea. Temple U Pr.

--Annual of the Modern Language Association Group on Children's Literature & the Children's Literature Association, Vol. 8. (Illus.). vi, 212p. 1980. 30.00x (ISBN 0-300-02452-5); pap. 9.95x (ISBN 0-300-02491-6). Yale U Pr.

--Children's Literature, Vol. 10. LC 79-66588. 272p. 1982. text ed. 30.00x (ISBN 0-300-02805-9); pap. 9.95x (ISBN 0-300-02806-7). Yale U Pr.

--Children's Literature: Annual of the Modern Language Association Division on Children's Literature & the Children's Literature Association, Vol. 9. LC 79-66588. (Illus.). 272p. 1981. text ed. 30.00x (ISBN 0-300-02623-4); pap. 9.95x (ISBN 0-300-02642-0). Yale U Pr.

Butler, Francelis & Higonnet, Margaret R., eds. Children's Literature: Annual of the Modern Language Association Division on Children's Literature & the Children's Literature Association, No. 13. LC 79-66588. 240p. 1985. text ed. 30.00 (ISBN 0-300-03319-2); pap. 9.95 (ISBN 0-300-03362-1). Yale U Pr.

Butler, Francella, ed. Masterworks of Children's Literature, Vol. I, & Vol. II: The Early Years 1550-1739, 2 vols. 1983. Vol. I. 37.50 ea. (ISBN 0-87754-375-5). Vol. II (ISBN 0-87754-376-3). Chelsea Hse.

Butler, Frances. Colored Reading: The Graphic Art of Frances Butler. (Lancaster-Miller Art Ser.). (Illus.). 1980. 8.95 (ISBN 0-89581-011-5). Asian Human Pr.

Butler, Francine. Biofeedback: A Survey of the Literature. LC 78-6159. 352p. 1978. 59.50x (ISBN 0-306-65173-4, IFI Plenum). Plenum Pub.

Butler, Francis G. History of Farmington. LC 83-62057. (Illus.). 764p. 1983. Repr. of 1885 ed. 45.00 (ISBN 0-89725-042-7). NE History.

Butler, Francis J. & Farrell, Catherine E. Foundation Guide for Religious Grant Seekers. LC 84-10593. (Handbook Ser.). 150p. 1984. pap. 11.95 (ISBN 0-89130-756-7, 00 15 02). Scholars Pr GA.

Butler, Frank. Muhammad Ali. (Profiles Ser.). (Illus.). 64p. (gr. 4-6). 1981. 7.95 (ISBN 0-241-10600-1, Pub. by Hamish Hamilton England). David & Charles.

Butler, Frank A. Improvement of Teaching in Secondary Schools. 3rd ed. LC 54-10718. 1954. 17.50x (ISBN 0-226-08533-9). U of Chicago Pr.

Butler, G. & Ison, H. C. Corrosion & Its Prevention in Waters. LC 76-30515. 310p. 1978. Repr. of 1966 ed. 21.00 (ISBN 0-88275-515-3). Krieger.

Butler, G. A. Native Gardens in Canberra. LC 79-54190. 113p. (Orig.). 1979. pap. text ed. 2.75 (ISBN 0-7081-1079-7, 1540, Pub. by ANUP Australia). Australia N U P.

Butler, G. D. Introduction to Community Recreation. 5th ed. 1975. text ed. 35.95 (ISBN 0-07-009361-X). McGraw.

Butler, G. J. & Mandeville, T. D. Regional Economics: An Australian Introduction. (Illus.). 139p. 1981. text ed. 15.50x (ISBN 0-7022-1594-5). U of Queensland Pr.

Butler, G. W. & Bailey, R. W., eds. Chemistry & Biochemistry of Herbage, 3 vols. Incl. Vol. 1. 1973. 90.00 (ISBN 0-12-148101-8); Vol. 2. 1974; Vol. 3. 1974. 55.00 (ISBN 0-12-148103-4). Acad Pr.

Butler, Gareth, jt. ed. see Butler, David.

Butler, Geoffrey. Studies in Statecraft. LC 79-110899. 1970. Repr. of 1920 ed. 15.00x (ISBN 0-8046-0882-2, Pub. by Kennikat). Assoc Faculty Pr.

Butler, George, jt. auth. see Gaines, Charles.

Butler, George & Kresta, Jiri E., eds. Cyclopolymerization & Polymers with Chain-Ring Structures. LC 82-11331. (ACS Symposium Ser.: No. 195). 454p. 1982. lib. bdg. 49.95x (ISBN 0-8412-0731-3). Am Chemical.

Butler, George B. & Berlin, K Darrell. Fundamentals of Organic Chemistry: Theory & Application. LC 79-128351. pap. 160.00 (ISBN 0-317-08668-5, 2012449). Bks Demand UMI.

Butler, George P., ed. Best Sermons, Nineteen Forty-Nine to Nineteen Fifty. facsimile ed. LC 74-134065. (Essay Index Reprint Ser). Repr. of 1949 ed. 23.50 (ISBN 0-8369-2488-6). Ayer Co Pubs.

--Best Sermons, 1946. LC 74-134065. (Essay Index Reprint Ser.). 1946. Repr. of 1946 ed. 19.50 (ISBN 0-8369-2757-5). Ayer Co Pubs.

--Best Sermons, 1947. facsimile ed. LC 74-134065. (Essay Index Reprint Ser). Repr. of 1947 ed. 23.50 (ISBN 0-8369-2487-8). Ayer Co Pubs.

Butler, George V. & Grey, Jerry, eds. Working in Space. LC 81-20528. (Illus.). 138p. 1981. 24.00 (ISBN 0-915928-57-4, AAS5); members 20.00 (ISBN 0-317-32208-7). AIAA.

Butler, George V., jt. ed. see Koelle, Dietrich E.

Butler, Grant C. Bali to Bahrein. 1969. 5.95 (ISBN 0-8159-5100-0). Devin.

--Beyond Arabian Sands. 1964. Devin.

--Kings & Camels. 1960. 9.95 (ISBN 0-8159-6000-X). Devin.

--Kings & Camels: An American in Saudi Arabia. LC 60-7601. (Illus.). pap. 57.80 (ISBN 0-317-11038-1, 2022708). Bks Demand UMI.

Butler, Gwendoline. A Coffin from the Past. (Scene of the Crime Ser.: No. 54). 1982. pap. 2.50 (ISBN 0-440-11590-6). Dell.

--Coffin in Malta. (Walker British Paperback Mysteries Ser.). 192p. 1985. pap. 2.95 (ISBN 0-8027-3111-2). Walker & Co.

--Nameless Coffin. 1985. pap. 2.95 (ISBN 0-8027-3081-7). Walker & Co.

Butler, H. The Embryology of the Lesser Galago (Galago senegalensis) (Contributions to Primatology: Vol. 19). (Illus.). vi, 158p. 1983. pap. 32.50 (ISBN 3-8055-3749-2). S Karger.

Butler, H. C. The Story of Athens. 59.95 (ISBN 0-8490-1127-2). Gordon Pr.

Butler, H. E. Post-Augustan Poetry from Seneca to Juvenal. 1909. 25.00 (ISBN 0-89984-036-1). Century Bookbindery.

Butler, H. E. & Scullard, H. H., eds. Livy, Bk. XX. (Classical Texts Ser.). 186p. pap. 9.95x (ISBN 0-904679-15-2). Basil Blackwell.

Butler, H. E., ed. see IAU Symposium, No. 36, Lunteren, Netherlands, June 1969.

Butler, H. E., tr. see Apuleius, Madaurensis.

Butler, H. E., tr. see Quintilianus, Marcus F.

Butler, Harold E. Post-Augustan Poetry. (Latin Poetry Ser.: Vol. 15). (LC 77-070766). 1977. Repr. of 1909 ed. lib. bdg. 40.00 (ISBN 0-8240-2964-X). Garland Pub.

--Post-Augustan Poetry from Seneca to Juvenal. facsimile ed. LC 70-99656. (Select Bibliographies Reprint Ser). 1909. 27.50 (ISBN 0-8369-5085-2). Ayer Co Pubs.

Butler, Henry M. Ten Great & Good Men. Repr. of 1912 ed. 25.00 (ISBN 0-686-19868-9). Ridgeway Bks.

--Ten Great & Good Men. Repr. of 1909 ed. 25.00 (ISBN 0-686-18791-1). Scholars Ref Lib.

Butler, Herbert J., ed. Antique Auto Body Leather Work for the Restorer. LC 82-62713. (Vintage Craft Ser.: No. 3). (Illus.). 1969. pap. 6.95 (ISBN 0-911160-03-5). Post-Era.

--Antique Auto Body Top Work for the Restorer. LC 76-18437. (Vintage Craft Ser.: No. 4). (Illus.). 1970. pap. 6.95 (ISBN 0-911160-04-3). Post-Era.

Butler, I. S. & Grosser, A. E. Relevant Problems for Chemical Principles. 4th, rev. ed. 1984. pap. 14.95 (ISBN 0-8053-1230-7). Benjamin-Cummings.

Butler, Isabel. The Song of Roland. LC 76-40196. 1904. Repr. 10.00 (ISBN 0-8414-1794-6). Folcroft.

Butler, Ivan. Choosing a Play for Your Amateur Group. LC 72-2194. 121p. 1972. pap. 2.95 (ISBN 0-8008-1500-9). Taplinger.

Butler, J. Sketches of Mexico. 1976. lib. bdg. 59.95 (ISBN 0-8490-2613-X). Gordon Pr.

Butler, J., tr. see Revesz, Geza.

Butler, J. A. Modern Biology & Its Human Implications. LC 76-27619. 119p. 1976. pap. 9.95x (ISBN 0-8448-1007-X). Crane-Russak Co.

Butler, J. A. & Noble, D., eds. Progress in Biophysics & Molecular Biology, Vols. 5-11, & 13-30. Incl. Vol. 5. 1955. Vol. 10. 62.50 (ISBN 0-08-009293-4); Vol. 6. 1956. write for info.; Vol. 7. 1957. write for info.; Vol. 8. 1958. write for info.; Vol. 9. 1959. write for info.; Vol. 10. 1960. write for info.; Vol. 11. 1961. write for info.; Vol. 13. 1963. 60.00 (ISBN 0-08-010028-7); Vol. 14. 1964. 60.00 (ISBN 0-08-010612-9); Vol. 15. 1965; Vol. 16. 1966. 10.50 (ISBN 0-08-011581-0); Vol. 17. 1967. 60.00 (ISBN 0-08-012046-6); Vol. 18. 1968. 60.00 (ISBN 0-08-012753-3); Vol. 19, Pt. 1. 1969. 31.00 (ISBN 0-08-013034-8); Vol. 19, Pt. 2. 1969. 31.00 (ISBN 0-08-006522-8); Vol. 19, Complete. 62.50 (ISBN 0-08-006523-6); Vol. 20. 1970. 62.50 (ISBN 0-08-006627-5); Vol. 21. 1970. 60.00 (ISBN 0-08-015696-7); Vol. 22. 1971. 60.00 (ISBN 0-08-016348-3); Vol. 23. 1971. 60.00 (ISBN 0-08-016740-3); Vol. 24. 1972. 60.00 (ISBN 0-08-016868-X); Vol. 25. 1972. 60.00 (ISBN 0-08-016935-X); Vol. 26. 1973. 62.50 (ISBN 0-08-017048-X); Vol. 27. 1973. 60.00 (ISBN 0-08-017142-7); Vol. 28. 1974. 60.00 (ISBN 0-08-018005-1); Vol. 29. 1975-76. Pt. 1. 60.00 (ISBN 0-08-019719-1); Vol. 29, Pt. 2, 1975. pap. 18.50 (ISBN 0-08-019784-1); Vol. 29, Pt. 3, 1975. pap. 18.50 (ISBN 0-08-019890-2); Vol. 29, Complete, 1976. 55.00 (ISBN 0-08-020201-2); Vol. 30. 1976. Pt. 1. 60.00 (ISBN 0-08-019972-0); Pts. 2-3. 55.00 (ISBN 0-08-020207-1); Vol. 30, Complete. pap. 22.00 (ISBN 0-686-66314-4). Pergamon.

--Progress in Biophysics & Molecular Biology, Vols. 31-33. Incl. Vol. 31. 1976-1977. Pt. 1. 60.00 (ISBN 0-08-021065-1); Vol, 31, Pt. 2. pap. 13.00 (ISBN 0-08-021415-0); Vol. 31, Pt. 3. pap. 14.00 (ISBN 0-08-021522-X); Vol. 31. Complete. 55.00 (ISBN 0-08-020293-4); Vol. 32, Pt. 1. 60.00 (ISBN 0-08-021547-5); Pt. 2. pap. 15.00 (ISBN 0-08-021554-8); Pt. 3, 1978. pap. 15.00 (ISBN 0-08-022656-6); Vol. 32 Complete 1978. 55.00 (ISBN 0-08-020295-0); Vol. 33. Date not set. Pt. 1. pap. 15.00 (ISBN 0-08-022675-2); Pt. 2. pap. 15.00 (ISBN 0-08-023166-7); Pt. 3. pap. 15.00 (ISBN 0-08-023184-5). Pergamon.

Butler, J. D. Air Pollution Chemistry. 1979. 69.50 (ISBN 0-12-147950-1). Acad Pr.

Butler, J. Douglas, jt. ed. see Walbert, David F.

Butler, J. K. Semiconductor Injection Lasers. LC 79-91615. 395p. 1980. 44.95x (ISBN 0-471-08156-6, Pub. by Wiley Interscience); pap. 29.50x (ISBN 0-471-08157-4). Wiley.

Butler, J. K., jt. auth. see Kressel, H.

Butler, J. K., ed. Semiconductor Injection Lasers. LC 79-91615. 1980. 46.75 (ISBN 0-87942-129-0, PC01248). Inst Electrical.

Butler, J. N. Carbon Dioxide Equilibria & Their Applications. 1982. pap. 13.95 (ISBN 0-201-10100-9). Addison-Wesley.

Butler, J. R. How Many Patients? 144p. 1980. pap. text ed. 11.25x (ISBN 0-7199-1041-2, Pub. by Bedford England). Brookfield Pub Co.

Butler, Jack. Hawk Gumbo & Other Stories. LC 82-70167. (Illus.). 156p. 1983. 14.95 (ISBN 0-935304-34-7); pap. 6.95 (ISBN 0-935304-35-5). August Hse.

--The Kid Who Wanted to Be a Spaceman: And Other Poems. LC 84-12429. 121p. 1984. 9.95 (ISBN 0-935304-75-4). August Hse.

--West of Hollywood: Poems from a Hermitage. LC 80-65468. 60p. 1980. 9.95 (ISBN 0-935304-10-X); pap. 4.95 (ISBN 0-935304-09-6). August Hse.

Butler, James. Fortune's Foot-Ball; or the Adventures of Mercutio, 2 vols. in one. LC 78-64068. Repr. of 1797 ed. 37.50 (ISBN 0-404-17394-2). AMS Pr.

--River of Death-Song Vam Sat. 1979. pap. 1.95 (ISBN 0-87881-089-7). Mojave Bks.

Butler, James, ed. see Wordsworth, William.

Butler, James D; see Vining, Edward P.

Butler, James L. The Master. 1982. 9.95 (ISBN 0-8062-1899-1). Carlton.

Butler, James N. Solubility & Ph Calculations. LC 64-15563. (Chemistry Ser). (Orig.). (gr. 9 up). 1964. pap. 6.95 (ISBN 0-201-00733-9). Addison-Wesley.

Butler, James N., et al. Studies of Sargassum & the Sargassum Community. (Bermuda Biological Station Special Publications: No. 22). (Illus.). 307p. 1983. pap. 10.00 (ISBN 0-917642-22-8). Bermuda Bio.

--Pelagic Tar from Bermuda & the Sargasso Sea. LC 73-175455. (Bermuda Biological Station Special Pubn.: No. 10). (Illus.). vi, 346p. pap. 8.00 (ISBN 0-917642-10-4). Bermuda Bio.

Butler, James R. M. Passing of the Great Reform Bill. 2nd ed. 454p. 1964. 32.50x (ISBN 0-7146-1459-9, F Cass Co). Biblio Dist.

Butler, Jan, jt. auth. see Bianchi, Susan.

Butler, Jan, tr. see Kozhenikov, Vadim.

Butler, Jan, tr. see Kuzmenko, Yuri.

Butler, Janet, jt. ed. see Tosi, Laura.

Butler, Janet, tr. see Alexandrov, V., et al.

Butler, Jeffrey, ed. Boston University Papers in African History, 2 vols. LC 64-15197. (Pub. by Boston U Pr). Vol. 1. 1964. 12.50x (ISBN 0-8419-8709-2, Africana); Vol. 2. 1966. 15.00x (ISBN 0-8419-8710-6). Holmes & Meier.

Butler, Jeffrey, jt. ed. see Thompson, Leonard.

Butler, Jeffrey, et al. The Black Homelands of South Africa: The Political & Economic Development of Bophuthatswana & Kwazulu. LC 76-7755. (Perspectives on Southern Africa: No. 21). 1977. pap. 4.95 (ISBN 0-520-03716-2). U of Cal Pr.
Butler, Jeffrey E., jt. auth. see Martello, William E.
Butler, Jerry. Swift to Hear, Slow to Speak. 1975. pap. 4.75 (ISBN 0-89137-511-2). Quality Pubns.
Butler, Jim. There Is a Time. 1983. 6.95 (ISBN 0-533-05294-7). Vantage.
Butler, Joan & Walker, Katherine S. Ballet for Boys & Girls. (Illus.). (gr. 3-7). 1979. 9.95x (ISBN 0-13-055574-6). P-H.
Butler, John. Christian Ways to Date, Go Steady, & Break up. (Mini Bible Studies). (Illus.). 1978. pap. 2.50 instructor (ISBN 0-87239-203-1, 88556); pap. 1.95 student (ISBN 0-87239-199-X, 88552). Standard Pub.
--TV, Movies & Morality: A Guide for Catholics. LC 84-60753. 144p. 1984. pap. 6.95 (ISBN 0-87973-602-X, 602). Our Sunday Visitor.
Butler, John E. Natural Disasters. 1976. pap. text ed. 8.50x (ISBN 0-435-34068-9). Heinemann Ed.
Butler, John E., ed. The Ruminant Immune System. LC 80-29702. (Advances in Experimental Medicine & Biology Ser.: Vol. 137). 915p. 1981. 95.00x (ISBN 0-306-40641-1, Plenum Pr). Plenum Pub.
Butler, John G. Joseph: Tried, True & Triumphant. 1977. pap. 0.95 (ISBN 0-87227-028-9); tchr's guide 3.95 (ISBN 0-87227-029-7). Reg Baptist.
Butler, John P., ed. Index of the Papers of the Continental Congress 1774-1789, 5 Vols. LC 78-23783. 1982. Repr. of 1978 ed. Set. lib. bdg. 200.00 (ISBN 0-89941-233-5). W S Hein.
Butler, John R. Who Goes Home? 75p. 1970. pap. text ed. 5.00x (ISBN 0-7135-1593-7, Pub. by Bedford England). Brookfield Pub Co.
Butler, John R. & Vaile, Michael S. Health & Health Services: An Introduction to Health Care in Britain. LC 83-27031. 256p. (Orig.). 1984. 15.95x (ISBN 0-7100-9902-9). Routledge & Kegan.
Butler, John S. Inequality in the Military: The Black Experience. LC 79-65253. 130p. 1980. 11.95 (ISBN 0-86548-002-8). R & E Pubs.
Butler, John T. Elements of Administration for Building Students. new ed. (Illus.). 221p. pap. text ed. 23.50x (ISBN 0-392-01119-0). Sportshelf.
Butler, Johnnella E. Black Studies: Pedagogy & Revolution; A Study of Afro-American Studies & the Liberal Arts Tradition through the Discipline of Afro-American Literature. LC 80-67213. 162p. 1981. lib. bdg. 21.75 (ISBN 0-8191-1568-1); pap. text ed. 10.00 (ISBN 0-8191-1569-X). U Pr of Amer.
Butler, Jon. The Huguenots in America: A Refugee People in New World Society. (Historical Monographs: No. 72). (Illus.). 272p. 1984. text ed. 25.00x (ISBN 0-674-41320-2). Harvard U Pr.
Butler, Jonathan L. Latin-inus, -ina, -inus, & -ineus: From Proto-Indo-European to the Romance Languages. LC 73-631070. (U. C. Publ. in Linguistics: Vol. 68). pap. 38.50 (ISBN 0-8357-9633-7, 2015099). Bks Demand UMI.
Butler, Joseph. The Analogy of Religion. 30.00 (ISBN 0-8274-1862-0). R West.
--Five Sermons. Darwall, Stephen, ed. LC 83-12577. (HPC Philosophical Classics Ser.). 86p. 1983. pap. text ed. 3.75 (ISBN 0-915145-61-8). Hackett Pub.
Butler, Joseph C. An Educational Approach to Modern Jazz Orchestration: Methods & Techniques. (Orig.). 1985. 35.00 (ISBN 0-932315-01-1). Butler Pub Hse.
--How to Think Positive & Achieve Great Success. (Orig.). 1984. 15.00 (ISBN 0-932315-00-3). Bulter Pub Hse.
Butler, Joseph H. Economic Geography: Spatial & Environmental Aspects of Economic Activity. LC 80-14542. 402p. 1980. 34.00 (ISBN 0-471-12681-0). Wiley.
Butler, Joseph T. Field Guide to American Antique Furniture. LC 83-14052. (Illus.). 399p. 1985. 24.95 (ISBN 0-8160-1008-0). Facts on File.
--Sleepy Hollow Restorations: A Cross-Section of the Collection. LC 82-16774. (Illus.). 344p. 1983. 39.95 (ISBN 0-912882-57-3). Sleepy Hollow.
--Van Cortlandt Manor. LC 77-17531. (A Sleepy Hollow Restorations Guidebook). (Illus.). 1978. pap. 1.95 (ISBN 0-912882-33-6). Sleepy Hollow.
Butler, Josephine. Woman's Work & Woman's Culture. 69.95 (ISBN 0-8490-1319-4). Gordon Pr.
Butler, Josephine, jt. auth. see Butler, Albert.
Butler, Josephine E. Personal Reminiscences of a Great Crusade. LC 74-33934. (Pioneers of the Woman's Movement: an International Perspective Ser.). 1976. Repr. 19.75 (ISBN 0-88355-257-4). Hyperion Conn.
Butler, Joyce. A Kennebunkport Album. LC 84-60405. (Illus.). 88p. 1984. pap. 11.95 (ISBN 0-9613275-0-2). Rosemary Hse.
--Wildfire Loose, the Week Maine Burned. (Illus., Orig.). 1978. 12.95 (ISBN 0-911764-21-6). Durrell.
Butler, Judy. Mystery of the Hidden Staircase. 1983. 6.95 (ISBN 0-8062-2031-7). Carlton.
Butler, Judy, tr. see Vilas, Carlos.
Butler, Julia. Spellbinding & Other Poems. 88p. (Orig.). 1985. pap. 5.99 (ISBN 0-9614049-0-6). Synergy Enter.
Butler, K. Meissen Porcelain of the 18th Century in the Hermitage: Catalogue. 379p. 1977. 32.00x (ISBN 0-317-14257-7, Pub. by Collet's). State Mutual Bk.
Butler, Karl D., jt. auth. see Palmer, Richard F.
Butler, Katherine G. & Wallach, Geraldine P. Language Disorders & Learning Disabilities, Topics in Language Disorders, Vol. 1, No.1. LC 82-1665. 118p. 1982. 18.50 (ISBN 0-89443-688-0). Aspen Systems.
Butler, Katy, jt. auth. see Vanguard Public Foundation.
Butler, Keith H. Fluorescent Lamp Phosphors. LC 79-11829. (Illus.). 1980. lib. bdg. 45.00x (ISBN 0-271-00219-0). Pa St U Pr.
Butler, Kurt & Rayner, Lynn. The Best Medicine: The Complete Health & Preventive Medicine Handbook. LC 84-48850. 800p. 1985. 31.68 (ISBN 0-06-250123-2, HarpR); pap. 17.26 (ISBN 0-06-250124-0, HarpR). Har-Row.
Butler, L. J. Thomas Hardy. LC 77-23532. (British Authors Ser.). 1978. 32.50 (ISBN 0-521-21743-1); pap. 11.95 (ISBN 0-521-29271-9). Cambridge U Pr.
Butler, Lance S. see St. John Butler, Lance.
Butler, Linda. The Role of Public Libraries in the Provision of Educational Guidance for Adults. (LIR Report 22). (Orig.). 1985. pap. 17.25 (ISBN 0-7123-3032-1, Pub. by British Lib). Longwood Pub Group.
Butler, Lindley S. The North Carolina Experience: An Interpretive & Documentary History. Watson, Alan D., ed. LC 83-27357. (Illus.). 475p. 1984. 29.95x (ISBN 0-8078-1609-4); pap. 9.95X (ISBN 0-8078-4124-2). U of NC Pr.
--Rockingham County: A Brief History. xiv, 92p. 1982. pap. 3.00 (ISBN 0-86526-198-9). NC Archives.
Butler, Lionel & Given-Wilson, Chris. Medieval Monasteries of Great Britain. (Illus.). 416p. 1980. 19.95 (ISBN 0-7181-1614-3, Pub. by Michael Joseph). Merrimack Pub Cir.
--Medieval Monasteries of Great Britain. (Illus.). 416p. 1984. pap. 14.95 (ISBN 0-7181-2368-9, Pub. by Michael Joseph). Merrimack Pub Cir.
Butler, Lord. The Art of Memory: Friends in Perspective. 175p. 1984. 18.95 (ISBN 0-340-26497-7, Pub. by Hodder & Stoughton UK). David & Charles.
Butler, Lucius A. & Youngs, Chaesoon T.compiled by. Films for Korean Studies. LC 77-86325. (Occasional Papers: No. 8). 167p. 1978. pap. 6.00x (ISBN 0-917536-12-6). Ctr Korean U HI at Manoa.
Butler, Lucy. Diana: The Fairy Tale Princess. LC 83-5109. (gr. 2-4). 1983. 6.95 (ISBN 0-671-47301-8). Summit Bks.
Butler, M., jt. ed. see Goddard, M.
Butler, Manley C., Jr. How to Get an FAA TSO for Parachutes. 112p. 1984. pap. text ed. 34.95x (ISBN 0-930747-00-3). Tech Info Pubn.
Butler, Mann. Valley of the Ohio. Clift, G. Glenn & Tapp, Hambleton, eds. 1971. 5.00 (ISBN 0-916968-01-4). Kentucky Hist.
Butler, Margaret & Greves, Beryl. Fabric Furnishings. 1972. 24.00 (ISBN 0-7134-2754-X, Pub. by Batsford). David & Charles.
Butler, Margaret G. Clothes: Their Choosing, Making & Care. 1978. (Pub. by Batsford England); pap. 12.95 (ISBN 0-7134-3035-4). David & Charles.
Butler, Marian, ed. Canadian Books in Print 1985: Author & Title Index. 1003p. 1985. 65.00 (ISBN 0-8020-4621-5). U of Toronto Pr.
--Canadian Books in Print 1985: Subject Index. 570p. 1985. 50.00 (ISBN 0-8020-4622-3). U of Toronto Pr.
Butler, Marilyn. Jane Austen & the War of Ideas. 1975. 34.00x (ISBN 0-19-812068-0). Oxford U Pr.
--Romantics, Rebels, & Reactionaries: English Literature & Its Background, 1760 to 1830. 1982. 19.95x (ISBN 0-19-520384-4); pap. 6.95x (ISBN 0-19-289132-4, OPUS). Oxford U Pr.
Butler, Marilyn, ed. Burke, Paine, Godwin & the Revolution Controversy. LC 83-15324. (English Prose Texts Ser.). 272p. 1984. 39.50 (ISBN 0-521-24386-6); pap. 13.95 (ISBN 0-521-28656-5). Cambridge U Pr.
Butler, Martin. Theatre & Crisis, Sixteen Thirty-Two to Sixteen Forty-Two. LC 83-15250. 1984. 39.50 (ISBN 0-521-24632-6). Cambridge U Pr.
Butler, Mary. Piedras Negras Pottery. LC 36-19557. (Piedras Negras Preliminary Papers: No. 4). pap. 25.00 (ISBN 0-317-26206-8, 2052124). Bks Demand UMI.
Butler, Mary & Butler, Trent. The John Allen Moores: Good News in War & Peace. (gr. 4-6). 1985. 5.50 (ISBN 0-8054-4295-2, 4242-95). Broadman.
Butler, Mary K. Papa's Old Trunk. LC 81-68812. (Illus.). 1981. 10.00 (ISBN 0-934530-03-3). Buck Pub.
Butler, Matilda & Paisley, William J. Knowledge Utilization Systems in Education. (Illus.). 320p. 1983. 27.50 (ISBN 0-8039-1944-1). Sage.
Butler, Matilda & Paisley, William, eds. Women & the Mass Media: Sourcebook for Research & Action. LC 79-16271. 432p. 1980. text ed. 34.95 (ISBN 0-87705-409-6); pap. text ed. 14.95 (ISBN 0-87705-419-3). Human Sci Pr.
Butler, Maureen, ed. see Emig, Janet.
Butler, Melvin A., et al. Students' Right to Their Own Language. 32p. 1974. pap. 1.50 (ISBN 0-8141-4806-9). NCTE.
Butler, Michael. The Novels of Max Frisch. 1976. text ed. 17.50x (ISBN 0-391-00687-8). Humanities.
--The Plays of Max Frisch. LC 84-17906. 144p. 1985. 22.50 (ISBN 0-312-61680-5). St Martin.
Butler, Mike. Ninety-Two Days in the Saddle. (Illus.). 1975. 9.95 (ISBN 0-88342-042-2). Old Army.
Butler, Montagu C. Esperanto-English Dictionary. (Esperanto & Eng.). 1967. 5.95x (ISBN 0-685-71601-5, 1065). Esperanto League North Am.
--Step by Step in Esperanto. 8th ed. 1979. 6.95x (ISBN 0-85230-071-9, 1019). Esperanto League North Am.
Butler, Natalie S. Dwight C. Sturges: Etcher of an Era. LC 74-20198. 1974. 12.95 (ISBN 0-87027-154-7); pap. 7.95 (ISBN 0-87027-155-5). Cumberland Pr.
Butler, Nathan. Kaheesh. 224p. (Orig.). 1983. pap. 2.50 (ISBN 0-449-12550-5, GM). Fawcett.
Butler, Neville, et al. Enciclopedia de la Vida, 5 vols. 6th ed. 2100p. (Espn.). 1978. Set. leather 175.00 (ISBN 84-02-00346-X, S-50570). French & Eur.
Butler, Neville R., jt. auth. see Davie, Ronald.
Butler, Nicholas M. The Effect of the War of 1812 Upon the Consolidation of the Nation. LC 78-63773. (Johns Hopkins University. Studies in the Social Sciences. Fifth Ser. 1887: 7). Repr. of 1887 ed. 11.50 (ISBN 0-404-61039-0). AMS Pr.
--The Effect of the War of 1812 Upon the Consolidation of the Union. 1973. pap. 9.00 (ISBN 0-384-06774-3). Johnson Repr.
--Is America Worth Saving? Addresses on National Problems & Party Policies. facsimile ed. LC 76-37772. (Essay Index Reprint Ser). Repr. of 1920 ed. 22.00 (ISBN 0-8369-2583-1). Ayer Co Pubs.
--Meaning of Education: Contributions to a Philosophy of Education. rev. & enl. facsimile ed. LC 72-142611. (Essay Index Reprint Ser). Repr. of 1915 ed. 21.50 (ISBN 0-8369-2219-0). Ayer Co Pubs.
--Scholarship & Service: The Policies & Ideals of a National University in a Modern Democracy. facsimile ed. LC 78-134066. (Essay Index Reprint Ser). Repr. of 1921 ed. 21.50 (ISBN 0-8369-2220-4). Ayer Co Pubs.
--Symbolism, Mysticism & the Unknowable, 2 vols. (Illus.). 305p. 1984. Repr. of 1896 ed. Set. 165.85 (ISBN 0-89901-166-7). Found Class Reprints.
--True & False Democracy. facsimile ed. LC 78-93323. (Essay Index Reprint Ser). 1907. 14.00 (ISBN 0-8369-1278-0). Ayer Co Pubs.
--Why Should We Change Our Form of Government: Studies in Practical Politics. LC 73-167321. (Essay Index Reprint Ser.). Repr. of 1912 ed. 17.00 (ISBN 0-8369-2758-3). Ayer Co Pubs.
--Why War? (Essay & General Literature Index Reprint Ser). 1969. Repr. of 1941 ed. 24.00x (ISBN 0-8046-0058-9, Pub. by Kennikat). Assoc Faculty Pr.
Butler, Nicholas M., ed. Education in the United States, 2 Vols. (American Studies). 1969. Repr. of 1900 ed. Set. lib. bdg. 80.00 (ISBN 0-384-06770-0). Johnson Repr.
--Education in the United States: A Series of Monographs, 2 Vols. LC 79-89159. (American Education: Its Men, Institutions & Ideas, Ser. 1). 1969. Repr. of 1900 ed. Set. 39.00 (ISBN 0-405-01396-5). Ayer Co Pubs.
Butler, Noble. A Practical & Critical Grammar of the English Language. 1874. 15.00 (ISBN 0-8274-3194-5). R West.
Butler, Octavia. Clay's Ark. LC 83-17766. 224p. 1984. 12.95 (ISBN 0-312-14321-4). St Martin.
--Kindred. 1981. pap. 2.75 (ISBN 0-671-83483-5). PB.
Butler, Octavia E. Clay's Ark. 208p. 1985. pap. 2.75 (ISBN 0-441-11089-4). Ace Bks.
--Wild Seed. 1981. pap. 2.75 (ISBN 0-671-43066-1, Timescape). PB.
Butler, Orton C. An Introductory Soils Laboratory Handbook. 1979. 8.00 (ISBN 0-682-49169-1, University). Exposition Pr FL.
Butler, Ovid, ed. see Schenck, Carl A.
Butler, P. F. A Student's Guide to Racine. 1974. pap. text ed. 5.00x (ISBN 0-435-37582-2). Heinemann Ed.
Butler, P. M. & Joysey, K. A., eds. Development, Function & Evolution of Teeth. 1978. 83.50 (ISBN 0-12-148050-X). Acad Pr.
Butler, P. T. Minor Prophets: The Prophets of the Decline: Hosea-Jonan. LC 79-1493. (Bible Study Textbook). 1968. 14.30 (ISBN 0-317-03548-7). College Pr Pub.
Butler, Pamela E. Self-Assertion for Women. rev. ed. LC 80-8904. (Illus.). 320p. (Orig.). 1981. pap. 8.61i (ISBN 0-06-250121-6, CN4011, HarpR). Har-Row.
--Talking to Yourself: Learning the Language of Self-Support. LC 82-48921. 1983. pap. text ed. 6.68i (ISBN 0-06-250122-4, CN4059, HarpR). Har-Row.
--Talking to Yourself: Learning to Communicate with the Most Important Person in Your Life. LC 80-6161. 192p. 1981. 12.95 (ISBN 0-8128-2779-1). Stein & Day.
Butler, Paul. Daniel. rev. ed. (The Bible Study Textbook Ser.). (Illus.). 1971. 16.00 (ISBN 0-89900-025-8). College Pr Pub.
--The Gospel of John. 3rd ed. LC 78-1789. (The Bible Study Textbook Ser.). (Illus.). 1965. 15.90 (ISBN 0-89900-035-5). College Pr Pub.
--Isaiah, Vol. III. (The Bible Study Textbook). (Illus.). 1978. 14.30 (ISBN 0-89900-022-3). College Pr Pub.
--Isaiah, Vol. I, II. (Bible Study Textbook). 694p. 1980. 15.90 (ISBN 0-89900-061-4). College Pr Pub.
--Luke. LC 81-68817. (Bible Study Textbook Ser.). 627p. 1981. 17.50 (ISBN 0-89900-062-2). College Pr Pub.
Butler, Paul F. Exercises in Pre-Algebra. (gr. 6-8). 1977. pap. text ed. 5.75x (ISBN 0-88334-041-0). Ind Sch Pr.
Butler, Paul T., jt. auth. see Ratzlaff, Ruben M.
Butler, Percy J. Portals to Peace. 1982. 5.95 (ISBN 0-533-05192-4). Vantage.
Butler, Perry. Gladstone: Church, State & Tractarianism, a Study of His Religious Ideas & Attitudes, 1809-1859. (Oxford Historical Monographs). 1982. 45.00x (ISBN 0-19-821890-7). Oxford U Pr.
Butler, Peter, ed. see Wagner, Richard.
Butler, Philip F., ed. see Racine, Jean B.
Butler, Philip H. Point Group Symmetry Applications: Methods & Tables. LC 80-17947. 578p. 1981. 75.00 (ISBN 0-306-40523-7, Plenum Pr). Plenum Pub.
Butler, Phyllis. Woman's Guide. Leonard, Jan, ed. LC 80-66585. (Savvy San Francisco Ser.). (Illus.). 64p. (Orig.). 1980. pap. 2.50 (ISBN 0-89395-047-5). Cal Living Bks.
Butler, Pierce. Analytical Questions on Shakespeare's Plays. 59.95 (ISBN 0-87968-620-0). Gordon Pr.
--Judah P. Benjamin. LC 80-20134. (American Statesmen Ser.). 460p. 1981. pap. 6.95 (ISBN 0-87754-198-1). Chelsea Hse.
--A Malady. 106p. 1982. pap. 5.95 (ISBN 0-905441-48-6, Pub. by Salem Hse Ltd.). Merrimack Pub Cir.
--Materials for the Life of Shakespeare. LC 71-113568. Repr. of 1930 ed. 16.00 (ISBN 0-404-01248-5). AMS Pr.
--Women of Medieval France. 75.00 (ISBN 0-87968-269-8). Gordon Pr.
Butler, Pierce, et al. Women in All Ages & All Nations, 10 vols. 1975. lib. bdg. 2000.00 (ISBN 0-8490-1322-4). Gordon Pr.
Butler, R., ed. Rodin in Perspective. 1980. 12.95 (ISBN 0-13-782326-6, Spec); pap. 5.95 (ISBN 0-13-782318-5, Spec). P-H.
Butler, R. A. The Art of the Possible. (Illus.). 288p. 1983. Repr. of 1971 ed. 21.00 (ISBN 0-241-10896-9, Pub. by Hamish Hamilton England). David & Charles.
Butler, R. R., jt. auth. see Higgins, P. C.
Butler, Ralph. Out of the Silence. 142p. 1978. pap. 5.00 (ISBN 0-7050-0059-1). Attic Pr.
Butler, Richard. Mind of Santayana. LC 68-21326. 1968. Repr. of 1955 ed. lib. bdg. 15.00 (ISBN 0-8371-0334-7, BUMS). Greenwood.
Butler, Richard O. Religious Vocation: An Unnecessary Mystery. LC 78-14365. 1979. Repr. of 1961 ed. lib. bdg. 18.75x (ISBN 0-313-21018-7, BURV). Greenwood.
Butler, Rita B., ed. Ascension Parish, Louisiana: 1890 Census. LC 83-62962. 260p. (Orig.). 1984. pap. 25.00 (ISBN 0-88127-027-X). Oracle Pr LA.
Butler, Robert A. Family Records of Revolutionary War Pension Applicants, Volume 1: Butler. LC 83-82119. vi, 102p. (Orig.). 1983. pap. 11.95x (ISBN 0-914769-00-6). Heritage Tech Serv.
--Handbook of Practical Writing. (Orig.). 1978. pap. text ed. 9.60 (ISBN 0-07-009341-5). McGraw.
Butler, Robert B. Architectural & Engineering Calculations Manual. (Illus.). 384p. 1983. 21.95 (ISBN 0-07-009363-6). McGraw.
--The Ecological House. 256p. 1981. pap. 9.95 (ISBN 0-87100-175-6, 2175). Morgan.
Butler, Robert M., ed. see Ovens, E. Albert.
Butler, Robert N. Why Survive? Being Old in America. LC 73-4066. 512p. 1975. 19.95i (ISBN 0-06-010591-7, HarpT); pap. 9.57i (ISBN 0-06-090872-6, CN-872, HarpT). Har-Row.
--Why Survive? Being Old in America. 510p. 1985. pap. 9.95i (ISBN 0-06-131997-X, TB 1997, Torch). Har-Row.
Butler, Robert N. & Gleason, Herbert P. Productive Aging. 1985. text ed. 25.95 (ISBN 0-8261-4810-7). Springer Pub.
Butler, Robert N. & Lewis, Myrna I. Aging & Mental Health. LC 82-22404. (Mosby Medical Library). (Illus.). 383p. 1983. pap. 8.95 (ISBN 0-452-25405-1, 1002-8). Mosby.
--Love & Sex After Sixty: A Guide for Men & Women in Their Later Years. 1977. pap. 2.95i (ISBN 0-06-080423-8, P423, PL). Har-Row.
--Sex After Sixty: A Guide for Men & Women for Their Later Years. LC 74-15815. (Illus.). 176p. 1976. 9.95i (ISBN 0-06-010593-3, HarpT). Har-Row.
Butler, Robert O. The Alleys of Eden. LC 81-82842. 1981. 12.95 (ISBN 0-8180-0631-5). Horizon.
--The Alleys of Eden. 256p. 1983. pap. 2.95 (ISBN 0-345-30774-7). Ballantine.
--Countrymen of Bones. LC 83-12822. 224p. 1983. 13.95 (ISBN 0-8180-0639-0). Horizon.
--Countrymen of Bones. 256p. 1985. pap. 2.95 (ISBN 0-345-32118-9). Ballantine.

--On Distant Ground. LC 84-48517. 256p. 1985. 14.45 (ISBN 0-394-54040-9). Knopf.
--On Distant Ground. 272p. 1986. pap. 3.95 (ISBN 0-345-32596-6). Ballantine.
--Sun Dogs. LC 82-48104. 250p. 1982. 12.95 (ISBN 0-8180-0636-6). Horizon.
--Sun Dogs. 240p. 1985. pap. 2.95 (ISBN 0-345-32125-1). Ballantine.
Butler, Robert W., ed. see Vaughan, Bill.
Butler, Rohan. Choiseul: Vol. 1; Father & Son, 1719-1754. (Illus.). 1981. 130.00x (ISBN 0-19-822509-1). Oxford U Pr.
Butler, Rohan D. The Roots of National Socialism 1783-1933. LC 78-63657. (Studies in Fascism: Ideology & Practice). 312p. Repr. of 1941 ed. 34.50 (ISBN 0-404-16917-1). AMS Pr.
Butler, Ron. Best of the West: The Texas Monthly Guidebook. Rodriquez, Barbara, ed. 224p. 1983. 9.95 (ISBN 0-932012-54-X). Texas Month Pr.
Butler, Ronnie. Balzac & the French Revolution. LC 83-9926. 280p. 1983. 28.50x (ISBN 0-389-20406-4, 07291). B&N Imports.
Butler, Roy F. The Meaning of Agapao & Phileo in the Greek New Testament. 1977. 6.50x (ISBN 0-87291-089-X). Coronado Pr.
Butler, Ruth. Western Sculpture: Definitions of Man. LC 79-1912. (Illus.). 1979. pap. 10.95xi (ISBN 0-06-430098-6, IN-98, HarpT). Har-Row.
Butler, Ruth L., ed. Guide to the Hispanic American Historical Review, 1918-1945. 14.00 (ISBN 0-527-36700-1). Kraus Repr.
Butler, Ruth M. Well-Being. (Illus.). 512p. Date not set. text ed. price not set (ISBN 0-86542-002-5). Blackwell Sci.
Butler, S. T., jt. auth. see Messel, H.
Butler, S. T., jt. ed. see Messel, H.
Butler, Samuel. Alps & Sanctuaries of Piedmont & the Canton Ticino. 376p. 1981. Repr. of 1882 ed. lib. bdg. 75.00 (ISBN 0-89984-067-1). Century Bookbindery.
--Butleriana. Bartholomen, A. T., ed. 172p. 1980. Repr. of 1932 ed. lib. bdg. 20.00 (ISBN 0-8492-3752-1). R West.
--Characters & Passages from Notebooks. 489p. Repr. of 1908 ed. 69.00 (ISBN 0-403-08911-5). Somerset Pub.
--Erewhon. (Classics Ser). (gr. 11 up). pap. 1.25 (ISBN 0-8049-0130-9, CL-130). Airmont.
--Erewhon. (English Library). 272p. 1970. pap. 3.95 (ISBN 0-14-043057-1). Penguin.
--Erewhon & Erewhon Revisited. 1979. Repr. of 1932 ed. 10.95 (Evman). Biblio Dist.
--Essays on Life, Art & Science. Streatfeild, R. A., ed. LC 77-95333. 1970. Repr. of 1908 ed. 26.00 (ISBN 0-8046-1345-1, Pub. by Kennikat). Assoc Faculty Pr.
--Essays on Life, Art & Science. 1908. 11.50 (ISBN 0-8274-2308-X). R West.
--Evolution, Old & New. 59.95 (ISBN 0-8490-0145-5). Gordon Pr.
--The Fair Haven: A Work in Defence of the Miraculous Element in Our Lord's Ministry Upon Earth. Wolff, Robert L., ed. LC 75-1503. (Victorian Fiction Ser.). 1975. Repr. of 1873 ed. lib. bdg. 73.00 (ISBN 0-8240-1578-9). Garland Pub.
--Further Extracts from the Note-Books of Samuel Butler. Bartholomew, A. T., ed. LC 75-136910. (Illus.). 414p. Repr. of 1934 ed. lib. bdg. 24.75x (ISBN 0-8371-5357-3, BUNB). Greenwood.
--Hudibras. Wilders, John, ed. (Oxford English Texts Ser.). (Illus.). 1967. 63.00x (ISBN 0-19-811844-9). Oxford U Pr.
--Humour of Homer, & Other Essays. facs. ed. Streatfield, R. A., ed. LC 67-30178. (Essay Index Reprint Ser). 1914. 18.00 (ISBN 0-8369-0268-8). Ayer Co Pubs.
--The Humour of Homer & Other Essays. Streatfeild, R. A., ed. 1978. Repr. of 1913 ed. lib. bdg. 20.00 (ISBN 0-8492-3547-2). R West.
--The Humour of Homer & Other Essays. Streatfeild, R. A., ed. 313p. 1982. Repr. of 1913 ed. lib. bdg. 25.00 (ISBN 0-8495-0492-9). Arden Lib.
--Prose Observations. De Quehen, Hugh, ed. (English Texts Ser.). (Illus.). 1979. text ed. 74.00x (ISBN 0-19-812728-6). Oxford U Pr.
--Satires & Miscellaneous Poetry & Prose. Lamar, Rene, ed. LC 76-29457. (BCL Ser. II). Repr. of 1928 ed. 33.50 (ISBN 0-404-15301-1). AMS Pr.
--Way of All Flesh. (Classics Ser). (gr. 11 up). pap. 2.50 (ISBN 0-8049-0090-6, CL-90). Airmont.
--The Way of All Flesh. Wolff, Robert L., ed. LC 75-1540. (Victorian Fiction Ser.). 1975. Repr. of 1903 ed. lib. bdg. 73.00 (ISBN 0-8240-1611-4). Garland Pub.
--Way of All Flesh. pap. 3.50 (ISBN 0-451-51867-5, CE1867, Sig Classics). NAL.
--The Way of All Flesh. Cochrane, James, ed. (English Library Ser.). 1966. pap. 4.95 (ISBN 0-14-043012-1). Penguin.
--The Way of All Flesh. 345p. 1983. Repr. lib. bdg. 317.95x (ISBN 0-89966-310-9). Buccaneer Bks.
--Works of Samuel Butler, 20 Vols. Jones, Henry F. & Bartholomew, A. T., eds. LC 77-181920. (BCL Ser. II). Repr. of 1926 ed. Set. 800.00 (ISBN 0-404-01320-1); 40.00 ea. AMS Pr.
Butler, Samuel, ed. Shakespeare's Sonnets Reconsidered. LC 76-136416. Repr. of 1899 ed. 15.00 (ISBN 0-404-01249-3). AMS Pr.
Butler, Sandra. Conspiracy of Silence: The Trauma of Incest. LC 78-1975. 288p. 1978. pap. 10.00 (ISBN 0-912078-65-0). Volcano Pr.
--Conspiracy of Silence: The Trauma of Incest. 208p. 1978. postpaid 11.50 (ISBN 0-318-17075-2). Kemper Nat Ctr.
Butler, Sharon, jt. auth. see Hieatt, Constance B.
Butler, Sherman. Hollywood Sherman. 1984. 6.95 (ISBN 0-8062-2353-7). Carlton.
Butler, Smedley. War Is a Racket. 59.95 (ISBN 0-87700-153-7). Revisionist Pr.
Butler, Stanley. Guide to the Best in Contemporary Piano Music: An Annotated List of Graded Solo Piano Music Published Since 1950, 2 vols. Incl. Vol. 1. Levels 1-5. 16.00 (ISBN 0-8108-0628-2); Vol. 2. Levels 6-8. 16.00 (ISBN 0-8108-0669-X). LC 73-5693. 368p. 1973. Set. Set 22.50 (ISBN 0-686-86727-0). Scarecrow.
Butler, Steven. Agricultural Mechanization in China: The Administrative Impact. (Occasional Papers of the East Asian Institute). 58p. 1978. pap. 3.00 (ISBN 0-317-17101-1). Columbia U E Asian Inst.
Butler, Stuart. Enterprise Zones. LC 80-54400. (Illus.). 192p. 1981. 12.95x (ISBN 0-87663-350-5); pap. text ed. 7.95 (ISBN 0-87663-579-6). Universe.
Butler, Stuart M. Enterprise Zones: Greenlining the Inner Cities. 183p. 1981. 12.95 (ISBN 0-87663-350-5). Heritage Found.
--Privatizing Federal Spending: A Strategy to Eliminate the Deficit. LC 84-8805. 176p. 1985. 14.95 (ISBN 0-87663-454-4). Universe.
Butler, Susan. A Trip to the Jungle. (Illus.). 40p. (Orig.). (ps-2). 1978. pap. 3.95 (ISBN 0-931416-00-0). Open Books.
Butler, T. G., jt. ed. see Kana, D. D.
Butler, Thomas. Monumenta Serbocroatica: A Bilingual Anthology of Serbian & Croatian Texts from the 12th to the 19th Century. (Joint Committee on Eastern Europe Ser.: No. 6). 1979. 15.00 (ISBN 0-930042-32-8). Mich Slavic Pubns.
Butler, Thomas A., jt. ed. see Knapp, Fern F.
Butler, Thomas C. Plague & Other Yersinia Infections. (Current Topics in Infectious Disease). 232p. 1983. 22.50x (ISBN 0-306-41414-7, Plenum Pr). Plenum Pub.
Butler, Thomas W., Jr., jt. auth. see Bacon, Frank R., Jr.
Butler, Tom. Mental Health, Social Policy & the Law. 224p. 1985. 19.00x (ISBN 0-333-37301-4, Pub. by Salem Acad). Merrimack Pub Cir.
Butler, Tommie & Smith, Edgar R. Tahoe Times-The Receptionist: Simulation. (gr. 9-12). 1985. 8.95 (ISBN 0-538-25820-9, Y82). SW Pub.
Butler, Trent, jt. auth. see Butler, Mary.
Butler, Trent C. Layman's Bible Book Commentary: Isaiah, Vol. 10. LC 80-68890. 1983. 5.75 (ISBN 0-8054-1180-1). Broadman.
Butler, Vera M. Education As Revealed by New England Newspapers Prior to 1850. LC 73-89160. (American Education: Its Men, Institutions & Ideas, Ser. 1). 1969. Repr. of 1935 ed. 21.00 (ISBN 0-405-01397-3). Ayer Co Pubs.
Butler, W. E. Apprenticed to Magic. 112p. 1962. pap. 6.95 (ISBN 0-85030-284-6, Pub. by Aquarian Pr England). Weiser.
--Collected Legislation of the U. S. S. R. Incl. Union Republic Legislation, 1 binder; Constitutions, 2 binders; U. S. S. R, 7 binders. LC 78-24391. 1980. Set. 700.00 (ISBN 0-379-20450-9). Oceana.
--Down Among the Sugar Cane. (Illus.). 266p. 1980. 24.95 (ISBN 0-89716-083-5). Superior Pub.
--How to Develop Clairvoyance. (Paths to Inner Power Ser). 1973. pap. 2.50 (ISBN 0-87728-092-4). Weiser.
--How to Develop Psychometry. (Paths to Inner Power Ser.). 1971. pap. 2.50 (ISBN 0-87728-088-6). Weiser.
--How to Read the Aura. (Paths to Inner Power Ser.). 96p. 1971. pap. 2.50 (ISBN 0-87728-090-8). Weiser.
--International Law in Comparative Perspective. 324p. 1980. 42.50x (ISBN 90-286-0089-2). Sijthoff & Noordhoff.
--Introduction to Telepathy. (Paths to Inner Power Ser.). 64p. (Orig.). pap. 2.50 (ISBN 0-85030-344-3, Pub. by Thorsons Pub). Weiser.
--Magic & the Qabbalah. 1972. pap. 6.95 (ISBN 0-85030-155-6). Weiser.
--Magic: Its Ritual Power & Purpose. 1972. pap. 5.95 (ISBN 0-85030-149-1). Weiser.
--Magician-His Training & Work. pap. 3.00 (ISBN 0-87980-212-X). Wilshire.
--The Soviet Legal System: Selected Contemporary Legislation & Documents. LC 78-2419. (Parker School Studies in Foreign & Comparative Law). 733p. 1978. 45.00 (ISBN 0-379-00791-6). Oceana.
Butler, W. E., ed. A Sourcebook on Socialist International Organizations. 1168p. 1980. 125.00x (ISBN 90-286-0798-6). Sijthoff & Noordhoff.
Butler, W. H., jt. ed. see Newberne, Paul M.
Butler, William. Butterfly Revolution. LC 67-10948. 1979. pap. 1.95 (ISBN 0-345-28686-3). Ballantine.
--How to Read the Aura, Practice Psychometry, Telepathy, & Clairvoyance. 335p. 3.50 (ISBN 0-446-82751-7). Inner Tradit.
--How to Read the Aura, Practice Psychometry, Telepathy & Clairvoyance. (Warner Destiny Book). (Orig.). 1978. pap. 3.95 (ISBN 0-446-32543-0). Warner Bks.
Butler, William see Marric, J. J., pseud.
Butler, William A. Mrs. Limber's Raffle, or a Church Fair & Its Victims. facs. ed. LC 71-137724. (American Fiction Reprint Ser). 1876. 14.00 (ISBN 0-8369-7023-3). Ayer Co Pubs.
Butler, William E. Bibliography on the Soviet Union & the Development of the Law of the Sea. 1985. loose leaf 75.00 (ISBN 0-317-20381-9). Oceana.
--The Mongolian Legal System. 1982. lib. bdg. 195.00 (ISBN 90-247-2685-9, Pub. by Martinus Nijhoff Netherlands). Kluwer Academic.
--Oil & Gas Law: The U. S. S. R, Release 2. 1984. looseleaf 85.00 (ISBN 0-379-10252-8). Oceana.
--U. S. S. R. Eastern Europe & the Development of the Law of the Sea. 1983. loose-leaf 100.00 (ISBN 0-317-30345-7). Oceana.
Butler, William E. see Simmonds, Kenneth R.
Butler, William E., ed. Anglo-Polish Legal Essays. LC 81-16259. 272p. 1982. lib. bdg. 30.00 (ISBN 0-941320-00-6). Transnatl Pubs.
--Basic Documents on the Soviet Legal System. LC 83-43157. (Studies on Socialist Legal Systems). 416p. 1984. lib. bdg. 35.00 (ISBN 0-379-20833-4). Oceana.
--International Commercial Arbitration: Soviet Commercial & Maritime Arbitration. LC 80-10606. 1980. looseleaf 100.00 (ISBN 0-379-10152-1). Oceana.
--Law of the Sea & International Shipping: Anglo-Soviet Post UNCLOS Perspectives. 1985. lib. bdg. 45.00 (ISBN 0-317-20384-3). Oceana.
--The Legal System of the Chinese-Soviet Republic 1931-1934. LC 83-460. (Transnational Studies in East-West Relations). 224p. 1983. lib. bdg. 35.00 (ISBN 0-941320-07-3). Transnatl Pubs.
--The Legal System of the Chinese Soviet Republic, 1931-34. 224p. 1983. 35.00 (ISBN 0-941320-07-3). Transnatl Pubs.
Butler, William E. & Kudriavtsev, W. N., eds. Comparative Law & Legal System: Historical & Socio-Legal Perspectives. 1985. lib. bdg. 20.00 (ISBN 0-379-20782-6). Oceana.
Butler, William E., tr. see Kuznetov, Anatolii.
Butler, William E., tr. see Kuznetsov, Anatoli.
Butler, William E., tr. see Kuznetsov, Anatolii.
Butler, William E., tr. see Tunkin, G. I.
Butler, William F. Confiscation in Irish History. LC 76-102594. (Irish Culture & History Ser). 1970. Repr. of 1917 ed. 25.00x (ISBN 0-8046-0771-0, Pub. by Kennikat). Assoc Faculty Pr.
--Lombard Communes. LC 68-25226. (World History Ser., No. 48). 1969. lib. bdg. 62.95x (ISBN 0-8383-0923-2). Haskell.
--Lombard Communes: A History of the Republics of North Italy. LC 69-13847. Repr. of 1906 ed. lib. bdg. 22.75x (ISBN 0-8371-2753-X, BULC). Greenwood.
--The Wild Northland, Being the Story of a Winter Journey, with Dogs, Across Northern North America. LC 72-2824. (American Explorers Ser.). Repr. of 1922 ed. 42.00 (ISBN 0-404-54904-7). AMS Pr.
Butler, William V. The Young Detective's Handbook. (Illus.). (gr. 3-7). 1981. 10.45i (ISBN 0-316-11888-5, Pub. by Atlantic Monthly Pr). Little.
Butler, William V. see Marric, J. J., pseud.
Butler-Bowdon, W. The Book of Margery Kempe: A Modern Version. 1978. Repr. of 1936 ed. lib. bdg. 25.00 (ISBN 0-8482-3353-0). Norwood Edns.
Butlin, A. G. & D'Oyly-Watkins, C., eds. Gas Chromatography Abstracts: Cumulative Indexes, 1958-1963, Inclusive. LC 63-22896. pap. 78.80 (ISBN 0-317-29011-8). Bks Demand UMI.
Butlin, J., jt. auth. see Lidgren, K.
Butlin, J. A., ed. The Economics of Environmental & Natural Resources Policy. 200p. 1981. lib. bdg. 33.00x (ISBN 0-86531-190-0); pap. 14.50x (ISBN 0-86531-196-X). Westview.
Butlin, L., et al, eds. Numerically Controlled or Special Purpose Machining I. (E.I.T.B. Training Manuals Ser.). (Illus.). 271p. 1984. pap. 49.95x spiral bdg. (ISBN 0-85083-542-9). Intl Ideas.
Butlin, Martin. The Later Works of JMW Turner. (Illus.). 32p. pap. 6.95 (ISBN 0-905005-96-1, Pub. by Salem Hse Ltd). Merrimack Pub Cir.
--The Paintings & Drawings of William Blake, 2 vols. LC 80-6221. (Paul Mellon Centre for Studies in British Art). (Illus.). 1408p. 1981. 300.00x (ISBN 0-300-02550-5). Yale U Pr.
--Turner at the Tate. (Illus.). 112p. 1985. 24.95 (ISBN 0-905005-74-0, Pub. by Salem Hse Ltd); pap. 16.95 (ISBN 0-905005-66-X). Merrimack Pub Cir.
--William Blake. (Tate Gallery: Little Art Book Ser.). (Illus.). 1977. 21.95 (ISBN 0-8120-5299-4); pap. 15.95 full size ed. o.p. (ISBN 0-8120-2038-3). Barron.
--William Blake. (Illus.). 80p. 1985. pap. 6.95 (ISBN 0-900874-23-6, Pub. by Salem Hse Ltd). Merrimack Pub Cir.
Butlin, Martin & Joll, Evelyn. The Paintings of J. M. W. Turner. rev. ed. LC 84-40182. (Studies in British Art). (Illus.). 944p. 1984. 195.00x (ISBN 0-300-03276-5). Yale U Pr.
Butlin, N. G. Our Original Aggression: Aboriginal Populations of Southeastern Australia, 1788-1850. 180p. 1984. pap. text ed. 14.95x (ISBN 0-86861-223-5). Allen Unwin.
Butlin, N G., et al. Government & Capitalism: Public & Private Choice in Twentieth Century Austraia. 376p. 1982. text ed. 37.50x (ISBN 0-86861-187-5); pap. text ed. 18.50 (ISBN 0-86861-195-6). Allen Unwin.
Butlin, R. A., ed. The Development of the Irish Town. (Illus.). 144p. 1977. 17.50x (ISBN 0-87471-979-8). Rowman.
Butlin, R. A., jt. ed. see Baker, Alan R.
Butlin, R. A., jt. ed. see Dodgshon, R. A.
Butlin, R. A., jt. ed. see Fox, H. S. A.
Butlin, Ron. The Exquisite Instrument: Imitations from the Chinese. 32p. 1982. 30.00x (ISBN 0-907540-13-9, Pub. by Salamander Pr Scotland); pap. 20.00x (ISBN 0-907540-14-7). State Mutual Bk.
Butlin, S. Foundations of the Australian Monetary System, 1788-1851. 1969. 27.00x (ISBN 0-424-05830-8, Pub. by Sydney U Pr). Intl Spec Bk.
Butman, Alexander M. Responding to the Mass Casualty Incident: A Guide for EMS Personnel. 1982. 8.95 (ISBN 0-940432-02-1, Pub. by Emergency Training); 15 or more copies 6.95 ea. Educ Direction.
Butman, Alexander M., et al. Advanced Skills in Emergency Care: A Text for the Intermediate EMT. 1982. 12.95 (ISBN 0-940432-01-3, Pub. by Emergency Training); 15 or more copies 10.95 ea. Educ Direction.
Butnarescu, G. F., et al. Perinatal Nursing: Reproductive Risk, Vol. 2. 553p. 1980. 38.50 (ISBN 0-471-04445-8). Wiley.
Butnarescu, Glenda F. Perinatal Nursing: Reproductive Health, Vol. 1. LC 77-25924. 296p. 1978. 38.50 (ISBN 0-471-04361-3, Pub. by Wiley Med). Wiley.
Butnarescu, Glenda F. & Tillotson, Delight M. Maternity Nursing: Theory to Practice. LC 82-17614. 798p. 1983. 32.00 (ISBN 0-471-07793-3, Pub. by Wiley Med); write for info tm (ISBN 0-471-87070-6). Wiley.
Butner, Alfred N. Surgery Specialty Board Review. 5th ed. 1973. spiral bdg. 21.50 (ISBN 0-87488-302-4). Med Exam.
--Surgery: Specialty Board Review. 6th ed. 1984. pap. text ed. write for info (ISBN 0-87488-200-1). Med Exam.
Butor, Michel. La Banlieue de Paris a l'Aurore, Mouvement Brownien. (Coll. Huit). 18.50 (ISBN 0-685-37243-X). French & Eur.
--Bryen en Temps Conjuges. 1975. 25.00 (ISBN 0-686-51940-X). French & Eur.
--Carte Commentee. 1974. 59.95 (ISBN 0-686-51941-8). French & Eur.
--A Change of Heart. 260p. 1984. pap. cancelled (ISBN 0-941324-04-4). Van Vactor & Goodheart.
--Une Chanson Pour Don Juan. 1973. 750.00 (ISBN 0-686-51939-6). French & Eur.
--Degres. (Coll. Soleil). 1960. 9.95 (ISBN 0-685-11130-X). French & Eur.
--Description de San Marco. pap. 7.50 (ISBN 0-685-37244-8). French & Eur.
--Dialogue avec Trente Trais Variations de Ludwig van Beethoven sur une Valse de Diabelli. (Coll. le Chemin). pap. 8.95 (ISBN 0-685-37245-6). French & Eur.
--Emploi du Temps. 1956. pap. 15.50 (ISBN 0-685-11158-X). French & Eur.
--Entretiens avec Georges Charbonnier. pap. 8.95 (ISBN 0-685-37246-4). French & Eur.
--Essais sur le Roman. 1969. pap. 3.95 (ISBN 0-686-50135-7). French & Eur.
--Essais sur les Essais. pap. 4.95 (ISBN 0-685-37247-2). French & Eur.
--Essais sur les Modernes. (Coll. Idees). pap. 3.95 (ISBN 0-685-37248-0). French & Eur.
--Le Genie du Lieu. pap. 8.95 (ISBN 0-685-37249-9). French & Eur.
--Le Genie du Lieu, II. 17.50 (ISBN 0-685-37250-2). French & Eur.
--Herold. pap. 7.95 (ISBN 0-685-37251-0). French & Eur.
--Une Histoire Extraordinaire. pap. 6.95 (ISBN 0-685-37252-9). French & Eur.
--Intervalle. 1973. pap. 8.95 (ISBN 0-686-51942-6). French & Eur.
--Letters from the Antipodes. Spencer, Michael, tr. from Fr. xii, 177p. 1981. lib. bdg. 21.95x (ISBN 0-8214-0659-0, 82-84291). Ohio U Pr.
--Matiere des Reves. 1975. pap. 15.95 (ISBN 0-686-51943-4). French & Eur.
--Mobile. 16.50 (ISBN 0-685-37254-5). French & Eur.
--Modification. 1957. pap. 5.95 (ISBN 0-685-11400-7). French & Eur.
--Les Mots Dans le Peinture. (Coll. Les Sentiers de la Creation). 39.50 (ISBN 0-685-37255-3). French & Eur.
--L' Oeil Ces Sangasses. 1972. 75.00 (ISBN 0-686-50136-5). French & Eur.
--Passage de Milan. 1954. pap. 14.95 (ISBN 0-686-51944-2). French & Eur.
--Passing Time. Stewart, Jean, tr. from Fr. 1980. pap. 4.95 (ISBN 0-7145-0436-6). Riverrun NY.
--Les Petits Miroirs. 1972. pap. 7.95 (ISBN 0-686-51945-0). French & Eur.
--Portraits de L'artiste en Jeune Singe. pap. 7.95 (ISBN 0-685-37256-1). French & Eur.
--Repertoire: Essais Critiques, 4 vols. 1960-64. Set. pap. 65.00 (ISBN 0-685-11526-7). French & Eur.

--Reseau Aerien. pap. 5.95 (ISBN 0-685-37257-X). French & Eur.
--La Rose Des Vents: 32 Rhumbs Pour Charles Fournier. (Coll. Le Chemin). pap. 6.95 (ISBN 0-685-37258-8). French & Eur.
--Les Sept Femmes de Gilbert le Mauvais. (Coll. Scholies). 10.95 (ISBN 0-685-37260-X). French & Eur.
--Six-Million Huit-Cent Dix Mille Litres D'eau Par Seconde. 12.50 (ISBN 0-685-37259-6). French & Eur.
--Travaux d'Approche. (Coll. Poesie). 3.95 (ISBN 0-685-37261-8). French & Eur.
Butow, R. J. C. Japan's Decision to Surrender. 1954. 20.00x (ISBN 0-8047-0460-0); pap. 6.95o.p (ISBN 0-8047-0461-9, SP55). Stanford U Pr.
--The John Doe Associates: Backdoor Diplomacy for Peace, 1941. LC 73-89857. (Illus.). xii, 480p. 1974. 32.50x (ISBN 0-8047-0852-5). Stanford U Pr.
--Tojo & the Coming of the War. (Illus.). 1961. 35.00x (ISBN 0-8047-0690-5); pap. 10.95x (ISBN 0-8047-0691-3). Stanford U Pr.
Butrica, James L. The Manuscript Tradition of Propertius. (Phoenix Supplementary Ser.: Vol. 17). 384p. 1984. text ed. 47.50x (ISBN 0-8020-5581-8). U of Toronto Pr.
Butrick, Lyn M. If This... & That.. Then What, 3 vols. Cooper, William R., ed. LC 83-50783. (My Read & Think Ser.). (Illus.). 27p. (gr. 1-3). 1983. Set. pap. 7.00 (ISBN 0-914127-06-3). Vol. 1 (ISBN 0-914127-04-7). Univ Class.
--Logic for Space Age Kids, Vol. II. Cooper, William H., ed. LC 84-50892. (My Read & Think Ser.). (Illus.). 32p. (gr. 3-6). 1984. pap. 7.95 (ISBN 0-914127-16-0). Univ Class.
Butrick, Richard. Deduction & Analysis. rev. ed. LC 80-6177. 121p. 1981. lib. bdg. 19.00 (ISBN 0-8191-1410-3); pap. text ed. 8.00 (ISBN 0-8191-1411-1). U Pr of Amer.
Butrick, Richard, Jr. Carnap on Meaning & Analyticity. LC 78-106469. (Janua Linguarum, Ser. Minor: No. 85). (Orig.). 1970. pap. text ed. 4.80x (ISBN 0-686-22409-4). Mouton.
Butrym, Zofia. Medical Social Work in Action. 128p. 1968. pap. text ed. 5.00x (ISBN 0-686-70850-4, Pub. by Bedford England). Brookfield Pub Co.
Butrym, Zofia & Horder, John. Health, Doctors, & Social Workers. (Library of Social Work). 192p. (Orig.). 1983. pap. 10.95x (ISBN 0-7100-9403-5). Routledge & Kegan.
Butsch, Albert F. Handbook of Renaissance Ornament: 1290 Designs from Decorated Books. Werner, Alfred, ed. LC 68-13685. Orig. Title: Die Bucherornamentik Der Renaissance. (Illus.). 1970. pap. 9.95 (ISBN 0-486-21998-4). Dover.
Butsch, Charlotte. American Labor Movement, Student Syllabus. 30p. 1976. pap. text ed. 4.25 (ISBN 0-89420-078-X, 330011); cassette recording 24.60 (ISBN 0-89420-206-5, 330000). Natl Book.
--Electronic Calculator: Student Guide. 1971. pap. text ed. 3.95 (ISBN 0-89420-055-0, 126877); cassette recordings 65.50 (ISBN 0-89420-143-3, 156780). Natl Book.
--The Printing Calculator: Student Guide. 2nd ed. 1971. pap. text ed. 3.85 (ISBN 0-89420-022-4, 126855); cassette recordings 50.20 (ISBN 0-89420-174-3, 156760). Natl Book.
Butsch, Charlotte, jt. auth. see Salser, Carl.
Butsch, Charlotte, ed. see Salser, Carl W., et al.
Butsch, Charlotte A., ed. see Salser, Carl W. & Yerian, C. Theo.
Butscher, Edward. Amagansett Cycle. LC 79-2525. (Poetry Ser.). (Illus., Orig.). 1979. 8.95x (ISBN 0-89304-033-9, CCC121); pap. 3.95x (ISBN 0-89304-034-7); signed ltd. ed. 15.00x (ISBN 0-89304-035-5). Cross Cult.
--Sylvia Plath: Method & Madness. 443p. (gr. 11 up). 1977. pap. 3.50 (ISBN 0-671-41518-2). WSP.
--Unfinished Sequence. Barkan, Stanley H., ed. (Cross-Cultural Review Chapbook 6: American Poetry 3). 20p. 1980. pap. 2.25 (ISBN 0-89304-805-4). Cross Cult.
Butscher, Edward, ed. Faces on the Barroom Floor. 202p. (Orig.). Date not set. 12.95 (ISBN 0-317-13522-8); pap. 6.95 (ISBN 0-317-13523-6). Cornerstone Pr.
--Sylvia Plath, The Woman & the Work. 256p. 1985. pap. 6.95 (ISBN 0-396-08732-9). Dodd.
Butson, Thomas G. Gorbachev: A Biography. LC 85-40232. 1985. 14.95 (ISBN 0-8128-3035-0). Stein & Day.
--The Tsar's Lieutenant: The Soviet Marshall. LC 84-47410. 224p. 1984. 27.95 (ISBN 0-03-070683-1). Praeger.
Butt. Practical Immunoassay. (Clinical & Biochemical Analysis Ser.). 360p. 1984. 55.00 (ISBN 0-8247-7094-3). Dekker.
Butt, Archibald W. Taft & Roosevelt, 2 Vols. LC 71-137968. (American History & Culture in the Twentieth Century Ser). 1971. Repr. of 1930 ed. Set. 65.00x (ISBN 0-8046-1425-3, Pub by Kennikat). Assoc Faculty Pr.
Butt, Arthur J. Etiologic Factors in Renal Lithiasis. (Illus.). 416p. 1956. photocopy ed. 39.75x (ISBN 0-398-04374-4). C C Thomas.
Butt, C. R. & Smith, R. E., eds. Conceptual Models in Exploration Geochemistry: Australia. (Developments in Economic Geology: Vol. 13). 276p. 1980. 68.00 (ISBN 0-444-41902-0). Elsevier.
Butt, Dorcas S. Psychology of Sport. LC 82-12661. 208p. 1982. Repr. of 1976 ed. lib. bdg. 14.95 (ISBN 0-89874-535-7). Krieger.
Butt, Herbert W. Tests of Eternal Life: Studies in First John. pap. 0.50 (ISBN 0-685-00745-6). Reiner.
Butt, J. Reaction Kinetic & Reactor Design. 1980. 41.95 (ISBN 0-13-753335-7). P-H.
Butt, J. & Clarke, I. F., eds. The Victorians & Social Protest: A Symposium. 243p. 1973. 19.50 (ISBN 0-208-01329-6, Archon). Shoe String.
Butt, J. E. see Gibson, S. & Holdsworth, William.
Butt, Jamshed. Shikar. 1967. pap. 2.35 (ISBN 0-88253-128-X). Ind-US Inc.
Butt, John. Industrial Archaeology of Scotland. LC 67-109342. (Illus.). 1967. 24.95x (ISBN 0-678-05749-4). Kelley.
--The Mid-Eighteenth Century, Vol. 8. Carnall, Geoffrey, ed. (Oxford History of English Literature Ser.). 1979. text ed. 49.95x (ISBN 0-19-812212-8). Oxford U Pr.
--Pope's Poetical Manuscripts. LC 74-3370. 1954. lib. bdg. 8.00 (ISBN 0-8414-3113-2). Folcroft.
--Writers & Politics in Modern Spain. LC 78-18704. (Writers & Politics Ser.). 75p. 1978. 14.50x (ISBN 0-8419-0432-X); pap. text ed. 9.50x (ISBN 0-8419-0415-4). Holmes & Meier.
Butt, John & Tillotson, Kathleen. Dickens at Work. (Library Reprints Ser.). 1982. 39.95x (ISBN 0-416-34030-X, NO. 3704). Methuen Inc.
Butt, John, ed. see Pope, Alexander.
Butt, John, tr. see De Voltaire, Francois M.
Butt, John, tr. see Voltaire, Francois.
Butt, John, et al. Industrial History in Pictures: Scotland. LC 68-23824. 1968. 17.95x (ISBN 0-678-05585-8). Kelley.
Butt, John E. The Augustan Age. LC 75-36092. 152p. 1976. Repr. of 1950 ed. lib. bdg. 18.75 (ISBN 0-8371-8621-8, BUAAG). Greenwood.
--Pope's Taste in Shakespeare. LC 75-17694. 1975. Repr. of 1936 ed. lib. bdg. 8.50 (ISBN 0-8414-3226-0). Folcroft.
Butt, John E., jt. auth. see Dyson, Henry V.
Butt, L. T. & Wright, D. C. Use of Polymers in Chemical Plant Construction. (Illus.). vii, 148p. 1981. 49.95x (ISBN 0-85334-914-2, Pub. by Elsevier Applied Sci England). Elsevier.
--Use of Polymers in Chemical Plant Construction. (Illus.). 156p. 1981. text ed. 28.00 (ISBN 0-85334-914-2, Pub. by Applied Sci England). J K Burgess.
Butt, Margaret G., ed. see Pierce, Barbara H.
Butt, Martha H. Anti-Fanaticism, a Tale of the South. LC 78-39571. Repr. of 1853 ed. 19.00 (ISBN 0-404-04575-8). AMS Pr.
Butt, W. R. Hormone Chemistry, 2 vols. 2nd ed. Incl. Vol. 1. Protein, Polypeptides & Peptide Hormones. 272p. 1975. 79.95x (ISBN 0-470-12770-8); Vol. 2. Steroids, Thyroid Hormones, Biogenic Amines & Prostaglandins. 272p. 1977. 69.95x (ISBN 0-470-98961-0). LC 75-16158. Halsted Pr.
Butt, William, jt. ed. see Strode, William.
Buttaci, Sal S. & Gerstle, Susan L., eds. Dreams of the Heroic Muse. 150p. 1982. 13.95 (ISBN 0-917398-11-4). New Worlds.
--Treasures of the Precious Moments. LC 85-61728. 140p. 1985. 18.98 (ISBN 0-917398-14-9). New Worlds.
Buttaci, Sal St. John & Gerstle, Susan L. Journeys of the Poet-Prophet. 150p. 1983. 15.95 (ISBN 0-917398-12-2). New Worlds.
Buttaci, Sal St. John see St. John Buttaci, Sal & Gerstle, Susan L.
Buttaci, Salvatore S. & Gerstle, Susan L., eds. Reflections of the Inward Silence. LC 76-19240. 1976. 9.95 (ISBN 0-917398-03-3); pap. 7.95 (ISBN 0-917398-04-1). New Worlds.
--Whispers of the Unchained Heart. LC 77-75496. 1977. 10.95 (ISBN 0-917398-05-X); pap. 8.95 (ISBN 0-917398-06-8). New Worlds.
Buttaci, Salvatore St. John. Coming-Home Poems: Stops & Pauses on the Scrapbook Express. 64p. 1974. pap. 2.00 (ISBN 0-917398-00-9). New Worlds.
Buttaci, Salvatore St. John & Gerstle, Susan L. Shadows of the Elusive Dream. LC 75-18323. 128p. 1975. 9.95 (ISBN 0-917398-02-5). New Worlds.
Buttaci, Salvatore St. John see Buttaci, Salvatore St. John.
Buttaci, Salvatore St. John see Buttaci, Salvatore St. John & Gerstle, Susan L.
Buttaci, Salvatore St. John & Gerstle, Susan L., eds. Echoes of the Unlocked Odyssey. 1974. pap. 7.95 (ISBN 0-917398-01-7). New Worlds.
Buttaravoli, Philip M. & Stair, Thomas O. Common Simple Emergencies. (Illus.). 320p. 1985. pap. text ed. 19.95 (ISBN 0-89303-371-5). Brady Comm.
Buttari, Juan J., jt. auth. see Salazar-Carillo, Jorge.
Butte Business Men's Association. Butte, Montana. facs. ed. (Shorey Historical Ser.). 35p. pap. 3.95 (ISBN 0-8466-0150-8, S150). Shorey.
Buttel, Frederick, jt. auth. see Humphrey, Craig.
Buttel, Frederick H., jt. auth. see Pearson, Arn H.
Buttel, Frederick H. & Newby, Howard, eds. The Rural Sociology of the Advanced Societies: Critical Perspectives. LC 79-5177. 538p. 1980. text ed. 22.50x (ISBN 0-916672-30-1); pap. text ed. 9.50x (ISBN 0-916672-34-4). Allanheld.
Buttel, Frederick H., et al, eds. Labor & the Environment: An Analysis of & Annotated Bibliography on Workplace Environmental Quality in the United States. LC 83-22575. viii, 148p. 1984. lib. bdg. 29.95 (ISBN 0-313-23935-5, BLE/). Greenwood.
Buttel, Paula W., ed. see Hellyer, Barbara.
Buttel, Robert. Seamus Heaney. (Irish Writers Ser.). 88p. 1975. 4.50 (ISBN 0-8387-1567-2). Bucknell U Pr.
Buttel, Robert, jt. ed. see Doggett, Frank.
Buttenwieser, Moses. The Psalms: Chronologically Treated with a New Translation. rev. ed. (Library of Biblical Studies Ser.). 1969. 59.50x (ISBN 0-87068-044-7). Ktav.
Butter, Anton J. An Introduction to Mini-Economics. 142p. (Orig.). 1985. pap. 20.00x (ISBN 90-6032-263-0, Pub. by B R Gruener Netherlands). Benjamins North Am.
Butter, F. J. Locks & Lockmaking. (Illus.). 135p. 1984. pap. text ed. 15.00 (ISBN 0-87556-392-9). Saifer.
Butter, Gwendoline. The Dull Dead. 1985. pap. 2.95 (ISBN 0-8027-3108-2). Walker & Co.
Butter, P. H., ed. Shelly--Alastor & Other Poems, Prometheus Unbound with Other Poems, Adonais. (Illus.). 368p. 1980. pap. 14.95x (ISBN 0-7121-0145-4). Trans-Atlantic.
--William Blake: Selected Poems. 288p. 1982. 25.00x (ISBN 0-460-01125-1, Pub. by J M Dent England). State Mutual Bk.
Butter, P. H., ed. see Blake, William.
Butter, Peter. Shelley's Idols of the Cave. LC 68-24118. (Studies in Shelley, No. 25). 1969. Repr. of 1954 ed. lib. bdg. 49.95x (ISBN 0-8383-0781-7). Haskell.
Butter, Peter H. Edwin Muir: Man & Poet. LC 76-11018. 1977. Repr. of 1966 ed. lib. bdg. 24.75 (ISBN 0-8371-8169-0, BUEM). Greenwood.
Butterfass, T. Patterns of Chloroplast Reproduction. (Cell Biology Monographs: Vol. 6). (Illus.). 1979. 69.00 (ISBN 0-387-81541-4). Springer-Verlag.
Butterfid, R. B., jt. ed. see Banerjee, P. K.
Butterfield, Arthur. Practical Spanish-English, English-Spanish Dictionary. (Practical Language Dictionaries Ser.). 400p. (Orig., Eng. & Span.). 1983. pap. 6.95 (ISBN 0-88254-814-X). Hippocrene Bks.
--Spanish-English, English-Spanish Dictionary. (Hippocrene Dictionaries Ser.). 400p. 1985. 12.95 (ISBN 0-88254-905-7). Hippocrene Bks.
Butterfield, B. G. & Meylan, B. Three-Dimensional Structure of Wood. 1980. 25.00 (ISBN 0-412-16320-9, NO. 6403, Pub by Chapman & Hall England). Methuen Inc.
Butterfield, B. G., jt. auth. see Meylan, B. A.
Butterfield, C. W. History of the Discovery of the Northwest by John Nicolet in 1634. LC 68-26262. 1969. Repr. of 1881 ed. 21.00x (ISBN 0-8046-0059-7, Pub. by Kennikat). Assoc Faculty Pr.
Butterfield, Clare. Recognitions. William, Johnston, et al, eds. Johnston, L. (Chapbook Ser.: No. 11). 18p. 1983. pap. 3.00 (ISBN 0-932884-10-5). Red Herring.
Butterfield, Consul W. Brule's Discoveries & Explorations. LC 73-90017. (Illus.). 186p. 1974. pap. 7.00 (ISBN 0-912382-13-9). Black Letter.
--History of Lt. Col. George Rogers Clark's Conquest of the Illinois & Wabash Towns. LC 72-8729. (American Revolutionary Ser.). Repr. of 1904 ed. lib. bdg. 45.00x (ISBN 0-8398-0188-2). Irvington.
Butterfield, Fox. China: Alive in the Bitter Sea. LC 81-52567. (Illus.). 480p. 1982. 24.95 (ISBN 0-8129-0927-5). Times Bks.
--China: Alive in the Bitter Sea. 1983. pap. 11.95 (ISBN 0-553-34219-3). Bantam.
Butterfield, H. Historical Novel. LC 72-187203. 1924. lib. bdg. 10.00 (ISBN 0-8414-0490-9). Folcroft.
Butterfield, Herbert. Christianity in European History: The Riddel Memorial Lectures, 1951. 1979. Repr. of 1952 ed. lib. bdg. 10.00 (ISBN 0-8482-3440-5). Norwood Edns.
--Herbert Butterfield on History. Winks, Robin W., ed. LC 83-49176. (History & Historiography Ser.). 204p. 1985. lib. bdg. 25.00 (ISBN 0-8240-6352-X). Garland Pub.
--International Conflict in the Twentieth Century. LC 74-6777. 123p. 1974. Repr. of 1960 ed. lib. bdg. 65.00 (ISBN 0-8371-7569-0, BUIC). Greenwood.
--Napoleon. 1962. pap. 3.95 (ISBN 0-02-001870-3, Collier). Macmillan.
--The Origins of History. LC 81-661117. 260p. 1981. 20.95 (ISBN 0-465-05344-0). Basic.
--Origins of Modern Science. rev. ed. 1965. pap. text ed. 10.95x (ISBN 0-02-905070-7). Free Pr.
--The Whig Interpretation of History. LC 75-41043. (BCL Ser. II). Repr. of 1931 ed. 16.00 (ISBN 0-404-14515-9). AMS Pr.
--Whig Interpretation of History. 1965. pap. 4.95 (ISBN 0-393-00318-3, Norton Lib). Norton.
--Writing on Christianity & History. 1979. 19.95x (ISBN 0-19-502454-0). Oxford U Pr.
Butterfield, James. Machine Language for the Commodore 64 & Other Commodore Computers. (Illus.). 336p. 1984. pap. 14.95 (ISBN 0-89303-652-8); kit 37.95 (ISBN 0-89303-653-6); diskette 25.00 (ISBN 0-89303-654-4). Brady Comm.
Butterfield, Jan. Frog Raising. 1983. pap. 2.95 (ISBN 0-440-52866-6, Dell Trade Pbks). Dell.
Butterfield, Jan, jt. auth. see Albright, Thomas.
Butterfield, Jan, et al, eds. see Meier, C. A.
Butterfield, John, et al. What Is Dungeons & Dragons? 240p. 1984. pap. 2.95 (ISBN 0-446-32212-1). Warner Bks.
Butterfield, L. H. see Adams, Charles F.
Butterfield, L. H., et al, eds. see Adams, Abigail & Adams, John.
Butterfield, L. H., et al, eds. see Adams, John.
Butterfield, Lyman, jt. auth. see Lumpkin, William L.
Butterfield, Oliver M. Love Problems of Adolescence. LC 70-176619. (Columbia University. Teachers College. Contributions to Education: No. 768). Repr. of 1939 ed. 22.50 (ISBN 0-404-55768-6). AMS Pr.
--Sex Life in Marriage. (Illus.). 8.95 (ISBN 0-87523-035-0). Emerson.
--Sexual Harmony in Marriage. LC 84-13625. (Illus.). 1984. pap. 2.45 (ISBN 0-89490-108-7). Enslow Pubs.
Butterfield, R., jt. auth. see Banerjee, P. K.
Butterfield, R., jt. ed. see Baerjee, P. K.
Butterfield, R., jt. ed. see Banerjee, P. K.
Butterfield, R. M. & May, N. D. Muscles of the Ox. (Illus.). 1966. 25.00x (ISBN 0-7022-0400-5). U of Queensland Pr.
Butterfield, R. W., ed. Modern American Poetry. LC 83-27507. (Critical Studies). 240p. 1984. 27.50x (ISBN 0-389-20460-9, 08021). B&N Imports.
Butterfield, Rex M., jt. auth. see Berg, Roy T.
Butterfield, Sherri. Value Tales Teacher's Resource Guide. (Illus.). 120p. 1981. pap. 9.95 (ISBN 0-916392-49-X, Dist. by Oak Tree Pubns). Value Comm.
Butterfield, Sherri M. & Kaplan, Sandra N. Developing IEPs for the Gifted-Talented. 71p. 4.95 (ISBN 0-318-15996-1, 19). NSLTIGT.
Butterfield, Sherri M., et al. Developing IEPs for the Gifted-Talented. 71p. 4.95 (ISBN 0-318-02135-8). NSLTIGT.
Butterfield, Stephen. Amway: The Cult of Free Enterprise. 195p. 1985. 25.00 (ISBN 0-89608-254-7); pap. 8.50 (ISBN 0-89608-253-9). South End Pr.
Butterfield, Stephen, ed. see Burton, Bruce A.
Butterfield, Stephen, ed. see Pohl, Frederick J.
Butterfield, William H. Bank Letters: How to Use Them in Public Relations. 64p. text ed. 2.25x (ISBN 0-8134-0309-X, 309). Interstate.
--Letters That Build Bank Business. 1953. text ed. 2.75x (ISBN 0-8134-0306-5, 306). Interstate.
Butterfiled, Jan, ed. see Selz, Peter.
Butterick. Vogue Christmas. LC 84-47560. (Illus.). 192p. 1984. 17.26i (ISBN 0-06-181126-2, HarpT). Har-Row.
--Vogue Fitting. LC 84-47561. (Illus.). 192p. 1984. 17.26i (ISBN 0-06-181127-0, HarpT). Har-Row.
--Vogue Sewing. LC 81-48031. (Illus.). 568p. 1982. 26.44i (ISBN 0-06-015001-7, HarpT). Har-Row.
Butterick, George. Editing the Maximus Poems. (Illus.). 125p. 1983. pap. 10.00 (ISBN 0-917590-09-0). Univ Conn Lib.
Butterick, George, ed. Charles Olson: Man & Poet. LC 85-61156. (Man & Poet Ser.). 480p. (Orig.). 1985. 28.50 (ISBN 0-915032-65-1); pap. 15.95 (ISBN 0-915032-66-X). Natl Poet Foun.
Butterick, George F. A Guide to the Maximus Poems of Charles Olson. LC 75-27921. 1978. 55.00x (ISBN 0-520-03140-7); pap. 14.95 (ISBN 0-520-04270-0). U of Cal Pr.
--Reading Genesis by the Light of a Comet. LC 76-43367. 1976. pap. 2.95 (ISBN 0-917488-01-6). Ziesing Bros.
--Rune Power. LC 83-417. 60p. 1983. pap. 4.00 (ISBN 0-9610604-0-9). Tin Man CT.
Butterick, George F., jt. auth. see Allen, Donald.
Butterick, George F., jt. ed. see Allen, Donald.
Butterick, George F., ed. & intro. by see Ferrini, Vincent.
Butterick, George F., ed. see Olson, Charles.
Butterick, George F., ed. see Olson, Charles, et al.
Butterick, George F., ed. see Olson, Charles & Creeley, Robert.
Butterick, George F., ed. see Olson, Charles F.
Butteriss, Margaret. New Management Tools: Ideas & Techniques to Help You As a Manager. LC 78-11826. (Illus.). 1978. (Spec) pap. 4.95 (ISBN 0-13-615187-6). P-H.
Butters, Dorothy G. The Bells of Freedom. (Illus.). (YA) 1984. 15.50 (ISBN 0-8446-6162-7). Peter Smith.
Butters, G., ed. Particulate Nature of PVC: Formation, Structure & Processing. (Illus.). xv, 240p. 1982. 40.75 (ISBN 0-85334-120-6, Pub. by Elsevier Applied Sci England). Elsevier.
Butters, Gordon, ed. Plastics Pneumatic Conveying & Bulk Storage. (Illus.). 296p. 1981. 57.50 (ISBN 0-85334-983-5, Pub. by Elsevier Applied Sci England). Elsevier.
Butters, H. C. Governors & Government in Early Sixteenth-Century Florence, 1502-1519. 420p. 1985. 34.50 (ISBN 0-19-822593-8). Oxford U Pr.
Butters, J. Keith, et al. Case Problems in Finance. 8th ed. 1981. 29.95x (ISBN 0-256-02500-2). Irwin.
Butters, J. N. Holography & its Technology. (IEE Monograph Series: No. 8). 236p. 1972. 36.00 (ISBN 0-901223-10-7, MO008). Inst Elect Eng.
Butters, John Neil. Holography & Its Technology. LC 73-179369. (Institution of Electrical Engineers, IIE Monograph Ser.: No. 8). (Illus.). pap. 59.00 (ISBN 0-317-08482-8, 2017592). Bks Demand UMI.

Butters, N. Selected Readings in Neuropsychology. 1972. text ed. 29.50x (ISBN 0-8422-5006-9); pap. text ed. 8.50x (ISBN 0-8422-0221-8). Irvington.

Butters, Nelson & Cermak, Laird S. Alcoholic Korsakoff's Syndrome: An Information Processing Approach to Amnesia. LC 79-6779. 1980. 24.50 (ISBN 0-12-148380-0). Acad Pr.

Butters, Nelson & Squire, Larry R., eds. Neuropsychology of Memory. LC 84-4642. 715p. 1984. 65.00 (ISBN 0-89862-638-2, 2638). Guilford Pr.

Butters, Roger. First Person Singular: A Review of the Life & Work of Mr. Sherlock Holmes, the Worlds First Consulting Detective. 1984. 10.00 (ISBN 0-533-05646-2). Vantage.

Butterweck, Joseph S. The Problem of Teaching High School Pupils How to Study. LC 75-176620. (Columbia University. Teachers College. Contributions to Education: No. 237). Repr. of 1926 ed. 22.50 (ISBN 0-404-55237-4). AMS Pr.

Butterworh, Neil. Dvorak: His Life & Times. 1981. 40.00x (ISBN 0-85936-142-X, Pub. by Midas Bks England). State Mutual Bk.

Butterworth & Stockdale. Danger in the Mountains. (Jim Hunter Ser.). 1977. pap. 3.72 (ISBN 0-8224-3782-1). Pitman Learning.

--The Desert Chase. (Jim Hunter Ser.). 1976. pap. 3.72 (ISBN 0-8224-3783-X). Pitman Learning.

--The Diamond Smugglers. (Jim Hunter Ser.). 1977. pap. 3.72 (ISBN 0-8224-3784-8). Pitman Learning.

--The Island of Helos. (Jim Hunter Ser.). 1976. pap. 3.72 (ISBN 0-8224-3785-6). Pitman Learning.

--Jim & the Dolphin. (Jim Hunter Ser.). 1975. pap. 3.72 (ISBN 0-8224-3786-4). Pitman Learning.

--Jim & the Sun Goddess. (Jim Hunter Ser.). 1975. pap. 3.72 (ISBN 0-8224-3787-2). Pitman Learning.

--Jim Hunter International Spy Stories. (gr. 6-12). 1975-82. pap. 56.00 boxed set of 16 bks. with tchrs. guide (ISBN 0-8224-3781-3). Pitman Learning.

--Jim in Training. (Jim Hunter Ser.). 1975. pap. 3.72 (ISBN 0-8224-3788-0). Pitman Learning.

--The Killer Rocket. (Jim Hunter Ser.). 1982. 3.72 (ISBN 0-8224-3797-X). Pitman Learning.

--The Missing Aircraft. (Jim Hunter Ser.). 1975. pap. 3.72 (ISBN 0-8224-3789-9). Pitman Learning.

--Prisoner of Pedro Cay. (Jim Hunter Ser.). 1978. pap. 3.72 (ISBN 0-8224-3790-2). Pitman Learning.

--Race for Gold. (Jim Hunter Ser.). 1982. 3.72 (ISBN 0-8224-3795-3). Pitman Learning.

--Rescue Mission. (Jim Hunter Ser.). 1982. 3.32 (ISBN 0-8224-3796-1). Pitman Learning.

--Sabotage in the Arctic. (Jim Hunter Ser.). 1982. 3.72 (ISBN 0-8224-3798-8). Pitman Learning.

--The Shipwreckers. (Jim Hunter Ser.). 1976. pap. 3.72 (ISBN 0-8224-3791-0). Pitman Learning.

--The Sniper at Zimba. (Jim Hunter Ser.). 1978. pap. 3.72 (ISBN 0-8224-3792-9). Pitman Learning.

--The Temple of Mantos. (Jim Hunter Ser.). 1976. pap. 3.48 (ISBN 0-8224-3793-7). Pitman Learning.

Butterworth, Adeline M. William Blake: Mystic. LC 74-8017. 1911. lib. bdg. 15.00 (ISBN 0-8414-3186-8). Folcroft.

Butterworth, B. Language Production: Vol. 1, Speech & Talk. 1980. 69.50 (ISBN 0-12-147501-8). Acad Pr.

Butterworth, B. & Hutchinson, Martha. Language Production: Development, Writing & Other Language Processes, Vol. 2. 1984. 49.00 (ISBN 0-12-147502-6). Acad Pr.

Butterworth, Bernard B. Laboratory Anatomy of the Human Body. 3rd ed. (Laboratory Anatomy Ser.). 130p. 1985. wire coil (ISBN 0-697-05125-0). Wm C Brown.

Butterworth, Bill. Peanut Butter Families Stick Together. pap. 4.95 (ISBN 0-8007-5181-7). Revell.

Butterworth, Bill & Nix, John. Farm Mechanisation for Profit. 288p. 1983. pap. 22.00x (ISBN 0-246-11562-9, Pub. by Granada England). Sheridan.

--Farm Mechanization for Profit. 269p. 1983. pap. text ed. 24.95 (ISBN 0-246-11562-9, Granada England). Brookfield Pub Co.

Butterworth, Bill, jt. auth. see Parry, John.

Butterworth, Byron E. Strategies for Short-Term Testing for Mutagens-Carcinogens. 160p. 1979. 56.00 (ISBN 0-8493-5661-X). CRC Pr.

Butterworth, C. E. & Hutchinson, Martha. Nutritional Factors in the Induction & Maintenance of Malignancy: Symposium. LC 83-5020. (Bristol-Myers Symposia Ser.: Vol. 2). 1983. 42.00 (ISBN 0-12-147520-4). Acad Pr.

Butterworth, C. E. & A. Abd Al-Magid Haridi, eds. Averroes's Middle Commentary on Aristotle's Topics. (American Research Center in Egypt, Publications Ser.: Vol. 1, a (6)). 247p. (Orig., Arabic & Eng.). 1979. pap. 5.00x (ISBN 0-686-30893-X, Pub. by Am Res Ctr Egypt). Undena Pubns.

Butterworth, C. E., Jr., jt. auth. see Weinsier, Roland L.

Butterworth, Charles, tr. see Rousseau, Jean J.

Butterworth, Charles A. & Skidmore, David A. Caring for the Mentally Ill in the Community. (Illus.). 126p. 1981. 21.00 (ISBN 0-7099-0071-6, Pub. by Croom Helm Ltd); pap. 9.95 (ISBN 0-7099-0072-4). Longwood Pub Group.

Butterworth, Charles C. The English Primers, Fifteen Twenty-Nine to Fifteen Forty-Five: Their Publication & Connection with the English Bible & the Reformation in England. 1970. lib. bdg. 26.00x (ISBN 0-374-91131-2). Octagon.

--Literary Lineage of the King James Bible, 1340-1611. LC 76-120241. 1971. Repr. lib. bdg. 30.50x (ISBN 0-374-91133-9). Octagon.

Butterworth, Charles E., jt. auth. see Weiss, Raymond L.

Butterworth, Charles E., ed. & tr. Averroes' Three Short Commentaries on Aristotle's Topics, Rhetoric, & Poetics. LC 75-4900. 1977. 49.50x (ISBN 0-87395-208-1). State U NY Pr.

Butterworth, Charles E., ed. see Rousseau, Jean-Jacques.

Butterworth, Charles E., tr. Averroe's Middle Commentaries on Aristotle's Categories & De Interpretations. LC 82-61359. 192p. 1983. 22.50 (ISBN 0-691-07276-0). Princeton U Pr.

Butterworth Company of Cape Cod Inc. Cape Cod & Islands Atlas & Guide Book, Vol. 6. rev. ed. (Illus.). 112p. 1984-1985. pap. 9.95 (ISBN 0-937338-03-6). Butterworth of Cape Cod.

Butterworth, Douglas & Chance, John K. Latin American Urbanization. LC 80-18486. (Urbanization in Developing Countries Ser.). (Illus.). 320p. 1981. text ed. 44.50 (ISBN 0-521-23713-0); pap. text ed. 12.95 (ISBN 0-521-28175-X). Cambridge U Pr.

Butterworth, Douglas S. The People of Buena Ventura: Relocation of Slum Dwellers in Post-Revolutionary Cuba. LC 79-11779. 304p. 1980. 14.95x (ISBN 0-252-00746-8). U of Ill Pr.

Butterworth, E. A. Some Traces of the Pre-Olympian World in Greek Literature & Myth. (Illus.). 1966. 23.80x (ISBN 3-11-005010-2). De Gruyter.

Butterworth Editorial Staff. Illinois Limitations Manual. 1982. looseleaf 37.50 (ISBN 0-86678-151-X). Butterworth MN.

Butterworth Editorial Staff. Dunnell Minnesota Digest. rev., 2nd ser. ed. (42 vols in course of publication). 1695.00 (ISBN 0-917126-21-1). Butterworth MN.

--Minnesota Criminal Law Digest, 3 vols. 1982. looseleaf 190.00 (ISBN 0-86678-037-8). Butterworth MN.

--Minnesota Insurance Law Digest. 1982. looseleaf 80.00 (ISBN 0-86678-035-1). Butterworth MN.

--Minnesota Limitations Manual. 1982. looseleaf 37.50 (ISBN 0-86678-033-5). Butterworth MN.

--Minnesota Probate Law Digest, 3 vols. 1982. looseleaf 185.00 (ISBN 0-86678-036-X). Butterworth MN.

Butterworth Editorial Staff, ed. Iowa Limitations Manual. 1982. looseleaf 37.50 (ISBN 0-86678-048-3). Butterworth MN.

--Nebraska Limitations Manual. 1982. looseleaf 37.50 (ISBN 0-86678-059-9). Butterworth MN.

Butterworth, Emma M. As the Waltz Was Ending. 224p. (YA) (gr. 7 up). 1985. pap. 2.50 (ISBN 0-317-17366-9, Point). Scholastic Inc.

--The Complete Book of Calligraphy. LC 79-7642. (Illus.). 164p. 1980. 14.95i (ISBN 0-690-01852-5). Har-Row.

--The Complete Book of Calligraphy. (Illus.). 164p. 1984. pap. 6.68i (ISBN 0-06-463595-3, EH 595). Har-Row.

Butterworth, Eric. Celebrate Yourself. 128p. 1984. 4.95 (ISBN 0-87159-180-4). Unity School.

--Discover the Power Within You. LC 68-17583. 1968. 12.45 (ISBN 0-06-061266-5, HarpR). Har-Row.

--In the Flow of Life. LC 82-50121. 181p. 1982. Repr. 4.95 (ISBN 0-87159-065-4). Unity School.

--Life Is for Loving. LC 73-6326. 128p. 1974. 10.53 (ISBN 0-06-061268-1, HarpR). Har-Row.

--Spiritual Economics--the Prosperity Process. 220p. 1983. 4.95 (ISBN 0-87159-142-1). Unity School.

--Unity: A Quest for Truth. (Orig.). 1965. pap. 3.00 (ISBN 0-8315-0020-4). Speller.

--You Make the Difference. LC 76-9959. 160p. 1984. 10.53 (ISBN 0-06-061271-1, HarpR). Har-Row.

Butterworth, F. Edward. Roots of the Reorganization: French Polynesia. LC 77-944. (Illus.). 1977. pap. 8.00 (ISBN 0-8309-0176-0). Herald Hse.

--Secrets of the Mighty Sioux. 1982. pap. 11.00 (ISBN 0-8309-0352-6). Ind Pr MO.

--Sword of Laban, 2 vols. rev. ed. 1985. Vol. 1. 25.00 (ISBN 0-8309-0422-0). Vol. 2. Herald Hse.

Butterworth, G. W., tr. see Origen.

Butterworth, George. Infancy & Epistemology: An Evaluation of Piaget's Theory. LC 81-18555. 1982. 30.00 (ISBN 0-312-41588-5). St Martin.

Butterworth, George & Light, Paul. Social Cognition: Studies of the Development of Understanding. LC 81-24075. 1982. lib. bdg. 20.00x (ISBN 0-226-08609-7). U of Chicago Pr.

Butterworth, George, jt. auth. see Sharp, Cecil J.

Butterworth, George, ed. The Child's Representation of the World. LC 77-1046. (Illus.). 251p. 1977. 29.50x (ISBN 0-306-31025-2, Plenum Pr). Plenum Pub.

Butterworth, George, et al, eds. Evolution & Developmental Psychology. LC 84-26277. 256p. 1985. 27.50 (ISBN 0-312-27253-7). St Martin.

Butterworth, H. The Story of the Hymns. 59.95 (ISBN 0-8490-1139-6). Gordon Pr.

Butterworth, H. E., jt. auth. see Hooker, R.

Butterworth, Hezekiah. In Old New England. LC 73-19716. 1974. Repr. of 1895 ed. 40.00x (ISBN 0-8103-3686-3). Gale.

--Story of Hymns & Tunes. 1981. Repr. lib. bdg. 79.00x (ISBN 0-403-00107-2). Scholarly.

--Traveller Tales of the Pan-American Countries. LC 71-130986. (Illus.). Repr. of 1902 ed. 19.00 (ISBN 0-404-01255-8). AMS Pr.

Butterworth, Ian. Staffing for Curriculum Needs: Teachers Shortages & Surpluses in Comprehensive Schools. 208p. 1983. 16.00x (ISBN 0-7005-0554-7, Pub. by NFER Nelson UK). Taylor & Francis.

Butterworth, J. Scott, et al. Cardiac Auscultation. 2nd enl. ed. LC 60-6018. (Illus.). 104p. 1960. 46.50 (ISBN 0-8089-0089-7, 790740). Grune.

Butterworth, Jenny. The Cat Came Back. 144p. (gr. 4-6). 1983. pap. 1.95 (ISBN 0-590-31807-1). Scholastic Inc.

Butterworth, John. A Book of Beliefs: Cults & New Faiths. 72p. 30.00x (ISBN 0-85648-249-8, Pub. by Lion Pub England). State Mutual Bk.

--Debt Collection Letters in Ten Languages. LC 79-65006. 1979. 35.00 (ISBN 0-8144-5577-8). AMACOM.

Butterworth, John, jt. auth. see Hutson, Thomas G.

Butterworth, Keen. A Critical & Textual Study of Faulkner's "A Fable". Litz, Walton, ed. LC 83-5030. (Studies in Modern Literature: No. 11). 134p. 1983. 34.95 (ISBN 0-8357-1420-9). UMI Res Pr.

Butterworth, Keen & Kibler, James E., Jr. William Gilmore Simms: A Reference Guide. 1980. lib. bdg. 28.50 (ISBN 0-8161-1059-X, Hall Reference). G K Hall.

Butterworth, Michael. Hit List. LC 82-48705. (Crime Club Ser.). 192p. 1985. 12.95 (ISBN 0-385-19459-5). Doubleday.

--Virgin on the Rocks. LC 85-1582. (Crime Club Ser.). 192p. 1985. 12.95 (ISBN 0-385-19994-5). Doubleday.

Butterworth, Michael, jt. auth. see Seymour, Janette.

Butterworth, Michael, jt. auth. see Seymour, Jeannette.

Butterworth, Nancy & Broad, Laura. Kits for Kids. (Illus.). 256p. 1980. 15.95 (ISBN 0-312-45701-4); pap. 7.95 (ISBN 0-312-45702-2). St Martin.

Butterworth, Nancy T., jt. auth. see Broad, Laura P.

Butterworth, Neil. A Dictionary of American Composers. LC 81-43331. (Reference Library of the Humanities: Vol. 296). 600p. 1985. lib. bdg. 83.00 (ISBN 0-8240-9311-9). Garland Pub.

--Dvorak: His Life & Times. expanded ed. (Life & Times Ser.). (Illus.). 176p. 1981. Repr. of 1980 ed. 12.95 (ISBN 0-87666-580-6, Z-49). Paganiniana Pubns.

--Haydn: His Life & Times. (Illus.). 1978. 16.95 (ISBN 0-8467-0417-X, Pub. by Two Continents); pap. 9.95 (ISBN 0-8467-0418-8). Hippocrene Bks.

--Haydn: His Life & Times. expanded ed. (Life & Times Ser.). (Illus.). 176p. 1980. Repr. of 1977 ed. 12.95 (ISBN 0-87666-645-4, Z-44). Paganiniana Pubns.

--Haydn: His Life & Times. 2nd ed. 144p. 1981. 40.00x (ISBN 0-85936-030-X, Pub. by Midas Bks England). State Mutual Bk.

Butterworth, Nick & Inkpen, Mick. The Nativity Play. (Illus.). 32p. (gr. k-3). 1985. 10.95 (ISBN 0-316-11903-2). Little.

Butterworth, Oliver. The Enormous Egg. 1978. pap. 2.50 (ISBN 0-440-42337-6, YB). Dell.

--The Enormous Egg. (gr. 4-6). 1956. 13.45i (ISBN 0-316-11904-0, Pub. by Atlantic Monthly Pr). Little.

Butterworth, P. J., jt. auth. see Moss, D. W.

Butterworth, Rod. The Perigee Visual Dictionary of Signing: An A-to-Z Guide of over 1200 Signs of American Sign Language. LC 83-9728. (Illus.). 416p. (Orig.). 1984. (G&D); pap. 8.95 (ISBN 0-399-50863-5). Putnam Pub Group.

Butterworth Staff. Arizona Statutory Time Limitations. 314p. 1984. looseleaf 40.00 (ISBN 0-409-20206-1). Butterworth Legal Pubs.

--Local Rules of the Circuit & District Courts: Oregon. 450p. 1984. looseleaf 55.00 (ISBN 0-409-20212-6). Butterworth Legal Pubs.

--Local Rules of the Superior Court: Washington State. 433p. 1984. looseleaf 55.00 (ISBN 0-409-23004-9). Butterworth Legal Pubs.

--Oregon BARS (Butterworth Advance Report Service) 1984. 85.00 (ISBN 0-409-20003-4). Butterworth Legal Pubs.

--Statutory Time Limitations: Washington State. 280p. 1984. looseleaf 45.00 (ISBN 0-409-23003-0). Butterworth Legal Pubs.

--Utah Statutory Time Limitations. 170p. 1981. Incl. 1982 supplement. looseleaf 40.00 (ISBN 0-317-12920-1). Butterworth Legal Pubs.

Butterworth Staff, jt. auth. see Criminal Justice Training Commission Staff.

Butterworth Staff, ed. Land Conservation & Development Commission Decisions (LCDC) Selected Decisions, 1974-1979, 3 vols. 1984. Set. write for info.; Individual vols. 40.00 (ISBN 0-317-12918-X). Butterworth Legal Pubs.

--Land Use Board of Appeals Decision (LUBA) 1984. Vols. 1-7 (Set) 150.00 (ISBN 0-317-12919-8); Vol. 8 & future vols. (3 vols. annually) 50.00 ea. Butterworth Legal Pubs.

--Land Use Board of Appeals Handbook. 136p. 1981. pap. 10.00 (ISBN 0-409-24952-1). Butterworth Legal Pubs.

Butterworth, Thomas & Ladda, Roger. Clinical Genodermatology, Vol. 1. LC 81-1006. 398p. 1981. 59.95x (ISBN 0-03-056127-2); with vol. II 100.00 set (ISBN 0-03-060048-0). Praeger.

--Clinical Genodermatology, Vol. 2. LC 81-1006. 380p. 1981. 59.95x (ISBN 0-03-059139-2). Praeger.

Butterworth, Vida. The Girls in White. LC 78-10862. 1979. pap. 6.50 (ISBN 0-8309-0230-9). Herald Hse.

Butterworth, W. E. Flunking Out. 256p. (gr. 7 up). 1982. pap. 1.95 (ISBN 0-590-32741-0). Scholastic Inc.

--LeRoy & the Old Man. (gr. 7 up). 1982. pap. 2.25 (ISBN 0-590-33830-7, Point). Scholastic Inc.

Butterworth, W. E., jt. auth. see Hooker, R.

Butterworth, William. Moose, the Thing, & Me. (gr. 5 up). 1982. 9.95 (ISBN 0-395-32077-1). HM.

--Next Stop, Earth. LC 77-18346. (Illus.). (gr. 2-4). 1978. 5.95 (ISBN 0-8027-6322-7); PLB 5.85 (ISBN 0-8027-6323-5). Walker & Co.

Butterworth, William E. The House on "Q" Street. (Men at War Ser.: No. 1). (Orig.). 1985. pap. write for info. (ISBN 0-671-49778-2). PB.

Butterworth, William E., jt. auth. see Hooker, R.

Buttery, P. J. & Lindsay, D. B. Protein Deposition in Animals. 29th ed. LC 80-49869. (Nottingham Easter School Ser.). (Illus.). 320p. 1980. text ed. 99.95 (ISBN 0-408-10676-X). Butterworth.

Buttery, Roger & Simpson, Robert K. Internal Audit in the Public Sector. LC 85-5330. 160p. 1985. 29.00 (ISBN 0-85941-262-8, Pub. by Woodhead-Faulkner). Longwood Pub Group.

Buttery, William A. & Miller, H. G. Carpentry. Vorndran, Richard A., ed. LC 83-51098. (South-Western Construction Technology Ser.). 448p. 1984. text ed. 15.50 (ISBN 0-538-33200-X, IE20); write for info tchrs. manual (ISBN 0-538-33201-8). SW Pub.

Butti, Ken & Perlin, John. The Golden Thread: 2500 Years of Solar Architecture & Technology. LC 79-25095. (Illus.). 1980. 19.95 (ISBN 0-917352-07-6); pap. 9.95 (ISBN 0-917352-08-4). Cheshire.

Buttigieg, Ray. Apocraphasis. pap. 5.50 (ISBN 0-932436-07-2). Cykx.

--Pastorale. 1978. pap. 4.99 (ISBN 0-685-63585-6). Cykx.

--Pellegunagg Ghas-Santwarjutal-Qalb. (Maltese.). 3.99 (ISBN 0-932436-03-X). Cykx.

--Rubaiyat Is-Cykx. (Maltese.). 1978. pap. 3.99 (ISBN 0-932436-00-5). Cykx.

--Windrythm. 1983. pap. 5.50 (ISBN 0-932436-06-4). Cykx.

Buttiker, Wilhelm. The Wildlife of Arabia. 96p. 1984. 89.00 (ISBN 0-317-14200-3, Pub. by Stacey Pubs UK). State Mutual Bk.

Buttimer, Anne. The Practice of Geography. LC 82-13091. (Illus.). 1984. text ed. 29.95 (ISBN 0-582-30087-8). Longman.

--Society & Milieu in the French Geographic Tradition. LC 72-158112. (Monograph: No. 6). 4.95 (ISBN 0-89291-085-2). Assn Am Geographers.

--Values in Geography. LC 74-76634. (CCG Resource Papers Ser.: No. 24). (Illus.). 1974. pap. text ed. 4.00 (ISBN 0-89291-071-2). Assn Am Geographers.

Buttimer, Anne & Seaman, David. The Human Experience of Space & Place. LC 80-12173. (Illus.). 1980. 29.00 (ISBN 0-312-39910-3). St Martin.

Buttimore, R. A., jt. auth. see Hodge, R. I.

Buttimore, R. I., jt. ed. see Hodge, R. A.

Buttino-Hare. The Remaking of a City: Rochester, New York 1964-1984. 464p. 1984. pap. text ed. 18.95 (ISBN 0-8403-3451-6). Kendall-Hunt.

Buttitta, Tony & Witham, Barry B. Uncle Sam Presents: A Memoir of the Federal Theatre, 1935-1939. LC 81-43517. (Illus.). 232p. 1982. 25.00x (ISBN 0-8122-7826-7). U of Pa Pr.

Buttlar, Lois, jt. auth. see Wynar, Lubomyr R.

Buttles, Arlene. From Dream to Reality. 2nd ed. LC 82-81059. (Illus.). 192p. (Orig.). 1984. pap. 9.95 (ISBN 0-9606240-5-8). Pearl-Win.

Buttner, Gottfried. Samuel Beckett's Novel "Watt". Dolan, Joseph, tr. LC 84-7234. (Illus.). 144p. 1984. 20.00 (ISBN 0-8122-7932-8). U of Pa Pr.

Buttner, Horst & Meissner, Gunter. Town Houses of Europe. (Illus.). 351p. 1982. 45.00 (ISBN 0-312-81157-8). St Martin.

Buttner, J., ed. History of Clinical Chemistry. LC 83-1968. (Illus.). 91p. 1983. 49.00 (ISBN 3-11-008912-2). De Gruyter.

Buttner-Ennever, J., ed. Neuroanatomy of the Oculomotor System. (Reviews of Oculomotor Research: No. 2). 1984. write for info. (ISBN 0-444-80484-6, Biomedical Pr). Elsevier.

Buttner-Kolisko, Agnes. Plankton Rotifers: Biology & Taxonomy. Kolisko, G., tr. from German. (Die Binnengewaesser). (Illus.). 146p. 1974. pap. text ed. 19.25x (ISBN 0-318-00462-3). Lubrecht & Cramer.

Buttolph, Philip, tr. see Dibelius, Martin & Conzelmann, Hans.

Button, Eric, ed. & illus. Personal Construct Theory & Mental Health: Theory, Research & Practice. 400p. 1985. 35.00 (ISBN 0-914797-15-8, Pub. by Croom Helm Ltd.). Brookline Book.

Button, H. Warren & Provenzo, Eugene F., Jr. History of Education & Culture in America. (Illus.). 400p. 1983. 26.95 (ISBN 0-13-390237-4). P-H.

Button, James E., et al. Communications Research in Learning Disabilities & Mental Retardation. LC 78-20825. (Illus.). 368p. 1979. pap. 19.00 (ISBN 0-8391-1262-9). Pro Ed.

Button, James W. Black Violence: Political Impact of the 1960's Riots. LC 78-51158. 1978. 29.00x (ISBN 0-691-07531-X). Princeton U Pr.

Button, John. Making Love Work. 160p. 1985. pap. 7.95 (ISBN 0-85500-206-9). Newcastle Pub.

Button, K. J. Transport Economics. viii, 295p. (Orig.). 1982. pap. text ed. 15.00x (ISBN 0-435-84093-2). Gower Pub Co.

Button, K. J. & Pearman, A. D. The Economics of Urban Freight Transport. 1981. text ed. 49.50x (ISBN 0-8419-5060-1). Holmes & Meier.

Button, K. J. & Gillingwater, D., eds. Transport, Location & Spatial Policy. 272p. 1983. text ed. 35.50x (ISBN 0-566-00527-1). Gower Pub Co.

Button, K. J. & Pearman, A. D., eds. The Practice of Transport Investment Appraisal. 272p. 1983. text ed. 46.00 (ISBN 0-566-00464-X). Gower Pub Co.

Button, K. J. & Pitfield, D. E., eds. International Railway Economics. 384p. 1985. text ed. write for info. (ISBN 0-566-00854-8). Gower Pub Co.

Button, K. J., et al. Car Ownership Modelling & Forecasting. 176p. 1981. text ed. 47.50x (ISBN 0-566-00320-1). Gower Pub Co.

Button, Kenneth. Road Haulage Licensing & EC Transport Policy. LC 84-6112. 127p. 1984. text ed. 32.95x (ISBN 0-566-00702-9). Gower Pub Co.

Button, Kenneth, ed. Infrared & Millimeter Waves: Millimeter Systems, Vol. 4. Wiltse, James. LC 79-6949. 1981. 64.00 (ISBN 0-12-147704-5). Acad Pr.

--Infrared & Millimeter Waves: Systems & Components, Vol. 6. 1982. 67.50 (ISBN 0-12-147706-1). Acad Pr.

Button, Kenneth J. Infrared & Millimeter Waves: Millimeter Components & Techniques, Pt. III, Vol. 11. LC 79-6949. 1984. 75.00 (ISBN 0-12-147711-8). Acad Pr.

--Infrared & Millimeter Waves: Vol. 9: Millimeter Components & Techniques, Pt. 1. LC 79-6949. 1983. 61.00 (ISBN 0-12-147709-6). Acad Pr.

Button, Kenneth J., ed. Infrared & Millimeter Waves: Coherent Sources & Applications, Vol. 5 Pt. 1. LC 79-6949. 1982. 59.50 (ISBN 0-12-147705-3). Acad Pr.

--Infrared & Millimeter Waves: Coherent Sources & Applications Pt. II, Vol. 7. 416p. 1983. 85.00 (ISBN 0-12-147707-X). Acad Pr.

--Infrared & Millimeter Waves: Instrumentation, Vol. II. LC 79-6949. 1979. 67.50 (ISBN 0-12-147702-9). Acad Pr.

--Infrared & Millimeter Waves: Sources of Radiation, Vol. 1. LC 79-6949. 1979. 65.00 (ISBN 0-12-147701-0). Acad Pr.

--Infrared & Millimeter Waves: Submillimeter Techniques, Vol. 3. 1980. 65.00 (ISBN 0-12-147703-7). Acad Pr.

--Infrared & Millimeter Waves, Vol. 10: Millimeter Components & Techniques, Pt. II. 1984. 65.00 (ISBN 0-12-147710-X). Acad Pr.

--Infrared & Millimeter Waves, Vol. 13: Millimeter Components & Techniques, Pt. IV. Date not set. price not set (ISBN 0-12-147713-4). Acad Pr.

--Infrared & Millimeter Waves, Vol. 8: Electromagnetic Waves in Matter, Pt. I. LC 79-6949. 1983. 69.50 (ISBN 0-12-147708-8). Acad Pr.

--Infrared Millimeter Waves, Vol. 14: Millimeter Components & Techniques, Pt. V. Date not set. price not set (ISBN 0-12-147714-2). Acad Pr.

--Reviews of Infrared & Millimeter Waves, Vol. 1. 365p. 1983. 55.00x (ISBN 0-306-41260-8, Plenum Pr). Plenum Pub.

Button, Robert. Managing Publications. 52p. 1982. 3.00 (ISBN 0-318-16332-2). Quill & Scroll.

Buttram, Harold E. Dangers of Immunization. 72p. (Orig.). 1983. pap. 2.95 (ISBN 0-916285-27-8). Humanitarian.

--Freedom of Choice in the Healing Arts. 50p. (Orig.). 1971. pap. 2.00 (ISBN 0-916285-28-6). Humanitarian.

--Today's Health Movement & the Future of America. 56p. 1982. pap. 2.45 (ISBN 0-916285-31-6). Humanitarian.

Buttram, Harold E. & Hoffman, John C. Vaccinations & Immune Malfunction. 3rd ed. 64p. (Orig.). 1985. pap. 3.95. Humanitarian.

Buttram, Harold E. & Ricchio, Paul P. Love, Sex & Marriage. 64p. (Orig.). 1985. pap. 4.95 (ISBN 0-916285-37-5). Humanitarian.

Buttram, Harold E., et al. Hidden Influences of Love, Touch & Affection. 121p. (Orig.). 1981. pap. 4.95 (ISBN 0-916285-29-4). Humanitarian.

Buttram, Veasy C., Jr. & Reiter, Robert C. Surgical Treatment of the Infertile Female. 350p. 1985. 55.00 (ISBN 0-683-01251-7). Williams & Wilkins.

Buttrell, Frederick J. Technology to Payoff: Managing the New Product from Creation to Customer. 200p. 1984. 29.95x (ISBN 0-915601-00-1). Cresheim Pubns.

Buttress, F. A., ed. World Guide to Abbreviations of Organizations. 7th ed. 750p. 1984. 115.00x (ISBN 0-8103-2049-5, Pub. by Grand River). Gale.

Buttrey, D. N., ed. Plastics in Furniture. (Illus.). 183p. 1976. 24.00 (ISBN 0-85334-647-X, Pub. by Elsevier Applied Sci England). Elsevier.

Buttrey, T. V., et al. Greek, Roman, & Islamic Coins From Sardis. LC 81-6774. (Archaeological Exploration of Sardis Monograph: No. 7). (Illus.). 320p. 1982. text ed. 30.00x (ISBN 0-674-36305-1). Harvard U Pr.

Buttrey, Theodore V., Jr., ed. Coinage of the Americas. (Illus.). 139p. 1973. pap. 7.50 (ISBN 0-89722-062-5). Am Numismatic.

Buttrick, David. Epiphany. LC 84-18756. (Proclamation 3 C Ser.). 64p. 1985. pap. 3.50 (ISBN 0-8006-4126-4). Fortress.

Buttrick, David, jt. auth. see Juel, Donald H.

Buttrick, George A. The Interpreter's Bible, 12 vols. Incl. Vol. 1. General Articles, Genesis, Exodus. 1952 (ISBN 0-687-19207-2); Vol. 2. Leviticus - Samuel. 1953 (ISBN 0-687-19208-0); Vol. 3. Kings - Job. 1954 (ISBN 0-687-19209-9); Vol. 4. Psalms, Proverbs. 1955 (ISBN 0-687-19210-2); Vol. 5. Ecclesiates - Jeremiah. 1956 (ISBN 0-687-19211-0); Vol. 6. Lamentations - Malachi. 1956 (ISBN 0-687-19212-9); Vol. 7. General Articles, Matthew, Mark. 1951 (ISBN 0-687-19213-7); Vol. 8. Luke, John. 1952 (ISBN 0-687-19214-5); Vol. 9. The Acts, Romans. 1954 (ISBN 0-687-19215-3); Vol. 10. Corinthians, Ephesians. 1953 (ISBN 0-687-19216-1); Vol. 11. Philippians - Hebrews. 1955 (ISBN 0-687-19217-X); Vol. 12. James - Revelation. 1957 (ISBN 0-687-19218-8). LC 51-12276. 1957. 21.95 (ISBN 0-686-76914-7); 255.00 (ISBN 0-687-19206-4). Abingdon.

--The Parables of Jesus. (Minister's Paperback Library Ser). 274p. 1973. pap. 6.95 (ISBN 0-8010-0597-3). Baker Bk.

--Prayer in Life: Life in Prayer. 1976. pap. 0.85x (ISBN 0-8358-0346-5). Upper Room.

Buttrick, George A. & Crim, Keith R., eds. The Interpreter's Dictionary of the Bible, 5 vols. LC 62-9387. 1976. Set. 112.00 (ISBN 0-687-19268-4). Abingdon.

Buttrill, Carrol O. & Reid, Louis E., Jr. The Buttrill Family: A Genealogy with Touches of Family History & Recollections. LC 83-72278. 416p. 1983. 21.50 (ISBN 0-9612214-0-2). Buttrill Reid.

Buttross, Waddad H. Waddad's Kitchen. 224p. (Orig.). 1982. pap. 7.95 (ISBN 0-939114-35-6). Wimmer Bks.

Butts, Allison. Metallurgical Problems. LC 79-9867. 462p. 1981. Repr. of 1943 ed. lib. bdg. 29.50 (ISBN 0-88275-915-9). Krieger.

Butts, Allison, ed. Silver, Economics, Metallurgy, & Use. LC 74-34002. 498p. 1975. Repr. of 1967 ed. 37.50 (ISBN 0-88275-278-2). Krieger.

Butts, Carrol. Troubleshooting the High School Band: How to Detect & Correct Common & Uncommon Performance Problems. LC 80-24776. 224p. 1981. 22.95x (ISBN 0-13-931105-X, Parker). P-H.

Butts, Carrol M. The High School Band Clinic: Drills & Exercises That Improve Performance. (Illus.). 1978. 17.95x (ISBN 0-13-387621-7, Parker). P-H.

Butts, D. P. A Summary of Research in Science Education 1979. 130p. 1981. pap. 28.95 (ISBN 0-471-86587-7). Wiley.

Butts, David, jt. auth. see Peterson, Rita W.

Butts, David P. Teaching Science in the Elementary School. LC 72-86790. (Orig.). 1973. pap. text ed. 7.95 (ISBN 0-02-905060-X). Free Pr.

Butts, Hugh F., jt. auth. see Haskins, James M.

Butts, Karen R. Breathing Exercises for Asthma. (Illus.). 66p. 1980. spiral 12.75x (ISBN 0-398-04104-0). C C Thomas.

Butts, M., ed. see Linker, Robert.

Butts, Mary. Scenes from the Life of Cleopatra. LC 74-11648. (Neglected Books of the Twentieth Century Ser.). 286p. 1974. 7.95 (ISBN 0-912946-14-8). Ecco Pr.

Butts, Nancy K., et al, eds. The Elite Athlete. LC 85-10744. (Sports Medicine & Health Science Ser.). 285p. 1985. text ed. 35.00 (ISBN 0-89335-228-4). SP Med & Sci Bks.

Butts, R. Freeman. The American Tradition in Religion & Education. LC 73-20903. 230p. 1974. Repr. of 1950 ed. lib. bdg. 15.00 (ISBN 0-8371-5875-3, BURE). Greenwood.

--College Charts Its Course: Historical Conceptions & Current Proposals. LC 73-165710. (American Education, Ser. 2). 1972. Repr. of 1939 ed. 24.50 (ISBN 0-405-03699-X). Ayer Co Pubs.

--The Revival of Civic Learning: A Rationale for Citizenship Education in American Schools. LC 80-81870. (Foundation Monograph Ser.). 170p. (Orig.). 1980. pap. 6.00 (ISBN 0-87367-423-5). Phi Delta Kappa.

Butts, R. Freeman & Peckenpaugh, Donald H. The School's Role as Moral Authority. LC 77-89087. 1977. pap. text ed. 4.50 (ISBN 0-87120-085-6, 611-77110). Assn Supervision.

Butts, Robert E. Kant & the Double Government Methodology. 1984. lib. bdg. 43.00 (ISBN 90-277-1760-5, Pub. by Reidel Holland). Kluwer Academic.

Butts, Robert E. & Hintikka, Jaakko, eds. Basic Problems in Methodology & Linguistics. (Western Ontario Ser: No. 11). 1977. lib. bdg. 53.00 (ISBN 90-277-0829-0, Pub. by Reidel Holland). Kluwer Academic.

--Foundational Problems in the Special Sciences. (Western Ontario Ser: No. 10). 1977. lib. bdg. 53.00 (ISBN 90-277-0710-3, Pub. by Reidel Holland). Kluwer Academic.

--Historical & Philosophical Dimensions of Logic, Methodology & Philosophy of Science. (Western Ontario Ser: No. 12). 1977. lib. bdg. 56.00 (ISBN 90-277-0831-2, Pub. by Reidel Holland). Kluwer Academic.

--Logic, Foundations of Mathematics & Computability Theory. (Western Ontario Ser: No. 9). 1977. lib. bdg. 53.00 (ISBN 90-277-0708-1, Pub. by Reidel Holland). Kluwer Academic.

Butts, Robert E. & Pitt, Joseph C., eds. New Perspectives on Galileo. (Western Ontario Ser: No. 14). 1978. lib. bdg. 39.50 (ISBN 90-277-0859-2, Pub. by Reidel Holland); pap. 15.80 (ISBN 90-277-0891-6). Kluwer Academic.

Butts, Robert F. American Education in International Development. facs. ed. LC 73-117763. (Essay Index Reprint Ser). 1963. 17.00 (ISBN 0-8369-1786-3). Ayer Co Pubs.

Butts, Robert F., jt. auth. see Roberts, Jane.

Butts, W. E. The Inheritance. (Illus.). 32p. (YA) 1981. pap. 5.00 (ISBN 0-939622-27-0). Four Zoas Night.

Butt-Thompson, F. W. West African Secret Societies: Their Organizations, Officials & Teaching. 1969. Repr. of 1929 ed. 10.00 (ISBN 0-87266-003-6). Argosy.

Butt-Thompson, Frederick W. West African Secret Societies, Their Organizations, Officials & Teaching. LC 70-109320. (Illus.). Repr. of 1929 ed. 22.50x (ISBN 0-8371-3585-0, BWA&). Greenwood.

Buttton, Kenneth J., et al, eds. Reviews of Infrared & Millimeter Waves: Vol. 2. Optically Pumped Far-Infrared Lasers. 492p. 1984. 69.50x (ISBN 0-306-41487-2, Plenum Pr). Plenum Pub.

Butturff, Diane & Coffman, Mary. French: Language & Life Styles. (Illus.). 512p. 1975. text ed. 30.95 (ISBN 0-07-009455-1, C). McGraw.

Butwell, Richard. U Nu of Burma. rev. ed. (Illus.). 1969. 27.50x (ISBN 0-8047-0155-5). Stanford U Pr.

Butwell, Richard, jt. auth. see Vandenbosch, Amry.

Butwell, Richard, ed. Foreign Policy & the Developing Nation. LC 68-55041. 244p. 1969. 20.00x (ISBN 0-8131-1185-4). U Pr of Ky.

Butwill, N., jt. auth. see Brown, James R.

Butwin, Frances. The Jews in America. rev. ed. LC 68-31501. (In America Bks.). (Illus.). (gr. 5-11). 1980. PLB 7.95 (ISBN 0-8225-0217-8). Lerner Pubns.

--Jews of America: History & Sources. Blecher, Arthur C., ed. LC 73-2253. (Illus.). 160p. (gr. 7-9). 1973. pap. text ed. 3.95x (ISBN 0-87441-062-2). Behrman.

Butwin, Miriam & Pirmantgen, Pat. Protest I. LC 76-128798. (Real World: Crisis & Conflict Bks). (Illus.). (gr. 5-11). 1972. PLB 4.95g (ISBN 0-8225-0623-8). Lerner Pubns.

Butz, Arthur R. The Hoax of the Twentieth Century. LC 77-78964. 12.00 (ISBN 0-911038-23-X); pap. 8.00 (ISBN 0-911038-00-0). Inst Hist Rev.

Butz, George, jt. auth. see DeRisi, William J.

Butz, Ralph, illus. Christmas in Aunt Lillies Kitchen. (Illus.). 100p. 1978. pap. 3.00 (ISBN 0-931440-03-3). Stoneback Pub.

Butz, Ralph & Ward, Linda, illus. From Aunt Lillies Pantry Shelf. (Illus.). 100p. 1977. pap. 3.00 (ISBN 0-931440-01-7). Stoneback Pub.

Butz, Richard. How to Carve Wood: A Book of Projects & Techniques. LC 83-50680. (Illus.). 224p. 1984. pap. 13.95 (ISBN 0-918804-20-5, Dist. by W W Norton). Taunton.

Butzer, et al, eds. Approximation Theory & Functional Analysis: Anniversary Volume. (International Series of Numerical Math: Vol. 65). 632p. 1984. text ed. 48.95x (ISBN 3-76431-574-1). Birkhauser.

Butzer, Karl & Freeman, Leslie G., eds. Hydraulic Civilization in Egypt. LC 75-36398. (Prehistoric Archaelogy & Ecology Ser). (Illus.). 1976. pap. 6.50x (ISBN 0-226-08635-6). U of Chicago Pr.

Butzer, Karl W. Archaeology As Human Ecology: Methods & Theory for a Contextual Approach. LC 81-21576. (Illus.). 380p. 1982. 34.50 (ISBN 0-521-24652-0); pap. 14.95 (ISBN 0-521-28877-0). Cambridge U Pr.

--Environment & Archeology: An Ecological Approach to Prehistory. 2nd ed. LC 74-115938. (Illus.). 703p. 1971. text ed. 39.95x (ISBN 0-202-33023-0). Aldine Pub.

--Geomorphology from the Earth. (Meinig Ser.). (Illus.). 512p. 1976. text ed. 31.50 scp (ISBN 0-06-041097-3, HarpC). Har-Row.

--Geomorphology of the Lower Illinois Valley As a Spatial-Temporal Context for the Koster Archaic Site. (Reports of Investigations Ser.: No. 34). (Illus.). 60p. 1977. pap. 3.50 (ISBN 0-89792-067-8). Ill St Museum.

--Quarternary Stratigraphy & Climate in the Near East. 1958. pap. 20.00 (ISBN 0-384-06790-5). Johnson Repr.

--Recent History of an Ethiopian Delta: The Omo River & the Level of Lake Rudolf. LC 70-184080. (Research Papers Ser.: No. 136). 184p. 1971. pap. 10.00 (ISBN 0-89065-043-8). U Chicago Dept Geog.

Butzer, Karl W. & Hansen, Carl L. Desert & River in Nubia: Geomorphology & Prehistoric Environments at the Aswan Reservoir. LC 67-20761. (Illus.). 1968. 45.00x (ISBN 0-299-04770-9); Set Of 15 Maps. 20.00x (ISBN 0-685-20706-4). U of Wis Pr.

Butzer, Karl W., et al. Dimensions of Human Geography: Essays on Some Familiar & Neglected Themes. LC 77-27874. (Research Papers Ser: No. 186). (Illus.). 1978. pap. 10.00 (ISBN 0-89065-093-4). U Chicago Dept Geog.

Butzer, P. L. & Berens, H. Semi-Groups of Operators & Approximation. LC 68-11980. (Grundlehren der Mathematischen Wissenschaften: Vol. 145). 1967. 39.00 (ISBN 0-387-03832-9). Springer-Verlag.

Butzer, P. L. & Korevaar, J. On Approximation Theory. 2nd ed. (International Series of Numerical Mathematics: No. 5). (Illus.). 262p. 1972. 39.95x (ISBN 0-8176-0189-9). Birkhauser.

Butzer, P. L., ed. Linear Spaces & Approximation: Proceedings. (International Ser. of Numerical Mathematics: No. 40). 688p. 1978. 81.95x (ISBN 0-8176-0979-2). Birkhauser.

Butzer, P. L. & Feher, F., eds. E. B. Christoffel: The Influence of His Work in Mathematics & the Physical Sciences. (Illus.). 656p. 1981. 52.95x (ISBN 0-8176-1162-2). Birkhauser.

Butzer, P. L. & Szokefalvi-Nagy, B., eds. Abstract Spaces & Approximation. (International Series of Numerical Mathematics: No. 10). 423p. 1969. 68.95x (ISBN 0-8176-0194-5). Birkhauser.

Butzer, P. L., et al, eds. Linear Operators & Approximation, 2 vols. (International Series of Numerical Mathematics: Nos. 20 & 25). 1973. Vol. 1, 506p. 71.95x (ISBN 0-8176-0590-8); Vol. 2, 608p.,1975. 69.95x (ISBN 0-8176-0760-9). Birkhauser.

Butzler, Jean-Paul, ed. Campylobacter Infection in Man & Animals. 256p. 1984. 68.00 (ISBN 0-8493-5446-3). CRC Pr.

Buurman, Peter, ed. Podzols: Temperate Regions. (Benchmark Papers in Soil Science). 464p. 1984. 49.50 (ISBN 0-442-21129-5). Van Nos Reinhold.

Buursma, Kathryn & Stickney, Mary. Official Special Olympics Celebrity Cook Book. 1980. 15.00 (ISBN 0-87832-046-6). Piper.

Buvanendran, V, jt. auth. see Mason, I. L.

Buvet, R. & Ponnamperuma, C., eds. Chemical Evolution & the Origin of Life. LC 75-146189. (Molecular Evolution Ser.: Vol. 1). (Illus.). 571p. 1971. 34.00 (ISBN 0-444-10093-8, North-Holland). Elsevier.

Buvinic, Mayra see Tinker, Irene & Bramsen, Michelle B.

Buvinic, Mayra & Lycette, Margaret A., eds. Women & Poverty in the Third World. LC 82-8992. 344p. 1983. 32.50x (ISBN 0-8018-2681-0). Johns Hopkins.

Buvinic, Mayra, jt. ed. see Tinker, Irene.

Bux, W. & Rudin, H., eds. Performance of Computer Communication Systems: Proceedings of the IFIP WG 7.3 TC 6 International Symposium on the Performance of Computer C ommunication Systems, Zurich, Switzerland, 21-23 March, 1984. 500p. 1985. 50.00 (ISBN 0-444-86883-6). Elsevier.

Bux, William & Clark, James F. Data Entry Activities for the Micro Computer. 1982. text ed. 4.40 wkbk. (ISBN 0-538-10050-8, J05). SW Pub.

Bux, William E. & Cunningham, Edward G. RPG & RPG II Programming: Applied Fundamentals. (Illus.). 1979. pap. text ed. 23.95 (ISBN 0-13-783423-3). P-H.

Buxbaum, Ann & Gussin, Gilda. Alcohol & Other Drugs: Using Skills to Make Tough Choices. (Self-discovery Ser.). (Illus.). 59p. (gr. 7-11). 1984. pap. text ed. 5.95 (ISBN 0-913723-10-X); tchrs' guide 5.95 (ISBN 0-913723-11-8). Mgmt Sci Health.

Buxbaum, Ann, jt. auth. see Gussin, Gilda.

Buxbaum, David C., ed. Chinese Family Law & Social Change in Historical & Comparative Perspective. LC 76-7781. (Asian Law Ser: No. 3). 582p. 1978. 30.00x (ISBN 0-295-95448-5). U of Wash Pr.

Buxbaum, David C., et al, eds. China Trade: Prospects & Perspectives. LC 81-11858. 448p. 1982. 49.95x (ISBN 0-03-056687-8). Praeger.

Buxbaum, Edith. Troubled Children in a Troubled World. LC 79-128623. 341p. (Orig.). 1970. text ed. 30.00 (ISBN 0-8236-6653-0). Intl Univs Pr.

--Your Child Makes Sense: A Guidebook for Parents. 204p. (Orig.). 1961. text ed. 20.00 (ISBN 0-8236-7040-6); pap. text ed. 9.95 (ISBN 0-8236-8350-8, 027040). Intl Univs Pr.

Buxbaum, Edwin C. Collector's Guide to the National Geographic Magazine. 3rd ed. 1971. 26.25 (ISBN 0-9600494-0-1). Buxbaum.

--The Greek American Group of Tarpon Springs, Florida: A Study of Ethnic Identification & Acculturation. Cordasco, Francesco, ed. LC 80-843. (American Ethnic Groups Ser.). 1981. lib. bdg. 49.50x (ISBN 0-405-13407-X). Ayer Co Pubs.

Buxbaum, Edwin C., ed. Collector's Guide to the National Geographic Magazine: 35th Anniversary. (Illus.). 1971. deluxe ed. 125.00 (ISBN 0-9600494-1-X). Buxbaum.

Buxbaum, James M. The Corporate Politeia: A Conceptual Approach to Business, Government & Society. LC 81-40313. (Illus.). 96p. (Orig.). 1981. text ed. 20.50 (ISBN 0-8191-1763-3); pap. text ed. 8.50 (ISBN 0-8191-1764-1). U Pr of Amer.

Buxbaum, Larry M. The Yoga Food Book: A Guide to Vegetarian Eating & Cooking. (Illus.). 115p. 1975. spiral bdg. 4.00 (ISBN 0-915594-01-3). Univ Great Brother.

Buxbaum, Melvin H. Benjamin Franklin & the Zealous Presbyterians. LC 74-14932. 320p. 1974. 28.75x (ISBN 0-271-01176-9). Pa St U Pr.

--Benjamin Franklin, 1721-1906: A Reference Guide. 1983. 36.50 (ISBN 0-8161-7985-9, Hall Reference). G K Hall.

Buxbaum, Richard M., jt. auth. see Jennings, Richard W.

Buxbaum, Susan K. & Gelman, Rita G. Body Noises: Where They Come from, Why They Happen. LC 83-320. (Illus.). 72p. (gr. 3-7). 1983. PLB 8.99 (ISBN 0-394-95771-7); 8.99 (ISBN 0-394-85771-2). Knopf.

Buxbaum, Susan K., jt. auth. see Gelman, Rita G.

Buxtehude, Dietrich. Dietrich Buxtehudes Werke. Incl. Vol. 1. Kirchenkantaten Fuer Sopranstimme Mit Instrumenten. Gurlitt, Wilibald, ed. 75.00 (ISBN 0-89371-011-3); Vol. 2. Solokantanten fuer Alt, Tenor oder Bass mit Instrumenten. Gurlitt, Wilibald, ed. 75.00 (ISBN 0-89371-012-1); Vol. 3. Kirchenkantaten Fuer Zwei Singstimmen Mit Instrumenten. Rieber, Karl F. & Harms, Gottlieb, eds. 75.00 (ISBN 0-89371-013-X); Vol. 4. Grosse Vokalwerke. Harms, Gottlieb & Trede, Hilmar, eds. (ISBN 0-89371-014-8); Vol. 5. Zwoelf Kantaten und Arien fuer zwei Soprane und Bass mit Continuo und Instrumenten. Harms, Gottlieb & Trede, Hilmar, eds. 75.00 (ISBN 0-89371-015-6); Vol. 6. Neun Kantaten und Arien fuer zwei Soprane und Bass mit Continuo und Instrumenten. Harms, Gottlieb & Trede, Hilmar, eds. 75.00 (ISBN 0-89371-016-4); Vol. 7. Elf Kirchenkantaten und eine Aria Fuer Drei Singstimmen und Instrumente. Harms, Gottlieb & Trede, Hilmar, eds. 75.00 (ISBN 0-89371-017-2); Vol. 8. Neun Kantaten Fuer Vier Singstimmen und Instrumente. Kilian, Dietrich, ed. 80.00 (ISBN 0-685-74765-4). 1977. Vols. 1-7. pap. 75.00x (ISBN 0-685-74764-6); pap. 475.00 set (ISBN 0-89371-010-5). Broude.

Buxton, Barry, et al, eds. see Jones, Loyal, et al.

Buxton, Calude E., ed. Points of View in the Modern History of Psychology. Date not set. price not set (ISBN 0-12-148510-2). Acad Pr.

Buxton, Charles R., ed. Towards a Lasting Settlement. LC 78-147578. (Library of War & Peace; Int'l. Organization, Arbitration & Law). 1972. lib. bdg. 46.00 (ISBN 0-8240-0343-8). Garland Pub.

Buxton, Claude E. Adolescents in School. LC 72-91290. pap. 47.50 (ISBN 0-317-07909-3, 2021986). Bks Demand UMI.

Buxton, Clyne. Minister's Service Manual. text ed. 7.95 (ISBN 0-87148-584-2). Pathway Pr.

Buxton, Clyne W. This Way to Better Teaching. 1974. 5.25 (ISBN 0-87148-835-3); pap. 4.25 (ISBN 0-87148-836-1). Pathway Pr.

--What about Tomorrow? 1974. pap. 4.25 (ISBN 0-87148-903-1). Pathway Pr.

Buxton, D. R., jt. auth. see Johnston, H. B.

Buxton, David. The Wooden Churches of Eastern Europe: An Introductory Survey. (Illus.). 384p. 1982. 87.50 (ISBN 0-521-23786-6). Cambridge U Pr.

Buxton, David, tr. see Mattelart, Armand.

Buxton, David, tr. see Mattelart, Armand & Schmucler, Hector.

Buxton, Ed, jt. auth. see Fulton, Sue.

Buxton, Edward. Creative People at Work. LC 73-37245. 292p. 1983. pap. 9.95 (ISBN 0-917168-04-6). Executive Comm.

--New Business Tactics. 1983. pap. 20.00 (ISBN 0-917168-01-1). Executive Comm.

Buxton, Frank & Owen, Bill. The Big Broadcast 1920-1950. (Illus.). 301p. 1973. pap. 4.45 (ISBN 0-380-01058-5, 16683). Avon.

Buxton, Gail. Craft Making for Love & Money. LC 83-81742. (Illus.). 144p. 1983. pap. 12.50 (ISBN 0-917168-08-9). Executive Comm.

Buxton, Graham. Effective Marketing Logistics: The Analysis Planning & Control of Distribution Operations. 256p. 1975. 45.00x (ISBN 0-8419-5007-5). Holmes & Meier.

Buxton, H. J. & Koehler, S. R. English Painters & American Painters. 1980. Repr. of 1883 ed. lib. bdg. 30.00 (ISBN 0-89341-368-2). Longwood Pub Group.

Buxton, H. J. & Poynter, Edward J. German, Flemish & Dutch Painting. LC 79-23257. 1980. Repr. of 1881 ed. lib. bdg. 30.00 (ISBN 0-89341-369-0). Longwood Pub Group.

Buxton, I. L., et al. Cargo Access Equipment for Merchant Ships. LC 78-70528. 366p. 1979. 36.95x (ISBN 0-87201-099-6). Gulf Pub.

Buxton, Ian. Big Gun Monitors: The History of the Design, Construction & Operation of the Royal Navy's Monitors. LC 80-81901. (Illus.). 215p. 1980. 21.95 (ISBN 0-87021-104-8). Naval Inst Pr.

--Big Gun Monitors: The History of the Design, Construction, & Operation of the Royal Navy's Monitors. (Illus.). 215p. 1980. 21.95 (ISBN 0-87021-104-8); bulk rates avail. Naval Inst Pr.

Buxton, John. Elizabethan Taste. 370p. 1983. text ed. 20.45x (ISBN 0-391-02832-4, Pub. by Harvester England); pap. text ed. 11.45x (ISBN 0-391-02821-9). Humanities.

--The Grecian Taste: The Literature in the Age of Neo-Classicism 1740-1820. LC 78-909. (Illus.). 188p. 1978. text ed. 28.50x (ISBN 0-06-490845-3, 06378). B&N Imports.

Buxton, John, ed. see Walton, Izaak & Cotton, Charles.

Buxton, L. H. Primitive Labour. LC 70-115315. 1971. Repr. of 1924 ed. 21.00x (ISBN 0-8046-1106-8, Pub. by Kennikat). Assoc Faculty Pr.

Buxton, Laurie. Do You Panic About Maths? Coping with Maths Anxiety. 168p. (Orig.). 1981. pap. text ed. 12.00x (ISBN 0-435-50101-1). Heinemann Ed.

--Mathematics for Everyone. LC 84-22236. (Illus.). 270p. 1985. 16.95 (ISBN 0-8052-3986-3). Schocken.

Buxton, Leonard H. China, the Land & the People: A Human Geography. LC 79-2818. (Illus.). 333p. 1981. Repr. of 1929 ed. 31.75 (ISBN 0-8305-0000-6). Hyperion Conn.

Buxton, Marilyn. Advanced Projects for Children. (Thinking-Learning-Creating: TLC for Growing Minds Ser.). 59p. (gr. 5-8). 1984. pap. text ed. 9.95 (ISBN 0-88193-105-5). Create Learn.

--Beginning Projects for Children. (Thinking-Learning-Creating: TLC for Growing Minds Ser.). (Illus.). 47p. (gr. 5-8). 1983. pap. text ed. 9.95 (ISBN 0-88193-101-2). Create Learn.

--Intermediate Projects for Children. (Thinking-Learning-Creating: TLC for Growing Minds Ser.). (Illus.). 60p. (gr. 5-8). 1983. pap. text ed. 9.95 (ISBN 0-88193-103-9). Create Learn.

Buxton, Marilyn & Buxton, Robin. PET, Vol. 3. (Thinking-Learning-Creating: TLC for Growing Minds Ser.). 58p. (gr. 5-12). 1983. pap. text ed. 9.95 (ISBN 0-88193-023-7). Create Learn.

--PET, Vol. 4. (Thinking-Learning-Creating: TLC for Growing Minds Ser.). 54p. (gr. 5-12). 1983. pap. text ed. 9.95 (ISBN 0-88193-024-5). Create Learn.

--VIC-20, Vol. 4. (Thinking-Learning-Creating: TLC for Growing Minds Ser.). 63p. (gr. 5-12). 1983. pap. text ed. 9.95 (ISBN 0-88193-064-4). Create Learn.

Buxton, Marilyn & Buxton, Tammy. TI 99-4A, Vol. 3. (Thinking-Learning-Creating: TLC for Growing Minds Ser.). 65p. (gr. 5-12). 1983. pap. text ed. 9.95 (ISBN 0-88193-053-9). Create Learn.

--TI 99-4A, Vol. 4. (Thinking-Learning-Creating: TLC for Growing Minds Ser.). 45p. (gr. 5-12). 1983. pap. text ed. 9.95 (ISBN 0-88193-054-7). Create Learn.

Buxton, Marilyn, jt. auth. see Buxton, Robin.

Buxton, Neil. The Economic Development of the British Coal Industry. 1979. 48.00 (ISBN 0-7134-1994-6, Pub. by Batsford England). David & Charles.

Buxton, Neil K. & Aldcroft, Derek. British Industry Between the Wars: Instability & Industrial Development 1919-39. 1979. 40.00 (ISBN 0-85967-383-9); pap. 15.00 (ISBN 0-317-12615-6). Scolar.

Buxton, Peter, jt. auth. see Reardon, Ray.

Buxton, R. G. Persuasion in Greek Tragedy: A Study of Peitho. LC 81-17073. (Illus.). 256p. 1983. 42.50 (ISBN 0-521-24180-4). Cambridge U Pr.

Buxton, Richard. Sculptured Garland: A Selection from the Lyrical Poems of Walter Savage Landor. 1948. lib. bdg. 17.50 (ISBN 0-8414-1610-9). Folcroft.

Buxton, Robin. Commodore 64, Vol. 1. (Thinking-Learning-Creating: TLC for Growing Minds Ser.). 50p. (gr. 5-12). 1983. pap. text ed. 9.95 (ISBN 0-88193-041-5). Create Learn.

--Commodore 64, Vol. 2. (Thinking-Learning-Creating: TLC for Growing Minds Ser.). 58p. (gr. 5-12). 1983. pap. text ed. 9.95 (ISBN 0-88193-042-3). Create Learn.

--Commodore 64, Vol. 5. (Thinking-Learning-Creating: TLC for Growing Minds Ser.). 66p. (gr. 5-12). 1984. pap. text ed. 9.95 (ISBN 0-88193-045-8). Create Learn.

--Commodore 64, Vol. 6. (Thinking-Learning-Creating: TLC for Growing Minds Ser.). 76p. (YA) (gr. 9-12). 1984. pap. text ed. 9.95 (ISBN 0-88193-046-6). Create Learn.

--PET, Vol. 1. (Thinking-Learning-Creating: TLC for Growing Minds Ser.). 51p. (gr. 5-12). 1983. pap. text ed. 9.95 (ISBN 0-88193-021-0). Create Learn.

--PET, Vol. 2. (Thinking-Learning-Creating: TLC for Growing Minds Ser.). 51p. (gr. 5-12). 1983. pap. text ed. 9.95 (ISBN 0-88193-022-9). Create Learn.

--PET, Vol. 5. (Thinking-Learning-Creating: TLC for Growing Minds Ser.). 72p. (gr. 5-12). 1984. pap. text ed. 9.95 (ISBN 0-88193-025-3). Create Learn.

--PET, Vol. 6. (Thinking-Learning-Creating: TLC for Growing Minds Ser.). 56p. (YA) (gr. 5-10). 1984. pap. text ed. 9.95 (ISBN 0-88193-026-1). Create Learn.

--VIC-20, Vol. 1. (Thinking-Learning-Creating: TLC for Growing Minds Ser.). 51p. (gr. 5-12). 1983. pap. text ed. 9.95 (ISBN 0-88193-061-X). Create Learn.

--VIC-20, Vol. 2. (Thinking-Learning-Creating: TLC for Growing Minds Ser.). 59p. (gr. 5-12). 1983. pap. text ed. 9.95 (ISBN 0-88193-062-8). Create Learn.

--VIC-20, Vol. 3. (Thinking-Learning-Creating: TLC for Growing Minds Ser.). 59p. (gr. 5-12). 1983. pap. text ed. 9.95 (ISBN 0-88193-063-6). Create Learn.

Buxton, Robin & Buxton, Marilyn. Commodore 64, Vol. 3. (Thinking-Learning-Creating: TLC for Growing Minds Ser.). 59p. (gr. 5-12). 1983. pap. text ed. 9.95 (ISBN 0-88193-043-1). Create Learn.

--Commodore 64, Vol. 4. (Thinking-Learning-Creating: TLC for Growing Minds Ser.). 59p. (gr. 5-12). 1983. pap. text ed. 9.95 (ISBN 0-88193-044-X). Create Learn.

Buxton, Robin, jt. auth. see Buxton, Marilyn.

Buxton, Sydney C. Finance & Politics: An Historical Study, 1783-1885 2 Vols. LC 66-21367. Repr. of 1888 ed. Set. 75.00x (ISBN 0-678-00164-2). Kelley.

Buxton, Tammy. TI 99-4A, Vol. 1. (Thinking-Learning-Creating: TLC for Growing Minds Ser.). 54p. (gr. 5-12). 1983. pap. text ed. 9.95 (ISBN 0-88193-051-2). Create Learn.

--TI 99-4A, Vol. 2. (Thinking-Learning-Creating: TLC for Growing Minds Ser.). 53p. (gr. 5-12). 1983. pap. text ed. 9.95 (ISBN 0-88193-052-0). Create Learn.

Buxton, Tammy, jt. auth. see Buxton, Marilyn.

Buxton, Thomas F. African Slave Trade & Its Remedy 1839-1840. 582p. 1967. Repr. of 1840 ed. 37.50x (ISBN 0-7146-1159-X, BHA-01159, F Cass Co). Biblio Dist.

Buxton, Warren H. The P.38 Pistol, Vol. 2: The Contract Pistols 1940-1945. LC 78-51018. (Illus.). 256p. 1985. 45.50 (ISBN 0-9614024-0-7). Ucross Bks.

Buyers, Rebecca. The Marvelous Macadamia Nut. LC 82-73616. (Illus.). 84p. (Orig.). 1982. pap. 12.95 (ISBN 0-941034-74-7). I Chalmers.

Buyers, W. J., ed. Moment Formation in Solids. (NATO ASI Series B, Physics: Vol. 117). 350p. 1984. 49.50x (ISBN 0-306-41834-7, Plenum Pr). Plenum Pub.

Buyeva, L. P., ed. Civilisation & the Historical Process. Carlile, Cynthia, tr. from Ger. 398p. 1983. 8.95 (ISBN 0-8285-2564-1, Pub. by Progress Pubs USSR). Imported Pubns.

Buys, Clifford R. Motor Carrier Management Systems. 150p. 1980. text ed. 20.00 (ISBN 0-88711-025-8). Am Trucking Assns.

Buyse, H. & Robert, J. Electrical Machines & Converters: Modelling & Simulation. 1985. 40.75 (ISBN 0-444-87596-4). Elsevier.

Buyse, H. & Robert, J., eds. Simulation of Electrical Machines: Proceedings of the Conference, Liege, Belgium, May 17-18, 1983. 1984. write for info. (North-Holland). Elsevier.

Buyse, Marc E., et al, eds. Cancer Clinical Trials: Methods & Practice. (Illus.). 481p. 1984. 47.50x (ISBN 0-19-261357-X). Oxford U Pr.

Buysschaert, J. Criteria for the Classification of English Adverbials. (Royal Flemish Academy of Science, Literature, Proceedings 1982 Ser.). 176p. (Orig.). 1982. pap. 17.00x (ISBN 90-6569-321-1, Pub by Brepols Belgium). Benjamins North Am.

Buysse, James L. The Definitive Guide on How Not to Quit Smoking. (Illus.). 63p. (Orig.). 1982. pap. 3.95 (ISBN 0-911435-00-X). King Freedom.

Buytaert, Eligius M., jt. auth. see Boehner, Philotheus.

Buytaert, Eligius M., ed. Peter Aureoli: Scriptum Super Primum Sententiarum, 2 vols. (Text Ser). 1956. Vol. 1, Prologue-dist. 1. 20.00 (ISBN 0-686-11547-3); Vol. 2, Dist. 2-8. 23.00 (ISBN 0-686-11548-1). Franciscan Inst.

--Saint John Damascene: De Fide Orthodoxa, Versions of Burgundio & Cerbanus. (Text Ser). 1955. 23.00 (ISBN 0-686-11554-6). Franciscan Inst.

Buytaert, Eligius M., jt. ed. see Hooper, Sr. M. Rachel.

Buytendijk, F. J. The Mind of the Dog. LC 73-2964. (Classics in Psychology Ser.). Repr. of 1936 ed. 18.00 (ISBN 0-405-05137-9). Ayer Co Pubs.

--Prologomena to an Anthropological Physiology. (Psychological Ser.: No. 6). 1974. text ed. 15.50x (ISBN 0-391-00332-1). Duquesne.

Buytendijk, Frederik J. Pain: Its Modes & Functions. O'Shiel, Eda, tr. LC 72-12494. 189p. 1973. Repr. of 1961 ed. lib. bdg. 18.75 (ISBN 0-8371-6741-8, BUPM). Greenwood.

Buytendijk, Jacobus J. Wesen und Sinn Des Spiels: The Essence & Meaning of Games. LC 75-35064. (Studies in Play & Games). (Illus., German Text.). 1976. Repr. 17.00x (ISBN 0-405-07915-X). Ayer Co Pubs.

Buyukmichi, Hope S., jt. auth. see Richards, Dorothy.

Buyze, Jean. The Tenth Muse: Women Poets Before Eighteen Hundred Six. 1980. pap. 5.95 (ISBN 0-915288-39-7). Shameless Hussy.

Buz, E. Z., jt. auth. see Downs, Chugger.

Buzacott, J. A., et al, eds. Scale in Production Systems: Based on an IIASA Workshop June 26-29, 1979. (IIASA Proceedings: Vol. 15). (Illus.). 256p. 1982. 55.00 (ISBN 0-08-028725-5). Pergamon.

Buzaglo, Jorge. Planning the Mexican Economy: Alternative Development Strategies. LC 83-24792. 288p. 1984. 27.50 (ISBN 0-312-61433-0). St Martin.

Buzaljko, Grace, ed. see Kroeber, Alfred L. & Gifford, E. W.

Buzan, B. G. & Jones, R. J., eds. Change & the Study on International Relations. 1981. 27.50x (ISBN 0-312-12858-4). St Martin.

Buzan, Barry. People, States & Fear: A Conceptual Introduction to the Role of Force in International Relations. LC 83-3559. vi, 262p. 1983. 24.95x (ISBN 0-8078-1572-1); pap. 8.95 (ISBN 0-8078-4113-7). U of NC Pr.

Buzan, Norma & Howell, Bert. Bed & Breakfast in Michigan & Surrounding Areas. (Illus.). 228p. 1985. pap. 8.25 (ISBN 0-943232-04-X). Betsy Ross Pub.

Buzan, Norma S. Bed & Breakfast North America: A Directory of Agencies & Small Inns & Guesthouses. 3rd ed. (Illus.). 350p. 1984. pap. 10.95 (ISBN 0-943232-03-1). Betsy Ross Pub.

Buzan, Tony. The Brain User's Guide: A Handbook for Sorting Out Your Life. (Illus.). 128p. 1983. pap. 7.95 (ISBN 0-525-48045-5, 0772-230). Dutton.

--Speed Reading. (Illus.). 171p. 1984. pap. 7.95 (ISBN 0-525-48076-5, 0772-230). Dutton.

--Use Both Sides of Your Brain. rev. ed. (Illus.). 160p. 1983. pap. 6.95 (ISBN 0-525-48011-0, 0674-210). Dutton.

--Use Your Perfect Memory: A Complete Program of New Techniques for Remembering. (Illus.). 288p. 1984. pap. 9.95 (ISBN 0-525-48112-5, 0966-290). Dutton.

Buzan, Tony, jt. auth. see Dixon, Terence.

Buzas, I., ed. see International Conference on Thermal Analysis.

Buzas, I., jt. ed. see Pugnor, E.

Buzas, I., jt. ed. see Pungor, E.

Buzas, Ladislaus. German Library History: Eight Hundred to Nineteen Forty-Five. Boyd, William D., tr. Wolfe, Irmgard H., contrib. by. LC 84-43197. 600p. 1985. lib. bdg. 55.00 (ISBN 0-89950-175-3). McFarland & Co.

Buzby, Beth. Data Entry: Concepts & Applications. 480p. 1981. pap. text ed. 21.95 (ISBN 0-574-21255-8, 13-4255); instructor's guide avail. (ISBN 0-574-21256-6, 13-4256). SRA.

Buzby, Walter J. & Paine, David. Hotel & Motel Security Management. LC 76-12555. 256p. 1976. 24.95 (ISBN 0-913708-24-0). Butterworth.

Buzett, Frederick, jt. auth. see Hanson, Shirley.

Buzo, Alexander. Martello Towers. (Australian Plays Ser.). (Illus.). 76p. (Orig.). 1985. pap. 6.95 (ISBN 0-87910-237-3). Limelight Edns.

--Three Plays: Norm & Ahmed, Rooted & the Roy Murphy Show. (Australian Plays Ser.). (Illus.). 142p. (Orig.). 1985. pap. 7.95 (ISBN 0-87910-236-5). Limelight Edns.

Buzuev, A. Transnational Corporations & Militarism. 256p. 1985. 7.95 (ISBN 0-8285-2972-8, Pub. by Progress Pubs USSR). Imported Pubns.

Buzzacott & Wymore. Bi-Sexual Man or Evolution of the Sexes. 2nd ed. (Illus.). 83p. 1912. pap. 5.95 (ISBN 0-88697-012-1). Life Science.

Buzzacott, Francis H. The Mystery of the Sexes. (Illus.). 183p. 1914. pap. 8.95 (ISBN 0-88697-015-6). Life Science.

Buzzard, Juanita, jt. auth. see Buzzard, Lynn.

Buzzard, Lynn. Schools: They Haven't Got a Prayer. (Issues & Insights Ser.). 1982. pap. 5.95 (ISBN 0-89191-713-6). Cook.

--With Liberty & Justice. 156p. 1984. pap. 4.95 (ISBN 0-88207-613-2). Victor Bks.

Buzzard, Lynn & Buzzard, Juanita. Readiness for Reconciliation. 36p. (Orig.). 1982. wkbk 3.00 (ISBN 0-686-39857-2). Chr Concil Serv.

Buzzard, Lynn & Campbell, Paula. Holy Disobedience: When Christians Must Resist the State. 160p. (Orig.). 1984. pap. 6.95 (ISBN 0-89283-184-7). Servant.

Buzzard, Lynn & Ericcson, Samuel. The Battle for Religious Liberty. (Issues & Insight Ser.). (Orig.). 1982. pap. 6.95 (ISBN 0-89191-552-4, 55525). Cook.

Buzzard, Lynn R. & Eck, Laurence. Tell It to the Church. 192p. (Orig.). 1985. pap. 6.95 (ISBN 0-8423-6986-4). Tyndale.

Buzzati, Dino. Catastrophe: And Other Stories. Landry, Judith & Jolly, Cynthia, trs. from Ital. 200p. 1982. pap. 9.95 (ISBN 0-7145-3914-7). Riverrun NY.

--Restless Nights. Venuti, Lawrence, tr. & intro. by. LC 82-73713. 144p. 1983. pap. 12.00 (ISBN 0-86547-100-2). N Point Pr.

--The Siren. Venuti, Lawrence, tr. from Ital. 160p. (Orig.). 1984. pap. 10.50. N Point Pr.

--The Tartar Steppe. 1980. pap. 2.75 (ISBN 0-380-50252-6, 50252-6, Bard). Avon.

Buzzati-Traverso, Adriano A. The Scientific Enterprise, Today & Tomorrow. (Illus.). 439p. 1978. 59.50 (ISBN 92-3-101268-1, U865, UNESCO). Unipub.

Buzzell, Robert D., ed. Marketing in an Electronic Age. LC 84-25166. (Illus.). 404p. 1985. 32.50 (ISBN 0-87584-159-7). Harvard Busn.

Buzzotta, V. R., et al. Effective Motivation Through Performance Appraisal. 360p. 1980. Repr. of 1977 ed. prof. ref. 29.95 (ISBN 0-88410-499-0). Ballinger Pub.

--Effective Selling Through Psychology: Dimensional Sales Management Strategies. LC 82-16308. 344p. 1982. prof. ref. 29.95 (ISBN 0-88410-393-5). Ballinger Pub.

Bverey, D., jt. auth. see Sanders, G.

Byabazaire, Deogratias M. The Contribution of the Christian Churches to the Development of Western Uganda 1894-1974: Theology. (European University Studies: Ser. 23, Vol. 112). 198p. 1979. pap. 21.95 (ISBN 3-261-02553-0). P Lang Pubs.

Byars, Betsy. After the Goat Man. (Illus.). 126p. (gr. 3-5). 1975. pap. 1.75 (ISBN 0-380-00437-2, 53314-6, Camelot). Avon.

--The Animal, the Vegetable, & John D. Jones. LC 81-69665. (Illus.). 160p. (gr. 4-6). 1982. 11.95 (ISBN 0-385-28015-7); PLB 11.95 (ISBN 0-385-28016-5). Delacorte.

--The Animal, the Vegetable, & John D. Jones. (Illus.). 160p. (gr. 5 up). 1983. pap. 2.25 (ISBN 0-440-40356-1, YB). Dell.

--Betsy Byars Boxed Set. (gr. 5-8). 1979. pap. 7.50 (ISBN 0-380-46748-8, 46748-8, Camelot). Avon.

--Betsy Byars Boxed Set. Incl. The Pinballs; The Cybil War; The TV Kid; The Two-Thousand-Pound Goldfish. (gr. 4-6). 1985. Set. pap. 8.40 (ISBN 0-590-63050-4, Apple Paperbacks). Scholastic Inc.

--The Cartoonist. 128p. (gr. k-6). 1981. pap. 2.25 (ISBN 0-440-41046-0, YB). Dell.

--Cracker Jackson. LC 84-24684. 168p. (gr. 5-7). 1985. 11.95 (ISBN 0-670-80546-7). Viking.

--The Cybil War. (Illus.). 144p. (gr. 4-6). 1982. pap. 2.25 (ISBN 0-590-33750-5, Apple Paperbacks). Scholastic Inc.

--The Eighteenth Emergency. (Puffin Story Bk.). (Illus.). 1981. pap. 3.50 (ISBN 0-14-031451-2, Puffin). Penguin.

--Go & Hush the Baby. (Illus.). (ps-3). 1982. pap. 2.95 (ISBN 0-14-050396-X, Puffin). Penguin.

--Good-Bye, Chicken Little. LC 78-19829. 112p. (gr. 5 up). 1979. 10.53i (ISBN 0-06-020907-0); PLB 10.89 (ISBN 0-06-020911-9). HarpJ.

--Goodbye, Chicken Little. 128p. (gr. 4-6). 1981. pap. 2.25 (ISBN 0-590-33941-9, Apple Paperbacks). Scholastic Inc.

--The House of Wings. 136p. (gr. 3-7). 1982. pap. 2.95 (ISBN 0-14-031523-3, Puffin). Penguin.

--The Midnight Fox. (gr. 3-7). 1975. pap. 1.50 (ISBN 0-380-00197-7, 46987, Camelot). Avon.

--The Midnight Fox. (Puffin Story Bks.). 160p. (gr. 3-7). 1981. pap. 3.50 (ISBN 0-14-031450-4, Puffin). Penguin.

--The Night Swimmers. LC 79-53597. 160p. (gr. 4-6). 1980. 9.95; PLB 11.95 (ISBN 0-385-28709-7). Delacorte.

--The Night Swimmers. 144p. (YA) (gr. 5-9). 1981. pap. 2.25 (ISBN 0-440-96766-X, LE). Dell.

--The Night Swimmers. (Illus.). 144p. (gr. 5-9). pap. 2.25 (ISBN 0-440-45857-9, YB). Dell.

--The Pinballs. LC 76-41518. 144p. (gr. 5 up). 1977. 10.53i (ISBN 0-06-020917-8); PLB 10.89 (ISBN 0-06-020918-6). HarpJ.

--The Pinballs. (gr. 4-6). 1979. pap. 2.25 (ISBN 0-590-33785-8, Apple Paperbacks). Scholastic Inc.

--Rama, the Gypsy Cat. (gr. 3-9). 1976. pap. 1.25 (ISBN 0-380-00630-8, 41608, Camelot). Avon.

--Trouble River. 112p. (gr. 4-6). 1982. pap. 2.25 (ISBN 0-590-33708-4, Apple Paperbacks). Scholastic Inc.

--The TV Kid. (gr. 4-6). 1982. pap. 1.95 (ISBN 0-590-32555-8, Apple Paperbacks). Scholastic Inc.

--The Two-Thousand-Pound Goldfish. LC 81-48652. 160p. (gr. 5 up). 1982. 10.53i (ISBN 0-06-020889-9); PLB 10.89g (ISBN 0-06-020890-2). HarpJ.

--Two-Thousand-Pound Goldfish. Date not set. pap. 1.95 (ISBN 0-590-32925-1). Scholastic Inc.

--The Winged Colt of Casa Mia. (Illus.). 132p. (gr. 3-7). 1975. pap. 1.95 (ISBN 0-380-00201-9, 57489-6, Camelot). Avon.

Byars, Betsy C. After the Goat Man. LC 74-8200. (Illus.). 128p. (gr. 5-9). 1974. 10.95 (ISBN 0-670-10908-8). Viking.

--After the Goat Man. (Illus.). (gr. 3-7). 1982. pap. 2.95 (ISBN 0-14-031533-0, Puffin). Penguin.

--The Cartoonist. LC 77-12782. (Illus.). 128p. (gr. 3-7). 1978. 11.95 (ISBN 0-670-20556-7). Viking.

--The Computer Nut. LC 84-7239. 144p. (gr. 3-7). 1984. 11.95 (ISBN 0-670-23548-2, Viking Kestrel). Viking.

--The Cybil War. LC 80-26912. (Illus.). 144p. (gr. 8-12). 1981. 10.50 (ISBN 0-670-25248-4). Viking.

--The Eighteenth Emergency. LC 72-91399. (Illus.). 128p. (gr. 4-6). 1973. PLB 12.95 (ISBN 0-670-29055-6, Viking Kestrel). Viking.

--The Glory Girl. LC 83-5927. 144p. (gr. 5-9). 1983. 11.95 (ISBN 0-670-34261-0). Viking.

--The Glory Girl. (ps-3). 1985. pap. 3.50 (ISBN 0-14-031785-6, Puffin). Penguin.

--Go & Hush the Baby. (Illus.). (gr. k-3). 1971. PLB 10.50 (ISBN 0-670-34270-X). Viking.

--The House of Wings. (Illus.). 160p. (gr. 4-6). 1972. PLB 10.95 (ISBN 0-670-38025-3). Viking.

--The Lace Snail. (Illus.). 32p. (gr. k-3). 1975. PLB 9.95 (ISBN 0-670-41614-2). Viking.

--Midnight Fox. LC 68-27566. (Illus.). (gr. 3-7). 1968. PLB 12.95 (ISBN 0-670-47473-8). Viking.

--The Summer of the Swans. 144p. 1981. pap. 2.95 (ISBN 0-14-031420-2, Puffin). Penguin.

--Summer of the Swans. (Illus.). (gr. 7 up). 1970. 10.95 (ISBN 0-670-68190-3). Viking.

--Trouble River. (Illus.). (gr. 3-7). 1969. PLB 10.95 (ISBN 0-670-73257-5). Viking.

--The TV Kid. (Illus.). 128p. (gr. 4-6). 1976. 11.95 (ISBN 0-670-73331-8). Viking.

--The Winged Colt of Casa Mia. (Illus.). 128p. (gr. 4-6). 1973. 9.95 (ISBN 0-670-77318-2). Viking.

Byars, Ed & Holbrook, Bill. Soaring Cross Country. new ed. LC 74-78637. (Illus.). 180p. 1974. 9.95 (ISBN 0-914600-00-1). Ridge Soaring.

Byars, Edward F., et al. Engineering Mechanics of Deformable Bodies. 4th ed. 548p. 1983. text ed. 33.95 scp (ISBN 0-06-041109-0, HarpC); solution manual avail. (ISBN 0-06-361100-7). Har-Row.

Byars, Emma L. Witchcraft. 1981. 4.50 (ISBN 0-8062-1580-1). Carlton.

Byars, J. C., Jr., ed. Black & White. facsimile ed. LC 75-173602. (Black Heritage Library Collection). Repr. of 1927 ed. 12.50 (ISBN 0-8369-8914-7). Ayer Co Pubs.

Byars, Lloyd. Concepts of Strategic Management: Planning & Implementation. 320p. 1984. pap. text ed. 16.50scp (ISBN 0-06-041095-7, HarpC). Har-Row.

Byars, Lloyd L. Concepts of Strategic Management: Planning & Implementation. 1984. 17.50 (ISBN 0-317-06890-3). Har-Row.

--Strategic Management: Planning & Implementation, Concepts & Cases. 896p. 1984. text ed. 28.95 scp (ISBN 0-06-041096-5, HarpC); write for info. instr's manual (ISBN 0-06-361101-5). Har-Row.

Byars, Lloyd L. & Rue, Leslie W. Human Resource & Personnel Management. 1984. 28.50x (ISBN 0-256-03013-8). Irwin.

--Personnel Management. 442p. 1979. 29.95. (ISBN 0-7216-2250-X); instr's. manual 10.00 (ISBN 0-03-057067-0). Dryden Pr.

Byars, Lloyd L., jt. auth. see Rue, Leslie W.

Byars, Lloyd L., et al. Readings & Cases in Personnel Management. 1979. 14.95x (ISBN 0-7216-2252-6). Dryden Pr.

Byars, Lloyd L., jt. auth. see Rue, Leslie W.

Byars, Robert, jt. auth. see Speare, Grace.

Byars, Robert S. & Love, Joseph L., eds. Quantitative Social Science Research on Latin America. LC 72-95001. (University of Illinois at Urbana-Champaign Center for Latin American & Caribbean Studies Monograph: No. 1). pap. 70.00 (ISBN 0-317-29006-1, 2020245). Bks Demand UMI.

Byatt, A. S. Wordsworth & Coleridge in Their Time. LC 73-82999. (Illus.). 288p. 1973. 19.50x (ISBN 0-8448-0040-6). Crane-Russak Co.

Byatt, Antonia. Still Life. 376p. 16.95 (ISBN 0-684-18577-6, ScribT). Scribner.

Byatt, Antonia, intro. by see Elliott, George P.

Byatt, I. C. The British Electrical Industry Eighteen Seventy-Five to Nineteen Fourteen. 1979. 42.00x (ISBN 0-19-828270-2). Oxford U Pr.

Byatt, William J., jt. auth. see Karni, Shlomo.

Bybee, Rodger. Activities for Teaching About Science & Society. 1984. pap. text ed. 12.95 (ISBN 0-675-20059-8). Merrill.

Bybee, Rodger W. Human Ecology: A Perspective for Biology Education. LC 84-29595. (Monograph Ser. II). 63p. 1984. pap. write for info. (ISBN 0-941212-04-1). Natl Assn Bio Tchrs.

Bybee, Rodger W. & Gee, E. Gordon. Violence, Values, & Justice in the Schools. 264p. 1982. 26.95x (ISBN 0-205-07387-5, 237387, Pub. by Longwood Div). Allyn.

Bybee, Rodger W., jt. auth. see Sund, Robert B.

Bybee, Roger & Sund. Piaget for Educators. 2nd ed. 288p. 1982. pap. text ed. 12.95 (ISBN 0-675-09838-6). Merrill.

Bychowski, Gustav. Dictators & Disciples. 1969. pap. text ed. 9.95 (ISBN 0-8236-8029-0, 021280). Intl Univs Pr.

--Evil in Man: Anatomy of Hate & Violence. LC 68-13447. 104p. 1968. pap. 24.50 (ISBN 0-8089-0090-0, 790750). Grune.

Bycina, jt. auth. see Richards.

Bycina, jt. ed. see Richards.

Byck, Robert. The Mood Modifiers. (Encyclopedia of Psychoactive Drugs Ser.). (Illus.). 1985. PLB 15.95x. Chelsea Hse.

Byck, Robert, ed. see Freud, Sigmund.

Byde, Alan. Canoe Building in Glass-Reinforced Plastic. (Illus.). 192p. 1974. 15.00 (ISBN 0-7136-1457-9). Transatlantic.

--Canoeing (Kayaking) (Illus.). 1978. 10.95 (ISBN 0-7136-1826-4). Transatlantic.

--Living Canoeing. 3rd ed. (Illus.). 266p. 1979. 18.00 (ISBN 0-7136-1912-0). Transatlantic.

Bye, A. E. Art into Landscape, Landscape into Art. LC 82-22406. (Illus.). 178p. 1983. 28.00 (ISBN 0-914886-19-3); pap. 19.75 (ISBN 0-914886-20-7). PDA Pubs.

Bye, G. C. Portland Cement: Composition, Production & Properties. (The Pergamon Materials Engineering Practice Ser.). (Illus.). 156p. 1983. 20.00 (ISBN 0-08-029965-2); pap. 11.50 (ISBN 0-08-029964-4). Pergamon.

Bye, M. P., et al. Holt Mathematics 3. (Holt Mathematics Ser.). (gr. 9). 1978. text ed. 10.00 (ISBN 0-03-920014-0, Pub. by HR&W Canada); Tchr's Ed. 14.44 (ISBN 0-03-920015-9). HR&W.

Bye, Ranulph. Vanishing Depot. 1984. 35.00 (ISBN 0-910702-11-X). Haverford.

Bye, Ranulph & Richie, Margaret B. Victorian Sketchbook. (Illus.). 128p. 1980. 35.00 (ISBN 0-910702-04-7). Haverford.

Bye, Raymond T. Capital Punishment in the United States. LC 82-45658. 1983. Repr. of 1919 ed. 22.50 (ISBN 0-404-62405-7). AMS Pr.

Byer, Carol, illus. Henny Penny. LC 80-28146. (Illus.). 32p. (gr. k-4). 1981. PLB 7.89 (ISBN 0-89375-490-0); pap. text ed. 1.95 (ISBN 0-89375-491-9). Troll Assocs.

Byer, Norman. The Peripheral Retina in Profile. (Illus.). 159p. 1982. incl. cassettes 295.00 (ISBN 0-9609428-0-7). Criterion Pr.

Byer, Trevor A., jt. auth. see Fallen-Bailey, Darrel G.

Byerlee, J. D. & Wyss, M. Rock Friction & Earthquake Prediction. (Contributions to Current Research in Geophysics: No. 6). (Illus.). 413p. 1978. 70.95x (ISBN 0-8176-1018-9). Birkhauser.

Byerly, Carolyn M. The Mother's Book: How to Survive the Incest of Your Child. 64p. 1985. saddlestich 4.80 (ISBN 0-8403-3640-3). Kendall Hunt.

Byerly, Greg. Online Searching: A Dictionary & Bibliographic Guide. 288p. 1983. lib. bdg. 27.50 (ISBN 0-87287-381-1). Libs Unl.

Byerly, Greg & Rubin, Richard E. The Baby Boom: A Selective Annotated Bibliography. LC 84-47904. (Special Books Series in Libraries & Libraianship). 240p. 1984. 25.00x (ISBN 0-669-08903-6). Lexington Bks.

Byerly, Greg & Rubin, Rick. Pornography: The Conflict over Sexually Explicit Materials in the United States. An Annotated Bibliography. LC 80-1436. (Garland Reference Library of Social Science). 162p. 1980. 24.00 (ISBN 0-8240-9514-6). Garland Pub.

Byerman, Keith E. Fingering the Jagged Grain: Tradition & Form in Recent Black Fiction. LC 85-1102. 328p. 1986. text ed. 30.00 (ISBN 0-317-20356-8). U of Ga Pr.

Byers, A. L. Birth of a Reformation: Life & Labours of D. S. Warner. (Illus.). 496p. Repr. 5.50 (ISBN 0-686-29104-2). Faith Pub Hse.

Byers, Barbara. County Government in Washington State. LC 57-9238. (Illus.). (gr. 9-12). text ed. 7.50 (ISBN 0-8323-0165-5). Binford.

Byers, C. Randall, jt. auth. see Schneider, Kenneth C.

Byers, Carolyn. Mary Andrews: Companion of Sorrow. Wheeler, Gerald, ed. LC 83-21121. (A Banner Bk.). (Illus.). 91p. (Orig.). (gr. 5 up). 1984. pap. 5.95 (ISBN 0-8280-0212-6). Review & Herald.

Byers, Charles W. Shales: Depositional Processes & Environments. (Illus.). 225p. 1986. text ed. write for info. (ISBN 0-934634-67-X). Intl Human Res.

Byers, Charles W. & Binkley, Harold R. Handbook on Student Organizations in Vocational Education. (Illus.). 246p. 1981. pap. text ed. 7.95 (ISBN 0-8134-2175-6). Interstate.

Byers, Charles W., jt. auth. see Binkley, Harold R.

Byers, Chester. Cowboy Roping & Rope Tricks. xiii, 99p. 1928. pap. 2.00 (ISBN 0-486-21535-0). Dover.

Byers, Cordia. Callista. 352p. (Orig.). 1986. pap. 3.50 (ISBN 0-449-12462-2, GM). Fawcett.

--Love Storm. 352p. (Orig.). 1986. pap. 3.95 (ISBN 0-449-12817-2, GM). Fawcett.

--Silk & Steel. 352p. 1985. pap. 3.50 (ISBN 0-449-12746-X, GM). Fawcett.

Byers, D. & Johnson, F. Two Sites on Martha's Vineyard, Vol. 1 No. 1. LC 40-3078. 1940. 4.00 (ISBN 0-939312-00-X). Peabody Found.

Byers, David M. & Quinn, Bernard. Readings for Town & Country Church Workers: An Annotated Bibliography. LC 74-77445. 120p. 1974. pap. 2.00x (ISBN 0-914422-00-6). Glenmary Res Ctr.

Byers, Douglas S. The Nevin Shellheap: Burial & Observations, Vol. 9. 1979. 6.00 (ISBN 0-939312-10-7). Peabody Found.

Byers, Douglas S. & MacNeish, R. S., eds. Prehistory of the Tehuacan Valley. Incl. Vol. 1. Environment & Subsistence. (Illus.). 339p. 1968. 35.00x (ISBN 0-292-73683-5); Vol. 2. The Non-Ceramic Artifacts. (Illus.). 272p. 1968. 30.00x (ISBN 0-292-73684-3). (Illus.). 1968. U of Tex Pr.

Byers, Dwight C. Better Health with Foot Reflexology. (Illus.). 263p. (Orig.). 1983. pap. 14.95 (ISBN 0-9611804-2-0). Ingham Pub.

Byers, E. E., jt. auth. see Root, Kathleen B.

Byers, Edward A. The Long Forgetting. 288p. 1985. pap. 2.95 (ISBN 0-317-27053-2, Pub. by Baen Bks). PB.

Byers, Edward E. Gregg Medical Shorthand Dictionary. 1975. 24.35 (ISBN 0-07-009504-3). McGraw.

--Ten Thousand Medical Words, Spelled & Divided for Quick Reference. 128p. 1972. text ed. 7.48 (ISBN 0-07-009503-5). McGraw.

Byers, Edward E., jt. auth. see Place, Irene.

Byers, Edward E., ed. see Rosenberg, R. Robert, et al.

Byers, G. H. Attack Death in the Skies Over the Middle East. 300p. (Orig.). pap. 8.95 (ISBN 0-916829-03-0). Apollo.

Byers, George F. The Valiant Scot. LC 79-54332. (Renaissance Drama Ser.). 350p. 1980. lib. bdg. 46.00 (ISBN 0-8240-4451-7). Garland Pub.

Byers, Horace R. Elements of Cloud Physics. LC 65-17282. (Illus.). 1965. 20.00x (ISBN 0-226-08697-6). U of Chicago Pr.

--General Meteorology. 4th ed. (Illus.). 550p. 1974. text ed. 45.95 (ISBN 0-07-009500-0). McGraw.

Byers, J. W. Parent & Child. 60p. pap. 0.50 (ISBN 0-686-29132-8). Faith Pub Hse.

--Sanctification. 96p. 0.75 (ISBN 0-686-29140-9). Faith Pub Hse.

Byers, Jack A., jt. auth. see Prisk, Berneice.

Byers, John R., Jr. & Owen, James J. A Concordance to the Five Novels of Nathaniel Hawthorne. LC 79-7910. 951p. 1979. lib. bdg. 152.00 (ISBN 0-8240-9545-6). Garland Pub.

Byers, Kenneth T., ed. Employee Training & Development in the Public Sector. new ed. (Public Sector Human Resources Management Ser: Vol. 1). 394p. 1974. 14.00 (ISBN 0-87373-005-4). Intl Personnel Mgmt.

Byers, Laura T. Hortus Librorum: Early Botanical Books at Bumbarton Oaks. LC 83-5697. (Illus.). 48p. 1983. pap. 6.00x (ISBN 0-88402-118-1). Dumbarton Oaks.

Byers, Mary & McBurney, Margaret. The Governor's Road: Early Buildings & Families from Mississauga to London. (Illus.). 334p. 1982. 19.95 (ISBN 0-8020-2483-1). U of Toronto Pr.

Byers, Mary, jt. auth. see McBurney, Margaret.

Byers, Patricia & Preston, Julia. The Kids' Money Book. LC 82-184275. (Illus.). 144p. 1983. pap. 4.95 (ISBN 0-89709-041-1). Liberty Pub.

Byers, Paul. Unto Him Be Glory. 1974. 4.95 (ISBN 0-89114-047-6); pap. 2.95 (ISBN 0-89114-046-8). Baptist Pub Hse.

Byers, Paul, jt. auth. see Mead, Margaret.

Byers, R. B., ed. Canadian Annual Review of Politics & Public Affairs, 1979. 1981. 50.00x (ISBN 0-8020-2407-6). U of Toronto Pr.

--Canadian Annual Review of Politics & Public Affairs, 1980. 400p. 1982. 48.50x (ISBN 0-8020-2462-9). U of Toronto Pr.

--Canadian Annual Review of Politics & Public Affairs, 1982. (Canadian Annual Review Ser.). 368p. 1984. 50.00 (ISBN 0-8020-2533-1). U of Toronto Pr.

--Deterrence in the 1980s. 256p. 1985. 29.95 (ISBN 0-312-19593-1). St Martin.

Byers, R. McCulloch. The Hard Hat Girl - Power Engineer. LC 76-29554. 1976. 5.95 (ISBN 0-9602048-0-6). Fairfield Hse.

Byers, Robert. Everyman's Data Base Primer. 1983. pap. text ed. 19.95 (ISBN 0-8359-1799-1). Reston.

Byers, Robert A. The dBASE II for Every Business. Thomson, Monet & Lincoln, Mary, eds. 339p. 1983. pap. 19.95 (ISBN 0-912677-03-1). Ashton-Tate Bks.

--The dBASE II for Every Business. 399p. 19.95 (ISBN 0-8359-1246-9). Reston.

--The dBASE III for Every Business. 300p. 1985. pap. 19.95 (ISBN 0-912677-32-5). Ashton-Tate Bks.

--Everyman's Database Primer: Featuring dBASE III. 300p. 1984. pap. 19.95 (ISBN 0-912677-31-7). Ashton-Tate Bks.

--Everyman's Database Primer: Featuring dBASE II. Barre, Virginia, ed. 295p. 1982. pap. 19.95 (ISBN 0-912677-00-7). Ashton-Tate Bks.

--Introduction to UNIX System V. 350p. 1985. pap. 17.95 (ISBN 0-912677-29-5). Ashton-Tate Bks.

Byers, Roland O. Flak Dodger. LC 85-60155. (Illus.). 256p. (Orig.). 1985. pap. 12.95 (ISBN 0-9614563-0-2). Pawpaw Pr.

--The Linchpin: The Oregon Trail in Eighteen Forty-Three. new ed. LC 83-51526. (GEM Book). (Illus.). 300p. (Orig.). 1984. pap. 12.95 (ISBN 0-89301-094-4). U Pr of Idaho.

Byers, Samuel H. M. With Fire & Sword. 1983. Repr. of 1911 ed. 16.95 (ISBN 0-89201-110-6). Zenger Pub.

Byers, T. J. Guide to Local Area Networks. (Illus.). 182p. 1985. 24.95 (ISBN 0-13-369679-0); pap. 15.95 (ISBN 0-13-369661-8). P-H.

--Inside the IBM PC AT. 288p. 1985. 19.95 (ISBN 0-07-009520-5, BYTE Bks). McGraw.

--Microprocessor Support Chips: Theory, Design & Applications. 302p. (Orig.). 1982. 38.00 (ISBN 0-942412-05-2). Micro Text Pubs.

--Microprocessor Support Chips: Theory, Design, & Applications. (Illus.). 300p. 1983. 39.50 (ISBN 0-07-009518-3). McGraw.

--Solar Cells: Understanding & Using Photovoltaics. 256p. (Orig.). 1982. pap. 14.95 (ISBN 0-942412-04-4). Micro Text Pubs.

--Twenty Selected Solar Projects: Making Photovoltaics Work for You. 1984. 19.95 (ISBN 0-13-934779-8); pap. 11.95 (ISBN 0-13-934761-5). P-H.

Byers, Tracy. Martha Berry, the Sunday Lady of Possum Trot. LC 72-159905. 1971. Repr. of 1932 ed. 40.00x (ISBN 0-8103-3783-5). Gale.

Byers, Vera S., jt. ed. see Baldwin, R. W.

Byers, Virginia B. Nursing Observation. 3rd ed. (Foundations of Nursing Ser.). 226p. 1977. pap. text ed. write for info. (ISBN 0-697-05542-6). Wm C Brown.

Byers, William N. & Kellom, John H. Hand-book to the Gold Fields of Nebraska & Kansas. LC 72-9432. (The Far Western Frontier Ser.). (Illus.). 122p. 1973. Repr. of 1859 ed. 11.00 (ISBN 0-405-04963-3). Ayer Co Pubs.

Byers-Brown, Betty. Speech Therapy: Principles & Practice. (Illus.). 272p. 1981. pap. text ed. 15.00 (ISBN 0-443-02099-X). Churchill.

Byfield, Brian & Orpin, Alan. Every Great Chess Player Was Once a Beginner. 1974. 24.95 (ISBN 0-8184-0203-2). Lyle Stuart.

Byfield, Judith S. Help with Business English. (gr. 10-12). 1984. pap. text ed. 4.16 (ISBN 0-395-34819-6); tchr's manual 1.00 (ISBN 0-395-34820-X). HM.

Byfield, Magdelina. In a Miniature Garden. 64p. pap. 6.95 (ISBN 0-87588-175-0). Hobby Hse.

Byfield, Richard, jt. auth. see Pike, James.

Byfield, Sue. To Be or Not to Be. (Harlequin Romances Ser.). 192p. 1983. pap. 1.50 (ISBN 0-373-02529-7). Harlequin Bks.

Bygott, Ursula M. With Pen & Tongue. 444p. 1980. 40.00x (ISBN 0-522-84150-3, Pub. by Melbourne U Pr Australia). Intl Spec Bk.

Bygrave, Stephen. Coleridge & the Self: Romantic Egotism. 224p. 1985. 27.50 (ISBN 0-312-14721-X). St Martin.

Byham, William, jt. auth. see Thornton, George, III.

Byham, William C., jt. ed. see Moses, Joseph L.

Bying, Lucy. Roumanian Stories. 1979. Repr. of 1921 ed. lib. bdg. 35.00 (ISBN 0-8495-0517-8). Arden Lib.

Byington, Cyrus. A Dictionary of the Choctaw Language. (Choctaw.). Repr. of 1915 ed. 79.00x (ISBN 0-403-03579-1). Scholarly.

Byington, Ezra H. The Puritan As a Colonist & Reformer. LC 75-31115. Repr. of 1899 ed. 34.50 (ISBN 0-404-13601-X). AMS Pr.

--The Puritan in England & New England: With a Chapter on Witchcraft in New England. 4th & enl. ed. LC 70-183241. (Research & Source Works Ser). (Illus.). 457p. 1972. Repr. of 1900 ed. lib. bdg. 29.50 (ISBN 0-8337-4017-2). B Franklin.

Byington, Margaret. Homestead: The Households of a Milltown. (Illus.). 1974. text ed. 19.95x (ISBN 0-8229-4200-3); pap. text ed. 7.95 (ISBN 0-8229-8250-1). U of Pittsburgh Pr.

Byington, Margaret F. Homestead: The Households of a Milltown. LC 70-89757. (American Labor, from Conspiracy to Collective Bargaining, Ser. 1). 307p. 1969. Repr. of 1910 ed. 20.00 (ISBN 0-405-02109-7). Ayer Co Pubs.

Byington, Steven, tr. see Striner, Max.

Byington, Steven T., tr. The Bible in Living English: Written by an Anarchist. (Men & Movements in the History & Philosophy of Anarchism Ser.). 1979. lib. bdg. 59.95 (ISBN 0-686-59576-9). Revisionist Pr.

Byington, Steven T., tr. see Eltzbacher, Paul.

Byington, Steven T., tr. see Stirner, Max.

Bykhovskii, Bernard. Kierkegaard. (Philosophical Currents Ser: No. 16). 122p. 1976. pap. text ed. 17.75x (ISBN 90-6032-070-0). Humanities.

Bykhovsky, B. Schopenhauser & the Ground Existence. (Philosophical Currents Ser.: Vol. 30). 194p. 1984. pap. text ed. 19.00x (ISBN 90-6032-208-8, Pub. by B R Gruner Netherlands). Humanities.

Bykhovsky, Isidor I. Fundamentals of Vibration Engineering. 2nd ed. Zhitomirsky, V., tr. from Russ. LC 77-20089. 384p. 1980. lib. bdg. 26.00 (ISBN 0-88275-550-1). Krieger.

Bykov, O., et al. Priorities of Soviet Foreign Policy Today. 214p. 1981. 5.00 (ISBN 0-8285-2151-4, Pub. by Progress Pubs USSR). Imported Pubns.

Bykov, Vasil. His Battalion & Live Until Dawn: Contemporary Russian Writing. Woodhouse, Jennifer & Woodhouse, Robert, trs. 412p. 1982. 14.95 (ISBN 0-7022-1605-4). U of Queensland Pr.

Bykov, Vasilii. Pack of Wolves. Solotaroff, Lynn, tr. from Rus. LC 80-2456. 192p. (gr. 7 up). 1981. 11.49i (ISBN 0-690-04114-4); PLB 11.89g (ISBN 0-690-04115-2). Crowell Jr Bks.

Bylander, E. G. Electronic Displays. LC 78-31849. (Illus.). 1979. 35.00 (ISBN 0-07-009510-8). McGraw.

Bylanski, P. & Ingram, D. G. Digital Transmission Systems. rev. ed. (IEE Telecommunications Ser.). 430p. pap. 35.00 (ISBN 0-906048-37-0, TE004, Pub. by Peregrinus England). Inst Elect Eng.

Bylebyl, Jerome J. Teaching the History of Medicine at a Medical Center. LC 82-148. 200p. 1982. 16.50x (ISBN 0-8018-2799-X). Johns Hopkins.

Byles, A. T., ed. The Book of the Ordre of Chyualry. (EETS, OS Ser.: No. 168). Repr. of 1926 ed. 13.00 (ISBN 0-527-00165-1). Kraus Repr.

Byles, Marie B. Footprints of Gautama the Buddha. LC 68-5855. (Illus.). 1967. pap. 1.75 (ISBN 0-8356-0399-7, Quest). Theos Pub Hse.

Byles, Mather. The Works of Mather Byles. LC 78-6439. 1978. 70.00x (ISBN 0-8201-1309-3). Schol Facsimiles.

Bylinsky, Gene. Life in Darwin's Universe: Evolution & the Cosmos. LC 80-2988. (Illus.). 256p. 1981. 17.95 (ISBN 0-385-17049-1). Doubleday.

Bylov, B. F., et al. Ten Papers on Analysis. LC 51-5559. (Translations Ser.: No. 2, Vol. 74). 1968. 35.00 (ISBN 0-8218-1774-4, TRANS 2-74). Am Math.

Byman, Isabelle Y. Piano Teacher's Art (Guideline for Successful Piano Teaching) De Vito, Albert K., ed. 1979. 13.50 (ISBN 0-934286-13-2). Kenyon.

Byne, M. Forgotten Shrines of Spain. 1976. lib. bdg. 59.95 (ISBN 0-8490-1859-5). Gordon Pr.

--The Sculptured Capital in Spain. 1976. lib. bdg. 59.95 (ISBN 0-8490-2577-X). Gordon Pr.

--Spanish Gardens & Patios. 1976. lib. bdg. 75.00 (ISBN 0-8490-2649-0). Gordon Pr.

--Spanish Ironwork. 1976. lib. bdg. 75.00 (ISBN 0-8490-2650-4). Gordon Pr.

Byng, Edward J. The World of the Arabs. LC 74-869. (Essay Index Reprint Ser.). Repr. of 1944 ed. 18.75 (ISBN 0-518-10144-4). Ayer Co Pubs.

Byng, Lucy M., tr. from Roumanian. Roumanian Stories. facsimile ed. LC 73-169543. (Short Story Reprint Ser.). Repr. of 1921 ed. 18.00 (ISBN 0-8369-4004-0). Ayer Co Pubs.

Byng-Hall, John, jt. ed. see Whiffen, Rosemary.

Bynjes, W E. Medical & Pharmaceutical Dictionary: German-English. 4th ed. 574p. 1981. 125.00 (ISBN 0-317-14289-5, Pub. by Holdan Bk Ltd UK). State Mutual Bk.

Bynner, Edwin L. Chase of the Meteor, & Other Stories. facs. ed. LC 79-81264. (Short Story Index Reprint Ser.). 1891. 17.00 (ISBN 0-8369-3016-9). Ayer Co Pubs.

Bynner, Witter. The Chinese Translations. 400p. 1978. pap. 9.95 (ISBN 0-374-51708-8). FS&G.

--Light Verse & Satires. Smith, Jay W., ed. 368p. 1978. 20.00 (ISBN 0-374-18740-1). FS&G.

--Prose Pieces. Kraft, James, ed. LC 78-11441. 430p. 1979. 25.00 (ISBN 0-374-23833-2). FS&G.

--Selected Letters. Kraft, James, ed. 304p. 1981. 30.00 (ISBN 0-374-18504-2). FS&G.

--Selected Poems. Wilbur, Richard, ed. 384p. 1978. 20.00 (ISBN 0-374-25863-5). FS&G.

--Take Away the Darkness. LC 83-45725. Repr. of 1947 ed. 22.50 (ISBN 0-404-20049-4). AMS Pr.

--Tiger. LC 77-70352. (One-Act Plays in Reprint Ser.). 1977. Repr. of 1913 ed. 13.50x (ISBN 0-8486-2013-5). Core Collection.

Bynner, Witter see Euripides.

Bynon, James, ed. Current Progress in Afro-Asiatic Linguistics: Papers from the Third International Hamito-Semitic Congress. (Current Issues in Linguistic Theory Ser.: Vol. 28). 505p. 1984. 58.00x (ISBN 90-272-3520-1). Benjamins North Am.

Bynon, James, ed. see Colloquium of Linguistics Association of Great Britain, Historical Section, Univ. of London, March 18-20, 1970.

Bynon, Theodora. Historical Linguistics. LC 76-62588. (Cambridge Textbooks in Linguistics Ser.). (Illus.). 1977. 47.50 (ISBN 0-521-21582-X); pap. 14.95 (ISBN 0-521-29188-7). Cambridge U Pr.

Bynon, Theodora, ed. see Colloquium of Linguistics Association of Great Britain, Historical Section, Univ. of London, March 18-20, 1970.

Bynum, Bill. Teaching Youth with Confidence. 48p. 1983. pap. 2.95 (ISBN 0-910566-41-0); seminar planbook 2.95 (ISBN 0-910566-42-9). Evang Tchr.

Bynum, Caroline W. Jesus as Mother: Studies in the Spirituality of the High Middle Ages. (Cal Ser.: No. 697). 279p. 1984. pap. text ed. 7.95 (ISBN 0-520-05222-6). U of Cal Pr.

Bynum, Curtis. Marriage Bonds of Tryon & Lincoln Counties, North Carolina. 184p. 1982. Repr. of 1962 ed. 17.50 (ISBN 0-89308-316-X). Southern Hist Pr.

Bynum, David E., ed. see Parry, Milman.

Bynum, Terrell W., ed. see Frege, Gottlob.

Bynum, W. F. & Porter, Roy, eds. William Hunter & the Eighteenth Century Medical World. 450p. Date not set. price not set. (ISBN 0-521-26806-0). Cambridge U Pr.

Bynum, William F., et al, eds. Dictionary of the History of Science. LC 81-47116. (Illus.). 528p. 1981. 50.00 (ISBN 0-691-08287-1); pap. 12.95 (ISBN 0-691-02384-0). Princeton U Pr.

Byny, Richard L., jt. ed. see Thompson, Troy L.

Byock, Jesse. Feud in the Icelandic Saga. LC 82-40098. (Illus.). 300p. 1982. 27.50x (ISBN 0-520-04564-5). U of Cal Pr.

Byon, Jae-Hyon. Local Gazetteers of Southwest China: A Handbook. (Parerga Ser.: No. 5). 154p. 1979. pap. 5.50x (ISBN 0-295-95702-6). U of Wash Pr.

Byram, H. M. Occupations for Youth in Agriculture. text ed. 4.00x (ISBN 0-8134-0492-4, 492). Interstate.

--Some Problems in the Provision of Professional Education for College Teachers. LC 79-176621. (Columbia University. Teachers College. Contributions to Education: No. 576). Repr. of 1933 ed. 22.50 (ISBN 0-404-55576-4). AMS Pr.

Byram, Harold M. Guidance in Agricultural Education. LC 65-25513. (Illus.). 298p. 1966. text ed. 7.95x (ISBN 0-8134-0521-1, 521). Interstate.

Byram, J. E., ed. see Arme, C., et al.

Byram, M. S. Tom Kristensen. (World Authors Ser.). 1982. lib. bdg. 18.50 (ISBN 0-8057-6491-7, Twayne). G K Hall.

Byram, Martin L. Theater for Development: A Guide to Training. (Training Notes Ser.). 65p. (Orig.). pap. text ed. 4.00 (ISBN 0-932288-76-6). Ctr Intl Ed U of MA.

Byram, Martin L., et al. Modules for Training Extension Workers. (Curriculum Aid Ser.). 85p. pap. text ed. 6.00 (ISBN 0-932288-77-4). Ctr Intl Ed U of MA.

Byram, Michael, jt. ed. see Goodings, Richard.

Byrant, Arthur. Pepys: Vol. I, The Man in the Making 1663-1669. 352p. 1985. pap. 8.95 (ISBN 0-586-06470-2, Pub. by Granada England). Academy Chi Pubs.

--Pepys: Vol. II, The Years of Peril 1669-1683. 384p. 1985. pap. 8.95 (ISBN 0-586-06471-0, Pub. by Granada England). Academy Chi Pubs.

--Pepys: Vol. III, The Savior of the Navy 1683-1689. 352p. 1985. pap. 8.95 (ISBN 0-586-06472-9, Pub. by Granada England). Academy Chi Pubs.

Byrd. The Edicts of Vulcan. LC 84-70521. 213p. 1984. pap. 10.95 (ISBN 0-9613299-0-4). Byrd SDI.

Byrd, jt. auth. see Abrams.

Byrd, et al see Beck, Syndey.

Byrd, Anita. Handwriting Analysis. LC 81-3461. (Illus.). 183p. 1981. 9.95 (ISBN 0-668-05307-0); pap. 5.95 (ISBN 0-668-05311-9). Arco.

Byrd, Anne. Omelettes & Souffles. Rich, Irene, ed. LC 81-68839. (Great American Cooking Schools Ser.). (Illus.). 84p. 1982. pap. 5.95 (ISBN 0-941034-08-9). I Chalmers.

--Omelettes & Souffles. LC 82-47860. (Great American Cooking Schools Ser.). (Illus.). 84p. 1982. 8.61i (ISBN 0-06-015065-3, HarpT). Har-Row.

Byrd, Ben. The Basketball: University of Tennessee Basketball. LC 74-21103. (College Sports Ser.). Orig. Title: Tennessee Basketball. 1980. 9.95 (ISBN 0-87397-052-7). Strode.

Byrd, Ben, jt. auth. see Campbell, Archie.

Byrd, Bobby. Here. 60p. 1975. pap. 25.00 (ISBN 0-913028-37-1). North Atlantic.

Byrd, C. L., tr. Soho. LC 80-2856. 528p. 1981. 16.95 (ISBN 0-385-17185-4). Doubleday.

Byrd, Cecil K. A Bibliography of Illinois Imprints, 1814-58. LC 65-24423. pap. 156.80 (ISBN 0-317-26164-9, 2024086). Bks Demand UMI.

Byrd, D. H. I'm an Endangered Species: The Autobiography of a Free Enterpriser. LC 78-62614. 122p. 1978. 6.95x (ISBN 0-88415-258-8, Pub. by Pacesetter Pr). Gulf Pub.

Byrd, Deborah. Under Texas Skies: Feeling at Home among the Planets & Stars. (Illus.). 100p. (Orig.). Date not set. pap. write for info. (ISBN 0-939722-27-5). Pressworks.

Byrd, Don. Aesop's Garden. 1976. pap. 4.00 (ISBN 0-913028-42-8). North Atlantic.

--Charles Olson's Maximus. LC 79-21788. 218p. 1980. 15.00x (ISBN 0-252-00779-4). U of Ill Pr.

Byrd, Donald R. & Cabetas, Isis C. React Interact: Situations for Communication. (Illus.). 100p. (gr. 10-12). 1980. pap. text ed. 5.95 (ISBN 0-88345-412-2, 18674). Regents Pub.

Byrd, Doris A., jt. auth. see Byrd, Robert L.

Byrd, Doris Elaine. Organizational Constraints on Psychiatric Treatment. Roth, Julius A., ed. (Research in the Sociology of Health Care: Supplement No. 1). 285p. 1981. 40.00 (ISBN 0-89232-176-8). Jai Pr.

Byrd, Elizabeth. The Famished Land. 1978. pap. 1.95 (ISBN 0-380-39313-1, 39313). Avon.

--I'll Get By. 204p. (gr. 7up). 1981. 9.95 (ISBN 0-670-39134-4). Viking.

--I'll Get By. 224p. 1982. pap. 1.95 (ISBN 0-449-70020-8, Juniper). Fawcett.

--It Had to Be You. LC 82-2604. 180p. (gr. 7 up). 1982. 11.95 (ISBN 0-670-40306-7). Viking.

--Lady of Monkton. LC 74-78519. 192p. 1975. pap. 2.50 (ISBN 0-8128-7053-0). Stein & Day.

--Rest Without Peace. 1975. pap. 1.50 (ISBN 0-380-00401-1, 26831). Avon.

--The Search for Maggie Hare. (Orig.). 1977. pap. 1.50 (ISBN 0-380-00925-0, 31872). Avon.

Byrd, Harold E. Cannot Plead Black Anymore. LC 78-67830. (Illus.). 1978. 9.95 (ISBN 0-9601972-0-6); pap. 6.95 (ISBN 0-9601972-1-4). Byrd.

Byrd Hoffman Foundation, New York, jt. auth. see Contemporary Arts Center, Cincinnati.

Byrd, J. & Moore, L. T. Decision Models for Management. 1982. 34.95x (ISBN 0-07-009511-6). McGraw.

Byrd, James F., jt. ed. see Carey, Floyd D.

Byrd, Jay. Animal Superstars. (Illus.). 128p. 1985. pap. 5.95 (ISBN 0-88188-398-0, 00183029, Pub. by H Leonard Bks). H Leonard Pub Corp.

--Huey Lewis & the News. (Illus.). 32p. 1985. 4.95 (ISBN 0-88188-328-X, Robus Books). H Leonard Pub Corp.

--Ratt. (Metal Mania Ser.). (Illus.). 32p. 1985. 4.95 (ISBN 0-88188-329-8, Robus Books). H Leonard Pub Corp.

Byrd, Joan F. Harvey K. Littleton: A Retrospective Exhibition. LC 84-80145. (Illus.). 112p. (Orig.). 1984. pap. 20.00x (ISBN 0-939802-20-1). High Mus Art.

Byrd, Leslie, tr. see Martinez De Toledo, Alfonso.

Byrd, M. L., jt. ed. see Ryder, O. A.

Byrd, Max. A California Thriller. 224p. 1984. 13.95 (ISBN 0-8052-8184-3, Pub. by Allison & Busby England). Schocken.

--Daniel Defoe: A Collection of Critical Essays. 1975. 12.95 (ISBN 0-13-197608-7, Spec). P-H.

--Finders Weepers. 192p. 1985. 13.95 (ISBN 0-8052-8236-X, Pub. by Allison & Busby England). Schocken.

--Fly Away, Jill. 342p. 1984. 13.95 (ISBN 0-8052-8198-3, Pub. by Allison & Busby, England). Schocken.

--Tristram Shandy. Rawson, Claude, ed. (Unwin Critical Library). 192p. 1985. text ed. 22.95x (ISBN 0-04-800033-7). Allen Unwin.

Byrd, Oliver E. Patient's Self-History Form. 0.35x (ISBN 0-8047-1063-5). Stanford U Pr.

Byrd, P., et al. Guide to Academic Libraries in the United States. 1981. pap. 13.95 (ISBN 0-13-367979-9). P-H.

Byrd, P. F. & Friedman, M. D. Handbook of Elliptic Integrals for Engineers & Scientists. 2nd ed. LC 72-146515. (Die Grundlehren der Mathematischen Wissenschaften: Vol. 67). (Illus.). 1971. 42.00 (ISBN 0-387-05318-2). Springer-Verlag.

Byrd, Patricia. Write on: A Student's Guide to Handwriting. 128p. (Orig.). 1985. pap. text ed. 10.00 (ISBN 0-8384-1301-3). Heinle & Heinle.

Byrd, Peggy. Windy Lindy. (Illus.). 1981. 4.50 (ISBN 0-8062-1702-2). Carlton.

Byrd, Richard E. Alone. (Illus.). 360p. 1984. Repr. of 1938 ed. 16.95 (ISBN 0-933280-24-6). Island CA.

--Discovery: The Story of the Second Byrd Antarctic Expedition. facsimile ed. LC 71-37874. (Select Bibliographies Reprint Ser). Repr. of 1935 ed. 36.00 (ISBN 0-8369-6711-9). Ayer Co Pubs.

--Discovery: The Story of the Second Byrd Antarctic Expedition. LC 76-159906. (Tower Bks). (Illus.). 1971. Repr. of 1935 ed. 47.00x (ISBN 0-8103-3904-8). Gale.

--A Guide to Personal Risk Taking. (AMACOM Executive Books). 1978. pap. 7.95 (ISBN 0-8144-7505-1). AMACOM.

--A Guide to Personal Risk Taking. LC 74-75169. pap. 64.00 (ISBN 0-317-29454-7, 2055936). Bks Demand UMI.

--Little America. 1930. 35.00 (ISBN 0-686-17225-6). Scholars Ref Lib.

Byrd, Robert. Marcella Was Bored. Amper, Julie, ed. LC 84-28674. (Illus.). 32p. (ps-2). 1985. 11.95 (ISBN 0-525-44156-5). Dutton.

Byrd, Robert L. & Byrd, Doris A. The Trumpet Sounds. 127p. (Orig.). 1981. pap. 2.50 (ISBN 0-87178-878-0). Brethren.

Byrd, Ronald James & Browning, Freddie Melton. A Laboratory Manual for Exercise Physiology. (Illus.). 168p. 1972. spiral bdg. 17.50x (ISBN 0-398-02459-6). C C Thomas.

Byrd, Russell A. Planet of Gold. (Illus.). 88p. 1983. pap. 5.95 (ISBN 0-911096-02-7). Pacific-West.

Byrd, Thomas L., Jr. The Early Poetry of W. B. Yeats: The Poetic Quest. (National University Pubns. Literary Criticism Ser.). 1978. 14.95x (ISBN 0-8046-9184-3, Pub. by Kennikat). Assoc Faculty Pr.

Byrd, Walter, jt. auth. see Horton, Marilee.

Byrd, William. China's Financial System: The Changing Role of Banks. LC 83-6610. (Replica Edition Ser.). 188p. 1982. softcover 24.00x (ISBN 0-86531-943-X). Westview.

--Histories of the Dividing Line Betwixt Virginia & North Carolina. LC 67-24220. 20.00 (ISBN 0-8446-1790-3). Peter Smith.

--London Diary, 1717-1721 & Other Writings. Wright, Louis B. & Tinglin, Marion, eds. LC 77-141208. (Research Library of Colonial Americana). (Illus.). 1971. Repr. of 1958 ed. 38.50 (ISBN 0-405-03305-2). Ayer Co Pubs.

--My Ladye Nevells Booke. Andrews, Hilda, ed. & intro. by. (Illus.). 292p. 1955. Repr. of 1926 ed. 25.00x (ISBN 0-8450-0101-9). Broude.

--My Ladye Nevells Booke of Virginal Music. Andrews, Hilda, ed. LC 68-55532. 1969. pap. 8.95 (ISBN 0-486-22246-2). Dover.

--Prose Works of William Byrd of Westover. 25.00x (ISBN 0-674-71650-7). Harvard U Pr.

--The Secret Diary of William Byrd of Westover 1709-1712. LC 72-141097. Repr. of 1941 ed. 38.50 (ISBN 0-405-03304-4, Blom Pubns). Ayer Co Pubs.

--Writings of Colonel William Byrd. Bassett, J. S., ed. LC 76-125631. (Research & Source Ser.: No. 518). (Illus.). 1970. Repr. of 1901 ed. lib. bdg. 32.00 (ISBN 0-8337-0442-7). B Franklin.

Byrd, William see Arkwright, G. E. P.

Byrd, William see Buck, P. C. & Fellowes, E. H.

Byrd, William, et al. Gradualia, Bks.1 & 2. Buck, P. C., ed. (Tudor Church Music: Vol. 7). 1963. Repr. of 1927 ed. 85.00x (ISBN 0-8450-1857-4). Broude.

--Masses, Cantiones, Motets. Buck, P. C., ed. (Tudor Church Music Ser.: Vol. 9). 1963. Repr. of 1928 ed. write for info. (ISBN 0-8450-1859-0). Broude.

--The Fitzwilliam Virginal Book, 2 vols. Maitland, J. A. & Squire, W. B., eds. (Illus.). 974p. 1949. Repr. of 1899 ed. 25.00x (ISBN 0-8450-0102-7). Broude.

--Parthenia, or the Maydenhead of the First Musicke that Ever Was Printed for the Virginalls. new ed. Stone, Kurt, ed. (Illus.). 62p. 1951. pap. 9.50x (ISBN 0-8450-6001-5). Broude.

Byrde, R. J., ed. see Long Ashton Research Station Symposium, University of Bristol, Sept. 1971.

Byrdsall, Fitzwilliam. History of the Loco-Foco or, Equal Rights Party. 1965. Repr. of 1842 ed. 19.00 (ISBN 0-8337-0443-5). B Franklin.

Byres, T. J., ed. Foreign Resources & Economic Development: Symposium on the Report of the Pearson Commission. 212p. 1972. 28.50x (ISBN 0-7146-2932-4, F Cass Co). Biblio Dist.

--Sharecropping & Sharecroppers. (Illus.). 284p. 1983. 32.00x (ISBN 0-7146-3223-6, F Cass Co). Biblio Dist.

Byres, Terence. Adam Smith, Malthus & Marx. Yapp, Malcolm, et al, eds. (World History Ser.). (Illus.). 32p. (gr. 10). 1980. lib. bdg. 6.95 (ISBN 0-89908-046-4); pap. text ed. 2.45 (ISBN 0-89908-021-9). Greenhaven.

Byrkit, James W. Forging the Copper Collar: Arizona's Labor-Management War, 1901-1921. LC 82-2075. 435p. 1982. 24.95 (ISBN 0-8165-0745-7). U of Ariz Pr.

Byrn, Stephen. Solid State Chemistry of Drugs. LC 82-13950. 349p. 1982. 60.00 (ISBN 0-12-148620-6). Acad Pr.

Byrne, Beverly. The Adventurer. 480p. 1982. pap. 2.95 (ISBN 0-449-14452-6, GM). Fawcett.

--Jason's People. 488p. 1985. pap. 3.95 (ISBN 0-449-12455-X, GM). Fawcett.

--Jemma. 512p. 1981. pap. 2.75 (ISBN 0-449-14375-9, GM). Fawcett.

--The Outcast. (The Griffin Saga Ser.: Vol. I). 512p. (Orig.). 1981. pap. 2.95 (ISBN 0-449-14396-1, GM). Fawcett.

--Women's Rites. LC 84-40486. 534p. 1985. 17.95 (ISBN 0-394-54274-6, Pub. by Villard Bks). Random.

Byrne, Charles L. Music Fundamentals: A Functional Approach. 240p. 1983. pap. text ed. 15.95 (ISBN 0-8403-3048-0). Kendall-Hunt.

Byrne, Claire J., et al. Laboratory Tests: Implications for Nurses & Allied Health Professionals. 1981. 21.95 (ISBN 0-201-00088-1, Med-Nurse). Addison-Wesley.

Byrne, D. & Wright, A. What Do You Think? (English As a Second Language Bk.). (Illus.). 1974. pap. text ed. 3.75x student bk. 1 (ISBN 0-582-52269-2); pap. text ed. 3.75x student bk. 2 (ISBN 0-582-52271-4); tchr's bk. 1 o.p. 3.50x (ISBN 0-582-52270-6); pap. text ed. 3.50x tchr's bk. 2 (ISBN 0-582-52272-2). Longman.

Byrne, D. & Fisher, W. A., eds. Adolescents, Sex & Contraception. 336p. 1983. 29.95x (ISBN 0-89859-217-8). L Erlbaum Assocs.

Byrne, David, et al. The Poverty of Education: A Study in the Politics of Opportunity. 204p. 1975. 17.50x (ISBN 0-87471-693-4). Rowman.

Byrne, Dawson. Story of Ireland's National Theatre. LC 70-119093. (Studies in Drama, No. 39). 1970. Repr. of 1929 ed. lib. bdg. 39.95x (ISBN 0-8383-1089-3). Haskell.

Byrne, Diana K., jt. auth. see Sutton-Smith, Brian.

Byrne, Donald E. No Foot of Land: Folklore of American Methodist Itinerants. LC 75-1097. (ATLA Monograph: No. 6). (Illus.). 370p. 1975. 21.00 (ISBN 0-8108-0798-X). Scarecrow.

Byrne, Donn. Messer Marco Polo. LC 79-10460. 1979. Repr. of 1922 ed. lib. bdg. 12.50x (ISBN 0-8376-0437-0). Bentley.

--Messer Marco Polo. 151p. 1982. Repr. of 1892 ed. lib. bdg. 30.00 (ISBN 0-89984-083-3). Century Bookbindery.

--Messer Marco Polo. 12.95 (ISBN 0-8488-0074-5, Pub. by Amereon Hse). Amereon Ltd.

--Progressive Picture Compositions: Student's Book. (Illus.). 55p. 1967. pap. 3.25 (ISBN 0-582-52126-2); 3.95 (ISBN 0-582-52127-0); picture 37.50 (ISBN 0-582-52128-9). Longman.

--Teaching Oral English. (Longman Handbooks for Language Teachers Ser.). (Illus.). 192p. 1976. pap. text ed. 9.95x (ISBN 0-582-55081-5). Longman.

--Teaching Writing Skills. (Handbooks for Language Teachers). (Illus.). 1980. pap. text ed. 9.95x (ISBN 0-582-74602-7). Longman.

--Using the Magnetboard. (Practical Language Teaching Ser.). (Orig.). 1980. pap. text ed. 6.95x (ISBN 0-435-28966-7). Heinemann Ed.

Byrne, Donn & Cornelius, Edwin T. Thirty Passages: Comprehension Practice for High Intermediate & Advanced Students. (English As a Second Language Bk.). (Illus.). 1978. pap. text ed. 4.25x (ISBN 0-582-79704-7). Longman.

Byrne, Donn & Kelley, Kathryn. Approaches to the Study of Sexual Behavior. 256p. 1986. text ed. 29.95 (ISBN 0-89859-677-7). L Erlbaum Assocs.

Byrne, Donn & Kelly, Kathryn. An Introduction to Personality. 3rd ed. (Illus.). 576p. 1981. text ed. 29.95 (ISBN 0-13-491605-0). P-H.

Byrne, Donn & Rixon, Shelagh. Communication Games. (ELT Guides Ser.). 100p. 1981. 20.00x (ISBN 0-317-18036-3, Pub. by NFER Nelson UK). Taylor & Francis.

Byrne, Donn see Allen, W. S.

Byrne, Donn, jt. auth. see Baron, Robert A.

Byrne, Donn, jt. auth. see Lindgren, Henry C.

Byrne, Donn B., pseud. Alley of Flashing Spears & Other Stories. facsimile ed. LC 70-103501. (Short Story Index Reprint Ser.). 1934. 17.00 (ISBN 0-8369-3243-9). Ayer Co Pubs.

--Daughter of the Medici, & Other Stories. LC 73-125207. (Short Story Index Reprint Ser). 1935. 17.00 (ISBN 0-8369-3574-8). Ayer Co Pubs.

--Hound of Ireland, & Other Stories. LC 70-116942. (Short Story Index Reprint Ser). 1935. 17.00 (ISBN 0-8369-3444-X). Ayer Co Pubs.

--Island of Youth, & Other Stories. LC 74-116943. (Short Story Index Reprint Ser.). 1933. 18.00 (ISBN 0-8369-3445-8). Ayer Co Pubs.

--Rivers of Damascus & Other Stories. facsimile ed. LC 72-106253. (Short Story Index Reprint Ser.). 1931. 18.00 (ISBN 0-8369-3290-0). Ayer Co Pubs.

--Stories Without Women & a Few with Women. facsimile ed. LC 74-103502. (Short Story Index Reprint Ser). 1931. 19.00 (ISBN 0-8369-3370-2). Ayer Co Pubs.

Byrne, Donn E. The Attraction Paradigm. (Personality & Psychopathology Ser.: Vol. 11). 1971. 75.00 (ISBN 0-12-148650-8). Acad Pr.

Byrne, E. H. Genoese Shipping in the Twelfth & Thirteenth Centuries. (Mediaeval Academy of America Publications). 1930. 27.00 (ISBN 0-527-01682-9). Kraus Repr.

Byrne, Edward. Along the Dark Shore. (New Poets of America Ser.: No. 3). 10.00 (ISBN 0-918526-09-4); pap. 5.00 (ISBN 0-918526-10-8). Boa Edns.

--Military Law. 3rd ed. LC 81-47857. 776p. 1981. text ed. 22.95x (ISBN 0-87021-389-X). Naval Inst Pr.

--Military Law. 3rd ed. (Illus.). 776p. 1981. 22.95 (ISBN 0-87021-389-X); bulk rates avail. Naval Inst Pr.

Byrne, Eileen M. Planning & Educational Inequality. 388p. 1974. 22.00x (ISBN 0-85633-039-6, Pub. by NFER Nelson). Taylor & Francis.

Byrne, F. L. Prophet of Prohibition: Neal Dow & His Crusade. 12.75 (ISBN 0-8446-0533-6). Peter Smith.

Byrne, Frank & Soman, Jean, eds. Your True Marcus: The Civil War Letters of a Jewish Colonel. LC 84-12266. 365p. 1985. 19.95 (ISBN 0-87338-306-0). Kent St U Pr.

Byrne, Frank L., ed. The View from Headquarters: Civil War Letters of Harvey Reid. LC 65-63010. (Illus.). 258p. 1965. 7.50 (ISBN 0-87020-004-6). State Hist Soc Wis.

Byrne, Gary C. & Marx, Paul. The Great American Convention: A Political History of Presidential Elections. LC 76-14102. 1977. 7.95 (ISBN 0-87015-220-3). Pacific Bks.

Byrne, George D. & Hall, Charles A., eds. Numerical Solution of Systems of Nonlinear Algebraic Equations. 1973. 60.00 (ISBN 0-12-148950-7). Acad Pr.

Byrne, Geraldine. Shakespeare's Use of the Pronoun of Address. LC 72-121150. (Studies in Shakespeare, No. 24). 1970. Repr. of 1936 ed. lib. bdg. 39.95x (ISBN 0-8383-1097-4). Haskell.

Byrne, H. W. A Christian Approach to Education: Educational Theory & Application. rev. ed. LC 76-56229. 1977. pap. text ed. 7.95 (ISBN 0-915134-20-9). Mott Media.

--Improving Church Education. LC 79-10852. 352p. (Orig.). 1979. pap. 12.95 (ISBN 0-89135-017-9). Religious Educ.

Byrne, Herbert W. Christian Education for the Local Church. 14.95 (ISBN 0-310-22230-3). Zondervan.

Byrne, Jack. Salmon Country. (Illus.). 224p. 1982. 15.95 (ISBN 0-00-216975-4, Pub. by W Collins New Zealand). Intl Spec Bk.

Byrne, James, jt. auth. see Wood, Douglas.

Byrne, Janet, ed. Key Issues: Issues & Events of 1979. LC 80-1717. (News in Print Ser.). (Illus.). 1980. lib. bdg. 27.45x (ISBN 0-405-12877-0). Ayer Co Pubs.

--The Middle East: Issues & Events of 1979. LC 80-1718. (News in Print Ser.). (Illus.). 1980. lib. bdg. 27.45x (ISBN 0-405-12878-9). Ayer Co Pubs.

Byrne, Janet S. Renaissance Ornament Prints & Drawings. Horbar, Amy, ed. LC 81-18806. (Illus.). 144p. 1981. 35.00 (ISBN 0-87099-288-0). Metro Mus Art.

Byrne, Jim, ed. see Feinberg, Wilbert.

Byrne, John. Cuttin' a Rug. (Paisley Patterns Trilogy). 40p. 1983. pap. 5.95 (ISBN 0-907540-21-X, NO.3985). Methuen Inc.

--The Slab Boys. (Paisley Patterns Trilogy). 44p. 1983. pap. 5.95 (ISBN 0-907540-20-1, NO.3990). Methuen Inc.

--Still Life. (Paisley Patterns Trilogy). 44p. 1983. pap. 5.95 (ISBN 0-907540-22-8, NO.3984). Methuen Inc.

Byrne, John & Cuti, Nicola. Rog Two Thousand. 32p. 1982. pap. 2.95 (ISBN 0-943128-00-5). Blue Dolphin.

Byrne, John & Wilson, Ron. Super Boxers. (Marvel Graphic Novel: No. 8). 5.95 (ISBN 0-939766-77-9). Marvel Comics.

Byrne, John see Milne, John.

Byrne, John, ed. Modern Sports Writers: A Collection of Prose. 72p. (gr. 7-10). 1982. 14.95 (ISBN 0-7134-4303-0, Pub. by Batsford England). David & Charles.

Byrne, John & Rich, Daniel, eds. Energy & Cities. (Energy Policy Studies: Vol. II). 171p. 1985. pap. 12.95 (ISBN 0-87855-813-6). Transaction Bks.

--Technology & Energy Choice. 160p. 1983. pap. 12.95 (ISBN 0-87855-812-8). Transaction Bks.

Byrne, John F. The Silent Years: An Autobiography with Memoirs of James Joyce & Our Ireland. LC 75-11682. xi, 307p. 1975. Repr. of 1953 ed. lib. bdg. 24.50x (ISBN 0-374-91144-4). Octagon.

Byrne, John J. The Hand: Its Anatomy & Diseases. (Illus.). 408p. 1959. photocopy ed. 36.50x (ISBN 0-398-00269-X). C C Thomas.

Byrne, John M., et al, eds. Families & the Energy Transition. (Marriage & Family Review Ser.: Vol. 9, Nos. 1-2). 328p. 1985. text ed. price not set (ISBN 0-86656-451-9); pap. price not set. Haworth Pr.

Byrne, Josefa H. Mrs. Byrne's Dictionary. 240p. 1984. pap. 3.50 (ISBN 0-671-49782-0). WSP.

--Mrs. Byrne's Dictionary of Unusual, Obscure, & Preposterous Words, Gathered from Numerous & Diverse Authoritative Sources. Byrne, Robert, ed. & intro. by. 1974. 12.50 (ISBN 0-8216-0203-9). Univ Bks.

Byrne, Josefa Heifetz. Mrs. Byrne's Dictionary of Unusual, Obscure, & Preposterous Words. Byrne, Robert, ed. & intro. by. 1976. pap. 7.95 (ISBN 0-8065-0498-6). Citadel Pr.

Byrne, Julia. Curiosities of the Search-Room. LC 70-78117. 1969. Repr. of 1880 ed. 40.00x (ISBN 0-8103-3573-5). Gale.

Byrne, Julianne M., ed. Fetal Pathology Laboratory Manual, Vol. 19, No. 2. LC 82-62707. (March of Dimes Ser.). 1983. 10.00 (ISBN 0-317-12041-7). A R Liss.

Byrne, Kathleen D. & Snyder, Richard C. Chrysalis: Willa Cather in Pittsburgh, 1896-1906. LC 80-80284. (Illus.). 160p. 1982. 14.95 (ISBN 0-936340-00-2). Hist Soc West Pa.

Byrne, L. S., tr. see Von Klarwill, Victor.

Byrne, Lee. Check List Materials for Public School Building Specifications, Covering the General Specifications. LC 71-178797. (Columbia University. Teachers College. Contributions to Education: No. 492). Repr. of 1931 ed. 22.50 (ISBN 0-404-55492-X). AMS Pr.

Byrne, Leo G. The Great Ambassador. LC 64-22404. 393p. 1965. 6.25 (ISBN 0-8142-0032-X). Ohio St U Pr.

Byrne, M. St. Clare, ed. see Arts Council Of Great Britain.

Byrne, M. St. Clare, ed. see Massinger, Philip.

Byrne, M. St. Clare, ed. see Pliny.

Byrne, Majorie L. & Thompson, Lida F. Key Concepts for the Study & Practice of Nursing. 2nd ed. LC 77-26957. (Illus.). 1978. pap. text ed. 11.95 (ISBN 0-8016-0920-8). Mosby.

Byrne, Margaret C. & Shervanian, Chris C. Introduction to Communicative Disorders. 1977. text ed. 24.75 scp (ISBN 0-06-041116-3, HarpC); instructor's manual avail. (ISBN 0-06-361132-5). Har-Row.

Byrne, Miles. Memoirs of Miles Byrne, 3 vols. in one. 1972. Repr. of 1863 ed. 40.00x (ISBN 0-7165-0027-2, Pub. by Irish Academic Pr). Biblio Dist.

Byrne, Muriel S., ed. The Lisle Letters, 6 vols. LC 80-12019. 1981. Set. 325.00x (ISBN 0-226-08801-4). U of Chicago Pr.

Byrne, Muriel S. & Boland, Bridget, eds. The Lisle Letters: An Abridgement. LC 82-15914. xxvi, 438p. 1985. 25.00 (ISBN 0-226-08800-6); pap. 12.95 (ISBN 0-226-08810-3). U of Chicago Pr.

Byrne, Muriel St. C. & Boland, Bridget, eds. The Lisle Letters: An Abridgement. LC 82-15914. 1985. 25.00 (ISBN 0-226-08800-6). U of Chicago Pr.

Byrne, Patrick. Irish Ghost Stories. 1969. pap. 4.50 (ISBN 0-85342-037-8, Co-dist. by Irish Bks Media). Irish Bk Ctr.

--Irish Ghost Stories, 2nd Book. 1971. pap. 3.95 (ISBN 0-85342-264-8, Co-dist. by Irish Bks Media). Irish Bk Ctr.

--Witchcraft in Ireland. 80p. 1967. pap. 4.95 (ISBN 0-85342-038-6, Pub. by Mercier Pr Ireland). Irish Bk Ctr.

Byrne, Patrick, ed. Irish Ghost Stories of LeFanu. 1973. pap. 3.95 (ISBN 0-85342-375-X, Co-dist. by Irish Bks Media). Irish Bk Ctr.

Byrne, Patrick B. & Rodono, Marcello, eds. Activity in Red-Dwarf Stars. 1983. lib. bdg. 85.00 (ISBN 90-277-1601-3, Pub. by Reidel Holland). Kluwer Academic.

Byrne, Patrick F., ed. Bedside Book of Irish Ghost Stories. 112p. (Orig.). 1980. pap. 4.95 (ISBN 0-85342-623-6, Pub. by Mercier Pr Ireland). Irish Bk Ctr.

Byrne, Phil. Inside Skiing. LC 78-24074. 214p. 1979. 17.95x (ISBN 0-88229-455-5). Nelson-Hall.

Byrne, Robert. Always a Catholic. 192p. (Orig.). 1982. pap. 2.50 (ISBN 0-523-42035-8). Pinnacle Bks.

--Byrne's Standard Book of Pool & Billiards. LC 80-25552. (Illus.). 352p. 1981. pap. 10.95 (ISBN 0-15-614972-9, Harv). HarBraceJ.

--Byrne's Treasury of Trick Shots in Pool & Billiards. LC 82-47676. (Illus.). 320p. 1982. 19.95 (ISBN 0-15-115224-1). HarBraceJ.

--Byrne's Treasury of Trick Shots in Pool & Billards. 1983. pap. 8.95 (ISBN 0-15-614973-7, Harv). HarBraceJ.

--Mc Goorty: The Story of a Billiard Bum. 224p. 1984. pap. 8.95 (ISBN 0-8065-0925-2). Citadel Pr.

--Memories of a Non-Jewish Childhood. 5.95 (ISBN 0-8184-0112-5). Lyle Stuart.

--Once a Catholic... 224p. 1981. pap. 2.25 (ISBN 0-523-41165-0). Pinnacle Bks.

--The Other Six Hundred & Thirty-Seven Best Things Anybody Ever Said. LC 84-45057. (Illus.). 192p. 1984. 10.95 (ISBN 0-689-11472-9). Atheneum.

--The Other Six Hundred Thirty-Seven Best Things Anybody Ever Said. 192p. 1985. pap. 2.95 (ISBN 0-449-20762-5, Crest). Fawcett.

--The Six Hundred Thirty-Seven Best Things Anybody Ever Said. LC 82-45172. 192p. 1982. 10.95 (ISBN 0-689-11300-5). Atheneum.

--Six Hundred Thirty-Seven Best Things Anybody Ever Said. 1985. pap. 2.95 (ISBN 0-449-20375-1, Crest). Fawcett.

--Skyscraper. LC 83-45514. 288p. 1984. 14.95 (ISBN 0-689-11430-3). Atheneum.

Byrne, Robert & Skelton, Teresa. Cat Scan: All the Best from the Literature of Cats. 208p. 1985. pap. 2.95 (ISBN 0-449-20640-8, Crest). Fawcett.

Byrne, Robert & Skelton, Teressa. Cat Scan: Three Thousand Years of the Best Things Ever Said about Cats. LC 83-45064. 208p. 1983. 11.95 (ISBN 0-689-11390-0). Atheneum.

Byrne, Robert, ed. & intro. by see Byrne, Josefa H.

Byrne, Robert, ed. & intro. by see Byrne, Josefa Heifetz.

Byrne, Robert, ed. see Rose, Louis J.

Byrne, Robert L. Writing Rackets. LC 69-17965. 1969. 4.00 (ISBN 0-8184-0095-1). Lyle Stuart.

Byrne, Seamus. Little City. (The Irish Play Ser.). Date not set. pap. 1.25x (ISBN 0-912262-16-8). Proscenium.

Byrne, Stephen. Irish Immigration to the United States: What It Has Been & What It Is. LC 69-18763. (American Immigration Collection Ser.: No. 1). (Illus.). 1969. Repr. of 1873 ed. 13.50 (ISBN 0-405-00511-3). Ayer Co Pubs.

Byrne, Vincent. Choices & Other Poems. 1981. pap. 6.95 (ISBN 0-8159-5223-6). Devin.

--Miracles & Other Poems. LC 78-65634. 1979. pap. 6.95 (ISBN 0-8159-6216-9). Devin.

Byrnes. Partial Differential Equations & Geometry. (Lecture Notes in Pure & Applied Math Ser.: Vol. 48). 1979. 55.00 (ISBN 0-8247-6775-6). Dekker.

Byrnes, Christopher, jt. ed. see Martin, Clyde F.

Byrnes, Christopher I., ed. see NATO ASI & AMS Summer Seminar in Applied Mathematics Held at Harvard University, Cambridge, Ma., June 18-29, 1979.

Byrnes, Dennis L., jt. auth. see Wingfield, Arthur.

Byrnes, Edward. Monarch Notes on Ibsen's Plays. (Orig.). pap. 3.50 (ISBN 0-671-00562-6). Monarch Pr.

Byrnes, Heidi, ed. Georgetown University Round Table on Languages & Linguistics 1982: Contemporary Perceptions of Language: Interdisciplinary Dimensions. LC 58-31607. (Georgetown University Round Table on Languages and Linguistics (GURT) Ser.). 260p. (Orig.). 1983. pap. text ed. 8.95 (ISBN 0-87840-117-2). Georgetown U Pr.

Byrnes, James F. Speaking Frankly. LC 74-4657. (Illus.). 324p. 1974. Repr. of 1947 ed. lib. bdg. 19.75x (ISBN 0-8371-7480-5, BYSF). Greenwood.

Byrnes, John. Emil Marriot: A Re-Evaluation Based on Her Short Fiction. LC 82-84613. (American Universtiy Studies: No. 1, Vol. 6). 285p. (Orig.). 1983. pap. text ed. 33.40 (ISBN 0-8204-0005-X). P Lang Pubs.

Byrnes, Jonathan. Diversification Strategies for Regulated & Deregulated Industries: Lessons from the Airlines. LC 83-48638. 160p. 1984. 19.00x (ISBN 0-669-07272-9). Lexington Bks.

Byrnes, Joseph F. The Psychology of Religion. LC 84-47854. 320p. 1984. 24.95x (ISBN 0-02-903580-5). Free Pr.

--The Virgin of Chartres: An Intellectual & Psychological History of the Work of Henry Adams. LC 78-75174. 128p. 1981. 19.50 (ISBN 0-8386-2369-7). Fairleigh Dickinson.

Byrnes, Laurence. History of the Ninety-Fourth Infantry Division in World War II. (Divisional Ser.: No. 22). (Illus.). 534p. 1982. Repr. of 1948 ed. 25.00 (ISBN 0-89839-064-8). Battery Pr.

Byrnes, Patricia & Krenz, Nancy. Southwestern Arts & Crafts Projects. Rev. ed. LC 77-18988. (Illus.). (gr. 1-8). 1979. pap. 9.95 (ISBN 0-913270-62-8). Sunstone Pr.

Byrnes, Robert F. Awakening American Education to the World: The Role of Archibald Cary Coolidge, 1866-1928. LC 81-40451. 256p. 1982. 24.95 (ISBN 0-268-00599-0). U of Notre Dame Pr.

--Bibliography of American Publications on East Central Europe, 1945-1957. LC 69-106305. (Indiana University Publications Russian & East European Ser.: Vol. 12). pap. 60.80 (ISBN 0-317-10611-2, 2050954). Bks Demand UMI.

--Pobedonostsev: His Life & Thought. LC 68-14598. Repr. of 1968 ed. 96.80 (ISBN 0-8357-9231-5, 2013022). Bks Demand UMI.

Byrnes, Robert F., ed. After Brezhnev: Sources of Soviet Conduct in the 1980's. LC 82-48614. (Midland Bks.: No. 306). 457p. 1983. 25.00x (ISBN 0-253-35392-0); pap. 12.50x (ISBN 0-253-20306-6). Ind U Pr.

--Communal Families in the Balkans: The Zadruga. LC 74-27892. 352p. 1976. 28.95 (ISBN 0-268-00569-9). U of Notre Dame Pr.

Byrns, James. Speak for Yourself. 2nd ed. 329p. 1985. pap. text ed. 12.95 (ISBN 0-394-34099-X, RanC). Random.

Byrns, James H. Speak for Yourself. 329p. 1981. pap. text ed. 14.00 (ISBN 0-394-32410-2, RanC). Random.

Byrns, John H. Where the Antiques Are in Britain & Ireland. (Illus.). 129p. 1972. pap. 6.50 (ISBN 0-8038-8056-1). Hastings.

Byrns, Ralph T. & Stone, Gerald W. An Economics Casebook: Applications from the Law. 1980. pap. 10.80x (ISBN 0-673-16162-5). Scott F.

--Great Ideas for Teaching Economics. 1984. pap. 9.40 (ISBN 0-673-17184-1). Scott F.

Byrns, Ralph T. & Stone, Gerald W., Jr. Economics. 2nd ed. 1984. text ed. 29.95x (ISBN 0-673-16626-0); Study Guide 10.95 (ISBN 0-673-16628-7). Scott F.

--Exploring Economics. 1984. pap. text ed. 19.50x (ISBN 0-673-16583-3); Study Guide 8.95 (ISBN 0-673-16584-1). Scott F.

--Macroeconomics. 2nd ed. 1984. pap. text ed. 18.60x (ISBN 0-673-16641-4). Scott F.

--Microeconomics. 2nd ed. 1984. pap. text ed. 18.60x (ISBN 0-673-16640-6). Scott F.

Byrnside, Ronald L. Music: Sound & Sense. 432p. 1984. pap. text ed. write for info (ISBN 0-697-08277-6); instr's manual avail. (ISBN 0-697-00227-6); recordings avail. (ISBN 0-697-00249-7). Wm C Brown.

Byrom, Fletcher L., jt. auth. see Fraser, Douglas A.

Byrom, Michael. Punch in the Italian Puppet Theatre. 1983. 50.00 (ISBN 0-900001-20-8, Pub. by Centaur Pr England). State Mutual Bk.

Byrom, N. A. & Hobbs, J. R., eds. Thymic Factor Therapy. (Serono Symposia Publications Ser.: Vol.16). 458p. 1984. text ed. 49.50 (ISBN 0-88167-041-3). Raven.

Byrom, Thomas, tr. The Dhammapada. 1976. pap. 5.95 (ISBN 0-394-72198-5, Vin). Random.

Byron. Byron: Poems. (Penguin Poetry Library). 352p. 1985. pap. 5.95 (ISBN 0-14-058507-9). Penguin.

--Byron: Selected Prose. Gunn, Peter, ed. (Penguin English Library). 1973. pap. 5.95 (ISBN 0-14-043080-6). Penguin.

--Poetical Works. rev. ed. Page, Frederick & Jump, John, eds. (Oxford Standard Author Ser.). (Illus.). 1979. Leatherbound 60.00 (ISBN 0-19-192822-4); pap. text ed. 10.95x (ISBN 0-19-281068-5). Oxford U Pr.

Byron & Hunt, Leigh. The Liberal Verse & Prose from the South: London, 4 vols. (Salzburger Studien zur Anglistik und Amerikanistik: No. 7). (Orig.). 1979. pap. text ed. 36.25x ea.; Bk. 1, 1822. pap. text ed. (ISBN 0-391-01334-3); Bk. 2, 1823. pap. text ed. (ISBN 0-391-01335-1); Bk. 3, 1823. pap. text ed. (ISBN 0-391-01336-X); Bk. 4, 1823. pap. text ed. (ISBN 0-391-01337-8). Humanities.

Byron, ed. Lord Byron: Selected Letters & Journals. 416p. 1982. 18.50x (ISBN 0-674-53915-X, Belknap Pr). Harvard U Pr.

Byron, Amanda. The Warning. (Twilight Bks.: No. 23). (gr. 5 up). pap. 2.25 (ISBN 0-440-99335-0, LFL). Dell.

Byron, Arthur. A Guide to London's Statues. 1981. 15.00x (ISBN 0-09-463430-0, Pub. by Constable Pubs). State Mutual Bk.

Byron, George G. Autographs Once in the Possession of Teresa Guicciolo, Don Juan, Cantos I-V, Vol. II. McGann, Jerome J. & Levine, Alice, eds. LC 83-49281. (The Manuscripts of the Younger Romantics & the Bodleian Shelley Manuscripts Ser.). 350p. 1984. lib. bdg. 80.00 (ISBN 0-8240-6251-5). Garland Pub.

--Byron. LC 76-17072. 1976. Repr. of 1941 ed. lib. bdg. 10.00 (ISBN 0-8414-9409-6). Folcroft.

--Byron: A Self-Portrait, 2 vols. Quennell, Peter, ed. 1967. Set. pap. text ed. 40.50x (ISBN 0-391-00480-8). Humanities.

--Byron & Greece. LC 76-29014. 1976. Repr. of 1924 ed. lib. bdg. 25.00 (ISBN 0-8414-7744-2). Folcroft.

--Byron's Letters & Journals, 12 vols. Marchand, Leslie A., ed. Incl. Vol. I. In My Hot Youth: Seventeen Ninety-Eight to Eighteen Ten. 288p. 1973. 16.50x (ISBN 0-674-08940-5); Vol. II. Famous in My Time: Eighteen Ten to Eighteen Twelve. 298p. 1974. 16.50x (ISBN 0-674-08941-3); Vol. III. Alas! the Love of Women: Eighteen Thirteen to Eighteen Fourteen. 285p. 1974. 16.50x (ISBN 0-674-08942-1); Vol. IV. Wedlock's the Devil: Eighteen Fourteen to Eighteen Fifteen. 369p. 1975. 18.50x (ISBN 0-674-08944-8); Vol. V. So Late into the Night. 320p. 1976. 17.50x (ISBN 0-674-08945-6); Vol. VI. The Flesh Is Frail: Eighteen Eighteen to Eighteen Nineteen. 289p. 1976. 16.50x (ISBN 0-674-08946-4); Vol. VII. Between Two Worlds: Eighteen Twenty. 282p. 1977. 16.50x (ISBN 0-674-08947-2); Vol. VIII. Born for Opposition: Eighteen Twenty-One. 384p. 1978. 18.50x (ISBN 0-674-08948-0); Vol. 9. In the Wind's Eye: 1821-1822. 248p. 1979. 15.00x (ISBN 0-674-08949-9); Vol. 10. A Heart for Every Fate: 1822-1823. 239p. 1980. 15.00x (ISBN 0-674-08952-9); Vol. 11. For Freedom's Battle. 256p. 15.00x (ISBN 0-674-08953-7); Vol. 12. The Trouble of an Index. LC 73-81853. 176p. 15.00x (ISBN 0-674-08954-5). Harvard U Pr.

--Byron's Poetry. McConnell, Frank D., ed. (Norton Critical Editions). 1978. 12.95 (ISBN 0-393-04452-1); pap. text ed. 9.95x (ISBN 0-393-09152-X). Norton.

--The Complete Poetical Works of Byron, Vol. 3. McGann, Jerome J., ed. (Oxford English Text Ser.). 1981. 105.00x (ISBN 0-19-812755-3); pap. 64.00x (ISBN 0-19-812765-0). Oxford U Pr.

--The Complete Poetical Works of Byron: Vol. 2, Childe Harold's Pilgrimage. McGann, Jerome J., ed. (Oxford English Text Ser.). (Illus.). 1980. 105.00x (ISBN 0-19-812754-5); pap. 64.00x (ISBN 0-19-812764-2). Oxford U Pr.

--Confessions of Lord Byron. Bettany, W. A., ed. LC 72-3739. (Studies in Byron, No. 5). 1972. Repr. of 1905 ed. lib. bdg. 55.95x (ISBN 0-8383-1578-X). Haskell.

--Confessions of Lord Byron. 1973. Repr. of 1905 ed. 20.00 (ISBN 0-8274-1161-8). R West.

--Don Juan. Marchand, L., ed. LC 58-14387. (YA) (gr. 9 up). 1958. pap. 6.50 (ISBN 0-395-05138-X, RivEd). HM.

--Fugitive Pieces. LC 73-13775. 1933. lib. bdg. 15.00 (ISBN 0-8414-3243-0). Folcroft.

--Fugitive Pieces. LC 72-3567. (Studies in Byron, No. 5). 1972. Repr. of 1933 ed. lib. bdg. 43.95x (ISBN 0-8383-1553-4). Haskell.

--Letters. Howarth, R. G., ed. 1971. Repr. of 1962 ed. 12.95x (ISBN 0-460-00931-1, Evman). Biblio Dist.

--Life Letters & Journals of Lord Byron. 1901. 79.00x (ISBN 0-403-00441-1). Scholarly.

--Lord Byron: Don Juan. Steffan, T. G., et al, eds. LC 81-3011. (Yale English Poets Ser.: No. 10). 760p. 1982. text ed. 31.00x (ISBN 0-300-02678-1); pap. 9.95x (ISBN 0-300-02686-2, YEP-10). Yale U Pr.

--Lord Byron in His Letters. Collins, V. H., ed. LC 72-3626. (Studies in Byron, No. 5). 1972. Repr. of 1927 ed. lib. bdg. 53.95x (ISBN 0-8383-1582-8). Haskell.

--Lord Byron in His Letters. 1973. Repr. of 1927 ed. 15.00 (ISBN 0-8274-1160-X). R West.

--The Poetical Works of Byron. Gleckner, Robert F., intro. by. LC 75-4909. (Cambridge Editions Ser.). 1975. 29.50 (ISBN 0-395-20431-3). HM.

--The Poetical Works of Lord Byron. Coleridge, E. H., ed. (Illus.). 1120p. 1972. Repr. of 1905 ed. text ed. 24.25x (ISBN 0-7195-0171-7). Humanities.

--Werner: A Tragedy. Bd. with A Facsimile of the Acting Version of William Charles Macready. 232p. 1970. soft cover 32.50x (ISBN 3-7705-0360-0). Adlers Foreign Bks.

Byron, George G. & Byron, Noel. The Ravenna Journal. LC 72-12938. 1974. Repr. of 1928 ed. lib. bdg. 15.00 (ISBN 0-8414-0993-5). Folcroft.

Byron, George N. Seventeen Letters of George Noel Gordon, Lord Byron, to an Unknown Lady. LC 76-41751. 1976. Repr. of 1930 ed. lib. bdg. 17.00 (ISBN 0-8414-6765-X). Folcroft.

Byron, Gilbert. Chesapeake Duke. LC 75-40037. (Illus.). 167p. 1975. pap. 5.00 (ISBN 0-87033-210-4). Tidewater.

--The Lord's Oysters. LC 74-9246. xiv, 330p. 1967. Repr. of 1957 ed. 30.00x (ISBN 0-8103-5032-7). Gale.

--The Lord's Oysters. LC 57-6442. 344p. 1977. pap. 6.95 (ISBN 0-8018-1959-8). Johns Hopkins.

--The War of Eighteen-Twelve on the Chesapeake Bay. (Illus.). 94p. 1964. 5.00 (ISBN 0-686-36633-6). Md Hist.

Byron, H. J. & Davis, Jim. Plays: Babes in the Wood, the Lancashire Lass, Our Boys & the Gaeity Gulliver. LC 83-7852. (British & American Playwrights Series, 1750-1920). (Illus.). 220p. 1984. 44.50 (ISBN 0-521-24175-8); pap. 15.95 (ISBN 0-521-28495-3). Cambridge U Pr.

Byron, James. Or Be He Dead. LC 81-48169. 224p. 1982. pap. 2.84i (ISBN 0-06-080585-4, P585, PL). Har-Row.

Byron, Janet. Selection Among Alternates in Language Standardization: The Case of Albanian. (Contributions to the Sociology of Language Ser.: No. 12). 1976. pap. text ed. 14.00x (ISBN 90-2797-542-6). Mouton.

Byron, Joseph. New York Interiors at the Turn of the Century. (Illus.). 192p. (Orig.). 1976. pap. 7.95 (ISBN 0-486-23359-6). Dover.

--New York Life at the Turn of the Century in Photographs. (New York City Ser.). 144p. 1985. pap. 9.95 (ISBN 0-486-24863-1). Dover.

Byron, Joseph & Lancaster, Clay. New York Interiors at the Turn of the Century: 131 Photographs from the Byron Collection of the Museum of the City of New York. 14.50 (ISBN 0-8446-5518-X). Peter Smith.

Byron, Lord. A Choice of Byron's Verse. Dunn, Douglas, ed. 164p. 1974. pap. 6.95 (ISBN 0-571-10589-0). Faber & Faber.

--Confessions: A Collection of His Private Opinions of Men & Matters. 59.95 (ISBN 0-87968-927-7). Gordon Pr.

Byron, Lord, jt. auth. see Gordon, George.

Byron, Lord see Byron, George G.

Byron, May. A Day with Elizabeth Barrett Browning. LC 77-21913. 1977. Repr. of 1911 ed. lib. bdg. 15.00 (ISBN 0-8414-9931-4). Folcroft.

--A Day with John Greenleaf Whittier. Repr. 10.00 (ISBN 0-8274-2150-8). R West.

--A Day with John Greenleaf Whittier. 1978. Repr. lib. bdg. 10.00 (ISBN 0-8492-3563-4). R West.

--A Day with John Keats. Repr. 10.00 (ISBN 0-8274-2151-6). R West.

--A Day with Nathaniel Hawthorne. LC 78-4080. Repr. 15.00 (ISBN 0-8414-0159-4). Folcroft.

--A Day with Samuel Taylor Coleridge. LC 78-14436. 1978. Repr. of 1912 ed. lib. bdg. 15.00 (ISBN 0-8414-1745-8). Folcroft.

--A Day with the Poet Shelley. 1973. 10.00 (ISBN 0-8274-0080-2). R West.

--A Day with William Wordsworth. 1942. Repr. 15.00 (ISBN 0-8414-0885-8). Folcroft.

--Jams & Jellies. 320p. 1975. pap. 4.95 (ISBN 0-486-23130-5). Dover.

Byron, May C. A Day with Byron. LC 77-21478. 1977. lib. bdg. 15.00 (ISBN 0-8414-4606-7). Folcroft.

--A Day with Charles Dickens. LC 77-13814. 1977. lib. bdg. 15.00 (ISBN 0-8414-0901-3). Folcroft.

--A Day with Charlotte Bronte. 50p. 1980. Repr. lib. bdg. 10.00 (ISBN 0-8495-0462-7). Arden Lib.

--A Day with Charlotte Bronte. LC 76-58442. 1977. lib. bdg. 15.00 (ISBN 0-8414-1653-2). Folcroft.

--A Day with John Milton. LC 77-21475. 1977. Repr. of 1912 ed. lib. bdg. 15.00 (ISBN 0-685-85840-5). Folcroft.

--A Day with Nathaniel Hawthorne. 1979. Repr. of 1912 ed. lib. bdg. 10.00 (ISBN 0-8482-3441-3). Norwood Edns.

--A Day with Sir Walter Scott. LC 77-7796. 1977. lib. bdg. 15.00 (ISBN 0-8414-9938-1). Folcroft.

--A Day with the Poet Percy Bysshe Shelley. LC 77-21977. 1977. Repr. of 1910 ed. lib. bdg. 15.00 (ISBN 0-8414-9935-7). Folcroft.

Byron, Noel, jt. auth. see Byron, George G.

Byron Preiss Visual Publications Inc. & Bischoff, David. Search for Dinosaurs. (Time Machine Ser.: No. 2). (Illus.). 144p. (Orig.). 1984. pap. 2.25 (ISBN 0-553-25399-9). Bantam.

Byron Preiss Visual Publications Inc. & Gasperini, Jim. Secret of the Knights. (Time Machine Bk.: No. 1). (Illus.). 144p. (gr. 4 up). 1984. pap. 2.25 (ISBN 0-553-23601-6). Bantam.

Byron, Robert. The Road to Oxiana. (Illus.). 1982. pap. 8.95 (ISBN 0-19-503067-2, GB 675, GB). Oxford U Pr.

--The Station: Athos: Treasures & Men. (Century Travellers). 272p. 1984. pap. 9.95 (ISBN 0-88254-914-6). Hippocrene Bks.

Byron, Stuart & Weis, Elisabeth, eds. Movie Comedy. 1977. pap. 5.95 (ISBN 0-14-004578-3). Penguin.

Byron, William. Cervantes: A Biography. (Illus.). 583p. 1979. 29.95x (ISBN 0-8464-1176-8). Beekman Pubs.

Byron, William, ed. The Causes of World Hunger. LC 82-60591. 1983. pap. 8.95 (ISBN 0-8091-2483-1). Paulist Pr.

Byron, William, tr. see Lenteric, Bernard.

Byron, William, tr. see Revel, Jean-Francois.

Byron, William J. Toward Stewardship: An Interim Ethic of Poverty, Power & Pollution. LC 74-30806. (Topics in Moral Argument Ser.). 1975. pap. 1.95 (ISBN 0-8091-1865-3). Paulist Pr.

Byrt, G. W. John Clifford: A Fighting Free Churchman. 192p. 1947. Repr. 4.50 (ISBN 0-87921-011-7). Attic Pr.

Byrt, W. J. The Australian Company: Studies in Strategy & Structure. 171p. 1981. 20.00 (ISBN 0-7099-0615-3, Pub. by Croom Helm Ltd). Longwood Pub Group.

Byrum, Douglas. Practical Drilling & Production Design. 528p. 1982. 49.95x (ISBN 0-87814-180-4). Pennwell Bks.

Byrum, E. E. The Secret of Salvation. 264p. pap. 2.50 (ISBN 0-686-29166-2). Faith Pub Hse.

Byrum, Isabel. Harry the Newsboy & Other Stories. 32p. 1982. pap. 0.35 (ISBN 0-686-36266-7). Faith Pub Hse.

--How John Became a Man. 64p. pap. 0.40 (ISBN 0-686-29118-2); pap. 1.00 3 copies (ISBN 0-686-29119-0). Faith Pub Hse.

--The Pilot's Voice. (Illus.). 146p. pap. 1.50 (ISBN 0-686-29159-X). Faith Pub Hse.

--The Poorhouse Waif & His Divine Teacher. 223p. pap. 2.00 (ISBN 0-686-29161-1). Faith Pub Hse.

Byrum, R. R. Christian Theology. rev. ed. Newell, Arlo F., ed. 1982. 14.95 (ISBN 0-87162-252-1, D3051). Warner Pr.

--Holy Spirit Baptism & the Second Cleansing. 108p. pap. 0.75 (ISBN 0-686-29114-X); pap. 2.00 3 copies (ISBN 0-686-29115-8). Faith Pub Hse.

--Shadows of Good Things, or the Gospel in Type. (Illus.). 144p. pap. 1.50 (ISBN 0-686-29141-7). Faith Pub Hse.

Byse, Fanny. Milton on the Continent: A Key to L'Allegro & Il Pensaroso. 1978. Repr. of 1903 ed. lib. bdg. 15.00 (ISBN 0-8495-0432-5). Arden Lib.

Byse, Frank. Milton on the Continent. LC 74-4225. 1903. lib. bdg. 15.00 (ISBN 0-8414-3134-5). Folcroft.

Bysiewicz, Shirley R. Monarch's Dictionary of Legal Terms. 192p. (Orig.). 1983. pap. 7.95 (ISBN 0-671-09232-4). Monarch Pr.

Byskov, A. G. & Peters, H., eds. Development & Function of Reproductive Organs: Proceedings of the Workshop on the Development & Function of the Reproduction Organs, 5th, Copenhagen, Jul. 6-9, 1981. (International Congress Ser.: No. 559). 450p. 1982. 73.75 (ISBN 0-444-90230-9, Excerpts Medica). Elsevier.

Bystrom, Adoree. The Tailoring Process: Custom & Simplified. Love, Carolyn J., ed. 128p. 1985. pap. text ed. 9.95 (ISBN 0-538-32310-8, HE31); tchr's ed. 3.00 (ISBN 0-538-32311-6). SW Pub.

Bystrom, Robert. Nature's Special Moments. Batts, H. Lewis, ed. & illus. (Illus.). 80p. 1975. 7.50 (ISBN 0-939294-01-X, QH-71-K3-A7). Beech Leaf.

Bysveen, Josef. Epic Tradition & Innovation in James Macphersons's Fingal. (Studia Anglistica Upsaliensia: No. 44). 146p. 1982. pap. text ed. 16.75x (ISBN 91-554-1332-3, Pub. by Almqvist & Wiksell Sweden). Humanities.

Byte, Maurice K., et al. How to Make Love to a Computer. 96p. (Orig.). 1984. pap. 3.95 (ISBN 0-671-50370-7). PB.

Bythell, Duncan. Handloom Weavers. LC 69-10487. (Illus.). 1969. 59.50 (ISBN 0-521-07580-7). Cambridge U Pr.

--The Sweated Trade: Outwork in Nineteenth Century Britain. LC 78-451. 1979. 27.50 (ISBN 0-312-77999-2). St Martin.

Bytheriver, Marylee, ed. see George, Llewellyn.

Bytheway, A., ed. Structured Methods. (Computer State of the Art Report, Series 12: No. 1). (Illus.). 250p. 1984. 460.00 (ISBN 0-08-028585-6). Pergamon.

Bytwerk, Randall L. Julius Streicher: The Man Who Persuaded a Nation to Hate Jews. LC 81-40814. (Illus.). 208p. 1982. 18.95 (ISBN 0-8128-2834-8). Stein & Day.

Bytyns'Kyi, Mykola. Mazepyntsi Po Poltavi. LC 75-561602. (Ukrainian.). 1974. 15.00 (ISBN 0-918884-19-5). Slavia Lib.

Byung-Nak, Song, jt. auth. see Fu-Chen.

Byung-Nak Song, jt. auth. see Mills, Edwin S.

Bywater, Hector C. Sea-Power in the Pacific: A Study of the American-Japanese Naval Problem. LC 75-111749. (American Imperialism: Viewpoints of United States Foreign Policy, 1898-1941). 1970. Repr. of 1921 ed. 22.00 (ISBN 0-405-02006-6). Ayer Co Pubs.

Bywater, Ingram. Aristotle on the Art of Poetry. 1909. Repr. 50.00 (ISBN 0-8274-3796-X). R West.

--Aristotle on the Art of Poetry. 2nd ed. LC 78-66550. (Ancient Philosophy Ser.). 435p. 1982. lib. bdg. 53.00 (ISBN 0-8240-9607-X). Garland Pub.

--Contributions to the Textual Criticism of Aristotle's Nicomachean Ethics. LC 72-9285. (The Philosophy of Plato & Aristotle Ser.). Repr. of 1892 ed. 9.00 (ISBN 0-405-04835-1). Ayer Co Pubs.

Bywater, Ingram, ed. see Aristotle.

Bywater, Ingram, tr. see Aristotle.

Bywater, Michael F. & Yamey, Basil S. Historic Accounting Literature: A Companion Guide. 1982. 70.00 (ISBN 0-85967-647-1). Scolar.

Bywater, Michael F., ed. Historic Accounting Literature: A Facsimile Collection, 50 vols. Repr. of 1979 ed. Set. 3000.00 (ISBN 0-317-12639-3). Scolar.

Bywater, R. Hardware-Software Design of Digital Systems. 1981. 38.95 (ISBN 0-13-383950-8). P-H.

Bywater, William G., Jr. Clive Bell's Eye. LC 74-23853. (Illus.). 249p. 1975. text ed. 13.95x (ISBN 0-8143-1534-8). Wayne St U Pr.

Bywaters, Phyllis K., jt. auth. see Streng, William P.

Bzang, Ye Shes Blo see Blo Bzang, Ye Shes.

Bzdega, A., et al. Podreczny Slownik Polsko-Niemiecki (Manual Dictionary Polish-German) 1018p. (Pol. & Ger.). 1977. leatherette 19.95 (ISBN 0-686-87194-4, M-0129). French & Eur.

Bzoch, K. Assessing Language Skills in Infancy. (Illus.). 68p. 1978. pap. text ed. 18.00 (ISBN 0-8391-1240-8). Univ Park.

Bzoch, Kenneth. Communicative Disorders Related to Cleft Lip & Palate. 2nd ed. 1979. 23.95 (ISBN 0-316-11936-9). Little.

C

C, Chester, jt. auth. see O'Brien, Bonnie B.

C. D. Howe Institute. Au dela de la reprise: l'adaptation au futur, Vol. 1984. (Commentaires sur la politique economique). 72p. 1984. 6.00 (ISBN 0-88806-120-X). Inst C D Howe.

--Beyond Recovery: Adjusting to the Future, Vol. 1984. (Policy Review & Outlook). 204p. 1984. 6.00 (ISBN 0-88806-120-X). Inst C D Howe.

--Recognizing Reality, Vol. 1982. (Policy Review & Outlook). 69p. 1982. 5.00 (ISBN 0-88806-112-9). Inst C D Howe.

C Q Press, jt. auth. see O'Toole, Lawrence.

C Q Press Staff. Politics in America 1984. LC 85-12777. 1758p. 1986. 29.95 (ISBN 0-87187-375-3). Congr Quarterly.

--Rational Politics: Decisions, Games & Strategies. LC 85-17117. 230p. 1985. pap. 16.95 (ISBN 0-87187-337-0). Congr Quarterly.

C Q Press Staff, jt. auth. see Baum, Lawrence.

C Q Press Staff, jt. auth. see Fishel, Jeff.

C Q Press Staff, jt. auth. see Nelson, Michael.

C Q Press Staff, jt. auth. see Parker, Glenn.

C Q Press Staff, jt. auth. see Rosenbaum, Walter.

CAB Books, ed. British Crop Protection Conference: Weeds, 3 vols. 1976. Set. 125.00x (ISBN 0-901436-40-2, Pub. by CAB Bks England). State Mutual Bk.

--Crop Loss Assessment Methods: FAO Manual on the Evaluation & Prevention of Losses by Pests, Disease & Weeds. 276p. 1971. 59.00x (ISBN 0-85198-185-2, Pub. by CAB Bks England). State Mutual Bk.

--Directory of Collections of Micro-Organisms Maintained in the United Kingdom. 1978. 40.00x (ISBN 0-85198-427-4, Pub. by CAB Bks England). State Mutual Bk.

--Herbicides in British Fruit Growing. 1973. 39.00x (ISBN 0-901436-29-1, Pub. by CAB Bks England). State Mutual Bk.

--Horticultural Research International Directory of Horticultural Research Institutes & Their Activiities in 61 countries. 698p. 1981. 130.00x (ISBN 90-220-0765-0, Pub. by CAB Bks England). State Mutual Bk.

--Lentils: International Center for Agricultural Research in Dry Areas. 216p. 1981. 99.00x (ISBN 0-85198-475-4, Pub. by CAB Bks England). State Mutual Bk.

--List of Research Workers. 658p. 1981. 89.00x (ISBN 0-85198-485-1, Pub. by CAB Bks England). State Mutual Bk.

--Livestock Management in the Arid Zone: V Squires. 271p. 1981. 90.00x (ISBN 0-909605-23-8, Pub. by CAB Bks England). State Mutual Bk.

Caba, Sid & Church, Norm. A Stroke of Genius: Graphic Programming in BASIC for the Apple Computer. (Illus.). 128p. (gr. 4 up). 1985. pap. 14.95 (ISBN 0-88056-311-7). Dilithium Pr.

Cabaj, Janice. The Elvis Image. (Illus.). 224p. 1982. 10.00 (ISBN 0-682-49837-8). Exposition Pr FL.

Caballero, Arturo. Flora Analitica de Espana. (Floras of the World Ser.: Vol. 3). (Illus.). 617p. (Span.). 1984. pap. text ed. 128.00 (ISBN 3-87429-214-2). Lubrecht & Cramer.

Caballero, Cesar. Chicano Organizations Directory. 221p. (Orig.). 1985. pap. 19.95 (ISBN 0-918212-65-0). Neal-Schuman.

Caballero, E., tr. see Benteen, John.

Caballero, E., tr. see Rosenberger, Joseph.

Caballero, E., tr. see Slade, Jack.

Caballero, Ernesto G. Don Quijote Ante el Mundo: (y Ante Mi) LC 77-87981. (Illus.). 1979. 15.00 (ISBN 0-913480-37-1); pap. 7.95 (ISBN 0-913480-38-X). Inter Am U Pr.

Caballero, Fernan. The Sea Gull: La Gaviota. MacLean, Joan, tr. from Span. LC 65-18177. (Orig.). (YA) 1965. pap. text ed. 3.95 (ISBN 0-8120-0124-9). Barron.

Caballero, Jane. Vanila Manilla Folder Games for Young Children. LC 80-83231. (Illus.). 113p. 1980. pap. 14.95 (ISBN 0-89334-059-6). Humanics Ltd.

Caballero, Jane & Christman-Rothlein, Liz. Back to Basics in Reading Made Fun. LC 80-83232. (Illus.). 113p. (Orig.). 1980. pap. 14.95 (ISBN 0-89334-060-X). Humanics Ltd.

Caballero, Jane A. Art Projects for Young Children. LC 79-65813. (Illus.). 142p. (Orig.). pap. 14.95 (ISBN 0-89334-051-0). Humanics Ltd.

--Handbook of Learning Activities for Young Children. LC 80-81660. (Illus.). 207p. 1981. pap. 14.95 (ISBN 0-89334-058-8). Humanics Ltd.

--Month by Month Activity Guide for the Primary Grades. LC 80-83230. (Illus.). 200p. 1980. pap. 14.95 (ISBN 0-89334-061-8). Humanics Ltd.

Caballero, Jane A. & Whordley, Derek. Children Around the World. 172p. (Orig.). 1983. pap. 14.95 (ISBN 0-89334-033-2). Humanics Ltd.

--Humanics National Infant & Toddler Handbook. LC 81-81660. 164p. (Orig.). 1981. pap. 14.95 (ISBN 0-89334-049-9). Humanics Ltd.

Caballero, Justo. Guia-Diccionario del Quijote. (Span.). 12.50 (ISBN 0-686-56697-1, S-5649). French & Eur.

Caballero, Romeo Flores see Flores Caballero, Romeo.

Cabana Committee of World Assoc. of Girl Guides & Girl Scouts. Canciones de Nuestra Cabana: Songs of Our Cabana. rev. ed. 112p. (Orig., Span. & Eng.). 1980. pap. 4.25 (ISBN 0-88441-366-7, 23-113). GS.

Cabanellas, Guillermo. Antitrust & Direct Regulation of International Transfer of Technology Transactions. (IIC Studies: Vol. 7). 175p. 1984. pap. 30.30x (ISBN 0-89573-076-6). VCH Pubs.

Cabanillas, Berta. Puerto Rican Dishes. 3rd ed. 1971. 9.75 (ISBN 0-8477-2776-9). Adlers Foreign Bks.

Cabanillas, Berta & Ginorio, Carmen. Puerto Rican Dishes. 4th ed. 5.60 (ISBN 0-8477-2776-9). U of PR Pr.

Cabanillas, Berta, et al. Cocine a Gusto. (Illus.). 1983. 9.00 (ISBN 0-8477-2775-0). U of PR Pr.

Cabanillas De Rodriguez, Berta. Folklore en la Alimentacion Puertorriquena. LC 80-25836. 197p. 1983. pap. 7.50 (ISBN 0-8477-2503-0). U of PR Pr.

Cabanis, Pierre J. On the Relations Between the Physical & Moral Aspects of Man, Vol. I. Saidi, Margaret D., tr. LC 80-21694. pap. 112.00 (ISBN 0-317-08229-9, 2019949). Bks Demand UMI.

Cabanis, Pierre J; see Whytt, Robert.

Cabaniss, Allen, ed. Charlemagne's Cousins: Contemporary Lives of Adalard & Wala. LC 67-26919. 1967. 14.95x (ISBN 0-8156-2115-9). Syracuse U Pr.

--Son of Charlemagne: A Contemporary Life of Louis the Pious. LC 61-1398. 1961. 16.95x (ISBN 0-8156-2031-4). Syracuse U Pr.

Cabaniss, Micki L. Atlas of Fetal Monitoring. (Illus.). 300p. 1985. text ed. 55.00 (ISBN 0-8391-2027-3, 21342). Univ Park.

Cabanne, Pierre. The Brothers Duchamp: Jacques Villon, Raymond Duchamp-Villon, Marcel Duchamp. LC 75-37285. (Illus.). 1976. 60.00 (ISBN 0-8212-0666-4, 109800). NYGS.

--Pablo Picasso: A Biography. 1977. 19.95 (ISBN 0-688-03232-X). Morrow.

--Pablo Picasso: His Life & Times. 2nd ed. Salemson, Harold J., tr. from Fr. LC 77-4984. (Illus.). 1979. pap. 6.95 (ISBN 0-688-08232-7, Quill). Morrow.

Cabannes, H., et al, eds. Sixth International Conference on Numerical Methods in Fluid Dynamics: Proceedings of the Conference, Held in Tbilisi (USSR) June 21-24, 1978. (Lecture Notes in Physics: Vol. 90). 1979. pap. 33.00 (ISBN 0-387-09115-7). Springer-Verlag.

Cabannes, Henri. Theoretical Magnetofluid-Dynamics. LC 75-117095. (Applied Mathematics & Mechanics Ser.: Vol. 13). 1970. 70.00 (ISBN 0-12-153750-1). Acad Pr.

Cabarga, Leslie. A Treasury of German Trademarks: 1850-1925, Vol. 1. LC 81-71799. (Illus.). 160p. 1982. 17.50 (ISBN 0-910158-89-4). Art Dir.

--A Treasury of German Trademarks, 1925-1950, Vol. 2. LC 81-71799. 156p. 17.50 (ISBN 0-88108-007-1). Art Dir.

Cabarrouy, Evaldo, et al. Principios de Macroeconomia. (Span.). 1983. text ed. 13.95 (ISBN 0-538-22140-2, V14). SW Pub.

--Principios de Microeconomia. (Span.). 1984. text ed. 11.95 (ISBN 0-538-22130-5, V13). SW Pub.

Cabasilas, Nicholas. Commentary on the Divine Liturgy. Hussey, J. M. & McNulty, P. A., trs. from Greek. LC 62-53410. 120p. 1977. pap. 5.95 (ISBN 0-913836-37-0). St Vladimirs.

--The Life in Christ. Decatanzaro, Carmino J., tr. 229p. 1974. pap. 7.95 (ISBN 0-913836-12-5). St Vladimirs.

Cabat, Erni. Arizona Cacti & Succulents, Bk. 2. 32p. Date not set. price not set (ISBN 0-913521-04-3). Cabat Studio Pubns.

--Arizona Wildflowers: And the Southwest, Bk. 2. Date not set. price not set (ISBN 0-913521-03-5). Cabat Studio Pubns.

Cabat, Erni & Cardon, Charlotte M. Life on the Tanque Verde: The History, Bk. 1. (Illus.). 1983. write for info. (ISBN 0-913521-00-0). Cabat Studio Pubns.

Cabat, Erni & Engard, Rodney G. Arizona Cacti & Succulents, Bk. 1. LC 83-63523. (Illus.). 32p. 1984. write for info. (ISBN 0-913521-01-9). Cabat Studio Pubns.

Cabat, Erni & Polzer, Charles W. Father Eusebio Francisco Kino & His Missions of the Pimeria Alta: Bk. II, The Main Altars, Book II. Prezelski, Carmen V., tr. LC 82-50219. (Illus.). 36p. (Orig.). 1983. pap. 5.00 (ISBN 0-915076-08-X). SW Mission.

Cabat, Erni, jt. auth. see Engard, Rodcey G.

Cabat, Ernie. Father Eusebio Francisco Kino & His Missions of the Primeria Alta: Bk. I, The Side Altars. Polzer, Charles W., ed. Prezelski, Carmen V., tr. LC 82-50219. (Illus.). 36p. (Orig.). 1982. pap. 5.00 (ISBN 0-915076-06-3). SW Mission.

Cabat, Ernii & Polzer, Charles W. Father Eusebio Francisco Kino & His Missions of the Pimeria Alta: Bk. II, Facing the Missions. Prezelski, Carmen V., tr. LC 82-50219. (Illus.). 36p. 1983. pap. 5.00 (ISBN 0-915076-09-8). SW Mission.

Cabat, Louis & Cabat, Robert. Diga! Diga! (gr. 7-12). 1974. pap. text ed. 5.67 (ISBN 0-87720-510-8). AMSCO Sch.

Cabat, Louis, jt. auth. see Cabat, Robert.

Cabat, Louis, et al. Barron's How to Prepare for the College Board Achievement Tests - French. 3rd ed. LC 75-151972. (gr. 11-12). 1982. pap. 7.95 (ISBN 0-8120-0941-X). Barron.

Cabat, Robert & Cabat, Louis. Momentos Hispanos. (gr. 11). 1978. pap. text ed. 5.50 (ISBN 0-87720-520-5). AMSCO Sch.

--Un Verano en Mexico. (Orig.). (gr. 7-12). 1975. pap. text ed. 6.25 (ISBN 0-87720-504-3). AMSCO Sch.

Cabat, Robert, jt. auth. see Cabat, Louis.

Cabaton, Antoine. Java, Sumatra & Other Islands of the Dutch East Indies. Miall, Bernard, tr. LC 77-86967. (Illus.). Repr. of 1911 ed. 31.00 (ISBN 0-404-16699-7). AMS Pr.

Cabaud. Simone Weil a New York et a Londres. 10.40 (ISBN 0-685-36635-9). French & Eur.

Cabeceiras, James. The Multimedia Library: Materials Selection & Use. (Library & Information Science). 1982. 26.50 (ISBN 0-12-153952-0). Acad Pr.

Cabeen, David C. & Brody, Jules, eds. Critical Bibliography of French Literature, Vol. 3: The Seventeenth Century. LC 47-3282. 1961. 34.95x (ISBN 0-8156-2007-1). Syracuse U Pr.

Cabeen, David C. & Havens, George R., eds. Critical Bibliography of French Literature, Vol. 4: The Eighteenth Century. LC 47-3282. 1951. text ed. 34.95x (ISBN 0-8156-2008-X). Syracuse U Pr.

Cabeen, David C. & Schutz, Alexander H., eds. Critical Bibliography of French Literature, Vol. 2: The Sixteenth Century. LC 47-3282. 1956. 34.95x (ISBN 0-8156-2006-3). Syracuse U Pr.

Cabeen, Richard M. Standard Handbook of Stamp Collecting. 3rd ed. LC 78-3297. (Illus.). 1979. 15.34i (ISBN 0-690-01773-1). T Y Crowell.

Cabeen, Richard M., jt. auth. see Chase, Carroll.

Cabelka, J., jt. auth. see Novak, P.

Cabell, David W., ed. Cabell's Directory of Publishing Opportunities in Business & Economics. rev., 3rd ed. 550p. (Orig.). 1985. pap. 29.95x (ISBN 0-911753-01-X). Cabell Pub.

--Cabell's Directory of Publishing Opportunities in Education. LC 84-231406. 490p. (Orig.). 1984. 24.95 (ISBN 0-911753-00-1). Cabell Pub.

Cabell, Edward J., jt. ed. see Turner, William H.

Cabell, James. The Witch Woman. 10.95 (ISBN 0-89190-273-2, Pub. by Am Repr). Amereon Ltd.

Cabell, James B. Beyond Life: Dizain Des Demiurges. LC 19-1362. (American Studies). 1970. Repr. of 1927 ed. lib. bdg. 27.00 (ISBN 0-384-06935-5). Johnson Repr.

--Chivalry. facs. ed. LC 71-140326. (Short Story Index Reprint Ser). 1909. 13.00 (ISBN 0-8369-3718-X). Ayer Co Pubs.

--The Cream of the Jest. Flora, Joseph M., ed. (Masterworks of Literature Ser.). 1973. pap. 5.95x (ISBN 0-8084-0396-6). New Coll U Pr.

--The Devil's Own Dear Son. 238p. Repr. of 1949 ed. lib. bdg. 14.95 (ISBN 0-88411-570-4, Pub. by Aeonian Pr). Amereon Ltd.

--Domnei. facs. ed. LC 75-133517. (Select Bibliographies Reprint Ser). 1920. 16.00 (ISBN 0-8369-5549-8). Ayer Co Pubs.

--Domnei: A Comedy of Woman - Worship. LC 76-131653. 1970. Repr. of 1925 ed. 19.00 (ISBN 0-403-00540-X). Scholarly.

--The High Place. 17.95 (ISBN 0-88411-795-2, Pub. by Aeonian Pr). Amereon Ltd.

--The High Place: A Comedy of Disenchantment. (Illus.). 1978. pap. 5.95 (ISBN 0-486-23670-6). Dover.

--Jurgen. (Illus.). 13.25 (ISBN 0-8446-5561-9). Peter Smith.

--Jurgen: A Comedy of Justice. 287p. Repr. of 1919 ed. lib. bdg. 18.95 (ISBN 0-88411-794-4, Pub. by Aeonian Pr). Amereon Ltd.

--Jurgen: A Comedy of Justice. LC 77-74612. (Illus.). 1978. pap. 5.95 (ISBN 0-486-23507-6). Dover.

--Ladies & Gentlemen: A Parcel of Reconsiderations. facs. ed. LC 68-14897. (Essay Index Reprint Ser). 1934. 18.00 (ISBN 0-8369-0269-6). Ayer Co Pubs.

--The Letters of James Branch Cabell. Wagenknecht, Edward C., ed. LC 74-5963. (Illus.). 400p. 1975. 19.95x (ISBN 0-8061-1220-4). U of Okla Pr.

--Line of Love, Dizain Des Mariages. facsimile ed. LC 79-996077. (Select Bibliographies Reprint Ser). 1921. 24.50 (ISBN 0-8369-5106-9). Ayer Co Pubs.

--The Nightmare Has Triplets: Smirt, Smith & Smire. LC 70-156179. 311p. 1972. Repr. of 1971 ed. lib. bdg. 47.50x (ISBN 0-8371-6122-3, CANT). Greenwood.

--Quiet, Please. 1952. 4.50 (ISBN 0-8130-0040-8). U Presses Fla.

--The Rivet in Grandfather's Neck, a Comedy of Limitations. LC 70-144930. Repr. of 1929 ed. 39.00 (ISBN 0-403-00892-1). Scholarly.

Cabell, James-Branch. The Eagle's Shadow. 69.95 (ISBN 0-87968-088-1). Gordon Pr.

--The Line of Love. 69.95 (ISBN 0-8490-0541-8). Gordon Pr.

--A Roundtable in Poictesme. 69.95 (ISBN 0-87968-234-5). Gordon Pr.

Cabellero, Jane A. Aerospace Projects for Young Children. rev. ed. (Illus.). 112p. (Orig.). (YA) 1983. pap. 12.95 (ISBN 0-89334-042-1). Humanics Ltd.

Cabestrero, Teofilo. Blood of the Innocent: Victims of the Contras' War in Nicaragua. Barr, Robert R., tr. from Span. LC 85-13658. 107p. (Orig.). 1985. pap. 6.95 (ISBN 0-88344-211-6). Orbis Bks.

--Ministers of God, Ministers of the People: Testimonies of Faith from Nicaragua. Barr, Robert R., tr. from Span. LC 83-6306. Orig. Title: Ministros De Dios, Ministros Del Pueblo. (Illus.). 144p. (Orig.). 1983. pap. 6.95 (ISBN 0-88344-335-X). Orbis Bks.

--Mystic of Liberation: A Portrait of Bishop Pedro Casaldaliga of Brazil. Walsh, Donald D., tr. from Span. & Fr. LC 80-25402. Orig. Title: Dialogos en Mato Grosso con Pedro Casadaliga. (Illus.). 176p. (Orig.). 1981. pap. 7.95 (ISBN 0-88344-324-4). Orbis Bks.

Cabestrero, Teofilo, ed. Faith: Conversations with Contemporary Theologians. Walsh, Donald D., tr. from Span. LC 80-1431. Orig. Title: Coversationes sobre la fe. 192p. (Orig.). 1980. pap. 7.95 (ISBN 0-88344-126-8). Orbis Bks.

Cabet, Etienne. Colonie icarienne aux Etats-Unis d'Amerique. (Research & Source Works Ser.: No. 840). 1971. Repr. of 1856 ed. lib. bdg. 21.00 (ISBN 0-8337-0444-3). B Franklin.

--History & Constitution of the Icarian Community. LC 72-2962. (Communal Societies of America Ser). Repr. of 1917 ed. 11.50 (ISBN 0-404-10726-5). AMS Pr.

--Voyage En Icarie. LC 69-16857. Repr. of 1848 ed. 50.00x (ISBN 0-678-00923-6). Kelley.

Cabetas, Isis C., jt. auth. see Byrd, Donald R.

Cabeza, Susana, tr. see Jones, Chris.

Cabeza de Baca, Fabiola. We Fed Them Cactus. LC 54-12881. (Zia Bks.). 208p. 1979. pap. 6.95 (ISBN 0-8263-0517-2). U of NM Pr.

Cabeza de Vaca, Alvar N. Adventures in the Unknown Interior of America. Covey, Cyclone, tr. from Span. (Zia Book Ser.). 168p. 1983. 7.95 (ISBN 0-8263-0656-X). U of NM Pr.

Cabezas, Omar. Fire from the Mountain: The Making of a Sandinista. Weaver, Kathleen, tr. from Span. LC 83-1305. 1985. 13.95 (ISBN 0-517-55800-9). Crown.

Cabezon. Antonio de Cabezon Gestamtausgabe 1969-1975, Pts. 1-3. Jacobs, Charles, ed. (Gesamtausgaben - Collected Works Ser.: No. 4). (Ger. & Eng.). Pt. 1, 80p. lib. bdg. 32.00 (ISBN 0-912024-60-7); Pt. 2, 80p. lib. bdg. 32.00 (ISBN 0-912024-61-5); Pt. 3, 80p. lib. bdg. 32.00 (ISBN 0-912024-62-3). Inst Mediaeval Mus.

Cabibbo, N. & Sertorio, L., eds. Hadronic Matter at Extreme Energy Density. LC 79-18446. (Ettore Majoana International Science Ser., Physical Sciences: Vol. 2). 365p. 1980. 59.50x (ISBN 0-306-40303-X, Plenum Pr). Plenum Pub.

Cabioch, L. & Glemare, M. Fluctuation & Succession in Marine Ecosystems. 224p. 1983. pap. 28.00 (ISBN 2-04-011898-5, Pub by Gauthier-Villars FR). Heyden.

Cable, jt. auth. see Nanney.

Cable, Carole. The Architecture of Houston, Texas: A Bibliography of Articles, 1978 to 1983, An Update to Architecture Ser: Bibliography A-2. (Architecture Ser.: Bibliogrаpy A 1325). 1985. pap. 2.00 (ISBN 0-89028-275-7). Vance Biblios.

--A Bibliography of Writings by & about Sir Reginald Theodore Bloomfield, 1856 to 1942. (Architecture Ser.: Bibliography A 1342). 1985. pap. 2.00 (ISBN 0-89028-312-5). Vance Biblios.

--Periodical Scholarship on Islamic Architecture Published 1973-1983: A Bibliography. (Architecture Ser. Bibliography A-1307). 7p. 1985. pap. 2.00 (ISBN 0-89028-237-4). Vance Biblios.

--The Publications of William Pain, 1730 to 1790: Architect & Carpenter. (Architecture Ser.: Bibliography A 1338). 1985. pap. 2.00 (ISBN 0-89028-308-7). Vance Biblios.

Cable, Carole A. Ove Arup; Ove Arup & Partners, Architectects; & Arup Associates: A Bibliography of Articles. (Architecture Ser.: Bibliography A 1343). 1985. pap. 2.00 (ISBN 0-89028-313-3). Vance Biblios.

Cable, Dana G. Death & Dying: The Universal Experiences. 105p. (Orig.). 1983. pap. 7.00 (ISBN 0-914547-00-3). Specialized Studies.

Cable, George W. Bonaventure. 1972. Repr. of 1888 ed. lib. bdg. 12.50 (ISBN 0-8398-0250-1). Irvington.

--Bylow Hill. LC 75-80625. (BCL Ser. I). (Illus.). Repr. of 1902 ed. 15.00 (ISBN 0-404-01355-4). AMS Pr.

--Bylow Hill. LC 2-14684. 1902. 13.00x (ISBN 0-403-00106-4). Scholarly.

--The Cavalier. 1901. lib. bdg. 15.00 (ISBN 0-8482-9956-6). Norwood Edns.

--Collected Works, 19 vols. Incl. Old Creole Days. 1879. Repr. 10.00x (ISBN 0-403-03056-0); The Grandissimes. 1880. Repr. 49.00x (ISBN 0-403-02979-1); Madame Delphine. 1881. Repr. 9.00x (ISBN 0-403-02287-8); The Creoles of Louisiana. 1884. Repr. 49.00x (ISBN 0-403-04550-9); Doctor Sevier. 1885. Repr. 19.00 (ISBN 0-403-02953-8); The Silent South. 1885. Repr. 9.00x (ISBN 0-403-04551-7); Bonaventure. 1888. Repr. 10.00x (ISBN 0-403-02974-0); Strange True Stories of Louisiana. 1889. Repr. 18.00 (ISBN 0-403-02952-X); The Negro Question. 1890. Repr. 18.00 (ISBN 0-403-04553-3); John March, Southerner. 1894. Repr. 20.00x (ISBN 0-403-04554-1); Strong Hearts. 1899. Repr. 29.00x (ISBN 0-403-02990-2); The Cavalier. 1901. Repr. 14.00x (ISBN 0-403-02956-2); Bylow Hill. 1902. Repr. 14.00x (ISBN 0-403-02297-5); Kinkaid's Battery. 1908. Repr. 49.00x (ISBN 0-403-04555-X); Posson Jone & Pere Raphael. 1909. Repr. 29.00 (ISBN 0-403-02950-3); Gideon's Band: A Tale of the Mississippi. 1914. Repr. 49.00x (ISBN 0-403-02959-7); The Amateur Garden. 1914. Repr. 49.00x (ISBN 0-686-01561-4); The Flower of the Chapdelaines. 1918. Repr. 49.00x (ISBN 0-403-02991-0); Lovers of Louisiana. 1918. Repr. 49.00x (ISBN 0-403-04557-6). Set. 695.00 (ISBN 0-686-01544-4). Somerset Pub.

--Creoles & Cajuns. Turner, Arlin, ed. 11.25 (ISBN 0-8446-1097-6). Peter Smith.

--Dr. Sevier. 1972. Repr. of 1884 ed. 20.00 (ISBN 0-8422-8016-2). Irvington.

--Doctor Sevier. LC 76-104426. lib. bdg. 16.50x (ISBN 0-8398-0251-X); pap. text ed. 9.95x (ISBN 0-89197-735-X). Irvington.

--The Grandissimes: The Story of Creole Life. 18.95 (ISBN 0-88411-796-0, Pub. by Aeonian Pr). Amereon Ltd.

--John March, Southerner. facs. ed. LC 72-83933. (Black Heritage Library Collection Ser). 1894. 26.50 (ISBN 0-8369-8529-X). Ayer Co Pubs.

--John March: Southerner. 1972. Repr. of 1894 ed. 22.50 (ISBN 0-8422-8019-7). Irvington.

--Madame Delphine. LC 74-80649. (BCL Ser. I). Repr. of 1896 ed. 11.50 (ISBN 0-404-01356-2). AMS Pr.

--Madame Delphine. LC 4-22066. 1896. 11.50x (ISBN 0-403-00039-4). Scholarly.

--Old Creole Days. 234p. 1980. Repr. of 1897 ed. lib. bdg. 30.00 (ISBN 0-89987-111-9). Century Bookbindery.

--Old Creole Days. 1972. Repr. of 1879 ed. lib. bdg. 9.00 (ISBN 0-8422-8184-3). Irvington.

--Old Creole Days, Pts. 1 & 2, 2 Vols. In 1. facs. ed. LC 79-83932. (Black Heritage Library Collection Ser). 1883. Set. 10.00 (ISBN 0-8369-8530-3). Ayer Co Pubs.

--Silent South: Including the Freedman's Case in Equity, the Convict Lease System & to Which Has Been Added Eight Hitherto Uncollected Essays by Cable on Prison & Asylum Reform & an Essay on Cable by Arlin Turner. LC 69-14915. (Criminology, Law Enforcement, & Social Problems Ser.: No. 57). 1969. 10.00x (ISBN 0-87585-057-X). Patterson Smith.

--Strange True Stories of Louisiana. LC 78-116944. (Short Story Index Reprint Ser). 1889. 22.00 (ISBN 0-8369-3446-6). Ayer Co Pubs.

--Strong Hearts. facsimile ed. LC 76-106254. (Short Story Index Reprint Ser.). 1899. 17.00 (ISBN 0-8369-3291-9). Ayer Co Pubs.

--Strong Hearts. 1972. Repr. of 1899 ed. lib. bdg. 13.00 (ISBN 0-8422-8020-0). Irvington.

Cable, Harold, tr. see Enstron, Federich, et al.

Cable, James. Britain's Naval Future. LC 82-73725. (Illus.). 240p. 1983. 24.95 (ISBN 0-87021-920-0). Naval Inst Pr.

--Diplomacy at Sea: Essays on Foreign & Naval Affairs. 200p. 1984. 24.95 (ISBN 0-87021-836-0). Naval Inst Pr.

--Gunboat Diplomacy. 2nd ed. 260p. 1981. 27.50 (ISBN 0-312-35346-4). St Martin.

Cable, James, tr. from Fr. Death of King Arthur. (Classics Ser.). 1972. pap. 3.95 (ISBN 0-14-044255-3). Penguin.

Cable, Sir James. The Royal Navy & the Siege of Bilbao. LC 78-73238. (Illus.). 1980. 24.95 (ISBN 0-521-22516-7). Cambridge U Pr.

Cable, John, jt. auth. see Nanney, Louis J.

Cable, John, et al. Algebra & Trigonometry. 1984. text ed. 32.14 (ISBN 0-205-08208-4, 568208); study guide avail. (568210). Allyn.

Cable, John C., jt. auth. see Nanney, J. L.

Cable, John L., jt. auth. see Bosstick, Maurice.

Cable, John L., jt. auth. see Nanney, J. Louis.

Cable, John R. Bank of the State of Missouri. LC 78-78008. (Columbia University Studies in the Social Sciences: No. 232). Repr. of 1923 ed. 23.50 (ISBN 0-404-51232-1). AMS Pr.

Cable, Lucy L. Lowell Day-by-Day. 1910. Repr. 30.00 (ISBN 0-8274-3004-3). R West.

Cable, Mary. Top Drawer: American High Society from the Gilded Age to the Roaring Twenties. LC 83-45513. (Illus.). 256p. 1984. 19.95 (ISBN 0-689-11431-1). Atheneum.

Cable, Mary B., jt. auth. see Burt, Mary E.

Cable, Mildred & French, Francesca. A Woman Who Laughed. 1984. pap. 3.95 (ISBN 0-7208-0568-6). OMF Bks.

Cable, Paul. Bob Dylan: His Unreleased Recordings. LC 79-57285. (Illus.). 1980. pap. 5.95 (ISBN 0-02-870360-X). Schirmer Bks.

Cable, Raymond M. An Illustrated Laboratory Manual of Parasitology. 5th ed. 1977. spiral bdg. 13.95x (ISBN 0-8087-0373-0). Burgess.

Cable, Thomas. A Companion to Baugh & Cable's History of the English Language. (Illus.). 144p. 1983. pap. text ed. 15.95 (ISBN 0-13-153585-4). P-H.

--The Meter & Melody of Beowulf. LC 72-97683. (Studies in Language & Literature Ser.: No. 64). Repr. of 1974 ed. 33.00 (ISBN 0-8357-9689-2, 2011130). Bks Demand UMI.

Cable, Thomas, jt. auth. see Baugh, Albert C.

Cable, Vincent. Economics & the Politics of Protection: Some Case Studies of Industries. (Staff Working Paper: No. 569). 80p. 1983. 3.00 (ISBN 0-8213-0199-3, WP 0569). World Bank.

Cable, Vincent & Rebelo, Ivonia. Britain's Pattern of Specialization in Manufactured Goods with Developing Countries & Trade Protection. (Working Paper: No. 425). 61p. 1980. 3.00 (ISBN 0-686-36204-7, WP-0425). World Bank.

Cable-Alexander, June, et al. Giving A Children's Party: Planning, Ideas, Food & Games For One to Ten Year Olds. (Illus.). 80p. 1984. laminated bds 12.95 (ISBN 0-7207-1482-6). Merrimack Pub Cir.

Cabot, A. N. Ships & Their Cargoes. 3rd ed. 41p. 1975. pap. 2.50x (ISBN 0-85174-073-1). Sheridan.

Cabot, A. Victor & Hartnett, Donald L. Introduction to Management Science. LC 76-20024. (Illus.). 1977. text ed. 38.95 (ISBN 0-201-02746-1). Addison-Wesley.

Cabot, Cain. Assault on Fellawi. 1972. pap. 1.50 (ISBN 0-380-00718-5, 28969). Avon.

Cabot, George. Life & Letters of George Cabot. Lodge, Henry C., ed. LC 71-124902. (American Public Figures Ser). xi, 617p. 1974. Repr. of 1877 ed. lib. bdg. 79.50 (ISBN 0-306-71001-3). Da Capo.

Cabot, Harriet R. Handbook of the Bostonian Society. 110p. pap. 3.50 (ISBN 0-317-33892-7); 10.00 (ISBN 0-317-33893-5). Bostonian Soc.

Cabot, Henry B., jt. auth. see Warner, Sam B.

Cabot, Hugh & Kahl, Joseph A. Human Relations: Concepts & Cases in Concrete Social Science, Vol. 2. LC 52-12256. pap. 70.80 (ISBN 0-317-08281-7, 2017744). Bks Demand UMI.

Cabot, Isabel. Enchanted Carousel. (YA) 1981. 8.95 (ISBN 0-686-74794-1, Avalon). Bouregy.

--Love Finds Dr. Shelly. (YA) 1978. 8.95 (ISBN 0-685-05590-6, Avalon). Bouregy.

--Nurse Hilary's Promise. (YA) (gr. 9-12). 1984. 8.95 (ISBN 0-8034-8456-9, Avalon). Bouregy.

--Nurse Lauren's Challenge. (YA) 1984. 8.95 (ISBN 0-8034-8406-2, Avalon). Bouregy.

--Nurse Mara's Fear. (YA) 1983. 8.95 (ISBN 0-8034-8326-0, Avalon). Bouregy.

--Share of Danger. (YA) 1980. 8.95 (ISBN 0-686-59801-6, Avalon). Bouregy.

--Summer of Discovery. (YA) 1980. 8.95 (ISBN 0-686-73940-X, Avalon). Bouregy.

Cabot, James E. Memoir of Ralph Waldo Emerson, 2 Vols. LC 78-97164. Repr. of 1887 ed. Set. 25.00 (ISBN 0-404-01357-0). Vol. 1 (ISBN 0-404-01358-9). Vol. 2 (ISBN 0-404-01359-7). AMS Pr.

Cabot, John M. Toward Our Common American Destiny. facsimile ed. LC 72-90621. (Essay Index Reprint Ser.). 1955. 20.00 (ISBN 0-8369-1553-4). Ayer Co Pubs.

Cabot, Natalie H. You Can't Count on Dying. Stein, Leon, ed. LC 79-8662. (Growing Old Ser.). 1980. Repr. of 1961 ed. lib. bdg. 25.50x (ISBN 0-405-12779-0). Ayer Co Pubs.

Cabot, Philippe S., ed. Juvenile Delinquency: A Critical Annotated Bibliography. LC 75-138580. 1971. Repr. of 1946 ed. lib. bdg. 19.75x (ISBN 0-8371-5779-X, CAJD). Greenwood.

Cabot, Richard C. Social Service & the Art of Healing. LC 73-84257. (NASW Classics Ser.). 192p. 1973. pap. text ed. 5.50 (ISBN 0-87101-062-3). Natl Assn Soc Wkrs.

--Social Work: Essays on the Meeting-Ground of Doctor & Social Worker. LC 76-180561. (Medicine & Society in America Ser.). 224p. 1972. Repr. of 1919 ed. 15.00 (ISBN 0-405-03940-9). Ayer Co Pubs.

Cabot, Stephen J. Labor Management Relations Act Manual: Annual Supplement. 1st ed. LC 78-60446. 1978. 64.00 (ISBN 0-88262-208-0). Warren.

Cabot, Thomas D. Beggar on Horseback: The Autobiography of Thomas D. Cabot. LC 78-70524. (Illus.). 1979. 12.50 (ISBN 0-87923-268-4). Godine.

Cabot, Tracy. How to Make a Man Fall in Love with You. 208p. 1984. pap. 10.95 (ISBN 0-312-39578-7). St Martin.

--How to Make a Man Fall in Love with You. 1985. pap. 5.95 (ISBN 0-440-53832-7, Dell Trade Pbks.). Dell.

Cabot, Tracy, jt. auth. see Wanderer, Zev.

Cabot, Val. Goldmining in Foreclosure Properties. 2nd ed. Golomb, Patricia C., ed. LC 82-82661. 207p. 1982. pap. 13.50 (ISBN 0-9601530-7-1). Impact Pub.

Cabral, Adolfo, ed. see Southey, Robert.

Cabral, Amilcar. Revolution in Guinea. 110p. 1974. 3.95, monthly (ISBN 0-317-36674-2). Africa Fund.

--Unity & Struggle: Speeches & Writings. LC 79-2337. 298p. 1979. 16.50 (ISBN 0-85345-510-4); pap. 10.00 (ISBN 0-85345-625-9). Monthly Rev.

Cabral, Amilcar see Africa Information Service.

Cabral, Olga. The Darkness in My Pockets. (Literary Chapbook Ser.). 48p. 1976. pap. 2.50 (ISBN 0-916300-03-X). Gallimaufry.

--In the Empire of Ice. LC 80-53808. (Illus.). 88p. (Orig.). 1980. pap. 3.25 (ISBN 0-931122-19-8). West End.

--Occupied Country. 1976. pap. 1.25 (ISBN 0-685-83035-7). New Rivers Pr.

--So Proudly She Sailed. (Illus.). (gr. 5-9). 1981. 8.95 (ISBN 0-395-31670-7). HM.

Cabral De Melo Neto, Joao. A Knife All Blade: Poetry. 1980. pap. 10.00 (ISBN 0-930502-01-9). Pine Pr.

Cabranes, Jose A. Citizenship & the American Empire. LC 78-65479. 1979. 16.00x (ISBN 0-300-02325-1). Yale U Pr.

Cabre, S. J., ed. Geodynamics of the Eastern Pacific Region, Caribbean & Scotia Arcs. (Geodynamics Ser.: Vol. 9). 170p. 1983. 24.00 (ISBN 0-87590-502-1). Am Geophysical.

Cabrera, Gilberto R. Fundamentos del Comercio Internacional. 7.50 (ISBN 0-8477-2602-9). U of PR Pr.

Cabrera, James C., jt. auth. see Morin, William J.

Cabrera, Lydia. El Monte. Marks, Morton, tr. from Span. (Illus.). 600p. 1985. 35.00 (ISBN 0-939544-16-4, 9662). Methuen Inc.

--El Monte. Marks, Morton, tr. 1984. 29.95 (ISBN 0-939544-16-4); pap. cancelled (ISBN 0-939544-17-2). Wildman Pr.

--Reglas De Congo-Palo Monte-Mayombe. LC 79-50627. (Coleccion Del Chicherku). 1979. pap. 15.00 (ISBN 0-686-59741-9). Ediciones.

Cabrera, Neonetta C. & Cunanan, Augustina S. Tagalog Beginning Course. Bowen, J. Donald, tr. 526p. 1968. with 33 audio cassettes 295.00x (ISBN 0-88432-103-7, TG10). J Norton Pubs.

Cabrera, Roberto & Meyers, Patricia. Classic Tailoring Techniques: A Construction Guide for Men's Wear. (Illus.). 260p. 1983. text ed. 20.00 (ISBN 0-87005-431-7). Fairchild.

--Classic Tailoring Techniques: A Construction Guide for Women's Wear. (Illus.). 285p. 1984. text ed. 22.50 (ISBN 0-87005-435-X). Fairchild.

Cabrera, Rosa M., jt. auth. see Zaldivar, Gladys.

Cabrera, Vicente. Juan Benet. (World Authors Ser.). 1983. lib. bdg. 18.95 (ISBN 0-8057-6532-8, Twayne). G K Hall.

--La Noche del Te: El Gaban. LC 84-50238. 80p. (Span.). 1984. pap. 10.00 (ISBN 0-89295-035-8). Society Sp & Sp-Am.

Cabrera, Vicente & Gonzalez-Del-Valle, Luis. Antonio Machado. LC 76-4181. (Span.). 1976. pap. 8.00 (ISBN 0-89294-000-X). Journal Span Stud.

Cabrera, Vicente, jt. auth. see Gonzalez Del Valle, L.

Cabrera, Vicente & Boyer, Harriet, eds. Critical Views on Vicente Aleixandre's Poetry. LC 79-65008. 1979. pap. 18.00 (ISBN 0-89295-006-4). Society Sp & Sp-Am.

Cabrera, Y. Arturo. Emerging Faces: The Mexican-Americans. LC 79-135153. 1978. pap. 5.95x (ISBN 0-932848-02-8). Sierra Pubns Co.

--Minorities in Higher Education. LC 78-68819. 1978. pap. 5.95x (ISBN 0-932848-01-X). Sierra Pubns Co.

Cabrera, Y. Arturo & Perea, Jose A. Community College Conflict: Chicano Under Fire. LC 78-56755. (Illus.). 1979. pap. 3.95x (ISBN 0-932848-03-6). Sierra Pubns Co.

Cabrera, Y. Arturo, ed. Strategies for the Education of Chicanos. LC 78-52129. 1978. pap. 5.95x (ISBN 0-932848-00-1). Sierra Pubns Co.

Cabrera Infante, G. View of Dawn in the Tropics. Levine, Suzanne J., tr. from Span. LC 76-5134. 150p. 1981. pap. 6.95 (ISBN 0-916870-37-5). Creative Arts Bk.

Cabrera Infante, Guillermo. View of Dawn in the Tropics. Levine, Suzanne J., tr. from Span. LC 76-5134. 1978. 8.95i (ISBN 0-06-010622-0, HarpT). Har-Row.

Caccamise, Frank & Garretson, Mervin, eds. Teaching ASL as a Second-Foreign Language: Proceedings of National Symposium on Sign Language Research & Teaching. 240p. (Orig.). 1982. pap. text ed. 15.95 (ISBN 0-913072-49-4). Natl Assn Deaf.

Caccamo, Domenico. Eretici Italiani in Moravia, Polonia, Transilvania (1558-1611) LC 72-3474. (Corpus Reformatorum Italicorum & Biblioteca Ser.). (Illus.). 286p. (Latin & It.). 1970. pap. 17.50 (ISBN 0-87580-511-6). N Ill U Pr.

Cacciari, E. & Prader, A., eds. Pathophysiology of Puberty. LC 80-40928. (Serono Symposia Ser.: No. 36). 1981. 66.00 (ISBN 0-12-154160-6). Acad Pr.

Cacciari, E., et al, eds. Obesity in Childhood. 1978. 44.00 (ISBN 0-12-154150-9). Acad Pr.

Caccioppo, John T., jt. auth. see Petty, Richard E.

Cacciotti, Tony. The Cacciotti Method. LC 82-42802. (Illus.). 256p. 1983. 17.95 (ISBN 0-394-52567-1). Random.

--The Cacciotti Method. 1985. pap. write for info. (ISBN 0-345-30717-8). Ballantine.

Caccoullos, T., ed. Discriminant Analysis & Applications: Proceedings. 1973. 65.00 (ISBN 0-12-154050-2). Acad Pr.

Caceres, Ana C. Introduccion a la Orientacion Individual. (UPREX, Pedagogia: No. 15). pap. 1.85 (ISBN 0-8477-0015-1). U of PR Pr.

--La Orientacion En Instituciones Educativas. LC 76-10359. 209p. (Orig.). 1976. pap. 4.35 (ISBN 0-8477-2737-8). U of PR Pr.

Caceres, C. A., ed. Biomedical Telemetry. 1965. 76.50 (ISBN 0-12-153850-8). Acad Pr.

--Clinical Electrocardiography & Computers: A Symposium Vol. 1970. 80.50 (ISBN 0-12-153840-0). Acad Pr.

--The Management of Technology in Health & Medical Care. LC 80-70587. (Artech Medical Library). (Illus.). 502p. 1981. 25.00 (ISBN 0-89006-101-7). Artech Hse.

--The Practice of Clinical Engineering. 1977. 75.00 (ISBN 0-12-153860-5). Acad Pr.

Caceres, C. A., et al, eds. Medical Devices Measurements, Quality Assurance, & Standards - STP 800. LC 82-72890. 298p. 1983. text ed. 38.00 (ISBN 0-8031-0235-6, 04-800000-54). ASTM.

Caceres, Cesar A. Management & Clinical Engineering. 470p. 1980. 25.00 (ISBN 0-89006-094-0). Artech Hse.

Caceres, Jose A. Sociologia y Educacion. 5th ed. LC 76-10842. 1976. 8.75 (ISBN 0-8477-2735-1); pap. 8.00 (ISBN 0-8477-2736-X). U of PR Pr.

Caceres, Raul S., intro. by. Del Cuerpo a las Palabras: La Narrativa de Antonio Skarmeta. 200p. 1983. 8.00 (ISBN 84-85594-05-3, 3004). Ediciones Norte.

Caceres Freire, Julian. Diccionario de Regionalismos de la Provincia de la Rioja. (Span.). 42.50 (ISBN 0-686-56673-4, S-33066). French & Eur.

Cachard, A., jt. ed. see Thomas, J. P.

Cachenmeyer, Charles. Organizational Politica. (Analysis Ser.). 74p. (Orig.). 1979. pap. text ed. 18.00 (ISBN 0-938526-00-6). Inst Analysis.

Cachera, J. P., ed. see European Society for Surgical Research, 10th, Paris, 1975.

Cachia, P. A., jt. auth. see Watt, W. M.

Cachia, Pierre. Al-Arif: A Dictionary of Grammatical Terms, Arabic-English, English-Arabic. 1974. 15.00x (ISBN 0-86685-119-4). Intl Bk Ctr.

Cachiaras, Dot. God Gives Us Seasons. (Happy Day Bks.). (Illus.). 24p. (ps-2). 1984. 1.39 (ISBN 0-87239-732-7, 3702). Standard Pub.

--I'm Glad God Thought of Mothers. (Happy Day Bks.). (Illus.). 24p. (gr. k-3). 1979. 1.39 (ISBN 0-87239-360-7, 3630). Standard Pub.

--Sharing Makes Me Happy. LC 82-80030. (Happy Day Bks.). (Illus.). 24p. (Orig.). (ps-3). 1982. pap. 1.39 (ISBN 0-87239-543-X, 3589). Standard Pub.

Cachin, Francoise, jt. ed. see Adhemar, Jean.

Cachin, Francoise, et al. Manet, 1832-1883. Walter, Emily, ed. (Illus.). 548p. 1983. 59.50 (ISBN 0-87099-359-3). Metro Mus Art.

Cachin, Francoise, et al, eds. Manet 1832-1883. (Illus.). 548p. 1984. 75.00 (ISBN 0-8109-1346-1). Abrams.

Caciagli, F., et al, eds. Developmental Neuroscience-Physiological, Pharmacological & Clinical Aspects: Proceedings of the International Meeting of the International Society for Developmental Neuroscience, 5th, Held in Chieti, Italy, 24-28 June, 1984. (Symposia of the Giovanni Lorenzini Foundation Ser.: Vol. 20). 404p. 1985. 83.50 (ISBN 0-444-80640-7). Elsevier.

Cacioppo, John T. & Petty, Richard E., eds. Perspectives in Cardiovascular Psychophysiology. LC 81-6766. 392p. 1982. 39.50 (ISBN 0-89862-613-7, 2613). Guilford Pr.

--Social Psychophysiology. LC 82-15575. 769p. 1983. text ed. 50.00 (ISBN 0-89862-626-9). Guilford Pr.

Cackavell, jt. auth. see Kaye.

Cacko, J., jt. auth. see Bily, M.

Cacoyannis, Michael, tr. see Euripides.

Cada, Lawrence, et al. Shaping the Coming Age of Religious Life. 2nd ed. LC 78-25987. 208p. 1985. pap. 7.95 (ISBN 0-89571-023-4). Affirmation.

Cadart-Richard, Odette. Les Gammas! Les Gammas! 548p. 1983. pap. text ed. write for info. (ISBN 0-02-319290-9). Macmillan.

Cadawallader, Sylvanus. Three Years with Grant: As Recalled by War Correspondent Sylvanus Cadwallader. Thomas, Benjamin P., ed. LC 80-21191. (Illus.). xiv, 361p. 1980. Repr. of 1955 ed. lib. bdg. 32.50x (ISBN 0-313-22576-1, CATY). Greenwood.

Cadbury, Edward. Experiments in Industrial Organization. Chandler, Alfred D., ed. LC 79-7534. (History of Management Thought & Practice Ser.). 1980. Repr. of 1912 ed. lib. bdg. 28.50x (ISBN 0-405-12316-7). Ayer Co Pubs.

Cadbury, Edward, et al. Women's Work & Wages. LC 79-56954. (The English Working Class Ser.). 1980. lib. bdg. 40.00 (ISBN 0-8240-0108-7). Garland Pub.

Cadbury, H. J. Style & Literary Method of Luke, 2 Vols. in 1. 1919-1920. 22.00 (ISBN 0-527-01006-5). Kraus Repr.

Cadbury, Henry J. Behind the Gospels. LC 68-8591. (Orig.). 1968. pap. 2.30x (ISBN 0-87574-160-6). Pendle Hill.

--The Character of a Quaker. 1983. pap. 5.00x (ISBN 0-87574-103-7, 103). Pendle Hill.

--Eclipse of the Historical Jesus. LC 64-12998. (Orig.). 1964. 5.00x (ISBN 0-87574-133-9, 133). Pendle Hill.

--Quaker Relief During the Siege of Boston. 1983. pap. 5.00x (ISBN 0-686-43965-1, 004). Pendle Hill.

Cadbury, Henry J., ed. see Fox, George.

Cadbury, Matheson S. Women's Work & Wages. 1976. lib. bdg. 59.95 (ISBN 0-8490-2836-1). Gordon Pr.

Cadbury, Rachel. The Choice Before Us. (FGC). 64p. 1957. 0.50 (ISBN 0-318-14144-2). Friends Genl Conf.

Cadbury, Warder, frwd. by. Journal of a Hunting Excursion to Louis Lake, 1851. (Illus.). 80p. 1961. 8.95 (ISBN 0-686-74832-8). Adirondack Mus.

Cadbury, Warder, intro. by. Journal of a Hunting Excursion to Louis Lake, 1851. (Illus.). 1961. 8.95 (ISBN 0-8156-8029-5, Pub. by Adirondack Museum). Syracuse U Pr.

Cadbury, Warder H. Arthur Fitzwilliam Tait. LC 82-40347. (Illus.). 480p. 1984. 65.00 (ISBN 0-87413-224-X). U Delaware Pr.

Cadbury, William & Poague, Leland. Film Criticism: A Counter Theory. (Illus.). 304p. 1982. 23.50x (ISBN 0-8138-0352-7). Iowa St U Pr.

Cadbury, William A. Labour in Portuguese West Africa. 2nd ed. LC 73-75542. (Illus.). Repr. of 1910 ed. 17.50x (ISBN 0-8371-0982-5, CAP&, Pub. by Negro U Pr). Greenwood.

Caddel. Burnt Aces & Shangri-las. signed ed o.p. 13.95x (ISBN 0-904461-50-5, Pub. by Ceolfrith Pr England). Intl Spec Bk.

Caddell, Foster. Keys to Painting Better Portraits: A Problem-Solving Guide for Painters in Oil & Pastel. (Illus.). 144p. 1982. 22.50 (ISBN 0-8230-2582-9). Watson-Guptill.

--Keys to Successful Color. (Illus.). 144p. 1979. 22.50 (ISBN 0-8230-2580-2). Watson-Guptill.

--Keys to Successful Landscape Painting. (Illus.). 160p. 1976. 22.50 (ISBN 0-8230-2579-9). Watson-Guptill.

Caddell, Foster, jt. auth. see Blake, Wendon.

Caddell, Gloria M., et al see Oakley, Carey.

Caddell, Laurie & Winfield, Mike. Superbikes. LC 81-81994. (Orig.). 1981. pap. 9.95 (ISBN 0-89586-067-8). H P Bks.

Caddell, Robert M. Deformation & Fracture of Solids. (Illus.). 1980. text ed. 37.95 (ISBN 0-13-198309-1). P-H.

Caddell, Robert M. & Hosford, William F. Metal Forming: Mechanics & Metallurgy. (Illus.). 352p. 1983. text ed. 37.95 (ISBN 0-13-577700-3). P-H.

Cadden, John Paul. The Historiography of the American Catholic Church: 1785-1943, No. 82. (Studies in Sacred Theology). 134p. 1984. Repr. of 1944 ed. 35.00x (ISBN 0-939738-33-3). Zubal Inc.

Cadden, Tom S. What a Bunch of Characters! An Entertaining Guide to Who Played What in the Movies. 320p. 1984. 19.95 (ISBN 0-13-951914-9); pap. 12.95 (ISBN 0-13-951906-8). P-H.

Caddick, James W. Production Improvement in a Rehabilitation Workshop. (Illus.). 106p. (Orig.). 1980. pap. 6.00x (ISBN 0-916671-24-0). Material Dev.

Caddy, Douglas. The Hundred Million Dollar Payoff: How Big Labor Buys Its Democrats. LC 74-5348. 412p. 1976. pap. 2.95 (ISBN 0-916054-30-6, Dist. by Kampmann). Green Hill.

--Legislative Trends in Insurance Regulation. LC 84-40562. 1986. 16.75 (ISBN 0-89096-222-7). Tex A&M Univ Pr.

--Understanding Texas Insurance. LC 83-40499. 208p. 1984. 14.95 (ISBN 0-89096-179-4). Tex A&M Univ Pr.

Caddy, Douglas & Dethloff, Henry C. Insurance Is Everybody's Business. (Series on Public Issues: No. 15). 26p. 1985. pap. 2.00 (ISBN 0-86599-051-4). Ctr Educ Res.

Caddy, Eileen. The Spirit of Findhorn. LC 75-36747. (Illus.). 1979. pap. 6.68i (ISBN 0-06-061291-6, RD 296, HarpR). Har-Row.

Caddy, Glenn R., ed. see Newman, Frederick L. & Sorenson, James E.

Caddy, Glenn R., ed. see Vincent, Ken, et al.

Caddy, J. F. Advances in Assessment of World Cephalopod Resources. (Fisheries Technical Papers: No. 231). 452p. (Orig., Eng., Fr., & Span.). 1984. pap. text ed. 33.50 (ISBN 92-5-001431-7, F2552, FAO). Unipub.

Cade, J. F., et al, eds. see Symposium, Hamilton, Ont., Oct. 1972.

Cade, Tom. The Falcons of the World. (Illus.). 192p. 1982. 38.50 (ISBN 0-8014-1454-7). Comstock.

Cade, Toni, ed. The Black Woman: An Anthology. 256p. 1974. pap. 3.95 (ISBN 0-451-62398-3, ME2068, Ment). NAL.

Cadell, Elizabeth. Around the Rugged Rock. 15.95 (ISBN 0-88411-390-6, Pub. by Aeonian Pr). Amereon Ltd.

--Canary Yellow. 15.95 (ISBN 0-88411-391-4, Pub. by Aeonian Pr). Amereon Ltd.

--The Cuckoo in Spring. 214p. 1976. Repr. of 1954 ed. lib. bdg. 13.95x (ISBN 0-89244-067-8, Pub. by Queens Hse). Amereon Ltd.

--Enter Mrs. Belchamber. 15.95 (ISBN 0-88411-392-2, Pub. by Aeonian Pr). Amereon Ltd.

--Gay Pursuit. 15.95 (ISBN 0-88411-393-0, Pub. by Aeonian Pr). Amereon Ltd.

--I Love a Lass. 15.95 (ISBN 0-88411-394-9, Pub. by Aeonian Pr). Amereon Ltd.

--The Lark Shall Sing. 15.95 (ISBN 0-88411-395-7, Pub. by Aeonian Pr). Amereon Ltd.

--A Lion in the Way. 330p. 1982. 13.50 (ISBN 0-688-01098-9). Morrow.

--A Lion in the Way. (General Ser.). 1982. lib. bdg. 15.95 (ISBN 0-8161-3425-1, Large Print Bks). G K Hall.

--The Marrying Kind. (General Ser.). 1980. lib. bdg. 12.95 (ISBN 0-8161-3083-3, Large Print Bks). G K Hall.

--Money to Burn. 14.95 (ISBN 0-88411-396-5, Pub. by Aeonian Pr). Amereon Ltd.

--Remains to Be Seen. LC 83-61741. 1983. 12.95 (ISBN 0-688-02177-8). Morrow.

--Remains to Be Seen. (General Ser.). 1984. lib. bdg. 12.95 (ISBN 0-8161-3650-5, Large Print Bks). G K Hall.

--Shadow on the Water. 14.95 (ISBN 0-88411-397-3, Pub. by Aeonian Pr). Amereon Ltd.

--Six Impossible Things. 15.95 (ISBN 0-88411-398-1, Pub. by Aeonian Pr). Amereon Ltd.

--The Waiting Game. Williams, Jennifer, ed. LC 84-62590. 224p. 1985. Repr. of 1984 ed. 15.95 (ISBN 0-688-04198-1). Morrow.

--The Yellow Brick Road. 14.95 (ISBN 0-88411-399-X, Pub. by Aeonian Pr). Amereon Ltd.

Cadell, H. M. Klondike & Yukon Goldfield in 1913. facs. ed. (Shorey Historical Ser.). 11p. pap. 1.95 (ISBN 0-8466-0027-7, S27). Shorey.

Cadell, James, tr. see Bosi, Roberto.

Cadenas, Vicente de. Diccionario Heraldico. 2nd ed. 304p. (Espn.). 1976. pap. 29.95 (ISBN 84-00-04294-8, S-50107). French & Eur.

Cadenet, J. J. de see Castro, Rene & De Cadenet, J. J.

Cadenhead, D. A., ed. Progress in Surface & Membrane Science, Vol. 13. (Serial Publication). 1979. 70.00 (ISBN 0-12-571813-6). Acad Pr.

Cadenhead, D. A. & Danielli, J. F., eds. Progress in Surface & Membrane Science, Vol. 14. (Serial Publication Ser.). 1981. 70.00 (ISBN 0-12-571814-4). Acad Pr.

Cadenhead, D. A. & Danielli, James F., eds. Progress in Surface & Membrane Science, Vol. 12. 1979. 71.50 (ISBN 0-12-571812-8). Acad Pr.

Cadenhead, I. E. Theodore Roosevelt: The Paradox of Progressivism. Colegrove, Kenneth, ed. LC 74-790. (Shapers of History Ser). (gr. 10 up). 1974. pap. text ed. 4.95 (ISBN 0-8120-0462-0). Barron.

Cadenhead, I. E., Jr., ed. see Michael, Franz.

Cadet, Felix. Histoire de l'economie politique, les precurseurs: Boisguilbert, Vauban, Quesnay, Turgot. LC 73-121598. (Research & Source Ser.: No. 503). (Fr). 1970. Repr. of 1869 ed. lib. bdg. 21.00 (ISBN 0-8337-0448-6). B Franklin.

--Pierre de Boisguilbert, precurseur des economistes, 1646-1714: sa vie, ses travaux, son influence. LC 68-56731. Repr. of 1870 ed. 25.50 (ISBN 0-8337-0449-4). B Franklin.

Cadet, Melissa L. Food Aid & Policy for Economic Development: An Annotated Bibliography & Directory. LC 80-53500. 178p. (Orig.). 1981. 29.95 (ISBN 0-938398-00-8); pap. 19.95 (ISBN 0-938398-01-6). Trans Tech Mgmt.

Cadez, Mary J., jt. auth. see Striefel, Sebastian.

Cadfryn-Roberts, John, ed. Old London. LC 79-81859. (Golden Ariels Ser). (Illus.). 1969. 3.95 (ISBN 0-8008-5690-2). Taplinger.

Cadieux, Charles. These Are the Endangered. LC 80-54448. (Illus.). 240p. 1981. 16.95 (ISBN 0-913276-35-9). Stone Wall Pr.

Cadieux, Charles L. Coyotes: Predators & Survivors. LC 82-62895. (Illus.). 240p. 1983. 16.95 (ISBN 0-913276-42-1). Stone Wall Pr.

--Goose Hunting. LC 79-19953. (Illus.). 1979. 16.95 (ISBN 0-913276-30-8). Stone Wall Pr.

--Goose Hunting. 208p. 1983. 9.95 (ISBN 0-88317-120-1). Stoeger Pub Co.

--Wildlife Management on Your Land: The Practical Owner's Manual on How, What, When & Why. Fish, Chet, ed. (Illus.). 320p. 1985. 29.95 (ISBN 0-8117-1877-8). Stackpole.

Cadillac Publishing Company & Shapiro, Max. Mathematics Encyclopedia. LC 76-23817. 1977. pap. 6.95 (ISBN 0-385-12427-9). Doubleday.

Cadilla De Martinez, Maria. Raices de la Tierra. LC 78-67694. (The Folktale). Repr. of 1941 ed. 22.50 (ISBN 0-404-16065-4). AMS Pr.

Cadkin, Alan V. & Motew, Martin N. Clinical Atlas of Gray Scale Ultrasonography in Obstetrics. (Illus.). 384p. 1979. photocopy ed. 78.50x (ISBN 0-398-03842-2). C C Thomas.

Cadman, B. D., jt. auth. see Bryne, P.

Cadman, Eileen, et al. Rolling Our Own: Women as Printers, Publishers, & Distributors. 35.00x (ISBN 0-906890-06-3, Pub. by Comedia England); pap. 25.00x (ISBN 0-906890-07-1). State Mutual Bk.

Cadman, John. Games for Hockey Training. (Illus.). 232p. 1985. 15.95 (ISBN 0-7207-1246-7, Pub. by Michael Joseph). Merrimack Pub Cir.

--Hockey Rules Illustrated. (Illus.). 112p. 1980. 18.00 (ISBN 0-7207-1112-6). Transatlantic.

Cadman, Samuel P. Charles Darwin & Other English Thinkers. facs. ed. LC 76-142612. (Essay Index Reprint Ser.). 1911. 18.00 (ISBN 0-8369-2040-6). Ayer Co Pubs.

Cadmus, Robert R. Caring for Your Aging Parents. 253p. 1984. 17.95 (ISBN 0-13-114786-2); pap. 7.95 (ISBN 0-13-114752-8). P-H.

--Hospitals Are Us. LC 79-66803. 184p. (Orig.). 1979. 15.95 (ISBN 0-931028-12-4); pap. 12.95 (ISBN 0-931028-11-6). Teach'em.

Cadmus, Spencer, tr. see Mikhailovsky, Nikolai K.

Cadnum, Michael. The Morning of the Massacre. 1982. 27.50x (ISBN 0-931460-19-0). Bieler.

Cadogan, Edward. Makers of Modern History. LC 75-112797. 1970. Repr. of 1905 ed. 19.50x (ISBN 0-8046-1064-9, Pub. by Kennikat). Assoc Faculty Pr.

Cadogan, Georges. Kondratieff & the Mastery of the Future Through the Theory of Cycles. (Illus.). 136p. 1983. 81.25x (ISBN 0-86654-076-8). Inst Econ Finan.

Cadogan, Gerald. Palaces of Minoan Crete. (Illus.). 168p. 1980. pap. 7.95x (ISBN 0-416-73160-0, 2878). Methuen Inc.

Cadogan, J. I., ed. Organophosphorus Reagents in Organic Synthesis. LC 79-50307. (Organic Chemistry Ser.). 1980. 95.00 (ISBN 0-12-154350-1). Acad Pr.

Cadogan, Peter. The Moon-Our Sister Planet. LC 80-41564. (Illus.). 400p. 1981. 72.50 (ISBN 0-521-23684-3); pap. 32.50 (ISBN 0-521-28152-0). Cambridge U Pr.

Cadogan, Peter H. From Quark to Quasar. (Illus.). 192p. Date not set. price not set (ISBN 0-521-30135-1). Cambridge U Pr.

Cadoret, Remi, jt. ed. see Sexias, Frank A.

Cadoux, Arthur T. Shakespearean Selves. 176p. 1981. Repr. of 1938 ed. lib. bdg. 30.00 (ISBN 0-89984-109-0). Century Bookbindery.

Cadoux, C. John. The Early Christian Attitude to War: A Contribution to the History of Christian Ethics. 304p. 1982. pap. 9.95 (ISBN 0-8164-2416-0, Pub. by Seabury). Winston Pr.

--The Early Christian Attitude Toward War. 69.95 (ISBN 0-87968-198-5). Gordon Pr.

--The Historic Mission of Jesus: A Constructive Re-Examination of the Eschatological Teaching in the Synoptic Gospels with an Extensive Bibliography. 1977. lib. bdg. 59.95 (ISBN 0-8490-1955-9). Gordon Pr.

Cadoux, Cecil J. Philip of Spain & the Netherlands: An Essay on Moral Judgments in History. xv, 251p. 1969. Repr. of 1947 ed. 20.00 (ISBN 0-208-00735-0, Archon). Shoe String.

Cadoux, Cecil J., ed. see Bartlet, James V.

Cadoux, R. Envolee. college ed. 1973. write for info. (ISBN 0-02-318020-X). Macmillan.

--L' Envolee, Level 3. 1972. 25.32 (ISBN 0-02-268660-6). Macmillan.

--Notre Monde, Level 2. 1971. 24.08 (ISBN 0-02-268580-4). Macmillan.

--Vous et Moi: En Avant. 1970. 19.28 (ISBN 0-02-268400-X). Macmillan.

--Vous et Moi: Premier Pas. 1970. 19.28 (ISBN 0-02-268300-3). Macmillan.

Cadoux, Remunda. Invitation Au Francais: Vous et Moi, Level One. 1970. 22.88 (ISBN 0-02-268500-6). Macmillan.

Cadoux, Remunda, jt. auth. see Finocchiaro, Mary.

Cadoux, T., pref. by. The Sorrowful & Immaculate Heart of Mary. 1974. pap. 3.00 (ISBN 0-913382-02-7, 101-2). Prow Bks-Franciscan.

Cadrain, Linda A., adapted by. The Diary of Anne Frank. (Contemporary Motivators Ser.). (Illus.). 32p. (Orig.). (YA) (gr. 4-12). 1979. pap. text ed. 1.95 (ISBN 0-88301-308-8). Pendulum Pr.

Caduto, Michael J. Pond & Brook: A Guide to Nature Study in Freshwater Environments. (Illus.). 256p. 1985. 21.95 (ISBN 0-13-685108-8); pap. 12.95 (ISBN 0-13-685090-1). P-H.

Cadwalader, Sandra L. & Deloria, Vine, Jr., eds. The Aggressions of Civilization: Federal Indian Policy Since the 1880s. LC 84-94. (Illus.). 272p. 1984. 34.95 (ISBN 0-87722-349-1). Temple U Pr.

Cadwallader, Donald E. Biopharmaceutics & Drug Interactions. 3rd ed. 162p. 1983. pap. 19.50 (ISBN 0-89004-704-9). Raven.

Cadwallader, Eva H. Searchlight on Values: Nicolai Hartmann's Twentieth-Century Value Platonism. LC 84-20898. 234p. (Orig.). 1985. lib. bdg. 22.50 (ISBN 0-8191-4369-3); pap. text ed. 11.25 (ISBN 0-8191-4370-7). U Pr of Amer.

Cadwallader, Martin. Analytical Urban Geography: Spatial Patterns & Theories. (Illus.). 336p. 1985. text ed. 33.95 (ISBN 0-13-034950-X). P-H.

Cadwallader, Sharon. Cooking Adventures for Kids. LC 74-9544. (A San Francisco Ser.). 101p. 1974. pap. 6.95 (ISBN 0-395-19980-8). HM.

--The Living Kitchen. LC 82-10763. (Tools for Today Ser.). (Illus.). 128p. (Orig.). 1983. pap. 7.95 (ISBN 0-87156-326-6). Sierra.

--Whole Earth Cookbook 2. LC 75-23317. 1975. 7.95 (ISBN 0-395-21984-1, Co-Pub. by San Francisco Bk. Co.). HM.

Cadwell, Jerry J. Nuclear Facility Threat Analysis & Tactical Response Procedures. (Illus.). 114p. 1983. 22.50x (ISBN 0-398-04778-2). C C Thomas.

Cadwell, Karin, jt. auth. see Tibbetts, Edith.

Cady. Computer Techniques in Cardiology. (Biomedical Engineering & Instrumentation Ser.: Vol. 4). 1979. 75.00 (ISBN 0-8247-6743-8). Dekker.

Cady, Blake, jt. auth. see Sedgwick, Cornelius E.

Cady, Dale R. Pilot's Bahamas Aviation Guide. (Illus.). 468p. 1984. ring bdg. 19.95 (ISBN 0-318-03984-2). Pilot Pubns.

--Pilot's Bahamas Aviation Guide 1980. (Illus.). 442p. 1979. ring bdg. 16.95 (ISBN 0-911721-68-1). Pilot Pubns.

--Pilot's Bahamas Aviation Guide, 1981. (Illus.). 480p. 1980. ring binding 12.95 (ISBN 0-686-31872-2). Pilot Pubns.

--Pilot's Bahamas Aviation Guide, 1982. (Illus.). 494p. 1981. ring binding 19.95 (ISBN 0-686-31873-0). Pilot Pubns.

--Pilot's Bahamas Aviation Guide, 1983. (Illus.). 494p. 1982. ring binding 19.95 (ISBN 0-686-40511-0). Pilot Pubns.

--Pilot's Bahamas Aviation Guide, 1984. (Illus.). 494p. 1983. ring binding 19.95 (ISBN 0-318-02794-1). Pilot Pubns.

Cady, Denise A., compiled by. Good Seats: Seating Diagrams of Los Angeles Area Theatres & Stadiums. (Illus.). 29p. 1983. pap. 5.00 (ISBN 0-9606976-0-8). Clearview Pr.

Cady, Denise A., ed. Good Seats: Seating Diagrams of Thirty Chicago Area Theatres & Stadiums. (Illus.). 43p. 1983. pap. 3.50 (ISBN 0-9606976-1-6). Clearview Pr.

Cady, E. H., ed. see Howells, William D.

Cady, Edwin H. The Big Game: College Sports & American Life. LC 78-6794. 1978. 21.50x (ISBN 0-87049-254-3). U of Tenn Pr.

--Stephen Crane. (Twayne's United States Authors Ser). 1962. pap. 5.95x (ISBN 0-8084-0284-6, T23, Twayne). New Coll U Pr.

--Stephen Crane. rev. ed. (United States Authors Ser.). 1980. lib. bdg. 13.50 (ISBN 0-8057-7299-5, Twayne). G K Hall.

--Young Howells & John Brown: Episodes in a Radical Education. LC 85-5013. 128p. 1985. 17.50x (ISBN 0-8142-0383-4). Ohio St U Pr.

Cady, Edwin H. & Cady, Norma W. Critical Essays on William Dean Howells, 1866-1920. (Critical Essays on American Literature Ser.). 312p. 1983. lib. bdg. 36.50 (ISBN 0-8161-8651-0). G K Hall.

Cady, Edwin H. & Wells, Lester G., eds. Stephen Crane's Love Letters to Nellie Crouse. 1954. 14.95x (ISBN 0-8156-2014-4). Syracuse U Pr.

Cady, Edwin H., ed. see Howells, William D.

Cady, Emilie H. God a Present Help. rev. ed. LC 84-5002010. 1985. 4.95 (ISBN 0-87159-044-1). Unity School.

Cady, Foster B., jt. auth. see Allen, David M.

Cady, Frank. Poems on a White Page. (Flowering Quince Poetry Ser.: No. 4). (Illus.). 24p. (Orig.). 1982. pap. 4.50 (ISBN 0-940592-13-4). Heyeck Pr.

Cady, H. Emilie. How I Used Truth. 1916. 4.95 (ISBN 0-87159-056-5). Unity School.

--Lessons in Truth. 1894. deluxe ed. 4.95 (ISBN 0-87159-084-0). Unity School.

Cady, Howard, ed. see Canning, Victor.

Cady, Howard, ed. see Hough, Richard.

Cady, Howard, ed. see Lodge, David.

Cady, Howard, ed. see Phillips, Wally.

Cady, Howard, ed. see Terry, Carolyn.

Cady, Jack. The Burning & Other Stories. LC 72-76304. (The Iowa School of Letters Award for Short Fiction Ser: No. 3). 157p. 1972. 11.00 (ISBN 0-87745-030-7). U of Iowa Pr.

--The Jonah Watch. 224p. 1983. pap. 2.75 (ISBN 0-380-62828-7, 62828-7). Avon.

--The Jonah Watch: A True-Life Ghost Story in the Form of a Novel. LC 81-66973. 1982. 12.95 (ISBN 0-87795-342-2). Arbor Hse.

--McDowell's Ghost. LC 81-66974. 256p. 1981. 14.50 (ISBN 0-87795-343-0). Arbor Hse.

--The Man Who Could Make Things Vanish. LC 82-72074. 288p. 1983. 14.95 (ISBN 0-87795-428-3). Arbor Hse.

--Singleton. LC 81-8117. 288p. 1981. 13.95 (ISBN 0-914842-63-3). Madrona Pubs.

--Tattoo. 1978. pap. 6.25 (ISBN 0-931594-01-4). Circinatum Pr.

--The Well. LC 80-67623. 1980. 11.95 (ISBN 0-87795-287-6). Arbor Hse.

Cady, John F. Contacts with Burma, 1935-1949: Personal Account. LC 82-90629. (Papers in International Studies, Southeast Asia Ser.: No. 61). 117p. 1983. pap. 9.00x monograph (ISBN 0-89680-114-4). Ohio U Pr.

--Foreign Intervention in the Rio De La Plata 1838-50: A Study of French, British, & American Policy in Relation to the Dictator Juan Manuel Rosas. LC 71-100817. (BCL Ser. II). Repr. of 1929 ed. 24.00 (ISBN 0-404-01360-0). AMS Pr.

--History of Modern Burma. (Illus.). 729p. 1958. 49.50x (ISBN 0-8014-0059-7). Cornell U Pr.

--The History of Post War Southeast Asia: Independence Problems. LC 74-82497. xxii, 720p. 1975. 30.00x (ISBN 0-8214-0160-2, 82-81594); pap. 15.00x (ISBN 0-8214-0175-0, 82-81602). Ohio U Pr.

--Restricted Advertising & Competition: The Case of Retail Drugs. 1976. pap. 2.25 (ISBN 0-8447-3207-9). Am Enterprise.

--The Southeast Asian World. LC 76-53353. (World of Asia Ser). (Illus.). 1977. pap. text ed. 5.95x (ISBN 0-88273-502-0). Forum Pr IL.

--The United States & Burma. 1976. text ed. 18.50x (ISBN 0-674-92320-0). Harvard U Pr.

Cady, John W. Magnetic & Gravity Anomalies in the Great Valley & Western Sierra Nevada Metamorphic Belt, California. LC 75-19540. (Geological Society of America Special Paper Ser.: No. 168). pap. 20.00 (ISBN 0-317-30055-5, 2025031). Bks Demand UMI.

Cady, Lanore. Houses & Letters: A Heritage in Architecture & Calligraphy. (Illus.). 70p. 1977. 35.00 (ISBN 0-87027-184-9). TBW Bks.

Cady, Lew. Beer Can Collecting. 224p. (Orig.). 1981. pap. 1.95 (ISBN 0-441-05274-6, Pub. by Charter Bks). Ace Bks.

Cady, Norma W., jt. auth. see Cady, Edwin H.

Cady, Richard A. Marine Hawser Towing Guide. (Illus.). 123p. (Orig.). Date not set. pap. text ed. 26.00 (ISBN 0-934114-65-X, BK-120). Marine Educ.

Cady, Wallace M. Regioanl Tectonic Synthesis of Northwestern New England & Adjacent Quebec. LC 77-98020. (Geological Society of America Ser.: No. 120). pap. 62.00 (ISBN 0-317-28385-5, 2025466). Bks Demand UMI.

Cadzow, James & Van Landingham, Hugh. Signals, Systems & Transforms. (Illus.). 384p. 1985. text ed. 34.95 (ISBN 0-13-809542-6). P-H.

Cadzow, James A. Discrete Time Systems: An Introduction with Interdisciplinary Applications. (Computer Applications in Electrical Engineering Ser.). (Illus.). 448p. 1973. ref. ed. 39.95 (ISBN 0-13-215996-1). P-H.

Cadzow, James A. & Martens, Hinrich R. Discrete Time & Computer Control Systems. (Electrical Engineering Ser). 1970. ref. ed. 39.95 (ISBN 0-13-216036-6). P-H.

Cadzow, John F. & Ludanyi, Andrew, eds. Transylvania: The Roots of Ethnic Conflict. LC 82-23354. (Illus.). 360p. 1984. 32.50x (ISBN 0-87338-283-8). Kent St U Pr.

Caelen, Genevieve. Structures prosodiques de la phrase enonciative simple et etendue. (Hamburger Phonetische Beitraege (HPB) Ser.: 34). 325p. (Orig., Fr.). 1981. pap. 26.00x (ISBN 3-87118-463-2, Pub. by Helmut Buske Verlag Hamburg). Benjamins North AM.

Caelleigh, Addeane, jt. auth. see Olson, William J.

Caelli, Terrence M., jt. ed. see Dodwell, Peter C.

Caelli, Terry. An Introduction to Modern Approaches in Visual Perception. LC 80-40167. (Illus.). 200p. 1981. 46.00 (ISBN 0-08-024420-3); pap. 22.00 (ISBN 0-08-024419-X). Pergamon.

Caemmerer, H. Paul. Life of Pierre Charles l'Enfant. LC 71-87546. (Architecture & Decorative Art Ser.: Vol. 33). 1970. Repr. of 1950 ed. lib. bdg. 55.00 (ISBN 0-306-71381-0). Da Capo.

Caemmerer, Richard R., Jr. Visual Art in the Life of the Church: Encouraging Creative Worship & Witness in the Congregation. LC 83-70504. 96p. (Orig.). 1983. pap. 9.50 (ISBN 0-8066-2010-2, 10-6855). Augsburg.

Caen, Herb. One Man's San Francisco. new ed. LC 75-14808. 1978. pap. 3.95 (ISBN 0-89174-031-7). Comstock Edns.

Caen, Maria T. Dining In San Franciso. 8.95 (ISBN 0-89716-130-0). Peanut Butter.

Caenegem, R. C. Van see Van Caenegem, R. C.

Caes, Charles. Stock Market Arithmetic: A Primer for New Investors. LC 81-85563. 112p. 1982. pap. 6.95 (ISBN 0-89526-868-X). Regnery-Gateway.

Caes, Charles J. Introduction to the Arguments for God. LC 82-82548. 1983. 8.95 (ISBN 0-686-97926-5). Libra.

Caesar. C. Iuli Caesaris de Bello Gallico, 7 vols. in 1. Connor, W. R., ed. LC 78-67135. (Latin Texts & Commentaries Ser.). (Latin & Eng.). 1979. Repr. of 1914 ed. lib. bdg. 64.50x (ISBN 0-405-11607-1). Ayer Co Pubs.

--Commentarii, 2 Vols. Du Pontet, R. L., ed. (O. C. T). 1900-1901. Vol. 1. 14.95x (ISBN 0-19-814602-7); Vol. 2. 14.95x (ISBN 0-19-814603-5). Oxford U Pr.

Caesar & Pompey. Caesar & Pompey. LC 77-133642. (Tudor Facsimile Texts. Old English Plays: No. 114). Repr. of 1913 ed. 49.50 (ISBN 0-404-53414-7). AMS Pr.

Caesar, C. Julius. Commentaries of Caesar, Translated in English, 2 Vols in 1. LC 77-161798. (The Augustan Translations: Restoration & Eighteenth Century English Translations of the Classics Ser.). Repr. of 1753 ed. 87.50 (ISBN 0-404-54104-6). AMS Pr.

Caesar, Caius Julius. Egypt Books of Caius Julius Caesar Conteyning His Martiall Exploytes in Gallia. Goldinge, Arthur, tr. LC 68-54623. (English Experience Ser.: No. 36). 1968. Repr. of 1565 ed. 42.00 (ISBN 90-221-0036-7). Walter J Johnson.

Caesar, Fred. Love Thine Enemy. 190p. 1984. 3.95 (ISBN 0-89697-147-3). Intl Univ Pr.

Caesar, Gaius J. Civil War. Gardner, Jane F., tr. from Roman. 400p. 1985. 16.95 (ISBN 0-88029-041-2, Pub. by Dorset Pr). Hippocrene Bks.

Caesar, Irving. Sing a Song of Friendship. Repr. 1.95 (ISBN 0-686-95023-2). ADL.

Caesar, Julius. The Ancient State of the Court of Requests. LC 76-57367. (English Experience Ser.: No. 785). 1977. Repr. of 1597 ed. lib. bdg. 17.50 (ISBN 90-221-0785-X). Walter J Johnson.

--The Battle for Gaul. Wiseman, Anne & Wiseman, Peter, trs. from Lat. LC 79-54955. (Illus.). 216p. 1980. 17.95 (ISBN 0-87923-306-0). Godine.

--Battle for Gaul. Wiseman, Anne, tr. LC 79-54955. 208p. 1985. pap. 12.95 (ISBN 0-87923-561-6). Godine.

--Caesar's Gallic War. Pearl, Joseph, tr. from Latin. (Orig.). (gr. 10 up). 1962. pap. text ed. 4.95 (ISBN 0-8120-0037-4). Barron.

--The Civil War. Mitchell, Jane F., tr. (Classics Ser.). 1976. pap. 4.95 (ISBN 0-14-044187-5). Penguin.

--Civil Wars. (Loeb Classical Library: No. 39). 12.50x (ISBN 0-674-99043-9). Harvard U Pr.

--The Conquest of Gaul. rev. ed. Handford, S. A., tr. 1983. pap. 4.95 (ISBN 0-14-044433-5). Penguin.

--Gallic War. (Loeb Classical Library: No. 72). 12.50x (ISBN 0-674-99080-3). Harvard U Pr.

Caesar, Michael & Hainsworth, Peter, eds. Writers & Society in Contemporary Italy: A Collection of Essays. LC 83-40503. 302p. 1984. 25.00 (ISBN 0-312-89350-7). St Martin.

Caesar, Sid. Where Have I Been? An Autobiography with Bill Davidson. 1983. pap. 3.50 (ISBN 0-451-12501-0, Sig). NAL.

Caesar, Sid & Davidson, Bill. Where Have I Been? An Autobiography. 288p. 1982. 3.98 (ISBN 0-517-54794-5). Crown.

Caesarius Of Arles, St. Sermons, Nos. 81-186. LC 56-3628. (Fathers of the Church Ser.: Vol. 47). 495p. 1964. 25.95x (ISBN 0-8132-0047-4). Cath U Pr.

--Sermons, Nos. 187-238. LC 56-3628. (Fathers of the Church Ser.: Vol. 66). 303p. 1973. 17.95x (ISBN 0-8132-0066-0). Cath U Pr.

--Sermons-One to Eighty. (Fathers of the Church Ser.: Vol. 31). 1956. 29.95x (ISBN 0-8132-0031-8). Cath U Pr.

Caesy, Bill, jt. auth. see McMullin, Rian E.

Caetani, Marquerite, ed. see Botteghe Oscure.

Cafagna, Albert C., et al, eds. Child Nurturance, Vol. 1: Philosophy, Children, & the Family. LC 82-3701. 392p. 1982. 39.50x (ISBN 0-306-41003-6, Plenum Pr). Plenum Pub.

Cafarelli, Eugene J. Developing New Products & Repositing Mature Brands: A Risk-Reduction System That Produces Investment Alternatives. (Marketing Management Ser.). 253p. 1980. 39.95 (ISBN 0-471-04634-5, Pub by Ronald Pr). Wiley.

Cafazzo, Veda M., ed. see Johnson, Norman F.

Cafazzo, Veda M., ed. see Stenzel, Jeffery R.

Cafazzo, Veda M., ed. see Weishaupt, Clara G.

Caffarel, Henri. Being Present to God: Letters on Prayer. LC 83-15459. 202p. 1983. pap. 6.95 (ISBN 0-8189-0462-3). Alba.

Caffarella, Edward. Spreadsheets Go to School: Applications for Administrators. 1985. 19.95 (ISBN 0-8359-7060-4). Reston.

Caffee, Gabrielle L., tr. see Van Gennep, Arnold.

Cafferky, Tony. Baulox. (Illus.). 175p. 1983. 11.95 (ISBN 0-86322-021-5, Pub. by Brandon Bks); pap. 5.95 (ISBN 0-86322-020-7). Longwood Pub Group.

Cafferty. Chess Openings for You. pap. 12.95 (ISBN 0-7134-1977-6, Pub. by Batsford England). David & Charles.

--A Complete Defence to IP-K4: A Study of Petroff's Defence. 2nd ed. 1967. 19.00 (ISBN 0-08-024089-5); pap. 9.95 (ISBN 0-08-024088-7). Pergamon.

Cafferty, Bernard. Spassky's One Hundred Best Games. 1973. pap. 16.95 (ISBN 0-7134-2409-5, Pub. by Batsford England). David & Charles.

Cafferty, Bernard & Hooper, David. A Complete Defence to 1d4: A Study of the Queen's Gambit Accepted. LC 79-41623. (Pergamon Chess Ser.). 160p. 1981. 19.00 (ISBN 0-08-024103-4); pap. 9.95 (ISBN 0-08-024102-6). Pergamon.

Cafferty, P. & Chiswick, Barry. The Dilemma of American Immigration: Beyond the Golden Door. LC 83-543. 230p. 1983. 24.95 (ISBN 0-87855-481-5); pap. 9.95 (ISBN 0-87855-935-3). Transaction Bks.

Cafferty, Pastora & McReady, William, eds. Hispanics in the United States: A New Social Agenda. 330p. 1985. 29.95 (ISBN 0-88738-018-2); pap. 12.95 (ISBN 0-87855-975-2). Transaction Bks.

Cafferty, Pastora S. & Chestang, Leon W., eds. The Diverse Society: Implications for Social Policy. LC 76-43633. 176p. 1976. pap. 8.95x (ISBN 0-87101-072-0). Natl Assn Soc Wkrs.

Cafferty, Pastora S. J. & Gail, Spangenberg. Backs Against the Wall: Urban-Oriented Colleges & Universities & the Urban Poor & Disadvantaged. LC 82-25124. (Ford Foundation Series on Higher Education in the Cities). 76p. (Orig.). 1983. pap. 4.00 (ISBN 0-916584-22-4). Ford Found.

Caffey, David L. The Old Home Place: Farming on the West Texas Frontier. (Illus.). 224p. 1981. 11.95 (ISBN 0-89015-283-7). Eakin Pubns.

Caffey, John. The Coming Out Party. 224p. (Orig.). 1982. pap. 2.50 (ISBN 0-523-41707-1). Pinnacle Bks.

Caffin, Caroline & Caffin, Charles H. Dancing & Dancers of Today. (Series in Dance). (Illus.). 1978. Repr. of 1912 ed. lib. bdg. 29.50 (ISBN 0-306-77579-4). Da Capo.

Caffin, Charles H. American Masters of Painting. facs. ed. LC 73-128217. (Essay Index Reprint Ser). 1902. 19.00 (ISBN 0-8369-1868-1). Ayer Co Pubs.

--American Masters of Sculpture. facs. ed. LC 75-84301. (Essay Index Reprint Ser). 1903. 21.50 (ISBN 0-8369-1253-5). Ayer Co Pubs.

--American Masters of Sculpture. 1980. lib. bdg. 65.00 (ISBN 0-8490-3156-7). Gordon Pr.

--Appreciation of the Drama. 1975. Repr. of 1908 ed. 25.00 (ISBN 0-8274-4107-X). R West.

--How to Study Pictures. facs. ed. Buselle, A., Jr., ed. LC 68-58776. (Essay Index Reprint Ser). 1941. 27.50 (ISBN 0-8369-0104-5). Ayer Co Pubs.

--Photography As a Fine Art. facsimile ed. LC 73-167715. 192p. 1981. pap. 12.95 (ISBN 0-87100-019-9, 2019). Morgan.

--The Story of American Painting: The Evolution of Painting in America from Colonial Times to the Present. LC 37-15304. (American Studies). 1970. Repr. of 1907 ed. 33.00 (ISBN 0-384-06955-X). Johnson Repr.

--Story of Spanish Painting. LC 72-100521. (BCL Ser. I). (Illus.). Repr. of 1910 ed. 17.50 (ISBN 0-404-01361-9). AMS Pr.

Caffin, Charles H., jt. auth. see Caffin, Caroline.

Caffrey, Dorothy C. Songs for Autumn Singing. LC 71-174492. 1971. 4.95 (ISBN 0-913264-02-4). Douglas-West.

Caffrey, Kate. Mayflower. LC 73-91855. 1975. pap. 5.95 (ISBN 0-8128-1857-1). Stein & Day.

Caffrey, Pat. Climbers Guide to Montana. (Illus.). 288p. 1985. pap. 9.95 (ISBN 0-87842-191-2). Mountain Pr.

Caffrey, Stephanie & Kenslea, Timothy. The Family That Wanted a Home. (Rainbow Books (Bible Story Books for Children)). (Orig.). 1978. pap. 1.00 (ISBN 0-8192-1235-0). Morehouse.

--How the World Began. (Rainbow Books (Bible Story Books for Children)). 16p. 1978. pap. 1.00 (ISBN 0-8192-1233-4). Morehouse.

--The Shepherds Find a King. (Rainbow Books (Bible Story Books for Children)). 16p. 1978. pap. 1.00 (ISBN 0-8192-1232-6). Morehouse.

Caffrey, Stephanie & Kenslea, Timothy, eds. The Boy in the Striped Coat. (Rainbow Books). 1978. pap. 1.00 (ISBN 0-8192-1234-2). Morehouse.

Cafky, Morris & Haney, John A. Pikes Peak Trolleys. LC 83-73227. (Illus.). 112p. 1984. 22.95 (ISBN 0-937080-13-6); pap. 16.95 (ISBN 0-937080-14-4). Century One.

Caflisch, Lucius, jt. auth. see Zacklin, Ralph.

Cafritz, E., jt. auth. see Chu, J.

Cagan, Maxwell S. Medianetics: Dynamic Living in Your Middle Years. LC 75-22570. 204p. 1975. 8.95 (ISBN 0-913264-20-2). Douglas-West.

Cagan, Phillip. The Channels of Monetary Effects on Interest Rates. (General Ser.: No. 97). 142p. 1972. 10.00x (ISBN 0-87014-235-6, Dist. by Columbia U Pr). Natl Bur Econ Res.

--Determinants & Effects of Changes in the Stock of Money, 1875-1960. (Business Cycles Ser.: No. 13). 408p. 1965. 25.00x (ISBN 0-87014-097-3, Dist. by Columbia U Pr). Natl Bur Econ Res.

--The Hydra-Headed Monster: The Problem of Inflation in the United States. LC 74-22830. (Orig.). 1974. pap. 4.25 (ISBN 0-8447-3143-9). Am Enterprise.

--Persistent Inflation. LC 79-1017. 280p. 1979. pap. 15.00x (ISBN 0-231-04729-0). Columbia U Pr.

--Recent Monetary Policy & Inflation, 1965 to August 1971. 1971. pap. 2.00 (ISBN 0-8447-1055-5). Am Enterprise.

Cagan, Phillip & Lipsey, Robert. The Financial Effects of Inflation. LC 78-13124. (National Bureau of Economic Research General Studies: No. 103). 96p. 1978. prof ref 20.00 (ISBN 0-88410-486-9). Ballinger Pub.

Cagan, Phillip & Moore, Geoffrey H. Consumer Price Index: Issues & Alternatives. 1981. pap. 4.25 (ISBN 0-8447-3446-2). Am Enterprise.

Cagan, Phillip, ed. New Look at Inflation. 1973. 8.50 (ISBN 0-8447-3130-7); pap. 3.75 (ISBN 0-8447-3113-7). Am Enterprise.

Cagan, Phillip, et al. Economic Policy & Inflation in the Sixties. 1972. 8.50 (ISBN 0-8447-3078-5). Am Enterprise.

Cagan, Robert H. & Kare, Morley R., eds. Biochemistry of Taste & Olfaction. (Nutrition Foundation Ser.). 1981. 55.00 (ISBN 0-12-154450-8). Acad Pr.

Cage, Bob N., jt. auth. see Wattenbarger, James L.

Cage, John. Empty Words. LC 78-27212. 189p. 1979. 20.00x (ISBN 0-8195-5032-9); pap. 12.95 (ISBN 0-8195-6067-7). Wesleyan U Pr.

--For the Birds. 240p. 1981. 20.00 (ISBN 0-7145-2690-8, Dist by Scribner); pap. 11.95 (ISBN 0-7145-2691-6). M Boyars.

--M: Writings '67-'72. LC 72-11051. (Illus.). 217p. 1974. pap. 10.95 (ISBN 0-8195-6035-9). Wesleyan U Pr.

--Silence: Lectures & Writings. LC 61-14238. 1961. pap. 10.95 (ISBN 0-8195-6028-6). Wesleyan U Pr.

--Themes & Variations. LC 81-13626. (Illus.). 150p. 25.00 (ISBN 0-930794-22-2); pap. 9.95 (ISBN 0-930794-23-0). Station Hill Pr.

--A Year from Monday: New Lectures & Writings. LC 67-24105. 1967. pap. 10.95 (ISBN 0-8195-6002-2). Wesleyan U Pr.

Cage, John & Barnard, Geoffrey. Conversation Without Feldman. (Illus.). 28p. 1980. pap. 2.00. Left Bank.

Cage, John, jt. auth. see Hoover, Kathleen O.

Cage, John, ed. X: Writings '79-'82. 176p. 1983. 25.95 (ISBN 0-8195-5090-6). Wesleyan U Pr.

Cage, John, et al. Poets Encyclopedia. (Illus.). 1980. pap. 4.95 (ISBN 0-934450-03-X). Unmuzzled Ox.

--The Poets' Encyclopedia. Andre, Michael & Rothenberg, Erika, eds. (Illus.). 1979. 14.95 (ISBN 0-934450-02-1). Unmuzzled Ox.

Cage, John M., jt. auth. see Oliver, Bernard M.

Cage, R. A. The Scottish Poor Law 1745-1845. 216p. 1981. 20.00x (ISBN 0-7073-0289-7, Pub. by Scottish Academic Pr Scotland). Columbia U Pr.

Cage, R. A., ed. The Scots Abroad: Labour, Capital, Enterprise, 1750- 1914. LC 84-19985. 288p. 1984. 31.00 (ISBN 0-7099-0833-4, Pub. by Croom Helm Ltd). Longwood Pub Group.

Cagg, Richard D. The Clouds & the Sea. 80p. 1980. pap. 4.00 (ISBN 0-9605636-0-1). Cagg.

--The Niche of Time. 80p. 1983. pap. 4.00 (ISBN 0-9605636-1-X). Cagg.

Caggiano, Biba. Northern Italian Cooking. LC 81-82276. 1981. 12.95 (ISBN 0-89586-127-5); pap. 7.95 (ISBN 0-89586-119-4). H P Bks.

Caggiano, J. The Complete Guide to Your Macintosh. 1984. 19.95 (ISBN 0-317-05711-1). SYBEX.

Caggiano, Joseph. The Macintosh: A Practical Guide. (Illus.). 280p. 1984. pap. 12.95 (ISBN 0-89588-216-7). SYBEX.

Caggiano, Philip, adapted by. The Ring: Four Plays for Children. 96p. 1982. pap. 2.50 (ISBN 0-380-79434-9, 79434-9, Bard). Avon.

Caggiano, Phyllis. Love's Fragile Flame. LC 83-22454. 144p. (Orig.). 1984. pap. 3.95 (ISBN 0-87123-582-X). Bethany Hse.

Caggiano, Rosemary & Martinez, Larry. The Circus. 48p. (gr. k-6). 1978. pap. 7.95 (ISBN 0-86704-000-9). Clarus Music.

Caggiano, Rosemary, jt. auth. see Fass, Bernie.

Caggiano, Rosemary, jt. auth. see Young, Roger.

Cagin, Seth & Dray, Philip. Hollywood Films of the Seventies: Sex, Drugs, Violence, Rock 'n Roll & Politics. LC 83-48332. (Illus.). 320p. (Orig.). 1984. pap. 9.57i (ISBN 0-06-091117-4, CN 1117, CN). Har-Row.

Cagle, Charles V. Handbook of Adhesive Bonding. Lee, Henry & Neville, Kris, eds. 754p. 1982. Repr. of 1973 ed. 64.50 (ISBN 0-07-009588-4). McGraw.

Cagle, Charles V., et al, eds. Handbook of Adhesive Bonding. 754p. 1982. Repr. of 1973 ed. 59.50 (ISBN 0-938648-18-7). T-C Pubns CA.

Cagle, Eldon B. Quadrangle: The History of Fort Sam Houston. (Illus.). 200p. 1985. 14.95 (ISBN 0-89015-463-5). Eakin Pubns.

Cagle, Malcolm W. & Manson, Frank A. The Sea War in Korea. LC 79-6104. (Navies & Men Ser.). (Illus.). 1980. Repr. of 1957 ed. lib. bdg. 57.50x (ISBN 0-405-13033-3). Ayer Co Pubs.

Cagle, Paul R., Jr. & Wallace, Mary H. The Curtain of Time. (Illus., Orig.). 1984. pap. 6.95 (ISBN 0-912315-76-8). Word Aflame.

Caglioti, G., ed. Atomic Structure & Mechanical Properties of Metals: Proceedings. (Enrico Fermi International Summer School of Physics Ser.: Vol. 61). 664p. 1976. 159.75 (ISBN 0-7204-0490-8, North-Holland). Elsevier.

Caglioti, G. & Milone, A. F., eds. Mechanical & Thermal Behaviour of Metallic Materials: Proceedings of the International School of Physics, "Enrico Fermi," Course LXXXII, Varenna, Italy, 30 June-10 July, 1981. (Enrico Fermi International Summer School of Physics Ser.: Vol. 82). 500p. 1983. 100.00 (ISBN 0-444-86500-4, North Holland). Elsevier.

Caglioti, Luciano & Giacconi, Mirella. The Two Faces of Chemistry: The Benefits & the Risks of Chemical Technology. LC 82-12706. 240p. 1985. Repr. of 1983 ed. 22.50 (ISBN 0-262-03088-8); pap. 8.95 (ISBN 0-262-53064-3). MIT Pr.

Cagnac, B. & Pebay-Peyroula, J. C. Modern Atomic Physics. Incl. Vol. 1. Fundamentals & Principles. LC 74-28161. text ed. 31.95x (ISBN 0-470-12920-4); Vol. 2. Quantum Theory & Its Application. LC 74-26875. 328p. 1975. Halsted Pr.

--Modern Atomic Physics: Quantum Theory & Its Application, Vol. 2. LC 74-26875. 253p. 21.00 (ISBN 0-470-12921-2). Krieger.

Cagnacci-Schwicker, Angelo. Dictionnaire International de Metallurgie, Mineralogie, Geologie et Industries Extractives, 2 vols. 1530p. (Fr.). 1969. Set. 95.00 (ISBN 0-686-56933-4, M-6054). French & Eur.

Cagnat, et al. Inscriptiones Graecae: Ad Res Romanas Pertinentes, 3 vols. 1975. 75.00 (ISBN 0-89005-072-4). Ares.

Cagnat, R. & Chapot, V. Manuel D'archeologie Romaine, 2 vols. (Illus., Fr.). Repr. of 1920 ed. lib. bdg. 150.00x (ISBN 0-89241-139-2). Vol. 1. 735p. Vol. 2, 574p. Caratzas.

Cagnat, Rene L. L' Armee Romaine d'Afrique et l'Occupation Militaire de lAfrique sous les Empereurs. LC 75-7306. (Roman History Ser.). (Illus., Fr.). 1975. Repr. 60.00x (ISBN 0-405-07187-6). Ayer Co Pubs.

Cagney, James. Cagney by Cagney. 1981. pap. 2.75 (ISBN 0-671-43056-4). PB.

Cagney, James, jt. auth. see Warren, Doug.

Cagno, Michael. Exercise Book for Italian: Level II. 1984. pap. 3.50x (ISBN 0-913298-00-X). S F Vanni.

--Exercise Book for Italian: Level III. 1984. pap. 3.95x (ISBN 0-913298-01-8). S F Vanni.

--Italian Review & Culture. 1977. pap. 4.50x (ISBN 0-913298-02-6). S F Vanni.

Cagno, Michael & D'Arlon, Ben. Rapid Italian for Students & Tourists. 1979. pap. 4.50x (ISBN 0-913298-05-0). S F Vanni.

Cagnon, Charles. Successful Business Ventures for Non-Profit Organizations. 1984. pap. 16.75 (ISBN 0-914977-04-0). Public Serv Materials.

Cagnon, Maurice, ed. Ethique et Esthetique Dans la Litterature Francaise Du XXe Siecle. (Stanford French & Italian Studies: No. 10). vi, 214p. 1978. pap. 25.00 (ISBN 0-915838-38-9). Anma Libri.

Cagnone, Nanni. What's Hecuba to Him or He to Hecuba? Verzoni, David, tr. LC 75-4969. 183p. (Eng. & Ital.). 1975. 7.95 (ISBN 0-915570-01-7). Oolp Pr.

Caha, J. & Kramsky, J. English-Czech Dictionary. 878p. (Eng. & Czech.). 1980. 50.00x (ISBN 0-569-00405-5, Pub. by Collet's). State Mutual Bk.

Cahagnet, Louis A. The Celestial Telegraph: Or, Secrets of the Life to Come Revealed Through Magnetism... LC 75-36832. (Occult Ser.). 1976. Repr. of 1850 ed. 33.00x (ISBN 0-405-07944-3). Ayer Co Pubs.

Cahalan, Don. Problem Drinkers: A National Survey. LC 73-133617. (Social & Behavioral Science Ser.). 1970. 21.95x (ISBN 0-87589-080-6). Jossey-Bass.

Cahalan, Don & Room, Robin. Problem Drinking Among American Men. 1974. 15.95x (ISBN 0-8084-0380-X). New Coll U Pr.

--Problem Drinking Among American Men. LC 72-619570. (Rutgers Center of Alcohol Studies: Monograph No. 7). 1974. 8.25 (ISBN 0-911290-38-9). Rutgers Ctr Alcohol.

Cahalan, Don, et al. American Drinking Practices: A National Study of Drinking Behavior & Attitudes. LC 70-626701. (Rutgers Center of Alcohol Studies: Monograph No. 6). 1969. pap. 10.95 (ISBN 0-911290-37-0). Rutgers Ctr Alcohol.

--American Drinking Practices. 1969. 10.95x (ISBN 0-8084-0412-1). New Coll U Pr.

Cahalan, James M. Great Hatred, Little Room: The Irish Historical Novel. (Irish Studies). 256p. 1983. text ed. 25.00x (ISBN 0-8156-2297-X). Syracuse U Pr.

Cahalan, M. J., intro. by. Advances in Extractive Metallurgy. 1023p. 1968. text ed. 40.25x (ISBN 0-686-32508-7). IMM North Am.

Cahalan, Peter. Belgian Refugee Relief in England During the Great War. Stansky, Peter & Hume, Leslie, eds. LC 81-48398. (Modern British History Ser.). 554p. 1982. lib. bdg. 79.00 (ISBN 0-8240-5152-1). Garland Pub.

Cahalane, Cornelius F. Policeman. LC 75-112529. (Rise of Urban America Ser.). 1970. Repr. of 1923 ed. 23.50 (ISBN 0-405-02440-1). Ayer Co Pubs.

Cahall, Raymond D. Sovereign Council of New France: A Study in Canadian Constitutional History. LC 15-13350. (Columbia University Studies in the Social Sciences: No. 156). Repr. of 1915 ed. 21.00 (ISBN 0-404-51156-2). AMS Pr.

Cahan, Abraham. The Imported Bridegroom & Other Stories of the New York Ghetto. 1972. Repr. of 1898 ed. 22.50 (ISBN 0-8422-8021-9). Irvington.

--Rise of David Levinsky. pap. 7.95xi (ISBN 0-06-131912-0, TB1912, Torch). Har-Row.
--Rise of David Levinsky. 12.00 (ISBN 0-8446-1794-6). Peter Smith.
--The White Terror & the Red: A Novel of Revolutionary Russia. facsimile ed. LC 74-27969. (Modern Jewish Experience Ser.). 1975. Repr. of 1905 ed. 34.50x (ISBN 0-405-06699-6). Ayer Co Pubs.
--Yekl & the Imported Bridegroom & Other Stories of the New York Ghetto. 1978. pap. 4.50 (ISBN 0-486-22427-9). Dover.
--Yekl & the Imported Bridegroom & Other Stories of the New York Ghetto. 11.25 (ISBN 0-8446-0048-2). Peter Smith.
Cahan, Judah L. Shtudies Vegn Yidisher Folksshafung. Weinreich, ed. 1952. 5.00 (ISBN 0-914512-05-6). Yivo Inst.
Cahan, Linda & Robinson, Joseph. A Practical Guide to Visual Merchandising. LC 83-16745. (Retailing-Fashion Merchandising Ser.: 1569). 368p. 1984. text ed. 25.95 (ISBN 0-471-86441-2, 1-565, Pub by Wiley). Wiley.
Cahe, L A., et al, eds. Antidromic Vasodilatation & Neurogenic Inflammation: Satellite Symposium of the 29th International Congress of Physiological Sciences Newcastle Australia 1983. 353p. 1984. 46.00 (Pub. by Akademiai Kiado Hungary). Heyden.
Cahen, Alfred. Statistical Analysis of American Divorce. LC 68-58553. (Columbia University Studies in the Social Sciences: No. 360). Repr. of 1932 ed. 14.50 (ISBN 0-404-51360-3). AMS Pr.
Cahen, Claude. La Regime Feodal De l'Italie Normande. LC 80-1995. Repr. of 1923 ed. 25.00 (ISBN 0-404-18555-X). AMS Pr.
Cahen, Gaston. Some Early Russo-Chinese Relations. 59.95 (ISBN 0-8490-1077-2). Gordon Pr.
Cahen, L., et al. The Geochronology & Evolution of Africa. (Illus.). 512p. 1984. 110.00x (ISBN 0-19-857544-0). Oxford U Pr.
Cahen, Leon. Condorcet et la Revolution Francaise. LC 76-159693. (History, Economics & Social Science Ser.: No. 288). 33.00 (ISBN 0-8337-4018-0). B Franklin.
Cahen, Leonard & Filby, Nikola. Class Size & Instruction: A Field Study. LC 82-20376. (Research on Teaching). (Illus.). 256p. 1983. text ed. 25.00x (ISBN 0-582-28325-6). Longman.
Cahen, M. & Flato, M., eds. Differential Geometry & Relativity. new ed. (Mathematical Physics & Applied Mathematics Ser: No. 3). 1976. lib. bdg. 42.00 (ISBN 90-277-0745-6, Pub. by Reidel Holland). Kluwer Academic.
Cahen, Michel & Parker, Monique. Pseudo-Riemannian Symmetric Spaces. LC 79-27541. (Memoirs Ser.: No. 229). 108p. 1980. pap. 10.00 (ISBN 0-8218-2229-2, MEMO-229). Am Math.
Cahgalan, D. & Cisin, I. H. American Drinking Practices: A National Study of Drinking Behavior & Attitudes. 260p. 1969. 10.95 (ISBN 0-318-15296-7). Natl Coun Alcoholism.
Cahill, A. L. The Thirteenth Gun. (Orig.). 1981. pap. 1.75 (ISBN 0-505-51587-3, Pub. by Tower Bks). Dorchester Pub Co.
Cahill, Bob, jt. auth. see Stephenson, John G.
Cahill, Bruce, ed. Bulletin of the UNESCO Regional Office for Education in Asia & the Pacific: June 1984. (Science Education Ser.: No. 25). 550p. 1985. pap. 27.50 (UB162 5071, UNESCO). Unipub.
Cahill, Donald R. & Orland, Matthew J. Atlas of Human Cross-Sectional Anatomy. LC 83-13613. (Illus.). 139p. 1984. text ed. 29.50 (ISBN 0-8121-0890-6). Lea & Febiger.
Cahill, E. Freemasonry & the Anti-Christian Movement. 59.95 (ISBN 0-8490-0195-1). Gordon Pr.
Cahill, E. D., jt. auth. see Cushman, J. A.
Cahill, F. J. Rare Bits of Humor. Repr. of 1906 ed. 10.00 (ISBN 0-8274-4149-5). R West.
Cahill, George F., Jr., jt. ed. see Skyler, Jay S.
Cahill, George F., Jr., ed. see Wechsler, Henry, et al.
Cahill, Holger. American Folk Art: The Art of the Common Man in America 1750-1900. LC 71-86427. (Museum of Modern Art Publications in Reprint Ser). (Illus.). 1970. Repr. of 1932 ed. 20.00 (ISBN 0-405-01530-5). Ayer Co Pubs.
--American Painting & Sculpture: 1862-1932. LC 79-86429. (Museum of Modern Art Publications in Reprint Ser). (Illus.). 1970. Repr. of 1932 ed. 20.00 (ISBN 0-405-01531-3). Ayer Co Pubs.
--American Sources of Modern Art. LC 78-86426. (Museum of Modern Art Publications in Reprint Ser). (Illus.). 1970. Repr. of 1933 ed. 18.00 (ISBN 0-405-01532-1). Ayer Co Pubs.
--New Horizons in American Art. LC 75-86428. (Museum of Modern Art Publications in Reprint Ser). (Illus.). 1970. Repr. of 1936 ed. 22.00 (ISBN 0-405-01533-X). Ayer Co Pubs.
Cahill, Holger & Barr, Alfred, eds. Art in America in Modern Times. facs. ed. LC 69-17569. (Essay Index Reprint Ser). 1934. 44.00 (ISBN 0-8369-0067-7). Ayer Co Pubs.
Cahill, Holger, et al. Masters of Popular Painting. LC 66-26120. (Museum of Modern Art Publications in Repr. Ser.). Repr. of 1938 ed. 14.00 (ISBN 0-405-01524-0). Ayer Co Pubs.
Cahill, Hope L. Old Age-a Balance Sheet. LC 80-54452. (Illus.). 102p. 1981. pap. 3.95 (ISBN 0-933174-13-6). Wide World-Tetra.
Cahill, James. The Art of Southern Sung China. LC 74-27411. (Asia Society Ser.). (Illus.). 1979. Repr. of 1962 ed. lib. bdg. 24.00x (ISBN 0-405-06560-4). Ayer Co Pubs.
--The Compelling Image: Nature & Style in Seventeenth-Century Chinese Painting. LC 81-1272. (The Charles Eliot Norton Lectures). (Illus.). 288p. 1982. text ed. 35.00x (ISBN 0-674-15280-8). Harvard U Pr.
--The Distant Mountains: Chinese Painting of the Late Ming Dynasty, 1570-1644. (Vol. 3). (Illus.). 336p. 1982. 49.95 (ISBN 0-8348-0174-4). Weatherhill.
--Fantastics & Eccentrics in Chinese Paintings. LC 74-27412. (Asia Society Ser.). (Illus.). 1979. Repr. of 1967 ed. lib. bdg. 33.00x (ISBN 0-405-06561-2). Ayer Co Pubs.
--Hills Beyond a River: Chinese Painting of the Yuan Dynasty, 1279-1368. LC 75-44083. (Illus.). 1976. 32.50 (ISBN 0-8348-0120-5). Weatherhill.
--Parting at the Shore: Chinese Painting of the Early & Middle Ming Dynasty, 1368-1580. LC 77-8682. (History of Later Chinese Painting Ser.: Vol. 2). (Illus.). 1978. 32.50 (ISBN 0-8348-0128-0). Weatherhill.
--Sakaki Hyakusen & Early Nanga Painting. (Japan Research Monograph: No. 3). (Illus.). 145p. (Orig.). 1983. pap. 10.00x (ISBN 0-912966-58-0). IEAS.
--Scholar Painters of Japan: The Nanga School. LC 74-27413. (Asia Society Ser.). (Illus.). 1979. Repr. of 1972 ed. lib. bdg. 33.00x (ISBN 0-405-06562-0). Ayer Co Pubs.
Cahill, James & Skira-Rizzoli. Chinese Painting. LC 76-62896. (Illus.). 216p. 1977. pap. 17.50 (ISBN 0-8478-0079-2). Rizzoli Intl.
Cahill, James, ed. The Works of Tomioka Tessai. (Illus.). 152p. (Orig.). 1968. pap. 5.00 (ISBN 0-88397-015-5, Pub. by Intl Exhibit Foun). C E Tuttle.
Cahill, James, compiled by. An Index of Early Chinese Painters & Painting: T'ang, Sung & Yuan. LC 77-85755. 1980. 38.50x (ISBN 0-520-03576-3). U of Cal Pr.
Cahill, Kevin, ed. The AIDS Epidemic. 192p. 1983. 12.95 (ISBN 0-312-01498-8); pap. 7.95 (ISBN 0-312-01499-6). St Martin.
--Famine. LC 81-19034. 160p. (Orig.). 1982. 15.95 (ISBN 0-88344-133-0); pap. 8.95 (ISBN 0-88344-132-2). Orbis Bks.
Cahill, Kevin M. Irish Essays. LC 80-80550. 140p. 1980. 9.00 (ISBN 0-89444-028-4). John Jay Pr.
--Tropical Diseases: A Handbook for Practitioners. LC 76-11951. (Illus.). 1976. 14.95 (ISBN 0-87762-199-3). Technomic.
Cahill, Kevin M., ed. The American Irish Revival: A Decade of the Recorder, 1974-1983. LC 84-2899. 807p. 1984. 35.00 (ISBN 0-8046-9359-5, 9359, Pub. by Natl U). Assoc Faculty Pr.
Cahill, Lawrence B. Environmental Audits. 3rd ed. (Illus.). 240p. 1984. pap. 49.00 (ISBN 0-86587-066-7). Gov Insts.
Cahill, Lisa S. Between the Sexes. 160p. (Orig.). 1985. pap. 7.95 (ISBN 0-8091-2711-3). Paulist Pr.
--Between the Sexes: Foundations for a Christian Ethics of Sexuality. LC 84-48717. 160p. 1985. pap. 7.95 (ISBN 0-8006-1834-3). Fortress.
Cahill, M. J. Debra Winger: Hollywood's Wild Child. 96p. 1985. pap. 9.95 (ISBN 0-312-18896-X). St Martin.
Cahill, Marion C. Shorter Hours: A Study of the Movement Since the Civil War. LC 68-54258. (Columbia University Studies in the Social Sciences: No. 380). 1971. Repr. of 1932 ed. 17.50 (ISBN 0-404-51380-8). AMS Pr.
Cahill, Mary Ann. Heart Has Its Own Reasons. (Illus.). 340p. 1983. pap. 6.50 (ISBN 0-912500-13-1). La Leche.
--The Heart Has It's Own Reasons: Mothers Wisdom for the 1980's. 1985. pap. 8.95 (ISBN 0-452-25690-9, Plume). NAL.
Cahill, Matthew, ed. Diagnostics. 2nd ed. (Nurse's Reference Library). (Illus.). 1152p. 1985. 23.95 (ISBN 0-916730-89-1). Springhouse Corp.
--Diseases. 2nd ed. (Nurse's Reference Library). (Illus.). 1374p. 1985. text ed. 23.95 (ISBN 0-916730-95-6). Springhouse Corp.
Cahill, P. Joseph. Mended Speech: The Crisis of Religious Study & Theology. 272p. 1982. 14.95 (ISBN 0-8245-0421-6). Crossroad NY.
Cahill, P. Joseph, tr. see Leon-Dufour, Xavier.
Cahill, Patrick. The English First Editions by the Author. 1978. Repr. of 1953 ed. lib. bdg. 25.00 (ISBN 0-8495-0764-2). Arden Lib.
--English First Editions of Hilaire Belloc. 1953. lib. bdg. 15.00 (ISBN 0-8414-3613-4). Folcroft.
Cahill, R. N., jt. ed. see Trnka, Z.
Cahill, Rick. Colorado Hot Springs Guide. (Illus.). 100p. (Orig.). 1983. pap. 7.50 (ISBN 0-87108-649-2). Pruett.
Cahill, Robert B. & Herbic, Herbert. How to Take an Essay Exam: Stack the Deck Writing Program Ser. 48p. 1981. pap. 2.50 (ISBN 0-933282-06-0). Stack the Deck.
Cahill, Robert B. & Herbic, Herbert J. Fan the Deck. rev. ed. 1980. pap. text ed. 5.00 (ISBN 0-933282-02-8). Stack the Deck.
Cahill, Robert B. & Hrebic, Herbert J. Cut the Deck. (Writing Program Ser.). (Illus.). (gr. 7-12). 1977. text ed. 8.00 (ISBN 0-933282-10-9); pap. 5.00 (ISBN 0-933282-01-X). Stack the Deck.
--Fan the Deck. (Writing Program Ser.). (gr. 9-12). 1978. pap. text ed. 8.00 (ISBN 0-933282-12-5). Stack the Deck.
--Stack the Deck. rev. ed. (Illus.). 1980. pap. 5.00 (ISBN 0-933282-00-1). Stack the Deck.
--Stack the Deck. (Writing Program Ser.). (gr. 9-12). 1973. text ed. 8.00 (ISBN 0-933282-11-7); pap. 5.00. Stack the Deck.
Cahill, Robert E. Finding New England's Shipwrecks & Treasures. (Collectible Classics Ser.: No. 6). (Illus.). 54p. (Orig.). 1984. pap. 3.95 (ISBN 0-916787-05-2). Chandler-Smith.
--New England's Ghostly Haunts. (Collectible Classics Ser.: No. 2). (Illus.). 50p. (Orig.). 1983. pap. 3.95 (ISBN 0-916787-01-X). Chandler-Smith.
--New England's Mad & Mysterious Men. (Collectible Classics Ser: No. 4). (Illus.). 50p. (Orig.). 1984. pap. 3.95 (ISBN 0-916787-03-6). Chandler-Smith.
--New England's Marvelous Monsters. (Collectible Classics Ser.: No. 3). (Illus.). 50p. 1983. pap. 3.95 (ISBN 0-916787-02-8). Chandler-Smith.
--New England's Strange Sea Sagas. (Collectible Classics Ser.: No. 5). (Illus.). 54p. 1984. pap. 3.95 (ISBN 0-916787-04-4). Chandler-Smith.
--New England's Visitors from Outer Space. (Collectible Classics Ser.: No. 8). (Illus.). 54p. (Orig.). 1985. pap. 3.95 (ISBN 0-916787-07-9). Chandler-Smith.
--New England's War Wonders. (Collectible Classics Ser: No. 7). (Illus.). 50p. (Orig.). 1984. pap. 3.95 (ISBN 0-916787-06-0). Chandler-Smith.
--New England's Witches & Wizards. (Collectible Classics Ser.: No. 1). (Illus.). 50p. (Orig.). 1983. pap. 3.95 (ISBN 0-916787-00-1). Chandler-Smith.
--The Old Irish of New England. (Collectible Classics Ser.: No. 10). (Illus.). 50p. (Orig.). 1985. pap. 3.95 (ISBN 0-916787-09-5). Chandler-Smith.
Cahill, S. J. Designing Microprocessor: Based Digital Circuitry. (Illus.). 192p. 1985. pap. text ed. 16.95 (ISBN 0-13-200601-4). P-H.
--Digital & Microprocessor Engineering. (Electrical & Electronic Engineering Ser.). 550p. 1982. 94.95x (ISBN 0-470-27301-1); pap. 34.95 (ISBN 0-470-20093-6). Halsted Pr.
Cahill, Susan. Motherhood: A Reader for Men & Women. 432p. 1982. pap. 3.95 (ISBN 0-380-79350-4, 79350-4, Discus). Avon.
--Women & Fiction, Vol. 2. (Orig.). 1978. pap. 3.95 (ISBN 0-451-62156-5, ME2156, Ment). NAL.
Cahill, Susan & Cahill, Thomas. A Literary Guide to Ireland. 352p. 1979. 13.95 (ISBN 0-905473-35-3, Pub. by Wolfhound Pr England); pap. 5.95 (ISBN 0-905473-36-1, Pub. by Wolfhound Pr England). Irish Bks Media.
Cahill, Susan, ed. Women & Fiction: Short Stories by & About Women. (YA) 1975. pap. 4.50 (ISBN 0-451-62411-4, ME2263, Ment). NAL.
Cahill, Thomas, jt. auth. see Cahill, Susan.
Cahill, Thomas A., jt. auth. see McCray, James A.
Cahill, Tim & Ewing, Russ. Buried Dreams. LC 85-47793. 320p. 1986. 16.95 (ISBN 0-553-05115-6). Bantam.
Cahill, Verna. But to the Hungry Soul. 1985. 6.50 (ISBN 0-8233-0401-9). Golden Quill.
Cahimite. Don't Git Hit by a Coconut. pap. 50.00 (ISBN 0-317-26232-7, 2055570). Bks Demand UMI.
Cahir, Stephen & Kovac, Ceil. Exploring Functional Language: It's Your Turn. (Exploring Functional Language Ser.). (Orig.). 1981. tchrs ed. 4.00x (ISBN 0-15-599021-7); wkbk. pap. 3.50x (ISBN 0-15-599022-5). Ctr Appl Ling.
--Exploring Functional Language: Teacher Talk Words. (Exploring Functional Language Ser.). (Orig.). 1981. tchrs ed. 4.00x (ISBN 0-15-599025-X); wkbk. pap. 3.50x (ISBN 0-15-599024-1). Ctr Appl Ling.
--Exploring Functional Language: When Is Reading? (Exploring Functional Language Ser.). (Orig.). 1981. tchrs ed. 4.00 (ISBN 0-15-599037-3); wkbk. pap. 3.50x (ISBN 0-15-599036-5). Ctr Appl Ling.
Cahir, Stephen R. & Kovac, Ceil. Exploring Functional Language: A Way With Words. (Exploring Functional Language Ser.). (Orig.). 1981. tchrs ed. 4.00x (ISBN 0-15-599030-6); wkbk. pap. 3.50x (ISBN 0-15-599032-2). Ctr Appl Ling.
--Exploring Functional Language: What's What With Questions. (Exploring Functional Language Ser.). (Orig.). 1981. tchrs ed. 4.00x (ISBN 0-15-599034-9); wkbk. pap. 3.50x (ISBN 0-15-599033-0). Ctr Appl Ling.
Cahir, Stephen R. & Kovac, Ciel. Exploring Functional Language: Transitions, Activity between Activities. (Exploring Functional Language Ser.). (Orig.). 1981. tchrs ed. 4.00x (ISBN 0-15-599027-6); wkbk. pap. 3.50 (ISBN 0-15-599029-2). Ctr Appl Ling.
Cahlander, Adele. Double Woven Treasures from Old Peru. 1985. 20.00 (ISBN 0-932394-05-1). Dos Tejedoras.
Cahlander, Adele, et al. Bolivian Tubular Edging & Crossed-Warp Techniques. 23p. (Orig.). 1978. pap. 3.00 (ISBN 0-937452-00-9). Colo Fiber.
--Sling Braiding of the Andes. 96p. (Orig.). 1980. pap. text ed. 10.00 (ISBN 0-937452-03-3). Colo Fiber.
Cahm, Eric & Fisera, Vladimir C., eds. Socialism & Nationalism in Contemporary Europe Eighteen Forty-Eight to Nineteen Forty-Five. 1983. Vol. 1, 116pgs. pap. text ed. 5.95x (ISBN 0-936508-04-3); Vol. 2, 132pgs. pap. 5.95x (ISBN 0-936508-05-1); Vol. 3, 132pgs. pap. 5.95x (ISBN 0-936508-06-X). Barber Pr.
Cahn. Romanesque Sculpture in American Collections, Vol. 1. (Illus.). 1979. lib. bdg. 38.50x (ISBN 0-89102-131-0). B Franklin.
Cahn, Ann F., ed. Women in the U. S. Labor Force. LC 78-22130. (Praeger Special Studies). 346p. 1979. 41.95 (ISBN 0-03-045646-0). Praeger.
Cahn, Cynthia. The Day the Sun Split. pap. 3.00 (ISBN 0-938078-14-3). Anhinga Pr.
Cahn, Dudley D., Jr., jt. auth. see Cushman, Donald P.
Cahn, Edgar, ed. Our Brother's Keeper: The Indian in White America. pap. 8.95 (ISBN 0-452-00706-2, F706, Mer). NAL.
Cahn, Edmond. The Moral Decision: Right & Wrong in the Light of American Law. LC 81-47586. (Midland Bks.: No. 273). 352p. 1981. 22.50x (ISBN 0-253-33875-1); pap. 7.95x (ISBN 0-253-20273-6). Ind U Pr.
Cahn, Edmond N. Confronting Injustice: The Edmond Cahn Reader. Cahn, Lenore L., ed. LC 72-8525. (Essay Index Reprint Ser.). 1972. Repr. of 1966 ed. 30.00 (ISBN 0-8369-7308-9). Ayer Co Pubs.
--The Predicament of Democratic Man. LC 78-16399. 1979. Repr. of 1961 ed. lib. bdg. 22.50x (ISBN 0-313-20597-3, CAPR). Greenwood.
Cahn, Edmond N., ed. Supreme Court & Supreme Law. LC 68-55629. (Illus.). 1968. Repr. of 1954 ed. lib. bdg. 22.50 (ISBN 0-8371-0335-5, CASC). Greenwood.
Cahn, Frances. Federal Employees in War & Peace: Selection, Placement, & Removal. LC 78-16400. 1978. Repr. of 1949 ed. lib. bdg. 20.75x (ISBN 0-313-20602-3, CAFE). Greenwood.
Cahn, Frances & Bary, Valeska. Welfare Activities of Federal, State, & Local Governments in California, 1850-1934. LC 75-17212. (Social Problems & Social Policy Ser.). 1976. Repr. of 1936 ed. 33.00x (ISBN 0-405-07484-0). Ayer Co Pubs.
Cahn, H. A. The Coins of the Sicilian City of Naxos: (Die Munzen der Sizilischen Stadt Naxos) (Illus.). 1978. 30.00 (ISBN 0-916710-37-8). Obol Intl.
--Munzen der Sizilischen Stadt Naxos. 1985. Repr. of 1940 ed. 30.00 (ISBN 0-89005-404-5). Ares.
Cahn, Herbert A. Knidos: Die Muenzen Des 6. und Des 5. Jahrhunderts V. Chr. (Illus., Ger.). 1970. 48.00x (ISBN 3-11-002538-8). De Gruyter.
Cahn, Julie. The Dating Book. Schneider, Meg, ed. (Just for Teens Ser.). 160p. 1983. pap. 3.50 (ISBN 0-671-46277-6). Wanderer Bks.
--The Dating Book. LC 82-23911. (Teen Survival Library). 160p. (gr. 9-12). 1983. PLB 9.29 (ISBN 0-671-46742-5). Messner.
--Holiday Romance. Schnedier, Meg & Schwartz, Betty, eds. (Dream Your Own Romance Ser.: No. 2). 128p. (Orig.). (gr. 4-5). 1983. pap. 2.95 (ISBN 0-671-46450-7). Wanderer Bks.
--Spotlight on Love. (Dream Your Own Romance Ser.: No. 3). (gr. 2-7). 1984. 2.95 (ISBN 0-671-52625-1). Wanderer Bks.
Cahn, L. R., ed. see International Academy of Oral Pathology, 4th.
Cahn, Lenore L., ed. see Cahn, Edmond N.
Cahn, Nguyen Van & Cooper, Earle. Vietnam under Communism. LC 83-10754. (Illus.). xvi, 312p. 1985. pap. 9.95 (ISBN 0-8179-7852-6). Hoover Inst Pr.
Cahn, R. W., ed. Physical Metallurgy. 2nd rev. ed. 1971. 127.75 (ISBN 0-444-10063-6, North-Holland). Elsevier.
Cahn, Robert. Footprints on the Planet: A Search for an Environmental Ethic. LC 78-56363. 1978. 12.50x (ISBN 0-87663-324-6). Universe.
--Footprints on the Planet: A Search for an Environmental Ethic. LC 78-56363. 1979. pap. 5.95x (ISBN 0-87663-988-0). Universe.
Cahn, Robert N. Semi-Simple Lie Algebras & Their Representations. 1984. 23.95 (ISBN 0-8053-1600-0, 31600). Benjamin Cummings.
Cahn, Robert N., ed. Annihilation: New Quarks & Leptons. (The Annual Reviews Special Collections Program.). 1984. 29.95 (ISBN 0-8053-1610-8). Benjamin Cummings.
Cahn, Rolf. Self-Defense for Gentle People. LC 73-88701. (Illus.). 183p. (Orig.). pap. 6.00 (ISBN 0-912528-07-9). John Muir.
Cahn, Sammy. The Songwriter's Rhyming Dictionary. (Illus.). 224p. 1983. 17.95 (ISBN 0-87196-765-0). Facts on File.
--The Songwriter's Rhyming Dictionary. 208p. 1984. pap. 8.95 (ISBN 0-452-00678-3, Mer). NAL.
Cahn, Stephen M. & Shatz, David, eds. Contemporary Philosophy of Religion. 1982. pap. text ed. 8.95x (ISBN 0-19-503009-5). Oxford U Pr.
Cahn, Steven M. Education & the Democratic Ideal. LC 78-27155. 116p. 1979. 19.95x (ISBN 0-88229-589-6); pap. 9.95x (ISBN 0-88229-661-2). Nelson-Hall.

--Saigon Commandos, No. 4: Cherry-Boy Body Bag. 272p. 1984. pap. 2.50 (ISBN 0-8217-1407-4). Zebra.

--Saigon Commandos, No. 5: Boonie-Rat Body Burning. 1984. pap. 2.50 (ISBN 0-317-06368-5). Zebra.

--Saigon Commandos: Sac Mau, Victor Charlie, No. 7. 1985. pap. 2.50 (ISBN 0-8217-1574-7). Zebra.

--You Die, Du Ma! (Saigon Commandos Ser.: No. 8). 1985. pap. 2.50 (ISBN 0-8217-1629-8). Zebra.

Cain, Katherine. Change Begins with Me. 7th ed. (Illus., Orig.). 1976. pap. 2.95 (ISBN 0-9603188-0-1). K Cain.

--Now Is the Time. (Illus., Orig.). 1979. pap. 2.95 (ISBN 0-9603188-1-X). K Cain.

Cain, Louis & Uselding, Paul, eds. Business Enterprise & Economic Change: Essays in Honor of H. F. Williamson. LC 72-92365. 350p. 1973. 15.00x (ISBN 0-87338-134-3). Kent St U Pr.

Cain, Louis P. Sanitation Strategy for a Lakefront Metropolis: The Case of Chicago. LC 76-14711. 173p. 1978. 15.00 (ISBN 0-87580-064-5). N Ill U Pr.

Cain, Louis P., jt. auth. see Aduddell, Robert M.

Cain, M. & Kulscar, K., eds. Disputes & the Law. 286p. 1983. text ed. 37.50x (ISBN 963-05-3379-0, Pub. by Kultura Hungary). Humanities.

Cain, Marvin R. Lincoln's Attorney General: Edward Bates of Missouri. LC 65-13690. 373p. 1965. 22.00 (ISBN 0-8262-0038-9). U of Mo Pr.

Cain, Mary. The Historical Development of State Normal Schools for White Teachers in Maryland. LC 72-176622. (Columbia University. Teachers College. Contributions to Education Ser.: No. 824). Repr. of 1941 ed. 22.50 (ISBN 0-404-55824-0). AMS Pr.

Cain, Mary A. Boys & Girls Together: Non-Sexist Activities for the Elementary School. LC 80-82020. 253p. (Orig.). 1980. 19.95 (ISBN 0-918452-28-7). Learning Pubns.

Cain, Maureen & Hunt, Alan. Marx & Engels on Law. (Law, State & Society Ser.). 1979. 37.50 (ISBN 0-12-154850-3); pap. 19.50 (ISBN 0-12-154852-X). Acad Pr.

Cain, Melinda, jt. ed. see Dauber, Roslyn.

Cain, Michael S. Co-Op Publishing Handbook. 1978. 8.95 (ISBN 0-913218-76-6). Dustbooks.

--An Intelligent Guide to Book Distribution. 250p. 1981. 12.50 (ISBN 0-913218-77-4). Dustbooks.

Cain, Mike. Autos of Interest. 1977. pap. 4.50 (ISBN 0-9601458-1-8). M Cain.

Cain, Nancy W., jt. auth. see Cain, Thomas.

Cain, Peter J. Economic Foundations of British Overseas Expansion 1815-1914. (Studies in Economic & Social History). 1980. pap. text ed. 6.00x (ISBN 0-333-23284-4). Humanities.

Cain, Priscilla, ed. see Glassman, Barbara.

Cain, Robert J., ed. Colonial Records of North Carolina: Records of the Executive Council, 1664-1734, Vol. VII. (Colonial Records of North Carolina Ser.: Second Ser.). (Illus.). lxvii, 763p. 1984. 25.00x (ISBN 0-86526-210-1). NC Archives.

Cain, Robert J. see Parker, Mattie E. & Price, William S., Jr.

Cain, Roy L. Studies of Coprophilous Sphaeriales in Ontario. (Illus.). 1968. Repr. of 1934 ed. 14.00 (ISBN 3-7682-0531-2). Lubrecht & Cramer.

Cain, Sandra E. & Evans, Jack M. Sciencing: An Involvement Approach to Elementary Science Methods. 350p. 1984. pap. text ed. 16.95 (ISBN 0-675-20055-5). Additional supplements may be obtained from publisher. Merrill.

Cain, Sandra G. & Evans, Jack M. Sciencing: An Involvement Approach to Elementary Science Methods. 1979. 17.95 (ISBN 0-675-08364-8). Merrill.

Cain, Seymour. Gabriel Marcel. LC 79-50156. 128p. 1979. pap. 3.95 (ISBN 0-89526-905-8). Regnery-Gateway.

Cain, T. G., ed. see Hilliard, Nicholas.

Cain, Thomas & Cain, Nancy W. Lotus 1-2-3 at Work. pap. text ed. 16.95 (ISBN 0-8359-5227-4). Reston.

--One-Two-Three at Work. (Illus.). 1984. pap. 16.95 (ISBN 0-8359-7862-1). Reston.

Cain, Thomas H. Praise in "The Faerie Queene". LC 78-8962. (Illus.). xvi, 229p. 1978. 19.95x (ISBN 0-8032-1405-7). U of Nebr Pr.

Cain, Tubal. Hardening, Tempering & Heat Treatment. (Workshop Practice Ser.: No. 1). (Illus.). 128p. 1984. pap. 13.95 (ISBN 0-85242-837-5, Pub. by Argus). Aztex.

--Milling Operations in the Lathe. (Workshop Practice Ser.: No. 5). (Illus.). 128p. (Orig.). 1984. pap. 9.95 (ISBN 0-85242-840-5, Pub. by Argus). Aztex.

--Model Engineers Handbook. rev. ed. (Illus.). 192p. 1982. pap. 9.95 (ISBN 0-85242-715-8). Aztex.

--Simple Workshop Devices. (Illus.). 144p. (Orig.). 1983. pap. 13.95 (ISBN 0-85242-827-8, Pub by ARGUS). Aztex.

--Soldering & Brazing, No. 9. (Workshop Practice Ser.). (Illus.). 136p. Date not set. pap. 11.95 (ISBN 0-85242-845-6, Pub. by Aztex Corp). Argus Bks.

Cain, William, ed. see Clark, Michael P.

Cain, William, ed. see Young, Thomas D.

Cain, William E. The Crisis in Criticism: Theory, Literature, & Reform in English Studies. LC 83-49197. 336p. 1984. 24.50x (ISBN 0-8018-3191-1). Johns Hopkins.

Cain, William E., ed. Philosophical Approaches to Literature. LC 82-48652. 256p. 1984. 29.50 (ISBN 0-8387-5055-9). Bucknell U Pr.

Cain, William E., ed. see Day, Frank.

Caine, Clifford. How to Get into College: A Step-by-Step Manual. 128p. 1985. pap. 7.95 (ISBN 0-86616-046-9). Greene.

Caine, H. Recollections of Rossetti. LC 72-6285. (English Literature Ser., No. 33). 267p. 1972. Repr. of 1928 ed. lib. bdg. 49.95x (ISBN 0-8383-1634-4). Haskell.

Caine, Hall. Cobwebs of Criticism. LC 71-39879. Repr. of 1883 ed. 21.00 (ISBN 0-404-07287-9). AMS Pr.

--The Deemster. LC 78-63983. (The Gay Experience). Repr. of 1897 ed. 29.50 (ISBN 0-404-61503-1). AMS Pr.

--Life of Christ. 1310p. 1985. Repr. of 1938 ed. lib. bdg. 45.00 (ISBN 0-89987-194-1). Darby Bks.

--The Manxman. LC 79-8243. Repr. of 1894 ed. 44.50 (ISBN 0-404-61801-4). AMS Pr.

--Recollections of Rossetti. 59.95 (ISBN 0-8490-0935-9). Gordon Pr.

--The Scapegoat: A Romance, 2 vols. in 1. LC 79-8244. Repr. of 1891 ed. 44.50 (ISBN 0-404-61802-2). AMS Pr.

Caine, Jackson. Hell Hound. 304p. (Orig.). 1984. pap. 2.75 (ISBN 0-446-32100-1). Warner Bks.

Caine, Jeffrey. Heathcliff. 1979. pap. 1.95 (ISBN 0-449-23898-9, Crest). Fawcett.

Caine, John B. Design of Ferrous Castings. (Illus.). 124p. 32.00 (ISBN 0-317-32616-3, FC8001); members 16.00 (ISBN 0-317-32617-1). Am Foundrymen.

Caine, Lynn. What Did I Do Wrong? Mothers, Children, Guilt. 1985. 15.95 (ISBN 0-87795-623-5). Arbor Hse.

--Widow. 192p. 1975. pap. 3.50 (ISBN 0-553-23957-0). Bantam.

Caine, M., ed. The Pharmacology of the Urinary Tract: Clinical Practice in Urology. (Illus.). 180p. 1984. 38.50 (ISBN 0-387-13238-4). Springer-Verlag.

Caine, Mitchell. Creole Surgeon. 1978. pap. 1.95 (ISBN 0-449-13924-7, GM). Fawcett.

--Worship the Wind. 1979. pap. 2.25 (ISBN 0-449-14178-0, GM). Fawcett.

Caine, Nancy, jt. ed. see Reite, Martin.

Caine, Nel. The Mountains of Northern Tasmania. 228p. 1983. lib. bdg. 25.00 (ISBN 90-6191-289-X, Pub. by Balkema RSA). IPS.

Caine, Stanley P. The Myth of a Progressive Reform: Railroad Regulation in Wisconsin, 1903-1910. LC 75-630131. (Illus.). 250p. 1970. 7.95 (ISBN 0-87020-110-7). State Hist Soc Wis.

Caine, Stanley P., ed. see Philipp, Emanuel L.

Caine, Sydney. Education As a Factor of Production. 114p. 1984. 97.50 (ISBN 0-86654-131-4). Inst Econ Finan.

--Paying for TV. (Institute of Economic Affairs, Hobart Papers Ser.: No. 43). (Illus., Orig.). 1969. pap. 2.50 technical (ISBN 0-255-69632-9). Transatlantic.

--The Price of Stability...? (Institute of Economic Affairs, Hobart Papers: No. 97). pap. 5.95 technical (ISBN 0-255-36160-2). Transatlantic.

Caine, T. H. My Story. 1973. Repr. of 1908 ed. 25.00 (ISBN 0-8274-1503-6). R West.

Caine, T. M. & Smail, D. J. Treatment of Mental Illness: Science, Faith & the Therapeutic Community. LC 78-88569. 192p. (Orig.). 1969. text ed. 22.50 (ISBN 0-8236-6648-4). Intl Univs Pr.

Caine, Thomas H. see Adderly, James G.

Caine, Tom, et al. Personal Styles in Neurosis: Implications for Small Group Psychotherapy & Behavior Therapy. (International Library of Group Psychotherapy & Group Process). 224p. 27.95x (ISBN 0-7100-0617-9). Routledge & Kegan.

Cainelli, G. & Cardillo, G. Chromium Oxidations in Organic Chemistry. (Reactivity & Structure, Concepts in Organic Chemistry: Vol. 19). (Illus.). 290p. 1984. 62.50 (ISBN 0-387-12834-4). Springer-Verlag.

Cainer, Jonathan. Love Signs: A Zodiac Guide to Romance. (Illus.). 64p. 1985. laminated boards 4.95 (ISBN 0-86188-315-2, Pub. by Salem Hse Ltd). Merrimack Pub Cir.

Caines, Jeannette. Abby. LC 73-5480. (Illus.). 32p. (ps-3). 1973. PLB 10.89 (ISBN 0-06-020922-4). HarpJ.

--Abby. LC 73-5480. (Trophy Picture Bk). (Illus.). 32p. (ps-3). 1984. pap. 3.80i (ISBN 0-06-443049-9, Trophy). HarpJ.

--Daddy. LC 76-21388. (Illus.). 32p. (gr. k-3). 1977. 11.06i (ISBN 0-06-020923-2); PLB 9.84 (ISBN 0-06-020924-0). HarpJ.

--Just Us Women. LC 81-48655. (Illus.). 32p. (gr. k-3). 1982. 10.10i (ISBN 0-06-020941-0); PLB 10.89g (ISBN 0-06-020942-9). HarpJ.

--Just Us Women. LC 81-48655. (Trophy Picture Bk.). (Illus.). 32p. (ps-3). 1984. pap. 3.80i (ISBN 0-06-443056-1, Trophy). HarpJ.

--Window Wishing. LC 79-2698. (Illus.). 32p. (gr. k-3). 1980. 9.57i (ISBN 0-06-020933-X); PLB 9.89 (ISBN 0-06-020934-8). HarpJ.

Caines, Joseph E., jt. auth. see McElroy, Jerome L.

Caines, Peter B. & Hermann, Robert. Geometry & Identification: Proceedings of APSM Workshop - On System Geometry, System Identification, Parameter Identification. (LIE Groups Ser.: Vol. 1; Pt. B). 1983. 23.00 (ISBN 0-915692-33-3). Math Sci Pr.

Cairas, David, tr. see Althaus, Paul.

Caircross, Andrew S. The Problem of Hamlet. 1978. Repr. of 1936 ed. lib. bdg. 20.00 (ISBN 0-8495-0765-0). Arden Lib.

Caird & Williamson. Eye & Its Disorders in the Elderly. 1986. price not set (ISBN 0-7236-0706-0). PSG Pub Co.

Caird, jt. auth. see Exton-Smith.

Caird, Edward. Critical Philosophy of Immanuel Kant, 2 Vols, Vol. 1. LC 4-196. 1968. Repr. of 1889 ed. Set. 58.00 (ISBN 0-527-14100-3). Kraus Repr.

--Essays on Literature & Philosophy, 2 Vols. in 1. LC 11-16433. 1968. Repr. of 1892 ed. 36.00 (ISBN 0-527-14110-0). Kraus Repr.

--Essays on Literature: Dante, Goethe, Rousseau, Carlyle, Wordsworth. 1973. Repr. of 1909 ed. 30.00 (ISBN 0-8274-1541-9). R West.

--Evolution of Religion, 2 Vols. in 1. LC 1-17697. (Gifford Lectures 1890-1892). 1968. Repr. of 1893 ed. 46.00 (ISBN 0-527-14120-8). Kraus Repr.

--Evolution of Theology in the Greek Philosophers, 2 Vols in 1. LC 4-16272. (Gifford Lectures 1900-1902). 1968. Repr. of 1904 ed. 46.00 (ISBN 0-527-14130-5). Kraus Repr.

--Evolution of Theology in the Greek Philosophers, the Gifford Lectures, 1900-1902, 2 Vols. 1968. 39.00x (ISBN 0-403-00116-1). Scholarly.

--Hegel. LC 71-181924. (BCL Ser. I). Repr. of 1883 ed. 22.50 (ISBN 0-404-01362-7). AMS Pr.

--Social Philosophy & Religion of Comte. LC 11-15832. 1968. Repr. of 1885 ed. 17.00 (ISBN 0-527-14140-2). Kraus Repr.

Caird, F. I. & Evans, J. Grimley. Advanced Geriatric Medicine, No. 1. 192p. text ed. cancelled (ISBN 0-272-79629-8, Pub. by Pitman Bks Ltd UK). Pitman Pub MA.

Caird, F. I. & Scott, P. J. Drug Induced Disorders: Geriatrics One. (Drug Induced Disorders Ser.: No. C1). 1984. write for info. (ISBN 0-444-90362-3, Excerpta Medica). Elsevier.

Caird, F. I. & Tallis, R. C. Advanced Geriatric Medicine Five. 200p. 1985. 42.50 (ISBN 0-272-79840-1, Pub. by Pitman Med UK). Urban & S.

Caird, F. I. & Evans, J. Grimley, eds. Advanced Geriatric Medicine, No. 2. 192p. cancelled (ISBN 0-272-79670-0, Pub. by Pitman Bks Ltd UK). Pitman Pub MA.

--Advanced Geriatric Medicine, Vol. 3. 202p. 1983. text ed. 37.50 (ISBN 0-272-79716-2, Pub. by Pitman Med. Uk). Urban & S.

Caird, F. I., jt. ed. see Evans, J. Grimley.

Caird, F. I., et al, eds. Cardiology in Old Age. LC 76-23094. (Illus.). 428p. 1976. 49.50x (ISBN 0-306-30927-0, Plenum Pr). Plenum Pub.

Caird, G. B. The Apostolic Age. (Studies in Theology). 222p. 1974. pap. 13.50x (ISBN 0-7156-0010-9, BPA-02530, Pub. by Duckworth England). Biblio Dist.

--The Language & Imagery of the Bible. LC 79-27586. 288p. 1980. 20.00 (ISBN 0-664-21378-2). Westminster.

--Our Dialogue with Rome: The Second Vatican Council & After. 7.25 (ISBN 0-8446-1797-0). Peter Smith.

--The Revelation of St. John the Divine. LC 66-20774. (New Testament Commentaries Ser.). 1966. 16.30i (ISBN 0-06-061296-7, HarpR). Har-Row.

--Saint Luke. LC 77-81622. (Westminster Pelican Commentaries Ser.). 272p. 1978. 10.95 (ISBN 0-664-21345-6). Westminster.

Caird, George B. The Gospel of St. Luke: Commentaries. (Orig.). 1964. pap. 6.95 (ISBN 0-14-020490-3, Pelican). Penguin.

--Paul's Letters from Prison (Elphesians, Phillipians, Colossians, Philemon) in the Revised Standard Edition. (New Clarendon Bible). (Orig.). 1976. pap. text ed. 17.00x (ISBN 0-19-836920-4). Oxford U Pr.

Caird, James. English Agriculture in Eighteen Fifty & Eighteen Fifty-One. LC 67-16347. Repr. of 1852 ed. 37.50x (ISBN 0-678-05033-3). Kelley.

--English Agriculture in 1850-51. 2nd ed. 550p. 1968. Repr. of 1852 ed. 35.00x (ISBN 0-7146-1281-2, F Cass Co). Biblio Dist.

--Landed Interest & the Supply of Food. 5th rev ed. 184p. 1967. 26.00x (ISBN 0-7146-1042-9, F Cass Co). Biblio Dist.

--Landed Interest & the Supply of Food. 4th ed. LC 67-16346. Repr. of 1880 ed. 25.00x (ISBN 0-678-05034-1). Kelley.

--Prairie Farming in America: With Notes by the Way on Canada & the United States. LC 72-89090. (Rural America Ser.). 1973. Repr. of 1859 ed. 15.00 (ISBN 0-8420-1479-9). Scholarly Res Inc.

Caird, John. The Fundamental Ideas of Christianity, 2 vols. LC 77-27231. (Gifford Lectures: 1892-93, 1895-96). Repr. of 1899 ed. Set. 49.50 (ISBN 0-404-60460-9). AMS Pr.

--Introduction to the Philosophy of Religion. LC 75-113569. (BCL Ser. I). Repr. of 1901 ed. 12.50 (ISBN 0-404-01363-5). AMS Pr.

--Spinoza. facsimile ed. LC 75-164593. (Select Bibliographies Reprint Ser). Repr. of 1888 ed. 21.00 (ISBN 0-8369-5877-2). Ayer Co Pubs.

Caird, Kenneth A. Cameraready. (Illus.). 400p. 1973. looseleaf 40.00x (ISBN 0-87703-066-9). Univelt Inc.

Cairncross, A. S., ed. Eight Essayists. 1979. Repr. of 1947 ed. lib. bdg. 15.00 (ISBN 0-8495-0777-4). Arden Lib.

Cairncross, Alec. Years of Recovery: British Economic Policy, 1945-1951. 544p. 1985. text ed. 59.95 (ISBN 0-416-37920-6, 9522). Methuen Inc.

Cairncross, Alec & Eichengreen, Barry. Sterling in Decline. 270p. 1985. pap. 12.95x (ISBN 0-631-13938-9); 34.95 (ISBN 0-631-13368-2). Basil Blackwell.

Cairncross, Alec, ed. Britain's Economic Prospects Reconsidered. LC 71-37996. 1972. 29.50x (ISBN 0-87395-174-3). State U NY Pr.

Cairncross, Alec & Puri, Mohinder, eds. Employment, Income Distribution & Development Strategy: Problems of the Developing Countries - Essays in Honour of H. W. Singer. LC 75-34052. 300p. 1976. text ed. 28.50x osi (ISBN 0-8419-0242-9). Holmes & Meier.

Cairncross, Alec, ed. see Clarke, Richard.

Cairncross, Alec, et al. Economic Policy for the European Community. LC 74-22006. 304p. 1975. text ed. 39.50x (ISBN 0-8419-0189-9). Holmes & Meier.

Cairncross, Alex. Inflation, Growth & International Finance. LC 75-20428. 136p. 1976. 29.50x (ISBN 0-87395-315-0). State U NY Pr.

Cairncross, Alexander. Control of Long-Term International Capital Movement. LC 73-12634. (Brookings Institution Staff Paper Ser.). pap. 29.50 (ISBN 0-317-20780-6, 2025367). Bks Demand UMI.

Cairncross, Alexander K. Essays in Economic Management. LC 78-37995. 219p. 1971. 29.50x (ISBN 0-87395-173-5). State U NY Pr.

--Home & Foreign Investment, 1870-1913. LC 74-17410. 251p. Repr. of 1953 ed. lib. bdg. 27.50x (ISBN 0-678-01023-4). Kelley.

Cairncross, Andrew S. Problem of Hamlet: A Solution. 1936. lib. bdg. 12.50 (ISBN 0-8414-1599-4). Folcroft.

Cairncross, Andrew S., ed. see Kyd, Thomas.

Cairncross, Andrew S., ed. see Shakespeare, William.

Cairncross, Chris. Ferrocement Boat Construction. LC 72-76553. (Illus.). pap. 48.00 (ISBN 0-317-08220-5, 2010131). Bks Demand UMI.

Cairncross, J. Population & Agriculture in the Developing Countries. (Economic & Social Development Papers: No. 15). 52p. (Eng., Fr. & Span.). 1981. pap. 7.50 (ISBN 92-5-100885-X, F2117, FAO). Unipub.

Cairncross, John. La Fontaine Fables, & Other Poems. 2nd, rev. ed. 143p. 1982. pap. text ed. 12.00x (ISBN 0-86140-122-0, Pub. by Colin Smythe). Humanities.

Cairncross, John, tr. see Corneille, Pierre.

Cairncross, John, tr. see Racine, Jean.

Cairncross, John, tr. see Racine, Jean B.

Cairncross, S. & Feachem, R. G. Environmental Health Engineering in the Tropics: An Introductory Text. 283p. 1983. 42.95 (ISBN 0-471-90001-X). Wiley.

Cairncross, Sandy, et al. Evaluation for Village Water Supply Planning. 179p. 1980. 34.95 (ISBN 0-471-27662-6, Pub. by Wiley-Interscience). Wiley.

Cairneross, Frances, ed. Changing Perceptions in Economic Policy: Essays in Honour of the Seventieth Birthday of Sir Alec Cairneross. 276p. 26.00 (ISBN 0-416-31550-X, NO. 3579). Methuen Inc.

Cairnes, J. E. The Slave Power: Its Character, Career, & Probable Designs. 12.00. Peter Smith.

Cairnes, John E. Character & Logical Method of Political Economy. 2nd ed. LC 65-20922. Repr. of 1875 ed. 25.00x (ISBN 0-678-00104-9). Kelley.

--Essays in Political Economy. LC 65-20923. Repr. of 1873 ed. 35.00x (ISBN 0-678-00105-7). Kelley.

--Examination into the Principles of Currency Involved in the Bank Charter Act of 1844. LC 65-2094. Repr. of 1854 ed. 15.00 (ISBN 0-678-00106-5). Kelley.

--Political Essays. LC 66-22615. Repr. of 1873 ed. 25.00x (ISBN 0-678-00206-1). Kelley.

--Slave Power: Its Character, Career & Probable Designs. LC 75-75548. Repr. of 1862 ed. 17.50x (ISBN 0-8371-1014-9, CAS&). Greenwood.

--Some Leading Principles of Political Economy Newly Expounded. LC 66-22617. Repr. of 1874 ed. 37.50x (ISBN 0-678-00205-3). Kelley.

Cairnie, A. B., ed. Stems Cells: Renewing Cell Population. 1976. 57.50 (ISBN 0-12-155050-8). Acad Pr.

Cairns. Conversations with Husserl & Fink. (Phaenomenologica Ser: No. 66). 1976. 31.50 (ISBN 90-247-1793-0, Pub. by Martinus Nijhoff Netherlands). Kluwer Academic.

--Guide for Translating Husserl. (Phaenomenologica Ser: No. 55). 1973. pap. 18.50 (ISBN 90-247-1452-4, Pub. by Martinus Nijhoff Netherlands). Kluwer Academic.

Cairns, Alison. New Year Resolution. 203p. 1985. 12.95 (ISBN 0-312-57112-7). St Martin.

--Strained Relations. 208p. 1983. 10.95 (ISBN 0-312-76382-4). St Martin.

Calahan, John C. Casual Realism: An Essay on Philosophical Method & the Foundations of Knowledge. Deely, John & Williams, Brooke, eds. LC 85-3309. (Sources in Semiotics Ser.: Vol. II). 516p. (Orig.). 1985. lib. bdg. 36.50 (ISBN 0-8191-4621-8, Sources Semiotics); pap. 19.25 (ISBN 0-8191-4622-6). U Pr of Amer.

Calahan, North. Peggy. LC 83-45139. 248p. 1983. 14.95 (ISBN 0-8453-4717-9). Cornwall Bks.

Calais, Aloy J. Consumer Legislation in France. 1981. 42.50 (ISBN 0-442-30415-3). Van Nos Reinhold.

Calais, Jean. Villon. 1981. pap. 4.95 (ISBN 0-915008-18-1). Duende.

Calais, Jean-Louis, et al, eds. Quantum Science: Methods & Structure. LC 76-21354. 595p. 1976. 85.00 (ISBN 0-306-30968-8, Plenum Pr). Plenum Pub.

Calamari. Contracts: Adaptable to Courses Utilizing Materials by Calamari. LC 82-240945. (Legalines Ser.). write for info. (Law & Business). HarBraceJ.

Calamari, John D. & Perillo, Joseph M. Contracts. 2nd ed. LC 77-81268. (Hornbook Ser.). 878p. 1977. 20.95 (ISBN 0-685-88129-6). West Pub.

--Contracts. LC 83-6605. (Black Letter Ser.). 397p. 1983. pap. text ed. 14.95 (ISBN 0-314-73225-X). West Pub.

--Contracts Cases & Problems. LC 78-18757. (American Casebook Ser.). 1061p. 1978. text ed. 26.95 (ISBN 0-8299-2010-2). West Pub.

Calame, O., ed. High-Precision Earth Rotation & Earth-Moon Dynamics. 1982. 54.50 (ISBN 90-277-1405-3, Pub by Reidel Holland). Kluwer Academic.

Calame-Griaule, Genevieve. Words & the Dogon World. LaPin, Deirdre, tr. from Fr. LC 84-25160. (Translations in Folklore Studies). (Illus.). 730p. 1985. text ed. 42.50 (ISBN 0-915980-95-9). ISHI PA.

Calandra, Denis. All's Well That Ends Well & The Merry Wives of Windsor Notes. 71p. (Orig.). 1985. pap. text ed. 3.25 (ISBN 0-8220-0004-0). Cliffs.

--Comedy of Errors Notes. Bd. with Love's Labour's Lost & The Two Gentlemen of Verona Notes. 88p. (Orig.). 1982. pap. 2.75 (ISBN 0-8220-0010-5). Cliffs.

--Fathers & Sons Notes. (Orig.). 1966. pap. 2.95 (ISBN 0-8220-0470-4). Cliffs.

--Macbeth Notes. (Orig.). 1979. pap. 2.95 (ISBN 0-8220-0046-6). Cliffs.

--New German Dramatists. LC 83-48310. (Modern Dramatists Ser.). (Illus.). 224p. 1984. 17.50 (ISBN 0-394-53499-9, GP-875); pap. 9.95 (ISBN 0-394-62487-4, E 866). Grove.

--Richard Second Notes. (Orig.). 1982. pap. 3.25 (ISBN 0-8220-0068-7). Cliffs.

Calandra, Denis, ed. see Fassbinder, Rainer W.

Calandra, Denis M. Crucible Notes. (Orig.). 1968. pap. 3.25 (ISBN 0-8220-0337-6). Cliffs.

--Lord of the Flies Notes. (Orig.). 1971. pap. 3.25 (ISBN 0-8220-0754-1). Cliffs.

Calandra, Denis M., jt. auth. see Roberts, James L.

Calandra, S., et al, eds. Liver & Lipid Metabolism: Proceedings of the Symposium on Liver & Lipid Metabolism, Modena, Italy, 17-18 November, 1983. (International Congress Ser.: No. 632). 228p. 1984. 59.25 (ISBN 0-444-80608-3, Excerpta Medica). Elsevier.

Calano, James & Salzman, Jeff. Real World One Hundred One. 256p. 1984. pap. 7.95 (ISBN 0-446-38077-6). Warner Bks.

Calasanti, Toni M., jt. auth. see Hendricks, Jon.

Calasibetta, Charlotte. Essential Terms of Fashion: A Collection of Definitions. (Illus.). 225p. 1985. pap. text ed. 12.50 (ISBN 0-87005-519-4). Fairchild.

Calasibetta, Charlotte M. Fairchild's Dictionary of Fashion. Davis, Lorraine & Goble, Ermina S., eds. LC 74-84805. (Illus.). 700p. 1975. 50.00 (ISBN 0-87005-133-4). Fairchild.

Calasso, M. G. & Mirak, M. L. A Reader in Electronics & Telecomunications, English-Italian. 470p. pap. 29.95 (ISBN 88-00-26311-9, M-9194). French & Eur.

Calavita, Kitty. U. S. Immigration Law & the Control of Labor, 1820-1924. LC 84-45222. (Law, State, & Society Ser.). 1984. 39.50 (ISBN 0-12-155052-4). Acad Pr.

Calaway, Bernie. Forty-Four Fun Fables. 96p. (Orig.). 1982. pap. 5.95 (ISBN 0-8192-1296-2). Morehouse.

Calba, Marti J. de see Martorell, Joanot & De Calba, Marti J.

Calbally, E. I. & Freney, J. R., eds. The Cycling of Carbon, Nitrogen, Sulfur, & Phosphorus in Terrestrial & Aquatic Ecosystems. 230p. 1982. 28.00 (ISBN 0-387-11272-3). Springer-Verlag.

Calbe, jt. auth. see Nanney.

CALC Staff. Living for Justice: A Study Guide to Hunger for Justice: the Politics of Food & Faith. 28p. (Orig.). 1982. pap. 1.00 (ISBN 0-88344-296-5). Orbis Bks.

Calcagno, P. L., jt. ed. see Pascual, J. F.

Calciati, Romolo. Corpus Numorrum Siculorum, the Bronze Coinage. 1983. Set. 180.00 (ISBN 0-318-03947-8); Vol. 1, Greek Sicilian Coinage. write for info; Vol.2, Syracusan Coinage. write for info. Numismatic Fine Arts.

Calcott, P. H. Freezing & Thawing Microbes. 74p. 1979. 40.00x (ISBN 0-904095-27-4, Pub. by Meadowfield Pr England). State Mutual Bk.

Calcott, Peter H. Continuous Cultures of Cells, 2 vols. 1981. Vol. 1, 208 pgs. 67.00 (ISBN 0-8493-5377-7); Vol. 2, 224 pgs. 70.00 (ISBN 0-8493-5378-5). CRC Pr.

Caldara, Antonio. Olimpiade. Brown, Howard M., ed. LC 76-20980. (Italian Opera 1640-1770 Ser.). 1978. lib. bdg. 77.00 (ISBN 0-8240-2631-4). Garland Pub.

Caldarera, Claudio M., et al, eds. Advances in Polyamine Research, Vol. 3. 512p. 1981. 79.00 (ISBN 0-89004-621-2). Raven.

Caldarini, E., jt. auth. see Du Bellay, Joachim.

Caldarola, Carlo, ed. Religion & Societies: Asia & the Middle East. (Religion & Society: No. 22). 688p. 1982. text ed. 50.00 (ISBN 90-279-3259-X); Pub. 1984. pap. 29.95 (ISBN 3-11-010021-5). Mouton.

Caldecott, Alfred. Church in the West Indies. 268p. 1970. Repr. of 1898 ed. 28.50x (ISBN 0-7146-1932-9, F Cass Co). Biblio Dist.

--Selections from the Literature of Theism. 1973. Repr. of 1904 ed. 45.00 (ISBN 0-8274-1540-0). R West.

Caldecott, Alfred & MacKintosh, H. R. Selections from the Literature of Theism. 1979. Repr. of 1909 ed. lib. bdg. 65.00 (ISBN 0-8495-0932-7). Arden Lib.

Caldecott, J. O. An Ecological & Behavioural Study of the Pig-Tailed Macaque. (Contributions to Primatology: Vol. 21). (Illus.). viii, 336p. 1985. 59.75 (ISBN 3-8055-4212-7). S Karger.

Caldecott, Leonie & Leland, Stephanie. Reclaim the Earth: Women Speak Out for Life on Earth. 245p. 1984. pap. 7.95 (ISBN 0-7043-3908-0, Pub. by The Women's Press). Merrimack Pub Cir.

Caldecott, Moyra. Adventures by Leaf Light. LC 79-105810. (Illus.). 48p. 1978. (Star & Elephant Bks.); pap. 10.95 (ISBN 0-914676-20-2). Green Tiger Pr.

--The Lily & the Bull. 192p. 1979. 9.95 (ISBN 0-8090-6572-X). Hill & Wang.

--Shadow on the Stones. 160p. 1979. 8.95 (ISBN 0-8090-8599-2). Hill & Wang.

Caldecott, Randolph see Aesop.

Caldeira, Ernesto. Jefferson Davis Coloring Book. (Illus.). 32p. (Orig.). (gr. 1-6). 1982. pap. 2.95 (ISBN 0-88289-256-8). Pelican.

Calder, A. B. Photometric Methods of Analysis. (Illus.). 1969. 43.50 (ISBN 0-9960017-0-0, Pub. by A Hilger England). Heyden.

Calder, Alexander. Animal Sketching. (Illus.). 64p. 1973. pap. 2.50 (ISBN 0-486-20129-5). Dover.

Calder, Alexander, jt. auth. see De La Fontaine, Jean.

Calder, Angus. Russia Discovered: Nineteenth-Century Fiction from Pushkin to Chekhov. LC 75-44752. 302p. 1976. text ed. 24.50x (ISBN 0-06-490924-7, 06379). B&N Imports.

Calder, Angus, ed. Summer Fires: New Poetry of Africa. (African Writers Ser.: No. 257). xii, 116p. 1984. pap. text ed. 7.00x (ISBN 0-435-90257-1). Heinemann Ed.

Calder, Angus, ed. see Dickens, Charles.

Calder, Angus, ed. see Scott, Walter.

Calder, Bobby J. & Marks, Amy S. Attitudes Toward Death & Funerals. 270p. (Orig.). pap. 4.95 (ISBN 0-9608220-0-3). Nat Res Info.

Calder, Bruce J. The Impact of Intervention: The Dominican Republic during the U. S. Occupation of 1916-1924. (Texas Pan American Ser.). (Illus.). 352p. 1984. text ed. 25.00x (ISBN 0-292-73830-7). U of Tex Pr.

Calder, Clarence A., ed. Mechanics of Materials Exam File. LC 84-24702. (Exam File Ser.). 378p. (Orig.). 1985. pap. 9.95 (ISBN 0-910554-46-3). Engineering.

Calder, D. G. & Allen, M. J. Sources & Analogues of Old English Poetry: The Major Latin Sources in Translation. LC 75-2240. 235p. 1976. 29.50 (ISBN 0-85991-013-X, Pub. by Boydell & Brewer). Longwood Pub Group.

Calder, Daniel C., ed. Old English Poetry: Essays on Style. (Contributions of the Center for Medieval & Renaissance Studies, UCLA: No. 10). 1979. 27.50x (ISBN 0-520-03830-4). U of Cal Pr.

Calder, Daniel G. & Forker, Charles. Edward Phillip's History of the Literature of England & Scotland. (Salzburg Studies in English Literature, Poetic Drama & Poetic Theory: No. 21). 134p. (A translation from the Compendios Enumeratio Poetarum). 1973. pap. text ed. 25.50x (ISBN 0-391-01338-6). Humanities.

Calder, Daniel G., jt. auth. see Greenfield, Stanley B.

Calder, Daniel G., et al, trs. Sources & Analogues of Old English Poetry II: The Major Germanic & Celtic Texts in Translation. LC 83-12288. 222p. 1983. 42.50x (ISBN 0-389-20434-X, 07320). B&N Imports.

Calder, G. The Principles & Techniques of Engineering Estimating. 180p. 1976. text ed. 28.00 (ISBN 0-08-019704-3); pap. 8.75 (ISBN 0-08-019703-5). Pergamon.

Calder, George, ed. Auraicept Na N-Eces. LC 78-72717. (Celtic Language & Literature: Goidelic & Brythonic). Repr. of 1917 ed. 47.50 (ISBN 0-404-17538-4). AMS Pr.

Calder, Isabel M. Colonial Captivities, Marches, & Journeys. LC 67-27581. 1935. Repr. 21.50x (ISBN 0-8046-0061-9, Pub. by Kennikat). Assoc Faculty Pr.

--New Haven Colony. vi, 301p. 1970. Repr. of 1934 ed. 22.50 (ISBN 0-208-00836-5, Archon). Shoe String.

Calder, Isabel M., ed. see Davenport, John.

Calder, J. M., tr. see Lange, Monique.

Calder, Jean. Walking: A Guide to Beautiful Walks & Trails in America. (Americans-Discover-America Ser.). 1977. 3.95 (ISBN 0-688-03131-5). Morrow.

Calder, Jenn, ed. Dr. Jekyll & Mr. Hyde. 1980. pap. 2.95 (ISBN 0-14-043117-9). Penguin.

Calder, Jenni. Robert Louis Stevenson: A Life Study. (Illus.). 1980. 27.50x (ISBN 0-19-520210-4). Oxford U Pr.

--Stevenson & Victorian England. 141p. 1981. 16.00x (ISBN 0-85224-399-5, Pub. by Edinburgh U Pr Scotland). Columbia U Pr.

--There Must Be a Lone Ranger: The American West in Film & in Reality. LC 74-20216. (Illus.). 256p. 1975. 8.95 (ISBN 0-8008-7636-9). Taplinger.

--There Must Be a Lone Ranger: The American West in Myth & Reality. (McGraw-Hill Paperbacks). 1977. pap. 3.95 (ISBN 0-07-009607-4). McGraw.

Calder, Jenni, ed. Robert Louis Stevenson: A Critical Celebration. (Illus.). 104p. 1980. 24.50x (ISBN 0-389-20145-6, 06916). B&N Imports.

Calder, John. Diabetes: Basic Principles of Treatment. (Orig.). 1980. pap. 5.50x (ISBN 0-85564-143-6, Pub. by U of W Austral Pr). Intl Spec Bk.

Calder, John, ed. Beckett at Sixty. 100p. 1967. 12.95 (ISBN 0-7145-0111-5). Dufour.

--Gambit: International Drama Review-French Issue, No. 30. (Orig.). 1980. pap. 5.00 (ISBN 0-7145-3745-4). Riverrun NY.

--Gambit: International Drama Review-German Theatre Issue, No. 39-40. 96p. (Orig.). 1983. pap. 9.00 (ISBN 0-7145-3909-0). Riverrun NY.

--Gambit: International Drama Review-Political Theatre Issue, No. 36. 96p. (Orig.). 1982. pap. 5.00 (ISBN 0-7145-3707-1). Riverrun NY.

--Gambit: International Drama Review-Simone Benmussa Issue, No. 35. 96p. (Orig.). 1982. pap. 5.00 (ISBN 0-7145-3706-3). Riverrun NY.

--Gambit: International Drama Review-Tom Stoppard Issue, No. 37. 96p. (Orig.). 1982. pap. 5.00 (ISBN 0-7145-3830-2). Riverrun NY.

--New Writing & Writers, 20. 1982. 13.95 (ISBN 0-7145-3868-X); pap. 6.95 (ISBN 0-7145-3869-8). Riverrun NY.

Calder, John, intro. by. A Nouveau Roman Reader. Date not set. pap. 5.95 (ISBN 0-7145-3720-9). Riverrun NY.

Calder, John, ed. Signature Anthology. pap. 4.95 (ISBN 0-7145-0491-2). Riverrun NY.

Calder, John, ed. see Schiascha, Leonardo, et al.

Calder, John A., jt. ed. see Hood, Donald W.

Calder, Julian & Garett, John. Fielding's the Travel Photographer's Handbook. (Illus.). 240p. (Orig.). 1985. pap. 14.95 (ISBN 0-688-04219-8). Fielding Travel Bks.

Calder, Julian & Garrett, John. The Thirty-Five MM Photographer's Handbook. (Illus.). 1979. 14.95 (ISBN 0-517-53917-9); pap. 11.95 (ISBN 0-517-53918-7). Crown.

Calder, Julian, et al. The Thirty-Five Millimeter Photographer's Handbook. rev. updated ed. 1983. pap. 11.95 (ISBN 0-517-55124-1). Crown.

Calder, K. J. Britain & the Origins of the New Europe, 1914-1918. LC 75-12161. (International Studies Ser.). 282p. 1976. 42.50 (ISBN 0-521-20897-1). Cambridge U Pr.

Calder, Kent E., jt. auth. see Hofheinz, Roy, Jr.

Calder, L., et al. The Correspondence of Lu: Samarin & Baroness Rahden (1861-1876) 267p. 1974. text ed. 12.00x (ISBN 0-88920-005-X, Pub. by Wilfrid Laurier U Pr Canada); pap. 8.50x (ISBN 0-88920-004-1). Humanities.

Calder, Lyn. Happy Birthday, Buddy Blue. (Rainbow Brite Story Bks.). (Illus.). 48p. (ps-2). 1985. write for info. (ISBN 0-307-16002-5, 16002, Pub. by Golden Bks). Western Pub.

Calder, Malcolm D. & Bernhardt, Peter. The Biology of Mistletoes. LC 83-71158. 1984. 55.00 (ISBN 0-12-155055-9). Acad Pr.

Calder, Nigel. The Comet Is Coming: The Ferverish Legacy of Mr. Halley. (Illus.). 1982. pap. 6.95 (ISBN 0-14-006069-3). Penguin.

--Einstein's Universe. 1980. pap. 5.95 (ISBN 0-14-005499-5). Penguin.

--Einstein's Universe. (Illus.). 1979. 15.95 (ISBN 0-670-29076-9). Viking.

--The Key to the Universe. (Large Format Ser.). 1978. pap. 8.95 (ISBN 0-14-005065-5). Penguin.

--Key to the Universe. 1977. 16.95 (ISBN 0-670-41270-8). Viking.

--Nineteen Eighty-Four & Beyond. (Penguin Nonfiction Ser.). 224p. 1984. pap. 5.95 (ISBN 0-14-007288-8). Penguin.

--Nineteen Eighty-Four & Beyond: Into the 21st Century. (Illus.). 208p. 1984. 14.95 (ISBN 0-670-51389-X). Viking.

--Nuclear Nightmares. 1981. pap. 4.95 (ISBN 0-14-005867-2). Penguin.

--Nuclear Nightmares: An Investigation into Possible Wars. (Illus.). 188p. 1980. 10.95 (ISBN 0-670-51820-4). Viking.

--Restless Earth: A Report on the New Geology. 1978. pap. 9.95 (ISBN 0-14-004902-9). Penguin.

--Spaceships of the Mind. 1979. pap. 6.95 (ISBN 0-14-005231-3). Penguin.

--Spaceships of the Mind. (Illus.). 1978. 14.95 (ISBN 0-670-66021-3). Viking.

--Timescale. Date not set. pap. 8.95 (ISBN 0-14-006342-0). Penguin.

--Timescale: An Atlas of the Fourth Dimension. LC 83-47874. (Illus.). 336p. 1983. 19.95 (ISBN 0-670-71571-9). Viking.

--The Violent Universe: An Eyewitness Account of the New Astronomy. LC 76-30435. (Illus.). 1977. pap. 8.95 (ISBN 0-14-004485-X). Penguin.

--Violent Universe: An Eyewitness Account of the New Astronomy. LC 73-83246. (Illus.). 1970. 14.95 (ISBN 0-670-74720-3). Viking.

--The Weather Machine. (Illus.). 144p. 1977. pap. text ed. 4.95 (ISBN 0-14-004489-2). Penguin.

--The Weather Machine. (Illus.). 1975. PLB 14.95 (ISBN 0-670-75425-0). Viking.

Calder, Philip T. see Tierney, Cornelius E.

Calder, Philip T. & Tierney, Cornelius E., eds. Governmental Accounting Procedures & Practices: A Comprehensive Study of the Financial Reporting Practices of over 500 Governmental Units. (GAPP 1983 Ser.). 225p. 1983. 59.00 (ISBN 0-444-00792-X, North Holland). Elsevier.

Calder, Raven, ed. see Brooke, Meridith & Rodrick, Leigh.

Calder, S. Hitch Hikers Manual: Britain. (Illus.). 144p. 1979. pap. 5.95 (ISBN 0-901205-68-0). Bradt Ent.

Calder, W., jt. auth. see Magison, E. C.

Calder, W. M., tr. see Maximilian - Prince Of Baden.

Calder, William A., III. Size, Function, & Life History. (Illus.). 448p. 1984. text ed. 32.50x (ISBN 0-674-81070-8). Harvard U Pr.

Calder, William M., III & Traill, David M., eds. Myth, Scandal & History: The Heinrich Schliemann Controversy & a First Edition of the Mycenaean Diary. 300p. 1985. 30.00 (ISBN 0-8143-1795-2). Wayne St U Pr.

Calderbank, V. J. Course in Programming in FORTRAN IV. 2nd ed. 1983. 25.00 (ISBN 0-412-24270-2, NO. 6737, Pub. by Chapman & Hall); pap. 9.95x (ISBN 0-412-23790-3, NO. 6738). Methuen Inc.

--A Course on Programming in FORTRAN. 2nd ed. 1983. 25.00 (ISBN 0-412-24270-2, NO.6737); pap. 9.95 (ISBN 0-412-23790-3, NO.6738). Methuen Inc.

Calderelli, David D. Pediatric Otolaryngology. (New Directions in Therapy Ser.). 1983. 35.00 (ISBN 0-87488-695-3). Med Exam.

Calderhead, James, ed. Hospitals for People: A Look at Some New Hospital Buildings in England. 64p. 1977. 30.00x (ISBN 0-900889-47-0, Pub. by Kings Fund). State Mutual Bk.

Calderini, G., jt. ed. see Toffano, G.

Calderon. The Great Stage of the World. Brandt, G. W., tr. from Span. (Classics of Drama in English Translation Ser.). 1976. pap. 6.50 (ISBN 0-7190-0571-X, Pub. by Manchester Univ Pr). Longwood Pub Group.

Calderon, A. P., ed. see Symposium in Pure Mathematics - Chicago - 1966.

Calderon, George. Eight One-Act Plays. LC 79-50020. (One-Act Plays in Reprint Ser.). 1980. Repr. of 1922 ed. 19.50x (ISBN 0-8486-2044-5). Core Collection.

Calderon, Pedro. Life Is a Dream. Colford, William E., tr. from Span. 1958. pap. text ed. 3.75 (ISBN 0-8120-0127-3). Barron.

Calderon, W. Frank. Animal Painting & Anatomy. LC 72-75583. (Illus.). 352p. 1975. pap. 6.95 (ISBN 0-486-22523-2). Dover.

--Animal Painting & Anatomy. (Illus.). 16.25 (ISBN 0-8446-5168-0). Peter Smith.

Calderon, Wilfredo, ed. Dinamicas de la Escuela Dominical. 108p. (Span.). 1973. pap. 3.25 (ISBN 0-87148-255-X). Pathway Pr.

Calderon De La Barca & Frances, E. Life in Mexico During a Residence of Two Years in That Country. LC 75-41046. Repr. of 1913 ed. 27.50 (ISBN 0-404-14517-5). AMS Pr.

Calderon de la Barca, Frances. Life in Mexico. (California Library Reprint Ser.: No. 116). (Illus.). 550p. 1982. 28.50x (ISBN 0-520-04661-7, CLRS 116); pap. 6.95 (ISBN 0-520-04662-5, CAL 568). U of Cal Pr.

Calderon de la Barca, Pedro. Beware of Still Waters. Gitlitz, David, tr. from Span. & Eng. LC 84-224. (Illus.). 216p. 1984. text ed. 25.00 (ISBN 0-939980-04-5); pap. 12.00x (ISBN 0-939980-08-8). Trinity U Pr.

--Four Comedies by Pedro Calderon de la Barca. Muir, Kenneth, tr. LC 80-14570. 304p. 1980. 26.00x (ISBN 0-8131-1409-8). U Pr of Ky.

--The Mayor of Zalamea: Or the Best Garroting Ever Done. 110p. 1983. pap. 7.95 (ISBN 0-907540-12-0, NO. 4051, Pub. by Salamander Press). Methuen Inc.

--The Surgeon of His Honour. Campbell, Roy, tr. from Span. LC 77-13711. 1978. Repr. of 1960 ed. lib. bdg. 24.75 (ISBN 0-8371-9871-2, CASU). Greenwood.

Calderone, Mary & Johnson, Eric. The Family Book About Sexuality. 330p. 1-5 copies 14.95 ea.; 6-25 copies 12.71 ea.; 26 copies or more 10.47 ea. Ed-U Pr.

Calderone, Mary, jt. auth. see Bride's Magazine Editors.

Calderone, Mary, jt. auth. see Newhall, Beaumont.

Calderone, Mary S. Manual of Family Planning & Contraceptive Practice. 2nd ed. LC 76-53723. 494p. 1977. Repr. of 1970 ed. 18.50 (ISBN 0-88275-270-7). Krieger.

Calderone, Mary S. & Ramey, James W. Talking with Your Child about Sex: Questions & Answers for Children from Birth to Puberty. LC 84-48319. 256p. 1983. 14.95 (ISBN 0-394-52124-2). Random.
--Talking with Your Child about Sex: Questions & Answers for Children from Birth to Puberty. 1984. pap. 2.95 (ISBN 0-345-31379-8). Ballantine.
Calderone, Mary S., jt. ed. see Rapp, Clyde E., Jr.
Calderwood, Ann, jt. ed. see Rossi, Alice S.
Calderwood, David. A Solution of Doctor Resolutus, His Resolutions for Kneeling. LC 79-84093. (English Experience Ser.: No. 913). 60p. 1979. Repr. of 1619 ed. lib. bdg. 8.00 (ISBN 90-221-0913-5). Walter J Johnson.
--The True History of the Church of Scotland: From the Beginnnings of the Reform to the End of the Reign of King James VI, 8 vols. Thomson, Thomas, ed. LC 83-45577. Date not set. Repr. of 1842 ed. Set. 525.00 (ISBN 0-404-19894-5). AMS Pr.
Calderwood, Henry. David Hume. LC 77-973. 1977. lib. bdg. 22.50 (ISBN 0-8414-3571-5). Folcroft.
--David Hume. 158p. 1980. Repr. of 1898 ed. lib. bdg. 22.50 (ISBN 0-8492-3862-5). R West.
Calderwood, James L. Metadrama in Shakespeare's Henriad: Richard II to Henry V. LC 77-93467. 1979. 24.50x (ISBN 0-520-03652-2). U of Cal Pr.
--Shakespearean Metadrama: The Argument of the Play in Titus Andronicus, Love's Labour's Lost, Romeo & Juliet, a Midsummer Night's Dream & Richard 2nd. LC 71-141839. 1971. 10.95x (ISBN 0-8166-0595-5). U of Minn Pr.
--To Be & Not to Be. LC 82-22214. 232p. 1983. 30.00x (ISBN 0-231-05628-1); pap. 14.50x (ISBN 0-231-05629-X). Columbia U Pr.
Caldicott, Helen. Missile Envy. 400p. (Orig.). 1985. pap. 4.50 (ISBN 0-553-25080-9). Bantam.
--Missile Envy: Helen Caldicott Speaks Out. LC 84-60198. 393p. 1984. 15.95 (ISBN 0-688-01954-4). Morrow.
--Nuclear Madness. 1981. pap. 3.50 (ISBN 0-553-22774-2). Bantam.
--Nuclear Madness. 120p. 3.95 (ISBN 0-318-15680-6). Natl Health Fed.
--Nuclear Madness: What You Can Do! 120p. 3.50 (ISBN 0-686-30388-1, Pub. by Bantam Books). WILPF.
Caldie, Roberta W. Dominance & Language: A New Perspective on Sexism. LC 81-40141. (Illus.). 130p. (Orig.). 1982. lib. bdg. 21.75 (ISBN 0-8191-1966-0); pap. text ed. 9.25 (ISBN 0-8191-1967-9). U Pr of Amer.
Caldirola, P., ed. Ergodic Theories. (Italian Physical Society: Course 14). 1962. 75.00 (ISBN 0-12-368814-0). Acad Pr.
Caldirola, P. & Knoepfel, H., eds. Physics of High Energy Density. (Italian Physical Society: Course 48). 1971. 80.00 (ISBN 0-12-368848-5). Acad Pr.
Caldwell. How You Can Stop Smoking Permanently. pap. 3.00 (ISBN 0-87980-074-7). Wilshire.
--Playing Chess. (Beginner's Guides Ser.). (gr. 4-9). 1980. 6.95 (ISBN 0-86020-408-1, Usborne-Hayes); PLB 11.95 (ISBN 0-88110-036-6); pap. 2.95 (ISBN 0-86020-407-3). EDC.
Caldwell & Hegner. Health Assistant. 3rd ed. LC 79-50661. (Illus.). 1980. pap. 13.80 (ISBN 0-8273-1337-3); instr's. guide 2.75 (ISBN 0-8273-1338-1). Delmar.
Caldwell & King. A Brief Course in Semimicro Qualitative Analysis. 3rd ed. write for info. Watts.
Caldwell, jt. ed. see Mulder.
Caldwell, A. D., ed. Rifamficin in Extra Pulmonary Tuberculosis. (Royal Society of Medicine International Congress & Symposium Ser.: No. 11). 72p. 1979. pap. 16.00 (ISBN 0-8089-1216-X, 790755). Grune.
Caldwell, A. D. & Lambert, H. P., eds. Pneumonia & Pneumococcal Infections. (Royal Society of Medicine International Congress & Symposium Ser.: No. 27). 1980. 19.50 (ISBN 0-8089-1287-9, 790756). Grune.
Caldwell, A. D., jt. ed. see Huskisson, E. C.
Caldwell, A. D., jt. ed. see Keen, H.
Caldwell, A. D., jt. ed. see Mezey, K. C.
Caldwell, A. D., jt. ed. see Neu, H. C.
Caldwell, A. D., jt. ed. see Newsom, S. W.
Caldwell, A. D., jt. ed. see Parsonage, M. J.
Caldwell, A. D., jt. ed. see Robertson, J. I.
Caldwell, A. D., jt. ed. see Simpson, S. T.
Caldwell, Anne E. Origins of Psychopharmacology: From CPZ to LSD. 240p. 1970. 19.50x (ISBN 0-398-00271-1). C C Thomas.
Caldwell, B. E., ed. Soybeans: Improvement, Production & Uses. (Illus.). 1973. 14.50 (ISBN 0-89118-017-6). Am Soc Agron.
Caldwell, Betty. The Vanderleigh Legacy. (Orig.). 1981. pap. 2.75 (ISBN 0-89083-813-5). Zebra.
Caldwell, Bettye & Ricciuti, Henry N. Review of Child Development Research, Vol. 3. 1974. pap. 7.95x (ISBN 0-226-09044-2, P680, Phoen). U of Chicago Pr.
Caldwell, Bettye & Stedman, Donald, eds. Infant Education. 1977. 9.95 (ISBN 0-8027-9042-9); pap. 8.95 (ISBN 0-8027-7110-6). Walker & Co.
Caldwell, Bill. Enjoying Maine. LC 77-78126. 1978. 12.95 (ISBN 0-930096-01-0). G Gannett.
--Islands of Maine: Where America Really Began. LC 81-81541. (Illus.). 240p. 1981. 12.95 (ISBN 0-930096-17-7). G Gannett.
--Maine Lighthouses. 1985. 15.95 (ISBN 0-930096-63-0); pap. 11.95 (ISBN 0-317-19636-7). G Gannett.
--Maine Magic. LC 79-88015. (Illus.). 334p. (Orig.). 1979. 14.95 (ISBN 0-930096-03-7). G Gannett.
--Rivers of Fortune. Snowman, Bob, ed. (Caldwell Ser.). (Illus.). 320p. 1983. text ed. 15.95 (ISBN 0-930096-45-2). G Gannett.
Caldwell, Brice & Caldwell, Craig, eds. Basic Bodywork & Painting. 5th ed. LC 73-79967. (Illus.). 192p. (Orig.). 1981. pap. 6.95 (ISBN 0-8227-5057-0, Dist. by Kampmann). Petersen Pub.
Caldwell, Bruce & Caldwell, Craig, eds. Best of Hot Rod. (Illus.). 192p. (Orig.). 1981. pap. 9.95 (ISBN 0-8227-5060-0, Dist. by Kampmann). Green Hill.
Caldwell, Bruce J. Beyond Positivism: Economic Methodology in the Twentieth Century. 288p. 1984. pap. text ed. 10.95 (ISBN 0-04-330342-0). Allen Unwin.
--Fuel Gas Energy Metering. (Gas Measurement Committee Reports: No. 5). 58p. 1970. pap. 2.00 (ISBN 0-318-12618-4, XQ0776). Am Gas Assn.
Caldwell, Bruce J., ed. Appraisal & Criticism in Economics: A Book of Readings. 400p. 1984. text ed. 29.50x (ISBN 0-04-330343-9); pap. text ed. 12.50x (ISBN 0-04-330344-7). Allen Unwin.
Caldwell, Celeste. Thirteen Towers. 1978. pap. 1.50 (ISBN 0-505-51286-6, Pub. by Tower Bks). Dorchester Pub Co.
Caldwell, Charles. Facts in Mesmerism. (Hypnosis & Altered States of Consciousness Ser.). 162p. 1982. Repr. of 1842 ed. lib. bdg. 19.50 (ISBN 0-306-76073-8). Da Capo.
Caldwell, Claire. Surf's Up for Laney. 187p. (YA) 1984. pap. 1.95 (ISBN 0-671-53390-8). PB.
Caldwell, Craig, jt. ed. see Caldwell, Brice.
Caldwell, Craig, jt. ed. see Caldwell, Bruce.
Caldwell, D. K. & Gohring, eds. Progress in Simulation, 2 vols. 1972. Vol. 1,382. 106.50 (ISBN 0-677-14890-9); Vol. 2, 380. 101.25 (ISBN 0-677-12490-2). Gordon.
Caldwell, Dan. American-Soviet Relations: From Nineteen Forty-Seven to the Nixon-Kissinger Grand Design. LC 80-27333. (Contributions in Political Science Ser.: No. 69). (Illus.). 288p. 1981. lib. bdg. 29.95 (ISBN 0-313-22538-9, CCC/). Greenwood.
Caldwell, Dan, ed. Henry Kissinger: His Personality & Policies. LC 83-5710. (Duke Press Policy Studies). 160p. 1983. text ed. 27.00 (ISBN 0-8223-0485-6). Duke.
--Soviet International Behavior & U. S. Policy Options. LC 84-48047. 304p. 1985. 30.00x (ISBN 0-669-09125-1); pap. text ed. 14.95x (ISBN 0-669-09124-3). Lexington Bks.
Caldwell, David, ed. Scottish Weapons & Fortifications, Eleven Hundred-Eighteen Hundred. (Illus.). 1980. text ed. 40.50x (ISBN 0-85976-047-2). Humanities.
Caldwell, David H. The Scottish Armoury. 78p. 1981. 10.00x (ISBN 0-85158-131-5, Pub. by Blackwood & Sons England). State Mutual Bk.
Caldwell, Douglas E. & Brierley, Corale L., eds. Planetary Ecology. (Illus.). 544p. 1985. 54.50 (ISBN 0-442-24007-4). Van Nos Reinhold.
Caldwell, E. The Complete Stories of Eskine Caldwell. 29.95 (ISBN 0-88411-455-4, Pub. by Aeonian Pr). Amereon Ltd.
Caldwell, E., jt. auth. see Bourke-White, M.
Caldwell, E. S. Only One Life. LC 75-22582. 1975. pap. 1.45 (ISBN 0-88243-562-0, 02-0562, Radiant Books). Gospel Pub.
--She's Gone. LC 75-43158. (Radiant Life Ser.). 128p. (Orig.). 1976. pap. 1.95 (ISBN 0-88243-893-X, 020893); teacher's ed 3.95 (ISBN 0-88243-167-6, 32-0167). Gospel Pub.
Caldwell, Erskine. The Black & White Stories of Erskine Caldwell. McIver, Ray, ed. LC 84-6092. 189p. 1984. 12.95 (ISBN 0-931948-63-0). Peachtree Pubs.
--Deep South: Memory & Observation. LC 80-16013. (Brown Thrasher Ser.). 270p. 1980. pap. 6,95 (ISBN 0-8203-0525-1). U of Ga Pr.
--God's Little Acre. pap. 2.95 (ISBN 0-451-51802-0, Sig Classics). NAL.
--God's Little Acre. Large Print ed. LC 81-21197. 335p. 1982. Repr. of 1933 ed. 12.95 (ISBN 0-89621-329-3). Thorndike Pr.
--Stories of Life, North & South. LC 82-9922. 1983. 14.95 (ISBN 0-396-08133-9). Dodd.
--This Very Earth. 10.95 (ISBN 0-89190-164-7, Pub. by Am Repr). Amereon Ltd.
--Tobacco Road. LC 78-55752. 1978. Repr. of 1932 ed. lib. bdg. 12.50x (ISBN 0-8376-0422-2). Bentley.
--Tobacco Road. 1970. pap. 2.95 (ISBN 0-451-12156-2, AE2156, Sig). NAL.
Caldwell, Erskine & Bourke-White, Margaret. North of the Danube. LC 77-1494. (Photography Ser.). (Illus.). 1977. Repr. of 1939 ed. lib. bdg. 35.00 (ISBN 0-306-70877-9). Da Capo.
--You Have Seen Their Faces. facsimile ed. McCurry, Dan C. & Rubenstein, Richard E., eds. LC 74-30622. (American Farmers & the Rise of Agribusiness Ser.). (Illus., With a new introductory note by Erskine Caldwell). 1975. Repr. of 1937 ed. 20.00x (ISBN 0-405-06769-0). Ayer Co Pubs.
Caldwell, Esther & Hegner, Barbara. Geriatrics: A Study of Maturity. 3rd ed. LC 79-55313. (Practical Nursing Ser.). (Illus.). 288p. 1981. pap. text ed. 14.00 (ISBN 0-8273-1935-5); instr's. guide 3.00 (ISBN 0-8273-1934-7). Delmar.
--Health Assistant. 3rd ed. 288p. 1981. 16.95 (ISBN 0-442-21850-8). Van Nos Reinhold.
--Health Care Assistant. 4th ed. LC 84-26021. 1985. pap. text ed. 16.00 (ISBN 0-8273-2453-7); instr's. guide 2.75 (ISBN 0-8273-2454-5). Delmar.
Caldwell, Esther & Hegner, Barbara R. Foundation for Medical Communication. (Illus.). 1978. text ed. 21.95 (ISBN 0-87909-299-8); instrs'. manual avail. (ISBN 0-8359-2080-1). Reston.
Caldwell, Esther, jt. ed. see Craney, Jan.
Caldwell, Francis E. The Ebb & the Flood: A History of the Halibut Producers Cooperative. Matsen, Bradford, ed. LC 80-51978. (Illus.). 144p. (Orig.). 1980. pap. 7.95 (ISBN 0-937288-00-4). Waterfront Pr.
--Pacific Troller: Life on the Northwest Fishing Grounds. LC 77-10324. (Illus.). 1978. pap. 5.95 (ISBN 0-88240-099-1). Alaska Northwest.
Caldwell, G. & Zanfagna, P. Fluoridation & Truth Decay. 4.95x (ISBN 0-686-29882-9). Cancer Control Soc.
Caldwell, Gladys & Zanfagna, P. E. Fluoridation & Truth Decay. McCoy, Caroline, ed. (Illus.). 301p. (Orig.). 1980. pap. 6.95 (ISBN 0-9607710-0-X). Top-Ecol Pr.
Caldwell, Guy A. Early History of the Ochsner Medical Center: The First Twenty-Two Years. (Illus.). 128p. 1965. photocopy ed. 14.75x (ISBN 0-398-00272-X). C C Thomas.
Caldwell, H. M. History of the Elyton Land Company & Birmingham, Ala. The Origin & Development of an American City. pap. 3.75 (ISBN 0-686-92272-7). Southern U Pr.
Caldwell, Happy. How to Live in Perilous Times. 96p. (Orig.). 1983. pap. 2.50 (ISBN 0-89274-258-5, HH-258). Harrison Hse.
--The Word System. 60p. 1981. pap. 1.50 (ISBN 0-89274-176-7). Harrison Hse.
Caldwell, Harry B. & Middleton, David L., eds. English Tragedy, Thirteen Seventy to Sixteen Hundred: Fifty Years of Criticism. LC 72-153857. (Checklists in the Humanities & Education Ser.). 89p. 1971. 6.00 (ISBN 0-911536-37-X). Trinity U Pr.
Caldwell, Helen. Machado de Assis: The Brazilian Master & His Novels. LC 76-89891. 1970. 27.50x (ISBN 0-520-01608-4). U of Cal Pr.
--Michio Ito: The Dancer & His Dances. LC 76-7756. (Illus.). 1977. 30.00 (ISBN 0-520-03219-5). U of Cal Pr.
Caldwell, Helen, tr. see De Assis, Machado.
Caldwell, Helen, tr. see Machado de Assis, Joaquim M.
Caldwell, Inga. Jonquils in December. LC 73-86339. 125p. 1973. 4.00 (ISBN 0-913264-12-1). Douglas-West.
Caldwell, J. The Book of Ultimates. 160p. 1983. 6.95 (ISBN 0-07-009608-2). McGraw.
Caldwell, J. & Paulson, G., eds. Foreign Compound Metabolism: Proceedings of the International Society for the Study of Xenobiotics Symposium, Florida, November 1983. 400p. 1984. 71.00x (ISBN 0-85066-271-0). Taylor & Francis.
Caldwell, J., jt. ed. see Mulder, G. J.
Caldwell, J. C. Food Production & Crisis in the West African Savannah. (Development Studies Centre - Occasional Papers: No. 25). 28p. 1981. pap. text ed. 2.00 (ISBN 0-909150-43-5, 0108, Pub. by ANUP Australia). Australia N U P.
--Theory of Fertility Decline. LC 81-68983. (Population & Social Structure Ser.). 1982. 29.50 (ISBN 0-12-155080-X). Acad Pr.
Caldwell, J. Edward. Business Simulation: Audio Tech Company. (gr. 9-12). 1984. 5.55 (ISBN 0-538-07165-6, G165). SW Pub.
Caldwell, J. J., jt. ed. see Atreya, S. K.
Caldwell, James A., jt. auth. see White, Alvin D.
Caldwell, James F. The History of a Brigade of South Carolinians: Known First as "Greggs" & Subsequently as "McGowan's Brigade". 247p. 1984. 25.00 (ISBN 0-89029-001-6). Pr of Morningside.
Caldwell, James R. Beauty Is Truth...Five Studies in Literature. (University of California Publication in English Vol. 8 No. 11). 1940. Repr. 20.00 (ISBN 0-8274-1919-8). R West.
Caldwell, Jan. A Re-Evaluation of the Hyla Bistincta Species Group, with Descriptions of Three New Species (Anura: Hylidae) (Occasional Papers: No. 28). 37p. 1974. pap. 3.00 color plate (ISBN 0-686-79835-X). U of KS Mus Nat Hist.
Caldwell, Joan G. & McDermott, Betty N. Handbook of the Collection. LC 80-81414. (Illus.). 220p. 1980. pap. 5.95 (ISBN 0-89494-009-0). New Orleans Mus Art.
Caldwell, John. Amphetamines & Related Stimulants, Vol. 1. 216p. 1980. 69.00 (ISBN 0-8493-5347-5). CRC Pr.
--Caldwell on Competitive Cross-Country Skiing. LC 79-18726. (Illus.). 1979. 10.95 (ISBN 0-8289-0359-X). Greene.
--Cross-Country Ski Book. rev. 6th ed. LC 81-13554. (Illus.). 192p. 1981. 12.95 (ISBN 0-8289-0454-5); pap. 7.95 (ISBN 0-8289-0455-3). Greene.
--The Cross-Country Ski Book. 7th ed. 196p. 1984. pap. 8.95 (ISBN 0-8289-0544-4). Greene.
--Desperate Voyage. 250p. 1985. pap. 11.50 (ISBN 0-246-12708-2, Pub. by Granada England). Sheridan.
--Editing Early Music. (Early Music Ser.: No. 5). 144p. 1985. 29.95 (ISBN 0-19-816143-3); pap. 12.95 (ISBN 0-19-816142-5). Oxford U Pr.
--English Keyboard Music Before the Nineteenth Century. (Music Bks.). 353p. 1985. pap. 6.95 (ISBN 0-486-24851-8). Dover.
--Excuses, Excuses: How to Get Out of Practically Anything. LC 81-43028. (Illus.). 48p. (gr. 3-6). 1981. PLB 8.89g (ISBN 0-690-04125-X). Crowell Jr Bks.
--George R. Stewart. LC 81-67300. (Western Writers Ser.: No. 46). (Illus., Orig.). 1981. pap. text ed. 2.00x (ISBN 0-88430-070-6). Boise St Univ.
--Joan Witek. (Illus.). 36p. 1984. pap. 4.95 (ISBN 0-88039-007-7). Carnegie.
--Medieval Music. LC 77-94060. (Illus.). 304p. 1978. 20.00x (ISBN 0-253-33731-3). Ind U Pr.
--Medieval Music. 306p. 1981. 40.00x (ISBN 0-09-120900-5, Pub. by Barrie & Jenkins England). State Mutual Bk.
--Mug Shots. 64p. (Orig.). 1980. pap. 2.95 (ISBN 0-938782-00-2). Fantaco.
--Rustlings Above Saururus Hollow. Brune, Genevieve A., ed. LC 85-60024. (Illus.). 90p. 1985. 8.00 (ISBN 0-932777-00-7). Caldwell Pubns.
Caldwell, John & Brady, Michael. Citizen Racing. (Illus.). 192p. (Orig.). 1982. pap. 9.95 (ISBN 0-89886-041-5). Mountaineers.
--Citizen Racing. 1983. 15.25 (ISBN 0-8446-6045-0). Peter Smith.
Caldwell, John & Jakoby, William B., eds. Biological Basis of Detoxification. LC 82-18933. (Biochemical Pharmacology & Toxicology). 1983. 59.50 (ISBN 0-12-155060-5). Acad Pr.
Caldwell, John, et al. Sean Scully. Maloy, Kate, ed. (Illus.). 36p. 1985. pap. write for info. (ISBN 0-88039-010-7). Mus Art Carnegie.
Caldwell, John C. African Rural-Urban Migration: The Movement to Ghana's Towns. LC 69-17496. 257p. 1969. 24.00x (ISBN 0-231-03269-2). Columbia U Pr.
--Let's Visit China Today. rev. ed. LC 72-12092. (Let's Visit Ser.). (Illus.). 96p. (gr. 3-7). 1973. lib. bdg. 9.89 (ISBN 0-685-25270-1, A42941, JD-J). Har-Row.
--South of Tokyo. 1978. Repr. of 1957 ed. lib. bdg. 20.00 (ISBN 0-8492-4018-2). R West.
Caldwell, John C. & Caldwell, Patricia. Limiting Population Growth: The Ford Foundation Contribution. 160p. 1985. 22.50 (ISBN 0-86187-576-1, Pub. by Frances Pinter). Longwood Pub Group.
Caldwell, John C., jt. auth. see Popescu, Julian.
Caldwell, John C., et al, eds. Population Growth & Socioeconomic Change in West Africa. LC 74-17409. 763p. (Orig.). 1975. text ed. write for info. Population Coun.
--Population Growth & Socioeconomic Change in West Africa. LC 74-17409. 736p. 1975. 47.00x (ISBN 0-231-03732-5). Columbia U Pr.
Caldwell, John E. Tour Through Part of Virginia in the Summer of 1808. Rachal, William M., ed. 1951. 2.00 (ISBN 0-685-09014-0). Dietz.
Caldwell, John R. Seven New Artists: Pittsburgh Today. 24p. (Orig.). 1984. pap. 5.00 (ISBN 0-88039-008-5). Carnegie.
Caldwell, John S. The Jumping Plant-Lice of Ohio (Homoptera: Chermidae) 1938. 1.00 (ISBN 0-86727-033-0). Ohio Bio Survey.
Caldwell, Joseph. The Deer at the River. 228p. 1984. 15.45i (ISBN 0-316-12438-9). Little.
--The Deer at the River. (Penguin Fiction Ser.). 256p. 1985. pap. 5.95 (ISBN 0-14-008269-7). Penguin.
--In Such Dark Places. 230p. 1978. 8.95 (ISBN 0-374-17648-5). FS&G.
--In Such Dark Places. 1984. pap. 6.95 (ISBN 0-932870-54-6). Alyson Pubns.
Caldwell, Joseph R. & Hall, Robert L., eds. Hopewellian Studies. facsimile ed. (Scientific Papers Ser.: Vol. XII). (Illus.). 156p. 1977. pap. 4.00 (ISBN 0-89792-026-0). Ill St Museum.
Caldwell, Justin. The Sleeping Porch. LC 78-17912. (Lost Roads Poetry Ser.: No. 16). 1979. pap. 4.00 (ISBN 0-918786-17-7). Lost Roads.
Caldwell, K. P. S., ed. Urinary Incontinence. (Illus.). 176p. 1975. 49.50 (ISBN 0-8089-0877-4, 790760). Grune.
Caldwell, Kathryn S. The Principle. 193p. 1983. 9.95 (ISBN 0-934126-39-9). Randall Bk Co.
Caldwell, Lawrence & Diebold, William, Jr. Soviet-American Relations in the 1980's: Super-Power Politics & East-West Trade. (Illus.). 1980. pap. 18.95 (ISBN 0-07-009616-3). McGraw.
Caldwell, Lawrence T. Soviet-American Relations: One-half Decade of Detente Problems & Issues. (The Atlantic Papers: No. 75/5). (Orig.). 1976. pap. text ed. 4.75x (ISBN 0-686-83640-5). Allanheld.
Caldwell, Lesley, jt. ed. see Day, Graham.
Caldwell, Louis. The Adventure of Becoming One. (Ultra Bks.). 80p. 1981. 5.95 (ISBN 0-8010-2334-3). Baker Bk.
--After the Tassel Is Moved. (Ultra Bks Ser.). 1968. 4.95 (ISBN 0-8010-2332-7). Baker Bk.

Caldwell, Louis O. Another Tassel Is Moved: Guidelines for College Graduates. (Ultra Books Ser). 1970. 4.95 (ISBN 0-8010-2343-2). Baker Bk.
--A Birthday Remembrance. LC 77-7043. (Illus.). pap. 20.00 (ISBN 0-8357-9001-0, 2016349). Bks Demand UMI.
--Congratulations: A Graduation Remembrance. (Ultra Books). 64p. 1983. 4.95 (ISBN 0-8010-2485-4). Baker Bk.
--Good Morning, Lord: Devotions for College Students. (Good Morning Lord Ser.). 1971. 4.95 (ISBN 0-8010-2324-6). Baker Bk.
--Good Morning, Lord: Meditations for Modern Marrieds. (Good Morning Lord Ser.). 1974. 3.95 (ISBN 0-8010-2351-3). Baker Bk.
--Something Good for Those Who Feel Bad: Positive Solutions for Negative Emotions. 1985. pap. 4.95 (ISBN 0-8010-2505-2). Baker Bk.
--You Can Develop a Positive Self-Image. (Christian Counseling Aids Ser.). pap. 1.25 (ISBN 0-8010-2503-6). Baker Bk.
--You Can Find Help Through Counseling: Christain Counseling Aids. 1983. pap. 0.95 (ISBN 0-8010-2484-6). Baker Bk.
--You Can Overcome Your Fears, Phobias, & Worries. 1985. pap. 1.25 (ISBN 0-8010-2506-0). Baker Bk.
--You Can Prevent or Overcome a Nervous Breakdown. (Christian Counseling Aids Ser.). 1978. pap. 0.95 (ISBN 0-8010-2415-3). Baker Bk.
--You Can Stop Feeling Guilty. (Christian Counseling Aids Ser.). 1978. pap. 1.25 (ISBN 0-8010-2414-5). Baker Bk.
Caldwell, Louise. Timothy: Young Pastor. (BibLearn Ser.). (gr. 1-6). 1978. 5.95 (ISBN 0-8054-4239-1, 4242-39). Broadman.
Caldwell, Lynne. Nutrition Education for the Patient: The Handout Manual. LC 84-50687. 150p. 1984. pap. 17.50 (ISBN 0-89313-043-5). G F Stickley Co.
Caldwell, Lynton K. International Environmental Policy: Emergence & Dimensions. (Duke Press Policy Studies). 450p. 1984. PLB 37.50x (ISBN 0-8223-0571-2); pap. text ed. 14.75x (ISBN 0-8223-0572-0). Duke.
--Man & His Environment: Policy & Administration. (Man & His Environment Ser.). 172p. 1975. pap. text ed. 14.00 scp (ISBN 0-06-041146-5, HarpC). Har-Row.
--Science & the National Environmental Policy Act: Redirecting Policy Through Procedural Reform. 1982. 18.50 (ISBN 0-8173-0111-9); pap. 8.75 (ISBN 0-8173-0112-7). U of Ala Pr.
Caldwell, Lynton K., et al. Citizens & the Environment: Case Studies in Popular Action. LC 75-31422. (Midland Books: No. 205). 480p. 1976. pap. 7.95x (ISBN 0-253-20205-1). Ind U Pr.
Caldwell, Mark & Kendrick, Walter, eds. The Treasury of English Poetry. LC 82-46028. 768p. 1984. 16.95 (ISBN 0-385-18533-2). Doubleday.
Caldwell, Martha B. Annals of Shawnee Methodist Mission & Indian Manual Labor School. 2nd ed. LC 39-28738. (Illus.). 120p. 1977. pap. 2.95 (ISBN 0-87726-005-2). Kansas St Hist.
Caldwell, Mary. Morning, Rabbit, Morning. LC 81-47724. (Illus.). 32p. (ps-1). 1982. 9.53i (ISBN 0-06-020939-9); PLB 9.89g (ISBN 0-06-020940-2). HarpJ.
Caldwell, Michael D., jt. auth. see Rombeau, John L.
Caldwell, Nancy L. A History of Brooke County. 1975. 4.00 (ISBN 0-87012-235-5). McClain.
Caldwell, Oliver J. A Secret War: Americans in China, 1944-1945. LC 73-7755. (Arcturus Books Paperbacks). 1973. pap. 2.65 (ISBN 0-8093-0650-6). S Ill U Pr.
Caldwell, Otis W. & Courtis, Stuart A. Then & Now in Education, Eighteen Forty-Five to Nineteen Twenty-Three. LC 77-165711. (American Education Ser, No. 2). 1971. Repr. of 1923 ed. 19.00 (ISBN 0-405-03700-7). Ayer Co Pubs.
Caldwell, Pablo. Diccionario de Modismos Ingleses. 496p. (Eng. & Span.). 1973. 17.50 (ISBN 0-686-56672-6, S-33065). French & Eur.
Caldwell, Patricia. The Puritan Conversion Narrative: The Beginnings of American Expression. LC 82-22772. (Cambridge Studies in American Literature & Culture). 192p. 1983. 19.95 (ISBN 0-521-25460-4). Cambridge U Pr.
Caldwell, Patricia, jt. auth. see Caldwell, John C.
Caldwell, Patsy, jt. auth. see Weinberg, Robert.
Caldwell, Peggy. Without a Brush. (Illus.). 76p. (Orig.). 1978. pap. 6.95 (ISBN 0-917119-38-X, 45-1209). Priscillas Pubns.
Caldwell, Peter. Draw Boats & Harbours. LC 78-14071. (Learn to Draw Ser.). (Illus.). 1980. pap. 2.25 (ISBN 0-8008-4578-1, Pentalic). Taplinger.
Caldwell, R. A Comparative Grammar of the Dravidian or South-Indian Family of Languages. Wyatt, J. L. & Pillai, T. Ramakrishna, eds. 640p. 1980. Repr. of 1913 ed. lib. bdg. 75.00 (ISBN 0-89760-111-4). Telegraph Bks.
Caldwell, R. L., jt. ed. see Lidicker, W. Z., Jr.
Caldwell, Ronald J. The Era of the French Revolution: A Bibliography of the History of Western Civilization, 1789-1799. LC 84-48397. (Reference Library of Social Science). 800p. 1985. lib. bdg. 200.00 (ISBN 0-8240-8794-1). Garland Pub.
Caldwell, S. F. Instead of Shooting Reagan: Love Poems to the Whirled. 1985. 5.95 (ISBN 0-533-06482-1). Vantage.
Caldwell, Stan R. & Crissman, Randy D., eds. Design for Ice Forces. LC 83-70400. 224p. 1983. pap. 21.25x (ISBN 0-87262-356-4). Am Soc Civil Eng.
Caldwell, Stephen A. A Banking History of Louisiana. Bruchey, Stuart, ed. LC 80-1137. (The Rise of Commercial Banking Ser.). 1981. Repr. of 1935 ed. lib. bdg. 12.00x (ISBN 0-405-13637-4). Ayer Co Pubs.
Caldwell, Taylor. Answer As a Man. 480p. 1981. pap. 3.95 (ISBN 0-449-24467-9, Crest). Fawcett.
--Answer As a Man. (General Ser.). 1984. lib. bdg. 15.95 (ISBN 0-8161-3746-3, Large Print Bks); pap. 11.95 (ISBN 0-8161-3766-8). G K Hall.
--Answer as a Man. 22.95 (ISBN 0-88411-143-1, Pub. by Aeonian Pr). Amereon Ltd.
--The Arm & the Darkness. 1974. Repr. of 1943 ed. lib. bdg. 27.95 (ISBN 0-88411-151-2, Pub. by Aeonian Pr). Amereon Ltd.
--The Arm & the Darkness. 608p. 1982. pap. 3.50 (ISBN 0-449-23616-1, Crest). Fawcett.
--The Balance Wheel. 1974. Repr. of 1951 ed. lib. bdg. 24.95 (ISBN 0-88411-153-9, Pub. by Aeonian Pr). Amereon Ltd.
--The Balance Wheel. 512p. 1985. pap. 4.50 (ISBN 0-515-08083-7). Jove Pubns.
--Bright Flows the River. 1984. pap. 3.95 (ISBN 0-449-20655-6, Crest). Fawcett.
--Captains & the Kings. LC 74-178831. 720p. 1972. 9.95 (ISBN 0-385-01309-4). Doubleday.
--Captains & the Kings. 1983. pap. 3.95 (ISBN 0-449-20562-2, Crest). Fawcett.
--Ceremony of the Innocent. 1978. pap. 3.50 (ISBN 0-449-23977-2, Crest). Fawcett.
--Ceremony of the Innocent. 1984. pap. 3.95 (ISBN 0-449-20626-2, Crest). Fawcett.
--Dear & Glorious Physician. 608p. 1984. pap. 3.95 (ISBN 0-553-22788-2). Bantam.
--The Devil's Advocate. 1976. Repr. of 1952 ed. lib. bdg. 19.95 (ISBN 0-88411-163-6, Pub. by Aeonian Pr). Amereon Ltd.
--The Devil's Advocate. 352p. 1984. pap. 3.50 (ISBN 0-515-07864-6). Jove Pubns.
--The Devil's Advocate. 352p. 1985. pap. 3.50 (ISBN 0-515-07864-6). Jove Pubns.
--Dialogues with the Devil. 1978. pap. 2.50 (ISBN 0-449-23714-1, Crest). Fawcett.
--Dialogues with the Devil. 15.95 (ISBN 0-89190-279-1, Pub. by Am Repr). Amereon Ltd.
--Dynasty of Death. 864p. 1985. pap. 3.95 (ISBN 0-515-08478-6). Jove Pubns.
--The Eagles Gather. 602p. Repr. of 1940 ed. lib. bdg. 27.95 (ISBN 0-88411-165-2, Pub. by Aeonian Pr). Amereon Ltd.
--The Eagles Gather. 448p. 1984. pap. 3.50 (ISBN 0-515-07868-9). Jove Pubns.
--The Earth Is the Lord's. 1985. pap. 4.50 (ISBN 0-515-08111-6). Jove Pubns.
--The Earth Is the Lord's: A Tale of the Rise of Genghis Kahn. 1974. Repr. of 1941 ed. lib. bdg. 25.95x (ISBN 0-88411-154-7, Pub. by Aeonian Pr). Amereon Ltd.
--The Final Hour. 1974. Repr. of 1944 ed. lib. bdg. 25.95x (ISBN 0-88411-152-0). Amereon Ltd.
--The Final Hour. 608p. (Orig.). 1981. pap. 3.50 (ISBN 0-449-24221-8, Crest). Fawcett.
--Glory & the Lightning. 544p. 1982. pap. 3.50 (ISBN 0-449-23972-1, Crest). Fawcett.
--Grandmother & the Priests. 432p. 1982. pap. 3.50 (ISBN 0-449-24027-4, Crest). Fawcett.
--Great Lion of God. 704p. 1982. pap. 3.50 (ISBN 0-449-24096-7, Crest). Fawcett.
--Late Clara Beame. 1978. pap. 1.95 (ISBN 0-449-23725-7, Crest). Fawcett.
--Let Love Come Last. 1974. Repr. of 1949 ed. lib. bdg. 20.95 (ISBN 0-88411-160-1, Pub. by Aeonian Pr). Amereon Ltd.
--Let Love Come Last. 448p. 1984. pap. 3.95 (ISBN 0-515-07919-7). Jove Pubns.
--The Listener. 288p. Repr. of 1960 ed. lib. bdg. 16.95 (ISBN 0-88411-166-0, Pub. by Aeonian Pr). Amereon Ltd.
--The Listener. 1978. pap. 3.95 (ISBN 0-553-24483-3). Bantam.
--Maggie: Her Marriage. 204p. Repr. of 1953 ed. lib. bdg. 14.95 (ISBN 0-88411-169-5, Pub. by Aeonian Pr). Amereon Ltd.
--Maggie: Her Marriage. 160p. 1977. pap. 2.50 (ISBN 0-449-24195-5, Crest). Fawcett.
--Melissa. 1974. Repr. of 1948 ed. lib. bdg. 20.95 (ISBN 0-88411-159-8, Pub. by Aeonian Pr). Amereon Ltd.
--Melissa. 1984. pap. 3.95 (ISBN 0-515-07882-4). Jove Pubns.
--Never Victorious Never Defeated. 1976. Repr. of 1954 ed. lib. bdg. 25.95x (ISBN 0-88411-162-8, Pub. by Aeonian Pr). Amereon Ltd.
--Never Victorious, Never Defeated. 576p. 1984. pap. 3.95 (ISBN 0-446-31076-X). Warner Bks.
--No One Hears But Him. 1977. pap. 2.50 (ISBN 0-449-24030-4, Crest). Fawcett.
--On Growing up Tough. 160p. Repr. of 1971 ed. lib. bdg. 13.95x (ISBN 0-88411-170-9, Pub. by Aeonian Pr.). Amereon Ltd.
--On Growing up Tough. 1979. pap. 1.95 (ISBN 0-449-24006-1, Crest). Fawcett.
--On Growing up Tough: An Irreverent Memoir. 160p. Date not set. pap. 9.95 (ISBN 0-8159-6402-1). Devin.
--A Pillar of Iron. 768p. 1982. pap. 3.50 (ISBN 0-449-23952-7, Crest). Fawcett.
--A Prologue to Love. 768p. 1980. pap. 3.95 (ISBN 0-553-24012-9). Bantam.
--The Sound of Thunder. 576p. 1981. pap. 4.50 (ISBN 0-553-24916-9). Bantam.
--Strong City. 1974. Repr. of 1942 ed. lib. bdg. 27.95x (ISBN 0-88411-158-X, Pub. by Aeonian Pr). Amereon Ltd.
--The Strong City. 544p. 1984. pap. 3.95 (ISBN 0-515-07873-5). Jove Pubns.
--Tender Victory. 512p. 1984. pap. 3.95 (ISBN 0-446-31082-4). Warner Bks.
--Testimony of Two Men. 704p. 1984. pap. 3.95 (ISBN 0-449-20572-X, Crest). Fawcett.
--Testimony of Two Men. 22.95 (ISBN 0-88411-171-7, Pub. by Aeonian Pr). Amereon Ltd.
--There Was a Time. 1974. Repr. of 1947 ed. lib. bdg. 23.95x (ISBN 0-88411-157-1, Pub. by Aeonian Pr). Amereon Ltd.
--There Was a Time. 512p. 1985. pap. 4.50 (ISBN 0-515-08175-2). Jove Pubns.
--This Side of Innocence. 1976. Repr. of 1946 ed. lib. bdg. 24.95x (ISBN 0-88411-164-4, Pub. by Aeonian Pr). Amereon Ltd.
--This Side of Innocence. 512p. 1984. pap. 3.95 (ISBN 0-446-31248-7). Warner Bks.
--Time No Longer. 1974. Repr. of 1941 ed. lib. bdg. 19.95x (ISBN 0-88411-161-X, Pub. by Aeonian Pr). Amereon Ltd.
--Time No Longer. 320p. 1984. pap. 3.50 (ISBN 0-515-07875-1). Jove Pubns.
--To Look & Pass. 288p. 1978. pap. 2.25 (ISBN 0-449-14055-5, GM). Fawcett.
--The Turnbulls. 1974. Repr. of 1943 ed. lib. bdg. 24.95x (ISBN 0-88411-155-5, Pub. by Aeonian Pr). Amereon Ltd.
--The Turnbulls. 512p. (Orig.). 1985. pap. 4.50 (ISBN 0-515-08044-6). Jove Pubns.
--Wicked Angel. 224p. Repr. of 1965 ed. lib. bdg. 14.95x (ISBN 0-88411-167-9, Pub. by Aeonian Pr). Amereon Ltd.
--Wicked Angel. 1980. pap. 1.95 (ISBN 0-449-23950-0, Crest). Fawcett.
--The Wide House. 1974. Repr. of 1945 ed. lib. bdg. 25.95 (ISBN 0-88411-156-3, Pub. by Aeonian Pr). Amereon Ltd.
--The Wide House. 560p. 1984. pap. 3.95 (ISBN 0-515-08057-8). Jove Pubns.
--Your Sins & Mine. 156p. Repr. of 1955 ed. lib. bdg. 11.95x (ISBN 0-88411-168-7, Pub. by Aeonian Pr). Amereon Ltd.
--Your Sins & Mine. 128p. 1984. pap. 2.50 (ISBN 0-446-31101-4). Warner Bks.
Caldwell, Taylor & Stearn, Jess. I, Judas. 1978. pap. 3.95 (ISBN 0-451-13295-5, Sig). NAL.
--The Romance of Atlantis. 272p. 1978. pap. 2.25 (ISBN 0-449-23787-7, Crest). Fawcett.
Caldwell, Thomas, ed. The Golden Book of Modern English Poetry: 1870-1920. 1978. Repr. of 1922 ed. lib. bdg. 25.00 (ISBN 0-8495-0755-3). Arden Lib.
Caldwell, Thomas, et al. An Akkadian Grammar: A Translation of Lehrbuch Des Akkadischen. 3rd ed. 1978. pap. 19.95 (ISBN 0-87462-444-4). Marquette.
Caldwell, Thomas D., ed. see Bellairs, Herbert J. & Helsel, James L.
Caldwell, Wallace E. Hellenic Conceptions of Peace. LC 19-18236. (Columbia University Studies in the Social Sciences: No. 195). Repr. of 1919 ed. 12.50 (ISBN 0-404-51195-3). AMS Pr.
Caldwell, William. Travel Babble. LC 72-95994. (Illus.). 196p. 5.00 (ISBN 0-8323-0209-0). Binford.
Caldwell, William E. Family Safari. LC 59-14340. (Illus.). 1959. 4.95 (ISBN 0-8323-0081-0). Binford.
Caldwell, William L. Cancer of the Urinary Bladder: With Emphasis on Treatment by Irradiation. LC 72-96980. (Illus.). 128p. 1970. 12.50 (ISBN 0-87527-003-4). Green.
Caldwell-Wilson, Marolyn. Flight into Danger. 192p. 1984. 12.95 (ISBN 0-8027-0778-5). Walker & Co.
--Whirlwind. (Judy Sullivance Romance Ser.). 1985. 14.95 (ISBN 0-8027-0850-1). Walker & Co.
Caleder, Alexander. Fables of Aesop According to Sir Roger L'Estrange. (Illus.). 124p. (gr. k-6). pap. 3.50 (ISBN 0-486-21780-9). Dover.
Calef, John, ed. Siege of Penobscot by the Rebels & the Proceedings of the General Assembly & of the Council of the State of Massachusetts Bay Relating to the Penobscot Expedition. LC 78-140857. (Eyewitness Accounts of the American Revolution Ser., No. 3). (Illus.). 1970. Repr. of 1780 ed. 9.50 (ISBN 0-405-01226-8). Ayer Co Pubs.
Calef, Wesley. Private Grazing & Public Lands. Bruchey, Stuart, ed. LC 78-56701. (Management of Public Land Law in the U. S. Ser.). 1979. Repr. of 1960 ed. lib. bdg. 25.50x (ISBN 0-405-11321-8). Ayer Co Pubs.
Calella, John. Cooking Naturally. LC 78-54342. (Illus.). 1978. pap. 5.95 (ISBN 0-915904-35-7). And-Or Pr.
Calendar, Richard, jt. auth. see Stent, Gunther S.
Calenko, M. S., et al. Twenty-Two Papers on Algebra, Number Theory, & Differential Geometry. LC 51-5559. (Translations Ser.: No. 2, Vol. 37). 1964. 34.00 (ISBN 0-8218-1737-X, TRANS 2-37). Am Math.
--Twelve Papers on Algebra, Number Theory & Topology. LC 80-20715. (Translations Ser.: No. 2, Vol. 58). 1966. 34.00 (ISBN 0-8218-1758-2, TRANS 2-58). Am Math.
Calenoff, Leonid. Radiology of Spinal Cord Injury. LC 80-27532. (Illus.). 573p. 1981. text ed. 89.50 (ISBN 0-8016-1114-8). Mosby.
Calero, Henry H. & Oskam, Bob. Negotiate the Deal You Want. 320p. 1983. 16.95 (ISBN 0-89696-191-5, An Everest House Book). Dodd.
Calero, Henry H., jt. auth. see Nierenberg, Gerard I.
Caleron, Eduardo, et al. Eduardo el Curandero: The Words of a Peruvian Healer. (Illus.). 200p. 1982. 20.00 (ISBN 0-913028-94-0); pap. 7.95 (ISBN 0-913028-95-9). North Atlantic.
Caley, Earle R. & Richards, John C. Theophrastus on Stones. 248p. 1956. 6.00 (ISBN 0-8142-0033-8). Ohio St U Pr.
Caley, Earle R., jt. ed. see Schwind-Belkin, Johanna.
Caley, Michael E., jt. auth. see Miller, Samuel K.
Caley, Ray L. The Ragged Statue & Other Stories. (Illus.). 75p. 1982. 12.95 (ISBN 0-910987-01-7); pap. 8.95 (ISBN 0-910987-00-9). Dragon's Lair.
Caley, Ray Leland. New & Original Opera Librettos. LC 83-70679. (Illus.). 283p. 1983. 20.00 (ISBN 0-910987-03-3). Dragon's Lair.
Calfa, Ambroise. Dictionnaire Armenien-Francais, 2 vols. 1038p. (Armenian & Fr.). 1973. Set. pap. 49.95 (ISBN 0-686-56934-2, M-6056). French & Eur.
Calfee, Robert C. & Drum, Priscilla A., eds. Teaching Reading in Compensatory Classes. (Orig.). 1979. pap. text ed. 6.50 (ISBN 0-87207-725-X, 725). Intl Reading.
Calfhill, James. An Answer to John Martiall's Treatise of the Cross. 1846. 31.00 (ISBN 0-384-07020-5). Johnson Repr.
Calhoon, Richard P., et al. Coaching in Supervision: Instructor's Manual. Rev. ed. 191p. 1981. 5.00 (ISBN 0-686-39475-5). U of NC Inst Gov.
--Coaching in Supervision: Student's Manual. Rev. ed. 98p. 2.00 (ISBN 0-686-39476-3). U of NC Inst Gov.
Calhoun, Bruce. Council Fires: A Story of the Chippewa Indians in the Mid-1800s & the Treaties of the Great White Father. 158p. pap. cancelled (ISBN 0-89404-009-X). Aztex.
Calhoun, C. Raymond. Typhoon: The Other Enemy: The Third Fleet & the Pacific Storm of December 1944. (Illus.). 261p. 1981. 16.95 (ISBN 0-87021-510-8); bulk rates avail. Naval Inst Pr.
Calhoun, Calfrey C. Managing the Learning Process in Business Education. 624p. 1980. text ed. write for info. (ISBN 0-534-00834-8). Wadsworth Pub.
Calhoun, Calfrey C., ed. see Rhodes, George S.
Calhoun, Catherine. Egyptian Designs. (The International Design Library). (Illus.). 48p. 1983. pap. 3.50 (ISBN 0-88045-012-6). Stemmer Hse.
Calhoun, Chad. The Hidden Princess. (Brad Spear Ser.: No. 6). (Orig.). 1982. pap. 2.25 (ISBN 0-440-03727-1, Banbury). Dell.
--The Lady Rustler. (Agent Brad Spear Ser.: No. 10). 304p. 1982. pap. 2.25 (ISBN 0-440-04628-9, Emerald). Dell.
Calhoun, Cheshire & Solomon, Robert C., eds. What Is an Emotion? Classic Readings in Philisophical Psychology. 1984. 24.95x (ISBN 0-19-503355-8); pap. 10.95x (ISBN 0-19-503304-3). Oxford U Pr.
Calhoun, Craig. The Question of Class Struggle: The Social Foundation of Popular Radicalism During the Industrial Revolution. LC 81-2018. xiv, 322p. 1982. lib. bdg. 25.00x (ISBN 0-226-09090-6, PHOEN); pap. 11.00x (ISBN 0-226-09091-4). U of Chicago Pr.
Calhoun, Daniel F. The United Front: The Tuc & the Russians, 1923-1928. LC 75-23486. (Soviet & East European Studies). pap. 115.50 (ISBN 0-317-20618-4, 2024572). Bks Demand UMI.
--The United Front: The TUC & the Russians, 1923-1928. LC 75-23846. (Soviet & East European Studies). pap. 115.30 (ISBN 0-317-26273-4, 2055703). Bks Demand UMI.
Calhoun, Daniel H. The Intelligence of a People. (Illus.). 392p. 1973. 42.50 (ISBN 0-691-04619-0, 400); pap. 11.50x (ISBN 0-691-00587-7). Princeton U Pr.
--Professional Lives in America: Structure & Aspiration, 1750-1850. LC 65-22042. (Center for the Study of the History of Liberty in America Ser). (Illus.). Repr. of 1965 ed. 61.80 (ISBN 0-8357-9174-2, 2017745). Bks Demand UMI.
Calhoun, D'Ann, ed. see Farr, Naunerle.
Calhoun, D'Ann, ed. see Verne, Jules.
Calhoun, David. Yearbook of Science & the Future 1984. 448p. 1983. write for info. Ency Brit Inc.
--Yearbook of Science & the Future 1984: 1985. 448p. 1984. write for info. Ency Brit Inc.
Calhoun, David, ed. Yearbook of Science & the Future, 1983. 448p. 1982. write for info. (ISBN 0-85229-384-4). Ency Brit Inc.
Calhoun, David, jt. ed. see Core, Lucy.
Calhoun, Don. Dando Shaft. LC 65-22273. 190p. 1974. pap. 1.50 (ISBN 0-8128-1748-6). Stein & Day.

--Is There Life After Advertising? 1984. pap. 2.95 (ISBN 0-8128-8031-5). Stein & Day.
--The Oceanic Quest: Toward a Religion Beyond Illusion. 1983. 10.95 (ISBN 0-533-05591-1). Vantage.
Calhoun, Donald W. Social Science in an Age of Change. 2nd ed. LC 77-489. (Illus.). 1978. text ed. 23.95 scp (ISBN 0-06-041148-1, HarpC); instructor's manual avail. (ISBN 0-06-361149-X); scp wkbk. 10.50 (ISBN 0-06-041149-X). Har-Row.
--Sport, Culture & Personality. LC 80-84355. (Illus.). 256p. (Orig.). 1981. pap. text ed. 12.95 (ISBN 0-918438-68-3). Leisure Pr.
Calhoun, Dorothy, ed. see Hardy, Thomas.
Calhoun, Elizabeth. Twenty Simple Solar Projects: Fun, Practical, Attractive, Easy-to-Build Projects, Powered by the Sun. (Illus.). 272p. 1983. 16.95 (ISBN 0-87857-476-X). Rodale Pr Inc.
Calhoun, Frances B. Miss Minerva & William Green Hill. LC 75-20498. (Tennesseana Editions Series). (Illus.). 286p. 1976. 9.50 (ISBN 0-87049-182-2). U of Tenn Pr.
Calhoun, Fred. Physics for Divers. (Illus.). 1978. pap. 4.50 (ISBN 0-916974-28-6). NAUI.
Calhoun, Fred & Christensen, Chris. A Divers Guide to Cape Ann. (Illus.). 36p. 1977. pap. 4.50 (ISBN 0-916974-25-1). NAUI.
Calhoun, Fryar, jt. auth. see Cassady, Jim.
Calhoun, George M. Athenian Clubs in Politics & Litigation. LC 74-125017. (Research & Source Works Ser.: No. 496). 1970. Repr. of 1913 ed. lib. bdg. 15.00 (ISBN 0-8337-0453-2). B Franklin.
--Business Life of Ancient Athens. LC 68-18490. 175p. 1968. Repr. of 1926 ed. 18.50 (ISBN 0-8154-0043-8). Cooper Sq.
--The Growth of Criminal Law in Ancient Greece. LC 73-10874. x, 149p. 1974. Repr. of 1927 ed. lib. bdg. 15.00x (ISBN 0-8371-7043-5, CACL). Greenwood.
Calhoun, George M. & Delamere, Catherine. A Working Bibliography of Greek Law. (Harvard Series of Legal Bibliographies: Vol. 1). xix, 144p. 1980. Repr. of 1927 ed. lib. bdg. 35.00 (ISBN 0-89941-133-9). W S Hein.
Calhoun, H. M. Twixt North & South. 1974. 10.00 (ISBN 0-87012-166-9). McClain.
Calhoun, Horace B. Two for the Show. LC 82-3725. (Muppet Press Bks.). (Illus.). 32p. (gr. 1-4). 1982. pap. 1.95 (ISBN 0-394-85409-8). Random.
Calhoun, J. & Acocella, J. Psychology of Adjustment. 2nd ed. LC 82-18078. 1983. text ed. 25.00 (ISBN 0-394-32906-6, RanC); study guide 8.95 (ISBN 0-394-33116-8). Random.
Calhoun, James & Kempe, Helen. Louisiana Almanac 1979-80. 10th ed. (Illus.). 1979. pap. 11.95 (ISBN 0-88289-182-0). Pelican.
Calhoun, James, jt. auth. see Jolly, Ellen R.
Calhoun, James, ed. Louisiana Sports Record Book. 104p. 1971. pap. 3.95 (ISBN 0-911116-55-9). Pelican.
--The Real Spiro Agnew. 127p. 1970. 10.00 (ISBN 0-911116-29-X). Pelican.
Calhoun, James & Kempe, Helen, eds. Louisiana Almanac, 1975-76 Ed. (Illus.). 496p. 1975. 11.95 (ISBN 0-88289-038-7, 039-5). Pelican.
Calhoun, James, jt. ed. see Calhoun, Nancy.
Calhoun, James, ed. see Reeves, Miriam G.
Calhoun, James, ed. see Schlappi, Elizabeth.
Calhoun, James F., jt. auth. see Goodstein, Leonard D.
Calhoun, Janes, jt. ed. see Calhoun, Nancy H.
Calhoun, John B., ed. Environment & Population: Problems of Adaptation. (Illus.). 508p. 1983. 71.00 (ISBN 0-03-063337-0). Praeger.
Calhoun, John C. Calhoun: Basic Documents. Anderson, John M., ed. 330p. 24.95x (ISBN 0-271-00322-7, Pub. by Bald Eagle). Pa St U Pr.
--A Disquisition on Government. 1958. 11.25 (ISBN 0-8446-1099-2). Peter Smith.
--Papers of John C. Calhoun, Vol. 4, 1819-1820. Hemphill, W. Edwin, ed. LC 59-10351. xxii, 802p. 1969. 34.95x (ISBN 0-87249-150-1). U of SC Pr.
--Papers of John C. Calhoun, Vol. 5, 1820-1821. Hemphill, W. Edwin, ed. LC 59-10351. (Illus.). xxxii, 762p. 1971. 34.95x (ISBN 0-87249-210-9). U of SC Pr.
--The Papers of John C. Calhoun, Vol. 7, 1822-1823. Hemphill, W. Edwin, ed. LC 59-10351. iiv, 610p. 1973. 34.95x (ISBN 0-87249-288-5). U of SC Pr.
--The Papers of John C. Calhoun, Vol. 9, 1824-1825. Hemphill, W. Edwin, ed. LC 59-10351. lxvi, 684p. 1976. 34.95x (ISBN 0-87249-337-7). U of SC Pr.
--The Papers of John C. Calhoun, Vol. 10, 1825-1829. Wilson, Clyde N. & Hemphill, W. Edwin, eds. LC 59-10351. xlii, 728p. 1977. 34.95x (ISBN 0-87249-349-0). U of SC Pr.
--The Papers of John C. Calhoun, Vol. 11, 1829-1832. Wilson, Clyde N., ed. LC 59-10351. xlii, 728p. 1978. lib. bdg. 34.95x (ISBN 0-87249-363-6). U of SC Pr.
--Papers of John C. Calhoun, Vol. 12: 1833-1835. Wilson, Clyde N., ed. LC 59-10351. xlvi, 618p. 1979. lib. bdg. 34.95x (ISBN 0-87249-382-2). U of SC Pr.
--The Papers of John C. Calhoun, Vol. 13, 1835-1837. Wilson, Clyde N., ed. LC 59-10351. 700p. 1980. lib. bdg. 34.95x (ISBN 0-87249-392-X). U of SC Pr.
--The Papers of John C. Calhoun, Vol. 14, 1837-1839. Wilson, Clyde N., ed. LC 59-10351. (Illus.). 730p. 1981. lib. bdg. 34.95x (ISBN 0-87249-409-8). U of SC Pr.
Calhoun, John C. A. Disquisition on Government & Selections from the Discourse. Post, C. Gordon, ed. 1953. pap. 7.20 scp (ISBN 0-672-60014-5, AHS10). Bobbs.
Calhoun, John C., Jr. Fundamentals of Reservoir Engineering. LC 60-14924. (Illus.). 426p. pap. 15.95x (ISBN 0-8061-1389-8). U of Okla Pr.
Calhoun, Karen S. see Turner, Samuel M., et al.
Calhoun, Karen S., et al. Innovative Treatment Methods in Psychopathology. LC 73-21968. 429p. 1974. 24.95 (ISBN 0-471-12995-X, Pub. by Wiley). Krieger.
Calhoun, Ken. Cabinetmaking. (Illus.). 304p. 1984. 23.95 (ISBN 0-13-110064-5). P-H.
Calhoun, Lawrence G. Dealing with Crisis: A Guide to Critical Life Problems. 1976. 14.95 (ISBN 0-13-197723-7, Spec); pap. 4.95 (ISBN 0-13-197715-6). P-H.
Calhoun, Lillian S. Desegregation Works: A Primer for Parents & Teachers. 1968. pap. 0.90 (ISBN 0-912008-19-9). Integrated Ed Assoc.
Calhoun, Mary. Adventures with Children: Exploring Ways of Learning & Teaching in the Church School. LC 78-715. 1978. pap. 5.50 (ISBN 0-687-00925-1). Abingdon.
--Audubon Cat. LC 80-16278. (Illus.). 32p. (gr. k-3). 1981. 11.25 (ISBN 0-688-22253-6); PLB 11.88 (ISBN 0-688-32253-0). Morrow.
--Big Sixteen. LC 83-1007. (Illus.). 32p. (gr. 1-3). 1983. 10.25 (ISBN 0-688-02350-9); lib. bdg. 10.88 (ISBN 0-688-02351-7). Morrow.
--Camels Are Meaner Than Mules. LC 72-141255. (Regional American Stories Ser.). (Illus.). 64p. (gr. 3-6). 1971. PLB 7.47 (ISBN 0-8116-4250-X). Garrard.
--Cross-Country Cat. (Illus.). (gr. k-3). 1979. 11.25 (ISBN 0-688-22186-6); PLB 11.88 (ISBN 0-688-32186-0). Morrow.
--Depend on Katie John. LC 61-7328. (Illus.). (gr. 3-6). 1961. PLB 10.89 (ISBN 0-06-020926-7). HarpJ.
--Depend on Katie John. LC 61-7328. (Illus.). (gr. 3-6). 1961. pap. 2.95 (ISBN 0-06-440029-8, Trophy). HarpJ.
--Honestly, Katie John. LC 63-8473. (Illus.). (gr. 3-6). 1963. PLB 10.89 (ISBN 0-06-020936-4). HarpJ.
--Honestly, Katie John. LC 63-8473. (Illus.). (gr. 3-6). 1963. pap. 2.95 (ISBN 0-06-440030-1, Trophy). HarpJ.
--Hot-Air Henry. LC 80-26189. (Illus.). 40p. (gr. k-3). 1981. 10.25 (ISBN 0-688-00501-2); PLB 10.88 (ISBN 0-688-00502-0); pap. 3.95 (ISBN 0-688-04068-3). Morrow.
--The House of Thirty Cats. (Illus.). (gr. 4-6). 1970. pap. 1.95 (ISBN 0-671-42064-X). Archway.
--Hungry Leprechaun. (Illus.). (gr. k-3). 1962. PLB 11.88 (ISBN 0-688-31713-8). Morrow.
--It's Getting Beautiful Now. LC 77-135777. (gr. 7 up). 1971. HarpJ.
--Katie John. LC 60-5775. (Illus.). (gr. 3-6). 1960. PLB 10.89 (ISBN 0-06-020951-8). HarpJ.
--Katie John. LC 60-5775. (Illus.). (gr. 3-6). 1960. pap. 2.95 (ISBN 0-06-440028-X, Trophy). HarpJ.
--Katie John & Heathcliff. LC 80-7770. 160p. (gr. 3-6). 1980. PLB 10.89 (ISBN 0-06-020932-1). HarpJ.
--Katie John & Heathcliff. LC 80-7770. 160p. (gr. 3-6). 1981. pap. 2.95 (ISBN 0-06-440120-0, Trophy). HarpJ.
--Medicine Show: Conning People & Making Them Like It. LC 75-25417. (Illus.). (gr. 5-8). 1976. PLB 9.89 (ISBN 0-06-020929-1); PLB 10.89 (ISBN 0-06-020930-5). HarpJ.
--White Witch of Kynance. LC 76-104757. (gr. 7 up). 1970. PLB 10.89 (ISBN 0-06-020957-7); pap. 2.95 (ISBN 0-686-76871-X). HarpJ.
--The Witch of Hissing Hill. (Illus.). (gr. k-3). 1964. PLB 11.88 (ISBN 0-688-31762-6). Morrow.
--The Witch Who Lost Her Shadow. (Illus.). (gr. k-3). 1979. PLB 11.89 (ISBN 0-06-020947-X). HarpJ.
--Wobble the Witch Cat. (Illus.). (gr. k-3). 1958. PLB 10.88 (ISBN 0-688-31621-2). Morrow.
Calhoun, Mary & Morrill, Leslie. The Night the Monster Came. LC 81-18712. (Illus.). 64p. 1982. 10.25 (ISBN 0-688-01167-5); lib. bdg. 10.88 (ISBN 0-688-01168-3). Morrow.
Calhoun, Mary E. Wall Street Warmup: How to Get Today's Most Sought-After Jobs in Business & Finance. LC 84-62660. (Illus.). 208p. 1985. pap. 8.95 (ISBN 0-932763-14-6). Overture Pub.
Calhoun, Mary E. & MacAlarney, Emma L. Readings from American Literature: A Textbook for Schools & Colleges. 1979. Repr. of 1915 ed. lib. bdg. 40.00 (ISBN 0-8495-0938-6). Arden Lib.
Calhoun, Mary L. & Hawisher, Margaret. Teaching & Learning Strategies for Physically Handicapped Students. LC 79-12255. (Illus.). 382p. 1979. pap. text ed. 14.00 (ISBN 0-8391-1394-3). Pro Ed.
Calhoun, Mary L., jt. auth. see Hawisher, Margaret F.
Calhoun, Nancy & Calhoun, James, eds. Pelican Guide to Plantation Homes of Louisiana. 5th ed. LC 75-162347. (Pelican Guide Ser.). (Illus.). 128p. 1980. pap. 4.95 (ISBN 0-911116-50-8). Pelican.
Calhoun, Nancy H. & Calhoun, Janes, eds. Guia Pelican a las Casas de Plantaciones de Louisiana. Smith, Josie, tr. LC 81-10646. (Pelican Guide Ser.). Orig. Title: Pelican Guide to Plantation Homes of Louisiana. (Illus.). 128p. (Span.). 1982. pap. 5.95 (ISBN 0-88289-292-4). Pelican.
Calhoun, R. B. In Search of the New Old: Redefining Old Age in America, 1945-1970. 27.50 (ISBN 0-444-99048-6, CIS/, Pub. by Elsevier). Greenwood.
Calhoun, Raymond C. Typhoon: The Other Enemy. LC 81-38384. 261p. 1981. 16.95 (ISBN 0-87021-510-8). Naval Inst Pr.
Calhoun, Richard J. & Hill, Robert W. James Dickey. (United States Authors Ser.: No. 451). 1983. lib. bdg. 15.95 (ISBN 0-8057-7391-6, Twayne). G K Hall.
Calhoun, Richard J., ed. James Dickey: The Expansive Imagination. LC 72-90914. 1973. lib. bdg. 12.00 (ISBN 0-912112-00-X). Everett-Edwards.
Calhoun, Robert K., et al. Speedy Trial: Practice & Procedures. LC 80-70118. (California Criminal Law Practice Ser.). xi, 158p. 1981. 30.00 (ISBN 0-88124-082-6). Cal Cont Ed Bar.
Calhoun, Robert M. Revolutionary America: An Interpretive Overview. (History of the United States Ser.). (Illus.). 212p. (Orig.). 1976. pap. text ed. 11.95 (ISBN 0-15-576712-7, HC). HarBraceJ.
Calhoun, Thomas O. Henry Vaughan: The Achievement of Silex Scintillans. LC 79-51851. 272p. 1981. 25.00 (ISBN 0-87413-165-0). U Delaware Pr.
Calhoun, William G. Fort Scott: A Pictorial History. LC 77-93303. (Illus., Orig.). pap. 8.50 (ISBN 0-9601568-1-X). Historic Pres Bourbon.
Calhoun, William P. The Caucasian & the Negro in the United States: They Must Separate, If Not, Then Extermination. a Proposed Solution: Colonization. Grob, Gerald, ed. LC 76-46070. (Anti-Movements in America). 1977. Repr. of 1902 ed. lib. bdg. 17.00x (ISBN 0-405-09944-4). Ayer Co Pubs.
Cali, Santo. Yossiph Shyryn. Scammacca, Nat, ed. 132p. (Ital. & Eng.). 1980. 20.00 (ISBN 0-89304-563-2); pap. 10.00 (ISBN 0-89304-564-0). Cross Cult.
Cali, Vincent M. The New Lower-Cost Way to End Gum Trouble Without Surgery. LC 81-14702. (Illus.). 206p. 1982. pap. 7.95 (ISBN 0-446-38139-X). Warner Bks.
Calia, Vincent F. & Wall, Bartholomew D. Pupil Personnel Administration: New Perspectives & Foundations. (Illus.). 344p. 1968. 24.50x (ISBN 0-398-00273-8). C C Thomas.
Calian, Carnegie S. Today's Pastor in Tomorrow's World. Rev. ed. LC 82-7114. 164p. 1982. pap. 8.95 (ISBN 0-664-24426-2). Westminster.
Caliandro, Arthur. You Can Make Your Life Count. LC 81-82120. 192p. 1981. 12.95 (ISBN 0-916392-79-1). Oak Tree Pubns.
Caliaro, Marco & Francesconi, Mario. John Baptist Scalabrini: Apostle to Emigrants. Zizzamia, Alba I., tr. from It. LC 76-44922. (Illus.). 1977. lib. bdg. 15.00x (ISBN 0-913256-24-2). Ctr Migration.
Calic, Edouard. Reinhard Heydrich: The Chilling Story of the Man Who Masterminded the Nazi Death Camps. Bair, Lowell, tr. LC 84-16486. (Illus.). 320p. 1984. 15.95 (ISBN 0-688-00481-4). Morrow.
Calicchio, David, tr. see Camon, Ferdinando.
Calico Museum, Ahmedabad. Treasures of Indian Textiles. (Illus.). 148p. 1980. 49.95x (ISBN 0-940500-44-2). Asia Bk Corp.
Calico Museum-Ahmedabad, ed. Treasures of Indian Textiles. 146p. 1980. text ed. 52.50x (ISBN 0-391-02523-6, Pub. by UBS India). Humanities.
Caliendo, Mary A. Nutrition & Preventative Health Care. (Illus.). 1981. text ed. write for info. (ISBN 0-02-318330-6). Macmillan.
--The Nutrition Crisis: Alternatives for Change. (Illus.). 1979. pap. text ed. write for info. (ISBN 0-02-318340-3). Macmillan.
Caliered, Andre. The Prose of Emerson. 1978. Repr. of 1936 ed. lib. bdg. 15.00 (ISBN 0-8495-0740-5). Arden Lib.
Calif, R. C. Rust. (Orig.). 1980. pap. 1.95 (ISBN 0-532-23198-8). Woodhill.
Calif, Ruth. The World of Wheels: An Illustrated History of the Bycycle & Its Relatives. LC 80-70511. (Illus.). 256p. 1981. 25.00 (ISBN 0-686-31325-9). Cornwall Bks.
Califana, Anthony & Levkov, Jerome S. Criminalistics for the Law Enforcement Officer. (Illus.). 1978. text ed. 29.95 (ISBN 0-07-009620-1). McGraw.
Califano, Joseph A., jt. ed. see Simons, Howard.
Califano, Joseph A., Jr. Report on Drug Abuse & Alcoholism, 1982. (Illus.). 312p. (Orig.). pap. 3.95 (ISBN 0-446-30625-8). Warner Bks.
--Student Revolution: A Global Confrontation. 1969. 3.95x (ISBN 0-393-05391-1, Norton Lib); pap. 1.50x (ISBN 0-393-00519-4). Norton.
Califano, Joseph, Jr. Presidential Nation. 1975. 3.95 (ISBN 0-393-09135-X). Norton.
Califano, S., et al. Lattice Dynamics of Molecular Crystals. (Lecture Notes in Chemistry Ser.: Vol. 26). 309p. 1981. pap. 24.50 (ISBN 0-387-10868-8). Springer-Verlag.
Califf, Robert M. & Wagner, Calen S., eds. Acute Coronary Care. 1985. lib. bdg. 99.50 (ISBN 0-89838-666-7, Pub. by Martinus Nijhoff Netherlands). Kluwer-Academic.
Califia, Pat. Sapphistry: The Book of Lesbian Sexuality. 2nd, rev. ed. (Illus.). 208p. (Orig.). 1983. pap. 7.95 (ISBN 0-930044-47-9). Naiad Pr.
Califonia Continuing Education of the Bar, jt. auth. see Browne, Allan.
California Academy of Sciences. The Elkus Collection: Southwestern Indian Art. LC 84-50906. (Illus.). 244p. (Orig.). 1984. pap. 19.95 (ISBN 0-295-96170-8, Pub. by Calif Acad Sci). U of Wash Pr.
California Coastal Commission. The California Coastal Access Guide. rev. & enl. ed. LC 82-45905. (Illus.). 288p. 1983. pap. 8.95 (ISBN 0-520-05051-7). U of Cal Pr.
California Continuing Eduacation of the Bar. California Juvenile Court Practice, 2 vols. 1122p. 1981. Set. 115.00 (ISBN 0-88124-085-0); Vol. 1. 60.00 (ISBN 0-88124-083-4); Vol. 2. 60.00 (ISBN 0-88124-084-2). Cal Cont Ed Bar.
California Continuing Education Bar, jt. auth. see Karplus, Curtis M.
California Continuing Education of the Bar, jt. auth. see Acret, James.
California Continuing Education of the Bar, jt. auth. see Chuan, Victor L.
California Continuing Education of the Bar, jt. auth. see Giacomini, Edward D.
California Continuing Education of the Bar., jt. auth. see Hargrove, John O.
California Continuing Education of the Bar, jt. auth. see Hargrove, John O.
California Continuing Education of the Bar, jt. auth. see Karplus, Curtis M.
California Continuing Education of the Bar, jt. auth. see Peyrat, Paul I.
California Continuing Education of the Bar, jt. auth. see Sigman, Harry C.
California Continuing Education of the Bar, jt. auth. see Walker, John R.
California Continuing Education ot the Bar, jt. auth. see Hosack, John L.
California Continuing Education of the Bar, ed. see Dean, Michael A., et al.
California Continuing Education of the Bar. Attorney's Directory of Services & Information. 4th ed. 383p. 1982. pap. 30.00 (ISBN 0-88124-100-8, MI-39040). Cal Cont Ed Bar.
--Attorney's Guide to Trade Secrets. LC 79-181871. 202p. 1971. 30.00 (ISBN 0-88124-014-1, BV-30030). Cal Cont Ed Bar.
--California Attorney's Damages Guide. LC 74-620090. 449p. 1975. pap. 55.00 (ISBN 0-88124-036-2, CP-31430). Cal Cont Ed Bar.
--California Attorney's Fees Award Practice. LC 82-73239. 239p. 1982. 55.00 (ISBN 0-88124-105-9). Cal Cont Ed Bar.
--California Civil Appellate Practice. LC 66-63134. 738p. 1966. 35.00 (ISBN 0-88124-001-X). Cal Cont Ed Bar.
California Continuing Education of the Bar & Peyrat, Paul I. California Civil Litigation Forms Manual. LC 80-65241. xv, 576p. 1980. 55.00 (ISBN 0-88124-069-9). Cal Cont Ed Bar.
California Continuing Education of the Bar & Freiser, Lawrence H. California Civil Procedure During Trial, Vol. 1. LC 81-68678. (Illus.). 578p. 90.00 (ISBN 0-88124-092-3). Cal Cont Ed Bar.
California Continuing Education of the Bar. California Civil Writs. LC 78-630838. 534p. 1970. 65.00 (ISBN 0-88124-011-7, CP-30260). Cal Cont Ed Bar.
California Continuing Education of the Bar & Smith, James B. California Commercial Law, 3 vols. 1966. Set. 75.00 (ISBN 0-88124-000-1). Cal Cont Ed Bar.
California Continuing Education of the Bar. California Corporate Securities Law Notebook. 356p. 40.00 (ISBN 0-88124-024-9, BV-71010). Cal Cont Ed Bar.
--California Decedent Estate Administration, Vol. 1. LC 70-635710. 885p. 1971. 65.00 (ISBN 0-88124-017-6). Cal Cont Ed Bar.
--California Eviction Defense Manual. LC 73-184152. 420p. 1971. pap. 55.00 (ISBN 0-88124-018-4). Cal Cont Ed Bar.
--California Judicial Council Forms Manual. LC 81-65171. 350p. 1981. 65.00 (ISBN 0-88124-081-8, CP-74000). Cal Cont Ed Bar.
--California Marital Disssolution Practice, Vol. 1. 573p. 1981. 70.00 (ISBN 0-88124-086-9, FA-35570). Cal Cont Ed Bar.
--California Mechanics' Liens & Other Remedies. LC 70-189671. 347p. 1972. 65.00 (ISBN 0-88124-022-2). Cal Cont Ed Bar.
--California Probate Workflow Manual, 2 vols. rev. ed. Blaine, William L., ed. LC 79-53359. Set 90.00 (ISBN 0-88124-072-9). Cal Cont Ed Bar.
--California Real Property Sales Transactions. LC 81-65233. 868p. 1981. 75.00 (ISBN 0-88124-089-3). Cal Cont Ed Bar.
--The CEB Style Manual. LC 80-67155. 1980. 50.00 (ISBN 0-88124-076-1). Cal Cont Ed Bar.
--Civil Trials Benchbook. LC 81-67564. (California Judges Benchbook Civil Trials Ser.). 776p. 65.00 (ISBN 0-88124-080-X, CP-34550). Cal Cont Ed Bar.

--Drafting Agreements for the Sale of Businesses. LC 79-176333. 284p. 1971. 65.00 (ISBN 0-88124-015-X, BV-30140). Cal Cont Ed Bar.
--Eminent Domain Law: With Conforming Changes in Codified Sections & Official Comments. 512p. 1976. 10.00 (ISBN 0-88124-046-X). Cal Cont Ed Bar.
--Estate Planning for the General Practitioner. 889p. 1979. 70.00 (ISBN 0-88124-064-8, ES-33320). Cal Cont Ed Bar.
--Estate Planning: 1980. LC 80-69720. 260p. 1980. 50.00 (ISBN 0-88124-073-7). Cal cont Ed Bar.
--Estate Planning: 1981. 320p. 1983. 65.00 (ISBN 0-88124-112-1). Cal Cont Ed Bar.
--Index to the CEB Business & Commercial Law Books. LC 79-51292. x, 408p. 1979. 35.00 (ISBN 0-88124-059-1). Cal Cont Ed Bar.
--Transcripts of Nineteen Eighty-Two Developments Tapes. LC 77-74476. 245p. 1982. pap. 40.00 (ISBN 0-88124-091-5). Cal Cont Ed Bar.
--Trial Attorney's Evidence Code Notebook. LC 82-73213. 481p. 1982. looseleaf 50.00 (ISBN 0-88124-107-5). Cal Cont Ed Bar.
California Continuing Education to the Bar. California Uninsured Motorist Practice. LC 72-619679. 349p. 1973. 40.00 (ISBN 0-88124-028-1, TO-30580). Cal Cont Ed Bar.
California Energy Commission. Model Ordinance for Small Wind Energy Conversion Systems. pap. 9.95x (W-065). Solar Energy Info.
California Farm Bureau Federation. Country Cooking...California Style. 320p. 1981. pap. 10.25 (ISBN 0-686-31491-3). Cal Farm Bureau.
California Fertilizer Association. Western Fertilizer Handbook. 7th ed. 312p. 1985. pap. text ed. 9.95x (ISBN 0-8134-2490-9, 2490). Interstate.
California Historical Society. Index to California Historical Society Quarterly, Vol. 1 To 40. 1965. pap. 10.00 (ISBN 0-910312-12-5). Calif Hist.
California Institute of Public Affairs. Academic Research & Public Service Centers in California: A Guide. Fleming, Lizanne, ed. LC 82-70806. (California Information Guides Ser.). 66p. (Orig.). 1983. pap. 18.50x (ISBN 0-912102-61-6). Cal Inst Public.
California Institute of Public Affairs Staff. Ethnic Groups in California: A Guide to Organizations & Information Resources. LC 81-67062. (California Information Guides Ser.). 58p. 1981. pap. 16.50x (ISBN 0-912102-56-X). Cal Inst Public.
California-International Arts Foundation Staff. Eileen Cowin & John Divola: New Work, No Fancy Titles. Bonner, Kathleen, ed. Hart, Jeanne, tr. (Illus.). 48p. (Eng. & Fr.). 1985. pap. write for info. (ISBN 0-917571-01-0). CA Intl Arts.
California Land-Use Task Force, ed. The California Land: Planning for People. LC 75-19439. (Illus.). 98p. 1975. pap. 4.50x (ISBN 0-913232-20-3). W Kaufmann.
California Landmark Publications. Occupational Licensing & Certification: A Guide to Requirement of Federal & State Agencies & National Associations. 1098p. 1984. loose-leaf binder 265.00 (ISBN 0-9613382-0-2). CA Landmark.
California Law Review, ed. Essays in Honor of Hans Kelsen Celebrating the 90th Anniversary of His Birth. (Illus.). 1971. text ed. 17.50x (ISBN 0-8377-0528-2). Rothman.
California Legislature Assembly, jt. auth. see Greenwood, Peter W.
California Linguistics Association Conference, Sixth. Proceedings. Underhill, Robert, ed. LC 77-83490. 1977. 5.50x (ISBN 0-916304-38-8). SDSU Press.
California Medical Association, ed. see Thurber, Packard.
California Optometric Assoc. COA Practice Reference Manual. 456p. 1982. 3 ring binders 85.00 (ISBN 0-8403-2668-8). Kendall-Hunt.
California Restaurant Association. Cuisine of California. 116p. 1984. pap. 9.95 (ISBN 0-939944-40-5). Marmac Pub.
California Spanish Language Data Base. Bilindex: A Bilingual Spanish-English Subject Heading List: Spanish Equivalents to Library of Congress Subject Headings. LC 83-25285. 1983. 65.00 (ISBN 0-915745-00-3). Floricanto Pr.
California, State Board of Control. California & the Oriental. Daniels, Roger, ed. LC 78-54809. (Asian Experience in North America Ser.). (Illus.). 1979. Repr. of 1922 ed. lib. bdg. 16.00x (ISBN 0-405-11265-3). Ayer Co Pubs.
California State Department of Education. Handbook for Planning an Effective Writing Program: Kindergarten Through Grade Twelve. rev. ed. 63p. 1982. 5.00 (ISBN 0-8141-2017-2). NCTE.
California State Department of Health. Leisure Time Activities for Deaf-Blind Children. LC 75-70066. 24.95 (ISBN 0-917002-06-7). Joyce Media.
California State Department of Health & Huffmann, Jeanne. Sign Language for Everyone. LC 75-70066. (Illus.). 10.95 (ISBN 0-917002-02-4). Joyce Media.
California State Department of Health. Talk with Me: Communication with the Multi-Handicapped Deaf. LC 75-70066. 24.95 (ISBN 0-917002-05-9). Joyce Media.
California State Legislature. California Synthetic Fuels Program: Final Report. 176p. 1980. pap. 19.95x (ISBN 0-89934-058-X, B001). Solar Energy Info.
California State University. Classroom Leadership Styles: Apple II Version. 1984. 49.95 (ISBN 0-07-831046-6). McGraw.
--Classroom Leadership Styles: IBM-PC Version. 1984. 49.95 (ISBN 0-07-831047-4). McGraw.
--Constructing the Paragraph: The Ramblestones on the Road for Use with Apple II. 1984. 39.95 (ISBN 0-07-831012-1). McGraw.
--Constructing the Paragraph: The Ramblestones on the Road for Use with IBM-PC. 1984. 39.95 (ISBN 0-07-831013-X). McGraw.
--Contestination: Developing Successful Estimating Abilities for Use with Apple II. 1984. 49.950 (ISBN 0-07-831020-2). McGraw.
--Contestination: Developing Successful Estimating Abilities for Use with IBM-PC. 1984. 49.95 (ISBN 0-07-831021-0). McGraw.
--Introduction to Language for Use with Apple II. 1984. 49.95 (ISBN 0-07-831034-2). McGraw.
--Introduction to Language for Use with IBM PC. 1984. 49.95 (ISBN 0-07-831035-0). McGraw.
--Miranda: Understanding Poetry-Alliteration & Assonance; Images; Metaphors; Similies & Symbols for Use with Apple II, Pt. 2. 1984. write for info. (ISBN 0-07-831002-4). McGraw.
--Miranda: Understanding Poetry-Alliteration & Assonance; Images; Metaphors; Similies & Symbols for Use with IBM-PC, Pt. 2. 1984. write for info. (ISBN 0-07-831003-2). McGraw.
--Miranda: Understanding Poetry-Meter, Rhythm, Rhyme for Use with Apple II, Pt. 1. 1984. write for info. (ISBN 0-07-831010-5). McGraw.
--Miranda: Understanding Poetry-Meter, Rhythm, Rhyme for Use with the IBM-PC, Pt. 1. 1984. write for info. (ISBN 0-07-831011-3). McGraw.
--Ten Common Inferences: Oscar-The Big Escape for Use with Apple II. 1984. write for info. (ISBN 0-07-831014-8). McGraw.
--Ten Common Inferences: Oscar-The Big Escape for Use with IBM-PC, Pt. 2. 1984. write for info. (ISBN 0-07-831015-6). McGraw.
California State University, Fullerton. Beatrice Wood Retrospective. (Illus.). 48p. (Orig.). 1983. pap. 12.00 (ISBN 0-935314-23-7). CSU Art Gallery.
--Charles Arnoldi & Laddie John Dill. (Orig.). 1983. pap. write for info. (ISBN 0-935314-24-5). CSU Art Gallery.
California Trial Lawyers Association. Damages Seminar. 216p. 1966. 10.00 (ISBN 0-913338-05-2). Condyne-Oceana.
California University at Los Angeles African Studies Center, jt. ed. see Kuper, Hilda.
California University Committee on International Relations. Problems of Hemispheric Defense. LC 77-167322. (Essay Index Reprint Ser.). Repr. of 1942 ed. 14.50 (ISBN 0-8369-2759-1). Ayer Co Pubs.
California University - Committee On International Relations. Problems of War & Peace in the Society of Nations. facs. ed. LC 67-23188. (Essay Index Reprint Ser). 1937. 17.00 (ISBN 0-8369-0270-X). Ayer Co Pubs.
California University Committee on International Relations. The Southwest Pacific & the War. LC 74-3750. 168p. 1974. Repr. of 1944 ed. lib. bdg. 22.50 (ISBN 0-8371-7473-2, CUSP). Greenwood.
California University - Committee on International Relations. United States Among the Nations. facs. ed. LC 68-54336. (Essay Index Reprint Ser). 1937. 15.00 (ISBN 0-8369-0271-8). Ayer Co Pubs.
California University - Department Of English. Essays in Criticism: First Series. facs. ed. LC 67-22083. (Essay Index Reprint Ser.). 1929. 18.00 (ISBN 0-8369-0272-6). Ayer Co Pubs.
--Essays in Criticism, Second Series. facs. ed. LC 67-22083. (Essay Index Reprint Ser.). 1934. 19.00 (ISBN 0-8369-1327-2). Ayer Co Pubs.
California University Library. Spain & Spanish America in the Libraries of the University of California, 2 vols. LC 68-56591. (Bibliography & Reference Ser.: No. 115). 1968. Repr. of 1928 ed. Set. 80.50 (ISBN 0-8337-4020-2). B Franklin.
California Weed Conference Staff. Principles of Weed Control in California. (Illus.). 500p. text ed. 29.95 (ISBN 0-913702-32-3). Thomson Pub Ca.
California Wine List Panel. A Consumer's Guide to One Hundred Sixty-One Jug Wines. Holzgang, David, ed. (California Wine List Ser.). 60p. (Orig.). 1981. pap. 4.95 (ISBN 0-932664-18-0). Wine Appreciation.
--Guide to One Hundred Twenty Chardonnays. Holzgang, David, ed. (California Wine List Ser.). 60p. 1981. pap. 4.95 (ISBN 0-932664-15-6). Wine Appreciation.
--Guide to One Hundred Twenty-Five Zinfandels. Holzgang, David, ed. (California Wine List Ser.). 60p. 1980. pap. 4.95 (ISBN 0-932664-16-4). Wine Appreciation.
California Winemakers. Adventures in Wine Cookery. 2nd ed. Bottrell, Donna, et al, eds. (The Wine Cookbook Ser.). (Illus.). 128p. 1980. pap. 5.95 (ISBN 0-932664-10-5). Wine Appreciation.
Caligari, Marc, tr. see Pope Paul VI.
Caligor, Judith, et al. Individual & Group Therapy: Combining Psychoanalytic Treatments. LC 83-46117. 272p. 1985. pap. 18.95x (ISBN 0-465-03250-8). Basic.
Caligor, Leopold. A New Approach to Figure Drawing: Based Upon an Interrelated Series of Drawings. (Illus.). 160p. 1957. photocopy ed. 14.75x (ISBN 0-398-04226-8). C C Thomas.
Caligor, Leopold, et al, eds. Clinical Perspectives on the Supervision of Psychoanalysis & Psychotheraphy. (Critical Issues in Psychiatry Ser.). 302p. 1984. 29.50x (ISBN 0-306-41403-1, Plenum Pr). Plenum Pub.
Caliguiri, L. A., jt. ed. see Came, P. E.
Calin, A., jt. ed. see Calabro, J. J.
Calin, Andrei. Differential Diagnosis in Rheumatology: An Atlas for the Physician. (Illus.). 272p. 1984. text ed. 36.75 (ISBN 0-397-52105-7, 65-07073, Lippincott Medical). Lippincott.
Calin, Andrei & Fries, James F. Ankylosing Spondylitis. (Contemporary Patient Management Ser.). 1978. spiral 14.00 (ISBN 0-87488-887-5). Med Exam.
Calin, Andrei, ed. Spondylathropathies. 432p. 1984. 59.50 (ISBN 0-8089-1613-0, 790763). Grune.
Calin, Harold. Attack In the Forest. 288p. 1982. pap. 2.75 (ISBN 0-8439-1176-X, Leisure Bks). Dorchester Pub Co.
--Diepe. 1978. pap. 1.75 (ISBN 0-505-51231-9, Pub. by Tower Bks). Dorchester Pub Co.
--The Indian Killer. 1981. pap. 1.95 (ISBN 0-505-51726-4, Pub. by Tower Bks). Dorchester Pub Co.
--Mercenary. 1977. pap. 1.50 (ISBN 0-685-78234-4, Leisure Bks). Dorchester Pub Co.
--Slave Ship. 1977. pap. 1.75 (ISBN 0-8439-0478-X, Leisure Bks). Dorchester Pub Co.
--White Forest Battle. 1979. pap. 1.75 (ISBN 0-8439-0624-3, Leisure Bks). Dorchester Pub Co.
--White Forest Battle. (Inflation Fighter). 208p. 1982. pap. 1.50 (ISBN 0-8439-1150-6, Leisure Bks). Dorchester Pub Co.
Calin, William. Crown, Cross & "Fleur-de-Lis". An Essay on Pierre Le Moyne's Baroque Epic "Saint Louis". (Stanford French & Italian Studies: No. 6). 1977. pap. 25.00 (ISBN 0-915838-34-6). Anma Libri.
--A Muse for Heroes: Nine Centuries of the Epic in France. (Romance Ser.). 527p. 1983. 47.50x (ISBN 0-8020-5599-0). U of Toronto Pr.
--A Poet at the Fountain: Essays on the Narrative Verse of Guillaume de Machaut. LC 72-91663. (Studies in Romance Languages: No. 9). 264p. 1974. 24.00x (ISBN 0-8131-1297-4). U Pr of Ky.
Calin, William C., ed. Chanson de Roland. LC 67-29335. (Medieval French Literature Ser.). (Fr.). 1968. pap. text ed. 8.95x (ISBN 0-89197-071-1). Irvington.
Calinescu, Matei. Faces of Modernity: Avant-Garde, Decadence, Kitsch. LC 77-72194. 352p. 1977. 22.50x (ISBN 0-253-32087-9). Ind U Pr.
Calingaert, Efrem F. & Serwer, Jacquelyn D. Pasta & Rice Italian Style. (Illus.). 256p. 1983. 16.95 (ISBN 0-684-17878-8, ScribT). Scribner.
--Pasta & Rice Italian Style. 1984. pap. 7.95 (ISBN 0-452-25618-6, Plume). NAL.
Calingaert, Peter. Assemblers, Compilers, & Program Translation. LC 78-21905. 270p. 1979. 28.95 (ISBN 0-914894-23-4). Computer Sci.
--Operating System Elements: A User Perspective. (Illus.). 304p. 1982. 26.95 (ISBN 0-13-637421-2). P-H.
Calinger, Ronald, ed. Classics of Mathematics. LC 80-15567. (Classics Ser.). (Orig.). 1982. pap. 20.00 (ISBN 0-935610-13-8). Moore Pub IL.
Calisch, Edward N. The Jew in English Literature As Author & Subject. 1980. lib. bdg. 64.95 (ISBN 0-8490-3132-X). Gordon Pr.
Calisher, Charles H. & Thompson, Wayne H. California Serogroup Viruses. LC 83-7936. (Progress in Clinical & Biological Research Ser.: Vol. 123). 428p. 1983. 42.00. A R Liss.
Calisher, Hortense. Mysteries of Motion. LC 82-45593. 528p. 1983. 17.95. Doubleday.
Calisher, Hortense. The Collected Stories of Hortense Calisher. 1984. pap. 9.95 (ISBN 0-87795-602-2). Arbor Hse.
--Saratoga Hot. LC 84-24695. 288p. 1985. 16.95 (ISBN 0-385-19975-9). Doubleday.
--Standard Dreaming. LC 78-82176. 1972. 5.95 (ISBN 0-87795-043-1). Arbor Hse.
--Standard Dreaming. 1983. 13.95 (ISBN 0-87795-043-1); pap. 5.95. Arbor Hse.
Calisher, Hortense & Ravenel, Shannon, eds. The Best American Short Stories, 1981. 1981. 12.95 (ISBN 0-395-31259-0). HM.
Calisse, Carlo. History of Italian Law. Register, Layton B., tr. LC 68-54745. (Continental Legal History Ser.: Vol. 8). Repr. of 1928 ed. 37.50x (ISBN 0-678-04509-7). Kelley.
--History of Italian Law. Register, Layton B., tr. (Continental Legal History Ser.: Vol. 8). lix, 827p. 1969. Repr. of 1928 ed. 37.50x (ISBN 0-8377-2002-8). Rothman.
Calisto & Melebea. Beauty & Good Properties of Women As Also Their Vices & Evil Conditions. LC 70-133640. (Tudor Facsimile Texts. Old English Plays: No. 10). Repr. of 1909 ed. 49.50 (ISBN 0-404-53310-8). AMS Pr.
Caliver, Ambrose. Background Study of Negro College Students. LC 76-82089. (Illus.). Repr. of 1933 ed. cancelled (ISBN 0-8371-3205-3, O, Pub. by Negro U Pr). Greenwood.
--Education of Negro Teachers. LC 70-82090. Repr. of 1933 ed. 19.75x (ISBN 0-8371-3206-1, CEN&, Pub. by Negro U Pr). Greenwood.
--A Personnel Study of Negro College Students: A Study of the Relations Between Certain Background Factors of Negro College Students & Their Subsequent Careers in College. LC 76-176623. (Columbia University. Teachers College. Contributions to Education: No. 484). Repr. of 1931 ed. 22.50 (ISBN 0-404-55484-9). AMS Pr.
--Personnel Study of Negro College Students: A Study of the Relations Between Certain Background Factors of Negro College Students & Their Subsequent Careers in College. LC 73-107470. Repr. of 1931 ed. cancelled (ISBN 0-8371-3749-7). Greenwood.
--Secondary Education for Negroes. LC 74-82091. (Illus.). Repr. of 1933 ed. 15.00x (ISBN 0-8371-2046-2, CSE&). Greenwood.
--Vocational Education & Guidance of Negroes. LC 78-82092. (Illus.). Repr. 17.50x (ISBN 0-8371-3208-8, CAV&). Greenwood.
Calixte, Demosthenes P. Haiti: The Calvary of a Soldier. LC 75-98715. Repr. of 1939 ed. 15.00x (ISBN 0-8371-2760-2, CAJ&, Pub. by Negro U Pr). Greenwood.
Caljon, A. G. Brackish-Water Phytoplankton of the Flemish Lowland. (Developments in Hydrobiology Ser.). 1984. lib. bdg. 74.50 (ISBN 90-6193-769-8, Pub. by Junk Pubs Netherlands). Kluwer-Academic.
Calkin, Ruth. Lord, I Keep Running Back to You. 1983. pap. 2.95 (ISBN 0-8423-3819-5). Tyndale.
Calkin, Ruth H. Letters to a Young Bride. 112p. 1985. 10.95 (ISBN 0-8423-2134-9). Tyndale.
--Lord, Could You Hurry a Little. 1983. pap. 2.95 (ISBN 0-8423-3816-0, 07-3816-0). Tyndale.
--Lord, It Keeps Happening...& Happening. LC 83-91404. 112p. 1984. pap. 2.95 (ISBN 0-8423-3823-3). Tyndale.
--Lord, You Love to Say Yes. (Living Books). 160p. (Orig.). 1985. pap. 2.95 (ISBN 0-8423-3824-1). Tyndale.
--Love Is So Much More, Lord. LC 79-51739. 1979. pap. 2.50 (ISBN 0-89191-187-1). Cook.
Calkins & White. Talk to God about The Sabbath. large type ed. 70p. 1984. pap. 8.50x (ISBN 0-914009-22-2). Chr Overeaters Bks.
Calkins, Alonzo. Opium & the Opium-Appetite. Grob, Gerald N., ed. LC 80-1215. (Addiction in America Ser.). 1981. Repr. of 1871 ed. lib. bdg. 35.00x (ISBN 0-405-13571-8). Ayer Co Pubs.
Calkins, Clinch. Spy Overhead: The Story of Industrial Espionage. LC 70-156408. (American Labor Ser., No. 2). 1971. Repr. of 1937 ed. 32.00 (ISBN 0-405-02917-9). Ayer Co Pubs.
Calkins, Donald A. Cases & Materials on Michigan Criminal Law, 2 vols. LC 74-12490. 1506p. 1974. text ed. 19.95x ea.; Vol. 1. text ed. (ISBN 0-8143-1535-6); Vol. 2. text ed. (ISBN 0-8143-1538-0). Wayne St U Pr.
Calkins, Earnest E. And Hearing Not: Annals of an Ad Man. LC 84-46060. (History of Advertising Ser.). 400p. 1985. lib. bdg. 45.00 (ISBN 0-8240-6754-1). Garland Pub.
--Louder Please: The Autobiography of a Deaf Man. LC 74-164148. 1971. Repr. of 1924 ed. 40.00x (ISBN 0-8103-3792-4). Gale.
--They Broke the Prairie: Being Some Account of the Settlement of the Upper Mississippi Valley by Religious & Educational Pioneers, Told in Terms of One City, Galesburg, & of One College, Knox. LC 75-138103. 1971. Repr. of 1937 ed. lib. bdg. 22.50x (ISBN 0-8371-5679-3, CABP). Greenwood.
Calkins, Earnest E. & Holden, Ralph. Modern Advertising. Assael, Henry & Craig, Samuel, eds. LC 84-46038. 378p. 1985. lib. bdg. 40.00 (ISBN 0-8240-6731-2). Garland Pub.
Calkins, Erling. Adventure at Beaver Falls. LC 79-15601. (Crown Ser.). (gr. 5-8). 1979. 4.95 (ISBN 0-8127-0223-9). Review & Herald.
Calkins, Evan. The Practice of Geriatric Medicine. (Illus.). 800p. Date not set. price not set (ISBN 0-7216-2329-8). Saunders.
Calkins, Fay. The CIO & the Democratic Party. (Midway Reprint Ser). 1975. pap. text ed. 6.50x (ISBN 0-226-09098-1). U of Chicago Pr.
Calkins, Fay G. My Samoan Chief. (Pacific Classics Ser.: No. 2). (Illus.). 207p. 1971. pap. 5.95 (ISBN 0-87022-932-X). UH Pr.
Calkins, Fern, et al. It's Your World Vegetarian Cookbook. rev. ed. (Illus.). 1980. wire bdg. 12.95 (ISBN 0-8280-0002-6). Review & Herald.
Calkins, Franklin W. Cougar-Tamer & Other Stories of Adventure. facsimile ed. LC 79-153541. (Short Story Index Reprint Ser). Repr. of 1898 ed. 15.50 (ISBN 0-8369-3795-3). Ayer Co Pubs.
--My Host the Enemy, & Other Tales. facs. ed. LC 72-81265. (Short Story Index Reprint Ser). 1901. 19.00 (ISBN 0-8369-3017-7). Ayer Co Pubs.
Calkins, H. W., jt. auth. see Tomlinson, R. F.
Calkins, John, ed. The Role of Solar Ultraviolet Radiation in Marine Ecosystems. LC 82-3792. (NATO Conference Series IV, Marine Sciences: Vol. 7). 740p. 1982. 89.50x (ISBN 0-306-40909-7, Plenum Pr). Plenum Pub.
Calkins, Kenneth R. Hugo Haase: Democrat & Revolutionary. LC 77-88657. 257p. 1979. lib. bdg. 22.75 (ISBN 0-89089-075-7); pap. 9.95 (ISBN 0-89089-073-0). Carolina Acad Pr.

Calkins, Leroy A., jt. auth. see Scammon, Richard.

Calkins, Lucy M. Lessons from a Child. LC 83-8599. (Illus.). 192p. (Orig.). 1983. pap. text ed. 10.00x (ISBN 0-435-08206-X). Heinemann Ed.

Calkins, Mary W. The Good Man & the Good: An Introduction to Ethics. LC 75-3093. Repr. of 1918 ed. 16.00 (ISBN 0-404-59090-X). AMS Pr.

--The Persistent Problems of Philosophy. LC 75-3096. (Philosophy in America). Repr. of 1925 ed. 44.50 (ISBN 0-404-59092-6). AMS Pr.

Calkins, Mary W. see Griffing, Arnold.

Calkins, Mary W., ed. see Hume, David.

Calkins, Michael. Tune-Up Service Manual. rev. ed. Phelps, Jo L. & Fennema, Roger, eds. (Apprentice Mechanics Ser.). (Illus.). 192p. 1985. pap. 8.75 wkbk. (ISBN 0-88098-002-8); quiz 3.45x (ISBN 0-88098-003-6). H M Gousha.

Calkins, Ray. Looking Back from the Hill: Recollections of Butte People. (Illus.). 92p. 1982. pap. 8.95 (ISBN 0-930683-00-5). Butte Hist Soc.

Calkins, Raymond. Substitutes for the Saloon: An Investigation Originally Made for the Committee of Fifty. LC 75-137181. (Poverty U.S.A. Historical Record Ser). 1971. Repr. of 1919 ed. 23.00 (ISBN 0-405-03119-X). Ayer Co Pubs.

Calkins, Richard M. Antitrust Guideline for the Business Executive. LC 81-65229. pap. 87.50 (ISBN 0-317-07971-9, 2021661). Bks Demand UMI.

Calkins, Robert G. Distribution of Labor: The Illuminators of the Hours of Catherine of Cleves & Their Workshop. LC 79-51537. (Transactions Ser.: Vol. 69, Pt. 5). 1979. 10.00 (ISBN 0-87169-695-9). Am Philos.

--The Franklin D. Murphy Lectures V: Programs of Medieval Illumination. LC 84-51249. (Illus.). 158p. 1984. 12.00 (ISBN 0-913689-12-2). Spencer Muse Art.

--Illuminated Books of the Middle Ages. (Illus.). 368p. 1983. 48.50x (ISBN 0-8014-1506-3). Cornell U Pr.

--Monuments of Medieval Art. LC 84-21504. (Illus.). 320p. (Orig.). 1985. pap. text ed. 14.95 (ISBN 0-8014-9306-4). Cornell U pr.

Call, Betty & Souther, Sheila. Children Can Worship, Bk. 3. (Orig.). (gr. 1-3). 1983. pap. text ed. 10.95 (ISBN 0-87148-178-2). Pathway Pr.

Call, Betty & Souther, Shelia. Children Can Worship: Book Two. (YA) 1982. pap. 9.95 (ISBN 0-87148-176-6). Pathway Pr.

Call, David M. Within Our Reach. LC 83-26162. 68p. 1984. 5.95 (ISBN 0-87747-975-5). Deseret Bk.

Call, Hughie. Golden Fleece. LC 80-39781. (Illus.). xx, 250p. 1981. 19.95x (ISBN 0-8032-1413-8); pap. 5.25 (ISBN 0-8032-6308-2, BB 760, Bison). U of Nebr Pr.

Call, Jack. The Latest Roundup. 60p. 1985. pap. 2.95 (ISBN 0-9613585-0-5). Spiraling Bks.

Call, Justin see Nospnitz, Joseph D.

Call, Justin D., jt. ed. see Galenson, Eleanor.

Call, Max. Hand of Death: The Henry Lee Lucas Story. 191p. 1985. 12.95 (ISBN 0-933451-00-8). Prescott Pr.

--Phoebe. 224p. 1984. pap. 6.95 (ISBN 0-310-60721-3, Pub by Chosen Bks). Zondervan.

Call, Stephen T. & Holahan, William L. Microeconomics. 2nd ed. 528p. 1983. text ed. write for info. (ISBN 0-534-01314-7). Wadsworth Pub.

Call, Val. Anything I Can Play, You Can Play Better. (Illus.). 105p. (Orig.). 1985. pap. 7.95 (ISBN 0-940076-03-9). Fiesta City.

Call, Vaughn R. & Otto, Luther B. Tracking Respondents: A Multi-Method Approach, Vol. II. LC 79-48034. (Entry into Careers Ser.). 176p. 1982. 22.00x (ISBN 0-669-03644-7). Lexington Bks.

Call, W. Vosco. William Tell. (Children's Theatre Playscript Ser.). 1963. pap. 2.00x (ISBN 0-88020-063-4). Coach Hse.

Calladine, Andrew, jt. auth. see Calladine, Carole.

Calladine, Carole. One Terrific Year: Supporting Your Kids Through the Ups & Downs of the School Year & Next Summer Too. (The Winston Family Handbooks Ser.). 96p. (Orig.). 1985. pap. 9.95 (ISBN 0-86683-862-7, Pub. by Seabury). Winston Pr.

Calladine, Carole & Calladine, Andrew. Raising Brothers & Sisters Without Raising the Roof. 216p. (Orig.). 1983. pap. 6.95 (ISBN 0-86683-803-1, AY8382). Winston Pr.

Calladine, Christopher R. Theory of Shell Structures. LC 82-4255. 700p. 1983. 140.00 (ISBN 0-521-23835-8). Cambridge U Pr.

Callaghan & Co., jt. auth. see Nichols, Clark A.

Callaghan & Company, jt. auth. see Michigan Supreme Court Staff.

Callaghan & Company, ed. see Henderson, James M.

Callaghan & Company Publisher's Staff & Latta, John D. Callaghan's Illinois Digest: 1955-1983, 63 vols. 3rd ed. LC 55-4775. 1983. Set. 1350.00 (ISBN 0-317-12062-X); Suppl., 1982. 767.50; Suppl., 1983. 728.00. Callaghan.

Callaghan & Company Publisher's Staff. Callaghan's Wisconsin Digest: 1950, 28 vols. LC 50-2898. Set. 925.00 (ISBN 0-317-12219-3); Suppl., 1981. 395.00; Suppl., 1982. 400.00. Callaghan.

Callaghan & Company Publishers' Staff. Horner Probate Practice & Estates: With Forms, 1976-1983, 8 vols. LC 40-9159. 1983. Set. 475.00 (ISBN 0-317-12065-4). Callaghan.

Callaghan, Barry. Black Queen Stories. 224p. 1982. 13.95 (ISBN 0-86538-017-1); pap. 7.95 (ISBN 0-86538-018-X). Ontario Rev NJ.

Callaghan, Brian, jt. auth. see Maleson, Alfred.

Callaghan, Catherine A. Plains Miwok Dictionary. LC 83-18034. (Linguistics Ser.: Vol. 105). 318p. 1984. lib. bdg. 19.00x (ISBN 0-520-09952-4). U of Cal Pr.

Callaghan, Christopher T., jt. ed. see Connors, Tracy D.

Callaghan, Dennis W., jt. auth. see Elkins, Arthur.

Callaghan, Dennis W., jt. ed. see Comerford, Robert A.

Callaghan, John. Geoffrey Boycott. (Profiles Ser.). (Illus.). 64p. (gr. 3-6). 1982. 7.95 (ISBN 0-241-10712-1, Pub. by Hamish Hamilton England). David & Charles.

Callaghan, Mary K., ed. Oregon State Fair Cookbook. (Illus.). 465p. 1983. 12.00 (ISBN 0-9612966-0-7). Oreg St Fair Expo Cntr.

Callaghan, Mary R. Confessions of a Prodigal Daughter. 224p. 1985. 14.95 (ISBN 0-7145-2830-7, Dist. by Scribner). M Boyars.

--Mothers. 244p. 1984. 12.95 (ISBN 0-7145-2806-4, Dist. by Scribner). M Boyars.

Callaghan, Morley. Native Argosy. facsimile ed. LC 70-106255. (Short Story Index Reprint Ser.). 1929. 18.00 (ISBN 0-8369-3292-7). Ayer Co Pubs.

--That Summer in Paris: Memories of Tangled Friendships with Hemingway, Fitzgerald & Some Others. (Illus.). 1979. pap. 3.95 (ISBN 0-14-005074-4). Penguin.

--A Time for Judas. 248p. 1984. 12.95 (ISBN 0-312-80513-6). St Martin.

Callaghan, N. & Galvin, R., eds. Recent Research in Neurology. (Progress in Neurology Ser.). 214p. 1984. text ed. 42.50 (ISBN 0-272-79761-8, Pitman Med UK). Urban & S.

Callaghan, Thomas. The Tramp's Chronicle. 220p. 1983. 15.95 (ISBN 0-85362-201-9, Oriel Press). Routledge & Kegan.

Callaghy, Thomas M. The State-Society Struggle: Zaire in Comparative Perspective. LC 84-5865. 515p. 1984. 45.00 (ISBN 0-231-05720-2); pap. 16.00x (ISBN 0-231-05721-0). Columbia U Pr.

Callaghy, Thomas M., ed. South Africa in Southern Africa: The Intensifying Vortex of Violence. 432p. 1983. 45.00x (ISBN 0-03-060306-4). Praeger.

Callaghy, Thomas M., jt. ed. see Rosberg, Carl G.

Callaham, Ludmilla I. Russian-English Chemical & Polytechnical Dictionary. 3rd ed. LC 75-5982. 852p. (Rus. & Eng.). 1975. 62.95x (ISBN 0-471-12998-4, Pub. by Wiley-Interscience). Wiley.

Callaham, Michael, jt. ed. see Dailey, Robert H.

Callahan, Anne, jt. auth. see Furber, Donald.

Callahan, Annice. Karl Rahner's Spirituality of the Pierced Heart: A Reinterpretation of Devotion to the Sacred Heart. LC 84-29170. 198p. (Orig.). 1985. lib. bdg. 22.75 (ISBN 0-8191-4568-8); pap. text ed. 11.50 (ISBN 0-8191-4569-6). U Pr of Amer.

Callahan, Arthur B., jt. auth. see Dinno, Mumtaz A.

Callahan, Betsy N. Assertiveness Training. LC 80-5954. 125p. 1980. 14.95 (ISBN 0-86618-003-6). Family Serv.

--Separation & Divorce. LC 78-21649. (Workshop Models for Family Life Education Ser.). 129p. 1979. plastic comb 14.95 (ISBN 0-87304-169-0). Family Serv.

Callahan, Betsy N. & Apgar, Kathryn. Four One-Day Workshops. 134p. 1980. 14.95 (ISBN 0-86618-004-4). Family Serv.

--Four One-Day Workshops. LC 80-5952. 134p. 1980. 12.95 (ISBN 0-86618-004-4). Family Serv.

Callahan, Betsy N. & Resource Communications Inc. Assertiveness Training. LC 80-5954. 125p. 1980. 12.95 (ISBN 0-86618-003-6). Family Serv.

Callahan, Betsy N., jt. auth. see Apgar, Kathryn.

Callahan, Betsy N., jt. auth. see Freeman, Vivian.

Callahan, Betsy W. Real Men Balance Budgets: A Primer on Federal Budget Management. 60p. (Orig.). 1984. pap. 5.95 (ISBN 0-931494-51-6). Brunswick Pub.

Callahan, Bob. Algonquin Woods. (New World Writing Ser.). (Illus., Orig.). 1978. 10.00 (ISBN 0-913666-26-2); pap. 4.95 (ISBN 0-913666-25-4). Turtle Isl Foun.

Callahan, Bob, ed. see De Angulo, Jaime.

Callahan, Bob, ed. & intro. by see Sauer, Carl O.

Callahan, Carolyn M., jt. auth. see Bear, George G.

Callahan, Charles C. Adverse Possession. LC 61-7300. (Law Forum Ser.: No. 1). 132p. 1961. 3.00 (ISBN 0-8142-0034-6). Ohio St U Pr.

Callahan, Christine. Two Score & Growing Up. 144p. 1985. 8.95 (ISBN 0-89962-456-1). Todd & Honeywell.

Callahan, Daniel. Abortion: Law, Choice & Morality. 1970. pap. 4.95 (ISBN 0-685-14564-6). Macmillan.

--Ethics & Population Limitation. LC 78-155736. 45p. (Orig.). 1971. pap. text ed. 3.95 (ISBN 0-87834-002-5). Population Coun.

--The Tyranny of Survival: And Other Pathologies of Civilized Life. LC 85-5316. (Illus.). 300p. 1985. pap. text ed. 10.75 (ISBN 0-8191-4636-6). U Pr of Amer.

Callahan, Daniel, ed. The Teaching of Ethics in Higher Education: A Report by the Hastings Center. LC 80-10294. (The Teaching of Ethics Ser.). 103p. 1980. pap. 5.00 xerox form only (ISBN 0-916558-09-6). Hastings Ctr Inst Soc.

Callahan, Daniel & Bok, Sissela, eds. Ethics Teaching in Higher Education. LC 80-24002. (Hastings Center Monograph Ser.). 332p. 1980. 22.50x (ISBN 0-306-40522-9). Plenum Pub.

Callahan, Daniel & Clark, Phillip G., eds. Ethical Issues of Population Aid: Culture, Economics & International Assistance. 1982. text ed. 29.50x (ISBN 0-8290-0364-9). Irvington.

Callahan, Daniel & Engelhardt, H. Tristram, Jr., eds. The Roots of Ethics. (The Hasting Center Series in Ethics). 464p. 1981. 29.50 (ISBN 0-306-40796-5, Plenum Pr). Plenum Pub.

Callahan, Daniel & Jennings, Bruce, eds. Ethics, The Social Sciences, & Policy Analysis. (The Hastings Center Series in Ethics). 408p. 1983. 29.50x (ISBN 0-306-41143-1, Plenum Pr). Plenum Pub.

Callahan, Daniel, jt. ed. see Callahan, Sidney.

Callahan, Daniel, jt. ed. see Caplan, Arthur L.

Callahan, Daniel, jt. ed. see Engelhardt, H. Tristram, Jr.

Callahan, Daniel, et al. Congress & the Media: The Ethical Connection. LC 85-11965. 52p. pap. 7.00 (ISBN 0-916558-22-3). Inst Soc Ethics.

Callahan, Dorothy. Ruffian. Schroeder, Howard, ed. LC 83-14382. (Horses (Pasture to Paddock) Ser.). (Illus.). 48p. (gr. 4 up). 1983. PLB 8.95 (ISBN 0-89686-231-3). Crestwood Hse.

--Thoroughbreds. Schroeder, Howard, ed. LC 83-7731. (Horses (Pasture to Paddock) Ser.). (Illus.). 48p. (gr. 4 up). 1983. PLB 8.95 (ISBN 0-89686-232-1). Crestwood Hse.

Callahan, Dorothy, jt. auth. see Payne, Alma.

Callahan, Ed. Fondue Cookbook. rev. ed. LC 77-670103. (Illus.). 104p. (Orig.). 1975. pap. 4.95 (ISBN 0-911954-01-5). Nitty Gritty.

Callahan, Edward J. & McCluskey, Kathleen, eds. Life-Span Development Psychology: Non-Normative-Life Events. LC 82-22784. 1983. 31.50 (ISBN 0-12-155140-7). Acad Pr.

Callahan, Edward W. List of Officers of the Navy of the U. S. & of the Marine Corps, 1775-1900. LC 68-31274. (Genealogy Ser., No. 43). 1969. Repr. of 1901 ed. lib. bdg. 58.95x (ISBN 0-8383-0327-7). Haskell.

Callahan, Genevieve & Richardson, Lou. Home Economics Show-How & Showmanship. (Illus.). 1966. 8.95x (ISBN 0-8138-1425-1). Iowa St U Pr.

Callahan, Genevieve, jt. auth. see Richardson, Louvice F.

Callahan, Harry. Eleanor, No. 35. Callaway, Nicholas & Kennedy, Anne, eds. LC 83-71130. (Illus.). 64p. 1984. pap. 16.00 (ISBN 0-933286-40-6). Friends Photography.

--Harry Callahan: Color. Tow, Robert & Winsor, Ricker, eds. (Illus.). 144p. 1980. 100.00 (ISBN 0-936554-00-2). Matrix Pubns.

Callahan, Helen, jt. auth. see Rowland, A. Ray.

Callahan, J. J. Science of Language. 1938. 15.00 (ISBN 0-8274-3338-7). R West.

Callahan, J. M. Neutrality of the American Lakes & Anglo-American Relations. 1973. Repr. of 1898 ed. 21.00 (ISBN 0-384-07195-3). Johnson Repr.

Callahan, James J., Jr. & Wallack, Stanley S., eds. Reforming the Long-Term-Care System: Financial & Organizational Options. LC 80-8366. (The University Health Policy Consortium Ser.). 272p. 1981. pap. 14.00x (ISBN 0-669-05547-6). Lexington Bks.

Callahan, James M. American Foreign Policy in Canadian Relations. LC 66-30786. 1937. 26.50 (ISBN 0-8154-0044-6). Cooper Sq.

--American Foreign Policy in Canadian Relations. 1937. 12.50x (ISBN 0-686-33257-1). R S Barnes.

--American Foreign Policy in Mexican Relations. LC 66-30787. 1932. 26.50 (ISBN 0-8154-0045-4). Cooper Sq.

--American Relations in the Pacific & the Far East, 1784-1900. LC 78-63879. (Johns Hopkins University. Studies in the Social Sciences. Nineteenth Ser. 1901: 1-3). Repr. of 1901 ed. 18.50 (ISBN 0-404-61134-6). AMS Pr.

--Cuba & International Relations. LC 76-39880. Repr. of 1899 ed. 28.50 (ISBN 0-404-01364-3). AMS Pr.

--Diplomatic History of the Southern Confederacy. LC 69-13849. Repr. of 1901 ed. lib. bdg. 15.75x (ISBN 0-8371-0336-3, CADH). Greenwood.

--The Neutrality of the American Lakes & Anglo-American Relations. LC 78-63862. (Johns Hopkins University. Studies in the Social Sciences. Sixteenth Ser. 1898: 1-4). Repr. of 1898 ed. 15.00 (ISBN 0-404-61118-4). AMS Pr.

Callahan, Jay. Night of the Wolf. 288p. 1985. pap. 3.25 (ISBN 0-8439-2269-9, Leisure Bks). Dorchester Pub Co.

Callahan, Jay C. Footprints of the Dead. (Twilight Ser.: No. 14). 160p. (Orig.). (YA) (gr. 5-9). 1983. pap. 1.95 (ISBN 0-440-92531-2, LFL). Dell.

Callahan, John F. Four Views of Time in Ancient Philosophy. LC 69-13850. Repr. of 1948 ed. lib. bdg. 15.00x (ISBN 0-8371-0337-1). Greenwood.

Callahan, John J. Needed: Professional Management in Data Processing. (Illus.). 240p. 1983. 30.00 (ISBN 0-13-610956-X). P-H.

Callahan, John W. & Lowden, J. Alexander, eds. Lysosomes & Lysosomal Storage Diseases. 455p. 1981. text ed. 71.50 (ISBN 0-89004-476-7). Raven.

Callahan, Joseph F. & Clark, Leonard H. Foundations of Education. 2nd ed. 384p. 1983. pap. text ed. write for info. (ISBN 0-02-318220-2). Macmillan.

--Introduction to American Education. 2nd ed. 352p. 1983. pap. text ed. write for info. (ISBN 0-02-318240-7). Macmillan.

--Teaching in the Elementary School: Planning for Competence. 1977. write for info. (ISBN 0-02-318070-6, 31807). Macmillan.

--Teaching in the Middle & Secondary School. 2nd ed. 1982. text ed. write for info. (ISBN 0-02-318260-1). Macmillan.

Callahan, Kennon L. Twelve Keys to an Effective Church. LC 83-47718. 1983. pap. 12.45 (ISBN 0-06-061297-5, HarpR). Har-Row.

Callahan, Leroy G., jt. auth. see Glennon, Vincent J.

Callahan, Leroy G., jt. auth. see Riedesel, C. Alan.

Callahan, Mrs. M. Mrs. M.'s Quick & Easy Refund & Rebate System. (Illus.). 12p. Date not set. pap. 4.95 (ISBN 0-915453-00-2). Info Bks.

Callahan, Michael T. & Bramble, Barry B. Discovery in Construction Litigation. 441p. 1983. 45.00 (ISBN 0-87215-588-9). Michie Co.

Callahan, Michael T. & Hohns, H. Murray. Construction Schedules: Analysis, Evaluation, and Interpretation of Schedules in Litigation. 314p. 1983. 45.00 (ISBN 0-87215-642-7). Michie Co.

Callahan, Neal & Young, David. Fill the Heavens with Commerce: Chicago Aviation 1855 to 1926. (Illus.). 250p. 1981. 15.00 (ISBN 0-914090-99-2). Chicago Review.

Callahan, Nelson J. Case for Due Process in the Church: Father Eugene O'Callaghan, American Pioneer of Dissent. LC 71-158570. 1971. 3.95 (ISBN 0-8189-0214-0). Alba.

Callahan, North. Carl Sandburg: Lincoln of Our Literature: A Biography. LC 76-92521. (Illus.). 1970. 25.00x (ISBN 0-8147-0069-1). NYU Pr.

--Daniel Morgan: Ranger of the Revolution. LC 71-161759. Repr. of 1961 ed. 14.50 (ISBN 0-404-09017-6). AMS Pr.

--Flight from the Republic: The Tories of the American Revolution. LC 75-42359. (Illus.). 208p. 1976. Repr. of 1967 ed. lib. bdg. 22.50x (ISBN 0-8371-7428-7, CAFR). Greenwood.

--TVA: Bridge Over Troubled Waters. LC 79-21586. (Illus.). 420p. 1980. 17.95 (ISBN 0-8453-2490-X). Cornwall Bks.

Callahan, North see Weaver, Glenn.

Callahan, P. J. How to Make a Will, How to Use Trusts. 4th ed. LC 78-7913. (Legal Almanac Ser.: No. 2). 128p. 1978. 5.95 (ISBN 0-379-11109-8). Oceana.

--Your Complete Guide to Estate Planning. rev. ed. LC 70-150939. (Legal Almanac Giant: No. 1). 399p. 1971. 8.50 (ISBN 0-379-10976-X). Oceana.

Callahan, Parnell J. How to Serve on a Jury. 2nd ed. LC 79-19272. (Legal Almanac Ser.: No. 31). 120p. (Orig.). 1979. 5.95 (ISBN 0-379-11122-5). Oceana.

--Law of Separation & Divorce. 4th ed. LC 78-25547. (Legal Almanac Ser.: No. 1). 128p. 1978. 5.95 (ISBN 0-379-11108-X). Oceana.

--Legal Status of Women. 2nd ed. LC 78-3469. (Legal Almanac Ser.: No. 53). 122p. 1978. 5.95 (ISBN 0-379-11115-2). Oceana.

--Protection Through the Law. 2nd ed. LC 78-808956. (Legal Almanac Ser.: No. 55). 128p. (Orig.). 1978. 5.95 (ISBN 0-379-11116-0). Oceana.

Callahan, Parnell J. & Nussbaum, Louis M. Real Estate Law for the Homeowner & Broker. Sloan, Irving J., ed. LC 79-28178. (Legal Almanac Ser.: No. 4). 128p. 1980. lib. bdg. 5.95 (ISBN 0-379-11121-7). Oceana.

Callahan, Patrick, et al, eds. Describing Foreign Policy Behavior. (Illus.). 416p. 1982. 32.50 (ISBN 0-8039-1708-2). Sage.

Callahan, Philip S. Birds & How They Function. LC 79-2109. (Illus.). 160p. (YA) 1979. 8.95 (ISBN 0-8234-0363-7). Holiday.

--Soul of the Ghost Moth: Paths of a Naturalist. (Illus.). 1980. 10.00 (ISBN 0-8159-6840-X). Devin.

--Tuning into Nature. (Illus.). 240p. 1976. 10.00 (ISBN 0-8159-6309-2). Devin.

Callahan, Raymond. The East India Company & Army Reform, 1783-1798. LC 70-188351. (Historical Monographs Ser: No. 67). (Illus.). 303p. 1972. 16.50x (ISBN 0-674-22410-8). Harvard U Pr.

Callahan, Raymond, jt. auth. see Payne, Howard E.

Callahan, Raymond A. Burma Nineteen Forty-Two to Nineteen Forty-Five. Frankland, Noble & Dowling, Christopher, eds. LC 79-52240. (The Politics & Strategy of the Second World War). 192p. 1979. 18.50 (ISBN 0-87413-162-6). U Delaware Pr.

--Churchill: Retreat from Empire. LC 83-20285. 288p. 1984. lib. bdg. 25.00 (ISBN 0-8420-2210-4). Scholarly Res Inc.

--The Worst Disaster: The Fall of Singapore. LC 75-29730. 293p. 1977. 25.00 (ISBN 0-87413-112-X). U Delaware Pr.

Callahan, Raymond E. Education & the Cult of Efficiency. LC 62-17961. 1962. 20.00x (ISBN 0-226-09148-1). U of Chicago Pr.

--Education & the Cult of Efficiency. 1962. pap. 11.00x (ISBN 0-226-09150-3, P149, Phoen). U of Chicago Pr.

Callahan, Robert, jt. ed. see Eron, Leonard D.

Callahan, Roger. Five Minute Phobia Cure. 1985. 12.95 (ISBN 0-913864-89-7). Enterprise Del.

Callahan, Roger & Levine, Karen. It Can Happen To You: The Practical Guide to Romantic Love. 1983. pap. 2.95 (ISBN 0-451-12270-4, Sig). NAL.

Callahan, Sean. Photographs of Margaret Bourke-White. LC 72-80415. (Illus.). 1975. pap. 11.95 (ISBN 0-8212-0656-7, 706655). NYGS.

Callahan, Sidney & Callahan, Daniel, eds. Abortion: Understanding Differences. (The Hastings Center Series in Ethics). 360p. 1984. 35.00x (ISBN 0-306-41640-9, Plenum Pr). Plenum Pub.

Callahan, Sidney, jt. ed. see Berger, Brigitte.

Callahan, Sterling G. Successful Teaching in Secondary Schools: A Guide for Student & In-Service Teachers. 2nd ed. 1971. text ed. 20.60x (ISBN 0-673-07720-9). Scott F.

Callahan, Thomas C. & Turner, Freda. Shadow of Death. LC 80-50008. (Illus.). 192p. 1980. 9.95 (ISBN 0-936354-01-1). Val-Hse Pub.

Callahan, Timothy R. Callahan's College Guide to Athletics & Academics in America: 1984 Edition. 1984. 17.95 (ISBN 0-06-015249-4); pap. 9.95 (ISBN 0-06-464081-7). Har-Row.

--Callahan's Compact College Guide to Athletics & Academics in America. LC 82-73347. 264p. 1982. 12.95 (ISBN 0-910967-00-8). Callahan's Guides.

Callahan, W. J. & Higgs, D. Church & Society in Catholic Europe of the Eighteenth Century. LC 78-12165. 1979. 27.95 (ISBN 0-521-22424-1). Cambridge U Pr.

Callahan, William. Song Leader's Handbook. 1980. pap. 7.95 (ISBN 0-915866-07-2). Am Cath Pr.

Callahan, William E., et al. The Continuing Quest: Introductory Readings in Philosophy. 1979. pap. text ed. 10.95 (ISBN 0-8403-2075-2). Kendall-Hunt.

Callahan, William J. Church, Politics, & Society in Spain, 1750-1874. (Harvard Historical Monographs: No. 73). (Illus.). 336p. 1984. text ed. 25.00x (ISBN 0-674-13125-8). Harvard U Pr.

Callan, Charles J. & Callan, Frank H. Excellence in English. 1924. 14.50 (ISBN 0-8159-5402-6). Devin.

Callan, Edward. Alan Paton. rev. ed. (World Authors Ser.). 1982. lib. bdg. 14.50 (ISBN 0-8057-6512-3, Twayne). G K Hall.

--Auden: A Carnival of Intellect. 1983. 25.00 (ISBN 0-19-503168-7). Oxford U Pr.

--Yeats on Yeats: The Last Introductions & 'Under Ben Bulben' (Illus.). 96p. 1980. pap. text ed. 23.00x (ISBN 0-85105-370-X, Dolmen Pr). Humanities.

Callan, Frank H., jt. auth. see Callan, Charles J.

Callan, Hilary & Ardener, Shirley, eds. The Incorporated Wife. LC 84-12743. 224p. 1984. (Pub. by Croom Helm Ltd); pap. 13.50 (ISBN 0-7099-0556-4). Longwood Pub Group.

Callan, Jamie. Over the Hill at Fourteen. 176p. pap. 1.95 (ISBN 0-451-13090-1, Sig Vista). NAL.

--The Young & the Soapy. 160p. 1984. pap. 2.25 (ISBN 0-451-12981-4, Sig Vista). NAL.

Callan, John F. The Military Laws of the United States 1776-1858. LC 70-165125. 488p. 1858. lib. bdg. 45.00 (ISBN 0-87821-085-7). Milford Hse.

Callan, John P. The Physician: A Professional Under Stress. 408p. 1983. 29.95 (ISBN 0-8385-7855-1). ACC.

--Your Guide to Mental Help. (People's Health Library). 200p. 1982. 9.50 (ISBN 0-89313-059-1). G F Stickley.

Callan, Laurence B., jt. auth. see Eisner, Victor.

Callan, Michael F. Julie Christie. (Illus.). 1985. 14.95 (ISBN 0-312-44851-1). St Martin.

--Sean Connery. 296p. Date not set. pap. 3.50 (ISBN 0-8128-8120-6). Stein & Day.

--Sean Connery: His Life & Times. LC 83-42827. 312p. 1983. 16.95 (ISBN 0-8128-2932-8). Stein & Day.

Callanan, Joseph. Communicating: How to Organize Meetings & Presentations. 272p. 1984. 15.95 (ISBN 0-531-09575-4). Watts.

Callander, Lee A. & Slivka, Ruth. Shawnee Home Life: The Painting of Earnest Spybuck. LC 84-70468. (Illus.). 32p. 1984. pap. 8.95 (ISBN 0-934490-42-2). Mus Am Ind.

Callander, Lee A., jt. auth. see Fawcett, David M.

Callander, R. A., jt. auth. see Stephenson, John.

Callander, Robin, jt. auth. see McNaught, Ann B.

Callao, David P. & Rowland, Benjamin M. America & the World Political Economy: Atlantic Dreams & National Realities. LC 73-173390. pap. 95.80 (ISBN 0-317-27944-0, 2056025). Bks Demand UMI.

Callard, D. A. Pretty Good for a Woman: The Engimas of Evelyn Scott. (Illus.). 1986. 14.95 (ISBN 0-393-02276-5). Norton.

Callarman, Frederick A. Paulevala: Land of Hurrahs. 88p. (Orig.). 1981. pap. 1.98 (ISBN 0-930092-01-5). Callarman Hse.

Callarman, Ruth. California Guide to Motel-Hotel Discounts. 104p. (Orig.). 1985. pap. 6.98x (ISBN 0-9613087-1-0). Potter Pubns.

--California Guide to Restaurant Discounts. 160p. (Orig.). 1985. pap. 8.98x (ISBN 0-9613087-2-9). Potter Pubns.

--Seniors Living It Up on a Budget: California Edition. 212p. (Orig.). 1983. pap. 10.00x (ISBN 0-9613087-0-2). Potter Pubns.

Callas, Evangelia & Blochman, Lawrence G. My Daughter Maria Callas. Farkas, Andrew, ed. LC 76-29928. (Opera Biographies). (Illus.). 1977. Repr. of 1960 ed. lib. bdg. 19.00x (ISBN 0-405-09671-2). Ayer Co Pubs.

Callaway, Archibald. Educational Planning & Unemployed Youth. (Fundamentals of Educational Planning: No. 14). 47p. (Orig.). 1971. pap. 5.00 (ISBN 92-803-1040-2, U206, UNESCO). Unipub.

Callaway, Archibald, et al. The Nigerian Political Scene. LC 62-18315. (Duke University Commonwealth-Studies Center Publications Ser.: No. 17). pap. 88.00 (ISBN 0-317-28829-6, 2017939). Bks Demand UMI.

Callaway, Cason J., Jr. & Flowers, Charles M., eds. A Southern Collection. LC 81-68298. (Illus.). 318p. (Orig.). 1979. pap. 10.00 (ISBN 0-9606300-0-7). Jr League Columbus.

Callaway, Enoch, jt. ed. see Lehmann, Dietrich.

Callaway, Enoch, et al, eds. Event-Related Brain Potentials in Man. (Behavioral Biology Ser.). 1978. 55.00 (ISBN 0-12-155150-4). Acad Pr.

Callaway, Frank, ed. Australian Composition in the Twentieth Century. Tunley, David. 1978. 52.00x (ISBN 0-19-550522-0). Oxford U Pr.

Callaway, Godfrey. Fellowship of the Veld: Sketches of Native Life in South Africa. LC 71-89027. (Illus.). Repr. of 1926 ed. cancelled (ISBN 0-8371-1913-8, CFV&, Pub. by Negro U Pr). Greenwood.

--Sketches of Kafir Life. LC 79-77192. (Illus.). Repr. 19.75x (ISBN 0-8371-1277-X, CAK&). Greenwood.

Callaway, Henry. Nursery Tales, Traditions, & Histories of the Zulus: In their Own Words, with a Translation. LC 72-132641. Repr. of 1868 ed. 22.50x (ISBN 0-8371-2493-X, CNT&, Pub. by Negro U Pr). Greenwood.

Callaway, Joseph. Electron Energy Bands in Solids. (Solid State Reprint Ser.). 1964. 21.50 (ISBN 0-12-608450-5). Acad Pr.

--Energy Band Theory. (Pure and Applied Physics: Vol. 16). 1964. 59.50 (ISBN 0-12-155250-0). Acad Pr.

--Pottery from Tombs at Ai. (Colt Archaeological Institute Monograph: No. 2). (Illus.). 56p. 1964. pap. text ed. 13.50x (ISBN 0-85668-066-4, Pub. by Aris & Phillips England). Humanities.

Callaway, Joseph, ed. Quantum Theory of the Solid State. 1976. 29.00 (ISBN 0-12-155256-X). Acad Pr.

Callaway, Joseph A. The Annual of the American Schools of Oriental Research, Vols. 47-48. Incl. Vol. 47: The Excavations at Araq El-Emir. Lapp, Nancy L., ed; Vol. 48: The Amman Airport Excavations, 1976. LC 83-11819. 1984. 30.00x (ISBN 0-89757-047-2, Am Sch Orient Res). Eisenbrauns.

--The Early Bronze Age Citadel & Lower City at Ai. LC 79-23011. (Report of the Joint Archaeological Expedition to Ai Ser.: Vol. 2). 295p. 1981. text ed. 25.00x (ISBN 0-89757-202-5, Am Sch Orient Res). Eisenbrauns.

Callaway, Joseph A. & Adams, J. McKee, eds. Biblical Backgrounds. rev. ed. 1966. 14.95 (ISBN 0-8054-1113-5). Broadman.

Callaway, Kathy. The Bloodroot Flower. LC 81-20799. 192p. (gr. 5-9). 1982. 9.95 (ISBN 0-394-85276-1); PLB 9.99 (ISBN 0-394-95276-6). Knopf.

--Heart of the Garfish. LC 81-70217. (Pitt Poetry Ser.). 60p. 1982. 12.95x (ISBN 0-8229-3458-2); pap. 5.95 (ISBN 0-8229-5338-2). U of Pittsburgh Pr.

Callaway, Lew L. Montana's Righteous Hangmen: The Vigilantes in Action. Callaway, Lew L., Jr., ed. LC 81-40282. (Illus.). 240p. 1982. 13.95 (ISBN 0-8061-1728-1). U of Okla Pr.

Callaway, Nicholas, ed. see Callahan, Harry.

Callaway, Sydney M., jt. auth. see Johnson, Broderick.

Callaway, Tucker N. Zen Way - Jesus Way. LC 76-6032. 1976. 11.00 (ISBN 0-8048-1190-3). C E Tuttle.

Callaway, William J., jt. auth. see Gurley, LaVerne T.

Callcott, Frank. The Supernatural in Early Spanish Literature. 158p. 1.00 (ISBN 0-318-14309-7). Hispanic Inst.

Callcott, George H. History in the United States, 1800-1860: Its Practice & Purpose. LC 74-88115. 247p. 1970. 23.50x (ISBN 0-8018-1099-X). Johns Hopkins.

--A History of the University of Maryland. LC 65-29087. 422p. 1966. casebound 9.75 (ISBN 0-686-86319-4). Maryland Hist Pr.

--Maryland & America, Nineteen Forty to Nineteen Eighty. LC 85-166. (Illus.). 416p. 1985. 27.50 (ISBN 0-8018-2492-3). Johns Hopkins.

Callcott, M. V. & Peters, Terry, eds. Mr. George, 2 pts. Incl. Pt. 1. In Victorian England; Pt. 2. In Pioneer Texas. (National History Ser.). (Illus.). Date not set. 22.95 (ISBN 0-89482-046-X); ltd. ed. 39.95 (ISBN 0-89482-048-6); pap. 12.95 (ISBN 0-89482-047-8); video cassette of Frank Callcott 165.00 (ISBN 0-89482-022-2). Stevenson Pr.

Callcott, W. H. South Carolina: Economic & Social Conditions in 1944. LC 74-34437. 248p. 1975. Repr. of 1945 ed. 12.50 (ISBN 0-87152-189-X). Reprint.

Callcott, Wilfrid H. Caribbean Policy of the United States, 1890-1920. 1967. lib. bdg. 40.00x (ISBN 0-374-91216-5). Octagon.

--Church & State in Mexico, 1822-1857. 1965. lib. bdg. 27.00x (ISBN 0-374-91235-1). Octagon.

--Liberalism in Mexico, 1857-1929. 1976. lib. bdg. 59.95 (ISBN 0-8490-2157-X). Gordon Pr.

--Liberalism in Mexico, 1857-1929. (Illus.). xiii, 410p. 1965. Repr. of 1931 ed. 29.50 (ISBN 0-208-00278-2, Archon). Shoe String.

--Santa Anna: The Story of an Enigma Who Once Was Mexico. LC 36-37514. pap. 101.30 (ISBN 0-317-28705-2, 2055509). Bks Demand UMI.

--The Western Hemisphere: Its Influence on United States Policies to the End of World War II. 520p. 1968. 30.00x (ISBN 0-292-78390-6). U of Tex Pr.

Calle, Paul. The Pencil. (Illus.). 1975. 17.50 (ISBN 0-8230-3990-0). Watson-Guptill.

--The Pencil. LC 74-83836. (Illus.). 160p. 1985. pap. 15.95 (ISBN 0-89134-118-8). North Light Pub.

Callebaut, M., et al. Meiosis: Current Research, 4 vols, Vol. 4. LC 72-6751. 244p. 1972. text ed. 24.50x (ISBN 0-8422-7041-8). Irvington.

Calleiro, Mary. Distancia de un Espacio Prometido. LC 84-73242. (Coleccion Espejo de Paciencia). (Illus.). 78p. (Orig., Span.). 1985. pap. 6.95 (ISBN 0-89729-365-7). Ediciones.

Callejo, Fernando. Music & Musicians of Puerto Rico. (Puerto Rico Ser.). 1979. lib. bdg. 59.95 (ISBN 0-8490-2974-0). Gordon Pr.

Callely, A., et al, eds. Treatment of Industrial Effluents. LC 76-54909. 378p. 1977. 42.95x (ISBN 0-470-98934-3). Halsted Pr.

Callely, A. G., jt. ed. see Bousfield, I. J.

Callen, Anna T. Anna Teresa Callen's Menus for Pasta. 1985. 12.95 (ISBN 0-517-55400-3). Crown.

--Science Fiction Puzzle Tales. Behrman, Marion, ed. 288p. 1981. 10.95 (ISBN 0-517-54380-X). Crown.

--The Wonderful World of Pizzas, Quiches, & Savory Pies. LC 80-23802. 288p. 1981. 5.98 (ISBN 0-517-53683-8). Crown.

Callen, Anthea. Courbet. 1981. 27.00x (ISBN 0-906379-42-3, Pub. by Jupiter England). State Mutual Bk.

--Renoir. LC 77-10354. (Oresko Art Book). (Illus.). 1978. 15.95 (ISBN 0-8467-0377-7, Pub. by Two Continents); pap. 9.95 (ISBN 0-8467-0378-5). Hippocrene Bks.

--Renoir. 1981. 27.00x (ISBN 0-905368-20-7, Pub. by Jupiter England). State Mutual Bk.

Callen, Barry L., ed. First Century: Church of God Reformation Movement, 2 vols. 1977. Set. 19.95 set (ISBN 0-317-18001-0). Vol. I (D1386). Vol. II (ISBN 0-87162-220-3, D1387). Warner Pr.

Callen, Donald M., ed. see Beardsley, Monroe C.

Callen, Herbert B. Thermodynamics: An Introduction to the Physical Theories of Equilibrium Thermostatics & Irreversible Thermodynamics. LC 60-5597. (Illus.). 376p. 1960. text ed. 35.50 (ISBN 0-471-13035-4). Wiley.

Callen, Jeffery P. Cutaneous Aspects of Internal Disease. 1980. 99.95 (ISBN 0-8151-1411-7). Year Bk Med.

Callen, Jeffrey P., et al. Manual of Dermatology: An Introduction to Diagnosis & Treatment. (Illus.). 1980. pap. 26.50 (ISBN 0-8151-1410-9). Year Bk Med.

Callen, Larry. The Deadly Mandrake. (Illus.). (gr. 3-7). 1978. 7.95 (ISBN 0-316-12496-6, Atlantic-Little, Brown). Little.

--If the World Ends. LC 83-6429. (Escapade Ser.). 128p. (gr. 3-7). 1983. 3.95 (ISBN 0-689-31372-1). Atheneum.

--The Just-Right Family. (Cabbage Patch Kids Ser.). (Illus.). 40p. 1984. 5.95 (ISBN 0-910313-26-1). Parker Bro.

--Muskrat War. 144p. (gr. 5 up). 1980. 8.95 (ISBN 0-316-12498-2, Pub. by Atlantic-Little Brown). Little.

--Pinch. (Illus.). 1976. 10.45i (ISBN 0-316-12495-8, Pub.by Atlantic Monthly Pr). Little.

--Sorrow's Song. LC 78-31789. (Illus.). (gr. 3-7). 1979. 10.70i (ISBN 0-316-12497-4, Pub by Atlantic Monthly Pr). Little.

--Who Kidnapped the Sheriff? Or, Tales From Tickfaw. Kroupa, Melanie, ed. LC 84-72596. (Illus.). 176p. (gr. 4 up). 1985. 13.95 (ISBN 0-87113-008-4). Atlantic Monthly.

Callen, Peter W. Ultrasonography in Obstetrics & Gynecology. (Illus.). 368p. 1983. 47.95 (ISBN 0-7216-2331-X). Saunders.

Callen, Richard W., jt. auth. see Hayen, Roger L.

Callenbach, Ernest. Ecotopia. (gr. 10 up). 1977. pap. 3.95 (ISBN 0-553-23471-4). Bantam.

--Ecotopia. LC 74-84366. 168p. (Orig.). 1975. 10.00 (ISBN 0-9604320-0-0); pap. 4.95 (ISBN 0-9604320-1-9). Banyan Tree.

--Ecotopia Emerging. LC 81-10821. 320p. (Orig.). 1981. lib. bdg. 18.00 (ISBN 0-9604320-4-3); pap. 7.95 (ISBN 0-9604320-3-5). Banyan Tree.

--The Ecotopian Encyclopedia for the Eighties. LC 81-2148. (Illus.). 352p. 1981. 9.95 (ISBN 0-915904-54-3). And-Or Pr.

Callenbach, Ernest & Phillips, Michael. A Citizen Legislature. LC 84-28377. 96p. (Orig.). 1985. pap. 6.00 (ISBN 0-9604320-5-1, Dist. by Bookpeople). Banyan Tree.

Callenbach, Ernest, jt. auth. see Leefeldt, Christine.

Callender, Charles & El Guindi, Fadwa. Life-Crisis Rituals among the Kenuz. (Illus.). 87p. 1985. pap. text ed. 6.95x (ISBN 0-317-19713-4). Waveland Pr.

Callender, E., tr. see Cazenave.

Callender, Edward B. Thaddeus Stevens, Commoner. LC 70-39881. Repr. of 1882 ed. 18.00 (ISBN 0-404-00011-8). AMS Pr.

Callender, G., ed. see Southey, Robert.

Callender, Guy S. Selections from the Economic History of the United States 1765-1860. LC 65-19646. Repr. of 1909 ed. 50.00x (ISBN 0-678-00080-8). Kelley.

Callender, J. Time-Saver Standards for Architectural Design Data. 6th ed. 1982. 75.00 (ISBN 0-07-009663-5). McGraw.

Callender, John. Historical Discourse on the Civil & Religious Affairs of the Colony of Rhode Island. facs. ed. LC 79-150172. (Select Bibliographies Reprint Ser.). 1843. 18.00 (ISBN 0-8369-5685-0). Ayer Co Pubs.

Callender, John, jt. auth. see De Chiara, Joseph.

Callender, John B. Studies in the Nominal Sentence in Egyptian & Coptic. LC 83-17961. (Near Eastern Studies: Vol. 24). 232p. 1984. lib. bdg. 22.00 (ISBN 0-520-09675-4). U of Cal Pr.

Callender, Willard D. How to Make a Friendly Call. 112p. 1982. pap. 4.95 (ISBN 0-8170-0947-7). Judson.

Calleo, David. The Atlantic Fantasy: The U. S., NATO, & Europe. (Studies in Int'l Affairs Series: No. 13). 192p. 1970. 17.00x (ISBN 0-8018-1222-4); pap. 3.95x (ISBN 0-8018-1196-1). Johns Hopkins.

--The German Problem Reconsidered. LC 78-9683. 1978. 29.95 (ISBN 0-521-22309-1). Cambridge U Pr.

--The German Problem Reconsidered. LC 78-9683. 208p. 1980. pap. 10.95 (ISBN 0-521-29966-7). Cambridge U Pr.

--The Imperious Economy. LC 81-20066. (Illus.). 304p. 1982. 18.50 (ISBN 0-674-44522-8); pap. 7.95 1983 272p. (ISBN 0-674-44521-X). Harvard U Pr.

Calleo, David P. American Political System. LC 69-17194. (Background Ser.). 1969. 7.95 (ISBN 0-8023-1210-1). Dufour.

--Europe's Future: The Grand Alternatives. 1967. pap. 1.95x (ISBN 0-393-00406-6, Norton Lib.). Norton.

Callery, Bernadette G. & Mosimann, E. A., eds. The Tradition of Fine Bookbinding in the Twentieth Century. (Illus.). 120p. 1979. 25.00x (ISBN 0-913196-28-2); unbd. o.p. 22.00 (ISBN 0-686-65642-3). Hunt Inst Botanical.

Callery, Michael. Commodore Magic. (Illus.). 256p. 1984. pap. 12.95 (ISBN 0-525-48120-6, 01258-370). Dutton.

Callery, Michael, jt. auth. see Schwartz, Roberta.

Callesen, Gerd & Logue, John. Social-Demokraten & Internationalism: The Copenhagen Social Democratic Newspaper's Coverage of International Labor Affairs, 1871-1958. (U. of Gothenburg (Sweden), Research Section Post-War History Publications: No. 8). (Illus.). 73p. 1979. pap. 3.95 (ISBN 0-933522-00-2). Kent Popular.

Callesen, Gerd, et al, eds. see Bryld, Claus, et al.

Callewaert, Denis M. & Genyea, Julien. Basic Chemistry: General, Organic, Biological. 1980. text ed. 28.95x (ISBN 0-87901-130-0). Worth.

--Fundamentals of College Chemistry. 1980. text ed. 24.95x (ISBN 0-87901-125-4). Worth.

--Fundamentals of Organic & Biological Chemistry. 1980. text ed. 25.95x (ISBN 0-87901-129-7). Worth.

Callewaert, Winand M. Bhagavadgitanuvada: A Study in Transcultural Translation. 1984. 26.00x (ISBN 0-8364-1148-X, Pub. by Satya Bharati Pub). South Asia Bks.

Callicott, J. Baird, jt. auth. see Overholt, Thomas W.

Callicutt, James W. & Lecca, Pedro J., eds. Social Work & Mental Health. LC 82-71734. 245p. 1983. 22.95x (ISBN 0-02-905830-9); pap. text ed. 12.95 (ISBN 0-02-905850-3). Free Pr.

Callie, M. K. Quien Me Robo a Mi Hija? De Torres, Jacinto, tr. from Eng. (Compadre Collection Ser). Orig. Title: Where Have All the Little Girls Gone. 160p. (Span.). 1974. pap. 0.85 (ISBN 0-88473-707-1). Fiesta Pub.

Callier, F. M. & Desoer, C. A. Multivariable Feedback Systems. (Springer Texts in Electrical Engineering). (Illus.). 275p. 1982. 42.00 (ISBN 0-387-90768-8); pap. 21.50 (ISBN 0-387-90759-9). Springer-Verlag.

Callies, David L. Regulating Paradise: Land Use Control in Hawaii. LC 84-8718. 253p. 1984. pap. text ed. 14.95x (ISBN 0-8248-0891-6). UH Pr.

Callies, Fritz A. Playing with Grown Ups. 1978. pap. 6.95 (ISBN 0-8100-0007-5, 11N0623). Northwest Pub.

Calligan, Edward L., ed. see Mencken, H. L.

Callihan, D. Jeanne & Nesmith, Samuel P. Our Mexican Ancestors, Vol. I. (Young Readers Ser.). (Illus.). 124p. (gr. 5-8). 8.95 (ISBN 0-933164-39-4); pap. 5.95 (ISBN 0-933164-38-6). U of Tex Inst Tex Culture.

Callihan, E. L. Grammar for Journalists. 3rd ed. LC 78-22114. 1979. pap. 9.95 (ISBN 0-8019-6823-2). Chilton.

Callimachi, Anne-Marie, tr. see Colette.

Callimachus. Aetia, Iambi, Lyric Poems, Hecale, Minor Epic & Elegiac Poems, Fragments of Epigrams, Fragments of Uncertain Location. (Loeb Classical Library: No. 421). 1958. 12.50x (ISBN 0-674-99463-9). Harvard U Pr.

--Callimachus, 2 vols. in 1. Pfeiffer, Rudolfus & Connor, W. R., eds. LC 78-18592. (Greek Texts & Commentaries Ser.). 1979. Repr. of 1953 ed. lib. bdg. 68.50x (ISBN 0-405-11433-8). Ayer Co Pubs.
--Hymns & Epigrams. Bd. with Poems. Lycophron; Poems. Aratus. (Loeb Classical Library: No. 129). 12.50x (ISBN 0-674-99143-5). Harvard U Pr.
Callinicos, Alex. Is There a Future for Marxism? 272p. 1981. (Pub. by Macmillan England); pap. text ed. 15.50x (ISBN 0-391-02360-8). Humanities.
--Marxism & Philosophy. (Marxist Introductions Ser.). 1983. 17.95x (ISBN 0-19-876126-0). Oxford U Pr.
--Southern Africa After Zimbabwe. 192p. pap. 5.95 (ISBN 0-86104-336-7). Pluto Pr.
Callinicos, Luli. Workers on the Rand: Factories, Townships & Popular Culture, 1886-1942. (A People's History of South Africa Ser.: Vol. II). 160p. 1985. pap. 8.95 (ISBN 0-86975-227-8, Pub. by Ravan Pr). Ohio U Pr.
Callis, Helmut G. Foreign Capital in Southeast Asia. LC 75-30051. (Institute of Pacific Relations Ser.). Repr. of 1942 ed. 27.50 (ISBN 0-404-59514-6). AMS Pr.
--Foreign Capital in Southeast Asia. Bruchey, Stuart & Bruchey, Eleanor, eds. LC 76-4998. (American Business Abroad Ser.). (Illus.). 1976. Repr. of 1942 ed. 17.00x (ISBN 0-405-09267-9). Ayer Co Pubs.
Callis, Robert, et al, eds. Ethical Standards Casebook. Rev. ed. 116p. 1982. pap. text ed. 9.75 (ISBN 0-911547-37-1, 72125W34). Am Assn Coun Dev.
Callison, C. Stuart. The Land-to-the-Tiller Program & Rural Resource Mobilization in the Mekong Delta of South Vietnam. LC 74-620183. (Papers in International Studies: Southeast Asia Ser.: No. 34). (Illus.). 1974. pap. 4.50x (ISBN 0-89680-020-2, 82-90355, Ohio U Ctr Intl). Ohio U Pr.
Callison, Charles H., ed. America's Natural Resources. rev. ed. LC 67-14482. pap. 56.80 (ISBN 0-317-28652-8, 2055092). Bks Demand UMI.
Callison, Charles S. Land-to-the-Tiller in the Mekong Delta: Economic, Social & Political Effects of Land Reform in Four Villages of South Vietnam. LC 83-6745. (Monograph Ser.: No. 23). (Illus.). 418p. (Orig.). 1983. lib. bdg. 30.25 (ISBN 0-8191-3252-7, Co-pub. by Ctr S&SE Asia Stud); pap. text ed. 17.50 (ISBN 0-8191-3253-5). U Pr of Amer.
Callison, Herbert G. Introduction to Community-Based Corrections. (McGraw-Hill Series in Criminology & Criminal Justice). (Illus.). 384p. 1982. text ed. 28.95 (ISBN 0-07-009637-6). McGraw.
Callison, William L. Using Computers in the Classroom. (Illus.). 192p. 1985. pap. 16.95 (ISBN 0-13-940214-4). P-H.
Callison, William L., jt. auth. see Iles, Robert H.
Callister, J. Herbert. Dress from Three Centuries. LC 76-14506. (Illus.). 86p. 1976. pap. 7.00 (ISBN 0-317-13585-6). Wadsworth Atheneum.
Callister, W. D. Materials Science & Engineering: An Introduction. 602p. 1985. 34.95 (ISBN 0-471-08145-0). Wiley.
Callistratus see Philostratus The Elder.
Callman, Ellen. Family Pride: The Italian Renaissance House & its Furnishings. LC 84-80552. 54p. pap. text ed. 3.00 (ISBN 0-9606718-2-X). Hyde Collect.
Callois, ed. see Corneille, Pierre.
Callot, Jacques. Callot's Etchings. Daniel, Howard, ed. (Illus., Orig.). 1974. 10.00 (ISBN 0-486-23081-3); pap. 8.00 (ISBN 0-486-23073-2). Dover.
Calloud, Jean & Patte, Daniel, trs. Structural Analysis of Narrative. 108p. 1976. pap. 8.95 (ISBN 0-317-35734-4, 06-06-04). Scholars Pr GA.
Callow, Alexander B. The Tweed Ring. LC 81-6528. (Illus.). xi, 351p. 1981. Repr. of 1966 ed. lib. bdg. 28.75x (ISBN 0-313-22761-6, CATR). Greenwood.
Callow, Alexander B., Jr., ed. American Urban History: An Interpretive Reader with Commentaries. 3rd ed. (Illus.). 1982. pap. text ed. 12.95x (ISBN 0-19-502981-X). Oxford U Pr.
Callow, Edward. The Phynodderree & Other Legends of the Isle of Man. LC 75-174441. (Illus.). Repr. of 1882 ed. 20.00 (ISBN 0-405-08336-X, Blom Pubns). Ayer Co Pubs.
Callow, J. A. Biochemical Plant Pathology. 484p. 1983. 69.95x (ISBN 0-471-90092-3, Pub. by Wiley-Interscience). Wiley.
Callow, J. A. & Woolhouse, H. W., eds. Advances in Botanical Research, Vol. 11. (Serial Publication Ser.). 1985. 55.00 (ISBN 0-12-005911-8). Acad Pr.
Callow, James T. & Reilly, Robert J. Guide to American Literature from Emily Dickinson to the Present. LC 75-39903. 272p. 1977. text ed. 24.50x (ISBN 0-06-480133-0, 06381). B&N Imports.
--Guide to American Literature from Its Beginnings Through Walt Whitman. LC 75-29621. 244p. 1976. text ed. 17.50x (ISBN 0-06-480132-2). B&N Imports.
Callow, Paul & Cornford, Jean, eds. La Cotte de St. Brelade: Excavations on Jersey by Charles McBurney, 1961-1978. (Studies in Archaeology). Date not set. price not set (ISBN 0-12-155270-5). Acad Pr.
Callow, Ridgeway, et al. You Can Make It: A Insider's Guide to a Hollywood Career. (Illus.). 88p. (Orig.). 1981. pap. 7.95 (ISBN 0-9606328-0-8). You Can Make It Ent.
Callow, Simon. Being an Actor. (Illus.). 224p. 1985. 15.95 (ISBN 0-413-52440-X, NO. 9187). Methuen Inc.
Calloway, jt. auth. see Igel.
Calloway, Doris H., jt. auth. see Briggs, George M.
Calloway, Doris H., jt. auth. see Carpenter, Kathy.
Calloway, Jan. The Trapnall Legacy. LC 81-67266. (Illus.). 112p. (Orig.). 1981. 9.95 (ISBN 0-9606278-0-4); pap. 5.95 (ISBN 0-9606278-1-2). AR Commemorative.
Calloway, Jo. All the Days to Come. (Candlelight Ecstasy Supreme Ser.: No. 70). 288p. pap. 2.50 (ISBN 0-440-10117-4). Dell.
--Ashes of Honor. 1978. pap. 2.25 (ISBN 0-532-22136-2). Woodhill.
--A Classic Love. (Candlelight Ecstasy Ser.: No. 220). 192p. (Orig.). 1984. pap. 1.95 (ISBN 0-440-11242-7). Dell.
--Dawn's Promise. (Candlelight Ecstasy Ser.: No. 121). (Orig.). 1983. pap. 1.95 (ISBN 0-440-11619-8). Dell.
--Heartbeats. (Candlelight Ecstasy Supreme Ser.: No. 238). (Orig.). 1984. pap. 1.95 (ISBN 0-440-13609-1). Dell.
--Illusive Lover. (Candlelight Ecstasy Ser.: No. 164). 192p. (Orig.). 1983. pap. 1.95 (ISBN 0-440-14526-0). Dell.
--Mirrors of Love. 224p. 1983. pap. 2.75 (ISBN 0-380-84434-6, 84434-6). Avon.
--One of a Kind. (Candlelight Ecstasy Ser.: No. 150). (Orig.). 1983. pap. 1.95 (ISBN 0-440-16689-6). Dell.
--Scattered Roses. (Candlelight Ecstasy Ser.: No. 273). 192p. (Orig.). 1984. pap. 1.95 (ISBN 0-440-17606-9). Dell.
--Somewhere in the Stars. (Candlelight Ecstasy Supreme Ser.: No. 24). (Orig.). 1984. pap. 2.50 (ISBN 0-440-18157-7). Dell.
--Southern Fire. (Candlelight Ecstasy Ser.: No. 376). (Orig.). 1985. pap. 2.25 (ISBN 0-440-18170-4). Dell.
--Special Sparrow. 1978. pap. 1.50 (ISBN 0-532-15350-2). Woodhill.
--Through the Eyes of Love. (Candlelight Ecstasy Ser.). (Orig.). 1985. pap. 2.25 (ISBN 0-440-18672-2). Dell.
--Time of a Winter Love. (Candlelight Ecstasy Supreme Ser.: No. 6). 288p. (Orig.). 1983. pap. 2.50 (ISBN 0-440-18915-2). Dell.
--To Catch the Wild Wind. (Candlelight Ecstasy Ser.: No. 82). (Orig.). 1982. pap. 1.95 (ISBN 0-440-11126-9). Dell.
--To Remember Love. (Candlelight Ecstacy Ser.: No. 282). (Orig.). 1984. pap. 1.95 (ISBN 0-440-18711-7). Dell.
--Touched by Fire. (Candlelight Ecstasy Supreme Ser.: No. 41). 288p. (Orig.). 1984. pap. 2.50 (ISBN 0-440-19015-0). Dell.
--Where the River Bends. (Candlelight Ecstasy Ser.: No. 109). (Orig.). 1983. pap. 1.95 (ISBN 0-440-19650-7). Dell.
--Windsong. (Candlelight Ecstasy Romance Ser.: No. 188). (Orig.). 1983. pap. 1.95 (ISBN 0-440-19495-4). Dell.
Calloway, P. H. Human Ecology in Space Flight, 3 Vols. Incl. Vol. 1. Proceedings of the First Conference. 286p. 1969. 63.95 (ISBN 0-677-65030-2); Vol. 2. Proceedings of the Second Conference. 298p. 1967. 63.95 (ISBN 0-677-65040-X); Vol. 3. Proceedings of the Third Conference. 246p. 1968. 55.00 (ISBN 0-677-65050-7). 830p. 1969. Set. 161.75 (ISBN 0-677-65220-8). Gordon.
Calloway, Stephen. English Prints for the Collector. LC 80-19370. (Illus.). 240p. 1981. 85.00 (ISBN 0-87951-120-6). Overlook Pr.
--English Prints for the Collector. 1981. 50.00x (ISBN 0-7188-2447-4, Pub. by Lutterworth Pr England). State Mutual Bk.
Callson, Oliver G., jt. auth. see Flood, Kenneth U.
Callum, Michael, tr. see Fernandez, Dominique.
Callvert, Isabel, jt. auth. see Beard, James A.
Callwell, C. E. Small Wars: Their Principles & Practices. (Illus.). 1977. Repr. of 1906 ed. 35.00x (ISBN 0-7158-1200-9). Charles River Bks.
Callwood, June. Emma: A True Story of Treason. (Illus.). 288p. 1985. 16.95 (ISBN 0-8253-0251-X). Beaufort Bks NY.
Calman, Kenneth C., jt. ed. see Mareel, Marc M.
Calman, Leslie J. Protest in Democratic India: Authority's Response to Challenge. (WVSS on East Asia Ser.). 250p. 1985. pap. 19.50x (ISBN 0-8133-7060-4). Westview.
Calman, Mel. Dr. Calman's Psychoanalysis Book. 48p. (Orig.). 1981. pap. 1.50 (ISBN 0-8431-0659-X). Price Stern.
Calman, Stephanie. Gentlemen Prefer My Sister. 192p. 1985. 14.95 (ISBN 0-434-10620-8, Pub. by W Heinemann Ltd). David & Charles.
Calmann, Marianne. The Carriere of Carpentras. (Litman Library of Jewish Civilization). (Illus.). 1984. 29.95x (ISBN 0-19-710037-6). Oxford U Pr.
Calmeil, Louis F. De la Paralysie Consideree Chez les Alienes. LC 75-16696. (Classics in Psychiatry Ser.). (Fr.). 1976. Repr. of 1826 ed. 34.50x (ISBN 0-405-07424-7). Ayer Co Pubs.
Calmeil, Louis-Florentin. De la Folie: Consideree Soys le Point De Vue Pathologique, Philosophique, Historique et Judiciai Re, 2 vols. in 1. LC 75-16695. (Classics in Psychiatry Ser.). (Fr.). 1976. Repr. of 1845 ed. 79.50x (ISBN 0-405-07423-9). Ayer Co Pubs.
Calmels, ed. see Pagnol, Marcel.
Calmenson, Stephanie. The After School Book. (Kindergarten Storybks.). (Illus.). 48p. (ps-1). 1984. 5.95 (ISBN 0-448-11227-2, G&D). Putnam Pub Group.
--All Aboard the Goodnight Train. (Illus.). (ps-1). 1984. 5.95 (ISBN 0-448-11226-4, G&D). Putnam Pub Group.
--The Birthday Hat. (Ready Readers). (Illus.). 32p. (gr. 1-3). 1983. pap. 3.50 (ISBN 0-448-21705-8, G&D). Putnam Pub Group.
--One Little Monkey. LC 82-7958. (Illus.). 48p. (gr. 1-5). 1982. pap. 5.95 (ISBN 0-8193-1091-3); PLB 5.95 (ISBN 0-8193-1092-1). Parents.
--Ten Furry Monsters. LC 84-4998. (Illus.). 48p. (ps-3). 1984. 5.95 (ISBN 0-8193-1128-6). Parents.
--Waggleby of Fraggle Rock. LC 84-16599. (Illus.). (ps-2). 1985. 5.95 (ISBN 0-03-003259-8). HR&W.
--Where Is Grandma Potamus. (Ready Readers). (Illus.). 32p. (gr. 1-3). 1983. pap. 3.50 (ISBN 0-448-21706-6, G&D). Putnam Pub Group.
--Where Will the Animals Stay? LC 83-13479. (Illus.). 48p. (ps-3). 1984. 5.95 (ISBN 0-8193-1119-7). Parents.
Calmenson, Stephanie, ed. Never Take a Pig to Lunch. LC 80-2040. (Illus.). 32p. (gr. 3). 1982. 8.95a (ISBN 0-385-15592-1); PLB (ISBN 0-385-15593-X). Doubleday.
Calmer, Ned. Bay of Lions. LC 78-72924. 1980. 9.95 (ISBN 0-87795-214-0). Arbor Hse.
Calmes, Robert, jt. auth. see Roth, Gerald I.
Calmet, A. Dictionnaire Historique, Archeologique, Philologique, Chronologique Geographique et Literal de la Bible, 4 vols. Migne, J. P., ed. (Encyclopedie Theologique First Ser.: Vols. 1-4). 2602p. (Fr.). Repr. of 1846 ed. lib. bdg. 332.50x (ISBN 0-89241-231-3). Caratzas.
Calmet, Augustin. The Phantom World, 2 vols. LC 79-8599. Repr. of 1850 ed. 69.50 set (ISBN 0-404-18452-9). AMS Pr.
Calmet, J., ed. Computer Algebra: EUROCAM 82, Marseille, France 1982. (Lecture Notes in Computer Science: Vol. 144). 301p. 1982. pap. 16.00 (ISBN 0-387-11607-9). Springer-Verlag.
Calmette, Joseph L. La Societe Feodale. LC 80-1994. Repr. of 1923 ed. 30.00 (ISBN 0-404-18556-8). AMS Pr.
Calmfors, Lars. Long-Run Effects of Short-Run Stabilization Policy. 276p. 1983. text ed. 33.00x (ISBN 0-333-33172-9, Pub. by Macmillan England). Humanities.
Calmon, C. & Gold, H. Ion Exchange for Pollution Control, 2 vols. 1979. Vol. 1, 272p. 76.50 (ISBN 0-8493-5153-7); Vol. 2, 288p. 81.50 (ISBN 0-8493-5154-5). CRC Pr.
Calmour, Alfred C. Fact & Fiction About Shakespeare. LC 70-39876. Repr. of 1894 ed. 22.50 (ISBN 0-404-01365-1). AMS Pr.
Calmus, Lawrence P. The Business Guide to Small Computers. LC 82-10080. (Illus.). 192p. 1983. 23.50 (ISBN 0-07-009662-7). McGraw.
Calna, J. The Hammersmith Nineteen Thirty-Five to Nineteen Eighty-Five. 1985. lib. bdg. 18.00 (ISBN 0-85200-910-0, Pub. by MTP Pr Netherlands). Kluwer Academic.
Calnan, jt. auth. see Levene.
Calnan, D. C., jt. auth. see Levene, G. M.
Calnan, J. Coping with Research: The Complete Guide for Beginners. 158p. (Orig.). 1984. pap. text ed. 15.00 (ISBN 0-433-05014-4, Pub. by W Heinemann Med Bks). Heinman.
--Talking with Patients: A Guide to Good Practice. (Illus.). 1983. pap. text ed. 15.00. Heinman.
--Talking with Patients: A Guide to Good Practice. 192p. 1983. pap. 9.00 (991430131, Pub. by Heinemann Medical). Heyden.
Calnan, James. One Way to do Research: The A-Z for Those Who Must. 1976. pap. 15.00 (ISBN 0-433-05012-8). Heinman.
Calnan, James & Barabas, Andras. Speaking at Medical Meetings: A Practical Guide. 2nd rev. & enl. ed. (Illus.). 1981. pap. 15.00 (ISBN 0-433-05001-2). Heinman.
--Writing Medical Papers: A Practical Guide. (Illus.). 1977. pap. 8.50 (ISBN 0-433-05005-5). Heinman.
Calnan, T. R. Molluscan Distribution in Copano Bay, Texas. (Report of Investigations Ser.: RI 103). (Illus.). 71p. 1980. 2.50 (ISBN 0-318-03236-8). Bur Econ Geology.
Calne, D. see Goldstein, Menek, et al.
Calne, D. B., et al, eds. Dopaminergic Mechanisms. LC 74-13904. (Advances in Neurology Ser: Vol. 9). 445p. 1975. 59.50 (ISBN 0-911216-93-6). Raven.
Calne, Donald B., et al, eds. Lisuride & Other Dopamine Agonists: Basic Mechanisms & Endocrine & Neurological Effects. (Illus.). 576p. 1983. text ed. 52.00 (ISBN 0-89004-867-3). Raven.
Calne, R. Y., ed. Transplantation Immunology. (Illus.). 1984. 64.00x (ISBN 0-19-261414-2). Oxford U Pr.
Calne, Roy Y. Liver Transplantation. 399p. 1983. 63.00 (ISBN 0-8089-1550-9, 790767). Grune.
--Surgical Procedures: Renal Transplantation, Vol. 13. (Single Surgical Procedures Ser.). 1984. 25.95 (ISBN 0-87489-523-5). Med Economics.
Calo, J., jt. auth. see Rodrigues, A.
Calo, J. M. & Henley, E. J., eds. Multicomponent Distillation. LC 80-25577. (AIChEMI Modular Instruction B. Ser.: Vol. 2). 76p. 1981. pap. 30.00 (ISBN 0-8169-0177-5, J-8); pap. 15.00 members (ISBN 0-317-03842-7). Am Inst Chem Eng.
--Stagewise & Mass Transfer Operations. (Modular Instruction Series B: Vol. 3). 61p. 1983. pap. 30.00 (ISBN 0-317-05081-8). Am Inst Chem Eng.
Calogero, F. Variable Phase Approach to Potential Scattering. (Mathematics in Science & Engineering Ser.: Vol. 35). 1967. 69.50 (ISBN 0-12-155550-X). Acad Pr.
Calogero, F. & Degasperis, A. Spectral Transform & Solutions: Tools to Solve & Investigate Evolution Equations. (Studies in Math & Its Applications: Vol. 13). 516p. 1982. 89.50 (ISBN 0-444-86368-0, North Holland). Elsevier.
Calogero, F., ed. Nonlinear Evolution Equations Solvable by the Spectral Transform. (Research Notes in Mathematics Ser.: No. 26). 257p. (Orig.). 1978. pap. text ed. 27.00 (ISBN 0-273-08402-X). Pitman Pub MA.
Calohoun, D'Ann, ed. see Farr, Naunerle.
Calomino, Salvatore. From Verse to Prose: The Barlaam & Josephat Legend in 15th Century Germany. (Ger.). 1984. 28.00 (ISBN 0-916379-04-3). Scripta.
Calonne, David S. William Saroyan: My Real Work Is Being. LC 83-1184. (Illus.). xii, 185p. 1983. 19.95x (ISBN 0-8078-1565-9). U of NC Pr.
Calore, Frank P. How They Train: High School Field Events. (Illus.). 1980. 6.00 (ISBN 0-911520-95-3). Tafnews.
Calore, Frank P., ed. How High School Runners Train. (Illus.). 128p. (gr. 10-12). 1982. pap. 7.00 (ISBN 0-911521-04-6). Tafnews.
Calow, P. Biological Machines: A Cybernetic Approach to Life. LC 76-27603. 133p. 1976. pap. 14.95x (ISBN 0-8448-1005-3). Crane-Russak Co.
--Invertebrate Biology: A Functional Approach. LC 81-6162. 224p. 1981. pap. 23.95x (ISBN 0-470-27238-4). Halsted Pr.
Calow, Peter. Evolutionary Principles. LC 82-17834. (Tertiary Level Biology Ser.). (Illus.). 108p. 1983. 35.00 (ISBN 0-412-00321-X, NO. 5032, Pub. by Chapman & Hall); pap. 15.95 (ISBN 0-412-00331-7, NO. 5033). Methuen Inc.
Calow, Peter, jt. ed. see Townsend, Colin R.
Calow, Peter, jt. ed. see Tyler, Peter.
Calsat, Jean-Henri & Sydler, Jean P. Vocabulaire International des Termes d'Urbanisme et d'Architecture. 350p. (Fr., Ger. & Eng.). 1970. 95.00 (ISBN 0-686-56935-0, M-6057). French & Eur.
Caltagirone, Carmen L. The Catechist as a Minister. LC 82-1605. 116p. (Orig.). 1982. pap. 4.95 (ISBN 0-8189-0430-5). Alba.
Calter, Paul. Mathematics for Computer Technology. (Illus.). 608p. 1986. text ed. 29.95 (ISBN 0-13-562190-9). P-H.
--Practical Math Handbook for the Building Trades. (Illus.). 288p. 1983. pap. 10.95 (ISBN 0-13-692228-7). P-H.
--Problem Solving with Computers. 1972. pap. text ed. 27.65 (ISBN 0-07-009648-1). McGraw.
--Schaum's Outline of Technical Mathematics. (Schaum's Outline Ser). (Illus.). 1979. pap. 9.95 (ISBN 0-07-009651-1). McGraw.
--Technical Mathematics. (Illus.). 688p. 1983. 29.95 (ISBN 0-13-598714-8). P-H.
--Technical Mathematics with Calculus. (Illus.). 1008p. 1984. 31.95 (ISBN 0-13-898312-7). P-H.
Calthorpe, Charles. The Relation Betweene the Lord of a Mannor & the Coppy-Holder His Tenent, Etc. LC 74-38163. (English Experience Ser.: No. 440). 100p. 1972. Repr. of 1635 ed. 15.00 (ISBN 90-221-0440-0). Walter J Johnson.
Calthrop, Dion C. I Will Be Good: Dickens, Etc. 1973. Repr. of 1929 ed. 12.50 (ISBN 0-8274-1771-3). R West.
Calthrop, Kenyon & Owens, Graham. Teachers for Tomorrow. 1971. pap. text ed. 6.50x (ISBN 0-435-80200-3). Heinemann Ed.
Caluori, Eleanor. The Cantatas of Luigi Rossi: Analysis & Thematic Index, 2 vols. Buelow, George, ed. LC 81-4749. (Studies in Musicology: No. 41). 530p. 1981. Set. 79.95 (ISBN 0-8357-1171-4). Vol. 1 (ISBN 0-8357-1191-9). Vol. 2 (ISBN 0-8357-1192-7). UMI Res Pr.
Calusaru, Aurelian. Electrodeposition of Metal Powders. (Materials Science Monographs: Vol. 3). 568p. 1980. 83.00 (ISBN 0-444-99781-4). Elsevier.
Calvacorlessi, Peter. Top Secret Ultra, No. 10. 160p. 1981. pap. 2.75 (ISBN 0-345-30069-6). Ballantine.
Calvan, Rita A., jt. auth. see Greene, Sherwin.
Calvani, Terry & Siegfried, John J. Economic Analysis of Antitrust Law. 1979. pap. 10.95 (ISBN 0-316-12500-8). Little.
Calvary Episcopal Church. The Cook's Book. 1972. 6.75 (ISBN 0-918544-41-6). Wimmer Bks.
Calve, Emma. My Life. Farkas, Andrew, ed. Gilder, Rosamond, tr. LC 76-29929. (Opera Biographies). (Illus.). 1977. Repr. of 1922 ed. lib. bdg. 30.00x (ISBN 0-405-09672-0). Ayer Co Pubs.

Calvello, Michael. Triangular Man. (Illus.). 1977. lib. bdg. 20.00 (ISBN 0-916908-39-9); pap. 3.00 (ISBN 0-916908-07-0). Place Herons.

Calver, James L. Mining & Mineral Resources. (Illus.). 132p. 1957. 1.00 (ISBN 0-318-17298-4, B 39). FL Bureau Geology.

Calver, William L. & Bolton, Reginald P. History Written with Pick & Shovel. LC 50-10740. (New York Historical Society Ser.). (Illus.). 1970. 8.00x (ISBN 0-685-73900-7). U Pr of Va.

Calverley, Charles S. Literary Remains with a Memoir by Sir Walter J. Sendall. 1979. Repr. of 1896 ed. lib. bdg. 30.00 (ISBN 0-8495-0931-9). Arden Lib.

Calverley, Charles S., tr. see Theocritus.

Calverley, E. E. The Mysteries of Worship in Islam. 1981. 6.50 (ISBN 0-686-97865-X). Kazi Pubns.

Calverley, E. E., tr. see Ghazzali, Al.

Calverley, Edwin E., ed. see Al-Ghazzali.

Calverly, Charles S. The Literary Remains of Charles Stuart Calverley. 1978. Repr. of 1885 ed. lib. bdg. 30.00 (ISBN 0-8495-0730-8). Arden Lib.

Calvero, Teofidez E., jt. auth. see Kapili, Pascual H.

Calvert, A. Leon, Burgos & Salamanca. 1976. lib. bdg. 59.95 (ISBN 0-8490-2149-9). Gordon Pr.

--Spain, 2 vols. 1976. Set. lib. bdg. 250.00 (ISBN 0-8490-2634-2). Gordon Pr.

--Toledo. 1976. lib. bdg. 59.95 (ISBN 0-8490-2752-7). Gordon Pr.

Calvert, Albert F. The Cameroons. 1976. lib. bdg. 59.95 (ISBN 0-8490-1564-2). Gordon Pr.

--German East Africa. LC 79-100259. (Illus.). Repr. of 1917 ed. 25.00x (ISBN 0-8371-2870-6, CGA&, Pub. by Negro U Pr). Greenwood.

--The Life of Cervantes. LC 76-10970. 1976. Repr. of 1905 ed. lib. bdg. 20.00 (ISBN 0-8414-3637-1). Folcroft.

--Nigeria & Its Tin Fields. Wilkins, Mira, ed. LC 76-29763. (European Business Ser.). (Illus.). 1977. Repr. of 1910 ed. lib. bdg. 32.00x (ISBN 0-405-09778-6). Ayer Co Pubs.

--South-West Africa, During the German Occupation, 1884-1914. LC 70-97418. Repr. of 1915 ed. 21.50x (ISBN 0-8371-2721-1, CSW&, Pub. by Negro U Pr). Greenwood.

Calvert, Alfred T. Mohammedan Architecture & Decoration in Spain with a Portfolio of Rare Plates in Full Colours & Gold of Typical Moorish, 3 vols. (Illus.). 425p. 1985. Set. 975.00x (ISBN 0-86650-160-6). Gloucester Art.

Calvert, Brian. Flying Concorde. LC 81-16745. (Illus.). 256p. 1982. 13.95 (ISBN 0-312-29685-1). St Martin.

--Flying Concorde. 272p. 1982. 39.00x (ISBN 0-906393-14-0, Pub. by Airlife England). State Mutual Bk.

Calvert, Brigadier M., jt. auth. see Young, Brigadier P.

Calvert, Cecil & Baron Baltimore. A Relation of the Successefull Beginnings of the Lord Baltimore's Plantation in Mary-Land. LC 77-6864. (English Experience Ser.: No. 857). 1977. Repr. of 1634 ed. lib. bdg. 3.50 (ISBN 90-221-0857-0). Walter J Johnson.

Calvert, Charles J. The Greatest Nudes of the Italian Renaissance with Pertinent Commentaries both Moral & Artistic. (Illus.). 123p. 1983. 125.25 (ISBN 0-89901-142-X). Found Class Reprints.

Calvert, D. R., jt. auth. see Simmons-Martin, A.

Calvert, David D. Making Your Own Stringed Instruments. (Illus.). 144p. (Orig.). 1982. pap. 8.95 (ISBN 0-8306-1379-X). TAB Bks.

Calvert, Donald. Descriptive Phonetics. LC 79-27737. 1980. 18.95 (ISBN 0-913258-70-9). Thieme Stratton.

Calvert, Donald R. Parent's Guide to Speech & Deafness. LC 84-70988. 80p. 1984. pap. text ed. 9.50 (ISBN 0-88200-155-8). Alexander Graham.

Calvert, Donald R. & Silverman, S. Richard. Speech & Deafness. rev. ed. 304p. 1983. pap. text ed. 16.95 (ISBN 0-88200-070-5). Alexander Graham.

Calvert, E., et al, eds. Injection Moulding. (E.I.T.B. Instruction Manuals Ser.). (Illus.). 163p. 1982. pap. 39.95x spiral bdg. (ISBN 0-85083-553-4). Intl Ideas.

Calvert, E. Roy. Capital Punishment in the Twentieth Century. 5th, rev. ed. Bd. with The Death Penalty Enquiry. 1931. LC 73-172571. (Criminology, Law Enforcement, & Social Problems Ser., No. 153). (Intro. added). 1973. Repr. 22.50x (ISBN 0-87585-153-3). Patterson Smith.

Calvert, G., jt. auth. see Mylroi, M. G.

Calvert, G. H. Cortina Handy Spanish-English, English-Spanish Dictionary. LC 81-47221. 546p. 1982. 7.95 (ISBN 0-06-464800-1, BN-4800). B&N NY.

--Spanish Dictionary. (Routledge Pocket Dictionaries Ser.). 560p. 1980. pap. 7.95 (ISBN 0-7100-0558-X). Routledge & Kegan.

Calvert, George H. Coleridge, Shelley, Goethe. 1978. Repr. lib. bdg. 30.00 (ISBN 0-8495-0816-9). Arden Lib.

--Coleridge, Shelley, Goethe. 1880. lib. bdg. 20.00 (ISBN 0-8414-1565-X). Folcroft.

--Goethe: His Life & Works. 1872. 35.00 (ISBN 0-8274-2420-5). R West.

--Goethe: His Life & Works. 276p. 1981. Repr. of 1872 ed. lib. bdg. 50.00 (ISBN 0-89760-155-6). Telegraph Bks.

--Goethe, His Life & Works: An Essay. (Illus.). 276p. 1981. Repr. of 1886 ed. lib. bdg. 45.00 (ISBN 0-8495-0866-5). Arden Lib.

--Wordsworth: A Biographic Aesthetic Study. 1878. lib. bdg. 20.00 (ISBN 0-8414-1551-X). Folcroft.

Calvert, Harry. Smythe's Mountains: The Climbs of F. S. Smythe. (Illus.). 192p. 1985. 28.00 (ISBN 0-575-03550-1, Pub. by Gollancz England). David & Charles.

Calvert, Harry, ed. Devolution. 80.00x (ISBN 0-903486-30-X, Pub. by Prof Bks England). State Mutual Bk.

Calvert, J. M. & McCausland, M. A. Electronics. LC 78-4113. (Manchester Physics Ser.). 615p. 1978. pap. 39.95 (ISBN 0-471-99639-4, Pub. by Wiley-Interscience). Wiley.

Calvert, Jack G. & Teasley, John I., eds. SO2, No, & NO2 Oxidation Mechanisms: Atmospheric Considerations. (Acid Precipitation Ser.: Vol. 3). 272p. 1984. text ed. 32.50 (ISBN 0-250-40568-7). Butterworth.

Calvert, James, jt. auth. see Williams, Thomas.

Calvert, Judith, jt. ed. see Jerse, Dorothy W.

Calvert, Laura. Francisco de Osuna & the Spirit of the Letter. (Studies in the Romance Languages & Literatures: No. 133). 176p. 1973. pap. 10.00x (ISBN 0-8078-9133-9). U of NC Pr.

Calvert, Lynne, illus. The Five-Petalled Blossom: Work by Women of the Milwaukee Chapter, Feminist Writers' Guild. 176p. (Orig.). 1982. pap. 6.95 (ISBN 0-9606982-0-5). Fem Writers Guild.

Calvert, M. Dawn over the Kennebec. (Illus.). 1984. 16.95 (ISBN 0-9609914-3-3). M Calvert.

Calvert, Mary. Maine Captured in Color. (Illus.). 120p. 1982. 12.95 (ISBN 0-9609914-0-9). M Calvert.

--Maine Captured in Color. Rev ed. (Illus.). 1983. 14.95 (ISBN 0-9609914-1-7). M Calvert.

--Maine's Nature Trails. (Illus.). 144p. 1983. write for info. (ISBN 0-9609914-2-5). Twin City.

--Nature Trails Captured in Color. (Illus.). 144p. 1983. 16.95 (ISBN 0-9609914-2-5). M Calvert.

Calvert, N. G. Windpower Principles: Their Applications on the Small Scale. LC 79-19706. 122p. 1979. 32.95x (ISBN 0-470-26867-0). Halsted Pr.

Calvert, P., jt. auth. see Dieppe, P.

Calvert, Patricia. Hadder MacColl. LC 85-40292. 160p. (gr. 6-8). 1985. 12.95 (ISBN 0-684-18447-8). Scribner.

--The Hour of the Wolf. LC 83-14184. 160p. (gr. 7 up). 1983. 11.95 (ISBN 0-684-17961-X, ScribJ). Scribner.

--Hour of the Wolf. 1985. pap. 2.50 (ISBN 0-451-13493-1, Sig Vista). NAL.

--The Money Creek Mare. 144p. (gr. 7 up). 1981. 9.95 (ISBN 0-684-17223-2, ScribJ). Scribner.

--The Money Creek Mare. 144p. 1983. pap. 2.50 (ISBN 0-451-13983-6, Sig Vista). NAL.

--The Snowbird. (YA) 1982. pap. 1.95 (ISBN 0-451-13353-6, AE1354, Sig Vista). NAL.

--The Snowbird. LC 80-19139. 192p. (gr. 5 up). 1980. 9.95 (ISBN 0-684-16719-0, ScribJ). Scribner.

--The Stone Pony. LC 83-10391. 176p. (gr. 7 up). 1982. 10.95 (ISBN 0-684-17769-2, ScribJ). Scribner.

--The Stone Pony. (gr. 7-9). 1983. pap. 2.50 (ISBN 0-451-13729-9, Sig Vista). NAL.

Calvert, Peter. The Concept of Class: An Historical Introduction. LC 82-10617. 256p. 1983. 25.00 (ISBN 0-312-15918-8). St Martin.

--The Concept of Class: An Historical Introduction. LC 82-10617. 1985. pap. 12.95 (ISBN 0-312-15919-6). St Martin.

--The Falklands Crisis. LC 82-42611. 1982. 20.00x (ISBN 0-312-27964-7). St Martin.

--The Mexicans: How They Live & Work. LC 74-17467. 168p. 1975. text ed. 9.95 (ISBN 0-275-26010-0, HoltC). HR&W.

--Politics, Power & Revolution: A Comparative Analysis of Contemporary Government. LC 82-16879. 208p. 1983. 22.50x (ISBN 0-312-62954-0). St Martin.

--Revolution & International Politics. LC 83-9640. 250p. 1983. 25.00 (ISBN 0-312-67985-8). St Martin.

--Understanding Comparative Politics. 1982. 65.00x (ISBN 0-7108-0196-3, Pub. by Harvester Pr England). State Mutual Bk.

Calvert, Peter A. Guatemala. 135p. 1985. 28.00x (ISBN 0-86531-572-8). Westview.

Calvert, R., ed. Polymer Latices & Their Applications. 1980. text ed. 40.00x (ISBN 0-02-949280-7). Macmillan.

Calvert, Raymond. The Ballad of William Bloat. 40p. (Orig.). 1982. pap. 3.95 (ISBN 0-85640-273-7, Pub. by Blackstaff Pr). Longwood Pub Group.

Calvert, Robert, ed. The Encyclopedia of Patent Practice & Invention Management. LC 74-1028. 880p. 1974. Repr. of 1964 ed. 49.50 (ISBN 0-88275-181-6). Krieger.

Calvert, Robert A., jt. ed. see Wooster, Ralph A.

Calvert, Robert A., jt. auth. see Rosaldo, Renato.

Calvert, Robert, Jr. Affirmative Action: A Comprehensive Recruitment Manual. LC 79-50634. 380p. 1979. pap. 15.00 (ISBN 0-912048-79-4). Garrett Pk.

Calvert, Robert, Jr. & Steel, John E. Planning Your Career. 1963. pap. 3.95 (ISBN 0-07-009658-9). McGraw.

Calvert, Rodger & Smith, Mike. Drive It! The Complete Book of Long-Circuit Karting. (Drive It Ser.). (Illus.). 128p. 1985. 9.95 (ISBN 0-85429-416-3, Pub. by G T Foulis Ltd). Interbook.

Calvert, Seymour & Englund, Harold M., eds. Handbook of Air Pollution Technology. LC 83-19797. 1066p. 1984. 84.95x (ISBN 0-471-08263-5, Pub. by Wiley-Interscience). Wiley.

Calvert, Sherry. Track & Field Drills for Women, Vol. 4: The Throwing Events, 4 bks. 66p. (Orig.). 1983. pap. 16.95 (ISBN 0-317-14593-2). Championship Bks.

Calvert, Thomas. The Strange Fibonacci Discoveries in Numerology for Greater Living Achievement. (Illus.). 245p. 1976. 99.15 (ISBN 0-89266-009-0). Am Classical Coll Pr.

Calvert, Thomas H. Regulation of Commerce Under the Federal Constitution. (Studies in Constitutional Law). xiv, 380p. 1981. Repr. of 1907 ed. lib. bdg. 32.50x (ISBN 0-8377-0429-4). Rothman.

Calvert, W. E., tr. see Birket-Smith, Kaj.

Calvert, W. E., tr. see Fischer-Moller, Knud.

Calverton, V. F. Bankruptcy of Marriage. LC 76-169403. (Family in America Ser). 344p. 1972. Repr. of 1928 ed. 26.50 (ISBN 0-405-03852-6). Ayer Co Pubs.

--Collected Writings, 6 vols. 600.00 (ISBN 0-87968-900-5). Gordon Pr.

--Modern Monthly & Quarterly Anthology, 10 vols. 1800.00 (ISBN 0-8490-0650-3). Gordon Pr.

--The Passing of the Gods. 1979. Repr. of 1935 ed. lib. bdg. 20.00 (ISBN 0-8495-0935-1). Arden Lib.

--The Passing of the Gods. 326p. 1982. Repr. of 1934 ed. lib. bdg. 35.00 (ISBN 0-89987-123-2). Darby Bks.

Calverton, V. F., ed. Anthology of American Negro Literature. Repr. of 1929 ed. 29.00 (ISBN 0-527-14500-9). Kraus Repr.

Calverton, V. F. & Schmalhausen, Samuel D., eds. New Generation: The Intimate Problems of Modern Parents & Children. LC 70-165712. (American Education, Ser. 2). (Illus.). 1971. Repr. of 1930 ed. 38.50 (ISBN 0-405-03701-5). Ayer Co Pubs.

Calverton, Victor F. The Liberation of American Literature. LC 73-404. 500p. 1973. Repr. lib. bdg. 37.50x (ISBN 0-374-91245-9). Octagon.

--The Newer Spirit: A Sociological Criticism of Literature. 1972. lib. bdg. 23.00x (ISBN 0-374-91246-7). Octagon.

Calverton, Victor F. & Schmalhausen, S. D., eds. Sex in Civilization. LC 72-9630. Repr. of 1929 ed. 39.50 (ISBN 0-404-57429-7). AMS Pr.

Calvet, Corinne. Has Corinne Been A Good Girl? The Intimate Memoirs of a French Actress in Hollywood. (Illus.). 360p. 1983. 16.95 (ISBN 0-312-36405-9). St Martin.

Calvet, Francoise, tr. see Ewing, A. F.

Calvey, T. N. & Williams, N. E. Principles & Practice of Pharmacology for Anaesthetists. 320p. 1983. 38.50 (ISBN 0-632-00868-7, B1159-8). Mosby.

Calvez, J. Y., et al. Conferences on the Chief Decrees of the Jesuit General Congregation XXXII: A Symposium by Some of Its Members. LC 76-2977. (Study Aids on Jesuit Topics Ser.: No. 4). 173p. 1976. smyth sewn 4.50 (ISBN 0-912422-17-3); pap. 3.50 (ISBN 0-912422-13-0). Inst Jesuit.

Calvez, Jean Y. The Social Thought of John Twenty-Third: Mater et Magistra. McKenzie, George J., tr. LC 75-40992. 1977. Repr. of 1965 ed. lib. bdg. 22.50 (ISBN 0-8371-8711-7, CASCJ). Greenwood.

Calvez, Jean-Yves. Politics & Society in the Third World. OConnell, Matthew J., tr. from Fr. LC 72-85792. 256p. (Orig.). 1973. pap. 6.95 (ISBN 0-88344-389-9). Orbis Bks.

Calvi, Guido. The Architectural Monuments of the Ancient Cities of Italy. (Illus.). 129p. 1982. Repr. of 1901 ed. 81.35 (ISBN 0-89901-056-3). Found Class Reprints.

Calvin. Decision-Making. 5.95 (ISBN 0-8298-0437-4). Pilgrim NY.

Calvin, Allen, ed. Perspectives on Education. LC 76-20019. (Illus.). 1977. pap. text ed. 10.95. Addison-Wesley.

Calvin, Allen D., ed. Programmed Instruction: Bold New Venture. LC 69-15993. pap. 65.00 (ISBN 0-317-07895-X, 2050121). Bks Demand UMI.

Calvin, Clyde L. & Knutson, Donald. Modern Home Gardening. LC 82-15978. 545p. 1983. text ed. 29.95 (ISBN 0-471-02486-4). Wiley.

Calvin, Henry. It's Different Abroad. LC 82-48241. 192p. 1983. pap. 2.84i (ISBN 0-06-080640-0, P 640, PL). Har-Row.

Calvin, I. The Lost White Race. 1982. lib. bdg. 59.95 (ISBN 0-87700-339-4). Revisionist Pr.

Calvin, Jean. Aphorismes of Christian Religion or a Verie Compendious Abridgement of M. I. Calvins Institutions Set Forth by M I Piscator. Holland, H., tr. LC 73-6107. (English Experience Ser.: No. 575). 1973. Repr. of 1596 ed. 26.00 (ISBN 90-221-0575-X). Walter J Johnson.

--Catechisms or, Manner to Teach-Children the Christian Religion. LC 68-54624. (English Experience Ser.: No. 46). 168p. 1968. Repr. of 1556 ed. 14.00 (ISBN 90-221-0046-4). Walter J Johnson.

--Certain Homilies Containing Profitable Admonition for This Time. LC 73-6108. (English Experience Ser.: No. 576). 120p. 1973. Repr. of 1553 ed. 8.00 (ISBN 90-221-0576-8). Walter J Johnson.

--Letters, Compiled from the Original Manuscripts & Edited with Historical Notes, 4 vols. Bonnet, Jules, ed. Gilchrist, M. R. & Constable, David, trs. from Lat. & Fr. LC 70-185936. 1973. Repr. of 1858 ed. Set. 110.00 (ISBN 0-8337-4021-0). B Franklin.

--Opera Quae Supersunt Omnia, 59 Vols. in 58. Baum, G., et al, eds. 1863-1900. Set. 2600.00 (ISBN 0-384-07195-3); 50.00 ea. Johnson Repr.

--Rallying to Win. (Illus.). 1974. 8.95 (ISBN 0-393-60002-5). Norton.

--Three French Treatises. Higman, Francis M., ed. (Renaissance Library). 171p. (Fr.). 1970. 36.50 (ISBN 0-485-13802-6, Pub. by Athlone Pr Ltd); pap. 16.95 (ISBN 0-485-12802-0). Longwood Pub Group.

Calvin, John. The Best of John Calvin. Dunn, Samuel, compiled by. (Best Ser.). 416p. 1981. pap. 5.95 (ISBN 0-8010-2467-6). Baker Bk.

--Calvin's Commentaries, 22 vols. 1979. Repr. Set. 495.00 (ISBN 0-8010-2440-4). Baker Bk.

--Calvin's Letters. pap. 5.45 (ISBN 0-85151-323-9). Banner of Truth.

--Calvin's New Testament Commentaries, 12 vols. Torrance, David W. & Torrance, Thomas F., eds. Incl. The Gospel According to St. John; Chapters 1-10. Parker, T. H., tr. 10.95 (ISBN 0-8028-2044-1); The Gospel According to St. John; Chapters 11-21. Parker, T. H., tr. 10.95 (ISBN 0-8028-2045-X); Acts of the Apostles, Vol. 1. McDonald, W. J., tr. 10.95 (ISBN 0-8028-2046-8); Acts of the Apostles, Vol. 2. Fraser, John W., tr. 10.95 (ISBN 0-8028-2047-6); The Epistle to the Romans & the Thessalonians. Mackenzie, R., tr. 9.95 (ISBN 0-8028-2048-4); The First Epistle to the Corinthians. Fraser, John W., tr. 10.95 (ISBN 0-8028-2049-2); Galatians, Ephesians, Philippians, Colossians. Parker, T. H., tr. 10.95 (ISBN 0-8028-2051-4); Hebrews and Peter First & Second. Johnson, W. B., tr. 10.95 (ISBN 0-8028-2052-2); Second Corinthians, Timothy, Titus. & Philemon. Smail, T. A. 10.95 (ISBN 0-8028-2050-6); Harmony of the Gospels, 3 Vols. Parker, T. H., tr. 10.95 ea. (ISBN 0-685-22779-0). Vol. 1 (ISBN 0-8028-2038-7). Vol. 2 (ISBN 0-8028-2039-5). Vol. 3 (ISBN 0-8028-2040-9). 1960. Set. 131.40 (ISBN 0-8028-2053-0). Eerdmans.

--Calvin's Selected Works: Tracts & Letters, 7 vols. Beveridge, Henry & Bonnet, Jules, eds. 1983. Repr. 99.95 (ISBN 0-8010-2493-5). Baker Bk.

--The Christian Life. Leith, John A., ed. LC 83-48978. 112p. 1984. 9.57 (ISBN 0-06-061298-3, HarpR). Har-Row.

--Concerning Scandals. Fraser, John W., tr. LC 78-8675. Repr. of 1978 ed. 24.90 (ISBN 0-8357-9126-2, 2012802). Bks Demand UMI.

--Concerning the Eternal Predestination of God. Reid, J. K., tr. 1961. pap. 13.95 (ISBN 0-227-67438-3). Attic Pr.

--Genesis. (Geneva Commentaries Ser.). 1979. 19.95 (ISBN 0-85151-093-0). Banner of Truth.

--Golden Booklet of the True Christian Life: Devotional Classic. (Summit Books). 1975. pap. 2.95 (ISBN 0-8010-2366-1). Baker Bk.

--Institutes of the Christian Religion: Beveridge Translation, 2 Vols. 1953. Set. pap. 16.95 (ISBN 0-8028-8026-6). Eerdmans.

--John Calvin's Sermons on the Ten Commandments. Farley, Benjamin W., ed. 544p. 1980. 12.95 (ISBN 0-8010-2443-9). Baker Bk.

--John Calvin's Treatises Against the Anabaptists & Against the Libertines. Farley, Benjamin W., tr. 360p. (Orig.). 1982. pap. 16.95 (ISBN 0-8010-2476-5). Baker Bk.

--Knowledge of God the Creator. 2.50 (ISBN 0-686-23485-5). Rose Pub MI.

--On God & Man. Strothmann, F. W., ed. LC 56-7500. (Milestones of Thought Ser.). 1965. 6.00 (ISBN 0-8044-5214-8); pap. 3.95 (ISBN 0-8044-6073-6). Ungar.

--On God & Political Duty. 2nd ed. LC 50-4950. 1956. pap. 5.99 scp (ISBN 0-672-60184-2, LLA23). Bobbs.

--Senecae libri duo de clementia commentariis illustrati. Battles, Ford L. & Hugo, Andre M., eds. 1969. write for info. Renaissance Soc Am.

--Sermons on Ephesians. 1979. 18.95 (ISBN 0-85151-170-8). Banner of Truth.

--Sermons on Timothy & Titus. 1983. 34.95 (ISBN 0-85151-374-3). Banner of Truth.

Calvin, John & Sadoleto, Jacopo, eds. A Reformation Debate. 1976. pap. 4.50 (ISBN 0-8010-2390-4). Baker Bk.

Calvin, Martin. Our Father's Before Us. 305p. (Orig.). 1983. pap. 4.95 (ISBN 0-914397-00-1). Cornell Des.

Calvin, Melvin, ed. Organic Chemistry of Life: Readings from Scientific American. LC 73-12475. (Illus.). 452p. 1973. text ed. 23.95 (ISBN 0-7167-0884-1); pap. text ed. 12.95 (ISBN 0-7167-0883-3). W H Freeman.

Calvin, Robert J. Profitable Sales Management & Marketing for Growing Businesses. 1984. 29.95 (ISBN 0-442-21502-9). Van Nos Reinhold.

Calvin, W. H. The Throwing Madonna: From Nervous Cells to Hominid Brains. 252p. 1983. 13.95 (ISBN 0-07-009665-1); pap. 7.95 (ISBN 0-07-009664-3). McGraw.

Calvin, William H. & Ojemann, George A. Inside the Brain. (Illus., Orig.). 1980. pap. 4.50 (ISBN 0-451-62397-5, ME2052, Ment). NAL.

--History & Topography of Ireland. O'Meara, John J., tr. (Dolmen Texts Ser.: No. 4). 1982. text ed. 21.50x (ISBN 0-391-01166-9, Dolmen Pr). Humanities.

Cambridge Book Editors. Increase Your Vocabulary, 2 Bks. (Illus.). pap. text ed. 4.87 ea.; Bk. 1. pap. text ed. (ISBN 0-8428-0008-5); Bk. 2. pap. text ed. (ISBN 0-8428-0009-3); Bk. 1. key 1.13 (ISBN 0-8428-0028-X); Bk. 2. key 1.13 (ISBN 0-8428-0029-8). Cambridge Bk.

--Spelling. (Illus.). pap. text ed. 6.00 (ISBN 0-8428-0076-X); key 2.00 (ISBN 0-8428-0027-1). Cambridge Bk.

Cambridge Communication Ltd. Anatomy & Physiology: A Self Instructional Course, 5 vols. (Illus.). 1985. Set. pap. text ed. 24.75 (ISBN 0-443-03395-1); Bk. 1. The Human Body & the Reproductive System. pap. text ed. 4.95 (ISBN 0-443-03170-3); Bk. 2. The Endocrine Glands & the Nervous System. pap. text ed. 4.95 (ISBN 0-443-03206-8); Bk. 3. The Locomotor System & the Special Senses. pap. text ed. 4.95 (ISBN 0-443-03207-6); BK. 5. The Urinary System & the Digestive System. pap. text ed. 4.95 (ISBN 0-443-03209-2). Churchill.

Cambridge Department of Criminal Science. Detention in Remand Homes: A Report of the Cambridge Department of Criminal Science on the Use of Sec. 54 of the Children & Young Persons Act, 1933. (Cambridge Studies in Criminology: Vol. 7). pap. 13.00 (ISBN 0-317-15572-5). Kraus Repr.

Cambridge Historical Commission. Survey of Architectural History in Cambridge. Incl. Report One: East Cambridge; Report Two: Mid Cambridge. 1967. pap. 8.95 o. p. (ISBN 0-262-53012-0); Report Three: Cambridgeport. 1971. pap. 8.95 (ISBN 0-262-53013-9); Report Four: Old Cambridge. 1973; Report Five: Northwest Cambridge. 1977. pap. 9.95 (ISBN 0-262-53032-5). pap. MIT Pr.

Cambridge Information & Research Services, Ltd. World Directory of Energy Information: Middle East, Africa & Asia Pacific, Vol. II. 336p. 1982. 85.00x (ISBN 0-87196-602-6). Facts on File.

--World Directory of Energy Information, Vol. I: Western Europe. 336p. 1981. 85.00x (ISBN 0-87196-563-1). Facts on File.

Cambridge School Classics Project. Cambridge Latin Course, 5 units. Incl. Unit 1. text ed. 7.95 (ISBN 0-521-07922-5); tchr's handbk. 7.95x (ISBN 0-521-07902-0); tape recording 18.50x (ISBN 0-521-08036-3); slides 45.00x (ISBN 0-521-08009-6); Unit 2. text ed. 7.95x (ISBN 0-521-08043-6); tchr's handbk. 7.50 (ISBN 0-521-08157-2); tape recording 18.50x (ISBN 0-521-08158-0); slides 45.00x (ISBN 0-521-08159-9); Unit 3. text ed. 8.95x (ISBN 0-521-08515-2); tchr's handbk. 7.50x (ISBN 0-521-08539-X); slides 49.00x (ISBN 0-521-08541-1); tape recording 18.50x (ISBN 0-521-08540-3); Unit 4. text ed. 7.50x (ISBN 0-521-08542-X); tchr's handbk. 9.50x (ISBN 0-521-08543-8); tape recordings 18.50x (ISBN 0-521-20231-0); limp bdg. 9.50x (ISBN 0-686-82874-7); Unit 5. 1977. tchr's handbk. 6.95x (ISBN 0-521-08544-6). LC 72-132282. (gr. 9-12). 1971-73. Cambridge U Pr.

--Cambridge Latin Course, 3 bklts, Unit 5, Pupils Books. Incl. Dido et Aeneas; Nero et Agrippina; Words & Phrases. (Illus.). 1974. pap. text ed. 4.50x (ISBN 0-521-08545-4). Cambridge U Pr.

--Foundation Course Folder III: Greek Religion. 1974. 13.95x (ISBN 0-521-08724-4). Cambridge U Pr.

--Foundation Course Folders One to Five: Teacher's Handbook. (Illus.). 160p. 1973. pap. 6.95x (ISBN 0-521-08548-9). Cambridge U Pr.

--Latin Course: Information About the Language, Units 4 & 5. 80p. (gr. 7-12). 1975. pap. 3.95x (ISBN 0-521-20822-X). Cambridge U Pr.

Cambridge School Classics Project Foundation Course. The Gauls. (Roman World Ser.). (Illus.). 1978. 2.95x (ISBN 0-521-21599-4). Cambridge U Pr.

--Gods of Olympus. Forrest, M., ed. (Roman World Ser.). (Illus.). 1973. text ed. 12.50x (ISBN 0-521-08469-5). Cambridge U Pr.

--Lugdunum. (Roman World Ser.). (Illus.). 1978. 2.95x (ISBN 0-521-21601-X). Cambridge U Pr.

--Troy & the Early Greeks. Forrest, M., ed. (Illus.). 1973. text ed. 12.50x (ISBN 0-521-08467-9). Cambridge U Pr.

--Two Journeys. (Roman World Ser.). (Illus.). 1978. 2.95x (ISBN 0-521-21603-6). Cambridge U Pr.

Cambridge Songs. The Cambridge Songs, a Goliard's Song Book of the 11th Century. Breul, Karl, ed. LC 77-178517. Repr. of 1915 ed. 24.50 (ISBN 0-404-56529-8). AMS Pr.

Cambridge Staff. Pre-GED Program in Language Skills. Mendyk, Dennis, ed. (Pre-GED Ser.). 224p. 1983. pap. text ed. 6.00 (ISBN 0-8428-9318-0); student wkbk. 3.93 (ISBN 0-8428-9323-7). Cambridge Bk.

--Pre-GED Program in Math Skills: 1984 Edition. (Pre-GED Ser.). 288p. 1984. pap. text ed. 6.00 (ISBN 0-8428-9325-3); student wkbk. 3.93 (ISBN 0-8428-9322-9). Cambridge Bk.

--Pre-GED Program in Reading Skills. Mendyk, Dennis, ed. (Pre-GED Ser.). 224p. 1983. pap. text ed. 6.00 (ISBN 0-8428-9320-2); wkbk 3.93 (ISBN 0-8428-9324-5). Cambridge Bk.

Cambridge Staff, ed. English Grammar: Kentucky Educational Television Study Guide. rev. ed. (GED Program Ser.). 218p. student videotext 6.50 (ISBN 0-317-31591-9, 893-687). Cambridge Bk.

--Mathematics: Kentucky Educational Television Study Guide. rev. ed. (GED Program Ser.). 218p. student videotext 6.50 (ISBN 0-317-31588-9, 893-660); tchr's. guide 4.40 (893-660). Cambridge Bk.

--Reading: Kentucky Educational Television Study Guide. rev. ed. (GED Program Ser.). 206p. student videotext 6.50 (ISBN 0-317-31594-3, 893-709). Cambridge Bk.

Cambridge Summer School in Mathematical Logic, 1971. Proceedings. Mathias, A. R. & Rogers, H., eds. LC 73-12410. (Lecture Notes in Mathematics Ser: Vol. 337). ix, 660p. 1973. pap. 30.00 (ISBN 0-387-05569-X). Springer-Verlag.

Cambridge University, Fitzwilliam Museum. Catalogue of Paintings, Vol. 3: British School by J. W. Goodison. LC 61-19559. pap. 96.30 (ISBN 0-317-26398-6, 2024455). Bks Demand UMI.

Cambridge University Library. Catalog of a Collection of Books on Logic Presented to the Library by John Venn. LC 74-165346. 1975. Repr. of 1889 ed. 29.50 (ISBN 0-8337-3624-8). B Franklin.

--Early English Printed Books in the University Library, 4 Vols. Repr. of 1907 ed. Set. 138.50 (ISBN 0-384-07221-6); Vols. 1-2. 40.00 ea.; Vols. 3-4. 40.00 ea. Johnson Repr.

Cambridge University Staff. Cambridge Essays. 308p. Repr. of 1855 ed. lib. bdg. 65.00 (ISBN 0-8495-0864-9). Arden Lib.

Cambridge. University. Trinity College. Library. Catalogue of the Books Presented by Edward Capell to the Library of Trinity College in Cambridge. Greg, Sir Walter W., ed. LC 77-4008. 1977. Repr. of 1903 ed. lib. bdg. 25.00 (ISBN 0-8414-4589-3). Folcroft.

Cambridge Women's Peace Collecive Staff, ed. My Country Is the Whole World: An Anthology of Women's Work on Peace & War. (Illus.). 306p. (Orig.). 1984. pap. 8.95 (ISBN 0-86358-004-1, Pandora Pr). Routledge & Kegan.

Cambridge Women's Study Group. Women in Society: Interdisciplinary Essays. 314p. 1983. pap. 9.95 (ISBN 0-86068-083-5, Pub. by Virago Pr). Merrimack Pub Cir.

Cambridge-Pickard, A. W. Demosthenes & the Last Days of Greek Freedom: 384-322 B. C. Vlastos, Gregory, ed. LC 78-19377. (Morals & Law in Ancient Greece Ser.). Repr. of 1914 ed. lib. bdg. 44.00x (ISBN 0-405-11566-0). Ayer Co Pubs.

Cambron, Jim. The First Primer of Microcomputer Telecommunications. (Illus.). 128p. (Orig.). 1984. 14.95 (ISBN 0-8306-0688-2, 1688); pap. 10.25 (ISBN 0-8306-1688-8). TAB Bks.

Cambron, Mark. Come, Lord Jesus. pap. 1.45 (ISBN 0-686-12745-5). Grace Pub Co.

Cambron, Mark G. Bible Doctrines. 1954. 14.95 (ISBN 0-310-22260-5). Zondervan.

Cambron, Nelda H., jt. auth. see McCarthy, Martha M.

Cambron-McCabe, Nelda H., ed. The Changing Politics of School Finance. (American Education Finance Association). 312p. 1982. prof ref 29.00x (ISBN 0-88410-896-1). Ballinger Pub.

Camburn, K. E., et al. The Haptobenthic Diatom Flora of Long Branch Creek, South Carolina. (Offprint from Nova Hedwigia Ser.: No. 30). (Illus.). 1979. 21.00x (ISBN 3-7682-1197-5). Lubrecht & Cramer.

Camden, Archie. Blow by Blow: The Memories of a Musical Rogue & Vagabond. (Illus.). 208p. 1983. text ed. 15.00x (ISBN 0-87663-421-8). Universe.

Camden Arts Centre Exhibition. Contemporary African Art. LC 70-108670. 40p. 1970. pap. 7.50x (ISBN 0-8419-0040-X, Africana). Holmes & Meier.

Camden, Carroll. The Elizabethan Woman. 333p. 1975. Repr. of 1952 ed. 15.00x (ISBN 0-911858-30-X). Appel.

Camden, K. R. A Revision Course in School Certificate Mathematics. pap. 6.50x (ISBN 0-392-08359-0, SpS). Sportshelf.

Camden, Kenneth. Graphical Work. pap. 8.50x (ISBN 0-392-08412-0, ABC). Sportshelf.

Camden Society. Camden Miscellany, 6 vols. LC 66-80313. (First Ser). Repr. of 1871 ed. 192.00 set (ISBN 0-404-50212-1); 32.00 ea. Vol. 39 (ISBN 0-404-50139-7). Vol. 55 (ISBN 0-404-50155-9). Vol. 61 (ISBN 0-404-50161-3). Vol. 73 (ISBN 0-404-50173-7). Vol. 87 (ISBN 0-404-50187-7). Vol. 104 (ISBN 0-404-50204-0). AMS Pr.

--Camden Miscellany, 3 vols, Vols 7-9. Repr. of 1875 ed. 27.00 ea. (ISBN 0-384-07228-3). Johnson Repr.

--Camden Society Publications: New Series, Vols. 1-62. Repr. of 1871 ed. Set. 1550.00 (ISBN 0-384-07232-1). Johnson Repr.

--Camden Society Publications: Series 1, Vols. 1-105. Repr. of 1838 ed. Set. 2850.00 (ISBN 0-384-07230-5). Johnson Repr.

Camden Society, London. Camden Society Publications, 1838 to 1872, 105 vols. Repr. of 1872 ed. Set. 2850.00 (ISBN 0-404-50100-1); write for info. AMS Pr.

Camden, Thomas M. The Job Hunter's Final Exam. LC 84-50165. 117p. (Orig.). 1984. pap. 4.95 (ISBN 0-9609516-2-8). Surrey Bks.

Camden, Thomas M. & Bishop, Nancy. How to Get a Job in Dallas-Ft. Worth: The Insider's Guide. LC 83-18137. (Illus.). 459p. (Orig.). 1984. pap. 13.95 (ISBN 0-9609516-1-X). Surrey Bks.

Camden, Thomas M. & Greene, Freda. How to Get a Job in Los Angeles-The Insider's Guide. (Illus.). 450p. (Orig.). 1984. pap. 13.95 (ISBN 0-9609516-4-4). Surrey Bks.

Camden, Thomas M. & Holland, Susan F. How to Get a Job in New York: The Insider's Guide. (Illus.). 458p. (Orig.). 1985. pap. 13.95 (ISBN 0-9609516-7-9). Surrey Bks.

Camden, Thomas M. & Schwartz, Susan. How to Get a Job in Chicago: The Insider's Guide. Rev., 2nd ed. (Illus.). 458p. (Orig.). 1985. pap. 13.95 (ISBN 0-9609516-6-0). Surrey Bks.

Camden, William. Britannia, 4 vols. (Illus.). Repr. of 1806 ed. Set. 539.00x (ISBN 3-4870-5492-2). Adlers Foreign Bks.

--Camden's Britannia. 1971. Repr. of 1695 ed. 110.00 (ISBN 0-384-07350-6). Johnson Repr.

--History of Elizabeth I: The History of the Renowned & Victorious Princess Elizabeth. 4th ed. LC 70-113570. Repr. of 1688 ed. 90.00 (ISBN 0-404-01366-X). AMS Pr.

--History of the Most Renowned & Victorious Princess Elizabeth Late Queen of England: Selected Chapters. MacCaffrey, Wallace T., ed. LC 74-115682. (Classics of British Historical Literature Ser). 1972. pap. 3.45x (ISBN 0-226-09219-4, P399, Phoen). U of Chicago Pr.

--Remaines Concerning Britain. LC 77-113572. (Illus.). Repr. of 1657 ed. 46.50 (ISBN 0-404-01367-8). AMS Pr.

--Remains Concerning Britain. 446p. 1974. Repr. of 1870 ed. 19.50x (ISBN 0-87471-543-1). Rowman.

--Remains Concerning Britain. Dunn, R. D., ed. 632p. 1984. 75.00x (ISBN 0-8020-2457-2). U of Toronto Pr.

Came, P. E. & Caliguiri, L. A., eds. Chemotherapy of Viral Infections. (Handbook of Experimental Pharmacology: Vol. 61). (Illus.). 610p. 1982. 171.00 (ISBN 0-387-11347-9). Springer-Verlag.

Came, P. E. & Carter, W. A., eds. Interferons & Their Applications. (Handbook of Experimental Pharmacology Ser.: Vol. 71). (Illus.). 640p. 1984. 180.00 (ISBN 0-387-12533-7). Springer-Verlag.

Cameens, Luiz Vaz De see De Cameens, Luis Vaz.

Camejo, Pedro & Murphy, Fred, eds. The Nicaraguan Revolution. LC 79-55833. (Illus.). 1979. lib. bdg. 8.00 (ISBN 0-87348-573-4). Path Pr NY.

Camejo, Pedro M. La Guerrilla: For Que "Fracaso" Como Estrategia. 48p. (Span.). 1974. pap. 0.85 (ISBN 0-87348-337-5). Path Pr NY.

Camejo, Peter. Liberalism, Ultraleftism or Mass Action. pap. 0.35 (ISBN 0-87348-188-7). Path Pr NY.

--Racism, Revolution, Reaction 1861-1877: The Rise & Fall of Radical Reconstruction. LC 76-24184. (Illus.). 23.00 (ISBN 0-913460-49-4, Dist. by Path Pr NY); pap. 6.95 (ISBN 0-913460-50-8, Dist. by Path Pr NY). Monad Pr.

--Who Killed Jim Crow? The Story of the Civil Rights Movement & Its Lessons for Today. pap. 0.75 (ISBN 0-87348-343-X). Path Pr NY.

Camejo, Peter, et al. The Lesser Evil? The Left Debates the Democratic Party & Social Change. 1978. cloth 14.00 (ISBN 0-87348-517-3); pap. 4.95 (ISBN 0-87348-518-1). Path Pr NY.

Cameli, Louis. Mary's Journey. 5.95 (ISBN 0-8215-9911-9). Sadlier.

Camellion, Richard. Assassination: Theory & Practice. 130p. 1977. pap. 10.00 (ISBN 0-87364-089-6). Paladin Pr.

--Behavior Modification. LC 78-2209. 140p. 1978. pap. 10.00 (ISBN 0-87364-100-0). Paladin Pr.

Camenisch, Paul. Grounding Professional Ethics in a Pluralistic Society. LC 83-83297. (Professional Ethics Ser.). 160p. (Orig.). 1983. pap. text ed. 14.50 (ISBN 0-930586-11-5). Haven Pubns.

Camenzind, Hans R. Electronic Integrated Systems Design. LC 78-12195. (Illus.). 342p. 1980. Repr. of 1972 ed. lib. bdg. 22.50 (ISBN 0-88275-763-6). Krieger.

Camerer, T. P. Camerer Cuss Book of Antique Watches. (Illus.). 1976. cancelled 49.50 (ISBN 0-902028-33-2). Apollo.

Camerer Cuss, T. P. The Camerer Cuss Book of Antique Watches. (Illus.). 332p. 1976. Repr. of 1967 ed. 49.50 (ISBN 0-902028-33-2). Antique Collect.

Camerini-Davalos, R. & Hanover, B., eds. Treatment of Early Diabetes. LC 79-16121. (Advances in Experimental Medicine & Biology: Vol. 119). 548p. 1979. 75.00x (ISBN 0-306-40194-0, Plenum Pr). Plenum Pub.

Camerini-Davalos, R. A. see Levine, R. & Tuft, R.

Camerini-Davalos, Rafael A. see Levine, R. & Tuft, R.

Camerini-Davalos, Rafael A., et al, eds. Atherogenesis, Vol. 275. (Annals of the New York Academy of Sciences). 1976. 47.00x (ISBN 0-89072-054-1). NY Acad Sci.

Cameron. How to Buy & Install Your Hi-Fi Stereo System. (Illus.). 112p. 1980. pap. 10.95 (ISBN 0-8359-2921-3). Reston.

--Political Strategy of America Poor. 1985. lib. bdg. 27.50 (ISBN 0-8240-9869-2). Garland Pub.

Cameron & Scaletta. Business Law: Text & Cases. 2nd ed. 1985. text ed. 30.95x (ISBN 0-256-03254-8); study guide 11.95x (ISBN 0-256-03255-6). Business Pubns.

Cameron, jt. auth. see Cohen.

Cameron, jt. auth. see Field.

Cameron, jt. auth. see Kerney.

Cameron, A. & Ettles, C. M. Basic Lubrication Theory. 3rd ed. (Engineering Science Ser.). 256p. 1983. pap. 34.95 (ISBN 0-470-27554-5). Halsted Pr.

Cameron, A. & Herrin, J., eds. Constantinople in the Early Eighth Century: The Parastaseis Syntomoi Chronikai. (Studies in the Classical Tradition: No. 10). 304p. 1984. text ed. 51.25x (ISBN 90-04-07010-9, Pub. by Brill Holland). Humanities.

Cameron, A. D. The Caledonian Canal. (Illus.). 1979. 20.00 (ISBN 0-900963-33-6, Pub. by Terence Dalton England). State Mutual Bk.

Cameron, A. E., ed. Determination of the Isotopic Composition of Uranium. AEC Technical Information Center. (National Nuclear Energy Ser.: Div. I, Vol. 13). 173p. 1950. pap. 16.00 (ISBN 0-87079-177-X, TID-5213); microfilm 10.00 (ISBN 0-87079-452-3, TID-5213). DOE.

Cameron, A. G., jt. auth. see Marsden, B. G.

Cameron, A. G., ed. Astrophysics Today. LC 84-70879. (Readings from Physics Today Ser.). (Illus.). 348p. 1984. pap. 25.00 (ISBN 0-88318-446-X). Am Inst Physics.

Cameron, A. G., jt. ed. see Brancazio, Peter J.

Cameron, A. G., jt. ed. see Jastrow, R.

Cameron, A. G., jt. ed. see Stein, R. F.

Cameron, A. G., ed. see Symposium on Cosmochemistry, Cambridge, Mass., Aug. 1972.

Cameron, A. G. W., ed. see Greisen, Kenneth.

Cameron, A. J. Mathematical Enterprises for Schools. 1966. 8.75 (ISBN 0-08-011833-X). Pergamon.

Cameron, A. V. Influence of Ariosto's Epic & Lyric Poetry on Ronsard & His Group. 1973. Repr. of 1930 ed. 19.00 (ISBN 0-384-07365-4). Johnson Repr.

Cameron, Alan. Circus Factions: Blues & Greens at Rome & Byzantium. 1976. 64.00x (ISBN 0-19-814804-6). Oxford U Pr.

--Porphyrius the Charioteer. (Illus.). 1973. 59.00x (ISBN 0-19-814805-4). Oxford U Pr.

Cameron, Alastair. The Principles of Lubrication. LC 67-70366. pap. 156.30 (ISBN 0-317-29446-6, 2055943). Bks Demand UMI.

Cameron, Alexander. Reliquiae Celticae, 2 vols. MacBain, Alexander & Kennedy, John K., eds. LC 78-72621. (Celtic Language & Literature: Goidelic & Brythonic). Repr. of 1894 ed. Set. 84.50 (ISBN 0-404-17543-0). AMS Pr.

Cameron, Alison S. Chinese Painting Techniques. LC 67-15140. (Illus.). 1967. 39.50 (ISBN 0-8048-0103-7). C E Tuttle.

Cameron, Allan. The Science of Food & Cooking. 3rd ed. (Illus.). 1973. pap. 19.95x (ISBN 0-7131-1791-5). Intl Ideas.

Cameron, Allan G., jt. auth. see Fox, Brian A.

Cameron, Allen. A Guide to New Jersey Legal Bibliography & Legal History. (Illus.). xxv, 636p. 1984. 75.00x (ISBN 0-8377-0217-8). Rothman.

Cameron, Angus & Jones, Judith. The L. L. Bean Game & Fish Cookbook. (Illus.). 640p. 1983. 19.95 (ISBN 0-394-51191-3). Random.

Cameron, Angus & Kingsmill, Allison, eds. Old English Word Studies: A Preliminary Word & Author List. (Old English Ser.). 208p. 1983. 60.00x (ISBN 0-8020-5526-5); fiche incl. U of Toronto Pr.

Cameron, Angus, jt. ed. see Frank, Roberta.

Cameron, Angus, intro. by. The Magic of Owls. LC 77-78130. 1977. 11.95 (ISBN 0-8027-0578-2); pap. 6.95 (ISBN 0-8027-7117-3). Walker & Co.

Cameron, Angus, et al, eds. Computers & Old English Concordances. (Toronto Old English Ser.). 1970. pap. 17.50x (ISBN 0-8020-4024-1). U of Toronto Pr.

Cameron, Ann. The Journey. 336p. 1982. pap. 5.95 (ISBN 0-380-79087-4, 79087-4). Avon.

--The Seed. LC 74-15296. (Illus.). 36p. (gr. k-4). 1975. PLB 5.99 (ISBN 0-394-93087-8). Pantheon.

--The Stories Julian Tells. LC 80-18023. (Illus.). 96p. (gr. k-5). 1981. 8.95 (ISBN 0-394-84301-0); PLB 8.99 (ISBN 0-394-94301-5). Pantheon.

Cameron, Archie & Grant, J. Robert. Credit Union Salary Administration. 202p. (Orig.). 1982. pap. 21.95 (ISBN 0-318-16993-2, 671). Credit Union Natl Assn.

Cameron, Averil. Continuity & Change in Sixth-Century Byzantium. 338p. 1981. 65.00x (ISBN 0-86078-090-2, Pub. by Variorum). State Mutual Bk.

--Procopius & the Sixth Century. (Transformation of the Classical Heritage Ser.: Vol. 10). 300p. 1985. 35.00x (ISBN 0-520-05517-9). U of Cal Pr.

Cameron, Averil & Kuhrt, Amelie, eds. Images of Women in Antiquity. LC 83-124030. 317p. 25.00 (ISBN 0-8143-1762-6); pap. 14.95 (ISBN 0-8143-1763-4). Wayne St U Pr.

Cameron, Averil, ed. see Corippus, Flavius C.

Cameron, Barbara. An Affair to Remember. 2nd ed. (Candlelight Ecstasy Ser.: No. 124). (Orig.). 1983. pap. 1.95 (ISBN 0-440-11405-5). Dell.

--Mahabote: The Little Key. 118p. 1981. 10.00 (ISBN 0-86690-014-4, 2409-01). Am Fed Astrologers.

--The Metal Mistress. (Candlelight Ecstasy Ser.). (Orig.). 1982. pap. 1.75 (ISBN 0-440-15636-X). Dell.
--Predictive Planetary Periods. 158p. 1984. 12.00 (ISBN 0-86690-235-X, 2645-01). Am Fed Astrologers.
--Turning the Tables. 128p. 1984. 10.00 (ISBN 0-86690-282-1, 2559-01). Am Fed Astrologers.
Cameron, Barry, ed. Carboniferous Basins of Southeastern New England. LC 79-51602. 1979. pap. 10.00 (ISBN 0-913312-14-2). Am Geol.
Cameron, Bevelry J. & Cameron, Norman E. Economics in Action. LC 83-50199. 192p. 1983. pap. text ed. 10.95 (ISBN 0-312-23656-5); instr's. manual avail. St Martin.
--Microeconomics in Action: An Applications Book. LC 83-61627. 99p. 1984. pap. text ed. 8.95 (ISBN 0-312-53183-4). St Martin.
Cameron, Beverly J. & Cameron, Norman E. Macroeconomics in Action: An Applications Book. LC 3-61628. 118p. 1984. pap. text ed. 8.95 (ISBN 0-312-50337-7). St Martin.
Cameron, Blair. Boss Lady. (Candlelight Supreme Ser.: No. 62). (Orig.). 1985. pap. 2.50 (ISBN 0-440-10763-6). Dell.
--Bright Flame, Distant Star. (Candlelight Ecstasy Supreme Ser.: No. 78). (Orig.). 1985. pap. 2.75 (ISBN 0-440-10832-2). Dell.
--Million Dollar Lover. (CandleLight Supreme Ser.: No. 98). (Orig.). 1985. pap. 2.75 (ISBN 0-440-15634-3). Dell.
Cameron, Bruce F., ed. see Miami Winter Symposium.
Cameron, Bruce M. Shaft Fractures & Pseudarthroses. (Illus.). 128p. 1966. photocopy ed. 17.50x (ISBN 0-398-00276-2). C C Thomas.
Cameron, Burgess. Input-Output Analysis & Resource Allocation. LC 68-21188. pap. 29.30 (ISBN 0-317-09707-5, 2050791). Bks Demand UMI.
Cameron, Catherine. The Name Givers: How They Influence Your Life. 230p. 1983. 13.95 (ISBN 0-13-609495-3); pap. 6.95 (ISBN 0-13-609487-2). P-H.
Cameron, Charles & Elusorr, Suzanne. T. G. I. M. (Thank God Its Monday) How to Find Fulfilling Work & How to Make Your Work Fulfilling. (Illus.). 208p. 1986. pap. cancelled (ISBN 0-87477-357-1). J P Tarcher.
Cameron, Charles, jt. auth. see Cleaves, Bennett.
Cameron, Charlotte. Mexico in Revolution. 1976. lib. bdg. 59.95 (ISBN 0-8490-0627-9). Gordon Pr.
Cameron, Clive A. Going Metric with the U. S. Printing Industry. 125p. 1972. pap. 11.00 (ISBN 0-317-14996-2). Tech & Ed Ctr Graph Arts RIT.
Cameron, Colin. The Displaced Homemaker: A Bibliography. (Public Administration Ser.: P-895). 48p. 1982. pap. 7.50 (ISBN 0-88066-135-6, P-895). Vance Biblios.
Cameron, Cyril T. Public Relations in the Emergency Department. LC 80-15894. 126p. 1980. text ed. 18.95 (ISBN 0-87619-746-2). Brady Comm.
Cameron, D. Arabic-English Dictionary. (Arabic & Eng.). 1979. 16.00x (ISBN 0-86685-084-8). Intl Bk Ctr.
Cameron, D. C., jt. ed. see Kramer, J. F.
Cameron, D. Ewen. Psychotherapy in Action. LC 68-16303. 240p. 1968. 49.50 (ISBN 0-8089-0091-9, 790770). Grune.
Cameron, D. G., jt. auth. see Clements, R. J.
Cameron, D. G., jt. ed. see Clements, R. J.
Cameron, David K. The Cornkister Days. (Illus.). 272p. 1984. 17.50 (ISBN 0-575-03492-0, Pub. by Gollancz England). David & Charles.
--Willie Gavin, Crofter Man. 1980. 18.95 (ISBN 0-575-02816-5, Pub. by Gollancz England). David & Charles.
Cameron, David M. Regionalism & Supranationalism. 136p. 1981. pap. text ed. 9.95x (ISBN 0-920380-74-3, Pub.by Inst Res Pub Canada). Brookfield Pub Co.
Cameron, Deborah. Feminism & Linguistic Theory. LC 84-15150. 205p. 1984. 22.50 (ISBN 0-312-28746-1). St martin.
Cameron, Derek. Advanced Electronic Troubleshooting. (Illus.). 1977. 24.95 (ISBN 0-87909-002-2). Reston.
Cameron, Don. Ballooning Handbook. (Illus.). 174p. 1981. 15.95 (ISBN 0-7207-1220-3, Pub. by Michael Joseph). Merrimack Pub Cir.
Cameron, Donald. My Tanganyika Service: And Some Nigeria. Huessler, Robert, ed. LC 82-8666. (Illus.). 308p. 1982. lib. bdg. 27.75 (ISBN 0-8191-2441-9); pap. text ed. 14.75 (ISBN 0-8191-2442-7). U Pr of Amer.
Cameron, Dorothy. Sculpture 'Sixty-Seven. (Illus.). 116p. pap. 7.95 (ISBN 0-88884-156-6, 56509-2, Pub. by Natl Mus Canada). Nat Gal Can.
Cameron, Eion M. Uranium Exploration in Athabaska Basin. 320p. 1983. pap. text ed. 49.95x (ISBN 0-660-11508-5, Pub. by Minister Supplies Canada). Brookfield Pub Co.
Cameron, Eleanor. Beyond Silence. LC 80-10350. (gr. 5-9). 1980. 10.25 (ISBN 0-525-26463-9, 0995-300). Dutton.
--Beyond Silence. (gr. k-12). 1985. pap. 2.75 (ISBN 0-440-90582-6, LFL). Dell.
--The Court of the Stone Children. (gr. 5-10). 1976. pap. 1.75 (ISBN 0-380-00681-2, 48942). Avon.
--The Court of the Stone Children. 208p. (gr. 5 up). 1973. 12.95 (ISBN 0-525-28350-1, 01258-370). Dutton.
--The Green & Burning Tree: On the Writing & Enjoyment of Children's Books. 377p. (gr. 8 up). 1969. pap. 3.95 (ISBN 0-316-12522-9, Pub. by Atlantic Monthly Pr). Little.
--Julia & the Hand of God. LC 77-4507. (Illus.). 1977. 9.95 (ISBN 0-525-32910-2). Dutton.
--Julia's Magic. LC 84-8118. (Illus.). 144p. (gr. 2-5). 1984. 10.95 (ISBN 0-525-44114-X, 01063-320). Dutton.
--Mr. Bass's Planetoid. (Illus.). (gr. 3-7). 1958. 12.45 (ISBN 0-316-12525-3, Pub. by Atlantic Monthly Pr). Little.
--A Room Made of Windows. (gr. 7 up). 1971. 14.45 (ISBN 0-316-12523-7, Pub. by Atlantic Monthly Pr). Little.
--Stowaway to the Mushroom Planet. (gr. 3-7). 1956. 12.45i (ISBN 0-316-12534-2, Atlantic-Little, Brown). Little.
--The Terrible Churnadryne. (Illus.). (gr. 4-6). 1959. 10.95 (ISBN 0-316-12535-0, Pub. by Atlantic Monthly Pr). Little.
--That Julia Redfern. LC 82-2405. 144p. (gr. 2-5). 1982. 9.95 (ISBN 0-525-44015-1, 0966-290). Dutton.
--Time & Mr. Bass. (Illus.). (gr. 4-6). 1967. 12.45i (ISBN 0-316-12536-9, Pub. by Atlantic Monthly Pr). Little.
--To the Green Mountains. 224p. (gr. 5 up). 1975. 9.95 (ISBN 0-525-41355-3). Dutton.
--The Wonderful Flight to the Mushroom Planet. (Illus.). (gr. 4-6). 1954. 13.45i (ISBN 0-316-12537-7, Pub. by Atlantic Monthly Pr). Little.
Cameron, Elisabeth & Lewis, Philippa. Potters on Pottery. (Illus.). 1976. 11.95 (ISBN 0-312-63280-0). St Martin.
Cameron, Elizabeth. Big Book of Real Trucks. (Grosset Picture Bks.). (gr. 1-5). 1970. 2.95 (ISBN 0-448-02240-0, G&D). Putnam Pub Group.
--A Floral ABC. LC 82-12450. (Illus.). 64p. 1983. 7.70 (ISBN 0-688-01821-1). Morrow.
--Shopping Guide for Large-Size Clothes. LC 80-85236. 128p. (Orig.). 1981. pap. 7.95 (ISBN 0-939006-00-6). Odyssey Ent.
--A Wild Flower Alphabet. (Illus.). 64p. 1984. 9.70 (ISBN 0-688-02525-0). Morrow.
Cameron, Elspeth. Hugh MacLennan: A Writer's Life. 424p. 1981. 30.00 (ISBN 0-8020-5556-7). U of Toronto Pr.
Cameron, Euan. The Reformation of the Heretics: The Waldenses of the Alps, 1480-1580. (Oxford Historical Monographs). (Illus.). 1984. 45.00x (ISBN 0-19-822930-5). Oxford U Pr.
Cameron, Eugene N., ed. The Mineral Position of the United States, 1975-2000. LC 72-7983. (Illus.). 182p. 1973. 15.00x (ISBN 0-299-06300-3); pap. 5.95x (ISBN 0-299-06304-6). U of Wis Pr.
Cameron, Eugene N., et al. Internal Structure of Granitic Pragmatites. (Economic Geology Monograph: No. 2). pap. 43.00 (ISBN 0-317-28808-3, 2020336). Bks Demand UMI.
Cameron, Evan W., ed. Sound & the Cinema: The Coming of Sound to American Film. xvi, 232p. (Orig.). 1980. pap. 12.50 (ISBN 0-913178-56-X). Redgrave Pub Co.
Cameron, Fiona, jt. auth. see Kristensen, Preben.
Cameron, Frank. Micro Guns. (Illus.). 48p. 1982. 24.00 (ISBN 0-88014-049-6). Mosaic Pr OH.
Cameron, G. Gordon, tr. see Urbanski, J., et al.
Cameron, George C. History of Early Iran. 1976. lib. bdg. 69.95 (ISBN 0-8490-1972-9). Gordon Pr.
Cameron, George D., jt. auth. see Scaletta, Phillip J.
Cameron, George D., III. The Soviet Lawyer & His System: A Historical & Bibliographic Study. LC 78-9652. (Michigan International Business Studies: No. 14). 1978. pap. 9.00 (ISBN 0-87712-185-0). U Mich Busn Div Res.
Cameron, George G., ed. see Chiera, Edward.
Cameron, Gladys. Tissue Culture Technique. 2nd ed. 1950. 39.00 (ISBN 0-12-156650-1). Acad Pr.
Cameron, Gordon C. Regional Economic Development: The Federal Role. LC 77-86390. (Resources for the Future Ser.). 176p. Repr. of 1970 ed. 27.50 (ISBN 0-404-60329-7). AMS Pr.
CAmeron, H. Chart Processing Functions of Regional Meteorological Centres. (World Weather Watch Planning Reports: No. 12). 46p. 1966. pap. 6.00 (ISBN 0-685-22294-2, W230, WMO). Unipub.
Cameron, I. M. & Rae, L. John. Atlas of the Battered Child Syndrome. LC 76-356148. (Illus.). 160p. 1975. text ed. 35.00 (ISBN 0-443-01253-9). Churchill.
Cameron, I. R. Nuclear Fission Reactors. LC 82-18128. 398p. 1982. 49.50x (ISBN 0-306-41073-7, Plenum Pr). PLenum Pub.
Cameron, Iain A. Crime & Represssion in the Auvergne & Guyenne, 1720-1790. LC 80-41953. (Illus.). 256p. 1982. 44.50 (ISBN 0-521-23882-X). Cambridge U Pr.
Cameron, Ian. The White Ship. 1977. pap. 1.50 (ISBN 0-380-01701-6, 33761). Avon.
Cameron, Ian R. & Bateman, Nigel T. Respiratory Disorders. (Illus.). 128p. 1984. pap. text ed. 16.00 (ISBN 0-8391-2021-4, 21296). Univ Park.
Cameron, Ivan L. & Jeter, James R., Jr., eds. Acidic Proteins of the Nucleus. 1974. 67.50 (ISBN 0-12-156930-6). Acad Pr.
Cameron, Ivan L. & Padilla, George M., eds. Cell Synchrony: Studies in Biosynthetic Regulation. 1966. 75.00 (ISBN 0-12-156950-0). Acad Pr.
--Developmental Aspects of the Cell Cycle. (Cell Biology Ser). 1971. 67.50 (ISBN 0-12-156960-8). Acad Pr.
Cameron, Ivan L. & Pool, Thomas B., eds. The Transformed Cell. (Cell Biology Ser.). 1981. 65.00 (ISBN 0-12-157160-2). Acad Pr.
Cameron, Ivan L. & Thrasher, Jack D., eds. Cellular & Molecular Renewal in the Mammalian Body. LC 76-137622. (Cell Biology Ser). 1971. 75.00 (ISBN 0-12-156940-3). Acad Pr.
Cameron, J. H., tr. see Girard, Paul F.
Cameron, J. M. On the Idea of a University. 1978. pap. 6.50 (ISBN 0-8020-6335-7). U of Toronto Pr.
Cameron, J. M. R. Ambition's Fire: The Agricultural Colonization of Pre-Convict Western Australia. 238p. 1982. pap. 27.00x (ISBN 0-85564-196-7, Pub. by U of W Austral Pr). Intl Spec Bk.
Cameron, J. Stewart, et al. Nephrology for Nurses - A Modern Approach to the Kidney. 2nd ed. 1977. 12.00 (ISBN 0-87488-869-7). Med Exam.
Cameron, James. The Making of Israel. LC 77-76041. (Illus.). 1977. 7.95 (ISBN 0-8008-5084-X). Taplinger.
--Nineteen Fourteen. LC 74-31338. 210p. 1975. Repr. of 1959 ed. lib. bdg. 15.00 (ISBN 0-8371-7861-4, CANI). Greenwood.
Cameron, James, jt. auth. see Fairbairns, Zoe.
Cameron, James B., et al. Advanced Accounting: Theory & Practice. LC 78-69529. (Illus.). 1979. text ed. 33.95 (ISBN 0-395-27446-X); solutions manual 5.50 (ISBN 0-395-27447-8); student check sheets. set of 100 2.50 (ISBN 0-395-27497-4). HM.
Cameron, James M. Images of Authority: A Consideration of the Concepts of "Regnum" & "Sacerdotium". LC 66-12489. pap. 24.30 (ISBN 0-8357-9261-7, 2016769). Bks Demand UMI.
Cameron, James R. Frederick William Maitland & the History of English Law. LC 77-677. xvi, 214p. 1977. Repr. of 1961 ed. lib. bdg. 19.75x (ISBN 0-8371-9499-7, CAFWM). Greenwood.
Cameron, Janet E. Double Crostic No. 19. 1983. 5.00 (ISBN 0-686-46625-X). Cameron & Co.
--Double Crostic No. 20. 1984. 5.00 (ISBN 0-686-46626-8). Cameron & Co.
--Double-Crostics, Vols. 5-18. Incl. Vol. 5 (ISBN 0-8317-2414-5); Vol. 6 (ISBN 0-8317-2415-3); Vol. 7 (ISBN 0-8317-2416-1); Vol. 8 (ISBN 0-8317-2417-X); Vol. 9 (ISBN 0-8317-2418-8); Vol. 10 (ISBN 0-8317-2419-6); Vol. 11 (ISBN 0-8317-2420-X); Vol. 12 (ISBN 0-8317-2421-8); Vol. 13 (ISBN 0-8317-2422-6); Vol. 14 (ISBN 0-8317-2411-0); Vol. 15 (ISBN 0-8317-2412-9); Vol. 16 (ISBN 0-8317-2413-7); Vol. 17 (ISBN 0-8317-2423-4); Vol. 18 (ISBN 0-8317-2424-2). 64p. 1982. pap. 5.00 ea. spiral bdg. Smith Pubs.
--Double Crostics, No. 12. 1979. 5.00 (ISBN 0-918684-09-9). Cameron & Co.
--Double Crostics, No. 13. 1980. 5.00 (ISBN 0-918684-12-9). Cameron & Co Inc.
--Double Crostics, No. 14. 1980. 5.00 (ISBN 0-918684-13-7). Cameron & Co Inc.
--Double Crostics, No. 16. 1981. 5.00 (ISBN 0-918684-15-3). Cameron & Co Inc.
--Double Crostics, No. 17. 1982. 5.00 (ISBN 0-918684-16-1). Cameron & Co.
--Double Crostics No. 10. 1978. 5.00 (ISBN 0-918684-06-4). Cameron & Co.
--Double Crostics, No. 11. 1979. 5.00 (ISBN 0-918684-07-2). Cameron & Co.
--Double Crostics, No. 15. 1981. 5.00 (ISBN 0-918684-14-5). Cameron & Co.
--Double Crostics, No 18. 1982. 5.00 (ISBN 0-918684-17-X). Cameron & Co.
--Double Crostics, No. 9. 1978. 5.00 (ISBN 0-918684-04-8). Cameron & Co.
--Double Crostics Nos. 5-8, 4 bks. 5.00 ea. Cameron & Co.
Cameron, Jean. For All That Has Been: Time to Live & Time to Die. 120p. 1982. pap. 9.50 (ISBN 0-02-521980-4). Macmillan.
Cameron, Jean W. The Orchids of Maine. 1976. pap. 3.50 (ISBN 0-89101-001-7). U Maine Orono.
Cameron, Jenks. The Bureau of Biological Survey: Its History, Activities & Organization. LC 72-3071. (Brookings Institution. Institute for Government Research. Service Monographs of the U.S. Government: No. 54). Repr. of 1929 ed. 42.50 (ISBN 0-404-57154-9). AMS Pr.
--The Bureau of Biological Survey: Its History, Activities, & Organization. LC 73-17805. (Natural Sciences in America Ser.). 354p. 1974. Repr. 24.50x (ISBN 0-405-05722-9). Ayer Co Pubs.
--The Bureau of Dairy Industry: Its History, Activities & Organization. LC 72-3072. (Brookings Institution. Institute for Government Research. Service Monographs of the U.S. Government: No. 55). Repr. of 1929 ed. 21.50 (ISBN 0-404-57155-7). AMS Pr.
--The Development of Governmental Forest Control in the United States. LC 79-38096. (Law, Politics, & History Ser.). 484p. 1972. Repr. of 1928 ed. lib. bdg. 55.00 (ISBN 0-306-70440-4). Da Capo.
--Development of Governmental Forest Control in the United States. (Brookings Institution Reprint Ser.). Repr. of 1928 ed. lib. bdg. 29.00x (ISBN 0-697-00153-9). Irvington.
--The National Park Service: Its History, Activities & Organization. LC 72-3024. (Brookings Institution. Institute for Government Research. Service Monographs of the U.S. Government: No. 11). Repr. of 1922 ed. 25.00 (ISBN 0-404-57111-5). AMS Pr.
Cameron, Jerry D. Kings of the Road. Halgerson, Alison, ed. LC 85-90693. 220p. 1985. 12.50x (ISBN 0-317-19555-7). Lyman Co Herald.
Cameron, John. JSP & JSD: The Jackson Approach to Software Development. 257p. 1983. 30.00 (ISBN 0-8186-8516-6). IEEE Comp Soc.
Cameron, John L. Current Surgical Therapy 1984-1985. 600p. 1984. casebound 58.00 (ISBN 0-317-01540-0). Mosby.
Cameron, John R. & Skofronick, James G. Medical Physics. LC 77-26909. 1978. 42.50 (ISBN 0-471-13131-8, Pub. by Wiley-Interscience). Wiley.
Cameron, John R. & Suntharalingam, N. Thermoluminescent Dosimetry. LC 68-16061. pap. 48.70 (ISBN 0-317-11063-2, 2012631). Bks Demand UMI.
Cameron, Kate. Kiss Me Kill Me. 1979. pap. 1.50 (ISBN 0-505-51384-6, Pub. by Tower Bks). Dorchester Pub Co.
--Music from the Past. (Holderly Hall Ser). (Orig.). 1975. pap. 0.95 (ISBN 0-685-53904-0, LB287ZK, Leisure Bks). Dorchester Pub Co.
--Voices in the Fog. (Holderly Hall Ser: No. 3). 1975. pap. 0.95 (ISBN 0-685-51410-2, LB230NK, Leisure Bks). Dorchester Pub Co.
Cameron, Keith. Rene Maran. (World Author Ser.). 1985. lib. bdg. 24.95 (ISBN 0-8057-6604-9, Twayne). G K Hall.
Cameron, Kenneth see Corrigan, Robert W.
Cameron, Kenneth M. & Gillespie, Patti P. The Enjoyment of Theatre. (Illus.). 1980. pap. text ed. write for info. (ISBN 0-02-318360-8). Macmillan.
Cameron, Kenneth M. & Hoffman, Theodore J. Guide to Theatre Study. 2nd ed. (Illus.). 384p. 1974. text ed. write for info. (ISBN 0-02-318350-0, 31835). Macmillan.
Cameron, Kenneth M., jt. auth. see Gillespie, Patti P.
Cameron, Kenneth N. Humanity & Society: A World History. LC 76-55618. 480p. 1977. pap. 6.50 (ISBN 0-85345-408-6). Monthly Rev.
--Man of Contradiction: Stalin, A Reexamination. 272p. 1985. 29.95 (ISBN 0-89935-048-8). Synthesis Pubns.
--Marxism: The Science of Society; An Introduction. LC 84-405. 240p. 1984. 27.95 (ISBN 0-89789-051-5); pap. text ed. 12.95 (ISBN 0-89789-086-8). Bergin & Garvey.
--Shelley: The Golden Years. LC 73-80566. 1974. text ed. 32.50x (ISBN 0-674-80605-0). Harvard U Pr.
--The Young Shelley: Genesis of a Radical. 437p. 1980. Repr. of 1951 ed. lib. bdg. 30.00 (ISBN 0-89984-107-4). Century Bookbindery.
Cameron, Kenneth N., ed. Romantic Rebels: Essays on Shelley & His Circle. LC 72-97087. (Carl H. Pforzheimer Library). 1973. 20.00x (ISBN 0-674-77937-1). Harvard U Pr.
--Shelley & His Circle: 1773-1822, 6 Vols. Incl. Vol. 1. (Illus.). l, 474p. 1961; Vol. 2. (Illus.). xvi, 545p. 1961. Vols. 1 & 2. boxed set 60.00x (ISBN 0-674-80610-7); Vol. 3. (Illus.). xxxvi, 485p. 1970; Vol. 4. (Illus.). xviii, 529p. 1970. Vols. 3 & 4. boxed set 60.00x (ISBN 0-674-80611-5); Vols. 5-6. (Illus.). 1973. boxed set 60.00x (ISBN 0-674-80612-3). LC 60-5393. (Carl H. Pforzheimer Library). Harvard U Pr.
Cameron, Kenneth N., ed. see Shelley, Percy B.
Cameron, Kenneth W. Emerson the Essayist: An Outline of His Philosophical Development Through 1836, 2 vols. LC 80-2529. Repr. of 1945 ed. Set. 92.00 (ISBN 0-404-19280-7). Vol. 1 (ISBN 0-404-19281-5). Vol. 2 (ISBN 0-404-19282-3). AMS Pr.
--Ralph Waldo Emerson's Readings. LC 72-10872. (American Biography Ser., No. 32). 1969. Repr. of 1941 ed. lib. bdg. 39.95x (ISBN 0-8383-0518-0). Haskell.
--Ralph Waldo Emerson's Readings. 1973. Repr. of 1941 ed. 8.75 (ISBN 0-8274-1305-X). R West.
Cameron, Kim S., jt. auth. see Whetten, David A.
Cameron, Kim S. & Whetten, David A., eds. Organizational Effectiveness: A Comparison of Multiple Models. 320p. 1982. 31.50 (ISBN 0-12-157180-7). Acad Pr.
Cameron, Lewis. Opportunity My Ally. (Illus.). 253p. 1965. 10.95 (ISBN 0-227-67706-4). Attic Pr.
Cameron, Lou. The Hot Car. 208p. (Orig.). 1981. pap. 2.25 (ISBN 0-380-78949-3, 78949). Avon.
Cameron, Luis de see De Cameron, Luis.
Cameron, M. Coleoptera - Staphylinidae: Staphylinidae, Vol. II. (Fauna of British India Ser.). (Illus.). vii, 260p. 1978. Repr. of 1931 ed. 30.00 (ISBN 0-88065-027-3, Pub. by Messers Today & Tomorrows Printers & Publishers India). Scholarly Pubns.
--Coleoptera - Staphylinidae: Staphylinidae, Vol. 1. (Fauna of British India Ser.). (Illus.). xviii, 478p. 1978. Repr. of 1930 ed. 30.00 (ISBN 0-88065-026-5, Pub. by Messers Today & Tommorrows Printers & Publishers India). Scholarly Pubns.

--Coleoptera - Staphylinoidea: Staphylinidae, Vol. 4, Pt. 2. (Fauna of British India Ser.). (Illus.). 691p. 1977. Repr. of 1939 ed. 40.00 (ISBN 0-88065-030-3, Pub. by Messers Today & Tomorrows Printers & Publishers India). Scholarly Pubns.

--Coleoptera-Staphylinoidea: Staphy-linoidea, Vol. 3. (Fauna 9f British India Ser.). (Illus.). 1978. Repr. of 1932 ed. 30.00 (ISBN 0-88065-028-1, Pub. by Messers Today & Tomorrows Printers & Publishers India). Scholarly Pubns.

--Coleoptera-Staphylinoidea: Staphylinodea, Vol. 4, Pt. 1. (Fauna of British India Ser.). (Illus.). Repr. of 1939 ed. 30.00 (ISBN 0-88065-029-X, Pub. by Messers Today & Tomorrows Printers & Publishers India). Scholarly Pubns.

Cameron, M. & Hofvander, Y. Manual on Feeding Infants & Young Children. 2nd ed. (Illus.). 184p. (2nd Printing 1980). 1976. pap. 9.95 (ISBN 0-685-92339-8, F1505, FAO). Unipub.

Cameron, Mabel W., ed. The Biographical Cyclopaedia of American Women, 2 vols. LC 24-7615. 408p. 1975. Repr. of 1924 ed. 110.00x (ISBN 0-8103-3990-0). Gale.

Cameron, Malcolm E. Pterygium Throughout the World. (Illus.). 208p. 1965. photocopy ed. 19.50x (ISBN 0-398-00277-0). C C Thomas.

Cameron, Margaret & Hofvander, Tngve. Manual on Feeding Infants & Young Children. 3rd ed. (Illus.). 1983. pap. 9.95x (ISBN 0-19-261403-7). Oxford U Pr.

Cameron, Margaret M., tr. see Lanctot, Gustave.

Cameron, Meribeth E. The Reform Movement in China: 1898-1912. LC 78-161506. (Standford University. Standford Studies in History, Economics & Political Science Ser. 3: No. 1). Repr. of 1931 ed. 22.00 (ISBN 0-404-50959-2). AMS Pr.

Cameron, Meribeth E., et al. China, Japan & the Powers: A History of the Modern Far East. 2nd ed. LC 60-7761. Repr. of 1960 ed. 120.00 (ISBN 0-8357-9857-7, 2012473). Bks Demand UMI.

Cameron, Miranda. Lord Cleary's Revenge. 1985. pap. 2.50 (ISBN 0-451-13762-0, Sig). NAL.

--The Meddlesome Heiress. 224p. (Orig.). 1983. pap. 2.25 (ISBN 0-451-12616-5, Sig). NAL.

--The Reluctant Abigail. 1984. pap. 2.50 (ISBN 0-451-13162-2, Sig). NAL.

--A Scandalous Bargain. 1983. pap. 2.25 (ISBN 0-451-12449-9, Sig). NAL.

Cameron, Morag, ed. see International Union for the Scientific Study of Population.

Cameron, Moven, ed. Voices of Our Kind: An Anthology of Contemporary Scottish Verse. 80p. 1975. 15.00x (ISBN 0-85411-000-3, Pub. by Saltire Soc). State Mutual Bk.

Cameron, Nigel. Barbarians & Mandarins: Thirteen Centuries of Western Travelers in China. (Illus.). 444p. 1976. pap. 7.95x (ISBN 0-226-09229-1, P681). U of Chicago Pr.

--Evolution & the Authority of the Bible. 128p. 1983. pap. 6.95 (ISBN 0-85364-326-1, Pub. by Paternoster UK). Attic Pr.

--The Face of China As Seen by Photographers or Travelers: 1860-1912. LC 78-53932. (Illus.). 160p. 1978. 25.00 (ISBN 0-89381-029-0); pap. 14.95 (ISBN 0-89381-031-2). Aperture.

--From Bondage to Liberation: East Asia 1860-1952. (Illus.). 1975. pap. 21.95x (ISBN 0-19-580735-9). Oxford U Pr.

Cameron, Noel. The Measurement of Human Growth. (Illus.). 208p. 1984. text ed. 32.50x (ISBN 0-7099-0731-1). Sheridan Med Bks.

Cameron, Nonnie & Phillips, Diane. Hors d'Oeuvres. 56p. (Orig.). 1984. pap. 2.95 (ISBN 0-942320-10-7). WRC Pub.

Cameron, Norman & Rychlak, Joseph F. Personality Development & Psychopathology. 2nd ed. LC 84-80710. 816p. 1984. text ed. 29.95 (ISBN 0-395-34387-9). HM.

Cameron, Norman, tr. see Stendhal.

Cameron, Norman E. Evolution of the Negro, 2 Vols in 1. LC 79-111568. Repr. of 1934 ed. 28.00x (ISBN 0-8371-4589-9, CNE&, Pub. by Negro U Pr). Greenwood.

Cameron, Norman E., jt. auth. see Cameron, Bevelry J.

Cameron, Norman E., jt. auth. see Cameron, Beverly J.

Cameron, P. Monograph of the British Phytophagous Hymenoptera, 4 Vols. 1882-1893. Set. 92.00 (ISBN 0-384-07240-2). Johnson Repr.

Cameron, P. J. Parallelisms of Complete Designs. LC 75-32912. (London Mathematical Society Lecture Note Ser.: No. 23). (Illus.). 1976. 22.95 (ISBN 0-521-21160-3). Cambridge U Pr.

Cameron, P. J. & Van Lint, J. H. Graphs, Codes & Designs. (London Mathematical Society Lecture Notes Ser.: No. 43). 180p. 1980. 24.95 (ISBN 0-521-23141-8). Cambridge U Pr.

Cameron, Pat. Crete. 4th ed. (Blue Guides Ser.). 1986. pap. 11.95 (ISBN 0-393-30078-1). Norton.

Cameron, Peter, ed. see British Combinatorial Conference, Sixth.

Cameron, Peter D. Property Rights & Sovereign Rights: The Case of North Sea Oil. (Law State & Society Ser.). 1984. 36.00 (ISBN 0-12-157060-6). Acad Pr.

Cameron, R. Great Comp & its Garden. 180p. 1982. 49.00x (ISBN 0-85974-100-1, Pub. by Bachman & Turner). State Mutual Bk.

Cameron, R. H. & Storvick, D. A. A Simple Definition of the Feynman Integral, with Applications. LC 83-15605. (Memoirs Ser.: No. 288). 48p. 1983. paper 9.00 (ISBN 0-8218-2288-8). Am Math.

Cameron, R. J., ed. Working Together: New Developments Incorporating the Portage Teaching Model. 12.00x (ISBN 0-85633-241-0, Pub. by NFER Nelson UK). Taylor & Francis.

Cameron, Robert. Above Hawaii. LC 77-88840. 1977. 19.95 (ISBN 0-918684-02-1). Cameron & Co.

--Above Los Angeles: A Collection of Nostalgic & Contemporary Aerial Photographs of Greater Los Angeles. LC 76-28657. 1977. 19.95 (ISBN 0-918684-03-X). Cameron & Co.

--Above San Francisco, Vol. II. LC 70-103848. 1977. 19.95 (ISBN 0-918684-05-6). Cameron & Co.

--Above Washington. LC 79-89078. 1979. 19.95 (ISBN 0-918684-08-0). Cameron & Co.

Cameron, Robert & Cooke, Alistair. Above London. LC 80-80944. 1980. 19.95 (ISBN 0-918684-10-2). Cameron & Co.

Cameron, Robert & Salinger, Pierre. Above Paris. 1984. 19.95 (ISBN 0-918684-19-6). Cameron & Co.

Cameron, Robert W. Above Yosemite. 1983. 19.95 (ISBN 0-918684-20-X). Cameron & Co.

--Alcatraz. 1983. 6.95 (ISBN 0-918684-19-6). Cameron & Co.

Cameron, Ron. Sayings Traditions in the Apocryphon of James. LC 84-45189. (Harvard Theological Studies). 160p. 1984. pap. 12.95 (ISBN 0-8006-7015-9). Fortress.

Cameron, Ron, ed. The Other Gospels: Non-Canonical Gospel Texts. LC 82-8662. 192p. 1982. pap. 11.95 (ISBN 0-664-24428-9). Westminster.

Cameron, Ron & Dewey, Arthur J., trs. The Cologne Mani Codex. LC 79-14743. (Society of Biblical Literature Texts & Translations, 15. Early Christian Literature Ser.: No. 3). 1979. pap. 8.95 (ISBN 0-89130-312-X, 060215). Scholars Pr GA.

Cameron, Rondo, ed. Civilization Since Waterloo: A Book of Source Readings. LC 75-108872. 1971. text ed. 24.95x (ISBN 0-88295-778-3); pap. text ed. 15.95x (ISBN 0-88295-779-1). Harlan Davidson.

Cameron, Roy & Spector, W. C. The Chemistry of the Injured Cell. (Illus.). 160p. 1961. 14.50x (ISBN 0-398-00278-9). C C Thomas.

Cameron, Roy, jt. auth. see Cohen, Donald.

Cameron, Sharon. The Corporeal Self: Allegories of the Body in Melville and Hawthorne. LC 81-47602. 176p. 1981. text ed. 16.50x (ISBN 0-8018-2643-8). Johns Hopkins.

--Lyric Time: Dickinson & the Limits of Genre. LC 78-9983. 296p. 1981. pap. 8.95x (ISBN 0-8018-2116-9). Johns Hopkins.

--Lyric Time: Dickinson & the Limits of Genre. LC 78-9983. 1979. text ed. 26.50x (ISBN 0-8018-2171-1). Johns Hopkins.

--Writing Nature: Henry Thoreau's Journal. 192p. 1985. 15.95 (ISBN 0-19-503570-4). Oxford U Pr.

Cameron, Sheila M. The Best from New Mexico Kitchens. LC 78-73806. (Illus.). 152p. (Orig.). 1979. pap. 6.95 (ISBN 0-937206-00-8, Pub. by NM Magazine). U of NM Pr.

--The Best from New Mexico Kitchens. (Illus.). 164p. (Orig.). 1978. pap. 6.95 (ISBN 0-937206-00-8). New Mexico Mag.

--Homemade Ice Cream & Sherbet. LC 69-16175. (Illus.). (YA) (gr. 9 up). 1969. pap. 3.50 (ISBN 0-8048-0258-0). C E Tuttle.

--More of the Best From New Mexico Kitchens. King, Scottie, ed. LC 82-62076. (Illus.). 160p. (Orig.). 1982. pap. 6.95 (ISBN 0-937206-02-4, Pub. by NM Magazine). U of NM Pr.

Cameron, Sheila M., jt. ed. see New Mexico Magazine Staff.

Cameron, Stewart. Kidney Disease: The Facts. (The Facts Ser.). (Illus.). 1981. text ed. 18.95x (ISBN 0-19-261329-4). Oxford U Pr.

Cameron, Thomas W. The Parasites of Man in Temperate Climates. 2nd ed. LC 43-17056. pap. 56.80 (ISBN 0-317-07799-6, 2016082). Bks Demand UMI.

Cameron, Verne L. Aquavideo: Locating Underground Water, a Complete Dowsing Method by the World Renowned Master. Cox, Bill, ed. LC 7-139236. (Illus.). 116p. 1970. pap. 6.95 (ISBN 0-88234-005-0). Life Understanding.

--Map Dowsing. (Dowser's Hdbk, Ser., No. 1). 40p. 1971. pap. 2.75 (ISBN 0-88234-003-4). Life Understanding.

--Oil Locating. (Dowser's Hdbk. Ser., No. 2). 40p. 1971. pap. 2.75 (ISBN 0-88234-004-2). Life Understanding.

Cameron, Verney L. Across Africa. LC 76-88425. (Illus.). Repr. of 1877 ed. 21.50x (ISBN 0-8371-1819-0, CAA&, Pub. by Negro U Pr). Greenwood.

--Across Africa, 2 Vols. LC 5-8821. 1971. Repr. of 1877 ed. Set. 40.00 (ISBN 0-384-07363-8, L141). Johnson Repr.

Cameron, Viola R. Emigrants from Scotland to America, 1774-1775. LC 61-40562. 117p. 1980. pap. 7.50 (ISBN 0-8063-0066-3). Genealog Pub.

Cameron, W. & Munday, Shirley. The Games Lesson in Primary & Junior Schools. LC 76-21014. (Illus.). 1977. limp bdg. 7.95 (ISBN 0-521-21426-2). Cambridge U Pr.

Cameron, W. J. Covenant People. 3.00 (ISBN 0-685-08801-4). Destiny.

Cameron, William E. Great Dramas of the Bible. LC 81-71560. 305p. 1982. 4.95 (ISBN 0-87159-047-6). Unity School.

Cameron, William E., compiled by. The Bible Treasure Book. (Quiz & Puzzle Bks). 1977. pap. 1.45 (ISBN 0-8010-2399-8). Baker Bk.

Cameron, William J., ed. Poems on Affairs of State: Augustan Satirical Verse 1660-1714, Vol. 5 1688-1697. LC 63-7983. (Illus.). 1972. 57.00x (ISBN 0-300-01190-3). Yale U Pr.

Cameron, Wm., jt. ed. see Cross, Frank L., Jr.

Cameron-Bandler, Leslie. Solutions: Practical & Effective Antidotes for Sexual & Relationship Problems. rev. ed. LC 85-70138. 258p. 1985. pap. 11.95 (ISBN 0-932573-01-0). Futurepace.

Cameron-Bandler, Leslie, et al. The Emprint Method: A Guide to Reproducing Competency. 250p. (Orig.). 1985. pap. 11.95 (ISBN 0-932573-02-9). Futurepace.

--Know How: Guided Programs for Inventing Your Own Best Future. LC 85-70138. 270p. (Orig.). 1985. pap. 11.95 (ISBN 0-932573-00-2). Futurepace.

Camesasca, Ettore. Mantegna (Andrea) (Illus.). 80p. (Orig.). 1981. pap. 12.50 (ISBN 0-935748-11-3). Scala Books.

Cametti, Alberto. Palestrina. LC 74-24055. Repr. of 1925 ed. 32.00 (ISBN 0-404-12878-5). AMS Pr.

Camfield, William A. & Martin, Jean-Hubert, eds. Tabu Dada: Jean Crotti & Suzanne Duchamp, 1915-1922. (Illus.). 140p. (Orig.). 1983. pap. 12.50 (ISBN 0-295-96133-3, Pub. by Museum of Fine Arts, Houston). U of Wash Pr.

Camhi, Jeffrey M. Neuroethology: Nerve Cells & the Natural Behavior of Animals. LC 83-14957. (Illus.). 360p. 1983. text ed. 32.50x (ISBN 0-87893-075-2). Sinauer Assoc.

Camhy, Cathy, jt. auth. see Harlowe, Clarissa.

Camic, Charles. Experience & Enlightenment: Socialization for Cultural Change in Eighteenth-Century Scotland. LC 83-4992. 304p. 1983. lib. bdg. 27.50x (ISBN 0-226-09238-0). U of Chicago Pr.

Camil, Jorge, jt. auth. see Herget, James E.

Camille, Cl. & Dehaine, M. Dictionnaire de l'Informatique, Francais-Anglais. 248p. (Fr. & Eng.). 1972. 22.50 (ISBN 0-686-56936-9, M-6058). French & Eur.

Camille, Saint Saens see Rameau, Jean Philippe.

Camiller, Patrick & Rothschild, Jon, eds. Power & Opposition in Post-Revolutionary Societies. Camiller, Patrick, tr. from Ital. Orig. Title: Potere e Opposizione Nelle Societa Post-rivoluzionare. 281p. 1979. 15.95 (ISBN 0-906133-18-1, Pub. by Ink Links Ltd.); pap. 6.95 (ISBN 0-906133-19-X). Longwood Pub Group.

Camiller, Patrick, tr. see Camiller, Patrick & Rothschild, Jon.

Camiller, Patrick, tr. see Pluto-Maspero Project.

Camilleri, Dorothy, jt. auth. see Grace, Helen K.

Camilleri, Joseph. Chinese Foreign Policy: The Maoist Era & Its Aftermath. LC 80-50686. (Illus.). 325p. 1980. 27.50 (ISBN 0-295-95776-X). U of Wash Pr.

Camilleri, Joseph A. Civilization in Crisis: Human Prospects in a Changing World. LC 76-4240. pap. 77.80 (ISBN 0-317-09276-6, 2022441). Bks Demand UMI.

--The State & Nuclear Power: Conflict & Control in the Western World. LC 83-19824. 366p. 1984. 25.00x (ISBN 0-295-96094-9). U of Wash Pr.

Camilli, Camillo. Impressions of Famous Men, 3 Vols. (Printed Sources of Western Art Ser.). (Illus., Latin.). 1981. pap. 50.00 slipcase (ISBN 0-915346-66-4). A Wofsy Fine Arts.

Camilli, Thomas. Make It Metric. (Illus.). 72p. (Orig.). 1982. 6.95 (ISBN 0-9607366-7-0, KP111). Kino Pubns.

Camillo, Philip L. & Pappin, Steven. Computer-Ease. (Illus.). 50p. (Orig.). (gr. 5-6). 1983. pap. text ed. 4.95 (ISBN 0-318-01034-8); lab manual 3.50 (ISBN 0-318-01035-6); tchrs' ed. 3.50. D Anderson Assoc.

Camillos, Lucille. Mother Let Go of That Burden. (Outreach Ser.). 1980. pap. 0.99 (ISBN 0-8163-0379-7). Pacific Pr Pub Assn.

Camillus, John C. Budgeting for Profit. (Better Business Ser.). 168p. 1985. 19.95 (ISBN 0-8019-7552-2). Chilton.

--Budgeting for Profit: How to Exploit the Potential of Your Business. (An Alexander Hamilton Institute Bk.). 192p. 1984. pap. 19.95 (ISBN 0-8019-7523-9). Chilton.

Camin, Betty J. Beaufort Orphans, Bk. A: Eighteen Hundred Eight to Eighteen Twenty-Eight. (Beaufort Orphans Ser.). 245p. 1985. 25.00 (ISBN 0-9614123-0-5). Camin.

Camina, A. R. & Whelan, E. A. Linear Groups & Permutations. (Research Notes in Mathematics Ser.: No. 118). 168p. 1985. pap. text ed. 15.95 (ISBN 0-273-08672-3). Pitman Pub Ma.

Camina, M. M. see Diamond, Donald R. & McLoughlin, J. B.

Caminha, Adolfo. Bom-Crioulo: The Black Man & the Cabin Boy. Lacey, E. A., tr. from Portuguese. 144p. 1982. 20.00 (ISBN 0-917342-89-5); pap. 7.95 (ISBN 0-917342-88-7). Gay Sunshine.

Çaminos, Horacio & Goethert, Reinhard. Urbanization Primer: Project Assessment, Site Analysis, Design Criteria for Site & Services & Similar Dwelling Environments in Developing Areas, with a Documentary Collection of Photographs on Urbanization. (Illus.). 1978. text ed. 42.50x (ISBN 0-262-03066-7). MIT Pr.

Caminos, R. A. Literary Fragments in the Hieratic Script. 112p. 1956. 75.00x (ISBN 0-900416-31-9, Pub. by Griffith Inst). State Mutual Bk.

Caminos, Ricardo A. Literary Fragments in the Hieratic Script. (Illus.). 72p. 1956. text ed. 56.50x (ISBN 0-900416-31-9, Pub. by Aris & Phillips England). Humanities.

--A Tale of Woe: Papyrus Pushkin, No. 127. 99p. 1977. text ed. 37.50x (ISBN 0-900416-09-2, Pub. by Aris & Phillips England). Humanities.

Caminos, Ricardo A. & Fischer, Henry G. Ancient Egyptian Epigraphy & Palaeography. (Illus.). 1976. pap. text ed. 3.50 (ISBN 0-87099-197-3). Metro Mus Art.

Camm, Frank A. Regulatory Rulemaking to Implement Congressional Legislature: Lessons from the Powerplant & Industrial Fuel Use Act of 1978. LC 83-11010. 1983. 7.50 (ISBN 0-8330-0510-3). Rand Corp.

Camm, Frederick J. Mathematical Tables & Formulae. pap. 0.95 (ISBN 0-685-19408-6, 21, WL). Citadel Pr.

Camm, John A., jt. ed. see Martin, Anthony.

Cammack, Emerson, jt. auth. see Mehr, Robert I.

Cammack, Floyd M., et al. Community College Library Instruction: Training for Self-Reliance in Basic Library Use. (Illus.). 283p. 1979. 22.50 (ISBN 0-208-01825-5, Linnet). Shoe String.

Cammack, Paul, jt. ed. see O'Brien, Philip.

Cammaerts, Emile. The Childhood of Christ: As Seen by the Primitive Masters. 1978. Repr. of 1922 ed. lib. bdg. 20.00 (ISBN 0-8495-0766-9). Arden Lib.

--Discoveries in England. 1930. Repr. 10.00 (ISBN 0-8274-2189-3). R West.

--The Laughing Prophet. 243p. 1979. Repr. of 1937 ed. lib. bdg. 30.00 (ISBN 0-8482-7582-9). Norwood Edns.

--The Laughing Prophet. 243p. 1980. Repr. of 1937 ed. lib. bdg. 30.00 (ISBN 0-8492-4047-6). R West.

--The Poetry Nonsense. 1978. Repr. of 1925 ed. lib. bdg. 25.00 (ISBN 0-8495-0769-3). Arden Lib.

--Poetry of Nonsense. lib. bdg. 17.50 (ISBN 0-8414-3548-0). Folcroft.

Camman, Karl. Working with Ion-Selective Electrodes. Schroeder, A. H., tr. from Ger. (Chemical Laboratory Practice Ser.). (Illus.). 1979. 49.00 (ISBN 0-387-09320-6). Springer-Verlag.

Camman, Schuyler. Trade Through the Himalayas. LC 74-90477. Repr. of 1951 ed. lib. bdg. 15.00 (ISBN 0-8371-3260-6, CAHI). Greenwood.

Cammarano, Nick. Winning at the Harness Races. 1977. pap. 5.00 (ISBN 0-87980-326-6). Wilshire.

Cammarata, Phil. Who Farted? (Orig.). 1984. pap. 3.95 (ISBN 0-671-50674-9, Long Shadow Bks). PB.

Cammell, Charles R. Dante Gabriel Rossetti & the Philosophy of Love. 1978. Repr. of 1933 ed. lib. bdg. 12.50 (ISBN 0-8495-0811-8). Arden Lib.

--Dante Gabriel Rossetti & the Philosophy of Love. 1972. Repr. of 1933 ed. lib. bdg. 10.00 (ISBN 0-8414-0733-9). Folcroft.

Cammell, Diarmid, tr. see Laroui, Abdallah.

Cammer, Leonard. Up from Depression. 1983. pap. 3.50 (ISBN 0-671-50188-7). PB.

Cammett, John, tr. see Hobsbawm, Eric.

Cammett, John M. Antonio Gramsci & the Origins of Italian Communism. LC 66-22983. xiv, 306p. 1967. 25.00x (ISBN 0-8047-0141-5). Stanford U Pr.

Cammett, John M., ed. The Italian American Novel. 1969. 9.95 (ISBN 0-686-21886-8). Am Italian.

Cammock, Ruth. Primary Health Care Buildings. (Illus.). 96p. 1981. 25.00 (ISBN 0-85139-962-2). Nichols Pub.

Camner, James. Great Composers in Historic Photographs. 1981. pap. 7.95 (ISBN 0-486-24132-7). Dover.

--Great Conductors in Historic Photographs: 193 Portraits. (Music Ser.). (Illus.). 96p. (Orig.). 1983. pap. 6.95 (ISBN 0-486-24397-4). Dover.

--The Great Instrumentalists in Historic Photographs: 275 Portraits from 1850 to 1950. (Illus.). 1980. pap. 7.95 (ISBN 0-486-23907-1). Dover.

--The Great Opera Stars in Historic Photographs: Three Hundred Thirty-Three Portraits from the 1850s to the 1940s. 16.50 (ISBN 0-8446-5672-0). Peter Smith.

Camner, James, jt. auth. see Appelbaum, Stanley.

Camner, James, ed. The Great Instrumentalists in Historic Photographs: 274 Portraits from 1850 to 1950. (Illus.). 19.00 (ISBN 0-8446-5741-7). Peter Smith.

--The Great Opera Stars in Historic Photographs: Three Hundred & Forty Three Portraits from the 1850's to the 1940's. LC 77-86260. (Illus.). 1978. pap. 7.50 (ISBN 0-486-23575-0). Dover.

Camner, James, jt. ed. see Applebaum, Stanley.

Camoens, Luis De see De Camoens, Luis.

Camoes, L. Camoes: Some Poems. 1976. pap. 2.00 (ISBN 0-685-79255-2, Pub. by Menard Pr). Small Pr Dist.

Camoes, L. De see De Camoes, L.

Camoes, Luiz De see De Camoes, Luiz.

Camoin, Francois. The End of the World Is Los Angeles: Stories. LC 81-69838. 112p. 1982. pap. 6.95 (ISBN 0-8262-0365-5). U of Mo Pr.
--Why Men Are Afraid of Women: Stories. LC 84-1374. (Flannery O'Connor Award for Short Fiction Ser.). 160p. 1984. 13.95 (ISBN 0-8203-0722-X). U of Ga Pr.
Camoin, Francois A. The Revenge Convention in Tourneur, Webster & Middleton. (Salzburg Studies in English Literature, Jacobean Drama Studies: No. 20). 1972. pap. text ed. 25.50x (ISBN 0-391-01339-4). Humanities.
Camon, Ferdinando. Memorial. Calicchio, David, tr. from Itl. LC 83-60549. Orig. Title: Un Altare per la madre. 128p. 1983. pap. 7.50 (ISBN 0-910395-07-1). Marlboro Pr.
--The Story of Sirio. Bentea, Cassandra, tr. from Italian. 144p. (Orig.). 1985. pap. 8.00 (ISBN 0-910395-12-8). Marlboro Pr.
Camosy, Art, jt. ed. see Zuerner, Frank.
Camougis, G. Environmental Biology for Engineers: A Guide to Environmental Assessment. 1980. 28.50 (ISBN 0-07-009677-5). McGraw.
Camougis, George. Nerves, Muscles, & Electricity: An Introductory Manual of Electrophysiology. LC 79-117053. 81p. 1970. pap. 12.50x (ISBN 0-306-50008-6, Plenum Pr). Plenum Pub.
Camp & Smay. Microprocessor Systems Engineering. (Illus.). 656p. 1979. 29.95 (ISBN 0-916460-26-6). Matrix Pub.
Camp, et al. Microcomputer Systems Principles Featuring the 6502-KIM. (Illus.). 560p. 1979. pap. 16.95 (ISBN 0-916460-27-4). Matrix Pub.
Camp, A. Cinema Mexicain. 1976. lib. bdg. 59.95 (ISBN 0-8490-1634-7). Gordon Pr.
Camp, Ann. Pen Lettering. pap. 3.95 (ISBN 0-8008-6272-4, Pentalic). Taplinger.
Camp, Anthony J. Everyone Has Roots: An Introduction to English Genealogy. LC 78-62818. 189p. 1978. 9.50 (ISBN 0-8063-0828-1). Genealog Pub.
Camp, Bill & Dougherty, Thomas. Managing Our Natural Resources. 1984. text ed. 18.95 (ISBN 0-8359-4199-X); instr's manual avail. (ISBN 0-8359-4200-7). Reston.
Camp, Bonnie, jt. auth. see Bash, Mary Ann.
Camp, Bonnie, jt. ed. see Frankenburg, William K.
Camp, Bonnie W. & Bash, Mary A. Think Aloud: Increasing Social & Cognitive Skills--A Problem-Solving Program for Children (Primary Level) LC 81-51871. (Illus.). 296p. 1981. 3-ring binder 49.95 (ISBN 0-87822-254-5, 2545). Res Press.
Camp, Bonnie W. & Bash, Mary Ann S. Think Aloud: Increasing Social & Cognitive Skills-A Problem-Solving Program for Children, Classroom Program, Grades 1 & 2. LC 85-61575. (Illus.). 300p. 1985. pap. 35.95 (ISBN 0-87822-240-5). Res Press.
Camp, Bonnie W., jt. auth. see Bash, Mary Ann S.
Camp, Bonnie W., ed. Advances in Behavioral Pediatrics, Vol. 1. 266p. 1980. 40.00 (ISBN 0-89232-076-1). Jai Pr.
--Advances in Behavioral Pediatrics, Vol. 2. 232p. 1981. 40.00 (ISBN 0-89232-185-7). Jai Pr.
Camp, C. L., ed. see White, Philo.
Camp, Catherine C. De see De Camp, L. Sprague & De Camp, Catherine C.
Camp, Catherine C. de see De Camp, L. Sprague & De Camp, Catherine C.
Camp, Catherine C. De see De Camp, Catherine C.
Camp, Charles L., et al. Bibliography of Fossil Vertebrates, 1964-1968. LC 79-190170. (Geological Society of America Memoir Ser.: No. 134). pap. 160.00 (ISBN 0-317-29133-5, 2025028). Bks Demand UMI.
Camp, Charles W. The Artisan in Elizabethan Literature. LC 73-159171. 180p. 1972. Repr. of 1924 ed. lib. bdg. 18.50x (ISBN 0-374-91261-0). Octagon.
Camp, Christopher. How to Play Ragtime Guitar. LC 75-16976. (Illus., Orig.). 1976. pap. 4.95 (ISBN 0-8256-2351-0, +012). Music Sales.
Camp, Debbie. Gateway to the Heart. (Orig.). 1980. pap. 1.95 (ISBN 0-532-23208-9). Woodhill.
Camp, Deborah. Tandem. (Orig.). 1980. pap. 1.95 (ISBN 0-532-23236-4). Woodhill.
Camp, Dennis, ed. see Lindsay, Vachel.
Camp, Diana Van. Basic Skills Human Body Workbook: Grade 5. (Basic Skills Workbooks). 32p. 1982. tchrs' ed. 0.99 (ISBN 0-8209-0420-1, HBW-F). ESP.
--Basic Skills Human Body Workbook: Grade 8. (Basic Skills Workbooks). 32p. 1982. tchrs' ed. 0.99 (ISBN 0-8209-0423-6, HBW-I). ESP.
--Basic Skills Human Workbook: Grade 6. (Basic Skills Workbooks). 32p. 1982. tchrs' ed. 0.99 (ISBN 0-8209-0421-X, HBW-G). ESP.
--Basic Skills Human Workbook: Grade 7. (Basic Skills Workbooks). 32p. 1982. tchrs' ed. 0.99 (ISBN 0-8209-0422-8, HBW-H). ESP.
Camp, Diana van see Van Camp, Diana.
Camp, Doug. Turkey Hunting: Spring & Fall. Taylor, Buck, ed. (Illus.). 176p. (Orig.). 1983. pap. 12.95 (ISBN 0-940022-01-X). Outdoor Skills.
Camp Farthest Out. Roots & Fruits of the Camp Farthest Out. 1980. 3.95 (ISBN 0-910924-89-9). Macalester.
Camp, Gerald, ed. Teaching Writing: Essays from the Bay Area Writing Project. 336p. (Orig.). 1983. pap. text ed. 11.50x (ISBN 0-86709-081-2). Boynton Cook Pubs.
Camp, Glen D., Jr., ed. Berlin in the East-West Struggle, 1958-61. LC 70-159689. (Interim History Ser.). pap. 64.50 (ISBN 0-317-20505-6, 2022897). Bks Demand UMI.
Camp, Henry R. Sequatchie County. Jones, Robert B., ed. (Tennessee County History Ser.: No. 77). (Illus.). 144p. 1985. 12.50x (ISBN 0-87870-166-4). Memphis St Univ.
Camp, J. E. de see Franz, Shepherd I.
Camp, James. Carnal Refreshment. (Burning Deck Poetry Ser.). 1975. 15.00 (ISBN 0-930900-02-2); pap. 4.00 (ISBN 0-930900-03-0). Burning Deck.
Camp, James, et al. Three Tenors, One Vehicle: A Book of Songs. LC 74-28757. (Open Places Poets Ser.: No. 2). 1975. pap. 2.50x (ISBN 0-913398-01-2). Open Places.
Camp, James L., jt. auth. see Haueisen, William D.
Camp, Jeffery. The Drawing Book. (Illus.). 256p. 1981. 24.95 (ISBN 0-03-059888-5). HR&W.
Camp, Joe. Oh Heavenly Dog! 144p. (Orig.). (gr. 7 up). 1980. pap. 1.95 (ISBN 0-590-31400-9). Scholastic Inc.
Camp, John. Discovering Bells & Bellringing. (Discovering Ser.: No. 29). (Illus.). 48p. 1985. pap. 3.50 (ISBN 0-85263-290-8, Pub. by Shire Pubns England). Seven Hills Bks.
--Magic, Myth & Medicine. LC 73-18793. 200p. 1974. 8.50 (ISBN 0-8008-5046-7). Taplinger.
--One Hundred Years of Medical Murder. 224p. 1983. 12.95 (ISBN 0-370-30354-7, Pub by the Bodley Head). Merrimack Pub Cir.
Camp, John M. Gods & Heroes in the Athenian Agora. (Excavations of the Athenian Agora Picture Bks.: No. 19). (Illus.). 1980. pap. 1.50x (ISBN 0-87661-623-6). Am Sch Athens.
Camp, John M., II & Dinsmoor, William B., Jr. Ancient Athenian Building Methods. (Excavations of the Athenian Agora Picture Bks.: No. 21). (Illus.). 32p. (Orig.). 1984. pap. text ed. 1.50 (ISBN 0-87661-626-0). Am Sch Athens.
Camp, Kay, ed. Listen to the Women for a Change. (Illus.). 55p. pap. 1.00 (ISBN 0-686-30399-7, Co-Pub. by Addams Peace). WILPF.
Camp, L. Sprague De see De Camp, L. Sprague.
Camp, L. Sprague de see DeCamp, L. Sprague.
Camp, L. Sprague De see De Camp, L. Sprague.
Camp, L. Sprague de see De Camp, L. Sprague.
Camp, L. Sprague De see De Camp, L. Sprague.
Camp, L. Sprague de see De Camp, L. Sprague.
Camp, L. Sprague De see De Camp, L. Sprague.
Camp, L. Sprague de see De Camp, L. Sprague.
Camp, L. Sprague de see De Camp, L. Sprague & Carter, Lin.
Camp, L. Sprague De see De Camp, L. Sprague & De Camp, Catherine C.
Camp, L. Sprague de see De Camp, L. Sprague & De Camp, Catherine C.
Camp, L. Sprague De see De Camp, L. Sprague & Pratt, Fletcher.
Camp, L. Sprague de see De Camp, L. Sprague & Pratt, Fletcher.
Camp, L. Sprague de see Howard, Robert E.
Camp, L. Sprague de see Howard, Robert E. & De Camp, L. Sprague.
Camp, L. Sprague De see Howard, Robert E. & Sprague De Camp, L.
Camp, L. Sprague de see Sprague de Camp, L.
Camp, L. Sprague de see De Camp, L. Sprague, et al.
Camp, Max W. Developing Piano Performance: A Teaching Philosophy. LC 80-84674. 211p. (Orig.). Date not set. 22.95 (ISBN 0-937276-01-4); pap. text ed. 14.95. Hinshaw Mus.
Camp, Maxime Du see Du Camp, Maxime.
Camp, Norma C. George Washington: Man of Courage & Prayer. LC 76-3084. (Sowers Ser.). (Illus.). (gr. 3-6). 1977. lib. bdg. 8.95 (ISBN 0-915134-98-5); pap. 4.95 (ISBN 0-915134-25-X). Mott Media.
Camp, Norman. Pensando con Dios. Orig. Title: Thinking with God. 128p. (Span.). 1981. pap. 2.95 (ISBN 0-8254-1100-9). Kregel.
Camp, Orville. The Forest Farmer's Handbook: A Guide to Natural Selection Forest Management. Roseland, Mark, ed. (Illus.). 72p. (Orig.). 1984. pap. 6.95 (ISBN 0-918475-00-7). Sky River Pr.
Camp, Pamela & Arms, Karen. Exploring Biology. 2nd ed. 1984. text ed. 32.95x (ISBN 0-03-063372-9, CBS C); lab manual 16.95 (ISBN 0-03-063373-7); study guide 11.95 (ISBN 0-03-063374-5); instr's manual 20.00 (ISBN 0-03-063708-2). SCP.
Camp, Pamela S., jt. auth. see Arms, Karen.
Camp, Piet van see Devreese, Josef T. & Van Camp, Piet.
Camp, R., jt. auth. see Hartley, A.
Camp, R. L. Papal Ideology of Social Reform: A Study in Historical Development, 1878-1967. 1969. 30.00 (ISBN 9-0040-4317-9). Heinman.
Camp, Raymond. Game Cookery in America & Europe. rev. ed. LC 58-10599. (Illus.). 192p. 1983. Repr. of 1958 ed. 29.95 (ISBN 0-318-00146-2). Wild Duck Pr.
Camp, Robert. Creating Arcade Games on the Commodore 64. 357p. 1984. 14.95 (ISBN 0-942386-36-1). Compute Pubns.
--Creating Arcade Games on the VIC. 185p. 1984. pap. 12.95 (ISBN 0-942386-25-6). Compute Pubns.
Camp, Roderic A. The Making of a Government: Political Leaders in Modern Mexico. LC 84-8811. 237p. 1984. 23.50x (ISBN 0-8165-0871-2). U of Ariz Pr.
--Mexican Political Biographies, Nineteen Thirty-Five to Nineteen Eighty-One. 2nd, rev., exp. ed. LC 82-2768. 447p. 1982. 35.00x (ISBN 0-8165-0743-0). U of Ariz Pr.
--Mexico's Leaders: Their Education & Recruitment. LC 79-19836. 259p. 1980. pap. text ed. 12.50x (ISBN 0-8165-0660-4). U of Ariz Pr.
Camp, S. C. Developing Editing Skill. 176p. 1985. 6.40 (ISBN 0-07-009638-4). McGraw.
Camp, Sprague L. de see De Camp, Sprague L.
Camp, Sprague L. de see De Camp, Sprague L. & Carter, Lin.
Camp, Sprague L. de see De Camp, Sprague L. & Howard, Robert E.
Camp, Sue C. Developing Proofreading Skill. Tinervia, Joseph, ed. LC 80-12596. (Illus.). 128p. (gr. 11-12). 1980. pap. text ed. 4.92 (ISBN 0-07-009635-X). McGraw.
Camp, Sylvia. I Wonder from Job. pap. 3.50 (ISBN 0-89315-127-0). Lambert Bk.
Camp, Sylvia L. Welcome to My World. pap. 3.95 (ISBN 0-89137-435-3). Quality Pubns.
Camp, Thomas & Meserve, Robert L. Water & Its Impurities. 2nd ed. LC 74-7012. (Illus.). 384p. 1974. 48.50 (ISBN 0-87933-112-7). Van Nos Reinhold.
Camp, W. H., et al. Plants Collected in Ecuador by W. H. Camp: Bromeliaceae, Cannaceae, Zingiberaceae, Musaceae, Marantaceae, Xyridaceae, Begoniaceae, Vacciniaceae, Vol. 8(1) (Memoirs of the New York Botanical Garden Series). 85p. 1952. 10.00 (ISBN 0-317-35524-4). NY Botanical.
Camp, Walter. American Football. LC 74-15732. (Popular Culture in America Ser.). 248p. 1975. Repr. of 1891 ed. 19.00x (ISBN 0-405-06367-9). Ayer Co Pubs.
Camp, Wesley D. Roots of Western Civilization, 2 vols. Incl. Vol. 1. From Ancient Times to 1715 (ISBN 0-394-34167-8); Vol. 2. From the Enlightenment to the 1980's (ISBN 0-394-34168-6). (Illus.). 1983. pap. text ed. 11.95 ea. (RanC). Random.
Camp, Wesley D., tr. see Egret, Jean.
Camp, Wesley D., et al, trs. see Diderot, Denis.
Camp, William. The Jacobs Park Killings: A Police Procedural Mystery. LC 78-57257. 1979. 8.95 (ISBN 0-8149-0803-9). Vanguard.
Campa, Arthur. Hispanic Folklore Studies of Arthur Campa: An Original Anthology. Cortes, Carlos E., ed. & intro. by. LC 76-1475. (Chicano Heritage Ser.). (Illus.). 1976. 42.00x (ISBN 0-405-09536-8). Ayer Co Pubs.
Campa, Arthur L. Hispanic Culture in the Southwest. LC 78-58135. (Illus.). 328p. 1979. 32.50 (ISBN 0-8061-1488-6). U of Okla Pr.
--Sayings & Riddles in New Mexico. LC 37-28299. 67p. 1982. lib. bdg. 22.95x (ISBN 0-89370-731-7). Borgo Pr.
--Spanish Religious Folktheatre in the Southwest, Second Series. LC 34-27430. 157p. 1982. lib. bdg. 29.95x (ISBN 0-89370-736-8). Borgo Pr.
--Treasure of the Sangre De Cristos: Tales & Traditions of the Spanish Southwest. LC 63-17162. (Illus.). 1963. pap. 6.95 (ISBN 0-8061-1176-3). U of Okla Pr.
Campagna, Andrew & Grundlehner, Philip. Points De Vue. LC 80-24800. 228p. (Orig.). 1981. text ed. 15.95 (ISBN 0-03-055546-9, HoltC). HR&W.
Campagna, Anthony S. Macroeconomics. 600p. 1981. text ed. 27.95x (ISBN 0-312-50333-4); instr's. manual avail.; study guide 8.95 (ISBN 0-312-50335-0). St Martin.
Campaign for Political Rights. U. S. Covert Operations Against Nicaragua: A Public Forum. (Illus.). 95p. pap. 5.00 (ISBN 0-910175-02-0). Campaign Political.
Campan, Madame. Memoirs of Marie Antoinette. Waller, A. R., ed. 442p. 1981. Repr. of 1823 ed. lib. bdg. 40.00 (ISBN 0-89987-116-X). Darby Bks.
Campana, A. M. Teacher of China Painting. (Illus.). 1959. 9.95 (ISBN 0-939608-00-6). Campana Art.
--Teacher of Drawing. (Illus.). 1954. 12.00 (ISBN 0-939608-13-8). Campana Art.
--Teacher of Firing China & Glass. (Illus.). 1961. 3.50 (ISBN 0-939608-02-2). Campana Art.
--Teacher of Flower & Fruit Painting. (Illus.). 1961. 14.95 (ISBN 0-939608-03-0). Campana Art.
--Teacher of Oil Painting. (Illus.). 1965. 6.60 (ISBN 0-939608-07-3). Campana Art.
--Teacher of Picture Frame Finishing. (Illus.). 1962. 12.95 (ISBN 0-939608-12-X). Campana Art.
--Teacher of Pottery, Clay Modeling, Casting, Sculpturing, Wood Carving. (Illus.). 1962. 5.40 (ISBN 0-939608-10-3). Campana Art.
--Teacher of Rose Painting. (Illus.). 1959. 10.95 (ISBN 0-939608-01-4). Campana Art.
--Teacher of Textile Painting. (Illus.). 3.50 (ISBN 0-939608-15-4). Campana Art.
--Teacher of Water Color Painting. (Illus.). 1955. 7.60 (ISBN 0-939608-08-1). Campana Art.
Campana, D. M. Amateur Artist' Encyclopedia. (Illus.). 9.95 (ISBN 0-939608-17-0). Campana Art.
--The Artist & the Decorator. (Illus.). 12.95 (ISBN 0-939608-16-2). Campana Art.
--Beginner in Water Color, Oil, & China Painting, 3 bks. (Illus.). 3.50 ea. Campana Art.
--Book of Monograms. (Illus.). 10.00 (ISBN 0-939608-06-5). Campana Art.
--Decorative Design, No. 4. (Illus.). 9.00 (ISBN 0-939608-22-7). Campana Art.
--Decorative Design, No. 5. (Illus.). 17.50 (ISBN 0-939608-23-5). Campana Art.
--Decorative Designs, No. 2. (Illus.). 7.50 (ISBN 0-939608-18-9). Campana Art.
--Decorative Designs: No. 1. (Illus.). 7.50 (ISBN 0-939608-20-0). Campana Art.
--Decorative Designs: No. 6. (Illus.). 8.85 (ISBN 0-939608-24-3). Campana Art.
--Decorative Designs: No. 7. (Illus.). 17.50 (ISBN 0-939608-19-7). Campana Art.
--Enamel Decorations for Porcelain & Glass. 3.50 (ISBN 0-939608-05-7). Campana Art.
--New Transparent Decorations. 5.75 (ISBN 0-939608-27-8). Campana Art.
--One Hundred Luster Color Effects. 1979. 3.50 (ISBN 0-939608-04-9). Campana Art.
--Picture Painting Self Taught. 9.50 (ISBN 0-939608-28-6). Campana Art.
--Teacher of Advertising & Lettering. (Illus.). 8.00 (ISBN 0-939608-29-4). Campana Art.
--Teacher of Animal Painting. (Illus.). 6.95 (ISBN 0-939608-14-6). Campana Art.
--Teacher of Geometrical Drawing. 6.95 (ISBN 0-939608-26-X). Campana Art.
--The Teacher of Jesso-Craft. (Illus.). 5.50 (ISBN 0-939608-21-9). Campana Art.
--Teacher of Linoleum Block Painting. 3.50 (ISBN 0-939608-25-1). Campana Art.
--Teacher of Pastel Painting. (Illus.). 8.45 (ISBN 0-939608-09-X). Campana Art.
--Teacher of Pottery Made at Home. (Illus.). 6.00 (ISBN 0-939608-11-1). Campana Art.
Campana, Dino. Orphic Songs. Wright, Charles, tr. from Italian. LC 83-63448. (Field Translation Ser.). 150p. (Orig.). 1984. 11.50 (ISBN 0-932440-16-9); pap. 6.50 (ISBN 0-932440-17-7). Field Translat.
Campana, Manny, illus. The Saggy Baggy Elephant's Great Big Counting Book. (Big Golden Story Books). (Illus.). 24p. (ps). 1983. 3.50 (ISBN 0-307-10442-7, 10442, Golden Bks). Western Pub.
Campana, R. J. & Stipes, R. J. Compendium of Elm Diseases. LC 81-67058. (Illus.). 96p. 1981. saddle stitched 17.00 (ISBN 0-89054-042-X). Am Phytopathol Soc.
Campanella see White, Frederic R.
Campanella, Anthony P., compiled by. Giuseppe Garibaldi e la Tradizione Garibaldina: Una Bibliografia dal 1807 al 1970, 2 vols. (Illus.). xxvii, 1311p. (Ital.). 1971. Set. 30.00x (ISBN 92-9013-001-6). Intl Inst Garibaldian.
Campanella, Anthony P., ed. Pages from the Garibaldian Epic. (Illus.). xxv, 368p. 1984. 22.50x (ISBN 92-9013-004-0). Intl Inst Garibaldian.
Campanella, Anthony P., ed. see Garibaldi, Giuseppe.
Campanella, Thomas. The Defense of Galileo. LC 74-26254. (History, Philosophy & Sociology of Science Ser.). 1975. Repr. 14.00 (ISBN 0-405-06582-5). Ayer Co Pubs.
--Spanish Conquest. 59.95 (ISBN 0-8490-1101-9). Gordon Pr.
Campanella, Tommaso. The City of the Sun: A Poetical Dialogue of Tommaso Campanella. Donno, Daniel J., ed. LC 80-20133. (Biblioteca Italiana Ser.). 1981. 19.50 (ISBN 0-520-04034-1); pap. 3.95x (ISBN 0-520-04036-8). U of Cal Pr.
Campanella, Tommasso. The Defense of Galileo of Thomas Campanella. McColley, Grant, tr. from Ital. LC 76-1114. (Smith College Studies in History). 93p. 1976. Repr. of 1937 ed. lib. bdg. 14.50x (ISBN 0-915172-20-8). Richwood Pub.
Campanelli, Louise D. Sex & All You Can Eat. 1975. 7.95 (ISBN 0-8184-0202-4). Lyle Stuart.
Campanini, G. & Carboni, G., eds. Vocabulario Latino-Italiano, Italiano-Latino. 1500p. (Lat. & Ital.). 1982. 59.50x (ISBN 0-913298-76-X). S F Vanni.
Campanis, Al. Play Ball with Roger the Dodger. (Illus.). 80p. (gr. 1-5). 1980. 3.95 (ISBN 0-399-20711-2, Putnam); pap. 3.95 (ISBN 0-399-20711-2, Peppercorn). Putnam Pub Group.
Campano, Giovanni. Antonio: Opera Omnia. 608p. 1495. Repr. of 1495 ed. text ed. 99.36 (ISBN 0-576-72225-1, Pub. by Gregg Intl Pubs England). Gregg Intl.
Campardon, Emile. L'Academie Royale de Musique au 18 Siecle, 2 Vols. LC 73-141152. (Music Ser). 1971. Repr. of 1884 ed. Set. lib. bdg. 95.00 (ISBN 0-306-70090-5). Da Capo.
Campbel, S. L. Singular Systems of Differential Equations. LC 79-20908. (Reserach Notes in Mathematics Ser.: No. 40). 176p. (Orig.). 1980. pap. text ed. 22.95 (ISBN 0-273-08438-0). Pitman Pub MA.
Campbell. EEC Competition Law: A Practitioner's Textbook. 346p. 1980. 64.00 (ISBN 0-444-85496-7, North-Holland). Elsevier.
--How to Really Love Your Teenager. LC 81-51515. 1982. 4.95 (ISBN 0-88207-274-9). Victor Bks.
--Picture Atlas. (Children's Guides Ser.). (gr. 3-6). 1976. pap. 4.95 (ISBN 0-86020-060-4, Usborne-Hayes). EDC.
Campbell & Fields. Introduction to Health Assessment. 1982. text ed. 28.95 (ISBN 0-8359-3191-9). Reston.
Campbell, jt. auth. see Tulley.
Campbell, et al. Commercial Agency. 1984. lib. bdg. 40.00 (ISBN 90-6544-181-6, Pub. by Kluwer Law Netherlands). Kluwer Academic.

Campbell, A. Old English Grammer. 29.95 (ISBN 0-19-811901-1); pap. 19.95 (ISBN 0-19-811943-7). Oxford U Pr.

--Santal Folk Tales. LC 78-67700. (The Folktale). Repr. of 1891 ed. 17.00 (ISBN 0-404-16066-2). AMS Pr.

Campbell, A., et al. Worker-Owners: The Mondragon Achievement. 69p. 1982. 25.00x (ISBN 0-905492-03-X, Pub. by Anglo-German England). State Mutual Bk.

Campbell, A. B. Queer Shipmates. (Illus.). (gr. 9 up). 10.00 (ISBN 0-392-04313-0, SpS). Sportshelf.

Campbell, A. C. The Larousse Guide to the Seashore & Shallow Seas of Britain & Europe. LC 80-82755. (Larousse Nature Guides Ser.). (Illus.). 320p. (Orig.). 1981. 10.95 (ISBN 0-88332-251-X, 8068). Larousse.

Campbell, A. E. Great Britain & the United States, 1895-1903. LC 73-19122. 216p. 1974. Repr. of 1960 ed. lib. bdg. 15.00 (ISBN 0-8371-7302-7, CAGB). Greenwood.

Campbell, A. H., ed. Justice: An Historical & Philosophical Essay. Vecchio, Giorgio Del. 236p. 1982. Repr. of 1953 ed. 26.00 (ISBN 0-317-31425-4). Rothman.

Campbell, A. H., ed. see Kantorowicz, Hermann.

Campbell, A. H., ed. see Vecchio, Giorgio del.

Campbell, A. H., tr. see Del Vecchio, Giorgio.

Campbell, A. K., jt. auth. see Ashley, C. C.

Campbell, A. M. Monoclonal Antibody Technology: Production & Characterization of Rodent & Human Hybridomas. (Laboratory Techniques in Biochemistry & Molecular Biology Ser.: Vol. 13). 1984. pap. 25.75 (ISBN 0-444-80575-3). Elsevier.

Campbell, A. M., jt. ed. see Work, T. S.

Campbell, Ada M. & Penfield, Marjorie. Experimental Study of Food. 2nd ed. LC 78-69535. (Illus.). 1979. text ed. 31.95 (ISBN 0-395-26666-1). HM.

Campbell, Alan. Common Market Law, Vol. 3. 2nd ed. 1973. 65.00 (ISBN 0-379-16063-3). Oceana.

--Common Market Law: Supplementary 1975. LC 75-80747. 1975. 105.00 (ISBN 0-379-16065-X). Oceana.

Campbell, Alan & Bowyer, John. Trade Unions & the Individual. 480p. 1981. 54.00x (ISBN 0-906214-05-X, Pub. by ESC Pub England). State Mutual Bk.

Campbell, Alan B. The Lanarkshire Miners: A Social History of Their Trade Unions, 1775-1874. 1980. text ed. 47.25x (ISBN 0-85976-048-0). Humanities.

Campbell, Alan D., jt. ed. see Boynton, Charles E., IV.

Campbell, Alastair, ed. The Graphic Designer's Handbook. LC 83-13983. (Illus.). 192p. 1983. lib. bdg. 24.80 (ISBN 0-89471-238-1); 14.95 (ISBN 0-89471-226-8). Running Pr.

Campbell, Alastair see Malone, Kemp & Schibsbye, Knud.

Campbell, Alastair V. Moral Dilemmas in Medicine. 3rd ed. (Illus.). 210p. 1983. pap. text ed. 9.75 (ISBN 0-443-02948-2). Churchill.

--Professionalism & Pastoral Care. LC 84-48710. (Theology & Pastoral Care Ser.). 128p. 1985. pap. 6.95 (ISBN 0-8006-1733-9, 1-1733). Fortress.

--Rediscovering Pastoral Care. LC 81-7547. 132p. 1981. pap. 7.95 (ISBN 0-664-24381-9). Westminster.

Campbell, Alastair W. Professional Care: Its Meaning & Practice. LC 84-4081. 160p. 1984. pap. 7.95 (ISBN 0-8006-1812-2). Fortress.

Campbell, Albert H. Report on the Pacific Wagon Roads. (Senate Exec. Doc. 36-1859). 1969. 14.95 (ISBN 0-87770-003-6). Ye Galleon.

Campbell, Alexander. Albyn's Anthology, 2 vols. 200p. 1980. Repr. of 1816 ed. Set. lib. bdg. 45.00 (ISBN 0-8495-0774-X). Arden Lib.

--Albyn's Anthology, 2 vols. (Folklore Ser). 45.00 (ISBN 0-88305-109-5). Norwood Edns.

--Alybn's Anthology, 2 vols. 1978. Repr. of 1816 ed. Set. lib. bdg. 40.00 (ISBN 0-8492-3852-8). R West.

--The Christian Bapist. rev. ed. 736p. 1983. Repr. of 1835 ed. 29.95 (ISBN 0-89900-232-3). College Pr Pub.

--The Christian System. LC 73-83412. (Religion in America Ser). 1969. Repr. of 1871 ed. 20.00 (ISBN 0-405-00233-5). Ayer Co Pubs.

--Heroes Then, Heroes Now. (Illus.). 89p. (Orig.). (gr. 1-6). 1981. pap. 12.95 (ISBN 0-940754-08-8). Ed Ministries.

--Stories of Jesus, Stories of Now. 80p. (Orig.). (gr. 1-6). 1980. pap. 12.95 (ISBN 0-940754-04-5). Ed Ministries.

Campbell, Alexander & Haff, Gerry. Live with Jesus. 90p. (Orig.). (gr. 1-6). 1984. pap. 12.95 (ISBN 0-940754-20-7). Ed Ministries.

--Live with Moses. 90p. (Orig.). (gr. 1-6). 1982. pap. 12.95 (ISBN 0-940754-13-4). Ed Ministries.

Campbell, Alice. Short History of Rosalia, Washington. 10p. 1970. pap. 1.00 (ISBN 0-87770-037-0). Ye Galleon.

Campbell, Alistair. Maori Legends. 60p. 1969. pap. 2.50 (ISBN 0-85467-017-3, Pub. by Viking New Zealand). Intl Spec Bk.

Campbell, Alistair, ed. see Brunanburh.

Campbell, Allan. Voodoo: Treasure in Bootle Bay, Vol. 1. (Illus.). 200p. 1985. 14.95 (ISBN 0-9613326-0-3). C I L Inc.

Campbell, Allan, jt. ed. see Roman, Herschel L.

Campbell, Allan, et al, eds. Annual Review of Genetics, Vol. 19. LC 67-29891. (Illus.). 600p. 1985. text ed. 27.00 (ISBN 0-8243-1219-8). Annual Reviews.

Campbell, Allan N. The Railroad Sirens. 1979. 8.95 (ISBN 0-533-03906-1). C I L Inc.

Campbell, Anabel L. Jeannie, a Cocker's Diary. 1981. 4.95 (ISBN 0-8062-1816-9). Carlton.

Campbell, Andrew & Martine, Roddy. The Swinging Sporran: A Lighthearted Guide to the Basic Steps of Scottish Reels & Country Dances. (Illus.). 120p. 1982. 10.95 (ISBN 0-904505-88-X, Pub. by Salem House). Merrimack Pub Cir.

Campbell, Angus. White Attitudes toward Black People. LC 74-161548. 177p. 1971. cloth 12.00x (ISBN 0-87944-007-4); pap. 8.00x (ISBN 0-87944-006-6). Inst Soc Res.

Campbell, Angus & Converse, Phillip E. Quality of American Life, Nineteen Seventy-Eight. LC 80-84081. 1980. write for info., codebk (ISBN 0-89138-951-2). ICPSR.

Campbell, Angus & Cooper, Homer C. Group Differences in Attitudes & Votes: A Study of the 1954 Congressional Election. LC 73-21339. (Survey Research Center Ser.: No. 15). 149p. 1974. Repr. of 1956 ed. lib. bdg. 22.50 (ISBN 0-8371-6185-1, CAGD). Greenwood.

Campbell, Angus & Converse, Philip E., eds. Human Meaning of Social Change. LC 75-169837. 548p. 1972. 16.00x (ISBN 0-87154-193-9). Russell Sage.

Campbell, Angus, et al. American National Election Study, 1956. 1974. write for info. codebook (ISBN 0-89138-066-3). ICPSR.

--American National Election Study, 1958. 1971. write for info. codebook (ISBN 0-89138-153-8). ICPSR.

--American National Election Study, 1960. 1974. write for info. codebook (ISBN 0-89138-067-1). ICPSR.

--The American Voter. LC 76-21115. (Midway Reprint Ser.). 576p. 1980. lib. bdg. 27.00x (ISBN 0-226-09254-2). U of Chicago Pr.

--The Quality of American Life: Perceptions, Evaluations & Satisfactions. LC 75-7176. 600p. 1976. 16.95x (ISBN 0-87154-194-7). Russell Sage.

--The Voter Decides. LC 73-138211. 242p. 1972. Repr. of 1954 ed. lib. bdg. 45.00x (ISBN 0-8371-5566-5, CAVD). Greenwood.

Campbell, Ann O. Archibald the Horse: A Children's Illustrated Story Book. (Illus.). 1982. 4.95 (ISBN 0-938686-25-9). H Spriggle.

Campbell, Anna M. Black Death & Men of Learning. LC 31-29792. Repr. of 1931 ed. 18.50 (ISBN 0-404-01368-6). AMS Pr.

Campbell, Anne. Girl Delinquents. 1981. 26.00x (ISBN 0-312-32727-7). St Martin.

--Girls in the Gang. (Illus.). 284p. 1984. 16.95x (ISBN 0-631-13374-7). Basil Blackwell.

Campbell, Anne, jt. auth. see Marsh, Peter.

Campbell, Annejet. Listen to the Children. 1981. 20.00x (ISBN 0-901269-39-5, Pub. by Grosvenor Bks England). State Mutual Bk.

Campbell, Anneke, jt. auth. see Marston, Elsa.

Campbell, Anson. A Matter of Degree. rev. ed. 1985. pap. text ed. 5.00 (ISBN 0-88734-203-5). Players Pr.

Campbell, Anthony K. Intracellular Calcium: Its Universal Role As Regulator. LC 82-8656. (Monographs in Molecular Biophysics & Biochemistry). 540p. 1983. 82.95x (ISBN 0-471-10488-4, Pub. by Wiley-Interscience). Wiley.

Campbell, Antony F. Of Prophets & Kings: A Late Ninth Century Document (1 Samuel 1-2 Kings 10, No. 17. Karris, Robert J., ed. LC 85-12791. (CBQMS Ser.). 256p. (Orig.). 1985. pap. write for info. (ISBN 0-915170-16-7). Catholic Bibl Assn.

Campbell, April, ed. see Brunner, Frank.

Campbell, Archibald. Journal of an Expedition Against the Rebels of Georgia in North America under the Orders of Archibald Campbell, Esquire, Lieut. Colonel of His Majesty's 71 Regiment, 1778. 1980. 25.00 (ISBN 0-937044-07-5); pap. 15.00 (ISBN 0-937044-08-3). Richmond Cty Hist Soc.

--Scottish Swords from the Battlefield at Culloden. Mowbray, Andrew, ed. (Illus.). 1971. 5.00 (ISBN 0-917218-04-3). Mowbray.

--Voyage Around the World from 1806 to 1812. (Fasc, of 1822 Ed). 1967. Repr. 8.95x (ISBN 0-87022-100-0). UH Pr.

Campbell, Archibald, ed. Craignish Tales & Others. LC 78-144454. (Waifs & Strays of Celtic Tradition: Argyllshire Ser.: No. 1). Repr. of 1889 ed. 11.50 (ISBN 0-404-53531-3). AMS Pr.

--Waifs & Strays of Celtic Tradition: Argyllshire Series, Vol. 1 To 5. Repr. of 1895 ed. Set. 89.50 (ISBN 0-404-53530-5); individual vols. avail. AMS Pr.

Campbell, Archibald Y. Horace, a New Interpretation. LC 70-109714. Repr. of 1924 ed. lib. bdg. 24.75x (ISBN 0-8371-4204-0, CAHO). Greenwood.

Campbell, Archie & Byrd, Ben. Archie Campbell: An Autobiography. (Illus.). 144p. 1981. 12.95 (ISBN 0-87870-205-9). Memphis St Univ.

Campbell, Arthur. John Day River Guide. (Illus.). 90p. (Orig.). 1980. pap. 9.95 (ISBN 0-936608-11-0). F Amato Pubns.

--Law of Sentencing, Vol. 1. LC 78-18626. 1978. 69.50 (ISBN 0-686-29233-2); Suppl. 1984. 21.00; Suppl. 1983. 17.00. Lawyers Co-Op.

Campbell, Arthur A., jt. auth. see Whelpton, Pascal K.

Campbell, Ashley S. Thermodynamic Analysis of Combustion Engines. LC 84-12203. 376p. 1985. Repr. of 1979 ed. lib. bdg. 40.00 (ISBN 0-89874-774-0). Krieger.

Campbell, B. Impressions of a White Tourist in the Caribbean. 1982. lib. bdg. 59.95 (ISBN 0-87700-331-9). Revisionist Pr.

Campbell, B. A., jt. ed. see Spear, N. E.

Campbell, Ballard. The Good Roads Movement in Wisconsin Eighteen Ninety to Nineteen Eleven. (Wisconsin Stories Ser). 24p. pap. 1.75 (ISBN 0-686-76152-9). State Hist Soc Wis.

Campbell, Ballard C. Representative Democracy: Public Policy & Midwestern Legislatures in the Late Nineteenth Century. 267p. 1980. text ed. 20.00x (ISBN 0-674-76275-4). Harvard U Pr.

Campbell, Barbara. A Girl Called Bob & a Horse Called Yoki. LC 81-68780. 170p. (gr. 3-7). 1982. 11.95 (ISBN 0-8037-3149-3, 01160-350, Dial); PLB 11.89 (ISBN 0-8037-3150-7). Dial Bks Young.

Campbell, Barbara, jt. ed. see Swansea, Charleen.

Campbell, Barbara, tr. see Barreiro, Alvaro.

Campbell, Barbara E., tr. see Richard, Pablo, et al.

Campbell, Barbara K. The "Liberated" Woman of 1914: Prominent Women in the Progressive Era. LC 78-27703. (Studies in American History & Culture: No. 6). 220p. 1979. 44.95 (ISBN 0-8357-0980-9). UMI Res Pr.

Campbell, Barry R., et al. The International Debt Problem & Its Impact on Finance & Trade: A Course Handbook. 241p. 1984. 35.00 (ISBN 0-317-11485-9, A4-4080). PLI.

Campbell, Bernard. Human Ecology. LC 84-16733. (Illus.). 208p. 1985. lib. bdg. 19.95 (ISBN 0-202-02025-8); pap. text ed. 8.95 (ISBN 0-202-02026-6). Aldine Pub.

--Human Evolution. 3rd ed. LC 85-1267. (Illus.). 477p. 1985. lib. bdg. 39.95x (ISBN 0-202-02023-1); pap. text ed. 16.95x (ISBN 0-202-02024-X). Aldine Pub.

Campbell, Bernard, ed. Sexual Selection & the Descent of Man. LC 70-169510. 388p. 1972. 39.95x (ISBN 0-202-02005-3). Aldine Pub.

Campbell, Bernard G. Humankind Emerging. 4th ed. 1985. pap. text ed. 23.95 (ISBN 0-316-12553-9); tchr's. ed. avail. (ISBN 0-316-12554-7). Little.

Campbell, Bernard G., ed. see Clark, W. E.

Campbell, Bob & Baldwin, Victor, eds. Severely Handicapped-Hearing Impaired Students: Strengthening Service Delivery. LC 81-10203. 280p. (Orig.). 1982. pap. text ed. 17.95 (ISBN 0-933716-24-9, 249). P H Brookes.

Campbell, Bonnie, jt. auth. see Bernstein, Henry.

Campbell, Bonnie, jt. auth. see Campbell, Will.

Campbell, Bruce & Campbell, Margaret, eds. The Countryman Bird Book. (Countryman Books). (Illus.). 200p. 1974. 5.95 (ISBN 0-7153-6418-9). David & Charles.

Campbell, Bruce & Lack, Elizabeth, eds. A Dictionary of Birds. LC 84-72101. (Illus.). 700p. 1985. 75.00 (ISBN 0-931130-12-3). Buteo.

Campbell, Bruce A. The American Electorate. LC 78-31154. 1979. pap. text ed. 11.95 (ISBN 0-275-85770-0, HoltC). HR&W.

Campbell, Bruce A. & Trilling, Richard J., eds. Realignment in American Politics: Toward a Theory. 393p. 1979. text ed. 25.00x (ISBN 0-292-77019-7). U of Tex Pr.

Campbell, Bruce F. Ancient Wisdom Revived: A History of the Theosophical Movement. LC 79-64664. 224p. 1980. 16.95 (ISBN 0-520-03968-8). U of Cal Pr.

Campbell, Bryn. Exploring Photography. LC 79-13440. (Illus.). 1979. 20.00 (ISBN 0-933920-01-6). Hudson Hills.

Campbell, Bryn, ed. Great Action Photography. (Illus.). 160p. 1983. 24.95 (ISBN 0-8174-3936-6, Amphoto). Watson-Guptill.

Campbell, Burt L. Marine Badges & Insignia of the World: Including Marines, Commandos & Naval Infantrymen. (Illus.). 160p. 1983. 16.95 (ISBN 0-7137-1138-8, Pub. by Blandford Pr England). Sterling.

Campbell, Byram. American Race Theorists. 1978. pap. 4.00x (ISBN 0-911038-33-7). Noontide.

--American Race Theorists. 1984. lib. bdg. 79.95 (ISBN 0-87700-638-5). Revisionist Pr.

Campbell, Byrn, ed. World Photography: Twenty-Five Contemporary Masters Write About Their Work, Techniques & Equipment. (Illus.). 320p. 1981. 49.95 (ISBN 0-87165-113-0, Amphoto). Watson-Guptill.

Campbell, Byron A., jt. ed. see Spear, Norman E.

Campbell, C. Bats, Mosquitoes & Dollar. 1981. 8.95 (ISBN 0-686-76725-X). B Of A.

Campbell, C., tr. see Dohm, Hedwig.

Campbell, C. L., jt. auth. see Lucas, G. B.

Campbell, C. Lee. The Fischer-Smith Controversy: Are There Bacterial Diseases of Plants. LC 80-85458. (Phytopathology Classic Ser.: No. 13). (Illus.). 65p. 1981. 8.50 (ISBN 0-89054-014-4). Am Phytopathol Soc.

Campbell, C. M. Destiny & Disease in Mental Disorders. 1977. lib. bdg. 59.95 (ISBN 0-8490-1710-6). Gordon Pr.

Campbell, C. M. & Robertson, E. F., eds. Groups: St. Andrew's 1981. LC 82-4427. (London Mathematical Society Lecture Note Ser.: No. 71). 360p. 1982. pap. 39.50 (ISBN 0-521-28974-2). Cambridge U Pr.

Campbell, Camille. Meditations with Teresa of Avila. 144p. (Orig.). 1985. pap. 6.95 (ISBN 0-939680-23-8). Bear & Co.

Campbell, Carl. Economic Growth, Capital Gains & Income Distribution: 1897-1956 (Doctoral Dissertation, University of California, Berkley, 1964) LC 76-39824. (Illus.). 1977. lib. bdg. 49.50x (ISBN 0-405-09904-5). Ayer Co Pubs.

Campbell, Carlos C. Birth of a National Park in the Great Smoky Mountains. rev. ed. LC 60-12223. (Illus.). 1978. 9.50 (ISBN 0-87049-029-X). U of Tenn Pr.

Campbell, Carlos C., et al. Great Smoky Mountains Wildflowers. 4th ed. LC 77-126938. (Illus.). 112p. 1977. spiral bdg. 4.95 (ISBN 0-87049-124-5). U of Tenn Pr.

Campbell, Caroline. Love Masque. 192p. 1982. 11.95 (ISBN 0-8027-0703-3). Walker & Co.

Campbell, Carolyn. American Celebration. Bonner, Jordan, ed. (Papa Jan Ser.: Bk. 3). (Illus.). 80p. (gr. 3 up). 1985. pap. 5.95 (ISBN 0-914007-05-X). Bonner Pub Co.

--Generation to Generation. Bonner, Jordan, ed. (Papa Jan Ser.: Bk. 9). (Illus.). 80p. (gr. 3 up). 1985. pap. 5.95 (ISBN 0-914007-11-4). Bonner Pub Co.

--Goodbye, Grandpa. Bonner, Jordan, ed. (Papa Jan Ser.: Bk. 10). (Illus.). 80p. (gr. 3 up). 1985. pap. 5.95 (ISBN 0-914007-12-2). Bonner Pub Co.

--In Competition. Bonner, Jordan, ed. (Papa Jan Ser.: Bk. 6). 80p. (gr. 3 up). 1985. pap. 5.95 (ISBN 0-914007-08-4). Bonner Pub Co.

--Kids, Inc. Bonner, Jordan, ed. (Papa Jan Ser.: Bk. 2). (Illus.). 80p. (Orig.). (gr. 3 up). 1985. pap. 5.95 (ISBN 0-914007-04-1). Bonner Pub Co.

--Merry Christmas Papa Jan. Bonner, Jordan, ed. Wilson, Marianne, tr. (Papa Jan Ser.: Bk. 5). 80p. (gr. 3 up). 1985. pap. 5.95 (ISBN 0-914007-07-6). Bonner Pub Co.

--My Hometown. Bonner, Jordan, ed. (Papa Jan Ser.: Bk. 7). (Illus.). 80p. (gr. 3 up). 1985. pap. 5.95 (ISBN 0-914007-09-2). Bonner Pub Co.

--Not in Vain. Bonner, Jordan, ed. (Papa Jan Ser.: Bk. 8). (Illus.). 80p. (gr. 3 up). 1985. pap. 5.95 (ISBN 0-914007-10-6). Bonner Pub Co.

--Small World. Bonner, Jordan, ed. (Papa Jan Ser.: Bk. 1). (Illus.). 80p. (Orig.). (gr. 3 up). 1985. pap. 5.95 (ISBN 0-914007-03-3). Bonner Pub Co.

Campbell, Carolyn & Thompson, Pat. On My Own. Bonner, Jordon, ed. (Papa Jan Ser.: Bk. 4). (Illus.). 80p. (gr. 3 up). 1985. pap. 5.95 (ISBN 0-914007-06-8). Bonner Pub Co.

Campbell, Catherine E. The French Procuress: Her Character in Renaissance Comedies. (American University Studies II (Romance Langauges & Literature): Vol. 21). 164p. 1985. text ed. 21.55 (ISBN 0-8204-0182-X). P Lang Pubs.

Campbell, Catherine H. & Blaine, Marcia S. New Hampshire Scenery: A Dictionary of Nineteenth Century Artists of New Hampshire Mountain Landscapes. LC 85-3700. 264p. 1985. 25.00 (ISBN 0-914659-12-X). Phoenix Pub.

Campbell, Charles. History of the Colony & Ancient Dominion of Virginia. LC 66-31942. 1966. Repr. of 1860 ed. 17.50 (ISBN 0-87152-027-3). Reprint.

Campbell, Charles, jt. auth. see Jahn, Penelope.

Campbell, Charles A. In Defense of Free Will. (Muirhead Library of Philosophy). 1967. text ed. 18.00x (ISBN 0-04-170003-1). Humanities.

Campbell, Charles D. Introduction to Washington Geology & Resources. (Information Circular Ser.: No. 22r). (Illus.). 44p. 1962. 0.25 (ISBN 0-686-34733-1). Geologic Pubns.

Campbell, Charles D., ed. The Surgical Treatment of Aortic Aneurysms. LC 81-69572. (Illus.). 208p. 1981. monograph 25.00 (ISBN 0-87993-162-0). Futura Pub.

Campbell, Charles F. Serving Time Together: Men & Women in Prison. LC 79-22496. 1980. pap. 10.00X (ISBN 0-912646-54-3). Tex Christian.

Campbell, Charles G. Race & Religion. LC 71-104256. Repr. of 1953 ed. lib. bdg. 15.00 (ISBN 0-8371-3262-2, CARR). Greenwood.

--Tales from the Arab Tribes. Dorson, Richard M., ed. LC 80-790. (Folklore of the World Ser.). (Illus.). 1980. Repr. of 1950 ed. lib. bdg. 23.00x (ISBN 0-405-13329-4). Ayer Co Pubs.

Campbell, Charles I., tr. see Muhammad & Ali, Hazrat.

Campbell, Charles S. The Transformation of American Foreign Relations 1865-1900. (New American Nation Ser.). 1976. pap. 5.95i (ISBN 0-06-090531-X, CN 531, CN). Har-Row.

--The Transformation of American Foreign Relations, 1865-1900. LC 75-23877. (New American Nation Ser.). (Illus.). 352p. (YA) 1976. 16.95i (ISBN 0-06-010618-2, HarpT). Har-Row.

Campbell, Charles S., Jr. Anglo-American Understanding: Eighteen Ninety-Eight to Nineteen Hundred Three. LC 79-25199. (Illus.). vii, 385p. 1980. Repr. of 1957 ed. lib. bdg. 32.50x (ISBN 0-313-22162-6, CAAA). Greenwood.

Campbell, Christiana M. The Farm Bureau & the New Deal: A Study of the Making of National Farm Policy, 1933 to 1940. LC 62-13210. Repr. of 1962 ed. 56.30 (ISBN 0-8357-9676-0, 2015026). Bks Demand UMI.

Campbell, Christopher. Nuclear Weapons Fact Book. LC 84-1977. (Illus.). 192p. 1984. 18.95 (ISBN 0-89141-208-5). Presidio Pr.

Campbell, Christopher S., jt. auth. see Hyland, Fay.

Campbell, Christy. Air Warfare. LC 84-9317. (Illus.). 192p. 1985. 16.95 (ISBN 0-668-06202-9, 6202). Arco.

--Weapons of War: Present & Future Weapons, Systems & Strategies. LC 83-71621. (Illus.). 304p. 1983. 19.95x (ISBN 0-911745-13-0). P Bedrick Bks.

Campbell, Civardi. Viking Raiders. (Time Travelers Books). (gr. 4-9). 1977. 7.95 (ISBN 0-86020-086-8, Usborne-Hayes); PLB 12.95 (ISBN 0-88110-102-8); pap. 4.95 (ISBN 0-86020-085-X). EDC.

Campbell, Claire. Nursing Diagnosis & Intervention in Nursing Practice. 2nd ed. LC 83-21836. 2000p. 1984. 44.95 (ISBN 0-471-08427-1, Pub. by Wiley Med). Wiley.

Campbell, Clarice T. & Rogers, Oscar A. Mississippi: The View from Tougaloo. LC 78-10229. 1979. 9.95x (ISBN 0-87805-091-4); pap. 4.95x (ISBN 0-87805-092-2). U Pr of Miss.

Campbell, Clark S. The O Three Springfields. LC 78-180733. (Illus.). 1978. 35.00 (ISBN 0-9603094-5-4). Ray Riling.

Campbell, Clyde. Toward Perfection in Learning. LC 68-59444. 142p. 1969. 5.50 (ISBN 0-686-70601-3). Pendell Pub.

Campbell, Colin. Do We Need a Bill of Rights. 1980. pap. 25.00x (ISBN 0-85117-205-9, Pub. by M Temple Smith). State Mutual Bk.

--Governments under Stress: Political Executives & Key Bureaucrats in Washington, London, & Ottawa. 400p. 1983. 27.50 (ISBN 0-8020-5622-9); pap. 14.95c (ISBN 0-8020-6572-4). U of Toronto Pr.

--New Directions in Suspension Design: Making the Fast Car Faster. LC 80-24348. (Illus.). 224p. 1981. 14.95 (ISBN 0-8376-0150-9). Bentley.

--The Sports Car: Its Design & Performance. 4th ed. LC 77-94089. (Illus.). 306p. 1979. 14.95 (ISBN 0-8376-0158-4). Bentley.

Campbell, Colin & Murphy, Allan. Things We Said Today: The Complete Lyrics & a Concordance to the Beatles' Songs, 1960-1970. LC 80-83203. (Rock & Roll Reference Ser.: No. 4). 1980. individuals 39.50 (ISBN 0-87650-104-8); institutions 49.50. Pierian.

Campbell, Colin & Wiles, Paul, eds. Law & Society. LC 78-73116. 310p. 1979. text ed. 28.50x (ISBN 0-06-490947-6, 06382). B&N Imports.

Campbell, Colin A., ed. see Weaver, Betsy & Frederick, Gary E.

Campbell, Colin D. Over-Indexed Benefits: The Decoupling Proposals for Social Security. 1976. pap. 2.25 (ISBN 0-8447-3211-7). Am Enterprise.

Campbell, Colin D. & Campbell, Rosemary G. An Introduction to Money & Banking. 5th ed. 544p. 1984. text ed. 32.95x (ISBN 0-03-063568-3). Dryden Pr.

Campbell, Colin D., ed. Controlling the Costs of Social Security. LC 83-48154. 288p. 1984. 26.00x (ISBN 0-669-06918-3). Lexington Bks.

--Financing Social Security. 1979. 16.25 (ISBN 0-8447-2140-9); pap. 8.25 (ISBN 0-8447-2139-5). Am Enterprise.

--Income Redistribution: Proceedings of a Conference. 1977. 15.25 (ISBN 0-8447-2099-2); pap. 7.25 (ISBN 0-8447-2098-4). Am Enterprise.

Campbell, Coyne H. Induced Delusions. 187p. 1981. Repr. of 1957 ed. 10.95x (ISBN 0-686-76737-3). B Of A.

Campbell, Craig. Reel America & World War I: A Comprehensive Filmography & History of Motion Pictures in the U. S., 1914-1920. LC 83-42890. (Illus.). 347p. 1985. lib. bdg. 29.95x (ISBN 0-89950-087-0). McFarland & Co.

Campbell, D. & Rohwer, C., eds. Legal Aspects of International Business Transactions. 476p. 1984. 57.75 (ISBN 0-444-87506-9, I-240-84). Elsevier.

Campbell, D. A., ed. Greek Lyric Poetry. (Gr). 1969. 19.95 (ISBN 0-312-34860-6). St Martin.

Campbell, D. J. & Forester, R. J., eds. Canadian Veterinary Pharmaceuticals & Biologicals 1984-1985. 512p. 1983. lib. bdg. 32.00 (ISBN 0-932036-13-9). Harwal Pub Co.

Campbell, D. J., tr. see Gogol, Nikolai.

Campbell, D. K., jt. ed. see Kostelecky, V. A.

Campbell, D. L. Comparative Law Yearbook, Vol. III. 294p. 1980. 47.50x (ISBN 90-286-0340-9). Sijthoff & Noordhoff.

Campbell, D. Ross. How to Really Love Your Child. LC 77-89470. 132p. 1977. pap. 4.95 (ISBN 0-88207-751-1). Victor Bks.

Campbell, D. S. Capacitors. Date not set. price not set (ISBN 0-677-05740-7). Gordon.

Campbell, Dale F., ed. Strengthening Financial Management. LC 84-82367. (Community College Ser.: No. 50). (Orig.). 1985. pap. text ed. 9.95x (ISBN 0-87589-740-1). Jossey-Bass.

Campbell, D'Ann. Women at War with America: Private Lives in a Patriotic Era. (Illus.). 320p. 1984. text ed. 20.00x (ISBN 0-674-95475-0). Harvard U Pr.

Campbell, David. All the Fulness. 173p. (Orig.). 1975. pap. 5.95 (ISBN 0-912315-08-3). Word Aflame.

--The Eternal Sonship: A Refutation According to Adam Clarke. (Illus.). 95p. (Orig.). 1977. pap. 1.95 (ISBN 0-912315-44-X). Word Aflame.

--A First History of English Literature. 1973. Repr. of 1905 ed. 15.00 (ISBN 0-8274-1543-5). R West.

--Flame & Shadow, Selected Stories. 1977. 14.95x (ISBN 0-7022-1394-2); pap. 7.95x (ISBN 0-7022-1400-0). U of Queensland Pr.

--Yet Not I. 88p. (Orig.). 1978. pap. 1.95 (ISBN 0-912315-39-3). Word Aflame.

Campbell, David & Van Velsor, Ellen. The Use of Personality Measures in the Leadership Development Program. (Special Report: No. 8). 1985. pap. 7.00 (ISBN 0-912879-57-2). Ctr Creat Leader.

Campbell, David & Draper, Rosalind, eds. Applications of Systemic Family Therapy: The Milan Approach (Complimentary Framework of Theory & Practice) 336p. 1985. 39.50 (ISBN 0-8089-1696-3, 790774). Grune.

Campbell, David & Rose, Harvey, eds. Order in Chaos: Proceedings. 370p. 1984. 53.75 (ISBN 0-444-86727-9, I-299-84, North-Holland). Elsevier.

Campbell, David, jt. ed. see Dverk, Donna.

Campbell, David, jt. tr. see Dobson, Rosemary.

Campbell, David A. The Golden Lyre: The Themes of the Greek Lyric Poets. 320p. 1983. 45.00x (ISBN 0-7156-1563-7, Pub. by Duckworth England). Biblio Dist.

Campbell, David P. Handbook for the Strong Vocational Interest Blank. LC 74-93495. 1971. 32.50x (ISBN 0-8047-0735-9). Stanford U Pr.

--If I'm in Charge, Why Is Everybody Laughing? 164p. 1984. pap. 3.50 (ISBN 0-912879-90-4). Ctr Creat Leader.

--If You Don't Know Where You're Going, You'll Probably End up Somewhere Else. LC 74-84711. 1974. pap. 3.50 (ISBN 0-913592-42-0). Argus Comm.

--Take the Road to Creativity & Get off Your Dead End. 136p. 1985. pap. 3.50 (ISBN 0-912879-91-2). Ctr Creat Leader.

Campbell, David P. & Hansen, Jo-Ida C. Manual for the Strong-Campbell Interest Inventory, Form T325 of the Strong Vocational Interest Blank. 3rd. ed. LC 80-54735. pap. prices on request (ISBN 0-8047-1104-6). Stanford U Pr.

Campbell, David P. & Strong, Edward K. Strong Vocational Interest Blank. prices on request (ISBN 0-8047-1069-4). Stanford U Pr.

Campbell, David P. & Strong, Edward K., Jr. Strong-Campbell Interest Inventory. prices on request (ISBN 0-8047-1068-6). Stanford U. Pr.

Campbell, David S., ed. The Denver Gathering Guide: A Directory of Activities for Singles & Other Sociable Critters. (Illus.). 70p. (Orig.). 1983. pap. 4.95 (ISBN 0-912849-00-2). Timberwind.

Campbell, Dennis. Authority & Renewal of American Theology. LC 75-40340. 156p. 1976. 8.95 (ISBN 0-8298-0303-3). Pilgrim NY.

--Legal Aspects of Doing Business in Asia & the Pacific. LC 84-11250. 1984. write for info. (ISBN 9-06-544982-5, Pub. by Kluwer Law Netherlands). Kluwer Academic.

--Legal Aspects of Doing Business in Europe, 2 Vols. 1983. lib. bdg. 76.00 (ISBN 90-6544-099-2, Pub. by Kluwer Law Netherlands). Kluwer Academic.

--The U. S. Legal System: A Practice Handbook. 1983. lib. bdg. 56.50 (ISBN 90-247-2782-0, Pub. by Martinus Nijhoff Netherlands). Kluwer Academic.

Campbell, Dennis, ed. International Handbook on Comparative Business Law. 1979. lib. bdg. 39.50 (ISBN 90-268-1074-1, Pub. by Kluwer Law Netherlands). Kluwer Academic.

--Legal Aspects of Alien Acquisitions of Real Property. 218p. 1980. lib. bdg. 42.00 (ISBN 90-2681-169-1, Pub. by Kluwer Law Netherlands). Kluwer Academic.

--Legal Aspects of Joint Ventures in Eastern Europe. 136p. 1982. 42.00 (ISBN 90-65-44034-8). Kluwer Academic.

Campbell, Dennis M. Doctors, Lawyers, Ministers: Christian Ethics in Professional Practice. 176p. 1982. pap. 7.95 (ISBN 0-687-11016-5). Abingdon.

Campbell, Diana. The Counterfeit Countess. 224p. (Orig.). 1983. pap. 2.25 (ISBN 0-451-12615-7, Sig). NAL.

--The Good Mixer Cookbook. LC 81-69077. (Illus.). 160p. 1982. 9.95 (ISBN 0-916752-49-6). Dorison Hse.

--Lord Margrave's Deception. 1982. pap. 2.50 (ISBN 0-451-13886-4, AE1460, Sig). NAL.

--Payment in Kind. 1985. pap. 2.50 (ISBN 0-451-13329-3, Sig). NAL.

--The Reluctant Cyprian. 1983. pap. 2.25 (ISBN 0-451-12338-7, Sig). NAL.

--Teaching Guide for Indian Literature, Vol. I. 110p. (gr. 4-8). 1983. 4.50x (ISBN 0-936008-14-8). Navajo Curr.

--Teaching Guide for Indian Literature, Vol. II. 69p. (gr. 6 up). 1983. 4.50 (ISBN 0-936008-20-2). Navajo Curr.

Campbell, Diane. Step-by-Step to Natural Food. 7.95x. Cancer Control Soc.

--Step-by-Step to Natural Food. 224p. comb bdg. 7.95 (ISBN 0-9603766-0-7). C C Pubs.

Campbell, Diane, jt. auth. see Cripe, Helen.

Campbell, Dianna & Meier, Terry R. Easy Writer: Basic Sentence Combining & Comprehensive Skills. 2nd ed. 238p. 1984. scp 12.50 (ISBN 0-06-041164-3, HarpC); write for info. instr's manual (ISBN 0-06-361155-4). Har-Row.

Campbell, Doah S., jt. auth. see Caswell, Hollis L.

Campbell, Doak S. Doak S. Campbell: Southern Educator, Selected Addresses. (Florida State U. Studies: No. 25). 1957. 5.00 (ISBN 0-8130-0469-1). U Presses Fla.

--El Maestro Eficiente. Rodriguez, Jose M., tr. from Eng. Orig. Title: When Do Teachers Teach. 160p. (Span.). 1980. pap. 3.25 (ISBN 0-311-11029-0). Casa Bautista.

--University in Transition: Florida State College for Women & Florida State University, 1941-1957. LC 64-64161. (Florida State U. Studies: No. 40). 1964. 7.00 (ISBN 0-8130-0478-0). U Presses Fla.

Campbell, Don. Police: The Exercise of Power. 128p. 1978. 27.50x (ISBN 0-7121-1678-8, Pub. by Macdonald & Evans Engalnd). Trans-Atlantic.

Campbell, Don, jt. auth. see Lynn, D. M.

Campbell, Don G. Introduction to the Musical Brain. (Illus.). 1983. pap. 14.00 (ISBN 0-918812-28-3). MMB Music.

--Master Teacher: Nadia Boulanger. (Illus.). 151p. 1984. text ed. 19.95 (ISBN 0-912405-03-1). Pastoral Pr.

Campbell, Donald & Spence, Alastair A. Norris & Campbell's Anaesthetics, Resuscitation, & Intensive Care. 5th ed. (Illus.). 1979. pap. text ed. 16.25 (ISBN 0-443-01573-2). Churchill.

Campbell, Donald, jt. auth. see Norris, Walter.

Campbell, Donald E. Arabian Medicine & Its Influence on the Middle Ages, 2 vols. LC 74-180330. Repr. of 1926 ed. Set. 40.00 (ISBN 0-404-56235-3). AMS Pr.

Campbell, Donald K. Nehemiah: Man in Charge. 1979. pap. 3.95 (ISBN 0-88207-781-3). Victor Bks.

--No Time for Neutrality. 144p. 1981. pap. 4.95 (ISBN 0-88207-337-0). Victor Bks.

Campbell, Donald K., ed. Walvoord: A Tribute. LC 81-16888. 396p. 1982. 15.95 (ISBN 0-8024-9227-4). Moody.

Campbell, Donald T. & Stanley, Julian C. Experimental & Quasi-Experimental Designs for Research. LC 81-80806. 1966. pap. text ed. 12.50 (ISBN 0-395-30787-2). HM.

Campbell, Donald T., jt. auth. see Cook, Thomas.

Campbell, Donald T., jt. auth. see Herskovits, Mellville.

Campbell, Donald T., jt. auth. see Webb, Eugene J.

Campbell, Dorothy W. Index to Black American Authors in Collective Biographies. 162p. 1983. lib. bdg. 27.50 (ISBN 0-87287-349-8). Libs Unl.

Campbell, Douglas & Higgins, John. Tales of the Comet: Digressions & Fantasies Concerning the Good Dr. Halley & the Wonderous Reappearances of His Celestial Namesake. (Illus.). 256p. (Orig.). 1985. 14.95 (ISBN 0-89793-039-8); pap. 9.95 (ISBN 0-89793-038-X). Hunter Hse.

Campbell, Douglas & Higgins, John, eds. Mathematics: People, Problems, Results. LC 83-17039. 900p. 1984. write for info. (ISBN 0-534-03199-4); pap. write for info. (ISBN 0-534-03202-8). Wadsworth Pub.

Campbell, Douglas G., ed. see Mills, Dick & Vevers, Gwynne.

Campbell, Douglas W., jt. auth. see O'Rourke, Vernon A.

Campbell, Dowling. The Intimate Grand: Inside Arizona's Grand Canyon. LC 84-62425. (Illus.). 84p. (Orig.). 1984. pap. 8.95 (ISBN 0-87358-373-6). Northland.

Campbell, Drusilla. Autumntide. 512p. (Orig.). 1984. pap. 3.95 (ISBN 0-440-00328-8). Dell.

--Broken Promises. (The Hopewell Saga: No. 1). (Orig.). 1982. pap. 2.95 (ISBN 0-440-00837-9, Banbury). Dell.

--Men Like Gods. 640p. (Orig.). 1984. pap. 3.95 (ISBN 0-440-05411-7). Dell.

--Reunions. (Orig.). 1985. pap. 3.95 (ISBN 0-440-07394-4, Emerald). Dell.

--Silent Dreams. (The Hopewell Saga: No. 2). (Orig.). 1982. pap. 2.95 (ISBN 0-440-08450-4, Banbury). Dell.

--Stolen Passions. 384p. 1982. pap. 2.95 (ISBN 0-440-08130-0, Banbury). Dell.

Campbell, Dugald. In the Heart of Bantuland. LC 70-79271. Repr. of 1922 ed. 25.00x (ISBN 0-8371-4835-9, CAB&, Pub. by Negro U Pr). Greenwood.

Campbell, Duncan. The Unsinkable Aircraft Carrier: American Military Power in Britain. (Illus.). 256p. 1984. 19.95 (ISBN 0-7181-2289-5, Pub. by Michael Joseph); pap. 11.95. Merrimack Pub Cir.

Campbell, Duncan C. & Rowan, Richard L. Multinational Enterprises & the OECD Industrial Relations Guidelines. LC 82-81083. (Multinational Industrial Relations Ser.: No. 11). 289p. (Orig.). 1983. pap. 22.00 (ISBN 0-89546-039-4). Indus Res Unit-Wharton.

Campbell, E. F., Jr., jt. ed. see Freedman, D. N.

Campbell, E. L. The Science of Law According to the American Theory of Government. viii, 375p. 1981. Repr. of 1887 ed. lib. bdg. 32.50x (ISBN 0-8377-0433-2). Rothman.

Campbell, Earl V. Confessions of Some Lonely Housewives: A Book on Marriage Problems. 106p. 1973. 4.95 (ISBN 0-686-02488-5). Dade Variety Pr.

Campbell, Edward D., Jr. The Celluloid South: Hollywood & the Southern Myth. LC 81-7457. (Illus.). 256p. 1981. 19.50x (ISBN 0-87049-327-2). U of Tenn Pr.

Campbell, Edward F. Ruth. LC 74-18785. (Anchor Bible Ser.: Vol. 7). (Illus.). 216p. 1975. 14.00 (ISBN 0-385-05316-9). Doubleday.

Campbell, Edward F., Jr. & Boling, Robert, eds. Essays in Honor of George Ernest Wright. 177p. 1976. text ed. 10.00x (ISBN 0-89757-003-0, Am Sch Orient Res). Eisenbrauns.

Campbell, Edward G. Reorganization of the American Railroad System, 1893-1900. LC 76-76643. (Columbia University Studies in the Social Sciences: No. 434). Repr. of 1938 ed. 26.00 (ISBN 0-404-51434-0). AMS Pr.

Campbell, Edward I. Outrage in Annapolis. LC 80-80608. 130p. (Orig.). 1980. pap. 5.95 (ISBN 0-936460-00-8). Camward Hse.

Campbell, Elisabeth, ed. see McKinzie, Harry & Tindimwebwa, Issy.

Campbell, Elizabeth. Jamestown: The Beginning. (Illus.). 96p. (gr. 4-6). 1974. 12.45i (ISBN 0-316-12599-7). Little.

Campbell, Elizabeth A. The Carving on the Tree. LC 67-21180. (Illus.). (gr. 1-3). 1968. 12.45i (ISBN 0-316-12564-4). Little.

Campbell, Elizabeth W. An Archelogical Survey of the Twenty-Nine Palms Region. 93p. 1963. Repr. of 1931 ed. 5.00 (ISBN 0-916561-05-4). Southwest Mus.

Campbell, Elizabeth W. & Campbell, William H. The Archeology of Pleistocene Lake Mohave. 118p. 1963. Repr. of 1937 ed. 5.00 (ISBN 0-916561-09-7). Southwest Mus.

--The Pinto Basin Site. 51p. 1963. Repr. of 1935 ed. 5.00 (ISBN 0-916561-55-0). Southwest Mus.

Campbell, Emily A. Publications Based on Project TALENT: An Annotated Bibliography. 1979. pap. 10.00 (ISBN 0-89785-628-7). Am Inst Res.

Campbell, Enid. Parliamentary Privilege in Australia. 1966. 17.50x (ISBN 0-522-83556-2, Pub. by Melbourne U Pr). Intl Spec Bk.

Campbell, Eric. Rallying Point. 1965. 14.00x (ISBN 0-522-83555-4, Pub. by Melbourne U Pr). Intl Spec Bk.

Campbell, Ernest Q. When a City Closes Its Schools. LC 75-16840. (Univ. of N. Carolina, Institute for Research in Social Science Monographs). 195p. 1975. Repr. of 1960 ed. lib. bdg. 15.00 (ISBN 0-8371-8193-3, CAWC). Greenwood.

Campbell, Ernest Q., ed. Racial Tensions & National Identity. LC 70-185873. (Illus.). 232p. 1972. 14.95x (ISBN 0-8265-1179-1). Vanderbilt U Pr.

Campbell, et al see Marier, Donald & Stoiaken, Larry.

Campbell, Eugene E., jt. auth. see Gowans, Fred R.

Campbell, Eva M. Satire in the Early English Drama. 1914. lib. bdg. 17.00 (ISBN 0-8414-3550-2). Folcroft.

Campbell, Ewing. The Rincon Triptych. 255p. 1984. 12.95 (ISBN 0-318-00074-1); pap. 7.95 (ISBN 0-318-00075-X). Latitudes Pr.

--The Way of Sequestered Places. 1982. pap. text ed. 4.00 (ISBN 0-918722-11-X). Nefertiti.

--Weave It Like Nightfall. LC 77-72760. 1977. 8.95 (ISBN 0-918722-00-4); pap. 3.95 (ISBN 0-918722-01-2). Nefertiti.

Campbell, Ewing, tr. see Ortega, Julio.

Campbell, F. Flowers of Literature: Lord Byron, Coleridge, Burns, Shelley. 1826. Repr. 40.00 (ISBN 0-8274-2351-9). R West.

Campbell, F. & Singer, G. Stress, Drugs & Health - Recent Brain-Behavior Research. (Illus.). 136p. 1983. pap. 13.70 (ISBN 0-08-024838-1). Pergamon.

Campbell, F. Gregory. Confrontation in Central Europe: Weimar Germany & Czechoslovakia. LC 74-11618. (Midway Reprint). 1978. pap. text ed. 14.00x (ISBN 0-226-09252-6). U of Chicago Pr.

Campbell, F. S. & Riley, R. J. Stanford's Sailing Companion: With 1975 Tide Tables. (Illus.). 228p. 1973. 15.95x (ISBN 0-8464-0882-1). Beekman Pubs.

Campbell, Faith F. Stanley Frodsham: Prophet with a Pen. LC 74-77406. 1974. pap. 1.25 (ISBN 0-88243-603-1, 02-0603). Gospel Pub.

Campbell, Farragher J., et al. Defense of Speeding, Reckless Driving & Vehicular Homicide Cases. LC 84-71307. (Illus.). 1984. 80.00. Bender.

Campbell, Ferdinand. Jamaica, Land We Love. 32p. 1983. 3.00 (ISBN 0-912444-26-6). Gaus.

--A Profile of Love. LC 78-62758. 96p. Repr. of 1978 ed. 6.00 (ISBN 0-912444-16-9). Gaus.

Campbell, Florence. Your Days Are Numbered. 21st ed. 246p. 1980. pap. 6.50 (ISBN 0-87516-422-6). De Vorss.

Campbell, Florence, jt. auth. see Randall, Edith.

Campbell, Florence, jt. auth. see Randall, Edith L.

Campbell, Francis S. The Menace of the Herd. Kuhnelt-Leddihn, Eric Von, ed. 1976. lib. bdg. 75.00 (ISBN 0-87968-372-4). Gordon Pr.

Campbell, Frank & Sinaer, George. Brain & Behaviour: Psychobiology of Everyday Life. (Illus.). 168p. 1980. 26.00 (ISBN 0-08-024788-1); pap. 13.50 (ISBN 0-08-024787-3). Pergamon.

Campbell, Frank D. John D. MacDonald & the Colorful World of Travis McGee. LC 77-773. (Milford Series Popular Writers of Today: Vol. 5). 1977. lib. bdg. 12.95x (ISBN 0-89370-108-4); pap. 4.95x (ISBN 0-89370-208-0). Borgo Pr.

Campbell, Frank R. God's Message in Troubled Times. LC 80-67462. 1981. pap. 4.50 (ISBN 0-8054-2239-0). Broadman.

Campbell, Frederick L., et al, eds. Teaching Sociology: The Quest for Excellence. LC 84-1107. 256p. 1984. lib. bdg. 24.95x (ISBN 0-8304-1097-X). Nelson-Hall.

Campbell, G. Doctor's Proven Home Cure for Arthritis. 4.95x. Cancer Control Soc.

Campbell, G. & Morgan. Studies in the Prophecy of Jeremiah. 288p. 13.95 (ISBN 0-8007-0298-0). Revell.

Campbell, G. D. Oral Hypoglycaemic Agents. (Medicinal Chemistry Ser.: Vol. 9). 1969. 76.50 (ISBN 0-12-157350-8). Acad Pr.

Campbell, G. D., et al, eds. Clinical Medicine & Health in Developing Africa. 632p. 1982. 28.00x (ISBN 0-908396-62-7, Pub. by David Philip Pub Africa). Humanities.

Campbell, G. S. An Introduction to Environmental Biophysics. LC 76-43346. (Heidelberg Science Library). 1977. pap. 17.00 (ISBN 0-387-90228-7). Springer-Verlag.

Campbell, Gail. Salt-Water Tropical Fish in Your Home. LC 76-1175. (Illus.). 160p. (YA) 1976. 11.95 (ISBN 0-8069-3730-0); PLB 14.49 (ISBN 0-8069-3731-9). Sterling.

Campbell, George. China Tea Clippers. (Illus.). 156p. 1985. 29.95 (ISBN 0-229-11525-X, Pub. by Adlard Coles). Sheridan.

--A Dissertation on Miracles, Containing an Examination of the Principles Advanced by David Hume, Esq. in an Essay on Miracles. LC 82-48331. (The Philosophy of David Hume Ser.). 300p. 1983. lib. bdg. 39.00 (ISBN 0-8240-5403-2). Garland Pub.

--First Poems: A New Edition with Additional Poems. LC 80-8529. 110p. 1981. lib. bdg. 31.00 (ISBN 0-8240-9455-7). Garland Pub.

--New Directions in Health Education. 250p. 1984. 31.00X (ISBN 0-905273-58-3, Pub. by Falmer Pr); pap. 18.00X (ISBN 0-905273-57-5, Pub. by Falmer Pr). Taylor & Francis.

--White & Black: The Outcome of a Visit to the United States. LC 72-77193. Repr. of 1879 ed. 19.75x (ISBN 0-8371-1281-8). Greenwood.

Campbell, George, tr. see Heller, Agnes.

Campbell, George A. The Knights Templars, Their Rise & Fall. LC 78-63330. (The Crusades & Military Orders: Second Ser.). Repr. of 1937 ed. 28.50 (ISBN 0-404-17005-6). AMS Pr.

--Strindberg. LC 71-163501. (Studies in Drama, No. 39). 1971. Repr. of 1933 ed. lib. bdg. 39.95x (ISBN 0-8383-1320-5). Haskell.

Campbell, George E. Airport Management & Operations. 1972. 15.00x (ISBN 0-87511-015-0). Claitors.

Campbell, George F., ed. Health Education & Youth: A Review of Research & Developments. (Curriculum Series for Teachers). 480p. 1984. 39.00x (ISBN 0-905273-54-0, Pub. by Falmer Pr); pap. 27.00x (ISBN 0-905273-53-2, Pub. by Falmer Pr). Taylor & Francis.

Campbell, George R. An Illustrated Guide to Some Poisonous Plants & Animals of Florida. LC 83-61760. (Illus.). 200p. 1983. 15.95 (ISBN 0-910923-04-3). Pineapple Pr.

Campbell, George R. & Winterbotham, Ann L. Jaws Too! The Natural History of Crocodillians with Emphasis on Sanibel Island's Alligators. LC 85-50388. (Illus.). 250p. 1985. price not set (ISBN 0-930942-06-X). Sutherland IA.

Campbell, Georgetta M. Extant Collections of Early Black Newspapers: A Research Guide to the Black Press, 1880-1915, with an Index to the Boston Guardian, 1902-1904. LC 80-51418. 433p. 1981. 28.50x (ISBN 0-87875-197-1). Whitston Pub.

Campbell, Gil L. I'll Never Forget What's Her Name. 24p. 1974. pap. 1.50 (ISBN 0-910584-74-5). Filter.

Campbell, Gil L. & Gorman, Martha. Everybody for President. (Illus.). 64p. 1984. 4.95 (ISBN 0-89480-761-7, 761). Workman Pub.

Campbell, Gilbert L. Wet Plates & Dry Gulches. LC 71-41602. (Wild & Woolly West Ser., No. 8). (Illus., Orig.). 1973. 8.00 (ISBN 0-910584-94-X); pap. 2.00 (ISBN 0-910584-11-7). Filter.

Campbell, Giraud W. & Stone, Robert B. A Doctor's Proven New Home Cure for Arthritis. 1973. 12.95 (ISBN 0-13-216929-0, Reward); pap. 4.95 (ISBN 0-13-217034-5). P-H.

Campbell, Gladys. The Sheep Boy. 193p. 1984. 7.60 (ISBN 0-317-19627-8). Intl Univ Pr.

Campbell, Gordon. Famous American Athletes of Today. 9th ed. (Essay Index Reprint Ser.). 1972. Repr. of 1945 ed. 29.00 (ISBN 0-8369-7313-5). Ayer Co Pubs.

Campbell, Grace. La Synphore Dans "la Jeune Parque" De Paul Valery. LC 74-28038. (Romance Monographs: No. 12). 1975. 9.00x (ISBN 84-399-3510-2). Romance.

Campbell, Greg. The Joy of Jumping: A Complete Jump-Rope Program for Health, Looks & Fun. (Illus.). 1978. (Marek); pap. 3.50 (ISBN 0-399-90010-1). Putnam Pub Group.

Campbell, H. C. Developing Public Library Systems & Services: A Guide to the Organization of National & Regional Public Library Systems as a Part of the Overall National Information Service Planning. (Documentation, Libraries & Archives: Studies & Research: No. 11). (Illus.). 186p. 1983. pap. text ed. 18.75 (ISBN 92-3-101995-3, U1280, UNESCO). Unipub.

--Public Libraries in the Urban Metropolitan Setting. (Management of Change Ser.). 298p. 1973. 22.50 (ISBN 0-208-01193-5, Linnet). Shoe String.

Campbell, H. S. Darkness & Daylight: Or, Lights & Shadows of New York Life. 59.95 (ISBN 0-87968-997-8). Gordon Pr.

Campbell, Hannah. Why Did They Name It. LC 64-12968. (Illus.). (gr. 7 up). 1964. 9.95 (ISBN 0-8303-0047-3). Fleet.

Campbell, Harold. Measuring the Abilities of Severely Handicapped Students. (Illus.). 94p. 1981. spiral bdg. 15.75x (ISBN 0-398-04526-7). C C Thomas.

Campbell, Harriet. Children's Literature. (Illus.). 64p. 1981. 24.00 (ISBN 0-88014-032-1). Mosaic Pr OH.

Campbell, Harry M. & Foster, Ruel E. Elizabeth Madox Roberts: American Novelist. 1956. 14.95 (ISBN 0-8061-0355-8). U of Okla Pr.

Campbell, Helen. Darkness & Daylight: Or, Lights & Shadows of New York Life: A Pictorial Record of Personal Experiences by Day & Night in the Great Metropolis with Hundreds of Thrilling Anecdotes & Incidents. LC 76-81511. 1969. Repr. of 1895 ed. 48.00x (ISBN 0-8103-3566-2). Gale.

--Prisoners of Poverty: Women Wage-Workers, Their Trades & Their Lives. 1972. lib. bdg. 23.50 (ISBN 0-8422-8176-2); pap. text ed. 8.50x (ISBN 0-8290-0665-6). Irvington.

--Women Wage-Earners: Their Past, Their Present, & Their Future. LC 72-2594. (American Women Ser: Images & Realities). 324p. 1972. Repr. of 1893 ed. 20.000 (ISBN 0-405-04451-8). Ayer Co Pubs.

Campbell, Helen S. Prisoners of Poverty: Women Wage-Workers, Their Trades & Their Lives. LC 76-88512. 257p. Repr. of 1887 ed. lib. bdg. 15.00 (ISBN 0-8371-4972-X, CAPP). Greenwood.

Campbell, Hilbert & Modlin, Charles E., eds. Sherwood Anderson: Centennial Studies. LC 76-21468. 1976. 12.50 (ISBN 0-87875-093-2). Whitston Pub.

Campbell, Hilbert H. James Thomson. (English Authors Ser.). 1979. lib. bdg. 15.95 (ISBN 0-8057-6715-0, Twayne). G K Hall.

--James Thomson: An Annotated Bibliography of Selected Writings & the Important Criticism. LC 75-24092. (Reference Library of the Humanities: Vol. 33). 158p. 1976. lib. bdg. 31.00 (ISBN 0-8240-9979-6). Garland Pub.

Campbell, Hope. Meanwhile, Back at the Castle. 256p. (gr. 6-10). 1973. pap. 0.95 (ISBN 0-448-05447-7, Tempo). Ace Bks.

--Mystery at Fire Island. 176p. (gr. 4-6). 1984. pap. 1.95 (ISBN 0-590-33205-8, Apple Paperbacks). Scholastic Inc.

Campbell, Howard E. Concepts of Algebra & Trigonometry. 656p. 1982. text ed. write for info. (ISBN 0-87150-332-8, 2651, Prindle). PWS Pubs.

--Concepts of College Algebra. 480p. 1982. text ed. write for info. (ISBN 0-87150-325-5, 33L 2591, Prindle). PWS Pubs.

--Concepts of Trigonometry. LC 80-22168. 249p. 1981. text ed. write for info. (ISBN 0-87150-299-2, 2351, Prindle). PWS Pubs.

Campbell, Howard E. & Dierker, Paul F. Calculus with Analytic Geometry. 3rd ed. 912p. 1982. text ed. write for info. (ISBN 0-87150-331-X, 2641, Prindle). PWS Pubs.

--Student Supplement to Accompany Calculus with Analytic Geometry. 3rd ed. 341p. 1982. pap. text ed. write for info. (ISBN 0-87150-353-0, 2646, Prindle). PWS Pubs.

Campbell, Hugh. Linear Algebra with Applications. 2nd ed. (Illus.). 1980. text ed. 28.95 (ISBN 0-13-536979-7). P-H.

Campbell, Hugh, et al. Voice Speech & Gesture. LC 72-5589. (Granger Index Reprint Ser). 1972. Repr. of 1895 ed. 52.00 (ISBN 0-8369-6381-4). Ayer Co Pubs.

Campbell, Hugh D. & Bauer, Camille. Programmed French Readers, 4 bks. Incl. Contes pour Debutants. 1965. pap. text ed. 10.50 (ISBN 0-395-04258-5); Arsene Lupin. 1965. pap. text ed. 10.50 (ISBN 0-395-04259-3); La Robe et le Couteau. 1966. pap. text ed. 10.50 (ISBN 0-395-04264-X); La Dynamite. 1970. pap. text ed. 10.50 (ISBN 0-395-04265-8). pap. HM.

Campbell, Hugh G. Introduction to Matrices, Vectors & Linear Programming. 2nd ed. LC 76-22757. (Illus.). 1977. text ed. 25.95 (ISBN 0-13-487439-0). P-H.

--Matrices with Applications. (Illus.). 1968. pap. text ed. 17.95 (ISBN 0-13-565424-6). P-H.

Campbell, Hugh H. Knock Vigorously to Be Heard. LC 65-26184. 1966. 4.00 (ISBN 0-8022-0211-X). Philos Lib.

Campbell, I. D. & Dwek, R. A. Biological Spectroscopy: Concepts, Applications & Problems. 1984. 39.95 (ISBN 0-8053-1847-X); pap. 26.95 (ISBN 0-8053-1849-6). Benjamin-Cummings.

Campbell, I. R. Kudrun: A Critical Appreciation. LC 77-1721. (Anglica Germanica Ser.: No. 2). 1978. 59.50 (ISBN 0-521-21618-4). Cambridge U Pr.

Campbell, Ian. Biomass, Catalysts, & Liquid Fuels. 169p. 1983. 36.00 (ISBN 0-87762-331-7). Technomic.

Campbell, Ian, ed. Nineteenth Century Scottish Fiction: Critical Essays. LC 79-51072. 165p. 1979. text ed. 24.50x (ISBN 0-06-490953-0, 06383). B&N Imports.

Campbell, Isaac see Bear, James A., Jr.

Campbell, Ivor E. & Sherwood, Edwin M., eds. High Temperature Materials & Technology. LC 67-13541. (Electrochemical Society Ser.). pap. 160.00 (ISBN 0-317-10450-0, 2051630). Bks Demand UMI.

Campbell, J. A. & Bewick, M. W. Neutron Activation Analysis. 36p. 1978. 40.00x (ISBN 0-85198-438-X, Pub. by CAB Bks England). State Mutual Bk.

Campbell, J. A., jt. auth. see Steels, L.

Campbell, J. B. The Emperor & the Roman Army: Thirty-One B.C. to A.D. Two Hundred Thirty-Five. 1984. 54.00x (ISBN 0-19-814834-8). Oxford U Pr.

Campbell, J. F. Leabhar Na Feinne. 272p. 1972. Repr. of 1872 ed. 36.00x (ISBN 0-7165-2060-5, Pub. by Irish Academic Pr Ireland). Biblio Dist.

Campbell, J. H., jt. auth. see Tersine, R. J.

Campbell, J. I., jt. auth. see Meadows, P. S.

Campbell, J. K. Honour, Family & Patronage: A Study of Institutions & Moral Values in a Greek Mountain Community. (Illus.). 1973. 37.50x (ISBN 0-19-823122-9); pap. text ed. 10.95x (ISBN 0-19-519756-9). Oxford U Pr.

Campbell, J. L. Canna: The Story of a Hebridean Island. (Illus.). 340p. 1985. 45.00x (ISBN 0-19-920137-4). Oxford U Pr.

Campbell, J. R. & Lasley, J. F. The Science of Animals That Serve Humanity. 3rd ed. LC 84-7950. 880p. 1984. 39.95 (ISBN 0-07-009700-3). McGraw.

Campbell, J. R. & Marshall, R. T. The Science of Providing Milk for Man. (Agricultural Sciences Ser). 1975. 39.95 (ISBN 0-07-009690-2). McGraw.

Campbell, J. S. Types of Parastatal Bodies Concerned with Fisheries Development & Their Financial Responsibilities. (Fisheries Technical Papers: No. 179). 45p. 1978. pap. 7.50 (ISBN 92-5-100560-5, F1433, FAO). Unipub.

Campbell, J. William, ed. see Washington University, Department of Medicine.

Campbell, Jacqueline C. & Humphreys, Janice C. Nursing Care of Victims of Family Violence. 1983. text ed. 25.00 (ISBN 0-8359-5042-5); pap. text ed. 18.95 (ISBN 0-8359-5041-7). Reston.

Campbell, James. Bomber Raid. 1978. pap. 1.75 (ISBN 0-505-51272-6, Pub. by Tower Bks). Dorchester Pub Co.

--The Bombing of Nuremberg. (World at War Ser.: No. 5). 1978. pap. 2.25 (ISBN 0-89083-356-7). Zebra.

--Essays in Anglo-Saxon History, 400-1200. (No. 26). 220p. 1985. 27.00 (ISBN 0-907628-32-X). Hambledon Press.

--Greek Fathers. LC 63-10279. (Our Debt to Greece & Rome Ser.). 167p. 1963. Repr. of 1930 ed. 18.50 (ISBN 0-8154-0046-2). Cooper Sq.

--Scotland From the Air. 160p. 1984. 25.00 (ISBN 0-517-55527-1). Crown.

--Two Plays (TWT) 1985. 6.50 (ISBN 0-8062-2484-3). Carlton.

Campbell, James, ed. The Anglo-Saxons. LC 81-70710. 272p. 1982. 39.95x (ISBN 0-8014-1482-2). Cornell U Pr.

Campbell, James B. Across the Wide Missouri: The Diary of a Journey from Virginia to Missouri in 1819 & Back Again in 1821, with a Description of the City of Cincinnati. Burgess, Mary W., ed. LC 84-268. (Stokvis Studies in Historical Chronology & Thought: No. 4). 144p. (Orig.). 1985. lib. bdg. 19.95x (ISBN 0-89370-169-6); pap. text ed. 9.95x (ISBN 0-89370-269-2). Borgo Pr.

Campbell, James B., jt. auth. see Hole, Francis D.

Campbell, James D. Samuel Taylor Coleridge. 2nd ed. 1973. Repr. of 1896 ed. lib. bdg. 39.50 (ISBN 0-8414-1846-2). Folcroft.

Campbell, James D., ed. see Coleridge, Samuel T.

Campbell, James E., ed. Pottery & Ceramics: A Guide to Information Sources. LC 74-11545. (Art & Architecture Information Guide Ser.: Vol. 7). 1978. 60.00x (ISBN 0-8103-1274-3). Gale.

Campbell, James K., ed. see Liliuokalani.

Campbell, James K., et al, eds. Kaulana na Pua: A Hawaiian Album, 1890-1930. LC 77-156041. (Illus.). 1977. pap. 6.95 (ISBN 0-917850-01-7). Pueo Pr.

Campbell, James M. Paul the Mystic. 1977. lib. bdg. 59.95 (ISBN 0-8490-2415-3). Gordon Pr.

Campbell, James M., intro. by. The Confessions of St. Augustine. 266p. 1981. Repr. of 1930 ed. lib. bdg. 35.00 (ISBN 0-89987-129-1). Darby Bks.

Campbell, James W. America in Her Centennial Year 1876. LC 79-6757. 272p. 1980. pap. text ed. 13.00 (ISBN 0-8191-0947-9). U Pr of Amer.

Campbell, Jane. The Retrospective Review (1820-1828) & the Revival of Seventeenth-Century Poetry. 76p. 1972. pap. text ed. 7.45x (ISBN 0-88920-001-7, Pub. by Wilfred Laurier U Pr Canada). Humanities.

Campbell, Jane, jt. auth. see Del Hierro, Audrey.

Campbell, Jane, jt. auth. see Lively, Virginia.

Campbell, Jane, jt. auth. see Middleton, John.

Campbell, Jane & Doyle, James, eds. The Practical Vision: Essays in Honour of Flora Roy. xvi, 163p. 1978. text ed. 12.00x (ISBN 0-88920-066-1, Pub. by Wilfred Laurier U Pr Canada). Humanities.

Campbell, Janis, jt. auth. see Deane, Donna.

Campbell, Jean. Dreams Beyond Dreaming. LC 79-26131. 1980. pap. 5.95 (ISBN 0-89865-015-1, Unilaw). Donning Co.

Campbell, Jean, ed. see Lonik, Larry J.

Campbell, Jean, ed. see Ridley, Gustave.

Campbell, Jean M. Reaching Out with Love: Encounters with Troubled Youth. LC 81-50354. 144p. (Orig.). 1981. pap. 3.95 (ISBN 0-87239-453-0, 3652). Standard Pub.

Campbell, Jefferson. Alive Polarity: Healing Yourself & Your Family. LC 81-70027. (Illus.). 272p. 1982. 24.95 (ISBN 0-941732-00-2); pap. 12.95 (ISBN 0-941732-01-0). Alive Polarity.

Campbell, Jefferson & Handelsman, Judith. Spiritual Non-Violence. 224p. 1985. write for info. (ISBN 0-941732-02-9); pap. write for info. (ISBN 0-941732-03-7). Alive Polarity.

Campbell, Jeffrey. The Homing. 256p. (Orig.). 1981. pap. 2.50 (ISBN 0-345-28793-2). Ballantine.

Campbell, Jeremy. Grammatical Man: Information, Entropy, Language, & Life. 320p. 1982. 16.95 (ISBN 0-671-44061-6). S&S.

--Grammatical Man: Information, Entropy, Language & Life. 320p. 1983. pap. 8.95 (ISBN 0-671-44062-4, Touchstone). S&S.

Campbell, Jerry, ed. see Davis, Larry.

Campbell, Jerry, ed. see Stern, Robert.

Campbell, Jim. Hold Fast: An Illustrated History of Sail. LC 83-82655. (Illus.). 288p. 1986. 29.95 (ISBN 0-89709-128-0). Liberty Pub.

Campbell, Jim, jt. auth. see Brock, Ted.

Campbell, Joan. The German Werkbund: The Politics of Reform in the Applied Arts. LC 77-71974. (Illus.). 1977. text ed. 37.50 (ISBN 0-691-05250-6). Princeton U Pr.

Campbell, Joanna. The Films of Steve McQueen. Castell, David, ed. (The Films of...Ser.). (Illus.). (gr. 7-12). 1978. Repr. of 1973 ed. PLB 6.95 (ISBN 0-912616-84-9). Greenhaven.

--Secret Identity. 1982. pap. 2.25 (ISBN 0-553-24327-6). Bantam.

Campbell, Joe. Mastering Serial Communications. 250p. 1985. pap. 19.95 (ISBN 0-89588-180-2). SYBEX.

--The RS-232 Solution. LC 83-51568. 194p. (Orig.). 1984. pap. 16.95 (ISBN 0-89588-140-3). SYBEX.

Campbell, Joe B., jt. auth. see Campbell, June M.

Campbell, Joe E. Pentecostal Holiness Church. pap. 6.00 (ISBN 0-911866-55-8). Advocate.

Campbell, John. An Account of the Spanish Settlements in America. LC 73-2680. (Illus.). Repr. of 1762 ed. 32.00 (ISBN 0-404-00276-5). AMS Pr.

--F. E. Smith: First Earl of Birkenhead. (Illus.). 839p. 1984. 35.00 (ISBN 0-224-01596-6, Pub. by Jonathan Cape). Merrimack Pub Cir.

--Introductory Cartography. (Illus.). 182p. 1984. 35.95 (ISBN 0-13-501304-6). P-H.

--Lloyd George: The Goat in the Wilderness; 1922-1931. (Illus.). 383p. 1977. 27.50x (ISBN 0-87471-813-9). Rowman.

--The Macintosh Connection. 1985. 17.95 (ISBN 0-8359-4172-8). Reston.

--Negro-Mania: Examination of the Falsely Assumed Equality of the Various Races of Men. facs. ed. LC 79-89420. (Black Heritage Library Collection Ser). 1851. 20.25 (ISBN 0-8369-8532-X). Ayer Co Pubs.

--Programming Tips & Techniques for the Apple II & IIe. LC 83-22363. (Illus.). 416p. 1984. pap. 19.95 (ISBN 0-89303-273-5); diskette 30.00 (ISBN 0-89303-782-6); bk. & diskette 49.95 (ISBN 0-89303-776-1). Brady Comm.

--Roy Jenkins: A Biography. LC 83-10927. (Illus.). 280p. 1983. 22.50 (ISBN 0-312-69460-1). St Martin.

--Speak Softly of Christmas. 1973. 5.00 (ISBN 0-682-47899-7). Exposition Pr FL.

--Thirty Years Experience of a Medical Officer in the English Convict Service. LC 83-49236. (Crime & Punishment in England, 1850-1922 Ser.). 139p. 1984. lib. bdg. 30.00 (ISBN 0-8240-6211-6). Garland Pub.

--The Travels & Adventures of Edward Brown, Esq. LC 75-170599. (Foundations of the Novel Ser.: Vol. 70). 1973. lib. bdg. 61.00 (ISBN 0-8240-0582-1). Garland Pub.

--Travels in South Africa, Undertaken at the Request of the London Missionary Society, 2 Vols. in 1. 1968. Repr. of 1822 ed. 55.00 (ISBN 0-384-07260-7). Johnson Repr.

Campbell, John & Goodman, Susan. High-Technology Employment in Texas: A Labor Market Analysis. 75p. (Orig.). 1985. pap. text ed. 6.00 (ISBN 0-87755-290-8). Bureau Busn UT.

Campbell, John A. Adding Logic to Fire Prevention Systems. 1982. 4.65 (ISBN 0-686-37669-2, TR 82-5). Society Fire Protect.

--Estimating the Magnitude of Macro-Hazards. 1981. 3.75 (ISBN 0-686-31894-3, TR 81-2). Society Fire Protect.

--Expanding Fire Safety Management Systems in High-Rise Buildings. 4.65 (ISBN 0-318-00406-2, TR83-4). Society Fire Protect.

--MODCOM: Speech Preparation. 2nd ed. Applbaum, Ronald & Hart, Roderick, eds. LC 13-5567. 1984. pap. text ed. 3.25 (ISBN 0-574-22567-6, 13-5567). SRA.
--Obstetrical Diagnosis by Radiographic, Ultrasonic & Nuclear Methods. LC 77-6448. 220p. 1977. 25.00 (ISBN 0-683-01416-1). Krieger.
Campbell, John A., ed. Implementation of Prolog. (Artificial Intelligence Ser.: I-381). 391p. 1984. text ed. 74.95x (ISBN 0-470-20044-8); pap. text ed. 29.95x (ISBN 0-470-20045-6). Halsted Pr.
Campbell, John A., Jr., ed. Campbell's List: A Directory of Selected Lawyers Since 1879. rev. ed. LC 34-11733. 320p. 1985. pap. 10.00 (ISBN 0-933089-00-7). Campbells List.
Campbell, John B. The Upper Palaeolithic of Britain: A Study of Man & Nature in the Late Ice Age, Vols. I & II. (Illus.). 1978. 84.00 set (ISBN 0-19-813188-7). Oxford U Pr.
Campbell, John B., jt. auth. see Willson, James D.
Campbell, John C. American Policy Toward Communist Eastern Europe: The Choices Ahead. LC 65-15982. pap. 37.50 (ISBN 0-317-29391-5, 2055846). Bks Demand UMI.
--Contemporary Japanese Budget Politics. LC 73-85782. 1977. 35.00x (ISBN 0-520-02573-3); pap. 8.95x (ISBN 0-520-04087-2, CAMPUS NO. 253). U of Cal Pr.
--French Influence & the Rise of Roumanian Nationalism, Generation of 1848: 1830-1857. LC 73-135839. (Eastern Europe Collection Ser.). 1970. Repr. of 1940 ed. 23.00 (ISBN 0-405-02781-8). Ayer Co Pubs.
--Houses of Gold. (Illus.). 228p. (Orig.). 1980. pap. 15.00 (ISBN 0-8310-7121-4). Howell North.
--Lives of the Lord Chancellors & Keepers of the Great Seal of England, 10 Vols. 5th ed. LC 74-39877. Repr. of 1868 ed. Set. 350.00 (ISBN 0-404-01380-5); 35.00 ea. AMS Pr.
--The Middle East in the Muted Cold War. (Monograph Series in World Affairs: Vol. 2, 1964-65, Bk. 1). (Orig.). 1964. 3.95 (ISBN 0-87940-003-X). Monograph Series.
--Shakespeare's Legal Acquirements Considered. LC 79-39811. Repr. of 1859 ed. 14.50 (ISBN 0-404-01369-4). AMS Pr.
--The Southern Highlander & His Homeland. LC 79-15028. (Illus.). 508p. 1969. pap. 13.00x (ISBN 0-8131-0121-2). U Pr of Ky.
--Two Dogs Plus. (Illus.). 95p. (Orig.). (gr. 8 up). 1984. pap. text ed. 9.95 (ISBN 0-9613596-0-9); pap. 7.95. Deer Creek Pr.
Campbell, John C., ed. Successful Negotiation: Trieste Ninteen Fifty-Four: An Appraisal by the Five Participants. LC 75-2981. 225p. 1975. 24.50x (ISBN 0-691-05658-7). Princeton U Pr.
Campbell, John D., jt. auth. see Leinbaugh, Harold P.
Campbell, John E. & Alabama ACEP. Basic Trauma Life Support. (Illus.). 224p. 1985. pap. text ed. 16.95 (ISBN 0-89303-361-8); instr's guide 14.95 (ISBN 0-89303-363-4). Brady Comm.
Campbell, John F. History & Bibliography of the New American Practical Navigator & the American Coast Pilot. LC 64-15742. (Illus.). 1964. 25.00 (ISBN 0-87577-006-1). Peabody Mus Salem.
--More West Highland Tales, 2 vols. Watson, W. J., et al, eds. McKay, John G., tr. LC 78-67695. (The Folktale). Repr. of 1940 ed. Set. 70.00 (ISBN 0-404-16070-0). AMS Pr.
--Popular Tales of the West Highlands, 4 Vols. LC 67-23921. 1969. Repr. of 1890 ed. 150.00x (ISBN 0-8103-3458-5). Gale.
Campbell, John G. Clan Traditions & Popular Tales of the Western Highlands & Islands. Wallace, Jessie & MacIsaac, Duncan, eds. LC 72-144458. (Waifs & Strays of Celtic Tradition: Argyllshire Ser.: No. 5). Repr. of 1895 ed. 14.50 (ISBN 0-404-53535-6). AMS Pr.
--Fians. LC 79-144457. (Waifs & Strays of Celtic Tradition: Argyllshire Ser.: No. 4). Repr. of 1891 ed. 18.00 (ISBN 0-404-53534-8). AMS Pr.
--Superstitions of the Highlands & Islands of Scotland. LC 71-173104. (Illus.). Repr. of 1900 ed. 18.00 (ISBN 0-405-08337-8, Blom Pubns). Ayer Co Pubs.
--Superstitions of the Highlands & Islands of Scotland. 1970. 43.00x (ISBN 0-8103-3589-1). Gale.
--Witchcraft & Second Sight in the Highlands & Islands of Scotland. 1976. Repr. 20.00x (ISBN 0-85409-978-6). Charles River Bks.
Campbell, John H. Logistics: Concepts & Applications. Nishi, Masao, ed. LC 82-84389. 328p. (Orig.). 1982. pap. 15.45 (ISBN 0-9610146-0-1). Leaseway Trans Corp.
--Logistics: Issues for the Eighties. Nishi, Masao, ed. LC 81-86565. 211p. 1981. pap. 15.45 (ISBN 0-86551-017-2). Leaseway Trans Corp.
Campbell, John J., jt. auth. see Brunner, Joseph F.
Campbell, John L. Highland Songs of the Forty-Five. LC 75-173105. Repr. of 1933 ed. 27.50 (ISBN 0-405-08338-6, Blom Pubns). Ayer Co Pubs.
--The Lives of the Chief Justices of England: From the Norman Conquest till the Death of Lord Tenterden, 3 vols. facsimile ed. LC 70-152976. (Select Bibliographies Reprint Ser). Repr. of 1857 ed. Set. 104.50 (ISBN 0-8369-5728-8). Ayer Co Pubs.
--Six Months in the New Gold-Diggings: Placer Gold Mining in Idaho Territory in 1863. 86p. 1980. 9.95 (ISBN 0-87770-225-X). Ye Galleon.
Campbell, John L. & Zimmerman, Lance. Programming the Apple II & IIe: A Structured Approach. rev. & enl. ed. LC 83-21441. (Illus.). 464p. 1984. pap. 19.95 (ISBN 0-89303-779-6); diskette 30.00 (ISBN 0-89303-780-X); bk. & diskette 49.95 (ISBN 0-89303-777-X). Brady Comm.
Campbell, John L., jt. auth. see Adams, Bert N.
Campbell, John L., ed. Highland Songs of the Forty-Five. (Illus.). 250p. 1984. 16.00 (ISBN 0-7073-0349-4, Pub. by Academic Pr Scotland). Columbia U Pr.
Campbell, John L. & Collinson, Francis, eds. Hebridean Folksongs, Vol. 3. 1981. 74.00 (ISBN 0-19-815215-9). Oxford U Pr.
Campbell, John M., ed. Prehistoric Cultural Relations Between the Arctic & Temperate Zones of North America. Repr. of 1962 ed. 16.00 (ISBN 0-384-07270-4). Johnson Repr.
Campbell, John M., ed. see MacNeill, Nigel.
Campbell, John P. Campbell's High School-College Quiz Book: The Quiz Contestant's Vade Mecum. rev. ed. LC 84-19012. 524p. 1984. pap. 14.95x (ISBN 0-9609412-3-1). Patricks Pr.
--Campbell's Middle School Quiz Book No. 1. (Middle School Ser.). 326p. (Orig.). (gr. 5-8). 1985. pap. 12.95x (ISBN 0-9609412-4-X). Patricks Pr.
--Campbell's Potpourri I of Quiz Bowl Questions. LC 83-83076. (Campbell's Potpourri Ser.). 318p. (Orig.). (gr. 7 up). 1984. pap. 12.95x (ISBN 0-9609412-1-5). Patricks Pr.
--Campbell's Potpourri II of Quiz Bowl Questions. LC 84-61238. (Campbell's Potpourri Ser.). 354p. (Orig.). 1984. pap. 12.95x (ISBN 0-9609412-2-3). Patricks Pr.
--Campbell's Potpourri III of Quiz Bowl Questions. (Campbell's Potpourri Ser.). 330p. (Orig.). (gr. 7-12). 1985. pap. 12.95x (ISBN 0-9609412-5-8). Patricks Pr.
Campbell, John P. & Daft, Richard L. What to Study: Generating & Developing Research Questions. (Studying Organizations: Innovations in Methodology). 168p. 1982. 17.95 (ISBN 0-8039-1871-2); pap. 8.95 (ISBN 0-8039-1872-0). Sage.
Campbell, John R. Dealing with Disaster: Hurricane Response in Fiji. 236p. 1984. pap. 9.00 (ISBN 0-86638-058-2). E W Center HI.
--Introductory Treatise on Lie's Theory. LC 65-28441. 16.95 (ISBN 0-8284-0183-7). Chelsea Pub.
Campbell, John R. & Lasley, John F. The Science of Animals That Serve Mankind. 2nd ed. (Agricultural Science Ser.). (Illus.). 736p. 1975. text ed. 39.95 (ISBN 0-07-009696-1). McGraw.
Campbell, John S. Improve Your Technical Communication. LC 76-8493. 216p. 1976. pap. text ed. 9.95x (ISBN 0-915668-26-2). G S E Pubns.
Campbell, John T. Our Twentieth Century's Greatest Poems. 700p. 1982. 59.95 (ISBN 0-910147-00-0). World Poetry Pr.
--Our Worlds Best Loved Poems. 608p. 1983. 69.95 (ISBN 0-910147-03-5). World Poetry Pr.
--Today's Greatest Poems. 665p. 1983. pap. 59.95 (ISBN 0-910147-01-9). World Poetry Pr.
Campbell, John T., ed. Our Western World's Greatest Poems. 450p. 1983. 69.95 (ISBN 0-317-03222-4); text ed. 69.95. World Poetry Pr.
Campbell, John W. Cloak of Aesir. LC 75-10664. (Classics of Science Fiction Ser.). 255p. 1976. 15.00 (ISBN 0-88355-359-7); pap. 3.95 (ISBN 0-88355-449-6). Hyperion-Conn.
--Who Goes There? Seven Tales of Science Fiction. LC 75-28850. (Classics of Science Fiction Ser.). 230p. 1976. 19.25 (ISBN 0-88355-365-1); pap. 3.95. Hyperion-Conn.
Campbell, John W., et al. Cosmos. Lupoff, Richard A., ed. 1980. Repr. of 1934 ed. 17.95t (ISBN 0-930800-03-6). Pennyfarthing.
Campbell, Jonathan A. & Ford, Linda S. Phylogenetic Relationships of the Colubrid Snakes of the Genus Adelphicos in the Highlands of Middle America. (Occasional Papers: No. 100). 22p. 1982. 2.25 (ISBN 0-317-04838-4). U of KS Mus Nat Hist.
Campbell, Joseph. The Flight of the Wild Gander. LC 70-183820. 256p. 1972. pap. 6.95 (ISBN 0-89526-914-7). Regnery-Gateway.
--Hero with a Thousand Faces. rev. ed. LC 49-8590. (Bollingen Ser.: No. 17). (Illus.). 1968. 37.50 (ISBN 0-691-09743-7); pap. 9.95 (ISBN 0-691-01784-0). Princeton U Pr.
--The Inner Reaches of Outer Space: Metaphor As Myth & As Religion. LC 84-40776. (Illus.). 160p. 1985. 16.95 (ISBN 0-912383-09-7). Van der Marck.
--The Masks of God: Creative Mythology. (Illus.). 730p. 1970. pap. 7.95 (ISBN 0-14-004307-1). Penguin.
--The Masks of God: Occidental Mythology. (Illus.). 564p. 1976. pap. 7.95 (ISBN 0-14-004306-3). Penguin.
--The Masks of God: Oriental Mythology. (Illus.). 576p. 1970. pap. 7.95 (ISBN 0-14-004305-5). Penguin.
--The Masks of God: Primitive Mythology. (Illus.). 528p. 1976. pap. 7.95 (ISBN 0-14-004304-7). Penguin.
--The Masks of God 1: Primitive Mythology. 1959. 19.95 (ISBN 0-670-46012-5). Viking.
--The Masks of God 2: Oriental Mythology. (Illus.). 1962. 19.95 (ISBN 0-670-46045-1). Viking.
--The Masks of God 4: Creative Mythology. 1968. 19.95 (ISBN 0-670-46111-3). Viking.
--The Mountainy Singer by Seosamh MacCathmhaoil. LC 74-64007. (Des Imagistes: Literature of the Imagist Movement). 88p. Repr. of 1909 ed. 15.00 (ISBN 0-404-17078-1). AMS Pr.
--Myths to Live by. 304p. 1973. pap. 4.50 (ISBN 0-553-25011-6). Bantam.
--The Portable Jung. (Viking Portable Library: No. 70). 1971. 14.95 (ISBN 0-670-41062-4). Viking.
--The Way of Animal Powers. LC 83-80561. (Historical Atlas of World Mythology Ser.: Vol. 1). (Illus.). 304p. 1983. 75.00 (ISBN 0-912383-00-3). Van der Marck.
--The Way of the Animal Powers, Vol. 1: Historical Atlas of World Mythology. 1983. 75.00 (ISBN 0-912383-00-3). Har-Row.
Campbell, Joseph & Abadie, M. J. The Mythic Image. LC 79-166363. (Bollingen Series C). (Illus.). 560p. 1981. pap. 19.95 (ISBN 0-691-01839-1). Princeton U Pr.
Campbell, Joseph & Roberts, Richard. Tarot Revelations. 2nd ed. LC 81-86684. (Illus.). 304p. 1982. pap. 8.95 (ISBN 0-942380-00-2). Vernal Equinox.
Campbell, Joseph, ed. Myths, Dreams, & Religion. 1970. pap. 6.50 (ISBN 0-525-47255-X, 0631-190). Dutton.
--Papers from Eranos Yearbooks, 6 vols. Manheim, Ralph & Hull, R. F., trs. Incl. Vol. 1. Spirit & Nature. (Illus.). 1954. 31.00 (ISBN 0-691-09736-4); pap. 9.95 (ISBN 0-691-01841-3); Vol. 2. The Mysteries. 1955. 28.50x (ISBN 0-691-09734-8); pap. 11.50x (ISBN 0-691-01823-5); Vol. 3. Man & Time. LC 72-1982. (Illus.). 440p. 1957. 33.00x (ISBN 0-691-09732-1); pap. 8.95x (ISBN 0-691-01857-X); Vol. 4. Spirtual Disciplines. (Illus.). 1960. 38.50x (ISBN 0-691-09737-2); Vol. 5. Man & Transformation. (Illus.). 1964. 36.00 (ISBN 0-691-09733-X); pap. 9.95 (ISBN 0-691-01834-0); Vol. 6. Mystic Vision. 1969. 44.00x (ISBN 0-691-09735-6). (Bollingen Ser.: No. 30). pap. 7.95x (ISBN 0-691-01842-1). Princeton U Pr.
--Spirit & Nature: Papers from the Eranos Yearbooks, Vol. 1. Manheim, Ralph & Hull, R. F., trs. from Ger. LC 54-5647. (Bollingen Ser.: No. XXX). (Illus.). 520p. (Orig.). 1982. 33.00x (ISBN 0-691-09736-4); pap. 9.95x (ISBN 0-691-01841-3). Princeton U Pr.
--Spiritual Disciplines: Papers from the Eranos Yearbooks, Vol. 4. Manheim, Ralph & Hull, R. F., trs. LC 54-5647. (Bollingen Ser.: Vol. 4). (Illus.). 560p. 1985. pap. 9.95x (ISBN 0-691-01863-4). Princeton U Pr.
Campbell, Joseph, ed. see Jung, Carl G.
Campbell, Joseph, ed. see Zimmer, Heinrich.
Campbell, Joseph X. Poems of Joseph Campbell. 1963. 3.95 (ISBN 0-900372-66-4). Irish Bk Ctr.
Campbell, Judith. Four Ponies. 9.50 (ISBN 0-392-09902-0, SpS). Sportshelf.
--Police Horses. pap. 2.00 (ISBN 0-87980-199-9). Wilshire.
--Royal Horses. (Illus.). 190p. 1984. 24.00 (ISBN 0-450-06001-2, New Eng Lib). David & Charles.
Campbell, Judy & Lowe, Susan. Twice the Heartache. LC 80-85034. 200p. (Orig.). 1983. 3.95 (ISBN 0-89896-050-9). Larksdale.
Campbell, Julie & Kenny, Katherine. Mystery of the Midnight Marauder, No. 30. (Trixie Belden Mysteries Ser.). 236p. (gr. 4-6). 1980. pap. 1.95 (ISBN 0-307-21551-2, Golden Bks.). Western Pub.
--Mystery of the Velvet Gown, No. 29. (Trixie Belden Mysteries Ser.). 236p. (gr. 4-6). 1980. pap. 1.95 (ISBN 0-307-21550-4, Golden Bks.). Western Pub.
Campbell, Julie & Kenny, Katheryn. Mystery at Maypenny's, No. 31. (Trixie Belden Mysteries). 236p. (gr. 4-6). 1980. pap. 1.50 (ISBN 0-307-21552-0, Golden Bks.). Western Pub.
Campbell, Julie & Kenny, Kathryn. Mystery of the Missing Millionaire, No. 34. (Trixie Belden Mysteries Ser.). 216p. (gr. 4-6). 1979. pap. 1.95 (ISBN 0-307-21555-5, Golden Bks.). Western Pub.
--Mystery of the Vanishing Victim, No. 33. (A Trixie Belden Mysteries Ser.). 216p. (gr. 4-6). 1979. pap. 1.95 (ISBN 0-307-21554-7, Golden Bks.). Western Pub.
--Mystery of the Whispering Witch, No. 32. (A Trixie Belden Mysteries Ser.). 216p. (gr. 4-6). 1979. pap. 1.50 (ISBN 0-307-21553-9, Golden Bks.). Western Pub.
Campbell, June M. & Campbell, Joe B. Laboratory Mathematics: Medical & Biological Applications. 3rd ed. LC 83-8203. (Illus.). 320p. 1984. text ed. 15.95 (ISBN 0-8016-0800-7). Mosby.
Campbell, Karel. Blue Jay & the Monster. LC 67-14952. (General Juvenile Bks). (Illus.). (gr. k-5). 1967. PLB 3.95g (ISBN 0-8225-0258-5). Lerner Pubns.
Campbell, Karlyn K. Critiques of Contemporary Rhetoric. 1971. pap. write for info. (ISBN 0-534-00135-1). Wadsworth Pub.
--The Rhetorical Act. 336p. 1981. text ed. write for info. (ISBN 0-534-01008-3). Wadsworth Pub.
Campbell, Karlyn K., jt. auth. see Jamieson, Kathleen H.
Campbell, Kate. One Hundred Ways to Amaze a Kid. LC 82-81464. (Illus.). 64p. (Orig.). 1982. pap. 3.95 (ISBN 0-938530-08-9). Lexikos.
Campbell, Kathleen. Then & Now. 1985. pap. 5.00 (ISBN 0-941150-29-1). Barth.
Campbell, Kathleen, ed. An Anthology of English Poetry: Dryden to Blake. facsimile ed. LC 75-168777. (Granger Index Reprint Ser.). Repr. of 1930 ed. 24.00 (ISBN 0-8369-6297-4). Ayer Co Pubs.
Campbell, Keith. Body & Mind. rev. ed. LC 84-13082. 176p. 1984. text ed. 10.95 (ISBN 0-268-00672-5); pap. text ed. 4.95. U of Notre Dame Pr.
Campbell, Keith O. Food for the Future: How Agriculture Can Meet the Challenge. LC 78-23982. xii, 178p. 1979. 15.95x (ISBN 0-8032-0965-7). U of Nebr Pr.
Campbell, Ken. Caribbean. LC 80-54668. (Countries Ser.). PLB 13.96 (ISBN 0-382-06415-1). Silver.
--Skungpoomery. 47p. 1984. pap. 4.95 (ISBN 0-413-33910-6, 4108, Pub. by Eyre Methuen England). Methuen Inc.
Campbell, Kimo, ed. see Speakman, Cummins E.
Campbell, Lee F., jt. auth. see Jericho, Eugene.
Campbell, Leon G. The Military & Society in Colonial Peru 1750-1810. LC 77-91650. (Memoirs Ser.: Vol. 123). 1978. pap. 10.00 (ISBN 0-87169-123-X). Am Philos.
Campbell, Leslie. Two Hundred Years of Pharmacy in Mississippi. LC 73-86313. 224p. 1974. 2.50x (ISBN 0-87805-058-2). U Pr of Miss.
Campbell, Leslie G. International Auditing: A Comparative Survey of Professional Requirements in Australia, Canada, France, Germany, Japan, the Netherlands, the U. K. & the U. S. A. LC 84-11643. 212p. 1984. 30.00 (ISBN 0-312-41969-4). St Martin.
Campbell, Lewis. Aeschylus: The Seven Plays in English Verse. 1906. 10.00 (ISBN 0-8274-1827-2). R West.
--A Guide to Greek Tragedy for English Readers. 1980. lib. bdg. 75.00 (ISBN 0-8490-3200-8). Gordon Pr.
--Religion in Greek Literature: A Sketch in Outline. facsimile ed. LC 79-148874. (Select Bibliographies Reprint Ser). Repr. of 1898 ed. 22.00 (ISBN 0-8369-5645-1). Ayer Co Pubs.
--The Theaetetus of Plato. 2nd ed. LC 78-66572. (Ancient Philosophy Ser.). 356p. 1980. lib. bdg. 43.00 (ISBN 0-8240-9606-1). Garland Pub.
Campbell, Lewis & Garnett, William. Life of James Clerk Maxwell. (Sources of Science, House Ser: No. 85). 1970. Repr. of 1882 ed. 50.00 (ISBN 0-384-07295-X). Johnson Repr.
Campbell, Lewis, ed. see Plato.
Campbell, Lewis, rev. by see Plato.
Campbell, Libby M. Make Me a Falcon. LC 74-33070. 100p. 1974. 3.95 (ISBN 0-89227-011-X). Commonwealth Pr.
Campbell, Liberty. Blue Dawn, Blue River. 48p. 1982. 5.95 (ISBN 0-89962-257-7). Todd & Honeywell.
--Haiku of Old Japan. LC 81-90433. 80p. 1983. 6.95 (ISBN 0-533-05185-1). Vantage.
--Lanternes-Cinquains-Cameos. (Contemporary Poets of Dorrance Ser.). 112p. 1983. 8.95 (ISBN 0-8059-2878-2). Dorrance.
--To a Far Province with Basho. 64p. 1983. pap. 3.95 (ISBN 0-939332-04-3). Pohl Assoc.
--Up to My Neck in Haiku. 76p. 1982. 6.00 (ISBN 0-682-49922-6). Exposition Pr FL.
Campbell, Lily. The Grotesque in the Poetry of Robert Browning. 1978. Repr. of 1907 ed. lib. bdg. 15.00 (ISBN 0-8495-0770-7). Arden Lib.
Campbell, Lily B. Divine Poetry & Drama in Sixteenth-century England. LC 59-3609. pap. 69.00 (ISBN 0-317-26043-X, 2024437). Bks Demand UMI.
--Divine Poetry & Drama in 16th Century England. LC 79-148614. 1972. Repr. of 1959 ed. text ed. 12.50x (ISBN 0-87752-143-3). Gordian.
--Grotesque in the Poetry of Robert Browning. 1907. lib. bdg. 15.00 (ISBN 0-8414-3506-5). Folcroft.
--Shakespeare's "Histories". Mirrors of Elizabethan Policy. LC 47-2108. 346p. 1978. pap. 7.50 (ISBN 0-87328-004-0). Huntington Lib.
Campbell, Lily B., ed. see Higgins, John & Blenerhasset, Thomas.
Campbell, Lily G. Shakespeare's Tragic Heroes: Slaves of Passion. 1960. 15.00 (ISBN 0-8446-1806-3). Peter Smith.
Campbell, Lindsey. Moonie & the Oil Search. (Illus.). 14.50x (ISBN 0-392-03985-0, ABC). Sportshelf.
Campbell, Lloyd. The Ebony Keys. (Private Library Collection). 1985. mini-bound 6.95 (ISBN 0-938422-18-9). SOS Pubns CA.
Campbell, Lorne. The Early Flemish Pictures in the Collection of Her Majesty the Queen. (Illus.). 250p. Date not set. price not set (ISBN 0-521-26523-1). Cambridge U Pr.
Campbell, Louis H. The Frightful Fate of Wilhelmina Worthington. 1984. pap. 1.75 (ISBN 0-912963-06-9). Eldridge Pub.
Campbell, Louisa. Ernie Gets Lost. (Sesame Street Growing-Up Bks.). (Illus.). 32p. (gr. k-3). 1985. 2.50 (ISBN 0-317-17819-9, Pub. by Golden Bks). Western Pub.
Campbell, Lowrie. Curtailing Inflation. 1983. 5.75 (ISBN 0-8062-2193-3). Carlton.

Campbell, Lucile M. To God Be the Glory. (Orig.). 1981. pap. 1.95 (ISBN 0-9607114-0-6). L M Campbell.
Campbell, Luke. Ridge Runner Rhymes. 75p. 1974. 2.00 (ISBN 0-914724-01-0). St Cuthberts.
Campbell, Lyle & Mithun, Marianne, eds. The Languages of Native America: Historical & Comparative Assessment. 1040p. 1979. text ed. 35.00x (ISBN 0-292-74624-5). U of Tex Pr.
Campbell, M., jt. ed. see Henson, J. B.
Campbell, M., jt. ed. see MacIntyre, R.
Campbell, Magda, et al. Child & Adolescent Psychopharmacology. 1985. 17.95 (ISBN 0-8039-2463-1); pap. 8.95 (ISBN 0-8039-2464-X). Sage.
Campbell, Malcolm. Pietro Da Cortona at the Pitti Palace: A Study of the Planetary Rooms & Related Projects. LC 76-3247. (Monographs in Art & Architecture: No. 41). (Illus.). 1976. text ed. 70.00x (ISBN 0-691-03891-0). Princeton U Pr.
Campbell, Malcolm, ed. Business Information Services. 2nd ed. 179p. 1981. 20.00 (ISBN 0-85157-321-5, Pub. by Bingley England). Shoe String.
Campbell, Malcolm J. Case Studies in Business Information Provision. 128p. 1984. 18.50 (ISBN 0-85157-353-3, Pub. by Bingley England). Shoe String.
Campbell, Malcolm J., ed. Manual of Business Library Practice. 2nd ed. 248p. 1985. lib. bdg. 19.50 (ISBN 0-85157-360-6, Pub. by Bingley England). Shoe String.
Campbell, Margaret. Dolmetsch: The Man & His Work. LC 75-4558. (Illus.). 336p. 1975. 25.00x (ISBN 0-295-95416-7). U of Wash Pr.
Campbell, Margaret, jt. ed. see Campbell, Bruce.
Campbell, Margaret, ed. see Stark, Raymond.
Campbell, Margaret W. Paper Toy Making. LC 75-2570. 96p. 1975. pap. 2.95 (ISBN 0-486-21662-4). Dover.
Campbell, Maria. Halfbreed. LC 82-8382. 157p. 1982. pap. 4.95 (ISBN 0-8032-6311-2, BB 816, Bison). U of Nebr Pr.
Campbell, Maria, ed. Revolutionary Services & Civil Life of General William Hull. 1972. Repr. of 1848 ed. lib. bdg. 29.50x (ISBN 0-8422-8022-7). Irvington.
Campbell, Marian. Medieval Enamels. (The Victoria & Albert Museum Introductions to the Decorative Arts). (Illus.). 48p. 1984. 9.95 (ISBN 0-88045-021-5). Stemmer Hse.
Campbell, Marie. Folks Do Get Born. Reverby, Susan, ed. LC 83-49143. (History of American Nursing Ser.). 245p. 1984. Repr. of 1946 ed. lib. bdg. 30.00 (ISBN 0-8240-6504-2). Garland Pub.
--Tales from the Cloud Walking Country. LC 76-14944. (Illus.). 1976. Repr. of 1958 ed. lib. bdg. 22.50x (ISBN 0-8371-8607-2, CATC). Greenwood.
Campbell, Marion. Towards a New Iron Age. (Illus.). 100p. (Orig.). 1984. pap. 5.95 (ISBN 0-905209-23-0, Pub. by Victoria & Albert Mus UK). Faber & Faber.
Campbell, Mary. The New England Butt'ry Shelf Almanac. LC 83-11589. 1983. 12.95 (ISBN 0-8289-0511-8). Greene.
Campbell, Mary B. The Business of Being Alive. Smith, Craig, designed by. LC 82-60107. (Illus.). 81p. (Orig.). 1982. pap. 6.00 (ISBN 0-932662-38-2). St Andrews NC.
Campbell, Mary C. & Stewart, Joyce L. The Medical Mycology Handbook. LC 80-11935. 436p. 1980. pap. 35.00x (ISBN 0-471-04728-7, Pub. by Wiley Med). Wiley.
Campbell, Mary E. Attitude of Tennesseans Toward the Union, Eighteen Forty-Seven to Eighteen Sixty-One. LC 60-53338. 1961. 7.50 (ISBN 0-910294-15-1). Brown Bk.
--Defoe's First Poem. 222p. 1938. 3.70 (ISBN 0-911536-06-X). Trinity U Pr.
Campbell, Mary J. & Quinones, Patricia. Volleyball. (Illus.). 21p. (Orig.). 1983. pap. text ed. 4.50 (ISBN 0-88136-015-5). Jostens.
Campbell, Mary J., jt. auth. see Anderson, Emma D.
Campbell, Mary L. Open Mandala Journey. LC 79-63633. (Illus.). 1980. 50.00 (ISBN 0-8048-1314-0). C E Tuttle.
Campbell, Mary M. The Butt'ry Shelf Cookbook. LC 82-9287. 1982. 12.95 (ISBN 0-8289-0490-1). Greene.
Campbell, Mary M., ed. A Basket of Herbs. LC 82-21130. (Illus.). 1983. text ed. 12.95 (ISBN 0-8289-0500-2). Greene.
Campbell, Mavis C. The Dynamics of Change in a Slave Society: A Sociopolitical History of the Free Colored's of Jamaica, 1800-1865. LC 74-4968. 393p. 1976. 32.50 (ISBN 0-8386-1584-8). Fairleigh Dickinson.
Campbell, Michael. The Call of a New Age. 88p. 1984. 3.95x (ISBN 0-931290-78-3). Alchemy Bks.
--Lord Dismiss Us. LC 83-18173. (Phoenix Fiction Ser.). 384p. 1984. pap. 9.95 (ISBN 0-226-09244-5). U of Chicago Pr.
Campbell, Michael D. & Lehr, Jay H. Water Well Technology. 681p. 43.75 (ISBN 0-318-15933-3); members 35.00 (ISBN 0-318-15934-1). Natl Water Well.
Campbell, Mike. Capitalism in the U. K. A Perspective from Marxist Political Economy. (Illus.). 204p. 1981. 28.00 (ISBN 0-7099-0089-9, Pub. by Croom Helm Ltd); pap. 8.95 (ISBN 0-7099-0090-2). Longwood Pub Group.
Campbell, Mike, jt. auth. see Burden, Tom.
Campbell, Mildred. The English Yeoman. 453p. Date not set. pap. 11.95 (ISBN 0-85036-289-X). Kapitan Szabo.
--English Yeoman under Elizabeth & the Early Stuarts. LC 68-4919. Repr. of 1942 ed. 37.50x (ISBN 0-678-08003-8). Kelley.
Campbell, Milton H., ed. High Level Radioactive Waste Management. LC 76-25020. (Advances in Chemistry Ser.: No. 153). 1976. 29.95 (ISBN 0-8412-0270-2). Am Chemical.
Campbell, Moran, jt. auth. see Jones, Norman L.
Campbell, Morgan G. Handbook for Bible Teachers & Preachers. (Paperback Reference Library). 312p. 1985. pap. 8.95 (ISBN 0-8010-6190-3). Baker Bk.
Campbell, Murdoch. From Grace to Glory: Meditations of the Psalms. 1979. pap. 4.45 (ISBN 0-85151-028-0). Banner of Truth.
Campbell, Nellie M. The Elementary School Teacher's Treatment of Classroom Behavior Problems. LC 70-176624. (Columbia University. Teachers College. Contributions to Education: No. 668). Repr. of 1935 ed. 22.50 (ISBN 0-404-55668-X). AMS Pr.
Campbell, Newell P. A Geologic Road Log over Chinook, White Pass & Ellensburg to Yakima Highways. (Information Circular Ser.: No. 54). 82p. 1975. 1.50 (ISBN 0-686-34718-8). Geologic Pubns.
Campbell, Norine D. Patrick Henry: Patriot & Statesman. (Illus.). 1969. 14.50 (ISBN 0-8159-6501-X). Devin.
Campbell, Norma L., jt. auth. see Christen, William.
Campbell, Norman R. What Is Science? 1921. pap. 4.50 (ISBN 0-486-60043-2). Dover.
Campbell, Olwen. Thomas Love Peacock. 104p. 1983. Repr. of 1953 ed. lib. bdg. 20.00 (ISBN 0-89987-143-7). Darby Bks.
Campbell, Olwen W. Shelley & the Unromantics. LC 68-1189. (Studies in Shelley, No. 25). 1969. Repr. of 1924 ed. lib. bdg. 51.95x (ISBN 0-8383-0652-7). Haskell.
--Thomas Love Peacock. LC 73-157327. (Select Bibliographies Reprint Ser.). 1972. Repr. of 1953 ed. 14.00 (ISBN 0-8369-5787-3). Ayer Co Pubs.
Campbell, Oscar J. Comedies of Holberg. LC 68-20216. 1968. Repr. of 1914 ed. 22.00 (ISBN 0-405-08339-4, Blom Pubns). Ayer Co Pubs.
--Comicall Satyre & Shakespeare's Troilus & Cressida. LC 39-1295. 246p. 1970. Repr. of 1938 ed. 10.00 (ISBN 0-87328-001-6). Huntington Lib.
--English Poetry of the Nineteenth Century. LC 75-154103. 1971. Repr. of 1929 ed. lib. bdg. 37.50x (ISBN 0-8371-6074-X, CAEP). Greenwood.
--Shakespeare's Satire. LC 74-159036. 1971. Repr. of 1943 ed. text ed. 12.50x (ISBN 0-87752-150-6). Gordian.
Campbell, Oscar J. & Pyre, J. F., eds. Great English Poets. facsimile ed. LC 77-152147. (Granger Index Reprint Ser). Repr. of 1928 ed. 60.50 (ISBN 0-8369-6250-8). Ayer Co Pubs.
Campbell, Oscar J. & Rice, Richard A., eds. Book of Narratives. LC 72-5901. (Short Story Index Reprint Ser). Repr. of 1917 ed. 27.50 (ISBN 0-8369-4196-9). Ayer Co Pubs.
Campbell, Oscar J., ed. see Alden, Raymond M.
Campbell, Oscar J., ed. see Bos, Lambert Van Den.
Campbell, Oscar J., et al. Studies in Shakespeare, Milton & Donne. McCartney, Eugene S., ed. LC 78-93244. (University of Michigan Publications: Vol. 1). 1970. Repr. of 1925 ed. 12.50x (ISBN 0-87753-020-3). Phaeton.
Campbell, P. & Marshall, R. D., eds. Essays in Biochemistry, Vol. 19. 1984. pap. 19.00 (ISBN 0-12-158119-5). Acad Pr.
Campbell, P. N. The Structure & Function of Animal Cell Components. 1966. 25.00 (ISBN 0-08-011819-4); pap. 10.75 (ISBN 0-08-011818-6). Pergamon.
Campbell, P. N., ed. Biology in Profile: An Introduction to the Many Branches of Biology. (Illus.). 148p. 1981. 21.00 (ISBN 0-08-026846-3); pap. 10.50 (ISBN 0-08-026845-5). Pergamon.
--Essays in Biochemistry, Vol. 18. 1983. pap. 15.00 (ISBN 0-12-158118-7). Acad Pr.
Campbell, P. N. & Kilby, B. A., eds. Basic Biochemistry for Medical Students. 1975. pap. 24.00 (ISBN 0-12-158150-0). Acad Pr.
Campbell, P. N. & Marshall, R. D., eds. Essays in Biochemistry, Vol. 16. 1981. 23.00 (ISBN 0-12-158116-0). Acad Pr.
--Essays in Biochemistry, Vol. 17. 1981. pap. 22.50 (ISBN 0-12-158117-9). Acad Pr.
--Essays in Biochemistry, Vol. 20. (Serial Publications). 1985. 18.00 (ISBN 0-12-158120-9). Acad Pr.
Campbell, Pamela, jt. auth. see Patton, Annie.
Campbell, Pat, jt. auth. see Fein, Gieta.
Campbell, Patricia B. Evaluating Youth Participation: A Program Operator's Guide. 59p. 1982. pap. 5.00 (ISBN 0-912041-14-5). Natl Comm Res Youth.
Campbell, Patricia J. Passing the Hat: Street Performance in America. LC 81-65502. 288p. 1981. 14.95 (ISBN 0-385-28773-9); pap. 7.95 (ISBN 0-385-28771-2). Delacorte.
--Presenting Robert Corimer. (Twayne Young Adult Authors Ser.: No. I). 176p. 1985. lib. bdg. 12.95 (ISBN 0-8057-8200-1, Twayne). G K Hall.
--Sex Education Books for Young Adults, 1892-1979. LC 79-1535. 1979. 19.95 (ISBN 0-8352-1157-6). Bowker.
Campbell, Patrick. From Silent Glens to Noisy Streets. 118p. (Orig.). 1983. pap. 4.95 (ISBN 0-85342-693-7, Pub. by Mercier Pr Ireland). Irish Bk Ctr.
--Patrick Campbell's Travels. LC 78-50738. (Illus.). 96p. 1978. 12.50x (ISBN 0-8139-0858-2). U Pr of Va.
--Travels in the Interior Inhabited Parts of North America in the Years 1791 & 1792. Langton, H. H., ed. LC 68-28611. 1968. Repr. of 1937 ed. lib. bdg. 24.00x (ISBN 0-8371-5061-2, CATI). Greenwood.
Campbell, Mrs. Patrick. My Life & Some Letters. LC 71-173104. (Illus.). 1922. Repr. of 1900 ed. 27.50 (ISBN 0-405-08340-8, Blom Pubns). Ayer Co Pubs.
Campbell, Patty G., jt. auth. see White, Jane F.
Campbell, Paul, jt. auth. see Conley, Patrick.
Campbell, Paul, ed. see Hopkins, Stephen.
Campbell, Paul N. Form & the Art of Theatre. LC 84-71037. 136p. 1984. 16.95 (ISBN 0-87972-279-7); pap. 8.95 (ISBN 0-87972-280-0). Bowling Green Univ.
Campbell, Paul N. & Greville, G. D., eds. Essays in Biochemistry, Vols. 1-5 & 8-15. Incl. Vol. 1. 1965. 25.00 (ISBN 0-12-158101-2); Vol. 2. 1966. 25.00 (ISBN 0-12-158102-0); Vol. 3. 1967. 25.00 (ISBN 0-12-158103-9); Vol. 4. 1968. 25.00 (ISBN 0-12-158104-7); Vol. 5. 1970. 25.00 (ISBN 0-12-158105-5); Vol. 8. 1972. 25.00 (ISBN 0-12-158108-X); Vol. 9. 1974. 25.00 (ISBN 0-12-158109-8); Vol. 10. 1974. 25.00 (ISBN 0-12-158110-1); Vol. 11. 1976. 25.00 (ISBN 0-12-158111-X); Vol. 12. 1977. 25.00 (ISBN 0-12-158112-8); Vol. 13. 1978. 25.00 (ISBN 0-12-158113-6); Vol. 14. 1978. 25.00 (ISBN 0-12-158114-4); Vol. 15. 1979. 25.00 (ISBN 0-12-158115-2). (Illus.). Acad Pr.
Campbell, Paul R., jt. auth. see Conley, Patrick T.
Campbell, Paula, jt. auth. see Buzzard, Lynn.
Campbell, Penelope. Maryland in Africa: The Maryland State Colonization Society, 1831-1857. LC 75-131058. 270p. 1971. 19.95x (ISBN 0-252-00133-8). U of Ill Pr.
Campbell, Persia. The Consumer Interest: A Study in Consumer Economics. LC 75-17213. (Social Problems & Social Policy Ser.). 1976. Repr. of 1949 ed. 49.50x (ISBN 0-405-07485-9). Ayer Co Pubs.
--Consumer Representation in the New Deal. LC 73-76637. (Columbia University Studies in the Social Sciences: No. 477). Repr. of 1940 ed. 18.50 (ISBN 0-404-51477-4). AMS Pr.
Campbell, Persia C. Chinese Coolie Emigration to Countries Within the British Empire. new ed. 240p. 1971. Repr. of 1923 ed. 28.50x (ISBN 0-7146-2000-9, F Cass Co). Biblio Dist.
--Chinese Coolie Emigration to Countries Within the British Empire. LC 70-88402. Repr. of 1923 ed. 19.75x (ISBN 0-8371-1751-8, CCE&, Pub. by Negro U Pr). Greenwood.
Campbell, Peter. French Electoral Systems & Elections since 1789. 2nd ed. 155p. 1965. 15.00 (ISBN 0-208-00394-0, Archon). Shoe String.
Campbell, Peter, jt. auth. see Ball, Richard.
Campbell, Peter, jt. auth. see McMahon, Edwin H.
Campbell, Peter A. & McMahon, Edwin M. Bio-Spirituality: Focusing As a Way to Grow. 1985. pap. 6.95 (ISBN 0-8294-0478-3). Loyola.
Campbell, Mrs. Praed. The Brother of the Shadow: A Mystery of Today. Reginald, R. & Menville, Douglas, eds. LC 76-1539. (Supernatural & Occult Fiction Ser.). 1976. Repr. of 1886 ed. 14.00x (ISBN 0-405-08162-6). Ayer Co Pubs.
Campbell, R. Complete Guide & Descriptive Books of Mexico. 1976. lib. bdg. 59.95 (ISBN 0-8490-1654-1). Gordon Pr.
--Microbial Ecology. 2nd ed. (Illus.). 202p. 1983. pap. text ed. 17.00x (ISBN 0-632-00988-8). Blackwell Pubns.
--Plant Microbiology. 200p. 1985. pap. text ed. write for info. (ISBN 0-7131-2892-5). E Arnold.
Campbell, R., tr. see Mutahhari, Ayatullah M.
Campbell, R., tr. see Shariati, Ali.
Campbell, R., tr. see Taleghani, Sayyid M.
Campbell, R. C. Statistics for Biologists. 2nd ed. (Illus.). 300p. 1974. 59.50 (ISBN 0-521-20381-3); pap. 15.95 (ISBN 0-521-09836-X). Cambridge U Pr.
Campbell, R. D. & Jones, J. The Microlight Flying Manual. 240p. (Orig.). 1982. pap. text ed. 21.95x (ISBN 0-246-11914-4, Pub. by Granada England). Brookfield Pub Co.
Campbell, R. G. State Supervision & Regulation of Budgetary Procedure in Public School Systems: An Evaluation of State Provisions for Budget-Making in Local School Systems. LC 73-176625. (Columbia University. Teachers College. Contributions to Education: No. 637). Repr. of 1935 ed. 22.50 (ISBN 0-404-55637-X). AMS Pr.
Campbell, R. H. The Rise & Fall of Scottish Industry: Seventeen Seven to Nineteen Thirty-Nine. 217p. 1980. text ed. 33.00x (ISBN 0-85976-054-5). Humanities.
--Scotland since Seventeen Hundred Seven. 260p. 1985. 24.25x (ISBN 0-85976-122-3, Pub. by John Donald Scotland). Humanities.
Campbell, R. H. & Skinner, A. The Origins & Nature of the Scottish Enlightenment. 240p. 1982. text ed. 32.00x (ISBN 0-85976-076-6, Pub. by John Donald). Humanities.
Campbell, R. H. & Skinner, A. S. Adam Smith. LC 82-3308. 231p. 1982. 27.50 (ISBN 0-312-00423-0). St Martin.
--Adam Smith. 231p. 1985. pap. 13.95 (ISBN 0-312-00424-9). St Martin.
Campbell, R. H., ed. see Smith, Adam.
Campbell, R. J. The Story of Christmas. 1977. lib. bdg. 59.95 (ISBN 0-8490-2677-6). Gordon Pr.
--Thomas Campbell. 1927. 17.50 (ISBN 0-8274-3601-7). R West.
Campbell, R. Joe. A Morphological Dictionary of Classical Nahuatl. 1985. write for info. Hispanic Seminary.
Campbell, R. K. The Church of the Living God. 8.95 (ISBN 0-88172-007-0). Believers Bkshelf.
--Divine Principles of Gathering. 40p. pap. 0.45 (ISBN 0-88172-015-1). Believers Bkshelf.
--Essentials of the Christian Life. 46p. pap. 0.50 (ISBN 0-88172-008-9). Believers Bkshelf.
--Headship & Headcovering. 32p. pap. 0.95 (ISBN 0-88172-166-2). Believers Bkshelf.
--Our Wonderful Bible. 417p. 15.95 (ISBN 0-88172-009-7); pap. 11.95 (ISBN 0-88172-010-0). Believers Bkshelf.
--Outside the Camp. 16p. pap. 0.30 (ISBN 0-88172-087-9). Believers Bkshelf.
--Parables in Matthew's Gospel. 1978. pap. 1.95 (ISBN 0-915374-42-0, 42-0). Rapids Christian.
--Parables in Matthew's Gospel: Matthew 13. tchr's lesson outline 3.75 (ISBN 0-88172-011-9). Believers Bkshelf.
--Prophetic History of Christendom. 6.95 (ISBN 0-88172-012-7). Believers Bkshelf.
--Things That Accompany Salvation. 40p. pap. 0.45 (ISBN 0-88172-013-5). Believers Bkshelf.
--Woman's Place. 32p. pap. 0.60 (ISBN 0-88172-014-3). Believers Bkshelf.
Campbell, R. M., jt. auth. see IFAC Symposium, Columbus, O., May 1982.
Campbell, R. N. & Smith, P. T., eds. Recent Advances in the Psychology of Language: Part A. Language Development & Mother-Child Interactions, Part A. (NATO Conference Series III, Human Factors: Vol. 4A). 499p. 1978. 39.50x (ISBN 0-306-32884-4, Plenum Pr). Plenum Pub.
--Recent Advances in the Psychology of Language: Part B. Formal & Experimental Approaches. (NATO Conference Series III, Human Factors: Vol. 4B). 446p. 1978. 39.50x (ISBN 0-306-32885-2, Plenum Pr). Plenum Pub.
Campbell, R. T. Bodies in a Bookshop. 192p. 1984. pap. 3.95 (ISBN 0-486-24720-1). Dover.
--Unholy Dying. 128p. 1985. pap. 3.95 (ISBN 0-486-24977-8). Dover.
Campbell, R. Wright. Circus Couronne. (General Ser.). 1978. lib. bdg. 13.50 (ISBN 0-8161-6594-7, Large Print Bks). G K Hall.
--Fat Tuesday. LC 82-19264. 384p. 1983. 15.95 (ISBN 0-89919-158-4). Ticknor & Fields.
--Killer of Kings. 1980. pap. 2.50 (ISBN 0-671-83209-3). PB.
--The Spy Who Sat & Waited. (gr. 11 up). 1979. pap. 2.50 (ISBN 0-671-82111-3). PB.
Campbell, Ramsey. Cold Print. (Illus.). 248p. 1985. lib. bdg. 17.50 (ISBN 0-910489-13-0). Scream Pr.
--Dark Companions. 258p. 1982. 13.95 (ISBN 0-02-521090-4). Macmillan.
--Dark Companions. 1985. pap. 3.50 (ISBN 0-8125-1652-4). Tor Bks.
--Demons by Daylight. 1973. 6.00 (ISBN 0-87054-062-9). Arkham.
--The Doll Who Ate His Mother. 288p. 1985. pap. 3.50 (ISBN 0-8125-1654-0, Dist. by Pinnacle Bks, Warner Pub Services & St. Martin). Tor Bks.
--Face That Must Die. (Illus.). 256p. 1984. 12.95 (ISBN 0-910489-01-7). Scream Pr.
--The Face That Must Die. 352p. 1985. Repr. 3.95 (ISBN 0-8125-1658-3, 51658-3). Tor Bks.
--The Height of the Scream. 1976. 8.95 (ISBN 0-87054-075-0). Arkham.
--The Incarnate. 320p. 1983. 14.95 (ISBN 0-02-521040-8). Macmillan.
--Incarnate. 512p. 1984. pap. 3.95 (ISBN 0-8125-1650-8). Tor Bks.
--The Nameless. 288p. 1984. pap. 3.50 (ISBN 0-671-44489-1). PB.
--The Nameless. 320p. 1985. pap. 3.50 (ISBN 0-8125-8125-3). Tor Bks.
--New Terrors, Vol. I. 1982. pap. 2.95 (ISBN 0-671-45116-2). PB.
--New Terrors I. 1984. pap. 3.50 (ISBN 0-671-53196-4). PB.
--New Terrors II. 1984. pap. 3.50 (ISBN 0-671-45117-0). PB.
--Obsession. GW & BO'B, eds. 272p. 1985. 16.95 (ISBN 0-02-521130-7). Macmillan.
--Obsession. 320p. 1986. pap. 3.95 (ISBN 0-8125-1656-7, Dist. by Warner Pub Services & St. Martin). Tor Bks.
--The Parasite. 1981. pap. 2.95 (ISBN 0-671-41905-6). PB.
Campbell, Randolph B. A Southern Community in Crisis: Harrison County, Texas, 1850-1880. 1983. 24.95 (ISBN 0-87611-061-8). Tex St Hist Assn.

Campbell, Randolph B. & Lowe, Richard G. Planters & Plainfolks: Farming in Antebellum Texas. Date not set. price not set (ISBN 0-87074-212-4). SMU Press.
--Wealth & Power in Antebellum Texas. LC 76-51652. 200p. 1977. 16.50x (ISBN 0-89096-030-5). Tex A&M Univ Pr.
Campbell, Reginald J. Livingstone. LC 77-138212. (Illus.). 295p. 1972. Repr. of 1930 ed. lib. bdg. 17.75x (ISBN 0-8371-5567-3, CALI). Greenwood.
Campbell, Regis I., jt. auth. see Gallo, Frank J.
Campbell, Rex R., jt. auth. see Johnson, Daniel M.
Campbell, Richard & Thompson, Mary. Working: Today & Tomorrow. (Illus.). 416p. (YA) (gr. 9-12). 1986. text ed. 17.95 (ISBN 0-8219-0190-7, 25802); tchr's ed. 20.00 (ISBN 0-8219-0191-5, 25657); wkbk. 4.95 (ISBN 0-8219-0192-3, 25901); Test Booklet 3.95 (ISBN 0-8219-0193-1). EMC.
Campbell, Richard D. I Did It My Way (Signed) God. 1982. 7.00 (ISBN 0-89536-577-4). CSS of Ohio.
--Old Tales with a New Twist. 1981. 3.00 (ISBN 0-89536-504-9). CSS of Ohio.
--The People of the Land of Flint. 130p. (Orig.). 1985. lib. bdg. 19.75 (ISBN 0-8191-4550-5); pap. text ed. 9.25 (ISBN 0-8191-4551-3). U Pr of Amer.
--Signs of a Lively Congregation. 1984. 3.00 (ISBN 0-89536-701-7, 4886). CSS of Ohio.
Campbell, Richard H. & Pitts, Michael R. The Bible on Film: A Checklist 1897-1980. LC 81-13560. 224p. 1981. 16.00 (ISBN 0-8108-1473-0). Scarecrow.
Campbell, Richard L. Historical Sketches of Colonial Florida. Dodson, Pat, ed. LC 75-14032. (FloridianaFacsimile & Reprint Ser.). 1975. Repr. of 1892 ed. 11.00 (ISBN 0-8130-0370-9). U Presses Fla.
Campbell, Richmond & Sowden, Lanning. Paradoxes of Rationality & Cooperation: Prisoner's Dilemma & Newcomb's Problem. 1985. 19.95 (ISBN 0-7748-0215-4). U BC Pr.
Campbell, Rita R. Drug Lag: Federal Government Decision Making. LC 76-26772. (Studies Ser.: No. 55). 1976. pap. 3.00x (ISBN 0-8179-3552-5). Hoover Inst Pr.
Campbell, Rita R. & Campbell, W. Glenn. Voluntary Health Insurance in the U. S. 46p. 1960. pap. 4.25 (ISBN 0-8447-3025-4). Am Enterprise.
Campbell, Rita Ricardo. Social Security: Promise & Reality. LC 77-83830. (Publication Ser: No. 179). 368p. 1977. 15.95x (ISBN 0-8179-6791-5). Hoover Inst Pr.
Campbell, Roald, et al. Organization & Control of American Schools. 470p. 1984. 27.95 (ISBN 0-675-20386-4). Merrill.
Campbell, Roald F. & Layton, Donald H. Policy Making for American Education. 1969. pap. 4.00 (ISBN 0-931080-03-7). U Chicago Midwest Admin.
Campbell, Roald F. & Mazzoni, Tim L., Jr. State Policy Making for the Public Schools. LC 75-31311. 476p. 1976. 27.25x (ISBN 0-8211-0224-9); text ed. 24.75x 10 or more copies. McCutchan.
Campbell, Roald F., ed. Strengthening State Departments of Education. Sroufe, Gerald E. & Layton, Donald H. LC 67-25738. 1967. pap. 4.00 (ISBN 0-931080-02-9). U Chicago Midwest Admin.
Campbell, Roald F. & Bunnell, Robert A., eds. Nationalizing Influences on Secondary Education. LC 63-11932. 1963. pap. 4.00 (ISBN 0-931080-01-0). U Chicago Midwest Admin.
Campbell, Roald F., et al. Introduction to Educational Administration. 6th ed. 1983. text ed. 33.57 (ISBN 0-205-07983-0, EDP 237983). Allyn.
Campbell, Robert. Fisherman's Guide: A Systems Approach to Creativity & Organization. LC 83-20064. (New Science Library). 320p. (Orig.). 1985. pap. 9.95 (ISBN 0-87773-265-5, 72334-1). Shambhala Pubns.
--Two Journals of Robert Campbell. (Shorey Historical Ser.). 151p. pap. 10.95 (ISBN 0-8466-0052-8, S52). Shorey.
Campbell, Robert & Sherer, Michael. Turn Us, Lord. 1985. 2.50 (ISBN 0-89536-728-9, 5812). CSS of Ohio.
Campbell, Robert, ed. Skeet Shooting with D. Lee Braun: A Remington Sportsmen's Library Bk. LC 67-10528. pap. 4.95 (ISBN 0-87502-068-2). Benjamin Co.
--Trapshooting with D. Lee Braun & the Remington Pros: A Remington Sportsmen's Library Bk. pap. 5.95 (ISBN 0-87502-069-0). Benjamin Co.
Campbell, Robert A., et al, eds. Advances in Polyamine Research, Vol. 1. 300p. 1978. text ed. 50.50 (ISBN 0-89004-189-X). Raven.
--Advances in Polyamine Research, Vol. 2. LC 77-83687. 395p. 1978. 59.00 (ISBN 0-89004-194-6). Raven.
Campbell, Robert B., jt. auth. see Remmling, Gunter W.
Campbell, Robert E. & Shaltry, Paul, eds. Perpectives on Adult Career Development & Guidance. 197p. 1980. 10.50 (ISBN 0-318-15530-3, RD181). Natl Ctr Res Voc Ed.
Campbell, Robert E., et al. Building Comprehensive Career Guidance Programs for Secondary Schools: A Handbook of Programs, Pratices & Models. 262p. 1978. 11.80 (ISBN 0-318-15399-8, RD147). Natl Ctr Res Voc Ed.
Campbell, Robert F. History of Basic Metals Price Control in World War Two. LC 77-76654. (Columbia University Studies in the Social Sciences: No. 541). Repr. of 1948 ed. 21.00 (ISBN 0-404-51541-X). AMS Pr.
Campbell, Robert G. Neutral Rights & Obligations in the Anglo-Boer War. LC 78-63926. (Johns Hopkins University. Studies in the Social Sciences. Twenty-Sixth Ser. 1908: 4-6). Repr. of 1908 ed. 17.50 (ISBN 0-404-61176-1). AMS Pr.
--The Panhandle Aspect of the Chaquaqua Plateau. (Graduate Studies: No. 11). (Illus.). 118p. (Orig.). 1976. pap. 5.00 (ISBN 0-89672-021-7). Tex Tech Pr.
Campbell, Robert J. Morality of Caring: Ethical Issues in Psychiatry. 265p. 1986. 17.95x (ISBN 0-88048-010-6, 48-010-6). Am Psychiatric.
Campbell, Robert J., ed. Psychiatric Dictionary. 5th ed. 1981. 37.95 (ISBN 0-19-502817-1). Oxford U Pr.
Campbell, Robert M. First Twenty-One: Life, History & Thoughts. 272p. (Orig.). 1984. pap. 6.95 (ISBN 0-9613542-0-8). R M Campbell.
Campbell, Robert N. The New Science: Self-Esteem Psychology. LC 84-5085. 354p. (Orig.). 1984. lib. bdg. 24.75 (ISBN 0-8191-3892-4); pap. text ed. 14.25 (ISBN 0-8191-3893-2). U Pr of Amer.
Campbell, Robert R. James Duncan Campbell: A Memoir by His Son, Robert R. Campbell. LC 72-123565. (East Asian Monographs Ser: No. 38). 1970. pap. 11.00x (ISBN 0-674-47131-8). Harvard U Pr.
Campbell, Robert W. The Economics of Soviet Oil & Gas. LC 68-22277. (Resources for the Future Ser). (Illus.). 294p. 1968. 24.95x (ISBN 0-8018-0105-2). Johns Hopkins.
--The Economics of Soviet Oil & Gas. 294p. 1968. 24.95 (ISBN 0-8018-0105-2). Resources Future.
--Soviet Energy Technologies: Planning, Policy, Research & Development. LC 80-7562. 288p. 1980. 25.00x (ISBN 0-253-15965-2). Ind U Pr.
--Trends in the Soviet Oil & Gas Industry. LC 76-15940. (Resources for the Future Ser). (Illus.). 144p. 1977. 12.00x (ISBN 0-8018-1870-2). Johns Hopkins.
--Trends in the Soviet Oil & Gas Industry. 142p. 1977. 12.00 (ISBN 0-8018-1870-2). Resources Future.
Campbell, Robin, ed. see Seneca.
Campbell, Rod. Baby Animals. (Play-Slots Ser.). (Illus.). 14p. (gr. 1-3). 1984. pap. 2.95 board bk. (ISBN 0-590-07942-5). Scholastic Inc.
--Book of Board Games. (Illus.). 12p. 1984. 5.95 (ISBN 0-13-079872-X). P-H.
--Buster's Afternoon. (Buster Bks.). (Illus.). 16p. (ps-1). 1984. 5.95 (ISBN 0-911745-74-2, Bedrick Blackie). P Bedrick Bks.
--Buster's Morning. (Buster Bks.). (Illus.). 16p. (ps-1). 1984. 5.95 (ISBN 0-911745-73-4, Bedrick Blackie). P Bedrick Bks.
--Circus Monkeys. (Play-Slots Ser.). (Illus.). 14p. (ps). 1984. board bks. 2.95 (ISBN 0-590-07941-7). Scholastic Inc.
--Henry's Busy Day. LC 83-25905. (Illus.). 18p. (ps-1). 1984. 6.95 (ISBN 0-670-80024-4, Viking Kestrel). Viking.
--Look Inside! All Kinds of Places. (Look Inside! Ser.). (Illus.). 16p. (ps). 1984. bds. 4.95 (ISBN 0-911745-72-6, Bedrick Blackie). P Bedrick Bks.
--Look Inside! Land, Sea, Air. (Look Inside! Ser.). (Illus.). 16p. (ps). 1984. bds. 4.95 (ISBN 0-911745-71-8, Bedrick Blackie). P Bedrick Bks.
--Misty's Mischief. LC 84-19617. 20p. (ps-1). 1985. 6.95 (ISBN 0-670-80149-6). Viking.
--Pet Shop. (Play-Slots Ser.). (Illus.). 14p. (gr. 1-3). 1981. bds. 2.95 (ISBN 0-590-07940-9). Scholastic Inc.
--Toy Soldiers. (Play-Slots Ser.). (Illus.). 14p. (ps). 1984. board 2.95 (ISBN 0-590-07943-3). Scholastic Inc.
--Wheels. (Illus.). 10p. (ps). 1985. board bk. 7.95 (ISBN 0-911745-95-5, Bedrick Blackie). P Bedrick Bks.
Campbell, Roderick. Israel & the New Covenant. LC 82-142978. 364p. 1982. Repr. of 1954 ed. 12.95 (ISBN 0-939404-01-X). Geneva Ministr.
--Israel & the New Covenant. 1982. 12.95 (ISBN 0-87552-161-4). Presby & Reformed.
Campbell, Roger. Justice Through Restitution: Making Criminals Pay. LC 77-6312. 1977. pap. 4.95 (ISBN 0-915134-10-1). Mott Media.
--Let's Communicate. (Orig.). 1979. pap. 3.50 (ISBN 0-87508-060-X). Chr Lit.
--Lord, I'm Afraid. (Orig.). 1980. pap. 2.50 (ISBN 0-87508-056-1). Chr Lit.
--Staying Positive in a Negative World. 132p. 1984. pap. 3.95 (ISBN 0-89693-377-6). Victor Bks.
--Weight! A Better Way to Lose. LC 76-14647. 128p. 1976. pap. 3.95 (ISBN 0-88207-735-X). Victor Bks.
--You Can Win. 132p. 1985. pap. 4.50 (ISBN 0-89693-317-2). Victor Bks.
Campbell, Roger F. Herbert W. Armstrong & His Worldwide Church of God. 1974. pap. 3.95 (ISBN 0-87508-061-8). Chr Lit.
--A Place to Hide. 108p. 1983. pap. 3.95 (ISBN 0-88207-383-4). Victor Bks.
--Prosperity in the End Time. 1983. pap. 2.95 (ISBN 0-87508-055-3). Chr Lit.
Campbell, Ron. Bovine Excrement. LC 84-91313. 51p. 1985. 6.95 (ISBN 0-533-06404-X). Vantage.
--Flying Training for the Private Pilot Licence: Instrument Flying, Radio Navigation & Instrument Approach Procedure. 1981. Instructor Manual, 308pp. pap. 18.00x (ISBN 0-246-11695-1, Pub. by Granada England); Student Manual, 200pp. pap. 18.00x (ISBN 0-246-11697-8). Sheridan.
--Flying Training for the Private Pilot Licence: Teaching & Learning. 80p. 1981. pap. 10.00x (ISBN 0-246-11694-3, Pub. by Granada England). Sheridan.
--Flying Training for the Private Pilot Licence. 1981. Teacher's Manual, 624pp. pap. 30.00x (ISBN 0-246-11688-9, Pub. by Granada England); Student Manual, Part 1, 256pp. pap. 13.00x (ISBN 0-246-11689-7); Student Manual, Part 2, 376pp. pap. 17.00x (ISBN 0-246-11690-0); Night Rating, 54pp. pap. 10.00x (ISBN 0-246-11691-9). Sheridan.
Campbell, Ron & Hall, Joss. PPL Revision: Twelve Hundred Questions & Answers for the Private Pilot. 200p. 1982. pap. cancelled (ISBN 0-246-11882-2, Pub. by Granada England). Sheridan.
Campbell, Ron & Tempest, Barry. Basic Aerobatics. 128p. 1984. 19.50x (ISBN 0-246-11705-2, Pub. by Granada England). Sheridan.
Campbell, Ronald F., et al. The Organization & Control of American Schools. 4th ed. (Educational Administration Ser.: No. C21). 520p. 1980. text ed. 26.95 (ISBN 0-675-08164-5). Merrill.
Campbell, Rosemary G., jt. auth. see Campbell, Colin D.
Campbell, Ross. How to Really Love Your Child. 1982. pap. 2.95 (ISBN 0-451-13437-0, Sig). NAL.
Campbell, Roy. Adamastor. LC 71-98828. 1971. Repr. of 1950 ed. lib. bdg. 15.00 (ISBN 0-8371-3079-4, CAAD). Greenwood.
--Broken Record, Reminiscenses. LC 70-131657. 1971. Repr. of 1934 ed. 29.00 (ISBN 0-403-00544-2). Scholarly.
--Flaming Terrapin. LC 74-131658. 1970. Repr. of 1924 ed. 29.00 (ISBN 0-403-00545-0). Scholarly.
--Flowering Reeds: Poems. LC 78-131659. 1971. Repr. of 1933 ed. 29.00x (ISBN 0-403-00546-9). Scholarly.
--Lorca: An Appreciation of His Poetry. LC 76-137665. (Studies in Poetry, No. 38). 1971. Repr. of 1952 ed. lib. bdg. 26.95x (ISBN 0-8383-1226-8). Haskell.
--Measuring the Sales & Profit Results of Advertising: A Managerial Approach. 133p. 1969. 10.00 (ISBN 0-318-13467-5, 19). Assn Natl Advertisers.
--Wayzgoose: A South African Satire. LC 72-131660. 1971. Repr. of 1928 ed. 29.00x (ISBN 0-403-00547-7). Scholarly.
Campbell, Roy & Connolly, Christopher. Mass at Dawn: A Poem Set to Music. 16p. 1984. pap. 25.00x (ISBN 0-930126-15-7). Typographeum.
Campbell, Roy & Alexander, Peter, eds. The Selected Poems of Roy Campbell. 1982. 22.50x (ISBN 0-19-211946-X). Oxford U Pr.
Campbell, Roy, tr. see Bentley, Eric.
Campbell, Roy, tr. see Calderon de la Barca, Pedro.
Campbell, Roy, tr. see Eca de Queiroz.
Campbell, Roy J. Janey. 192p. 1982. 9.00 (ISBN 0-682-49875-0). Exposition Pr FL.
--Peggy. 187p. 1983. 10.00 (ISBN 0-682-49952-8). Exposition Pr FL.
Campbell, Russell. Cinema Strikes Back: Radical Filmmaking in the United States, 1930-1942. Kirkpatrick, Diane, ed. LC 82-4819. (Studies in Cinema: No. 20). 398p. 1982. 44.95 (ISBN 0-8357-1330-X). Univ Microfilms.
Campbell, Russell, compiled by. Photographic Theory for the Motion Picture Cameraman. LC 70-130298. (Illus.). 160p. 1981. pap. 6.95 (ISBN 0-498-07776-4). A S Barnes.
Campbell, Russell N. & Lindfors, Judith W. Insights into English Structure: A Programmed Course. 1969. pap. text ed. 14.95 (ISBN 0-13-467571-1). P-H.
Campbell, Russell N., jt. auth. see King, Harold V.
Campbell, S., ed. Sampling & Analysis of Rain - STP 823. 96p. 1984. pap. 18.00 (ISBN 0-8031-0266-6, 04-823000-17). ASTM.
Campbell, S. C. Only Begotten Sonnets: A Reconstruction of Shakespeare's Sonnet Sequence. 241p. 1978. 21.50x (ISBN 0-8476-6135-0). Rowman.
Campbell, S. C., ed. see Shakespeare, William.
Campbell, S. L. Singular Systems of Differential Equations, Vol. 2. (Research Notes in Mathematics Ser.: No. 61). 200p. 1982. pap. text ed. 22.95 (ISBN 0-273-08516-6). Pitman Pub MA.
Campbell, S. L. & Meyer, C. D. Generalized Inverses of Linear Transformations. (Surveys & References Ser.: No. 4). 284p. 1979. text ed. 54.50 (ISBN 0-273-08422-4). Pitman Pub MA.
Campbell, S. L., ed. Recent Applications of Generalized Inverses. (Research Notes in Mathematics Ser.: No. 66). 300p. 1982. pap. text ed. 27.95 (ISBN 0-273-08550-6). Pitman Pub MA.
Campbell, Sally. Microcomputer Software Design: How to Develop Complex Application Programs. (Illus.). 232p. 1983. 21.95 (ISBN 0-13-580639-9); pap. 12.95 (ISBN 0-13-580621-6). P-H.
Campbell, Sally R. The Confident Consumer. LC 81-20013. (Illus.). 368p. 1982. text ed. 16.00 (ISBN 0-87006-403-7). Goodheart.
--The Confident Consumer. rev. ed. (Illus.). 368p. 1984. text ed. 17.00 (ISBN 0-87006-486-X); wkbk. 4.00 (ISBN 0-87006-427-4). Goodheart.
Campbell, Sandy. B: Twenty-Nine Letters from Coconut Grove. (Illus.). 1974. wrappers, ltd. ed. 20.00x (ISBN 0-917366-03-4). S Campbell.
Campbell, Sara, ed. The Blue Four: Galka Scheyer Collection. LC 76-13890. (Illus.). 160p. 1976. pap. 14.95 (ISBN 0-295-95959-2, Pub by Norton Simon Mus). U of Wash Pr.
Campbell, Sarah F., ed. see Piaget, Jean.
Campbell, Scott. AMX: A Source Book. (Illus.). 144p. (Orig.). (YA) 1981. pap. 12.95 (ISBN 0-934780-08-0). Bookman Dan.
--Javelin: A Source Book. (Illus.). 144p. 1983. pap. 12.95 (ISBN 0-934780-17-X). Bookman Dan.
Campbell, Scott D. The Complete Book of Birdhouse Construction for Woodworkers. (Crafts Ser.). 48p. (Orig.). 1984. pap. 1.95 (ISBN 0-486-24407-5). Dover.
Campbell, Sid. Falcon Claw: The Motion Picture. Morales, Mahi, ed. 115p. 1980. pap. 7.50 (ISBN 0-937610-01-1). Dimond Pubs.
--Ninja Shuriken Throwing: The Weapon of Stealth. (Illus.). 152p. (Orig.). 1984. pap. 12.00 (ISBN 0-87364-273-2). Paladin Pr.
--Shadows of Darkness: Secrets of the Night Fighter. (Illus.). 176p. (Orig.). 1985. pap. 12.00 (ISBN 0-87364-329-1). Paladin Pr.
Campbell, Sid & Logsdon, Jim. This Book Could Save Your Life. (Illus.). 16p. pap. 1.80x (ISBN 0-686-36029-X). Self Defense.
Campbell, Sid & Warren, Nelson. The Bay Area Roller Skaters Guide. (Illus.). 80p. 1985. pap. 28.00 (ISBN 0-318-04543-5). Gong Prods.
Campbell, Sid, jt. auth. see Lee, Greglon Y.
Campbell, Sid, et al. Two Thousand & One Martial Arts Questions, Kung Fu, Karate, Tae Kwon Do, Kenpo Students Should Know. LC 80-67769. (Illus.). 150p. 1980. pap. text ed. 8.95 (ISBN 0-686-28062-8). Dimond Pubs.
Campbell, Stafford. The Yachting Book of Celestial Navigation. (Triton Sailing Bks.). (Illus.). 160p. 1984. pap. 9.95 (ISBN 0-396-08388-9). Dodd.
--The Yachting Book of Coastwise Navigation. 192p. 1984. pap. 9.95 (ISBN 0-396-08356-0). Dodd.
--The Yachting Book of Practical Navigation. (Illus.). 320p. 1985. 23.95 (ISBN 0-396-08561-X). Dodd.
Campbell, Stan. Any Old Time, Bk. 3. 80p. 1985. pap. 5.95 (ISBN 0-317-18832-1). Victor Bks.
--Any Old Time, Bk. 4. 80p. 1985. pap. 5.95 (ISBN 0-89693-640-6). Victor Bks.
Campbell, Stanley W. Slave Catchers: Enforcement of the Fugitive Slave Law, 1850-1860. 1972. pap. 1.95x (ISBN 0-393-00626-3, Norton Lib). Norton.
--The Slave Catchers: Enforcement of the Fugitive Slave Law, 1850-1860. LC 79-109463. ix, 236p. 1970. 20.00 (ISBN 0-8078-1141-6). U. of NC Pr.
Campbell, Stephanie, ed. As We Seek God: International Reflections on Contemporary Benedictine Monasticism. (Cistercian Studies Ser.: No. 70). 1983. pap. 7.95 (ISBN 0-87907-868-5). Cistercian Pubns.
Campbell, Stephen K. Flaws & Fallacies in Statistical Thinking. LC 73-5655. (Illus.). 192p. 1974. pap. 15.95 (ISBN 0-13-322214-4). P-H.
Campbell, Stu. Home Water Supply: How to Find, Filter, Store & Conserve It. Griffith, Roger, ed. LC 83-1635. (Illus.). 280p. (Orig.). 1983. pap. 12.95 (ISBN 0-88266-324-0). Garden Way Pub.
--Let It Rot! The Gardener's Guide to Composting. LC 74-75469. (Illus.). 152p. 1975. pap. 5.95 (ISBN 0-88266-049-7). Garden Way Pub.
--The Underground House Book. LC 80-14992. (Illus.). 208p. (Orig.). 1980. pap. 10.95 (ISBN 0-88266-166-3). Garden Way Pub.
Campbell, Stuart. Ski with the Big Boys. LC 77-22846. 1977. pap. 8.95 (ISBN 0-8120-0875-8). Barron.
Campbell, Stuart L. The Second Empire Revisited: A Study in French Historiography. LC 77-20247. 1978. 28.00x (ISBN 0-8135-0856-8). Rutgers U Pr.
Campbell, Susan. Earth Community. (Illus.). 250p. 1985. pap. 8.95 (ISBN 0-939508-11-7). Mindbody.
--Expanding Your Teaching Potential: A Role Clarification Guide for Educators & Human Service Workers. enl. ed. LC 76-58637. (Mandala Series in Education). 1983. pap. 12.95 (ISBN 0-8290-0349-5). Irvington.
Campbell, Susan, ed. see McQuilkin, Robert.
Campbell, Susan M. Beyond the Power Struggle: Dealing with Conflict in Love & Work. LC 84-11846. 256p. (Orig.). 1984. pap. 7.95 (ISBN 0-915166-46-1). Impact Pubs Cal.
Campbell, Suzann K., ed. Pediatric Neurologic Physical Therapy. (Clinics in Physical Therapy Ser.: Vol. 5). (Illus.). 448p. 1984. text ed. 29.00 (ISBN 0-443-08241-3). Churchill.
Campbell, T. E. Colonial Caroline: A History of Caroline County, Virginia. 1974. Repr. 20.00 (ISBN 0-685-47895-5). Dietz.
Campbell, T. R., jt. auth. see Paterson, W. E.
Campbell, T. S. Financial Institutions, Markets & Economic Activity. 1982. 33.95x (ISBN 0-07-009691-0). McGraw.
Campbell, T. W., jt. auth. see Stille, John K.
Campbell, Terry L., jt. auth. see Gleim, Irvin N.

Campbell, Tessa. Children's Picture Atlas. LC 77-17968. (Children's Guides Ser.). (Illus.). (gr. 3 up). 1978. PLB 7.95 (ISBN 0-88436-465-8, 35464). EMC.

Campbell, Thomas. Complete Poetical Works of Thomas Campbell. Robertson, J. Logie, ed. LC 68-24901. (Studies in Poetry, No. 38). 1969. Repr. of 1907 ed. lib. bdg. 41.95x (ISBN 0-8383-0924-0). Haskell.

--Cyclopaedia of English Poetry. 1977. Repr. of 1874 ed. 50.00 (ISBN 0-89984-160-0). Century Bookbindery.

--An Essay on English Poetry: With Notices of the British Poets. 1973. Repr. of 1848 ed. 35.00 (ISBN 0-8274-1542-7). R West.

--Life & Times of Petrarch: With Notices of Boccaccio & His Illustrious Contemporaries, 2 vols. 1843. Repr. 100.00 (ISBN 0-8274-2875-8). R West.

--Life of Petrarch. 444p. 1981. Repr. of 1841 ed. lib. bdg. 150.00 (ISBN 0-89987-119-4). Darby Bks.

--The Poetical Works. Hill, Alfred, ed. LC 73-39665. (Select Bibliographies Reprint Ser). 1972. Repr. of 1875 ed. 19.75 (ISBN 0-8369-9932-0). Ayer Co Pubs.

Campbell, Thomas, ed. see Shakespeare, William.

Campbell, Thomas C. & Reierson, Gary B. The Gift of Adminstration. LC 80-24594. 138p. 1981. pap. 6.95 (ISBN 0-664-24357-6). Westminster.

Campbell, Thomas F. Daniel E. Morgan, 1877-1949: The Good Citizen in Politics. (Illus.). 1966. 10.00 (ISBN 0-8295-0054-5). UPB.

Campbell, Thomas J. Jesuits: Fifteen Thirty-Four to Nineteen Twenty-One. LC 77-82144. (Reprints Ser). 1970. Repr. of 1921 ed. lib. bdg. 45.00 (ISBN 0-87821-018-0). Milford Hse.

--The Jesuits, 1534-1921, 2 vols. 1977. lib. bdg. 250.00 (ISBN 0-8490-2093-X). Gordon Pr.

Campbell, Thomas L., tr. from Gr. Dionysius the Pseudo-Areopagite: The Ecclesiastical Hierarchy. LC 81-40140. 236p. (Orig.). 1981. lib. bdg. 24.75 (ISBN 0-8191-1798-6); pap. text ed. 12.25 (ISBN 0-8191-1799-4). U Pr of Amer.

Campbell, Thomas M. Masquerade Peace: America's UN Policy, 1944-1945. LC 72-93328. 226p. 1973. 12.00 (ISBN 0-8130-0425-X). U Presses Fla.

--Movable School Goes to the Negro Farmer. Cremin, Lawrence A. & Barnard, Frederick A., eds. LC 78-101403. (American Education: Its Men, Institutions & Ideas, Ser. 1). 1969. Repr. of 1936 ed. 14.00 (ISBN 0-405-01398-1). Ayer Co Pubs.

Campbell, Thrane Lucille, ed. Correspondence Education Moves to the Year 2000: National Invitational Forum on Correspondence Education. 187p. 1984. 16.50 (ISBN 0-318-17783-8, SN47). Natl Ctr Res Voc Ed.

Campbell, Toby H. & Bendick, Marc, Jr. A Public Assistance Data Book. 344p. 1977. pap. 12.00x (ISBN 0-87766-207-X, 20300). Urban Inst.

Campbell, Tom. The Contemplative Stroller. (Illus.). 96p. 1982. pap. 4.95 (ISBN 0-9607506-1-4). News Rev Pub.

--The Left & Rights: A Conceptual Analysis of the Idea of Socialist Rights. (International Library of Welfare & Philosophy). 296p. (Orig.). 1983. pap. 12.95x (ISBN 0-7100-9085-4). Routledge & Kegan.

--Seven Theories of Human Society. 1981. text ed. 22.50x (ISBN 0-19-876104-X); pap. text ed. 8.95x (ISBN 0-19-876105-8). Oxford U Pr.

Campbell, Tom & Sinatra, Frank. Las Vegas. (Illus.). 1984. 15.95 (ISBN 0-19-540619-2). Skyline Press.

Campbell, Tony. Early Maps. LC 80-24787. (Illus.). 148p. 1981. 45.00 (ISBN 0-89659-191-3). Abbeville Pr.

Campbell, Viola, ed. Programas Para Reuniones Sociales y Banquetes. (Illus.). 64p. 1985. pap. 1.80 (ISBN 0-311-11011-8). Casa Bautista.

Campbell, Viola D. Juguemos. (Illus.). 199p. 1983. pap. 2.75 (ISBN 0-311-11006-1). Casa Bautista.

--Recreation Cristiana. (Illus.). 160p. (Span.). 1981. pap. 4.25 (ISBN 0-311-11037-1). Casa Bautista.

Campbell, Vivian, ed. A Christmas Anthology of Poetry & Painting. LC 79-51963. (Granger Poetry Library). 1980. Repr. of 1947 ed. 27.50x (ISBN 0-89609-181-3). Granger Bk.

Campbell, W., jt. auth. see Clark, S. H.

Campbell, W. Glenn, jt. auth. see Campbell, Rita R.

Campbell, W. H., jt. ed. see Matsushita, S.

Campbell, W. J. Medical School Admission Interviews: A Success System That Works! 144p. (Orig.). 1984. pap. 5.95 (ISBN 0-668-06005-0, 6005-0). Arco.

Campbell, W. John. Henry VI, Parts 1, 2, 3 Notes. 65p. (Orig.). 1985. pap. text ed. 3.25 (ISBN 0-8220-0032-6). Cliffs.

--Henry VIII Notes. 52p. (Orig.). 1984. pap. 3.95 (ISBN 0-8220-0038-5). Carlton.

--Lysistrata, the Birds, the Clouds, the Frogs Notes. 78p. 1984. pap. text ed. 3.25 (ISBN 0-8220-0776-2). Cliffs.

--No Exit & the Flies Notes. 54p. 1983. pap. text ed. 2.95 (ISBN 0-8220-0904-8). Cliffs.

Campbell, W. L., ed. see Nagarjuna.

Campbell, Walter S. Mountain Men. LC 77-99620. (Essay Index Reprint Ser). 1937. 25.00 (ISBN 0-8369-1397-3). Ayer Co Pubs.

Campbell, Wanza J. Runaway Rapture. 1983. pap. 3.75 (ISBN 0-8217-1231-4). Zebra.

Campbell, Wilfred. At the Mermaid Inn: Wilfred Campbell, Archibald Lampman, Duncan Campbell Scott in the Globe, 1892-93. LC 79-313103. (Literature of Canada, Poetry & Prose in Reprint Ser.: No. 21). pap. 94.30 (ISBN 0-317-27023-0, 2023642). Bks Demand UMI.

Campbell, Will & Campbell, Bonnie. God on Earth: The Lord's Prayer for Our Time. (Illus.). 128p. 1983. pap. 12.95 (ISBN 0-8245-0586-7). Crossroad NY.

Campbell, Will D. Brother to a Dragonfly. 1980. pap. 8.95 (ISBN 0-8264-0032-9). Continuum.

Campbell, William. Formosa Under the Dutch. LC 77-86948. Repr. of 1903 ed. 40.00 (ISBN 0-404-16700-4). AMS Pr.

--Villi the Clown. 272p. 1983. 15.95 (ISBN 0-571-11794-5). Faber & Faber.

Campbell, William, ed. Materials for a History of the Reign of Henry VII from Original Documents Preserved in the Public Record Office, 2 vols. (Rolls Ser.: No. 60). Repr. of 1877 ed. Set. 120.00 (ISBN 0-317-16783-9). Kraus Repr.

Campbell, William A. North Carolina Guidebook for Registers of Deeds. 4th ed. 109p. 1982. 7.00 (ISBN 0-686-39431-3). U of NC Inst Gov.

--North Carolina Privilege License Taxation. 70p. 1981. 6.50 (ISBN 0-686-39440-2). U of NC Inst Gov.

--Notary Public Guidebook for North Carolina. 5th ed. 73p. 1984. 4.00 (ISBN 0-686-39479-8). U of NC Inst Gov.

--Property Tax Collection in North Carolina. 2nd. Rev. ed. 334p. 1974. 5.00 (ISBN 0-686-39435-6). U of NC Inst Gov.

Campbell, William A. & Soto, Victoria H. The Constitutionality of in Rem Tax Lien Foreclosures: Recent Cases. LC 81-621042. (Property Tax Bulletin: No. 54). 1980. 1.00. U of NC Inst Gov.

Campbell, William A., ed. Guidebook for North Carolina Registers of Deeds. rev. ed. 109p. 1982. pap. 7.00 (ISBN 0-686-17568-9). U of NC Inst Gov.

Campbell, William C., ed. Trichinella & Trichinosis. 606p. 1983. 95.00x (ISBN 0-306-41140-7, Plenum Pr). Plenum Pub.

Campbell, William E. Behavior Problems in Dogs. (Illus.). 306p. 1975. 20.00 (ISBN 0-939674-03-3). Am Vet Pubns.

Campbell, William G., et al. Form & Style: Theses, Reports, Term Papers. 6th ed. LC 81-82571. 1981. pap. 11.50 (ISBN 0-395-31689-8). HM.

Campbell, William H. Anthropology for the People: A Refutation of the Theory of the Adamic Origin of All Races. LC 72-6467. (Black Heritage Library Collection Ser). 1972. Repr. of 1891 ed. 21.00 (ISBN 0-8369-9154-0). Ayer Co Pubs.

Campbell, William H., jt. auth. see Campbell, Elizabeth W.

Campbell, Zerah A. Wait Don't Pull That Plug: The Story of Timmy. 96p. 1979. 5.00 (ISBN 0-682-49278-7). Exposition Pr FL.

Campbell-Adams, Neville. The Development of An Executive Training Program in a Medium-Sized Bank. 1983. 7.75 (ISBN 0-8062-2223-9). Carlton.

Campbell-Allen, D., jt. auth. see Davis, E. H.

Campbell-Ferguson, H. J., jt. auth. see Lowrie, R. S.

Campbell-Harding, Valerie. Textures in Embroidery. (Illus.). 96p. 1985. pap. 8.95 (ISBN 0-7134-4625-0, Pub. by Batsford England). David & Charles.

Campbell-Johnson, Alan. Mission with Mountbatten. rev. ed. 1951. pap. 2.45 (ISBN 0-88253-129-8). Ind-US Inc.

--Mission with Mountbatten. LC 85-4019. 400p. 1985. pap. 10.95 (ISBN 0-689-70697-9, 329). Atheneum.

--Mission with Mountbatten. 400p. 1985. 10.95 (ISBN 0-689-70697-9). Atheneum.

Campbell-Jones, Simon, ed. At the Edge of the Universe. LC 83-6680. (Illus.). 172p. 1983. 9.95x (ISBN 0-87663-433-1). Universe.

--At the Frontiers of Medicine. LC 83-4914. (Illus.). 172p. 1983. 9.95x (ISBN 0-87663-435-8). Universe.

Campbell-Kelley, M. An Introduction to Macros. (Computer Monograph Ser.: Vol. 21). 114p. 1973. 24.75 (ISBN 0-444-19563-7). Elsevier.

Campbell-Kelly, Martin. The Charles Babbage Institute Reprint Series for the History of Computing. 1983. write for info. limited edition (ISBN 0-938228-01-3). Tomash Pubs.

Campbell-Kelly, Martin & Williams, M. R., eds. The Moore School Lectures. (Charles Babbage Institute Reprint Series for the History of Computing). (Illus.). 736p. 1985. text ed. 50.00x (ISBN 0-262-03109-4). MIT Pr.

Campbell-Morgan, G. Minor Prophets. 160p. 1960. 10.95 (ISBN 0-8007-0208-5). Revell.

Campbell Reid, D. A. & Tubiang, R. Mutilating Injuries of the Hand. 2nd ed. (G. E. M. Monographs: Vol. 3). (Illus.). 1984. text ed. 55.00 (ISBN 0-443-02369-7). Churchill.

Campden-Main, Simon M. A Field Guide to the Snakes of South Vietnam. (Illus.). 1983. pap. 9.95 (ISBN 0-9612494-0-4). Herpetological Search.

Campderros, Daniel. Bosquejos Biblicos, Tomo III. 96p. 1981. pap. 2.50 (ISBN 0-311-43033-3). Casa Bautista.

--Bosquejos Biblicos Tomo I: Antiguo Testamento. 96p. 1981. pap. 2.50 (ISBN 0-311-43025-2). Casa Bautista.

--Bosquejos Biblicos Tomo II. 96p. 1981. pap. 2.50 (ISBN 0-311-43026-0). Casa Bautista.

Campe-Aguilar, Patricia, ed. see Clark, Jeff.

Campell, Eva M. Satire in the Early English Drama. 1978. Repr. of 1914 ed. lib. bdg. 17.50 (ISBN 0-8495-0813-4). Arden Lib.

Campell, J. E. & Inderwood, J. H., eds. Application of Fracture Mechanics for Selection of Metallic Structural Materials. 1982. 83.00 (ISBN 0-87170-136-7). ASM.

Campell, James B. Mapping the Land: Ariel Imagery for Land Use Information. Knight, C. Gregory, ed. 85p. (Orig.). 1983. pap. 5.00 (ISBN 0-89291-167-0). Assn Am Geographers.

Campell, John H. Logistics: Issues for the Eighties. Nishi, Masao, et al, eds. 223p. 1982. pap. 15.45 (ISBN 0-86551-017-2). Corinthian.

Campell, Leslie L. Galvanomagnetic & Thermogmagnetic Effects: The Hall & Allied Phenomena. (Illus.). 1923. 23.00 (ISBN 0-384-07280-1). Johnson Repr.

Campen. The Selection Administration & Content of Health Insurance Plans for Public School District Personnel. (Research Bulletin: No. 23). pap. 0.69 (ISBN 0-685-57186-6). Assn Sch Busn.

Campen, Henry & Drennan, James C. A Manual for North Carolina Jury Commissioners. 2nd ed. (Illus.). 22p. 1983. 4.00. U of NC Inst Gov.

Campen, Joseph A. Van see Sholiton, Robert D. & Van Campen, Joseph A.

Campen, Richard N. Architecture of the Western Reserve, 1800-1900. LC 70-116382. (Illus.). 272p. 1971. 15.00 (ISBN 0-8295-0196-7). Kent St U Pr.

--Chautauqua Impressions: Architecture & Ambience. LC 83-451028. (Illus.). 144p. 1984. pap. 14.95 (ISBN 0-9601356-3-4). West Summit.

--Outdoor Sculpture in Ohio. LC 79-57393. (Illus.). 176p. 1980. 20.00 (ISBN 0-9601356-2-6). West Summit.

--Sanibel & Captiva-Enchanting Islands. 3rd ed. LC 77-76136. (Illus.). 96p. 1982. 8.95 (ISBN 0-9601356-0-X). West Summit.

Campen, S. I. Van see Van Campen, S. I.

Campenhausen, Hans Von. Virgin Birth in the Theology of the Ancient Church. LC 64-55217. (Studies in Historical Theology: No. 2). 1964. pap. 10.00x (ISBN 0-8401-0322-0). A R Allenson.

Campenhausen, Hans von see Von Campenhausen, Hans.

Campenhausen, Hansvon see Von Campenhausen, Hans.

Camper, Frank. The Mission. (Orig.). 1979. pap. 1.75 (ISBN 0-532-17243-4). Woodhill.

--Sand Castles. (Orig.). 1980. pap. 2.25 (ISBN 0-532-23132-5). Woodhill.

Campese, V. M. & Hsueh, W. A., eds. The Kidney in Hypertension. (Journal: American Journal of Nephrology: Vol. 3, No. 2-3). (Illus.). vi, 140p. 1983. pap. 43.50 (ISBN 3-8055-3648-8). S Karger.

Campfield, Regis W. Estate Planning & Drafting. 1104p. 1984. pap. 45.00 (ISBN 0-317-19188-8, 4836). Commerce.

--Estate Planning & Drafting. LC 84-71854. (Illus.). 1055p. write for info. Amer Bar Assn.

--Instruments & Forms Supplement to Estate Planning & Drafting. 224p. 1985. pap. 20.00 (ISBN 0-317-19189-6, 4835). Commerce.

Camphor, Alexander P. Missionary Story Sketches: Folk-Lore from Africa. facsimile ed. LC 79-173603. (Black Heritage Library Collection). Repr. of 1909 ed. 20.00 (ISBN 0-8369-8915-5). Ayer Co Pubs.

Campillo, A. Algebroid Curves in Positive Characteristic. (Lecture Notes in Mathematics Ser.: Vol. 813). 168p. 1980. pap. text ed. 15.00 (ISBN 0-387-10022-9). Springer-Verlag.

Campinchi, R., et al. Uveitis: Immunologic & Allergic Phenomena. Golden, Bruce & Givoiset, Mariette, trs. (Illus.). 836p. 1973. photocopy ed. 116.75x (ISBN 0-398-02710-2). C C Thomas.

Camping, Elizabeth. Living Through History: The Russian Revolution. (Living Through History Ser.). (Illus.). 72p. (gr. 7-12). 1985. 14.95 (ISBN 0-7134-4671-4, Pub. by Batsford England). David & Charles.

Campio, L., et al, eds. Role of Medroxyprogesterone in Endocrine-Related Tumors, Vol. 2. 230p. 1983. text ed. 32.00 (ISBN 0-89004-865-7). Raven.

Campion, Alan. Bees at the Bottom of the Garden. (Illus.). 112p. 1985. pap. 6.95 (ISBN 0-7136-2433-7, Pub. by A & C Black UK). Sterling.

Campion, C. T., tr. see Schweitzer, Albert.

Campion, Daniel. Calypso. (Illus.). 40p. (Orig.). 1981. pap. 3.00 (ISBN 0-9603794-1-X). Syncline.

Campion, Donald R. & Louapre, Albert C., eds. Documents of the Thirty-Third General Congregation of the Society of Jesus: An English Translation of the Official Latin Texts. LC 84-80080. 116p. pap. 3.00 (ISBN 0-912422-64-5). Inst Jesuit.

Campion, Edith. Back to Back. (Orig.). 1986. pap. 8.95 (ISBN 0-89407-041-X). Strawberry Hill.

Campion, Edmund. A Historie of Ireland. LC 41-6539. 1977. Repr. of 1633 ed. 35.00x (ISBN 0-8201-1191-0). Schol Facsimiles.

Campion, Frank. The AMA & U. S. Health Policy since 1940. (Illus.). 512p. 1984. 25.00 (ISBN 0-914091-57-3). Chicago Review.

Campion, Joan. Gisi Fleischmann & the Jewish Fight for Survival. (Illus.). 150p. (Orig.). 1983. pap. 11.95 (ISBN 0-686-39695-2). Dvorion Bks.

--To Save the Rest of Them: Gisi Fleischmann & the Rescue of Central European Jews. 2nd, rev. ed. (Illus.). 196p. 1985. lib. bdg. 18.95 (ISBN 0-9614649-0-9); pap. text ed. 10.95 (ISBN 0-9614649-1-7). G Hein.

Campion, John, tr. see De la Cruz, Sov J.

Campion, Kathy, jt. auth. see Campion, Mike.

Campion, Lee. Photo Montage. 1980. 10.95 (ISBN 0-85936-199-3, Pub. by Midas Bks England). Intl Spec Bk.

Campion, Leslie. The Family of Edmund Campion. 58p. 1975. 7.50 (ISBN 0-7050-0034-6). Attic Pr.

Campion, Margaret R. Hydrotheraphy in Paediatrics. 256p. 1985. 31.00 (ISBN 0-87189-106-9, Pub by W. Heinemann). Aspen Systems.

--Hydrotherapy in Paediatrics. 256p. 1985. 31.00 (ISBN 0-87189-106-9, Pub. by W. Heinemann). Aspen Systems.

Campion, Michael & Zehr, Wilmer. Especially for Grandparents. (When Was the Last Time Ser.). (Illus.). 112p. (Orig.). 1980. pap. 5.95 (ISBN 0-87123-141-7, 210141). Bethany Hse.

--Especially for Husbands. (When Was the Last Time Ser.). (Illus.). 112p. 1978. pap. 5.95 (ISBN 0-87123-136-0, 210136). Bethany Hse.

--Especially for Parents. (When Was the Last Time Ser.). (Illus.). 112p. 1978. pap. 5.95 (ISBN 0-87123-137-9, 210137). Bethany Hse.

Campion, Mike & Campion, Kathy. Don't Bite the Dinosaur. (Andrew Ser.: No. 2). 1982. text ed. 1.95 (ISBN 0-8024-9447-1). Moody.

--The Very Special Stone. (Andrew Ser.: No. 4). 1982. pap. 1.95 (ISBN 0-8024-9449-8). Moody.

--Where Does the White Go When the Snow Melts? (Andrew Ser.: No. 1). 1982. 1.95 (ISBN 0-8024-9446-3). Moody.

Campion, Thomas. The Description of a Maske, in Honour of the Lord Hayes. LC 75-25214. (English Experience Ser.: No. 153). 20p. 1969. Repr. of 1607 ed. 8.00 (ISBN 90-221-0153-3). Walter J Johnson.

--Observations in the Art of English Poesie. LC 78-38164. (English Experience Ser.: No. 441). 52p. 1972. Repr. of 1602 ed. 7.00 (ISBN 90-221-0441-9). Walter J Johnson.

--The Selected Songs of Thomas Campion. Auden, W. H., ed. LC 71-152794. (Illus.). 168p. 1972. 15.00x (ISBN 0-87923-037-1); ltd. ed. 40.00 (ISBN 0-87923-036-3); pap. 10.00 (ISBN 0-87923-091-6). Godine.

--Songs & Masques: With Observations in the Art of English Poesy. Bullen, A. H., ed. 1973. Repr. of 1889 ed. lib. bdg. 30.00 (ISBN 0-8414-0150-0). Folcroft.

--Works of Thomas Campion. Davis, Walter R., ed. (Seventeenth Century Ser.). 1970. pap. 2.95x (ISBN 0-393-00439-2, Norton Lib). Norton.

Campion, Thomas, et al see Arkwright, G. E. P.

Campion, Walter A. The Six Ideas Which Govern & Shape the Growth of Civilizations. (A Managerial & Inventiveness Science Ser. Bk.). (Illus.). 1979. 77.55 (ISBN 0-89266-187-9). Am Classical Coll Pr.

Campkin, Marie. The Technique of Marquetry. (Illus.). 120p. 1984. pap. 9.95 (ISBN 0-7134-4624-2, Pub. by Batsford England). David & Charles.

Camplin, Paul. A New History of Muhlenberg County. LC 84-71350. (Illus.). 304p. 1985. 28.95 (ISBN 0-9613634-0-1). Caney Station Bks.

Campling, Elizabeth. Africa in the Twentieth Century. (Twentieth Century World History Ser.). (Illus.). 72p. (gr. 7 up). 1980. 14.95 (ISBN 0-7134-2492-3, Pub. by Batsford England). David & Charles.

Campling, Elizabeth, jt. auth. see Campling, Robert.

Campling, Jo, ed. Image of Ourselves: Women with Disabilities Talking. 160p. 1981. pap. 9.95x (ISBN 0-7100-0822-8). Routledge & Kegan.

Campling, Robert & Campling, Elizabeth. Living Through History: The French Revolution. (Living Through History Ser.). (Illus.). 72p. (gr. 7-12). 1984. 14.95 (ISBN 0-7134-3848-7, Pub. by Batsford England). David & Charles.

Campman, M. S., jt. auth. see McMurrey, David A.

Campo & Carpenter. William Everson: Poet from the San Joaquin. 1978. 10.00 (ISBN 0-912950-43-9); pap. 5.00 (ISBN 0-912950-44-7). Blue Oak.

Campo, Allan, jt. auth. see Bartlett, Lee.

Campo, Vincent, et al. The Middle of the Journey. (Twice a Year, but Last Two Years One Issue Only Ser.). 156p. write for info. V Campo.

Campo-Flores, Filemon, jt. auth. see Chang, Y. N.

Campolo, Anthony. Ideas for Social Action. 160p. (gr. 9-12). 1985. pap. 6.95 (ISBN 0-310-45251-1, 11375P, Pub. by Youth Specialities). Zondervan.

--Partly Right. 192p. 1985. 10.95 (ISBN 0-8499-0368-8, 0368-8). Word Bks.

--A Reasonable Faith. 208p. 1985. write for info. (ISBN 0-8499-3040-5, 3040-5). Word Bks.

--A Reasonable Faith: Responding to Secularism. 1983. 8.95 (ISBN 0-8499-0325-4). Word Bks.

--The Success Fantasy. LC 79-67852. 144p. 1980. pap. 4.95 (ISBN 0-88207-796-1). Victor Bks.

Campolo, Anthony, Jr. The Power Delusion. 168p. 1983. pap. 4.95 (ISBN 0-88207-292-7). Victor Bks.

Campos, Anthony J., ed. Mexican Folk Tales. LC 77-10603. 136p. 1977. pap. 4.95 (ISBN 0-8165-0560-8). U of Ariz Pr.

Campos, Emilio C., ed. Sensory Evaluation of Strabismus & Amblyopia in a Natural Environment. (Documenta Ophthalmologica Proceedings Ser.). 1984. lib. bdg. 34.50 (ISBN 90-6193-508-3, Pub. by Junks Pubs Netherlands). Kluwer Academic.

Campos, German J. B. The Argentine Supreme Court: The Court of Constitutional Guarantees. Brisk, William J., tr. from Span. viii, 143p. 1982. pap. 15.00x (ISBN 9-500621-14-2). Rothman.

Campos, Joachim J. History of the Portuguese in Bengal. LC 75-179176. (Illus.). Repr. of 1919 ed. 22.50 (ISBN 0-404-54806-7). AMS Pr.

Campos, John. Only a Little Planet. LC 84-90335. (The Poems & Drawings of John Campos Ser.). (Illus.). 78p. (Orig.). 1984. pap. 4.95 (ISBN 0-917021-00-2). Lighthouse Pr.

Campos, Joseph J., jt. auth. see Lamb, Michael E.

Campos, Jules. The Sculpture of Jose De Creeft. LC 72-16688. (Illus.). 238p. 1972. lib. bdg. 49.50 (ISBN 0-306-70294-0). Da Capo.

Campos, Pedro A. Economic Independence. (Puerto Rico Ser.). 1979. lib. bdg. 59.95 (ISBN 0-8490-2907-4). Gordon Pr.

--Writings of Pedro Albizu Campos. (Puerto Rico Ser.). 1979. lib. bdg. 69.95 (ISBN 0-8490-3016-1). Gordon Pr.

Campos, S., jt. auth. see Ford, S. F.

Campos-Boralevi, Lea. Bentham & the Oppressed. LC 84-14951. (European University Institute Series C: Political & Social Sciences No. 1). xii, 248p. 1984. 35.20x (ISBN 3-11-009974-8). De Gruyter.

Campos-De Metro, Joseph. The Slugger Heart & Other Stories. 172p. 1984. 12.95 (ISBN 0-15-183100-9). HarBraceJ.

Campos-Lopez, Enrique, ed. Renewable Resources: A Systematic Approach. 1980. 45.00 (ISBN 0-12-158350-3). Acad Pr.

Campos-Lopez, Enrique & Anderson, Robert J., eds. Natural Resources & Development in Arid & Semi-Arid Regions. 350p. 1982. lib. bdg. 29.00x (ISBN 0-86531-418-7). Westview.

Campra, Andre. L' Europe Galante. De Lajarte, Theodore, ed. (Chefs-d'Oeuvre Classiques de l'Opera Francais Ser: Vol. 4). (Illus.). 196p. (Fr.). 1972. pap. 25.00x (ISBN 0-8450-1104-9). Broude.

--Les Festes Venitiennes. Guilmant, Alexandre, ed. (Chefs-d'oeuvre classiques de l'opera francais Ser: Vol. 5). (Illus.). 346p. (Fr.). 1972. pap. 27.50x (ISBN 0-8450-1105-7). Broude.

--Tancrede. Guilmant, Alexandre, ed. (Chefs-d'oeuvre classiques de l'opera francais Ser.: Vol. 6). (Illus.). 354p. (Fr.). 1972. pap. 27.50x (ISBN 0-8450-1106-5). Broude.

Camp-Randolph, I. Lillian. I, Lillian, Here. LC 84-50157. 36p. (Orig.). 1985. pap. 6.00 (ISBN 0-934172-09-9). WIM Pubns.

Camps, jt. auth. see Gree.

Camps, et al. Gradwohl's Legal Medicine. 3rd ed. 742p. 1978. 83.50 (ISBN 0-7236-0310-3). PSG Pub Co.

Camps, Arnulf. Partners in Dialogue: Christianity & Other World Religions. Drury, John, tr. from Dutch. LC 82-18798. 272p. (Orig.). 1983. pap. 10.95 (ISBN 0-88344-378-3). Orbis Bks.

Camps, Luis, jt. auth. see Gree, Alain.

Camps, Miriam. First World Relationships: The Role of the OECD. 56p. (Orig.). 1975. pap. text ed. 4.75x (ISBN 0-686-83638-3). Allanheld.

Camps, Miriam & Diebold, William, Jr. The New Multilateralism: Can the World Trading System Be Saved. 72p. 1983. pap. 6.95 (ISBN 0-87609-003-X). Coun Foreign.

Camps, Miriam & Gwin, Catherine. Collective Management: The Reform of Global Economic Organizations. 371p. 1982. 21.95 (ISBN 0-07-009708-9). McGraw.

Camps, Miriam & Hirono, Ryokichi. The Trilateral Countries in the International Economy of the 1980's. 1982. write for info. Trilateral Comm.

Camps, W. A. An Introduction to Homer. 1980. 19.95x (ISBN 0-19-872099-8); pap. 8.95x (ISBN 0-19-872101-3). Oxford U Pr.

--An Introduction to Virgil's Aeneid. (Orig.). 1969. pap. 10.95x (ISBN 0-19-872024-6). Oxford U Pr.

Camps, W. A., ed. see Propertius.

Campsey, B. J. & Brigham, Eugene F. Introduction to Financial Management. 704p. 1985. text ed. 32.95x (ISBN 0-03-059666-1); instr's. manual 19.95x (ISBN 0-03-059667-X); study guide 12.95x (ISBN 0-03-059668-8). Dryden Pr.

Campus Crusade for Christ. How to Make Your Mark. 540p. (Orig.). 1983. pap. 8.95 (ISBN 0-86605-142-2). Campus Crusade.

Campus Crusade for Christ Staff. Discovery II. 1980. pap. 2.95 saddlestitched (ISBN 0-918956-63-3). Campus Crusade.

--Game Plan II. 100p. 1980. pap. text ed. 3.50 (ISBN 0-918956-64-1). Campus Crusade.

Campus Crusade Staff. Insights: Building a Successful Youth Ministry, Vol. I. (Insight Ser.). (Orig.). 1981. pap. text ed. 5.95 (ISBN 0-86605-017-5). Campus Crusade.

Campwell, Olwen W. Thomas Love Peacock. 1978. Repr. of 1953 ed. lib. bdg. 25.00 (ISBN 0-8482-3531-2). Norwood Edns.

Camras, Marvin, ed. Magnetic Tape Recording. (Illus.). 512p. 1985. 54.50 (ISBN 0-442-21774-9). Van Nos Reinhold.

Camurati, Mireya. Enfoques: Temas De Comentario Oral y Escrito. 1980. pap. text ed. 10.95 (ISBN 0-669-01919-4). Heath.

Camus. The Stranger. (Book Notes Ser.). 1985. pap. 2.50 (ISBN 0-8120-3543-7). Barron.

Camus, A. L'etranger. Bree, G. & Lynes, C., eds. 1955. pap. 13.95 (ISBN 0-13-530790-2). P-H.

Camus, A. Le see Le Camus, A.

Camus, Albert. Actuelles, 3 tomes. Incl. Tome I. (1944-1948) pap. 7.95 (ISBN 0-685-37263-4); Tome II. (1948-1953) pap. 10.50 (ISBN 0-685-37264-2); Tome III. Chroniques Algeriennes (1939-1958) pap. 7.50 (ISBN 0-685-37265-0). pap. French & Eur.

--Caligula. Bd. with Malentendu. (Coll. Folio). pap. 3.95 (ISBN 0-685-23889-X). French & Eur.

--Caligula & Three Other Plays. Gilbert, Stuart, tr. Incl. Misunderstanding; State of Siege; Just Assassin. (YA) 1962. pap. 3.95 (ISBN 0-394-70207-7, V-207, Vin). Random.

--Carnets, 2 tomes. Incl. Tome I. Mai 1935-Fevrier 1942; Tome II. Janvier 1942-Mars 1951. 1962-64. 12.95 ea. French & Eur.

--Chute. (Coll. Soleil). 1956. 10.95 (ISBN 0-685-11081-8); pap. 3.95 (ISBN 0-686-66417-5). French & Eur.

--Discours De Suede. 1958. pap. 3.95 (ISBN 0-685-11146-6). French & Eur.

--L' Envers et 'Endroit: Essai. 1958. pap. 3.95 (ISBN 0-685-11164-4). French & Eur.

--Essais. 1965. leather bdg. 45.00 (ISBN 0-685-11168-7). French & Eur.

--Etat De Siege. (Coll. Soleil). 1949. 13.50 (ISBN 0-685-11172-5). French & Eur.

--L' Ete: Essai. 1954. pap. 6.50 (ISBN 0-685-11173-3). French & Eur.

--Etranger. (Coll. Blanche). 1942. 7.50 (ISBN 0-685-11174-1); pap. 3.95 (ISBN 0-686-66418-3). French & Eur.

--Exil et le Royaume: Nouvelles. (Coll. Soleil). 1957. 13.25 (ISBN 0-685-11177-6); pap. 3.95 (ISBN 0-686-66419-1). French & Eur.

--Exile & the Kingdom. (YA) 1965. pap. 3.95 (ISBN 0-394-70281-6, V281, Vin). Random.

--Fall. 1957. 10.95 (ISBN 0-394-42424-7). Knopf.

--Fall. O'Brien, Justin, tr. (YA) 1963. pap. 1.95 (ISBN 0-394-70223-9, V223, Vin). Random.

--A Happy Death: A Novel. LC 72-8028. 224p. (YA) 1973. pap. 3.95 (ISBN 0-394-71865-8, V865, Vin). Random.

--L' Homme Revolte. (Coll. Idees). pap. 4.95 (ISBN 0-685-37266-9). French & Eur.

--Homme Revolte: Essai. (Coll. Soleil). 1951. 16.50 (ISBN 0-685-11234-9); pap. 4.95 (ISBN 0-686-66425-6). French & Eur.

--Justes: Theatre. (Coll. Soleil). 1950. 13.95 (ISBN 0-685-11283-7); pap. 3.95 (ISBN 0-686-66428-0). French & Eur.

--Lettres a un Ami Allemand: Essai. 1948. pap. 6.95 (ISBN 0-685-11289-6). French & Eur.

--Lyrical & Critical Essays. LC 67-18621. 384p. (YA) 1970. pap. 3.95 (ISBN 0-394-70852-0, V626, Vin). Random.

--La Mort Heureuse. (Cahiers Albert Camus). 12.50 (ISBN 0-685-37268-5); pap. 3.95 (ISBN 0-686-66857-X). French & Eur.

--Myth of Sisyphus & Other Essays. 1959. pap. 1.95 (ISBN 0-394-70075-9, V75, Vin). Random.

--Mythe De Sisyphe. (Coll. Soleil). 1942. 11.50 (ISBN 0-685-11412-0). French & Eur.

--Neither Victims nor Executioners. MacDonald, Dwight, tr. 64p. 1980. pap. 2.95 (ISBN 0-8264-0001-9). Continuum.

--Neither Victims nor Executioners. MacDonald, Dwight, tr. (Modern Classics of Peace Ser). 1968. pap. 2.95 (ISBN 0-912018-04-6). World Without War.

--Noces et l'ete. (Coll. Soleil). 1959. 15.75 (ISBN 0-685-11423-6). French and Eur.

--Notebooks: Nineteen Thirty-Five to Nineteen Forty-Two. LC 77-16226. 225p. 1978. pap. 3.95 (ISBN 0-15-667400-9, Harv). HarBraceJ.

--Notebooks: 1935-1942. 1965. 3.95 (ISBN 0-394-60349-4). Modern Lib.

--La Peste. (Coll. Folio). pap. 3.95 (ISBN 0-685-37269-3). French & Eur.

--Peste. (Coll. Soleil). 1942. 15.75 (ISBN 0-685-11487-2). French and Eur.

--La Peste. (Documentation thematique). (Illus., Fr.). pap. 2.95 (ISBN 0-685-14031-8, 38). Larousse.

--The Plague. (YA) 1948. 14.95 (ISBN 0-394-44061-7). Knopf.

--The Plague. Gilbert, Stuart, tr. (Modern Library College Editions). 1965. pap. 1.95 (ISBN 0-394-30969-3, T69, RanC). Random.

--The Plague. 228p. 1972. pap. 2.95 (ISBN 0-394-71258-7, V258, Vin). Random.

--Possedees: Theatre. 1959. pap. 3.95 (ISBN 0-685-11508-9). French & Eur.

--Possessed: A Modern Dramatization of Dostoevsky's Novel. O'Brien, Justin, tr. 1964. pap. 3.95 (ISBN 0-394-70245-X, V245, Vin). Random.

--Rebel. 1954. 13.50 (ISBN 0-394-44232-6). Knopf.

--Rebel: An Essay on Man in Revolt. Bower, Anthony, tr. 1956. pap. 3.95 (ISBN 0-394-70030-9, V30, Vin). Random.

--Requiem Pour une Nonne: Theatre. 1956. pap. 7.50 (ISBN 0-685-11527-5). French & Eur.

--Resistance, Rebellion & Death. LC 73-14867. 1974. pap. 3.95 (ISBN 0-394-71966-2, V-966, Vin). Random.

--Stranger. 1946. 10.95 (ISBN 0-394-44748-4). Knopf.

--Stranger. Gilbert, Stuart, tr. 1954. pap. 2.95 (ISBN 0-394-70002-3, V2, Vin). Random.

--The Stranger. Griffith, Kate, tr. from Fr. LC 81-40927. 110p. (Orig.). 1982. lib. bdg. 21.75 (ISBN 0-8191-2141-X); pap. text ed. 9.00 (ISBN 0-8191-2142-8). U Pr of Amer.

--The Stranger. Laredo, Joseph, tr. LC 83-48885. Date not set. 12.95 (ISBN 0-394-53305-4). Knopf.

--The Stranger. 13.95 (ISBN 0-89190-220-1, Pub. by Am Repr). Amereon Ltd.

--Theatre, Recits et Nouvelles, 2 vols. (Bibl. De la Pleiade). 1962. Set. leather bdg set 89.95 (ISBN 0-685-11586-0). French & Eur.

--Youthful Writings. 1977. pap. 2.95 (ISBN 0-394-72404-6, Vin). Random.

Camus, Albert see Otten, Anna.

Camus, Pierre-Albert, tr. see Schell, Rolfe. F.

Camus, Raoul F. Military Music of the American Revolution. LC 75-38947. (Illus.). xii, 210p. 1976. 19.50x (ISBN 0-8078-1263-3). U of NC Pr.

Camus, Renaud. Tricks. 320p. 1982. pap. 3.25 (ISBN 0-441-82425-0). Ace Bks.

Camuse, Ruth. Parent & Child Computer. 1986. 14.95 (ISBN 0-317-05656-5). Reston.

Camuse, Ruth, ed. Fourth Annual Microcomputers in Education Conference: Literacy Plus. LC 84-17597. 465p. 1984. text ed. 35.00 (ISBN 0-88175-077-8). Computer Sci.

Camuse, Ruth A., jt. auth. see Bitter, Gary G.

Camuti, Louis J. All My Patients Are under the Bed. 1980. 14.95 (ISBN 0-671-24271-7). S&S.

--All My Patients Are under the Bed. 1985. pap. 5.95 (ISBN 0-671-55450-6, Fireside). S&S.

Camy-Peyret, C., jt. auth. see Flaud, J. M.

CAN Task Force, National Research Council. Feeding Value of Ethanol Production by-Products. 79p. 1981. pap. text ed. 6.50 (ISBN 0-309-03136-2). Natl Acad Pr.

Cana Conference of Chicago. Marriage: Discoveries & Encounters. 1978. pap. 1.35 (ISBN 0-915388-10-3). Buckley Pubns.

--Perspectives on Money. 1973. pap. 0.40 (ISBN 0-915388-11-1). Buckley Pubns.

Cana, Frank R. South Africa from the Great Trek to the Union. LC 70-97398. Repr. of 1909 ed. 22.50x (ISBN 0-8371-2652-5, CSA&). Greenwood.

Cana, Proinsias Mac see Mac Cana, Proinsias.

Canaan, Gilbert. Heinrich Heine's Memoirs, 2 vols. Karpeles, Gustav, ed. Repr. of 1893 ed. 17.00 (ISBN 0-8274-3846-X). R West.

Canaan, L. A. The Doctor's Quartet & More. 1980. 8.95 (ISBN 0-533-04693-9). Vantage.

--The Lament of Sophocles & Other Works. 1979. 7.95 (ISBN 0-533-04321-2). Vantage.

--Odds & Ends. 1983. 8.95 (ISBN 0-533-05334-X). Vantage.

Canaan, Lionel A. Ajax the Athenian & Other Tales. 1978. 6.95 (ISBN 0-533-03524-4). Vantage.

--Stories for the Sophisticated. 1981. 7.95 (ISBN 0-533-04871-0). Vantage.

Canada, et al. Surviving the First Year of Law School. 1979. Lord Pub.

Canada Department of Agriculture Staff Belleville, Ontario. Biological Control Programmes Against Insects & Weeds in Canada, 1959-1968. 266p. 1971. 35.00x (ISBN 0-85198-018-X, Pub. by CAB Bks England). State Mutual Bk.

Canada Department of Labour. Two Reports on Japanese Canadians in World War II, 2 vols. in 1. Daniels, Roger, ed. LC 78-7079. (Asian Experience in North America Ser.). (Illus.). 1979. Repr. of 1947 ed. lib. bdg. 12.00x (ISBN 0-405-11266-1). Ayer Co Pubs.

Canada, John R. & White, John A., Jr. Capital Investment Decision Analysis for Management & Engineering. 1980. text ed. 34.95 (ISBN 0-13-113555-4). P-H.

Canada, Lena. To Elvis with Love. (gr. 7-12). 1979. pap. 1.95 (ISBN 0-590-05779-0). Scholastic Inc.

Canada-Public Archives. Documents Relating to Canadian Currency, Exchange & Finance During the French Period, 2 Vols. Shortt, Adam, ed. (Fr. & Eng.). 1925. Set. 63.00 (ISBN 0-8337-3256-0). B Franklin.

Canada Royal Commission on Chinese & Japanese Immigration. Report of the Royal Commission on Chinese & Japanese Immigration. Daniels, Roger, ed. LC 78-54812. (Asian Experience in North America Ser.). 1979. Repr. of 1902 ed. lib. bdg. 30.50x (ISBN 0-405-11268-8). Ayer Co Pubs.

Canada, Thomas. Accounting Systems of U. S. Government Agencies. 1983. 22.00 (ISBN 0-87771-013-9). Grad School.

Canaday, John. The Artful Avocado. 1975. pap. 1.95 (ISBN 0-346-12179-5). Cornerstone.

--Baroque Painters. 1972. pap. write for info. (ISBN 0-393-00665-4, Norton Lib). Norton.

--Late Gothic to Renaissance Painters. 1972. pap. 2.95 (ISBN 0-393-00664-6, Norton Lib). Norton.

--Lives of the Painters, 4 Vols. LC 67-17666. (Illus.). 1969. 24.95x (ISBN 0-393-04231-6). Norton.

--Mainstreams of Modern Art. 2nd ed. LC 80-25696. 484p. 1981. pap. text ed. 33.95x (ISBN 0-03-057638-5, HoltC). HR&W.

--Neoclassic to Post-Impressionist Painters. 1972. pap. 2.95 (ISBN 0-393-00666-2, Norton Lib). Norton.

--Richard Estes: The Urban Landscape. LC 78-59702. 1979. 16.95 (ISBN 0-87846-126-4, 760668). NYGS.

--What Is Art? An Introduction to Painting, Sculpture & Architecture. 1980. 30.00 (ISBN 0-394-50320-1); text ed. 25.00 (ISBN 0-394-32450-1). Knopf.

Canaday, John, ed. Western Painting Illustrated: Giotto to Cezanne. (Illus.). 1972. pap. 3.50 (ISBN 0-393-00667-0, Norton Lib). Norton.

Canaday, Ouida. Georgia Sketch Book. LC 81-84168. (Illus.). 1981. 4.99 (ISBN 0-931948-29-0). Peachtree Pubs.

Canadian-American Committee. Bilateral Relations in an Uncertain World Context: Canada-U.S. Relations in 1978. LC 78-71435. (Canadian-American Committee Ser.). 112p. 1978. 4.00 (ISBN 0-88806-044-0). Natl Planning.

--The New Environment for Canadian-American Relations. LC 72-86374. 80p. 1974. 1.50 (ISBN 0-89068-018-3). Natl Planning.

Canadian Association of Oilwell Drilling Contractors. Drilling Rig Task Details & Performance Standards, 5 vols. (Orig.). 1982. Set. 42.25x (ISBN 0-87201-927-6). Rig Manager (ISBN 0-87201-929-2). Driller (ISBN 0-87201-930-6). Derrickhand (ISBN 0-87201-931-4). Motorhand (ISBN 0-87201-932-2). Floorhand (ISBN 0-87201-933-0). Gulf Pub.

--An Introduction to Oilwell Drilling & Servicing. LC 82-12027. 98p. (Orig.). 1982. pap. 6.95x (ISBN 0-87201-202-6). Gulf Pub.

--Servicing Rig Task Details & Performance Standards, 4 vols. (Orig.). 1982. Set. pap. 33.80x (ISBN 0-87201-928-4). Rig Manager (ISBN 0-87201-934-9). Rig Operator (ISBN 0-87201-935-7). Derrickhand (ISBN 0-87201-936-5). Floorhand (ISBN 0-87201-937-3). Gulf Pub.

--SI Drilling Manual. LC 82-15466. 820p. 1982. three ring binder 175.00x (ISBN 0-87201-211-5). Gulf Pub.

Canadian Broadcasting Corporation. Thirty-Four Biographies of Canadian Composers. LC 75-166224. 1964. Repr. 39.00x (ISBN 0-403-01351-8). Scholarly.

Canadian Cancer Conference. Proceedings, 5 vols. Begg, R. W., ed. Incl. Vol. 1. 1st Conference, 1954. 1955 (ISBN 0-12-149001-7); Vol. 2. 2nd Conference, 1956. 1957 (ISBN 0-12-149002-5); Vol. 3. 3rd Conference, 1958. 1959 (ISBN 0-12-149003-3); Vol. 4. 4th Conference, 1960. 1961 (ISBN 0-12-149004-1); Vol. 5. 5th Conference, 1962. 1963 (ISBN 0-12-149005-X). 75.00 ea. Acad Pr.

Canadian Centre for Films on Art for the Federation of Arts, ed. Films on Art. (Illus.). 240p. 1977. 17.95 (ISBN 0-8230-1780-X). Watson-Guptill.

Canadian Christian Movement for Peace Staff. Economic Rights & Human Development. (People Living for Justice Ser.). 240p. 1984. pap. 29.95 (ISBN 0-697-01932-2). Wm C Brown.

--Militarism & Hope. (People Living for Justice Ser.). 1983. pap. text ed. 29.95 (ISBN 0-697-01919-5). Wm C Brown.

--Political & Social Rights & Human Dignity. (People Living for Justice Ser.). 208p. 1984. pap. text ed. 29.95 (ISBN 0-317-19703-7). Wm C Brown.

--Women & Human Wholeness. (People Living for Justice Ser.). 160p. 1983. pap. text ed. 29.95 (ISBN 0-697-01920-9). Wm C Brown.

--Work & Co-Creation. (People Living for Justice Ser.). 160p. 1983. pap. text ed. 29.95 (ISBN 0-697-01921-7). Wm C Brown.

Canadian Government. Never Say Die: The Canadian Air Force Survival Manual. (Illus.). 208p. 1979. pap. 8.00 (ISBN 0-87364-112-4). Paladin Pr.

--Winning Low Energy Building Designs. 651p. 1980. text ed. 35.00x (ISBN 0-660-50675-0, Pub. by Inst Engeering Australia). Brookfield Pub Co.

Canadian Government Publishing Centre. Architecture of the Picturesque in Canada. 183p. 1985. pap. 18.50 (ISBN 0-660-11641-3, SSC185 5071, SSC). Unipub.

--Climatic Atlas - Canada: A Series of Maps Portraying Canada's Climate. (Map Series 1: Temperature & Degree Days). 22p. 1985. pap. 15.00 (ISBN 0-660-52683-2, SSC180 5071, SSC). Unipub.

--Directory of Labour Organizations in Canada - 1984. 245p. (Eng. & Fr.). 1985. pap. 13.00 (ISBN 0-660-52793-6, SSC189 5071, SSC). Unipub.

--Economic Review - April 1984. 236p. 1985. pap. 19.50 (ISBN 0-660-11642-1, SSC179 5071, SSC). Unipub.

--Ethical Conduct in the Public Sector. 348p. 1985. pap. 28.75 (ISBN 0-660-11572-7, SSC190 5071, SSC). Unipub.

--Guide to Canadian Photographic Archives. 727p. (Eng. & Fr.). 1985. 65.00 (ISBN 0-660-52274-8, SSC192 5071, SSC). Unipub.

--Men & Meridians, 3 vols. Incl. Vol. 1. The History of Surveying & Mapping in Canada Prior to 1867. 345p. 18.75 (SSC186 5071); Vol. 2. The History of Surveying & Mappong in Canada 1867-1917. 18.75 (SSC187 5071); Vol. 3. The History of Surveying & Mapping in Canada 1917-1947. 370p. 15.00 (SSC194 5071). 1985 (SSC). Unipub.

--Mortality Atlas of Canada, 3 vols. Incl. Vol. 1. Cancer. pap. 33.25 (ISBN 0-660-50443-X, SSC184 5071); Vol. 2. General Mortality. pap. 33.25 (ISBN 0-660-50584-3, SSC183 5071); Vol. 3. Urban Mortality. 139p. (Eng. & Fr.). pap. 35.25 (ISBN 0-660-52650-6, SSC182 5071). 1985 (SSC). Unipub.

--Report of the Committee on Sexual Offences Against Children & Youths: Sexual Offences Against Children, 2 vols. 1314p. 1985. Set. pap. 46.50 (ISBN 0-660-11639-1, SSC193 5071, SSC). Unipub.

--Royal Commission on the Ocean Ranger Marine Disaster: Report One: The Loss of the Semisubmersible Drill Rig & Its Crew. 400p. 1985. pap. 55.25 (ISBN 0-660-11682-0, SSC191 5071, SSC). Unipub.

--The Totem Poles & Monuments of Gitwangak Village. 160p. 1985. pap. 17.25 (ISBN 0-660-11560-3, SSC188 5071, SSC). Unipub.

--Western Transition: Economic Council Report. 260p. 1985. pap. 18.50 (ISBN 0-660-11693-6, SSC178 5071, SSC). Unipub.

Canadian Kennel Club Staff. The Canadian Kennel Club Book of Dogs. (Illus.). 836p. 1982. 29.95 (ISBN 0-7736-0104-X). Howell Bk.

Canadian Manufacturers Association. Canadian Trade Index 1982. 72nd ed. LC 14-21699. 1400p. (Orig.). 1982. pap. 82.50x (ISBN 0-919102-02-6). Intl Pubns Serv.

--Canadian Trade Index, 1983. 73rd ed. LC 14-21699. 1210p. (Orig.). 1983. pap. 105.00x (ISBN 0-919102-03-4). Intl Pubns Serv.

Canadian Mathematical Society, NSERC & the University of Waterloo, June 1978, et al. Algebraic Topology: Proceedings. Hoffman, P., ed. (Lecture Notes in Mathmatics: Vol. 741). 1979. pap. 37.00 (ISBN 0-387-09545-4). Springer-Verlag.

Canadian Polish Millenium Fund. Poland's Millenium of Christianity. 50p. (Eng. & Fr.). 1966. 1.00 (ISBN 0-940962-29-2). Polish Inst Arts.

Canadian Press Association. A History of Canadian Journalism in the Several Portions of the Dominion. LC 75-41047. Repr. of 1908 ed. 24.50 (ISBN 0-404-14745-3). AMS Pr.

Canadian Reliability Engineers. Reliability Engineering, 1975. pap. 32.00 (ISBN 0-08-019977-1). Pergamon.

Canadian Reliabilty Engineers, ed. Reliability Engineering 1980: Proceedings of the 1980 Canadian SRE Reliability Symposium, Ottawa, Ontario, Canada May 15-16 1980. 170p. 1981. pap. 39.00 (ISBN 0-08-026163-9). Pergamon.

Canadian Solar Energy Society. Energex 82 Technical Conference: Proceedings. 1228p. 1983. pap. text ed. 120.00x (ISBN 0-89553-120-8). Am Solar Energy.

Canadian SRE Reliability Symposium, Ottawa, Ontario, Canada, October 1978. Reliability Engineering Nineteen Seventy-Eight: Proceedings. LC 78-10571. 1979. pap. 26.00 (ISBN 0-08-023228-0). Pergamon.

Canadian-U. S. Conference on Communications Policy. Cultures in Collision: The Interaction of Canadian & U.S. Broadcasting Policies. LC 83-19232. 224p. 1984. text ed. 27.95x (ISBN 0-03-069533-3). Praeger.

Canadian Universities Travel Services. Budget Travel in Canada. Rev. ed. (Illus.). 336p. 1984. pap. 10.95 (ISBN 0-312-10751-X). St Martin.

Canady, John E. Embattled Critic: Views on Modern Art. LC 72-8492. (Essay Index Reprint Ser.). 1972. Repr. of 1962 ed. 24.50 (ISBN 0-8369-7309-7). Ayer Co Pubs.

Canady, Robert L. & Seyfarth, John T. How Parent-Teacher Conferences Build Partnerships. LC 79-66527. (Fastback Ser.: No. 132). (Orig.). 1979. pap. 0.75 (ISBN 0-87367-132-5). Phi Delta Kappa.

Canal Library-Museum. Panama Subject Catalog of the Special Panama Collection of the Canal Zone Library-Museum. 1964. lib. bdg. 78.00 (ISBN 0-8161-0675-4, Hall Library). G K Hall.

Canal, Veronique, tr. see Potter, Beatrix.

Canale, Andrew. Understanding the Human Jesus: A Journey in Scripture & Imagination. LC 84-61027. 208p. 1985. pap. 7.95 (ISBN 0-8091-2654-0). Paulist Pr.

Canale, R. P., jt. auth. see Chapra, S. C.

Canales, Luis. Contos Tristes. (Illus.). 60p. 1982. pap. 2.95 (ISBN 0-933704-25-9). Dawn Pr.

--Japan: Bewitching & Alienating. (Illus.). 110p. 1982. pap. 2.95 (ISBN 0-933704-24-0). Dawn Pr.

Canales, Nemesio. Antologia Nueva De Nemesio Canales, 4 bks. Montana Palaez, Servando, ed. Incl. Bk. 21. Glosario (ISBN 0-8477-0021-6); Bk. 22. Meditaciones Acres (ISBN 0-8477-0022-4); Bk. 23. Boberias (ISBN 0-8477-0023-2); Bk. 24. Hacia un Lejano Sol (ISBN 0-8477-0024-0). (UPREX, Puerto Rico Ayer). pap. 2.00 ea. U of PR Pr.

Canaletto. Drawings in the Royal Collection. 3000.00 (ISBN 0-384-07315-8). Johnson Repr.

--Views of Venice by Canaletto. 8.50 (ISBN 0-8446-0050-4). Peter Smith.

Canaletto, Antonio. Views of Venice by Canaletto. (Illus.). pap. 7.95 (ISBN 0-486-22705-7). Dover.

Canals, Salvatore. Jesus as Friend. 117p. (Orig.). 1979. pap. 6.95 (ISBN 0-906127-11-4). Scepter Pubs.

Canan. Qualified Retirement Plans. (West's Handbook Ser.). write for info. West Pub.

Canan, Craig T. Southern Progressive Periodicals Directory. LC 80-644934. 1983. 4.00 (ISBN 0-935396-01-2). Prog Educ.

--U. S. Progressive Periodicals Directory. LC 81-85888. 1983. 8.00 (ISBN 0-935396-02-0). Prog Educ.

Canan, James. War in Space. LC 81-48032. 192p. 1982. 13.41i (ISBN 0-06-038022-5, HarpT). Har-Row.

--War in Space. 272p. 1984. pap. 3.50 (ISBN 0-425-06848-X). Berkley Pub.

Canan, Janine. Of Your Seed. 1977. sewn in wrappers 2.00 (ISBN 0-685-80004-0). Oyez.

Canape, Charlene. How to Profit from the Video Revolution. LC 83-26534. 200p. 1984. 16.95 (ISBN 0-03-070343-3). HR&W.

Canard, M., et al, eds. Biology of Chrysopidae. (Entomological Ser.). 1984. lib. bdg. 57.50 (ISBN 90-6193-137-1, Pub. by Junk Pubs Netherlands). Kluwer-Academic.

Canard, Marius. Miscellaneous Orientalia. 556p. 1973. 60.00x (ISBN 0-902089-51-X, Pub. by Variorum). State Mutual Bk.

Canard, Marius, intro. by see Rozen, V. R.

Canario, Jack. Be Ad-Wise. (Money Matters). (Illus.). 64p. (YA) (gr. 7-12). 1981. pap. 3.95 (ISBN 0-915510-54-5). Janus Bks.

--The Big Hassle: Getting along with Authority. (Read on! Write on! Ser.). (Illus.). 64p. (gr. 6-12). 1980. 3.95 (ISBN 0-915510-38-3). Janus Bks.

--The Put-Down Pro: Getting along With Friends. (Read on! - Write on! Ser.). (Illus.). 64p. (gr. 6-12). 1980. pap. text ed. 3.95 (ISBN 0-915510-39-1). Janus Bks.

Canario, Jack & Mathias, Marilynne. Help! First Steps to First Aid. Katz, Elaine, ed. (Survival Guides Ser.). (Illus.). 64p. (gr. 7 up). 1980. pap. text ed. 3.95 (ISBN 0-915510-46-4). Janus Bks.

Canario, Jack, ed. see Kelsey, Keenan & Gundlach, Pat.

Canart, Paul. Studies in Comparative Semantics. 1979. 19.95x (ISBN 0-312-77087-1). St Martin.

Canary, Brenda. Home to the Mountains. LC 74-82167. 192p. 1975. pap. 7.95 (ISBN 0-8027-0474-3). Walker & Co.

Canary, Brenda B. The Voice of the Clown. 288p. 1982. pap. 2.95 (ISBN 0-380-79624-4, 79624-4). Avon.

Canary, Robert. The Cabell Scene. (James Branch Cabell Ser.). 300p. 1975. lib. bdg. 69.95 (ISBN 0-87700-236-3). Revisionist Pr.

--T. S. Eliot: The Poet & His Critics. 392p. 1982. lib. bdg. 30.00x (ISBN 0-8389-0355-X). ALA.

Canary, Robert H. & Kozicki, Henry, eds. The Writing of History: Literary Form & Historical Understanding. LC 78-4590. 182p. 1978. 29.50x (ISBN 0-299-07570-2). U of Wis Pr.

Canas, Dionisio. Que Dice el Periodico. (Lecturas Faciles Ser.). 70p. (Spanish.). 1983. pap. text ed. 3.75 (ISBN 0-88345-522-6, 21268). Regents Pub.

Canavaggio, Pierre. Dictionnaire Raisonne Des Superstitions et Des Croyances Populaires. 247p. (Fr.). 1977. pap. 19.95 (ISBN 0-686-56937-7, M-6059). French & Eur.

Canavan, Bernard. Economists for Beginners. 11.95 (ISBN 0-906495-51-2). Writers & Readers.

Canavan, Francis. Freedom of Expression: Purpose As Limit. LC 83-71826. 181p. 1984. lib. bdg. 19.75 (ISBN 0-89089-269-5); pap. text ed. 9.75 (ISBN 0-89089-270-9). Carolina Acad Pr.

Canavan, Francis S. & Cole, R. T., eds. The Ethical Dimensions of Political Life: Essays in Honor of John H. Hallowell. LC 83-1772. 295p. 1983. 27.75 (ISBN 0-8223-0490-2). Duke.

Canavan, Jean. Midwinter's Night. 1985. pap. 2.95 (ISBN 0-671-54686-4). PB.

--The Shadow of the Flame. 304p. 1984. pap. 2.95 (ISBN 0-380-86504-1, 86504). Avon.

Canavan, John R. The English Tense System: A Study of Temporal Meaning & Reference. (Wuppertaler Schriftenreihe Linguistik: Vol. 5). 200p. 1983. 24.00x (ISBN 3-416-01760-9, Pub. by Bouvier Verlag W Germany). Benjamins North Am.

Canavan, Michael M. Product Liability for Supervisors & Managers. 1981. text ed. 18.95 (ISBN 0-8359-5630-X). Reston.

Canavan, P J. Paragraphs & Themes. 4th ed. 510p. 1983. pap. text ed. 13.95 (ISBN 0-669-05273-6); 1.95 (ISBN 0-669-05271-X). Heath.

Canavan, P. Joseph. The Effective Writer's Companion. 1981. pap. text ed. 13.65x (ISBN 0-673-15449-1). Scott F.

--Rhetoric & Literature. 352p. (Orig.). 1974. text ed. 20.95 (ISBN 0-07-009705-4). McGraw.

Canavarro, Marie de S. The Aztec Chief. 1977. lib. bdg. 59.95 (ISBN 0-8490-1464-6). Gordon Pr.

Canavor, Natalie. Sell Your Photographs: The Complete Marketing Strategy for the Freelancer. LC 79-18958. 320p. 1979. 17.95 (ISBN 0-914842-40-4). Madrona Pubs.

--Sell Your Photographs: The Complete Marketing Strategy for the Freelancer. 1982. pap. 7.95 (ISBN 0-452-25638-0, Plume). NAL.

Canavos, George C. Applied Probability & Statistical Methods. 1984. text ed. 29.95 (ISBN 0-316-12778-7); solutions manual avail. (ISBN 0-316-12779-5). Little.

Canberra Nat'l. Library of Australia. Australian National Bibliography, 1979, 2 vols. 19th ed. LC 63-33739. 1980. Set. 67.50x (ISBN 0-8002-1860-4). Intl Pubns Serv.

Canby, Courtland & Carruth, Gorton. The Encyclopedia of Historic Places, 2 vols. (Illus.). 1200p. 1983. Set. 120.00x (ISBN 0-87196-125-3). Facts on File.

Canby, Courtland, et al, eds. The World of History. LC 83-49178. (History & Historiography Ser.). 224p. 1985. lib. bdg. 25.00 (ISBN 0-8240-6353-8). Garland Pub.

Canby, Courtlandt. The Encyclopedia of Historic Places, 2 Vols. Carruth, Gorton, ed. LC 80-25121. (A Hudson Group Bk.). (Illus.). 1052p. 1984. Set. 120.00x (ISBN 0-87196-126-1). Facts on File.

--The Past Displayed: A Journey Through the Ancient World. 188p. 1980. 50.00x (ISBN 0-7148-1915-8, Pub. by Phai don Pr). State Mutual Bk.

Canby, Henry S. Alma Mater: The Gothic Age of the American College. facsimile ed. LC 75-1835. (Leisure Class in America Ser.). (Illus.). 1975. Repr. of 1936 ed. 20.00x (ISBN 0-405-06904-9). Ayer Co Pubs.

--Better Writing. 141p. 1981. pap. 20.00 (ISBN 0-8495-0857-6). Arden Lib.

--Better Writing. 141p. 1981. Repr. of 1926 ed. lib. bdg. 20.00 (ISBN 0-89984-112-0). Century Bookbindery.

--The Brandywine. 2nd ed. 285p. 1977. 9.95 (ISBN 0-916838-06-4). Schiffer.

--College Sons & College Fathers. facs. ed. LC 68-16917. (Essay Index Reprint Ser). 1968. Repr. of 1915 ed. 18.00 (ISBN 0-8369-0274-2). Ayer Co Pubs.

--Seven Years Harvest. LC 66-25902. Repr. of 1936 ed. 23.50x (ISBN 0-8046-0065-1, Pub. by Kennikat). Assoc Faculty Pr.

--A Study of the Short Story. Dashiell, Alfred, ed. LC 83-45726. Repr. of 1935 ed. 33.00 (ISBN 0-404-20050-8). AMS Pr.

--Thomas Hardy: Notes on His Life & Work. LC 74-11144. 1925. lib. bdg. 10.00 (ISBN 0-8414-3515-4). Folcroft.

--Turn West, Turn East: Mark Twain & Henry James. LC 65-23485. 1951. 18.00x (ISBN 0-8196-0154-3). Biblo.

--Walt Whitman: An American. LC 72-106663. Repr. of 1943 ed. lib. bdg. 22.50x (ISBN 0-8371-3421-8, CAWW). Greenwood.

Canby, Henry S., ed. Harper Essays. LC 69-16483. (Essay & General Literature Reprint Ser). 1969. Repr. of 1927 ed. 23.50x (ISBN 0-8046-0520-3, Pub. by Kennikat). Assoc Faculty Pr.

Canby, Henry S., et al. Saturday Papers, Essays on Literature from the Literary Review. 1969. Repr. of 1921 ed. 15.00 (ISBN 0-384-07310-7). Johnson Repr.

--Thomas Hardy: Notes on His Life & Work. 1978. Repr. lib. bdg. 10.00 (ISBN 0-8495-0812-6). Arden Lib.

Canby, Jeanny. Ancient Near East in the Walters Art Gallery. LC 75-310215. (Illus.). 1974. pap. 4.00 (ISBN 0-911886-01-X). Walters Art.

Canby, Jeanny V., et al. Ivory: The Sumptuous Art. (Illus.). 1983. pap. 5.00 (ISBN 0-911886-27-3). Walters Art.

Canby, Jeanny V., jt. auth. see Bergman, Robert P.

Canby, William C., Jr. American Indian Law. LC 81-3066. (Nutshell Ser.). 288p. 1981. pap. text ed. 7.95 (ISBN 0-314-59473-6). West Pub.

Cancalon, Elaine D. Fairy-Tale Structures & Motifs in le Grand Meaulnes. 89p. (Fr.). 1975. pap. 11.75 (ISBN 3-261-01607-8). P Lang Pubs.

Cancalon, Paul, jt. ed. see Elam, John S.

Cancellieri, Giovanni, jt. auth. see Ravaioli, Umberto.

Cancer Care, Inc. & National Cancer Foundation, Inc. Catastrophic Illness in the Seventies, Critical Issues & Complex Decision: Proceedings. 1971. 2.00 (ISBN 0-9606494-0-9). Cancer Care.

Cancer Care, Inc. & National Cancer Foundation Inc. Listen to the Children: A Study of the Impact on the Mental Health of Children of a Parent's Catastrophic Illness. LC 77-94376. 1977. 2.50 (ISBN 0-9606494-1-7). Cancer Care.

Cancian, F. What Are Norms? A Study of Beliefs & Action in a Maya Community. LC 74-77833. 256p. 1975. 34.50 (ISBN 0-521-20536-0). Cambridge U Pr.

Cancian, Frank. Change & Uncertainty in a Peasant Community: The Maya Corn Farmers of Zinacantan. LC 72-153814. (Illus.). 1972. 17.50x (ISBN 0-8047-0787-1). Stanford U Pr.

--Economics & Prestige in a Maya Community: The Religious Cargo System in Zinacantan. (Illus.). 1965. 18.50x (ISBN 0-8047-0259-4); pap. 7.95 (ISBN 0-8047-0260-8, SP90). Stanford U Pr.

--The Innovator's Situation: Upper-Middle-Class Conservatism in Agricultural Communities. LC 78-65327. xvi, 159p. 1979. 14.00x (ISBN 0-8047-1017-1); pap. 5.95 (ISBN 0-8047-1111-9, SP27). Stanford U Pr.

Canclini, Arnoldo. Onesimo. 204p. 1982. pap. 3.75 (ISBN 0-89922-215-3). Edit Caribe.

Canclini, Arnoldo, tr. see Geisler, Norman.

Canclini, Arnoldo, tr. see Jones, J. Estill.

Canclini, Arnoldo, tr. see Jungel, Eberhard.

Canclini, Arnoldo, tr. see Ladd, George E.

Canclini, Arnoldo, tr. see Stagg, Frank.

Canclini, Santiago. Alzare Mis Ojos. 316p. (Span.). 1984. pap. 7.95 (ISBN 0-311-40047-7). Casa Bautista.

Cancogni, Annapaola. The Mirage in the Mirror: Nabokov's Ada & Its French Pre-Texts. Wilhelm, James J., ed. LC 84-48373. (Comparative Literature Ser.). 350p. 1985. lib. bdg. 40.00 (ISBN 0-8240-6702-9). Garland Pub.

Cancogni, Annapaoloa, tr. see Benni, Stefano.

Cancro, R., et al, eds. Strategic Intervention in Schizophrenia: Current Developments in Treatment. LC 74-1201. 326p. 1974. text ed. 34.95 (ISBN 0-87705-133-X). Human Sci Pr.

Cancro, Robert, ed. Annual Review of the Schizophrenic Syndrome, 5 vols. Incl. Vol. 1. 1971; Vol. 2. 1972 (ISBN 0-87630-058-1); Vol. 3. 1973; Vol. 4. 1974-75 (ISBN 0-87630-108-1); Vol. 5. 1976-77 (ISBN 0-87630-160-X). LC 76-156466. Orig. Title: Schizophrenic Syndrome. 40.00 ea. Brunner-Mazel.

--Intelligence: Genetic & Environmental Influences. LC 79-153576. 300p. 1971. 49.50 (ISBN 0-8089-0689-5, 790775). Grune.

Cancro, Robert & Dean, Stanley R., eds. Research in the Schizophrenic Disorders: The Stanley R. Dean Award Lectures, Vol. 1. LC 84-20603. 291p. 1985. text ed. 47.50 (ISBN 0-89335-211-X). SP Med & Sci Bks.

--Research in the Schizophrenic Disorders: The Stanley R. Dean Award Lectures, Vol. 2. LC 84-20603. 376p. 1985. text ed. 57.50 (ISBN 0-89335-212-8). SP Med & Sci Bks.

Cancro, Robert & Taintor, Zebulen, eds. Towards a New Psychology of Women & Men: A Special Issue of Journal of Psychiatric Education. 85p. 1984. 9.95 (ISBN 0-89885-223-4). Human Sci Pr.

Cancro, Robert, et al, eds. Progress in Functional Psychoses. new ed. LC 78-31828. (Illus.). 250p. 1979. 30.00 (ISBN 0-89335-072-9). SP Med & Sci Bks.

Candau de Cevallos, Maria del C. Historia de la Lengua Espanola. (Span.). 1985. 33.00 (ISBN 0-916379-22-1). Scripta.

Cande, Roland de. Dictionnaire Des Musiciens. 288p. (Fr.). 1974. pap. 8.95 (ISBN 0-686-56882-6, F-17742). French & Eur.

Candea, Dan, jt. auth. see Hax, Arnoldo C.

Candea, Virgil, jt. auth. see Bodea, Cornelia.

Candee, Richard M. Atlantic Heights: A World War I Shipbuilders Community. (Illus.). 136p. 1985. 19.95 (ISBN 0-915819-06-6). Portsmouth Marine Soc.

Candelaria, Cordelia. Ojo de la Cueva. Alurista & Xelina, eds. (Serie Milpa Poetica). 64p. (Orig.). 1985. pap. 5.00x (ISBN 0-939558-08-4). Maize Pr.

Candelaria, Nash. Memories of the Alhambra. LC 76-26410. 192p. 1982. pap. 9.00x (ISBN 0-916950-32-8). Biling Rev-Pr.

--Memories of the Alhambra. LC 76-26410. 192p. 1977. 16.95x (ISBN 0-9601086-1-0). Biling Rev-Pr.

--Not by the Sword. LC 81-71731. 235p. 1982. 16.95x (ISBN 0-916950-30-1); pap. 10.00x (ISBN 0-916950-31-X). Biling Rev-Pr.

Candi, Giovanni P; see Brown, Howard M.

Candland, Shelby V. How to Communicate Ideas. Knipe, D. L., ed. (Illus.). 150p. (Orig.). 1982. 19.95x (ISBN 0-911703-00-4). Comm Skills.

--Writers Reference Book. 30p. (Orig.). 1982. 9.95x (ISBN 0-911703-01-2). Comm Skills.

Candler, Allen D., ed. see Georgia Colony.

Candler, Allen D., ed. see Georgia General Assembly.

Candler, Edmund. The Long Road to Baghdad, 2 vols. LC 77-7002. 1977. Repr. of 1919 ed. lib. bdg. 65.00 (ISBN 0-89341-253-8). Longwood Pub Group.

Candler, John. Brief Notices of Hayti. 13.00 (ISBN 0-8369-9219-9, 9074). Ayer Co Pubs.

Candler, Wilfred C., jt. auth. see Heady, Earl O.

Candlish, J. K. A Medical Biochemistry for the Tropics. 1978. pap. text ed. 16.95 (ISBN 0-7216-0709-8, Pub. by Bailliere-Tindall). Saunders.

Candlish, Robert S. First Epistle of John. LC 79-14801. (Kregel Bible Study Classics Ser.). 1979. 18.95 (ISBN 0-8254-2320-1). Kregel.

--Studies in Genesis, 2 vols. in one. LC 79-14084. (Kregel Bible Study Classics Ser.). 1979. 19.95 (ISBN 0-8254-2315-5). Kregel.

C&MA Home Department Board. The Pastor's Handbook. 102p. 3.95 (ISBN 0-87509-118-0). Chr Pubns.

Candoli, Carl I., et al. School Business Administration: A Planning Approach. 3rd ed. 421p. 1984. write for info. Allyn.

Candoli, Conte, ed. The Greatest Jazz Solos-Trumpet. 1978. pap. 7.95 (ISBN 0-89705-000-2). Almo Pubns.

Candoli, I. Carl, et al. School Business Administration: A Planning Approach. 3rd ed. 421p. 1984. 30.95x (ISBN 0-205-08152-5, Pub. by Longwood Div). Allyn.

Candolle, A. De. Memoires sur la Famille des Legumineuses. (Illus.). 1966. Repr. of 1825 ed. 78.40 (ISBN 3-7682-0299-2). Lubrecht & Cramer.

Candolle, A. P. de see De Candolle, A. P.

Candolle, Alphonse de see De Candolle, Alphonse.

Candolle, Augustin P. De see De Candolle, Augustin P. & Sprengel, Kurt.

Candragomin. Difficult Beginnings: Three Works on the Bodhisattva Path. Tatz, Mark, tr. LC 83-2317. 121p. 1985. 22.50 (ISBN 0-87773-317-1, 54530-3). Shambhala Pubns.
Candullo, C. System Developments Standards. 544p. 1985. 49.95 (ISBN 0-07-009724-0). McGraw.
Candy, David J. Biological Functions of Carbohydrates. LC 80-18668. (Tertiary Level Biology Ser.). 197p. 1980. 49.95x (ISBN 0-470-27038-1). Halsted Pr.
Candy, Edward. Bones of Contention. LC 82-45964. (Crime Club Ser.). 192p. 1983. 11.95 (ISBN 0-385-18804-8). Doubleday.
--Bones of Contention. 192p. 1984. pap. 2.95 (ISBN 0-345-31698-3). Ballantine.
--Voices of Children. 1980. 13.95 (ISBN 0-575-02735-5, Pub. by Gollancz England). David & Charles.
--Which Doctor. LC 83-25365. (Crime Club Ser.). 192p. 1984. 11.95 (ISBN 0-385-18942-7). Doubleday.
--Which Doctor. 224p. 1985. pap. 2.95 (ISBN 0-345-32082-4). Ballantine.
--Words for Murder Perhaps. 192p. 1985. pap. 2.75 (ISBN 0-345-31952-4). Ballantine.
Candy, Hugh C. Milton: The Individualist in Metre. 1978. Repr. of 1924 ed. lib. bdg. 12.50 (ISBN 0-8495-0771-5). Arden Lib.
--Milton: The Individualist in Metre. 49p. 1980. Repr. lib. bdg. 8.50 (ISBN 0-89987-112-7). Darby Bks.
--Milton: The Individualist in Metre. 1930. lib. bdg. 7.50 (ISBN 0-8414-3630-4). Folcroft.
--Some Newly-Discovered Stanzas Written by John Milton on Engraved Scenes Illustrating Ovid's Metamorphoses. 1972. Repr. of 1924 ed. lib. bdg. 20.00 (ISBN 0-8414-0912-9). Folcroft.
Candy, J. V. Signal Processing: Model Based Approach. 256p. 1986. price not set (ISBN 0-07-009725-9). McGraw.
Candy, Robert. Getting the Most from Your Game & Fish. LC 78-1777. (Illus.). 278p. (Orig.). 1984. pap. 12.95 flexible bdg. (ISBN 0-911469-01-X). A C Hood Pub.
Cane. Case Studies in Critical Care Medicine. 1985. 29.95 (ISBN 0-8151-1421-4). Year Bk Med.
Cane, B. S., jt. auth. see Hilsum, S.
Cane, Bill. Through Crisis to Freedom. LC 79-89874. (Orig.). 1980. pap. 3.25 (ISBN 0-914070-14-2). ACTA Found.
Cane, Edmund du see Du Cane, Edmund.
Cane, Florence. The Artist in Each of Us. LC 83-14347. (Illus.). 380p. 1983. pap. 18.95 (ISBN 0-9611462-0-6). Art Therapy.
Cane, Hubert Du see Prussia.
Cane, Melville. Snow Toward Evening: Poems. LC 74-13258. 117p. (Orig.). 1974. pap. 3.50 (ISBN 0-15-683400-6, Harv). HarBraceJ.
--To Build a Fire: Recent Poems & a Prose Piece. LC 64-14640. 1964. 9.95 (ISBN 0-15-190478-2). HarBraceJ.
Cane, Melville, et al, eds. Golden Year. facsimile ed. LC 73-76941. (Granger Index Reprint Ser). 1960. 23.50 (ISBN 0-8369-6004-1). Ayer Co Pubs.
Cane, Mike. The Computer Phone Book. 1983. pap. 14.95 (ISBN 0-452-25446-9, Plume). NAL.
--Computer Phone Book Online Guide for the Commodore Computers. 496p. 1984. pap. 9.95 (ISBN 0-451-82084-3, Sig). NAL.
Cane, Peter, jt. auth. see Trindade, Francis.
Canedo, Lino G., ed. Cronica De los Colegios De Propaganda Fide De la Nueva Espana, De Fr. Isidro Felix De Espinosa. (Franciscan Historical Classics). (Illus.). 1964. deluxe ed. 35.00 (ISBN 0-88382-154-0); pap. 12.00 (ISBN 0-88382-152-4). AAFH.
--Cronica Franciscana De las Provincias Del Peru De Fr. Diego De Cordoba Salinas. (Franciscan Historical Classics). (Illus., Span.). 1957. deluxe ed. 40.00 (ISBN 0-88382-151-6). AAFH.
Canedy, Norman W. The Roman Sketchbook of Girolano Da Garpi. 1977. 115.00x (ISBN 0-686-79322-6, Pub. by U of London England). State Mutual Bk.
Canegham, Michel van see Van Canegham, Michel & Warren, David D.
Canemaker, John. The Animated Raggedy Ann & Andy: The Story Behind the Movie. LC 76-53289. (Illus.). 1977. 25.00 (ISBN 0-672-52329-9); pap. 12.95 (ISBN 0-672-52330-2). Bobbs.
Canenbley, C., ed. Enforcing Antitrust Against Foreign Enterprises: Procedural Problems in the Extraterritorial Application of Antitrust Laws. 300p. 1981. 60.00 (ISBN 90-654-4014-3, Pub. by Kluwer Law Netherlands). Kluwer Academic.
Canes, Michael, ed. see Markun, Patricia M.
Canestano, James C. Real Estate Financial Feasibility Analysis Handbook & Workbook. 280p. 1982. Set. 25.00 (ISBN 0-318-03322-4); wkbk. (ISBN 0-936954-04-3); handbk. (ISBN 0-936954-05-1). Natl Assoc Realtors.
Canetta, Robert. Photo Language Stimulation for Aphasic Patients. LC 74-76839. 1974. pap. text ed. 14.50x (ISBN 0-8134-1641-8, 1641). Interstate.
Canetti, Elias. Auto-Da-Fe. 1979. 17.50 (ISBN 0-8264-0210-0); pap. 11.95 (ISBN 0-8264-0068-X). Continuum.
--Auto-da-Fe. Wedgewood, D. V., tr. from Ger. 464p. 1984. pap. 10.95 (ISBN 0-374-51879-3). FS&G.
--Comedy of Vanity & Life-Terms. Honegger, Gitta, tr. LC 82-62100. 1983. 18.95 (ISBN 0-933826-30-3); pap. 7.95 (ISBN 0-933826-31-1). Performing Arts.
--The Conscience of Words. Neugroschel, Joachim, tr. from Ger. 1979. 12.95 (ISBN 0-8264-0081-7). Continuum.
--The Conscience of Words. Neugroschel, Joachim, tr. from Ger. 246p. 1984. pap. 8.95 (ISBN 0-374-51881-5). FS&G.
--Crowds & Power. 495p. 1982. 17.50 (ISBN 0-8264-0211-9); pap. 11.95 (ISBN 0-8264-0089-2). Continuum.
--Crowds & Power. Stewart, Carol, tr. from Ger. 496p. 1984. pap. 8.95 (ISBN 0-374-51820-3). FS&G.
--Earwitness: Fifty Characters. 1979. 7.95 (ISBN 0-8264-0096-5). Continuum.
--The Human Province. Neugroschel, Joachim, tr. from Ger. LC 78-3826. 1978. 12.95 (ISBN 0-8264-0114-7). Continuum.
--Kafka's Other Trial: The Letters to Felice. Middleton, Christopher, tr. from Ger. LC 74-3048. 128p. (Orig.). 1982. 11.95 (ISBN 0-8052-3553-1); pap. 5.95 (ISBN 0-8052-0705-8). Schocken.
--The Play of the Eyes. Manheim, Ralph, tr. from Ger. 1985. 17.95 (ISBN 0-374-23434-5). FS&G.
--The Plays of Elias Canetti. Manheim, Ralph, tr. 300p. 1986. 17.95 (ISBN 0-374-23434-5). FS&G.
--The Tongue Set Free: Remembrance of a European Childhood. Neugroschel, Joachim, tr. from Ger. 1980. 14.95 (ISBN 0-8264-0165-1). Continuum.
--The Torch in My Ear. Neugroschel, Joachim, tr. from Ger. 384p. 1982. 16.50 (ISBN 0-374-27847-4); pap. 9.95 (ISBN 0-374-51804-1). FS&G.
--The Voices of Marrakesh: A Record of a Visit. 103p. 1982. pap. 5.95 (ISBN 0-8264-0213-5). Continuum.
--The Voices of Marrakesh: A Record of a Visit. Underwood, J. A., tr. from Ger. LC 78-9776. 1978. 9.95 (ISBN 0-8264-0170-8). Continuum.
--The Voices of Marrakesh: A Record of a Visit. Underwood, J. A., tr. from Ger. 104p. 1984. pap. 5.95 (ISBN 0-374-51823-8). FS&G.
Canetti, Elias & Neugroschel, Joachim. The Tongue Set Free: Remembrance of a European Childhood. 268p. 1983. pap. 9.95 (ISBN 0-374-51802-5). FS&G.
Caneva-Decevska, N., ed. see Stamov, Stefan & Angreova, R.
Canevari, Leonore. I'll Always Love You-Frankie. 252p. (Orig.). 1983. softcover 7.95 (ISBN 0-9611120-0-X). Casino.
Caney, John C. The Modernisation of Somali Vocabulary with Particular Reference to the Period from 1972 to the Present. (Hamburger Philologische Studien: No. 59). 389p. (Orig.). 1984. pap. write for info. (ISBN 3-87118-663-5, Pub. by Helmut Buske Verlag Hamburg). Benjamins North Am.
Caney, R. W. & Reynolds, J. E., eds. Reed's Marine Distance Tables. 4th ed. 1978. pap. 22.50 (ISBN 0-900335-51-3). Heinman.
Caney, Steven. Inventions, Concoctions & Contraptions. (Illus.). 1985. pap. 7.95 (ISBN 0-89480-076-0, 406). Workman Pub.
--Kids' America. LC 77-27465. (Illus.). 416p. (gr. k-9). 1978. pap. 9.95 (ISBN 0-911104-80-1, IBM 1147). Workman Pub.
--Steve Caney's Toybook. LC 75-8814. (Illus.). 176p. (gr. 3 up). 1972. 8.95 (ISBN 0-911104-15-1, 022); pap. 6.95 (ISBN 0-911104-17-8, 023). Workman Pub.
--Steven Caney's Invention Book. LC 78-73723. (Illus.). 224p. (Orig.). (gr. 3-7). 1985. 12.95 (ISBN 0-89480-077-9, 315); pap. 7.95 (ISBN 0-89480-076-0, 406). Workman Pub.
--Steven Caney's Playbook. LC 75-9816. (Illus.). 240p. (ps-7). 1975. pap. 8.95 (ISBN 0-911104-38-0, 050). Workman Pub.
Canfield, Anita. Self-Esteem & the Physical You. 293p. 1983. 8.95 (ISBN 0-934126-21-6). Randall Bk Co.
--Self-Esteem & the Social You. 140p. 1983. 7.95 (ISBN 0-934126-26-7). Randall Bk Co.
--Self-Esteem for the Latter-Day Saint Woman. 2nd ed. 135p. 1983. 7.95 (ISBN 0-934126-15-1). Randall Bk Co.
--The Young Woman & Her Self-Esteem. 93p. 1983. 9.95 (ISBN 0-934126-41-0). Randall Bk Co.
Canfield, Anita, jt. auth. see Flynn, Johanna.
Canfield, Arthur G. The Reappearing Characters in Balzac's "Comedie Humaine". Ham, Edward B., ed. LC 77-14166. (Studies in Romance Languages & Literature: No. 37). 1977. Repr. of 1961 ed. lib. bdg. 24.75 (ISBN 0-8371-9836-4, CARC). Greenwood.
Canfield, Arthur G., ed. French Lyrics. 382p. 1982. Repr. of 1899 ed. lib. bdg. 35.00 (ISBN 0-8495-0958-0). Arden Lib.
Canfield, Betty M. The Bible World Maps of the Old & New Testaments. (Illus.). 24p. (Orig.). 1983. pap. text ed. 4.95 (ISBN 0-9611756-0-5). Humble Pub Co.
Canfield, Cass. The Incredible Pierpont Morgan: Financier & Art Collector. LC 73-15000. (Illus.). 176p. 1974. 17.50i (ISBN 0-06-010599-2, HarpT). Har-Row.
--Samuel Adams's Revolution, 1765-1776: With the Assistance of George Washington, Thomas Jefferson, Benjamin Franklin, John Adams, George III, & the People of Boston. LC 75-29937. (Illus.). 160p. 1976. 12.45i (ISBN 0-06-010619-0, HarpT). Har-Row.
--Up & Down & Around: A Publisher Recollects the Time of His Life. LC 73-156512. (Illus.). 228p. 1971. 10.00i (ISBN 0-06-121540-6). Har-Row.
Canfield-ChekChart. Automotive Electrical Systems, 2 vols. 294p. 1978. pap. text ed. 21.50 (ISBN 0-06-454000-6, HarpC); instructors manual avail. (ISBN 0-06-454004-9). Har-Row.
--Fuel Systems & Emission Controls, 2 vols. 248p. 1978. pap. text ed. 21.50 scp (ISBN 0-06-454002-2, HarpC); instructors manual avail. (ISBN 0-06-454005-7). Har-Row.
Canfield, Curtis, ed. Plays of the Irish Renaissance, 1880-1930. LC 73-4881. (Play Anthology Reprint Ser.). Repr. of 1929 ed. 31.00 (ISBN 0-8369-8248-7). Ayer Co Pubs.
Canfield, D. Lincoln. East Meets West, South of the Border: Essays on Spanish American Life & Attitudes. LC 67-10723. (Latin American Classics Ser.). 160p. 1968. 6.50x (ISBN 0-8093-0306-X). S Ill U Pr.
--Spanish Pronunciation in the Americas. LC 80-23664. 128p. 1981. 4.95 (ISBN 0-226-09263-1, Phoen). U of Chicago Pr.
--Spanish Pronunciation in the Americas. LC 80-23664. (Illus.). 1981. lib. bdg. 15.00x (ISBN 0-226-09262-3). U of Chicago Pr.
Canfield, D. Lincoln & Davis, J. Cary. East Meets West: An Introduction to Romance Linguistics. LC 74-34260. (Illus.). 230p. 1975. 15.95x (ISBN 0-8093-0677-8). S Ill U Pr.
Canfield, De Los Lincoln. Spanish Literature in Mexican Languages as a Source for the Study of Spanish Pronunciation. 257p. 3.00 (ISBN 0-318-14306-2). Hispanic Inst.
Canfield, Dorothea F. see Fisher, Dorothea F.
Canfield, Dorothy. The Bent Twig. 334p. 1981. Repr. PLB 17.95x (ISBN 0-89966-343-5). Buccaneer Bks.
--The Bent Twig. 340p. 1981. Repr. PLB 13.95x (ISBN 0-89967-018-0). Harmony Raine.
--The Home Maker. 320p. pap. 6.95 (ISBN 0-89733-069-2). Academy Chi Pubs.
--Understood Betsy. 219p. 1981. Repr. PLB 14.95 (ISBN 0-89966-342-7). Buccaneer Bks.
--Understood Betsy. 213p. 1980. Repr. PLB 17.95x (ISBN 0-89967-016-4). Harmony Raine.
Canfield, Gae W. Sarah Winnemucca of the Northern Paiutes. LC 82-40448. (Illus.). 336p. 1983. 19.95 (ISBN 0-8061-1814-8). U of Okla Pr.
Canfield, George L. & Dalzell, George W. The Law of the Sea: A Manual of the Principles of Admiralty Law for Students, Mariners & Ship Operators. xvi, 315p. 1983. Repr. of 1926 ed. lib. bdg. 35.00x (ISBN 0-8377-0442-1). Rothman.
Canfield, J. Douglas. Nicholas Rowe & Christian Tragedy. LC 76-39917. 1977. 10.00 (ISBN 0-8130-0545-0). U Presses Fla.
Canfield, J. Douglas, ed. Sanctuary: A Collection of Critical Essays. 145p. 1982. 10.95 (ISBN 0-13-791228-5); pap. 4.95 (ISBN 0-13-791210-2). P-H.
Canfield, Jack, jt. auth. see Wells, Harold C.
Canfield, James D., jt. auth. see Dethlefsen, Merle.
Canfield, James L. A Case of Third Party Activism: The George Wallace Campaign Worker & the American Independent Party. (Illus.). 130p. (Orig.). 1983. lib. bdg. 20.50 (ISBN 0-8191-3720-0); pap. text ed. 8.75 (ISBN 0-8191-3721-9). U Pr of Amer.
Canfield, Jane W. Swan Cove. LC 77-11832. (Early I Can Read Bk.). (Illus.). 32p. 1978. PLB 8.89 (ISBN 0-06-020949-6). HarpJ.
Canfield, Jimmie. Ain't No Bears Out Tonight. 1984. 5.00 (ISBN 0-934834-42-3). White Pine.
Canfield, John V. Wittgenstein: Language & World. LC 81-4522. 240p. 1981. lib. bdg. 18.50x (ISBN 0-87023-318-1); pap. 8.95x (ISBN 0-87023-319-X). U of Mass Pr.
Canfield, Leon H. The Early Persecutions of the Christians. LC 68-54259. (Columbia University Studies in the Social Sciences: No. 136). Repr. of 1913 ed. 14.50 (ISBN 0-404-51136-8). AMS Pr.
--Presidency of Woodrow Wilson. LC 66-24796. (Illus.). 299p. 1968. 28.50 (ISBN 0-8386-6744-9). Fairleigh Dickinson.
Canfield, Michael & Weberman, Alan J. Coup d'Etat in America: The CIA & the Assassination of John F. Kennedy. LC 75-4360. (Illus.). 340p. 1975. 12.95 (ISBN 0-89388-204-6). Okpaku Communications.
Canfield, Muriel. Anne. LC 83-73597. (Heartsong Bks.). 160p. (YA) (gr. 8-12). 1984. pap. 2.95 (ISBN 0-87123-423-8). Bethany Hse.
--I Wish I Could Say, "I Love You". 204p. (Orig.). 1983. pap. 4.95 (ISBN 0-87123-265-0). Bethany Hse.
Canfield Press Chek-Chart. Automatic Transmissions, 2 vols. 1979. pap. text ed. 21.50 scp (ISBN 0-06-454001-4, HarpC); instructors manual avail. (ISBN 0-06-454007-3). Har-Row.
Canfield Press-Chek-Chart. Engine Performance Diagnosis & Tune-up, 2 vols. 1978. pap. text ed. 21.50 scp (ISBN 0-06-454003-0, HarpC); instructors manual avail. (ISBN 0-06-454006-5). Har-Row.
Canfield, Richard A. Blackjack Your Way to Riches. (Illus.). 1979. Repr. 12.00 (ISBN 0-8184-0273-3). Lyle Stuart.
Canfield, Robert, intro. by. The Encyclopedia of Mankind. (Illus.). 2712p. 1984. lib. bdg. 324.95x (ISBN 0-86307-231-3). M Cavendish Corp.
Canfield, Robert L. Faction & Conversion in a Plural Society: Religious Alignments in the Hindu Kush. (Anthropological Papers: No. 50). 1973. 3.00x (ISBN 0-932206-48-4). U Mich Mus Anthro.
Canfield, Robert L., jt. ed. see Shahrani, M. Nazif.
Canfield, Rosemary, ed. Perspectives: The Alabama Heritage. LC 78-64441. 1978. 15.00x (ISBN 0-916624-27-7). Troy State Univ.
Cange, Charles D. Du Fresne Du see Du Cange, Charles D.
Cangelosi, James S. Cooperation in the Classroom: Students & Teachers Together. 64p. 1984. 6.95 (ISBN 0-8106-1690-4). NEA.
--Measurement & Evaluation: An Inductive Approach for Teachers. 448p. 1982. pap. write for info. (ISBN 0-697-06065-9); instr's manual avail. (ISBN 0-697-06067-5). Wm C Brown.
Cangelosi, Vincent E. & Taylor, Phillip H. Basic Statistics: A Real World Approach. 3rd ed. (Illus.). 550p. 1983. text ed. 27.95 (ISBN 0-314-69637-7); study guide available 9.95 (ISBN 0-314-71082-5); solutions manual avail. (ISBN 0-314-71083-3). West Pub.
Cangelosi, Vincent E., et al. Basic Statistics: A Real World Approach. 2nd ed. (Illus.). 1979. pap. text ed. 15.95 international ed. (ISBN 0-8299-0268-6). West Pub.
Cangemi, Joseph P. Higher Education & the Development of Self-Actualizing Personalities. (Illus.). 1977. 9.95 (ISBN 0-8022-2175-0). Philos Lib.
Cangemi, Joseph P. & Kowalski, Casimir J. Perspectives in Higher Education. LC 80-81695. 128p. 1983. 9.95 (ISBN 0-8022-2369-9). Philos Lib.
Cangemi, Joseph P., jt. auth. see Kowalski, Casimir J.
Cangemi, Joseph P. & Guttschalk, George E., eds. Effective Management: A Humanistic Perspective. LC 78-61106. 1980. 8.50 (ISBN 0-8022-2229-3). Philos Lib.
Cangemi, Joseph P., jt. auth. see Kowalski, Casimir J.
Canger, Raffaele, ed. see Epilepsy International Symposium, 11th., et al.
Cangialosi, Karen, jt. auth. see Paffrath, Jim.
Canh, Nguyen Van see Cahn, Nguyen Van & Cooper, Earle.
Canh, Nguyen van see Van Canh, Nguyen.
Canham, Elizabeth. Pilgrimage to Priesthood. 128p. (Orig.). 1985. pap. 9.95 (ISBN 0-8164-2492-6, 8603, Pub. by Seabury). Winston Pr.
Canham, Erwin D. Ethics of United States Foreign Relations. LC 66-14031. 101p. 1966. 6.00x (ISBN 0-8262-0044-3). U of Mo Pr.
Canham, Erwin D., ed. see Christian Science Monitor.
Canham, Geoffrey R. Foundations of Chemistry. 320p. 1983. pap. 10.95 lab manual (ISBN 0-201-10416-4); instr's. guide 2.50 (ISBN 0-201-10418-0). Addison-Wesley.
Canham, Kingsley, jt. auth. see Denton, Clive.
Canham, Marsha. Bound by the Heart. (Avon Romance Ser.). 400p. 1984. pap. 2.95 (ISBN 0-380-88732-0). Avon.
--China Rose. 288p. 1984. pap. 2.95 (ISBN 0-380-85985-8, 85985). Avon.
Caniff, Milton. The China Journey. Chadbourne, Bill, ed. LC 77-75667. (Milton Caniff's Terry & the Pirates Ser.: Vol. 1). (Illus.). 1977. pap. 6.95 (ISBN 0-685-81984-1). Nostalgia Pr.
--Enter the Dragon Lady. Chadbourne, Bill, ed. LC 77-75670. (Milton Coniff's Terry & the Pirates Ser.: Vol. 4). (Illus.). 1977. pap. 6.95 (ISBN 0-87897-016-9). Nostalgia Pr.
--The Normandie Affair. Chadbourne, Bill, ed. LC 77-75668. (Milton Caniff's Terry & the Pirates Ser.: Vol. 2). (Illus.). 1977. pap. 6.95 (ISBN 0-685-81985-X). Nostalgia Pr.
--Terry & the Pirates: Enter the Dragon Lady. (Illus.). 1976. pap. 6.95 (ISBN 0-517-52734-0). Crown.
--Terry & the Pirates (1934-1935, Vol. 1. Blackbeard, Bill, ed. LC 84-60900. 224p. 1984. Repr. 30.00x (ISBN 0-918348-06-4). NBM.
--Terry & the Pirates (1935-1936, Vol. 2. Blackbeard, Bill, ed. LC 84-60900. 224p. 1984. Repr. 32.50x (ISBN 0-918348-07-2). NBM.
--Terry & the Pirates (1936-1937, Vol. 3. Blackbeard, Bill, ed. LC 84-60900. 288p. 1985. Repr. 32.50x (ISBN 0-918348-08-0). NBM.
--Terry & the Pirates (1937-1938, Vol. 4. Blackbeard, Bill, ed. 288p. 1985. Repr. 32.50x (ISBN 0-918348-09-9). NBM.
--Terry & The Pirates (1938-1939, Vol. 5. Blackbeard, Bill, ed. LC 84-60900. 288p. 1985. Repr. 34.50x (ISBN 0-918348-10-2). NBM.
--Terry & the Pirates (1939-1940, Vol. 6. Blackbeard, Bill, ed. LC 84-60900. 288p. 1985. Repr. 34.50 (ISBN 0-918348-12-9, Pub. by Flying Buttress Classics). NBM.
Canino, Marcelino J. El Cantar Folklorico De Puerto Rico: Estudio y Florilegio. pap. 5.00 (ISBN 0-8477-0501-3). U of PR Pr.

Canino, Robert. The Divorcee's Kitchen Give You Servings from One to Six. 1985. 11.95 (ISBN 0-533-06508-9). Vantage.

Canino, Thomas L. Mountain Man Cookbook: Venison & Other Recipies. LC 85-90129. 85p. (Orig.). 1985. pap. 7.95 (ISBN 0-9614922-0-1). TLC Enterprises.

--Mountainman Cookbook: Venison & Other Recipies. (Orig.). 1985. pap. 7.95 (ISBN 0-317-19108-X). TLC Enterprises.

Canino Salgado, Marcelino. Gozos Devocionales En la Tradicion De Puerto Rico. (UPREX, Folklore: No. 32). pap. 1.85 (ISBN 0-8477-0032-1). U of PR Pr.

Canis, Wayne F., et al. Living with the Alabama-Mississippi Shore. (Living with the Shore Ser.). 1984. 24.75 (ISBN 0-8223-0510-0); pap. 11.75 (ISBN 0-8223-0511-9). Duke.

Canizares, Orlando. A Manual of Dermatology for Developing Countries. (Illus.). 1982. text ed. 39.50x (ISBN 0-19-261366-9); pap. text ed. 14.95x (ISBN 0-19-261185-2). Oxford U Pr.

Canjar, Lawrence & Manning, Francis. Thermodynamic Properties & Reduced Correlations for Gases. LC 66-30022. 222p. 1967. pap. text ed. 6.95x abridged student (ISBN 0-87201-868-7). Gulf Pub.

Canjar, Lawrence N. & Manning, Francis S. Thermodynamic Properties & Reduced Correlations for Gases. LC 66-30022. pap. 64.50 (ISBN 0-317-08041-5, 2051874). Bks Demand UMI.

Canler, Louis. Autobiography of a French Detective from 1818 to 1858: Most Curious Revelations of the French Detective Police System. LC 75-32738. (Literature of Mystery & Detection Ser.). 1976. Repr. of 1862 ed. 24.50x (ISBN 0-405-07866-8). Ayer Co Pubs.

Cann, Christian. A Scriptural & Allegorical Glossary to Milton's Paradise Lost. 1978. Repr. of 1828 ed. lib. bdg. 35.00 (ISBN 0-8495-0807-X). Arden Lib.

--Scriptural & Allegorical Glossary to Milton's Paradise Lost. Repr. of 1828 ed. 32.50 (ISBN 0-8414-0566-2). Folcroft.

Cann, Kevin. David Bowie. LC 83-25411. (Illus.). 239p. 1984. pap. 8.95 (ISBN 0-671-50537-8, Fireside). S&S.

Cannadine, David. Lords & Landlords: The Aristocracy & the Towns, 1774-1967. 494p. 1981. text ed. 50.00x (ISBN 0-7185-1152-2, Leicester). Humanities.

Cannadine, David, ed. Patricians, Power & Politics in Nineteenth Century Towns. LC 82-42544. 240p. 1982. 35.00x (ISBN 0-312-59803-3). St Martin.

Cannadine, David, ed. see Dyos, H. J.

Cannady, Criss, ed. see Felipe, Leon.

Cannady, Joan. Black Images in American Literature. (gr. 10 up). 1977. pap. text ed. 7.50x (ISBN 0-8104-5795-4). Boynton Cook Pubs.

Cannan, Edwin. The History of Local Rates in England. LC 79-1574. 1980. Repr. of 1912 ed. 18.00 (ISBN 0-88355-880-7). Hyperion Conn.

--History of the Theories of Production & Distribution in English Political Economy from 1776 to 1848. 3rd ed. LC 66-22618. Repr. of 1917 ed. 32.50x (ISBN 0-678-00284-3). Kelley.

--Wealth: A Brief Explanation of the Causes of Economic Welfare. LC 79-1575. 1981. Repr. of 1928 ed. 22.50 (ISBN 0-88355-881-5). Hyperion Conn.

Cannan, Edwin, ed. Paper Pound of 1797-1812. 2nd ed. 72p. 1970. Repr. of 1925 ed. 28.50x (ISBN 0-7146-1210-3, F Cass Co). Biblio Dist.

--Paper Pound of 1797-1821. 2nd ed. LC 67-24748. Repr. of 1925 ed. 25.00x (ISBN 0-678-00536-2). Kelley.

--Review of Economic Theory, 1929. 2nd ed. 448p. 1964. Repr. of 1929 ed. 30.00x (ISBN 0-7146-1211-1, BHA-01211, F Cass Co). Biblio Dist.

Cannan, Edwin, ed. see Smith, Adam.

Cannan, Edwin, ed. & intro. by see Smith, Adam.

Cannan, G. Samuel Butler: A Critical Study. LC 70-133284. (English Biography Ser., No. 31). 1970. Repr. of 1925 ed. lib. bdg. 39.95x (ISBN 0-8383-1183-0). Haskell.

Cannan, Gilbert. The Joy of the Theatre. 1973. 10.00 (ISBN 0-8274-1773-X). R West.

--Samuel Butler: A Critical Study. 194p. 1980. Repr. of 1915 ed. lib. bdg. 20.00 (ISBN 0-8495-0796-0). Arden Lib.

--Samuel Butler: A Critical Study. 1915. lib. bdg. 20.00 (ISBN 0-8414-3537-5). Folcroft.

--Satire. lib. bdg. 15.00 (ISBN 0-8414-3535-9). Folcroft.

Cannan, Gilbert, tr. see Chekhov, Anton P.

Cannan, Joanna. The Body in the Beck. Barzun, J. & Taylor, W. H., eds. LC 81-47393. (Crime Fiction 1950-1975 Ser.). 2097p. 1982. lib. bdg. 18.00 (ISBN 0-8240-4954-3). Garland Pub.

Cannar, K. The Theory & Practice of Motor Insurance. 1978. text ed. 89.00x (ISBN 0-900886-24-2, Pub. by Witherby & Co. Ltd). State Mutual Bk.

Cannar, Kenneth S. Essential Cases in Insurance Law. LC 84-20846. 224p. 1985. 29.00 (ISBN 0-85941-284-9, Pub. by Woodhead-Faulkner). Longwood Pub Group.

Cannata, F. & Ueberall, H. Giant Resonance Phenomena in Intermediate-Energy Nuclear Reactions. (Springer Tracts in Modern Physics: Vol. 89). (Illus.). 112p. 1980. 35.00 (ISBN 0-387-10105-5). Springer-Verlag.

Cannatella, David C. A Review of the Phyllomedusa Buckleyi Group: (Anura: Hylidae) (Occasional Papers: Vol. 87). 40p. 1980. 2.25 (ISBN 0-317-04840-6). U of KS Mus Nat Hist.

Cannatella, Mary M. & Arnold, Rita E. Plants of the Texas Shore: A Beachcomber's Guide. LC 84-40553. (Illus.). 96p. 1985. pap. 5.95 (ISBN 0-89096-214-6). Tex A&M Univ Pr.

Cannavale, Frank J. & Falcon, William D. Witness Cooperation. 1978. pap. text ed. 8.95x (ISBN 0-669-01063-4). Heath.

Cannegieter, C. A. Human Aspects of Economics: A Human Treatise of Unemployment, Inflation & World Poverty. (Illus.). 224p. 1982. 12.50 (ISBN 0-682-49751-7, University). Exposition Pr FL.

Cannell, Charles F. & Marquis, Kent H. A Summary of Research Studies of Interviewing Methodology, 1959-1970. (Ser. 2: No. 69). 70p. 1976. pap. text ed. 2.00 (ISBN 0-8406-0062-3). Natl Ctr Health Stats.

Cannell, Charles F., jt. auth. see Kahn, Robert L.

Cannell, Charles F., et al. Experiments in Interviewing Techniques: Field Experiments in Health Reporting, 1971-1977. 446p. (Orig.). 1979. pap. 18.00x (ISBN 0-87944-247-6). Inst Soc Res.

--A Technique for Evaluating Interviewer Performance: A Manual for Coding & Analyzing Interviewer Behavior from Tape Recordings of Household Interviews. LC 74-620203. 138p. 1975. pap. 10.00x (ISBN 0-87944-174-7). Inst Soc Res.

Cannell, Dorothy. Down the Garden Path: A Pastoral Mystery. 304p. 1985. 14.95 (ISBN 0-312-21869-9). St Martin.

--The Thin Woman. (Crime Monthly Ser.). 256p. 1985. pap. 3.50 (ISBN 0-14-007947-5). Penguin.

--The Thin Woman: An Epicurean Mystery. 288p. 1984. 13.95 (ISBN 0-312-80005-3). St Martin.

Cannell, G. H., et al, eds. Agriculture in Semi-Arid Environments. (Ecological Studies: Vol. 34). (Illus.). 1979. 60.00 (ISBN 0-387-09414-8). Springer-Verlag.

Cannell, J. Secrets of Houdini. 3.00x (ISBN 0-685-47573-5). Wehman.

Cannell, J. C. The Secrets of Houdini. LC 72-93609. (Illus.). 288p. 1973. pap. 5.95 (ISBN 0-486-22913-0). Dover.

Cannell, M. G., ed. World Forest Biomass & Primary Production Data. 1982. 55.00 (ISBN 0-12-158780-0). Acad Pr.

Cannell, M. G. & Last, F. T., eds. Tree Physiology & Yield Improvement. 1977. 80.50 (ISBN 0-12-158750-9). Acad Pr.

Cannell, Michael T. & Zimmer, Judith. Free Weights. LC 84-4060. (AT Home Gym Ser.). 64p. 1985. pap. 2.95 (ISBN 0-394-72974-9, Pub. by Villard Bks). Random.

--Rowing. Wallach, Susan, ed. LC 84-40601. (The At Home Gym Ser.). 64p. 1985. pap. 2.95 (ISBN 0-394-72971-4, Pub. by Villard Bks). Random.

--Stationary Bicycles. Wallach, Susan, ed. LC 84-40600. (The At Home Gym Ser.). 64p. 1985. pap. 2.95 (ISBN 0-394-72973-0, Pub. by Villard Bks). Random.

--Weight Machines. Wallach, Susan, ed. LC 84-40602. (The At Home Gym Ser.). 64p. 1985. pap. 2.95 (ISBN 0-394-72974-9, Pub. by Villard Bks). Random.

Canner, Mark, jt. ed. see Collins, Dana.

Canner, Norma. And a Time to Dance. new ed. (Illus.). 1975. 8.95 (ISBN 0-8238-0171-3). Plays.

Canney, John, et al. Working on Words. viii, 260p. (Orig.). 1981. pap. text ed. 17.95x (ISBN 0-913580-72-4). Gallaudet Coll.

Canney, Maragret, et al, eds. Catalogue of the Goldsmiths' Library of Economic Literature, Vol. 4. 449p. 1983. 160.00 (ISBN 0-485-15013-1, Pub. by Athlone Pr Ltd). Longwood Pub Group.

Canney, Margaret, et al, eds. Catalogue of the Goldsmiths' Library of Economic Literature, 4 vols. 1983. Set. 550.00 (ISBN 0-485-15016-6, Pub. by Athlone Pr Ltd). Longwood Pub Group.

--Catalogue of the Goldsmiths' Library of Economic Literature, Vol. 1. 838p. 1970. 130.00 (ISBN 0-485-15014-X, Pub. by Athlone Pr Ltd). Longwood Pub Group.

--Catalogue of the Goldsmiths' Library of Economic Literature, Vol. 3. 223p. 1982. 130.00 (ISBN 0-485-15012-3, Pub. by Athlone Pr Ltd). Longwood Pub Group.

--Catalogue of the Goldsmiths' Library of Economic Literature, Vol. 2. 772p. 1975. 130.00 (ISBN 0-485-15015-8, Pub. by Athlone Pr Ltd). Longwood Pub Group.

Canney, Maurice A. Encyclopaedia of Religions. LC 75-123370. 1970. Repr. of 1921 ed. 58.00 (ISBN 0-8103-3856-4). Gale.

Cannie, Joan K. The Woman's Guide to Management Success: How to Win Power in the Real Organizational World. (Illus.). 1979. 12.95 (ISBN 0-13-961771-X, Spec); pap. 4.95 (ISBN 0-13-961763-9). P-H.

Cannie, John K. Take Charge: Success Tactics for Business & Life. (Illus.). 1980. 12.95 (ISBN 0-13-882621-8, Spec); pap. 4.95 (ISBN 0-13-882613-7, Spec). P-H.

Canniff, Kiki. Free Campgrounds of Washington & Oregon. (Illus.). 80p. (Orig.). 1985. pap. 5.95 (ISBN 0-9608744-4-5). KITwo Enter.

Canniff, William. The Medical Profession in Upper Canada, 1753-1850. LC 75-23690. Repr. of 1894 ed. 56.50 (ISBN 0-404-13242-1). AMS Pr.

Canning, Albert & Stratford, George. History in Fact & Fiction. LC 76-10788. 1976. Repr. of 1897 ed. lib. bdg. 25.00 (ISBN 0-8414-3497-2). Folcroft.

--Literary Influence in British History. LC 76-10959. 1976. Repr. of 1904 ed. lib. bdg. 25.00 (ISBN 0-8414-3495-6). Folcroft.

Canning, Albert S. British Writers on Classic Lands. 1973. lib. bdg. 30.00 (ISBN 0-8414-3480-8). Folcroft.

--British Writers on Classic Lands. 296p. 1980. Repr. of 1907 ed. lib. bdg. 27.50 (ISBN 0-8482-3574-6). Norwood Edns.

--Dickens & Thackeray Studied in Three Novels. 1911. 9.45 (ISBN 0-8274-2179-6). R West.

--History in Fact & Fiction. 336p. 1980. Repr. of 1897 ed. lib. bdg. 38.50 (ISBN 0-8492-3863-3). R West.

--Literary Influence in British History. 202p. 1980. Repr. of 1904 ed. lib. bdg. 30.00 (ISBN 0-8495-0627-1). Arden Lib.

--Philosophy of the Waverly Novels. 1973. Repr. of 1879 ed. 25.00 (ISBN 0-8274-1784-5). R West.

Canning, B. W. Raise the Speed, Reduce the Errors. (Pitman Secretarial Science Ser.). 96p. 1975. spiral bdg. 9.95x (ISBN 0-8464-0782-5). Beekman Pubs.

Canning, E. V. & Wright, C. A., eds. Behavioural Aspects of Parasite Transmission. (Zoological Journal of the Linean Society Ser.: Vol. 5). 1973. 47.50 (ISBN 0-12-158650-2). Acad Pr.

Canning, G. Some Official Correspondence, 1812-1827, 2 Vols. in 1. Stapleton, E. J., ed. Repr. of 1887 ed. 36.00 (ISBN 0-527-14811-3). Kraus Repr.

Canning, George. George Canning & His Friends, Containing Hitherto Unpublished Letters, Jeux D'espirit, Etc, 2 Vols. in 1. Bagot, J., ed. LC 9-14585. 1969. Repr. of 1909 ed. 41.00 (ISBN 0-527-14800-8). Kraus Repr.

--The Occasional Horseman. (Illus.). 4.50 (ISBN 0-85131-188-1, BL212, Dist. by Miller). J A Allen.

Canning House Library. Catalogues of the Canning House Library: Author & Subject Catalogues, 2 pts. Incl. Pt. 1. Hispanic Catalogues, 4 vols. Hispanic Council. 1967. 325.00 (ISBN 0-8161-0741-6); First Supplement, 1973. 115.00 (ISBN 0-8161-1125-1); Pt. 2. Luso-Brazilian Catalogues. Luso-Brazilian Council. 1967. 100.00 (ISBN 0-8161-0126-4); First Supplement, 1973. lib. bdg. 110.00 (ISBN 0-8161-1100-6). Hall Library). G K Hall.

Canning, Jeremiah W., ed. Values in an Age of Confrontation: A Symposium Sponsored by the Religion in Education Foundation. LC 72-109054. (Studies of the Person). pap. 41.10 (ISBN 0-317-09226-X, 2055239). Bks Demand UMI.

Canning, John. Fifty True Mysteries of the Sea. LC 80-5498. (Illus.). 478p. 1980. 14.95 (ISBN 0-8128-2734-1). Stein & Day.

--Fifty True Mysteries of the Sea. 480p. 1984. pap. 3.95 (ISBN 0-8128-8044-7). Stein & Day.

Canning, John, ed. Fifty Great Horror Stories. 512p. (gr. 9 up). 1973. pap. 3.50 (ISBN 0-553-24404-3). Bantam.

--One Hundred Great Kings, Queens & Rulers of the World. LC 68-23429. 1978. pap. 7.95 (ISBN 0-8008-5776-3). Taplinger.

--One Hundred Great Modern Lives. 29.95 (ISBN 0-88411-286-1, Pub. by Aeonian Pr). Amereon Ltd.

Canning, John B. The Economics of Accountancy: A Critical Analysis of Accounting Theory. Brief, Richard P., ed. LC 77-16723. (Development of Contemporary Accounting Thought Ser). 1978. Repr. of 1929 ed. lib. bdg. 32.00x (ISBN 0-405-10948-2). Ayer Co Pubs.

Canning, Paul. British Policy Towards Ireland, Nineteen Twenty-One to Nineteen Forty-One. (Illus.). 360p. 1985. 29.95 (ISBN 0-19-820068-4). Oxford U Pr.

Canning, R. G. & Leeper, N. C. So You Are Thinking about a Small Business Computer. 203p. 1982. 22.95 (ISBN 0-13-823625-9); pap. 10.95 (ISBN 0-13-823617-8). P-H.

Canning, Victor. Birds of a Feather. Cady, Howard, ed. LC 84-62518. 192p. (Orig.). 1985. 13.95 (ISBN 0-688-04220-1). Morrow.

--The Crimson Chalice. 1979. pap. 2.50 (ISBN 0-441-12190-X, Pub. by Charter Bks). Ace Bks.

--The Doomsday Carrier. 320p. 1978. pap. 1.95 (ISBN 0-441-15865-X, Pub. by Charter Bks). Ace Bks.

--Doubled in Diamonds. 224p. 1980. pap. 2.25 (ISBN 0-441-16024-7, Pub. by Charter Bks). Ace Bks.

--The Dragon Tree. 1980. pap. 2.25 (ISBN 0-441-16659-8, Pub. by Charter Bks). Ace Bks.

--Fall from Grace. LC 80-83325. 224p. 1981. 9.95 (ISBN 0-688-00195-5). Morrow.

--The Melting Man. 272p. 1980. pap. 2.50 (ISBN 0-441-52426-5, Pub. by Charter Bks). Ace Bks.

--Raven's Wind. LC 83-61372. 192p. 1983. 11.95 (ISBN 0-688-02133-6). Morrow.

--The Runaways. 1972. 6.95 (ISBN 0-688-00114-9). Morrow.

--Scorpio Letter. 272p. 1981. pap. 2.50 (ISBN 0-441-75519-4, Pub. by Charter Bks). Ace Bks.

--Vanishing Point. LC 82-18845. 224p. 1983. 10.95 (ISBN 0-688-01107-1). Morrow.

Cannings, C. & Thompson, E. A. Genealogical & Genetic Structure. LC 81-6100. (Cambridge Studies in Mathematical Biology: No. 3). (Illus.). 150p. 1981. 42.50 (ISBN 0-521-23946-X); pap. 16.95 (ISBN 0-521-28363-9). Cambridge U Pr.

Cannistraro, Philip V., ed. Historical Dictionary of Fascist Italy. LC 81-4493. (Illus.). xxix, 657p. 1982. lib. bdg. 49.95 (ISBN 0-313-21317-8, CFA/). Greenwood.

Cannistraro, Philip V., intro. by see Salvemini, Gaetano.

Cannistraro, Philip V., et al, eds. see Biddle, A. J. Drexel, Jr.

Cannizarro, Marilyn. Cooking with Abstinence: An Inspirational Cookbook for the Compulsive Overeater. LC 81-43898. (Illus.). 96p. 1983. pap. 5.95 (ISBN 0-385-18140-X, Dolp). Doubleday.

Cannizzo, Cindy, ed. The Gun Merchants: Politics & Policies of the Major Arms Suppliers. (Pergamon Policy Studies). 1980. 32.00 (ISBN 0-08-024632-X). Pergamon.

Cannom, Robert. Van Dyke & the Mythical City, Hollywood. LC 76-52096. (Classics of Film Literature Ser.: Vol. 8). (Illus.). 1977. Repr. of 1948 ed. lib. bdg. 26.00 (ISBN 0-8240-2870-8). Garland Pub.

Cannon. The One-Dimensional Heat Equation. 1984. 68.00 (ISBN 0-201-13522-1). Cambridge U Pr.

Cannon & Hanson. Clean Water Act Permit Manual. 1984. pap. 125.00 (ISBN 0-88057-136-5). Exec Ent Inc.

Cannon, Ann. My Home Has One Parent. LC 81-86637. (gr. 7-12). 1983. pap. 4.95 (ISBN 0-8054-5337-7, 4253-37). Broadman.

Cannon, Anthon S., et al, eds. Popular Beliefs & Superstitions from Utah. 526p. 1984. 45.00x (ISBN 0-87480-236-9). U of Utah Pr.

Cannon, Aubrey, jt. auth. see Hayden, Brian.

Cannon, Barrie R. & Cannon, George W. Coming into the Light: An Invitation. (Illus.). 1979. pap. 12.95 (ISBN 0-9603020-0-X). Voyager Pubns.

Cannon, Beekman C. Johann Mattheson, Spectator in Music. (Illus.). xi, 244p. 1968. Repr. of 1947 ed. 18.50 (ISBN 0-208-00311-8, Archon). Shoe String.

Cannon, Betty, jt. ed. see Krolick, Sanford.

Cannon, Bill. How to Cast Small Metal & Rubber Parts. (Illus.). 1979. 11.95 (ISBN 0-8306-9869-8); pap. 8.95 (ISBN 0-8306-1105-3, 1105). TAB Bks.

Cannon, C. J. The Transfer of Spectral Line Radiation. (Illus.). 650p. 1985. 99.50 (ISBN 0-521-25995-9). Cambridge U Pr.

Cannon, Calvin, ed. Modern Spanish Poems. 1965. 7.95x (ISBN 0-02-318870-7). Macmillan.

Cannon, Carl L. American Book Collectors & Collecting from Colonial Times to the Present. LC 76-6149. 1976. Repr. of 1941 ed. lib. bdg. 32.50x (ISBN 0-8371-8841-5, CAAB). Greenwood.

Cannon, Chapman R. & Cannon, Donnie. How We Made Millions & Never Left the Ghetto. 1983. 6.95 (ISBN 0-8062-1956-4). Carlton.

Cannon, Charles D. A Warning for Fair Women: A Critical Edition. LC 73-81080. (Studies in English Literature: No. 86). 241p. 1975. text ed. 27.20 (ISBN 90-2793-134-8). Mouton.

Cannon, Dianne. Kathleen. LC 76-13241. 1977. 14.95 (ISBN 0-87949-072-1). Ashley Bks.

Cannon, Don L. Fundamentals of Microcomputer Design. LC 81-51951. (Illus.). 584p. 1982. pap. 15.00 (ISBN 0-89512-050-X, MBP30A). Tex Instr Inc.

--Sixteen-Bit Microprocessor Systems. (Solid-State Electronics Technology Bks.). 505p. 49.50 (ISBN 0-317-06598-X). Tex Instr Inc.

--Understanding Digital Troubleshooting. 2nd ed. Luecke, Gerald, et al, eds. LC 84-51468. (Understanding Ser.). (Illus.). 272p. 1984. pap. 14.95 (ISBN 0-89512-165-4, LCB8473). Tex Instr Inc.

--Understanding Electronic Control of Energy Systems. Luecke, Gerald & Battle, Charles, eds. LC 81-85602. (Understanding Ser.). (Illus.). 272p. 1982. pap. 9.95 (ISBN 0-89512-051-8, LCB6642). Tex Instr Inc.

--Understanding Solid Electronics, Vol. II. Battle, Charles W. & Luecke, Gerald, eds. (Understanding Ser.). (Illus.). 256p. (Orig.). 1985. pap. 14.95 (ISBN 0-89512-183-2). Tex Instr Inc.

Cannon, Don L. & Luecke, G. Understanding Microprocessors. 2nd ed. LC 84-51247. (The Understanding Ser.). 288p. 1984. pap. text ed. 14.95 (ISBN 0-89512-160-3, LCB8451). Tex Instr Inc.

Cannon, Don L. & Luecke, Gerald. Understanding Communications Systems. 2nd ed. Mansir, Leslie, et al, eds. LC 84-51469. (Understanding Ser.). (Illus.). 288p. 1984. pap. 14.95 (ISBN 0-89512-166-2, LCB8474). Tex Instr Inc.

Cannon, Donald Q., jt. auth. see Cook, Lyndon W.

Cannon, Donald Q. & Cook, Lyndon W., eds. Far West Record. LC 82-23476. 318p. 1983. 10.95 (ISBN 0-87747-901-1). Deseret Bk.

Cannon, Donald W., jt. auth. see Cook, Lyndon W.

Cannon, Donnie, jt. auth. see Cannon, Chapman R.

Cannon, Elaine. Putting Life in Your Life Story. LC 77-15451. 1977. pap. 3.95 (ISBN 0-87747-679-9). Deseret Bk.

Cannon, Enid S. Golden Opportunities: A History of Perenjori Western Australia. (Illus.). 230p. 1983. 26.25 (ISBN 0-9592847-0-2, Pub. by U of W Austral Pr). Intl Spec Bk.

Cannon, Frances A., ed. see Petz, Richard A.

Cannon, Frank, ed. see Vincent, James E.

Cannon, Garland. An Integrated Transformational Grammar of the English Language. (Costerus New Ser.: No. 8). 1978. pap. text ed. 34.75x (ISBN 90-6203-400-4). Humanities.

--Sir William Jones: A Bibliography of Primary & Secondary Sources. (Library & Information Sources in Linguistics Ser.: No. 7). xiv, 73p. 1979. 16.00x (ISBN 90-272-0998-7). Benjamins North Am.

Cannon, Garland H. Sir William Jones, Orientalist: An Annotated Bibliography of His Works. LC 52-7595. (Pacific Area Bibliographies Ser.). pap. 26.50 (ISBN 0-317-09239-1, 2001352). Bks Demand UMI.

Cannon, Geoffrey & Einzig, Hetty. Dieting Makes You Fat: A Guide to Energy, Food, Fitness & Health. 363p. 1985. 15.95 (ISBN 0-671-53072-0). S&S.

Cannon, George C. The Use of Traditional Material in Colossians: Their Significance for the Problem of Authenticity. LC 83-8181. viii, 253p. 1983. 17.95x (ISBN 0-86554-074-8, H51). Mercer Univ Pr.

Cannon, George Q. Writings from the "Western Standard". Repr. of 1864 ed. 25.00 (ISBN 0-404-01379-1). AMS Pr.

Cannon, George W., jt. auth. see Cannon, Barrie R.

Cannon, Gwenda L. Financial & Estate Planning Applications, 2 Vols. (Huebner School Ser.). (Illus.). 463p. (Orig.). 1983. Vol. 1. pap. text ed. 36.00 (ISBN 0-943590-05-1); Vol. 2. pap. text ed. 40.00 (ISBN 0-943590-06-X). Amer College.

Cannon, Gwenda L., ed. Readings in Estate & Gift Tax Planning. (Huebner School Ser.). 400p. 1982. pap. text ed. 25.00 (ISBN 0-943590-02-7). Amer College.

Cannon, H. Graham. Lamarck & Modern Genetics. LC 75-10211. 152p. 1975. Repr. of 1959 ed. lib. bdg. 27.50x (ISBN 0-8371-8173-9, CALA). Greenwood.

Cannon, Hal, ed. Cowboy Poetry. (Illus.). 192p. 1985. 14.95 (ISBN 0-87905-204-X); pap. 9.95 (ISBN 0-87905-208-2). Gibbs M Smith.

Cannon, Hal, compiled by. The Grand Beehive. (Illus.). 88p. (Orig.). 1980. pap. 8.95 (ISBN 0-87480-190-7). U of Utah Pr.

Cannon, Helen. A Better Place I Know. 1979. pap. 2.25 (ISBN 0-380-75002-3, 75002). Avon.

--Seasons Change. 320p. 1981. pap. 2.50 (ISBN 0-380-01438-6, 77164). Avon.

Cannon, Helen L. & Hopps, Howard C., eds. Environmental Geochemistry in Health & Disease: American Association for Advancement of Science Symposium. LC 78-111440. (Geological Society of America Ser.: No. 123). pap. 60.00 (ISBN 0-317-28384-7, 2025465). Bks Demand UMI.

Cannon, Helen S., jt. auth. see Cannon, Raymond S.

Cannon, J. Parliamentary Reform: 1640-1832. LC 72-83588. (Illus.). 288p. 1973. pap. 15.95 (ISBN 0-521-09736-3). Cambridge U Pr.

Cannon, J. T. & Dostrovsky, S. The Evolution of Dynamics: Vibration Theory from 1687 to 1742. (Studies in the History of Mathematics & Physical Sciences: Vol. 6). (Illus.). 584p. 1981. 45.00 (ISBN 0-387-90626-6). Springer-Verlag.

Cannon, Jack, ed. see Cannon, Jimmy.

Cannon, James G. Clearing-Houses: Their History, Methods & Administration. Bruchey, Stuart, ed. LC 80-1138. (The Rise of Commercial Banking Ser.). (Illus.). 1981. Repr. of 1908 ed. lib. bdg. 35.00x (ISBN 0-405-13638-2). Ayer Co Pubs.

Cannon, James P. America's Road to Socialism. LC 74-26234. 128p. 1975. pap. 3.95 (ISBN 0-87348-417-7). Path Pr NY.

--The Communist League of America 1932-1934. Stanton, Fred & Taber, Michael, eds. (James P. Cannon: Writings & Speeches). 480p. (Orig.). 1985. lib. bdg. 30.00 (ISBN 0-913460-98-2); pap. 9.95 (ISBN 0-913460-99-0). Monad Pr.

--The First Ten Years of American Communism. new ed. LC 73-88411. (Illus.). 352p. (Orig.). 1974. 25.00 (ISBN 0-87348-352-9); pap. 6.95 (ISBN 0-87348-353-7). Path Pr NY.

--History of American Trotskyism. new rev. ed. LC 72-78439. 1972. pap. 6.95 (ISBN 0-87348-268-9). Path Pr NY.

--The Left Opposition in the U. S. 1928 to 1931. Stanton, ed. 446p. 1981. lib. bdg. 30.00 (ISBN 0-913460-86-9); pap. 8.95 (ISBN 0-913460-87-7). Monad Pr.

--Letters from Prison. Lavan, George, ed. LC 73-79781. 1968. cloth 25.00 (ISBN 0-87348-006-6). Path Pr NY.

--Letters from Prison. 2nd ed. Weissman, George L., ed. LC 73-79781. (Illus.). 384p. 1973. pap. 7.95 (ISBN 0-87348-307-3). Path Pr NY.

--Notebook of an Agitator. 2nd ed. LC 73-79782. (Illus.). 384p. 1974. 25.00 (ISBN 0-87348-304-9); pap. 7.95 (ISBN 0-87348-305-7). Path Pr NY.

--The Revolutionary Party: Its Role in the Struggle. pap. 0.50 (ISBN 0-87348-346-4). Path Pr NY.

--Socialism on Trial. LC 73-86630. 1969. cloth 17.00 (ISBN 0-87348-009-0). Path Pr NY.

--Socialism on Trial. 2nd ed. LC 73-86630. 192p. 1973. pap. 3.95 (ISBN 0-87348-317-0). Path Pr NY.

--The Socialist Workers Party in World War Two: Writings and Speeches, Nineteen Forty to Nineteen Forty-Three. Breitman, George & Evans, Les, eds. LC 75-20719. (Illus.). 48p. 1975. 33.00 (ISBN 0-87348-456-8); pap. 8.95 (ISBN 0-87348-457-6). Path Pr NY.

--Speeches for Socialism. Weissman, George L., ed. LC 70-156380. 1971. 33.00 (ISBN 0-87348-196-8); pap. 7.95 (ISBN 0-87348-198-4). Path Pr NY.

--Speeches to the Party. LC 73-86189. 352p. 1973. 27.00 (ISBN 0-87348-320-0); pap. 8.95 (ISBN 0-87348-321-9). Path Pr NY.

--The Struggle for a Proletarian Party. 2nd, rev. ed. Wright, John G., ed. LC 73-133396. 320p. 1972. pap. 6.95 (ISBN 0-87348-260-3). Path Pr NY.

--The Struggle for Socialism in the "American Century". Writings & Speeches, 1945-1947. Evans, Les, ed. LC 75-20719. (Writings & Speeches of James P. Cannon). 1977. 33.00 (ISBN 0-87348-550-5); pap. 9.95 (ISBN 0-87348-551-3). Path Pr NY.

Cannon, James P., intro. by see Trotskii, Lev.

Cannon, James S. A Clear View: Guide to Industrial Pollution Control. LC 75-15321. (Illus.). 1975. pap. 3.95 (ISBN 0-686-70491-6). INFORM.

--Coal Conversion at New Jersey Utilities: A Study of the Conversion Prospects & Obstacles at Seven Power Plants. Srtyker, Perrin, ed. LC 83-82880. 1983. pap. 15.00 (ISBN 0-918780-25-X). INFORM.

--Converting New York State Utilities to Coal: A Study of the Costs & Environmental Impacts of Conversion. 1982. pap. 10.00 (ISBN 0-918780-26-8). INFORM.

Cannon, James S. & Armentrout, Frederick S. Environmental Steel Update: Pollution in the Iron & Steel Industry. Schwartz, Wendy C., ed. LC 77-86496. 1977. pap. 42.00 (ISBN 0-87871-006-X). CEP.

Cannon, James S., jt. auth. see Inform Inc.

Cannon, Janet. The Last Night in New York. (Voices in the Wind: No. 4). 52p. (Orig.). 1984. pap. 5.00 (ISBN 0-938392-06-9). Homeward Pr.

Cannon, Jim, et al. The Contemporary World: Conflict or Co-Operation? (Illus.). 128p. (Orig.). (gr. 9-12). 1979. pap. text ed. 9.50 (ISBN 0-05-003159-7); resource bk. 3.95 (ISBN 0-05-003676-9). Longman.

Cannon, Jimmy. Nobody Asked Me but... The World of Jimmy Cannon. Cannon, Jack & Cannon, Tom, eds. (Penguin Sports Library). 320p. 1983. pap. 5.95 (ISBN 0-14-006617-9). Penguin.

Cannon, Joan B. & Smith, Ed. Resources for Affirmative Action: An Annotated Directory of Books, Periodicals, Films, Training Aids, & Consultants on Equal Opportunity. LC 82-83304. 190p. (Orig.). 1982. pap. 11.95 (ISBN 0-912048-28-X). Garrett Pk.

Cannon, Joe. Uncle Joe Cannon: The Story of a Pioneer American. Busbey, L. White, ed. LC 77-144924. (Illus.). 1971. Repr. of 1927 ed. 29.00 (ISBN 0-403-00887-5). Scholarly.

Cannon, John. Aristocratic Century: The Peerage of Eighteenth Century England. 208p. 1985. 34.50 (ISBN 0-521-25729-8). Cambridge U Pr.

Cannon, John, ed. The Historian at Work. 216p. (Orig.). 1980. text ed. 25.00x (ISBN 0-04-901025-5); pap. text ed. 8.95x (ISBN 0-04-901026-3). Allen Unwin.

--The Whig Ascendancy: Colloquies on Hanoverian England. 1981. 25.00x (ISBN 0-312-86761-1). St Martin.

Cannon, John, ed. see Junius.

Cannon, John R. Encyclopedia of Mathematics & Its Applications: The One-Dimensional Heat Equation, Vol. 23. 1984. 59.50 (ISBN 0-317-14401-4, 30243-9). Cambridge U Pr.

Cannon, Joseph L. For Missionaries Only. 96p. 1975. pap. 2.95 (ISBN 0-8010-2347-5). Baker Bk.

Cannon, Le Grand. Personal Reminiscences of the Rebellion 1861-1866. facs. ed. LC 78-157363. (Black Heritage Library Collection Ser). 1895. 17.50 (ISBN 0-8369-8801-9). Ayer Co Pubs.

Cannon, Lee. Quick & Easy Cookbook. LC 79-88365. (Illus.). 256p. 1979. 17.26i (ISBN 0-8487-0509-2). Oxmoor Hse.

Cannon, Lou. Reporting: An Inside View. LC 77-79691. 1977. 9.955 (ISBN 0-930302-12-5); pap. 4.95 (ISBN 0-930302-13-3). Cal Journal.

Cannon, M. Samuel, jt. auth. see Sucheston, Martha E.

Cannon, Margaret H., compiled by. South Carolina Magazine Index of Ancestral Research: Volumes I-X, 1973-1982. LC 85-8314. 392p. 1985. 35.00 (ISBN 0-87152-408-2). Reprint.

Cannon, Mark W. & O'Brien, David M. Views from the Bench: The Judiciary & Constitutional Politics. LC 85-9990. (Chatham House Series on Change in American Politics). 352p. 1985. 25.00 (ISBN 0-934540-34-9); pap. text ed. 12.95x (ISBN 0-934540-33-0). Chatham Hse Pubs.

Cannon, Mary A. The Education of Women During the Renaissance. LC 79-2933. 182p. 1981. Repr. of 1916 ed. 16.00 (ISBN 0-8305-0100-2). Hyperion Conn.

Cannon, Melissa. Sister Fly Goes to Market. LC 80-21120. (Illus., Orig.). 1980. pap. 1.95 (ISBN 0-937212-01-6). Truedog.

Cannon, Michael. Land Boomers. 1973. pap. 10.00x (ISBN 0-522-83788-3, Pub. by Melbourne U Pr Australia). Intl Spec Bk.

--That Damned Democrat. 186p. 1981. 18.50x (ISBN 0-522-84215-1, Pub. by Melbourne U Pr Australia). Intl Spec Bk.

Cannon, Miles. Waiilatpu, Its Rise & Fall. 1969. 12.00 (ISBN 0-87770-004-4). Ye Galleon.

Cannon, Minuha. The Fructose Cookbook. LC 79-4902. (Illus.). 128p. (Orig.). 1979. pap. 5.95 (ISBN 0-914788-18-3). East Woods.

--Sweets Without Guilt. LC 80-18133. (Illus.). 150p. (Orig.). 1980. pap. 5.95 (ISBN 0-914788-30-2). East Woods.

Cannon, Nancy M., et al. Manual of Hand Splinting. (Illus.). 118p. (Orig.). 1985. pap. text ed. 18.00 (ISBN 0-443-08451-3). Churchill.

Cannon, P. H. Pulptime! LC 84-50724. (Illus.). 96p. 1985. 15.00 (ISBN 0-932445-07-1); pap. 5.00 (ISBN 0-932445-06-3). Ganley Pub.

Cannon, Poppy. Fast Gourmet Cookbook. pap. 2.50 (ISBN 0-87980-034-8). Wilshire.

Cannon, R., jt. auth. see Newble, D. I.

Cannon, R. D. Electron Transfer Reactions. LC 79-41278. 1981. text ed. 89.95 (ISBN 0-408-10646-8). Butterworth.

Cannon, Raymond S. & Cannon, Helen S. Kearney County Cemeteries. 275p. 1985. 30.00 (ISBN 0-916170-24-1). J-B Pub.

Cannon, Robert H. Dynamics of Physical Systems. 1967. text ed. 48.00 (ISBN 0-07-009754-2). McGraw.

Cannon, Robert L. & Banks, Michael A. The Rocket Book: A Guide to Building & Launching Model Rockets for Teachers & Students Of the Space Age. (Illus.). 240p. 1985. 22.95 (ISBN 0-13-782251-0); pap. 12.95 (ISBN 0-13-782244-8). P-H.

Cannon, Roderick D. A Bibliography of Bagpipe Music. 1980. text ed. 39.50x (ISBN 0-85976-024-3). Humanities.

Cannon, Sharol. Social Functioning Patterns in Families of Offspring Receiving Treatment for Drug Abuse. LC 75-42602. 1975. 6.95 (ISBN 0-87212-040-6). Libra.

Cannon, Steve, intro. by. The Deluxe Show: Exhibition Catalog. LC 75-117924. (Publication of Rice University Institute of the Arts). (Illus.). 74p. 1971. pap. 4.00 (ISBN 0-913456-85-3). Interbk Inc.

Cannon, Taffy. Convictions: A Novel of the Sixties. Lister, Laurie, ed. LC 84-29468. 384p. 1985. 18.95 (ISBN 0-688-04343-7). Morrow.

Cannon, Terence. Revolutionary Cuba. LC 77-26587. (Illus.). 368p. (gr. 9 up). 1981. 16.95i (ISBN 0-690-01307-8). Crowell Jr Bks.

Cannon, Tim. Distribution Research. 1973. pap. text ed. 17.95x (ISBN 0-7002-0232-3). Intl Ideas.

Cannon, Timothy L. & Whitmore, Nancy F. Ghosts & Legends of Fredrick County. LC 79-64285. (Illus., Orig.). 1979. pap. 2.95 (ISBN 0-9602816-0-6). T L Cannon & N F Whitmore.

Cannon, Tom. Advertising Research. 1973. 17.95x (ISBN 0-7002-0220-X). Intl Ideas.

--Advertising: The Economic Implications. 1974. text ed. 24.95x (ISBN 0-7002-0242-0). Intl Ideas.

--How to Win Profitable Business. (Building Your Business Ser.). 239p. 1984. text ed. 18.95x (ISBN 0-09-151840-7, Pub. by Busn Bks England). Brookfield Pub Co.

--New Product Development. 1978. 90.00x (ISBN 0-905440-58-7, Pub. by MCB Pubns). State Mutual Bk.

Cannon, Tom & Brown, Daniel. International Marketing. 1980. 89.00x (ISBN 0-86176-026-3, Pub. by MCB Pubns). State Mutual Bk.

Cannon, Tom, ed. see Cannon, Jimmy.

Cannon, Walter B. The Way of an Investigator. 1945. 30.00 (ISBN 0-8274-4190-8). R West.

--The Way of an Investigator: A Scientist's Experiences in Medical Research. 1984. pap. 5.95 (ISBN 0-393-30125-7). Norton.

--Wisdom of the Body. (Illus.). 1963. pap. 6.95x (ISBN 0-393-00205-5, Norton Lib). Norton.

--The Wisdom of the Body. 2nd ed. (Illus.). 18.25 (ISBN 0-8446-0536-0). Peter Smith.

Cannon, Wendell E., jt. auth. see Meyers, Edward C.

Cannon, William A. & Fox, Fred K. Studebaker: The Complete Story. (Illus.). 368p. 1982. 39.95 (ISBN 0-8306-2064-8, 2064). TAB Bks.

Cannon, William R. A Disciple's Profile of Jesus. LC 75-2956. 1975. 2.95x (ISBN 0-8358-0322-8). Upper Room.

--The Gospel of John. 128p. (Orig.). 1985. pap. 4.95 (ISBN 0-8358-0511-5). Upper Room.

--The Gospel of Matthew. LC 82-50948. 128p. (Orig.). 1983. pap. 4.95 (ISBN 0-8358-0450-X). Upper Room.

--History of Christianity in the Middle Ages. (Twin Brooks Ser.). 1983. pap. 9.95 (ISBN 0-8010-2492-7). Baker Bk.

--Jesus the Servant: From the Gospel of Mark. LC 78-62578. 1978. pap. text ed. 2.95x (ISBN 0-8358-0376-7). Upper Room.

--The Theology of John Wesley: With Special Reference to the Doctrine of Justification. 284p. 1984. pap. text ed. 12.50 (ISBN 0-8191-4001-5). U Pr of Amer.

Cannon-Alfred, C., jt. auth. see Alfred, J. Tyrone.

Cannon-Alfred, C., jt. auth. see J. Tyrone.

Cannon-Bonventre, Kristina & Kahn, Janet R. The Ecology of Help-Seeking Behavior among Adolescent Parents. 99p. 1979. pap. 6.00 (ISBN 0-89785-006-8). Am Inst Res.

Cannon-Brookes, Peter. Czech Sculpture Eighteen Hundred - Nineteen Thirty-Eight. 128p. 1983. pap. text ed. 13.00x (ISBN 0-86294-043-5, Pub. by Trefoil Bks Ltd UK). Humanities.

--Emile Antoine Bourdelle: An Illustrated Commentary. (Illus.). 128p. 1983. pap. text ed. 13.00x (ISBN 0-86294-039-7, Pub. by Trefoil Bks Ltd UK). Humanities.

Cannons, Harry G. Bibliography of Library Economy. LC 73-122221. (Bibliography & Reference Ser.: No. 350). 1971. Repr. of 1920 ed. lib. bdg. 41.50 (ISBN 0-8337-0458-3). B Franklin.

Cannum. Deluxe on Farts. (Illus.). 8p. 1979. pap. 2.95 (ISBN 0-89708-032-7). And Bks.

--On Farts. (Illus.). 8p. 1979. pap. 0.95 (ISBN 0-89708-002-5). And Bks.

Canny, Nicholas. The Upstart Earl: A Study of the Social & Mental World of Richard Boyle, First Earl of Cork, 1566-1643. LC 81-21687. 208p. 1982. 37.50 (ISBN 0-521-24416-1). Cambridge U Pr.

Cano, Fray A. Manche & Peten: The Hazards of Itza Deceit & Barbarity. Bowditch, Charles P. & Rivera, Guillermo, trs. from Span. 32p. 1984. pap. 8.00x (ISBN 0-911437-02-9). Labyrinthos.

Cano, Raul J. & Colome, Jaime S. Microbiology. (Illus.). 1000p. 1985. text ed. 36.95 (ISBN 0-314-85223-9). West Pub.

Canobbio, E., ed. Heating in Toroidal Plasmas II: Proceedings of the 2nd Joint Grenoble-Varenna International Symposium, 2 vols. (Committee of the European Communities Ser.). 1230p. 1982. pap. 165.00 (ISBN 0-08-029347-6, C135, B120). Pergamon.

Canobbio, Mary M., jt. auth. see Pollack-Latham, Christine L.

Canoles, Marian l. The Creative Copycat. (Illus.). 265p. 1982. lib. bdg. 18.50x (ISBN 0-87287-340-4). Libs Unl.

--Creative Copycat II. 175p. 1985. lib. bdg. 18.50 (ISBN 0-87287-436-2). Libs Unl.

Canon, Bradley & Johnson, Charles. Judicial Policies: Implementation & Impact. LC 83-26303. 288p. 1984. pap. 11.95 (ISBN 0-87187-284-6). Congr Quarterly.

Canon, Claudia Von see Von Canon, Claudia.

Canon, Harry J. & Brown, Robert D., eds. Applied Ethics in Student Services. LC 84-82379. (Student Services Ser.: No. 30). (Orig.). 1985. pap. text ed. 9.95x (ISBN 0-87589-768-1). Jossey-Bass.

Canon, Jack. A Hangman for Paradise. (Paradise Ser.). 256p. (Orig.). 1980. pap. 1.95 (ISBN 0-441-31634-4, Pub. by Charter Bks). Ace Bks.

--Sable & Gold. 288p. (Orig.). 1981. pap. 2.50 (ISBN 0-523-41105-7). Pinnacle Bks.

Canon Law Society of America Staff, tr. from Latin. The Code of Canon Law: Latin-English Edition. Orig. Title: Codex Iuris Canonici. xlii, 668p. (Orig.). 1983. 15.00 (ISBN 0-943616-20-4); pap. 12.00 (ISBN 0-943616-19-0). Canon Law Soc.

Canon Law Society of Great Britain & Ireland. Index to the Code of Canon Law. 104p. (Orig.). 1985. pap. 3.50 (ISBN 0-8028-0067-X). Eerdmans.

Canon Law Society of Great Britain, Ireland Staff, ed. The Code of Canon Law in English Translation. 1983. pap. 9.95 (ISBN 0-8028-1978-8). Eerdmans.

Canon, Mary. The Defiant. (The O'Hara Dynasty Ser.). 1982. pap. 2.95 (ISBN 0-373-89001-X). Harlequin Bks.

--The Renegades. (The O'Hara Dynasty Ser.). 1982. pap. 2.95 (ISBN 0-373-89003-6). Harlequin Bks.

--The Survivors. (The O'Hara Dynasty Ser.). 1982. pap. 2.95 (ISBN 0-373-89002-8). Harlequin Bks.

Canonico & Margison, G. P., eds. Carcinogenesis, Vol. 1. (Illus.). 1979. 80.00 (ISBN 0-08-024379-7). Pergamon.

Canonico, et al, eds. Cancer Control: International Cancer Congress, 12th, Buenos Aires, 1978, Vol. 2. LC 79-40704. (Advances in Medical Oncology, Research & Education: Vol. II). (Illus.). 80.00 (ISBN 0-08-024385-1). Pergamon.

Canonico, A., ed. Biological Basis for Cancer Diagnosis, Vol. 4. (Illus.). 1979. 80.00 (ISBN 0-08-024387-8). Pergamon.

Canonico, A., et al. Clinical Cancer: Principle Sites 2. (Advances in Medical Oncology Ser.: Vol. 11). 1979. 80.00 (ISBN 0-08-024394-0). Pergamon.

--Digestive Cancer. (Advances in Medical Oncology Ser.: Vol. 9). 1979. 80.00 (ISBN 0-08-024392-4). Pergamon.

--Leukemia & Non-Hodgkin Lymphoma. (Advances in Medical Oncology Ser.: Vol. 7). 1979. 80.00 (ISBN 0-08-024390-8). Pergamon.

Canonico, A., et al, eds. Clinical Cancer - Principal Sites One: International Cancer Congress, 12th, Buenos Aires, 1978. LC 79-40710. (Advances in Medical Oncology, Research & Education: Vol. X). (Illus.). 1979. 80.00 (ISBN 0-08-024393-2). Pergamon.

Canonico, P. G., jt. ed. see Powanda, M. C.

Canosa, C. A., et al, eds. see International Symposium, Valencia, May 1973.

Canot, Theodore. Adventures of an African Slaver. (Illus.). 9.50 (ISBN 0-8363-0000-9). Jenkins.

--Adventures of an African Slaver. 11.50 (ISBN 0-8446-0537-9). Peter Smith.

Canouts, Veletta, et al. Cultural Frontiers in the Upper Cache Valley, Illinois. LC 82-72482. (Research Paper Ser.: No. 16). (Illus.). 258p. 1984. pap. 8.50 (ISBN 0-88104-004-5). Center Archaeo.

Canovan, Margaret. Populism. LC 80-22245. 1981. 17.95 (ISBN 0-15-173078-4). Harbracej.

Canright, D. M. El Adventismo Del Septimo Dia. Correa, F. G., tr. 1981. pap. 1.85 (ISBN 0-311-05601-6). Casa Bautista.

--Seventh Day Adventism in a Nutshell. 2.75 (ISBN 0-89225-162-X). Gospel Advocate.

--Seventh Day Adventism Renounced. 1982. pap. 5.95. Gospel Advocate.

Canright, David. Ships & the River. Cambell, Janet, ed. (Illus.). 32p. (gr. 2-6). 1975. pap. 2.00 (ISBN 0-913344-22-2). South St Sea Mus.

Cansler, Philip T. Twentieth-Century Music for Trumpet & Organ: An Annotated Bibliography. LC 84-20422. (Research Ser.: No. 11). 1984. pap. 8.00 (ISBN 0-914282-30-1). Brass Pr.

Canstantopoulos, E. Stories from Greek Mythology. (Illus.). (gr. 3-4). 3.20 (ISBN 0-686-79632-2). Divry.

Canstatt, Carl. Die Krankheiten des Hoheren Alters unt Ihre Heilung, 2 vols. in one. Kastenbaum, Robert, ed. LC 78-22187. (Aging & Old Age Ser.). (Illus., Ger.). 1979. Repr. of 1839 ed. lib. bdg. 48.50x (ISBN 0-405-11805-8). Ayer Co Pubs.

Cant, H. J., tr. see Hedin, Sven A.

Cant, M. The Villages of Edinburgh: North Edinburgh, Vol. 1. (Illus.). 200p. 1985. text ed. 11.50x (ISBN 0-85976-131-2, Pub. by Donald Scotland). Humanities.

Cant, R. C., jt. ed. see Aylmer, G. E.

Cantacuzene, Princess. Revolutionary Days: Recollections of Romanoffs & Bolsheviki 1914-1917. LC 76-115515. (Russia Observed, Ser.1). 1970. Repr. of 1919 ed. 21.00 (ISBN 0-405-03012-6). Ayer Co Pubs.

Cantacuzino, S., ed. Charles Correa. 127p. 1984. text ed. 37.25x (ISBN 9971-83-887-7, Pub. by A Mimar Bk Sl). Humanities.

Cantacuzino, Sherban. Architecture in Continuity: Building in the Islamic World Today. price not set. Aperture.

--Howell Killick Partridge & Amis: Architecture. (Illus.). 128p. 1985. 30.00x (ISBN 0-8390-0346-3). Abner Schram Ltd.

Cantacuzino, Sherban & Brandt, Susan. Saving Old Buildings. (Illus.). 240p. 1981. 67.50x (ISBN 0-85139-498-1). Nichols Pub.

Cantacuzino, Sherban, ed. Architectural Conservation in Europe. (Illus.). 144p. 1975. 20.00 (ISBN 0-8230-7044-1, Whitney Lib). Watson-Guptill.

Cantarella, Michele. Prosatori del Novecento. (For 4th-5th semesters). (gr. 10-12). 1967. text ed. 16.95 (ISBN 0-03-055190-0, HoltC). HR&W.

Cantarino, Vicente. Civilacion y Cultura de Espana. LC 80-24839. 416p. 1981. text ed. 17.95 (ISBN 0-02-319010-8, Pub. by Scribner). Macmillan.

--Syntax of Modern Arabic Prose. Incl. Vol. 1. The Simple Sentence. 184p. 1974. 20.00x (ISBN 0-253-39504-6); Vol. 2. The Expanded Sentence. 544p. 1976. 25.00x (ISBN 0-253-39505-4); Vol. 3. The Compound Sentence. (Oriental Ser.). 424p. 1976. 22.50x (ISBN 0-253-39506-2). LC 69-16996. (Oriental Ser.: Vol. 4). Set. 55.00x (ISBN 0-253-39507-0). Ind U Pr.

Cantarow, Ellen, et al. Moving the Mountain: Women Working for Social Change. (Women's Lives-Women's Work Ser.). (Illus.). 166p. (gr. 11 up). 1980. pap. 8.95 (ISBN 0-912670-61-4); pap. 4.00 teaching guide (ISBN 0-912670-75-4). Feminist Pr.

Cantelo, William W. & Webb, Raymond E. Insects & Diseases of Vegetables in the Home Garden. 54p. pap. 4.25 (ISBN 0-318-11794-0). Gov Printing Office.

Cantelon, Hart & Gruneau, Richard, eds. Sport, Culture, & the Modern State: Papers Presented at a Conference Held at Queen's University, Kingston, Ont., Oct. 1979. 315p. 1982. 30.00x (ISBN 0-8020-2494-7); pap. 12.95 (ISBN 0-8020-6493-0). U of Toronto Pr.

Cantelon, Philip L. & Williams, Robert C. Crisis Contained: The Department of Energy at Three Mile Island. LC 81-21413. (Science & International Affairs Ser.). (Illus.). 243p. 1982. 17.50 (ISBN 0-8093-1079-1). S Ill U Pr.

Cantelon, Philip L., jt. ed. see Williams, Robert C.

Cantelon, Willard. The Baptism in the Holy Spirit. 34p. 1951. pap. 1.00 (ISBN 0-88243-692-9, 02-0692). Gospel Pub.

--The Day the Dollar Dies: Biblical Prophecy of a New World System in the End Times. LC 72-94186. 190p. 1973. (Haven Bks); pap. 2.95 (ISBN 0-88270-170-3). Bridge Pub.

--Money Master of the World. LC 75-38197. 1976. pap. 2.95 (ISBN 0-88270-152-5, Pub. by Logos). Bridge Pub.

--New Money or None. LC 79-90400. 1979. pap. 2.95 pocketsize (ISBN 0-88270-388-9, Pub. by Logos). Bridge Pub.

Cantelupe, Eugene, jt. ed. see Mates, Julian.

Canter, Bram D., jt. auth. see Hamann, Richard G.

Canter, D., ed. Facet Theory: Approaches to Social Research. (Springer Series in Social Psychology). (Illus.). 330p. 1985. 35.00 (ISBN 0-387-96016-3). Springer-Verlag.

Canter, David. Fires & Human Behaviour. LC 79-41489. 338p. 1980. 44.95 (ISBN 0-471-27709-6, Pub. by Wiley-Interscience). Wiley.

--Psychology for Architects. LC 74-30415. 171p. 1975. 34.95x (ISBN 0-470-13460-7). Halsted Pr.

--Psychology for Architects. (Illus.). 171p. 1982. 26.00 (ISBN 0-85334-115-X, Pub. by Elsevier Applied Sci England). Elsevier.

--The Psychology of Place. LC 77-73621. (Illus.). 1977. 22.50 (ISBN 0-312-65322-0). St Martin.

Canter, David & Donald, Ian. Person Environmental Connections. 200p. 1986. text ed. price not set (ISBN 0-566-05085-4). Gower Pub Co.

Canter, David, jt. auth. see Canter, Sandra.

Canter, David, ed. Environmental Interaction. LC 75-37077. 374p. (Orig.). 1976. 32.50 (ISBN 0-8236-1685-1). Intl Univs Pr.

Canter, David, tr. see Levy-Leboyer, Claude.

Canter, David, et al. The Cranks Recipe Book: From Europe's Leading Gourmet Vegetarian Restaurant. (Illus.). 204p. (Orig.). 1985. pap. 12.95 (ISBN 0-7225-0959-6). Thorsons Pubs.

--Action & Place, Vol. 1. 275p. 1985. text ed. write for info (ISBN 0-566-05080-3). Gower Pub Co.

--Action & Place, Vol. 2. 275p. 1986. text ed. price not set (ISBN 0-566-05081-1). Gower Pub Co.

Canter, Howard V. Rhetorical Elements in the Tragedies of Seneca. Repr. of 1925 ed. 15.00 (ISBN 0-384-07325-5). Johnson Repr.

Canter, Howard V., jt. auth. see Oldfather, William A.

Canter, L. W. Acid Precipitation & Dry Deposition. (Illus.). 400p. 1985. 49.95 (ISBN 0-87371-016-9). Lewis Pubs Inc.

--Environmental Impact of Water Resources Projects. (Illus.). 400p. 1985. 39.95 (ISBN 0-87371-015-0). Lewis Pubs Inc.

--Ground Water Quality Management. (Illus.). 450p. 1985. 49.95 (ISBN 0-87371-018-5). Lewis Pubs Inc.

--River Water Quality Monitoring. (Illus.). 230p. 1985. 28.00 (ISBN 0-87371-011-8). Lewis Pubs Inc.

Canter, Larry. Environmental Impact Assessment. (McGraw-Hill Series in Environmental Engineering & Water Resources). (Illus.). 1977. text ed. 45.00 (ISBN 0-07-009764-X). McGraw.

Canter, Larry W. Environmental Impact Statements on Municipal Wastewater Programs. LC 79-53112. vi, 95p. (Orig.). 1979. pap. 15.00 (ISBN 0-87815-026-9). Info Resources.

Canter, Larry W. & Knox, R. C. Effect of Septic Tank Systems on Ground Water Quality. LC 84-23280. (Illus.). 336p. 1985. 29.95 (ISBN 0-87371-012-6). Lewis Pubs Inc.

--Ground Water Pollution Control. (Illus.). 529p. 1985. 49.95 (ISBN 0-87371-014-2). Lewis Pubs Inc.

Canter, Larry W., et al. Environmental Impact of Growth. LC 84-26187. (Illus.). 600p. 1985. 44.80 (ISBN 0-87371-013-4). Lewis Pubs Inc.

Canter, Lee & Canter, Marlene. Assertive Discipline: A Take-Charge Approach for Today's Educator. LC 76-42182. 1976. pap. text ed. 6.95 (ISBN 0-9608978-0-1). Canter & Assoc.

--Assertive Discipline: Elementary Resource Materials Workbook. 88p. 1985. wkbk. 6.95 (ISBN 0-9608978-6-0). Canter & Assoc.

--Assertive Discipline Follow-Up Guide. (Illus.). 1981. wkbk. 6.95 (ISBN 0-9608978-2-8). Canter & Assoc.

--Assertive Discipline for Parents. LC 82-74174. 206p. 1982. 12.95 (ISBN 0-06-859835-1); pap. 7.95 144 pgs. (ISBN 0-06-859836-X). Canter & Assoc.

--Assertive Discipline Resource Guide for Parents. (Illus.). 112p. 1985. wkbk. 7.95 (ISBN 0-9608978-7-9). Canter & Assoc.

--Assertive Discipline: Secondary Resource Materials Workbook. (Illus.). 72p. (gr. 7-12). 1984. 6.95 (ISBN 0-9608978-5-2). Canter & Assoc.

Canter, Lee & Schadlow, Barbara. The Parent Conference Book. 1984. wkbk. 6.95 (ISBN 0-9608978-4-4). Canter & Assoc.

Canter, Marlene, jt. auth. see Canter, Lee.

Canter, Miriam. Dazzling Desserts: Over 100 Delicious Recipes. (Illus.). 40p. 1983. pap. 2.95 (ISBN 0-941016-08-0). Penfield.

Canter, Sandra & Canter, David. Psychology in Practice: Perspectives on Professional Psychology. 361p. 1982. pap. 24.95 (ISBN 0-471-10411-6, Pub. by Wiley-Interscience). Wiley.

Canter, Sandra, jt. auth. see Wilkinson, Jill.

Canterbery, Ray, jt. auth. see Bell, Frederick.

Canterbury England Prerogative Court. Wills from Doctors' Commons, 1495-1695. 1863. 19.00 (ISBN 0-384-07345-X). Johnson Repr.

Cantieni, Benita. Little Elephant & Big Mouse. Gadsby, Oliver E., tr. from Ger. LC 82-183307. Orig. Title: Der Kleine Elefant und die Grosse Maus. (Illus.). 32p. 1981. 9.95 (ISBN 0-907234-09-7, Pub. by Picture Bk Studio USA). Neugebauer Pr.

Cantilli, E. J., ed. see Furioso.

Cantillon, Richard. Essai sur La Nature Du Commerce En General. Higgs, Henry, ed. LC 65-10365. Repr. of 1931 ed. 37.50x (ISBN 0-678-00059-X). Kelley.

--Essai sur la Nature Du Commerce En General: 1755 with English Translation-Essay on the Nature of Trade 1931. Higgs, Henry, tr. 1981. write for info. (ISBN 0-08-027645-8, HE 021); microfiche 25.00 (ISBN 0-686-79341-2). Pergamon.

Cantin, M., ed. Cell Biology of the Secretory Process. (Illus.). viii, 624p. 1983. 127.00 (ISBN 3-8055-3619-4). S Karger.

Cantin, M., jt. ed. see Jasmin, G.

Cantin, Marc & Seelig, Mildred S., eds. Magnesium in Health & Disease. LC 78-13181. (Monographs of the Am College of Nutrition: Vol. 4). (Illus.). 1154p. 1980. 225.00 (ISBN 0-89335-055-9). SP Med & Sci Bks.

Cantine, Marguerite J. Beggar T. Bear: The History, Significance, Manufacture, Promotion, Identification Guide, Photographs & Current Values of the American Teddy Bear Circa 1903-1945. (Illus.). 64p. 1981. pap. 5.95x (ISBN 0-940548-00-3). Cantine & Kilpatrick.

Cantino, E. C., jt. auth. see Myers, R. B.

Cantlay, Jed, jt. auth. see Hoffman, Robert.

Cantle, A. Pleas of Quo Waranto for the County of Lancaster. 1937. 24.00 (ISBN 0-384-07370-0). Johnson Repr.

Cantle, J. E. Atomic Absorption Spectrometry: Techniques & Instrumentation in Analytical Chemistry. 448p. 1982. 89.50 (ISBN 0-444-42015-0). Elsevier.

Cantleberry, Lillian. Jacob: God's Plain Man. 1984. pap. 7.95 (ISBN 0-570-03928-2, 12-2863). Concordia.

--Moses: Prince, Servant, Prophet. 208p. (Orig.). 1985. pap. 7.95 (ISBN 0-570-03970-3, 12-3005). Concordia.

--Sarah's Story. (Continued Applied Christianity Ser.). 1983. pap. 7.95 (ISBN 0-570-03898-7, 12-2980). Concordia.

Cantlie, Audrey. The Assamese: Religion, Caste & Sect in an Indian Village. 240p. 1983. 39.00x (ISBN 0-7007-0149-4, Pub. by Curzon England). State Mutual Bk.

--The Assamese: Religion, Caste & Sect in an Indian Village. (Illus.). 340p. 1984. 27.00x (ISBN 0-7007-0149-4, Pub. by Salem Hse Ltd). Merrimack Pub Cir.

Cantlie, Audrey, jt. ed. see Burghart, Richard.

Cantlie, James. Degeneration Amongst Londoners. Lees, Lynn H. & Lees, Andrew, eds. (The Rise of Urban Britain Ser.). 35.00 (ISBN 0-317-26209-2). Garland Pub.

Canto, Julio P. Economic & Social Progress of the Republic of Chile. 1977. lib. bdg. 59.95 (ISBN 0-8490-1745-9). Gordon Pr.

Canto, Victor. Foundations of Supply-Side Economics: Theory & Evidence. 284p. 1983. 39.50 (ISBN 0-12-158820-3). Acad Pr.

Canto, Victor A. The Determinants & Consequences of Trade Restrictions in the U. S. Economy. LC 85-12211. Date not set. price not set (ISBN 0-03-004964-4). Praeger.

Canton, Alan N. Computermoney: How to Make It in Data Processing Consulting. Kent, Richard S., ed. 189p. 1981. pap. 25.00 (ISBN 0-935730-00-1). DLM CPA.

Canton, Dario. Poamorio. Stroud, Drew M., tr. LC 84-51027. 160p. (Orig.). 1984. pap. text ed. 6.95 (ISBN 0-935086-01-3). Saru.

Canton, Eli. Love Letters. 1979. 8.95 (ISBN 0-517-53707-9). Crown.

Canton, Frank M. Frontier Trails: The Autobiography of Frank M. Canton. Dale, Edward E., ed. LC 66-13415. (Western Frontier Library: Vol. 30). Repr. of 1966 ed. 47.70 (ISBN 0-8357-9728-7, 2016200). Bks Demand UMI.

Canton, H. J., et al, eds. New Scientific Aspect. LC 61-642. (Advances in Polymer Science: Vol. 20). (Illus.). 200p. 1976. 43.00 (ISBN 0-387-07631-X). Springer-Verlag.

Canton, Wilberto. Nosotros Somos Dios: Pieza En Dos Actos. Trifilo, S. S. & Soto-Ruiz, Luis, eds. (Span). 1966. pap. text ed. 10.95 scp (ISBN 0-06-046365-1, HarpC). Har-Row.

Cantoni, Louise. St. Germaine. rev. ed. (gr. 4-8). 1973. 1.75 (ISBN 0-8198-0262-X). Dghtrs St Paul.

Cantoni, Louise B. Leaving Matters to God. (Illus.). 164p. (gr. 3-8). 1984. 3.00 (ISBN 0-8198-4424-1); pap. 2.00 (ISBN 0-8198-4425-X). Dghtrs St Paul.

Cantor, Alfred J. Doctor Cantor's Longevity Diet. 1982. pap. 4.95 (ISBN 0-13-216549-X, Reward). P-H.

Cantor, Alfred U. Doctor Cantor's Longevity Diet: How to Slow Down Aging & Prolong Youth & Vigor. 1967. 16.50 (ISBN 0-13-216267-9, Parker). P-H.

Cantor, Benjamin J., jt. auth. see Hughes, Kenneth B.

Cantor, Bill. Fire: Prevention, Protection, Escape. (Illus.). 96p. (Orig.). 1985. pap. 3.95 (ISBN 0-345-32190-1). World Almanac.

Cantor, Bill & Burger, Chester. Experts in Action: Inside Public Relations. LC 83-17558. (Public Communications Ser.). 480p. 1984. text ed. 29.95 (ISBN 0-582-28437-6); pap. text ed. 18.95 (ISBN 0-582-28438-4). Longman.

Cantor, Charles R. & Schimmel, Paul R. Biophysical Chemistry, Part I: The Conformation of Biological Macromolecules. LC 79-22043. (Illus.). 365p. 1980. 40.95 (ISBN 0-7167-1042-0); pap. text ed. 23.95 (ISBN 0-7167-1188-5). W H Freeman.

--Biophysical Chemistry, Part II: Techniques for the Study of Biological Structure & Function. LC 79-24854. (Illus.). 554p. 1980. text ed. 46.95 (ISBN 0-7167-1189-3); pap. text ed. 26.95 (ISBN 0-7167-1190-7). W H Freeman.

--Biophysical Chemistry, Part III: The Behavior of Biological Macromolecules. LC 79-27860. (Illus.). 597p. 1980. 49.95 (ISBN 0-7167-1191-5); pap. text ed. 29.95 (ISBN 0-7167-1192-3). W H Freeman.

Cantor, D., et al, eds. Selected Papers of Theodore S. Motzkin. 1983. text ed. 65.00x (ISBN 0-8176-3087-2). Birkhauser.

Cantor, Daniel J. Law Office Employment Guide. 2nd ed. 72p. 1980. spiral bound 12.95 (ISBN 0-686-35740-X). D J Cantor.

Cantor, Dorothy W. & Drake, Ellen A. Divorced Parents & Their Children: A Guide for Mental Health Professionals. 192p. 1983. text ed. 21.95 (ISBN 0-8261-3560-9). Springer Pub.

Cantor, Eddie. Caught Short! 8.95 (ISBN 0-89190-984-2, Pub. by Am Repr). Amereon Ltd.

Cantor, Edward B. Female Urinary Stress Incontinence. (Illus.). 360p. 1979. 30.25x (ISBN 0-398-03819-8). C C Thomas.

Cantor, Eli. Enemy in the Mirror. 1981. pap. 3.50 (ISBN 0-89083-842-9). Zebra.

--Love Letters. 1982. pap. 3.50 (ISBN 0-8217-1068-0). Zebra.

Cantor, Fitzgerald Collection Inc. Rodin & Balzac: Bronzes from the Cantor, Fitzerald Collection, Inc. (Illus.). 72p. 1973. pap. 4.00x (ISBN 0-685-46516-0). Norton Art.

Cantor, Fred R. The Graduates: They Came Out of New York's Public Schools. (Illus.). 80p. (Orig.). 1982. pap. 3.75 (ISBN 0-9612238-0-4). Hall Fame Mgt.

Cantor, G. N. Optics after Newton: Theories of Light in Britain & Ireland, 1704-1840. LC 83-7954. 256p. 1984. 25.00 (ISBN 0-7190-0938-3, Pub. by Manchester Univ Prr). Longwood Pub Group.

Cantor, G. N. & Hodge, M. J. Conceptions of Ether: Studies in the History of Ether Theories 1740 to 1900. LC 80-21174. (Illus.). 350p. 1981. 67.50 (ISBN 0-521-22430-6). Cambridge U Pr.

Cantor, Georg. Contributions to the Founding of the Theory of Transfinite Numbers. Jourdain, Philip E., tr. pap. 4.95 (ISBN 0-486-60045-9). Dover.

--Contributions to the Founding of the Theory of Transfinite Numbers. Jourdain, P. E., tr. ix, 220p. 1952. 19.95 (ISBN 0-87548-157-4). Open Court.

Cantor, George. The Great Lakes Guidebook: Lake Huron & Eastern Lake Michigan. LC 77-13606. (Illus.). 1979. pap. 6.95 (ISBN 0-472-19651-0). U of Mich Pr.

--The Great Lakes Guidebook: Lake Superior & Western Lake Michigan. 1980. pap. 6.95 (ISBN 0-472-19652-9). U of Mich Pr.

--The Great Lakes Guidebook: Lakes Ontario & Erie. 2nd ed. 240p. 1984. pap. 7.95 (ISBN 0-472-06361-8). U of Mich Pr.

Cantor, Gilbert M. The Lawyer's Complete Guide to the Perfect Will. 1984. pap. 47.50 (ISBN 0-916621-00-6). Cato Pr.

Cantor, Gilbert M., jt. auth. see Rothkopf, Nancy.

Cantor, Gordon N. Race & Sex Effects in the Conformity Behavior of Children. (Augustana College Library Occasional Paper Ser.: No. 14). 16p. 1978. pap. 1.00x (ISBN 0-910182-37-X). Augustana Coll.

Cantor, Harvey, et al. Regulation of the Immune System. (UCLA Symposium on Molecular & Cellular Biology, New Ser.: Vol. 18). 1008p. 1984. 160.50 (ISBN 0-8451-2617-2). A R Liss.

Cantor, Howard V., jt. auth. see Oldfather, William A.

Cantor, Irwin & Smith, Charles M. Arizona Marriage Dissolution Manual. LC 83-112484. 510p. 1982. 34.35 (ISBN 0-910039-01-1). Az Law Inst.

Cantor, Jay. The Death of Che Guevara. LC 83-47777. (Illus.). 576p. 1983. 17.95 (ISBN 0-394-51767-9). Knopf.

--The Death of Che Guevara. 592p. 1984. pap. 8.95 (ISBN 0-394-72592-1, Vin.). Random.

--The Space Between: Literature & Politics. LC 81-47600. 160p. 1982. text ed. 16.50x (ISBN 0-8018-2672-1). Johns Hopkins.

Cantor, Jay E. Winterthur. (Illus.). 240p. 1985. 49.50 (ISBN 0-317-19102-0). Abrams.

Cantor, Leonard & Roberts, I. F. Further Education Today. rev. ed. 256p. 1983. pap. text ed. 14.95x (ISBN 0-7100-9501-5). Routledge & Kegan.

Cantor, Leonard M., ed. The English Medieval Landscape. LC 82-50174. (Middle Ages Ser.). (Illus.). 224p. 1982. 27.50x (ISBN 0-8122-7841-0). U of Pa Pr.

Cantor, Louis. Prologue to the Protest Movement: The Missouri Sharecropper Roadside Demonstrations of 1939. LC 70-86480. 204p. 1969. 16.75 (ISBN 0-8223-0215-2). Duke.

Cantor, Marjorie A., ed. see Lewis, Christine L., et al.

Cantor, Marjorie H. & Kamerman, Sheila. Strengthening Informal Supports for the Aging: Theory, Practice, & Policy Implications. 59p. (Orig.). 1981. pap. 4.00 (ISBN 0-88156-007-3). Comm Serv Soc NY.

Cantor, Marjorie M. Achieving Nursing Care Standards: Internal & External. LC 78-53072. 180p. 1978. 29.00 (ISBN 0-913654-47-7). Aspen Systems.

Cantor, Milton. Max Eastman. LC 71-120012. (Twayne's United States Authors Ser.). 1970. lib. bdg. 15.95 (ISBN 0-89197-844-5). Irvington.

Cantor, Milton, ed. American Working Class Culture: Explorations in American Labor & Social History. LC 78-59260. (Contributions in Labor History: No. 7). 1979. lib. bdg. 35.00 (ISBN 0-313-20611-2, CAW/). Greenwood.

--Black Labor in America. LC 74-111265. (Contributions in Afro-American & African Studies, No. 2). 1969. 29.95 (ISBN 0-8371-4667-4, CLM&, Pub. by Negro U Pr). Greenwood.

Cantor, Milton & Laurie, Bruce, eds. Class, Sex, & the Woman Worker. LC 76-15304. (Contributions in Labor History Ser.: No. 1). 1977. lib. bdg. 27.50 (ISBN 0-8371-9032-0, CCS/). Greenwood.

--Class, Sex, & the Woman Worker. LC 76-15304. (Contributions in Labor History Ser.: No. 1). ix, 253p. 1980. pap. text ed. 7.95 (ISBN 0-313-22733-0, CSS/). Greenwood.

Cantor, Milton, jt. ed. see Quint, Howard H.

Cantor, Moritz B. Vorlesungen Ueber Geschichte der Mathematik, 4 Vols. 1900-08. 195.00 (ISBN 0-384-07380-8). Johnson Repr.

Cantor, Morton B. & Glucksman, Myron L. Affect: Psychoanalytic Theory & Practice (Selected Papers from the Journal of the American Academy of Psychoanalysis) 726p. 1983. 28.95 (ISBN 0-471-88071-X). Wiley.

Cantor, Muriel G. Prime-Time Television: Content & Control. LC 80-12288. (The Sage Commtext Ser: No. 3). 143p. 1980. 17.50 (ISBN 0-8039-1316-8); pap. 8.95 (ISBN 0-8039-1317-6). Sage.

Cantor, Muriel G. & Pingree, Suzanne. The Soap Opera. (CommText 12 Ser.). 168p. 1983. 17.50 (ISBN 0-8039-2004-0); pap. 9.95 (ISBN 0-8039-2005-9). Sage.

Cantor, Muriel G., jt. auth. see Stewart, Phyllis L.

Cantor, Myron. Open & Operate Your Own Small Store. (Illus.). 230p. 1982. 15.95 (ISBN 0-13-637496-4); pap. 7.95 (ISBN 0-13-637488-3). P-H.

Cantor, N. & Kihlstrom, J., eds. Personality, Cognition, & Social Interaction. LC 81-208. 384p. 1981. text ed. 36.00x (ISBN 0-89859-057-4). L Erlbaum Assocs.

Cantor, Nathaniel. Dynamics of Learning. LC 71-166546. 1950. 10.00x (ISBN 0-87586-026-5). Agathon.

Cantor, Norman, et al, eds. Notebooks in Cultural Analysis, Vol. 1. (Illus.). 238p. 1984. lib. bdg. 35.00 (ISBN 0-8223-0617-4); pap. 12.75 (ISBN 0-8223-0618-2). Duke.

Cantor, Norman F. Church, Kingship & Lay Investiture in England, 1089-1135. 1969. lib. bdg. 26.00x (ISBN 0-374-91273-4). Octagon.

--Medieval History: The Life & Death of a Civilization. 2nd ed. 1975. pap. write for info. (ISBN 0-02-319020-5). Macmillan.

--Medieval World: Three Hundred to Thirteen Hundred. 2nd ed. (Orig.). 1968. pap. text ed. write for info. (ISBN 0-02-319110-4, 31911). Macmillan.

--Western Civilization: Its Genesis & Destiny, 2 bks. Incl. Bk. 2 (ISBN 0-673-07574-5); Bk. 3. pap. 13.20 (ISBN 0-673-07575-3). 1970. pap. 13.65x ea. Scott F.

Cantor, Norman F. & Schneider, Richard I. How to Study History. LC 67-14303. (Orig.). pap. 7.95x (ISBN 0-88295-709-0). Harlan Davidson.

Cantor, Norman F. & Berner, Samuel, eds. Ancient & Medieval Europe: To Fifteen Hundred. LC 70-101941. (Problems in European History Ser.: Vol. 1). 1970. pap. 12.95x (ISBN 0-88295-706-6). Harlan Davidson.

--The Modern Era: Eighteen Fifteen to the Present. LC 70-101941. (Problems in European History Ser.: Vol. 3). 1970. pap. 12.95x (ISBN 0-88295-708-2). Harlan Davidson.

Cantor, Norman F. & Werthman, Michael S., eds. Ancient Civilizations: Four Thousand B. C. to Four Hundred A. D. 2nd ed. LC 72-76355. (Structure of European History Ser.: Vol. 1). 284p. 1972. pap. text ed. 6.95x (ISBN 0-88295-710-4). Harlan Davidson.

--Making of the Modern World: Eighteen Fifteen to Nineteen Fourteen. LC 67-16644. (Structure of European History Ser.: Vol. 5). 240p. 1967. pap. text ed. 6.95x (ISBN 0-88295-714-7). Harlan Davidson.

--Medieval Society: Four Hundred to Fourteen Fifty. 2nd ed. LC 72-76355. (Structure of European History Ser.: Vol. 2). 303p. 1972. pap. text ed. 6.95x (ISBN 0-88295-711-2). Harlan Davidson.

--Renaissance, Reformation, & Absolutism: 1450 to 1650. 2nd ed. LC 72-76355. (Structure of European History Ser.: Vol. 3). 319p. 1972. pap. text ed. 6.95x (ISBN 0-88295-712-0). Harlan Davidson.

--Twentieth Century: Nineteen Fourteen to the Present. LC 67-16644. (Structure of European History Ser.: Vol. 6). 251p. 1967. pap. text ed. 6.95 (ISBN 0-88295-715-5). Harlan Davidson.

Cantor, Norman F., ed. see Mandelbaum, Seymour J.

Cantor, Norman F., et al, eds. Notebooks in Cultural Analysis: An Annual Review, Vol. 2. (Notebooks in Cultural Analysis Ser.). (Illus.). 238p. 1985. 35.00x (ISBN 0-8223-0661-1); pap. 12.75x (ISBN 0-8223-0694-8). Duke.

Cantor, Paul A. Creature & Creator: Myth-Making & English Romanticism. LC 83-14255. 250p. 1984. 34.50 (ISBN 0-521-25831-6). Cambridge U Pr.

--Creature & Creator: Myth-Making & the English Romanticism. 250p. Date not set. pap. price not set (ISBN 0-521-31362-7). Cambridge U Pr.

--Shakespeare's Rome: Republic & Empire. LC 75-36522. 248p. 1976. 26.95x (ISBN 0-8014-0967-5). Cornell U Pr.

Cantor, Robert C. And a Time to Live: Toward Emotional Well-Being During the Crisis of Cancer. LC 76-26216. 1980. pap. 6.68i (ISBN 0-06-090746-0, CN 746, CN). Har-Row.

Cantor, Robert D. Introduction to International Politics. LC 75-17314. (Illus., Orig.). 1976. text ed. 19.95 (ISBN 0-87581-189-2). Peacock Pubs.

--Voting Behavior & Presidential Elections. LC 74-83751. (Illus.). 139p. (Orig.). 1975. pap. text ed. 4.95 (ISBN 0-87581-173-6). Peacock Pubs.

Cantor, Robert D., ed. American Government Reader. (Illus.). 1978. pap. text ed. 11.95 scp (ISBN 0-06-041171-6, HarpC). Har-Row.

Cantor, S. M. see Pigman, Ward & Wolfrom, Melville L.

Cantor, Shelia. The Schizophrenic Child: A Primer for Parents & Professionals. 130p. 1982. pap. 6.95 (ISBN 0-920792-13-8). Eden Pr.

Cantor, Sidney M., ed. Use of Sugars & Other Carbohydrates in the Food Industry. LC 55-4135. (Advances in Chemistry Ser: No. 12). 1955. pap. 10.95 (ISBN 0-8412-0013-0). Am Chemical.

Cantore, Bill, jt. auth. see Cantore, Virginia.

Cantore, Enrico. Atomic Order: An Introduction to the Philosophy of Microphysics. 1970. pap. text ed. 8.95x (ISBN 0-262-53028-7). MIT Pr.

--Scientific Man: The Humanistic Significance of Science. xviii, 487p. 1985. text ed. 20.00 (ISBN 0-917392-01-9). W I S H.

Cantore, Virginia & Cantore, Bill. Creative Picture Framing: How to Frame Your Artwork, Needlework, Mirrors & 3-D Displays. 129p. 1981. 12.95 (ISBN 0-13-190645-3); pap. 6.95 (ISBN 0-13-190637-2). P-H.

Cantori, Louis J. & Harik, Iliya, eds. Local Politics & Development in the Middle East. (Special Studies on the Middle East). 350p. 1984. lib. bdg. 25.75x (ISBN 0-86531-169-2). Westview.

Cantos, Irene. Oh! What's the Use! 1984. 5.95 (ISBN 0-8062-2157-7). Carlton.

Cantow, H. J., ed. Polydiacetylenes. (Advances in Polymer Science: Fortschritte der Hochpolymeren-Forschung: Vol. 63). (Illus.). 160p. 1984. 40.00 (ISBN 0-387-13414-X). Springer-Verlag.

--Polymer Chemistry. LC 61-642. (Advances in Polymer Science: Vol. 25). (Illus.). 1977. 55.00 (ISBN 0-387-08389-8). Springer-Verlag.

Cantow, H. J., ed. see Casale, A., et al.

Cantow, H. J., ed. see Henrici-Olive, G., et al.

Cantow, H. J., et al. Behavior of Macromolecules. (Advances in Polymer Science Ser.: Vol. 46). (Illus.). 170p. 1982. 42.00 (ISBN 0-387-11640-0). Springer-Verlag.

--Light Scattering from Polymers. (Advances in Polymer Science Ser.: Vol. 48). (Illus.). 167p. 1983. 41.50 (ISBN 0-387-12030-0). Springer-Verlag.

--Polymers: Syntheses, Reactivities, Properties. (Advances in Poymer Science: Vol. 32). (Illus.). 1979. 56.00 (ISBN 0-387-09442-3). Springer-Verlag.

--Unusual Properties of New Polymers. (Advances in Polymer Science: Vol. 50). (Illus.). 149p. 1983. 39.00 (ISBN 0-387-12048-3). Springer-Verlag.

Cantow, H. J., et al, eds. Chemistry. LC 61-642. (Advances in Polymer Science: Vol. 31). (Illus.). 1979. 54.00 (ISBN 0-387-09200-5). Springer-Verlag.

--Luminescence. (Advances in Polymer Science: Vol. 40). (Illus.). 200p. 1981. 45.00 (ISBN 0-387-10550-6). Springer-Verlag.

--Polymer Products. (Advances in Polymer Science Ser.: Vol. 39). (Illus.). 230p. 1981. 59.50 (ISBN 0-387-10218-3). Springer-Verlag.

--Polymerization Processes. (Advances in Polymer Sciences Ser.: Vol. 38). (Illus.). 180p. 1981. 48.00 (ISBN 0-387-10217-5). Springer-Verlag.

--Polymerization Reactions. LC 61-642. (Advances in Polymer Science: Vol. 28). (Illus.). 1978. 51.00 (ISBN 0-387-08885-7). Springer-Verlag.

--Specialty Polymers. (Advances in Polymer Science Ser.: Vol. 41). (Illus.). 186p. 1981. 58.00 (ISBN 0-387-10554-9). Springer-Verlag.

--Synthesis & Degradation-Rheology & Extrusion. (Advances in Polymer Science: Vol. 47). (Illus.). 170p. 1982. 39.00 (ISBN 0-387-11774-1). Springer-Verlag.

--Analysis - Reactions - Morphology. (Advances in Polymer Science Ser.: Vol. 71). (Illus.). 220p. 1985. 55.00 (ISBN 0-387-15482-5). Springer-Verlag.

Cantow, H. T., ed. Polymerizations & Polymer Properties. (Advances in Polymer Science Ser.: Vol. 43). (Illus.). 240p. 1982. 52.00 (ISBN 0-387-11048-8). Springer-Verlag.

Cantow, M. J., ed. Polymer Fractionation. 1967. 92.50 (ISBN 0-12-158850-5). Acad Pr.

Cantraine, G. & Destin, E. J., eds. New Systems & Services in Telecommunications II: Proceedings of the 2nd International Conference on New Systems & Services in Telecommunications, Liege, Belgium, Nov. 16-18, 1984. 470p. 1984. 55.75 (ISBN 0-444-87550-6, North-Holland). Elsevier.

Cantraine, G. & Destine, J., eds. New Systems & Services in Telecommunications. 368p. 1981. 64.00 (ISBN 0-444-86206-4, North Holland). Elsevier.

Cantrell, Charles L. & Blair, Chris. Oklahoma Criminal Practice Manual. Date not set. price not set looseleaf (ISBN 0-409-25069-4). Butterworth TX.

Cantrell, David P. Psychology: Strategies for Success. LC 83-70800. (Illus.). 174p. (Orig.). 1983. pap. 5.95 (ISBN 0-913011-01-0). Ambleside.

Cantrell, Jacqueline P. Ancient Mexico: Art, Architecture, & Culture in the Land of the Feathered Serpent. 152p. 1984. 11.95 (ISBN 0-8403-3399-4). Kendall-Hunt.

Cantrell, James C. Geometric Topology. LC 78-31631. 1979. 67.50 (ISBN 0-12-158860-2). Acad Pr.

Cantrell, John A. James Nasmyth & the Bridgewater Foundry: A Study of Entrepreneurship in the Early Engineering Industry. LC 84-25415. (Chetham Society Ser.). 1985. 33.00 (ISBN 0-7190-1339-9, Pub. by Manchester Univ Pr). Longwood Pub Group.

Cantrell, Leon. Bards, Bohemians & Bookmen: Essays in Australian Literature. 1977. 24.95x (ISBN 0-7022-1321-7). U of Queensland Pr.

Cantrell, Leon, ed. The Eighteen Nineties Stories, Verses & Essays. (Portable Australian Authors Ser.). 1978. 30.00x (ISBN 0-7022-1037-4); pap. 12.95x (ISBN 0-7022-1038-2). U of Queensland Pr.

Cantrell, R., jt. ed. see Matlon, P.

Cantrell, Ray. Alpha Motivation. (Illus.). 120p. 1982. 5.00 (ISBN 0-940178-13-3). Sitare Inc.

Cantrelle, P., ed. Population in African Development, 2 Vols. 899p. 1975. Set. pap. 50.00 (ISBN 0-685-90712-0, ORD8, ORDINA). Unipub.

Cantril, Albert H., jt. auth. see Roll, Charles W., Jr.

Cantril, H. The Invasion from Mars. 1982. 24.00 (ISBN 0-691-09399-7); pap. 6.95 (ISBN 0-691-02827-3). Princeton U Pr.

Cantril, H. see Peak, Helen.

Cantril, Hadley. Human Dimension: Experiences in Policy Research. 1967. 20.00x (ISBN 0-8135-0538-0). Rutgers U Pr.

--The Pattern of Human Concerns. 1966. 35.00x (ISBN 0-8135-0510-0). Rutgers U Pr.

--Pattern of Human Concerns Data, 1957-1963. 1977. codebk. write for info. (ISBN 0-89138-115-5). ICPSR.

--The Psychology of Social Movements. LC 73-89079. 288p. 1973. pap. text ed. 10.50 (ISBN 0-88275-133-6). Krieger.

Cantril, Hadley & Allport, Gordon W. Psychology of Radio. LC 72-161159. (History of Broadcasting: Radio to Television Ser). 1971. Repr. of 1935 ed. 23.50 (ISBN 0-405-03574-8). Ayer Co Pubs.

Cantril, Hadley, ed. Public Opinion, Nineteen Thirty-Five to Nineteen Forty-Six. LC 78-12745. 1978. Repr. of 1951 ed. lib. bdg. 98.50x (ISBN 0-313-21165-5, CAUE). Greenwood.

Cantu, Caesar C. Cortes & the Fall of the Aztec Empire. (Illus.). 1966. 12.95 (ISBN 0-685-16803-4, 0-910978-1-3). Modern World.

--Mexico: All About the Country & Its People. (Illus.). 10.95 (ISBN 0-685-16804-2, 0-910978-3-4). Modern World.

Cantu, Elizabeth C. Loneliness for Sale. 183p. 1985. 7.30 (ISBN 0-89697-244-5). Intl Univ Pr.

Cantu, Norma E., ed. see Aguilar-Henson, Marcela.

Cantu, Rita. Great Smoky Mountains: The Story Behind the Scenery. LC 78-78123. (Illus.). 1979. 8.95 (ISBN 0-916122-60-3); pap. 3.75 (ISBN 0-916122-59-X). KC Pubns.

Cantu, Robert. Toward Fitness: Guided Exercise for Those with Health Problems. LC 79-27686. 258p. 1980. 19.95 (ISBN 0-87705-496-7). Human Sci Pr.

Cantu, Robert C. Clinical Sports Medicine. LC 83-70135. 224p. 1983. 19.95 (ISBN 0-669-06842-X, Collamore). Heath.

--Diabetes & Exercise: A Practical, Positive Way to Control Diabetes. LC 81-19463. (Illus.). 192p. 1982. 13.50 (ISBN 0-525-93235-6, 01311-390). Dutton.

--Exercise Injuries: Prevention & Treatment. LC 83-50359. (Illus.). 220p. (Orig.). 1983. pap. 12.95 (ISBN 0-913276-45-6). Stone Wall Pr.

--Regaining Health & Fitness: Guided Exercises to Recover from Heart Attack, Lower Back Pain, Obesity, & Diabetes for Inactive Adults Under Sixty, the Physically Disabled, & the Aged. LC 82-2883. 1982. pap. 8.95 (ISBN 0-8289-0474-X). Greene.

--Sports Medicine in Primary Care. LC 81-70166. 240p. 1982. 24.95 (ISBN 0-669-04593-4, Collamore); pap. 16.95 (ISBN 0-669-05429-1, Collamore). Heath.

Cantu, Robert C. & Gillespie, W. Jay. Sports Medicine, Sports Science: Bridging the Gap. LC 81-70165. 252p. 1982. 18.95 (ISBN 0-669-05226-4, Collamore). Heath.

Cantu, Robert C. & Higdon, Hal. The Complete Diabetic Exercise & Diet Guide. (Illus.). 224p. 1982. cancelled (ISBN 0-8027-0670-3). Walker & Co.

Cantu, Robert C., ed. The Exercising Adult. LC 81-65129. 192p. 1981. text ed. 14.95 (ISBN 0-669-04509-8, Collamore Pr). Heath.

--Health Maintenance Through Physical Conditioning. LC 80-15622. 180p. 1981. 13.00 (ISBN 0-88416-312-1). PSG Pub Co.

Cantu, Robert C., et al. Ventriculocisternostomy: Long-Term Experiences. (Illus.). 152p. 1970. photocopy ed. 14.75x (ISBN 0-398-00282-7). C C Thomas.

Cantwell, Aileen, jt. auth. see Polon, Linda.

Cantwell, Alan, Jr. AIDS: The Mystery & the Solution. LC 84-70662. (Illus.). 250p. 1984. 14.95x (ISBN 0-917211-19-7); pap. text ed. 9.95 (ISBN 0-917211-17-0). Aries Rising.

Cantwell, Allan R., Jr. AIDS: The Mystery & the Solution. 300p. 1984. 17.50x (ISBN 0-932426-34-4). Trado-Medic.

Cantwell, Anne M., et al, eds. The Research Potential of Anthropological Museum Collections. (Annals of The New York Academy of Science Ser.: Vol. 376). 585p. 1981. lib. bdg. 115.00x (ISBN 0-89766-141-9); pap. 115.00x (ISBN 0-89766-142-7). NY Acad Sci.

Cantwell, Anne-Marie. Dickson Camp & Pond: Two Early Havana Tradition Sites in the Central Illinois Valley. (Reports of Investigations Ser.: No. 36). (Illus.). 174p. 1980. pap. 6.00 (ISBN 0-89792-086-4). Ill St Museum.

Cantwell, Anne-Marie, ed. see Goodman, Claire G.

Cantwell, Aston. Tease for Two. 240p. (Orig.). 1983. pap. 2.75 (ISBN 0-446-30293-7). Warner Bks.

--Twin Spin. 256p. (Orig.). 1983. pap. 2.75 (ISBN 0-446-30633-9). Warner Bks.

Cantwell, Becky & Luce, Don. Made in Taiwan: A Human Rights Investigation. 19p. 2.00 (ISBN 0-686-36615-8). Asia Resource.

Cantwell, D. & Carlson, G., eds. Affective Disorders in Childhood & Adolescence: An Update. (Child Behavior & Development Ser.: Vol. 5). 480p. 1983. 35.00 (ISBN 0-89335-189-X). SP Med & Sci Bks.

Cantwell, Donald W., jt. auth. see Isakson, Hans R.

Cantwell, George, ed. Insect Diseases, Vol. 1. LC 73-90772. 326p. 1974. 59.75 (ISBN 0-8247-6117-0). Dekker.

--Insect Diseases, Vol. 2. 312p. 1974. 59.75 (ISBN 0-8247-6118-9). Dekker.

Cantwell, John D. Stay Young at Heart. LC 75-25958. (Illus.). 212p. 1975. 17.95 (ISBN 0-88229-247-1). Nelson-Hall.

Cantwell, John D., jt. auth. see Apple, David F.

Cantwell, John D., jt. auth. see Fletcher, Gerald F.

Cantwell, Lois. Freedom. (An American Values First Bk.). (Illus.). (gr. 7-9). 1985. PLB 9.40 (ISBN 0-531-10040-5). Watts.

--Money & Banking. (First Bks.). (Illus.). 72p. 1984. lib. bdg. 8.90 (ISBN 0-531-04827-6). Watts.

Cantwell, Mary. Saint Patrick's Day. LC 67-10070. (Holiday Ser.). (Illus.). (gr. k-3). 1967. PLB 10.89 (ISBN 0-690-71673-7). Crowell Jr Bks.

Cantwell, Robert. Bluegrass Breakdown: The Making of the Old Southern Sound. LC 83-4861. (Music in American Life Ser.). 328p. 1984. 19.95 (ISBN 0-252-01054-X). U of Ill Pr.

--The Land of Plenty. LC 73-83664. 400p. 1971. 10.00 (ISBN 0-8093-0457-0). S Ill U Pr.

--Land of Plenty: Toward a Pluralistic Criticism. LC 65-19771. (Crosscurrents-Modern Critiques Ser.). 219p. 1965. 7.95 (ISBN 0-8093-0179-2). S Ill U Pr.

--Nathaniel Hawthorne: The American Years. LC 77-159172. xiv, 499p. 1971. Repr. of 1948 ed. lib. bdg. 34.50x (ISBN 0-374-91277-7). Octagon.

Cantwell, Zita M. & Svajian, Pergrouhi. Adolescence. LC 73-85769. (Orig.). 1974. pap. text ed. 12.50 (ISBN 0-87581-165-5). Peacock Pubs.

Canty, Donald, ed. The Annual of American Architecture, 1980. (Annual of American Architecture). (Illus.). 124p. 1980. 21.95x (ISBN 0-913962-30-9). Am Inst Arch.

Canty, Jerome, jt. auth. see France, Richard.

Canty, Timothy G., et al. Ultrasonography of Pediatric Surgical Disorders. 288p. 1981. 61.00 (ISBN 0-8089-1395-6, 790783). Grune.

Cantzlaar, George L., jt. auth. see Brussel, James A.

Canudo, Eugene R. Marriage, Divorce & Adoption: New York. 1979. pap. 5.50x (ISBN 0-87526-222-8). Gould.

--New York Corporations. 112p. 1969. pap. text ed. 5.50x (ISBN 0-87526-215-5). Gould.

--New York Criminal Law. 600p. (Supplemented annually). looseleaf 20.00 (ISBN 0-87526-201-5). Gould.

--New York Evidence Laws. 260p. (Supplemented annually). looseleaf 12.00 (ISBN 0-87526-175-2). Gould.

Canuto, V., jt. auth. see Gordon, C. W.

Canuto, V., ed. Role of Magnetic Fields in Physics & Astrophysics, Vol. 257. (Annals of the New York Academy of Sciences). 226p. 1975. 38.00x (ISBN 0-89072-012-6). NY Acad Sci.

Canutt, Yakima & Drake, Oliver. Stunt Man: The Autobiography of Hollywood's Greatest. LC 78-58869. 1979. 14.95 (ISBN 0-8027-0613-4). Walker & Co.

Canvas Products Association International. Practical Application of Air-Supported Structures International Conference: Proceedings. 220p. 1974. 18.00 (ISBN 0-318-14389-5). Indus Fabrics.

Canzona, Nicholas A., jt. auth. see Montross, Lynn.

Canzoneri, Robert. Watch Us Pass. LC 68-20364. 106p. 1968. 5.00 (ISBN 0-8142-0035-4). Ohio St U Pr.

Cao, Antonio & Carcassi, Ugo, eds. Thalassemia: Recent Advances in Detection & Treatment. LC 82-16179. (Birth Defects: Original Article Ser.: Vol. 18, No. 7). 400p. 1982. 74.00 (ISBN 0-8451-1051-9). A R Liss.

Cao, Lan, et al. Flavors of Southeast Asia. LC 79-22341. (Illus.). 168p. (Orig.). 1979. pap. 5.95 (ISBN 0-89286-159-2). One Hund One Prods.

Cao, Xuegin. A Dream of Red Mansions, Vol. 1. Yang, Hsien-Yi, et al, trs. from Chinese. (Illus.). 599p. 1978. 15.95 (ISBN 0-917056-66-3, Pub. by Foreign Lang Pr China). Cheng & Tsui.

--A Dream of Red Mansions, Vol. 3. Yang, Hsien-Yi, et al, trs. from Chinese. (Illus.). 586p. 1980. 15.95 (ISBN 0-917056-68-X, Pub. by Foreign Lang Pr China). Cheng & Tsui.

--The Story of the Stone (The Dream of the Red Chamber, 4 vols. Set. 92.00 (ISBN 0-253-19266-8). Ind U Pr.

--The Story of the Stone, Vol. 1: The Golden Days. Hawkes, David, tr. (Classics Ser.). 1974. pap. 8.95 (ISBN 0-14-044293-6). Penguin.

--The Story of the Stone, Vol. 2: The Crab-Flower Club. Hawks, David, tr. (Classics Ser.). 1977. pap. 8.95 (ISBN 0-14-044326-6). Penguin.

Cao, Xuegin & Gao E. The Story of the Stone, Vol. 4: The Debt of Tears. Minford, John, tr. 1982. pap. 8.95 (ISBN 0-14-044371-1). Penguin.

Cao, Xuegin see Cao Xuequin.

Cao, Xueqin. The Story of the Stone (The Dream of the Red Chamber), Vol. 1: The Golden Days. Hawkes, David, tr. from Chinese. LC 78-20279. (Chinese Literature in Translation Ser.). 544p. 1979. 25.00x (ISBN 0-253-19261-7). Ind U Pr.

--The Story of the Stone (The Dream of the Red Chamber), Vol. 2: The Crab-Flower Club. Hawkes, David, tr. from Chinese. LC 78-20279. (Chinese Literature in Translation Ser.). 608p. 1979. 25.00x (ISBN 0-253-19262-5). Ind U Pr.

--The Story of the Stone (The Dream of the Red Chamber), Vol. 3: The Warning Voice. Hawkes, David, tr. LC 78-20279. (Chinese Literature in Translation Ser.). 640p. 1981. 35.00x (ISBN 0-253-19263-3). Ind U Pr.

--The Story of the Stone (The Dream of the Red Chamber), Vol. 4: The Debt of Tears. E, Gao, ed. Minford, John, tr. LC 78-20279. (Chinese Literature in Translation Ser.). 400p. (Chinese.). 1983. 30.00X (ISBN 0-253-19264-1). Ind U Pr.

Cao, Xueqin, et al. A Dream of Red Mansions, Vol. 2. Yang, Hsien-Yi & Yang, Gladys, trs. from Chinese. (Illus.). 701p. 1978. 15.95 (ISBN 0-917056-67-1, Pub. by Foreign Lang Pr China). Cheng & Tsui.

Cao, Z., et al. Incline Algebra & Its Applications. (Mathematics & Its Applications Ser.). 165p. 1984. 36.95 (ISBN 0-470-20116-9). Halsted Pr.

Cao-Garcia, Ramon J. Explorations Toward an Economic Theory of Political Systems. LC 83-1147. (Illus.). 192p. (Orig.). 1983. lib. bdg. 23.50 (ISBN 0-8191-3055-9); pap. text ed. 11.25 (ISBN 0-8191-3056-7). U Pr of Amer.

Cao Garcia, Ramon J. see Garcia, Ramon J. & Hailstones, Thomas J.

Cao Garcia, Ramon J. see Garcia, Ramon J., et al.

Cao-Ky, Nguyen. Twenty Years & Twenty Days. LC 75-35895. 1976. 8.95 (ISBN 0-8128-1908-X). Stein & Day.

Cao Ky, Nguyen see Ky, Nguyen C.

Cao-Pinna, Vera & Shatalin, Stanislav S. Consumption Patterns in Eastern & Western Europe. 1979. 44.00 (ISBN 0-08-021808-3). Pergamon.

Caorsin, Gulielmus. To the Most Excellente Kyng, Kyng Edward 4th Cohan Kay Hys Humble Poete Lawreate, Etc. LC 72-179. (English Experience Ser.: No. 236). 48p. 1970. Repr. of 1482 ed. 21.00 (ISBN 90-221-0236-X). Walter J Johnson.

Caoursin, Guillaume see Aesopus.

Cao Xueqin. The Persian Expedition. rev. ed. Warner, Rex, tr. (Classics Ser.). 1950. pap. 4.95 (ISBN 0-14-044007-0). Penguin.

Cao Xuequin. The Story of the Stone, Vol. 3: The Warning Voice. Hawkes, David, tr. 1981. pap. 8.95 (ISBN 0-14-044370-3). Penguin.

Cap, Ferdinand. Handbook of Plasma Instabilities, Vol. I. 1976. 55.00 (ISBN 0-12-159101-8). Acad Pr.

--Handbook on Plasma Instabilities, Vol. 2. 1978. 57.00 (ISBN 0-12-159102-6). Acad Pr.

Cap, Ferdinand, tr. see Karpman, V. I.

Cap, Orest, jt. ed. see Warmbrod, Catherine P.

Capa, Cornell. Lewis W. Hine. LC 72-11010. (Library of Photographers Ser.). (Illus.). 96p. 1974. 14.95 (ISBN 0-670-42742-X, Grossman). Viking.

Capa, Cornell, ed. Concerned Photographer No. 2. LC 68-31898. (Illus.). 1972. 19.95 (ISBN 0-670-23556-3, Grossman). Viking.

--Robert Capa. (Library of Photographers Ser.). (Illus.). 1974. 16.95 (ISBN 0-670-60095-4, Grossman). Viking.

Capablanca, Jose R. Chess Fundamentals. LC 22-127. (Illus.). 1938. 12.95 (ISBN 0-15-117045-2). HarBraceJ.

--Chess Fundamentals. (Illus.). 1967. pap. 6.95 (ISBN 0-679-14004-2, 27, Tartan). McKay.

--My Chess Career. (Illus.). 1965. pap. 4.50 (ISBN 0-486-21548-2). Dover.

--Primer of Chess. LC 35-3374. (Illus.). 1977. pap. 5.95 (ISBN --15-673900-3, Harv). HarBraceJ.

--World's Championship Matches: 1921 & 1927. LC 76-28101. 1977. pap. 3.50 (ISBN 0-486-23189-5). Dover.

Capacchione, Lucia. The Creative Journal: The Art of Finding Yourself. LC 78-51590. (Illus.). 180p. 1979. pap. 12.95 (ISBN 0-8040-0798-5, 82-79527, Pub. by Swallow). Ohio U Pr.

Capaccio, Albert, jt. auth. see Sloan, Annette.

Capaccioli, Massimo, ed. Astronomy with Schmidt-Type Telescopes. 1984. lib. bdg. 84.00 (ISBN 90-277-1756-7, Pub. by Reidel Holland). Kluwer Academic.

Capachi, Nick. Excavation & Grading Handbook. LC 78-3850. 1978. pap. 15.25 (ISBN 0-910460-54-X). Craftsman.

Capacino, W. F., et al. Modern Logistics Management: Integrating Marketing, Manufacturing & Physical Distribution. (Marketing Management Ser.). 1985. 29.95 (ISBN 0-471-81261-7). Wiley.

Capalari, Steve, tr. see Heisenberg, Elisabeth.

Capaldi. Membrane Proteins in Energy Transduction. (Membrane Proteins Ser.: Vol. 2). 1979. 85.00 (ISBN 0-8247-6817-5). Dekker.

Capaldi, G., et al, eds. Uranium Geochemistry, Mineralogy, Geology, Exploration & Resources. 201p. 1984. pap. text ed. 63.00X (ISBN 0-900488-70-0). Imm North Am.

Capaldi, I. G., tr. see Pellico, Silvio.

Capaldi, N., jt. ed. see Norton, D. F.

Capaldi, Nicholas. The Art of Deception. 2nd ed. LC 75-21077. 192p. 1979. pap. text ed. 8.95 (ISBN 0-87975-058-8). Prometheus Bks.

--Out of Order: Affirmative Action & the Crisis of Doctrinaire Liberalism. LC 84-43181. 201p. 1985. 17.95 (ISBN 0-87975-279-3). Prometheus Bks.

Capaldi, Nicholas, et al. An Invitation to Philosophy. LC 81-81131. 295p. (Orig.). 1981. pap. text ed. 14.95 (ISBN 0-87975-162-2). Prometheus Bks.

Capaldi, Nicholas, et al, eds. Journeys Through Philosophy. Rev. ed. LC 81-85574. 484p. 1982. pap. text ed. 15.95 (ISBN 0-87975-171-1). Prometheus Bks.

Capaldi, Roderick A., ed. Membrane Proteins & Their Interaction with Lipids. (Membranes: Structure & Techniques Ser.: Vol. 1). 1977. 59.75 (ISBN 0-8247-6595-8). Dekker.

Capano, Carmela, ed. see Gansert, Robert.

Caparosa, Ralph J. An Atlas of Surgical Anatomy & Techniques of the Temporal Bone. (Illus.). 136p. 1972. photocopy ed. 23.75x (ISBN 0-398-02253-4). C C Thomas.

Capart, Jean. Egyptian Art: Introductory Studies. facsimile ed. Dawson, Warren R., tr. from Fr. (Select Bibliographies Reprint Ser). Repr. of 1923 ed. 29.00 (ISBN 0-8369-6638-4). Ayer Co Pubs.

Caparulo, Frank, jt. auth. see London, Kathy.

Capasso, V., et al, eds. Mathematics in Biology & Medicine. (Lecture Notes in Biomathematics Ser.: Vol. 57). xviii, 524p. pap. 36.00 (ISBN 0-387-15200-8). Springer-Verlag.

Capbell, William H., jt. auth. see Koch, Hugo.

Capdevila Font, Juan. Diccionario Actualizado de la Lengua Espanola. 3rd ed. 392p. (Span.). 1976. 10.50 (ISBN 84-85117-06-9, S-50266); pap. 9.25 (ISBN 84-85117-28-X, S-50265). French & Eur.

--Diccionario Actualizado De Sinonimos y Contrarios De la Lengua Espanola. 2nd ed. 513p. (Span.). 1978. pap. 13.95 (ISBN 84-7176-301-X, S-50267). French & Eur.

--Diccionario de Citas. 132p. (Span.). 1977. pap. 13.95 (ISBN 84-85117-43-3, S-50580). French & Eur.

--Diccionario de la Lengua Espanola y Enciclopedia Escolar. 2nd ed. 407p. (Span.). 1975. pap. 7.95 (ISBN 84-85117-32-8, S-50451). French & Eur.

--Diccionario de la Lengua Espanola y Enciclopedia Escolar Distein. 2nd ed. 407p. (Span.). 1975. 8.95 (ISBN 84-85117-09-3, S-50459). French & Eur.

--Diccionario de la Literatura Universal. 536p. (Span.). 1977. 22.50 (ISBN 84-85117-41-7, S-50261). French & Eur.

--Diccionario de la Vida Sexual. 200p. (Span.). 1976. 9.95 (ISBN 84-85117-21-2, S-50262). French & Eur.

--Diccionario De Matematicas. 160p. (Span.). 1976. 9.75 (ISBN 84-85117-39-5, S-50263). French & Eur.

--Diccionario Enciclopedico Distein 2, 2 vols. 992p. (Espn.). 1976. Set. leather 29.50 (ISBN 84-85117-24-7, S-50450). French & Eur.

--Diccionario Escolar De Sinonimos y Contrarios De la Lengua Espanola. 499p. (Span.). 1978. 12.25 (ISBN 84-7176-302-8, S-50268). French & Eur.

--Diccionario Ideologico Manual de la Lengua Espanola. 900p. (Span.). 1976. 18.75 (ISBN 84-85117-22-0, S-50264). French & Eur.

--Diccionario Practico Escolar de la Lengua Espanola. 500p. (Span.). 1976. pap. 3.25 (ISBN 84-85117-38-7, S-50256). French & Eur.

--Diccionario Simultaneo en 6 Idiomas. 192p. (Span., Eng., Fr., Ital., Ger. & Port.). 1975. pap. 6.75 (ISBN 84-85117-14-X, S-31467). French & Eur.

--Moderna Enciclopedia Universal Distein. 600p. (Espn.). 1974. pap. 15.75 (ISBN 84-85117-31-X, S-50448). French & Eur.

Capdevila i Valls, Roser. Gerry Goes to Town. LC 84-40801. (Stories from Around the World Ser.). (Illus.). 28p. (ps-3). 1985. pap. 3.95 (ISBN 0-382-09048-9). Silver.

--Gerry Takes a Trip. LC 85-61400. (Stories from Around the World Ser.). (Illus.). 28p. (ps-3). 1985. pap. 3.95 (ISBN 0-382-09157-4). Silver.

Capdevila Font, Juan. Diccionario Basico Escolar de la Lengua Espanola. 2nd ed. 398p. (Span.). 1975. 6.75 (ISBN 84-85117-17-4, S-50254). French & Eur.

--Diccionario Basico Escolar de la Lengua Espanola. 2nd ed. 398p. (Span.). 1975. pap. 4.75 (ISBN 84-85117-29-8, S-50255). French & Eur.

--Diccionario De la Lengua Espanola y Enciclopedia Escolar. 6th ed. 437p. (Span.). 1978. 7.50 (ISBN 84-7176-273-0, S-50252); pap. 5.953 (ISBN 84-85117-33-6, S-50253). French & Eur.

--Diccionario Simultaneo en 21 Idiomas. 416p. (Span., Eng., Fr., Ger., Ital., Port., Catalan, Czech, Danish, Esparanto, Finnish, Gr., Dutch, Hungarian, Malaysian, Pol., Rumanian, Rus., Swedish & Turkish.). 1977. pap. 18.75 (ISBN 0-686-57350-1, S-31466). French & Eur.

Cape of Good Hope, Public Record Office, London. Records of the Cape Colony, 36 vols. LC 74-8329. (Illus.). Repr. of 1905 ed. Set. 1240.00 (ISBN 0-404-11750-3); 34.50 ea. AMS Pr.

Cape, Peter. Please Touch: A Survey of the Three-Dimensional Arts in New Zealand. (Illus.). 160p. 1980. 29.95 (ISBN 0-00-216957-6, Pub. by W Collins New Zealand). Intl Spec Bk.

Cape, Ronald D., et al, eds. Fundamentals of Geriatric Medicine. 480p. 1983. 38.50 (ISBN 0-89004-845-2); pap. 21.50 (ISBN 0-89004-877-0). Raven.

Cape, Ronald D. T. & Coe, Rodney M. Fundamentals of Geriatric Medicine. (Illus.). 468p. 1983. 35.96 (ISBN 0-89004-845-2, 1215); pap. 21.70 (ISBN 0-89004-877-0). Gerontological Soc.

Cape, W. H. Constitutional Revision in South Dakota. 1957. write for info. U of Sd Gov Res Bur.

--Public Employee Retirement Plans in South Dakota. 1956. write for info. U of SD Gov Res Bur.

Cape, W. H. & Felt, F. O. A Handbook for South Dakota Municipal Officials. 1954. write for info. U of SD Gov Res Bur.

Cape, William H., jt. auth. see Farber, W. O.

Capeci, Dominic J., Jr. The Harlem Riot of 1943. LC 77-70328. 278p. 1977. 32.95 (ISBN 0-87722-094-8). Temple U Pr.

--Race Relations in Wartime Detroit: The Soujourner Truth Housing Controversy, 1937-1942. 328p. 1984. lib. bdg. 37.95 (ISBN 0-87722-339-4). Temple U Pr.

Capek. And So Ad Infinitum: The Life of the Insects. 1923. 27.50 (ISBN 0-932062-42-3). Sharon Hill.

Capek, Josef & Capek, Karel. R.U.R. Bd. with The Insect Play. 1961. pap. 5.95x (ISBN 0-19-281010-3). Oxford U Pr.

Capek, Karel. The Absolute at Large. Del Rey, Lester, ed. LC 75-397. (Library of Science Fiction). 1975. lib. bdg. 21.00 (ISBN 0-8240-1403-0). Garland Pub.

--The Gardener's Year. LC 84-40203. (Illus.). 160p. (Orig.). 1984. 12.95 (ISBN 0-299-10020-0); pap. 7.95 (ISBN 0-299-10024-3). U of Wis Pr.

--Intimate Things. facs. ed. LC 68-54337. (Essay Index Reprint Ser). 1936. 15.00 (ISBN 0-8369-0275-0). Ayer Co Pubs.

--Krakatit. LC 74-16389. (Science Fiction Ser). 416p. 1975. Repr. of 1925 ed. 23.00x (ISBN 0-685-51338-6). Ayer Co Pubs.

--Letters from England. Selver, Paul, tr. 192p. 1980. Repr. of 1926 ed. lib. bdg. 25.00 (ISBN 0-8495-0952-1). Arden Lib.

--Letters from Spain. 192p. 1980. Repr. of 1931 ed. lib. bdg. 30.00 (ISBN 0-8495-0999-8). Arden Lib.

--Makropoulos Secret. Burrell, Randal C., ed. (Orig.). 1925. pap. 2.50 (ISBN 0-8283-1447-0, 41). Branden Pub Co.

--Money & Other Stories. facsimile ed. LC 73-106256. (Short Story Index Reprint Ser.). 1930. 18.00 (ISBN 0-8369-3293-5). Ayer Co Pubs.

--President Masaryk Tells His Story. LC 71-135797. (Eastern Europe Collection Ser). 1970. Repr. of 1935 ed. 25.50 (ISBN 0-405-02739-7). Ayer Co Pubs.

--War with the Newts. Weatherall, M. & Weatherall, R., trs. from Czech. LC 75-41049. (BCL Ser. II). Repr. of 1937 ed. 19.00 (ISBN 0-404-14649-X). AMS Pr.

--War with the Newts. 360p. Date not set. 8.95 (ISBN 0-8101-0663-9). Northwestern U Pr.

Capek, Karel, jt. auth. see Capek, Josef.

Capek, Karel see Dent, Anthony.

Capek, Leslie. Transforming Your Office. LC 81-68395. (Illus.). 200p. (Orig.). 1981. pap. 6.95 (ISBN 0-89708-080-7). And Bks.

Capek, M. Bergson & Modern Physics: A Re-Interpretation & Re-Evaluation. LC 79-146967. (Synthese Library: No. 37). 414p. 1971. 42.00 (ISBN 90-277-0186-5, Pub. by Reidel Holland). Kluwer Academic.

Capek, M., ed. Boston Studies in the Philosophy of Science, Vol. 22: The Concepts of Space & Time - Their Structure & Their Development. LC 73-75761. (Synthese Library: No. 74). 564p. 1975. 58.00 (ISBN 90-277-0355-8, Pub. by Reidel Holland); pap. 26.00 (ISBN 90-277-0375-2). Kluwer Academic.

Capek, Thomas. Czechs & Bohemeians in America. LC 69-18764. (American Immigration Collection Ser., No. 1). (Illus.). 1969. Repr. of 1920 ed. 18.00 (ISBN 0-405-00512-1). Ayer Co Pubs.

--Czechs & Bohemians in America. LC 79-90095. (Illus.). Repr. of 1920 ed. 12.50 (ISBN 0-404-01391-0). AMS Pr.

Capel, Lee M., tr. see Kierkegaard, Soren.

Capel, Vivian. Public Address Handbook. 224p. 1981. 40.00x (ISBN 0-907266-02-9, Pub. by Dickson England). State Mutual Bk.

--Radio Servicing Pocket Book. 3rd ed. 8.35 (ISBN 0-408-00144-5, NB 27, Pub. by Newnes-Technical). Hayden.

Capel, Will. Story of the World Cup. (Heinemann Guided Readers Ser.). (Orig.). 1981. pap. text ed. 2.00x (ISBN 0-435-27083-4). Heinemann Ed.

Capelia, M. E. & Wienstock, M. Games Ti's Plays. 14.95 (ISBN 0-317-05649-2). P-H.

Capell, A. A Survey of New Guinea Languages. LC 68-21925. (Illus.). 158p. 1971. 27.00x (ISBN 0-424-05420-5, Pub. by Sydney U Pr). Intl Spec Bk.

Capell, A. & Hinch, H. E. Maung Grammar, Texts & Vocabulary. (Janua Linguarum, Ser. Practica: No. 98). 1970. pap. text ed. 27.20x (ISBN 0-686-22447-7). Mouton.

Capell, Arthur. The Linguistic Position of South-Eastern Papua. LC 75-32803. Repr. of 1943 ed. 23.50 (ISBN 0-404-14107-2). AMS Pr.

Capell, Edward. Notes & Various Readings to Shakespeare, 3 Vols. LC 70-39873. Repr. of 1783 ed. Set. 97.50 (ISBN 0-404-01400-3). AMS Pr.

Capell, Edward, ed. Notes & Various Readings to Shakespeare, 3 vols. LC 70-80245. 1970. Repr. of 1783 ed. Set. text ed. 78.00 (ISBN 0-8337-0465-6). B Franklin.

Capell, Edward, ed. see Shakespeare, William.

Capell, Elizabeth A. Constitutional Officers, Agencies, Boards & Commissions in California State Government: 1849-1975. (Research Report: 77-1). 1977. pap. 3.50x (ISBN 0-685-87444-3). Inst Gov Stud Berk.

Capell, H., et al. Rheumatic Disease. (Treatment in Clinical Medicine Ser.). (Illus.). 210p. 1983. pap. 19.00 (ISBN 0-387-12622-8). Springer-Verlag.

Capell, H. A., et al. Auranofin. (Current Clinical Practice Ser.: Vol. 7). 1983. 149.00 (ISBN 0-444-90334-8, I-364-83). Elsevier.

Capell, Richard. Opera. 1979. Repr. of 1930 ed. lib. bdg. 12.50 (ISBN 0-8495-0925-4). Arden Lib.

--Opera. LC 78-66894. (Encore Music Editions Ser.). 1981. Repr. of 1948 ed. 14.95 (ISBN 0-88355-730-4). Hyperion Conn.

--Schubert's Songs. LC 77-5524. (Music Reprint Ser.). 1977. Repr. of 1928 ed. lib. bdg. 32.50 (ISBN 0-306-77422-4). Da Capo.

Capella, Joseph N., jt. ed. see Monge, Peter R.

Capella, Mark & Weinstock, Mike. Games Commodore 64s Play. (Games Computers Play Ser.). pap. 14.95 (ISBN 0-88190-121-0). Datamost.

Capella, Mark, jt. auth. see Weinstock, Mike.

Capella, Mark J. & Weinstock, Michael D. Games Apples Play. (Illus.). 272p. (Orig.). 1983. pap. text ed. 14.95 (ISBN 0-88190-060-5, BO060). Datamost.

Capellan, Angel. Hemingway & the Hispanic World. Litz, A. Walton, ed. LC 85-8421. (Studies in Modern Literature: No. 51). 343p. 1985. 44.95 (ISBN 0-8357-1665-1). UMI Res Pr.

Capellanus, Andreas. Art of Courtly Love. abr ed. Locke, F. W., ed. Parry, John J., tr. LC 56-12400. (Milestones of Thought Ser.). 6.00 (ISBN 0-8044-2108-0); pap. 2.95 (ISBN 0-8044-6075-2). Ungar.

Capellaro, Helen, jt. auth. see Donahue, Parnell.

Capelle, Carl. Volistaendiges Woerterbuch Ueber die Gedichte des Homores und der Homeriden. 9th ed. (Ger.). 1968. 48.00 (ISBN 3-534-03408-2, M-7681, Pub. by Wissenschaftl Buchgesells). French & Eur.

Capelle, G. Basic Dictionary of English. 2nd ed. (Illus.). 176p. 1983. pap. text ed. 2.95 (ISBN 0-88345-542-0, 21422). Regents Pub.

Capelle, Ronald G. Changing Human Systems. 1984. 11.95x (ISBN 0-9690171-0-3). BDR Learn Prods.

Capeller, Carl. Sanskrit-Woerterbuch. 2nd ed. rev ed. (Ger). 1966. 28.80x (ISBN 3-11-000191-8). De Gruyter.

Capello, Hermenegildo C. & Ivens, Roberto. From Benguella to the Territory of Yacca, 2 Vols. Elwes, Alfred, tr. LC 76-77194. (Illus.). Repr. Set. 39.00x (ISBN 0-8371-3794-2, CBY&, Pub. by Negro U Pr). Greenwood.

Capellos, C. & Walker, R. F., eds. Fast Reactions in Energetic Systems. 759p. 1981. 89.50 (ISBN 90-277-1299-9, Pub. by Reidel Holland). Kluwer Academic.

Capellos, Christos & Bielski, Benon H. Kinetic Systems: Mathematical Description of Chemical Kinetics in Solution. LC 80-11940. 152p. 1980. pap. 9.50 (ISBN 0-89874-141-6). Krieger.

Capelo, Antonio, jt. auth. see Baiocchi, Claudio.

Capen, Edward W. Historical Development of the Poor Law of Connecticut. LC 71-76674. (Columbia University. Studies in the Social Sciences Ser.: No. 57). Repr. of 1905 ed. 34.50 (ISBN 0-404-51057-4). AMS Pr.

Capers, Charlotte. The Capers Papers. LC 81-22013. 128p. 1982. 9.95 (ISBN 0-87805-152-X). U Pr of Miss.

Capers, Gerald M. John C. Calhoun, Opportunist. LC 60-15788. 1960. 8.00 (ISBN 0-8130-0274-5). U Presses Fla.

--Stephen A. Douglas: Defender of the Union. (The Library of American Biography). 239p. 1972. pap. 6.95 (ISBN 0-316-12814-7). Little.

Capers, Gerald M., Jr. The Biography of a River Town: Memphis--Its Heroic Age. 2nd ed. (Illus.). 318p. 1980. Repr. of 1966 ed. 17.95 (ISBN 0-937130-09-5); signed ltd. ed. 27.95 (ISBN 0-937130-10-9). Burke's Bk Store.

Capers, Roberta M. & Maddox, J. Images & Imagination: An Introduction to Art. LC 65-11698. (Illus.). Repr. of 1965 ed. 58.80 (ISBN 0-8357-9909-3, 2012474). Bks Demand UMI.

Caperton, Thomas J. Rogue! Life & High Times of Stephen W. Dorsey. 1978. pap. 1.95 (ISBN 0-89013-114-7). Museum NM Pr.

Caperton, Thomas J. & Fry, LoRheda. Links to the Past: New Mexico's State Monuments. (Illus.). 1977. pap. 2.50 (ISBN 0-89013-120-1). Museum NM Pr.

Capes, Bernard. Historical Vignettes. (Orig.). 1962. pap. 3.00 (ISBN 0-8283-1439-X, 30, IPL). Branden Pub Co.

--Historical Vignettes. Repr. of 1910 ed. 20.00 (ISBN 0-686-20655-X). Lib Serv Inc.

Capes, Bernard E. At a Winter's Fire. facsimile ed. LC 78-101793. (Short Story Index Reprint Ser). 1899. 18.00 (ISBN 0-8369-3181-5). Ayer Co Pubs.

Capes, Edward C., et al, eds. Coal Processing. LC 74-26744. (Energy Ser.). 1976. text ed. 28.00x (ISBN 0-8422-7265-8). Irvington.

Capes, Harriett, ed. see Conrad, Joseph.

Capes, M. Harriett. Wisdom & Beauty from Conrad. 1973. lib. bdg. 17.50 (ISBN 0-8414-1803-9). Folcroft.

Capes, W. W. The Age of Antonines. 1897. 10.00 (ISBN 0-8482-7254-4). Norwood Edns.

--The Early Empire. 1899. 20.00 (ISBN 0-8482-3561-4). Norwood Edns.

Capes, William W. English Church in the Fourteenth & Fifteenth Centuries, 1272-1486. LC 2-21441. (History of the English Church: No. 3). Repr. of 1900 ed. 29.50 (ISBN 0-404-50753-0). AMS Pr.

--Stoicism. 1976. lib. bdg. 59.95 (ISBN 0-8490-2669-5). Gordon Pr.

--University Life in Ancient Athens. LC 77-445. 1977. Repr. of 1922 ed. lib. bdg. 17.50 (ISBN 0-8414-3561-8). Folcroft.

--University Life in Ancient Athens. 134p. 1980. Repr. of 1922 ed. lib. bdg. 17.50 (ISBN 0-8492-3864-1). R West.

Capesius, P. & Babin, A. E. Radiculosaccography with Water-Soluble Contrast Media. LC 77-26014. (Illus.). 1978. 63.00 (ISBN 0-387-08562-9). Springer-Verlag.

Capestany, Edward J. The Dialectic of the Little Prince. LC 81-43025. 90p. (Orig.). 1982. pap. text ed. 7.50 (ISBN 0-8191-2213-0). U Pr of Amer.

Capetanakis, Demetrio. Demetrios Capetanakis. facs. ed. LC 73-148208. (Biography Index Reprint Ser.). 1947. 18.00 (ISBN 0-8369-8055-7). Ayer Co Pubs.

Capetanakis, Demetrios. Shores of Darkness. facs. ed. LC 73-76897. (Essay Index Reprint Ser). 1949. 17.00 (ISBN 0-8369-0010-3). Ayer Co Pubs.

Capetanos, Leon, jt. auth. see Mazursky, Paul.

Capetti, Giselda, ed. Cronistoria, 5 vols. 400p. (Orig.). 1980. Set. pap. 40.00 (ISBN 0-89944-043-6); Vol. 1. pap. (ISBN 0-89944-044-4); Vol. 2. pap. (ISBN 0-89944-045-2); Vol. 3. pap. (ISBN 0-89944-046-0); Vol. 4. pap. (ISBN 0-89944-047-9); Vol. 5. pap. (ISBN 0-89944-048-7). Don Bosco Multimedia.

Capey, Ernest F. Erasmus. 1902. 25.00 (ISBN 0-8274-2284-9). R West.

Capgrave, J. Lives of St. Augustine & St. Gilbert of Sempringham. (EETS, OS Ser.: No. 140). Repr. of 1910 ed. 40.00 (ISBN 0-527-00137-6). Kraus Repr.

Capgrave, John. Liber de Illustribus Henricis. Hingeston, Francis C., ed. (Rolls Ser.: No. 7). Repr. of 1858 ed. 44.00 (ISBN 0-317-16654-9). Kraus Repr.

--The Life of St. Katharine of Alexandria. Horstmann, Carl, ed. (EETS, OS Ser.: No. 100). Repr. of 1893 ed. 70.00 (ISBN 0-527-00102-3). Kraus Repr.

--Ye Solace of Pilgrimes. Mills, C. A., ed. LC 78-63453. (The Crusades & Military Orders: Second Ser.). Repr. of 1911 ed. 25.00 (ISBN 0-404-16375-0). AMS Pr.

Capie, Forrest. Depression & Protectionism: Britain Between the Wars. 192p. 1983. text ed. 27.50x (ISBN 0-04-330338-2). Allen Unwin.

Capie, Forrest & Collins, Michael. The Inter-War British Economy: A Statistical Abstract. LC 83-5413. 118p. 1983. 24.00 (ISBN 0-7190-0901-4, Pub. by Manchester Univ Pr). Longwood Pub Group.

Capie, Forrest & Webber, Alan. A Monetary History of the United Kingdom, 1870-1982: Data, Sources, Methods, Vol. I. 1985. text ed. 50.00x (ISBN 0-04-332097-X). Allen Unwin.

Capildeo, Rudy, jt. auth. see Rose, Clifford.

Capildeo, Rudy, jt. ed. see Findley, Lesley.

Capildeo, Rudy, jt. ed. see Rose, F. Clifford.

Capirola, Vincenzo. Vincenzo Capirola Lute Book. Gombosi, Otto, ed. (Music Ser.). 236p. 1982. Repr. of 1955 ed. lib. bdg. 65.00 (ISBN 0-306-76100-9). Da Capo.

Capitaine, Jean L. & Charton, Balthazar. Le Affiche De Cinema. (Illus.). 159p. (Orig., Fr.). 1983. pap. 40.00 (ISBN 0-317-06234-4, 2390099, Pub. by Editions de l'Amateur FR). Seven Hills Bks.

Capital Conference on Graph Theory & Conbinatorics, George Washington University, June 18-22, 1973. Graphs & Combinatorics: Proceedings. Bari, R. A. & Harary, F., eds. LC 74-13955. (Lecture Notes in Mathematics: Vol. 406). viii, 355p. 1974. pap. 20.00 (ISBN 0-387-06854-6). Springer-Verlag.

Capital Planning Information. National Repository Plans & Programmes: A Comparative Study of Existing Plans & Possible Models. 133p. 1982. 56.00x (ISBN 0-7123-2001-6, Pub. by Pubns Sec Brit Lib England). State Mutual Bk.

Capital Planning Information Staff. Availability of Publications in the United Kingdom: A State of the Art Review. (BNB RF Report 12). (Illus.). 96p. (Orig.). 1984. pap. 18.75 (ISBN 0-7123-3039-9, Pub. by British Lib). Longwood Pub Group.

Capitan, A. Nature, Peace, Equality. LC 81-90639. 95p. 1983. 7.95 (ISBN 0-533-05263-7). Vantage.

Capitanchik, David & Eichenberg, Richard. Defense & Public Opinion. (Chatham House Papers on Foreign Policy). 96p. (Orig.). 1984. pap. 10.95x (ISBN 0-7100-9356-X). Routledge & Kegan.

Capitman, Barbara. American Trademark Designs: A Survey with 732 Marks, Logos & Corporate-Identity Symbols. 1976. pap. 6.00 (ISBN 0-486-23259-X). Dover.

Capitman, Barbara B. American Trademark Designs: A Survey of 732 Marks, Logos & Corporate Indentity Symbols. 14.75 (ISBN 0-8446-5517-1). Peter Smith.

Capitol Enquiry Staff, compiled by. Pocket Directory of the California Legislature. 64p. (Orig.). Date not set. Annual. text ed. cancelled (ISBN 0-917982-30-4); pap. 4.95. Capitol Enquiry.

Capizzi, Joseph, jt. auth. see Larew, Hiram.

Caplan, Ann P. Choice & Constraint in a Swahili Community: Property Hierarchy & Cognatic Descent on the East African Coast. (International African Institute Ser.). (Illus.). 1975. 29.95x (ISBN 0-19-724195-6). Oxford U Pr.

Caplan, Annette, ed. see Shapiro, Jack J. & Caplan, Marla S.

Caplan, Arnold I., jt. ed. see Fallon, John F.

Caplan, Arthur, jt. ed. see Engelhardt, Tristram H., Jr.

Caplan, Arthur L., jt. auth. see Rosen, Bernard.

Caplan, Arthur L., ed. The Sociobiology Debate. 1979. pap. 10.00ix (ISBN 0-06-131995-3, TB 1995, TB). Har-Row.

Caplan, Arthur L. & Callahan, Daniel, eds. Ethics in Hard Times. LC 81-17728. (The Hastings Center Series in Ethics). 311p. 1981. text ed. 25.00 (ISBN 0-306-40790-6, Plenum Pr). Plenum Pub.

Caplan, Arthur L. & Jennings, Bruce, eds. Darwin, Marx, & Freud: Their Influence on Moral Theory. (Hastings Center Series in Ethics). 258p. 1984. 25.00x (ISBN 0-306-41530-5, Plenum Pr). Plenum Pub.

Caplan, Arthur L., et al. Concepts of Health & Disease: Interdisciplinary Perspectives. 608p. 1981. pap. text ed. 41.95 (ISBN 0-201-00973-0, Med-Nurse). Addison-Wesley.

Caplan, David, ed. Biological Studies of Mental Processes. 352p. 1980. pap. text ed. 10.95x (ISBN 0-262-53041-4). MIT Pr.

--Biological Studies of Mental Processes. (Illus.). 1980. 35.00x (ISBN 0-262-03061-6). MIT Pr.

Caplan, David, jt. ed. see Studdert-Kennedy, Michael.

Caplan, David, et al, eds. Biological Perspectives on Language. (Neuropsyche-Neurolinguistic Ser.). (Illus.). 432p. 1984. text ed. 40.00x (ISBN 0-262-03101-9). MIT Pr.

Caplan, Edwin H. Management Accounting & Behavioral Science. LC 72-150575. (Business & Economics Ser). 1971. pap. 10.50 (ISBN 0-201-00891-2). Addison-Wesley.

Caplan, Edwin H. & Champoux, Joseph E. Cases in Management Accounting: Context & Behavior. 88p. 1983. 9.95 (ISBN 0-86641-049-X, 78101). Natl Assn Accts.

Caplan, Edwin H. & Landekich, Stephen. Human Resource Accounting: Past, Present, & Future. 156p. 16.95 (ISBN 0-86641-055-4, 7465). Natl Assn Accts.

Caplan, Frank. The Quality System: A Sourcebook for Managers & Engineers. LC 80-969. 256p. 1980. 38.50 (ISBN 0-8019-6972-7). Chilton.

Caplan, Frank & Caplan, Theresa. The Power of Play. LC 68-10557. 336p. 1973. pap. 4.50 (ISBN 0-385-09935-5, Anch). Doubleday.

--The Second Twelve Months of Life. LC 77-78748. (Illus.). 1979. pap. 10.95 (ISBN 0-399-50776-0, G&D). Putnam Pub Group.

--The Second Twelve Months of Life: A Kaleidoscope of Growth. (Illus.). 1983. 10.95 (ISBN 0-399-50776-0, G&D,Perige). Putnam Pub Group.

Caplan, Frank, jt. auth. see Caplan, Theresa.

Caplan, Frank, ed. The First Twelve Months of Life. 1978. pap. 4.95 (ISBN 0-553-24233-4). Bantam.

--The Second Twelve Months of Life. 1980. pap. 4.95 (ISBN 0-553-23249-5). Bantam.

Caplan, Frank, ed. see Princeton Center for Infancy.

Caplan, Gerald. Arab & Jew in Jerusalem: Explorations in Community Mental Health. LC 79-27832. 1980. text ed. 20.00x (ISBN 0-674-04315-4). Harvard U Pr.

--Principles of Preventive Psychiatry. LC 64-10248. 1964. 13.95x (ISBN 0-465-06344-6). Basic.

--Support Systems & Community Mental Health. LC 73-12398. 267p. 1974. text ed. 29.95 (ISBN 0-87705-119-4). Human Sci Pr.

--Theory & Practice of Mental Health Consultation. LC 77-103089. 1970. text ed. 18.50x (ISBN 0-465-08450-8). Basic.

Caplan, Gerald & Killilea, Marie, eds. Support Systems & Mutual Help. LC 76-7473. (Illus.). 336p. 1976. 56.00 (ISBN 0-8089-0927-4, 790785). Grune.

Caplan, Gerald M. & Police Foundation, eds. ABSCAM Ethics: Moral Issues & Deceptions in Law Enforcement. LC 82-74444. 168p. 1983. 22.50 (ISBN 0-88410-634-9). Ballinger Pub.

Caplan, H. H., ed. Classified Directory of Artists' Signatures, Symbols & Monograms. 2nd ed. 850p. 1982. 220.00x (ISBN 0-8103-0977-7). Gale.

Caplan, Harry, tr. & notes by see Pico della Mirandola, Giovanni.

Caplan, Jonathan, jt. auth. see Price, Christopher.

Caplan, Lincoln. The Insanity Defense & the Trial of John W. Hinckley, Jr. LC 84-47658. 160p. 1984. 13.95 (ISBN 0-87923-533-0). Godine.

Caplan, Lionel. Administration & Politics in a Nepalese Town. (Illus.). 1975. 17.95x (ISBN 0-19-713585-4). Oxford U Pr.

Caplan, Marc. Ralph Nader Presents a Citizens' Guide to Lobbying. LC 83-2022. 1983. 13.50 (ISBN 0-934878-26-9); pap. 6.95 (ISBN 0-934878-27-7). Dembner Bks.

Caplan, Marla S., jt. auth. see Shapiro, Jack J.

Caplan, Neil. Futile Diplomacy: Early Arab-Zionist Negotiation Attempts, 1913-1931, Vol. 1. (Illus.). 296p. 1983. text ed. 32.00x (ISBN 0-7146-3214-7, F Cass Co). Biblio Dist.

--Palestine Jewry & the Arab Question, 1917-1925. 268p. 1978. 28.50x (ISBN 0-7146-3110-8, F Cass Co). Biblio Dist.

Caplan, Patricia & Bujra, Janet M. Women United, Women Divided: Comparative Studies of Ten Contemporary Cultures. LC 78-14085. (Midland Bks.: Bk. 297). 288p. 1982. pap. 8.95 (ISBN 0-253-20297-3); 22.50x (ISBN 0-253-12215-5). Ind U Pr.

Caplan, Paula. Barriers Between Women. LC 80-12983. 167p. 1981. 19.95 (ISBN 0-89335-103-2). SP Med & Sci Bks.

Caplan, Paula, jt. auth. see Kinsbourne, Marcel.

Caplan, Paula J. The Myth of Women's Masochism. 256p. 1985. 16.95 (ISBN 0-525-24361-5, 01646-490). Dutton.

Caplan, Ralph. By Design: Why There are No Locks on the Bathroom Doors in the Hotel Louis XIV & Other Object Lessons. (Illus.). 192p. 1982. 16.95 (ISBN 0-312-11085-5). St Martin.

Caplan, Ralph, pref. by. Graphis Packaging Four. (Illus.). 304p. 1984. 59.50 (ISBN 0-8230-2154-8, Visual Communication). Watson-Guptill.

Caplan, Robert D., et al. Adhering to Medical Regimens: Pilot Experiments in Patient Education & Social Support. LC 76-620035. 284p. 1976. pap. 14.00x (ISBN 0-87944-207-7). Inst Soc Res.

--Job Demands & Worker Health. 358p. (Orig.). 1980. pap. 17.00x (ISBN 0-87944-265-4). Inst Soc Res.

--Social Support & Patient Adherence: Experimental & Survey Findings. 834p. (Orig.). 1980. pap. 16.00x (ISBN 0-87944-260-3). Inst Soc Res.

--Tranquilizer Use & Well-Being: A Longitudinal Study of Social & Psychological Effects. (ISR Research Report Ser.). 512p. (Orig.). 1984. pap. text ed. 25.00x (ISBN 0-87944-296-4). Inst Soc Res.

Caplan, Ron, jt. ed. see Sinclair, John.

Caplan, Ronald M. Pregnant Is Beautiful. (Orig.). 1985. pap. 3.95 (ISBN 0-671-53259-6). PB.

--Principles of Obstetrics. (Illus.). 322p. 1982. pap. text ed. 19.95 (ISBN 0-683-01436-6). Williams & Wilkins.

Caplan, S. Roy & Essig, Alvin. Bioenergetics & Linear Nonequilibrium Thermodynamics: The Steady State. (Harvard Books in Biophysics: No. 3). (Illus.). 448p. 1983. text ed. 37.50x (ISBN 0-674-07352-5). Harvard U Pr.

Caplan, Samuel & Ribalow, Harold. The Great Jewish Books. 1983. pap. 10.95 (ISBN 0-8180-1135-1). Horizon.

Caplan, Simon, jt. auth. see Levy, James.

Caplan, Theresa & Caplan, Frank. The Early Childhood Years: The Two to Six Year Old. 560p. 1984. pap. 3.95 (ISBN 0-553-24496-5). Bantam.

--The Early Childhood Years: The 2 to 6 Year Old. (Illus.). 320p. (Orig.). 1983. (G&D); pap. 9.95 (ISBN 0-399-50862-7, G&D). Putnam Pub Group.

Caplan, Theresa, jt. auth. see Caplan, Frank.

Caplan, Thomas. Line of Chance. 416p. 1981. pap. 2.95 (ISBN 0-671-83137-2). PB.

Caple, John. Careercycles: A Guidebook to Success in the Passages & Challenge of Your Work Life. (Illus.). 248p. 1983. 15.95 (ISBN 0-13-114587-8); pap. 7.95 (ISBN 0-13-114579-7). P-H.

Caple, Kathy. The Biggest Nose. LC 84-19745. (Illus.). 32p. (gr. k-3). 1985. 12.95 (ISBN 0-395-36894-4). HM.

Caplen, R. H. A Practical Approach to Quality Control. 4th ed. 326p. 1983. pap. text ed. 17.00x (ISBN 0-09-147451-5, Pub. by Busn Bks England). Brookfield Pub Co.

Caples, C. B., et al. A Medieval Miscellany. (Rice University Studies: Vol. 62, No. 2). (Illus.). 120p. (Orig.). 1976. pap. 10.00x (ISBN 0-89263-228-3). Rice Univ.

Caples, J. Tested Advertising Methods. 4th ed. 318p. 1974. 14.95 (ISBN 0-13-906909-7, Busn); pap. 6.95 (ISBN 0-13-906891-0). P-H.

Caples, John. Advertising Ideas: A Practical Guide to Methods That Make Advertisements Work. LC 84-46051. (History of Advertising Ser.). 218p. 1985. lib. bdg. 25.00 (ISBN 0-8240-6745-2). Garland Pub.

--How to Make Your Advertising Make Money. LC 83-4455. (Illus.). 383p. 1983. 19.95 (ISBN 0-13-423608-4); pap. 6.95 (ISBN 0-13-423590-8). P-H.

--Making Ads Pay. 1957. pap. 5.00 (ISBN 0-486-21575-X). Dover.

Caplin, A. D. Electronic Structure of Solids. (Structure & Properties of Solids Ser.). 148p. 1976. pap. text ed. 17.50 (ISBN 0-7131-2527-6). E Arnold.

Caplin, Lee E., ed. The Business of Art. 1982. 20.00 (ISBN 0-13-106518-1, Busn); pap. 9.95 (ISBN 0-13-106500-9). P-H.

Caplin, Lee Evan, ed. The Business of Art. 383p. pap. 9.95 (ISBN 0-317-36356-5, NO. 205). Am Council Arts.

Caplin, Maxwell. The Tuberculin Test in Clinical Practice. (Illus.). 1980. pap. text ed. 18.50 (ISBN 0-7216-0710-1, Pub. by Bailliere-Tindall). Saunders.

Caplinger, Timothy E., jt. auth. see Feldman, Ronald A.

Caplis, M. E., et al, eds. Drug Mechanisms. (Journal: Clinical Physiology & Biochemistry: Vol. 3, No. 2-3). (Illus.). 96p. 1985. pap. 35.75 (ISBN 3-8055-4051-5). S Karger.

Caplovitz, David. Consumers in Trouble: Study of Debtors in Default. LC 73-14747. 1974. 10.95 (ISBN 0-02-905260-2). Free Pr.

--Poor Pay More: Consumer Practices of Low Income Families. LC 63-18312. 1967. pap. text ed. 13.95 (ISBN 0-02-905250-5). Free Pr.

--The Stages of Social Research. 434p. 1983. 24.95x (ISBN 0-471-08781-5, Pub. by Wiley-Interscience). Wiley.

--Student-Faculty Relations in Medical School: A Study of Professional Socialization. Zuckerman, Harriet & Merton, Robert K., eds. LC 79-8980. (Dissertations on Sociology Ser.). 1980. lib. bdg. 26.50x (ISBN 0-405-12956-4). Ayer Co Pubs.

--The Working Addict. LC 77-94070. 168p. 1978. 22.50 (ISBN 0-87332-116-2). M E Sharpe.

Caplovitz, David, jt. auth. see Bradburn, Norman M.

Caplow, Harriet M. Michelozzo. LC 76-23604. (Outstanding Dissertations in the Fine Arts - 2nd Series - 15th Century). (Illus.). 1977. Repr. of 1970 ed. lib. bdg. 140.00 (ISBN 0-8240-2678-0). Garland Pub.

Caplow, Theodore. Managing an Organization: A Manual of Practical Sociology. 2nd ed. 1984. pap. text ed. 15.95 (ISBN 0-03-059729-3). HR&W.

--The Sociology of Work. LC 77-18112. (Illus.). 1978. Repr. of 1954 ed. lib. bdg. 32.00 (ISBN 0-313-20111-0, CASOW). Greenwood.

Caplow, Theodore & Reece, J. McGee. The Academic Marketplace. Merrager, Walter P., ed. LC 76-55171. (The Academic Profession Ser.). (Illus.). 1977. Repr. of 1958 ed. lib. bdg. 20.00x (ISBN 0-405-10002-7). Ayer Co Pubs.

Caplow, Theodore, et al. All Faithful People: Change & Continuity in Middletown's Religion. LC 82-24759. x, 380p. 1983. 19.50 (ISBN 0-8166-1230-7). U of Minn Pr.

--Middletown Families: Fifty Years of Change & Continuity. LC 81-14757. (Illus.). 400p. 1982. 18.95 (ISBN 0-8166-1073-8). U of Minn Pr.

Caplow-Linder, et al. Therapeutic Dance Movement: Expressive Activities for Older Adults. LC 78-1093. 283p. 1979. 29.95 (ISBN 0-87705-340-5); pap. 12.95 (ISBN 0-87705-347-2). Human Sci Pr.

Capno, A. De see DeCaprio, A.

Capobianco, Joseph F. Italy. LC 80-27851. (World Education Ser.). (Illus.). 101p. (Orig.). 1981. pap. text ed. 2.00 (ISBN 0-910054-59-2). Am Assn Coll Registrars.

Capobianco, M. & Molluzzo, J. C. Examples & Counter Examples in Graph Theory. 260p. 1978. 41.00 (ISBN 0-444-00255-3, North-Holland). Elsevier.

Capobianco, M., et al, eds. see New York City Graph Theory Conference, 1st, 1970.

Capobianco, R. J., jt. auth. see Dunn, L.

Capobianco, S., jt. ed. see Samis, H. V.

Capocaccia, L., et al, eds. The Epidemiology & Prevention of Gallstone Disease. 1984. lib. bdg. 47.75 (ISBN 0-318-03679-7, Pub. by MTP Pr England). Kluwer Academic.

Capocaccia, Livio, et al, eds. Hepatic Encephalopathy in Chronic Liver Failure. 398p. 1984. 65.00x (ISBN 0-306-41702-2, Plenum Pr). Plenum Pub.

Capon, B. & Rees, C. W., eds. Organic Reaction Mechanisms, 1969: An Annual Survey Covering the Literature Dated December 1968 Through November 1969. LC 66-23143. pap. 160.00 (ISBN 0-317-28687-0, 2051618). Bks Demand UMI.

Capon, Brian. Investigations into the Biology of Plants. 1981. coil bdg. 8.95 (ISBN 0-88252-041-5). Paladin Hse.
Capon, Brian, ed. Neighboring Group Participation, Vol. 1. LC 76-17812. (Illus.). 280p. 1976. 42.50x (ISBN 0-306-35027-0, Plenum Pr). Plenum Pub.
Capon, Edmond. Art & Archeology in China. 1977. pap. 9.95 (ISBN 0-262-53034-1). MIT Pr.
Capon, Jack. Perceptual Motor Development Series, 5 bks. Incl. Balance Activities (ISBN 0-8224-5302-9); Ball, Rope, Hoop Activities (ISBN 0-8224-5301-0); Basic Movement Activities (ISBN 0-8224-5300-2); Beanbag, Rhythm-Stick Activities (ISBN 0-8224-5303-7); Tire, Parachute Activities (ISBN 0-8224-5304-5). (ps-3). 1975. pap. 4.95 ea. Pitman Learning.
--Perceptual-Motor Lesson Plans - Level 1: Basic & "Practical" Lesson Plans for Perceptual-Motor Programs in Preschool & Elementary Grades. 5th ed. Alexander, Frank, ed. (Illus.). 76p. 1975. tchr's manual 6.95 (ISBN 0-915256-03-7). Front Row.
--Perceptual-Motor Lesson Plans Level 2: Basic & "Practical" Lesson Plans for Perceptual-Motor Programs in Preschool & Elementary Grades. 2nd ed. Alexander, Frank, ed. (Illus.). 1976. tchrs' manual 6.95 (ISBN 0-915256-04-5). Front Row.
--Successful Movement Challenges: Movement Activities for the Developing Child. Alexander, Frank & Alexander, Diane, eds. (Illus.). 129p. (Orig.). 1981. pap. 7.95 (ISBN 0-915256-07-X). Front Row.
Capon, Paul, tr. see Duplessis, Yves.
Capon, Robert F. Between Noon & Three: A Parable of Romance, Law, & the Outrage of Grace. LC 81-47832. 192p. 1982. 11.49i (ISBN 0-06-061308-4, HarpR). Har-Row.
--Capon on Cooking. (Illus.). 182p. 1983. 14.95 (ISBN 0-395-34393-3). HM.
--Hunting the Divine Fox: Images & Mystery in the Christian Faith. 176p. 1977. pap. 6.95 (ISBN 0-8164-2137-4, AY7359, Pub. by Seabury). Winston Pr.
--An Offering of Uncles: The Priesthood of Adam & the Shape of the World. (The Crossroad Paperback Ser.). 192p. 1982. pap. 5.95 (ISBN 0-8245-0422-4). Crossroad NY.
--The Parables of the Kingdom. 192p. 1985. 10.95 (ISBN 0-310-42670-7, Pub. by Zondervan Bks). Zondervan.
--The Supper of the Lamb: A Culinary Reflection. LC 78-14937. 1979. pap. 3.95 (ISBN 0-15-686893-8, Harv). HarBracej.
--The Youngest Day: Nature & Grace on Shelter Island. LC 82-48414. (Illus.). 160p. 1983. 11.49i (ISBN 0-06-061309-2, HarpR). Har-Row.
Capon, Robin. Basic Drawing. (Illus.). 128p. 1984. 12.95 (ISBN 0-8052-3924-3). Schocken.
--Papier Mache. LC 76-39676. (Illus.). 1977. 9.75 (ISBN 0-87192-090-5). Davis Mass.
Capone, Annette. Skin Deep. (Wildfire Extra Ser.). 96p. (Orig.). (gr. 6 up). 1984. pap. 2.25 (ISBN 0-590-33458-1, Wildfire). Scholastic Inc.
--Your Fourteen Day Total Shape-up Plan. 128p. (gr. 7 up). 1984. pap. 1.95 (ISBN 0-590-30913-7, Wildfire). Scholastic Inc.
Capone, Donald, jt. auth. see Cheyney, Arnold.
Capone, Douglas G., jt. ed. see Carpenter, Edward J.
Capone, Robert J., jt. auth. see Boden, William E.
Caponegro, Mary. Tales from the Next Village, No. 28. Wright, C. D. & Gander, Forrest, eds. 90p. (Orig.). 1985. pap. 6.95 (ISBN 0-918786-32-0). Lost Roads.
Caponera, D. A. Water Laws in Moslem Countries, Vol. 1. (Irrigation & Drainage Papers: No. 20-21). 229p. 1973. pap. 15.00 (ISBN 0-686-92952-7, F989, FAO). Unipub.
--Water Laws in Moslem Countries, Vol. 2. (Irrigation & Drainage Papers: No. 20-2). 314p. (Eng. & Fr.). 1978. pap. 20.50 (ISBN 92-5-100536-2, F1507, FAO). Unipub.
Caponera, Dante A. The Law of International Water Resources. (Legislative Studies: No. 23). 335p. (Eng., Fr. & Span.). 1980. pap. 24.00 (ISBN 92-5-101036-6, F2186, FAO). Unipub.
--Water Law in Selected African Countries: Benin, Burundi, Ethopia, Gabon, Kenya, Mauritius, Sierra Leone, Swaziland, Upper Volta, Zambia. (Legislative Studies: No. 17). 273p. (Eng., Fr. & Span.). 1979. pap. 19.75 (ISBN 92-5-100748-9, F1620, FAO). Unipub.
Caponetto, Salvatore, ed. Benedetto Da Mantova: Il Beneficio Di Cristo. LC 72-3471. (Corpus Reformatorum Italicorum & Biblioteca Ser.). (Illus.). 558p. (Latin & It.). 1972. 40.00 (ISBN 0-87580-035-1). N Ill U Pr.
Caponigri, A. Robert. A History of Western Philosophy. Incl. Vol. 4. Philosophy from the Romantic Age to the Age of Positivism. LC 63-20526. 342p (ISBN 0-268-00415-3). pap. (ISBN 0-268-00508-7); Vol. 5. Philosophy from the Age of Positivism to the Age of Analysis. LC 63-20526. 380p (ISBN 0-268-00439-0). pap. (ISBN 0-268-00509-5). LC 63-20526. 1971. 25.00 ea.; pap. 4.95x ea. U of Notre Dame Pr.
--Time & Idea: The Theory of History in Giambattista Vico. 1968. pap. 6.95x (ISBN 0-268-00277-0). U of Notre Dame Pr.
Caponigri, A. Robert, tr. see Pico Della Mirandola, Giovanni.
Caponigri, A. Robert, tr. see Zubiri, Xavier.
Caponigri, Aloysius R. Modern Catholic Thinkers: An Anthology. (Essay Index Reprint Ser.). 650p. Repr. of 1960 ed. lib. bdg. 34.00 (ISBN 0-8290-0784-9). Irvington.
Caponigri, Aloysius R., ed. Modern Catholic Thinkers. facs. ed. LC 78-117775. (Essay Index Reprint Ser). 1960. 38.50 (ISBN 0-8369-1787-1). Ayer Co Pubs.
Caporale, Rocco & Grumelli, Antonio, eds. The Culture of Unbelief: Studies & Proceedings from the First International Symposium on Belief, Held in Rome, March 22-27, 1969. LC 75-138513. 1971. 36.00x (ISBN 0-520-01856-7). U of Cal Pr.
Caporaso, James A. & Roos, Leslie L., Jr., eds. Quasi-Experimental Approaches: Testing Theory & Evaluating Policy. LC 72-96703. Repr. of 1973 ed. 97.00 (ISBN 0-8357-9467-9, 2011468). Bks Demand UMI.
Capossela, Jim. Fifty Secrets of Success: A Common Sense Approach. 24p. 1982. pap. 1.95 (ISBN 0-942990-03-X). Northeast Sportsmans.
--Good Fishing Close to New York City: A Guide to the Great Close-to-Home Angling of the Metropolitan Region. LC 85-60313. (The "Good Fishing in New York" Ser.). (Illus.). 244p. (Orig.). 1985. 15.95 (ISBN 0-942990-06-4); pap. 9.95 (ISBN 0-942990-07-2). Northeast Sportsmans.
--How to Catch Crabs by the Bushel: The Manual of Sport Crabbing. LC 82-90080. (Illus.). 72p. 1982. pap. 3.95 (ISBN 0-942990-01-3). Northeast Sportsman.
--How to Write for the Outdoors Magazines: A Concise Guide to Writing Fishing, Hunting & Other Outdoor Articles. (Illus.). 72p. 1984. pap. 3.95 (ISBN 0-942990-05-6). Northeast Sportsmans.
--Part Time Cash for the Sportsman: Twenty-Five Ways for the Fisherman & Hunter to Earn Extra Money. LC 82-80911. 72p. 1984. pap. 3.95 (ISBN 0-942990-05-6). Northeast Sportsmans.
Capossela, Jim & Capossela, Josephine. Festive Christmas Recipes. 36p. 1982. pap. 1.95 (ISBN 0-942990-04-8). Northeast Sportsmans.
Capossela, Josephine, jt. auth. see Capossela, Jim.
Capostosto, John. Basic Carpentry. 2nd ed. (Illus.). 1980. text ed. 24.95 (ISBN 0-8359-0368-0). Reston.
Capotasto, John. Residential Carpentry for the 1980's. 1982. text ed. 25.95 (ISBN 0-8359-6648-8). Reston.
Capote, Truman. Breakfast at Tiffany's. 1959. pap. 2.50 (ISBN 0-451-12042-6, Sig). NAL.
--Breakfast at Tiffany's. 1958. 13.95 (ISBN 0-394-41770-4). Random.
--Christmas Memory. 1966. slip-case 14.95 (ISBN 0-394-41931-6). Random.
--A Christmas Memory. (Christmas Stories Ser.). 32p. 1983. 8.95 (ISBN 0-87191-956-7). Creative Ed.
--The Dogs Bark: Private Places & Public People. 1973. 10.95 (ISBN 0-394-48751-6). Random.
--The Dogs Bark: Public People & Private Places. 1977. pap. 8.95 (ISBN 0-452-25389-6, Z5389, Plume). NAL.
--The Grass Harp, & A Tree of Night & Other Short Stories. pap. 2.75 (ISBN 0-451-12043-4, AE2043, Sig). NAL.
--In Cold Blood. 1971. pap. 3.95 (ISBN 0-451-12198-8, AE2198, Sig). NAL.
--In Cold Blood. 1966. 18.95 (ISBN 0-394-43023-9). Random.
--Miriam: A Classic Story of Loneliness. (Classic Short Stories Ser.). (Illus.). (gr. 4 up). PLB 8.95 (ISBN 0-317-30966-8). Creative Ed.
--Music for Chameleons. 1981. pap. 3.95 (ISBN 0-451-13880-5, E9934, Sig). NAL.
--Music for Chameleons. 1980. 11.95 (ISBN 0-394-50826-2). Random.
--Music for Chameleons. 1983. pap. 6.95 (ISBN 0-452-25463-9, Plume). NAL.
--One Christmas. 1983. slipcased 12.95 (ISBN 0-394-53266-X). Random.
--Other Voices Other Rooms. pap. 2.95 (ISBN 0-451-13451-6, J9961, Sig). NAL.
--Other Voices, Other Rooms. 1968. 13.95 (ISBN 0-394-43949-X). Random.
--Selected Writings of Truman Capote. 1963. 13.95 (ISBN 0-394-44467-1). Random.
--Selected Writings of Truman Capote. LC 83-42946. 1963. 6.95 (ISBN 0-394-60495-4). Modern Lib.
--The Thanksgiving Visitor. 1968. 14.95 (ISBN 0-394-44824-3). Random.
--Three by Truman Capote. Date not set. price not set. Random.
Capotosto, John. Step-by-Step Home Carpentry. (Illus.). 1977. pap. 10.95 (ISBN 0-87909-794-9). Reston.
Capotosto, Rosario. Capotosto's Woodworking Techniques & Projects. 1982. pap. 25.95 (ISBN 0-442-21671-8). Van Nos Reinhold.
--Capotosto's Woodworking Wisdom: Five Hundred Original Jigs, Shop Aids & Tool Techniques for the Home Craftsman. 1983. 29.95 (ISBN 0-442-21696-3). Van Nos Reinhold.
--The Complete Book of Woodworking. LC 74-27319. (A Popular Science Ser). (Illus.). 448p. 1975. 18.22i (ISBN 0-06-010613-1, HarpT). Har-Row.
Capouya, Emile & Tompkins, Keitha, eds. The Essential Kropotkin. 296p. 1975. pap. 3.95x (ISBN 0-87140-400-1). Liveright.
Capouya, Emile, tr. see Waechter, Friedrich K.
Capozzi, Angelo. Change of Face: What You Should Know If You Choose Cosmetic Surgery. 1985. 13.95 (ISBN 0-942294-14-9). Kampmann & Co.
Capozziello, Vincent, Jr. Planning My Career, Occupational Guidance. LC 75-20074. (gr. 7 up). 1979. 3.75 (ISBN 0-912486-43-0). Finney Co.
Capozzoli, Tom. Coaching Football for Young Athletes. 133p. 7.95 (ISBN 0-8092-7009-9). Contemp Bks.
Capp, Al & Van Buren, Raeburn. Abbie an' Slats. Galewitz, Herb, ed. (U. S. Classics Ser.). (Illus.). 80p. (Orig.). 1983. pap. 5.95 (ISBN 0-912277-14-9). K Pierce Inc.
Capp, Al & Wallace, George. Great Issues: A Forum on Important Questions Facing the American Public. 1970. 5.95x (ISBN 0-686-29368-1). Troy State Univ.
Capp, Al, et al. Abbie an 'Slats, Vol. 2. Galewitz, Herb, ed. (U. S. Classics Ser.). (Illus.). 80p. (Orig.). 1984. pap. 5.95 (ISBN 0-912277-24-6). K Pierce Inc.
Capp, Bernard. English Almanacs: Fifteen Hundred to Eighteen Hundred: Astrology & the Popular Press. LC 78-74212. (Illus.). 416p. 1979. 55.00x (ISBN 0-8014-1229-3). Cornell U Pr.
Capp, Glenn R., et al. Basic Oral Communication. 4th ed. (Illus.). 336p. 1986. pap. text ed. 17.95 (ISBN 0-13-065921-5). P-H.
--Basic Oral Communication. 3rd ed. (Illus.). 416p. 1981. pap. text ed. 19.95 (ISBN 0-13-065979-7). P-H.
Capp, M. Paul. Digital Radiographic Imaging. (Illus.). 500p. Date not set. price not set (ISBN 0-7216-1117-6). Saunders.
Capp, Richard. Crown of Thorns. Young, Billie, ed. LC 77-78802. 1979. 15.95 (ISBN 0-87949-096-9). Ashley Bks.
Capp, Robert A. & Bush, Robert G. Glass Etching: Fifty-Two Patterns with Complete Instructions. (Crafts Ser.). 64p. (Orig.). 1984. pap. 2.95 (ISBN 0-486-24578-0). Dover.
Cappa, Alphonse. Fatima: Cove of Wonders. 1980. 4.50 (ISBN 0-8198-0569-6); pap. 3.25 (ISBN 0-8198-0570-X). Dghtrs St Paul.
Cappa, Cornell, ed. International Center of Photography Encyclopedia of Photography. LC 84-1856. (Illus.). 672p. 1984. 50.00 (ISBN 0-517-55271-X). Crown.
Cappacciio, Albert, jt. auth. see Sloan, Annette.
Cappadelta, Luigi, tr. see Von Funk, Franz X.
Cappadona, Diane A., ed. The Sacred Play of Children. 160p. 1983. pap. 9.95 (ISBN 0-8164-2427-6, Pub. by Seabury). Winston Pr.
Cappalli, Richard. Federal Grants & Cooperative Agreements: Law, Policy, & Practice, 3 vols. LC 82-17699. 1982. 240.00; Suppl., 1983. 45.00. Callaghan.
Cappallini, V., et al. Digital Filters & Their Applications. (Techniques of Physics Ser.). 1979. 69.50 (ISBN 0-12-159250-2). Acad Pr.
Cappel, Robert P. S. W. A. T. Team Manual. (Illus.). 150p. 1979. pap. 12.00 (ISBN 0-87364-169-8). Paladin Pr.
Cappelens. English-Norse Dictionary. deluxe ed. 100.00 (ISBN 0-317-19064-4, N461). Vanous.
Cappelens, ed. Engelsk-Norsk: Rettskriuning-Orddeling Uttale-Synonymer. 304p. (Eng. & Norwegian.). 1975. pap. 9.75 (ISBN 0-317-18994-8, N548). Vanous.
--Norsk-Engelsk: Twenty-Five Thousand Sentrale Norske. 304p. (Norwegian & Eng.). 1975. pap. 11.50 (ISBN 0-317-18991-3, N547). Vanous.
Cappelini, V. & Constantinides, A. G., eds. Digital Signal Processing. 1980. 59.50 (ISBN 0-12-159080-1). Acad Pr.
Cappell, Charles L., jt. auth. see Halliday, Terence C.
Cappell, Ralph & Howard, Ethel M. Reading & Writing about Health Careers. 1984. wkbk. 3.95 (ISBN 0-910307-02-4). Comp Pr.
Cappell, Ralph, jt. auth. see Howard, Ethel M.
Cappellanus, George. Latin Can Be Fun. Needham, Peter, tr. (Lat.). 1977. 7.95x (ISBN 0-285-62161-0, Pub. by Souvenir Pr). Intl Spec Bk.
Cappellari, Marjorie, jt. ed. see Walsh, Don.
Cappelletti, M. Procedure Orale et Procedure Ecrite: Oral & Written Procedure in Civil Litigation. (Studi di Diritto Comparato: No. 4). 968p. 1971. 12.00 (ISBN 0-379-00032-6). Oceana.
Cappelletti, Mauro. Judicial Review in the Contemporary World. 133p. 1971. pap. 6.50 (ISBN 0-672-81757-8, Bobbs-Merrill Law). Michie Co.
--Oral & Written Procedure in Civil Litigation. 116p. (Fr. & Eng.). 1976. 12.00 (ISBN 0-317-30237-X). Oceana.
Cappelletti, Mauro & Tallon, Denis, eds. Fundamental Guarantees of Parties in Civil Litigation: Studies in National & Comparative Law. LC 73-762. (Studies in Comparative Law: No. 5). 821p. (Eng. & Fr.). 1973. lib. bdg. 35.00 (ISBN 0-379-00007-5). Oceana.
Cappelletti, Mauro, et al. The Italian Legal System: An Introduction. 1967. 32.50x (ISBN 0-8047-0285-3). Stanford U Pr.
--Toward Equal Justice: A Comparative Study of Legal Aid in Modern Societies. LC 75-18519. (Studies in Comparative Law: No. 13). 756p. 1975. text ed. 35.00 (ISBN 0-379-00213-2). Oceana.
Cappelli, G., jt. auth. see Borgioli, A.
Cappelli, William S., ed. see Gartner Group, Inc. Staff.
Cappellini, V., ed. Data Compression & Error Control Techniques with Applications. Date not set. price not set (ISBN 0-12-159260-X). Acad Pr.
Cappellini, V. & Constantinides, A. G., eds. Digital Signal Processing-84: Proceedings of the International Conference Held in Florence, Italy, 5-8 September 1984. 886p. 1985. 98.00 (ISBN 0-444-87583-2, North-Holland). Elsevier.
Capper, Arthur. The Agricultural Bloc. LC 78-136848. 171p. 1972. Repr. of 1922 ed. lib. bdg. 15.00 (ISBN 0-8371-5282-8, CAAG). Greenwood.
Capper, H., jt. ed. see Frederick, S. H.
Capper, John, et al. Chesapeake Waters: Pollution, Public Health, & Public Opinion, 1607-1972. LC 83-40102. 217p. 1983. 19.95 (ISBN 0-87033-310-0). Tidewater.
Capper, P. L. & Cassie, W. F. Mechanics of Engineering Soils: SI Version. 6th ed. 1976. pap. 15.95 (ISBN 0-419-10990-0, NO. 6052, Pub. by E & FN Spon). Methuen Inc.
Capper, P. L., et al. Problems in Engineering Soils. 3rd ed. 1980. 14.95x (ISBN 0-419-11840-3, NO. 2966, Pub. by E & FN Spon). Methuen Inc.
Capper, W. M. & Johnson, D., eds. The Faith of a Surgeon: Belief & Experience in the Life of Arthur Rendle Short. 160p. 1976. pap. 5.95 (ISBN 0-85364-198-6). Attic Pr.
Cappiello, Frank. Super Stock Source Book. 64p. 1983. pap. 4.95 (ISBN 0-89709-100-0). Liberty Pub.
Cappiello, Frank A., Jr. Finding the Next Super Stock. LC 81-84999. (Illus.). 160p. 1982. 12.95 (ISBN 0-89709-048-9); pap. 6.95 (ISBN 0-89709-031-4). Liberty Pub.
Cappiello, Rose. Oh Lucky Country: pb. Rando, Gaetano, tr. from Ital. 236p. 1985. 12.95 (ISBN 0-7022-1789-1). U of Queensland Pr.
Cappon, Alexander. Scope of Shelley's Philosophical Thinking. 1938. lib. bdg. 10.00 (ISBN 0-8414-3646-0). Folcroft.
Cappon, Alexander P. About Wordsworth & Whitehead. LC 81-80237. 1982. 14.95 (ISBN 0-8022-2386-9). Philos Lib.
--Action, Organism & Philosophy in Wordsworth & Whitehead. LC 84-14897. 1985. 25.00 (ISBN 0-8022-2468-7). Philos Lib.
--Aspects of Wordsworth & Whitehead. LC 82-18904. 283p. 1983. 19.95 (ISBN 0-8022-2412-1). Philos Lib.
--The Scope of Shelley's Philosophical Thinking. 1978. Repr. of 1935 ed. lib. bdg. 8.50 (ISBN 0-8495-0809-6). Arden Lib.
Cappon, Daniel. Eating, Loving & Dying: A Psychology of Appetites. LC 72-97151. pap. 32.50 (ISBN 0-317-07779-1, 2019165). Bks Demand UMI.
--Technology & Perception. (Illus.). 282p. 1971. 24.75x (ISBN 0-398-00284-3). C C Thomas.
Cappon, J. Bliss Carman & the Literary Currents & Influences of His Time. 59.95 (ISBN 0-87968-759-2). Gordon Pr.
Cappon, James. Britain's Title in South Africa. Repr. of 1901 ed. 23.00 (ISBN 0-527-15000-2). Kraus Repr.
Cappon, Lester, ed. Atlas of Early American History: The Revolutionary Era, 1760-1790. 1976. 200.00 (ISBN 0-911028-00-5). Newberry.
Cappon, Lester J. Atlas of Early American History: The Revolutionary Era, 1760-1790. LC 75-2982. 1975. 200.00x (ISBN 0-691-04634-4). Princeton U Pr.
Cappon, Lester J. & Duff, Stella F. Virginia Gazette Index, 2 vols. LC 51-15336. 1314p. 1950. lib. bdg. 65.00 (ISBN 0-910776-00-8). Inst Early Am.
Cappon, Rene J., jt. ed. see Associated Press Staff.
Capps. Alaska Peninsula & Aleutian Islands. facsimile ed. (Shorey Prospecting Ser.). (Illus.). 14p. Shorey.
Capps, B. The Indians. LC 72-93991. (Old West Ser). (Illus.). (gr. 7 up). 1973. 17.27 (ISBN 0-8094-1455-4, Pub. by Time-Life). Silver.
Capps, Bemjamin. The Trail to Ogallala. LC 85-4721. (The Texas Traditon Ser.: No. 3). 288p. 1985. 16.95 (ISBN 0-87565-012-0); pap. 9.95 (ISBN 0-87565-013-9). Tex Christian.
Capps, Ben. The Indians. (The Old West Ser.). (Illus.). 1973. 14.95 (ISBN 0-8094-1454-6). Time-Life.
Capps, Benjamin. The Great Chiefs. LC 75-744. (The Old West). (Illus.). (gr. 7 up). 1975. 17.27 (ISBN 0-8094-1494-5, Pub. by Time-Life). Silver.
--Woman Chief. 256p. 1981. pap. 2.50 (ISBN 0-441-90804-7). Ace Bks.
--A Woman of the People. LC 84-11884. 292p. 1985. pap. 8.95 (ISBN 0-8263-0782-5). U of NM Pr.
Capps, Charles. Angels. 224p. (Orig.). 1984. pap. 3.95 (ISBN 0-89274-308-5, HH-308). Harrison Hse.
--Authority in Three Worlds. 247p. 1980. pap. text ed. 3.95 (ISBN 0-89274-160-0). Harrison Hse.
--Authority (Special Edition) Word of Faith Bible School. rev. ed. 192p. 1984. write for info. (ISBN 0-89274-319-0). Harrison Hse.
--Can Your Faith Fail? 1978. pap. 1.75 (ISBN 0-89274-105-8). Harrison Hse.
--Changing the Seen & Shaping the Unseen. 1981. pap. 1.95 (ISBN 0-89274-220-8, HH-220). Harrison Hse.
--Dynamics of Faith & Confession. 288p. (Orig.). 1983. pap. 6.95 (ISBN 0-914307-05-3). Word Faith.

--God's Creative Power Will Work for You. 30p. 1976. minibook 0.75 (ISBN 0-89274-024-8). Harrison Hse.
--Kicking over Sacred Cows. 132p. (Orig.). 1984. pap. 3.95 (ISBN 0-914307-18-5). Word Faith.
--Paul's Thorn in the Flesh. 60p. (Orig.). 1983. pap. text ed. 4.95 (ISBN 0-914307-09-6). Word Faith.
--Releasing the Ability of God Through Prayer. 159p. 1978. pocketbook 2.95 (ISBN 0-89274-075-2). Harrison Hse.
--Success Motivation Through the Word. 272p. 1982. pap. 3.95 (ISBN 0-89274-183-X, HH-183). Harrison Hse.
--The Tongue-a Creative Force. rev. ed. 1976. pocket size 3.25 (ISBN 0-89274-061-2). Harrison Hse.
--Why Tragedy Happens to Christians. 187p. (Orig.). 1980. pap. 3.25 (ISBN 0-89274-175-9, HH-175). Harrison Hse.
Capps, Claudius M., ed. Blue & the Gray. facsimile ed. LC 70-75710. (Granger Index Reprint Ser). 1943. 17.00 (ISBN 0-8369-6005-X). Ayer Co Pubs.
Capps, Donald. Biblical Approaches to Pastoral Counseling. LC 81-11473. 214p. 1981. pap. 9.95 (ISBN 0-664-24388-6). Westminster.
--Life Cycle Theory & Pastoral Care. LC 83-5585. (Theology & Pastoral Care Ser.). 128p. 1983. pap. 6.95 (ISBN 0-8006-1726-6, 1-1726). Fortress.
--Pastoral Care: A Thematic Approach. LC 78-15093. (Illus.). 162p. 1979. softcover 8.95 (ISBN 0-664-24222-7). Westminster.
--Pastoral Care & Hermeneutics. LC 84-47909. (Theology & Pastoral Care Ser.). 128p. 1984. pap. 6.95 (ISBN 0-8006-1732-0). Fortress.
--Pastoral Counseling & Preaching: A Quest for an Integrated Ministry. LC 80-18502. 156p. 1980. pap. 8.95 (ISBN 0-664-24342-8). Westminster.
Capps, Donald, jt. ed. see Reynolds, Frank E.
Capps, Donald, et al. Encounter with Erikson: Historical Interpretation & Religious Biography. LC 76-44434. (American Academy of Religion, Formative Contemporary Thinkers Ser.: No. 2). 1977. pap. 13.50 (ISBN 0-89130-037-6, 010402). Scholars Pr GA.
Capps, Donald, et al, eds. Psychology of Religion: A Guide to Information Sources. LC 73-17530. (Philosophy & Religion Information Guide Ser.: Vol. 1). vii, 380p. 1976. 60.00x (ISBN 0-8103-1356-1). Gale.
Capps, Edward. From Homer to Theocritus: A Manual of Greek Literature. text ed. 22.00 (ISBN 0-8369-8184-7, 8322). Ayer Co Pubs.
Capps, Edward, ed. see Menander.
Capps, Finis H. From Isolation to Involvement: The Swedish Immigrant Press in America, 1914-1945. 238p. 1966. 3.00 (ISBN 0-318-16616-X, SP13). Swedish-Am.
--From Isolationism to Involvement: The Swedish Immigrant Press in America. 1966. 3.00 (ISBN 0-318-03683-5). Swedish Am.
Capps, Howard. Take the Wrists Out: A Life in Golf. LC 85-60492. 158p. (Orig.). 1985. pap. 7.00 (ISBN 0-937088-12-9). Illum Pr.
Capps, Jack L. Emily Dickinson's Reading, 1836-1886. LC 66-14439. 1966. 16.50x (ISBN 0-674-25050-8). Harvard U Pr.
Capps, Marcia M. Light & Shadow. iii, 63p. 1984. pap. 5.05 (ISBN 0-932269-09-5). Wyndham Hall.
Capps, Randall & O'Connor, J. Regis. Fundamentals of Effective Speech Communication. 272p. 1984. pap. text ed. 13.25 (ISBN 0-8191-3534-8). U Pr of Amer.
Capps, Walter. The Monastic Impulse. LC 82-14866. 224p. 1982. 10.95 (ISBN 0-8245-0490-9). Crossroad NY.
Capps, Walter H. The Unfinished War: Vietnam & the American Conscience. LC 81-66193. 192p. 1983. pap. 6.68 (ISBN 0-8070-0401-4, BP 657). Beacon Pr.
Capps, Walter H., ed. Seeing with a Native Eye: Contributions to the Study of Native American Religion. LC 76-9980. 1976. pap. 6.95xi (ISBN 0-06-061312-2, RD-177, HarpR). Har-Row.
Capps, Walter H. & Wright, Wendy M., eds. Silent Fire. LC 78-3366. (Forum Bk.). 1978. pap. 7.95x (ISBN 0-06-061314-9, RD 290, HarpR). Har-Row.
Cappuccinelli, P. Motility of Living Cells. 80p. 1980. pap. 7.50x (ISBN 0-412-15770-5, NO. 2887, Pub. by Chapman & Hall England). Methuen Inc.
Cappucino, James C. & Sherman, Natalie. Microciology Laboratory Manual. LC 82-18509. (Biology Ser.). (Illus.). 480p. 1983. pap. text ed. 19.95 (ISBN 0-201-11160-8). Addison-Wesley.
Capra, Christine L., jt. auth. see Poleman, Charlotte L.
Capra, Frank. The Name above the Title: An Autobiography. 1985. 9.95 (ISBN 0-394-71205-6, Vin). Random.
Capra, Fritjof. The Tao of Physics. 1977. pap. 3.95 (ISBN 0-553-24013-7). Bantam.
--The Tao of Physics. 2nd ed. LC 82-42679. (New Science Library Ser.). (Illus.). 308p. 1975. pap. 7.95 (ISBN 0-87773-246-9, 71612-4). Shambhala Pubns.
--The Turning Point: Science, Society & the Rising Culture. 1982. 18.50 (ISBN 0-671-24423-5). S&S.
Capra, Fritjof & Spretnak, Charlene. Green Politics: The Global Promise. LC 83-27474. 224p. 1984. 12.95 (ISBN 0-525-24231-7, 01258-370). Dutton.
Capra, J. Donald, jt. auth. see Kindt, Thomas J.
Capretta, Laura. Beginning Math Skills 1-10. (Let's Learn Ser.). (Illus.). 32p. (ps-1). 1984. pap. 1.79 (ISBN 0-88724-089-5, CD-7028). Carson-Dellos.
Capri, Anton Z. & Kamal, Abdul N., eds. Particles & Fields 2. 695p. 1983. 97.50x (ISBN 0-306-41162-8, Plenum Pr). Plenum Pub.
Capri, Antonio. Il Settecento Musicale in Europa. LC 77-5523. (Music Reprint Ser). 1977. Repr. of 1936 ed. lib. bdg. 42.50 (ISBN 0-306-77413-5). Da Capo.
Caprino, Luciano, ed. Platelet Aggregation & Drugs. 1975. 55.00 (ISBN 0-12-158950-1). Acad Pr.
Caprio. Sexually Adequate Female. pap. 3.00 (ISBN 0-87980-146-8). Wilshire.
--Sexually Adequate Male. pap. 3.00 (ISBN 0-87980-147-6). Wilshire.
Caprio, Anthony, jt. auth. see Carton, Dana.
Caprio, Betsy. Experiments in Prayer. (Illus.). 192p. 1973. pap. 4.95 (ISBN 0-87793-054-6). Ave Maria.
--The Woman Sealed in the Tower: A Psychological Approach to Feminine Spirituality. 1983. pap. 5.95 (ISBN 0-8091-2486-6). Paulist Pr.
Caprio, Betsy & Hedberg, Thomas. Coming Home: A Handbook for Exploring the Sanctuary Within. 176p. (Orig.). 1986. pap. 7.95 (ISBN 0-8091-2739-3). Paulist Pr.
Caprio, Frank, jt. auth. see Wilbur, L. Perry.
Caprio, Frank S. How to Solve Your Sex Problems with Self-Hypnosis. pap. 5.00 (ISBN 0-87980-064-X). Wilshire.
Caprio, Frank S. & Berger, Joseph R. Helping Yourself with Self-Hypnosis. LC 63-10671. 1963. pap. 4.95 (ISBN 0-13-386623-8, Reward). P-H.
--Helping Yourself with Self-Hypnosis. 1968. pap. 3.50 (ISBN 0-446-30598-7). Warner Bks.
Caprio, Frank S., jt. auth. see London, Louis S.
Caprione, Carol. Opportunities in Food Services. (VGM Career Bks.). (Illus.). 160p. 1983. 7.95 (ISBN 0-8442-6252-8, 6252-8, Passport Bks.); pap. 5.95 (ISBN 0-8442-6253-6, 6253-6). Natl Textbk.
Capron, Alexander M., jt. auth. see Katz, Jay.
Capron, Alexander M., et al, eds. Genetic Counseling: Fact, Values & Norms. LC 79-1736. (Alan R. Liss Ser.: Vol. 15, No. 2). 1979. 41.00 (ISBN 0-8451-1025-X). March of Dimes.
--Genetic Counseling: Facts, Values, & Norms. LC 79-1736. (Birth Defects Original Article Ser.: Vol. 15, No. 2). 346p. 1979. 45.00 (ISBN 0-8451-1025-X). A R Liss.
Capron, E. W. Modern Spiritualism: Its Facts & Fanaticisms. LC 75-36833. (Occult Ser.). 1976. Repr. of 1855 ed. 32.00x (ISBN 0-405-07945-1). Ayer Co Pubs.
Capron, H. & Williams, B. Computers & Data Processing. 1982. text ed. 28.95 (ISBN 0-8053-2201-9); instr's. guide 4.95; trans. 40.00; study guide 9.95. Benjamin-Cummings.
Capron, H. L. & Williams, Brian K. Computers & Data Processing. 2nd ed. 1984. 28.95 (ISBN 0-8053-2214-0); instr's guide 5.95 (ISBN 0-8053-2215-9); study guide 8.95 (ISBN 0-8053-2216-7); guide to testing 5.95 (ISBN 0-8053-2217-5); transparency masters 40.00 (ISBN 0-8053-2218-3); instr's resource manual (3-ring binder) 150.00 (ISBN 0-8053-2219-1); guide to subscriptions, films & videos 5.95 (ISBN 0-8053-2222-1); transparencies 150.00 (ISBN 0-8053-2223-X). Benjamin-Cummings.
Capron, J. Hugh. Wood Laminating. rev. ed. (gr. 11-12). 1972. 16.64 (ISBN 0-87345-046-9). McKnight.
Capron, Jean F. Never Say No. (Sweet Dreams Ser.: No. 78). 176p. 1985. pap. 2.25 (ISBN 0-553-24384-5). Bantam.
Caproni, Gianni. Gli Aeroplane Caproni: Studi-Progetti-Realizzazioni dal 1908 al 1935. Gilbert, James, ed. LC 79-7234. (Flight: Its First Seventy-Five Years Ser.). (Illus.). 1979. Repr. of 1936 ed. lib. bdg. 62.00x (ISBN 0-405-12150-4). Ayer Co Pubs.
Capstick, M. Economics of Agriculture. 672p. 1971. 20.00 (ISBN 0-312-22645-4). St Martin.
Capstick, Peter. Death in the Silent Places. 320p. 1981. 13.95 (ISBN 0-312-18618-5). St Martin.
Capstick, Peter H. Death in the Dark Continent. (Illus.). 320p. 1983. 14.95 (ISBN 0-312-18615-0). St Martin.
--Death in the Long Grass. LC 77-9224. (Illus.). 1978. 14.95 (ISBN 0-312-18613-4). St Martin.
--Maneaters. (Illus.). 200p. 1981. 17.95 (ISBN 0-8227-3023-5). Petersen Pub.
--Safari - The Last Adventure: How You Can Share in It. (Illus.). 352p. 1984. 15.95 (ISBN 0-312-69657-4). St Martin.
Capt, E. Raymond. The Glory of the Stars. LC 79-116390. (Illus.). 144p. (Orig.). 1976. pap. 5.00 (ISBN 0-934666-02-4). Artisan Sales.
--The Great Pyramid Decoded. rev. ed. LC 78-101677. (Illus.). 96p. 1978. pap. 3.00 (ISBN 0-934666-01-6). Artisan Sales.
--Jacob's Pillar. LC 79-116385. (Illus.). 96p. 1977. pap. 3.00 (ISBN 0-934666-03-2). Artisan Sales.
--King Solomon's Temple. LC 79-54774. (Illus.). 96p. 1979. pap. 3.00 (ISBN 0-934666-05-9). Artisan Sales.
--Lost Chapter of Acts of the Apostles. 32p. 1982. pap. 2.00 (ISBN 0-934666-09-1). Artisan Sales.
--Missing Links Discovered in Assyrian Tablets. (Illus.). 256p. 1985. 15.00 (ISBN 0-934666-17-2); pap. 10.00 (ISBN 0-934666-15-6). Artisan Sales.
--Our Great Seal-Symbols of Our Heritage & Our Destiny. LC 79-53862. 96p. (Orig.). 1979. pap. 3.00 (ISBN 0-934666-00-8). Artisan Sales.
--Scottish Declaration of Independence. (Illus.). 32p. 1983. pap. 2.00 (ISBN 0-934666-11-3). Artisan Sales.
--Stonehenge & Druidism. rev. ed. LC 79-54773. (Illus.). 96p. 1979. pap. 3.00 (ISBN 0-934666-04-0). Artisan Sales.
--The Stones in the Breastplate. (Illus.). 48p. (Orig.). 1985. pap. cancelled (ISBN 0-934666-18-0). Artisan Sales.
--The Traditions of Glastonbury. LC 82-72525. (Illus.). 128p. (Orig.). 1983. pap. 5.00 (ISBN 0-934666-10-5). Artisan Sales.
Captain Comal's Staff. Cartridge Graphics & Sound. (The Amazing Adventures of Captain Comal Ser.). (Illus.). 64p. (Orig.). (gr. 6 up). 1984. pap. 9.95 (ISBN 0-928411-02-8). Comal Users.
Captain, Philip A. Eight Stages of Christian Growth: Human Development in Psycho-Spiritual Terms. (Illus.). 240p. 1984. 13.95 (ISBN 0-13-246679-1); pap. 6.95 (ISBN 0-13-246661-9). P-H.
Captain Marryat, see Marryat, Captain.
Captiva Civic Association. Voices from the Past... True Tales of Old Captiva. Robb, Bunty, ed. LC 84-52565. (Illus.). 368p. 1985. 13.33 (ISBN 0-930942-05-1). Sutherland IA.
Captor, Renee S. Library Research for the Analysis of Public Policy. (Learning Packages in the Policy Sciences Ser.: No. 19). 36p. (Orig.). 1979. pap. text ed. 2.75x (ISBN 0-936826-08-8). Pol Stud Assocs.
Capua, A. G. De see De Capua, A. G.
Capuchin, John A. Padre Pio. 1983. 9.50 (ISBN 0-8199-0864-9). Franciscan Herald.
Capurro, L. R. & Reid, Joseph L., eds. Contributions on the Physical Oceanography of the Gulf of Mexico. LC 71-135998. (Texas A&M University Oceanographic Studies on the Gulf of Mexico: Vol. 2). 288p. 1972. 29.95x (ISBN 0-87201-347-2). Gulf Pub.
Capurro, Luis R. Oceanography for Practicing Engineers. LC 71-126339. 184p. 1970. pap. 10.95 (ISBN 0-8436-0323-2). Van Nos Reinhold.
Capus, Joseph see Mocarski, S. & Pietrocini, T.
Capusan, I., et al. Systemic Sclerosis: Current Research, Vol. 2. 1974. text ed. 29.50x (ISBN 0-8422-7203-8). Irvington.
Caput, J., jt. auth. see Caput, J. P.
Caput, J. P. & Caput, J. Dictionnaire des verbes francais. (Fr., Fr). 27.50 (ISBN 0-685-13871-2, 3622). Larousse.
Caput, Jean-Pol. La Langue francaise, Vol. 2. (Collection "L"). 287p. (Orig., Fr.). 1975. pap. 13.95 (ISBN 2-03-036009-0). Larousse.
Capute, Arnold J., et al. Primitive Reflex Profile. LC 77-27294. (Illus.). 114p. 1977. text ed. 21.00 (ISBN 0-8391-1181-9). Univ Park.
Caputi, Anthony. Buffo: The Genius of Vulgar Comedy. LC 78-15992. (Illus.). 256p. 1979. 17.95x (ISBN 0-8143-1606-9). Wayne St U Pr.
--John Marston, Satirist. 289p. 1976. Repr. of 1961 ed. lib. bdg. 24.00x (ISBN 0-374-91286-6). Octagon.
--Storms & Son. LC 84-45614. 224p. 1985. 13.95 (ISBN 0-689-11526-1). Atheneum.
Caputi, Anthony, ed. Modern Drama: Annotated Texts. Bd. with Desire Under the Elms. O'Neill, Eugene; Devil's Disciple. Shaw, George B; Dream Play. Strindberg, August; Henry Fourth. Pirandello, Luigi; Three Sisters. Chekhov, Anton; Wild Duck. Ibsen, Henrik. (Critical Editions). 1966. pap. text ed. 11.95x (ISBN 0-393-09664-5). Norton.
Caputi, Natalino. Guide to the Unconscious. LC 83-24620. 172p. (Orig.). 1984. pap. 14.95 (ISBN 0-89135-042-X). Religious Educ.
--Unconscious: A Guide to the Sources. LC 85-1979. (ATCA Bibliography Ser.: No. 16). 161p. 1985. 15.00 (ISBN 0-8108-1798-5). Scarecrow.
Caputo, A., ed. Biological Basis of Clinical Effect of Bleomycin. (Progress in Biochemical Pharmacology: Vol. 11). (Illus.). 200p. 1976. 54.25 (ISBN 3-8055-2338-6). S Karger.
Caputo, A., jt. ed. see Silvestrini, B.
Caputo, Carmela C. Hairatage Beauty Salon Practice Set: Practical Accounting Procedures. 2nd ed. (Illus.). 320p. 1984. wkbk. 10.95 (ISBN 0-13-688177-7). P-H.
Caputo, David A. Urban America: The Policy Alternatives. LC 76-7351. (Illus.). 1976. text ed. 22.95 (ISBN 0-7167-0556-7). W H Freeman.
Caputo, David A., ed. The Politics of Policy Making in America: Five Case Studies. LC 77-24516. (Illus.). 189p. 1977. text ed. 22.95 (ISBN 0-7167-0194-4); pap. text ed. 11.95 (ISBN 0-7167-0193-6). W H Freeman.
Caputo, Flora. The Stranger Inside & a Band of Hoods. LC 82-91042. 1984. 6.95 (ISBN 0-533-05892-9). Vantage.
Caputo, Janette S. The Assertive Librarian. LC 83-43252. 256p. 1984. pap. 22.50 (ISBN 0-89774-085-8). Oryx Pr.
Caputo, John D. Heidegger & Aquinas: An Essay on Overcoming Metaphysics. LC 82-71398. xii, 308p. 1982. 35.00 (ISBN 0-8232-1097-9); pap. 17.50 (ISBN 0-8232-1098-7). Fordham.
--The Mystical Element in Heidegger's Thought. LC 77-92251. xvi, 292p. 1978. 28.95x (ISBN 0-8214-0372-9, 82-82667). Ohio U Pr.
--The Mystical Element in Heidegger's Thought. xvi, 292p. 1986. pap. 10.00 (ISBN 0-8232-1153-3). Fordham.
Caputo, Luciano V. Questioned Document Case Studies. LC 82-3563. (Illus.). 100p. 1982. text ed. 38.95x (ISBN 0-88229-259-5). Nelson-Hall.
Caputo, M., jt. ed. see Coulomb, J.
Caputo, Michele. Gravity Field of the Earth: Classical & Modern Methods. (International Geophysics Ser.: Vol. 10). 1967. 49.50 (ISBN 0-12-159050-X). Acad Pr.
Caputo, Philip. Del Corso's Gallery. LC 83-156. 374p. 1983. 15.95 (ISBN 0-03-058277-6). HR&W.
--Delcorso's Gallery. 368p. 1984. pap. 3.95 (ISBN 0-440-11842-5). Dell.
--Horn of Africa. LC 79-27513. 528p. 1980. 12.95 (ISBN 0-03-042136-5). HR&W.
--Horn of Africa. 544p. 1983. pap. 4.95 (ISBN 0-440-33675-9, LE). Dell.
--A Rumor of War. 1986. pap. 3.95 (ISBN 0-345-33122-2). Ballantine.
--A Rumor of War. LC 76-29900. 1977. 10.00 (ISBN 0-03-017631-X). HR&W.
Caputo, Ralph J., jt. auth. see Wong, James I.
Caputo, Rudolph R., jt. auth. see Aubry, Arthur S., Jr.
Caputo, Thomas H. Fifty Selected Poems. LC 77-3600. 1977. pap. 3.00x (ISBN 0-914476-63-7). Thorp Springs.
Caputto, R. & Marsan, C. Ajmone, eds. Neural Transmission, Learning, & Memory. (International Brain Research Organization Monographs: Vol. 10). (Illus.). 286p. 1983. text ed. 76.00 (ISBN 0-89004-860-6). Raven.
Capuzzi, Frank, tr. see Heidegger, Martin.
Capuzzi, Frank A., tr. see Heidegger, Martin.
Capwell, Charles. The Music of the Bauls of Bengal. LC 84-27824. (Illus.). 330p. 1985. 32.50x (ISBN 0-87338-317-6). Kent St U Pr.
Caquot, Andre & Cohen, D., eds. Actes Du Premier Congres International De Linguistique Semitique et Chamito-Semitique, Paris, 16-19 Juillet 1969. (Janua Linguarum, Series Practica: No. 159). 1974. pap. 59.20x (ISBN 90-2792-670-0). Mouton.
Carabine, Keith, ed. see Conrad, Joseph.
Carabis, Anne. The Magic Rocking Chair. (Illus.). 28p. (Orig.). (gr. 2-6). 1980. pap. 3.00 (ISBN 0-9605802-0-4). Carabis.
Caraboolad, Clemens J. Mysticism & Zen: An Introduction. LC 77-18492. 1978. pap. text ed. 9.25 (ISBN 0-8191-0422-1). U Pr of Amer.
Caradec, Francois. Dictionnaire du Francais Argotique et Populaire. 255p. (Fr.). 1977. pap. 6.95 (ISBN 0-686-56879-6, M-4968). French & Eur.
Caradoc Of Llancarfan. The Historie of Cambria, Now Called Wales. Lhoyd, H., tr. LC 70-26025. (English Experience Ser.: No. 163). 402p. 1969. Repr. of 1584 ed. 49.00 (ISBN 90-221-0163-0). Walter J Johnson.
Caradog-Jones, D., jt. auth. see Carr-Saunders, A. M.
Caradon & Goldberg, Arthur J. U. N. Security Council Resolution 242: A Case Study in Diplomatic Ambiguity. LC 81-1671. 64p. 1981. 4.00 (ISBN 0-934742-11-1, Inst Study Diplomacy). Geo U Sch For Serv.
Caradus, S. R. Calkin Algebras & Algebras of Banach Spaces. (Pure & Applied Math Ser.: Vol. 9). 1974. 35.00 (ISBN 0-8247-6246-0). Dekker.
Caraeff, Ed. Dolly: Close Up. (Illus.). 96p. (Orig.). 1982. pap. 9.95 (ISBN 0-933328-58-3). Delilah Bks.
Caraeff, Eddie J. The Gourmet Cabbie: High Class Eats at Street Smart Prices. (Illus.). 96p. (Orig.). 1984. pap. 5.95 (ISBN 0-933328-26-5). Delilah Bks.
Carafa, Michelle. Le Nozze di Lammermoor. (Italian Opera 1810-1840 Ser.). 360p. 1985. lib. bdg. 85.00 (ISBN 0-8240-6551-4). Garland Pub.
Carafiol, Peter C. Transcendent Reason: James Marsh & the Forms of Romantic Thought. LC 82-13617. xviii, 222p. 1982. 23.00 (ISBN 0-8130-0732-1). U Presses Fla.
Carafoli, E. Wing Theory in Supersonic Flow. 1969. 105.00 (ISBN 0-08-012330-9). Pergamon.
Carafoli, E., ed. Membrane Transport of Calcium. LC 81-68980. 1982. 49.50 (ISBN 0-12-159320-7). Acad Pr.
Carafoli, E. & Semenza, G., eds. Membrane Biochemistry: A Laboratory Manual on Transport & Bioenergetics. (Illus.). 175p. 1979. pap. 19.50 (ISBN 0-387-09844-5). Springer-Verlag.
Carafoli, E., jt. ed. see Semenza, G.
Carafoli, Ernesto, jt. ed. see Scarpa, Antonio.
Caragata, Patrick J. National Resources & International Bargaining Power: Canada's Mineral Policy Options. 188p. 1984. pap. text ed. 20.00x (ISBN 0-88757-036-4, Pub. by Ctr Resource Stud Canada). Brookfield Pub Co.
Caraher, Patrick. Hands On: A Book of Art Activities. 56p. (ps). 1985. pap. write for info. (ISBN 0-916197-02-6). Jayell Ent.
Caraion, Ion. Ion Caraion: Poems. Dorian, Marguerite & Urdang, Elliott B., trs. from Romanian. LC 81-4847. vii, 112p. 1981. 17.95x (ISBN 0-8214-0608-6, 82-83947); pap. 8.95 (ISBN 0-8214-0620-5, 82-83954). Ohio U Pr.

Caraley, Demetrios. City Governments & Urban Problems: A New Introduction to Urban Politics. LC 76-28327. (Illus.). 1977. 27.95 (ISBN 0-13-134973-2). P-H.

--Doing More with Less: Cutback Management in New York City. 160p. (Orig.). Date not set. pap. 7.00x (ISBN 0-910955-01-8). Grad Program.

Caraley, Demetrios, ed. American Political Institutions in the 1970's: A Political Science Quarterly Reader. LC 76-8494. 407p. 1976. 34.00x (ISBN 0-231-04106-3); pap. 17.00x (ISBN 0-231-04107-1). Columbia U Pr.

--The Politics of Military Unifieation: A Study of Conflict & the Policy Process. LC 66-15762. (Institute of War & Peace Studies). 345p. 1966. 31.00x (ISBN 0-231-02885-7). Columbia U Pr.

Caraman, P. N-Dimensional Quasiconformal Mappings. 1974. 44.00 (ISBN 0-9961002-0-2, Pub. by Abacus England). Heyden.

Caraman, Philip. The University of the Nations. LC 80-84512. (Illus.). 232p. (Orig.). 1981. pap. 6.95 (ISBN 0-8091-2355-X). Paulist Pr.

Caraman, Philip S. The Lost Empire. 192p. 1985. 16.95x (ISBN 0-317-30280-9, 85-12766, Dist. by Har-Row). U of Notre Dame Pr.

Caraman, Phillip, ed. Saints & Ourselves: A Selection of Saints' Lives. 226p. 1982. pap. 7.95 (ISBN 0-89283-123-5). Servant.

Caramazza, Alfonso & Zurif, Edgar, eds. Language Acquisition & Language Breakdown: Parallels & Divergencies. LC 77-4789. (Illus.). 1978. text ed. 33.00x (ISBN 0-8018-1948-2). Johns Hopkins.

Caramello, Charles. Silverless Mirrors: Book, Self, & Postmodern American Fiction. LC 83-14841. 1983. o. p. 25.00 (ISBN 0-8130-0769-0); pap. 12.00x (ISBN 0-8130-0772-0). U Presses Fla.

Caramillo, Albert, Jr. Chicanos in California. Hundley, Norris & Schutz, John, eds. (Golden State Ser.). 145p. (Orig.). 1984. pap. 6.95x (ISBN 0-87835-128-0). Boyd & Fraser.

Caran, S. C., et al. Lineament Analysis & Inference of Geologic Structure: Examples from the Balcones-Ouachita Trent of Texas. (Geological Circular Ser.: GC 82-1). 1982. Repr. 1.00 (ISBN 0-686-37545-9). Bur Econ Geology.

Caranasos, George J., jt. auth. see Cluff, Leighton E.

Carandente, Giovanni. Balthus: Drawings & Watercolors. (Illus.). 120p. 1983. 29.45i (ISBN 0-8212-1529-9, 080691). NYGS.

Caranfa, Angelo. Machiavelli Rethought: A Critique of Strauss' Machiavelli. LC 77-94393. 1978. pap. text ed. 8.25 (ISBN 0-8191-0421-3). U Pr of Amer.

Caranfa, Angelo, jt. ed. see Gendreau, Francis R.

Carano, Paul & Sanchez, Pedro C. A Complete History of Guam. LC 64-21619. (Illus.). 1964. 20.50 (ISBN 0-8048-0114-2). C E Tuttle.

Caras, Roger. A Celebration of Dogs. 1982. 13.95 (ISBN 0-8129-1029-X); pap. 6.95 (ISBN 0-8129-6335-0). Times Bks.

--The Custer Wolf. 175p. 1966. 14.95 (ISBN 0-317-27105-9). Yankee Peddler.

--The Endless Migrations: The Epic Voyages of Living Things Across the North American Continent. 1985. 20.00 (ISBN 0-525-24341-0, 01942-580). Dutton.

--The Forest. 1980. pap. 4.95 (ISBN 0-395-29611-0). HM.

--Mara Simba: The African Lion. 240p. 1985. 15.95 (ISBN 0-03-016611-X). HR&W.

--The Roger Caras Dog Book. LC 79-17757. (Illus.). 304p. 1980. 16.95 (ISBN 0-275-23540-8). HR&W.

Caras, Roger, ed. Harper's Illustrated Handbook of Cats: A Guide to Every Breed Recognized in America. LC 85-1331. (Illus.). 192p. (Orig.). 1985. pap. 9.95 (ISBN 0-06-091199-9, PL 1199, PL). Har-Row.

--Harper's Illustrated Handbook of Dogs. LC 85-1330. (Illus.). 320p. (Orig.). 1985. pap. 9.95 (ISBN 0-06-091198-0, PL 1198, PL). Har-Row.

Caras, Roger A. Dangerous to Man. (Illus.). 432p. pap. 7.95 (ISBN 0-88317-034-5). Stoeger Pub Co.

Caras, Roger A., ed. Dog Owner's Bible. (Illus.). 480p. pap. 7.95 (ISBN 0-88317-089-2). Stoeger Pub Co.

Caras, Steven, photos by. Balanchine: Photo Album & Memoir. LC 85-43061. (Illus.). 64p. 1985. pap. 14.95 (ISBN 0-8478-0656-1). Rizzoli Intl.

Caras, Tracy, jt. auth. see Gagne, Cole.

Carasov, Victor. Two Gentlemen to See You, Sir: The Autobiography of a Villain. LC 76-155091. 1971. 5.50 (ISBN 0-8008-7920-1). Taplinger.

Carasso, Alfred & Stone, Alex P., eds. Improperly Posed Boundary Value Problems. (Research Notes in Mathematics Ser.: No. 1). 157p. 1975. pap. text ed. 20.50 (ISBN 0-273-00105-1). Pitman Pub MA.

Caratelli, Sebastian. A Musicians Odyssey. 1983. 10.95 (ISBN 0-533-05688-8). Vantage.

Caratheodory, C. Funktionentheorie, 2 vols. rev. 2nd ed. (Mathematische Reihe: Nos. 8 & 9). (Ger.). 1961. Vol 1, 288p. 32.95x (ISBN 0-8176-0064-7); Vol. 2, 194p. 24.95x (ISBN 0-8176-0065-5). Birkhauser.

--Mass und Integral und Ihre Alebraisierung. Finsler, P., et al, eds. (Mathematische Reihe Ser.: No. 10). (Illus.). 337p. (Ger.). 1956. 41.95x (ISBN 0-8176-0066-3). Birkhauser.

Caratheodory, Constantin. Calculus of Variations & Partial Differential Equations of the First Order. 2nd ed. LC 81-71519. (Illus.). 421p. 1982. text ed. 25.00 (ISBN 0-8284-0318-X). Chelsea Pub.

--Theory of Functions. 2nd ed. LC 60-16838. Vol. 1. 12.95 (ISBN 0-8284-0097-0); Vol. 2. 12.95 (ISBN 0-8284-0106-3). Chelsea Pub.

--Vorlesungen Ueber Reelle Funktionen. 3rd ed. LC 63-11321. (Ger). 1968. 17.95 (ISBN 0-8284-0038-5). Chelsea Pub.

Caratin, Roger, ed. Sciences Sociales, 2: Linguistique. 160p. (Fr.). 1971. 29.95 (ISBN 0-686-57219-X, M-6511). French & Eur.

Caratini, Roger, ed. Sciences Sociales, 1. 160p. (Fr.). 1971. 29.95 (ISBN 0-686-57218-1, M-6510). French & Eur.

Caratzas, A. D., ed. see Herrad Of Landsberg.

Caratzas, Stam C. Les Tzacones. (Supplementa Byzantina: Vol. 4). 1976. 148.00x (ISBN 3-11-004799-3). De Gruyter.

Caravale, G. A., ed. The Legacy of Ricardo. 320p. 1985. 45.00x (ISBN 0-631-13617-7). Basil Blackwell.

Caravan, Bernard. Economists for Beginners. 1982. pap. 3.95 (ISBN 0-394-73939-6). Pantheon.

Caravella, Joseph R. Minicalculators in the Classroom. 64p. 1977. pap. 4.95 (ISBN 0-8106-1812-5). NEA.

--Minicalculators in the Classroom. LC 76-41213. 64p. 1977. pap. 4.40 (ISBN 0-8106-1812-5). NCTM.

Carawan, Candie, jt. ed. see Carawan, Guy.

Carawan, Guy & Carawan, Candie, eds. Voices from the Mountains. LC 82-8657. (Illus.). 256p. 1982. pap. 13.95x (ISBN 0-252-01006-X). U of Ill Pr.

Caraway, Caren. African Designs of Guinea Coast. (International Design Library). (Illus.). 48p. 1985. pap. 3.50 (ISBN 0-88045-064-9). Stemmer Hse.

--African Designs of Nigeria & the Cameroons. (International Design Library). (Illus.). 48p. (Orig.). 1984. pap. 3.50 (ISBN 0-88045-060-6). Stemmer Hse.

--Aztec & Other Mexican Indian Designs. (International Design Library). (Illus.). 48p. (Orig.). 1984. pap. 3.50 (ISBN 0-88045-051-7). Stemmer Hse.

--Beauty & the Beast. (A Stemmer House Story-to-Color Book). (Illus.). (ps up). 1980. pap. 2.95 (ISBN 0-916144-46-1). Stemmer Hse.

--Cinderella. (A Stemmer House Story-to-Color Bk.). (Illus.). 32p. (Orig.). (ps-4). 1981. pap. 2.95 (ISBN 0-916144-85-2). Stemmer Hse.

--Designs of the South Pacific. (International Design Library). (Illus.). 48p. (Orig.). 1983. pap. 3.50 (ISBN 0-88045-036-3). Stemmer Hse.

--Dick Whittington & His Cat. (Story-to Color Books Ser.). (Illus.). 32p. (gr. 2 up). 1982. pap. 2.95 (ISBN 0-916144-99-2). Stemmer Hse.

--Eastern Woodland Indian Designs. (International Design Library). (Illus.). 48p. (Orig.). 1984. pap. 3.50 (ISBN 0-88045-057-6). Stemmer Hse.

--Hansel & Gretel: Story-to-Color. (Story to Color Ser.). 32p. (ps up). 1982. pap. 2.95 (ISBN 0-88045-017-7). Stemmer Hse.

--Hawaiian & Easter Island Designs. (The International Design Library). (Illus.). 48p. (Orig.). 1985. pap. 3.50 (ISBN 0-88045-071-1). Stemmer Hse.

--Mayan Designs. (International Design Library). (Illus.). 56p. 1981. pap. 3.50 (ISBN 0-916144-80-1). Stemmer Hse.

--The Mola Design Coloring Book. (International Design Library). (Illus.). 48p. 1981. pap. 3.50 (ISBN 0-916144-71-2). Stemmer Hse.

--Northwest Indian Designs. (International Design Library). (Illus.). 48p. 1982. pap. 3.50 (ISBN 0-916144-98-4). Stemmer Hse.

--Peruvian Textile Designs. (The International Design Library). (Illus.). 48p. 1983. pap. 3.50 (ISBN 0-88045-026-6). Stemmer Hse.

--Pieced Quilts. (International Design Library). (Illus.). 48p. 1981. pap. 3.50 (ISBN 0-916144-79-8). Stemmer Hse.

--Plains Indian Designs. (International Design Library). (Illus.). 48p. (Orig.). 1984. pap. 3.50 (ISBN 0-88045-050-9). Stemmer Hse.

--Sleeping Beauty. (Story to Color Ser.). pap. 2.95 (ISBN 0-916144-81-X). Stemmer Hse.

--Snow White & the Seven Dwarfs. (Stemmer House Story-to-Color Bks). (Illus.). 32p. (ps up). 1980. pap. 2.95 (ISBN 0-916144-57-7). Stemmer Hse.

--Southeast Asian Textile Designs. (International Design Library). (Illus.). 48p. (Orig.). 1983. pap. 3.50 (ISBN 0-88045-034-7). Stemmer Hse.

--Southeastern Woodland Indian Designs. (The International Design Library). (Illus.). 48p. (Orig.). 1985. pap. 3.50 (ISBN 0-88045-072-X). Stemmer Hse.

--Southwest American Indian Design. (International Design Library). (Illus.). 48p. (Orig.). 1983. pap. 3.50 (ISBN 0-88045-035-5). Stemmer Hse.

--Tarot Designs. (International Design Library). (Illus.). 48p. 1980. pap. 3.50 (ISBN 0-916144-56-9). Stemmer Hse.

--Zodiac Designs. (International Design Library). (Illus.). 48p. 1980. pap. 3.50 (ISBN 0-916144-47-X). Stemmer Hse.

Caraway, Caren & International Design Library. Applique Quilts. (The International Design Library). (Illus.). 56p. (Orig.). pap. 3.50 (ISBN 0-916144-78-X). Stemmer Hse.

Caraway, Hattie W. Silent Hattie Speaks: The Personal Journal of Senator Hattie Caraway. Kincaid, Diane D., ed. LC 78-22136. (Contributions in Women's Studies: No. 9). (Illus.). 1979. lib. bdg. 27.50 (ISBN 0-313-20820-4, KSI/). Greenwood.

Carayon, Jean. Essai sur les rapports du pouvoir politique et du pouvoir religieux chez Montesquieu. LC 75-168919. (Fr.). 1973. Repr. of 1903 ed. lib. bdg. 15.00 (ISBN 0-8337-4024-5). B Franklin.

Carballido, Emilio. The Golden Thread & Other Plays. Peden, Margaret S., tr. from Sp. (Texas Pan American Ser). 255p. 1970. 11.95 (ISBN 0-292-70039-3). U of Tex Pr.

--The Norther. Peden, Margaret S., tr. from Sp. (Texas Pan American Ser.). Orig. Title: El Norte. (Illus.). 101p. 1968. 7.95x (ISBN 0-292-78389-2). U of Tex Pr.

Carballido y Zuniga, Andres Gonzalez de Barcia see Barcia Carballido Y Zuniga, Andres Gonzalez de.

Carballo, Manuel & Bane, Mary J. The State & the Poor in the Nineteen Eighties. 350p. 1984. pap. 16.00 (ISBN 0-86569-118-5); 24.95 (ISBN 0-86569-064-2). Auburn Hse.

Carballosa, Evis L. Daniel y el Reino Mesianico. Orig. Title: Daniel & the Messianic Kingdom. 320p. 1979. pap. 7.95 (ISBN 0-8254-1101-7). Kregel.

--La Deidad de Cristo. Orig. Title: The Deity of Christ. 168p. (Span.). 1982. pap. 3.25 (ISBN 0-8254-1102-5). Kregel.

--El Dictador del Futuro. Orig. Title: The Future Dictator. 80p. (Span.). 1978. pap. 2.25 (ISBN 0-8254-1103-3). Kregel.

--Filipenses: Un Comentario Exegetico y Practico. Orig. Title: Phillippians: Commentary. 140p. (Span.). 1973. pap. 1.95 (ISBN 0-8254-1105-X). Kregel.

--Santiago: La Fe en Accion. Orig. Title: James: Faith in Action. 384p. (Orig., Span.). 1985. pap. 10.95 (ISBN 0-8254-1112-2). Kregel.

Carbarga, Leslie. The Fleischer Story. LC 73-94123. (Illus.). 1977. 12.50 (ISBN 0-87897-032-0). Nostalgia Pr.

Carbato, Charles E. Bouger Gravity Anomalies of the San Fernando Valley, California. LC 65-63511. (University of California Publications in Geological Services: Vol. 46, No. 1). pap. 20.00 (ISBN 0-317-09122-0, 2011792). Bks Demand UMI.

Carbaugh. International Economics. 2nd ed. 1984. write for info. (ISBN 0-534-03831-X). Wadsworth Pub.

Carbaugh, Robert J. & Fan, Liang-Shing. The International Monetary System: History, Institutions, Analyses. LC 75-38829. (Illus.). 176p. 1976. 19.95x (ISBN 0-7006-0141-4). U Pr of KS.

Carberry, James J. Chemistry & Catalytic Reaction Engineering. (Chemical Engineering Ser.). (Illus.). 1976. 45.00 (ISBN 0-07-009790-9). McGraw.

Carberry, John. The Book of the Rosary. LC 83-62424. 120p. (Orig.). 1983. pap. 4.50 (ISBN 0-87973-610-0, 610). Our Sunday Visitor.

--Mary Queen & Mother. 1979. 5.50 (ISBN 0-8198-0584-X); pap. 3.95 (ISBN 0-8198-0585-8). Dghtrs St Paul.

--Reflections & Prayers for Visits with Our Eucharistic King. pap. 0.50 (ISBN 0-8198-0315-4). Dghtrs St Paul.

Carberry, M., et al. Foundations of Computer Science. LC 78-27891. 317p. 1979. text ed. 28.95 (ISBN 0-914894-18-8). Computer Sci.

Carberry, Patrick R. CAD-CAM with Personal Computers. 189p. 1985. 21.95 (ISBN 0-8306-0852-4, 1852); pap. 14.95 (ISBN 0-8306-1852-X). TAB Bks.

Carbery, Eithne. In the Irish Past. 79p. 1978. pap. 3.95 (ISBN 0-85342-546-9, Pub. by Mercier Pr Ireland). Irish Bk Ctr.

Carbery, Mary. The Farm by Lough Gur. 286p. 1982. pap. 5.95 (ISBN 0-85342-370-9, Pub. by Mercier Pr Ireland). Irish Bks Media.

Carbery, Thomas F. Consumers in Politics. LC 68-56547. 1969. 27.50x (ISBN 0-678-06754-6). Kelley.

Carbino, Rosemarie. Foster Parenting: An Updated Review of the Literature. (Orig.). 1980. pap. text ed. 4.95 (ISBN 0-87868-178-7, F-56). Child Welfare.

Carbo, Margarete & Barras, Diane M. Arnie the Darling Starling. 208p. 1985. pap. 2.95 (ISBN 0-449-20654-8, Crest). Fawcett.

Carbo, Marie, et al. Teaching Students to Read Through Their Individual Learning Styles. rev. ed. 1985. text ed. 23.95 (ISBN 0-8359-7517-7). Reston.

Carbo, Marie L. & Carbo, Nicholas A. La Historia De Mi Familia: My Family History. (Illus.). (gr. 2-6). 1977. wkbk. in Span. 4.50x (ISBN 0-930804-02-3); wkbk. in Eng. 4.50x (ISBN 0-930804-01-5). World Rec Pubns.

Carbo, Nicholas A., jt. auth. see Carbo, Marie L.

Carbo, R. & Riera, J. M. A General SFC Theory. (Lecture Notes in Chemistry Ser.: Vol. 5). 1978. pap. 18.00 (ISBN 0-387-08535-1). Springer-Verlag.

Carbo, R., ed. Current Aspects of Quantum Chemistry, 1981. (Studies in Physical & Theoretical Chemistry: Vol. 21). 464p. 1982. 106.50 (ISBN 0-444-42119-X). Elsevier.

Carbon Dioxide Assessment Committee, National Research Council. Changing Climate: Report of the Carbon Dioxide Assessment Committee. 1983. pap. text ed. 29.50 (ISBN 0-309-03425-6). Natl Acad Pr.

Carbon, Susan B. & Berkson, Larry C. Judicial Retention Elections in the United States. LC 80-69565. 90p. (Orig.). 1980. pap. 4.00 (ISBN 0-938870-01-7, 8566). Am Judicature.

Carbon, Susan B., jt. auth. see Berkson, Larry C.

Carbonara, Nancy T. Techniques for Observing Normal Child Behavior. LC 61-9991. 1961. pap. 2.50x (ISBN 0-8229-5043-X). U of Pittsburgh Pr.

Carbone, Maria. Born to Be Mellow: A Guide to the Laid Back Life. LC 83-18095. (Illus.). 96p. (Orig.). 1984. pap. 3.95 (ISBN 0-943392-37-3). Tribeca Comm.

Carbone, Peter F. The Social & Educational Thought of Harold Rugg. LC 75-36176. pap. 59.50 (ISBN 0-317-20094-1, 2023374). Bks Demand UMI.

Carbone, Robert. Presidential Passages. 1981. 17.00 (ISBN 0-8268-1454-9). ACE.

Carbone, Salvatore & Gueze, Raoul. Draft Model Law on Archives: Descriptions & Text. LC 72-82782. (Documentation, Libraries & Archives: Studies & Research: No. 1). 225p. (Orig.). 1972. pap. 8.75 (ISBN 92-3-100962-1, U171, UNESCO). Unipub.

Carbonell, Jaime G. Subjective Understanding: Computer Models of Belief Systems. Stone, Harold S., ed. LC 81-11528. (Computer Science Ser.: Artificial Intelligence: No. 5). 304p. 1981. 49.95 (ISBN 0-8357-1212-5). UMI Res Pr.

Carbonell, Maria G. Volver. (Coleccion Espejo de Paciencia). 122p. (Orig., Span.). 1980. pap. 5.95 (ISBN 0-89729-290-1). Ediciones.

Carboni, David K. Geriatric Medicine in the United States & Great Britain. LC 82-9245. (Contributions to the Study of Aging Ser.: No. 1). (Illus.). 159p. 1983. lib. bdg. 35.00 (ISBN 0-313-23437-X, CAO/). Greenwood.

Carboni, G., jt. ed. see Campanini, G.

Carboni, R. Eureka Stockade. 1975. pap. 4.50x (ISBN 0-522-83945-2, Pub. by Melbourne U Pr). Intl Spec Bk.

Carbonneau, Denis, ed. Annual Report of the American Rare, Antiquarian & Out-of-Print Book Trade 1978-1979. 1980. pap. 9.95 (ISBN 0-930986-03-2). Three Mtn Pr.

Carbonneau, Thomas E., jt. auth. see Robert, Jean.

Carbonneau, Thomas E., ed. see Sokol Colloquium.

Carby-Hall, J. R. Studies in Labour Law. 1976. 90.00x (ISBN 0-903763-43-5, Pub. by MCB Pubns). State Mutual Bk.

Carby-Hall, Jo. The Closed Shop in Britain: A Human Rights Issue. 1980. 79.00x (ISBN 0-86176-054-9, Pub. by MCB Pubns). State Mutual Bk.

Carby-Hall, Joseph R. Worker Participation in Europe. LC 77-4863. 271p. 1977. 23.50x (ISBN 0-87471-992-5). Rowman.

Carcamo, L. Dictionnaire pour Ingenieurs et Techniciens: Francais-Espagnol, Espagnol-Francais. 1106p. (Fr. & Span.). 1981. 95.00 (ISBN 0-686-92423-1, M-7669). French & Eur.

Carcaraded, Maria de see De Carcaradec, Maria.

Carcassi, M. Classical Guitar Method. rev. ed. 128p. 1962. pap. 5.95 (ISBN 0-8258-0049-8, 0762). Fischer Inc NY.

Carcassi, Ugo, jt. ed. see Cao, Antonio.

Carcasson. The Butterflies of Africa. 29.95 (ISBN 0-00-219783-9, Collins Pub England). Greene.

Carcasson, R. H. Catalogue of the African Sphingidae with Descriptions of the East African Species. rev. ed. 148p. 1968. 40.00x (ISBN 0-317-07051-7, Pub. by EW Classey UK). State Mutual Bk.

--The Swallowtail Butterflies of East Africa. 1984. 30.00x (ISBN 0-317-07177-7, Pub. by FW Classey UK). State Mutual Bk.

Carchedi, Guglielmo. Problems in Class Analysis. 300p. (Orig.). 1983. pap. 14.95x (ISBN 0-7100-9426-4). Routledge & Kegan.

Carcich, Theodore. So What's There to Live for? (Better Living Ser.). 64p. 1972. pap. 0.95 (ISBN 0-8127-0064-3). Review & Herald.

Carcione, Joe. The Greengrocer Cookbook. LC 75-9083. (Illus.). 1975. pap. 6.95 (ISBN 0-89087-055-1). Celestial Arts.

Carcione, Joe & Lucas, Bob. The Greengrocer. LC 72-85171. (Illus.). 1978. pap. 6.95 (ISBN 0-87701-113-3). Chronicle Bks.

Carcopino, Jerome. Daily Life in Ancient Rome: The People & the City at the Height of the Empire. Rowell, Henry T., ed. Lorimer, E. O., tr. (Illus., Fr.). 1940. pap. 7.95x 1960 (ISBN 0-300-00031-6, Y28). Yale U Pr.

Card, Emily. Staying Solvent: A Comprehensive Guide to Equal Credit for Women. LC 84-4537. 256p. 1985. 15.95 (ISBN 0-03-062954-3). HR&W.

Card, James Van Dyck. An Anatomy of Penelope. LC 82-49195. 168p. 1984. 24.50 (ISBN 0-8386-3158-4). Fairleigh Dickinson.

Card, Josefina J. Lives after Vietnam: The Personal Impact of Military Service. 208p. 1983. 26.00x (ISBN 0-669-06420-3). Lexington Bks.

Card, Orson S. Ainge. 104p. (Orig.). 1982. pap. 3.95 (ISBN 0-941214-02-8). Signature Bks.

--Dragons of Darkness. 320p. (Orig.). 1981. pap. 6.95 (ISBN 0-441-16662-8). Ace Bks.

--Dragons of Darkness. 288p. 1983. pap. 2.95 (ISBN 0-441-16664-4, Pub. by Ace Science Fiction). Ace Bks.

--Ender's Game. 368p. 1985. 13.95 (ISBN 0-312-93208-1). Tor Bks.
--Ender's Game. 368p. 1986. pap. 3.50 (ISBN 0-8125-3253-8, Dist. by Warner Pub Services & St. Martin). Tor Bks.
--Hart's Hope. 272p. 1983. pap. 2.75 (ISBN 0-425-05819-0). Berkley Pub.
--A Planet Called Treason. 1980. pap. 2.50 (ISBN 0-440-16897-X). Dell.
--Saintspeak. 64p. (Orig.). 1981. pap. 3.95 (ISBN 0-941214-00-1). Signature Bks.
--A Woman of Destiny. 800p. 1984. pap. 3.95 (ISBN 0-425-06476-X). Berkley Pub.
--The Worthing Chronicle. 272p. 1983. pap. 2.75 (ISBN 0-441-91810-7, Pub. by Ace Science Fiction). Ace Bks.
Card, Orson S., ed. Dragons of Light. 1983. pap. 2.95 (ISBN 0-441-16661-X, Ace Science Fiction). Ace Bks.
Card, Richard, jt. auth. see Taylor, Raymond G.
Card, Stuart K., et al. The Psychology of Human-Computer Interaction. 488p. 1983. text ed. 39.95 (ISBN 0-89859-243-7). L Erlbaum Assocs.
Cardamone, Donna G. The "Canzone villanesca alla napolitana" & Related Forms, 1537-1570, 2 vols. Buelow, George, ed. LC 81-4750. (Studies in Musicology: No. 45). 616p. 1981. Set. 84.95 (ISBN 0-8357-1184-6). Vol. 1 (ISBN 0-8357-1203-6). Vol. 2 (ISBN 0-8357-1204-4). UMI Res Pr.
Cardamone, Tom. Adverstising Agency & Studio Skills: A Guide to the Preparation of Art & Mechanicals for Reproduction. 3rd ed. (Illus.). 160p. 1981. 12.95 (ISBN 0-8230-0151-2). Watson-Guptill.
--Advertising Agency & Studio Skills: A Guide to the Preparation of Art & Mechanicals for Reproduction. rev. ed. (Illus.). 1970. 12.95 (ISBN 0-8230-0151-2). Watson-Guptill.
--Mechanical Color Separation Skills for the Commercial Artist. 1980. pap. 14.95 (ISBN 0-442-21487-1). Van Nos Reinhold.
Cardano, Girolamo. Cardanus Comforte. Bedingfield, T., ed. LC 77-6565. (English Experience Ser.: No. 82). 204p. 1969. Repr. of 1576 ed. 25.00 (ISBN 90-221-0082-0). Walter J Johnson.
--Opera Omnia, 10 vols. Repr. of 1663 ed. 34.50 ea.; Set. 445.00 (ISBN 0-384-07500-2). Johnson Repr.
Cardarelli, Nate F. Controlled Release Pesticides Formulations. LC 75-46632. (Uniscience Ser.). 224p. 1976. 66.00 (ISBN 0-8493-5114-6). CRC Pr.
Carde, Ring T., jt. ed. see Bell, William T.
Cardella, Carol A. Builders Guide to Merchandising. 55p. 1978. pap. 8.00 (ISBN 0-86718-012-9); pap. 6.00 members. Natl Assn Home.
--Salespersons Guide to Merchandising. 44p. 1978. pap. 8.00 (ISBN 0-86718-041-2); pap. 6.00 members. Natl Assn Home.
Cardelle, Gustavo. Reflejos Sobre la Nieve. LC 78-59838. (Senda Poetica Ser.). (Span.). 1978. pap. 3.95 (ISBN 0-918454-07-7). Senda Nueva.
Carden, A. E., ed. see American Society for Testing & Materials, et al.
Carden & Cherry Advertising Agency, Inc. Staff, ed. see Worrell, Ernest P.
Carden, Jerry A., jt. auth. see Korb, Ruth H.
Carden, Joy C. Music in Lexington Before Eighteen Forty. LC 80-83683. 148p. 1980. pap. 9.95 (ISBN 0-912839-05-8). Lexington-Fayette.
Carden, Karen W., jt. auth. see Metcalf, Calvin S.
Carden, Maren L. Feminism in the Mid 1970s: The Non-Establishment the Establishment, & the Future. LC 77-4367. 63p. 1977. pap. 4.50 (ISBN 0-916584-04-6). Ford Found.
--The New Feminist Movement. LC 73-83889. 226p. 1974. 9.95x (ISBN 0-87154-196-3). Russell Sage.
Carden, Richard. The Papyrus Fragments of Sophocles: An Edition with Prolegomena & Commentary. (Texte und Kommentare: Vol. 7). 261p. 1974. 80.00x (ISBN 3-11-003833-1). De Gruyter.
Carden, Robert W., tr. see Buonarroti, Michelangelo.
Cardenal, Ernesto. Apocalypse, & Other Poems. Pring-Mill, Robert & Walsh, Donald D., eds. LC 77-7280. 1977. pap. 4.95 (ISBN 0-8112-0661-0). New Directions.
--Flights of Victory: Songs in Celebration of the Nicaraguan Revolution. Zimmerman, Marc, ed. & tr. LC 84-5278. 123p. (Orig., Span. & Eng.). pap. 9.95 (ISBN 0-88344-131-4). Orbis Bks.
--The Gospel in Solentiname, 4 vols. Walsh, Donald D., tr. from Span. LC 76-2681. Orig. Title: El Evangelio en Solentiname. (Orig.). 1982. Vol. 1, 288p. pap. 8.95 (ISBN 0-88344-176-4); Vol. 2, 272p. pap. 8.95 (ISBN 0-88344-175-6); Vol. 3, 320p. pap. 8.95 (ISBN 0-88344-174-8); Vol. 4, 288p. pap. 8.95 (ISBN 0-88344-173-X). Orbis Bks.
--Homage to the American Indians. Altschul, Carlos & Altschul, Monique, trs. LC 73-8111. pap. 30.80 (ISBN 0-317-09702-4, 2020497). Bks Demand UMI.
--In Cuba. Walsh, Donald D., tr. from Span. & pref. by. LC 74-8493. 352p. 1974. 10.50 (ISBN 0-8112-0537-1); pap. 3.95 (ISBN 0-8112-0538-X, NDP377). New Directions.
--Love. 160p. 1981. pap. 4.95 (ISBN 0-8245-0043-1). Crossroad NY.
--Psalms. 96p. 1981. pap. 3.95 (ISBN 0-8245-0044-X). Crossroad NY.
--With Walker in Nicaragua & Other Early Poems. Cohen, Jonathan, tr. 1985. 17.00x (ISBN 0-8195-5123-6); pap. 8.95 (ISBN 0-8195-6118-5). Wesleyan U Pr.
--Zero Hour & Other Documentary Poems. Walsh, Donald D., ed. Borgeson, Paul W. & Cohen, Jonathan, trs. from Span. LC 80-36817. 1980. pap. 5.95 (ISBN 0-8112-0766-8). New Directions.
Cardenas, Alfonso F. Data Base Management Systems. 2nd ed. 704p. 1984. text ed. 37,44 net (ISBN 0-205-08191-6, 208191); write for info. Allyn.
Cardenas, Alfonso F., et al. Computer Science. LC 71-169162. pap. 101.50 (ISBN 0-8357-9861-5, 2055172). Bks Demand UMI.
Cardenas, Gilberto, jt. auth. see Weintraub, Sidney.
Cardenas, Reyes. Survivors of the Chicano Titanic. LC 81-81742. 80p. 1982. lib. bdg. 20.00 (ISBN 0-916908-20-8); pap. 5.95 (ISBN 0-916908-15-1). Place Herons.
Cardenas-Ruiz, Manuel, ed. & tr. from Fr. Cronicas Francesas de los Indios Caribes. LC 79-11655. (Illus.). xii, 624p. (Orig., Span.). 1982. pap. 20.00 (ISBN 0-8477-0852-7). U of PR Pr.
Cardenas-Ruiz, Manuel, ed. see Labat, Jean B.
Carder, Clarence A., ed. Lees-McRae College Recipe Book. (Illus.). 1984. 5.50. Puddingstone.
Carder, James N. Art Historical Problems of a Roman Land. LC 77-94730. (Outstanding Dissertations in the Fine Arts Ser.). 1979. lib. bdg. 40.00 (ISBN 0-8240-3218-7). Garland Pub.
Carder, Mary E., et al. Productive Reading & Study Skills: A Student's Guide. 1979. pap. text ed. 11.95 (ISBN 0-8403-1997-5). Kendall-Hunt.
Carder, Polly, jt. auth. see Landis, Beth.
Carder, R. W., jt. ed. see Kopal, Z.
Carder, Shirl. Nut Lover's Cookbook. 160p. 1984. pap. 6.95 (ISBN 0-89087-405-0). Celestial Arts.
Cardes, Alfred. The Water Bearer. LC 78-70264. 1980. 7.95 (ISBN 0-87212-117-8). Libra.
Cardew, Cornelius, ed. Scratch Music. 128p. 1974. pap. 3.95x (ISBN 0-262-53025-2). MIT Pr.
Cardew, Cornelius, tr. see Eimert, Herbert & Stockhausen, Karlheinz.
Cardew, Cornelius, tr. see Reich, Willi.
Cardew, Cornelius, tr. see Webern, Anton.
Cardew, G. F. Bengal Native Army to Year Eighteen Ninety-Five: A Sketch of the Services. (Illus.). 576p. 1971. Repr. 10.00 (ISBN 0-88065-025-7, Pub. by Messers Today & Tomorrows Printers & Publishers India). Scholarly Pubns.
Cardew, Richard V. & Langdale, John V., eds. Why Cities Change: Urban Development & Economic Change in Sydney. 304p. 1983. text ed. 37.50x (ISBN 0-86861-252-9). Allen Unwin.
Cardi, Carola. Das Kinderschauspiel der Aufklaerungszeit. (European University Studies Ser.: No. 1, Vol. 693). 352p. (Ger.). 1983. 41.60 (ISBN 3-8204-7715-2). P Lang Pubs.
Cardiff, Gladys. To Frighten a Storm. (Copperhead Chapbook Ser.). 24p. (Orig.). 1975. pap. 5.00 (ISBN 0-914742-13-2). Copper Canyon.
Cardiff, Ira, ed. Wisdom of George Santayana. LC 64-16360. 1964. 7.50 (ISBN 0-8022-1481-9). Philos Lib.
Cardiff, Ira D. What Great Men Think of Religion. LC 71-161322. (Atheist Viewpoint Ser). 504p. 1972. Repr. of 1945 ed. 29.00 (ISBN 0-405-03625-6). Ayer Co Pubs.
Cardiff, John. Farming & the Computer. Mahony, Ciaran O., ed. LC 85-9880. (Illus.). 230p. (Orig.). 1985. pap. 14.95 (ISBN 0-934125-00-7). Group Four Pubns.
Cardillo, G., jt. auth. see Cainelli, G.
Cardin, D. J., et al. Organometallic Compounds of the Lanthanides, Actinides, & Early Transition Metals. (Chemistry Sourcebooks Ser.). 454p. 49.95x (ISBN 0-412-26830-2, 9549, Pub. by Chapman & Hall). Methuen Inc.
Cardinal, Andre. Etude Sur les Ectocarpacees de la Manche. (Illus.). 1965. pap. 21.00 (ISBN 3-7682-5415-1). Lubrecht & Cramer.
Cardinal, Marie. The Words to Say It. Goodheart, Pat, tr. from Fr. 320p. 1983. 16.50 (ISBN 0-941324-02-8). Van Vactor & Goodheart.
--Words to Say It. Goodheart, Pat, tr. from Fr. 320p. 1984. pap. 7.95 (ISBN 0-941324-09-5). Van Vactor & Goodheart.
Cardinal, Roger. Figures of Reality: A Perspective on the Poetic Imagination. (Illus.). 245p. 1981. 26.50x (ISBN 0-389-20064-6, 06834). B&N Imports.
Cardinal, Roger, ed. Sensibility & Creation: Studies in Twentieth-Century French Poetry. LC 76-40876. 252p. 1977. text ed. 26.50x (ISBN 0-06-490957-3, 06385). B&N Imports.
Cardinale, Susan, compiled by. Anthologies by & About Women: An Analytical Index. LC 81-13423. xxvii, 922p. 1982. lib. bdg. 49.95 (ISBN 0-313-22180-4, CAB/). Greenwood.
Cardinal Gibbons. Faith of Our Fathers. LC 80-51331. 352p. 1980. pap. 9.00 (ISBN 0-89555-158-6). Tan Bks Pubs.
Cardinall, Allan W. Bibliography of the Gold Coast. LC 74-109321. Repr. of 1932 ed. cancelled (ISBN 0-8371-3587-7, CGC&, Pub. by Negro U Pr). Greenwood.
--In Ashanti & Beyond. LC 77-106868. (Illus.). Repr. of 1927 ed. 20.75x (ISBN 0-8371-3285-1, CBE&, Pub. by Negro U Pr). Greenwood.
--In Ashanti & Beyond: The Record of a Resident Magistrate's Many Years in Tropical Africa. LC 27-24653. 1971. Repr. of 1927 ed. 30.00 (ISBN 0-384-07520-7). Johnson Repr.
--Natives of the Northern Territories of the Gold Coast. LC 76-90109. (Illus.). Repr. of 1920 ed. 17.50x (ISBN 0-8371-2025-X, CAL&, Pub. by Negro U Pr). Greenwood.
Cardiovascular Conference, 3rd, Aspen, Colo., Jan. 1972. Myocardial Infarction: A New Look at an Old Subject. Vogel, J. H., ed. (Advances in Cardiology: Vol. 9). 1973. 41.75 (ISBN 3-8055-1373-9). S Karger.
Cardiovascular Conference, 4th, Aspen, Colo., Jan. 1973. A Perspective on New Techniques in Congenital & Acquired Heart Disease: Proceedings. Vogel, J., ed. (Advances in Cardiology: Vol. 11). 1974. 46.50 (ISBN 3-8055-1654-1). S Karger.
Cardiovascular Conference, 5th, Snowmass-at-Aspen, Colorado, Jan. 1974. Integrated Medical-Surgical Care in Acute Coronary Artery Disease: Proceedings. Vogel, J. H., ed. (Advances in Cardiology: Vol. 15). x, 199p. 1975. 46.00 (ISBN 3-8055-2098-0). S Karger.
Cardiovascular Conference, 7th, Snowmass, Aspen, 1976. Future Directions in the Management of Cardiac Disease: A Bicentennial Viewpoint, Proceedings. Vogel, H. K., ed. (Advances in Cardiology: Vol. 20). 1977. 32.00 (ISBN 3-8055-2412-9). S Karger.
Cardiovascular Congress at Snowmass-at-Aspen, 8th, Aspen, Colorado, January 10-14, 1977. Results & Evaluation of New Methodology in Cardiology: Proceedings. Vogel, J. H., ed. (Advances in Cardiology: Vol. 22). 1977. 57.50 (ISBN 3-8055-2748-9). S Karger.
Cardiovascular Disease Conference, 1st, Snowmass-at-Aspen, Colorado, 1970. Hypoxia, High Altitude & the Heart: Proceedings. Vogel, J. H., ed. (Advances in Cardiology:: Vol. 5). 1970. 30.25 (ISBN 3-8055-0728-3). S Karger.
Cardiovascular Disease 6th Conference in Snowmass at Aspen, Colorado, January 1975. Clinical Application of Current Techniques & Treatment in Cardiology: Proceedings. Vogel, H. K., ed. (Advances in Cardiology: Vol. 17). 1976. 53.75 (ISBN 3-8055-2267-3). S Karger.
Cardon, A. & Fransen, L. Dynamic Semiconductor RAM Structures. (European Patent Office Ser.: Vol. 1). (Illus.). 488p. 1984. 95.00 (ISBN 0-08-030578-4). Pergamon.
Cardon, Charlotte M., jt. auth. see Cabat, Erni.
Cardon, F., et al, eds. Photovoltaic & Photoelectrochemical Solar Energy Conversion. LC 81-10666. (NATO ASI Series B, Physics: Vol. 69). 436p. 1981. 65.00 (ISBN 0-306-40800-7, Plenum Pr). Plenum Pub.
Cardona, Consuelo M., tr. see Lovato, Rebecca.
Cardona, Francisco J. & Cardona, Maria E. Handbook of Latin American Studies, Author Index to Numbers 1-28. LC 36-32633. 1968. 32.50x (ISBN 0-8130-0265-6). U Presses Fla.
Cardona, George. On Haplology in Indo-European. LC 68-21552. (Haney Foundation Ser). 1968. 15.00x (ISBN 0-8122-7570-5). U of Pa Pr.
--Panini: A Survey of Research. (Trends in Linguistics: State-of-the-Art Reports: No. 6). 1976. pap. 42.00x (ISBN 90-2793-435-5). Mouton.
Cardona, George, et al, eds. Indo-European & Indo-Europeans: Papers Presented at the Third Indo-European Conference at the University of Pennsylvania. LC 68-21551. (Haney Foundation Ser.). (Illus.). 1971. text ed. 40.00x (ISBN 0-8122-7574-8). U of Pa Pr.
Cardona, Luis A. An Annotated Bibliography on Puerto Rican Materials & Other Sundry Matters. LC 83-50536. (Illus.). 154p. (Orig.). 1983. text ed. 36.95 (ISBN 0-914199-00-5). Carreta Pr.
Cardona, Luis A., ed. A Manifest of Puerto Rican Materials: Annotated Bibliography Part II. LC 84-70827. (Illus.). 200p. 1984. text ed. 36.95 (ISBN 0-914199-01-3). Carreta Pr.
--A Selected Directory of Audio Visual Materials on Puerto Rico & the Puerto Ricans. 70p. (Orig.). 1984. pap. text ed. 8.95 (ISBN 0-914199-02-1). Carreta Pr.
Cardona, M. Modulation Spectroscopy. (Solid State Physics: Suppl. 11). 1969. 76.00 (ISBN 0-12-607771-1). Acad Pr.
Cardona, M., ed. Light Scattering in Solids I. 2nd ed. (Topics in Applied Physics Ser.: Vol. 8). (Illus.). 363p. 1983. pap. 32.00 (ISBN 0-387-11913-2). Springer-Verlag.
Cardona, M. & Guentherodt, G., eds. Light Scattering in Solids II: Basic Concept & Instrumentation. (Topics in Applied Physics Ser.: Vol. 50). (Illus.). 251p. 1982. 48.00 (ISBN 0-387-11380-0). Springer-Verlag.
--Light Scattering in Solids III: Recent Results. (Topics in Applied Physics: Vol. 51). (Illus.). 305p. 1982. 47.00 (ISBN 0-387-11513-7). Springer-Verlag.
Cardona, M. & Guntherodt, G., eds. Light Scattering in Solids IV: Electronic Scattering, Spin Effects, SERS & Morphic Effects. LC 83-13095. (Topics in Applied Physics: Vol. 54). (Illus.). 560p. 1984. 47.50 (ISBN 0-387-11942-6). Springer-Verlag.
Cardona, M. & Ley, L., eds. Photoemission in Solids I: General Principles. LC 78-2503. (Topics in Applied Physics: Vol. 26). (Illus.). 1978. 52.00 (ISBN 0-387-08685-4). Springer-Verlag.
Cardona, M., jt. ed. see Ley, L.
Cardona, Maria E., jt. auth. see Cardona, Francisco J.
Cardona, Mariana R. De see De Cardona, Mariana R.
Cardona, Rudolph, ed. see Perez Galdos, Benito.
Cardona, Virginia, ed. Trauma Reference Manual. 416p. 1984. pap. text ed. 19.95 (ISBN 0-89303-900-4). Brady Comm.
Cardona, Virginia D., ed. Trauma Nursing. 275p. 1984. pap. 17.95 (ISBN 0-87489-341-0). Med Economics.
Cardona-Hine, Alvara, jt. auth. see Pena, Alfredo C.
Cardona-Hine, Alvaro. When I Was a Father. LC 82-80604. (Minnesota Voices Project Ser.: No. 7). (Illus.). 73p. 1982. pap. 4.00 (ISBN 0-89823-036-5). New Rivers Pr.
--Words on Paper. 1974. pap. 2.50 (ISBN 0-88031-013-8). Invisible-Red Hill.
Cardona-Hine, Alvaro, tr. see Vallejo, Cesar.
Cardonda, Nicolas de see De Cardonda, Nicolas.
Cardone, Samuel, jt. auth. see Corsini, Raymond J.
Cardoso, Bill. The Maltese Sangweech & Other Heroes. LC 83-45501. 288p. 1984. 15.95 (ISBN 0-689-11443-5). Atheneum.
Cardoso, Ersillo, jt. auth. see Rouse.
Cardoso, Fernando E. & Faletto, Enzo. Dependency & Development in Latin America. Urquidi, Marjory M., tr. LC 75-46033. 1979. 38.50x (ISBN 0-520-03193-8); pap. 6.95x (ISBN 0-520-03527-5). U of Cal Pr.
Cardoso, Gerald. Negro Slavery in the Sugar Plantations of Veracruz & Pernambuco, 1550-1680: A Comparative Study. LC 82-21731. 224p. (Orig.). 1983. lib. bdg. 24.25 (ISBN 0-8191-2926-7); pap. text ed. 12.25 (ISBN 0-8191-2927-5). U Pr of Amer.
Cardoso, Lawrence. Mexican Emigration to the United States, 1897-1931. LC 74-20029. 192p. 1980. pap. 8.95x (ISBN 0-8165-0659-0). U of Ariz Pr.
Cardot, J. Cryptogamic Botany. (Harriman Alaska Expedition: Vol. 5). Repr. of 1904 ed. 41.00 (ISBN 0-527-38165-9). Kraus Repr.
Cardoza, A. L. Agrarian Elites & Italian Fascism: The Province of Bologna, 1901-1926. 1982. 45.00 (ISBN 0-691-05360-X). Princeton U Pr.
Cardoza, Anne & Vlk, Suzee. High-Paying Jobs in Six Months or Less. 160p. (Orig.). 1984. pap. 7.95 (ISBN 0-671-50414-2, Pub. by Monarch Pr). S&S.
Cardoza, Anne & Vlk, Suzee J. Robotics. (Illus.). 160p. 1985. 16.95 (ISBN 0-8306-0858-3, 1858); pap. 10.95 (ISBN 0-8306-1858-9). TAB Bks.
Cardoza, Anne, et al. One Hundred One Ways to Make Money with Application Software. 288p. 1985. pap. 9.95 (ISBN 0-671-50384-7, Pub. by Computer Bks). S&S.
Cardoza, Avery D. Casino Craps for the Winner. (Illus.). 56p. 1982. pap. 3.95 (ISBN 0-9607618-1-0). Cardoza Sch Blackjk.
--Winning Casino Blackjack for the Non-Counter. (Illus.). 56p. 1981. pap. 3.95 (ISBN 0-9607618-0-2). Cardoza Sch Blackjk.
Cardoza, Lida L., jt. auth. see Kindersley, David.
Cardozo, Arlene. Jewish Family Celebrations. (Illus.). 288p. 1985. pap. 6.95 (ISBN 0-312-44232-7). St Martin.
Cardozo, Arlene R. Jewish Family Celebrations: Shabbat, Festivals & Traditional Ceremonies. LC 82-5566. (Illus.). 288p. 1982. 17.50 (ISBN 0-312-44231-9). St Martin.
Cardozo, Benjamin N. The Growth of the Law. LC 73-8154. xvi, 145p. 1973. Repr. of 1963 ed. lib. bdg. 25.00x (ISBN 0-8371-6953-4, CAGL). Greenwood.
--Nature of the Judicial Process. (Storrs Lectures Ser.). 1921. pap. 5.95x (ISBN 0-300-00033-2, Y21). Yale U Pr.
--The Paradoxes of Legal Science. LC 76-104241. 142p. Repr. of 1928 ed. lib. bdg. 16.50x (ISBN 0-8371-3263-0, CALS). Greenwood.
--Selected Writings of Benjamin N. Cardozo. 1947. 12.50 (ISBN 0-685-02517-9). Bender.
--Women's Annotated Legal Bibliography. 1984. 45.00 (ISBN 0-87632-349-2). Boardman.
Cardozo, Harold G. The March of a Nation: Spain's Civil War. 59.95 (ISBN 0-8490-0584-1). Gordon Pr.
Cardozo, Jacob L. The Contemporary Jew in the Elizabethan Drama. (Research & Source Works Ser: No. 175). Repr. of 1925 ed. 15.00 (ISBN 0-8337-0466-4). B Franklin.
Cardozo, Jacob N. Notes on Political Economy. LC 72-187225. Repr. of 1826 ed. 35.00x (ISBN 0-678-00860-4). Kelley.
Cardozo, Lida L., jt. auth. see Kindersley, David.
Cardozo, Manoel D. The Portuguese in America, 590 BC-1974: A Chronology & Fact Book. LC 75-45203. (Ethnic Chronology Ser.: No. 22). 154p. 1976. lib. bdg. 8.50 (ISBN 0-379-00520-4). Oceana.
Cardozo, Peter. The Whole Kids Do-It-Yourself Scrapbook. (Illus.). 1979. spiral bdg. 7.95 (ISBN 0-553-01181-2). Bantam.
Cardozo, Richard N. Product Policy: Cases & Concepts. LC 78-67939. 1979. text ed. 33.95 (ISBN 0-201-00888-2). Addison-Wesley.

Cardozo-Freeman, Inez. The Joint: Language & Culture in a Maximum Security Prison. LC 83-9266. 602p. 1984. 52.75x (ISBN 0-398-04911-4). C C Thomas.
Carducci, Dewey & Carducci, Judy. The Caring Classroom. 232p. 1984. 12.95 (ISBN 0-915950-61-8); pap. 7.95 (ISBN 0-915950-62-6). Bull Pub.
Carducci, Giosue. Odi Barbare: Italian Text with English Prose. Smith, William F., tr. 1950. 7.50 (ISBN 0-913298-40-9). S F Vanni.
Carducci, Joshua. The Best Poems by Joshua Carducci Translated from the Italian. Trinidad, Montgomery, tr. from Ital. (Illus.). 1979. 47.45 (ISBN 0-89266-211-5). Am Classical Coll Pr.
--The Inspired Poetry by Joshua Carducci. Corradini, V., tr. (The Most Meaningful Classics in the World Culture Ser.). (Illus.). 137p. 1982. Repr. of 1916 ed. 67.45 (ISBN 0-89901-074-1). Found Class Reprints.
Carducci, Judy, jt. auth. see Carducci, Dewey.
Carduner, Jean & Carduner, Sylvie. Contextes: A French College Reader. 1975. pap. text ed. 9.95x (ISBN 0-669-73627-9). Heath.
Carduner, Jean, jt. auth. see Benamou, Michel.
Carduner, Jean, ed. see Bucher, Bernadette, et al.
Carduner, Sylvie & Hagiwara, Peter M. D'Accord: La Prononciation Du Francais International: Acquisition et Perfectionnement. LC 81-13123. 304p. 1982. text ed. 23.50x (ISBN 0-471-09729-2); tapes 76.00 (ISBN 0-471-86551-6); cassettes avail. 51.00 (ISBN 0-471-86757-8). Wiley.
Carduner, Sylvie, jt. auth. see Carduner, Jean.
Cardus, D. & Vallbona, C., eds. Computers & Mathematical Models in Medicine: Proceedings. (Lecture Notes in Medical Information Ser.: Vol. 9). 315p. 1981. pap. 28.50 (ISBN 0-387-10278-7). Springer-Verlag.
Cardus, David, jt. ed. see Blocker, William, Jr.
Cardus, Neville. Autobiography. LC 75-37825. (Illus.). 288p. 1976. Repr. of 1947 ed. lib. bdg. 22.50x (ISBN 0-8371-8577-7, CAAU). Greenwood.
--Composers Eleven. facsimile ed. (Essay Index Reprint Ser.). 1958. 21.50 (ISBN 0-8369-1554-2). Ayer Co Pubs.
--Neville Cardus: Autobiography. (Illus.). 288p. 1984. pap. 9.95 (ISBN 0-241-11286-9, Pub. by Hamish Hamilton England). David & Charles.
--Talking of Music. LC 74-14112. 320p. 1975. Repr. of 1957 ed. lib. bdg. 18.00x (ISBN 0-8371-7786-3, CAMU). Greenwood.
Cardwell. Elections & Ethics. (The Law in Florida Ser.). incl. latest pocket part supplement 24.95 (ISBN 0-686-90237-8); separate pocket part supplement, 1981 11.45 (ISBN 0-686-90238-6). Harrison Co GA.
--Turning Points in Western Technology. 256p. 1972. pap. text ed. 8.95 (ISBN 0-88202-003-X, Sci Hist). Watson Pub Intl.
Cardwell, Cardwell, ed. From the Heart of a Poet, 2 Vols. (Illus.). 225p. (Orig.). 1984. pap. 8.45 ea. (FH-1). Vol. 1 (ISBN 0-916395-12-X). Vol. 2 (ISBN 0-916395-15-4). Set (ISBN 0-916395-18-9). Hieroglyphics.
Cardwell, Carolyn, ed. Odes to a Cockroach, Vol. 2. (Illus.). 250p. 1985. pap. 8.45 (ISBN 0-916395-03-0, OC-2). Hieroglyphics.
Cardwell, Carolyn E. Kids, Cats & Puppydogs, Vol. 1. (Illus.). 250p. (Orig.). 1985. pap. 8.45 (ISBN 0-916395-14-6, KC-1). Hieroglyphics.
--Sands of Time, Vol. 1. (Illus.). 225p. (Orig.). 1986. pap. 8.45 (ISBN 0-916395-21-9, ST-1). Hieroglyphics.
--Sands of Time, Vol. 2. (Illus.). 225p. (Orig.). 1985. pap. 8.45 (ISBN 0-916395-23-5, ST-2). Hieroglyphics.
--Scratch-ings to a Flea, Vol. 1. (Illus.). 225p. (Orig.). 1985. pap. 8.45 (ISBN 0-916395-13-8, SF-l). Hieroglyphics.
--Scratch-ings to a Flea, Vol. 2. (Illus.). 225p. (Orig.). 1985. pap. 8.45 (ISBN 0-916395-16-2, SF-2). Hieroglyphics.
--Tidings to a Tick, Vol. 1. (Illus.). 225p. (Orig.). 1985. pap. 8.45 (ISBN 0-916395-17-0, TT-1). Hieroglyphics.
Cardwell, Carolyn E., ed. Dreams & Wishes, 2 Vols. (Illus.). 225p. (Orig.). Vol. 1, 01/1986. pap. 8.45 (ISBN 0-916395-20-0, DW-1); Vol. 2, 03/1986. pap. 8.45 (ISBN 0-916395-22-7). Hieroglyphics.
--My Heart Speaks to Thee, Vol. 1. (Illus.). 250p. 1985. pap. 8.45 (ISBN 0-916395-02-2, MH-1). Hieroglyphics.
--My Heart Speaks to Thee, Vol. 2. (Illus.). 250p. (Orig.). 1985. pap. 8.45 (ISBN 0-916395-05-7, MH-2). Hieroglyphics.
--My Heart Speaks to Thee, Vol. 3. (Illus.). 250p. (Orig.). 1985. pap. cancelled (ISBN 0-916395-08-1). Hieroglyphics.
Cardwell, Carolyn E., pref. by. Odes to a Cockroach, Vol. 1. (Illus.). 250p. (Orig.). 1984. pap. 8.45 (ISBN 0-916395-00-6, 0C-1). Hieroglyphics.
Cardwell, Carolyn E., ed. Odes to a Cockroach, Vol. 3. (Illus.). 250p. 1985. pap. 8.45 (ISBN 0-916395-06-5, 0C-3). Hieroglyphics.
--Teardrops & Laughter, 3 vols. (Illus.). 250p. (Orig.). 1984. Set. pap. write for info. (ISBN 0-916395-10-3); Vol. 1. pap. 8.45 (ISBN 0-916395-01-4, TD-1); Vol. 2. pap. 8.45 (ISBN 0-916395-04-9, TD-2); Vol. 3, 04/1985. pap. 8.45 (ISBN 0-916395-07-3, TD-3). Hieroglyphics.
Cardwell, Charles E. Argument & Inference: An Introduction to Symbolic Logic. (Philosophy Ser.). 1978. 14.95 (ISBN 0-675-08368-0). Merrill.
Cardwell, D. S. The Organization of Science in England. 2nd ed. 1972. pap. text ed. 10.00x (ISBN 0-435-54154-4). Heinemann Ed.
Cardwell, D. S., ed. Artisan to Graduate. 1974. 23.50 (ISBN 0-7190-1272-4). Manchester.
Cardwell, Edward, ed. see Peel, Robert.
Cardwell, Guy, ed. see Twain, Mark.
Cardwell, Jerry D. Mass Media Christianity: Televangelism & the Great Commission. 234p. (Orig.). 1985. lib. bdg. 22.75 (ISBN 0-8191-4323-5); pap. text ed. 10.75 (ISBN 0-8191-4324-3). U Pr of Amer.
--A Rumor of Trumpets: The Return of God to Secular Society. 118p. (Orig.). 1985. lib. bdg. 19.75 (ISBN 0-8191-4791-5); pap. text ed. 8.75 (ISBN 0-8191-4792-3). U Pr of Amer.
--The Social Context of Religiosity. LC 80-67216. 174p. 1980. pap. text ed. 10.75 (ISBN 0-8191-1136-8). U Pr of Amer.
--Social Psychology: A Symbolic Interaction Perspective. LC 75-158650. pap. 6.95x (ISBN 0-88295-203-X). Harlan Davidson.
Cardwell, Jerry D., jt. auth. see Vernon, Glenn M.
Cardwell, Julia C. The Moonshine Special. (Illus.). 1983. 5.75 (ISBN 0-8062-1908-4). Carlton.
Cardwell, Kenneth H. Bernard Maybeck: Artisan, Architect, Artist. LC 77-13773. (Illus.). 260p. 1984. pap. 19.95 (ISBN 0-87905-148-5, Peregrine Smith). Gibbs M Smith.
Cardwell, Margaret, ed. see Dickens, Charles.
Cardwell, Paul, Jr. Index of Model Periodicals: 1971 Through 1975. LC 77-1737. 789p. 1977. 40.00 (ISBN 0-8108-1027-1). Scarecrow.
Cardwell, Rick D., et al, eds. Aquatic Toxicology & Hazard Assessment-STP 854: Seventh Symposium. LC 84-70338. (Illus.). 590p. 1985. text ed. 60.00 (ISBN 0-8031-0410-3, 04-854000-16). ASTM.
Cardy, Lynn & Dart, Alan. Kids' Clothes: Making a Complete Wardrobe from Babyhood to Eleven Years. (Illus.). 128p. 1984. pap. 8.95 (ISBN 0-7135-1296-2, Pub. by Salem Hse Ltd). Merrimack Pub Cir.
--Maternity Clothes: Simple Patterns to Make While You Wait. (Illus.). 128p. 1985. pap. 9.95 (ISBN 0-7135-1313-6, Pub. by Salem Hse Ltd). Merrimack Pub Cir.
Cardy, Wayne C., jt. auth. see Arnold, Wesley F.
Care, Henry. English Liberties, or The Free-Born Subject's Inheritance. 6th ed. LC 75-31087. Repr. of 1774 ed. 28.50 (ISBN 0-404-13505-6). AMS Pr.
Care, Norman S. & Grimm, Robert H., eds. Perception & Personal Identity: Proceedings of the 1967 Oberlin Colloquium in Philosophy. LC 68-9427. (Oberlin Colloquium in Philosophy Ser). 1969. 20.00 (ISBN 0-8295-0145-2). UPB.
Care, Norman S., et al, eds. Readings in the Theory of Action. LC 68-27339. pap. 111.50 (ISBN 0-317-08105-5, 2050050). Bks Demand UMI.
Care, Norman S., et al, eds. see Oberlin Colloquim in Philosophy.
Career Associates. Career Choices for Undergraduates Considering Law. LC 83-40448. 1984. 11.95 (ISBN 0-8027-0795-5) (ISBN 0-8027-7241-2). Walker & Co.
Career Institute Staff. Photography for Fun & Profit, 18 vols. pap. 29.95 boxed (ISBN 0-911744-54-1). Career Pub IL.
Careers Research & Advisory Centre, ed. Graduate Studies 1982-83: The Guide to Postgraduate Study in the UK. 1013p. 1982. 150.00x (ISBN 0-86021-343-9). Intl Pubns Serv.
Carefoot, Jean, jt. auth. see Gracy, David.
Carefoot, Thomas. Pacific Seashores: A Guide to Intertidal Ecology. LC 76-7782. (Illus.). 192p. 1977. pap. 14.95x (ISBN 0-295-95522-8). U of Wash Pr.
Carek, Donald J. Principles of Child Psychotherapy. 240p. 1972. 25.75x (ISBN 0-398-02254-2). C C Thomas.
Careles, Rick. The Ferry Guide. 36p. 1982. pap. 4.95 (ISBN 0-88826-090-3). Superior Pub.
Careless, Anthony. Initiative & Response: The Adaptation of Canadian Federalism to Regional Economic Development. (Canadian Public Administration Ser). 1977. 17.50x (ISBN 0-7735-0280-7); pap. 8.50 (ISBN 0-7735-0294-7). McGill-Queens U Pr.
Careless, J. M., ed. The Pre-Confederation Premiers: Ontario Government Leaders 1841 to 1867. (Ontario Historical Studies). 368p. 1985. 14.95 (ISBN 0-8020-6590-2). U of Toronto Pr.
Careless, James M. Canada: A Story of Challenge. rev. ed. (Illus.). 1969. pap. 14.95 (ISBN 0-312-11620-9). St Martin.
Careless, John. Trenchard's Brat. 301.00x (ISBN 0-86116-673-6, Pub by New Horizon England). State Mutual Bk.
Carelius, Norman & Kidd, Verna. The Last Sunrise. 432p. 1984. pap. 3.50 (ISBN 0-515-07530-2). Jove Pubns.
Carell, Paul. Invasion: They're Coming. 304p. (Orig.). 1984. pap. 3.95 (ISBN 0-553-24164-8). Bantam.
Carelli, Adriano. Three Hundred & Sixty Degrees of the Zodiac. 208p. 1982. 5.50 (ISBN 0-86690-063-2, 1032-01). Am Fed Astrologers.
Carelli, M. Dino, ed. A New Look at the Relation Between School Education and Work: Second All-European Conference for Directors of Educational Research Institutions, Madrid 11-13 Sept. 79. (International Studies in Education Ser.: No. 37). vi, 164p. 1980. pap. text ed. 11.50 (ISBN 90-265-0355-5, Pub. by Swets & Zeitlinger Netherlands). Hogrefe Intl.
Carelli, M. Dino, ed. see All-European Conference for Directors of National Research Institutions in Education, 1st, Hamburg 1976.
Carelli, M. Dino, compiled by see Becker, H. A. & Dueuzeide, H.
Carelli, M. Dino, ed. see Directors of National Research Institutions in Education Colloquy, 3rd, Hamburg, 12-14 September 1978.
Carello, Claudia A., jt. auth. see Michaels, Claire F.
Carelman, Jacques. The Catalogue of Fantastic Inventions. (Illus.). 128p. 1984. pap. 9.95 (ISBN 0-312-12363-9). St Martin.
Carels, Edward, et al. The Physician & Cost Control. LC 79-21736. 196p. 1979. text ed. 35.00 (ISBN 0-89946-005-4). Oelgeschlager.
Carels, Peter E. The Satiric Treatise in Eighteenth Century Germany. (Germanic Studies in America: Vol. 24). 170p. 1977. 22.20 (ISBN 3-261-01931-X). P Lang Pubs.
Carelse, Xavier. Making Science Laboratory Equipment: A Manual for Students & Teachers in Developing Countries. 273p. 1983. pap. 24.95 (ISBN 0-471-10353-5, Pub. by Wiley-Interscience). Wiley.
Careme, Maurice. The Peace. Neumeyer, Helen, tr. (Illus.). 8p. (Orig.). 1982. pap. 2.50 (ISBN 0-914676-68-7, Pub. by Envelope Bks). Green Tiger Pr.
Carenas, F. & Ferrando, Jose. La Sociedad Espanola en la Novela de la Postguerra. 1971. 10.95 (ISBN 0-88303-997-4). E Torres & Sons.
Carens, James F. Surpassing Wit: Oliver St. John Gogarty, His Poetry & His Prose. LC 78-12644. 304p. 1979. 26.00x (ISBN 0-231-04642-1). Columbia U Pr.
Carens, James F., jt. ed. see Bowen, Zack R.
Carens, James F., ed. see Sullivan, Eileen.
Carens, Joseph H. Equality, Moral Incentives, & the Market. LC 80-36774. (Illus.). 264p. 1981. lib. bdg. 19.00x (ISBN 0-226-09269-0). U of Chicago Pr.
Carenza, L. & Zichella, L., eds. Emotion & Reproduction, Pt. A. (Serono Symposia Ser.). 1979. 89.50 (ISBN 0-12-159401-7). Acad Pr.
Carenza, L., ed. see International Congress of Psychosomatic Obstertrics& Gynecology, 5th.
Carenza, L., et al, eds. Clinical Psychoneuroendocrinology in Reproduction. (Proceedings of the Serono Symposia Ser.). 1979. 66.00 (ISBN 0-12-159450-5). Acad Pr.
Careri. Order & Disorder in Matter. 1984. 38.95 (ISBN 0-8053-1700-7); pap. 19.95 (ISBN 0-8053-1725-2). Benjamin-Cummings.
Careri, G., ed. Liquid Helium. (Italian Physical Society: Course 21). 1964. 85.00 (ISBN 0-12-368821-3). Acad Pr.
Careri, Giorgio. Order & Disorder on Matter. 1983. text ed. 38.95 (ISBN 0-8053-1700-7); pap. 19.95 (ISBN 0-8053-1725-2). Benjamin-Cummings.
Caress, Jay. Hank Williams. LC 78-23942. (Illus.). 1979. 10.95 (ISBN 0-8128-2583-7). Stein & Day.
--Hank Williams: Country Music's Tragic King. LC 78-23942. (Illus.). 288p. 1982. pap. 9.95 (ISBN 0-8128-6109-4). Stein & Day.
Caress, Jay, jt. auth. see Hybels, Bill.
Caret, jt. auth. see Wingrove.
Caret, Robert L., jt. auth. see Wingrove, Alan S.
Carew, Anthony. The Lower Deck of the Royal Navy, 1900-39: The Invergordon Mutiny in Perspective. (Illus.). 256p. 1982. 25.00 (ISBN 0-7190-0841-7, Pub. by Manchester Univ Pr). Longwood Pub Group.
Carew, Bampfylde-Moore. The King of the Beggars, Bampfylde-Moore Carew. Wilkinson, C. H., ed. LC 80-2471. Repr. of 1931 ed. 39.50 (ISBN 0-404-19103-7). AMS Pr.
Carew, Henry. The Vampires of the Andes. Reginald, R. & Menville, Douglas, eds. LC 77-84206. (Lost Race & Adult Fantasy Ser.). 1978. Repr. of 1925 ed. lib. bdg. 26.50x (ISBN 0-405-10962-8). Ayer Co Pubs.
Carew, J. & Chan, I. Observing Intelligence in Young Children: Eight Case Studies. (Early Childhood Education Ser.). (Illus.). 192p. 1976. pap. 18.95 (ISBN 0-13-628982-7). P-H.
Carew, Jan. Children of the Sun. (Illus.). 40p. (gr. k up). 1980. 9.95 (ISBN 0-316-12848-1). Little.
--The Third Gift. (Illus.). 32p. (gr. k-3). 1974. 10.45i (ISBN 0-316-12847-3). Little.
Carew, Jean. Cara's Masquerade. (Sharon Romance Ser.). 128p. (Orig.). 1981. pap. 2.25 (ISBN 0-89531-135-6, 0198-96). Sharon Pubns.
--Stage Struck. (Contemporary Teens Ser.). 224p. (Orig.). 1981. pap. 2.25 (ISBN 0-89531-137-2, 0146-96). Sharon Pubns.
Carew, Jean V. & Lightfoot, Sara L. Beyond Bias: Perspectives on Classrooms. LC 78-20997. (Illus.). 1979. text ed. 17.50x (ISBN 0-674-06882-3). Harvard U Pr.
Carew, Joycelyn. Pavilion of Passion. 320p. 1983. pap. 2.95 (ISBN 0-380-84681-0, 84681-0). Avon.
Carew, R., tr. see Huarte Navarro, Juan de Dios.
Carew, Richard. The Survey of Cornwall. LC 70-6074. (English Experience Ser.: No. 100). 338p. 1969. Repr. of 1602 ed. 35.00 (ISBN 90-221-0100-2). Walter J Johnson.
Carew, Thomas. Poems of Thomas Carew. Vincent, Arthur, ed. LC 76-38343. (Selected Bibliographies Reprint Ser.). 1899. 17.00 (ISBN 0-8369-6760-7). Ayer Co Pubs.
--Poems of Thomas Carew. Dunlap, Rhodes, ed. (Oxford English Texts Ser). 1949. 42.00x (ISBN 0-19-811804-X). Oxford U Pr.
Carey. Wuthering Heights (Bronte) (Book Notes Ser.). 1984. pap. 2.50 (ISBN 0-8120-3448-1). Barron.
Carey & Perry. Zodiac & the Salts of Salvation. LC 77-166412. 1971. 15.00 (ISBN 0-87728-143-2). Weiser.
Carey, ed. see Roxburgh, W.
Carey, A. G., jt. auth. see Benson, John H.
Carey, Andrew G., jt. auth. see Carey, Jane P.
Carey, Anna K., jt. auth. see Harvey, Nancy L.
Carey, Anne. The Children's Pharmacy. 272p. 1985. pap. 9.95 (ISBN 0-446-38014-8). Warner Bks.
--The Children's Pharmacy: Everything You Should Know about Medicines for Your Children. LC 82-20712. 264p. 1984. 15.95 (ISBN 0-672-52727-8). Bobbs.
Carey, Art. In Defense of Marriage. LC 83-40434. 158p. 1984. 11.95 (ISBN 0-8027-0764-5). Walker & Co.
Carey, Bernard, jt. auth. see Painter, Martin.
Carey, Betsy, ed. WomanSource: A Guide to Women's Resources in Metropolitan Denver. LC 81-71997. (Illus.). 184p. (Orig.). 1982. pap. 4.95 (ISBN 0-9608012-0-0). Metro Source Pubns.
--WomanSource: A Guide to Women's Resources in Metropolitan Denver. 2nd ed. LC 84-51362. (Illus.). 200p. 1984. pap. 6.95 (ISBN 0-9608012-1-9). Metro Source Pubns.
Carey, C., ed. see Demosthenes.
Carey, Charles H. General History of Oregon. 3rd ed. LC 70-140122. (Illus.). 1971. 25.00 (ISBN 0-8323-0221-X). Binford.
Carey, Christopher. A Commentary of Five Odes of Pindar. rev. ed. Connor, W. R., ed. LC 80-2644. (Monographs in Classical Studies). 1981. lib. bdg. 26.00 (ISBN 0-405-14032-0). Ayer Co Pubs.
Carey, David. Aeroplane: How It Works. (Illus.). (gr. 5 up). 2.50 (ISBN 0-7214-0129-5). Merry Thoughts.
--Motor Car: How It Works. (Illus.). (gr. 5 up). 2.50 (ISBN 0-7214-0127-9). Merry Thoughts.
--Motor Cars. rev. ed. (gr. 5 up). 1968. 2.50 (ISBN 0-7214-0185-6). Merry Thoughts.
--Motor Cycle: How It Works. (Illus.). (gr. 5 up). 2.50 (ISBN 0-7214-0224-0). Merry Thoughts.
--Rocket: How It Works. (Illus.). (gr. 5 up). 2.50 (ISBN 0-7214-0128-7). Merry Thoughts.
--Story of the Motor Car. (Illus.). (gr. 4 up). 2.50 (ISBN 0-7214-0135-X). Merry Thoughts.
--Television: How It Works. (Illus.). (gr. 5 up). 1968. 2.50 (ISBN 0-7214-0130-9). Merry Thoughts.
Carey, Elizabeth. Debt of Honour. 192p. (Orig.). 1982. pap. 1.50 (ISBN 0-449-50308-9, Coventry). Fawcett.
--Marriage by Bequest. (Coventry Romance Ser.: No. 165). 224p. 1982. pap. 1.50 (ISBN 0-449-50265-1, Coventry). Fawcett.
Carey, Ernestine, jt. auth. see Gilbreth, Frank B., Jr.
Carey, Ernestine G., jt. auth. see Gilbreth, Frank.
Carey, Ernestine G., jt. auth. see Gilbreth, Frank B.
Carey, Ernestine G., jt. auth. see Gilbreth, Frank B., Jr.
Carey, Floyd D. Teenagers Pocket Companion, No. 2. 1962. pap. 0.25 (ISBN 0-87148-828-0). Pathway Pr.
--Teenagers Pocket Companion, No. 3. 1962. pap. 0.25 (ISBN 0-87148-829-9). Pathway Pr.
Carey, Floyd D., ed. Sunday School Basics. 1976. 5.25 (ISBN 0-87148-778-0); pap. 4.25 (ISBN 0-87148-777-2). Pathway Pr.
Carey, Floyd D. & Byrd, James F., eds. Manna: A Book of Table Devotions. 1973. pap. 3.95 (ISBN 0-87148-564-8). Pathway Pr.
Carey, Floyd D., Jr. Teen-Agers' Treasure Chest. 100p. 1963. pap. 1.25 (ISBN 0-87148-830-2). Pathway Pr.
Carey, Frances & Griffiths, Antong. The Print in Germany. 272p. 1985. pap. write for info. (ISBN 0-8419-1025-1). Holmes & Meier.
Carey, Francis A. Advanced Organic Chemistry, 2 Pts. LC 76-54956. Pt. A - Structure & Mechanisms. pap. 152.30 (ISBN 0-317-30351-1, 2024720); Pt. B - Reactions & Synthesis. pap. 136.80 (ISBN 0-317-30352-X). Bks Demand UMI.
Carey, Francis A. & Sundberg, Richard J. Advanced Organic Chemistry, 2 pts. Incl. Pt. A: Structure & Mechanisms. 583p (ISBN 0-306-25003-9); Pt. B: Reactions & Synthesis. 521p (ISBN 0-306-25004-7). LC 76-54956. 1977. softcover, ea. 13.95x (ISBN 0-686-64927-3, Rosetta). Plenum Pub.
--Advanced Organic Chemistry, Part A: Structure & Mechanisms. LC 76-26090. (Illus.). 583p. 1977. 49.50x (ISBN 0-306-35116-1, Plenum Pr). Plenum Pub.
--Advanced Organic Chemistry, Part B: Reactions & Synthesis. LC 76-54956. (Illus.). 521p. 1977. 49.50x (ISBN 0-306-35117-X, Plenum Pr). Plenum Pub.

--Advanced Organic Chemistry: Structure & Mechanism, Pt. A. 2nd ed. 744p. 1984. 59.50x (ISBN 0-306-41087-7, Plenum Pr); pap. 19.95x (ISBN 0-306-41198-9). Plenum Pub.

Carey, G. F., jt. auth. see Martin, Harold C.

Carey, G. K. Romeo & Juliet Notes. (Orig.). 1979. pap. 2.75 (ISBN 0-8220-0074-1). Cliffs.

Carey, Gary. Brothers Karamazov Notes. (Orig.). 1967. pap. 2.95 (ISBN 0-8220-0265-5). Cliffs.

--Great Expectations Notes. (Orig.). 1979. pap. 2.95 (ISBN 0-8220-0551-4). Cliffs.

--Katharine Hepburn: A Hollywood Yankee. LC 83-3356. (Illus.). 284p. 1983. 14.95 (ISBN 0-312-45089-3). St Martin.

--Katharine Hepburn: A Hollywood Yankee. 1984. pap. 3.95 (ISBN 0-440-14412-4). Dell.

--Katharine Hepburn: A Hollywood Yankee. large print ed. LC 84-21. 419p. 1984. Repr. of 1983 ed. 14.95 (ISBN 0-89621-522-9). Thorndike Pr.

--Marlon Brando: The Only Contender. 1985. 14.95 (ISBN 0-312-51543-X). St Martin.

--Mrs. Dalloway Notes. (Orig.). 1969. pap. 2.95 (ISBN 0-8220-0855-6). Cliffs.

--Plague Notes. (Orig.). 1967. pap. 2.50 (ISBN 0-8220-1039-9). Cliffs.

--Stranger Notes. (Orig.). 1979. pap. 2.75 (ISBN 0-8220-1229-4). Cliffs.

--Sun Also Rises Notes. (Orig.). 1968. pap. 2.95 (ISBN 0-8220-1237-5). Cliffs.

Carey, Gary & Jorgenson, Paul A. Othello Notes. (Orig.). 1980. pap. 2.95 (ISBN 0-8220-0063-6). Cliffs.

Carey, Gary K. The Old Man & the Sea Notes. 59p. (Orig.). 1973. pap. 3.25 (ISBN 0-8220-0935-8). Cliffs.

--The Red Pony "Chrysanthemums" "Flight" Notes. (Orig.). 1978. pap. text ed. 2.75 (ISBN 0-8220-1135-2). Cliffs.

Carey, George. Biochemic Pathology of Disease. 1981. pap. 7.95x (Regent House). B of A.

--A Faraway Time & Place: Lore of the Eastern Shore. Dorson, Richard M., ed. LC 77-70586. (International Folklore Ser.). (Illus.). 1977. Repr. of 1971 ed. lib. bdg. 22.00x (ISBN 0-405-10086-8). Ayer Co Pubs.

--I Believe in Man. LC 77-13426. pap. 4.95 (ISBN 0-8028-1711-4). Eerdmans.

--Relation of Mineral Salts of the Body. 1979. pap. 7.95 (ISBN 0-317-07304-4, Regent House). B of A.

--A Tale of Two Churches: Can Protestants & Catholics Get Together? LC 84-28858. 180p. (Orig.). 1985. pap. 5.95 (ISBN 0-87784-972-2). Inter-Varsity.

--Twelve Cell Salts of Zodiac. 1981. pap. 9.95x (ISBN 0-317-07280-3, Regent House). B of A.

Carey, George G. Maryland Folklore & Folklife. LC 71-142189. (Illus.). 110p. 1970. pap. 6.50 (ISBN 0-87033-154-X). Tidewater.

Carey, George G., ed. A Sailor's Songbag: An American Rebel in an English Prison,1777-1779. LC 75-32483. (Illus.). 176p. 1976. lib. bdg. 12.00x (ISBN 0-87023-200-2). U of Mass Pr.

Carey, George W. The Political Science Reviewer. 320p. annual 8.00 (ISBN 0-318-14487-5); back issues 8.00 ea. Intercoll Studies.

--A Vignette of the New York-New Jersey Metropolitan Region. LC 76-4796. (Contemporary Metropolitan Analysis Ser.). (Illus.). 96p. 1976. pap. 14.95 prof ref (ISBN 0-88410-436-2). Ballinger Pub.

Carey, George W., jt. auth. see Kendall, Willmoore.

Carey, George W., ed. Freedom & Virtue: The Conservative Libertarian Debate. LC 84-19637. 164p. (Orig.). 1985. lib. bdg. 22.75 (ISBN 0-8191-4334-0, Co-Pub. by Intercollegiate Studies); pap. text ed. 9.25 (ISBN 0-8191-4335-9, Co-pub. by Intercollegiate Studies). U Pr of Amer.

Carey, George W. & Schall, James V., eds. Essays on Christianity & Political Philosophy. (The ISI Roots of Western Culture Ser.). 144p. (Orig.). 1985. 21.50 (ISBN 0-8191-4275-1, Co-pub. by Intercollegiate Studies); pap. text ed. 9.25 (ISBN 0-8191-4276-X). U Pr of Amer.

Carey, George W., jt. ed. see Hyneman, Charles S.

Carey, Glen O. Edward Payson Roe. (United States Author Ser.). 1985. lib. bdg. 19.95 (ISBN 0-8057-7421-1, Twayne). G K Hall.

Carey, Glenn O. Faulkner: the Unappeased Imagination: A Collection of Critical Essays. 290p. 1980. 18.50x (ISBN 0-87875-181-5, 57440). Whitston Pub.

Carey, Graham, jt. auth. see Abbs, Peter.

Carey, Graham F. & Oden, J. Tinsley. Finite Elements: A Second Course, Vol. II. (Illus.). 336p. 1983. text ed. 37.95 (ISBN 0-13-317065-9). P-H.

--Finite Elements: Computational Aspects, Vol. III. (Illus.). 240p. 1984. text ed. 37.95 (ISBN 0-13-317107-8). P-H.

Carey, Graham F., jt. auth. see Oden, J. Tinsley.

Carey, Helen. How to Use Maps & Globes. (Social Studies Skills Ser.). 96p. (YA) (gr. 7 up). 1983. lib. bdg. 9.40 (ISBN 0-531-04673-7). Watts.

--How to Use Your Community as a Resource. (Social Studies Skills Ser.). 96p. (YA) (gr. 7 up). 1983. lib. bdg. 9.40 (ISBN 0-531-04675-3). Watts.

Carey, Helen & Greenberg, Judith. How to Use Primary Sources. (Social Studies Skills Ser.). 96p. (YA) (gr. 7 up). 1983. lib. bdg. 9.40 (ISBN 0-531-04674-5). Watts.

Carey, Helen & Greenberg, Judith E. How to Read a Newspaper. (Social Studies Skills Ser.). 96p. (YA) (gr. 7 up). 1983. lib. bdg. 9.40 (ISBN 0-531-04672-9). Watts.

Carey, Helen, jt. auth. see Greenberg, Judith E.

Carey, Helen, ed. Playing with Energy. 106p. (Orig.). 1981. pap. 5.00 (ISBN 0-87355-020-X). Natl Sci Tchrs.

Carey, Helen H. Producing Energy. (First Books-Economics Ser.). 72p. (gr. 4-8). 1984. lib. bdg. 9.40 (ISBN 0-531-04830-6). Watts.

Carey, Helen H., jt. auth. see Greenberg, Judith E.

Carey, Henry. Musical Century in 100 English Ballads on Various Subjects & Occasions, 2 vols. in 1. (Monuments of Music & Music Literature in Facsimile: Series I, Vol. 22). 256p. 1976. Repr. of 1737 ed. 45.00x (ISBN 0-8450-2022-6). Broude.

--The Plays of Henry Carey. Macey, Samuel C., ed. LC 78-66613. (Eighteenth Century English Drama Ser.). 1980. lib. bdg. 73.00 (ISBN 0-8240-3580-1). Garland Pub.

Carey, Henry C. Collected Works, 6 vols. 600.00 (ISBN 0-87968-885-8). Gordon Pr.

--Credit System in France, Great Britain & the United States. LC 73-18238. Repr. of 1838 ed. 19.50x (ISBN 0-678-01024-2). Kelley.

--Essay of the Rate of Wages. LC 77-119647. Repr. of 1835 ed. 7.00 (ISBN 0-404-01392-9). AMS Pr.

--Essay on the Rate of Wages. LC 64-66155. Repr. of 1835 ed. x 25.00 (ISBN 0-678-00081-6). Kelley.

--Harmony of Interests: Agricultural, Manufacturing & Commercial. LC 68-18572. Repr. of 1851 ed. 27.50x (ISBN 0-678-00246-0). Kelley.

--Miscellaneous Works of Henry C. Carey, 2 vols. 1966. Repr. of 1883 ed. Set. 60.50 (ISBN 0-8337-0473-7). B Franklin.

--Past, the Present, & the Future. LC 67-18573. Repr. of 1847 ed. 37.50x (ISBN 0-678-00245-2). Kelley.

--Principles of Political Economy, 3 Vols. LC 65-16983. Repr. of 1837 ed. Set. 87.50x (ISBN 0-678-00071-9). Kelley.

--Principles of Social Science, 3 Vols. LC 63-22257. Repr. of 1859 ed. Set. 125.00x (ISBN 0-678-00013-1). Kelley.

--Slave Trade: Domestic & Foreign. LC 67-18574. Repr. of 1853 ed. 37.50x (ISBN 0-678-00248-7). Kelley.

--Unity of Law: As Exhibited in the Relation of Physical, Social, Mental & Moral Science. LC 67-18575. (Illus.). Repr. of 1872 ed. 37.50x (ISBN 0-678-00247-9). Kelley.

Carey, Howard R. Journey into Light & Joy. LC 79-53905. (Illus.). 180p. 1979. pap. 4.50 (ISBN 0-87516-380-7). De Vorss.

Carey, Hugh. Duet for Two Voices. LC 78-62115. (Illus.). 1980. 34.50 (ISBN 0-521-22312-1). Cambridge U Pr.

--Mansfield Forbes & His Cambridge. (Illus.). 172p. 1984. 29.95 (ISBN 0-521-25680-1). Cambridge U Pr.

Carey, Iskandar. Orang Asli: The Aboriginal Tribes of Peninsular Malaysia. 1976. 29.95x (ISBN 0-19-580270-5). Oxford U Pr.

Carey, J., jt. auth. see Franck, T. M.

Carey, J., ed. see Taubenfeld, Howard J. & Taubenfeld, Rita.

Carey, James. When the Doors Break. 1982. 7.75 (ISBN 0-8062-1870-3). Carlton.

Carey, James C. Kansas State University: The Quest for Identity. LC 77-392. (Illus.). 1977. 12.95x (ISBN 0-7006-0156-2). U Pr of KS.

--The Mexican Revolution in Yucatan, Nineteen Fifteen to Nineteen Twenty-Four. (A Westview Replica Ser.). 250p. 1984. pap. 22.50x (ISBN 0-86531-877-8). Westview.

--Peru & the United States, 1900-1962. 1964. 15.95x (ISBN 0-268-00206-1). U. of Notre Dame Pr.

Carey, James E., et al, eds. CRC Manual of Nuclear Medicine Procedures. 248p. 1983. 39.50 (ISBN 0-8493-0708-2). CRC Pr.

Carey, James T. Introduction to Criminology. 1978. ref. ed. 29.95 (ISBN 0-13-481143-7). P-H.

Carey, James T. & McAnany, Patrick D. Introduction to Juvenile Delinquency: Youth & the Law. LC 83-10997. 1982. 26.95 (ISBN 0-13-485458-6). P-H.

Carey, Jane P. & Carey, Andrew G. The Web of Modern Politics. LC 68-28394. (Illus.). 240p. 1968. 26.00x (ISBN 0-231-03170-X). Columbia U Pr.

Carey, Jocelyn E. Handbook of Selected Poems. 1984. 5.75 (ISBN 0-8062-2363-4). Carlton.

Carey, John. English Renaissance Studies: Presented to Dame Helen Gardner in Honour of Her Seventieth Birthday. (Illus.). 1980. 49.00x (ISBN 0-19-812093-1). Oxford U Pr.

--Hand to Hand. LC 83-7851. 48p. 1983. pap. 4.50 (ISBN 0-915306-40-9). Curbstone.

--International Protection of Human Rights. LC 68-27153. (Hammarskjold Forum Ser.: No. 12). 128p. 1968. 10.00 (ISBN 0-379-11812-2). Oceana.

--John Donne: Life, Mind & Art. 1981. 25.00x (ISBN 0-19-520242-2). Oxford U Pr.

--Thackeray: Prodigal Genius. 212p. (Orig.). 1980. pap. 7.95 (ISBN 0-571-11505-5). Faber & Faber.

--UN Protection of Civil & Political Rights, Vol. 8. (Procedural Aspects of International Law Ser.). 205p. 1970. 20.00x (ISBN 0-8156-2146-9). U Pr of Va.

--The Violent Effigy. LC 74-160359. 184p. 1979. pap. 5.95 (ISBN 0-571-11370-2). Faber & Faber.

Carey, John & Fowler, Alastair. Poems of Milton. (Longman Annotated English Poets Ser.). 1181p. 1980. text ed. 60.00x (ISBN 0-582-48443-X). Longman.

Carey, John, ed. John Milton: Complete Shorter Poems. (Longman Annotated English Poets Ser.). (Illus.). 1971. pap. text ed. 14.50x (ISBN 0-582-48456-1). Longman.

Carey, John, ed. see Hogg, James.

Carey, John, ed. see Levie, H. S.

Carey, John, ed. see Metzger, Stanley D.

Carey, John see Milton, John.

Carey, John A. Judical Reform in France Before the Revolution of 1789. LC 81-6463. (Historical Studies: No. 99). (Illus.). 176p. 1981. text ed. 22.50x (ISBN 0-674-48878-4). Harvard U Pr.

Carey, John J. Carlyle Marney: A Pilgrim's Progress. LC 80-82573. xii, 156p. 1980. pap. 7.95 (ISBN 0-86554-001-2). Mercer Univ Pr.

--Kairos & Logos: Studies in the Roots & Implications of Tillich Society. LC 84-6738. 306p. 1984. Repr. of 1978 ed. 15.95x (ISBN 0-86554-106-X, MUP/H100). Mercer Univ Pr.

Carey, John J., ed. Theonomy & Autonomy: Studies in Paul Tillich's Engagement with Modern Culture. LC 83-25847. xxii, 287p. 1984. Repr. of 1978 ed. 21.95x (ISBN 0-86554-105-1, MUP/H99). Mercer Univ Pr.

Carey, John L. From Technician to Professional 1896-1936. 387p. Vol. I. 16.50 (ISBN 0-317-32892-1). Am Inst CPA.

--Professional Ethics of Public Accounting. Brief, Richard P., ed. LC 80-1476. (Dimensions of Accounting Theory & Practice Ser.). 1981. Repr. of 1946 ed. lib. bdg. 14.00x (ISBN 0-405-13506-8). Ayer Co Pubs.

--The Rise of the Accounting Profession, 2 vols. 1969. Set. 36.50 (ISBN 0-685-05617-1). Am Inst CPA.

Carey, John L. & Skousen, K. Fred. Getting Acquainted with Accounting. 2nd ed. LC 76-10904. (Illus.). 1977. pap. text ed. 13.95 (ISBN 0-395-24513-3). HM.

Carey, Jonathan S., jt. ed. see Ahlstrom, Sydney E.

Carey, Joshua see Crosby, Elizabeth C., et al.

Carey, Karen L. The Last Voyage of Odysseus: A Novel. LC 82-3970. (Illus.). xii, 187p. 1983. text ed. 16.95x (ISBN 0-8214-0683-3, 82-84515); pap. 9.95 (ISBN 0-8214-0749-X, 82-84523). Ohio U Pr.

Carey, Katherine & Burdick, Holly, eds. Drug Interactions. LC 84-5639. (Nursing Now Ser.). (Illus.). 136p. 1984. text ed. 13.95 (ISBN 0-916730-78-6). Springhouse Corp.

Carey, Katherine & Perkins, Alice, eds. Shock. LC 83-20068. (Nursing Now Ser.). 136p. 1984. text ed. 13.95 (ISBN 0-916730-63-8). Springhouse Corp.

Carey, Katherine W., ed. Pain. (Nursing Now Ser.). (Illus.). 128p. 1985. text ed. 13.95 (ISBN 0-916730-81-6). Springhouse Corp.

Carey, Katherine W. & West, Richard S., eds. Professional Guide to Diseases. LC 81-19996. (Illus.). 1300p. 1982. text ed. 22.95 (ISBN 0-916730-36-0). Springhouse Corp.

Carey, Kay. The Awakening Notes. (Cliffs Notes Ser.). 74p. (Orig.). 1980. pap. text ed. 3.75 (ISBN 0-8220-0218-3). Cliffs.

Carey, Ken. Notes to My Children: A Simplified Metaphysics. Gross, Jim, ed. (Illus.). 160p. (Orig.). 1984. pap. 8.95 (ISBN 0-912949-01-5). Uni-Sun.

--Terra Christa: The Global Spiritual Awakening. Gross, Jim, ed. 256p. (Orig.). 1985. pap. 7.95t (ISBN 0-912949-02-3). Uni-Sun.

Carey, Larry L. Colonial & Revolutionary American Literature: Recent Scholarship, Since Nineteen Seventy-Five. 74p. 1985. text ed. 17.95x (ISBN 0-8290-0742-3); pap. text ed. 8.95x (ISBN 0-8290-1534-5). Irvington.

Carey, Len. Doberman Pinschers. (Illus.). 80p. 1984. pap. 3.95 (ISBN 0-86622-249-9, PB-107). TFH Pubns.

Carey, Lou, jt. auth. see Dick, Walter.

Carey, Lou M. & Marsh, David D. University Roles in Inservice Education: Planning for Change. 102p. (Orig.). 1980. pap. text ed. write for info. (ISBN 0-89333-018-3). AACTE.

Carey, M. V. Alfred Hitchcock & the Three Investigators in the Mystery of the Magic Circle. LC 78-55915. (Alfred Hitchcock & the Three Investigators Ser.: No. 27). (Illus.). (gr. 4-7). 1978. (BYR); PLB 5.39 (ISBN 0-394-93607-8). Random.

--Alfred Hitchcock & the Three Investigators in the Mystery of Death Trap Mine. LC 76-8135. (Illus.). (gr. 4-7). 1976. lib. bdg. 2.95 (ISBN 0-394-83321-X, BYR); PLB 5.99 (ISBN 0-394-93321-4). Random.

--Alfred Hitchcock & the Three Investigators in the Mystery of the Flaming Footprints. Hitchcock, Alfred, ed. (Three Investigators Ser.: No. 15). (Illus.). (gr. 4-7). 1971. 2.95 (ISBN 0-394-83776-2, BYR). Random.

--Alfred Hitchcock & the Three Investigators in the Mystery of the Singing Serpent. Hitchcock, Alfred, ed. (Three Investigators Ser.: No. 17). (Illus.). (gr. 4-7). 1972. (BYR); PLB 5.99 (ISBN 0-394-92408-8). Random.

--Alfred Hitchcock & the Three Investigators in the Mystery of Monster Mountain. Hitchcock, Alfred, ed. (Three Investigators Ser.: No. 20). (Illus.). (gr. 4-7). 1973. (BYR). Random.

--Alfred Hitchcock & the Three Investigators in the Secret of the Haunted Mirror. LC 74-5750. (Tree Investigators Ser.). (Illus.). 160p. (gr. 4-7). 1974. (BYR). Random.

--The Mystery of Monster Mountain. LC 79-11372. (gr. 4-7). 1979. pap. 1.95 (ISBN 0-394-84259-6, BYR). Random.

--The Mystery of the Blazing Cliffs. Hitchcock, Alfred, ed. LC 80-10954. (The Three Investigators Mystery Ser.: No. 32). 192p. (gr. 4-7). 1981. PLB 5.99 (ISBN 0-394-94504-2); pap. 1.95 (ISBN 0-394-84504-8). Random.

--The Mystery of the Creep-Show Crooks. LC 85-2237. (The Three Investigators Mystery Ser.). (Illus.). 192p. (gr. 4-7). 1985. pap. 1.95 (ISBN 0-394-87382-3, BYR); PLB 5.99 (ISBN 0-394-97382-8). Random.

--The Mystery of the Invisible Dog. LC 79-27778. (Alfred Hitchcock & the Three Investigators Ser.). 160p. (gr. 4-7). 1981. pap. 1.95 (ISBN 0-394-86423-9). Random.

--The Mystery of the Magic Circle. LC 79-27657. (Alfred Hitchcock & the Three Investigators Ser.). 160p. (gr. 4-7). 1981. pap. 1.95 (ISBN 0-394-84490-4). Random.

--The Mystery of the Missing Mermaid. LC 83-3030. (The Three Investigators Mystery Ser.: No.36). (Illus.). 192p. (gr. 4-7). 1983. pap. 1.95 (ISBN 0-394-85875-1); PLB 5.99 (ISBN 0-394-95875-6). Random.

--The Mystery of the Scar-Faced Beggar. LC 81-4040. (The Three Investigators Mystery Ser.: No. 31). 192p. (gr. 4-7). 1981. PLB 5.39 (ISBN 0-394-94903-X); pap. 1.95 (ISBN 0-394-84903-5). Random.

--The Mystery of the Trail of Terror. LC 84-1952. (The Three Investigators Mystery Ser.: No. 39). (Illus.). 192p. (gr. 4-7). 1984. pap. 1.95 (ISBN 0-394-86609-6, Pub. by BYR); lib. bdg. 5.99 GLB (ISBN 0-394-96609-0). Random.

--The Mystery of the Wandering Cave Man. LC 82-3667. (The Three Investigators Mystery Ser.: No. 34). (Illus.). 192p. (gr. 4-7). 1982. PLB 5.99 (ISBN 0-394-95278-2); pap. 1.95 (ISBN 0-394-85278-8). Random.

Carey, MacDonald. Out of Heart. Adler, Andrew & Adler, Roger, eds. 1979. 5.95 (ISBN 0-916844-04-8). Turtle Pr.

Carey, Margaret S. & Hainline, Patricia H. Brownsville: Linn County's Oldest Town. (Illus.). 48p. 1976. pap. 3.95 (ISBN 0-934784-01-9). Calapooia Pubns.

--Sweet Home in the Oregon Cascades. (Illus.). 140p. 1979. pap. 6.95 (ISBN 0-934784-04-3). Calapooia Pubns.

Carey, Mary. Caverns of Fear. (Golden Super Adventure Books). (Illus.). 24p. (gr. k-3). 1983. pap. 1.95 (ISBN 0-307-11794-4, 11794, Golden Bks). Western Pub.

--A Place for Allie. 160p. (gr. 2-7). 1985. PLB 11.95 (ISBN 0-396-08583-0). Dodd.

--Walt Disney's Happy, Healthy Pooh Book. (Look-Look Ser.). (Illus.). 24p. (ps-3). 1977. pap. 1.50 (ISBN 0-307-11832-0, Golden Bks). Western Pub.

--Walt Disney's Peter Pan & Captain Hook. (Disney's Wonderful World of Reading Ser.: No. 4). (Illus.). (ps-3). 1973. 5.95 (ISBN 0-394-82517-9, BYR); PLB 4.99 (ISBN 0-394-92517-3). Random.

Carey, Mary & Sherman, George. A Compendium of Bunk or How to Spot a Con Artist: A Handbook for Fraud Investigators, Bankers & Other Custodians of the Public Trust. 216p. 1976. 16.50x (ISBN 0-398-03498-2); pap. 11.50x (ISBN 0-398-03501-6). C C Thomas.

Carey, Mary, jt. auth. see McCormick, Harry.

Carey, Mary, ed. see Massachusetts General Hospital Department of Dietetics Staff.

Carey, Mary B., ed. Napa Valley Guide, 1985. (Illus.). 112p. 1985. pap. text ed. 3.75 (ISBN 0-931973-01-5). Vintage Pubns.

--Napa Valley Guide, 1986. (Illus.). 112p. 1986. pap. text ed. 3.95 (ISBN 0-931973-03-1). Vintage Pubns.

--Sonoma Guide: 1985-1986. (Illus.). 96p. 1985. pap. text ed. 3.95 (ISBN 0-931973-02-3). Vintage Pubns.

Carey, Mary K. How Long Must I Hide. 240p. 1983. 12.95 (ISBN 0-89015-412-0). Eakin Pubns.

Carey, Mathew. Addresses of the Philadelphia Society for the Promotion of National Industry. Hudson, Michael, ed. Bd. with Essay on Expediency & Practicability of Improving or Creating Home Markets for the Sale of Agricultural Productions & Raw Materials. Tibbits, George. (The Neglected American Economists Ser.). 1974. lib. bdg. 61.00 (ISBN 0-8240-1000-0). Garland Pub.

--Autobiographical Sketches. LC 70-125683. (American Journalists Ser.). 1970. Repr. of 1829 ed. 20.00 (ISBN 0-405-01660-3). Ayer Co Pubs.

--Essays on Banking: With a Selection of His Other Writings on Banking. LC 68-27850. Repr. of 1816 ed. lib. bdg 37.50x (ISBN 0-678-00801-9). Kelley.

--Olive Branch: or, Faults on Both Sides, Federal & Democratic. facsimile ed. LC 69-16848. (Select Bibliographies Reprint Ser). 1818. 26.50 (ISBN 0-8369-5002-X). Ayer Co Pubs.

--Short Account of the Malignant Fever, Lately Prevalent in Philadelphia. LC 73-112531. (Rise of Urban America). 1970. Repr. of 1794 ed. 12.00 (ISBN 0-405-02441-X). Ayer Co Pubs.

Carey, Matthew. Essays on Political Economy. LC 66-21660. Repr. of 1822 ed. 47.50x (ISBN 0-678-00285-1). Kelley.

--Miscellaneous Essays, 2 Vols. in 1. 1966. Repr. of 1830 ed. 32.00 (ISBN 0-8337-0469-9). B Franklin.

Carey, Maureen, et al. Deciding on the Human Use of Power. LC 73-83110. (Decision-Making Skills Ser.). (Illus.). 130p. (Orig.). (gr. 10-12). 1974. 4.89 (ISBN 0-88343-672-8). McDougal-Littell.

Carey, Michael. THe Noise the Earth Makes. (Iowa Poets Ser.: No. 1). (Illus.). 56p. (Orig.). 1985. 25.00 (ISBN 0-931757-19-3); pap. 15.00 (ISBN 0-931757-20-7). Pterodactyl Pr.

Carey, Michael J., jt. ed. see Balaam, David N.

Carey, Neil G. A Guide to the Queen Charlotte Islands. 6th ed. LC 81-12794. (Illus.). 82p. 1985. pap. 4.95 (ISBN 0-88240-252-8). Alaska Northwest.

Carey, Omer & Olson, Dean. Financial Tools for Small Business. 1983. 19.95 (ISBN 0-8359-2043-7); pap. 14.95 (ISBN 0-8359-2042-9). Reston.

--Opportunity Management: Strategic Planning for Small Business. 1984. text ed. 21.95 (ISBN 0-8359-5260-6); pap. 14.95 (ISBN 0-8359-5259-2). Reston.

--Opportunity Management: Strategic Planning for Smaller Business. price not set. P-H.

Carey, P. B., ed. The Archive of Yogyakarta, Vol.1. (British Academy Ser.). (Illus.). 1980. 84.00x (ISBN 0-19-725997-9). Oxford U Pr.

Carey, P. R. Biochemical Applications of Raman & Resonance Raman Spectroscopies. (Molecular Biology Ser.). 1982. 44.00 (ISBN 0-12-159650-8). Acad Pr.

Carey, Patrick. An Immigrant Bishop: John England's Adaptation of Irish Catholicism to American Republicanism. LC 79-63860. (USCHS Monograph: Vol. 36). (Illus.). ix, 236p. 1982. 14.95x (ISBN 0-930060-16-4). US Cath Hist.

Carey, Patrick, ed. see Ignatow, David.

Carey, Patrick D. Chicanismo: Hypothesis, Thesis & Argument. (Philosophy Ser.). 200p. (Orig.). 1983. pap. text ed. 10.95 (ISBN 0-941018-11-3). Martin Pr CA.

Carey, Peggie L., jt. ed. see Holden, David F.

Carey, Peter. Bliss. LC 81-47881. 304p. 1982. 13.41i (ISBN 0-06-014959-0, HarpT). Har-Row.

--Illywhacker. LC 84-48583. 512p. 1985. 18.22 (ISBN 0-06-015425-X, HarpT). Har-Row.

Carey, Raymond G., jt. auth. see Posavac, Emil J.

Carey, Robert J., jt. auth. see Coulacos, Spero.

Carey, Robert K. I've Never Known a Happily Married Couple. O'Connell, Patrick, ed. 1969. pap. 1.25 (ISBN 0-911776-03-6). Hogarth.

Carey, Robert K., jt. auth. see Wong, Helen H.

Carey, Robert L. Daniel Webster As an Economist. LC 29-15020. (Columbia University Studies in the Social Sciences: No. 313). Repr. of 1929 ed. 16.00 (ISBN 0-404-51313-1). AMS Pr.

Carey, Robert M., jt. auth. see Edwards, C. R.

Carey, Robin. Beautiful Mt. Hood. LC 78-102323. (Illus.). 1977. 12.95 (ISBN 0-915796-27-9); pap. 7.95 (ISBN 0-915796-26-0). Beautiful Am.

Carey, Roy & Isaac, E. D. Magnetic Domains & Techniques for Their Observation. 1966. 52.50 (ISBN 0-12-159550-1). Acad Pr.

Carey, Sandra H. Sexual Harrassment: A Management Issue. Date not set. text ed. price not set (ISBN 0-8290-1055-6). Irvington.

--Social Stress & Mortality. 400p. Date not set. text ed. price not set (ISBN 0-8290-1542-6). Irvington.

Carey, Susan. Conceptual Change in Childhood. (LDCC Learning, Development, & Conceptual Change Ser.). (Illus.). 168p. 1985. text ed. 15.00x (ISBN 0-262-03110-8, Pub. by Bradford). MIT Pr.

Carey, Valerie S. Harriet & William & the Terrible Creature. (Illus.). 32p. (ps-1). 1985. 11.95 (ISBN 0-525-44154-9, 01160-350). Dutton.

Carey, W. S. The Expanding Earth. (Developments in Geotectonics Ser.: Vol. 10). 488p. 1976. 61.75 (ISBN 0-444-41485-1). Elsevier.

Carey, William, jt. ed. see Hutton, Laurence.

Carey, William T. Law Students: How to Get a Job When There Aren't Any. 102p. (Orig.). 1985. lib. bdg. 10.75 (ISBN 0-89089-301-2); pap. 5.75 (ISBN 0-89089-300-4). Carolina Acad Pr.

Carey, Zenja & Habeeb, Virginia. The Complete Blender Cookbook. LC 78-52133. 1978. 9.95 (ISBN 0-87502-059-3); pap. 4.95 (ISBN 0-87502-060-7). Benjamin Co.

Careyhill, T. Arthur, et al. The Scientist's Answer to the Problem of Weight Loss, Weight Control & Dieting. (Illus.). 192p. 15.95 (ISBN 0-943792-00-2); pap. 11.95 (ISBN 0-943792-01-0). Pacific Scientific.

Carey Jones, N. S. The Pattern of a Dependent Economy: The National Income of British Honduras. LC 77-157955. (Illus.). 162p. Repr. of 1953 ed. lib. bdg. 15.00 (ISBN 0-8371-6178-9, CADE). Greenwood.

Carey-Jones, N. S., et al. Politics, Public Enterprise & the Industrial Development Agency: Industrialisation Policies & Practices. 248p. 1975. 22.50x (ISBN 0-8419-5500-X). Holmes & Meier.

Carfagno, Vincent R., tr. see Reich, Wilhelm.

Carfardi, Nicholas P., jt. auth. see Maida, Adam J.

Carfi, John & Carle, Cliff. Getting Even with the Answering Machine. (Illus.). 96p. (Orig.). 1985. pap. 2.95 (ISBN 0-918259-01-0). CCC Pubns.

--No Hang-Ups: Funny Answering Machine Messages. (Illus.). 132p. (Orig.). 1984. pap. 2.95 (ISBN 0-918259-00-2). CCC Pubns.

Cargan. Marriage & Family: Coping with Change. write for info. (ISBN 0-534-04410-7). Wadsworth Pub.

Cargan & Ballantine. Sociological Footprints: Introductory Readings in Sociology. 3rd ed. 1984. write for info. (ISBN 0-534-03669-4). Wadsworth Pub.

Cargan, Leonard & Melko, Matthew. Singles: Myths & Realities. (Sage Library of Social Research). (Illus.). 256p. 1982. 25.00 (ISBN 0-8039-1806-2); pap. 12.50 (ISBN 0-8039-1807-0). Sage.

Cargas. A Christian Response to the Holocaust. 1981. 10.95 (ISBN 0-937050-16-4). Stonehenge.

--Conversations with Elie Wiesel. 1982. 9.95 (ISBN 0-937050-18-0). Stonehenge.

Cargas, Harry. I Lay Down My Life. 1964. 2.50 (ISBN 0-8198-0063-5); pap. 1.50 (ISBN 0-8198-0064-3). Dghtrs St Paul.

Cargas, Harry J. Daniel Berrigan & Contemporary Protest Poetry. 1972. pap. 5.95x (ISBN 0-8084-0352-4). New Coll U Pr.

Cargas, Harry J. & Corrigan, John T. The Holocaust: An Annotated Bibliography. 1977. pap. text ed. 4.00 (ISBN 0-87507-005-1). Cath Lib Assn.

Cargas, Harry J. & Radley, Roger J. Keeping a Spiritual Journal. LC 80-2072. 128p. 1981. pap. 2.75 (ISBN 0-385-17439-X, Im). Doubleday.

Cargas, Harry J., jt. auth. see Erazmus, Edward T.

Cargas, Harry J., ed. Responses to Elie Wiesel. LC 77-94055. 1978. o. p. 15.00 (ISBN 0-89255-031-7); pap. 5.95 (ISBN 0-89255-032-5). Persea Bks.

--Responses to Elie Wiesel. 286p. 15.00 (ISBN 0-686-95081-X); pap. 5.95 (ISBN 0-686-99458-2). ADL.

Cargas, Henry J., ed. When God & Man Failed: Non-Jewish Views of the Holocaust. 320p. 1981. 16.95 (ISBN 0-02-521300-8). Macmillan.

Cargile, J. Paradoxes. LC 78-67299. (Cambridge Studies in Philosophy). 1979. 39.50 (ISBN 0-521-22475-6). Cambridge U Pr.

Cargile, Wayne. Bible Melodies Chosen. 1971. pap. 1.00 (ISBN 0-87012-106-5). McClain.

--Random Giblets Written. 1973. 1.50 (ISBN 0-87012-162-6). McClain.

--Three Bells Told Again. 1973. 2.00 (ISBN 0-87012-155-3). McClain.

Cargill & Brown. Signos Para el Ingles Exacto: A Book for Spanish-Speaking Families of Deaf Children in Schools Using Signing Exact English. LC 82-61647. (Illus.). 160p. 1983. pap. 10.95 (ISBN 0-916708-06-3). Modern Signs.

Cargill, Burton F., jt. auth. see O'Brien, Michael.

Cargill, Jack. The Second Athenian League: Empire or Free Alliance? 325p. 1981. 36.50x (ISBN 0-520-04069-4). U of Cal Pr.

Cargill, Jennifer S. & Alley, Brian. Practical Approval Plan Management. 104p. 1980. lib. bdg. 29.95x (ISBN 0-912700-52-1). Oryx Pr.

Cargill, Jennifer S., jt. auth. see Alley, Brian.

Cargill, Morris. A Gallery of Nazis. (Illus.). 1978. 12.00 (ISBN 0-8184-0256-3). Lyle Stuart.

--Jamaica Farewell. 1978. 8.95 (ISBN 0-8184-0269-5). Lyle Stuart.

Cargill, Oscar. Drama & Liturgy. LC 73-86272. 1969. Repr. of 1930 ed. lib. bdg. 17.00x (ISBN 0-374-91292-0). Octagon.

Cargill, Thomas & Garcia, Gillian. Financial Deregulation & Monetary Control: Historical Perspective & Impact of the 1980 Act. (Publication Ser.: No. 259). (Illus.). 168p. 1982. pap. 8.95x (ISBN 0-8179-7592-6). Hoover Inst Pr.

Cargill, Thomas F. Money, the Financial System, & Monetary Policy. 2nd ed. (Illus.). 608p. 1983. 29.95 (ISBN 0-13-600361-3). P-H.

--Money, the Financial System & Monetary Policy. 3rd ed. (Illus.). 560p. 1986. text ed. 29.95 (ISBN 0-13-600495-4). P-H.

Cargill, Thomas F. & Garcia, Gillian G. Financial Reform in the 1980s. (Publication Ser.: No. 313). xx, 214p. 1985. pap. text ed. 10.95 (ISBN 0-8179-8132-2); 19.95 (ISBN 0-8179-8131-4). Hoover Inst Pr.

Cargill-Thompson, W. D. The Political Thought of Martin Luther. Broadhead, Philip, ed. LC 83-27521. 204p. 1984. 27.50x (ISBN 0-389-20468-4, 08029). B&N Imports.

Cargill Thompson, W. D. Studies in the Reformation: Luther to Hooker. Dugmore, C. W., ed. 259p. 1980. 58.50 (ISBN 0-485-11187-X, Pub. by Athlone Pr Ltd). Longwood Pub Group.

Cargo, David N. & Mallory, Bob F. Man & His Geologic Environment. 2nd ed. LC 76-7655. 1977. text ed. 29.95 (ISBN 0-201-00894-7). Addison-Wesley.

Cargo, Douglas B. Solid Wastes: Factors Influencing Generation Rates. LC 78-16823. (Research Papers Ser.: No. 174). (Illus.). 1978. pap. 10.00 (ISBN 0-89065-081-0). U Chicago Dept Geog.

Cargo, Robert T. Baudelaire Criticism Nineteen Fifty to Nineteen Sixty-Seven: A Bibliography with Critical Commentary. LC 68-13737. 171p. 1968. 13.50 (ISBN 0-8173-9509-1). U of Ala Pr.

--A Concordance to Baudelaire's "les Fleurs Du Mal". LC 73-15399. 417p. 1975. Repr. of 1965 ed. lib. bdg. 27.50x (ISBN 0-8371-7197-0, CACB). Greenwood.

--Concordance to Baudelaire's Petits Poemes En Prose. LC 76-135707. 480p. 1971. 25.00 (ISBN 0-8173-9601-2). U of Ala Pr.

Carhart, Alfreda. Masoud the Bedouin. facsimile ed. LC 76-150541. (Short Story Index Reprint Ser.). (Illus.). Repr. of 1915 ed. 18.00 (ISBN 0-8369-3838-0). Ayer Co Pubs.

Carhart, Jane M., jt. ed. see Kline, Linda J.

Carhart, Margaret S. The Life & Work of Joanna Baillie. 1923. Repr. 25.00 (ISBN 0-8274-2905-3). R West.

--Life & Work of Joanna Baillie. LC 74-91178. (Yale Studies in English Ser.: No. 64). 215p. 1970. Repr. of 1923 ed. 17.50 (ISBN 0-208-00917-5, Archon). Shoe String.

Cariaga, Roman R. The Filipinos in Hawaii: Thesis. LC 74-76757. 1974. spiral bdg. 9.95 (ISBN 0-88247-224-0). R & E Pubs.

Caribbean Geological Conference (5th: 1968: St. Thomas, Virgin Islands) Staff. Caribbean Geophysical, Tectonic & Petrological Studies. Donnelly, Thomas D., ed. LC 74-165441. (Geological Society of America Memoir Ser.: No. 130). pap. 68.50 (ISBN 0-317-29126-2, 2025025). Bks Demand UMI.

Caribbean Seminar on Science & Technology Policy & Planning, 2nd. Proceedings. (Studies on Scientific & Technological Development: No. 28). 1977. pap. text ed. 4.00 (ISBN 0-8270-6000-9). OAS.

Carico, Charles C. College Algebra & Trigonometry. LC 82-11055. 500p. 1983. text ed. 29.50x (ISBN 0-471-07700-3); student ed. 13.45 (ISBN 0-471-09269-X). Wiley.

--College Algebra with Analytic Geometry. LC 83-12419. 382p. 1984. text ed. 26.95 (ISBN 0-471-88748-X); 9.95 (ISBN 0-471-80055-4); solutions manual 12.50 (ISBN 0-471-87912-6). Wiley.

Carico, Charles C. & Drooyan, Irving. Analytic Geometry. LC 79-21633. 310p. 1980. 31.50x (ISBN 0-471-06435-1); student supplement, 175 p. 14.45 (ISBN 0-471-06378-9). Wiley.

Caridi, Ronald J. Korean War & American Politics: The Republican Party As a Case Study. LC 68-9738. 1969. 15.00x (ISBN 0-8122-7581-0). U of Pa Pr.

Carigan, William. Flying Game. LC 74-13775. 1974. 7.95 (ISBN 0-9605986-1-8). Juniper Pubs.

--Staves for Louisville. LC 81-81067. 1981. 10.95 (ISBN 0-9605986-0-X). Juniper Pubs.

Carillo, Mary. Rick Elstein's Tennis Kinetics with Martina Navratilova. Date not set. price not set. S&S.

Carillo, Mary, jt. auth. see Navratilova, Martina.

Carillon, Annie & Goutel, Beatrice. Grand Dictionnaire du Scrabble. 875p. (Fr.). 1978. 39.95 (ISBN 0-686-56938-5, M-6060). French & Eur.

Carillon, Annie & Goutel, Beatrice de. Dictionnaire du Scrabble. 215p. (Fr.). 1976. pap. 12.95 (ISBN 0-686-56872-9, M-6650). French & Eur.

Carim, Enver, ed. Africa Review, 1985. (World of Information Ser.). pap. 24.95 (ISBN 0-911818-31-6). World Almanac.

Carimed, Envers. Asia & Pacific. 322p. 1984. 24.95. World Almanac.

--Latin America & Pacific. 338p. 1984. cancelled. World Almanac.

Carin, Arthur & Sund, Robert. Teaching Modern Science. 4th ed. 336p. 1984. pap. 16.95 (ISBN 0-675-20221-3). Merrill.

--Teaching Science Through Discovery. 5th ed. 512p. 1985. 25.95 (ISBN 0-675-20387-2). Additional supplements may be obtained from publisher. Merrill.

Carin, Arthur A. & Sund, Robert B. Discovery Activities for Elementary Science. (Elementary Education Ser.: No. C22). 296p. 1980. pap. text ed. 14.50 (ISBN 0-675-08089-4). Merrill.

--Teaching Modern Science. 3rd ed. (Elementary Education Ser.: No. C22). 352p. 1980. pap. text ed. 17.95 (ISBN 0-675-08193-9). Merrill.

Carin, V. S., et al. Nine Papers on Foundations, Algebra, Topology, Functions of a Complex Variable. (Translations Ser.: No. 2, Vol. 15). 1960. 29.00 (ISBN 0-8218-1715-9, TRANS 2-15). Am Math.

Carinat, Alois. The Fully Illustrated Book in Colours of the Crucifixion. (Illus.). 101p. 1983. 275.50x (ISBN 0-86650-078-2). Gloucester Art.

Carington, Whately. Matter, Mind & Meaning. facsimile ed. LC 78-111818. (Essay Index Reprint Ser.). 1949. 21.50 (ISBN 0-8369-1596-8). Ayer Co Pubs.

Carini, Anselmo, tr. see Goguel, Catherine M. & Viatte, Francoise.

Carini, E. Take Another Look. (ps-3). 1969. pap. 1.50. P-H.

Carini, Geraldine & Birmingham, Jacqueline. Traction Made Manageable: A Self Learning Module. (Illus.). 1980. pap. text ed. 24.00 (ISBN 0-07-009841-7). McGraw.

Carini, Louis. The Theory of Symbolic Transformations: A Humanistic Scientific Psychology. LC 83-1049. (Illus.). 176p. (Orig.). 1983. lib. bdg. 23.50 (ISBN 0-8191-3053-2); pap. text ed. 11.25 (ISBN 0-8191-3054-0). U Pr of Amer.

--Three Axioms for a Theory of Conduct: Philosophy, & the Humanistic Science of Psychology. 108p. (Orig.). 1984. pap. text ed. 7.25 (ISBN 0-8191-3971-8). U Pr of Amer.

Carini, P., jt. ed. see Kalman, G.

Carini, Patricia V., jt. auth. see Lewis, Elizabeth N.

Carino, Benjamin V. Filipinos on Oahu, Hawaii. LC 81-5382. (Papers of the East-West Population Institute: No. 72). vii, 46p. (Orig.). 1981. pap. text ed. 1.50 (ISBN 0-86638-019-1). E W Center HI.

Caris, John. Reality Inspector. (Illus.). 1982. pap. 3.95 (ISBN 0-9607320-0-4). Westgate Hse.

Caris, Susan L. Community Attitudes Toward Pollution. LC 78-13164. (Research Papers Ser.: No. 188). (Illus.). 1978. pap. 10.00 (ISBN 0-89065-095-0). U Chicago Dept Geog.

Carisson, C. & Kochetkov, Y., eds. Theory & Practice of Multiple Criteria Decision Making: Collection of Papers Presented at a Workshop, Moscow, May 1981. x, 170p. 1983. 42.75 (ISBN 0-444-86579-9, I-004-83, North-Holland). Elsevier.

Caristi, Anthony J. Electronic Telephone Projects. LC 79-63868. 168p. 1979. pap. 8.95 (ISBN 0-672-21618-3, 21618). Sams.

Caritt, E. F., tr. see Croce, Benedetto.

Carkeet, David. Double Negative. 246p. 1982. pap. 3.50 (ISBN 0-14-006070-7). Penguin.

--The Greatest Slump of All Time. LC 83-48334. 256p. 1984. 14.37i (ISBN 0-06-015250-8, HarpT). Har-Row.

--The Greatest Slump of All Time. (Penguin Fiction Ser.). 240p. 1985. pap. 5.95 (ISBN 0-14-007909-2). Penguin.

--I Been There Before. LC 84-48584. 384p. 1985. 19.22 (ISBN 0-06-015426-8, HarpT). Har-Row.

Carkhuff, Robert. Productive Problem Solving. 150p. 1985. pap. text ed. 15.00 (ISBN 0-87425-019-6). Human Res Dev Pr.

--Productive Program Development. 150p. 1985. 15.00 (ISBN 0-87425-020-X). Human Res Dev Pr.

Carkhuff, Robert, et al. The Skills of Helping: An Introduction to Counseling. LC 78-73987. 262p. 1979. text ed. 15.00 (ISBN 0-914234-09-9); pap. 11.95x (ISBN 0-914234-87-0). Human Res Dev.

--The Skills of Teaching: Interpersonal Skills. (The Skills of Teaching Series: Vol. 1). (Illus., Orig.). 1977. pap. text ed. 9.95x (ISBN 0-914234-20-X); Tchrs. Guide. pap. text ed. 15.00x (ISBN 0-914234-51-X). Human Res Dev Pr.

--The Art of Helping, IV. 4th ed. LC 79-91075. (Life Skills). 243p. pap. text ed. 10.95x (ISBN 0-914234-10-2, CAH4); tchrs. guide 12.95 (ISBN 0-914234-11-0); wkbk. 6.95 (ISBN 0-914234-12-9). Human Res Dev Pr.

Carkhuff, Robert R. Art of Helping Five. (Illus.). 302p. 1983. pap. text ed. 15.00x (ISBN 0-914234-16-1); trainer's guide 10.95 (ISBN 0-914234-66-8); student wkbk. 10.00x (ISBN 0-914234-17-X). Human Res Dev Pr.

--Cry Twice! from Custody to Treatment: Story of Operation Changeover. LC 74-75371. (HRD Perspective Ser.). 142p. 1974. pap. text ed. 10.95x (ISBN 0-914234-80-3). Human Res Dev Pr.

--The Exemplar. 250p. 1984. pap. 25.00 (ISBN 0-914234-79-X). Human Res Dev Pr.

--How to Help Yourself: The Art of Program Development. LC 74-18144. (Life Skills Ser.). (Illus.). 172p. 1974. pap. text ed. 10.00x (ISBN 0-914234-02-1). Human Res Dev Pr.

--Interpersonal Skills & Human Productivity. 120p. 1983. pap. 15.00 (ISBN 0-914234-19-6). Human Res Dev Pr.

--Productive Parenting Skills. 175p. 1985. pap. 15.00 (ISBN 0-87425-018-8). Human Res Dev Pr.

--The Productive Teacher II: An Introduction to Instruction. 232p. 1984. pap. text ed. 20.00 (ISBN 0-914234-78-1). Human Res Dev Pr.

--The Productive Teacher 1: An Introduction to Curriculum Development. 319p. 1984. pap. text ed. 20.00 (ISBN 0-914234-77-3). Human Res Dev Pr.

--The Skilled Teacher: A System Approach to Teaching Skills. (Illus.). 184p. 1981. pap. 15.00 (ISBN 0-914234-52-8). Human Res Dev Pr.

--Sources of Human Productivity. (Illus.). 250p. 1983. 35.00 (ISBN 0-686-45957-1). Human Res Dev Pr.

--Toward Actualizing Human Potential. (Illus.). 184p. 1981. 15.00x (ISBN 0-914234-15-3). Human Res Dev Pr.

Carkhuff, Robert R. & Berenson, Bernard G. Beyond Counseling & Therapy. 2nd ed. LC 76-16184. 295p. 1977. text ed. 23.95 (ISBN 0-03-089812-9, HoltC). HR&W.

Carkhuff, Robert R. & Bernson, Bernard G. Teaching As Treatment. LC 75-40865. (Support Ser.). 150p. 1976. pap. text ed. 11.95x (ISBN 0-914234-84-6). Human Res Dev Pr.

Carkhuff, Robert R. & Fisher, Sharon G. Instructional Systems Design I: Designing the Instructional System. 151p. 1984. pap. text ed. 25.00 (ISBN 0-914234-71-4). Human Res Dev Pr.

--Instructional Systems Design II: Evaluating the Instructional System. 151p. 1984. pap. text ed. 25.00 (ISBN 0-914234-72-2). Human Res Dev Pr.

Carkhuff, Robert R. & Pierce, Richard. Training Delivery Skills I: Preparing the Training Delivery. 281p. 1984. pap. text ed. 25.00. Human Res Dev Pr.

Carkhuff, Robert R. & Pierce, Richard M. Helping Begins at Home. LC 75-40866. (Support Ser.). 121p. 1976. pap. text ed. 10.00x (ISBN 0-914234-05-6). Human Res Dev Pr.

--Training Delivery Skills II: Making the Training Delivery. 209p. 1984. pap. text ed. 25.00 (ISBN 0-914234-74-9). Human Res Dev Pr.

Carkhuff, Robert R., jt. auth. see Collingwood, Tom.

Carkhuff, Robert R., jt. auth. see Friel, Theodore W.

Carkhuff, Robert R., jt. auth. see Truax, Charles B.

Carkhuff, Robert R., et al. GETAJOB. LC 75-1498. 178p. 1975. pap. text ed. 8.95x (ISBN 0-914234-44-7). Human Res Dev Pr.

Carl, Angela, jt. auth. see Lang, June.

Carl, Angela R. A Matter of Choice. 32p. 1984. 4.95 (ISBN 0-317-06084-8). Victor Bks.

--A Matter of Choice. LC 84-7040. (Illus.). 32p. (gr. 2-3). 1984. lib. bdg. 4.95 (ISBN 0-89693-223-0). Dandelion Hse.

Carl, Angela R. & Holmes, Alice C. Growing with Bible Heroes: Grade 4. rev. ed. Miller, Marge, ed. (Basic Bible Readers Ser.). (Illus.). 128p. (gr. 4). 1983. text ed. 7.95 (ISBN 0-87239-664-9, 2954). Standard Pub.

Carl, Ann. The Small World of Long-Distance Sailors. (Illus.). 240p. 1985. pap. 22.95 (ISBN 0-396-08519-9). Dodd.

Carl, Beverly M. A Guide to Incentives for Investing in Brazil. LC 72-95288. vi, 58p. 1972. pap. 3.95 (ISBN 0-87074-133-0). SMU Press.

Carl, Joseph B. Jesus in Our Affluent Society. 208p. 1981. 9.95 (ISBN 0-938234-01-3); pap. 5.95 (ISBN 0-938234-00-5). Ministry Pubns.

Carl, Lillian S. Sabazel. 256p. 1985. pap. 2.75 (ISBN 0-441-74522-9, Pub. by Ace Science Fiction). Ace Bks.

Carl, Linda. The Alumni College Movement. 1977. pap. 10.50 (ISBN 0-89964-001-X). Coun Adv & Supp Ed.

--The Alumni College Movement. 63p. 1977. 10.50 (ISBN 0-89964-001-X). Coun Adv & Supp Ed.

Carl, Mary K. & Kramer, Marlene. Curriculum in Graduate Education in Nursing: Part I - Factors Influencing Curriculum in Graduate Education in Nursing. 61p. 1975. 5.95 (ISBN 0-88737-188-4, 15-1596). Natl League Nurse.

Carl Vinson Institute of Government, et al. Handbook for Georgia Mayors & Council Members. LC 84-5094. 1984. 14.95 (ISBN 0-89854-096-8). U of Ga Inst Govt.

Carl, William J., II. Preaching Christian Doctrine. LC 83-48923. pap. 8.95 (ISBN 0-8006-1788-6). Fortress.

Carl, William J., III, jt. auth. see Pervo, Richard I.

Carl, William J., III, jt. auth. see Vawter, Bruce.

Carland, John. The Colonial Office & Nigeria Eighteen Ninety-Five to Nineteen Fourteen. (Publication Ser.: 314). 200p. 1985. lib. bdg. 26.95x (ISBN 0-8179-8141-1). Hoover Inst Pr.

Carlander, Kenneth D. Handbook of Freshwater Fishery Biology, Vol. 2. 1977. text ed. 21.50x (ISBN 0-8138-0670-4). Iowa St U Pr.

Carlaw, Raymond W., ed. Perspectives on Community Health Education: A Series of Case Studies. LC 80-54741. 224p. 1982. pap. text ed. 7.95x (ISBN 0-89914-007-6). Third Party Pub.

Carlberg, Bo Casten. The Creative Cooperation Movement: The Swedish Cutting Edge to Productivity & Quality Work Life. LC 82-60736. 120p. 1982. softcover 8.95 (ISBN 0-913420-13-1). Olympus Pub Co.

Carlberg, David M. Essentials of Bacterial & Viral Genetics. (Illus.). 336p. 1976. photocopy ed. 45.50x (ISBN 0-398-03493-1). C C Thomas.

Carlbom, Ingrid. High-Performance Graphics System Architecture: A Methodology for Design & Evaluation. Stone, Harold S., ed. LC 84-2673. (Computer Science: Systems Programming Ser.: No. 21). 182p. 1984. 39.95 (ISBN 0-8357-1595-7). UMI Res Pr.

Carle, Cliff, jt. auth. see Carfi, John.

Carle, Don De see DeCarle, Don.

Carle, Eric. Catch the Ball. 10p. 1982. 4.95 (ISBN 0-399-20885-2, Philomel). Putnam Pub Group.

--Do You Want to Be My Friend? LC 70-140643. (Very First Step to Reading Bk). (Illus.). (gr. k-3). 1971. 11.49i (ISBN 0-690-24276-X); PLB 11.89 (ISBN 0-690-43307-7). Crowell Jr Bks.

--The Grouchy Ladybug. LC 77-3170. (Illus.). (ps). 1977. 10.53i (ISBN 0-690-01391-4); PLB 10.89 (ISBN 0-690-01392-2). Crowell Jr Bks.

--The Honeybee & the Robber: A Moving Picture Book. (Illus.). 16p. (gr. 4-8). 1981. 10.95 (ISBN 0-399-20767-8, Philomel). Putnam Pub Group.

--I See a Song. LC 72-9249. (Illus.). (ps-2). 1973. PLB 11.49i (ISBN 0-690-43307-7). Crowell Jr Bks.

--Let's Paint a Rainbow. 10p. 1982. 4.95 (ISBN 0-399-20881-X, Philomel). Putnam Pub Group.

--The Mixed-up Chameleon. LC 75-5505. (Illus.). (gr. k-2). 1975. 10.53i (ISBN 0-690-00605-5). Crowell Jr Bks.

--The Mixed-Up Chameleon. 2nd ed. LC 83-45950. (Illus.). 32p. (ps-3). 1984. 12.02i (ISBN 0-690-04396-1); PLB 11.89g (ISBN 0-690-04397-X). Crowell Jr Bks.

--My Very First Book of Colors. LC 72-83776. (My Very First Library). (Illus.). 10p. (ps). 1985. 2.95i (ISBN 0-690-57365-0). Crowell Jr Bks.

--My Very First Book of Numbers. LC 72-83777. (My Very First Library). (Illus.). 10p. (ps). 1985. 2.95i (ISBN 0-690-57366-9). Crowell Jr Bks.

--My Very First Book of Shapes. LC 72-83778. (My Very First Library). (Illus.). 10p. (ps). 1985. 2.95i (ISBN 0-690-57367-7). Crowell Jr Bks.

--My Very First Book of Words. LC 72-83779. (My Very First Library). (Illus.). 10p. (ps). 1985. 2.95i (ISBN 0-690-57368-5). Crowell Jr Bks.

--Secret Birthday Message. LC 75-168726. (Illus.). (ps-3). 1972. 11.49i (ISBN 0-690-72347-4); PLB 11.89 (ISBN 0-690-72348-2). Crowell Jr Bks.

--The Very Busy Spider. LC 84-5907. (Illus.). 32p. (ps-2). 1984. 14.95 (ISBN 0-399-21166-7, Philomel). Putnam Pub Group.

--Very Hungry Caterpillar. LC 70-82764. (Ger). (ps-2). 1981. 12.95 (ISBN 0-399-20853-4, Philomel). Putnam Pub Group.

--What's for Lunch? 10p. 1982. 4.95 (ISBN 0-399-20897-6, Philomel). Putnam Pub Group.

Carle, Erica. Give Us the Young. LC 81-71144. 96p. (Orig.). 1982. pap. 4.00 (ISBN 0-942130-00-6). Echoes & Shadows.

Carle, Teet, jt. auth. see Webb, Richard.

Carlebach, Julius. Karl Marx & the Radical Critique of Judaism. (LLJC Ser.). 478p. 1978. 43.00x (ISBN 0-19-710031-7). Oxford U Pr.

Carlebach, Shlomo. Holy Beggar Teachings: Jewish Hasidic Stories, 1975-1977. Maimes, Steven L. & Rappaport, Elana, eds. 1979. pap. 4.95 (ISBN 0-917246-06-3). Maimes.

Carlen, Pat. Women's Imprisonment: The Meanings of Women's Imprisonment in Scotland. 192p. (Orig.). 1983. pap. 10.50x (ISBN 0-7100-9441-8). Routledge & Kegan.

Carlen, Pat, ed. The Sociology of Law. LC 78-323107. (Sociological Review Monograph: No. 23). 250p. 1976. pap. 23.50x (ISBN 0-8476-2296-7). Rowman.

Carlen, Pat & Collison, Mike, eds. Radical Issues in Criminology. 212p. 1980. 28.50x (ISBN 0-389-20083-2, 06856). B&N Imports.

Carlen, Pat, et al, eds. Criminal Women: Some Autobiographical Accounts. 252p. 1985. 24.95x (ISBN 0-7456-0087-5); pap. 8.95x (ISBN 0-7456-0088-3). Basil Blackwell.

Carleon, A. The May Spoon. LC 81-6101. 207p. 1981. 10.95 (ISBN 0-8253-0059-2). Beaufort Bks NY.

Carles, A. B. Sheep Production in the Tropics. (Tropical Handbooks). (Illus.). 1983. 31.95x (ISBN 0-19-859449-6). Oxford U Pr.

Carleson, Lennart, jt. auth. see Salem, Raphael.

Carless, Geoff. Advanced Motorcycling. 128p. 1982. 25.00x (ISBN 0-7158-0776-5, Pub. by EP Pub England). State Mutual Bk.

Carleton & Agalloco. Practical Pharmceutic Aseptic Production. 736p. 1986. price not set (ISBN 0-8247-7362-4). Dekker.

Carleton, A. J. Absorption of Odours: Summary Report, 1979. 1981. 65.00x (ISBN 0-686-97007-1, Pub. by W Spring England). State Mutual Bk.

--Odour Control by Thermal Incineration, 1978. 1981. 75.00x (ISBN 0-686-97130-2, Pub. by W Spring England). State Mutual Bk.

Carleton, A. J. & French, R. J. Hydraulic Transport of Limestone Aggregates & Colliery Spoil, 1978. 1981. 80.00x (ISBN 0-686-97086-1, Pub. by W Spring England). State Mutual Bk.

Carleton, Ardis, ed. Guide to Microforms in Print: Author-Title 1980. LC 61-7082. 1980. 49.50x (ISBN 0-913672-35-1). Microform Rev.

--Guide to Microforms in Print: Subject. 1980. LC 61-7082. 1980. 49.50x (ISBN 0-913672-36-X). Microform Rev.

Carleton, Ardis V. Guide to Microforms in Print: 1983 Supplement. 200p. 1983. 50.00x (ISBN 0-930466-74-8). Meckler Pub.

Carleton, Ardis V., ed. Guide to Microforms in Print: Author-Title, 1981. LC 61-7082. 900p. 1981. 84.50x (ISBN 0-913672-40-8). Microform Rev.

--Guide to Microforms in Print: Author-Title. 1200p. 1983. 102.50x (ISBN 0-930466-78-0). Meckler Pub.

--Guide to Microforms in Print: Subject. 1500p. 1983. 109.50x (ISBN 0-930466-79-9). Meckler Pub.

--Guide to Microforms in Print: Subject, 1981. LC 61-7082. 1400p. 1981. 89.50x (ISBN 0-913672-44-0). Microform Rev.

--Guide to Microforms in Print, 1982. 1200p. 1982. Vol. 1, subject. 89.50x (ISBN 0-930466-51-9); Vol. 2, Author-Title. 84.50x (ISBN 0-930466-50-0). Meckler Pub.

--Microform Market Place Nineteen Eighty to Nineteen Eighty-One. 4th ed. 250p. 1980. pap. text ed. 20.95x (ISBN 0-913672-37-8). Microform Rev.

Carleton, Don E. Red Scare. Lubeck, Scott, ed. 1985. 18.95 (ISBN 0-932012-90-6). Texas Month Pr.

Carleton, Frances B. The Dramatic Monologue: Vox Humana. (Salzburg Studies in English Literature: Romantic Reassessment: 64). 1977. pap. text ed. 25.50x (ISBN 0-391-01340-8). Humanities.

Carleton, George. Jurisdiction Regall, Episcopall, Papall. LC 68-54625. (English Experience Ser.: No. 34). 302p. 1969. Repr. of 1610 ed. 30.00 (ISBN 90-221-0034-0). Walter J Johnson.

--The Madness of Astrologers: Or, an Examination of Sir C. Heydons Booke. LC 68-54626. (English Experience Ser.: No. 53). 124p. 1968. Repr. of 1624 ed. 16.00 (ISBN 90-221-0053-7). Walter J Johnson.

Carleton, George W., ed. Suppressed Book About Slavery. LC 68-28987. (American Negro: His History & Literature Ser., No. 1). (Illus.). 1968. Repr. of 1864 ed. 19.00 (ISBN 0-405-01806-1). Ayer Co Pubs.

Carleton, J. Henry. The Prarie Logbooks: Dragoon Campaigns to the Pawnee Villages in 1844, & to the Rocky Mountains in 1845. Pelzer, Louis, ed. (Illus.). xviii, 295p. 1983. 22.95x (ISBN 0-8032-1422-7); pap. 7.50 (ISBN 0-8032-6314-7, BB 845, Bison). U of Nebr Pr.

Carleton, Jetta. The Moonflower Vine. 352p. (Orig.). 1984. pap. 3.95 (ISBN 0-553-24422-1). Bantam.

Carleton, John L. & Mahlendorf, Ursula. Man for Man: A Multidisciplinary Workshop on Affecting Man's Social & Psychological Nature Through Community Action. 384p. 1973. 39.75x (ISBN 0-398-02754-4). C C Thomas.

Carleton, John L. & Mahlendorf, Ursula R., eds. Dimensions of Social Psychiatry. new ed. LC 78-4347. (Illus.). 1979. lib. bdg. 39.00 (ISBN 0-89500-014-8). Sci Pr.

Carleton, Marjorie. Vanished. LC 81-47092. 256p. 1981. pap. 2.40i (ISBN 0-06-080559-5, P 559, PL). Har-Row.

Carleton, Mark T. Politics & Punishment: The History of the Louisiana State Penal System. LC 78-165067. xii, 216p. 1971. pap. 14.95x (ISBN 0-8071-1219-4). La State U Pr.

Carleton, Patrick. Buried Empires: The Earliest Civilizations of The Middle East. LC 78-14110. (Illus.). 1979. Repr. of 1939 ed. 26.50 (ISBN 0-88355-782-7). Hyperion Conn.

Carleton, R. Milton. Vegetables for Today's Gardens. pap. 2.00 (ISBN 0-87980-226-X). Wilshire.

Carleton, R. O., jt. auth. see Jaffe, A.

Carleton, Ralph A. Biological & Ethical Deviations in Human Beings. (Illus.). 1980. 67.75 (ISBN 0-89920-007-9). Am Inst Psych.

Carleton, William. The Black Prophet. 408p. 1972. Repr. of 1899 ed. 20.00 (ISBN 0-7165-1798-1, BBA 02225, Pub by Irish Academic Pr). Biblio Dist.

--Fardorougha the Miser; or, the Convicts of Lisnamona. LC 79-8245. Repr. of 1839 ed. 44.50 (ISBN 0-404-61805-7). AMS Pr.

--The Tithe Proctor: Being a Tale of the Tithe Rebellion in Ireland. LC 79-8246. Repr. of 1849 ed. 44.50 (ISBN 0-404-61806-5). AMS Pr.

--Traits & Stories of the Irish Peasantry: With Illustrations by Phiz, Wrightson Lee & Others, 4 vols. facsimile ed. LC 79-163022. (Short Story Index Reprint Ser.). (Illus.). Repr. of 1853 ed. Set. 80.00 (ISBN 0-8369-3936-0). Ayer Co Pubs.

--Valentine M'Clutchy, the Irish Agent: The Chronicles of Castle Cumber Property, with the Pious Aspirations of Solomon M'Slime, 3 vols. in 2. LC 79-8247. Repr. of 1845 ed. 84.50 set (ISBN 0-404-61807-3). AMS Pr.

--Works of William Carleton, 2 Vols. facsimile ed. LC 77-106257. (Short Story Index Reprint Ser.). 1881. Set. 88.00 (ISBN 0-8369-3294-3). Ayer Co Pubs.

Carleton, William G. Technology & Humanism: Some Exploratory Essays for Our Times. LC 70-112601. 1970. 17.95x (ISBN 0-8265-1154-6). Vanderbilt U Pr.

Carley, Ed. Way of the Cross. (gr. 4-6). 1985. 9.95 (ISBN 0-89837-101-5, Pub. by Pflaum Press). Peter Li.

Carley, Eliane. Classics from a French Kitchen: Delicious Recipes, Both Ancient & Modern, Together with Savory History & Gastronomic Lore in the Grand Tradition of the Cuisine of France. 1983. 8.98 (ISBN 0-517-54919-0). Crown.

Carley, Isabel M. Simple Settings of American Folk Songs and Rhymes for Orff Ensemble, Book 1. 1972. pap. 2.00 (ISBN 0-918812-06-2). MMB Music.

--Simple Settings of American Folk Songs and Rhymes for Orff Ensemble Book 2. 1974. pap. 2.00 (ISBN 0-918812-07-0). MMB Music.

Carley, James P. The Chronicle of Glastonbury Abbey: An Edition, Translation & Study of John of Glastonbury's Cronica Sive Antiquitates Glastoniensis Ecclesie. Townsend, David, tr. 320p. 1985. 44.25 (ISBN 0-85115-409-3, Pub. by Boydell & Brewer). Longwood Pub Group.

Carley, K. W. The Book of the Prophet Ezekiel. LC 73-94352. (Cambridge Bible Commentary on the New English Bible Ser.). (Illus.). 340p. (Orig.). 1974. 34.50 (ISBN 0-521-08653-1); pap. 13.95 (ISBN 0-521-09755-X). Cambridge U Pr.

Carley, Keith W. Ezekiel Among the Prophets: A Study of Ezekiel's Place in Prophetic Tradition. (Studies in Biblical Theology, 2nd Ser.: No. 31). 1975. pap. text ed. 10.00x (ISBN 0-8401-3081-3). A R Allenson.

Carley, Ken. Gems & Stones: Scientific Properties & Aspects of Twenty Two-A Comparative Study Based upon the Edgar Cayce Psychic Readings. rev. ed. 1979. pap. 4.95 (ISBN 0-87604-110-1). ARE Pr.

Carley, Kenneth. Minnesota in the Civil War. 10.00 (ISBN 0-87018-006-1). Ross.

--The Sioux Uprising of 1862. rev. ed. LC 76-16499. (Illus.). 102p. 1976. 7.95 (ISBN 0-87351-102-6); pap. 4.95 (ISBN 0-87351-103-4). Minn Hist.

Carley, Larry. The Mechanics Guide to Front Wheel Drive. (Illus.). 240p. 1983. 24.95 (ISBN 0-13-569822-7). P-H.

Carley, Larry W. Chrysler K-Cars, Nineteen Eighty to Nineteen Eighty-Four: Do-It-Yourself Car Care. (Illus.). 352p. (Orig.). 1984. pap. 11.95 (ISBN 0-8306-2123-7, 2123). TAB Bks.

--Ford Escort-Mercury Lynx Cars, Nineteen Eighty-One to Nineteen Eighty-Four: Do-it-Yourself Car Care. (Illus.). 352p. (Orig.). 1984. pap. 11.95 (ISBN 0-8306-2133-4, 2133). TAB Bks.

--How to Make Your Own Alcohol Fuels. 2nd ed. (Modern Automotive Ser.). (Illus.). 182p. 1983. 13.95o.p (ISBN 0-8306-0047-7); pap. 7.95 (ISBN 0-8306-2084-2, 2084). TAB Bks.

--Propane Conversion of Cars, Trucks & RVs. (Illus.). 224p. 1982. 14.95 (ISBN 0-8306-3103-8); pap. 9.95 (ISBN 0-8306-2103-2, 2103). TAB Bks.

Carley, Larry W. & Freudenberger, Robert. The Mechanic's Guide to Electronic Emission Control & Tune-Up. (Illus.). 240p. 1986. text ed. 24.95 (ISBN 0-13-569815-4). P-H.

Carley, Lionel & Threlfall, Robert. Delius. (Illus.). 103p. 1984. pap. 9.95 (ISBN 0-87663-856-6). Universe.

--Delius: A Life in Pictures. (Illus.). 1977. 21.95x (ISBN 0-19-315437-4). Oxford U Pr.

Carley, Lionel, ed. Delius: A Life in Letters, 1862-1908. (Illus.). 500p. 1984. text ed. 35.00x (ISBN 0-674-19570-1). Harvard U Pr.

Carley, Lionel, ed. see Delius, F.

Carley, Maurine, jt. auth. see Trenholm, Virginia C.

Carley, Michael. Rational Techniques in Policy Analysis. 1980. text ed. 40.95x (ISBN 0-435-83801-6); pap. text ed. 17.95x (ISBN 0-435-83802-4). Gower Pub Co.

--Social Measurement & Social Indicators: Issues of Policy & Theory. (Contemporary Social Research Ser.: No. 1). (Illus.). 208p. 1981. text ed. 28.50x (ISBN 0-04-310009-0); pap. text ed. 12.50x (ISBN 0-04-310010-4). Allen Unwin.

Carley, Michael J. Revolution & Intervention: The French Government & the Russian Civil War, 1917-1919. 288p. 1983. 30.00x (ISBN 0-7735-0408-7). McGill-Queens U Pr.

Carley, Michael J. & Derow, Ellan O. Social Impact Assessment: A Cross-Disciplinary Guide to the Literature. (Social Impact Assessment Ser.). 250p. 1984. 32.50x (ISBN 0-86531-529-9). Westview.

Carley, Royal V., compiled by. & Lord's Prayer for Today. LC 73-86686. 30p. 1974. 4.95 (ISBN 0-8378-2005-7). Gibson.

Carley, Royal V., ed. Twenty-Third Psalm for Today. LC 73-101450. (Illus.). 1971. 4.95 (ISBN 0-8378-2001-4). Gibson.

Carley, V. A. Student Aid in the Secondary Schools of the United States. LC 77-176626. (Columbia University. Teachers College. Contributions to Education: No. 594). Repr. of 1933 ed. 22.50 (ISBN 0-404-55594-2). AMS Pr.

Carley, Wayne. Alone Is No Fun. LC 72-1921. (Venture Ser.). (Illus.). 64p. (gr. 2). 1972. PLB 7.68 (ISBN 0-8116-6966-1). Garrard.

--Charley the Mouse Finds Christmas. LC 72-1770. (Venture Ser.). (Illus.). 64p. (gr. 2). 1972. PLB 7.68 (ISBN 0-8116-6953-X). Garrard.

--Color My World. LC 73-21584. (Easy Venture Ser.). (Illus.). 32p. (gr. k-2). 1974. PLB 7.47 (ISBN 0-8116-6056-7). Garrard.

--Is Anybody Listening. LC 73-157997. (Venture Ser.). (Illus.). (gr. 1). 1971. 7.47 (ISBN 0-8116-6712-X). Garrard.

--Mixed-up Magic. LC 70-157999. (Venture Ser.). (Illus.). (gr. 1). 1971. PLB 7.47 (ISBN 0-8116-6711-1). Garrard.

--Percy the Parrot Strikes Out. LC 77-157998. (Venture Ser.). (Illus.). (gr. 1). 1971. PLB 7.47 (ISBN 0-8116-6710-3). Garrard.

--Percy the Parrot Yelled Quiet! LC 73-21585. (Easy Venture Ser.). (Illus.). 32p. (gr. k-2). 1974. PLB 7.47 (ISBN 0-8116-6058-3). Garrard.

--Puppy Love. LC 75-161027. (Venture Ser.). (Illus.). (gr. 1). 1971. PLB 7.47 (ISBN 0-8116-6716-2). Garrard.

Carley-Macauly, K. W., ed. Radioactive Waste: Advanced Management Methods for Medium-Active Liquid Waste. (Radioactive Waste Management Ser.). 352p. 1981. 79.25 (ISBN 3-7186-0060-9). Harwood Academic.

Carlgren, M. W. Swedish Foreign Policy During the Second World War. LC 77-78681. (Illus.). 1977. 25.00x (ISBN 0-312-78058-3). St Martin.

Carli. Sienese Painting. pap. 12.50 (ISBN 0-935748-25-3). Scala Books.

Carli, Enzo. Sienese Paintings. (Illus.). 80p. 12.50 (ISBN 0-935748-25-3, Dist by Scala Books). Sotheby Pubns.

Carli, Franco De see De Carli, Franco.

Carlier, Auguste. Marriage in the United States. LC 70-169376. (Family in America Ser.). 200p. 1972. Repr. of 1867 ed. 20.00 (ISBN 0-405-03853-4). Ayer Co Pubs.

Carlier, Robert, et al, eds. Larousse des citations: Francaises et etrangeres. new ed. 895p. (Fr.). 1975. 31.50x (ISBN 2-03-021001-3, 3932). Larousse.

Carlile, Candy. Book Report Big Top. (Reading Ser.). 48p. (gr. 1-3). 1980. 4.95 (ISBN 0-88160-009-1, LW 111). Learning Wks.
Carlile, Clancy. Honkytonk Man. 320p. 1982. pap. 2.95 (ISBN 0-515-07125-0). Jove Pubns.
--Spore Seven. 288p. 1979. pap. 2.25 (ISBN 0-380-49031-5, 49031). Avon.
Carlile, Clark S. Project Text for Public Speaking. 4th ed. 276p. 1981. pap. text ed. 11.50 scp (ISBN 0-06-041182-1, HarpC). Har-Row.
--Thirty Eight Basic Speech Experiences. 7th ed. 235p. 1982. pap. text ed. 7.75 (ISBN 0-931054-07-9). Clark Pub.
Carlile, Cynthia, tr. see Buyeva, L. P.
Carlile, Henry. Rough-Hewn Table: Poems. LC 70-167918. (Breakthrough Bks). 72p. 1971. pap. 6.95 (ISBN 0-8262-0114-8). U of Mo Pr.
--Running Lights. LC 80-67971. 66p. 1981. 9.00 (ISBN 0-937872-00-8); pap. 5.00 (ISBN 0-937872-01-6). Dragon Gate.
Carlile, M. J., et al. Molecular & Cellular Aspects of Microbial Evolution. LC 80-42172. (Society for General Microbiology Ser.: Symposium 32). (Illus.). 400p. 1981. 77.50 (ISBN 0-521-24108-1). Cambridge U Pr.
Carlile, William W. Evolution of Modern Money. LC 68-56766. (Research & Source Works Ser.: No. 251). 1968. Repr. of 1901 ed. lib. bdg. 20.50 (ISBN 0-8337-0475-3). B Franklin.
--Evolution of Modern Money. LC 69-17029. Repr. of 1901 ed. 35.00x (ISBN 0-678-00467-6). Kelley.
Carlin, Angela G. & Schwartz, Richard W., eds. Merrick-Rippner, Ohio Probate Law. 3rd ed. (Baldwin's Ohio Practice Ser.). 2944p. 1978. Includes annual cumulative supp. bdr. 125.00 (ISBN 0-8322-0021-2). Banks-Baldwin.
--Merrick-Rippner, Ohio Probate Law, 3 Vols. 3rd. rev. ed. (Baldwin's Ohio Practice Ser.). 1978. 160.00 (ISBN 0-8322-0055-7). Banks-Baldwin.
Carlin, Cathy. Jesus, What Are You Doing Tonight? (Outreach Ser.). 32p. 1982. pap. 0.99 (ISBN 0-8163-0492-0). Pacific Pr Pub Assn.
Carlin, George. Carlin: Sometimes a Little Brain Damage Can Help. LC 84-15081. (Illus.). 32p. (Orig.). 1984. pap. 5.95 (ISBN 0-89471-271-3); lib. bdg. 19.80 (ISBN 0-89471-272-1). Running Pr.
Carlin, Harriette L. Medical Secretary Medispeller: A Transcription Aid. 260p. 1973. pap. 25.75x spiral (ISBN 0-398-02579-7). C C Thomas.
Carlin, Jerome E. Lawyers on Their Own: A Study of Individual Practitioners in Chicago. 1962. 22.00x (ISBN 0-8135-0412-0). Rutgers U Pr.
Carlin, Joseph M. A Food Service Guide to the Nutrition Program for the Elderly. rev. ed. 1975. pap. text ed. 6.50 (ISBN 0-89634-013-9, 023). New England Geron.
--Nutrition Education for the Elderly: The Technique. (Serving the Elderly Ser.: Pt. 4). 1978. pap. text ed. 4.00 (ISBN 0-89634-009-0, 046). New England Geron.
Carlin, Mark S., jt. auth. see Criminal Practice Institute.
Carlin, R. L., ed. Transition Metal Chemistry: A Series of Advances, Vol. 4. 1968. 75.00 (ISBN 0-8247-1079-7). Dekker.
Carlin, Richard L. Transition Metal Chemistry, Vol. 3. LC 65-27431. pap. 92.80 (ISBN 0-317-08346-5, 2017696). Bks Demand UMI.
Carlin, Richard L., ed. Transition Metal Chemistry: A Series of Advances, Vol. 5. 1969. 75.00 (ISBN 0-8247-1080-0). Dekker.
--Transition Metal Chemistry: A Series of Advances, Vol. 6. LC 65-27431. 1970. 75.00 (ISBN 0-8247-1081-9). Dekker.
Carlin, Vivian F. & Mansberg, Ruth. If I Live to Be One Hundred: Congregate Housing for Later Life. 216p. 1984. 17.95 (ISBN 0-13-450387-2, Parker); pap. 8.95 (ISBN 0-13-450379-1). P-H.
Carline, Jan, et al. Mountaineering First Aid. 3rd ed. (Illus.). 136p. 1985. pap. 4.95 (ISBN 0-89886-092-X). Mountaineers.
Carline, Richard. Pictures in the Post: The Story of the Picture Postcard. LC 70-190038. 128p. 1971. 10.95 (ISBN 0-913782-04-1); pap. 7.95 (ISBN 0-318-01131-X). Deltiologists Am.
Carling, E. B. & Kopal, Z., eds. Photometric & Spectroscopic Binary Systems. xii, 546p. 1982. 69.50 (ISBN 90-277-1281-6, Pub. by Reidel Holland). Kluwer Academic.
Carling, Finn & Haecker, Theodor. And Yet We Are Human & Kierkegaard: The Cripple, 2 vols. in 1. Bruyn, C. V., tr. from Norwegian. Phillips, William R. & Rosenberg, Janet, eds. LC 79-6897. (Physically Handicapped in Society Ser.). (Illus.). 1980. Repr. of 1962 ed. lib. bdg. 23.00x (ISBN 0-405-13108-9). Ayer Co Pubs.
Carlino, G. A. Economies of Scale in Manufacturing Location. (Studies in Applied Regional Science: Vol. 12). 1978. pap. 15.00 (ISBN 90-207-0721-3, Pub. by Martinus Nijhoff Netherlands). Kluwer Academic.
Carlino, Lawrence L. The Proto-Spin Theory of the Universe. LC 82-90017. (Illus.). 124p. 1984. 10.95 (ISBN 0-533-05344-7). Vantage.
Carlinsky, Dan. Celebrity Yearbook. 96p. (Orig.). 1982. pap. 5.95 (ISBN 0-8431-0619-0). Price Stern.
--Do You Know Your Boss? 48p. 1983. pap. 1.75 (ISBN 0-8431-0913-0). Price Stern.
--Do You Know Your Husband? (Illus., Orig.). 1979. pap. 1.75 (ISBN 0-8431-0495-3). Price Stern.
--Do You Know Your Parents? 48p. (gr. 3-12). 1983. pap. 1.75 (ISBN 0-8431-0623-9). Price Stern.
--Do You Know Your Wife? (Illus., Orig.). 1979. pap. 1.75 (ISBN 0-8431-0496-1). Price Stern.
Carlinsky, Dan & Goodgold, Ed. The Game of Status: The Book You Can Play to Rate Your Status. 1985. cancelled (ISBN 0-517-55573-5). Crown.
Carlinsky, Dan & Heim, David. Bicycle Tours in & Around New York. LC 75-4036. 1975. pap. 2.95 (ISBN 0-02-938850-3). Hagstrom Map.
--Twenty Bicycle Tours in & Around New York City. (Bicycle Tours Ser.). 136p. 1984. pap. 6.95 (ISBN 0-942440-21-8). Backcountry Pubns.
Carlisle, A., jt. auth. see Maini, J. S.
Carlisle, A. L. Beautiful New England. (Illus.). 72p. 1984. 14.95 (ISBN 0-89802-395-5); pap. 7.95 (ISBN 0-89802-394-7). Beautiful Am.
Carlisle, Amanda. Southland. 448p. (Orig.). 1982. pap. 3.50 (ISBN 0-523-41686-5). Pinnacle Bks.
Carlisle, Anthony. An Essay on the Disorders of Old Age, & on the Means for Prolonging Human Life. Kastenbaum, Robert, ed. LC 78-22183. (Aging & Old Age Ser.). 1979. Repr. of 1818 ed. lib. bdg. 12.00x (ISBN 0-405-11802-3). Ayer Co Pubs.
Carlisle, Brian, jt. auth. see Bowey, Angela.
Carlisle, Charles R., ed. Beyond the Rivers: An Anthology of Twentieth Century Paraguayan Poetry. LC 77-3497. text ed. 10.00x (ISBN 0-914476-73-4); pap. 5.00x (ISBN 0-914476-64-5). Thorp Springs.
Carlisle, Cynthia, tr. see Kollantai, Alexandra.
Carlisle, Douglas H. Venezuelan Foreign Policy: Its Organization & Beginning. LC 78-57979. 1978. pap. text ed. 12.00 (ISBN 0-8191-0317-9). U Pr of Amer.
Carlisle, E. Fred. Loren Eiseley: The Development of a Writer. LC 82-8459. 216p. 1983. 15.95x (ISBN 0-252-00987-8). U of Ill Pr.
Carlisle, Earl C. Little Known Facts & Secrets About Real Estate. 4th ed. LC 71-183787. 81p. 1973. pap. 2.95 (ISBN 0-9600344-2-0). Carlisle Indus.
Carlisle, Elliott. Dialogues on "MAC" Management Organization. (New Press Ser.). 144p. 1983. 10.95 (ISBN 0-07-009843-3). McGraw.
--MAC: Managers Talk about Managing People. 144p. 1985. pap. 5.95 (ISBN 0-14-007315-9). Penguin.
Carlisle, Fred E. The Uncertain Self: Whitman's Drama of Identity. 1973. 8.50 (ISBN 0-87013-172-9). Mich St U Pr.
Carlisle, G. L. & Stanbury, Percy. Shotgun & Shooter. Rev. ed. 232p. 1981. 35.00x (ISBN 0-686-87325-4, Pub. by Hutchinson). State Mutual Bk.
Carlisle, Henry. The Jonah Man. LC 83-48869. (Illus.). 260p. 1984. 13.95 (ISBN 0-394-52942-1). Knopf.
--The Jonah Man. 272p. 1985. pap. 5.95 (ISBN 0-14-008110-0). Penguin.
Carlisle, Howard M. Management: Concepts, Methods & Applications. 2nd ed. 656p. 1982. text ed. 27.95 (ISBN 0-574-19515-7, 13-2515); instr. guide avail. (ISBN 0-574-19516-5, 13-2516). SRA.
Carlisle, Janice. The Sense of an Audience: Dickens, Thackeray & George Eliot at Mid-Century. LC 81-435. 262p. 1981. 22.00x (ISBN 0-8203-0559-6). U of Ga Pr.
Carlisle, Jim. Oh No! It's the Game Warden. 1984. 6.95 (ISBN 0-8062-2240-9). Carlton.
Carlisle, Jody, jt. auth. see Cook, Carole.
Carlisle, Jody, et al. Classroom Nursery Rhymes Activities Kit. 232p. 1983. comb-bound 16.50x (ISBN 0-87628-228-1). Ctr Appl Res.
Carlisle, Lilian B. Hat Boxes & Bandboxes at Shelburne Museum. (Museum Pamphlet Ser.: No. 4). (Illus., Orig.). 1960. pap. 4.50 (ISBN 0-939384-02-7). Shelburne.
Carlisle, Madelyn, jt. auth. see Carlisle, Norman.
Carlisle, Michael, tr. see Andreyev, Olga C.
Carlisle, Nicholas. A Concise Description of the Endowed Grammar Schools in England & Wales. 1896p. 1984. Repr. of 1818 ed. 110.00x (ISBN 0-317-07149-1, Pub. by Richmond Pub England). State Mutual Bk.
--Endowed Grammar Schools: Lancashire & Yorkshire. 248p. 1984. Repr. of 1818 ed. 40.00x (ISBN 0-85546-186-1, Pub. by Richmond Pub England). State Mutual Bk.
--Endowed Grammar Schools: Leicestershire Northamptonshire, Rutland, Staffordshire, Warwickshire & Worcestershire. 250p. 1984. Repr. of 1818 ed. 45.00x (ISBN 0-85546-189-6, Pub. by Richmond Pub England). State Mutual Bk.
--Endowed Grammar Schools: London, Middlesex, Essex, Kent & Surrey. 320p. 1984. Repr. of 1818 ed. 49.00 (ISBN 0-85546-185-3, Pub. by Richmond Pub England). State Mutual Bk.
Carlisle, Norman. Treasure Hunting in the U. S. A. 17.95 (ISBN 0-89190-324-0, Pub. by Am Repr). Amereon Ltd.
Carlisle, Norman & Carlisle, Madelyn. Bridges. LC 82-17874. (New True Bks.). (Illus.). 48p. (gr. k-4). 1983. PLB 10.60 (ISBN 0-516-01677-6); pap. 3.95 (ISBN 0-516-41677-4). Childrens.
--Rivers. LC 81-38448. (New True Bks.). (Illus.). 48p. (gr. k-4). 1982. PLB 10.60 (ISBN 0-516-01645-8). Childrens.
Carlisle, Olga. Island in Time: A Memoir of Childhood. LC 79-9434. (Illus.). 240p. 1980. 12.95 (ISBN 0-03-053326-0). HR&W.
Carlisle, Richard G., jt. auth. see Freilich, Robert H.
Carlisle, Robert A., ed. UNITAS Twenty-Five: A Silver Anniversary. Schiavo, Alex, tr. (Illus.). 160p. (Span. & Port.). 1985. 23.00 (ISBN 0-318-11836-X). Gov Printing Office.
Carlisle, Rodney P. Hearst & the New Deal: The Progressive as Reactionary. Freidel, Frank, ed. LC 78-62378. (Modern American History Ser.: Vol. 4). 240p. 1979. lib. bdg. 34.00 (ISBN 0-8240-3628-X). Garland Pub.
--Sovereignty for Sale. LC 81-607020. 278p. 1981. 21.95 (ISBN 0-87021-668-6). Naval Inst Pr.
--Sovereignty for Sale. (Illus.). 278p. 1981. 21.95 (ISBN 0-87021-668-6); bulk rates avail. Naval Inst Pr.
Carlisle, Sarah. Cleopatra's Carpet. (Regency Love Story). 1979. pap. 1.75 (ISBN 0-449-50009-8, Coventry). Fawcett.
--Daphne. (Coventry Romance Ser.: No. 67). 224p. 1980. pap. 1.75 (ISBN 0-449-50098-5, Coventry). Fawcett.
--Kit & Kitty. 224p. 1981. pap. 1.95 (ISBN 0-449-50202-3, Crest). Fawcett.
--Mlle. Cecie. 224p. (Orig.). 1980. pap. 1.75 (ISBN 0-449-50038-1, Coventry). Fawcett.
--Penny Wise. 224p. 1981. pap. 1.95 (ISBN 0-449-50176-0, Coventry). Fawcett.
Carlisle, Thomas. Bonstonofavitch! LC 74-78089. (Illus.). 176p. (Orig.). 1974. pap. 3.95 (ISBN 0-914580-00-0). Angst World.
--A Ride on the Wave of the Future: An Essay on Human Potential. LC 78-55736. (Illus.). 1978. saddlestich 2.00 (ISBN 0-914580-08-6). Angst World.
Carlisle, Thomas J. Eve & After: Old Testament Woman in Portrait. 160p. (Orig.). 1984. pap. 5.95 (ISBN 0-8028-1970-2). Eerdmans.
--Journey with Job: Poems. LC 75-34230. pap. 17.90 (ISBN 0-8357-9129-7, 2012830). Bks Demand UMI.
--Journey with Jonah. rev. ed. 96p. 1984. pap. 1.95 (ISBN 0-88028-035-2). Forward Movement.
--You! Jonah! LC 68-20587. (Illus.). pap. 20.00 (ISBN 0-8357-9134-3, 2012750). Bks Demand UMI.
Carlisle, Wendy. Siblings of the Mentally Ill. 160p. (Orig.). 1984. pap. 8.95 (ISBN 0-317-13561-9). R & E Pubs.
Carll, Barbara & Richard, Nancy. One Piece of the Puzzle: A School Readiness Manual. rev. ed. LC 77-76434. (Illus.). 1977. pap. text ed. 8.75x (ISBN 0-932950-00-0). Athena Pubns.
Carlmichael, Carrie, jt. auth. see Storch, Marcia L.
Carlo. The Juggling Book. (Illus.). 112p. (Orig.). 1974. pap. 6.95 (ISBN 0-394-71956-5, Vin). Random.
Carlo & Murphy. Merchandising Mathmematics. 179p. 1981. pap. 11.80 (ISBN 0-8273-1416-7); instructor's guide 3.60 (ISBN 0-8273-1417-5). Delmar.
Carlo, Joyce W. Trammels, Trenchers & Tartlets. (Illus.). 144p. (Orig.). 1982. pap. 7.95 (ISBN 0-933614-13-6). Peregrine Pr.
Carlo, Mona W., jt. auth. see Scott, Gwendolyn D.
Carlock, Jesse C., jt. auth. see Frey, Diane.
Carlock, L. L. The Electronic Office & You: Managing Your Productivity. 192p. 1985. 7.04 (ISBN 0-07-027978-0). McGraw.
Carlon & Howland. High Frequency Ventilation. (Lung & Biology Ser.). 328p. 1985. 57.50 (ISBN 0-8247-7364-0). Dekker.
Carlo-Rota, Gian & Moser, Jurgen, eds. Fritz John: Collected Works, 2 vols. (Contemporary Mathematicians Ser.). 1985. Set. write for info. (ISBN 0-8176-3267-0). Vol. 1 (ISBN 0-8176-3265-4). Vol. 2 (ISBN 0-8176-3266-2). Birkhauser.
Carlos. Albear: The Dog Who Could Talk. (Illus.). 64p. (gr. k-2). 1981. 5.00 (ISBN 0-682-49748-7). Exposition Pr FL.
Carlos, Alberto J., ed. see Hernandez, Jose.
Carlos, Alberto J., tr. see Hernandez, Jose.
Carlos, Peter. Praise the High Grass. 1977. 1.50 (ISBN 0-918476-01-1). Cornerstone Pr.
Carlova, John, jt. auth. see Belli, Melvin M., Sr.
Carlova, John, jt. auth. see Horsley, Jack E.
Carlow, Joyce. Succession. 1984. pap. 3.50 (ISBN 0-451-13152-5, Sig). NAL.
Carlozzi, Carl G. The Episcopal Way. 1977. pap. text ed. 4.95x (ISBN 0-8192-4073-7); tchrs ed. 4.95x (ISBN 0-8192-4074-5). Morehouse.
--Promises & Prayers for Healing: Hope for the Future. (Pocketpac Books). 128p. (Orig.). 1985. pap. 2.50 (ISBN 0-87788-336-X). Shaw Pubs.
Carlozzi, Carl G. & Parkes, Ellen. Pocket Parables. 80p. (Orig.). 1985. pap. 2.50 (ISBN 0-8423-4919-7). Tyndale.
Carlquist, Sherwin. Ecological Strategies of Xylem Evolution. LC 74-76382. (Illus.). 1975. 36.50x (ISBN 0-520-02730-2). U of Cal Pr.
--Island Biology. LC 73-4643. (Illus.). 660p. 1974. 60.00x (ISBN 0-231-03562-4); pap. 20.00x (ISBN 0-231-08364-5). Columbia U Pr.
Carlsen. Encyclopedia of Business Charts. 1977. 55.00 (ISBN 0-13-275321-9). P-H.
Carlsen, Clarence J., tr. see Hallesby, O.
Carlsen, D. & Tryon, V. Communication: Graphic Arts. 1976. pap. 8.84 (ISBN 0-13-153189-1). P-H.
Carlsen, Darvey. Graphic Arts. (gr. 7-12). 1977. text ed. 14.64 (ISBN 0-02-664280-8); tchr's guide 2.00 (ISBN 0-02-664290-5). Bennett IL.
Carlsen, Fran, ed. Harris Ohio Industrial Directory. (Illus.). 950p. 79.50 (ISBN 0-916512-61-4). Harris Pub.
--Ohio Buyers Industrial Directory. 720p. 25.00 (ISBN 0-916512-60-6). Harris Pub.
Carlsen, G. R. English Literature: A Chronological Approach. 976p. 1985. 23.96 (ISBN 0-07-009845-X). McGraw.
Carlsen, G. R. & Gilbert, Miriam. British & Western Literature. 3rd ed. (Themes & Writers Ser.). (Illus.). 1979. text ed. 24.20 (ISBN 0-07-009871-9). McGraw.
Carlsen, G. R., et al. American Literature: A Chronological Approach. 896p. 1985. 22.64 (ISBN 0-07-009844-1). McGraw.
--American Literature: A Thematic Approach. 4th ed. 1984. 22.64 (ISBN 0-07-009817-4). McGraw.
--British & Western Literature: A Thematic Approach. 4th ed. 800p. 1984. 23.96 (ISBN 0-07-009821-2). McGraw.
--Encounters. 832p. 21.32 (ISBN 0-07-009813-1). McGraw.
--Focus: Themes in Literature. 2nd ed. 1975. 21.76 (ISBN 0-07-009907-3). McGraw.
--Perception: Themes in Literature. 2nd ed. 1975. 21.76 (ISBN 0-07-009908-1). McGraw.
Carlsen, G. Robert. Books & the Teenage Reader: A Guide for Teachers, Librarians & Parents. 2nd, rev. ed. LC 78-2117. 1980. 15.34i (ISBN 0-06-010626-3, HarpT). Har-Row.
--Encounters: Themes in Literature. 3rd ed. (Themes & Writers Ser.). (Illus.). (gr. 10). 1979. text ed. 22.32 (ISBN 0-07-009863-8). McGraw.
--Focus: Themes in Literature. 3rd ed. (Themes & Writers Ser.). (Illus.). (gr. 7). 1979. text ed. 20.96 (ISBN 0-07-009851-4). McGraw.
--Perception: Themes in Literature. 3rd ed. Rothermich, John A., ed. (Themes & Writers Ser.). (Illus.). (gr. 8). 1979. text ed. 20.96 (ISBN 0-07-009855-7). McGraw.
Carlsen, G. Robert & Tovatt, A. Insights: Themes in Literature. 3rd ed. (Themes & Writers Ser.). (Illus.). 1979. pap. text ed. 22.32 (ISBN 0-07-009859-X). McGraw.
Carlsen, G. Robert, et al. Western Literature: Themes & Writers. 2nd ed. (Themes & Writers Ser.). (Illus.). 768p. (gr. 12). 1975. text ed. 25.72 (ISBN 0-07-009906-5). McGraw.
--American Literature: Themes & Writers. 3rd ed. (Illus.). (gr. 11). 1979. text ed. 23.64 (ISBN 0-07-009867-0). McGraw.
Carlsen, G. Robert, et al, eds. Encounters: Themes in Literature. 2nd ed. Tovatt. (Themes & Writers Ser). (Illus.). 768p. (gr. 10). 1972. text ed. 24.32 (ISBN 0-07-009904-9). McGraw.
--American Literature: Themes & Writers. 2nd ed. (Illus.). 768p. (gr. 11). 1972. text ed. 25.72 (ISBN 0-07-009905-7). McGraw.
Carlsen, John. Economic & Social Transformation in Rural Kenya. (Centre for Development Research Ser.: No. 4). (Illus.). 230p. 1983. pap. text ed. 9.50x (ISBN 0-8419-9759-4, Africana). Holmes & Meier.
Carlsen, Martin, et al. Student Workbook for Introduction to the Administration of Justice. 1978. pap. text ed. 10.95 (ISBN 0-8403-1921-5). Kendall-Hunt.
Carlsen, Melody A., jt. auth. see Cooper, Robert D.
Carlsen, R. G. Focus. 4th ed. (Themes & Writers Ser.). (Illus.). 640p. (gr. 7). 1984. text ed. 19.96 (ISBN 0-07-009801-8). McGraw.
--Insights. 4th ed. (Themes & Writers Ser.). (Illus.). 800p. (gr. 9). 1984. text ed. 21.32 (ISBN 0-07-009809-3). McGraw.
--Perception. 4th ed. (Themes & Writers Ser.). (Illus.). 640p. (gr. 8). 1984. text ed. 19.96 (ISBN 0-07-009805-0). McGraw.
Carlsen, Robert & McHugh, James. Handbook of Research & Development Forms & Formats. (Illus.). 1978. pap. 39.95 (ISBN 0-13-380766-5, Busn). P-H.
Carlsen, Robert D. Handbook & Portfolio of Successful Sales Proposals. LC 82-15085. 506p. looseleaf bdg. 125.00 (ISBN 0-13-380808-4, Busn). P-H.
Carlsen, Robert D. & Lewis, James A. The Systems Analysis Workbook: A Complete Guide to Project Implementation & Control. 2nd ed. 288p. 1979. 45.00 (ISBN 0-686-98491-9). P-H.
Carlsen, Robert D. & McHugh, James F. Handbook of Production Management Forms & Formats. (Illus.). 1978. 54.95 (ISBN 0-13-380618-9, Busn). P-H.
--Handbook of Sales & Marketing Forms & Formats. (Illus.). 1978. 64.95 (ISBN 0-13-380857-2, Busn). P-H.
Carlsen-Jones, M. Introduction to Logic. 624p. 1983. 28.95 (ISBN 0-07-032890-0). McGraw.
Carlsmith, J. Merrill, et al. Methods of Research in Social Psychology. 336p. 1976. text ed. 22.95 (ISBN 0-394-34804-4, RanC). Random.
Carlsnaes, Walter. The Concept of Ideology & Political Analysis: A Critical Examination of Its Usage by Marx, Lenin, & Mannheim. LC 80-1202. (Contributions in Philosophy Ser.: No. 17). xii, 274p. 1981. lib. bdg. 35.00 (ISBN 0-313-22267-3, CCI/). Greenwood.

Carlson. A Christmas Lullaby. (Arch Bks.). 24p. (gr. k-4). 1985. pap. 0.99 (ISBN 0-570-06195-4, 59-1296). Concordia.
--Spring Designers Handbook. (Mechanical Engineering Ser.: Vol. 1). 1978. 59.75 (ISBN 0-8247-6623-7). Dekker.
--Spring Manufacturing Handbook. (Mechanical Engineering Ser.). 344p. 1982. 55.00 (ISBN 0-8247-1678-7). Dekker.
--Springs: Troubleshooting & Failure Analysis. (Engineering Troubleshooting Ser.: Vol. 1). 216p. 1980. 39.75 (ISBN 0-8247-1003-7). Dekker.
Carlson & Lassey. Rural Society & Environment in America. (Agricultural Science Ser.). (Illus.). 448p. 1981. text ed. 29.95 (ISBN 0-07-009959-6). McGraw.
Carlson, A., jt. auth. see Youtz, H.
Carlson, A. B. Communications Systems. 2nd ed. (Electrical & Electronic Engineering Ser.). 1974. text ed. 44.00 (ISBN 0-07-009957-X). McGraw.
--Communications Systems. 3rd ed. (Electrical Engineering Ser.). 704p. 1985. price not set (ISBN 0-07-009960-X). McGraw.
Carlson, A. Bruce & Gisser, David G. Electrical Engineering: Concepts & Applications. LC 80-21519. (Electrical Engineering Ser.). 640p. 1981. text ed. 39.95 (ISBN 0-201-03940-0); solutions manual 4.00 (ISBN 0-201-03941-9). Addison-Wesley.
Carlson, A. Bruce, jt. auth. see Frederick, Dean K.
Carlson, Albert D., jt. auth. see Soucek, Branko.
Carlson, Andrew R. Anarchism in Germany, Vol. 1: The Early Movement. LC 78-186946. 455p. 1972. 20.00 (ISBN 0-8108-0484-0). Scarecrow.
--German Foreign Policy, Eighteen Ninety to Nineteen Fourteen & Colonial Policy to 1914: A Handbook & Annotated Bibliography. LC 72-9539. 333p. 1970. 10.00 (ISBN 0-8108-0296-1). Scarecrow.
Carlson, Ann D. Early Childhood Literature-Sharing Programs in Libraries. 120p. (Orig.). 1985. text ed. 19.50 (ISBN 0-208-02068-3, Lib Prof Pubns); pap. text ed. 13.50 (ISBN 0-208-02074-8, Lib Prof Pubns). Shoe String.
Carlson, Anna L. The Candy Cruncher. 2nd. ed. LC 80-83738. (Illus.). 24p. (gr. k-4). 1983. pap. 1.95 (ISBN 0-939938-03-0). Karwyn Ent.
--The Cookie Looker. 2nd. ed. LC 80-82182. (Illus.). (gr. k-4). 1983. pap. 1.95 (ISBN 0-939938-01-4). Karwyn Ent.
--Homer Bear's Secret. 1st. ed. (Illus.). 24p. (Orig.). (gr. k-4). 1983. pap. 1.95 (ISBN 0-939938-05-7). Karwyn Ent.
--The Mouse Family's Christmas. 1st. ed. (Illus.). 24p. (Orig.). (gr. k-4). 1983. pap. 1.95 (ISBN 0-939938-04-9). Karwyn Ent.
--Stories to Treasure. (Illus.). 24p. (Orig.). (ps-5). 1984. pap. 62.40 (ISBN 0-939938-06-5). Karwyn Ent.
--Toady Tales. 2nd. ed. LC 80-83018. 24p. (gr. k-4). 1983. pap. 1.95 (ISBN 0-939938-02-2). Karwyn Ent.
Carlson, Anna L. & Wynne, Diana. My Brother & I Like Cookies. 2nd. ed. LC 80-81624. (Illus.). 96p. (Orig.). (gr. 1-7). 1983. pap. 4.95 (ISBN 0-939938-00-6). Karwyn Ent.
Carlson, Anton J., et al. The Machinery of the Body. rev. & enl. ed. LC 61-14536. 1961. 30.00x (ISBN 0-226-09279-8). U of Chicago Pr.
Carlson, Arthru E., et al. Accounting Essentials for Career Secretaries. 1983. text ed. 10.00 (ISBN 0-538-01070-3, A07). SW Pub.
Carlson, Arthur E., et al. Boyds Clothiers: Automated Accounting for the Microcomputer. 1983. 8.00 (ISBN 0-538-01150-5, A15). SW PUb.
Carlson, Avis D. Small World, Long Gone. LC 75-25212. (Illus.). 1977. 7.95 (ISBN 0-914090-29-1). Chicago Review.
Carlson, B. C., ed. Special Functions of Applied Mathematics. 1977. 37.00 (ISBN 0-12-160150-1). Acad Pr.
Carlson, Bernice W. Let's Find the Big Idea. LC 81-19121. 128p. (gr. 4-6). 1982. 8.95g (ISBN 0-687-21430-0). Abingdon.
--Listen & Help Tell the Story. (Illus.). (gr. k-2). 1965. 9.95 (ISBN 0-687-22096-3). Abingdon.
--Quick Wits & Nimble Fingers. LC 79-10035. (Illus.). 128p. (gr. 3-7). 1979. 9.95 (ISBN 0-687-35199-5). Abingdon.
Carlson, Bernice W., jt. auth. see Ginglend, David R.
Carlson, Bernice W., jt. auth. see Hunt, Kari.
Carlson, Betty. A New Song from L'Abri. LC 75-16653. 1979. pap. 3.95 (ISBN 0-89107-177-6). Good News.
--The Unhurried Chase That Ended at L'Abri. LC 83-62688. 158p. 1984. pap. 5.95 (ISBN 0-89107-304-3). Good News.
Carlson, Bruce M. Patten's Foundations of Embryology. 4th, rev. ed. (Organismal Biology Ser.). (Illus.). 608p. 1981. text ed. 38.95 (ISBN 0-07-009875-1). McGraw.
Carlson, Bruce M., tr. see Polezhaev, L. V.
Carlson, C. C., jt. auth. see Lindsey, Hal.
Carlson, C. Lennart. The First Magazine. LC 74-3762. 281p. 1975. Repr. of 1938 ed. lib. bdg. 24.75x (ISBN 0-8371-7464-3, CAFM). Greenwood.
Carlson, Carole. A Light in Babylon. 256p. 1985. 12.95 (ISBN 0-8499-0452-8, 0452-8). Word Bks.
Carlson, Carole C. Corrie Ten Boom: Her Life, Her Faith. (Illus.). 224p. 1982. 12.95 (ISBN 0-8007-1293-5). Revell.
--Corrie Ten Boom: Her Life, Her Faith. (Illus.). 224p. 1984. pap. 3.50 (ISBN 0-8007-8490-1, Spire Bks). Revell.
--Corrie Ten Boom: Her Life, Her Faith. (Illus.). 240p. 1984. pap. 2.95 (ISBN 0-515-08061-6). Jove Pubns.
Carlson, Carole C., jt. auth. see Rogers, Dale E.
Carlson, Carole C., jt. auth. see Ross, Skip.
Carlson, Carolyn E. & Blackwell, Betty. Behavioral Concepts & Nursing Intervention. 2nd ed. LC 78-8761. 1978. 15.50x (ISBN 0-397-54217-8, 64-00287, Lippincott Nursing). Lippincott.
Carlson, Charles R. A Financial Efficiency Model: Long-Range Financial Planning. LC 74-620206. xi, 88p. 1975. pap. 5.00 (ISBN 0-87744-128-6). Mich St U Pr.
Carlson, D. & Shield, R., eds. Finite Elasticity. 1982. lib. bdg. 79.00 (ISBN 90-247-2629-8, Pub. by Martinus Nijhoff Netherlands). Kluwer Academic.
Carlson, Dale. Boys Have Feelings Too. LC 80-12895. (Illus.). 160p. (gr. 7 up). 1980. 9.95 (ISBN 0-689-30770-5). Atheneum.
--Call Me Amanda. 80p. (gr. 4-6). 1981. 9.50 (ISBN 0-525-27355-7, 0922-280). Dutton.
--Call Me Amanda. 96p. (gr. 5 up). 1983. pap. 1.95 (ISBN 0-590-32725-9). Scholastic Inc.
--The Case of the Triple Girl. (James Budd Mysteries Ser.: No. 6). (Illus.). 144p. (gr. 3-7). 1985. pap. 2.95 (ISBN 0-307-21661-6, 21661, Pub. by Golden Bks). Western Pub.
--Charlie the Hero. (Illus.). 80p. (gr. 4-6). 1983. 9.95 (ISBN 0-525-44072-0, 0966-290). Dutton.
--The Frog People. (Illus.). 80p. (gr. 7 up). 1982. 8.95 (ISBN 0-525-45107-2, 0869-260, Skinny Bk). Dutton.
--Girls Are Equal Too: The Women's Movement for Teenagers. LC 73-76333. (Illus.). 160p. (YA) (gr. 6-9). 1973. 9.95 (ISBN 0-689-30106-5); pap. 2.95 (ISBN 0-689-70433-X). Atheneum.
--Loving Sex for Both Sexes: Straight Talk for Teen-Agers. (YA) (gr. 9 up). 1979. PLB 9.90 (ISBN 0-531-02872-0). Watts.
--The Mountain of Truth. LC 78-17550. (gr. 5-9). 1972. 5.95 (ISBN 0-689-30023-9). Atheneum.
--The Mystery of Galaxy Games. LC 83-83329. (James Budd Mysteries Ser.: No. 4). (Illus.). 144p. (gr. 3-7). 1984. pap. 2.95 (ISBN 0-307-21579-2, 21579, Golden Bks). Western Pub.
--The Mystery of the Lost Princess. LC 83-83327. (James Budd Mysteries Ser.: No. 3). (Illus.). 144p. (gr. 3-7). 1984. pap. 2.95 (ISBN 0-307-21581-4, 21581, Golden Bks). Western Pub.
--The Mystery of the Madman at Cornwall Crag. LC 83-83326. (James Budd Mysteries Ser.: No. 1). (Illus.). 144p. (gr. 3-7). 1984. pap. 2.95 (ISBN 0-307-21582-2, 21582, Golden Bks). Western pub.
--The Mystery of the Shining Children. (Jenny Dean Science Fiction Mystery Ser.). (Illus.). (gr. 3-7). 1983. 2.95 (ISBN 0-448-19001-X, G&D). Putnam Pub Group.
--The Mystery of the Vanished Palace. (James Budd Mysteries Ser.: No. 7). (Illus.). 144p. (gr. 3-7). 1985. pap. 2.95 (ISBN 0-307-21662-4, 21662, Pub. by Golden Bks). Western Pub.
--The Plant People. 96p. (YA) (gr. 5 up). 1979. pap. 1.75 (ISBN 0-440-96959-X, LFL). Dell.
--The Secret of Operation Brain. LC 83-83328. (James Budd Mysteries: No. 2). (Illus.). 144p. (gr. 3-7). 1984. pap. 2.95 (ISBN 0-307-21580-6, 21580, Golden Bks). Western Pub.
--The Secret of the Circus of Terror. (James Budd Mysteries Ser.: No. 5). (Illus.). 144p. (gr. 3-7). 1985. pap. 2.95 (ISBN 0-307-21660-8, 21660, Pub. by Golden Bks). Western Pub.
--The Secret of the Invisible City. LC 84-80178. (Jenny Dean Mystery Ser.). (Illus.). (gr. 3-7). 1984. pap. 2.95 (ISBN 0-448-19004-4, G&D). Putnam Pub Group.
--The Secret of the Third Eye. (Jenny Dean Science Fiction Mystery Ser.). (Illus.). 140p. (gr. 3-7). 1983. 2.95 (ISBN 0-448-19003-6, G&D). Putnam Pub Group.
--The Space Plague Mystery. (James Budd Mysteries Ser.: No. 8). (Illus.). 144p. (gr. 3-7). 1985. pap. 2.95 (ISBN 0-307-21663-2, 21663, Pub. by Golden Bks). Western Pub.
Carlson, Dale & Carlson, Danny. The Shining Pool. LC 78-13636. 1979. 6.95 (ISBN 0-689-30614-8, Argo). Atheneum.
Carlson, Dale & Fitzgibbon, Dan. Manners That Matter: For People Under Twenty-One. LC 82-9761. 144p. (gr. 7-12). 1983. 9.95 (ISBN 0-525-44008-9, 0966-290). Dutton.
Carlson, Dale Bick. Where's Your Head? LC 77-2292. (Illus.). 224p. (gr. 6-12). 1977. 8.95 (ISBN 0-689-30578-8). Atheneum.
Carlson, Danny, jt. auth. see Carlson, Dale.
Carlson, David. Ready-to-Use Outdoor Recreations Spot Illustrations. (Clip Art Ser.). 64p. 1985. pap. 2.95 (ISBN 0-486-24784-8). Dover.
--Ready-to-Use Sports Illustrations (Clip Art) (Pictorial Archive Ser.). (Illus.). 64p. (Orig.). 1982. pap. 2.95 (ISBN 0-486-24344-3). Dover.
Carlson, David, ed. see Instrument Society of America Staff.
Carlson, David B. & Heinberg, John D. How Housing Allowances Work: Integrated Findings to Date from the Experimental Housing Allowance Program. 95p. 1978. pap. 10.00x (ISBN 0-87766-215-0, 21300). Urban Inst.
Carlson, Deborah, ed. see Mason, Karen & Lacey, Carol.
Carlson, Delbert G. & Giffin, James M. Cat Owner's Home Veterinary Handbook. LC 82-23383. (Illus.). 392p. 1985. 18.95 (ISBN 0-87605-814-4). Howell Bk.
--Dog Owner's Home Veterinary Handbook. LC 80-13912. (Illus.). 384p. 1985. 16.95 (ISBN 0-87605-764-4). Howell Bk.
Carlson, Dennis G. African Fever: A Study of British Science, Technology, & Politics in West Africa, 1787-1864. LC 81-5621. 1984. 15.95 (ISBN 0-88202-196-6). Watson Pub Intl.
Carlson, Dick. Modern Management. (Orig.). 1967. pap. text ed. 3.95 (ISBN 0-87252-006-4). Tinnon-Brown.
--Modern Management Guides for Improving the Profits of Any Small Business. 1969. pap. 2.95 (ISBN 0-87252-018-8). Tinnon-Brown.
--Modern Management: Principles & Practices. 184p. 1962. 7.00x (ISBN 0-686-14670-0). OECD.
Carlson, Don, ed. Automation in Housing & Systems Building News: Dictionary of Industrialized Manufactured Housing. (Illus.). 1981. 15.00 (ISBN 0-9607408-0-5). Automation in Housing Mag.
--Peace Trek: Reclaiming Our Future. Comstock, Craig. (Illus.). 300p. (Orig.). 1985. pap. 19.95 (ISBN 0-317-19166-7). Ark Comm Inst.
Carlson, Doug. Hill of Sacrifice: The National Memorial Cemetery of the Pacific at Punchbowl. LC 81-83482. (Illus.). 64p. (Orig.). 1982. pap. 4.95 (ISBN 0-89610-085-5). Island Herit.
Carlson, Douglas W., et al. Guide to the Papers in the John Hunter Walker Collection, 1911-1953. LC 80-16678. (Robert B. Downs Publication Fund Ser.: No. 6). 114p. 1980. pap. 15.00 (ISBN 0-87845-056-4). U of Ill Lib Info Sci.
Carlson, Dwight L. Guilt-Free: How to Release the Tension in Your Life. 2nd ed. 1985. pap. 4.95 (ISBN 0-89081-375-2). Harvest Hse.
--Overcoming Hurts & Anger. LC 80-83852. 1981. pap. 4.95 (ISBN 0-89081-277-2). Harvest Hse.
Carlson, E. D., et al. Display Generation & Management Systems (DGMS) for Interactive Business Applications. 15.00 (ISBN 0-9940013-8-X, Pub. by Vieweg & Sohn Germany). Heyden.
Carlson, Edgar M. The Church & the Public Conscience. LC 79-8710. xii, 104p. 1981. Repr. of 1956 ed. lib. bdg. 19.25x (ISBN 0-313-22195-2, CACH). Greenwood.
Carlson, Edgar M., tr. see Wingren, Gustaf.
Carlson, Edward. Kids & the Franklin. (Illus.). 200p. 19.95 (ISBN 0-8359-3664-3). P-H.
--Kids & the IBM. 1984. pap. 19.95 (ISBN 0-8359-3675-9). Reston.
Carlson, Edward H. Compute's Kids & the Apple. Orig. Title: Kids & the Apple. (Illus., Orig.). 1984. pap. 12.95 (ISBN 0-942386-76-0). Compute Pubns.
--Compute's Kids & the Commodore 64. rev. ed. (Illus., Orig.). 1984. pap. 12.95 (ISBN 0-942386-77-9). Compute Pubns.
--Kids & the Commodore 64. (Illus.). (gr. 6-8). 1984. pap. 19.95 (ISBN 0-8359-3667-8). Reston.
--Kids & the IBM PC & PCjr. rev. ed. Compute Editors, ed. 272p. (Orig.). 1985. pap. 12.95 (ISBN 0-942386-93-0). Compute Pubns.
Carlson, Effie B. A Bio-Bibliographical Dictionary of Twelve-Tone & Serial Composers. LC 79-8959. pap. 58.30 (ISBN 0-317-09921-3, 2012347). Bks Demand UMI.
Carlson, Ellsworth C. The Foochow Missionaries, 1847-1880. LC 72-97832. (East Asian Monographs Ser: No. 51). 1973. pap. 20.00x (ISBN 0-674-30735-6). Harvard U Pr.
--Kaiping Mines, Eighteen Seventy-Seven to Nineteen Twelve. rev. 2nd ed. LC 71-148943. (East Asian Monographs Ser: No. 3). 1971. pap. 11.00x (ISBN 0-674-49700-7). Harvard U Pr.
Carlson, Elof A. Human Genetics. 528p. 1983. text ed. 26.95 (ISBN 0-669-05559-X). Heath.
Carlson, Elof A., ed. see Muller, Hermann J.
Carlson, Elof Axel. Genes, Radiation & Society: The Life and Work of H. J. Muller. LC 81-5486. (Illus.). 496p. 1981. 35.00 (ISBN 0-8014-1304-4). Cornell U Pr.
Carlson, Elwood & Carlson, Ruth. Navy Marriages & Deployment. 114p. (Orig.). 1984. lib. bdg. 18.75 (ISBN 0-8191-4158-5); pap. text ed. 9.25 (ISBN 0-8191-4159-3). U Pr of Amer.
Carlson, Eric D., jt. auth. see Sprague, Ralph H., Jr.
Carlson, Eric T., ed. Classics in Psychiatry Ser, 46 vols. 1976. 1985.50x (ISBN 0-405-07410-7). Ayer Co Pubs.
Carlson, Eric T., et al, eds. Benjamin Rush's Lectures on the Mind. LC 80-70300. (Memoir Ser.: Vol. 144). 1981. 20.00 (ISBN 0-87169-144-2). Am Philos.
Carlson, Eric W., ed. see Emerson, Ralph Waldo.
Carlson, Estelle. The I'm Too Busy Cook Book: Recipes for Busy People Who Love to Cook. (Illus.). 59p. (Orig.). 1981. pap. 5.95 (ISBN 0-686-31754-8). Pot of Gold.
Carlson, Evans F. The Chinese Army. LC 74-10097. (China Studies: from Confucius to Mao Ser). (Illus.). 142p. 1975. Repr. of 1940 ed. 17.60 (ISBN 0-88355-162-4). Hyperion Conn.
--Twin Stars of China. LC 74-10098. (China Studies: from Confucius to Mao Ser). (Illus.). xiv, 331p. 1975. Repr. of 1940 ed. 31.00 (ISBN 0-88355-163-2). Hyperion Conn.
Carlson, Evelyn, et al. Vintage. Traxler, Patricia, ed. (Illus.). 104p. (Orig.). 1984. pap. 5.00 (ISBN 0-932199-00-3). Smoky Hill.
Carlson, Faith. Alternate Methods of Communication. 109p. 1981. pap. text ed. 3.95x (ISBN 0-8134-2237-X). Interstate.
--PICSYMS Categorical Dictionary. LC 84-72946. (Illus.). 192p. 1985. pap. 25.00 (ISBN 0-932591-01-9); small symbol packet 10.00 (ISBN 0-932591-02-7); reg. symbol packet 15.00 (ISBN 0-932591-03-5); large symbol packet 20.00 (ISBN 0-932591-04-3). Baggeboda Pr.
Carlson, Fred A. & Seawall, Frank. Coal Traffic on the Ohio River System. 1962. pap. 2.00x (ISBN 0-87776-107-8, R107). Ohio St U Admin Sci.
Carlson, Frederick L. Thoughts in Time. Jones, Michael P., intro. by. (Illus.). 61p. 1984. limited edition 20.00 (ISBN 0-89904-006-3). Crumb Elbow Pub.
Carlson, G., jt. ed. see Cantwell, D.
Carlson, G. A., jt. auth. see Reichelderfer, K. H.
Carlson, G. E., jt. auth. see Putnam, R.
Carlson, G. E., jt. auth. see Putnam, R. E.
Carlson, G. Raymond. The Acts Story. LC 78-57178. (Radiant Life Ser.). 128p. (Orig.). 1978. pap. 2.50 (ISBN 0-88243-913-8, 02-0913); tchr's. ed 2.50 (ISBN 0-88243-184-6, 32-0184). Gospel Pub.
--The Life Worth Living. LC 75-22607. (Radiant Life Ser.). 128p. 1975. pap. 2.50 (ISBN 0-88243-876-X, 02-0876); teacher's ed. 2.50 (ISBN 0-88243-160-9, 32-0160). Gospel Pub.
--Our Faith & Fellowship. LC 77-75023. (Radiant Life Ser.). 128p. 1977. pap. 2.50 (ISBN 0-88243-908-1, 02-0908); teacher's ed. 2.50 (ISBN 0-88243-178-1, 32-0178). Gospel Pub.
--Prayer & the Christian's Devotional Life. LC 80-83522. (Radiant Life Ser.). 128p. (Orig.). 1981. 1.95 (ISBN 0-88243-878-6, 02-0878); teacher's ed. 3.95 (ISBN 0-88243-190-0, 32-0190). Gospel Pub.
--Preparing to Teach God's Word. LC 75-5221. (Illus.). 128p. 1975. pap. 1.25 (ISBN 0-88243-579-5, 02-0579). Gospel Pub.
--Spiritual Dynamics. LC 76-5633. (Radiant Life Ser.). 128p. 1976. pap. 2.50 (ISBN 0-88243-894-8, 02-0894); teacher's ed 3.95 (ISBN 0-88243-168-4, 32-0168). Gospel Pub.
Carlson, Gayle F. Archeological Investigations at Fort Atkinson: Washington County, Nebraska 1956-1971. (Publications in Anthropology: No. 8). 251p. 1979. 9.00 (ISBN 0-686-27209-9). Nebraska Hist.
Carlson, Gayle F. & Jensen, Richard E. Archeological Salvage & Survey in Nebraska. (Publications in Anthropology: No. 5). 191p. 1973. pap. 6.00 (ISBN 0-686-20018-7). Nebraska Hist.
Carlson, Gayle F. & Steinacher, Terry L. Nebraska Highway Archaeological & Historical Investigations, 1969-1975. (Publications in Archaeology Ser.: No. 10). 191p. 1984. 10.00. Nebraska Hist.
Carlson, Gene, ed. see IFSTA Committee.
Carlson, Gene P., ed. see IFSTA Committee.
Carlson, Gene P., ed. see IFSTA Committee & Walker, Lorrin.
Carlson, Gene P., et al. Haz Mat Response Team Leak & Spill Guide. (Illus.). 56p. (Orig.). 1984. pap. text ed. 4.00 (ISBN 0-87939-053-0). Intl Fire Serv.
Carlson, George. Crossword Adventures. LC 76-43215. (Busyback Bks). (Illus.). (gr. 2-6). 1977. pap. 1.95 (ISBN 0-448-48005-0, G&D). Putnam Pub Group.
--Crossword Puzzles. LC 76-54385. (Busyback Bks). (Illus.). (gr. 2-6). 1977. pap. 1.95 (ISBN 0-448-48004-2, G&D). Putnam Pub Group.
Carlson, Gerald P. & Blackwell, E. Harold. Bowling Basics. 162p. 1982. pap. text ed. 8.95 (ISBN 0-8403-2683-1). Kendall-Hunt.
Carlson, Glenn. Airplane Talk. 276p. 1982. pap. 16.95 (ISBN 0-686-43398-X, Pub. by Watosh Pub). Aviation.
Carlson, Glenn E. Air Plane Talk. 276p. (Orig.). 1982. pap. 16.95 (ISBN 0-9611954-0-1). Watosh Pub.
Carlson, Greg N. Reference to Kinds in English. Hankamer, Jorge, ed. LC 79-6619. (Outstanding Dissertations in Linguistics Ser.). 300p. 1985. text ed. 40.00 (ISBN 0-8240-4551-3). Garland Pub.
Carlson, Harold E. Endocrinology. (UCLA Series of Internal Medicine Today: A Comprehensive Postgraduate Library). 308p. 1983. 38.00x (ISBN 0-471-09553-2, Pub. By Wiley Med). Wiley.
Carlson, Harriet. New Horizons for the Housewife. LC 75-85822. 47p. (Orig.). 1969. pap. 2.00 (ISBN 0-87576-024-4). Pilot Bks.
Carlson, Harry C., ed. see Lamm, Martin.
Carlson, Harry G. Strindberg & the Poetry of Myth. LC 81-12989. 252p. 1982. 23.50x (ISBN 0-520-04442-8). U of Cal Pr.
Carlson, Harry G., tr. see Friis, Erik J., et al.
Carlson, Harry G., tr. see Strindberg, August.

Carlson, Helen S. Nevada Place Names: A Geographical Dictionary. 2nd ed. LC 74-13877. (Illus.). 282p. 1985. pap. 15.00 (ISBN 0-87417-094-X). U of Nev Pr.

Carlson, Helen V., et al, eds. An Annotated Bibliography of Technical Writing, Editing, Graphics, & Publishing 1966-1980. 500p. 1983. text ed. 40.00x (ISBN 0-914548-45-X). Soc Tech Comm.

Carlson, Jack & Graham, Hugh. The Economic Importance of Exports to the United States, No. 5. LC 80-66694. (Significant Issues Ser.: Vol. 2). 134p. 1980. 5.95 (ISBN 0-89206-019-0). CSI Studies.

Carlson, Jean. The Cup. LC 81-86002. 1982. 2.50 (ISBN 0-8323-0401-8). Binford.

Carlson, Joanna M. How to Start a Quality Drop-In Child Care Center & Make Money Doing It. LC 82-61480. 100p. (Orig.). 1984. pap. text ed. 9.95 (ISBN 0-88247-706-4). R & E Pubs.

Carlson, Jody. George C. Wallace & the Politics of Powerlessness. LC 79-65225. 332p. 1981. 22.95 (ISBN 0-87855-344-4). Transaction Bks.

Carlson, Joel. No Neutral Ground. 4.95 (ISBN 0-7043-3158-6, Pub. by Quartet England). Charles River Bks.

Carlson, John. Getting More From Your Bible Reading. LC 82-14563. 137p. (Orig.). 1982. pap. 3.95 (ISBN 0-87123-256-1, 210256). Bethany Hse.

--Nineteen Eighty Census Fact Book: Nineteen Eighty Census of Population-Housing Summary Tape File 1-A, B Dallas-Ft. Worth SMSA, Vol. II. 214p. (Orig.). 1982. pap. 30.00 (ISBN 0-936440-41-4). Inst Urban Studies.

Carlson, John F. Carlson's Guide to Landscape Painting. (Illus.). 144p. 1973. pap. 4.95 (ISBN 0-486-22927-0). Dover.

--Carlson's Guide to Landscape Painting. 1984. 15.75 (ISBN 0-8446-6102-3). Peter Smith.

--Nineteen-Eighty Census of Population & Housing: Analysis of Household Size & Occupancy Rates for the State of Texas. 22p. (Orig.). 1981. pap. text ed. 7.00 (ISBN 0-936440-66-X). Inst Urban Studies.

Carlson, Jon. Muscatine: A Pictorial History. (Illus.). 200p. 25.00x (ISBN 0-940286-03-3). Quest Pub IL.

Carlson, Jon & Thorpe, Casey. The Growing Teacher: How to Become the Teacher You've Always Wanted to Be. 220p. 1984. 13.95 (ISBN 0-13-366709-X); pap. 6.95 (ISBN 0-13-366691-3). P-H.

Carlson, Jon, jt. auth. see Dinkmeyer, Don C.

Carlson, Jon, jt. auth. see Hendricks, Gay.

Carlson, Jon, et al, eds. The Consulting Process. (APGA Reprint Ser.: No. 7). 1975. pap. 7.25 (ISBN 0-911547-20-7, 72099W34); pap. 4.50 (ISBN 0-686-34287-9). Am Assn Coun Dev.

Carlson, Judith H., et al. Nursing Diagnosis. (Illus.). 258p. 1982. 15.95 (ISBN 0-7216-2392-1). Saunders.

Carlson, Karen & Meyers, Alan. Speaking with Confidence. 1977. pap. 14.70x (ISBN 0-673-15022-4). Scott F.

Carlson, Katherine. Casualties. LC 82-61652. (Minnesota Voices Project Ser.: No. 9). (Illus.). 124p. 1982. pap. 5.00. New Rivers Pr.

Carlson, Kenneth N. College Football Scorebook. 2nd, rev. ed. (Illus.). 926p. 1984. pap. 14.75 (ISBN 0-938428-05-5). Rain Belt.

--Manual for Travel Counsellors. rev. 14th ed. (Illus.). 276p. 1985. pap. text ed. 17.50 (ISBN 0-938428-06-3). Rain Belt.

--Pro Football Scorebook. (Illus.). 346p. (Orig.). 1982. pap. 6.50 (ISBN 0-938428-02-0). Rain Belt.

--Rugby Football Scorebook. (Illus.). 242p. (Orig.). 1984. pap. 4.75 (ISBN 0-938428-04-7). Rain Belt.

Carlson, Lars A. & Olsson, Anders G., eds. Treatment of Hyperlipoproteinemia. 304p. 1984. text ed. 58.50 (ISBN 0-89004-341-8). Raven.

Carlson, Lars A. & Pernow, Bengt, eds. Metabolic Risk Factors in Ischemic Cardiovascular Disease. 264p. 1982. text ed. 42.50 (ISBN 0-89004-614-X). Raven.

Carlson, Lars A., et al, eds. see International Conference on Atherosclerosis, Milan, November 1977.

Carlson, Lauri. Dialogue Games. 1982. lib. bdg. 49.50 (ISBN 90-277-1455-X, Pub. by Reidel Holland). Kluwer Academic.

Carlson, Lee W., ed. Christian Parenting. 80p. 1984. pap. 8.95 (ISBN 0-8170-1072-6). Judson.

Carlson, Leland H. Martin Marprelate, Gentleman. LC 80-26442. (Illus.). 462p. 1981. 25.00 (ISBN 0-87328-112-8). Huntington Lib.

Carlson, Leonard A. Indians, Bureaucrats, & Land: The Dawes Act & the Decline of Indian Farming. LC 80-1709. (Contributions in Economics & Economic History Ser.: No. 36). xii, 219p. 1981. lib. bdg. 29.95 (ISBN 0-313-22533-8, CDA/). Greenwood.

Carlson, Linda. The Publicity & Promotion Handbook: A Complete Guide for Small Business. 272p. 1982. 21.50 (ISBN 0-8436-0865-X). Van Nos Reinhold.

Carlson, Loren M. Bibliography of South Dakota Government. 1951. write for info. U of SD Gov Res Bur.

--Dakota Preposition: Panacea or Nightmare for South Dakota? 1980. write for info. U of SD Gov Res Bur.

--South Dakota Budgetary Developments: Process & Trends, 1967-1983. 1984. write for info. U of SD Gov Res Bur.

--State Budgeting in South Dakota. 1967. write for info. U of SD Gov Res Bur.

Carlson, Lorentz. Here Come the Littles. (Illus.). 64p. (Orig.). (gr. 1 up). 1984. pap. 5.95 (ISBN 0-590-33149-3). Scholastic Inc.

Carlson, Luis. The Nexus: Test Results to Insights for Remediation. 1978. pap. text ed. 15.00x binder with 2nd addenda (ISBN 0-87879-147-7). Acad Therapy.

Carlson, Luis A. Language-Structured Auditory Retention Span Test (LARS) 1975. manual 10.00 (ISBN 0-87879-097-7); forms a & b in packs of 25 7.00 ea. Acad Therapy.

Carlson, Margaret B. & Shafer, Ronald G. How to Get Your Car Repaired Without Getting Gypped. LC 72-11811. (Illus.). 288p. 1973. 11.49i (ISBN 0-06-010612-3, HarpT). Har-Row.

Carlson, Maria, tr. see Prokofiev, Sergei.

Carlson, Marifran. Feminismo: The Women's Movement in Argentina from Its Beginnings to Evita Peron. 225p. 16.95 (ISBN 0-89733-152-4); pap. 8.95 (ISBN 0-89733-180-X). Academy Chi Pubs.

--Women in Argentina. 1985. 14.95 (ISBN 0-89733-152-4); pap. 6.95 (ISBN 0-89733-168-0). Academy Chi Pubs.

Carlson, Marthena, et al. A Computer-Assisted Instructional System for Elementary Mathematics. 78p. 1974. 1.00 (ISBN 0-318-14702-5, ED 104 667). Learn Res Dev.

Carlson, Marvin. Italian Stage from Goldoni to D'Annunzio. LC 80-10554. 239p. 1981. lib. bdg. 21.95x (ISBN 0-89950-000-5). McFarland & Co.

--Theories of the Theater: A Historical & Critical Survey, from the Greeks to the Present. LC 84-7658. 528p. 1984. 49.50x (ISBN 0-8014-1678-7). Cornell U Pr.

--Theories of the Theatre: A Historical & Critical Survey from the Greeks to the Present. LC 84-7658. 528p. (Orig.). 1985. pap. text ed. 14.95x (ISBN 0-8014-9337-4). Cornell U Pr.

Carlson, Marvin, tr. see Antoine, Andre.

Carlson, Marvin A. Goethe & the Weimar Theatre. (Illus.). 328p. 1978. 29.95x (ISBN 0-8014-1118-1). Cornell U Pr.

Carlson, Morry, jt. auth. see Anderson, Ken.

Carlson, Nancy. Bunnies & Their Hobbies. LC 83-23161. (Illus.). 32p. (ps-2). 1984. PLB 8.95 (ISBN 0-87614-257-9). Carolrhoda Bks.

--Bunnies & Their Hobbies. LC 84-26458. (Illus.). 32p. (ps-3). 1985. pap. 3.95 (ISBN 0-14-050538-5, Puffin). Penguin.

--Harriet & the Garden. LC 81-18136. (Illus.). 32p. (ps-3). 1982. lib. bdg. 8.95g (ISBN 0-87614-184-X). Carolrhoda Bks.

--Harriet & the Garden. (Illus.). 32p. (ps-3). 1985. pap. 3.95 (ISBN 0-14-050466-4, Puffin). Penguin.

--Harriet & the Garden. (Illus.). (gr. k-3). 1985. bk. & cassette 19.95 (ISBN 0-941078-66-3); pap. 12.95 bk. & cassette (ISBN 0-317-14686-6); cassette, 4 paperbacks & guide 27.95 (ISBN 0-317-14687-4). Live Oak Media.

--Harriet & the Roller Coaster. LC 81-18138. (Illus.). 32p. (ps-3). 1982. lib. bdg. 8.95g (ISBN 0-87614-183-1). Carolrhoda Bks.

--Harriet & the Roller Coaster. (Picture Puffins). 32p. (gr. k-3). 1984. pap. 3.95 (ISBN 0-14-050467-2, Puffin). Penguin.

--Harriet & the Roller Coaster. (Illus.). (gr. k-3). 1985. bk. & cassette 19.95 (ISBN 0-941078-56-6); pap. 12.95 bk. & cassette (ISBN 0-941078-54-X); cassette, 4 paperbacks & guide 27.95 (ISBN 0-941078-55-8). Live Oak Media.

--Harriet & Walt. LC 81-18137. (Illus.). 32p. (ps-3). 1982. lib. bdg. 8.95g (ISBN 0-87614-185-8). Carolrhoda Bks.

--Harriet & Walt. (Picture Puffins Ser.). 32p. (gr. k-3). 1984. pap. 3.95 (ISBN 0-14-050463-X, Puffin). Penguin.

--Harriet & Walt. (Illus.). (gr. k-3). 1984. bk. & cassette 19.95 (ISBN 0-941078-59-0); pap. 12.95 bk. & cassette (ISBN 0-317-14688-2); cassette, 4 paperbacks & guide 27.95 (ISBN 0-317-14689-0). Live Oak Media.

--Harriet's Halloween Candy. LC 81-18140. (Illus.). 32p. (ps-3). 1982. lib. bdg. 8.95g (ISBN 0-87614-182-3). Carolrhoda Bks.

--Harriet's Halloween Candy. (Picture Puffins Ser.). 32p. (gr. k-3). 1984. pap. 3.95 (ISBN 0-14-050465-6, Puffin). Penguin.

--Harriet's Halloween Candy. (Illus.). (gr. k-3). 1985. bk. & cassette 19.95 (ISBN 0-941078-53-1); pap. 12.95 bk. & cassette (ISBN 0-941078-51-5); cassette, 4 paperbacks & guide 27.95 (ISBN 0-941078-52-3). Live Oak Media.

--Harriet's Recital. LC 81-18135. (Illus.). 32p. (ps-3). 1982. lib. bdg. 8.95g (ISBN 0-87614-181-5). Carolrhoda Bks.

--Harriet's Recital. (Illus.). 32p. (ps-3). 1985. pap. 3.95 (ISBN 0-14-050464-8, Puffin). Penguin.

--Harriet's Recital. (Illus.). (gr. k-3). 1985. bk. & cassette 19.95 (ISBN 0-941078-69-8); pap. 12.95 bk. & cassette (ISBN 0-941078-67-1); cassette, 4 paperbacks & guide 27.95 (ISBN 0-941078-68-X). Live Oak Media.

--Loudmouth George & the Big Race. LC 83-5191. (Illus.). 32p. (gr. k-3). 1983. PLB 8.95g (ISBN 0-87614-215-3). Carolrhoda Bks.

--Loudmouth George & the Cornet. LC 82-22171. (Illus.). 32p. (gr. k-3). 1983. PLB 8.95g (ISBN 0-87614-214-5). Carolrhoda Bks.

--Loudmouth George & the Cornet. LC 84-18121. (Illus.). 32p. (ps-3). 1985. 3.95 (ISBN 0-14-050509-1, Puffin). Penguin.

--Loudmouth George & the Fishing Trip. LC 82-22159. (Illus.). 32p. (gr. k-3). 1983. PLB 8.95g (ISBN 0-87614-213-7). Carolrhoda Bks.

--Loudmouth George & the Fishing Trip. LC 84-18119. (Illus.). 32p. (ps-3). 1985. 3.95 (ISBN 0-14-050508-3, Puffin). Penguin.

--Loudmouth George & the New Neighbors. LC 83-7298. (Illus.). 32p. (gr. k-3). 1983. PLB 8.95g (ISBN 0-87614-216-1). Carolrhoda Bks.

--Loudmouth George & the Sixth-Grade Bully. LC 83-7178. (Illus.). 32p. (gr. k-3). 1983. PLB 8.95g (ISBN 0-87614-217-X). Carolrhoda Bks.

--Loudmouth George & the Sixth Grade Bully. LC 84-18120. (Illus.). 32p. (ps-3). 1985. 3.95 (ISBN 0-14-050510-5, Puffin). Penguin.

--Making the Team. LC 85-3775. (Illus.). 32p. (ps-3). 1985. PLB 8.95 (ISBN 0-87614-281-1). Carolrhoda Bks.

--The Mysterious Valentine. LC 85-3757. (Illus.). 32p. (ps-3). 1985. PLB 8.95 (ISBN 0-87614-282-X). Carolrhoda Bks.

--The Perfect Family. LC 85-4123. (Illus.). 32p. (ps-3). 1985. PLB 8.95 (ISBN 0-87614-280-3). Carolrhoda Bks.

--The Talent Show. LC 85-4122. (Illus.). 32p. (ps-3). 1985. PLB 8.95 (ISBN 0-87614-284-6). Carolrhoda Bks.

--Witch Lady. LC 85-3756. (Illus.). 32p. (ps-3). 1985. PLB 8.95 (ISBN 0-87614-283-8). Carolrhoda Bks.

Carlson, Nancy, ed. see Pederson, Rolf A.

Carlson, Natalie S. Ann Aurelia & Dorothy. LC 68-10781. (gr. 4-8). 1968. PLB 10.89 (ISBN 0-06-020959-3). HarpJ.

--Carnival in Paris. LC 62-13319. (Illus.). (gr. 2-6). PLB 13.89 (ISBN 0-06-020971-2). HarpJ.

--Empty Schoolhouse. LC 65-11452. (Illus.). (gr. 2-6). 1965. PLB 11.89 (ISBN 0-06-020981-X). HarpJ.

--Family Under the Bridge. LC 58-5292. (Illus.). (gr. 3-7). 1958. PLB 13.89 (ISBN 0-06-020991-7). HarpJ.

--The Ghost in the Lagoon. LC 83-25114. (Illus.). 40p. (gr. 2-4). 1984. 9.75 (ISBN 0-688-03794-1); lib. bdg. 9.12 (ISBN 0-688-03795-X). Lothrop.

--A Grandmother for the Orphelines. LC 80-7769. (Illus.). 96p. (gr. 3-6). 1980. 10.53i (ISBN 0-06-020993-3). HarpJ.

--The Half Sisters. LC 75-105463. (Illus.). (gr. 5 up). 1974. pap. 2.95 (ISBN 0-06-440017-4, Trophy). HarpJ.

--Happy Orpheline. LC 57-9260. (Illus.). (gr. 3-6). 1957. PLB 13.89 (ISBN 0-06-021007-9). HarpJ.

--King of the Cats & Other Tales. LC 79-7861. (Illus.). (ps-3). 1980. PLB 7.95a (ISBN 0-385-15428-3). Doubleday.

--Luvvy & the Girls. LC 77-145999. (Illus.). (gr. 4-8). 1971. HarpJ.

--Marie Louise & Christopher at the Carnival. (Illus.). 32p. (gr. k-3). 1981. 11.95 (ISBN 0-684-17014-0, ScribJ). Scribner.

--Marie Louise's Heyday. LC 75-8345. (Illus.). 32p. (ps-3). 1975. (ScribJ); pap. 0.79 encore ed. (ISBN 0-684-17408-1). Scribner.

--Orphelines in the Enchanted Castle. LC 63-14368. (Illus.). (gr. 3-7). 1964. HarpJ.

--Runaway Marie Louise. LC 77-9448. (Illus.). 32p. (gr. k-3). 1977. 9.95 (ISBN 0-684-15045-X, ScribJ). Scribner.

--Spooky & the Ghost Cat. LC 84-17146. (Illus.). 32p. (ps-1). 1985. 11.75 (ISBN 0-688-04316-X); lib. bdg. 11.88 (ISBN 0-688-04317-8). Lothrop.

--Spooky Night. LC 82-54. 32p. (ps-3). 1982. 11.75 (ISBN 0-688-00934-4); PLB 11.88 (ISBN 0-688-00935-2). Lothrop.

--The Surprise in the Mountains. LC 82-47716. (Illus.). 32p. (gr. 1-3). 1983. 9.57i (ISBN 0-06-021008-7); PLB 9.89g (ISBN 0-06-021009-5). HarpJ.

--Talking Cat & Other Stories of French Canada. LC 52-5429. (Illus.). (gr. 3-6). 1952. PLB 10.89 (ISBN 0-06-021081-8). HarpJ.

--Time for the White Egret: Encore Edition. LC 78-17226. (Illus.). (gr. 1-3). 1978. reinforced bdg 7.95 (ISBN 0-684-15990-2, ScribJ). Scribner.

--Tomahawk Family. LC 60-8348. (Illus.). (gr. 2-6). 1960. PLB 9.89 (ISBN 0-06-021096-6). HarpJ.

Carlson, Neal. To Die is Gain. (Solace Ser.). 1983. pap. 1.25 (ISBN 0-8010-2487-0). Baker Bk.

Carlson, Neal, jt. auth. see Crane, Dale.

Carlson, Neil. Psychology: The Science of Behavior. 1983. text ed. 31.83 (ISBN 0-205-08038-3, 798038); write for info. tchr's manual (ISBN 0-205-08039-1); student guide 13.36 (ISBN 0-205-08040-5, 798040). Allyn.

Carlson, Neil R. Physiology of Behavior. 2nd ed. 704p. 1981. text ed. 32.84 (ISBN 0-205-07262-3, 797262-8); tchr's. ed. avail. (ISBN 0-205-07263-1); wkbk. 15.24 (ISBN 0-205-07264-X, 797264). Allyn.

Carlson, Nola. PB: A New Face in the Mirror. 176p. 1983. pap. 1.95 (ISBN 0-441-57122-0). Ace Bks.

--Sixteen Summer. (Capric Romance Ser.: No. 62). 160p. 1985. pap. 2.25 (ISBN 0-441-76864-4, Pub. by Tempo). Ace Bks.

--Spring Dreams. (Caprice Ser.: No. 41). 160p. 1984. pap. 1.95 (ISBN 0-441-77836-4). Ace Bks.

--Three's a Crowd. 192p. 1982. pap. 1.95 (ISBN 0-448-16921-5). Ace Bks.

Carlson, Norman, ed. Iowa Trolleys: Bulletin No. 114. LC 73-90937. (Illus.). 304p. 1975. 25.00 (ISBN 0-915348-14-4). Central Electric.

Carlson, Norman & Peterson, Arthur, eds. Remember When-Trolley Wires Spanned the Country: Bulletin No. 119. LC 78-74495. (Illus.). 154p. 1980. 30.00 (ISBN 0-915348-20-9). Central Electric.

Carlson, Oliver. Brisbane: A Candid Biography. LC 75-98829. Repr. of 1937 ed. lib. bdg. 19.75x (ISBN 0-8371-2980-X, CABR). Greenwood.

Carlson, Oliver & Bates, Ernest S. Hearst, Lord of San Simeon. LC 70-98830. Repr. of 1936 ed. lib. bdg. 18.75 (ISBN 0-8371-2847-1, CAHE). Greenwood.

--Hearst, Lord of San Simeon. (American Studies). 1969. Repr. of 1936 ed. 24.00 (ISBN 0-384-07575-4). Johnson Repr.

Carlson, P. M. Audition for Murder. 225p. 1985. pap. 2.75 (ISBN 0-380-89538-2). Avon.

Carlson, Paul F., ed. Introduction to Applied Optics for Engineers. 1977. 43.00 (ISBN 0-12-160050-5). Acad Pr.

Carlson, Paul H. Texas Woollybacks: The Range Sheep & Goat Industry. LC 82-40311. (Illus.). 256p. 1982. 19.50 (ISBN 0-89096-133-6). Tex A&M Univ Pr.

Carlson, Paul R. O Christian! O Jew! LC 74-78937. 256p. (Orig.). 1974. pap. 1.95 (ISBN 0-912692-39-1). Cook.

Carlson, Per & Trower, W. Peter, eds. Physics in Collision: High ee-ep-pp Interactions, Vol. 2. 430p. 1983. 69.50 (ISBN 0-306-41249-7, Plenum Press). Plenum Pub.

Carlson, Peter. Roughneck: The Life & Times of Big Bill Haywood. (Illus.). 1983. 17.50 (ISBN 0-393-01621-8). Norton.

--Roughneck: The Life & Times of Big Bill Haywood. (Illus.). 352p. 1984. pap. 6.95 (ISBN 0-393-30208-3). Norton.

Carlson, Peter S. The Biology of Crop Productivity. LC 79-28261. 1980. 52.50 (ISBN 0-12-159850-0). Acad Pr.

Carlson, R. & Granstrom, B., eds. The Representation of Speech in the Peripheral Auditory System: Proceedings of the Symposium, Stockholm, Sweden, May, 1982. 294p. 1982. 63.00 (ISBN 0-444-80447-1, Biomedical Pr). Elsevier.

Carlson, R. F., et al. North American Apples: Varieties, Rootstocks, Outlook. (Illus.). 197p. 1971. text ed. 8.50x (ISBN 0-87013-157-5). Mich St U Pr.

Carlson, R. W., ed. see Vollrath, H. K.

Carlson, R. W., ed. see Wood, S. R. & Nichols, H. E.

Carlson, Ray. Getting Your Baby into Modeling & TV Commercials. LC 84-9420. (Illus.). 32p. (Orig.). 1984. pap. 3.50 (ISBN 0-87576-113-5). Pilot Bks.

Carlson, Ray, jt. auth. see Millkie, Ron.

Carlson, Raymond. Guide to Collecting & Selling Comic Books. LC 76-2461. 24p. 1976. pap. 2.00 (ISBN 0-87576-056-2). Pilot Bks.

Carlson, Raymond, ed. National Directory of Budget Motels 1985-86. rev. ed. LC 75-11992. 78p. 1985. pap. 3.95 (ISBN 0-87576-051-1). Pilot Bks.

--National Directory of Free Tourist Attractions. LC 77-3251. 71p. 1979. pap. 2.95 (ISBN 0-87576-057-0). Pilot Bks.

--National Directory of Free Vacation & Travel Information. rev. ed. LC 78-6456. 48p. 1986. pap. 3.95 (ISBN 0-87576-120-8). Pilot Bks.

--National Directory of Low-Cost Tourist Attractions. LC 79-12044. 71p. 1979. pap. 3.50 (ISBN 0-87576-080-5). Pilot Bks.

--National Directory of Theme Parks & Amusement Areas. LC 78-15725. 47p. 1978. pap. 2.95 (ISBN 0-87576-073-2). Pilot Bks.

Carlson, Reynold E. British Block Grants & Central-Local Finance. LC 78-64203. (Johns Hopkins University. Studies in the Social Sciences. Sixty-Fifth, 1947: 1). 224p. 1980. Repr. of 1947 ed. 24.50 (ISBN 0-404-61309-8). AMS Pr.

Carlson, Reynold E., jt. auth. see MacLean, Janet R.

Carlson, Richard E. Meterology Manual & Lecture Guide. 112p. 1983. pap. text ed. 7.95 (ISBN 0-8403-2992-X). Kendall-Hunt.

Carlson, Richard J., ed. Issues of Electoral Reforms. 170p. 1974. 1.75 (ISBN 0-318-15803-5). Citizens Forum Gov.

Carlson, Richard O. Adoption of Educational Innovations. LC 65-64647. 1965. Ctr Educ Policy Mgmt.

--Orderly Career Opportunities. LC 79-54079. 1979. 4.95 (ISBN 0-936276-09-6). Ctr Educ Policy Mgmt.

Carlson, Rick J. The End of Medicine. LC 75-6856. (Health, Medicine & Society Ser.). pap. 75.80 (ISBN 0-317-28097-X, 2055729). Bks Demand UMI.

Carlson, Robert A. Conceptual Learning: From Mollusks to Adult Education. LC 73-72. (Ocassional Paper Ser.: No. 35). 1973. pap. 2.00 (ISBN 0-87060-058-3, OCP 35). Syracuse U Cont Ed.

Carlson, Robert E. Liverpool & Manchester Railway Project, 1821-1831. LC 76-86621. (Illus.). 1969. 27.50x (ISBN 0-678-05540-8). Kelley.
--The Nurse's Guide to Better Communication. (PROCOM Ser.). 1983. pap. 9.95 (ISBN 0-673-15552-8). Scott F.
Carlson, Robert S., et al. International Finance: Cases & Simulation. LC 80-81213. 400p. 1980. pap. text ed. 17.95 (ISBN 0-201-00903-X); instrs' manual o.p. 6.95. Addison-Wesley.
Carlson, Rodger D. The Economics for the Profitable Mining & Marketing of Gold, Silver, Copper, Lead & Zinc Ores. LC 81-40818. (Illus.). 88p. (Orig.). 1982. lib. bdg. 20.75 (ISBN 0-8191-2021-9); pap. text ed. 8.00 (ISBN 0-8191-2022-7). U Pr of Amer.
--The Economics of Geothermal Power in California. Bruchey, Stuart, ed. LC 78-22666. (Energy in the American Economy Ser.). (Illus.). 1979. lib. bdg. 16.00x (ISBN 0-405-11970-4). Ayer Co Pubs.
Carlson, Ron. Betrayed by F. Scott Fitzgerald. 224p. 1984. pap. 6.95 (ISBN 0-393-30168-0). Norton.
Carlson, Ronald L. Criminal Justice Procedure. 3rd ed. 372p. 1985. pap. text ed. 19.95 (ISBN 0-87084-130-0). Anderson Pub Co.
--Criminal Justice Procedure: Text Discussion. 3rd ed. (Criminal Justice Studies). write for info. Amer Bar Assn.
--Successful Techniques for Civil Trials. LC 83-81617. 1983. 69.50 (ISBN 0-318-00076-8); Suppl. 1984. 17.00. Lawyers Co-Op.
Carlson, Roy, ed. Contemporary Northwest Writing: A Collection of Poetry & Fiction. 208p. 1979. text ed. 12.95 (ISBN 0-87071-324-8); pap. text ed. 9.95x (ISBN 0-87071-323-X). Oreg St U Pr.
Carlson, Roy L., ed. Indian Art Traditions of the Northwest Coast. (Illus.). 214p. 1984. pap. 14.95 (ISBN 0-295-96101-5). U of Wash Pr.
Carlson, Ruth. Writing Aids Through the Grades: One Hundred Eighty-Six Developmental Writing Activities. LC 77-108775. 1970. pap. 5.95x (ISBN 0-8077-1141-1). Tchrs Coll.
Carlson, Ruth, jt. auth. see Carlson, Elwood.
Carlson, Ruth K. Sparkling Words. 1979. 8.95 (ISBN 0-88252-009-1). Paladin Hse.
--Speaking Aids Through the Grades. LC 74-14719. 1975. pap. text ed. 4.95x (ISBN 0-8077-2421-1). Tchrs Coll.
Carlson, Ruth Kearney. Sparkling Words: Three Hundred & Fifteen Practical & Creative Writing Ideas. rev. ed. 312p. 1979. 13.00 (ISBN 0-8141-4617-1); members 10.00 (ISBN 0-317-35319-5). NCTE.
Carlson, Sevinc. China's Oil: Problems & Prospects. LC 79-92159. (CSIS Monograph). 128p. 1979. 77.00 (ISBN 0-89206-010-7). CSI Studies.
--Venezuela's Oil Plans & Potential for the 1980's. LC 81-85374. 154p. (Orig.). 1983. pap. 77.00 (ISBN 0-07-606796-3). McGraw.
Carlson, Stephen P., jt. auth. see Schneider, Fred W.
Carlson, Sune. Executive Behaviour: A Study of the Workload & the Working Methods of Managing Directors. Chandler, Alfred D., ed. LC 79-7535. (History of Management Thought & Practice Ser.). 1980. Repr. of 1951 ed. lib. bdg. 16.00x (ISBN 0-405-12317-5). Ayer Co Pubs.
--Study on the Pure Theory of Production. LC 65-18333. Repr. of 1939 ed. 17.50x (ISBN 0-678-00009-3). Kelley.
Carlson, Susan. Women of Grace: James's Plays & the Comedy of Manners. Litz, A. Walton, ed. LC 84-23932. (Studies in Modern Literature Ser.: No. 48). 200p. 1984. 34.95 (ISBN 0-8357-1617-1). UMI Res Pr.
Carlson, Sylvia, jt. auth. see Carlson, Verne.
Carlson, T. A. X-Ray Photoelectron Spectroscopy. LC 77-28499. (Benchmark Papers in Physical Chemistry & Chemical Physics: Vol. 2). 341p. 1978. 51.00 (ISBN 0-87933-325-1). Van Nos Reinhold.
Carlson, Theodore L. The Illinois Military Tract. Bruchey, Stuart, ed. LC 78-56707. (Management of Public Lands in the U. S. Ser.). (Illus.). 1979. Repr. of 1951 ed. lib. bdg. 17.00 (ISBN 0-405-11322-6). Ayer Co Pubs.
Carlson, Thomas A. Photoelectron & Auger Spectroscopy. LC 72-28025. (Modern Analytical Chemistry Ser.). (Illus.). 417p. 1975. 55.00 (ISBN 0-306-33901-3, Plenum Pr). Plenum Pub.
Carlson, Vada. Broken Pattern: Sunlight & Shadows of Hopi History. (Illus.). 176p. 12.95 (ISBN 0-87961-148-0); pap. 6.95 (ISBN 0-87961-149-9). Naturegraph.
Carlson, Vada & Witherspoon, Gary. Black Mountain Boy. LC 68-27160. (Illus.). 81p. 1982. pap. 4.50 (ISBN 0-89019-008-9). Navajo Curr.
Carlson, Verne. Translation of Film-Video Terms Into Series, 5 Bks. Incl. French (ISBN 0-943288-00-2); German (ISBN 0-943288-01-0); Italian (ISBN 0-943288-02-9); Spanish (ISBN 0-943288-03-7); Japanese (ISBN 0-943288-04-5). LC 84-203565. 1982. pap. 17.95 ea.; 59.95 set (ISBN 0-943288-05-3). Double C Pub.
Carlson, Verne & Carlson, Sylvia. Professional Cameraman's Handbook. 3rd, rev. ed. (Illus.). 575p. 1980. 24.95 (ISBN 0-8174-5548-5). Focal Pr.
--Professional Lighting Handbook. (Illus.). 224p. 1985. 22.95 (ISBN 0-240-51721-0). Focal Pr.
Carlson, Victor I. Picasso Drawings & Watercolors, 1899-1907 in the Collection of the Baltimore Museum of Art. LC 76-41022. 1977. pap. 25.00 (ISBN 0-912298-43-X); pap. 17.50 (ISBN 0-912298-42-1). Baltimore Mus.
Carlson, Victor I., intro. by. Matisse As a Draughtsman. LC 82-82229. (Illus.). 191p. 1983. 35.00 (ISBN 0-87817-291-2). Hacker.
Carlson, William H. In a Grand & Awful Time. LC 67-16715. (Illus.). 160p. 1967. pap. 9.95x (ISBN 0-87071-309-4). Oreg St U Pr.
Carlsson, A., et al, eds. Current Topics in Extrapyramidal Disorders. (Journal of Neural Transmission Supplementum: No. 16). (Illus.). 240p. 1980. 57.90 (ISBN 0-387-81570-8). Springer-Verlag.
Carlsson, Erik, jt. ed. see Higgins, Charles B.
Carlsson, J., ed. Mechanical Behaviour of Materials: Proceedings of the Fourth International Conference on Mechanical Behaviour of Materials, Stockholm, Sweden, August 15-19, 1983, 2 Vols, No. IV. (International Series on Strength & Fracture of Materials & Structures). (Illus.). 1175p. 1984. 225.00 (ISBN 0-08-029340-9). Pergamon.
Carlsson, Jerker. The Limits to Structural Change: A Comparative Study of Foreign Direct Investments in Liberia & Ghana, 1950-1971. 299p. 1982. pap. text ed. 29.50x (ISBN 0-8419-9740-3, Africana). Holmes & Meier.
Carlsson, Jerker, ed. Recession in Africa. 203p. 1982. 29.50x (ISBN 0-8419-9765-9, Africana). Holmes & Meier.
Carlsson-Paige, Nancy & Levin, Diana. Helping Children Understand Peace, War & the Nuclear Threat. LC 84-63040. 1985. 3.00 (NAEYC#321). Natl Assn Child Ed.
Carlsson-Paige, Nancy & Levin, Diane E. Helping Young Children Understand Peace, War & the Threat. LC 84-63040. 1985. pap. 3.00 (ISBN 0-912674-93-8, NAEYC#321). Natl Assn Child Ed.
Carlstein, Tommy. Time Resources, Society & Ecology. (Preindustrial Society Ser.: Vol. 1). (Illus.). 300p. 1983. text ed. 35.00x (ISBN 0-04-300082-7); pap. text ed. 15.95x (ISBN 0-04-300083-5). Allen Unwin.
Carlstein, Tommy, et al, eds. Timing Space & Spacing Time, 3 vols. Incl. Vol. I. Making Sense of Time. 150p. 32.95x (ISBN 0-470-26511-6); Vol. II. Human Activity & Time Geography. 286p. 53.95x (ISBN 0-470-26513-2); Vol. III. Time & Regional Dynamics. 120p. 32.95x (ISBN 0-470-26512-4). 1979. Halsted Pr.
Carlsten, Arne & Grimby, Gunner. The Circulatory Response to Muscular Exercise in Man. (Illus.). 144p. 1966. 14.75x (ISBN 0-398-00285-1). C C Thomas.
Carlston, Charles. Epiphany. Achtemeier, Elizabeth, ed. LC 84-6012. (Proclamation 3: Aids for Interpreting the Lessons of the Church Year Series B). 64p. 1984. pap. 3.50 (ISBN 0-8006-4102-7). Fortress.
Carlston, D. E., jt. auth. see Wyer, R. S.
Carlston, Doug. Applesoft Isn't Hard: BASIC Programming for the Apple II. 232p. 1983. pap. 19.95 (ISBN 0-88701-002-4); disk 9.95; disk & book 27.95. Softalk Pub.
Carlston, Kenneth S. Law & Structures of Social Action. LC 80-19159. (The Library of World Affairs Ser.: No. 30). xii, 288p. 1980. Repr. of 1956 ed. lib. bdg. 32.50x (ISBN 0-313-20837-9, CALW). Greenwood.
--The Process of International Arbitration. LC 74-152591. 318p. 1972. Repr. of 1946 ed. lib. bdg. 19.75x (ISBN 0-8371-6024-3, CAIA). Greenwood.
--Social Theory & African Tribal Organization: The Development of Socio-Legal Theory. LC 68-13226. 473p. 1968. 37.50x (ISBN 0-252-72729-0). U of Ill Pr.
Carlton, Bea. In the House of the Enemy. 192p. (Orig.). 1984. pap. 5.95 (ISBN 0-89636-122-5). Accent Bks.
--The Mystery Book. LC 84-72788. 210p. (Orig.). 1985. pap. 6.95 (ISBN 0-89636-153-5). Accent Bks.
Carlton, Bob. Return to the Forbidden Planet. (Methuen Theatrescripts Ser.). 48p. (Orig.). 1985. pap. 4.95 (ISBN 0-413-57970-0, 9371). Methuen Inc.
Carlton, Charles. Bigotry & Blood: Documents on the Ulster Troubles. LC 76-17018. 160p. 1977. 18.95x (ISBN 0-88229-278-1). Nelson-Hall.
--Charles I: The Personal Monarch. 426p. 1984. pap. 8.95 (ISBN 0-7448-0016-1, Ark Paperbks). Routledge & Kegan.
--Charles the First: The Personal Monarch. (Illus.). 432p. 1983. 27.95x (ISBN 0-7100-9485-X); pap. 8.95 (ISBN 0-7448-0016-1). Routledge & Kegan.
--Descriptive Syntax of the Old English Charters. LC 73-102955. (Janua Linguarum Ser. Practica: No. 111). (Illus., Orig.). 1970. pap. text ed. 25.60x (ISBN 90-2790-744-7). Mouton.
Carlton, Charles M. A Linguistic Analysis of a Collection of Late Latin Documents Composed in Ravenna Between A. D. 445-700: A Quantitative Approach. LC 72-91400. (Janua Linguarum Ser.: No. 89). (Illus.). 1973. pap. 44.00x (ISBN 90-2792-488-0). Mouton.
Carlton, David. Mill & Town in South Carolina, Eighteen Eighty to Nineteen Twenty. LC 82-7753. 313p. 1982. text ed. 32.50x (ISBN 0-8071-1042-6); pap. text ed. 14.95x (ISBN 0-8071-1059-0). La State U Pr.
Carlton, David & Schaerf, Carlo. The Hazards of the International Energy Crisis. LC 80-22412. 300p. 1982. 22.50x (ISBN 0-312-36479-2). St Martin.
Carlton, David & Schaerf, Carlo, eds. The Arms Race in the Nineteen Eighties. LC 81-21303. 256p. 1982. 29.00 (ISBN 0-312-04946-3). St Martin.
--Contemporary Terror: Studies in Sub-State Violence. 1981. 29.95 (ISBN 0-312-16841-1). St Martin.
--The Dynamics of the Arms Race. LC 74-20106. 244p. 1975. 39.95x (ISBN 0-470-13480-1). Halsted Pr.
--Reassessing Arms Control: Studies in Disarmament & Conflicts. LC 84-40339. 232p. 1985. 27.50 (ISBN 0-312-66545-8). St Martin.
--South-Eastern Europe after Tito: A Powder-Keg for the 1980s? LC 82-7352. 250p. 1983. 22.50x (ISBN 0-312-74730-6). St Martin.
Carlton, Dennis W. Market Behavior under Uncertainty. LC 80-8617. (Outstanding Dissertations in Economics Ser.). 215p. 1985. lib. bdg. 31.00 (ISBN 0-8240-4174-7). Garland Pub.
Carlton, Eric. Patterns of Belief, 2 vols. Incl. Vol. 1. Peoples & Religion. 130p (ISBN 0-04-377004-5); Vol. 2. Religions in Society. 140p. pap. 6.95 2 vols. (ISBN 0-04-377005-3). 1973. pap. 6.95 ea. Attic Pr.
--Sexual Anxiety: A Study of Male Impotence. LC 79-56651. 197p. 1980. 27.50x (ISBN 0-06-490960-3, 06386). B&N Imports.
Carlton, Fran. A Time for Fitness: A Daily Exercise Guide for the Christian. LC 76-5719. 1976. 1.75 (ISBN 0-8499-4144-X, 80464). Word Bks.
Carlton, Frank. Marine Recreational Fisheries, Vol. 6. Clepper, Henry, ed. Date not set. 15.00. Sport Fishing.
Carlton, Frank E. Marine Recreational Fisheries, Vol. 3. Clepper, Henry, ed. LC 76-22389. 1978. 15.00 (ISBN 0-686-65030-1). Sport Fishing.
--Marine Recreational Fisheries, Vol. 4. Clepper, Henry, ed. LC 76-22389. 1979. 15.00 (ISBN 0-686-65031-X). Sport Fishing.
--Marine Recreational Fisheries, Vol. 5. Clepper, Henry, ed. LC 76-22389. 1980. 15.00 (ISBN 0-686-70340-5). Sport Fishing.
--Marine Recreational Fisheries, Vol. 9. Clepper, Henry, ed. Date not set. 15.00 (ISBN 0-317-30084-9). Sport Fishing.
--Marine Recreational Fisheries, Vol. 7. Clepper, Henry, ed. Date not set. 15.00. Sport Fishing.
Carlton, Frank T. Economic Influences upon Educational Progress in the United States 1820-1850. LC 66-11657. (Classics in Education Ser.). (Orig.). 1966. pap. text ed. 5.00x (ISBN 0-8077-1140-3). Tchrs Coll.
Carlton, Geoff, jt. auth. see Moore, Jeff.
Carlton, James T., ed. see Light, S. F.
Carlton, Jan. Richmond Receipts. Browder, Robyn, ed. (Regional Cookbook Ser.). (Illus.). 300p. (Orig.). 1985. pap. 8.95 (ISBN 0-89865-322-3). Donning Co.
Carlton, Jan, ed. Apron Strings. (Illus.). 396p. 1983. pap. 9.95 (ISBN 0-9613752-0-5). Womens Com Rich.
Carlton, Jay. The Economical Economy. 64p. 1984. 6.00 (ISBN 0-682-40203-6). Exposition Pr FL.
--Neurology of Mentality. 45p. 1984. 5.00 (ISBN 0-682-40145-5). Exposition Pr FL.
Carlton, Joseph R. Carlton's Complete Reference Book of Music. LC 44-181. (Illus.). 729p. 1980. PLB 40.00 (ISBN 0-937348-00-7). Carlton Pubns CA.
Carlton, Lowis. Famous Florida Recipes. LC 72-170802. (Illus.). 80p. 1972. pap. 1.95 (ISBN 0-8200-0804-4). Great Outdoors.
Carlton, Malcolm. Music in Education. (Woburn Education Ser.). 1985. 22.50x (ISBN 0-7130-0155-0, Woburn Pr England). Biblio Dist.
Carlton, Mitchell. Hot Oil. (Orig.). 1980. pap. 1.75 (ISBN 0-505-51477-X, Pub. by Tower Bks). Dorchester Pub Co.
Carlton, N., ed. Astrophysics, Pt. A: Optical & Infrared Astronomy. (Methods of Experimental Physics Ser.: Vol. 12). 1974. 80.00 (ISBN 0-12-475912-2). Acad Pr.
Carlton, Peter L. A Primer of Behavioral Pharmacology. LC 83-9083. (Illus.). 320p. 1983. text ed. 25.95 (ISBN 0-7167-1450-7); pap. text ed. 16.95 (ISBN 0-7167-1451-5). W H Freeman.
Carlton, Rich. Salvation. (The Road Knights Ser.: No. 2). 224p. (Orig.). 1985. pap. 2.50 (ISBN 0-523-42229-6). Pinnacle Bks.
Carlton, Robert, jt. auth. see Rubin, Barbara.
Carlton, Susan, ed. see Fifield, Sarah A.
Carlton, Thomas. Clinical Social Work in Health Settings: A Guide to Professional Practice with Exemplars. (Springer Series on Social Work: Vol. 4). 320p. 1984. 24.95 (ISBN 0-8261-4400-4). Springer Pub.
Carlton, Tom. One, Two, Three Financial Macros. 250p. 1985. pap. 19.95 (ISBN 0-88022-205-0, 187). Que Corp.
Carlton, W. N. English Literature. 1973. Repr. of 1925 ed. 15.00 (ISBN 0-8274-1545-1). R West.
Carlton, Wendy. In Our Professional Opinion... The Primacy of Clinical Judgment Over Moral Choice. LC 78-51524. 1978. text ed. 12.95x (ISBN 0-268-01143-5). U of Notre Dame Pr.
Carlucci, Nicola A., jt. auth. see Benedict, Robert P.
Carluccio, Luigi. Domenico Gnoli. LC 74-82606. (Illus.). 168p. 1975. 75.00 (ISBN 0-87951-026-9). Overlook Pr.
Carlut, Charles. A Concordance to Flaubert's Bouvard et Pecuchet. LC 79-7915. 1021p. 1980. lib. bdg. 121.00 (ISBN 0-8240-9518-9). Garland Pub.
--A Concordance to Flaubert's "Madame Bovary", 2 vols. LC 77-83409. (Library of Humanities Reference Bks.: No. 109). 1185p. 1978. Set. lib. bdg. 145.00 (ISBN 0-8240-9832-3). Garland Pub.
--Correspondance de Flaubert: Etude et Repertoire Critique. 845p. (Fr). 1969. 10.00 (ISBN 0-8142-0010-9). Ohio St U Pr.
Carlut, Charles & Meiden, Walter. French for Oral Written Review. 3rd ed. 1983. text ed. 19.95 (ISBN 0-03-062318-9); practice manual 11.95 (ISBN 0-03-062319-7); tapes 180.00 (ISBN 0-03-062321-9). HR&W.
Carlut, Charles, et al. A Concordance to Flaubert's L'education Sentimentale, 2 vols. LC 78-68262. (Reference Library of the Humanities: Vol. 125). 1979. Set. lib. bdg. 169.00 (ISBN 0-8240-9795-5). Garland Pub.
--A Concordance to Flaubert's La Tentation de Saint Antoine. LC 79-7914. (Garland Reference Library of the Humanities: No. 180). 1980. lib. bdg. 73.00 (ISBN 0-8240-9547-2). Garland Pub.
--A Concordance to Flaubert's Salammbo, 2 vols. LC 78-68268. (Garland Reference Library of the Humanities: No. 148). 1979. Set. lib. bdg. 121.00 (ISBN 0-8240-9794-7). Garland Pub.
--A Concordance to Flaubert's Trois Contes. LC 79-17347. (Garland Reference Library of the Humaities: No. 178). 1980. lib. bdg. 73.00 (ISBN 0-8240-9548-0). Garland Pub.
Carlwright, jt. auth. see Rawson.
Carlyle, A., ed. see Carlyle, Thomas.
Carlyle, A. J., jt. auth. see Carlyle, R. W.
Carlyle, Alexander. An Argument to Prove That the Tragedy of Douglas Ought to Be Publickly Burned by the Hands of the Hangman. Bd. with The Justice & Necessity of the War with Our American Colonies Examined. Repr. of 1977 ed; The Usefulness & Necessity of a Liberal Education for Clergymen. Repr. of 1793 ed. LC 78-67650. Repr. of 1977 ed. 24.50 (ISBN 0-404-17185-0). AMS Pr.
--Autobiography of the Rev. Dr. Alexander Carlyle: Containing Memorials of Men & Events of His Time. Burton, John H., ed. LC 78-67649. Repr. of 1860 ed. 44.50 (ISBN 0-404-17179-6). AMS Pr.
Carlyle, Alexander, jt. auth. see Crichton-Browne, James.
Carlyle, Alexander, ed. see Carlyle, Jane B.
Carlyle, Alexander, ed. see Carlyle, Jane W.
Carlyle, Alexander, ed. see Carlyle, Thomas.
Carlyle, Alexander J. Christian Church & Liberty. LC 68-56734. (Research & Source Works Ser.: No. 214). 1968. Repr. of 1924 ed. 14.50 (ISBN 0-8337-0476-1). B Franklin.
--Political Liberty. 220p. 1963. 26.00x (ISBN 0-7146-1551-X, F Cass Co). Biblio Dist.
--Political Liberty: A History of the Conception in the Middle Ages & Modern Times. LC 80-18967. viii, 220p. 1980. Repr. of 1963 ed. lib. bdg. 22.50x (ISBN 0-313-21482-4, CAPL). Greenwood.
Carlyle, E. I. William Cobbett. 59.95 (ISBN 0-8490-1301-1). Gordon Pr.
Carlyle, Jane B. Letters & Memorials of Jane Welsh Carlyle, 3 vols. LC 79-37683. 1168p. 1983. Repr. of 1883 ed. Set. 120.00 (ISBN 0-404-56709-6). AMS Pr.
--New Letters & Memorials of Jane Welsh Caryle, 2 vols. Carlyle, Alexander, ed. LC 78-37672. (Illus.). 1983. Repr. of 1903 ed. 87.50 set (ISBN 0-404-56724-X). AMS Pr.
--New Letters & Memorials of Jane Welsh Carlyle, 2 vols. Carlyle, Alexander, ed. 1903. 38.00 set (ISBN 0-8274-3022-1). R West.
Carlyle, Jane W. I Too Am Here: Selections from the Letters of Jane Welsh Carlyle. LC 76-11093. pap. 81.80 (ISBN 0-317-28139-9, 2022471). Bks Demand UMI.
--New Letters & Memorials of Jane Welsh Carlyle: Volumes I & II. Carlyle, Alexander, ed. 1979. Repr. of 1903 ed. Set. lib. bdg. 50.00 (ISBN 0-8495-0934-3). Arden Lib.
Carlyle, Ken. Challenging & Highly Profitable Business Careers for the New College Graduate Eager for Success & Adventure. (Illus.). 1977. 47.50 (ISBN 0-89266-078-3). Am Classical Coll Pr.
Carlyle, R. W. & Carlyle, A. J. A History of Medieval Political Theory in the West, 6 vols. 1979. Repr. Set. lib. bdg. 400.00 (ISBN 0-8495-0919-X). Arden Lib.
Carlyle, Thomas. A Carlyle Reader. Tennyson, G. B., ed. LC 83-21024. 544p. 1984. 44.50 (ISBN 0-521-26238-0); pap. 9.95 (ISBN 0-521-27873-2). Cambridge U Pr.
--Critical & Miscellaneous Essays: Collected & Republished, 2 Vols. 337p. Repr. of 1984 ed. Set. lib. bdg. 65.00 (ISBN 0-89984-047-7). Century Bookbindery.

--The Early Letters of Thomas Carlyle, 2 vols. in 1. Norton, Charles E., ed. LC 77-88563. 1977. Repr. of 1886 ed. lib. bdg. 65.00 (ISBN 0-89341-460-3). Longwood Pub Group.
--History of Friedrich II of Prussia, Called Frederick the Great. CLive, John, ed. LC 79-82375. (Classic European Historians Ser.). pap. 129.80 (ISBN 0-317-28204-2, 2020042). Bks Demand UMI.
--Lectures on the History of Literature: April to July 1838. Greene, J. Reay, ed. 263p. 1983. Repr. of 1892 ed. lib. bdg. 45.00 (ISBN 0-89987-139-9). Darby Bks.
--Lectures on the History of Literature Delivered by Thomas Carlyle: April to July 1838. Greene, J. Reay, ed. 1978. Repr. of 1892 ed. lib. bdg. 25.00 (ISBN 0-8495-0754-5). Arden Lib.
--Letters of Thomas Carlyle. 1971. Repr. of 1923 ed. 39.00x (ISBN 0-403-00897-2). Scholarly.
--Letters of Thomas Carlyle, Eighteen Twenty-Six to Eighteen Thirty-Six, 2 vols. Norton, Charles E., ed. LC 70-39194. (Select Bibliographies Reprint Ser.). 1888. Set. 48.50 (ISBN 0-8369-6796-8). Ayer Co Pubs.
--Letters of Thomas Carlyle: Eighteen Twenty-Six to Nineteen Thirty-Six, 2 vols. Norton, Charles Eliot, ed. 1888. 45.00 set (ISBN 0-8274-2847-2). R West.
--The Letters of Thomas Carlyle to His Brother Alexander, with Related Family Letters. Marrs, Edwin W., Jr., ed. LC 68-21978. (Illus.). 40.00x (ISBN 0-674-52612-0). Harvard U Pr.
--Letters of Thomas Carlyle to John Stuart Mill, John Sterling & Robert Browning. LC 77-95420. (English Biography Ser., No. 31). 1969. Repr. of 1923 ed. lib. bdg. 51.95x (ISBN 0-8383-0964-X). Haskell.
--Letters to His Youngest Sister. Copeland, C. T., ed. (Illus.). 1968. Repr. of 1899 ed. 27.00x (ISBN 3-4870-2208-7). Adlers Foreign Bks.
--The Life of Friedrich Schiller. 1973. Repr. of 1901 ed. 16.50 (ISBN 0-8274-1504-4). R West.
--The Life of John Sterling. 1851. Repr. 25.00 (ISBN 0-8274-2890-1). R West.
--The Love Letters of Thomas Carlyle & Jane Welsh, 2 vols. Carlyle, Alexander, ed. LC 75-30016. (Illus.). Repr. of 1909 ed. 80.00 set (ISBN 0-404-14050-5). AMS Pr.
--Montaigne: And Other Essays, Chiefly Biographical. LC 72-13208. (Essay Index Reprint Ser.). Repr. of 1897 ed. 23.00 (ISBN 0-8369-8149-9). Ayer Co Pubs.
--New Letters, 2 Vols. Carlyle, A., ed. (Illus.). 1969. Repr. of 1904 ed. Set. 62.00x (ISBN 3-4870-2525-6). Adlers Foreign Bks.
--New Letters of Thomas Carlyle, 2 vols. Carlyle, Alexander, ed. 1904. Set. 60.00 (ISBN 0-8274-3023-X). R West.
--New Letters of Thomas Carlyle, 2 Vols. Carlyle, Alexander, ed. LC 75-108465. 1970. Repr. of 1904 ed. Set. 49.00x (ISBN 0-403-00204-4). Scholarly.
--The Nigger Question. August, Eugene R., ed. Bd. with The Negro Question. Mill, John S. LC 73-14584. (Crofts Classics Ser.). 1971. text ed. 5.95x (ISBN 0-88295-021-5); pap. text ed. 1.25x (ISBN 0-88295-020-7). Harlan Davidson.
--On Heroes, Hero-Worship & the Heroic in History. Niemeyer, Carl, ed. LC 66-12130. (Illus.). xxviii, 259p. 1966. pap. 6.95x (ISBN 0-8032-5030-4, BB 334, Bison). U of Nebr Pr.
--Past & Present. 1976. Repr. of 1912 ed. 8.95x (ISBN 0-460-00608-8, Evman). Biblio Dist.
--Past & Present. Altick, Richard D., ed. LC 77-70381. (Gotham Library). 294p. 1977. pap. 9.50x (ISBN 0-8147-0562-6). NYU Pr.
--The Psychological Theory of the Hero in History & in Politics. (The Essential Library of the Great Philosophers Ser.). (Illus.). 121p. 1983. 71.85 (ISBN 0-686-82208-0). Am Inst Psych.
--The Psychology of the Hero As the Most Powerful Force Determining the Course of History, 2 vols. (Illus.). 375p. 1985. Set. 187.75 (ISBN 0-89920-088-5). Am Inst Psych.
--Reminiscences, 2 vols. Froude, James A., ed. 1881. 21.50 set (ISBN 0-8274-3268-2). R West.
--Reminiscences, 2 vols. Froude, James A., ed. LC 71-144936. (Literature Ser.). 1972. Repr. of 1881 ed. 29.00x (ISBN 0-403-00898-0). Scholarly.
--Reminiscences. Froude, James A., ed. 352p. 1983. Repr. of 1881 ed. lib. bdg. 30.00 (ISBN 0-89987-138-0). Darby Bks.
--Sartor Resartus. 272p. 1981. Repr. of 1921 ed. lib. bdg. 20.00 (ISBN 0-8495-0858-4). Arden Lib.
--Sartor Resartus. Bd. with On Heroes & Hero Worship. 1954. 8.95x (ISBN 0-460-00278-3, Evman); pap. 3.50x (ISBN 0-460-01278-9, Evman). Biblio Dist.
--Sartor Resartus & On Heroes & Hero-Worship. 1967. Repr. of 1908 ed. 11.95 (Evman). Biblio Dist.
--Selected Writings. Shelston, Alan, ed. (Penguin English Library). 310p. 1980. pap. 4.95 (ISBN 0-14-043065-2). Penguin.
--Thomas Carlyle: Letters to His Wife. Bliss, Trudy, ed. 1953. 20.00 (ISBN 0-8274-3603-3). R West.
--Works of Thomas Carlyle, 30 Vols. Traill, H. D., ed. LC 79-22238. (BCL Ser. II). Repr. of 1899 ed. Set. 1200.00 (ISBN 0-404-09800-2); 40.00 ea. AMS Pr.

Carlyle, Thomas & Emerson, Ralph Waldo. The Correspondence of Thomas Carlyle & Ralph Waldo Emerson 1834-1872, 2 vols. 1980. Repr. of 1894 ed. Set. lib. bdg. 65.00 (ISBN 0-89341-481-6). Longwood Pub Group.
Carlyle, Thomas & Greene, J. Reay. Lectures on the History of Literature. 1979. Repr. of 1892 ed. lib. bdg. 25.00 (ISBN 0-89987-101-1). Darby Bks.
Carlyle, Thomas & Mims, Edwin. Past & Present. 363p. 1981. Repr. of 1918 ed. lib. bdg. 20.00 (ISBN 0-8495-8770-0). Arden Lib.
Carlyle, Thomas see Copeland, Charles Townsend.
Carlyle, Thomas, jt. auth. see Emerson, Ralph Waldo.
Carlyle, Thomas see Hedge, F. H. & Noa, L.
Carlyle, Thomas, ed. Latter- Day Pamphlets. LC 72-37771. (Essay Index Reprint Ser.). Repr. of 1853 ed. 21.00 (ISBN 0-8369-2584-X). Ayer Co Pubs.
Carlyle, Thomas, tr. Goethe's Wilhelm Meister's Apprenticeship & Travels, 2 vols. 889p. 1985. Repr. of 1890 ed. Set. lib. bdg. 75.00 (ISBN 0-8414-4316-5). Folcroft.
Carlyle, Thomas, tr. see Von Goethe, Johann W. & Steiner, Rudolf.
Carlyle, William. A Comprehensive Outline Guide to Ancient Empires. 1983. 8.95 (ISBN 0-533-05166-5). Vantage.
Carlyon, Richard. The Dark Lord of Pengersick. LC 80-13360. (Illus.). 176p. (gr. 4 up). 1980. 10.95 (ISBN 0-374-31700-3). FS&G.
--The Dark Lord of Pengersick. 176p. 1985. pap. 2.75 (ISBN 0-441-13786-5). Ace Bks.
Carmack, Daniel F. Ohio Probate: Ohio Practice Systems Library Selection. LC 79-91159. 87.50; Suppl. 1984. 31.00; Suppl. 1983. 28.00. Lawyers Co-Op.
Carmack, Paul A., jt. auth. see Crocker, Lionel.
Carmack, Robert & Cofacci, Gino. Desserts with Spirit! LC 84-45056. 244p. 1985. 15.95 (ISBN 0-689-11473-7). Atheneum.
Carmack, Robert M. The Quiche Mayas of Utatlan: The Evolution of a Highland Guatemala Kingdom. LC 80-5241. (The Civilization of the American Indian Ser.: No. 155). (Illus.). 400p. 1981. 29.50 (ISBN 0-8061-1546-7). U of Okla Pr.
--Quichean Civilization: The Ethnohistoric, Ethnographic & Archaelogical Sources. LC 70-149948. (Illus.). 1973. 45.00x (ISBN 0-520-01963-6). U of Cal Pr.
Carmack, William, et al. Native American Research Information Service. 275p. 1983. pap. 15.00 (ISBN 0-935626-11-5). U Cal AISC.
Carman & Saunders. Modern Technical Math. 1984. write for info. (ISBN 0-534-02739-3). Wadsworth Pub.
--Modern Technical Math with Calculus. write for info. (ISBN 0-534-04305-4). Wadsworth Pub.
Carman, Barry & McPherson, John, eds. Bimbashi McPherson: A Life in Egypt. (Illus.). 316p. 1985. 19.95 (ISBN 0-88186-027-1). Parkwest Pubns.
Carman, Bliss. James Whitcomb Riley: An Essay. LC 76-53562. 1977. Repr. of 1925 ed. lib. bdg. 15.00 (ISBN 0-8414-3464-6). Folcroft.
--The Poetry of Life: Longfellow, Emerson, Swinburne. 1973. Repr. of 1905 ed. 20.00 (ISBN 0-8274-1544-3). R West.
Carman, Bliss & Hovey, Richard. Last Songs from Vagabondia. 59.95 (ISBN 0-87968-316-3). Gordon Pr.
--More Songs from Vagabondia. 59.95 (ISBN 0-87968-315-5). Gordon Pr.
--Songs from Vagabondia. 59.95 (ISBN 0-87968-314-7). Gordon Pr.
--Songs from Vagabondia. LC 68-57593. Repr. of 1895 ed. lib. bdg. 24.75 (ISBN 0-8371-1800-X, CASO). Greenwood.
--Songs from Vagabondia. (American Studies). (Illus.). 1969. Repr. of 1907 ed. lib. bdg. 12.00 (ISBN 0-384-07590-8). Johnson Repr.
Carman, Bliss, compiled by. Canadian Poetry in English. LC 76-22428. 456p. 1976. Repr. of 1954 ed. lib. bdg. 32.50x (ISBN 0-8371-9008-8, CACP). Greenwood.
Carman, Bliss, ed. The World's Best Poetry, 10 vols. 1975. Set. lib. bdg. 1200.00 (ISBN 0-87968-323-6). Gordon Pr.
--The World's Best Poetry, 10 Vols. LC 81-83524. (The Granger Anthology, Series I). 4944p. 1982. Repr. of 1904 ed. lib. bdg. 399.50x (ISBN 0-89609-300-X). Granger Bk.
Carman, Harry J. Social & Economic History of the United States, 2 Vols. 1930-34. 100.00 (ISBN 0-384-07600-9). Johnson Repr.
--Street Surface Railway Franchises of New York City. LC 76-77998. (Columbia University Studies in the Social Sciences: No. 200). Repr. of 1919 ed. 20.00 (ISBN 0-404-51200-3). AMS Pr.
Carman, Harry J. & Thompson, Arthur W. A Guide to the Principal Sources for American Civilization, 1800-1900, in the City of New York: Manuscripts. LC 60-6935. pap. 125.30 (ISBN 0-317-10490-X, 2013209). Bks Demand UMI.
Carman, Harry J., ed. Jesse Buel, Agricultural Reformer: Selections from His Writings. LC 72-2835. (Use & Abuse of America's Natural Resources Ser). 650p. 1972. Repr. of 1947 ed. 37.50 (ISBN 0-405-04503-4). Ayer Co Pubs.
Carman, Harry J., ed. see Eliot, Jared.

Carman, J. Neale. A Study of the Pseudo-Map Cycle of Arthurian Romance to Investigate Its Historico-Geographic Background & to Provide a Hypothesis As to Its Fabrication. LC 72-88008. 144p. 1973. 19.95x (ISBN 0-7006-0100-7). U Pr of KS.
Carman, J. Neale, tr. From Camelot to Joyous Guard: The Old French La Mort le Roi Artu. LC 73-18242. xxii, 172p. 1974. 19.95x (ISBN 0-7006-0121-X). U Pr of KS.
Carman, John B., jt. auth. see Luke, P. Y.
Carman, John B., jt. ed. see Dawe, Donald G.
Carman, John S. Obstacles to Mineral Development: A Pragmatic View. Varon, Benison, ed. LC 78-26807. (Illus.). 1979. 33.00 (ISBN 0-08-023904-8). Pergamon.
Carman, M. J., jt. auth. see Carman, R. A.
Carman, Marilyn J., jt. auth. see Carman, Robert A.
Carman, Michael D. U. S. Customs & the Madero Revolution. (Southwestern Studies Ser.: No. 48). 1976. 3.00 (ISBN 0-87404-105-8). Tex Western.
Carman, R. A. & Carman, M. J. Basic Algebra: A Guided Approach. 2nd ed. 575p. 1982. pap. text ed. 27.45 (ISBN 0-471-04174-2); solutions manual 12.00 (ISBN 0-471-08688-6); tapes 209.45 (ISBN 0-471-08686-X). Wiley.
Carman, Robert A. & Adams, Royce W., Jr. Study Skills: A Student's Guide for Survival. 2nd ed. LC 83-5925. (Self-Teaching Guides: No. 1-581). 272p. 1984. pap. 6.95 (ISBN 0-471-88911-3, 1-591). Wiley.
Carman, Robert A. & Adams, W. Royce, Jr. Study Skills: A Student's Guide for Survival. LC 72-4506. (Wiley-Self Teaching Guides). 256p. 1972. 6.95x (ISBN 0-471-13491-0, Pub. by Wiley Pr). Wiley.
Carman, Robert A. & Carman, Marilyn J. Basic Mathematical Skills: A Guided Approach. 2nd ed. LC 80-19121. 576p. 1981. pap. text ed. 27.45x (ISBN 0-471-03608-0). Wiley.
--Intermediate Algebra: A Guided Approach. 575p. 1980. text ed. 27.45x (ISBN 0-471-02104-0); student ed. 13.45 (ISBN 0-471-07912-X). Wiley.
--Quick Arithmetic: A Self-Teaching Guide. 2nd ed. LC 83-3531. 286p. 1984. pap. 7.95 (ISBN 0-471-88966-0, 1-581, Pub. by Wiley Press). Wiley.
Carman, Robert A. & Saunders, Hal M. Mathematics for the Trades: A Guided Approach. LC 79-11491. 580p. 1981. pap. text ed. 27.95x (ISBN 0-471-13481-3); tchr's. manual 7.00 (ISBN 0-471-07791-7). Wiley.
Carman, W. Y. Richard Simkin's Uniforms of the British Army: The Cavalry Regiments. 222p. 1982. 24.45 (ISBN 0-906671-13-2). Webb & Bower.
Carman, W. Y., intro. by. Dress Regulations Nineteen Hundred. (Illus.). 198p. 1983. 23.95 (ISBN 0-85368-044-2, Arms & Armour Pr). Sterling.
Carmean, E. A. Bellows: The Boxing Pictures. LC 82-8161. (Illus.). 1982. pap. 1.00 (ISBN 0-89468-028-5). Natl Gallery Art.
Carmean, E. A., jt. auth. see Monod-Fontaine, Isabelle.
Carmean, E. A., Jr. The Great Decade of American Abstraction: The Modernist Art, 1960-1970. LC 73-94140. (Illus.). 140p. 1973. pap. 14.95 (ISBN 0-295-96068-X). U of Wash Pr.
--The Morton G. Neumann Family Collection: Picasso Prints & Drawings, Vol. 3. LC 81-14151. (Illus.). pap. 2.00 (ISBN 0-89468-042-0). Natl Gallery Art.
Carmean, Patrice. Site Value Taxation. (Research & Information Ser.). 67p. 1980. 13.00 (ISBN 0-88329-020-0). Intl Assess.
Carmean, Patricia. Property Tax Incentives for Alternative Energy Devices. (Research & Information Ser.). 108p. 1980. 17.00 (ISBN 0-88329-041-3). Intl Assess.
Carmel, Abraham. So Strange My Path. LC 64-17487. 1977. pap. 5.95 (ISBN 0-8197-0066-5). Bloch.
Carmel, Herman. Black Days, White Nights. LC 84-10866. 320p. 1984. 17.95 (ISBN 0-88254-998-7). Hippocrene Bks.
Carmel, Hesi, jt. auth. see Derogy, Jacques.
Carmel, Simon J. International Hand Alphabet Charts. 2nd ed. LC 81-90361. (Illus.). 136p. 1982. pap. 10.95 (ISBN 0-9600886-2-8). S Carmel.
Carmeli. Statistical Theory & Random Matrices. (Pure & Applied Mathematics Ser.). 184p. 1983. 45.00 (ISBN 0-8247-1779-1). Dekker.
Carmeli, M., et al, eds. Relativity. LC 74-112865. 381p. 1970. 55.00x (ISBN 0-306-30475-9, Plenum Pr). Plenum Pub.
Carmeli, Moshe. Classical Fields: General Relativity & Gauge Theory. 650p. 1982. 52.95 (ISBN 0-471-86437-4, Pub. by Wiley-Interscience). Wiley.
--Group Theory & General Relativity. (Pure & Applied Physics Ser.). (Illus.). 1977. text ed. 56.95x (ISBN 0-07-009986-3). McGraw.
Carmelite Sisters of Cristo Rey Carmel, San Francisco, tr. see Carmelite Sisters of Noto, Italy.
Carmelite Sisters of Noto, Italy. God's Word to His Church. Carmelite Sisters of Cristo Rey Carmel, San Francisco, tr. from Ital. LC 81-83568. 144p. (Orig.). 1982. pap. text ed. 7.95 (ISBN 0-89870-016-7). Ignatius Pr.

Carmell. Aids to Talmud Study. 1979. write for info. (ISBN 0-87306-181-0). Feldheim.
Carmell, Aryeh & Domb, Cyril, eds. Challenge. 1978. 13.95 (ISBN 0-87306-174-8); pap. 7.95 (ISBN 0-87306-165-9). Feldheim.
Carmell, Aryeh, tr. see Dessler, E. E.
Carmell, Aryeh, jt. tr. see Mallin, Shlomo.
Carmelli, Moshe & Malin, Shimon. Representations of the Rotation & Lorentz Groups: An Introduction. (Lecture Notes in Pure & Applied Mathematics Ser.: Vol. 16). 1976. 35.00 (ISBN 0-8247-6449-8). Dekker.
Carmen, Arlene & Moddy, Howard. Working Women: The Subterranean World of Street Prostitution. LC 84-48585. 256p. 1985. 15.34 (ISBN 0-06-039040-9, C&M Bessie Bk). Har-Row.
Carmen, G. E., et al. Residue Reviews, Vol. 62. LC 62-18595. (Residue Review Ser.). (Illus.). 176p. 1976. 29.50 (ISBN 0-387-90158-2). Springer-Verlag.
Carmen, Ira H. Cloning & the Constitution: An Inquiry into Govermental Policy Making & Genetic Engineering. LC 85-40363. (Illus.). 240p. 1985. text ed. 22.50x (ISBN 0-299-10340-4). U of Wis Pr.
Carmen, Richard. Positive Solutions to Hearing Loss. 212p. 1983. 15.95 (ISBN 0-13-687590-4); pap. 7.95 (ISBN 0-13-687582-3). P-H.
Carmen, Richard, jt. auth. see Hurvitz, Joel.
Carmen, Vicente F. see Del Carmen, Vicente F.
Carmer, Carl. Stars Fell on Alabama. LC 85-8107. (Illus.). xxii, 294p. (Orig.). 1985. 22.50 (ISBN 0-8173-0236-0); pap. 10.95 (ISBN 0-8173-0235-2). U of Ala Pr.
Carmer, Carl, jt. auth. see Carmer, Elizabeth.
Carmer, Carl L. For the Rights of Men. facs. ed. LC 75-86740. (Essay Index Reprint Ser). 1947. 15.00 (ISBN 0-8369-1175-X). Ayer Co Pubs.
Carmer, Elizabeth & Carmer, Carl. Captain Abner & Henry Q. LC 65-10059. (American Folktales Ser.). (gr. 2-5). 1965. PLB 7.47 (ISBN 0-8116-4001-9). Garrard.
--The Susquehanna: From New York to the Chesapeake. LC 64-10245. (Rivers of the World Ser.). (Illus.). (gr. 4-7). 1964. PLB 4.47 (ISBN 0-8116-6360-4). Garrard.
Carmi, A., ed. Euthanasia. LC 84-3099. (Medicolegal Library: Vol. 2). 160p. 1984. pap. 32.10 (ISBN 0-387-13251-1). Springer Verlag.
Carmi, A. & Schneider, S., eds. Nursing Law & Ethics. (Medicolegal Library: Vol. 4). 225p. 1985. pap. 59.00 (ISBN 0-387-15253-9). Springer-Verlag.
Carmi, A. & Zimrin, H., eds. Child Abuse. (Medicolegal Library: Vol. 1). (Illus.). 224p. 1984. 39.50 (ISBN 0-387-12471-3). Springer-Verlag.
Carmi, A., et al, eds. Disability. (Medicolegal Library: Vol. 3). 225p. 1984. pap. 42.20 (ISBN 0-387-13421-2). Springer-Verlag.
Carmi, S., jt. ed. see Peterson, F.
Carmi, T. At the Stone of Losses. Schulman, Grace, tr. from Hebrew. (Jewish Poetry Ser.). (Illus.). 192p. (Orig.). 1983. 13.95 (ISBN 0-520-05106-8); pap. 8.95 (ISBN 0-520-05107-6). U of Cal Pr.
--The Penguin Book of Hebrew Verse. 1981. 25.00 (ISBN 0-670-36507-6). Viking.
Carmi, T., ed. The Penguin Book of Hebrew Verse. 448p. (Orig., Hebrew & Eng.). 1981. pap. 9.95 (ISBN 0-14-042197-1). Penguin.
Carmichael. Auditing Service 1985. (Professional Accounting & Business Ser.). 1985. 90.00 (ISBN 0-471-82334-1). Wiley.
--Reassessing Canada's Potential Economic Growth. (Canadian Studies). 75p. 1979. 30.00 (ISBN 0-317-34006-9, CS-59); members 10.00 (ISBN 0-317-34007-7). Conference Bd.
Carmichael, A. C. Domestic Manners & Social Condition of the White, Coloured, & Negro Population of the West Indies. LC 74-88403. Repr. of 1833 ed. 31.00x (ISBN 0-8371-2477-8, CDM&, Pub. by Negro U Pr). Greenwood.
Carmichael, A. Douglas. Ocean Engineering Power Systems. LC 74-4343. (Illus.). 201p. 1974. pap. 8.00x (ISBN 0-87033-192-2). Cornell Maritime.
Carmichael, Alasdair. Kintyre. (Island Ser.). 1974. 16.95 (ISBN 0-7153-6317-4). David & Charles.
Carmichael, Amy. Candles in the Dark. 1982. pap. text ed. 3.50 (ISBN 0-87508-085-5). Chr Lit.
--Edges of His Ways. 1955. pap. 5.95 (ISBN 0-87508-062-6). Chr Lit.
--Figures of the True. 1968. pap. 1.50 (ISBN 0-87508-065-0). Chr Lit.
--God's Missionary. 1957. pap. 1.25 (ISBN 0-87508-066-9). Chr Lit.
--Gold by Moonlight. 1960. 7.95 (ISBN 0-87508-067-7). Chr Lit.
--Gold Cord. 1957. pap. 5.95 (ISBN 0-87508-068-5). Chr Lit.
--His Thoughts Said...His Father Said. 1958. pap. 2.95 (ISBN 0-87508-069-3). Chr Lit.
--Mimosa. 1958. pap. 2.95 (ISBN 0-87508-074-X). Chr Lit.
--Rose from Brier. 1972. 4.95 (ISBN 0-87508-078-2); pap. 2.95 (ISBN 0-87508-077-4). Chr Lit.
--Thou Givest...They Gather. 1970. pap. 3.95 (ISBN 0-87508-083-9). Chr Lit.
--Toward Jerusalem. 1961. pap. 2.95 (ISBN 0-87508-080-4). Chr Lit.
--Whispers of His Power. new ed. 256p. 1983. 10.95 (ISBN 0-8007-1360-5). Revell.

Carmichael, Amy W. If. (Illus.). 64p. 1980. 3.95 (ISBN 0-310-42202-7). Zondervan.

Carmichael, Ava & Carmichael, David. From White Knuckles to Cockpit Cool. LC 77-83055. 1977. pap. 7.95 (ISBN 0-8168-5850-0). Aero.

Carmichael, Betty. You Can't Borrow from Tomorrow. 1984. 8.95 (ISBN 0-8062-2410-X). Carlton.

Carmichael, Bill & Carmichael, Nancie. Answers to the Questions Christian Women Are Asking. 1984. text ed. 10.95 (ISBN 0-89081-446-5); pap. 6.95 (ISBN 0-89081-442-2). Harvest Hse.

Carmichael, C. Women, Law, & the Genesis Tradition. 112p. 1979. 16.50x (ISBN 0-85224-364-2, Pub. by Edinburgh U Pr Scotland). Columbia U Pr.

Carmichael, C., ed. see Kent, R. T.

Carmichael, Calum M. Law & Narrative in the Bible: The Evidence of the Deuteronomic Laws & the Decalogue. LC 85-4214. 352p. 1985. text ed. 35.00x (ISBN 0-8014-1792-9). Cornell U Pr.

--The Laws of Deuteronomy. LC 73-19206. 277p. 1974. 29.50x (ISBN 0-8014-0824-5). Cornell U Pr.

Carmichael, Carol. Dynasty of Desire. 544p. (Orig.). 1984. pap. 3.95 (ISBN 0-8439-2141-2, Leisure Bks). Dorchester Pub Co.

Carmichael, Carolyn W. see Cullinan, Bernice E.

Carmichael, Carrie. BigFoot: Man, Monster, or Myth? LC 77-21317. (Great Unsolved Mysteries). (Illus.). (gr. 4-5). 1977. PLB 14.25 (ISBN 0-8172-1052-0). Raintree Pubs.

--Bigfoot: Man, Monster, or Myth? LC 77-13297. (Great Unsolved Mysteries Ser.). (Illus.). 48p. (gr. 4up). 1983. pap. 9.27 (ISBN 0-8172-2154-9). Raintree Pubs.

--Non-Sexist Childraising. LC 76-48497. 1977. pap. 6.95 (ISBN 0-8070-2739-1, BP579). Beacon Pr.

--Secrets of the Great Magicians. LC 77-13297. (Myth, Magic & Superstition). (Illus.). (gr. 4-5). 1977. PLB 14.25 (ISBN 0-8172-1031-8). Raintree Pubs.

Carmichael, D. Erskine. The Pap Smear: Life of George N. Papanicolaou. (Illus.). 140p. 1973. photocopy ed. 11.25x (ISBN 0-398-02716-1). C C Thomas.

Carmichael, D. G. Structural Modelling & Optimization. (Engineering Science Ser.). 306p. 1981. 74.95 (ISBN 0-470-27114-0). Halsted Pr.

Carmichael, D. R. The Auditor's Reporting Obligation: Meaning & Implementation of the Fourth Standard of Reporting. 2nd ed. (Auditing Research Monographs: No. 1). 188p. 1978. pap. 9.50 (ISBN 0-685-58470-4). Am Inst CPA.

Carmichael, D. R. & Benis, Martin. Wiley-Ronald Auditing Service. LC 83-25935. (Wiley Ronald Series in Professional Accounting & Business: 1-560). 600p. 1984. Spiral 85.00x (ISBN 0-471-09616-4, Pub. by Ronald Pr). Wiley.

Carmichael, D. R. & Willingham, John J. Perspectives in Auditing. 3rd ed. 1979. pap. text ed. 17.95 (ISBN 0-07-009991-X). McGraw.

--Perspectives in Auditing. 4th ed. 1984. 17.95 (ISBN 0-07-009988-X). McGraw.

Carmichael, D. R. & Makela, Ben, eds. Corporate Financial Reporting: The Benefits & Problems of Disclosure. 288p. 1976. 12.00 (ISBN 0-685-58499-2). Am Inst CPA.

Carmichael, David. Guide to the Records of the American Crystal Sugar Company. (Orig.). 1985. pap. 5.00 (ISBN 0-87351-179-4). Minn Hist.

Carmichael, David, jt. auth. see Carmichael, Ava.

Carmichael, Douglas R., jt. auth. see Seidler, Lee L.

Carmichael, Edward A. Tackling the Federal Deficit. (Observation: No. 26). 183p. 1984. 8.00 (ISBN 0-88806-124-2). Inst C D Howe.

--Time for Decisions, Vol. 1985. (Policy Review & Outlook). 94p. 1985. 6.00 (ISBN 0-88806-128-5). Inst C D Howe.

Carmichael, Edward A. & Dobson, Wendy. Achieving a Realistic Recovery. (Policy Review & Outlook). 65p. 1983. 6.00 (ISBN 0-88806-114-5). Inst C D Howe.

Carmichael, Fitzhugh L. & Nassimbene, Raymond. Changing Aspects of Urban Relief. LC 72-173446. (FDR & the Era of the New Deal Ser.). 94p. 1971. Repr. of 1939 ed. lib. bdg. 19.50 (ISBN 0-306-70370-X). Da Capo.

Carmichael, G. Quilts to Grow on. 1986. cancelled (ISBN 0-442-22532-6). Van Nos Reinhold.

Carmichael, Hoagy. Stardust Road. LC 79-94603. Repr. of 1948 ed. lib. bdg. 19.00x (ISBN 0-8371-2451-4, CASR). Greenwood.

--The Stardust Road. LC 82-48583. (Midland Bks.: No. 296). (Illus.). 160p. 1983. pap. 6.95 (ISBN 0-253-20296-5). Ind U Pr.

Carmichael, Hoagy & Longstreet, Stephen. Sometimes I Wonder. LC 76-7577. (Roots of Jazz Ser.). 1976. Repr. of 1965 ed. lib. bdg. 29.50 (ISBN 0-306-70809-4). Da Capo.

Carmichael, Hogie B., jt. auth. see Garrison, Everett.

Carmichael, Joel. Arabs Today. LC 76-41554. 240p. 1977. pap. 2.95 (ISBN 0-385-11351-X, Anch). Doubleday.

--The Death of Jesus. 296p. (Orig.). 1982. pap. 8.95 (ISBN 0-8180-0826-1). Horizon.

--Open Letter to Moses & Mohammed. LC 68-9705. (Open Letter Ser). (Orig.). 1968. pap. 2.25 (ISBN 0-685-11973-4, 18). Heineman.

Carmichael, Joel, ed. see Sukhanov, N. N.

Carmichael, Joel, tr. see Aldanov, Mark.

Carmichael, Joel, tr. see Tolstoy, Leo.

Carmichael, John. Vacant Possessions. (Institute of Economic Affairs, Hobart Papers Ser.: No. 28). (Illus., Orig.). 1969. pap. 2.50 technical (ISBN 0-255-69578-0). Transatlantic.

Carmichael, John, Jr. & Bulmer, Charles. Labor & Employment Policy. (Orig.). 1979. pap. 8.00 (ISBN 0-918592-35-6). Policy Studies.

Carmichael, John L., jt. auth. see Bulmer, Charles.

Carmichael, John P., jt. ed. see Griesbach, Marc F.

Carmichael, Katherine. Critical Edition of the Early Poems of John Keats with a Philosophical Supplement. 1944. lib. bdg. 7.50 (ISBN 0-8414-3533-2). Folcroft.

Carmichael, Mary C. Oh, Boy! Joy Roy! 23p. 1985. 4.95 (ISBN 0-533-05795-7). Vantage.

Carmichael, Nancie, jt. auth. see Carmichael, Bill.

Carmichael, Oliver C. Graduate Education: A Critique & a Program. LC 77-4229. 1977. Repr. of 1961 ed. lib. bdg. 18.50x (ISBN 0-8371-9585-3, CAGE). Greenwood.

--Universities: Commonwealth & American; a Comparative Study. LC 70-167323. (Essay Index Reprint Ser.). Repr. of 1959 ed. 20.25 (ISBN 0-8369-2760-5). Ayer Co Pubs.

Carmichael, Patrick H., ed. Understanding the Books of the New Testament. rev. ed. LC 61-9583. 1961. pap. 6.25 (ISBN 0-8042-3304-7). John Knox.

--Understanding the Books of the Old Testament. rev. ed. LC 61-9223. 1961. pap. 6.25 (ISBN 0-8042-3316-0). John Knox.

Carmichael, Peter A. Reasoning: A Textbook of Elementary Logic. LC 77-80132. (Illus.). 1978. 12.50 (ISBN 0-8022-2206-4). Philos Lib.

Carmichael, R. CRC Handbook of Physical Properties of Rocks, Vol. I. 416p. 1981. 71.50 (ISBN 0-8493-0226-9). CRC Pr.

Carmichael, R. D. The Logic of Discovery. LC 74-26255. (History, Philosophy & Sociology of Science Ser). 1975. Repr. 22.00x (ISBN 0-405-06583-3). Ayer Co Pubs.

Carmichael, Ralph. He's Everything to Me: Autobiography. 1985. 9.95 (ISBN 0-8499-0094-8). Word Bks.

Carmichael, Robert D. & Smith, Edwin R. Mathematical Tables & Formulas. 1931. pap. 3.75 (ISBN 0-486-60111-0). Dover.

Carmichael, Robert S., ed. CRC Handbook of Physical Properties of Rocks, Vol. III. 360p. 1984. 60.00 (ISBN 0-8493-0228-5). CRC Pr.

Carmichael, Ronald L., jt. auth. see Eckles, Robert W.

Carmichael, Standrod, ed. see Knight, Tanis & Lewin, Larry.

Carmichael, Stephen. The Adrenal Medulla, Vol. 1. Horrobin, D. F., ed. (Annual Research Reviews). 1979. 20.00 (ISBN 0-88831-051-X). Eden Pr.

Carmichael, Stephen W. The Adrenal Medulla, Vol. 2. Horrobin, David F., ed. (Annual Research Reviews). 118p. 1981. 18.00 (ISBN 0-88831-108-7). Eden Pr.

--The Adrenal Medulla, Vol. 3. Horrobin, D. F., ed. (Annual Research Reviews). 223p. 1984. 38.00 (ISBN 0-88831-168-0). Eden Pr.

Carmichael, Stokely S. & Hamilton, Charles V. Black Power: The Politics of Liberation in America. 1967. pap. 5.95 (ISBN 0-394-70033-3, V33, Vin). Random.

Carmichael, Viola S. Science Experiences for Young Children. Reed, R., ed. LC 81-85434. (Orig.). 1982. pap. 6.95 (ISBN 0-88247-633-5). R & E Pubs.

Carmichael, W. W., ed. The Water Environment: Algal Toxins & Health. (Environmental Science Research Ser.: Vol. 20). 504p. 1981. 69.50 (ISBN 0-306-40756-6, Plenum Pr). Plenum Pub.

Carmichel, Jim. The Compleat Just Jim. 2nd ed. Wolfe, Dave, ed. (Illus.). 128p. 1981. text ed. 13.50 (ISBN 0-935632-09-3). Wolfe Pub Co.

--Do-It-Yourself Gunsmithing. LC 77-12450. (Outdoor Life Book). (Illus.). 1978. 18.22i (ISBN 0-06-010638-7, HarpT). Har-Row.

--Women's Guide to Handguns. 190p. 1983. pap. 8.95 (ISBN 0-88317-118-X). Stoeger Pub Co.

Carmignac, Jean. The Birth of the Synoptic Gospels. Wrenn, Michael J., tr. 1985. 9.50 (ISBN 0-8199-0887-8). Franciscan Herald.

Carmigniani, Juan C., jt. auth. see Lachouque, Henry.

Carmilly-Weinberger, Moshe. Censorship & Freedom of Expression in Jewish History. LC 77-79828. 1979. pap. 8.95 (ISBN 0-87203-088-1). Hermon.

Carmines, Christine. Celluloid Warrior. (Illus.). pap. 11.95 (ISBN 0-931945-00-3). Thinking Gnomes.

Carmines, E. G., jt. auth. see Zeller, R. A.

Carmines, Edward G. & Zeller, Richard A. Reliability & Validity Assessment. LC 79-67629. (Quantitative Applications in the Social Sciences: No. 17). (Illus.). 70p. 1979. pap. 5.00 (ISBN 0-8039-1371-0). Sage.

Carmines, Edward G., jt. auth. see McIver, John P.

Carmines, Edward G., jt. auth. see Zeller, Richard A.

Carmo, M. Do, ed. Geometry & Topology. (Lecture Notes in Mathematics: Vol. 597). 1977. 35.00 (ISBN 0-387-08345-6). Springer-Verlag.

Carmo, Manfredo Do see Do Carmo, Manfredo.

Carmo, Pamela B. Do. see Do Carmo, Pamela B. & Patterson, Angelo T.

Carmody & Carmody. Shamans, Prophets & Sages: A Concise Intro to World Religion. 1984. write for info. (ISBN 0-534-04263-5). Wadsworth Pub.

Carmody, Denise L. Caring for Marriage. 176p. (Orig.). 1985. pap. 7.95 (ISBN 0-8091-2721-0). Paulist Pr.

--Feminism & Christianity: A Two-Way Reflection. LC 82-1709. 192p. (Orig.). 1982. pap. 9.95 (ISBN 0-687-12914-1). Abingdon.

--The Oldest God: Archaic Religion Yesterday & Today. LC 80-25499. 192p. (Orig.). 1981. pap. 7.50 (ISBN 0-687-28813-4). Abingdon.

--Seizing the Apple: A Feminist Spirituality of Personal Growth. 176p. (Orig.). 1984. pap. 10.95 (ISBN 0-8245-0652-9). Crossroad NY.

--What Are They Saying about Non-Christian Faith? (WATSA Ser.). 96p. (Orig.). 1982. pap. 3.95 (ISBN 0-8091-2432-7). Paulist Pr.

--Women & World Religions. LC 79-102. 1979. pap. 7.50 (ISBN 0-687-45954-0). Abingdon.

Carmody, Denise L. & Carmody, John. Religion: The Great Questions. 176p. 1983. pap. 9.95 (ISBN 0-8164-2476-4, Pub. by Seabury). Winston Pr.

Carmody, Denise L. & Carmody, John T. Becoming One Flesh. LC 84-50841. 160p. (Orig.). 1984. pap. 6.95 (ISBN 0-8358-0486-0). Upper Room.

--Christianity: An Introduction. 288p. 1982. pap. text ed. write for info (ISBN 0-534-01181-0). Wadsworth Pub.

--Western Ways to the Center: An Introduction to Religions of the West. 272p. 1982. pap. text ed. write for info. (ISBN 0-534-01328-7). Wadsworth Pub.

Carmody, Denise L. & Caromody, John T. Eastern Ways to the Centers: An Introduction to Asian Religions. 256p. 1982. pap. text ed. write for info. (ISBN 0-534-01342-2). Wadsworth Pub.

Carmody, Denise L., jt. auth. see Carmody, John T.

Carmody, Dennis L. & Carmody, John T. Ways to the Center: An Introduction to World Religions. 432p. 1981. text ed. write for info. (ISBN 0-534-00890-9). Wadsworth Pub.

Carmody, Edmond, et al. Automation in the Marriage Tribunal: A Report from a Special Committee of the Canon Law Society of America. viii, 90p. (Orig.). pap. 9.95 (ISBN 0-943616-27-1). Canon Law Soc.

Carmody, John. Ecology & Religion: Toward a New Christian Theology of Nature. LC 82-62412. 1983. pap. 6.95 (ISBN 0-8091-2526-9). Paulist Pr.

--The Heart of the Christian Matter: An Ecumenical Approach. 304p. (Orig.). 1983. pap. 12.95 (ISBN 0-687-16765-5). Abingdon.

--Holistic Spirituality. 160p. 1984. pap. 7.95 (ISBN 0-8091-2564-1). Paulist Pr.

--How to Make It Through the Day. LC 84-51826. 112p. (Orig.). 1985. pap. 5.95 (ISBN 0-8358-0491-7). Upper Room.

--Maturing a Christian Conscience. 160p. (Orig.). 1985. pap. 6.95 (ISBN 0-8358-0510-7). Upper Room.

--Reexamining Conscience. 144p. (Orig.). 1982. pap. 8.95 (ISBN 0-8164-2405-5, Pub. by Seabury). Winston Pr.

Carmody, John, jt. auth. see Carmody, Denise L.

Carmody, John, et al. Exploring the New Testament. (Illus.). 448p. 1986. text ed. 24.95 (ISBN 0-13-297276-X). P-H.

Carmody, John T. & Carmody, Denise L. Contemporary Catholic Theology. rev. ed. LC 84-48213. 256p. 1985. pap. 14.95x (ISBN 0-06-061316-5, HarpR). Har-Row.

--Contemporary Catholic Theology: An Introduction. LC 80-7743. 256p. (Orig.). 1980. pap. text ed. 14.95x (ISBN 0-06-061317-3, RD340, HarpR). Har-Row.

Carmody, John T., jt. auth. see Carmody, Denise L.

Carmody, John T., jt. auth. see Carmody, Dennis L.

Carmody, Leie & Conheim, Cathy. So Who's a Ten in a World of One to Nine? (Illus.). 64p. (Orig.). 1985. pap. 9.95 (ISBN 0-317-18239-0). Ventures Intl.

Carmona, J. & Vergne, M., eds. Non-Commutative Analysis: Proceedings. (Lecture Notes in Mathematics: Vol. 728). 1979. pap. 17.00 (ISBN 0-387-09516-0). Springer-Verlag.

--Non-Commutative Harmonic Analysis. (Lecture Notes in Mathematics Ser.: Vol. 587). 1977. soft cover 18.00 (ISBN 0-387-08245-X). Springer-Verlag.

--Non Commutative Harmonic Analysis & Lie Groups. (Lecture Notes in Mathematics Ser.: 1020). 187p. 1983. pap. 12.00 (ISBN 0-387-12717-8). Springer-Verlag.

--Non-Commutative Harmonic Analysis & Lie Group: Proceedings. (Lecture Notes in Mathematics Ser.: Vol. 830). 553p. 1981. pap. 32.00 (ISBN 0-387-10872-6). Springer-Verlag.

Carmona, J., et al, eds. Non-Commutative Harmonic Analysis. 231p. 1975. pap. 16.00 (ISBN 0-387-07183-0). Springer-Verlag.

Carmona-Agosto, Vivian, ed. The Bit. Albornoz, Fernando, tr. (Rotary Drilling Ser.: Unit I, Lesson 2). (Illus.). 59p. (Orig., Span.). 1981. pap. text ed. 5.00 (ISBN 0-88698-030-5, 2.10232). PETEX.

--Safety on the Rig. rev. ed. Albornoz, Fernando, tr. from Eng. (Rotary Drilling Ser.: Unit I, Lesson6). (Illus.). 77p. (Span.). 1981. pap. text ed. 5.00 (ISBN 0-88698-038-0, 2.11032). PETEX.

Carmona-Agosto, Vivian, tr. see Albornoz, Fernando.

Carmona-Agosto, Vivian, et al, eds. Wind, Waves, & Weather. Rossman, Marcela, tr. from Eng. (Rotary Drilling Series, Unit V: Lesson 1). (Illus.). 44p. (Span.). 1982. pap. text ed. 4.50 (ISBN 0-88698-046-1, 2.50112). PETEX.

Carmony, Lowell A. & Holliday, Robert L. Macintosh BASIC. LC 84-23051. (Illus.). Date not set. pap. 19.95 (ISBN 0-88175-082-4). Computer Sci.

--Macintosh Pascal. LC 84-19901. (Illus.). 315p. 1985. pap. 19.95 (ISBN 0-88175-081-6); student's diskette 20.00 (ISBN 0-88175-088-3); solutions diskette 15.00 (ISBN 0-88175-089-1). Computer Sci.

Carmony, Lowell A., et al. Apple Pascal: A Self-Study Guide for the Apple II Plus, IIe, & IIc. LC 84-19950. (Illus.). 233p. 1985. pap. text ed. 18.95 (ISBN 0-88175-076-X); diskette 15.00 (ISBN 0-88175-095-6). Computer Sci.

--Problem Solving in Apple Pascal: Teacher's Guide & Solution Manual. (gr. 10-12). 1984. 15.00 (ISBN 0-88175-021-2). Computer Sci.

Carmony, Marvin, jt. auth. see Baker, Ronald L.

Carmony, Neil B. & Brown, David E., eds. Tales from Tiburon: An Anthology of Adventures in Seriland. LC 82-51171. (Illus.). 146p. (Orig.). 1983. 15.95 (ISBN 0-9610126-1-7); pap. 9.95 (ISBN 0-9610126-0-9). SW Nat Hist Assn.

Carmouche, William J. Crisis in Space: Enunciation of Non-Inertial Phenomenon. LC 83-61832. (Illus.). 127p. 1984. 24.00 (ISBN 0-317-02458-2). Revelation Pr.

Carmoy, Guy De see De Carmoy, Guy.

Carn, John. Shaw's Nam. LC 84-70275. 224p. (Orig.). 1984. pap. 3.95 (ISBN 0-916967-00-X). Benjamin Bks.

Carn, Neil, jt. auth. see Hinds, Dudley.

Carnac, Nicholas. Indigo. 448p. 1982. 14.95 (ISBN 0-312-41413-7). St Martin.

--Tournament of Shadows. 352p. 1981. pap. 2.75 (ISBN 0-345-28772-X). Ballantine.

Carnahan, Brice & Wilkes, James O. Digital Computing & Numerical Methods with FORTRAN IV WATFOR & WATFIV Programming. LC 72-13010. 477p. 1973. text ed. 45.45 (ISBN 0-471-13500-3). Wiley.

Carnahan, Brice, et al. Applied Numerical Methods. LC 67-27555. 604p. 1969. 45.50 (ISBN 0-471-13507-0). Wiley.

Carnahan, Charles W. Conflict of Law & Life Insurance Contracts. 2nd ed. LC 58-11622. xviiii, 768p. 1958. lib. bdg. 25.00 (ISBN 0-89941-361-7). W S Hein.

Carnahan, David H. Prologue in the Old French & Provencal Mystery. LC 68-55160. (Studies in French Literature, No. 45). 1969. Repr. of 1905 ed. lib. bdg. 46.95x (ISBN 0-8383-0519-9). Haskell.

Carnall, C. A. The Evaluation of Organisational Change. 136p. 1982. text ed. 31.00x (ISBN 0-566-00519-0). Gower Pub Co.

Carnall, Geoffrey, ed. see Butt, John.

Carnall, William T. & Choppin, Gregory R., eds. Plutonium Chemistry. LC 83-6057. (Symposium Ser.: No. 216). 484p. 1983. lib. bdg. 51.95 (ISBN 0-8412-0772-0). Am Chemical.

Carnap, Rudolf. Foundations of Logic & Mathematics. (Foundations of the Unity of Science Ser: Vol. 1, No. 3). 1937. pap. 4.50x (ISBN 0-226-57578-0, P402, Phoen). U of Chicago Pr.

--Introduction to Semantics & Formalization of Logic. LC 58-13846. 1959. 30.00x (ISBN 0-674-46200-9). Harvard U Pr.

--Introduction to Symbolic Logic & Its Applications. 1958. pap. 4.95 (ISBN 0-486-60453-5). Dover.

--The Logical Structure of the World & Pseudoproblems in Philosophy. George, Rolf A., tr. LC 66-13604. Orig. Title: Logische Aufbau der Welt. 1967. pap. 9.95x (ISBN 0-520-01417-0, CAL184). U of Cal Pr.

--Logical Syntax of Language. (International Library of Psychology & Philosophy & Scientific Method). 1964. text ed. 30.50x (ISBN 0-7100-3125-4). Humanities.

--Meaning & Necessity: A Study in Semantics & Modal Logic. 2nd ed. LC 56-9132. 1956. pap. 4.95 (ISBN 0-226-09346-8, P30, Phoen). U of Chicago Pr.

--Philosophy & Logical Syntax. LC 75-41050. (BCL Ser. II). Repr. of 1935 ed. 11.50 (ISBN 0-404-14518-3). AMS Pr.

--Two Essays on Entropy. Shimony, Abner, ed. LC 73-94444. 1978. 28.50x (ISBN 0-520-02715-9). U of Cal Pr.

Carnap, Rudolf & Gardner, Martin, eds. Introduction to the Philosophy of Science. LC 66-16499. pap. 8.95x (ISBN 0-465-09517-8, TB-5018). Basic.

Carnarvon, Earl. No Regrets: Memoirs of the Earl of Carnarvon. (Illus.). 227p. 1976. Repr. of 1978 ed. 17.00x (ISBN 0-297-77246-5, GWN 03581, Pub. by Weidenfeld & Nicolson England). Biblio Dist.

Carnarvon, Henry J. Portugal & Galicia: Review of the Social & Political State of the Basque Provinces. 3rd ed. LC 77-87712. Repr. of 1848 ed. 27.50 (ISBN 0-404-16578-8). AMS Pr.

Carnazza, Joseph. Succession-Replacement Planning: Programs & Practices. 1982. pap. 12.00 (ISBN 0-317-11511-1). Columbia U Res.

Carne, Barbara & Mills, Bruce. A Basic Guide to Horse Care & Management. LC 78-12794. 304p. 1979. 12.95 (ISBN 0-668-04498-5). Arco.

Carne, E. Bryan. Modern Telecommunications. (Applications of Communications Theory Ser.). 306p. 1984. 29.50x (ISBN 0-306-41841-X, Plenum Pr). Plenum Pub.

Carne, Judy. Laughing on the Outside Crying on the Inside: The Bittersweet Saga of the Sock-It-to-Me Girl. (Illus.). 1985. 15.95 (ISBN 0-89256-271-4). Rawson Assocs.

Carne, Marcel. Children of Paradise. (Lorrimer Classic Screenplay Ser.). (Illus.). pap. 10.95 (ISBN 0-8044-6076-0). Ungar.

--Le Jour Se Leve. (Lorrimer Classic Screenplay Ser.). (Illus.). 10.95 (ISBN 0-8044-2110-2); pap. 6.95 (ISBN 0-8044-6077-9). Ungar.

--Les Visiteurs Du Soir. (Bibliotheque Des Classiques Du Cinema). (Illus.). 255p. (Fr.). 1981. 19.95 (ISBN 0-8044-2114-5). Ungar.

Carne, Marcel, jt. auth. see Prevert, Jacques.

Carne, P. B. & Crawford, L. D. Scientific & Common Names of Insects & Allied Forms Occuring in Australia. 98p. 1980. pap. 7.25 (ISBN 0-643-00386-X, C059, CSIRO). Unipub.

Carnegie, Andrew. Empire of Business. LC 68-23280. 1968. Repr. of 1933 ed. lib. bdg. 55.00x (ISBN 0-8371-0037-2, CAEB). Greenwood.

--James Watt. 164p. 1984. Repr. of 1984 ed. lib. bdg. 40.00 (ISBN 0-89987-195-X). Darby Books.

--Miscellaneous Writings. facs. ed. Hendrick, B. J., ed. LC 68-58777. (Essay Index Reprint Ser). 1933. 40.00 (ISBN 0-8369-0105-3). Ayer Co Pubs.

--Problems of To-Day: Wealth - Labor - Socialism. 1908. 15.00 (ISBN 0-686-17693-6). Quality Lib.

--Triumphant Democracy. 1971. Repr. of 1886 ed. 37.00 (ISBN 0-384-07697-1). Johnson Repr.

--Triumphant Democracy; or, Fifty Year's March of the Republic. 1888. 30.00 (ISBN 0-8482-7584-5). Norwood Edns.

Carnegie Council, jt. auth. see DeLone, Richard.

Carnegie Council on Children, jt. auth. see Keniston, Kenneth.

Carnegie Council on Policy Studies in Higher Education. The Carnegie Council on Policy Studies in Higher Education: A Summary of Reports & Recommendations. LC 80-7999. (Higher Education Ser. & the Carnegie Council Ser.). 1981. text ed. 29.95x (ISBN 0-87589-474-7). Jossey-Bass.

--Faculty Bargaining in Public Higher Education: A Report & Two Essays. LC 76-50728. (Higher Education Ser. & the Carnegie Council Ser.). (Illus.). 1977. text ed. 19.95x (ISBN 0-87589-322-8). Jossey-Bass.

--Fair Practices in Higher Education: Rights & Responsibilities of Students & Their Colleges in a Period of Intensified Competition for Enrollments. LC 79-84232. (Higher Education Ser. & the Carnegie Council Ser.). 1979. 18.95x (ISBN 0-87589-415-1). Jossey-Bass.

--The Federal Role in Postsecondary Education: Unfinished Business, 1975-1980: A Report. 1st ed. LC 75-4482. (The Carnegie Council Ser.). pap. 27.80. Bks Demand UMI.

--Giving Youth a Better Chance: Options for Education, Work, & Service. LC 79-90851. (Higher Education Ser. & the Carnegie Council Ser.). 1980. 19.95x (ISBN 0-87589-441-0). Jossey-Bass.

--Low or No Tuition: The Feasibility of a National Policy for the First Two Years of College: An Analytical Report. 1st ed. LC 75-4276. pap. 24.00 (ISBN 0-317-27210-1, 2023873). Bks Demand UMI.

--Making Affirmative Action Work in Higher Education: An Analysis of Institutional & Federal Policies with Recommendations. LC 75-27205. (Higher Education Ser. & the Carnegie Council Ser.). (Illus.). 1975. 21.95x (ISBN 0-87589-270-1). Jossey-Bass.

--Next Steps for the Nineteen Eighties in Student Financial Aid: A Fourth Alternative. LC 78-62576. (Higher Education Series & Carnegie Council Ser.). 1979. 21.95x (ISBN 0-87589-395-3). Jossey-Bass.

Carnegie Council on Policy Studies in Higher Education Staff. Progress & Problems in Medical & Dental Education: Federal Support Versus Federal Control. LC 76-11964. (Carnegie Council Ser.). pap. 48.00 (ISBN 0-317-26053-7, 2023780). Bks Demand UMI.

--Selective Admissions in Higher Education: Public Policy & Academic Policy, the Pursuit of Fairness in Admissions to Higher Education, the Status of Selective Admissions. 1st ed. LC 77-88501. pap. 68.00. Bks Demand UMI.

--Three Thousand Futures: The Next Twenty Years for Higher Education. LC 79-9675. (Higher Education Ser. & the Carnegie Council Ser.). 1980. text ed. 19.95x (ISBN 0-87589-453-4). Jossey- Bass.

Carnegie, Dale. Dale Carnegie's Biographical Roundup. facs. ed. LC 77-117764. (Essay Index Reprint Ser). 1944. 17.00. Ayer Co Pubs.

--How to Develop Self-Confidence & Influence People by Public Speaking. 1984. pap. 3.95. PB.

--How to Enjoy Your Life & Your Job. 1983. pap. 2.95 (ISBN 0-671-49269-1). PB.

--How to Enjoy Your Life & Your Job. rev. ed. 1985. 12.95 (ISBN 0-671-54644-9). S&S.

--How to Stop Worrying. 1984. pap. 3.95 (ISBN 0-671-53267-7). PB.

--How to Stop Worrying & Start Living. rev. ed. 1984. 15.95 (ISBN 0-671-50619-6). S&S.

--How to Win Friends & Influence People. rev. & updated ed. 1983. pap. 3.95 (ISBN 0-671-49408-2). PB.

--Quick & Easy Ways to Effective Speaking. (gr. 10 up). 1983. pap. 3.50 (ISBN 0-671-49891-6). PB.

Carnegie, Dale & Carnegie, Dorothy. How to Win Friends & Influence People. rev. ed. 1981. 12.95 (ISBN 0-671-42517-X). S&S.

Carnegie, David. Among the Matabele. LC 74-97399. (Illus.). Repr. of 1894 ed. 15.00x (ISBN 0-8371-5094-9, CTM&, Pub. by Negro U Pr). Greenwood.

--A Scot in Wales & the West Country. Fraser, Duncan, ed. 1980. 35.00x (ISBN 0-900871-33-4, Pub. by Standard Scotland). State Mutual Bk.

Carnegie, Dorothy. Don't Grow Old, Grow Up. 1956. 9.95 (ISBN 0-525-09455-5, 0966-290). Dutton.

Carnegie, Dorothy, jt. auth. see Carnegie, Dale.

Carnegie Endowment for International Peace, jt. auth. see Leiken, Robert S.

Carnegie Endowment for International Peace. American Labor in a Changing World Economy. Morehouse, Ward, ed. LC 78-15545. (Praeger Special Studies). 362p. 1978. 49.95 (ISBN 0-03-045281-3). Praeger.

Carnegie Endowment for International Peace, Washington. Division of International Law. Monograph Ser. 1937-45. Repr. Set. 240.00 (ISBN 0-384-07699-8). Johnson Repr.

Carnegie Endowment for International Peace. A Repertoire of League of Nations Documents, 1919-1947, 2 vols. Ghebali, Victor-Yves, ed. LC 73-7839. 773p. 1973. lib. bdg. 85.00 (ISBN 0-379-00371-6); lib. bdg. 42.50 ea. Oceana.

Carnegie Endowment for International Peace, Division of International Law. The Sino-Japanese Negotiations of 1915: Japanese & Chinese Documents & Chinese Official Statement. LC 75-36222. Repr. of 1921 ed. 16.50 (ISBN 0-404-14473-X). AMS Pr.

Carnegie Endowment for International Peace. Treaties & Agreements with, & Concerning China, 1919-29. LC 75-39021. (China Studies: Perspectives on the Revolution Ser.). xiv, 282p. 1977. Repr. of 1929 ed. 21.00 (ISBN 0-88355-378-3). Hyperion Conn.

--United Nations Studies, 11 vols. (Repr. of 1947-1964 ed.). 1978. lib. bdg. 238.50x (ISBN 0-313-20320-2, UNSS). Greenwood.

Carnegie Foundation for the Advancement of Teaching Staff. The Control of the Campus: A Report on the Governance of Higher Education. LC 82-18772. 126p. 1982. pap. text ed. 6.95 (ISBN 0-931050-21-9). Carnegie Found Adv Teach.

Carnegie Foundation for the Advancement of Teaching. The Financial Status of the Professor in America & in Germany, No. 2. Metzger, Walter P., ed. LC 76-55175. (The Academic Profession Ser.). (Illus.). 1977. Repr. of 1908 ed. lib. bdg. 14.00x (ISBN 0-405-10003-5). Ayer Co Pubs.

Carnegie Foundation for the Advancement of Teaching & Boyer, Ernest L. High School: A Report on Secondary Education in America. 1985. pap. 8.61i (ISBN 0-06-091224-3, CN 1224, CN). Har-Row.

Carnegie Foundation for the Advancement of Teaching. Missions of the College Curriculum: A Contemporary Review with Suggestions. LC 77-84320. (Higher Education Ser. & the Carnegie Council Ser.). (Illus.). 1977. text ed. 18.95x (ISBN 0-87589-360-0). Jossey-Bass.

--More Than Survival: Prospects for Higher Education in a Period of Uncertainty. LC 75-4481. (Higher Education Ser. & the Carnegie Council Ser.). (Illus.). 192p. 1975. 19.95x (ISBN 0-87589-258-2). Jossey-Bass.

--The States & Higher Education: A Proud Past & a Vital Future: A Commentary of the Carnegie Foundation for the Advancement of Teaching. LC 76-11958. (The Carnegie Council Ser.). pap. 28.00 (ISBN 0-317-26531-8, 2023982). Bks Demand UMI.

Carnegie Institute. American Painting in the Nineteen Forties, 8 vols. (Illus.). 1982. Set. pap. 110.00 (ISBN 0-915346-80-X). A Wofsy Fine Arts.

--American Painting: 1670-1940. (Illus.). 306p. 1982. pap. 25.00 (ISBN 0-915346-77-X). A Wofsy Fine Arts.

--Painting in the Late Nineteen Twenties, 4 Vols. (Illus.). 600p. 1982. pap. 55.00 (ISBN 0-915346-78-8). A Wofsy Fine Arts.

--Painting in the Nineteen Thirties, 7 vols. (Illus.). 1982. Set. pap. 95.00 (ISBN 0-686-79694-2). A Wofsy Fine Arts.

Carnegie Institute Exhibition Catalogues. Pittsburgh Internationals: A Selection of 5 of the Annual Exhibition of Paintings Catalogues from the 1920s-1930s, 5 vols. 150p. Set. 75.00 (ISBN 0-686-87742-X). A Wofsy Fine Arts.

Carnegie Institute of Technology, Department of English, ed. see Broes, Arthur T.

Carnegie Institute of Technology & Hayes, Ann L. Studies in Faulkner. LC 72-1325. (Essay Index Reprint Ser.). Repr. of 1961 ed. 14.00 (ISBN 0-8369-2839-3). Ayer Co Pubs.

Carnegie Institute of Technology Department of English, ed. Lovers Meeting: Discussions of Five Plays by Shakespeare. LC 72-1335. (Essay Index Reprint Ser.). Repr. of 1964 ed. 12.00 (ISBN 0-8369-2836-9). Ayer Co Pubs.

--Six Novelists: Stendhal, Dostoevski, Tolstoy, Hardy, Dreiser & Proust. LC 72-1311. (Essay Index Reprint Ser.). Repr. of 1959 ed. 15.00 (ISBN 0-8369-2837-7). Ayer Co Pubs.

Carnegie Institute of Technology Department of English. Six Satirists. LC 72-1315. (Essay Index Reprint Ser.). Repr. of 1965 ed. 12.00 (ISBN 0-8369-2838-5). Ayer Co Pubs.

Carnegie Institute Of Washington. Floras of Yellowstone National Park & Southeastern Oregon. Repr. of 1933 ed. 19.00 (ISBN 0-685-02250-1). Johnson Repr.

--Notes on Middle American Archaeology & Ethnology, 5 vols. Repr. of 1957 ed. Set. write for info. (ISBN 0-685-78166-6). AMS Pr.

Carnegie Institution Of Washington. Additions to the Palaeontology of the Pacific Coast & Great Basin Regions of North America. Repr. of 1927 ed. 28.00 (ISBN 0-685-02200-5). Johnson Repr.

--Albany Catalogue of Twenty Thousand Eight Hundred Eleven Stars for the Epoch Nineteen Hundred Ten: Prepared at the Dudley Observatory, Albany, New York. LC 32-5590. (Carnegie Institution of Washington Publication Ser.: No. 419). pap. 121.00 (ISBN 0-317-07801-1, 2006084). Bks Demand UMI.

--Contributions to American Archaeology, 12 vols. LC 77-11501. (Vols. 5-12: Contributions to American Anthropology & History). Repr. of 1960 ed. Set. 390.00 (ISBN 0-404-16250-9). AMS Pr.

--Contributions to Paleontology. Repr. of 1930 ed. 19.00 (ISBN 0-685-02235-8). Johnson Repr.

--Eocene Flora of Western America. Repr. of 1937 ed. 28.00 (ISBN 0-685-02242-0). Johnson Repr.

--Marine Mammals. Repr. of 1934 ed. 19.00 (ISBN 0-685-02195-5). Johnson Repr.

--Miocene & Pliocene Floras of Western North America. Repr. of 1938 ed. 23.00 (ISBN 0-685-02185-8). Johnson Repr.

--Papers Concerning the Palaeontology of California, Arizona & Idaho. Repr. of 1934 ed. 19.00 (ISBN 0-685-02119-X). Johnson Repr.

--Papers Concerning the Palaeontology of California, Nevada & Oregon. Repr. of 1935 ed. 19.00 (ISBN 0-685-02120-3). Johnson Repr.

--Papers Concerning the Palaeontology of California, Oregon & the Northern Great Basin Province. Repr. of 1932 ed. 19.00 (ISBN 0-685-02121-1). Johnson Repr.

--Papers Concerning the Palaeontology of the Cretaceous & Later Tertiary of Oregon, of the Pliocene of North-Western Nevada, & of the Late Miocene & Pleistocene of California. Repr. of 1928 ed. 19.00 (ISBN 0-685-02122-X). Johnson Repr.

--Papers Concerning the Palaeontology of the Pleistocene of California & the Tertiary of Oregon. Repr. of 1925 ed. 19.00 (ISBN 0-685-02123-8). Johnson Repr.

--Studies of Tertiary & Quaternary Mammals of North America. Repr. of 1936 ed. 19.00 (ISBN 0-685-02165-3). Johnson Repr.

--Studies of the Pleistocene Palaeobotany of California. Repr. of 1934 ed. 19.00 (ISBN 0-685-02051-7). Johnson Repr.

--Studies of the Pliocene Palaeobotany of California. Repr. of 1933 ed. 19.00 (ISBN 0-685-02164-5). Johnson Repr.

--Studies on Cenozoic Vertebrates of Western America. Repr. of 1938 ed. 28.00 (ISBN 0-685-02176-9). Johnson Repr.

--Studies on the Fossil Flora & Fauna of the Western United States. Repr. of 1925 ed. 19.00 (ISBN 0-685-02175-0). Johnson Repr.

Carnegie Institution Of Washington - Dept. Of Meridian Astronomy. General Catalogue of Thirty Three Thousand Three Hundred Forty-Two Stars for the Epoch 1950, 5 vols. Boss, Benjamin, et al, eds. 1937. Set. 150.00 (ISBN 0-384-07706-4). Johnson Repr.

Carnegie, James. Jonas Fisher: A Poem in Brown & White. Freedman, William, et al, eds. (The Victorian Muse Ser.). 35.00 (ISBN 0-8240-8621-X). Garland Pub.

--Suomiria: A Fantasy. Reginald, R. & Menville, Douglas, eds. LC 75-46307. (Supernatural & Occult Fiction Ser.). 1976. Repr. of 1899 ed. lib. bdg. 24.50x (ISBN 0-405-08170-7). Ayer Co Pubs.

Carnegie-Mellon University & DeGroot, Morris H. Probability & Statistics. 2nd ed. LC 84-6269. 1985. text ed. write for info. (ISBN 0-201-11366-X). Addison-Wesley.

Carnegie Symposium on Cognition, Eighth Annual. Visual Information Processing: Proceedings. Chase, William G., ed. 1973. 49.50 (ISBN 0-12-170150-6). Acad Pr.

Carnegy, Patrick. Faust As Musician: A Study of Thomas Mann's Novel 'Dr. Faustus' LC 73-78718. 192p. 1973. 9.25 (ISBN 0-8112-0515-0). New Directions.

Carneiro, Cecilio J. The Bonfire: A Fogueira. Poore, Dudley, tr. from Port. LC 75-139127. 334p. 1972. Repr. of 1944 ed. lib. bdg. 19.75x (ISBN 0-8371-5743-9, CABF). Greenwood.

Carneiro, F. L., et al. Offshore Structures Engineering, Vol. 5. LC 84-80880. (Offshore Structures Engineering Ser.). 832p. 1984. 49.95x (ISBN 0-87201-607-2). Gulf Pub.

Carneiro, F. L., et al, eds. Offshore Structures Engineering, Vol. 2. LC 78-74102. (Offshore Structures Engineering Ser.). 600p. 1980. 49.95x (ISBN 0-87201-609-9). Gulf Pub.

--Offshore Structures Engineering, Vol. 4. LC 82-81336. (Offshore Structures Engineering Ser.). 584p. 1982. 49.95x (ISBN 0-87201-612-9). Gulf Pub.

Carneiro, Jose, jt. auth. see Junqueira, Luis C.

Carnell, C. Mitchell, Jr. Development, Management, & Evaluation of Community Speech & Hearing Centers. (Illus.). 148p. 1976. 17.25x (ISBN 0-398-03524-5). C C Thomas.

Carnell, Edward J. Christian Commitment: An Apologetic. (Twin Brooks Ser.). 330p. 1982. pap. 9.95 (ISBN 0-8010-2473-0). Baker Bk.

--A Philosophy of the Christian Religion. (Twin Brooks Ser.). 525p. 1981. pap. 10.95 (ISBN 0-8010-2464-1). Baker Bk.

Carnell, Hilary, jt. auth. see Eagle, Dorothy.

Carnell, Hilary, jt. ed. see Eagle, Dorothy.

Carnell, Lois. Beyond the Flight of Birds. (Harlequin American Romance Ser.). 256p. 1983. pap. 2.25 (ISBN 0-373-16028-3). Harlequin Bks.

Carnemark, Curt & Biderman, Jaime. The Economic Analysis of Rural Road Projects. (Working Paper: No. 241). 92p. 1976. 5.00 (ISBN 0-686-36217-9, WP-0241). World Bank.

Carner, Chas. Tawny. LC 77-17411. 160p. (gr. 6 up). 1978. 10.95 (ISBN 0-02-716700-3, 71670). Macmillan.

Carner, Mosco. Alban Berg. 2nd rev. ed. (Illus.). 255p. 1983. text ed. 42.50x (ISBN 0-8419-0841-9). Holmes & Meier.

--Alban Berg: The Man & the Work. LC 76-30457. (Illus.). 1977. text ed. 39.50x (ISBN 0-8419-0301-8). Holmes & Meier.

--Giacomo Puccini: Tosca. (Cambridge Opera Handbooks). (Illus.). 160p. Date not set. price not set (ISBN 0-521-22824-7); pap. price not set (ISBN 0-521-29661-7). Cambridge U Pr.

--Hugo Wolf Songs. LC 81-71301. (BBC Music Guides Ser.). 72p. (Orig.). 1983. pap. 4.95 (ISBN 0-295-95851-0). U of Wash Pr.

--Madam Butterfly. LC 79-67164. (Masterworks of Opera Ser.). 15.96 (ISBN 0-382-06313-9). Silver.

--Major & Minor. LC 79-27481. (Illus.). 267p. 1980. text ed. 45.00x (ISBN 0-8419-0600-9). Holmes & Meier.

--Puccini: A Critical Biography. 2nd ed. LC 76-30456. (Illus.). 519p. 1977. text ed. 55.00x (ISBN 0-8419-0302-6). Holmes & Meier.

Carner, Mosco, jt. auth. see Lenormand, Rene.

Carne-Ross, D. S. Instaurations: Essays in & Out of Literature, Pindar to Pound. LC 77-91772. 1979. 29.50x (ISBN 0-520-03619-0). U of Cal Pr.

--Pindar. LC 84-40668. (Hermes Bk.). 224p. 1985. text ed. 25.00x (ISBN 0-300-03383-4); 7.95x (ISBN 0-300-03393-1, Y-531). Yale U Pr.

Carnes, Bruce. Ken Kesey. LC 74-1971. (Western Writers Ser: No. 12). 1974. pap. 2.00x (ISBN 0-88430-011-0). Boise St Univ.

Carnes, Del. How to Make Money in Cake Decorating: Owning & Operating a Successful Business in Your Home. 2nd ed. (How to Profit Ser.: Vol. 1). (Illus.). 192p. 1982. pap. 9.95. Deco Pr Pub.

Carnes, Del, ed. see Murphy, Esther.

Carnes, John. Axiomatics & Dogmatics. (Theology & Scientific Culture Ser.). 1982. 14.95x (ISBN 0-19-520377-1). Oxford U Pr.

Carnes, Joshua A. Journal of a Voyage from Boston to the West Coast of Africa. LC 78-88404. Repr. of 1852 ed. cancelled (ISBN 0-8371-1816-6, CVA&, Pub. by Negro U Pr). Greenwood.

--Journal of a Voyage from Boston to the West Coast of Africa with a Full Description of the Manner of Trading with the Natives on the Coast. LC 16-9118. (Landmarks in Anthropology Ser). 1970. Repr. of 1852 ed. 42.00 (ISBN 0-384-07760-9). Johnson Repr.

Carnes, Mark C., ed. see Bowerman, Guy E., Jr.

Carnes, Pack. Fable Scholarship: An Annotated Bibliography. LC 82-48494. 480p. 1985. 40.00 (ISBN 0-8240-9229-5). Garland Pub.

Carnes, Patrick. Out of the Shadows: Understanding Sexual Addiction. LC 85-4195. 185p. 1985. pap. 8.95 (ISBN 0-89638-086-6). CompCare.

Carnes, Patrick J. Counseling the Sexual Addict. 150p. 1984. postponed (ISBN 0-89638-059-9). CompCare.

--Sexual Addiction. LC 83-8137. 215p. 1983. 12.95 (ISBN 0-89638-058-0); pap. 8.95 (ISBN 0-89638-066-1). CompCare.

Carnes, Ralph & Carnes, Valerie. Bodypower: The Complete Guide to the Use of Health Club Exercise Machines & Home Gym Equipment. (Illus.). 288p. 1982. 6.95 (ISBN 0-312-08734-9). St Martin.

--Bodysculpture. (Illus.). 192p. 1981. pap. 6.95 (ISBN 0-312-08735-7). St Martin.

--The Essential College Survival Handbook: An Insider's Guide to Making College Work for You. 224p. 1981. (Playboy); pap. 7.25 (ISBN 0-87223-694-3). Putnam Pub Group.

Carnes, Ralph, jt. auth. see Carnes, Valerie.

Carnes, Valerie & Carnes, Ralph. Bodysculpture Plus: The Aerobic Resistance Bodyshaping System for Women. (Illus.). 224p. 1985. pap. 7.95 (ISBN 0-312-08739-X). St Martin.

--Wonder in Aliceland. (Illus.). 130p. 1982. pap. 9.95 (ISBN 0-942488-01-6). Wholeo Bks.

Carolino, Pedro, pseud. Fractured English As She Is Spoke. abr. ed. LC 74-75099. 114p. 1969. pap. 2.95 (ISBN 0-486-22329-9). Dover.

Caromody, John T., jt. auth. see Carmody, Denise L.

Caron, Aimery P. & Highfield, Arnold R. St. Croix under French Dominion: 1650-1733. (Illus.). 200p. (Orig.). 1984. pap. text ed. 10.00 (ISBN 0-916611-00-0). Antilles Pr.

Caron, David D. & Buderi, L. O., eds. Perspectives on U. S. Policy Toward the Law of the Sea: Prelude to the Final Session of the Third U. N. Conference of the Sea, OP35 Occasional Paper No. 35. 1985. 10.00 (ISBN 0-911189-12-2). Law Sea Inst.

Caron, Denis R. Connecticut Foreclosures: An Attorney's Manual of Practice & Procedure. 2nd ed. 229p. 1982. 35.00 (ISBN 0-910051-00-3). CT Law Trib.

Caron, Denis R. & Grafstein, Joel M. Connecticut Foreclosures: An Attorney's Manual of Practice & Procedure, 1984 Supplement. 197p. 1984. pap. 30.00 (ISBN 0-910051-01-1). CT Law Trib.

Caron, Fabien, ed. see Universite Laval,Centre d'Etudes Nordiques, Quebec.

Caron, Francois. An Economic History of Modern France. Bray, Barbara, tr. from Fr. (Columbia Economic History of the Modern World). 360p. 1979. 29.00x (ISBN 0-231-03860-7). Columbia U Pr.

--Histoire De L'exploitation D'un Grand Reseau: La Compagnie Du Chemin De Fer Du Nord, 1846-1937. (Industrie et Artisanat: No. 7). 1973. pap. 34.40x (ISBN 90-2797-198-6). Mouton.

Caron, Louis. The Draft Dodger. Homel, David T., tr. from Fr. (Fiction Ser: No. 42). 150p. (Orig.). 1980. pap. 8.95 (ISBN 0-88784-085-X, Pub. by Hse Anansi Pr Canada). U of Toronto Pr.

Caron, P. F. & Golen, S. P. Developing the Internal Auditors Leadership Skills. (Illus.). 1983. pap. text ed. 12.00 (ISBN 0-89413-105-2). Inst Inter Aud.

Carona, Philip. Basic Science Skills. (Pre-GED Basic Skills Ser.). 1979. pap. 5.95 (ISBN 0-07-010138-8). McGraw.

--Chemistry & Cooking. LC 75-11532. (Illus.). (gr. 3-7). 1975. 5.95 (ISBN 0-13-129460-1). P-H.

--Numbers. LC 82-4455. (New True Bks.). (gr. k-4). 1982. 10.60 (ISBN 0-516-01634-2); pap. 3.95 (ISBN 0-516-41634-0). Childrens.

--Power Skills in Science. 1979. pap. 4.95 (ISBN 0-07-010134-5). McGraw.

Carona, Philip B. Microscope & How to Use It. LC 73-131927. (Illus.). 63p. (Orig.). 1970. pap. 7.95x (ISBN 0-87201-563-7). Gulf Pub.

Carone, Pasquale, ed. Addictive Disorders Update: Alcoholism, Drug Abuse, Gambling. Kieffer, Sherman, et al. LC 81-6880. (Problems of Industrial Psychiatric Medicine Ser.: Vol. VII). 192p. 1982. 24.95 (ISBN 0-89885-034-7). Human Sci Pr.

Carone, Pasquale, et al, eds. The Emotionally Troubled Employee: A Challenge to Industry. LC 76-26603. 1976. 29.50x (ISBN 0-87395-801-2). State U NY Pr.

--History of Mental Health & Industry: The Last Hundred Years. (Problems of Industrial Psychiatric Medicine Ser.: Vol. 10). 112p. 1984. 16.95 (ISBN 0-89885-207-2). Human Sci Pr.

Carone, Pasquale A. & Krinsky, Leonard W. Drug Abuse in Industry. (Illus.). 192p. 1973. 25.50x (ISBN 0-398-02801-X). C C Thomas.

Carone, Pasquale A., et al, eds. Mental Health Problems of Workers & Their Families. (Problems of Industrial Psychiatric Medicine Ser.: Vol. 11). 160p. 1985. 24.95 (ISBN 0-89885-227-7). Human Sci Pr.

Caronni, Ernesto P. Craniofacial Surgery. 620p. Date not set. text ed. 75.00 (ISBN 0-317-18201-3). Little.

Caroselli, Remus F. Mystery at Long Crescent Marsh. LC 84-15716. (gr. 4-7). 1985. 11.95 (ISBN 0-03-001414-X). HR&W.

Caroselli, Susan L. The Casa Marliani & Palace Building In Late Quattrocento Lombardy. Freedberg, S. J., ed. (Outstanding Dissertations in Fine Arts Ser.). (Illus.). 360p. 1985. Repr. of 1980 ed. 50.00 (ISBN 0-8240-6850-5). Garland Pub.

Caroso, Fabritio. Nobilta Di Dame: A Treatise on Courtly Dance, Translated from the Edition of 1600. Sutton, Julia, ed. (Illus.). 1984. 39.95x (ISBN 0-19-311917-X). Oxford U Pr.

Carosso. Technical Communications. 1986. text ed. write for info. Wadsworth Pub.

Carosso, Rebecca B. & Stanford, Judith D. The Writing Connection. (Illus.). 448p. 1983. pap. 15.95 (ISBN 0-13-970541-4). P-H.

Carosso, Vincent P. The California Wine Industry: A Study of the Formative Years, 1830-1895. (California Library Reprint Ser.). 1976. 32.00x (ISBN 0-520-03178-4). U of Cal Pr.

--Investment Banking in America: A History. Sears, Martin V. & Katz, Irving, eds. LC 70-99515. (Studies in Business History: No. 25). 1970. 32.50x (ISBN 0-674-46574-1). Harvard U Pr.

Carosso, Vincent P., ed. The Boston Stock Exchange: An Original Anthology. LC 75-2622. (Wall Street & the Security Market Ser.). 1975. 32.00x (ISBN 0-405-06949-9). Ayer Co Pubs.

--The Chicago Securities Market: An Original Arno Press Anthology. LC 75-2627. (Wall Street & the Security Markets Ser.). 1975. 15.00x (ISBN 0-405-06953-7). Ayer Co Pubs.

--Finance & Industry: The New York Stock Exchange: Banks, Bankers, Business Houses, & Moneyed Institutions of the Great Metropolis of the United States. facsimile ed. LC 75-2620. (Wall Street & the Security Markets Ser.). 1975. Repr. of 1886 ed. 23.50x (ISBN 0-405-06947-2). Ayer Co Pubs.

--The New York Stock Market: An Original Anthology. LC 75-2656. (Wall Street & the Security Market Ser.). 1975. 47.50x (ISBN 0-405-06981-2). Ayer Co Pubs.

--Regulation of the Security Markets: An Original Anthology. facsimile ed. LC 75-2662. (Wall Street & the Security Market Ser.). 1975. 32.00x (ISBN 0-405-06986-3). Ayer Co Pubs.

--Two Private Banking Partnerships: An Original Anthology. LC 75-2676. (Wall Street & the Security Market Ser.). (Illus.). 1975. 45.50x (ISBN 0-405-07238-4). Ayer Co Pubs.

--Wall Street & the Security Markets, 58 vols. facsimile ed. 1975. Repr. Vols. 1-29. 2103.00x (ISBN 0-405-12493-7); Vols. 30-58. 770.00x (ISBN 0-405-19007-7). Ayer Co Pubs.

Carosso, Vincent P. & Bruchey, Stuart, eds. The Survival of Small Business. new ed. LC 78-18155. (Small Business Enterprise in America Ser.). 1979. lib. bdg. 25.50x (ISBN 0-405-11512-1). Ayer Co Pubs.

Carosso, Vincent P., jt. ed. see Bruchey, Stuart.

Carosso, Vincent P., ed. see Bruchey, Stuart W.

Carosso, Vincent P., ed. see Bunn, Verne A.

Carosso, Vincent P., ed. see Bunzel, John A.

Carosso, Vincent P., ed. see Carpenter, Walter H., Jr. & Handler, Edward.

Carosso, Vincent P., ed. see Christensen, Roland C.

Carosso, Vincent P., ed. see Commerce Clearing House, Inc.

Carosso, Vincent P., ed. see Daughters, Charles G.

Carosso, Vincent P., ed. see Flink, Salomon J.

Carosso, Vincent P., ed. see Glover, John D.

Carosso, Vincent P., ed. see Haas, Harold M.

Carosso, Vincent P., ed. see Hollander, Edward, et al.

Carosso, Vincent P., ed. see Howard, Marshall C.

Carosso, Vincent P., ed. see Kaplan, Abraham D.

Carosso, Vincent P., ed. see Konopa, Leonard J.

Carosso, Vincent P., ed. see Lumer, Wilfred.

Carosso, Vincent P., ed. see McGee, John S.

Carosso, Vincent P., ed. see Merwin, Charles L.

Carosso, Vincent P., ed. see Morris, Bruce R.

Carosso, Vincent P., ed. see Neifeld, Morris R.

Carosso, Vincent P., ed. see Pepper, Roger S.

Carosso, Vincent P., ed. see Proxmire, William.

Carosso, Vincent P., ed. see Richards, Max D.

Carosso, Vincent P., ed. see Schor, Stanley S.

Carosso, Vincent P., ed. see Still, Jack W.

Carosso, Vincent P., ed. see Tosiello, Rosario J.

Carosso, Vincent P., ed. see U. S. House of Representatives, Committee No. 1 of the Select Committee on Small Business.

Carosso, Vincent P., ed. see United States House of Representatives, Select Committee on Small Business.

Carosso, Vincent P., ed. see U. S. House of Representatives, Select Committee on Small Business.

Carosso, Vincent P., ed. see U. S. House of Representatives, Subcommittee No. 1 of the Select Committee on Small Business.

Carosso, Vincent P., ed. see United States House of Representatives, Subcommittee No. 2 of the Select Committee on Small Business.

Carosso, Vincent P., ed. see U. S. House of Representatives, Subcommittee No. 4 on Distribution Problems Affecting Small Business.

Carosso, Vincent P., ed. see U. S. Senate Subcommittee of the Committee on Banking & Currency.

Carosso, Vincent P., ed. see U. S. Senate, Subcommittee on Monopoly of the Select Committee on Small Business.

Carosso, Vincent P., ed. see Vatter, Harold G.

Carosso, Vincent P., ed. see Vatter, Paul A.

Carosso, Vincent P., ed. see Weissman, Rudolph L.

Carosso, Vincent P., ed. see Zeigler, Harmon.

Carotenuto, Aldo. A Secret Symmetry: Sabina Spielrein Between Jung & Freud. 1982. 16.45 (ISBN 0-394-51530-7). Pantheon.

--A Secret Symmetry: Sabina Spielrein Between Jung & Freud. Bettelheim, Bruno, commentary by. Pomerans, Arno, et al, trs. 1984. pap. 8.95 (ISBN 0-394-72295-7). Pantheon.

Carotenuto, Rosine & Bullock, John. Physical Assessment of the Gerontologic Client. LC 80-15247. 157p. 1981. pap. text ed. 10.95x (ISBN 0-8036-1680-5). Davis Co.

Carothers, Diane F. Self-Instruction Manual for Filing Catalog Cards. LC 81-3606. 128p. 1981. pap. 9.00x (ISBN 0-8389-0326-6). ALA.

Carothers, Doris. Chronology of the Federal Emergency Relief Administration: May 12, 1933 to December 31, 1935. LC 70-165681. (Research Monograph: Vol. 6). 1971. Repr. of 1937 ed. lib. bdg. 19.50 (ISBN 0-306-70338-6). Da Capo.

Carothers, J. Edward. Caring for the World. (Orig.). 1978. pap. 4.95 (ISBN 0-377-00078-7). Friend Pr.

--Living with the Parables: Jesus & the Reign of God. 141p. (Orig.). 1984. pap. 9.95 (ISBN 0-377-00146-5). Friend Pr.

Carothers, James B. William Faulkner's Short Stories. Litz, Walton, ed. LC 85-8523. (Studies in Modern Literature: No. 34). 166p. 1985. 39.95 (ISBN 0-8357-1500-0). UMI Res Pr.

Carothers, James E. & Gasten, Ruth S. Helping Children to Like Themselves: Activities for Building Self-Esteem. 1978. pap. 4.95 (ISBN 0-9602090-1-8). RJ Assocs.

Carothers, John C. African Mind in Health & Diseases: A Study in Ethnopsychiatry. LC 73-100260. Repr. of 1953 ed. 17.50x (ISBN 0-8371-2864-1, CMI&, Pub. by Negro U Pr). Greenwood.

Carothers, L. The Public Accommodations Law of 1964: Arguments, Issues & Attitudes in a Legal Debate. LC 67-21036. (Edwin H. Land Prize Essays). 1968. 2.00 (ISBN 0-87391-003-6). Smith Coll.

Carothers, Merlin R. Answers to Praise. 169p. (Orig.). 1972. pap. 4.95 (ISBN 0-943026-07-5). Carothers.

--The Bible on Praise. 32p. (Orig.). 1981. pap. 2.25 (ISBN 0-943026-03-2). Carothers.

--Bringing Heaven into Hell. 120p. (Orig.). 1976. pap. 4.95 (ISBN 0-943026-10-5). Carothers.

--More Power to You. 143p. (Orig.). 1982. pap. 4.95 (ISBN 0-943026-00-8). Carothers.

--Power in Praise. 143p. 1972. pap. 4.95 (ISBN 0-943026-01-6). Carothers.

--Praise Works. 161p. (Orig.). 1973. pap. 4.95. Carothers.

--Prison to Praise. 106p. (Orig.). 1970. pap. 2.95 (ISBN 0-943026-02-4). Carothers.

--Prison to Praise: Giant Print. 106p. (Orig.). 1970. pap. 3.95 (ISBN 0-943026-08-3). Carothers.

--Victory on Praise Mountain. 175p. (Orig.). 1979. pap. 4.95 (ISBN 0-943026-04-0). Carothers.

--Walking & Leaping. 129p. (Orig.). 1974. pap. 4.95 (ISBN 0-943026-05-9). Carothers.

--What's on Your Mind. 1984. 4.95 (ISBN 0-943026-13-X). Carothers.

Carothers, Neil. Fractional Money: A History of the Small Coins & Fractional Paper Currency of the United States. LC 65-26361. Repr. of 1930 ed. 35.00x (ISBN 0-678-00253-3). Kelley.

Carothers, Robert. John Calvin's Favorite Son. (Illus.). 24p. (Orig.). 1980. pap. 3.95 (ISBN 0-935306-07-2). Barnwood Pr.

Carothers, Steven W., et al. Breeding Birds of the San Francisco Mountain Area & the White Mountains, Arizona. (MNA Technical Ser.: No. 12). 1973. pap. 3.00 (ISBN 0-685-76472-9). Mus Northern Ariz.

Carouge, Scott & Meyer, Jackie M. I Loathe New York: A Humorous Look at the Rotten Apple. (Illus.). 96p. 1982. pap. 3.95 (ISBN 0-02-040370-4) (ISBN 0-02-040380-1). Macmillan.

Carovillano, R. L. & Forbes, J. M., eds. Solar-Terrestial Physics: Principles & Theoretical Foundations. 1983. lib. bdg. 115.00 (ISBN 90-277-1632-3, Pub. by Reidel Holland). Kluwer Academic.

Carovillano, R. L., ed. see Conference on Physics of the Magnetosphere, Boston College, 1967.

Carovillano, Robert L. & Skehan, James W., eds. Science & the Future of Man. 1st u.s. ed. 1971. 22.50x (ISBN 0-262-03031-4). MIT Pr.

Carozza, Davy A. European Baroque. 1978. lib. bdg. 27.50 (ISBN 0-8414-9977-2). Folcroft.

--European Baroque: A Selective Bibliography. 226p. 1980. Repr. of 1976 ed. lib. bdg. 20.00 (ISBN 0-8492-4048-4). R West.

Carozzi, A. V., tr. see Cayeux, L.

Carozzi, Albert V. Microscopic Sedimentary Petrography. LC 60-6447. 498p. 1972. Repr. of 1960 ed. 28.50 (ISBN 0-88275-061-5). Krieger.

Carozzi, Albert V., jt. auth. see Ward, Frederick.

Carozzi, Albert V., ed. see Argand, Emile.

Carp, Augustus. Augustus Carp, Esq. 244p. 1985. pap. 6.95 (ISBN 0-317-17254-9, Pub. by Boydell England). Academy Chi Pubs.

Carp, E. Wayne. To Starve the Army at Pleasure: Continental Army Administration & American Political Culture, 1775-1783. LC 83-19697. (Illus.). xv, 305p. 1984. 29.00 (ISBN 0-8078-1587-X). U of NC Pr.

Carp, Eric. A Directory of Western Palearctic Wetlands. (Illus.). 506p. 1980. pap. 27.50 (ISBN 2-8803-2300-2, IUCN87, IUCN). Unipub.

Carp, Frances M. A Future for the Aged: Victoria Plaza & Its Residents. (Hogg Foundation Research Series). (Illus.). 308p. 1966. 16.95x (ISBN 0-292-73609-6). U of Tex Pr.

Carp, Robert A. & Rowland, C. K. Policymaking & Politics in the Federal District Courts. LC 82-13462. (Illus.). 220p. 1983. text ed. 17.95x (ISBN 0-87049-369-8). U of Tenn Pr.

Carp, Robert A. & Stidham, Ronald. The Federal Courts. LC 85-17095. 260p. 1985. pap. 12.95 (ISBN 0-87187-349-4). Congr Quarterly.

Carpanini, Rudolf, tr. see Baldini, Umberto.

Carpegna, N. Di see Di Carpegna, N.

Carpenito. Handbook of Nursing Diagnosis. LC 64-4339. 1984. 10.75 (ISBN 0-397-54493-6, Lippincott Nursing). Lippincott.

Carpenito, Lynda J. Nursing Diagnosis: Application to Clinical Practice. (Illus.). 656p. 1983. pap. text ed. 21.50 (ISBN 0-397-54377-8, 64-03190, Lippincott Nursing). Lippincott.

Carpenito, Lynda J. & Duespohl, T. Audean. A Guide in Effective Clinical Instruction. 2nd ed. 250p. 1984. 26.00 (ISBN 0-89443-573-6). Aspen Systems.

Carpenter. The Captain Hook Affair. Date not set. price not set. HM.

--Elephants Don't Bounce. Date not set. price not set. HM.

--The Joshers: Or London to Birmingham with Albert & Victoria. Date not set. price not set. HM.

--The Solitary Volcano. Date not set. price not set. HM.

--The Wind in the Willows. Date not set. price not set. HM.

Carpenter & Prichard, Mari. The Oxford Companion to Children's Literature. Date not set. price not set. HM.

Carpenter, jt. auth. see Campo.

Carpenter, Allan. Alabama. LC 77-13920. (New Enchantment of America State Bks). (Illus.). 96p. (gr. 4 up). 1978. PLB 12.65 (ISBN 0-516-04101-0). Childrens.

--Alaska. LC 78-12419. (New Enchantment of America State Bks.). (Illus.). 96p. (gr. 4 up). 1979. PLB 12.65 (ISBN 0-516-04102-9). Childrens.

--Arizona. LC 79-11802. (New Enchantment of America State Bks.). (Illus.). 96p. (gr. 4 up). 1979. PLB 12.65 (ISBN 0-516-04103-7). Childrens.

--Arkansas. LC 78-3786. (New Enchantment of America State Bks.). (Illus.). 96p. (gr. 4 up). 1978. PLB 12.65 (ISBN 0-516-04104-5). Childrens.

--California. LC 77-21101. (New Enchantment of America State Bks). (Illus.). 96p. (gr. 4 up). 1978. PLB 12.65 (ISBN 0-516-04105-3). Childrens.

--Colorado. LC 77-13921. (New Enchantment of America State Bks). (Illus.). 96p. (gr. 4 up). 1978. PLB 12.65 (ISBN 0-516-04106-1). Childrens.

--Connecticut. LC 79-4173. (New Enchantment of America State Bks.). (Illus.). 96p. (gr. 4 up). 1979. PLB 12.65 (ISBN 0-516-04107-X). Childrens.

--Delaware. LC 78-15915. (New Enchantment of America State Bks). (Illus.). 96p. (gr. 4 up). 1979. PLB 12.65 (ISBN 0-516-04108-8). Childrens.

--District of Columbia. new ed. LC 78-31683. (New Enchantment of America State Bks.). (Illus.). 96p. (gr. 4 up). 1979. PLB 12.65 (ISBN 0-516-04151-7). Childrens.

--Far-Flung America. new ed. LC 79-12505. (New Enchantment of America State Bks.). (Illus.). 96p. (gr. 4 up). 1979. PLB 12.65 (ISBN 0-516-04152-5). Childrens.

--Florida. LC 78-8108. (New Enchantment of America State Bks.). (Illus.). 96p. (gr. 4 up). 1979. PLB 12.65 (ISBN 0-516-04109-6). Childrens.

--Georgia. LC 79-12095. (New Enchantment of America State Bks.). (Illus.). 96p. (gr. 4 up). 1979. PLB 12.65 (ISBN 0-516-04110-X). Childrens.

--Hawaii. LC 79-9991. (New Enchantment of America State Bks.). (Illus.). 96p. (gr. 4 up). 1979. PLB 12.65 (ISBN 0-516-04111-8). Childrens.

--Idaho. new ed. LC 79-9804. (New Enchantment of America State Bks.). (Illus.). 96p. (gr. 4 up). 1979. PLB 12.65 (ISBN 0-516-04112-6). Childrens.

--Illinois. new ed. LC 78-32064. (New Enchantment of America State Bks.). (Illus.). 96p. (gr. 4 up). 1979. PLB 12.65 (ISBN 0-516-04113-4). Childrens.

--Indiana. new ed. LC 78-12459. (New Enchantment of America State Bks). (Illus.). 96p. (gr. 4 up). 1979. PLB 12.65 (ISBN 0-516-04114-2). Childrens.

--Iowa. LC 79-11802. (New Enchantment of America State Bks.). (Illus.). 96p. (gr. 4 up). 1979. PLB 12.65 (ISBN 0-516-04115-0). Childrens.

--Kansas. new ed. LC 79-12433. (New Enchantment of America State Bks.). (Illus.). 96p. (gr. 4 up). 1979. PLB 12.65 (ISBN 0-516-04116-9). Childrens.

--Kentucky. new ed. LC 79-12696. (New Enchantment of America State Bks.). (Illus.). 96p. (gr. 4 up). 1979. PLB 12.65 (ISBN 0-516-04117-7). Childrens.

--Louisiana. LC 78-3390. (New Enchantment of America State Bks.). (Illus.). 96p. (gr. 4 up). 1978. PLB 12.65 (ISBN 0-516-04118-5). Childrens.

--Maine. new ed. LC 79-10804. (New Enchantment of America State Bks.). (Illus.). 96p. (gr. 4 up). 1979. PLB 12.65 (ISBN 0-516-04119-3). Childrens.

--Maryland. new ed. LC 78-14892. (New Enchantment of America State Bks.). (Illus.). 96p. (gr. 4 up). 1979. PLB 12.65 (ISBN 0-516-04120-7). Childrens.

--Massachusetts. new ed. LC 78-3785. (New Enchantment of America State Bks.). (Illus.). 96p. (gr. 4 up). 1978. PLB 12.65 (ISBN 0-516-04121-5). Childrens.

--Michigan. LC 78-8001. (New Enchantment of America State Bks.). (Illus.). 96p. (gr. 4 up). 1978. PLB 12.65 (ISBN 0-516-04122-3). Childrens.

--Minnesota. new ed. LC 78-8000. (New Enchantment of America State Bks.). (Illus.). 96p. (gr. 4 up). 1978. PLB 12.65 (ISBN 0-516-04123-1). Childrens.

--Mississippi. LC 78-3400. (New Enchantment of America State Bks.). (Illus.). 96p. (gr. 4 up). 1978. PLB 12.65 (ISBN 0-516-04124-X). Childrens.

--Missouri. LC 78-3551. (New Enchantment of America State Bks.). (Illus.). 96p. (gr. 4 up). 1978. PLB 12.65 (ISBN 0-516-04125-8). Childrens.

--Montana. new ed. LC 79-683. (New Enchantment of America State Bks.). (Illus.). 96p. (gr. 4 up). 1979. PLB 12.65 (ISBN 0-516-04126-6). Childrens.

--Nebraska. LC 78-10480. (New Enchantment of America State Bks). (Illus.). 96p. (gr. 4 up). 1979. PLB 12.65 (ISBN 0-516-04127-4). Childrens.

--Nevada. LC 79-4355. (New Enchantment of America State Bks.). (Illus.). 96p. (gr. 4 up). 1979. PLB 12.65 (ISBN 0-516-04128-2). Childrens.

--New Hampshire. LC 79-11454. (New Enchantment of America State Bks.). (Illus.). 96p. (gr. 4 up). 1979. PLB 12.65 (ISBN 0-516-04129-0). Childrens.

--New Jersey. LC 78-14891. (New Enchantment of America State Bks). (Illus.). 96p. (gr. 4 up). 1979. PLB 12.65 (ISBN 0-516-04130-4). Childrens.

--New Mexico. LC 78-2695. (Enchantment of America State Books Ser.). (Illus.). 96p. (gr. 4 up). 1978. PLB 12.65 (ISBN 0-516-04131-2). Childrens.

--New York. new ed. LC 78-3395. (New Enchantment of America State Bks.). (Illus.). 96p. (gr. 4 up). 1978. PLB 12.65 (ISBN 0-516-04132-0). Childrens.

--North Carolina. new ed. LC 79-682. (New Enchantment of America State Bks.). (Illus.). 96p. (gr. 4 up). 1979. PLB 12.65 (ISBN 0-516-04133-9). Childrens.

--North Dakota. new ed. LC 79-11470. (New Enchantment of America State Bks.). (Illus.). 96p. (gr. 4 up). 1979. PLB 12.65 (ISBN 0-516-04134-7). Childrens.

--Ohio. new ed. LC 78-16162. (New Enchantment of America State Bks). (Illus.). 96p. (gr. 4 up). 1979. PLB 12.65 (ISBN 0-516-04135-5). Childrens.

--Oklahoma. new ed. LC 79-10592. (New Enchantment of America State Bks.). (Illus.). 96p. (gr. 4 up). 1979. PLB 11.95 (ISBN 0-516-04136-3). Childrens.

--Oregon. new ed. LC 78-13955. (New Enchantment of America State Bks). (Illus.). 96p. (gr. 4 up). 1979. PLB 12.65 (ISBN 0-516-04137-1). Childrens.

--Pennsylvania. new ed. LC 78-5089. (New Enchantment of America State Bks.). (Illus.). 96p. (gr. 4 up). 1978. PLB 12.65 (ISBN 0-516-04138-X). Childrens.

--Rhode Island. LC 78-16446. (New Enchantment of America State Bks). (Illus.). 96p. (gr. 4 up). 1979. PLB 12.65 (ISBN 0-516-04139-8). Childrens.

--South Carolina. LC 79-11453. (New Enchantment of America State Bks.). (Illus.). 96p. (gr. 4 up). 1979. PLB 12.65 (ISBN 0-516-04140-1). Childrens.

--South Dakota. new ed. LC 78-3385. (New Enchantment of America State Bks.). (Illus.). 96p. (gr. 4 up). 1978. PLB 12.65 (ISBN 0-516-04141-X). Childrens.

--Tennessee. LC 78-11522. (New Enchantment of America State Bks). (Illus.). 96p. (gr. 4 up). 1979. PLB 12.65 (ISBN 0-516-04142-8). Childrens.

--Texas. LC 78-18430. (New Enchantment of America State Bks). (Illus.). 96p. (gr. 4 up). 1979. PLB 12.65 (ISBN 0-516-04143-6). Childrens.

--Utah. new ed. LC 79-12433. (New Enchantment of America State Bks.). (Illus.). 96p. (gr. 4 up). 1979. PLB 12.65 (ISBN 0-516-04144-4). Childrens.

--Vermont. new ed. LC 79-829. (New Enchantment of America State Bks.). (Illus.). 96p. (gr. 4 up). 1979. PLB 12.65 (ISBN 0-516-04145-2). Childrens.

--Virginia. LC 78-8002. (New Enchantment of America State Bks.). (Illus.). 96p. (gr. 4 up). 1978. PLB 12.65 (ISBN 0-516-04146-0). Childrens.

--Washington. LC 79-13390. (New Enchantment of America State Bks.). (Illus.). 96p. (gr. 4 up). 1979. PLB 12.65 (ISBN 0-516-04147-9). Childrens.

--West Virginia. new ed. LC 79-12900. (New Enchantment of America State Bks.). (Illus.). 96p. (gr. 4 up). 1979. PLB 12.65 (ISBN 0-516-04148-7). Childrens.

--Wisconsin. new ed. LC 77-13666. (New Enchantment of America State Bks.). (Illus.). 96p. (gr. 4 up). 1978. PLB 12.65 (ISBN 0-516-04149-5). Childrens.

--Wyoming. new ed. LC 78-32135. (New Enchantment of America State Bks.). (Illus.). 96p. (gr. 4 up). 1979. PLB 12.65 (ISBN 0-516-04150-9). Childrens.

Carpenter, Andrew, ed. Place, Personality & the Irish Writer. (Irish Literary Studies: No. 1). 199p. 1977. text ed. 28.50x (ISBN 0-06-490727-9, 06387). B&N Imports.

Carpenter, Andrew & Fallon, Peter, eds. The Writers: A Sense of Ireland. LC 80-12681. 1980. 20.00 (ISBN 0-8076-0970-6). Braziller.

Carpenter, Anne N. Ma's Ram & Other Poems. LC 85-1893. (Eileen W. Barnes Award Ser.). 80p. 1985. pap. 6.50 (ISBN 0-938158-06-6). Saturday Pr.

Carpenter, B. Stephen, ed. Computers in Activation Analysis & Gamma-Ray Spectroscopy: Proceedings. LC 79-19600. (DOE Symposium Ser.). 904p. 1979. pap. 30.50 (ISBN 0-87079-117-6, CONF-780421); microfiche 4.50 (ISBN 0-87079-169-9, CONF-780421). DOE.

Carpenter, Barry K. Determination of Organic Reaction Mechanisms. 247p. 1984. 34.95x (ISBN 0-471-89369-2, Pub. by Wiley-Interscience). Wiley.

Carpenter, Blyth, jt. auth. see Carpenter, Russell.

Carpenter, Bogdana. The Poetic Avant-Garde in Poland, 1918-1939. LC 83-1126. (Publications on Russia & Eastern Europe of the School of International Studies: No. 11). (Illus.). 254p. 1983. 22.50x (ISBN 0-295-95996-7). U of Wash Pr.

Carpenter, Bogdana, tr. see Herbert, Zbigniew.

Carpenter, Bruce. The Way of the Drama. 1975. Repr. of 1929 ed. 25.00 (ISBN 0-8274-4108-8). R West.

Carpenter, C. R. Naturalistic Behavior of Nonhuman Primates. LC 64-15065. (Illus.). 1964. 27.50x (ISBN 0-271-73084-6). Pa St U Pr.

Carpenter, C. R., ed. Behavioral Regulators of Behavior in Primates. LC 72-3602. (Illus.). 303p. 1974. 30.00 (ISBN 0-8387-1099-9). Bucknell U Pr.

Carpenter, Carmen, compiled by see U. S. Congress-Senate Library.

Carpenter, Carmen, ed. see U. S. Congress-Senate Library.

Carpenter, Carol B. & Rakow, Sue F. Say it in Sign: A Workbook of Sign Language Exercises. (Illus.). 266p. 1983. pap. 21.75x spiral (ISBN 0-398-04779-0). C C Thomas.

Carpenter, Carole H., jt. auth. see Fowke, Edith.

Carpenter, Cecelia S. They Walked Before: The Indians of Washington State. LC 77-81590. (Illus.). 71p. 1977. pap. 6.00 (ISBN 0-917048-04-0). Wash St Hist Soc.

Carpenter, Charles, ed. Clinical Histocompatibility Testing, Vol. 2. (Transplantation Proceedings Reprint Ser.). 244p. 1978. 52.00 (ISBN 0-8089-1095-7, 790792). Grune.

Carpenter, Charles A. Modern British Drama. LC 76-4654. (Goldentree Bibliographies in Language & Literature). 1979. pap. text ed. 14.95x (ISBN 0-88295-559-4). Harlan Davidson.

Carpenter, Charles B., ed. Clinical Histocompatibility Testing, Vol. 3. 320p. 1979. 52.00 (ISBN 0-8089-1207-0, 790793). Grune.

--Clinical Histocompatibility Testing, Vol. 4. (Transplantation Proceedings Reprint Ser.). 336p. 1980. 52.00 (ISBN 0-8089-1275-5, 790794). Grune.

Carpenter, Charles B. & Miller, William V., eds. Clinical Histocompatibility - Testing, Vol. 1. (Transplantation Proceedings Reprint Ser.). 248p. 1977. 52.00 (ISBN 0-8089-1022-1, 790791). Grune.

Carpenter, Charles C. Comparative Display Behavior in the Genus Sceloporus (Iguanidae) 71p. 1978. 4.50 (ISBN 0-89326-032-0). Milwaukee Pub Mus.

Carpenter, Charles F. The Purchasing Role: A View from the Top. LC 77-6349. (AMA Management Briefing Ser.). pap. 20.00 (ISBN 0-317-29943-3, 2051698). Bks Demand UMI.

Carpenter, Charles H., Jr. Gorham Silver. LC 82-2359. 1983. 34.95 (ISBN 0-396-08068-5). Dodd.

Carpenter, Charles H., Jr. & Carpenter, Mary G. Tiffany Silver. (Illus.). 1978. 25.00 (ISBN 0-396-07547-9). Dodd.

--Tiffany Silver. (Illus.). 296p. 1984. pap. text ed. 13.95 (ISBN 0-396-08338-2). Dodd.

Carpenter, Charles W. The Systematic Exploitation of the Verbal Calque in German: German Language & Literature, Vol. 65. (European University Studies: Ser. 1). 132p. 1973. pap. 18.25 (ISBN 3-261-00748-6). P Lang Pubs.

Carpenter, Clarence R. A Field Study in Siam of the Behavior & Social Relations of the Gibbon. LC 76-44702. (Illus.). 224p. Repr. of 1941 ed. 37.50 (ISBN 0-404-15855-2). AMS Pr.

--A Field Study of the Behavior & Social Relations of Howling Monkeys. LC 76-44703. 1985. Repr. of 1934 ed. 35.00 (ISBN 0-404-15854-4). AMS Pr.

Carpenter, Cyndy. Rapture's Heaven. (Orig.). 1983. pap. 3.50 (ISBN 0-8217-1218-7). Zebra.

Carpenter, D. M. & Ruddiman, K. W. Looking at Society. 2nd ed. (Illus.). 184p. (Orig.). 1975. pap. 12.95x (ISBN 0-8464-0579-2). Beekman Pubs.

Carpenter, David O. Cellular Pacemakers: Function in Normal & Disease States, Vol. 2. 371p. 1982. 64.50 (ISBN 0-471-09608-3). Wiley.

--Cellular Pacemakers: Mechanisms of Pacemaker Generation, Vol. 1. LC 81-11711. 332p. 1982. 64.50 (ISBN 0-471-06509-9, Pub. by Wiley-Interscience). Wiley.

Carpenter, Delburn. The Radical Pietists. LC 72-13586. (Illus.). 19.00 (ISBN 0-404-11008-8). AMS Pr.

Carpenter, Delores B., ed. The Life of Lidian Jackson Emerson by Ellen Tucker Emerson. (American Literary Manuscripts Ser.). 1980. lib. bdg. 26.00 (ISBN 0-8057-9651-7, Twayne). G K Hall.

Carpenter, Don. The Class of Forty-Nine. 200p. 1985. 14.50 (ISBN 0-86547-213-0). N Point Pr.

Carpenter, Dorr & Mayborn, Mitch. Ryan Guidebook. rev., 2nd ed. LC 75-1687. (American Aircraft Ser: Bk. 3). (Illus.). 120p. 1975. 14.95 (ISBN 0-912470-23-2); pap. 9.95 (ISBN 0-912470-18-6). Flying Ent.

Carpenter, Edith. Lorenzo DeMedici: An Historical Portrait. 1978. Repr. of 1893 ed. lib. bdg. 22.50 (ISBN 0-8495-0760-X). Arden Lib.

Carpenter, Edmund J. Roger Williams. LC 72-13. (Select Bibliographies Reprint Ser). 1972. Repr. of 1909 ed. 17.25 (ISBN 0-8369-9955-X). Ayer Co Pubs.

Carpenter, Edward. Animals & Ethics. 48p. 1980. 6.00x (ISBN 0-7224-0180-9, Pub. by Watkins England). State Mutual Bk.

--The Art of Creation. 1978. Repr. of 1904 ed. lib. bdg. 45.00 (ISBN 0-8495-0814-2). Arden Lib.

--The Art of Creation. 1912. lib. bdg. 32.00 (ISBN 0-8414-3611-8). Folcroft.

--A Bibliography of Edward Carpenter. 1973. Repr. of 1949 ed. lib. bdg. 25.00 (ISBN 0-8414-3357-7). Folcroft.

--A Bibliography of Edward Carpenter. 59.95 (ISBN 0-87968-737-1). Gordon Pr.

--Civilization: Its Cause & Cure. 44p. pap. 2.50 (ISBN 0-934676-01-1). Greenlf Bks.

--Civilization: Its Cause & Cure & Other Essays. 1978. Repr. of 1921 ed. lib. bdg. 30.00 (ISBN 0-8495-0768-5). Arden Lib.

--Collected Works. 600.00 (ISBN 0-87968-886-6). Gordon Pr.

--Days with Walt Whitman: With Some Notes on His Life & Work. LC 78-22293. (The Gay Experience). Repr. of 1906 ed. 21.50 (ISBN 0-404-61522-8). AMS Pr.

--Friends of Walt Whitman. 1977. 16.50 (ISBN 0-685-81155-7). Porter.

--Homogenic Love, & Its Place in a Free Society. LC 78-63984. (The Gay Experience). Repr. of 1894 ed. 11.50 (ISBN 0-404-61523-6). AMS Pr.

--The Intermediate Sex: A Study of Some Transitional Types of Men & Women. 2nd ed. LC 78-22294. (The Gay Experience). Repr. of 1909 ed. 22.50 (ISBN 0-404-61524-4). AMS Pr.

--Intermediate Types Among Primative Folk. LC 75-12308. (Homosexuality). 1975. Repr. of 1919 ed. 17.00x (ISBN 0-405-07352-6). Ayer Co Pubs.

--Intermediate Types Among Primitive Folk: A Study in Social Evolution. 185p. 1982. Repr. of 1919 ed. lib. bdg. 50.00 (ISBN 0-89987-131-3). Darby Bks.

--Iolaus: An Anthology of Friendship. 3rd ed. LC 76-174018. 1971. Repr. of 1920 ed. 30.00x (ISBN 0-8103-3790-8). Gale.

--Love's Coming-of-Age. 1912. lib. bdg. 40.00 (ISBN 0-8414-1559-5). Folcroft.

--Pagan & Christian Creeds. 59.95 (ISBN 0-8490-0794-1). Gordon Pr.

--Selected Writings, Vol. 1: Sex. (Gay Modern Classics Ser.). 320p. (Orig.). 1984. 32.50 (ISBN 0-907040-44-6, Pub. by GMP England); pap. 10.95 (ISBN 0-907040-43-8). Alyson Pubns.

--Some Friends of Walt Whitman: A Study in Sex-Psychology. lib. bdg. 17.50 (ISBN 0-8414-3467-0). Folcroft.

--Visit to a Gnani. 65p. 1971. Repr. of 1902 ed. 4.00 (ISBN 0-911662-44-8). Yoga.

Carpenter, Edward & Barnefield, George. Psychology of the Poet Shelley. LC 72-1334. (English Literature Ser., No. 33). 1972. Repr. of 1925 ed. lib. bdg. 39.95x (ISBN 0-8383-1431-7). Haskell.

Carpenter, Edward & Barnfield, George. Psychology of the Poet Shelley. 1925. lib. bdg. 17.50 (ISBN 0-8414-3590-1). Folcroft.

Carpenter, Edward, jt. auth. see Cunninghame Graham, R. B.

Carpenter, Edward, ed. Iolaus: An Anthology of Friendship. (Illus.). 202p. 1982. lib. bdg. 25.00 (ISBN 0-943742-01-3); pap. 8.95 (ISBN 0-943742-00-5). Pagan Pr.

Carpenter, Edward C., jt. auth. see Otter, Floyd L.

Carpenter, Edward J. & Capone, Douglas G., eds. Nitrogen in the Marine Environment. LC 83-2829. 1983. 59.00 (ISBN 0-12-160280-X). Acad Pr.

Carpenter, Edward K. Thirty-Seven Design & Environment Projects: First Annual Review. (Illus.). 96p. 1976. 13.95 (ISBN 0-8230-7456-0, Whitney Lib). Watson-Guptill.

Carpenter, Edwin H., Jr., jt. ed. see Skeel, Emily E.

Carpenter, Esther B. South County Studies: Of Some Eighteenth Century Persons, Places & Conditions. in That Portion of Rhode Island Called Narragansett. facsimile ed. LC 75-160961. (Select Bibliographies Reprint Ser). Repr. of 1924 ed. 21.00 (ISBN 0-8369-5829-2). Ayer Co Pubs.

Carpenter, F. I. English Lyric Poetry, Fifteen Hundred to Seventeen Hundred. facs. ed. LC 77-76942. (Granger Index Reprint Ser). 1906. 18.00 (ISBN 0-8369-6006-8). Ayer Co Pubs.

--A Reference Guide to Edmund Spenser. 1980. 11.50 (ISBN 0-8446-1102-6). Peter Smith.

Carpenter, F. M., et al. Coal Age Fossils from Mazon Creek. (Scientific Papers Ser.: Vol. III, Nos. 1-4). (Illus.). 147p. 1979. pap. 4.00 (ISBN 0-89792-082-1). Ill St Museum.

Carpenter, Finlay. The Skinner Primer: Behind Freedom & Dignity. LC 73-16603. 1974. 14.95 (ISBN 0-02-905290-4); pap. 4.95 (ISBN 0-02-905310-2). Free Pr.

Carpenter, Frances. Tales of a Chinese Grandmother. LC 72-77514. (Illus.). 302p. (gr. 3-8). 1972. pap. 6.95 (ISBN 0-8048-1042-7). C E Tuttle.

--Tales of a Korean Grandmother. LC 72-77515. (Illus.). (gr. 3-8). 1972. pap. 7.50 (ISBN 0-8048-1043-5). C E Tuttle.

Carpenter, Francis. Tales of a Chinese Grandmother. 293p. Repr. of 1937 ed. lib. bdg. 18.95x (ISBN 0-89190-481-6, Pub. by River City Pr). Amereon Ltd.

Carpenter, Francis B. Six Months with Lincoln in the White House. LC 60-15560. 7.00 (ISBN 0-87282-017-3). CHB-ALF.

Carpenter, Frank G. How the World Is Fed. 1977. lib. bdg. 59.95 (ISBN 0-8490-2021-2). Gordon Pr.

Carpenter, Franklin I., ed. see Cox, Leonard.

Carpenter, Frederic I. Eugene O'Neill. rev. ed. (United States Authors Ser.). 1979. lib. bdg. 13.50 (ISBN 0-8057-7267-7, Twayne). G K Hall.

--Metaphor & Simile in Minor Elizabethan Drama. LC 67-30900. 1967. Repr. of 1901 ed. 9.00x (ISBN 0-87753-007-6). Phaeton.

--Metaphor & Simile in the Minor Elizabethean Drama. 1979. Repr. of 1895 ed. lib. bdg. 30.00 (ISBN 0-8495-0928-9). Arden Lib.

--Robinson Jeffers. (Twayne's United States Authors Ser.). 1962. pap. 5.95x (ISBN 0-8084-0269-2, T22, Twayne). New Coll U Pr.

Carpenter, Frederic I., ed. see Cox, Leonard.

Carpenter, Frederick. American Literature & the Dream. facs. ed. LC 68-57310. (Essay Index Reprint Ser). 1955. 18.00 (ISBN 0-8369-0276-9). Ayer Co Pubs.

--Eugene O'Neill. (United States Authors Ser.). 192p. (Orig.). pap. 5.95 (ISBN 0-8057-7428-9, Twayne). G K Hall.

Carpenter, Frederick I. Emerson & Asia. LC 67-30810. (Studies in Comparative Literature, No. 35). 1969. Repr. of 1930 ed. lib. bdg. 75.00 (ISBN 0-8383-0710-8). Haskell.

--Metaphor & Simile in the Minor Elizabethan Drama. LC 77-136372. (Chicago. University. English Studies: No. 4). Repr. of 1895 ed. 24.00 (ISBN 0-404-50264-4). AMS Pr.

Carpenter, Fredrick I., ed. Metaphor & Simile in Minor Elizabethan Drama. 1895. lib. bdg. 12.00 (ISBN 0-8414-3457-3). Folcroft.

Carpenter, G., jt. auth. see Jones, A. J.

Carpenter, G. Russell, jt. auth. see Gove, Walter R.

Carpenter, Gaylene M., jt. auth. see Howe, Christine Z.

Carpenter, George R. American Prose. 1907. Repr. 25.00 (ISBN 0-8274-1856-6). R West.

--Daniel Defoe's Journal of the Plague Year. 253p. 1978. Repr. of 1895 ed. 16.50 (ISBN 0-87928-091-3). Corner Hse.

--Henry Wadsworth Longfellow. 1901. lib. bdg. 10.00 (ISBN 0-8414-3471-9). Folcroft.

--Model English Prose. 1905. lib. bdg. 12.50 (ISBN 0-8414-1571-4). Folcroft.

Carpenter, George R., ed. see Steele, Richard.

Carpenter, George W. Encounter of the Faiths. (Orig.). 1967. pap. 1.75 (ISBN 0-377-37001-0). Friend Pr.

Carpenter, Gilbert C., jt. ed. see Eddy, Mary B.

Carpenter, Gilbert C., Sr. & Carpenter, Gilbert C., Jr. Mary Baker Eddy: Her Spiritual Footsteps. 290p. 1985. pap. 17.50 (ISBN 0-930227-02-6). Bookmark CA.

Carpenter, Humphrey. The Inklings. 256p. 1981. pap. 3.50 (ISBN 0-345-29552-8). Ballantine.

--Jesus. (Past Masters Ser.). 1980. pap. 3.95 (ISBN 0-19-283016-3). Oxford U Pr.

--OUDS: A Centenary History of the Oxford University Drama Society 1885-1985. (Illus.). 256p. 1985. 19.95x (ISBN 0-19-212241-X). Oxford U Pr.

--Secret Gardens: A Study of the Golden Age of Children's Literature. (Illus.). 235p. 1985. 16.95 (ISBN 0-395-35293-2). HM.

--Tolkien: A Biography. 1985. pap. 3.50 (ISBN 0-345-27256-0). Ballantine.

--Tolkien: A Biography. 1977. 10.00 (ISBN 0-395-25360-8). HM.

--W. H. Auden: A Biography. (Illus.). 476p. 1981. 10.95 (ISBN 0-395-32439-4). HM.

Carpenter, Humphrey & Prichard, Mari. The Oxford Companion to Children's Literature. LC 83-15130. (Illus.). 1984. 35.00 (ISBN 0-19-211582-0). Oxford U Pr.

Carpenter, Humphrey & Tolkien, Christopher, eds. The Letters of J. R. R. Tolkien. 464p. 1981. 16.95 (ISBN 0-395-31555-7). HM.

Carpenter, Inta G. A Latvian Storyteller: The Repertoire of Janis Plavnieks. Dorson, Richard M., ed. LC 80-725. (Folklore of the World Ser.). 1980. lib. bdg. 25.50x (ISBN 0-405-13306-5). Ayer Co Pubs.

Carpenter, Inta G. & Dorson, Richard M., eds. Folklore in the Calumet Region: Special Issue, Indiana Folklore, Vol. 10, No. 2. LC 80-7779. (Folklore of the World Ser.). (Illus.). 1980. Repr. of 1977 ed. lib. bdg. 16.00x (ISBN 0-405-13341-3). Ayer Co Pubs.

Carpenter, J. A., ed. Drug Interactions: The Effects of Alcohol & Meprobamate Applied Singly & Jointly in Human Subjects. (Journal of Studies on Alcohol: Suppl. No. 7). 1975. 10.00 (ISBN 0-911290-02-8). Rutgers Ctr Alcohol.

Carpenter, J. Estlin. The Life and Work of Mary Carpenter. 2nd ed. LC 77-172564. (Criminology, Law Enforcement & Social Problems Ser.: No. 145). (Illus.). 420p. (Index added). 1974. Repr. of 1881 ed. lib. bdg. 20.00x (ISBN 0-87585-145-2). Patterson Smith.

--Theism in Medieval India. 1977. Repr. of 1921 ed. 22.50x (ISBN 0-89684-457-9). Orient Bk Dist.

Carpenter, James M. Visual Art: A Critical Introduction. 289p. 1982. pap. text ed. 20.95 (ISBN 0-15-594935-7, HC). HarBraceJ.

Carpenter, Jan. A Chairman's Guide to Effective Committee Management. 53p. 1981. 5.00 (ISBN 0-317-36324-7). Natl Conf State Legis.

Carpenter, Jesse T. Competition & Collective Bargaining in the Needle Trades, 1910-1967. LC 79-630987. (Cornell Studies in Industrial & Labor Relations: No. 17). 936p. 1972. 17.50 (ISBN 0-87546-035-6). ILR Pr.

Carpenter, John. A Most Excellent Instruction for Keeping Merchants Bookes of Accounts. LC 76-57368. (English Experience Ser.: No. 786). 1977. Repr. of 1632 ed. lib. bdg. 23.00 (ISBN 90-221-0786-8). Walter J Johnson.

--Poetry & Space. price not set. U of Wash Pr.

Carpenter, John, jt. ed. see Treacher, Andrew.

Carpenter, John, tr. see Herbert, Zbigniew.

Carpenter, Johonet H. The Well of Understanding. LC 82-61176. (Illus.). 136p. 1982. 13.00 (ISBN 0-9609378-0-3). Sophia Pr.

Carpenter, Joseph E. Theism in Medieval India. LC 77-27152. (Hibbert Lectures: 1919). Repr. of 1921 ed. 38.50 (ISBN 0-404-60419-6). AMS Pr.

Carpenter, Juliet W., tr. see Abe, Kobo.

Carpenter, Juliet W., tr. see Enchi, Fumiko.

Carpenter, K. Theism in Medieval India. 1977. 22.50x (ISBN 0-8364-0100-X). South Asia Bks.

Carpenter, Kathy & Calloway, Doris H. Nutrition & Health. 1981. text ed. 28.95 (ISBN 0-03-057711-X, HoltC) (ISBN 0-03-058274-1). HR&W.

Carpenter, Kenneth, ed. Pellagra. LC 81-6514. (Benchmark Papers in Biochemistry Ser.: Vol. 2). 416p. 1981. 52.95 (ISBN 0-87933-364-2). Van Nos Reinhold.

Carpenter, Kenneth E. Books & Society in History. 254p. 1983. 29.95 (ISBN 0-8352-1675-6). Bowker.

--Speculation in Gold & Silver. LC 74-367. (Vol. 14). 1974. gold 13.00x (ISBN 0-405-05928-0). Ayer Co Pubs.

Carpenter, Kenneth E., ed. British Labour Struggles: Contemporary Pamphlets, 1727-1850, 32 bks. 1972. Set. 693.00 (ISBN 0-405-04410-0). Ayer Co Pubs.

--Gold & Silver in the Presidential Campaign of 1896. LC 74-366. (Vol. 5). 1974. 23.50x (ISBN 0-405-05927-2). Ayer Co Pubs.

--Gold Mining Company Prospect Uses: California, Alaska, Arizona, Colorado, Idaho, Utah, 2 pts. LC 74-365. (Vol. 6). (Illus.). 1974. gold 32.00 (ISBN 0-405-05926-4). Ayer Co Pubs.

Carpenter, Kenneth E., ed. see Coughlin.

Carpenter, Kevin. Penny Dreadfuls & Comics: English Periodicals for Children from Victorian Times to the Present Day. (Illus.). 128p. (Orig.). pap. 17.95 (ISBN 0-905209-47-8, Pub. by Victoria & Albert Mus UK). Faber & Faber.

Carpenter, L. G., ed. Vacuum Technology. 2nd ed. 1983. 25.00 (ISBN 0-9960026-8-5, Pub. by A Hilger England). Heyden.

Carpenter, Linda J. Gymnastics for Girls & Women. LC 84-19064. 207p. 1984. 18.95 (ISBN 0-13-371808-5, Busn); pap. 7.95 (ISBN 0-13-371790-9). P-H.

Carpenter, Malcolm. Core Text of Neuroanatomy. 3rd ed. 375p. 1985. 22.95 (ISBN 0-683-01455-2). Williams & Wilkins.

--Study Guide & Self Assessment Review for the Core Text of Neuro-Anatomy. 3rd ed. 100p. 1985. pap. 15.95 (ISBN 0-683-14560-6). Williams & Wilkins.

Carpenter, Malcolm B. & Sutin, Jerome. Human Neuroanatomy. 8th ed. (Illus.). 906p. 1982. text ed. 45.50 (ISBN 0-683-01461-7). Williams & Wilkins.

Carpenter, Margaret. Season's of Change. 56p. 1983. 22.00 (ISBN 0-942494-60-1). Coleman Pub.

Carpenter, Margaret H. A Gift for the Princess of Springtime. LC 63-7621. (Illus.). 27p. 1964. 9.95 (ISBN 0-913110-02-7). Pentelic Pr.

--Sara Teasdale: A Biography. LC 77-81159. (Illus.). 1977. Repr. of 1960 ed. 14.95 (ISBN 0-913110-03-5). Pentelic Pr.

Carpenter, Mark, ed. see Culver, Robert D.

Carpenter, Mark, ed. see Lyon, Harold C., Jr. & Lyon, Edith A.

Carpenter, Mary. Juvenile Delinquents, Their Condition & Treatment. LC 76-108224. (Criminology, Law Enforcement, & Social Problems Ser.: No. 107). (With essay by Katharine Lenroot & index added). 1970. Repr. of 1953 ed. lib. bdg. 15.00x (ISBN 0-87585-107-X). Patterson Smith.

--Our Convicts, 2 vols. in 1. LC 69-16229. (Criminology, Law Enforcement, & Social Problems Ser.: No. 88). 1969. Repr. of 1864 ed. 25.00x (ISBN 0-87585-080-4). Patterson Smith.

--Reformatory Prison Discipline As Developed by the Rt. Hon. Sir Walter Crofton in the Irish Convict Prisons. LC 67-26667. (Criminology, Law Enforcement, & Social Problems Ser.: No. 2). 1967. Repr. of 1872 ed. 10.00x (ISBN 0-87585-002-2). Patterson Smith.

--Reformatory Schools for the Children of the Perishing & Dangerous Classes & for Juvenile Offenders. (Social History of Education Ser.: First Series, No. 2). 1968. Repr. of 1851 ed. 27.50x (ISBN 0-7130-0018-X, Pub. by Woburn Pr England). Biblio Dist.

--Reformatory Schools for the Children of the Perishing & Dangerous Classes. LC 75-5684. (Social History of Education). Repr. of 1851 ed. 27.50x (ISBN 0-678-08451-3). Kelley.

--Reformatory Schools for the Children of the Perishing & Dangerous Classes & for Juvenile Offenders. Lenroot, Katharine, contrib. by. LC 72-108223. (Criminology, Law Enforcement, & Social Problems Ser.: No. 106). 1970. Repr. of 1851 ed. lib. bdg. 15.00x (ISBN 0-87585-106-1). Patterson Smith.

Carpenter, Mary G., jt. auth. see Carpenter, Charles H., Jr.

Carpenter, Maryann, jt. auth. see Bench, Carson E.

Carpenter, Maurice. The Indifferent Horseman. 368p. 1980. Repr. of 1954 ed. lib. bdg. 30.00 (ISBN 0-8482-3552-5). Norwood Edns.

--The Indifferent Horseman: The Divine Commedy of Samuel Taylor Coleridge. 1973. lib. bdg. 20.00 (ISBN 0-8414-9981-0). Folcroft.

Carpenter, Max H. & Waldo, Wayne M. Real Time Method of Radar Plotting. (Illus.). 48p. 1975. pap. 10.50x (ISBN 0-87033-204-X). Cornell Maritime.

Carpenter, Max H., jt. auth. see Van Wyck, Samuel M.

Carpenter, Michael & Svenonius, Elaine, eds. Foundations of Cataloging: A Sourcebook. 270p. 1985. PLB 27.50 (ISBN 0-87287-511-3). Libs Unl.

Carpenter, Michael A. Corporate Authorship: Its Role in Library Cataloging. LC 80-1026. (Contributions in Librarianship & Information Science Ser.: No. 34). x, 200p. 1981. lib. bdg. 29.95 (ISBN 0-313-22065-4, CAU/). Greenwood.

Carpenter, Mimi G. What the Sea Left Behind. LC 81-66251. (Illus.). 32p. (gr. 2-3). 1981. pap. 7.95 (ISBN 0-89272-123-5). Down East.

Carpenter, Myron, jt. auth. see Beckman, Neal.

Carpenter, Nan. A Quiver of Quizzes for Quidnuncs. 1985. pap. 6.95 (ISBN 0-8158-0420-2). Chris Mass.

Carpenter, Nan Cooke. Music in the Medieval & Renaissance Universities. LC 70-171380. (Music Ser). (Illus.). 394p. 1972. Repr. of 1958 ed. lib. bdg. 39.50 (ISBN 0-306-70453-6). Da Capo.

Carpenter, Nancy & Sperath, Albert, eds. Total Recall: An Anthology. LC 80-620037. 12p. (Orig.). 1980. pap. 3.00 (ISBN 0-939058-00-6). Kentucky Arts.

Carpenter, Nathanael. Achitophel, or Toe Picture of a Wicked Politician. LC 79-84094. (English Experience Ser.: No. 914). 76p. 1979. Repr. of 1629 ed. lib. bdg. 9.00 (ISBN 90-221-0914-3). Walter J Johnson.

--Geography Delineated Forth in Two Books. LC 76-57369. (English Experience Ser.: No. 787). 1977. Repr. of 1625 ed. lib. bdg. 58.00 set (ISBN 90-221-0787-6). Walter J Johnson.

Carpenter, Niles. Immigrants & Their Children, 1920. Ozer, Jerome S., ed. LC 70-78038. (American Immigration Collection Ser., No. 1). 1969. Repr. of 1927 ed. 18.00 (ISBN 0-405-00504-0). Ayer Co Pubs.

--Nationality, Color, & Economic Opportunity in the City of Buffalo. LC 70-107480. Repr. of 1927 ed. 25.00x (ISBN 0-8371-3782-9, CCB&, Pub. by Negro U Pr). Greenwood.

Carpenter, P. A., jt. ed. see Just, M. A.

Carpenter, Pearl E. The Duck Book One & Two: Basics for Painting Wood-Carved Ducks & Birds. (Illus., Orig.). 1984. wkbk. 12.75 (ISBN 0-9614021-0-5). Shades Mother Nat.

Carpenter, Philip L. Immunology & Serology. 3rd ed. LC 74-31833. (Illus.). 495p. 1975. text ed. 32.95 (ISBN 0-7216-3422-2). HR&W.

--Microbiology. 4th ed. LC 76-27056. (Illus.). 1977. text ed. 35.95 (ISBN 0-7216-2438-3); instr's manual 6.95 (ISBN 0-03-057068-9). HR&W.

--Residential Landscaping II. LC 81-18833. (Illus.). 143p. 1983. 21.50 (ISBN 0-914886-21-5); pap. 14.50 (ISBN 0-914886-22-3). PDA Pubs.

Carpenter, Philip L., et al. Plants in the Landscape. LC 74-32292. (Illus.). 481p. 1975. text ed. 33.95 (ISBN 0-7167-0778-0). W H Freeman.

Carpenter, Philip P. Catalogue of the Collection of Mazatlan Shells in the British Museum. (Illus.). 576p. Repr. of 1857 ed. 8.00 (ISBN 0-87710-371-2); illustrations 8.00, 110p. (ISBN 0-87710-372-0). Paleo Res.

Carpenter, R. H. Movements of the Eyes. 420p. 1977. 38.50x (ISBN 0-85086-063-6, NO. 2923, Pub. by Pion England). Methuen Inc.

--Neurophysiology. (Physiological Principles in Medicine Ser.). 350p. 1984. pap. text ed. 24.00 (ISBN 0-8391-2047-8, 21571). Univ Park.

Carpenter, Ray L. Statistical Methods for Librarians. LC 78-3476. 134p. 1978. lib. bdg. 15.00x (ISBN 0-8389-0256-1). ALA.

Carpenter, Rebecca O., et al. Demographic Projections of Non-English-Language-Background & Limited-English Proficient Persons in the United States. LC 84-61164. 132p. 1984. 6.50 (ISBN 0-89763-100-5). Natl Clearinghse Bilingual Ed.

Carpenter, Renee, ed. see Sherman, Jory.

Carpenter, Rhys. Folk Tale, Fiction & Saga in the Homeric Epics. LC 55-7555. (Sather Classical Lectures Ser.: No. 20). 1974. 24.50x (ISBN 0-520-02808-2). U of Cal Pr.

--Greek Sculpture. LC 60-14233. (Illus.). 1971. pap. 12.95 (ISBN 0-226-09475-8, P436, Phoen). U of Chicago Pr.

--Greeks in Spain. LC 74-161505. Repr. of 1925 ed. 17.50 (ISBN 0-404-01394-5). AMS Pr.

--Humanistic Value of Archaeology. LC 72-138582. 1971. Repr. of 1933 ed. lib. bdg. 15.00 (ISBN 0-8371-5781-1, CAHV). Greenwood.

Carpenter, Richard A. Natural Systems Development. 1983. 41.00 (ISBN 0-02-949290-4). Macmillan.

Carpenter, Richard C. Thomas Hardy. (English Authors Ser.). 1964. lib. bdg. 13.50 (ISBN 0-8057-1244-5, Twayne). G K Hall.

Carpenter, Richard E. Parental Duties & You. 1981. 6.50 (ISBN 0-8062-1849-5). Carlton.

Carpenter, Rita Jean. Chicken Delight Cookbook. 1984. 9.75 (ISBN 0-8062-2226-3). Carlton.

Carpenter, Robert D. Thanks Doctor. LC 72-78231. 200p. 1972. pap. text ed. 5.95 (ISBN 0-9600576-1-7). RDC Pubs.

--Why Can't I Learn. LC 73-76060. 1972. 7.95 (ISBN 0-8307-0226-1); pap. 5.95 (ISBN 0-8307-0224-5). RDC Pubs.

Carpenter, Ronald H. The Eloquence of Frederick Jackson Turner. LC 83-8370. 238p. 1983. 20.00 (ISBN 0-87328-078-4). Huntington Lib.

Carpenter, Russell & Carpenter, Blyth. Fish Watching in Hawaii. (Illus.). 120p. (Orig.). 1981. pap. 7.95 (ISBN 0-939560-00-3). Natural World.

Carpenter, S. C. Taxonomic Revision of the Genus Crocicreas & a Reassessment of Genera Previously Assigned to Phialeoideae, No. 33. (Memoirs of the New York Botanical Garden Ser.). 264p. 1981. 35.00 (ISBN 0-317-35535-X). NY Botanical.

Carpenter, Samuel T. Structural Mechanics. LC 75-31671. 550p. 1976. Repr. of 1966 ed. 30.50 (ISBN 0-88275-363-0). Krieger.

Carpenter, Sharan. Scissor Sorcery: Cutting Activities for Early Childhood Programs. (Orig.). 1984. pap. 16.95 (ISBN 0-89334-076-6). Humanics Ltd.

Carpenter, Shirley. Atlas of Man & His World. (Horizons of Knowledge Ser.). (Illus.). 1980. 24.95 (ISBN 0-87196-412-0). Facts on File.

Carpenter, Stanley B., jt. ed. see De Vore, R. William.

Carpenter, Stanley J. & Lacasse, Walter J. Mosquitoes of North America. (California Library Reprint Ser.). (Illus.). 1974. Repr. 66.00x (ISBN 0-520-02638-1). U of Cal Pr.

Carpenter, Steve & Wallerstein, Ed. Ribbons & Haywire. 256p. (Orig.). 1985. pap. 2.50 (ISBN 0-8125-7665-9, Dist. by Pinnacle Bks, Warner Pub Services & St. Martin). Tor Bks.

Carpenter, Steven E. Monograph of Crocicreas: Ascomycetes, Helotiales, Helotiaceae, Vol. 33. (Memoirs of the New York Botanical Garden Ser.). (Illus.). 1981. pap. 35.00x (ISBN 0-89327-230-2). NY Botanical.

Carpenter, Susan & Jones, Peter, eds. Recent Advances in Travel Demand Analysis: First Int'l Conference, Oxford University, England - July, 1981. 488p. 1983. text ed. 54.00x (ISBN 0-566-00601-4). Gower Pub Co.

Carpenter, Ted. Calling the Tune: Communications Technology for Working, Learning, & Living. 90p. 1980. 15.00 (ISBN 0-318-15732-2). Natl Inst Work.

Carpenter, Thomas, et al. Results from the First Mathematics Assessment of the National Assessment of Educational Progress. LC 78-2345. 144p. 1978. pap. 9.00 (ISBN 0-87353-123-X). NCTM.

Carpenter, Thomas D. Pasadena: Resort Hotels & Paradise. (Illus.). 1984. 24.95 (ISBN 0-317-12073-5). M Sheldon Pub.

Carpenter, Thomas H. & Gula, Robert J. Mythology: Greek & Roman. (Illus.). (gr. 10). 1977. pap. text ed. 6.50x (ISBN 0-88334-089-5). Ind Sch Pr.

Carpenter, Thomas P., et al. Addition & Subtraction: A Cognitive Perspective. 265p. 1982. text ed. 24.95x (ISBN 0-89859-171-6). L Erlbaum Assocs.

Carpenter, Victor, tr. see Lehrmann, Charles C.

Carpenter, W. B., et al. Introduction to the Study of the Foraminifera. 1965. Repr. of 1862 ed. 37.50 (ISBN 0-934454-52-3). Lubrecht & Cramer.

Carpenter, W. Boyd. The Spiritual Message of Dante. 1973. Repr. of 1914 ed. 20.00 (ISBN 0-8274-1506-0). R West.

Carpenter, Walter H., Jr. & Handler, Edward. Small Business & Pattern Bargaining. Bruchey, Stuart & Carosso, Vincent P., eds. LC 78-18953. (Small Business Enterprise in America Ser.). 1979. Repr. of 1961 ed. lib. bdg. 19.00x (ISBN 0-405-11461-3). Ayer Co Pubs.

Carpenter, Wayne. The Voyage of Kristina. 239p. 1983. 17.95 (ISBN 0-913179-01-9). Azimuth Pr.

Carpenter, William. The Hours of Morning: Poems, 1976-1979. LC 81-7452. xii, 71p. 1981. 9.95x (ISBN 0-8139-0909-0). U Pr of Va.

--The Life & Times of John Milton. 171p. 1980. Repr. of 1836 ed. lib. bdg. 22.50 (ISBN 0-8495-0795-2). Arden Lib.

--Political Letters & Pamphlets by William Carpenter, Nos. 1-34. Repr. of 1830 ed. lib. bdg. 53.00x (ISBN 0-8371-9136-X, BC00). Greenwood.

--Rain. 70p. (Orig.). 1985. pap. 4.95x (ISBN 0-930350-80-4). NE U Pr.

--The Unfinished Business of Civil Service Reform. LC 72-86539. 136p. 1973. Repr. of 1952 ed. 19.50x (ISBN 0-8046-1748-1, Pub by Kennikat). Assoc Faculty Pr.

Carpenter, William B. Nature & Man: Essays Scientific & Philosophical. LC 78-72791. (Brainedness, Handedness, & Mental Ability Ser.). Repr. of 1888 ed. 34.50 (ISBN 0-404-60855-8). AMS Pr.

--On the Use & Abuse of Alcoholic Liquors, in Health & Disease. Grob, Gerald N., ed. LC 80-1216. (Addiction in America Ser.). 1981. Repr. of 1853 ed. lib. bdg. 15.00x (ISBN 0-405-13572-6). Ayer Co Pubs.

--Principles of Mental Physiology: With Their Applications to the Training & Discipline of the Mind & the Study of Its Morbid Conditions. rev. ed. LC 78-72792. Repr. of 1900 ed. 55.00 (ISBN 0-404-60856-6, BF161). AMS Pr.

--The Spiritual Message of Dante. 19.00 (ISBN 0-8369-7103-5, 7937). Ayer Co Pubs.

Carpenter, William S. The Development of American Political Thought. LC 70-1623. 1980. Repr. of 1930 ed. 19.25 (ISBN 0-88355-928-5). Hyperion Conn.

--Foundations of Modern Jurisprudence. LC 58-5314. 1958. 26.50x (ISBN 0-89197-174-2); pap. text ed. 14.95x (ISBN 0-89197-175-0). Irvington.

--The Unfinished Business of Civil Service Reform. LC 79-16863. 1980. Repr. of 1952 ed. lib. bdg. 19.75x (ISBN 0-313-22051-4, CACS). Greenwood.

Carpenter, William T., jt. auth. see Strauss, John S.

Carpenter, William W. Certain Phases of the Administration of High School Chemistry. LC 70-176627. (Columbia University. Teachers College. Contributions to Education: No. 191). Repr. of 1925 ed. 22.50 (ISBN 0-404-55191-2). AMS Pr.

Carpenter-Turner, Barbara. A History of Hampshire. (The Darwen County History Ser.). (Illus.). 128p. 1978. Repr. of 1963 ed. 18.00x (ISBN 0-8476-2312-2). Rowman.

Carpentier, Alejo. The Lost Steps. 1979. pap. 2.50 (ISBN 0-380-46177-3, 46177-3, Bard). Avon.

--Reasons of State. Patridge, Frances, tr. from Span. 320p. 1981. pap. 4.95 (ISBN 0-904613-52-6). Writers & Readers.

Carpentier, Didier & Bachelet, Joel. Painting on Glass. 64p. 1982. 25.00x (ISBN 0-7158-0805-2, Pub. by EP Pub England). State Mutual Bk.

--Painting on Glass. LC 84-3021. (Hobbycraft Bks.). (Illus.). 64p. 1984. pap. 4.95 (ISBN 0-668-06237-1, 6237-1). Arco.

Carpentier, Hortense, tr. see Onetti, Juan C.

Carpentier, Hortense, tr. see Valenzuela, Luisa.

Carpentier, James & Cazamian, Pierre. Night Work: Its Effects on the Health & Welfare of the Worker. x, 82p. (Eng., Fr. & Span., 2nd Impression (with Modifications)). 1978. 10.00 (ISBN 92-2-101729-X, ILO15, ILO); pap. 10.00 (ISBN 92-2-101676-5). Unipub.

Carpentier, L. J., ed. New Developments in Phosphate Fertilizer Technology: Proceedings of the 1976 Technical Conference, The Hague, Sept. 1976. 454p. 1977. 95.75 (ISBN 0-444-41535-1). Elsevier.

Carpentier, Michael H. Radars-New Concepts. rev. ed. LC 66-27987. 282p. 1968. 80.95 (ISBN 0-677-01760-X). Gordon.

Carpentier, Posey. Posey Carpentier's Master Plan for Real Estate Selling Success. (Illus.). 186p. 1984. 19.95 (ISBN 0-13-687716-8, Busn). P-H.

Carper, James C. & Hunt, Thomas C., eds. Religious Schooling in America. LC 84-1942. 257p. (Orig.). 1984. pap. 14.95 (ISBN 0-89135-043-8). Religious Educ.

Carper, Janice M. Between the Bays: Somerset, Wicomico & Worcester Counties Maryland. LC 78-71245. (Illus.). 86p. 1979. pap. 13.00 (ISBN 0-914440-74-8). EPM Pubns.

Carper, Jean. The National Medical Directory. (Orig.). 1985. pap. 11.95 (ISBN 0-671-49974-2). PB.

Carper, Jean & Eyton, Audrey. The Revolutionary Seven-Unit Low-Fat Diet. LC 80-5982. 1981. 3.95 (ISBN 0-89256-156-4). Rawson Assocs.

--The Revolutionary Seven Unit Low Fat Diet. 256p. (Orig.). 1985. pap. 3.50 (ISBN 0-553-23113-8). Bantam.

Carper, Jean & Krause, Patricia A. The All-in-One Calorie Counter. rev. ed. 304p. (Orig.). 1980. pap. 3.95 (ISBN 0-553-24756-5). Bantam.

--The All-in-One Carbohydrate Gram Counter. rev. ed. 304p. 1980. pap. 3.95 (ISBN 0-553-24475-2). Bantam.

Carper, L. Dean. GIB. 111p. 1985. pap. 6.00 (ISBN 0-8309-0413-1). Herald Hse.

Carper, Robert S. America's New Railroads. LC 77-84563. (Illus.). 256p. 1980. 25.00 (ISBN 0-498-02179-3). A S Barnes.

Carpiceci, A. C. Pompeii Two Thousand Years Ago. (Bonechi Guides Ser.). (Illus.). 160p. pap. 11.95 (ISBN 0-88332-335-4, 8271). Larousse.

Carpini, Michael Delli see Delli Carpini, Michael X.

Carpinisan, Mariana, tr. see Stanescu, Nichita.

Carpino, Pasquale. Recipes from Pasquale's Kitchen. LC 84-10251. (Illus.). 212p. 1985. 17.95 (ISBN 0-385-19306-8); pap. 9.95 (ISBN 0-385-19307-6). Doubleday.

Carpino, Pasquale & Drynan, Judith. Italian Gourmet Cooking: La Cucina di Pasquale. (Illus.). 239p. 1984. pap. 9.95 (ISBN 0-919157-01-7, Pub. by Summerhill CN). Sterling.

Carpinteri, A., ed. Fracture Mechanics of Concrete: Material Characterization & Testing. 1984. lib. bdg. 49.50 (ISBN 90-247-2959-9, Pub. by Martinus Nijhoff Netherlands). Kluwer Academic.

Carpio, L. F. De Vega see De Vega Carpio, L. F.

Carpou, Mary, ed. Greek Cookery: Marin. LC 75-41189. (Orig.). 1981. pap. text ed. 7.50 (ISBN 0-9611164-0-4). Ladies Philo.

Carpovich, Eugene A. Russian-English Atomic Dictionary: Physics, Mathematics, Nucleonics. rev. ed. 2nd ed. LC 57-8256. (Rus. & Eng.). 1959. 15.00 (ISBN 0-911484-00-0). Tech Dict.

--Russian-English Biological & Medical Dictionary. 2nd ed. LC 58-7915. (Rus. & Eng.). 1960. 25.00 (ISBN 0-911484-01-9). Tech Dict.

--Russian-English Chemical Dictionary. 2nd ed. LC 61-11700. (Rus. & Eng.). 1963. 25.00 (ISBN 0-911484-03-5). Tech Dict.

--Russian-English Metals & Machines Dictionary. LC 60-12013. (Rus. & Eng.). 1960. 15.00x (ISBN 0-911484-02-7). Tech Dict.

Carpovich, Vera V. Solzhenitsyn's Peculiar Vocabulary, Russian-English Glossary. LC 76-3932. (Rus. & Eng.). 1976. 15.00 (ISBN 0-911484-04-3). Tech Dict.

Carpozi, George, Jr. Andrew Young: The Impossible Man. 1978. pap. 1.95 (ISBN 0-532-19202-8). Woodhill.

--The Distinguished Performers. (That's Hollywood Ser.: No. 5). (Orig.). 1979. pap. 1.95 (ISBN 0-532-19230-3). Woodhill.

--The Fabulous Life of Bing Crosby. 1978. pap. 1.95 (ISBN 0-532-19171-4). Woodhill.

--Frank Sinatra: Is This Man Mafia? (Orig.). 1979. pap. 2.25 (ISBN 0-532-23282-8). Woodhill.

--The Gangland Killers. (Orig.). 1979. pap. 1.95 (ISBN 0-532-19256-7). Woodhill.

--Great Crimes of the Century, No. 3. (Orig.). 1979. pap. 1.95 (ISBN 0-532-19231-1). Woodhill.

--Great Crimes of the Century, No. 4. (Orig.). 1979. pap. 2.25 (ISBN 0-686-62759-8). Woodhill.

--Great Crimes of the Century No. 1. 1979. pap. 1.95 (ISBN 0-532-19217-6). Woodhill.

--Great Crimes of the Century No. 2. 1979. pap. 1.95 (ISBN 0-532-19224-9). Woodhill.

--Great Crimes of the Century, No. 5: The Senseless Slayers. (Orig.). 1979. pap. 1.95 (ISBN 0-532-23165-1). Woodhill.

--Great Crimes of the Century, No. 6: The Weird Murderers. (Orig.). 1979. pap. 1.95 (ISBN 0-532-23113-9). Woodhill.

--Great Crimes of the Century, No. 7: The Savage Killers. (Orig.). 1980. pap. 1.95 (ISBN 0-532-23129-5). Woodhill.

--Great Crimes of the Century, No. 8: Murderers Leave Clues. (Orig.). 1980. pap. 1.95 (ISBN 0-532-23130-9). Woodhill.

--Ordeal by Trial: The Alice Crimmins Case. LC 75-186179. 352p. (gr. 9-12). 1972. 7.95 (ISBN 0-8027-0374-7). Walker & Co.

--Son of Sam: The .44 Caliber Killer. 1977. pap. 2.25 (ISBN 0-532-22112-5). Woodhill.

--That's Hollywood: Beautiful & Special People, No. 7. (Orig.). 1980. pap. 1.95 (ISBN 0-532-23281-X). Woodhill.

--That's Hollywood: The Clossal Cowboys, No. 6. (Orig.). 1980. pap. 1.95 (ISBN 0-532-23222-4). Woodhill.

--That's Hollywood: The Great Ladies of Hollywood, No. 4. 1978. pap. 1.95 (ISBN 0-532-19214-1). Woodhill.

--That's Hollywood: The Love Goddesses, No. 2. 1978. pap. 1.95 (ISBN 0-532-19191-9). Woodhill.

--That's Hollywood: The Magnificent Entertainers, No. 3. 1978. pap. 1.95 (ISBN 0-532-19194-3). Woodhill.

--That's Hollywood: The Matinee Idols, No. 1. 1978. pap. 1.95 (ISBN 0-532-19190-0). Woodhill.

Carque, Otto. Vital Facts About Foods. LC 75-18697. 240p. 1975. pap. 3.50 (ISBN 0-87983-113-8). Keats.

Carr. The Radio Hobbyist's Handbook. (Illus.). 392p. 1982. 19.95 (ISBN 0-8306-1346-3, 1346). TAB Bks.

Carr & Greenberg. Treasury of Modern Fantasy. 1981. pap. 8.95 (ISBN 0-380-77115-2, 77115-2). Avon.

Carr & Paquet. God, I've Got to Talk to You Again! LC 59-1315. (Arch Bks.). 24p. (Orig.). (gr. k-4). 1985. pap. 0.99 (ISBN 0-570-06197-0, 59-1315). Concordia.

Carr & Ruffino. The Promotable Woman. 2nd ed. 1985. pap. write for info. (ISBN 0-534-05052-2). Wadsworth Pub.

Carr, et al. No Mind of Man. 1976. pap. 1.50 (ISBN 0-532-15220-4). Woodhill.

Carr, jt. auth. see Cochran, Clarke E.

Carr, A. H. Finding Maubee. Barzun, J. & Taylor, W. H., eds. LC 81-47334. (Crime Fiction 1950-1975 Ser.). 222p. 1982. lib. bdg. 18.00 (ISBN 0-8240-4977-2). Garland Pub.

Carr, A. W. Angels & Principalities. (Society for the New Testament Studies Monographs: No. 42). 240p. 1982. 32.50 (ISBN 0-521-23429-8). Cambridge U Pr.

Carr, Albert H. How to Attract Good Luck. pap. 5.00 (ISBN 0-87980-054-2). Wilshire.

--Juggernaut: The Path of Dictatorship. LC 79-180393. Repr. of 1939 ed. 42.00 (ISBN 0-404-56109-8). AMS Pr.

--Juggernaut, the Path of Dictatorship. facs. ed. LC 75-93325. (Essay Index Reprint Ser). 1939. 27.50 (ISBN 0-8369-1280-2). Ayer Co Pubs.

Carr, Allan, jt. auth. see Sun Yun Chiang, Cecilia.

Carr, Anna. Good Neighbors: Companion Planting for Gardeners. Nelson, Suzanne, ed. (Illus.). 1985. 19.95 (ISBN 0-87857-530-8). Rodale Pr Inc.

Carr, Anne. The Theological Method of Karl Rahner. LC 76-51639. (American Academy of Religion, Dissertation Ser.: No. 19). pap. 72.30 (ISBN 0-317-08410-0, 2017556). Bks Demand UMI.

Carr, Anne, ed. Academic Study of Religion: Proceedings. LC 74-14212. (American Academy of Religion. Section Papers). Repr. of 1974 ed. 40.50 (ISBN 0-8357-9563-2, 2017552). Bks Demand UMI.

Carr, Anne, et al. Academic Study of Religion, 1975: Public Schools Religion-Studies. LC 75-26653. (American Academy of Religion. Section Papers). 1975. pap. 9.95 (ISBN 0-89130-023-6, 01-09-17). Scholars Pr Ga.

Carr, Archie. Handbook of Turtles: The Turtles of the United States, Canada, & Baja California. (HANH Ser.). (Illus.). 557p. 1952. 45.00x (ISBN 0-8014-0064-3). Comstock.

--So Excellent a Fish: Tales of Sea Turtles. (Illus.). 320p. 1984. 15.95 (ISBN 0-684-18008-1, ScribT). Scribner.

--The Windward Road: Adventures of a Naturalist on Remote Caribbean Shores. LC 79-23624. (Illus.). xl, 258p. 1979. pap. 6.95 (ISBN 0-8130-0639-2). U Presses Fla.

Carr, Arthur, et al. Bernard Schoenberg: Contributions to Psychiatry, Education of the Health Professional, Thanatology, & Ethical Values. 250p. 1985. 25.00 (ISBN 0-930194-28-4); pap. 17.95 (ISBN 0-930194-27-6). Ctr Thanatology.

Carr, Arthur C., jt. auth. see Frazier, Shervert.

Carr, Arthur C., ed. Tolstoi's: Ivan Ilych & Commentary. 94p. 1973. pap. 1.95 (ISBN 0-930194-75-6). Ctr Thanatology.

Carr, Arthur C., et al. The Prediction of Overt Behavior Through the Use of Projective Techniques. (Illus.). 192p. 1960. photocopy ed. 16.75x (ISBN 0-398-04227-6). C C Thomas.

Carr, Arthur C., et al, eds. Grief: Selected Readings. 155p. 1974. pap. 7.50 (ISBN 0-930194-76-4). Ctr Thanatology.

Carr, Arthur J. & Steinhoff, William R., eds. Points of Departure: Essays & Stories for College English. facsimile ed. LC 74-167324. (Essay Index Reprint Ser). Repr. of 1960 ed. 35.50 (ISBN 0-8369-2449-5). Ayer Co Pubs.

Carr, Arthur S., ed. Victorian Poetry: Clough to Kipling. 1982. Repr. of 1972 ed. text ed. cancelled (ISBN 0-8290-0597-8). Irvington.

Carr, Audrey, jt. auth. see Sohl, Robert.

Carr, Audrey, jt. ed. see Sohl, Robert.

Carr, B. History of England from the Close of the Saxon Heptarchy to the Declaration of Independence. 10.00x (ISBN 0-87556-047-4). Saifer.

Carr, Benjamin. Musical Miscellany in Occasional Numbers. (Early American Music Ser.: No. 21). 1982. Repr. of 1825 ed. 49.50 (ISBN 0-306-79547-7). Da Capo.

Carr, Brian, jt. auth. see O'Connor, D. J.

Carr, Bruce, jt. ed. see Winter, Robert.

Carr, C. J., jt. auth. see Wright, M.

Carr, C. T. The General Principles of the Law of Corporations: Being the Yorke Prize Essay for the Year 1902. xiii, 211p. 1984. Repr. of 1905 ed. lib. bdg. 25.00x (ISBN 0-8377-2006-0). Rothman.

Carr, C. T. see Barker, M. L. & Homeyer, H.

Carr, Carolyn, jt. auth. see Link, O. Winston.

Carr, Carolyn K., ed. Ohio: A Photographic Portrait 1935-1941 - Farm Security Administration Photographs. LC 80-65227. (Illus.). 96p. 1980. pap. 12.00 (ISBN 0-87338-244-7). Kent St U Pr.

Carr, Cecil T. Concerning English Administrative Law. LC 70-38958. Repr. of 1941 ed. 17.50 (ISBN 0-404-01395-3). AMS Pr.

Carr, Cecil T., ed. Select Charters of Trading Companies A.D. 1530-1707. LC 76-130593. (Research & Source Works: No. 551). 1970. Repr. of 1913 ed. lib. bdg. 24.00 (ISBN 0-8337-0479-6). B Franklin.

Carr, Charles C. Alcoa, an American Enterprise. LC 72-5039. (Technology & Society Ser.). (Illus.). 292p. 1972. Repr. of 1952 ed. 24.50 (ISBN 0-405-04692-8). Ayer Co Pubs.

Carr, Charles C., jt. auth. see Gause, Frank A.

Carr, Charlotte, jt. auth. see Romness, Kirsten.

Carr, Christopher. For Concordance in Archaeological Analysis: Bridging Data Structure, Quantitative Technique & Theory. (Illus.). 684p. 1985. text ed. 75.00 (ISBN 0-933701-00-4). Westport Pubs.

--Handbook on Soil Resistivity Surveying. LC 82-4277. (Research Ser.: No. 2). (Illus.). 704p. 1982. 27.50 (ISBN 0-942118-13-8, CC79.S6C37); microfiche incl. Ctr Amer Arche.

Carr, Christopher, ed. The Analysis of Archaeological Data Structures. (Studies in Archaeology). Date not set. price not set (ISBN 0-12-160520-5). Acad Pr.

Carr, Clare, ed. The Gathering of Souls. Freelander, Iris. LC 81-69576. 240p. 1981. pap. 10.00 (ISBN 0-910378-17-7). Christward.

Carr, Claudia J. Pastoralism in Crisis: The Desanetch & Their Ethiopian Lands. LC 77-1252. (Research Papers Ser.: No. 180). (Illus.). 1977. pap. 10.00 (ISBN 0-89065-087-X). U Chicago Dept Geog.

Carr, D. J., ed. Sydney Parkinson: Artist of Cook's Endeavor Voyage. (Illus.). 315p. 1983. text ed. 45.00X (ISBN 0-8248-0889-4). UH Pr.

Carr, D. J. & Carr, S. G., eds. People & Plants in Australia. 450p. 1981. 50.00 (ISBN 0-12-160720-8); pap. 40.00 (ISBN 0-12-160722-4). Acad Pr.

--Plants & Man in Australia. 350p. 1981. 40.00 (ISBN 0-12-160723-2); pap. 35.00 (ISBN 0-12-160724-0). Acad Pr.

Carr, D. J., jt. ed. see Barlow, P. W.

Carr, D. J., ed. see International Conference on Plant Growth Substances, 7th, Canberra, 1970.

Carr, Dan. Cheating. (God I Need to Talk to You About...Ser.). (Illus.). 1984. pap. 0.75 (ISBN 0-570-08725-2, 56-1469). Concordia.

--The Ennead of Set-Heru. (Illus.). 20p. 1981. 25.00x (ISBN 0-939622-23-8). Four Zoas Night.

--Hurting Others. (God I Need to Talk to You about...Ser.). (Illus.). 1984. pap. 0.75 (ISBN 0-570-08727-9, 56-1471). Concordia.

--Lying. (God I Need to Talk to You About...Ser.). (Illus.). 1984. pap. 0.75 (ISBN 0-570-08732-5, 56-1476). Concordia.

--My Bad Temper. (God I Need to Talk to You About...Ser.). (Illus.). 1984. pap. 0.75 (ISBN 0-570-08730-9, 56-1474). Concordia.

--Our Savior Is Born. 1984. 5.95 (ISBN 0-570-04092-2, 56-1460). Concordia.

--Paying Attention. (God I Need to Talk to You About...Ser.). (Illus.). 1984. pap. 0.75 (ISBN 0-570-08729-5, 56-1473). Concordia.

--Sharing. (God I Need to Talk to You About...Ser.). (Illus.). 1984. pap. 0.75 (ISBN 0-570-08728-7, 56-1472). Concordia.

--Stealing. (God I Need to Talk to You About...Ser.). (Illus.). 1984. pap. 0.75 (ISBN 0-570-08731-7, 56-1475). Concordia.

--Vandalism. (God I Need to Talk to You About...Ser.). (Illus.). 1984. pap. 0.75 (ISBN 0-570-08726-0, 56-1470). Concordia.

Carr, David. Foreign Investment & Development in Egypt. LC 79-1230. 159p. 1979. 38.95 (ISBN 0-03-048351-4). Praeger.

--The Gardener's Handbook, 2 bks. Incl. Vol. 1. Broad-Leaved Trees. (Illus.). 144p. 24.00 (ISBN 0-7134-1306-9); pap. 12.50; Vol. 2. Conifers. (Illus.). 144p. 24.00 (ISBN 0-7134-1307-7). (Illus.). 1980 (Pub. by Batsford England). David & Charles.

--Phenomenology & the Problem of History: A Study of Husserl's Transcendental Philosophy. LC 73-94429. (Studies in Phenomenology & Existential Philosophy). 1974. text ed. 22.95 (ISBN 0-8101-0449-0); pap. 9.95 (ISBN 0-8101-0609-4). Northwestern U Pr.

Carr, David, tr. see Husserl, Edmund.

Carr, Donald E. Death of the Sweet Waters. (Illus.). 1966. 6.95 (ISBN 0-393-06354-2). Norton.

--The Sky Is Still Falling. 1982. 14.95 (ISBN 0-393-01508-4). Norton.

Carr, Dorothy, jt. auth. see Dickens, Arthur G.

Carr, E. H. Britain. 1939. 10.00 (ISBN 0-8482-3556-8). Norwood Edns.

--The Comintern & the Spanish Civil War. Deutscher, Tamara, ed. Date not set. 14.45 (ISBN 0-394-53550-2); pap. 7.95 (ISBN 0-394-72263-9). Pantheon.

--Foundations of a Planned Economy Nineteen Twenty-Six to Nineteen Twenty-Nine. (A History of Soviet Russia Ser.: No. 14). 1097p. 1978. text ed. 42.50x (ISBN 0-333-19493-4, Pub. by Macmillan England). Humanities.

--From Napoleon to Stalin & Other Essays. 1980. 26.00 (ISBN 0-312-30774-8). St Martin.

--The Russian Revolution. LC 79-2295. (Illus.). 1979. 16.95 (ISBN 0-02-905140-1). Free Pr.

--The Twenty Years' Crisis Nineteen Nineteen to Nineteen Thirty-Nine. 244p. 1981. Repr. of 1939 ed. text ed. 19.45x (ISBN 0-333-06913-7, Pub. by Macmillan England). Humanities.

Carr, Edward G. How to Teach Sign Language to Developmentally Disabled Children. 54p. 1981. 6.00 (ISBN 0-89079-063-9). Pro Ed.

Carr, Edward H. The Bolshevik Revolution Nineteen Seventeen to Nineteen Twenty-Three, 3 vols. 1985. Vol. 1. pap. 11.95 (ISBN 0-393-30195-8); Vol. 2. pap. 11.95 (ISBN 0-393-30197-4); Vol. 3. pap. 12.95 (ISBN 0-393-30199-0). Norton.

--Dostoevsky (1821-1881) A New Biography. LC 77-25843. 1977. Repr. of 1931 ed. lib. bdg. 40.00 (ISBN 0-8414-1104-2). Folcroft.

--German-Soviet Relations Between the Two World Wars, 1919-1939. LC 83-12572. ix, 146p. 1983. Repr. of 1951 ed. lib. bdg. 27.50x (ISBN 0-313-24117-1, CAGS). Greenwood.

--A History of Soviet Russia, 7 vols. Incl. Vol. 1-3. The Bolshevik Revolution. 1951-53. 12.95 ea. Vol. 1 o.p (52169). Vol. 2 (52175). Vol. 3 o.p (52181); Vol. 4. The Interregnum. 1954. 12.95 (ISBN 0-685-22917-3, 52187); Vols. 5-6. Socialism in One Country. 1958-60. 12.95 ea. Vol. 5 (52193). Vol. 6 (52199); Vol. 7. Socialism in One Country. 1964. 14.95 (ISBN 0-685-22919-X). Pt. 2 (52202). Set. 29.95 (ISBN 0-686-66600-3, 52200). Macmillan.

--International Relations Between the Two World Wars: 1919-1939. (Illus.). 1969. 22.50 (ISBN 0-312-42315-2). St Martin.

--The Romantic Exiles. 391p. 1975. Repr. of 1933 ed. lib. bdg. 27.50x (ISBN 0-374-91297-1). Octagon.

--The Romantic Exiles: A Nineteenth-Century Portrait Gallery. 392p. 1981. pap. 9.95 (ISBN 0-262-53040-6). MIT Pr.

--Twenty Years' Crisis, Nineteen Nineteen to Nineteen Thirty Nine: An Introduction to the Study of International Relations. pap. 5.95xi (ISBN 0-06-131122-7, TB1122, Torch). Har-Row.

--Twilight of the Comintern, 1930-1935. 436p. 1983. 22.00 (ISBN 0-394-52512-4). Pantheon.

--What Is History. 1967. pap. 4.95 (ISBN 0-394-70391-X, V391, Vin). Random.

Carr, Edwin H. The Happy Phrase. 1915. 20.00 (ISBN 0-8274-2468-X). R West.

Carr, Edwin H., compiled by. Putnam's Minute-a-Day English for Busy People. 316p. 1983. Repr. of 1921 ed. text ed. 40.00 (ISBN 0-89984-148-1). Century Bookbindery.

--Putnam's Phrase Book: An Aid to Social Letter Writing & to Ready & Effective Conversation. 327p. 1983. Repr. of 1919 ed. text ed. 40.00 (ISBN 0-89984-147-3). Century Bookbindery.

Carr, Elizabeth B. Da Kine Talk: From Pidgin to Standard English in Hawaii. LC 70-151455. 208p. 1972. 10.00x (ISBN 0-8248-0209-8). UH Pr.

Carr, Ellen F., jt. auth. see Jeffers, Susan J.

Carr, Francis. Ivan the Terrible. (Illus.). 200p. 1981. 27.50x (ISBN 0-389-20150-2, 06921). B&N Imports.

--Mozart & Constanze. 192p. 1984. 12.95 (ISBN 0-531-09820-6). Watts.

--Mozart & Constanze. 192p. 1985. pap. 3.95 (ISBN 0-380-69884-6, Discus). Avon.

Carr, G. Lloyd & Wiseman, D. J. The Song of Solomon. LC 83-22651. (Tyndale Old Testament Commentaries Ser.). 240p. 1984. 10.95 (ISBN 0-87784-918-8); pap. 6.95 (ISBN 0-87784-268-X). Inter-Varsity.

Carr, G. P. & Montemerlo, M., eds. Aerospace Crew Station Design: Proceedings of a Course Presented by the School of Biomechanics of the Center for Transportation Studies, Amalfi, Italy, 19-22 Oct. 1983. 1984. 57.75 (ISBN 0-444-87569-7, North-Holland). Elsevier.

Carr, Gary L. The Left Side of Paradise: The Screenwriting of John Howard Lawson. Kirkpatrick, Diane M., ed. LC 84-2551. (Studies in Cinema: No. 26). 138p. 1984. 34.95 (ISBN 0-8357-1570-1). UMI Res Pr.

Carr, Gerald F., jt. ed. see Rauch, Irmengard.

Carr, Gerald L. Frederic Edwin Church: The Icebergs. (Illus.). 117p. 1981. pap. 12.95 (ISBN 0-292-72439-X). U of Tex Pr.

Carr, Gerry. Tackle Hockey. (Tackle Ser). (Illus.). pap. text ed. 8.95x (ISBN 0-09-127551-2, SpS). Sportshelf.

Carr, Glynn. Death Finds a Foothold. Barzun, J. & Taylor, W. H., eds. LC 81-47395. (Crime Fiction 1950-1975 Ser.). 224p. 1982. lib. bdg. 18.00 (ISBN 0-8240-4961-6). Garland Pub.

Carr, H. Old Mother Mexico. 1976. lib. bdg. 59.95 (ISBN 0-8490-2369-6). Gordon Pr.

Carr, H. Wildon. Time & History in Contemporary Philosophy with Special Reference to Bergson & Croce. 1974. lib. bdg. 59.95 (ISBN 0-8490-2750-0). Gordon Pr.

Carr, H. Wildon, tr. see Bergson, Henri.

Carr, Harriet. Mystery of the Aztec Idol. (gr. 4-6). 1967. pap. 0.79 (ISBN 0-02-042270-9). Macmillan.

Carr, Harvey see Judd, Charles H.

Carr, Herbert W. The General Principle of Relativity in Its Philosophical & Historical Aspect. LC 75-3099. Repr. of 1922 ed. 11.50 (ISBN 0-404-59096-9). AMS Pr.

--Henri Bergson. LC 70-103174. 1970. Repr. of 1912 ed. 14.50x (ISBN 0-8046-0811-3, Pub. by Kennikat). Assoc Faculty Pr.

--A Theory of Monads. LC 75-3101. Repr. of 1922 ed. 24.00 (ISBN 0-404-59098-5). AMS Pr.

--The Unique Status of Man. 1977. Repr. of 1928 ed. lib. bdg. 20.00 (ISBN 0-8492-0496-8). R West.

Carr, Herman Y. & Weidner, Richard T. Physics from the Ground Up, Pt. 1, 2, 3. LC 78-22000. 296p. 1979. Repr. Pt. 1. text ed. 10.50 (ISBN 0-88275-791-1); Pt. 2. text ed. 10.50 (ISBN 0-89874-021-5); Pt. 3. text ed. 10.50 (ISBN 0-89874-213-7). Krieger.

Carr, Hobart C. Early History of Iowa Railroads. Bruchey, Stuart, ed. LC 80-1277. (Railroads Ser.). 1981. lib. bdg. 15.00x (ISBN 0-405-13752-4). Ayer Co Pubs.

Carr, Howard & Simon, Marllin. Physics: A Laboratory Textbook. 2nd ed. (Illus.). 1981. pap. text ed. 15.95x lab manual (ISBN 0-89892-039-6). Contemp Pub Co of Raleigh.

Carr, Hugh. Encounter in the Wilderness. (Irish Play Ser.). pap. 2.95x (ISBN 0-912262-65-6). Proscenium.

Carr, Ian. Miles Davis: A Biography. (Illus.). 336p. 1984. pap. 6.95 (ISBN 0-688-02198-0, Quill). Morrow.

--Miles Davis: A Critical Biography. LC 82-6469. (Illus.). 324p. 1982. 14.95 (ISBN 0-688-01321-X). Morrow.

Carr, Ian & Daems, W. T., eds. The Reticuloendothalial System--A Comprehensive Treatise, Vol. 1: Morphology. (Illus.). 818p. 1980. 69.50x (ISBN 0-306-40291-2, Plenum Pr). Plenum Pub.

Carr, Ian, et al. Lymphoreticular Disease: An Introduction for the Pathologist & Oncologist. 1978. soft cover 21.95 (ISBN 0-397-60436-X, Pub. by Blackwell Scientific). Mosby.

Carr, Isobel, jt. auth. see Gorton, Keith.

Carr, J. Applications of Centre Manifold Theory. (Applied Mathematical Sciences Ser.: Vol. 35). 160p. 1981. pap. 17.50 (ISBN 0-387-90577-4). Springer-Verlag.

Carr, J. Comyns. Some Eminent Victorians: Personal Recollections in the World of Art & Letters. 1908. Repr. 25.00 (ISBN 0-8274-3453-7). R West.

Carr, J. D., et al. Classic Short Stories of Crime & Detection. Barzun, J. & Taylor, W. H., trs. LC 81-47406. (Crime Fiction 1950-1975 Ser.). 290p. 1982. lib. bdg. 18.00 (ISBN 0-8240-4975-6). Garland Pub.

Carr, J. E. & Dengerink, H. A., eds. Behavioral Science in the Practice of Medicine. 560p. 1983. 32.00 (ISBN 0-444-00784-9, Biomedical Pr). Elsevier.

Carr, J. G. Information Technology & the Accountant: An Accountancy Sector Study Jointly Sponsored by the Chartered Association of Certified Accountants & the Department of Industry. 318p. 1985. pap. text ed. 89.95x set (ISBN 0-566-02568-X). Gower Pub Co.

Carr, J. G., jt. auth. see Skinner, F. A.

Carr, J. G., jt. ed. see Skinner, F. A.

Carr, J. L. Carr's Illustrated Dictionary of Extra-Ordinary Cricketers. (Illus.). 96p. (Orig.). 1983. pap. 4.95 (ISBN 0-7043-3432-1, Pub. by Quartet Bks). Merrimack Pub Cir.

--A Month in the Country. LC 83-7494. 128p. 1983. 9.95 (ISBN 0-312-54680-7). St Martin.

--A Month in the Country. 110p. 1984. 5.95 (ISBN 0-89733-124-9). Academy Chi Pubs.

Carr, Jack. Advanced Table Tennis. 1979. pap. 2.95 (ISBN 0-346-12384-4). Cornerstone.

Carr, Jacquelyn B. Communicating & Relating. 2nd ed. 392p. 1984. pap. text ed. write for info (ISBN 0-697-00130-X); instr's. manual avail. (ISBN 0-697-00178-4); journal avail. (ISBN 0-697-00142-3). Wm C Brown.

--Communicating with Myself: A Journal. 208p. 1984. pap. text ed. write for info (ISBN 0-697-00142-3). Wm C Brown.

Carr, James G. Criminal Procedure Handbook, 1985. 1985. pap. 37.50 (ISBN 0-87632-440-5). Boardman.

--The Law of Electronic Surveillance. LC 76-56748. 1977. 65.00 (ISBN 0-87632-108-2). Boardman.

Carr, James G., jt. auth. see McCarthy, Francis B.

Carr, James G., ed. Criminal Law Review 1985. (Criminal Law Ser.). 1984. 57.50 (ISBN 0-317-18867-4). Boardman.

Carr, James H. Crisis & Constraints in Municipal Finance: Local Fiscal Prospects in a Period of Uncertainty. 256p. 1983. pap. text ed. 14.95x (ISBN 0-88285-092-X). Ctr Urban Pol Res.

Carr, James H. & Duensing, Edward. Land Use Issues of the 1980s. LC 83-1888. 325p. 1983. 12.95 (ISBN 0-88285-085-7). Ctr Urban Pol Res.

Carr, James H., ed. Crisis & Constraint in Municipal Finance. 424p. 1984. pap. 12.95 (ISBN 0-88285-092-X). Transaction Bks.

Carr, James H. & Duensing, Edward E., eds. Land Use Issues of the Nineteen Eighty's. 344p. 1983. pap. 12.95 (ISBN 0-88285-085-7). Transaction Bks.

Carr, Jan, jt. auth. see Flettrich, Terry.

Carr, Janet, jt. ed. see Yule, William.

Carr, Janet H. & Shepherd, Roberta B. Early Care of the Stroke Patient: A Positive Approach. 55p. 1979. 8.50 (ISBN 0-89443-812-3). Aspen Systems.

--A Motor Relearning Programme for Stroke. 175p. 1983. 28.00 (ISBN 0-89443-931-6). Aspen Systems.

--Physiotherapy in Disorders of the Brain. 408p. 1980. 31.00 (ISBN 0-89443-656-2). Aspen Systems.

Carr, Jayge. Treasure in the Heart of the Maze. LC 85-6740. (Science Fiction Ser.). 192p. 1985. 12.95 (ISBN 0-385-18831-5). Doubleday.

Carr, Jayge, et al. Pandora, No. 5. Wickstrom, Lois, ed. (Illus.). 60p. (Orig.). 1980. pap. 2.50 (ISBN 0-916176-10-X). Sproing.

--Pandora, an Original Anthology of Role-Expanding Science Fiction & Fantasy. Wickstrom, Lois, ed. (Illus., Orig.). 1979. pap. 2.50 (ISBN 0-916176-08-8); Vol.1,No.3. pap. 1.50 (ISBN 0-916176-07-X). Sproing.

Carr, Jean. Another Story: Women & the Falklands War. 192p. 1984. 13.95 (ISBN 0-241-11391-1, Pub. by Hamish Hamilton England); pap. 6.50 (ISBN 0-241-11354-7, Pub. by Hamish Hamilton England). David & Charles.

--Mowing the Rabbits. (Illus.). 48p. (Orig.). 1976. pap. 5.00 (ISBN 0-942908-03-1). Pancake Pr.

Carr, Jean F., ed. see Emerson, Ralph Waldo.

Carr, Jess. Birth of a Book. LC 74-84706. 151p. 1974. 6.95 (ISBN 0-89227-010-1). Commonwealth Pr.

--A Creature Was Stirring & Other Stories. 128p. 1970. 3.95 (ISBN 0-89227-022-5). Commonwealth Pr.

--Frost of Summer. LC 75-4257. 248p. 1975. 7.95 (ISBN 0-89227-046-2). Commonwealth Pr.

--How a Book Is Born. LC 78-59112. 1978. 10.95 (ISBN 0-89227-041-1). Commonwealth Pr.

--Millie & Cleve. 1979. pap. 2.25 (ISBN 0-8439-0615-4, Leisure Bks). Dorchester Pub Co.

--The Moonshiners. LC 77-71601. 1977. 9.95 (ISBN 0-89227-042-X). Commonwealth Pr.

--Murder on the Appalachian Trail. LC 84-72458. (Illus.). 401p. 1985. 16.95 (ISBN 0-89227-106-X). Commonwealth Pr.

--The Saint of the Wilderness. LC 74-77781. 441p. 1974. 8.95 (ISBN 0-89227-008-X); pap. 4.95 (ISBN 0-89227-026-8). Commonwealth Pr.

--The Second Oldest Profession. LC 70-172277. 252p. 1978. 9.95 (ISBN 0-89227-031-4). Commonwealth Pr.

--Ship Ride Down the Spring Branch. LC 78-60480. 200p. 1978. 8.95 (ISBN 0-89227-048-9). Commonwealth Pr.

--A Star Rising. (Orig.). 1980. pap. 3.50 (ISBN 0-505-51575-X, Pub. by Tower Bks). Dorchester Pub Co.

Carr, Jo. Beyond Fact: Nonfiction for Children & Young People. LC 82-1601. 236p. 1982. pap. 12.50x (ISBN 0-8389-0348-7). ALA.

--Beyond Fact: Nonfiction for Children & Young People. LC 82-1601. pap. 59.30 (ISBN 0-317-27979-3, 2025609). Bks Demand UMI.

--Living on Tiptoe. (Orig.). 1972. pap. 2.95x (ISBN 0-8358-0269-8). Upper Room.

--Touch the Wind. LC 74-33831. (gr. 3-6). 1975. 2.50x (ISBN 0-8358-0321-X). Upper Room.

--Trouble with Tikki. LC 71-115459. (Illus.). (gr. k-2). 1970. 6.19 (ISBN 0-8313-0013-2). Lantern.

Carr, Jo & Cash, Donna. Advent: A Calendar of Devotions, 1984. 48p. (Orig.). 1984. pap. 30.00 per 100 (ISBN 0-687-00883-2). Abingdon.

Carr, Jo & Sorley, Imogene. Bless This Mess & Other Prayers. (Festival Books). 1976. pap. 3.25 (ISBN 0-687-03618-6). Abingdon.

--Plum Jelly & Stained Glass & Other Prayers. 1981. pap. 2.50 (ISBN 0-687-31660-X, Festival). Abingdon.

--Too Busy Not to Pray. (Festival Books). 1978. pap. 3.25 (ISBN 0-687-42380-5). Abingdon.

Carr, Jo, jt. auth. see Norwood, Frederick A.

Carr, John. Poems. 1809. Reiman, Donald H., ed. LC 75-31177. (Romantic Context Ser.: Poetry 1789-1830). 1977. lib. bdg. 57.00 (ISBN 0-8240-2129-0). Garland Pub.

Carr, John, jt. ed. see Cornell, James.

Carr, John C. The Craft of Crime: Conversations with Crime Writers. LC 83-133. 349p. 1983. 15.95 (ISBN 0-395-33120-X); pap. 8.95 (ISBN 0-395-33121-8). HM.

Carr, John C., jt. auth. see Grambs, Jean D.

Carr, John C., et al, eds. The Organization & Administration of Pastoral Counseling Centers. LC 80-22416. 304p. 1981. 17.50 (ISBN 0-687-29430-4). Abingdon.

Carr, John D. The Arabian Nights Murder. Dorszynski, Alexia, ed. 320p. 1985. pap. 3.50 (ISBN 0-02-018600-2, Collier). Macmillan.

--Captain Cut-Throat. 232p. 1980. pap. 1.95 (ISBN 0-441-09134-2, Pub. by Charter Bks). Ace Bks.

--The Case of the Blind Barber. 256p. 1984. pap. 3.50 (ISBN 0-02-018300-3, Collier). Macmillan.

--Case of the Constant Suicides. 1962. pap. 3.95 (ISBN 0-02-018470-0, Collier). Macmillan.

--The Case of the Constant Suicides. Dorszynski, Alexia, ed. 192p. 1985. pap. 3.50 (ISBN 0-02-018860-9, Collier). Macmillan.

--The Corpse in the Waxworks. 192p. 1984. pap. 3.50 (Collier). Macmillan.

--The Crooked Hinge. 256p. 1984. pap. 3.50 (ISBN 0-02-018840-4, Collier). Macmillan.

--Death Turns the Tables. 200p. 1985. pap. 4.95 (ISBN 0-930330-22-6). Intl Polygonics.

--The Four False Weapons. 256p. 1984. pap. 3.50 (ISBN 0-02-018650-9, Collier). Macmillan.

--The Life of Sir Arthur Conan Doyle. 20.95 (ISBN 0-317-28498-3, Pub. by Am Repr). Amereon Ltd.

--Lost Gallows. 344p. 1986. pap. 3.50 (ISBN 0-88184-202-8). Carroll & Graf.

--The Mad Hatter Mystery. 288p. 1984. pap. 3.95 (ISBN 0-02-018820-X, Collier). Macmillan.

--The Murder of Sir Edmund Godfrey. LC 74-10426. (Classics of Crime & Criminology Ser). (Illus.). 352p. 1975. Repr. of 1936 ed. 26.25 (ISBN 0-88355-193-4). Hyperion Conn.

--Poison in Jest. 1965. pap. 1.95 (ISBN 0-02-018800-5, Collier). Macmillan.

--Poison in Jest. 224p. 1985. pap. 3.50 (ISBN 0-02-018400-X, Collier). MacMillan.

--The Problem of the Wire Cage. 224p. 1982. 20.00x (ISBN 0-7278-0249-6, Pub. by Severn Hse). State Mutual Bk.

--The Sleeping Sphinx. 199p. 1985. 4.95 (ISBN 0-930330-24-2). Intl Polygonics.

--The Three Coffins. 1979. lib. bdg. 11.95 (ISBN 0-8398-2533-1, Gregg). G K Hall.

--Till Death Do Us Part. 200p. 1985. pap. 4.95 (ISBN 0-930330-21-8). Intl Polygonics.

--To Wake the Dead. 256p. 1984. pap. 3.50 (ISBN 0-02-018750-5). Macmillan.

Carr, John D., jt. auth. see Doyle, Arthur Conan.

Carr, John F. Carnifex Mardi Gras. (Illus.). 218p. 1982. 12.00 (ISBN 0-937912-00-X). Pequod Press.

Carr, John F., jt. auth. see Green, Roland.

Carr, John F., ed. The Worlds of H. Beam Piper. 1983. pap. 2.75 (ISBN 0-441-91052-1). Ace Bks.

Carr, John F., jt. ed. see Pournelle, Jerry.

Carr, John F., ed. see Pournelle, Jerry.

Carr, John W. Factors Affecting Distribution of Trained Teachers Among Rural White Elementary Schools of North Caroline. LC 74-176628. (Columbia University. Teachers College. Contributions to Education Ser.: No. 269). Repr. of 1927 ed. 22.50 (ISBN 0-404-55269-2). AMS Pr.

Carr, Johnny. The Cardman. 271p. 1983. 9.95 (ISBN 0-949894-01-X); pap. 4.95 (ISBN 0-949894-01-X). Lionheart.

Carr, Jonathan. Helmut Schmidt: Helmsman of Germany. LC 84-24190. 224p. 1985. 29.95 (ISBN 0-312-36744-9). St Martin.

Carr, Joseph. Digital Interfacing with an Analog World. (Illus.). 1978. pap. 14.95 (ISBN 0-8306-1070-7, 1070). TAB Bks.

--Elements of Electronic Instrumentation & Measurement. (Illus.). 1979. text ed. 26.95 (ISBN 0-8359-1650-2). Reston.

--The Twisted Cross. LC 84-62776. 310p. (Orig.). 1985. pap. 7.95 (ISBN 0-910311-22-6). Huntington Hse Inc.

--Z80 User's Manual. (Illus.). 352p. 1980. text ed. 21.95 O.P. (ISBN 0-8359-9517-8); pap. text ed. 16.95 (ISBN 0-8359-9516-X). Reston.

Carr, Joseph J. Antenna Data Reference Manual-Including Dimension Tables. (Illus.). 1979. 15.95 (ISBN 0-8306-9738-1); pap. 7.95o.p (ISBN 0-8306-1152-5, 1152). TAB Bks.

--Christian Heroes of the Holocaust. LC 85-70538. 1985. pap. 3.50 (ISBN 0-88270-582-2). Bridge Pub.

--CMOS-TTL-A: User's Guide with Projects. (Illus.). 336p. 1984. 19.95 (ISBN 0-8306-0650-5); pap. 13.50 (ISBN 0-8306-1650-0, 1650). TAB Bks.

--The Complete Handbook of Amplifiers, Oscillators & Multivibrators. (Illus.). 364p. 1981. pap. 11.50 (ISBN 0-8306-1230-0, 1230). TAB Bks.

--Designing & Building Electronic Gadgets, with Projects. (Illus.). 406p. (Orig.). 1984. 19.95 (ISBN 0-8306-0690-4); pap. 12.95 (ISBN 0-8306-1690-X, 1690). TAB Bks.

--Designing Microprocessor-Based Instrumentation. 29.95 (ISBN 0-8359-1270-1). Reston.

--Eight-Bit & Sixteen-Bit Microprocessor Cookbook. (Illus.). 308p. 1983. 19.95 (ISBN 0-8306-0643-2, 1643); pap. 13.50 (ISBN 0-8306-1643-8, 1643). TAB Bks.

--How to Troubleshoot & Repair Amateur Radio Equipment. (Illus.). 448p. (Orig.). 1980. pap. 9.95 (ISBN 0-8306-1194-0, 1194). TAB Bks.

--Interfacing Your Microcomputer to Virtually Anything. LC 84-8709. (Illus.). 336p. (Orig.). 1984. 21.95 (ISBN 0-8306-0890-7); pap. 13.95 (ISBN 0-8306-1890-2, 1890). TAB Bks.

--Linear-IC-OP Amp Handbook. 2nd ed. (Illus.). 350p. (Orig.). 1983. 21.95 (ISBN 0-8306-0150-3, 1550); pap. 13.95 (ISBN 0-8306-1550-4). TAB Bks.

--Microcomputer Interfacing Handbook: A-D & D-A. (Illus.). 287p. o.p 18.95 (ISBN 0-8306-9704-7, 1271); pap. 10.95 (ISBN 0-8306-1271-8). TAB Bks.

--Microprocessor Interfacing. (Illus.). 252p. 1982. 14.95 (ISBN 0-8306-0064-7); pap. 7.95 o.p (ISBN 0-8306-1396-X, 1396). TAB Bks.

--Sixty-Eight Scientific & Engineering Programs for the Apple II & IIe. 1984. 19.95 (ISBN 0-8359-6920-7). Reston.

--The TAB Handbook of Radio Communications. (Illus.). 1056p. (Orig.). 1984. 45.00 (ISBN 0-8306-0636-X, 1636); pap. 29.50 (ISBN 0-8306-1636-5). TAB Bks.

Carr, Joseph J. & Brown, John M. Introduction to Biomedical Equipment Technology. LC 80-6218. (Electronic Technology Ser.). 430p. 1981. 32.95x (ISBN 0-471-04143-2); tchr's manual avail. (ISBN 0-471-04144-0). Wiley.

Carr, Joseph L. Sixty-Eight Scientific & Engineering Programs for the IBM PC & PC XT. 1984. 19.95 (ISBN 0-8359-6921-5). Reston.

Carr, Josephine. No Regrets. LC 82-70194. 192p. (gr. 7 up). 1982. 10.95 (ISBN 0-8037-6721-8). Dial Bks Young.

Carr, K., jt. ed. see Hodges, G.

Carr, K. E. & Toner, P. G. Cell Structure: An Introduction to Biomedical Electron Microscopy. LC 81-67939. (Illus.). 388p. 1983. text ed. 48.00 (ISBN 0-443-02324-7). Churchill.

Carr, Laura & Palmer, Ursula. An Intermediate Sign Language Workbook of Text Analysis. 1984. pap. 11.95 (ISBN 0-932666-21-3). T J Pubs.

Carr, Lillian. Lions at Large. LC 83-90275. 141p. 1984. 10.95 (ISBN 0-533-05773-6). Vantage.

Carr, Lucien. Missouri, a Bone of Contention. LC 72-3761. (American Commonwealth: No. 11). Repr. of 1888 ed. 34.00 (ISBN 0-404-57211-1). AMS Pr.

Carr, Lucile, compiled by. A Catalogue of the Vanderpoel Dickens Collection at the University of Texas. LC 68-65506. (Tower Bibliographical Ser: No. 1). 1968. 16.50 (ISBN 0-87959-077-7). U of Tex H Ransom Ctr.

Carr, Marilyn. Blacksmith, Baker, Roofingsheet Maker: Employment for Rural Women in Developing Countries. (Illus.). 144p. (Orig.). 1984. pap. 11.50x (ISBN 0-946688-15-X, Pub. by Intermediate Tech England). Intermediate Tech.

--Developing Small Scale Industries in India: An Integrated Approach. (Illus.). 87p. (Orig.). 1981. pap. 10.75x (ISBN 0-903031-81-7, Pub. by Intermediate Tech England). Intermediate Tech.

Carr, Marilyn, ed. The AT Reader: Theory & Practice of Appropriate Technology. (Illus.). 468p. (Orig.). 1985. pap. 19.50x (ISBN 0-942850-03-3, Pub. by Intermediate Tech England). Intermediate Tech.

Carr, Marilyn, compiled by. Economically Appropriate Technologies for Developing Countries: An Annotated Bibliography. rev. ed. 123p. (Orig.). 1981. pap. 11.50x (ISBN 0-903031-75-2, Pub. by Intermediate Tech England). Intermediate Tech.

Carr, Mary J. Children of the Covered Wagon. rev. ed. LC 56-13460. (Illus.). (gr. 3-7). 1957. Crowell Jr Bks.

Carr, Maurice, tr. see Kreitman, Esther S.

Carr, Micheline, jt. auth. see Crouch, James.

Carr, Mike. Robbers & Robots. LC 83-50049. (Top Secret Endless Quest Bk.). 160p. (gr. 5up). 1983. pap. 2.00 (ISBN 0-394-72100-4). Random.

Carr, N. G. & Whitton, B. A. Biology of Cyanobacteria. LC 82-1906. (Botanical Monographs: Vol. 19). (Illus.). 700p. 1982. 78.50x (ISBN 0-520-04717-6). U of Cal Pr.

Carr, N. G., jt. ed. see Kelly, D. P.

Carr, N. L. Viscosities of Natural Gas Components & Mixtures. (Research Bulletin Ser.: No. 23). iv, 59p. 1953. 5.00 (ISBN 0-317-34319-X). Inst Gas Tech.

Carr, Nick. America's Secret Service Ace: The Operator 5 Story. 64p. 1985. Repr. lib. bdg. 19.95x (ISBN 0-89370-564-0). Borgo Pr.

--America's Secret Service Ace: The Operator 5 Story. (Pulp & Dime Novel Studies: No. 2). (Illus.). 63p. (Orig.). 1985. 19.95x (ISBN 0-930261-70-4); pap. 9.95x (ISBN 0-930261-73-9). Starmont Hse.

--The Flying Spy: A History of G-8. 160p. 1985. Repr. lib. bdg. 19.95x (ISBN 0-89370-562-4). Borgo Pr.

--The Flying Spy: A History of G-8. (Pulp & Dime Novel Studies: No. 3). (Illus.). 160p. (Orig.). 1985. 19.95x (ISBN 0-930261-72-0); pap. 9.95x (ISBN 0-930261-75-5). Starmont Hse.

Carr, Nicole. Make Your Dreams Come True, No. 3: Worthy Opponents. 192p. (Orig.). 1984. pap. 2.25 (ISBN 0-446-32037-4). Warner Bks.

--Make Your Dreams Come True, No. 6: Holiday of Love. 192p. (Orig.). 1984. pap. 2.25 (ISBN 0-446-30728-9). Warner Bks.

Carr, Norma & Ruffino. The Promotable Woman. (Wadsworth Series inContinuing Education). 450p. 1982. pap. write for info. (ISBN 0-534-01059-8). Wadsworth Pub.

Carr, P. J., et al. Community Psychiatric Nursing. (Illus.). 1980. pap. text ed. 15.75 (ISBN 0-443-01550-3). Churchill.

Carr, Pat. Mimbres Mythology. (Southwest Studies Ser.: No. 56). 1984. Repr. of 1979 ed. 3.00 (ISBN 0-87404-114-7). Tex Western.

--The Women in the Mirror. LC 77-24965. (Iowa School of Letters Short Fiction Ser.: No. 8). 152p. 1977. 11.95 (ISBN 0-87745-081-1); pap. 6.95 (ISBN 0-87745-082-X). U of Iowa Pr.

Carr, Pat & Tracey, Steve. Enchantments. (Mindstrechers Level Two). (gr. 4-6). pap. 4.95 (ISBN 0-8224-4508-5). Pitman Learning.

--Great Explorations. (Mindstrechers Level Two). (gr. 4-6). pap. 4.95 (ISBN 0-8224-4507-7). Pitman Learning.

--Mindstretchers: Level 2, 4 vols. Incl. Star Gazing. pap. 4.95 (ISBN 0-8224-4505-0); Who Done It? pap. 4.95 (ISBN 0-8224-4506-9); Great Explorations. pap. 4.95 (ISBN 0-8224-4507-7); Enchantments. pap. 4.95 (ISBN 0-8224-4508-5). (gr. 4-6). 1983. Set. pap. 19.80 (ISBN 0-8224-4510-7). Pitman Learning.

--Star Gazing. (Mindstrechers Level Two). (gr. 4-6). 4.95 (ISBN 0-8224-4505-0). Pitman Learning.

--Who Done It? (Mindstrechers: Level Two). (gr. 4-6). pap. 4.95 (ISBN 0-8224-4506-9). Pitman Learning.

Carr, Pat & Tracy, Steve. Monterey Peninsula Walking Tours. (Illus.). 48p. (Orig.). 1984. pap. 4.95 (ISBN 0-917837-00-2). Hampton-Brown.

Carr, Patricia A., jt. auth. see Dignan, Mark B.

Carr, Patrick. Word Trip Games for the (l), (r), & (s) Sounds. 1974. text ed. 11.75x (ISBN 0-8134-1603-5). Interstate.

Carr, Patrick & Gardner, George. Gun People. LC 84-26014. (Illus.). 144p. 1985. pap. 16.95 (ISBN 0-385-19193-6, Dolp). Doubleday.

Carr, Peter & Bowers, Larry D. Immobilized Enzymes in Analytical & Clinical Chemistry: Fundamentals & Applications. LC 80-13694. (Chemical Analysis: A Series of Monographs on Analytical Chemistry & Its Applications). 460p. 1980. 75.95 (ISBN 0-471-04919-0, Pub. by Wiley-Interscience). Wiley.

Carr, Philip. English Are Like That. facs. ed. LC 70-142613. (Essay Index Reprint Ser.). 1941. 20.00 (ISBN 0-8369-2041-4). Ayer Co Pubs.

Carr, Philippa. The Adulteress. (General Ser.). 1983. PLB 19.95 (ISBN 0-8161-3513-4, Large Print Bks). G K Hall.

--The Adulteress. 1983. pap. 3.50 (ISBN 0-449-20143-0, Crest). Fawcett.

--Knave of Hearts. 288p. 1983. 13.95 (ISBN 0-399-12810-7, Putnam). Putnam Pub Group.

--Knave of Hearts. (General Ser.). 490p. 1983. lib. bdg. 16.95 (ISBN 0-8161-3589-4, Large Print Bks). G K Hall.

--Lament for a Lost Lover. 1985. pap. 3.95 (ISBN 0-449-20771-4, Crest). Fawcett.

--The Lion Triumphant. 384p. 1985. pap. 3.50 (ISBN 0-449-20857-5, Crest). Fawcett.

--Love Child. 352p. 1985. pap. 3.50 (ISBN 0-449-20865-6, Crest). Fawcett.

--The Return of the Gypsy. LC 84-24768. 1985. 16.95 (ISBN 0-399-13064-0, Putnam). Putnam Pub Group.

--Saraband for Two Sisters. 1985. pap. 3.50 (ISBN 0-449-20768-4, Crest). Fawcett.

--The Song of the Siren. 352p. 1985. pap. 3.50 (ISBN 0-449-20772-2, Crest). Fawcett.

Carr, Philippa, pseud. Voices in a Haunted Room. 1984. lib. bdg. 16.95 (ISBN 0-8161-3780-3, Large Print Bks). G K Hall.

Carr, Philippa. Voices in a Haunted Room. 1985. pap. 3.95 (ISBN 0-449-20629-7, Crest). Fawcett.

--Will You Love Me in September. 320p. 1985. pap. 3.50 (ISBN 0-449-20774-9, Crest). Fawcett.

--The Witch from the Sea. 320p. 1985. pap. 3.50 (ISBN 0-449-20767-6). Fawcett.

Carr, R. Anarchism in France: The Case of Octove Mirbeau. (French Language & Literature Ser.). 224p. 1977. cancelled (ISBN 0-7190-0668-6, Pub. by Manchester Univ Pr). Longwood Pub Group.

Carr, R., et al. Portable Programs: Games & Utilities for the TRS-80 Model 100. 1984. write for info. NAL.

Carr, R. K. The House Committee on un-American Activities, Nineteen Forty-Five to Nineteen Fifty. 1979. Repr. of 1952 ed. lib. bdg. 37.50x (ISBN 0-374-91295-5). Octagon.

Carr, Rachel. Arthritis: Relief Beyond Drugs. (Illus.). 160p. 1983. pap. 6.68i (ISBN 0-06-464054-X, BN 4054). B&N NY.

--Be a Frog, a Bird, or a Tree. LC 72-92198. (Illus.). 1977. pap. 6.68i (ISBN 0-06-090570-0, CN 570, CN). Har-Row.

--Wheel, Camel, Fish & Plow: Yoga for You. (Illus.). (gr. 5 up). 1981. 9.95 (ISBN 0-13-956045-9). P-H.

--Yoga for All Ages. (Illus.). 160p. 1975. pap. 4.95 (ISBN 0-671-22151-5, Fireside). S&S.

Carr, Rachel, jt. auth. see Saibull, Solomon.

Carr, Raymond. Modern Spain, 1875-1980. 1981. 22.00x (ISBN 0-19-215828-7); Oxford Paperback University Ser. pap. 12.50x (ISBN 0-19-289090-5). Oxford U Pr.

--Puerto Rico: A Colonial Experiment. (Twentieth Century Fund Studies). 477p. 1984. 25.00x (ISBN 0-8147-1389-0). NYU Pr.

--Puerto Rico: A Colonial Experiment. (Twentieth Century Fund Study). 477p. 1984. pap. 9.95 (ISBN 0-394-72431-3, Vin). Random.

--Spain: 1808-1975. 2nd ed. (Oxford History of Modern Europe Ser.). 1982. pap. 14.95x (ISBN 0-19-822128-2). Oxford U Pr.

Carr, Raymond & Fusi, Juan P. Spain: Dictatorship to Democracy. 2nd ed. 304p. 1981. pap. text ed. 10.95x (ISBN 0-04-946014-5). Allen Unwin.

Carr, Richard & O'Con, Robert. Welding Practices & Procedures. (Illus.). 416p. 1983. text ed. 23.95 (ISBN 0-13-948059-5). P-H.

Carr, Richard, jt. auth. see O'Con, Robert.

Carr, Richard, jt. auth. see Sutton, Ann.

Carr, Richard, tr. see Guillen, Nicholas.

Carr, Richard A. Pierre Boaistuau's Histoires "Tragiques". A Study of Narrative Form & Tragic Vision. (Studies in the Romance Languages & Literatures: No. 210). 258p. 1979. 14.00x (ISBN 0-8078-9210-6). U of NC Pr.

Carr, Richard W. Virtual Memory Management. Stone, Harold, ed. LC 84-140. (Computer Science: Systems Programming Ser.: No. 20). 186p. 1984. 39.95 (ISBN 0-8357-1533-7). UMI Res Pr.

Carr, Robert, ed. see Kosinski, D. S.

Carr, Robert F. & Hazard, James E. Tikal Report No. 11: Map of the Ruins of Tikal, El Peten, Guatemala. (University Museum Monographs: No. 21). (Illus.). iv, 24p. 1961. pap. 15.00x (ISBN 0-934718-13-X). Univ Mus of U PA.

Carr, Robert H., ed. see Conference of the Cryogenic Society of America, 5th, 1972.

Carr, Robert K. Supreme Court & Judicial Review. LC 74-98215. xiv, 304p. Repr. of 1942 ed. lib. bdg. 29.75 (ISBN 0-8371-3261-4, CAJR). Greenwood.

Carr, Robert W. Government of Michigan: Under the 1964 Constitution. rev. & enl. ed. LC 67-14740. 1967. pap. 3.95x (ISBN 0-472-08196-9). U of Mich Pr.

Carr, Robyn. The Braeswood Tapestry. 1984. 14.45i (ISBN 0-316-12975-5). Little.

--Chelynne. 1985. pap. 3.50 (ISBN 0-671-50176-3). PB.

--The Troubadour's Romance. 288p. 1985. 16.45i (ISBN 0-316-12976-3). Little.

Carr, Roland T. To Sea in Haste. LC 75-13944. 1975. 12.50 (ISBN 0-87491-204-0). Acropolis.

Carr, Ron, et al. Games & Utilities for the TRS-80 Model 100. 1984. 16.95 (ISBN 0-452-25577-5, Plume). NAL.

Carr, Roy & Murray, Charles S. David Bowie: An Illustrated Record. 120p. 1981. pap. 12.95 (ISBN 0-380-77966-8, 60164-8). Avon.

Carr, Roy & Tyler, Tony. The Beatles: An Illustrated Record. rev. 3rd ed. (Illus.). 176p. 1981. pap. 4.98 (ISBN 0-517-54493-8, Harmony). Crown.

--The Beatles: An Illustrated Record. rev. ed. (Illus.). 1978. (Harmony); pap. 9.95 (ISBN 0-517-53367-7). Crown.

--The Beatles: An Illustrated Record. (Illus.). 176p. 1975. 15.00 (ISBN 0-517-52010-9, Harmony); pap. 4.98 (ISBN 0-517-54493-8). Crown.

Carr, S. G., jt. ed. see Carr, D. J.

Carr, Sally B., ed. see Fisher, Terry.

Carr, Sally B., ed. see Superior, Irving.

Carr, Sam, ed. Hymns As Poetry. 1980. 17.95 (ISBN 0-7134-3447-3, Pub. by Batsford England). David & Charles.

Carr, Samuel. The Batsford Book of Romantic Poetry. (Illus.). 128p. 1982. 14.95 (ISBN 0-7134-3903-3, Pub. by Batsford England). David & Charles.

--Birds, Beasts & Fishes: Animal Verse for Children. (Illus.). 96p. (gr. 1-3). 1982. 14.95 (ISBN 0-7134-4151-8, Pub. by Batsford England). David & Charles.

--Poetry of the Railways. 1978. 15.50 (ISBN 0-7134-0222-9, Pub. by Batsford England). David & Charles.

Carr, Samuel, ed. Poetry of Flowers. LC 77-26728. 1977. 7.50 (ISBN 0-8008-6393-3). Taplinger.

--The Poetry of Horses. (Illus.). 128p. 1980. 15.50 (ISBN 0-7134-2594-6, Pub. by Batsford England). David & Charles.

--The Poetry of the Countryside. (Illus.). 96p. 1984. 16.95 (ISBN 0-7134-1848-6, Pub by Batsford England). David & Charles.

Carr, Sandy. The Simon & Schuster Pocket Guide to Cheese. (Illus.). 1981. 5.95 (ISBN 0-671-42475-0). S&S.

Carr, Sherry. Let Passion Soar, No. 116. 192p. 1983. pap. 1.95 (ISBN 0-515-07204-4). Jove Pubns.

Carr, Stephen. City Signs & Lights: Prepared for the Boston Redevelopment Authority & U. S. Dept of Housing & Urban Development. 1973. 17.50x (ISBN 0-262-02087-4). MIT Pr.

Carr, Stephen L. The Historical Guide to Utah Ghost Towns. 166p. 1972. pap. 7.95 (ISBN 0-914740-02-4). Western Epics.

Carr, T. R. & Colston, Stephanie. State & Urban Policy Analysis: An Annotated Bibliography. 1975. 3.50 (ISBN 0-686-18643-5). Univ OK Gov Res.

Carr, T. R., et al. Quantitative Research in Public Administration & Policy Analysis: A Methodologically Annotated Bibliography. 1977. 4.50 (ISBN 0-686-22970-3). Univ OK Gov Res.

Carr, Terry. The Best from Universe. LC 82-45318. (Science Fiction Ser.). 224p. 1984. 11.95 (ISBN 0-385-17512-4). Doubleday.

--Fantasy Annual III. 304p. (Orig.). 1981. pap. 2.95 (ISBN 0-671-41272-8, Timescape). PB.

--Universe Eleven. LC 80-2790. (Science Fiction Ser.). 192p. 1981. 10.95 (ISBN 0-385-17226-5). Doubleday.

--Universe Fourteen. LC 83-20785. (Science Fiction Ser.). 192p. 1984. 11.95 (ISBN 0-385-19134-0). Doubleday.

--Universe Thirteen. 256p. 1985. pap. 2.95 (ISBN 0-8125-3269-4). Tor Bks.

Carr, Terry, ed. The Best Science Fiction of the Year, No. 9. (Orig.). 1980. pap. 2.50 (ISBN 0-345-28601-4). Ballantine.

--The Best Science Fiction of the Year, No. 10. (Orig.). 1981. pap. 3.50 (ISBN 0-671-42262-6, Timescape). PB.

--The Best Science Fiction of the Year, No. 11. (Orig.). 1982. pap. 3.95 (ISBN 0-671-44483-2, Timescape). PB.

--The Best Science Fiction of the Year, No. 12. 179p. 1983. pap. 3.95 (ISBN 0-671-46680-1, Timescape). PB.

--The Best Science Fiction of the Year, No. 13. 384p. 1984. pap. 3.50 (ISBN 0-671-55901-X). PB.

--Best Science Fiction of the Year, No. 14. 384p. 1985. 16.95 (ISBN 0-575-03714-8, Pub. by Gollancz England). David & Charles.

--The Best Science Fiction of the Year, 1984. (Orig.). 1985. pap. 3.50 (ISBN 0-8125-3273-2). Tor Bks.

--Classic Science Fiction: The First Golden Age. LC 74-1798. 1978. 14.95i (ISBN 0-06-010634-4, HarpT). Har-Row.

--Dream's Edge: Science Fiction Stories About the Future of Planet Earth. LC 80-13389. 320p. 1980. 14.95 (ISBN 0-87156-232-4); pap. 5.95 (ISBN 0-87156-238-3). Sierra.

--An Exaltation of Stars: Transcendental Adventures in Science Fiction. Silverberg, Robert, et al. LC 72-89253. 191p. 1973. 15.00 (ISBN 0-671-21469-1). Ultramarine Pub.

--Fantasy Annual, No. IV. 1981. pap. 3.50 (ISBN 0-671-41273-6, Timescape). PB.

--Fantasy Annual V. 1982. pap. 2.95 (ISBN 0-671-45436-6, Timescape). PB.

--Terry Carr's Best Science Fiction of the Year. 1985. 3.50 (ISBN 0-8125-3273-2). Tor Bks.

--Universe, No. 10. 1982. pap. 2.50 (ISBN 0-8217-1114-8). Zebra.

--Universe, No. 11. 1983. pap. 2.50 (ISBN 0-8217-1143-1). Zebra.

--Universe Fifteen. LC 85-4346. (Science Fiction Ser.). 192p. 1985. 12.95 (ISBN 0-385-19890-6). Doubleday.

--Universe Thirteen. LC 82-45351. (Science Fiction Ser.). (Illus.). 192p. 1983. 11.95 (ISBN 0-385-18288-0). Doubleday.

--Universe Twelve. LC 81-43900. (Science Fiction Ser.). 192p. 1982. 10.95 (ISBN 0-385-17923-5). Doubleday.

--Universe Twelve. 1983. pap. 2.95 (ISBN 0-8217-1303-5). Zebra.

Carr, Terry, ed. see Asimov, Isaac.

Carr, Terry, ed. see Gibson, William.

Carr, Terry, ed. see Robinson, Kim S.

Carr, Thomas H., ed. The Development of Reading Skills. LC 84-80838. (Child Development Ser.: No. 27). (Orig.). 1985. pap. text ed. 9.95x (ISBN 0-87589-794-0). Jossey-Bass.

Carr, Timothy W., ed. Plasma Chromatography. 274p. 1984. 37.50x (ISBN 0-306-41432-5, Plenum Pr). Plenum Pub.

Carr, Vikki. Los Exitos de Hoy. (Span.). pap. 3.50 (ISBN 0-686-09061-6, Pub. by Peer-Southern). Columbia Pictures.

Carr, Virginia. Toybox Tales. LC 82-455. (Illus.). 150p. 1982. 21.95 (ISBN 0-87108-623-9). Pruett.

Carr, Virginia M. The Drama As Propaganda: A Study of The Troublesome Reign of King John. (Salzburg Studies in English Literature, Elizabethan & Renaissance Studies: No. 28). 185p. 1974. pap. text ed. 25.50x (ISBN 0-391-01341-6). Humanities.

Carr, Virginia S. Dos Passos: A Life. LC 79-7230. (Illus.). 648p. 1984. 24.95 (ISBN 0-385-12964-5). Doubleday.

--The Lonely Hunter: A Biography of Carson McCullers. 600p. 1985. pap. 12.95 (ISBN 0-88184-123-4). Carroll & Graf.

Carr, Virginia Spencer. The Lonely Hunter: A Biography of Carson McCullers. LC 74-9478. 1976. pap. 5.95 (ISBN 0-385-12289-6, Anch). Doubleday.

Carr, W. J., Jr. AC Loss & Macroscopic Theory of Superconductors. 170p. 1983. 57.50 (ISBN 0-677-05700-8). Gordon.

Carr, Walter H. The World & William Walker. LC 75-18354. (Illus.). 289p. 1975. Repr. of 1963 ed. lib. bdg. 20.75x (ISBN 0-8371-8328-6, CAWWW). Greenwood.

Carr, William. Arms, Autarky, & Aggression. (Foundations of Modern History Ser.). 136p. 1973. 7.00 (ISBN 0-393-05486-1); pap. 1.95 (ISBN 0-393-09361-1). Norton.

--A History of Germany Eighteen Fifteen to Nineteen Forty-Five. 2nd ed. LC 79-20108. (Illus.). 1979. 25.00x (ISBN 0-312-37871-8); pap. 14.95 (ISBN 0-312-37872-6). St Martin.

Carr, William G. Collecting My Thoughts. LC 80-82881. (Foundation Monograph). 101p. 1980. pap. 5.00 (ISBN 0-87367-424-3). Phi Delta Kappa.

--The Conspiracy to Destroy All Governments & Religions. 1982. lib. bdg. 59.95 (ISBN 0-87700-358-0). Revisionist Pr.

--Pawns in the Game. 193p. pap. 4.00 (ISBN 0-913022-34-9). Angriff Pr.

--Pawns in the Game. 1978. pap. 4.00x (ISBN 0-911038-29-9). Noontide.

--Red Fog Over America. 280p. pap. 4.00 (ISBN 0-913022-35-7). Angriff Pr.

--Red Fog Over America. 1978. pap. 4.00x (ISBN 0-911038-30-2). Noontide.

Carr, William N. & Mize, Jack P. MOS-LSI Design & Application. LC 72-7407. (Texas Instruments Electronics Ser.). (Illus.). 320p. 1972. 54.50 (ISBN 0-07-010081-0). McGraw.

Carra, Andrew J., ed. Camping. LC 77-8745. (Illus.). 1978. pap. 4.95 (ISBN 0-8128-2117-3). Stein & Day.

Carra, Lawrence, jt. auth. see Dean, Alexander.

Carrabis, Joseph-David. The dBASE III Advanced Programming. LC 85-60691. 300p. 1985. pap. 19.95 (ISBN 0-88022-169-0, 194). Que Corp.

Carrada-Bravo, Francisco. Oil, Money, & the Mexican Economy: A Macroeconometric Analysis. LC 82-50687. (Replica Edition Ser.). 146p. 1982. softcover 19.50x (ISBN 0-86531-902-2). Westview.

Carra de Vaux, Bernard. Les Penseurs de l'Islam, 5 vols. LC 80-2197. Repr. of 1926 ed. Set. 200.00 (ISBN 0-404-18990-3). AMS Pr.

Carrafiello, Vincent A. Paths of the Law: The Pursuit of Justice in a Time of Transition, 1960-1980. LC 83-50006. 280p. (Orig.). 1983. lib. bdg. 24.75 (ISBN 0-8191-3291-8); pap. text ed. 13.25 (ISBN 0-8191-3292-6). U Pr of Amer.

Carraher, Ann M., ed. see Carraher, Philip J.

Carraher, Charles E., jt. auth. see Millich, Frank.

Carraher, Charles E., jt. auth. see Seymour, Raymond B.

Carraher, Charles E. & Sheats, John, eds. Organometallic Polymers. 1978. 49.50 (ISBN 0-12-160850-6). Acad Pr.

Carraher, Charles E. & Tsuda, Minoru, eds. Modification of Polymers. LC 79-28259. (ACS Symposium Ser.: No. 121). 1980. 49.95 (ISBN 0-8412-0540-X). Am Chemical.

Carraher, Charles E., jt. ed. see Millich, Frank.

Carraher, Charles E., Jr. & Gebelein, Charles G., eds. Biological Activities of Polymers. LC 82-3988. (ACS Symposium Ser.: No. 186). 1982. 39.95 (ISBN 0-8412-0719-4). Am Chemical.

Carraher, Charles E., Jr. & Moore, James, eds. Modification of Polymers. 390p. 1983. 57.50x (ISBN 0-306-41387-6, Plenum Pr). Plenum Pub.

Carraher, Charles E., Jr. & Preston, Jack, eds. Interfacial Synthesis: Vol. III: Recent Advances. (Illus.). 408p. 1982. 65.00 (ISBN 0-8247-1725-2). Dekker.

Carraher, Charles E., Jr. & Sheats, John E., eds. Advances in Organometallic & Inorganic Polymer Science. (Illus.). 472p. 1982. 67.50 (ISBN 0-8247-1610-8). Dekker.

Carraher, Charles E., Jr. & Sperling, L. H., eds. Polymer Applications of Renewable-Resource Materials. LC 82-10127. (Polymer Science & Technology Ser.: Vol. 17). 484p. 1983. 69.50 (ISBN 0-306-41033-8, Plenum Pr). Plenum Pub.

Carraher, Charles E., Jr., jt. ed. see Gebelein, Charles G.

Carraher, Charles E., Jr., jt. ed. see Mathias, Lon J.

Carraher, Philip J. The Scarlet Wreath: The Murder of Jeanne Anderson. Carraher, Ann M., ed. LC 85-80039. (Orig.). 1985. 11.95 (ISBN 0-9615097-0-8); pap. 5.50 (ISBN 0-9615097-1-6). Phian Bks.

Carran, Archie B. Genic Psychology: Method & Theory. 183p. 1972. 29.50x (ISBN 0-8422-5011-5); pap. text ed. 9.95x (ISBN 0-8422-0189-0). Irvington.

Carranco, Juan C. The Pearl Hunters in the Gulf of California, 1668. Mathes, W. Michael, tr. from Span. 36.00 (ISBN 0-317-11545-6). Dawsons.

Carranco, Lynwood. The Redwood Lumber Industry. (Illus.). 218p. 35.95 (ISBN 0-87095-084-3). Golden West.

Carranco, Lynwood & Beard, Estle. Genocide & Vendetta: The Round Valley Wars in Northern California. LC 81-40279. (Illus.). 414p. 1981. 24.95 (ISBN 0-8061-1549-1). U of Okla Pr.

Carranco, Lynwood & Labbe, John. Logging the Redwoods. LC 72-80989. (Illus.). 144p. 1975. boxed 17.95 (ISBN 0-87004-236-X). Caxton.

Carranza & Kenney. Prevention of Periodontal Disease. 1981. 28.00 (ISBN 0-931386-51-9). Quint Pub Co.

Carranza, et al. Scanning Electron Microscope: Atlas of Periodontal Biology & Pathology. 1986. price not set. Ishiyaku Euro.

Carranza, Fermin A. Glickman's Clinical Periodontology. 6th ed. (Illus.). 100p. 1984. 55.00 (ISBN 0-7216-2441-3). Saunders.

Carrara, Antonio, jt. auth. see Frassica, Pietro.

Carras, Helen. Passion's Rogue. (Ecstasy Ser.: No. 396). (Orig.). 1986. pap. 2.25 (ISBN 0-440-16894-5). Dell.

Carras, J. N. & Johnson, G. M., eds. The Urban Atmosphere, Sydney: A Case Study. (Illus.). 654p. (Orig.). 1983. pap. text ed. 26.95 (ISBN 0-643-03479-X, Pub. by CSIRO). Intl Spec Bk.

Carras, Mary C. Dynamics of Indian Political Factions: A Study of District Councils in the State of Maharashtra. LC 76-186250. (Cambridge South Asian Studies: No. 12). (Illus.). 288p. 1972. 39.50 (ISBN 0-521-08521-7). Cambridge U Pr.

--Indira Gandhi in the Crucible of Leadership. LC 78-19598. 256p. 1980. pap. 6.95 (ISBN 0-8070-0243-7, BP-607). Beacon Pr.

--Indira Gandhi in the Crucible of Leadership. LC 78-19598. 1979. 16.50x (ISBN 0-8070-0242-9). Beacon Pr.

Carrasco, David. Quetzalcoatl & the Irony of Empire: Myth & Prophecies in the Aztec Tradition. LC 82-13356. (Illus.). xii, 234p. 1984. lib. bdg. 22.50x (ISBN 0-226-09487-1); pap. 7.95 (ISBN 0-226-09489-8). U of Chicago Pr.

Carrasco, David & Swanberg, Jane M., eds. Waiting for the Dawn: Mircea Eliade in Perspective. (Academy of Independent Scholars Retrospective Ser.). 128p. 1985. 20.00x (ISBN 0-8133-0148-3). Westview.

Carrasco, Pedro, ed. see Nutini, Hugo G.

Carrasco Martinez, Castulo. Diccionario de Medicina, Farmacia Veterinaria y Quimica. 1040p. (Span.). 1978. pap. 49.95 (ISBN 84-7391-013-3, S-50123). French & Eur.

Carravetta, Peter, tr. see Oberto, Martino.

Carraway, Mary. Jill. 144p. (Orig.). (gr. 6-9). 1985. pap. 2.95 (ISBN 0-87123-847-0). Bethany Hse.

Carre, Antonio. Necker et la question des grains a la fin du XVIIIe siecle. LC 79-147152. 220p. 1973. Repr. of 1903 ed. 21.00 (ISBN 0-8337-0481-8). B Franklin.

Carre, Bernard. Graphs & Networks. (Oxford Applied Mathematics & Computing Science Ser.). (Illus.). 1979. 55.00x (ISBN 0-19-859615-4); pap. 21.95x (ISBN 0-19-859622-7). Oxford U Pr.

Carre, E. G. Praying Hyde. LC 82-73972. 183p. 1983. pap. 4.95 (ISBN 0-88270-541-5). Bridge Pub.

Carre, J. J., et al. French Economic Growth. Hatfield, John P., tr. from French. LC 74-82775. Orig. Title: Croissance Francaise. 608p. 1975. 37.50x (ISBN 0-8047-0878-9). Stanford U Pr.

Carre, Jean M. Goethe. Hard, Eleanor, tr. 1973. Repr. of 1929 ed. 20.00 (ISBN 0-8274-0082-9). R West.

--Robert Louis Stevenson: The Frail Warrior. facsimile ed. Hard, Eleanor, tr. from Fr. LC 78-165619. (Select Bibliographies Reprint Ser). Repr. of 1930 ed. 18.00 (ISBN 0-8369-5926-4). Ayer Co Pubs.

--A Season in Hell: The Life of Arthur Rimbaud. Josephson, Hannah & Josephson, Matthew, trs. from Fr. LC 77-10254. Repr. of 1931 ed. 27.50 (ISBN 0-404-16309-2). AMS Pr.

Carre, John Le see Le Carre, John.

Carre, John le see Le Carre, John.

Carre, John Le see Le Carre, John.
Carre, John le see Le Carre, John.
Carre, Meyrick H. Phases of Thought in England. LC 72-7858. 392p. 1973. Repr. of 1949 ed. lib. bdg. 19.25x (ISBN 0-8371-6537-7, CAPT). Greenwood.
Carre, Raymond. Maximum Effort. (Orig.). 1984. pap. 6.95 (ISBN 0-86666-196-4). Natl Lit Guild.
Carreck, Carole. Star Rider. (The Starlight Adventure Ser.). (Illus.). 356p. (gr. 7 up). 1985. pap. 2.95 (ISBN 0-14-031840-2, Puffin). Penguin.
Carreck, Michael. Blaze of Glory. 208p. 1983. 10.95 (ISBN 0-312-08366-1). St Martin.
Carreira, Antonio. The People of the Cape Verde Islands: Exploitation & Emigration. ix, 224p. 1982. 21.50 (ISBN 0-208-01988-X, Archon Bks). Shoe String.
Carrell, A. Super Handyman's Encyclopedia of Home Repair Hints: Better, Faster, Cheaper, & Easier Ideas for House & Workshop. 1971. pap. 4.95 (ISBN 0-13-875914-6). P-H.
Carrell, Al. The Handy Dan Guide to Home Plumbing. 96p. 1982. pap. text ed. 4.95 (ISBN 0-8403-2695-5). Kendall-Hunt.
--A Super Handyman's Do-It-Quick but Do-It Right Home Repair Hints. LC 80-24659. 1981. 9.95 (ISBN 0-13-875906-5). P-H.
--The Superhandyman's Fix & Finish Furniture Guide. 180p. 1982. pap. 5.95 (ISBN 0-13-875971-5); 7.95 (ISBN 0-13-875997-9). P-H.
Carrell, Bob, jt. auth. see Newsom, Doug.
Carrell, J. B., ed. Group Actions & Vector Fields: Vancouver, Canada, 1981, Proceedings. (Lecture Notes in Mathematics: Vol. 956). 144p. 1982. pap. 10.00 (ISBN 0-387-11946-9). Springer-Verlag.
Carrell, James, jt. auth. see Tiffany, William R.
Carrell, James B., jt. auth. see Dieudonne, J. A.
Carrell, James B., et al. Topics in the Theory of Algebraic Groups. LC 82-17329. (Notre Dame Mathematical Lectures Ser.: No. 10a). 192p. (Orig.). 1982. pap. text ed. 9.95x (ISBN 0-268-01843-X, 85-18433). U of Notre Dame Pr.
Carrell, John, jt. auth. see Andrews, Michael.
Carrell, Mary J. Learning Math Skills. 1978. pap. text ed. 3.00x (ISBN 0-88323-139-5, 228). Richards Pub.
--Understanding the Metric System. 1978. pap. text ed. 3.00x (ISBN 0-88323-140-9, 229). Richards Pub.
Carrell, Mary Jane. Understanding English. rev. ed. 1982. pap. 2.75x (ISBN 0-88323-182-4, 197). Richards Pub.
Carrell, Michael R. & Heavrin, Christina. Collective Bargaining & Labor Relations. 544p. 1985. text ed. 26.95 (ISBN 0-675-20302-3). Additional supplements may be obtained from publishers. Merrill.
Carrell, Michael R. & Kuzmits, Frank E. The Management of Human Resources. 712p. 1981. text ed. 26.95 (ISBN 0-675-09927-7). Additional supplements may be obtained from publisher. Merrill.
Carrell, Michael R. & Smith, Jerald. Labor Management Simulation. 72p. 1985. pap. 10.95 (ISBN 0-675-20298-1). Additional supplements may be obtained from publisher. Merrill.
Carrell, Norman. Bach the Borrower. LC 79-26050. 396p. 1980. Repr. of 1967 ed. lib. bdg. 32.50x (ISBN 0-313-22205-3, CABB). Greenwood.
--Bach's Brandenburg Concerts. Repr. lib. bdg. 39.00x (ISBN 0-403-08968-9). Scholarly.
Carrell, Susan L. Le Soliloque de la Passion Feminine, ou le Dialogue Illusoire: Etude d'une Formule Monophonique de la Litterature Epistolaire. (Etudes Litteraires Francaise Ser.: No. 12). 137p. (Orig., Fr.). 1982. pap. 19.00x (ISBN 3-87808-891-4). Benjamins North Am.
Carrenno, Josephine & Larson, Diane. Spanish: Practical Communication for Health Professionals. 2nd ed. 1981. 14.00 (ISBN 0-87488-722-4). Med Exam.
Carreno, Teresa. Selected Works: Piano Music & String Quartet. (Women Composers Ser.: No. 15). 235p. 1985. lib. bdg. 32.50 (ISBN 0-306-76193-9). Da Capo.
Carreras, J., et al. Shear Zones in Rocks: Papers Presented at the International Conference Held at the University of Barcelona, May 1979. 200p. 1980. pap. 44.00 (ISBN 0-08-026244-9). Pergamon.
Carrere, Claude. Barcelone: Centre Economique a L'epoque Des Difficultes, 1380-1462, 2 vols. (Civilisations et Societes: No. 5). 1967. pap. 72.00x (ISBN 90-2796-076-3). Mouton.
Carrere, Felix. Le Theater de Thomas Kyd Contribution: A L'Etude du Drame Elizabethain. 462p. 1984. Repr. of 1951 ed. lib. bdg. 85.00 (ISBN 0-8492-4100-6). R West.
Carrere, Jean. Degeneration in the Great French Masters. facs. ed. McCabe, J., tr. LC 67-26722. (Essay Index Reprint Ser). 1922. 20.00 (ISBN 0-8369-0277-7). Ayer Co Pubs.
--The Pope: An Analysis of the Office of the Pope & the Roman Church & City. 1977. lib. bdg. 59.95 (ISBN 0-8490-2453-6). Gordon Pr.
Carrere, Jean & Dessaigne, Jacques. Lexique des Termes Usuels de Psychiatrie. 114p. (Fr.). 1976. pap. 17.50 (ISBN 0-686-56939-3, M-6061). French & Eur.
Carrero, Jaime. El Hombre Que No Sudaba. LC 81-68070. 205p. (Span.). 1981. pap. 7.50 (ISBN 0-934770-14-X). Arte Publico.
--Los Nombres. (UPREX, Ficcion: No. 13). pap. 1.85 (ISBN 0-8477-0013-5). U of PR Pr.
--Teatro. 200p. Date not set. 7.50 (ISBN 0-317-06975-6). Arte Publico.
Carrero, Jean P. The Deceivers. LC 83-90830. 175p. 1984. 10.95 (ISBN 0-533-05841-4). Vantage.
Carret, Philip L. The Art of Speculation. rev. ed. LC 75-2625. (Wall Street & the Security Markets Ser.). 1975. Repr. of 1930 ed. 31.00x (ISBN 0-405-06951-0). Ayer Co Pubs.
Carreter, Fernando L. Diccionario de Terminos Filologicos. 5th ed. 444p. (Span.). 1977. pap. 17.95 (ISBN 84-249-1111-3, S-12048, French & Eur). French & Eur.
--Diccionario de Terminos Filologicos. 3rd ed. 444p. (Span.). 1977. 22.25 (ISBN 84-249-1112-1, S-50129, French & Eur). French & Eur.
Carrett, Philip L. The Art of Speculation. 1979. Repr. of 1930 ed. flexible cover 14.00 (ISBN 0-87034-050-6). Fraser Pub Co.
Carretta, Vincent. The Snarling Muse: Verbal & Visual Political Satire from Pope to Churchill. LC 83-6979. (Illus.). 304p. 1983. 25.00x (ISBN 0-8122-7885-2). U of Pa Pr.
Carretto, Carlo. Blessed Are You Who Believed. Wall, Barbara, tr. from Ital. LC 82-22504. (Illus.). 96p. (Orig.). 1983. pap. 4.95 (ISBN 0-88344-038-5). Orbis Bks.
--The Desert in the City. (The Crossroad Paperback Ser.). 112p. 1982. pap. 4.95 (ISBN 0-8245-0423-2). Crossroad NY.
--The God Who Comes. Hancock, Rose M., tr. from It. LC 73-89358. (Illus.). 254p. (Orig.). 1974. pap. 6.95 (ISBN 0-88344-160-8). Orbis Bks.
--I, Francis. Barr, Robert R., tr. from Ital. LC 81-16913. Orig. Title: Io Francesco. 144p. (Orig.). 1982. pap. 5.95 (ISBN 0-88344-200-0). Orbis Bks.
--I Sought & I Found: My Experience of God & of the Church. Barr, Robert R., tr. from Ital. 144p. 1984. pap. 6.95 (ISBN 0-88344-202-7). Orbis Bks.
--Letters from the Desert. 1976. pap. write for info (ISBN 0-515-09573-7). Jove Pubns.
--Letters from the Desert. Hancock, Rose, tr. from Ital. LC 72-85791. Orig. Title: Lettres dal deserto. 146p. (Orig.). 1982. pap. 5.95 (ISBN 0-88344-280-9). Orbis Bks.
--Love Is for Living. Moiser, Jeremy, tr. from Ital. LC 76-49878. Orig. Title: Cio Che Conta E Amare. 158p. 1977. pap. 5.95 (ISBN 0-88344-293-0). Orbis Bks.
--Made in Heaven. 4.95 (ISBN 0-87193-135-4). Dimension Bks.
--Summoned by Love. Neame, Alan, tr. from Italian. LC 78-962. Orig. Title: Padre Mio me abbandono a Te. 1978. pap. 5.95 (ISBN 0-88344-472-0). Orbis Bks.
Carrey, Dixieann W. First Impressions: A Guide to More Profitable Direct Mail Advertising. LC 77-155433. (Illus.). 1978. 12.95 (ISBN 0-931882-02-8). D W Carrey.
Carrey, John, jt. auth. see Conley, Cort.
Carrez, Maurice & Morel, Francois. Dictionnaire Grec-Francais du Nouveau Testament. 276p. (Fr.-Gr.). 37.50 (ISBN 0-686-56940-7, M-6062). French & Eur.
Carr-Gregg, Charlotte. Japanese Prisoners of War in Revolt: The Outbreaks at Featherston & Cowra During World War II. LC 78-2103. (Illus.). 1978. 22.50x (ISBN 0-312-44060-X). St Martin.
--Kicking the Habit: Four Australian Therapeutic Communities. LC 83-26118. 186p. 1985. text ed. 25.00x (ISBN 0-7022-1748-4). U of Queensland Pr.
Carr-Hill, Roy & Stern, Nicholas. Crime, the Police & Criminal Statistics: An Analysis of Official Statistics for England & Wales Using Economic Methods. (Quantitative Studies in Social Relations). 1979. 46.00 (ISBN 0-12-160350-4). Acad Pr.
Carr-Hill, Roy A. & Pritchard, Colin W. The Development & Exploitation of Empirical Birthweight Standards. (Illus.). 208p. 1985. 80.00x (ISBN 0-943818-08-7). Stockton Pr.
Carrick, A. Computers & Instrumentation. Thomas, L. C., ed. 256p. 1979. casebound 49.95 (ISBN 0-471-25624-2, Pub. by Wiley Heyden). Wiley.
Carrick, Carol. The Accident. LC 76-3532. (Illus.). 32p. (ps-3). 1976. 7.95 (ISBN 0-395-28774-X, Clarion); pap. 3.45 (ISBN 0-89919-041-3). HM.
--Beach Bird. LC 72-703. (Pied Piper Book). (Illus.). 32p. (ps-3). 1978. pap. 1.95 (ISBN 0-8037-0416-X). Dial Bks Young.
--Ben & the Porcupine. (Illus.). 32p. 1981. 8.95 (ISBN 0-395-30171-8). HM.
--Ben & the Porcupine. LC 80-214020. (Illus.). 32p. (ps-3). 1985. pap. 4.95 (ISBN 0-89919-348-X, Clarion). HM.
--The Climb. 32p. (gr. k-4). 1980. 8.95 (ISBN 0-395-29431-2, Clarion). HM.
--The Crocodiles Still Wait. LC 79-23519. (Illus.). 32p. (gr. 1-4). 1980. 8.95 (ISBN 0-395-29102-X, Clarion). HM.
--Dark & Full of Secrets. LC 83-21017. (Illus.). 32p. (ps-4). 1984. PLB 11.95 (ISBN 0-89919-271-8, Clarion). HM.
--The Empty Squirrel. LC 80-16475. (Greenwillow Read-Alone Bks.). (Illus.). 64p. (gr. 1-3). 1981. 8.75 (ISBN 0-688-80293-1); PLB 8.88 (ISBN 0-688-84293-3). Greenwillow.
--The Foundling. LC 77-1587. (Illus.). 32p. (ps-4). 1977. 7.95 (ISBN 0-395-28775-8, Clarion). HM.
--The Longest Float in the Parade. LC 81-6701. (Read-Alone Bks.). (Illus.). 56p. (gr. 1-3). 1982. 9.25 (ISBN 0-688-00918-2); PLB 8.88 (ISBN 0-688-00919-0). Greenwillow.
--Lost in the Storm. LC 74-1051. (Illus.). 32p. (ps-3). 1974. 7.95 (ISBN 0-395-28776-6, Clarion). HM.
--Octopus. LC 77-12769. (Illus.). 32p. (gr. 1-4). 1978. 7.95 (ISBN 0-395-28777-4, Clarion). HM.
--Old Mother Witch. LC 75-4609. (Illus.). 32p. (ps-4). 1975. 11.95 (ISBN 0-395-28778-2, Clarion). HM.
--Patrick's Dinosaurs. LC 83-2049. (Illus.). 32p. (gr. k-3). 1983. PLB 10.95 (ISBN 0-89919-189-4, Clarion). HM.
--Patrick's Dinosaurs. LC 83-2049. (Illus.). (ps-3). 1985. pap. 4.95 (ISBN 0-89919-402-8, Clarion). HM.
--Paul's Christmas Birthday. LC 77-28408. (Illus.). 32p. (gr. k-3). 1978. PLB 11.88 (ISBN 0-688-84159-7). Greenwillow.
--Sand Tiger Shark. LC 76-40206. (gr. 1-5). 1976. 9.95 (ISBN 0-395-28779-0, Clarion). HM.
--Sleep Out. (Illus.). 32p. (ps-3). 1982. pap. 3.45 (ISBN 0-89919-083-9, Clarion). HM.
--Sleep Out. LC 72-88539. (Illus.). 32p. (gr. 1-3). 1973. 7.95 (ISBN 0-395-28780-4, Clarion). HM.
--Some Friend! LC 79-11490. (Illus.). 112p. (gr. 6 up). 1979. 8.95 (ISBN 0-395-28966-1, Clarion). HM.
--Stay Away from Simon. LC 84-14289. (Illus.). 64p. (gr. 2-5). 1985. pap. 10.95 (ISBN 0-89919-343-9, Clarion). HM.
--Two Coyotes. (Illus.). 32p. (gr. 1-5). 1982. 11.50 (ISBN 0-89919-078-2, Clarion). HM.
--The Washout. LC 78-8135. (Illus.). 32p. (gr. 1-4). 1978. 8.95 (ISBN 0-395-28781-2, Clarion). HM.
--What a Wimp! (Illus.). 96p. (gr. 3-6). 1983. 10.95 (ISBN 0-89919-139-8, Clarion). HM.
Carrick, Donald. Harald & the Giant Knight. 32p. (gr. 1-3). 1982. 10.95 (ISBN 0-89919-060-X, Clarion). HM.
--Milk. LC 84-25879. (Illus.). 24p. (ps-1). 1985. 11.75 (ISBN 0-688-04822-6); lib. bdg. 11.88 (ISBN 0-688-04823-4). Greenwillow.
--Morgan & the Artist. LC 84-14267. (Illus.). 32p. (ps-4). 1985. pap. 12.95 (ISBN 0-89919-300-5, Clarion). HM.
Carrick, Edward, ed. Art & Design in the British Film: A Pictorial Directory of British Art Directors & Their Work. LC 76-169340. (Arno Press Cinema Program). (Illus.). 144p. 1972. Repr. of 1948 ed. 17.00 (ISBN 0-405-03913-1). Ayer Co Pubs.
Carrick, J. C. Wycliffe & the Lollards. 1977. lib. bdg. 59.95 (ISBN 0-8490-2824-8). Gordon Pr.
Carrick, Malcolm. Happy Jack. LC 78-19476. (I Can Read Bk.). (Illus.). 64p. (gr. k-3). 1979. PLB 8.89 (ISBN 0-06-021122-9). HarpJ.
--I'll Get You! LC 78-19490. (gr. 5-8). 1979. HarpJ.
--Mr. Todd's Trap. LC 79-2012. (I Can Read Bks.). (Illus.). 64p. (gr. k-3). 1980. PLB 9.89 (ISBN 0-06-021114-8). HarpJ.
--Today Is Shrew's Day. LC 77-11836. (I Can Read Bk.). (Illus.). 64p. (gr. k-3). 1978. o.p 6.95 (ISBN 0-06-021119-9). HarpJ.
Carrick, Peter. Encyclopaedia of Motor-Cycle Sport. 224p. 1982. 40.00x (ISBN 0-7091-8874-9, Pub. by Robert Hale England). State Mutual Bk.
--A Tribute to Fred Astaire. (Illus.). 188p. 1985. 14.95 (ISBN 0-88162-081-5, Pub. by Salem Hse Ltd). Merrimack Pub Cir.
Carrick, Peter, compiled by. Encyclopedia of Motor Cycle Sport. Rev. ed. (Illus.). 240p. 1982. 19.95 (ISBN 0-312-24868-7). St Martin.
Carrick, R. J. East-West Technology Transfer in Perspective. LC 78-78134. (Policy Papers in International Affairs Ser.: No. 9). 1978. pap. 5.50x (ISBN 0-87725-509-1). U of Cal Intl St.
Carrick, Robert & Henderson, Richard. John G. Alden & His Yacht Designs. LC 77-85407. (Illus.). 464p. 1983. 65.00 (ISBN 0-87742-089-0, J456); ltd. ed. 150.00. Intl Marine.
Carrick, Valery. Tales of Wise & Foolish Animals. LC 69-17674. (Illus.). v, 97p. (gr. k-4). 1969. pap. 3.50 (ISBN 0-486-21997-6). Dover.
Carrico, Charles J., jt. auth. see Shires, George T.
Carrico, Clayton H. Refrigeration Licenses: (Contractor-Journeyman-Operator) Unlimited. 1980. text ed. 29.95x (ISBN 0-912524-20-0). Busn News.
Carrie, Christopher. Adventure at the Pirates' Cave. (Crayola Activity Storybooks). (Illus.). 48p. (Orig.). (gr. k-4). 1980. pap. 1.32 (ISBN 0-86696-025-2). Binney & Smith.
--Adventure of the Haunted Mansion. (Crayola Activity Storybooks). (Illus.). 48p. (Orig.). (gr. k-4). 1980. pap. 1.32 (ISBN 0-86696-030-9). Binney & Smith.
--Adventure of the Space Robots. (Crayola Activity Storybooks). (Illus.). 48p. (Orig.). (gr. k-4). 1980. pap. 1.32 (ISBN 0-86696-027-9). Binney & Smith.
--Amazing Cars. (Crayola Laugh & Play Bks.). (Illus.). 48p. (Orig.). (gr. k-4). 1981. pap. 1.32 (ISBN 0-86696-033-3). Binney & Smith.
--Astounding Animals. (Crayola Laugh & Play Bks.). (Illus.). 48p. (Orig.). (gr. k-4). 1981. pap. 1.32 (ISBN 0-86696-032-5). Binney & Smith.
--Exciting Outer Space. (Crayola Laugh & Play Books). (Illus.). 48p. (Orig.). (gr. k-4). 1981. pap. 1.32 (ISBN 0-86696-036-8). Binney & Smith.
--Fantastic Airplanes. (Crayola Laugh & Play Bks.). (Illus.). 48p. (Orig.). (gr. k-4). 1981. pap. 1.32 (ISBN 0-86696-035-X). Binney & Smith.
--Friendly Monsters. (Crayola Laugh & Play Bks.). (Illus.). 48p. (Orig.). (gr. k-4). 1981. pap. 1.32 (ISBN 0-86696-034-1). Binney & Smith.
--Mystery of Dinosaur Island. (Crayola Activity Storybooks). (Illus.). 48p. (Orig.). (gr. k-4). 1980. pap. 1.32 (ISBN 0-86696-029-5). Binney & Smith.
--Mystery of the Missing Wand. (Crayola Activity Storybooks). (Illus.). 48p. (Orig.). (gr. k-4). 1980. pap. 1.32 (ISBN 0-86696-028-7). Binney & Smith.
--Mystery of the Stolen Gold. (Crayola Activity Storybooks). (Illus.). 48p. (Orig.). (gr. k-4). 1980. pap. 1.32 (ISBN 0-86696-026-0). Binney & Smith.
--Surprising People. (Crayola Laugh & Play Bks.). (Illus.). 48p. (Orig.). (gr. k-4). 1981. pap. 1.32 (ISBN 0-86696-031-7). Binney & Smith.
Carrie, Jacques. Bridge of Movie Producer Louis King. LC 80-67977. 187p. (Orig.). 1981. pap. 6.95 (ISBN 0-937578-00-2). Fablewaves.
--Intrepid Visions. LC 81-67260. (Illus.). 208p. (Orig.). 1985. pap. 6.95 (ISBN 0-937578-01-0). Fablewaves.
Carrier. Manual de Aire Acondicionado. 848p. (Espn.). 1977. 75.95 (ISBN 84-267-0115-9, S-30875). French & Eur.
Carrier Air Conditioning Co. Handbook of Air Conditioning System Design. 1965. 74.50 (ISBN 0-07-010090-X). McGraw.
Carrier, Constance, tr. see Propertius.
Carrier, Constance, tr. see Tibullus, Albius.
Carrier, David, jt. auth. see Roskill, Mark.
Carrier, Else H. Water & Grass: Study in the Pastoral Economy of Southern Europe. LC 77-87717. Repr. of 1932 ed. 41.50 (ISBN 0-404-16579-6). AMS Pr.
Carrier, Esther J. Fiction in the Public Libraries, Nineteen Hundred to Nineteen Fifty. 300p. 1985. lib. bdg. 27.50 (ISBN 0-87287-459-1). Libs Unl.
Carrier, Franklin H. Begin to Keep Bees. (Illus.). 234p. 1981. text ed. 14.95 (ISBN 0-9607550-0-4). Carrier's Bees.
--Keeping Bees: A Handbook for the Hobbyist Beekeeper. (Illus.). 1983. 15.95 (ISBN 0-9607550-1-2). Carriers Bees.
Carrier, John, jt. ed. see Bowker, Gordon.
Carrier, Lark. There Was a Hill... LC 84-25536. (Illus.). 40p. (ps up). 1985. 10.95 (ISBN 0-907234-70-4, Pub. by Picture Bk Studio USA). Neugebauer Pr.
Carrier, Leonard S. Experience & the Objects of Perception. LC 81-40068. 188p. 1981. lib. bdg. 22.75 (ISBN 0-8191-1673-4); pap. text ed. 11.25 (ISBN 0-8191-1674-2). U Pr of Amer.
Carrier, Lois, jt. auth. see Gooch, Bill.
Carrier, Lyman. Agriculture in Virginia, Sixteen Hundred Seven to Sixteen Ninety-Nine. (Illus.). 41p. 1974. pap. 2.95 (ISBN 0-8139-0138-3). U Pr of Va.
--The Beginnings of Agriculture in America. 1976. lib. bdg. 59.95 (ISBN 0-8490-1485-9). Gordon Pr.
--Beginnings of Agriculture in America. (History of American Economy Ser). 1968. Repr. of 1923 ed. 24.00 (ISBN 0-384-07771-4). Johnson Repr.
Carrier, Oliver, Jr. & Shibata, Shoji, eds. Factors Influencing Vascular Reactivity. LC 77-91590. (Illus.). 296p. 1977. 41.00 (ISBN 0-89640-024-7). Igaku-Shoin.
Carrier, Rick. Ultralights: The Complete Book of Flying, Training & Safety. LC 83-40143. (Illus.). 144p. 1985. pap. 12.95 (ISBN 0-385-19290-8, Dolp). Doubleday.
Carrier, Robert. Menu Planner. (Illus.). 310p. 1985. 29.95 (ISBN 0-317-28930-6). Little.
Carrier, Roch. Le Chandail de Hockey. (Illus., Orig., Fr.). (gr. 5). 1985. pap. 7.95 (ISBN 0-88776-176-3, Dist. by U of Toronto Pr). Tundra Bks.
--Floralie, Where Are You? Fischman, Sheila, tr. from Fr. LC 75-524113. (Anansi Fiction Ser.: No. 17). 108p. 1971. pap. 5.95 (ISBN 0-88784-317-4, Pub. by Hse Anansi Pr Canada). U of Toronto Pr.
--The Garden of Delights. Fischman, Sheila, tr. from Fr. (Anansi Fiction Ser.: No. 38). 173p. (Orig.). 1978. pap. 7.95 (ISBN 0-88784-066-3, Pub. by Hse Anansi Pr Canada). U of Toronto Pr.
--La Guerre, Yes Sir! Fischman, Sheila, tr. from Fr. (Anansi Fiction Ser.: No. 10). 113p. 1970. 9.95 (ISBN 0-88784-410-3, Pub. by Hse Anansi Pr Canada); pap. 5.95 (ISBN 0-88784-310-7); study guide by Peter Carver 1.00x (ISBN 0-88784-068-X). U of Toronto Pr.
--The Hockey Sweater. Fischman, Sheila, tr. from Fr. (Illus.). 24p. (gr. 2-5). 1984. text ed. 14.95 (ISBN 0-88776-169-0, Dist. by U of Toronto Pr). Tundra Bks.
--The Hockey Sweater. Fischman, Sheila, tr. from Fr. (Illus.). 24p. (gr. 5). 1985. pap. 7.95 (ISBN 0-88776-174-7, Dist. by U of Toronto Pr). Tundra Bks.
--The Hockey Sweater & Other Stories. Fischman, Sheila, tr. from Fr. (Anansi Fiction Ser.: No. 40). 160p. (Orig.). 1979. pap. 6.95 (ISBN 0-88784-078-7, Pub. by Hse Anansi Pr Canada). U of Toronto Pr.

--Is It the Sun, Philibert? Fischman, Sheila, tr. from Fr. LC 75-190705. (Anansi Fiction Ser.: No. 20). 100p. 1972. pap. 5.95 (ISBN 0-88784-321-2, Pub. by Hse Anansi Pr Canada). U of Toronto Pr.
--Lady With Chains. Fischman, Sheila, tr. from Fr. (Anansi Fiction Ser.: AF 47). 152p. (Orig.). 1984. pap. 8.95 (ISBN 0-88784-139-2, Pub. by Hse Anansi Pr Canada). U of Toronto Pr.
--No Country Without Grandfathers. Fischman, Sheila, tr. from Fr. (Anansi Fiction Ser.: No. 45). Orig. Title: Il NY a Pas De Pays Sans Grand-Pere. 156p. (Orig.). 1981. pap. 8.95 (ISBN 0-88784-090-6, Pub. by Hse Anansi Pr Canada). U of Toronto Pr.
--They Won't Demolish Me! Fischman, Sheila, tr. from Fr. (Anansi Fiction Ser.: No. 30). 134p. (Orig.). 1974. pap. 6.95 (ISBN 0-88784-328-X, Pub. by Hse Anansi Pr Canada). U of Toronto Pr.
Carrier, Warren. Leave Your Sugar for the Cold Morning. 65p. (Orig.). 1977. pap. 4.00 (ISBN 0-932662-19-6). St Andrews NC.
Carrier, Warren & Neumann, Bonnie, eds. Literature from the World. LC 80-53528. 550p. (gr. 11-12). 1981. text ed. 14.95 (ISBN 0-684-16754-9). Scribner.
Carrier, Warren & Oliver, Kenneth, eds. Guide to World Literature. 237p. (Orig.). 1980. pap. 11.00 (ISBN 0-8141-1949-2). NCTE.
Carriere, Anne-Marie. Le Dictionnaire des Hommes. 252p. (Fr.). 1962. 8.95 (ISBN 0-686-56845-1, M-6623). French & Eur.
Carriere, Dean & Day, Fraser. Solar Houses for a Cold Climate. (Illus.). 1982. pap. 4.50 Encore (ISBN 0-684-17424-3, ScribT). Scribner.
Carriere, G. Dictionary of Surface Active Agents, Cosmetics & Toiletries. 198p. 1978. 36.25 (ISBN 0-444-99809-8). Elsevier.
--Lexicon of Detergents, Cosmetics & Toiletries. (Elsevier Lexica Ser.: No. 8). viii, 203p. 1966. 36.25 (ISBN 0-444-40099-0). Elsevier.
Carriere, Joseph M. Tales from the French Folk-Lore of Missouri. LC 79-128989. (Northwestern University. Humanities Ser.: No. 1). Repr. of 1937 ed. 24.00 (ISBN 0-404-50701-8). AMS Pr.
Carrieri, Mario, photos by. The Vatican & Christian Rome. (Illus.). 522p. 1979. 100.00 (ISBN 0-89860-025-1). Eastview.
Carriero, Joe. How to Hit Slowpitch Softball: The Fundamentals & Psychology of Hitting. LC 84-50194. (Illus., Orig.). 1984. pap. 3.95 (ISBN 0-916533-00-X). Sports Info Pr.
Carrig, Carol. The Re-Evaluation Counseling Community. 1972. pap. 0.50 (ISBN 0-911214-19-4). Rational Isl.
Carrigan, Ana. Salvador Witness: The Life & Calling of Jean Donovan. 320p. 1984. 16.95 (ISBN 0-671-47992-X). S&S.
Carrigan, Andrew, et al. Book 3. 1972. 7.50 (ISBN 0-912090-20-0); pap. 2.45 (ISBN 0-912090-19-7). Sumac Mich.
Carrigan, Arnold. How Your IRA Can Make You a Millionaire. 1982. 9.95 (ISBN 0-517-54917-4, Harmony Bks); pap. 3.95 (ISBN 0-517-54918-2). Crown.
Carrigan, J. A., ed. see Fortier, Alcee.
Carrigan, R. A., et al, eds. see AIP Conference Proceedings No. 87, Fermilab School,.
Carrigan, R. A., Jr. & Huson, F. R., eds. The State of Particle Accelerators & High Energy Physics (Fermilab Summer School, 1981) LC 82-73861. (AIP Conference Proceedings Ser.: No. 92). 337p. 1982. lib. bdg. 33.75 (ISBN 0-88318-191-6). Am Inst Physics.
Carrigan, Richard A. & Trower, W. Peter, eds. Magnetic Monopoles. (NATO ASI Series B, Physics: Vol. 102). 348p. 1983. 47.50x (ISBN 0-306-41399-X, Plenum Pr). Plenum Pub.
Carrighar, Sally. The Glass Dove. 1977. pap. 1.75 (ISBN 0-380-01829-2, 36194). Avon.
--One Day at Teton Marsh. LC 78-26679. (Illus.). xii, 239p. 1979. pap. 4.25 (ISBN 0-8032-6302-3, BB 692, Bison). U of Nebr Pr.
--One Day on Beetle Rock. LC 78-18854. viii, 196p. 1978. pap. 3.25 (ISBN 0-8032-6301-5, BB 691, Bison). U of Nebr Pr.
Carril, Bonifacio Del see Saint-Exupery, Antione De.
Carrill, John H., ed. see Douglas, Henry K.
Carrillo, David L., jt. auth. see Ritchie, Michael J.
Carrillo, Fred, illus. Heroic Warriors. (Masters of the Universe Giant Picture Bks.). (Illus.). 24p. (gr. k-5). 1984. pap. 3.50 (ISBN 0-307-11363-9, 11363, Golden Bks). Western Pub.
Carrillo, Frederico M. The Development of a Rationale & Model Program to Prepare Teachers for the Bilingual-Bicultural Secondary School Programs. LC 77-81021. 1977. soft bdg. 11.00 (ISBN 0-88247-473-1). R & E Pubs.
Carrillo, Lawrence W. Teaching Reading. 1976. pap. 11.95 (ISBN 0-312-78750-2). St Martin.
Carrillo, Santiago. Eurocommunism & the State. Green, Nan & Elliott, A. M., trs. LC 78-51455. 180p. 1978. 8.95 (ISBN 0-88208-093-8). Lawrence Hill.
Carrillo-Beron, Carmen. Changing Adolescent Sex-Role Ideology Through Short Term Bicultural Group Process. LC 76-55961. 1977. soft bdg. 9.95 (ISBN 0-88247-435-9). R & E Pubs.
--A Comparison of Chicano & Anglo Women: Thesis. LC 74-77167. 1974. soft bdg. 10.95 (ISBN 0-88247-241-0). R & E Pubs.
Carrillo Romero, Ricarda, jt. auth. see Cerezo de Ponce, Engracia.
Carrilo, Salvador. Power from on High: The Holy Spirit in the Gospels & the Acts. Mishler, Carolyn, tr. from Sp. 1978. pap. 2.95 (ISBN 0-89283-060-3). Servant.
Carrin, Guy. The Economic Evaluation of Health Care. LC 83-23068. 340p. 1984. 23.95 (ISBN 0-312-23231-4). St Martin.
Carringer, Robert, jt. auth. see Allen, Nancy.
Carringer, Robert, et al. Film Study Guides. 1977. pap. text ed. 3.80x (ISBN 0-87563-155-X). Stipes.
Carringer, Robert L. The Making of Citizen Kane. LC 84-8777. 1985. 22.50 (ISBN 0-520-05367-2). U of Cal Pr.
Carringer, Robert L., ed. The Jazz Singer. LC 78-53295. (Screenplay Ser.). (Illus.). 1979. 17.50x (ISBN 0-299-07660-1); pap. 6.95x (ISBN 0-299-07664-4). U of Wis Pr.
Carringer, Robert L. & Sabath, Barry, eds. Ernst Lubitch: A Guide to References & Resources. 1978. lib. bdg. 26.50 (ISBN 0-8161-7895-X, Hall Reference). G K Hall.
Carrington. Computers for Spectroscopists. LC 74-12526. 275p. 1975. 54.95x (ISBN 0-470-13581-6). Halsted Pr.
--Pepper & Jam. (Illus.). 32p. (gr. 1-3). 1985. 11.95 (ISBN 0-224-02139-7, Pub. by Jonathan Cape). Merrimack Pub Cir.
Carrington, A. & Ramsay, D. A., eds. Molecules in Interstellar Space: Proceedings. (Royal Society of London Ser.). (Illus.). 167p. 1982. text ed. 51.00x (ISBN 0-85403-180-4, Pub. by Royal Soc London). Scholium Intl.
Carrington, Alan. Microwave Spectroscopy of Free Radicals. 1974. 49.50 (ISBN 0-12-160750-X). Acad Pr.
Carrington, Charles E. An Exposition of Empire. LC 75-41051. (BCL Ser. II). Repr. of 1947 ed. 15.00 (ISBN 0-404-14650-3). AMS Pr.
--A Subaltern's War: Being a Memoir of the Great War from the Point of View of a Romantic Young Man. LC 72-4273. (World Affairs Ser.: National & International Viewpoints). (Illus.). 236p. 1972. Repr. of 1930 ed. 20.00 (ISBN 0-405-04562-X). Ayer Co Pubs.
Carrington, David & Stephenson, Richard, eds. Map Collections in the United States & Canada. 4th ed. 180p. 1985. 35.00 (ISBN 0-87111-306-6). SLA.
Carrington, David K. & Stephenson, Richard W. Map Collections in the United States & Canada: A Directory. 3rd ed. LC 77-26685. pap. 60.00 (ISBN 0-317-30406-2, 2024960). Bks Demand UMI.
Carrington, Delores, ed. see Haddock, Durwood & Miller, Ron.
Carrington, Elsie R., jt. auth. see Willson, J. Robert.
Carrington, Fitzroy, ed. The King's Lyrics: Lyrical Poems of the Reigns of King James I & King Charles I. 1978. Repr. of 1899 ed. lib. bdg. 20.00 (ISBN 0-8495-0847-9). Arden Lib.
--Prints & Their Makers. 1979. Repr. of 1912 ed. lib. bdg. 100.00 (ISBN 0-8482-7565-9). Norwood Edns.
--The Quiet Hour. facsimile ed. LC 71-160901. (Granger Index Reprint Ser). Repr. of 1915 ed. 17.00 (ISBN 0-8369-6264-8). Ayer Co Pubs.
--The Quiet Hour. LC 78-74813. (Granger Poetry Library). (Illus.). 1979. Repr. of 1915 ed. 17.00x (ISBN 0-89609-131-7). Granger Bk.
Carrington, Frances C. My Army Life. facs. ed. LC 72-150173. (Select Bibliographies Reprint Ser). 1910. 25.00 (ISBN 0-8369-5686-9). Ayer Co Pubs.
Carrington, Frank. Crime & Justice: A Conservative Strategy. LC 83-81877. (Critical Issues Ser.). xiii, 73p. 1983. 3.00 (ISBN 0-89195-035-4). Heritage Found.
Carrington, Frank & Lambie, William. The Defenseless Society. LC 76-32544. 160p. (Orig.). 1976. pap. 1.95 (ISBN 0-916054-11-X, Dist. by Kampmann). Green Hill.
Carrington, George C., Jr. The Dramatic Unity of "Huckleberry Finn". LC 76-939. (Illus.). 219p. 1976. 12.00x (ISBN 0-8142-0238-1). Ohio St U Pr.
--The Immense Complex Drama: The World & Art of the Howells Novel. LC 66-16764. 259p. 1966. 6.25 (ISBN 0-8142-0036-2). Ohio St U Pr.
Carrington, George C., Jr. & Carrington, Ildiko. Plots & Characters in the Fiction of William Dean Howells. (Plots & Characters Ser.). xxii, 306p. 1976. 24.50 (ISBN 0-208-01461-6, Archon). Shoe String.
Carrington, Harold. Drive Suite. (Heritage Ser). 1970. pap. 2.50x (ISBN 0-685-26074-7). Broadside.
Carrington, Henry, ed. Anthology of French Poetry. (Poetry Library). 318p. 1985. Repr. of 1900 ed. 27.50x (ISBN 0-89609-247-X). Granger Bk.
Carrington, Henry B. Battle Maps & Charts of the American Revolution. LC 74-8018. 96p. 1974. Repr. of 1877 ed. 35.00 (ISBN 0-405-05540-4). Ayer Co Pubs.
--Battles of the American Revolution, 1775-1781: Historical & Military Criticism, 2 vols in 1. Incl. Battle Maps & Charts of the American Revolution. Repr. of 1881 ed. LC 67-29047. (Eyewitness Accounts of the American Revolution, Ser. 1). Repr. of 1877 ed. 29.00 (ISBN 0-405-01107-5). Ayer Co Pubs.
--Beacon Lights of Patriotism. facs. ed. LC 74-133068. (Granger Index Reprint Ser). 1894. 23.00 (ISBN 0-8369-6196-X). Ayer Co Pubs.
--The Indian Question. (Illus.). 1985. 10.00 (ISBN 0-914074-04-0, Pub. by J M C & Co). Ameereon Ltd.
Carrington, Hereward. Death: The Causes & Phenomena with Special Reference to Immortality. Kastenbaum, Robert, ed. LC 76-19563. (Death & Dying Ser.). 1977. lib. bdg. 27.50 (ISBN 0-405-09559-7). Ayer Co Pubs.
--Fasting for Health & Long Health. 1981. pap. 9.95x (ISBN 0-317-06969-1, Regent House). B of A.
--Higher Psychical Development. LC 83-22469. 310p. 1983. Repr. lib. bdg. 16.95x (ISBN 0-89370-670-1). Borgo Pr.
--Higher Psychical Development. 310p. 1983. pap. 6.95 (ISBN 0-87877-070-4). Newcastle Pub.
--Laboratory Investigations into Psychic Phenomena. LC 75-7370. (Perspectives in Psychical Research Ser.). (Illus.). 1975. Repr. of 1939 ed. 21.00x (ISBN 0-405-07021-7). Ayer Co Pubs.
--Save Your Life by Fasting. 1981. write for info (Regent House). B of A.
--World of Psychic Research. pap. 2.00 (ISBN 0-87980-254-5). Wilshire.
--Your Psychic Powers & How to Develop Them. LC 80-24076. 358p. 1980. Repr. of 1975 ed. lib. bdg. 17.95x (ISBN 0-89370-633-7). Borgo Pr.
--Your Psychic Powers & How to Develop Them. (Occult Ser.). 358p. 1975. pap. 7.95 (ISBN 0-87877-033-X, P-33). Newcastle Pub.
Carrington, Hereward & Whitehead, Willis F. Keys to the Occult: Two Guides to Hidden Wisdom. LC 80-23835. 182p. 1980. Repr. of 1977 ed. lib. bdg. 14.95x (ISBN 0-89370-641-8). Borgo Pr.
--Keys to the Occult: Two Guides to Hidden Wisdom. (Newcastle Arcana Ser.). 1977. pap. 4.95 (ISBN 0-87877-041-0, F-41). Newcastle Pub.
Carrington, Hereward, jt. auth. see Buckland, Raymond.
Carrington, Hereward, jt. auth. see Ernst, Bernard M.
Carrington, Hereward, jt. auth. see Muldoon, Sylvan.
Carrington, Hereward, jt. auth. see Muldoon, Sylvia.
Carrington, Hugh, ed. see Robertson, George.
Carrington, Ildiko, jt. auth. see Carrington, George C., Jr.
Carrington, Joanna. Landscape Painting for Beginners. LC 79-84664. (Start to Paint Ser.). (Illus.). 1979. pap. 3.95 (ISBN 0-8008-4543-9, Pentalic). Taplinger.
Carrington, John C. & Edwards, George T. Financing Industrial Investment. LC 78-65708. 300p. 1979. 47.95 (ISBN 0-03-049761-2). Praeger.
--Reversing Economic Decline. LC 79-24035. 224p. 1981. 27.50 (ISBN 0-312-67931-9). St Martin.
Carrington, John F. Talking Drums of Africa. LC 70-77195. (Illus.). Repr. of 1949 ed. 19.75 (ISBN 0-8371-1292-3, CDA&, Pub. by Negro U Pr). Greenwood.
--Talking Drums of Africa. (Illus.). 96p. 1949. 14.00. G Vanderstoel.
Carrington, Lawrence D. St. Lucian Creole: A Descriptive Analysis of Its Phonology & Morpho-Syntax. (Kreolische Bibliothek: No. 6). 180p. (Orig.). 1984. pap. 17.00x (ISBN 3-87118-667-8, H Buske). Benjamins North Am.
Carrington, Leonara. The Hearing Trumpet. 160p. 1985. 13.95 (ISBN 0-87286-170-8, Dist. by Subterranean Co); pap. 6.95 (ISBN 0-87286-169-4). City Lights.
Carrington, Leonora. Down Below. (Illus.). 56p. 1982. pap. 4.95 (ISBN 0-941194-17-5). Black Swan Pr.
Carrington, Margaret I. Absaraka: Home of the Crows. LC 83-6951. (Illus.). iv, 284p. 1983. 21.50x (ISBN 0-8032-1423-5); pap. 6.95 (ISBN 0-8032-6315-5, BB 856, Bison). U of Nebr Pr.
Carrington, Noel. Carrington: Paintings, Drawings & Decorations. (Illus.). 96p. 1980. 8.98 (ISBN 0-500-09143-9). Thames Hudson.
Carrington, Patricia. Freedom in Meditation. LC 76-6240. 384p. 1977. pap. 8.00. Pace Ed Syst.
--Releasing: The New Behavioral Science Method for Dealing with Pressure Situations. LC 83-15143. 256p. 1984. 13.95 (ISBN 0-688-02139-5). Morrow.
Carrington, Paul. Carrington's Corner: A Book of Poetry. (Orig.). 1979. pap. 2.00 (ISBN 0-686-24998-4). J & A Enterprises.
Carrington, Paul & Babcock, Barbara. Civil Procedure: Cases & Comments on the Process of Adjudication. 3rd ed. 1250p. 1983. 34.00 (ISBN 0-316-12988-7). Little.
--Civil Procedure: Statutes & Rules of the Court. 2nd ed. 1983. pap. text ed. 12.00 (ISBN 0-316-12974-7). Little.
Carrington, Paul D., et al. Justice on Appeal. 263p. 1976. write for info. West Pub.
Carrington, R. A. Computers for Spectroscopists. LC 74-12526. 275p. 1974. 27.50 (ISBN 0-470-13581-6, Pub. by Wiley). Krieger.
Carrington, Timothy. The Year They Sold Wall Street. (Illus.). 384p. 1985. 17.95 (ISBN 0-395-34394-1). HM.
Carrington, Ulrich S. The Making of an American: An Adaptation of Memorable Tales by Charles Sealsfield. LC 74-77736. (Bicentennial Series in American Studies: No. 2). 1974. 10.95 (ISBN 0-87074-143-8). SMU Press.
Carrino, Frank G., ed. see Hernandez, Jose.
Carrino, Frank G., tr. see Hernandez, Jose.
Carrino, Frank G., et al, trs. see Hernandez, Jose.
Carrio, Genaro R., tr. see Silving, Helen.
Carrion, Arturo M. Puerto Rico: A Political & Cultural History. (Illus.). 400p. 1984. pap. text ed. 8.95x (ISBN 0-393-30193-1). Norton.
--Puerto Rico & the Non-Hispanic Caribbean: A Study in the Decline of Spanish Exclusivism. pap. 3.10 (ISBN 0-8477-0835-7). U of PR Pr.
Carrion, Arturo M., et al. Puerto Rico: A Political & Cultural Odyssey. (Illus.). 1983. 19.50 (ISBN 0-393-01740-0). Norton.
Carris, Bill & Wolfe, Bob. Inside Commodore 64 BASIC. 12.95 (ISBN 0-8359-3087-4). Reston.
--Inside Commodore 64 BASIC. (Illus.). 192p. 12.95 (ISBN 0-317-13066-8). P-H.
Carris, Joan. Pets, Vets & Marty Howard. LC 84-47635. (Illus.). 192p. (gr. 5 up). 1984. 11.06i (ISBN 0-397-32092-2); PLB 10.89g (ISBN 0-397-32093-0). Lipp Jr Bks.
--Rusty Timmons' First Million. LC 85-40096. (Illus.). 192p. (gr. 5-9). 1985. 11.06i (ISBN 0-397-32154-6); PLB 11.50g (ISBN 0-397-32155-4). Lipp Jr Bks.
--When the Boys Ran the House. LC 82-47762. (Illus.). 160p. (gr. 4-7). 1982. 9.57i (ISBN 0-397-32019-1); PLB 10.89g (ISBN 0-397-32020-5). Lipp Jr Bks.
--Witch-Cat. LC 83-48448. (Illus.). 160p. (gr. 5 up). 1984. 10.53i (ISBN 0-397-32067-1); PLB 10.89g (ISBN 0-397-32068-X). Lipp Jr Bks.
Carris, Joan D. The Revolt of Ten-X. LC 80-7980. (gr. 4-6). 1980. 7.95 (ISBN 0-15-266462-9, HJ). HarBraceJ.
Carris, Joan D. & Crystal, Michael R. SAT Success: Peterson's Study Guide to English & Math Skills for College Entrance Examinations: SAT, ACT, PSAT. LC 82-16165. 380p. (Orig.). 1982. pap. 8.95 (ISBN 0-87866-208-1). Petersons Guides.
Carrithers, David W., ed. see Montesquieu.
Carrithers, Gale H. Donne at Sermons. LC 74-171183. 1972. 39.50x (ISBN 0-87395-122-0). State U NY Pr.
Carrithers, Michael. The Buddha. LC 83-8004. (Past Masters Ser.). 102p. 1983. 12.95x (ISBN 0-19-287590-6); pap. 3.95 (ISBN 0-19-287589-2). Oxford U Pr.
--Forest Monks of Sri Lanka: An Anthropological & Historical Study. (Illus.). 306p. 1983. 32.50 (ISBN 0-19-561389-9). Oxford U Pr.
Carrithers, Micheal & Collins, Steven, eds. The Category of the Person. 304p. Date not set. price not set (ISBN 0-521-25909-6); pap. price not set (ISBN 0-521-27757-4). Cambridge U Pr.
Carritt, E. F. The Theory of Morals: An Introduction to Ethical Philosophy. 144p. 1982. Repr. of 1928 ed. lib. bdg. 30.00 (ISBN 0-89984-118-X). Century Bookbindery.
Carritt, Edgar F. Ethical & Political Thinking. LC 73-3020. 186p. 1973. Repr. of 1947 ed. lib. bdg. 15.00x (ISBN 0-8371-6826-0, CAET). Greenwood.
--The Theory of Beauty. LC 77-9622. 1977. Repr. of 1962 ed. lib. bdg. 32.50 (ISBN 0-8414-1805-5). Folcroft.
--The Theory of Morals. LC 73-3021. 144p. 1974. Repr. of 1928 ed. lib. bdg. 15.00 (ISBN 0-8371-6827-9, CATM). Greenwood.
Carritt, Edgar F., ed. Philosophies of Beauty, from Socrates to Robert Bridges. LC 76-5885. 334p. 1976. Repr. of 1931 ed. lib. bdg. 60.00 (ISBN 0-8371-8812-1, CAPB). Greenwood.
Carrodeguas, Andy, ed. see Bennett, Dennis & Bennett, Rita.
Carrol, Freida. Creative Financing for Education, Housing, Automobiles, Vacations, Medical Care Etc. A Bibliography. 60p. 1983. pap. text ed. 5.95 (ISBN 0-939476-58-4, Pub. by Biblio Pr GA). Prosperity & Profits.
--Factory Outlet Directories: A Directory. 50p. 1983. pap. text ed. 2.95 (ISBN 0-939476-91-6, Pub. by Biblio Pr GA). Prosperity & Profits.
--Unemployment Challenge Log Workbook. 60p. 1983. pap. 2.00 (ISBN 0-939476-86-X, Pub. by Biblio Pr GA). Prosperity & Profits.
Carrol, Freida, compiled by. Registering Agents Services for Delaware Incorporators: A Directory. 150p. 1983. pap. text ed. 2.95 (ISBN 0-939476-87-8, Pub. by Biblio Pr GA). Prosperity & Profits.
Carrol, Frieda. Barter Poetry, Bk. 1. 16p. 1984. pap. text ed. 3.00 (ISBN 0-317-04043-X, Pub. by Barter Pub). Prosperity & Profits.
--Boom Businesses U. S. A. 50p. 1983. 3.95 (ISBN 0-939476-75-4, Pub. by Biblio Pr GA). Prosperity & Profits.
--Boom Cities & Towns: U. S. A. Workbook. 50p. 1983. 8.95 (ISBN 0-939476-51-7, Pub. by Biblio Pr GA). Prosperity & Profits.
--Boom Towns U. S. A. LC 81-68664. 50p. 1981. pap. text ed. 2.95 (ISBN 0-939476-31-2, Pub. by Biblio Pr GA). Prosperity & Profits.
--The Consumer Survival Notebook. LC 80-70456. 1980. 3.00 (ISBN 0-939476-02-9, Pub. by Biblio Pr GA); pap. 5.95 (ISBN 0-9605246-2-2). Prosperity & Profits.
--Continuing Education Alternatives. LC 80-68549. 1981. 49.95 (ISBN 0-939476-14-2, Pub. by Biblio Pr GA); pap. 39.95 (ISBN 0-939476-15-0). Prosperity & Profits.
--Continuing Education Alternatives Workbook. 50p. 1983. 4.95 (ISBN 0-939476-85-1, Pub. by Biblio Pr GA). Prosperity & Profits.

--Creative Uses for the Barter Card. 16p. 1983. pap. 4.95 (ISBN 0-911617-56-6, Pub. by Barter Pub). Prosperity & Profits.

--Guide for the Unemployed Cookbook. 20p. 1984. pap. text ed. 2.00 (ISBN 0-317-01654-7, Pub. by Biblio Pr GA). Prosperity & Profits.

--Guide for the Unemployed: Keeping Busy Until... LC 80-70495. 103p. 1981. 9.95 (ISBN 0-939476-01-0, Pub. by Biblio Pr GA); pap. 6.95 (ISBN 0-9605246-5-7). Prosperity & Profits.

--Guide for the Unemployed Workbook. 60p. Date not set. 6.95 (ISBN 0-939476-80-0, Pub. by Biblio Pr GA). Prosperity & Profits.

--How to Get Something for Almost Nothing & More. LC 78-59909. 52p. (Orig.). 1981. pap. text ed. 5.00 (ISBN 0-9605246-0-6, Pub. by Biblio Pr GA). Prosperity & Profits.

--The Joys of Saving & Economizing. LC 80-70794. 1981. 6.95 (ISBN 0-9605246-8-1, Pub. by Biblio Pr GA); pap. 3.95 (ISBN 0-939476-08-8). Prosperity & Profits.

--New & Useful Forms, Stationery & Greetings to Duplicate & Use. 50p. Date not set. pap. text ed. 10.95 (ISBN 0-939476-84-3, Pub. by Biblio Pr GA). Prosperity & Profits.

--People's Money Pages. 1st ed. LC 80-70419. 50p. 1981. 6.95 (ISBN 0-9605246-3-0, Pub. by Biblio Pr GA); pap. 4.95 (ISBN 0-686-96676-7). Prosperity & Profits.

--Pick Your Own Fruits & Vegetables & More: A Reference Guide. LC 80-70861. 1981. 7.95 (ISBN 0-939476-12-6, Pub. by Biblio Pr GA); pap. 4.95 (ISBN 0-939476-11-8); wkbk. 6.95 (ISBN 0-939476-82-7). Prosperity & Profits.

--Prescriptions for Survival. LC 78-72312. 148p. 1981. pap. text ed. 12.95 (ISBN 0-9605246-1-4, Pub. by Biblio Pr GA). Prosperity & Profits.

--Scentouri Potpourri Recipe Book. 15p. 1983. pap. 3.95 (ISBN 0-939476-94-0, Pub. by Biblio Pr GA). Prosperity & Profits.

--Small Business Entrepreneural Services: Suggestions for a Small Business Entrepreneural Service Center. 20p. 1983. pap. text ed. 3.95 (ISBN 0-939476-95-9, Pub. by Biblio Pr GA). Prosperity & Profits.

--Smorgasboard U. S. A. 150p. (Orig.). 1982. pap. text ed. 9.95 (ISBN 0-939476-49-5, Pub. by Biblio Pr GA). Prosperity & Profits.

--Survival Handbook for Small Business. LC 80-70496. 73p. 1981. 16.95 (ISBN 0-9605246-4-9, Pub. by Biblio Pr GA); pap. 12.95 (ISBN 0-686-96677-5); 8.95 (ISBN 0-939476-79-7). Prosperity & Profits.

--The Traveler's Workbook: Based on the People's Travel Book Index. 50p. 1983. 3.95 (ISBN 0-939476-52-5). Biblio Pr GA.

Carrol, Frieda, ed. Continuing Education Alternatives Index. LC 82-70343. 150p. 1982. pap. text ed. 10.95 (ISBN 0-939476-41-X, Pub. by Biblio PR GA). Prosperity & Profits.

Carrol, Frieda, compiled by. Corporation Registering Agents: An International Directory. 300p. 1983. text ed. 15.95 (ISBN 0-913597-02-3, Pub. by Alpha Pyramis); pap. text ed. 9.95. Prosperity & Profits.

--Directory of Barter Directories. LC 83-90673. 100p. 1983. pap. 19.95 (ISBN 0-911617-55-8, Pub. by Barter Pub). Prosperity & Profits.

--International Directory of Barter Associations & Organizations. LC 83-90672. 200p. 1983. pap. 19.95 (ISBN 0-911617-54-X, Pub. by Barter Pub). Prosperity & Profits.

--Meditation & Yoga Retreats: An International Directory. 200p. 1983. text ed. 4.75 (ISBN 0-913597-06-6, Pub. by Alpha Pyramis). Prosperity & Profits.

--The People's Travel Book. LC 80-70869. 115p. 1981. 39.95 (ISBN 0-939476-05-3, Pub. by Biblio PR GA); pap. 29.95 (ISBN 0-939476-06-1). Prosperity & Profits.

Carrol, Frieda, ed. The People's Travel Book Index. LC 82-70342. 58p. 1981. pap. text ed. 12.95 (ISBN 0-939476-42-8, Pub. by Biblio Pr GA). Prosperity & Profits.

Carrol, Frieda, compiled by. Private Postal Boxes, Mail Addresses & Mail Forwarding Services: An International Directory. 250p. 1983. (Pub. by Alpha Pyramis); pap. text ed. 19.95 (ISBN 0-913597-11-2). Prosperity & Profits.

--Thrift Stores: An International Directory. 150p. 1983. text ed. 17.95 (ISBN 0-913597-13-9, Pub. by Alpha Pyramis). Prosperity & Profits.

Carrol, Frieda, ed. U. S. Directory of Business Start Up Fees. LC 83-90726. 1983. text ed. 59.95 50 pg. (ISBN 0-911569-13-8, Pub. by Data Notes); pap. text ed. 29.95 160 pg. (ISBN 0-911569-08-1). Prosperity & Profits.

Carrol, Frieda, compiled by. The Woman's Index. LC 80-70675. 200p. 1981. 11.95 (ISBN 0-939476-04-5, Pub. by Biblio Pr GA); pap. 6.95 (ISBN 0-9605246-6-5). Prosperity & Profits.

Carrol, James. Fault Lines. 1982. pap. 3.50 (ISBN 0-440-12436-0). Dell.

Carrol, Ricki, jt. auth. see Carrol, Robert.

Carrol, Robert & Carrol, Ricki. Cheesemaking Made Easy: Sixty Delicious Varieties. LC 82-9300. (Illus.). 128p. 1982. pap. 6.95 (ISBN 0-88266-267-8). Garden Way Pub.

Carrol, Shana. Live for Love. 352p. (Orig.). 1985. pap. 3.95 (ISBN 0-515-07385-7). Jove Pubns.

--Paxton Pride. 448p. 1984. pap. 3.95 (ISBN 0-515-07884-0). Jove Pubns.

--Raven. 512p. 1983. pap. 3.95 (ISBN 0-515-07883-2). Jove Pubns.

--Rebels in Love. 384p. 1985. pap. 3.95 (ISBN 0-515-08249-X). Jove Pubns.

--Yellow Rose. 416p. 1985. pap. 3.95 (ISBN 0-515-07885-9). Jove Pubns.

Carroll. Controlling White Collar Crime: White & Audit for Systems Security. 193p. 1982. text ed. 21.95 (ISBN 0-409-95065-3). Butterworth.

--Learning God's Word, 3 bks. 1971. Bk. 1. pap. 1.75 (ISBN 0-87148-502-8); Bk. 2. pap. 1.35 (ISBN 0-87148-503-6); Bk. 3. pap. 1.35 (ISBN 0-87148-504-4). Pathway Pr.

--Thirty-Two Super Salads. (Illus.). 64p. 1983. 4.95 (ISBN 0-8120-5529-2). Barron.

Carroll, jt. auth. see Wicklow.

Carroll, Alan. Pirate Subdivisions & the Market for Residential Lots in Bogota. (Working Paper: No. 435). 116p. 1980. 5.00 (ISBN 0-686-36229-2, WP-0435). World Bank.

Carroll, Albert. Crosswords for the Connoisseur Omnibus: A New Jumbo Collection. (Orig.). 1985. pap. 6.95 (ISBN 0-399-51131-8, Perigee). Putnam Pub Group.

Carroll, Alexander. Women of Early Christianity. 75.00 (ISBN 0-87968-268-X). Gordon Pr.

Carroll, Alice M., abridged by see Morris, Milton D. & Mayio, Albert.

Carroll, Anne K., jt. auth. see Cooper, Darien B.

Carroll, Anne Kristin. Together Forever: For Healthy Marriages, or for Strained, or Broken Ones. 256p. (Orig.). 1982. pap. 7.95 (ISBN 0-310-45021-7). Zondervan.

Carroll, Archie B. Business & Society: Managing Corporate Social Performance. text ed. 21.95 (ISBN 0-316-13010-9); tchr's. manual avail. (ISBN 0-316-13011-7). Little.

Carroll, Archie B., jt. auth. see Huseman, Richard C.

Carroll, Archie B., jt. auth. see Watson, Hugh H.

Carroll, Archie B., jt. auth. see Watson, Hugh J.

Carroll, Archie B., ed. Managing Corporate Social Responsibility. pap. text ed. 13.95 (ISBN 0-316-13008-7). Little.

Carroll, B. H., et al. Introduction to Photographic Theory: The Silver Halide Process. LC 79-26802. 355p. 1980. 45.95X (ISBN 0-471-02562-3, Pub. by Wiley Interscience). Wiley.

Carroll, B. J. General English Tests Advanced One Pack. (Illus.). 8p. 1982. pap. 100.00 (ISBN 0-08-029431-6). Pergamon.

--General English Tests Elementary One Pack. (Illus.). 8p. 1982. pap. 100.00 (ISBN 0-08-029432-4). Pergamon.

--General English Tests Instruction Booklet. (Illus.). 14p. 1982. pap. 2.00 (ISBN 0-08-028659-3). Pergamon.

--General Tests Instruction Booklet. 2nd ed. (Pergamon Oxford English Tests Ser.). 1984. pap. 2.00 (ISBN 0-08-031533-X). Pergamon.

--Specific Test in English for Everyday International Use: SEVI One. 40p. 1983. Complete Kit. 45.00 (ISBN 0-08-030340-4); Instr's. manual & marking card. 2.70 (ISBN 0-08-030338-2); Twenty magazine booklets. 27.00 (ISBN 0-08-030337-4); Twenty answer booklets. 18.00 (ISBN 0-08-030336-6); Cassette. 10.60 (ISBN 0-08-030339-0). Pergamon.

Carroll, Bartholomew R., compiled by. & intro. by. Historical Collections of South Carolina: Embracing Many Rare & Valuable Pamphlets, & Other Documents, Relating to the History of That State, from Its First Discovery to Its Independence in the Year 1776, 2 vols. LC 72-14376. Repr. of 1836 ed. Set. 105.00 (ISBN 0-404-11056-8). AMS Pr.

Carroll, Berenice A. Design for Total War: Arms & Economics in the Third Reich. LC 68-15527. (Studies in European History: Vol. 17). 1968. text ed. 32.00x (ISBN 90-2790-299-2). Mouton.

Carroll, Berenice A., ed. Liberating Women's History: Theoretical & Critical Essays. LC 74-45451. 448p. 1976. 24.95x (ISBN 0-252-00441-8); pap. 10.00x (ISBN 0-252-00569-4). U of Ill Pr.

Carroll, Berenice A., et al. Peace & War: A Guide to Bibliographies. LC 81-4980. (War-Peace Bibliography Ser.: No.16). 488p. 1983. lib. bdg. 42.50 (ISBN 0-87436-322-5). ABC-Clio.

Carroll, Betty De, ed. see Petter, Hugo M.

Carroll, Bill. Auto Mechanics Basic Engineering Guide. LC 70-102903. (Performance Engineering Handbooks Ser.). (Illus.). 228p. 1974. pap. 9.95 (ISBN 0-910390-19-3). Auto Bk.

--Ford V8 Performance Guide. (Performance Engineering Handbooks). (Illus., Orig.). (YA) (gr. 7 up). 1972. 7.95 (ISBN 0-910390-17-7). Auto Bk.

--Honda Civic Guide. LC 74-75225. (Performance Engineering Handbooks Ser.). (Illus.). 214p. 1975. pap. 9.95 (ISBN 0-910390-21-5). Auto Bk.

Carroll, Bonnie. Job Satisfaction. rev. ed. (Key Issues Ser.: No. 3). 60p. 1973. pap. 2.00 (ISBN 0-87546-206-5). ILR Pr.

Carroll, C. Jean. Female Difficulties. 208p. (Orig.). 1985. 10.95 (ISBN 0-553-05088-5). Bantam.

Carroll, Carroll. Carroll's First Book of Proverbs or Life Is a Fortune Cookie. (Illus.). 80p. 1981. pap. 4.95 (ISBN 0-87786-004-1). Gold Penny.

Carroll, Charles. Journal of Charles Carroll of Carrollton During His Visit to Canada in 1776, As One of the Commissioners from Congress. Mayer, Brantz & Decker, Peter, eds. LC 70-76557. (Eyewitness Accounts of the American Revolution Ser., No. 2). (Illus.). 1969. Repr. of 1876 ed. 11.50 (ISBN 0-405-01147-4). Ayer Co Pubs.

--Negro a Beast. facs. ed. LC 74-89419. (Black Heritage Library Collection Ser). 1900. 18.75 (ISBN 0-8369-8533-8). Ayer Co Pubs.

Carroll, Charles & Miller, Dean. Health: The Science of Human Adaptation. 3rd ed. 720p. 1982. pap. text ed. write for info. (ISBN 0-697-07393-9); instructor's manual avail. (ISBN 0-697-07394-7); transparencies avail. (ISBN 0-697-07395-5). Wm C Brown.

Carroll, Charles F. The Timber Economy of Puritan New England. LC 73-7122. (Illus.). 235p. 1973. pap. 18.00x (ISBN 0-87057-142-7). U Pr of New Eng.

Carroll, Charles H. Organization of Debt into Currency: & Other Papers. Simmons, Edward C., ed. LC 70-172207. (Right Wing Individualist Tradition in America Ser). 1972. Repr. of 1964 ed. 30.00 (ISBN 0-405-00418-4). Ayer Co Pubs.

Carroll, Charles J. Eighty Practical Time-Saving Programs for the TRS-80. (Illus.). 252p. o.p 15.95 (ISBN 0-8306-0010-8, 1293); pap. 11.50 (ISBN 0-8306-1293-9, 1293). TAB Bks.

Carroll, Charles R. Alcohol: Use, Nonuse, & Abuse. 2nd ed. (Contemporary Topics in Health Science Ser.). 94p. 1975. pap. text ed. write for info. (ISBN 0-697-07345-9). Wm C Brown.

--Drugs in Modern Society. 448p. 1985. pap. write for info. (ISBN 0-697-00139-3); instr's. manual avail. (ISBN 0-697-00558-5). Wm C Brown.

Carroll, D. Living with Dying: A Loving Guide for Family & Close Friends. 400p. 1985. 17.95 (ISBN 0-07-010098-5). McGraw.

Carroll, D., jt. auth. see Baxter, R. R.

Carroll, D., jt. ed. see O'Callaghan, A. J.

Carroll, D. Allen & Williams, Gary Jay. A Midsummer Night's Dream. LC 83-48272. 300p. 1985. lib. bdg. 40.00 (ISBN 0-8240-9073-X). Garland Pub.

Carroll, D. Allen, ed. see Guilpin, Everard.

Carroll, D. M., ed. Euroanalysis III. (Illus.). 429p. 1979. 90.75 (ISBN 0-85334-847-2, Pub. by Elsevier Applied Sci England). Elsevier.

Carroll, Daniel B. Henri Mercier & the American Civil War. LC 77-132235. 1971. 42.00 (ISBN 0-691-04585-2). Princeton U Pr.

Carroll, David. Chinua Achebe. LC 79-57249. 180p. 1980. 16.95x (ISBN 0-312-13386-3). St Martin.

--The Complete Book of Natural Foods. 1985. pap. 8.95 (ISBN 0-671-47517-7). Summit Bks.

--The Complete Book of Natural Medicines. LC 80-11332. (Illus.). 416p. 1980. 17.95 (ISBN 0-671-24418-3); pap. 7.95 (ISBN 0-671-41623-5). Summit Bks.

--The Dictionary of Foreign Terms in the English Language. 1979. pap. 4.95 (ISBN 0-8015-2053-3, Hawthorn). Dutton.

--The Magic Makers. LC 73-91503. 1974. 8.95 (ISBN 0-87795-080-6). Arbor Hse.

--Make Your Own Chess Set. (Illus.). (gr. 5 up). 1975. (Pub. by Treehouse); pap. 2.95 (ISBN 0-13-547786-7). P-H.

--The Matinee Idols. LC 72-184882. (Illus.). 160p. 1972. 10.00 (ISBN 0-87795-031-8, A4320); pap. 4.95 (ISBN 0-87795-060-1, A4320P). Arbor Hse.

--The Subject in Question: The Languages of Theory & the Strategies of Fiction. LC 82-1995. 240p. (Orig.). 1982. lib. bdg. 26.00x (ISBN 0-226-09493-6); pap. 9.00x (ISBN 0-226-09494-4). U of Chicago Pr.

--Telecommunications for the IBM PCjr. 224p. 1984. pap. 15.95 (ISBN 0-13-902503-0). P-H.

Carroll, David & Saxe, Barry. Natural Magic. LC 75-31073. 1977. 9.95 (ISBN 0-87795-143-8); pap. 4.95 (ISBN 0-87795-152-7). Arbor Hse.

Carroll, David, jt. auth. see Simenauer, Jacqueline.

Carroll, David W. Multiplan for Your Commodore 64. LC 84-22352. 200p. 1985. pap. 14.95 (ISBN 0-13-605130-8). P H.

--Ohio Administrative Law. (Baldwin's Ohio Handbook Ser.). 1985. write for info. (ISBN 0-8322-0069-7). Banks-Baldwin.

--Psychology of Language. (Psychology Ser.). 500p. 1985. text ed. 22.50 (pub net) (ISBN 0-534-05640-7). Brooks-Cole.

Carroll, Dennis. Australian Contemporary Drama 1909-1982: A Critical Introduction. (American University Studies IV (English Language & Literature): Vol. 25). 271p. 1985. text ed. 31.20 (ISBN 0-318-04578-8). P Lang Pubs.

Carroll, Dennis, ed. Kumu Kahua Plays. LC 82-23724. 270p. (Orig.). 1983. pap. text ed. 10.95x (ISBN 0-8248-0805-3). UH Pr.

Carroll, Dewey E., ed. see Clinic on Library Applications of Data Processing, 1968.

Carroll, Dewey E., ed. see Clinic on Library Applications of Data Processing, 1969.

Carroll, Diahann & Firestone, Ross. Diahann. 1985. 16.95 (ISBN 0-316-13019-2). Little.

Carroll, Don & Carroll, Marie. Focus on Special Effects: Locating Pictures That Exist Only in Your Mind. (Illus.). 184p. 1982. 24.95 (ISBN 0-8174-3885-8, Amphoto). Watson-Guptill.

Carroll, Donald. The Best Excuse. 176p. 1983. 14.95 (ISBN 0-698-11219-9, Coward). Putnam Pub Group.

--Why Didn't I Say That? 1982. pap. 2.25 (ISBN 0-671-44582-0). PB.

Carroll, Donald, ed. New Poets of Ireland. LC 76-56145. 1977. Repr. of 1963 ed. lib. bdg. 18.75 (ISBN 0-8371-9424-5, CANPI). Greenwood.

Carroll, Donald C. see Sheppard, C. Stewart.

Carroll, Dorothy. Rock Weathering. LC 77-107534. 203p. 1970. 35.00x (ISBN 0-306-30434-1, Plenum Pr). Plenum Pub.

Carroll, Douglas. Biofeedback in Practice. LC 83-9399. (Applied Psychology Ser.). 160p. (Orig.). 1984. pap. text ed. 9.95 (ISBN 0-582-29616-1). Longman.

Carroll, Douglas, jt. auth. see Green, Paul E.

Carroll, E. Jean. Female Difficulties: Sorority Sisters, Rodeo Queens, Frigid Women, Smut Stars & Other Modern Girls. LC 84-91732. 1985. 10.95 (ISBN 0-553-05088-5). Bantam.

Carroll, E. Malcolm. French Public Opinion & Foreign Affairs, 1870-1914. viii, 348p. 1964. Repr. of 1931 ed. 23.50 (ISBN 0-208-00414-9, Archon). Shoe String.

--Germany & the Great Powers, 1866-1914: A Study in Public Opinion & Foreign Policy. 852p. 1975. Repr. of 1938 ed. lib. bdg. 54.50x (ISBN 0-374-91299-8). Octagon.

Carroll, Eber M. Origins of the Whig Party. 12.75 (ISBN 0-8446-1104-2). Peter Smith.

Carroll, Elizabeth. Summer Love, No. 1. (Dream your own Romance Ser.). 128p. (gr. 3-7). 1983. pap. 2.95 (ISBN 0-671-46449-3). Wanderer Bks.

Carroll, Eudora. San Francisco Nights. (Orig.). 1983. pap. 1.95 (ISBN 0-87067-169-3, BH169). Holloway.

Carroll, Eugene A. The Drawings of Rosso Fiorentino, 2 vols. LC 75-23786. (Outstanding Dissertations in the Fine Arts - 16th Century). (Illus.). 1976. Set. lib. bdg. 146.00 (ISBN 0-8240-1982-2). Garland Pub.

Carroll, Faye. South West Africa & the United Nations. LC 75-3984. 123p. 1975. Repr. of 1967 ed. lib. bdg. 22.50 (ISBN 0-8371-7441-4, CASWA). Greenwood.

Carroll, Frances. A Book of Devotions for Today's Woman. 192p. 1983. 14.95 (ISBN 0-13-080036-8); pap. 5.95 (ISBN 0-13-080028-7). P-H.

--How to Talk with Your Children about God. 1985. pap. 6.95 (ISBN 0-317-18129-7). P-H.

Carroll, Frances, tr. see Szechter, Szymon.

Carroll, Frances L. The Christian's Diary: A Personal Journal for Bible Study, Prayer & Spiritual Growth. 304p. 1984. 15.95 (ISBN 0-13-133801-3); pap. 9.95 (ISBN 0-13-133793-9). P-H.

--Frustration: How Christians Can Deal with It. 156p. 1984. 12.95 (ISBN 0-13-330812-X); pap. 6.95 (ISBN 0-13-330804-9). P-H.

--Promises: A Guide to Christian Commitment. 228p. 1985. 14.95 (ISBN 0-13-731076-5); pap. 7.95 (ISBN 0-13-731068-4). P H.

--Recent Advances in School Librarianship. (Recent Advances in Library & Information Science Ser.). (Illus.). 250p. 1981. 33.00 (ISBN 0-08-026084-5). Pergamon.

--Temptation: How Christians Can Deal with It. 192p. 1984. 13.95 (ISBN 0-13-903229-0); pap. 5.95 (ISBN 0-13-903211-8). P-H.

Carroll, Frances L. & Meacham, Mary, eds. Exciting, Funny, Scary, Short, Different, & Sad Books Kids Like about Animals, Science, Sports, Families, Songs & Other Things. LC 84-20469. 168p. 1985. pap. text ed. 10.00x (ISBN 0-8389-0423-8). ALA.

Carroll, Frances Laverne & Beilke, Patricia F. Guidelines for the Planning & Organization of School Library Media Centres. Rev. ed. 52p. 1982. pap. 9.50 (ISBN 0-686-95502-1, UPB116, UNESCO). Unipub.

Carroll, Francis Laverne & Meacham, Mary, eds. Exciting, Funny, Scary, Short, Different, & Sad Books Kids Like about Animals, Science, Sports, Families, Songs, & Other Things. 168p. 1984. 10.00 (ISBN 0-317-36982-2). ALA.

Carroll, Francis M. American Opinion & the Irish Question: 1910-1923. LC 78-58897. 1978. 26.00x (ISBN 0-312-02890-3). St Martin.

Carroll, Frank L. Brief Bible Studies for Busy People. 144p. 1985. 13.95 (ISBN 0-13-081993-X); pap. 6.95 (ISBN 0-13-081985-9). P-H.

Carroll, Gerry. Creation, Christ & Credibility: How & Why Mankind Has Failed to Discredit the Bible. LC 83-72663. (Illus.). 204p. (Orig.). 1983. pap. 5.95 (ISBN 0-914569-01-5). Creat Pubns B P C M.

Carroll, Glenn & Vogel, David, eds. Strategy & Organization: A West Coast Perspective. 193p. 1984. text ed. 15.95 (ISBN 0-273-02186-9). Pitman Pub Ma.

Carroll, H. Bailey & Haggard, J. Villasana, eds. Three New Mexico Chronicles. Incl. Exposicion. Pino, Pedro B; Ojeada. Barreiro, Antonio; Addition. De Escudero, Jose A. LC 67-24722. (Quivira Society Publications Ser). 342p. 1967. Repr. of 1942 ed. 17.00 (ISBN 0-405-00085-5). Ayer Co Pubs.

Carroll, H. Bailey, jt. ed. see Webb, Walter P.

Carroll, Harry. OS Data Processing with Review of OS-VS. LC 74-2047. pap. 56.70 (ISBN 0-317-09196-4, 2013881). Bks Demand UMI.

Carroll, Harry J. The Art of Greece & Rome. (Illus.). 12p. 1972. 1.00 (ISBN 0-915478-30-7). Galleries Coll.

Carroll, Harry J., Jr., et al. The Development of Civilization: A Documentary History of Politics, Society & Thought, 2 vols. 2nd. ed. 1969. pap. 13.65x ea.; Vol. 1. (ISBN 0-673-05784-4); Vol.2. (ISBN 0-673-05785-2). Scott F.

Carroll, Henry K. Report on the Island of Porto Rico. LC 74-14223. (The Puerto Rican Experience Ser). (Illus.). 817p. 1975. Repr. 59.50x (ISBN 0-405-06213-3). Ayer Co Pubs.

Carroll, Herbert A. Generalization of Bright & Dull Children: A Comparative Study with Special Reference to Spelling. LC 78-176629. (Columbia University. Teachers College. Contributions to Education: No. 439). Repr. of 1930 ed. 22.50 (ISBN 0-404-55439-3). AMS Pr.

--Mental Hygiene: Dynamics of Adjustment. 5th ed. 1969. text ed. 26.95x O.P. (ISBN 0-13-576314-2). P-H.

Carroll, Holbert N. The House of Representatives & Foreign Affairs. LC 84-6718. vii, 366p. 1984. Repr. of 1958 ed. lib. bdg. 41.00x (ISBN 0-313-24523-1, CAHR). Greenwood.

Carroll, Howard. Twelve Americans: Their Lives & Times. facsimile ed. LC 70-37154. (Essay Index Reprint Ser.). Repr. of 1883 ed. 30.00 (ISBN 0-8369-2489-4). Ayer Co Pubs.

Carroll, Hugh J. & Oh, Man S. Water Electrolyte & Acid-Base Metabolism: Diagnosis & Management. LC 78-15563. 1978. 30.75 (ISBN 0-397-50394-6, 65-00649, Lippincott Medical). Lippincott.

Carroll, J. B. & Freedle, R. O., eds. Language Comprehension & the Acquisition of Knowledge. LC 72-6708. Repr. of 1972 ed. 99.00 (ISBN 0-8357-9147-5, 2050706). Bks Demand UMI.

Carroll, J. Frank. Meeting Singles: Where French Is Spoken. LC 85-50429. (Illus.). 60p. (Orig.). 1985. pap. 6.95 (ISBN 0-933571-00-3). Ure Pr.

Carroll, Jackson & Wilson, Robert. Too Many Pastors? the State of the Clergy Job Market. LC 80-16037. 1980. pap. 6.95 (ISBN 0-8298-0405-6). Pilgrim NY.

Carroll, Jackson W. & Hargrove, Barbara J. Women of the Cloth: New Opportunity for the Churches. LC 82-47740. 288p. 1983. 14.37i (ISBN 0-06-061321-1, HarpR). Har-Row.

Carroll, James. Eleven Hundred Powerful Words. 107p. 1982. pap. 2.95 (ISBN 0-89826-008-6). Natl Paperback.

--Family Trade. 1982. 14.95 (ISBN 0-316-13013-3). Little.

--Family Trade. (General Ser.). 1983. lib. bdg. 18.95 (ISBN 0-8161-3483-9, Large Print Bks). G K Hall.

--Family Trade. 1983. pap. 3.95 (ISBN 0-451-12325-5, Sig). NAL.

--Fault Lines. 288p. 1980. 11.95 (ISBN 0-316-13012-5). Little.

--Madonna Red. 1976. 7.95 (ISBN 0-316-13007-9). Little.

--Mortal Friends. 1981. pap. 4.95 (ISBN 0-440-15790-0). Dell.

--Nature's Basic Law of Economics. 92p. 1982. pap. 2.95 (ISBN 0-89826-009-4). Natl Paperback.

--Prince of Peace. 512p. 1984. 17.45i (ISBN 0-316-13014-1). Little.

--Prince of Peace. 1985. pap. 4.95 (ISBN 0-451-13847-3, Sig). NAL.

--Utopia Now. 160p. 1977. pap. 1.95 (ISBN 0-89826-001-9). Natl Paperback.

--Wonder & Worship. LC 70-133469. 168p. 1970. pap. 1.95 (ISBN 0-8091-1871-8). Paulist Pr.

Carroll, James & Overton, Barbara. Be Sure Your Child Learns to Read. 160p. 1976. pap. 1.95 (ISBN 0-89826-000-0). Natl Paperback.

Carroll, James D. & Zuck, Alfred M., eds. The Study of Administration Revisited: A Report on the Centennial Agendas Project of the American Society for Public Administration. 1983. 5.00 (ISBN 0-936678-07-0). Am Soc Pub Admin.

Carroll, James D., jt. ed. see Smith, Bruce L.

Carroll, James J., ed. see Hartmann, Frederick H.

Carroll, James J., ed. see Phillips, James, et al.

Carroll, James L., ed. Contemporary School Psychology: Readings from Psychology in the Schools. 2nd ed. 1981. pap. text ed. 12.95 (ISBN 0-88422-014-1). Clinical Psych.

Carroll, James M. The Problem with Public Education Is Administrative. 70p. 1984. pap. 3.95 (ISBN 0-89826-012-4). Natl Paperback.

--Three Steps to Success. 86p. (Orig.). 1984. pap. 4.95 (ISBN 0-89826-011-6). Natl Paperback.

Carroll, Janet F., jt. auth. see Wolfart, H. Christoph.

Carroll, Jay, jt. auth. see Hardy, Gordon.

Carroll, Jean & Lofthouse, Peter. Creative Dance for Boys. (Illus.). 1979. Repr. of 1969 ed. 12.50 (ISBN 0-7121-0318-X). Dufour.

Carroll, Jean G. Patient Care Audit Criteria: Standards for Hospital Quality Assurance. LC 82-73622. 250p. 1983. 55.00 (ISBN 0-87094-392-8). Dow Jones-Irwin.

--Restructuring Hospital Quality Assurance: The New Guide for Health Care Providers. LC 84-71132. 225p. 1984. 19.95 (ISBN 0-87094-541-6). Dow Jones-Irwin.

Carroll, Jeffrey. Climbing to the Sun. LC 77-8617. 128p. (gr. 6 up). 1977. 6.95 (ISBN 0-395-28898-3, Clarion). HM.

Carroll, Jeri. Learning Centers for Little Kids. (Illus.). 64p. (ps-2). 1983. wkbk. 5.95 (ISBN 0-86653-103-3, GA 458). Good Apple.

Carroll, Jerry. A Pilgrimage to St. Jean. 1978. pap. 1.50 (ISBN 0-532-15364-2). Woodhill.

Carroll, Jim. Living at the Movies. 100p. 1981. pap. 4.95 (ISBN 0-14-042290-0). Penguin.

Carroll, Joellyn. A Flight of Splendor. (Candlelight Ecstasy Ser.: No. 159). (Orig.). 1983. pap. 1.95 (ISBN 0-440-12858-7). Dell.

--Run Before the Wind. (Candlelight Ecstasy Ser.: No. 131). (Orig.). 1983. pap. 1.95 (ISBN 0-440-17880-0). Dell.

Carroll, John. Guilt: The Grey Eminence behind Character, History & Culture. 288p. 1985. 36.00x (ISBN 0-7102-0357-8). Routledge & Kegan.

--How to Handicap the Claiming Races Professionally. 1983. 10.00 (ISBN 0-533-05233-5). Vantage.

--Intruders in the Bush: The Australian Quest for Identity. 1982. pap. 13.95x (ISBN 0-19-554308-4). Oxford U Pr.

--Learning to Fly Radio Control Model Airplanes. Hayden, Bob, ed. (Illus.). 88p. (Orig.). 1985. pap. 9.95 (ISBN 0-89024-070-1). Kalmbach.

--Sceptical Sociology. 256p. 1980. 26.00x (ISBN 0-7100-0587-3). Routledge & Kegan.

Carroll, John, ed. Computer Simulation in Emergency Planning. (Simulation Series: Vol. 11, No. 2). 1983. 30.00 (ISBN 0-686-38791-0). Soc Computer Sim.

--Samuel Richardson: A Collection of Critical Essays. LC 69-17372. (Twentieth Century Views Ser). 1969. 12.95t (ISBN 0-13-791160-2, Spec); (Spec). P-H.

Carroll, John A. & Ashworth, Mary W. George Washington: A Biography First In Peace, Vol. 7. LC 75-4504. (Illus.). xxiv, 729p. 1981. Repr. of 1957 ed. lib. bdg. 37.50x (ISBN 0-678-02833-8). Kelley.

Carroll, John A. & Faulk, Odie B. Home of the Brave: A Patriot's Guide to American History. (Illus.). 416p. 1984. pap. text ed. 16.75 (ISBN 0-8191-3628-X). U Pr of Amer.

Carroll, John A. see Freeman, Douglas S.

Carroll, John B., ed. Language, Thought & Reality: Selected Writings of Benjamin Lee Whorf. 1956. pap. 7.95x (ISBN 0-262-73006-5). MIT Pr.

Carroll, John B. & Chall, Jeanne, eds. Toward a Literate Society: A Report from the National Academy of Education. 352p. 1975. 24.95 (ISBN 0-07-010130-2). McGraw.

Carroll, John B., jt. ed. see Anderson, Lorin W.

Carroll, John C., jt. auth. see Leech, Harper.

Carroll, John E. Acid Rain: An Issue in Canadian-American Relations. LC 82-82205. (Canadian-American Committee). 98p. (Orig.). 1982. pap. 6.00 (ISBN 0-89068-064-7). Natl Planning.

--Environmental Diplomacy: An Examination & a Perspective of Canadian-U. S. Transboundary Environmental Relations. 402p. 1983. 22.50 (ISBN 0-472-10029-7). U of Mich Pr.

Carroll, John E. & Logan, Roderick M. The Garrison Diversion Unit: A Case Study in Canadian-U.S. Environmental Relations. (Canadian-U. S. Prospect Ser.). 60p. 1980. 5.00 (ISBN 0-88806-070-X). Natl Planning.

--The Garrison Diversion Unit: A Case Study in Canadian-U.S. Environmental Relations. (Canada-U.S. Prospects: No. 7). 56p. 1980. 5.00 (ISBN 0-88806-070-X). Inst C D Howe.

Carroll, John E., jt. auth. see Curtis, Kenneth M.

Carroll, John, Jr. Solutions for the Major Problems That Face America Today & Beyond. 1984. 7.50 (ISBN 0-533-05414-1). Vantage.

Carroll, John L. & Ignatius, Keith L. Youth Ministry: Sunday, Monday, & Every Day. LC 72-3236. 64p. (Orig.). 1972. pap. 3.95 (ISBN 0-8170-0577-3). Judson.

Carroll, John M. Cavalry Scraps: The Writings of Frederick Benteen. 1985. 149.00 (ISBN 0-317-28083-X, Pub. by J M C & Co). Amereon Ltd.

--Computer Security. LC 77-10615. (Illus.). 400p. 1977. 27.50 (ISBN 0-913708-28-3). Butterworth.

--Confidential Information Sources: Public & Private. LC 74-20177. (Illus.). 320p. 1975. 27.50 (ISBN 0-913708-19-4). Butterworth.

--Data Base & Computer Systems Security. Curtice, Robert M., ed. (Data Base Monograph: No. 4). 1976. pap. 15.00 (ISBN 0-89435-002-1). QED Info Sci.

--List of Field Officers of the Confederate Army. 22.95 (ISBN 0-317-28544-0, Pub. by J M C & Co). Amereon Ltd.

--List of Staff Officers of the Confederate Army. 22.95 (ISBN 0-317-28545-9, Pub. by J M C & Co). Amereon Ltd.

--Managing Risk. 288p. 1984. text ed. 19.95 (ISBN 0-409-95109-9). Butterworth.

--The Medal of Honor: History & Recipients for the Indian Wars. 1985. pap. 15.00 (ISBN 0-317-28081-3, Pub. by J M C & Co). Amereon Ltd.

--Register of Naval Officers of the Confederate Navy. 22.95 (ISBN 0-317-28547-5, Pub. by J M C & Co). Amereon Ltd.

--Roster of General Officers of the Confederate Service During the Civil War. 22.95 (ISBN 0-317-28542-4, Pub. by J M C & Co). Amereon Ltd.

--The Seventh Cavalry's Own Colonel Tommy Tompkins: A Military Heritage & Tradition. (Illus.). 39.95 (ISBN 0-8488-0013-3, Pub. by J M C & Co). Amereon Ltd.

--Toward a Structural Psychology of Cinema. (Approaches to Semiotics Ser.: No. 55). 224p. 1980. 22.40 (ISBN 90-279-3447-9). Mouton.

--What's in a Name? An Essay in the Psychology of Reference. LC 85-6726. (Psychology Ser.). (Illus.). 204p. 1985. text ed. 23.95 (ISBN 0-7167-1687-9). W H Freeman.

Carroll, John M., jt. auth. see Baker, William J.

Carroll, John M., ed. The Benteen-Goldin Letters on Custer & His Last Battle. 1985. pap. 16.95 (ISBN 0-8488-0032-X, Pub. by J M C & Co). Amereon Ltd.

--The Black Military Experience in the American West. 1974. pap. 3.95 (ISBN 0-87140-285-8). Liveright.

--Calvalry Bits: Custer & the Seventh Calvalry, 7 Vols. Incl. Vol. I. The Civil War Custer. Hanson, Joseph M; Vol. II. Custer & the Battle of the Washita. Godfrey, Edward S. (Illus.); Vol. III. Custer & the Yellowstone Expedition of 1873. Braden, Charles. (Illus.); Vol. IV, Pt. 1. The Battle of the Little Big Horn. Graham, W. A. & Godfrey, Edward S. (Illus.); Vol. V, Pt. 2. The Battle of the Little Big Horn. Godfrey, Edward S. & Gram, W. A. (Illus.); Vol. VI. Wounded Knee. Scott, E. D. & Arnold, Frazer. (Illus.); Vol. VII. A Custer Potpourri. McBlain, John F. & Tallmadge, Frank.. 1985. each 29.95 (ISBN 0-317-28167-4, Pub. by J M C & Co). Amereon Ltd.

--Custer in the Civil War. text ed. 29.95 (ISBN 0-89141-049-X, Pub. by J M C & Co); pap. 16.59 (ISBN 0-8488-0025-7). Amereon Ltd.

--General Custer & the Battle of the Little Big Horn: The Federal View. 1985. 25.00 (ISBN 0-8488-0017-6, Pub. by J M C & Co); pap. 10.00 (ISBN 0-8488-0018-4). Amereon Ltd.

--I, Varnum: The Autobiographical Reminiscences of Custer's Chief of Scouts. Including His Testimony at the Reno Court of Inquiry. 1985. pap. 9.95 (ISBN 0-8488-0027-3, Pub. by J M C & Co). Amereon Ltd.

--The Indian Wars Campaign Medal: Its History & Its Recipients. 73p. 1985. pap. 12.50 (ISBN 0-317-28134-8, Pub. by JMC & Co). Amereon Ltd.

--The Papers of the Order of the Indian Wars. (Illus.). 1975. 27.50 (ISBN 0-88342-040-6). Old Army.

Carroll, John M., intro. by. The Sand Creek Massacre: A Documentary History, 1865-1867. 1985. 34.95 (ISBN 0-914074-03-2, Pub. by J M C & Co). Amereon Ltd.

Carroll, John M., ed. The Two Battles of the Little Horn. 1985. pap. 12.95 (ISBN 0-8488-0029-X, Pub. by J M C & Co). Amereon Ltd.

Carroll, John M. & Aldrich, Robert, eds. The Reno Court of Inquiry: Proceedings of a Court of Inquiry in the Case of Major Marcus A. Reno, January 13, 1879, Chicago, Illinois, Concerning His Conduct at the Battle of the Little Big Horn River, June 25-26, 1876. 1985. 125.00 (ISBN 0-317-28326-X, Pub. by J M C & Co); pre-Publication 65.00. Amereon Ltd.

Carroll, John M. & Horn, W. Donald, eds. The Custer Genealogies. 1985. 19.95 (ISBN 0-317-28078-3, Pub. by J M C & Co). Amereon Ltd.

Carroll, John M., ed. see Anders, Frank L.

Carroll, John M., jt. ed. see Asay, Karol.

Carroll, John M., jt. ed. see Bever, Thomas.

Carroll, John M., ed. see Carter, Robert G.

Carroll, John M., ed. see Remsburg, John E. & Remsburg, George J.

Carroll, John M., ed. see Thian, Raphael P.

Carroll, John R. Physical & Technical Aspects of Fire & Arson Investigation. (Illus.). 470p. 1983. 44.50x (ISBN 0-398-03785-X). C C Thomas.

Carroll, John S. In Patria: An Exposition of Dante's Paradiso. 1973. Repr. of 1911 ed. 14.00 (ISBN 0-8274-1191-X). R West.

--Prisoners of Hope. LC 70-118407. 1971. Repr. of 1906 ed. 36.50x (ISBN 0-8046-1184-X, Pub. by Kennikat). Assoc Faculty Pr.

Carroll, John S. & Payne, John W. Cognition & Social Behavior. LC 76-48939. 290p. 1976. text ed. 29.95x (ISBN 0-89859-111-2). L Erlbaum Assocs.

Carroll, Johnathan. Voice of Our Shadow. pap. 2.75 (ISBN 0-441-86584-4, Pub. by Ace Science Fiction). Ace Bks.

Carroll, Jonathan. The Land of Laughs. 252p. 1980. 10.95 (ISBN 0-670-41755-6). Viking.

--The Land of Laughs. 256p. 1983. pap. 2.50 (ISBN 0-441-46987-6). Ace Bks.

--The Voice of Our Shadow. LC 82-70560. 168p. 1983. 13.50 (ISBN 0-670-49240-X). Viking.

Carroll, Joseph. The Cultural Theory of Matthew Arnold. LC 81-23996. 296p. 1982. 23.50x (ISBN 0-520-04616-1). U of Cal Pr.

Carroll, Joseph C. Slave Insurrections in the United States, 1800-1865. LC 68-55874. Repr. of 1938 ed. cancelled (ISBN 0-8371-0341-X). Greenwood.

Carroll, K. K., ed. Lipids & Tumors. (Progress in Biochemical Pharmacology: Vol. 10). (Illus.). 300p. 1974. 63.00 (ISBN 3-8055-1708-4). S Karger.

Carroll, Karen J., ed. A Baby Is a Special Blessing. (Illus.). 32p. 1984. pap. 4.95 (ISBN 0-8378-2039-1). Gibson.

Carroll, Kay. The Ewoks Save the Day. LC 83-60330. (Return of the Jedi Ser.). (Illus.). 12p. (gr. 1-3). 1983. 2.95 (ISBN 0-394-86118-3). Random.

--Han Solo's Rescue. LC 83-60329. (Return of the Jedi Ser.). (Illus.). 12p. (gr. 1-3). 1983. 2.95 (ISBN 0-394-86112-4). Random.

Carroll, Kenneth. Quakerism on the Eastern Shore. LC 70-112986. (Illus.). 328p. 1970. 15.00x (ISBN 0-938420-15-1). Md Hist.

Carroll, Kent, ed. see Rechy, John.

Carroll, L. Alice's Adventures in Wonderland. (Illus.). 285p. (gr. 4 up). 1969. pap. 7.95 (ISBN 0-312-01821-5, Papermac). St Martin.

Carroll, L. Patrick & Dyckman, Katharine M. Inviting the Mystic, Supporting the Prophet: An Introduction to Spiritual Direction. LC 81-80053. 112p. (Orig.). 1981. pap. 4.95 (ISBN 0-8091-2378-9). Paulist Pr.

Carroll, L. Patrick, jt. auth. see Dyckman, Katherine M.

Carroll, Lewis. Alice au pays de merveilles. (Fr.). (gr. 3-8). 5.50 (ISBN 0-685-28445-X). French & Eur.

--The Alice Birthday Book. (Illus.). 144p. (gr. 2 up). 1984. bds. 3.95 (ISBN 0-517-55457-7). Crown.

--Alice in Wonderland. (Illus.). 160p. (gr. 4 up). 1979. pap. 1.25 (ISBN 0-448-17048-5, Pub. by Tempo). Ace Bks.

--Alice in Wonderland. 215p. 1981. Repr. PLB 15.95x (ISBN 0-89966-345-1). Buccaneer Bks.

--Alice in Wonderland. 299p. 1981. Repr. PLB 12.95x (ISBN 0-89967-019-9). Harmony Raine.

--Alice in Wonderland. Gray, Donald J., ed. (Critical Editions Ser). (Illus.). 1971. 10.00 (ISBN 0-393-04343-6); pap. 6.95x (ISBN 0-393-09977-6). Norton.

--Alice in Wonderland. (Illus.). 108p. 1973. (C N Potter Bks); pap. 3.95 (ISBN 0-517-50858-3, C N Potter). Crown.

--Alice in Wonderland. (Illus.). (gr. 4-6). 1972. pap. 1.95 (ISBN 0-590-08503-4). Scholastic Inc.

--Alice in Wonderland. LC 84-60958. (Classics Ser.). (Illus.). 162p. (gr. 2 up). 1984. Repr. of 1940 ed. 12.95 (ISBN 0-88088-902-0, 889020). Peter Pauper.

--Alice in Wonderland. (Illus.). 160p. (ps up). 1985. pap. 2.25 (ISBN 0-590-33960-5). Scholastic Inc.

--Alice in Wonderland & Alice Through the Looking Glass. LC 81-16048. (Illus.). 256p. 1982. 14.79 (ISBN 0-671-45649-0). Messner.

--Alice in Wonderland & Other Favorites. 288p. 1983. pap. 2.95 (ISBN 0-671-46688-7). WSP.

--Alice in Wonderland & Through the Looking Glass. (Illus.). (gr. 4-6). 1946-63. 10.95 (ISBN 0-448-06004-3, G&D). Putnam Pub Group.

--The Alice in Wonderland Pop-up. LC 80-7615. (Illus.). 12p. (gr. k-4). 1980. 7.95 (ISBN 0-385-28038-6). Delacorte.

--Alice in Wonderland: Through the Looking Glass. (Classics Ser.). 346p. (gr. 2 up). 1984. Repr. of 1940 ed. Boxed Set. 25.00 (ISBN 0-88088-903-9, 889039). Peter Pauper.

--Alice in Wonderland-Through the Looking Glass. LC 62-293. (Illus.). 315p. (gr. 4-6). 1963. pap. 1.95x (ISBN 0-02-042350-0). Macmillan.

--Alice Through the Looking Glass & What Alice Found There. (Illus.). 144p. 1973. (C N Potter); pap. 3.95 (ISBN 0-517-50858-3, C N Potter Bks). Crown.

--Alice's Abenteuer im Wunderland. Zimmermann, Antonie, tr. from Ger. (Illus.). 178p. 1974. Repr. of 1869 ed. 4.00 (ISBN 0-486-20668-8). Dover.

--Alice's Adventures in Wonderland. Bd. with Through the Looking Glass. (Classics Ser.). (gr. 5 up). pap. 1.75 (ISBN 0-8049-0079-5, CL-79). Airmont.

--Alice's Adventures in Wonderland. Bd. with Through the Looking Glass. (Reader's Request). 1980. PLB 10.95 (ISBN 0-8161-3070-1, Large Print Bks). G K Hall.

--Alice's Adventures in Wonderland. Bd. with Through the Looking Glass. (gr. 1-8). 1962. pap. 1.95 (ISBN 0-02-042350-0, Collier). Macmillan.

--Alice's Adventures in Wonderland. Bd. with Through the Looking Glass. 1950. pap. 2.25 (ISBN 0-14-030169-0, Puffin). Penguin.

--Alice's Adventures in Wonderland. Bd. with Through the Looking Glass: And What Alice Found There; The Hunting of the Snark: An Agony in Eight Fits. LC 77-17651. (Illus.). 1978. pap. 5.95 (ISBN 0-8052-0594-2). Schocken.

--Alice's Adventures in Wonderland. (Bambi Classics Ser.). (Illus.). 256p. (Orig.). 1981. pap. 3.95 (ISBN 0-89531-059-7, 0221-48). Sharon Pubns.

--Alice's Adventures in Wonderland, No. I. Pennyroyal ed. (Illus.). 148p. 1982. 24.95 (ISBN 0-520-04815-6); deluxe ed. 195.00 (ISBN 0-520-04820-2). U of Cal Pr.

--Alice's Adventures in Wonderland. Bd. with Through the Looking Glass. (Bantam Classics Ser.). (Illus.). 256p. (gr. 6-12). 1981. pap. 1.95 (ISBN 0-553-21173-0). Bantam.

--Alice's Adventures in Wonderland. LC 83-47783. (Illus.). 1983. 16.95 (ISBN 0-394-53227-9). Knopf.

--Alice's Adventures in Wonderland. LC 84-15540. (Illus.). 160p. (gr. 3 up). 1985. 10.95 (ISBN 0-517-55591-3). Crown.

--Alice's Adventures in Wonderland. (Puffin Classic Ser.). (Illus.). (gr. 7 up). 1985. 2.25 (ISBN 0-14-035038-1). Penguin.

--Alice's Adventures in Wonderland. LC 85-856. (Illus.). 120p. 1985. 14.95 (ISBN 0-03-002037-9). HR&W.

--Alice's Adventures in Wonderland & Through the Looking Glass. (RL 4). 1973. pap. 1.75 (ISBN 0-451-51477-7, CE1477, Sig Classics). NAL.

--Alice's Adventures in Wonderland & Through the Looking Glass. LC 79-64115. (Illus.). (gr. 3-9). 1979. lib. bdg. 9.95x (ISBN 0-8052-3716-X). Schocken.

--Alice's Adventures in Wonderland & Through the Looking Glass. Barish, Wendy, ed. (Illus.). 256p. 1982. 14.95 (ISBN 0-671-43788-7). Wanderer Bks.

--Alice's Adventures in Wonderland & Through the Looking-Glass. Green, Roger L., ed. (World's Classics Ser.). (Illus.). 1982. pap. 2.25 (ISBN 0-19-281620-9). Oxford U Pr.

--Alice's Adventures in Wonderland & Through the Looking Glass & What Alice Found There, 2 vols. (Illus.). 1983. Boxed Set. 38.50 (ISBN 0-520-05053-3). Vol. 1: Alice, Adventures in Wonderland 148 pg. Vol. 2: Through the Looking Glass, 198 pg. U of Cal Pr.

--Alice's Adventures in Wonderland & Through the Looking Glass. (Childrens Illustrated Classics Ser.). (Illus.). 246p. 1975. Repr. of 1954 ed. 11.00x (ISBN 0-460-05029-X, BKA 01583, Pub. by J, M, Dent England). Biblio Dist.

--Alice's Adventures in Wonderland & Through the Looking Glass & What Alice Found There. (Illus.). (gr. k up). 1984. 2 vol. slipcased boxed set 27.95 (ISBN 0-394-86936-2); Wonderland, 208 p. 13.95 (ISBN 0-394-86915-X); Looking-Glass, 234 p. 13.95 (ISBN 0-394-86916-8). Knopf.

--Alice's Adventures in Wonderland: Through the Looking Glass. Repr. of 1929 ed. text ed. 10.95x (ISBN 0-460-00836-6, Evman). Biblio Dist.

--Alice's Adventures in Wonderland: Through the Looking Glass & the Hunting of the Snark. (Illus.). 292p. 1982. 12.95 (ISBN 0-370-10927-9, Pub. by the Bodley Head). Merrimack Pub Cir.

--Alice's Adventures Under-Ground. 13.50 (ISBN 0-8446-1813-6). Peter Smith.

--Alice's Adventures Underground. (Illus.). 128p. (gr. 4-9). 1965. pap. 2.95 (ISBN 0-486-21482-6). Dover.

--Alice's Adventures Underground. (Facsimile Classics Ser.). (Illus.). 96p. 1981. 7.95 (ISBN 0-8317-0240-0, Rutledge Pr). Smith Pubs.

--Anderson's Alice: Walter Anderson Illustrates Alice's Adventures in Wonderland by Lewis Carroll. LC 83-14643. (Illus.). 128p. 1983. 14.95 (ISBN 0-87805-188-0). U Pr of Miss.

--Ania V Strane Chudes. Nabokov, Vladimir, tr. 1982. 17.00 (ISBN 0-88233-658-4); pap. 6.50 (ISBN 0-88233-659-2). Ardis Pubs.

--Annotated Alice: Alice's Adventures in Wonderland & Through the Looking Glass. Gardner, Martin, ed. (Illus.). pap. 5.95 (ISBN 0-452-00665-1, F665, Mer). NAL.

--Anya V Stranye Chudes. Nabokov, Vladimir, tr. from Rus. LC 75-43371. (Illus.). 128p. 1976. pap. 3.95 (ISBN 0-486-23316-2). Dover.

--Aventures D'Alice au Pays des Merveilles. Bue, Henri, tr. from Eng. (Illus.). 196p. (Fr.). (gr. 4-8). 1972. pap. 3.95 (ISBN 0-486-22836-3). Dover.

--The Complete Illustrated Works of Lewis Carroll. Guiliano, Edward, ed. (Illus.). 900p. (YA) 1982. 7.98 (ISBN 0-517-37155-3, Avenel); jacketed ed. 7.98 (ISBN 0-517-38566-X). Outlet Bk Co.

--Complete Works. 1976. pap. 9.95 (ISBN 0-394-71661-2, Vin). Random.

--The Complete Works of Lewis Carroll. LC 36-27494. 1936. 10.95 (ISBN 0-394-60485-7). Modern Lib.

--Feeding the Mind. 1973. Repr. of 1907 ed. lib. bdg. 17.50 (ISBN 0-8414-1818-7). Folcroft.

--For the Train: Five Poems & a Tale. 1973. Repr. of 1932 ed. lib. bdg. 17.50 (ISBN 0-8414-1821-7). Folcroft.

--Humorous Verse of Lewis Carroll. Orig. Title: Collected Verse of Lewis Carroll. (Illus.). 446p. (gr. 1 up). 1933. pap. 6.50 (ISBN 0-486-20654-8). Dover.

--Humorous Verse of Lewis Carroll. (Illus.). 14.25 (ISBN 0-8446-1814-4). Peter Smith.

--The Humorous Verse of Lewis Carroll. 23.95 (ISBN 0-89190-687-8, Pub. by Am Repr). Amereon Ltd.

--The Hunting of the Snark: An Agony in Eight Fits. (Illus.). 46p. 1978. 4.95 (ISBN 0-7011-0605-0, Pub. by Chatto & Windus). Merrimack Pub Cir.

--The Hunting of the Snark: An Agony in Eight Fits. (Facsimile Classics Ser.). (Illus.). 83p. 1981. 7.95 (ISBN 0-8317-4750-1, Rutledge Pr). Smith Pubs.

--The Hunting of the Snark: Annotated by Martin Gardner. Tanis, James & Dooley, John, eds. LC 81-17212. (Illus.). 294p. 1981. collector's ed. 60.00 (ISBN 0-913232-98-X); subscriber's ed. 395.00 (ISBN 0-913232-51-3); 18.95 (ISBN 0-913232-36-X). W Kaufmann.

--Jabberwocky. LC 77-75040. (Illus.). (gr. 1 up). 1977. 11.95 (ISBN 0-7232-6145-8). Warne.

--Jabberwocky. Tucker, Kathleen, ed. LC 84-17339. (Illus.). 32p. (gr. k up). 1985. PLB 9.95 (ISBN 0-8075-3747-0). A Whitman.

--The Letters of Lewis Carroll, 2 vols. Cohen, Morton H. & Green, Roger L., eds. (Illus.). 1979. Set. 75.00x (ISBN 0-19-520090-X). Oxford U Pr.

Carroll, Lewis, pseud. Lewis Carroll & the Kitchins. Cohen, Morton N., tr. LC 79-92406. (Carroll Studies: No. 4). (Illus.). 80p. (Orig.). pap. 15.00 (ISBN 0-930326-04-0). Lewis Carroll Soc.

Carroll, Lewis. The Lewis Carroll Centenary in London. 75.00 (ISBN 0-8490-0515-9). Gordon Pr.

--Lewis Carroll's Symbolic Logic: Part I & Part II. Bartley, W. W., ed. (Illus.). 1978. pap. 6.95 (ISBN 0-517-52383-3, C N Potter Bks). Crown.

--Novelty & Romancement. 1973. Repr. of 1925 ed. lib. bdg. 17.50 (ISBN 0-8414-1825-X). Folcroft.

--The Nursery "Alice". (Illus.). xxiii, 67p. (gr. 4-9). pap. 4.95 (ISBN 0-486-21610-1). Dover.

--Nursery Alice. (Illus.). 9.00 (ISBN 0-8446-1815-2). Peter Smith.

--The Nursery Alice. LC 79-12419. (Facsimile Classics). (Illus.). 1979. Repr. of 1890 ed. 6.95 (ISBN 0-8317-6478-3, Mayflower Bks). Smith Pubs.

--The Philosopher's Alice: Alice's Adventures in Wonderland & Through the Looking-Glass. Heath, Peter, ed. (Illus.). 256p. 1982. pap. 8.95 (ISBN 0-312-60518-8). St Martin.

--The Pig-Tale. (Illus.). 32p. (gr. 4-6). 1975. 7.95 (ISBN 0-316-13006-0). Little.

--Pillow Problems & A Tangled Tale. pap. 4.95 (ISBN 0-486-20493-6). Dover.

--Poems of Lewis Carroll. Livingston, Myra C., compiled by. LC 73-7914. (Poets Ser.). (Illus.). (gr. 6 up). 1973. Crowell Jr Bks.

--The Rectory Magazine. facsimile ed. LC 75-37212. 128p. 1976. 8.95 (ISBN 0-292-77010-3). U of Tex Pr.

--The Rectory Umbrella & Mischmasch. (Illus.). 1932. pap. 3.50 (ISBN 0-486-21345-5). Dover.

--The Russian Journal & Other Selections from the Works of Lewis Carroll. McDermott, John F., ed. LC 77-84529. 1978. pap. 4.50 (ISBN 0-486-23569-6). Dover.

--The Russian Journal & Other Selections from the Works of Lewis Carroll. McDermott, J. F., ed. 11.25 (ISBN 0-8446-5682-8). Peter Smith.

--The Story of Sylvie & Bruno. (Mayflower Facsimilie Classics Ser.). (Illus.). 344p. 1980. 8.95 (ISBN 0-8317-8602-7, Mayflower Bks). Smith Pubs.

--Symbolic Logic & the Game of Logic. pap. 4.95 (ISBN 0-486-20492-8). Dover.

--Through the Looking Glass. 1979. pap. 1.95x (ISBN 0-460-01018-2, Evman). Biblio Dist.

--Through the Looking Glass. LC 77-77325. (Illus.). (gr. 4 up). 1977. 7.95 (ISBN 0-312-80374-5). St Martin.

--Through the Looking Glass. 1981. Repr. lib. bdg. 15.95x (ISBN 0-89966-419-9). Buccaneer Bks.

--Through the Looking Glass. (Puffin Classic Ser.). 176p. (gr. 7 up). 1985. pap. 2.25 (ISBN 0-14-035039-X, Puffin). Penguin.

--Through the Looking Glass, & What Alice Found There. LC 84-60960. (Classics Ser.). (Illus.). 184p. (gr. 2 up). 1984. Repr. of 1941 ed. 12.95 (ISBN 0-88088-991-8, 889918). Peter Pauper.

--Useful & Instructive Poetry. 1954. lib. bdg. 17.50 (ISBN 0-8414-3638-X). Folcroft.

Carroll, Lewis & Cohen, Morton. Alice's Adventures Underground. ltd. ed. (Illus.). 112p. 1979. hand bound leather 236.00 (ISBN 0-904351-11-4). Genesis Pubns.

Carroll, Lewis & Harper, Don. Songs from Alice. LC 79-11314. (Illus.). 48p. 1979. reinforced bdg. 8.95 (ISBN 0-8234-0358-0); cassette 9.95 (ISBN 0-8234-0421-8). Holiday.

Carroll, Lewis & Moser, Barry. Through the Looking-Glass & What Alice Found There: The California Edition of the Pennyroyal Press Book. Incl. Deluxe Edition. 198p. 195.00 (ISBN 0-520-05026-6). LC 83-47520. (Illus.). 198p. 1983. 24.50 (ISBN 0-520-05039-8). U of Cal Pr.

Carroll, Lewis & Tenniel, Sir John. Alice's Adventures in Wonderland. LC 77-77324. (Illus.). (gr. 5 up). 1977. 8.95 (ISBN 0-312-01821-5). St Martin.

Carroll, Lewis see Howe, D. H.

Carroll, Lewis see Swan, D. K.

Carroll, M., compiled by. Acronyms Relating to International Development. 162p. (Fr., Eng. & Span.). 1980. pap. 9.00 (ISBN 0-88936-208-4, IDRC138, IDRC). Unipub.

Carroll, M. E. & Garner, D. R. Gymnastics Seven-Eleven: A Lesson by Lesson Approach. (Curriculum Series for Teachers Monograph). (Illus.). 130p. 1984. pap. 16.00x (ISBN 0-905273-43-5, Pub. by Falmer Pr). Taylor & Francis.

Carroll, Malachy, tr. see Briciamer, Serge.

Carroll, Malachy, tr. see De Margerie, Bertrand.

Carroll, Malcolm E. Origins of the Whig Party: A Dissertation. LC 72-112705. (Law, Politics & History Ser). 1970. Repr. of 1925 ed. lib. bdg. 37.50 (ISBN 0-306-71917-7). Da Capo.

Carroll, Malissa. Match Made in Heaven. (Candlelight Ecstasy Ser.: No. 281). 192p. (Orig.). 1984. pap. 1.95 (ISBN 0-440-15573-8). Dell.

Carroll, Margaret D. & Abraham, Sidney. Dietary Intake Source Data: United States, 1976-80. Olmstead, Mary, ed. (Ser. 11: No. 231). 50p. 1982. pap. text ed. 1.75 (ISBN 0-8406-0265-0). Natl Ctr Health Stats.

Carroll, Marie, jt. auth. see Carroll, Don.

Carroll, Marilyn. PCP: The Deadly Angel. (Encyclopedia of Psychoactive Drugs Ser.). (Illus.). 1985. PLB 15.95x (ISBN 0-87754-753-X). Chelsea Hse.

Carroll, Marilyn & Gallo, Gary. Quaaludes: The Quest for Oblivion. (Encyclopedia of Psychoactive Drugs Ser.). (Illus.). 1985. PLB 15.95x (ISBN 0-87754-766-1). Chelsea Hse.

Carroll, Mary, et al. Learner Language & Control, Vol. 637. (European University Studies Ser.: No. 1). 130p. 1982. pap. 19.45 (ISBN 3-8204-7501-X). P Lang Pubs.

Carroll, Mary A. Catholic History of Alabama & the Floridas. facs. ed. LC 70-124228. (Select Bibliographies Reprint Ser). 1908. 18.00 (ISBN 0-8369-5417-3). Ayer Co Pubs.

Carroll, Mary A. & Humphrey, Richard A. Moral Problems in Nursing: Case Studies. 1979. pap. text ed. 12.00 (ISBN 0-8191-0705-0). U Pr of Amer.

Carroll, Mary A., et al. Ethics in the Practice of Psychology. 224p. 1985. pap. text ed. 12.50 (ISBN 0-13-290610-4). P-H.

Carroll, Mary B. Overworked & Underpaid: How to Go from Being a Low-Paid Secretary to Being a High-Paid Secretary to Having Your Own Secretary. LC 84-90845. (Illus.). 240p. 1984. pap. 6.95 (ISBN 0-449-90132-7). Fawcett.

Carroll, Maryrose. Alice's Book. 1982. pap. 5.00 (ISBN 0-916384-02-0). TriQuarterly.

Carroll, Melissa, ed. Flight Into Fantasy: A Collection of Vietnamese Folk Tales. Tran, Minh C., tr. LC 85-61338. 60p. 1985. pap. 5.95 (ISBN 0-931323-02-9). Mini-World Pubns.

Carroll, Michael M., jt. ed. see Cowin, Stephen C.

Carroll, Mitchell. Greek Women. 69.95 (ISBN 0-87968-326-0). Gordon Pr.

Carroll, Mitchell B. Global Perspectives of an International Tax Lawyer. 1978. 8.00 (ISBN 0-682-49133-0). Exposition Pr FL.

--A Ring of Jingles. (Illus.). 64p. 1979. 4.00 (ISBN 0-682-49282-5). Exposition Pr FL.

Carroll, Mollie R. Labor & Politics. LC 74-89723. (American Labor: From Conspiracy to Collective Bargaining Ser., No. 1). 1969. Repr. of 1923 ed. 17.00 (ISBN 0-405-02110-0). Ayer Co Pubs.

Carroll, Noel. Sport in Ireland. (Aspects of Ireland Ser.: Vol. 6). (Illus.). 105p. 1979. pap. 5.95 (ISBN 0-906404-06-1, Pub. by Dept Foreign Ireland). Irish Bks Media.

Carroll, P. Thomas, ed. Annotated Calendar of the Letters of Charles Darwin in the Library of the American Philosophical Society. LC 75-29739. 1976. Repr. 31.00 (ISBN 0-8420-2077-2). Scholarly Res Inc.

Carroll, Paul. New & Selected Poems. 1978. 7.95 (ISBN 0-916328-11-2); pap. 3.50 (ISBN 0-916328-10-4). Yellow Pr.

Carroll, Paul, ed. The Earthquake on Ada Street: An Anthology of Poems from the "Sculpture Factory". LC 79-20159. xii, 93p. (Orig.). 1979. pap. 5.00x (ISBN 0-933104-06-5). Jupiter Pr.

Carroll, Paul, ed. see Dahlberg, Edward.

Carroll, Paul V. Goodbye to the Summer. (The Lost Play Ser.). Date not set. pap. 1.25x (ISBN 0-912262-21-4). Proscenium.

--Irish Stories & Plays. 9.95 (ISBN 0-8159-5818-8). Devin.

Carroll, Peter & Noble, David W. The Restless Centuries: A History of the American People. 2nd ed. LC 78-67974. 1979. pap. text ed. 18.95x (ISBN 0-8087-2920-9). Burgess.

Carroll, Peter N. Famous in America: Jane Fonda, George Wallace, Phyllis Schafly, John Glenn. 352p. 1985. 17.95 (ISBN 0-525-24363-1, 01743-520, W Abrahams Bk.). Dutton.

--It Seemed Like Nothing Happened: The Tragedy & Promise in America of the 1970s. 1982. 19.95 (ISBN 0-03-058319-5). HR&W.

--It Seemed Like Nothing Happened: The Tragedy & Promise of America in the 1970s. 1984. pap. 9.95 (ISBN 0-03-071057-X). HR&W.

--The Other Samuel Johnson: A Psychohistory of Early New England. LC 77-74413. 247p. 1978. 22.50 (ISBN 0-8386-2059-0). Fairleigh Dickinson.

Carroll, Phil. How to Chart Data. 2nd ed. LC 60-6963. pap. 67.50 (ISBN 0-317-10891-3, 2010381). Bks Demand UMI.

Carroll, Quinn B. Fuchs's Principles of Radiographic Exposure, Processing & Quality Control. 3rd ed. (Illus.). 394p. 1985. 29.75x (ISBN 0-398-05081-3); lab manual 12.75x (ISBN 0-398-05082-1); instr's. manual 9.75x (ISBN 0-398-05117-8). C C Thomas.

Carroll, R. Transmutation, Scattering Theory & Special Functions. (Mathematics Studies: Vol. 69). 458p. 1982. 64.00 (ISBN 0-444-86426-1, North Holland). Elsevier.

Carroll, R. L. & Kuhn, O. Batrachosauria (Anthrosauria), Gephyrostegida-Chronlosuchide. (Encyclopedia of Paleoherpetology Ser.: Pt. 5-B). (Illus.). 81p. 1972. text ed. 27.25 (ISBN 3-437-30136-5). Lubrecht & Cramer.

Carroll, R. Leonard. Stewardship: Total Life Commitment. 144p. 1967. 5.25 (ISBN 0-87148-754-3); pap. 4.25 (ISBN 0-87148-755-1). Pathway Pr.

Carroll, R. W. Transmutation & Operator Differential Equations. (Mathematics Studies: Vol. 37). 246p. 1979. 47.00 (ISBN 0-444-85328-6, North Holland). Elsevier.

Carroll, R. W. & Showalter, R. E. Singular & Degenerate Cauchy Problems. 1976. 47.50 (ISBN 0-12-161450-6). Acad Pr.

Carroll, Raymond. Anwar Sadat. (Impact Biographies Ser.). (Illus.). 128p. (gr. 7 up). 1982. PLB 9.90 (ISBN 0-531-04480-7). Watts.

--The Caribbean: Issues in U. S. Relations. (Impact Bks.). 96p. 1984. lib. bdg. 9.90 (ISBN 0-531-04852-7). Watts.

--The Future of the U. N. (Impact Ser.). (Illus.). 128p. (gr. 7-12). 1985. PLB 10.90 (ISBN 0-531-10062-6). Watts.

--The Palestine Question. (Impact Ser.). 96p. (gr. 7 up). 1983. PLB 9.90 (ISBN 0-531-04549-8). Watts.

Carroll, Robert & Gaskill, Pamela. The Order Microsauria. LC 78-56735. (Memoirs Ser.: Vol. 126). (Illus.). pap. 20.00 (ISBN 0-87169-126-4). Am Philos.

Carroll, Robert P. An Experimental Study of Comprehension in Reading with Special Reference to the Reading of Directions. LC 72-176630. (Columbia University. Teachers College. Contributions to Education: No. 245). Repr. of 1926 ed. 22.50 (ISBN 0-404-55245-5). AMS Pr.

--From Chaos to Covenant: Prophecy in the Book of Jeremiah. 288p. 1981. 14.95 (ISBN 0-8245-0106-3). Crossroad NY.

Carroll, Rosalyn. Enchanted Encore. (Rapture Romance Ser.: No. 67). 192p. 1984. pap. 1.95 (ISBN 0-451-12871-0, Sig). NAL.

Carroll, Rosalynn. Enchanted Encore. (Rapture Romance Ser.: No. 63). 192p. 1984. pap. 1.95 (ISBN 0-451-12867-2, Sig). NAL.

Carroll, S. J. & Park, R. E. The Search for Equity in School Finance. LC 82-11510. 200p. 1983. prof ref 25.00 (ISBN 0-88410-840-6). Ballinger Pub.

Carroll, St. Thomas M. Aliens. 70p. 1975. 5.00 (ISBN 0-87881-021-8). Mojave Bks.

Carroll, Sidney W. Some Dramatic Opinions. LC 68-8217. 1968. Repr. of 1923 ed. 22.50x (ISBN 0-8046-0069-4, Pub. by Kennikat). Assoc Faculty Pr.

Carroll Staff. Career Guide to Professional Associations: A Directory of Organizations by Occupational Field. 2nd ed. LC 80-13268. 288p. 1980. 19.95 (ISBN 0-910328-06-4). Carroll Pr.

Carroll, Stephen J. & Schneier, Craig E. Performance Appraisal: A Systems Approach. (The Scott, Foresman Series in Management & Organizations). 1982. pap. text ed. 13.65x (ISBN 0-673-16006-8). Scott F.

Carroll, Stephen J. & Schuler, Randall S. Human Resources Management in the 1980s: 1983 Supplement to ASPA Handbook of Personal & Industrial Relations. 272p. 1983. pap. text ed. 20.00 (ISBN 0-87179-401-2). BNA.

Carroll, Stephen J. & Tosi, Henry L. Organizational Behavior. (St. Clair Series in Management & Organizational Behavior). (Illus.). 590p. 1977. 36.45 (ISBN 0-471-06234-0). Wiley.

Carroll, Stephen J., jt. auth. see Tosi, Henry L.

Carroll, Stephen J., Jr. & Paine, Frank T. Management Process: Cases & Readings. 2nd ed. 448p. 1977. pap. text ed. write for info. (ISBN 0-02-319520-7, 31952). Macmillan.

Carroll, Susan J. Women As Candidates in American Politics. LC 84-42836. (Illus.). 272p. cancelled (ISBN 0-253-36615-1). Ind U Pr.

Carroll, Susanne, jt. auth. see Gregory, Michael.

Carroll, Sydney W. Some Dramatic Opinions. 1975. Repr. of 1923 ed. 11.50 (ISBN 0-8274-4109-6). R West.

Carroll, T. Owen. Decision Power with Supersheets. 300p. 1985. pap. 19.95 (ISBN 0-87094-679-X). Dow Jones-Irwin.

Carroll, Terence. Diary of a Fox-Hunting Man. (Illus.). 209p. 1985. 26.00 (ISBN 0-241-11361-X, Pub. by Hamish Hamilton England). David & Charles.

Carroll, Theodus C. The Lost Christmas Star. (Mystery Ser.: Gr. 3). (Illus., Based on a story by Elizabeth Yates). (gr. 3-6). 1979. PLB 7.68 (ISBN 0-8116-6409-0, 79-12224). Garrard.

Carroll, Thomas J. Blindness: What It Is, What It Does, & How to Live with It. 382p. 1961. pap. 7.00 (ISBN 0-316-12999-2). Little.

Carroll, Thomas K. Preaching the Word. (Message of the Fathers of the Church Ser.: Vol. 11). 15.00 (ISBN 0-89453-351-7); pap. 8.95 (ISBN 0-89453-322-3). M Glazier.

Carroll, Thomas M. The Abomination of Desolation: The Great Persecution. 96p. 1983. pap. 5.95 (ISBN 0-87881-103-6). Mojave Bks.

--Microeconomic Theory: Concepts & Applications. LC 82-60454. 675p. 1983. text ed. 26.95 (ISBN 0-312-53178-8); write for info. instr's manual; study guide 7.95 (ISBN 0-312-53179-6). St Martin.

Carroll, Vern & Soulik, Tobias. Nukuoro Lexicon. LC 73-78975. (PALI Language Texts: Polynesia). 859p. (Orig., Pali.). 1973. pap. text ed. 17.50x (ISBN 0-8248-0250-0). UH Pr.

Carroll, Vern, ed. Adoption in Eastern Oceania. LC 77-89650. (Association for Social Anthropology in Oceania Monographs: No. 1). (Illus.). 432p. 1970. text ed. 17.50x (ISBN 0-87022-110-8). UH Pr.

--Pacific Atoll Populations. LC 75-1264. (Asao Monograph Ser.: No. 3). (Illus.). 547p. 1975. text ed. 22.50x (ISBN 0-8248-0354-X, Eastwest Ctr). UH Pr.

Carroll, W. The Great Feast of Language in Love's Labour's Lost. 1976. 30.00 (ISBN 0-691-06309-5). Princeton U Pr.

Carroll, W. H. How to Put Money in Your Pockets Every Day. LC 77-79402. 1977. 12.95 (ISBN 0-930238-01-X). Merritt Pubs.

Carroll, W. H., et al. Reasons for Hope. rev. ed. 254p. 1982. pap. 6.95 (ISBN 0-931888-07-7, Chris. Coll. Pr.). Christendom Pubns.

Carroll, Walter J., ed. Educational Media Catalogs on Microfiche: 1983-84. 175.00x set (ISBN 0-88367-301-0). Olympic Media.

--Educational Media Catalogs on Microfiche. 1985. 87.50x (ISBN 0-88367-305-3). Olympic Media.

--Media Profiles: The Audiovisual Marketing Newsletter, 1985, Vol. 2. 1985. 48.00x (ISBN 0-88367-376-2). Olympic Media.

--Media Profiles: The Career Development Edition, 1985, Vol. 16. 1985. 185.00 (ISBN 0-88367-016-X). Olympic Media.

--Media Profiles: The Career Development Edition, 1976-1984, Vols. 11-16. abr. ed. 1983. 496.00x set (ISBN 0-88367-000-3). Olympic Media.

--Media Profiles: The Health Science Edition, Vols. 3-11. 1984. 496.00x set (ISBN 0-88367-236-7). Olympic Media.

--Media Profiles: The Health Science Edition, 1984, Vol. 12. 1985. 87.50 (ISBN 0-88367-211-1). Olympic Media.

--Media Profiles: The Whole Earth Edition, 1984, Vol. 1. 1984. 18.00x (ISBN 0-88367-350-9). Olympic Media.

--Patient Education Media Handbook, 1983. 1983. 34.50x (ISBN 0-88367-475-0). Olympic Media.

--The Sales Trainer's Media Handbook. new ed. 1985. 28.00x (ISBN 0-88367-375-4). Olympic Media.

Carroll, Warren H. The Founding of Christendom. (History of Christendom Ser.: Vol. 1). 605p. 1985. 24.95 (ISBN 0-931888-21-2); pap. 12.95 (ISBN 0-931888-21-2). Christendom Pubns.

--Nineteen Seventeen: Red Banners, White Mantle. 168p. (Orig.). 1981. pap. 4.95 (ISBN 0-931888-05-0). Christendom Pubns.

--Our Lady of Guadalupe & the Conquest of Darkness. 123p. (Orig.). pap. 4.95 (ISBN 0-931888-12-3). Christendom Pubns.

Carroll, William. Automotive Troubleshooting: Glossary. 144p. (Orig.). 1973. pap. 5.95 (ISBN 0-910390-18-5, 118). Auto Bk.

--San Marcos: A Brief History. LC 75-26259. (Illus.). 1977. 15.00 (ISBN 0-910390-24-X, Pub by Coda Publications). Auto Bk.

Carroll, William C. The Metamorphoses of Shakespearean Comedy. LC 84-42877. 290p. 1985. text ed. 28.00x (ISBN 0-691-06633-7). Princeton U Pr.

Carroll, William E., ed. see Weisheipl, James A.

Carroll, William K., jt. auth. see Arnolds, Edward B.

Carroll, William M. Animal Conventions in English Renaissance Non-Religious Prose. 166p. 1974. Repr. of 1954 ed. lib. bdg. 24.75 (ISBN 0-8371-6186-X, CAAN). Greenwood.

Carroll-Najder, Halina, tr. see Conrad, Joseph, et al.

Carroll-Porczynski, C. Z. Flammability of Composite Fabrics. (Illus.). 1976. 45.00 (ISBN 0-8206-0246-9). Chem Pub.

Carron, Alan J., jt. auth. see Packard, Sidney.

Carron, Albert V. Social Psychology of Sport. 1980. text ed. 22.95 (ISBN 0-932392-06-7); pap. 16.95. Mouvement Pubns.

--Social Psychology of Sport: An Experiential Approach. 1981. pap. text ed. 7.95 (ISBN 0-932392-09-1). Mouvement Pubns.

Carron, Andrew S. The Plight of the Thrift Institutions. LC 81-71434. (Regulation of Economic Activity Ser.). 120p. 1982. 16.95 (ISBN 0-8157-1299-5); pap. 6.95 (ISBN 0-8157-1300-2). Brookings.

--Reforming the Bank Regulatory Structure. LC 84-45847. 50p. 1985. pap. 6.95 (ISBN 0-8157-1303-7). Brookings.

--The Rescue of the Thrift Industry. LC 83-71590. 1983. pap. 5.95 (ISBN 0-8157-1301-0). Brookings.

--Transition to a Free Market: Deregulation of the Air Cargo Industry. LC 81-10244. (Studies in the Regulation of Economic Activity). 73p. 1981. pap. 6.95 (ISBN 0-8157-1297-9). Brookings.

Carron, Andrew S. & MacAvoy, Paul W. Decline of Service in the Regulated Industries. 1980. pap. 4.25 (ISBN 0-8447-3417-9). Am Enterprise.

Carron, G. & Bordia, A., eds. Issues in Planning & Implementing National Literacy Programmes. 385p. 1985. pap. 29.75 (ISBN 92-803-1118-2, U1456, UNESCO). Unipub.

Carron, Gabriel & Chau, Ta Ngoc. Reduction of Regional Disparaties: The Role of Educational Planning. (Illus.). 126p. (Co-published with Kogan Page Ltd.). 1981. pap. 15.00 (ISBN 92-803-1100-X, U1195, UNESCO). Unipub.

Carron, Gabriel & Chau, Ta Ngoc, eds. Regional Disparities in Educational Development: A Controversial Issue. (Illus.). 257p. 1980. pap. 18.75 (ISBN 92-803-1085-2, U1048, UNESCO). Unipub.

--Regional Disparities in Educational Development: Diagnosis & Policies for Reduction. (Illus.). 409p. 1980. pap. 18.75 (ISBN 92-803-1086-0, U1049, UNESCO). Unipub.

Carron, Gwenda L. Readings in Estate & Gift Tax Planning. 4th ed. LC 83-71860. (Huebner School Ser.). 1985. 25.00 (ISBN 0-943590-02-7). Amer College.

Carron, Harold & McLaughlin, Robert E. Management of Low Back Pain. (Illus.). 258p. 1982. 33.50 (ISBN 0-7236-7001-3). PSG Pub Co.

Carron, Harold, et al. Regional Anesthesia: Techniques & Clinical Applications. 208p. 1984. 39.50 (ISBN 0-8089-1654-8, 790797). Grune.

Carron, L P. How to Break into the Computer Field. LC 81-69763. (Illus.). 140p. 1981. pap. 7.95 (ISBN 0-9607242-0-6). Carron Pubs.

Carron, L. Peter, Jr. Computers: How to Break into the Field. LC 82-82844. (Illus.). 160p. (gr. 11-12). 1982. pap. 6.95 (ISBN 0-89709-034-9). Liberty Pub.

--The World below Five Hundred Kilohertz. (Illus.). 62p. (Orig.). 1986. pap. 4.95 (ISBN 0-9607242-1-4). Carron Pubs.

Carrothers, George E. The Physical Efficiency of Teachers: An Analytical Study of Some Factors Affecting the Health & Physical Efficiency of Public School Teachers. LC 76-176631. (Columbia University. Teachers College. Contributions to Education: No. 155). Repr. of 1924 ed. 22.50 (ISBN 0-404-55155-6). AMS Pr.

Carrothers, W. A. Emigration from the British Isles. 328p. 1965. Repr. 29.50x (ISBN 0-7146-1282-0, F Cass Co). Biblio Dist.

Carrott, Richard G. The Egyptian Revival: Its Sources, Monuments, & Meaning, 1808-1858. LC 76-24579. (Illus.). 1978. 44.50x (ISBN 0-520-03324-8). U of Cal Pr.

Carrow, Milton M. Licensing Power in New York City. (Illus.). 223p. 1968. pap. 12.50x (ISBN 0-8377-0401-4). Rothman.

Carrow, Milton M., jt. ed. see Nyhart, J. D.

Carrow-Wolfolk, Elizabeth & Lynch, Joan I., eds. An Integrative Approach to Language Disorders in Children. 512p. 1985. pap. 24.50 (792878). Grune.

Carrow-Woolfolk, Elizabeth & Lynch, Joan. Integrative Approach to Language Disorders in Children. 512p. 1981. 37.00 (ISBN 0-8089-1406-5, 790799). Grune.

Carrozza-Martin, Fay, jt. ed. see Hauser-Cram, Penny.

Carr-Ruffino, N. Writing Short Business Reports. 1979. pap. text ed. 14.15 (ISBN 0-07-010155-8). McGraw.

Carr-Ruffino, Norma. The Promotable Woman: Becoming a Successful Manager. 1983. 18.95 (ISBN 0-442-21669-6). Van Nos Reinhold.

Carr-Saunders, A. M. The Population Problem: A Study in Human Evolution. LC 73-14150. (Perspectives in Social Inquiry Ser.). 520p. 1974. Repr. 27.00x (ISBN 0-405-05496-3). Ayer Co Pubs.

Carr-Saunders, A. M. & Caradog-Jones, D. A Survey of the Social Structure of England & Wales. 246p. 1985. lib. bdg. 30.00 (ISBN 0-8240-7606-0). Garland Pub.

Carr-Saunders, Alexander M. World Population. (Illus.). 336p. 1964. 32.50x (ISBN 0-7146-1283-9, F Cass Co). Biblio Dist.

Carr-Saunders, Alexander M. & Wilson, Paul A. The Professions. 536p. 1964. Repr. 35.00x (ISBN 0-7146-1576-5, F Cass Co). Biblio Dist.

Carr-Saunders, Sir Alexander M. New Universities Overseas. LC 77-7518. (Illus.). 1977. Repr. of 1961 ed. lib. bdg. 19.75x (ISBN 0-8371-9665-5, CSNU). Greenwood.

Carruth. The Theory of Topological Semigroups. (Pure & Applied Mathematics Ser.). 183p. 1986. price not set (ISBN 0-8247-7320-9). Dekker.

Carruth & Hildebrandt. The Theory of Topological Semigroups. (Monographs & Textbooks in Pure & Applied Mathematics). 408p. 1983. 45.00 (ISBN 0-8247-1795-3). Dekker.

Carruth, Ella K. She Wanted to Read: The Story of Mary Macleod Bethune. (Illus.). (gr. 3-7). 1966. 6.50 (ISBN 0-687-38353-6). Abingdon.

Carruth, Frances W. Fictional Rambles in & About Boston. 1973. Repr. of 1902 ed. 30.00 (ISBN 0-8274-1536-2). R West.

Carruth, Gorton, jt. auth. see Brownstone, David M.

Carruth, Gorton, jt. auth. see Canby, Courtland.

Carruth, Gorton, jt. auth. see Ehrlich, Eugene.

Carruth, Gorton, ed. see Canby, Courtlandt.

Carruth, Gorton, et al. The Transcriber's Handbook: With the Dictionary of Sound-Alike Words. LC 84-40307. 519p. 1984. 32.00x (ISBN 0-471-08876-5, Pub. by Wiley-Interscience). Wiley.

Carruth, Gorton, et al, eds. The Encyclopedia of American Facts & Dates. 7th rev. ed. LC 78-4757. 1979. 14.95i (ISBN 0-690-01669-7); suppl. of the 70's incl. T Y Crowell.

Carruth, Hayden. Asphalt Georgics. LC 84-25499. 96p. 1985. 15.00 (ISBN 0-8112-0937-7); pap. 6.95 (ISBN 0-8112-0938-5, NDP591). New Directions.

--The Bloomingdale Papers. LC 74-75938. (Contemporary Poetry Ser.). 90p. 1974. pap. 5.95 (ISBN 0-8203-0360-7). U of Ga Pr.

--Brothers, I Loved You All. LC 77-95138. 100p. 1978. 8.95 (ISBN 0-8180-1543-8); pap. 3.95 (ISBN 0-8180-1544-6). Sheep Meadow.

--Brothers, I Loved You All. 100p. 1982. pap. 7.95 (ISBN 0-935296-35-2). Sheep Meadow.

--Dark World. 1974. pap. 2.00 (ISBN 0-87711-052-2). Kayak.

--Effluences from the Sacred Caves: More Selected Essays & Reviews. (Poets on Poetry Ser.). 1983. pap. 7.95 (ISBN 0-472-06349-9). U of Mich Pr.

--For You. LC 71-122103. 1970. 5.95 (ISBN 0-8112-0256-9); pap. 1.95 (ISBN 0-8112-0016-7, NDP298). New Directions.

--From Snow & Rock, from Chaos. LC 72-93973. 1973. pap. 2.25 (ISBN 0-8112-0469-3, NDP349). New Directions.

--If You Call This Cry a Song. 108p. 1983. 12.95 (ISBN 0-88150-009-7); pap. 7.50 (ISBN 0-88150-008-9). Countryman.

--Lighter Than Air Craft. Wheatcroft, John, ed. (Bucknell University Fine Editions: Series in Contemporary Poetry). (Illus.). 56p. 1985. ltd. ed 85.00 (ISBN 0-916375-02-1). Press Alley.

--The Mythology of Dark & Light. (Illus.). 28p. 1982. 12.00 (ISBN 0-918092-33-7); signed 35.00 (ISBN 0-918092-32-9). Tamarack Edns.

--The Selected Poetry of Hayden Carruth. 160p. 1986. 18.95 (ISBN 0-02-522290-2); pap. 9.95 (ISBN 0-02-069310-9). MacMillan.

--The Sleeping Beauty. LC 82-47518. 144p. 1982. 11.49i (ISBN 0-06-015021-1, HarpT); pap. 6.68i (ISBN 0-06-090973-0, CN973). Har-Row.

--Working Papers: Selected Essays & Reviews by Hayden Carruth. Weissman, Judith, ed. LC 81-4404. 264p. 1982. 21.95x (ISBN 0-8203-0583-9). U of Ga Pr.

Carruth, Hayden, ed. Voice That Is Great Within Us. (Bantam Classic Edition Ser). (Orig.). (gr. 10-12). 1970. pap. 4.95 (ISBN 0-553-24136-2). Bantam.

Carruth, J. H., jt. auth. see Eaves, Edgar D.

Carruth, William A. Verse Writing: A Practical Handbook for College Classes & Private Guidance. 1973. Repr. of 1917 ed. 25.00 (ISBN 0-8274-1546-X). R West.

Carruth, William H. Verse Writing. 123p. 1980. Repr. of 1925 ed. lib. bdg. 17.50 (ISBN 0-8482-3554-1). Norwood Edns.

--Verse Writing: A Practical Handbook for College Classes & Private Guidance. 1979. Repr. of 1925 ed. lib. bdg. 20.00 (ISBN 0-8414-9987-X). Folcroft.

Carruthers, jt. auth. see D'Agenais.

Carruthers, B. J. Labour Market Services in Britain & Germany: Employer & Trade Union Participation. 53p. 1979. 25.00x (ISBN 0-905492-16-1, Pub. by Anglo-German Found England). State Mutual Bk.

Carruthers, Christopher. Biochemistry of Skin in Health & Disease. (Illus.). 284p. 1962. photocopy ed. 31.75x (ISBN 0-398-00288-6). C C Thomas.

Carruthers, Douglas, ed. The Desert Route to India. (Hakluyt Society Works Ser.: No. 2, Vol. 63). (Illus.). Repr. of 1928 ed. 25.00 (ISBN 0-317-16776-6). Kraus Repr.

Carruthers, Ian & Stoner, Roy. Economic Aspects & Policy Issues in Ground Water Development, No. 496. 110p. 1981. pap. 5.00 (ISBN 0-686-39634-0, WP-0496). World Bank.

Carruthers, Ian, ed. Social & Economic Perspectives on Irrigation. 100p. 1981. pap. 24.00 (ISBN 0-08-026780-7). Pergamon.

Carruthers, Ian D., ed. see OECD.

Carruthers J. Bruce II, Business Info. Display, Inc. The Energy Decade: Nineteen Seventy to Nineteen Eighty. LC 81-22884. 558p. 1982. prof ref 150.00 (ISBN 0-88410-873-2). Ballinger Pub.

Carruthers, M., ed. see Annual Conference for Psychosomatic Research, 20th, London, Nov. 15-16, 1976.

Carruthers, Mary. The Search for St. Truth. 1974. 14.95 (ISBN 0-8101-0422-9). Northwestern U Pr.

Carruthers, Mary J. & Kirk, Elizabeth D., eds. Acts of Interpretation: The Text in Its Context. 1982. 32.95 (ISBN 0-937664-60-X). Pilgrim Bks OK.

Carruthers, N. Bermuda 1985. (Fisher Annotated Travel Guides Ser.). 128p. 1984. 9.95 (ISBN 0-8116-0067-X). NAL.

Carruthers, N., jt. auth. see Brooks, Charles E.

Carruthers, N. B., jt. auth. see Houghton, E. I.

Carruthers, N. B., jt. auth. see Houghton, E. L.

Carruthers, P., jt. auth. see Brout, R.

Carruthers, P., ed. The Coming Age of Psychosomatics: Proceedings of the 21st Annual Conference of the Society of Psychosomatic Research, November 21-22 1977, Royal College of Physicians. (Illus.). 163p. 1979. 31.00 (ISBN 0-08-023736-3). Pergamon.

Carruthers, Peter A. Spin & Isospin in Particle Physics. LC 72-160021. (Illus.). 268p. 1971. 69.50 (ISBN 0-677-02580-7). Gordon.

Carruthers, W. Some Modern Methods of Organic Synthesis. 2nd ed. LC 77-77735. (Cambridge Texts in Chemistry & Biochemistry Ser.). (Illus.). 1978. pap. 24.95 (ISBN 0-521-29241-7). Cambridge U Pr.

Carruthers, W., jt. auth. see Cook, J.

Carry, Virginia. Double Duty Decorating: Design Ideas to Help You Get the Most Out of Your Limited Space. (Illus.). 192p. 1983. 17.95 (ISBN 0-684-17949-0, ScribT). Scribner.

Carryl, Charles E. River Syndicate & Other Stories. facsimile ed. LC 70-106258. (Short Story Index Reprint Ser.). 1899. 18.00 (ISBN 0-8369-3295-1). Ayer Co Pubs.

Carryl, Guy W. Grimm Tales Made Gay. LC 73-104428. (Illus.). Repr. of 1902 ed. lib. bdg. 14.50x (ISBN 0-8398-0253-6). Irvington.

--Zut, & Other Parisians. facs. ed. LC 76-81266. (Short Story Index Reprint Ser.). 1903. 18.00 (ISBN 0-8369-3018-5). Ayer Co Pubs.

Carsaniga, Giovanni. Italiano Espresso. 256p. 1982. pap. 11.95 (ISBN 0-521-28220-9); of 4 cassettes 65.00 set (ISBN 0-521-23777-7). Cambridge U Pr.

--Leopardi. 129p. 1977. 14.00x (ISBN 0-85224-297-2, Pub. by Edinburgh U Pr Scotland). Columbia U Pr.

Carsberg, Bryan V. Introduction to Mathematical Programming for Accountants. LC 71-95609. 1969. lib. bdg. 17.50x (ISBN 0-678-06006-1). Kelley.

Carse, Adam. The History of Orchestration. (Illus.). 1935. pap. 5.00 (ISBN 0-486-21258-0). Dover.

--History of Orchestration. (Illus.). 13.50 (ISBN 0-8446-1816-0). Peter Smith.

--Musical Wind Instruments: A History of the Wind Instruments Used in European Orchestras & Wind Bands, from the Later Middle Ages up to the Present Time. 2nd ed. LC 65-18502. (Music Ser). 1965. Repr. of 1939 ed. 39.50 (ISBN 0-306-70906-6). Da Capo.

--Musical Wind Instruments: A History of the Wind Instruments Used in European Orchestras & Wind-Bands from the Later Middle Ages up to the Present Time. LC 74-20868. (Illus.). xxvi, 381p. 1975. pap. 6.95 (ISBN 0-306-80005-5). Da Capo.

--The Orchestra from Beethoven to Berlioz. new ed. (Illus.). 528p. 1949. 15.00x (ISBN 0-8450-2550-3). Broude.

--The Orchestra in the XVIIIth Century. (Illus.). 184p. 1969. 10.00x (ISBN 0-8450-2551-1). Broude.

Carse, Adam V. Eighteenth Century Symphonies: A Short History of the Symphony in the 18th Century. LC 78-66900. (Encore Music Editions Ser.). (Illus.). 1979. Repr. of 1951 ed. 15.00 (ISBN 0-88355-731-2). Hyperion Conn.

--The History of Orchestration. 59.95 (ISBN 0-8490-0342-3). Gordon Pr.

Carse, Adam Von Ahn. The Orchestra from Beethoven to Berlioz. LC 79-181122. 514p. 1948. Repr. 69.00 (ISBN 0-403-01521-9). Scholarly.

--Orchestral Conducting, a Textbook for Students & Amateurs. LC 78-109716. (Illus.). iv, 100p. Repr. of 1929 ed. lib. bdg. 15.00x (ISBN 0-8371-4206-7, CAOC). Greenwood.

Carse, James P. Death & Existence: A Conceptual History of Human Mortality. LC 79-24830. (Contemporary Religious Movements: a Wiley-Interscience Ser.). 473p. 1980. 37.95 (ISBN 0-471-13704-9, Pub. by Wiley-Interscience). Wiley.

--The Silence of God: Meditations on Prayer. 97p. 1985. 11.95 (ISBN 0-02-521490-X). Macmillan.

Carse, Stephen, et al. The Financing Procedures of British Foreign Trade. LC 79-18146. 160p. 1980. 32.50 (ISBN 0-521-22534-5). Cambridge U Pr.

Carskadon, Thomas G. Using Psychology to Teach Psychology. 1984. pap. 11.95 (ISBN 0-935652-11-6). Ctr Applications Psych.

Carsky, P. & Urban, M. Ab Initio Calculations: Methods & Applications in Chemistry. (Lecture Notes in Chemistry: Vol. 16). (Illus.). 247p. 1980. pap. 25.00 (ISBN 0-387-10005-9). Springer-Verlag.

Carsky, P., jt. auth. see Zahradnik, R.

Carsky, Petr, jt. auth. see Zahradnik, Rudolf.

Carslaw, H. S., ed. see Bonola, Roberto.

Carslaw, Horatio S. Introduction to the Theory of Fourier's Series & Integrals. 3rd ed. (Illus.). 1952. pap. 7.50 (ISBN 0-486-60048-3). Dover.

Carslaw, Horatio S. & Jaeger, J. C. Conduction of Heat in Solids. 2nd ed. (Illus.). 1959. 45.00x (ISBN 0-19-853303-9). Oxford U Pr.

Carslaw, Horatio S; see Ball, W. Rouse, et al.

Carsley, Alexander C. One-Hundred-One Proof. 80p. 1982. special signed ltd. ed. 19.95 (ISBN 0-915520-48-6); pap. 5.95 (ISBN 0-915520-49-4). Ross-Erikson.

Carsley, Anne. Defiant Desire. (Orig.). 1982. pap. 3.50 (ISBN 0-440-12019-5). Dell.

--The Golden Savage. 352p. (Orig.). 1984. pap. 3.50 (ISBN 0-523-42143-5). Pinnacle Bks.

--Tempest. 384p. (Orig.). 1985. pap. 3.50 (ISBN 0-523-42232-6). Pinnacle Bks.

Carson, et al. Late Roman Bronze Coinage. 1977. 18.00 (ISBN 0-685-51531-1, Pub by Spink & Son England). S J Durst.

Carson, A. Domestic Tragedy in English, 2 vols. (Salzburg Poetic Drama Ser.: No. 67). 465p. 1982. Set. pap. text ed. 50.75x (ISBN 0-391-03000-0, Pub. by Salzburg Austria). Vol. 1 (ISBN 0-391-03001-9). Vol. 2 (0-391-03002-7). Humanities.

Carson, Alex. Confidence in God in Times of Danger. pap. 2.75 (ISBN 0-685-88371-X). Reiner.

Carson, Alexander. Baptism: It's Mode & Subjects. Young, John, ed. LC 80-8067. 1981. 14.95 (ISBN 0-8254-2324-4). Kregel.

Carson, Ann. The Memoirs of the Celebrated & Beautiful Mrs. Ann Carson, Daughter of an Officer of the U. S. Navy & Wife of Another, Whose Life Terminated in the Philadelphia Prison, 2 vols. in 1. rev. ed. Baxter, Annette K., ed. LC 79-8780. (Signal Lives Ser.). 1980. Repr. of 1838 ed. lib. bdg. 43.00x (ISBN 0-405-12829-0). Ayer Co Pubs.

Carson, Arthur B. General Excavation Methods. LC 79-23811. 400p. 1980. Repr. of 1961 ed. lib. bdg. 37.50 (ISBN 0-89874-067-3). Krieger.

Carson, Arthur L. The Story of Philippine Education. 1978. pap. 10.25x (ISBN 0-686-23915-6, Pub. by New Day Pub). Cellar.

Carson, Barbara. A Basis for Composition. 416p. 1982. pap. text ed. 13.95 (ISBN 0-675-09848-3). Additional Supplements May Be Obtained From Publisher. Merrill.

Carson, Barbara, jt. auth. see Wheatland, David.

Carson, Ben, jt. auth. see Martin, Betty.

Carson, Byrta, et al. How You Plan & Prepare Meals. 3rd ed. (Illus.). 1980. text ed. 20.36 (ISBN 0-07-010162-0). McGraw.

Carson, Charles. Mountain Troubadour. 3.00 (ISBN 0-87505-127-8). Borden.

Carson, Charles R. Managing Employee Honesty. LC 76-51836. (Illus.). 1977. 29.95 (ISBN 0-913708-27-5). Butterworth.

Carson, Christopher, et al, eds. see Pabst, William R.

Carson, Ciaran. The New Estate. (Illus.). 42p. 1976. pap. 3.25 (ISBN 0-916390-02-0). Wake Forest.

Carson, Clarence B. American Tradition. 306p. 1970. pap. 4.00 (ISBN 0-910614-17-2). Foun Econ Ed.

--Flight from Reality. 568p. 1969. pap. 4.00 (ISBN 0-910614-18-0). Foun Econ Ed.

--The Trouble with Farming. 1983. pap. 2.50 (ISBN 0-915513-02-1). Ctr Futures Ed.

Carson, Clayborne. In Struggle: SNCC & the Black Awakening of the Nineteen Sixties. LC 80-16540. (Illus.). 384p. 1981. text ed. 25.00x (ISBN 0-674-44725-5); pap. text ed. 8.95 (ISBN 0-674-44726-3). Harvard U Pr.

Carson, D. A. Divine Sovereignty & Human Responsibility: Biblical Perspectives in Tension. Toon, Peter & Martin, Ralph, eds. LC 79-27589. (New Foundations Theological Library). 228p. 1981. 12.95 (ISBN 0-8042-3707-7); pap. 11.95 (ISBN 0-8042-3727-1). John Knox.

--Exegetical Fallacies. 1984. text ed. 7.95p (ISBN 0-8010-2499-4). Baker Bk.

--The Farewell Discourse & the Final Prayer of Jesus: An Exposition of John 14-17. LC 80-68769. 196p. 1981. 9.95 (ISBN 0-8010-2460-9). Baker Bk.

--King James Version Debate. LC 79-50443. 1978. pap. 4.50 (ISBN 0-8010-2427-7). Baker Bk.

--Sermon on the Mount: An Evangelical Exposition of Matthew 5-7. LC 77-93260. 1978. 4.95 (ISBN 0-8010-2480-3). Baker Bk.

Carson, D. A., ed. Biblical Interpretation & the Church. 232p. 1985. pap. 6.95 (ISBN 0-8407-7501-6). Nelson.

--From Sabbath to Lord's Day. 432p. (Orig.). 1982. pap. 10.95 (ISBN 0-310-44531-0). Zondervan.

Carson, Dale. Native New England Cooking. (Illus., Orig.). 1980. pap. 5.95 (ISBN 0-933614-05-5). Peregrine Pr.

Carson, David, et al. The Sound of Wonder: Interviews from "The Science Fiction Radio Show", 2 vols. 1985. pap. 18.50 ea. Vol. 1, 184pgs (ISBN 0-89774-175-7). Vol. 2, 184pgs (ISBN 0-89774-233-8). Oryx Pr.

Carson, Donald A. From Triumphalism to Maturity: An Exposition of II Corinthians 10-13. 1984. 12.95 (ISBN 0-8010-2489-7). Baker Bk.

Carson, E. R., jt. auth. see Finkelstein, L.

Carson, E. R. & Cramp, D. G., eds. Computers & Control in Clinical Medicine. 274p. 1984. 39.50x (ISBN 0-306-41892-4, Plenum Pr). Plenum Pub.

Carson, E. R., et al. The Mathematical Modeling of Metabolic & Endocrine Systems: Model Formulation, Identification & Validation. (Biomedical Engineering & Health Systems Ser.). 394p. 1983. 57.50 (ISBN 0-471-08660-6). Wiley.

Carson, E. W., Jr., ed. The Plant Root & Its Environment. LC 72-92877. (Illus.). xxiii, 425p. 1974. 25.00x (ISBN 0-8139-0411-0). U Pr of Va.

Carson, Edward. The Ancient & Rightful Customs: A History of the English Customs Service. 336p. 1972. 24.00 (ISBN 0-208-01271-0, Archon). Shoe String.

Carson, Ewart R., jt. auth. see Finkelstein, Ludwick.

Carson, George B., jt. auth. see Brown, Louise F.

Carson, George B., Jr. Russia since 1917: The Once & Future Utopia. LC 72-89540. (AHA Pamphlets: No. 427). 1972. pap. text ed. 1.50 (ISBN 0-87229-007-7). Am Hist Assn.

Carson, Gerald. Cornflake Crusade. LC 75-39240. (Getting & Spending: the Consumer's Dilemma). (Illus.). 1976. Repr. of 1957 ed. 25.50x (ISBN 0-405-08013-1). Ayer Co Pubs.

--The Golden Egg: The Personal Income Tax, Where It Came from, How It Grew. 1977. 10.00 (ISBN 0-395-25177-X). HM.

--The Polite Americans: A Wide-Angle View of Our More or Less Good Manners over 300 Years. LC 80-11824. (Illus.). xvi, 346p. 1980. Repr. of 1966 ed. lib. bdg. 32.50x (ISBN 0-313-22417-X, CAPO). Greenwood.

--The Social History of Bourbon: An Unhurried Account of Our Star-Spangled American Drink. LC 84-2216. (Illus.). 312p. 1984. Repr. of 1963 ed. 22.00 (ISBN 0-8131-1509-4). U Pr of KY.

Carson, Gordon B., et al, eds. Production Handbook. 3rd ed. (Illus.). 1450p. 1972. 80.50 (ISBN 0-471-06651-6, 12602, Pub. by Ronald Pr). Wiley.

Carson, H. G. Cache Hunting. 108p. (Orig.). 1984. pap. text ed. 6.95 (ISBN 0-941620-32-8). Cache Pr.

Carson, H. G., jt. auth. see Boyd, L. M.

Carson, H. Glenn. Coinshooting, How & Where to Do It: Using a Metal Detector Effectively. (Illus.). 63p. (Orig.). 1981. pap. text ed. 4.95 (ISBN 0-941620-30-1). H G Carson Ent.

--Coinshooting II: Digging Deeper Coins. (Illus.). 106p. (Orig.). 1982. pap. 5.95 (ISBN 0-941620-17-4). H G Carson Ent.

--Hedge Yourself Against Disaster. 47p. 1973. pap. 1.75 (ISBN 0-941620-25-5). H G Carson Ent.

--Hunting the Ghost Towns. (Illus.). 1977. pap. 4.00 (ISBN 0-941620-08-5). H G Carson Ent.

--The Malpais Gold. (Illus.). 148p. 1978. pap. 2.50 (ISBN 0-941620-09-3). H G Carson Ent.

--Treasure Hunting: A Modern Search for Adventure. (Illus.). 82p. 1981. pap. 4.95 (ISBN 0-941620-05-0). H G Carson Ent.

Carson, H. Glenn, compiled by. Treasure Hunting Annual, Vol. 1. (Illus.). 160p. 1979. pap. 7.95 (ISBN 0-941620-11-5). H G Carson Ent.

--Treasure Hunting Annual, Vol. 2. (Illus.). 164p. 1980. pap. 7.95 (ISBN 0-941620-22-0). H G Carson Ent.

Carson, H. L. see Ashburner, M., et al.

Carson, Hampton L. Pedigrees in the Ownership of Law Books. Mersky, Roy M. & Jacobstein, J. Myron, eds. (Classics in Legal History Reprint Ser.: Vol. 2). 31p. 1968. Repr. of 1916 ed. lib. bdg. 30.00 (ISBN 0-89941-001-4). W S Hein.

Carson, Hampton L. see Mueller-Dombois, Dieter.

Carson, Herbert M. Epistles of Paul to the Colossians & to Philemon. (Tyndale Bible Commentaries). 1960. pap. 3.95 (ISBN 0-8028-1411-5). Eerdmans.

Carson, J. H. Early Recollections of the Mines. 59.95 (ISBN 0-8490-0074-2). Gordon Pr.

Carson, J. W. & Rickards, T. Industrial New Product Development: A Manual for the 1980's. LC 79-65781. 166p. 1979. 44.95x (ISBN 0-470-26821-2). Halsted Pr.

Carson, James. Deserts & People. LC 82-50396. (Nature's Landscape Ser.). 91p. (gr. 5 up). PLB 15.96 (ISBN 0-382-06669-3). Silver.

Carson, James M. The Yosemite in Winter: An 1892 Account. Jones, William R., ed. (Illus.). 1978. pap. 1.00 (ISBN 0-89646-053-3). Outbooks.

Carson, James P., jt. auth. see Petigru, James L.

Carson, Jane. Colonial Virginia Cookery. 1985. Repr. of 1983 ed. 9.95. U Pr of Va.

--James Innes & His Brothers of the F.H.C. LC 65-26594. (Williamsburg Research Studies). Repr. of 1965 ed. 46.00 (ISBN 0-8357-9804-6, 2013414). Bks Demand UMI.

Carson, Janet. Tell Me about Your Picture: Art Activities to Help Children Communicate. 176p. 1984. 17.95 (ISBN 0-13-903139-1); pap. 9.95 (ISBN 0-13-903121-9). P-H.

Carson, Joan, jt. auth. see Carson, Peter.

Carson, Joan C. & Carson, Peter. Any Teacher Can: Practical Strategies for Effective Classroom Management. 232p. 1984. 19.50x (ISBN 0-398-04867-3); spiral, student workbook 9.75 (ISBN 0-398-04917-3). C C Thomas.

--Freeing Yourself to Love: How to Make the Most of Your Intimate Relations. 200p. (Orig.). 1984. pap. 8.95 (ISBN 0-89769-056-7, Dist. by Caroline Hse). Pine Mntn.

Carson, Joan C., jt. auth. see Carson, Peter.

Carson, John, jt. auth. see Banks, Jerry.

Carson, John H. Design of Microprocessor Systems. (Tutorial Texts Ser.). 262p. 1979. 18.00 (ISBN 0-8186-0260-0, Q260). IEEE Comp Soc.

Carson, John H., jt. auth. see Liebowitz, Burt H.

Carson, Jonathan E. Making College Pay: How to Earn Money While You're Still in School. LC 83-11903. 1983. pap. 6.95 (ISBN 0-201-10820-8). Addison-Wesley.

Carson, Julius M. & Banks, Lacy. Winning Boxing. (Winning Ser.). 1980. pap. 5.95 (ISBN 0-8092-7151-6). Contemp Bks.

Carson, Katherine F., jt. auth. see Schutz, Susan P.

Carson, Kelton. Simplified Computer Programming: Including the Easy RPG Way. LC 73-90739. (Illus.). 240p. 1974. pap. 8.95 (ISBN 0-8306-3676-5, 676). TAB Bks.

Carson, Kit. Kit Carson's Autobiography. Quaife, Milo M., ed. LC 66-4130. (Illus.). xxxii, 192p. 1966. pap. 4.95 (ISBN 0-8032-5031-2, BB 325, Bison). U of Nebr Pr.

Carson, Leonard C. Pursue & Destroy. (Illus.). 1978. text ed. 19.95 (ISBN 0-913194-05-0). Sentry.

Carson, M. A. The Mechanics of Erosion. (Monographs in Spatial & Environmental Systems Analysis). (Illus.). 174p. 1971. 16.95x (ISBN 0-85086-029-6, NO. 2946, Pub. by Pion England). Methuen Inc.

Carson, M. A. & Kirkby, M. J. Hillslope Form & Process. (Cambridge Geographical Studies). 67.50 (ISBN 0-521-08234-X). Cambridge U Pr.

Carson, Mary. Handbook of Treasure Signs & Symbols. (Illus.). 60p. (Orig.). 1980. pap. 4.95 (ISBN 0-941620-33-6). H G Carson Ent.

Carson, Matt. Casino Gambling-Plain & Simple. (Illus.). 224p. (Orig.). 1983. pap. text ed. 14.95 incl. 60-min. audio cassette (ISBN 0-913013-01-3). Arnold & Co.

Carson, Neil. Arthur Miller. LC 81-84704. (Modern Dramatists Ser.). 184p. (Orig.). 1982. pap. 6.95 (ISBN 0-394-17966-8, E-794, Ever). Grove.

Carson, O. E. The Trolley Titans: A Mobile History of Atlanta. Sebree, Mac, ed. LC 81-8312. (Interurbans Special Ser.: No. 76). (Illus.). 178p. 1981. 27.95 (ISBN 0-916374-46-7). Interurban.

Carson, Patti & Dellosa, Janet. Alphabet Sounds & Pictures. (Let's Learn Ser.). (Illus.). 32p. (ps-1). 1983. pap. 1.79 (ISBN 0-88724-003-8, CD-7004). Carson-Dellos.

--Basics about Money. (Let's Learn Ser.). (Illus.). 32p. (gr. 1-2). 1984. pap. 1.79 (ISBN 0-88724-094-1, CD-7033). Carson-Dellos.

--Beginning Money Skills. (Let's Learn Ser.). (Illus.). 32p. (ps-k). 1984. pap. 1.79 (ISBN 0-88724-087-9, CD-7026). Carson-Dellos.

--Beginning Numbers: One Through Ten. (Stick-Out-Your-Neck Ser.). (Illus.). 20p. (ps-2). 1984. pap. 4.95 (ISBN 0-88724-136-0, CD-0570). Carson Dellos.

--Capital & Lower Case Letters. (Let's Learn Ser.). (Illus.). 32p. (ps-1). 1983. pap. 1.79 (ISBN 0-88724-004-6, CD-7005). Carson-Dellos.

--Cat Fun Book. (Stick-Out-Your-Neck Ser.). (Illus.). 32p. (ps-2). 1984. pap. 1.25 (ISBN 0-88724-021-6, CD-8036). Carson-Dellos.

--Christmas Fun Book. (Stick-Out-Your-Neck Ser.). (Illus.). 32p. (ps-2). 1981. pap. 1.25 (ISBN 0-88724-053-4, CD-8008). Carson-Dellos.

--Christmas Preschool & Kindergarten Practice. (Stick-Out-Your-Neck Ser.). (Illus.). 32p. (ps-k). 1983. pap. 1.79 (ISBN 0-88724-049-6, CD-8025). Carson-Dellos.

--Christmas Primary Reading & Art Activities. (Stick-Out-Your-Neck Ser.). (Illus.). 32p. (gr. 1-3). 1983. pap. 1.79 (ISBN 0-88724-038-0, CD-8029). Carson-Dellos.

--Circus Fun Book. (Stick-Out-Your-Neck Ser.). (Illus.). 32p. (ps-1). 1982. pap. 1.25 (ISBN 0-88724-056-9, CD-8011). Carson-Dellos.

--Consonants: Cut & Paste & More. (Let's Learn Ser.). (Illus.). 32p. (ps-1). 1983. pap. 1.79 (ISBN 0-88724-008-9, CD-7009). Carson-Dellos.

--Doggone Good Fun Book. (Stick-Out-Your-Neck Ser.). (Illus.). 32p. (ps-1). 1982. pap. 1.25 (ISBN 0-88724-055-0, CD-8010). Carson-Dellos.

--Easter Preschool-K Practice. (Stick-Out-Your-Neck Ser.). (Illus.). 32p. (ps-k). 1984. pap. 1.79 (ISBN 0-88724-017-8, CD-8032). Carson-Dellos.

--Easter Primary Reading & Art Activities. (Stick-Out-Your-Neck Ser.). (Illus.). 32p. (gr. 1-3). 1984. pap. 1.79 (ISBN 0-88724-027-5, CD-8042). Carson-Dellos.

--Fall Primary Reading & Art Activities. (Stick-Out-Your-Neck Ser.). (Illus.). 32p. (gr. 1-3). 1983. pap. 1.79 (ISBN 0-88724-035-6, CD-8026). Carson-Dellos.

--Fish Fun Book. (Stick-Out-Your-Neck Ser.). (Illus.). 32p. (ps-2). 1984. pap. 1.25 (ISBN 0-88724-013-5, CD-8012). Carson-Dellos.

--Fun with Numbers. (Let's Learn Ser.). (Illus.). 32p. (gr. k-1). 1984. pap. 1.79 (ISBN 0-88724-075-5, CD-7018). Carson-Dellos.

--General Patterns. (Stick-Out-Your-Neck Ser.). (Illus.). 32p. (ps-1). 1984. pap. 1.98 (ISBN 0-88724-033-X, CD-0914). Carson-Dellos.

--Halloween Preschool & Kindergarten Practice. (Stick-Out-Your-Neck Ser.). (Illus.). 32p. (ps-k). 1983. pap. 1.79 (ISBN 0-88724-047-X, CD-8023). Carson-Dellos.

--Halloween Primary Reading & Art Activities. (Stick-Out-Your-Neck Ser.). (Illus.). 32p. (gr. 1-3). 1983. pap. 1.79 (ISBN 0-88724-036-4, CD-8027). Carson-Dellos.

--Letters & the Sounds They Make. (Let's Learn Ser.). (Illus.). 21p. (gr. k-1). 1984. pap. 1.79 (ISBN 0-88724-074-7, CD-7017). CArson-Dellos.

--March Primary Reading & Art Activities. (Stick-Out-Your-Neck Ser.). (Illus.). 32p. (gr. 1-3). 1984. pap. 1.79 (ISBN 0-88724-024-0, CD-8039). Carson-Dellos.

--Numbers, Number Words & Sets. (Let's Learn Ser.). (Illus.). 32p. (ps-1). 1983. pap. 1.79 (ISBN 0-88724-005-4, CD-7006). Carson-Dellos.

--Numbers, Number Words & Sets. (Stick-Out-Your-Neck Ser.). (Illus.). 20p. (ps-2). 1984. pap. 4.95 (ISBN 0-88724-153-0, CD-0576). Carson-Dellos.

--Pre School & Kindergarten Skills. (Let's Learn Ser.). (Illus.). 24p. (ps-k). 1984. pap. 1.79 (ISBN 0-88724-072-0, CD7015). CArson-Dellos.

--Seasonal Blank Reproducible Worksheets. (Stick-Out-Your-Neck Ser.). (Illus.). 96p. (gr. 1 up). 1984. pap. 6.95 (ISBN 0-88724-025-9, CD-0918). Carson-Dellos.

--Shapes: Circle, Triangle, Square, Rectangle, Diamond. (Let's Learn Ser.). (Illus.). 32p. (ps-1). 1983. pap. 1.79 (ISBN 0-88724-006-2, CD-7007). Carson-Dellos.

--Spooky Fun Book. (Stick Out Your Neck Ser.). (Illus.). 32p. (ps-1). 1981. pap. 1.25 (ISBN 0-88724-051-8, 8006). Carson-Dellos.

--Sporty Blank Reproducible Worksheets. (Stick-Out-Your-Neck Ser.). (Illus.). 96p. (gr. 1-6). pap. 6.95 (ISBN 0-88724-031-3, 0919). Carson-Dellos.

--Spring Fun Book. (Stick-Out-Your-Neck Ser.). (Illus.). 32p. (ps-2). 1984. pap. 1.25 (ISBN 0-88724-059-3, CD-8047). Carson-Dellos.

--Spring Preschool-K Practice. (Stick-Out-Your-Neck Ser.). (Illus.). 32p. (ps-k). 1984. pap. 1.79 (ISBN 0-88724-019-4, CD-8034). Carson-Dellos.

--Spring Primary Reading & Art Activities. (Stick-Out-Your-Neck Ser.). (Illus.). 32p. (gr. 1-3). 1984. pap. 1.79 (ISBN 0-88724-066-6, CD-8046). Carson-Dellos.

--Subtraction Facts: Differences to Ten. (Let's Learn Ser.). (Illus.). 32p. (gr. 1-2). 1984. pap. 1.79 (ISBN 0-88724-078-X, CD-7021). Carson-Dellos.

--Thanksgiving Primary Reading & Art Activities. (Stick-Out-Your-Neck Ser.). (Illus.). 32p. (gr. 1-3). 1983. pap. 1.79 (ISBN 0-88724-037-2, CD-8028). Carson-Dellos.

--Transportation Fun Book. (Stick-Out-Your-Neck Ser.). (Illus.). 32p. (ps-2). 1984. pap. 1.25 (ISBN 0-88724-022-4, CD-8037). Carson-Dellos.

--Valentine Day Fun Book. (Stick-Out-Your-Neck Ser.). (Illus.). 32p. (ps-1). 1982. pap. 1.25 (ISBN 0-88724-054-2, CD-8009). Carson-Dellos.

--Valentine-February Primary Reading & Art Activities. (Stick-Out-Your-Neck Ser.). (Illus.). 32p. (gr. 1-3). 1984. pap. 1.79 (ISBN 0-88724-026-7, CD-8041). Carson-Dellos.

--Valentine Preschool-K Practice. (Stick-Out-Your-Neck Ser.). (Illus.). 32p. (ps-k). 1984. pap. 1.79 (ISBN 0-88724-018-6, CD-8033). Carson-Dellos.

--Winter Preschool-K Practice. (Stick-Out-Your-Neck Ser.). (Illus.). 32p. (ps-k). 1984. pap. 1.79 (ISBN 0-88724-016-X, CD-8031). Carson-Dellos.

--Winter Primary Reading & Art Activities. (Stick-Out-Your-Neck Ser.). (Illus.). 32p. (gr. 1-3). 1984. pap. 1.79 (ISBN 0-88724-023-2, CD-8038). Carson-Dellos.

Carson, Patti, jt. auth. see Dellosa, Janet.

Carson, Patti, et al. A to Z Alphabet Kids. (Let's Learn Ser.). (Illus.). 32p. (ps-1). 1984. pap. 1.79 (ISBN 0-88724-090-9, CD-7029). Carson-Dellos.

--Days, Months, Seasons. (Stick-Out-Your-Neck Ser.). (Illus.). 20p. (gr. 2-4). 1984. pap. 4.95 (ISBN 0-88724-098-4, CD-0568). Carson-Dellos.

Carson, Peter & Carson, Joan. Don't Say You Can't When You Mean You Won't: How to Act in Your Own Best Interest. 163p. 1982. 12.95 (ISBN 0-13-218438-9); pap. 5.95 (ISBN 0-13-218420-6). P-H.

Carson, Peter & Carson, Joan C. Don't Say You Can't When You Mean You Won't. 165p. pap. 8.95 (ISBN 0-89769-091-5, Dist. by Caroline Hse). Pine Mntn.

Carson, Peter, jt. auth. see Carson, Joan C.

Carson, Peter, jt. auth. see Twiford, Rainer.

Carson, R. A. & Kraay, C. M. Scripta Numaria Romana. 1979. 40.00 (ISBN 0-686-63876-X, Pub. by Spink & Son England). S J Durst.

Carson, R. A., jt. auth. see Sutherland, C. H.

Carson, Rachael. Silent Spring. 304p. 1978. pap. 2.95 (ISBN 0-449-23871-7, Crest). Fawcett.

Carson, Rachel. The Edge of the Sea. (Illus.). 1979. pap. 9.95 (ISBN 0-395-28519-4). HM.

--Sea Around Us. rev. ed. (gr. 10 up). 1961. 19.95x (ISBN 0-19-500500-7). Oxford U Pr.

--The Sense of Wonder. 1965. 12.95i (ISBN 0-06-010645-X, HarpT); PLB 10.87i (ISBN 0-06-010646-8). Har-Row.

--Silent Spring. (Illus.). 1962. 16.95 (ISBN 0-395-07506-8). HM.

Carson, Rachel L. Sea Around Us. 1954. pap. 3.95 (ISBN 0-451-62164-6, ME2164, Ment). NAL.

Carson, Ralph M., jt. auth. see Goodrich, Herbert F.

Carson, Ralph S. High-Frequency Amplifiers. 2nd ed. LC 75-8780. 291p. 1975. 34.95x (ISBN 0-471-86832-9, Pub. by Wiley-Interscience); 29.95. Wiley.

Carson, Ray F. & Patterson, Buel R. Principles of Championship Wrestling. 1978. 2.95 (ISBN 0-346-12371-2). Cornerstone.

Carson, Ray F., ed. Championship Wrestling: An Anthology. LC 73-94015. (Illus.). 1974. 14.95 (ISBN 0-686-09318-6). R Carson.

Carson, Richard D. Taming Your Gremlin: A Guide to Enjoying Yourself. (Illus.). 112p. (Orig.). 1984. pap. 12.50 (ISBN 0-914915-00-2). Family Res.

Carson, Robert B. American Economy in Conflict. LC 74-135858. 415p. 1971. pap. text ed. 7.95x (ISBN 0-669-50815-2). Heath.

--Economic Issues Today: Alternative Approaches. 3rd ed. LC 82-60455. 375p. 1983. pap. text ed. 11.95 (ISBN 0-312-23428-7). instr's. manual avail. St Martin.

--Enterprise: An Introduction to Business. 664p. 1985. text ed. 25.95x (ISBN 0-15-522800-5, HC); test manual avail. (ISBN 0-15-522803-X); wkbk. avail. (ISBN 0-15-522805-6); study guide 10.95 (ISBN 0-15-522801-3); instr's manual avail. (ISBN 0-15-522802-1); transparency masters avail. (ISBN 0-15-522804-8); teaching transparencies avail. (ISBN 0-15-522807-2). HarBraceJ.

--Macroeconomic Issues Today: Alternative Approaches. 3rd ed. LC 82-60456. 300p. 1983. pap. text ed. 9.95 (ISBN 0-312-50327-X); instr's manual avail. St Martin.

--Main Line to Oblivion: The Disintegration of the New York Railroads in the Twentieth Century. LC 75-139352. (American Studies Ser.). 1971. 21.00x (ISBN 0-8046-9003-0, Pub. by Kennikat). Assoc Faculty Pr.

--Microeconomic Issues Today, Alternative Approaches. 3rd ed. LC 82-60457. 275p. 1983. pap. text ed. 9.95 (ISBN 0-312-53174-5); write for info. instr's. manual. St Martin.

--Whatever Happened to the Trolley? 1977. pap. text ed. 9.50 (ISBN 0-8191-0330-6). U Pr of Amer.

Carson, Robert B., ed. Business Issues Today: Alternative Perspectives. LC 83-61610. 348p. 1984. pap. text ed. 10.95 (ISBN 0-312-10905-9); instructor's manual avail. St Martin.

Carson, Robert B., ed. see Pacific Northwest Conference on Higher Education, 1978.
Carson, Robert B., et al. Government in the American Economy. 1973. pap. text ed. 9.95x (ISBN 0-669-83261-8). Heath.
Carson, Robert R., jt. auth. see Rose, Elizabeth A.
Carson, Rosalind. Le Chant du Desir. (Harlequin Seduction Ser.). 332p. 1983. pap. 3.25 (ISBN 0-373-45023-0). Harlequin Bks.
--Song of Desire. (Superromances Ser.). 384p. 1982. pap. 2.50 (ISBN 0-373-70040-7, Pub. by Worldwide). Harlequin Bks.
--Such Sweet Magic. (Superromances Ser.). 384p. 1983. pap. 2.95 (ISBN 0-373-70091-1, Pub. by Worldwide). Harlequin Bks.
--This Dark Enchantment. (Superromances Ser.). 384p. 1982. pap. 2.50 (ISBN 0-373-70016-4, Pub. by Worldwide). Harlequin Bks.
Carson, Rubin. The Coward's Guide to Vasectomy. 192p. 1982. pap. 2.50 (ISBN 0-523-41717-9). Pinnacle Bks.
Carson, Ruby L., jt. auth. see Tebeau, Charlton W.
Carson, Russell M. L. Peaks & People of the Adirondacks. (Illus.). 1973. pap. 6.95 (ISBN 0-935272-06-2). ADK Mtn Club.
Carson, S. McB, ed. Environmental Education-Principles & Practice. (Illus.). 1978. pap. 24.95x (ISBN 0-7131-0133-4). Intl Ideas.
Carson, Steven L. Canadian Ben. LC 79-51132. (Illus.). 238p. 1979. 9.95 (ISBN 0-918628-25-3); pap. 5.95 (ISBN 0-918628-26-1). Bunkhouse.
Carson, Thomas L. The Status of Morality. 1984. lib. bdg. 34.50 (ISBN 0-318-00889-0, Pub. by Reidel Holland). Kluwer Academic.
Carson, Tom. Twisted Kicks. LC 81-67560. 264p. 1981. 12.95 (ISBN 0-934558-03-5); pap. 5.95 (ISBN 0-934558-05-1). Entwhistle Bks.
--Twisted Kicks. LC 81-22901. 260p. 1982. pap. 5.95 (ISBN 0-915904-62-4). And-Or Pr.
Carson, W. E. Mexico, the Wonderland of the South. 1977. lib. bdg. 59.95 (ISBN 0-8490-2252-5). Gordon Pr.
Carson, W. G. The Other Price of Britain's Oil: Safety & Control in the North Sea. 352p. 1982. 27.50x (ISBN 0-8135-0957-2). Rutgers U Pr.
--The Other Price of Britain's Oil: Safety & Control in the North Sea. 220p. 1981. 40.00x (ISBN 0-85520-392-7, Pub. by Robertson & Co England). State Mutual Bk.
Carson, William. Crying Out, Silently: On Getting Along with Others. Barrington, Thomas, ed. 100p. 1985. pap. 8.50 (ISBN 0-911519-09-2). Richelieu Court.
Carson, William G. Managers in Distress: The St. Louis Stage, 1840-1844. (Illus.). 1949. 20.00 (ISBN 0-405-08341-6, Blom Pubns). Ayer Co Pubs.
--Peter & Brownie Follow the Trace. (Illus.). vii, 141p. 1965. 3.95 (ISBN 0-935284-33-8). Patrice Pr.
--Theatre on the Frontier: The Early Years of the St. Louis Stage. rev. ed. LC 65-16229. (Illus.). 1965. Repr. of 1932 ed. 20.00 (ISBN 0-405-08342-4, Blom Pubns). Ayer Co Pubs.
Carson, William M., jt. auth. see Connor, John J.
Carstairs, Andrew M. Short History of Electoral Systems in Western Europe. 256p. 1980. text ed. 28.50x (ISBN 0-04-324006-2). Allen Unwin.
Carstairs, G. M. & Kapur, R. L. The Great Universe of Kota: Stress, Change & Mental Disorder in an Indian Village. LC 75-13151. 1976. 30.00x (ISBN 0-520-03024-9). U of Cal Pr.
Carstarphen. Windjammer World. 1979. pap. 6.95 (ISBN 0-89272-066-2). Down East.
Carstarphen, Dee. The Conch Book. LC 81-90632. (Illus.). 80p. 1981. pap. 6.95 (ISBN 0-9607544-0-7). Pen & Ink.
--The Conch Book. LC 81-90632. (Illus.). 80p. 1981. pap. 6.95 (ISBN 0-9607544-0-7). Banyan Bks.
--Maverick Sea Fare. LC 78-107177. (Illus.). 64p. 1982. pap. 5.95 (ISBN 0-9607544-2-3). Pen & Ink.
--Maverick Sea Fare: A Caribbean Cook Book. LC 78-107177. 60p. 1982. pap. 5.95 (ISBN 0-916224-74-0). Banyan Bks.
Carstarphen, James. My Trip to California in 1849. 8p. 1971. Repr. pap. 2.00 (ISBN 0-87770-038-9). Ye Galleon.
Carsten, F. L. Britain & the Weimar Republic. LC 84-5613. 352p. 1984. 21.50 (ISBN 0-8052-3940-5). Schocken.
--Reichswehr & Politics: Nineteen Eighteen to Nineteen Thirty-Three. 1974. pap. 8.50x (ISBN 0-520-02492-3). U of Cal Pr.
--Revolution in Central Europe, Nineteen Eighteen to Nineteen Nineteen. LC 78-165225. 1972. 40.00x (ISBN 0-520-02084-7). U of Cal Pr.
--The Rise of Fascism. 2nd ed. LC 80-51592. 1980. 22.50 (ISBN 0-520-04307-3); pap. 7.95 (ISBN 0-520-04643-9). U of Cal Pr.
--War Against War: British & German Radical Movements in the First World War. LC 81-69812. 300p. 1982. 24.50 (ISBN 0-520-04581-5). U of Cal Pr.
Carsten, F. L. & Phil, D. Essays in German History. 400p. 1985. 40.00 (ISBN 0-907628-67-2). Hambledon Press.
Carsten, F. L., et al, eds. The Hapsburg Monarchy, 2 vols. LC 81-14902. (Studies in Russian & East European History). Date not set. text ed. 28.50x ea. Vol. 1, Austria & Bohemia 1835-1918 (ISBN 0-389-20248-7). Vol. 2, Hungary 1835-1918 (ISBN 0-389-20249-5, 06389). B&N Imports.
Carsten, Francis L. The Origins of Prussia. LC 81-17866. 309p. 1982. Repr. of 1954 ed. lib. bdg. 29.75x (ISBN 0-313-23220-2, CAOP). Greenwood.
Carsten, Franz L. Reichswehr & Politics: Nineteen Eighteen to Nineteen Thirty-Three. 1966. 39.95x (ISBN 0-19-821457-X). Oxford U Pr.
Carstenpen, J. Thuro, jt. auth. see Leeson, Lewis J.
Carstens, A. L., jt. auth. see Cronkite, E. P.
Carstens, Christoper & Mahedy, William H. Right Here, Right Now: Spiritual Exercises for Busy Christians. 1985. 9.95 (ISBN 0-345-31802-1, Pub. by Ballantine Epiphany). Ballantine.
Carstens, Christopher & Mahedy, William. Right Here, Right Now: Spiritual Exercises for Busy Christians. 1985. 9.95 (ISBN 0-345-31801-3, Pub. by Ballantine Epiphany). Ballantine.
Carstens, Harold & Schopp, William. Complete Layout Plans. rev. ed. (Carstens Hobby Bks: C-17). 1974. pap. 2.50 (ISBN 0-911868-07-0). Carstens Pubns.
Carstens, Harold H. Lionel Standard Gauge Era. LC 64-56883. (Carstens Hobby Bks.: C-13). 1974. pap. 3.00 (ISBN 0-911868-13-5). Carstens Pubns.
--Traction Planbook. 2nd ed. (Carstens Hobby Bks.: C-16). (Illus.). 1969. pap. 6.00 (ISBN 0-911868-16-X). Carstens Pubns.
Carstens, Harold H., ed. Circus Trains & Modelling. LC 75-8473. (Rail-Craft Library: C-29). (Illus.). 1975. pap. 3.00 (ISBN 0-911868-29-1). Carstens Pubns.
Carstens, Sharon, ed. Cultural Identity in Northern Peninsular Malaysia. (CIS Southeast Asia Ser.: No. 63). 109p. 1985. pap. text ed. 9.00x (ISBN 0-89680-116-0, Ohio U Ctr Intl). Ohio U Pr.
Carstens, W. Peter. The Social Structure of a Cape Coloured Reserve. LC 75-3985. (Illus.). 264p. 1975. Repr. of 1966 ed. lib. bdg. 22.50x (ISBN 0-8371-7431-7, CACR). Greenwood.
Carstensen, E. L. Biological Effects on Transmission Line Fields. 300p. 1984. write for info. (ISBN 0-444-00891-8). Elsevier.
Carstensen, Fred V. American Enterprise in Foreign Markets: Singer & International Harvester in Imperial Russia. LC 83-17069. vi, 289p. 1984. 29.95 (ISBN 0-8078-1585-3). U of NC Pr.
Carstensen, Fred V. see Guroff, Gregory.
Carstensen, Jens T. Pharmaceutics of Solids & Solid Dosage Forms. LC 76-22754. 256p. 1977. 44.50 (ISBN 0-471-13726-X, Pub. by Wiley-Interscience). Wiley.
--Solid Pharmaceutics: Mechanical Properties & Rate Phenomena. LC 79-6805. 1980. 52.50 (ISBN 0-12-161150-7). Acad Pr.
--Theory of Pharmaceutical Systems, 2 vols. 1972. Vol. 1. 60.00 (ISBN 0-12-161101-9); Vol. 2, 1973. 60.00 (ISBN 0-12-161102-7). Acad Pr.
Carstensen, Russell V. EMI Control in Boats & Ships. White, Donald R., ed. LC 80-51209. (Illus.). 280p. 1981. text ed. 37.00 (ISBN 0-932263-20-8). White Consult.
Carstensen, Vernon. Farms of Forests. Bruchey, Stuart, ed. LC 78-36706. (Management of Public Lands in the U. S. Ser.). (Illus.). 1979. Repr. of 1958 ed. lib. bdg. 12.00x (ISBN 0-405-11323-4). Ayer Co Pubs.
Carstensen, Vernon, ed. Public Lands: Studies in the History of the Public Domain. 548p. 1963. pap. 9.95x (ISBN 0-299-02754-6). U of Wis Pr.
Carstenson, Cecil C. The Craft & Creation of Wood Sculpture. (Illus.). 192p. 1981. pap. 4.50 (ISBN 0-486-24094-0). Dover.
Carston, Rachel. Devil's Claw Root & Other. 1981. pap. 8.95x (ISBN 0-317-06967-5, Regent House). B of A.
Carswell, C. The Life of Robert Burns. 59.95 (ISBN 0-8490-0535-3). Gordon Pr.
Carswell, Catherine. Life of Robert Burns. LC 78-164157. (Illus.). 1971. Repr. of 1931 ed. 42.00x (ISBN 0-8103-3788-6). Gale.
--The Life of Robert Burns. 1973. Repr. of 1936 ed. 14.50 (ISBN 0-8274-1500-1). R West.
--Robert Burns. 1973. Repr. of 1933 ed. 10.00 (ISBN 0-8274-1505-2). R West.
--The Savage Pilgrimage: A Narrative of D. H. Lawrence. LC 81-3891. 330p. 1981. 39.50 (ISBN 0-521-23975-3); pap. 13.95 (ISBN 0-521-28386-8). Cambridge U Pr.
--The Tranquil Heart: Portrait of Giovanni Boccaccio. 1978. Repr. of 1937 ed. 27.50 (ISBN 0-8492-3934-6). R West.
Carswell, Catherine M. The Savage Pilgrimage: A Narrative by D. H. Lawrence. LC 75-144937. 307p. 1972. Repr. of 1932 ed. 39.00 (ISBN 0-403-01760-2). Scholarly.
--The Tranquil Heart: Boccacio. LC 76-8895. 1976. Repr. of 1937 ed. lib. bdg. 27.50 (ISBN 0-8414-3639-8). Folcroft.
Carswell, D. Life of Sir Walter Scott. LC 70-176490. (English Biography Ser., No. 31). 1971. lib. bdg. 54.95x (ISBN 0-8383-1365-5). Haskell.
Carswell, Donald. Scott & His Circle. facsimile ed. LC 72-175692. (Select Bibliographies Reprint Ser). Repr. of 1930 ed. 19.00 (ISBN 0-8369-6607-4). Ayer Co Pubs.
Carswell, E. A. & Rommetveit, R. Social Context of Messages. (European Monographs in Social Psychology). 1972. 31.50 (ISBN 0-12-161250-3). Acad Pr.
Carswell, John. The Exile. (Illus.). 216p. 1983. 19.95 (ISBN 0-571-13135-2). Faber & Faber.
--Lives & Letters: A. R. Orage; Beatrice Hastings; Katherine Mansfield; John Middleton Murray; S. S. Koteliansky. LC 77-15986. (Illus.). 1978. 15.00 (ISBN 0-8112-0681-5). New Directions.
Carta. Israel Motor Atlas. rev. ed. (Illus.). 1978. pap. 15.00x (ISBN 0-930038-06-1). Arbit.
--Jerusalem Guide & Map. rev. ed. (Illus.). 1978. pap. 7.50x (ISBN 0-930038-08-8). Arbit.
--Map of the Middle East. rev. ed. (Illus.). 1978. pap. 9.95x (ISBN 0-930038-09-6). Arbit.
Carta Staff. Carta's Israel Road & Touring. 8th ed. (Illus.). 175p. 1985. pap. 14.95 (ISBN 965-220-067-0, Pub. by Carta Maps & Guides Pub. Israel). Hippocrene Bks.
Cartagena, Rafael. Una Agenda para la Excelencia Academica. LC 84-681. (Illus.). 128p. (Orig.). 1984. pap. 9.95 (ISBN 0-913480-60-6). Inter Am U Pr.
Cartan, Elie. Geometry of Riemannian Spaces. (LIE Groups Ser.: Vol. XIII). 506p. 1983. 55.00 (ISBN 0-317-18190-4, 991600010). Math Sci Pr.
--On Manifolds with Affine Connections & General Relativity. (Monographs & Textbooks in Physical Sciences). 150p. 1984. text ed. 45.50x (ISBN 88-7088-086-9, Pub. by Bibliopolis, Italy). Humanities.
--The Theory of Spinors. 160p. 1981. pap. 5.00 (ISBN 0-486-64070-1). Dover.
Cartan, H. & Eilenberg, S. Homological Algebra. (Mathematical Ser.: Vol. 19). 1956. 46.00 (ISBN 0-691-07977-3). Princeton U Pr.
Cartan, Paul. Simple Vegetarian Cookery. 1974. lib. bdg. 69.95 (ISBN 0-685-51356-4). Revisionist Pr.
Cartari, Vincenzo. The Fountaine of Ancient Fiction. Linche, Richard, tr. from It. LC 73-6109. (English Experience Ser.: No. 577). 206p. 1973. Repr. of 1599 ed. 20.00 (ISBN 90-221-0577-6). Walter J Johnson.
--Le Imagini...Degli Dei. LC 75-27855. (Renaissance & the Gods Ser.: Vol. 12). (Illus.). 602p. 1976. Repr. of 1571 ed. lib. bdg. 88.00 (ISBN 0-8240-2061-8). Garland Pub.
Cartarius, Ulrich, ed. Bibliograhie Widerstand: Forshungsgemeinschaft 20. Juli e. V. 326p. 1984. lib. bdg. 50.00 (ISBN 3-598-10468-5). K G Saur.
Cartcart, W. George, jt. auth. see Cathcart, Gloria.
Carte, Elaine A., jt. auth. see Carte, Gene E.
Carte, Gene E. & Carte, Elaine A. Police Reform in the United States: The Era of August Vollmer, 1905-1932. LC 73-87248. 390p. 1976. 24.50x (ISBN 0-520-02599-7). U of Cal Pr.
Cartee, Clifford. The Three Horns of Daniel Seven. 32p. 1983. 3.95 (ISBN 0-317-00594-4). Dorrance.
Cartellieri, Otto. Court of Burgundy. LC 70-132437. (World History Ser.: No. 48). 1970. Repr. of 1929 ed. lib. bdg. 49.95x (ISBN 0-8383-1197-0). Haskell.
Carter. The Control & Assurance of Quality, Reliability & Safety. 345p. 26.95 (ISBN 0-318-13203-6, P41). Am Soc QC.
--Corrosion Testing for Metal Finishing. 1982. text ed. 29.95 (ISBN 0-408-01194-7). Butterworth.
--Quality Assurance, Quality Control & Inspection Handbook. 3rd ed. 112p. 6.40 (ISBN 0-318-13232-X, P30). Am Soc QC.
Carter & Mayo. Key for Writing. Date not set. 2.50 (ISBN 0-317-20156-5). Campus.
Carter, jt. auth. see Hubert, J. J.
Carter, jt. auth. see Kricka.
Carter, A. & Brody, A., eds. Contributions to Input-Output Analysis, 2 vols. 1970. Vol. 1: Techniques Geneva 1968. 70.25 (ISBN 0-444-10044-X, North-Holland); Vol. 2: Applications to Input Output Analysis. 70.25 (ISBN 0-444-10029-6). Elsevier.
Carter, A. H., ed. see Burns, D. T. & Townshend, A.
Carter, Adam. A Day in the Life of a Medical Detective. LC 84-8851. (A Day in the Life of Ser.). (Illus.). 32p. (gr. 4-8). 1985. PLB 9.79 (ISBN 0-8167-0097-4); pap. text ed. 2.50 (ISBN 0-8167-0098-2). Troll Assocs.
Carter, Albert E. Miracles of Rebound Exercise. rev. ed. LC 80-134465. 188p. 1980. pap. 3.95 (ISBN 0-938302-01-9). NIRH.
Carter, Alden. Growing Season. 280p. 1985. pap. 2.50 (ISBN 0-425-08427-2, Pub. by Berkley-Pacer). Berkley Pub.
Carter, Alden R. Growing Season. 300p. (gr. 6 up). 1984. 13.95 (ISBN 0-698-20599-5, Coward); pap. 2.25 (ISBN 0-448-47749-1). Putnam Pub Group.
--Wart, Son of Toad. 208p. (gr. 7 up). 1985. 12.95 (ISBN 0-448-47770-X, Putnam). Putnam Pub Group.
Carter, Alden R. & Leblanc, Wayne J. Supercomputers. (Impact Ser.). 128p. (gr. 7 up). 1985. PLB 10.90 (ISBN 0-531-04931-0). Watts.
Carter, Alice C. Dutch Republic in Europe in the Seven Years War. LC 74-154553. 1971. 10.00x (ISBN 0-87024-203-2). U of Miami Pr.
Carter, Amanda. Write Me a Murder. (Mystery Puzzler Ser.: No. 19). (Illus., Orig.). 1979. pap. 1.95 (ISBN 0-89083-454-7). Zebra.
Carter, Angela. The Bloody Chamber. LC 79-2645. 176p. 1981. pap. 3.95i (ISBN 0-06-090836-X, CN836, CN). Har-Row.
--The Bloody Chamber. LC 79-2645. 1980. 9.57i (ISBN 0-06-010708-1, HarpT). Har-Row.
--Fireworks: Nine Stories in Various Disguises. LC 80-8706. 144p. 1981. 10.53i (ISBN 0-06-014852-7, HarpT). Har-Row.
--Nights at the Circus. LC 84-40459. 304p. 1985. 15.95 (ISBN 0-670-80375-8). Viking.
--The Sadeian Woman: And the Ideaology of Pornography. LC 78-20412. 1980. pap. 3.50i (ISBN 0-06-090768-1, CN 768, CN). Har-Row.
--The War of Dreams. 1977. pap. 1.95 (ISBN 0-380-00933-1, 31948-9, Bard). Avon.
Carter, Angela, tr. Sleeping Beauty & Other Favourite Fairy Tales. LC 84-1451. (Illus.). 128p. (gr. 1-8). 1984. 12.95 (ISBN 0-8052-3921-9). Schocken.
Carter, Anjean, jt. auth. see Marshall, Eleanor.
Carter, Anjean B. Do Community Health Centers Save Money? 42p. (Orig.). 1984. pap. 3.50 (ISBN 0-88156-019-7). Comm Serv Soc NY.
Carter, Anne. God Loved the Muddle. (Concept Ser. II). (Illus.). (gr. 1-4). 1978. pap. 3.50 (ISBN 0-570-07787-7, 56-1310). Concordia.
Carter, Anne, tr. see Rodinson, Maxime.
Carter, Anne P. Structural Change in the American Economy. LC 73-95516. (Studies in Technology & Society). 1970. 20.00x (ISBN 0-674-84370-3). Harvard U Pr.
Carter, Anne P., ed. Energy & the Environment: A Structural Analysis. LC 74-15447. (Illus.). 280p. 1976. 25.00x (ISBN 0-87451-112-7). U Pr of New Eng.
Carter, Anthony. World Bayonets, Eighteen Hundred to the Present. (Illus.). 1984. 12.95 (ISBN 0-85368-628-9, Arms & Armour Pr). Sterling.
Carter, Anthony M., jt. auth. see Svendsen, Per.
Carter, April. Democratic Reform in Yugoslavia. LC 81-47910. 288p. 1982. 29.00 (ISBN 0-691-09397-0). Princeton U Pr.
--Direct Action: A Method of Non-Violently Opposing Wars, Tyranny & Other Forms of Oppression. 30p. 1983. lib. bdg. 12.95 (ISBN 0-88286-139-5); pap. 2.50 (ISBN 0-88286-114-X). C H Kerr.
--Direct Action & Liberal Democracy. 1973. 13.95x (ISBN 0-7100-7594-4). Routledge & Kegan.
Carter, Arnold. Communicate Effectively! LC 78-9397. 128p. 1978. 10.00 (ISBN 0-88289-201-0). Pelican.
Carter, Art, photos by. Southeast Coast. LC 85-71193. (Illus.). 160p. (Text by George Reiger). 1985. 37.50 (ISBN 0-912856-95-5). Graphic Arts Ctr.
Carter, Ashley. Heritage of Blackoaks. 1981. pap. 2.95 (ISBN 0-449-14424-0, GM). Fawcett.
--Master of Blackoaks. 1978. pap. 2.95 (ISBN 0-449-13585-3, GM). Fawcett.
--Panama. 1978. pap. 2.25 (ISBN 0-449-14025-3, GM). Fawcett.
--Rogue of Falconhurst. 384p. 1983. pap. 3.50 (ISBN 0-449-12514-9, GM). Fawcett.
--Scandal of Falconhurst. (Orig.). 1980. pap. 2.50 (ISBN 0-449-14334-1, GM). Fawcett.
--Secret of Blackoaks. 1978. pap. 2.95 (ISBN 0-449-13960-3, GM). Fawcett.
--Sword of the Golden Stud. 1977. pap. 2.95 (ISBN 0-449-13842-9, GM). Fawcett.
--Taproots of Falconhurst. 1979. pap. 2.25 (ISBN 0-449-14090-3, GM). Fawcett.
Carter, Ashton & Schwartz, David N., eds. Ballistic Missile Defense. LC 83-24064. 446p. 1984. 32.95 (ISBN 0-8157-1312-6); pap. 12.95 (ISBN 0-8157-1311-8). Brookings.
Carter, B., et al, eds. With One Single Voice: The Stories of Salvadoran Women. (Illus.). 200p. 1986. pap. 8.00 (ISBN 0-942638-13-1, 31L). Solidarity.
Carter, Barbara B., tr. see Montessori, Maria.
Carter, Barbara L. The Copts in Egyptian Politics Nineteen Eighteen to Nineteen Fifty-Two. 256p. 1985. 34.50 (ISBN 0-7099-3417-3, Pub. by Croom Helm Ltd). Longwood Pub Group.
Carter, Barbara L., ed. Computed Tomography of the Head & Neck. (Contemporary Issues in Computed Tomography Ser.: Vol. 5). (Illus.). 344p. 1985. text ed. 44.50 (ISBN 0-443-08380-0). Churchill.
Carter, Barton T., jt. auth. see Franklin, Marc A.
Carter, Ben. Where to Buy Everything Wholesale: A Book of Lifetime Savings. 32p. 1984. pap. 5.95 (ISBN 0-934650-06-3). Sunnyside.
Carter, Bernard, jt. auth. see Singleton, Fred.
Carter, Boake. Why Meddle in Europe & the Orient, 2 vols. Set. 250.00 (ISBN 0-8490-1298-8). Gordon Pr.
Carter, Boyd G. & Carter, Mary E., eds. Manuel Gutierrez Najera: Escritos Ineditos de Sabor Satirico. "Plato del Dia". LC 75-158074. 277p. 1972. 24.00x (ISBN 0-8262-0122-9). U of Mo Pr.
Carter, Bruce. Buzzbugs. 133p. (gr. 5-9). 1979. pap. 1.50 (ISBN 0-380-43323-0, 43323-0, Camelot). Avon.
Carter, Burnham, Jr., et al. Writing Laboratory. 1964. pap. 9.75x (ISBN 0-673-05218-4). Scott F.
Carter, C. C., jt. ed. see Sasser, J. N.
Carter, C. E. The Astrology of Accidents. 1978. pap. 10.00 (ISBN 0-7229-5045-4). Quest Edns.
--Encyclopedia of Psychological Astrology. 4th ed. 1964. pap. 6.75 (ISBN 0-8356-5124-X). Theos Pub Hse.
--Zodiac & the Soul. 59.95 (ISBN 0-8490-1349-6). Gordon Pr.
Carter, C. E., jt. ed. see Alvord, C. W.

Carter, C. F. The Wedding Day in Literature & Art. 59.95 (ISBN 0-8490-1280-5). Gordon Pr.

Carter, C. F. & Ford, J. L., eds. Uncertainty & Expectations in Economics: Essays in Honour of G.L.S. Schakle. LC 72-184239. 299p. 1972. lib. bdg. 35.00x (ISBN 0-678-06277-3). Kelley.

Carter, Candy, ed. Literature-News That Stays News: Fresh Approaches to the Classics. (Classroom Practices in Teaching English Ser.). 120p. (Orig.). 1984. pap. 8.50 (ISBN 0-8141-3012-7); pap. 6.65 members. NCTE.

Carter, Candy & Committee on Classroom Practices, eds. Non-Native & Nonstandard Dialect Students: Classroom Practices in Teaching English, 1982-1983. LC 82-14502. (Classroom Practices in Teaching English Ser.). 112p. 1982. pap. 7.00 (ISBN 0-8141-3351-7); members 6.00. NCTE.

Carter, Candy & Rashkis, Zora, eds. Ideas for Teaching English in the Junior High & Middle School. LC 80-25921. 320p. 1980. 15.00 (ISBN 0-8141-2253-1); members 13.50. NCTE.

Carter, Candy, et al. Structuring for Success in the English Classroom: Classroom Practices in Teaching English, 1981-1982. LC 82-2309. 1982. pap. 10.50 (ISBN 0-8141-4760-7). NCTE.

Carter, Carolle J. The Shamrock & the Swastika: German Espionage in Ireland in World War II. LC 76-14103. (Illus.). 1977. 12.95 (ISBN 0-87015-221-1). Pacific Bks.

Carter, Carrol J. Pike in Colorado. LC 78-60399. (Illus.). 1978. 12.95 (ISBN 0-88342-058-9); pap. 5.95 (ISBN 0-88342-241-7). Old Army.

Carter, Cedric O., ed. Developments in Human Reproduction & Their Eugenic & Ethical Implications. 1983. 36.00 (ISBN 0-12-161860-9). Acad Pr.

Carter, Charles. The Complete Practical Cook: Seventeen Thirty. (Illus.). 316p. 1985. text ed. 42.50x (ISBN 0-907325-20-3, Pub. by Prospect England). U Pr of Va.

Carter, Charles & Pinder, John. Policies for a Constrained Economy. (Policy Studies Institute Ser.). x, 196p. 1982. text ed. 34.00x (ISBN 0-435-84260-9). Gower Pub Co.

Carter, Charles, ed. Industrial Policy & Innovation. (Joint Studies in Public Policy). 1981. text ed. 40.00x o. p. (ISBN 0-435-83115-1); pap. text ed. 16.50x (ISBN 0-435-83116-X). Gower Pub Co.

Carter, Charles E. Principles of Astrology. LC 79-154829. 5.75 (ISBN 0-8356-0423-3, Quest). Theos Pub Hse.

Carter, Charles F. Stories of the Old Missions of California. LC 71-116945. (Short Story Index Reprint Ser). 1917. 14.00 (ISBN 0-8369-3447-4). Ayer Co Pubs.

--The Wedding Day in Literature & Art: A Collection of the Best Descriptions of Wedding from the Works of the World's Leading Novelists & Poets. LC 74-86598. 1969. Repr. of 1900 ed. 30.00x (ISBN 0-8103-0154-7). Gale.

Carter, Charles F., jt. auth. see Barroitt, Denis P.

Carter, Charles F., et al. The Measurement of Production Movements. LC 50-7304. (University of Cambridge, Dept. of Applied Economics, Monographs: 1). pap. 35.80 (ISBN 0-317-26036-7, 2024435). Bks Demand UMI.

Carter, Charles H. Handbook of Mental Retardation Syndromes. 3rd ed. (Illus.). 432p. 1979. photocopy ed. 40.75x (ISBN 0-398-03090-1). C C Thomas.

--Medical Aspects of Mental Retardation. 2nd ed. (Illus.). 912p. 1978. 72.00x (ISBN 0-398-03613-6). C C Thomas.

Carter, Charlotte A. Media in the Courts. 128p. pap. 6.00 (ISBN 0-317-35129-X, R0055). Natl Ctr St Courts.

Carter, Christine A., ed. Indianapolis Dining Guide, 1985. rev. ed. (Illus., Orig.). 1984. pap. 6.95 (ISBN 0-9607968-4-3). Shepard Poorman.

--Indianapolis Dining Guide, 1986. rev. ed. (Illus.). 240p. (Orig.). 1985. pap. 7.95 (ISBN 0-9607968-6-X). Shepard Poorman.

Carter, Ciel. Guide to Reference Sources in the Computer Sciences. LC 72-82745. 1974. 25.00 (ISBN 0-02-468300-0). Macmillan Info.

Carter, Clarence E. Great Britain & the Illinois Country 1763-74. facsimile ed. LC 79-164594. (Select Bibliographies Reprint Ser). Repr. of 1910 ed. 19.00 (ISBN 0-8369-5878-0). Ayer Co Pubs.

--Great Britain & the Illinois Country, 1763-1774. LC 73-120870. (American Bicentennial Ser). 1970. Repr. of 1910 ed. 24.00x (ISBN 0-8046-1263-3, Pub. by Kennikat). Assoc Faculty Pr.

Carter, Clarence E., ed. General Introduction to the Series. Bd. with The Territory Northwest of the River Ohio, 1787-1803. (The Territorial Papers of the United States: Vols. 1 & 2). Repr. of 1934 ed. 69.50 (ISBN 0-404-01451-8). AMS Pr.

--Territorial Papers of the United States, 26 vols. in 25. LC 76-38840. Repr. of 1962 ed. Set. lib. bdg. 1737.50 (ISBN 0-404-01450-X); lib. bdg. 69.50 ea. AMS Pr.

--The Territory Northwest of the River Ohio, 1787-1803. (The Territorial Papers of the United States: Vol. 3). Repr. of 1934 ed. 69.50 (ISBN 0-404-01453-4). AMS Pr.

--The Territory of Alabama, 1817-1819. (The Territorial Papers of the United States: Vol. 18). Repr. of 1952 ed. 69.50 (ISBN 0-404-01468-2). AMS Pr.

--The Territory of Arkansas, 1819-1836. (The Territorial Papers of the United States: Vol. 19). Repr. of 1953 ed. 69.50 (ISBN 0-404-01469-0). AMS Pr.

--The Territory of Arkansas, 1825-1829. (The Territorial Papers of the United States: Vol. 20). Repr. of 1954 ed. 69.50 (ISBN 0-404-01470-4). AMS Pr.

--The Territory of Arkansas, 1829-1836. (The Territorial Papers of the United States: Vol. 21). Repr. of 1954 ed. 69.50 (ISBN 0-404-01471-2). AMS Pr.

--The Territory of Florida, 1821-1825. (The Territorial Papers of the United States: Vol. 22). Repr. of 1956 ed. 69.50 (ISBN 0-404-01472-0). AMS Pr.

--The Territory of Florida, 1824-1828. (The Territorial Papers of the United States: Vol. 23). Repr. of 1958 ed. 69.50 (ISBN 0-404-01473-9). AMS Pr.

--The Territory of Florida, 1828-1834. (The Territorial Papers of the United States: Vol. 24). Repr. of 1959 ed. 69.50 (ISBN 0-404-01474-7). AMS Pr.

--The Territory of Florida, 1834-1839. (The Territorial Papers of the United States: Vol. 25). Repr. of 1960 ed. 69.50 (ISBN 0-404-01475-5). AMS Pr.

--The Territory of Florida, 1839-1845. (The Territorial Papers of the United States: Vol. 26). Repr. of 1962 ed. 69.50 (ISBN 0-404-01476-3). AMS Pr.

--The Territory of Illinois, 1809-1814. (The Territorial Papers of the United States: Vol. 16). Repr. of 1948 ed. 69.50 (ISBN 0-404-01466-6). AMS Pr.

--The Territory of Illinois, 1814-1818. (The Territorial Papers of the United States: Vol. 17). Repr. of 1950 ed. 69.50 (ISBN 0-404-01467-4). AMS Pr.

--The Territory of Indiana, 1800-1810. (The Territorial Papers of the United States: Vol. 7). Repr. of 1939 ed. 69.50 (ISBN 0-404-01457-7). AMS Pr.

--The Territory of Indiana, 1810-1816. (The Territorial Papers of the United States: Vol. 8). Repr. of 1939 ed. 69.50 (ISBN 0-404-01458-5). AMS Pr.

--The Territory of Louisiana-Missouri, 1803-1806. (The Territorial Papers of the United States: Vol. 13). Repr. of 1948 ed. 69.50 (ISBN 0-404-01463-1). AMS Pr.

--The Territory of Louisiana-Missouri, 1806-1814. (The Territorial Papers of the United States: Vol. 14). Repr. of 1949 ed. 69.50 (ISBN 0-404-01464-X). AMS Pr.

--The Territory of Louisiana-Missouri, 1815-1821. (The Territorial Papers of the United States: Vol. 15). Repr. of 1951 ed. 69.50 (ISBN 0-404-01465-8). AMS Pr.

--The Territory of Michigan, 1805-1820. (The Territorial Papers of the United States: Vol. 10). Repr. of 1942 ed. 69.50 (ISBN 0-404-01460-7). AMS Pr.

--The Territory of Michigan, 1820-1829. (The Territorial Papers of the United States: Vol. 11). Repr. of 1943 ed. 69.50 (ISBN 0-404-01461-5). AMS Pr.

--The Territory of Michigan, 1829-1837. (The Territorial Papers of the United States: Vol. 12). Repr. of 1945 ed. 69.50 (ISBN 0-404-01462-3). AMS Pr.

--The Territory of Mississippi, 1798-1817. (The Territorial Papers of the United States: Vol. 5). Repr. of 1937 ed. 69.50 (ISBN 0-404-01455-0). AMS Pr.

--The Territory of Mississippi, 1809-1817. (The Territorial Papers of the United States: Vol. 6). Repr. of 1938 ed. 69.50 (ISBN 0-404-01456-9). AMS Pr.

--The Territory of Orleans, 1803-1812. (The Territorial Papers of the United States: Vol. 9). Repr. of 1940 ed. 69.50 (ISBN 0-404-01459-3). AMS Pr.

--The Territory South of the River Ohio, 1790-1796. (The Territorial Papers of the United States: Vol. 4). Repr. of 1936 ed. 69.50 (ISBN 0-404-01454-2). AMS Pr.

Carter, Clarence E., jt. ed. see Alvord, Clarence W.

Carter, Codell K. A Contemporary Introduction to Logic with Applications. 1977. text ed. write for info. (ISBN 0-02-471500-X). Macmillan.

Carter, Colin A., ed. see Schmitz, Andrew, et al.

Carter, Craig. How to Use the Power of Mind in Everyday Life. 96p. 1976. pap. 4.50 (ISBN 0-911336-65-6). Sci of Mind.

--Your Handbook for Healing. 64p. 1981. pap. 6.95 (ISBN 0-911336-86-9). Sci of Mind.

Carter, Curtis I. & Flew, Anthony, eds. Skepticism & Moral Principles: Modern Ethics in Review. 9.95 (ISBN 0-89044-017-4); pap. 4.95 (ISBN 0-686-78724-2). Precedent Pub.

Carter, Curtis L., ed. Skepticism & Moral Principles: Modern Ethics in Review. LC 73-79477. (Studies in Ethics & Society Ser.: Vol. 1). 1973. 9.95 (ISBN 0-89044-017-4); pap. 4.95 (ISBN 0-89044-018-2). New Univ Pr.

--Skepticism & Moral Principles: Modern Ethics in Review. 143p. 1973. 9.95; pap. 4.95. Transaction Bks.

Carter, Cyril A., jt. auth. see Jacks, Brian.

Carter, D. C. & Polk, Hiram C. BIMR Surgery Vol. 1: Trauma. 1981. text ed. 39.95 (ISBN 0-407-02316-X). Butterworth.

Carter, Dagny. China Magnificent: Five Thousand Years of Chinese Art. LC 78-114493. (Illus.). 225p. 1973. Repr. of 1935 ed. lib. bdg. 18.25x (ISBN 0-8371-4777-8, CACM). Greenwood.

Carter, Dan T. Scottsboro: A Tragedy of the American South. LC 79-1090. (Illus.). 512p. 1979. 35.00x (ISBN 0-8071-0568-6); pap. 7.95x (ISBN 0-8071-0498-1). La State U Pr.

--When the War Was Over: The Failure of Self-Reconstruction in the South, 1865-1867. 369p. 1985. text ed. 27.50x (ISBN 0-8071-1192-9); pap. text ed. 12.95x (ISBN 0-8071-1207-0). La State U Pr.

Carter, Dan T., ed. see Mayo, A. D.

Carter, Daniela B., jt. auth. see Pease, Antonella.

Carter, Darryl. Interpretation of Breast Biopsies. (Biopsy Interpretation Ser.). (Illus.). 212p. 1984. text ed. 41.50 (ISBN 0-88167-022-7). Raven.

Carter, David. Build It Underground: A Guide for the Self-Builder & Building Professional. LC 81-85021. (Illus.). 224p. 1982. pap. 7.95 (ISBN 0-8069-7582-2). Sterling.

--Butterflies & Moths in Britain & Europe. (Illus.). 192p. 1982. 31.50 (ISBN 0-434-10965-7, Pub. by W Heinemann Ltd). David & Charles.

--Cheap Shelter. LC 84-2759. (Illus.). 160p. (Orig.). 1985. pap. 7.95 (ISBN 0-8069-7896-1). Sterling.

--Designing Corporate Identity Programs for Small Corporations. LC 82-71809. (Illus.). 338p. 1982. 35.00 (ISBN 0-686-91925-4). Art Dir.

Carter, David & Phillips, Roger, eds. Butterflies & Moths of Britain & Europe. (Illus.). 192p. (Orig.). 1982. pap. text ed. 14.95x (ISBN 0-916422-37-2, Pub. by Pan Bks England). Mad River.

Carter, David E. Best Financial Advertising, No. 2. LC 79-50633. (Illus.). 424p. 1981. 30.00 (ISBN 0-910158-74-6). Art Dir.

--Best Financial Advertising, No. 3. LC 79-50633. (Best Financial Advertising Ser.). 400p. 1984. 30.00 (ISBN 0-88108-013-6). Art Dir.

--Letterheads, No. 3. LC 81-65825. (Illus.). 326p. 1981. 30.00 (ISBN 0-910158-71-1). Art Dir.

Carter, David E., ed. Best Financial Advertising, No. 1. LC 79-50633. (Illus.). 1979. 30.00 (ISBN 0-910158-56-8). Art Dir.

--The Book of American Trade Marks, No. 1. LC 72-76493. (Trade Marks Ser.). 1978. Repr. of 1972 ed. 14.50 ea.; Vol. 1. (ISBN 0-910158-27-4); Vol. 2. (ISBN 0-910158-28-2); Vol. 3. (ISBN 0-910158-29-0). Art Dir.

--Book of American Trade Marks, Vol. 4. LC 72-76493. (Illus.). 232p. 1976. 16.50 (ISBN 0-910158-30-4). Art Dir.

--Book of American Trade Marks, Vol. 5. LC 72-76493. (Illus.). 1977. 16.50 (ISBN 0-910158-31-2). Art Dir.

--Book of American Trademarks, Vol. 6. LC 72-76493. (Illus.). 1979. 16.50 (ISBN 0-910158-39-8). Art Dir.

--Book of American Trademarks, Vol. 8. LC 72-76493. (Illus.). 1983. 16.50 (ISBN 0-910158-94-0). Art Dir.

--Corporate Identity Manuals. new ed. LC 75-44679. (Illus.). 460p. 1978. Repr. of 1976 ed. 32.50 (ISBN 0-910158-33-9). Art Dir.

--Designing Corporate Symbols. LC 74-29013. (Illus.). 1978. Repr. of 1975 ed. 11.95 (ISBN 0-910158-32-0). Art Dir.

--Evolution of Design. LC 83-73399. 282p. 1985. 37.50 (ISBN 0-88108-005-5). Art Dir.

--Letterheads, No. 4. LC 81-65825. (Letterheads Ser.). 304p. 1984. 30.00 (ISBN 0-88108-002-0). Art Dir.

--Letterheads: The International Annual of Letterhead Design, No. 1. LC 78-58439. (Illus.). 1977. 30.00 (ISBN 0-910158-42-8). Art Dir.

--Letterheads: The Second International Annual of Letterhead Design, No. 2. LC 78-58439. (Letterheads Ser.). (Illus.). 1979. 30.00 (ISBN 0-910158-57-6). Art Dir.

--LOGO International. LC 84-71451. 260p. 1984. 28.50 (ISBN 0-88108-012-8). Art Dir.

Carter, David E., ed. see Annual of Trade Mark Design.

Carter, David J. Pest Lepidopters of Europe. (Entomologica Ser.). 1984. lib. bdg. 89.50 (ISBN 90-6193-504-0, Pub. by Junk Pubs Netherlands). Kluwer Academic.

Carter, David L., jt. auth. see Sapp, Allen D.

Carter, David S. & Vogt, Andrew. Collinearity-Preserving Functions Between Affine Desarguesian Planes. LC 80-20427. (Memoirs: No. 235). 98p. 1980. pap. 9.00 (ISBN 0-8218-2235-7). Am Math.

Carter, Deane G. The Fraternity of Alpha Zeta: A Seventy-five Year History. (Illus.). 122p. (Index & Appendix). 1972. pap. text ed. 5.00 (ISBN 0-318-16923-1). Alpha Zeta.

Carter, Debby L. Clipper. LC 80-8937. (Illus.). 32p. (ps-3). 1981. 8.95 (ISBN 0-06-021127-X); PLB 8.89g (ISBN 0-06-021128-8). HarpJ.

Carter, Dennis, jt. auth. see Wauer, Roland H.

Carter, Dianne K., jt. auth. see Rawlings, Edna I.

Carter, Dilford C. & Dolan, Patricia G. Catalogue of Type Specimens of Neotropical Bats in Selected European Museums. (Special Publications, Museum: No. 15). 136p. 1978. pap. 8.00 (ISBN 0-89672-063-2). Tex Tech Pr.

Carter, Donald. Backgammon: How to Play & Win. (Orig.). 1973. pap. 2.00 (ISBN 0-87067-616-4, BH616). Holloway.

Carter, E. A. & Seaquist, V. G. Extreme Weather History & Climate Atlas from Alabama. 350p. (Orig.). 1984. 15.95 (ISBN 0-317-04384-6); pap. 10.95. Strode.

Carter, E. Dale, Jr. & Bas, Joe, eds. Cuentos Argentinos de Misterio. LC 68-13434. (Orig., Span). (gr. 9 up). 1968. pap. text ed. 7.95x (ISBN 0-89197-119-X). Irvington.

Carter, E. Eugene. College Financial Management: Basics for Administrators. LC 80-7465. 1980. 24.00x (ISBN 0-669-03700-1). Lexington Bks.

Carter, E. Eugene, jt. auth. see Rodriguez, Rita M.

Carter, E. F. Dictionary of Inventions & Discoveries. rev. 2nd ed. LC 75-37058. 208p. 1976. 14.50x (ISBN 0-8448-0867-9). Crane-Russak Co.

Carter, E. M., jt. auth. see Srivastava, M. S.

Carter, E. R. Biographical Sketches of Our Pulpit. LC 72-99355. 1969. Repr. of 1888 ed. lib. bdg. 14.00 (ISBN 0-8411-0026-8). Metro Bks.

Carter, Edward. Jesus, I Want to Talk with You: Contemporary Prayers. LC 73-75617. (Illus.). 1977. pap. 1.95 (ISBN 0-8189-1142-5, Pub. by Alba Bks). Alba.

--Response to God's Love: A View of the Spiritual Life. 184p. 1984. 9.95 (ISBN 0-317-14585-1). Loyola.

Carter, Edward C., ed. see Latrobe, Benjamin.

Carter, Edward C., et al, eds. see Latrobe, Benjamin H.

Carter, Edward C., II, et al, eds. Enterprise & Entrepreneurs in Nineteenth & Twentieth Century France. LC 75-36936. (Illus.). 240p. 1976. 23.00x (ISBN 0-8018-1717-X). Johns Hopkins.

Carter, Edward H., ed. New Past, & Other Essays on the Development of Civilization. facs. ed. LC 68-8446. (Essay Index Reprint Ser). 1968. Repr. of 1925 ed. 17.00 (ISBN 0-8369-0278-5). Ayer Co Pubs.

Carter, Edward R. The Black Side. facsimile ed. LC 78-170692. (Black Heritage Library Collection). Repr. of 1894 ed. 30.75 (ISBN 0-8369-8882-5). Ayer Co Pubs.

Carter, Eleanor-Jean. Doll Modes: Doll Fashions with Patterns. LC 72-76726. 112p. 1972. pap. 15.00 (ISBN 0-9604404-0-2). Carter Craft.

Carter, Elizabeth. Emerald Love. 448p. (Orig.). 1983. pap. 2.95 (ISBN 0-440-02270-3, Emerald). Dell.

--Letters from Mrs. Elizabeth Carter to Mrs. Montagu Between the Years 1755-1800, 3 vols. LC 73-178402. Repr. of 1817 ed. Set. 127.50 (ISBN 0-404-56720-7). AMS Pr.

--The Marriage Mart. 256p. (Orig.). 1983. pap. 2.25 (ISBN 0-449-20082-5, Crest). Fawcett.

--Memoirs of the Life of Mrs. Elizabeth Carter, 2 vols. 4th ed. Pennington, M., ed. LC 75-37674. Repr. of 1825 ed. 90.00 (ISBN 0-404-56727-4). AMS Pr.

--Series of Letters Between Mrs. Elizabeth Carter & Miss Catherine Talbot from the Year 1741 to 1770, 4 vols. Repr. of 1809 ed. Set. 170.00 (ISBN 0-404-56730-4); 42.50 ea. AMS Pr.

Carter, Elizabeth & Pearce, John L. A Canoeing & Kayaking Guide to the Streams of Florida, Vol. 1. Williams, Barbara E., ed. (Illus., Orig.). 1985. pap. 12.95 (ISBN 0-89732-033-6). Menasha Ridge.

Carter, Elizabeth & Stolper, Matthew W. ELAM: Surveys of Political History & Archaeology. LC 83-18005. (Near Eastern Studies: Vol. 25). 342p. 1984. lib. bdg. 23.50 (ISBN 0-520-09950-8). U of Cal Pr.

Carter, Elizabeth A. The Family Life Cycle: A Framework for Family Therapy. McGoldrick, Monica, ed. 1980. text ed. 29.50 (ISBN 0-89876-028-3). Gardner Pr.

Carter, Elton & Fife, Iline. Learning Your Way Through College. 96p. 1963. 9.50x (ISBN 0-398-00292-4). C C Thomas.

Carter, Eneida & Mikalac, Miriam. Break Dance: The Free & Easy Way! 32p. 1984. pap. 9.95 (ISBN 0-916391-00-0). Carter's Free & Easy Pub.

Carter, Ernest. British Steam Locomotives. pap. 7.50x (ISBN 0-392-08880-0, SpS). Sportshelf.

--Let's Look at Trains. 9.50x (ISBN 0-392-08037-0, SpS). Sportshelf.

Carter, Evelyn & Choy, Leona. No Ground. LC 78-73008. 1978. 4.95 (ISBN 0-88270-291-2, Pub. by Logos). Bridge Pub.

Carter, Everett. The American Idea: The Literary Response to American Optimism. LC 76-13867. ix, 276p. 1977. 24.00 (ISBN 0-8078-1279-X). U of NC Pr.

Carter, Everett & Homburger, Wolfgang S. Introduction to Transportation Engineering: Highways & Transit. (Illus.). 1978. text. ref. ed. 26.95 (ISBN 0-87909-388-9). Reston.

Carter, Everett, ed. see Frederic, Harold.

Carter, F. D. H. Lawrence & the Body Mystical. LC 68-910. (Studies in D. H. Lawrence, No. 20). 1969. Repr. of 1932 ed. lib. bdg. 29.95x (ISBN 0-8383-0653-5). Haskell.

Carter, F. W., ed. An Historical Geography of the Balkans. 1977. 93.00 (ISBN 0-12-161750-5). Acad Pr.

Carter, Forrest. The Vengeance Trail of Josey Wales. 1980. pap. 2.25 (ISBN 0-440-19344-3). Dell.

--Watch for Me on the Mountain. 1983. pap. 3.95 (ISBN 0-440-39065-6, LE). Dell.

Carter, Forrest L., ed. Molecular Electronic Devices. 424p. 1982. 65.00 (ISBN 0-8247-1676-0). Dekker.

Carter, Forrest S., jt. auth. see Mentzer, John T.

Carter, Frances M. Psychosocial Nursing. 3rd ed. 1981. text ed. 25.95 (ISBN 0-02-319660-2). Macmillan.

Carter, Frank, jt. auth. see Trevillian, Bob.

Carter, Frank B., Jr. Mendacity Without Scruples. Ashton, Sylvia, ed. LC 77-78384. 1978. 14.95 (ISBN 0-87949-093-4). Ashley Bks.

Carter, Fred F. Free & Easy: Male & Female Poses. 1978. pap. 11.95 (ISBN 0-87314-075-3). Peter Glenn.

Carter, Frederick. D. H. Lawrence & the Body Mystical. 1978. Repr. lib. bdg. 10.00 (ISBN 0-8495-0823-1). Arden Lib.

Carter, Frederick D. D. H. Lawrence: The Body Mystical. 1932. lib. bdg. 12.50 (ISBN 0-8414-3356-9). Folcroft.

Carter, G. A. J. L. Hobbs' Local History & the Library. 2nd, rev. ed. 352p. 1973. 20.00x (ISBN 0-233-95615-8, 05773-8, Pub. by Gower Pub Co England). Lexington Bks.

Carter, G. R. Diagnostic Procedures in Veterinary Bacteriology & Mycology. 4th ed. (Illus.). 526p. 1984. 39.50x (ISBN 0-398-04870-3). C C Thomas.

--Essentials of Veterinary Bacteriology & Mycology. 1982. 15.50 (ISBN 0-87013-201-6). Mich St U Pr.

Carter, G. R., jt. auth. see Roberts, A. Wayne.

Carter, G. S. A General Zoology of the Invertebrates. (Illus.). 1965. text ed. 17.95 (ISBN 0-8464-1166-0). Beekman Pubs.

--Structure & Habit in Vertebrate Evolution. LC 67-25160. (Biology Ser.). (Illus.). 544p. 1967. 20.00x (ISBN 0-295-95121-4). U of Wash Pr.

Carter, G. W. & Richardson, A. Techniques of Circuit Analysis. LC 79-183222. (Illus.). 544p. 1972. 47.50 (ISBN 0-521-08435-0). Cambridge U Pr.

Carter, Genevieve W., jt. auth. see Steinberg, Raymond M.

Carter, Geoffrey W. The Electromagnetic Field in Its Engineering Aspects. 2nd ed. LC 79-355853. (Electrical Engineering Ser.). pap. 97.00 (ISBN 0-317-09839-X, 2006978). Bks Demand UMI.

Carter, George. The Story of Milton's Paradise. 1909. lib. bdg. 15.00 (ISBN 0-8414-1590-0). Folcroft.

Carter, George, jt. auth. see Sippl, Charles J.

Carter, George E. & Ripley, C. Peter, eds. Black Abolitionist Papers, 1830-1865. 572p. 1981. pap. text ed. 30.00 (ISBN 0-667-00630-3). Microfilming Corp.

Carter, George F. Earlier Than You Think: A Personal View of Man in America. LC 79-5280. 368p. 1980. 22.50x (ISBN 0-89096-091-7). Tex A&M Univ Pr.

--Pleistocene Man at San Diego. LC 77-74811. Repr. of 1957 ed. 37.00 (ISBN 0-404-14885-9). AMS Pr.

Carter, George W. Zoroastrianism & Judaism. LC 70-112489. 1970. Repr. of 1918 ed. 14.00 (ISBN 0-404-01396-1). AMS Pr.

Carter, Georgia H. The Second Best of Granny: Family Recipes. 1985. 7.95 (ISBN 0-533-06268-3). Vantage.

Carter, Gerald. Data Entry Skills: Additional Problems. 2nd ed. 103p. (gr. 9-12). 1978. pap. text ed. 14.00 (ISBN 0-9610582-1-8). Apollo Com.

Carter, Gerald L. & Minkema, Douglas D. Data Entry Skills-Key Disk Machine. 3rd ed. (Data Entry Skills-Key Disk Machine & Additional Problems Ser.). 97p. (gr. 9-12). 1977. pap. text ed. 14.50 (ISBN 0-9610582-0-X). Apollo Com.

--Data Entry Skills Teacher's Guide. text ed. 32.00 (ISBN 0-9610582-4-2). Apollo Com.

Carter, Gerald L., jt. auth. see Minkema, Douglas D.

Carter, Giles F. Principles of Physical & Chemical Metallurgy. 1979. 59.00 (ISBN 0-87170-080-8). ASM.

--Principles of Physical & Chemical Metallurgy. LC 79-19184. pap. 111.80 (ISBN 0-317-20682-6, 2025146). Bks Demand UMI.

Carter, Giles F., ed. Archaeological Chemistry, Vol. II. LC 78-26128. (Advances in Chemistry Ser.: No. 171). 1978. 54.95 (ISBN 0-8412-0397-0). Am Chemical.

Carter, Gwendolen M. British Commonwealth & International Security. LC 71-114494. 1971. Repr. of 1947 ed. lib. bdg. 21.25x (ISBN 0-8371-4731-X, CABC). Greenwood.

--National Unity & Regionalism in Eight African States: Nigeria, Niger, the Congo, Gabon, Central African Republic. LC 66-12113. pap. 145.30 (ISBN 0-317-10941-3, 2005457). Bks Demand UMI.

Carter, Gwendolen M., ed. African Independence: The First Twenty-Five Years. O'Meara, Patrick. LC 84-48457. (Illus.). 416p. 1985. 29.95x (ISBN 0-253-30255-2). Ind U Pr.

Carter, Gwendolen M. & Karis, Thomas, eds. South African Political Materials: A Catalogue of the Carter-Karis Collection. LC 77-74449. 830p. 1977. 35.00x (ISBN 0-253-35396-3). Ind U Pr.

Carter, Gwendolen M. & Morgan, E. Philip, eds. From the Frontline: Speeches of Sir Seretse Khama. (Special Project Ser.: No. 27). 252p. 1980. 26.95x (ISBN 0-8179-4271-8). Hoover Inst Pr.

Carter, Gwendolen M. & O'Meara, Patrick, eds. International Politics in Southern Africa. LC 81-48325. (Midland Bks.: No. 281). (Illus.). 288p. 1982. 32.50x (ISBN 0-253-34285-6); pap. 9.95 (ISBN 0-253-20281-7). Ind U Pr.

--Southern Africa: The Continuing Crisis. 2nd ed. LC 81-48324. (Midland Bks.: No. 280). 416p. 1982. 35.00x (ISBN 0-253-35400-5); pap. 12.95x (ISBN 0-253-20280-9). Ind U Pr.

Carter, Gwendolen M. & Paden, Ann, eds. Expanding Horizons in African Studies: Program of African Studies, Northwestern University, Proceedings of the Twentieth Anniversary Conference, 1968. 1969. 19.95x (ISBN 0-8101-0265-X). Northwestern U Pr.

--Expanding Horizons in African Studies: Program of African Studies, Northwestern University, Proceedings of the 20th Anniversary Conference 1968. LC 72-89823. pap. 95.00 (ISBN 0-317-29809-7, 2016704). Bks Demand UMI.

Carter, Gwendolen M., ed. see Hess, Robert L.

Carter, Gwendolyn & Karis, Thomas. Suoth Africa's Transkei, the Politics of Domestic Colonialism. LC 67-15937. pap. 53.50 (ISBN 0-317-27594-1, 2014773). Bks Demand UMI.

Carter, Gwendolyn M. Southern Africa: Prospects for Change. LC 73-93659. (Headline Ser.: No. 219). (Illus., Orig.). 1974. pap. 3.00 (ISBN 0-87124-024-6). Foreign Policy.

Carter, Gwendolyn M. & O'Meara, Patrick, eds. Southern Africa in Crisis. LC 76-48534. pap. 69.80 (ISBN 0-317-27939-4, 2056027). Bks Demand UMI.

Carter, H. & Partington, I. Applied Economics in Banking & Finance. 3rd ed. 1984. 29.95x (ISBN 0-19-877230-0); pap. 11.95x (ISBN 0-19-877229-7). Oxford U Pr.

Carter, H. & Wheatley, S. Merthyr Tydfil in Eighteen Fifty-One: A Study of the Spartial Structure of a Welsh Industrial Town. (Social Science Monographs: No. 7). (Illus.). 100p. 1982. pap. text ed. 11.00x (ISBN 0-7083-0825-2, Pub. by Univ of Wales Pr England). Humanities.

Carter, H. B. Sir Joseph Banks & the Plant Collection from Kew Sent to the Empress Catherine II of Russia 1795. (Bulletin of the British Museum Natural History, Historical Ser.: Vol. 4, No. 5). (Illus.). 1975. text ed. 20.00x (ISBN 0-565-00768-8, Pub. by Brit Mus Nat Hist); pap. text ed. 22.00x (ISBN 0-8277-4351-3). Sabbot-Natural Hist Bks.

Carter, H. W., et al. Clinical Applications of the Scanning Electron Microscope. Johari, Om & Becker, R. P., eds. (Illus.). 1980. pap. 10.00x (ISBN 0-931288-16-9). Scanning Electron.

Carter, Harley. Diccionario de Electronica. 416p. (Span.). 1962. 19.95 (ISBN 0-686-56716-1, S-33049). French & Eur.

Carter, Harold. An Introduction to Urban Historical Geography. 320p. 1983. pap. text ed. 18.95 (ISBN 0-7131-6386-0). E Arnold.

--Social Areas in Cities: Past & Future. 1984. pap. 3.00. U MD Geography.

--Social Areas in Cities: Past & Future. pap. text ed. write for info. (ISBN 0-913749-01-X). U MD Inst.

--The Study of Urban Geography. 2nd ed. LC 76-22730. 398p. 1976. 26.95x (ISBN 0-470-98911-4). Wiley.

--The Study of Urban Geography. 3rd ed. 434p. 1981. pap. text ed. 18.95 (ISBN 0-7131-6235-X). E Arnold.

Carter, Harold A. Myths That Mire the Ministry. 1980. pap. 5.95 (ISBN 0-8170-0845-4). Judson.

Carter, Harold B., ed. The Sheep & Wool Correspondence of Sir Joseph Banks, 1781-1820. (Illus.). xxx, 641p. 1979. 94.00x (ISBN 0-565-00802-1, Pub. by Brit Mus Nat Hist England). Sabbot-Natural Hist Bks.

Carter, Harry. A History of the Oxford University Press, (Vol. 1 to 1780. (Illus.). 1975. text ed. 47.50x (ISBN 0-19-951032-6). Oxford U Pr.

Carter, Harry, jt. auth. see Fournier, Pierre S.

Carter, Harvey L. Far Western Frontiers. LC 72-77078. (AHA Pamphlets: No. 222). (Illus.). 1972. pap. text ed. 1.50 (ISBN 0-87229-004-2). Am Hist Assn.

Carter, Harvey L., jt. auth. see Guild, Thelma S.

Carter, Helen. Bridge of Dreams. (Second Chance at Love Ser.: No. 241). 192p. 1985. pap. 1.95 (ISBN 0-425-07768-3). Berkley Pub.

--Tender Is the Night. (Second Chance At Love Ser.: No. 307). 192p. 1985. pap. 2.25 (ISBN 0-425-08675-5). Berkley Pub.

--Touched by Lightning. (Second Chance at Love Ser.: No. 194). 192p. 1984. pap. 1.95 (ISBN 0-515-07810-7). Jove Pubns.

--Words of Endearment. (Second Chance at Love Ser.: No. 251). 192p. 1985. pap. 1.95 (ISBN 0-425-07976-7). Berkley Pub.

Carter, Henry H. Dictionary of Middle English Musical Terms. Gerhard, George B., et al, eds. LC 61-63413. (Indiana University Humanities Ser: No. 45). 1961. 39.00 (ISBN 0-527-15150-5). Kraus Repr.

--The Portuguese Book of Joseph of Arimathea. (Studies in the Romance Languages & Literatures: No. 71). 464p. 1968. pap. 19.00x (ISBN 0-8078-9071-5). U of NC Pr.

Carter, Hobart C. Modern Basic Mathematics. LC 63-19876. (Illus.). 1964. 26.00x (ISBN 0-89197-305-2). Irvington.

Carter, Hodding. The Angry Scar: The Story of Reconstruction. LC 73-10751. 425p. 1974. Repr. of 1959 ed. lib. bdg. 29.75 (ISBN 0-8371-7022-2, CAAS). Greenwood.

--The Commandos of World War II. LC 80-21142. (Landmark Bks.). (Illus.). 160p. (gr. 5-9). 1981. 2.95 (ISBN 0-394-84735-0, BYR). Random.

--First Person Rural. LC 77-10014. 1977. Repr. lib. bdg. 20.00x (ISBN 0-8371-9727-9, CAFI). Greenwood.

--South Strikes Back. Repr. of 1959 ed. cancelled (ISBN 0-8371-5178-3). Greenwood.

Carter, Hodding, ed. Louisiana Almanac 1968. (Illus.). 1968. pap. 12.95 (ISBN 0-911116-48-6). Pelican.

--Louisiana Almanac, 1969. 1969. pap. 11.95 (ISBN 0-911116-49-4). Pelican.

Carter, Hodding, intro. by. Past As Prelude: New Orleans 1718-1968. LC 68-25161. (Illus.). 1968. 10.00 (ISBN 0-911116-02-8). Pelican.

Carter, Horace, jt. auth. see Hannon, Douglas.

Carter, Howard. Questions & Answers on Spiritual Gifts. 127p. 1976. pocket bk. 2.95 (ISBN 0-89274-007-8). Harrison Hse.

--Spiritual Gifts & Their Operation. 96p. 1968. pap. 1.95 (ISBN 0-88243-593-0, 02-0593). Gospel Pub.

Carter, Howard & Mace, A. C. The Discovery of the Tomb of Tutankhamen. LC 77-71042. (Illus.). 382p. 1977. pap. 5.50 (ISBN 0-486-23500-9). Dover.

--The Discovery of the Tomb of Tutankhamen. (Illus.). 13.75 (ISBN 0-8446-5562-7). Peter Smith.

--Tomb of Tut-Ankh-Amen, 3 Vols. LC 63-17462. (Illus.). Repr. of 1954 ed. Set. 85.00 (ISBN 0-8154-0048-9). Cooper Sq.

Carter, Howard M. The Jurisdiction of Federal Courts, as Limited by the Citizenship & Residence of the Parties. xxviii, 303p. 1983. Repr. of 1899 ed. lib. bdg. 32.50x (ISBN 0-8377-0445-6). Rothman.

Carter, Hugh. Social Theories of L. T. Hobhouse. LC 67-27609. 1927. Repr. 15.00x (ISBN 0-8046-0070-8, Pub. by Kennikat). Assoc Faculty Pr.

Carter, Hugh & Glick, Paul C. Marriage & Divorce: A Social & Economic Study. rev. ed. LC 79-105369. (Vital & Health Statistics Monographs, American Public Health Association). 1970. 25.00x (ISBN 0-674-55075-7). Harvard U Pr.

Carter, Huntly. New Spirit in the Cinema. LC 76-112580. (Literature in Cinema, Ser. 1). Repr. of 1930 ed. 19.00 (ISBN 0-405-01605-0). Ayer Co Pubs.

--The New Spirit in the Cinema. 59.95 (ISBN 0-8490-0724-0). Gordon Pr.

--New Spirit in the Russian Theatre Nineteen Seventeen to Nineteen Twenty-Eight. LC 77-112583. (Literature of Cinema, Ser. 1). Repr. of 1929 ed. 17.00 (ISBN 0-405-01606-9). Ayer Co Pubs.

--New Theatre & Cinema of Soviet Russia. LC 74-124001. (Literature of Cinema, Ser. 1). Repr. of 1924 ed. 17.00 (ISBN 0-405-01607-7). Ayer Co Pubs.

--Theatre of Max Reinhardt. LC 64-14700. (Illus.). 1914. 22.00 (ISBN 0-405-08344-0, Blom Pubns). Ayer Co Pubs.

Carter, I. R. Alien Blossom: A Japanese-Australian Love Story. 14.50x (ABC). Sportshelf.

--Southern Cloud. 15.00x (ISBN 0-392-06644-0, SpS). Sportshelf.

Carter, Ian, ed. Aberdeenshire Peasant Life: William Alexander-Scottish Peasant Life. (Library of Peasant Studies: No. 5). 1985. 28.00x (ISBN 0-7146-3087-X, BHA-03087, F Cass Co). Biblio Dist.

Carter, Ian R. Farm Life in North East Scotland, 1840-1914: The Poo Man's Country. (Illus.). 1979. text ed. 33.00x. Humanities.

Carter, Irl, jt. auth. see Anderson, Ralph E.

Carter, J. E., ed. Physical Structure of Olympic Athletes. (Medicine & Sport Science Ser.: Vol. 18). (Illus.). viii, 248p. 1984. 67.00 (ISBN 3-8055-3871-5). S Karger.

Carter, J. M. Suetonius: Divus Augustus. 300p. 30.00x (ISBN 0-906515-55-6, Pub. by Bristol Classical Pr). State Mutual Bk.

Carter, J. P., ed. La Famine En Afrique: Rapports de Conference d'un Groupe de Travail sur la Famine en Afrique a Kinshasa au Zaire en janvier 1980. 46p. 1982. pap. 11.00 (ISBN 0-08-028885-5, H120). Pergamon.

--Famine in Africa: Proceedings of a Conference of a Working Group on Famine in Africa, Kinshasa, Zaire, January 1980. 46p. 1982. 11.00 (ISBN 0-08-027998-8, H120). Pergamon.

Carter, J. R. Investors in Saudi Araia. 452p. 1982. 250.00x (ISBN 0-905906-32-2, Pub. by Scorpion Comm England). State Mutual Bk.

--Tribes in Oman. 176p. 1982. 110.00x (ISBN 0-907151-02-7, Pub. by Scorpion Comm England). State Mutual Bk.

Carter, J. R., ed. see Desikachar, T. K.

Carter, Jack, ed. Sunflower Science & Technology. 1978. 17.50 (ISBN 0-89118-054-0). Am Soc Agron.

Carter, James. Law: Its Origin, Growth & Function. LC 74-6413. (American Constitutional & Legal History Ser.). 1974. Repr. of 1907 ed. lib. bdg. 42.50 (ISBN 0-306-70631-8). Da Capo.

Carter, James E. Help for the Evangelistic Preacher. LC 83-70371. 1985. pap. 6.50 (ISBN 0-8054-6243-0). Broadman.

--Layman's Bible Book Commentary: John, Vol. 18. LC 81-65391. 1984. 5.75 (ISBN 0-8054-1188-7). Broadman.

--People Parables. (Pocket Pulpit Library). 128p. 1981. pap. 2.95 (ISBN 0-8010-2348-3). Baker Bk.

--A Sourcebook for Stewardship Sermons. LC 78-74768. 1979. pap. 5.50 (ISBN 0-8054-6403-4). Broadman.

Carter, James G. Essays upon Popular Education. LC 70-89162. (American Education: Its Men, Institutions & Ideas, Ser. 1). 1969. Repr. of 1826 ed. 10.00 (ISBN 0-405-01399-X). Ayer Co Pubs.

--Letters to the Honorable William Prescott, LL.D., on the Free Schools of New England. LC 77-89161. (American Education: Its Men, Institutions & Ideas, Ser. 1). 1969. Repr. of 1824 ed. 13.00 (ISBN 0-405-01400-7). Ayer Co Pubs.

Carter, James J. Love-Affinity. (Illus.). 60p. (Orig.). 1984. pap. 9.95 (ISBN 0-317-02694-1). Carter Pub.

--Nasty People: All You Ever Wanted to Know about SOB's but Were Afraid to Ask Them. (Illus.). 60p. (Orig.). pap. 9.95 (ISBN 0-317-02693-3). Carter Pub.

--Prose, Poetry, & Flows. (Illus., Orig.). 1979. pap. 4.95 (ISBN 0-937004-01-4). Carter Pub.

--Self Analysis: The Book About Life. (Illus., Orig.). 1979. pap. 4.95 (ISBN 0-937004-00-6). Carter Pub.

Carter, James J. & Bucks County Community College. Introduction to DEC-10 Assembler. (Illus., Orig.). 1984. pap. 9.95 (ISBN 0-317-02675-5). Carter Pub.

Carter, James L. & Rankin, Ernest H., eds. North to Lake Superior: Journal of Charles W. Penny, 1840. LC 74-80875. 1970. 4.95 (ISBN 0-938746-02-2). Marquette Cnty.

Carter, James L., ed. see Castle, Beatrice H.

Carter, James L., ed. see Van Riper, Charles.

Carter, James M. The Norman Conquest in English Historiography. 115p. 1980. pap. 12.00x (ISBN 0-89126-086-2). MA-AH Pub.

Carter, James R. Computer Mapping: Progress in the Eighties. LC 84-70007. (Resource Publications in Geography). 100p. 1984. pap. 5.00 (ISBN 0-89291-175-1). Assn Am Geographers.

Carter, Jan. Day Services for Adults Somewhere to Go. (National Institute Social Services Library: No. 40). 352p. 1981. text ed. 28.50x (ISBN 0-04-362035-3). Allen Unwin.

--Day Services for Adults: Somewhere to Go. 1981. 60.00x (ISBN 0-317-05820-7, Pub. by Natl Inst Social Work). State Mutual Bk.

Carter, Jan, jt. auth. see Edwards, Carol.

Carter, Jane Burr see Burr Carter, Jane.

Carter, Janette. Living with Memories. (Illus.). 83p. 12.00x (ISBN 0-318-00547-6). Pub Ctr Cult Res.

--Living with Memories. (Illus.). 96p. 1983. 12.00; pap. 4.00 (ISBN 0-89062-177-2). Carter Fam.

Carter, Jared. Early Warning. 16p. (Orig.). 1979. pap. 5.00 (ISBN 0-935306-06-4). Barnwood Pr.

--Fugue State. 16p. (Orig.). 1984. pap. 2.50 (ISBN 0-935306-16-1). Barnwood Pr.

--Pincushion's Strawberry. (Illus.). 31p. (Orig.). 1984. pap. 3.50 (ISBN 0-914946-43-9). Cleveland St Univ Poetry Ctr.

--Work, for the Night Is Coming. 64p. 1981. 10.95 (ISBN 0-02-522090-X); pap. 5.95 (ISBN 0-02-069290-0). Macmillan.

Carter, Jean & Ogden, Jess. Everyman's Drama. 1938. 15.00 (ISBN 0-8482-3563-0). Norwood Edns.

Carter, Jenny. The Scottish Field Colour Book of Scotland. 152p. 1983. 45.00x (ISBN 0-906391-26-1, Pub. by Mainstream). State Mutual Bk.

Carter, Jenny & Hardley, Dennis. The Highlands & Islands of Scotland in Colour. (Illus.). 64p. 1983. 12.50 (ISBN 0-7134-3825-8, Pub. by Batsford England). David & Charles.

Carter, Jesse B. Religious Life of Ancient Rome. 270p. 1972. Repr. of 1911 ed. lib. bdg. 27.50 (ISBN 0-8154-0429-8). Cooper Sq.

Carter, Jessie. Make Your Dreams Come True, No. 8: Special Friends. (Orig.). 1985. pap. cancelled (ISBN 0-446-32386-1). Warner Bks.

Carter, Jimmy. The Blood of Abraham: Insights into the Middle East. (Illus.). 236p. 1985. 15.95 (ISBN 0-395-37722-6). HM.

--Keeping Faith: Memoirs of a President. 1983. pap. 9.95 (ISBN 0-553-34017-4). Bantam.

--Letters to Hon. William Prescott. 1977. lib. bdg. 59.95 (ISBN 0-8490-2156-1). Gordon Pr.

--Negotiation: The Alternative to Hostility. LC 84-10720. (The Carl Vinson Memorial Lecture Ser.). (Illus.). xxxiii, 57p. 1984. 12.95x (ISBN 0-86554-137-X, MUP/H128). Mercer Univ Pr.

--Why Not the Best? LC 75-22730. (Illus.). 156p. 1975. 5.95 (ISBN 0-8054-5561-2); pap. 1.95 (ISBN 0-8054-5564-7); presidential ed. 8.95 (ISBN 0-8054-5582-5). Broadman.

Carter, Jo A., jt. auth. see Baker, Betty S.

Carter, Joan H., et al. Standards of Nursing Care: A Guide for Evaluation. 2nd ed. LC 72-75096. 292p. 1976. text ed. 22.50 (ISBN 0-8261-1361-3). Springer Pub.

Carter, John. A B C for Book-Collectors. rev. ed. (Illus.). 1963. 11.95 (ISBN 0-394-41403-9). Knopf.

--Taste & Technique in Book Collecting. 256p. 1982. 60.00x (ISBN 0-686-79275-0, Pub. by Private Libs England). State Mutual Bk.

Carter, John & Pollard. Enquiry into the Nature of Nineteen Century Pamphlets. LC 76-164659. (English Literature Ser., No. 33). 1971. Repr. of 1934 ed. lib. bdg. 49.95x (ISBN 0-8383-1261-6). Haskell.

Carter, John & Pollard, Graham. An Enquiry into the Nature of Certain Nineteenth Century Pamphlets. Barker, Nicolas & Collins, John, eds. (Illus.). 464p. 1984. Repr. of 1934 ed. 40.00 (ISBN 0-85967-637-4). Scolar.

Carter, John & Sparrow, John. A.E. Housman: A Bibliography. rev. ed. Orig. Title: A. E. Housman: An Annotated Handlis t. 94p. 1982. 27.50x (ISBN 0-906795-05-2, Pub. by St Pauls Biblios England). U Pr of Va.

Carter, John, jt. auth. see Narramore, Bruce.

Carter, John, ed. Fiji Handbook & Travel Guide. 304p. 1980. pap. 13.95 (ISBN 0-85807-046-4, 3012, Pub. by Pacific Pubns Australia). Australia N U P.

--Fiji Handbook & Travel Guide. LC 81-159471. (Illus.). 304p. (Orig.). 1980. 27.50x (ISBN 0-85807-046-4). Intl Pubns Serv.

--New Paths in Book Collecting: Essays by Various Hands. facs. ed. LC 67-30179. (Essay Index Reprint Ser). 1934. 16.00 (ISBN 0-8369-0279-3). Ayer Co Pubs.

--Pacific Islands Yearbook, 1981. 14th ed. LC 32-24429. (Illus.). 560p. 1981. 47.50x (ISBN 0-85807-049-9). Intl Pubns Serv.

Carter, John, illus. Texas Wildlife Coloring Book. 40p. 1984. 2.95 (ISBN 0-89015-483-X). Eakin Pubns.

Carter, John D. The Warren Court & the Constitution: A Critical View of Judicial Activism. LC 73-7828. 176p. 1972. 10.00 (ISBN 0-911116-98-2). Pelican.

Carter, John D., jt. auth. see Barber, Cyril J.

Carter, John D., jt. ed. see Fleck, J. Roland.

Carter, John E. Solomon D. Butcher: Photographing the American Dream. LC 85-5835. (Illus.). 144p. 1985. 28.95 (ISBN 0-8032-1404-9). U of Nebr Pr.

Carter, John F. American Messiahs by the Unofficial Observer. LC 68-26232. 1968. Repr. of 1935 ed. 19.00x (ISBN 0-8046-0010-4, Pub by Kennikat). Assoc Faculty Pr.

--Layman's Harmony of the Gospel. 1961. 12.95 (ISBN 0-8054-1326-X). Broadman.

--The New Dealers: By the Unofficial Observer. LC 74-23461. (FDR & the Era of the New Deal Ser.). ix, 414p. 1975. Repr. of 1934 ed. lib. bdg. 45.00 (ISBN 0-306-70710-1). Da Capo.

--What We Are about to Receive. facs. ed. LC 68-29196. (Essay Index Reprint Ser). 1968. Repr. of 1932 ed. 18.00 (ISBN 0-8369-0280-7). Ayer Co Pubs.

Carter, John F., Jr. The Destroyers. LC 74-22771. Repr. of 1907 ed. 21.00 (ISBN 0-404-58410-1). AMS Pr.

Carter, John H. Log of Commodore Rollingpin: His Adventures Afloat & Ashore. LC 74-166690. (Illus.). 1971. Repr. of 1874 ed. 29.00 (ISBN 0-403-01452-2). Scholarly.

Carter, John L. & Carter, Ruth C. Bibliography & Index of North American Carboniferous Brachiopoda 1898-1968. LC 74-129146. (Geological Society of America Ser.: No. 128). pap. 98.00 (ISBN 0-317-27889-4, 2025460). Bks Demand UMI.

Carter, John M. Arms & the Man: Studies in Roman & Medieval Warfare & Society. 1983. pap. 9.50x (ISBN 0-89126-123-0). MA-AH Pub.

--Ludi Medi Aevi: Studies in the History of Medieval Sport. 1981. pap. 20.00x (ISBN 0-89126-102-8). MA-AH Pub.

--Medieval Institutions: Study-Lecture Notes, Vol. 1. 205p. 1983. 25.00x (ISBN 0-89126-125-7). MA-AH Pub.

--The Military & Social Significance of Ballad Singing in the English Civil War, 1642-1649. 95p. 1980. pap. text ed. 9.50x (ISBN 0-89126-095-1). MA-AH Pub.

--Rape in Medieval England: An Historical & Sociological Study. 196p. (Orig.). 1985. lib. bdg. 22.50 (ISBN 0-8191-4503-3); pap. text ed. 11.00 (ISBN 0-8191-4504-1). U Pr of Amer.

--War & Military Reform in the Roman Republic: 578-589 B.C. 1980. pap. text ed. 9.50x (ISBN 0-89126-096-X). MA-AH Pub.

Carter, John M. & Feeney, Joan. Starting at the Top: America's New Achievers. LC 85-4826. 286p. 1985. 15.95 (ISBN 0-688-04520-0). Morrow.

Carter, John R. Dhamma: Western Academic & Sinhalese Buddhist Interpretations: A Study of a Religious Concept. 1978. 32.75 (ISBN 0-89346-014-1, Pub. by Hokuseido Pr.). Heian Intl.

Carter, John R. & Bond, George D. The Threefold Refuge in the Theravada Buddhist Tradition. 1983. 3.95x (ISBN 0-89012-030-7). Anima Pubns.

Carter, John S. American Traders in European Ports. LC 82-303. (Illus.). 56p. 1982. write for info. (ISBN 0-87577-067-3); pap. 12.50 (ISBN 0-87577-068-1). Peabody Mus Salem.

Carter, John S., ed. Contemporary Marine Art. LC 81-5916. (Illus.). 80p. (Orig.). 1981. pap. 9.95 (ISBN 0-87577-065-7); 20.00 (ISBN 0-686-86588-X). Peabody Mus Salem.

Carter, John S., ed. see Shirley, James.

Carter, Joseph B., jt. auth. see Teachey, William G.

Carter, Joseph C. The Sculpture of Taras. LC 75-19514. (Transactions Ser: Vol. 65, Pt. 7). (Illus.). 1975. 18.00 (ISBN 0-87169-657-6). Am Philos.

Carter, Juanita E. & Young, Darroch. Electronic Calculators: A Mastery Approach Year. 1981. 15.50 (ISBN 0-395-29621-8); instr's manual 1.00 (ISBN 0-395-29622-6). HM.

Carter, Juanita E. & Young, Darroch F. Calculating Machines: A Ten-Key Approach. 1975. pap. text ed. 19.95 (ISBN 0-395-18594-7); instrs.' manual 1.50 (ISBN 0-395-18805-9). HM.

Carter, Judith Q., compiled by. Herbert L. Fink: Graphic Artist. Carter, Richard D. & Gardner, John. LC 80-39918. (Illus.). 158p. 1981. 29.95 (ISBN 0-8093-1016-3). S Ill U Pr.

Carter, K. Codell, ed. see Godwin, William.

Carter, K. Codell, tr. see Semmelweis, Ignaz.

Carter, Katharine J. Oceans. LC 81-17093. (New True Bks.). (Illus.). 48p. (gr. k-4). 1982. PLB 10.60 (ISBN 0-516-01639-3); pap. 3.95 (ISBN 0-516-41639-1). Childrens.

Carter, Katherine. Houses. LC 82-4431. (New True Bks.). (Illus.). (gr. k-4). 1982. PLB 10.60 (ISBN 0-516-01672-5). Childrens.

--Ships & Seaports. LC 82-4463. (New True Bks.). (Illus.). (gr. k-4). 1982. PLB 10.60 (ISBN 0-516-01656-3). Childrens.

Carter, Kathryn T. At the Battle of San Jacinto: With Rip Cavitt. (Illus.). 64p. 5.95 (ISBN 0-89015-374-4). Eakin Pubns.

--Stagecoach Inns of Texas. 1982. 17.50 (ISBN 0-87244-067-2). Texian.

Carter, Kenneth. Photography Simplified for Archivists. Gill, Rowland P., ed. (A Collegiate Guide to Archival Science Ser.: No. 5). 16p. (Orig.). 1948. pap. text ed. 3.75 (ISBN 0-910653-10-0, 8101-K). Archival Servs.

Carter, Kenneth J. I Was a Giant Last Night, Mom. (Illus.). 44p. (gr. k-5). 1983. PLB 9.95 (ISBN 0-911247-00-9). Calif Cam.

Carter, Kit, jt. auth. see Clark, I. E.

Carter, Kit C. & Mueller, Robert. The Army Air Forces in World War II: Combat Chronology 1941-1945. Gilbert, James, ed. LC 79-7235. (Flight: Its First Seventy-Five Years Ser.). 1979. Repr. of 1973 ed. lib. bdg. 80.00x (ISBN 0-405-12151-2). Ayer Co Pubs.

Carter, L. B., et al. Arco's Comprehensive State Board Examination Review for Nurses. LC 79-28537. 357p. (Orig.). 1980. pap. 11.95 (ISBN 0-668-04925-1). ACC.

Carter, L. J. & Bainum, Peter M., eds. Space: A Developing Role for Europe, 18th European Space Symposium. (Science & Technology Ser.: Vol. 56). (Illus.). 278p. 1984. lib. bdg. 45.00x (ISBN 0-87703-193-2, Pub. by Am Astro Soc); pap. text ed. 35.00 (ISBN 0-87703-194-0); fiche suppl. 20.00 (ISBN 0-87703-195-9). Univelt Inc.

Carter, L. L. & Cashwell, E. D. Particle-Transport Simulation with the Monte Carlo Method. LC 75-25993. (ERDA Critical Review Ser.). 124p. 1975. pap. 11.00 (ISBN 0-87079-021-8, TID-26607); microfiche 4.50 (ISBN 0-87079-382-9, TID-26607). DOE.

Carter, L. P., jt. auth. see Bishop, D.

Carter, L. Phillip, jt. auth. see Spetzler, Robert F.

Carter, L. R. & Huzan, E. Learn Computer Programming with the Commodore VIC-20. 1983. pap. 5.95 (ISBN 0-679-10537-9). Mckay.

--Teach Yourself Computer Programming in BASIC. (Teach Yourself Ser.). 174p. 1981. pap. 5.95 (ISBN 0-679-10535-2). McKay.

--Teach Yourself Computer Programming with the Commodore 64. 192p. 1983. pap. 6.95 (ISBN 0-679-10538-7). McKay.

Carter, Lanie. Congratulations! You're Going to Be a Grandmother. LC 80-1345. 1980. PLB 5.95 (ISBN 0-916392-48-1); pap. 3.95 (ISBN 0-916392-53-8). Oak Tree Pubns.

Carter, Lark P., jt. auth. see Chapman, Stephen R.

Carter, Lawrence T. Eubie Blake: Keys of Memory. LC 79-12430. 1979. 8.00 (ISBN 0-913642-10-X). Balamp Pub.

Carter, Lawson A. Zola & the Theater. LC 77-6784. (Yale Romantic Studies, English Ser.). 1977. Repr. of 1963 ed. lib. bdg. 24.75x (ISBN 0-8371-9659-0, CAZO). Greenwood.

Carter, Lee. Fifty Programs for the Timex-Sinclair 1000. 72p. 1983. pap. 6.95 (ISBN 0-916688-23-2, 15T). Creative Comp.

--Lucifer's Handbook. LC 76-55893. 1977. pap. text ed. 5.95 (ISBN 0-918260-01-9). Acad Assoc.

Carter, Les. Good 'n' Angry. 128p. 1983. 8.95 (ISBN 0-8010-2488-9); pap. 5.95 (ISBN 0-8010-2481-1). Baker Bk.

--Mind over Emotions. 1985. pap. 5.95 (ISBN 0-8010-2504-4). Baker Bk.

--The Push-Pull Marriage. 1984. 7.95 (ISBN 0-8010-2497-8); pap. 5.95 (ISBN 0-8010-2490-0). Baker Bk.

--Will the Defense Please Rest? A Guide to Marital Harmony. Anderson, Marty, ed. 200p. (Orig.). 1985. pap. 8.95 (ISBN 0-933629-07-9). Today Pubs.

Carter, Les, et al. Why Be Lonely? A Guide to Meaningful Relationships. 176p. (Orig.). 1982. 5.95 (ISBN 0-8010-2474-9, 2474-9); 8.95 (ISBN 0-8010-2475-7). Baker Bk.

Carter, Lief. Reason in Law. 2nd ed. 1984. 12.95 (ISBN 0-316-13049-4). Little.

Carter, Lief H. Administrative Law & Politics: Cases & Commentaries. 1983. text ed. 28.95 (ISBN 0-316-13047-8); write for info tchr's. manual avail. (ISBN 0-316-13048-6). Little.

--Contemporary Constitutional Lawmaking: The Supreme Court & the Art of Politics. (Pergamon Government & Politics Ser.). (Illus.). 256p. 1985. 29.50 (ISBN 0-08-030970-4); pap. 12.95 (ISBN 0-08-030969-0). Pergamon.

Carter, Lin. As the Green Star Rises. 176p. 1983. pap. text ed. 2.25 (ISBN 0-87997-811-2). DAW Bks.

--Beyond the Gates of Dream. (Inflation Fighters Ser.). 160p. 1982. pap. 1.50 (ISBN 0-8439-1082-8, Leisure Bks). Dorchester Pub Co.

--By the Light of the Green Star. (Science Fiction Ser.). 1974. pap. 2.25 (ISBN 0-87997-742-6, UE1742). DAW Bks.

--Down to a Sunless Sea. 1984. pap. 2.50 (ISBN 0-87997-937-2). DAW Bks.

--Dragonrouge: Further Adventures in Terra Magica. 224p. 1984. pap. 2.50 (ISBN 0-87997-982-8). DAW Bks.

--Dreams from R'lyeh. LC 74-78131. 1975. 5.00 (ISBN 0-87054-067-X). Arkham.

--Found Wanting. 1985. pap. 2.75 (ISBN 0-88677-050-5). DAW Bks.

--Invisible Death. LC 75-9219. 173p. 1975. 15.00 (ISBN 0-385-08768-3). Ultramarine Pub.

--Kellory the Warlock. LC 82-45283. (Science Fiction Ser.). 192p. 1984. 11.95 (ISBN 0-385-17315-6). Doubleday.

--Renegade of Callisto. 1978. pap. 1.75 (ISBN 0-440-14377-2). Dell.

--Tara of the Twilight. (Orig.). 1979. pap. 2.25 (ISBN 0-89083-428-8). Zebra.

--Tower at the Edge of Time. (Inflation Fighter Ser.). 144p. 1982. pap. 1.50 (ISBN 0-8439-1097-6, Leisure Bks). Dorchester Pub Co.

--Under the Green Star. (Science Fiction Ser.). (Orig.). 1972. pap. 1.50 (ISBN 0-87997-433-8, UY1433). DAW Bks.

Carter, Lin, jt. auth. see DeCamp, L. Sprague.

Carter, Lin, jt. auth. see De Camp, L. Sprague.

Carter, Lin, jt. auth. see De Camp, Sprague L.

Carter, Lin, jt. auth. see Sprague de Camp, L.

Carter, Lin, ed. Weird Tales, No. 1. 288p. (Orig.). 1981. pap. 2.50 (ISBN 0-89083-714-7). Zebra.

--Weird Tales, No. 2. 288p. (Orig.). 1981. pap. 2.50 (ISBN 0-89083-715-5). Zebra.

--Weird Tales, Vol. 4. 1983. pap. 2.95 (ISBN 0-8217-1238-1). Zebra.

--Weird Tales, No. 3. (YA) 1981. pap. 2.50 (ISBN 0-89083-803-8). Zebra.

Carter, Linda & Culinary Arts Institute Staff. The Food Processor Cookbook. Finnegan, Edward G., ed. LC 78-54620. (Adventures in Cooking Ser). (Illus.). 1980. pap. write for info (ISBN 0-8326-0607-3, 2517). Delair.

Carter, Linda B. Fundamentals of Nursing Review. LC 79-1088. (Arco Nursing Review Ser.). 1979. pap. text ed. 7.00x (ISBN 0-668-04512-4). Arco.

--Fundamentals of Nursing Review. 208p. 1979. pap. 10.95 (ISBN 0-668-04512-4). ACC.

Carter, Loretta M. & Yaman, Peter. Dental Instruments. LC 80-28707. (Illus.). 190p. 1981. pap. text ed. 12.95 (ISBN 0-8016-0980-1). Mosby.

Carter, Luther. The Florida Experience: Land & Water Policy in a Growth State. 376p. 1974. 24.00 (ISBN 0-8018-1646-7); pap. 10.95 (ISBN 0-8018-1896-6). Resources Future.

Carter, Luther J. The Florida Experience: Land & Water Policy in a Growth State. LC 74-6816. (Resources for the Future Ser.). 376p. 1976. o. p. 24.00x (ISBN 0-8018-1646-7); pap. 10.95x (ISBN 0-8018-1896-6). Johns Hopkins.

Carter, Lynn R. An Analysis of Pascal Programs. Stone, Harold, ed. LC 82-4925. (Computer Science: Systems Programming: No. 6). 202p. 1982. 44.95 (ISBN 0-8357-1331-8). UMI Res Pr.

Carter, Lynn T., et al. The Thinking Skills Workbook: A Cognitive Skills Remediation Manual for Adults. 2nd ed. 234p. 1984. pap. 19.75x spiral (ISBN 0-398-04992-0). C C Thomas.

Carter, M. Geotechnical Engineering Handbook. (Illus.). 244p. 1982. 35.00 (ISBN 0-412-00341-4, NO. 5041, Chapman & Hall). Methuen Inc.

Carter, M. & Maddock, R. Rational Expectations: Macroeconomics for the 1980s? 165p. 1984. text ed. 33.50x (ISBN 0-333-33143-5, Pub. by Macmillan England); pap. text ed. 11.50x (ISBN 0-333-33144-3). Humanities.

Carter, M. G., ed. Arab Linguistics: An Introductory Classical Text with Translation & Notes. (Studies in the History of Linguistics: No. 24). x, 485p. 1981. 50.00x (ISBN 90-272-4506-1). Benjamins North Am.

Carter, Madison H. An Annotated Catalog of Composers of African Ancestry. 1985. 13.95 (ISBN 0-533-06613-1). Vantage.

Carter, Margaret L. Vampirism in Literature: Shadow of a Shade. 1974. lib. bdg. 69.95 (ISBN 0-87968-225-6). Gordon Pr.

Carter, Marion E. Role of the Symbol in French Romantic Poetry. LC 77-94178. (Catholic University of America. Studies in Romance Languages & Literatures: No. 32). Repr. of 1946 ed. 19.00 (ISBN 0-404-50332-2). AMS Pr.

Carter, Martin & Mayblin, Munday. Systems Management & Change. 1984. pap. text ed. 7.00 (ISBN 0-06-318272-6). Har-Row.

Carter, Mary E. Edgar Cayce on Prophecy. 208p. 1968. pap. 3.50 (ISBN 0-446-32712-3). Warner Bks.

--Essential Fiber Chemistry. (Fiber Science Ser.: Vol. 2). 1971. 65.00 (ISBN 0-8247-1088-6). Dekker.

Carter, Mary E. & McGarey, William A. Edgar Cayce on Healing. 208p. 1972. pap. 2.95 (ISBN 0-446-30861-7). Warner Bks.

Carter, Mary E., jt. ed. see Carter, Boyd G.

Carter, Melvin W., et al, eds. Management of Low-Level Radioactive Waste, 2 vols. 1979. 180.00 (ISBN 0-08-023907-2). Pergamon.

Carter, Michael. George Orwell & the Problem of Authentic Existence. LC 85-6166. 256p. 1985. 24.75x (ISBN 0-389-20578-8). B&N Imports.

Carter, Michael & Leahy, William, eds. New Directions in Labor Economics & Industrial Relations. LC 81-50457. 214p. 1981. text ed. 18.95 (ISBN 0-268-01458-2); pap. text ed. 6.95 (ISBN 0-268-01459-0). U of Notre Dame Pr.

Carter, Mildred. Body Reflexology: Healing at Your Fingertips. LC 83-2422. 234p. 1983. 18.95 (ISBN 0-13-079699-9, Parker); pap. 5.95 (ISBN 0-13-079681-6). P-H.

--Hand Reflexology: Key to Perfect Health. 1975. 12.95 (ISBN 0-13-383612-6, Reward); pap. 4.95 (ISBN 0-13-383604-5). P-H.

--Helping Yourself with Foot Reflexology. Orig. Title: Helping Yourself to Vibrant Health Through Secrets of Foot Reflexology. (Illus.). 1969. 10.95 (ISBN 0-13-386680-7, Reward); pap. 4.95 (ISBN 0-13-386532-0). P-H.

Carter, Morris. Isabella Stewart Gardner & Fenway Court. LC 72-5539. (Select Bibliographies Reprint Ser.). (Illus.). 1972. Repr. of 1925 ed. 31.00 (ISBN 0-8369-6901-4). Ayer Co Pubs.

--Isabella Stewart Gardner & Fenway Court. 3rd ed. LC 72-5539. (Illus.). 265p. 1981. Repr. of 1925 ed. 12.00 (ISBN 0-914660-07-1). I S Gardner Mus.

Carter, N. Routine Circumcision: The Tragic Myth. 1982. lib. bdg. 59.75 (ISBN 0-87700-398-X). Revisionist Pr.

Carter, N. & Dixon, A. F. Cereal Aphid Population: Biology, Simulation & Prediction. 94p. 1982. pap. 14.50 (ISBN 90-220-0804-5, PDC252, Pudoc). Unipub.

Carter, N. F. History of Pembroke, 2 Vols. 1976. Repr. of 1895 ed. 45.00X (ISBN 0-89725-032-X). NH Pub Co.

Carter, N. L. & Friedman, M., eds. Mechanical Behavior of Crustal Rocks. (Geophysical Monograph Ser.: Vol. 24). 326p. 1981. 42.00 (ISBN 0-87590-024-0). Am Geophysical.

Carter, Nancy M. & Cullen, John B. The Computerization of Newspaper Organizations: The Impact of Technology on Organizational Structuring. (Illus.). 146p. (Orig.). 1983. lib. bdg. 22.25 (ISBN 0-8191-3378-7); pap. text ed. 9.75 (ISBN 0-8191-3379-5). U Pr of Amer.

Carter, Nevada. Frontier Steel. 160p. 1982. 10.95 (ISBN 0-8027-4008-1). Walker & Co.

--Frontier Steel. large print ed. LC 82-19693. 212p. 1983. Repr. of 1965 ed. 11.95 (ISBN 0-89621-431-1). Thorndike Pr.

Carter, Nicholas. The Late Great Book: The Bible. McCalden, David, ed. 230p. (Orig.). 1985. pap. 10.00 (ISBN 0-910607-01-X). Truth Missions.

--Routine Circumcision: The Tragic Myth. 1979. pap. 4.00 (ISBN 0-911038-26-4). Noontide.

--The Stolen Pay Train. LC 74-15733. (Popular Culture in America Ser.). 128p. 1975. Repr. 13.00 (ISBN 0-405-06368-7). Ayer Co Pubs.

Carter, Nicholas, ed. Development, Growth & Aging. 176p. 1980. 27.50 (ISBN 0-85664-861-2, Pub. by Croom Helm Ltd); pap. 9.75 (ISBN 0-85664-862-0). Longwood Pub Group.

Carter, Nick. The Algarve Affair, No. 185. 208p. 1984. pap. 2.50 (ISBN 0-441-01276-0). Ace Bks.

--Appointment in Haiphong. (Illus.). 224p. 1982. pap. 2.50 (ISBN 0-441-02592-7, Pub. by Charter Bks). Ace Bks.

--The Assassin Convention, No. 204. 208p. 1985. pap. 2.50 (ISBN 0-441-03211-7). Ace Bks.

--Assignment: Rio. 208p. 1984. pap. 2.50 (ISBN 0-441-03223-0). Ace Bks.

--Beirut Incident. (Nick Carter Ser.). 192p. (Orig.). 1981. pap. 2.25 (ISBN 0-441-05381-5, Pub. by Charter Bks). Ace Bks.

--Blood of the Scimitar, No. 205. 208p. 1985. pap. 2.50 (ISBN 0-441-06790-5). Ace Bks.

--The Blue Ice Affair, No. 97. 208p. 1985. pap. 2.50 (ISBN 0-441-06861-8). Ace Bks.

--The Cairo Mafia. 224p. 1982. pap. 2.50 (ISBN 0-441-09028-1). Ace Bks.

--Caribbean Coup. 208p. 1984. pap. 2.50 (ISBN 0-441-09157-1). Ace Bks.

--Cauldron of Hell. (Nick Carter Ser.). 224p. (Orig.). 1981. pap. 2.50 (ISBN 0-441-09274-8). Ace Bks.

Carter, Thomas P., jt. ed. see Willey, Ann M.
Carter, Timothy, et al, eds. Rural Crime: Integrating Research & Prevention. 294p. 1982. 33.95 (ISBN 0-318-02914-6). Biblio Dist.
Carter, Timothy J., et al, eds. Rural Crime: Integrating Research & Prevention. LC 81-65018. (Illus.). 294p. 1982. text ed. 33.95x (ISBN 0-86598-023-3). Allanheld.
Carter, Tom. The Victorian Garden. (Illus.). 192p. 1985. 19.95 (ISBN 0-88162-120-X, Pub. by Salem Hse Ltd). Merrimack Pub Cir.
Carter, V. L. Arkansas Baptist College: A Historical Prospective. 1981. text ed. 12.00 (ISBN 0-918464-38-2). D Armstrong.
Carter, Velma T. & Leavenworth, J. Lynn. Putting the Pieces Together. LC 77-4124. 1977. text ed. 6.95 (ISBN 0-8170-0746-6); pap. 3.95 (ISBN 0-8170-0747-4). Judson.
Carter, Velma T. & Leavenworth, Lynn J. Caught in the Middle: Children of Divorce. 176p. 1985. pap. 9.50 (ISBN 0-8170-1037-8). Judson.
Carter, Vernon G. & Dale, Tom. Topsoil & Civilization. rev. ed. (Illus.). 240p. 1974. 12.95 (ISBN 0-8061-0332-9); pap. 8.95x (ISBN 0-8061-1107-0). U of Okla Pr.
--Topsoil & Civilization. (Illus.). 308p. pap. 8.95 (ISBN 0-8061-1107-0). U of Okla Pr.
Carter, Vernon G., jt. auth. see Dale, Tom.
Carter, Virginia B. A Handbook of Metal Threads for the Embroiderer. rev. ed. (Illus.). 50p. 1979. 8.00 (ISBN 0-9603862-1-1). V B Carter.
--I'm Going to Be a Missionary. (Orig.). 1978. pap. 2.95 (ISBN 0-89036-103-7). Hawkes Pub Inc.
Carter, Virginia L., ed. Annual Fund Ideas. 48p. 1979. pap. 10.50 (ISBN 0-89964-016-8). Coun Adv & Supp Ed.
--How to Cut Publications Costs. 98p. 1984. 14.50 (ISBN 0-89964-231-4). Coun Adv & Supp Ed.
Carter, Virginia L., compiled by. How to Survey Your Readers. 48p. 1981. 14.50 (ISBN 0-89964-189-X). Coun Adv & Supp Ed.
Carter, Virginia L., ed. A Marketing Approach to Student Recruitment. 79p. 1979. pap. 14.50 (ISBN 0-89964-031-1). Coun Adv & Supp Ed.
--A Marketing Approach to Student Recruitment. 79p. 1979. pap. 14.50 (ISBN 0-89964-031-1). Coun Adv & Supp Ed.
Carter, Virginia L. & Alberger, Patricia, eds. Building Your Alumni Program. 122p. 1980. 14.50 (ISBN 0-89964-165-2). Coun Adv & Supp Ed.
Carter, Virginia L. & Garigan, Catherine S., eds. Planned Giving Ideas. 30p. 1979. pap. 9.50 (ISBN 0-89964-039-7). Coun Adv & Supp Ed.
Carter, Virginia L. & LaSalle Alberger, Patricia, eds. How to Cut Publications Costs. rev. ed. 98p. 1984. 14.50 (ISBN 0-89964-231-4). Coun Adv & Supp Ed.
Carter, Virginia L., jt. ed. see Alberger, Patricia L.
Carter, W. A., ed. Selective Inhibitors of Viral Functions. LC 73-81479. (Uniscience Ser). 377p. 1973. 64.00 (ISBN 0-87819-027-9). CRC Pr.
Carter, W. A., jt. ed. see Came, P. E.
Carter, W. D. & Engman, E. T., eds. Remote Sensing from Satellites: Proceedings of Workshops I & IX of the COSPAR Interdisciplinary Scientific Commission A (Meetings A2) of the COSPAR 25th Plenary Meeting Held in Graz, Austria 25 June - 7 July 1974. 264p. 1985. pap. 49.50 (ISBN 0-08-032751-6, Pub. by P P L). Pergamon.
Carter, W. Horace. Creatures & Chronicles from Cross Creek. LC 80-68460. (Illus.). 286p. (Orig.). 1981. pap. text ed. 5.95 (ISBN 0-937866-02-4). Atlantic Pub Co.
--Nature's Masterpiece at Homosassa. (Illus.). 288p. (Orig.). 1984. 7.95 (ISBN 0-937866-07-5). Atlantic Pub Co.
--Wild & Wonderful Santee Cooper Country. LC 1-67210. (Illus.). 392p. (Orig.). 1981. pap. 6.95 (ISBN 0-686-75381-X). Atlantic Pub Co.
Carter, W. Horace, jt. auth. see Faircloth, Rudy.
Carter, W. Horace, jt. auth. see Hamlet, John N.
Carter, W. Horace, ed. see Stone, C R.
Carter, W. Nick. Procedures & Guidelines for Disaster Preparedness & Response. vi, 189p. Date not set. pap. 13.00 (ISBN 0-86638-063-9). E W Center HI.
Carter, Walter. Insects in Relation to Plant Disease. 2nd ed. LC 73-4362. pap. 160.00 (ISBN 0-317-28102-X, 2055731). Bks Demand UMI.
Carter, Warren B. Locomotives of the Jersey Central 1-999. rev. ed. (Illus.). 105p. (Orig.). 1978. pap. 7.50 (ISBN 0-941652-02-5). Railroadians.
Carter, William A., jt. ed. see Doumeingts, Guy.
Carter, William C. & Vines, Robert F., eds. A Concordance to the Oeuvres Completes of Arthur Rimbaud. LC 75-36985. xiv, 810p. 1978. 45.00x (ISBN 0-8214-0216-1, 82-82220). Ohio U Pr.
Carter, William D. Study Abroad & Educational Development. (Fundamentals of Educational Planning: No. 19). 49p. (Orig.). 1973. pap. 5.00 (ISBN 92-803-1059-3, U636, UNESCO). Unipub.
Carter, William E. South America. rev. ed. (First Bks.). (Illus.). 72p. (gr. 4 up). 1983. PLB 8.90 (ISBN 0-531-04531-5). Watts.
Carter, William E., ed. Cannabis in Costa Rica: A Study of Chronic Marihuana Use. LC 80-14726. (Illus.). 344p. 1980. text ed. 19.95 (ISBN 0-89727-008-8). ISHI PA.
Carter, William E., jt. ed. see Margolis, Maxine L.
Carter, William J., et al. A Catalog of Dental Collectibles & Antiques, Vol. 2. LC 84-72258. (Illus.). 72p. (Orig.). 1984. pap. 9.95 (ISBN 0-930989-00-7). Dental Folk.
Carter, William S. Let Us Pray: Series A. (Orig.). 1974. pap. 3.00 (ISBN 0-89536-129-9). CSS of Ohio.
--Let Us Pray: Series B. 1975. pap. 3.00 (ISBN 0-89536-130-2). CSS of Ohio.
--Let Us Pray: Series C. 1976. pap. 3.00 (ISBN 0-89536-128-0). CSS of Ohio.
Carter, Winifred. Dr. Johnson's "Dear Mistress". Repr. 17.50 (ISBN 0-8274-2199-0). R West.
Carterette, Edward C. & Jones, Margaret H. Informal Speech: Alphabetic & Phonemic Text. LC 73-92376. 1975. 60.00x (ISBN 0-520-01476-6). U of Cal Pr.
Carterette, Edward C. & Friedman, Morton P., eds. Handbook of Perception. Incl. Vol. 1. 1974. 50.00 (ISBN 0-12-161901-X); Vol. 2. 1974. 60.00 (ISBN 0-12-161902-8); Vol. 4. Hearing. 1978. 60.00 (ISBN 0-12-161904-4); Vol. 5. 1975. 60.00 (ISBN 0-12-161905-2); Vol. 6, 2 pts. 1978. Pt. A, Testing & Smelling. 43.00 (ISBN 0-12-161906-0); Pt. B, Feeling & Hurting. 45.00 (ISBN 0-12-161922-2); Vol. 7. 1976. 60.00 (ISBN 0-12-161907-9); Vol. 8. Perceptual Coding. 1978. 50.00 (ISBN 0-12-161908-7); Vol. 9. Perceptual Processing. 1978. 50.00 (ISBN 0-12-161909-5); Vol. 10. Perceptual Ecology. 1978. 60.00 (ISBN 0-12-161910-9). Acad Pr.
Carter Ewel, Katherine & Odum, Howard T., eds. Cypress Swamps. LC 84-5230. (Center for Wetlands Research, University of Florida). 490p. 1985. 25.00 (ISBN 0-8130-0714-3). U Presses Fla.
Carteron, Henri. La Notion De Force Dans le Systeme D' Aristote. LC 78-66622. (Ancient Philosophy Ser.). 193p. 1979. lib. bdg. 34.00 (ISBN 0-8240-9605-3). Garland Pub.
Carter-Ruck, Peter. Libel & Slander. xxx, 448p. 1973. 32.50 (ISBN 0-208-01321-0, Archon). Shoe String.
Carter-Ruck, Peter see Carter-Ruck, Peter.
Carter Southard, Edna see Southard, Edna C.
Cartesius, Hugo. Individual & Society: Nature-Marx-Mao. 158p. 1977. 12.40 (ISBN 3-261-02063-6). P Lang Pubs.
Cartey, Wilfred & Kilson, Martin, eds. Africa Reader, 2 vols. Incl. Vol. 1. Colonial Africa. pap. 3.95 (ISBN 0-394-70854-7, V-628); Vol. 2. Independent Africa. pap. 3.95 (ISBN 0-394-70855-5, V-629). LC 79-102316. 1970. pap. (Vin). Random.
Carthach, St. The Monastic Rule of St. Carthach: St. Mochuda the Younger. pap. 1.50 (ISBN 0-686-05656-6). Eastern Orthodox.
Carthew, John A. Physical Geography Workbook. rev. ed. (Illus.). 68p. 1981. pap. text ed. 7.00x (ISBN 0-89179-218-X). Tam's Bks.
Carthy, Margaret. A Cathedral of Suitable Magnificence: St. Patrick's Cathedral, New York. 1983. 15.00 (ISBN 0-89453-372-X); pap. 6.95 (ISBN 0-89453-373-8). M Glazier.
Carthy, Mary P. Old St. Patrick's: New York's First Cathedral. (Monograph Ser.: No. 23). (Illus.). 1947. 10.00x (ISBN 0-930060-05-9). US Cath Hist.
Cartier. Boccaccio's Revenge. 1977. pap. 18.50 (ISBN 90-247-1961-5, Pub. by Martinus Nijhoff Netherlands). Kluwer Academic.
Cartier, Francis A. & Todaro, Martin T. The Phonetic Alphabet. 3rd ed. 112p. 1982. pap. text ed. write for info. (ISBN 0-697-04218-9); avail. instr's. guide & answer key (ISBN 0-697-04231-6). Wm C Brown.
Cartier, J. P., jt. auth. see Groueff, S.
Cartier, Jacques. A Shorte & Briefe Narration of the Two Navigations to Newe Fraunce. Florio, J., tr. LC 73-6110. (English Experience Ser.: No. 718). 1975. Repr. of 1580 ed. 8.00 (ISBN 90-221-0718-3). Walter J Johnson.
Cartier, Lynn. Heart & Soul. (Orig.). 1982. pap. 3.50 (ISBN 0-440-13594-X). Dell.
--Intimates. 304p. (Orig.). 1984. pap. 3.50 (ISBN 0-440-14066-8). Dell.
Cartier, Michel. Une Reforme Locale En Chine Au XVIe Siecle: Hai Rui a Chun'an, 1558-1562. (Le Monde D'outre-Mer Passe et Present, Etudes: No. 39). 1973. pap. 12.80x (ISBN 0-686-20925-7). Mouton.
Cartier, N. R. Aquila, Vol. 3. (Aquila Chestnut Hill Studies in Modern Languages & Literatures). 1976. pap. 34.00 (ISBN 90-247-1797-3). Kluwer Academic.
Cartier, R. Colposcopie Pratique. (Illus., Fr.). 1977. 98.00 (ISBN 3-8055-2820-5). S Karger.
--Practical Colposcopy. (Illus.). 1977. 52.00 (ISBN 3-8055-2808-6). S Karger.
Cartier, Raymond, ed. see Groueff, S. & Cartier, J. P.
Cartier-Bresson, Henri. Henri Cartier-Bresson: Photographer. LC 79-88493. (Illus.). 1979. 75.00 (ISBN 0-8212-0756-3, 357715). NYGS.
Cartin, Roger J. & Osborne, Wilma M. Guidance on Software Maintenance. (National Bureau of Standards Special Publications 500-105. Computer Science & Technology Ser.). 72p. (Orig.). 1983. pap. 2.50 (ISBN 0-318-11727-4). Gov Printing Office.
Cartinhour, Gaines T. & Westerfield, Ray B. Branch, Group & Chain Banking & Historical Survey of Branch Banking in the United States, 2 vols. in 1. Bruchey, Stuart, ed. LC 80-1139. (The Rise of Commercial Banking Ser.). (Illus.). 1981. Repr. of 1939 ed. lib. bdg. 39.00x (ISBN 0-405-13639-0). Ayer Co Pubs.
Cartland, Barbara. Alone & Afraid. (Camfield Ser.: No. 21). 192p. 1985. pap. 2.50 (ISBN 0-515-08185-X). Jove Pubns.
--As Eagles Fly. 12.95 (ISBN 0-317-27746-4, Pub. by Am Repr). Amereon Ltd.
--Barbara Cartland's Book of Celebrities. (Illus.). 160p. 1983. pap. 9.95 (ISBN 0-7043-3395-3, Pub. by Quartet Bks). Merrimack Pub Cir.
--The Bitter Winds of Love. 12.95 (ISBN 0-89190-899-4, Pub. by Am Repr). Amereon Ltd.
--Bride to a Brigand. (Camfield Ser.: No. 7). 192p. 1984. pap. 2.50 (ISBN 0-515-07308-3). Jove Pubns.
--Count the Stars. (Barbara Cartland Ser.: No. 10). 192p. (Orig.). 1981. pap. 1.75 (ISBN 0-515-05860-2). Jove Pubns.
--Danger by the Nile. 1967. pap. 1.25 (ISBN 0-380-00314-7, 23325). Avon.
--The Dangerous Dandy. 13.95 (ISBN 0-317-28194-1, Pub. by Am Repr). Amereon ltd.
--The Devilish Deception. (Camfield Ser.: No. 24). 176p. 1985. pap. 2.50 (ISBN 0-515-08326-7). Jove Pubns.
--The Duchess Disappeared. LC 79-21293. 1979. 6.95 (ISBN 0-87272-084-5, Duron Bks). Brodart.
--The Frightened Bride. 13.95 (ISBN 0-89190-897-8, Pub. by Am Repr). Amereon Ltd.
--Fugitive from Love. LC 77-25534. 1978. 6.95 (ISBN 0-87272-033-0, Duron Bks.). Brodart.
--Getting Older, Growing Younger. (Illus.). 192p. 1984. 15.95 (ISBN 0-396-08372-2). Dodd.
--A Heart Is Broken. (Romance Ser.: No. 20). 288p. 1983. pap. 2.25 (ISBN 0-515-06392-4). Jove Pubns.
--The Horizons of Love. (Barbara Cartland Ser.). (Orig.). pap. 1.75 (ISBN 0-515-05569-7). Jove Pubns.
--The Island of Love. (Camfield Ser.: No. 15). 192p. 1984. pap. 2.50 (ISBN 0-515-07911-1). Jove Pubns.
--The Kiss of Paris. 224p. pap. 2.25 (ISBN 0-515-06391-6). Jove Pubns.
--Light of the Gods. (Camfield Ser.: No. 6). 192p. 1982. pap. 1.95 (ISBN 0-515-06297-9). Jove Pubns.
--A Light to the Heart, No. 56. 256p. 1982. pap. 1.95 (ISBN 0-515-06387-8). Jove Pubns.
--Look With Love. (Camfield Ser.: No. 28). 176p. 1985. pap. 2.50 (ISBN 0-515-08419-0). Jove Pubns.
--Lord Ravenscar's Revenge. LC 78-6464. 1978. 6.95 (ISBN 0-87272-040-3, Duron Bks). Brodart.
--Love Climbs in. LC 79-21292. 1979. 6.95 (ISBN 0-87272-082-9, Duron Bks). Brodart.
--Love Comes West. (Camfield Ser.: No. 8). 192p. 1984. pap. 2.50 (ISBN 0-515-07607-4). Jove Pubns.
--Love Has His Way. LC 80-108. 1979. 6.95 (ISBN 0-87272-085-3, Duron Bks). Brodart.
--Love Is a Gamble. 10/1985 ed. (Camfield Ser.: No. 26). 192p. pap. 2.50 (ISBN 0-515-08364-X). Jove Pubns.
--Love Is Heaven. (Camfield Ser.: No. 7). 192p. 1985. pap. 2.50 (ISBN 0-515-08079-9). Jove Pubns.
--Love Leaves at Midnight. LC 78-3825. 1978. 6.95 (ISBN 0-87272-038-1, Duron Bks). Brodart.
--Lucky in Love. (Camfield Romance Ser.: No. 13). (Orig.). 1982. pap. 1.95 (ISBN 0-515-06292-8). Jove Pubns.
--The Magic of Love. 12.95 (ISBN 0-89190-898-6, Pub. by Am Repr). Amereon Ltd.
--Miracle for a Madonna. (Camfield Ser.: No. 18). 192p. 1985. pap. 2.50 (ISBN 0-515-08105-1). Jove Pubns.
--Moonlight on the Sphinx. (Camfield Ser.: No. 12). 192p. (Orig.). 1984. pap. 2.50 (ISBN 0-515-07732-1). Jove Pubns.
--The Naked Battle. 1977. 6.95 (ISBN 0-87272-028-4, Duron Bks.). Brodart.
--A Nightingale Sang. LC 79-21752. 1979. 6.95 (ISBN 0-87272-083-7, Duron Bks). Brodart.
--No Escape from Love. LC 77-21225. 1977. 6.95 (ISBN 0-87272-029-2, Duron Bks.). Brodart.
--Open Wings, No. 37. 256p. 1982. pap. 1.95 (ISBN 0-515-06388-6). Jove Pubns.
--Paradise Found. (Camfield Ser.: No. 25). 192p. 1985. pap. 2.50 (ISBN 0-515-08340-2). Jove Pubns.
--The Peril & the Prince, No. 20. (Canfield Ser.). 192p. 1985. pap. 2.50 (ISBN 0-515-08171-X). Jove Pubns.
--Princess to the Rescue. (Illus.). 1984. 9.95 (ISBN 0-531-03782-7). Watts.
--The Prisoner of Love. LC 79-13513. 1979. 6.95 (ISBN 0-87272-080-2, Duron Bks). Brodart.
--Revenge of the Heart. (Camfield Ser.: No. 14). 192p. 1984. pap. 2.50 (ISBN 0-515-07879-4). Jove Pubns.
--Romance of Food. LC 83-40137. (Illus.). 176p. 1984. 14.95 (ISBN 0-385-19269-X). Doubleday.
--Royal Punishment. (Camfield Ser.: No. 23). 192p. 1985. pap. 2.50 (ISBN 0-515-08229-5). Jove Pubns.
--The Runaway Heart, No. 69. 224p. 1983. pap. 2.25 (ISBN 0-515-06389-4). Jove Pubns.
--A Runaway Star. LC 78-19107. 1978. 6.95 (ISBN 0-87272-042-X, Duron Bks). Brodart.
--Secrets. (Camfield Ser.: No. 10). 192p. 1984. pap. 2.50 (ISBN 0-515-07625-2). Jove Pubns.
--A Serpent of Satan. LC 79-13514. 1979. 6.95 (ISBN 0-87272-077-2, Duron Bks). Brodart.
--The Sign of Love. LC 77-17353. 1977. 6.95 (ISBN 0-87272-032-2, Duron Bks.). Brodart.
--The Storms of Love. (Camfield Ser.: No. 11). 192p. 1984. pap. 2.50 (ISBN 0-515-07649-X). Jove Pubns.
--Sweet Adventure, No. 17. Date not set. pap. 2.25 (ISBN 0-515-06390-8). Jove Pubns.
--Temptation of a Teacher. (Camfield Ser.: No. 22). 192p. 1985. pap. 2.50 (ISBN 0-515-08252-X). Jove Pubns.
--Theresa & a Tiger. (Camfield Ser.: No. 16). 192p. 1984. pap. 2.50 (ISBN 0-515-08053-5). Jove Pubns.
--The Treasure Is Love. LC 79-13511. 1979. 6.95 (ISBN 0-87272-079-9, Duron Bks). Brodart.
--The Unknown Heart. 1979. pap. 1.75 (ISBN 0-515-05859-9). Jove Pubns.
--A Very Unusual Wife, No. 19. (Campfield Ser.). 192p. 1985. pap. 2.50 (ISBN 0-515-08040-3). Jove Pubns.
--A Victory for Love. (Camfield Ser.: No. 27). 192p. 1985. pap. 2.50 (ISBN 0-515-08393-3). Jove Pubns.
--White Lilac. (Camfield Ser.: No. 13). 192p. 1984. pap. 2.50 (ISBN 0-515-07745-3). Jove Pubns.
--Who Can Deny Love. LC 79-28822. 1979. 6.95 (ISBN 0-87272-086-1, Duron Bks). Brodart.
--A Witch's Spell. (Camfield Ser.: No. 9). 192p. 1984. pap. 2.75 (ISBN 0-515-07602-3). Jove Pubns.
Cartland, Fernando G. Southern Heroes, or the Friends in Wartime. Bd. with Conscript Quakers. Foster, Ethan. (Library of War & Peace; Conscrip. & Cons. Object.). 1972. lib. bdg. 42.00 (ISBN 0-8240-0424-8). Garland Pub.
Cartledge, J. A., compiled by. List of Glees, Madrigals, Part-Songs, Etc. in the Henry Watson Music Library. LC 74-80247. (Bibliography & Reference Ser.: No. 362). 1970. Repr. of 1913 ed. lib. bdg. 24.50 (ISBN 0-8337-0483-4). B Franklin.
Cartledge, Paul. Sparta & Lakonia: A Regional History Thirteen Hundred to Three Sixty-Two B.C. (States & Cities of Ancient Greece Ser.). 1979. 30.00x (ISBN 0-7100-0377-3). Routledge & Kegan.
Cartledge, Sue & Ryan, Joanna, eds. Sex & Love: New Thoughts on Old Contradictions. 256p. (Orig.). 1984. pap. 7.95 (ISBN 0-7043-3913-7, Pub. by Quartet Bks). Merrimack Pub Cir.
Cartlidge, Barbara. Twentieth-Century Jewelry. (Illus.). 198p. 1985. 60.00 (ISBN 0-8109-1685-1). Abrams.
Cartlidge, David R. & Dungan, David L. Documents for the Study of the Gospels. LC 79-21341. 300p. (Orig.). 1980. 16.95 (ISBN 0-8006-0640-X, 1-640); pap. 9.95 (ISBN -08006-1640-5, 1-1640). Fortress.
Cartlidge, Michelle. A Mouse's Diary. LC 80-17060. (Illus.). 32p. (ps-3). 1982. 10.25 (ISBN 0-688-41987-9); PLB 10.88 (ISBN 0-688-51987-3). Lothrop.
--Munch & Mixer's Puppet Show. (Illus.). 12p. (gr. k-3). 1983. 9.50 (ISBN 0-13-605345-9). P-H.
--Teddy Trucks. LC 81-82508. (Illus.). 32p. (ps-1). 1982. 11.75 (ISBN 0-688-00904-2); PLB 11.88 (ISBN 0-688-00905-0). Lothrop.
Cartlidge, N. E., jt. auth. see Bates, D.
Cartlidge, Niall & Shaw, David. Head Injury. (Major Problems in Neurology Ser.: Vol. 10). 1981. text ed. 35.00 (ISBN 0-7216-2443-X). Saunders.
Cartmail, Keith St. Exodus Indochina. (Illus.). 309p. pap. text ed. 12.50x (ISBN 0-86863-408-5). Heinemann Ed.
Cartmell & Fowles. Valency & Molecular Structure. 4th ed. 1977. 19.95 (ISBN 0-408-70809-3). Butterworth.
Cartmell, ed. see Henry, O.
Cartmell, Thomas K. Shenandoah Valley Pioneers & Their Descendants. LC 64-1062. (Illus.). 572p. Repr. of 1909 ed. write for info. (ISBN 0-686-63647-3). Va Bk.
Cartmell, Van H. The Amateur Theater Handbook. 203p. 1981. Repr. of 1945 ed. lib. bdg. 30.00 (ISBN 0-89760-154-8). Telegraph Bks.
Cartmell, Van H., ed. Plot Outlines of One Hundred Famous Plays. 11.25 (ISBN 0-8446-0539-5). Peter Smith.
Cartmell, Van H. & Cerf, Bennett, eds. Twenty-Four Favorite One-Act Plays. LC 58-13274. pap. 6.95 (ISBN 0-385-06617-1, C423, Dolp). Doubleday.
Cartmell, Van H. & Cerf, Bennett A., eds. Famous Plays of Crime & Detection: From Sherlock Holmes to Angel Street. LC 76-173621. (Play Anthology Reprint Ser). Repr. of 1946 ed. 41.00 (ISBN 0-8369-8220-7). Ayer Co Pubs.
Cartmell, Van H., jt. ed. see Cerf, Bennett.
Cartmell, Van H., ed. see Cerf, Bennett.
Cartmell, Van H., jt. ed. see Cerf, Bennett.

Carto, W. Profiles in Populism. 1982. 12.95 (ISBN 0-8159-6518-4); pap. 7.95 (ISBN 0-8159-6519-2). Devin.

Carto, Willis A., ed. Profiles in Populism: The Story of Henry Ford, Charles A. Lindbergh, Bob Lafollette, Burton K. Wheeler, Hamilton Fish & Father Coughlin. 1983. lib. bdg. 79.95 (ISBN 0-87700-466-8). Revisionist Pr.

Cartographic Publishing House Staff, ed. Map of the People's Republic of China-Relief. 1981. pap. 3.95 (ISBN 0-8351-1035-4). China Bks.

Carton & Dimon. Discovering BASIC with Wozzy: For the Apple II Plus, IIe, & IIc. 1985. 9.95 (ISBN 0-8104-6302-4). Hayden.

Carton, Cyril. As the Tree Grows. 13.95 (ISBN 0-317-18257-9); pap. 7.95 (ISBN 0-317-18258-7). C Barton.

Carton, D. S., et al, eds. Rocket Propulsion Technology. LC 61-15168. 374p. 1961. 32.50x (ISBN 0-306-30149-0, Plenum Pr). Plenum Pub.

Carton, Dana & Caprio, Anthony. En Francais: French for Communication. 3rd ed. 448p. 1985. text ed. 21.95 (ISBN 0-8384-1285-8); instr's. manual avail. (ISBN 0-8384-1287-4); wkbk manual 10.95 (ISBN 0-8384-1286-6); tapes 125.00 (ISBN 0-8384-1288-2). Heinle & Heinle.

Carton, Evan. The Rhetoric of American Romance: Dialectic & Identity in Emerson, Dickinson, Poe, & Hawthorne. LC 84-27770. 304p. 1985. text ed. 25.00x (ISBN 0-8018-2544-X). Johns Hopkins.

Carton, Jo-Anne & Dimon, Cecile. Ready, Set, Run My Apple. 128p. (gr. 1-4). 1982. pap. 9.95 (6302). Hayden.

Carton, Lonnie. Raise Your Kids Right. 1984. pap. 2.95 (ISBN 0-671-42125-5). PB.

Cartoon Archetypical Slogan Theatre. Confessions of a Socialist. 32p. 1981. pap. 3.95 (ISBN 0-86104-200-X, NO. 4121). Pluto Pr.

Cartoun, Susan. The Complete New York Guide for Singles. 256p. 1983. pap. 7.95 (ISBN 0-02-097360-8). Macmillan.

Cartron, Jean-Pierre, jt. auth. see Salmon, Charles.

Cartter, Allan. PH. D.'s & the Academic Labor Market. LC 75-38700. pap. 70.00 (ISBN 0-317-29023-1, 2020884). Bks Demand UMI.

Cartter, Allan M. The Redistribution of Income in Postwar Britain. LC 72-86540. 256p. 1973. Repr. of 1955 ed. 24.50x (ISBN 0-8046-1750-3, Pub. by Kennikat). Assoc Faculty Pr.

--Theory of Wages & Employment. LC 75-31357. (Illus.). 193p. 1976. Repr. of 1959 ed. lib. bdg. 17.00x (ISBN 0-8371-8512-2, CATW). Greenwood.

Cartwheel, Rosemary. Love's Reckless Rash: A Charlatan Romance. 128p. 1984. pap. 3.95 (ISBN 0-312-49971-X). St Martin.

Cartwright & Rawson. Gnomes, Goblins & Fairies. (Story Books). (gr. k-4). 1980. 6.95 (ISBN 0-86020-385-9, Usborne-Hayes); PLB 11.95 (ISBN 0-88110-054-4); pap. 2.95 (ISBN 0-86020-384-0). EDC.

--Princes & Princesses. (Story Bks.). (gr. k-4). 1980. 6.95 (ISBN 0-86020-383-2, Usborne-Hayes); PLB 11.95 (ISBN 0-88110-053-6); pap. 2.95 (ISBN 0-86020-382-4). EDC.

--Princes, Wizards & Gnomes. (Story Books). (gr. k-4). 1980. 10.95 (ISBN 0-86020-508-8, Usborne-Hayes). EDC.

--Wizards. (Story Books). (gr. k-4). 1980. 6.95 (ISBN 0-86020-381-6, Usborne-Hayes); PLB 11.95 (ISBN 0-88110-052-8); pap. 2.95 (ISBN 0-86020-380-8). EDC.

Cartwright, et al. Educating Special Learners. 2nd ed. 1984. write for info. (ISBN 0-534-03675-9). Wadsworth Pub.

Cartwright, Ann. The Dignity of Labour? A Study of Childbearing & Induction. 1979. 29.95x (ISBN 0-422-76690-9, NO.2039, Pub by Tavistock England). Methuen Inc.

--Health Surveys in Practice & in Potential: A Critical Review of Their Scope & Methods. 1983. 19.95x (ISBN 0-19-724623-0). Oxford U Pr.

Cartwright, Ann & Anderson, Robert. General Practice Revisited: A Second Study of Patients & Their Doctors. 1981. 28.95x (ISBN 0-422-77360-3, NO. 3440, Pub. by Tavistock). Methuen Inc.

Cartwright, Ann & Cartwright, Reg. Norah's Ark. (Illus.). 32p. (gr. k-2). 1984. PLB 11.97 (ISBN 0-671-52540-9). Messner.

--Norah's Ark. 1984. pap. 9.95 (ISBN 0-671-50763-X, Little Simon). S&S.

Cartwright, Ann, jt. auth. see Bowling, Ann.

Cartwright, B. O., tr. see Turpin, Francois H.

Cartwright, Calhoun. Bread Baking Can Be Easy (& Fun Too) 1979. Repr. of 1977 ed. spiral bdg. 4.95 (ISBN 0-917234-13-8). Kitchen Harvest.

Cartwright, Carol A. & Cartwright, Phillip G. Developing Observation Skills. 2nd ed. Smith, Robert M., ed. (Special Education Ser.). 176p. 1984. pap. text ed. 15.95 (ISBN 0-07-010185-X). McGraw.

Cartwright, Carol A., jt. auth. see Seaver, Judith W.

Cartwright, Charles. Cartwright's Choice Chuckles. LC 68-31127. (Church Humor Ser). (Illus., Orig.). 1968. pap. 1.95 (ISBN 0-8254-2306-6). Kregel.

Cartwright, Colbert S. The Lord's Prayer Comes Alive. LC 73-2816. (Orig.). 1973. pap. 1.00 (ISBN 0-8272-2112-6). CBP.

Cartwright, D. E., tr. see Marchuk, G. I. & Kagan, B. A.

Cartwright, Donald. Extensions of Positive Operators Between Banach Lattices. LC 75-19496. (Memoirs: No. 164). 48p. 1975. pap. 12.00 (ISBN 0-8218-1864-3, MEMO-164). Am Math.

Cartwright, Donald G. Official Language Populations in Canada: Patterns & Contracts. 160p. 1980. pap. text ed. 4.95x (ISBN 0-920380-56-5, Pub. by Inst Res Pub Canada). Brookfield Pub Co.

Cartwright, Dorwin & Zander, Alvin, eds. Group Dynamics: Research & Theory. 3rd ed. LC 68-12274. 1968. text ed. 26.50 scp (ISBN 0-06-041201-1, HarpC). Har-Row.

Cartwright, Dorwin, ed. see Lewin, Kurt.

Cartwright, Dorwin P., ed. Studies in Social Power. LC 59-63036. 225p. 1959. 12.00x (ISBN 0-87944-230-1). Inst Soc Res.

Cartwright, F. D., ed. see Cartwright, John.

Cartwright, Frances D., ed. see Cartwright, John.

Cartwright, G. Philip, et al. Activities, Guidelines & Resources for Teachers of Special Learners. 272p. 1981. pap. text ed. write for info (ISBN 0-534-00940-9). Wadsworth Pub.

Cartwright, Gary. Blood Will Tell. 1984. pap. 4.50 (ISBN 0-671-50898-9). PB.

--Confessions of a Washed-Up Sportswriter: Including Various Digressions about Sex, Crime, & Other Hobbies. Rodriguez, Barbara, ed. 288p. 1983. 15.95 (ISBN 0-932012-39-6). Texas Month Pr.

--Dirty Dealing: A True Story of Smuggling & Murder. LC 81-69130. (Illus.). 352p. 1984. 16.95 (ISBN 0-689-11243-2). Atheneum.

Cartwright, Hilary. Ballet & Contemporary Dance: Dancing for a Living. 127p. 1982. 27.00x (ISBN 0-85225-755-4, Pub. by Careers Con England). State Mutual Bk.

Cartwright, J. & Critchley, J. Cruise, Pershing & SS-20: The Search for Consensus: Nuclear Weapons in Europe. 188p. 1985. 22.75 (ISBN 0-08-031201-2, Pub by BDP); pap. 12.50 (ISBN 0-08-031202-0). Pergamon.

Cartwright, J. J., ed. see Pococke, Richard.

Cartwright, John. Commonwealth in Danger. 1968. Repr. of 1795 ed. 24.50 (ISBN 0-8337-0486-9). B Franklin.

--Life & Correspondence of Major Cartwright, 2 Vols. Cartwright, Frances D., ed. (Research & Source Works Ser.: No. 192). 1969. Repr. of 1926 ed. Set. 33.50 (ISBN 0-8337-0489-3). B Franklin.

--Life & Correspondence of Major Cartwright, 2 Vols. Cartwright, F. D., ed. LC 68-57728. Repr. of 1826 ed. 75.00x (ISBN 0-678-00449-8). Kelley.

Cartwright, John, ed. American Independence: The Interest & Glory of Great Britain. LC 78-124309. (Research & Source Ser.: No. 487). (Illus.). 1970. Repr. of 1776 ed. lib. bdg. 24.50 (ISBN 0-8337-0484-2). B Franklin.

Cartwright, John M. Farm & Ranch Real Estate Law. LC 70-189071. 1972. 64.50 (ISBN 0-686-14537-2); Suppl. 1984. 21.00; Suppl. 1983. 19.00. Lawyers Co-Op.

--Glossary of Real Estate Law. LC 76-189072. 1972. 20.00 (ISBN 0-686-14538-0). Lawyers Co-Op.

Cartwright, John R. Political Leadership in Africa. LC 82-23151. 310p. 1983. 27.50 (ISBN 0-312-62314-3). St Martin.

--Political Leadership in Sierra Leone. LC 79-300056. pap. 77.00 (ISBN 0-317-26934-8, 2023602). Bks Demand UMI.

--Politics in Sierra Leone, 1947-67. LC 71-18592. pap. 74.00 (ISBN 0-317-11262-7, 2055459). Bks Demand UMI.

Cartwright, Joseph H. The Triumph of Jim Crow: Tennessee Race Relations in the 1880s. LC 76-2009. 296p. 1976. 21.50x (ISBN 0-87049-192-X). U of Tenn Pr.

Cartwright, Julia. Beatrice D'Este: Duchess of Milan, 1475-1497. 1977. Repr. of 1920 ed. lib. bdg. 27.50 (ISBN 0-8495-0717-0). Arden Lib.

--Beatrice D'Este: Duchess of Milan, 1475-1497; a Study of the Renaissance. LC 73-38345. (Select Bibliographies Reprint Ser.). 1899. 22.00 (ISBN 0-8369-6762-3). Ayer Co Pubs.

--Isabella D'Este Marchioness of Mantua, 1474-1539, 2 vols. 1977. Repr. of 1903 ed. 50.00 set (ISBN 0-8274-4296-3). R West.

--The Painters of Florence: From the Thirteenth to the Sixteenth Century. 1979. Repr. of 1911 ed. lib. bdg. 40.00 (ISBN 0-8495-0916-5). Arden Lib.

--Sacharissa: Some Account of Dorothy Sidney, Countess of Sunderland, Her Family & Friends, 1617-1684. 1978. Repr. lib. bdg. 22.50 (ISBN 0-8492-3901-X). R West.

Cartwright, L. E., jt. auth. see Goodhew, P. J.

Cartwright, N. P. Candidceces-Versos Spanish Poetry. LC 83-76. 91p. (Eng. & Span.). 1983. pap. text ed. 4.00 (ISBN 0-9601482-3-X). N P Cartwright.

Cartwright, Nancy. How the Laws of Physics Lie. (Illus.). 1983. pap. 9.95x (ISBN 0-19-824704-4). Oxford U Pr.

Cartwright, Nellie P. Bless the Nightingale: Ama Al ruisenor. rev. ed. LC 77-85799. 105p. (Eng. & Span.). 1977. pap. text ed. 4.00 (ISBN 0-9601482-2-1). N P Cartwright.

--New Moon - Luna Nueva. LC 70-38. 85p. (Orig., Span. & Eng.). 1982. pap. text ed. 4.00 (ISBN 0-9601482-4-8). N P Cartwright.

Cartwright, Peter. Autobiography of Peter Cartwright: The Backwoods Preacher. Strickland, W. P., ed. LC 70-38344. (Select Biographies Reprint Ser.). 1856. 24.00 (ISBN 0-8369-6761-5). Ayer Co Pubs.

Cartwright, Phillip G., jt. auth. see Cartwright, Carol A.

Cartwright, R. Y. & Hirsch, H. A., eds. Antifungals in Gynecology: Focus on Terconazole. (Journal: Gynaekologische Rundschau: Vol. 25, Supplement 1). (Illus.). iv, 120p. 1985. pap. 16.25 (ISBN 3-8055-4041-8). S Karger.

Cartwright, Ralph & Russell, R. T. The Welshpool & Lanfair Light Railway. LC 80-70290. (Illus.). 208p. 1981. 16.95 (ISBN 0-7153-8151-2). David & Charles.

Cartwright, Reg, jt. auth. see Cartwright, Ann.

Cartwright, Richard M., ed. Design of Urban Space: A GLC Manual. LC 80-21537. 163p. 1980. 59.95x (ISBN 0-470-27066-7). Halsted Pr.

Cartwright, Rosalind D. Night Life: Explorations in Dreaming. (Illus.). 1977. 11.95 (ISBN 0-13-622324-9, Spec); pap. 4.95 (ISBN 0-13-622316-8). P-H.

Cartwright, Sally. What's in a Map? LC 76-10694. (Illus.). (gr. k-3). 1976. PLB 6.99 (ISBN 0-698-30635-X, Coward). Putnam Pub Group.

Cartwright, Steve R. Developing Video Training Programs. 165p. 1985. 34.95 (ISBN 0-86729-132-X, 530-BW). Knowledge Indus.

--Training with Video. (Video Bookshelf Ser.). 165p. 1985. 34.50 (ISBN 0-86729-132-X). Knowledge Indus.

Cartwright, Thomas. A Briefe Apologie Against M. Sutcliffe. LC 78-25890. (English Experience Ser.: No. 237). 28p. 1970. Repr. of 1596 ed. 7.00 (ISBN 90-221-0237-8). Walter J Johnson.

--The Christian Letter of Certaine English Protestants Unto Mr. R. Hooker. LC 72-180. (English Experience Ser.: No. 202). 50p. 1969. Repr. of 1599 ed. 8.00 (ISBN 90-221-0202-5). Walter J Johnson.

--A Confutation of the Rhemists Translation, Glosses & Annotations on the New Testament. LC 71-171737. (English Experience Ser.: No. 364). 830p. 1971. Repr. of 1618 ed. 114.00 (ISBN 90-221-0364-1). Walter J Johnson.

--Diary. 1843. 19.00 (ISBN 0-384-07815-X). Johnson Repr.

--Diary of Dr. Thomas Cartwright, Bishop of Chester October 1687. (Camden Society, London. Publications. First Ser.: No. 22). Repr. of 1843 ed. 19.00 (ISBN 0-404-50122-2). AMS Pr.

Cartwright, William & Hamilton, William B., eds. Duke University Centennial Conference on Teacher Training. LC 70-115993. (Duke University. Trinity College Historical Society. Historical Papers: No. 30). pap. text ed. 17.50 (ISBN 0-404-51780-3). AMS Pr.

Cartwright, William H. & Watson, Richard L., eds. The Reinterpretation of American History & Culture. LC 73-84548. 1973. 8.50 (ISBN 0-87986-010-3, 491-15272). Nat Coun Soc Studies.

Carty, Anthony. The Decay of International Law: A Reappraisal of the Limits of Legal Imagination in International Affairs. (Melland Schill Monographs in International Law). 200p. 1986. 30.00 (ISBN 0-7190-1850-1, Pub. by Manchester Univ Pr). Longwood Pub Group.

Carty, Charles, jt. auth. see O'Connell, Patrick.

Carty, Charles M. Padre Pio: The Stigmatist. (Illus.). 1971. pap. 8.50 (ISBN 0-89555-054-7, 115). TAN Bks Pubs.

--Stigmata & Modern Science. 31p. 1974. pap. 0.65 (ISBN 0-89555-104-7). TAN Bks Pubs.

--Who Is Teresa Neumann? 1974. pap. 1.25 (ISBN 0-89555-093-8). TAN Bks Pubs.

--Why Squander Illness? 1974. pap. 1.50 (ISBN 0-89555-051-2). TAN Bks Pubs.

Carty, Charles M., jt. auth. see Rumble, Leslie.

Carty, Ciaran. Robert Ballagh. (Illus.). 224p. 1985. 39.95 (ISBN 0-907085-70-9, Pub. by Ward River Pr Ireland). Irish Bks Media.

Carty, Joan, jt. auth. see Dale, Sheila.

Carty, Margaret F. Christmas in Vermont: Three Stories. LC 83-62750. (Illus.). 48p. (Orig.). 1983. pap. 2.95 (ISBN 0-933050-21-6). New Eng Pr VT.

Carty, Mickey D. Searching in Indiana: A Reference Guide to Public & Private Records. LC 85-60284. (ISC State Search Bks.: No. 4). 278p. (Orig.). 1985. pap. text ed. 14.95 (ISBN 0-942916-06-9). ISC Pubns.

Carty, R. K. Party & Parish Pump: Electoral Politics in Ireland. 207p. 1981. text ed. 15.45x (ISBN 0-88920-105-6, Pub. by Wilfrid Laurier U Pr). Humanities.

Carty, R. Kenneth & Ward, W. Peter, eds. Entering the Eighties: Canada in Crisis. 1980. pap. 8.95x (ISBN 0-19-540364-9). Oxford U Pr.

Carty, Richard. Visual Merchandising -- Principles & Practice. 1982. text ed. 9.92 (ISBN 0-87350-262-0); wkbk. 5.60 (ISBN 0-87350-263-9). Milady.

Carty, Sally C. How to Make Braided Rugs. LC 76-49513. (Illus.). 1977. pap. 6.95 (ISBN 0-07-010196-5). McGraw.

--How to Make Braided Rugs. 1983. 14.25 (ISBN 0-8446-6061-2). Peter Smith.

Carty, Tony & Smith, Alexander M. Power & Maneuverability. 1978. text ed. 18.75x (ISBN 0-905470-04-4). Humanities.

Caruana, Russell A. A Guide to Organizing a Health Care Fiscal Services Division with Job Descriptions for Key Functions. 2nd ed. 94p. 1981. pap. 8.50 (ISBN 0-930228-13-8). Healthcare Fin Man Assn.

Carus, Carl G. Psyche, on the Development of the Soul, Pt. 1: 1846. Hillman, James, ed. & intro. by. (Dunquin Ser.: No. 3). 1970. pap. 5.00 (ISBN 0-88214-203-8). Spring Pubns.

Carus, Julius V. Geschichte der Zoologie Bis Auf Johann Mueller und Charles Darwin. Repr. of 1872 ed. 50.00 (ISBN 0-384-07825-7). Johnson Repr.

Carus, Paul. Amitabha: A Story of Buddhist Theology. 1977. Repr. 29.00x (ISBN 0-403-07255-7). Scholarly.

--The Bride of Christ. 118p. 1908. 15.95 (ISBN 0-87548-218-X). Open Court.

--Buddhism & Its Christian Critics. 59.95 (ISBN 0-87968-801-7). Gordon Pr.

--Chinese Astrology. LC 73-20411. (Illus.). 114p. 1974. pap. 4.95 (ISBN 0-87548-155-8). Open Court.

--Chinese Thought: An Exposition of the Main Characteristic Features of the Chinese World Conception. LC 7-14567. (Illus.). pap. 52.30 (ISBN 0-317-11337-2, 2050917). Bks Demand UMI.

--The Dharma; or, the Religious Enlightenment; an Exposition of Buddhism. 5th rev. & enl. ed. LC 78-72393. Repr. of 1907 ed. 19.00 (ISBN 0-404-17253-9). AMS Pr.

--The Ethical Problem: Three Lectures on Ethics As a Science. 2nd enl ed. LC 75-3103. Repr. of 1899 ed. 25.50 (ISBN 0-404-59100-0). AMS Pr.

--The Foundations of Mathematics: A Contribution to the Philosophy of Geometry. LC 75-3104. Repr. of 1908 ed. 18.00 (ISBN 0-404-59101-9). AMS Pr.

--Friedrich Schiller: A Sketch of His Life & an Appreciation of His Poetry. 102p. 1905. 19.95 (ISBN 0-87548-269-4). Open Court.

--Fundamental Problems. 59.95 (ISBN 0-8490-0207-9). Gordon Pr.

--God: An Enquiry & a Solution. iv, 253p. 1943. 19.95 (ISBN 0-87548-223-6); pap. 7.95 (ISBN 0-87548-224-4). Open Court.

--Goethe: With Special Consideration of His Philosophy. 1973. Repr. of 1915 ed. 30.00 (ISBN 0-8274-0083-7). R West.

--Goethe: With Special Consideration of His Philosophy. (Illus.). 376p. 1981. pap. 17.00 (ISBN 0-89540-121-5, SB-121). Sun Pub.

--Gospel of Buddha. (Illus.). 1979. pap. 6.95 (ISBN 0-89744-195-8). Auromere.

--The Gospel of Buddha. 59.95 (ISBN 0-8490-0252-4). Gordon Pr.

--Gospel of Buddha. rev. & enl. ed. LC 17-29837. (Illus.). 331p. 1973. deluxe ed. 24.95 (ISBN 0-87548-226-0); pap. 9.95 (ISBN 0-87548-228-7). Open Court.

--History of the Devil & the Idea of Evil. (Illus.). 496p. 1974. pap. 14.95 (ISBN 0-87548-307-0). Open Court.

--Kant & Spencer. 59.95 (ISBN 0-8490-0468-3). Gordon Pr.

--Karma: A Story of Buddhist Ethics. 52p. 1951. pap. 4.95 (ISBN 0-87548-262-7). Open Court.

--Karma; Nirvana: Two Buddhist Tales. LC 73-82781. (Illus.). 160p. 1973. 15.95 (ISBN 0-87548-249-X); pap. 6.95 (ISBN 0-87548-359-3). Open Court.

--The Mechanistic Principle & the Non-Mechanical: An Inquiry into Fundamentals with Extracts from Representatives of Either Side. 125p. 9.95 (ISBN 0-912050-69-1). Open Court.

--Nietzsche. LC 72-2039. (Studies in German Literature, No. 13). 1972. Repr. of 1914 ed. lib. bdg. 39.95x (ISBN 0-8383-1464-3). Haskell.

--Nietzsche & Other Exponents of Individualism. LC 14-1736. (Illus.). pap. 42.80 (ISBN 0-317-09075-5, 2009077). Bks Demand UMI.

--Nirvana, a Story of Buddhist Psychology. LC 78-72395. (Illus.). Repr. of 1902 ed. 17.50 (ISBN 0-404-17254-7). AMS Pr.

--Personality. 68p. 6.95 (ISBN 0-912050-67-5). Open Court.

--Philosophy As a Science. LC 75-3106. Repr. of 1909 ed. 14.00 (ISBN 0-404-59103-5). AMS Pr.

--The Philosophy of Form. LC 75-3108. Repr. of 1911 ed. 15.00 (ISBN 0-404-59104-3). AMS Pr.

--The Philosophy of Form: An Expanded Reprint of the Author's Introduction to His "Philosophy As a Science". LC 80-12865. (Philosophy in America Ser.). Repr. of 1911 ed. 15.00 (ISBN 0-404-59104-3). AMS Pr.

--Point of View. Cook, Catherine E., ed. (Illus.). xvi, 227p. 1927. 16.95 (ISBN 0-87548-268-6). Open Court.

--The Principle of Relativity in the Light of the Philosophy of Science. LC 75-3109. Repr. of 1913 ed. 18.00 (ISBN 0-404-59105-1). AMS Pr.

--The Principle of Relativity in the Light of the Philosophy of Science. 105p. 5.95 (ISBN 0-912050-66-7). Open Court.

--The Religion of Science. 3rd ed. 145p. 6.95 (ISBN 0-912050-68-3). Open Court.

--The Soul of Man. 59.95 (ISBN 0-8490-1090-X). Gordon Pr.

--The Venus of Milo: An Archaeological Study of the Goddess of Womanhood. 1977. lib. bdg. 59.95 (ISBN 0-8490-2796-9). Gordon Pr.

--Whence & Whither. 59.95 (ISBN 0-8490-1289-9). Gordon Pr.

Carus, Paul, ed. Yin Chih Wen: The Tract of the Quiet Way. Suzuki, Teitaro & Carus, Paul, trs. from Chinese. 52p. 1906. pap. 4.95 (ISBN 0-87548-245-7). Open Court.
Carus, Paul, ed. see Lao-Tze.
Carus, Paul, tr. see Carus, Paul.
Carus, Paul, tr. see Kant, Immanuel.
Carus, Paul, tr. see Kant, Immanuel, et al.
Carus, Paul, tr. see Kant, Immanuel.
Carus, Paul, tr. see Lao Tze.
Carus, Paul, tr. see Yin Chih Wen.
Carusi, Andrea & Valsecchi, Giovanni B., eds. Dynamics of Comets: Their Origin & Evolution. (Astrophysics & Space Science Library). 1985. lib. bdg. 59.00 (ISBN 90-277-2047-9, Pub. by Reidel Holland). Kluwer-Academic.
Caruso, Domenick & Weidenborner, Stephen. Creating Contexts: A Practical Approach to Writing. LC 76-55159. (Illus.). 1977. pap. text ed. 6.95x (ISBN 0-393-09101-5); tchrs manual gratis (ISBN 0-393-09107-4). Norton.
Caruso, Domenick, jt. auth. see Weidenborner, Stephen.
Caruso, Enrico. Caruso's Caricatures. LC 77-77704. (Illus.). 217p. 1977. pap. 7.50 (ISBN 0-486-23528-9). Dover.
--Caruso's Caricatures. (Illus.). 16.50 (ISBN 0-8446-5563-5). Peter Smith.
Caruso, Enrico & Tetrazzini, Louisa. The Art of Singing: How to Sing, 2 vols. in 1. LC 74-23417. (Music Reprint Ser.). 1975. Repr. of 1909 ed. lib. bdg. 25.00 (ISBN 0-306-70674-1). Da Capo.
Caruso, Enrico & Tetrazzini, Luisa. Caruso & Tetrazzini on the Art of Singing. LC 74-84048. 80p. 1975. pap. 2.50 (ISBN 0-486-23140-2). Dover.
Caruso, Guiseppe & Ludin, Hans-Peter, eds. Electromyography in the Diagnosis & Management of Peripheral Nerve Injuries. (Illus.). 130p. (Orig.). 1983. pap. text ed. 25.00 (ISBN 3-456-81289-2, Pub. by Hans Huber Switzerland). J K Burgess.
Caruso, J. A. The Liberators of Mexico. (Illus.). 13.25 (ISBN 0-8446-1105-0). Peter Smith.
Caruso, Joseph G. Happyville. (Illus.). 24p. 1981. pap. 1.50 (ISBN 0-88680-079-X); royalty 25.00 (ISBN 0-317-03596-7). I E Clark.
--The Phantom of the Old Opera House. 48p. 1982. pap. 2.50 (ISBN 0-88680-153-2); royalty 35.00 (ISBN 0-317-03574-6). I E Clark.
Caruso, Mary G. Reflection & Its Consequences. 64p. (Orig.). 1985. pap. text ed. 3.50 (ISBN 0-910727-07-4). Golden Phoenix.
Caruso, Peter. Destination. LC 72-118307. 1970. 10.00 (ISBN 0-8022-2342-7). Philos Lib.
Carus-Wilson, E. M., ed. & pref. by. The Overseas Trade of Bristol in the Later Middle Ages. (Illus.). 1967. Repr. of 1937 ed. lib. bdg. 27.50 (ISBN 0-678-08063-1). Kelley.
Caruth, Donald L. Work Measurement in Banking. 2nd ed. 234p. 1984. text ed. 42.00 (ISBN 0-87267-045-7). Bankers.
Caruth, Donald L., et al. Office & Administrative Management. 3rd ed. 1970. P-H.
Caruthers, Clifford M., ed. Letters from Ring. LC 78-71297. 305p. 1979. pap. 6.95 (ISBN 0-911938-09-5). N Ill U Pr.
Caruthers, Clifford M., ed. & intro. by. Ring Around Max: The Correspondence of Ring Lardner & Maxwell Perkins. LC 72-6919. (Illus.). 192p. 1973. 10.00 (ISBN 0-87580-041-6); pap. 4.50 (ISBN 0-87580-512-4). N Ill U Pr.
Caruthers, Clifford M., ed. see Lardner, Ring.
Caruthers, Harold. For Lovers of Little Creatures. 1983. 7.95 (ISBN 0-533-05736-1). Vantage.
Caruthers, J. W. Fundamentals of Marine Acoustics. (Elsevier Oceanography Ser.: Vol. 18). 154p. 1977. 49.00 (ISBN 0-444-41552-1). Elsevier.
Caruthers, Madeline, jt. auth. see Tucker, Dennis.
Caruthers, William A. The Cavaliers of Virginia. LC 68-23715. (Americans in Fiction Ser.). lib. bdg. 29.50 (ISBN 0-8398-0254-4); pap. text ed. 12.95x (ISBN 0-89197-693-0). Irvington.
--The Kentuckian in New York. LC 68-23714. (Americans in Fiction Ser.). lib. bdg. 15.00 (ISBN 0-8398-0255-2); pap. text ed. 5.50x (ISBN 0-89197-817-8). Irvington.
Carvajal, Arnold J., jt. auth. see Louvau, Gordon E.
Carvajal, Gaspar de. Discovery of the Amazon According to the Accounts of Friar Gaspar De Carvajal & Other Documents. Heaton, H. C. & Lee, Bertram T., eds. LC 77-120567. Repr. of 1934 ed. 31.50 (ISBN 0-404-01404-6). AMS Pr.
Carvajal, M. De see De Carvajal, M.
Carvajal, M. J. & Geithman, David T. Family Planning & Family Size Determination: The Evidence from Seven Latin American Cities. LC 75-37700. (University of Florida Latin American Monographs: No. 18). (Illus.). 1976. 7.50 (ISBN 0-8130-0526-4). U Presses Fla.
Carvalho, David N. Forty Centuries of Ink, or a Chronological Narrative Concerning Ink & Its Backgrounds. 1971. Repr. of 1904 ed. lib. bdg. 24.50 (ISBN 0-8337-0490-7). B Franklin.
Carvalho, Joseph. Black Families in Hampden County, Massachusetts, 1650-1855. LC 83-22044. 211p. 1984. lib. bdg. 16.65 (ISBN 0-88082-006-3). New Eng Hist.
Carvalho, Manoel J., Jr. In Search of Being. Wald, Susan, tr. from Fr. LC 84-19079. 217p. 1985. 15.00 (ISBN 0-8022-2424-5). Philos Lib.
Carvalho, S. N. Incidents of Travel & Adventure in the Far West. Repr. of 1954 ed. 21.00 (ISBN 0-527-15200-5). Kraus Repr.
Carvalho, Sergio de see De Carvalho, Sergio.
Carvalho, Solomon N. Incidents of Travel & Adventure in the Far West, with Colonel Fremont's Last Expedition Across the Rocky Mountains. LC 72-9434. (The Far Western Frontier Ser.). 384p. 1973. Repr. of 1857 ed. 24.50 (ISBN 0-405-04964-1). Ayer Co Pubs.
Carvell, H. T. & Svartvik, J. Computational Experiments in Grammatical Classification. LC 68-23805. (Janua Linguarum, Ser. Minor: No. 61). (Orig.). 1969. pap. text ed. 23.20x (ISBN 90-2790-682-3). Mouton.
Carvely, A. Institutionalizing Revolution: Egypt & Libya. write for info. (ISBN 0-686-11964-9). Bks Intl DH-TE.
Carvely, Andrew. U. S.-UAR Diplomatic Relations. LC 73-86351. 1969. pap. 2.00 (ISBN 0-686-05635-3). Bks Intl DH-TE.
Carvely, Andrew, et al, eds. Nonaligned Third World Annual. LC 74-89628. (Illus.). 1970-1971. 14.00 (ISBN 0-686-00055-2); pap. 8.50 (ISBN 0-686-00056-0). Bks Intl DH-TE.
--Nonaligned Third World Annual 1972-1975: The Politics of Ideas, Part 2. LC 74-89628. 1975. 10.00 (ISBN 0-686-11962-2). Bks Intl DH-TE.
Carver, jt. auth. see Bowles.
Carver, C. C. Church of God Doctrines. 180p. 1948. pap. 2.00 (ISBN 0-686-29106-9). Faith Pub Hse.
Carver, C. S. & Scheier, M. F. Attention & Self Regulation: A Control-Theory Approach to Human Behavior. (Springer Series in Social Psychology). (Illus.). 403p. 1981. 36.00 (ISBN 0-387-90553-7). Springer-Verlag.
Carver, Caroline. Canadian Christmas Book: A Handsel from Our Victorian Past. LC 75-30483. (Illus.). 1975. pap. 4.95 (ISBN 0-912766-30-1). Tundra Bks.
Carver, Craig R., ed. Federal Oil & Gas Leasing & Operations - Onshore- 60.00 (ISBN 0-318-02017-3). IED Pub Hse.
Carver, D. K. Computers & Data Processing: Introduction with BASIC. 3rd ed. LC 78-19131. 366p. 1983. text ed. 24.95 (ISBN 0-471-09834-5). wkbk. 11.95 (ISBN 0-471-86252-5). Wiley.
Carver, D. Keith. Beginning BASIC. LC 79-20457. 1980. pap. text ed. 17.50 pub net (ISBN 0-8185-0368-8). Brooks-Cole.
--Beginning BASIC. 260p. pap. write for info. Wadsworth Pub.
--Beginning Structured COBOL. 2nd ed. LC 84-11340. (Computer Science Ser.). 500p. 1984. pap. text ed. 20.00 pub net (ISBN 0-534-03795-X). Brooks-Cole.
--Structured COBOL for Microcomputers. LC 82-20573. (Computer Science Ser.). 418p. 1983. pap. text ed. 18.00 pub net (ISBN 0-534-01421-6). Brooks-Cole.
--Structured COBOL for Microcomputers. 150p. 1983. pap. write for info. Wadsworth Pub.
Carver, Deenie B., jt. auth. see Dillow, Louise B.
Carver, Estelle C. Newness of Life. rev. ed. Helms, Hal M., ed. 150p. pap. 4.95 (ISBN 0-941478-19-X). Paraclete Pr.
Carver, Everett I. When Jesus Comes Again. 1979. 7.95 (ISBN 0-87552-159-2). Presby & Reformed.
Carver, Field M. The Apostles of Mobility: The Theory & Practice of Armoured Warfare. LC 79-16678. (Illus.). 108p. 1979. text ed. 15.00x (ISBN 0-8419-0539-8). Holmes & Meier.
Carver, Field Marshall Lord. The Seven Ages of the British Army. (Illus.). 344p. 1985. 22.50 (ISBN 0-8253-0241-2). Beaufort Bks NY.
Carver, Frank. Beacon Small-Group Bible Studies, Matthew, Vol. I: To Be a Disciple. Wolf, Earl C., ed. (Beacon Small-Group Bible Study). 96p. (Orig.). 1984. pap. 2.50 (ISBN 0-8341-0870-4). Beacon Hill.
Carver, Fred D., jt. auth. see Sergiovanni, Thomas J.
Carver, George. The Catholic Tradition in English Literature. 59.95 (ISBN 0-87968-820-3). Gordon Pr.
--The Catholic Tradition in English Literature. 1977. Repr. lib. bdg. 25.00 (ISBN 0-8492-3819-6). R West.
Carver, George, ed. The Catholic Tradition in English Literature. 1982. Repr. of 1926 ed. lib. bdg. 40.00 (ISBN 0-89987-121-6). Darby Bks.
--Periodical Essays of the Eighteenth Century. facsimile ed. LC 70-99621. (Essay Index Reprint Ser.). 1930. 25.50 (ISBN 0-8369-1555-0). Ayer Co Pubs.
Carver, George A., Jr., ed. The View from the South: A U. S. Perspective on Key Bilateral Issues Affecting U. S.-Canadian Relations, Vol VII. (Significant Issues Ser.: No. 4). 52p. 1985. 6.95 (ISBN 0-89206-081-6). CSI Studies.
Carver, George T. & Lee, Eugene. Beginning Photography. (Illus.). 160p. 1985. pap. text ed. 12.95 (ISBN 0-13-071440-2). P-H.
Carver, H. E., jt. auth. see Reynolds, Steve.
Carver, Henry C., jt. auth. see Glover, James W.
Carver, Humphrey. Cities in the Suburbs. LC 63-1664. (Illus.). 1962. pap. 6.50 (ISBN 0-8020-6049-8). U of Toronto Pr.
Carver, Jeffrey A. The Infinity Link. 544p. 1984. 16.95 (ISBN 0-312-94233-8); cancelled signed, ltd. ed. (ISBN 0-312-94234-6). Bluejay Bks.
--Infinity Link. 544p. 1985. pap. 3.50 (ISBN 0-8125-3300-3, Dist. by Warner Pub Services & St. Martin). Tor Bks.
Carver, John N. & Carver, Nellie E. The Family of the Retarded Child. LC 72-85384. (Segregated Settings & the Problem of Change Ser.: No. 2). 156p. 1972. 12.00x (ISBN 0-8156-8079-1). Syracuse U Pr.
Carver, Joyce S. Jonny Lincoln & His Three Dogs. (Illus.). 38p. 1982. 5.50 (ISBN 0-682-49920-X). Exposition Pr FL.
Carver, Larry, ed. see Kelly, Hugh.
Carver, Leona P., ed. You Can't Get the Coons All up One Tree: True Life Story of John N. Jones. 244p. (Orig.). 1980. pap. 7.95x (ISBN 0-686-36932-7). Coltharp Pub.
Carver, M. O., et al. Riverside Structures & a Well in Skeldergate & Buildings in Bishophill. (Archaeology of York the Colonia Ser.: Vol. 4). (Illus.). 55p. 1978. pap. text ed. 15.45X (ISBN 0-900312-59-9, Pub. by Coun Brit Archaeological). Humanities.
Carver, Marjorie L. Grampa Gomez' Garden. Riffel, Maria, tr. from Span. LC 77-92711. (Illus.). 36p. (gr. 1-12). 1977. pap. text ed. 3.00 (ISBN 0-918536-04-9). Margaritas Bks Brown.
--Lovely Lana, the Hula Champion. (Illus.). 20p. (gr. k-12). 1978. pap. text ed. 3.00 (ISBN 0-918536-06-5). Margaritas Bks Brown.
--The Practically Purple Pumpkin. McKenna, Helen, ed. (Illus., Span. & Eng.). (gr. 1-6). 1977. pap. text ed. 1.95 (ISBN 0-918536-03-0). Margaritas Bks Brown.
--Willy Worm & His New Friend. LC 78-52409. (Companion Books: English, Spanish, French Ser.). (Illus.). (gr. k-4). 1978. pap. text ed. 2.50 (ISBN 0-918536-05-7). Margaritas Bks Brown.
Carver, Michael. War Since Nineteen Forty-Five. (Illus.). 336p. 1980. 17.95x (ISBN 0-297-77846-3, GWN 04977, Pub. by Weidenfeld & Nicolson England). Biblio Dist.
Carver, Nellie E., jt. auth. see Carver, John N.
Carver, Norman F., Jr. Iberian Villages: Portugal & Spain. (Illus.). 192p. 1982. 26.95 (ISBN 0-932076-02-5); pap. 19.95 (ISBN 0-932076-03-3). Documan.
--Italian Hilltowns. 3rd ed. (Illus.). 192p. 1979. 26.95 (ISBN 0-932076-00-9); pap. 19.95 (ISBN 0-932076-01-7). Documan.
--Japanese Folkhouses. (Illus.). 200p. 1984. 26.95 (ISBN 0-932076-04-1); pap. 19.95 (ISBN 0-932076-05-X). Documan.
Carver, P. L., ed. see Gnaphaeus, Gulielmus.
Carver, Raymond. Cathedral. LC 83-47779. 1983. 13.95 (ISBN 0-394-52884-0). Knopf.
--Cathedral. LC 84-40009. (Vintage Contemporaries Ser.). 240p. 1984. pap. 4.95 (ISBN 0-394-71281-1, Vin). Random.
--Fires: Essays, Poems, Stories. 1984. pap. 3.95 (ISBN 0-394-72299-X, Vin). Random.
--Fires: Essays, Poems, Stories 1966-1982. LC 82-22210. 192p. 1983. ltd. ed. 30.00 (ISBN 0-88496-195-8); 18.95 (ISBN 0-88496-195-8). Capra Pr.
--If It Please You. 25p. 1984. deluxe ed. 50.00 Deluxe Signed Ed. (ISBN 0-935716-28-9). Lord John.
--The Pheasant. (Metacom Limited Edition Ser.: No. 7). 24p. 1982. lt d. 37.50 (ISBN 0-911381-06-6). Metacom Pr.
--What We Talk about When We Talk about Love. LC 80-21752. 176p. 1981. 9.95 (ISBN 0-394-51684-2). Knopf.
--What We Talk About When We Talk About Love. LC 81-52447. 176p. pap. 2.95 (ISBN 0-394-75080-2, Vin). Random.
--Where Water Comes Together with Other Water. Date not set. 13.45 (ISBN 0-394-54470-6). Random.
--Will You Please Be Quiet, Please? (McGraw-Hill Paperbacks Ser.). 1978. pap. 5.95 (ISBN 0-07-010194-9). McGraw.
Carver, Raymond, jt. auth. see Le Guin, Ursula K.
Carver, Raymond, et al. A Celebration for Stanley Kunitz by Twenty-Five Poets. 150p. (Orig.). 1985. pap. 8.95 (ISBN 0-935296-59-X). Sheep Meadow.
Carver, Robert C. & Thiess, Susan. The Creator's World. (gr. k-3). 1978. 4.95x (ISBN 0-8192-4082-6); parent pupil packet 4.95x (ISBN 0-8192-4083-4). Morehouse.
Carver, Robert E., ed. Procedures in Sedimentary Petrology. LC 75-138907. 653p. 1971. 85.00 (ISBN 0-471-13855-X, Pub. by Wiley-Interscience). Wiley.
Carver, Ronald P. Reading Comprehension & Rauding Theory. (Illus.). 224p. 1981. 23.75x (ISBN 0-398-04495-3). C C Thomas.
--Writing a Publishable Research Report: In Education, Psychology, & Related Disciplines. 156p. 1984. spiral bdg. 18.75x (ISBN 0-398-04986-6). C C Thomas.
Carver, Sally S. American Postcard Guide to Tuck. rev. ed. (Illus.). 1982. pap. 8.95 (ISBN 0-686-38919-0). Carves.
Carver, Terrel. Marx's Social Theory. (Oxford Paperback University Ser.). 1983. 17.95x (ISBN 0-19-219170-5); pap. 6.95x (ISBN 0-19-289158-8). Oxford U Pr.
Carver, Terrell. Engels. (Past Masters Ser.). 1981. pap. 3.95 (ISBN 0-19-287548-5). Oxford U Pr.
--Marx & Engels: The Intellectual Relationship. LC 83-48679. 172p. 1984. 25.00x (ISBN 0-253-33681-3). Ind U Pr.
Carver, Terrell, ed. & tr. see Zeleny, Jindrich.
Carver, Terrell, tr. see Bekerman, Gerard.
Carver, Thomas N. The Distribution of Wealth. LC 79-51858. 1980. Repr. of 1904 ed. 24.75 (ISBN 0-88355-951-X). Hyperion Conn.
--Essays in Social Justice. facsimile ed. LC 79-105003. (Essay Index Reprint Ser.). 1915. 26.50 (ISBN 0-8369-1456-2). Ayer Co Pubs.
--The Essential Factors of Social Evolution. LC 73-14151. (Perspectives in Social Inquiry Ser.). 580p. 1974. Repr. 33.00x (ISBN 0-405-05497-1). Ayer Co Pubs.
--Essential Factors of Social Evolution. 1935. 17.50. Brown Bk.
--The Essential Factors of Social Evolution. (Harvard Sociological Studies). (Illus.). 564p. 1974. Repr. 17.50x (ISBN 0-89020-007-6). Crofton Pub.
--Sociology & Social Progress. 1905. 17.50 (ISBN 0-8482-3598-3). Norwood Edns.
--Sociology & Social Progress. 1905. 17.50 (ISBN 0-686-17694-4). Quality Lib.
Carver, Tina & Fotinos, Sandra. A Conversation Book: English in Everyday Life, Bk. I. 2nd ed. (Illus.). 224p. 1985. pap. text ed. 10.95 (ISBN 0-13-172362-6). P-H.
Carver, Tina, et al. A Writing Book: English in Everyday Life. 200p. 1982. pap. text ed. 10.95 (ISBN 0-13-970129-X). P-H.
Carver, Tina K. & Fotinos, S. Douglas. A Conversation Book: English in Everyday Life, Bk. 1. (Illus.). 1977. pap. text ed. 9.95 (ISBN 0-13-172239-5). P-H.
--A Conversation Book: English in Everyday Life, Bk. 2. (Illus.). 1977. pap. text ed. 9.95 (ISBN 0-13-172247-6). P-H.
Carver, Vida, ed. Child Abuse: A Study Text. 312p. 1978. pap. 18.00x (ISBN 0-335-00231-5, Pub. by Open Univ Pr). Taylor & Francis.
Carver, Vida & Liddiard, Penny, eds. An Ageing Population: A Reader & Sourcebook. LC 78-26607. 434p. 1979. text ed. 34.50x (ISBN 0-8419-0474-X). Holmes & Meier.
Carver, Wayne, et al. Greening Wheat: Fifteen Mormon Short Stories. Peterson, Levi S., ed. 216p. (Orig.). 1983. pap. 5.95 (ISBN 0-941214-12-5, Eden Hill Pub). Signature Bks.
Carvic, Heron. Odds on Miss Seton. 279p. 1981. Repr. lib. bdg. 16.95x (ISBN 0-89966-307-9). Buccaneer Bks.
Carvill, Barbara M. Der Verfuehrte Leser: Johann Karl August Musaeus' Romane und Romankritiken. (Canadian Studies in German Language & Literature: Vol. 31). 342p. (Ger.). 1985. text ed. 25.50 (ISBN 0-8204-0224-9). P Lang Pubs.
Carville, Geraldine. Norman Splendour: Duiske Abbey, Graignamanagh. (Illus.). 120p. 1979. 13.95 (ISBN 0-85640-171-4, Pub. by Blackstaff Pr). Longwood Pub Group.
--The Occupation of Celtic Sites in Medieval Ireland by the Canons Regular of St Augustine & the Cistercians. (Cistercian Studies Ser.: Nbr. 56). (Illus.). 1983. 13.95 (ISBN 0-87907-856-1). Cistercian Pubns.
Carvounis, Chris C. The Debt Dilemma of Developing Nations: Issues & Cases. LC 84-1981. 256p. 1984. lib. bdg. 35.00 (ISBN 0-89930-062-6, CDD/, Quorum). Greenwood.
Carwardine, Richard. Transatlantic Revivalism: Popular Evangelicalism in Britain & America, 1790-1865. LC 77-94740. (Contributions in American History Ser.: No. 75). 1978. lib. bdg. 35.00 (ISBN 0-313-20308-3, CTR/). Greenwood.
Carwardine, William H. The Pullman Strike. LC 73-77550. (Illus.). 176p. 1973. lib. bdg. 17.95 (ISBN 0-88286-003-8). C H Kerr.
Carwell, Catherine M. The Savage Pilgrimage: A Narrative by D. H. Lawrence. 1932. Repr. 19.00 (ISBN 0-8274-3325-5). R West.
Carwell, Hattie. Blacks in Science: Astrophysicist to Zoologist. (Illus.). 96p. 1977. 6.50 (ISBN 0-682-48911-5). Exposition Pr FL.
Carwell, L'Ann. Baby's First Bible Story Book. (Illus.). 1979. 1.25 (ISBN 0-570-08003-7, 56-1328). Concordia.
--Baby's First Book About Christmas. (Illus.). 1979. 1.25 (ISBN 0-570-08002-9, 56-1327). Concordia.
--Baby's First Book About Creation. (Illus.). 1979. 1.25 (ISBN 0-570-08000-2, 56-1325). Concordia.
--Baby's First Book About Jesus. (Illus.). 1979. 1.25 (ISBN 0-570-08001-0, 56-1326). Concordia.
Carwelti, Gordon. Vitalizing the High School: A Curriculum Critique of Major Reform Proposals. new ed. LC 74-19625. 61p. 1974. pap. 3.50 (ISBN 0-87120-067-8, 611-74026). Assn Supervision.
Carwile, Ruth, ed. see Gold, David T.
Carwile, Ruth H., ed. see Karter, Michael J.
Carwile, Ruth H., ed. see National Fire Protection Association.
Carwin, Merle A. Supervised Occupational Experience Manual. 2nd ed. 242p. 1982. pap. text ed. 4.50x (ISBN 0-8134-2228-0, 2228). Interstate.
Cary, Alice & Cary, Phoebe. Ballads for Little Folk. facs. ed. LC 73-109136. (Granger Index Reprint Ser.). 1873. 14.00 (ISBN 0-8369-6120-X). Ayer Co Pubs.
Cary, Allen S., jt. auth. see Mackin, J. Hoover.

Cary, Barbara. Meet Abraham Lincoln. (Step-up-Books Ser.). (Illus.). (gr. 2-6). 1965. 4.95 (ISBN 0-394-80057-5, BYR); PLB 5.99 (ISBN 0-394-90057-X). Random.

Cary, Beth, jt. auth. see McCarthy, Liz.

Cary, Bob. The Big Wilderness Canoe Manual. LC 83-8729. (Illus.). 192p. 1983. 14.95 (ISBN 0-668-05847-1); pap. 7.95 (ISBN 0-668-05852-8). Arco.

Cary, Carl. Salish Songs & Rituals. 1969. pap. 2.00 (ISBN 0-686-14907-6); pap. 15.00 deluxe ed. (ISBN 0-686-14908-4). Goliards Pr.

Cary, Cecile W. & Limouze, Henry S., eds. Shakespeare & the Arts: A Collection of Essays from the Ohio Shakespeare Conference, Wright State University, Dayton, Ohio, 1981. LC 82-17486. (Illus.). 256p. (Orig.). 1983. lib. bdg. 26.75 (ISBN 0-8191-2819-8); pap. text ed. 13.25 (ISBN 0-8191-2820-1). U Pr of Amer.

Cary, Diane M. Master. 1981. 9.95 (ISBN 0-8062-1763-4). Carlton.

Cary, E. & Peratis, K. W. Woman & the Law. Haiman, Franklyn S., ed. (To Protect These Rights Ser.). 216p. 1983. pap. 10.00 (ISBN 0-8442-6005-3, 6005-3, Passport Bks.). Natl Textbk.

Cary, E. L. Browning: Poet & the Man. LC 74-30337. (Studies in Browning, No. 4). 1974. lib. bdg. 49.95x (ISBN 0-8383-1876-2). Haskell.

Cary, Edward. George W. Curtis. 343p. 1980. Repr. of 1894 ed. lib. bdg. 20.00 (ISBN 0-8492-4045-X). R West.

--George William Curtis. 1894. lib. bdg. 13.50 (ISBN 0-8414-1596-X). Folcroft.

--George William Curtis. 1894. 12.00x (ISBN 0-403-00006-8). Scholarly.

Cary, Elisabeth L. The Works of James McNeill Whistler. facsimile ed. LC 77-157328. (Select Bibliographies Reprint Ser). Repr. of 1907 ed. 24.50 (ISBN 0-8369-5788-1). Ayer Co Pubs.

Cary, Elisabeth Luther. The Works of James McNeill Whistler. LC 77-6969. 1977. Repr. of 1913 ed. lib. bdg. 35.00 (ISBN 0-89341-217-1). Longwood Pub Group.

Cary, Elizabeth L. Browning, Poet & Man: A Survey. 1973. Repr. of 1899 ed. 30.00 (ISBN 0-8274-1501-X). R West.

--Emerson: Poet & Thinker. 1904. lib. bdg. 35.00 (ISBN 0-8414-3420-4). Folcroft.

--Novels of Henry James: A Study. LC 72-10933. (Studies in Henry James, No. 17). 1969. Repr. of 1905 ed. lib. bdg. 49.95x (ISBN 0-8383-0520-2). Haskell.

--The Rossettis. LC 74-30190. (Studies in the Rossettis, No. 81). 1974. lib. bdg. 57.95x (ISBN 0-8383-1943-2). Haskell.

--William Morris: Poet, Craftsmen, Socialist. LC 74-18124. 74. Repr. of 1902 ed. lib. bdg. 35.00 (ISBN 0-8414-3545-6). Folcroft.

Cary, Emily. The Ghost of Whitaker Mountain. (YA) 1979. 8.95 (ISBN 0-685-65270-X, Avalon). Bouregy.

Cary, Eve. What Every Teacher Should Know about Student Rights. LC 75-19038. pap. 20.00 (ISBN 0-317-29208-0, 2022231). Bks Demand UMI.

Cary, Henry. The Poems of Henry Carey. LC 83-45727. Repr. of 1930 ed. 27.00 (ISBN 0-404-20051-6). AMS Pr.

Cary, Henry F. The Early French Poets. LC 72-103219. 1970. Repr. of 1923 ed. 19.00x (ISBN 0-8046-0856-3, Pub.by Kennikat). Assoc Faculty Pr.

--Lives of English Poets from Johnson to Kirke White. 1973. Repr. of 1846 ed. 45.00 (ISBN 0-8274-1772-1). R West.

Cary, Henry F., tr. see Alighieri, Dante.

Cary, Howard B. Modern Welding Technology. LC 78-2966. (Illus.). 1979. 32.95 (ISBN 0-13-599290-7). P-H.

Cary, Jane R. How to Create Interiors for the Disabled: A Guidebook for Family & Friends. LC 77-88781. 1978. 15.00; pap. 5.95 (ISBN 0-394-73595-1). Pantheon.

Cary, Jere. Building Your Own Kitchen Cabinets. LC 82-51260. (Illus.). 152p. 1983. pap. 11.95 (ISBN 0-918804-15-9, Dist. by W W Norton). Taunton.

Cary, John H., et al. The Social Fabric: American Life from Sixteen Hundred Seven Reconstruction, Vol. I. 4th ed. 1983. 12.95 (ISBN 0-316-13072-9). Little.

--The Social Fabric: American Life from the Civil War to the Present, Vol. II. 4th ed. 1983. 12.95 (ISBN 0-316-13073-7). Little.

Cary, John M. Data Security & Performance Overhead in a Distributed Architecture System. Stone, Harold S., ed. LC 81-11638. (Computer Science: Distributed Database Systems Ser.: No. 9). 188p. 1981. 39.95 (ISBN 0-8357-1225-7). UMI Res Pr.

Cary, John W. The Organization & History of the Chicago, Milwaukee & St. Paul Railway Company. Bruchey, Stuart, ed. LC 80-1296. (Railroads Ser.). 1981. Repr. of 1893 ed. lib. bdg. 35.00x (ISBN 0-405-13766-4). Ayer Co Pubs.

Cary, Joyce. Art & Reality: Ways of the Creative Process. facsimile ed. LC 77-128218. (Essay Index Reprints - World Perspectives Ser.: Vol. 20). Repr. of 1958 ed. 20.00 (ISBN 0-8369-1906-8). Ayer Co Pubs.

--The Captive & the Free. 19.95 (ISBN 0-88411-309-4, Pub. by Aeonian Pr). Amereon Ltd.

--Except the Lord. LC 85-10601. (Second Trilogy Ser.: Bk. 2). 288p. 1985. pap. 7.95 (ISBN 0-8112-0965-2, NDP607). New Directions.

--Except the Lord. 16.95 (ISBN 0-88411-310-8, Pub. by Aeonian Pr). Amereon Ltd.

--A Fearful Joy, a Novel. LC 73-428. 343p. 1973. Repr. of 1949 ed. lib. bdg. 66.00x (ISBN 0-8371-6777-9, CAFJ). Greenwood.

--Herself Surprised. 275p. 1976. Repr. of 1948 ed. lib. bdg. 16.95 (ISBN 0-89244-070-8, Pub. by Aeonian Pr). Amereon Ltd.

--Herself Surprised. 1980. pap. 4.95 (ISBN 0-7145-0270-7). Riverrun NY.

--The Horse's Mouth. 1965. pap. 3.80i (ISBN 0-06-080046-1, P46, PL). Har-Row.

--The Horse's Mouth. 17.95 (ISBN 0-88411-311-6, Pub. by Aeonian Pr). Amereon Ltd.

--Not Honour More. LC 85-10601. (Second Trilogy Ser.: Bk. 3). 320p. 1985. pap. 7.95 (ISBN 0-8112-0966-0, NDP608). New Directions.

--Not Honour More. 17.95 (ISBN 0-88411-312-4, Pub. by Aeonian Pr). Amereon Ltd.

--Prisoner of Grace. LC 52-7281. (Second Trilogy Ser.: Bk. 1). 320p. pap. 8.95 (ISBN 0-8112-0964-4, NDP606). New Directions.

--Prisoner of Grace. 16.95 (ISBN 0-88411-313-2, Pub. by Aeonian Pr). Amereon Ltd.

--To Be a Pilgrim. 18.95 (ISBN 0-88411-314-0, Pub. by Aeonian Pr). Amereon Ltd.

Cary, Lee J., ed. Community Development As a Process. LC 74-130669. 1983. Repr. of 1970 ed. 15.00x (ISBN 0-8262-0415-5). U of Mo Pr.

--Community Development As a Process. LC 74-130669. 224p. 1983. pap. text ed. 8.50x (ISBN 0-8262-0415-5). U of Mo Pr.

Cary, Lorin L., jt. auth. see Boryczka, Raymond.

Cary, M. & Scullard, H. H. A History of Rome. 3rd ed. LC 74-24818. (Illus.). 640p. 1976. text ed. 27.95 (ISBN 0-312-38395-9). St Martin.

Cary, Mara. Basic Baskets. LC 75-14222. 127p. 1975. pap. 9.95 (ISBN 0-395-21989-2). HM.

--Useful Baskets. 1977. 11.95 (ISBN 0-395-25707-7); pap. 9.95 (ISBN 0-395-25950-9). HM.

Cary, Margaret M. Are Your Meetings Held in the Life. 1983. pap. 5.00x (ISBN 0-87574-037-5, 037). Pendle Hill.

Cary, Max. Documentary Sources of Greek History. LC 78-90478. Repr. of 1927 ed. lib. bdg. 15.00x (ISBN 0-8371-2215-5, CADS). Greenwood.

--The Geographic Background of Greek & Roman History. LC 81-7170. vi, 331p. 1981. Repr. of 1949 ed. lib. bdg. 37.50x (ISBN 0-313-23187-7, CAGH). Greenwood.

--A History of the Greek World: 323-146 B.C. 2nd rev. ed. (History of the Greek & Roman World Ser). (Illus.). 446p. 1972. pap. 16.95x (ISBN 0-416-70200-7, NO. 2125). Methuen Inc.

Cary, Meredith. Different Drummers: A Study of Cultural Alternatives in Fiction. LC 84-1346. 300p. 1984. 20.00 (ISBN 0-8108-1689-X). SCARECROW.

Cary, Norman D., jt. auth. see Book, Albert C.

Cary, Norman R. Christian Criticism in the Twentieth Century. (National University Publications Literary Criticism Ser.). 1976. 13.50x (ISBN 0-8046-9104-5, Pub. by Kennikat). Assoc Faculty Pr.

Cary, O., et al. War-Wasted Asia: Letters, 1945-46. LC 75-11395. (Illus.). 322p. 16.95x (ISBN 0-87011-257-0). Kodansha.

Cary, Otis. A History of Christianity in Japan: Roman Catholic & Greek Orthodox Missions, 2 vols. LC 75-28972. (Illus.). 1975. Repr. of 1909 ed. boxed 32.50 (ISBN 0-8048-1177-6). C E Tuttle.

--History of Christianity in Japan, Roman Catholic & Greek Orthodox Missions, 2 Vols. 1971. Repr. of 1909 ed. Set. 18.00 (ISBN 0-403-00252-4). Scholarly.

Cary, Otis, ed. From a Ruined Empire: Letters-Japan, China, Korea 1945-1946. LC 75-11395. 322p. 1984. pap. 5.25 (ISBN 0-87011-638-X). Kodansha.

Cary, Phoebe, jt. auth. see Cary, Alice.

Cary, R., jt. auth. see Roberts, G.

Cary, Richard. Early Reception of Edwin Arlington Robinson: The First Twenty Years. 1974. 12.50 (ISBN 0-910394-12-1). Colby.

--Mary N. Murfree. (Twayne's United States Authors Ser). 1967. pap. 5.95x (ISBN 0-8084-0216-1, T121, Twayne). New Coll U Pr.

--Mary N. Murfree. LC 67-24762. (Twayne's United States Authors Ser.). 1967. lib. bdg. 12.50 (ISBN 0-89197-839-9); pap. 2.95 (ISBN 0-89197-990-5). Irvington.

--Sarah Orne Jewett. (Twayne's United States Authors Ser). 1962. pap. 5.95x (ISBN 0-8084-0272-2, T19, Twayne). New Coll U Pr.

Cary, Richard, ed. Appreciation of Edwin Arlington Robinson: Twenty-Eight Interpretive Essays. 1969. 8.00 (ISBN 0-910394-08-3). Colby.

--Uncollected Poems & Prose of Edwin Arlington Robinson. 1975. 10.00 (ISBN 0-910394-13-X). Colby.

Cary, Richard, ed. see Jewett, Sarah O.

Cary, Richard, ed. see Robinson, Edwin A.

Cary, Sylvia. It Must Be Five O'Clock Somewhere. 225p. (Orig.). 1985. pap. 8.95 (ISBN 0-89638-094-7). CompCare.

Cary, Thomas G. Memoir of Thomas Handasyd Perkins. LC 77-164040. (Research & Source Works Ser.: No. 591). 1971. Repr. of 1856 ed. lib. bdg. 21.00 (ISBN 0-8337-0491-5). B Franklin.

Cary, William & Eisenberg, Melvin A. Casese & Materials on Corporations. 5th, unabridged ed. LC 80-18042. (University Casebook Ser.). 1753p. 1980. text ed. 27.50 (ISBN 0-88277-012-8). Foundation Pr.

Cary, William L. & Eisenberg, Melvin A. Cases & Materials on Corporations. abr. 5th ed. LC 80-68866. (University Casebook Ser.). 1030p. 1980. text ed. 22.50 (ISBN 0-88277-017-9). Foundation Pr.

Cary, William L., jt. auth. see Eisenberg, Melvin A.

Cary-Elwes, Columbia. Law, Liberty & Love. 1950. 5.00 (ISBN 0-8159-6104-9). Devin.

Caryl, Charles W. New Era. LC 78-154432. (Utopian Literature Ser). (Illus.). 1971. Repr. of 1897 ed. 18.00 (ISBN 0-405-03515-2). Ayer Co Pubs.

Caryle, A. J., ed. see Crabbe, George.

Caryle, R. M., ed. see Crabbe, George.

Carylon, Richard. A Guide to the Gods. 1982. 16.95 (ISBN 0-688-01332-5); pap. 8.25 (ISBN 0-688-01333-3). Morrow.

Carylye, J. A., ed. see Irving, David.

Carynnk, Marco, tr. see Kotsiubynsky, Mykhailo.

Carynnyk, Marco, ed. see Dovzhenko, Alexander.

Carynnyk, Marco, tr. see Dovzhenko, Alexander.

Carynnyk, Marco, tr. see Nekipelov, Victor.

Carynnyk, Marco, tr. see Osadchy, Mykhaylo.

Carynnyk, Maro, tr. see Osadchy, Mykhaylo.

Carzou, J. M. Paris. Henderson, S. D., tr. (Illus.). 144p. (French.). 1982. 29.95 (ISBN 2-03-523102-7, 8222). Larousse.

--Paris. (Illus.). 144p. (Fr.). 1983. 29.95 (ISBN 2-03-523101-9, 2228). Larousse.

Casa, Frank P. Dramatic Craftsmanship of Moreto. LC 66-18244. (Studies in Romance Languages: No. 29). 1966. 12.50x (ISBN 0-674-21550-8). Harvard U Pr.

Casa, Giovanni della see Della Casa, Giovanni.

Casa-Alvero, E., et al, eds. Algebraic Geometry: Sitges (Barcelona) 1983. (Lecture Notes in Mathematics: Vol. 1124). xi, 416p. pap. 25.80 (ISBN 0-387-15232-6). Springer Verlag.

Casabonne, Richard, ed. Official Apple Computer Club Books: First Three Handbooks in a Series. 19.95 ea.; pap. 12.95 ea. P-H.

Casad, Dede, jt. auth. see Driskill, Frank A.

Casad, Dede W. Becoming by Being. 144p. 1984. pap. 8.95 (ISBN 0-89015-427-9). Eakin Pubns.

Casad, Eugene. Dialect Intelligibility Testing. (Publications in Linguistics & Related Fields Ser.: No. 38). 201p. 1974. pap. 8.00 (ISBN 0-88312-040-2); microfiche (3) 3.80 (ISBN 0-88312-440-8). Summer Inst Ling.

Casad, Mary B. Bluebonnet at the Alamo. 40p. 1984. 6.95 (ISBN 0-89015-445-7). Eakin Pubns.

--Bluebonnet of the Hill Country. (Illus.). (gr. k-4). 1983. 6.95 (ISBN 0-89015-395-7). Eakin Pubns.

Casad, Robert C. Civil Judgment Recognition & the Integration of Multiple-State Associations: Central America, the United States of America, & the European Economic Community. LC 81-11926. xiv, 258p. 1982. 29.95x (ISBN 0-7006-0218-6). U Pr of KS.

--Jurisdiction in Civil Actions. 1983. 84.00 (ISBN 0-88262-891-7). Warren.

--Res Judicata. (Nutshell Ser.). 310p. 1976. 7.95 (ISBN 0-317-00004-7). West Pub.

Casad, Robert C. & Montagne, Rogelio S. Expropriation in Central America & Panama: Processes & Procedures. LC 74-21957. xiii, 188p. 1975. lib. bdg. 35.00 (ISBN 0-930342-10-0). W S Hein.

Casad, Robert C. & Simon, Peter N. Civil Procedure: Cases & Materials. LC 84-60853. (Contemporary Legal Education Ser.). xxiv, 815p. 1984. 30.00 (ISBN 0-87215-788-1). Michie Co.

Casada, James, ed. see Boucher, Philip P.

Casada, James A. Dr. David Livingstone & Henry Morton Stanley: An Annotated Bibliography with Commentary. LC 75-24101. (Reference Library of Social Science: Vol. 21). 225p. 1976. lib. bdg. 31.00 (ISBN 0-8240-9967-2). Garland Pub.

Casada, James A., ed. African & Afro-American History. LC 77-15305. 200p. 1978. pap. 15.00 (ISBN 0-914970-38-0). Conch Mag.

Casada, James A., ed. see Musiker, Naomi & Musiker, Reuben.

Casado, Dario. Psicologia: Curso Basico. LC 81-65574. (Coleccion Textos Ser.). 384p. (Orig., Span.). 1984. pap. 12.00 (ISBN 0-89729-285-5). Ediciones.

Casady, Cleo, jt. auth. see Casady, Mona.

Casady, Cleo, et al. Basic Typewriting Applications. (gr. 9-12). 1984. text ed. 5.45 (ISBN 0-538-20900-3, T90). SW Pub.

Casady, Cort, jt. auth. see Davidson, John.

Casady, Edwin E. Henry Howard, Earl of Surrey. (MLA Rev. Fund Ser.). 1938. 22.00 (ISBN 0-527-15250-1). Kraus Repr.

--Henry Howard, Earl of Surrey. 1938. Repr. 15.00 (ISBN 0-8482-3569-X). Norwood Edns.

Casady, Mona. Word Information Processing Concepts. (gr. 9-12). 1984. text ed. 5.30 wkbk. (ISBN 0-538-23610-8, W61). SW Pub.

Casady, Mona & Casady, Cleo. Business Letter Typing. (gr. 9-12). 1983. text ed. 4.85 (ISBN 0-538-20930-5, T93). SW Pub.

Casady, Mona J. Competitive Edge - Production Typing: Simulation. 1983. 13.80 (ISBN 0-538-20380-3, T38). SW Pub.

Casady, R. B. & Jawin, P. B. Commerical Rabbit Raising. (Shorey Lost Arts Ser.). (Illus.). 69p. pap. 3.95 (ISBN 0-8466-6054-7, U54). Shorey.

Casagrande, Bob. Better Black & White Darkroom Techniques. (Master Class Photography Ser.). (Illus.). 176p. 1984. pap. 8.95 (ISBN 0-13-071324-4). P-H.

Casagrande, Diane O. & Casagrande, Roger D. Oral Communication: A Tool for Technical Success. 300p. 1985. pap. text ed. write for info. (ISBN 0-534-05532-X). Wadsworth Pub.

Casagrande, Jean. The Sound System of French. 240p. 1984. lexotone 19.95 (ISBN 0-87840-085-0). Georgetown U Pr.

Casagrande, Jean, ed. The Linguistic Connection. 340p. (Orig.). 1984. lib. bdg. 27.75 (ISBN 0-8191-3588-7); pap. text ed. 14.50 (ISBN 0-8191-3589-5). U Pr of Amer.

Casagrande, Louis B. & Bourns, Phillips. Side Trips: The Photography of Sumner W. Matteson. LC 83-61682. (Illus.). 249p. 1983. 24.95 (ISBN 0-89326-095-9). Milwaukee Pub Mus.

--Side Trips: The Photography of Sumner W. Matteson, 1898-1908. 256p. 1983. pap. 24.95 (ISBN 0-295-96097-3). U of Wash Pr.

Casagrande, Louise B. & Ringheim, Melissa M. Straight Tongue: Minnesota Indian Art from the Bishop Whipple Collections. LC 80-53670. (Illus.). 94p. (Orig.). 1980. pap. 9.95 (ISBN 0-295-96032-9). U of Wash Pr.

Casagrande, Peter J. Unity in Hardy's Novels: "Repetitive Symmetries". xii, 252p. 1982. 29.95x (ISBN 0-7006-0209-7). U Pr of KS.

Casagrande, Robert. Better Black & White Darkroom Techniques. (Illus.). 176p. 1982. 14.95 (ISBN 0-13-071332-5). P-H.

Casagrande, Roger D., jt. auth. see Casagrande, Diane O.

Casale, A., et al. Advances in Polymer Science: Polymerization, Vol. 17. Cantow, H. J., ed. LC 61-642. (Illus.). 120p. 1975. 35.00 (ISBN 0-387-07111-3). Springer-Verlag.

Casale, Anne. Italian Family Cooking: Like Mama Used to Make. 384p. (Orig.). 1984. pap. 9.95 (ISBN 0-449-90133-5, Columbine). Fawcett.

Casale, Antonio & Porter, Roger S. Polymer Stress Reactions, 2 vols. Vol. 1, 1978. 42.00 (ISBN 0-12-162801-9); Vol. 2, 1979. 65.00 (ISBN 0-12-162802-7). Acad Pr.

Casale, James F., jt. ed. see Gant, Wanda.

Casale, James F., et al, eds. Papers & Proceedings of Syntopican XII: Anthology. (Illus., Orig.). 1984. pap. 30.00 (ISBN 0-935220-11-9). Assn Info Sys.

Casale, Mick. Elm Circle. 1984. pap. 3.85x (ISBN 0-317-17215-8). Dramatists Play.

Casale, Ottavio M. A Leopardi Reader. Leopardi, Giacomo., ed. LC 80-29068. 300p. 1981. 24.95x (ISBN 0-252-00824-3); pap. 8.95x (ISBN 0-252-00892-8). U of Ill Pr.

Casali, Dan & Diness, Madelynne. The New Henning's Guide to Fishing in Oregon. 6th, rev ed. LC 84-80050. (Illus.). 170p. 1984. pap. 10.95 (ISBN 0-916473-01-5). Flying Pubns.

Casalis, George. Correct Ideas Don't Fall from the Skies: Elements for an Inductive Theology. Lyons, Jeanne M. & John, Michael, trs. from Fr. LC 83-19374. 240p. (Orig.). 1984. pap. 8.95 (ISBN 0-88344-023-7). Orbis Bks.

--Portrait of Karl Barth. Brown, Robert M., tr. LC 80-25829. viii, 135p. 1981. Repr. of 1963 ed. lib. bdg. 19.25x (ISBN 0-313-22775-6, CAKB). Greenwood.

Casalis, Jacques. Dictionnaire Laitier: Francais, Allemand, Anglais. (Fr., Ger. & Eng.). 1963. 49.95 (ISBN 0-686-56941-5, M-6063). French & Eur.

Casals, Felipe G. The Syncretic Society. Meyer, Alfred G., ed. Daniels, Guy, tr. from Fr. LC 80-5455. 100p. 1980. 22.50 (ISBN 0-87332-176-6). M E Sharpe.

Casamassa, J. V. & Bent, R. D. Jet Aircraft Power Systems. 3rd ed. 1965. text ed. 28.20 (ISBN 0-07-010199-X). McGraw.

Casanave, Christine P. Strategies for Readers: A Reading Communication Text for Students of ESL, Bk. 1. (Illus.). 192p. 1986. pap. text ed. 8.95 (ISBN 0-13-850728-7). P H.

--Strategies for Readers: A Reading Communication Text for Students of ESL, Bk. 2. (Illus.). 144p. 1986. pap. text ed. 8.95 (ISBN 0-13-850744-9). P H.

Casanova, Jacques. Life & Memoirs of Casanova. Gribble, George, ed. Machen, Arthur, tr. (Da Capo Quality Paperbacks Ser.). 750p. 1984. pap. 13.95 (ISBN 0-306-80208-2). Da Capo.

Casanova, M. A. The Concurrency Control Problem for Database Systems. (Lecture Notes in Computer Science: Vol. 116). 175p. 1981. pap. 14.00 (ISBN 0-387-10845-9). Springer-Verlag.

Casanova, Olivier & Casanova, Patrice. Short Cuts: Styling & Caring for Short Hair. 1985. pap. 7.95 (ISBN 0-671-55375-5, Pub. by Fireside). S&S.

Casanova, Pablo G., ed. La Sociologie Du Developpement Latino-Americain: Tendances Actuelles De la Recherche et Bibliographie, 2 pts. Incl. Pt. 1. Etudes Generales. (No. 18). 1971. pap. 7.20x (ISBN 0-686-22179-6); Pt. 2. Etudes Sectorielles. (No. 19). 1973. pap. 12.00x (ISBN 90-2797-218-4). (La Sociologie Contemporaine). pap. Mouton.

Casanova, Patrice, jt. auth. see Casanova, Olivier.

Casanova, Patrice, jt. auth. see Geutary, Helene.

Casanova, Richard L. & Ratkevich, Ronald P. Illustrated Guide to Fossil Collecting. rev., 3rd ed. LC 81-18788. (Illus.). 240p. 1981. lib. bdg. 12.95 (ISBN 0-87961-112-X); pap. 6.95 (ISBN 0-87961-113-8). Naturegraph.

Casanova De Seingalt, Jacques. Casanova's "Icosameron", or the Story of Edward & Elizabeth: Who Spent 81 Years in the Land of the Megamicres, Original Inhabitants of Protocosmos in the Interior of Our Globe. Zurer, Rachel, tr. from Fr. LC 83-82006. 240p. 1985. o. p. 14.50 (ISBN 0-941752-02-X); pap. 9.50 (ISBN 0-941752-00-3). Jenna Pr.

Casares, Adolfo B. The Invention of Morel & Other Stories. Simms, Ruth L. C., tr. (Texas Pan American Ser.). (Illus.). 245p. 1985. pap. 9.95 (ISBN 0-292-73840-4). U of Tex Pr.

Casares, Angel, tr. see Rosenfeld, Erwin & Geller, Harriet.

Casares, Angel J. Curso de Filosofia. rev., 2nd ed. 238p. 1980. text ed. 12.00 (ISBN 0-8477-2821-8); pap. text ed. 9.00 (ISBN 0-8477-2822-6). U of PR Pr.

--Dos Palabras Sobre las Palabras: Apuntes sobre la traduccion y sus problemas. LC 82-4938. 118p. (Span.). 1982. pap. 6.25x (ISBN 0-8477-3503-6). U of PR Pr.

--Sobre la Esencia del Hombre. LC 78-15645. 1979. pap. 6.00 (ISBN 0-8477-2818-8). U of PR Pr.

Casares, Julio. Diccionario Ideologico De la Lengua Espanola. 2nd ed. 1444p. (Espn.). 1977. leatherette 56.00 (ISBN 84-252-0592-1, S-12240). French & Eur.

Casares Sanchez, Julio. Diccionario Ideologico De la Lengua Espanola. 2nd ed. 1444p. (Espn.). 1977. pap. 50.95 (ISBN 84-252-0126-8, S-50270). French & Eur.

Casarett, Alison P. Radiation Biology. (Illus.). 1968. 32.95 (ISBN 0-13-750356-3). P-H.

Casarett, George W. Radiation Histopathology, 2 vols. 1981. Vol. 1, 160p. 54.00 (ISBN 0-8493-5357-2); Vol. 2, 176p. 56.00 (ISBN 0-8493-5358-0). CRC Pr.

Casarett, George W., jt. auth. see Rubin, Phillip.

Casart, Jonathan, tr. see Uribe, Armando.

Casas, Arnold J., ed. see Wenger, J. C.

Casas, Arnoldo J., ed. see Wenger, J. C.

Casas, Bartholome De Las. The Spanish Colonie, or Briefe Chronicle or the Acts & Gestes of the Spaniardes in the West Indies. LC 77-6866. (English Experience Ser.: No. 859). 1977. Repr. of 1583 ed. lib. bdg. 14.00 (ISBN 90-221-0859-7). Walter J Johnson.

Casas, Celso A. De see De Casas, Celso A.

Casas, Don Fray Bartolome de Las see De Las Casas, Don Fray Bartolome.

Casas, Myrna. La Trampa. Bd. with El Impromptu De San Juan. (UPREX, Teatro y Cine: No. 36). pap. 1.85 (ISBN 0-8477-0036-4). U of PR Pr.

Casas, Penelope. Foods & Wines of Spain. LC 82-47830. (Illus.). 1982. 18.95 (ISBN 0-394-51348-7). Knopf.

--Tapas: The Little Dishes of Spain. LC 85-40160. (Illus.). 256p. (Orig.). 1985. 22.95 (ISBN 0-394-54086-7); pap. 12.95 (ISBN 0-394-74235-4). Knopf.

Casasayas, Josefina & Llibre, Jaume. Qualitative Analysis of the Anistropic Kepler Problem. LC 84-18521. (Memoirs of the American Mathematical Society: No. 312). 115p. 1984. pap. 13.00 (ISBN 0-8218-2309-4). Am Math.

Casasent, D., ed. Optical Data Processing: Applications. (Topics in Applied Physics: Vol. 23). (Illus.). 1978. 57.00 (ISBN 0-387-08453-3). Springer-Verlag.

Casasent, David. Digital Electronics. (Illus.). 276p. 1982. 13.95 (ISBN 0-13-212340-1). P-H.

--Electronic Circuits. (Illus.). 400p. 1982. pap. 13.95 (ISBN 0-13-250233-X). P-H.

Casasnovas, Sonia, tr. see Edwards, Gabrielle I. & Cimmino, Marion.

Casasnovas, Sonia, tr. see Rosenfeld, Erwin & Geller, Harriet.

Casasnovas, Sonia, tr. see Rosenfeld & Geller.

Casas-Vazquez, J., et al, eds. Recent Developments in Nonequilibrium Thermodynamics: Proceedings of the Meeting Held at Bellaterra School of Thermodynamics, Autonomous University of Barcelona, Spain, Sept. 26-30, 1983. (Lecture Notes in Physics Ser.: Vol. 199). xiii, 485p. 1984. pap. 24.00 (ISBN 0-387-12927-8). Springer-Verlag.

Casati, G., ed. Chaotic Behavior in Quantum Systems: Theory & Applications. (NATO ASI Series B, Physics: Vol. 120). 380p. 1985. 59.50x (ISBN 0-306-41898-3, Plenum Pr). Plenum Pub.

Casati, G., ed. see Volta Memorial Conference, Como, Italy, 1977.

Casati, Gaetano. Ten Years in Equatoria & the Return with Emin Pasha, 2 Vols. Clay, J. Randolph, tr. LC 73-76854. (Illus.). Repr. of 1891 ed. 46.00x (ISBN 0-8371-3795-0, CEO&). Greenwood.

Casaubon, George E. Card Sorcery with Salt. 95p. 1979. pap. 7.50 (ISBN 0-915926-36-9). Magic Ltd.

Casaubon, Isaac. De Satyrica Graecorum Poesi & Romanorum Satira. LC 72-13784. 392p. (Lat.). 1973. Repr. of 1605 ed. lib. bdg. 60.00x (ISBN 0-8201-1115-5). Schol Facsimiles.

Casaubon, Meric. The Golden Book of Marcus Aurelius. 1979. Repr. of 1906 ed. lib. bdg. 12.50 (ISBN 0-8482-7564-0). Norwood Edns.

--A Letter of Meric Casaubon to Peter du Moulin Concerning Natural Experimental Philosophie. LC 76-47045. 1976. Repr. of 1669 ed. 90.00x (ISBN 0-8201-1284-4). Schol Facsimiles.

--Of Credulity & Incredulity; In Things Divine & Spiritual. LC 79-8097. Repr. of 1670 ed. 30.00 (ISBN 0-404-18408-1). AMS Pr.

--Treatise Concerning Enthusiasme. LC 77-119864. 1970. Repr. of 1656 ed. 45.00x (ISBN 0-8201-1077-9). Schol Facsimiles.

Casaus, Victor, et al. Somos-We Are: Five Contemporary Cuban Poets. Whitney, Anita, ed. (Illus., Orig.). 1971. pap. 1.00 (ISBN 0-87810-000-8). Times Change.

Casavant, Helen. Christmas By Mail: A Series of Letters. 27p. 1985. 4.95 (ISBN 0-533-06324-8). Vantage.

Casavant, Kenneth & Infanger, Craig. Economics & Agricultural Management: An Introduction. 1984. text ed. 23.95 (ISBN 0-8359-1578-6); instr's manual avail. Reston.

Casaverde, Mateo, jt. auth. see Forbush, Scott E.

Casavola, Franco. Tommaso Traetta di Bitonto (1727-1779) La Vita e le Opere. LC 80-22630. Repr. of 1957 ed. 22.50 (ISBN 0-404-18816-8). AMS Pr.

Casazza, jt. auth. see Ransom.

Casazza, John A. Condominium Conversions. LC 82-70139. (Illus.). 157p. 1982. 28.00 (ISBN 0-87420-606-5, C19); members 21.00. Urban Land.

Casazza, John A., jt. auth. see O'Mara, W. Paul.

Casazza, John A., jt. auth. see Wrenn, Douglas M.

Casberg, Melvin A. Death Stalks the Punjab. LC 80-23558. (Illus.). 240p. (Orig.). 1981. pap. 6.95 (ISBN 0-89407-045-2). Strawberry Hill.

--Dowry of Death. (Illus.). 240p. (Orig.). 1984. pap. 6.95 (ISBN 0-89407-062-2). Strawberry Hill.

--Five Rivers to Death. LC 82-5814. (Illus.). 240p. (Orig.). 1982. pap. 6.95 (ISBN 0-89407-051-7). Strawberry Hill.

Casberg, Olivia. Mission Through a Woman's Eyes. LC 84-27232. 120p. (Orig.). 1985. pap. 6.95 (ISBN 0-933380-31-3). Olive Pr Pubns.

--Women of My Other Worlds. LC 84-27221. 100p. (Orig.). 1985. pap. 5.95 (ISBN 0-933380-30-5). Olive Pr Pubns.

Cascade Graphics Development. Cascadet Student Manual. 1985. write for info. McGraw.

Cascardi, Andrea E. Good Books to Grow on: A Guide to Building Your Childs Library from Birth to Age Five. 144p. 1985. pap. 6.95 (ISBN 0-446-38173-X). Warner Bks.

Cascardi, Anthony J. The Bounds of Reason: Cervantes, Dostoevsky, Flaubert. 288p. 1985. 29.50x (ISBN 0-231-06212-5). Columbia U Pr.

--The Limits of Illusion: A Critical Study of Calderon. (Cambridge Iberian & Latin American Studies). 196p. 1984. 39.95 (ISBN 0-521-26281-X). Cambridge U Pr.

Casci, Corrado, ed. Recent Advances in the Aerospace Sciences. 454p. 1985. 55.00x (ISBN 0-306-41079-6, Plenum Pr). Plenum Pub.

Casciani, C. U. & Adorno, D., eds. Tissue Typing & Kidney Transplantation, 1978 Report. (Illus.). 57p. 1980. 20.00 (ISBN 8-8212-0032-9, Pub. by Piccin Italy). J K Burgess.

Casciani, Patricia N. The Lizards of Trianada. 1983. 10.00 (ISBN 0-533-05500-8). Vantage.

Casciato & Horsfall. TI 99-4A: Twenty-Four BASIC Programs. LC 83-50831. 224p. 1983. pap. 12.95 (ISBN 0-672-22247-7, 22247); incl. tape 19.95 (ISBN 0-672-26172-3, 26172). Sams.

Casciato, Carol A. & Horsfall, Donald. Panasonic Sr. Partner Users Guide. LC 84-51464. 18.95 (ISBN 0-672-22381-3). Sams.

--TI-99 4A BASIC Reference Manual. LC 83-51181. 17.95 (ISBN 0-672-22246-9). Sams.

Casciato, Carol Ann & Horsfall, Donald J. The TI 99-4A User's Guide. LC 83-61067. 192p. 1983. pap. 11.95 (ISBN 0-672-22071-7, 22071). Sams.

Casciato, Dennis A. & Bennet, Lowitz Barry B. Manual of Bedside Oncology. (SPIRAL Manual Ser.). 699p. 1983. spiralbound 17.95 (ISBN 0-316-13068-0). Little.

Casciero, Albert J. & Roney, Raymond G. Introduction to AV for Technical Assistants. LC 81-13690. (Library Science Text). (Illus.). 250p. 1981. lib. bdg. 28.00 (ISBN 0-87287-232-7); 20.00 (ISBN 0-87287-281-5). Libs Unl.

Cascio, Dorothy, jt. auth. see Hodgetts, Richard M.

Cascio, Wayne. Applied Psychology in Personnel Management. 2nd ed. (Illus.). 496p. 1982. text ed. 34.95 (ISBN 0-8359-0282-X); instr's. manual avail. (ISBN 0-8359-0283-8). Reston.

Cascio, Wayne F. Costing Human Resources. LC 82-15228. (Human Resources Management Ser.). 224p. 1982. pap. text ed. write for info. (ISBN 0-534-01158-6). Kent Pub Co.

--Costing Human Resources: The Financial Impact of Behavior in Organizations. 256p. 1983. 21.95 (ISBN 0-442-21501-0). Van Nos Reinhold.

Cascio, Wayne F. & Awad, Elias M. Human Resources Management: An Information Systems Approach. 450p. 1981. text ed. 29.95 (ISBN 0-8359-3008-4); student activities guide o.p. 7.95 (ISBN 0-8359-3010-6). Reston.

Casciato, Arthur D. & West, James L., III, eds. Critical Essays on William Styron. (Critical Essays on American Literature Ser.). 1982. lib. bdg. 34.00 (ISBN 0-8161-8261-2). G K Hall.

Cascone, Gina. Pagan Babies & Other Catholic Memories. 160p. 1982. 9.95 (ISBN 0-312-59418-6). St Martin.

--Pagan Babies & Other Catholic Memories. 160p. 1983. pap. 4.95 (ISBN 0-312-59419-4). St Martin.

Casdaglis, Emmanuel C., ed. Cyprus Seventy-Four: Aphrodite's Face. (Illus.). 221p. 35.00 (ISBN 0-89241-081-7). Caratzas.

Casdorph, Herman R. Treatment of the Hyperlipidemic States. (Illus.). 464p. 1971. photocopy ed. 44.50x (ISBN 0-398-02255-0). C C Thomas.

Casdorph, Paul. The Letters of John Brown. 150p. Date not set. 15.95 (ISBN 0-934750-35-1). Jalamap.

Casdorph, Paul D. Republicans, Negroes, & Progressives in the South, Nineteen Twelve to Nineteen Sixteen. LC 80-15398. (Illus.). ix, 262p. 1981. text ed. 19.75 (ISBN 0-8173-0048-1). U of Ala Pr.

Case, jt. auth. see Barrows.

Case, Albert F., Jr. Information Systems Development: Principles of Software Engineering & Computer-Aided Software Engineering. (Illus.). 240p. 1986. text ed. 30.00 (ISBN 0-13-464520-0). P-H.

Case, Arthur E. Bibliography of English Poetical Miscellanies, Fifteen Twenty-One to Seventeen Fifty. 1935. lib. bdg. 50.00 (ISBN 0-8414-3008-X). Folcroft.

--Four Essays on Gulliver's Travels. 11.25 (ISBN 0-8446-1106-9). Peter Smith.

Case, Arthur E., jt. ed. see Nettleton, George H.

Case, Betsy, jt. auth. see Dennis, Ben.

Case, Bill. Life Begins at Sixty. LC 85-40719. 204p. 1985. 14.95 (ISBN 0-8128-3023-7). Stein & Day.

Case, C. E. Beachhead. 1983. pap. 3.95 (ISBN 0-8217-1219-5). Zebra.

Case, C. M. South Asian History, Seventeen Fifty to Nineteen Fifty: A Guide to Periodicals, Dissertations & Newspapers. 1967. 62.50x (ISBN 0-691-03059-6). Princeton U Pr.

Case, Carlton B. The Big Toast Book & After Dinner Stories. 0.75 (ISBN 0-685-02626-4, 00545163). Stein Pub.

Case Centennial Symposium on Large Scale Systems, Cleveland, O., July 1980. Large Scale Systems: Proceedings. Haimes, Yacov Y., ed. (Studies in Management Sciences & Systems: Vol. 7). 184p. 1982. 42.75 (ISBN 0-444-86367-2, I-112-82, North-Holland). Elsevier.

Case, Charles C. Culture, the Human Plan: Essays in the Anthropological Interpretation of Human Behavior. 186p. (Orig.). 1977. pap. text ed. 11.25 (ISBN 0-8191-0268-7). U Pr of Amer.

--Talking Trees & Singing Whales. Woolsey, Raymond H., ed. (Devotional Ser.). 365p. (gr. 5 up). 1985. 7.95 (ISBN 0-8280-0285-1). Review & Herald.

--The Yankee Generations: A History of the Case Family in America. LC 81-40638. (Illus.). 338p. (Orig.). 1982. lib. bdg. 28.75 (ISBN 0-8191-1947-4); pap. text ed. 15.75 (ISBN 0-8191-1948-2). U Pr of Amer.

Case, Charles J. Stock Market Arithmetic: A Home Study Course for Investors. rev., & enl. ed. 1985. pap. 8.95 (ISBN 0-89526-805-1). Regnery-Gateway.

Case, Charles W. & Matthes, William A., eds. Colleges of Education: Perspectives on Their Future. LC 84-61701. (National Society for the Study of Education Publication Ser.). 206p. 1985. text ed. 23.00x (ISBN 0-8211-0230-3). McCutchan.

Case, Christine & Johnson, Ted. Laboratory Exercises in Microbiology. 1984. 20.95 (ISBN 0-8053-5040-3); instr's guide 6.95 (ISBN 0-8053-5041-1). Benjamin-Cummings.

Case, Clarence M. Essays in Social Values. facs. ed. LC 67-30201. (Essay Index Reprint Ser). 1944. 15.00 (ISBN 0-8369-0281-5). Ayer Co Pubs.

--Non-Violent Coercion: A Study in Methods of Social Pressure. LC 78-137530. (Peace Movement in America Ser). viii, 423p. 1972. Repr. of 1923 ed. lib. bdg. 22.95x (ISBN 0-89198-058-X). Ozer.

--Outlines of Readings in Social Science. 1924. 20.00 (ISBN 0-8482-3588-6). Norwood Edns.

Case, D. H. Modern Mathematical Topics. 1968. 5.00 (ISBN 0-8022-0217-9). Philos Lib.

Case, David. The Fighting Breed. (Orig.). 1979. pap. 1.95 (ISBN 0-89083-541-1). Zebra.

--Gold Fever. 224p. (Orig.). 1982. pap. 2.25 (ISBN 0-505-51763-9, Pub. by Tower Bks). Dorchester Pub Co.

--Plumb Drilling. 208p. 1984. pap. 2.50 (ISBN 0-8128-8054-4). Stein & Day.

--The Third Grave. (Illus.). 192p. 1981. 10.95 (ISBN 0-87054-089-0). Arkham.

--Wolf Tracks. (Orig.). 1980. pap. 1.95 (ISBN 0-505-51485-0, Pub. by Tower Bks). Dorchester Pub Co.

--Wolf Tracks. 240p. 1984. pap. 2.95 (ISBN 0-8439-2166-8, Leisure Bks). Dorchester Pub Co.

Case, David, et al, eds. Captopril & Hypertension. LC 80-23373. (Topics in Cardiovascular Disease Ser.). 248p. 1980. 32.50x (ISBN 0-306-40532-6, Plenum Pr). Plenum Pub.

Case, David B., et al. Advances in Potassium Suplementation. write for info. (ISBN 0-911741-06-2). Advanced Thera Comm.

Case, David S. Alaska Natives & American Laws. LC 84-80796. 608p. 1984. 25.00 (ISBN 0-912006-08-0); pap. 15.00 (ISBN 0-912006-09-9). U of Alaska Pr.

Case, Doug & Davey, John. Developing Writing Skills in English. 1982. pap. text ed. 4.00x (ISBN 0-435-28021-X); tchr's. ed. 6.00x (ISBN 0-435-28022-8); wkbk. 2.00x (ISBN 0-435-28023-6). Heinemann Ed.

Case, Doug & Wilson, Ken. Off-Stage. (Orig.). 1979. pap. text ed. 6.50x (ISBN 0-435-28032-5); tchr's ed. 12.95x (ISBN 0-435-28033-3); cassette 24.00x (ISBN 0-435-28035-X). Heinemann Ed.

Case, Elinor. Humphrey, Wimsey & Doo. (Illus.). 48p. (Orig.). (ps-6). 1984. pap. 5.95 (ISBN 0-910781-02-8). G Whittell Mem.

Case, Everett N. & Case, Josephine Y. Owen D. Young & American Enterprise: A Biography. LC 80-83945. (Illus.). 992p. 1982. 25.00 (ISBN 0-87923-360-5). Godine.

Case, F., jt. auth. see Kaufman, A.

Case, Fred E. Professional Real Estate Investing: How to Evaluate Complex Investment Alternatives. 326p. 1983. 22.95 (ISBN 0-13-725861-5); pap. 12.95 (ISBN 0-13-725853-4). P-H.

--Real Estate Brokerage: A System's Approach. 2nd ed. (Illus.). 416p. 1982. 30.95 (ISBN 0-13-762344-5). P-H.

Case, Frederick E. & Clapp, John M. Real Estate Financing. LC 77-27938. 417p. 1978. text ed. 41.45 (ISBN 0-471-07248-6); tchr's. manual 8.00 (ISBN 0-471-04411-3). Wiley.

Case, Frederick E., jt. auth. see Kahn, Sanders A.

Case, Frederick W., Jr. Orchids of the Western Great Lakes Region. rev. ed. Bartz, Christine E., ed. LC 64-25251. (Bulletin Ser.: No. 48). (Illus.). 150p. 1985. write for info. (ISBN 0-87737-036-2). Cranbrook.

Case, Gerard R. A Pictorial Guide to Fossils. LC 81-10504. (Illus.). 514p. 1982. 29.95 (ISBN 0-442-22651-9). Van Nos Reinhold.

Case, H. J. & Whittle, A. W. Settlement Patterns in the Oxford Region. 1982. 90.00x (ISBN 0-900090-85-5, Pub. by Ashmolean Mus UK). State Mutual Bk.

Case, H. J. & Whittle, A. W., eds. Settlement Patterns in the Oxford Region: The Abingdon Causewayed Enclosure & Other Sites. (CBA Research Report Ser.: No. 44). 170p. 1982. pap. text ed. 40.50x (ISBN 0-906780-14-4, Pub. by Coun Brit Archaeology England). Humanities.

Case, J. M., et al, eds. Secretion: Mechanisms & Control. LC 84-5733. 416p. 1984. 35.00 (ISBN 0-7190-0975-8, Pub. by Manchester Univ Pr). Longwood Pub Group.

Case, James L. Clinical Management of Voice Disorders. LC 84-2858. 341p. 1984. 31.00 (ISBN 0-89443-587-6). Aspen Systems.

Case, James L., jt. auth. see Mowrer, Donald E.

Case, John. Digital Future: The Personal Computer Explosion-Why It's Happening & What It Means. LC 84-20775. 180p. 1985. 12.95 (ISBN 0-688-01101-2). Morrow.

--Understanding Inflation. LC 80-29139. (Illus.). 224p. 1981. 9.95 (ISBN 0-688-00399-0). Morrow.

--Understanding Inflation. 1982. pap. 4.95 (ISBN 0-14-006082-0). Penguin.

Case, John & Chilver, A. H. Strength of Materials & Structures: An Introduction to the Mechanics of Solids & Structures. 2nd ed. (Illus.). 1971. pap. text ed. 32.50x (ISBN 0-7131-3244-2). Intl Ideas.

Case, John, jt. auth. see Sevareid, Eric.

Case, John & Taylor, Rosemary C., eds. Co-Ops, Communes, & Collectives: Experiments in Social Change in the 1960s & 1970s. LC 78-51798. 1979. pap. 5.95 (ISBN 0-394-73621-4). Pantheon.

Case, Josephine Y., jt. auth. see Case, Everett N.

Case, Karl E. Property Taxation: The Need for Reform. LC 78-9850. 144p. 1978. prof ref 25.00 (ISBN 0-88410-485-0). Ballinger Pub.

Case, Kenneth E. & Jones, Lynn L. Profit Through Quality: Quality Assurance Programs for Manufacturers. 1978. pap. text ed. 15.00 (ISBN 0-89806-005-2); pap. text ed. 9.00 members. Inst Indus Eng.

Case, Laurel, ed. Guide to the Management of Infectious Diseases. X ed. (Mongraphs in Family Medicine). 256p. 1982. 35.50 (ISBN 0-8089-1506-1, 790801). Grune.

Case, Lloyd A. Laboratory Physics. LC 76-7374. (Illus.). 144p. 1976. pap. text ed. 6.00x (ISBN 0-8422-0535-7). Irvington.

Case, Lynn M. Franco-Italian Relations, 1860-1865. LC 75-121289. (BCL Ser. I). Repr. of 1932 ed. 24.50 (ISBN 0-404-01405-4). AMS Pr.

--French Opinion on War & Diplomacy During the Second Empire. LC 70-120242. 1972. Repr. of 1954 ed. lib. bdg. 26.00x (ISBN 0-374-91302-1). Octagon.

Case, Lynn M. & Spencer, Warren F. The United States & France: Civil War Diplomacy. LC 75-105108. 680p. 1970. 30.00x (ISBN 0-8122-7604-3). U of Pa Pr.

Case, Lynn M., ed. French Opinion on the United States & Mexico: Extracts from the Reports of the Procureurs Generaux. LC 69-19212. xxiii, 452p. 1969. Repr. of 1936 ed. 29.50 (ISBN 0-208-00791-1, Archon). Shoe String.

Case, Lynn M., jt. ed. see Thomas, Daniel H.

Case, Lynn M., tr. see De Bertier De Sauvigny, Guillaume.

Case, M., ed. European Pancreatic Club (EPC) 17th Meeting, Manchester, September 1985: Abstracts. (Illus.). 64p. 1985. pap. 23.50 (ISBN 3-8055-4203-8). S Karger.

Case, Marshall T. Look What I Found: The Young Conservationist's Guide to the Care & Feeding of Small Wildlife. 95p. 1983. pap. 9.95 (ISBN 0-8159-6119-7). Devin.

Case, Matthew H. Northwest Frontier. LC 82-73309. (Illus.). 1983. pap. 12.95 (ISBN 0-938416-02-2). BCS Educ Aids.

Case, Maurice. Recreation for Blind Adults: Organized Programs in Specialized Settings. (Illus.). 228p. 1965. photocopy ed. 17.50x (ISBN 0-398-00294-0). C C Thomas.

Case, Maynard, et al, eds. Electrolyte & Water Transport Across Gastrointestinal Epithelia. 335p. 1982. text ed. 53.50 (ISBN 0-89004-765-0). Raven.

Case, Patricia A. How to Write Your Autobiography: Preserving Your Family Heritage. LC 77-72670. (Orig.). 1977. pap. 4.95 (ISBN 0-912800-38-0). Woodbridge Pr.

Case, Patricia J., ed. The Alternative Press Annual, 1983. 288p. 1985. lib. bdg. 34.95 (ISBN 0-87722-355-6). Temple U Pr.

--Alternative Press Annual, 1984. 432p. 1985. lib. bdg. 34.95 (ISBN 0-87722-392-0). Temple U Pr.

Case, Paul F. Book of Tokens - Tarot Meditations. rev. ed. enl. ed. (Illus.). 1974. 6.50 (ISBN 0-938002-00-7). Builders of Adytum.

--The Great Seal of the United States. (Illus.). 1976. 2.25 (ISBN 0-938002-01-5). Builders of Adytum.

--Highlights of Tarot. rev. ed. 1970. 2.00 (ISBN 0-938002-02-3). Builders of Adytum.

--The Magical Language. LC 82-60162. 320p. 1986. pap. 8.95 (ISBN 0-87728-526-8). Weiser.

--The Masonic Letter G. 80p. 1983. pap. 5.50 (ISBN 0-88053-066-9). Macoy Pub.

--The Name of Names. 1981. 2.00 (ISBN 0-938002-04-X). Builders of Adytum.

--The True & Invisible Rosicrucian Order. LC 85-3185. (Illus.). 352p. Date not set. 22.50 (ISBN 0-87728-608-6). Weiser.

Case, Paul Foster. The Tarot: A Key to the Wisdom of the Ages. 1977. Repr. s.p. 6.95 (ISBN 0-685-70965-5). Macoy Pub.

--Tarot: A Key to the Wisdom of the Ages. 1981. Repr. of 1977 ed. 6.95 (ISBN 0-88053-767-1). Macoy Pub.

Case Publishing Staff. Case Collection 1983: Bibliography Containing Detailed Case Abstracts of over 300 Cases. 300p. (Orig.). 1983. pap. text ed. 10.00 (ISBN 0-930204-17-4, Case Pub). Lord Pub.

Case, R. H., ed. see Marlowe, Christopher.

Case, R. M., ed. Variations in Human Physiology. LC 84-11301. (Integrative Studies in Human Physiology). 241p. 1985. text ed. 21.00 (ISBN 0-7190-1086-1, Pub. by Manchester Univ Pr); pap. text ed. 9.00 (ISBN 0-7190-1732-7). Longwood Pub Group.

Case, Richard, et al. The Money Diet: Biblical Prescriptions for Financial Success. Anderson, Marty, ed. 127p. (Orig.). pap. 8.95 (ISBN 0-933629-03-6). Today Pubs.

Case, Robbie. Intellectual Development: Birth to Adulthood. Monograph ed. (Developmental Psychology Ser.). 1985. 39.50 (ISBN 0-12-162880-9). Acad Pr.

Case, Robert H. English Epithalamies. 1973. Repr. of 1869 ed. lib. bdg. 27.50 (ISBN 0-8414-0400-3). Folcroft.

Case, S. G., et al. Electronic Measurement & Control Applications, 3 vols. (Illus.). 1981. Set. 154.00x (ISBN 0-87683-015-7); Vol. 1; 370p. looseleaf 60.00x (ISBN 0-87683-016-5); Vol. 2; lab. manual; 175p. looseleaf 47.00x (ISBN 0-87683-017-3); Vol. 3; solutions maual; 175p. looseleaf 47.00x (ISBN 0-87683-018-1); looseleaf & lesson plans 1250.00x (ISBN 0-317-11867-6). G P Courseware.

Case, Shirley J. Experience with the Supernatural in Early Christian Times. LC 75-174851. Repr. of 1929 ed. 26.50 (ISBN 0-405-08345-9, Blom Pubns). Ayer Co Pubs.

--Jesus, a New Biography. LC 70-95149. (BCL Ser. II). Repr. of 1927 ed. 17.50 (ISBN 0-404-01406-2). AMS Pr.

--Jesus: A New Biography. LC 68-57594. 1968. Repr. of 1927 ed. lib. bdg. 20.50x (ISBN 0-8371-0342-8, CAJE). Greenwood.

--Jesus, a New Biography. 1928. 30.00 (ISBN 0-932062-36-9). Sharon Hill.

--Social Origins of Christianity. LC 74-84544. 263p. 1975. Repr. of 1923 ed. lib. bdg. 28.50 (ISBN 0-8154-0501-4). Cooper Sq.

--The Social Triumph of the Ancient Church. facsimile ed. LC 76-164596. (Select Bibliographies Reprint Ser). Repr. of 1933 ed. 18.00 (ISBN 0-8369-5880-2). Ayer Co Pubs.

--Studies in Early Christianity. 1928. 35.00 (ISBN 0-932062-35-0). Sharon Hill.

Case, Ted J. & Cody, Martin L., eds. Island Biogeography in the Sea of Cortez. LC 82-16036. (Illus.). 400p. 1983. text ed. 45.00x (ISBN 0-520-04799-0). U of Cal Pr.

Case, Thomas E., ed. A Critical & Annotated Edition of Lope de Vega's "las Almas de Toro". (Studies in the Romance Languages & Literatures: No. 104). 218p. 1971. pap. 12.00x (ISBN 0-8078-9104-5). U of NC Pr.

Case, Virginia A., ed. see Abrams, Kathleen & Abrams, Lawrence.

Case, Walter. In Their Pea Green Boat. 128p. 1983. 7.95 (ISBN 0-89962-340-9). Todd & Honeywell.

Case, Walter H. History of Long Beach & Vicinity. LC 73-2901. (Metropolitan America Ser.). (Illus.). 692p. 1974. Repr. 43.00x (ISBN 0-405-05387-8, Blom Pubns). Ayer Co Pubs.

Case Western Reserve University. Die Casting of Copper Alloys. 115p. 1973. 17.25 (ISBN 0-317-34514-1, 189). Intl Copper.

Case Western Reserve University. Center for Criminal Justice, jt. auth. see Ohio.

Casear, Paul. Postural Behavior in Newborn Infants. (Clinics in Developmental Medicine Ser.: Vol. 72). 120p. 1979. text ed. 22.50 (ISBN 0-433-05148-5, Pub. by Spastics Intl England). Lippincott.

Casebeer, Beverly. Using the Right-Left Brains: Auditory Imagery Program. 112p. 1982. 7.00 (ISBN 0-87879-333-X). Acad Therapy.

Casebeer, Beverly B. Casebeer Program: Developing Motor Skills for Early Childhood Education. 1978. pap. 5.00 manual (ISBN 0-87879-203-1); test record forms (25 pkg.) 2.00. Acad Therapy.

Casebere, James. In the Second Half of the Twentieth Century. (Illus.). 16p. (Orig.). 1982. pap. 4.00 (ISBN 0-939784-01-7). CEPA Gall.

Casebier, Allen & Casebier, Janet J., eds. Social Responsibilities of the Mass Media. LC 78-58603. 1978. pap. text ed. 13.00 (ISBN 0-8191-0539-2). U Pr of Amer.

Casebier, Dennis G. Camp Beale's Springs & the Hualpai Indians. LC 79-92835. (Illus.). 240p. (Orig.). 1980. 18.50 (ISBN 0-914224-08-5). Tales Mojave Rd.

--Camp El Dorado: Arizona Territory. 1970. pap. 3.00 (ISBN 0-910152-04-7). AZ Hist Foun.

--Camp Rock Spring California. new ed. LC 72-98119. (Illus.). 144p. 1973. pap. 6.00 (ISBN 0-914224-02-6). Tales Mojave Rd.

--Fort Pah-Ute California. new ed. LC 74-75521. (Illus.). 160p. 1974. pap. 7.50 (ISBN 0-914224-03-4). Tales Mojave Rd.

--Guide to the Mojave Road. LC 83-70868. (Illus.). 264p. 1983. 25.00 (ISBN 0-914224-10-7). Tales Mojave Rd.

--Nissan on the Mojave Road. LC 83-70971. (Illus.). 24p. 1983. 10.00 (ISBN 0-914224-11-5). Tales Mojave Rd.

Casebier, Eleanor. Managerial Statistics. LC 77-70316. 1977. pap. text ed. 7.95x (ISBN 0-8134-1946-8, 1946). Interstate.

Casebier, Janet J., jt. ed. see Casebier, Allen.

Casebooks Publishing Company Inc. Sex Discrimination: Adaptable to Courses Utilizing Babcock, Freedman, Norton & Ross Casebook on Sex Discrimination & the Law. Goldenberg, Norman S., et al, eds. (Legal Briefs Ser.). 1979. pap. write for info. (ISBN 0-87457-125-1, 1530). Casenotes Pub.

--Taxation: Adaptable to Courses to Bittker & Clark's Casenotes on Estate & Gift Taxation. Tenen, Peter, et al, eds. (Legal Briefs Ser.). 1984. pap. write for info. (ISBN 0-87457-128-6, 1217). Casenotes Pub.

Caseley, Judith. Molly Pink. LC 84-4169. (Illus.). 32p. (gr. k-3). 1985. 10.25 (ISBN 0-688-04004-7); PLB 10.88 (ISBN 0-688-04005-5). Greenwillow.

--Molly Pink Goes Hiking. LC 84-25335. (Illus.). 32p. (gr. k-3). 1985. 11.75 (ISBN 0-688-05699-7); lib. bdg. 11.88 (ISBN 0-688-05700-4). Greenwillow.

Casella, Alfredo. Music in My Time: The Memoirs of Alfredo Casella. Norton, Spencer, ed. (Illus.). 1955. 14.50x (ISBN 0-8061-0311-6). U of Okla Pr.

Casella, Dolores. THe Complete Vegetable Cookbook. (Illus.). 229p. 1983. 18.95 (ISBN 0-87250-033-0). D White.

--The New Book of Breads. (Illus.). 1979. 9.95 (ISBN 0-87250-032-2). D White.

--World of Baking. 1968. 12.95 (ISBN 0-87250-027-6); pap. 9.95 (ISBN 0-87250-040-3). D White.

--World of Breads. (Illus.). 1966. pap. 8.95 (ISBN 0-87250-041-1). D White.

Casella, Frank A. The Girls, Errol Flynn & Me. LC 81-68789. (Illus.). 200p. 1981. text ed. 4.95 (ISBN 0-9606850-0-6). Anthony Pr CA.

Casella, Jeanne & Barnett, Carolyn. English Plain & Simple. (gr. 6-9). 1982. 5.50 (ISBN 0-87720-396-2). AMSCO Sch.

Caselli, Giovanni. The First Civilizations. LC 84-6179. (History of Everyday Things Ser.). (Illus.). 48p. 1985. 12.95 (ISBN 0-911745-59-9). P Bedrick Bks.

--The Roman Empire & the Dark Ages. LC 84-6480. (History of Everyday Things Ser.). (Illus.). 48p. 1985. 12.95 (ISBN 0-911745-58-0). P Bedrick Bks.

Caselli, Joseph, tr. see Aubry, Joseph.

Casement, Gray, tr. see Fernandez Guardia, Ricardo.

Casement, Patrick. On Learning from the Patient. 232p. (Orig.). 1985. text ed. 26.00 (ISBN 0-422-79190-3, NO. 9234); pap. text ed. 13.95 (ISBN 0-422-79200-4, NO. 9235). Methuen Inc.

Casement, Richard. Man Suddenly Sees to the Edge of the Universe. 204p. 1984. 12.95 (ISBN 0-87548-418-2). Open Court.

Casenote Publishing Company Inc. Admiralty: Adaptable to Courses Utilizing Healy & Sharpe's Casebook on Admiralty. Goldenberg, Norman S., et al, eds. (Legal Briefs Ser.). 1983. pap. write for info. (ISBN 0-87457-005-0, 1290). Casenotes Pub.

Casenotes Publishig Company Inc. Staff. Taxation: Adaptable to Courses Utilizing Bittker & Stone's Casebook on Federal Income, Estate & Gift Taxation. Goldenberg, Norman S., et al, eds. (Legal Briefs Ser.). 1983. pap. write for info. (ISBN 0-87457-127-8, 1210). Casenotes Pub.

Casenotes Publishing Co., Inc. Staff. Taxation: Adaptable to Courses Utilizing Kahn & Waggoner's Casebook on Basic Federal Taxation of Gifts, Trusts, & Estates. Goldenberg, Norman S., et al, eds. (Legal Briefs Ser.). 1982. pap. write for info. (ISBN 0-87457-131-6, 1214). Casenotes Pub.

--Torts: Adaptable to Courses Utilizing Epstein, Gregory & Kalven's Casebook on Torts. Tenen, Peter, et al, eds. (Legal Briefs Ser.). 1984. pap. write for info. (ISBN 0-87457-134-0, 1003). Casenotes Pub.

Casenotes Publishing Co. Staff. Property: Adaptable to Courses Utilizing Haar and Liebman's Casebook on Property and Law. Goldenberg, Norman, et al, eds. (Casenote Legal Briefs). 1982. pap. write for info (ISBN 0-87457-118-9, 1034). Casenotes Pub.

Casenotes Publishing Company Inc. Accounting: Adaptable to Courses Utilizing Fiflis & Kripke's Casebook on Accounting for Lawyers. (Legal Briefs Ser.). 1978. pap. write for info. (ISBN 0-87457-000-X, 1380). Casenotes Pub.

--Administrative Law: Adaptable to Courses Utilizing Breyer & Stewart's Casebook on Administrative Law & Regulatory Policy. Goldenberg, Norman S., et al, eds. (Legal Briefs Ser.). 1984. pap. write for info. (ISBN 0-87457-001-8, 1263). Casenotes Pub.

--Administrative Law: Adaptable to Courses Utilizing Davis' Casebook on Administrative Law. Goldberg, Norman S., et al, eds. (Legal Briefs Ser.). 1980. pap. write for info. (ISBN 0-87457-002-6, 1261). Casenotes Pub.

--Administrative Law: Adaptable to Courses Utilizing Gelhorn & Byse's Casebook on Administrative Law. Goldenberg, Norman S., et al, eds. (Legal Briefs Ser.). 1983. pap. write for info. (ISBN 0-87457-003-4, 1260). Casenotes Pub.

--Administrative Law: Adaptable to Courses Utilizing Schwartz's Casebook on Administrative Law. Goldenberg, Norman S., et al, eds. (Legal Briefs Ser.). 1984. pap. write for info. (ISBN 0-87457-004-2, 1262). Casenotes Pub.

--Admiralty: Adaptable to Courses Utilizing Lucas' Casebook on Admiralty. Goldenberg, Norman S., et al, eds. (Legal Briefs Ser.). 1983. pap. write for info. (ISBN 0-87457-006-9, 1291). Casenotes Pub.

--Antitrust: Adaptable to Courses Utilizing Areeda's Casebook on Antitrust. Goldenberg, Norman S., et al, eds. (Legal Briefs Ser.). 1981. pap. write for info. (ISBN 0-87457-008-5, 1280). Casenotes Pub.

--Antitrust: Adaptable to Courses Utilizing Handler, Blake, Pitofsky & Goldschmid's Casebook on Trade Regulation. Goldenberg, Norman S., et al, eds. (Legal Briefs Ser.). 1983. pap. write for info. (ISBN 0-87457-009-3, 1281). Casenotes Pub.

--Antitrust: Adaptable to Courses Utilizing Oppenheim, Weston & McCarthy's Casebook on Federal Antitrust Laws. Goldenberg, Norman S., et al, eds. (Legal Briefs Ser.). 1982. pap. write for info. (ISBN 0-87457-010-7, 1282). Casenotes Pub.

--Business Planning: Adaptable to Courses Utilizing Herwitz' Casebook on Planning of Corporate Transactions. Goldenberg, Norman S., et al, eds. (Legal Briefs Ser.). 1980. pap. write for info. (ISBN 0-87457-011-5, 1440). Casenotes Pub.

--Civil Procedure: Adaptable to Courses Utilizing Carrington & Babcock's Casebook on Civil Procedure. Goldenberg, Norman S., et al, eds. (Legal Briefs Ser.). 1980. pap. write for info. (ISBN 0-87457-012-3, 1045). Casenotes Pub.

--Civil Procedure: Adaptable to Courses Utilizing Cound, Friedenthal & Miller's Casebook on Civil Procedure. Goldenberg, Norman S., et al, eds. (Legal Briefs Ser.). 1984. pap. write for info. (ISBN 0-87457-013-1, 1040). Casenotes Pub.

--Civil Procedure: Adaptable to Courses Utilizing Field, Kaplan & Clermont's Casebook on Civil Procedure. Goldenberg, Norman S., et al, eds. (Legal Briefs Ser.). pap. write for info. (ISBN 0-87457-014-X, 1043). Casenotes Pub.

--Civil Procedure: Adaptable to Courses Utilizing Karlen, Meisenholder, Stevens & Vestal's Casebook on Civil Procedure. Goldenberg, Norman S., et al, eds. (Legal Briefs Ser.). 1981. pap. write for info. (ISBN 0-87457-015-8, 1042). Casenotes Pub.

--Civil Procedure: Adaptable to Courses Utilizing Landers & Martin's Casebook on Civil Procedure. Goldenberg, Norman S., et al, eds. (Legal Briefs Ser.). 1985. pap. write for info. (ISBN 0-87457-016-6, 1046). Casenotes Pub.

--Civil Procedure: Adaptable to Courses Utilizing Louisell, Hazard & Tait's Casebook on Pleading & Procedure. Goldenberg, Norman S., et al, eds. (Legal Briefs Ser.). 1985. pap. write for info. (ISBN 0-87457-017-4, 1041). Casenotes Pub.

--Civil Procedure: Adaptable to Courses Utilizing Rosenberg, Weinstein, Smit & Korn's Casebook on Civil Procedure. Goldenberg, Norman S., et al, eds. (Legal Briefs Ser.). 1981. pap. write for info. (ISBN 0-87457-018-2, 1044). Casenotes Pub.

--Commercial Law: Adaptable to Courses Utilizing Farnsworth & Honnald's Casebook on Commercial Law. Goldenberg, Norman S., et al, eds. (Legal Briefs Ser.). 1982. pap. write for info. (ISBN 0-87457-019-0, 1311). Casenotes Pub.

--Commercial Law: Adaptable to Courses Utilizing Jordan & Warren's Casebook on Commercial Law, Secured Transactions & Commercial Paper. Goldenberg, Norman S., et al, eds. (Legal Briefs Ser.). 1983. pap. write for info. (ISBN 0-87457-020-4, 1312). Casenotes Pub.

--Commercial Paper: Adaptable to Courses Utilizing Spiedel, Summers & White's Casebook on Commercial & Consumer Law. Goldenberg, Norman S., et al, eds. (Legal Briefs Ser.). 1982. pap. write for info. (ISBN 0-87457-021-2, 1310). Casenotes Pub.

--Community Property: Adaptable to Courses Utilizing Verrall & Bird's on California Community Property. Goldenberg, Norman S., et al, eds. (Legal Briefs Ser.). 1984. pap. write for info. (ISBN 0-87457-022-0, 1320). Casenotes Pub.

--Conflicts: Adaptable to Courses Utilizing Cramton, Currie & Kay's Casebook on Conflict of Laws. Goldenberg, Norman S., et al, eds. (Legal Briefs Ser.). 1983. pap. write for info. (ISBN 0-87457-023-9, 1071). Casenotes Pub.

--Conflicts: Adaptable to Courses Utilizing Reese & Rosenberg's Casebook on Conflict of Laws. Goldenberg, Norman S., et al, eds. (Legal Briefs Ser.). 1982. pap. write for info. (ISBN 0-87457-024-7, 1070). Casenotes Pub.

--Constitutional Law: Adaptable to Courses Utilizing Barrett's & Cohen's on Constitutional Law. Goldenberg, Norman S., et al, eds. (Legal Briefs Ser.). 1984. pap. write for info. (ISBN 0-87457-025-5, 1082). Casenotes Pub.

--Constitutional Law: Adaptable to Courses Utilizing Brest & Levinson's Casebook on Processes of Constitutional Decision-Making. Goldenberg, Norman S., et al, eds. (Legal Briefs Ser.). 1984. pap. write for info. (ISBN 0-87457-026-3, 1086). Casenotes Pub.

--Constitutional Law: Adaptable to Courses Utilizing Freund, Sutherland, Howe & Brown's Casebook on Constitutional Law. Goldenberg, Norman S., et al, eds. (Legal Briefs Ser.). 1981. pap. write for info. (ISBN 0-87457-027-1, 1083). Casenotes Pub.

--Constitutional Law: Adaptable to Courses Utilizing Gunther's Casebook on Constitutional Law. Goldenberg, Norman S., et al, eds. (Legal Briefs Ser.). 1984. pap. write for info. (ISBN 0-87457-028-X, 1080). Casenotes Pub.

--Constitutional Law: Adaptable to Courses Utilizing Kauper & Beytagh's Casebook on Constitutional Law. Goldenberg, Norman S., et al, eds. (Legal Briefs Ser.). 1982. pap. write for info. (ISBN 0-87457-029-8, 1084). Casenotes Pub.

--Constitutional Law: Adaptable to Courses Utilizing Lockhart, Kamisar & Choper's Casebook on Constitutional Law. Goldenberg, Norman S., et al, eds. (Legal Briefs Ser.). 1983. pap. write for info. (ISBN 0-87457-030-1, 1081). Casenotes Pub.

--Constitutional Law: Adaptable to Courses Utilizing Rotunda's Casebook on Modern Constitutional Law. Goldenberg, Norman S., et al, eds. (Legal Briefs Ser.). 1984. pap. write for info. (ISBN 0-87457-031-X, 1085). Casenotes Pub.

--Consumer Protection: Adaptable to Courses Utilizing McCall's Casebook on Consumer Protection. Goldenberg, Norman S., et al, eds. (Legal Briefs Ser.). 1978. pap. write for info. (ISBN 0-87457-032-8, 1490). Casenotes Pub.

--Contracts: Adaptable to Courses Utilizing Calamari & Perillo's Casebook on Contracts, Cases & Problems. Goldenberg, Norman S., et al, eds. (Legal Briefs Ser.). 1983. pap. write for info. (ISBN 0-87457-033-6, 1017). Casenotes Pub.

--Contracts: Adaptable to Courses Utilizing Dawson & Harvey's Casebook on Contracts. Goldenberg, Norman S., et al, eds. (Legal Briefs Ser.). 1984. pap. write for info. (ISBN 0-87457-034-4, 1014). Casenotes Pub.

--Contracts: Adaptable to Courses Utilizing Fuller & Eisenberg's Casebook on Contracts. Goldenberg, Norman S., et al, eds. (Legal Briefs Ser.). 1984. pap. write for info. (ISBN 0-87457-036-0, 1011). Casenotes Pub.

--Contracts: Adaptable to Courses Utilizing Farnsworth, Young & Jones' Casebook on Contracts. Goldenberg, Norman S., et al, eds. (Legal Briefs Ser.). 1985. pap. write for info. (ISBN 0-87457-035-2, 1010). Casenotes Pub.

Casenotes Publishing Company, Inc. Contracts: Adaptable to Courses Utilizing Kessler & Gilmore's Casebook on Contracts. Goldenberg, Norman S., et al, eds. (Legal Briefs Ser.). 1983. pap. write for info. (ISBN 0-87457-037-9, 1013). Casenotes Pub.

Casenotes Publishing Company Inc. Contracts: Adaptable to Courses Utilizing Knapp's Casebook on Problems in Contract Law. Goldenberg, Norman S., et al, eds. (Legal Briefs Ser.). 1982. pap. write for info. (ISBN 0-87457-038-7, 1016). Casenotes Pub.

--Contracts: Adaptable to Courses Utilizing Murphy & Speidel's Casebook on Contract Law. Goldenberg, Norman S., et al, eds. (Legal Briefs Ser.). 1985. pap. write for info. (ISBN 0-87457-041-7, 1012). Casenotes Pub.
--Contracts: Adaptable to Courses Utilizing Mueller, Rosett & Lopez's Casebook on Contracts Law & Its Application. Goldenberg, Norman S., et al, eds. (Legal Briefs Ser.). 1984. pap. write for info. (ISBN 0-87457-040-9, 1015). Casenotes Pub.
--Contracts: Adaptable to Courses Utilizing Vernon's Casebook on Contracts: Theory & Practice. Goldenberg, Norman S., et al, eds. (Legal Briefs Ser.). 1981. pap. write for info. (ISBN 0-87457-043-3, 1019). Casenotes Pub.
--Copyright: Adaptable to Courses Utilizing Kaplan & Brown's Caesbook on Copyright. Goldenberg, Norman S., et al, eds. (Legal Briefs Ser.). 1979. pap. write for info. (ISBN 0-87457-044-1, 1500). Casenotes pub.
--Copyright: Adaptable to Courses Utilizing Nimmer's Casebook on Copyright & Other Aspects of Law Pertaining to Literary, Musical & Artistic Works. Goldenberg, Norman S., et al, eds. (Legal Briefs Ser.). 1980. pap. write for info. (ISBN 0-87457-045-X, 1501). Casenotes Pub.
--Corporations: Adaptable to Courses Utilizing Cary & Eisenberg's Casebook on Corporations. Goldenberg, Norman S., et al, eds. (Legal Briefs Ser.). 1984. pap. write for info. (ISBN 0-87457-046-8, 1050). Casenotes Pub.
--Corporations: Adaptable to Courses Utilizing Frey, Choper, Leech & Morris' Casebook on Corporations. Goldenberg, Norman S., et al, eds. (Legal Briefs Ser.). 1981. pap. write for info. (ISBN 0-87457-047-6, 1054). Casenotes Pub.
--Corporations: Adaptable to Courses Utilizing Henn's Casebook on Corporations. Goldenberg, Norman S., et al, eds. (Legal Briefs Ser.). 1980. pap. write for info. (ISBN 0-87457-049-2, 1051). Casenotes Pub.
--Corporations: Adaptable to Courses Utilizing Hamilton's Casebook on Corporations-Including Partnerships & Limited Partnerships. Goldenberg, Norman S., et al, eds. (Legal Briefs Ser.). 1981. pap. write for info. (ISBN 0-87457-048-4, 1053). Casenotes Pub.
--Corporations: Adaptable to Courses Utilizing Vagt's Casebook on Basic Corporation Law. Goldenberg, Norman S., et al, eds. (Legal Briefs Ser.). 1983. pap. write for info. (ISBN 0-87457-051-4, 1052). Casenotes Pub.
--Corporations: Jennings & Buxbaum's Casebook on Corporations. Goldenberg, Norman s., et al, eds. (Casenote Legal Briefs Ser.). 1980. pap. write for info. (ISBN 0-87457-050-6, 1055). Casenotes Pub.
--Creditors' Rights: Adaptable to Courses Utilizing Reisenfeld's Casebook on Creditors' Remedies & Debtors' Protection. Goldenberg, Norman S., et al, eds. (Legal Briefs Ser.). 1983. pap. write for info. (ISBN 0-87457-052-2, 1300). Casenotes Pub.
--Criminal Justice: Adaptable to Courses Utilizing Weinreb's Casebook on Criminal Justice. Goldenberg, Norman S., et al, eds. (Legal Briefs Ser.). 1982. pap. write for info. (ISBN 0-87457-053-0, 1550). Casenotes Pub.
--Criminal Law: Adaptable to Courses Utilizing Dix & Sharlot's Casebook on Criminal Law. Goldenberg, Norman S., et al, eds. (Legal Briefs Ser.). 1984. pap. write for info. (ISBN 0-87457-054-9, 1024). Casenotes Pub.
--Criminal Law: Adaptable to Courses Utilizing Foote & Levy's Casebook on Criminal Law. Goldenberg, Norman S, et al, eds. (Legal Briefs Ser.). 1982. pap. write for info. (ISBN 0-87457-055-7, 1025). Casenotes Pub.
--Criminal Law: Adaptable to Courses Utilizing Kadish, Schulhofer & Paulsen's Casebook on Criminal Law & Its Processes. Goldenberg, Norman S., et al, eds. (Legal Briefs Ser.). 1985. pap. write for info. (ISBN 0-87457-056-5, 1021). Casenotes Pub.
--Criminal Law: Adaptable to Courses Utilizing LaFave's casebook of Modern Criminal Law. Goldenberg, Norman S., et al, eds. (Legal Briefs Ser.). 1983. pap. write for info. (ISBN 0-87457-057-3, 1023). Casenotes Pub.
--Criminal Law: Adaptable to Courses Utilizing Perkins & Boyce's Casebook on Criminal Law. Goldenberg, Norman S., et al, eds. (Legal Briefs Ser.). 1985. pap. write for info. (ISBN 0-87457-058-1, 1020). Casenotes Pub.
--Criminal Law: Adaptable to Courses Utilizing Weinreb's Casebook on Criminal Law. Goldenberg, Norman S., et al, eds. (Legal Briefs Ser.). 1981. pap. write for info. (ISBN 0-87457-059-X, 1022). Casenotes Pub.
--Criminal Procedure: Adaptable to Courses Utilizing Goldstein & Orland's Casebook on Criminal Procedure. Goldenberg, Norman S., et al, eds. (Legal Briefs Ser.). 1977. pap. write for info. (ISBN 0-87457-061-1, 1201). Casenotes Pub.
--Criminal Procedure: Adaptable to Courses Utilizing Inbau, Thompson, Haddad, Zagel & Starkman's Casebook on Criminal Procedure. Goldenberg, Norman, et al, eds. (Legal Briefs Ser.). 1977. pap. write for info. (ISBN 0-87457-060-3, 1202). Casenotes Pub.
--Criminal Procedure: Adaptable to Courses Utilizing Kamisar, LaFave & Israel's Casebook on Criminal Procedure. Goldenberg, Norman S., et al, eds. (Legal Briefs Ser.). 1984. pap. write for info. (ISBN 0-87457-062-X, 1200). Casenotes Pub.
--Criminal Procedure: Adaptable to Courses Utilizing Weinreb's Casebook on Criminal Process. Goldenberg, Norman S., et al, eds. (Casenote Legal Briefs). 1982. pap. write for info. (ISBN 0-87457-064-6, 1203). Casenotes Pub.
--Debtor-Creditor: Adaptable to Courses Utilizing Epstein & Lander's Casebook on Debtors & Creditors. Goldenberg, Norman S., et al, eds. 1984. pap. write for info. (ISBN 0-87457-066-2, 1302). Casenotes Pub.
--Debtor-Creditor: Adaptable to Courses Utilizing Warren & Hogan's Casebook on Debtor-Creditor Law. Goldenberg, Norman S., et al, eds. (Legal Briefs Ser.). 1982. pap. write for info. (ISBN 0-87457-067-0, 1301). Casenotes Pub.
--Decedents' Estates: Adaptable to Courses Utilizing Ritchie, Alford & Effland's Casebook on Decedents' Estates & Trusts. Goldenberg, Norman S., et al, eds. (Legal Briefs Ser.). 1984. pap. write for info. (ISBN 0-87457-069-7, 1224). Casenotes Pub.
--Decedents' Estates: Adaptable to Courses Utilizing Scoles & Halbach's Casebook on Decedents' Estates & Trusts. Goldenberg, Norman S., et al, eds. (Legal Briefs Ser.). 1984. pap. write for info. (ISBN 0-87457-070-0, 1222). Casenotes Pub.
--Descendents' Estates: Adaptable to Courses Utilizing Dukeminier & Johanson's Casebook on Family Wealth Transactions: Wills, Trusts, Future Interests & Estate Planning. Goldenberg, Norman S., et al, eds. (Casenote Legal Briefs). 1983. pap. write for info. (ISBN 0-87457-068-9, 1223). Casenotes Pub.
--Enterprise Organizations: Adaptable to Courses Utilizing Conard, Knauss & Siegel's Casebook on Enterprise Organizations. Goldenberg, Norman S., et al, eds. (Legal Briefs Ser.). 1985. pap. write for info. (ISBN 0-87457-007-7, 1350). Casenotes Pub.
--Environmental Law: Adaptable to Courses Utilizing Findley & Farber's casebook on Environmental Law. Goldenberg, Norman S., et al, eds. (Legal Briefs Ser.). 1982. pap. write for info. (ISBN 0-87457-071-9, 1341). Casenotes Pub.
--Environmental Law: Adaptable to Courses Utilizing Hanks, Tarlock & Hanks' Casebook on Environmental Law & Policy. Goldenberg, Norman S., et al, eds. (Legal Briefs Ser.). 1977. pap. write for info. (ISBN 0-87457-072-7, 1340). Casenotes Pub.
--Equity: Adaptable to Courses Utilizing Childres & Johnson's Casebook on Equity, Restitution & Damages. Goldenberg, Norman S., et al, eds. (Legal Briefs Ser.). 1981. pap. write for info. (ISBN 0-87457-073-5, 1251). Casenotes Pub.
--Estate Planning: Adaptable to Courses Utilizing Westfall's Casebook on Estate Planning Problems. Goldenberg, Norman, et al, eds. (Legal Briefs Ser.). 1977. pap. write for info. (ISBN 0-87457-074-3, 1400). Casenotes Pub.
--Ethics: Adaptable to Courses Utilizing Persig & Kirwin's Casebook on Professional Responsibility. Goldenber, Norman S., et al, eds. (Legal Briefs Ser.). 1981. pap. write for info. (ISBN 0-87457-075-1, 1090). Casenotes Pub.
--Evidence: Adaptable to Courses Utilizing Cleary & Strong's Casebook on Evidence. Goldenberg, Norman S., et al, eds. (Legal Briefs Ser.). 1982. pap. write for info. (ISBN 0-87457-076-X, 1064). Casenotes Pub.
--Evidence: Adaptable to Courses Utilizing Kaplan & Waltz's Casebook on Evidence. Goldenberg, Norman S., et al, eds. (Legal Briefs Ser.). 1984. pap. write for info. (ISBN 0-87457-079-4, 1061). Casenotes Pub.
--Evidence: Adaptable to Courses Utilizing Lempert & Saltzburg's Casebook on Test Problems, Transcripts & Cases. Goldenberg, Norman S., et al, eds. (Legal Briefs Ser.). 1980. pap. write for info. (ISBN 0-87457-078-6, 1063). Casenotes Pub.
--Evidence: Adaptable to Courses Utilizing McCormick, Elliot & Sutton's Casebook on Evidence. Goldenberg, Norman S., et al, eds. (Legal Briefs Ser.). 1983. pap. write for info. (ISBN 0-87457-081-6, 1062). Casenotes Pub.
--Evidence: Adaptable to Courses Utilizing Weinstein, Mansfield, Abrams & Berger's Casebook on Evidence. Goldenberg, Norman S., et al, eds. (Legal Briefs Ser.). 1984. pap. write for info. (ISBN 0-87457-080-8, 1060). Casenotes Pub.
--Family Law: Adaptable to Courses Utilizing Clark's Casebook on Domestic Relations. Goldenberg, Norman S., et al, eds. (Legal Briefs Ser.). 1983. pap. write for info. (ISBN 0-87457-082-4, 1242). Casenotes Pub.
--Family Law: Adaptable to Courses Utilizing Foote, Levy & Sander's Casebook on Family Law. Goldenberg, Norman S., et al, eds. (Legal Briefs Ser.). 1981. pap. write for info. (ISBN 0-87457-083-2, 1241). Casenotes Pub.
--Family Law: Adaptable to Courses Utilizing Krause's Casebook on Family Law. Goldenberg, Norman S., et al, eds. (Legal Briefs Ser.). 1981. pap. write for info. (ISBN 0-87457-084-0, 1243). Casenotes Pub.
--Family Law: Adaptable to Courses Utilizing Wadlington's Is Casebook on Domestic Relations. Goldenberg, Norman S., et al, eds. (Legal Briefs Ser.). 1984. pap. write for info. (ISBN 0-87457-085-9, 1240). Casenotes Pub.
--Federal Courts: Adaptable to Courses Utilizing Bator, Mishkin, Shapiro, & Weschler's Casebook on the Federal Courts & the Federal System. Goldenberg, Norman S., et al, eds. (Legal Briefs Ser.). 1985. pap. write for info. (ISBN 0-87457-086-7, 1360). Casenotes Pub.
--Federal Courts: Adaptable to Courses Utilizing Currie's casebook on Federal Courts. Goldenberg, Norman S., et al, eds. (Legal Briefs Ser.). 1981. pap. write for info. (ISBN 0-87457-087-5, 1362). Casenotes Pub.
--Federal Courts: Adaptable to Courses Utilizing McCormick, Chadbourn & Wright's Casebook on Federal Courts. Goldenberg, Norman S., et al, eds. (Legal Briefs Ser.). 1983. pap. write for info. (ISBN 0-87457-088-3, 1361). Casenotes Pub.
--Gratuitous Transfers: Adaptable to Courses Utilizing Clark, Lusky & Murphy's Casebook on Gratuitous Transfers, Wills, Intestate Succession, Trusts, Gifts, & Future Interests. Goldenberg, Norman S., et al, eds. (Legal Briefs Ser.). 1983. pap. write for info. (ISBN 0-87457-089-1, 1510). Casenotes Pub.
--Insurance Law: Adaptable to Courses Utilizing Keeton's Casebook on Basic Insurance Law. Goldenberg, Norman S., et al, eds. (Legal Briefs Ser.). 1983. pap. write for info. (ISBN 0-87457-090-5, 1371). Casenotes Pub.
--Insurance Law: Adaptable to Courses Utilizing Young's Casebook on Insurance. Goldenberg, Norman S., et al, eds. (Legal Briefs Ser.). 1983. pap. write for info. (ISBN 0-87457-091-3, 1370). Casenotes Pub.
--International Law: Adaptable to Courses Utilizing Henkin, Pugh, Schacter & Smit's Casebook on International Law. Goldenberg, Norman S., et al, eds. (Legal Briefs Ser.). 1985. pap. write for info. (ISBN 0-87457-093-X, 1392). Casenotes Pub.
--International Law: Adaptable to Courses Utilizing Steiner & Vagt's Casebook on Transnational Problems. Goldenberg, Norman S., et al, eds. (Legal Briefs Ser.). 1979. pap. write for info. (ISBN 0-87457-092-1, 1391). Casenotes Pub.
--International Law: Adaptable to Courses Utilizing Sweeney Oliver & Loech's Casebook on the International Legal System. Goldenberg, Norman S., et al, eds. (Legal Briefs Ser.). 1982. pap. write for info. (ISBN 0-87457-094-8, 1390). Casenotes Pub.
--Juvenile Justice: Adaptable to Courses Utilizing Miller, Dawson & Dix's Casebook on the Juvenile Justice Process. Goldenberg, Norman S., et al, eds. (Legal Briefs Ser.). 1979. pap. write for info. (ISBN 0-87457-095-6, 1460). Casenotes Pub.
--Labor Law: Adaptable to Courses Utilizing Cox, Bok & Gorman's Casebook on Labor Law. Goldenberg, Norman S., et al, eds. (Legal Briefs Ser.). 1985. pap. write for info. (ISBN 0-87457-096-4, 1331). Casenotes Pub.
--Labor Law: Adaptable to Courses Utilizing Leslie's Casebook on Labor Relations Law. Goldenberg, Norman S., et al, eds. (Legal Briefs Ser.). 1979. pap. write for info. (ISBN 0-87457-097-2, 1333). Casenotes Pub.
--Labor Law: Adaptable to Courses Utilizing Meltzer's Casebook on Labor Law. Goldenberg, Norman S., et al, eds. (Legal Briefs Ser.). 1978. pap. write for info. (ISBN 0-87457-098-0, 1332). Casenotes Pub.
--Labor Law: Adaptable to Courses Utilizing Smith, Merrifield & St. Antoine's Casebook on Labor Relations. Goldenberg, Norman S., et al, eds. (Legal Breifs Ser.). 1982. pap. write for info. (ISBN 0-87457-099-9, 1330). Casenotes Pub.
--Land Finance: Adaptable to Courses Utilizing Axelrod, Berger & Johnstone's Casebook on Land Transfer & Finance. Goldenberg, Norman S., et al, eds. (Casenote Legal Briefs). 1983. pap. write for info. (ISBN 0-87457-100-6, 1471). Casenotes Pub.
--Land Finance: Adaptable to Courses Utilizing Penney & Broude's Casebook on Land Financing. Goldenberg, Norman S., et al, eds. (Legal Briefs Ser.). 1981. pap. write for info. (ISBN 0-87457-101-4, 1470). Casenotes Pub.
--Land Use: Adaptable to Courses Utilizing Haar's Casebook on Land Use Planning. Goldenberg, Norman S. & Tenen, Peter, eds. (Legal Briefs Ser.). 1979. pap. write for info. (ISBN 0-87457-103-0, 1451). Casenotes Pub.
--Land Use: Adaptable to Courses Utilizing Wright & Gitelman's Casebook on Land Use. Goldenberg, Norman S., et al, eds. (Legal Briefs Ser.). 1978. pap. write for info. (ISBN 0-87457-102-2, 1450). Casenotes Pub.
--Legislation: Adaptable to Courses Utilizing Nutting & Dickerson's Casebook on Legislation. Goldenberg, Norman S., et al, eds. (Legal Briefs Ser.). 1978. pap. write for info. (ISBN 0-87457-104-9, 1420). Casenotes Pub.
--Local Government: Adaptable to Courses Utilizing Valente's Casebook on Local Government Law. Goldenberg, Norman S., et al, eds. (Legal Briefs Ser.). 1984. pap. write for info. (ISBN 0-87457-105-7, 1590). Casenotes Pub.
--Mass Media: Adaptable to Courses Utilizing Franklin's Casebook on Mass Media Law. Goldenberg, Norman S., et al, eds. (Legal Briefs Ser.). 1979. pap. write for info. (ISBN 0-87457-106-5, 1480). Casenotes Pub.
--Medicine & Law: Adaptable to Courses Utilizing Sharpe's Casebook on Law & Medicine. Goldenberg, Norman S., et al, eds. (Legal Briefs Ser.). 1980. pap. write for info. (ISBN 0-87457-107-3, 1520). Casenotes Pub.
--Negotiable Instruments: Adaptable to Courses Utilizing Whaley's casebook on Negotiable Instruments. Goldenberg, Norman S., et al, eds. (Legal Briefs Ser.). 1984. pap. write for info. (ISBN 0-87457-108-1, 1600). Casenotes Pub.
--New York Practice: Adaptable to Courses Utilizing Peterfreund & McLaughlin's Casebook on New York Practice. Goldenberg, Norman S., et al, eds. (Legal Briefs Ser.). 1982. pap. write for info. (ISBN 0-87457-109-X, 1570). Casenotes Pub.
--Oil & Gas: Adaptable to Courses Utilizing Williams, Maxwell & Myer's Casebook on Oil & Gas. Goldenberg, Norman S., et al, eds. (Legal Briefs Ser.). 1983. pap. write for info. (ISBN 0-87457-110-3, 1540). Casenotes Pub.
--Patent Law: Adaptable to Courses Utilizing Choate's Casebook on Patent Law. Goldenberg, Norman S., et al, eds. (Legal Briefs Ser.). 1981. pap. write for info. (ISBN 0-87457-111-1, 1560). Casenotes Pub.
--Products Liability: Adaptable to Courses Utilizing Keeton, Owen & Montgomery's Casebook on Products Liability & Safety. Goldenberg, Norman S., et al, eds. (Legal Briefs Ser.). 1984. pap. write for info. (ISBN 0-87457-113-8, 1431). Casenotes Pub.
--Products Liability: Adaptable to Courses Utilizing Noel & Phillip's Casebook on Product Liability. Goldenberg, Norman S., et al, eds. (Legal Briefs Ser.). 1984. pap. write for info. (ISBN 0-87457-112-X, 1430). Casenotes Pub.
--Property: Adaptable to Courses Utilizing Browder, Cunningham & Julian's Casebook on Basic Property Law. Goldenberg, Norman S., et al, eds. (Legal Briefs Ser.). 1982. pap. write for info. (ISBN 0-87457-114-6, 1033). Casenotes Pub.
--Property: Adaptable to Courses Utilizing Cribbet & Johnson's Casebook on Property. Goldenberg, Norman S., et al, eds. (Legal Briefs Ser.). 1985. pap. write for info. (ISBN 0-87457-116-2, 1031). Casenotes Pub.
--Property: Adaptable to Courses Utilizing Casner & Leach's Casebook on Property. Goldenberg, Norman S., et al, eds. (Legal Briefs Ser.). 1985. pap. write for info. (ISBN 0-87457-115-4, 1030). Casenotes Pub.
--Property: Adaptable to Courses Utilizing Dukeminier & Krier's Casebook on Property. Goldenberg, Norman S., et al, eds. (Legal Briefs Ser.). 1984. pap. write for info. (ISBN 0-87457-117-0, 1035). Casenotes Pub.
--Property: Adaptable to Courses Utilizing Rabin's Casebook on Real Property Law. Goldenberg, Norman S., et al, eds. (Legal Briefs Ser.). 1981. pap. write for info. (ISBN 0-87457-119-7, 1032). Casenotes Pub.
--Remedies: Adaptable to Courses Utilizing Leavell, Love & Nelson's Casebook on Equitable Remedies & Restitution. Goldenberg, Norman S., et al, eds. (Legal Briefs Ser.). 1983. pap. write for info. (ISBN 0-87457-120-0, 1253). Casenotes Pub.
--Remedies: Adaptable to Courses Utilizing Re's Casebook on Equity & Equitable Remedies. Goldenberg, Norman S., et al, eds. (Legal Briefs Ser.). 1983. pap. write for info. (ISBN 0-87457-121-9, 1252). Casenotes Pub.
--Remedies: Adaptable to Courses Utilizing York & Bauman's Casebook on Remedies. Goldenberg, Norman S., et al, eds. (Legal Briefs Ser.). 1983. pap. write for info. (ISBN 0-87457-122-7, 1250). Casenotes Pub.
--Securities Regulation: Adaptable to Courses Utilizing Ratner's Casebook on Securities Regulation. Goldenberg, Norman S., et al, eds. (Legal Brief Ser.). 1983. pap. write for info. (ISBN 0-87457-124-3, 1271). Casenotes Pub.
--Securities Regulations: Adaptable to Courses Utilizing Jennings & Marsh's Casebook on Securities Regulation. Goldenberg, Norman S., et al, eds. (Legal Briefs Ser.). 1984. pap. write for info. (ISBN 0-87457-123-5, 1270). Casenotes Pub.
--Taxation: Adaptable to Courses Utilizing Andrew's Casebook on Basic Federal Income Taxation. Goldenberg, Norman S., et al, eds. (Legal Briefs Ser.). 1984. pap. write for info. (ISBN 0-87457-126-X, 1215). Casenotes Pub.
--Taxation: Adaptable to Courses Utilizing Kragen & McNulty's Casebook on Federal Income Taxation, Vol. 1. Tenen, Peter & Switzer, Robert J., eds. (Legal Briefs Ser.). 1980. pap. write for info. (ISBN 0-87457-132-4, 1216). Casenotes Pub.
--Taxation: Adaptable to Courses Utilizing Surrey, Warren, McDaniel & Gutman's Casebook on Federal Wealth Transfer Taxation. Tenen, Peter, et al, eds. (Legal Briefs Ser.). 1982. pap. write for info. (ISBN 0-87457-133-2, 1213). Casenotes Pub.

--Torts: Adaptable to Courses Utilizing Franklin's & Rabin's Casebook on Tort Law & Alternatives. Tenen, Peter, et al, eds. (Legal Briefs Ser.). 1984. pap. write for info. (ISBN 0-87457-135-9, 1004). Casenotes Pub.

--Torts: Adaptable to Courses Utilizing Henderson & Pearson's Casebook on the Torts Process. Tenen, Peter, et al, eds. (Legal Briefs Ser.). 1981. pap. write for info. (ISBN 0-87457-136-7, 1001). Casenotes Pub.

--Torts: Adaptable to Courses Utilizing Keeton, Keeton, Sargentich & Steiner's Casebook on Torts. Tenen, Peter, et al, eds. (Legal Briefs Ser.). 1983. pap. write for info. (ISBN 0-87457-137-5, 1002). Casenotes Pub.

--Torts: Adaptable to Courses Utilizing Prosser, Wade & Schwartz's Casebook on Torts. Tenen, Peter, et al, eds. (Legal Briefs Ser.). 1985. pap. write for info. (ISBN 0-87457-138-3, 1000). Casenotes Pub.

--Torts: Adaptable to Courses Utilizing Shulman, James & Grey's Casebook on Torts. Tenen, Peter, et al, eds. (Legal Briefs Ser.). 1979. pap. write for info. (ISBN 0-87457-139-1, 1005). Casenotes Pub.

--Trusts: Adaptable to Courses Utilizing Bogert & Oak's Casebook on Law of Trusts. Tenen, Peter, et al, eds. (Legal Briefs Ser.). 1982. pap. write for info. (ISBN 0-87457-140-5, 1230). Casenotes Pub.

--U.C.C. Adaptable to Courses Utilizing Epstein & Martin's Casebook on Basic Uniform Commercial Code. Goldenberg, Norman S., et al, eds. (Legal Briefs Ser.). 1982. pap. write for info. (ISBN 0-87457-142-1, 1410). Casenotes Pub.

--Water Law: Adaptable to Courses Utilizing Trelease's Casebook on Water Law. Goldenberg, Norman S., et al, eds. (Legal Briefs Ser.). 1982. pap. write for info. (ISBN 0-87457-143-X, 1410). Casenotes Pub.

--Wills: Adaptable to Courses Utilizing Mechem & Atkinson's Casebook on Wills & Administration. Goldenberg, Norman S., et al, eds. (Legal Briefs Ser.). 1980. pap. write for info. (ISBN 0-87457-144-8, 1220). Casenotes Pub.

--Wills: Adaptable to Courses Utilizing Mennell's Casebook on California Decedents' Estates. Goldenberg, Norman S., et al, eds. (Legal Briefs Ser.). 1976. pap. write for info. (ISBN 0-87457-145-6, 1221). Casenotes Pub.

Casenotes Publishing Company Inc. Staff. Taxation: Adaptable to Courses Utilizing Freeland, Lind & Stephens' Casebook on Fundamentals of Federal Income Taxation. Goldenberg, Norman S., et al, eds. (Legal Briefs Ser.). 1985. pap. write for info. (ISBN 0-87457-129-4, 1212). Casenotes Pub.

--Taxation: Adaptable to Courses Utilizing Graetz's Casebook on Federal Income Taxation. Goldenberg, Norman S., et al, eds. (Legal Briefs Ser.). 1979. pap. write for info. (ISBN 0-87457-130-8, 1211). Casenotes Pub.

Casensky, B., jt. auth. see Strouf, O.

Caserio, M. C., jt. auth. see Roberts, John D.

Caserio, Robert L. Plot, Story, & the Novel: From Dickens & Poe to the Modern Period. LC 79-4321. 1979. 29.00x (ISBN 0-691-06382-6). Princeton U Pr.

Casero, F., jt. auth. see Haensch, G.

Caserta, Ernesto. Giacomo Leopardi: The War of the Mice & the Crabs. (Studies in the Romance Languages & Literatures Ser: No. 164). 112p. 1976. 8.00x (ISBN 0-8078-9164-9). U of NC Pr.

Caserta, John G. The Golden Guitar. 1985. 7.50 (ISBN 0-682-40212-5). Exposition Pr FL.

Caserta, John S. The Red Brigades. 1978. pap. 1.95 (ISBN 0-532-19196-X). Woodhill.

Casese, Antonio. The New Humanitarian Law of Armed Conflict, 2 vols. 1974-1981. Set. lib. bdg. 88.00; lib. bdg. 44.00 ea. Vol. 1 (ISBN 0-379-20458-4). Vol. 2 (ISBN 0-379-20468-1). Oceana.

Casewit, Curtis. Graphology Handbook. (Illus.). 168p. (Orig.). 1980. pap. 9.95 (ISBN 0-914918-15-X). Para Res.

--Quit Smoking: Forty Major Techniques to Help You Stop Smoking. Werkman, Sidney L., intro. by. LC 83-60346. 160p. 1983. pap. 7.95 (ISBN 0-914918-44-3). Para Res.

--Strategies for Getting the Job You Want Now. LC 76-2079. 48p. 1976. pap. 2.50 (ISBN 0-87576-053-8). Pilot Bks.

Casewit, Curtis W. The Diary: A Complete Guide to Journal Writing. LC 81-69698. 120p. (Orig.). 1981. pap. 2.95 (ISBN 0-89505-060-9, 21055). Argus Comm.

--Foreign Jobs: The Most Popular Countries. 160p. 1984. pap. 8.95 (ISBN 0-671-49295-0). Monarch Pr.

--Freelance Writing: Advice from the Pros. new rev. ed. 304p. 1985. pap. 8.95 (ISBN 0-02-079610-2). Macmillan.

--How to Get a Job Overseas. 3rd ed. LC 83-21453. 160p. (Orig.). 1984. lib. bdg. 11.95 (ISBN 0-668-06015-8); pap. 6.95 (ISBN 0-668-05755-6). Arco.

--Making a Living in the Fine Arts: Advice from the Pros. 160p. 1981. 10.95 (ISBN 0-02-522420-4). Macmillan.

--Making a Living in the Fine Arts: Advice from the Pros. 176p. 1984. 5.95 (ISBN 0-02-079330-8, Collier). Macmillan.

--The Saga of the Mountain Soldiers: The Story of the Tenth Mountain Division. LC 81-9662. (Illus.). 160p. (gr. 7 up). 1981. PLB 9.79 (ISBN 0-671-41630-8). Messner.

--Skiing Colorado: A Complete Guide to America's Number 1 Ski State. LC 75-21060. 160p. 1975. pap. 4.95 (ISBN 0-85699-123-6). Chatham Pr.

Casey, jt. auth. see Kraft.

Casey, jt. auth. see Paris.

Casey, Bernard & Bruche, Gert. Work or Retirement? 200p. 1983. text ed. 31.00x (ISBN 0-566-00618-9). Gower Pub Co.

Casey, Betty. The Complete Book of Square Dancing (& Round Dancing) LC 75-40718. (Illus.). 394p. 1976. 12.50 (ISBN 0-385-03603-5). Doubleday.

--Dance Across Texas. (Illus.). 144p. 1985. 17.95 (ISBN 0-292-71540-4); pap. 8.95 (ISBN 0-292-71551-X). U of Tex Pr.

Casey, Bill & McMullin, Rian E. Cognitive Restructuring Therapy Package. 53p. 1976. 50.00 (ISBN 0-318-12060-7). Counseling Res.

Casey, Bill, jt. auth. see McMullin, Rian E.

Casey, Bill, jt. auth. see Paris, Claudine.

Casey, Bob, jt. auth. see Ryan, Tom.

Casey, Brigid & Haugh, Wendy. Sled Dogs. (Illus.). (gr. 4 up). 1983. 9.95 (ISBN 0-396-08225-4). Dodd.

Casey, Brigid, jt. auth. see Lavine, Sigmund A.

Casey, Cindy, jt. auth. see Miller, Shirley.

Casey, Clifford B. A Baker's Dozen: We Were Thirteen, the Caseys of Tuscola, Taylor County, Texas. (Illus.). 262p. 1974. 9.75 (ISBN 0-933512-21-X). Pioneer Bk Tx.

--Sul Ross State University: The Cultural Center of Trans-Pecos Texas 1917-1975. (Illus.). 416p. 1976. 9.50 (ISBN 0-933512-25-2). Pioneer Bk Tx.

Casey, D. E., et al, eds. Dyskinesia: Research & Treatment. (Psychopharmacology Supplementum: No. 2). (Illus.). 235p. 1985. 39.50 (ISBN 0-387-15009-9). Springer-Verlag.

Casey, Daniel. Benedict Kiely. (Irish Writers Ser.). 107p. 1975. 4.50 (ISBN 0-8387-7936-0); pap. 1.95 (ISBN 0-8387-7970-0). Bucknell U Pr.

Casey, Daniel J. & Rhodes, Robert E., eds. Friends & Relations: Twenty-One Irish-American Short Stories. 368p. 1985. 19.95 (ISBN 0-8159-5519-7). Devin.

--Irish-American Fiction: Essays in Criticism. LC 78-18944. (AMS Studies in Modern Literature: No. 4). 1979. 34.50 (ISBN 0-404-16036-0); pap. 11.95 (ISBN 0-404-16037-9). AMS Pr.

--Views of the Irish Peasantry, 1800-1916. (Illus.). 225p. 1977. 19.00 (ISBN 0-208-01630-9, Archon). Shoe String.

Casey, Denise. Black-Footed Ferret. (Skylight Bk.). (Illus.). 64p. (gr. 2-5). 1985. PLB 9.95 (ISBN 0-396-08625-X). Dodd.

Casey, Douglas. Strategic Investing. 1983. pap. 3.95 (ISBN 0-671-43886-7). PB.

Casey, Douglas R. Crisis Investing. 1983. pap. 3.50 (ISBN 0-671-42678-8). PB.

--Crisis Investing. 2nd ed. LC 79-64112. 1980. 12.50 (ISBN 0-936906-00-6). Stratford Pr.

Casey, E. S., tr. see Dufrenne, Mikel.

Casey, Edward S. Imagining: A Phenomenological Study. LC 76-12370. (Studies in Phenomenology & Existential Philosophy). 256p. 1976. 20.00x (ISBN 0-253-32912-4); pap. 9.95x (ISBN 0-253-20228-0). Ind U Pr.

Casey, Edward S., tr. see Dufrenne, Mikel.

Casey, Elizabeth T. The Lucy Truman Aldrich Collection of European Porcelain Figures of the Eighteenth Century. LC 65-28229. (Illus.). 1965. 9.00 (ISBN 0-87821-231-0). Mus of Art RI.

Casey, Genevieve M. Library Services for the Aging. xiv, 161p. 1984. 18.50 (ISBN 0-208-01946-4, Lib Prof Pubns); pap. 13.50x (ISBN 0-208-01947-2). Shoe String.

Casey, Gerard. Natural Reason: A Study of the Notions of Inference, Assent, Intuition, & First Principles in the Philosophy of John Henry Cardinal Newman. (American University Studies V Philosophy: Vol. 4). 345p. 1984. 37.00 (ISBN 0-8204-0078-5). P Lang Pubs.

Casey, H. C., Jr. & Panish, M. B. Heterostructure Lasers, 2 pts. Incl. Pt. A. Fundamental Principles. 49.50 (ISBN 0-12-163101-X); Pt. B. Materials & Operating Characteristics. 60.00 (ISBN 0-12-163102-8). (Quantum Electronics Ser.). 1978. Acad Pr.

Casey, Helen & Clark, Mary T. Logic: A Practical Approach. (gr. 9-12). 1966. pap. text ed. 4.50 (ISBN 0-87505-313-0, Pub. by Lawrence). Borden.

Casey, J. The Kingdom of Valencia in the Seventeenth Century. LC 77-88669. (Cambridge Studies in Early Modern History). (Illus.). 1979. 44.50 (ISBN 0-521-21939-6). Cambridge U Pr.

Casey, James F. Fire Service Hydraulics. 2nd ed. (Illus.). 1970. 22.95 (ISBN 0-912212-05-5). Fire Eng.

Casey, James F., ed. The Fire Chief's Handbook. 4th ed. (Illus.). 1978. 24.95 (ISBN 0-912212-04-7). Fire Eng.

Casey, James P. Pulp & Paper: Chemistry & Chemical Technology, 4 vols. 3rd ed. 1983. Set. 305.00 (ISBN 0-471-88186-4, Pub. by Wiley-Interscience). Wiley.

--Pulp & Paper: Chemistry & Technology, Vol. 4. 3rd ed. LC 79-13435. 2609p. 1983. 81.00 (ISBN 0-471-03178-X, Pub. by Wiley-Interscience). Wiley.

Casey, James P., ed. Pulp & Paper: Chemistry & Chemical Technology, 2 vols. 3rd ed. LC 79-13435. 820p. 1980. Vol. 1, 820 p. 96.50 (ISBN 0-471-03175-5, Pub. by Wiley-Interscience); Vol. 2, 625 p. 91.00 (ISBN 0-471-03176-3). Wiley.

Casey, Jane A., ed. see Nalin, David R.

Casey, Joan D. Bordeaux, Colonial Port of Nineteenth Century France. Bruchey, Stuart, ed. LC 80-2798. (Dissertations in European Economic History II). 1981. lib. bdg. 38.50x (ISBN 0-405-13982-9). Ayer Co Pubs.

Casey, Joseph H. From Why to Yes: Pain Uncovers the Meaningful Life to a Philosopher. LC 81-43471. 108p. (Orig.). 1982. pap. text ed. 9.25 (ISBN 0-8191-2205-X). U Pr of Amer.

Casey, Joseph H., ed. see Grisez, Germain & Shaw, Russell.

Casey, Juanita. A Sampling. (Chapbook Ser.). pap. 2.95x (ISBN 0-912262-72-9). Proscenium.

Casey, Judy I., jt. auth. see Duchesneau, Vicki L.

Casey, Juliana. Hebrews. (New Testament Message Ser.: Vol. 18). 8.95 (ISBN 0-89453-206-5); pap. 4.95 (ISBN 0-89453-141-7). M Glazier.

Casey, June. Infidel of Love. (Superromances Ser.). 384p. 1982. pap. 2.50 (ISBN 0-373-70025-3, Pub. by Worldwide). Harlequin Bks.

Casey, Karen & Vanceburg, Martha. The Promise of a New Day. 400p. 1983. pap. 5.95 (ISBN 0-89486-203-0). Hazelden.

--The Promise of a New Day. 400p. pap. 5.95 (ISBN 0-86683-502-4). Winston Pr.

Casey, Karen, ed. Venture Capital Investment: 1982. 1983. pap. 925.00 (CPC101, Capital). Unipub.

Casey, Kevin, et al. A Community-Based System for the Mentally Retarded: The ENCOR Experience. LC 84-13126. xvi, 217p. 1985. 21.50x (ISBN 0-8032-4147-X). U of Nebr Pr.

Casey, Lawrence. Casey Federal Tax Practice: 1977-1983, 6 vols. LC 77-18109. Set. 35.00 (ISBN 0-317-11936-2). Callaghan.

Casey, Lydian. Outdoor Gardening. LC 74-11890. (Early Craft Bks.). (Illus.). 32p. (gr. 1-4). 1975. PLB 4.95 (ISBN 0-8225-0864-8). Lerner Pubns.

Casey, M. Beth, jt. auth. see Abramson, David I.

Casey, Marion. Charles McCarthy: Librarianship & Reform. LC 81-15022. 260p. 1982. 16.00x (ISBN 0-8389-0347-9). ALA.

Casey, Mary C., jt. auth. see Bate, Marjorie D.

Casey, Michael. Obscenities. LC 78-179470. (Younger Poets of Sixty-Seven Ser.). 64p. 1972. 12.95x (ISBN 0-300-01546-1); pap. 5.95x (ISBN 0-300-01548-8, Y-253). Yale U Pr.

Casey, P. A. Try Us: Washington Artillery in World War 2. 1971. 15.00 (ISBN 0-87511-588-8). Claitors.

Casey, P. A., tr. see Freuler, F., et al.

Casey, P. A., tr. see Henche, H. R.

Casey, P. A., tr. see Liechti, R.

Casey, P. J. Roman Coinage in Britian. (Archaeology Ser.: No. 12). 1985. pap. 5.95 (ISBN 0-85263-671-7, Pub. by Shire Pubns England). Seven Hills Bks.

Casey, Patricia. Autumn Days. (The Seasons Ser.). (Illus.). 20p. 1984. pap. 4.95 (ISBN 0-399-21171-3, Philomel). Putnam Pub Group.

--Spring Days. (The Seasons Ser.). (Illus.). 20p. 1984. pap. 4.95 (ISBN 0-399-21034-2, Philomel). Putnam Pub Group.

--Winter Days. (The Seasons Ser.). (Illus.). 20p. 1984. pap. 4.95 (ISBN 0-399-21036-9, Philomel). Putnam Pub Group.

Casey, Patrick A., jt. auth. see Aeberhard, Peter.

Casey, Paul F. The Susanna Theme in German Literature. (Abhandlungen zur Kunst-, Musik- und Literaturwissenschaft: Vol. 214). 260p. (Orig.). 1976. pap. 18.00x (ISBN 3-416-01250-X, Pub. by Bouvier Verlag W Germany). Benjamins North Am.

Casey, R., jt. auth. see Thompson, R.

Casey, R., ed. see International Symposium on the Boreal Lower Cretaceous (1972: London) Staff.

Casey, Ralph D., ed. The Press in Perspective. LC 63-16657. pap. 58.80 (ISBN 0-317-30011-3, 2051876). Bks Demand UMI.

Casey, Richard G. Friends & Neighbors. 1955. 3.00 (ISBN 0-87013-010-2). Mich St U Pr.

Casey, Rita, jt. auth. see Sowell, Evelyn.

Casey, Robert J. Four Faces of Siva. 1929. 25.00 (ISBN 0-8482-3565-7). Norwood Edns.

Casey, Robert L. Journey to the High Southwest: A Traveler's Guide. 2nd, rev. ed. LC 84-25366. (Illus.). 400p. 1985. pap. 14.95 (ISBN 0-914718-96-7). Pacific Search.

Casey, Robert P., ed. see Serapion, Saint.

Casey, Sara. Two by Two Romance, No. 1: Cassie & Chris. 192p. (Orig.). 1983. pap. 1.95 (ISBN 0-446-30801-3). Warner Bks.

Casey, Stephen, jt. auth. see Listokin, David.

Casey, T. J., et al, eds. Methods of Characterization of Sewage Sludge. 164p. 1984. lib. bdg. 29.00 (ISBN 90-277-1782-6, Pub. by Reidel Holland). Kluwer Academic.

Casey, Therese. PMS & Alcoholism. 20p. (Orig.). 1984. pap. 0.85 (ISBN 0-89486-247-2). Hazelden.

Casey, Thomas A., et al. Corneal Grafting: Principles & Practice. 2nd ed. (Illus.). 352p. 1984. 85.00 (ISBN 0-7216-2448-0). Saunders.

Casey, Todd. Dinobots Strike Back: Find Your Fate Junior-Transformers. (No. 1). 80p. (Orig.). 1985. pap. 1.95 (ISBN 0-345-32669-5). Ballantine.

Casey, W. W. How to Meet Men (For Ladies Only) 16p. pap. 3.00x (ISBN 0-943462-01-0). CaseCo.

--You, Too can Beat Police Radar & Avoid Speeding Tickets. 220p. pap. 19.95x (ISBN 0-943462-02-9). CaseCo.

Casey, W. Wilson. TV Trivia Quiz. 32p. pap. 1.95x (ISBN 0-686-36931-9). CaseCo.

--TV Trivia Teasers. 1984. 9.50 (ISBN 0-87650-164-1). Pierian.

Casey, William, ed. Thomas Morley's First Book of Consort Lessons, 6 vols. LC 81-80729. 1982. pap. 45.00x spiral bdg. (ISBN 0-918954-27-4). Baylor Univ Pr.

Casey, William L., Jr. & Marthinsen, John E. Entrepreneurship, Productivity & the Freedom of Information Act: Protecting Circumstantially Relevant Business Information. LC 82-48609. 240p. 1983. 26.50x (ISBN 0-669-06349-5). Lexington Bks.

Casey-Gaspar, Jeff, et al. The State of Hispanic America, Vols. I-IV. (Orig.). pap. text ed. 14.00 ea. Natl His Univ.

Casgrain, jt. ed. see Laverdiere.

Cash, Adam. How to Make Money in the Underground Economy. 150p. (Orig.). 1985. pap. 9.95 (ISBN 0-915179-25-3). Loompanics.

Cash, Alan. The Fifth Penguin Book of the Times Crosswords. (Penguin Nonfiction Ser.). 144p. 1984. pap. 2.95 (ISBN 0-14-006554-7). Penguin.

--The Fourth Penguin Book of the "Times" Crosswords. 144p. 1983. pap. 3.50 (ISBN 0-14-006553-9). Penguin.

Cash, Alan, ed. The Daily Telegraph Ninth Crossword Puzzle Book. 224p. 1984. pap. 2.95 (ISBN 0-14-001744-5). Penguin.

--The Daily Telegraph Sixteenth Crossword Puzzle Book. 144p. 1984. pap. 2.95 (ISBN 0-14-005873-7). Penguin.

--The Daily Telegraph Thirteenth Crossword Puzzle Book. 192p. 1984. pap. 2.95 (ISBN 0-14-004153-2). Penguin.

--The Daily Telegraph Twelfth Crossword Puzzle Book. 192p. (Orig.). 1984. pap. 2.95 (ISBN 0-14-003872-8). Penguin.

Cash, Arthur H. Laurence Sterne: The Early & Middle Years. LC 75-18378. (Illus.). 1975. 60.00x (ISBN 0-416-82210-X, NO. 2126). Methuen Inc.

Cash, Arthur H. & Stedmond, John, eds. Winged Skull: Papers of the Laurence Sterne Bicentenary Conference. LC 70-114668. (Illus.). 334p. 1971. 21.00x (ISBN 0-87338-102-5). Kent St U Pr.

Cash, Audrey. The Southern Literary Cookbook. 1978. 6.95 (ISBN 0-685-39051-9). Hope Ent Fla.

Cash, Donna, jt. auth. see Carr, Jo.

Cash, E. A. John A. Williams: The Evolution of a Black Writer. LC 73-92796. 1974. 10.00 (ISBN 0-89388-142-2). Okpaku Communications.

Cash, J. To Be an Indian. LC 79-174548. 251p. 1971. pap. 7.50 (ISBN 0-03-086372-4, Pub. by HR&W). Krieger.

Cash, J. & Hopkinson, J. British Freshwater Rhizopoda & Heliozoa, 5 Vols. 1905-21. Set. 92.00 (ISBN 0-384-07835-4). Johnson Repr.

Cash, J. R. Stable Recursions: With Applications to the Numerical Solution of Stiff Systems. LC 79-50521. (Computational Mathematics & Application Ser.). 1980. 55.00 (ISBN 0-12-163050-1). Acad Pr.

Cash, James I., Jr., et al. Corporate Information Systems Management: Text & Cases. 1983. text ed. 32.50x (ISBN 0-256-02912-1). Irwin.

Cash, Jonathan. The Sleepers of Erin. (Crime Monthly Ser.). 224p. 1984. pap. 3.50 (ISBN 0-14-006970-4). Penguin.

Cash, Joseph H. Working the Homestake. (Illus.). 142p. 1973. 6.95 (ISBN 0-8138-0755-7). Iowa St U Pr.

Cash, Joseph H., et al. The Practice of Oral History: A Handbook. Hoover, Herbert T., ed. LC 73-93526. 98p. 1975. 8.50 (ISBN 0-88455-001-X). Microfilming Corp.

Cash, Kathy. Designing & Using Simulations for Training. (Technical Note Ser.: No. 20). 34p. (Orig.). 1982. pap. 1.50 (ISBN 0-932288-66-9). Ctr Intl Ed U of MA.

Cash, Kevin. Who the Hell Is William Loeb? 1975. 8.95 (ISBN 0-686-15518-1); pap. 5.95 (ISBN 0-686-15519-X). Amoskeag Pr.

Cash, McKinley. Final Accounting: The Collected Rimes & Recollections of Alabama's Premier Folk Poet. 1985. 12.50 (ISBN 0-916620-75-1). Portals Pr.

Cash, Paul, ed. see Brunton, Paul.

Cash, Paul, et al, eds. see Brunton, Paul.

Cash, Philip. Medical Men at the Siege of Boston, April, 1775 - April, 1776: Problems of the Massachusetts & Continental Armies. LC 73-79578. (Memoirs Ser.: Vol. 98). (Illus.). 1973. pap. 4.00 (ISBN 0-87169-098-5). Am Philos.

Cash, Philip, et al, eds. Medicine in Colonial Massachusetts, 1620-1820. LC 80-68589. (Illus.). xxiv, 425p. 1980. 30.00x (ISBN 0-8139-0908-2, Colonial Soc MA). U Pr of Va.

Cash, Phyllis. How to Prepare for the Miller Analogies Test (MAT) (McGraw-Hill Paperbacks). (Orig.). 1979. pap. 5.95 (ISBN 0-07-010222-8). McGraw.

--How to Write a Research Paper. (How to Ser.). 128p. (Orig.). 1983. pap. 5.95 (ISBN 0-671-47093-0). Monarch Pr.

Cash, Wilbur J. Mind of the South. 1960. 17.95 (ISBN 0-394-43623-7). Knopf.

--Mind of the South. 1960. pap. 3.95 (ISBN 0-394-70098-8, Vin, V98). Random.

Cash, William B., Jr., jt. auth. see Stewart, Charles J.

Cash, William M. & Howorth, Lucy S., eds. My Dear Nellie: The Civil War Letters of William L. Nugent to Eleanor Smith Nugent. LC 77-24597. (Illus.). 1977. 3.95x (ISBN 0-87805-036-1). U Pr of Miss.

Cashatt, Everett & Schuberth, Christopher J. Natural History Tour to Horseshoe Lake & Shawnee National Forest. (Guidebooklet Ser.: No. 1). (Illus.). 36p. 1977. pap. 2.25 (ISBN 0-89792-069-4). Ill St Museum.

Cashdan, Sheldon. Abnormal Psychology. LC 70-39029. (Foundations of Modern Psychology Ser.). (Illus.). 160p. 1972. 12.95 (ISBN 0-13-000802-8). P-H.

--Interactional Psychotherapy: Stages & Strategies in Behavioral Change. LC 73-5764. (Illus.). 168p. 1973. 37.00 (ISBN 0-8089-0809-X, 790800). Grune.

Cashdollar, Pat & Fabian, Miriam, eds. Ohio Almanac Nineteen Eighty. 9th ed. LC 68-3162. (Illus.). 544p. 1980. lib. bdg. 8.95 (ISBN 0-686-29709-1, B-14); pap. 4.95 (ISBN 0-686-29710-5). Kids Special.

Cashel Diocesan Library. County Tipperary, Republic of Ireland. Catalogue of the Cashel Diocesan Library. 1973. 100.00 (ISBN 0-8161-1065-4, Hall Library). G K Hall.

Cashel, Sue, jt. auth. see Boreta, Anne.

Cashell, G. T. & Durran, I. M. Handbook of Orthoptic Principles. 4th ed. (Illus.). 1981. pap. text ed. 15.50 (ISBN 0-443-02200-3). Churchill.

Cashen, Richard A. Solitude in the Thought of Thomas Merton. (Cistercian Studies: No. 40). 208p. 1981. 15.50 (ISBN 0-87907-840-5); pap. 5.50 (ISBN 0-87907-940-1). Cistercian Pubns.

Cashen, William. Man Folk-Lore. (Folklore Ser.). Repr. 17.50 (ISBN 0-8482-3583-5). Norwood Edns.

--William Cashen's Manx Folk-Lore. LC 77-22640. 1977. Repr. of 1912 ed. lib. bdg. 25.00 (ISBN 0-8414-1835-7). Folcroft.

Cashin, Edward J. & Robertson, Heard. Augusta & the American Revolution: Events in the Georgia Back Country, 1773-1783. LC 74-28968. (Illus.). 1975. pap. 7.00 (ISBN 0-686-15798-2). Richmond Cty Hist Soc.

Cashin, Herschel V., et al. Under Fire with the Tenth U. S. Cavalry. LC 69-18550. (American Negro: His History & Literature Ser., No. 2). 1969. Repr. of 1899 ed. 16.00 (ISBN 0-405-01854-1). Ayer Co Pubs.

Cashin, J. A. & Neuwirth, P. D. Cashin's Handbook for Auditors. 2nd ed. 1986p. 1985. price not set (ISBN 0-07-010264-3). McGraw.

Cashin, J. A., jt. auth. see Polimeni, R.

Cashin, J. A., jt. auth. see Wiseman, J. A.

Cashin, James & Polimeni, Ralph S. Cost Accounting. 1981. 34.95 (ISBN 0-07-010213-9). McGraw.

Cashin, James A. Handbook for Auditors. 1971. 85.00 (ISBN 0-07-010200-7). McGraw.

Cashin, James A. & Lerner, Joel J. Schaum's Outline of Accounting I. 2nd ed. (Schaum's Outline Ser.). 1980. pap. 8.95 (ISBN 0-07-010251-1). McGraw.

Cashin, James A. & Owens, Garland C. Auditing. 2nd ed. LC 63-9246. pap. 160.00 (ISBN 0-317-10056-4, 2012393). Bks Demand UMI.

Cashin, James A., jt. auth. see Moss, Morris H.

Cashin, James A., et al. Intermediate Accounting, Pt. 1. (Schaum's Outline Ser.). 256p. 1975. pap. text ed. 7.95 (ISBN 0-07-010202-3). McGraw.

--Schaum's Outline of Cost Accounting Two. (Schaum's Outline Ser.). Orig. Title: Schaum's Outline of Advanced Cost Accounting. 240p. 1982. pap. 8.95 (ISBN 0-07-010207-4). McGraw.

Cashion, Barbara G., jt. auth. see Eshleman, J. Ross.

Cashion, Jerry. Guide to North Carolina Historical Highway Markers. (Illus.). 262p. 1979. pap. 3.00 (ISBN 0-86526-079-6). NC Archives.

Cashion, Kathy, jt. ed. see Smith, C. Carter.

Cashman, jt. auth. see Shelly.

Cashman, Dennis. Prohibition in America: The Lie of the Land. (Illus.). 300p. 1981. 17.95 (ISBN 0-02-905730-2). Macmillan.

--Prohibition: The Lie of the Land. 1981. 17.95x (ISBN 0-317-30516-6). Free Pr.

Cashman, Diane C. Cape Fear Adventure: An Illustrated History of Wilmington. LC 82-50188. (Illus.). 128p. 1982. 22.95 (ISBN 0-89781-057-0). Windsor Pubns Inc.

Cashman, Greer F. Jewish Days & Holidays. LC 79-66167. (Illus.). 64p. 1979. Repr. of 1976 ed. 9.95 (ISBN 0-89961-000-5). SBS Pub.

Cashman, John R. Hazardous Materials Emergencies. LC 82-74318. 400p. 1983. 45.00 (ISBN 0-87762-324-4). Technomic.

Cashman, Marc, ed. Cincinnati Companion. 2nd ed. (Illus., Orig.). 1977. pap. text ed. 3.95 (ISBN 0-685-85679-8). Tom Tuttle.

Cashman, Norine D. & Braunstein, Mark M., eds. Slide Buyers' Guide. 5th ed. 200p. 1985. lib. bdg. 25.00 (ISBN 0-87287-471-0). Libs Unl.

Cashman, Richard. Patrons, Players & the Crowd: The Phenomenon of Indian Cricket. 202p. 1981. 30.00x (Pub. by Orient Longman India). State Mutual Bk.

Cashman, Richard I. The Myth of the Lokamanya: Tilak & Mass Politics in Maharashtra. LC 72-97734. 1975. 36.00x (ISBN 0-520-02407-9). U of Cal Pr.

Cashman, Seamus, jt. auth. see Quinn, Bridie.

Cashman, Seamus & Gaffney, Sean, eds. Proverbs & Sayings of Ireland. rev. ed. (Illus.). 1985. pap. 4.95 (ISBN 0-86327-073-5, Pub. by Wolfhound Pr Ireland). Irish Bks Media.

Cashman, Seamus, jt. ed. see Gaffney, Sean.

Cashman, Seamus, jt. ed. see Quinn, Bridie.

Cashman, Sean D. America in the Gilded Age: From the Death of Lincoln to the Rise of Theodore Roosevelt. (Illus.). 384p. 1984. 35.00x (ISBN 0-8147-1386-6); pap. 14.50x (ISBN 0-8147-1387-4). NYU Pr.

Cashman, Thomas J. & Shelly, Gary B. IBM System-360 Assembler Language Workbook. LC 75-23969. (Illus.). 237p. 1973. pap. text ed. 11.95 (ISBN 0-88236-051-5). Anaheim Pub Co.

--Introduction to Computer Programming IBM System-360 Assembler Language. LC 75-4790. 327p. 1969. pap. text ed. 24.95x (ISBN 0-88236-050-7). Anaheim Pub Co.

Cashman, Thomas J., jt. auth. see Shelly, Gary B.

Cashman, Thomas J, jt. auth. see Shelly, Gary B.

Cashman, Thomas J., jt. auth. see Shelly, Gary B.

Cashmore, E. & Mullan, B. Approaching Social Theory. 235p. 1983. text ed. 28.25x (ISBN 0-435-82167-9, Pub. by Heinemann Ed England); pap. text ed. 11.00x (ISBN 0-435-82168-7). Humanities.

Cashmore, E. Ellis. No Future: Youth & Society. 120p. (Orig.). 1984. pap. text ed. 10.00x (ISBN 0-435-82163-6). Gower Pub Co.

Cashmore, Ellis. Dictionary of Race & Ethnic Relations. LC 84-11730. 1985. 34.95x (ISBN 0-7100-9904-5). Routledge & Kegan.

Cashmore, Ernest. Black Sportsmen. 224p. (Orig.). 1982. pap. 13.95x (ISBN 0-7100-9054-4). Routledge & Kegan.

--Having to: The World of One Parent Families. 1985. text ed. 20.00x (ISBN 0-04-301098-9); pap. text ed. 9.95x (ISBN 0-04-301099-7). Allen Unwin.

--Rastaman: The Rastafarian Movement in England. (Counterpoint Ser.). 263p. 1983. pap. 7.95 (ISBN 0-04-301164-0). Allen Unwin.

Cashmore, Ernest E. & Troyna, Barry. Introduction to Race Relations. 256p. (Orig.). 1983. pap. 10.95x (ISBN 0-7100-9930-4). Routledge & Kegan.

Cashwell, E. D., jt. auth. see Carter, L. L.

Casida, John E., ed. Pyrethrum: The Natural Insecticide. 1973. 59.50 (ISBN 0-12-162950-3). Acad Pr.

Casida, John E., jt. ed. see Pallos, Ferenc M.

Casillo, Peter C., jt. auth. see Simon, James C.

Casimaty, Nina, ed. India & Nepal: A Travel Handbook. 1979. pap. 4.00x (ISBN 0-686-19964-2). Intl Learn Syst.

Casimir, Hendrik B. Haphazard Reality: Half a Century of Science. LC 82-48112. (Sloan Foundation Books). 356p. 1983. 19.23i (ISBN 0-06-015028-9, HarpT). Har-Row.

--Haphazard Reality: Half A Century of Science. LC 83-48112. 368p. 1984. pap. 7.64i (ISBN 0-06-091104-2, CN 1104, CN). Har-Row.

Casimir, M. & Bament, R. C. An Outbreak of the Australian Plague Locust, (Hortoicetes Terminiferal Walk.), During 1966-67 & the Influence of Weather on Swarm Flight. 1974. 35.00x (ISBN 0-85135-062-3, Pub. by Centre Overseas Research). State Mutual Bk.

Casini, G. Plasma Physics for Thermonuclear Fusion Reactors. (Ispra Courses on Nuclear Engineering & Technology Ser.). 496p. 1982. 75.00 (ISBN 3-7186-0091-9). Harwood Academic.

Casini, G., ed. Engineering Aspects of Thermonuclear Fusion Reactors. (Ispra Courses on Nuclear Engineering & Technology Ser.). 642p. 1982. 97.00 (ISBN 3-7186-0090-0). Harwood Academic.

Casjens, Sherwood. Virus Structure & Assembly. 356p. 1985. text ed. write for info. (ISBN 0-86720-044-8). Jones & Bartlett.

Caskey, C. Thomas & Robbins, D. Christopher, eds. Somatic Cell Genetics. LC 82-7604. (NATO ASI Series A, Life Sciences: Vol. 50). 226p. 1982. 35.00x (ISBN 0-306-41018-4, Plenum Pr). Plenum Pub.

Caskey, C. Thomas & White, Raymond, eds. Banbury Report 14: Recombinant DNA Applications to Human Disease. LC 82-19712. (Banbury Report Ser.: Vol. 14). 371p. 1983. 55.00x (ISBN 0-87969-214-6). Cold Spring Harbor.

Caskey, Clark. Balance in Management. LC 68-57174. 1968. 10.95 (ISBN 0-912164-06-9). Masterco Pr.

Caskey, Jefferson D., compiled by. Index to Poetry in Popular Periodicals, 1955-1959. LC 83-22584. xv, 269p. 1984. lib. bdg. 29.95 (ISBN 0-313-22227-4, CIP/). Greenwood.

Caskey, Jefferson D. & Stapp, Melinda M., eds. Samuel Taylor Coleridge: A Selective Bibliography of Criticism, 1935-1977. LC 78-57765. 1978. lib. bdg. 35.00 (ISBN 0-313-20564-7, CCO/). Greenwood.

Caskey, John H. The Life & Works of Edward Moore. (Yale Studies in English Ser.: No. 75). iv, 197p. 1973. Repr. of 1927 ed. 18.00 (ISBN 0-208-01125-0, Archon). Shoe String.

Caskey, Marie. Chariot of Fire: Religion & the Beecher Family. LC 77-5291. (Historical Publications Ser.). (Illus.). 1978. 38.00x (ISBN 0-300-02007-4). Yale U Pr.

Caskey, Owen L. Suggestive-Accelerative Learning & Teaching. Langdon, Danny G., ed. LC 79-26386. (Instructional Design Library). 136p. 1980. 19.95 (ISBN 0-87778-156-7). Educ Tech Pubns.

Caskey, Owen L., jt. auth. see Trang, Myron L.

Caskey, Willie M. Secession & Restoration of Louisiana. LC 78-75302. (American Scene Ser). (Illus.). 1970. Repr. of 1938 ed. lib. bdg. 39.50 (ISBN 0-306-71263-6). Da Capo.

Caskoden, Edwin, pseud. When Knighthood Was in Flower, or, the Love Story of Charles Brandon & Mary Tudor the King's Sister, & Happening in the Reign of His August Majesty, King Henry VIII. LC 77-145160. (Illus.). 310p. 1972. Repr. of 1898 ed. 39.00x (ISBN 0-403-01088-8). Scholarly.

Casler, Darwin J. & Crockett, James R. Operational Auditing: An Introduction. Holman, Richard, ed. (Illus.). 80p. pap. text ed. 27.00 (ISBN 0-89413-097-8). Inst Inter Aud.

Casler, John O. Four Years in the Stonewall Brigade. (Civil War Heritage Ser.: No. 7). (Illus.). 1975. 20.00 (ISBN 0-89029-003-2); pap. 8.95. Pr of Morningside.

Casler, L. Maternal Deprivation, a Critical Review of the Literature. (SRCD.M). 1961. pap. 14.00 (ISBN 0-527-01589-X). Kraus Repr.

Casler, Lawrence. Is Marriage Necessary? LC 73-18236. 249p. 1974. text ed. 24.95 (ISBN 0-87705-132-1). Human Sci Pr.

--NRJD on Three Eighty Seven Glizzits a Day. (Illus.). 64p. 1986. 5.95 (ISBN 0-87795-732-0, Pub. by Timbre Bks.). Arbor Hse.

Casler, Melyer. Journal Giving the Incidents of a Journey to California in the Summer of 1859, by the Overland Route. 1970. Repr. 14.95 (ISBN 0-87770-039-7). Ye Galleon.

Casler, Robin E., ed. see American Pharmaceutical Association.

Casley, D. J. & Lury, D. A. Data Collection in Developing Countries. (Illus.). 1981. 47.50x (ISBN 0-19-877123-1); pap. 13.95x (ISBN 0-19-877124-X). Oxford U Pr.

Casley, Dennis J. & Lury, Denis A. Monitoring & Evaluation of Agriculture & Rural Development Projects. LC 82-7126. (World Bank Ser.). 160p. 1983. pap. 8.50x (ISBN 0-8018-2910-0). Johns Hopkins.

Caslon, William. Caslon Old Face: Roman & Italic. (Illus.). 64p. 1979. 80.00x (ISBN 0-85667-075-8, Pub. by Sotheby Pubns England). Biblio Dist.

Caslow, Dan. Christian Disciple, No. 2. 1984. pap. 1.75 (ISBN 0-8163-0497-1). Pacific Pr Pub Assn.

--Church Fellowship. 1984. pap. 1.75 (ISBN 0-8163-0499-8). Pacific Pr Pub Assn.

--New Life, No. 1. 1984. pap. 1.75 (ISBN 0-317-30423-2). Pacific Pr Pub Assn.

--Personal Ministry, No. 3. 1984. pap. 1.75 (ISBN 0-8163-0498-X). Pacific Pr Pub Assn.

--Profiles. 1984. pap. 1.75 (ISBN 0-317-30412-7). Pacific Pr Pub Assn.

Caslow, Daniel E. Winning. 1981. pap. 5.95 (ISBN 0-8163-0462-9). Pacific Pr Pub Assn.

Caslow, Don. Profiles. 1984. pap. 3.50 Manual (ISBN 0-8163-0495-5). Pacific Pr Pub Assn.

Casner, A. James. American Law of Property: 1976 Supplement. 1976. pap. 70.00 (ISBN 0-316-13138-5). Little.

--An Estate Family Plan for Mr. & Mrs. Harry S. Black. 4th ed. 1983. pap. 18.00 (ISBN 0-316-13162-8). Little.

--Estate Planning, 6 vols. 5th ed. Set. 275.00 (ISBN 0-316-13154-7); 1982 supplement 60.00, (ISBN 0-317-27316-7); 1983 supplement 60.00, (ISBN 0-317-27317-5). Little.

--Estate Planning, Vols. 1-6. 1980. text ed. 275.00 (ISBN 0-316-13148-2). Vol. 1. Vol. 2 (ISBN 0-316-13149-0). Vol. 3 (ISBN 0-316-13150-4). Vol. 4 (ISBN 0-316-13151-2). Vol. 5 (ISBN 0-316-13152-0). Vol. 6 (ISBN 0-316-13153-9). Little.

--Estate Planning: Student Edition. 4th ed. 1150p. 1979. 31.00 (ISBN 0-316-13173-3). Little.

--Estate Planning: Volume I Revision. 5th ed. LC 83-80449. 488p. 1984. 67.50 (ISBN 0-316-13197-0). Little.

--Estate Planning: 1982 Supplement. 4th ed. 1982. pap. 9.95 (ISBN 0-316-13171-7). Little.

--Estate Planning: 1984 Supplement, Lawyers Edition. LC 79-91935. 750p. 1984. 65.00 (ISBN 0-316-13160-1). Little.

--The Irrevocable Trust: No. B320. rev. ed. 48p. 1977. pap. write for info. Am Law Inst.

--The Revocable Trust. rev. ed. 67p. 1977. pap. 3.00 (ISBN 0-317-32256-7, B318). Am Law Inst.

Casner, A. James & Leach, W. Barton. Cases & Text on Property. 3rd ed. LC 83-82695. 1427p. 1984. text ed. 34.00 (ISBN 0-316-13183-0). Little.

Casner, A. James, jt. auth. see American Law Institute.

Casner, A. James, ed. American Law of Property, 8 vols. LC 52-10235. 1952. Set. 395.00 (ISBN 0-316-13145-8). Little.

Caso, Adolph. Alfieri's Ode to America's Independence. LC 76-6244. 1976. pap. 5.00 (ISBN 0-8283-1667-8). Branden Pub Co.

--America's Italian Founding Fathers. 1975. 12.00 (ISBN 0-8283-1610-4). Branden Pub Co.

--Bilingual Two Language Battery of Tests. (Span., Fr., Ital., Portuguese, Eng. & Vietnamese.). 1983. pap. 15.00 tchr's manual (ISBN 0-8283-1857-3). Branden Pub Co.

--Lives of Italian Americans: Fifty Biographies. (Illus.). 1979. 12.50 (ISBN 0-8283-1699-6). Branden Pub Co.

--Mass Media vs. the Italian Americans. LC 80-66885. (Illus.). 278p. 1980. 12.00 (ISBN 0-8283-1737-2). Branden Pub Co.

--Mass Media vs. the Italian Americans. 1984. pap. 4.95 (ISBN 0-8283-1831-X). Branden Pub Co.

--Water & Life: Poetry in English & Italian. 1976. pap. 5.00 (ISBN 0-8283-1682-1). Branden Pub Co.

Caso, Adolph, jt. auth. see Kinney, Joseph.

Caso, Alfonso. Aztecs: People of the Sun, Vol. 50. Dunham, Lowell, tr. (Civilization of the American Indian Ser.: No. 50). (Illus.). 142p. 1978. Repr. of 1958 ed. 21.95 (ISBN 0-8061-0414-7). U of Okla Pr.

--Thirteen Masterpieces of Mexican Archaeology; Trece Obras Maestras De Arqueologia Mexicana. N. Mackie, Edith & Acosta, Jorge R., trs. from Span. LC 76-25239. (Illus., Eng. & Span.). 1976. Repr. of 1938 ed. 12.00 (ISBN 0-87917-057-3). Ethridge.

Caso, Alolph. Issues in Foreign Language & Bilingual Education. LC 77-94784. 1979. pap. 7.50 (ISBN 0-8283-1721-6). Branden Pub Co.

Caso, Antonio. Thirteen Masterpieces of Mexican Archaeology. 1976. lib. bdg. 59.95 (ISBN 0-8490-1194-9). Gordon Pr.

Caso, Jacques de see Rodin, Auguste.

Casola, Matteo A. Successful Mass Catering & Volume Feeding. rev. ed. Darveau, Mary, ed. LC 80-66708. 329p. 1980. Repr. of 1969 ed. text ed. 24.95 (ISBN 0-916096-25-4). Continental CA.

Casolaro, Daniel. The Ice King. LC 81-52154. 168p. 1981. 8.95 (ISBN 0-87426-052-3). Whitmore.

Cason, Clarence. Ninety Degrees in the Shade. LC 74-106851. (Illus.). Repr. of 1935 ed. 19.75x (ISBN 0-8371-3473-0, CNS&, Pub. by Negro U Pr). Greenwood.

--Ninety Degrees in the Shade. (Illus.). 240p. 1983. 22.50 (ISBN 0-8173-0186-0); pap. text ed. 11.75 (ISBN 0-8173-0170-4). U of Ala Pr.

Cason, Eloise M. Mechanical Methods for Increasing the Speed of Reading: An Experimental Study at the Third Grade Level. LC 77-176693. (Columbia University. Teachers College. Contributions to Education: No. 878). Repr. of 1943 ed. 22.50 (ISBN 0-404-55878-X). AMS Pr.

Cason, H. see Lepley, William M.

Cason, H. see Ruckwick, Christian A.

Cason, J. C. Treatment of Burns. 1981. 50.50 (ISBN 0-8151-1443-5). Year Bk Med.

Cason, James & Rapoport, Henry. Laboratory Text in Organic Chemistry. 3rd ed. (Chemistry Ser). 1970. pap. 26.95 ref. ed. O.P. (ISBN 0-13-521435-1). P-H.

Cason, Mabel Earp. Spotted Boy & Commanches. LC 63-21050. (Dest Ser.). 1984. pap. 4.95 (ISBN 0-317-28327-8). Pacific Pr Pub Assn.

Casona, Alejandro. Barca Sin Pescador. Balseiro, J. A. & Owre, J., eds. (YA) (gr. 9 up). 1955. pap. 6.95x (ISBN 0-19-501984-9). Oxford U Pr.

--Corona de Amor y Muerte. Balseiro, Jose & Owre, J. Riis, eds. (Orig., Span). 1960. pap. 8.95x (ISBN 0-19-500844-8). Oxford U Pr.

--La Dama Del Alba. Rodriquez-Castellano, J., ed. 207p. (Span.). 1947. pap. text ed. 8.95 (ISBN 0-684-41194-6, ScribT). Scribner.

Casona, Alejandro & Castellano, Juan R. La Dama del Alba. 207p. 1972. pap. text ed. price not set (ISBN 0-02-325140-9, Pub. by Scribner). Macmillan.

Casoni, Frederick J. Best Wishes, Richard Nixon: The Handwriting of Richard M. Nixon. LC 82-50677. (Illus.). 64p. (Orig.). 1982. pap. 6.00 (ISBN 0-9608816-0-3). Univ Autograph.

Casoni, Jennifer. Sincerely, Lyndon: The Handwriting of Lyndon Baines Johnson. LC 83-6956. 100p. (Orig.). 1983. pap. 14.95 (ISBN 0-9608816-1-1). Univ Autograph.

Casorti. The Technic of the Bow Op. 50 for Violin. (Carl Fischer Music Library Ser.: No. L-345). (Ger. & Fr.). pap. 6.00 (ISBN 0-8258-0042-0, L-345). Fischer Inc NY.

Casotti, Fred. Colorado Football: The Golden Buffaloes. LC 80-53023. (College Sports Ser.). (Illus.). 225p. 1980. 9.95 (ISBN 0-87397-173-6). Strode.

Caspar, Franz. Die Tupari: Ein Indianerstamm in Westbrasilien. (Monographien Zur Voelkerkunde: Vol. 7). 1975. 108.00x (ISBN 3-11-003756-4). De Gruyter.

Caspar, Gerhard & Posner, Richard A. The Workload of the Supreme Court. xiii, 131p. 1976. pap. 5.00 (ISBN 0-910058-78-4). Amer Bar Assn.

Caspar, Paul, ed. Chicago Talent Source Book, 1986. (Illus.). 525p. 1986. pap. 45.00 (ISBN 0-942454-07-3). R Silver.

Caspari, jt. auth. see Schauer.

Caspari, E. W. & Ravin, A. W., eds. Genetic Organization, Vol. 1. 1969. 77.00 (ISBN 0-12-163301-2). Acad Pr.

Caspari, E. W. see Demerec, M.

Caspari, Vera. Laura. 237p. pap. cancelled (ISBN 0-88184-153-6). Carroll & Graf.

Caspary, Gerard E. Politics & Exegesis: Origen & the Two Swords. LC 77-71058. 1979. 38.50x (ISBN 0-520-03445-7). U of Cal Pr.

Caspary, Vera. Laura. 1977. Repr. of 1943 ed. lib. bdg. 16.95x (ISBN 0-89244-066-X, Pub. by Queens Hse). Amereon Ltd.

Caspary, W. F., jt. auth. see Becker, H. D.

Caspel, Venita van see Van Caspel, Venita.

Casper. Urban America: A Bibliography. 1985. lib. bdg. 34.00 (ISBN 0-8240-8815-8). Garland Pub.

Casper & Kurland, eds. Landmark Briefs & Arguments of the Supreme Court of the United States: Constituitional Law Nineteen Seventy-Seven Term Supplement, Vol. 101-105. 5000p. 1977. 290.00 (ISBN 0-89093-277-8). U Pubns Amer.

--Landmark Briefs & Arguments of the Supreme Court of the United States: Constitutional Law Nineteen Seventy-Eight Term Supplement, Vol. 106-112. 7000p. 1978. 430.00 (ISBN 0-89093-299-9). U Pubns Amer.

--Landmark Briefs & Arguments of the Supreme Court of the United States: Constitutional Law Nineteen Seventy-Nine Term Supplement, Vol. 113-119. 7000p. 1980. 430.00 (ISBN 0-89093-474-6). U Pubns Amer.

--Landmark Briefs & Arguments of the Supreme Court of the United States: Constitutional Law Nineteen Seventy-Four Term Supplement, Vol. 81-82. 2000p. 1974. 115.00 (ISBN 0-89093-130-5). U Pubns Amer.

--Landmark Briefs & Arguments of the Supreme Court of the United States: Constitutional Law 1975 Term Supplement, Vol.83-90. 8000p. 1975. 460.00 (ISBN 0-89093-131-3). U Pubns Amer.

--Landmark Briefs & Arguments of the Supreme Court of the United States: Constitutional Law Nineteen Seventy-Six Term Supplement, Vol. 91-98. 8000p. 1976. 460.00 (ISBN 0-89093-185-2). U Pubns Amer.

--Landmark Briefs & Arguments of the Supreme Court of the United States: Constitutional Law Nineteen Seventy-Seven Term Supplement, Vol. 99-100. 2000p. 1977. 115.00 (ISBN 0-89093-197-6). U Pubns Amer.

Casper & Pinchback, eds. Geothermal Scaling & Corrosion - STP 717. 268p. 1980. 29.50 (ISBN 0-8031-0705-6, 04-717000-27). ASTM.

Casper, Barry M. & Noer, Richard J. Revolutions in Physics. (Illus.). 1972. text ed. 20.95x (ISBN 0-393-09992-X); instructor's guide free (ISBN 0-393-09405-7). Norton.

Casper, Barry M. & Wellstone, Paul D. Powerline: The First Battle of America's Energy War. LC 80-25903. (Illus.). 328p. 1981. lib. bdg. 20.00x (ISBN 0-87023-320-3); pap. 9.95 (ISBN 0-87023-321-1). U of Mass Pr.

Casper, Billy & Barkow, Al. The Good Sense of Golf. 1980. 9.95 (ISBN 0-13-360511-6). P-H.

--The Good Sense of Golf. 160p. 1982. pap. 6.95 (ISBN 0-13-360529-9). P-H.

Casper, Dale E. The Community Experiences of Immigrant Minorities: A Selected Bibliography. (Public Administration Series Bibliography: P-1610). 10p. 1985. pap. 2.00 (ISBN 0-89028-260-9). Vance Biblios.

--The English Urban Environment: Recent Writings, 1980-1983. (Public Administration Ser.: Bibliography P 1643). 1985. pap. 2.00 (ISBN 0-89028-333-8). Vance Biblios.

--Equal Opportunity in the Workplace: A Checklist, 1980-1983. (Public Administration Ser.: Bibliography P 1633). 1985. pap. 2.25 (ISBN 0-89028-303-6). Vance Biblios.

--Housing & Community Development: Recent Writings, 1980-1983. (Architecture Ser.: Bibliography A 1347). 1985. pap. 2.00 (ISBN 0-89028-317-6). Vance Biblios.

--Laboring Class Movements in the United States: Historical Perspectives. (Public Administration Ser.: Bibliography P 1632). 1985. pap. 2.25 (ISBN 0-89028-302-8). Vance Biblios.

--Public Pressures & the Practice of U. S. Foreign Policy: A Checklist, 1979 to 1983. (Public Administration Ser.: Bibliography P 1645). 1985. pap. 2.00 (ISBN 0-89028-335-4). Vance Biblios.

--Spatial Distribution of Urban Populations: A Bibliography. (Public Administration Ser.: Bibliography P-1609). 15p. 1985. pap. 2.25 (ISBN 0-89028-259-5). Vance Biblios.

Casper, Gerhard & Posner, Richard A. The Workload of the Supreme Court: A Theoretical & Empirical Study. Sikes, Bette, ed. 131p. 1976. pap. 5.00 (ISBN 0-910058-78-4). Am Bar Foun.

Casper, Gerhard, jt. ed. see Kurland, Philip B.

Casper, J. American Criminal Justice: The Defendent's Perspective. 1972. pap. 3.95 (ISBN 0-13-024026-5, Spec). P-H.

Casper, John A. Stanley Donen. LC 83-2913. (Filmmakers Ser.: No. 5). 300p. 1983. 19.50 (ISBN 0-8108-1615-6). Scarecrow.

Casper, Jonathan D. Lawyers Before the Warren Court: Civil Liberties & Civil Rights, 1957-66. LC 74-186342. 1972. 12.95 (ISBN 0-252-00244-X). U of Ill Pr.

--Lawyers Before the Warren Court: Civil Liberties & Civil Rights, Nineteen-Fifty Seven to Nineteen Sixty-Six. LC 74-186342. pap. 43.90 (ISBN 0-317-07951-4, 2015029). Bks Demand UMI.

Casper, K. see Binks, Robert, et al.

Casper, Kurland, ed. Landmark Briefs & Arguments of the Supreme Court of the United States: Constitutional Law, Vols. 134-142. (Nineteen Eighty-Two Term Supplement Ser.). 1984. 650.00 (ISBN 0-89093-652-8). U Pubns Amer.

Casper, Lawrence A. & Powell, Cedric J., eds. Industrial Applications of Surface Analysis. LC 82-16290. (ACS Symposium Ser.: No. 199). 438p. 1982. lib. bdg. 54.95x (ISBN 0-8412-0735-6). Am Chemical.

Casper, Leonard. A Lion Unannounced: Twelve Stories & a Fable. LC 75-128125. (Illus.). 1971. 12.95 (ISBN 0-87074-028-8). SMU Press.

--Robert Penn Warren: The Dark & Bloody Ground. LC 71-90479. Repr. of 1960 ed. lib. bdg. 22.50x (ISBN 0-8371-2131-0, CAPW). Greenwood.

Casper, M. E. Energy-Saving Techniques for the Food Industry. LC 77-71931. (Energy Technology Rev. 13; Food Technology Rev. 42). (Illus.). 657p. 1977. 39.00 (ISBN 0-8155-0663-5). Noyes.

Casper, Max, jt. ed. see Alissi, Albert.

Casper, S. J. & Krausch, H. D. Suesswasserflora von Mitteleuropa: Pteridophyta und Antophyta, Part 1 - Lycopodiaceae bis Orchidaceae, Vol. 23. Pascher, A., et al, eds. (Illus.). 403p. (Ger.). 1980. lib. bdg. 37.00 (ISBN 0-318-00460-7). Lubrecht & Cramer.

Casper, S. Jost, ed. Lake Stachlin. (Monographiae Biologicae). 1985. lib. bdg. 95.00 (ISBN 90-6193-512-1, Pub. by Junk Pubs Netherlands). Kluwer Academic.

Casper, Ursula H. Joy & Comfort Through Stretching & Relaxing: For Those Who Are Unable to Exercise. (Illus.). 128p. (Orig.). 1982. pap. 8.95 (ISBN 0-8164-2403-9, Pub. by Seabury). Winston Pr.

Casper, W. W., jt. ed. see Charnes, A.

Caspersson, Torbjorn & Zech, Lore, eds. Chromosome Identification. 1973. 67.50 (ISBN 0-12-163550-3). Acad Pr.

Caspi, Dan. Media Decentralization: The Case of Israel's Local Newspapers. (Illus.). 150p. 1985. 19.95 (ISBN 0-88738-055-7). Transaction Bks.

Caspi, Dan, jt. ed. see Gutmann, Emanuel.

Caspi, M. M., ed. Jewish Tradition in the Diaspora: Studies in Memory of Professor Walter J. Fischel. 314p. 1981. 19.95 (ISBN 0-943376-16-5). Magnes Mus.

Caspi, Mishael M., tr. Daughters of Yemen. (Arabic.). Date not set. price not set. U of Cal Pr.

Cass. Negro Freemasonry & Segregation. 11.00 (ISBN 0-685-19494-9). Powner.

Cass, Angelcia W. Reading Power: Book 2. 126p. (Orig.). 1984. pap. 5.95 (ISBN 0-668-05969-9). Arco.

Cass, Angelica W. Reading Power: Book 1. 128p. (Orig.). 1984. pap. 5.95 (ISBN 0-668-05968-0). Arco.

--Reading Power: Book 3. 160p. (Orig.). 1984. pap. 5.95 (ISBN 0-668-05970-2). Arco.

--Reading Power: Book 4. 192p. (Orig.). 1984. pap. 5.95 (ISBN 0-668-05971-0). Arco.

Cass, Bettina & Baldock, Cora V., eds. Women, Social Welfare & the State. 220p. 1983. text ed. 30.00 (ISBN 0-86861-158-1). Allen Unwin.

Cass, Bettina, et al. Why So Few? Women Academics in Australian Universities. 253p. (Orig.). 1983. pap. 14.95x (ISBN 0-424-00095-4, Pub. by Sydney U Pr). Intl Spec Bk.

Cass, D. A. Negro Freemasonry. 9.95x (ISBN 0-685-22057-5). Wehman.

Cass, David & Shell, Karl, eds. The Hamiltonian Approach to Dynamic Economics. (Economic Theory, Econometrics, & Mathematical Economics Ser.). 1976. 33.00 (ISBN 0-12-163650-X). Acad Pr.

Cass, David B. In the Studio: The Making of Art in Nineteenth Century France. (Illus.). 48p. pap. 6.95 (ISBN 0-931102-06-5). S & F Clark Art.

Cass, David B. & Floss, Michael M. Alexandre Gabriel Decamps, 1803-1860. LC 84-50229. (Illus.). 68p. (Orig.). 1984. pap. 5.95 (ISBN 0-931102-11-1). S&F Clark Art.

Cass, David B. & Wetenhall, John. Italian Paintings 1850-1910 from Collections in the Northeastern United States. (Illus.). 83p. (Orig.). 1982. pap. 6.95 (ISBN 0-931102-10-3). S & F Clark Art.

Cass, Eugene L. & Zimmer, Frederick G., eds. Man & Work in Society. 313p. (Orig.). 1975. 17.50. Moffat Pub.

Cass, Graham. Stylistic Deficiency in the English of German Advanced Learners in Teacher Education. (Tuebinger Beitraege Zur Liguistik Ser.: TBL 227). 264p. (Orig.). 1983. pap. 24.00x (ISBN 3-87808-227-4). Benjamins North Am.

Cass, James. Education U. S. A. LC 73-8866. (Great Contemporary Issues Ser). 1973. 35.00, subscribers 35.00 (ISBN 0-405-01292-6, New York Times). Ayer Co Pubs.

Cass, James & Birnbaum, Max. Comparative Guide to American Colleges. LC 83-47529. 874p. 1983. 26.87i (ISBN 0-06-015183-8, HarpT). Har-Row.

--Comparative Guide to American Colleges. 11th ed. LC 83-47529. 784p. 1983. pap. 12.45i (ISBN 0-06-091039-9, CN1039, CN). Har-Row.

--Comparative Guide to American Colleges. 12th ed. LC 85-42557. 800p. 1985. 28.80 (ISBN 0-06-015463-2, HarpT). Har-Row.

--Comparative Guide to American Colleges. 12th ed. LC 85-42557. 800p. 1985. pap. 14.95 (ISBN 0-06-096022-1, PL). Har-Row.

Cass, James, jt. ed. see Woodring, Paul.

Cass, Jeannette. Rudiments of Music: A Detailed Study in Music Essentials. (Illus., Orig.). 1956. pap. text ed. 23.95 (ISBN 0-13-783654-6). P-H.

Cass, Joan, ed. A Book of Dragons. (Illus.). 64p. (gr. k-3). 1985. 12.95 (ISBN 0-7182-2161-3, Pub. by Kaye & Ward). David & Charles.

Cass, Joan E. The Role of the Teacher in the Nursery School. 97p. 1975. pap. text ed. 7.75 (ISBN 0-08-018281-X). Pergamon.

--The Significance of Children's Play. 1977. 14.95 (ISBN 0-7134-0689-5, Pub. by Batsford England). David & Charles.

Cass, Jules S. Laboratory Animals: An Annotated Bibliography. 1971. 23.95x (ISBN 0-02-842640-1). Hafner.

Cass, Lee H. & Anderson, Karen E. Look Like a Winner! Why, When & Where to Wear What. LC 84-15027. (Illus.). 1985. 17.95 (ISBN 0-399-12999-5, Putnam). Putnam Pub Group.

Cass, Lewis. Considerations on the Present State of the Indians, & Their Removal to the West of the Mississippi. facsimile ed. LC 75-91. (Mid-American Frontier Ser.). 1975. Repr. of 1828 ed. 13.50 (ISBN 0-405-06858-1). Ayer Co Pubs.

Cass, Loretta K. & Thomas, Carolyn B. Childhood Pathology & Later Adjustment: The Question of Prediction. LC 78-31857. (Personality Processes Ser.). 1979. 30.95 (ISBN 0-471-04553-5, Pub. by Wiley-Interscience). Wiley.

Cass, M. T. Speech Habilitation in Cerebral Palsy. 1965. Repr. of 1951 ed. 15.95x (ISBN 0-02-842630-4). Hafner.

Cass, Martin. The Pilot in Command. 220p. 1981. 35.00x (ISBN 0-906393-05-1, Pub. by Airlife England). State Mutual Bk.

Cass, Ronald. Revolution in the Wasteland. LC 81-10283. viii, 238p. 1981. 12.95x (ISBN 0-8139-0900-7). U Pr of Va.

Cass, Rosemary H., jt. auth. see Manser, Gordon.

Cassady. METAFORTH. 30.00 (ISBN 0-318-01352-5). Mountain View Pr.

--Super Bowl: Pro Football Great Games. 1985. pap. 1.95 (ISBN 0-590-31784-9). Scholastic Inc.

Cassady, Jim & Calhoun, Fryar. California White Water: A Guide to the Rivers. (Illus.). 300p. (Orig.). 1984. pap. 17.95 (ISBN 0-9613650-0-5). Cassady & Calhoun.

Cassady, John M. & Douros, John D., eds. Anticancer Agents Based on Natural Product Models. LC 79-6802. (Medicinal Chemistry Ser.). 1980. 67.50 (ISBN 0-12-163150-8). Acad Pr.

Cassady, Marsh. Playwriting Step-By-Step. 152p. 1984. pap. 8.95 (ISBN 0-89390-056-7). Resource Pubns.

Cassady, Marshall. Characters in Action: A Guide to Playwriting. 126p. (Orig.). 1984. lib. bdg. 19.50 (ISBN 0-8191-3843-6); pap. text ed. 9.25 (ISBN 0-8191-3844-4). U Pr of Amer.

Cassady, Marshall & CAssady, Par. Theatre: A View of Life. 1982p. pap. text ed. 21.95 (ISBN 0-03-050551-8). HR&W.

Cassady, Neal. The First Third & Other Writings. LC 74-88229. 1971. pap. 6.95 (ISBN 0-87286-005-1). City Lights.

CAssady, Par, jt. auth. see Cassady, Marshall.

Cassady, Ralph. Exchange by Private Treaty. LC 73-20659. (Studies in Marketing: No. 19). 1974. pap. 8.00 (ISBN 0-87755-183-9). Bureau Busn UT.

Cassady, Ralph, Jr. Auctions & Auctioneering. LC 67-25051. 1967. 27.50x (ISBN 0-520-03978-5). U of Cal Pr.

--Price Warfare in Business Competition: A Study of Abnormal Competitive Behavior. LC 63-63619. 1963. pap. 2.75 (ISBN 0-87744-054-9). Mich St U Pr.

Cassady, Ralph, Jr., jt. auth. see Waite, Warren C.

Cassady, Stephen. Spanning the Gate: Building the Golden Gate Bridge. LC 77-83284. (Illus.). 132p. 1979. 20.00 (ISBN 0-916290-06-9). Squarebooks.

Cassagneres, Ev. The Spirit of Ryan. (Illus.). 256p. 1982. pap. 11.95 (ISBN 0-8306-2333-7, 2333). TAB Bks.

Cassan, Stanley M., jt. ed. see Tashkin, Donald P.

Cassandre. Life When Jesus Was a Boy. 48p. 1981. pap. 7.95 (ISBN 0-8170-0913-2). Judson.

--Making All Things Beautiful. LC 79-10286. 1979. pap. 3.95 (ISBN 0-8170-0833-0). Judson.

Cassanea de Mondonville, Jos. Masters of the Violin, Vol 5. Banat, Gabriel, ed. 75.00 (ISBN 0-384-03185-4). Johnson Repr.

Cassanelli, Lee V. The Shaping of Somali Society: Reconstructing the History of a Pastoral People, 1600 to 1900. LC 81-43520. (Illus.). 328p. 1982. 32.50x (ISBN 0-8122-7832-1). U of Pa Pr.

Cassano, C. & Andreoli, M., eds. Current Topics in Thyroid Research. 1966. 95.00 (ISBN 0-12-163750-6). Acad Pr.

Cassar, George H. The Tragedy of Sir John French. LC 82-49302. (Illus.). 320p. 1984. 35.00 (ISBN 0-87413-241-X). U Delaware Pr.

Cassara, Ernest. Hosea Ballou: The Challenge to Orthodoxy. LC 81-40859. 236p. 1982. lib. bdg. 25.00 (ISBN 0-8191-2271-8); pap. text ed. 12.25 (ISBN 0-8191-2272-6). U Pr of Amer.

Cassara, Ernest, ed. History of the United States of America: A Guide to Information Sources. LC 73-17551. (American Studies Information Guide: Vol. 3). 1977. 60.00x (ISBN 0-8103-1266-2). Gale.

--Universalism in America. 1984. pap. 5.95 (ISBN 0-933840-21-7). Unitarian Univ.

Cassara, Ernest, ed. see Ballou, Hosea.

Cassard, Daniel W., et al. Approved Practices in Feeds & Feeding. 5th ed. LC 76-62743. (Illus.). 444p. (gr. 9-12). 1977. 18.60 (ISBN 0-8134-1901-8, 1901); text ed. 13.95x. Interstate.

Cassarino, Ray & Parrasino, Len. Chord Construction & Analysis: Elements of Jazz & Pop, Vol. 1. 1978. pap. 6.95 (ISBN 0-8256-4073-3). Music Sales.

Cassart, C. & Moirant, R. Dictionnaire du Cheval et du Chevalier. 288p. (Fr.). 1979. 49.95 (ISBN 0-686-56942-3, M-6064). French & Eur.

Cassata, Mary & Skill, Thomas. Life on Daytime Television. Voigt, Melvin J., ed. LC 84-2853. (Communication & Information Science Ser.). 272p. 1983. text ed. 34.50 (ISBN 0-89391-138-0); pap. text ed. 19.95 (ISBN 0-89391-180-1). Ablex Pub.

Cassata, Mary B. & Skill, Thomas D. Television: A Guide to the Literature. LC 83-43236. 144p. 1985. lib. bdg. 32.50 (ISBN 0-89774-140-4). Oryx Pr.

Cassata, Mary B. & Totten, Herman L., eds. The Administrative Aspects of Education for Librarianship: A Symposium. LC 75-15726. 425p. 1975. 21.00 (ISBN 0-8108-0829-3). Scarecrow.

Cassavant, Sharron G. John Middleton Murry: The Critic As Moralist. (Illus.). 173p. 1982. text ed. 18.75 (ISBN 0-8173-0107-0). U of Ala Pr.

Cassavetti, Eillen. The Lion & the Lilies: The Stuarts & France. 1977. text ed. 21.25x (ISBN 0-354-04136-3). Humanities.

Cass-Beggs, Barbara. A Musical Calender of Festivals: Folk Songs of Feast-Days & Holidays from Around the World. (Ward Lock Educational Ser.). 29.00x (ISBN 0-7062-4226-2, Pub. by Ward Lock Educational England). State Mutual Bk.

--Your Baby Needs Music. (Illus.). 144p. 1980. pap. 5.95 (ISBN 0-312-89768-5). St Martin.

Cass-Beggs, Rosemary. Penguin Book of Rounds. 1982. pap. 4.95 (ISBN 0-14-070835-9). Penguin.

Casscells, S. Ward, ed. Arthroscopy: Diagnostic & Surgical Practice. LC 83-11289. (Illus.). 192p. 1984. text ed. 40.00 (ISBN 0-8121-0888-4). Lea & Febiger.

Casse, L. R., ed. Combinatorial Mathematics X. (Lecture Notes in Mathematics: Vol. 1036). xi, 419p. 1983. pap. 20.00 (ISBN 0-387-12708-9). Springer-Verlag.

Casse, L. R., ed. see Fourth Australian Conference, University of Adelaide, 27-29 Aug. 1976.

Casse, Pierre. Training for the Cross-Cultural Mind. 2nd ed. (Illus.). 190p. 1981. pap. 15.00 (ISBN 0-933934-06-8). Soc Intercult Ed Train & Res.

--Training for the Multicultural Manager. (Illus.). 191p. 1982. pap. 15.00 (ISBN 0-933934-09-2). Soc Intercult Ed Train & Res.

Casse, Pierre & Deol, Surinda. Managing Intercultural Negotiations: Guidelines for Trainers & Negotiators. (Orig.). pap. 15.00x (ISBN 0-933934-11-4). Soc Intercult Ed Train & Res.

Cassedy, David & Shrott, Gail. William Sidney Mount: Annotated Bibliography & Listings of Archival Holdings of the Museums at Stony Brook. (Illus., Orig.). 1983. pap. 7.00 (ISBN 0-943924-05-7). Mus Stony Brook.

--William Sidney Mount: Works in the Collection of the Museums at Stony Brook. (Illus.). 96p. (Orig.). 1983. pap. 13.50 (ISBN 0-943924-06-5). Mus Stony Brook.

Cassedy, Ellen & Nussbaum, Karen. Nine to Five: The Working Woman's Guide to Office Survival. 192p. (Orig.). 1983. pap. 5.95 (ISBN 0-14-006751-5). Penguin.

Cassedy, James H. American Medicine & Statistical Thinking, 1800-1860. LC 83-12831. (Illus.). 306p. 1984. text ed. 22.50x (ISBN 0-674-02560-1). Harvard U Pr.

Cassedy, Steven, ed. & tr. Selected Essays of Andrew Bely. LC 84-23919. 380p. 1985. 35.00x (ISBN 0-520-05273-0). U of Cal pr.

Cassedy, Sylvia. Behind the Attic Wall. LC 82-45922. 320p. (gr. 3-7). 1983. 11.49i (ISBN 0-690-04336-8); PLB 11.89g (ISBN 0-690-04337-6). Crowell Jr Bks.

--Behind the Attic Wall. 320p. (gr. 4 up). 1985. pap. 2.95 (ISBN 0-380-69843-9, Camelot). Avon.

--In Your Own Words. LC 78-1237. 216p. (YA) (gr. 7 up). 1979. 8.95 (ISBN 0-385-14036-3). Doubleday.

Cassee. In the Best Interest of the Child: An Evaluation of Assessment Centers. 125p. 1982. 17.50 (ISBN 0-08-028108-7). Pergamon.

Cassee, E. & Reuland, R., eds. The Management of Hospitality. LC 82-18610. (International Series in Hospitality Management). (Illus.). 236p. 1983. 28.00 (ISBN 0-08-028107-9). Pergamon.

Cassel & Swanson. FORTRAN Made Easy. text ed. 17.95 (ISBN 0-8359-2090-9); pap. 22.95 (ISBN 0-8359-2089-5). Reston.

Cassel, C. K. & Walsh, J. R., eds. Geriatric Medicine: Vol. 1-Medical, Psychiatric & Pharmacological Topics. (Illus.). 590p. 1984. 72.50 (ISBN 0-387-90944-3). Springer Verlag.

--Geriatric Medicine: Vol. 2-Fundamentals of Geriatric Care. (Illus.). 415p. 1984. 59.50 (ISBN 0-387-90958-3). Springer Verlag.

Cassel, Christine, et al, eds. Nuclear Weapons & Nuclear War: A Source Book for Health Professionals. Abraham, Henry. LC 83-24511. 564p. 1984. 29.95 (ISBN 0-03-063872-0); pap. 12.95 (ISBN 0-03-063873-9). Praeger.

Cassel, Christine K., jt. auth. see Purtilo, Ruth B.

Cassel, Claes-Magnus, et al. Foundations of Inference in Survey Sampling. LC 77-5114. (Probability & Mathematical Statistics Ser., Probability & Statistics Section). 192p. 1977. 41.95 (ISBN 0-471-02563-1, Pub. by Wiley-Interscience). Wiley.

Cassel, Don. BASIC & Problem Solving Made Easy. 1985. pap. text ed. 18.95 (ISBN 0-8359-0402-4); tchr's. manual avail. (ISBN 0-8359-0403-2). Reston.

--BASIC Programming for the Commodore 64. 1984. 16.95 (ISBN 0-697-09912-1); incl. diskette 27.95 (ISBN 0-697-00338-8). Wm C Brown.

--BASIC 4.0 Programming for the Commodore PET-CBM. (Micropower Ser.). 224p. 1983. plastic comb 16.95 (ISBN 0-697-08265-2); incl. disk o.p. 29.95 (ISBN 0-697-09908-3). Wm C Brown.

--Computers Made Easy. 1984. text ed. 25.95 (ISBN 0-8359-0859-3); pap. text ed. 18.95 (ISBN 0-8359-0858-5). Reston.

--The dBASE II Simplified for the IBM Personal Computer. (Illus.). 176p. 1985. text ed. 22.95 (ISBN 0-13-195942-5); 14.95 (ISBN 0-13-195934-4). P-H.

--EasyWriter Simplified for the IBM Personal Computer. 208p. 1984. text ed. 21.95 (ISBN 0-13-222449-6); pap. text ed. 12.95 (ISBN 0-13-222431-3). P-H.

--Graphics, Sound, & Music for the Commodore 64. (Microcomputer Power Ser.). 140p. 1984. deluxe ed. 27.95 plastic comb bdg. (ISBN 0-697-00422-8); pap. 15.95 (ISBN 0-697-00423-6); incl. diskette 27.95. Wm C Brown.

--Lotus 1-2-3 Simplified for the IBM Personal Computer. (Illus.). 208p. 1985. pap. 14.95 (ISBN 0-13-541012-6). P-H.

--Programming Language One: A Structural Approach with PLC. 1978. pap. 19.95 (ISBN 0-87909-650-0). Reston.

--The Structured Alternative: Programming Style, Debugging & Verification. 1982. text ed. 25.95 (ISBN 0-8359-7084-1); solutions manual avail. free (ISBN 0-8359-7085-X). Reston.

--WordStar Simplified for the IBM Personal Computer. (Illus.). 160p. 1984. text ed. 22.95 (ISBN 0-13-963620-X); pap. text ed. 12.95 (ISBN 0-13-963612-9). P-H.

--WordStar Simplified with WordStar 3.3: MailMerge, Spellstar & StarIndex. 176p. 1985. text ed. 22.95 (ISBN 0-13-963646-3); 14.95 (ISBN 0-13-963638-2). P-H.

Cassel, Don & Jackson, Martin. Introduction to Computers & Information Processing: Language Edition. 1981. pap. text ed. 23.95 (ISBN 0-8359-3150-1). Reston.

Cassel, Gustav. Downfall of the Gold Standard. 262p. 1966. 30.00x (ISBN 0-7146-1213-8, F Cass Co). Biblio Dist.

--Economic Essays in Honour of Gustav Cassel: October 20, 1933. 720p. 1967. 47.50x (ISBN 0-7146-1214-6, F Cass Co). Biblio Dist.

--Foreign Investments. Wilkins, Mira, ed. LC 78-3902. (International Finance Ser.). 1978. Repr. of 1928 ed. lib. bdg. 20.00x (ISBN 0-405-11207-6). Ayer Co Pubs.

--Fundamental Thoughts in Economics. LC 71-137933. (Economic Thought, History & Challenge Ser.). 1971. Repr. of 1925 ed. 20.50x (ISBN 0-8046-1438-5, Pub. by Kennikat). Assoc Faculty Pr.

--Money & Foreign Exchange After 1914. LC 72-4266. (World Affairs Ser.: National & International Viewpoints). 294p. 1972. Repr. of 1922 ed. 19.00 (ISBN 0-405-04563-8). Ayer Co Pubs.

--Nature & Necessity of Interest. LC 77-147898. Repr. of 1903 ed. 22.50x (ISBN 0-678-00848-5). Kelley.

--Theory of Social Economy. rev. ed. Barron, S. L., tr. LC 67-19584. Repr. of 1932 ed. 47.50x (ISBN 0-678-00241-X). Kelley.

Cassel, J., et al. Education & Training of Engineers for Environmental Health. 152p. 1970. 8.00 (ISBN 92-4-156004-5, 526). World Health.

Cassel, John C., jt. auth. see Kaplan, Berton H.

Cassel, Russell N. Drug Abuse Education. 1970. 8.95 (ISBN 0-8158-0245-5). Chris Mass.

Cassel, Russell N. & Heichberger, Robert L., eds. Leadership Development: Theory & Practice. 352p. 1975. 9.75 (ISBN 0-8158-0319-2). Chris Mass.

Cassell. Cassell's Colloquials, 4 bks. Incl. French. 160p. pap. 4.95 (ISBN 0-02-079420-7); German. 176p. pap. 3.95 (ISBN 0-02-079410-X); Spanish. 304p. pap. 4.95 (ISBN 0-02-079430-4); Italian. 192p. pap. 3.95 (ISBN 0-02-079440-1). 1981. pap. Macmillan.

--Cassell's New Dutch Dictionary: English-Dutch, Dutch-English. 729p. (Eng. & Dutch.). 1982. 34.95 (ISBN 0-02-522940-0). Macmillan.

Cassell, Abayomi. Liberia: History of the First African Republic, 2 vols. 1985. Vol. 1. 34.50x (ISBN 0-8290-1307-5); Vol. 2. 34.50x (ISBN 0-8290-1308-3). Irvington.

--Liberia: History of the First African Republic, Vol. 1. (Illus.). 457p. 15.00 (ISBN 0-685-41741-7). Fountainhead.

Cassell & the Publishers Association, ed. Directory of Publishing in Great Britain, the Commonwealth, Ireland, Pakistan, & South Africa. 448p. 1983. pap. 35.00 (ISBN 0-304-30913-3). Bradford Mtn Bk.

Cassell, Anthony K. Dante's Fearful Art of Justice. 224p. 1984. 20.00x (ISBN 0-8020-2504-8). U of Toronto Pr.

Cassell, Anthony K., ed. & tr. see Boccaccio, Giovanni.

Cassell, Carol. Swept Away: Why Women Confuse Love & Sex... & How They Can Have Both. 1985. pap. 3.95 (ISBN 0-317-19771-1). Bantam.

--Swept Away: Why Women Fear their Own Sexuality. 224p. 1984. 14.95 (ISBN 0-671-45238-X). S&S.

Cassell, Christine. Teaching Poor Readers in the Secondary School. (Special Education Ser.). (Illus.). 72p. 1982. pap. 13.00 (ISBN 0-7099-0294-8, Pub. by Croom Helm Ltd). Longwood Pub Group.

Cassell, Clark, ed. President Reagan's Quotations: A Collection by Braddock Publications. (Illus.). 181p. 1984. 14.95x (ISBN 0-931147-00-X); pap. 2.95x (ISBN 0-931147-01-8). Braddock Pubns.

--The President's Point of View: Ronald Reagan Speaks. (Illus.). 181p. 1985. 14.95x (ISBN 0-931147-06-9). Braddock Pubns.

Cassell, Dana K. Guide to Florida Writers, 1985-86. 1985. write for info. Cassell Commun Inc.

--How to Advertise & Promote Your Retail Store. LC 83-45209. 224p. 1983. 25.95 (ISBN 0-8144-5775-4). AMACOM.

--How to Advertise & Promote Your Retail Store. 202p. 1985. pap. 14.95 (ISBN 0-8144-7637-6). AMACOM.

--Making Money with Your Home Computer. 128p. 1984. pap. 5.95 (ISBN 0-396-08448-6). Dodd.

Cassell, Dana K., ed. Directory of Florida Markets for Writers. 96p. 1985. 12.95. Cassell Commun Inc.

Cassell, Douglas. Microcomputer & Modern Control Engineering. 1983. text ed. 31.95 (ISBN 0-8359-4365-8). Reston.

Cassell, Douglas A. Introduction to Computer-Aided Manufacturing in Electronics. LC 73-177882. 248p. 1972. 21.50 (ISBN 0-471-14053-8, Pub. by Wiley). Krieger.

Cassell, Eric & Siegler, Mark, eds. Changing Values in Medicine. 275p. 1984. 24.00x (ISBN 0-89093-574-2). U Pubns Amer.

Cassell, Eric J. The Healer's Art. 240p. 1985. pap. 7.95 (ISBN 0-262-53062-7). MIT Pr.

--The Place of the Humanities in Medicine. 1984. 7.00 (ISBN 0-317-07448-2). Inst Soc Ethics.

--Talking with Patients, Vol. 1: The Theory of Doctor-Patient Communication. (Illus.). 215p. 1985. text ed. 20.00x (ISBN 0-262-03111-6); pap. text ed. 9.95 (ISBN 0-262-53055-4). MIT Pr.

--Talking with Patients, Vol. 2: Clinical Technique. 215p. 1985. text ed. 20.00x (ISBN 0-262-03112-4); pap. text ed. 9.95x (ISBN 0-262-53056-2). MIT Pr.

Cassell, Frank A. Merchant Congressman in the Young Republic: Samuel Smith of Maryland, 1752-1839. LC 79-157390. (Illus.). 298p. 1971. 30.00x (ISBN 0-299-06000-4). U of Wis Pr.

Cassell, Frank H. Public Employment Service: Organization in Change. LC 68-27448. (Orig.). 1968. pap. 4.50x (ISBN 0-87736-310-2). U of Mich Inst Labor.

Cassell, Jack L. Rehabilitation Caseload Management. LC 85-3385. 350p. 1985. pap. text ed. 18.00 (ISBN 0-936104-67-8). Pro Ed.

Cassell, Phyllis, jt. ed. see McCoy, Vivian.

Cassell, Richard A. Ford Madox Ford: A Study of His Novels. LC 76-57731. 1977. Repr. of 1962 ed. lib. bdg. 24.75x (ISBN 0-8371-9465-2, CAFF). Greenwood.

Cassells, et al. Cassell's Italian Dictionary: Italian-English, English-Italian. LC 77-7405. (Ital. & Eng.). 1977. thumb indexed 23.95 (ISBN 0-02-522540-5); standard 19.95 (ISBN 0-02-522530-8). Macmillan.

Cassells, Cyrus. The Mud Actor. LC 81-13450. (National Poetry Ser.). 104p. (Orig.). 1982. 14.50 (ISBN 0-03-061371-X); pap. 7.95 (ISBN 0-03-061369-8, Owl Bks). HR&W.

Cassells, E. Steve. Archaeology of Colorado. LC 83-82868. (Illus.). 330p. 1983. 22.95 (ISBN 0-933472-76-5); pap. 14.95. Johnson Bks.

Casselman, Barry. Language, a Magical Enterprise, the Body. (Paperplay Ser. Mini-Bks.: Vol. 7). (Illus.). 16p. 1978. saddle-stitched 2.50 (ISBN 0-939044-13-7). Lingua Pr.

Casselman, Karen L. The Craft of the Dyer: Color from Plants & Lichens of the North East. 1980. 30.00 (ISBN 0-8020-2362-2). U of Toronto Pr.

Casselman, Lucy. Thanos Island. 1978. pap. 1.75 (ISBN 0-532-17192-6). Woodhill.

Cassels, Alan. Fascism. LC 73-13716. (Illus.). 1975. pap. 15.95x (ISBN 0-88295-718-X). Harlan Davidson.

--Fascist Italy. LC 68-9740. (Europe Since 1500Ser.). (Illus.). 1968. pap. 7.95x (ISBN 0-88295-719-8). Harlan Davidson.

--Fascist Italy: Europe since 1500. 2nd, rev. ed. 160p. 1985. pap. text ed. 8.95 (ISBN 0-88295-828-3). Harlan Davidson.

--Italian Foreign Policy, Nineteen Eighteen to Nineteen Forty-Five: A Guide to Research & Research Materials. Kimmich, Christoph M., ed. LC 80-53890. 275p. 1982. lib. bdg. 20.00 (ISBN 0-8420-2177-9). Scholarly Res Inc.

Cassels, Bruce K., tr. see Breitmaier, Eberhard & Bauer, Gerhard.

Cassels, Donald E. The Ductus Arteriosus. (Illus.). 356p. 1973. photocopy ed. 37.50x (ISBN 0-398-02720-X). C C Thomas.

Cassels, Donald E., ed. Heart & Circulation in the Newborn & Infant: A Symposium. LC 66-12966. (Illus.). 440p. 1966. 58.00 (ISBN 0-8089-0096-X, 790812). Grune.

Cassels, Donald E. & Ziegler, Robert, eds. Electrocardiography in Infants & Children: A Symposium. LC 65-25510. (Illus.). 376p. 1966. 87.50 (ISBN 0-8089-0095-1, 790810). Grune.

Cassels, J. M. Basic Quantum Mechanics. 2nd ed. (Illus.). 206p. 1982. pap. text ed. 17.00x (ISBN 0-333-31768-8). Scholium Intl.

Cassels, J. W. Economics for Mathematicians. LC 81-15461. (London Mathematical Society Lecture Note Ser.: No. 62). 150p. 1982. pap. 16.95 (ISBN 0-521-28614-X). Cambridge U Pr.

--Introduction to Diophantine Approximation. (Cambridge Tracts Ser.: No. 45). 1972. Repr. of 1957 ed. 9.95x (ISBN 0-02-842650-9). Hafner.

--Introduction to the Geometry of Numbers. 2nd ed. LC 75-154801. (Grundlehren der Mathematischen Wissenschaften: Vol. 99). (Illus.). 1971. 47.00 (ISBN 0-387-02397-6). Springer-Verlag.

--Local Fields. (London Mathematical Society Student Texts: No. 3). 200p. Date not set. price not set (ISBN 0-521-30484-9); pap. price not set (ISBN 0-521-31525-5). Cambridge U Pr.

--Rational Quadratic Forms. (London Mathematical Society Monograph). 1979. 70.00 (ISBN 0-12-163260-1). Acad Pr.

Cassels, J. W., ed. see Littlewood, J. E.

Cassels, John M. A Study of Fluid Milk Prices. LC 75-39237. (Getting & Spending: the Consumer's Dilemma). (Illus.). 1976. Repr. of 1937 ed. 26.50x (ISBN 0-405-08014-X). Ayer Co Pubs.

Cassels, Lavender. The Archduke & the Assassin: Sarajevo, June 28, 1914. LC 84-40709. 248p. 1985. 19.95 (ISBN 0-8128-3021-0). Stein & Day.

Cassels, Louis. Christian Primer. 112p. 1981. pap. 1.50 (ISBN 0-88028-012-3). Forward Movement.

--The Reality of God. LC 71-150879. 128p. (YA) 1972. pap. 0.95 (ISBN 0-8361-1681-X). Herald Pr.

--The Reality of God. LC 71-150879. 128p. 1972. pap. 0.95 (ISBN 0-8361-1681-X). Herald Hse.

Cassem, jt. auth. see Hackett.

Cassem, Ned H., jt. auth. see Hackett, Thomas P.

Cassen, R. H. India: Population, Economy, Society. LC 77-16217. 419p. 1978. text ed. 45.00x (ISBN 0-8419-0300-X); pap. text ed. 19.50x (ISBN 0-8419-0648-3). Holmes & Meier.

Cassen, Robert & Jolly, Richard, eds. Rich Country Interests & Third World Development. LC 81-42561. 1982. 35.00 (ISBN 0-312-68101-1). St Martin.

Cassen, Thomas. Chemistry Laboratory Manual for Nurses. 1983. Paladin Hse.

--Chemistry 101 L Lab Manual. 1981. coil binding 15.95 (ISBN 0-88252-092-X). Paladin Hse.

Casseres, Benjamin De see De Casseres, Benjamin.

Casserley, J. V. Langmead. No Faith of My Own & Graceful Reason: The Contribution of Reason to Theology. 408p. 1984. pap. text ed. 16.75 (ISBN 0-8191-3793-6). U Pr of Amer.

Casserly, jt. auth. see Johnston.

Casserly, H. C. British Locomotive Names of the 20th Century. 25.00x (ISBN 0-392-07681-0, SpS). Sportshelf.

Casserly, H. C. & Dorman, C. C. Railway History in Pictures: The Midlands. LC 78-77871. (Illus.). 1969. 17.95x (ISBN 0-678-05557-2). Kelley.

Casserly, John J. The Ford White House: The Diary of a Speechwriter. LC 77-82185. (Illus.). 1977. 15.00 (ISBN 0-87081-106-1). Colo Assoc.

Casserly, Michael D., et al. School Vandalism: Strategies for Prevention. LC 80-8118. 1980. 23.00x (ISBN 0-669-03956-X). Lexington Bks.

Cassese, A. Parliamentary Control Over Foreign Policy. 216p. 1980. 32.50x (ISBN 90-286-0019-1). Sijthoff & Noordhoff.

Cassese, A., ed. U. N. Law-Fundamental Rights: Two Topics in International Law. 268p. 1979. 38.00x (ISBN 90-286-0828-1). Sijthoff & Noordhoff.

Cassesse, Antonio. Control of Foreign Policy in Western Democracies: Comparative Study of Parliamentary Foreign Affairs Committees, 3 vols. 1983. lib. bdg. 20.00 ea.; Set. lib. bdg. 60.00 (ISBN 0-379-20040-6). Vol. 1; Parliamentary Foreign Affairs Committees: The National Setting, 381 pgs. Vol. 2; The Transnational Setting: The European Parliament & Its Foreign Affairs Committee, 161pgs (ISBN 0-379-20041-4). Vol. 3; The Impart on Foreign Affairs Committee on Foreign Policy 142 pgs (ISBN 0-379-20042-2). Oceana.

Cassetty, Judith. Standards for Child-Support Payments: Intra-Family Transfers. LC 81-47441. write for info. (ISBN 0-669-04592-6). Lexington Bks.

Cassetty, Judith, ed. The Parental Child-Support Obligation: Research, Practice, & Social Policy. LC 81-48464. 320p. 1982. 31.50x (ISBN 0-669-05376-7). Lexington Bks.

Cassian, St. John. Teachings of St. John Cassian. pap. 4.95 (ISBN 0-686-05665-5). Eastern Orthodox.

Cassian, Nina. Blue Apple. Barkan, Stanley H., ed. Feiler, Eva, tr. (Cross-Cultural Review Chapbook 13: Romanian Poetry 1). 16p. (Romanian & Eng.). 1981. pap. 2.00 (ISBN 0-89304-812-7). Cross Cult.

Cassianus, Joannes. De Institutis Coenobiorum et De Octo Principalium Remediis Libri Xii: De Incarnatione Domini Contra Nestorium Libri Vii, Bk. 12. (Corpus Scriptorum Ecclesiasticorum Latinorum Ser: Vol. 17). (Cat). 1888. 50.00 (ISBN 0-384-07850-8). Johnson Repr.

--Spiritual Life, a Guide for Those Seeking Perfection. 1977. pap. 4.95 (ISBN 0-686-19234-6). Eastern Orthodox.

Cassianus, Johannes. Opera, Pt. 2. Petschenig, M., ed. (Corpus Scriptorum Ecclesiasticorum Latinorum Ser: Vol. 13). 1886. 50.00 (ISBN 0-384-07860-5). Johnson Repr.

Cassiday, Bruce. Dinah! 1980. pap. 2.50 (ISBN 0-425-04675-3). Berkley Pub.

Cassiday, Bruce, ed. Roots of Detection: The Art of Deduction before Sherlock Holmes. (Recognitions). 225p. 1983. 12.95 (ISBN 0-8044-2113-7); pap. 6.95 (ISBN 0-8044-6065-5). Ungar.

Cassiday, Joan, jt. auth. see Hotchkiss, John F.

Cassidy. Thermally Stable Polymers. 392p. 1980. 65.00 (ISBN 0-8247-6969-4). Dekker.

Cassidy, jt. auth. see Robertson.

Cassidy, Bruce, jt. auth. see Takahashi, Yoko I.

Cassidy, Daniel J. & Alves, Michael J., eds. The Scholarship Book: The Complete Guide to Private Sector Scholarships, Grants, & Loans for Undergraduates. LC 84-11683. 391p. 1984. 29.95 (ISBN 0-13-792342-2, Busn); pap. 14.95 (ISBN 0-13-792334-1). P-H.

Cassidy, David, jt. ed. see Baker-Cassidy, Martha.

Cassidy, Diane. Circus Animals. 10/1985 ed. (Lift-the-Flap Bks.). (Illus.). (ps up). pap. 6.95 (ISBN 0-316-13241-1). Little.

--Circus People. (Lift-the-Flap Bks.). (Illus.). (ps up). 1985. pap. 6.95 (ISBN 0-316-13243-8). Little.

Cassidy, F. G. The Place-Names of Dane County, Wisconsin. (Publications of the American Dialect Society Ser., No. 7). 255p. 1947. pap. 8.25 (ISBN 0-8173-0607-2). U of Ala Pr.

Cassidy, F. G. & Duckert, A. R. A Method for Collecting Dialect. (Publications of the American Dialect Society: No. 20). 96p. 1970. pap. 2.75 (ISBN 0-8173-0620-X). U of Ala Pr.

Cassidy, F. J. & Ringler, R. Bright's Old English Grammar. 3rd ed. LC 76-179921. 1972. text ed. 24.95 (ISBN 0-03-084713-3, HoltC). HR&W.

Cassidy, Frederic G. The ADS Dictionary - How Soon? Bd. with The Linguistic Atlas of New England Revisited. (Publications of the American Dialect Society: No. 39). 27p. 1963. pap. 1.40 (ISBN 0-8173-0639-0). U of Ala Pr.

Cassidy, Frederic G; see Reed, Carroll E.

Cassidy, Frederic G; see Wood, Gordon R.

Cassidy, Frederic G., ed. Dictionary of American Regional English, Vol. 1 A-C. (Illus.). 1056p. 1985. 60.00 (ISBN 0-674-20511-1, Belknap Pr); pre-Jan 1986 49.95 (ISBN 0-317-20044-5). Harvard U Pr.

Cassidy, Frederick G. & Le Page, R. B., eds. Dictionary of Jamaican English. 2nd ed. LC 78-17799. 1980. 95.00 (ISBN 0-521-22165-X). Cambridge U Pr.

Cassidy, G. E. & Linnegar, S. Growing Irises. (Illus.). 160p. 1982. 16.95 (ISBN 0-917304-42-X). Timber.

Cassidy, George. King of the Mountain. 1980. pap. 1.75 (ISBN 0-8439-0717-7, Leisure Bks). Dorchester Pub Co.

Cassidy, Harold G. Science Restated: Physics & Chemistry for the Non-Scientist. LC 72-119371. (Illus.). 538p. 1970. text ed. 12.00x (ISBN 0-87735-007-8). Freeman Cooper.

Cassidy, Harold G., jt. auth. see Haskell, Edward F.

Cassidy, Henry J. Using Econometrics: A Beginner's Guide. 1981. text ed. 26.95 (ISBN 0-8359-8135-5); instr's. manual free (ISBN 0-8359-8136-3). Reston.

Cassidy, Hope & Flaherty, Linda. Caring Relationships: Guide for Families of Nursing Home Residents. 24p. (Orig.). 1982. pap. 1.75 (ISBN 0-8066-1966-X, 10-0969). Augsburg.

Cassidy, J. J., jt. auth. see Hjelmfelt, A. T., Jr.

Cassidy, Jack. Winning at Poker & Games of Chance. 1977. pap. 3.00 (ISBN 0-915596-20-2). West Coast.

Cassidy, Jack, et al. A Shortcut Through Adventureland. (Illus.). 168p. (gr. 6-12). 1984. pap. 9.95 (ISBN 0-88190-317-5, BO317). Datamost.

--Shortcut Through Adventureland, Vol. I. Date not set. price not set. P-H.

Cassidy, James A. Study of Browning's Ring & the Book. LC 74-117581. (Studies in Browning, No. 4). 1970. Repr. of 1924 ed. lib. bdg. 39.95x (ISBN 0-8383-1014-1). Haskell.

Cassidy, James T. Textbook of Pediatric Rheumatology. LC 82-4951. 684p. 1982. 55.00 (ISBN 0-471-09925-2, Pub. by Wiley Med). Wiley.

Cassidy, Joan H., jt. auth. see Hotchkiss, John F.

Cassidy, John. The Aerobie Book. (Illus., Orig.). 1985. pap. 12.95 (ISBN 0-932592-11-2). Klutz Pr.

--The Boomerang Book. (Illus.). 64p. (Orig.). 1985. pap. 12.95 (ISBN 0-932592-07-4). Klutz Pr.

--The Hacky Sack Book. 80p. 1982. pap. 9.95 (ISBN 0-932592-05-8). Klutz Pr.

--Knots: For Squares & Others. (Illus.). 12p. (Orig.). 1985. pap. 6.95 (ISBN 0-932592-10-4). Klutz Pr.

--Paperwings: The Book of Excellent Paper Airplanes. 96p. 1984. pap. cancelled (ISBN 0-932592-09-0). Klutz Pr.

--Pumping Plastic: The Jump Rope Fitness Plan. (Illus.). 96p. (Orig.). 1983. pap. 9.95 (ISBN 0-932592-06-6). Klutz Pr.

--A Station in the Delta. 320p. 1981. pap. 2.50 (ISBN 0-345-28846-7). Ballantine.

Cassidy, John & Rimbeaux, B. C. Juggling for the Complete Klutz. 2nd ed. (Illus.). 1980. pap. 9.95 (ISBN 0-932592-00-7). Klutz Pr.

Cassidy, Jude, jt. ed. see Spears, Ross.

Cassidy, Jules, jt. auth. see Stewart-Park, Angela.

Cassidy, Laurence L. Existence & Presence: The Dialectics of Divinity. LC 80-5881. 246p. 1981. lib. bdg. 21.75 (ISBN 0-8191-1486-3); pap. text ed. 11.75 (ISBN 0-8191-1487-1). U Pr of Amer.

Cassidy, Michael. Bursting the Wineskins: Spiritual Odyssey of a Peacemaker. 280p. 1983. pap. 6.95 (ISBN 0-87788-094-8). Shaw Pubs.

Cassidy, Norma C. Favorite Novenas & Prayers. LC 72-91456. 144p. 1972. pap. 2.95 (ISBN 0-8091-1761-4, Deus). Paulist Pr.

Cassidy, Pat & Close, Jim. BASIC Computer Programming for Kids. (Illus.). 192p. 1984. 17.95 (ISBN 0-13-057927-0, Spec); pap. 11.95 (ISBN 0-13-057919-X). P-H.

--Kids, BASIC & the Coleco Adam. (Illus.). 200p. 1984. 17.95 (ISBN 0-13-515446-4); pap. 11.95 (ISBN 0-13-515438-3). P-H.

--Kids, BASIC & the Coleco Adam. (Illus.). 200p. 11.95 (ISBN 0-317-13077-3). P-H.

--Kids, BASIC & the PCjr. 200p. 1984. 17.95 (ISBN 0-13-515461-8); pap. 11.95 (ISBN 0-13-515453-7). P-H.

Cassidy, Richard J. Jesus. Politics, & Society: A Study of Luke's Gospel. LC 78-735. 238p. (Orig.). 1978. 15.95 (ISBN 0-88344-238-8); pap. 7.95 (ISBN 0-88344-237-X). Orbis Bks.

Cassidy, Richard J. & Scharper, Philip J., eds. Political Issues in Luke-Acts. LC 82-19060. 192p. (Orig.). 1983. 16.95 (ISBN 0-88344-390-2); pap. 9.95 (ISBN 0-88344-385-6). Orbis Bks.

Cassidy, Robert. Margaret Mead: A Voice for the Century. LC 81-43435. 176p. 1982. 12.50x (ISBN 0-87663-376-9). Universe.

--Margaret Mead: A Voice for the Century. LC 81-4335. 176p. 1984. pap. 7.95 (ISBN 0-87663-850-7). Universe.

--Margaret Mead: A Voice for the Century. large print ed. LC 84-98. 309p. 1984. Repr. of 1982 ed. 14.95 (ISBN 0-89621-526-1). Thorndike Pr.

Cassidy, S. Current problems In Pediatrics, Prader Willis Syndrome. 55p. 7.50 (ISBN 0-318-17738-2); members 6.00 (ISBN 0-318-17739-0). Prader-Willi.

Cassidy, Samuel M., ed. Elements of Practical Coal Mining. LC 72-86921. pap. 155.50 (ISBN 0-317-29750-3, 2017419). Bks Demand UMI.

Cassidy, Sheila A. A Prayer for Pilgrims: A Book About Prayer for Ordinary People. (The Crossroad Paperback Ser.). 192p. 1982. pap. 6.95 (ISBN 0-8245-0420-8). Crossroad NY.

Cassidy, Vincent & Simpson, Amos. Traveling Man: The Life Story of Henry Watkins Allen. 1967. 4.50 (ISBN 0-87511-017-7). Claitors.

Cassidy, William. Memorial of William Cassidy. LC 73-125684. (American Journalists Ser). 1970. Repr. of 1874 ed. 17.00 (ISBN 0-405-01661-1). Ayer Co Pubs.

Cassidy, William L. Knife Digest: Second Edition. 2nd ed. (Illus.). 178p. 1976. pap. 12.95 (ISBN 0-87364-059-4). Paladin Pr.

--Political Kidnapping. 70p. 1978. pap. 6.00 (ISBN 0-87364-141-8). Paladin Pr.

--Quick or Dead. (Illus.). 160p. 1978. 12.95 (ISBN 0-87364-148-5). Paladin Pr.

Cassidy, William L., ed. Official History of the Office of Strategic Services Schools & Training Branch. 216p. 1984. 45.00x (ISBN 0-86695-036-2). Interserv Pub.

Cassidy-Brinn, Ginny, jt. auth. see Federation of Feminist Women's Health Centers Staff.

Cassie, Dhyan. Auditory Training Handbook for Good Listeners. LC 75-26439. 1976. pap. text ed. 3.25x (ISBN 0-8134-1762-7, 1762). Interstate.

--So Who's Perfect! LC 84-12948. 248p. (Orig.). 1984. pap. 12.95 (ISBN 0-8361-3372-2). Herald Pr.

Cassie, Dyan. The Three Bears & Other Plays. LC 76-48596. 1977. pap. text ed. 2.95x (ISBN 0-8134-1886-0, 1886). Interstate.

Cassie, W. F. Structural Analysis: The Solution of Statically Indeterminate Structures. 3rd ed. LC 67-72611. pap. 73.80 (ISBN 0-317-11039-X, 2004914). Bks Demand UMI.

Cassie, W. F., jt. auth. see Capper, P. L.

Cassie, W. Fisher. Statics, Structure & Stress: A Teaching Text for Problem-Solving in Theory of Structures & Strength of Materials. LC 74-158981. (Longman Text Ser.). pap. 141.30 (ISBN 0-317-09285-5, 2016309). Bks Demand UMI.

Cassiers, Juan. The Hazards of Peace: A European View of Detente. (Harvard Studies in International Affairs: No. 34). 94p. 1984. pap. text ed. 7.25 (ISBN 0-8191-4019-8). U Pr of Amer.

Cassil, John F. Here's Europe. LC 83-80973. 1984. pap. 6.95 (ISBN 0-86666-106-9). Natl Lit Guild.

Cassileth, Barrie R., ed. The Cancer Patient: Social & Medical Aspects of Care. LC 79-11338. (Illus.). 332p. 1979. pap. 12.50 (ISBN 0-8121-0672-5). Lea & Febiger.

Cassileth, Barrie R. & Cassileth, Peter A., eds. Clinical Care of the Terminal Cancer Patient. LC 82-15222. 274p. 1982. text ed. 24.00 (ISBN 0-8121-0854-X). Lea & Febiger.

Cassileth, P. A., jt. auth. see Webster, G. D.

Cassileth, Peter, et al. Practical Approaches to Hematology-Oncology. (Practical Points Ser.). 1982. pap. text ed. 30.95 (ISBN 0-87488-717-8). Med Exam.

Cassileth, Peter A., jt. ed. see Cassileth, Barrie R.

Cassilis, Robert. Winding Sheet. 222p. 1980. 16.95 (ISBN 0-241-89863-3, Pub. by Hamish Hamilton England). David & Charles.

Cassill, Kay. The Complete Handbook for Freelance Writers. LC 81-254. 400p. 1981. 14.95 (ISBN 0-89879-044-1). Writers Digest.

--Twins: Nature's Amazing Mystery. LC 81-69126. 336p. 1984. pap. 7.95 (ISBN 0-689-70663-4, 305). Atheneum.

Cassill, R. V. After Goliath. LC 84-16225. 224p. 1985. 14.95 (ISBN 0-89919-325-0). Ticknor & Fields.

--Flame. LC 80-66505. 1980. 11.95 (ISBN 0-87795-280-9). Arbor Hse.

--Labors of Love. LC 79-56020. 1980. 10.95 (ISBN 0-87795-261-2). Arbor Hse.

--Norton Anthology of Short Fiction. 3rd ed. 1986. pap. text ed. price not set complete ed.; pap. text ed. price not set shorter ed.; instr.'s. handbook avail. (ISBN 0-393-95482-X). Norton.

--Three Stories. LC 82-82012. 75p. (Orig.). 1982. pap. 4.50 (ISBN 0-9605008-1-2). Hermes Hse.

--Writing Fiction. 2nd ed. 192p. 1975. pap. 4.95 (ISBN 0-13-970103-6, Spec). P-H.

Cassill, R. V., ed. The Norton Anthology of Short Fiction. 2nd. ed. 1981. text ed. 13.95x (ISBN 0-393-95178-2); shorter ed. 12.95x (ISBN 0-393-95182-0); instrs. handbook 3.95x (ISBN 0-393-95186-3). Norton.

--The Norton Anthology of Short Fiction. 1472p. 1977. pap. text ed. 8.95x shorter edition (ISBN 0-393-09075-2); instr.'s handbook 2.50x (ISBN 0-393-09050-7). Norton.

Cassill, Ronald V. The Happy Marriage & Other Stories. LC 66-63480. 122p. 1966. 3.50 (ISBN 0-911198-11-3). Purdue U Pr.

Cassimati, Nina. Travelaid Guide to East Africa. 2nd ed. (Illus.). 191p. 1985. pap. 9.95 (ISBN 0-317-14674-2, Pub. by Travelaid England). Hippocrene Bks.

Cassin, Barbara & Solomon, Sheila. Dictionary of Eye Terminology. (Illus., Orig.). 1984. 14.95x (ISBN 0-937404-07-1). Triad Pub FL.

Cassin, Elena. La Splendeur Divine: Introduction a L'etude De la Mentalite Mesopotamienne. (Civilisations et Societes: No. 8). pap. 18.40x (ISBN 90-2796-077-1). Mouton.

Cassin, Elena & Glassner, Jean-Jacques. Anthroponymie et Anthropologie De Nuzi. 187p. (Fr.). 1977. 40.00x (ISBN 0-89003-024-3). Undena Pubns.

Cassin, John. United States Exploring Expedition During the Years 1838, 1839, 1840, 1841, 1842 Under the Command Charles Wilkes, U.S.N, 2 vols, Vol. 8. Sterling, Keir B., ed. LC 77-81079. (Biologists & Their World Ser.). (Illus.). 1978. Repr. of 1858 ed. lib. bdg. 48.00x (ISBN 0-405-10656-4). Ayer Co Pubs.

Cassin, Maxine. A Touch of Recognition. LC 72-179825. (New Poetry Ser.). Repr. of 1962 ed. 16.00 (ISBN 0-404-56025-3). AMS Pr.

Cassin, Maxine, ed. see Black, Charles.

Cassin, Maxine, ed. see McFerren, Martha.

Cassin, Maxine, ed. see Maddox, Everette.

Cassin, Maxine, ed. see Miller, Vassar.

Cassin, Maxine, et al, eds. The Maple Leaf Rag: An Anthology of New Orleans Poetry. 116p. (Orig.). 1980. pap. 4.95x (ISBN 0-938498-01-0). New Orleans Poetry.

Cassin, Riccardo. Fifty Years of Alpinism. Sottile, Renato, tr. LC 81-84329. (Illus.). 288p. 1982. 17.50 (ISBN 0-89886-060-1). Mountaineers.

Cassina, Edward B. & Cassina, Shirley E. Dicky: A True Story of a California Valley Quail. LC 84-90003. (Illus.). (gr. 1 up). 1985. 7.95 (ISBN 0-533-06099-0). Vantage.

Cassina, Shirley E., jt. auth. see Cassina, Edward B.

Cassinari, Valentino & Pagni, Carlo A. Central Pain: A Neurosurgical Survey. LC 68-54017. (Illus.). 1969. text ed. 10.00x (ISBN 0-674-10540-0). Harvard U Pr.

Cassinelli, C. W. Total Revolution: A Comparative Study of Germany under Hitler, the Soviet Union Under Stalin, & China Under Mao. LC 76-10302. (Studies in International & Comparative Politics: No. 10). 252p. 1976. pap. 11.75 (ISBN 0-87436-228-8); pap. 11.75 o. p. (ISBN 0-87436-228-8). ABC-Clio.

Cassinelli, Gianni. Encyclopedia of Mathematics & Its Applications: The Logic of Quantum Mechanics, Vol. 15. 1984. 37.50 (ISBN 0-317-14391-3, 30235-8). Cambridge U Pr.

Cassini, Igor. Pay the Price. 1983. pap. 3.95 (ISBN 0-8217-1234-9). Zebra.

Cassini, J. Now You Can Dance. (Ballroom Dance Ser.). 1985. lib. bdg. 62.00 (ISBN 0-87700-854-X). Revisionist Pr.

Cassinis, R., ed. Problems & Methods for Lithospheric Exploration. (Ettore Majorana International Science Series, Physical Sciences: Vol. 19). 230p. 1984. 49.50x (ISBN 0-306-41721-9, Plenum Pr). Plenum Pub.

--The Solution of the Inverse Problem in Geophysical Interpretation. LC 81-4067. 392p. 1981. 65.00x (ISBN 0-306-40735-3, Plenum Pr). Plenum Pub.

Cassin-Scott, Jack. Costumes & Settings for Historical Plays: The Nineteenth Century, Vol. 5. LC 79-56537. (Illus.). 96p. 1980. 16.95 (ISBN 0-7134-1710-2, Pub. by Batsford England). David & Charles.

--Costumes & Settings for Staging Historical Plays. Incl. Vol. 1. The Classical Period. 1979 (ISBN 0-8238-0231-0); Vol. 2. The Medieval Period. 1979 (ISBN 0-8238-0232-9); Vol. 3. The Elizabethan & Restoration Period. 1979 (ISBN 0-8238-0236-1); Vol. 4. The Georgian Period. 1979 (ISBN 0-8238-0237-X). (Illus.). 10.95 ea. Plays.

--Making Model Soldiers of the World. 1977. pap. 5.95 (ISBN 0-8120-0822-7). Barron.

Cassiodorus. Introduction to Divine & Human Readings. Jones, L. W., tr. 1966. lib. bdg. 20.50x (ISBN 0-374-94275-7). Octagon.

Cassirer, Ernst. Essay on Man: An Introduction to a Philosophy of Human Culture. 1962. pap. 7.95 (ISBN 0-300-00034-0, Y52). Yale U Pr.

--Individual & the Cosmos in Renaissance Philosophy. Domandi, Mario, tr. 1972. pap. 9.95x (ISBN 0-8122-1036-0, Pa. Paperbacks). U of Pa Pr.

--Kant's Life & Thought. Haden, James, tr. from Ger. LC 81-3354. 464p. 1981. 36.00x (ISBN 0-300-02358-8); pap. text ed. 12.95x (ISBN 0-300-02982-9). Yale U Pr.

--Language & Myth. Langer, Susanne K., tr. 1946. pap. 2.50 (ISBN 0-486-20051-5). Dover.

--Language & Myth. 13.50 (ISBN 0-8446-1820-9). Peter Smith.

--Myth of the State. 1961. pap. 7.95x (ISBN 0-300-00036-7, y33). Yale U Pr.

--The Myth of the State. LC 82-18392. xii, 303p. 1983. Repr. of 1946 ed. lib. bdg. 29.75x (ISBN 0-313-23790-5, CAMO). Greenwood.

--Philosophy of Symbolic Forms, Vol. 1, Language. Manheim, Ralph, tr. 1965. pap. 8.95x (ISBN 0-300-00037-5, Y146). Yale U Pr.

--Philosophy of Symbolic Forms, Vol. 2, Mythical Thought. Manheim, Ralph, tr. 1955. pap. 8.95x (ISBN 0-300-00038-3, Y147). Yale U Pr.

--The Philosophy of Symbolic Forms, Vol. 3, The Phenomenology Of Knowledge. Manheim, Ralph, tr. 1965. pap. 9.95x (ISBN 0-300-00039-1, Y148). Yale U Pr.

--The Philosophy of the Enlightenment. Koelin, F. & Pettegrove, J., trs. from Fr. 1951. pap. 8.95x (ISBN 0-691-01963-0). Princeton U Pr.

--Platonic Renaissance in England. LC 71-128186. 1970. Repr. of 1954 ed. text ed. 12.50x (ISBN 0-87752-128-X). Gordian.

--Problem of Knowledge: Philosophy, Science, & History Since Hegel. Woglom, William H. & Hendel, Charles W., trs. 1950. pap. 8.95x (ISBN 0-300-01098-2, Y211). Yale U Pr.

--Rousseau, Kant, & Goethe. 1970. 22.00x (ISBN 0-691-07168-3); pap. 7.95 (ISBN 0-691-01970-3). Princeton U Pr.

--Substance & Function & Einstein's Theory of Relativity. pap. 7.95 (ISBN 0-486-20050-7). Dover.

--Symbol, Myth & Culture: Essays & Lectures of Ernst Cassirer 1935-45. Verne, Donald P., ed. LC 78-9887. 1979. 38.50x (ISBN 0-300-02306-5); pap. 10.95x (ISBN 0-300-02666-8). Yale U Pr.

Cassirer, Ernst, jt. auth. see Lipton, David R.

Cassirer, Ernst, et al, eds. Renaissance Philosophy of Man. LC 48-9358. 1956. pap. 9.95 (ISBN 0-226-09604-1, P1, Phoen). U of Chicago Pr.

Cassirer, H. W. Kant's First Critique: An Appraisal of the Significance of Kant's Critique of Pure Reason. (Muirhead Library of Philosophy Ser.). 1978. Repr. of 1954 ed. text ed. 18.00x (ISBN 0-391-00868-4). Humanities.

Cassirer, Sidonie, ed. Female Studies: Teaching about Women in the Foreign Languages, No. 9. 237p. 1976. pap. 7.95x (ISBN 0-912670-38-X). Feminist Pr.

Cassis, A. F. Graham Greene: An Annotated Bibliography of Criticism. LC 81-770. (Scarecrow Author Bibliographies Ser.: No. 55). 423p. 1981. 27.50 (ISBN 0-8108-1418-8). Scarecrow.

--The Twentieth-Century English Novel. LC 76-24735. (Library of Humanities Reference Bks.: No. 56). 1977. lib. bdg. 55.00 (ISBN 0-8240-9942-7). Garland Pub.

Cassissi, Nicholas J., jt. auth. see Million, Rodney R.

Cassity, Joan. Flight Plan: Aquarius. Ashton, Sylvia, ed. LC 77-86488. 1979. 14.95 (ISBN 0-87949-088-8). Ashley Bks.

--Now & Again. 480p. 1984. pap. 2.95 (ISBN 0-380-87353-2, 87353-2). Avon.

Cassity, Michael J. Chains of Fear: American Race Relations Since Reconstruction. LC 82-21092. (Grass Roots Perspectives on American History Ser.: No. 3). xxx, 253p. 1984. lib. bdg. 35.00 (ISBN 0-313-21324-0, CRR/). Greenwood.

--Legacy of Fear: American Race Relations to Nineteen Hundred. LC 84-8981. (Grass Roots Perspectives on American History Ser.: No. 4). (Illus.). xxiv, 248p. 1985. lib. bdg. 35.00 (ISBN 0-313-24553-3, CLF/). Greenwood.

Cassity, Turner. The Defense of the Sugar Islands. 28p. 1979. s & l, wrappers 25.00 (ISBN 0-936576-01-4). Symposium Pr.

--Keys to Mayerling. (Orig.). 1983. pap. 4.00 (ISBN 0-941150-14-3). Barth.

--Steeplejacks in Babel. LC 73-76686. 72p. 1973. pap. 5.95 (ISBN 0-87923-070-3); 12.95 (ISBN 0-87923-100-9). Godine.

--Watchboy, What of the Night? LC 66-23920. (Wesleyan Poetry Program Ser.: Vol. 31). (Orig.). 1966. 15.00x (ISBN 0-8195-2031-4); pap. 6.95. Wesleyan U Pr.

--Yellow for Peril, Black for Beautiful. LC 74-21627. 80p. 1975. 6.95 (ISBN 0-8076-0775-4); pap. 3.95 (ISBN 0-8076-0776-2). Braziller.

Cassius, pseud. Give All the Flowers Smiles. (Libraries-School Libraries). (Illus.). 64p. (Orig.). 1985. pap. 5.00 (ISBN 0-915199-15-7). Pen-Dec.

--Glacial Blue Slippers on a Tear. (Libraries-School Libraries). (Illus.). 64p. 1985. pap. 5.00 (ISBN 0-915199-12-2). Pen-Dec.

--Lasers in a Closed Sparkle Spin. (Libraries-School Libraries). (Illus.). 64p. 1985. pap. 5.00 (ISBN 0-915199-14-9). Pen-Dec.

--Night Ballon Fever Rising. (Libraries-School Libraries). 64p. 1985. pap. 5.00 (ISBN 0-915199-10-6). Pen-Dec.

Cassizzi, Vic. Overlook: A Castle in the Kingdom. (Illus.). 1981. 3.95 (ISBN 0-686-30374-1). Cassizzi.

Casso, Evans J. Lorenzo: The Casso Family in Louisiana. LC 73-189735. (Illus.). 208p. 1972. 10.00 (ISBN 0-911116-61-3). Pelican.

--Louisiana Legacy: History of the National Guard. LC 76-10175. (Illus.). 300p. 1976. 19.50 (ISBN 0-88289-107-3); special ed. 75.00 (ISBN 0-88289-162-6). Pelican.

Cassola, Carlo. La Ragazza Di Bube. (Easy Readers, C). (Illus.). 1976. pap. text ed. 4.25 (ISBN 0-88436-284-1, 55259). EMC.

Casson, Dan P. From Rock to Rock of Ages. (Daybreak Ser.). 80p. 1982. pap. 4.95 (ISBN 0-8163-0474-2). Pacific Pr Pub Assn.

Casson, H. History of the Telephone. 1977. lib. bdg. 59.95 (ISBN 0-8490-2007-7). Gordon Pr.

Casson, Herbert N. Cyrus Hall McCormick: His Life & Work. LC 74-152977. (Select Bibliographies Reprint Ser.). 1972. Repr. of 1909 ed. 24.50 (ISBN 0-8369-5729-6). Ayer Co Pubs.

--Factory Efficiency: How to Increase Output, Wages, Dividends & Good-Will. Chandler, Alfred D., ed. LC 79-7537. (History of Management Thought & Practice Ser.). 1980. Repr. of 1917 ed. lib. bdg. 17.00x (ISBN 0-405-12322-1). Ayer Co Pubs.

--The History of the Telephone. facsimile ed. LC 76-175693. (Select Bibliographies Reprint Ser). Repr. of 1910 ed. 27.50 (ISBN 0-8369-6608-2). Ayer Co Pubs.

--The Romance of Steel: Story of a Thousand Millionaires. facsimile ed. LC 72-179510. (Select Bibliographies Reprint Ser). Repr. of 1907 ed. 37.50 (ISBN 0-8369-6639-2). Ayer Co Pubs.

Casson, Hugh. Hugh Casson's London. (Illus.). 128p. 1985. 18.95 (ISBN 0-460-04591-1, BKX 05277, Pub. by J M Dent England). Biblio Dist.

Casson, Hugh, intro. by. The Royal Academy of Arts Year Book 1981. (Illus.). 1981. 35.00 (ISBN 0-8390-0281-5). Abner Schram Ltd.

Casson, J., jt. auth. see Bennison, M.

Casson, J; see Institute of Marine Engineers.

Casson, Lionel. Ancient Trade & Society. LC 85-198800. 284p. 1984. 19.95 (ISBN 0-8143-1740-5). Wayne St U Pr.

Casson, Lionel & Price, Martin. Coins, Culture, & History in the Ancient World: Numismatic & Other Studies in Honor of Bluma L. Trell. LC 81-104910. (Illus.). 205p. 1981. 22.50 (ISBN 0-8143-1684-0). Wayne St U Pr.

Casson, Lionel, jt. auth. see Burriss, Eli E.

Casson, Lionel, ed. The Plays of Menander. LC 76-171347. 1971. 27.00x (ISBN 0-8147-1353-X). NYU Pr.

Casson, Lionel, ed. & tr. see Lucian.

Casson, Lionel, ed. see Plautus.

Casson, Lionel, et al. Ancient History. 640p. Date not set. pap. text ed. 25.95 (ISBN 0-394-33556-2, KnopfC). Knopf.

Casson, M. Introduction to Mathematical Economics. 1973. pap. 19.95 (ISBN 0-442-30718-7). Van Nos Reinhold.

Casson, Mark. Economics of Unemployment: An Historical Perspective. LC 83-62502. 298p. 1984. text ed. 37.50x (ISBN 0-262-03106-X). MIT Pr.

--The Entrepreneur: An Economic Theory. LC 82-13802. (Illus.). 432p. 1982. text ed. 29.95x (ISBN 0-389-20328-9, 07168). B&N Imports.

--Unemployment: A Disequilibrium Approach. LC 81-4442. 263p. 1981. 32.95x (ISBN 0-470-27179-5). Halsted Pr.
--Youth Unemployment. LC 79-11242. 141p. 1979. text ed. 27.75x (ISBN 0-8419-5050-4). Holmes & Meier.
Casson, Mark, jt. auth. see Buckley, Peter J.
Casson, Mark, ed. The Growth of International Business. 288p. 1983. text ed. 28.50x (ISBN 0-04-330333-1). Allen Unwin.
Casson, Michael. The Craft of the Potter. LC 78-15013. (Illus.). (gr. 10-12). 1979. pap. 10.95 (ISBN 0-8120-2028-6). Barron.
Casson, Patricia, ed. see Casson, Sybil T.
Casson, Paul. Decoys Simplified. (Illus.). 132p. 1973. 14.95 (ISBN 0-88395-016-2). Freshet Pr.
Casson, Ronald W. Language, Culture & Cognition: Readings in Cognitive Anthropology. 1981. write for info. (ISBN 0-02-320050-2). Macmillan.
Casson, S., ed. Essay in Aegean Archaeology: Presented to Sir Arthur Evans in Honor of His 75th Birthday. LC 72-309. (Essay Index Reprint Ser.). Repr. of 1927 ed. 23.50 (ISBN 0-8369-2791-5). Ayer Co Pubs.
--Essays in Aegean Archaeology: Presented to Sir Arthur Evans in Honour of His 75th Birthday. 1978. Repr. of 1927 ed. lib. bdg. 45.00 (ISBN 0-8495-0762-6). Arden Lib.
Casson, Stanley. Ancient Cyprus, Its Art & Archaeology. LC 70-95086. Repr. of 1937 ed. lib. bdg. 15.00x (ISBN 0-8371-3080-8, CAAC). Greenwood.
--Ancient Cyprus, Its Art & Archaeology. (Illus.). 1976. 15.00 (ISBN 0-916710-29-7). Obol Intl.
--Ancient Cyprus: Its Art & Archaeology. 1937. Repr. of 1937 ed. 15.00 (ISBN 0-89005-403-7). Ares.
--Archaeology. 1978. Repr. of 1930 ed. lib. bdg. 10.00 (ISBN 0-8492-3846-3). R West.
--Macedonia, Thrace & Illyria: Their Relations to Greece from the Earliest Times Down to the Time of Philip, Son of Amyntas. LC 75-114495. (Illus.). 1971. Repr. of 1926 ed. lib. bdg. 22.00x (ISBN 0-8371-4727-1, CAMT). Greenwood.
--Some Modern Sculptors. facs. ed. LC 67-28746. (Essay Index Reprint Ser). 1928. 18.00 (ISBN 0-8369-0282-3). Ayer Co Pubs.
--Twentieth Century Sculptors. facs. ed. LC 67-23189. (Essay Index Reprint Ser). 1930. 19.00 (ISBN 0-8369-0283-1). Ayer Co Pubs.
Casson, Sybil T. My Dear One: A Victorian Courtship. Casson, Patricia, ed. 160p. 1985. 13.95 (ISBN 0-531-09773-0). Watts.
Casson, Thomas. Lecture on the Pedal Organ. 1976. lib. bdg. 29.00x (ISBN 0-403-03627-5). Scholarly.
Cassone, Diane, jt. auth. see Cassone, Philip.
Cassone, Philip & Cassone, Diane. Hand Jobs. (Illus.). 56p. (Orig.). 1982. pap. 6.95 (ISBN 0-9610082-0-2). Cassone Pr.
Cassorla, Albert. The Skateboarder's Bible: Technique, Equipment, Stunts, Terms, Etc. LC 76-28511. (Illus.). 128p. (Orig.). (YA) 1976. lib. bdg. 12.90 (ISBN 0-914294-59-8); pap. 4.95 (ISBN 0-914294-60-1). Running Pr.
--The Suntan Book. LC 78-606. (Illus.). 1983. lib. bdg. cancelled (ISBN 0-89471-027-3); pap. cancelled (ISBN 0-89471-026-5). Running Pr.
Cassou, Jean & Read, Herbert. Jan Le Witt. (Illus.). 172p. 1971. 39.95x (ISBN 0-912050-17-9). Open Court.
Casstevens, Thomas B., jt. ed. see Shrivastava, B. K.
Cassuto, Alexander E., jt. auth. see Baird, Charles W.
Cassuto, Nelda, ed. see Eis, Ruth.
Cassuto, U. Biblical & Oriental Studies: Bible, Vol. 1. Abrahams, Israel, tr. from Hebrew. (Illus.). 298p. 1973. text ed. 25.50x (Pub. by Magnes Israel). Humanities.
--Biblical & Oriental Studies: Bible & Ancient Oriental Texts, Vol. 2. Abrahams, Israel, tr. from Hebrew. 286p. 1975. text ed. 30.50x (Pub. by Magnes Israel). Humanities.
--A Commentary on the Book of Exodus. 2nd ed. Abrahams, Israel, tr. from Hebrew. 509p. 1974. Repr. of 1967 ed. text ed. 35.50x (ISBN 965-223-456-7, Pub. by Magnes Israel). Humanities.
--The Documentary Hypothesis. Abrahams, Israel, tr. from Hebrew. 117p. 1972. Repr. of 1961 ed. text ed. 15.50x (Pub. by Magnes Israel). Humanities.
--From Adam to Noah: A Commentary on the Book of Genesis, Part 1. 3rd ed. 323p. 1978. Repr. of 1961 ed. text ed. 30.50x (Pub. by Magnes Israel). Humanities.
--From Noah to Abraham: A Commentary on the Book of Genesis, Pt. 2. 3rd ed. 386p. 1974. Repr. of 1964 ed. text ed. 36.50x (Pub. by Magnes Israel). Humanities.
--The Goddess Anath. Abrahams, Israel, tr. from Hebrew. (Illus.). 194p. 1971. Repr. of 1951 ed. text ed. 30.50x (Pub. Magnes Israel). Humanities.
Cast, David. The Calumny of Apelles: A Study in the Humanist Tradition. LC 80-26378. (Publication in the History of Art Ser.: No. 28). (Illus.). 320p. 1981. text ed. 41.00x (ISBN 0-300-02575-0). Yale U Pr.
Castagna, Edwin. Caught in the Act: The Decisive Reading of Some Notable Men & Women & Its Influence on Their Actions & Attitudes. LC 82-10276. 228p. 1982. 15.00 (ISBN 0-8108-1566-4). Scarecrow.
Castagnaro, R. Anthony. Vinte Contos Brasileiros. 218p. 1980. pap. text ed. 8.95 (ISBN 0-87840-079-6). Georgetown U Pr.
Castagnasso, J. M., ed. see Braithwaite, Gary M., et al.
Castagno, Margaret F. Historical Dictionary of Somalia. LC 75-25681. (African Historical Dictionary Ser.: No. 6). 243p. 1975. 20.00 (ISBN 0-8108-0830-7). Scarecrow.
Castagnola, Lawrence. Parables for Little People. (Illus.). 101p. (Orig.). (gr. 4 up). 1982. pap. 5.56 (ISBN 0-89390-034-6); pap. text ed. 7.95. Resource Pubns.
Castagnoli, E., tr. see Zollinger, H. U., et al.
Castagnoli, N., Jr., jt. ed. see Frigerio, A.
Castaing, C. & Valadier, M. Convex Analysis & Measurable Multifunctions. (Lecture Notes in Mathematics: Vol. 580). 1977. soft cover 18.00 (ISBN 0-387-08144-5). Springer-Verlag.
Castaing, D., et al. Hepatic & Portal Surgery in the Rat. (Illus.). 184p. 1980. 41.50x (ISBN 0-89352-101-9). Masson Pub.
Castaldi, Alfred J. & Kender, Joseph P., eds. Lehigh Reading Conference: Proceedings. LC 62-4990. 1972. pap. text ed. 2.50x (ISBN 0-8134-1460-1, 1460). Interstate.
Castaldi, Basil. Educational Facilities: Planning, Modernization & Management. 2nd ed. 350p. 1982. 24.71x (ISBN 0-205-07745-5, 237745, Pub. by Longwood Div). Allyn.
Castaldi, Cosmo R. & Brass, George A. Dentistry for the Adolescent. LC 77-88308. pap. 153.00 (ISBN 0-317-26413-3, 2024965). Bks Demand UMI.
Castaldo, George, ed. see Doane, Jim.
Castaldo, George, ed. see Von Normann, Bob.
Castandea, Alfredo, jt. auth. see Ramirez, Manuel, 3rd.
Castaneda, Alfredo, et al, eds. Mexican Americans & Educational Change. LC 73-14196. (The Mexican American Ser.). 424p. 1974. 29.00x (ISBN 0-405-05671-0). Ayer Co Pubs.
Castaneda, Carlos. The Eagle's Gift. 1982. pap. 3.95 (ISBN 0-671-44226-0). PB.
--Eagle's Gift. 1983. pap. text ed. 6.95 (ISBN 0-671-47070-1, Touchstone Bks). S&S.
--The Fire from Within. 320p. 1984. 17.95 (ISBN 0-671-49205-5). S&S.
--Fire from Within. 1985. pap. 4.50 (ISBN 0-671-54214-1). PB.
--Journey to Ixtlan. 1983. pap. 3.95 (ISBN 0-671-49668-9). PB.
--Journey to Ixtlan. 1973. pap. 8.95 (ISBN 0-671-21639-2, Touchstone Bks). S&S.
--The Second Ring of Power. (gr. 10-12). 1981. pap. 3.50 (ISBN 0-671-44781-5). PB.
--Separate Reality. 1983. pap. 3.95 (ISBN 0-671-50728-1). PB.
--Tales of Power. 1982. pap. 3.50 (ISBN 0-671-44780-7). PB.
--Tales of Power. 287p. 1975. pap. 4.95 (ISBN 0-671-22144-2, Touchstone Bks). S&S.
--Teachings of Don Juan. 1982. pap. 3.50 (ISBN 0-671-45800-0). PB.
--The Teachings of Don Juan: A Yaqui Way of Knowledge. LC 68-17303. 1968. 13.95 (ISBN 0-520-00217-2); pap. 5.95 (ISBN 0-520-02258-0, CAL253). U of Cal Pr.
Castaneda, Carlos E., ed. see Morfi, Fray J.
Castaneda, Carlos E., ed. see Texas University Institute of Latin American Studies.
Castaneda, H. N., jt. auth. see Philosophical Foundations of Institutions.
Castaneda, Hector-Neri, ed. Intentionality, Minds, & Perception: Discussions on Contemporary Philosophy. LC 66-19546. (Waynebooks Ser: No. 30). 402p. 1967. pap. text ed. 5.95x (ISBN 0-8143-1299-3). Wayne St U Pr.
Castaneda, Hector-Neri & Nakhnikian, George, eds. Morality & the Language of Conduct. LC 62-17557. (Waynebooks Ser: No. 11). 375p. 1963. pap. 5.95x (ISBN 0-8143-1209-8). Wayne St U Pr.
Castaneda, Jorge. Mexico & the United Nations. LC 74-6705. (National Studies on International Organization Ser.). 244p. 1975. Repr. of 1958 ed. lib. bdg. 17.00x (ISBN 0-8371-7548-8, CAME). Greenwood.
Castaneda-Zuniga, Wilfirdo. Transluminal Angioplasty. (Illus.). 207p. 1983. 41.00 (ISBN 0-86577-057-3). Thieme-Stratton.
Castano, Abel. La Ramera Fogosa. (Pimienta Collection Ser.). 1977. pap. 1.00 (ISBN 0-88473-268-1). Fiesta Pub.
Castano, Francis A. & Alden, Betsey, eds. Handbook of Clinical Dental Auxiliary Practice. 2nd ed. LC 79-18202. 290p. 1980. text ed. 25.20 (ISBN 0-397-54285-2, 64-01921, Lippincott Medical). Lippincott.
Castano, Wilfredo. Small Stones Cast upon the Tender Earth. 1981. pap. 3.00 (ISBN 0-915016-28-1). Second Coming.
Castanos, O., et al, eds. Introduction to Supersymmetry in Particle & Nuclear Physics. 196p. 1984. 29.50x (ISBN 0-306-41612-3, Plenum Pr). Plenum Pub.
Castanza, Philip. The Films of Jeanette MacDonald & Nelson Eddy. (Illus.). 224p. 1981. pap. 7.95 (ISBN 0-8065-0771-3). Citadel Pr.
--Films of Jeannette MacDonald & Nelson Eddy. (Citadel Press Film Ser.). (Illus.). (gr. 7 up). 1978. 14.95 (ISBN 0-8065-0600-8). Citadel Pr.
Castberg, A. Didvick, jt. ed. see Rosenblum, Victor G.
Castberg, C., jt. auth. see Adler, L. W.
Castberg, Frede. The European Convention on Human Rights. LC 73-85760. 230p. 1974. lib. bdg. 24.00 (ISBN 0-379-00202-7). Oceana.
Castedo, Leopoldo. The Cuzco Circle. LC 76-381383. (Illus.). 144p. 1980. 16.50x (ISBN 0-295-95738-7). U of Wash Pr.
Casteel, David A., et al. Basic Collision Analysis & Scene Documentation, Vol. I. Moss, David L., ed. (Illus.). 208p. 1983. text ed. 34.95 (ISBN 0-914509-00-4). D L Moss Pubns.
Casteel, J. Doyle. Learning to Think & Choose: Decision Making Episodes for the Middle Grades. LC 77-16050. 1978. 14.95 (ISBN 0-673-16385-7); pap. 12.95 (ISBN 0-673-16386-5). Scott F.
Casteel, J. Doyle, et al. Cross-Cultural Models of Teaching: Latin American Examples. LC 76-13369. 1976. pap. 7.50x (ISBN 0-8130-0558-2). U Presses Fla.
Casteel, R. W., ed. Fish Remains in Archaeology. 1977. 33.00 (ISBN 0-12-163850-2). Acad Pr.
Casteele, Dennis. The Cars of Oldsmobile. Dammann, George H., ed. LC 76-5767. (Automotive Ser.). (Illus.). 416p. 1981. 29.95 (ISBN 0-912612-11-8). Crestline.
--Four-Four-Two: A Source Book. (Illus.). 144p. 1982. pap. 12.95 (ISBN 0-934780-12-9). Bookman Dan.
Castegnaro, M., et al, eds. Laboratory Decontamination & Destruction of Aflatoxins, B1, B2, G1, G2 in Laboratory Wastes. (IARC Ser.). (Illus.). 68p. 1980. pap. 9.95x (ISBN 0-19-723037-7). Oxford U Pr.
--Laboratory Decontamination & Destruction of Carcinogens in Laboratory Wastes: Some Hydrazines. (International Agency for Research on Cancer Scientific Publications Ser.: No. 54). 1983. pap. 12.95x (ISBN 0-19-723053-9). Oxford U Pr.
--Laboratory Decontamination & Destruction of Carcinogens in Laboratory Wastes: Some N-Nitrosamines. (IARC). (Illus.). 82p. 1982. text ed. 10.95x (ISBN 0-19-723043-1). Oxford U Pr.
--Laboratory Decontamination & Destruction of Carcinogens in Laboratory Wastes: Some N-Nitrosamines. (IARC Ser.). (Illus.). 74p. 1983. pap. 12.95x (ISBN 0-19-723054-7). Oxford U Pr.
--Laboratory Decontamination & Destruction of Carcinogens in Laboratory Wastes: Some Polycyclic Aromatic Hydrocarbons. (IARC Ser.). (Illus.). 86p. 1983. pap. 12.95x (ISBN 0-19-723049-0). Oxford U Pr.
--Laboratory Decontamination & Destruction of Carcinogens in Laboratory Wastes: Some Haloethers. (International Agency for Research on Cancer Scientific Publications Ser.: No. 61). 1984. pap. 11.95x (ISBN 0-19-723061-X). Oxford U Pr.
Castel, Albert. The Presidency of Andrew Johnson. LC 79-11050. (The American Presidency Ser.). 1979. 19.95x (ISBN 0-7006-0190-2). U Pr of KS.
Castel, Albert & Gibson, Scott L. The Yeas & the Nays: Key Congressional Decisions 1774-1945. 1975. 7.95 (ISBN 0-932826-15-6). New Issues MI.
Castel, Albert E. A Frontier State at War: Kansas, Eighteen Sixty-One to Eighteen Sixty-Five. LC 78-26281. 1979. Repr. of 1958 ed. lib. bdg. 24.75x (ISBN 0-313-20863-8, CAFS). Greenwood.
Castel, B., et al, eds. Common Problems in Low & Medium-Energy Nuclear Physics. LC 79-17039. (NATO ASI Series B, Physics: Vol. 45). 1979. 95.00x (ISBN 0-306-40281-5, Plenum Pr). Plenum Pub.
Castel, Boris, jt. auth. see El-Baz, Edgard.
Castel, Christine du see Du Castel, Christine.
Castel, Francois. History of Israel & Judah: From the Beginnings to the Second Century A. D. 288p. (Orig.). 1985. pap. 8.95 (ISBN 0-8091-2701-6). Paulist Pr.
Castel, Francoise & Castel, Robert. The Psychiatric Society. Goldhammer, Arthur, tr. from Fr. (European Perspectives Ser.). 368p. 1982. 30.00x (ISBN 0-231-05244-8). Columbia U Pr.
Castel, Robert, jt. auth. see Castel, Francoise.
Castelain, Daniel. Sentimental Talks. Bowles, Patrick, tr. from Fr. Incl. Unlikely Meeting; A Sentimental Talk. LC 79-131217. 128p. (Orig.). 1971. 4.95 (ISBN 0-87376-014-X). Red Dust.
Castelain, Daniel, et al. New Writers, No. 5. 1980. pap. 6.00 (ISBN 0-7145-0405-X). Riverrun NY.
Castelein, A. Congo State: Its Origin, Rights - Duties. LC 77-75543. Repr. of 1907 ed. 19.75x (ISBN 0-8371-0983-3, CCS&, Pub. by Negro U Pr). Greenwood.
Casteleiro, Juan. Las Millonarias Lascivas. (Pimienta Collection Ser). (Illus.). 1976. pap. 1.25 (ISBN 0-88473-250-9). Fiesta Pub.
Casteleyn, Mary. Planning Library Training Programmes. 176p. 1972. 20.00x (ISBN 0-233-97338-9, 05774-6, Pub. by Gower Pub Co England). Lexington Bks.
Castell, Alburey. An Introduction to Modern Philosophy: Examining the Human Condition. 4th ed. 656p. 1983. text ed. write for info. (ISBN 0-02-320080-4). Macmillan.
Castell, Alburey, ed. Paine: The Age of Reason, Vol. 1. 1957. pap. text ed. write for info. (ISBN 0-02-320160-6). Macmillan.
Castell, Alburey, ed. see Huxley, Thomas H.
Castell, Alburey, ed. see James, William.
Castell, Alburey, ed. see Mill, John S.
Castell, Alburey, ed. see Paine, Thomas.
Castell, C. P., et al. British Caenozoic Fossils: Tertiary & Quaternary. 5th ed. (Illus.). vi, 132p. 1975. pap. 8.50x (ISBN 0-686-27501-2, Pub. by Brit Mus Nat Hist). Sabbot-Natural Hist Bks.
Castell, D. O. & Johnson, L. F., eds. Esophageal Function in Health & Disease. (Clinical Topics in Gastroenterology Ser.). xviii, 372p. 1983. 34.00 (ISBN 0-444-00762-8, Biomedical Pr). Elsevier.
Castell, David. The Films of Barbra Streisand. (The Films of...Ser.). (Illus.). (gr. 7-12). 1978. Repr. of 1974 ed. PLB 6.95 (ISBN 0-912616-78-4). Greenhaven.
--The Films of Robert Redford. (The Films of...Ser.). (Illus.). (gr. 7-12). 1978. Repr. of 1973 ed. PLB 6.95 (ISBN 0-912616-77-6). Greenhaven.
--Richard Attenborough: A Pictorial Film Biography. (Illus.). 128p. (Orig.). 1984. 19.95 (ISBN 0-370-30986-3, Pub. by the Bodley Head); pap. 12.95 (ISBN 0-370-30989-8). Merrimack Pub Cir.
Castell, David, ed. see Andrews, Emma.
Castell, David, ed. see Baxter, Brian.
Castell, David, ed. see Braithwaite, Bruce.
Castell, David, ed. see Campbell, Joanna.
Castell, David, ed. see D'Arcy, Susan.
Castell, David, ed. see McAsh, Iain F.
Castell, David, ed. see Thompson, Kenneth.
Castell, David, ed. see Whitman, Mark.
Castell, David, ed. see Williams, John.
Castell, Donald, jt. ed. see Dubois, Andre.
Castell, Donald O., et al, eds. Gastro-Esophageal Reflux Disease: Pathogenesis, Diagnosis, Therapy. (Illus.). 320p. 1985. monograph 42.50 (ISBN 0-87993-239-2). Futura Pub.
Castell, L., et al. Quantum Theory & the Structures of Time & Space, 2 vols. LC 77-83924. 252p. 1977. pap. text ed. 14.00x ea. Vol. 1 (ISBN 0-916672-95-6). Vol. 2 (ISBN 0-916672-96-4). Allanheld.
Castellan, Gilbert W. Physical Chemistry. 3rd ed. LC 82-22754. (Chemistry Ser.). (Illus.). 960p. 1983. text ed. 38.95 (ISBN 0-201-10386-9); solutions manual 9.95 (ISBN 0-201-10387-7). Addison-Wesley.
Castellan, Jr. & Restle, Frank, eds. Cognitive Theory, Vol. 3. LC 75-14293. (Cognitive Theory Ser.). 319p. 1978. 19.95x (ISBN 0-470-26375-X). Halsted Pr.
Castellan, Jr., et al, eds. Cognitive Theory, Vol. 2. LC 75-14293. (Cognitive Theory Ser.). 342p. 1977. 19.95x (ISBN 0-470-99025-2). Halsted Pr.
Castellan, N. J., Jr & Pisoni, D. B., eds. Cognitive Theory, Vol. 2. 342p. 1977. 36.00x (ISBN 0-89859-437-5). L Erlbaum Assocs.
Castellan, N. J., Jr & Restle, F., eds. Cognitive Theory, Vol. 3. 336p. 1978. 36.00x (ISBN 0-89859-438-3). L Erlbaum Assocs.
Castellani, A., ed. Research in Photobiology. LC 77-2189. 792p. 1977. 95.00x (ISBN 0-306-31034-1, Plenum Pr). Plenum Pub.
Castellani, A. & Quercia, I. F., eds. Synchrotron Radiation Applied to Biophysical & Biochemical Research. LC 79-16560. (NATO ASI Series A, Life Sciences: Vol. 25). 402p. 1979. 52.50x (ISBN 0-306-40284-X, Plenum Pr). Plenum Pub.
Castellani, Amleto, ed. Lymphocyte Stimulation: Differential Sensitivity to Radiation, Biochemical & Immunological Processes. LC 80-19883. 196p. 1980. 35.00x (ISBN 0-306-40475-3, Plenum Pr). Plenum Pub.
--The Use of Human Cells for the Evaluation of Risk from Physical & Chemical Agents. (NATO ASI Series, Series A, Life Science: Vol. 60). 822p. 1983. 110.00x (ISBN 0-306-41274-8, Plenum Pr). Plenum Pub.
Castellani, C., et al, eds. Disordered Systems & Localization: Proceedings. (Lecture Notes in Physics Ser.: Vol. 149). 308p. 1981. pap. 22.00 (ISBN 0-387-11163-8). Springer-Verlag.
Castellano, Carmine C. & Seitz, Clifford P. Basic Mathematics Skills. LC 81-2210. 272p. (Orig.). 1982. pap. 6.95 (ISBN 0-668-05126-4, 5126). Arco.
--You Fix It: Lawn Mowers. (Illus.). 192p. 1974. pap. 6.95 (ISBN 0-668-02705-3). Arco.
Castellano, Juan R., jt. auth. see Casona, Alejandro.
Castellano-Giron, Hernan. Twilights of Anthony Wayne Drive. Reinhart, Rodney E., pref. by. Efthimides, Emil, tr. from Span. (Illus.). 60p. (Orig.). 1984. pap. 6.00 (ISBN 0-931081-00-9). Operation DOME.
Castellanos, Agustin, ed. Cardiac Arrhythmias: Mechanisms & Management. LC 79-24345. (Cardiovascular Clinics Ser.: Vol. 11, No. 1). (Illus.). 296p. 1980. text ed. 40.00x (ISBN 0-8036-1684-8). Davis Co.
Castellanos, Henry C. New Orleans As It Was. Reinecke, George F., ed. LC 78-13014. (Louisiana Bicentennial Reprint Ser.). xxx, 394p. 1979. 20.30x (ISBN 0-8071-0457-4). La State U Pr.
Castellanos, Javier, tr. see Piaget, Jean, et al.
Castellanos, Jorge. Placido, Poeta Social y Politico. LC 83-82303. (Coleccion Polymita Ser.). 141p. (Orig., Span.). 1984. pap. 10.00 (ISBN 0-89729-341-X). Ediciones.
Castellanos, Juan. Compartamos Mi Esposa. new ed. (Pimienta Collection Ser). (Illus.). 160p. (Span.). 1975. pap. 1.25 (ISBN 0-88473-237-1). Fiesta Pub.
--La Doctora En Lujuria. new ed. (Pimienta Collection Ser). (Illus.). 160p. (Span.). 1976. pap. 1.25 (ISBN 0-88473-247-9). Fiesta Pub.

--Labios Devoradores. new ed. (Pimienta Collection Ser). (Illus.). 160p. (Span.). 1976. pap. 1.25 (ISBN 0-88473-246-0). Fiesta Pub.

--El Psicologo Perverso. new ed. (Pimienta Collection Ser). 160p. 1974. pap. 1.00 (ISBN 0-88473-194-4). Fiesta Pub.

Castellanos, Juan, tr. see Gray, Rod.

Castellanos Alentorn, Prado, jt. auth. see Guisset Poch, Consuelo.

Castellanos Llorenc, Carles & Castellanos Llorenc, Rafael. Diccionario Catala-Frances, Frances-Catala. 1096p. (Catalan & Fr.). 1979. 44.95 (ISBN 0-686-57353-6, S-50453). French & Eur.

Castellanos Llorenc, Rafael, jt. auth. see Castellanos Llorenc, Carles.

Castelli, Jim. Bishops & the Bomb: Waging Peace in a Nuclear Age. LC 82-48706. 288p. 1983. pap. 7.95 (ISBN 0-385-18760-2, IM). Doubleday.

Castelli, Jim, et al. The Abortion Issue in the Political Process: A Briefing for Catholic Legislators. Jackman, Paul, ed. 19p. pap. 3.00 (ISBN 0-915365-08-1). Cath Free Choice.

Castelli, Joseph R. Basques in the Western United States: A Functional Approach to Determination of Cultural Presence in the Geographical Landscape. Cordasco, Francesco, ed. LC 80-844. (American Ethnic Groups Ser.). 1981. lib. bdg. 21.00x (ISBN 0-405-13408-8). Ayer Co Pubs.

Castelli, K., tr. see Grohmann, Gerbert.

Castelli, Louis & Cleeland, Caryn L. David Lean: A Guide to References & Resources. 1980. lib. bdg. 21.00 (ISBN 0-8161-7933-6, Hall Reference). G K Hall.

Castellini, John. Rudiments of Music. (Illus.). 1962. 15.95x (ISBN 0-393-09573-8, NortonC). Norton.

Castellio, Sebastian. Advice to a Desolate France: 1562. new ed. Valkhoff, Maurius F., ed. Valkhoff, Wouter, tr. LC 75-16650. (Illus.). xiv, 50p. 1975. 12.95x (ISBN 0-915762-00-5). Patmos Pr.

Castelliz, K., tr. see Lauer, Hans E.

Castello, Jorge, tr. see Valenzuela, Luisa.

Castellon, Guillermo, tr. see Garbee, Ed & Van Dyke, Henry.

Castellon, Ninoska Perez. Dulcamara. LC 82-82596. (Espejo de Paciencia Ser.). 77p. (Orig., Span. & Eng.). 1982. pap. 5.00 (ISBN 0-89729-317-7). Ediciones.

Castellon, Rolando, ed. see Lobos, Amilcar & Mellot, Leland.

Castells, Manuel. The City & the Grassroots: A Cross-Cultural Theory of Urban Social Movements. LC 82-40099. (California Ser. in Urban Development: Vol. 2). (Illus.). 450p. 1983. 29.95 (ISBN 0-520-04756-7). U of Cal Pr.

--City, Class & Power. Lebas, Elizabeth, tr. from Fr. 1979. 25.00 (ISBN 0-312-13989-6). St Martin.

--City, Class & Power. LC 78-2978. 198p. 1982. 9.95 (ISBN 0-312-13991-8). St Martin.

--The Economic Crisis & American Society. LC 79-3194. (Illus.). 285p. 1980. 28.00 (ISBN 0-691-04220-9); pap. 9.95 (ISBN 0-691-00361-0). Princeton U Pr.

--High Technology, Space & Society. 1985. 29.95 (ISBN 0-8039-2415-1); pap. 14.95 (ISBN 0-8039-2414-3). Sage.

--The Urban Question: A Marxist Approach. 1977. pap. 12.50x (ISBN 0-262-53035-X). MIT Pr.

Castells, Manuel & Godard, Francis. Monopolville: L'entreprise, L'etat, L'urbain. LC 73-90935. (Lab Recherche Urbaine Ser.: No. 6). 496p. (Fr.). 1974. pap. text ed. 18.80x (ISBN 0-686-22581-3). Mouton.

Castells, Matilde O. Mundo Hispano: Lengua y Cultura. LC 80-23698. 402p. 1981. 26.00x (ISBN 0-471-03396-0); wkbk. 14.00x (ISBN 0-471-03397-9). Wiley.

Castells, Matilde O. de see De Castells, Matilde O. & Lionetti, Harold E.

Castellucci, Nicholas T. Seafood Creations by an Italian Gourmet. 1978. 7.95 (ISBN 0-682-49141-1, Banner). Exposition Pr FL.

Castellucis. Microcomputer System Analysis & Design. 1982. text ed. 19.95 (ISBN 0-8359-4368-2); solutions manual free (ISBN 0-8359-4369-0). Reston.

Castellucis, Richard, jt. auth. see Prensky, Sol.

Castellucis, Richard L. Digital Circuits & Systems. 356p. 1981. text ed. 28.95 (ISBN 0-8359-1297-3); instrs. manual avail. (ISBN 0-8359-1298-1). Reston.

Castelman, Harry & Podrazik, Walter J. Five Hundred Five Radio Questions Your Friends Can't Answer. (Five Hundred Five Quiz Ser.). 160p. 1983. pap. 3.95 (ISBN 0-8027-7211-0). Walker & Co.

Castelnuovo-Tedesco, Pietro. The Twenty-Minute Hour. 184p. 1965. 22.50 (ISBN 0-316-13178-4). Little.

Castelnuovo-Tedesco, Pietro, ed. Psychiatric Aspects of Organ Transplantation. LC 78-158947. 172p. 1971. 49.50 (ISBN 0-8089-0720-4, 790818). Grune.

Castelo Matran, Julio. Diccionario Basico De Seguros. 312p. (Span.). 1978. pap. 18.50 (ISBN 84-7100-049-0, S-50036). French & Eur.

Castelot, Andre. King of Rome. LC 74-6778. (Illus.). 396p. 1974. Repr. of 1960 ed. lib. bdg. 22.50x (ISBN 0-8371-7571-2, CAKR). Greenwood.

--Turbulent City: Paris 1783 to 1871. facs. ed. Folliot, Denise, tr. LC 76-117867. (Select Bibliographies Reprint Ser). 1962. 25.50 (ISBN 0-8369-5320-7). Ayer Co Pubs.

Castelvecchi, Tony. Little Friends. LC 79-13194. (Illus.). 40p. (gr. 1-6). 1980. 7.95 (ISBN 0-937150-00-2). A & M Bks.

Castelyn, Mary. A History of the Literacy & Libraries In Ireland: The Long Traced Pedigree. LC 83-15412. 255p. (Orig.). 1984. text ed. 34.50x (ISBN 0-566-03478-6). Gower Pub Co.

Castenada, Carlos E., tr. see Cortes, Carlos E.

Castenada Shular, A., et al. Literatura Chicana: Texto & Contexto. 1972. ref. ed. o.p. 12.95 (ISBN 0-13-537563-0); 16.95 (ISBN 0-13-537555-X). P-H.

Casteneda, Carlos E. Our Catholic Heritage in Texas, 1519-1936, 7 vols. LC 76-1471. (Chicano Heritage Ser.). (Illus.). 1976. Repr. Set. 248.00 (ISBN 0-405-09484-8). Ayer Co Pubs.

Caster, Lee E. Hunter's Folly. (Orig.). 1979. pap. 1.95 (ISBN 0-532-23288-7). Woodhill.

Caster, Paul. Reunion in Hell. (Illus.). 80p. 1983. pap. 25.00x (ISBN 0-937486-02-7). Perimeter Pr.

Casteret, Norbert. Ten Years under the Earth. Massey, Burrows, tr. LC 75-26892. (Illus.). 255p. 1975. 10.95 (ISBN 0-914264-06-0); pap. 6.50 (ISBN 0-914264-07-9). Cave Bks MO.

Casterline, Gail F. Archives & Manuscripts: Exhibits. LC 80-80072. (SAA Basic Manual Ser.). 72p. 1980. pap. 7.00 (ISBN 0-931828-18-X). Soc Am Archivists.

Casterline, Gail F. & Pederson, Ann. Archives & Manuscripts: Public Programs. (SAA Basic Archival Manual Ser.). 96p. (Orig.). 1982. pap. 7.00x (ISBN 0-931828-31-7). Soc Am Archivists.

Casterline, Gail F., jt. auth. see Darling, Sharon S.

Castetter, Edward F. & Bell, Willis. Pima & Papago Indian Agriculture. LC 76-43674. Repr. of 1942 ed. 21.00 (ISBN 0-404-15510-3). AMS Pr.

Castetter, Edward F. & Underhill, Ruth. The Ethnobiology of the Papago Indians. LC 76-43676. (University of New Mexico Bulletin Biological Ser.: Vol. 4). Repr. of 1935 ed. 14.00 (ISBN 0-404-15509-X). AMS Pr.

Castetter, William B. Personnel Function in Educational Administration. 3rd ed. 1981. text ed. write for info. (ISBN 0-02-320140-1). Macmillan.

--The Personnel Function in Educational Administration. 4th ed. 561p. 1986. text ed. price not set (ISBN 0-02-320170-3). Macmillan.

Castetter, William B. & Felker, Donald S. Planning the Financial Compensation of School Administrative Personnel. LC 65-20646. (Illus.). 1965. pap. text ed. 2.50x (ISBN 0-8134-6828-0, 6828). Interstate.

Castex, ed. see De Balzac, Honore.

Castex, P. & Surer, P. Manuel Des Etudes Litteraires Francaises, 6 tomes. (Illus.). Tome 1, Moyen Age. 5.95 (ISBN 0-685-11344-2); Tome, 2 16e Siecle. 5.95 (ISBN 0-685-11345-0); Tome 3, 17e Siecle. 7.95 (ISBN 0-685-11346-9); Tome 4, 18e Siecle. 7.95 (ISBN 0-685-11347-7); Tome 5, 19e Siecle. 8.95 (ISBN 0-685-11348-5); Tome 6, 20e Siecle. 8.95 (ISBN 0-685-11349-3). French & Eur.

Castex, Pierre Georges, jt. auth. see Balzac, Honore De.

Casti, jt. auth. see Larson.

Casti, John, tr. see Salukvadze, M.

Casti, John L. Nonlinear System Theory. (Mathematics Science & Engineering Ser.). 1985. 45.00 (ISBN 0-12-163452-3). Acad Pr.

Casti, John L., jt. auth. see Larson, Robert E.

Casti, John L., tr. see Gabasov, R. & Kirillova, F.

Castiglione, Baldassare. Book of the Courtier. Hoby, Thomas, tr. LC 1-7785. (Tudor Translations. First Ser.: No. 23). Repr. of 1900 ed. 45.00 (ISBN 0-404-51854-0). AMS Pr.

--The Book of the Courtier. Hoby, Thomas, tr. 1975. 10.95x (ISBN 0-460-10807-7, Evman); pap. 4.95x (ISBN 0-460-11807-2, Evman). Biblio Dist.

Castiglione, Baldesar. Book of the Courtier. LC 59-12883. (Illus.). 1959. pap. 6.50 (ISBN 0-385-09421-3, Anch). Doubleday.

--The Book of the Courtier. Bull, George, tr. (Classics Ser.). 368p. 1976. pap. 4.95 (ISBN 0-14-044192-1). Penguin.

--Book of the Courtier. abr. ed. Simpson, Friench, tr. LC 59-15520. (Milestones of Thought Ser.). 1959. pap. 2.95 (ISBN 0-8044-6078-7). Ungar.

Castiglione, Pierina B. Italian Phonetics, Diction & Intonation. 103p. pap. 9.50x (ISBN 0-913298-48-4); Castiglione tape set 23.95 (ISBN 0-686-77593-7). S F Vanni.

Castiglioni, Arturo. Italian Medicine. Krumbhaar, E. B., tr. LC 75-23656. (Clio Medica: No. 6). (Illus.). Repr. of 1932 ed. 12.00 (ISBN 0-404-58906-5). AMS Pr.

Castile, George P. & Kushner, Gilbert, eds. Persistent Peoples: Cultural Enclaves in Perspective. LC 81-10476. 274p. 1981. pap. text ed. 10.50x (ISBN 0-8165-0750-3). U of Ariz Pr.

Castile, George P., ed. & intro. by see Eells, Myron.

Castile, Rand. Shiko Munakata, 1903-1975: Works on Paper (Exhibition Catalogue) (Illus.). 48p. 1982. soft-bdg. 7.50 (ISBN 0-686-37057-0). Japan Soc.

--The Way of Tea. LC 70-157271. (Illus.). 1971. 27.50 (ISBN 0-8348-0059-4). Weatherhill.

Castilejo, Jose. The War of Ideas in Spain: Philosophy, Politics & Education. 1976. lib. bdg. 59.95 (ISBN 0-8490-2806-X). Gordon Pr.

Castilla, Ramon, et al, trs. see Gomez, Luis O. & Torretti, Roberto.

Castille, Olivier De see Oliver de Castille.

Castille, Philip & Osborne, William. Southern Literature in Transition: Heritage & Promise. 176p. 1984. pap. text ed. 12.50x (ISBN 0-87870-209-1). Memphis St Univ.

Castille, Vernon De see De Castille, Vernon.

Castillejo, Irene Claremont De see Claremont De Castillejo, Irene.

Castillo, Adelaida Del see Mora, Magdalena & Del Castillo, Adelaida.

Castillo, Ana. Women Are Not Roses. LC 83-72580. 64p. (Orig.). 1984. 5.00 (ISBN 0-934770-28-X). Arte Publico.

Castillo, Ana H. Del see Hernandez Del Castillo, Ana.

Castillo, Andres V. Spanish Mercantilism: Geronimo de Uztariz-Economist. LC 79-20392. 1980. Repr. of 1930 ed. lib. bdg. 19.50x (ISBN 0-87991-858-6). Porcupine Pr.

Castillo, Bernal Diaz Del see Diaz Del Castillo, Bernal.

Castillo, Carlos & Bond, Otto F. Spanish-English Dictionary. (Span. & Eng.). 1983. pap. 3.95 (ISBN 0-671-50853-9). PB.

--University of Chicago Spanish Dictionary. 3rd rev. enl. ed. (Span.). 1977. 15.95 (ISBN 0-226-09673-4, Phoen); pap. 5.95 (ISBN 0-226-09674-2). U of Chicago Pr.

Castillo, Debra A. The Translated World: A Postmodern Tour of Libraries in Literature. LC 84-17200. 368p. 1985. pap. 18.00 (ISBN 0-8130-0792-5). U Presses Fla.

Castillo, G. T. Beyond Manila: Philippine Rural Problems in Perspective. 420p. 1979. pap. 20.00 (ISBN 0-88936-191-6, IDRC116, IDRC). Unipub.

Castillo, Gloria. Left-Handed Teaching. 2nd ed. LC 77-85508. 1978. pap. 16.95 (ISBN 0-03-040266-2, HoltC); professional ed. 16.95 (ISBN 0-03-043066-6). HR&W.

Castillo, Hernando Del see Del Castillo, Hernando.

Castillo, Homero, et al. Sequential Spanish Readers, 3 bks. Incl. Bk. 1. Primeras Lecturas en Espanol. LC 72-11246. pap. text ed. 5.24 (ISBN 0-395-13389-0); Bk. 2. Aventuras en la Ciudad. LC 72-11248. pap. text ed. 8.96 (ISBN 0-395-14737-9); Bk. 3. El Hidalgo de la Mancha: Aventuras de Don Quijote. LC 72-11249. pap. text ed. 8.68 (ISBN 0-395-13390-4). (Span.). 1973. pap. HM.

Castillo, Otto R. Let's Go. Randall, Margaret, tr. 1984. 7.50 (ISBN 0-915306-44-1). Curbstone.

Castillo, Pedro & Rios, Antonio. Mexican Los Angeles: A Pictorial History. (Monograph: No. 12). 1985. pap. text ed. 15.95 (ISBN 0-89551-053-7). UCLA Chicano Stud.

Castillo, Richard G. Del see Del Castillo, Richard G.

Castillo, Richard Griswold del see Griswold del Castillo, Richard.

Castillo, Ronald. Commodity Futures Trading: The Essential Knowledge. new enl. ed. (Illus.). 111p. 1983. 75.45x (ISBN 0-89266-406-1). Am Classical Coll Pr.

Castillo-Feliu, Guillermo. Cuentos y Microcuentos. LC 77-12972. 1978. pap. text ed. 15.95 (ISBN 0-03-021796-2, HoltC). HR&W.

Castillo-Feliu, Guillermo & Mullen, Edward J. Lecturas Basicas: A Literary Reader. 2nd ed. (Span.). 1981. pap. text ed. 11.95 (ISBN 0-03-058108-7). HR&W.

Castillo-Feliu, Guillermo I. Malevolent Tales. 184p. 1983. text ed. 22.50x (ISBN 0-8290-0721-0); pap. text ed. 9.95x (ISBN 0-8290-1533-7). Irvington.

Castillo Solorzano, Alonso De. The Spanish Pole-Cat: The Adventures of Seniora Rufina. L'Estrange, Roger & Ozell, John, eds. LC 80-2472. Repr. of 1717 ed. 62.50 (ISBN 0-404-19104-5). AMS Pr.

Castino & Harmathy, eds. Fire Risk Assessment - STP 762. 112p. 1982. pap. 15.00 (ISBN 0-8031-0724-2, 04-762000-31). ASTM.

Castino, Anthony P. ProCommentator. (ProCom Ser.). 1986. pap. 19.95 (ISBN 0-673-18202-9). Scott F.

Castino, G. T., ed. see American Society for Testing & Materials.

Castle. Statistics in Operation 1E. 1979. pap. text ed. 8.25 (ISBN 0-443-01951-7). Churchill.

Castle, et al. The Business Insurance Handbook. LC 80-70437. 600p. 1981. 50.00 (ISBN 0-87094-237-9). Dow Jones-Irwin.

Castle, Allen F., tr. see Lang, C., et al.

Castle, Barbara. Castle Diaries Nineteen Seventy-Four to Seventy-Six. 788p. 1981. text ed. 54.50 (ISBN 0-8419-0689-0). Holmes & Meier.

Castle, Beatrice H. The Grand Island Story. Carter, James L., ed. LC 71-11186. 1974. 4.95 (ISBN 0-938746-01-4). Marquette Cnty.

Castle, Caroline. The Hare & the Tortoise. LC 84-9569. (Illus.). 32p. (ps-3). 1985. 10.95 (ISBN 0-8037-0138-1, 01063320). Dial Bks Young.

Castle, Charles. La Belle Otero: The Last Great Courtesan. (Illus.). 192p. 1983. 14.95 (ISBN 0-7181-1935-5, Pub by Michael Joseph). Merrimack Pub Cir.

--The Folies Bergeres. 320p. 1985. 18.95. Watts.

Castle, Coralie. The Complete Book of Steam Cookery. 224p. 1985. 16.95 (ISBN 0-87477-366-0); pap. 9.95. J P Tarcher.

--The Hors d'Oeuvre Book. rev. ed. Orig. Title: Hors d'Oeuvre Etc. (Illus.). 200p. 1985. pap. 8.95 (ISBN 0-89286-258-0). One Hund One Prods.

--Leftovers. LC 83-17203. (Illus.). 192p. (Orig.). 1983. pap. 8.95 (ISBN 0-89286-218-1). One Hund One Prods.

--Soup. rev. ed. LC 81-11277. (Illus.). 192p. 1981. pap. 7.95 (ISBN 0-89286-195-9). One Hund One Prods.

Castle, Coralie & Killeen, Jacqueline. Country Inns Cookery: The Best of American Regional Cooking. LC 82-61102. (Illus.). 160p. 1982. pap. 6.95 (ISBN 0-89286-202-5). One Hund One Prods.

Castle, Coralie & Newton, Astrid. The Art of Cooking for Two. LC 76-6892. (Illus.). 192p. (Orig.). 1976. pap. 7.95 (ISBN 0-912238-76-3). One Hund One Prods.

Castle, Coralie, jt. auth. see Baylis, Maggie.

Castle, Damon. Starbright. 240p. 1983. pap. 2.50 (ISBN 0-8439-2058-0, Leisure Bks). Dorchester Pub Co.

Castle, E. F. & Owens, N. P. Principles of Accounts. 6th ed. 448p. 1981. pap. text ed. 16.95x (ISBN 0-7121-1692-3, Pub. by Macdonald & Evans England). Intl Ideas.

--Principles of Accounts. 7th ed. 401p. 1984. pap. text ed. 19.95x (ISBN 0-7121-1769-5). Trans-Atlantic.

Castle, Edward J. Shakespeare, Bacon, Jonson & Greene. LC 77-113363. 1970. Repr. of 1897 ed. 24.00x (ISBN 0-8046-1010-X, Pub. by Kennikat). Assoc Faculty Pr.

Castle, Emery N. & Hemmi, Kenzo, eds. United States-Japanese Agriculture Trade Relations. LC 81-48245. 456p. 1982. 35.00x (ISBN 0-8018-2815-5); pap. 14.95x (ISBN 0-8018-2814-7). Johns Hopkins.

Castle, Emery N. & Price, Ken A., eds. U. S. Interests & Global Natural Resources: Energy, Minerals, Food. LC 83-42905. 160p. 1983. pap. 6.95x (ISBN 0-8018-3106-7). Johns Hopkins.

Castle, Emory N. & Becker, Manning H. Farm Business Management: The Decision-Making Process. 2nd ed. (Illus.). 320p. 1972. text ed. write for info. (ISBN 0-02-320250-5, 32025). Macmillan.

Castle, Frederick T. Anticipation. LC 83-14931. 352p. 1984. 22.50 (ISBN 0-914232-60-6); pap. 12.50 (ISBN 0-914232-65-7); limited ed. 50.00 (ISBN 0-914232-61-4). McPherson & Co.

--Gilbert Green: The Real Right Way to Dress for Spring. 256p. 1985. 16.95 (ISBN 0-914232-76-2); deluxe edition 50.00 (ISBN 0-914232-77-0). McPherson & Co.

Castle, Gladys C., jt. auth. see Gunn, Jack W.

Castle, H. G. Fire over England. (Illus.). 254p. 1982. 22.50 (ISBN 0-436-08900-9, Pub. by Secker & Warburg UK). David & Charles.

Castle, Irene. Castles in the Air. (Illus.). 264p. 1980. pap. 6.95 (ISBN 0-306-80122-1). Da Capo.

--My Husband. (Series in Dance). (Illus.). 1979. Repr. of 1919 ed. lib. bdg. 25.00 (ISBN 0-306-79505-1). Da Capo.

Castle, Irene, jt. auth. see Castle, Vernon.

Castle, Jayne. Affair of Risk. (Candlelight Ecstasy Ser.: No. 55). (Orig.). 1982. pap. 1.95 (ISBN 0-440-10054-2). Dell.

--Bargain with the Devil. (Candlelight Ecstasy Ser.: No. 26). (Orig.). 1981. pap. 1.75 (ISBN 0-440-10423-8). Dell.

--Conflict of Interest. (Candlelight Ecstasy Ser.: No. 130). (Orig.). 1983. pap. 1.95 (ISBN 0-440-10927-2). Dell.

--Double Dealing. 384p. (Orig.). 1984. pap. 3.95 (ISBN 0-440-12121-3). Dell.

--A Man's Protection. (Candlelight Ecstasy Ser.: No. 36). (Orig.). 1982. pap. 1.75 (ISBN 0-440-15188-0). Dell.

--A Negotiated Surrender. (Candlelight Ecstasy Ser.: No. 68). (Orig.). 1982. pap. 1.95 (ISBN 0-440-16498-2). Dell.

--Power Play. (Candlelight Ecstasy Ser.: No. 79). (Orig.). 1982. pap. 1.95 (ISBN 0-440-17067-2). Dell.

--Relentless Adversary. (Candlelight Ecstasy Ser.: No. 45). (Orig.). 1982. pap. 1.75 (ISBN 0-440-17290-X). Dell.

--Right of Possession. (Candlelight Ecstasy Ser.: No. 23). (Orig.). 1981. pap. 1.75 (ISBN 0-440-17441-4). Dell.

--Spellbound. (Candlelight Ecstasy Ser.: No. 91). (Orig.). 1982. pap. 1.95 (ISBN 0-440-18034-1). Dell.

--Trading Secrets. 1985. pap. 3.50 (ISBN 0-440-19053-3). Dell.

--Wagered Weekend. (Candlelight Ecstacy Ser.: No. 17). (Orig.). 1981. pap. 1.75 (ISBN 0-440-19413-X). Dell.

Castle, Jeffrey Lloyd. How Not to Lose at Poker. 1970. pap. 3.00 (ISBN 0-87980-346-0). Wilshire.

Castle, John, jt. auth. see Hailey, Arthur.

Castle, John N. Manufacturer in the Auto Parts Industry. 18.75. Northwood Campus Bkstore.

Castle, Joseph, tr. see Ehrenburg, Ilya.

Castle, Kate. Ballet Company: The Royal Ballet. (Illus.). 48p. (gr. 1-6). 1985. PLB 9.90 (ISBN 0-531-10023-5). Watts.

Castle, Kathryn. Infant & Toddler Handbook: Invitations for Optimum Early Development. 107p. 1983. pap. 12.95 (ISBN 0-89334-038-3). Humanics Ltd.

Castle, Kathryn, jt. ed. see Swick, Kevin.

Castle, Leon W. A Year of Children's Sermons. LC 76-6717. (Illus.). 144p. 1976. pap. 4.95 (ISBN 0-8054-4918-3). Broadman.

Castle, Malcolm & Watkins, Paul. Modern Milk Production. (Illus.). 320p. 1979. 18.95 (ISBN 0-571-11312-5); pap. 13.50 (ISBN 0-571-11347-8). Faber & Faber.

Castle, Mary. Hospital Infection Control: Principles & Practices. LC 80-13424. 251p. 1980. 28.95x (ISBN 0-471-05395-3, Pub. by Wiley Med). Wiley.

Castle, Mort. Mulbray. (Illus.). 1976. pap. 1.00 (ISBN 0-686-20633-9). Samisdat.

--The Strangers. 320p. (Orig.). 1984. pap. 3.50 (ISBN 0-8439-2174-9, Leisure Bks). Dorchester Pub Co.

Castle, Raymond N., ed. Pyridazines, Vol. 28. LC 72-13270. (Hetercyclic Compounds Ser.). 905p. 1973. 109.00 (ISBN 0-471-38213-2). Krieger.

--Topics in Heterocyclic Chemistry. LC 71-78478. pap. 69.00 (ISBN 0-317-08776-2, 2011959). Bks Demand UMI.

Castle, Sue. The Complete New Guide to Preparing Baby Foods. 1983. pap. 4.50 (ISBN 0-553-24752-2). Bantam.

--Nutrition for Your Child's Most Important Years: Birth to Age Three. Paton, Kathi, ed. (Illus.). 192p. (Orig.). 1984. pap. 8.95 (ISBN 0-671-49403-1, Fireside). S&S.

Castle, Ted & Ballerini, Julia. Carolee Schneemann: Early & Recent Work. LC 82-72833. (Illus.). 52p. 1983. 20.00 (ISBN 0-914232-56-8, Documentext); limited ed. 60.00 (ISBN 0-914232-57-6). McPherson & Co.

Castle, Ted, et al. Essays on Art. 3.00 (ISBN 0-931106-03-6). TVRT.

Castle, Terry. Clarissa's Ciphers: Meaning & Disruption in Richarson's "Clarissa". LC 82-2460. (Illus.). 204p. 1982. 22.50x (ISBN 0-8014-1495-4). Cornell U Pr.

Castle, Tony, ed. The New Book of Christian Quotations. LC 82-25253. 272p. 1983. pap. 9.95 (ISBN 0-8245-0551-4). Crossroad NY.

Castle, Vernon. Modern Dancing. (Ballroom Dance Ser.). 1985. lib. bdg. 79.95 (ISBN 0-87700-758-6). Revisionist Pr.

Castle, Vernon & Castle, Irene. Modern Dancing. (Series in Dance). 1980. Repr. of 1914 ed. 22.50 (ISBN 0-306-76050-9). Da Capo.

Castle, Wanda. The Vicarious Image. Ingraham, Steve, ed. 108p. (Orig.). 1985. pap. 1.45 (ISBN 0-916835-00-6, 600). C & I Pubns.

Castle, Wendell & Hunter-Stiebel, Penelope. The Fine Art of the Furniture Maker. Bayer, Patricia, ed. LC 81-83164. (Illus.). 1981p. (Orig.). pap. 17.95 (ISBN 0-295-96209-7). U of Wash Pr.

Castle, Wilfrid T. Syrian Pageant: The History of Syria & Palestine, 1000 B.C. to A.D. 1945. 1977. lib. bdg. 59.95 (ISBN 0-8490-2716-0). Gordon Pr.

Castle, William B., jt. ed. see Finland, Maxwell.

Castle, William E. The Effect of Selective Narrow-Band Filtering on the Perception of Certain English Vowels. (Janua Linguarum, Series Practica: No. 13). 1964. pap. 25.60x (ISBN 0-686-20926-5). Mouton.

Castle, Winifred M. Statistics in Small Doses. rev. 2nd ed. LC 76-8430. (Illus.). 1977. pap. text ed. 12.50 (ISBN 0-443-01491-4). Churchill.

Castlehaven, James T. The Earl of Castlehaven's Memoirs of the Irish Wars with the Earl of Anglesey's: A Letter from a Person of Honour in the Country. LC 74-3345. 332p. 1974. Repr. of 1684 ed. lib. bdg. 45.00x (ISBN 0-8201-1128-7). Schol Facsimiles.

Castleman, Barry. Asbestos: Medical & Legal Aspects. 608p. 1984. 55.00 (ISBN 0-15-100002-6). HarBraceJ.

Castleman, Benjamin, et al. The Massachusetts General Hospital, 1955-1980. 410p. 1983. text ed. 25.00 (ISBN 0-316-13185-7). Little.

Castleman, Craig. Getting Up: Subway Graffiti in New York. (Illus.). 164p. 1982. 16.50x (ISBN 0-262-03089-6). MIT Pr.

--Getting Up: Subway Graffitti in New York. (Illus.). 212p. 1982. pap. 6.95 (ISBN 0-262-53051-1). MIT Pr.

Castleman, Deke, ed. see Stanley, David.

Castleman, H. & Podrazik, W. J. Watching TV: Four Decades of American Television. 320p. 1982. 22.95 (ISBN 0-07-010268-6); pap. 14.95 (ISBN 0-07-010269-4). McGraw.

Castleman, Harry & Podrazik, Walter. The Beatles Again. LC 77-92320. (Rock & Roll Reference Ser.: No. 2). 280p. 1977. individuals 14.95 (ISBN 0-87650-086-6); institutions 17.95. Pierian.

Castleman, Harry & Podrazik, Walter J. All Together Now: First Complete Beatles Discography, 1961-75. LC 77-92320. (Rock & Roll Reference Ser.: No. 1). 410p. 1976. individual 16.95 (ISBN 0-87650-075-0); institutions 22.95. Pierian.

--All Together Now: The First Complete Beatles Discography, 1961-1975. 1980. pap. 7.95 (ISBN 0-345-29794-6). Ballantine.

--The End of the Beatles? (Rock & Roll Reference Ser.: No. 10). 1985. (individuals) 29.50 (ISBN 0-87650-162-5); (institutions) 39.50. Pierian.

--Five Hundred Five Television Questions Your Friends Can't Answer. 1983. pap. 3.95 (ISBN 0-8027-7210-2). Walker & Co.

Castleman, Kenneth R. Digital Image Processing. LC 78-27578. (Illus.). 1979. text ed. 44.95 (ISBN 0-13-212365-7). P-H.

Castleman, Michael. Crime Free. 1984. 16.95 (ISBN 0-671-45172-3). S&S.

Castleman, Riva. American Impressions: Prints since Pollock. Ralston, Susan, ed. LC 84-47690. (Illus.). 224p. 1985. 40.00 (ISBN 0-394-53683-5). Knopf.

--Printed Art: A View of Two Decades. LC 79-56089. (Illus.). 144p. 1979. 17.50 (ISBN 0-87070-531-8); pap. 9.95 (ISBN 0-87070-541-5). Museum Mod Art.

--Prints from Blocks: Gauguin to Now. (Illus.). 84p. 1983. pap. 8.95 (ISBN 0-87070-561-X). Museum Mod Art.

--Prints of the Twentieth Century: A History. LC 76-9219. (Illus.). 1976. pap. 10.95x (ISBN 0-19-519888-3). Oxford U Pr.

Castleman, Riva, intro. by. Latin American Prints from the Museum of Modern Art. (Illus.). 64p. 1974. pap. 3.00 (ISBN 0-913456-24-1, Pub. by Ctr Inter-Am Rel). Interbk Inc.

Castleman, Robbie. David: Man after God's Own Heart, 2 vols. (Fisherman Bible Studyguide). 1981. saddle stitched 2.95 ea. Vol. 1, 70p (ISBN 0-87788-164-2). Vol. 2, 63p (ISBN 0-87788-165-0). Shaw Pubs.

Castleman, William J. Beauty & the Mission of the Teacher. 144p. 1982. 7.50 (ISBN 0-682-49853-X, University). Exposition Pr FL.

Castles, Alex C. Australia: A Chronology & Fact Book, 1606-1976. LC 77-21516. (World Chronology Ser.). 151p. 1978. 8.50 (ISBN 0-379-16313-6). Oceana.

Castles, Francis G. The Social Democratic Image of Society: A Study of the Achievements & Origins of Scandinavian Social Democracy in Comparative Perspective. 1978. 21.95x (ISBN 0-7100-8870-1). Routledge & Kegan.

Castles, Francis G., ed. The Impact of Parties: Politics & Policies in Democratic Capitalist States. LC 81-85190. (Illus.). 370p. 1982. 27.50 (ISBN 0-8039-9787-6). Sage.

Castles, Stephen & Kosack, Godula. Immigrant Workers & Class Structure in Western Europe. 2nd ed. 1984. 32.00x (ISBN 0-19-878018-4); pap. 14.95x (ISBN 0-19-878017-6). Oxford U Pr.

Castles, Stephen, et al. Here for Good: Western Europe's New Ethnic Minorities. 259p. (Orig.). 1984. pap. 11.25 (ISBN 0-86104-752-4, Pub. by Pluto Pr). Longwood Pub Group.

Castleton, Kenneth B. Petroglyphs & Pictographs of Utah, Vol. 2. (Illus.). 1980. 15.00 (ISBN 0-686-26976-4). Utah Mus Natural Hist.

Castleton, Virginia. Handbook of Natural Beauty. LC 75-25828. 1975. 12.95 (ISBN 0-87857-100-0). Rodale Pr Inc.

--Handbook of Natural Beauty. 1978. pap. 8.95 (ISBN 0-87857-217-1). Rodale Pr Inc.

--Secrets of Natural Beauty. LC 72-76464. 1978. 5.95; pap. 2.25 (ISBN 0-87983-167-7). Keats.

Castlewitz, D. M. VisiCalc Made Easy. 160p. 1983. 12.95 (ISBN 0-931988-89-6, Osborne-McGraw). McGraw.

Castlewitz, David M. The VisiCalc Program Made Easy. 160p. (Orig.). 1983. pap. 12.95 (ISBN 0-07-931089-3, 89-3). Osborne-McGraw.

Castley, A. Business Situation German. 97p. (Ger. & Eng.). 1980. pap. 13.95 (ISBN 0-582-35161-8, M-9206). French & Eur.

Castner, Charles S. One of a Kind, Milton Snavely Hershey, 1857-1945. LC 83-73169. 356p. 1984. 29.95 (ISBN 0-9612586-0-8). Derry Lit.

Castner, Jane F., jt. auth. see Dreier, William A.

Casto, Glendon, ed. CAMS Training Manual. LC 79-64723. (Curriculum & Monitoring System Ser.). 102p. 1979. tchrs. ed. 9.70x (ISBN 0-8027-9061-5). Walker & Co.

Casto, Glendon, ed. see Douglass, Vonda & Baer, Richard.

Casto, Glendon, ed. see Mitchell, Helen & Hoagland, Victoria.

Casto, Glendon, ed. see Peterson, Adrienne & Sedjo, Karen.

Casto, Glendon, ed. see Sedjo, Karen & Baer, Richard.

Casto, James E. Huntington: An Illustrated History. 160p. 1985. 22.95 (ISBN 0-89781-101-1). Windsor Pubns Inc.

Castoire, Marie & Posner, Richard. The Gold Shield. 320p. 1984. pap. 2.95 (ISBN 0-523-42122-2). Pinnacle Bks.

Caston, Don. Easy-to-Make Aids for Your Handicapped Child: A Guide for Parents & Teachers. (Illus.). 144p. 1982. 14.95 (ISBN 0-13-223081-X); pap. 6.95 (ISBN 0-13-223073-9). P-H.

--Easy-to-Make Aids for Your Handicapped Child. 176p. 27.00x (ISBN 0-686-87159-6, Pub. by Souvenir Pr). State Mutual Bk.

Castonguay, C. Meaning & Existence in Mathematics. LC 72-96052. (Library of Exact Philosophy: Vol. 9). 159p. 1972. 26.00 (ISBN 0-387-81110-9). Springer-Verlag.

Castonguay, Russell. A Comparative Guide to Classification Schemes for Local Government Document Collections. LC 83-26594. xv, 143p. 1984. lib. bdg. 35.00 (ISBN 0-313-24208-9, CCG/). Greenwood.

Castor, G., ed. see De Ronsard, P.

Castor, Graham & Cave, Terrence, eds. Neo-Latin & the Vernacular in Renaissance France. (Illus.). 1984. 45.00x (ISBN 0-19-815780-0). Oxford U pr.

Castoriadis, Cornelius. Crossroads in the Labyrinth. Soper, Kate & Ryle, Martin, trs. from Fr. LC 83-62319. 339p. 1984. text ed. 30.00x (ISBN 0-262-03105-1). MIT Pr.

Castoro, Laura. Emerald & Sapphire. (Tapestry Romance Ser.). (Orig.). 1983. pap. 2.50 (ISBN 0-671-46415-9). PB.

Castoro, Laura, jt. auth. see Bailey, David.

Castracane Degli Antelminelli, F. Report on the Diatoms Collected During the Voyage of H.M.S. Challenger. (Illus.). 1966. Repr. of 1886 ed. 33.60 (ISBN 3-7682-0293-3). Lubrecht & Cramer.

Castres, Elizabeth De see De Castres, Elizabeth.

Castries, Armand-Charles Augustin de La Croix. A Middle Passage: The Journal of Armand-Charles Augustin de la Croix de Castries, Duc de Castries, Comtes de Charlus & Baron Croix. Jackman, Sydney W., ed. xv, 113p. 1970. 10.00 (ISBN 0-934552-26-6). Boston Athenaeum.

Castries, Duc de see De Castries, Duc.

Castro, Adolph de. Portrait of Ambrose Bierce. LC 74-610. (Illus.). 1974. Repr. 18.50x (ISBN 0-8464-0737-X). Beekman Pubs.

Castro, Americo. Iberoamerica. 4th ed. (Span). (gr. 10-12). 1971. pap. text ed. 16.95 (ISBN 0-03-069170-2, HoltC). HR&W.

--An Idea of History: Selected Essays of Americo Castro. Gilman, Stephen & King, Edmund L., eds. LC 76-41762. 353p. 1977. 12.50x (ISBN 0-8142-0220-9). Ohio St U Pr.

--The Spaniards: An Introduction to Their History. King, Willard F. & Margaretten, Selma, trs. from Sp. LC 67-14000. 638p. 1980. pap. 15.95x (ISBN 0-520-04177-1). U of Cal Pr.

Castro, Angel. Cubano..., Go Home! 1972. pap. 3.00 (ISBN 0-685-48631-1). E Torres & Sons.

--Cuentos De Nueva York. 1973. pap. 2.50 (ISBN 84-399-0644-7). Ediciones.

--Cuentos Yanquis. 1972. pap. 2.50 (ISBN 0-89729-137-9). Ediciones.

--Refugiados. 1971. pap. text ed. 4.00 (ISBN 0-685-48630-3). E Torres & Sons.

Castro, Carol C. Welcoming God's Forgiveness. 120p. 1978. pap. text ed. 3.95 (ISBN 0-697-01681-1); leader's guide 4.50 (ISBN 0-697-01682-X); classroom tchr's guide .75 (ISBN 0-697-01907-1); adult resource book, pack/10,10.25 1.05 (ISBN 0-697-01685-4). Wm C Brown.

--Welcoming Jesus. 120p. 1979. pap. 3.95 (ISBN 0-697-01702-8); leader's guide 4.50 (ISBN 0-697-01703-6); classroom teacher's guide .75 (ISBN 0-697-01909-8); adult resource book, pack/10, 10.25 1.05 (ISBN 0-697-01704-4). Wm C Brown.

Castro Colonies Heritage Association, Inc., ed. The History of Medina County, Texas, Vol. I. (Illus.). 600p. 1983. 57.00 (ISBN 0-88107-010-6). Natl ShareGraphics.

Castro Colonies Heritage Association, ed. History of Medina County, Texas. (Illus.). 600p. 1985. Repr. 65.00 (ISBN 0-88107-031-9). Natl ShareGraphics.

Castro, Daniel. In That Stillness... LC 79-92054. 201p. (Orig.). 1980. pap. 4.95 (ISBN 0-918038-12-X). Journey Pubns.

Castro, Emilio. Sent Free: Mission & Unity in the Perspective of the Kingdom. 112p. (Orig.). 1985. pap. 5.95 (ISBN 0-8028-0068-8). Eerdmans.

Castro, F. First Congress of CP of Cuba. 211p. 1978. pap. 5.45 (ISBN 0-8285-0456-3, Pub. by Progress Pubs USSR). Imported Pubns.

Castro, Fernando. Five Rolls of Plus-X: An Urban Photography Vision of Peru. Bilingual ed. (Span. & Eng.). 1983. 8.00 (ISBN 0-934840-08-3). Studia Hispanica.

Castro, Fidel. The Cuban Revolution, National Liberation & the Soviet Union: Two Speeches by Fidel Castro. 40p. 1974. pap. 0.70 (ISBN 0-87898-109-8). New Outlook.

--Fidel Castro Speeches: Building Socialism in Cuba, Vol. 2. Taber, Michael, ed. 400p. 1983. lib. bdg. 30.00X (ISBN 0-87348-624-2); pap. 7.95 (ISBN 0-87348-650-1). Path Pr NY.

--Fidel Castro Speeches Nineteen Eighty-Four-Nineteen Eighty-Five: War & Crisis in the Americas. Taber, Michael, ed. (Fidel Castro Speeches Ser.: Vol. 3). 270p. (Orig.). 1985. lib. bdg. 23.00 (ISBN 0-87348-656-0); pap. 6.95 (ISBN 0-87348-657-9). Path Pr NY.

--Revolutionary Struggle: Volume One (1947-1958) of the Selected Works of Fidel Castro. Bonachea, Rolando & Valdes, Nelson P., eds. 1972. pap. 7.95x (ISBN 0-262-52027-3). MIT Pr.

--The World Crisis: Its Economic & Social Impact on the Underdeveloped Countries. (Illus.). 224p. 1984. 21.75x (ISBN 0-86232-250-2, Pub. by Zed Pr England); pap. 5.95 (ISBN 0-86232-251-0, Pub. by Zed Pr England). Biblio Dist.

Castro, Fidel, et al. Fidel by Fidel: A New Interview with Dr. Fidel Castro Ruz, President of the Republic of Cuba. (Great Issues of the Day: No. 3). 160p. 1985. lib. bdg. 16.95x (ISBN 0-89370-330-3); pap. text ed. 8.95x (ISBN 0-89370-430-X); signed, ltd. ed. 100.00x (ISBN 0-89370-010-X). Borgo Pr.

--Fidel by Fidel: A New Interview with Dr. Fidel Castro Ruz, President of the Republic of Cuba. 160p. 1985. pap. 8.95 (ISBN 0-87877-430-0). Newcastle Pub.

Castro, J. Paul D. see Fielding, Henry.

Castro, Jan G. The Art & Life of Georgia O'Keeffe. (Illus.). 1985. 30.00 (ISBN 0-517-55058-X). Crown.

Castro, Jose I. The Sharks of North American Waters. LC 82-45892. (W. L. Moody, Jr., Natural History Ser.: No. 5). (Illus.). 194p. (Orig.). 1983. 19.50 (ISBN 0-89096-140-9); pap. 9.95 (ISBN 0-89096-143-3). Tex A&M Univ Pr.

Castro, Josue De see De Castro, Josue.

Castro, Karen G., tr. see Ferreiro, Emilia & Teberosky, Ana.

Castro, Margarita O., tr. see Rosenberger, Joseph.

Castro, Margarita O., tr. see Sapir, Richard & Murphy, Warren.

Castro, Mercedes. Noche Callada (Poemas) (Illus.). 79p. (Orig., Span.). pap. 3.75 (ISBN 0-9604748-0-3). Castro.

Castro, Michael. Ghost Hiways & Other Homes. 1976. 2.50 (ISBN 0-918476-03-8). Cornerstone Pr.

--Interpreting the Indian: Twentieth-Century Poets & the Native American. LC 83-14539. 224p. 1983. 22.50x (ISBN 0-8263-0672-1). U of NM Pr.

Castro, Norma S. de see DeCastro, Norma S.

Castro, Oscar & Kimbrough, Victoria. In Touch: A Beginning American English Series. Incl. students bk. 1, 1979 (ISBN 0-582-79742-X); tchr's manual 1 (ISBN 0-582-79743-8); workbook 1 (ISBN 0-582-79744-6); cassette 1; students bk. 2 (ISBN 0-582-79746-2); tchr's manual 2 (ISBN 0-582-79747-0); workbook 2 (ISBN 0-582-79748-9); cassette 2 (ISBN 0-582-79749-7); students bk. 3 (ISBN 0-582-79750-0); tchr's manual 3 (ISBN 0-582-79753-5); workbook 3 (ISBN 0-582-79752-7); cassette 3 (ISBN 0-582-79751-9). (English As a Second Language Bk.). (Illus.). 1980. pap. text ed. 5.75x ea. student bk.; tchr's manual 7.95x ea.; wkbk. 3.50x ea.; cassette 24.50 ea. Longman.

Castro, Rene & De Cadenet, J. J. Welding Metallurgy of Stainless & Heat-Resisting Steels. LC 74-676582. pap. 50.00 (ISBN 0-317-26032-4, 2024434). Bks Demand UMI.

Castro De Davila, Maria D. Arquitectura en San Juan de Puerto Rico (Siglo XIX) LC 78-21582. (Illus.). 1979. 20.00 (ISBN 0-8477-2110-8). U of PR Pr.

Castro-Magana, Mariano, jt. auth. see Collipp, Platon J.

Castronovo, David. Edmund Wilson. (Literature & Life Ser.). 250p. 1984. 15.50 (ISBN 0-8044-2116-1). Ungar.

Castroverde, Waldo de see De Castroverde, Waldo.

Castro Y Bellius, Guillem De see De Castro Y Bellius, Guillem.

Castro Y Rossi, Aldolfo De. The History of the Jews in Spain: From the Time of Their Settlement in That Country till the Commencement of the Present Century. Kirwan, Edward D., tr. from Span. LC 70-97273. (Judaica Ser). (Illus.). vii, 276p. 1972. Repr. of 1851 ed. lib. bdg. 15.00x (ISBN 0-8371-2593-6, CAJS). Greenwood.

Casty, Alan. Act of Writing & Reading: A Combined Text. (Orig.). 1966. pap. text ed. 15.95 (ISBN 0-13-003780-X). P-H.

--Improving Writing: A Positive Approach. (Illus.). 400p. 1982. 15.95 (ISBN 0-13-453399-2). P-H.

--Let's Make It Clear! A Workbook & Anthology for Concrete & Accurate Writing. 374p. (Orig.). 1977. pap. text ed. 11.95 (ISBN 0-15-550580-7, HC); answer key avail. (ISBN 0-15-550581-5). HarBraceJ.

--Mass Media & Mass Man. 2nd ed. LC 81-40917. 318p. 1982. pap. text ed. 14.25 (ISBN 0-8191-2261-0). U Pr of Amer.

--A Mixed Bag: A New Collection for Understanding & Response. 2nd ed. (Illus.). 256p. 1975. pap. text ed. 15.95 (ISBN 0-13-586016-4). P-H.

Casty, Alan & Dodge, Richard. The Writing Project: A Collection of Contemporary Prose. 384p. 1981. pap. text ed. write for info. (ISBN 0-534-01081-4). Wadsworth Pub.

Casty, Alan & Tighe, Donald J. Staircase to Writing & Reading. 3rd ed. (Illus.). 1979. 16.95 (ISBN 0-13-840579-4). P-H.

Casty, Alan H. The Shape of Fiction. 2nd ed. 448p. 1975. pap. text ed. 12.95 (ISBN 0-669-91066-X). Heath.

Casualty Surgeons Association of Great Britain. Care of the Acutely Ill & Injured: Proceedings, International Congress of Emergency Surgery, Brighton, 5th, 1981. Wilson, David H. & Marsden, Andrew K., eds. LC 82-1836. 300p. 1982. 60.00 (ISBN 0-471-10238-5, Pub. by Wiley Med). Wiley.

Casullo, Daniel P. & Matarazzo, Francis S. The Preparation & Restoration of the Multi-Rooted Tooth with Furcation Involvement. Cohen, D. Walter, ed. (Continuing Dental Education Series). 108p. 1980. 18.00 (ISBN 0-931386-20-9). Quint Pub Co.

Casurella, Frank. How Race Fans Lose Millions. LC 73-76623. 1974. pap. 3.25 (ISBN 0-914878-00-X). Charlotte Pubs.

--Twentieth Century Country Music Stars, & the Hall of Fame. new ed. LC 73-86073. (Illus.). 350p. 1974. pap. text ed. write for info. (ISBN 0-685-50219-8). Charlotte Pubs.

Caswall, Henry. America, & the American Church. LC 77-83413. (Religion in America Ser). 1969. Repr. of 1839 ed. 21.00 (ISBN 0-405-00234-3). Ayer Co Pubs.

Casway, Jerrold I. Owen Roe O'Neill & the Struggle for Catholic Ireland. LC 83-5901. (Illus.). 344p. 1984. 40.00 (ISBN 0-8122-7895-X). U of Pa Pr.

Caswell, Austin B., ed. Bacilly: A Commentary Upon the Art of Proper Singing. (Musical Theorists in Translation Ser.: Vol. 7). 1968. lib. bdg. 50.00 (ISBN 0-912024-27-5). Inst Mediaeval Mus.

Caswell, Christopher. Trailerable Sailboats. (Illus.). 1982. 19.95 (ISBN 0-393-03271-X). Norton.

Caswell, Hal. Evolutionary Demography: Matrix Models & Their Interpretation. 300p. 1985. 45.00. Macmillan.

Caswell, Helen R. God's World Makes Me Feel So Little. 32p. (gr. k-3). 1985. paper over board 5.95 (ISBN 0-687-15510-X). Abingdon.

--Shadows from the Singing House: Eskimo Folk Tales. LC 68-13867. (Illus.). (gr. 2-6). 1968. 8.95 (ISBN 0-8048-0523-7). C E Tuttle.

Caswell, Hollis L. City School Surveys: An Interpretation & Appraisal. LC 70-176632. (Columbia University. Teachers College. Contributions to Education Ser.: No. 358). Repr. of 1929 ed. 22.50 (ISBN 0-404-55358-3). AMS Pr.

Caswell, Hollis L. & Campbell, Doah S. Readings in Curriculum Development. 753p. 1984. Repr. of 1937 ed. lib. bdg. 65.00 (ISBN 0-89987-197-6). Darby Books.

Caswell, Lucy S. & Loomis, George A., Jr. Billy Ireland. LC 81-119198. (Illus.). 235p. (Orig.). 1980. pap. 18.95 (ISBN 0-88215-051-0). Ohio St U Lib.

Caswell, Robert W. The Compass of the Heart. 1978. 20.00 (ISBN 0-913028-59-2); pap. 4.00 (ISBN 0-913028-52-5). North Atlantic.

Caswell, W. E. & Snow, G. A. Particles & Fields, APS-DPF, University of Maryland, 1982: AIP Conference Proceedings No. 98, Particles & Fields Subseries, 29th. LC 83-70807. 413p. 1983. lib. bdg. 37.75 (ISBN 0-88318-197-5). Am Inst Physics.

Casy, A. F., ed. PMR Spectroscopy in Medicinal & Biological Chemistry. 1972. 67.00 (ISBN 0-12-164050-7). Acad Pr.

Catabzaro, Ronald J., ed. Alcoholism: The Total Treatment Approach. 508p. 1968. 28.50 (ISBN 0-318-15292-4). Natl Coun Alcoholism.

Catacalos, Rosemary. Again for the First Time. 72p. 1984. pap. 5.00 (ISBN 0-940510-07-3). Tooth of Time.

Catach. L' Orthographe Francaise a L'epoque de la Renaissance. (Publ. Romanes et Franc.). 72.00 (ISBN 0-685-36649-9). French & Eur.

Catala, Rafael. Cienciapoesia. LC 83-62040. (Serie de Poesia Guampara: No. 1). 80p. (Orig., Spa.). 1984. pap. text ed. 5.95 (ISBN 0-910235-04-X). Prisma Bks.

--Copulantes. LC 83-62039. (Serie de Poesia Guampara: No. 2). 80p. (Orig., Spa.). 1984. pap. text ed. 5.95 (ISBN 0-910235-03-1). Prisma Bks.

--Index of American Periodical Verse: 1981. LC 73-3060. 406p. 1983. 29.50 (ISBN 0-8108-1602-4). Scarecrow.

Catala, Rafael & Anderson, James D., eds. Index of American Periodical Verse: 1982. LC 73-3060. 669p. 1984. 37.50 (ISBN 0-8108-1731-4). Scarecrow.

Catala, Rafael & Lugo, Roberto, eds. Soles Emellis. LC 83-61864. 160p. (Orig., Spa.). 1983. pap. text ed. 6.95 (ISBN 0-910235-02-3). Prisma Bks.

Catala, Rafael, et al. Index of American Periodical Verse, 1983. LC 73-3060. 711p. 1985. 37.50 (ISBN 0-8108-1832-9). Scarecrow.

Catalado, Michael F., jt. auth. see Rodgers, Joan E.

Catalan, Jose, jt. auth. see Hawton, Keith.

Catalan Lafuente, Jose. Diccionario Tecnico Del Agua. 301p. (Span.). 1977. pap. 29.95 (ISBN 84-400-2913-6, S-50098). French & Eur.

Catalano, Gary. Remembering the Rural Life. (Paperback Poets Ser.). 1979. 9.95x (ISBN 0-7022-1308-X); pap. 4.95x (ISBN 0-7022-1309-8). U of Queensland Pr.

--Slow Tennis: Poems, Nineteen Eighty to Nineteen Eighty-Three. LC 84-11980. 62p. 1985. 9.95 (ISBN 0-7022-1775-1). U of Queensland Pr.

--The Years of Hope: Australian Art & Criticism 1959-1968. (Illus.). 1981. 37.50x (ISBN 0-19-554220-7). Oxford U Pr.

Catalano, Joseph S. A Commentary of Jean-Paul Sartre's "Being & Nothingness". LC 79-21234. (Midway Reprint Ser.). 1980. pap. 13.00x (ISBN 0-226-09699-8, P862, Phoen). U of Chicago Pr.

Catalano, Ralph. Health, Behavior & the Community: An Ecological Perspective. LC 78-23714. (Pergamon General Psychology Ser.: Vol. 76). (Illus.). 1979. text ed. 35.00 (ISBN 0-08-022972-7); pap. text ed. 11.00 (ISBN 0-08-022971-9). Pergamon.

Cataldo. Parent Education for Early Childhood. cancelled (ISBN 0-8391-1837-6, 20036). Pro Ed.

Cataldo, Bernard F., et al. Introduction to Law & the Legal Process. 3rd ed. LC 79-13193. 866p. 1980. 40.45x (ISBN 0-471-14082-1); T M 7.50 (ISBN 0-471-02267-5). Wiley.

Cataldo, Christine Z. Infant & Toddler Programs: A Guide to Very Early Childhood Education. LC 82-11418. (Illus.). 240p. 1983. pap. text ed. 11.50 (ISBN 0-201-11020-2). Addison-Wesley.

Cataldo, Corinne B. & Whitney, Eleanor N. Nutrition & Dietary Therapy: Principles & Practice. (Illus.). 550p. 1985. pap. text ed. 26.96 (ISBN 0-314-93160-0). West Pub.

Cataldo, Corrine, jt. auth. see Whitney, Eleanor N.

Cataldo, John. Pen Calligraphy. LC 78-72583. (Illus.). 1979. 16.95 (ISBN 0-87192-108-1). Davis Mass.

Cataldo, John W. Lettering. 1983. 12.95 (ISBN 0-87192-015-8, Davis Pubns); pap. 9.95 (ISBN 0-87192-146-4). Sterling.

--Lettering: A Guide for Teachers. new ed. LC 58-13613. (Illus.). 111p. 1974. 13.95 (ISBN 0-87192-015-8). Davis Mass.

Cataldo, Leonard & Pelletier, Robert. The Astrologer's Handbook: A Guide to Constructing a Natal Chart for Yourself or Friends. 256p. (Orig.). 1983. pap. 11.45i (ISBN 0-316-13198-9). Little.

Cataldo, Michael F., jt. auth. see Rodgers.

Cataldo, Peter J., ed. The Dynamic Character of Christian Culture: Essays on Dawsonian Themes. 242p. (Orig.) 1984. lib. bdg. 23.50 (ISBN 0-8191-3959-9, Soc Christ Cult); pap. text ed. 11.50 (ISBN 0-8191-3960-2). U Pr of Amer.

Cataldo, Susan. Brooklyn-Queens Day. Owen, Maureen, ed. (Summer Ser.). 48p. (Orig.). 1982. pap. 3.00 (ISBN 0-916382-30-3). Telephone Bks.

Catalina, Lynn J. How to Speak Air Force: A Basic Survival Guide. LC 84-91011. (Illus.). 96p. (Orig.). 1984. pap. 5.25 (ISBN 0-9613769-0-2). L J Catalina.

Catallozzi, Joseph P. Simply Sweet & Sometimes Sour. 48p. 1983. 6.95 (ISBN 0-89962-307-7). Todd & Honeywell.

Catallus. The Poems of Catallus. Whigham, Peter, tr. from Lat. (Classics Ser.). 1980. pap. 4.95 (ISBN 0-14-044180-8). Penguin.

Catalogues of the Library of the Marine Biological Association of the United Kingdom. Marine Biological Association of the United Kingdom, Library. 1978. lib. bdg. 1500.00 (ISBN 0-8161-0076-4, Hall Library). G K Hall.

Catalona, W. & Ratliff, T., eds. Urologic Oncology. (Cancer Treatment & Research Ser.). 1984. lib. bdg. 69.50 (ISBN 0-89838-628-4, Pub. by Martinus Nijhoff Netherlands). Kluwer Academic.

Catalona, William J. Prostate Cancer. 224p. 1984. 39.50 (ISBN 0-8089-1648-3, 790819). Grune.

Catalyst Editors. Upward Mobility. LC 81-4967. 312p. 1982. 15.95 (ISBN 0-03-056163-9). HR&W.

Catalyst Group. Marketing Yourself. 224p. 1981. pap. 3.95 (ISBN 0-553-23751-9). Bantam.

Catalyst Staff. It's Your Future! Catalyst's Career Guide for High School Girls. 344p. (Orig.). 1984. pap. 9.95 (ISBN 0-87866-280-4). Petersons Guides.

--Making the Most of Your First Job. 240p. 1982. pap. 2.75 (ISBN 0-345-30160-9). Ballantine.

--What to Do with the Rest of Your Life. 1981. pap. 11.95 (ISBN 0-671-25071-X, Touchstone Bks). S&S.

--When Can You Start? The Complete Job Search Guide for Women of All Ages. 148p. 1982. 9.95 (ISBN 0-02-522960-5). Macmillan.

Catalytic Inc. Study of the Effects of Reduced Occupational Radiation Exposure Limits on the Nuclear Power Industry (AIF-NESP-017) (National Environmental Studies Project: NESP Reports). 62p. 1980. 45.00 (ISBN 0-318-13594-9); NESP sponsors 15.00 (ISBN 0-318-13595-7). Atomic Indus Forum.

Catan, John R., ed. see Owens, Joseph.

Catan, John R., tr. see Reale, Giovanni.

Catan, Omero C. Secrets of Shuffleboard Strategy. 2nd enl ed. LC 72-91761. (Illus.). 224p. 1973. lib. bdg. 6.00 buckram (ISBN 0-9600618-1-9). Catan.

Catanach, I. J. Rural Credit in Western India, 1875-1930: Rural Credit & the Co-Operative Movement in the Bombay Presidency. LC 72-94986. 1970. 38.50x (ISBN 0-520-01595-9). U of Cal Pr.

Catanese, Anthony J. The Politics of Planning & Development. LC 84-8334. 231p. 1984. 29.00 (ISBN 0-8039-2314-7); pap. 14.50 (ISBN 0-8039-2315-5). Sage.

--Scientific Methods of Urban Analysis. LC 71-160384. (Illus.). 336p. 1972. 19.95 (ISBN 0-252-00185-0). U of Ill Pr.

Catanese, Anthony J. & Farmer, Paul W. Personality, Politics, & Planning: How City Planners Work. 277p. 1978. 17.50 (ISBN 0-318-13121-8); 15.50 (ISBN 0-318-13122-6). Am Plan Assn.

Catanese, Anthony J. & Snyder, James C. Introduction to Urban Planning. (Illus.). 1979. text ed. 39.00 (ISBN 0-07-010228-7). McGraw.

Catanese, Anthony J., et al. Urban Planning: A Guide to Information Sources. LC 78-13462. (Urban Studies Information Guide Ser.: Vol. 2). 165p. 1979. 60.00x (ISBN 0-8103-1399-5). Gale.

Catanese, Anthony James. Planners & Local Politics: Impossible Dreams. LC 73-94287. (Sage Library of Social Research: Vol. 7). 224p. 1974. 24.00 (ISBN 0-8039-0397-9); pap. 12.00 (ISBN 0-8039-0378-2). Sage.

Catania, A. Charles. Learning. (Century Psychology Ser.). (Illus.). 1979. P-H.

--Learning. 2nd ed. (Illus.). 416p. 1984. 27.95 (ISBN 0-13-527697-7). P-H.

Catania, A. Charles & Brigham, T. A., eds. Handbook of Applied Behavior Analysis: Social & Instructional Processes. LC 77-20991. (Century Psychology Ser.). 750p. 1979. 39.50x (ISBN 0-470-99347-2). Halsted Pr.

Catania, A. Charles & Brigham, Thomas A., eds. Handbook of Applied Behavior Analysis: Social & Instructional Processes. 750p. 1978. text ed. 44.50x (ISBN 0-8290-0857-8). Irvington.

Catania, Charles A. & Brigham, Thomas A., eds. Handbook of Applied Behavior Analysis: Social & Instructional Processes. 750p. 1982. pap. text ed. 24.95x (ISBN 0-8290-1034-3). Irvington.

Catania, Patrick J., et al. Agricultural Options: A Primer for Producers. (Illus.). 88p. (Orig.). 1984. pap. 7.95 (ISBN 0-932250-21-1). Doane Pub.

Catanius, Charles S., ed. The Greatest Flower Paintings in Full Colours by the Greatest Artists of All Times. (Illus.). 98p. 1983. 225.45x (ISBN 0-86650-072-3). Gloucester Art.

Catanzano, Raymond A. & Whitman, Douglas. Modern Business Law. 432p. 1984. Student Course Mastery Guide 11.95 (ISBN 0-394-34009-4, RanC). Random.

Catanzariti, John & Ferguson, E. James. The Papers of Robert Morris, 1781-1784: Volume 6, July 22-October 31, 1782. LC 72-91107. (Robert Morris Papers). (Illus.). 1984. 45.00x (ISBN 0-8229-3485-X). U of Pittsburgh Pr.

Catanzariti, John, jt. ed. see Ferguson, E. James.

Catanzaro, Denys De see De Catanzaro, Denys.

Catanzaro, Ronald J., ed. Alcoholism: The Total Treatment Approach. (Illus.). 528p. 1977. 35.50x (ISBN 0-398-00295-9). C C Thomas.

Catchings, Paul D. Thirty-One Financial Secrets. LC 85-50642. (Illus.). 274p. 1985. 39.95 (ISBN 0-9614410-0-3); manuscript 49.95 (ISBN 0-9614410-1-1). Long Range Planners.

Catchings, Waddill & Roos, Charles F. Money, Men & Machines. 1953. 12.50 (ISBN 0-686-17719-3). Quest Edns.

Catchpole, Brian. Clash of Cultures. (Orig.). 1981. pap. text ed. 10.00x (ISBN 0-435-31097-6). Heinemann Ed.

--A Map History of Modern China. (Illus.). 1977. pap. text ed. 8.00x (ISBN 0-435-31095-X). Heinemann Ed.

--Map History of Our Own Times: From the 1950's to the Present Day. viii, 148p. (Orig.). 1983. pap. text ed. 8.00x (ISBN 0-435-31099-2). Heinemann Ed.

--A Map History of Russia. 1974. pap. text ed. 8.00x (ISBN 0-435-31157-3). Heinemann Ed.

--A Map History of the British People Since 1700. 2nd ed. 1975. pap. text ed. 9.00x (ISBN 0-435-31160-3). Heinemann Ed.

--A Map History of the Modern World. 3rd ed. 1982. pap. text ed. 8.00x (ISBN 0-435-31098-4). Heinemann Ed.

--A Map History of the United States. 1972. pap. text ed. 8.00x (ISBN 0-435-31158-1). Heinemann Ed.

Catchpole, Clive. Deserts. LC 83-7757. (Illus.). 32p. (gr. 1-4). 1984. 10.95 (ISBN 0-8037-0035-0, 01063-320). Dial Bks Young.

--Deserts. LC 83-7757. (Pied Piper Book). (Illus.). 32p. (ps-4). 1985. 4.95 (ISBN 0-8037-0037-7, 0481140). Dial Bks Young.

--Grasslands. LC 83-27123. (Illus.). (ps-4). 1984. 10.95 (ISBN 0-8037-0082-2, 01063-320). Dial Bks Young.

--Grasslands. LC 83-27123. (Illus.). 32p. (gr. k-4). 1985. pap. 4.95 (ISBN 0-8037-0083-0, Pied Piper). Dial Bks Young.

--Jungles. LC 83-7796. (Illus.). 32p. (gr. 1-4). 1984. 10.95 (ISBN 0-8037-0034-2). Dial Bks Young.

--Jungles. LC 83-7796. (Pied Piper Book). (Illus.). 32p. (ps-4). 1985. 4.95 (ISBN 0-8037-0036-9, 0481140). Dial Bks Young.

--Mountains. LC 83-25273. (Illus.). 32p. (ps-4). 1984. 10.95 (ISBN 0-8037-0086-5, 01063-320). Dial Bks Young.

--Mountains. LC 83-25273. (Illus.). 32p. (gr. k-4). 1985. pap. 4.95 (ISBN 0-8037-0087-3, Pied Piper). Dial Bks Young.

--Owls. LC 77-8371. (New Biology Ser.). (Illus.). (gr. 4-9). 1978. 7.95 (ISBN 0-07-010232-5). McGraw.

Catchpole, Joan M. Watercolour Painting: A Beginner's Guide. (Illus.). 1975. 21.00x (ISBN 0-7188-2162-9). Intl Ideas.

Catchside, D. G. Genetics of Recombination. (Genetics Principles & Perspectives Ser.). 182p. 1977. pap. text ed. 19.95 (ISBN 0-7131-2613-2). E Arnold.

Catcott, E. J., ed. Animal Health Technology. LC 77-85491. (Illus.). 480p. 1977. 32.00 (ISBN 0-939674-10-6). Am Vet Pubns.

--Canine Medicine, Vols. I & II. LC 79-53900. (Illus.). 1400p. 1979. 92.50 (ISBN 0-939674-05-X). Am Vet Pubns.

Catcott, E. J., jt. ed. see Archibald, J.

Cate, Curtis. George Sand: A Biography. (YA) 1976. pap. 3.95 (ISBN 0-380-00700-2, 56242-1, Discus). Avon.

--George Sand: A Biography. LC 75-8680. 864p. 1975. 17.50 (ISBN 0-395-19954-9). HM.

--The War of the Two Emperors: The Confrontation Between Napoleon & Tzar Alexander. LC 84-42506. (Illus.). 423p. 1985. pap. 24.95 (ISBN 0-394-53670-3). Random.

Cate, Curtis, jt. auth. see Goldovsky, Boris.

Cate, Curtis, tr. see Saint-Exupery, Antoine De.

Cate, George A., ed. The Correspondence of Thomas Carlyle & John Ruskin. LC 81-50784. 272p. 1982. 30.00x (ISBN 0-8047-1114-3). Stanford U Pr.

Cate, James L. & Anderson, E. N. Medieval & Historiographical Essays in Honor of James Westfall Thompson. LC 66-25904. Repr. of 1938 ed. 34.50x (ISBN 0-8046-0072-4, Pub. by Kennikat). Assoc Faculty Pr.

Cate, James L., jt. auth. see Craven, Wesley F.

Cate, James L., jt. ed. see Craven, Wesley F.

Cate, Joan M. How to Start Your Own Home Typing Business. (Illus.). 102p. (Orig.). 1984. pap. 21.95 (ISBN 0-930025-00-8). Calabasas Pub.

Cate, Margaret D. Our Todays & Yesterdays, a Story of Brunswick & the Coastal Islands. LC 77-187380. (Illus.). 302p. 1972. Repr. of 1930 ed. 20.00 (ISBN 0-87152-075-3). Reprint.

Cate, Phillip D. & Gill, Susan. Theophile-Alexandre Steinlen. (Illus.). 166p. 1982. pap. 15.00 (ISBN 0-87905-129-9, Peregrine Smith). Gibbs M Smith.

Cate, Phillip D. & Hitchings, Sinclair H. The Color Revolution. 1985. pap. 12.00 (ISBN 0-87905-032-2). Boston Public Lib.

Cate, Phillip D., jt. auth. see Schimmel, Herbert D.

Cate, Phillip D., jt. ed. see Weisberg, Gabriel P.

Cate, Rikki. A Cat's Tale. LC 81-6997. (Illus.). 48p. (gr. 5-9). 1982. 9.95 (ISBN 0-15-215538-4, HJ). HarBraceJ.

Cate, Robert. Help in Ages Past, Hope for Years to Come: Daily Devotions from the Old Testament. 201p. 1983. 13.95 (ISBN 0-13-387449-4); pap. 5.95 (ISBN 0-13-387431-1). P-H.

--How to Interpret the Bible. LC 81-66638. (Orig.). 1983. pap. 6.95 (ISBN 0-8054-1142-9). Broadman.

Cate, Robert L. Layman's Bible Book Commentary: Exodus, Vol. 2. LC 78-59976. 1979. 5.75 (ISBN 0-8054-1172-0). Broadman.

--Old Testament Roots for New Testament Faith. LC 80-70914. 1982. pap. 7.95 (ISBN 0-8054-1220-4). Broadman.

--These Sought a Country. 1985. pap. 9.95 (ISBN 0-8054-1232-8). Broadman.

Cate, Ten. Hypertrophic Cardiomyopathy: Clinical Recognition & Management. (Basic & Clinical Cardiology Ser.). 256p. 1985. 55.00 (ISBN 0-8247-7374-8). Dekker.

Cate, Ten A. Richard see Ten Cate, A. Richard.

Catel, Charles-Simon. Les Bayaderes. D'Indy, Vincent, ed. (Chefs-d'oeuvre classiques de l'opera francais Ser: Vol. 7). (Illus.). 440p. (Fr.). 1972. pap. 32.50x (ISBN 0-8450-1107-3). Broude.

Catel, Jean. Rhythme et Language Dans la Primiere Edition Des Leaves of Grass. 1930. lib. bdg. 27.50 (ISBN 0-8414-3377-1). Folcroft.

--Rythme et Langage Dans la L'Edition Des "Leaves of Grass". 1979. Repr. of 1930 ed. lib. bdg. 32.50 (ISBN 0-8482-0469-7). Norwood Edns.

--Walt Whitman: La Naissance Du Poete. (Tr, from Fr). 1971. Repr. of 1929 ed. 39.00 (ISBN 0-403-00900-6). Scholarly.

Cately, George. Heathcliff Himself. 1984. pap. 4.95 (ISBN 0-671-50490-8, Wallaby). S&S.

Cateora, Philip R. International Marketing. 5th ed. 1983. 29.95x (ISBN 0-256-02844-3). Irwin.

--Strategic International Marketing. 450p. 1985. 37.50 (ISBN 0-87094-641-2). Dow Jones-Irwin.

Cateora, Philip R. & Richardson, Lee, eds. Readings in Marketing: The Qualitative & Quantitative Areas. LC 67-10928. (Illus., Orig.). 1967. pap. text ed. 6.95x (ISBN 0-89197-373-7). Irvington.

Cateora, Philip R., jt. ed. see Andersen, Clifton R.

Cater, Douglas & Lee, Philip R. Politics of Health. LC 77-28732. 248p. 1979. Repr. of 1972 ed. lib. bdg. 15.00 (ISBN 0-88275-640-0). Krieger.

Cater, Douglass & Strickland, Stephen P. TV Violence & the Child: The Evolution & Fate of the Surgeon General's Report. LC 74-83207. 168p. 1975. 7.95x (ISBN 0-87154-203-X). Russell Sage.

Cater, Douglass, jt. auth. see Childs, Marquis W.

Cater, Douglass & Nyhan, Michael J., eds. The Future of Public Broadcasting. LC 76-8889. 382p. 1976. text ed. 39.95 (ISBN 0-275-56990-X); pap. text ed. 18.95 (ISBN 0-275-64590-8). Praeger.

Cater, Gwendolyn M. Which Way Is South Africa Going? LC 79-3658. pap. 43.50 (ISBN 0-317-27941-6, 2056026). Bks Demand UMI.

Cater, John C. Electronically Speaking: Computer Speech Generation. 232p. 1982. pap. 14.95 (ISBN 0-672-21947-6, 21947). Sams.

Cater, John P. Electronically Hearing Computer Speech Recognition. LC 84-50051. 13.95 (ISBN 0-672-22173-X). Sams.

Cater, Nick. Operation Vendetta. 192p. 1983. pap. 2.50 (ISBN 0-441-63430-3). Ace Bks.

--War from the Clouds. 224p. (Orig.). 1980. pap. 2.25 (ISBN 0-441-87192-5, Pub. by Charter Bks). Ace Bks.

Caterinicchio, Russell. DRG's: What They Are & How to Survive. LC 84-50589. 150p. 1984. pap. text ed. 16.50 (ISBN 0-943432-30-8). Slack Inc.

Caterson, Lucile P. Handbook of Florida Flowers. (Orig.). pap. 1.95 (ISBN 0-8200-0405-7). Great Outdoors.

Cates, Bill, ed. see Whalen, Nana.

Cates, Clifford. Air Force Collecting. LC 82-60731. (Illus.). 1983. 14.95 (ISBN 0-912958-43-X); pap. 9.95 (ISBN 0-912958-44-8). MCN Pr.

Cates, Donald W. Index to J. C. Flanigan's Volume II History of Gwinnett County, Georgia 1818-1960. McCabe, Alice S., ed. 120p. 1985. 10.00. Gwinnett Hist.

--Index to Volume Two History of Gwinnett County, Ga, 1818-1960. 1984. 10.00. Gwinnett Hist.

Cates, Ed. I Can't Understand Why My Biscuits Never Turn Out Right I Make Them the Same Way Every Time. 96p. 1985. 7.95 (ISBN 0-89962-470-7). Todd & Honeywell.
Cates, Edwin H. English in America. rev. ed. LC 66-10145. (In America Bks.). (Illus.). (gr. 5-11). 1978. PLB 7.95 (ISBN 0-8225-0205-4). Lerner Pubns.
Cates, G. Truett & Swaffar, Janet K. Reading a Second Language. (Language in Education Ser.: No. 20). 32p. 1979. pap. 3.95x (ISBN 0-15-599045-4). Ctr Appl Ling.
Cates, Jerry R. Insuring Inequality: Administrative Leadership in Social Security, 1935-1954. 216p. 1982. text ed. 18.50x (ISBN 0-472-10026-2). U of Mich Pr.
Cates, Judith N. & Sussman, Marvin B., eds. Family Systems & Inheritance Patterns. LC 82-15790. (Marriage & Family Review Ser.: Vol. 5, No. 3). 116p. 1983. text ed. 19.95 (ISBN 0-86656-158-7, B158); pap. text ed. 9.95 (ISBN 0-86656-214-1). Haworth Pr.
Cates, Paul W. Bible ABC's: Four & Five Year Old's. (ps). write for info. (ISBN 0-686-22195-8). Freedom Univ-FSP.
--Bible ABC's: Three Year Old's. (ps). 4.95 (ISBN 0-686-22196-6). Freedom Univ-FSP.
--Neurological Impairment. 30.00 (ISBN 0-686-22194-X). Freedom Univ-FSP.
--Pre-School Curriculum. 24.95 (ISBN 0-686-22197-4). Freedom Univ-FSP.
--Test & Measurement. 30.00 (ISBN 0-686-22193-1). Freedom Univ-FSP.
Cates, Rosalie. Branded. LC 79-19211. 1981. 14.95 (ISBN 0-87949-147-7). Ashley Bks.
Cates, W. L., tr. see Merle d'Aubigne, Jean H.
Cates, Ward M. A Practical Guide to Educational Research. (Illus.). 224p. 1985. pap. text ed. 19.95 (ISBN 0-13-690678-8). P-H.
Catesby, Mark. Natural History of Carolina, Florida & the Bahama Islands, Catalogue Volume. (Illus.). 50.00 (ISBN 0-384-07865-6). Johnson Repr.
--Natural History of Carolina, Florida & the Bahama Islands. (Illus.). Repr. 575.00 (ISBN 0-384-07315-8). Johnson Repr.
Catford, J. C. Fundamental Problems in Phonetics. LC 76-47168. (Midland Bks Ser.: No. 294). (Illus.). 288p. 1977. 22.50x (ISBN 0-253-32520-X); pap. 8.95x (ISBN 0-253-20294-9). Ind U Pr.
Cath, Stanley, et al. Father & Child: Developmental & Clinical Perspectives. 1982. text ed. 29.50 (ISBN 0-316-13196-2). Little.
Cath, Stanley H., jt. ed. see Berezin, Martin A.
Cathcart, Charles D. Money, Credit & Economic Activity. 1982. 24.50x (ISBN 0-256-02491-X). Irwin.
Cathcart, Daniel C. Aircrash Litigation Techniques. (Contemporary Litigation Ser.). 300p. 1985. 65.00 (ISBN 0-87215-880-2). Michie Co.
Cathcart, Dwight. Doubting Conscience: Donne & the Poetry of Moral Argument. LC 74-78985. 1975. 10.00x (ISBN 0-472-08198-5). U of Mich Pr.
Cathcart, E., tr. see Savigny, Friedrich K.
Cathcart, George. Correspondence of Lieutenant-General the Honorable Sir George Cathcart. LC 70-75544. (Illus.). Repr. of 1856 ed. 23.75x (ISBN 0-8371-0984-1, CAO&, Pub. by Negro U Pr). Greenwood.
Cathcart, Glee. Apple Music for Apple II Plus, IIe & IIc. (Computer Fun Ser.). (Illus.). 48p. 1984. pap. 3.95 (ISBN 0-86582-167-4, EN79253). Enrich.
Cathcart, Gloria & Cartcart, W. George. Programming Exercises in BASIC for Microcomputers. 128p. 1984. 8.75 (ISBN 0-7715-1012-8). Forkner.
Cathcart, Gloria M. & Cathcart, W. George. Learning About Computers. 192p. 1984. 10.95x (ISBN 0-7715-3681-X). Forkner.
Cathcart, Helen. Prince Charles: The Making of a Prince. LC 77-73686. (Illus.). 1977. 8.50 (ISBN 0-8008-6555-3). Taplinger.
Cathcart, J., jt. auth. see Alessandra, A.
Cathcart, Jacqueline. Love's Fine Edge. 1983. 8.95 (ISBN 0-686-84732-6, Avalon). Bouregy.
Cathcart, Kevin J. Nahum in the Light of Northwest Semetic. (Biblica et Orientalia: Vol. 26). 1973. pap. 25.00 (ISBN 88-7653-326-5). Loyola.
Cathcart, Linda. The Martha Jackson Collection at the Albright-Knox Art Gallary. LC 75-24230. (Illus.). 1975. pap. 4.95 (ISBN 0-914782-04-5). Buffalo Acad.
Cathcart, Linda & Brutvan, Cheryl A. Texas on Paper. (Illus.). 37p. 1982. 6.00 (ISBN 0-916365-05-0). Ind Curators.
Cathcart, Linda, jt. auth. see Tucker, Marcia.
Cathcart, Linda L. Alfred Jensen: Paintings & Diagrams from the Years 1957-1977. LC 77-83756. 12.50 (ISBN 0-914782-15-0). Buffalo Acad.
--American Painting of the Seventies. LC 78-21790. (Illus.). 1978. 18.50 (ISBN 0-914782-22-3). Buffalo Acad.
--American Still Life: Nineteen Forty-Five to Nineteen Eighty-Two. 1983. pap. 19.18i (ISBN 0-06-430131-1). Har-row.
--Charles Simonds. LC 77-81577. (Illus.). 1977. 1.00 (ISBN 0-914782-14-2). Buffalo Acad.
--Nancy Graves: A Survey 1969 to 1980. LC 80-13227. (Illus.). 1980. pap. 15.00 (ISBN 0-914782-34-7). Buffalo Acad.
Cathcart, M. K., jt. ed. see Krakauer, R. S.
Cathcart, Rex. The Most Contrary Region: The BBC in Northern Ireland, 1924-1984. 306p. 1985. pap. 8.95 (ISBN 0-85640-323-7, Pub. by Blackstaff Pr). Longwood Pub Group.
Cathcart, Robert. Post Communication: Rhetorical Analysis & Evaluation. LC 80-36842. (Speech Communication Ser.). 144p. 1981. pap. text ed. 8.40 scp (ISBN 0-672-61520-7). Bobbs.
--Post-Communication: Rhetorical Analysis & Evaluation. 2nd ed. 144p. 1980. pap. text ed. write for info. (ISBN 0-02-319690-4). Macmillan.
Cathcart, Robert, jt. ed. see Gumpert, Gary.
Cathcart, Robert S., et al. Small Group Communication: A Reader. 4th ed. 520p. 1984. pap. text ed. write for info (ISBN 0-697-04189-1). Wm C Brown.
Cathcart, Ruth & Strong, Michael. Beyond the Classroom. (Gateway to English Program). (Illus.). 208p. (Orig.). 1981. pap. 7.95 (ISBN 0-88377-170-5). Newbury Hse.
Cathcart, W. George, jt. auth. see Cathcart, Gloria M.
Cathcart, W. George, ed. The Mathematics Laboratory: Readings from the Arithmetic Teacher. LC 77-341. (Illus.). 232p. 1977. pap. 6.20 (ISBN 0-87353-073-X). NCTM.
Cathedralite, Inc. Geodesic Floor Plans. (Illus.). 96p. 1981. pap. text ed. 10.95 (ISBN 0-8403-2528-2). Kendall-Hunt.
Cathell, D. W. The Physician Himself & What He Should Add to His Scientific Acquirements. 2nd ed. LC 70-180562. (Medicine & Society in America Ser). 216p. 1972. Repr. of 1882 ed. 16.00 (ISBN 0-405-03941-7). Ayer Co Pubs.
Cather. My Antonia. (Book Notes). 1985. pap. 2.50 (ISBN 0-8120-3528-3). Barron.
Cather, Willa. Alexander's Bridge. Repr. lib. bdg. 9.95x (ISBN 0-89190-520-0, Pub. by River City Pr). Amereon Ltd.
--Alexander's Bridge. LC 76-56439. xxx, 138p. 1977. pap. 5.50 (ISBN 0-8032-5863-1, BB 635, Bison). U of Nebr Pr.
--April Twilights. 11.95 (ISBN 0-88411-127-X, Pub by. Aeonian Pr). Amereon Ltd.
--April Twilights (Nineteen Hundred Three) rev. ed. Slote, Bernice, ed. LC 62-8899. (Illus.). xlviii, 88p. 1968. 11.95x (ISBN 0-8032-0011-0). U of Nebr Pr.
--Death Comes for the Archbishop. (YA) 1927. 16.95 (ISBN 0-394-42154-X). Knopf.
--Death Comes for the Archbishop. (YA) 1971. pap. 3.95 (ISBN 0-394-71679-5, Vin). Random.
--Death Comes for the Archbishop. LC 83-22034. 1984. 8.95 (ISBN 0-394-60503-9). Modern Lib.
--Death Comes for the Archbishop. Large Print ed. LC 83-18096. 374p. 1984. Repr. of 1971 ed. 14.95 (ISBN 0-89621-506-7). Thorndike Pr.
--Death Comes for the Archbishop. 1984. pap. 8.95 (ISBN 0-394-60503-9, Vin). Random.
--Early Stories of Willa Cather. Bennett, Mildred R., ed. 288p. 1983. pap. 7.95 (ISBN 0-396-08268-8). Dodd.
--Five Stories. (YA) 1956. pap. 4.95 (ISBN 0-394-70028-7, Vin, V28). Random.
--The Kingdom of Art: Willa Cather's First Principles & Critical Statements, 1893-1896. Slote, Bernice, ed. LC 65-15275. (Illus.). xiv, 489p. 1967. 27.95x (ISBN 0-8032-0012-9). U of Nebr Pr.
--A Lost Lady. 1973. 14.95 (ISBN 0-394-48558-0). Knopf.
--A Lost Lady. 192p. (YA) 1972. 12.95 (ISBN 0-394-48558-0, V705, Vin); pap. 3.95 (ISBN 0-394-71705-8). Random.
--Lucy Gayheart. (YA) 1976. pap. 3.95 (ISBN 0-394-71756-2, Vin). Random.
--My Antonia. 16.95 (ISBN 0-395-07514-9); pap. 5.95 (ISBN 0-395-08356-7, SenEd). HM.
--My Antonia. 19.95 (ISBN 0-88411-287-X, Pub. by Aeonian Pr). Amereon Ltd.
--My Mortal Enemy. 1961. pap. 3.95 (ISBN 0-394-70200-X, V200, Vin). Random.
--Obscure Destinies. LC 74-5323. 1974. pap. 4.95 (ISBN 0-394-71179-3, V-179, Vin). Random.
--The Old Beauty & Others. LC 76-7362. 1976. pap. 3.95 (ISBN 0-394-72122-5, Vin). Random.
--One of Ours. LC 22-26887. 1971. pap. 4.95 (ISBN 0-394-71252-8, V252, Vin). Random.
--The Professor's House. LC 72-10470. 288p. 1973. pap. 4.95 (ISBN 0-394-71913-1, Vin). Random.
--Sapphira & the Slave Girl. LC 74-20797. 1975. pap. 4.95 (ISBN 0-394-71434-2, Vin). Random.
--Shadows on the Rock. (YA) 1931. 13.95 (ISBN 0-394-44506-6). Knopf.
--Shadows on the Rock. 1971. pap. 5.95 (ISBN 0-394-71680-9, Vin). Random.
--Shadows on the Rock. large print ed. LC 82-19485. (American Authors (Fiction) Ser.). 330p. 1983. Repr. of 1931 ed. 13.95 (ISBN 0-89621-413-3). Thorndike Pr.
--The Song of the Lark. 1983. pap. 8.95 (ISBN 0-395-34530-8). HM.
--The Song of the Lark. 27.95 (ISBN 0-88411-288-8, Pub. by Aeonian Pr). Amereon Ltd.
--The Troll Garden. 160p. 1984. pap. 3.95 (ISBN 0-452-00714-3, Mer). NAL.
--The Troll Garden: A Definitive Edition. Woodress, James L., ed. LC 82-20138. xxx, 176p. 1983. 15.95 (ISBN 0-8032-1417-0). U of Nebr Pr.
--Uncle Valentine & Other Stories: Willa Cather's Uncollected Short Fiction, 1915-1929. Slote, Bernice, ed. LC 72-83755. xxx, 183p. 1973. 16.95x (ISBN 0-8032-0820-0). U of Nebr Pr.
--Willa Cather's Collected Short Fiction, 1892-1912. rev. ed. Faulkner, Virginia, ed. LC 73-126046. xlii, 601p. 1970. 23.95x (ISBN 0-8032-0770-0). U of Nebr Pr.
--The World & the Parish: Willa Cather's Articles & Reviews, 1893-1902, 2 Vols. Curtin, William M., ed. LC 65-10548. 1970. Set. 39.50x (ISBN 0-8032-0706-9). Vol. 1; xii, 502. Vol. 2; xii, 538. U of Nebr Pr.
--Youth & the Bright Medusa. LC 75-11560. 1975. pap. 3.95 (ISBN 0-394-71684-1, Vin). Random.
Catherall, Arthur. Kidnapped by Accident. LC 69-14319. (Illus.). (gr. 4-6). 1969. 10.00 (ISBN 0-688-40990-3). Lothrop.
Catherall, Ed. Clocks & Time. LC 82-50141. (Fun with Science Ser.). 12.68 (ISBN 0-382-06651-0). Silver.
--Electric Power. LC 81-86270. (Fun with Science Ser.). 12.68 (ISBN 0-382-06629-4). Silver.
--Hearing. LC 82-50142. (Fun with Science Ser.). 12.68 (ISBN 0-382-06649-9). Silver.
--Investigating Graphs. (Investigating Mathematics Ser.). (Illus.). 32p. (gr. 3-6). PLB 11.00 (ISBN 0-516-02281-4). Childrens.
--Investigating Numbers. (Investigating Mathematics). (Illus.). 32p. (gr. 3-6). 1983. PLB 11.00 (ISBN 0-516-02282-2). Childrens.
--Magnets & Magnetism. LC 82-50138. (Fun with Science Ser.). 12.68 (ISBN 0-382-06652-9). Silver.
--Sight. LC 82-50143. (Fun with Science Ser.). 12.68 (ISBN 0-382-06650-2). Silver.
--Solar Power. LC 81-86269. (Fun with Science Ser.). 12.68 (ISBN 0-382-06627-8). Silver.
--Taste & Smell. LC 82-50140. (Fun with Science Ser.). 12.68 (ISBN 0-382-06647-2). Silver.
--Touch. LC 82-50139. (Fun with Science Ser.). 12.68 (ISBN 0-382-06648-0). Silver.
--Water Power. LC 81-86272. (Fun with Science Ser.). 12.68 (ISBN 0-382-06630-8). Silver.
Cathers, David. Furniture of the American Arts & Crafts Movement. 1982. pap. 9.95 (ISBN 0-452-25374-8, Plume). NAL.
Catherwood, Benjamin F. Basic Theories of Distribution. facs. ed. LC 71-121454. (Essay Index Reprint Ser). 1939. 20.00 (ISBN 0-8369-1700-6). Ayer Co Pubs.
Catherwood, Christopher. Five Evangelical Leaders. 240p. 1985. pap. 7.95 (ISBN 0-87788-274-6); 12.95 (ISBN 0-87788-257-6). Shaw Pubs.
Catherwood, Fred. On the Job: The Christian Nine to Five. 192p. 1983. pap. 5.95 (ISBN 0-310-37261-5). Zondervan.
Catherwood, Frederick. First Things First: The Ten Commandments in the 20th Century. LC 81-51. 160p. 1981. pap. 5.95 (ISBN 0-87784-472-0). Inter Varsity.
Catherwood, Mary. Chase of Saint-Castin, & Other Stories of the French in the New World. LC 77-128723. (Short Story Index Reprint Ser). 1894. 17.00 (ISBN 0-8369-3614-0). Ayer Co Pubs.
--Romance of Dollard. facs. ed. LC 75-137725. (American Fiction Reprint Ser). 1889. 18.00 (ISBN 0-8369-7024-1). Ayer Co Pubs.
Catherwood, Mary H. Lower Illinois Valley Local Sketches of Long Ago. 55p. 1980. Repr. 3.00 (ISBN 0-686-27587-X). E S Cunningham.
--Mackinac & Lake Stories. 1972. Repr. of 1899 ed. lib. bdg. 19.50 (ISBN 0-8422-8023-5). Irvington.
--The Queen of the Swamp & Other Plain Americans. 1972. Repr. of 1899 ed. lib. bdg. 22.50 (ISBN 0-8422-8024-3). Irvington.
Cathey, Bill V. A New Day in Church Revivals. LC 83-70645. 1984. pap. 6.95 (ISBN 0-8054-6244-9). Broadman.
Cathey, Gerald M. Dental Anatomy. (Dental Laboratory Technology Manuals Ser). viii, 236p. 1972. pap. 12.50x (ISBN 0-8078-7905-3). U of NC Pr.
Cathey, James F., jt. auth. see Valfells, Sigrid.
Cathey, W. Thomas. Optical Information Processing & Holography. LC 73-14604. (Pure & Applied Optics Ser). 398p. 1974. 40.95 (ISBN 0-471-14078-3, Pub. by Wiley-Interscience). Wiley.
Cathie, Bruce L. & Temm, Peter N. UFOs & Anti-Gravity. LC 77-8718. (A Walnut Hill Book). (Illus.). 1971. pap. 6.95 (ISBN 0-89407-011-8). Strawberry Hill.
Cathie, John. The Political Economy of Food Aid. LC 81-9151. 200p. 1982. 25.00x (ISBN 0-312-62259-7). St Martin.
Cathles, Lawrence M. The Viscosity of the Earth's Mantle. LC 74-16162. (Illus.). 400p. 1975. 47.50x (ISBN 0-691-08140-9). Princeton U Pr.
Catholic Biblical Association of America, tr. The Gospel & Epistles According to John: Taken from the New Testament of the New American Bible. (Orig.). (gr. 6-12). 1983. pap. text ed. 0.75 (ISBN 0-686-23772-2). US Catholic.
Catholic Bishops of England & Wales. A Catechism of Christian Doctrine. LC 82-50599. 72p. 1982. pap. 2.00 (ISBN 0-89555-176-4). TAN Bks Pubs.
Catholic Church. The Roman & British Martyrology. 1980. lib. bdg. 79.95 (ISBN 0-8490-3128-1). Gordon Pr.
Catholic Church-Sacred Congregation of Divine Worship. Celebrating the Saints. International Committee on English in the Liturgy, tr. from Latin. 1978. pap. 10.00 (ISBN 0-916134-30-X). Pueblo Pub Co.
Catholic Church, Sacred Congregation for Divine Worship. The Study Edition (Lectors' Guide) of the Lectionary for Mass, Cycle A Sundays & Solemnities. International Committee on English in the Liturgy, tr. (The Study Edition (Lector's Guide) of the Lectionary for Mass Ser.: Texts from the New American Bible). 1977. pap. 6.95 (ISBN 0-916134-04-0). Pueblo Pub Co.
--The Study Edition (Lectors' Guide) of the Lectionary for Mass, Cycle B Sundays & Solemnities. 1978. pap. 6.95 (ISBN 0-916134-05-9). Pueblo Pub Co.
Catholic Church, Sacred Congregaton of Divine Worship. Lectionary for Mass: Cycle C, Sundays & Solemnities. Hartdegen, Steven J., ed. International Committee on English in the Liturgy Confraternity of Christian Doctrine for the New American Bible, tr. from Lat. (Lectionary for Mass). 1973. 27.50 (ISBN 0-916134-03-2). Pueblo Pub Co.
Catholic Health Association. Health Care Ministry Assessment: A Basic Accountability Process for Sponsors of Catholic Health Facilities. LC 83-10066. 80p. 1983. pap. 4.00 (ISBN 0-87125-087-X). Cath Health.
--The Ministry of Healing: Readings in the Catholic Health Care Ministry. LC 81-12201. 120p. 1981. pap. 7.50 (ISBN 0-686-85771-2). Cath Health.
Catholic Health Association Division of Legal Services. You Mean I Can't Do This? 2nd ed. LC 81-15457. (Illus.). 40p. 1981. pap. text ed. 0.50 (ISBN 0-87125-067-5). Cath Health.
Catholic Heritage Press, jt. auth. see Tiso, Francis.
Catholic Library Association. C L A: Handbook & Membership Directory. 30.00 ea. Cath Lib Assn.
--Guide to Catholic Literature, 6 vols. Romig, Walter, ed. Incl. 20.00 (ISBN 0-685-22623-9); 10.00; Vols. 3-5. 1944-1955. 15.00 ea.; Vol 6. 1956-1959. 17.50 (ISBN 0-685-22626-3); Vol. 7. 1960-1963. 25.00 (ISBN 0-685-22627-1); Vol. 8. 1964-1967. 25.00 (ISBN 0-685-22628-X). Cath Lib Assn.
Catholic University Of America. Catholic University Studies in German, 19 Vols. Repr. of 1943 ed. Set. 430.00 (ISBN 0-404-50220-2). AMS Pr.
--Catholic University Studies in Romance Languages & Literatures, 60 Vols. Repr. of 1959 ed. Set. 1429.50 (ISBN 0-404-50300-4). AMS Pr.
--New Catholic Encylopedia, 17 vols. LC 66-22292. 712p. 1981. Repr. of 1967 ed. Set. 550.00 (ISBN 0-07-010235-X). Publishers Guild.
--Psychological Counseling of Adolescents: The Proceedings. Steimel, Raymond J., ed. LC 62-6111. pap. 44.00 (ISBN 0-317-10527-2, 2005212). Bks Demand UMI.
--Studies in American Church History. Repr. of 1942 ed. 662.50 (ISBN 0-404-57750-4). AMS Pr.
Catholic University of America, Music Education Workshop. Music Pedagogy: The Proceedings of the Workshop on Music Pedagogy, Conducted at the Catholic University of America, June 15-16, 1962. Werder, Richard H., ed. LC 64-66051. pap. 24.00 (ISBN 0-317-09949-3, 2005359). Bks Demand UMI.
Catholic University Of America - School Of Law. Jubilee Law Lectures. facs. ed. LC 71-134067. (Essay Index Reprint Ser). 1939. 17.00 (ISBN 0-8369-1907-6). Ayer Co Pubs.
Catholic University of America, Washington, D. C. Catalog of the Oliveira Lima Library, 2 vols. 1970. Set. 200.00 (ISBN 0-8161-0873-0, Hall Library). G K Hall.
Catholic University of America, Washington, D.C., June 11-14, 1963. Proceedings of the Plasma Space Science Symposium. Chang, C. C. & Huang, S. S., eds. (Astrophysics & Space Science Library: No.3). 377p. 1965. lib. bdg. 60.50 (ISBN 90-277-0112-1, Pub. by Reidel Holland). Kluwer Academic.
Catholicon Anglicum. An English Latin Wordbook. (EETS, OS Ser.: No. 75). Repr. of 1881 ed. 63.00 (ISBN 0-527-00074-4). Kraus Repr.
Cathon, Laura E., ed. Stories to Tell to Children. 145p. 3.95 (ISBN 0-318-15101-4, A105). Natl Assn Preserv & Perpet Storytelling.
Cathon, Laura E., et al, eds. Stories to Tell to Children: A Selected List. LC 73-13317. (Illus.). 168p. 1974. pap. 4.95 (ISBN 0-8229-5246-7). U of Pittsburgh Pr.
Cathy, S. Truett. Mr. Chick-Fil-A. 192p. 1985. pap. 9.95 (ISBN 0-8407-9030-9). Nelson.
Catich, Edward M. Reed, Pen & Brush Alphabets for Writing & Lettering. (Visual Communications Bks.). (Illus.). 64p. (Orig.). 1980. pap. 8.95 (ISBN 0-8038-5891-4). Hastings.
Cativiela, A., tr. see Bonnet, L. & Schroeder, A.
Cativiela, A., tr. see Schroeder, A. & Bonnet, L.
Cativiela, A., tr. see Schroeder, L. Bonnet A.
Catledge, Oraien E. & Coles, Robert. Cabbagetown. (Illus.). 112p. 1985. 24.95 (ISBN 0-292-71094-1). U of Tex Pr.
Catledge, Turner, jt. auth. see Alsop, Joseph.
Catlett, Joyce, jt. auth. see Firestone, Robert.
Catlett, Robert H. Readings in Animal Energetics. LC 73-11003. 237p. 1973. text ed. 29.50x (ISBN 0-8422-7119-8); pap. text ed. 9.75x (ISBN 0-8290-0668-0). Irvington.
Catlett, Robert H., ed. Readings of Biological Concern. LC 72-6695. 84p. 1972. pap. text ed. 4.75x (ISBN 0-8422-0239-0). Irvington.

Catley, Bryan. Art Deco & Other Figures. (Illus.). 344p. 1978. 79.50 (ISBN 0-902028-57-X). Antique Collect.
--Art Deco & Other Figures. (Illus.). 1978. 79.50. Apollo.
Catley, Lucille M., jt. auth. see Wright, Jessie L.
Catley, Melanie. Forest of Dreams. (Candelight Ecstasy Ser.: No. 366). (Orig.). 1985. pap. 2.25 (ISBN 0-440-12630-4). Dell.
--Hired Husband. (Candlelight Supreme Ser: No. 101). (Orig.). 1985. pap. 2.75 (ISBN 0-440-13646-6). Dell.
--Star Attraction. (Candlelight Ecstasy Ser.: No. 248). 192p. (Orig.). 1984. pap. 1.95 (ISBN 0-440-18295-6). Dell.
--A Vision of Love. (Candlelight Ecstasy Ser.: No. 336). 192p. (Orig.). 1985. pap. 2.25 (ISBN 0-440-18483-5). Dell.
Catlin, Alan. Animal Acts. 92p. (Orig.). 1983. pap. 3.95 (ISBN 0-934040-10-9). Quality Ohio.
--Visiting Day on the Psychiatric Ward. 3.50 (ISBN 0-318-04451-X). Pudding.
Catlin, Daniel, Jr. Liberal Education at Yale: The Yale College Course of Study 1945-1978. LC 82-17576. 264p. (Orig.). 1983. lib. bdg. 27.25 (ISBN 0-8191-2796-5); pap. text ed. 13.25 (ISBN 0-8191-2797-3). U Pr of Amer.
Catlin, David T. A Naturalist's Blue Ridge Parkway. LC 83-26003. 234p. (Orig.). 1984. text ed. 18.95x (ISBN 0-87049-426-0); pap. 7.95 (ISBN 0-87049-430-9). U of Tenn Pr.
Catlin, F. S., ed. see Betz, C. E.
Catlin, George. Catlin's North American Indian Portfolio: A Reproduction. 1844 ed. LC 78-132585. 1970. Repr. of 1844 ed. 250.00 (ISBN 0-8040-0029-8, 82-70191, SB). Ohio U Pr.
--George Catlin: Episodes from "Life Among the Indians" & "Last Rambles". Ross, Marvin C., ed. LC 59-7959. 1980. pap. 14.95 (ISBN 0-8061-1693-5). U of Okla Pr.
--Kissinger's Atlantic Charter. 144p. 1974. 13.50x (ISBN 0-87471-694-2). Rowman.
--Letters & Notes on the Manners, Customs & Conditions of the North American Indians, Vol. 1. LC 64-18844. (Illus.). 264p. 1973. pap. 6.95 (ISBN 0-486-22118-0). Dover.
--Letters & Notes on the Manners, Customs & Conditions of the North American Indians, Vol. 2. LC 64-18844. (Illus.). 266p. 1973. pap. 6.95 (ISBN 0-486-22119-9). Dover.
--The Story of the Political Philosophers, 2 vols. Set. 250.00 (ISBN 0-87968-436-4). Gordon Pr.
Catlin, George & Hasrick, Peter. Drawings of the North American Indian. LC 83-45238. (Illus.). 480p. 1984. slipcased ed. 125.00 (ISBN 0-385-19119-7). Doubleday.
Catlin, George E. Science & Method of Politics. xii, 360p. 1964. Repr. of 1927 ed. 23.00 (ISBN 0-208-00535-8, Archon). Shoe String.
Catlin, Robin J. Appleton's Review for National Boards, Pt. II. 448p. 1984. pap. 29.95. ACC.
Catlin, Stanton L., frwd. by. Latin American Paintings & Drawings. (Illus.). 1971. pap. 3.00 (ISBN 0-88397-057-0, Pub. by Intl Exhibit Foun). C E Tuttle.
Catlin, Stanton L. & Grieder, Terence, eds. Art of Latin America Since Independence. rev. ed. (Illus.). 246p. 1966. pap. 5.00 (ISBN 0-913456-01-2, Pub. by Ctr Inter-Am Rel). Interbk Inc.
Catlin, Stanton L., intro. by. Pissarro in Venezuela. LC 68-21908. (Illus.). 1968. pap. 2.00 (ISBN 0-913456-05-5, Pub. by Ctr Inter-Am Rel). Interbk Inc.
Catlin, Stanton L. Latin American Paintings from the Solomon R. Guggenheim Museum. (Illus.). 1969. pap. 3.00 (ISBN 0-913456-07-1, Pub. by Ctr Inter-Am Rel). Interbk Inc.
Catlin, Stanton L., intros. by. Artists of the Western Hemisphere: Precursors of Modernism, 1860-1930. LC 67-29739. (Illus.). 60p. 1968. pap. 2.00 (ISBN 0-913456-02-0, Pub. by Ctr Inter-Am Rel). Interbk Inc.
Catlin, Warren B. The Progress of Economics: A History of Economic Thought. LC 61-15681. 788p. 1962. text ed. 64.50x (ISBN 0-8290-0200-6); pap. text ed. 19.50x (ISBN 0-8290-0680-X). Irvington.
Catling, D. M. & Graywon, J. Identification of Vegetable Fibers. LC 81-18186. 1982. 35.00 (ISBN 0-412-22300-7, NO. 6683, Pub. by Chapman & Hall). Methuen Inc.
Catling, Patrick S. The Chocolate Touch. (Skylark Ser.). 96p. 1981. pap. 2.25 (ISBN 0-553-15287-4). Bantam.
--The Chocolate Touch. LC 78-31100. (Illus.). (gr. 4-6). 1979. Repr. of 1952 ed. PLB 10.88 (ISBN 0-688-32187-9). Morrow.
Catlow, C. R. & Mackrodt, W. C., eds. Computer Simulation of Solids. (Lecture Notes in Physics Ser.: Vol. 166). 320p. 1982. pap. 19.00 (ISBN 0-387-11588-9). Springer-Verlag.
Cato & Varro. On Agriculture. (Loeb Classical Library: No. 283). 12.50x (ISBN 0-674-99313-6). Harvard U Pr.
Cato, Ingemar, jt. auth. see Olausson, Eric.
Cato, Nancy. All the Rivers Run. 640p. 1984. pap. 3.50 (ISBN 0-451-12535-5, AE2535, Sig). NAL.
--Chindera. 1985. pap. 3.95 (ISBN 0-451-14033-8, Sig). NAL.
--Forefathers. 704p. 1983. 15.95 (ISBN 0-312-29831-5). St Martin.
--Forefathers. 1984. pap. 3.95 (ISBN 0-451-12798-6, Sig). NAL.
Cato, Nathaniel J. Le see Le Cato, Nathaniel J.
Cato, Sid. Coping with Grief: Healing Life's Great Hurts. 64p. 1984. 5.95 (ISBN 0-914091-51-4). Chicago Review.
--Healing Life's Great Hurts. 64p. 5.95 (ISBN 0-914091-51-4). Chicago Review.
Cato The Censor. On Farming. Brehaut, Ernest, tr. 1968. lib. bdg. 16.50x (ISBN 0-374-90969-5). Octagon.
Catoe, Lynn E., ed. UFOs & Related Subjects: An Annotated Bibliography. LC 78-26124. 1979. Repr. of 1969 ed. 66.00x (ISBN 0-8103-2021-5). Gale.
Catoir, John. Catholics & Broken Marriage. LC 78-74434. 72p. 1979. pap. 1.95 (ISBN 0-87793-176-3). Ave Maria.
--Gozad del Senor. (Span.). 3.50 (ISBN 0-318-02209-5). Christophers NY.
Catoir, John T. Enjoy the Lord. 1979. pap. 2.95 (ISBN 0-88479-023-1). Arena Lettres.
--World Religions: Beliefs Behind Today's Headlines. 1985. pap. price not set (ISBN 0-940518-04-X). Guildhall Pubs.
Caton, Carol L. Management of Chronic Schizophrenia. (Illus.). 1984. 19.95x (ISBN 0-19-503346-9). Oxford U Pr.
Caton, Charles E. Philosophy & Ordinary Language. LC 63-7250. pap. 65.00 (ISBN 0-317-09788-1, 2020860). Bks Demand UMI.
Caton, Hiram. The Origin of Subjectivity: An Essays on Descartes. LC 72-91291. pap. 66.00 (ISBN 0-317-09043-7, 2010557). Bks Demand UMI.
Caton, John D. The Antelope & Deer of America: A Scientific Treatise upon the Natural History, Habits, Affinities & Capacity for Domestication of the Antilocapra & Cervidae of North America. LC 73-17896. (Natural Sciences in America Ser.). (Illus.). 428p. 1974. Repr. 30.00x (ISBN 0-405-05723-7). Ayer Co Pubs.
Caton, Joseph H. The Utopian Vision of Moholy-Nagy. Kirkpatrick, Diane, ed. LC 83-18182. (Studies in Photography: No. 5). 200p. 1984. 39.95 (ISBN 0-8357-1528-0). UMI Res Pr.
Caton, R. L., et al, eds. Rotating Electrical Equipment Testing, 2 vols. (Engineering Craftsmen: No. G22). (Illus.). 1969. Set. spiral bdg. 69.95x (ISBN 0-85083-072-9). Intl Ideas.
Catone, Marc A. As I Write This Letter: An American Generation Remembers the Beatles. LC 81-86107. (Rock & Roll Remembrances Ser.: No. 1). 1982. 19.50 (ISBN 0-87650-137-4). Pierian.
Catoni, Guiliano, jt. auth. see Falassi, Alessandro.
Caton-Thompson, Gertrude. Zimbabwe Culture: Ruins & Reactions. LC 79-100283. Repr. 21.50x (ISBN 0-8371-2936-2). Greenwood.
Caton-Thompson, Gertrude & Gardner, Elinor W. The Desert Fayum, 2 vols. LC 77-86428. (Royal Anthropological Institute of Great Britain & Ireland. Publication). Repr. of 1934 ed. 65.00 set (ISBN 0-404-16630-X). AMS Pr.
Caton-Thompson, Gertrude, jt. auth. see Brunton, Guy.
Cator, George. Trust Companies in the United States. LC 78-63889. (Johns Hopkins University. Studies in the Social Sciences. Twentieth Ser. 1902: 5-6). Repr. of 1902 ed. 24.50 (ISBN 0-404-61143-5). AMS Pr.
Catovsky, Daniel. The Leukemic Cell. (Methods in Hematology: Vol. 2). (Illus.). 230p. 1981. text ed. 37.50 (ISBN 0-443-01911-8). Churchill.
Catrambone, Gene. The Golden Touch: Frankie Carle. LC 80-80901. 1982. 10.95 (ISBN 0-87212-124-0). Libra.
Catran, Jack. Is There Intelligent Life on Earth? LC 80-80016. 240p. 1981. 12.95 (ISBN 0-936162-29-5, L42). Lidiraven Bks.
Catrice, R., jt. auth. see Lane, A.
Catrina, Christian, jt. auth. see Frei, Daniel.
Catron, Donald G. The Anesthesiologist's Handbook. 3rd ed. LC 83-6489. (Illus.). 288p. 1983. pap. text ed. 15.00 (ISBN 0-8391-1822-8, 19879). Univ Park.
Catron, Louis E. Writing, Producing & Selling Your Play: The Complete Guide for the Beginning & Advanced Playwright. 360p. 1984. 17.95 (ISBN 0-13-971995-4); pap. 8.95 (ISBN 0-13-971987-3). P-H.
Catrou, Paul G., jt. auth. see Beeler, Myrton F.
Catroux, G., jt. auth. see Hucker, T. W.
Catrow, David J., III, illus. The Story of the Oregon Trail. LC 83-23997. 31p. (gr. 3-5). 1984. 6.75 (ISBN 0-516-04668-3). Children.
Cats, A., jt. ed. see Bonta, I.
Catsch, Alexander. Radioactive Metal Mobilization in Medicine. Kawin, Bergene, tr. (Illus.). 184p. 1964. 17.50x (ISBN 0-398-00296-7). C C Thomas.
Catsimpoolas, N. N., ed. Physical Aspects of Protein Interactions. (Developments in Biochemistry Ser.: Vol. 3). 308p. 1979. 68.50 (ISBN 0-444-00304-5, Biomedical Pr). Elsevier.
Catsimpoolas, Nicholas. Immunological Aspects of Food. (Illus.). 1977. lib. bdg. 60.00 (ISBN 0-87055-203-1). AVI.
Catsimpoolas, Nicholas & Drysdale, James. Biological & Biomedical Applications of Isoelectric Focusing. LC 77-10776. (Biological Separations Ser.). (Illus.). 367p. 1977. 39.50x (ISBN 0-306-34603-6, Plenum Pr). Plenum Pub.
Catsimpoolas, Nicholas, ed. Cell Analysis, Vol. 1. LC 82-5289. 349p. 1982. text ed. 37.50 (ISBN 0-306-40864-3, Plenum Pr). Plenum Pub.
--Isoelectric Focusing. 1976. 55.00 (ISBN 0-12-163950-9). Acad Pr.
--Methods of Cell Separation, 3 vols. LC 77-11018. (Biological Separations Ser.). (Illus.). Vol. 1, 375p, 1977. 39.50x (ISBN 0-306-34604-4, Plenum Pr); Vol. 2, 315p, 1979. 39.50x (ISBN 0-306-40094-4); Vol. 3, 215p, 1980. 35.00x (ISBN 0-306-40377-3). Plenum Pub.
--Methods of Protein Separation, Vol. 1. LC 75-17684. (Biological Separations Ser.). (Illus.). 282p. 1975. 35.00x (ISBN 0-306-34601-X, Plenum Pr). Plenum Pub.
--Methods of Protein Separation, Vol. 2. LC 75-17684. (Biological Separations Ser.). (Illus.). 344p. 1976. 39.50x (ISBN 0-306-34602-8, Plenum Pr). Plenum Pub.
Catsky, J., jt. ed. see Sestak, Z.
Catt, J. A. see Bowen, D. Q.
Catt, K. J. An ABC of Endocrinology. 154p. 1972. 12.95 (ISBN 0-316-13190-3). Little.
Catt, K. J. & Dufau, Maria L., eds. Hormone Action & Testicular Function. (Annals of The New York Academy of Science Ser.: Vol. 438). 708p. 1984. lib. bdg. 163.00x (ISBN 0-89766-270-9); pap. 163.00x (ISBN 0-89766-271-7). NY Acad Sci.
Catt, Richard. Building Maintenance Techniques for Building Aftercare. 224p. 1986. 30.00x (ISBN 0-246-12219-6, Pub. by Granada England). Sheridan.
Catt, Stephen E. & Miller, Donald S. Supervisory Management & Communication. 1985. pap. 17.95x (ISBN 0-256-03137-1). Irwin.
Cattabeni, F. & Nicosia, S., eds. Principles & Methods in Receptor Binding. (NATO ASI Series A, Life Sicences: Vol. 72). 276p. 1984. 42.50x (ISBN 0-306-41613-1, Plenum Pr). Plenum Pub.
Cattafi, Bartolo. Cattafi Selected Poems. Swann, Brian & Feldman, Ruth, trs. from Ital. 228p. 1982. 17.50 (ISBN 0-931556-04-X); pap. 7.50 (ISBN 0-931556-05-8). Translation Pr.
Cattan, H. The Law of Oil Concessions in the Middle East & North Africa. LC 67-14400. 224p. 1967. 15.00 (ISBN 0-379-00319-8). Oceana.
Cattan, Henry. The Garden of Joys. 11.95 (ISBN 0-7043-2219-6, Pub. by Quartet England). Charles River Bks.
--Jerusalem. 240p. 1981. 25.00 (ISBN 0-312-44182-7). St Martin.
Cattan, I. & Smith, R. N., eds. Natural Convection. (HTD Ser.: Vol. 16). 150p. 1981. 24.00 (ISBN 0-686-34495-2, G00205). ASME.
Cattaneo, Anne, tr. see Strauss, Botho.
Cattaneo, Frank. Shop Made Easy. (Illus.). 1971. pap. text ed. 3.75x (ISBN 0-88323-064-X, 188). Richards Pub.
Cattano, Vincent. A to Z Personal Guidance. 40p. 1956. pap. 1.00x (ISBN 0-87542-101-6). Llewellyn Pubns.
Cattaui, Georges. Marcel Proust. Hall, Ruth, tr. from Fr. 125p. 1967. text ed. 10.95 (ISBN 0-686-78406-5). Beekman Pubs.
Cattaui, Georges & Kolb, Philip, eds. Entretiens Sur Marcel Proust: Decades Du Centre Culturel International De Cerisy-la-Salle. (Nouvelle Series: No. 2). 1966. pap. 12.80x (ISBN 90-2796-013-5). Mouton.
Cattaui, Georges & Madaule, Jacques, eds. Entretiens Sur Paul Claudel: Decades Du Centre Culturel International De Cerisy-la-Salle. (Nouvelle Series: No. 11). 1968. pap. 14.00x (ISBN 90-2796-249-9). Mouton.
Cattell, Ann. Dictionary of Esoteric Words. (Orig.). 1967. pap. 1.75 (ISBN 0-8065-0175-8, C205). Citadel Pr.
Cattell, David T. Communism & the Spanish Civil War. 1955. 30.00 (ISBN 0-384-07900-8); pap. 24.00 (ISBN 0-685-13391-5). Johnson Repr.
--Soviet Diplomacy & the Spanish Civil War. 1957. 26.00 (ISBN 0-384-07910-5); pap. 20.00 (ISBN 0-685-13596-9). Johnson Repr.
Cattell, Everett L. Christian Mission: A Matter of Life. 160p. (Orig.). 1981. 11.95 (ISBN 0-913408-76-X); pap. 8.95 (ISBN 0-913408-68-9). Friends United.
Cattell, J. & Fotos, J. Selected French Stories of the Nineteenth & Twentieth Centuries. 20.00 (ISBN 0-89987-094-5). Darby Bks.
Cattell, J. McKeen. University Control. Metzger, Walter P., ed. LC 76-55179. (The Academic Profession Ser.). 1977. Repr. of 1913 ed. lib. bdg. 36.50x (ISBN 0-405-10007-8). Ayer Co Pubs.
Cattell, N. R. New English Grammar. 1969. pap. 7.95x (ISBN 0-262-53010-4). MIT Pr.
Cattell, Nancy G. & Sharp, Shirley I. College & Career: Adjusting to College & Selecting an Occupation. LC 78-111101. (Orig.). 1970. pap. text ed. 12.95x (ISBN 0-89197-085-1). Irvington.
Cattell, Psyche. Measurement of Intelligence of Infants & Young Children. (Illus.). 1960. 27.50 (ISBN 0-384-07925-3). Johnson Repr.
--Raising Children with Love & Limits. LC 77-187810. 240p. 1972. 19.95x (ISBN 0-911012-20-6). Nelson-Hall.
Cattell, R., ed. Syntax & Semantics: Vol. 17, Composite Predicates in English. 310p. 1984. 42.00 (ISBN 0-12-613517-7). Acad Pr.
Cattell, R. B. Description & Measurement of Personality. 1969. Repr. of 1946 ed. 37.00 (ISBN 0-384-07935-0). Johnson Repr.
Cattell, R. B. & Kline, P. The Scientific Analysis of Personality & Motivation. (Personality & Psychopathology Ser.). 1977. 61.00 (ISBN 0-12-164250-X). Acad Pr.
Cattell, R. G. Formalization & Automatic Derivation of Code Generators. Stone, Harold S., ed. LC 82-4802. (Computer Science: Systems Programming Ser.: No. 3). 158p. 1982. 34.95 (ISBN 0-8357-1316-4). UMI Res Pr.
Cattell, Raymond B. Crooked Personalities in Childhood & After: An Introduction to Psychotherapy. 215p. 1982. Repr. of 1938 ed. PLB 45.00 (ISBN 0-8495-0977-7). Arden Lib.
--Factor Analysis. LC 72-10689. 462p. 1973. Repr. of 1952 ed. lib. bdg. 32.50x (ISBN 0-8371-6615-2, CAFA). Greenwood.
--Human Motivation & the Dynamic Calculus. 176p. 1985. 29.95 (ISBN 0-03-072009-5). Praeger.
--The Inheritance of Personality & Ability: Research Methods & Findings. LC 80-70667. (Personality & Psychopathology Ser.). 1982. 49.50 (ISBN 0-12-164260-7). Acad Pr.
--A New Morality from Science: Beyondism. 1973. 42.00 (ISBN 0-08-016956-2). Pergamon.
--Personality & Learning Theory: A Systems Theory of Maturation & Structured Learning, 2 vols, Vol. 2. LC 79-594. 1980. text ed. 49.00 (ISBN 0-8261-2124-1); text ed. 75.00 set. Springer Pub.
--Personality & Learning Theory: The Structure of Personality in Its Environment, 2 vols, Vol. 1. LC 79-593. 1979. text ed. 34.50 (ISBN 0-8261-2120-9); text ed. 75.00 set. Springer Pub.
--Personality & Mood by Questionnaire. LC 73-1853. (Jossey-Bass Behavioral Science Ser.). pap. 138.00 (ISBN 0-317-26038-3, 2023783). Bks Demand UMI.
--Personality & Social Psychology: Papers. LC 64-21698. 1964. text ed. 18.95 (ISBN 0-912736-01-1). EDITS Pubs.
--Structured Personality Learning Theory: A Holistic Multivariate Research Approach. LC 83-16103. (Centennial Psychology Ser.). 480p. 1983. 48.95 (ISBN 0-03-059731-5). Praeger.
Cattell, Raymond B. & Butcher, H. J. The Prediction of Achievement & Creativity. LC 67-18662. 1968. 32.50x (ISBN 0-672-60641-0); pap. text ed. 9.95x (ISBN 0-89197-900-X). Irvington.
Cattell, Raymond B. & Schuerger, James M. Personality Theory in Action: Handbook for the Objective-Analytic (O-A) Battery. LC 78-50146. 1978. 37.50 (ISBN 0-918296-11-0). Inst Personality & Ability.
Cattell, Raymond B., ed. The Scientific Use of Factor Analysis in Behavioral & Life Sciences. LC 77-10695. (Illus.). 640p. 1978. 49.50x (ISBN 0-306-30939-4, Plenum Pr). Plenum Pub.
Cattell, Raymond B. & Johnson, Ronald C., eds. Functional Psychological Testing: Principles & Instruments. 600p. 1985. 60.00 (ISBN 0-87630-363-7). Brunner-Mazel.
Cattell, Raymond B., et al. Intelligence & National Achievement. (Mankind Quarterly Monograph Ser.). 1984. 45.00 (ISBN 0-941694-14-3). Inst Study Man.
Cattell, Raymond B., et al, eds. Human Affairs. facs. ed. LC 70-128219. (Essay Index Reprint Ser). 1937. 25.50 (ISBN 0-8369-1943-2). Ayer Co Pubs.
Catter, Angela. Moonshadow. (Illus.). 32p. (ps-1). 1983. 10.50 (ISBN 0-575-03026-7, Pub. by Gollancz England). David & Charles.
Catterall, Anthony. Legg-Calve-Perthes's Disease. (Current Problems In Orthopedis Ser.). (Illus.). 1982. 40.00 (ISBN 0-443-01942-8). Churchill.
Catterall, Calvin D. & Gazda, George M. Strategies for Helping Students. (Illus.). 416p. 1978. 22.75x (ISBN 0-398-03686-1). C C Thomas.
Catterall, Calvin D., ed. Psychology in the Schools in International Perspective, 3 Vols. 1976. Vol. I, pap. text ed. 7.50 (ISBN 0-917668-02-2); Vol. II, 1977. pap. text ed. 7.50 (ISBN 0-917668-01-4); Vol. III, 253P. 1979. pap. 7.50 (ISBN 0-917668-00-6). Intl Schl Psych.
Catterall, E. Growing Begonias. (Illus.). 132p. 1984. 17.95 (ISBN 0-917304-88-8). Timber.
Catterall, Helen H., ed. Judicial Cases Concerning American Slavery & the Negro, 5 Vols. LC 68-55875. 1926-1937. Set. 155.00x (ISBN 0-8371-0343-6, CAC&, Pub. by Negro U Pr). Greenwood.
Catterall, James S. Education Vouchers. LC 84-61204. (Fastback Ser.: No. 210). 50p. (Orig.). 1984. pap. 0.75 (ISBN 0-87367-210-0). Phi Delta Kappa.
--Tuition Tax Credits: Fact & Fiction. LC 82-63057. (Fastback Ser.: No. 188). 50p. 1983. pap. 0.75 (ISBN 0-87367-188-0). Phi Delta Kappa.
Catterall, James S., ed. Economic Evaluation of Public Programs. LC 84-82377. (Program Evaluation Ser.: No. 26). (Orig.). 1985. pap. text ed. 9.95x (ISBN 0-87589-764-9). Jossey-Bass.
Catterall, Mary & Bewley, David K. Fast Neutrons in the Treatment of Cancer. 394p. 1979. 69.50 (ISBN 0-8089-1205-4, 790820). Grune.
Catterall, R. D., ed. Sexually Transmitted Diseases. 1976. 55.00 (ISBN 0-12-164150-3). Acad Pr.

Cattermole, K. W. Mathematical Foundations for Communication Engineering, Vol. 1. 29.95 (ISBN 0-470-20176-2). Halsted Pr.

--Mathematical Foundations for Communication Engineering, Vol. 2. 29.95 (ISBN 0-470-20177-0). Halsted Pr.

Cattermole, Kenneth W. Transistor Circuits. 2nd ed. 488p. 1964. 106.50 (ISBN 0-677-00990-9). Gordon.

Cattermole, Kenneth W. & O'Reilly, eds. Mathematical Topics in Telecommunications: Optimisation in Electronics & Communications, Vol. 1. 176p. 1984. text ed. 24.95x (ISBN 0-471-80765-6, Pub. by Wiley Interscience). Wiley.

Cattermole, Kenneth W. & O'Reilly, John J., eds. Mathematical Topics in Telecommunications: Problems of Randomness in Communication Engineering, Vol. 2. 352p. 1984. text ed. 32.50x (ISBN 0-471-80763-X, Pub. by Wiley Interscience). Wiley.

Cattermole, Peter & Moore, Patrick. The Story of the Earth. (Illus.). 224p. 1985. 24.95 (ISBN 0-521-26292-5). Cambridge U Pr.

Cattermole, Richard, ed. Sacred Poetry of the Seventeenth Century: Including the Whole of Giles Fletcher's Christ's Victory & Triumph, 2 vols. (Research & Source Works Ser.: No. 346). 1969. Repr. of 1835 ed. Set. 44.50 (ISBN 0-8337-0499-0). B Franklin.

Catterns, David, ed. see Boguslavsky, M. M.

Catterson, R. Smith. Drawing from Memory. (Illus.). 1979. deluxe ed. 77.75 (ISBN 0-930582-44-6). Gloucester Art.

Catterson, Robert A. How to Draw from Memory. (Illus.). 1980. 81.25 (ISBN 0-930582-58-6). Gloucester Art.

Cattier, Michel. The Life & Work of Wilhelm Reich. 1973. pap. 1.65 (ISBN 0-380-01327-4, 14928). Avon.

Cattin, Giulio. Music of the Middle Ages I. Botterill, Steven, tr. (Illus.). 256p. 1985. 34.50 (ISBN 0-521-24161-8); pap. 14.95 (ISBN 0-521-28489-9). Cambridge U Pr.

Cattle, Dorothy J. & Schwerin, Karl H., eds. Food Energy in Tropical Ecosystems. (Food & Nutrition in History & Anthropology Ser.: Vol. 4). 344p. 1985. text ed. 55.00 (ISBN 2-88124-036-4). Gordon.

Cattle, Edward, tr. see Elwenspoek, Curt.

Cattley, S. R., ed. see Foxe, John.

Catto, G. R. & Smith, J. A. Clinical Aspects of Renal Physiology. (Illus.). 160p. 1981. 19.95 (ISBN 0-7216-0711-X, Pub. by Bailliere-Tindall). Saunders.

Catto, Max. King Oil. 1982. 15.00x (ISBN 0-7274-0257-9, Pub. by Severn Hse). State Mutual Bk.

Catto, Mike. Art in Ulster, No. 2. (Illus.). 198p. (Orig.). 1977. pap. 13.00 (ISBN 0-85640-129-3, Pub. by Blackstaff Pr). Longwood Pub Group.

Catto, William T. Semi-Centenary Discourse. facs. ed. LC 78-154073. (Black Heritage Library Collection). 1857. 14.25 (ISBN 0-8369-8784-5). Ayer Co Pubs.

Catton, Bruce. America Goes to War. LC 58-13602. (Illus.). 1958. pap. 8.95 (ISBN 0-8195-6016-2). Wesleyan U Pr.

--American Heritage Short History of the Civil War. 288p. 1982. pap. 3.95 (ISBN 0-440-30123-8, LE). Dell.

--Banners at Shenandoah. 14.95 (ISBN 0-89244-019-8, Pub. by J M C & Co). Amereon Ltd.

--Civil War. 1971. pap. 6.95 (ISBN 0-07-010265-1). McGraw.

--The Civil War. LC 85-3969. (The American Heritage Library). (Illus.). 320p. 1985. pap. 8.95 (ISBN 0-8281-0305-4, Dist. by H M). Am Heritage.

--The Civil War. (Illus.). 320p. 1985. pap. 8.95 (ISBN 0-8281-0305-4). HM.

--Coming Fury. LC 61-12502. (Centennial History of the Civil War Ser.: Vol. 1). 1961. 17.95 (ISBN 0-385-09813-8). Doubleday.

--The Coming Fury, Vol. 1. (The Centennial History of the Civil War Ser.). 624p. 1972. pap. 3.95 (ISBN 0-671-43414-4). WSP.

--Confederates. 448p. 1983. pap. 3.95 (ISBN 0-425-06542-1). Berkley Pub.

--Gettysburg: The Final Fury. LC 73-11896. (Illus.). 128p. 1974. slipcased 17.95 (ISBN 0-385-02060-0). Doubleday.

--Gettysburg: The Final Fury. 128p. 1982. pap. 6.95 (ISBN 0-425-05758-5). Berkley Pub.

--Glory Road: The Bloody Route from Fredericksburg to Gettysburg. LC 62-1070. 1962. 12.95 (ISBN 0-385-04167-5). Doubleday.

--Grant Moves South. (Illus.). 1960. 24.50i (ISBN 0-316-13207-1). Little.

--Grant Takes Command. LC 69-12632. 1969. 24.50i (ISBN 0-316-13210-1). Little.

--Michigan. (States & the Nation Ser.). (Illus.). 224p. 1976. 14.95 (ISBN 0-393-05572-8, Co-Pub by AASLH). Norton.

--Mister Lincoln's Army. LC 62-1068. 1960. 12.95 (ISBN 0-385-04310-4). Doubleday.

--Never Call Retreat, Vol. III. LC 61-12502. (Centennial History of the Civil War Ser.). 1965. 17.95 (ISBN 0-385-02615-3). Doubleday.

--Never Call Retreat, Vol. 3. (The Centennial Histiry of the Civil War Ser.). 560p. 1969. pap. 3.95 (ISBN 0-671-43416-0). WSP.

--Reflections on the Civil War. Leekley, John, ed. LC 79-6164. (Illus.). 272p. 1981. 17.95 (ISBN 0-385-06347-4). Doubleday.

--Reflections on the Civil War. Leekley, John, ed. 272p. 1984. pap. 3.95 (ISBN 0-425-07699-7). Berkley Pub.

--Stillness at Appomattox. LC 62-1069. 1953. 16.95 (ISBN 0-385-04451-8). Doubleday.

--A Stillness at Appomattox. 512p. 1970. pap. 3.95 (ISBN 0-671-42385-1). WSP.

--Terrible Swift Sword, Vol. II. LC 62-15937. 17.95 (ISBN 0-385-02614-5). Doubleday.

--Terrible Swift Sword, Vol. 2. (The Centennial History of the Civil War Ser.). 592p. 1967. pap. 4.95 (ISBN 0-671-44925-7). WSP.

--This Hallowed Ground. 576p. 1969. pap. 3.95 (ISBN 0-671-44362-3). WSP.

--This Hallowed Ground: The Story of the Union Side of the Civil War. LC 56-5960. 17.95 (ISBN 0-385-04664-2). Doubleday.

--U. S. Grant & the American Military Tradition. (The Library of American Biography Ser.). (Orig.). 1972. pap. text ed. 6.95 (ISBN 0-316-13206-3). Little.

--U. S. Grant & the American Military Tradition. 1985. 15.95 (ISBN 0-8488-0279-9, Pub. by J M C & Co). Amereon Ltd.

--Waiting for the Morning Train: An American Boyhood. LC 72-76134. (Illus.). 256p. 1972. 12.95 (ISBN 0-385-07460-3). Doubleday.

--War Lords of Washington. LC 70-90481. Repr. of 1948 ed. lib. bdg. 22.25 (ISBN 0-8371-2149-3, CAWL). Greenwood.

Catton, Bruce & American Heritage Editors. The American Heritage Picture History of the Civil War. LC 60-10751. 1960. 24.95 (ISBN 0-385-00907-0, Pub. by Am Heritage). Doubleday.

Catton, Bruce & Catton, William B. The Bold & Magnificient Dream: America's Founding Years, 1492-1815. LC 77-25581. (Illus.). 1978. 6.50 (ISBN 0-385-00341-2). Doubleday.

Catton, Bruce, jt. auth. see Catton, William.

Catton, Chris & Gray, James. The Incredible Heap: A Guide to Compost Gardening. (Illus.). 64p. 1984. pap. 7.95 (ISBN 0-312-41187-1). St Martin.

Catton, I. & Torrance, K. E., eds. Natural Convection in Enclosures. (Bound Conference Volumes in Heat Transfer Ser.: Vol. 26). 113p. 1983. pap. text ed. 24.00 (ISBN 0-317-02635-6, H00270). ASME.

--Natural Convection in Enclosures: HTD, Vol.8. 128p. 1980. 20.00 (ISBN 0-317-33570-7, G00168); members 10.00 (ISBN 0-317-33571-5). ASME.

Catton, Margaret M. Social Service in Hawaii. LC 58-14378. (Illus.). 1959. 14.95x (ISBN 0-87015-088-X). Pacific Bks.

Catton, William & Catton, Bruce. Two Roads to Sumter. 1971. pap. 5.95 (ISBN 0-07-010255-4). McGraw.

Catton, William B., jt. auth. see Catton, Bruce.

Catton, William B., jt. auth. see Link, Arthur S.

Catton, William R., Jr. Overshoot: The Ecological Basis of Revolutionary Change. LC 80-13443. (Illus.). 250p. 1980. 16.50 (ISBN 0-252-00818-9); pap. 8.95x (ISBN 0-252-00988-6). U of Ill Pr.

Cattonar, Nell, tr. see Vidali, Vittorio.

Cattrell & Dougherty. Iran's Quest for Security: U.S. Arms Transfers & the Nuclear Option. 1977. pap. 5.00 (IFPA6, IFPA). Unipub.

Catts, Paul E., jt. auth. see Furman, Deane P.

Catty, F. B., tr. see Guth, W.

Catty, F. B., tr. see Laege, F. K.

Catudal, Honore M., Jr. The Exclave Problem of Western Europe. LC 78-24487. (Illus.). 150p. 1979. 12.50 (ISBN 0-8173-4729-1). U of Ala Pr.

Catullus. Carmina. Mynors, R. A., ed. (Oxford Classical Texts Ser). 1958. 9.95x (ISBN 0-19-814604-3). Oxford U Pr.

--Catullus. Merrill, Elmer T., ed. 1965. Repr. of 1893 ed. 16.50x (ISBN 0-674-10350-5). Harvard U Pr.

--The Catullus of William Hull. Hull, William, tr. 8.00 (ISBN 0-89253-791-4); flexible cloth 4.00 (ISBN 0-89253-792-2). Ind-US Inc.

--Lesbia. pap. 1.65 (ISBN 0-685-19405-1, 101, WL). Citadel Pr.

--Liber. 100p. 1985. Repr. of 1923 ed. 15.00 (ISBN 0-89005-453-3). Ares.

--Odi Et Amo: The Complete Poetry of Catussus. Swanson, Roy A., tr. LC 59-11685. 1959. pap. 5.99 scp (ISBN 0-672-60314-4, LLA114). Bobbs.

--The Poems of Catullus. bilingual ed. Whigham, Peter, tr. & intro. by. LC 69-19556. 1969. 18.95x (ISBN 0-520-01513-4). U of Cal Pr.

--The Poems of Catullus: A Bilingual Edition. Whigham, Peter, tr. (California Library Reprint: Vol. 123). 1983. Repr. text ed. 25.00x (ISBN 0-520-05082-7). U of Cal Pr.

--Selections from Catullus. Lyne, R. O., ed. (Latin Texts Ser.). 48p. 1973. 4.95 (ISBN 0-521-20267-1). Cambridge U Pr.

Catyrsse. Diderot et la Mystification. 22.50 (ISBN 0-685-34036-8). French & Eur.

Catz, Boris. Thyroid Case Studies. 2nd ed. 1981. 22.50 (ISBN 0-87488-038-6). Med Exam.

Catzel, Pincus & Olver, Richard. The Paediatric Prescriber. 5th ed. (Illus.). 360p. 1981. pap. text ed. 15.50 (ISBN 0-632-00586-6, B 1141-5). Mosby.

Cau, P., et al. Morphogenesis of Thyroid Follicles in Vitro. (Advances in Anatomy Embryology & Cell Biology: Vol. 52, Pt. 2). 1976. pap. 34.30 (ISBN 0-387-07654-9). Springer-Verlag.

Cauble, Chris, jt. auth. see Burk, Dale A.

Caucci, Al & Nastasi, Bob. Instant Mayfly Identification Guide. (Illus.). 64p. (Orig.). 1984. pap. 9.95 (ISBN 0-914521-00-4). Comparahatch.

Caucci, Al & Natasi, Bob. Hatches II: A Complete Guide to Fishing the Hatches of North American Trout Streams. rev. ed. 320p. 1985. 28.95 (ISBN 0-8329-0400-7, Pub. by Winchester Pr). New Century.

Caucett, Allen, ed. Focus: Elementary Art Education. 96p. 1975. 7.95 (ISBN 0-937652-18-0). Natl Art Ed.

Cauchi, Maurice N., et al, eds. The Clinical Pathology of Pregnancy & the Newborn Infant. (Illus.). 384p. 1984. text ed. 49.50 (ISBN 0-8391-2023-0, 21385). Univ Park.

Cauchie, Maurice. Thematic Index of the Works of Francois Couperin. LC 74-24057. Repr. of 1949 ed. 14.50 (ISBN 0-404-12879-3). AMS Pr.

Cauchois, Y., et al, eds. Wavelengths of X-Ray Emission Lines & Absorption Edges. LC 78-40419. 1978. 175.00 (ISBN 0-08-022448-2); pap. text ed. 80.00. Pergamon.

Cauchon, Joseph. L' Union Des Provinces De L'amerique Britannique Du Nord, (Quebec, 1865) (Canadiana Avant 1867: No. 6). 1968. 11.20x (ISBN 90-2796-334-7). Mouton.

Cauchon, Joseph E. Union Des Provinces De L'amerique Britannique Du Nord. 1865. 14.00 (ISBN 0-384-07945-8). Johnson Repr.

Cauchy, Augustin. Ordinary Differential Equations. 24.50 (ISBN 0-384-07950-4). Johnson Repr.

Caudano, R. & Verbist, J., eds. Electron Spectroscopy. 1136p. 1975. 149.00 (ISBN 0-444-41291-3). Elsevier.

Caudano, R., et al, eds. Vibrations at Surfaces. LC 81-15830. 596p. 1981. 89.50x (ISBN 0-306-40824-4, Plenum Pr). Plenum Pub.

Caudill, Harry M. A Darkness at Dawn: Appalachian Kentucky & the Future. LC 74-7871. (Kentucky Bicentennial Bookshelf Ser.). 88p. 1976. 6.95 (ISBN 0-8131-0218-9). U Pr of Ky.

--The Mountain, the Miner & the Lord, & Other Tales from a Country Law Office. LC 80-51012. 192p. 1980. 16.00 (ISBN 0-8131-1403-9). U Pr of Ky.

--Night Comes to the Cumberlands: Biography of a Depressed Area. 1963. pap. 9.70i (ISBN 0-316-13212-8, Pub. by Atlantic Monthly Pr). Little.

--Theirs Be the Power: The Moguls of Eastern Kentucky. LC 83-5771. (Illus.). 198p. 1983. 13.95 (ISBN 0-252-01029-9). U of Ill Pr.

Caudill, Paul R. First Corinthians: A Translation with Notes. LC 82-71220. 1983. 4.95 (ISBN 0-8054-1391-X). Broadman.

--Hebrews: A Translation with Notes. LC 84-21415. 1985. pap. 4.95 (ISBN 0-8054-1395-2). Broadman.

--Seven Steps to Peace. LC 81-71254. 1982. pap. 3.95 (ISBN 0-8054-1527-0). Broadman.

Caudill, R. Paul. Modern Acts of the Holy Spirit. LC 81-67992. 1982. pap. 5.50 (ISBN 0-8054-6936-2). Broadman.

--The Mountain Preacher. LC 84-71992. 1984. pap. 2.98 (ISBN 0-938980-02-5). Blue Ridge.

--Mountain Preacher, Vol. 2. pap. 2.98 (ISBN 0-938980-03-3). Blue Ridge.

--Philippians: A Translation with Notes. LC 80-70403. (Orig.). 1981. pap. 2.25 (ISBN 0-938980-00-9). Blue Ridge.

Caudill, Rebecca. Certain Small Shepherd. LC 65-17604. 48p. (gr. 2-6). 1965. reinforced bdg. 8.95 (ISBN 0-03-089755-6); pap. 3.95 (ISBN 0-03-080107-9). HR&W.

--Did You Carry the Flag Today, Charley! LC 66-11422. (Illus.). 94p. (gr. 2-4). 1971. reinforced bdg. 9.95 (ISBN 0-03-089753-X); pap. 3.95 (ISBN 0-03-086620-0). HR&W.

--A Pocketful of Cricket. LC 64-12617. (Illus.). 48p. (gr. k-4). 1964. reinforced bdg. 7.95 (ISBN 0-03-089752-1); pap. 2.95 (ISBN 0-03-086619-7). HR&W.

--Wind, Sand & Sky. (Illus.). 32p. (gr. k-6). 1976. 8.95 (ISBN 0-525-42899-2). Dutton.

Caudill, William. Effects of Social & Cultural Systems in Reactions to Stress. LC 58-10875. 1958. pap. 1.00 (ISBN 0-527-03302-2). Kraus Repr.

Caudill, William W., et al. Architecture & You: How to Experience & Enjoy Buildings. (Illus.). 176p. 1978. (Whitney Lib); pap. 14.95 (ISBN 0-8230-7041-7). Watson-Guptill.

Caudle, Hal M. The Hanging at Bahia Mar. (Illus.). 1975. 5.95 (ISBN 0-87482-077-4). Wake-Brook.

Caudrey, P. J., jt. ed. see Bullough, R. K.

Caudwell, Christopher. Illusion & Reality. LC 48-5327. 370p. 1973. pap. 2.25 (ISBN 0-7178-0374-0). Intl Pubs Co.

--Illusion & Reality: Study of the Sources of Poetry. 370p. 1973. pap. 8.95x (ISBN 0-8464-1109-1). Beekman Pubs.

--Studies & Further Studies in a Dying Culture. LC 77-142989. 544p. 1972. pap. 9.50 (ISBN 0-85345-218-0). Monthly Rev.

Caudwell, Christopher & Sprigg, C. St. John. Romance & Realism: A Study in English Bourgeois Literature. LC 78-120752. 1970. 19.00x (ISBN 0-691-06195-5). Princeton U Pr.

Caudwell, H. The Creative Impulse in Writing & Painting. 162p. 1981. Repr. of 1953 ed. lib. bdg. 25.00 (ISBN 0-89987-117-8). Darby Bks.

Caudwell, Irene. Damien of Molokai, Eighteen Forty to Eighteen Eighty-Nine. 1979. Repr. of 1932 ed. lib. bdg. 20.00 (ISBN 0-8492-4041-7). R West.

Caudwell, Sarah. The Shortest Way to Hades. 208p. 1985. 12.95 (ISBN 0-684-18292-0, ScribT). Scribner.

--Thus Was Adonis Murdered. 1982. pap. 3.50 (ISBN 0-14-006310-2). Penguin.

Caudy, Don W., jt. auth. see Hackman, Donald J.

Cauet, Fernand, jt. auth. see Bornecque, Henri.

Cauffield, Joyce V. & Banfield, Carolyn E., eds. The River Book: Cincinnati & the Ohio. (Illus.). 228p. (gr. 7-12). Repr. of 1981 ed. 29.95x (ISBN 0-9608200-0-0). Prog Cincinnati.

Caufield, Catherine. In the Rainforest. LC 84-47644. 1985. 16.95 (ISBN 0-394-52701-1). Knopf.

Caufield, Page, jt. ed. see Jacobson, Alex.

Caughey. Decisions for Independent Living. (gr. 9-12). 1983. text ed. 7.52 (ISBN 0-02-663190-3). Bennett IL.

Caughey, C. A. Depositional Systems in the Paluxy Formation (Lower Cretaceous), Northeast Texas: Oil, Gas, & Ground-Water Resources. (GC 77-8). (Illus.). 59p. 1977. Repr. 2.50 (ISBN 0-686-29327-4, GC 77-8). Bur Econ Geology.

Caughey, J. E. & Myrianthopoulos, N. C. Dystrophia Myotonica & Related Disorders. (Illus.). 300p. 1963. photocopy ed. 24.75x (ISBN 0-398-00297-5). C C Thomas.

Caughey, John. The California Gold Rush. Orig. Title: Gold Is the Cornerstone. (Illus.). 1976. pap. 5.95 (ISBN 0-520-02763-9). U of Cal Pr.

--To Kill a Child's Spirit: The Tragedy of School Segregation in Los Angeles. LC 72-89724. (Illus.). 255p. (Orig.). 1973. pap. text ed. 9.95 (ISBN 0-87581-146-9). Peacock Pubs.

Caughey, John & Caughey, LaRee. Los Angeles: Biography of a City. LC 75-17300. 1976. 20.00 (ISBN 0-520-03079-6); pap. 6.95 (ISBN 0-520-03410-4). U of Cal Pr.

Caughey, John L. Imaginary Social Worlds: A Cultural Approach. LC 83-6702. viii, 280p. 1984. 16.95 (ISBN 0-8032-1421-9). U of Nebr Pr.

Caughey, John W. Bernardo de Galvez in Louisiana: 1776-1783. 2nd ed. LC 72-86562. 290p. 1972. Repr. of 1934 ed. 20.00 (ISBN 0-911116-78-8). Pelican.

--California: A Remarkable State's Life History. 3rd ed. LC 73-118334. (History Ser). 1970. text ed. 21.95 (ISBN 0-13-112482-X). P-H.

--California: The Life History of a Remarkable State's Life History. 4th ed. (Illus.). 512p. 1982. 28.95 (ISBN 0-13-112482-X). P-H.

Caughey, John W., ed. see Rice, William B.

Caughey, LaRee, jt. auth. see Caughey, John.

Caughey, Mildred. Through the Eyes of a Child. 83p. 1979. 7.50 (ISBN 0-87770-224-1). Ye Galleon.

Caughey, Winslow, ed. Clinical & Biochemical Aspects of Hemoglobin Abnormalities. 1978. 69.50 (ISBN 0-12-164350-6). Acad Pr.

Caughey, Winslow S., ed. Biochemical & Clinical Aspects of Oxygen. LC 79-23522. 1979. 67.50 (ISBN 0-12-164380-8). Acad Pr.

Caughie, John, ed. Theories of Authorship. (B. F. I. Readers in Film Studies). (Illus.). 320p. 1981. 29.95x (ISBN 0-7100-0649-7); pap. 14.95x (ISBN 0-7100-0650-0). Routledge & Kegan.

Caughill, Rita E. The Dying Patient: A Supportive Approach. LC 75-30280. 1976. pap. text ed. 9.95 (ISBN 0-316-13216-0). Little.

Caughlan, Lar. Yoga: The Spirit of Union. 96p. 1981. pap. text ed. 8.95 (ISBN 0-8403-2487-1). Kendall-Hunt.

Caughley, Graeme. Analysis of Vertebrate Populations. LC 76-913. 1977. 53.95 (ISBN 0-471-01705-1, Pub. by Wiley-Interscience). Wiley.

--The Deer Wars: The Story of Deer in New Zealand. (Illus.). 187p. 1983. 15.00x (ISBN 0-86863-389-5, Pub. by Heinemann Pub New Zealand). Intl Spec Bk.

Cauhape, Elizabeth. Fresh Starts: Men & Women after Divorce. 227p. 1983. 16.50 (ISBN 0-465-02553-6). Basic.

Cauhe, Joana Raspall De see Raspall de Cauhe, Joana, et al.

Caujolle, Claude, jt. auth. see Price, Betty G.

Caulaincourt, Armand. No Peace with Napoleon. Hanoteau, Jean, ed. Libaire, George, tr. LC 74-29631. 286p. 1975. Repr. of 1936 ed. lib. bdg. 16.00x (ISBN 0-8371-7984-X, CANP). Greenwood.

Caulaincourt, Armand A. With Napolean in Russia: The Memoirs of General De Caulaincourt, Duke of Vicenza. Hanoteau, Jean & Libaire, George, eds. LC 75-40914. 1976. Repr. of 1935 ed. lib. bdg. 31.50x (ISBN 0-8371-8689-7, CAWN). Greenwood.

Caulcutt, R. & Boddy, R. Statistics for Analytical Chemists. 1983. 49.95 (ISBN 0-412-23730-X, NO. 6806, Pub. by Chapman & Hall). Methuen Inc.

Caulcutt, Roland. Statistics in Research & Development. 352p. 1982. 49.95 (ISBN 0-412-23720-2, NO. 6784, Pub. by Chapman & Hall). Methuen Inc.

Cauldrette. Romans of Partenay or of Lusignen. Skeat, W. W., ed. (EETS, OS Ser.: No. 22). Repr. of 1866 ed. 40.00 (ISBN 0-527-00022-1). Kraus Repr.

Cauldwell, Samuel M. Chocolate Cake & Black Sand & Two Other Plays. LC 79-50021. (One-Act Plays in Reprint Ser.). 1980. Repr. of 1917 ed. 18.50x (ISBN 0-8486-2045-3). Core Collection.

Cauley, Lorinda B. The Cock, the Mouse & the Little Red Hen. (Illus.). 32p. 1982. 9.95 (ISBN 0-399-20740-6, Putnam); pap. 4.95 (ISBN 0-399-20930-1). Putnam Pub Group.

--Goldilocks & the Three Bears. (Illus.). 32p. (ps-2). 1981. 10.95 (ISBN 0-399-20794-5, Putnam); pap. 4.95 (ISBN 0-399-20795-3). Putnam Pub Group.

--The Goose & the Golden Coins. LC 80-24591. (Illus.). 48p. (ps-3). 1981. pap. 5.95 (ISBN 0-15-232207-8, VoyB). HarBraceJ.

--Jack & the Beanstalk. (Illus.). (gr. k-4). 1983. 10.95 (ISBN 0-399-20901-8, Putnam); pap. 4.95 (ISBN 0-399-20902-6). Putnam Pub Group.

--The New House. LC 81-611. (A Let Me Read Bk.). (Illus.). 48p. (gr. 1-5). 1981. pap. 3.50 (ISBN 0-15-257041-1, VoyB). HarBraceJ.

--The Three Little Kittens. (Illus.). 32p. 1982. 7.95 (ISBN 0-399-20855-0, Putnam); pap. 3.95 (ISBN 0-399-20856-9). Putnam Pub Group.

--The Town Mouse & the Country Mouse. LC 84-11532. (Illus.). 32p. (ps-3). 1984. 11.95 (ISBN 0-399-21123-3, Putnam); pap. 4.95 (ISBN 0-399-21126-8). Putnam Pub Group.

--The Ugly Duckling. LC 79-12340. (Illus.). 48p. (gr. k-3). 1979. pap. 5.95 (ISBN 0-15-692528-1, VoyB). HarBraceJ.

Caulfeild, S. F. & Saward, Blanche. Encyclopedia of Victorian Needlework, 2 vols. 1985. pap. 10.95 ea. Vol. 1 (ISBN 0-486-22800-2). Vol. 2 (ISBN 0-486-22801-0). Dover.

Caulfield, Betty, jt. auth. see Sakoian, Frances.

Caulfield, C., ed. see Satue, Francisco J.

Caulfield, Carlota. Oscuridad Divina. (Poetry Ser.). (Illus.). 64p. (Orig., Span.). 1985. pap. 5.00 (ISBN 0-932367-02-X). Ediciones El.

Caulfield, Don & Caulfield, Joan. The Incredible Detectives. (Illus.). (gr. 4-6). 1972. pap. 1.50 (ISBN 0-380-01282-0, 50443, Camelot). Avon.

Caulfield, H. Winning the Fire Service Leadership Game. 1985. 19.95 (ISBN 0-912212-09-8). Fire Eng.

Caulfield, H. J. & Lu, Sun. The Applications of Holography. LC 77-107585. 138p. 1970. 16.50 (ISBN 0-471-14080-5, Pub. by Wiley). Krieger.

Caulfield, H. J., ed. Handbook of Optical Holography. LC 79-51672. 1979. 69.50 (ISBN 0-12-165350-1). Acad Pr.

Caulfield, H. John, et al. Holography Works. LC 83-62984. (Illus.). 72p. 1984. pap. 25.00 (ISBN 0-936210-13-3). Mus Holography.

Caulfield, James, jt. ed. see Sperelakis, Nicholas.

Caulfield, Joan, jt. auth. see Caulfield, Don.

Caulfield, Malachy. The Easter Rebellion. LC 74-5550. 375p. 1975. Repr. of 1963 ed. lib. bdg. 21.00x (ISBN 0-8371-7507-0, CAER). Greenwood.

Caulfield, Richard, ed. see Davies, Rowland.

Caulfield, Sean. The Experience of Praying. LC 79-92428. 88p. 1980. 2.95 (ISBN 0-8091-2358-4). Paulist Pr.

--In Praise of Chaos. LC 81-82335. 96p. (Orig.). 1981. pap. 3.50 (ISBN 0-8091-2396-7). Paulist Pr.

--Under the Broom Tree. LC 82-60593. 80p. 1983. pap. 3.95 (ISBN 0-8091-2493-9). Paulist Pr.

Caulfield, Sophia F. House Mottoes & Inscriptions. LC 68-21758. 1968. Repr. of 1908 ed. 35.00x (ISBN 0-8103-3322-8). Gale.

Caulfield, Thomas B. The Story of a Cancer Cure: Book I. 224p. 1983. lib. bdg. 16.95 (ISBN 0-9611788-0-9). Ctr Adv Psychic Res.

Caulkins, Frances M. History of New London, Connecticut: From the First Survey of the Coast in 1612 to 1860. 4th ed. (Illus.). 824p. 1985. Repr. of 1890 ed. text ed. 45.00 (ISBN 0-9607744-0-8). New London County.

Caulkins, Frank. The Long Riders' Winter. 224p. 1985. pap. 2.50 (ISBN 0-345-32124-3). Ballantine.

Caulkins, Janet. A Picture Life of Mikhail Gorbachev. (Picture Life Ser.). (Illus.). 48p. (gr. 1-8). 1985. PLB 9.90 (ISBN 0-531-10085-5). Watts.

Caullery, Maurice. French Science & Its Principle Discoveries since the Seventeenth Century. LC 74-26256. (History, Philosophy & Sociology of Science Ser). (Illus.). 1975. Repr. of 1934 ed. 20.00x (ISBN 0-405-06584-1). Ayer Co Pubs.

--Universities & Scientific Life in the United States. LC 74-26257. (History, Philosophy & Sociology of Science Ser). 1975. Repr. of 1922 ed. 24.50x (ISBN 0-405-06585-X). Ayer Co Pubs.

Caullery, Maurice J. Universities & Scientific Life in the United States. LC 72-94312. (The American Scientific Community, 1790-1920 Ser.). 1973. Repr. of 1922 ed. lib. bdg. 28.00 (ISBN 0-8420-1677-5). Scholarly Res Inc.

Caum, E. L. Check-List of Hawaiian Land & Freshwater Mollusca. (BMB Ser.: No. 56). Repr. of 1928 ed. 11.00 (ISBN 0-527-02162-8). Kraus Repr.

Caum, E. L., jt. auth. see Christophersen, E.

Cauman, Leigh, et al, eds. How Many Questions? Essays in Honor of Sidney Morgenbesser. 516p. 30.00 (ISBN 0-915145-59-6); pap. text ed. 15.00 (ISBN 0-915145-58-8). Hackett Pub.

Cauman, Samuel, jt. auth. see Janson, H. W.

Caunitz, William. One Police Plaza. 1984. 14.95 (ISBN 0-517-55029-6). Crown.

Caunitz, William J. One Police Plaza. 384p. 1985. pap. 3.95 (ISBN 0-553-24746-8). Bantam.

Caunt, A. E., jt. auth. see Taylor-Robinson, D.

Caunter, C. F. The Light Car: A Technical History of Cars with Engines of Less Than 1600cc. 14.95 (ISBN 0-8376-0053-7). Bentley.

Cauper, Eunice. Story of Christopher Columbus & Our October 12th Holiday for Elementary Children. (Illus.). (gr. k). 1986. pap. 2.95 (ISBN 0-8283-1992-8). Branden Pub Co.

--The Story of the Pilgrims & Their Indian Friends: A Thanksgiving Story for Children. 3rd ed. (Illus.). (gr. k). 1984. pap. 3.95 (ISBN 0-8283-1899-9). Branden Pub Co.

Cauquil, J. Cotton Boll Rot. 1981. 45.00x (ISBN 0-686-76631-8, Pub. by Oxford & IBH India). State Mutual Bk.

Caus, Isaac. Wilton Gardens: New & Rare Inventions of Water-Works. Hunt, John D., ed. LC 79-57005. (The English Landscape Garden Ser.). (Illus.). 91p. 1982. lib. bdg. 19.00 (ISBN 0-8240-0178-8). Garland Pub.

Causa-Steindler, Mariangel, tr. Giovanni Boccaccio: The Elegy of Lady Fiammetta. LC 83-48243. (Medieval Studies). 170p. 1985. lib. bdg. 30.00 (ISBN 0-8240-9440-9). Garland Pub.

Causby, Ralph E., jt. auth. see Baucom, Marta E.

Cause RFP Committee. Computer-Related Acquisitions. (Cause Monographs). 16.00 (ISBN 0-933783-02-7). CAUSE.

Causer, H. Phillip. M.I.A. (Missing in Action) LC 77-88747. (Illus.). 1977. 9.95 (ISBN 0-918442-00-1). Phipps Pub.

Causey, Andrew. Edward Burra. (Illus.). 208p. 1985. 75.00 (ISBN 0-7148-2323-6, Pub by Salem Hse Ltd). Merrimack Pub Cir.

--Paul Nash. (Illus.). 1980. 105.00x (ISBN 0-19-817348-2). Oxford U Pr.

Causey, Andrew & Colvin, Clare. Paul Nash's Photographs Document & Image. (Illus.). 124p. 12.95 (ISBN 0-900874-59-7, Pub. by Salem Hse Ltd). Merrimack Pub Cir.

Causey, Denzil Y. Accounting for Decision Making. LC 77-78479. (Grid Series in Accounting). pap. 142.80 (ISBN 0-317-30123-3, 2025306). Bks Demand UMI.

--Duties & Liabilities of Public Accountants. rev ed. LC 82-70156. (Illus.). 1982. 29.95 (ISBN 0-87094-325-1). Dow Jones-Irwin.

Causey, Denzil Y., Jr. Duties & Liabilities of Public Accountants. 3rd ed. 256p. 1986. Repr. lib. bdg. 39.95 (ISBN 0-930001-01-X). Accountants Pr.

--The Tax Practitioner: Legal & Ethical Rights & Responsibilities. 256p. 1984. 39.95 (ISBN 0-930001-00-1). Accountants Pr.

Causey, G. Donald, et al. Development of the Speech Reception. Cox, Klaudia, ed. (Ser. 2: No. 71). 1977. pap. text ed. 1.50 (ISBN 0-8406-0088-7). Natl Ctr Health Stats.

Causey, Leo. Home to Count the Memories. 1984. 5.95 (ISBN 0-8062-2191-7). Carlton.

Causey, Robert L. Unity of Science. (Synthese Library: No. 109). 1977. lib. bdg. 34.00 (ISBN 90-277-0779-0, Pub. by Reidel Holland). Kluwer Academic.

Causley, Charles. The Batsford Book of Stories in Verse for Children. 1979. 17.95 (ISBN 0-7134-1529-0, Pub by Batsford England). David & Charles.

--Collected Poems 1951-1975. LC 74-30906. 294p. 1975. 17.95x (ISBN 0-87923-139-4); pap. 7.95 (ISBN 0-87923-168-8). Godine.

--Hands to Dance & Skylark. 192p. 1982. pap. 7.50 (ISBN 0-907746-13-6, Pub. by A Mott Ltd). Longwood Pub Group.

Causley, Charles, ed. Modern Folk Ballads. (Pocket Poet Ser.). 1966. pap. 2.00 (ISBN 0-8023-9043-9). Dufour.

Causley, Marguerite. An Introduction to Benesh: Movement Notation. LC 79-7755. (Dance Ser.). (Illus.). 1980. Repr. of 1967 ed. lib. bdg. 14.00x (ISBN 0-8369-9280-6). Ayer Co Pubs.

Caussade, Jean-Pierre de see De Caussade, Jean-Pierre.

Caussy, Fernand, ed. see Voltaire.

Causton. Biometry of Plant Growth. (Illus.). 320p. 1982. text ed. 59.50 (ISBN 0-7131-2812-7). Univ Park.

Causton, David & Venus, Jill. Biometry of Plant Growth. 320p. 1981. text ed. 59.50 (ISBN 0-7131-2812-7). E Arnold.

Causton, David R. A Biologist's Basic Mathematics. (Contemporary Biology Ser.). (Illus.). 224p. 1983. pap. text ed. 14.50 (ISBN 0-7131-2879-8). E Arnold.

Causton, David R. & Venus, Jill C. The Biometry of Plant Growth. 272p. 1981. 90.00x (ISBN 0-7131-2812-7, Pub. by E Arnold England). State Mutual Bk.

Causton, Eric E. Militarism & Foreign Policy in Japan. LC 78-63658. (Studies in Fascism: Ideology & Practice). Repr. of 1936 ed. 26.00 (ISBN 0-404-16918-X). AMS Pr.

Caute, David. Under the Skin: The Death of White Rhodesia. 447p. 1983. 19.95 (ISBN 0-8101-0658-2). Northwestern U Pr.

Cautela, Joseph R. Behavior Analysis Forms for Clinical Intervention, Vol. 1. LC 76-52358. 1977. spiral bdg. 32.95 (ISBN 0-87822-135-2). Res Press.

Cautela, Joseph R. & Cautela, Julie. Forms for Behavior Analysis with Children. LC 82-62572. 199p. (Orig.). 1983. spiral bdg. 28.95 ea. (ISBN 0-87822-267-7, 2677). Res Press.

Cautela, Joseph R. & Groden, June. Relaxation: A Comprehensive Manual for Adults, Children, & Children with Special Needs. LC 78-62906. (Illus., Orig.). 1978. spiral 12.95 (ISBN 0-87822-186-7, 1867). Res Press.

Cautela, Joseph R., jt. ed. see Upper, Dennis.

Cautela, Julie, jt. auth. see Cautela, Joseph R.

Cauter, E. van see Van Cauter, E. & Copinschi, G.

Cauthen, Charles E., ed. State Records of South Carolina: Journals of the South Carolina Executive Councils of 1861 & 1862. LC 56-63363. xviii, 336p. 1956. 34.95x (ISBN 0-87249-913-8). U of SC Pr.

Cauthen, Henry, jt. auth. see Briggs, William J.

Cauthen, Irby B., Jr., jt. auth. see Dameron, J. Lasley.

Cauthen, John K. Speaker Blatt: His Challenges Were Greater. 1978. pap. 17.95x (ISBN 0-87249-369-5). U of SC Pr.

Cauthen, Joseph C. Lumbar Spine Surgery: Indications, Techniques, Failures & Alternatives. (Illus.). 225p. 1983. lib. bdg. 46.25 (ISBN 0-683-01500-1). Williams & Wilkins.

Cauthen, Kenneth. The Impact of American Religious Liberalism. 2nd ed. LC 82-23902. 308p. 1983. pap. text ed. 14.25 (ISBN 0-8191-2762-0). U Pr of Amer.

--Process Ethics: A Constructive System. LC 84-16662. (Toronto Studies in Theology: Vol. 18). 365p. 1985. 59.95x (ISBN 0-88946-764-1). E Mellen.

Cauthery, Philip, et al. Loving Sex: A Lifetime Guide. LC 83-40582. (Illus.). 444p. 1984. 19.95 (ISBN 0-8128-2968-9). Stein & Day.

Cautley, H. Munro. Norfolk Churches. (Illus.). 1979. 30.00 (ISBN 0-85115-022-5, Pub. by Boydell & Brewer). Longwood Pub Group.

--Suffolk Churches. 5th ed. (Illus.). 448p. 1982. 45.00 (ISBN 0-85115-143-4, Pub. by Boydell & Brewer). Longwood Pub Group.

Cautley, Patricia W. New Foster Parents: The First Experience. LC 80-10937. 287p. 1980. 29.95x (ISBN 0-87705-495-9). Human Sci Pr.

Cauvin, Jean-Pierre & Baker, Mary J. Panache Litteraire: Textes Du Monde Francophone. 1978. pap. text ed. 13.50 scp (ISBN 0-06-041205-4, HarpC). Har-Row.

Cauvin, Jean-Pierre, tr. see Breton, Andre.

Cauwels, Janice M. The Body Shop: Bionic Revolutions in Medicine. 1985. 12.95 (ISBN 0-8016-0944-5). Mosby.

--Bulimia: The Binge-Purge Compulsion. LC 82-45538. 288p. 1983. 14.95 (ISBN 0-385-18377-1). Doubleday.

Cauwenberghe, A. Van see IFAC Conference, 4th, Ghent, Belgium, June 1980.

Cauwenberghe, A. van see Van Cauwenberghe, A.

Cauwenberghe, Marc Van see Kushi, Michio & Van Cauwenberghe, Marc.

Cauwen Bergue, A. R. Van see Van Cauwenbergue, A. R.

Caux, Len De see De Caux, Len.

Cava, Ester, et al, eds. A Pediatrician's Guide to Child Behavior Problems. LC 79-88727. 223p. 1979. text ed. 26.00x (ISBN 0-89352-075-6). Masson Pub.

Cava, Michael P. & Mitchell, M. J. Cyclobutadiene & Related Compounds. (Organic Chemistry Ser.: Vol. 10). 1967. 89.50 (ISBN 0-12-164450-2). Acad Pr.

Cava, Ralph Della see Della Cava, Ralph.

Cavaco-Silva, Anibal A. Economic Effects of Public Debt. LC 77-74813. 1977. 25.00x (ISBN 0-312-23222-5). St Martin.

Cavada, F. F. Libby Life: Experience of a Prisoner of War in Richmond, Va., 1863-64. (Illus.). 266p. 1985. pap. text ed. 12.50 (ISBN 0-8191-4166-6). U Pr of Amer.

Cavafy, C. Complete Poems of Cavafy. expanded ed. Dalven, Rae, tr. LC 76-22804. 311p. 1976. pap. 5.95 (ISBN 0-15-619820-7, Harv). HarBraceJ.

Cavafy, C. P. C. P. Cavafy: Collected Poems. Savidis, George, ed. Keeley, Edmund & Sherrard, Philip, trs. from Gr. LC 74-2977. (Lockert Library of Poetry in Translation). 508p. (Eng. & Gr.). 1975. 40.00x (ISBN 0-691-06279-X); pap. 8.95 (ISBN 0-691-01320-9). Princeton U Pr.

--The Greek Poems of C. P. Cavafy. Kolaitis, Memas, tr. from Modern Greek. 480p. 1985. write for info. (ISBN 0-89241-400-6). Caratzas.

Cavagnaro, Charles, jt. auth. see Sorrels, William W.

Cavagnaro, David & Lanting, Frans, photos by. Feathers. LC 82-82344. (Illus.). 96p. (Text by David Cavagnaro). 1982. pap. 12.95 (ISBN 0-912856-79-3). Graphic Arts Ctr.

Cavaiani, Mabel. The Low Cholestrol Cookbook. LC 74-183813. 256p. 1972. 15.95 (ISBN 0-8092-9573-3). Contemp Bks.

--The New Diabetic Cookbook. (Illus.). 320p. 1984. 16.95 (ISBN 0-8092-5524-3). Contemp Bks.

Cavaiani, Mabel, et al. Simplified Quantity Regional Recipes. 1979. 16.75 (ISBN 0-8104-9453-1). Hayden.

Cavaignac, Godegroy, jt. auth. see Lemaitre, Jules.

Cavaioli, Frank J. & Lagumina, Salvatore J. The Peripheral Americans. LC 82-14019. 250p. 1984. pap. 9.50 (ISBN 0-89874-542-X). Krieger.

Cavalcanti, Guido. The Sonnets & Ballate of Guido Calvalcanti. LC 78-20454. 1980. Repr. of 1912 ed. 24.00 (ISBN 0-88355-834-3). Hyperion Conn.

Cavalcanti, Pedro & Piccone, Paul, eds. History, Philosophy & Culture in the Young Gramsci. LC 74-82995. 160p. (Orig.). 1975. 12.00 (ISBN 0-914386-07-7). Telos Pr.

Cavalcaselle, Giovanni B., jt. auth. see Crowe, Joseph A.

Cavalchini, Mariella, ed. see Tasso, Torquato.

Cavaletto, M., et al. Dizionario Italiano-Bulgaro. 967p. (Ital. & Bulgarian.). 1979. leatherette 35.00 (ISBN 0-686-97340-2, M-9835). French & Eur.

Cavalier, Julien. Classic American Railroad Stations. LC 78-69669. (Illus.). 1980. 20.00 (ISBN 0-498-02216-1). A S Barnes.

Cavalier, Peter & Silcock, Geof. Visions of Steam: The Four Seasons of Steam in Industrial South Wales. 120p. 1984. 32.00x (ISBN 0-86093-031-9, Pub. by ORPC Ltd UK). State Mutual Bk.

Cavalier, Richard. Sales Meetings That Work: Planning & Managing Meetings to Achieve Your Goals. LC 82-72764. 250p. 1983. 21.95 (ISBN 0-87094-364-2). Dow Jones-Irwin.

Cavalier, Robert J. Ludwig Wittgenstein's Tractatus Logico-Philosophicus: A Transcendental Critique of Ethics. LC 79-3724. 1980. text ed. 20.50 (ISBN 0-8191-0915-0); pap. text ed. 12.00 (ISBN 0-8191-0916-9). U Pr of Amer.

Cavaliere, A. R., et al. Field Guide to the Conspicuous Flora & Fauna of Bermuda. (Special Publication: No. 26). 60p. (Orig.). 1983. pap. 6.00 (ISBN 0-917642-26-0). Bermuda Bio.

Cavaliere, Alfredo, ed. see Raimon, Peire.

Cavalieri, Grace. Creature Comforts. LC 82-51068. 56p. 1982. pap. text ed. 5.95 (ISBN 0-915380-16-1). Word Works.

--Swan Research. LC 78-64529. (Illus.). 1979. perfect bdg. 5.95 (ISBN 0-915380-08-0). Word Works.

--Why I Cannot Take a Lover. (Ser. One). 1975. pap. 2.00 (ISBN 0-931846-01-3). Wash Writers Pub.

Cavalieri, Liebe F. The Double-Edged Helix: Genetic Engineering in the Real World. Anshen, Ruth N., ed. LC 84-17890. (Convergence Ser.). 208p. 1984. pap. 9.95 (ISBN 0-03-000998-7). Praeger.

--The Double-Edged Helix: Science in the Real World. Anshen, Ruth N., ed. (Convergence Ser.: Vol. II). 207p. 1981. 20.00x (ISBN 0-231-05306-1). Columbia U Pr.

Cavaliero, Glen. Charles Williams: Poet of Theology. 199p. 1983. 8.95 (ISBN 0-8028-3579-1). Eerdmans.

--A Reading of E. M. Forster. 187p. 1979. 23.50x (ISBN 0-8476-6191-1). Rowman.

--The Rural Tradition in the English Novel, 1900-1939. 240p. 1977. 19.50x (ISBN 0-87471-952-6). Rowman.

Cavaliero, Roderick. The Last of the Crusaders. LC 78-63337. (The Crusades & Military Orders: Second Ser.). Repr. of 1960 ed. 27.50 (ISBN 0-404-17006-4). AMS Pr.

Cavalier-Smith, T. & Smith. The Evolution of Genome Size. 1985. 59.95 (ISBN 0-471-10272-5). Wiley.

Cavallari, Ford, ed. Micro on the Apple Series, 3 vols. with disk 24.95 ea. (ISBN 0-938222-05-8). Vol. 1 (ISBN 0-938222-06-6). Vol. 2 (ISBN 0-938222-08-2). Vol. 3. Set. 59.95 (ISBN 0-686-46817-1). Computerist.

Cavallaro, A., jt. ed. see Stipa, S.

Cavallaro, Ann. Blimp. 192p. (gr. 12 up). 1983. 11.95 (ISBN 0-525-67139-0, 01160-350). Lodestar BKs.

--Careers in Food Services. 160p. (YA) 1981. 10.25 (ISBN 0-525-66698-2, 0995-300). Lodestar Bks.

Cavallaro, Lenny, jt. auth. see Kortchnoi, Viktor.

Cavallaro, Michael, ed. see Mohawk Valley Community College, Advertising Design Department.

Cavalleri, B., jt. ed. see Breccia, A.

Cavalletti, Sofia. The Religious Potential of the Child. 224p. 1982. pap. 10.95 (ISBN 0-8091-2389-4). Paulist Pr.

Cavalli, F., et al, eds. Proceedings of the International Symposium on Medroxyprogesterone Acetate: Geneva, Switzerland, February 24-26, 1982. (International Congress Ser.: No. 611). 632p. 1982. 95.75 (ISBN 0-444-90297-X, Excerpta Medica). Elsevier.

Cavalli, Ferdinando. Scienza politica in Italia, 4 Vols. LC 68-7283. (Research & Source Works Ser.: No. 219). 1968. Repr. of 1865 ed. Set. 110.00 (ISBN 0-8337-0505-9). B Franklin.

Cavalli, Francesco. Gli Amori d'Apollo e di Dafne. Brown, Howard M., ed. LC 76-21071. (Italian Opera 1640-1770 Ser.). 1978. lib. bdg. 77.00 (ISBN 0-8240-2600-4). Garland Pub.

--Scipione Africano. Brown, Howard M., ed. LC 76-20963. (Italian Opera 1640-1770 Ser.). 1978. lib. bdg. 77.00 (ISBN 0-8240-2604-7). Garland Pub.

Cavalli, Francesco, jt. auth. see Il Giasone.

Cavallini, D., et al, eds. Natural Sulfur Compounds: Novel Biochemical & Structural Aspects. 565p. 1980. 69.50x (ISBN 0-306-40335-8, Plenum Pr). Plenum Pub.

Cavallini, Ernesto. Thirty Caprices for the Clarinet. 64p. 1909. pap. 5.00 (ISBN 0-8258-0238-5, 0106). Fischer Inc NY.

Cavallini, Giuliana. St. Martin De Porres-Apostle of Charity. Holland, Caroline, tr. from It. LC 79-65530. (Cross & Crown Series of Spirituality). 1979. pap. 7.00 (ISBN 0-89555-092-X). TAN Bks Pubs.

Cavalli-Sforza. Atlas of Human Genetics. 27.50 (ISBN 0-317-14206-2). Princeton U Pr.

Cavalli-Sforza, L. L. Elements of Human Genetics. 2nd ed. LC 76-58969. 1977. text ed. 26.95 (ISBN 0-8053-1872-0); pap. text ed. 14.95 (ISBN 0-8053-1874-7). Benjamin-Cummings.

--The Genetics of Human Races. Head, J. J., ed. LC 83-71166. (Carolina Biology Readers Ser.). (Illus.). 16p. (gr. 10 up). 1983. pap. 1.60 (ISBN 0-89278-321-4, 45-9721). Carolina Biological.

Cavalli-Sforza, L. L. & Bodmer, Walter F. The Genetics of Human Populations. LC 79-120302. (Biology Ser.). (Illus.). 965p. 1978. pap. text ed. 30.95x (ISBN 0-7167-1018-8, 1018-8). W H Freeman.

Cavalli-Sforza, L. L. & Feldman, M. W. Cultural Transmission & Evolution: A Quantitative Approach. Robert, M., ed. LC 80-8539. (Monographs in Population Biology: No. 16). (Illus.). 368p. 1981. 33.00 (ISBN 0-691-08280-4); pap. 15.50 (ISBN 0-691-08283-9). Princeton U Pr.

Cavalli-Sforza, L. L., jt. auth. see Ammerman, Albert J.

Cavalli-Sforza, L. L., jt. auth. see Bodmer, W. F.

Cavalli-Sforza, Luigi L., ed. African Pygmies. Date not set. price not set (ISBN 0-12-164480-4). Acad Pr.

Cavallo, Adolph S. Needlework. Gilchrist, Brenda, ed. LC 78-62725. (Smithsonian Illustrated Library of Antiques). (Illus.). 128p. (Orig.). 1979. 9.95 (ISBN 0-910503-34-6). Cooper-Hewitt Museum.

Cavallo, Dominick. Muscles & Morals: Organized Playgrounds & Urban Reform, 1880-1920. LC 80-50689. 240p. 1981. 23.50x (ISBN 0-8122-7782-1). U of Pa Pr.

Cavallo, Dominick, jt. auth. see Albin, Mel.

Cavallo, Robert & Kahan, Stuart. The Business of Photography. 1981. Outlet 3.98 (ISBN 0-517-53945-4, Michelman Books). Crown.

Cavallo, Robert M., jt. auth. see Kahan, Stuart.

Cavallo, Roger. The Role of Systems Methodology in Social Science Research. (Frontiers in Systems Research Ser.: Vol. 1). 1979. lib. bdg. 22.00 (ISBN 0-89838-005-7, Pub. by Martinus Nijhoff Netherlands). Kluwer Academic.

--Systems Methodology in Social Science Research: Recent Developments. (Frontiers in Systems Research Ser.). 1982. lib. bdg. 35.50 (ISBN 0-89838-044-8). Kluwer-Nijhoff.

Cavalloro, R., ed. Aphid Antagonists: Proceedings of a Meeting of the EC Experts' Group, Portici, Nov. 23-24, 1982. 152p. 1983. lib. bdg. 20.00 (ISBN 90-6191-505-8, Pub. by Balkema RSA). IPS.

--Varroa Jacobsonioud Affecting Honey Bees-Present Status & Needs: Proceedings of a Meeting of the EC Experts Group, Wageningen 7-9 Feb. 1983. 107p. 1984. lib. bdg. 19.00 (ISBN 90-6191-524-4, Pub. by Balkema RSA). IPS.

Cavan, Ruth S. & Burgess, Ernest W. Personal Adjustment in Old Age. Kastenbaum, Robert, ed. LC 78-22188. (Aging & Old Age Ser). (Illus.). 1979. Repr. of 1949 ed. lib. bdg. 17.00x (ISBN 0-405-11806-6). Ayer Co Pubs.

Cavan, Ruth S. & Ferdinand, Theodore N. Juvenile Delinquency. 4th ed. 448p. 1981. pap. text ed. 20.95 scp (ISBN 0-06-041206-2, HarpC). Har-Row.

Cavan, Ruth S. & Ranck, Katherine H. Family & the Depression: A Study of One Hundred Chicago Families. facsimile ed. LC 79-102229. (Select Bibliographies Reprint Ser). 1938. 22.00 (ISBN 0-8369-5114-X). Ayer Co Pubs.

Cavan, Ruth S. & Das, Man S., eds. Communes: Historical & Contemporary. 1979. text ed. 30.00x (ISBN 0-7069-0786-8, Pub. by Vikas India). Advent NY.

Cavan, Sherri. Twentieth Century Gothic: America's Nixon. LC 79-65722. (Illus.). 1979. 17.50 (ISBN 0-934594-00-7). Wigan Pier.

Cavanagh, jt. ed. see Smith.

Cavanagh, Deirdre, tr. see Guyot, Charles.

Cavanagh, Denis & Marsden, Donald E. Gynecologic Cancer: A Clinical Pathologic Approach. 400p. 1985. 49.50 (ISBN 0-8385-3530-5). ACC.

Cavanagh, Denis & Woods, Ralph F., eds. Obstetric Emergencies. 3rd ed. (Illus.). 480p. 1982. pap. text ed. 28.75 (ISBN 0-06-140627-9, 14-06271, Harper Medical). Lippincott.

Cavanagh, Dennis, et al. Septic Shock in Obstetrics & Gynecology. LC 76-50147. (Major Problems in Obstetrics & Gynecology: Vol. 11). (Illus.). 1977. text ed. 15.00 (ISBN 0-7216-2455-3). Saunders.

Cavanagh, Eileen, jt. auth. see Harelson, Randy.

Cavanagh, Gerald, jt. auth. see Purcell, Theodore.

Cavanagh, Gerald F. American Business Values. 2nd ed. (Illus.). 256p. 1984. pap. text ed. 15.95 (ISBN 0-13-024159-8). P-H.

Cavanagh, H. Dwight. Modern Soft Contact Lenses. Date not set. write for info. (ISBN 0-89004-433-3, 493). Raven.

Cavanagh, Helen. Angel. 176p. (Orig.). (gr. 7 up). 1984. pap. 2.25 (ISBN 0-590-32284-2, Wildfire). Scholastic Inc.

--Honey. (gr. 7 up). 1980. pap. 1.95 (ISBN 0-590-32451-9, Wishing Star Bks). Scholastic Inc.

--Just a Summer Girl. 192p. (Orig.). (gr. 7 up). 1982. pap. 1.95 (ISBN 0-590-31962-0, Wildfire). Scholastic Inc.

--Kiss & Tell. 176p. (Orig.). (gr. 7 up). 1984. pap. 2.25 (ISBN 0-590-32536-1, Wildfire). Scholastic Inc.

--A Place for Me. 160p. (Orig.). (gr. 7 up). 1981. pap. 1.95 (ISBN 0-590-31765-2, Wildfire). Scholastic Inc.

--Second Best. (YA) (gr. 7 up). 1979. pap. 1.95 (ISBN 0-590-32313-X, Wildfire). Scholastic Inc.

Cavanagh, Helen M. Funk of Funk's Grove. 1968. 5.50 (ISBN 0-912226-10-2). Ill St Hist Soc.

Cavanagh, John & Clairmonte, Frederick F. Alcoholic Beverages: Dimensions of Corporate Power. LC 84-27708. 192p. 1985. 25.00 (ISBN 0-312-01714-6). St Martin.

Cavanagh, John, jt. auth. see Clairmonte, Frederick.

Cavanagh, Mary. Blends & Digraphs. (Illus.). 24p. (gr. 1-3). 1980. pap. 6.95 (ISBN 0-933358-65-2). Enrich.

--Favorite Menus. (Illus.). 13p. (gr. 3-5). 1980. pap. 5.95 (ISBN 0-933358-70-9). Enrich.

--Telephone Power. (Illus.). 13p. (gr. 3-5). 1980. pap. 5.95 (ISBN 0-933358-71-7). Enrich.

Cavanagh, Maura, jt. auth. see Smithies, Richard H.

Cavanagh, Michael E. The Counseling Experience: Understanding & Living It. LC 81-17050. (Psychology - Counseling Ser.). 552p. 1982. text ed. 19.50 pub net (ISBN 0-8185-0509-5). Brooks-Cole.

--Make Your Tomorrow Better: A Psychological Resource for Singles, Parents & the Entire Family. LC 80-80638. 360p. (Orig.). 1980. pap. 8.95 (ISBN 0-8091-2293-6). Paulist Pr.

Cavanagh, Peter. The Running Shoe Book. LC 80-20365. (Illus.). 400p. 1980. pap. 11.95 (ISBN 0-89037-182-2). Anderson World.

Cavanagh, Richard E., jt. auth. see Clifford, Donald K., Jr.

Cavanagh, Thomas E. Inside Black America: A National Survey of Political Attitudes. (Election '84 Report: No. 5). (Orig., Sold through publisher only). Date not set. pap. 4.95 (ISBN 0-941410-47-1). Jt Ctr Pol Studies.

Cavanagh, Thomas E., ed. Race & Political Strategy. LC 83-22189. 60p. (Orig.). 1983. pap. 4.95 (ISBN 0-941410-33-1). Jt Ctr Pol Studies.

--Strategies for Black Voter Mobilization: Four Case Studies. (Orig.). Date not set. pap. 4.95 (ISBN 0-941410-48-X). Jt Ctr Pol Studies.

Cavanah, Frances. Abe Lincoln Gets His Chance. (Illus.). (gr. 4-6). pap. 1.95 (ISBN 0-590-08501-8, Schol Pap). Scholastic Inc.

--Jenny Lind & Her Listening Cat. LC 61-15483. (Illus.). (gr. 3-6). 1961. 6.95 (ISBN 0-8149-0289-8). Vanguard.

--The Truth about the Man Behind the Book That Sparked the War Between the States. LC 75-11566. (Illus.). 188p. (gr. 3-7). 1975. 7.95 (ISBN 0-664-32572-6). Westminster.

Cavanah, Frances, ed. Favorite Christmas Stories. (gr. 3 up). 1948. 5.95 (ISBN 0-448-02376-8, G&D). Putnam Pub Group.

Cavanaugh, Ann. The Computer Primer. (Illus.). 481p. (gr. 4-9). 1983. pap. 12.95 (ISBN 0-89824-046-8). Trillium Pr.

--The Computer Primer: A Complete Guide for Gifted Beginners. LC 84-26274. (Illus.). 128p. (gr. 4 up). lib. bdg. 19.95 (ISBN 0-516-00532-4). Childrens.

Cavanaugh, Cam. Saving the Great Swamp: The People, the Power Brokers & an Urban Wilderness. LC 78-8132. (Illus.). 1978. 11.95 (ISBN 0-914366-11-4). Columbia Pub.

Cavanaugh, Catherine, jt. auth. see Feinstein, Barbara.

Cavanaugh, D. C., jt. auth. see Bahmanyar, M.

Cavanaugh, G. M., et al. Formulae & Methods. 1964. 6.00 (ISBN 0-685-52858-8). Marine Bio.

Cavanaugh, Gerald J., jt. ed. see Gay, Peter.

Cavanaugh, Helen. Superflirt. 176p. (Orig.). (gr. 7 up). 1980. pap. 1.95 (ISBN 0-590-30951-X, Wildfire). Scholastic Inc.

Cavanaugh, J. Albert. Lettering & Alphabets. 1946. pap. 3.75 (ISBN 0-486-20053-1). Dover.

--Lettering & Alphabets. (Illus.). 14.75 (ISBN 0-8446-0541-7). Peter Smith.

Cavanaugh, Jim. The Theatre Student: Organization & Management of Non-Professional Theatre. LC 72-75222. (Illus.). (gr. 7-12). 1973. PLB 15.00 (ISBN 0-8239-0259-5). Rosen Group.

Cavanaugh, Joan & Forseth, Pat. More of Jesus, Less of Me. 1976. pap. 3.95 (ISBN 0-88270-174-6, Pub. by Logos). Bridge Pub.

Cavanaugh, John T., ed. see Braly, Scott A. & Kay, Robert S.

Cavanaugh, Joseph H. Evidence for Our Faith. 3rd ed. 1959. 8.00x (ISBN 0-268-00092-1). U. of Notre Dame Pr.

Cavanaugh, Margery. Withering into Truth. (Juniper Bk.: No. 41). 1983. pap. 4.00 (ISBN 0-686-84329-0). Juniper Pr WI.

Cavanaugh, Merry, The Preschool & Daycare Book. 88p. 1984. 6.95x (ISBN 0-9614212-0-7). Cavanaugh.

Cavanaugh, Robin, ed. see Shannon, Terry.

Cavanaugh, Sara. A Woman in Space. (Orig.). 1981. pap. 1.75 (ISBN 0-8439-8023-0, Tiara Bks). Dorchester Pub Co.

Cavanaugh, Tom R. & Thomas, Payne E. Bannerstone House: A Frank Lloyd Wright House, Springfield, Illinois. 48p. 1979. pap. 3.75x (ISBN 0-398-00299-1). C C Thomas.

Cavander, Kenneth, jt. auth. see Barton, John.

Cavanilles, A. J. Icones & Descriptiones Plantarum Quae Aut Sponte in Hispania Crescunt Aut in Hortis Hospitantur 1791-1801, 6pts. in 2 vols. 1965. 280.00 (ISBN 3-7682-0292-5). Lubrecht & Cramer.

Cavanna, Betty. Almost Like Sisters. (gr. 7 up). 1963. 12.50 (ISBN 0-688-21014-7). Morrow.

--Ballet Fever. LC 78-3684. 144p. 1978. 8.95 (ISBN 0-664-32631-5). Westminster.

--The Boy Next Door. (gr. 7 up). 1956. PLB 12.88 (ISBN 0-688-31116-4). Morrow.

--Catchpenny Street. LC 75-2397. (Illus.). 222p. (gr. 6 up). 1975. 7.50 (ISBN 0-664-32574-2). Westminster.

--Going on Sixteen. (Illus.). 220p. (gr. 7-10). 1946. Westminster.

--Going on Sixteen. 224p. (gr. 5-9). 1985. Repr. of 1971 ed. 10.25 (ISBN 0-688-05892-2, Morrow Junior Books). Morrow.

--Paintbox Summer. 212p. 1981. Repr. PLB 16.95 (ISBN 0-89966-357-5). Buccaneer Bks.

--Paintbox Summer. 239p. 1981. Repr. PLB 12.95x (ISBN 0-89967-031-8). Harmony Raine.

--Petey. LC 73-4351. (Illus.). 144p. (gr. 3-6). 1973. 5.50 (ISBN 0-664-32532-7). Westminster.

--Romance on Trial. LC 84-10415. 96p. (gr. 6-9). 1984. 10.95 (ISBN 0-664-32715-X). Westminster.

--Ruffles & Drums. LC 75-9630. (Illus.). (gr. 7-9). 1975. 11.25 (ISBN 0-688-22035-5). Morrow.

--Spice Island Mystery. LC 72-83531. (gr. 7 up). 1969. 11.25 (ISBN 0-688-21706-0). Morrow.

--Stamp Twice for Murder. LC 81-8291. 224p. (gr. 7-9). 1981. pap. 11.25 (ISBN 0-688-00700-7); PLB 11.88 (ISBN 0-688-00701-5). Morrow.

--Storm in Her Heart. LC 82-20237. (A Hiway Book: A High Interest - Low Reading Level Book). 94p. (gr. 7-10). 1983. 9.95 (ISBN 0-664-32700-1). Westminster.

--The Surfer & the City Girl. LC 80-25901. (A Hiway Bk.: A High Interest-Low Reading Level Book). 96p. (gr. 7-9). 1981. 8.95 (ISBN 0-664-32679-X). Westminster.

--Two's Company. (Illus.). 190p. (gr. 5-9). 1951. 6.95 (ISBN 0-664-32080-5). Westminster.

--Wanted: A Girl for the Horses. LC 83-19289. 224p. (gr. 7 up). 1984. 9.50 (ISBN 0-688-02757-1). Morrow.

--You Can't Take Twenty Dogs on a Date. (YA) (gr. 7-12). 1979. pap. 1.95 (ISBN 0-590-05784-7). Scholastic Inc.

--You Can't Take Twenty Dogs on a Date. LC 77-432. 180p. (gr. 5-9). 1977. 8.95 (ISBN 0-664-32613-7). Westminster.

Cavanna, Roberto & Servadio, Emilio. ESP Experiments with LSD Twenty-Five & Psilocybin. LC 64-24271. (Parapsychological Monograph No. 5). 1964. pap. 3.00 (ISBN 0-912328-08-8). Parapsych Foun.

Cavanna, Roberto, ed. see International Conference on Hypnosis, Drugs, Dreams, & Psi, France, June 9-12, 1967.

Cavanna, Roberto, ed. see Of An International Conference on Methodology in Psi Research, France, Sept. 2-6, 1968.

Cavarnos, Constantine. Anchored in God. 2nd ed. LC 75-35432. (Illus.). 230p. 1975. 10.00 (ISBN 0-914744-30-5); pap. 6.50 (ISBN 0-914744-31-3). Inst Byzantine.

--Byzantine Sacred Music. 31p. 1981. pap. 1.00 (ISBN 0-914744-23-2). Inst Byzantine.

--Byzantine Thought & Art. 2nd ed. LC 68-21884. (Illus.). 139p. 1974. pap. 4.50 (ISBN 0-914744-22-4). Inst Byzantine.

--The Classical Theory of Relations. LC 75-2659. 116p. 1975. pap. 3.75 (ISBN 0-914744-28-3). Inst Byzantine.

--A Dialogue on G. E. Moore's Ethical Philosophy: Together with an Account of Three Talks with Moore on Diverse Philosophical Questions. LC 79-65479. 1979. 5.95 (ISBN 0-914744-43-7); pap. 2.95 (ISBN 0-914744-44-5). Inst Byzantine.

--The Future Life According to Orthodox Teaching. Auxentios, Hieromonk & Chrysostomos, Archimandrite, trs. from Gr. 100p. (Orig.). 1985. pap. 6.50 (ISBN 0-911165-06-1). Ctr Trad Orthodox.

--The Holy Mountain. 2nd ed. LC 73-84103. (Illus.). 172p. 1977. pap. 6.50 (ISBN 0-914744-38-0). Inst Byzantine.

--Modern Greek Philosophers on the Human Soul. (Illus.). 111p. 1967. 7.00 (ISBN 0-914744-06-2). Inst Byzantine.

--Modern Greek Thought. LC 71-93095. 115p. 1969. 7.00 (ISBN 0-914744-10-0). Inst Byzantine.

--Modern Orthodox Saints: Vol. 1-St. Cosmas Aitolos. 2nd ed. LC 73-157457. 118p. 1975. pap. 2.95 (ISBN 0-914744-29-1). Inst Byzantine.

--Modern Orthodox Saints: Vol. 2-St. Macarios of Corinth. 2nd ed. LC 72-85116. (Illus.). 1977. pap. 4.50 (ISBN 0-914744-35-6). Inst Byzantine.

--Modern Orthodox Saints: Vol. 3-St. Nicodemos the Hagiorite. 2nd ed. LC 78-71478. (Illus.). 167p. 1979. 8.00 (ISBN 0-914744-41-0); pap. 4.50. Inst Byzantine.

--Modern Orthodox Saints: Vol. 4-St. Nikephoros of Chios. LC 76-3152. (Illus.). 124p. 1976. pap. 8.00 (ISBN 0-914744-32-1). Inst Byzantine.

--Modern Orthodox Saints: Vol. 6-St. Arsenios of Paros. LC 78-54384. (Illus.). 123p. 1978. 8.00 (ISBN 0-914744-39-9); pap. 4.50 (ISBN 0-914744-40-2). Inst Byzantine.

--Modern Orthodox Saints: Vol. 7-St. Nectarios of Aegina. LC 81-82963. (Illus.). 222p. 1981. 10.00 (ISBN 0-914744-53-4); pap. 7.00 (ISBN 0-914744-54-2). Inst Byzantine.

--Orthodox Iconography. LC 77-74606. (Illus.). 76p. 1977. 8.00 (ISBN 0-914744-36-4); pap. 4.50 (ISBN 0-914744-37-2). Inst Byzantine.

--Plato's Theory of Fine Art. 98p. 1973. 6.00 (ISBN 0-914744-45-3); pap. 3.50 (ISBN 0-914744-46-1). Inst Byzantine.

--Plato's View of Man. LC 74-27242. 95p. 1975. pap. 3.50 (ISBN 0-914744-26-7). Inst Byzantine.

Cavarnos, Constantine, ed. Modern Orthodox Saints, Vol. 1: St. Cosmas Aitolos. 3rd. rev. & enl. ed. LC 85-80440. (Illus.). 118p. 1985. 8.50 (ISBN 0-914744-64-X); pap. 5.50 (ISBN 0-914744-65-8). Inst Byzantine.

--Modern Orthodox Saints: Vol. 8, St. Savvas the New. LC 85-60117. (Illus.). 144p. 1985. 8.95 (ISBN 0-914744-62-3); pap. 5.95 (ISBN 0-914744-63-1). Inst Byzantine.

Cavarnos, Constantine, ed. see Kontoglou, Photios.

Cavarnos, Constantine, compiled by. & t see Kontoglou, Photios.

Cavarnos, Constantine, tr. see Damascene, John & Oecuminical Synod Seventh.

Cavarnos, Constatine & Zeldin, Mary B. Modern Orthodox Saints: Vol. 5-St. Seraphim of Sarov. LC 80-80124. (Illus.). 167p. 1980. 9.00 (ISBN 0-914744-47-X); pap. 6.00 (ISBN 0-914744-48-8). Inst Byzantine.

Cavarnos, John P. The Dramatic Poetry of Demetrios N. Vernardakis. 244p. (Gr.). 1962. 8.50 (ISBN 0-914744-66-6); pap. 5.00 (ISBN 0-914744-67-4). Inst Byzantine.

--St. Gregory of Nyssa on the Origin & Destiny of the Soul. 12p. 1982. pap. 0.90 (ISBN 0-914744-60-7). Inst Byzantine.

Cavasina, Richard G. A Self Instructional Module Regarding the Effects of Abused Drugs. Reed, R., ed. LC 81-83632. (Illus.). 125p. 1982. pap. 5.95 (ISBN 0-88247-607-6). R & E Pubs.

Cavazza, Fabio L., et al. Television & Political Life. Smith, Anthony, ed. 1981. 15.00x (ISBN 0-333-24328-5, Pub. by Index on Censorship England). State Mutual Bk.

Cave, Alfred A. Jacksonian Democracy & the Historians. LC 80-13384. (University of Florida Monographs, Social Sciences: No. 22). 86p. 1980. Repr. of 1964 ed. lib. bdg. 18.75x (ISBN 0-313-22418-8, CAJA). Greenwood.

--Jacksonian Democracy & the Historians. LC 64-63899. (University of Florida Social Sciences Monographs: No. 22). 1964. pap. 3.50 (ISBN 0-8130-0044-0). U Presses Fla.

Cave, C. H., tr. see Jeremias, Joachim.

Cave, Cyril & Maddison, Pamela. A Survey of Recent Research in Special Education. 236p. 1978. 22.00x (ISBN 0-85633-160-0, Pub. by NFER Nelson UK). Taylor & Francis.

Cave, Emma. The Blood Bond. 192p. 1981. pap. 2.50 (ISBN 0-449-24402-4, Crest). Fawcett.

--Blood Bond. LC 78-20200. 1979. 12.45i (ISBN 0-06-010627-1, HarpT). Har-Row.

Cave, F. H., tr. see Jeremias, Joachim.

Cave, Frank & Terrell, David. Digital & Microprocessor Technology. 448p. 1981. text ed. 26.95 (ISBN 0-8359-1326-0); instrs. manual avail. (ISBN 0-8359-1327-9). Reston.

Cave, Hugh. A Summer Romance. Eyre, A. G., ed. (Longman Simplified English Ser.). 76p. 1980. pap. 1.95x (ISBN 0-582-52647-7). Longman.

Cave, Hugh see Eyre, A. G.

Cave, Hugh B. Long Were the Nights: The Saga of a PT Squadron in the Solomons. Repr. of 1943 ed. 15.00 (ISBN 0-89201-091-6). Zenger Pub.

--Murgunstrumm & Others. (Illus.). 475p. 1977. 15.00 (ISBN 0-913796-02-6). Carcosa.

--Shades of Evil. 320p. 1982. pap. 3.25 (ISBN 0-441-75986-6). Ace Bks.

Cave, Hugh B., jt. auth. see Miller, Norman M.

Cave, Hugh B., jt. auth. see Morris, Colton G.

Cave, J. Ronald. Trucks. (What About Ser.). (Illus.). 32p. (ps-3). 1982. PLB 7.90 (ISBN 0-531-04421-1). Watts.

Cave, Jane, tr. see Kuczynski, Waldemar.

Cave, Joyce & Cave, Ronald. Aircraft. (What about Ser.). (Illus.). 32p. (gr. k-3). 1982. PLB 7.90 (ISBN 0-531-04418-1, Gloucester Pr). Watts.

--Cars. (What About Ser.). (Illus.). 32p. (gr. k-3). 1982. PLB 7.90 (ISBN 0-531-04419-X, Gloucester Pr). Watts.

--Motorbikes. (What About Ser.). (Illus.). 32p. (gr. k-3). 1982. PLB 7.90 (ISBN 0-531-04420-3, Gloucester Pr). Watts.

Cave, Joyce, jt. auth. see Cave, Ron.

Cave, Kathryn, ed. see Farington, Joseph.

Cave, Martin. Computers & Economic Planning. LC 79-7659. (Soviet & East European Studies). 1980. 37.50 (ISBN 0-521-22617-1). Cambridge U Pr.

Cave, Martin & Hare, Paul. Alternating Approaches to Economic Planning. 1981. 32.50 (ISBN 0-312-02147-X). St Martin.

Cave, Martin, et al, eds. New Trends in Soviet Economics. Cave, Martin, tr. from Rus. LC 82-835. 425p. 1982. 40.00 (ISBN 0-87332-206-1). M E Sharpe.

Cave, Oenoen & Hodges, Jean. Smocking: Traditional & Modern. (Illus.). 120p. 1985. 14.95 (ISBN 0-7134-4229-8, Pub. by Batsford England). David & Charles.

Cave, Oenone. Cut-Work Embroidery & How to Do It. (Illus.). 96p. 1982. pap. 3.00 (ISBN 0-486-24267-6). Dover.

Cave, Peter. Fireflood. 256p. 1982. 20.00x (ISBN 0-7278-0734-X, Pub. by Severn Hse). State Mutual Bk.

--Foxbat. 288p. 1982. 20.00x (ISBN 0-7278-0521-5, Pub. by Severn Hse). State Mutual Bk.

--Siege. 288p. 1982. 20.00 (ISBN 0-7278-0628-9, Pub. by Severn Hse). State Mutual Bk.

Cave, Peter L., compiled by. Five Hundred Games. (Illus.). 160p. 1983. PLB 4.59 (ISBN 0-448-13619-8, G&D); (G&D). Putnam Pub Group.

Cave, Richard. Terence Gray & the Cambridge Festival Theatre. (Theatre in Focus Ser.). (Illus.). 90p. (Orig.). 1980. pap. text ed. 55.00x incl. slides (ISBN 0-85964-069-8). Chadwyck-Healey.

Cave, Richard, jt. auth. see Pine, Richard.

Cave, Richard, ed. see Moore, George.

Cave, Richard A. A Study of the Novels of George Moore. LC 78-3471. (Irish Literary Studies: No. 3). 271p. 1978. text ed. 28.50x (ISBN 0-06-491014-8, 06390). B&N Imports.

Cave, Roderick. The Private Press. 2nd ed. LC 83-7163. 389p. 1983. 59.95 (ISBN 0-8352-1695-0). Bowker.

--Rare Book Librarianship. 2nd rev. ed. 162p. 1982. 20.00 (ISBN 0-85157-328-2, Pub. by Bingley England). Shoe String.

Cave, Ron & Cave, Joyce. What About... Fighters. (What About Ser.). (Illus.). 32p. (gr. k-3). 1983. PLB 7.90 (ISBN 0-531-03468-2). Watts.

--What About... Missiles. (What About Ser.). (Illus.). 32p. (gr. k-3). 1983. PLB 7.90 (ISBN 0-531-03469-0). Watts.

--What About-Racing Cars? LC 82-81166. (What About Ser.). (Illus.). 32p. (gr. k-3). 1982. PLB 7.90 (ISBN 0-531-03464-X). Watts.

--What about-Space Shuttle? LC 82-81167. (What About Ser.). (Illus.). 32p. (gr. k-3). 1982. PLB 7.90 (ISBN 0-531-03465-8). Watts.

--What about Submarines? LC 82-81168. (What About Ser.). (Illus.). 32p. (gr. k-3). 1982. PLB 7.90 (ISBN 0-531-03466-6). Watts.

--What about... Tanks. (What About Ser.). (Illus.). 32p. (gr. k-3). 1983. PLB 7.90 (ISBN 0-531-03470-4). Watts.

--What about-Trains? LC 82-81169. (What About Ser.). 32p. (gr. k-3). 1982. lib. bdg. 7.90 (ISBN 0-531-03467-4). Watts.

--What about... War Ships. (What About Ser.). 32p. (gr. k-3). 1983. PLB 7.90 (ISBN 0-531-03471-2). Watts.

Cave, Ronald, jt. auth. see Cave, Joyce.

Cave, Roy C. & Coulson, Herbert H. Source Book for Medieval Economic History. LC 64-25840. 1936. 12.00x (ISBN 0-8196-0145-4). Biblo.

Cave, Sydney. Redemption, Hindu & Christian: The Religious Quest of India. facsimile ed. LC 73-102230. (Select Bibliographies Reprint Ser). 1919. 24.50 (ISBN 0-8369-5115-8). Ayer Co Pubs.

Cave, T., ed. see De Ronsard, P.

Cave, Terence. The Cornucopian Text: Problems of Writing in the French Renaissance. 1979. 57.00x (ISBN 0-19-815752-5). Oxford U Pr.

Cave, Terrence, jt. ed. see Castor, Graham.

Cave, William, jt. auth. see Chesler, Mark A.

Cave, William C. & Mayman, Gilbert W. Software Lifecycle Management: The Incremental Method. (Atre Ser.). 300p. 1984. pap. 27.95 (ISBN 0-02-949210-6). Macmillan.

Cavedon, Joelcira, jt. auth. see Third National Conference.

Cavel, Michael P. Nebraska Legal Forms: Workmen's Compensation. 1981. looseleaf 27.50 (ISBN 0-86678-023-8). Butterworth MN.

Cavell, S. Must We Mean What We Say? LC 75-32911. 365p. 1976. 39.50 (ISBN 0-521-21116-6); pap. 14.95 (ISBN 0-521-29048-1). Cambridge U Pr.

Cavell, Stanley. The Claim of Reason: Wittgenstein, Skepticism, Morality, & Tragedy. 1979. 24.95x (ISBN 0-19-502571-7). Oxford U Pr.

--The Claim of Reason: Wittgenstein, Skepticism, Morality, & Tragedy. 1979. pap. 9.95 (ISBN 0-19-503195-4, GB 704, GB). Oxford U Pr.

--Pursuits of Happiness: The Hollywood Comedy of Remarriage. (Harvard Film Studies). (Illus.). 320p. 1981. text ed. 18.50x (ISBN 0-674-73905-1). Harvard U Pr.

--Pursuits of Happiness: The Hollywood Comedy of Remarriages. (Harvard Film Studies). 296p. 1984. pap. 8.95 (ISBN 0-674-73906-X). Harvard U Pr.

--The Senses of Walden. expanded ed. LC 80-28315. 184p. 1981. 15.00 (ISBN 0-86547-031-6); pap. 8.50 (ISBN 0-86547-032-4). N Point Pr.

--Themes Out of School: Effects & Causes. 288p. 1984. 20.00 (ISBN 0-86547-146-0). N Point Pr.

--The World Viewed: Reflections on the Ontology of Film. enl. ed. (Paperback Ser.: No. 151). 1980. 17.50x (ISBN 0-674-96197-8); pap. 6.95 (ISBN 0-674-96196-X). Harvard U Pr.

Cavelti, Peter C. New Profits in Gold, Silver, & Strategic Metals: A Complete Investment Guide. 1984. 15.95 (ISBN 0-07-010288-0). McGraw.

Caven, Brian. The Punic Wars. LC 80-7467. (Illus.). 320p. 1980. 27.50 (ISBN 0-312-65580-0). St Martin.

Cavenagh, F. A., ed. see Mill, James & Mill, John S.

Cavenar, Jesse O. & Brodie, Keith H., eds. Critical Problems in Psychiatry. (Illus.). 512p. 1982. text ed. 34.50 (ISBN 0-397-50490-X, 65-06323, Lippincott Medical). Lippincott.

Cavenar, Jesse O., Jr. & Brodie, Keith H., eds. Signs & Symptoms in Psychiatry. (Illus.). 608p. 1983. text ed. 31.00 (ISBN 0-397-50489-6, 65-06315, Lippincott Medical). Lippincott.

Cavender, Finis L., jt. auth. see Somani, Satu M.

Cavender, Gray. Parole: A Critical Analysis. (Multidisciplinary Studies in Law & Jurisprudence). 130p. 1982. 16.50x (ISBN 0-8046-9296-3, 9296, Pub. by Kennikat). Assoc Faculty Pr.

Cavender, Nancy M. & Weiss, Leonard A. Thinking in Sentences: A Guide to Clear Writing. LC 81-82572. 1982. pap. 13.50 (ISBN 0-395-31690-1); instr's. manual 1.00 (ISBN 0-395-31691-X). HM.

Cavendish, Arthur M. The Guidebook to British Nobility: The History of the Great English Families. (The Memoirs Collections of Significant Historical Personalities Ser.). (Illus.). 99p. 1983. 79.85 (ISBN 0-89901-086-5). Found Class Reprints.

Cavendish, Butch. How to Cheat on College Exams & Get Away with It. 1983. pap. 4.95 (ISBN 0-317-03305-0). Loompanics.

Cavendish, George. The Life of Cardinal Wolsey. 1887. Repr. 15.00 (ISBN 0-8274-2879-0). R West.

--Metrical Visions. Edwards, Anthony S., ed. (Renaissance English Text Society Ser.: Vol. 9). 1980. 19.50 (ISBN 0-911028-19-6). Newberry.

Cavendish, George see Sylvester, Richard S. & Harding, Davis P.

Cavendish, Henry. Government of Canada: Debates of the House of Commons in the Year 1774. 1966. 24.00 (ISBN 0-384-07955-5). Johnson Repr.

Cavendish Laboratory, Electron Microscopy Section, jt. auth. see Saxton, W. O.

Cavendish, Marshall, ed. Step by Step to Better Knitting & Crochet. LC 81-67434. (Illus.). 288p. 1982. 19.95 (ISBN 0-668-05343-7, 5343). Arco.

Cavendish, Richard. A History of Magic. LC 76-56613. (Illus.). 1980. pap. 5.95 (ISBN 0-8008-3887-4). Taplinger.

--King Arthur & the Grail: The Arthurian Legends & Their Meaning. LC 79-14034. 238p. 1985. pap. 6.95 (ISBN 0-8008-4466-1). Taplinger.

Cavendish, Richard, ed. Legends of the World. LC 82-5525. (Illus.). 432p. 1982. 29.95 (ISBN 0-8052-3805-0). Schocken.

--Man, Myth & Magic: The Illustrated Encyclopedia of Mythology, Religion & the Unknown. 2nd ed. (Illus.). 3268p. 1983. lib. bdg. 399.95x (ISBN 0-86307-041-8). M Cavendish Corp.

Cavendish, Ruth. Women on the Line. 166p. 1982. pap. 12.50x (ISBN 0-7100-0987-9). Routledge & Kegan.

Cavendish, Thomas. The Last Voyage of Thomas Cavendish, 1591-1592. Quinn, David B., ed. LC 74-11619. (Studies in the History of Discoveries Ser). x, 166p. 1976. text ed. 22.50x (ISBN 0-226-09819-2). U of Chicago Pr.

Caveney, Philip. Tiger, Tiger. 400p. 1984. 15.95 (ISBN 0-312-80448-2). St Martin.

Caveney, Sylvia & Stern, Simon. Inside Mom. LC 76-46380. (Illus.). 93p. 1977. 6.95 (ISBN 0-312-41877-9). St Martin.

Caveny, Leonard H. Orbit-Raising & Maneuvering Propulsion: Research Status & Needs. 72.00 (ISBN 0-915928-82-5). AIAA.

Caveny, Sylvia & Giesen, Rosemary. Where Am I? LC 76-22476. (First Facts Books Ser). (Illus.). (gr. k-3). 1977. PLB 4.95 (ISBN 0-8225-1365-X). Lerner Pubns.

Cavera, Anthony La see Thomas, George & La Cavera, Anthony.

Caverly, D. J., jt. auth. see Eagle, D. J.

Caverly, Philip W. & Goldstein, Philip. Introduction to Ada: A Top-Down Approach for Programmers. 250p. 1985. pap. 16.25 (ISBN 0-534-05820-5). Brooks-Cole.

Caverly, Sandra see Ralov, Kirsten.

Caverni, Raffaello. Storia Del Metodo Sperimentale in Italia, 6 vols. xxii, 3478p. 1972. Repr. of 1891 ed. 300.00 (ISBN 0-384-07965-2). Johnson Repr.

Cavers, David F. The Choice-of-Law Process. LC 65-21050. (Michigan Legal Publications). xiv, 336p. 1983. Repr. of 1965 ed. lib. bdg. 32.50 (ISBN 0-89941-316-1). W S Hein.

--The Choice of Law: Selected Essays, 1933-1983. LC 84-24747. 448p. 1985. 45.00 (ISBN 0-8223-0626-3). Duke.

Cavers, Mars, jt. auth. see Stier, Wayne.

Cavert, C. Keep It Running. 1985. 74.25 (ISBN 0-07-079272-0). McGraw.

Cavert, C. Edward & Metcalf, Richard M. Accounting. 467p. 1982. text ed. 17.95x student guide (ISBN 0-931920-43-4). Dame Pubns.

Cavert, C. Edward, et al. Keep It Running: A Study Guide. (Illus.). 1978. pap. text ed. 16.95 (ISBN 0-07-009880-8). McGraw.

Cavert, Edward C., et al. Students Guide to Accounting, 2 vols. 512p. 1980. pap. text ed. 15.95 (ISBN 0-8403-2223-2). Kendall-Hunt.

Cavert, Samuel M. On the Road to Christian Unity: An Appraisal of the Ecumenical Movement. LC 78-12452. 1979. Repr. of 1961 ed. lib. bdg. 19.75x (ISBN 0-313-21184-1, CAOR). Greenwood.

Cavert, Walter D. With Jesus on the Scout Trail. (Orig.). 1970. pap. 3.75 (ISBN 0-687-45849-8). Abingdon.

Caves. CPC Study Program. 72p. pap. 9.50 (ISBN 0-317-36564-9); pap. 7.00 members (ISBN 0-317-36565-7). NAPC.

Caves, Richard. American Industry: Structure, Conduct, Performance. 5th ed. LC 82-495. (Illus.). 160p. 1982. 16.95 (ISBN 0-13-027656-1). P-H.

Caves, Richard, et al. Competition in the Open Economy: A Model Applied to Canada. LC 79-23908. (Harvard Economic Studies: No. 150). 1980. text ed. 30.00x (ISBN 0-674-15425-8). Harvard U Pr.

Caves, Richard E. Air Transport & Its Regulators: An Industry Study. LC 62-17216. (Economic Studies: No. 120). 1962. 25.00x (ISBN 0-674-01301-8). Harvard U Pr.

--Multinational Enterprise & Economic Growth. LC 82-4543. (Cambridge Surveys of Economic Literature Ser.). 352p. 1983. 37.50 (ISBN 0-521-24990-2); pap. 10.95 (ISBN 0-521-27115-0). Cambridge U Pr.

--Trade & Economic Structure: Models & Methods. LC 60-5389. (Economic Studies: No. 115). (Illus.). 1960. 20.00x (ISBN 0-674-89881-8). Harvard U Pr.

Caves, Richard E. & Jones, Ronald W. World Trade & Payments: An Introduction. 4th ed. LC 84-19396. 1984. text ed. 27.95 (ISBN 0-316-13227-6). Little.

Caves, Richard E. & Reuber, Grant L. Capital Transfers & Economic Policy: Canada, 1951-1962. LC 79-129123. (Economic Studies: No. 135). 1971. 25.00x (ISBN 0-674-09485-9). Harvard U Pr.

Caves, Richard E. & Uekusa, Masu. Industrial Organization in Japan. 1976. 22.95 (ISBN 0-8157-1324-X); pap. 8.95 (ISBN 0-8157-1323-1). Brookings.

Caves, Richard E. & Krause, Lawrence B., eds. The Australian Economy: A View from the North. LC 84-17074. 415p. 1984. 32.95 (ISBN 0-8157-1326-6); pap. 12.95 (ISBN 0-8157-1325-8). Brookings.

--Britain's Economic Performance. 1980. 29.95 (ISBN 0-8157-1320-7); pap. 11.95 (ISBN 0-8157-1319-3). Brookings.

Caves, Richard E. & Roberts, Marc J., eds. Regulating the Product: Quality & Variety. LC 74-18123. 256p. 1975. prof ref 27.50 (ISBN 0-88410-272-6). Ballinger Pub.

Caves, Richard E., frwd. by see Comanor, William S. & Wilson, Thomas A.

Caves, Richard E., et al. Britain's Economic Prospects. 1968. 24.95 (ISBN 0-8157-1322-3). Brookings.

Cavett, Dick & Porterfield, Christopher. Eye on Cavett. (Illus.). 256p. 1983. 15.95 (ISBN 0-87795-463-1). Arbor Hse.

Caviani, Mabel, et al. Simplified Quantity Ethnic Recipies. (Ahrens Ser.). 272p. 1980. 17.50 (ISBN 0-8104-9474-4). Hayden.

Caviedes, Cesar. The Southern Cone: Realities of the Authoritarian State in South America. LC 83-17842. 222p. 1984. text ed. 34.95x (ISBN 0-86598-109-4). Rowman & Allanheld.

Caviers, Luis M., jt. auth. see Bruch, Hans A.

Cavill, David. All about Showing Dogs. (All About Dogs Ser.). (Illus.). 144p. 1984. 14.95 (ISBN 0-7207-1480-X, Pub. by Michael Joseph). Merrimack Pub Cir.

--All about the Spitz Breeds. (Illus.). 168p. 1984. 14.95 (ISBN 0-7207-1113-4, Pub by Michael Joseph). Merrimack Pub Cir.

Cavill, I. Quality Control. LC 81-68801. (Methods in Hematology Ser.: Vol. 4). (Illus.). 191p. 1982. text ed. 28.00 (ISBN 0-443-02229-1). Churchill.

Cavin, Ruth. Famous Brands Cookbook. LC 81-20045. (Illus.). 384p. 1982. 14.95 (ISBN 0-8437-3393-4); pap. 9.95 (ISBN 0-8437-3394-2). Hammond Inc.

Cavin, Ruth, ed. see Wilson Learning Corporation.

Cavin, Susan. Lesbian Origins. rev. ed. Orig. Title: An Historical & Cross-Cultural Analysis of Sex Ratios, Female Sexuality, & Homosexual Segregation Versus Heterosexual Integration Patterns in Relation to the Liberation of Women. (Illus.). 227p. 1985. 28.00 (ISBN 0-910383-16-2); pap. 9.00 (ISBN 0-910383-15-4). ISM Pr.

Cavin, Thomas F. Champion of Youth: Daniel A. Lord, S. J. 1977. 6.50 (ISBN 0-8198-0398-7); pap. text ed. 5.00 (ISBN 0-8198-0399-5). Dghtrs St Paul.

Cavinato, Joseph L. Finance for Transportation & Logistics Managers. LC 77-80191. 1977. text ed. 22.50 (ISBN 0-87408-008-8). Traffic Serv.

--Purchasing & Materials Management: Integrative Strategies. (Illus.). 550p. 1984. text ed. 30.95 (ISBN 0-314-77869-1); instr's. manual avail. (ISBN 0-314-77870-5). West Pub.

Cavinato, Joseph L., ed. Transportation-Logistics Dictionary. 2nd ed. 323p. 1982. 14.00 (ISBN 0-87408-022-3). Traffic Serv.

Cavinato, Joseph L., Jr., ed. A Correspondence Course. Orig. Title: Transportation-Distribution Costs and Cost Analysis. 114p. 1982. pap. 225.00 (ISBN 0-318-16888-X); pap. 175.00 for members (ISBN 0-318-16889-8). Am Soc Transport.

Cavinder, Fred D. The Indiana Book of Records, Firsts, & Fascinating Facts. LC 84-43155. (Illus.). 400p. 1985. 27.50 (ISBN 0-253-14001-3); pap. 12.50 (ISBN 0-253-28320-5). Ind U Pr.

Caviness, Madeline H. The Early Stained Glass of Canterbury Cathedral: 1175-1220. (Illus.). 1978. text ed. 65.00x (ISBN 0-691-03927-5). Princeton U Pr.

--Great Britain, Vol. 1: The Windows of Christ Church, Canterbury. (Illus.). 1981. text ed. 395.00x (ISBN 0-19-725995-2). Oxford U Pr.

--The Windows of Christ Church Cathedral Canterbury. 372p. 1981. 500.00x (Pub. by Brit Acad England). State Mutual Bk.

Caviness, Madeline H. & Staudinger, Evelyn R. Stained Glass Before 1540: An Annotated Bibliography. 1983. lib. bdg. 49.00 (ISBN 0-8161-8332-5, Hall Reference). G K Hall.

Caviness, Madeline H., jt. ed. see Hayward, Jane.

Cavitch, David. My Soul & I: The Inner Life of Walt Whitman. LC 85-47525. (Illus.). 224p. 1985. 18.95 (ISBN 0-8070-7000-9). Beacon Pr.

Cavitch, David, ed. Life Studies: A Thematic Reader. LC 82-60460. 600p. 1983. pap. text ed. 11.95 (ISBN 0-312-48484-4); write for info. instr's. manual (ISBN 0-312-48485-2). St Martin.

Cavnar, Rebecca. Winning at Losing: A Complete Program for Losing Weight & Keeping it off. (Illus.). 182p. 1983. pap. 6.95 (ISBN 0-89283-157-X). Servant.

Cavoski, Kosta, jt. auth. see Kostunica, Vojislav.

Cavoto, Nino, tr. see Grillo, Salvatore.

Cavusgil, S. T. & Nevin, John R., eds. International Marketing: An Annotated Bibliography. LC 82-8753. 139p. (Orig.). 1983. pap. text ed. 8.00 (ISBN 0-87757-160-0). Am Mktg.

Caw, James L., jt. auth. see Crockett, W. S.

Cawasjee, Saos, ed. Stories from the Raj. 272p. pap. 4.95 (ISBN 0-586-05625-4, Pub. by Granada England). Academy Chi Pubs.

Cawdrey, Robert. A Table Alphabeticall of English Wordes. LC 73-25889. (English Experience Ser.: No. 226). 132p. 1970. Repr. of 1604 ed. 11.50 (ISBN 90-221-0226-2). Walter J Johnson.

--A Treasurie or Store-House of Similies. LC 75-171738. (English Experience Ser.: No. 365). 880p. 1971. Repr. of 1600 ed. 120.00 (ISBN 90-221-0365-X). Walter J Johnson.

Cawdry, Robert. Table Alphabet of Hard Usual English Words. LC 66-12119. 1977. Repr. 35.00x (ISBN 0-8201-1007-8). Schol Facsimiles.

Cawein, Madison, ed. Book of Love. facsimile ed. LC 79-116395. (Granger Index Reprint Ser). 1911. 17.00 (ISBN 0-8369-6136-6). Ayer Co Pubs.

Cawelti, Gordon, jt. auth. see Roberts, Arthur D.

Cawelti, John G. Adventure, Mystery & Romance: Formula Stories As Art & Popular Culture. LC 75-5077. 344p. 1976. 17.50x (ISBN 0-226-09866-4). U of Chicago Pr.

--Adventure, Mystery, & Romance: Formula Stories As Art & Popular Culture. LC 75-5077. (Phoenix Ser.). 1977. pap. 5.95 (ISBN 0-226-09867-2, P732). U of Chicago Pr.

--Apostles of the Self-Made Man. LC 65-25123. 1968. pap. 4.95x (ISBN 0-226-09865-6, P292, Phoen). U of Chicago Pr.

--Six-Gun Mystique. 148p. 1970. 7.95 (ISBN 0-87972-007-7); pap. 4.95 (ISBN 0-87972-008-5). Bowling Green Univ.

--The Six Gun Mystique. 2nd ed. LC 84-72052. 155p. 1984. 17.95 (ISBN 0-87972-313-0); pap. 8.95 (ISBN 0-87972-314-9). Bowling Green Univ.

Cawelti, John O. Apostles of the Self-Made Man. LC 65-25123. 1965. 15.00x (ISBN 0-226-09864-8). U of Chicago Pr.

Cawfield, Norman. Reconstructing Your Personality. 180p. (Orig.). 1985. pap. 3.50 (ISBN 0-88368-172-2). Whitaker Hse.

Cawker, Ruth, jt. auth. see Bernstein, William.

Cawl, Farrax M. Ignorance Is the Enemy of Love: A Novel. Andrzejewski, tr. from Somali. 128p. 1982. pap. 9.95x (ISBN 0-905762-86-X, Pub. by Zed Pr England). Biblio Dist.

Cawley. Hematology. (Intergrated Clinical Science Ser.). 1984. 19.95 (ISBN 0-8151-1459-1). Year Bk Med.

Cawley, ed. Everyman & Medieval Miracle Plays. pap. 4.50 (ISBN 0-525-47036-0, 0437-130). Dutton.

Cawley, A. C. & Stevens, Martin. The Towneley Cycle. Fasc. ed. LC 75-42854. 332p. 1976. pap. 12.00 (ISBN 0-87328-113-6). Huntington Lib.

Cawley, A. C., ed. Everyman. (Old & Middle English Texts). 47p. 1978. pap. 9.95x (ISBN 0-06-491012-1, 06391). B&N Imports.

--Everyman & Medieval Miracle Plays. 9.95x (ISBN 0-460-10381-4, Evman). Biblio Dist.

--The Wakefield Pageants in the Towneley Cycle. (Old & Middle English Texts). 187p. 1958. pap. 10.95x (ISBN 0-06-491013-X, 06392). B&N Imports.

Cawley, A. C. & Anderson, J. J., eds. Pearl Cleanness, Patience, & Sir Gawain & the Green Knight. 1970. 12.95x (ISBN 0-460-00346-1, Evman); pap. 2.95x (ISBN 0-460-11346-1, Evman). Biblio Dist.

Cawley, A. C. & Gaines, Barry, eds. A Yorkshire Tragedy. LC 85-7098. (Revels Plays Ser.). 1985. 30.00 (ISBN 0-7190-1535-9, Pub. by Manchester Univ Group). Longwood Pub Group.

Cawley, Clifford C. Sky Is Falling. LC 72-148962. 196p. 1971. 6.00 (ISBN 0-87787-005-5). Mara.

Cawley, Frederick D., jt. ed. see Waite, Diana S.

Cawley, J. C., et al, eds. Hairy Cell Leukaemia. (Recent Results in Cancer Research Ser.: Vol. 72). (Illus.). 180p. 1980. 37.00 (ISBN 0-387-09920-4). Springer-Verlag.

Cawley, James & Cawley, Margaret. Along the Delaware & Raritan Canal. LC 79-85760. (Illus.). 128p. 1970. 12.00 (ISBN 0-8386-7529-8). Fairleigh Dickinson.

--The First New York-Philadelphia Stage Road. LC 78-75175. (Illus.). 120p. 1980. 14.50 (ISBN 0-8386-2331-X). Fairleigh Dickenson.

Cawley, James, jt. auth. see Cawley, Margaret.

Cawley, John F., ed. Developmental Teaching of Mathematics for the Learning Disabled. LC 84-6247. 329p. 1984. 31.50 (ISBN 0-89443-581-7). Aspen Systems.

--Practical Mathematics Appraisal of the Learning Disabled. LC 84-20499. 350p. 1984. 31.50 (ISBN 0-89443-559-0). Aspen Systems.

--Secondary School Mathematics for the Learning Disabled. LC 84-16946. 327p. 1984. 31.50 (ISBN 0-89443-597-3). Aspen Systems.

Cawley, John F., et al, eds. Cognitive Functional Math. 264p. 1985. write for info. (ISBN 0-87189-120-4). Aspen Systems.

Cawley, M., jt. auth. see Bouyer, L.

Cawley, Margaret & Cawley, James. Exploring the Little Rivers of New Jersey. 3rd rev. ed. 1971. pap. 8.95 (ISBN 0-8135-0685-9). Rutgers U Pr.

Cawley, Margaret, jt. auth. see Cawley, James.

Cawley, Robert & Yost, George. Studies in Sir Thomas Browne. LC 65-29995. 1965. 5.00 (ISBN 0-87114-011-X). U of Oreg Bks.

Cawley, Robert R. Henry Peacham: His Contribution to English Poetry. LC 71-127387. 185p. 1971. 22.50x (ISBN 0-271-01130-0). Pa St U Pr.

--Milton & the Literature of Travel. LC 72-114095. (Princeton Studies in English: No. 32). 1970. Repr. of 1951 ed. text ed. 10.00x (ISBN 0-87752-015-1). Gordian.

--Milton's Literary Craftsmanship: A Study of a Brief History of Muscovia. LC 65-25136. (Princeton Studies in English: No. 24). 1965. Repr. of 1941 ed. 7.50x (ISBN 0-87752-016-X). Gordian.

--Unpathed Waters: Studies in the Influence of the Voyagers on Elizabethan Literature. 1967. Repr. lib. bdg. 20.50x (ISBN 0-374-91349-8). Octagon.

--Voyagers & Elizabethan Drama. (MLA.MS). 1938. 34.50 (ISBN 0-527-15400-8). Kraus Repr.

Cawood, Charles. Vintage Tractors. (Shire Album Ser.: No. 48). (Illus.). 32p. 1985. pap. 3.50 (ISBN 0-85263-499-4, Pub. by Shire Pubns England). Seven Hills Bks.

Cawood, Diana. Assertiveness for Managers. 208p. (Orig.). 1983. pap. 8.95 (ISBN 0-88908-562-5, 9516, Pub. by Intl Self-Counsel Pr). TAB Bks.

Caws, Mary A. The Eye in the Text: Essays on Perception, Mannerist to Modern. LC 80-8540. (Princeton Essays on the Arts Ser.: No. 11). (Illus.). 334p. 1981. 25.00 (ISBN 0-691-06453-9); pap. 9.95 (ISBN 0-691-01377-2). Princeton U Pr.

--A Metapoetics of the Passage: Architextures in Surrealism & After. LC 80-54468. 218p. 1981. 20.00x (ISBN 0-87451-194-1). U Pr of New Eng.

--Reading Frames in Modern Fiction. LC 84-16092. 275p. 1985. text ed. 27.50x (ISBN 0-691-06625-6). Princeton U Pr.

--Yves Bonnefoy. (World Authors Ser.: No. 702). 150p. 1984. lib. bdg. 18.95 (ISBN 0-8057-6549-2, Twayne). G K Hall.

Caws, Mary A., ed. About French Poetry from Dada to "Tel Quel". Text & Theory. LC 74-10962. 298p. 1974. text ed. 14.95x (ISBN 0-8143-1520-8). Wayne St U Pr.

--Writing in a Modern Temper: Essays on French Literature & Thought, in Honor of Henri Peyre. (Stanford French & Italian Studies: Vol. 33). 224p. 1984. pap. 25.00 (ISBN 0-915838-04-4). Anma Libri.

Caws, Mary A. & Riffaterre, Hermine, eds. The Prose Poem in France: Theory & Practice. 256p. 1983. 32.00x (ISBN 0-231-05434-3); pap. 13.50x (ISBN 0-231-05435-1). Columbia U Pr.

Caws, Mary A., ed. & intro. by see Mallarme, Stephane.

Caws, Mary A., ed. see Perse, Saint-John.

Caws, Mary A., tr. see Breton, Andre.

Caws, Mary Ann. The Inner Theatre of Recent French Poetry: Cendrars, Tzara, Peret, Artaud, Bonnefoy. LC 72-166364. (Princeton Essays in Literature). 132p. 1972. 23.50 (ISBN 0-691-06212-9). Princeton U Pr.

--The Presence of Rene Char. LC 75-30188. 1976. 37.50 (ISBN 0-691-06305-2). Princeton U Pr.

--The Surrealist Voice of Robert Desnos. LC 76-25145. (Illus.). 208p. 1977. 13.50x (ISBN 0-87023-223-1). U of Mass Pr.

Caws, Mary Ann & Terry, Patricia, eds. Roof Slates & Other Poems of Pierre Reverdy. LC 80-26806. (Illus.). 273p. 1981. 18.95x (ISBN 0-930350-09-X). NE U Pr.

Caws, Mary Ann & Griffin, Jonathan, trs. Poems of Rene Char. LC 75-30189. (Locket Library of Poetry in Translation). 1976. 32.00 (ISBN 0-691-06297-8). Princeton U Pr.

Caws, Mary Ann & Terry, Patricia, trs. from Fr. Roof Slates & Other Poems of Pierre Reverdy. LC 80-26806. 273p. 1983. pap. 10.95 (ISBN 0-930350-52-9). NE U Pr.

Caws, Mary Ann, tr. from Fr. & see Tzara, Tristan.

Caws, Mary Ann, tr. see Tzara, Tristan.

Caws, Peter. Sartre. (Arguments of the Philosophers Ser.). (Illus.). 1979. 26.95x (ISBN 0-7100-0314-5). Routledge & Kegan.

--Sartre. (Arguments of the Philosophers Ser.). 224p. 1984. pap. 10.50x (ISBN 0-7102-0233-4). Routledge & Kegan.

Caws, Peter & Ripley, S. Dillon. The Bankruptcy of Academic Policy. Ritterbush, Philip C., ed. LC 72-75040. (Prometheus: First Ser.). (Illus.). 1972. pap. 3.50 (ISBN 0-87491-500-7). Acropolis.

Caws, Peter, ed. Two Centuries of Philosophy: American Philosophy Since the Revolution -- Papers from the Bicentennial Symposium. (American Philosophical Quarterly Library of Philosophy). 381p. 1980. 30.00x (ISBN 0-8476-6249-7). Rowman.

Caws, Peter, tr. see Bochenski, J. M.

Cawson, Alan. Corporatism & Welfare: Social Policy & State Intervention in Britain. (Studies in Social Policy & Welfare: No. XVII). 145p. 1983. text ed. 27.50x (ISBN 0-435-82136-9). Gower Pub Co.

Cawson, Broderick A., jt. auth. see McCracken, Alexander W.

Cawson, R. A. Essentials of Dental Surgery & Pathology. 4th ed. (Dental Ser.). (Illus.). 1984. pap. text ed. 33.00 (ISBN 0-443-02653-X). Churchill.

Cawson, R. A. & Spector, R. G. Clinical Pharmacology in Dentistry. 4th ed. 1985. pap. 15.00 (ISBN 0-443-03279-3). Churchill.

Cawson, R. A., jt. auth. see Scully, C.

Cawson, Roderick A. & McCracken, Alexander W. Pathologic Mechanisms & Human Disease. LC 81-16832. (Illus.). 594p. 1982. pap. text ed. 26.95 (ISBN 0-8016-0939-9). Mosby.

Cawston, George & Keane, A. H. Early Chartered Companies: A.D. 1296-1858. LC 68-57901. (Research & Source Works Ser.: No. 140). (Illus.). 1968. Repr. of 1896 ed. 22.50 (ISBN 0-8337-0506-7). B Franklin.

Cawston, Vee. Matuk, the Eskimo Boy. (Illus.). (gr. 1-2). 1965. PLB 6.19 (ISBN 0-8313-0014-0). Lantern.

Cawte, E. C. Ritual Animal Disguise. (Folklore Society Mistletoe Ser.). (Illus.). 293p. 1978. 17.50x (ISBN 0-8476-6005-2). Rowman.

Cawte, John. Cruel, Poor & Brutal Nations: The Assessment of Mental Health in an Australian Aboriginal Community by Short-Stay Psychiatric Field Team Methods. LC 72-188979. (Illus.). 198p. 1972. 15.00x (ISBN 0-8248-0207-1). UH Pr.

--Medicine Is the Law: Studies in Psychiatric Anthropology of Australian Tribal Societies. LC 73-77011. 284p. 1974. text ed. 17.00x (ISBN 0-8248-0251-9). UH Pr.

Cawthorne, Barbara. Instant Success for Classroom Teachers: New & Substitute Teachers. LC 81-82947. (Illus.). 112p. (Orig.). 1981. pap. 7.95 (ISBN 0-9606666-0-5). Greenfield Pubns.

Cawthra, Bruce I. Industrial Property Rights in the European Economic Community. 1973 ed. 250p. 27.00 (ISBN 0-686-37377-4). Beekman Pubs.

Caxton Society. Publications of the Caxton Society, 16 Vols. 1966. Repr. of 1854 ed. Set. 320.00 (ISBN 0-8337-0507-5). B Franklin.

Caxton, W., tr. Here Begynneth a Lityll Treatise Spekynge of the Arte & Crafte to Knowe Well to Dye. LC 72-169. (English Experience Ser.: No. 221). 28p. Repr. of 1490 ed. 14.00 (ISBN 90-221-0221-1). Walter J Johnson.

Caxton, W., tr. see Jerome, Saint.

Caxton, William. Begin Two A. LC 72-5980. (English Experience Ser.: No. 508). 1973. Repr. of 1480 ed. 61.00 (ISBN 90-221-0508-3). Walter J Johnson.

--Caxton's Blanchardon & Eglantine. 1890. 65.00 (ISBN 0-8274-2014-5). R West.

--Dialogues in French & English. Bradley, H., ed. (EETS, ES Ser.: No. 79). pap. 12.00 (ISBN 0-527-00281-X). Kraus Repr.

--The Epic of the Beast: Consisting of English Translations of the History of Reynard the Fox & Physiologus. Broadway, tr. 30.00 (ISBN 0-8274-2281-4). R West.

--The Prologue & Epilogues of William Caxton. Crotch, W. J., ed. (EETS, OS Ser.: No. 176). Repr. of 1927 ed. 22.00 (ISBN 0-527-00173-2). Kraus Repr.

--Prologues & Epilogues of William Caxton. Crotch, Walter J., ed. LC 70-170185. (Research & Source Works Ser.: No. 829). 1971. Repr. of 1928 ed. lib. bdg. 22.50 (ISBN 0-8337-0738-8). B Franklin.

Caxton, William, ed. Quatre Fils Aimon, 2 pts. (EETS, ES Ser.: Nos. 44-45). Repr. of 1885 ed. Pt. 1. 26.00 (ISBN 0-527-00253-4); Pt. 2. 35.00 (ISBN 0-527-00254-2). Kraus Repr.

Caxton, William, tr. The Book of the Order of Chivalry. LC 76-57359. (English Experience Ser.: No. 778). 1977. Repr. of 1484 ed. lib. bdg. 11.50 (ISBN 90-221-0778-7). Walter J Johnson.

Caxton, William, tr. from Dutch. The History of Reynard the Fox. Blake, N. F., ed. (Early English Text Society Ser.). (Illus.). 1970. text ed. 21.95x (ISBN 0-19-722267-6). Oxford U Pr.

Caxton, William, tr. see Deguilleville, Guillaume de.

Caxton, William, tr. see Du Castel, Christine.

Caxton, William, tr. see Furvinall, F. J. & Meyer, P.

Caxton, William, tr. see Heraclius.

Caxton, William, tr. see Jacobus De Varagine.

Caxton, William, tr. see Lefevre, Raoul.

Caxton, William, tr. see Lull, Ramon.

Caxton, William, tr. see Vincentius, Bellovacensis.

Cayce, Edgar. Auras: An Essay on the Meaning of Colors. 1973. pap. 1.95 (ISBN 0-87604-012-1). ARE Pr.

--Revelation: A Commentary on the Book, Based on the Study of Twenty Four Psychic Discourses of Edgar Cayce. (Twenty-Six Interpretive Readings). 1969. pap. 8.95 (ISBN 0-87604-003-2). ARE Pr.

--Secrets of Beauty Through Health. 1981. pap. 5.95x (ISBN 0-317-06944-6, Regent House). B of A.

Cayce, Edgar & Cayce, Hugh L. God's Other Door & the Continuity of Life. 1976. pap. 2.95 (ISBN 0-87604-007-5). ARE Pr.

Cayce, Edgar E. Edgar Cayce on Atlantis. Cayce, Hugh L., ed. 176p. 1968. pap. 3.50 (ISBN 0-446-32694-1). Warner Bks.

Cayce, H. L. Gifts of Healing. 1976. pap. 1.95 (ISBN 0-87604-070-9). ARE Pr.

Cayce, Hugh L. Earth Changes Update. LC 80-116599. 134p. (Orig.). 1980. pap. 5.95 (ISBN 0-87604-121-7). ARE Pr.

--The Jesus I Knew. 81p. (Orig.). 1984. pap. 4.95 (ISBN 0-87604-156-X). ARE Pr.

--Venture Inward: Edgar Cayce's Story & the Mysteries of the Unconscious Mind. LC 85-42772. 256p. Date not set. pap. 6.95 (ISBN 0-06-250131-3, HarpR). Har-Row.

Cayce, Hugh L., jt. auth. see Cayce, Edgar.

Cayce, Hugh L., ed. The Edgar Cayce Reader. 192p. 1969. pap. 3.50 (ISBN 0-446-32561-9). Warner Bks.

Cayce, Hugh L., ed. see Bro, Harmon H.

Cayce, Hugh L., ed. see Cayce, Edgar E.

Cayce, Hugh L., ed. see Read, Anne, et al.

Cayce, Hugh L., et al. Dreams, Language of the Unconscious. rev. ed. 1971. pap. 4.95 (ISBN 0-87604-047-4). ARE Pr.

Caycedo, Bernardo J. The Life & Times of Juan Jose d'Elhuyar: Discoverer of Tungsten in 18th Century New Granada. Schufle, J. A., tr. from Span. (Illus.). 290p. 1981. 15.00x (ISBN 0-87291-149-7). Coronado Pr.

Caye, Derry. Single Entry Bookkeeping System for Small Scale Manufacturing Businesses. 55p. 1977. prfct. bnd. 5.50 (ISBN 0-86619-046-5, 11029-BK). Vols Tech Asst.

Cayen, Ron, jt. auth. see Dalton, David.

Cayer, N. Joseph. Managing Human Resources: An Introduction to Public Personnel Administration. 237p. 1980. text ed. 20.95x (ISBN 0-312-51244-9). St Martin.

--Public Personnel Administration in the United States. LC 74-23046. 200p. (Orig.). 1975. pap. text ed. 10.95 (ISBN 0-312-65520-7). St Martin.

Cayer, N. Joseph & Dickerson, SHerry S. Labor Management Relations in the Public Sector: An Annotated Bibliography. LC 82-49152. (Public Affairs & Administration Ser.: Vol. 7). 650p. 1983. lib. bdg. 35.00 (ISBN 0-8240-9153-1). Garland Pub.

Cayeux, Andre De see De Cayeux, Andre.

Cayeux, L. Carbonate Rocks, Limestone & Dolmites, Sedimentary Rocks of France. Carozzi, A. V., tr. (Illus.). 1969. Repr. 53.95x (ISBN 0-02-842660-6). Hafner.

Cayford, John E. All about Maine. 68p. 1982. 7.50 (ISBN 0-941216-00-4). Cay Bel.

--All about Maine: Historical Facts About People, Places & Events. LC 81-69087. 64p. 7.50 (ISBN 0-941216-00-4); pap. 4.95 (ISBN 0-941216-01-2). Cay-Bel.

--Fort Knox-Fortress in Maine. LC 83-71723. (Illus.). 104p. (Orig.). 1983. 17.50 (ISBN 0-941216-10-1); pap. 12.50 (ISBN 0-941216-14-4). Cay Bel.

--Maine Firsts. LC 79-56551. (Orig.). (gr. 4-8). 1980. PLB 1.50 (ISBN 0-918768-03-9). Historical Times.

--Maine Firsts. 3rd, rev. & enl. ed. LC 79-56551. 68p. (Orig.). pap. text ed. 2.00 (ISBN 0-941216-11-X); tchrs. ed. 2.00 (ISBN 0-941216-12-8). Cay-Bel.

--Maine's Hall of Fame, Vol. 1. 300p. 1983. write for info. Cay Bel.

--The Penobscot Expedition. LC 76-21153. (Illus., Orig.). 1976. 7.95 (ISBN 0-918768-00-4); pap. 5.95 (ISBN 0-918768-01-2). Cay-Bel.

--Underwater Work: A Manual of Scuba Commercial Salvage & Construction Operations. 2nd ed. LC 66-28081. (Illus.). 271p. 1966. 13.50x (ISBN 0-87033-129-9). Cornell Maritime.

Cayford, John E. & Scott, Ronald E. Underwater Logging. LC 64-18585. (Illus.). 92p. 1964. pap. 3.00 (ISBN 0-87033-128-0). Cornell Maritime.

Caygill, Marjorie. Treasures of the British Museum. (Illus.). 240p. 1985. 29.95 (ISBN 0-8109-1687-8). Abrams.

Caygill, Wayne M., jt. ed. see Kimura, Samuel J.

Cayless, M. A. & Marsden, A. M. Lamps & Lighting. 3rd ed. 640p. 1984. text ed. 49.50 (ISBN 0-7131-3487-9). E Arnold.

Cayley, Arthur. Collected Mathematical Papers, Vols. 1-13. 1889-1897. with index 700.00 (ISBN 0-384-07970-9); 55.00 ea.; Vol. suppl. 30.00 (ISBN 0-685-13389-3). Johnson Repr.

Cayley, E. S. On Commercial Economy. (Development of Industrial Society Ser.). 280p. 1971. Repr. of 1830 ed. 25.00x (ISBN 0-7165-1577-6, Pub. by Irish Academic Pr). Biblio Dist.

Caylor, H. W. & Pickle, Joe. H. W. Caylor: Frontier Artist. LC 80-6112. (Illus.). 130p. 1981. 29.50 (ISBN 0-89096-108-5). Tex A&M Univ Pr.

Caynor, Avis. Bridgeport: The Town & Its People. 1976. 4.00 (ISBN 0-87012-255-X). McClain.

Cayot, Billie J., et al. How to Select a Business Computer. LC 81-85927. (Successful Business Library). 150p. 1982. 29.95 (ISBN 0-916378-17-9, Oasis). PSI Res.

Cayre, Henri. Agriculture Plenty: A Monograph. 176p. 1980. 40.00x (ISBN 0-85614-070-8, Pub. by Gentry England). State Mutual Bk.

Cayton, Horace R. & Mitchell, George S. Black Workers & the New Unions. LC 71-129941. 473p. 1939. Repr. cancelled (ISBN 0-8371-3355-6, RET&, Pub. by Negro U Pr). Greenwood.

--Black Workers & the New Unions. 15.00 (ISBN 0-405-18493-X). Ayer Co Pubs.

Caywood, Nancy L., jt. ed. see Houck, Rudolph A., III.

Cazacu, A. Theorie der Funktionen Mehrerer Komplexer Veranderlicher. (Mathematische Reihe Ser.: No. 51). 360p. (Ger.). 1975. 74.95x (ISBN 0-8176-0770-6). Birkhauser.

Cazacu, C. A., et al, eds. Romanian-Finnish Seminar on Complex Analysis. (Lecture Notes in Mathematics: Vol. 743). 713p. 1979. pap. 40.00 (ISBN 0-387-09550-0). Springer-Verlag.

--Complex Analysis-Fifth Romanian--Finnish Seminar, Pt. I. (Lecture Notes in Mathematics: Vol. 1013). 393p. 1983. pap. 21.00 (ISBN 0-387-12682-1). Springer-Verlag.

--Complex Analysis-Fifth Romanian--Finnish Seminar, Pt. II. (Lecture Notes in Mathematics: Vol. 1014). 338p. 1983. 19.00 (ISBN 0-387-12683-X). Springer-Verlag.

Cazalas, Mary W. Nursing & the Law. 3rd ed. LC 78-24253. 294p. 1979. text ed. 24.50 (ISBN 0-89443-075-0). Aspen Systems.

Cazalet-Keir, Thelma, ed. Homage to P. G. Wodehouse. (Illus.). 146p. 1973. text ed. 9.50x (ISBN 0-214-66880-0). Humanities.

Cazamian, Louis. Development of English Humor, 2 pts. in 1. LC 75-181925. Repr. of 1952 ed. 18.50 (ISBN 0-404-01441-0). AMS Pr.

Cazamian, Louis see Legouis, Emile H.

Cazamian, Louis F. Carlyle. Brown, E. K., tr. ix, 289p. 1966. Repr. of 1932 ed. 22.00 (ISBN 0-208-00012-7, Archon). Shoe String.

--Criticism in the Making. LC 77-1286. 1977. lib. bdg. 25.00 (ISBN 0-8414-3588-X). Folcroft.

--Le Roman Social En Angleterre, 1830-1850: Dickens, Disraeli, Mrs. Gaskell, Kingsley, 2 Vols. in One. rev. ed. LC 66-27050. (Fr). 1967. Repr. of 1934 ed. 13.50x (ISBN 0-8462-0986-1). Russell.

Cazamian, Madeleine L. Le Roman et les Idees en Angleterre L'Influence de la Science. 1923. 50.00 (ISBN 0-8274-3298-4). R West.

Cazamian, Pierre, jt. auth. see Carpentier, James.

Cazden, Courtney B., ed. Language in Early Childhood Education. rev. ed. LC 81-82158. (Illus.). 170p. 1981. pap. text ed. 6.00 (ISBN 0-912674-74-1, NAEYC 131). Natl Assn Child Ed.

--Language in Early Childhood Education. rev. ed. LC 81-82158. 161p. 1981. 6.00 (ISBN 0-912674-74-1, NAEYC 131). Natl Assn Child Ed.

Cazden, Courtney B & John, Vera P., eds. Functions of Language in the Classroom. 394p. 1985. pap. 11.95x (ISBN 0-88133-151-1). Waveland Pr.

Cazden, Elizabeth. Antoinette Brown Blackwell: A Biography. LC 82-4986. (Illus.). 315p. 1983. 16.95 (ISBN 0-935312-00-5); pap. 9.95 (ISBN 0-935312-04-8). Feminist Pr.

Cazden, Norman & Haufrecht, Herbert. Notes & Sources for Folk Songs of the Catskills. LC 81-14610. 1982. 49.50x (ISBN 0-87395-582-X). State U NY Pr.

Cazden, Norman & Studer, Norman. Folk Songs of the Catskills. 650p. 20.00 (ISBN 0-318-17314-X). Hudson Clearwater.

Cazden, Norman, et al. Folk Songs of the Catskills. LC 81-14610. 600p. 1982. 69.50x (ISBN 0-87395-580-3); pap. 19.95 (ISBN 0-87395-581-1). State U NY Pr.

Cazden, Robert. German Exile Literature in America, 1933-1960: A History of the Free German Press & Book Trade. LC 76-98639. pap. 65.50 (ISBN 0-317-26822-8, 2024200). Bks Demand UMI.

Cazden, Robert E. A History of the German Book Trade in America to the Civil War, 2 pts. LC 81-70545. (Studies in German Literature, Linguistics, & Culture: Vol. 1). (Illus.). 801p. 1984. 75.00 (ISBN 0-938100-09-2). Camden Hse.

Cazeau, C. J. & Scott, S. D. Exploring the Unknown: Great Mysteries Re-Examined. LC 78-27413. (Illus.). 295p. 1979. (full discount avail.) 18.95 (ISBN 0-306-40210-6, Plenum Pr). Plenum Pub.

Cazeau, Charles J. & Scott, Stuart D., Jr. Exploring the Unknown: Great Mysteries Re-Examined. (Quality Paperbacks Ser.). (Illus.). 1981. pap. 8.95 (ISBN 0-306-80139-6). Da Capo.

Cazeau, Charles J. & Siemankowski, Francis T. Physical Geology Laboratory Manual. 3rd ed. 1982. wire coil bdg. 12.95 (ISBN 0-8403-2791-9, 40279101). Kendall-Hunt.
Cazeaux, Isabelle, tr. see De Commynes, Philippe.
Cazelles, Brigitte. La Faiblesse Chez Gautier De Coinci. (Stanford French & Italian Studies: No. 14). viii, 180p. (Fr.). 1978. pap. 25.00 (ISBN 0-915838-27-3). Anma Libri.
Cazelles, Brigitte, jt. auth. see Johnson, Phyllis.
Cazelles, H., et al. Supplement au Dictionnaire de la Bible, 7 vols. 128p. (Fr.). 1967. Set. 595.50 (ISBN 0-686-56943-1, M-6065). French & Eur.
Cazemajou, Jean. Stephen Crane. (Pamphlets on American Writers Ser: No. 76). (Orig.). 1969. pap. 1.25x (ISBN 0-8166-0526-2, MPAW76). U of Minn Pr.
Cazenave, ed. Science & Consciousness: Two Views of the Universe. Hall, A. & Callender, E., trs. (Illus.). 550p. 1984. 70.00 (ISBN 0-08-028127-3, 0720, 2601, 3505, 3506). Pergamon.
Cazenave, Pierre-Andre, jt. auth. see Bona, Constantin.
Cazenove, Theophile. Cazenove Journal, 1794: A Journey Through New Jersey & Pennsylvania. Kelsey, Rayner W., ed. (Haverford Coll. Studies: No. 13). 1922. 17.50x (ISBN 0-686-17388-0). R S Barnes.
Cazes. Liquid Chromatography of Polymers & Related Materials, Part III. (Chromatographic Science Ser., Vol. 19). 232p. 1981. 40.00 (ISBN 0-8247-1514-4). Dekker.
Cazes & De La Marre. Liquid Chromatography of Polymers & Related Materials Part II. (Chromatographic Science Ser.: Vol. 13). 232p. 1980. 44.50 (ISBN 0-8247-6985-6). Dekker.
Cazes, J. Liquid Chromatography of Polymers & Related Materials, Pt. I. (Chromatgraphic Science Ser.: Vol. 8). 1977. 45.00 (ISBN 0-8247-6592-3). Dekker.
Cazet, Denys. Big Shoe, Little Shoe. LC 83-21362. (Illus.). 32p. (ps-2). 1984. PLB 12.95 (ISBN 0-02-717820-X). Bradbury Pr.
--Christmas Moon. LC 84-10969. (Illus.). 32p. (ps-2). 1984. PLB 12.95 (ISBN 0-02-717810-2). Bradbury Pr.
--The Duck with Squeaky Feet. LC 80-18018. (Illus.). 32p. (gr. k-2). 1980. 8.95 (ISBN 0-02-717850-1). Bradbury Pr.
--Lucky Me. LC 81-7711. (Illus.). 32p. (ps-2). 1983. PLB 10.95 (ISBN 0-02-717870-6). Bradbury Pr.
--Mudbaths for Everyone. LC 80-39830. (Illus.). 32p. (ps-2). 1981. PLB 9.95 (ISBN 0-02-717860-9). Bradbury Pr.
--The Non-Coloring Book: A Drawing Book for Mind Stretching & Fantasy Building. 64p. 1973. pap. 3.95 (ISBN 0-88316-501-5). Chandler & Sharp.
--Saturday. LC 84-24306. (Illus.). 64p. (ps-2). 1985. PLB 10.95 (ISBN 0-02-717800-5). Bradbury Pr.
--You Make the Angels Cry. LC 82-9581. (Illus.). 32p. (ps-k). PLB 12.95 (ISBN 0-02-717830-7). Bradbury Pr.
Cazimero, Momi, ed. see Belknap, Jodi P.
Cazire, jt. auth. see Shelley, Victor.
Cazort, Jean E. & Hobson, Constance T. Born to Play: The Life & Career of Hazel Harrison. LC 82-12169. (Contributions to the Study of Music & Dance Ser.: No. 3). (Illus.). 200p. 1983. lib. bdg. 27.95 (ISBN 0-313-23643-7, CBO/). Greenwood.
Cazort, Mary & Johnson, Catherine. Bolognese Drawings in North American Collections 1500-1800. (National Gallery of Canada Ser.). (Illus.). 304p. 1982. 35.00 (ISBN 0-88884-476-X, 56295-6). U of Chicago Pr.
Cazort, Mimi, intro. by see Jackson, H. A.
Cazzaroli, Gianni. Dictionnaire de la Navication. 392p. (Fr.). 1973. 23.50 (ISBN 0-686-56803-6, M-4650). French & Eur.
--Enciclopedia Del Mar y De la Navegacion Deportiva. 396p. (Espn.). 1975. 37.50 (ISBN 84-279-4516-7, S-50490). French & Eur.
Cazziol, Roger J. Gloire D'Afrique. (Illus.). 1971. text ed. 2.50 (ISBN 0-521-08181-5). Cambridge U Pr.
--Kone. (Illus.). 1971. text ed. 2.50 (ISBN 0-521-07955-1). Cambridge U Pr.
--Paul et Remi. (Illus.). 40p. (Fr.). 1974. pap. text ed. 2.50 (ISBN 0-521-20433-X). Cambridge U Pr.
--Safari En Cote d'Ivoire. (Illus.). 40p. 1974. pap. 2.50 (ISBN 0-521-20434-8). Cambridge U Pr.
--Vacances au Senegal. (Illus.). 1971. text ed. 2.50x (ISBN 0-521-08180-7). Cambridge U Pr.
Cazzola, Gus. To Touch the Deer. LC 81-10452. 130p. (gr. 5-9). 1981. 9.95 (ISBN 0-664-32684-6). Westminster.
CB Test Labs Staff. How to Select & Install CB Antennas. (Illus.). (gr. 10 up). 1976. pap. 5.35 (ISBN 0-8104-0861-9). Hayden.
CBE Committee on Economics of Publication. Economics of Scientific Journals. LC 82-19926. (Illus.). 106p. 1982. pap. text ed. 11.95 (ISBN 0-914340-03-4). Coun Biology Eds.
CBE Committee on Graduate Training in Scientific Writing. Scientific Writing for Graduate Students. LC 68-56104. (Illus.). 190p. 1968. pap. text ed. 9.75 (ISBN 0-914340-01-8). Coun Biology Eds.
CBE Style Manual Committee. CBE Style Manual. rev., 5th ed. LC 83-7172. (Council of Biology Editors Style Manual Ser.). (Illus.). 324p. 1983. text ed. 24.00 (ISBN 0-914340-04-2). Coun Biology Eds.
CBEMA (Computer & Business Equipment Manufacturers Assn) Minimum COBOL. LC 77-12007. (Computer & Data Processing Professionals Ser). (Illus.). 1977. pap. text ed. 12.50 (ISBN 0-89433-054-3). Petrocelli.
CBEMA Inc. Computer & Business Equipment Market Book. 1985. 49.95 (ISBN 0-8104-6349-0). Hayden.
CBI Publishing Co., Inc. The Professional Host. 1981. 19.95 (ISBN 0-8436-2154-0). Van Nos Reinhold.
CBL Staff, ed. see Wenzel, William, Jr.
CBS Inc. Sixty Minutes Verbatim. LC 80-23836. (Illus.). 1981. lib. bdg. 20.00x (ISBN 0-405-13723-0). Ayer Co Pubs.
CBS, Inc. & Fury, Kathleen. Dear Sixty Minutes. 256p. (Orig.). 1985. pap. 4.95 (ISBN 0-671-50753-2, Fireside). S&S.
CBS News & New York Times. CBS News-New York Times Election Day Surveys, 1982. 2nd ed. LC 84-81926. 1984. write for info. codebook (ISBN 0-89138-895-8). ICPSR.
--CBS News-New York Times National Surveys, 1983. 2nd ed. LC 84-81221. 1984. write for info. codebook (ISBN 0-89138-897-4). ICPSR.
--CBS News-The New York Times Election Surveys 1980, 2 vols. LC 82-81160. 1982. Set. write for info. codebook (ISBN 0-89138-931-8, ICPSR 7812); Vol. I. write for info. codebook (ISBN 0-89138-933-4); Vol. II. write for info. codebook (ISBN 0-89138-932-6). ICPSR.
--CBS News- New York Times National Surveys, 1981. 1983. write for info. codebook (ISBN 0-89138-919-9). ICPSR.
CCI Source Listing. Nova Fig-FORTH. 15.00 (ISBN 0-318-01358-4). Mountain View Pr.
C. C. Li. First Course in Population Genetics. (Illus.). 1976. pap. 14.95x (ISBN 0-910286-42-6). Boxwood.
Cea, J., jt. auth. see Haug, E. J.
Cea, J., ed. Optimization Techniques Modeling & Optimization in the Service of Man: Pt. 2. LC 76-9857. (Lecture Notes in Computer Science: Vol. 41). 1976. pap. 29.00 (ISBN 0-387-07623-9). Springer-Verlag.
--Optimization Techniques: Modeling & Optimization in the Service of Man, Pt. 1. LC 76-9857. (Lecture Notes in Computer Science Ser.: Vol. 40.). 1976. pap. 39.00 (ISBN 0-387-07622-0). Springer-Verlag.
Ceadel, Eric B. Japanese-English Dictionary, 2 vols. (Japanese & Eng.). romanized 39.50 (ISBN 0-87557-048-8, 048-8). Saphrograph.
Ceadel, Martin. Pacifism in Britain Nineteen Fourteen to Nineteen Forty-Five: The Defining of a Faith. 1980. 39.95x (ISBN 0-19-821882-6). Oxford U Pr.
Cearley, Buster, jt. auth. see Cope, Eddie.
Ceasar, James W., jt. auth. see David, Paul T.
Ceaser, J. W., et al. American Government: Origins, Institutions & Public Policy. 144p. 1984. text ed. 28.95 study guide (ISBN 0-07-010275-9); 10.95 (ISBN 0-07-010276-7). McGraw.
Ceaser, James W. Presidential Selection: Theory & Development. LC 78-70282. 1979. 33.00 (ISBN 0-691-07602-2); pap. 9.95 (ISBN 0-691-02188-0). Princeton U Pr.
--Reforming the Reforms: A Critical Analysis of the Presidential Selection Process. LC 81-21638. 216p. 1982. 24.95 (ISBN 0-88410-884-8). Ballinger Pub.
Ceasor, Ebraska, et al. Blacks in Ohio: Seven Portraits. McCluskey, John, ed. (Orig.). (gr. 7-12). 1976. pap. 4.25x (ISBN 0-913678-13-9). New Day Pr.
Ceasor, Frank G., Sr. see McCluskey, John.
Ceaucescu, Nicolae. Builder of Modern Romania. LC 83-2266. (Leaders of the World Ser.). 1983. 17.50 (ISBN 0-08-028181-8). Pergamon.
Ceausescu, E. Sterospecific Polymerization of Isoprene. (Illus.). 300p. 1983. 60.00 (ISBN 0-08-029987-3). Pergamon.
Ceausescu, E., ed. Nouvelles Recherches dans le Domaine des Composes Macromoleculaires. (Illus.). 460p. 1984. 72.00 (ISBN 0-08-030725-6). Pergamon.
Ceausescu, Ilie. War, Revolution, & Society in Romania: The Road to Independence. (East European Monographs: No. 135). 298p. 1983. 30.00x (ISBN 0-88033-023-6). East Eur Quarterly.
Ceausescu, Ilie, et al. A Turning Point in World War II: August 23, 1944 in Romania. 224p. 1985. 22.50x (ISBN 0-88033-084-8, Dist. by Columbia U Pr). East Eur Quarterly.
Ceausescu, V., et al, eds. Critical Phenomena: 1983 Brasov School Conference. (Progress in Physics Ser.: Vol. 11). 436p. 1985. text ed. write for info. (ISBN 0-8176-3289-1). Birkhauser.
Cebeci, T. & Bradshaw, P. Physical & Computational Aspects of Convective Heat Transfer. (Illus.). 345p. 1984. 57.00 (ISBN 0-387-12097-1). Springer-Verlag.
Cebeci, T., ed. Numerical & Physical Aspects of Aerodynamic Flows, Pt. II. (Illus.). 500p. 1964. 64.00 (ISBN 0-387-12659-7). Springer-Verlag.
--Numerical & Physical Aspects of Aerodynamic Flows, California State University 1981: Proceedings. (Illus.). 636p. 1983. 84.00 (ISBN 0-387-11044-5). Springer-Verlag.
Cebeci, Tuncer & Smith, A. M. Analysis of Turbulent Boundary Layers. 1974. 80.50 (ISBN 0-12-164650-5). Acad Pr.
Cebes. Cebe's Tablet. new ed. Sider, Sandra, ed. & intro. by. (Renaissance Text Ser.: No. 6). (Illus.). iv, 230p. 1979. 9.95 (ISBN 0-9602696-2-2). Renaissance Soc Am.
--Tablet of Cebes. Orgel, Stephen, ed. LC 78-68186. (Philosophy of Images Ser.). 1980. lib. bdg. 80.00 (ISBN 0-8240-3693-X). Garland Pub.
Cebik, L. B. Concepts, Events, & History. LC 78-64825. 1978. pap. text ed. 12.00 (ISBN 0-8191-0639-9). U Pr of Amer.
--Fictional Narrative & Truth: An Epistemic Analysis. 260p. (Orig.). 1984. lib. bdg. 23.75 (ISBN 0-8191-3894-0); pap. text ed. 13.25 (ISBN 0-8191-3895-9). U Pr of Amer.
--Setting Up & Using Your Own Ham Shack. LC 81-9136. (Illus.). 308p. 1981. pap. 10.95 (ISBN 0-8306-1223-8, 1223). TAB Bks.
Cebollero, Pedro A. A School Language Policy for Puerto Rico. LC 74-14224. (The Puerto Rican Experience Ser). (Illus.). 148p. 1975. Repr. 10.00x (ISBN 0-405-06214-1). Ayer Co Pubs.
Cebula, James E. James Cox: Journalist & Politician. Burke, Robert E. & Freidel, Frank, eds. (Modern American History Ser.). 30.00 (ISBN 0-8240-5666-3). Garland PUb.
Cebula, Joseph P., jt. auth. see Bertrand, Arthur.
Cebula, Richard J. Geographic Living-Cost Differentials. LC 82-48096. 208p. 1983. 29.50x (ISBN 0-669-05968-4). Lexington Bks.
Cebulak, W. et al. see Mocarski, S. & Pietrocini, T.
Cebulash. The Spring Street Boys Go All Out. LC 82-73652. (Spring Street Boys Ser.). 64p. 1982. 7.95 (ISBN 0-89813-048-4). Childrens Bk Co.
--The Spring Street Boys Go All Out. (The Spring Street Boys Ser.). (Illus.). 64p. (gr. 4-8). 1985. 7.95 (ISBN 0-317-31257-X). Creative Ed.
--The Spring Street Boys Hit the Road. LC 82-73649. (Spring Street Boys Ser.). 64p. 1982. 7.95 (ISBN 0-89813-047-6). Childrens Bk Co.
--The Spring Street Boys Hit the Road. (The Spring Street Boys Ser.). (Illus.). 64p. (gr. 4-8). 1985. 7.95 (ISBN 0-317-31253-7). Creative Ed.
--The Spring Street Boys Settle a Score. LC 82-73651. (Spring Street Boys Ser.). 64p. 1982. 7.95 (ISBN 0-89813-049-2). Childrens Bk Co.
--The Spring Street Boys Settle a Score. (The Spring Street Boys Ser.). (Illus.). 64p. (gr. 4-8). 1985. 7.95 (ISBN 0-317-31258-8). Creative Ed.
--The Spring Street Boys Team Up. LC 82-73630. (Spring Street Boys Ser.). 64p. 1982. 7.95 (ISBN 0-89813-046-8). Childrens Bk Co.
--The Spring Street Boys Team Up. (The Spring Street Boys Ser.). (Illus.). 64p. (gr. 4-8). 1985. 7.95 (ISBN 0-317-31259-6). Creative Ed.
Cebulash, Mel. The Ball That Wouldn't Bounce. (Illus.). (gr. k-3). 1972. pap. 1.50 (ISBN 0-590-09297-9); pap. 3.95 bk. & record (ISBN 0-590-31073-9). Scholastic Inc.
--Baseball Players Do Amazing Things. (Step-up Bks: No. 21). (Illus.). (gr. 2-5). 1973. 3.95 (ISBN 0-394-82611-6, BYR); PLB 4.99 (ISBN 0-394-92611-0). Random.
--Basketball Players Do Amazing Things. LC 76-8127. (Step-up Bks.: No. 23). (Illus.). (gr. 2-3). 1976. 4.95 (ISBN 0-394-83184-5, BYR); PLB 4.99 (ISBN 0-394-93184-X). Random.
--Benny's Nose. (Illus.). (gr. k-3). 1972. pap. 1.50 (ISBN 0-590-09298-7); pap. 3.95 bk. & record (ISBN 0-590-04352-8). Scholastic Inc.
--The Champion's Jacket. (Challenge Bks). (Illus.). (gr. 4-8). 1979. PLB 7.95 (ISBN 0-87191-687-8). Creative Ed.
--Football Players Do Amazing Things. LC 73-3686. (Step-up Bk: No. 22). (Illus.). 72p. (gr. 2-5). 1975. 4.95 (ISBN 0-394-82677-9, BYR); PLB 5.99 (ISBN 0-394-92677-3). Random.
--Herbie Rides Again. (Illus.). (gr. 7-9). 1974. pap. 1.95 (ISBN 0-590-08821-1). Scholastic Inc.
--I'm an Expert: Motivating Independent Study Projects for Grades 4-6. 1982. pap. 7.95 (ISBN 0-673-16570-1). Scott F.
--Ruth Marini: Dodger Ace. LC 82-20383. (Ruth Marini on the Mound Ser.). 144p. (gr. 4up). 1983. PLB 8.95 (ISBN 0-8225-0726-9). Lerner Pubns.
--Ruth Marini of the Dodgers. LC 82-20403. (Ruth Marini on the Mound Ser.). 144p. (gr. 4up). 1983. PLB 8.95 (ISBN 0-8225-0725-0). Lerner Pubns.
--Ruth Marini: World Series Star. (Ruth Marini on the Mound Ser.). 144p. (gr. 5 up). 1985. 8.95 (ISBN 0-8225-0727-7). Lerner Pubns.
Cebulska, Marcia. Sayings & Stories. (Literacy Volunteers of America Readers Ser.). 32p. (Orig.). 1983. pap. 2.46 (ISBN 0-8428-9622-8). Cambridge Bk.
--Time for a Change. (Literacy Volunteers of America Readers Ser.). 32p. (Orig.). 1983. pap. 2.46 (ISBN 0-8428-9606-6). Cambridge Bk.
Cebulski, Frank. Corm. 1974. 5.00 (ISBN 0-685-48373-8); pap. 2.50 (ISBN 0-685-48374-6). Oyez.
Ceccaldi, Mathieu. Dictionnaire Corse-Francais, Pierre d'Evisa. 464p. (Corsican & Fr.). 1974. pap. 29.95 (ISBN 0-686-56944-X, M-6066). French & Eur.
Ceccarelli, B., ed. see International Symposium on Cell Biology & Cytopharmacology, First.
Ceccarelli, B., et al, eds. see NATO Advanced Study Institution, et al.
Ceccato, Silvio, ed. Linguistic Analysis & Programming for Mechanical Translation. (Illus.). 246p. 1961. 46.25 (ISBN 0-677-00110-X). Gordon.
Ceccerini, P. V., jt. auth. see Barlotti, A.
Cecchetti, Giovanni, tr. see Verga, Giovanni.
Cecchetti, Giovanni del, tr. see Leopardi, Giacomo.
Cecchettini, Philip A. CLEP Resource Manual: Introduction to Sociology. 1979. pap. 13.95 (ISBN 0-07-010306-2). McGraw.
--CLEP Resource Manual: Introduction to Business Management. (Illus.). 1979. pap. 13.95 (ISBN 0-07-010308-9). McGraw.
--CLEP Resourse Manual: Introduction to Humanities. 1979. text ed. 13.95 (ISBN 0-07-010307-0). McGraw.
--CLEP Resourse Manual: Introduction to General Psychology. 1979. pap. 13.95 (ISBN 0-07-010305-4). McGraw.
--CLEP Resourse Manual: Introduction to Natural Science. 1979. pap. text ed. 13.95 (ISBN 0-07-010309-7). McGraw.
Cecchi, Anna. La Struttura Del Sistema Bancario Toscano Dal 1815 Al 1859, 2 vols. Bruchey, Stuart, ed. LC 80-2804. (Dissertations in European Economic History II). (Illus.). 1981. lib. bdg. 35.50x (ISBN 0-405-13988-8). Ayer Co Pubs.
Cecchi, Dario. Titian. Wydenbruck, Nora, tr. from Italian. LC 72-13188. (Biography Index Reprint Ser). Repr. of 1958 ed. 19.50 (ISBN 0-8369-8143-X). Ayer Co Pubs.
Cecchi, Giovan Maria. The Horned Owl: L'assiuolo. Eisenbichler, Konrad, tr. from Ital. 80p. 1981. pap. text ed. 6.25x (ISBN 0-88920-116-1, Pub. by Wilfrid Laurier U Pr). Humanities.
Cecchini, Tina. Enciclopedia de las Hierbas y de las Plantas Medicinales. 3rd ed. 536p. (Espn.). 1978. pap. 23.75 (ISBN 84-315-0372-6, S-13663). French & Eur.
--Enciclopedia Practica de Floricultura y Jardineria. 2nd ed. 588p. (Espn.). 1978. pap. 28.50 (ISBN 84-315-0972-4, S-14572). French & Eur.
Ceccio, Cathy M., jt. auth. see Ceccio, Joseph F.
Ceccio, Joseph F. & Ceccio, Cathy M. Effective Communication in Nursing: Theory & Practice. LC 81-15999. 315p. 1982. pap. 16.95 (ISBN 0-471-07911-1, Pub. by Wiley Med). Wiley.
Cecco, John P. de see De Cecco, John P.
Cecco, Marcello de see De Cecco, Marcello.
Cecconi, J. P. & Zolezzi, T., eds. Mathematical Theories of Optimization: Proceedings, S. Margherita Ligure, Genova, Italy, 1981. (Lecture Notes in Mathematics: Vol. 979). 268p. 1983. pap. 17.00 (ISBN 0-387-11999-X). Springer-Verlag.
Cecela, Agnes. Word Processing Skills & Applications Using the Wang Systems. 2nd ed. 1985. pap. text ed. 21.95 (ISBN 0-8359-8824-4); instr's manual avail. (ISBN 0-8359-8825-2). Reston.
Cecelski, Elizabeth, et al. Household Energy & the Poor in the Third World: Domestic Energy Consumption for Low-Income Groups in Development Areas. LC 79-4863. (Resources for the Future Ser.). 1979. 6.75x (ISBN 0-8018-2283-1). Johns Hopkins.
--Household Energy & the Poor in the Third World. 160p. 1979. Research Paper R-15. 6.75 (ISBN 0-8018-2283-1). Resources Future.
Cech, E. Point Sets. 1969. 65.00 (ISBN 0-12-164850-8). Acad Pr.
Cech, John, ed. American Writers for Children, Nineteen Hundred to Nineteen Sixty. LC 83-14199. (Dictionary of Literary Biography Ser.: Vol. 22). (Illus.). 412p. 1983. 85.00x (ISBN 0-8103-1146-1). Gale.
Cech, Joseph J., jt. auth. see Moyle, Peter B.
Cech, O., jt. ed. see Weber, B. G.
Ceci, Stephen J., ed. Handbook of Cognitive, Social, & Neuropsychological Aspects of Learning Disabilities, 2 vols. in 1, Vols I & II. 500p. text ed. 59.95 (ISBN 0-89859-682-3). L Erlbaum Assocs.
Cecil see Jenkins, S. H.
Cecil, jt. auth. see Matacia.
Cecil, Algernon. British Foreign Secretaries, Eighteen Seven to Nineteen Sixteen. LC 70-118463. 1971. Repr. of 1927 ed. 28.50x (ISBN 0-8046-1212-9, Pub. by Kennikat). Assoc Faculty Pr.
--The Way of Peace: Essays & Addresses. LC 68-15818. 1968. Repr. of 1938 ed. 19.00x (ISBN 0-8046-0073-2, Pub. by Kennikat). Assoc Faculty Pr.
Cecil, Andrew R. The Foundations of a Free Society. (The Andrew R. Cecil Lectures on Moral Values in a Free Society Ser. Supplement). 190p. 1984. text ed. 14.95x (ISBN 0-292-72447-0). U of Tex Pr.
--The Third Way: Enlightened Capitalism & the Search for a New Social Order. (The Andrew R. Cecil Lectures on Moral Values in a Free Society Ser.: Vol. I). 175p. 1980. 9.95x (ISBN 0-292-78041-9, Pub. by U of Tex. at Dallas). U of Tex Pr.
Cecil, Andrew R., et al. Conflict & Harmony. (Andrew R. Cecil Lectures on Moral Values in a Free Society: Vol. III). 228p. 1982. text ed. 14.50x (ISBN 0-292-71081-X, Pub. by U of Tex. at Dallas). U of Tex Pr.
Cecil, Anthony C., Jr. The Theological Development of Edwards Amasa Park: Last of the "Consistent Calvinists". LC 74-83338. (American Academy of Religion. Dissertation Ser.). 1974. pap. 9.95 (ISBN 0-88420-118-X, 010101). Scholars Pr GA.

Cecil, C. Grandiosity. 1985. pap. 0.85 (ISBN 0-89486-296-0). Hazelden.
Cecil, D., ed. see De La Mare, Walter.
Cecil, David. Jane Austen. 1978. Repr. of 1935 ed. lib. bdg. 15.00 (ISBN 0-8495-0817-7). Arden Lib.
--Jane Austen. 1935. lib. bdg. 10.00 (ISBN 0-8414-3622-3). Folcroft.
--Max: A Biography of Max Beerbohm. LC 84-45637. (Illus.). 528p. 1985. pap. 13.95 (ISBN 0-689-70683-9, 323). Atheneum.
--Melbourne. (Power & Personality Ser.). (Illus.). 1979. pap. 2.98 (ISBN 0-517-53782-6, Harmony). Crown.
--Melbourne. LC 76-138583. 1971. Repr. of 1954 ed. lib. bdg. 22.50x (ISBN 0-8371-5782-X, CEME). Greenwood.
--Poetry of Thomas Gray: A Lecture. Repr. of 1945 ed. lib. bdg. 5.00 (ISBN 0-8414-3620-7). Folcroft.
--Poets & Story-Tellers. 201p. 1980. Repr. of 1968 ed. lib. bdg. 30.00 (ISBN 0-8495-0852-5). Arden Lib.
--Poets & Story-Tellers. 1979. Repr. of 1949 ed. lib. bdg. 15.00 (ISBN 0-8482-7580-2). Norwood Edns.
--A Portrait of Charles Lamb. LC 84-51157. (Illus.). 192p. 1984. 19.95 (ISBN 0-684-18226-2, ScribT). Scribner.
--A Portrait of Jane Austen. (Illus.). 208p. 1979. 25.00 (ISBN 0-8090-7811-2); pap. 9.95 (ISBN 0-8090-1392-4). Hill & Wang.
--Reading As One of the Fine Arts. 1949. lib. bdg. 9.50 (ISBN 0-8414-3517-0). Folcroft.
--The Stricken Deer or the Life of Cowper. 1929. 20.00 (ISBN 0-8274-3528-2). R West.
--Two Quiet Lives, Dorothy Osborne & Thomas Gray. 182p. 1981. Repr. of 1949 ed. lib. bdg. 30.00 (ISBN 0-8495-0854-1). Arden Lib.
--Visionary & Dreamer: Two Poetic Painters, Samuel Palmer & Edward Burne-Jones. LC 68-57088. (Bollingen Ser.: No. 35). (Illus.). 177p. 1970. 47.50x (ISBN 0-691-09853-0); pap. 14.50 (ISBN 0-691-01858-8). Princeton U Pr.
--Walter De la Mare. 1978. 18.50 (ISBN 0-685-87742-6). Porter.
--Walter De La Mare, a Checklist. 1956. lib. bdg. 10.00 (ISBN 0-8414-3636-3). Folcroft.
--Walter Pater: Scholar Artist. 1955. lib. bdg. 10.00 (ISBN 0-8414-3632-0). Folcroft.
Cecil, David, ed. Modern Biography. 229p. 1980. Repr. of 1938 ed. lib. bdg. 15.00 (ISBN 0-8492-3971-0). R West.
Cecil, David, ed. see Tennyson, Alfred L.
Cecil, David L. William Cowper. 1932. 10.00 (ISBN 0-8414-0313-9). Folcroft.
Cecil, David R. Debugging BASIC Programs. 176p. (Orig.). cancelled (ISBN 0-8306-0813-3); pap. 9.95 (ISBN 0-8306-1813-9, 1813). TAB Bks.
Cecil, Edward. A Journall & Relation of the Action Which E. Lord Cecil Did Vndertake Vpon the Coast of Spaine. LC 68-54643. (English Experience Ser.: No. 27). 1968. Repr. of 1625 ed. 7.00 (ISBN 90-221-0027-8). Walter J Johnson.
--Leisure of an Egyptian Official. (Century Travel Classics Ser.). 285p. 1985. pap. 9.95 (ISBN 0-7126-0444-8, Pub. by Century Pubs UK). Hippocrene Bks.
Cecil, Mrs. Evelyn. London Parks & Gardens. 1981. Repr. of 1907 ed. lib. bdg. 75.00 (ISBN 0-8495-0759-6). Arden Lib.
Cecil, Gwendolen. Life of Robert, Marquis of Salisbury: By His Daughter, 4 Vols. in 2. Repr. of 1932 ed. Set. 65.00 (ISBN 0-527-15550-0). Kraus Repr.
Cecil, Joe S., jt. auth. see Boruch, Robert F.
Cecil, Joe S., jt. ed. see Boruch, Robert F.
Cecil, Kay W. Financial Management Problems of Local Governments in Texas: Proceedings. 148p. (Orig.). 1980. pap. text ed. 6.00 (ISBN 0-936440-00-7). Inst Urban Studies.
Cecil, Kay W., jt. auth. see Wilkes, Stanley E., Jr.
Cecil, Lamar. The German Diplomatic Service, Eighteen Seventy-One to Nineteen Fourteen. 1976. text ed. 39.00 (ISBN 0-691-05235-2). Princeton U Pr.
Cecil, M. Ruby the Donkey: A Winter Story. 119p. 1980. 3.95 (ISBN 0-07-010321-6). McGraw.
Cecil, Martin. Being Where You Are. 1974. 2.95. Cole-Outreach.
--Meditations on the Lord's Prayer. 2nd ed. 1982. 10.95 (ISBN 0-686-27652-3). Cole-Outreach.
--On Eagle's Wings. 1977. 7.00 (ISBN 0-7051-0257-2); pap. 2.95 (ISBN 0-7051-0258-0). Cole-Outreach.
Cecil, Michael, et al. Spirit of Sunrise. 1979. 7.00 (ISBN 0-7051-0270-X); pap. 2.95 (ISBN 0-7051-0271-8). Cole-Outreach.
Cecil, Mirabel. Blue Bear's Race. LC 81-1105. (Illus.). 18p. (gr. 1-3). 1982. 6.95 (ISBN 0-316-13251-9). Little.
--Cora the Crow, a Spring Story. LC 79-22538. (A New Ser. of Nature Bks.). (Illus.). (gr. k-3). 1980. 3.95 (ISBN 0-07-010320-8). McGraw.
--Spiky the Hedgehog. LC 79-26358. (Illus.). 32p. (gr. k-3). 1980. 3.95 (ISBN 0-07-010322-4). McGraw.
Cecil, P. B. Word Processing in the Modern Office. 2nd ed. 1980. pap. 21.95 (ISBN 0-8053-1758-9); instrs manual 4.95 (ISBN 0-8053-1760-0); student wkbk 7.95 (ISBN 0-8053-1761-9). Benjamin-Cummings.
Cecil, Paula B. Management of Word Processing Operations. 1980. 32.95 (ISBN 0-8053-1759-7); instr's guide 4.95 (ISBN 0-8053-1762-7). Benjamin-Cummings.
--Office Automation: Concepts & Application. 3rd ed. 1984. 23.95 (ISBN 0-8053-1763-5); instr's guide 7.95 (ISBN 0-8053-1764-3); study guide 6.95 (ISBN 0-8053-1765-1). Benjamin-Cummings.
Cecil, Richard. Life of John Newton. (Summit Bks). 1978. pap. 3.95 (ISBN 0-8010-2418-8). Baker Bk.
Cecil, Robert. Letters from Sir Robert Cecil to Sir George Carew. 1864. 19.00 (ISBN 0-384-53140-7). Johnson Repr.
Cecil, Robert & Rieu, Richard, eds. The King's Son: Readings in the Contemporary Psychologies & Contemporary Thoughts on Man. 181p. 1981. 14.95 (ISBN 0-900860-88-X, Pub. by Octagon Pr England). Ins Study Human.
Cecil, T. E. & Ryan, P. J. Tight & Taut Immersions of Manifolds. (Research Notes in Mathematics Ser.: No. 107). 300p. 1985. pap. text ed. 22.95 (ISBN 0-273-08631-6). Pitman Pub MA.
Cecil, V. Minton "Majolica". (Illus.). 80p. 1982. pap. text ed. 15.75x (ISBN 0-86294-029-X, Pub. by Trefoil Bks Ltd UK). Humanities.
Cecil, Viscount. A Letter to an M.P. on Disarmament. 1932. 10.00 (ISBN 0-932062-33-4). Sharon Hill.
Cecil, William. A Declaration of the Favourable Dealing of Her Maiesties Commissioners Appointed for the Examination of Certaine Traitours. LC 73-25637. (English Experience Ser.: No. 113). 1969. Repr. of 1583 ed. 7.00 (ISBN 90-221-0113-4). Walter J Johnson.
--Execution of Justice in England. Incl. A True Sincere & Modest Defense of English Catholics. Allen, William. Kingdon, Robert M., ed. (Document Ser). 16.00 (ISBN 0-918016-41-X). Folger Bks.
Cecil, William W. The List. (Illus.). 7.95 (ISBN 0-9602766-0-2). Whitten Pub Co.
Cecille, L. & Simon, R., eds. Acid Digestion Process for Radioactive Waste. LC 83-10792. (Radioactive Waste Management Ser.: No. XII). (Illus.). 122p. 1984. 35.00 (ISBN 3-7186-0174-5). Harwood Academic.
Cecotti, Loralie. Pacific Northwest Writers Conference Story. (Illus.). 60p. (Orig.). 1983. pap. 6.95 (ISBN 0-933992-27-0). Coffee Break.
--Seattle Center. (Color-a-Story Ser.). (Illus.). 24p. (Orig.). (gr. 1-4). 1983. pap. 2.75 (ISBN 0-933992-30-0). Coffee Break.
--Washington Wildlife. (Color-a-Story Ser.). (Illus.). 24p. (Orig.). (gr. k-5). 1984. pap. text ed. 2.75 (ISBN 0-318-04105-7). Coffee Break.
Cedar Bog Symposium, Urbana College, Nov. 3, 1973. Proceedings. King, Charles C. & Frederick, Clara M., eds. 1974. 3.00 (ISBN 0-686-86536-7). Ohio Bio Survey.
Cedar, Paul. Becoming a Lover. 1978. 1.25 (ISBN 0-8423-0120-8). Tyndale.
Cedar, Paul, tr. see Ruhle, Otto.
Cedar, Paul A. The Communicator's Commentary-James First; Second, Peter, Jude, Vol. 2. Ogilvie, Lloyd J., ed. (The Communicator's Commentaries Ser.). 1983. 15.95 (ISBN 0-8499-0164-2). Word Bks.
Cedar Rapids Community College. Improving Spelling Performance: Student Edition Block II. 136p. 1981. pap. text ed. 2.55 (ISBN 0-8403-2417-0). Kendall-Hunt.
--Improving Spelling Performance: Student Edition Block III. 136p. 1981. pap. text ed. 2.55 (ISBN 0-8403-2418-9). Kendall-Hunt.
--Improving Spelling Performance: Student Edition Block IV. 136p. 1981. pap. text ed. 2.55 (ISBN 0-8403-2419-7). Kendall-Hunt.
--Improving Spelling Performance: Student Edition Block V. 136p. 1981. pap. text ed. 2.55 (ISBN 0-8403-2420-0). Kendall-Hunt.
Cedar Rapids Community District School. Improving Spelling Performance: Administrator's Guide Block One. 88p. 1981. shrink wrapped 5.00 (ISBN 0-8403-2410-3). Kendall-Hunt.
Cedar Rapids Community School District. Improving Spelling Performance: Administrator's Guide Block Four. 136p. 1981. 5.50 (ISBN 0-8403-2413-8). Kendall-Hunt.
--Improving Spelling Performance: Administrator's Guide Block Five. 136p. 1981. 5.50 (ISBN 0-8403-2414-6). Kendall-Hunt.
--Improving Spelling Performance: Administrator's Guide Block Three. 136p. 1981. shrink wrapped 5.50 (ISBN 0-8403-2412-X). Kendall-Hunt.
--Improving Spelling Performance: Adminisrator's Guide Secondary. 168p. 1981. shrink wrapped 6.00 (ISBN 0-8403-2415-4). Kendall-Hunt.
--Improving Spelling Performance: Student Edition Block I. 80p. 1981. pap. text ed. 2.40 (ISBN 0-8403-2416-2). Kendall-Hunt.
--Improving Spelling Performance: Student Edition Block Secondary. 136p. 1981. pap. 2.55 (ISBN 0-8403-2421-9). Kendall-Hunt.
Cedarbaum, Sophia. A First Book of Jewish Holidays. (Illus.). 80p. (gr. 1-3). 1984. pap. text ed. 6.00 (ISBN 0-8074-0274-5, 301500). UAHC.
Cedeno & Lazar. The Exercise Plus Pregnancy Program: Exercises for Before, During & after Pregnancy. LC 80-14278. (Illus.). 192p. 1980. pap. 5.95 (ISBN 0-688-08697-7, Quill). Morrow.
Cederbaums, Juris. Wiretapping & Electronic Eavesdropping, the Law & Its Implications: A Comparative Study. (New York University Criminal Law Education & Research Center Monograph: No. 2). 77p. (Orig.). 1969. pap. text ed. 8.50x (ISBN 0-8377-0402-2). Rothman.
Cederberg, Herbert. An Economic Analysis of English Settlement in North America (1583-1635) Bruchey, Stuart, ed. LC 76-39825. (Continuing Ser. for American Dissertations). (Illus.). 1977. Repr. lib. bdg. 32.00x (ISBN 0-405-09905-3). Ayer Co Pubs.
Cederberg, William E. On the Solution of the Differential Equations of Motion of a Double Pendulum. LC 24-3604. (Augustana College Library Publications: No. 9). 62p. 1923. pap. 0.75 (ISBN 0-910182-06-X). Augustana Coll.
Cederblom, J. B. & Blizek, William L., eds. Justice & Punishment. LC 77-3378. 1977. prof ref 22.00 (ISBN 0-88410-752-3). Ballinger Pub.
Cederblom, Jerry & Paulsen, David. Critical Reasoning. 2nd ed. 272p. 1985. pap. text ed. write for info. (ISBN 0-534-05616-4). Wadsworth Pub.
Cedergren, Harry R. Drainage of Highway & Airfield Pavements. LC 74-13400. (Illus.). 285p. 1974. 47.95 (ISBN 0-471-14181-X, Pub. by Wiley-Interscience). Wiley.
--Seepage, Drainage & Flow Nets. 2nd ed. LC 77-3664. 534p. 1977. 60.95 (ISBN 0-471-14179-8, Pub. by Wiley-Interscience). Wiley.
Cederholm, Theresa. Afro-American Artists: A Bio-Bibliographical Directory. 1973. 10.00 (ISBN 0-89073-007-5). Boston Public Lib.
Cedering, Siv. Letters from the Floating World: New & Selected Poems. LC 84-5222. (Pitt Poetry Ser.). 196p. 1984. 14.95x (ISBN 0-8229-3499-X); pap. 6.95 (ISBN 0-8229-5363-3). U of Pittsburgh Pr.
Cedering, Siv, tr. see Aspenstrom, Werner.
Cedering-Fox, Siv. The Blue Horse & Other Night Poems. LC 78-12793. (Illus.). 32p. (ps-3). 1979. 8.95 (ISBN 0-395-28952-1, Clarion). HM.
Cederroth, En. The Spell of the Ancestors & the Power of Mekkah: A Sasak Community on Lombok. (Gothenburg Studies in Social Anthropology: No. 3). 315p. 1981. pap. text ed. 25.75x (ISBN 91-7346-094-X, Pub. by Acta-Universitatis Sweden). Humanities.
Cedoline, Anthony J. The Effect of Affect. 1977. pap. 3.00x (ISBN 0-87879-166-3). Acad Therapy.
--Job Burnout in Public Education: Symptoms, Causes, & Survival Skills. 1982. text ed. 19.95x (ISBN 0-8077-2694-X). Tchrs Coll.
Cedrins, Inara, ed. Contemporary Latvian Poetry. Ivask, Ivar, et al, trs. from Latvian. LC 84-8800. (Iowa Translation Ser.). 224p. (Orig.). 1984. pap. 15.00 (ISBN 0-87745-128-1). U of Iowa Pr.
Cedrins, Inara, tr. see Bels, Albert.
Cedrins, Inara, tr. see Ivask, Astrid.
Cee Cee, pseud. Inside My Head. (gr. 5-6). 1985. 6.50 (ISBN 0-8062-2521-1). Carlton.
Ceely, Jonatha, et al. Writing a Research Paper. new ed. 1978. pap. text ed. 3.25x (ISBN 0-88334-108-5). Ind Sch Pr.
Ceely, Robert. Electronic Music Resource Book. LC 81-82292. (Illus.). 370p. 1981. pap. 21.50 (ISBN 0-9606426-1-7). NEV Multimedia Pubs.
Ceen, Allan. The Quartiere de Banchi: Urban Planning in Rome in the First Half of the Cinquecento. Freedberg, S. J., ed. (Outstanding Dissertations in Fine Arts Ser.). (Illus.). 295p. 1985. Repr. of 1977 ed. 50.00 (ISBN 0-8240-6884-X). Garland Pub.
Cefalo, Robert, jt. ed. see Bishop, Edward.
Cefola, Paul J., jt. ed. see Friedlander, Alan L.
Cegelka, Patricia T. & Prehm, Herbert J. Mental Retardation: From Categories to People. 448p. 1982. 25.50 (ISBN 0-675-09831-9). Additional Supplements May Be Obtained From Publisher. Merrill.
Cegelka, Patricia T., jt. auth. see Berdine, William H.
Cegielka, Francis A. Toward a New Spring of Humankind. 1985. 8.95 (ISBN 0-8158-0427-X). Chris Mass.
Ceglowski, W. S. & Friedman, Herman, eds. Virus Tumorigenesis & Immunogenesis. 1973. 55.00 (ISBN 0-12-165050-2). Acad Pr.
Cehovic, G. & Robison, G. A. Cyclic Nucleotides & Therapeutic Perspectives. 52.00 (ISBN 0-08-023760-6). Pergamon.
Cei, Jose M. A New Species of Liolaemus (Sauria: Iguanidae) from the Andean Mountains of the Southern Mendoza Volcanic Region of Argentina. (Occasional Papers: Vol. 76). 6p. 1978. 1.25 (ISBN 0-317-04841-4). U of KS Mus Nat Hist.
--A New Species of Tropidurus (Sauria, Iguanidae) from the Arid Chacoan & Western Regions of Argentina. (Occasional Papers: No. 97). 10p. 1982. 1.75 (ISBN 0-317-04843-0). U of KS Mus Nat Hist.
Ceitin, G. S., et al. Five Papers on Logic & Foundations. LC 51-5559. (Translations Ser.: No. 2, Vol. 98). 292p. 1971. text ed. 35.00 (ISBN 0-8218-1798-1, TRANS 2-98). Am Math.
--Five Papers on Logic & Foundations. new ed. LC 51-5559. (Translations Ser.: No. 2, Vol. 99). 280p. 1972. 33.00 (ISBN 0-8218-1799-X, TRANS 2-99). Am Math.
--Fourteen Papers on Logic, Geometry, Topology, & Algebra. LC 72-2350. (Translations Ser.: No. 2, Vol. 100). 1972. 48.00 (ISBN 0-8218-3050-3, TRANS 2-100). Am Math.
Ceja, Manuel V. Methods of Orientation of Spanish-Speaking Children to an American School. LC 73-76005. pap. 10.95 (ISBN 0-88247-207-0). R & E Pubs.
Cekalska, K., tr. see Bienkowska, B.
Cekanovskii, E. R., et al. Five Papers on Functional Analysis. LC 51-5559. (Translations Ser.: No. 2, Vol. 62). 1967. 36.00 (ISBN 0-8218-1762-0, TRANS 2-62). Am Math.
Cela, Camilo J. Family of Pascual Duarte. 144p. 1972. pap. 2.95 (ISBN 0-380-01175-1, 60749-2, Bard). Avon.
--The Hive. LC 81-11540. (Neglected Books of the 20th Century Ser.). 257p. 1983. pap. 6.95 (ISBN 0-686-82496-2). Ecco Pr.
--Journey to the Alcarria. Lopez-Morillas, Frances M., tr. (Illus.). 160p. 1964. 21.50x (ISBN 0-299-03250-7). U of Wis Pr.
--Mazurca para Dos Muertos. (Span.). 1983. pap. 8.50 (ISBN 84-322-0484-6, 3014). Ediciones Norte.
Celac, Mariana, jt. auth. see Botez, Mihai C.
Celada, Franco, et al, eds. Protein Conformation As an Immunological Signal. 510p. 1983. 69.50x (ISBN 0-306-41463-5, Plenum Pr). Plenum Pub.
Celan, Paul. Paul Celan: Poems. Hamburger, Michael, tr. from Ger. LC 79-9117. (Poetry in Translation Ser.). 286p. (Orig.). 1981. pap. 7.95 (ISBN 0-89255-060-0). Persea Bks.
Celano, Thomas. St. Francis of Assisi. 1963. pap. 10.50 (ISBN 0-8199-0098-2). Franciscan Herald.
Celant, Germano. Rauschenberg. (Illus.). 264p. Date not set. 65.00 (ISBN 0-933920-57-1). Hudson Hills.
Celant, Germano, jt. auth. see D'Harnoncourt, Anne.
Celant, Germano, ed. The European Iceberg. LC 85-43051. (Illus.). 372p. 1985. pap. 25.00 (ISBN 0-8478-0657-X). Rizzoli Intl.
Celarie, Henriette. Behind Moroccan Walls. Morris, Constance L., tr. LC 74-106259. (Short Story Index Reprint Ser.). 1931. 19.00 (ISBN 0-8369-3296-X). Ayer Co Pubs.
Cela Trulock, Camilo J. Diccionario Secreto, 3 vols. 2nd ed. 1184p. (Span.). 1975. Set. pap. 20.95 (ISBN 84-206-1997-3, S-29231). French & Eur.
Celaya, G., jt. ed. see Turnbull, P.
Celce-Murcia, Marianne & Larsen-Freeman, Diane. The Grammar Book: An ESL-EFL Teacher's Course. 655p. 1983. 29.95 (ISBN 0-88377-290-6). Newbury Hse.
Celce-Murcia, Marianne, ed. Teaching English As a Second or Foreign Language. 1979. pap. text ed. 15.95 (ISBN 0-88377-125-X). Newbury Hse.
Celebrity Kitchens Staff. The Art of Budget Cooking: The Minute Rice Cookbook. 1976. pap. 1.50 (ISBN 0-380-00692-8, 29207). Avon.
Celebrity Publishing Inc. Business to Business National Toll-Free Directory: Business Listings By Category, 1984 Edition, Vol. 3. 600p. (Orig.). 1983. pap. 30.00 (ISBN 0-943406-09-9). Celebrity Pub.
--The Business to Business National Toll-Free Directory: 1984, Vol. 2. (Business Communications, Services, Supplies Ser.). 600p. (Orig.). 1983. pap. 30.00 (ISBN 0-943406-08-0). Celebrity Pub.
--The National Directory of Toll-Free Phone Numbers. (Illus.). 544p. (Orig.). 1982. pap. 8.95 (ISBN 0-943406-00-5, 711-702). Celebrity Pub.
--The Shop at Home Toll-Free Directory. 272p. pap. 6.95 (ISBN 0-943406-03-X). Celebrity Pub.
--The Shop at Home Toll-Free Phone Directory. (Illus.). 220p. (Orig.). 1982. pap. 6.95 (ISBN 0-943406-02-1, 711-701). Celebrity Pub.
--Toll-Free Travel-Vacation Phone Directory. (Illus.). 378p. (Orig.). 1982. pap. 6.95 (ISBN 0-943406-01-3, 711-700). Celebrity Pub.
Celebrity Publishing Inc., ed. The Business to Business National Toll-Free Directory: Transportation & Travel, 1984, Vol. 1. 600p. (Orig.). 1983. pap. 30.00 (ISBN 0-943406-07-2). Celebrity Pub.
--The Business to Business Toll-Free Directories: 1984 Edition, 3 vols. 1800p. (Orig.). 1983. pap. 90.00 set (ISBN 0-943406-10-2). Celebrity Pub.
Celebrity Research Group. The Bedside Book of Celebrity Gossip: One Thousand Five Hundred Outrageous Barbs from One Celebrity Gossip to Another. 1983. pap. 1.98 (ISBN 0-517-55172-1). Crown.
Celebuski, Carin, jt. auth. see Cherlin, Andrew.
Celehar. Kitchens & Kitchenware: 1900 to 1950. LC 84-51254. 208p. 1985. 15.95 (ISBN 0-87069-425-1). Wallace Homestead.
Celehar, Jane. Kitchens & Gadgets Nineteen Twenty to Nineteen Fifty. 144p. 12.95 (ISBN 0-87069-358-1). Wallace-Homestead.
Celender, Donald. Musical Instruments in Art. LC 65-29037. (Fine Art Books). (Illus.). (gr. 5-11). 1966. PLB 5.95 (ISBN 0-8225-0160-0). Lerner Pubns.
Celenko, Theodore. A Treasury of African Art from the Harrison Eiteljorg Collection. LC 82-47954. (Illus.). 240p. 1984. 57.50x (ISBN 0-253-11057-2). Ind U Pr.
Celenza, Frank V. Occlusal Morphology. 110p. 1980. pap. 18.00 (ISBN 0-931386-33-0). Quint Pub Co.
Celenza, Frank V. & Nasedkin, John N. Occlusion, the State of the Art. (Illus.). 165p. 1978. 42.00 (ISBN 0-931386-00-4). Quint Pub Co.
Celeste, Emily, jt. auth. see Courtney, Elise.

Celestial Arts, ed. see Rinder, Walter.

Celestin, L. R., jt. ed. see Watson, A.

Celeyran, Mary Tapie De see Beaute, Georges & Tapie de Celeyran, Mary.

Celieres, Andre. Prose Style of Emerson. 1936. lib. bdg. 15.00 (ISBN 0-8414-3624-X). Folcroft.
--The Prose Style of Emerson. 59.95 (ISBN 0-8490-0903-0). Gordon Pr.
--The Prose Style of Emerson. 87p. 1983. Repr. of 1936 ed. lib. bdg. 25.00 (ISBN 0-89760-169-6). Telegraph Bks.

Celine, Louis-Ferdinand. Death on the Installment Plan. Manheim, Ralph, tr. LC 48-6410. 1971. pap. 9.95 (ISBN 0-8112-0017-5, NDP330). New Directions.
--Guignol's Band. Frechtman & Nile, trs. LC 54-10186. 1969. pap. 7.95 (ISBN 0-8112-0018-3, NDP278). New Directions.
--Journey to the End of Night. Manheim, Ralph, tr. LC 82-7970. 1983. 19.95 (ISBN 0-8112-0846-X); pap. 8.95 (ISBN 0-8112-0847-8, NDP542). New Directions.
--Rigadoon. Manheim, Ralph, tr. from Fr. 304p. 1975. pap. 4.95 (ISBN 0-14-004083-8). Penguin.

Celine, Louis-Ferdinand D. Ballets Sans Musique. 1959. pap. 3.95 (ISBN 0-686-51949-3). French & Eur.
--Casse-Pipe. 1975. pap. 3.95 (ISBN 0-686-51950-7). French & Eur.
--D'un Chateau a l'autre. 1973. pap. 4.95 (ISBN 0-686-51951-5). French & Eur.
--L' Eglise. 1952. pap. 15.95 (ISBN 0-686-50139-X). French & Eur.
--Entratiens avec le Professeur Y. 1976. pap. 12.95 (ISBN 0-686-50140-3). French & Eur.
--Feerie Pour une Autre Fois, 2 vols. Set. pap. 14.95 (ISBN 0-686-51952-3). French & Eur.
--Guignol's Band. 1972. pap. 4.95 (ISBN 0-686-51946-9). French & Eur.
--Mort a Credit. 1972. 22.50 (ISBN 0-686-51947-7); pap. 4.95 (ISBN 0-686-51948-5). French & Eur.
--Nord. 1972. 16.95 (ISBN 0-686-50137-3); pap. 4.95 (ISBN 0-686-50138-1). French & Eur.
--Oeuvres, 4 tomes. Set. 691.25 (ISBN 0-685-37273-1). French & Eur.
--Le Pont de Londres. 1964. 13.95 (ISBN 0-686-51953-1); pap. 4.95 (ISBN 0-686-51954-X). French & Eur.
--Progres. 1978. pap. 14.95 (ISBN 0-686-51955-8). French & Eur.
--Rigodon. 14.95 (ISBN 0-686-51956-6); pap. 4.95 (ISBN 0-686-51957-4). French & Eur.

Celine, Louis-Ferdinand D. Voyage Au Bout De la Nuit, 2 vols. Incl. Mort a Credit. (Bibliotheque de la Pleiade). Vol. I. 37.50 (ISBN 0-685-37271-5); Vol. II. 45.00 (ISBN 0-685-37272-3). French & Eur.

Celis, J. E. & Smith, J. D., eds. Nonsense Mutations & RNA Suppressors. 1979. 59.50 (ISBN 0-12-164550-9). Acad Pr.

Celis, J. E., et al, eds. Transfer of Cell Constituents into Eukaryotic Cells. (NATO ASI Series A, Life Sciences: Vol. 31). 450p. 1980. 59.50x (ISBN 0-306-40425-7, Plenum Pr). Plenum Pub.

Celis, Julio E. & Bravo, R. Two-Dimensional Gel Electrophoresis of Proteins: Methods & Applications. LC 83-5022. 1984. 69.50 (ISBN 0-12-164720-X). Acad Pr.

Celiz, Fray F. Diary of the Alarcon Expedition into Texas 1718-1719. Hoffman, Fritz L., ed. LC 67-24717. (Quivira Society Publications, Vol. 5). 1967. Repr. of 1935 ed. 17.00 (ISBN 0-405-00075-8). Ayer Co Pubs.

Cell, C. P., ed. Revolution at Work: Mass Campaigns in China. (Studies in Social Discontinuity). 1977. 42.50 (ISBN 0-12-164750-1). Acad Pr.

Cell, Derek. Doktor Bey's Book of Brats. 1978. pap. 4.95 (ISBN 0-380-46425-X, 46425). Avon.

Cell, Edward. Language, Existence & God: Interpretations of Moore, Russell, Ayer, Wittgenstein, Wisdom, Oxford Philosophy & Tillich. 1978. Repr. of 1971 ed. text ed. 18.00x (ISBN 0-391-00921-4). Humanities.
--Learning to Learn from Experience. 280p. 1984. 34.50x (ISBN 0-87395-832-2); pap. 10.95x (ISBN 0-87395-833-0). State U NY Pr.

Cell, George C. The Rediscovery of John Wesley. LC 83-6505. 438p. 1983. pap. text ed. 15.25 (ISBN 0-8191-3222-5). U Pr of Amer.

Cell, Gillian, ed. Great Britain's Indies, English Attempts to Colonise Newfoundland, 1617-31. 1980. 60.00x (ISBN 0-686-79475-3, Pub. by Hakluyt Soc England). State Mutual Bk.

Cell, John W. The Highest Stage of White Supremacy: The Origins of Segregation in South Africa & the American South. LC 82-4312. 320p. 1982. 39.50 (ISBN 0-521-24096-4); pap. 9.95 (ISBN 0-521-27061-8). Cambridge U Pr.

Cell, John W., ed. By Kenya Possessed: The Correspondence of J. H. Oldham & Norman Leys, 1918-1926. LC 75-27894. (Studies in Imperialism Ser). 382p. 1976. lib. bdg. 23.00x (ISBN 0-226-09971-7). U of Chicago Pr.

Cella, C. Ronald. Mary Johnston. (United States Authors Ser.). 1981. lib. bdg. 13.50 (ISBN 0-8057-7340-1, Twayne). G K Hall.

Cella, Charles P. & Lane, Rodney, eds. Basic Issues in Coordinating Family & Child Welfare Programs. 1964. 29.50x (ISBN 0-317-27416-3). Elliots Bks.

Cellar, G. K., jt. ed. see Appleton, B. R.

Cellard, J. & Key, A. Dictionnaire du Francais non Conventionnel. 893p. (Fr.). 1980. 65.00 (ISBN 2-01-007382-7). French & eur.

Celler, Morton M. Giraudoux et la Metaphore: Une Etude Des Images Dans Ses Romans. (De Proprietatibus Litterarum, Series Practica: No. 54). 1974. pap. 13.60x (ISBN 0-686-20927-3). Mouton.

Celli, Angelo. The History of Malaria in the Roman Campagna from Ancient Times. Celli-Fraentzel, Anna, ed. LC 75-23694. Repr. of 1933 ed. 19.00 (ISBN 0-404-13243-X). AMS Pr.

Celli, Elisa. The Pasta Diet. 272p. 1985. pap. 3.95 (ISBN 0-446-32862-6). Warner Bks.

Cellier, ed. see Hugo, Victor.

Cellier, Elizabeth. The Matchless Rogue: A Brief Account of the Life of Don Thomazo, the Unfortunate Son. LC 80-2473. Repr. of 1680 ed. 23.50 (ISBN 0-404-19105-3). AMS Pr.

Cellier, F. E., ed. Progress in Modelling & Simulation. 1982. 60.00 (ISBN 0-12-164780-3). Acad Pr.

Cellier, Francois & Bridgeman, Cunningham. Gilbert & Sullivan & Their Operas. LC 72-91479. (Illus.). 1914. 33.00 (ISBN 0-405-08346-7, Blom Pubns). Ayer Co Pubs.

Cellier, Leon, ed. see Sand, George.

Celli-Fraentzel, Anna, ed. see Celli, Angelo.

Cellina, A., jt. auth. see Aubin, J. P.

Cellini. Autobiography. (Classic Ser.). 1956. pap. 4.95 (ISBN 0-14-044049-6). Penguin.

Cellini, Benvenuto. The Autobiography of Benvenuto Cellini. Hope, Charles & Nova, Alessandro, eds. (Illus.). 224p. 1984. 19.95 (ISBN 0-312-06140-4). St Martin.
--Due trattati. (Documents of Art & Architectural History Series 2: Vol. 3). 148p. (Italian.). 1980. Repr. of 1569 ed. 27.50x (ISBN 0-89371-203-5). Broude Intl Edns.
--Treatises of Benvenuto Cellini on Goldsmithing & Sculpture. Ashbee, C. R., tr. (Illus.). 1966. pap. 6.95 (ISBN 0-486-21568-7). Dover.
--Treatises of Benvenuto Cellini on Goldsmithing & Sculpture. Ashbee, C. R., tr. (Illus.). 13.25 (ISBN 0-8446-1828-4). Peter Smith.

Cellini, Joseph. How to Choose a Computer Camp. (Handy Guide Ser.). 64p. (Orig.). 1984. pap. 3.50 (ISBN 0-88284-266-8). Alfred Pub.

Cello, Robert M., jt. auth. see Tabbara, Khalid F.

Celluci, Anthony J. & DeVries, David L. Measuring Managerial Satisfaction: A Manual for the MJSQ. (Technical Report Ser.: No. 11). 49p. 1978. pap. 7.00 (ISBN 0-912879-10-6). Ctr Creat Leader.

Celmer, Albert B., jt. auth. see Labor Relations Press Staff.

Celmina, Helene. Women in Soviet Prisons. (Illus.). 256p. 1985. 17.95 (ISBN 0-913729-04-3). Paragon Hse.

Celms, Theodor. Der Phanomenologische Idealismus Husserls. Natanson, ed. LC 78-66733. (Phenomenology: Vol. 3). 192p. 1979. lib. bdg. 26.00 (ISBN 0-8240-9567-7). Garland Pub.

Celorio, C. A. Essay on Reinforced Concrete Design for Flexure: Tables for the Design of Slabs, Formulas for the Design of Beams. (Illus.). 1976. pap. 4.00 (ISBN 0-918168-00-7). C A Celorio.

Celorio, Cesar A. Mathematics Applied to Structural Engineering: Part One, Design for Lateral Forces. 1978. pap. 6.50 (ISBN 0-918168-03-1). C A Celorio.

Celorio, Marta & Barlow, Annette C. Handbook of Spanish Idioms. 460p. (gr. 12 up). 1974. pap. text ed. 7.75 (ISBN 0-88345-216-2, 18112). Regents Pub.

Celotti, F., et al, eds. Metabolism of Hormonal Steroids in the Neuroendocrine Structures. (Serono Symposia Publications: Vol. 13). 216p. 1984. text ed. 46.00 (ISBN 0-317-02466-3). Raven.

Celsus. De Medicina, 3 Vols. (Loeb Classical Library: No. 292, 304, 336). 12.50x ea. Vol. 1 (ISBN 0-674-99322-5). Vol. 2 (ISBN 0-674-99335-7). Vol. 3 (ISBN 0-674-99370-5). Harvard U Pr.

Cember, H. Introduction to Health Physics. 2nd ed. 1969. 60.00 (ISBN 0-08-030129-0). Pergamon.

Cember, Herman. Introduction to Health Physics. (Illus.). 475p. 1983. pap. 29.50 (ISBN 0-08-030936-4). Pergamon.

Cembuna, Al, jt. auth. see Avery, Constance.

Cembura, Al & Avery, Constance. A Guide to Jim Beam Bottles. 10th ed. (Illus.). 192p. 1981. pap. 10.95 (ISBN 0-912454-16-4). Cembura.
--Guide to Jim Beam Bottles. 11th ed. (Illus.). 208p. 1983. pap. 14.95 (ISBN 0-912454-17-2). Cembura.
--Guide to Jim Beam Bottles. 12th ed. (Illus.). 208p. 1985. pap. 17.95 (ISBN 0-912454-19-9). Cembura.
--Jim Bean Regal China Go-Withs. (Illus.). 96p. 1979. pap. 6.95 (ISBN 0-912454-15-6). Cembura.

Cembureau (European Cement Association), ed. Cement Standards of the World. 2nd ed. (Illus.). 177p. (Orig.). 1980. pap. 75.00x (ISBN 0-8002-2965-7). Intl Pubns Serv.

Cembureau (European Cement Association) World Cement Directory 1980, 2 vols. 6th ed. LC 75-15776. (Illus.). 341p. (Orig.). 1980. Set. pap. 147.50x (ISBN 0-8002-2776-X). Intl Pubns Serv.

Cena, K. & Clark, J. A., eds. Bioengineering, Thermal Physiology & Comfort. (Studies in Environmental Science: Vol. 10). 290p. 1981. 64.00 (ISBN 0-444-99761-X). Elsevier.

Cenac, Arnaud, jt. auth. see Perlemuter, Leon.

Cence, R. J. & Ma, E., eds. Proceedings of the Ninth Topical Conference in Particle Physics. LC 83-18126. (Particle Physics Conference Proceedings Ser.). 396p. 1984. pap. 30.00x (ISBN 0-8248-0949-1). UH Pr.

Cence, R. J., et al, eds. Proceedings of the Seventh Hawaii Topical Conference in Particle Physics, 1977. LC 77-27006. (Particle Physics Conference Proceedings Ser). 488p. 1978. pap. text ed. 20.00x (ISBN 0-8248-0619-0). UH Pr.

Cence, Robert J. Pion-Nucleon Scattering. LC 66-11964. (Investigations in Physics Ser.: No. 11). (Illus.). 1969. 22.50x (ISBN 0-691-08068-2). Princeton U Pr.

Cencini, Alvaro. Time & Macroeconomic Analysis of Income. LC 83-40201. 260p. 1984. 27.50 (ISBN 0-312-80502-0). St Martin.

Cencov, N. N. Statistical Decision Rules & Optimal Inference. LC 81-15039. (Mathematical Monographs: Vol. 53). 88.00 (ISBN 0-8218-4502-0, MMONO). Am Math.

Cendrars, Blaise. African Saga. Bianco, Margery, tr. LC 75-97359. (Fr). Repr. of 1927 ed. 25.00x (ISBN 0-8371-2419-0, CEA&, Pub. by Negro U Pr). Greenwood.
--Complete Postcards from the Americas: Poems of Road & Sea. LC 73-94445. 1976. 27.50x (ISBN 0-520-02716-7). U of Cal Pr.
--Gold, the Marvelous History of General John Augustus Sutter. Rootes, Nina, tr. from Fr. LC 83-16253. 1984. 16.95 (ISBN 0-935576-08-8); pap. 8.95 (ISBN 0-935576-09-6). Kesend Pub Ltd.
--Moravagine. 12.95x (ISBN 0-8464-0642-X). Beekman Pubs.
--Night in the Forest. Ewing, Margaret K., tr. from Fr. LC 84-19634. (ALTA Ser.: No. 2). 96p. 1985. text ed. 8.50 (ISBN 0-8262-0466-X). U of Mo Pr.
--Selected Writings of Blaise Cendrars. Albert, Walter, ed. LC 78-14223. 1978. Repr. of 1966 ed. lib. bdg. 27.50x (ISBN 0-313-21020-9, CESW). Greenwood.
--Shadow. Marcia, Brown, tr. from Fr. & illus. Orig. Title: La Feticheuse. (Illus.). 40p. (gr. 1 up). 1982. 12.95 (ISBN 0-684-17226-7, ScribJ). Scribner.

Cenini, S., jt. auth. see Malatesta, Li.

Cenker, William. The Hindu Personality in Education: Tagore, Gandhi, & Aurobindo. LC 76-52211. 1976. 12.50x (ISBN 0-88386-759-1). South Asia Bks.
--A Tradition of Teachers: Sankara & the Jagadgurus Today. 1983. 18.50 (ISBN 0-8364-0944-2); text ed. 13.00 (ISBN 0-8364-1058-0). South Asia Bks.

Cennini, C. D'Andrea. The Craftsman's Handbook. Thompson, D. V., Jr., tr. 14.00 (ISBN 0-8446-0542-5). Peter Smith.

Cennini, Cennino A. Craftsman's Handbook. 1933. pap. 3.50 (ISBN 0-486-20054-X). Dover.

Cennini, Cennino D. Il Libro Dell'Arte: Introduction in English. Thompson, Daniel V., ed. (Ital.). 1932. 59.50x (ISBN 0-317-27510-0). Elliots Bks.

Cenone, Anna, jt. auth. see Somerville, Edith.

Censer, Jane T. North Carolina Planters & Their Children, 1800-1860. LC 83-19966. 361p. 1984. text ed. 20.00x (ISBN 0-8071-1135-X). La State U Pr.

Censoni, Bob. Ready-to-Use Christmas Silhouettes. 64p. (Orig.). 1985. pap. 3.50 (ISBN 0-486-24954-9). Dover.
--Ready-to-Use Silhouette Spot Illustrations. 64p. 1984. pap. 2.95 (ISBN 0-486-24711-2). Dover.

Censoni, Robert, illus. Ready-To-Use Humorous Spot Illustrations. (Clip Art Ser.). 64p. 1984. pap. 2.95 (ISBN 0-486-24644-2). Dover.

Censor, pseud. Don't: Or, Direction for Avoiding Improprieties in Conduct & Common Errors of Speech. (Illus.). 69p. 1984. pap. 5.95 (ISBN 0-912697-05-9). Algonquin Bks.

Centaur Press Ltd., ed. The Dialectics of Diotima. 176p. 1970. 11.95x (ISBN 0-8464-0325-0). Beekman Pubs.

Centenary Committee. Champion of Liberty: Charles Bradlaugh. LC 75-161323. (Atheist Viewpoint Ser). (Illus.). 384p. 1972. Repr. of 1934 ed. 25.50 (ISBN 0-405-03626-4). Ayer Co Pubs.

Centennial Colloquim on Thomas Mann Staff. Thomas Mann in Context: Papers of the Clark University Centennial Colloquim. Hughes, Kenneth, ed. LC 77-26366. pap. 34.50 (ISBN 0-317-27753-7, 2015545). Bks Demand UMI.

Centeno, Augusto. Corazon de Espana. (Illus.). (gr. 9-12). 1957. text ed. 21.95 (ISBN 0-03-015080-9, HoltC). HR&W.

Centeno, Augusto, jt. auth. see Tarr, F. C.

Centeno-Beltran, Violeta. Look-I'm Flat Again. 1985. 10.95 (ISBN 0-533-06520-8). Vantage.

Centeno Roman, Jose M. Enciclopedia de la Cocina, 3 vols. 840p. (Espn.). 1977. Set. 58.50 (ISBN 84-221-0395-8, S-50461). French & Eur.

Center, Allen H. & Walsh, Frank E. Public Relations Practices: Managerial Case Studies & Problems. 3rd ed. (Illus.). 400p. 1985. pap. text ed. 19.95 (ISBN 0-13-738691-5). P-H.

Center, Allen H., jt. auth. see Walsh, Frank E.

Center, Elizabeth M., ed. see Gans, Carl, et al.

Center for Academic Publications Japan. Current Contents of Academic Journals in Japan, 1977. 17th ed. LC 72-623679. 344p. (Orig.). 1979. pap. 50.00xcancelled (ISBN 0-8002-2322-5). Intl Pubns Serv.

Center for Academic Publications Japan, ed. Current Contents of Academic Journals in Japan, 1978. 18th ed. LC 72-623679. 392p. (Orig.). 1980. pap. 55.00xcancelled (ISBN 0-8002-2740-9). Intl Pubns Serv.

Center for Academic Publications, Japan. Current Contents of Academic Journals in Japan 1974-75. LC 72-623679. 1973. pap. cancelled (ISBN 0-8002-0311-9). Intl Pubns Serv.

Center for Advanced Computation. Energy Flow Through the United States Economy: A Wall Chart. 1976. 15.00x (ISBN 0-252-00637-2). U of Ill Pr.

Center for Afro-American & African Studies. Black Immigration & Ethnicity in the United States: An Annotated Bibliography. University of Michigan Staff, ed. LC 84-12886. (Bibliographies & Indexes in Afro-American & African Studies: No. 2). xi, 170p. 1985. lib. bdg. 29.95 (ISBN 0-313-24366-2, SBI/). Greenwood.

Center for Appl. Ling., LORC Staff. From the Classroom to the Workplace: Teaching ESL to Adults. 170p. (Orig.). 1983. pap. 9.95 (ISBN 0-15-599018-7). Ctr Appl Ling.

Center for Applied Linguistics. Bilingual Education, Current Perspectives No. 3: Law. LC 77-80381. 75p. 1977. pap. text ed. 9.95x (ISBN 0-15-599273-2). Ctr Appl Ling.
--Bilingual Education, Current Perspectives No. 1: Social Science. LC 77-80381. 136p. 1977. pap. text ed. 9.95x (ISBN 0-15-599068-3). Ctr Appl Ling.
--Bilingual Education, Current Perspectives No. 2: Linguistics. LC 77-80381. 182p. 1977. pap. text ed. 9.95 (ISBN 0-15-599281-3). Ctr Appl Ling.
--Bilingual Education, Current Perspectives No. 4: Education. LC 77-80381. 140p. 1977. pap. text ed. 9.95x (ISBN 0-15-599015-2). Ctr Appl Ling.
--Bilingual Education, Current Perspectives No. 5: Synthesis. LC 77-80381. 140p. (Orig.). 1978. pap. 9.95x (ISBN 0-15-599251-1). Ctr Appl Ling.

Center for Applied Linguistics, jt. auth. see Language & Orientation Resource Center.

Center for Applied Linguistics, Washington D.C. Dictionary Catalog of the Library of the Center for Applied Linguistics, Washington, D. C, 4 vols. 1974. Set. lib. bdg. 370.00 (ISBN 0-8161-1114-6, Hall Library). G K Hall.

Center for Arts Information. New York City Arts Funding Guide. 72p. 1982. pap. 10.00 (ISBN 0-935654-04-6). Ctr for Arts Info.

Center for Attitudinal Healing. Another Look at the Rainbow. 1983. pap. 7.95 (ISBN 0-89087-341-0). Celestial Arts.
--There Is a Rainbow Behind Every Dark Cloud. 1979. pap. 7.95 (ISBN 0-89087-253-8). Celestial Arts.

Center for Auto Safety Staff, jt. auth. see Goodman, Richard M.

Center for Business & Economic Research. Economic Abstract of Alabama, 1982. Sawyer, Carolyn, ed. (Illus.). 386p. 1982. 10.00x (ISBN 0-943394-01-5). U of Ala Ctr Bus.
--Economic Abstract of Alabama: 1984. rev. ed. Fowler, Steve & Watters, Annette, eds. (Illus.). 430p. 1984. reference 30.00x (ISBN 0-943394-02-3). U of Ala Ctr Bus.

Center for Business Information Staff, ed. Appropriate Technology Organizations: A Worldwide Directory. LC 83-43053. 149p. 1984. pap. 29.95x (ISBN 0-89950-098-6). McFarland & Co.

Center for Compliance Information. Noise Control in the Workplace. LC 78-65759. 1978. text ed. 18.75 (ISBN 0-89443-084-X). Aspen Systems.

Center for Conflict Resolution. A Manual for Group Facilitators. 89p. 4.50 (ISBN 0-318-17938-5, E03A). NASCO.

Center for Contemporary European Studies. Europe Today & Tomorrow. Freeman, Peggotty, ed. (Illus.). 1977. pap. text ed. 11.50x (ISBN 0-582-35170-7). Longman.

Center for Curriculum Design, ed. Somewhere Else: A Living-Learning Catalog. LC 72-91916. 214p. 1972. pap. 6.95 (ISBN 0-8040-0610-5, 82-75117, Pyb. by Swallow). Ohio U Pr.

Center for Design Planning. Streetscape Equipment Sorcebook 2: Lighting; Paving & Fixtures; Traffic Safety & Control; Housekeeping & Amenity; Signage; Communication & Safety Devices; Shelters; Recreation & Play; Miscellaneous. LC 79-56221. pap. 61.00 (ISBN 0-317-20033-X, 2023241). Bks Demand UMI.

Center for Disease Control, U.S. Public Health Service. Microbial Diseases: Notes, Reports, Summaries, Trends, 1980. May, Carl W., ed. LC 82-122209. 334p. 1980. text ed. 15.00x (ISBN 0-913232-85-8); pap. text ed. 9.95x (ISBN 0-913232-87-4). W Kaufmann.

Center for Editions of American Authors, ed. see Melville, Herman.

Center for Editions of American Authors, et al, eds. see Melville, Herman.

Center for Environmental & Consumer Justice Staff. Discrimination in Private Employment in Puerto Rico (Color, Sex & National Origin) LC 79-16965. 450p. Date not set. pap. price not set (ISBN 0-8477-2454-9). U of PR Pr.

Center for Environmental Education Staff. The Ocean-Consider the Connections: Educational Activities for Children. Maraniss, Linda, ed. (Illus.). 100p. (gr. 3-7). 1985. pap. write for info. (ISBN 0-9615294-0-7). Ctr Env Educ.
Center for Equal Education. Covering the Desegregation Story. LC 76-45286. 1976. 3.00 (ISBN 0-912008-12-1). Integrated Ed Assoc.
--Whites in Desegregated Schools. LC 76-24186. 1976. 4.50 (ISBN 0-912008-11-3). Integrated Ed Assoc.
--Worlds of Children. 1981. 7.50 (ISBN 0-912008-20-2). Integrated Ed Assoc.
Center for Equal Education & Egerton, John. Education & Desegregation in Eight Schools. LC 77-80528. 1977. pap. 3.60 (ISBN 0-912008-14-8). Integrated Ed Assoc.
Center for Inter-American Relations & American Federation of Arts. El Dorado: The Gold of Ancient Columbia. LC 74-175969. (Illus.). 150p. 1980. pap. 14.95 (ISBN 0-295-95736-0). U of Wash Pr.
Center for International & Strategic Affairs, Univ. of California, Los Angeles, jt. ed. see Spiegel, Steven.
Center for International Education, ed. see Kindervatter, Susan.
Center for International Policy. Voyage of the Mekong Dragon. (Illus.). 48p. 1985. write for info. (ISBN 0-912661-06-2). Woodsong Graph.
Center for Korean Studies. Korean Studies, Vol. I. (Korean Studies). 284p. 1977. pap. text ed. 13.50x (ISBN 0-8248-0560-7). UH Pr.
--Korean Studies, Vol. 4. 176p. 1982. 13.50x (ISBN 0-8248-0816-9). UH Pr.
Center for Learning. Advanced Composition. 280p. 1983. wire coil bdg. 29.95 (ISBN 0-697-01926-8); pap. text ed. 3.25 (ISBN 0-697-01875-X). Wm C Brown.
--Advanced Placement English. 272p. 1984. wire coil bdg. 29.95 (ISBN 0-697-01943-8). Wm C Brown.
--American Literature: Beginnings Through Civil War, Vol. 1. 280p. 1984. wire coil bdg. 29.95 (ISBN 0-697-02004-5). Wm C Brown.
--American Literature: Civil War to Present, Vol. 2. 280p. 1984. wire coil bdg. 29.95 (ISBN 0-697-02005-3). Wm C Brown.
--Basic Composition. 280p. 1983. wire coil bdg. 29.95 (ISBN 0-697-01925-X); wkbk. 2.95 (ISBN 0-697-01872-5). Wm C Brown.
--British Literature I. 280p. 1984. wire coil bdg. 29.95 (ISBN 0-697-02017-7). Wm C Brown.
--British Literature II. 280p. 1984. wire coil bdg. 29.95 (ISBN 0-697-02018-5). Wm C Brown.
--Experiencing Drama. 272p. 1983. wire coil bdg. 29.95 (ISBN 0-697-01888-1). Wm C Brown.
--Experiencing Shakespeare I. 188p. 1983. wire coil bdg. 29.95 (ISBN 0-697-01885-7). Wm C Brown.
--Experiencing Shakespeare II. 228p. 1983. wire coil bdg. 29.95 (ISBN 0-697-01886-5). Wm C Brown.
--Experiencing the Novel. 304p. 1983. wire coil bdg. 29.95 (ISBN 0-697-01889-X). Wm C Brown.
--Research Paper. 280p. 1984. wire coil bdg. 29.95 (ISBN 0-697-01936-5). Wm C Brown.
--Speech. 288p. 1984. wire coil bdg. 29.95 (ISBN 0-697-02001-0). Wm C Brown.
--Tools of Fiction. 248p. 1983. wire coil bdg. 29.95 (ISBN 0-697-01890-3). Wm C Brown.
--Tools of Nonfiction. 340p. 1983. wire coil bdg. 29.95 (ISBN 0-697-01891-1). Wm C Brown.
--Writing Creatively. 272p. 1984. wire coil bdg. 29.95 (ISBN 0-697-01935-7). Wm C Brown.
Center for Learning Staff. Classical Literature. 1982. pap. text ed. 29.95 (ISBN 0-697-01884-9). Wm C Brown.
--Participating in the Poem. 240p. 1983. wire coil bdg. 29.95 (ISBN 0-697-01887-3). Wm C Brown.
--Prewriting & Rewriting. 1983. pap. text ed. 29.95 (ISBN 0-697-01878-4). Wm C Brown.
--Shakespearean Comedies. 280p. 1984. wire coil bdg. 29.95 (ISBN 0-697-01982-9). Wm C Brown.
--Success with Practical Writing. 1982. pap. text ed. 29.95 (ISBN 0-697-01879-2). Wm C Brown.
--World Literature I. 1985. pap. text ed. 29.95 (ISBN 0-697-02073-8). Wm C Brown.
--World Literature II. 1985. pap. text ed. 29.95 (ISBN 0-697-02074-6). Wm C Brown.
Center for Migration Studies. Images: A Pictorial History of Italian Americans. Tomasi, Silvano M., ed. LC 81-67218. (Illus.). 348p. 1981. 29.95x (ISBN 0-913256-38-2). Ctr Migration.
Center for Migration Studies Staff. New Immigrants in Brooklyn & Queens: Policy Implications, Especially with Regard to Housing. (Occasional Papers & Documentation). (Illus.). 165p. 1983. pap. text ed. 75.00 (ISBN 0-913256-63-3). Ctr Migration.
Center for National Policy Review Staff. Breaking down Barriers: New Evidence on the Impact of Metropolitan School Desegregation on Housing Patterns. 1980. 5.00 (ISBN 0-318-03070-5). CU Law Natl.
--Civil Rights under General Revenue Sharing. 195p. 1975. 2.50 (ISBN 0-318-03074-8). CU Law Natl.
--Equal Opportunity under General Revenue Sharing. 51p. 1975. 1.00 (ISBN 0-318-03071-3). CU Law Natl.
--Equity under CETA: Issues & Problems Facing Minorities, Women & the Poor under the Comprehensive Employment & Training Act. 82p. 1978. 2.50 (ISBN 0-318-03067-5). CU Law Natl.
--Fair Mortgage Lending: A Handbook for Community Groups. 1978. 2.00 (ISBN 0-318-03068-3). CU Law Natl.
--Feminization of Poverty: Women, Work & Welfare. 10p. 1978. 2.50 (ISBN 0-318-03073-X). CU Law Natl.
--Justice Delayed & Denied: HEW & Northern School Desegregation. 117p. 1974. 3.00 (ISBN 0-318-03075-6). CU Law Natl.
--A Territorial Issue: A Study of Women in the Construction Trades. 75p. 1982. 5.00 (ISBN 0-318-03069-1). CU Law Natl.
--Trends in Black Segregation: 1970-74. write for info. (UD-016767). CU Law Natl.
--Without Justice: Report on Civil Rights Division of Department of Justice. 1982. 3.00 (ISBN 0-318-03076-4). CU Law Natl.
--Women & Children Alone & in Poverty. 1981. 2.50 (ISBN 0-318-03072-1). CU Law Natl.
Center for Ocean Management Studies. Comparative Marine Policy. 272p. 1981. 29.95x (ISBN 0-686-77546-5). Bergin & Garvey.
Center for Ocean Management Studies, ed. Comparative Marine Policy: Perspectives from Europe, Scandinavia, Canada & the United States. LC 80-21455. 336p. 1981. 42.95x (ISBN 0-03-058307-1). Praeger.
Center for Ocean Management Studies. Impact of Marine Pollution on Society. (Illus.). 320p. 1982. 29.95x (ISBN 0-686-86218-X). Bergin & Garvey.
Center for Oceans Law & Policy, University of Virginia. Ocean Policy Study Series. (Ocean Study Ser.). 1984. Six Studies Annually. looseleaf 150.00 (ISBN 0-379-20860-1). Oceana.
Center for Photographic Images of Medicine & Health Care. Illustrated Catalogue of the Slide Archive of Historical Medical Photographs at Stony Brook. LC 83-22626. (Illus.). 464p. 1984. lib. bdg. 55.00 (ISBN 0-313-24169-4, FCM/). Greenwood.
Center for Political Studies. American National Election Series: 1972, 1974, 1976, 5 vols. LC 79-84172. 1979. Set. write for info. codebk. (ISBN 0-89138-977-6). Vol. 1 (ISBN 0-89138-976-8). Vol. 2 (ISBN 0-89138-975-X). Vol. 3 (ISBN 0-89138-974-1). Vol. 4 (ISBN 0-89138-973-3). Vol. 5 (ISBN 0-89138-972-5). ICPSR.
--American National Election Study, 1970. 1972. codebook write for info. (ISBN 0-89138-051-5). ICPSR.
Center for Professional Responsibility Staff. Model Rules of Professional Conduct & Code of Judicial Conduct. 152p. 1983. pap. 5.00 (ISBN 0-317-16867-3). Amer Bar Assn.
Center for Professional Responsibility (American Bar Association) Survey of Lawyer Disciplinary Procedures in the United States. LC 84-250556. 355p. Date not set. price not set. Amer Bar Assn.
Center for Public Resources. Corporate Dispute Management, Nineteen Eighty-Two: A Manual of Innovative Corporate Strategies for the Avoidance & Resolution of Legal Disputes. LC 82-73068. (Illus.). 1982. 80.00. Bender.
Center for Real Estate & Urban Economic Studies of the University of Connecticut, jt. auth. see Galonska, Michael L.
Center for Renewable Resources. Renewable Energy in Cities. LC 83-23455. (Illus.). 376p. 1984. 38.50 (ISBN 0-442-21654-8). Van Nos Reinhold.
Center for Research & Documentation on World Language Problems & Esperantic Studies Foundation. World Communications Year 1983: Language & Language Learning. 95p. 1983. 7.50 (ISBN 0-317-37236-X). CRDWLP.
Center for Research in Ambulatory Health Care Administration, ed. see Schafer, Eldon L., et al.
Center for Research in Ambulatory Health Care Administration. Manual on Insurance. 142p. 1974. 6.00 (ISBN 0-317-34837-X, 13-0000-909); members 3.00 (ISBN 0-317-34838-8); corresp. subscr. 4.80 (ISBN 0-317-34839-6). Med Group Mgmt.
--Practical Financial Management for Medical Groups. 800p. 1979. 55.00 (ISBN 0-317-34845-0, 50-0000-916). Med Group Mgmt.
Center for Research in Ambulatory Health Care Administration Staff & Lawson, James G. Starting & Managing Your Practice: A Guide Book for Physicians. LC 82-2253. 288p. 1983. text ed. 30.00 (ISBN 0-89946-091-7). Oelgeschlager.
Center for Research in Cognition & Effect - 3rd Conference - New York City - 1971. Adaptive Functions of Imagery. Segal, Sydney J., ed. 1971. 47.50 (ISBN 0-12-635450-2). Acad Pr.
Center for Research Libraries. The Center for Research Libraries Handbook, 1984 Supplement. 1984. 2.00 (ISBN 0-932486-29-0). Ctr Res Lib.
--Cooperative Africana Microform Project: Cumulative Supplement. 246p. 1979. pap. text ed. 3.50 (ISBN 0-932486-18-5). Ctr Res Lib.
--Cooperative Africana Microform Project: 1981 Cumlative Supplement Edition. 151p. (Orig.). 1981. pap. text ed. 3.50 (ISBN 0-932486-26-6). Ctr Res Lib.
--Scientific & Technical Journals Listing, 1981. 142p. (Orig.). 1981. pap. text ed. 10.00 (ISBN 0-932486-24-X); members free. Ctr Res Lib.
Center for Research Libraries, ed. Monograph Catalog: The Center for Research Libraries Catalog, 5 vols. 1979. 332.00 set (ISBN 0-932486-13-4). Ctr Research Lib.
Center for Research of Aggression, Staff, Syracuse University. Prevention & Control of Aggression Principles, Practices & Research. 384p. 1983. 45.00 (ISBN 0-08-029375-1). Pergamon.
Center for Science in the Public Interest Staff, jt. auth. see Lipske, Michael.
Center for Science in the Public Interest. Ninety-Nine Ways to a Simple Lifestyle. 381p. 3.50 (ISBN 0-317-32274-5). Alternatives.
Center for Self-Sufficiency. Baby Kimono Basic Self-Sufficiency Poem with Pattern Bibliography. 1985. pap. text ed. 2.00 (ISBN 0-318-04297-5, Pub. by Center Self Suff). Prosperity & Profits.
--Fundraising Self-Sufficiency: A Bibliography. 20p. 1985. pap. text ed. 4.95 (ISBN 0-318-04299-1, Pub. by Center Self Suff). Prosperity & Profits.
--Home Business, Odd Job & Part Time Helpers Directory: Pennsylvania Edition. 40p. 1985. pap. text ed. 2.00 (Pub. by Center Self Suff). Prosperity & Profits.
--Recipe Ingredient Replacement As a Method for Food Self-Sufficiency. 20p. 1985. pap. text ed. 2.50 (ISBN 0-318-04300-9, Pub. by Center Self Suff). Prosperity & Profits.
--Recipe Ingredient Replacement for Small Business, Caterers, Small Restaurants, Deli Shops, Etc. 20p. 1985. pap. text ed. 6.95 (ISBN 0-318-04301-7, Pub. by Center Self Suff). Prosperity & Profits.
--Telephone Recyling Suggestions. 1985. pap. 1.50 (ISBN 0-318-04303-3, Pub. by Center Self Suff). Prosperity & Profits.
--Telephone Repair Service Suggestions. 1985. pap. text ed. 1.75 (ISBN 0-318-04304-1, Pub. by Center Self Suff). Prosperity & Profits.
Center for Self-Sufficiency Business Research Division. Considering a Catering Service? Catering Service Ideas. 50p. 1983. pap. text ed. 2.75 (ISBN 0-910811-62-8, Pub. by Center Self Suff). Prosperity & Profits.
--Considering a Referral Service? Referral Service Ideas. 25p. 1983. pap. text ed. 2.75 (ISBN 0-910811-64-4, Pub. by Center Self Suff). Prosperity & Profits.
--Considering a Secretarial Service? Possibilities for Income. 25p. 1983. pap. text ed. 2.75 (ISBN 0-910811-63-6, Pub. by Center Self Suff). Prosperity & Profits.
--Domestic Help Services: Suggestive Ideas for Services. 50p. 1983. pap. text ed. 1.95 (ISBN 0-910811-49-0, Pub. by Center Self Suff). Prosperity & Profits.
--Suggestions for Types of Recycling Businesses. 50p. 1984. pap. text ed. 2.75 (ISBN 0-910811-34-2, Pub. by Center Self Suff). Prosperity & Profits.
--Thrift Stores & Resale Shops: Suggestive Ideas for Specialized Thrift Stores. 50p. 1983. pap. text ed. 4.95 (ISBN 0-910811-46-6, Pub. by Center Self Suff). Prosperity & Profits.
Center for Self-Sufficiency Educational Division. Finding Temporary Shelter: A Workbook. 40p. 1984. pap. text ed. 3.75 (Pub. by Center Self Suff). Prosperity & Profits.
--Food Bank Creating: A Workbook. 25p. 1984. pap. text ed. 2.95 (Pub. by Center Self Suff). Prosperity & Profits.
Center for Self Sufficiency Learning Institute Staff. At Your Own Pace Bibliography on Food Preservation. 40p. 1985. pap. text ed. 2.95 (ISBN 0-910811-65-2, Pub. by Center Self Suff). Prosperity & Profits.
--At Your Own Pace Bibliography on Herb & Spice Plant Growing. 35p. 1985. pap. text ed. 2.75 (ISBN 0-910811-68-7, Pub. by Center Self Suff). Prosperity & Profits.
--At Your Own Pace Bibliography on Making Your Own Furniture. 35p. 1983. pap. text ed. 2.75 (ISBN 0-910811-70-9, Pub. by Center Self Suff). Prosperity & Profits.
--At Your Own Pace Bibliography on Meditation. 30p. 1985. pap. text ed. 2.75 (ISBN 0-910811-71-7, Pub. by Center Self Suff). Prosperity & Profits.
--At Your Own Pace Bibliography on Natural Foods & Nutrition. 50p. 1983. pap. text ed. 2.75 (ISBN 0-910811-67-9, Pub. by Center Self Suff). Prosperity & Profits.
Center for Self-Sufficiency Learning Institute. Clothing Alterations & Design: Self Paced Reading Bibliography. 1984. pap. 1.95 (ISBN 0-910811-75-X, Pub. by Center Self Suff). Prosperity & Profits.
Center For Self-Sufficiency Learning Division. Food Self-Sufficiency Seminar-Workshop Workbook. 35p. 1984. 9.95 (ISBN 0-910811-94-6, Pub. by Center Self Suff). Prosperity & Profits.
Center for Self-Sufficiency Learning Institute. Holistic Healing: Self Paced Reading Bibliography. 1983. pap. 1.50 (ISBN 0-910811-76-8, Pub. by Center Self Suff). Prosperity & Profits.
Center for Self-Sufficiency Learning Division. Home Businesses Seminar-Workshop Workbook. 28p. 1984. 9.95 (ISBN 0-910811-93-8, Pub. by Center Self Suff). Prosperity & Profits.
Center for Self Sufficiency Learning Institute. Housing Alternatives Self Paced Reading Bibliography. 1983. pap. 2.75 (ISBN 0-910811-74-1, Pub. by Center Self Suff). Prosperity & Profits.
Center for Self-Sufficiency Learning Division. Recycling Seminar-Workshop: Workbook. 25p. 1984. wkbk 5.95 (ISBN 0-910811-90-3, Pub. by Center Self Suff). Prosperity & Profits.
Center for Self-Sufficiency Learning Institute. Self Paced Reading: Bibliography on Food Preservation. 1983. pap. 4.95 (ISBN 0-910811-77-6, Pub. by Center Self Suff). Prosperity & Profits.
Center for Self Sufficiency Research Division. The A to Z Small Business Bibliography Encyclopedia. 2000p. 1983. Set. text ed. 650.00 (ISBN 0-910811-17-2, Pub. by Center Self Suff). Prosperity & Profits.
--Almost Coffee: Rhyming Coffee Substitutes Recipe Book. 30p. 1983. pap. text ed. 2.50 (ISBN 0-910811-66-0, Pub. by Center Self Suff). Prosperity & Profits.
--Aloe Vera Formula Use Bibliography. 20p. 1983. pap. text ed. 1.95 (ISBN 0-910811-39-3, Pub. by Center Self Suff). Prosperity & Profits.
Center for Self-Sufficiency Research Division. The Alternative Cooking Facilities Cookbook. LC 83-90718. 50p. 1983. pap. text ed. 3.95 (ISBN 0-910811-08-3, Pub. by Center Self Suff). Prosperity & Profits.
Center for Self-Sufficiency Research Division, ed. The Barter Index. LC 83-90717. 60p. 1985. pap. text ed. 9.95 (ISBN 0-910811-09-1, Pub. by Center Self Suff). Prosperity & Profits.
Center for Self Sufficiency Research Division. Business Recycling Suggestions. 26p. 1983. pap. text ed. 2.75 (ISBN 0-910811-24-5, Pub. by Center Self Suff). Prosperity & Profits.
--Center for Self Sufficiency Catalog of Recycling Books. 1984. pap. 1.00 (ISBN 0-910811-83-0, Pub. by Center Self Suff). Prosperity & Profits.
Center for Self-Sufficiency Research Division. Center for Self Sufficiency Catalog of Recycled Business Books. 12p. 1984. pap. 1.00 (ISBN 0-910811-81-4, Pub. by Center Self Suff). Prosperity & Profits.
--Center for Self-Sufficiency Catalog of Recycled Designer Patterns. 15p. 1983. pap. 1.00 (ISBN 0-910811-80-6, Pub. by Center Self Suff). Prosperity & Profits.
--Center for Self Sufficiency Catalog of Recycled Programmed Learning Books. 1984. pap. 1.00 (ISBN 0-910811-78-4, Pub. by Center Self Suff). Prosperity & Profits.
--Center for Self-Sufficiency: Directory of Mail Order Crafts, Arts, and Handmade Items & Gifts from the Original Artists. 20p. 1984. pap. 2.00 (ISBN 0-910811-85-7, Pub. by Center Self Seff). Prosperity & Profits.
Center for Self-Sufficiency, Research Division. Considering a Creative Advertising Agency? Suggestions for a Creative Advertising Agency. 25p. 1983. pap. text ed. 2.75 (ISBN 0-910811-61-X, Pub. by Center Self Suff). Prosperity & Profits.
Center for Self Sufficiency Research Division. Creative Suggestions on Obtaining Company Benefits for a Small Business. 26p. 1983. pap. text ed. 2.75 (ISBN 0-910811-21-0, Pub. by Center Self Suff). Prosperity & Profits.
Center for Self Sufficiency Research Division Staff. Creativity Productivity & Positivity. 50p. 1983. pap. text ed. 2.50 (ISBN 0-910811-15-6, Pub. by Center Self Suff). Prosperity & Profits.
Center for Self Sufficiency Research Division. Directory of New Topics for Future Research. 60p. 1984. pap. text ed. 0.25 (ISBN 0-317-03486-3, Pub. by Center Self Suff). Prosperity & Profits.
--Finding Bargains by Using the Newspapers & or Telephone Directory: A Workbook. 21p. pap. 1.95 (ISBN 0-686-47684-0, Pub. by Center Self Suff). Prosperity & Profits.
Center for Self-Sufficiency Research Division. Finding Temporary Shelter in New York: State of New York Edition. 50p. 1984. pap. text ed. 3.75 (Pub. by Center Self Suff). Prosperity & Profits.
Center for Self-Sufficiency Research Division, compiled by. The Food Preservation Index. LC 83-90716. 50p. 1982. pap. text ed. 5.95 (ISBN 0-910811-10-5, Pub. by Center Self Suff). Prosperity & Profits.
Center for Self-Sufficiency Research Division. Food Self-Sufficiency: A Bibliography. 21p. 1984. pap. text ed. 3.75 (ISBN 0-910811-95-4, Pub. by Center Self Suff). Prosperity & Profits.
--Food Self-Sufficiency References in American Literature. 25p. 1985. pap. text ed. 3.00 (ISBN 0-318-04298-3, Pub. by Center Self Suff). Prosperity & Profits.
Center for Self Sufficiency Research Division. Fruit Drinks Recipe Bibliography. 30p. 1983. pap. text ed. 9.95 (ISBN 0-910811-41-5, Pub. by Center Self Suff). Prosperity & Profits.
--Guide to Alternative Craft, Quilt, Drapery Etc. Pattern Sources. 35p. 1984. pap. text ed. 1.75 (ISBN 0-910811-31-8, Pub. by Center Self Suff). Prosperity & Profits.
--Health Care Alternatives: An Index. 60p. 1983. pap. 7.95 (ISBN 0-910811-37-7, Pub. by Center Self Suff). Prosperity & Profits.

Centre de Documentation De l'Armement, ed. Lexique des Mots-Cles, Descripteurs et Identificateurs, Francais et Anglais, a Utiliser Pour la Recherche Documentaire, 3 vols. 2001p. (Fr. & Eng., Lexicon of Key Words, Descriptions and Identification to be Used for Documentary Research, English-French). 1976. Set. pap. 95.00 (ISBN 0-686-56758-7, M-6360). French & Eur.

Centre De Documentation De L'Armement. Lexique Thematique des Descripteurs et Identificateurs. 151p. (Fr.). 1976. pap. 35.00 (ISBN 0-686-56742-0, M-6371). French & Eur.

Centre De Mathematique Sociale Ecole Des Hautes Etudes En Sciences Sociales. Combinatorics Graphs & Algebra. (Methods & Models in the Social Sciences: No. 5). (Illus., Orig.). 1976. text ed. 16.80x (ISBN 90-2797-511-6). Mouton.

Centre De Recherche et D'information Socio-Politiques see Gerard-Libois, J. & Verhaegen, B.

Centre de Recherche Pour un Tresor de la Langue Francaise, ed. Dictionnaire des Frequences, Vocabulaire Litteraire Des 19th et 20th Siecles, 4 vols. 2284p. (Fr.). 1976. pap. 110.00 (ISBN 0-686-56841-9, M-6620). French & Eur.

Centre de Recherche pour un Tresor de la Langue Francaise. Tresor de la Francaise: Dictionnaire du XIXe et du XXe Siecles (1789-1960, 4 vols. Set. 175.00 (ISBN 0-685-36650-2). French & Eur.

Centre d'etudes de la Musique Francaise aux XVIII et XIX Siecles Universite de Paris-Sorbonne, ed. Catalogue Thematique des Sources du Grand Motet Francais 1663-1792. 234p. 1984. lib. bdg. 33.00 (ISBN 3-598-10561-4). K G Saur.

Centre for Advanced Study in the Developmental Sciences Study Group. The Origins of Human Social Relations: Proceedings. Schaffer, H. R., ed. 1971. 49.50 (ISBN 0-12-622550-8). Acad Pr.

Centre for Contemporary Cultural Studies. The Empire Strikes Back: Race & Racism in 70's Britain. 324p. 1984. pap. 10.95 (ISBN 0-09-149381-1, Pub. by Hutchinson Educ). Longwood Pub Group.

--On Ideology. 265p. 1984. pap. 10.95 (ISBN 0-09-134151-5, Pub. by Hutchinson Educ). Longwood Pub Group.

--Unpopular Education: Schooling & Social Democracy in England Since 1944. (Illus.). 312p. 1984. pap. 10.95 (ISBN 0-09-138961-5, Pub. by Hutchinson Educ). Longwood Pub Group.

Centre for Information on Language Teaching & Research, ed. Language Teaching & Linguistics. LC 77-88671. 1978. 13.95 (ISBN 0-521-21926-4). Cambridge U Pr.

Centre for Scientific Culture Ettore Majorana, International School of Electron Microscopy. Electron Microscopy in Material Science. Valdre, U., ed. 1972. 107.00 (ISBN 0-12-780584-2). Acad Pr.

Centre for the Analysis of Conflict, London. International Relations Theory: A Critical Bibliography. Groom, A. J. & Mitchell, C. R., eds. 222p. 1978. 27.50 (ISBN 0-89397-026-3); pap. 17.50 (ISBN 0-903804-17-4). Nichols Pub.

Centre international de synthese, Paris. Encyclopedie et les encyclopedistes. 1971. Repr. of 1932 ed. lib. bdg. 26.50 (ISBN 0-8337-1059-1). B Franklin.

Centre International Du Droit Des Affaires (CIDA) Lexique Pratique Commercial. (Fr.). 1973. pap. 25.00x (ISBN 2-85273-001-4). Marlin.

Centre, Michael. In Search of God-the Solar Connection. LC 78-73706. (Illus.). 1978. pap. 4.95 (ISBN 0-932876-01-3). Centre Ent.

Centre National de la Recherce Scientifique, ed. Annuaire Francais de Droit International: 1981, Vol. XXVII (1981) LC 57-28515. 1206p. (Fr.). 1982. cancelled (ISBN 2-222-03121-4). Intl Pubns Serv.

Centre National de la Recherche Scientifique. Annuaire Francais de Droit International: Vol. 26. LC 57-28515. 1316p. 1981. cancelled (ISBN 2-222-02909-0). Intl Pubns Serv.

Centre National De la Recherche Scientifique, ed. Annuaire Francais de Droit International, Vol. 25. LC 57-28515. 1288p. 1979. cancelled (ISBN 2-222-02737-3). Intl Pubns Serv.

Centre National de la Recherche Scientifique. Ionic Bombardment: Theory & Applications. (Illus.). 360p. 1964. 93.75 (ISBN 0-677-10040-X). Gordon.

--Mechanics of Turbulence. (Illus.). 490p. 1964. 129.50 (ISBN 0-677-10050-7). Gordon.

--New Methods of Instrumental Spectroscopy. 210p. 1972. 57.75 (ISBN 0-677-30240-1). Gordon.

--New Physical & Chemical Properties of Metals of Very High Purity. (Illus.). 502p. 1965. 132.95 (ISBN 0-677-10060-4). Gordon.

Centre on Transnational Corporations United Nations. Main Features & Trends in Petroleum & Mining Agreements: A Technical Paper. (Illus.). write for info. Amer Bar Assn.

Centrella, Joan, et al, eds. Numerical Astrophysics. 548p. 1985. text ed. write for info (ISBN 0-86720-048-0). Jones & Bartlett.

Centro Internationale Mathematico Estivo. Bifurcation Theory & Applications: Lectures Given at the Second Session of the Centro Internationale Mathematico Estivo held at Montecatini, Italy, June 24-July 2, 1983. Salvadori, L., ed. (Lecture Notes in Mathematics Ser.: Vol. 1057). vii, 223p. 1984. pap. 12.50 (ISBN 0-387-12931-6). Springer-Verlag.

Centro Nuclear De Puerto Rico. Simposio Sobre Energia Nuclear y el Desarrollo De Latinoamerica. pap. 3.75 (ISBN 0-8477-2304-6). U of PR Pr.

CEntro Pedagogico, Inc. Staff, ed. see Velez, Rigoberto P.

Centro Studi e Laboratori Telecomumicazioni. Optical Fiber Communication. (Illus.). 928p. 1981. 54.50 (ISBN 0-07-014882-1). McGraw.

Centuori, Walter J. A Concordance to the Poets of the Dolce Stil Novo, 5 vols. LC 77-294. 1977. 185.00 (ISBN 0-8032-0929-0). U of Nebr Pr.

Century Association, New York. Robert Henri & Five of His Pupils: Loan Exhibition of Paintings, April 5, to June 1, 1946. LC 74-160918. (Biography Index Reprint Ser). Repr. of 1946 ed. 16.00 (ISBN 0-8369-8081-6). Ayer Co Pubs.

CEP & Boothe, Norris. Cleaning up: The Cost of Refinery Pollution Control. Haley, Mary J., ed. LC 75-10535. 1975. pap. 25.00 (ISBN 0-87871-002-7). CEP.

CEP & Komanoff, Charles. Power Plant Performance: Nuclear & Coal Capacity Factors & Economics. Armentrout, Fred, ed. LC 76-50521. 1976. pap. 300.00 (ISBN 0-87871-004-3). CEP.

CEP & Simich, Tina L. Shortchanged Update: Minorities & Women in Banking. Schwartz, Wendy C., ed. LC 76-50522. 1976. pap. 39.95 (ISBN 0-87871-005-1). CEP.

CEP & White, Ronald. The Price of Power Update: Electric Utilities & the Environment. LC 77-92111. 1977. pap. 25.00 (ISBN 0-87871-007-8). CEP.

CEP, et al. Cracking Down: Oil Refining & Pollution Control. Haley, Mary J., ed. LC 75-10534. 1975. pap. 45.00 (ISBN 0-685-83301-1). CEP.

Cepeda, Orlando & Markus, Robert. High & Inside: Orlando Cepeda's Story. (Illus.). 1984. 13.95 (ISBN 0-89651-302-5). Icarus.

Cepede, M. & Abensour, E. S. Rural Problems in the Alpine Region: An International Study. 201p. (Orig.). 1961. pap. 7.25 (ISBN 92-5-101667-4, F416, FAO). Unipub.

Cepek, Dick & Wheelock, Walt. Rough Riding. (Illus.). 1969. wrappers 1.00 (ISBN 0-910856-29-X). La Siesta.

Ceperley, Gordon. A Promised Land for a Chosen People. LC 79-65616. (Illus., Orig.). 1979. pap. 2.50 (ISBN 0-915540-25-8). Friends Israel-Spearhead Pr.

Cepican, Bob & Ali, Waleed. Yesterday... Came Suddenly: The Definitive History of the Beatles. (Illus.). 320p. (Orig.). 1984. pap. 12.95 (ISBN 0-87795-620-0, Pub. by Priam). Arbor Hse.

Ceplair, Larry & Englund, Steven. The Inquisition in Hollywood: Politics in the Film Community, 1930-1960. 550p. 1983. pap. 9.95 (ISBN 0-520-04886-5). U of Cal Pr.

Ceppede, Jean de La see De la Ceppede, Jean.

Cera, Mary J. & Bisignano, Judith. Creating Your Future: Level 1. (Illus.). 72p. 1982. 6.95 (ISBN 0-910141-00-2, KP107). Kino Pubns.

Ceram, C. W. Gods, Graves, & Scholars: The Story of Archaeology. rev. ed. LC 67-11119. (Illus.). 1967. 20.00 (ISBN 0-394-42661-4). Knopf.

--The Secret of the Hittites: The Discovery of an Ancient Empire. (Illus.). 312p. 1973. pap. 4.95 (ISBN 0-8052-0397-4). Schocken.

Cerami & Washington. Sickle Cell Anemia. LC 72-93681. 1973. 8.95 (ISBN 0-89388-068-X). Okpaku Communications.

Cerami, Charles A. More Profit, Less Risk. 225p. 1984. 8.95 (ISBN 0-346-16012-X). Cornerstone.

--More Profits, Less Risk: Your New Financial Strategy. LC 82-7775. 240p. 1982. 14.95 (ISBN 0-07-010324-0). McGraw.

Ceraskin, Emanuel, et al. The Vitamin C Connection. LC 82-48657. 256p. 1983. 13.41i (ISBN 0-06-038024-1, HarpT). Har-Row.

Ceravolo, Joseph. Millenium Dust. 7.00x (ISBN 0-318-04051-4); pap. 3.50x (ISBN 0-318-04052-2). Human Res Inst.

--Spring in This World of Poor Mutts. LC 68-56371. (Frank O'Hara Award Ser.). 1978. 17.95 (ISBN 0-916190-20-X); pap. 6.00 (ISBN 0-916190-21-8). Full Court NY.

--Transmigration Solo. LC 79-1068. 1979. signed 15.00 (ISBN 0-915124-22-X, Pub. by Toothpaste); pap. 4.00 (ISBN 0-915124-21-1). Coffee Hse.

Cerboni, Giuseppe. Primi Saggi di Logismografia Presentati, All' XI Congresso Degli Scienziati Italiani in Roma. Brief, Richard P., ed. LC 80-1477. (Dimensions of Accounting Theory & Practice Ser.). (Ital.). 1981. Repr. of 1873 ed. lib. bdg. 14.00x (ISBN 0-405-13507-6). Ayer Co Pubs.

Cerchione, Angelo J., et al, eds. Master Planning the Aviation Environment. LC 74-125171. pap. 56.00 (ISBN 0-317-28053-8, 2025553). Bks Demand UMI.

Cercignani, C., ed. Kinetic Theories & the Boltzmann Equation: Lectures Given at the 1st Session of the Centro Interrazionale Matematico Estivo (C. I. M. E.) Held at Montecatini, Italy, June 10-18, 1981. (Lecture Notes in Mathematics: Vol. 1048). vii, 248p. 1984. pap. 15.50 (ISBN 0-387-12899-9). Springer-Verlag.

Cercignani, Carlo. Mathematical Methods in Kinetic Theory. LC 69-15832. (Illus.). 227p. 1969. 29.50x (ISBN 0-306-30386-8, Plenum Pr). Plenum Pub.

Cercignani, Fausto. Shakespeare's Works & Elizabethan Pronunciation. 1981. 95.00x (ISBN 0-19-811937-2). Oxford U Pr.

Cercone, N. J., ed. Computational Linguistics. (International Series in Modern Applied Mathematics & Computer Science: Vol. 5). (Illus.). 200p. 1983. 37.50 (ISBN 0-08-030253-X). Pergamon.

Cerdic Colloquium, 4th, Strasbourg, May 10-12, 1973. Liberation Theology & the Message of Salvation: Proceedings. Metz, Rene & Schlick, Jean, eds. Gelzer, David G., tr. LC 78-7540. (Pittsburgh Theological Monographs: No. 20). 1978. pap. 8.75 (ISBN 0-915138-26-3). Pickwick.

Cerdonio, M. & Noble, R. W. Introductory Biophysics. 220p. 1984. 26.00 (ISBN 9971-966-33-6). Taylor & Francis.

Cereijido, Marcelino & Rotunno, Catalina A. Introduction to the Study of Biological Membranes. 272p. 1970. 56.75 (ISBN 0-677-02410-X). Gordon.

Ceres. The Healing Power of Herbal Teas: A Guide to Growing, Preparing, & Using Herbs for Alleviating Minor Ailments. (Illus.). 128p. 1985. pap. 6.95 (ISBN 0-7225-0885-9). Thorsons Pubs.

Ceresa, R. J. Block & Graft Copolymerization, Vol. 1. LC 72-5713. pap. 97.30 (ISBN 0-317-29348-6, 2024001). Bks Demand UMI.

Ceresa, R. J., ed. Block & Graft Copolymerization, 2 vols. LC 72-5713. 402p. 1976. Vol. 2. 89.95x (ISBN 0-471-14228-X, Pub. by Wiley-Interscience). Wiley.

--Block & Graft Copolymerization, Vol. 2. LC 72-5713. pap. 105.00 (ISBN 0-317-30330-9, 2024808). Bks Demand UMI.

Cereteli, I. G. Vospominanija O Fevral'skoj Revoljucii, 2 vols. (Etudes Sur L'histoire L'economie et la Sociologie Des Pays Slaves: No. 7). 1963. pap. 50.40x (ISBN 90-2796-127-1). Mouton.

Cerezo de Ponce, Engracia & Carrillo Romero, Ricarda. La Comunicacion Escrita: Manual de Redaccion. rev. ed. (UPREX, Manuales: No. 17). pap. 2.50 (ISBN 0-8477-0017-8). U of PR Pr.

Cerf, ed. see Henry, O.

Cerf, Aleeza. Say It in Modern Hebrew. (Orig.). pap. 2.50 (ISBN 0-486-20805-2). Dover.

Cerf, Bennett. At Random: The Reminiscences of Bennett Cerf. LC 77-1867. 1977. 12.95 (ISBN 0-394-47877-0). Random.

--Sixteen Famous British Plays. Cartmell, Van H., ed. 39.95 (ISBN 0-88411-265-9, Pub. by Aeonian Pr). Amereon Ltd.

--Stories to Make You Feel Better. (General Ser.). 1973. lib. bdg. 9.95 (ISBN 0-8161-6081-3, Large Print Bks). G K Hall.

--Stories to Make You Feel Better. 1972. 12.45 (ISBN 0-394-47553-4, BYR). Random.

Cerf, Bennett, ed. Famous Ghost Stories. 1956. pap. 3.95 (ISBN 0-394-70140-2, Vin, V140). Random.

--Four Contemporary American Plays. Incl. Tenth Man. Chayevsky, Paddy; Raisin in the Sun. Lansberry, Lorraine; Toys in the Attic. Hellman, Lillian; Andersonville Trial. Levitt, Sail. (Orig.). 1961. pap. 4.95 (ISBN 0-394-70203-4, V-203, Vin). Random.

--Great Modern Short Stories. (YA) 1955. pap. 6.95 (ISBN 0-394-70127-5, Vin, V127). Random.

--Plays of Our Time. 1967. 22.95 (ISBN 0-394-40661-3, BYR). Random.

--Riddle-De-Dee. 1962. 10.95 (ISBN 0-394-44304-7, BYR). Random.

Cerf, Bennett & Cartmell, Van H., eds. Favorite One Act Plays. 22.95 (ISBN 0-88411-264-0, Pub. by Aeonian Pr). Amereon Ltd.

--Thirty Famous One-Act Plays. LC 49-9032. 1943. 6.95 (ISBN 0-394-60473-3). Modern Lib.

Cerf, Bennett, jt. ed. see Cartmell, Van H.

Cerf, Bennett A. Bennett Cerf's Book of Animal Riddles. LC 64-11246. (gr. 2-3). 1964. PLB 5.99 (ISBN 0-394-90034-0). Beginner.

--Bennett Cerf's Book of Laughs. LC 59-13387. (Illus.). (gr. 1-2). 1959. PLB 5.99 (ISBN 0-394-90011-1). Beginner.

--Bennett Cerf's Book of Riddles. LC 60-13492. (Illus.). (gr. 1-2). 1960. 4.95 (ISBN 0-394-80015-X); PLB 5.99 (ISBN 0-394-90015-4). Beginner.

--Famous Ghost Stories. Repr. lib. bdg. 19.95 (ISBN 0-88411-146-6, Pub. by Aeonian Pr). Amereon Ltd.

--More Riddles. LC 61-11727. (Illus.). (gr. k-3). 1961. 4.95 (ISBN 0-394-80024-9); PLB 5.99 (ISBN 0-394-90024-3). Beginner.

Cerf, Bennett A., jt. ed. see Cartmell, Van H.

Cerf, Bennettt A., et al, eds. The Fireside Book of War Humor. 254p. Repr. lib. bdg. 14.40x (ISBN 0-88411-177-6, Pub. by Aeonian Pr). Amereon Ltd.

Cerf, C., jt. auth. see Lerner, S.

Cerf, Christopher & Navasky, Victor. The Experts Speak. LC 83-47741. (Illus.). 400p. 1984. 19.45 (ISBN 0-394-52061-0); pap. 9.95 (ISBN 0-394-71334-6). Pantheon.

Cerf, Kenneth, ed. see Hester, William.

Cerf, Martin, jt. auth. see Atkinson, Terry.

Cerf, Vinton G., jt. auth. see McQuillan, John M.

Cerf, Walter, ed. see Hegel.

Cerf, Walter, tr. see Hegel.

Cerfberr, Anatole & Christophe, Jules. Repertory of the Comedies Humaines of Balzac. 75.00 (ISBN 0-87968-319-8). Gordon Pr.

CERI, jt. auth. see OECD.

Ceri, jt. auth. see OECD Staff.

Ceri, S. Methodology & Tools for Data Design. 256p. 1983. 42.75 (ISBN 0-444-86557-8, 1-33-83, North-Holland). Elsevier.

Ceri, S. & Pelagatti, G. Distributed Databases: Principles & Systems. 1984. 37.50 (ISBN 0-07-010829-3). McGraw.

CERI Staff, jt. auth. see OECD Staff.

Ceriani, Roberto L., ed. Monoclonal Antibodies & Breast Cancer. (Developments in Onocology Ser.). 1985. lib. bdg. 47.50 (ISBN 0-89838-739-6, Pub. by Martinus Nijhoff Netherlands). Kluwer Academic.

Cerimele, Decio. Kaposi's Sarcoma. LC 84-13423. (Illus.). 168p. 1985. text ed. 35.00 (ISBN 0-89335-208-X). SP Med & Sci Bks.

Cerio, Edwin. That Capri Air. 25.00 (ISBN 0-89984-007-8). Century Bookbindery.

Cerkasov, I. D., et al. Eighteen Papers on Statistics & Probability. LC 61-9803. (Selected Translations on Mathematical Statistics & Probability Ser.: Vol. 3). 1963. 29.00 (ISBN 0-8218-1453-2, STAPRO-3). Am Math.

Cerling, Charles. The Divorced Christian. 1984. 9.95 (ISBN 0-8010-2495-1); pap. 5.95 (ISBN 0-8010-2486-2). Baker Bk.

--Freedom from Bad Habits. LC 84-62384. 141p. (Orig.). 1984. pap. 5.95 (ISBN 0-89840-079-1). Heres Life.

Cerling, Charles E. Assertiveness & the Christian. 140p. 1983. pap. 4.95 (ISBN 0-8423-0083-X). Tyndale.

Cermak. How to Repair Your Own 35mm Camera. 224p. 1981. o.p 14.95 (ISBN 0-8306-9637-7); pap. 10.25 (ISBN 0-8306-1270-X, 1270). TAB Bks.

Cermak, J. E., ed. Wind Engineering: Proceedings of the 5th International Conference, Colorado State University, USA, July 8-14, 1979, 2 vols. LC 80-40753. (Illus.). 1400p. 1980. Set. 235.00 (ISBN 0-08-024745-8). Pergamon.

Cermak, Jack E. Applications of Fluid Mechanics to Wind Engineering: Presented at the Winter Annual Meeting of ASME, New York, N. Y. November 17-21, 1974. pap. 20.00 (ISBN 0-317-08137-3, 2016871). Bks Demand UMI.

Cermak, L. S. & Craik, F. I., eds. Levels of Processing in Human Memory. 496p. 1979. 45.00x (ISBN 0-89859-357-3). L Erlbaum Assocs.

Cermak, Laird S. Human Memory & Amnesia. LC 80-395860. 416p. 1982. text ed. 39.95x (ISBN 0-89859-095-7). L Erlbaum Assocs.

--Improving Your Memory. LC 76-26011. (McGraw-Hill Paperbacks). 1976. pap. 5.95 (ISBN 0-07-010325-9). McGraw.

--Psychology of Learning: Research & Theory. LC 74-22534. (Illus.). pap. 77.90 (ISBN 0-8357-9970-0, 2012475). Bks Demand UMI.

Cermak, Laird S., jt. auth. see Butters, Nelson.

Cermak, V. & Haenel, R., eds. Geothermics & Geothermal Energy: Symposium Held During the Joint General Assemblies of EGS & ESC, Budapest, August 1980. (Illus.). 299p. 1982. pap. text ed. 36.00 (ISBN 3-510-65109-X). Lubrecht & Cramer.

Cermak, V. & Rybach, L., eds. Terrestrial Heat Flow in Europe. (Illus.). 1979. 59.00 (ISBN 0-387-09440-7). Springer-Verlag.

Cerminara, Gina. Edgar Cayce Revisited & Other Candid Commentaries. Horwege, Richard A., ed. LC 83-16321. 160p. (Orig.). 1984. pap. 5.95 (ISBN 0-89865-324-X, Unilaw). Donning Co.

--Insights for the Age of Aquarius. LC 76-6173. 314p. 1976. pap. 5.75 (ISBN 0-8356-0483-7, Quest). Theos Pub Hse.

--Many Lives, Many Loves. 3rd ed. LC 63-13710. 245p. 1981. pap. 6.95 (ISBN 0-87516-429-3). De Vorss.

--Many Mansions. 1972. pap. 3.50 (ISBN 0-451-12728-5, AE2728, Sig). NAL.

Cernada, George P. Knowledge into Action. (Community Health Education Monographs: Vol. 1). 168p. 1982. pap. text ed. 9.95x (ISBN 0-89503-031-4). Baywood Pub.

Cerna-Heyrovska, J., jt. auth. see Knobloch, E.

Cernak, Anne, jt. auth. see Basile, Leonard.

Cernea, Michael M. Measuring Project Impact: Monitoring & Evaluation in the PIDER Rural Development Project - Mexico. (Working Paper: No. 332). vi, 131p. 1979. 5.00 (ISBN 0-686-36071-0, WP-0332). World Bank.

Cernea, Michael M. & Tepping, Benjamin J. A System of Monitoring & Evaluating Agricultural Extension Projects. (Working Paper: No. 272). vi, 115p. 1977. 5.00 (ISBN 0-686-36079-6, WP-0272). World Bank.

Cernea, Michael M., ed. Putting People First: Sociological Dimensions of Rural Development. 1985. 24.95 (ISBN 0-19-520465-4). Oxford U Pr.

Cernea, Michael M., et al, eds. Agricultural Extension By Training & Visit: The Asian Experience. 176p. 13.50 (ISBN 0-318-02828-X, WP0301). World Bank.

Cernevak, Michael M. Continuing Education Log Book for Emergency Medical Technicians-Ambulance. 99p. 1978. pap. 7.50 (ISBN 0-8151-1519-9). Year Bk Med.

Cerney, J. Handbook of Unusual & Unorthodox Healing Methods. 1977. 12.95 (ISBN 0-13-382739-9, Reward); pap. 3.95 (ISBN 0-13-382721-6). P-H.

Cerney, J. V. Acupuncture Without Needles. 1975. pap. 5.95 (ISBN 0-346-12351-8). Cornerstone.

--Complete Book of Athletic Taping Techniques. LC 76-156762. 1971. 16.95x (ISBN 0-13-155572-3, Parker). P-H.

--Dynamic Laws of Thinking Rich. 1967. pap. 4.95 (ISBN 0-13-221374-5, Reward). P-H.

Cerney, Joseph, ed. Nuclear Spectroscopy & Reactions, 4 pts. Set. 274.50; Pt. A 1974. 92.00 (ISBN 0-12-165201-7); Pt. B 1974. 94.00 (ISBN 0-12-165202-5); Pt. C 1974. 94.00 (ISBN 0-12-165203-3); Pt. D 1975. 65.00 (ISBN 0-12-165204-1). Acad Pr.

Cernica, John N. Geotechnical Engineering. 1982. text ed. 40.95 (ISBN 0-03-059182-1). HR&W.

--Strength of Materials. 2nd ed. LC 76-57840. 1977. text ed. 34.95 (ISBN 0-03-077090-4, HoltC). HR&W.

Cernikov, S. N., et al. Algebra. (Translations Ser.: No. 1, Vol. 1). 1968. 24.00 (ISBN 0-8218-1601-2, TRANS 1-1). Am Math.

--Fourteen Papers on Groups & Semigroups. LC 51-5559. (Translations Ser.: No. 2, Vol. 36). 1964. 32.00 (ISBN 0-8218-1736-1, TRANS 2-36). Am Math.

--Seven Papers on Algebra. LC 51-5559. (Translations Ser.: No. 2, Vol. 69). 1968. 34.00 (ISBN 0-8218-1769-8, TRANS 2-69). Am Math.

--Twelve Papers on Algebra, Algebraic Geometry & Topology. LC 51-5559. (Translations Ser.: No. 2, Vol. 84). 1969. 36.00 (ISBN 0-8218-1784-1, TRANS 2-84). Am Math.

--Twelve Papers on Algebra & Real Functions. LC 51-5559. (Translations Ser.: No. 2, Vol. 17). 1961. 30.00 (ISBN 0-8218-1717-5, TRANS 2-17). Am Math.

Cernobous, Wayne J. Millie Milkweed Seed Meets the Genny Geranium Gang. (Illus.). 46p. (Orig.). (gr. k-5). 1984. pap. 5.95 (ISBN 0-9615065-0-4). Kinnickinnic Pr.

Cernovodeanu, Paul, jt. auth. see Stanciu, Ion.

Cernuda, Luis. Selected Poems of Luis Cernuda. Gibbons, Reginald, tr. from Span. LC 75-3767. 1976. 24.00x (ISBN 0-520-02984-4). U of Cal Pr.

Cernuda, Ralph & Lawson, Greg, photos by. California. LC 82-90775. (Illus.). 72p. (Orig., Eng., Span., Fr., Ger., Jap.). 1983. pap. 9.95 (ISBN 0-9606704-6-7). First Choice.

Cernuschi, Alberto. The Constructive Manifesto. LC 82-18903. 1983. 8.50 (ISBN 0-8022-2411-3). Philos Lib.

Cernuschi, Felix. Experimento, Razonamiento y Creacion en Fisica. 3rd ed. (Serie de Fisica Monografia: No. 5). 151p. 1981. pap. text ed. 3.50 (ISBN 0-8270-1417-1). OAS.

Cerny, J. Hieratic Inscriptions from the Tomb of Tut Ankhamun. 37p. 30.00x (ISBN 0-900416-11-4, Pub. by Griffith Inst). State Mutual Bk.

--Paper & Books in Ancient Egypt. 1985. pap. 5.00 (ISBN 0-89005-205-0). Ares.

Cerny, Jaroslav. Ancient Egyptian Religion. LC 78-9931. 1979. Repr. of 1957 ed. lib. bdg. 24.75x (ISBN 0-313-21104-3, CEAE). Greenwood.

--Coptic Etymological Dictionary. LC 69-10192. 350p. 1976. 195.00 (ISBN 0-521-07228-X). Cambridge U Pr.

--Egyptian Stelae in the Bankes Collection. (Bankes Collection Bks.). 33p. 1958. pap. text ed. 11.00x (ISBN 0-900416-07-6, Pub. by Aris & Philips England). Humanities.

--Hieratic Inscriptions from the Tomb of Tutankhamun. (Tutankhamun's Tomb Ser.: Vol. II). 29p. 1965. text ed. 24.50x (ISBN 0-900416-11-4, Pub. by Aris & Phillips England). Humanities.

Cerny, Jaroslav & Gardiner, Alan. Hieratic Ostraca, Vol. I. 35p. 1957. text ed. 80.50x (ISBN 0-900416-36-X, Pub. by Aris & Philips England). Humanities.

Cerny, Jerome A., jt. auth. see Ollendick, Thomas H.

Cerny, Johni & Eakle, Arlene. Ancestry's Guide to Research: Case Studies in American Genealogy. LC 84-72694. 364p. (Orig.). 1985. pap. 10.95 (ISBN 0-916489-01-9). Ancestry.

Cerny, Johni, jt. ed. see Eakle, Arlene H.

Cerny, Karl, ed. Scandinavia at the Polls. 1977. pap. 8.25 (ISBN 0-8447-3240-0). Am Enterprise.

Cerny, Karl H., ed. Germany at the Polls: The Bundestag Election of 1976. 1978. pap. 7.25 (ISBN 0-8447-3310-5). Am Enterprise.

Cerny, Ladislav. Elementary Statics & Strength of Materials. LC 80-20442. 1981. 38.00x (ISBN 0-07-010339-9). McGraw.

Cerny, Lothar. Erinnerung Bei Dickens. (Bochum Studies in English: No. 3). (Illus.). 284p. (Ger.). 1975. pap. 16.00 (ISBN 90-6032-063-8). Benjamins North Am.

Cerny, Philip & Schain, Martin, eds. French Politics & Public Policy. 1980. 27.50 (ISBN 0-312-30509-5). St Martin.

--Socialism: The State & Public in France. 220p. (Orig.). 29.95 (ISBN 0-416-01131-4, 9384); pap. 12.95 (ISBN 0-416-01161-6, 9416). Methuen Inc.

Cerny, Philip, jt. ed. see Howorth, Jolyon.

Cerny, Philip G. The Politics of Grandeur: Ideological Aspects of De Gaulle's Foreign Policy. LC 83-23725. 319p. 1984. pap. 10.50 (ISBN 0-86187-360-2). F Pinter Pubs.

--Social Movements & Protest in France. LC 81-21217. 270p. 1982. 25.00x (ISBN 0-312-73310-0). St Martin.

Cerny, Philip G., ed. Social Movements & Protest in France. 270p. 1982. pap. 12.00 (ISBN 0-86187-214-2). F Pinter Pubs.

Cerny, Philip G. & Schain, Martin A., eds. French Politics & Public Policy. 1981. pap. 10.95x (ISBN 0-416-30850-3, NO. 2381). Methuen Inc.

Cerny, Phillip G. The Politics of Grandeur. LC 79-50232. 1980. 42.50 (ISBN 0-521-22863-8). Cambridge U Pr.

Cernyak-Spatz, Susan E. German Holocaust Literature. LC 83-49045. (American University Studies I (Germanic Languages & Literature): Vol. 29). 115p. 1985. text ed. 19.00 (ISBN 0-8204-0072-6). P Lang Pubs.

Ceron, J. D., Jr. Children of the Devil. 1983. 11.95 (ISBN 0-533-05656-X). Vantage.

Cerovski, John S., ed. see Naunton, Robert.

Cerqueira-Gomes, M., ed. see International Symposium, Portugal, July, 1973.

Cerquiglini, S., et al, eds. see International Seminar on Biomechanics, 3rd, Rome, 1971.

Cerra. The Minnesota Manual of Critical Care. 1985. 25.00 (ISBN 0-8016-1010-9). Mosby.

--The Minnesota Manual of Hospital Based Nutritional Support. 1984. 20.00 (ISBN 0-8016-0937-2). Mosby.

Cerra, Frank J., ed. see Wiatrowski, Claude A. & House, Charles H.

Cerreta, Florindo, tr. The Deceived: A Comedy of the Italian Renaissance. (Renaissance Sources in Translation). (Illus.). 1978. lib. bdg. 15.95 (ISBN 0-89102-107-8). B Franklin.

Cerretelli, P., et al, eds. High Altitude Deterioration. (Medicine & Sport Science: Vol. 19). (Illus.). xvi, 228p. 1985. 61.75 (ISBN 3-8055-3972-X). S Karger.

Cerreto, Frank. Power Skills in Mathematics II. (Illus.). 1979. pap. 4.95 (ISBN 0-07-010338-0). McGraw.

Cerretti, Elena R., jt. auth. see Schanne, Otto F.

Cerro Copper & Brass Company. Investigation of Materials for Use in Copper Alloy Die Casting Dies. 150p. 1966. 22.50 (ISBN 0-317-34533-8, 59). Intl Copper.

Certeau, Michel de. The Practice of Everyday Life. Rendall, Steven F., tr. from Fr. LC 83-18070. 260p. 1985. 24.95x (ISBN 0-520-04750-8). U of Cal Pr.

Certigny, Henry. Le Douanier Rousseau en Son Temps: Biographie et Catalogue Raisonne, 2 vols. (Illus.). 699p. (Fr.). 1984. Set. 395.00 (ISBN 0-87817-305-6). Hacker.

Certo, Dominic N. Success-Pure & Simple (How to Make it in Business, Sports & the Arts) LC 83-90470. (Illus.). 203p. 1983. pap. 9.95x (ISBN 0-915755-00-9). Hillside Pubns.

--The Valor of Francesco D'Amini. (Orig.). 1979. pap. 2.25 (ISBN 0-532-23111-2). Woodhill.

Certo, Nick, et al, eds. Public School Integration of Severely Handicapped Students: Rational Issues & Progressive Alternatives. LC 83-15212. (Illus.). 343p. (Orig.). 1984. pap. text ed. 19.95 (ISBN 0-933716-35-4, 354). P H Brookes.

Certo, Samuel C. Principles of Modern Management. 3rd ed. 608p. 1986. text ed. price not set (ISBN 0-697-00285-3); price not set instr's. manual (ISBN 0-697-00512-7); price not set study guide (ISBN 0-697-00511-9); price not set test item file (ISBN 0-697-00514-3); price not set transparencies (ISBN 0-697-00513-5); price not set lecture enrichment kit (ISBN 0-697-00518-6); price not set planning guide (ISBN 0-697-00517-8). Wm C Brown.

--Principles of Modern Management: Functions & Systems. 2nd ed. 608p. 1983. text ed. write for info (ISBN 0-697-08084-6); instrs.' manual avail. (ISBN 0-697-08179-6); Experiential Wkbk. avail. (ISBN 0-697-08092-7); Bk of Readings avail. (ISBN 0-697-08090-0); Lecture Enrichment Kit avail. (ISBN 0-697-08099-4); instr's. manual - Readings avail. (ISBN 0-697-08091-9); transparencies avail. (ISBN 0-697-08190-7); Test Manual avail. (ISBN 0-697-08197-4); instructional planning guide avail. (ISBN 0-697-08268-7). Wm C Brown.

Certo, Samuel C. & Applebaum, Steven H. Principles of Modern Management: A Canadian Perspective. 608p. 1983. text ed. write for info. (ISBN 0-697-08168-0); instrs.' manual avail. (ISBN 0-697-08174-5). Wm C Brown.

Certo, Samuel C. & Graf, Lee A. Experiencing Modern Management Workbook. 2nd ed. 352p. 1983. pap. text ed. write for info. (ISBN 0-697-08092-7). Wm C Brown.

Certo, Samuel C., et al. Business. 656p. 1984. text ed. write for info (ISBN 0-697-08239-3); test item file avail. (ISBN 0-697-08266-0); lecture enrichment kit avail. (ISBN 0-697-00189-X); instructional planning guide avail. (ISBN 0-697-00186-5); study guide avail. (ISBN 0-697-08242-3); annotated business documents avail. (ISBN 0-697-00241-1); annotated film resource kit avail. (ISBN 0-697-08234-2); transparencies avail. (ISBN 0-697-00261-6); instr's. manual avail. (ISBN 0-697-08244-X). Wm C Brown.

Certon, M. J. & Davidson, H. F. Industrial Technology Transfer, No. 19. (NATO Advanced Study Applied Science Ser.). 480p. 1977. 45.50x (ISBN 90-286-0426-X). Sijthoff & Noordhoff.

Certon, Pierre see Expert, Henry.

Cerullo, John J. The Secularization of the Soul: Psychical Research in Modern Britain. LC 81-13322. 200p. 1982. text ed. 21.00 (ISBN 0-89727-028-2). ISHI PA.

Cerullo, Morris. From Judaism to Christianity. 96p. (Eng. & Sp.). 1976. 1.50 (ISBN 0-318-16871-5). World Evangelism.

Cerutti, Peter A., jt. ed. see Harris, Curtis C.

Cerutti, Toni. Guide to Composition in Italian. 1966. text ed. 8.95 (ISBN 0-521-04593-2). Cambridge U Pr.

Ceruzzi, Paul E. Reckoners: The Prehistory of the Digital Computer, From Relays to the Stored Program Concept, 1935-1945. LC 82-20980. (Contributions to the Study of Computer Science Ser.: No. 1). (Illus.). 240p. 1983. lib. bdg. 29.95 (ISBN 0-313-23382-9, CED/). Greenwood.

Cervantes. Don Quijote De la Mancha: Primer Parte. (Easy Reader, D). pap. 4.25 (ISBN 0-88436-056-3, 70275). EMC.

--The History of Don Quixote, 2 vols. Clark, J. W., ed. Set. 200.00 (ISBN 0-686-17755-X). Ridgeway Bks.

--The Spanish Ladie & Two Other Stories from Cervantes. Mabble, James, tr. (Illus.). 197p. 1981. Repr. of 1928 ed. lib. bdg. 45.00 (ISBN 0-89987-770-2). Darby Bks.

Cervantes see Allen, W. S.

Cervantes, Alex & Cervantes, E. DeMichael. Saturday with Daddy. LC 78-73527. (Illus.). (gr. k-4). Date not set. pap. price not set (ISBN 0-89799-079-X); pap. text ed. price not set (ISBN 0-89799-161-3). Dandelion Pr.

Cervantes, Alex, jt. auth. see Cervantes, Esther De Michael.

Cervantes, E. DeMichael, jt. auth. see Cervantes, Alex.

Cervantes, Esther De Michael & Cervantes, Alex. Senora Pepino & Her Bad Luck Cats: Senora Pepino y Sus Gatos de Mala Suerte. LC 76-4818. (Illus., Eng. & Span.). (gr. k-3). 1976. 5.95 (ISBN 0-87917-052-2). Ethridge.

Cervantes, Hermes, jt. auth. see Baca, Leonard.

Cervantes, Irma H. The Gifts. (Illus.). 50p. 1984. pap. 5.95x (ISBN 0-9609600-2-3). Five Windmills.

--Sparks, Flames & Cinders. (Illus.). 96p. 1982. 9.95x (ISBN 0-9609600-0-7). Five Windmills.

--Wing of Love. (Illus.). 72p. 1984. pap. 4.75x (ISBN 0-9609600-1-5). Five Windmills.

Cervantes, Jorge. Indoor Marijuana Horticulture. Bushwell, John & Greengenes, eds. (Illus.). 288p. 1984. pap. 14.95 (ISBN 0-932331-01-7). Interport U S A.

Cervantes, Lorna D. Emplumada. LC 80-54063. (Pitt Poetry Ser.). 77p. 1981. 12.95 (ISBN 0-8229-3436-1); pap. 5.95 (ISBN 0-8229-5327-7). U of Pittsburgh Pr.

Cervantes, M. Don Quixote. abr. ed. Starkie, Walter, tr. (YA) (RL 7). pap. 2.95 (ISBN 0-451-61987-0, ME1987, Ment). NAL.

Cervantes, Miguel. Don Quixote. Putnam, Samuel, tr. & intro. by. LC 83-42941. 1949. 10.95 (ISBN 0-394-60438-5). Modern Lib.

--El Ingenioso Hidalgo Don Quixote de la Mancha, I (1605) & II (1615, 2 vols. facsimile ed. 650p. 1968. Set. pap. 75.00 (ISBN 0-317-00542-1, Pub. by Hispanic Soc). Interbk Inc.

Cervantes, Miguel de. The Adventures of Don Quixote de la Mancha. (Children's Illustrated Classics Ser.). (Illus.). 384p. 1983. Repr. of 1953 ed. 15.00x (ISBN 0-460-05024-9, Pub. by J M Dent England). Biblio Dist.

--Aventuras de Don Quijote: Relatos Ilustrados. (Span.). 9.00 (ISBN 84-241-5412-6). E Torres & Sons.

--Don Quijote. LC 84-52573. (Classics for Kids Ser.). (Illus.). 32p. (Span.). (gr. 3 up). 1985. pap. 3.60 (ISBN 0-382-09023-3). Silver.

--Don Quixote. 1981. Repr. lib. bdg. 37.95 (ISBN 0-89966-383-4). Buccaneer Bks.

--Novelas Ejemplares. (Span.). 7.95 (ISBN 84-241-5613-7). E Torres & Sons.

--Rinconete & Cortadillo. pap. 2.50 (ISBN 0-8283-1453-5, IPL). Branden Pub Co.

Cervantes, Miguel de see Bentley, Eric.

Cervantes, Miguel De see De Cervantes, Miguel.

Cervantes, Miguel de see De Cervantes, Miguel.

Cervantes, Miguel De see De Cervantes, Miguel.

Cervantes, Miquel De. Don Quixote. LC 84-50432. (Classics for Kids Ser.). 1984. 5.96 (ISBN 0-382-06814-9). Silver.

Cervantes de Saavedra, Miguel. The Adventures of Don Quixote. Jones, Olive, ed. Cohen, J. M., tr. from Span. LC 79-23512. (Illus.). 1980. 10.95 (ISBN 0-416-87910-1, NO.0189). Methuen Inc.

Cervantes De Salazar, Francisco. Life in the Imperial & Loyal City of Mexico in New Spain. Shepard, Minnie L., tr. LC 79-100224. Repr. of 1953 ed. lib. bdg. 15.00x (ISBN 0-8371-3033-6, CELM). Greenwood.

Cervantes Gimeno, Fernando, ed. see Laplanche, Jean & Pontalis, Jean-Bertrand.

Cervantes Saavedra. The Portable Cervantes. Putnam, Samuel, tr. (Viking Portable Library: P57). 1976. pap. 7.95 (ISBN 0-14-015057-9). Penguin.

Cervantes Saavedra, Meguel. The History of Don Quixote of La Mancha Preceded by a Short Notice of the Life & Works of Motteux by Henri Vannlaun, 4 Vols. Lockhart, John G., ed. Motteux, tr. from Span. 1624p. 1983. Repr. of 1880 ed. lib. bdg. 100.00 set (ISBN 0-89987-148-8). Darby Bks.

Cervantes Saavedra, Miguel de. History of Don Quixote of the Mancha, 4 Vols. Shelton, Thomas, tr. LC 9-3440. (Tudor Translations, First Ser.: Nos. 13-16). Repr. of 1896 ed. Set. 180.00 (ISBN 0-404-51880-X); 40.00 ea. Vol. 1 (ISBN 0-404-51881-8). Vol. 2 (ISBN 0-404-51882-6). Vol. 3 (ISBN 0-404-51883-4). Vol. 4 (ISBN 0-404-51884-2). AMS Pr.

--Two Humorous Novels: A Diverting Dialogue Between Scipio & Bergansa & the Comical History of Rinconete & Cortadillo. Goadby, Robert, tr. LC 80-2474. Repr. of 1741 ed. 49.50 (ISBN 0-404-19106-1). AMS Pr.

Cervantes Saavedra, Miguil de. Interludes of Cervantes. Morley, S. Griswold, tr. LC 69-13852. 1948. lib. bdg. 39.75x (ISBN 0-8371-0976-0, CEIN). Greenwood.

Cervantes Saavedra, Miquel de. Three Exemplary Novels. Putnam, Samuel, tr. LC 81-20235. Orig. Title: Novelas Ejemplares. (Illus.). xxi, 232p. 1982. Repr. of 1950 ed. lib. bdg. 27.50x (ISBN 0-313-23346-2, CETN). Greenwood.

Cerve, Wishar S. Lemuria, el Continente Perdido del Pacifico. AMORC Staff, tr. from Eng. (Illus.). 191p. (Orig., Span.). 1980. pap. 7.00 (ISBN 0-912057-68-8, GS-512). AMORC.

--Lemuria: The Lost Continent of the Pacific. 17th ed. LC 31-34377. 1982. 12.50 (ISBN 0-912057-09-2, G-512). AMORC.

Cervenka, Edward J., jt. auth. see Saitz, Robert L.

Cervenka, Exene, jt. auth. see Lunch, Lydia.

Cervenka, Jaroslav & Koulischer, Lucien. Chromosomes in Human Cancer. (Illus.). 212p. 1973. photocopy ed. 21.50x (ISBN 0-398-02629-7). C C Thomas.

Cervenka, Zdenek, jt. auth. see Widstrand, Carl.

Cerveny, George. Mark the Wind's Power. 299p. 1982. 10.95 (ISBN 0-87770-272-1); pap. 5.95 (ISBN 0-87770-273-X). Ye Galleon.

Cervera, Alejo De see De Cervera, Alejo.

Cervera, Alejo de see De Cervera, Alejo.

Cervera, Joseph P. Modernismo: the Catalan Renaissance of the Arts. LC 75-23787. (Outstanding Dissertations in the Fine Arts - 19th Century). (Illus.). 1976. lib. bdg. 58.00 (ISBN 0-8240-1983-0). Garland Pub.

Cervera Tomas, Vicente, jt. ed. see Sills, David L.

Cerveri De Girona. Obras Completas. LC 80-2175. Repr. of 1947 ed. 72.50 (ISBN 0-404-19005-7). AMS Pr.

Cervetto, L., jt. ed. see Borsellino, A.

Cervical Spine Research Editorial Subcommittee, et al, eds. The Cervical Spine. (Illus.). 642p. 1983. text ed. 62.50 (ISBN 0-397-50510-8, 65-06554, Lippincott Medical). Lippincott.

Cervin, David R., ed. see Frey, Albert R.

Cervos-Navarro, J. & Ferszt, R., eds. Brain Edema. (Advances in Neurology: Vol. 28). (Illus.). 539p. 1980. text ed. 86.00 (ISBN 0-89004-482-1). Raven.

Cervos-Navarro, J. & Fritschka, E., eds. Cerebral Microcirculation & Metabolism. 500p. 1981. text ed. 79.00 (ISBN 0-89004-590-9). Raven.

Cervos-Navarro, J. & Sarkander, H. I., eds. Brain Aging: Neuropathology & Neuropharmacology. (Aging Ser.: Vol. 21). 454p. 1983. text ed. 83.50 (ISBN 0-89004-739-1). Raven.

Cervos-Navarro, J., et al, eds. The Cerebral Vessel Wall. LC 75-25110. 288p. 1976. 45.50 (ISBN 0-89004-071-0). Raven.

--Pathology of Cerebrospinal Microcirculation. LC 77-84125. (Advances in Neurology Ser.: Vol. 20). 632p. 1978. 80.50 (ISBN 0-89004-237-3). Raven.

Cervos-Navarro, J., et al, eds. see International Symposium, Berlin, Sep, 1973.

Cerwinske, Laura. Tropical Deco: The Architecture & Design of Old Miami Beach. LC 80-51596. (Illus.). 96p. (Orig.). 1980. pap. 14.95 (ISBN 0-8478-0345-7). Rizzoli Intl.

Cerwinske, Laura, jt. auth. see Rachlin, Norman S.

CES Industries. Ed-Lab Eight Hundred Exercise Manual: Programming for Ohm's Law, Unit 1. (Illus., Orig.). 1982. write for info. (ISBN 0-86711-029-5). CES Industries.

--Ed-Lab Eight Hundred Series Reference Manual: Operations & BASIC. (Illus., Orig.). 1983. write for info. (ISBN 0-86711-067-8). CES Industries.

--Ed-Lab Experiment Manual: Student Guide to Test Points; TV Trainer. (Illus., Orig.). (gr. 9-12). 1983. write for info. (ISBN 0-86711-044-9). CES Industries.

CES Industries, Inc. Ed-Lab Eight Hundred Exercise Manual: Interfaces, Unit 2. (Illus., Orig.). (gr. 9-12). 1982. write for info. (ISBN 0-86711-030-9). CES Industries.

--Ed-Lab Eight Hundred Experiment & Exercise Manual: Programming in BASIC. Rev. ed. (Illus.). (gr. 9-12). 1983. write for info. (ISBN 0-86711-029-5). CES Industries.

--Ed-Lab Eight Hundred Experiment Manual: Contactor Sensor Operation. (Illus., Orig.). (gr. 9-12). 1983. write for info. (ISBN 0-86711-048-1). CES Industries.

--Ed-Lab Eight Hundred Experiment Manual: EPROM Programming. (Illus., Orig.). (gr. 9-12). 1984. pap. write for info. (ISBN 0-86711-084-8). CES Industries.
--Ed-Lab Eight Hundred Experiment Manual: Infra-Red Sensor. (Illus., Orig.). (gr. 9-12). 1983. write for info. (ISBN 0-86711-047-3). CES Industries.
--Ed-Lab Eight Hundred Experiment Manual: Photocell Sensor. (Illus., Orig.). (gr. 9-12). 1983. write for info. (ISBN 0-86711-049-X). CES Industries.
--Ed-Lab Eight Hundred Experiment Manual: Robotics Interfacing. (Illus., Orig.). (gr. 9-12). 1983. write for info. (ISBN 0-86711-046-5). CES Industries.
--Ed-Lab Eight Hundred Experiment Manual: Talker Interfacing. (Illus., Orig.). (gr. 9-12). 1983. write for info. (ISBN 0-86711-069-4). CES Industries.
--Ed-Lab Eight Hundred Experiment Manual: Thermal Probe Sensor. (Illus., Orig.). (gr. 9-12). 1983. pap. write for info. (ISBN 0-86711-073-2). CES Industries.
--Ed-Lab Eight Hundred Experiment Manual: Touch Sensor. (Illus., Orig.). (gr. 9-12). 1983. write for info. (ISBN 0-86711-068-6). CES Industries.
--Ed-Lab Eighty Experiment Manual: Infra-Red Sensor. (Illus., Orig.). 1983. write for info. (ISBN 0-86711-065-1). CES Industries.
--Ed-Lab Eighty Experiment Manual: Photocell Sensor. (Illus., Orig.). (gr. 9-12). 1983. write for info. (ISBN 0-86711-036-8). CES Industries.
--Ed-Lab Eighty Experiment Manual: Printer Interfacing. (Illus., Orig.). (gr. 9-12). 1983. write for info. (ISBN 0-86711-033-3). CES Industries.
--Ed-Lab Eighty Experiment Manual: Thermal Probe Sensor. (Illus., Orig.). 1983. write for info. (ISBN 0-86711-041-4). CES Industries.
--Ed-Lab Eighty Experiment Manual: Touch Sensor. (Illus., Orig.). (gr. 9-12). 1983. write for info. (ISBN 0-86711-040-6). CES Industries.
--Ed-Lab Experiment Manual: CES 211 Breadboard Lab Manual. (Illus.). 1983. write for info. (ISBN 0-86711-066-X). CES Industries.
--Ed-Lab Experiment Manual: CES 303 Synchro-Servo Mechanism. (Illus.). (gr. 9-12). 1981. write for info. (ISBN 0-86711-012-0). CES Industries.
--Ed-Lab Experiment Manual: CES 307 Torque Synchros. (Illus.). (gr. 9-12). 1981. write for info. (ISBN 0-86711-011-2). CES Industries.
--Ed-Lab Experiment Manual: CES 308 Resolvers. (Illus.). (gr. 9-12). 1981. write for info. (ISBN 0-86711-013-9). CES Industries.
--Ed-Lab Experiment Manual: CES 309 Motor Speed Control Servo. (Illus.). (gr. 9-12). 1981. write for info. (ISBN 0-86711-009-0). CES Industries.
--Ed-Lab Experiment Manual: CES 310 Potentiometer Position Servo. (Illus.). (gr. 9-12). 1981. write for info. (ISBN 0-86711-010-4). CES Industries.
--Ed-Lab Experiment Manual: CES 380 Microprocessors. (Illus.). 162p. (gr. 9-12). 1980. 11.50 (ISBN 0-86711-007-4). CES Industries.
--Ed-Lab Experiment Manual: CES 380-85 Microprocessors. (Illus., Orig.). (gr. 9-12). 1984. pap. write for info. (ISBN 0-86711-076-7). CES Industries.
--Ed-Lab Experiment Manual: CES 6016 Telephone Modem. (Illus., Orig.). (gr. 9-12). 1984. pap. write for info. (ISBN 0-86711-085-6). CES Industries.
--Ed-Lab Experiment Manual: Instructor Guide to Troubles: TV Trainer. (Illus., Orig.). 1983. write for info. (ISBN 0-86711-045-7). CES Industries.
--Ed-Lab Nine Hundred Experiment Manual: Advanced Digital Systems. (Illus.). (gr. 9-12). 1981. 12.50 (ISBN 0-86711-008-2). CES Industries.
--Ed-Lab Seven Hundred Experiment Manual: Digital Systems. (Illus.). 304p. (gr. 9-12). 1979. 12.50 (ISBN 0-86711-001-5). CES Industries.
--Ed-Lab Six Hundred & Fifty Experiment Manual: Basic Electronics Concepts, Book O. (Illus.). 206p. (gr. 9-12). 1980. 11.50 (ISBN 0-86711-002-3). CES Industries.
--Ed-Lab Six Hundred & Fifty Experiment Manual: Communications, Bk. III. (Illus.). (gr. 9-12). 1982. 11.50 (ISBN 0-86711-026-0). CES Industries.
--Ed-Lab Six Hundred & Fifty Experiment Manual: Electricity-Electronics AC-DC, Bk. I. (Illus.). 288p. (gr. 9-12). 1981. 12.50 (ISBN 0-86711-015-5). CES Industries.
CES Industries Inc. Ed-Lab Six Hundred & Fifty Experiment Manual: Electricity-Electronics Solid-State, Bk. II. (Illus.). 304p. (gr. 9-12). 1981. 12.50 (ISBN 0-86711-014-7). CES Industries.
CES Industries, Inc. Ed-Lab Six Hundred & Fifty Experiment Manual: Operational Amplifiers, Bk. IV. (Illus.). 148p. (gr. 9-12). 1979. 9.50 (ISBN 0-86711-016-3). CES Industries.
CES Industries, Inc. & Nesenoff, Norman. Ed-Lab Eighty Experiment Manual: EPROM Programming. (Illus.). 1983. write for info. (ISBN 0-86711-038-4). CES Industries.
--Ed-Lab Eighty Experiment Manual: Robotics Interfacing. (Illus., Orig.). 1983. write for info. (ISBN 0-86711-034-1). CES Industries.
--Ed-Lab Experiment Manual: Mechanical Module. (Illus., Orig.). (gr. 9-12). 1980. write for info. (ISBN 0-86711-037-6). CES Industries.
--Ed-Lab Experiment Manual: Optics Trainer. (Illus., Orig.). 1983. write for info. (ISBN 0-86711-042-2). CES Industries.
CES Industries, Inc. Staff. Ed-Lab Eight Hundred Experiment Manual: Printer Interfacing. (Illus., Orig.). (gr. 9-12). 1984. write for info. (ISBN 0-86711-070-8). CES Industries.
--Ed-Lab Eighty Exercise Manual: DC-AC Electronics Programming. (Illus.). (gr. 9-12). 1982. write for info. (ISBN 0-86711-062-7). CES Industries.
--Ed-Lab Eighty Exercise Manual: Interfaces, Unit 2. (Illus.). (gr. 9-12). 1982. write for info. (ISBN 0-86711-057-0). CES Industries.
--Ed-Lab Eighty Exercise Manual: Programming for Ohm's Law. (Illus.). (gr. 9-12). 1982. write for info. (ISBN 0-86711-058-9). CES Industries.
--Ed-Lab Eighty Experiment Manual: Contactor Sensor Operation. (Illus.). (gr. 9-12). 1982. write for info. (ISBN 0-86711-063-5). CES Industries.
--Ed-Lab Eighty Reference Manual: Using the Ed-Lab 80 & the Basic Language. (Illus.). (gr. 9-12). 1982. write for info. (ISBN 0-86711-061-9). CES Industries.
--Ed-Lab Experiment Manual: CES 311 Transducers. (Illus.). (gr. 9-12). 1982. write for info. (ISBN 0-86711-050-3). CES Industries.
--Ed-Lab Experiment Manual: CES 318 Relay Module. (Illus.). (gr. 9-12). 1981. write for info. (ISBN 0-86711-024-4). CES Industries.
--Ed-Lab Experiment Manual: CES 349 Counter Timer Module; Troubleshooting System. (Illus.). (gr. 9-12). 1982. write for info. (ISBN 0-86711-031-7). CES Industries.
--Ed-Lab Experiment Manual: CES 6010 Microwave Training System. (Illus., Orig.). (gr. 9-12). 1984. pap. write for info. (ISBN 0-86711-083-X). CES Industries.
--Ed-Lab Experiment Manual: Microprocessor; Student Guide. (Illus.). (gr. 9-12). 1981. write for info. (ISBN 0-86711-018-X). CES Industries.
--Ed-Lab Instructor's Guide: I-O Module CES 342; A-D Converter Latch-Module CES 343. (Illus.). (gr. 9-12). 1982. write for info. (ISBN 0-86711-060-0). CES Industries.
--Ed-Lab Nine Hundred & Eighty Appendicies: Microcomputer Technology. (Illus.). (gr. 9-12). 1981. 11.50 (ISBN 0-86711-023-6). CES Industries.
--Ed-Lab Nine Hundred & Eighty Experiment Manual: Microcomputer Technology, Unit 2. (Unit 2). (Illus.). (gr. 9-12). 11.50 (ISBN 0-86711-022-8). CES Industries.
--Ed-Lab Nine Hundred & Eighty Experiment: Projects & Interfacing. (Illus.). (gr. 9-12). 1982. 9.50 (ISBN 0-86711-025-2). CES Industries.
--Ed-Lab Nine Hundred & Eighty: Microprocessor Concepts, Unit 1. (Illus.). (gr. 9-12). 1981. 9.50 (ISBN 0-86711-021-X). CES Industries.
--Ed-Lab Six Hundred & Fifty Experiment Manual: Pulses & Waveshaping, Bk.V. (Ed-Lab 650 Experiment Manual Ser.). (Illus.). (gr. 9-12). 1982. lab manual 11.50 (ISBN 0-86711-052-X). CES Industries.
--Ed-Lab Sixty Three Experiment Manual: Basic Electronics; User's Manual. (Illus.). (gr. 9-12). 1982. write for info. (ISBN 0-86711-028-7). CES Industries.
Cesaire, Aime. Aime Cesaire: The Collected Poetry. Smith, Annette & Eshleman, Clayton, trs. from Fr. LC 82-17394. (Illus.). 432p. 1985. pap. 9.95 (ISBN 0-520-05320-6, CAL 667). U of Cal Pr.
--Les Armes Miraculeuses. (Coll. Poesie). pap. 4.50 (ISBN 0-685-35647-7). French & Eur.
--Cadastre. Bd. with Soleil Cou Coupe; Corps Perdu. pap. 6.50 (ISBN 0-685-35646-9). French & Eur.
--Cadastre. Snyder, Emile, tr. from Fr. LC 75-169155. 160p. 1973. 7.95 (ISBN 0-89388-070-1); pap. 5.95 (ISBN 0-89388-085-X). Okpaku Communications.
--Cahier d'un Retour au Pays Natal: Return to My Native Land. (Livre-Poche Bilingue). pap. 4.50 (ISBN 0-685-35624-8). French & Eur.
--Discours sur le Colonialisme. pap. 4.50 (ISBN 0-685-35625-6). French & Eur.
--Discourse on Colonialism. Pinkham, Joan, tr. LC 72-178714. 96p. 1972. pap. 2.95 (ISBN 0-85345-226-1). Monthly Rev.
--Et les Chiens se Taisaient. pap. 7.95 (ISBN 0-685-35626-4). French & Eur.
--Ferrements. pap. 8.95 (ISBN 0-685-33975-0). French & Eur.
--Une Saison au Congo. 1975. pap. 3.95 (ISBN 0-686-51958-2). French & Eur.
--A Tempest. Miller, Richard, tr. from Fr. (Orig.). 1986. pap. text ed. 6.25 (ISBN 0-913745-15-4). Ubu Repertory.
--Une Tempete. 1975. pap. 3.95 (ISBN 0-686-51959-0). French & Eur.
--Textes. Mercier, R. & Battestini, M., eds. (Classique du Monde, Litterature Africaine). pap. 3.50 (ISBN 0-685-35627-2). French & Eur.
--La Tragedie du Roi Christophe. pap. 4.50 (ISBN 0-685-35628-0). French & Eur.
Cesaire, Aime see Harrison, Paul C.
Cesar, Joseph V. The Teaching of the Master. 120p. (Orig.). pap. text ed. 5.95 (ISBN 0-937816-01-9). Tech Data.
Cesara, Manda. No Hiding Place: Reflections of a Woman Anthropologists. (Studies in Anthropology Ser.). 1982. 27.50 (ISBN 0-12-164880-X). Acad Pr.
Cesare, Mario A. De see Ruiz, Juan.
Cesare, Mario A. Di see Mignani, Rigo & Di Cesare, Mario A.
Cesare, Mario Di see Di Cesare, Mario.
Cesares, Angeles, tr. see Rosenfeld, Erwin & Geller, Harriet.
Cesaresco, Evelyn M. Glimpses of Italian Society in the Eighteenth Century from the Journey' of Mrs. Piozzi. 1892. Repr. 25.00 (ISBN 0-8274-2415-9). R West.
--Italian Characters in the Epoch of Unification: Patriotti Italiani. 1901. 40.00 (ISBN 0-932062-51-2). Sharon Hill.
--Liberation of Italy, Eighteen Fifteen to Eighteen Seventy. LC 72-2563. (Select Bibliographies Reprint Ser.). 1972. Repr. of 1895 ed. 24.50 (ISBN 0-8369-6850-6). Ayer Co Pubs.
Cesaresco, Evelyn M., ed. Italian Characters. 1891. 15.00 (ISBN 0-8482-3573-8). Norwood Edns.
Cesaretti, C. A. & Commins, Stephen, eds. Let the Earth Bless the Lord: A Christian Perspective on Land Use. 160p. (Orig.). 1981. pap. 6.95 (ISBN 0-8164-2296-6, Pub. by Seabury). Winston Pr.
Cesaretti, Charles A. & Vitale, Joseph T., eds. Rumors of War: A Moral & Theological Perspective on the Arms Race. 128p. (Orig.). 1982. pap. 6.95 (ISBN 0-8164-2365-2, Pub. by Seabury). Winston Pr.
Cesari, Aura. Night Journeys. (Illus.). 12p. 1985. pap. 2.50 (ISBN 0-88138-053-9, Pub. by Envelope Bks). Green Tiger Pr.
Cesari, L. Surface Area. (Annals of Mathematics Studies: No. 35). 1956. 37.00 (ISBN 0-527-02752-9). Kraus Repr.
Cesari, L., jt. ed. see Bednarek, A. R.
Cesari, Lamberto. Optimization Theory & Applications: Problems with Ordinary Differential Equations. (Applications of Mathematics: Vol. 17). (Illus.). 544p. 1983. 69.50 (ISBN 0-387-90676-2). Springer-Verlag.
Cesari, Lamberto & Kannan, Rangacesari, eds. Nonlinear Analysis: A Collection of Papers in Honor or Eric Rothe. 1978. 55.00 (ISBN 0-12-165550-4). Acad Pr.
Cesari, Lamberto, et al. Dynamical Systems: An International Symposium, Vol. I. 1976. 82.50 (ISBN 0-12-164901-6). Acad Pr.
Cesari, Lamberto, et al, eds. Dynamical Systems: An International Symposium, Vol. 2. 1976. 81.00 (ISBN 0-12-164902-4). Acad Pr.
--Nonlinear Functional Analysis & Differential Equations: Proceedings of the Michigan State University Conference. (Lecture Notes in Pure and Applied Math Ser.: Vol. 19). 1976. 65.00 (ISBN 0-8247-6452-8). Dekker.
Cesaro, Ernesto. Vorlesungen Ueber Natuerliche Geometrie. (Bibliotheca Mathematica Teubneriana Ser: No. 36). (Ger). 1969. Repr. of 1921 ed. 33.00 (ISBN 0-384-08090-1). Johnson Repr.
Cescinsky & Webster. English Domestic Clocks. (Illus.). 353p. 1976. Repr. of 1913 ed. 49.50 (ISBN 0-902028-37-5). Antique Collect.
Cescinsky, H. English Furniture from Gothic to Sheraton. (Illus.). 22.50 (ISBN 0-8446-1829-2). Peter Smith.
--Gentle Art of Faking Furniture. (Illus.). 16.50 (ISBN 0-8446-1830-6). Peter Smith.
Cescinsky, Herbert. English Furniture: From Gothic to Sheraton. (Illus.). 1968. pap. 11.50 (ISBN 0-486-21929-1). Dover.
Ceserani, Gian, jt. auth. see Venture, Piero.
Ceserani, Gian P. Christopher Columbus. LC 77-86146. (Illus.). (gr. k-3). 1979. 3.95 (ISBN 0-394-93907-7, BYR); PLB 4.99. Random.
--Grand Constructions. (Illus.). 108p. (gr. 5 up). 1983. pap. 12.95 (ISBN 0-399-20942-5, Putnam). Putnam Pub Group.
--Marco Polo. (Illus.). 40p. 1982. 9.95 (ISBN 0-399-20843-7, Philomel). Putnam Pub Group.
Ceserani, Gian P., jt. auth. see Ventura, Piero.
Ceserani, V., jt. auth. see Kinton, R.
Ceserani, Victor & Kinton, Ronald. Practical Cookery. 5th ed. (Illus.). 432p. 1981. 19.95x (ISBN 0-7131-0509-7). Intl Ideas.
Ceserani, Victor, jt. auth. see Kinton, Ronald.
Cespedes, Alba de. Remorse. Weaver, William, tr. from Ital. LC 78-14003. 1978. lib. bdg. 27.50x (ISBN 0-313-20731-3, CERE). Greenwood.
Cespedes, Guillermo. Latin America: History. 1974. 9.00 (ISBN 0-394-31810-2, KnopfC). Knopf.
Cespedes y Meneses, Gonzalo. Gerardo the Unfortunate Spaniard: A Pattern for Lascivious Lovers. Digges, Leonard, tr. LC 80-2475. 1981. Repr. of 1622 ed. 142.40 (ISBN 0-404-19107-X). AMS Pr.
Cess, R. D., jt. auth. see Sparrow, E. M.
Cessac, Jean. Science Teaching in the Secondary Schools of Tropical Africa. (Orig.). 1963. pap. 5.00 (ISBN 92-3-100517-0, U583, UNESCO). Unipub.
Cessario, Romanus. Christian Satisfaction in Aquinas: Towards a Personalist Understanding. LC 81-43836. 390p. (Orig.). 1982. lib. bdg. 28.75 (ISBN 0-8191-2557-1); pap. text ed. 15.50 (ISBN 0-8191-2558-X). U Pr of Amer.
Cessaris, Ann. Pita: The Traditional Way. 1981. pap. 4.95x (ISBN 0-317-06941-1, Regent House). B of A.
Cessna Aircraft Co. Cessna, 1977 Model, 150 "Commuter" Pilot's Operating Handbook. (Illus.). 1977. pap. 15.00x (ISBN 0-911720-50-2, Cessna). Aviation.
--Cessna 1977 Model, 172 "Skyhawk" Pilot's Operating Handbook. pap. 15.00x (ISBN 0-911720-44-8, Cessna). Aviation.
Cesti. Italian Opera Librettos, Vol. XIV. Brown, Howard & Weimer, Eric, eds. (Italian Opera Ser., 1640-1770: No. 2). 83.00 (ISBN 0-317-20355-X). Garland Pub.
Cesto, Danilo. Goce Ahora, Pague Despues. (Pimienta Collection Ser). (Sp.). 1977. pap. 1.00 (ISBN 0-88473-253-3). Fiesta Pub.
--Hembra Caliente. (Pimienta Collection Ser.). 1977. pap. 1.00 (ISBN 0-88473-266-5). Fiesta Pub.
--La Maestra Pervertida. (Pimienta Collection Ser.). (Illus.). 160p. (Span.). 1976. pap. 1.25 (ISBN 0-88473-245-2). Fiesta Pub.
--Magnifica Secretaria... En la Cama. new ed. (Pimienta Collection Ser.). (Illus.). 160p. (Span.). 1976. pap. 1.25 (ISBN 0-88473-248-7). Fiesta Pub.
--Noches de Vudu. new ed. (Pimienta Collection). (Illus.). 160p. (Span.). pap. 1.25 (ISBN 0-88473-239-8). Fiesta Pub.
--Turistas Eroticos. (Pimienta Collection Ser). (Illus.). 1976. pap. 1.25 (ISBN 0-88473-251-7). Fiesta Pub.
Cesto, Danilo, tr. see Chase, Glenn.
Cesto, Danilo, tr. see Hytes, Jason.
Cestre, Charles. An Introduction to Edwin Arlington Robinson. 59.95 (ISBN 0-8490-0415-2). Gordon Pr.
--La Revolution Francaise et les Poetes Anglais, 1789-1809. 1972. Repr. of 1906 ed. lib. bdg. 50.00 (ISBN 0-8414-0108-X). Folcroft.
Cetnar, Jean, jt. auth. see Cetnar, William.
Cetnar, William & Cetnar, Jean. Questions for Jehovah's Witnesses. 1983. pap. 3.00 (ISBN 0-87552-162-2). Presby & Reformed.
Cetron, M. The Future of American Business in World Competition. 272p. 1985. 15.95 (ISBN 0-07-010349-6). McGraw.
Cetron, M. & Appel, M. Jobs of the Future: The 500 Best Jobs - Where They'll Be & How to Get Them. 276p. 1985. pap. price not set (ISBN 0-07-010352-6). McGraw.
Cetron, M., et al. Schools of the Future: Education into the Twenty-First Century. 176p. 1985. 12.95 (ISBN 0-07-010350-X). McGraw.
Cetron, Marvin & Appel, Marcia. Jobs of the Future: The Five Hundred Best Jobs--Where They'll Be & How to Get Them. 256p. 1984. 15.95 (ISBN 0-07-010342-9). McGraw.
Cetron, Marvin J. Technological Forecasting: A Practical Approach. 372p. 1969. 76.50 (ISBN 0-677-02140-2). Gordon.
Cetron, Marvin J. & Ralph, Christine A. Industrial Applications of Technological Forecasting. LC 80-20243. 582p. 1983. Repr. of 1971 ed. text ed. 49.50 (ISBN 0-89874-238-2). Krieger.
Cetron, Marvin J. & Bartocha, Bodo, eds. Technology Assessment in a Dynamic Environment. LC 72-75869. 1050p. 1973. 217.50 (ISBN 0-677-13150-X). Gordon.
Cetron, Marvin J., et al. Technical Resource Management: Quantitative Methods. 1970. 27.50x (ISBN 0-262-03034-9). MIT Pr.
Cetron, Marvin J., et al, eds. Methodology of Technology Assessment. 1969. pap. write for info. (ISBN 0-677-15315-5). Gordon.
--Quantitative Decision Aiding Techniques for Research & Development Management. LC 70-129677. (Illus.). 214p. 1972. 46.25 (ISBN 0-677-14250-1). Gordon.
Cetrulo, Curtis L., et al, eds. The Problem-Oriented Medical Record for High-Risk Obstetrics. 470p. 1983. 55.00x (ISBN 0-306-41325-6, Plenum Pr). Plenum Pub.
Ceuleman, Mieke & Fauconnier, Guido. Mass Media: The Image, Role, & Social Conditions of Women: A Collection & Analysis Research Materials. (Reports & Papers on Mass Communication: No. 84). 78p. 1979. pap. 5.00 (ISBN 92-3-101648-2, U977, UNESCO). Unipub.
Ceulemans, P. Question Arabe et le Congo, 1883-1892. (Academie Royale des Sciences d'Outre-Mer, Memoires Ser: Vol. 22, No. 1, N.S.). (Fr). 1969. Repr. of 1959 ed. 33.00 (ISBN 0-384-28459-0). Johnson Repr.
Cevasco, G. A. J. K. Huysman: A Reference Guide to English Translations of his Works & Studies of His Life & Literature Published in England & America, 1880-1978. 1980. lib. bdg. 25.50 (ISBN 0-8161-8235-3, Hall Reference). G K Hall.
--John Gray. (English Authors Ser.). 1982. lib. bdg. 18.95 (ISBN 0-8057-6839-4, Twayne). G K Hall.
--Oscar Wilde: British Author, Poet & Wit. Rahmas, D. Steve, ed. LC 72-89209. (Outstanding Personalities Ser.: No. 45). 32p. 1972. lib. bdg. 3.50 incl. catalog cards (ISBN 0-87157-541-8); pap. 1.95 vinyl laminated covers (ISBN 0-87157-041-6). SamHar Pr.
--The Population Problem. (Topics of Our Times Ser.: No. 8). 32p. lib. bdg. 3.50 incl. catalog cards (ISBN 0-87157-809-3); pap. 1.95 vinyl laminated covers (ISBN 0-87157-309-1). SamHar Pr.

--Salvador Dali: Master of Surrealism & Modern Art. Rahmas, D. Steve, ed. LC 79-185661. (Outstanding Personalities Ser.: No. 5). 32p. 1972. lib. bdg. 3.50 incl. catalog cards (ISBN 0-87157-505-1); pap. 1.95 vinyl laminated covers (ISBN 0-87157-005-X). SamHar Pr.

Ceyhan, A., et al. A Brief Review of the World Lube Oils Industry. (Energy Industries Report Ser.: No. 1). (Illus.). 58p. (Orig.). 1982. pap. 3.00 (ISBN 0-8213-0054-7). World Bank.

Ceynar, Marvin E., et al, eds. Creativity in the Communicative Arts: A Selected Bibliography, 1960-1970. LC 74-18202. vii, 120p. 1975. 8.50x (ISBN 0-87875-062-2). Whitston Pub.

Cezairliyan, A., ed. Recent Developments in Thermophysical Properties Research: Presented at the Winter Annual Meeting of the ASME, Washington, D. C., Dec. 1, 1971. LC 76-180675. (American Society of Mechanical Engineers. Heat Transfer Division HTD: Vol. 3). pap. 20.00 (ISBN 0-317-08191-8, 2016902). Bks Demand UMI.

Cezanne. A Collection of the Major Paintings by Cezanne in Full Colours. (Illus.). 89p. 1985. 88.55 (ISBN 0-86650-136-3). Gloucester Art.

Cezanne, Paul. A Cezanne Sketchbook: Figures, Portraits, Landscapes & Still Lives. (Fine Art Ser.). 144p. 1985. pap. 5.95 (ISBN 0-486-24790-2). Dover.

--Drawings of Cezanne. Longstreet, Stephen, ed. (Master Draughtsman Ser). (Illus., Orig.). treasure trove bdg. 9.95x (ISBN 0-87505-001-8); pap. 4.95 (ISBN 0-87505-154-5). Borden.

--Paul Cezanne, Letters. Rewald, John, ed. LC 83-45728. (Illus.). Repr. of 1941 ed. 49.50 (ISBN 0-404-20053-2). AMS Pr.

--Paul Cezanne Sketchbook. 1982. 500.00 (ISBN 0-384-08095-2). Johnson Repr.

CFK, Ltd. School Climate Improvement: A Challenge to the School Administrator. 141p. 1974. 3.00 (ISBN 0-87367-753-6). Phi Delta Kappa.

CFK Ltd. Editorial Staff. School Climate Improvement: A Challenge to the School Administrator. (Illus.). 141p. 1974. pap. 3.00 (ISBN 0-87367-753-6). Phi Delta Kappa.

Cha, Theresa H. Dictee. 176p. 1982. 13.95 (ISBN 0-934378-10-X); pap. 6.95 (ISBN 0-934378-09-6). Tanam Pr.

Cha, Theresa H., ed. see Barthes, et al.

Chaadaev, Peter Y. Philosophical Letters & Apology of a Madman. LC 79-88186. pap. 54.80 (ISBN 0-317-08084-9, 2019675). Bks Demand UMI.

Chaadaev, Petr. Filosoficheskie Pis'ma: Polnoe Sobranie. 200p. (Rus.). 1985. 22.50 (ISBN 0-88233-895-1). Ardis Pubs.

Chaback, Elaine. The Complete Calorie Counter. 1979. pap. 3.50 (ISBN 0-440-11134-X). Dell.

Chaback, Elaine & Fortunato, Pat. The Official Kids' Survival Kit: How to Do Things on Your Own. 1981. 17.45i (ISBN 0-316-13532-1); pap. 9.70 (ISBN 0-316-13531-3). Little.

Chabak, Michael. Speedx Reference Guide to the Utilities. 237p. (Orig.). 1985. pap. 11.75 looseleaf (ISBN 0-934705-05-4). Speedx.

Chabal, Patrick. Amilcar Cabral; Revolutionary Leadership & People's War. LC 82-14632. (African Studies: No. 37). (Illus.). 280p. 1983. 47.50 (ISBN 0-521-24944-9); pap. 17.95 (ISBN 0-521-27113-4). Cambridge U Pr.

Chaballe, L. Y. Elsevier's Sugar Dictionary: In English, French, Spanish, Dutch & German. 1984. 79.75 (ISBN 0-444-42376-1, I-410-84). Elsevier.

Chaballe, L. Y. & Masuy, L. Elsevier's Oil & Gas Field Dictionary. 672p. (in 6 languages plus Arabic suppl.). 1980. 138.50 (ISBN 0-444-41833-4). Elsevier.

Chaballe, L. Y. & Vandenberghe, J. P. Elsevier's Dictionary of Building Tools & Materials. 720p. (Eng., Fr., Span., Ger. & Dutch.). 1982. 138.50 (ISBN 0-444-42047-9, I-261-82). Elsevier.

Chaballe, L. Y., jt. ed. see Vandenberghe, J. P.

Chaban, Jane. Wang Word Processing Training Program. (Illus.). 272p. 1986. pap. text ed. 22.95 (ISBN 0-13-944729-6). P-H.

Chabaud, Jacqueline. Education & Advancement of Women. 155p. (Orig., 2nd Printing 1974). 1970. pap. 6.00 (ISBN 92-3-100842-0, U182, UNESCO). Unipub.

Chabersky, Stephen G., jt. auth. see Krasner, Michael A.

Chabert, M. de. Voyage Fait Par Ordre Du Roi En 1750 et 1751 Dans L'amerique Septentrionale, (Paris, 1753. (Canadianna Avant 1867: No. 7). 1966. 18.80x (ISBN 90-2796-326-6). Mouton.

Chabert De Cogolin, Joseph B. Voyage Fait Par Ordre Du Roi En 1750 et 1751, Dans l'Amerique Septentrionale. 1753. 20.00 (ISBN 0-384-08185-1). Johnson Repr.

Chabliss, Madelon. Musings in the Night. 240p. (Orig.). 1983. pap. 6.95 (ISBN 0-9612420-1-9). Madelon Chamb.

Chabner & Pinedo. Cancer Pharmacology Annual, Vol. 3. 1985. 33.50 (ISBN 0-444-90400-X). Elsevier.

Chabner, B. A., jt. auth. see Pinedo, H. M.

Chabner, B. A. & Pinedo, H. M., eds. The Cancer Pharmacology Annual. 1983. No. 1. 34.00 (ISBN 0-444-90325-9); No. 2. 30.50 (ISBN 0-444-90348-8, I-184-84). Elsevier.

Chabner, B. A., jt. ed. see Pinedo, H. M.

Chabner, Bruce A. Pharmacologic Principles of Cancer Treatment. (Illus.). 480p. 1982. 68.00 (ISBN 0-7216-2477-4). Saunders.

Chabner, Bruce A., jt. ed. see Fox, C. Fred.

Chabner, Davi-Ellen. The Language of Medicine: A Write-in Text Explaining Medical Terms. 2nd ed. (Illus.). 600p. 1981. pap. 21.95 (ISBN 0-7216-2479-0); audiotapes 75.00 (ISBN 0-7216-9960-X). Saunders.

Chaboseau, Augustin. De Babeuf a la Commune. LC 70-101232. (Research & Source Works: No. 389). (Fr). 1970. Repr. of 1911 ed. text ed. 14.00 (ISBN 0-8337-0508-3). B Franklin.

Chabot, ed. see Bernanos, Georges.

Chabot, Brain F. & Mooney, Hal. A, eds. Physiological Ecology Of North American Plant Communities. 400p. 1985. 39.95 (ISBN 0-412-23240-5, NO. 6536, Pub. by Chapman & Hall England). Methuen Inc.

Chabot, C. Barry. Freud on Schreber: Psychoanalytic Theory & the Critical Act. LC 81-16476. 192p. 1982. lib. bdg. 17.50x (ISBN 0-87023-348-3). U of Mass Pr.

Chabot, Frederick C., tr. see Morfi, Juan A.

Chabot, Leon, jt. auth. see Mallow, Alex.

Chabran, Richard, jt. ed. see Garcia-Ayvens, Francisco.

Chabrol, Claude. Le Recit Feminin: Contribution a L'Analyse Semiologique Du Courrier Du Coeur et Des Entreveuves Ou Enquetes Sur La Femme Dans La Presse Feminine Actuelle. (Approaches to Semiotics Ser.: No. 15). (Fr.). 1971. text ed. 15.60x (ISBN 90-2791-787-6). Mouton.

Chabrol, Claude, jt. auth. see Rohmer, Eric.

Chabrol, Claude, jt. auth. see Sagan, Francoise.

Chabrowe, Leonard. Ritual & Pathos: The Theater of O'Neill. 226p. 1976. 20.00 (ISBN 0-8387-1575-3). Bucknell U Pr.

Chabrowe, Leonard see Smith Experimental Fiction Project.

Chabrowski, O. Waclaw. Madonny. 46p. 1965. 2.50 (ISBN 0-940962-13-6). Polish Inst Art & Sci.

Chabrowski, T., jt. auth. see Waclaw, O.

Chacalos, Elias H. Dialogues on Time, Being & Awareness. LC 75-25220. 1976. 12.50 (ISBN 0-917262-01-8). Potomac Pr.

Chace, Fenner. The Caridean Shrimps (Crustacea Decapoda) of the Albatross Philippine Expedition, 1907-1910, Pt. 2: Families Glyphocrangonidae & Crangonidae. LC 83-600061. (Smithsonian Contributions to Zoology: No. 397). pap. 20.00 (ISBN 0-317-20103-4, 2023164). Bks Demand UMI.

Chace, Fenner A. The Atya-like Shrimps of the Indo-Pacific Region (Decapoda: Atyidae) LC 83-600083. (Smithsonian Contributions to Zoology: No: 384). pap. 20.00 (ISBN 0-317-29611-6, 2021866). Bks Demand UMI.

Chace, Fenner A., Jr., jt. ed. see Pequegnat, Willis E.

Chace, G. Earl. Rattlesnakes. (A Skylight Bk.). (Illus.). 64p. (gr. 2-5). 1984. PLB 7.95 (ISBN 0-396-08453-2). Dodd.

--The World of Lizards. (Illus.). 144p. (gr. 6 up). 1982. PLB 10.95 (ISBN 0-396-08043-X). Dodd.

Chace, Isobel. To Marry A Tiger, The Tartan Touch, Cadence of Portugal. (Harlequin Romances Ser.). 576p. 1982. pap. 3.50 (ISBN 0-373-20065-X). Harlequin Bks.

Chace, James. Endless War: How We Got Involved in Central America & What Can Be Done. LC 84-48004. 120p. (Orig.). 1984. pap. 3.95 (ISBN 0-394-72779-7, Vin). Random.

--Solvency: The Price of Survival. LC 82-40159. 128p. 1982. pap. 3.95 (ISBN 0-394-71242-0, Vin). Random.

Chace, James & Ravenal, Earl C., eds. Atlantis Lost: U.S.-European Relations after the Cold War. LC 75-15128. 1976. 27.00x (ISBN 0-8147-1361-0). NYU Pr.

Chace, W. G. & Moore, H. K., eds. Exploding Wires, 4 vols. Incl. Vol. 1. 373p. 1959. 32.50x (ISBN 0-306-37521-4); Vol. 2. 321p. 1962. 32.50x (ISBN 0-306-37522-2); Vol. 3. 410p. 1964. 37.50x (ISBN 0-306-37523-0); Vol. 4. 348p. 1968. 39.50x (ISBN 0-306-37524-9). LC 59-14822 (Plenum Pr). Plenum Pub.

Chace, William M. Lionel Trilling: Criticism & Politics. LC 78-66173. xiv, 207p. 1980. 17.50x (ISBN 0-8047-1032-5). Stanford U Pr.

--The Political Identities of Ezra Pound & T. S. Eliot. LC 73-80620. 256p. 1973. 17.50x (ISBN 0-8047-0843-6). Stanford U Pr.

Chace, William M. & Collier, Peter. An Introduction to Literature. 1097p. 1985. pap. text ed. 15.95x (ISBN 0-15-543034-3, HC); instr's manual avail. (ISBN 0-15-543035-1). HarBraceJ.

Chace, William M., ed. Joyce: A Collection of Critical Essays. LC 73-18496. (Illus.). 192p. 1973. 12.95 (ISBN 0-13-511303-2, Spec); pap. 4.95 (ISBN 0-13-511295-8, Spec). P-H.

Chacel, Julian, et al. Brazil's Economic & Political Future. (Special Studies Ser.). 1985. 24.00 (ISBN 0-8133-0268-4). Westview.

Chacey, C., jt. auth. see Chambers, H.

Chacholiades, Miltiades. International Monetary Theory & Policy. (Illus.). 1977. 37.95 (ISBN 0-07-010340-2). McGraw.

--Principles of International Economics. (Illus.). 656p. 1981. text ed. 33.95 (ISBN 0-07-010345-3). McGraw.

Chachra, V., et al. Applications of Graph Theory Algorithms. 422p. 1979. 35.75 (ISBN 0-444-00268-5, North-Holland). Elsevier.

Chackerian, Richard & Abcarian, Gilbert. Bureaucratic Power in Society. LC 83-17267. (Illus.). 216p. 1984. lib. bdg. 23.95x (ISBN 0-8304-1004-X); pap. text ed. 11.95x (ISBN 0-8304-1116-X). Nelson-Hall.

Chackett, K. Radionuclide Technology. 1981. 42.50 (ISBN 0-442-30170-7); pap. 19.95 (ISBN 0-442-30171-5). Van Nos Reinhold.

Chacko, Chirakaikaran J. International Joint Commission Between the United States of America & the Dominion of Canada. LC 68-58554. (Columbia University. Studies in the Social Sciences: No. 358). Repr. of 1932 ed. 30.00 (ISBN 0-404-51358-1). AMS Pr.

Chacko, David, jt. auth. see Allen, Dick.

Chacko, G. K. Applied Operations Research: Systems Analysis in Hierarchial Decision-Making, 2 vols. Incl. Vol. 1. Systems Approach to Public & Private Sector Problems; Vol. 2. Operations Research to Problem Formulation & Solution. (Studies in Management Science & Solution: Vol. 3). 1976. Set. 127.75 (ISBN 0-444-10768-1, North-Holland). Elsevier.

Chacko, G. K., ed. Health Handbook: An International Reference on Care & Cure. 1104p. 1979. 170.25 (ISBN 0-444-85254-9, North Holland). Elsevier.

Chacko, George K. India: Toward an Understanding. 9.95 (ISBN 0-8084-0401-6); pap. 6.95x (ISBN 0-8084-0402-4). New Coll U Pr.

--Management Information Systems. (Illus.). 454p. text ed. 29.95 (ISBN 0-89433-095-0). Petrocelli.

--Robotics-Artificial Intelligence-Productivity. (Illus.). 360p. 1985. text ed. 39.95 (ISBN 0-89433-228-7). Petrocelli.

--Robotics-Artificial Intelligence-Productivity: Japan & the USA. (Illus.). 340p. 1985. 39.95 (ISBN 0-317-31197-2). Van Nos Reinhold.

Chacko, Ranjit C. The Chronic Mental Patient in a Community Context. LC 84-24542. (Clinical Insights Monograph). 96p. 1985. pap. text ed. 12.00X (ISBN 0-88048-076-9, 48-076-9). Am Psychiatric.

Chacon, Joaquin Armando. Las Amarras Terrestres. 149p. (Span.). 1982. pap. 8.00 (ISBN 0-910061-08-4, 1107). Ediciones Norte.

Chacon, Louis, et al. Bilingual Business Grammar. (Span. & Eng.). 1981. text ed. 9.30 (ISBN 0-538-22610-2, V61). SW Pub.

--Personal Business. (Span.). 1983. text ed. 9.30 (ISBN 0-538-22620-X, V62). SW Pub.

Chacon, R., ed. see International Cancer Congress, 12th, Buenos Aires, 5-11 October 1978.

Chaconas, D. J. Danger in the Swamp. (Illus.). (gr. 1-4). 1971. PLB 6.19 (ISBN 0-8313-0015-9). Lantern.

Chaconas, Spiro J., ed. Orthodontics. LC 79-20126. (Illus.). 326p. 1980. text ed. 37.00 (ISBN 0-88416-155-2). PSG Pub Co.

Chaconas, Stephen G. Adamantios Koraïs: A Study in Greek Nationalism. LC 68-58555. (Columbia University Studies in the Social Sciences: No. 490). Repr. of 1942 ed. 22.50 (ISBN 0-404-51490-1). AMS Pr.

Chacour, Elias & Hazard, David. Blood Brothers. 224p. 1984. 9.95 (ISBN 0-310-60810-4, 13180, Pub. by Chosen Bks). Zondervan.

Chadam, J. M., ed. Nonlinear Partial Differential Equations & Applications: Proceedings of a Special Seminar Held at Indiana University, 1976-1977. (Lecture Notes in Mathematics: Vol. 648). 1978. pap. 16.00 (ISBN 0-387-08759-1). Springer-Verlag.

Chadan, K. & Sabatier, P. C. Inverse Problems in Quantum Scattering Theory. (Texts & Monographs in Physics). (Illus.). 1977. 49.00 (ISBN 0-387-08092-9). Springer-Verlag.

Chadbourn, James H. Lynching & the Law. LC 33-32207. (Basic Afro-American Reprint Library). 1970. Repr. of 1933 ed. 13.00 (ISBN 0-384-08205-X). Johnson Repr.

Chadbourn, James H. see Wigmore, John H.

Chadbourn, W. R. How to Speak L.A. 24p. 1984. pap. 1.50 (ISBN 0-317-02700-X). Price Stern.

Chadbourne, et al. Summary of Publications & Hearings, Vol. 4. (Municipal Securities Regulation Ser.). 1977. pap. text ed. 70.00 (ISBN 0-916450-11-2). Coun on Municipal.

--Federal Legislative Background & Four Legal Memoranda, Vols. 5 & 6. (Municipal Securites Regulation Ser.). 1978. Set. pap. text ed. 65.00 (ISBN 0-916450-35-X). Vol. 5 (ISBN 0-916450-12-0). Vol. 6 (ISBN 0-916450-13-9). Coun on Municipal.

--State Laws, Vol. 8. (Municipal Securities Regulation Ser.). 1978. pap. text ed. 50.00x (ISBN 0-916450-19-8). Coun on Municipal.

Chadbourne, Ava H. The Beginnings of Education in Maine. LC 73-176633. (Columbia University. Teachers College. Contributions to Education: No. 336). Repr. of 1928 ed. 22.50 (ISBN 0-404-55336-2). AMS Pr.

--Maine Place Names & the Peopling of its Towns: Cumberland County. Date not set. pap. 4.95 (ISBN 0-87027-131-8). Cumberland Pr.

--Maine Place Names & the Peopling of Its Towns: Hancock County. Wheelwright, Thea, ed. LC 77-115159. (Illus.). 1970. pap. 1.95 (ISBN 0-87027-112-1). Cumberland Pr.

--Maine Place Names & the Peopling of Its Towns: Lincoln County. Wheelwright, Thea, ed. LC 77-115159. 1970. pap. 1.95 (ISBN 0-87027-113-X). Cumberland Pr.

--Maine Place Names & the Peopling of Its Towns: Washington County. LC 77-115159. (Illus.). 1971. pap. 1.95 (ISBN 0-87027-114-8). Cumberland Pr.

--Maine Place Names & the Peopling of Its Towns: York County. LC 77-115159. (Illus., Orig.). 1971. pap. 1.95 (ISBN 0-87027-118-0). Cumberland Pr.

Chadbourne, Bill, ed. see Caniff, Milton.

Chadbourne, Bill, ed. see Coniff, Milton.

Chadbourne, Bill, ed. see Sickles, Noel.

Chadbourne, Richard & Dahlie, Hallvard, eds. The New Land: Studies in Literary Theme. 160p. 1978. pap. text ed. 8.50x (ISBN 0-88920-065-3, Pub. by Wilfrid Laurier U Pr Canada). Humanities.

Chadbourne, Richard M. Ernest Renan. LC 67-25197. (World Authors Ser.). 1968. lib. bdg. 15.95 (ISBN 0-8057-2754-X). Irvington.

Chadbourne, Robert L., jt. auth. see Wright, Ruth V.

Chadbourne, Thomas L. The Autobiography of Thomas L. Chadbourne, Esq. LC 83-13469. (Ingram Documents in Legal History Ser.). 301p. (Orig.). 1985. lib. bdg. 35.00 (ISBN 0-379-20846-6). Oceana.

Chadda, H. C., ed. Seeing Is Above All: Sant Darshan Singh's First Indian Tour. (Illus.). 1977. pap. 3.00 (ISBN 0-918224-04-7). Sawan Kirpal Pubns.

Chadda, Maya. Paradox of Power: The U. S. in Southwest Asia. 250p. 1985. lib. bdg. 35.00 (ISBN 0-87436-454-X); pap. text ed. 20.00 (ISBN 0-87436-455-8). ABC Clio.

Chadderdon, H. Determining Effectiveness of Teaching Home Economics. LC 74-78396. 1971. pap. 2.50 (ISBN 0-686-00147-8, 261-08408). Home Econ Educ.

Chadderton, L. T., jt. ed. see Jain, S. C.

Chadderton, Lewis T., jt. ed. see Eisen, Fred H.

Chaddock, D. H. The Quorn: Universal Tool & Cutter Grinder. (Illus.). 128p. (Orig.). 1984. pap. 16.95 (ISBN 0-85242-832-4, Pub by ARGUS). Aztex.

Chaddock, Robert E. Ohio Before Eighteen Fifty. LC 8-18567. (Columbia University Studies in the Social Sciences: No. 82). Repr. of 1908 ed. 16.50 (ISBN 0-404-51082-5). AMS Pr.

Chaddock, Robert E., jt. auth. see Dewey, Davis R.

Chadeayne, Leander. The Chadeayne Family in America. 65p. 1984. 15.00 (ISBN 0-318-17306-9). Huguenot Hist.

Chadeayne, Lee, tr. see Luthi, Max.

Chadeev, V. M., jt. auth. see Rajbman, N. S.

Chader, G. J., jt. ed. see Osborne, N. N.

Chader, G. J., jt. ed. see Osborne, N. O.

Chadha, K. L. & Randhawa, G. S., eds. International Symposium on Tropical & Sub-Tropical Horticulture, 3rd: Vol. 2, Use of Growth Regulators in Horticultural, Plantation & Medicinal Crops. (Illus.). 266p. 1978. 20.00 (ISBN 0-88065-238-1, Pub. by Messers Today & Tomorrow Printers & Publishers). Scholarly Pubns.

Chadha, Kumkum. The Indian Jail: A Contemporary Document. x, 252p. 1983. text ed. 30.00x (ISBN 0-7069-2300-6, Pub. by Vikas India). Advent NY.

Chadi, J. D. & Harrison, W. A., eds. Proceedings of the Seventeenth International Conference on the Physics of Semiconductors. (Illus.). 1600p. 1985. 135.00 (ISBN 0-387-96108-9). Springer-Verlag.

Chadman, Charles E. A Treatise on Criminal Law & Criminal Procedure. LC 77-156008. (Foundations of Criminal Justice Ser). Repr. of 1906 ed. 64.00 (ISBN 0-404-09108-3). AMS Pr.

Chadman, Charles E., ed. White House Hand-Book of Oratory. LC 77-88075. (Granger Poetry Library Ser.). 1977. Repr. of 1889 ed. 22.50x (ISBN 0-89609-062-0). Granger Bk.

Chadney, James G. The Sikhs of Vancouver. rev. ed. LC 83-45350. (Immigrant Communities & Ethnic Minorities in the U. S. & Canada Ser.: No. 1). (Illus.). 291p. 1984. 71.50 (ISBN 0-404-19403-6). AMS Pr.

Chadsey, Charles E. Struggle Between President Johnson & Congress Over Reconstruction. LC 79-181926. (Columbia University Studies in the Social Sciences: No. 19). Repr. of 1896 ed. 11.50 (ISBN 0-404-51019-1). AMS Pr.

Chadwell, David. Christian Perspectives on Dating & Marriage. 1980. pap. 4.95 (ISBN 0-89137-523-6). Quality Pubns.

Chadwell, Patricia. Missouri Land Claims. 1976. 17.50 (ISBN 0-686-20882-X). Polyanthos.

Chadwich-Jones, J. K. & Brown, Colin. Social Psychology of Absenteeism. LC 81-23395. 176p. 1982. 29.95 (ISBN 0-03-056652-5). Praeger.

Chadwick. Twenty-Five Mornings & Evenings. pap. 3.95 (ISBN 0-686-12924-5). Schmul Pub Co.

Chadwick, jt. auth. see Middleton.

Chadwick, Annie H., jt. ed. see Chadwick, John W.

Chadwick, Barbra. Shades of Green & Grey. (Illus.). 32p. 1980. 5.95 (ISBN 0-89962-033-7). Todd & Honeywell.

Chadwick, Bruce A., et al. Social Science Research Methods. (Illus.). 448p. 1984. text ed. 27.95 (ISBN 0-13-818336-8). P-H.

Chadwick, C. Rimbaud. (French Poets Ser.). 152p. 1979. 32.50 (ISBN 0-485-14610-X, Pub. by Athlone Pr Ltd); pap. 14.95 (ISBN 0-485-12210-3). Longwood Pub Group.

--Verlaine. (French Poets Ser.). 132p. 1973. 32.50 (ISBN 0-485-14603-7, Pub. by Athlone Pr Ltd); pap. 14.95 (ISBN 0-485-12203-0). Longwood Pub Group.
Chadwick, C., ed. see Verlaine, Paul.
Chadwick, Charles. Symbolism. (Critical Idiom Ser.). 1971. pap. 5.50x (ISBN 0-416-60910-4, 2129). Methuen Inc.
Chadwick, Donna see Clark, Cynthia.
Chadwick, Douglas H. A Beast the Color of Winter: The Mountain Goat Observed. LC 83-4737. (Illus.). 288p. 1983. 15.95 (ISBN 0-87156-805-5). Sierra.
Chadwick, E. Report on the Sanitary Condition of the Labouring Population of Great Britain, 1842. Flinn, M., ed. 443p. 1965. 28.00x (ISBN 0-85224-145-3, Pub. by Edinburgh U Pr Scotland). Columbia U Pr.
Chadwick, Edward M. Ontarian Families: Genealogies of United Empire Loyalist & Other Pioneer Families of Upper Canada, 2 vols. in 1. 1983. Repr. of 1898 ed. lib. bdg. 21.00 (ISBN 0-912606-08-8). Hunterdon Hse.
Chadwick, Edward W. Pastoral Preaching of Paul. LC 84-7123. 416p. 1984. 10.95 (ISBN 0-8254-2325-2). Kregel.
Chadwick, Eileen. The Craft of Hand Spinning. (Illus.). 168p. 1985. pap. 11.95 (ISBN 0-7134-1012-4, Pub. by Batsford England). David & Charles.
Chadwick, Enid M. At God's Altar. Schuler, Eugenia, ed. (Illus.). 1978. pap. 1.50x (ISBN 0-934502-00-5). Thursday Pubs.
--At God's Altar: Rite One. Schuler, Eugenia, ed. (Illus.). 1978. pap. 1.50x (ISBN 0-934502-01-3). Thursday Pubs.
Chadwick, Esther A. In the Footsteps of the Brontes. LC 70-159488. (English Literature Ser., No. 33). 1971. Repr. of 1895 ed. lib. bdg. 67.95x (ISBN 0-8383-1272-1). Haskell.
--In the Footsteps of the Brontes. 1973. Repr. of 1895 ed. 19.75 (ISBN 0-8274-1711-X). R West.
--Mrs. Gaskell. 1973. 25.00 (ISBN 0-8274-0084-5). R West.
Chadwick, French E. The Relations of the United States & Spain: Diplomacy. LC 68-25054. 610p. 1968. Repr. of 1909 ed. 16.00x (ISBN 0-8462-1230-7). Russell.
Chadwick, French E., ed. Graves Papers & Other Documents Relating to the Naval Operations of the Yorktown Campaign, July to October 1781. LC 76-29044. (Eyewitness Accounts of the American Revolution Ser., No. 1). 1968. Repr. of 1916 ed. 17.00 (ISBN 0-405-01108-3). Ayer Co Pubs.
Chadwick, G. A. & Smith, D. A., eds. Grain Boundary Structure & Properties. (Material Science & Technology Ser.). 1976. 67.00 (ISBN 0-12-166250-0). Acad Pr.
Chadwick, George. Harmony: A Course of Study, 2 vols. in 1. Incl. A Key to Chadwick's Harmony. vii, 103p. LC 74-36316. (Music Reprint Ser). xiv, 231p. 1975. Repr. of 1897 ed. lib. bdg. 37.50 (ISBN 0-306-70663-6). Da Capo.
--A Systems View of Planning: Towards a Theory of the Urban & Regional Planning Process. 2nd ed. (Urban & Regional Planning Ser.: Vol. 2). (Illus.). 1978. text ed. 59.50 (ISBN 0-08-020626-3); pap. text ed. 19.75 (ISBN 0-08-020625-5). Pergamon.
Chadwick, George H. Rocks of Greene County. 1973. pap. 2.00 (ISBN 0-685-40640-7). Hope Farm.
Chadwick, George W. Horatio Parker. LC 72-1392. Repr. of 1921 ed. 11.00 (ISBN 0-404-08304-8). AMS Pr.
--Judith: Lyric Drama for Solo, Chorus, & Orchestra. LC 70-169727. (Earlier American Music Ser.: Vol. 3). 176p. 1972. Repr. of 1901 ed. lib. bdg. 27.50 (ISBN 0-306-77303-1). Da Capo.
--Symphony No. Two: In B Flat, Opus 21. facsimile ed. LC 71-170930. (Earlier American Music Ser.: No. 3). 216p. 1972. Repr. of 1888 ed. 29.00 (ISBN 0-306-77304-X). Da Capo.
Chadwick, H., ed. Origen: Contra Celsum. LC 78-73132. 1980. 80.00 (ISBN 0-521-05866-X); pap. 29.95 (ISBN 0-521-29576-9). Cambridge U Pr.
Chadwick, H. M. Studies in Old English. 1978. Repr. of 1899 ed. lib. bdg. 40.00 (ISBN 0-8495-0844-4). Arden Lib.
--Studies in Old English. LC 73-20322. Repr. of 1899 ed. lib. bdg. 30.00 (ISBN 0-8414-3538-3). Folcroft.
Chadwick, H. M. & Chadwick, Nora K. Growth of Literature, 2 vols. 1969. Vol. 2. 84.00 (ISBN 0-521-07423-1); Vol. 3. 87.00 (ISBN 0-521-07424-X). Cambridge U Pr.
Chadwick, H. Munro. The Heroic Age. LC 73-7696. (Illus.). 474p. 1974. Repr. of 1912 ed. lib. bdg. 27.50x (ISBN 0-8371-6939-9, CHHA). Greenwood.
--The Nationalities of Europe & the Growth of National Ideologies. LC 72-88264. (Illus.). viii, 209p. 1973. Repr. of 1945 ed. lib. bdg. 19.50 (ISBN 0-8154-0446-8). Cooper Sq.
--The Origin of the English Nation. 232p. 1983. Repr. of 1907 ed. 35.00x (ISBN 0-941694-09-7). Cliveden Pr.
Chadwick, Hector M. Old English Studies. 265p. 1980. Repr. of 1899 ed. lib. bdg. 40.00 (ISBN 0-89987-105-4). Darby Bks.
Chadwick, Henry. Early Christian Thoughts & the Classical Tradition: Studies in Justin, Clement & Origan. 182p. 1984. pap. text ed. 11.50x (ISBN 0-19-826673-1). Oxford U Pr.
--Early Christian Church, Pelican History of the Church, Vol. 1. (Orig.). 1968. pap. 4.95 (ISBN 0-14-020502-0, Pelican). Penguin.
--The Game of Base Ball: How to Learn It, How to Play It, & How to Teach It. LC 83-70285. (Library of Baseball Classics: Vol. 1). (Illus.). 180p. 1983. Repr. of 1868 ed. 30.00x (ISBN 0-938100-11-4). Camden Hse.
--History & Thought of the Early Church: Eighteen Studies in English 1948-81. 344p. 1982. 75.00x (ISBN 0-86078-112-7, Pub. by Variorum England). State Mutual Bk.
--Priscillian of Avila: The Occult & the Charismatic in the Early Church. 1976. 39.95x (ISBN 0-19-826643-X). Oxford U Pr.
Chadwick, Henry, ed. Alexandrian Christianity. LC 54-10257. (Library of Christian Classics). 472p. 1977. softcover 8.95 (ISBN 0-664-24153-0). Westminster.
--Boethius: The Consolations of Music, Logic, Theology, & Philosophy. 1981. text ed. 42.00x (ISBN 0-19-826447-X). Oxford U Pr.
Chadwick, Henry, tr. see Lessing, Gotthold.
Chadwick, Ian. Mapping the Atari. 194p. 1983. 14.95 (ISBN 0-942386-09-4). Compute Pubns.
--Mapping the Atari. rev. ed. Compute Editors, ed. (Orig.). 1985. pap. 16.95 (ISBN 0-87455-004-1). Compute Pubns.
Chadwick, J. The Mycenaean World. (Illus.). 224p. 1976. 49.50 (ISBN 0-521-21077-1); pap. 12.95 (ISBN 0-521-29037-6). Cambridge U Pr.
Chadwick, J., jt. auth. see Ventris, M.
Chadwick, J., tr. see Lloyd, G. E.
Chadwick, Janet. How to Live on Almost Nothing & Have Plenty. LC 79-2246. (Illus.). 1979. 12.95 (ISBN 0-394-42811-0); pap. 7.95 (ISBN 0-394-73753-9). Knopf.
--The No-Time-To-Cook Book: An Afternoon of Cooking... A Week of Meals. LC 85-70194. (Illus.). 160p. 1984. 14.95 (ISBN 0-88266-394-1); pap. 6.95 (ISBN 0-88266-393-3). Garden Way Pub.
Chadwick, Janet B. The Busy Person's Guide to Preserving Food. LC 82-1022. 160p. (Orig.). 1982. pap. 5.95 (ISBN 0-88266-263-5). Garden Way Pub.
--The Country Journal Woodburner's Cookbook. (Illus.). 1981. pap. 9.95 (ISBN 0-393-00076-1). Norton.
Chadwick, Jenniffer, jt. auth. see Chadwick, Oliver.
Chadwick, John. Decipherment of Linear B. (Illus.). 1970. 34.50 (ISBN 0-521-04599-1); pap. 10.95x (ISBN 0-521-09596-4, 596). Cambridge U Pr.
--Mycenae Tablets Three. (Transactions Ser.: Vol. 52, Pt. 7). (Illus.). 1963. pap. 3.00 (ISBN 0-87169-527-8). Am Philos.
--The Unofficial Commonwealth: The Story of the Commonwealth Foundation, 1965-1980. 280p. 1982. text ed. 37.50x (ISBN 0-04-341021-9). Allen Unwin.
Chadwick, John & Chadwick, Suzanne. The Chadwick System: Discovering the Perfect Hairstyle for You. LC 82-10461. (Illus.). 250p. 1982. 18.95 (ISBN 0-671-44016-0). S&S.
Chadwick, John, jt. ed. see Tett, Norman.
Chadwick, John W. Computing for Executives. (Illus.). 240p. (Orig.). 1984. 19.95 (ISBN 0-8306-0796-X); pap. 12.95 (ISBN 0-8306-1796-5, 1796). TAB Bks.
--George William Curtis. 1973. Repr. of 1893 ed. 12.50 (ISBN 0-8274-1402-1). R West.
--Theodore Parker: Preacher & Reformer. LC 72-144939. 1971. Repr. of 1900 ed. 39.00x (ISBN 0-403-00925-1). Scholarly.
Chadwick, John W. & Chadwick, Annie H., eds. Lovers' Treasury of Verse. facs. ed. LC 70-139758. (Granger Index Reprint Ser). 1891. 16.00 (ISBN 0-8369-6212-5). Ayer Co Pubs.
--Out of the Heart. facsimile ed. LC 70-86795. (Granger Index Reprint Ser). 1891. 17.00 (ISBN 0-8369-6072-6). Ayer Co Pubs.
--Treasury of Helpful Verse. facsimile ed. LC 73-76933. (Granger Index Reprint Ser). 1896. 17.00 (ISBN 0-8369-6007-6). Ayer Co Pubs.
Chadwick, John White. William Ellery Channing: Minister of Religion. 1903. 40.00 (ISBN 0-8274-3707-2). R West.
Chadwick, Joselyn. Evil Is the Night. 1974. pap. 0.95 (ISBN 0-380-00012-1, 19224). Avon.
Chadwick, Joseph. A Town to Tame. 1979. pap. 1.50 (ISBN 0-449-14234-5, GM). Fawcett.
Chadwick, K. H. & Leenhouts, H. P. The Molecular Theory of Radiation Biology. (Monographs on Theoretical & Applied Genetics: Vol. 5). (Illus.). 377p. 1981. 69.50 (ISBN 0-387-10297-3). Springer-Verlag.
Chadwick, Kenneth E. A Hear Do'n Sing Book: Little Bitty You Little Bitty Me. (Illus.). (ps). 1979. 4.25 (ISBN 0-9603698-0-5). Bet-Ken Prods.
Chadwick, Lee. Cuba Today. LC 75-43185. (Illus.). 224p. 1976. 7.95 (ISBN 0-88208-065-2); pap. 5.95 (ISBN 0-88208-066-0). Lawrence Hill.
Chadwick, Leigh, tr. see Stumpke, Harald.
Chadwick, Leigh E., tr. see Von Frisch, Karl.
Chadwick, M. H., jt. ed. see Goodman, G. T.
Chadwick, M. J. & Goodman, G. T. The Ecology of Resource Degradation & Renewal. LC 75-5776. (British Ecological Society Symposia Ser.). 480p. 1975. 64.95x (ISBN 0-470-14295-2). Halsted Pr.
Chadwick, M. J., jt. auth. see Bradshaw, A. D.
Chadwick, M. J. & Lindman, N., eds. Environmental Implications of Expanded Coal Utilization. LC 81-23560. (Illus.). 304p. 1982. 61.00 (ISBN 0-08-028734-4). Pergamon.
Chadwick, Martin M., jt. auth. see Fitzhugh, Robert J.
Chadwick, Maureen V. Mycobacteria. (Institute of Medical Laboratory Sciences Monographs). 128p. 1983. pap. text ed. 13.00 (ISBN 0-7236-0595-5). PSG Pub Co.
Chadwick, N. Kershaw. Poetry & Prophecy: Oral Literature, Poetic Inspiration & Shamanism. 1942. lib. bdg. 22.50 (ISBN 0-8414-3381-X). Folcroft.
Chadwick, Neil. A Descriptive Study of the Djingili Language. (AIAS Regional Ser.: No. 2). (Illus., Orig.). 1975. pap. text ed. 5.75x (ISBN 0-85575-040-5). Humanities.
Chadwick, Nora. Celts. 1971. pap. 4.95 (ISBN 0-14-021211-6, Pelican). Penguin.
Chadwick, Nora K. Poetry & Prophecy. 1978. Repr. of 1924 ed. lib. bdg. 22.50 (ISBN 0-8495-0820-7). Arden Lib.
Chadwick, Nora K. & Zhirmunsky, Victor. Oral Epics of Central Asia. LC 68-21189. 1969. 92.50 (ISBN 0-521-07053-8). Cambridge U Pr.
Chadwick, Nora K., jt. auth. see Chadwick, H. M.
Chadwick, Nora K., ed. & tr. Russian Heroic Poetry. LC 64-10386. (Illus.). 1964. Repr. of 1932 ed. 12.50x (ISBN 0-8462-0491-6). Russell.
Chadwick, Nora K., et al. Studies in the Early British Church. vii, 374p. 1973. Repr. of 1958 ed. 25.00 (ISBN 0-208-01315-6, Archon). Shoe String.
Chadwick, Norah. The Beginnings of Russian History: An Enquiry into Sources. LC 75-41052. (BCL Ser. II). Repr. of 1946 ed. 16.50 (ISBN 0-404-14651-1). AMS Pr.
Chadwick, Norah K. An Early Irish Reader. LC 78-72634. (Celtic Language & Literature: Goidelic & Brythonic). Repr. of 1927 ed. 14.50 (ISBN 0-404-17559-7). AMS Pr.
Chadwick, O., jt. ed. see Nuttall, Geoffrey F.
Chadwick, Oliver & Chadwick, Jenniffer. Fifty Ways to Meet Your Lover. Jenny, Brian P., ed. (Illus.). 119p. (Orig.). 1984. pap. 3.95 (ISBN 0-915765-00-4). Natl Pr Inc.
Chadwick, Owen. Catholicism & History. LC 77-77740. 1978. 24.95 (ISBN 0-521-21708-3). Cambridge U Pr.
--John Cassian. 2nd ed. 1968. 32.50 (ISBN 0-521-04607-6). Cambridge U Pr.
--Newman. (Past Masters Ser.). 1983. 12.95x (ISBN 0-19-287567-1); pap. 3.95 (ISBN 0-317-04413-3). Oxford U Pr.
--The Popes & European Revolution. (Oxford History of the Christian Church Ser.). 1981. 84.00x (ISBN 0-19-826919-6). Oxford U Pr.
--Reformation, Vol. 3. (History of the Church Ser.). (Orig.). 1964. pap. 4.95 (ISBN 0-14-020504-7, Pelican). Penguin.
--The Secularization of the European Mind in the Nineteenth Century. LC 77-88670. (The Gifford Lectures in the University of Edinburgh Ser.: 1973-1974). 278p. 1976. 42.50 (ISBN 0-521-20892-0); pap. 13.95 (ISBN 0-521-29317-0). Cambridge U Pr.
--The Victorian Church, Pt. I. 3rd ed. (Ecclesiastical History of England Ser.). 1971. text ed. 30.00x (ISBN 0-06-491025-3, 06393). B&N Imports.
--The Victorian Church, Pt. II. 2nd ed. (Ecclesiastical History of England Ser.). 510p. 1972. text ed. 28.50x (ISBN 0-06-491026-1, 06394). B&N Imports.
Chadwick, Owen, ed. The Mind of the Oxford Movement. 1961. 18.50x (ISBN 0-8047-0342-6); pap. 3.95_O.P. (ISBN 0-8047-0343-4, SP41). Stanford U Pr.
--Western Asceticism. LC 58-8713. (Library of Christian Classics). 364p. 1979. softcover 8.95 (ISBN 0-664-24161-1). Westminster.
Chadwick, Ronald P. Teaching & Learning: An Integrated Approach to Christian Education. 256p. 1982. 14.95 (ISBN 0-8007-1267-6). Revell.
Chadwick, Roxane. Ameila Earhart: Aviation Pioneer. (Achievers Ser.). (Illus.). (gr. 4-10). 1986. PLB 6.95 (ISBN 0-8225-0484-7). Lerner Pubns.
--Anne Morrow Lindbergh: Pilot & Poet. (Achievers Ser.). (Illus.). 56p. (gr. 4-10). 1986. PLB 6.95 (ISBN 0-8225-0488-X). Lerner Pubns.
--Don't Shoot. LC 78-6101. (Real Life Bks). (Illus.). (gr. 2-9). 1978. PLB 5.95 (ISBN 0-8225-0706-4). Lerner Pubns.
Chadwick, Samuel. Path of Prayer. 1963. pap. 2.50 (ISBN 0-87508-095-2). Chr Lit.
--Way to Pentecost. 1960. pap. 2.50 (ISBN 0-87508-096-0). Chr Lit.
Chadwick, Suzanne, jt. auth. see Chadwick, John.
Chadwick, Whitney. Myth in Surrealist Painting, 1929-1939. Foster, Stephen, ed. LC 79-26713. (Studies in the Fine Arts: The Avant-Garde, No. 1). 262p. 1980. 39.95 (ISBN 0-8357-1057-2). UMI Res Pr.
Chadwick, William. Life & Times of Daniel Defoe. LC 68-58464. (Research & Source Ser.: No. 328). 1969. Repr. of 1859 ed. 26.50 (ISBN 0-8337-0509-1). B Franklin.
Chadwick, William J. & Bachelder, Joseph E. Administration & Enforcement of Titles I & II of ERISA: No. B373. (Procedural Law Affecting Qualified Plans Ser.). 18p. 1978. pap. 4.50 (ISBN 0-317-31248-0). Am Law Inst.
Chadwick, William J. & Hass, Lawrence J. The Annotated Fiduciary: Materials on Fiduciary Responsibility and Prohibited Transactions Under ERISA. 2nd ed. 487p. 1980. 35.00 (ISBN 0-89154-121-7). Intl Found Employ.
Chadwick-Jones, J. K. Brain, Environment, & Social Psychology. (Illus.). 224p. 1979. pap. text ed. 12.95 (ISBN 0-8391-1323-4). Univ Park.
Chadwin, Mark L. Warhawks: American Interventionists Before Pearl Harbor. Orig. Title: Hawks of World War Two. 1970. pap. 1.95x (ISBN 0-393-00546-1, Norton Lib). Norton.
Chadwyck-Healey, Charles, intro. by. Catalogue of British Official Publications not Published by HMSO 1980. 256p. 1981. lib. bdg. 140.00 (ISBN 0-85964-101-5). Chadwyck-Healey.
Chadwyck-Healey, Charles, pref. by. Catalogue of British Official Publications Not Published by HMSO, 1982. xxiii, 437p. 1983. lib. bdg. 160.00 (ISBN 0-85964-114-7). Chadwyck-Healey.
--Catalogue of British Official Publications Not Published by HMSO, 1981. 303p. 1983. lib. bdg. 140.00 (ISBN 0-85964-102-3). Chadwyck-Healey.
Chadzynski, Martin & Lakland, Carli. The Runaway! LC 79-14284. (gr. 7 up). 1979. 9.95 (ISBN 0-07-010360-7). McGraw.
Chae. Lebesque Integration. (Lecture Notes in Pure & Applied Mathematics Ser.: Vol. 58). 328p. 1980. 55.00 (ISBN 0-8247-6983-X). Dekker.
Chaet, Bernard. The Art of Drawing. 3rd ed. LC 82-15404. 1983. pap. 25.95 (ISBN 0-03-062028-7, HoltC, HoltC). HR&W.
--An Artist's Notebook: Techniques & Materials. LC 78-11274. 1979. pap. text ed. 21.95 (ISBN 0-03-040726-5, HoltC). HR&W.
Chafe, Wallace, ed. The Pear Stories: Cognitive, Cultural & Linguistic Aspects of Narrative Production, Vol. 3. (Advances in Discourse Processes Ser.: Vol. 3). (Illus.). 1980. text ed. 39.50x (ISBN 0-89391-032-5). Ablex Pub.
Chafe, Wallace L. The Caddoan, Iroquoian, & Siouan Languages. (Trends in Linguistics, State-of-the Art Reports Ser.: No. 3). 1976. pap. text ed. 13.20x (ISBN 90-2793-443-6). Mouton.
--Meaning & Structure of Language. LC 79-114855. x, 360p. 1975. pap. 11.00x (ISBN 0-226-10056-1, Phoen). U of Chicago Pr.
--Meaning & the Structure of Language. LC 79-114855. 1971. text ed. 20.00x (ISBN 0-226-10055-3). U of Chicago Pr.
Chafe, William H. American Woman: Her Changing Social, Economic & Political Roles, 1920-1970. 1974. pap. 8.95 (ISBN 0-19-501785-4, GB406). Oxford U Pr.
--Civilities & Civil Rights: Greensboro, North Carolina, & the Black Struggle for Freedom. (Illus.). 1980. 22.50x (ISBN 0-19-502625-X). Oxford U Pr.
--Civilities & Civil Rights: Greensboro, North Carolina, & the Black Struggle for Freedom. (Illus.). 1980. pap. 8.95 (ISBN 0-19-502919-4, GB 644, GB). Oxford U Pr.
--The Unfinished Journey: America Since World War II. (Illus.). 480p. 1986. 24.95 (ISBN 0-19-503639-5). Oxford U pr.
--Women & Equality: Changing Patterns in American Culture. LC 76-42639. 1977. 19.95x (ISBN 0-19-502158-4). Oxford U Pr.
--Women & Equality: Changing Patterns in American Culture. LC 76-42639. 1977. pap. 7.95 (ISBN 0-19-502365-X, GB531, GB). Oxford U Pr.
Chafe, William H. & Sitkoff, Harvard, eds. A History of Our Time: Readings on Postwar America. 1983. pap. 11.95x (ISBN 0-19-503174-1). Oxford U Pr.
Chafee, Zechariah. The Blessings of Liberty. LC 72-8237. 350p. 1973. Repr. of 1956 ed. lib. bdg. 17.50x (ISBN 0-8371-6536-9, CHBL). Greenwood.
--The Inquiring Mind. LC 74-699. (American Constitutional & Legal History Ser.). 276p. 1974. Repr. of 1928 ed. lib. bdg. 32.50 (ISBN 0-306-70641-5). Da Capo.
Chafee, Zechariah, Jr., et al. Third Degree. LC 70-90169. (Mass Violence in America Ser). 1969. Repr. of 1931 ed. 14.00 (ISBN 0-405-01304-3). Ayer Co Pubs.
Chafer, Lewis S. Grace. pap. 9.95 (ISBN 0-310-22331-8). Zondervan.
--He That Is Spiritual. 1918. 4.95 (ISBN 0-310-22341-5, Pub. by Dunham). Zondervan.
--Salvation. 160p. 1972. pap. 4.95 (ISBN 0-310-22351-2). Zondervan.
--Satan. 1977. pap. 4.95 (ISBN 0-310-22361-X). Zondervan.
--Systematic Theology, 8 vols. 2700p. 1981. Repr. 89.95 (ISBN 0-310-22378-4). Zondervan.
--True Evangelism. pap. 4.95 (ISBN 0-310-22381-4). Zondervan.
Chafer, Lewis S. & Walvoord, John F. Major Bible Themes. rev. ed. 11.95 (ISBN 0-310-22390-3). Zondervan.
Chafets, Ze'ev. Double Vision: How the Press Distorts America's View of the Middle East. LC 84-6742. 384p. 1984. 16.95 (ISBN 0-688-03977-4). Morrow.

Chafetz, Janet S. Masculine-Feminine or Human: An Overview of the Sociology of Gender Roles. 2nd ed. LC 77-83425. 275p. 1978. pap. text ed. 11.50 (ISBN 0-87581-231-7). Peacock Pubs.

--A Primer on the Construction & Testing of Theories in Sociology. LC 77-83430. 132p. 1978. pap. text ed. 7.95 (ISBN 0-87581-232-5). Peacock Pubs.

--Sex & Advantage: A Comparative, Macro-Structural Theory of Sex Stratification. LC 83-19077. 142p. 1984. 23.50x (ISBN 0-86598-159-0); pap. 11.95x (ISBN 0-86598-161-2). Rowman & Allanheld.

Chafetz, M. E., jt. ed. see Blane, H. T.

Chafetz, Marion C. Health Education: An Annotated Bibliography on Lifestyle, Behavior, & Health. 272p. 1981. 35.00x (ISBN 0-306-40754-X, Plenum Pr). Plenum Pub.

Chafetz, Morris, jt. ed. see O'Brien, Robert.

Chafetz, Morris E. The Alcoholic Patient: Diagnosis & Management. 240p. 1983. 24.95 (ISBN 0-87489-276-7). Med Economics.

Chaffe, Beatrice, jt. auth. see Hovelsrud, Joyce.

Chaffee, Dorcas, jt. ed. see Goodwin, Del.

Chaffee, Ellen E., et al. Basic Physiology & Anatomy. 4th ed. LC 79-15976. 628p. 1980. text ed. 27.50x (ISBN 0-397-54227-5, Lippincott Nursing). Lippincott.

Chaffee, John. Thinking Critically. 352p. 1984. pap. text ed. write for info. (ISBN 0-395-34105-1); instr's. manual avail. (ISBN 0-395-34106-X). HM.

Chaffee, John W. The Thorny Gates of Learning: A Social History of Examinations in Sung China (960-1279 AD) (Cambridge Studies in Chinese History, Literature & Institutions). 250p. Date not set. price not set. (ISBN 0-521-30207-2). Cambridge U Pr.

Chaffee, Margaret, jt. auth. see Bunker, Andrew F.

Chaffee, S. & Petrick, M. Using the Mass Media: Communication Problems in American Society. 1975. 27.95 (ISBN 0-07-010375-5). McGraw.

Chaffee, Steven H., ed. Political Communication. LC 75-14629. (Sage Annual Reviews of Communication Research: Vol. 4). 319p. 1975. 25.00 (ISBN 0-8039-0505-X); pap. 12.50 (ISBN 0-8039-0507-6). Sage.

Chaffee, Suzy & Adler, Bill. The I Love New York Fitness Book. LC 83-60414. (Illus.). 224p. 1983. 17.95 (ISBN 0-688-02040-2). Morrow.

Chaffee, Wilber A., jt. ed. see Ross, Stanley R.

Chaffee, Wilber A., Jr. & Griffin, Honor M. Dissertations on Latin America by U. S. Historians, 1960-1970: A Bibliography. (ILAS Guides & Bibliographies Ser.: No. 7). 74p. 1973. pap. 3.50x (ISBN 0-292-71503-X). U of Tex Pr.

Chaffer, J. & Taylor, Lawrence. History & the History Teacher. 136p. 1975. 12.95x (ISBN 0-8464-1260-8). Beekman Pubs.

Chaffers, William. Collectors Handbook of Marks & Monograms on Pottery & Porcelain. 8.50 (ISBN 0-87505-066-2). Borden.

--Marks & Monograms on European & Oriental Pottery & Porcelain. 39.95 (ISBN 0-87505-067-0). Borden.

Chaffetz, David. A Journey Through Afghanistan: A Memorial. LC 84-2623. (Illus.). xviii, 254p. 1984. pap. 9.95 (ISBN 0-226-10063-4). U of Chicago Pr.

Chaffetz, David & Rapoport, Mitchell, eds. The Middle East: Issues & Events of 1978 from The New York Times Information Bank. LC 78-32140. (News in Print Ser.). 300p. 1979. lib. bdg. 27.45x (ISBN 0-405-12875-4). Ayer Co Pubs.

Chaffin, Bethany. Caring for Those You Love: A Guide to Compassionate Care for the Aged. 1985. 7.95. Horizon Utah.

--Whence Comes the Rain. LC 83-81724. 114p. 1983. 6.95 (ISBN 0-88290-230-X). Horizon-Utah.

Chaffin, Charles, jt. auth. see Neufeld, Herm.

Chaffin, Don B. & Andersson, Gunnar B. Occupational Biomechanics. LC 84-3000. 454p. 1984. text ed. 29.50x (ISBN 0-471-87634-8, Pub. by Wiley Interscience). Wiley.

Chaffin, Don B., jt. auth. see Greenberg, Leo.

Chaffin, James B. The Wolfer. 1980. pap. 1.50 (ISBN 0-505-51461-3, Pub. by Tower Bks). Dorchester Pub Co.

Chaffin, Kenneth L. The Reluctant Witness. LC 74-84548. 1975. 6.95 (ISBN 0-8054-5550-7). Broadman.

Chaffin, Lillie D. Tommy's Big Problem. PLB 6.19 (ISBN 0-8313-0016-7). Lantern.

--Up Hatfield Holler. 40p. (Orig.). 1981. pap. 4.50 (ISBN 0-937992-04-6). Ashford Pr CT.

Chaffin, Verner F. The Rule Against Perpetuities in Georgia. 249p. 1984. 30.00 (ISBN 0-87215-746-6). Michie Co.

--Studies in the Georgia Law of Decendents Estates & Future Inte rest. 478p. 1979. 35.00 (ISBN 0-87215-221-9). Michie Co.

Chaffurin, L. Parfait Secretaire. (Fr). pap. 9.95 (ISBN 0-685-14021-0, 3922). Larousse.

Chaffurin, L. & Mergault, J. Dictionnaire Bilingue Larousse, Francais-Anglais, Anglais-Francais. (Apollo). (Fr. & Eng.). 10.95 (ISBN 0-685-13856-9, 3767). Larousse.

Chafin, Kenneth L. Tell All the Little Children. 1976. pap. 0.75 (ISBN 0-8054-6211-2). Broadman.

Chafin, Kenneth L. & Ogilvie, Lloyd J. The Communicator's Commentary: Corinthians First; Second, Vol. 7. 1983. 15.95 (ISBN 0-8499-0347-5). Word Bks.

Chafin, M. B. & Turner, M. Malissa. Badminton Everyone. (Illus.). 148p. (Orig.). 1984. pap. text ed. 6.95x (ISBN 0-88725-013-0). Hunter Textbks.

Chafin, M. B., jt. auth. see Moore, Clancy.

Chagall, Bella. First Encounter. Bray, Barbara, tr. from Fr. (Illus.). 348p. 1983. 16.95 (ISBN 0-8052-3768-2). Schocken.

Chagall, David. Diary of a Deaf Mute. 1971. pap. 3.50 (ISBN 0-916538-01-X). Millenium Hse.

--The New Kingmakers. LC 80-7932. 1981. 14.95 (ISBN 0-15-165203-1). HarBraceJ.

Chagall, Marc. Chagall's Daphnis & Chloe. LC 77-6207. (Illus.). 232p. 1977. 70.00 (ISBN 0-8076-0880-7). Braziller.

Chaganti, R. S. & German, James L., III, eds. Genetics in Clinical Oncology. (Illus.). 288p. 1985. 37.50 (ISBN 0-19-503609-3). Oxford U Pr.

Chaghaghi, F. S. Time Series Package (TSPACK) (Lecture Notes in Computer Science Ser.: Vol. 187). iii, 305p. 1985. pap. 18.70 (ISBN 0-387-15202-4). Springer-Verlag.

Chagnon, Jacqui & Luce, Don, eds. Of Quiet Courage: Poems from Viet-Nam. (Illus.). 150p. 1974. 3.00 (ISBN 0-686-36613-1). Asia Resource.

Chagnon, Napolean. Yanomamo: The Fierce People. 3rd ed. LC 83-313. 224p. 1984. pap. text ed. 10.95 (ISBN 0-03-062328-6). HR&W.

Chahine, Robert A., ed. Coronary Artery Spasm. (Illus.). 288p. 1983. monograph 34.50 (ISBN 0-87993-192-2). Futura Pub.

Chai, Chu & Chai, Winberg. The Story of Chinese Philosophy. LC 75-17196. (Illus.). 252p. 1975. Repr. of 1961 ed. lib. bdg. 22.50x (ISBN 0-8371-8289-1, CHSC). Greenwood.

Chai, Ch'U & Chai, Winberg, eds. Li Chi: Book of Rites, 2 Vols. 1966. 25.00 (ISBN 0-8216-0107-5). Univ Bks.

Chai, Henry, jt. auth. see Chai, Winchung.

Chai, Hong-Chan. Planning Education for a Plural Society. (Fundamentals of Educational Planning: No. 16). 67p. (Orig.). 1971. pap. 5.00 (ISBN 92-803-1042-9, U449, UNESCO). Unipub.

Chai, Mary Ann P. Herb Walk: Medicinal Guide. (Illus.). 127p. 1978. pap. text ed. 6.00 perfect bdg. (ISBN 0-935596-01-1). Gluten Co.

Chai, Winberg, jt. auth. see Chai, Chu.

Chai, Winberg, jt. auth. see Ch'u Chai.

Chai, Winberg, jt. ed. see Chai, Ch'U.

Chai, Winberg, jt. ed. see Hsiung, James C.

Chai, Winchung & Chai, Henry. Programming Standard COBOL. 1976. 18.50i (ISBN 0-12-166550-X). Acad Pr.

Chaianov, Aleksandr. Istoriia Parikmakherskoi Kukly I Drugie Sochineniia Botanika Kh. LC 82-60919. 450p. 1982. pap. 15.00 (ISBN 0-89830-028-2). Russica Pubs.

Chaichian, M. & Nelipa, N. F. Introduction to Gauge Field Theories. Estrin, J., tr. (Texts & Monographs in Physics). (Illus.). 350p. 1984. 43.00 (ISBN 0-387-13008-X). Springer-Verlag.

Chaigne, Louis. Paul Claudel: The Man & the Mystic. LC 78-5951. 1978. Repr. of 1961 ed. lib. bdg. 24.75x (ISBN 0-313-20465-9, CHCL). Greenwood.

Chaij, Fernando. Preparation for the Final Crisis. LC 66-29118. 1966. pap. 5.95 (ISBN 0-8163-0137-9, 16510-0). Pacific Pr Pub Assn.

Chaika, Elaine. Language: The Social Mirror. 272p. 1982. pap. 13.95 (ISBN 0-88377-203-5). Newbury Hse.

Chaiken, Irwin M., et al. Affinity Chromatography & Biological Recognition (Symposium) 1983. 47.00 (ISBN 0-12-166580-1). Acad Pr.

Chaiken, Jan M., jt. auth. see National Institute of Justice.

Chaiken, William E. & Harper, Mary J. Mainstreaming the Learning Disabled Adolescent: A Staff Development Guide. (Illus.). 162p. 1979. 16.75x (ISBN 0-398-03871-6). C C Thomas.

Chaikin, Joseph. The Presence of the Actor. LC 70-175287. (Illus.). 1972. pap. text ed. 4.95x (ISBN 0-689-70338-4, 194). Atheneum.

Chaikin, Joseph, jt. auth. see Malpede, Karen.

Chaikin, Judy, ed. see Hurwitz, Sadie W.

Chaikin, Milton. Right Words in Right Places: A Workbook in Diction & Sentence Style. 1979. pap. text ed. 9.95 (ISBN 0-8403-2080-9). Kendall-Hunt.

Chaikin, Miriam. Ask Another Question: The Story & Meaning of Passover. LC 84-12744. (Illus.). 96p. (gr. 3-7). 1985. pap. 13.95 (ISBN 0-89919-281-5, Clarion). HM.

--Finders Weepers. LC 79-9608. (Illus.). 128p. (gr. 3-6). 1980. 11.06i (ISBN 0-06-021176-8); PLB 10.89 (ISBN 0-06-021177-6). HarpJ.

--Getting Even. LC 81-48647. (A Charlotte Zolotow Bks.). (Illus.). 128p. (gr. 3-7). 1982. 10.53i (ISBN 0-06-021164-4); PLB 10.89g (ISBN 0-06-021165-2). HarpJ.

--How Yossi Beat the Evil Urge. LC 82-47705. (A Charlotte Zolotow Bk.). (Illus.). 64p. (gr. 3-5). 1983. 9.57i (ISBN 0-06-021184-9); PLB 8.89g (ISBN 0-06-021185-7). HarpJ.

--I Should Worry, I Should Care. 112p. (gr. 3-6). 1982. pap. 1.75 (ISBN 0-440-44149-8, YB). Dell.

--I Should Worry, I Should Care. LC 78-19480. (Illus.). (gr. 3-6). 1979. PLB 10.89 (ISBN 0-06-021175-X). HarpJ.

--Joshua in the Promised land. (Illus.). (gr. 3-8). 1982. 11.50 (ISBN 0-89919-120-7, Clarion). HM.

--Light Another Candle: The Story & Meaning of Hanukkah. LC 80-28137. (Illus.). 80p. (gr. 3-6). 1981. 10.50 (ISBN 0-395-31026-1, Clarion); pap. 3.95 (ISBN 0-89919-057-X). HM.

--Lower! Higher! You're a Liar! LC 83-48445. (A Charlotte Zolotow Bk.). (Illus.). 160p. (gr. 3-7). 1984. 11.49i (ISBN 0-06-021186-5); PLB 11.89g (ISBN 0-06-021187-3). HarpJ.

--Make Noise, Make Merry: The Story & Meaning of Purim. (Illus.). 96p. (gr. 3-6). 1983. 11.95 (ISBN 0-89919-140-1, Clarion). HM.

--Shake a Palm Branch: The Story & Meaning of Sukkot. LC 84-5022. (Illus.). 80p. (gr. 3-6). 1984. PLB 12.95 (ISBN 0-89919-254-8, Clarion). HM.

--Yossi Asks the Angels for Help. LC 84-48351. (Charlotte Zolotow Bk.). (Illus.). 64p. (gr. 3-5). 1985. 8.61i (ISBN 0-06-021195-4); PLB 8.89g (ISBN 0-06-021196-2). HarpJ.

Chaikin, Miriam & Frampton, David. The Seventh Day: The Story of the Jewish Sabbath. LC 82-16987. (Illus.). 48p. (Orig.). 1983. pap. 4.95 (ISBN 0-8052-0743-0). Schocken.

Chaikin, Richard. Elements of Surgical Treatment in the Delivery of Periodontal Therapy. (Illus.). 177p. 1978. 64.00 (ISBN 3-87652-661-2). Quint Pub Co.

Chaikin, Sol C. A Labor Viewpoint. LC 80-12784. (Illus.). 250p. (Orig.). 1980. pap. 10.95 (ISBN 0-912526-26-2). Lib Res.

Chaiklin, J. B., et al. Hearing Measurement: A Book of Readings. 2nd ed. 466p. 1982. 29.95 (ISBN 0-471-87864-2). Wiley.

Chaillet, Jean-Paul & Vincent, Elizabeth. Francis Ford Coppola. (Illus.). 128p. 1985. pap. 9.95 (ISBN 0-312-30317-3). St Martin.

Chailley, Jacques. Forty Thousand Years of Music: Man in Search of Music. Myers, Rollo, tr. from Fr. LC 74-31227. (Music Reprint Ser). (Illus.). xiv, 229p. 1975. Repr. of 1964 ed. lib. bdg. 29.50 (ISBN 0-306-70661-X). Da Capo.

--The Magic Flute, Masonic Opera. Weinstock, Herbert, tr. from Fr. (Music Reprint Ser.). xii, 336p. 1982. Repr. of 1971 ed. lib. bdg. 35.00 (ISBN 0-306-76149-1). Da Capo.

Chailley-Bert, Joseph. Les Compagnies de colonisation sous l'ancien regime. 1967. Repr. of 1898 ed. 22.50 (ISBN 0-8337-0510-5). B Franklin.

--Java et ses habitants. LC 77-86968. Repr. of 1900 ed. 27.50 (ISBN 0-404-16701-2). AMS Pr.

Chaillie, Jean H. I Never Wanted to Be Anything but Blue. (Illus.). 96p. (Orig.). 1985. pap. 8.95 (ISBN 0-933299-00-1). Le Chateau.

Chaillie, Paul E. Du see Du Chaillu, Paul.

Chaillie, Paul E. Du see Du Chaillu, Paul E.

Chaillou, Jacques. Hyperbolic Differential Polynomials & Their Singular Perturbations. Nienhuys, J. W., tr. from Fr. (Mathematics & Its Applications Ser.: No. 3). 1980. lib. bdg. 31.50 (ISBN 90-277-1032-5, Pub. by Reidel Holland). Kluwer Academic.

Chaillu, Paul B. Du see Du Chaillu, Paul.

Chaillu, Paul B. Du see Du Chaillu, Paul B.

Chaillu, Paul Du see Du Chaillu, Paul.

Chaim, B. A Bibliography of Mutualism & Individualist Anarchism. 1979. lib. bdg. 42.95 (ISBN 0-686-25748-0). Mutualist Pr.

Chaim, B., ed. Films of Charley Chase. (Cinema Ser.). (Illus.). 1979. lib. bdg. 69.95 (ISBN 0-685-99610-7). Revisionist Pr.

--Neturei Karta; Voice of Anti-Zionist Judaism: A Study. 1980. 75.00 (ISBN 0-87700-273-8). Revisionist Pr.

Chaim, Bezalel. Against the Tide: Jewish Nonconformist Views of Israel & Zionism. 1979. lib. bdg. 42.95 (ISBN 0-686-24783-3). M Buber Pr.

--Economics of Scarcity. 1979. lib. bdg. 39.95 (ISBN 0-87700-293-2). Revisionist Pr.

--Hugo Bilgram & Louis Levy: The Battle Against the Money Monopoly. 1980. lib. bdg. 49.95 (ISBN 0-686-26596-3). Mutualist Pr.

Chaim, Bezalel, ed. A Bio-Bibliographical Dictionary of Mutualist & Individualist Anarchist Authors. 1980. lib. bdg. 49.95 (ISBN 0-686-26595-5). Mutualist Pr.

--Toward Jewish-Arab Rapprochement: A History of Ihud. 1979. lib. bdg. 44.95 (ISBN 0-686-24785-X). M Buber Pr.

Chaim, Chafetz, pseud. Ahavath Chesed: The Love of Kindness As Required by G-D. Oschry, Leonard, tr. from Hebrew. 1978. pap. 4.95 (ISBN 0-87306-167-5). Feldheim.

Chaim, Lazar. Destruction & Resistance. LC 84-52354. (Illus.). 240p. 1985. pap. 13.95 (ISBN 0-88400-113-X). Shengold.

Chain, Steve, jt. auth. see Boas, Max.

Chain Store Guide Staff. Directory of Auto Aftermarket Suppliers, 1985-86. (Chain Store Guide Ser.). 1984. 149.00 (ISBN 0-86730-022-1, Pub. by Bus Guides Inc). Lebhar Friedman.

--Directory of Chain Restaurant Operators, 1985. (Chain Store Guide Ser.). 1985. 169.99 (ISBN 0-86730-012-4, Pub. by Bus Guides Inc). Lebhar Friedman.

--Directory of Computer & Software Retailers, 1985. (Chain Store Guide Ser.). 1985. 389.00 (ISBN 0-86730-010-8, Pub. by Bus Guides Inc). Lebhar Friedman.

--Directory of Cooperative Chains, Voluntary Chains & Wholesale Grocers, 1985. (Chain Store Guide Ser.). 1984. 159.00 (ISBN 0-86730-019-1, Pub. by Bus Guides Inc). Lebhar Friedman.

--Directory of Department Stores, 1985. (Chain Store Guide Ser.). 1984. 169.00 (ISBN 0-86730-020-5, Pub. by Bus Guides Inc). Lebhar Friedman.

--Directory of Discount Stores, 1985. (Chain Store Guide Ser.). 1985. 169.00 (ISBN 0-86730-023-X, Pub. by Bus Guides Inc). Lebhar Friedman.

--Directory of Drug Stores & HBA Chains, 1985. (Chain Store Guide Ser.). 1984. 169.00 (ISBN 0-86730-021-3, Pub. by Bus Guides Inc). Lebhar Friedman.

--Directory of Food Service Distributors, 1985. (Chain Store Guide Ser.). 1985. 159.00 (ISBN 0-86730-013-2, Pub. by Bus Guides Inc). Lebhar Friedman.

--Directory of General Merchandise, Variety Chains & Specialty Stores, 1985. (Chain Store Guide Ser.). 1985. 159.00 (ISBN 0-86730-011-6, Pub. by Bus Guides Inc). Lebhar Friedman.

--Directory of Hardware & Housewares Distributors, 1985-86. (Chain Store Guide Ser.). 1985. 149.00 (ISBN 0-86730-024-8, Pub. by Bus Guides Inc). Lebhar Friedman.

--Directory of Home Center Operators & Hardware Chains, 1985. (Chain Store Guide Ser.). 1985. 149.00 (ISBN 0-86730-014-0, Pub. by Bus Guides Inc). Lebhar Friedman.

--Directory of Men's & Boy's Wear Specialty Stores TM, 1985. (Chain Store Guide Ser.). 1984. 129.00 (ISBN 0-86730-017-5, Pub. by Bus Guides Inc). Lebhar Friedman.

--Directory of Supermarket, Grocery & Convenience Store Chains, 1985. (Chain Store Guide Ser.). 1984. 169.00 (ISBN 0-86730-015-9, Pub. by Chain Store Guide). Lebhar Friedman.

--Directory of VARS (Value Added Resellers), 1985. (Chain Store Guide Ser.). 1985. 289.00 (ISBN 0-86730-018-3, Pub. by Chain Store Guide). Lebhar Friedman.

--Directory of Women's & Children's Wear Specialty Stores TM, 1985. (Chain Store Guide Ser.). 1984. 129.00 (ISBN 0-86730-016-7, Pub. by Bus Guides Inc). Lebhar Friedman.

Chaintrier, Louis. Balloon Post of the Siege of Paris, Eighteen Seventy to Eighteen Seventy-One. 163p. (Eng.). 12.50 (ISBN 0-318-12356-8); members 10.00 (ISBN 0-318-12357-6). Am Air Mail.

Chairanya, Krishna. Freedom & Transcendence. 1983. 28.00x (ISBN 0-8364-0953-1, Pub. by Manohar India). South Asia Bks.

Chairman of Inquiry Commission, jt. ed. see Asmal, Kadmar.

Chairman Ronald. Quotations from Chairman Ronald. 96p. 1982. vinyl cover 4.00 (ISBN 0-939478-02-1). Calif Irvine.

Chais, Pamela. Final Cut. 304p. 1983. pap. 2.95 (ISBN 0-441-23540-9). Ace Bks.

Chaison, Gary N. & Rose, Joseph B., eds. Readings in Canadian Industrial Relations. LC 74-11073. 299p. 1974. text ed. 28.50x (ISBN 0-8422-5191-X); pap. text ed. 8.75x (ISBN 0-8422-0441-5). Irvington.

Chai-Song, Hong. Syntaxe des Verbes de mouvement en Coreen Contemporain. (Lingvisticae Investigationes Supplementas: No. 12). 309p. (French.). 1984. 32.00x (ISBN 90-272-3122-2). Benjamins North Am.

Chaisson, Dick. Hometown Chronicles. LC 84-62926. (Illus.). 160p. (Orig.). 1985. pap. 6.95 (ISBN 0-912395-05-2). Millers River Pub Co.

Chaisson, Eric. Cosmic Dawn: The Origins of Matter & Life. (Illus.). 320p. 1981. 18.45i (ISBN 0-316-13590-9, Pub. by Atlantic Monthly Pr). Little.

--Cosmic Dawn: The Origins of Matter & Life. 320p. 1984. pap. 3.95 (ISBN 0-425-06165-5). Berkley Pub.

Chaisson, Eric J., jt. auth. see Field, George B.

Chaisson-Stewart, G. Maureen, ed. Depression in the Elderly: An Interdisciplinary Approach. 377p. 1985. 21.95 (ISBN 0-471-87059-5). Wiley.

Chait, Richard P. & Ford, Andrew T. Beyond Traditional Tenure: A Guide to Sound Policies & Practices. LC 81-23606. (Higher Education Ser.). 1982. text ed. 19.95x (ISBN 0-87589-519-0). Jossey-Bass.

Chaitanya, Deva B. An Introduction to Indian Music. 149p. 1981. 9.95 (ISBN 0-317-12340-8, Pub. by Pubns Div India). Asia Bk Corp.

Chaitanya, K. A Profile of Indian Culture. 184p. 1982. text ed. 39.25x (ISBN 0-391-02914-2). Humanities.

Chaitanya, Krishna. A History of Arabic Literature. 1983. 18.00x (ISBN 0-8364-1045-9, Pub. by Manohar India). South Asia Bks.

--A History of Indian Painting: Pahari Traditions, Vol. 4. (Illus.). 150p. 1983. text ed. 68.00x (ISBN 0-391-03007-8). Humanities.

--A History of Indian Painting: The Mural Tradition. LC 76-900494. 1976. 28.50x (ISBN 0-88386-786-9). South Asia Bks.

--A History of Indian Painting: The Mural Tradition, Vol. 1. (Illus.). 92p. 1976. text ed. 23.50x (ISBN 0-391-02590-2, Pub. by Abhinav India). Humanities.

--A History of Indian Painting: The Rajasthani Traditions, Vol. 3. 134p. 1982. text ed. 50.50x (ISBN 0-391-02413-2, Pub. by Abhinav India). Humanities.

--A History of Indian Painting, Vol. 2: Manuscript, Moghul & Deccani Traditions. (Illus.). 92p. 1979. text ed. 36.50x (ISBN 0-391-02591-0, Pub. by Abhinav India). Humanities.

--A History of Malayalam Literature. 1971. 27.50x (ISBN 0-8046-8805-2, Pub. by Kennikat). Assoc Faculty Pr.

--Rohanta & Nandriya. (Nehru Library for Children). (Illus.). (gr. 1-9). 1979. pap. 2.00 (ISBN 0-89744-179-6). Auromere.

--Sociology of Freedom. 1978. 18.50x (ISBN 0-8364-0008-9). South Asia Bks.

Chaitanya, Krishna see Nair, K. K., pseud.

Chaitanya, Swami Christ, ed. see Rajneesh, Bhagwan Shree.

Chaitanya Yati, Guru N. Bhagavad Gita: A Sublime Hymn of Yoga. Nataraja Guru, tr. 550p. 1980. text ed. 50.00x (ISBN 0-7069-1129-6, Pub. by Vikas India). Advent NY.

Chaithiraphan, S. Current Concept in the Therapy of Hypertension with Beta-Blockers. (Journal: Cardiology Series: Vol. 66, Suppl. 1). (Illus.). vi, 62p. 1980. pap. 14.00 (ISBN 3-8055-0912-X). S Karger.

Chaitin, P. The Coastal War. LC 84-165. (Civil War Ser.). (gr. 7 up). 1984. lib. bdg. 19.94 (ISBN 0-8094-4733-9, Pub. by Time-Life). Silver.

Chaitin, Rebecca D., jt. auth. see Knowlton, Judith M.

Chaitkin, Anton. Treason in America: From Aaron Burr to Averell Harriman. (Illus.). 317p. (Orig.). 1984. pap. 5.95 (ISBN 0-933488-32-7). New Benjamin.

Chaitow, Alkimini. Greek Vegetarian Cooking: Colorful Dishes from the Eastern Shore of the Mediterranean. 128p. (Orig.). 1984. pap. 6.95 (ISBN 0-7225-0725-9). Thorsons Pubs.

Chaitow, Boris R. My Healing Secrets. 128p. 1980. 14.95 (ISBN 0-8464-1066-4). Beekman Pubs.

--My Healing Secrets. 1980. 11.75x (ISBN 0-85032-163-8, Pub. by Daniel Co England). State Mutual Bk.

Chaitow, Leon. The Acupuncture Treatment of Pain: Safe & Effective Methods for Using Acupuncture in Pain Relief. 188p. (Orig.). 1984. pap. text ed. 9.95 (ISBN 0-7225-0811-5). Thorsons Pubs.

--Amino Acids in Therapy: A Guide to the Therapeutic Application of Protein Constituents. 96p. (Orig.). 1985. pap. 7.95 (ISBN 0-7225-0998-7). Thorsons Pubs.

--Candida Albicans. 80p. (Orig.). 1985. pap. 3.95 (ISBN 0-7225-1144-2). Thorsons Pubs.

--An End to Cancer. 1978. 6.95x (ISBN 0-7225-0473-X). Cancer Control Soc.

--An End to Cancer? The Nutritional Approach to its Prevention & Control. 160p. (Orig.). 1985. pap. 6.95 (ISBN 0-7225-0927-8). Thorsons Pubs.

--Instant Pain Control. (Illus.). 96p. 1983. pap. 6.95 (ISBN 0-671-49168-7, Wallaby). S&S.

--Neuro-Muscular Technique: A Practitioner's Guide to Soft Tissue Manipulation. 144p. 1984. text ed. 29.95 (ISBN 0-7225-0586-8). Thorsons Pubs.

--Osteopathy: A Complete Health Care System. (Alternative Therapies Ser.). (Illus.). 112p. (Orig.). 1985. pap. 6.95 (ISBN 0-7225-0745-3). Thorsons Pubs.

--Relaxation & Meditation Techniques: A Complete Stress-Proofing System. 128p. 1983. pap. 6.95 (ISBN 0-7225-0737-2). Thorsons Pubs.

--Your Complete Stress-Proofing Program: How to Protect Yourself Against the Ill-Effects of Stress. 128p. (Orig.). 1985. pap. 4.95 (ISBN 0-7225-0983-9). Thorsons Pubs.

Chaix-Ruy, Jules. La Formation de la Pensee Philosophique de G. B. Vico. Mayer, J. P., ed. LC 78-67339. (European Political Thought Ser.). (Fr.). 1979. Repr. of 1943 ed. lib. bdg. 23.00x (ISBN 0-405-11684-5). Ayer Co Pubs.

Chajes. Student's Guide Through the Talmud. 10.95 (ISBN 0-87306-089-X). Feldheim.

Chajes, Alexander. Principles of Structural Stability Theory. (Civil Engineering & Engineering Mechanics Ser.). (Illus.). 288p. 1974. 41.95 (ISBN 0-13-709964-9). P-H.

--Structural Analysis. (Illus.). 384p. 1983. 35.95 (ISBN 0-13-853408-X). P-H.

Chakabarti, Ajit K. A Treatise on Book Selection. 300p. 1983. text ed. 32.50x (ISBN 0-86590-129-5). Apt Bks.

Chakela, Q. K. Soil Erosion & Reservoir Sedimentation in Lesotho. 1981. text ed. 29.50x (ISBN 0-8419-9737-3, Africana). Holmes & Meier.

Chakeres, John A. Traces: An Investigation in Reason. LC 76-47816. (Illus., Orig.). 1977. pap. 7.95 (ISBN 0-917924-00-2). Nuance Pr.

Chakeres, John A., jt. auth. see Manusos, Mary.

Chakerian, G. D., et al. Geometry: A Guided Inquiry. rev. ed. 557p. 1984. text ed. 16.50 (ISBN 0-916327-08-6); tchr's. ed. 18.50 (ISBN 0-916327-09-4). Davis Math Pr.

--Geometry: A Guided Inquiry. rev. ed. 1984. solutions key, 89 p. 6.00 (ISBN 0-916327-10-8); test questions, 44 p. 4.00 (ISBN 0-916327-11-6). Davis Math Pr.

Chaki-Sircar, Manjusri. Women of the Manipur Valley: Lai Harouba Ritual. 1984. text ed. 35.00 (Pub. By Vikas India). Advent NY.

Chakoo, B. L. Aldous Huxley & Eastern Wisdom. 308p. 1981. text ed. 16.75x (ISBN 0-391-02910-X). Humanities.

Chakotin, Serge. Rape of the Masses: The Psychology of Totalitarian Political Propaganda. LC 77-157553. (Studies in Philosophy, No. 40). 1971. lib. bdg. 49.95x (ISBN 0-8383-1264-0). Haskell.

Chakrabart, C. L., ed. Progress in Analytical Atomic Spectroscopy, Vol. 1, Pt. 1. 1978. 40.00 (ISBN 0-08-022924-7). Pergamon.

Chakrabarti, C. L. Progress in Analytical Atomic Spectroscopy, 2 vols. (Illus.). 282p. 1981. Set. 84.00 (ISBN 0-08-027126-X). Pergamon.

Chakrabarti, C. L., ed. Progress in Analytical Atomic Spectroscopy, Vol. 3. 368p. 1981. 84.00 (ISBN 0-08-029081-7, E130). Pergamon.

--Progress in Analytical Atomic Spectroscopy, Vol. 4. 440p. 1982. 115.00 (ISBN 0-08-029659-9). Pergamon.

--Progress in Analytical Atomic Spectroscopy, Vol. 5. (Illus.). 470p. 1983. 114.00 (ISBN 0-08-030418-4). Pergamon.

Chakrabarti, C. L. & Sturgeon, R. E., eds. Progress in Analytical Atomic Spectroscopy, Vol. 6. (Illus.). 444p. 1985. 132.00 (ISBN 0-08-032307-3). Pergamon.

Chakrabarti, Jayanta. Techniques in Indian Mural Painting. (Illus.). 134p. 1981. text ed. 28.50x (ISBN 0-391-02499-X). Humanities.

Chakrabarti, Kisor K. The Logic of Gotama. LC 77-13853. (Society for Asian & Comparative Philosophy Monograph: No. 5). 168p. 1978. pap. text ed. 7.00x (ISBN 0-8248-0601-8). UH Pr.

Chakrabarti, Nirendranath. The Naked King & Other Poems. Mukherjee, Sujit & Mukherjee, Meenakshi, trs. from Bengali. (Saffronbird Bk). 53p. 8.00 (ISBN 0-88253-833-0); pap. 4.80 (ISBN 0-88253-834-9). Ind-US Inc.

Chakrabarti, Prafulla. Social Profile of Tarakeswar. 1984. 14.00x (ISBN 0-8364-1244-3, Pub. by Mukhopadhyay India). South Asia Bks.

Chakrabarti, Radharaman. The Political Economy of India's Foreign Policy. 1983. 12.75 (ISBN 0-8364-1004-1, Pub. by KP Bagchi India). South Asia Bks.

Chakrabarty, A. M. Genetic Engineering. (Uniscience Ser.). 208p. 1978. 66.00 (ISBN 0-8493-5259-2). CRC Pr.

Chakrabarty, A. M., ed. Biodegradation & Detoxification of Environmental Pollutants. 160p. 1982. 50.00 (ISBN 0-8493-5524-9). CRC Pr.

Chakrabarty, B. N. Industrial Chemistry. 1981. 40.00x (ISBN 0-686-72953-6, Pub. by Oxford & IBH India). State Mutual Bk.

Chakrabarty, S. C. Imagery of Physical Beauty in Tennyson. 1978. Repr. of 1962 ed. lib. bdg. 12.50 (ISBN 0-8495-0750-2). Arden Lib.

Chakrabarty, Saroj. With West Bengal Chief Ministers: Memoirs, 1962-1977. cancelled (ISBN 0-86131-117-5, Orient Longman). South Asia Bks.

Chakraberti, Kanchan. Society, Religion & Art of the Kushana India: A Historico-Symbiosis. (Illus.). 116p. 1981. text ed. 32.75x (ISBN 0-391-02501-5). Humanities.

Chakraberty, Chandra. A Comparative Hindu Materia Medica. 198p. 1983. Repr. of 1923 ed. text ed. 30.00x (ISBN 0-86590-166-X). Apt Bks.

--An Interpretation of Ancient Hindu Medicine. 599p. 1983. Repr. of 1923 ed. text ed. 75.00x (ISBN 0-86590-190-2). Apt Bks.

Chakraborti, Haripada. Trade & Commerce of Ancient India. 354p. 1966. 15.00x (ISBN 0-87471-305-6). Rowman.

Chakraborti, S. K. Behaviour of Prices in India, Nineteen Fifty-Two to Nineteen Seventy. 1976. 12.50x (ISBN 0-333-90148-7). South Asia Bks.

Chakraborty, A. K. Jawaharlal Nehru's Writings. 1981. 15.00x (ISBN 0-685-59378-9). South Asia Bks.

Chakraborty, Amalendu. Mrinal Sen's in Search of Famine. Bandhyopadhyay, Samik, tr. (Illus., Orig.). 1984. pap. text ed. 8.95 (ISBN 0-86132-044-1, Pub. by Seagull Bks India). Apt Bks.

Chakraborty, D., jt. auth. see Ghosh, A.

Chakraborty, J. & Dhande, S. G. Kinematics & Geometry of Planer & Spatial CAM Mechanisms. LC 76-50585. 162p. 1977. 18.95x (ISBN 0-470-15069-6). Halsted Pr.

Chakraborty, Kishore, jt. auth. see Skinner, Wickham.

Chakraborty, R., jt. ed. see Schull, W. J.

Chakraborty, S. C. Imagery of Physical Beauty in Tennyson. 1947. lib. bdg. 8.50 (ISBN 0-8414-3449-2). Folcroft.

--Sentiment & Sensibility, Their Use & Significance in English Literature. lib. bdg. 8.50 (ISBN 0-685-25637-5). Folcroft.

Chakraborty, S. K. Management by Objectives. rev. ed. 1981. 12.50x (ISBN 0-8364-0739-3, Pub. by Macmillan India). South Asia Bks.

--Managerial Development & Appraisal: Empirical Perspectives India. 1978. 15.00x (ISBN 0-8364-0135-2). South Asia Bks.

--New Perspectives in Management Accounting. 1979. 9.50x (ISBN 0-8364-0374-6). South Asia Bks.

Chakraborty, Tapan K. Hume's Theory of Causality. 1979. 8.50x (ISBN 0-8364-0560-9, Pub. by Minerva Associates). South Asia Bks.

Chakrapani, Chuck. Financial Freedom on Five Dollars a Day. 2nd ed. 224p. 1984. pap. 6.95 (ISBN 0-88908-587-0, 9514, Pub. by Intl Self-Counsel Pr). TAB Bks.

--The Money Spinner: A Super Easy System for Making Money. 2nd ed. (Illus.). 113p. 1981. pap. 14.95 (ISBN 0-88908-081-X). Self Counsel Pr.

Chakravarthy, Balaji S. Managing Coal: A Challenge in Adaption. LC 80-24891. 220p. 1981. 44.50x (ISBN 0-87395-467-X); pap. 21.95x (ISBN 0-87395-468-8). State U NY Pr.

Chakravarti, Aravinda. Human Population Genetics. 1984. 39.50 (ISBN 0-442-21745-5). Van Nos Reinhold.

Chakravarti, D., jt. ed. see Agrawal, D.

Chakravarti, I. M., ed. Asymptotic Theory of Statistical Tests & Estimation: In Honor of Wassily Hoeffding. 1980. 39.50 (ISBN 0-12-166650-6). Acad Pr.

Chakravarti, K. C. A Study in Robert Browning. 1973. lib. bdg. 10.00 (ISBN 0-8414-3011-X). Folcroft.

Chakravarti, P. C. Integrals & Sums. 89p. 1970. 39.50 (ISBN 0-485-11114-4, Pub. by Athlone Pr Ltd). Longwood Pub Group.

Chakravarti, Prithvindra. Prettier Than the Black Pea Flower. (Redbird Bk.). 1976. lib. bdg. 8.00 (ISBN 0-89253-092-8); flexible bdg. 4.80 (ISBN 0-89253-147-9). Ind-US Inc.

Chakravarti, S. C. Bauls: The Spiritual Vikings. 1981. 10.00x (ISBN 0-8364-0671-0, Pub. by Mukhopadhyay India). South Asia Bks.

Chakravarti, Sri S. Be Your Own Guru. 1971. pap. 2.50 (ISBN 0-685-58384-8). Ranney Pubns.

--Samadhi & Beyond. LC 74-79444. 1974. pap. 3.50 (ISBN 0-87707-135-7). Ranney Pubns.

--Scientific Yoga for the Man of Today. 1971. pap. 3.50 (ISBN 0-685-58385-6). Ranney Pubns.

Chakravarti, Sri S., ed. Hidden Treasure of the Gospel of Sri Ramakrishna. 1975. Repr. of 1907 ed. 6.25 (ISBN 0-685-58386-4). Ranney Pubns.

Chakravarti, Surath. Mysterious Samadhi. 1984. 16.00x (ISBN 0-8364-1182-X, Pub. by Mukhopadhyaya India). South Asia Bks.

Chakravartinayanan, A., ed. see Kundakunda Acharya.

Chakravarty, A. S. Introduction to the Magnetic Properties of Solids. LC 80-12793. 696p. 1980. 99.50 (ISBN 0-471-07737-2, Pub. by Wiley-Interscience). Wiley.

Chakravarty, Amiya. Dynasts & the Post-War Age in Poetry. 1938. lib. bdg. 13.50 (ISBN 0-8414-3634-7). Folcroft.

--Dynasts & the Post War Age in Poetry. LC 74-111328. 1970. Repr. of 1938 ed. lib. bdg. 19.00x (ISBN 0-374-91362-5). Octagon.

--The Dynasts & the Post-War Age of Poetry. 1978. Repr. of 1938 ed. lib. bdg. 13.50 (ISBN 0-8495-0826-6). Arden Lib.

--The Indian Testimony. 1983. pap. 5.00x (ISBN 0-87574-072-3, 072). Pendle Hill.

Chakravarty, Amiya, ed. see Tagore, Rabindranath.

Chakravarty, K. Art of India Khajuraho. (Illus.). 176p. 1984. text ed. 60.00x (ISBN 0-391-03222-4, Pub. by Arnold Heinemann India). Humanities.

--Art of India Orchha. (Illus.). 176p. 1984. text ed. 90.50x (ISBN 0-391-03224-0, Pub. by Arnold Heinemann India). Humanities.

--Gwalior Fort: Art, Culture, & History. (Illus.). 156p. 1984. text ed. 40.50x (ISBN 0-391-03223-2, Pub. by Arnold Heinemann India). Humanities.

Chakravarty, K., ed. Rock Art of India. 480p. 1984. text ed. 90.50x (ISBN 0-391-03219-4, Pub. by Arnold Heinemann India). Humanities.

Chakravarty, Sarat C. Nag Mahasaya: A Saintly Householder Disciple of Sri Ramakrishna. 1978. pap. 2.25 (ISBN 0-87481-481-2). Vedanta Pr.

Chakravarty, Sharat C. Talks with Swami Vivekananda. 6.50 (ISBN 0-87481-156-2). Vedanta Pr.

Chakravarty, Suhash. From Khyber to Oxus. 306p. 1981. 30.00x (ISBN 0-686-78884-2, Pub. by Orient Longman India). State Mutual Bk.

--From Khyber to Oxus: A Study in Imperial Expansion. 286p. 1976. text ed. 18.95x (ISBN 0-86125-077-X). Apt Bks.

Chakravarty, Sukhamoy. Alternative Approaches to a Theory of Economic Growth: Marx, Marshall & Schumpeter. (R. C, Dutt Lectures on Political Economy Ser.: 1980). 1982. pap. text ed. 4.95x (ISBN 0-86131-355-0, Pub. by Orient Longman Ltd India). Apt Bks.

--Capital & Development Planning. 1969. 27.50x (ISBN 0-262-03027-6). MIT Pr.

Chakravorty, A. K., jt. ed. see Scott, K. J.

Chakravorty, Basuda. Jyotindra Nath Mukherjee: The Humanist Revolutionary. 1982. 8.00 (ISBN 0-8364-0919-1, Pub. by Minerva India). South Asia Bks.

Chakravorty, Birendra C. British Relations with the Hill Tribes of Assam Since Eighteen Fifty-Eight. 1981. 12.50x (ISBN 0-8364-0705-9, Pub. by Mukhopadhyay). South Asia Bks.

Chakravorty, M., ed. Molecular Basis of Host-Virus Interaction. LC 77-16743. (Illus.). 1979. lib. bdg. 65.00 (ISBN 0-89500-009-1). Sci Pr.

Chakrin, Lawrence W. & Bailey, Denis M., eds. Leukotrienes. (Medicinal Chemistry Ser.). 1984. 52.00 (ISBN 0-12-166750-2). Acad Pr.

Chalaguina, I. Dicionario de Bolso Portugues-Russo. 343p. (Rus. & Port.). 1976. 4.95 (ISBN 0-686-92579-3, M-9103). French & Eur.

Chalandon, Ferdinand. Essai sur le Regne d'Alexis Premier Comnene, 1081-1118. LC 61-33899. (Research & Source Works Ser.: No. 3). 1971. Repr. of 1900 ed. lib. bdg. 26.00 (ISBN 0-8337-0511-3). B Franklin.

--Histoire de la domination normande en Italie et en Sicilie, 2 Vols. 1969. Repr. of 1912 ed. Set. 55.50 (ISBN 0-8337-0514-8). B Franklin.

--Histoire de la premiere croisade jusqu'a l'election de Godefroi de Bouillon. 380p. 1972. Repr. of 1925 ed. lib. bdg. 25.50 (ISBN 0-8337-0515-6). B Franklin.

--Jean Deuxieme Comnene, 1118-1143 et Manuel Premier Comnene, 1143-1180, 2 Vols. LC 61-2244. (Research & Source Works Ser.: No. 2). 1971. Repr. of 1912 ed. Set. lib. bdg. 50.50 (ISBN 0-8337-0518-0). B Franklin.

Chalazonitis, N. & Boisson, M., eds. Abnormal Neuronal Discharges. LC 76-58750. 447p. 1978. 54.50 (ISBN 0-89004-238-1). Raven.

Chalberg, Dana, ed. see Kass-Annese, Barbara & Danzer, Hal C.

Chaleff, R. S. Genetics of Higher Plants: Applications of Cell Culture. (Development & Cell Biology Monographs: No. 9). 208p. 1981. 47.50 (ISBN 0-521-22731-3). Cambridge U Pr.

Chalemrs, Patrick R. At the Tail of the Weir. (Modern Fishing Classics Ser.). (Illus.). 277p. 1985. pap. 10.95 (ISBN 0-233-97690-6, Pub. A Deutsch England). David & Charles.

Chalfant, Edward. Both Sides of the Ocean - A Biography of Henry Adams, Vol. I: His First Life, 1838-1862. 475p. 1982. 32.50 (ISBN 0-208-01901-4, Archon). Shoe String.

Chalfant, Fran C. Ben Jonson's London: A Jacobean Placename Dictionary. LC 75-32125. 224p. 1978. 20.00x (ISBN 0-8203-0392-5). U of Ga Pr.

Chalfant, H. Paul. Sociological Aspects of Poverty: A Bibliography. (Public Administration Ser.: Bibliograpy P-414). 77p. 1980. pap. 8.00 (ISBN 0-88066-054-6). Vance Biblios.

Chalfant, H. Paul, jt. auth. see Kurtz, Richard.

Chalfant, H. Paul, compiled by. Social & Behavioral Aspects of Female Alcoholism: An Annotated Bibliography. LC 80-1021. xvi, 145p. 1980. lib. bdg. 29.95 (ISBN 0-313-20947-2, CAL/). Greenwood.

Chalfant, Henry, jt. auth. see Cooper, Martha.

Chalfant, James C. & Van Dusen Pysh, Margaret. The Compliance Manual: A Guide to the Rules & Regulations of P.L. 94-142. LC 79-90320. (Illus.). 100p. (Orig.). 1980. pap. 9.95 (ISBN 0-933922-01-9, P501). PEM Pr.

Chalfant, James C., jt. auth. see Kirk, Samuel A.

Chalfant, James C., jt. auth. see Van Dusen Pysh, Margaret.

Chalfant, James M., ed. see Stanton, Robert B.

Chalfant, Paul H. Sociology of Poverty in the United States: An Annotated Bibliography, No. 3. LC 84-25191. (Bibliographies & Indexes in Sociology Ser.). xxii, 187p. 1985. lib. bdg. 35.00 (ISBN 0-313-23929-0, CHS/). Greenwood.

Chalfant, Paul H. & Beckley, Robert E. Religion in Contemporary Society. Palmer, C. Eddie, ed. 490p. 1981. Repr. text ed. 21.95 (ISBN 0-87484-611-0). Mayfield Pub.

Chalfant, W. A. Gold, Guns & Ghost Towns. 12.95 (ISBN 0-912494-33-6); pap. 7.95. Chalfant Pr.

--The Story of Inyo. 1980. 18.95 (ISBN 0-912494-34-4); pap. 12.50 (ISBN 0-912494-35-2). Chalfant Pr.

Chalfant, William B. Primer of Free Government. 1959. 5.00 (ISBN 0-8022-0229-2). Philos Lib.

Chalfant, William B., ed. Ancient Champions of Oneness. Rev. ed. (Illus.). 156p. 1982. pap. 5.95 (ISBN 0-912315-41-5). Word Aflame.

Chalford, G. Inner Personalities of the Chart. 10.95 (ISBN 0-86690-040-3). Am Fed Astrologers.

Chalford, Ginger. Pluto, Planet of Magic & Power. 200p. 1984. 16.50 (ISBN 0-86690-270-8, 2524-01). Am Fed Astrologers.

Chaliand, Gerald & Rageau, Jean-Pierre. Strategic Atlas: A Comparative Geopolitics of the World's Powers. Berrett, Tony, tr. from Fr. LC 84-48143. (Illus.). 224p. 1985. pap. 14.37i (ISBN 0-06-091220-0, CN 1220, CN). Har-Row.

--Strategic Atlas: A Comparative Geopolitics of the World's Powers. Berrett, Tony, tr. LC 84-48143. (Illus.). 224p. 1985. 23.99 (ISBN 0-06-015387-3, HarpT). Har-Row.

Chaliand, Gerard. Armed Struggle in Africa: With the Guerrillas in "Portuguese" Guinea. LC 72-81789. 160p. 1969. pap. 2.95 (ISBN 0-85345-179-6). Monthly Rev.

--Guerrilla Strategies: An Historical Anthology from the Long March to Afghanistan. LC 81-16347. 808p. 1982. 32.00x (ISBN 0-520-04444-4); pap. 7.95 (ISBN 0-520-04443-6). U of Cal Pr.

--Report from Afghanistan. Jacoby, Tamar, tr. LC 81-21963. (Illus.). 120p. 1982. 13.95 (ISBN 0-670-59473-3). Viking.

--Report from Afghanistan. Jacoby, Tamar, tr. from Fr. 1982. pap. 5.95 (ISBN 0-14-006516-4). Penguin.

--Revolution in the Third World. 1978. pap. 5.95 (ISBN 0-14-004796-4). Penguin.

--The Struggle for Africa: Politics of the Great Powers. LC 82-5967. 1982. 16.95 (ISBN 0-312-76868-0). St Martin.

Chaliand, Gerard & Ternon, Yves. The Armenians: From Genocide to Resistance. (Illus.). 136p. 1983. 23.25x (Pub. by Zed Pr England); pap. 9.25 (ISBN 0-86232-160-3). Biblio Dist.

Chaliand, Gerard, ed. & intro. by. People Without a Country: The Kurds & Kurdistan. 292p. (Orig.). 1980. 33.00x (ISBN 0-905762-69-X, Pub. by Zed Pr England); pap. 8.50x (ISBN 0-905762-74-6, Pub. by Zed Pr England). Biblio Dist.

Chalidze, Valery. The Soviet Human Rights Movement: A Memoir. LC 84-72146. xii, 50p. 1984. pap. 2.50 (ISBN 0-87495-064-3). AM Jewish Comm.

Chalif, Don & Bender, Roger J. Military Pilot & Aircrew Badges of the World: 1870 to Present, Vol. 1. (Illus.). 224p. 1982. 24.95 (ISBN 0-912138-26-2). Bender Pub CA.

Chalif, Edward L., jt. auth. see Peterson, Roger T.

Chalif, L. H. The Dancing Book. (Ballroom Dancing Ser.). 1985. lib. bdg. 69.95 (ISBN 0-87700-756-X). Revisionist Pr.

Chalif, Louis H. Chalif Textbook of Dancing. (Ballroom Dance Ser.). 1985. lib. bdg. 75.00 (ISBN 0-87700-757-8). Revisionist Pr.

Chalk, Alfred. Still Searching... Holley, Barbara, ed. Orig. Title: The Rose Also Fades. 80p. pap. 4.50 (ISBN 0-933494-22-X). Earthwise Pubs.

Chalk, Gary, jt. auth. see Denver, Joe.

Chalk, Gary, jt. auth. see Dever, Joe.

Chalk, John, ed. see Garrod, Stan.

Chalk, John A. Jesus' Church. Thomas, J. D., ed. (Twentieth Century Sermons Ser.). 1969. 11.95 (ISBN 0-89112-303-2). Bibl Res Pr.

Chalk, L., jt. auth. see Metclfe, C. R.

Chalk, L., jt. ed. see Metcalfe, C. R.

Chalk, Rosemary & Frankel, S. Professional Ethics Activities of Scientific & Engineering Societies: AAAS Professional Ethics Report. 224p. 1980. 4.00 (ISBN 0-317-31967-1). AAAS.

Chalk, William, jt. auth. see Levens, Alexander.

Chalker. Soul Rider II: Empires of Flux & Anchor. 2.95 (ISBN 0-317-31893-4). Tor Bks.

Chalker, J., ed. see Swift, Jonathan.

Chalker, Jack. The Devil's Voyage. 224p. 1985. pap. 3.50 (ISBN 0-931773-38-5). Critics Choice Paper.

--Soul Rider III. (Masters of Flux & Anchor Ser.). 432p. (Orig.). 1985. pap. 2.95 (ISBN 0-8125-3281-3). Tor Bks.

--Spirits of Flux & Anchor. (Soul Rider: Bk. 1). 320p. (Orig.). 1984. pap. 2.95 (ISBN 0-8125-3275-9, Pinnacle Bks). Tor Bks.

Chalker, Jack L. And the Devil Will Drag You Under. 1984. pap. 2.95 (ISBN 0-345-32334-3, Del Rey Bks). Ballantine.

--The Birth of Flux & Anchor. 384p. (Orig.). 1985. pap. 3.50 (ISBN 0-8125-3284-8, Dist. by Warner Pub Services & St. Martin). Tor Bks.

--Cerberus: A Wolf in the Fold. (Four Lords of the Diamond Ser.: Bk. 2). 240p. 1982. pap. 2.50 (ISBN 0-345-29371-1, Del Rey). Ballantine.

--Charon: A Dragon at the Gate, Bk. 3. (Orig.). 1982. pap. 2.95 (ISBN 0-345-29370-3, Del Rey). Ballantine.

--Dancers in the Afterglow. 1982. pap. 2.50 (ISBN 0-345-30493-4, Del Rey). Ballantine.

--Demons of Dancing Gods. (Orig.). 1985. pap. 2.95 (ISBN 0-345-30893-X, Del Rey). Ballantine.

--Downtiming the Night Side. 288p. (Orig.). 1985. pap. 2.95 (ISBN 0-8125-3288-0). Tor Bks.

--Empires of Flux & Anchor. (Soul Rider Ser.: No. II). 320p. (Orig.). 1984. pap. 2.95 (ISBN 0-8125-3277-5). Tor Bks.

--An Informal Biography of Scrooge McDuck. (Illus.). 1974. pap. 5.00 (ISBN 0-88358-502-2). Mirage Pr.

--A Jungle of Stars. 1976. pap. 2.50 (ISBN 0-345-28960-9). Ballantine.

--Lilith: A Snake in the Grass, Bk. 1. (The Four Lords of the Diamond). 1981. pap. 2.50 (ISBN 0-345-29369-X, Del Rey). Ballantine.

--Medusa: A Tiger by the Tail. (The Four Lords of the Diamond Ser.: Bk. 4). 304p. (Orig.). 1983. pap. 2.95 (ISBN 0-345-29372-X, Del Rey). Ballantine.

--The Messiah Choice. 16.95 (ISBN 0-312-94301-6, Dist. by St. Martin). Bluejay Bks.

--Midnight at the Well of Souls. LC 76-56148. (Del Rey Bks). 1978. pap. 2.50 (ISBN 0-345-29769-5). Ballantine.

--Quest for the Well of Souls. 1978. pap. 2.95 (ISBN 0-345-32450-1, Del Rey Bks). Ballantine.

--The River of Dancing Gods. 1985. pap. 2.95 (ISBN 0-345-30892-1, Del Rey). Ballantine.

--Twilight at the Well of Souls: The Legacy of Nathan Brazil. (The Saga of the Well World: Vol. 5). 320p. 1984. pap. 2.95 (ISBN 0-345-32162-6). Ballantine.

--Vengeance of the Dancing Gods. (Dancing Gods Ser.). 1985. pap. 3.50 (ISBN 0-345-31549-9, Del Rey). Ballantine.

--A War of Shadows. 320p. 1984. pap. 2.95 (ISBN 0-441-87196-8, Pub. by Ace Science Fiction). Ace Bks.

--The Web of the Chozen. 1982. pap. 2.50 (ISBN 0-345-30455-1, Del Rey). Ballantine.

Chalker, Kenneth W. Dare to Defy: Challenging Sterotypes & Looking at Relationships in a Christian Context. LC 80-54478. 144p. 1981. pap. 4.50x (ISBN 0-8358-0418-6). Upper Room.

Chalkley, Lyman. Chronicles of the Scotch-Irish Settlement in Virginia: Extracted from the Original Court Records of Augusta County, 1745-1800, 3 vols. LC 65-15361. 1988p. 1980. Repr. of 1912 ed. Set. 75.00 (ISBN 0-8063-0069-8). Genealog Pub.

Chalkley, Thomas. The Journal of Thomas Chalkley. LC 75-31088. (Incl. a collection of author's works). Repr. of 1808 ed. 45.00 (ISBN 0-404-13506-4). AMS Pr.

--Your Eyes. 2nd ed. (Illus.). 144p. 1982. pap. 9.75x (ISBN 0-398-04629-8). C C Thomas.

Chalklin, C. W. The Provincial Towns of Georgian England: A Study of the Building Process, 1740-1820. (Studies in Urban History: No. 3). (Illus.). 416p. 1974. 25.00x (ISBN 0-7735-0200-9). McGill-Queens U Pr.

Chall, J. S. An Analysis of Textbooks in Relation to Declining SAT Scores. 1977. 5.00 (ISBN 0-87447-001-3, 251709). College Bd.

Chall, Jeanne. Reading 1967-1977: A Decade of Change & Promise. LC 77-89841. (Fastback Ser.: No. 97). 1977. pap. 0.75 (ISBN 0-87367-097-3). Phi Delta Kappa.

Chall, Jeanne, jt. ed. see Carroll, John B.

Chall, Jeanne S. Learning to Read: The Great Debate. 1967. pap. 4.95 (ISBN 0-07-010391-7). McGraw.

Challa, Krishna. Investment & Returns in Exploration & the Impact on the Supply of Oil & Natural Gas Reserves. Bruchey, Stuart, ed. LC 78-22667. (Energy in the American Economy Ser.). (Illus.). 1979. lib. bdg. 16.00x (ISBN 0-405-11971-2). Ayer Co Pubs.

Challamel, Augustin. Les Clubs Contre-Revolutionnaires. LC 72-38038. (Collection de documents relatifs a l'histoire de Paris pendant la Revolution francaise). Repr. of 1895 ed. 70.00 (ISBN 0-404-52552-0). AMS Pr.

Challand, Helen. Activities in the Earth Sciences. LC 82-9444. (Science Activities Ser.). (Illus.). (gr. 5 up). 1982. PLB 11.95g (ISBN 0-516-00506-5). Childrens.

--Activities in the Life Sciences. LC 82-9442. (Science Activities Ser.). (Illus.). (gr. 5 up). 1982. PLB 11.95g (ISBN 0-516-00507-3). Childrens.

--Earthquakes. LC 82-9699. (New True Bks.). (Illus.). (gr. k-4). 1982. PLB 10.60 (ISBN 0-516-01636-9); pap. 3.95 (ISBN 0-516-41636-7). Childrens.

Challand, Helen J. Activities in the Physical Sciences. LC 83-26224. (Science Activities Ser.). (Illus.). 96p. (gr. 5 up). 1984. lib. bdg. 11.95 (ISBN 0-516-00504-9). Childrens.

--Volcanoes. LC 82-17888. (New True Bks.). (Illus.). 48p. (gr. k-4). 1983. PLB 10.60 (ISBN 0-516-01690-3); pap. 3.95 (ISBN 0-516-41690-1). Childrens.

Challem, Jack & Challem, Renate. What Herbs Are All About. 1981. pap. 5.95 (ISBN 0-686-76752-7). B Of A.

Challem, Jack & Lewin-Challem, Renate. What Herbs Are All about. LC 80-82913. 150p. (Orig.). 1980. pap. 2.95 (ISBN 0-87983-204-5). Keats.

Challem, Jack J. Spirulina. (Good Health Guide Ser.). 1982. pap. 1.45 (ISBN 0-87983-262-2). Keats.

--Vitamin C Updated. Passwater, Richard A. & Mindell, Earl, eds. (Good Health Guide Ser.). 36p. 1983. pap. text ed. 1.45 (ISBN 0-87983-285-1). Keats.

Challem, Renate, jt. auth. see Challem, Jack.

Challen, D. W. & Hagger, A. J. Macroeconomic Systems: Construction, Evaluation & Applications. LC 83-2856. 249p. 1983. 35.00 (ISBN 0-312-50315-6). St Martin.

Challen, Don, et al. Unemployment & Inflation in the U. K. (Illus.). 448p. 1984. 21.95 (ISBN 0-582-29618-8). Longman.

Challender, Craig. The Family. 32p. (Orig.). 1983. pap. 5.00 (ISBN 0-910429-02-2). Stronghold Pr.

Challener, Richard D. Admirals, Generals & American Foreign Policy, 1898-1914. LC 72-732. 448p. 1973. 44.00x (ISBN 0-691-06916-6). Princeton U Pr.

--Extension of the European Recovery Program, 1949. 385p. 1979. lib. bdg. 56.00 (ISBN 0-8240-3039-7). Garland Pub.

--French Theory of the Nation in Arms, 1866-1939. LC 64-66394. 1965. Repr. of 1952 ed. 8.50x (ISBN 0-8462-0565-3). Russell.

Challener, Richard D., ed. Economic Assistance to China & Korea: 1949-50 (March, June, June, July 1949; January 1950) (Legislative Origins of American Foreign Policy Ser.: Vol. 7). 1979. lib. bdg. 37.00 (ISBN 0-8240-3036-2). Garland Pub.

--The Legislative Origins of American Foreign Policy, 5 vols. Incl. Vol. 1. Proceedings, April 7, 1913 to March 7, 1923. 415p. lib. bdg. 53.00 (ISBN 0-8240-3030-3); Vol. 2. Proceedings, December 3, 1923 to March 3, 1933. 279p. lib. bdg. 37.00 (ISBN 0-8240-3031-1); Vol. 3. Legislative Origins of the Truman Doctrine, March to April, 1947. 235p. 30.00 (ISBN 0-8240-3032-X); Vol. 4. Foreign Relief Aid, 1947. 401p. lib. bdg. 48.00 (ISBN 0-8240-3033-8); Vol. 5. Foreign Relief Assistance Act of 1948. 809p. lib. bdg. 86.00 (ISBN 0-8240-3034-6). (The Senate Foreign Relations Committee's Historical Ser.). 1979. Garland Pub.

--Nineteen Twenty (Feb. Seventh - April Ninth, 1920) (United States Military Intelligence 1917-1927 Ser.). 1979. lib. bdg. 60.50 (ISBN 0-8240-3011-7). Garland Pub.

--Reviews of the World Situation: 1949-50. (Legislative Origins of American Foreign Policy Ser.: Vol. 8). 1979. lib. bdg. 67.00 (ISBN 0-8240-3037-0). Garland Pub.

--The Vandenberg Resolution & the North Atlantic Treaty (May, June, 1948; February, March, April & June, 1949) (Legislative Origins of American Foreign Policy Ser.: Vol. 6). 1979. lib. bdg. 56.00 (ISBN 0-8240-3035-4). Garland Pub.

Challenge, Jack. St. Mick. LC 81-5867. 305p. 1981. 13.95 (ISBN 0-915520-38-9); pap. 6.95 (ISBN 0-915520-41-9). Ross-Erikson.

Challenor, Bernard, et al. Physician's Assistant Examination Review Book. 1975. pap. 16.00 (ISBN 0-87488-422-5). Med Exam.

Challenor, John, jt. auth. see Blenkinsopp, Joseph.

Challet, Gilbert L. & Keller, Justine, eds. Directory of Mosquito Control Agencies in the United States & Canada, 1981. 2nd ed. 39p. 1981. 10.00 (ISBN 0-9606210-3-2). Am Mosquito.

Challgren, Patricia, jt. auth. see Kennedy, Belle C.

Challgren, Patricia, ed. see Lohr, Andrew.

Challice, Annie E. Illustrious Women of France, Seventeen Ninety to Eighteen Seventy-Three. 17.25 (ISBN 0-8369-7212-0, 8011). Ayer Co Pubs.

Challice, C. E. & Viragh, S., eds. Ultrastructure of the Mammalian Heart. (Ultrastructure in Biological Systems Series). 1973. 47.50 (ISBN 0-12-170050-X). Acad Pr.

Challifour, John L. Generalized Functions & Fourier Analysis: An Introduction. (Math Lecture Notes Ser.: No. 49). 188p. 1972. 16.95 (ISBN 0-8053-1875-5, Adv Bk Prog). Benjamin-Cummings.

Challinor, Joan R., jt. auth. see Lichtman, Allan J.

Challinor, John. A Dictionary of Geology. 5th ed. 1978. text ed. 14.95x (ISBN 0-19-520063-2). Oxford U Pr.

Challinor, John, jt. auth. see Platt, John.

Challinor, Raymond. The Origins of British Bolshevism. 291p. 1977. 19.75x (ISBN 0-87471-985-2). Rowman.

Challis, Chris. Quest for Kerouac. 250p. (Orig.). 1984. pap. 7.95 (ISBN 0-571-13356-8). Faber & Faber.

Challis, James & Elliman, David. Child Workers Today. 170p. 1981. 25.00x (ISBN 0-905898-06-0, Pub. by Quartermaine England). State Mutual Bk.

Challis, L. J., et al, eds. Phonon Scattering in Solids. LC 75-40492. 439p. 1976. 65.00 (ISBN 0-306-30908-4, Plenum Pr). Plenum Pub.

Challoner, H. K. The Path of Healing. LC 76-3660. 175p. 1976. pap. 3.25 (ISBN 0-8356-0480-2, Quest). Theos Pub Hse.

Challoner, Rupert. Jamaica Passage. 1982. pap. 2.95 (ISBN 0-671-44308-9, Timescape). PB.

Chalmers, A., ed. General Biographical Dictionary, 32 vols. rev ed. 1812-1817. Set. 1160.00 (ISBN 0-527-15900-X). Kraus Repr.

Chalmers, A. F. What Is This Thing Called Science? An Assessment of the Nature & Status of Science & Its Methods. 1976. pap. text ed. 12.25x (ISBN 0-7022-1341-1). Humanities.

Chalmers, Alan. What Is This Thing Called Science? (Paperbacks Ser.). 179p. 1985. pap. 8.95 (ISBN 0-7022-1831-6). U of Queensland Pr.

Chalmers, Alexander. The Works of English Poets, from Chaucer to Cowper, 21 Vols. 1971. Repr. of 1810 ed. Set. 1400.00x (ISBN 3-4870-2603-1). Adlers Foreign Bks.

--Works of the English Poets from Chaucer to Cowper: Including the Series Ed., with Prefaces Biographical & Critical, by Dr. S. Johnson & the Most Approved Translations, 21 Vols. Johnson, S., ed. (English Literary Reference Ser.). 1969. Repr. of 1810 ed. Set. 825.00 (ISBN 0-384-08322-6). Johnson Repr.

Chalmers, Alexander, ed. General Biographical Dictionary, 32 vols. rev. ed. LC 54-51862. Repr. of 1817 ed. Set. 1200.00 (ISBN 0-404-01490-9). AMS Pr.

--Works of the English Poets from Chaucer to Cowper, 21 Vols. LC 69-13853. 1969. Repr. of 1810 ed. Set. lib. bdg. 605.00x (ISBN 0-8371-0344-4, CHEP). Greenwood.

Chalmers, Amanda J., jt. auth. see McCormack, James E.

Chalmers, B., ed. Progress in Materials Science, Vol. 23. 280p. 1980. 105.00 (ISBN 0-08-024846-2). Pergamon.

Chalmers, B., et al, eds. Progress in Materials Science, Vols. 15-21. Incl. Vol. 15, Pt. 1. 1971. pap. 15.50 (ISBN 0-08-015869-2); Vol. 15, Pt. 2. 1972. pap. 15.50 (ISBN 0-08-016824-8); Vol. 15, Pt. 3. 1972. pap. 15.50 (ISBN 0-08-016877-9); Vol. 15, Pt. 4. 1973. pap. 15.50 (ISBN 0-08-017132-X); Vol. 15, Complete. 85.00 (ISBN 0-08-017154-0); Vol. 16. 1972. 85.00 (ISBN 0-08-016866-3); Vol. 17. 1972. 31.00 (ISBN 0-08-017011-0); Vol. 18. 1974. 85.00 (ISBN 0-08-017155-9); Vol. 19. 1974. 85.00 (ISBN 0-08-017964-9); Vol. 20. 1977. 300.00 (ISBN 0-08-021143-7); Vol. 21, Pt. 1. 1975. pap. 12.00 (ISBN 0-08-018172-4); Vol. 21, Pt. 2. 1976. pap. 15.50 (ISBN 0-08-019831-7); Vol. 21, Pts. 3 & 4. pap. 33.00 (ISBN 0-08-019987-9); Vol. 21, Complete. 1977. 85.00 (ISBN 0-08-018171-6). pap. write for info. Pergamon.

--Progress in Materials Science, Vols. 6-10, 12-13. Incl. Vol. 6. 1956. 85.00 (ISBN 0-08-009035-4); Vol. 7. 1958; Vol. 8. 1959. 60.00 (ISBN 0-08-009294-2); Vol. 9, Pt. 1. 1961; Vol. 9, Pt. 2. 1962; Vol. 9, Pt. 3. Effects of Environment on Mechanical Properties of Metals. 1962; Vol. 9, Pt. 4. 1962; Vol. 9, Pt. 5. 1962; Vol. 10, Pt. 1. Alloy Phases of the Noble Metals. 1963. pap. 15.50 (ISBN 0-08-009618-2); Vol. 10, Complete. 1963. 67.50 (ISBN 0-08-010981-0); Vol. 12, Pt. 1. 1963; Vol. 12, Pt. 2. 1964. pap. 12.50 (ISBN 0-08-010035-X); Vol. 13, Pt. 1. write for info. Pergamon.

Chalmers, B. L., jt. auth. see Haynes, J. H.

Chalmers, Bruce. Physical Metallurgy. LC 59-14983. (Wiley Series on the Science & Technology of Materials). pap. 117.00 (ISBN 0-317-10463-2, 2055140). Bks Demand UMI.

--Principles of Solidification. LC 76-18772. 336p. 1977. Repr. of 1964 ed. 22.50 (ISBN 0-88275-446-7). Krieger.

--The Structure & Properties of Solids: An Introduction to Materials Science. 155p. 1982. 25.95x (ISBN 0-471-26214-5, Pub. by Wiley Heyden). Wiley.

Chalmers, David M. Hooded Americanism: The History of the Ku Klux Klan. 2nd ed. 1981. pap. 7.95 (ISBN 0-531-05632-5). Watts.

--The Muckrake Years. LC 79-22780. 176p. 1980. pap. 6.95 (ISBN 0-89874-066-5). Krieger.

--Social & Political Ideas of the Muckrakers. facs. ed. LC 70-117765. (Essay Index Reprint Ser). 1964. 14.95 (ISBN 0-8369-1745-6). Ayer Co Pubs.

Chalmers, David M., ed. see Tarbell, Ida M.

Chalmers, Eric B. International Interest Rate War. LC 74-185905. 1972. 25.00 (ISBN 0-312-42280-6). St Martin.

Chalmers, George. Another Account of the Incidents, from Which the Title, & a Part of the Story of Shakspeare's Tempest Were Derived. LC 72-1051. Repr. of 1815 ed. 11.50 (ISBN 0-404-01442-9). AMS Pr.

--Apology for the Believers in the Shakespeare Papers. LC 77-96373. (Eighteenth Century Shakespeare). Repr. of 1797 ed. lib. bdg. 45.00x (ISBN 0-678-05140-2). Kelley.

--Apology for the Believers in the Shakespeare Papers Which Were Exhibited in Norfolk Street. 628p. 1971. Repr. of 1797 ed. 45.00x (ISBN 0-7146-2531-0, F Cass Co). Biblio Dist.

--Considerations on Commerce, Bullion, & Coin, Circulation & Exchanges. LC 68-55502. Repr. of 1811 ed. 27.50x (ISBN 0-678-00431-5). Kelley.

--Estimate of the Comparative Strength of Great Britain. new ed. LC 67-29496. Repr. of 1794 ed. 45.00x (ISBN 0-678-00415-3). Kelley.

--Introduction to the History of the Revolt of the American Colonies. LC 70-141083. (Research Library of Colonial Americana). 1971. Repr. of 1845 ed. 66.00 (ISBN 0-405-03278-1). Ayer Co Pubs.

--An Introduction to the History of the Revolt of the American Colonies, 2 vols. LC 75-119049. (Era of the American Revolution Ser.). 1971. Repr. of 1845 ed. Set. lib. bdg. 85.00 (ISBN 0-306-71948-7). Da Capo.

--The Life of Daniel DeFoe. 1978. Repr. of 1841 ed. lib. bdg. 20.00 (ISBN 0-8495-0845-2). Arden Lib.

--Life of Daniel DeFoe. 1841. lib. bdg. 25.00 (ISBN 0-8414-0670-7). Folcroft.

--The Life of Thomas Ruddiman, A. M. LC 78-67651. (Scottish Enlightenment Ser.). Repr. of 1794 ed. 46.50 (ISBN 0-404-17186-9). AMS Pr.

--Opinions of Eminent Lawyers on Various Points of English Jurisprudence, Chiefly Concerning the Colonies, Fisheries & Commerce of Great Britain, 2 Vols. LC 70-173704. (Research & Source Works Ser.: No. 842). 1971. Repr. of 1814 ed. Set. 41.00 (ISBN 0-8337-0519-9). B Franklin.

--Political Annals of the Present United Colonies, from Their Settlement to the Peace of 1763, 2 vols. 1. LC 68-56753. (Research & Source Works Ser.: No. 238). 1968. Repr. of 1780 ed. 54.00 (ISBN 0-8337-0520-2). B Franklin.

--Supplemental Apology for the Believers in the Shakespeare Papers. 656p. 1971. Repr. of 1799 ed. 45.00x (ISBN 0-7146-2536-1, F Cass Co). Biblio Dist.

--Supplemental Apology for the Believers in the Shakespeare-Papers. LC 70-96374. (Eighteenth Century Shakespeare). Repr. of 1799 ed. lib. bdg. 45.00x (ISBN 0-678-05141-0). Kelley.

Chalmers, George, ed. see Henryson, Robert.

Chalmers, Helena. Clothes, On & Off the Stage: A History of Dress from the Earliest Times to the Present Day. LC 73-180965. (Illus.). xx, 292p. 1976. Repr. of 1928 ed. 46.00x (ISBN 0-8103-4033-X). Gale.

Chalmers, John I., jt. ed. see Chalmers, Patrick.

Chalmers, Kenneth E., jt. auth. see Biron, Henry C.

Chalmers, L. & Bathe, P. Household & Industrial Chemical Specialties: Polishes, Disinfectants, Adhesives, Abrasives, Paints, Aerosols, Household Toiletries, Vol. 2. 1979. 32.50 (ISBN 0-8206-0250-7). Chem Pub.

--Household & Industrial Chemical Specialties: Soap, Detergents & Laundry Products, House Pest Control, Vol. 1. 1978. 25.50 (ISBN 0-8206-0222-1). Chem Pub.

Chalmers, Malcolm. Paying for Defence: Military Spending & British Decline. 176p. (Orig.). 1985. pap. 6.75 (ISBN 0-7453-0023-5, Pub. by Pluto Pr). Longwood Pub Group.
Chalmers, Margaret T. Colonial Fireplace Cooking & Early American Recipes. (Illus.). 96p. (Orig.). 1979. pap. 4.95 (ISBN 0-932296-04-1). Eberly Pr.
Chalmers, Mary. Be Good, Harry. LC 67-16230. (A Trophy Picture Bk.). (Illus.). 32p. (ps-3). 1981. pap. 1.50 (ISBN 0-06-443027-8, Trophy). HarpJ.
--Come to the Doctor, Harry. LC 80-7910. (Illus.). 32p. (ps-1). 1981. 8.61i (ISBN 0-06-021178-4). HarpJ.
--Merry Christmas, Harry. LC 76-58715. (Trophy Picture Bk.). (Illus.). 32p. (ps-3). 1981. pap. 1.50 (ISBN 0-06-443029-4, Trophy). HarpJ.
--Take a Nap, Harry. LC 64-11838. (Trophy Picture Bk.). (Illus.). 32p. (ps-3). 1981. pap. 1.50 (ISBN 0-06-443028-6, Trophy). HarpJ.
--Throw a Kiss, Harry. LC 58-5294. (Trophy Picture Bk.). (Illus.). 32p. (ps-3). 1981. pap. 1.50 (ISBN 0-06-443030-8, Trophy). HarpJ.
Chalmers, Neil. Social Behavior in Primates. (Contemporary Biology Ser.). (Illus.). 264p. 1979. pap. text ed. 21.50 (ISBN 0-8391-1463-X). Univ Park.
Chalmers, P. D., jt. auth. see Etue, E.
Chalmers, Patrick. Ancient Sculptured Monuments of the County of Angus. LC 72-1052. (Bannatyne Club, Edinburgh. Publications: No. 88). Repr. of 1848 ed. 145.00 (ISBN 0-404-52818-X). AMS Pr.
Chalmers, Patrick & Chalmers, John I., eds. Registrum Episcopatus Brechinensis, 2 Vols. LC 72-39524. (Bannatyne Club, Edinburgh. Publications: No. 102). Repr. of 1856 ed. Set. 110.00 (ISBN 0-404-52855-4). AMS Pr.
Chalmers, Patrick, ed. see Arbroath Abbey.
Chalmers, R. A. Microprocessors in Analytical Chemistry, Vol. 27, No. 7b. 64p. 1982. pap. 25.00 (ISBN 0-08-026284-8). Pergamon.
Chalmers, R. A. & Cresser, M. S. Quantative Chemical Analysis: A Laboratory Manual. 4th ed. (Analytical Chemistry Ser.). 420p. 1983. 79.95x (ISBN 0-470-27228-7). Halsted Pr.
Chalmers, R. A. & Lawson, A. M. Organic Acids in Man. LC 81-11342. 1982. 68.00x (ISBN 0-412-14890-0, NO. 6573, Pub. by Chapman & Hall). Methuen Inc.
Chalmers, R. A. & Masson, M. R. Microchemical Techniques, Pt. 2. pap. 31.00 (ISBN 0-08-022004-5). Pergamon.
Chalmers, R. A., ed. Gains & Losses: Errors in Trace Analysis. 90p. 1983. pap. 27.50 (ISBN 0-08-030239-4). Pergamon.
Chalmers, Robert K., jt. ed. see Banker, Gilbert S.
Chalmers, Stephen. The Penny Piper of Saranac: An Episode in Stevenson's Life. 1973. Repr. of 1916 ed. 15.00 (ISBN 0-8274-0085-3). R West.
Chalmers, Thomas. On Political Economy. LC 67-19707. Repr. of 1832 ed. 45.00x (ISBN 0-678-00370-X). Kelley.
Chalmers, Thomas C., jt. ed. see Berk, Paul D.
Chalmers, W. E. & Cormick, G. W., eds. Racial Conflict & Negotiations: Perspectives & First Case Studies. LC 72-634167. (Orig.). 1971. 12.00x (ISBN 0-87736-313-7); pap. 5.95x (ISBN 0-87736-314-5). U of Mich Inst Labor.
Chalmers, W. Ellison. Racial Negotiations: Potentials & Limitations. LC 74-78509. 1974. 15.00 (ISBN 0-87736-321-8). U of Mich Inst Labor.
Chalmers, Wilma G. Two Dollars at the Door: Folk, Ethnic, & Bluegrass Music in the Northwest. Laursen, John, ed. LC 81-68883. (Books for Listeners Ser.). (Illus.). 1982. pap. 10.95 (ISBN 0-941142-00-0). Broadsheet Pubns.
Chalmers, Wm. P. Charakteristische Eigenschaften von R. L. Stevensons Stil. 1973. lib. bdg. 15.00 (ISBN 0-8414-3436-0). Folcroft.
Chalmers-Hunt, B. L., jt. auth. see Haynes, J. H.
Chalmers Hunt, B. L., jt. auth. see Haynes, J. H.
Chalmers-Hunt, B. L., jt. auth. see Haynes, J. H.
Chalmers-Hunt, B. L, jt. auth. see Haynes, J. H.
Chalmers-Hunt, B. L., jt. auth. see Haynes, J. H.
Chalmers-Hunt, J. M., ed. Natural History Auctions, Seventeen Hundred to Nineteen Seventy-Two: A Register of Sales in the British Isles. 192p. 1976. 45.00x (ISBN 0-85667-021-9, Pub. by Sotheby Pubns England). Biblio Dist.
Chalmers-Hunt, R. L., jt. auth. see Haynes, J. H.
Chalmers-Hunt, B. L., jt. auth. see Haynes, J. H.
Chalofshy, N. & Lincoln, C. I. Up the HRD Ladder: A Guide to Professional Growth. 1983. text ed. 17.95 (ISBN 0-201-04998-8). Addison-Wesley.
Chalon, Jack, et al. Humidification of Anesthetic Gases. (Illus.). 152p. 1981. 17.50x (ISBN 0-398-04461-9). C C Thomas.
Chalon, Jean. Portrait of a Seductress: The World of Natalie Barney. Barko, Carol, tr. (Illus.). 1978. 10.95 (ISBN 0-517-53264-6). Crown.
Chaloner, David. Chocolate Sauce. 1973. pap. 3.00 (ISBN 0-686-05255-2, Pub. by Ferry Pr). Small Pr Dist.
Chaloner, John. Bottom Line. 288p. 1984. 13.95 (ISBN 0-312-09333-0). St Martin.
Chaloner, W. H. The Coming Confrontation. (Institute of Economic Affairs Ser.: Hobart Paperback 12). 1979. pap. 9.25 technical (ISBN 0-255-36116-5). Transatlantic.
--Social & Economic Development of Crewe, Seventeen Eighty to Nineteen Twenty-Three. LC 73-1616. Repr. of 1950 ed. 29.50x (ISBN 0-678-06788-0). Kelley.
Chaloner, W. H. & Ratcliffe, Barrie M., eds. Trade & Transport: Essays in Economic History in Honour of T.S. Willan. 293p. 1977. 29.50x (ISBN 0-8476-6013-3). Rowman.
Chaloner, W. H. & Richardson, R. C., eds. Bibliography of British Economic & Social History. 2nd ed. LC 83-12045. 290p. 1984. 37.50 (ISBN 0-7190-0888-3, Pub. by Manchester Univ Pr). Longwood Pub Group.
Chaloner, W. H., ed. see Bamford, Samuel.
Chaloner, W. H., ed. & intro. by see Bamford, Samuel.
Chaloner, W. H., jt. ed. see Redford, A.
Chaloner, W. H., ed. see Redford, Arthur.
Chaloner, W. H., tr. see D'Eichthal, Gustave.
Chaloner, W. H., tr. see Engels, Friedrich.
Chaloner, W. H., tr. see Hoffmann, Walther G.
Chaloner, William H. People & Industries. (Illus.). 151p. 1963. 24.00x (ISBN 0-7146-1284-7, F Cass Co). Biblio Dist.
Chalpin, Lila. A New Look at Microwave Cooking. LC 76-41144. (Illus.). 1976. 9.95 (ISBN 0-916752-04-6). Dorison Hse.
--William Sansom. (English Authors Ser.). 1980. lib. bdg. 13.50 (ISBN 0-8057-6781-9, Twayne). G K Hall.
Chalres, Celestin & Bougle, Alfred. Oeuvre d'Henri de Saint-Simon & Saint Simon und die Okonomische Geschichtstehorie, 2 vols. in one. Mayer, J. P., ed. LC 78-67334. (European Political Thought Ser.). (Fr. & Ger.). 1979. Repr. of 1906 ed. lib. bdg. 25.50x (ISBN 0-405-11682-9). Ayer Co Pubs.
Chalutz, Edo, jt. ed. see Fuchs, Yoram.
Chalvet, O., ed. Localization & Delocalization in Quantum Chemistry; Ionized & Excited States: Proceedings, Vol.2. lib. bdg. 60.50 (ISBN 90-277-0661-1, Pub. by Reidel Holland). Kluwer Academic.
Chalvet, O., et al, eds. Localization & Delocalization in Quantum Chemistry, Vol. 1: Atoms & Molecules in the Ground State. LC 75-2437. vii, 350p. 1975. lib. bdg. 68.50 (ISBN 90-277-0559-3, Pub. by Reidel Holland). Kluwer Academic.
Chamala, Shankarish, jt. auth. see Crouch, Bruce R.
Chamala, Shankarish, jt. ed. see Crouch, Bruce R.
Chaman, Jain L., jt. ed. see Migliaro, Al.
Chambadal, Lucien. Diccionario de las Matematicas Modernas. 2nd ed. 264p. (Span.). 1976. pap. 5.25 (ISBN 84-01-90307-6, S-12248). French & Eur.
--Dictionnaire des Mathematiques Modernes. rev. ed. 250p. (Fr.). 1972. pap. 6.95 (ISBN 0-686-56847-8, M-6625). French & Eur.
Chamber, John. A Treatise Against Iudicial Astrologie, 2 pts. LC 77-6872. (English Experience Ser.: No. 860). 1977. Repr. of 1601 ed. lib. bdg. 20.00 (ISBN 90-221-0860-0). Walter J Johnson.
Chamber Of Commerce Of The State Of New York. Papers & Proceedings of the Committee on the Police Problem, City of New York. LC 79-154581. (Police in America Ser). 1971. Repr. of 1905 ed. 46.50 (ISBN 0-405-03364-8). Ayer Co Pubs.
Chamber of Commerce, Philadelphia. Giant Houseparty Cookbook. 385p. 1981. pap. 10.95 (ISBN 0-686-31495-6). COC.
Chamberas, Peter A., tr. see Kalokyris, Constantine D.
Chamberlain. When Can a Child Believe. LC 73-80778. pap. 4.95 (ISBN 0-8054-6208-2). Broadman.
Chamberlain, Alexander F. The Child & Childhood in Folk-Thought. LC 77-23737. 1977. Repr. of 1896 ed. lib. bdg. 45.00 (ISBN 0-8414-1827-6). Folcroft.
Chamberlain, Arthur. John Dos Passos: A Biographical & Critical Essay. 1939. Repr. 15.00 (ISBN 0-8482-3577-0). Norwood Edns.
Chamberlain, Arthur B. George Romney. facsimile ed. LC 70-157329. (Select Bibliographies Reprint Ser). Repr. of 1910 ed. 38.50 (ISBN 0-8369-5789-X). Ayer Co Pubs.
Chamberlain, Arthur H. Standards in Education. 1979. Repr. of 1908 ed. lib. bdg. 12.50 (ISBN 0-8492-4026-3). R West.
Chamberlain, B. H. Ainu Folktales. 1976. lib. bdg. 59.95 (ISBN 0-8490-1407-7). Gordon Pr.
Chamberlain, Barbara. Ride the West Wind. LC 78-73150. (YA) 1979. pap. 1.95 (ISBN 0-89191-133-2). Cook.
Chamberlain, Barbara B. These Fragile Outposts. 327p. 1981. pap. 9.95 (ISBN 0-940160-12-9). Parnassus Imprints.
Chamberlain, Basil H. Aino Folk Tales. (Folk Lore Society, London Ser.: Vol. 221). pap. 12.00 (ISBN 0-317-16256-X). Kraus Repr.
--Japanese Things: Being Notes on Various Subjects Connected with Japan. LC 76-87791. 1970. pap. 8.50 (ISBN 0-8048-0713-2). C E Tuttle.
Chamberlain, Basil H., tr. from Jap. The Kojiki: Records of Ancient Matters. LC 81-52934. 612p. 1982. pap. 10.00 (ISBN 0-8048-1439-2). C E Tuttle.
Chamberlain, Betty. The Artist's Guide to the Art Market. 4th ed. 263p. 1983. 12.95 (ISBN 0-8230-0328-0). Watson-Guptill.
--The Artist's Guide to the Market. rev. ed. 176p. 1975. 12.95 (ISBN 0-8230-0326-4). Watson-Guptill.
--The Artist's Guide to the Market. rev. & enl. ed. 1979. 16.95. Watson-Guptill.
Chamberlain, Beverly, jt. auth. see Bates, Virginia T.
Chamberlain, Bobby J. & Harmon, Ronald M. A Dictionary of Informal Brazilian Portuguese: With English Index. LC 84-13735. 724p. 1984. text ed. 22.95 (ISBN 0-87840-091-5). Georgetown U Pr.
Chamberlain, Charles J. Gymnosperms: Structure & Evolution. (Illus.). 1935. 40.00 (ISBN 0-384-08415-X). Johnson Repr.
Chamberlain, Chris. Class Consciousness in Australia. (Studies in Society: No. 13). 184p. 1983. text ed. 28.50x o. p. (ISBN 0-86861-021-6); pap. 15.50 (ISBN 0-86861-029-1). Allen Unwin.
Chamberlain, Chriss & Chamberlain, Margaret. The Buttercup Buskers' Rainy Day. (Illus.). 24p. (ps-1). 1983. 8.95 (ISBN 0-434-93115-2, Pub. by W Heinemann Ltd). David & Charles.
Chamberlain, Clint. Marinas: Recommendations for Design, Construction & Management, Vol. 1. 200p. 35.00 (ISBN 0-318-17794-3). Natl Marine Mfrs.
Chamberlain, Colette E. Heat of Passion. 1984. 6.95 (ISBN 0-8062-2261-1). Carlton.
Chamberlain, Craig. All about the Commodore 64, Vol. 1. 237p. (Orig.). 1984. pap. 12.95 (ISBN 0-942386-40-X). Compute Pubns.
--All about the Commodore 64, Vol. 2. Compute! Staff, ed. (Orig.). 1985. pap. 16.95 (ISBN 0-942386-45-0). Compute Pubns.
Chamberlain, Dorothy & Wilson, Robert, eds. The Otis Ferguson Reader. LC 82-71391. 327p. 1982. pap. 10.00x (ISBN 0-913204-14-5). December Pr.
Chamberlain, E. R. Florence in the Time of the Medici. Reeves, Marjorie, ed. (Then & There Ser.). (Illus.). 96p. (Orig.). (gr. 7-12). 1982. pap. 3.75 (ISBN 0-582-20489-5). Longman.
Chamberlain, Edward M. Freud's Incredible Conception of the Contemporary Female. (Illus.). 1979. deluxe ed. 67.45 (ISBN 0-930582-38-1). Gloucester Art.
Chamberlain, Elaine R. Pictures from the Bee House. 1978. 3.50 (ISBN 0-934834-10-5). White Pine.
Chamberlain, Elsie. Essays Old & New. 1926. 10.00 (ISBN 0-8495-0875-4). Arden Lib.
Chamberlain, Elwyn M. Gates of Fire. 350p. 1984. pap. 9.95 (ISBN 0-938190-21-0); 20.00 (ISBN 0-938190-20-2). North Atlantic.
--Hound Dog. 320p. 1984. 16.95 (ISBN 0-938190-25-3). North Atlantic.
Chamberlain, Essie, ed. Essays Old & New. 460p. 1985. Repr. of 1926 ed. lib. bdg. 35.00 (ISBN 0-918377-72-2). Russell Pr.
Chamberlain, Eugene. Jesus: God's Son, Saviour, Lord. (BibLearn Ser.). (gr. 1-6). pap. 5.95 (ISBN 0-8054-4226-X, 4242-26). Broadman.
--Loyd Corder: Traveler for God. LC 82-73663. (Meet the Missionary Ser.). (gr. 4-6). 1983. 5.50 (ISBN 0-8054-4284-7, 4242-84). Broadman.
Chamberlain, Eugene, jt. auth. see Buchanan, Neal C.
Chamberlain, G. & Winston, R. Tubal Infertility. 1982. 29.95 (ISBN 0-632-00785-0, B0948-8). Mosby.
Chamberlain, G. V., jt. auth. see Hytten, F. E.
Chamberlain, Gary, tr. The Psalms: A New Translation for Prayer & Worship. LC 84-50842. 192p. (Orig.). 1984. pap. 6.95 (ISBN 0-8358-0485-2). Upper Room.
--Psalms for Singing: Twenty-Six Psalms with Musical Settings for Congregation & Choir. LC 84-50778. 141p. (Orig.). 1984. pap. 7.50 (ISBN 0-8358-0495-X). Upper Room.
Chamberlain, Geoffery. Trading in Options. 3rd ed. 160p. 1985. 22.50 (ISBN 0-85941-287-3, Pub. by Woodhead-Faulkner). Longwood Pub Group.
Chamberlain, Geoffrey. Contemporary Obstetrics & Gynaecology, Vol. 1. 440p. 90.00x (ISBN 0-7198-2546-6, Pub. by Northwood Bks). State Mutual Bk.
--Practice of Obstetrics & Gynaecology. 250p. 1977. 40.00x (ISBN 0-272-79388-4, Pub. by Pitman Bks England). State Mutual Bk.
--Trading in Options: An Investor's Guide to Making High Profits in the Traded Options Market. 2nd ed. 163p. (Orig.). 1982. 19.50 (ISBN 0-85941-218-0). Woodhead-Faulkner.
Chamberlain, Geoffrey & Dewhurst, C. J. Practice of Obstetrics & Gynecology. (Illus.). 271p. 1977. 21.00x (ISBN 0-8464-1120-2). Beekman Pubs.
Chamberlain, Geoffrey & Dewhurst, John. A Practice of Obstetrics & Gynaecology. 2nd ed. 204p. (Orig.). 1984. pap. text ed. 22.50 (ISBN 0-272-79755-3, Pub. by Pitman Bks Ltd UK). Urban & S.
Chamberlain, Geoffrey, ed. Contemporary Gynaecology. (Illus.). 320p. (Orig.). 1984. pap. text ed. 35.00 (ISBN 0-407-00289-8). Butterworth.
--Contemporary Obstetrics. (Illus.). 320p. (Orig.). 1984. pap. text ed. 39.95. Butterworth.
Chamberlain, Geoffrey, jt. ed. see Zander, Luke.
Chamberlain, George W. Genealogies of Early Families of Weymouth, Massachusetts. LC 84-80081. 846p. 1984. Repr. of 1923 ed. 40.00. Genealog Pub.
Chamberlain, George W., jt. auth. see Chase, John C.
Chamberlain, H. S. Immanuel Kant, 2 vols. 250.00 (ISBN 0-8490-0387-3). Gordon Pr.
Chamberlain, Henry R. Six Thousand Tons of Gold. LC 76-42721. Repr. of 1894 ed. 25.50 (ISBN 0-404-60056-5). AMS Pr.
Chamberlain, Hugh, tr. see Marceau, Francis.
Chamberlain, J. Mister Chamberlain's Speeches, 2 Vols. in 1. Boyd, Charles W., ed. Repr. of 1914 ed. 27.00 (ISBN 0-527-16000-8). Kraus Repr.
--Principles of Interferometric Spectroscopy. LC 78-13206. 347p. 1979. 94.95 (ISBN 0-471-99719-6). Wiley.
Chamberlain, Jacob C. A Bibliography of the First Editions in Book Form of the Writings of Henry Wadsworth Longfellow. LC 72-3116. (American Literature Ser., No. 49). 1972. Repr. of 1908 ed. lib. bdg. 39.95x (ISBN 0-8383-1513-5). Haskell.
Chamberlain, John. The Enterprising Americans: A Business History of the United States. enl. ed. LC 73-4069. (Illus.). 304p. (YA) 1974. 16.30i (ISBN 0-06-010702-2, HarpT). Har-Row.
--Letters Written by John Chamberlain During the Reign of Queen Elizabeth. Williams, Sarah, ed. (Camden Society, London. Publications. First Ser.: No. 79). Repr. of 1861 ed. 28.00 (ISBN 0-404-50179-6). AMS Pr.
--Letters Written by John Chamberlain During the Reign of Queen Elizabeth. 1861. 28.00 (ISBN 0-384-08425-7). Johnson Repr.
--A Life with the Printed Word. LC 81-85567. 204p. 1982. 12.95 (ISBN 0-89526-656-3). Regnery-Gateway.
--The Roots of Capitalism. LC 76-58035. 1977. 9.00 (ISBN 0-913966-23-1, Liberty Pr); pap. 3.00 (ISBN 0-913966-24-X). Liberty Fund.
Chamberlain, John, jt. auth. see Kirk, Russell.
Chamberlain, John B., et al. The Sea Urchin: Molecular Biology, 3 vols, Vol. 2. 188p. 1973. text ed. 28.50x (ISBN 0-8422-7121-X). Irvington.
Chamberlain, John S. Ibsen: The Open Vision. 233p. 1984. 36.50 (ISBN 0-485-11227-2, Pub. by Athlone Pr Ltd); pap. 14.95 (ISBN 0-485-12044-5, Pub. by Athlone Pr Ltd). Longwood Pub Group.
Chamberlain, Jonathan M. Eliminate Your SDBS: Self-Defeating Behaviors. LC 77-27634. (Illus.). 1978. pap. 7.95 (ISBN 0-8425-0998-4). Brigham.
Chamberlain, Joseph. A Political Memoir, 1880-92. Howard, C. H., ed. LC 75-7235. (Illus.). 340p. 1975. Repr. of 1953 ed. lib. bdg. 20.75x (ISBN 0-8371-8101-1, CHPOM). Greenwood.
Chamberlain, Joseph, ed. Chemistry & Physics of the Stratosphere. 171p. 1976. pap. 3.00 (ISBN 0-87590-221-9). Am Geophysical.
--Reviews of Lunar Sciences. (Illus.). 540p. 1977. pap. 5.00 (ISBN 0-87590-220-0). Am Geophysical.
Chamberlain, Joseph E. The "IFS" of History. (Illus.). 147p. 1985. Repr. of 1907 ed. 77.75 (ISBN 0-89901-205-1). Found Class Reprints.
Chamberlain, Joseph P. Regime of the International Rivers: Danube & Rhine. LC 68-57565. (Columbia University Studies in the Social Sciences: No. 237). Repr. of 1923 ed. 22.50 (ISBN 0-404-51237-2). AMS Pr.
Chamberlain, Joseph P., et al, eds. Judicial Function in Federal Administrative Agencies. facs. ed. LC 79-128875. (Select Bibliographies Reprint Ser). 1942. 19.00 (ISBN 0-8369-5495-5). Ayer Co Pubs.
Chamberlain, Joseph W. Motion of Charged Particles in the Earth's Magnetic Field. (Documents on Modern Physics Ser.). (Illus.). 42p. 1964. 16.50 (ISBN 0-677-00120-7). Gordon.
--Theory of Planetary Atmospheres: An Introduction to Their Physics & Chemistry. (International Geophysics Ser.). 1978. 35.00 (ISBN 0-12-167250-6). Acad Pr.
Chamberlain, Joshua L. Passing of the Armies. (Civil War Heritage Ser.: No. 4). 1985. 30.00. Pr of Morningside.
Chamberlain, Joy. Michelle Mustn't Know. 272p. 1983. pap. 2.95 (ISBN 0-515-05699-5). Jove Pubns.
Chamberlain, Judy & Chamberlain, Tom. Atari (400, 800, & XL Series) for the Beginning Beginner. (Illus.). 128p. (gr. 5 up). 1983. Atari 400, 800 & XL Models. pap. 8.95 (ISBN 0-86582-119-4, EN79222). Enrich.
Chamberlain, Lawrence. The Work of the Bond House. facsimile ed. LC 75-2626. (Wall Street & the Security Market Ser.). 1975. Repr. of 1912 ed. 18.00x (ISBN 0-405-06952-9). Ayer Co Pubs.
Chamberlain, Lawrence H. Loyalty & Legislative Action: A Survey of Activity by the New York State Legislature 1919-1949. 1951. 19.00 (ISBN 0-384-08435-4). Johnson Repr.
--President, Congress & Legislation. LC 72-181927. (Columbia University Studies in the Social Sciences: No. 523). Repr. of 1946 ed. 24.50 (ISBN 0-404-51523-1). AMS Pr.
Chamberlain, Lyle B. You Can Break Your Own Horse. (Illus.). 1970. 5.00 (ISBN 0-914208-07-1). Longhorn Pr.
Chamberlain, Lyn & Chamberlin, Tony. Guide to Cross-Country Skiing in New England. LC 80-82792. (Illus.). 224p. (Orig.). 1985. pap. 8.95 (ISBN 0-87106-856-7). Globe Pequot.
Chamberlain, M. C. Grandma's Quilting Primer. LC 85-117500. (Illus.). 50p. 1985. pap. 3.50 (ISBN 0-318-04041-7). Basis Bks.
Chamberlain, M. E. The Scramble for Africa. LC 74-177119. (Seminar Studies in History). 1974. pap. text ed. 6.25x (ISBN 0-582-35204-5). Longman.
Chamberlain, Marcia & Crockett, Candace. Beyond Weaving. (Illus.). 192p. 1974. 19.95 (ISBN 0-8230-0486-4). Watson-Guptill.
Chamberlain, Margaret, jt. auth. see Chamberlain, Chriss.

Chamberlain, Margaret, illus. Sing a Song of Sixpence. LC 83-22510. (Nursery Rhyme Press-Out Bks.). (Illus.). 8p. (gr. k-2). 1984. 4.95 (ISBN 0-911745-29-7, Bedrick Blackie). P Bedrick Bks.

Chamberlain, Mary. Fenwomen: A Portrait of Women in an English Village. 3.95 (ISBN 0-7043-3806-8, Pub. by Quartet England). Charles River Bks.

--Fenwomen: A Portrait of Women in an English Village. (History Workshop Ser.). (Illus.). 192p. 1983. pap. 9.95 (ISBN 0-7100-9567-8). Routledge & Kegan.

--Old Wives Tales: Their History, Remedies, & Spells. 236p. 1983. pap. 7.95 (ISBN 0-86068-016-9, Pub. by Virago Pr). Merrimack Pub Cir.

Chamberlain, Mildred M. The Rhode Island 1777 Military Census. LC 84-82485. 181p. 1985. 20.00 (ISBN 0-8063-1107-X). Genealog Pub.

Chamberlain, Muriel. Decolonization: The Fall of the European Empires. (Historical Association Studies). 96p. 1985. pap. 6.95 (ISBN 0-631-13935-4). Basil Blackwell.

Chamberlain, Muriel E. Lord Aberdeen: A Political Biography. LC 82-273. (Illus.). 583p. 1983. 50.00x (ISBN 0-582-50462-7). Longman.

Chamberlain, N. & Kuhn, J. Collective Bargaining. 3rd ed. 512p. 1986. 31.95 (ISBN 0-07-010441-7). McGraw.

Chamberlain, N. H. Samuel Sewall & the World He Lived in. 319p. 1980. Repr. of 1897 ed. lib. bdg. 30.00 (ISBN 0-89987-110-0). Darby Bks.

Chamberlain, Narcissa. Old Rooms for New Living. (Illus.). 1977. 13.95 (ISBN 0-8038-5346-7). Hastings.

--Old Rooms for New Living. 1982. pap. 9.95 (ISBN 0-8038-5395-5). Hastings.

--Omelette Book. (Illus.). 1952. 13.95 (ISBN 0-394-40158-1). Knopf.

--The Omelette Book. LC 55-10130. (Illus.). 192p. 1976. pap. 3.95 (ISBN 0-07-010450-6). McGraw.

Chamberlain, Narcissa & Chamberlain, Narcisse. The Flavor of France. (Illus.). 1978. 15.95 (ISBN 0-8038-2326-6). Hastings.

Chamberlain, Narcissa G. & Chamberlain, Narcisse. French Menus for Parties. (Illus.). 9.95 (ISBN 0-8038-2256-1). Hastings.

Chamberlain, Narcissa G. & Kingsland, Jane F. The Prints of Samuel Chamberlain N.A. 1984. 75.00 (ISBN 0-317-13423-X). Boston Public Lib.

Chamberlain, Narcissa G., jt. auth. see Chamberlain, Samuel.

Chamberlain, Narcisse, jt. auth. see Chamberlain, Narcissa.

Chamberlain, Narcisse, jt. auth. see Chamberlain, Narcissa G.

Chamberlain, Narcisse, tr. see Guerard, Michael.

Chamberlain, Neil, et al. The Labor Sector. 3rd rev. ed. (Illus.). 1980. text ed. 29.95 (ISBN 0-07-010435-2). McGraw.

Chamberlain, Neil W. & Kuhn, J. W. Collective Bargaining. 2nd ed. 1965. 30.95 (ISBN 0-07-010437-9). McGraw.

Chamberlain, Neil W. & Schilling, Jane M. Impact of Strikes: Their Social & Economic Costs. LC 73-11841. 257p. 1973. Repr. of 1954 ed. lib. bdg. 20.50x (ISBN 0-8371-7066-4, CHIS). Greenwood.

Chamberlain, Neville. In Search of Peace. facsimile ed. LC 77-156627. (Essay Index Reprint Ser). Repr. of 1939 ed. 18.00 (ISBN 0-8369-2274-3). Ayer Co Pubs.

Chamberlain, Newell D. The Call of Gold. LC 81-50164. (Illus.). 185p. 1981. pap. 4.95 (ISBN 0-934136-12-2). Western Tanager.

--The Call of Gold. (Illus.). 1977. pap. 4.95 (ISBN 0-913548-11-1, Valley Calif). Western Tanager.

Chamberlain, Nugent F. The Practice of NMR Spectroscopy: With Spectra-Structure Correlations for Hydrogen-One. LC 74-11479. (Illus.). 424p. 1974. 55.00 (ISBN 0-306-30766-9, Plenum Pr). Plenum Pub.

Chamberlain, Nugent F. & Reed, J. J. The Analytical Chemistry of Sulfur & Its Compounds: Nuclear Magnetic Resonance Data of Sulfur Compounds, Pt. 3. Karchmer, J. H., ed. LC 77-84969. (Chemical Analysis Ser.: Vol. 29). pap. 80.00 (ISBN 0-317-09773-3, 2012433). Bks Demand UMI.

Chamberlain, P. D. Anagrams. 1984. 25.00x (ISBN 0-686-87393-9, Pub. by Selecteditions). State Mutual Bk.

Chamberlain, Paul. Its About Time: Catalog of Watches at Chicago Art Institute. 40.00 (ISBN 0-87556-574-3). Saifer.

Chamberlain, Peter. Winning Golf. (Illus.). 160p. 1985. 19.95 (ISBN 0-8069-4192-8); pap. 12.95 (ISBN 0-8069-6216-X). Sterling.

Chamberlain, Peter & Doyle, Hilary L. Encyclopedia of German Tanks of World War II. LC 77-29061. (Illus.). 1978. 14.95 (ISBN 0-668-04565-5, 4565). Arco.

Chamberlain, Peter & Ellis, Chris. British & American Tanks of World War II. LC 69-13591. (Illus.). 1977. pap. 8.95 (ISBN 0-668-04304-0). Arco.

--Pictorial History of Tanks of the World, 1915-1945. (Illus.). 1981. 24.95 (Arms & Armour Pr). Sterling.

Chamberlain, Peter & Gander, Terry. Weapons of the Third Reich. LC 78-20293. 1979. 12.50 (ISBN 0-385-15090-3). Doubleday.

Chamberlain, Peter, jt. auth. see Ellis, Chris.

Chamberlain, Peter, jt. auth. see Milson, John.

Chamberlain, R. & Diallo, A. Toward a Language Policy for Namibia: English As the Official Language, Perspectives & Strategies. LC 82-102557. (Namibia Studies: No. 4). (Illus.). viii, 123p. Date not set. price not set (UN). Unipub.

Chamberlain, Robert L. George Crabbe. LC 64-8326. (English Authors Ser.). 1965. lib. bdg. 8.95 (ISBN 0-89197-768-6); pap. text ed. 4.95x (ISBN 0-89197-991-3). Irvington.

Chamberlain, Robert S. Conquest & Colonization of Honduras, 1502-1550. 1967. lib. bdg. 20.00x (ISBN 0-374-91368-4). Octagon.

Chamberlain, Rudolph W. There Is No Truce. facs. ed. LC 74-124229. (Select Bibliographies Reprint Ser). 1935. 23.50 (ISBN 0-8369-5418-1). Ayer Co Pubs.

Chamberlain, Samuel. Clementine in the Kitchen. rev. ed. 1963. 10.95 (ISBN 0-8038-1100-4). Hastings.

--Domestic Architecture in Rural France. (Illus.). 96p. (Orig.). 1981. pap. 7.95 (ISBN 0-8038-1578-6). Architectural.

--Etched in Sunlight: Fifty Years in the Graphic Arts. (Illus.). 1968. 25.00 (ISBN 0-89073-036-9). Boston Public Lib.

--Old Marblehead: A Camera Impression. rev. ed. (Illus.). 96p. 1975. 6.95 (ISBN 0-8038-5378-5). Hastings.

--Small House in the Sun. 1936. 13.95 (ISBN 0-8038-6704-2). Hastings.

--Stroll Through Historic Salem. LC 78-79738. (Illus.). 1969. student ed. 9.95 (ISBN 0-8038-6689-5). Hastings.

--This Realm, This England. 1941. 13.95 (ISBN 0-8038-7063-9). Hastings.

--A Tour of Old Sturbridge Village. rev. ed. 72p. 1972. pap. 1.50 (ISBN 0-8038-7128-7). Hastings.

Chamberlain, Samuel & Chamberlain, Narcissa G. The Chamberlain Selection of New England Rooms, 1639-1863. 1973. 20.00 (ISBN 0-8038-1176-4). Hastings.

Chamberlain, Samuel & Flynt, Henry N. Historic Deerfield: Houses & Interiors. 1979. 16.95 (ISBN 0-8038-3027-0). Hastings.

Chamberlain, Samuel, compiled by. Genealogical Notes of the Chamberlain Family of Maryland. LC 70-175217. 1973. Repr. 20.00 (ISBN 0-686-26999-3). Polyanthos.

Chamberlain, Samuel, et al. Chamberlain Sampler of American Cooking. (Illus.). 1961. 9.95 (ISBN 0-8038-1088-1). Hastings.

Chamberlain, Tom, jt. auth. see Chamberlain, Judy.

Chamberlain, V. Teen Guide to Homemaking. 5th ed. 1982. 23.28 (ISBN 0-07-007843-2). McGraw.

Chamberlain, V. B., 3rd, jt. ed. see Rogers, Robert S.

Chamberlain, V. M. & Buddinger, Peyton B. Teen Guide. 6th ed. O'Neill, Martha, ed. (Illus.). 528p. (YA) 1985. 23.28 (ISBN 0-07-007842-4). McGraw.

Chamberlain, Valerie. Personal Skills: For Home, School, Work, 1984. (gr. 9-12). 1984. text ed. 11.36 (ISBN 0-02-665360-5). Bennett Il.

Chamberlain, Valerie & Kelly, Joan. Creative Home Economics Instruction. 2nd ed. O'Neill, Martha, ed. (Illus.). 256p. 1980. pap. text ed. 16.68 (ISBN 0-07-010424-7). McGraw.

Chamberlain, Valerie, jt. auth. see Kelly, Joan.

Chamberlain, Von Del see Von Del Chamberlain.

Chamberlain, Von Del, jt. ed. see Hanle, Paul A.

Chamberlain, Walter. The Thames & Hudson Manual of Etching & Engraving. (Illus.). 1978. pap. 10.95f (ISBN 0-500-68001-9). Thames Hudson.

--The Thames & Hudson Manual of Wood Engraving. (Illus.). 1979. 18.95 (ISBN 0-500-67018-8). Thames Hudson.

Chamberlain, William. Multidisciplinary Child Abuse & Neglect Team Manual. 77p. 3.50 (ISBN 0-318-16356-X, B10). Regional Inst Social Welfare.

--Trumpets of Company K. 1982. pap. 1.95 (ISBN 0-345-30551-5). Ballantine.

Chamberlain, William D. Exegetical Grammar of the Greek New Testament. 1979. pap. 7.95 (ISBN 0-8010-2438-2). Baker Bk.

Chamberlain, William H. America's Second Crusade. 1962. pap. 2.00 (ISBN 0-911956-07-7). Constructive Action.

Chamberlain, William J. Fighting for Peace: The War Resistance Movement. (Library of War & Peace; Non-Resis. & Non-Vio.). lib. bdg. 46.00 (ISBN 0-8240-0373-X). Garland Pub.

Chamberlane, C. G., ed. The Vestry Book of Petsworth Parish, Glouster County, Virginia, 1670-1793. LC 79-13640. xv, 429p. 1979. Repr. of 1933 ed. 10.00 (ISBN 0-88490-032-0). VA State Lib.

Chamberlayne, C. G. The Vestry Book & Register of St. Peter's Parish, New Kent & James City Counties, Virginia, 1684-1786. xxvi, 840p. 1973. Repr. of 1937 ed. 12.50 (ISBN 0-88490-037-1). VA State Lib.

Chamberlayne, C. G., ed. The Vestry Book of Blisland (Blissland) Parish, New Kent & James City Counties, Virginia, 1721-1786. LC 79-16401. ixii, 277p. 1979. Repr. of 1935 ed. 10.00 (ISBN 0-88490-030-4). VA State Lib.

--The Vestry Book of St. Paul's Parish, Hanover County, Virginia, 1706-1786. xx, 672p. 1973. Repr. of 1940 ed. 12.50 (ISBN 0-88490-038-X). VA State Lib.

Chamberlayne, Churchill G. Births from the Bristol Parish Register of Henrico, Prince George & Dinwiddie Counties, Virginia, 1720-1798. LC 74-8784. 133p. 1980. pap. 10.00 (ISBN 0-8063-0627-0). Genealog Pub.

Chamberlian, Peter & Gander, Terry. Eighty-Eight Flak & Pak. (Illus.). 80p. 1976. pap. 5.95 (ISBN 0-85383-092-4). Hippocrene Bks.

Chamberlin. A Glossary of West Worcestershire Words. (English Dialect Society Publications Ser.: No. 36). pap. 15.00 (ISBN 0-317-15880-5). Kraus Repr.

--Social Strategy & Corporate Structure. 192p. 1982. text ed. 24.95 (ISBN 0-02-905810-4). Free Pr.

Chamberlin, Bill F. & Brown, Charlene. The First Amendment Reconsidered. LC 81-11799. (Longman Series in Public Administration). 1982. text ed. 27.95x (ISBN 0-582-28303-5). Longman.

Chamberlin, Brewster, jt. ed. see Foner, Philip S.

Chamberlin, D. G., jt. auth. see Chamberlin, G. J.

Chamberlin, E. R. Great English Houses. 14.95 (ISBN 0-517-55086-5, Harmony). Crown.

--Librarian & His World. 1969. 6.00 (ISBN 0-8022-2265-X). Philos Lib.

--Loot! The Heritage of Plunder. LC 83-1525. (Illus.). 248p. 1983. 19.95 (ISBN 0-87196-259-4). Facts on File.

--The National Trust Book of English Country Towns. (Illus.). 240p. 1983. 25.50 (ISBN 0-03-064174-8). HR&W.

--The World of the Italian Renaissance. (Illus.). 176p. 1982. 25.00 (ISBN 0-04-900035-7). Allen Unwin.

--The World of the Italian Renaissance. (Illus.). 311p. 1983. pap. text ed. 9.95x (ISBN 0-04-900036-5). Allen Unwin.

Chamberlin, Edward H. Theory of Monopolistic Competition: A Re-Orientation of the Theory of Value. 8th ed. LC 63-649. (Economic Studies: No. 38). 1962. 25.00x (ISBN 0-674-88125-7). Harvard U Pr.

--Towards a More General Theory of Value. LC 82-6259. xii, 318p. 1982. Repr. of 1957 ed. lib. bdg. 35.00x (ISBN 0-313-23590-2, CHTO). Greenwood.

Chamberlin, Edward J. & Gilman, Sander L., eds. Degeneration: The Myth of Progress. 320p. 1985. 40.00x (ISBN 0-231-05196-4). Columbia U Pr.

Chamberlin, Edwin M. The Sovereigns of Industry. LC 75-308. (The Radical Tradition in America Ser). 165p. 1975. Repr. of 1875 ed. 17.00 (ISBN 0-88355-212-4). Hyperion Conn.

Chamberlin, Everett. Chicago & Its Suburbs. LC 73-2902. (Metropolitan America Ser.). (Illus.). 474p. 1974. Repr. 30.00x (ISBN 0-405-05388-6). Ayer Co Pubs.

Chamberlin, F. The Balearics. 1976. lib. bdg. 59.95 (ISBN 0-8490-1473-5). Gordon Pr.

Chamberlin, G. J. & Chamberlin, D. G. Colour: Its Measurement, Computation, & Application. (International Topics in Science Ser.). 148p. 1980. 34.95 (ISBN 0-471-25625-0, Pub. by Wiley Heyden). Wiley.

Chamberlin, Hal. Musical Applications of Microprocessors. 672p. 1983. pap. 21.95 (ISBN 0-317-00362-3). Hayden.

Chamberlin, Henry H., tr. see Horace.

Chamberlin, J. Gordon. The Educating Act: A Phenomenological View. LC 80-6076. 202p. 1981. lib. bdg. 22.75 (ISBN 0-8191-1449-9); pap. text ed. 10.50 (ISBN 0-8191-1450-2). U Pr of Amer.

--I Don't Have No Education & Other Reflections. 138p. 1984. 11.75 (ISBN 0-915481-01-4); pap. 7.75 (ISBN 0-915481-00-6). Ed Pr.

Chamberlin, Jane, illus. Saloons of San Francisco: The Great & Notorious. LC 82-12763. (Illus.). 128p. (Orig.). 1982. pap. 8.95 (ISBN 0-88496-186-9). Capra Pr.

Chamberlin, John S. Increase & Multiply: Arts of Discourse Procedure in the Preaching of John Donne. LC 76-6998. xiv, 192p. 1976. 18.00x (ISBN 0-8078-1266-8). U of NC Pr.

Chamberlin, Joseph. Nomads & Listeners. facs. ed. Waxman, S. M., ed. LC 68-22905. (Essay Index Reprint Ser). 1937. 17.00 (ISBN 0-8369-0287-4). Ayer Co Pubs.

Chamberlin, Joseph E. Boston Transcript: A History of Its First Hundred Years. facsimile ed. LC 76-103646. (Select Bibliographies Reprint Ser). 1930. 26.50 (ISBN 0-8369-5146-8). Ayer Co Pubs.

--Boston Transcript, a History of Its First Hundred Years. (American Studies). 1969. Repr. 22.00 (ISBN 0-384-08445-1). Johnson Repr.

Chamberlin, Judi. On Our Own: Patient-Controlled Alternatives to the Mental Health System. 1979. pap. 5.95 (ISBN 0-07-010451-4). McGraw.

Chamberlin, L. J. & Carnot, J. B. Improving School Discipline. 244p. 1974. 24.75x (ISBN 0-398-02812-5). C C Thomas.

Chamberlin, Leslie J. Coping with Today's Kids. (Illus.). 236p. 1984. pap. 19.75x (ISBN 0-398-04988-2). C C Thomas.

Chamberlin, M., jt. ed. see Losick, R.

Chamberlin, Michael. Promenades. 1976. signed ed. 6.00 (ISBN 0-685-79237-4, Pub. by Grosseteste); pap. 2.00 (ISBN 0-685-79238-2). Small Pr Dist.

Chamberlin, Michael J., ed. see Rodriguez, Raymond L.

Chamberlin, Ralph V. Ethno-Botany of the Gosiute Indians of Utah. LC 14-11549. 1911. 11.00 (ISBN 0-527-00510-X). Kraus Repr.

Chamberlin, Robert, jt. auth. see Hymovich, Debra P.

Chamberlin, Roxanna, ed. see Shell, Harvey.

Chamberlin, Russell. English Market Town. 1985. 16.95 (ISBN 0-517-55670-7). Crown.

--Everyday Life in the Nineteenth Century. LC 83-60889. (Everyday Life Ser.). 64p. (gr. 4 up). 1983. 13.72 (ISBN 0-382-06696-0). Silver.

Chamberlin, Susan. Hedges, Screens & Espaliers: How to Select, Grow & Enjoy. 176p. 1982. pap. 9.95 (ISBN 0-89586-190-9). H P Bks.

Chamberlin, Susan & Pollock, Janet. Fences, Gates & Walls: How to Design, Build & Enjoy. 160p. 1983. pap. 9.95 (ISBN 0-89586-189-5). H P Bks.

Chamberlin, Tony, jt. auth. see Chamberlain, Lyn.

Chamberlin, Vernon A. & Schulman, Ivan A. La Rivista Ilustrada de Nueva York: History, Anthology, & Index of Literary Selections. LC 75-35891. 212p. 1976. 22.00x (ISBN 0-8262-0189-X). U of Mo Pr.

Chamberlin, Waldo. Industrial Relations in Germany 1914-1939. LC 75-180664. Repr. of 1942 ed. 35.00 (ISBN 0-404-56400-3). AMS Pr.

Chamberlin, Waldo, jt. auth. see Hovet, Thomas.

Chamberlin, Willard J. Entomological Nomenclature & Literature. 3rd rev. & enl. ed. LC 79-108387. vii, 141p. Repr. of 1952 ed. lib. bdg. 24.75x (ISBN 0-8371-3810-8, CHNO). Greenwood.

Chamberlin, William C. Economic Development of Iceland Through World War Two. LC 73-76653. (Columbia University Studies in the Social Sciences: No. 531). Repr. of 1947 ed. 15.00 (ISBN 0-404-51531-2). AMS Pr.

Chamberlin, William H. America's Second Crusade. 1962. pap. 2.00 (ISBN 0-87926-000-9). R Myles.

--Russia's Iron Age. LC 73-115517. (Russia Observed, Series I). 1970. Repr. of 1934 ed. 23.50 (ISBN 0-405-03013-4). Ayer Co Pubs.

--Soviet Planned Economic Order. LC 70-107342. (BCL Ser.: No. I). 1970. Repr. of 1931 ed. 11.50 (ISBN 0-404-00595-0). AMS Pr.

--Soviet Planned Economic Order. LC 77-95088. Repr. of 1931 ed. lib. bdg. 25.00x (ISBN 0-8371-2544-8, CHSE). Greenwood.

Chamberlyne, C. G., ed. The Vestry Book of Stratton Major Parish, King & Queen County, Virginia, 1729-1783. LC 80-14672. xxi, 257p. 1980. Repr. of 1933 ed. 10.00 (ISBN 0-88490-087-8). VA State Lib.

Chambers. Gerard de Nerval et la Poetique du Voyage. 34.95 (ISBN 0-685-34959-4). French & Eur.

Chambers, jt. auth. see Wells.

Chambers, A. Internal Auditing: Theory & Practice. 360p. 1981. 45.00x (ISBN 0-273-01632-6, Pub. by Pitman Bks England). State Mutual Bk.

--Our Life After Death. 59.95 (ISBN 0-8490-0784-4). Gordon Pr.

Chambers, A., jt. auth. see Geddes, W. H.

Chambers, A. B., et al see Dryden, John.

Chambers, Aidan. Breaktime. LC 78-19472. (gr. 7 up). 1979. 9.57i (ISBN 0-06-021256-X). HarpJ.

--Dance on My Grave. LC 82-48258. (Charlotte Zolotow Bk.). 256p. (YA) (gr. 7 up). 1983. 13.41i (ISBN 0-06-021253-5); PLB 12.89g (ISBN 0-06-021254-3). HarpJ.

--Introducing Books to Children. 2nd ed. 224p. 1983. 22.00 (ISBN 0-87675-284-9); pap. 14.00 (ISBN 0-87675-285-7). Horn Bk.

--Out of Time. LC 85-42631. (A Charlotte Zolotow Bk.). 192p. (YA) (gr. 7 up). 1985. 11.49i (ISBN 0-06-021201-2); PLB 10.89g (ISBN 0-06-021202-0). HarpJ.

--The Present Takers. LC 83-48470. (A Charlotte Zolotow Bk.). 160p. (gr. 5 up). 1984. 10.53i (ISBN 0-06-021251-9); PLB 10.89g (ISBN 0-06-021252-7). HarpJ.

--Seal Secret. LC 80-8456. 128p. (gr. 5 up). 1981. 8.95 (ISBN 0-06-021258-6); PLB 9.89g (ISBN 0-06-021259-4). HarpJ.

Chambers, Albert S. A Name Index to the Eighteen Seventy-Eight History of Montgomery & Fulton Counties, New York. 1979. 10.00x (ISBN 0-932334-30-X). Heart of the Lakes.

Chambers, Andrew D. Computer Auditing. 256p. 1981. 24.50 (ISBN 0-317-04274-2, 5047). Commerce.

--Internal Auditing. 378p. 1981. 27.50 (ISBN 0-317-04285-8, 5048). Commerce.

Chambers, Andrew J. Recollections. Bd. with Reminiscences. Chambers, Margaret W. 1975. 6.00 (ISBN 0-87770-156-3). Ye Galleon.

Chambers, Anne. Chieftain to Knight: Tibbott-Ne-Long Bourke (1567-1629), First Viscount Mayo. (Illus.). 250p. 1983. 14.95 (ISBN 0-86327-008-5, Pub. by Wolfhound Pr Ireland). Irish Bks Media.

--Granuaile: The Life & Times of Grace O'Malley. (Illus.). 212p. 1983. 13.95 (ISBN 0-905473-31-0, Pub. by Wolfhound Pr Ireland); pap. 6.95 (ISBN 0-86327-007-7, Pub. by Wolfhound Pr Ireland). Irish Bks Media.

Chambers, Anthony H., tr. see Tanizaki, Junichiro.

Chambers, B. & Chambers, E. J. Bulking of Activated Sludge: Preventative & Remedial Methods. 279p. 1982. 74.95x (ISBN 0-470-27299-6). Halsted Pr.

Chambers, Bruce W. Art & Artists of the South: The Robert P. Coggins Collection. (Illus.). 210p. 1984. 40.00 (ISBN 0-87249-432-2). U of SC Pr.

Chambers, Calvin H. In Spirit & in Truth: Charismatic Worship & the Reformed Tradition. 168p. 1980. 7.95 (ISBN 0-8059-2686-0). Dorrance.

Chambers, Carl D. & Heckman, Richard D. Employee Drug Abuse: A Manager's Guide for Action. LC 73-183372. 240p. 1972. 19.95 (ISBN 0-8436-0718-1). Van Nos Reinhold.

Chambers, Carl D. & Brill, Leon, eds. Methadone: Experiences & Issues. LC 72-6122. 411p. 1973. text ed. 34.95 (ISBN 0-87705-072-4). Human Sci Pr.

Chambers, Carl D., jt. ed. see Inciardi, James A.

Chambers, Carol & Maidens, Melinda, eds. Our Aging Population: Burden or Resource. (Illus.). 196p. 1983. 19.95x (ISBN 0-87196-875-4). Facts on File.

Chambers, Catherine. The Measure of a Man. Clanton, Charles, ed. (Illus.). 194p. 1978. 7.95 (ISBN 0-912315-24-5). Word Aflame.

Chambers, Catherine, jt. auth. see Morgan, Nell.

Chambers, Catherine, ed. see Coleman, Kenneth.

Chambers, Catherine E. California Gold Rush: Search for Treasure. LC 83-18280. (Adventures in Frontier America Ser.). (Illus.). 32p. (gr. 5-9). 1984. PLB 8.79 (ISBN 0-8167-0051-6); pap. text ed. 1.95 (ISBN 0-8167-0052-4). Troll Assocs.

--Daniel Boone & the Wilderness Road. LC 83-18291. (Adventures in Frontier America Ser.). (Illus.). 32p. (gr. 5-9). 1984. PLB 8.79 (ISBN 0-8167-0037-0); pap. text ed. 1.95 (ISBN 0-8167-0038-9). Troll Assocs.

--Flatboats on the Ohio: Westward Bound. LC 83-18278. (Adventures in Frontier America Ser.). (Illus.). 32p. (gr. 5-9). 1984. PLB 8.79 (ISBN 0-8167-0049-4); pap. text ed. 1.95 (ISBN 0-8167-0050-8). Troll Assocs.

--Frontier Dream: Life on the Great Plains. LC 83-18282. (Adventures in Frontier America Ser.). (Illus.). 32p. (gr. 5-9). 1984. PLB 8.79 (ISBN 0-8167-0039-7); pap. text ed. 1.95 (ISBN 0-8167-0040-0). Troll Assocs.

--Frontier Farmer: Kansas Adventures. LC 83-18279. (Adventures in Frontier America Ser.). (Illus.). 32p. (gr. 5-9). 1984. PLB 8.79 (ISBN 0-8167-0053-2); pap. text ed. 1.95 (ISBN 0-8167-0054-0). Troll Assocs.

--Frontier Village: A Town Is Born. LC 83-18271. (Adventures in Frontier America Ser.). (Illus.). 32p. (gr. 5-9). 1984. PLB 8.79 (ISBN 0-8167-0045-1); pap. text ed. 1.95 (ISBN 0-8167-0046-X). Troll Assocs.

--Indiana Days: Life in a Frontier Town. LC 83-18283. (Adventures in Frontier America Ser.). (Illus.). 32p. (gr. 5-9). 1984. PLB 8.79 (ISBN 0-8167-0055-9); pap. text ed. 1.95 (ISBN 0-8167-0056-7). Troll Assocs.

--Log-Cabin Home: Pioneers in the Wilderness. LC 83-18277. (Adventures in Frontier America Ser.). (Illus.). 32p. (gr. 5-9). 1984. PLB 8.79 (ISBN 0-8167-0041-9); pap. text ed. 1.95 (ISBN 0-8167-0042-7). Troll Assocs.

--Texas Roundup: Life on the Range. LC 83-18281. (Adventures in Frontier America Ser.). (Illus.). 32p. (gr. 5-9). 1984. PLB 8.79 (ISBN 0-8167-0047-8); pap. text ed. 1.95 (ISBN 0-8167-0048-6). Troll Assocs.

--Wagons West: Off to Oregon. LC 83-18276. (Adventures in Frontier America Ser.). (Illus.). 32p. (gr. 5-9). 1984. PLB 8.79 (ISBN 0-8167-0043-5); pap. text ed. 1.95 (ISBN 0-8167-0044-3). Troll Assocs.

Chambers, Claire. The Siecus Circle. LC 75-41650. 1977. pap. 6.95 (ISBN 0-88279-119-2). Western Islands.

Chambers, Clarke A. Seedtime of Reform: American Social Service & Social Action, 1918 to 1933. LC 80-36788. xviii, 326p. 1980. Repr. of 1963 ed. lib. bdg. 32.50x (ISBN 0-313-22666-0, CHRE). Greenwood.

--Seedtime of Reform: American Social Service & Social Action, 1918-1933. LC 63-23058. pap. 86.50 (ISBN 0-317-29390-7, 2055847). Bks Demand UMI.

Chambers, Clarke A., jt. auth. see Hinding, Andrea.

Chambers, Clytia, jt. auth. see Efron, Edith.

Chambers, Colin. Other Spaces: New Theatre & the Royal Shakespeare Company. 80p. 1981. pap. 7.95 (ISBN 0-413-46880-1, NO. 2121). Methuen Inc.

Chambers, Constance. The Book of English Desserts. (Illus.). 1965. 17.95 (ISBN 0-911202-01-3). Radio City.

Chambers, D. S., ed. Patrons & Artists in the Italian Renaissance. LC 78-145530. (History in Depth Ser). 1971. 12.95x (ISBN 0-87249-220-6); pap. 7.95x (ISBN 0-87249-221-4). U of SC Pr.

Chambers, David. Lucien Pissarro: Notes on a Selection of Wood-blocks Held at the Ashmolean Museum, Oxford. 47p. 1980. 35.00x (ISBN 0-900090-75-8, Pub. by Ashmolean Mus UK). State Mutual Bk.

Chambers, David & Martineau, Jane. Splendours of the Gonzaga. (Illus.). 360p. (Orig.). 1984. pap. 25.00 (ISBN 0-317-30092-X, Pub. by Victoria & Albert Mus UK). Faber & Faber.

Chambers, David, jt. auth. see Mosley, James.

Chambers, David L. Making Fathers Pay: The Enforcement of Child Support. LC 79-11953. 1979. 32.50x (ISBN 0-226-10077-4). U of Chicago Pr.

--Metre of Macbeth. LC 78-113575. Repr. of 1903 ed. 9.50 (ISBN 0-404-01443-7). AMS Pr.

--Metre of Macbeth. 1903. lib. bdg. 10.00 (ISBN 0-8414-3012-8). Folcroft.

Chambers, Donald E. Social Policy & Social Programs: A Method for the Practical Public Policy Analyst. 294p. 1986. text ed. price not set (ISBN 0-02-320580-6). Macmillan.

Chambers, Donald L. How to Gold-Leaf Antiques & Other Art Objects. (Arts & Crafts Ser.). (Illus.). 96p. 1973. pap. 9.95 (ISBN 0-517-54217-X). Crown.

Chambers, E. J., jt. auth. see Chambers, B.

Chambers, E. K. English Pastorals. facs. ed. LC 70-76943. (Granger Index Reprint Ser). 1906. 18.00 (ISBN 0-8369-6008-4). Ayer Co Pubs.

Chambers, E. K. & Sidgwick, F. Early English Lyrics. 1967. 6.95 (ISBN 0-8079-0039-7); pap. 2.95 (ISBN 0-8079-0040-0). October.

Chambers, E. K., ed. Early English Lyrics: Amorous, Divine, Moral & Trivial. Sidgwick, F. LC 76-173857. Repr. of 1926 ed. 24.50 (ISBN 0-405-08347-5, Blom Pubns). Ayer Co Pubs.

Chambers, Edmund K. The Disintegration of Shakespeare. 1980. Repr. of 1924 ed. lib. bdg. 10.00 (ISBN 0-8495-0798-7). Arden Lib.

--Distintegration of Shakespeare. 1924. lib. bdg. 6.00 (ISBN 0-8414-3438-7). Folcroft.

--Early English Lyrics, Amorous, Divine, Moral & Trivial. LC 70-178518. Repr. of 1921 ed. 34.50 (ISBN 0-404-56531-X). AMS Pr.

--English Literature at the Close of the Middle Ages. (Oxford History of English Literature Ser.). 1945. 42.00x (ISBN 0-19-812203-9). Oxford U Pr.

--English Pastorals. 1978. Repr. of 1906 ed. lib. bdg. 30.00 (ISBN 0-8495-0824-X). Arden Lib.

--English Pastorals. 1906. lib. bdg. 35.00 (ISBN 0-8414-3013-6). Folcroft.

--The History & Motives of Literary Forgeries Being the Chancellor's English Essay for 1891. LC 68-56729. (Research & Source Works Ser.: No. 209). 1968. Repr. of 1891 ed. 12.50 (ISBN 0-8337-0522-9). B Franklin.

--History & Motives of Literary Forgeries. 1891. lib. bdg. 10.00 (ISBN 0-8414-3397-6). Folcroft.

--Notes on the History of the Revels Office Under the Tudors. LC 68-56727. (Research & Source Works Ser.: No. 207). 1968. Repr. of 1906 ed. 14.50 (ISBN 0-8337-0523-7). B Franklin.

--Samuel Taylor Coleridge: A Biographical Study. LC 78-19152. 1978. Repr. of 1967 ed. lib. bdg. 27.50x (ISBN 0-313-20539-6, CHST). Greenwood.

--Shakespearean Gleanings. LC 74-153312. Repr. of 1944 ed. 14.00 (ISBN 0-404-01444-5). AMS Pr.

--Shakespearean Gleanings. 1944. lib. bdg. 20.00 (ISBN 0-8414-3523-5). Folcroft.

--Sheaf of Studies. facsimile ed. LC 74-99622. (Essay Index Reprint Ser.). 1942. 18.00 (ISBN 0-8369-1398-1). Ayer Co Pubs.

--Sheaf of Studies. LC 74-12168. 1942. lib. bdg. 20.00 (ISBN 0-8414-3371-2). Folcroft.

--Sir Thomas Malory. Repr. of 1922 ed. lib. bdg. 10.00 (ISBN 0-8414-3431-X). Folcroft.

--The Timelessness of Poetry. 1940. lib. bdg. 10.00 (ISBN 0-8414-3582-0). Folcroft.

Chambers, Edmund K., ed. Oxford Book of Sixteenth Century Verse. 1932. 45.00x (ISBN 0-19-812126-1). Oxford U Pr.

Chambers, Edward L., jt. auth. see Chambers, Robert.

Chambers, Eric. Reproduction Photography for Lithography. (Illus.). 340p. 1979. avail. (1504) (ISBN 0-88362-057-X). Graphic Arts Tech Found.

Chambers, Eric G. Psychology & the Industrial Worker. LC 53-5436. pap. 49.80 (ISBN 0-317-10280-X, 2050766). Bks Demand UMI.

Chambers, Erve. Applied Anthropology: A Practical Guide. 300p. 1985. pap. text ed. 21.95 (ISBN 0-13-039371-1). P-H.

Chambers, Frances. France. (World Bibliographical Ser.: No. 13). 175p. 1980. lib. bdg. 31.50 (ISBN 0-903450-25-9). ABC Clio.

--Haiti. (World Bibliography Ser.: No. 39). 177p. 1983. lib. bdg. 27.00 (ISBN 0-903450-69-0). ABC-Clio.

Chambers, Frances, jt. auth. see Purvis, Douglas.

Chambers, Francis T., Jr. The Drinker's Addiction: Its Nature & Practical Treatment. (Illus.). 164p. 1968. 15.75x (ISBN 0-398-00301-7). C C Thomas.

Chambers, Frank. Prosateurs Francais XVIE Siecle. 1976. pap. 17.95 (ISBN 0-669-00016-7). Heath.

Chambers, Frank M. Proper Names in the Lyrics of the Troubadours. (Studies in the Romance Languages & Literatures: No. 113). 272p. 1972. pap. 13.00x (ISBN 0-8078-9113-4). U of NC Pr.

Chambers, Frank P. History of Taste: An Account of the Revolutions of Art Criticism & Theory in Europe. LC 76-136057. (Illus.). 1971. Repr. of 1932 ed. lib. bdg. 27.25x (ISBN 0-8371-5207-0, CHHT). Greenwood.

--The War Behind the War, 1914-1918: A History of the Political & Civilian Fronts. LC 72-4267. (World Affairs Ser.: National & International Viewpoints). (Illus.). 638p. 1972. Repr. of 1939 ed. 36.00 (ISBN 0-405-04564-6). Ayer Co Pubs.

Chambers, Frederick, compiled by. Black Higher Education in the United States: A Selected Bibliography on Negro Higher Education & Historically Black Colleges & Universities. LC 77-91100. 1978. lib. bdg. 29.95 (ISBN 0-313-20037-8, CBH/). Greenwood.

Chambers, George. Chambersburg. (Jupnier Bk.: No. 9). 1972. pap. 4.00 (ISBN 0-686-61865-3). Juniper Pr WI.

--Null Set. LC 76-47788. 1977. 8.95 (ISBN 0-914590-34-0); pap. 3.95 (ISBN 0-914590-35-9). Fiction Coll.

Chambers, George F. The Story of Eclipses. 1904. 15.00 (ISBN 0-686-17419-4). Ridgeway Bks.

Chambers, Ginger. Call It Love. (Candlelight Ecstasy Ser.: No. 40). (Orig.). 1982. pap. 1.75 (ISBN 0-440-11128-5). Dell.

--A Fire of the Soul. (Candlelight Ecstasy Ser.: No. 83). (Orig.). 1982. pap. 1.95 (ISBN 0-440-12540-5). Dell.

--Game of Hearts. (Harlequin American Romance Ser.). 256p. 1983. pap. 2.25 (ISBN 0-373-16032-1). Harlequin Bks.

--Harbor of Dreams. (Candlelight Ecstasy Supreme Ser.: No. 43). 288p. (Orig.). 1984. pap. 2.50 (ISBN 0-440-13446-3). Dell.

--A Heart Divided. (Candlelight Ecstasy Supreme Ser.: No. 18). 288p. (Orig.). 1984. pap. 2.50 (ISBN 0-440-13509-5). Dell.

--The Kindred Spirit. (Orig.). 1981. pap. 1.50 (ISBN 0-440-14395-0). Dell.

--Sweet Persuasion. (Candlelight Ecstasy Ser.: No. 102). (Orig.). 1982. pap. 1.95 (ISBN 0-440-17524-0). Dell.

--Too Close for Comfort. (CandleLight Supreme Ser.: No. 96). (Orig.). 1985. pap. 2.75 (ISBN 0-440-18740-0). Dell.

Chambers, Glen & Fisher, Gene. United States History for Christian Schools. (Heritage Studies for Christian Schools Ser.). (Illus.). 656p. (gr. 11). 1982. text ed. 26.60 (ISBN 0-89084-176-4); tchr's ed. 19.50 (ISBN 0-89084-177-2). Bob Jones Univ Pr.

Chambers, Glen, jt. auth. see Fisher, Gene.

Chambers, Graham, jt. auth. see Peacock, James.

Chambers, H. & Chacey, C. Drafting & Manual Programming for Numerical Control. 1980. 32.95 (ISBN 0-13-219113-X). P-H.

Chambers, H. A., compiled by. A Shakespeare Song Book. (Illus.). 64p. 1985. 12.95 (ISBN 0-7137-1504-9, Pub. by Blandford England); pap. 6.95 (ISBN 0-7137-1503-0). Sterling.

Chambers, H. E. Constitutional History of Hawaii. 1973. pap. 9.00 (ISBN 0-384-08450-8). Johnson Repr.

Chambers, Harold C. The Compaq Compatible Software Guide. 1984. 21.95 (ISBN 0-317-06185-2). P-H.

Chambers, Harry. Making the Most of Word Processing. 192p. 1982. 55.00x (ISBN 0-686-44697-6, Pub. by Hutchinson). State Mutual Bk.

Chambers, Harry T. Copying, Duplication & Microfilm. 192p. 1972. 17.95x (ISBN 0-8464-0291-2). Beekman Pubs.

--Making the Most of Word Processing. 189p. 1982. text ed. 31.75 (ISBN 0-09-147420-5, Busn Bks England). Brookfield Pub Co.

--The Management of Small Offset Print Departments. 2nd ed. 217p. 1979. text ed. 31.50x (ISBN 0-220-67007-2, Pub. by Busn Bks England). Brookfield Pub Co.

Chambers, Henry A., ed. Treasury of Negro Spirituals. LC 63-14218. (Illus.). 126p. (Orig.). (gr. 7 up). 1983. 12.95 (ISBN 0-87523-145-4). Emerson.

Chambers, Henry E. Constitutional History of Hawaii. LC 78-63846. (Johns Hopkins University. Studies in the Social Sciences. Fourteenth Ser. 1896: 1). Repr. of 1896 ed. 11.50 (ISBN 0-404-61103-6). AMS Pr.

--West Florida & Its Relations to the Historical Cartography of the United States. LC 78-63863. (Johns Hopkins University. Studies in the Social Sciences. Sixteenth Ser. 1898: 5). Repr. of 1898 ed. 11.50 (ISBN 0-404-61119-2). AMS Pr.

--West Florida & Its Relations to the Historical Cartography of the United States. 1973. pap. 9.00 (ISBN 0-384-08451-6). Johnson Repr.

Chambers, Iain. Urban Rhythms: Pop Music & Popular Culture. LC 84-22848. (Illus.). 288p. 1985. 29.95 (ISBN 0-312-83469-1). St Martin.

Chambers, J. D. & Mingay, G. E. The Agricultural Revolution. 1975. pap. 16.95 (ISBN 0-7134-1358-1, Pub. by Batsford England). David & Charles.

Chambers, J. D., jt. auth. see Bell, I. E.

Chambers, J. K. & Trudgill, P. Dialectology. LC 79-41604. (Cambridge Textbooks in Linguistics). (Illus.). 210p. 1980. pap. 13.95 (ISBN 0-521-29473-8). Cambridge U Pr.

Chambers, Jack. Milestones I: The Music & Times of Miles Davis to 1960. (Illus.). 357p. 1983. 24.95 (ISBN 0-8020-2499-8). U of Toronto Pr.

--Milestones One: The Music & Times of Miles Davis to 1960. LC 85-70574. (Illus.). 368p. 1985. Repr. of 1983 ed. 17.95 (ISBN 0-688-02635-4, Pub. by Beech Tree Bks). Morrow.

--Milestones Two: The Music & Times of Miles Davis since 1960. LC 85-70574. (Illus.). 432p. 1985. 17.95 (ISBN 0-688-04646-0, Pub. by Beech Tree Bks). Morrow.

Chambers, Jack & Sprecher, Jerry. Computer Assisted Instruction: Its Use in the Classroom. (Illus.). 240p. 1983. 19.95 (ISBN 0-13-164384-3); pap. 13.95 (ISBN 0-13-164376-2). P-H.

Chambers, James. The Devil's Horsemen: The Mongol Invasion of Europe. LC 78-22055. (Illus.). 208p. 1985. pap. 7.95 (ISBN 0-689-70693-6, 330). Atheneum.

--The Norman Kings. (Kings & Queens of England Ser.). (Illus.). 224p. 1981. text ed. 17.50x (ISBN 0-297-77964-8, GWN 04665, Pub. by Weidenfeld & Nicolson England). Biblio Dist.

Chambers, James, jt. auth. see Gore, Alan.

Chambers, Jane. Burning. LC 77-91248. 160p. 1983. pap. 6.95 (ISBN 0-935672-10-9). JH Pr.

--Chasin' Jasin. write for info. JH Pr.

--Last Summer at Bluefish Cove. LC 81-86655. (Illus.). 120p. (Orig.). 1982. 25.00 (ISBN 0-935672-04-4); pap. 6.95 (ISBN 0-935672-05-2). JH Pr.

--My Blue Heaven. (Illus.). 96p. (Orig.). 1981. pap. 4.95 (ISBN 0-935672-03-6). JH Pr.

--Warrior at Rest. 88p. 1984. pap. 5.95 (ISBN 0-935672-12-5). JH Pr.

Chambers, Janice E. & Yarbrough, James D., eds. Effects of Chronic Exposures to Pesticides on Animal Systems. 262p. 1982. text ed. 71.50 (ISBN 0-89004-756-1). Raven.

Chambers, Jay G. & Hartman, William T., eds. Special Education Policies: Their History, Implementation & Finance. LC 82-10515. 301p. 1982. text ed. 34.95 (ISBN 0-87722-280-0). Temple U Pr.

Chambers, Jessie. D. H. Lawrence: A Personal Record, by E. T. LC 80-40254. 223p. 1980. pap. 11.95 (ISBN 0-521-29919-5). Cambridge U Pr.

--D. H. Lawrence Personal Record, 1935. 2nd ed. 242p. 1965. Repr. of 1935 ed. 24.00x (ISBN 0-7146-2059-9, F Cass Co). Biblio Dist.

Chambers, Joan. Castro. (World Leaders: Past & Present Ser.). (Illus.). 112p. 1985. lib. bdg. 15.95x. Chelsea Hse.

Chambers, Joanna F. Hey,Miss! You Got a Book for ME? A Model Multicultural Resource Collection. rev. ed. LC 81-135242. 91p. 1981. pap. 12.95 (ISBN 0-940048-01-9). Austin Bilingual Lang Ed.

Chambers, John. Finder. LC 80-23928. 168p. (gr. 4-6). 1981. PLB 11.95 (ISBN 0-689-30803-5). Atheneum.

--Fritzi's Winter. LC 79-14672. (Illus.). 128p. (gr. 4-8). 1979. 9.95 (ISBN 0-689-30727-6). Atheneum.

--Showdown at Apple Hill. LC 81-10774. 180p. (gr. k-1). 1982. PLB 9.95 (ISBN 0-689-30897-3). Atheneum.

Chambers, John, jt. ed. see Susman, Warren.

Chambers, John C., et al. An Executive's Guide to Forecasting. LC 83-160. 320p. 1984. Repr. of 1974 ed. text ed. 28.50 (ISBN 0-89874-585-3). Krieger.

Chambers, John H. The Achievement of Education: An Examination of Key Concepts in Educational Practice. 190p. 1983. pap. text ed. 10.50 scp (ISBN 0-06-041237-2, HarpC). Har-Row.

Chambers, John M. Computational Methods for Data Analysis. LC 77-9493. (Wiley Ser. in Probability & Mathematical Statistics: Applied Section). 268p. 1977. 34.95 (ISBN 0-471-02772-3, Pub. by Wiley-Interscience). Wiley.

Chambers, John M. & Cleveland, William S. Graphical Methods for Data Analysis. LC 83-3660. (Statistics-Probability Ser.). 395p. 1983. write for info. (ISBN 0-534-98052-X). Wadsworth Pub.

Chambers, John M., jt. auth. see Becker, Richard A.

Chambers, John M., et al. Graphical Methods for Data Analysis. 416p. 1983. pap. text ed. write for info (ISBN 0-87150-413-8, 5020, Duxbury Pr). PWS Pubs.

Chambers, John W. The Colonel & Me. LC 84-20440. 192p. (gr. 5-9). 1985. 11.95 (ISBN 0-689-31087-0). Atheneum.

--Fire Island Forfeit. LC 84-5671. 192p. (gr. 4-6). 1984. 11.95 (ISBN 0-689-31043-9). Atheneum.

--The Tyranny of Change: America in the Progressive Era, 1900-1917. (Twentieth Century United States History Ser.). 280p. 1980. pap. text ed. 11.95 (ISBN 0-312-82758-X). St Martin.

Chambers, John W., ed. Black English: Educational Equity & the Law. xii, 210p. 1983. pap. 14.50 (ISBN 0-89720-065-9). Karoma.

Chambers, Jonathan D. Nottinghamshire in the Eighteenth Century. new ed. 377p. 1966. 30.00x (ISBN 0-7146-1285-5, F Cass Co). Biblio Dist.

--Population, Economy, & Society in Pre-Industrial England. (Oxford Paperbacks University Ser). 1972. pap. 4.95x (ISBN 0-19-888085-5). Oxford U Pr.

--The Workshop of the World: British Economic History from 1820 to 1880. 2nd ed. (Oxford Paperbacks University Ser.). 1968. pap. 6.95x (ISBN 0-19-888032-4). Oxford U Pr.

Chambers, Jonh W. Footlight Summer. LC 83-2628. 204p. (gr. 5-9). 1983. 10.95 (ISBN 0-689-30980-5). Atheneum.

Chambers, Karen, jt. auth. see Cowart, Jack.

Chambers, Karen S., et al. Selections from the Permanent Collection of the Vent Haven Museum. (Illus.). 1977. 1.50 (ISBN 0-917562-05-4). Contemp Arts.

Chambers, Kate. The Case of the Dog Lover's Legacy. (Diana Winthrop Ser.: No. 3). 160p. (gr. 7-9). 1983. pap. 2.25 (ISBN 0-451-12495-2, Sig Vista). NAL.

--Danger in the Old Fort. (Diana Winthrop Mystery Ser.: No. 2). 1983. pap. 2.25 (ISBN 0-451-12392-1, Sig Vista). NAL.

--The Legacy of Lucian Van Zandt. (Diana Winthrop Mystery Ser.: No. 5). 160p. 1984. pap. 2.25 (ISBN 0-451-12979-2, Sig Vista). NAL.

--The Secret of the Singing Strings. (Diana Winthrop Mystery Ser.: No. 1). 1983. pap. 2.25 (ISBN 0-451-12392-1, Sig Vista). NAL.
--The Secrets of Beacon Hill. (Diana Winthrop Mystery Ser.: No. 4). (gr. 7-9). 1984. pap. 2.25 (ISBN 0-451-12577-0, Sig Vista). NAL.
--The Threat of the Pirate Ship. (Diana Winthrop Ser.: No. 6). 1984. pap. 2.25 (ISBN 0-451-13066-9, Sig Vista). NAL.
Chambers, Kenneth. The Country Lover's Guide to Wildlife: Mammals, Amphibians, & Reptiles of the Northeastern United States. LC 79-4338. (Illus.). 248p. 1979. 18.50 (ISBN 0-8018-2207-6). Johns Hopkins.
Chambers, Kenneth A. A Country Lover's Guide to Wildlife. (Illus.). 1980. pap. 8.95 (ISBN 0-452-25239-3, Plume). NAL.
Chambers, Kenton L., ed. see Biology Colloquium, 29th, Oregon State University 1968.
Chambers, Lisa. Real Women Never Pump Iron. (Illus.). 96p. 1982. pap. 3.95 (ISBN 0-943392-10-1). Tribeca Comm.
Chambers, Lyn, ed. see Wallach, Harold C.
Chambers, M. M. Above High School. LC 71-18973. 68p. 1970. pap. text ed. 2.50x (ISBN 0-8134-1224-2, 1224). Interstate.
--Colleges & the Courts: The/Faculty & Staff Before the Bench. LC 72-96730. 260p. 1973. text ed. 8.75x (ISBN 0-8134-1544-6, 1544). Interstate.
--Higher Education & State Governments, 1970-1975. 1974 ed. LC 73-91359. 290p. text ed. 8.95 (ISBN 0-8134-1629-9, 1629). Interstate.
--Higher Education in the Fifty States. LC 70-107847. 452p. 1970. text ed. 10.00x (ISBN 0-8134-1149-1, 1149). Interstate.
--Keep Higher Education Moving. LC 76-3834. 348p. 1976. text ed. 12.95x (ISBN 0-8134-1797-X, 1797). Interstate.
Chambers, Margaret W; see Chambers, Andrew J.
Chambers, Mary D. Secret of Better Baking. (Illus.). 1975. pap. 1.00 (ISBN 0-89166-007-0). Cobblesmith.
Chambers, Mary D., jt. auth. see Esenwein, J. Berg.
Chambers, Merritt M. Chance & Choice in Higher Education. LC 62-21741. 120p. 1962. pap. text ed. 2.50x (ISBN 0-8134-0088-0, 88). Interstate.
Chambers, Merritt M., jt. ed. see Elliott, Edward C.
Chambers, Mortimer. Ancient Greece. LC 73-75443. (AHA Pamphlets Ser.: No. 311). 60p. (Orig.). 1973. pap. text ed. 1.50 (ISBN 0-87229-012-3). Am Hist Assn.
Chambers, Mortimer, ed. Fall of Rome: Can It Be Explained? 2nd ed. LC 75-135290. (gr. 11 up). 1971. pap. text ed. 13.95 (ISBN 0-03-084478-9, HoltC). HR&W.
Chambers, Mortimer, et al. The Western Experience. 3rd ed. LC 82-17096. 1982. text ed. 28.00 (ISBN 0-394-33086-2, KnopfC); Vol. 1, to 1715. pap. text ed. 18.00 (ISBN 0-394-33085-4); Vol. 2, since 1600. pap. text ed. 18.00 (ISBN 0-394-33096-X); Vol. 1, to 1500. pap. text ed. 15.00 (ISBN 0-394-33084-6); Vol. 2, 1300-1815. pap. text ed. 15.00 (ISBN 0-394-33098-6); Vol. 3, 1789-Present. pap. text ed. 15.00 (ISBN 0-394-33097-8); Vol. 1. study guide 7.00 (ISBN 0-394-33225-3); Vol. 2. study guide 7.00 (ISBN 0-394-33226-1). Knopf.
Chambers, Nancy, ed. The Signal Approach to Children's Books. LC 81-8824. 352p. 1981. 17.50 (ISBN 0-8108-1447-1). Scarecrow.
Chambers, Oswald. Approved unto God. 1973. pap. 2.50 (ISBN 0-87508-132-0). Chr Lit.
--Baffled to Fight Better. 1973. pap. 2.50 (ISBN 0-87508-134-7). Chr Lit.
--Biblical Ethics. 1964. 2.50 (ISBN 0-87508-102-9). Chr Lit.
--Biblical Psychology. 1973. pap. 3.95 (ISBN 0-87508-099-5). Chr Lit.
--Bringing Sons unto Glory. 1973. pap. 1.95 (ISBN 0-87508-104-5). Chr Lit.
--Called of God. 1965. pap. 2.25 (ISBN 0-87508-105-3). Chr Lit.
--Christian Discipline, 2 Vols. 1965. pap. 2.50 ea. Vol. 1 (ISBN 0-87508-106-1). Vol. 2 (ISBN 0-87508-107-X). Chr Lit.
--Christian Disciplines. 320p. 1985. pap. 8.95 (ISBN 0-310-61011-7, Pub. by Chosen Bks). Zondervan.
--Conformed to His Image. 1971. pap. 2.50 (ISBN 0-87508-133-9). Chr Lit.
--Conformed to His Image. 112p. 1985. pap. 4.95 (ISBN 0-310-60961-5, Pub. by Chosen Bks). Zondervan.
--Daily Thought for Disciples. 256p. 1983. pap. 5.95 (ISBN 0-310-22401-2). Zondervan.
--Daily Thoughts-Disciples. 1983. pap. 5.95 (ISBN 0-87508-143-6). Chr Lit.
--Daily Thoughts for Disciples. 208p. 1985. 8.95 (ISBN 0-310-30470-9, Pub. by Daybreak). Zondervan.
--Disciples Indeed. 1960. pap. 1.95 (ISBN 0-87508-109-6). Chr Lit.
--God's Workmanship. 1960. 2.50 (ISBN 0-87508-110-X). Chr Lit.
--He Shall Glorify Me. 1965. 2.50 (ISBN 0-87508-111-8). Chr Lit.
--Highest Good. 1965. pap. 2.50 (ISBN 0-87508-112-6). Chr Lit.
--If Thou Wilt Be Perfect. 1962. pap. 2.50 (ISBN 0-87508-113-4). Chr Lit.
--If Ye Shall Ask. 1965. pap. 2.50 (ISBN 0-87508-114-2). Chr Lit.
--If Ye Shall Ask. 128p. 1985. pap. 4.95 (ISBN 0-310-60951-8, Pub. by Chosen Bks). Zondervan.
--Knocking at God's Door. 1957. pap. 1.95 (ISBN 0-87508-115-0). Chr Lit.
--Knocking at God's Door. 128p. (Orig.). 1985. pap. 4.95 (ISBN 0-317-19418-6, Pub. by Chosen Bks). Zondervan.
--Love of God. 1965. pap. 2.50 (ISBN 0-87508-116-9). Chr Lit.
--The Love of God. 128p. 1985. pap. 4.95 (ISBN 0-310-60971-2, Pub. by Chosen Bks). Zondervan.
--Moral Foundations of Life. 1961. pap. 2.50 (ISBN 0-87508-117-7). Chr Lit.
--My Utmost for His Highest. large print ed. 640p. 1983. pap. 9.95 (ISBN 0-8007-1397-4). Revell.
--My Utmost for His Highest. 376p. 1985. deluxe ed. 15.95 special 50th anniversary ed. (ISBN 0-396-08640-3). Dodd.
--My Utmost for His Highest: The Golden Book of Oswald Chambers. 7.95 (ISBN 0-396-00241-2); deluxe ed. 15.95 (ISBN 0-396-08640-3). Dodd.
--Not Knowing Whither. 1957. pap. 2.50 (ISBN 0-87508-118-5). Chr Lit.
--Our Brilliant Heritage. 1965. pap. 2.50 (ISBN 0-87508-120-7). Chr Lit.
--Our Portrait in Genesis. 1973. pap. 1.95 (ISBN 0-87508-135-5). Chr Lit.
--Philosophy of Sin. 1961. pap. 1.95 (ISBN 0-87508-122-3). Chr Lit.
--Place of Help. 1973. pap. 2.95 (ISBN 0-87508-139-8). Chr Lit.
--Psychology of Redemption. 1955. pap. 2.50 (ISBN 0-87508-124-X). Chr Lit.
--Run Today's Race. 1968. pap. 1.95 (ISBN 0-87508-125-8). Chr Lit.
--Servant As His Lord. 1973. pap. 2.50 (ISBN 0-87508-137-1). Chr Lit.
--Shade of His Hand. 1961. pap. 2.50 (ISBN 0-87508-127-4). Chr Lit.
--Shadow of an Agony. 1965. pap. 2.50 (ISBN 0-87508-128-2). Chr Lit.
--So Send I You. 1973. pap. 2.95 (ISBN 0-87508-138-X). Chr Lit.
--Still Higher for His Highest. 192p. 1970. 6.95 (ISBN 0-87508-142-8). Chr Lit.
--Still Higher for His Highest. LC 75-120048. 1970. Repr. of 1970 ed. 7.95 (ISBN 0-310-22410-1); large print kivar 6.95 (ISBN 0-310-22417-9). Zondervan.
--Studies in the Sermon on the Mount. 1973. pap. 2.95 (ISBN 0-87508-136-3). Chr Lit.
--Studies in the Sermon on the Mount. 128p. (Orig.). 1985. pap. 4.95 (ISBN 0-310-60991-7, Pub. by Chosen Bks). Zondervan.
--Workmen of God. 1965. pap. 2.50 (ISBN 0-87508-131-2). Chr Lit.
Chambers, P. L. & Klinger, W., eds. Further Studies in the Assessment of Toxic Actions: Proceedings. (Archives of Toxicology Supplementum Ser.: No. 4). (Illus.). 507p. 1981. pap. 64.00 (ISBN 0-387-10191-8). Springer-Verlag.
Chambers, P. L., et al. Disease, Metabolism & Reproduction in the Toxic Response to Drugs & Other Chemicals: Proceedings of the European Society of Toxicology Meeting Held in Rome, March 28-30, 1983. (Archives of Toxicology Ser.: Supplement No. 7). (Illus.). 400p. 1984. pap. 50.00 (ISBN 0-387-12452-7). Springer-Verlag.
Chambers, P. L., et al, eds. Toxicology in the Use, Misuse, & Abuse of Food, Drugs & Chemicals. (Archives of Toxicology: Suppl. 6). (Illus.). 380p. 1983. pap. 55.00 (ISBN 0-387-12392-X). Springer-Verlag.
Chambers, Patricia. River Runner's Recipes. LC 83-19644. 132p. 1984. pap. 6.95 (ISBN 0-914718-85-1). Pacific Search.
Chambers, Q., jt. auth. see Hatsumi, M.
Chambers, Quintin, jt. auth. see Draeger, Donn F.
Chambers, Quintin, jt. auth. see Hatsumi, Masaaki.
Chambers, Quintin T., jt. auth. see Draeger, Donn F.
Chambers, R. Popular Rhymes of Scotland. 59.95 (ISBN 0-8490-0879-4). Gordon Pr.
Chambers, R., ed. Twentieth Century Interpretations of All the Kings Men. 1977. 9.95 (ISBN 0-13-022434-0, Spec); pap. 3.45 (ISBN 0-13-022426-X, Spec). P-H.
Chambers, R., tr. see Weissman, A., et al.
Chambers, R. J. Accounting is Disarray: A Case for the Reform of Company Accounts. LC 82-48354. (Accountancy in Transition Ser.). 258p. 1982. lib. bdg. 28.00 (ISBN 0-8240-5307-9). Garland pub.
Chambers, R. L. Novels of Virginia Woolf. LC 73-139909. 1971. Repr. of 1947 ed. 15.00x (ISBN 0-8462-1575-6). Russell.
Chambers, R. W. Chapters on the Exeter Book. 1973. Repr. of 1933 ed. lib. bdg. 50.00 (ISBN 0-8414-0388-0). Folcroft.
--Jacobean Shakespeare & Measure for Measure. 1937. lib. bdg. 8.50 (ISBN 0-8414-3427-1). Folcroft.
--King Lear. LC 74-7384. 1940. lib. bdg. 10.00 (ISBN 0-8414-3644-4). Folcroft.
--King Lear: The First W. P. Ker Memorial Lecture Delivered in the University of Glasgow 27th Nov., 1939. 1978. Repr. of 1940 ed. lib. bdg. 15.00 (ISBN 0-8492-0509-3). R West.
--On the Continuity of English Prose. (EETS OS Ser.: Vol. 199A). Repr. of 1932 ed. 15.00 (ISBN 0-317-15671-3). Kraus Repr.
--Place of Saint Thomas More in English Literature & History. LC 65-15870. (English Biography Ser., No. 31). 1969. Repr. of 1937 ed. lib. bdg. 39.95x (ISBN 0-8383-0523-7). Haskell.
--Poets & Their Critics: Langland & Milton. 1942. lib. bdg. 8.50 (ISBN 0-685-10478-8). Folcroft.
--Ruskin (& Others) on Byron. 1925. lib. bdg. 8.50 (ISBN 0-8414-3507-3). Folcroft.
--The Saga & the Myth of Sir Thomas More. 1978. Repr. of 1927 ed. lib. bdg. 10.00 (ISBN 0-8495-0744-8). Arden Lib.
--Text of Piers Plowman. LC 72-195253. lib. bdg. 8.50 (ISBN 0-8414-3015-2). Folcroft.
Chambers, R. W. & Grattan, J. H. The Text of Piers Plowman. 1978. Repr. of 1931 ed. lib. bdg. 10.00 (ISBN 0-8495-0825-8). Arden Lib.
Chambers, R. W., jt. ed. see Hitchcock, Elsie V.
Chambers, R. W., jt. ed. see Wyatt, Alfred J.
Chambers, Raymond J. Accounting, Evaluation & Economic Behavior. LC 66-13944. 1975. Repr. of 1966 ed. text ed. 15.00 (ISBN 0-914348-15-9). Scholars Bk.
Chambers, Raymond W. England Before the Norman Conquest. LC 75-109718. Repr. of 1926 ed. lib. bdg. 17.00x (ISBN 0-8371-4208-3, CHNC). Greenwood.
--Jacobean Shakespeare & Measure for Measure, Read 21 April 1937 - Annual Shakespeare Lecture. facsimile ed. LC 73-109641. (Oxford Paperbacks Ser.). 1937. 12.00 (ISBN 0-8369-5250-2). Ayer Co Pubs.
--Man's Unconquerable Mind. LC 67-30811. (Studies in Poetry, No. 38). (Illus.). 1969. Repr. of 1939 ed. lib. bdg. 49.95x (ISBN 0-8383-0711-6). Haskell.
--Ruskin & Others on Byron. (English Literature Ser., No. 33). 1970. pap. 11.95x (ISBN 0-8383-0012-X). Haskell.
--Saga & Myth of Sir Thomas More. 1926. lib. bdg. 8.50 (ISBN 0-8414-3642-8). Folcroft.
--The Teaching of English in the Universities of England. 1922. lib. bdg. 9.50 (ISBN 0-8414-3359-3). Folcroft.
--Thomas More. 1958. pap. 6.95x (ISBN 0-472-06018-X, 18, AA). U of Mich Pr.
Chambers, Raymond W., ed. Beowulf: An Introduction. 1959. 65.00 (ISBN 0-521-04615-7). Cambridge U Pr.
Chambers, Richard D. Fluorine in Organic Chemistry. LC 73-7824. (Interscience Monographs on Organic Chemistry). pap. 101.50 (ISBN 0-317-26348-X, 2055982). Bks Demand UMI.
Chambers, Richard L. & Kut, Gunay, eds. Contemporary Turkish Short Stories: An Intermediate Reader. LC 76-21045. (Middle Eastern Languages & Linguistics, 3). 1977. 14.00x (ISBN 0-88297-013-5). Bibliotheca.
Chambers, Richard L., jt. ed. see Polk, William R.
Chambers, Robert. A Biographical Dictionary of Eminent Scotsmen, 4 vols. 1979. Repr. of 1847 ed. lib. bdg. 150.00 (ISBN 0-8495-0941-6). Arden Lib.
--Cyclopedia of English Literature: A History, Critical & Biographical, of British Authors, from the Earliest to the Present Times, 3 vols. (Illus.). 1979. Repr. of 1938 ed. Set. 210.00x (ISBN 0-8103-4213-8). Gale.
--The King in Yellow. 288p. 1982. pap. 2.50 (ISBN 0-441-44482-2). Ace Bks.
--Managing Rural Development: Ideas & Experience from East Africa. (Scadinanian Institute of African Studies, Uppsala). 216p. 1974. pap. text ed. 19.50x (ISBN 0-8419-9716-0). Holmes & Meier.
--Popular Rhymes of Scotland. LC 68-58902. 1969. Repr. of 1870 ed. 40.00x (ISBN 0-8103-3828-9). Gale.
--Popular Rhymes of Scotland. 1870. 20.00 (ISBN 0-686-17672-3). Quaker City.
--The Romantic Scottish Ballads. LC 76-58428. 1977. Repr. of 1849 ed. lib. bdg. 15.00 (ISBN 0-8414-3430-1). Folcroft.
--The Romantic Scottish Ballads: Their Epoch & Authorship. (Folklore Ser). 15.00 (ISBN 0-8482-3595-9). Norwood Edns.
--Rural Development. LC 83-977. 1983. pap. text ed. 5.95 (ISBN 0-582-64443-7). Longman.
--Rural Poverty Unperceived: Problems & Remedies. (Working Paper: No. 400). 51p. 1980. 3.00 (ISBN 0-686-36076-1, WP-0400). World Bank.
--The Scottish Ballads. LC 77-144549. Repr. of 1829 ed. 24.50 (ISBN 0-404-08628-4). AMS Pr.
--Traditions of Edinburgh. (Illus.). 377p. 1983. 20.00 (ISBN 0-550-21292-2, Pub. by Salem Hse Ltd). Merrimack Pub Cir.
--Twelve Romantic Scottish Ballads, with the Original Airs. LC 77-17101. 1977. Repr. of 1844 ed. lib. bdg. 16.50 (ISBN 0-8414-1824-1). Folcroft.
Chambers, Robert & Chambers, Edward L. Explorations into the Nature of the Living Cell. LC 61-8845. (Commonwealth Fund Publications Ser). (Illus.). 1961. 22.50x (ISBN 0-674-28000-8). Harvard U Pr.
Chambers, Robert, ed. Book of Days: A Miscellany of Popular Antiquities in Connection with the Calendar, Including Anecdote, Biography & History, Curiosities of Literature, & Oddities of Human Life & Character, 2 Vols. LC 67-13009. (Illus.). 1967. Repr. of 1862 ed. 120.00x (ISBN 0-8103-3002-4). Gale.
--Scottish Songs, 2 vols. in 1. LC 70-144547. Repr. of 1829 ed. 49.50 (ISBN 0-404-08624-1). AMS Pr.
--The Songs of Scotland Prior to Burns. LC 73-144548. Repr. of 1862 ed. 27.50 (ISBN 0-404-08627-6). AMS Pr.
Chambers, Robert, et al, eds. Seasonal Dimensions to Rural Poverty. LC 81-2838. 276p. 1981. text ed. 28.50x (ISBN 0-86598-057-8). Allanheld.
--Seasonal Dimensions to Rural Poverty. 259p. 1981. pap. 10.50 (ISBN 0-86187-334-3). F Pinter Pubs.
Chambers, Robert W. Better Man. facsimile ed. LC 78-157773. (Short Story Index Reprint Ser.). Repr. of 1916 ed. 20.50 (ISBN 0-8369-3885-2). Ayer Co Pubs.
--The Gay Rebellion. LC 74-15953. (Science Fiction Ser.). (Illus.). 299p. 1975. Repr. of 1913 ed. 17.00x (ISBN 0-685-51337-8). Ayer Co Pubs.
--Haunts of Men. facsimile ed. LC 78-103503. (Short Story Index Reprint Ser.). 1898. 19.00 (ISBN 0-8369-3245-5). Ayer Co Pubs.
--In Search of the Unknown. LC 73-13249. (Classics of Science Fiction Ser.). 300p. 1973. 12.50 (ISBN 0-88355-105-5); pap. 10.00 (ISBN 0-88355-134-9). Hyperion Conn.
--King in Yellow. facs. ed. LC 72-75775. (Short Story Index Reprint Ser.). 1895. 17.00 (ISBN 0-8369-3000-2). Ayer Co Pubs.
--Maker of Moons. facsimile ed. LC 75-98565. (Short Story Index Reprint Ser.). 1896. 22.00 (ISBN 0-8369-3139-4). Ayer Co Pubs.
--Mystery of Choice. facsimile ed. LC 73-94710. (Short Story Index Reprint Ser). 1897. 18.00 (ISBN 0-8369-3089-4). Ayer Co Pubs.
--The Slayer of Souls. Reginald, R. & Melville, Douglas, eds. LC 77-84207. (Lost Race & Adult Fantasy Ser.). 1978. Repr. of 1920 ed. lib. bdg. 26.50x (ISBN 0-405-10963-6). Ayer Co Pubs.
--Young Man in a Hurry & Other Short Stories. facsimile ed. LC 71-103504. (Short Story Index Reprint Ser). 1904. 19.00 (ISBN 0-8369-3246-3). Ayer Co Pubs.
Chambers, Rosalind, ed. see Wootton, Barbara.
Chambers, Ross. Meaning & Meaningfulness: Studies in the Analysis & Interpretation of Texts. LC 79-50280. (French Forum Monographs: No. 15). 197p. 1979. pap. 12.50x (ISBN 0-917058-14-3). French Forum.
--Story & Situation: Narrative Seduction & the Power of Fiction. LC 83-14787. (Theory & History of Literature Ser.: No. 12). 279p. 1984. pap. 14.95 (ISBN 0-8166-1298-6). U of Minn Pr.
Chambers, Ross, ed. see Felman, Shoshana, et al.
Chambers, S. Allen, Jr. Lynchburg, an Architectural History. LC 81-3000. (Illus.). xiv, 576p. 1982. 27.50x (ISBN 0-8139-0882-5). U Pr of Va.
Chambers, Sue. Rachz: The True Story of a Fox. (Illus.). 160p. 1985. 16.00 (ISBN 0-85362-217-5, Oriel). Routledge & Kegan.
Chambers, Ted. The History of Athletics & Physical Education at Howard University. 1985. 12.95 (ISBN 0-533-06512-7). Vantage.
Chambers, Theodore F. Early Germans of New Jersey: Their History, Churches & Genealogies. LC 75-85697. (Illus.). 1982. Repr. of 1895 ed. 35.00 (ISBN 0-8063-0070-1). Genealog Pub.
Chambers, Thomas A. United States Foreign Policy & Soviet Union Foreign Policy: A Comparative Analysis. (Illus.). 121p. 1980. 77.75x (ISBN 0-930008-63-4). Inst Econ Pol.
Chambers, W. N. & Burnham, Walter D., eds. The American Party Systems. rev. 2nd ed. (Illus.). 1975. pap. 9.95x (ISBN 0-19-501917-2). Oxford U Pr.
Chambers, W. Walker & Wilkie, John R. A Short History of the German Language. 1970. pap. 11.95x (ISBN 0-416-18220-8, NO. 2130). Methuen Inc.
Chambers, Whittaker. Witness. 1952. 15.00 (ISBN 0-394-45233-X). Random.
--Witness. 808p. 1978. pap. 10.95 (ISBN 0-89526-915-5). Regnery-Gateway.
--Witness. 816p. 1983. pap. text ed. 13.50 (ISBN 0-8191-3554-2). U Pr of Amer.
Chambers, Whittaker, tr. see Salten, Felix.
Chambers, Whittaker, tr. see Weirauch, Anna E.
Chambers, Whittaker, tr. see Werfel, Franz.
Chambers, Wicke & Asher, Spring, eds. The Celebration Book of Great American Traditions. LC 82-48113. (Illus.). 192p. 1983. 14.37i (ISBN 0-06-015095-5, HarpT). Har-Row.
Chambers, William. American Slavery & Colour. LC 68-58050. Repr. of 1857 ed. 17.50x (ISBN 0-8371-0345-2, CHC&, Pub. by Negro U Pr). Greenwood.
--American Slavery & Colour. LC 76-99356. 1969. Repr. of 1857 ed. lib. bdg. 10.75 (ISBN 0-8411-0027-6). Metro Bks.
--Atlas of Lake Champlain, Seventeen Seventy-Nine to Seventeen Eighty. LC 84-51173. (Illus.). 112p. 1984. 49.50 (ISBN 0-911853-04-9); limited ed. incl. portofolio 200.00 (ISBN 0-911853-05-7); pap. 29.50 (ISBN 0-911853-05-7). Vermont Herit Pr.
--Designs of Chinese Buildings, Furniture, Dresses, Machines & Utensils. LC 68-17156. (Illus.). 1968. Repr. of 1757 ed. 55.00 (ISBN 0-405-08348-3, Blom Pubns). Ayer Co Pubs.
--Things As They Are in America. LC 68-58051. Repr. of 1854 ed. cancelled (ISBN 0-8371-0346-0). Greenwood.
--Treatise on Civil Architecture. 3rd ed. Harris, John, ed. LC 68-17154. (Illus.). Repr. of 1791 ed. 38.50 (ISBN 0-405-08349-1, Blom Pubns). Ayer Co Pubs.

Chambers, William N., ed. see Washington University, St. Louis, Dept. of Political Science.

Chambers-Schiller, Lee V. Liberty, a Better Husband: Single Women in America; The Generations of 1780-1840. LC 84-3524. 304p. 1984. 22.50x (ISBN 0-300-03164-5). Yale U Pr.

Chamblain De Marivaux, Pierre C. De see De Chamblain De Marivaux, Pierre C.

Chamblee, Ronald F. & Evans, Marchsll C. Transax: The NCHS System for Producing Multiple Cause-of-Death Statistics, 1968-78. Madison, Eddie, ed. 55p. 1982. pap. text ed. 1.75 (ISBN 0-8406-0269-3). Natl Ctr Health Stats.

Chambless, Dianne L. & Goldstein, Alan J. Agoraphobia: Multiple Perspectives on Theory & Treatment. LC 82-7087. (Personality Processes Ser.). 227p. 1982. 29.95 (ISBN 0-471-07947-2, Pub. by Wiley-Interscience). Wiley.

Chambliss, J. E. Life & Labors of David Livingstone. LC 76-132642. (Illus.). Repr. of 1875 ed. 36.00x (ISBN 0-8371-3636-9, CDL&, Pub. by Negro U Pr). Greenwood.

Chambliss, J. J. Boyd H. Bode's Philosophy of Education. LC 63-20334. (Studies in Educational Theory of the John Dewey Society: No. 2). 110p. 1964. 4.00 (ISBN 0-8142-0037-0). Ohio St U Pr.

Chambliss, Madelon. Our Defenses Are Down. LC 83-91231. 200p. (Orig.). 1983. pap. 10.00 (ISBN 0-9612420-2-7). Madelon Chamb.

--Writing to Eat. 88p. 1983. 6.95x (ISBN 0-9612420-0-0). Madelon Chamb.

Chambliss, Rollin. Social Thought: From Hammurabi to Comte. LC 54-10267. 469p. 1982. pap. text ed. 19.95x (ISBN 0-8290-0147-6). Irvington.

Chambliss, W. J., jt. auth. see Block, A. A.

Chambliss, W. J., jt. auth. see Brock, A. A.

Chambliss, Will. In, Wilma. LC 80-68881. (Illus., Orig.). 1981. pap. 3.95 (ISBN 0-938108-00-X). Crystal Pr.

--In, Wilma. 2nd ed. (Illus.). 1982. Write for Info. (ISBN 0-938108-01-8). Crystal Pr.

Chambliss, William. Chiaraijima Village: Land Tenure, Taxation, & Local Trade, 1818-1884. LC 64-17266. (Association for Asian Studies Monograph: No. 19). 159p. 1965. 10.95x (ISBN 0-8165-0148-3). U of Ariz Pr.

Chambliss, William & Seidman, Robert. Law, Order & Power. 2nd ed. (Sociology Ser.). (Illus.). 384p. 1982. text ed. 23.95 (ISBN 0-201-10126-2). Addison-Wesley.

Chambliss, William J. Crime & the Legal Process. (Sociology Ser.). 1968. pap. text ed. 28.95 (ISBN 0-07-010461-1). McGraw.

--Criminal Law in Action. 2nd ed. LC 83-14722. 461p. 1983. pap. text ed. 17.95 (ISBN 0-471-89678-0). Wiley.

--Criminology. Date not set. 20.00 (ISBN 0-471-14473-8). Wiley.

--Harry King: A Professional Thief's Journey. (Deviance & Criminology Ser.). 151p. 1984. pap. 9.95 (ISBN 0-471-87152-4). Wiley.

--On the Take: From Petty Crooks to Presidents. LC 77-15213. (Midland Bks.: Bk. 298). 288p. 1982. pap. 7.95x (ISBN 0-253-20298-1); 22.50x (ISBN 0-253-34244-9). Ind U Pr.

Chambliss, William J. & Ryther, Thomas E. Sociology: The Discipline & Its Direction. (Illus.). 480p. 1975. text ed. 31.95 (ISBN 0-07-010465-4); pap. text ed. 25.95 (ISBN 0-07-010466-2). McGraw.

Chambliss, William J., ed. Sociological Readings in the Conflict Perspective. LC 72-579. 1973. pap. text ed. 13.95 (ISBN 0-201-00959-5). Addison-Wesley.

Chambliss-Rigie, Jane. The Real Mother Goose Clock Book. (Illus.). pap. 4.95 (ISBN 0-528-82329-9). Rand.

Chambonnieres, Jacques C. Oeuvres Completes. Brunold, Paul & Tessier, Andre, eds. Restout, Denise, tr. (Illus.). 170p. 1967. Repr. of 1925 ed. 37.50x (ISBN 0-8450-1001-8). Broude.

Chambost, Edouard. Bank Accounts: A World Guide to Confidentiality. 450p. 1983. 31.95 (ISBN 0-471-90076-1, Pub. by Wiley-Interscience). Wiley.

Chambre, H. Le Developpement du Bassin du Kuznetsk (Sous la Direction De...) (Economies et Societes Series G: No. 8). 1960. pap. 34.00 (ISBN 0-317-16846-0). Kraus Repr.

Chambre, Tim, jt. auth. see Hounsome, Terry.

Chambrun, Adolphe De see De Chambrun, Adolphe.

Chambrun, Clara. Shakespeare: A Portrait Restored. facsimile ed. LC 77-109642. (Select Bibliographies Reprint Ser). 1957. 29.00 (ISBN 0-8369-5251-0). Ayer Co Pubs.

--Shakespeare: A Portrait Restored. 1957. Repr. 17.00 (ISBN 0-8274-3368-9). R West.

Chambrun, Clara L. De see De Chambrun, Clara L.

Chambrun, Clara Longworth De see Longworth de Chambrun, Clara.

Chambrun, Rene De see De Chambrun, Rene.

Chamchanya, K. C. Makulata: The African Miss. 1985. 9.95 (ISBN 0-8062-2474-6). Carlton.

Chamelin, Neil C., jt. auth. see Swanson, Charles R.

Chamelin, Neil C. & Truzzi, Marcello, eds. Criminal Law for Police Officers. 3rd ed. (Criminal Justice Ser.). 352p. 1981. text ed. 27.95 (ISBN 0-13-193821-5). P-H.

Chamelin, Neil C., et al. Introduction to Criminal Justice. 2nd ed. (Criminal Justice Ser.). (Illus.). 1979. ref. 28.95 (ISBN 0-13-480145-8). P-H.

Chamerovzow, L. A., ed. see Brown, John.

Chamers-Hunt, B. L., jt. auth. see Haynes, J. H.

Chametzky, Jules & Kaplan, Sidney, eds. Black & White in American Culture: An Anthology from "The Massachusetts Review". LC 74-76045. (Illus.). 496p. 1969. 17.50x (ISBN 0-87023-046-8). U of Mass Pr.

Chamfort. Products of the Perfected Civilization: Selected Writings of Chamfort. Merwin, W. S., tr. from Fr. 288p. 1984. pap. 12.50 (ISBN 0-86547-145-2). N Point Pr.

Chami, Joseph G. Days of Tragedy: Lebanon Nineteen Seventy-Five to Nineteen Seventy-Six, Vol. I. (Illus.). 400p. 1980. 69.95 (ISBN 0-88738-036-0). Transaction Bks.

--Days of Tragedy: Lebanon Nineteen Seventy-Five to Nineteen Seventy-Six, 2 vols, Vol. 1. Bd. with Vol. II. Days of Wrath: Lebanon Nineteen Seventy-Seven to Nineteen Eighty-Two. (Illus.). 400p. 1983. Set. 99.95 (ISBN 0-88738-038-7). Transaction Bks.

--Days of Wrath: Lebanon Nineteen Seventy-Seven to Nineteen Eighty-Two, Vol. II. (Illus.). 400p. 1983. 69.95 (ISBN 0-88738-037-9). Transaction Bks.

Chamie, Joseph. Religion & Fertility: Arab Christian-Muslim Differentials. LC 80-19787. (ASA Rose Monograph). (Illus.). 176p. 1981. 29.95 (ISBN 0-521-23677-0); pap. 9.95 (ISBN 0-521-28147-4). Cambridge U Pr.

Chamier, Adrian C., ed. Les Actes des Colloques des Eglises Francaises et des Synodes: Huguenot Society, Vols. 2-4. Bd. with Register of the Protestant Church at Guisnes. Minet, William, ed. Repr. of 1891 ed; Registre Des Baptesmes, Mariages & Mortz. Marett, Humphrey, ed. Repr. of 1890 ed. 93.00 (ISBN 0-317-16330-2). Kraus Repr.

Chamier, Frederick. Ben Brace, the Last of Nelson's Agamemnons, 3 vols. in 2. LC 79-8248. Repr. of 1836 ed. 84.50 set (ISBN 0-404-61811-1). AMS Pr.

--Jack Adams, or the Mutiny of the 'bounty, 3 vols. in 1. LC 79-8249. Repr. of 1838 ed. 44.50 (ISBN 0-404-61814-6). AMS Pr.

Chamier, John. Safety & Seamanship. 1979. 14.95x (ISBN 0-8464-0067-7). Beekman Pubs.

Chaminade, Cecile. Album of Songs, Vol. I. (Women Composers Ser.: No. 17). 96p. 1985. Repr. of 1893 ed. lib. bdg. 22.50 (ISBN 0-306-76245-5). Da Capo.

--Three Piano Works. Incl. Sonata in C Minor, Opus 21; Etude Symphonique, Opus 28; Six Concert Etudes, Opus 35. (Women Composers Ser.: No. 2). 1979. Repr. of 1895 ed. 24.50 (ISBN 0-306-79551-5). Da Capo.

Chamine, Susan. About-Cider Vinegar. 1981. pap. 4.95x (ISBN 0-317-06964-0, Regent House). B of A.

Chamis, C., ed. Test Methods & Design Allowables for Fibrous Composites - STP 734. 429p. 1981. 44.00 (ISBN 0-8031-0700-5, 04-734000-33). ASTM.

Chamis, C. C. see Broutman, L. J., et al.

Chamisso, Adelbert. Peter Schlemihl: The Shadowless Man. 147p. 1981. Repr. lib. bdg. 35.00 (ISBN 0-89760-151-3). Telegraph Bks.

Chamisso, Adelbert Von. Werke, 3 vols. LC 75-41053. (BCL Ser.: No. II). 1976. Repr. of 1908 ed. 72.50 set (ISBN 0-404-14850-6). AMS Pr.

Chamisso, Adelbert von see Von Chamisso, Adelbert.

Chamj, Deborah R. & Wolde, Menbere. Laubach Collection. 1974. 5.00 (ISBN 0-317-18234-X, MSS 19). Syracuse U Cont Ed.

Chamlin, Susan, jt. auth. see Ratner, Marilyn.

Chammah, Albert M., jt. auth. see Rapoport, Anatol.

Chammari, Abderraouf, jt. auth. see Beenhakker, Henri L.

Chamness, Danford. The Hollywood Guide to Film Budgeting & Script Breakdown. 3rd ed. Brooks, Susan & Brooks, Stanley J., eds. 224p. 1981. Repr. of 1977 ed. 20.00x (ISBN 0-941806-02-2). S J Brooks.

--The Hollywood Guide to Film Budgeting & Script Breakdown. (Illus.). 224p. 1977. pap. 19.95 (ISBN 0-240-51724-5). Focal Pr.

Chamot, A., tr. see Leskov, Nikolai S.

Chamot, A. E., tr. see Chekhov, Anton P.

Chamot, Emile & Mason, Clyde W. Handbook of Chemical Microscopy, Vol. 1. 3rd ed. LC 58-12706. pap. 125.50 (ISBN 0-317-28588-2, 2055183). Bks Demand UMI.

Chamot, Mary. The Early Works of J. M. W. Turner. (Illus.). 32p. pap. 6.95 (ISBN 0-905005-91-0, Pub by Salem Hse Ltd). Merrimack Pub Cir.

--Goncharova: Stage Designs & Paintings. (Oresko-Jupiter Art Bks). (Illus.). 1980. 17.95 (ISBN 0-905368-52-5, Pub. by Oresko-Jupiter England). Hippocrene Bks.

Champ, B. R. & Dyte, C. E. Report of the FAO Global Survey of Pesticide Susceptibility of Stored Grain Pests. (Plant Production & Protection Papers: No. 5). 297p. 1976. pap. 10.00 (ISBN 92-5-100022-0, F1394, FAO). Unipub.

Champ, Michael A. & Park, P. K. Global Marine Pollution Bibliography: Ocean Dumping of Municipal & Industrial Wastes. LC 82-28060. 424p. 1982. 75.00x (ISBN 0-306-65205-6, Consultants). Plenum Pub.

Champ, R. C. The Sunbeam Motorcycle. 205p. 18.95 (ISBN 0-85429-258-6, F258). Haynes Pubns.

Champa, Kermit S. Mondrian Studies. LC 85-980. (Illus.). 184p. 1985. 29.95 (ISBN 0-226-10078-2). U of Chicago Pr.

--Studies in Early Impressionism. LC 70-151569. (Publications in the History of Art Ser.: No. 22). (Illus.). Repr. of 1973 ed. 58.00 (ISBN 0-8357-1111-0, 2011110). Bks Demand UMI.

--Studies in Early Impressionism. LC 84-81040. (Illus.). 106p. 1985. Repr. of 1973 ed. lib. bdg. 75.00 (ISBN 0-87817-299-8). Hacker.

Champa, Shirley A. Kentucky Workers' Compensation. LC 82-244109. xiiii, 163p. 1982. 39.95. Harrison Co Ga.

Champagne, Anthony. Congressman Sam Rayburn. LC 83-4454. 230p. 1984. 19.95 (ISBN 0-8135-1012-0). Rutgers U Pr.

Champagne, Anthony & Dawes, Rosemary N. Courts & Modern Medicine. 274p. 1983. 29.75x (ISBN 0-398-04834-7). C C Thomas.

Champagne, Anthony & Harpham, Edward. The Attack on the Welfare State. (Illus.). 209p. (Orig.). 1984. pap. text ed. 9.95x (ISBN 0-88133-045-0). Waveland Pr.

Champagne, Audrey B. & Klopfer, Leo F. Criteria for Effective Energy Education. 91p. 1977. 1.50 (ISBN 0-318-14706-8). Learn Res Dev.

Champagne, Audrey B, et al. Content Structure in Science Instructional Materials & Knowledge Structure in Student's Memories. 59p. 1978. 1.50 (ISBN 0-318-14705-X). Learn Res Dev.

Champagne, Audrey B., et al. Interactions of Students' Knowledge with Their Comprehension & Design of Science Experiments. (Illus.). 90p. 1980. 1.50 (ISBN 0-318-14718-1). Learn Res Dev.

Champagne, David W. & Goldman, Richard M. Handbook for Managing Individualized Learning in the Classroom. LC 75-14101. 214p. 1975. pap. 24.95 (ISBN 0-87778-081-1). Educ Tech Pubns.

Champagne, Lenora. French Theatre Experiment since 1968. Beckerman, Bernard, ed. LC 84-60. (Theater & Dramatic Studies: No. 18). 194p. 1984. 39.95 (ISBN 0-8357-1538-8). UMI Res Pr.

Champagne, R. Beyond the Structuralist Myth of Ecriture. 1977. 18.00 (ISBN 90-279-3166-6). Mouton.

Champagne, Roland A. Literary History in the Wake of Roland Barthes: Re-Defining the Myths of Reading. LC 83-50516. 158p. 1984. pap. 13.00 (ISBN 0-917786-36-X). Summa Pubns.

Champaign County Historical Archives Staff see Schlipf, Frederick A.

Champaign County Historical Archives. Index to the Combined Eighteeen Ninety-Three, Nineteen Thirteen & Nineteen Twenty-Nine Atlases of Champaign County. Schlipf, Frederick A., ed. LC 84-72778. (Champaign County Historical Archives Historical Publications Ser.: No. 9). 116p. 1984. 15.00x (ISBN 0-9609646-4-9). Champaign County.

Champaigne, Deborah E., jt. auth. see Keith, Mary E.

Champailler, ed. see Bossuet, Jacques-Benigne.

Champakalakshmi, A. Vaisnava Iconography in the Tamil Country. 135p. 1981. text ed. 50.00 (ISBN 0-86131-216-3, Pub. by Orient Longman Ltd India). Apt Bks.

Champakalakshmi, R. Vaishnava Iconography in the Tamil Nadu. 370p. 1982. cloth 60.00x (Pub. by Sangam Bks England). State Mutual Bk.

--Vaisnava Iconography in the Tamil Country. cancelled (ISBN 0-686-81463-0, Orient Longman). South Asia Bks.

Champaklal. Champaklal Speaks. (Illus.). 275p. 1975. pap. 7.25 (ISBN 0-89071-278-6). Matagiri.

--Champaklal's Treasures. (Illus.). 234p. 1976. pap. 5.25 (ISBN 0-89071-279-4). Matagiri.

Champaud, Jacques. Mom: Terroir Bassa (Cameroun) (Atlas Des Structures Agraires Au Sud Du Sahara: No. 9). (Illus.). 1973. pap. 19.20x (ISBN 90-2797-223-0). Mouton.

Champe, Flavia W. The Matachines Dance of the Upper Rio Grande: History, Music, & Choreography. LC 82-10892. (Illus.). xii, 101p. 1983. 19.95x (ISBN 0-8032-1419-7). U of Nebr Pr.

Champe, P. C., jt. ed. see Prockop, D. J.

Champeney, D. C. Fourier Transforms & Their Physical Applications. (Techniques of Physics Ser.: No. 1). 1973. 47.50 (ISBN 0-12-167450-9). Acad Pr.

--Fourier Transforms in Physics. (Student Monographs in Physics). 64p. (Orig.). 1985. pap. text ed. 5.00 (ISBN 0-85274-794-2, 990300609, Pub. by Adam Hilger Techo Hse UK). Heyden.

Champernowne, Irene. A Memoir of Toni Wolff. pap. 3.50 (ISBN 0-317-13545-7). C G Jung Frisco.

Champigneulle, B. Art Nouveau. Eisler, B., tr. LC 76-8467. 1976. pap. text ed. 12.95 (ISBN 0-8120-0667-4). Barron.

Champigny, Robert. Humanism & Human Racism: A Critical Study of Essays by Sartre & Camus. LC 77-189701. (De Proprietatibus Litterarum, Ser. Practica: No. 41). 82p. (Orig.). 1973. pap. text ed. 10.40x (ISBN 90-2792-373-6). Mouton.

--Ontology of the Narrative. (De Proprietatibus Litterarum, Ser. Minor: No. 12). 1972. pap. text ed. 11.60x (ISBN 90-2792-366-3). Mouton.

--Sartre & Drama. 123p. 1982. 12.95 (ISBN 0-917786-31-9). Summa Pubns.

--Sense, Antisense, Nonsense. LC 83-26007. (University of Florida Humanities Monographs: No. 57). 128p. 1985. pap. 11.00 (ISBN 0-8130-0791-7). U Presses Fla.

--What Will Have Happened: A Philosophical & Technical Essay on Mystery Stories. pap. 47.80 (ISBN 0-317-27937-8, 2056028). Bks Demand UMI.

Champigny, Robert R. Portrait of a Symbolist Hero. 1954. 15.00 (ISBN 0-527-16100-4). Kraus Repr.

--Stages on Sartre's Way, 1938-52. LC 59-67200. (Indiana University Humanities Ser.: No. 42). 1959. 20.00 (ISBN 0-527-16110-1). Kraus Repr.

Champigny, Victor De see De Champigny, Victor.

Champine, G. Distributed Computer Systems: Impact on Management Design & Analysis. 380p. 1980. 44.75 (ISBN 0-444-86109-2, North-Holland). Elsevier.

Champine, G. A. Computer Technology Impact on Management. 292p. 1978. 38.50 (ISBN 0-444-85179-8, North-Holland). Elsevier.

Champion, A. G., jt. ed. see Goddard, J. B.

Champion, Anthony G., jt. ed. see Davies, Ross L.

Champion, Brian. Advanced Weapons Systems: An Annotated Bibliography of the Cruise Missile, MX Missile, Laser & Space Weapons, & Stealth Technology. LC 84-48398. (Referance Library of Social Science). 100p. 1985. lib. bdg. 35.00 (ISBN 0-8240-8792-3). Garland Pub.

Champion, Dean. Basic Statistics for Social Research. 2nd ed. 1981. text ed. write for info. (ISBN 0-02-320600-4). Macmillan.

Champion, Dean J., jt. auth. see Black, James A.

Champion, Dean J., et al. Introduction to Sociology. 1984. text ed. 26.95 (ISBN 0-317-07014-2). HR&W.

Champion, H. R., jt. auth. see Sacco, W. J.

Champion, Ivan F. Across New Guinea from the Fly to the Sepik. LC 75-32804. (Illus.). 1976. Repr. of 1932 ed. 27.50 (ISBN 0-404-14108-0). AMS Pr.

Champion, Jackson R. Blacks in the Republican Party? LC 75-29732. (Illus.). 1976. 7.50 (ISBN 0-917230-03-5). LenChamps Pubs.

Champion, James J. The Periphrastic Futures Formed by the Romance Reflexes of Valdo (Ad) Plus Infinitive. (Studies in the Romance Languages & Literatures: No. 202). 80p. 1978. 6.00x (ISBN 0-8078-9202-5). U of NC Pr.

Champion, John M. & James, John H. Critical Incidents in Management. 4th ed. 1980. pap. 15.95x (ISBN 0-256-02269-0). Irwin.

Champion, K. S. W., jt. auth. see Schmidtke, G.

Champion, Larry S. Ben Jonson's "Dotages". A Reconsideration of the Late Plays. LC 67-29338. 168p. 1967. 15.00x (ISBN 0-8131-1143-9). U Pr of Ky.

--Evolution of Shakespeare's Comedy: A Study in Dramatic Perspective. LC 73-105370. 1970. pap. 4.95x (ISBN 0-674-27141-6). Harvard U Pr.

--King Lear: An Annotated Bibliography, 2 Vols. LC 80-8489. (The Garland Shakespeare Bibliographies). 900p. 1981. lib. bdg. 121.00 (ISBN 0-8240-9498-0). Garland Pub.

--Thomas Dekker & the Traditions of English Drama. (American University Studies IV, (English Language & Literature): Vol. 27). 260p. 1985. text ed. 25.15 (ISBN 0-8204-0214-1). P Lang Pubs.

Champion, Pierre. Louis the Eleventh. facs. ed. Whale, Winifred S., tr. LC 73-109617. (Select Bibliographies Reprint Ser). 1929. 24.50 (ISBN 0-8369-5226-X). Ayer Co Pubs.

Champion, Richard G. Go on Singing. LC 76-20889. (Radiant Life). 128p. 1976. tchr's ed 3.95 (ISBN 0-88243-169-2, 32-0169); pap. 1.95 (ISBN 0-88243-895-6, 02-0895). Gospel Pub.

Champion, Sara. Dictionary of Terms & Techniques in Archaeology. (Illus.). 144p. 1982. pap. 7.95 (ISBN 0-89696-162-1, An Everest House Book). Dodd.

--A Dictionary of Terms & Techniques in Archaeology. LC 80-66774. pap. 36.00 (ISBN 0-317-20683-4, 2025147). Bks Demand UMI.

Champion, Selwyn G. The Eleven Religions & Their Proverbial Lore: A Comparative Study. 1979. Repr. of 1945 ed. lib. bdg. 30.00 (ISBN 0-8492-3856-0). R West.

--The Eleven Religions & Their Proverbial Lore: A Comparative Study. 340p. 1985. Repr. of 1945 ed. lib. bdg. 75.00 (ISBN 0-8492-4102-2). R West.

Champion, Selwyn G. & Mavrogordato, Ethel. Wayside Sayings. 284p. Repr. of 1924 ed. Set. lib. bdg. 75.00 (ISBN 0-89984-142-2). Century Bookbindery.

Champion, T. C. & Megaw, J. V., eds. Settlement & Society: Aspects of West Europe Prehistory in the First Millennnium B.C. 238p. 1985. 29.95 (ISBN 0-312-71317-7). St Martin.

Champion, Timothy, et al. Prehistoric Europe. 1984. casebound 45.00 (ISBN 0-12-167550-5); pap. 23.50 (ISBN 0-12-167552-1). Acad Pr.

Champion, Vici. Yet Forty Days. LC 82-99807. 59p. 1983. 6.95 (ISBN 0-533-05443-5). Vantage.

Champlain, Samuel. Voyages of Samuel De Champlain, 3 Vols. Slafter, Edmund F., ed. Otis, Charles P., tr. (Illus.). Set. 62.00 (ISBN 0-8337-3287-0). B Franklin.

Champlain, Samuel De. Narrative of a Voyage to the West Indies & Mexico in the Years 1599-1602. Shaw, Norton, ed. Wilmere, Alice, tr. LC 61-30806. (Illus.). 48p. 1859. Repr. 26.00 (ISBN 0-8337-0524-5). B Franklin.

--The Voyages & Explorations of Samuel De Champlain, Sixteen Four to Sixteen Sixteen, 2 vols. LC 72-2825. (Illus.). Repr. of 1922 ed. Set. 55.00 (ISBN 0-404-54905-5). AMS Pr.

Chance, Jane. Woman As Hero in Old English Literature. (Illus.). 192p. 1985. text ed. 25.00x (ISBN 0-8156-2345-3); pap. text ed. 12.50x (ISBN 0-8156-2346-1). Syracuse U Pr.

Chance, Jane & Wells, R. O., Jr., eds. Mapping the Cosmos. LC 84-62986. (New Ser.: No. 4). (Illus.). 180p. 1985. text ed. 19.95x (ISBN 0-89263-258-5). Rice Univ.

Chance, Jeanne L. Ma Chance's French Caribbean Creole Cooking. Kelly, June, ed. (Illus.). 16.95 (ISBN 0-399-13035-7). Putnam Pub Group.

--Ma Chances' French Creole Cooking. Kelly, June, ed. (Illus.). 1985. 16.95 (Putnam). Putnam Pub Group.

Chance, John K. Race & Class in Colonial Oaxaca. LC 76-48011. 1978. 20.00x (ISBN 0-8047-0937-8). Stanford U Pr.

Chance, John K., jt. auth. see Butterworth, Douglas.

Chance, Joseph E. The Second Texas Infantry: From Shiloh to Vicksburg. 192p. 1984. 12.95 (ISBN 0-89015-435-X). Eakin Pubns.

Chance, Lisbeth. Cutting Edge. 150p. 1985. 13.95 (ISBN 0-8027-0833-1). Walker & Co.

Chance, Michael R. & Larsen, Ray R., eds. The Social Structure of Attention. LC 76-15675. (Illus.). 1976. pap. 87.30 (ISBN 0-317-08030-X, 2017801). Bks Demand UMI.

Chance, Norman A. China's Urban Villagers. LC 83-12849. (Case Studies in Cultural Anthropology Ser.). 165p. 1984. pap. text ed. 9.95 (ISBN 0-03-060329-3). HR&W.

--Eskimo of North Alaska. LC 66-13590. (Case Studies in Cultural Anthropology). 1966. pap. text ed. 9.95 (ISBN 0-03-057160-X, HoltC). HR&W.

Chance, Paul. Learning & Behavior. 1979. pap. text ed. write for info. (ISBN 0-534-00700-7). Wadsworth Pub.

--Thinking in the Classroom: A Survey of Programs. 160p. (Orig.). 1985. pap. text ed. 10.95x (ISBN 0-8077-2794-6). Tchrs Coll.

Chance, Paul, ed. Learning Through Play. (PRT Ser.: No. 3). 60p. (Orig.). 1979. pap. 6.00 (ISBN 0-931562-02-3). J & J Child Develop.

Chancellar, Ann L. Costumes, Creatures & Characters. (Illus.). 16p. 1980. pap. 2.00 (ISBN 0-9603146-2-8). New Eng SF Assoc.

Chancellor, Betty. A Child's Christmas Cookbook. (Illus.). 40p. (Orig.). (gr. 1-8). 1969. pap. 3.00 (ISBN 0-914510-00-2). Evergreen.

Chancellor, E. Bereford. Essays & Studies, Literature & Historical. 1891. Repr. 15.00 (ISBN 0-8274-2299-7). R West.

Chancellor, E. Beresford. Literary Types. LC 76-105770. 1970. Repr. of 1895 ed. 19.00x (ISBN 0-8046-0943-8, Pub. by Kennikat). Assoc Faculty Pr.

--Literary Types. 1973. Repr. of 1895 ed. 15.00 (ISBN 0-8274-0597-9). R West.

--Literary Types, Being Essays in Criticism. 192p. 1979. Repr. lib. bdg. 22.50 (ISBN 0-8414-9989-6). Folcroft.

--The London of Charles Dickens. 1976. lib. bdg. 59.95 (ISBN 0-8490-2182-0). Gordon Pr.

--The London of Thackeray. 1923. lib. bdg. 30.00 (ISBN 0-8414-9986-1). Folcroft.

Chancellor, E. Beresford, ed. see Defoe, Daniel.

Chancellor, Edwin B. Dickens & His Times. LC 76-46454. 1976. Repr. of 1932 ed. lib. bdg. 20.00 (ISBN 0-8414-3551-0). Folcroft.

--The London of Charles Dickens. LC 78-14818. 1978. Repr. of 1924 ed. lib. bdg. 35.00 (ISBN 0-8414-0053-9). Folcroft.

Chancellor, G. J., jt. ed. see Hawtin, G. C.

Chancellor, J. & Mears, W. R. News Business. 1984. pap. 3.95 (ISBN 0-451-62309-6, Ment). NAL.

Chancellor, John. Charles Darwin. LC 76-5175. (Illus.). (YA) (gr. 10 up). 13.95 (ISBN 0-8008-1434-7). Taplinger.

--Flowers & Fruits of the Bible. LC 81-69042. (Illus.). 64p. 1982. 14.95 (ISBN 0-8253-0085-1). Beaufort Bks NY.

--The Life & Times of Edward I. (Kings & Queens of England Ser.). (Illus.). 224p. 1981. 17.50x (ISBN 0-297-77840-4, GWN 03689, Pub. by Weidenfeld & Nicolson England). Biblio Dist.

--On Telling the Truth in Public. LC 82-82496. (Orig.). 1982. pap. 1.00 (ISBN 0-934742-18-9, Inst Study Diplomacy). Geo U Sch For Serv.

Chancellor, John & Hawkins, Austin. The Maritime Paintings of John Chancellor. (Illus.). 80p. 1984. 60.00 (ISBN 0-7153-8598-4). David & Charles.

Chancellor, John & Mears, Walter R. The News Business: Getting & Writing the News as Two Top Journalists Do It. LC 82-48126. 224p. 1983. 12.45i (ISBN 0-06-015104-8, HarpT). Har-Row.

Chancellor, Philip, tr. see Lavier, J.

Chancellor, Phillip. Handbook on the Bach Flower Remedies. LC 79-93435. 254p. (Orig.). 1980. pap. 6.95 (ISBN 0-87983-196-0). Keats.

Chancellor, R. J. Garden Weeds & Their Control. 93p. 1981. 24.00x (ISBN 0-909605-21-1, Pub. by Richmond Pub England). State Mutual Bk.

Chancellor, Robin, tr. see Dutourd, Jean.

Chancellor, Valerie E., ed. Master & Artisan in Victorian England. LC 69-17619. 1969. 25.00x (ISBN 0-678-07501-8). Kelley.

Chancellor, William E. Educational Sociology. 1979. Repr. of 1919 ed. lib. bdg. 20.00 (ISBN 0-8492-4027-1). R West.

Chand, et al. Regional Planning in India. LC 83-3146. 1984. 12.00x (ISBN 0-8364-1168-4, Pub. by Allied India). South Asia Bks.

Chand, Attar. Disarmament, Detente & World Peace: A Bibliography with Selected Abstracts, 1916-1981. 167p. 1982. 22.95x (ISBN 0-940500-49-3, Pub. by Sterling India). Asia Bk Corp.

--Non-Aligned Nations: Challenges of the Eighties. 312p. 1983. 39.95 (ISBN 0-317-12336-X, Pub. by Select Bk Serv India). Asia Bk Corp.

--Tibet: Past & Present, 1600-1981. 257p. 1982. text ed. 25.00x (ISBN 0-391-02695-X, Pub. by Sterling India). Humanities.

Chand, Meira. The Bonsai Tree. LC 82-19615. 240p. 1983. 12.95 (ISBN 0-89919-166-5). Ticknor & Fields.

--The Gossamer Fly. 192p. 8.95 (ISBN 0-317-35811-1, 509). Soc Intercult Ed Train & Res.

Chand, Prem. The Chess-Players. Mallick, Gurdial, tr. (Orient Paperbacks Ser.). 174p. 1967. pap. 2.50 (ISBN 0-86578-079-X). Ind-US Inc.

Chand, Ramesh, ed. Symmetries & Quark Models. 420p. 1970. 80.95 (ISBN 0-677-13880-6). Gordon.

Chanda, Nayan. Brother Enemy: A History of Indochina Since the Fall of Saigon. (Illus.). 352p. 1986. 17.95 (ISBN 0-15-114420-6). HarBraceJ.

Chanda, Ram P. The Indo Aryan Races. 274p. 1978. Repr. of 1916 ed. 17.00 (ISBN 0-89684-152-9, Pub. by Cosmo Pubns India). Orient Bk Dist.

Chandebois, R. Histogenesis & Morphogenesis in Planarian Regeneration. Wolsky, A., ed. (Monographs in Developmental Biology: Vol. 11). (Illus.). 200p. 1976. 38.50 (ISBN 3-8055-2285-1). S Karger.

Chandebois, Rosine & Faber, J., eds. Automation in Animal Development. (Monographs in Developmental Biology: Vol. 16). (Illus.). xii, 204p. 1983. 70.25 (ISBN 3-8055-3666-6). S Karger.

Chander, Jagdish. George Eliot: The Law of Antecedents & Consequents in Her Novels. LC 77-16380. 1977. Repr. of 1964 ed. lib. bdg. 7.50 (ISBN 0-8414-1201-4). Folcroft.

--The Licentious Comedy of the Restoration Age. LC 73-474. 1973. lib. bdg. 6.50 (ISBN 0-8414-1419-X). Folcroft.

Chander, Krishan. The Dreamer & Other Stories. Ratan, Jai, tr. 160p. 1970. pap. 3.00 (ISBN 0-88253-025-9, 4027). Ind-US Inc.

--Mr. Ass Comes to Town. Bouman, Helen H., tr. 167p. 1968. pap. 1.95 (ISBN 0-88253-026-7). Ind-US Inc.

Chander, M., jt. auth. see Ravindranath, B.

Chander, Romesh & Karnik, Kiran. Planning for Satellite Broadcasting: The Indian Instructional Television Experiment. (Reports & Papers on Mass Communication: No. 78). 71p. 1976. pap. 5.00 (ISBN 92-3-101392-0, U453, UNESCO). Unipub.

Chander Grover, Subhash. Paths to Profits. 146p. (Orig.). 1985. pap. 8.95 (ISBN 0-930383-04-4). Monument Pr.

Chandernagor, Francoise. The King's Way: Recollections of Francoise d'Aubigne, Marquise de Maintenon, Wife to the King of France. Bray, Barbara, tr. (Penguin Fiction Ser.). 496p. 1985. pap. 8.95 (ISBN 0-14-007699-9). Penguin.

--The King's Way: The Life of Madame de Maintenon. Bray, Barbara, tr. (A Helen & Kurt Wolff Bk.). 512p. 1984. 15.95 (ISBN 0-15-147274-2). HarBraceJ.

Chandhry, M. H., jt. ed. see Martin, C. S.

Chandler. Atlas of Military Strategy. 208p. 1980. 29.95 (ISBN 0-02-905750-7). Macmillan.

--Tournament Chess, Vol. 1. Miles, A. J., ed. 128p. 1981. pap. 19.95 (ISBN 0-08-026888-9). Pergamon.

--The Trial of Jesus. (Illus.). 19.95 (ISBN 0-686-90784-1); deluxe edition 37.95 (ISBN 0-686-90785-X); pap. 9.95 (ISBN 0-686-90786-8). Harrison Co GA.

Chandler, A. B., ed. see McDonald, T. F.

Chandler, A. B., et al, eds. The Thrombotic Process in Atherogenesis. LC 78-18939. (Advances in Experimental Medicine & Biology Ser.: Vol. 104). 562p. 1978. 69.50x (ISBN 0-306-40022-7, Plenum Pr). Plenum Pub.

Chandler, A. Bertram. Beyond the Galactic Rim, Vol. 4. (Rim Worlds Ser.). 144p. 1983. 13.95 (ISBN 0-8052-8122-3, Pub. by Allison & Busby England). Schocken.

--Big Black Mark. (Science Fiction Ser). pap. 2.50 (ISBN 0-87997-726-4, UE1726). DAW Bks.

--Bring Back Yesterday. (Rim World Ser.: Vol. 3). 153p. 1982. 12.95 (ISBN 0-8052-8103-7, Pub. by Allison & Busby England). Schocken.

--Far Traveller. (Science Fiction Ser). (Orig.). 1979. pap. 2.25 (ISBN 0-87997-855-4, UE1855). DAW Bks.

--Frontier of the Dark. 240p. 1984. pap. 2.75 (ISBN 0-441-25504-3). Ace Bks.

--The Inheritors: Gateway to Never. 384p. 1981. pap. 2.50 (ISBN 0-441-37064-0). Ace Bks.

--Into the Alternate Universe: Contraband from Outer Space. 320p. 1981. pap. 2.75 (ISBN 0-441-37109-4). Ace Bks.

--The Last Amazon. 1984. pap. 2.95 (ISBN 0-87997-936-4). DAW Bks.

--Matilda's Stepchildren. 176p. 1983. pap. 2.50 (ISBN 0-87997-845-7). Daw Bks.

--The Rim of Space. 192p. 1981. 12.95 (ISBN 0-8052-8090-1, Pub. by Allison & Busby England). Schocken.

--The Road up to the Rim: The Hard Way up. 352p. 1981. pap. 2.75 (ISBN 0-441-73102-3). Ace Bks.

--Star Courier. (Science Fiction Ser.). 1977. pap. 1.95 (ISBN 0-87997-834-1). DAW Bks.

--To Keep the Ship. (Science Fiction Ser.). (Orig.). 1983. pap. 2.50 (ISBN 0-87997-827-9). DAW Bks.

--The Way Back. (Science Fiction Ser). (Orig.). 1978. pap. 2.25 (ISBN 0-87997-663-2, UE1663). DAW Bks.

--When the Dream Dies. 160p. 1981. 12.95 (ISBN 0-8052-8089-8, Pub. by Allison & Busby, England). Schocken.

--The Wild Ones. 253p. 1985. pap. 2.95 (ISBN 0-88677-031-9). DAW Bks.

Chandler, A. Bertram & Hoffman, Lee. Up to the Sky in Ships: In & Out of Quandry. Hitchcock, Charles J., ed. 172p. 1982. 13.00 (ISBN 0-915368-16-1). New Eng SF Assoc.

Chandler, A. Bertrom. Kelly Country. 1985. pap. 3.50 (ISBN 0-88677-066-1). DAW Bks.

Chandler, Albert R. Beauty & Human Nature: Elements of Psychological Aesthetics. LC 75-3110. Repr. of 1934 ed. 26.00 (ISBN 0-404-59106-X). AMS Pr.

--Beauty & Human Nature: Elements of Psychological Aesthetics. 1977. Repr. of 1934 ed. lib. bdg. 30.00 (ISBN 0-8495-0712-X). Arden Lib.

Chandler, Albert R. & Barnhart, Edward N. Bibliography of Psychological & Experimental Aesthetics, Eighteen Sixty-Four to Nineteen Thirty-Seven. LC 75-3111. Repr. of 1938 ed. 32.50 (ISBN 0-404-59107-8). AMS Pr.

Chandler, Alfred, ed. Pioneers in Modern Factory Management: An Original Anthology. LC 79-7526. (History of Management Thought & Practice Ser.). 1980. lib. bdg. 19.00x (ISBN 0-405-12310-8). Ayer Co Pubs.

Chandler, Alfred D. & Tedlow, Richard S. The Coming of Managerial Capitalism. 1985. 31.95x (ISBN 0-256-03285-8). Irwin.

Chandler, Alfred D., ed. The Application of Modern Systematic Management: An Original Anthology. LC 79-7522. (History of Management Thought & Practice Ser.). (Illus.). 1980. lib. bdg. 17.00x (ISBN 0-405-12307-8). Ayer Co Pubs.

--History of Management Thought & Practice, 32 bks. (Ser.). (Illus.). 1980. Set. lib. bdg. 1182.00x (ISBN 0-405-12306-X). Ayer Co Pubs.

--Management Thought in Great Britain: An Original Anthology. LC 79-7523. (History of Management Thought & Practice Ser.). 1980. lib. bdg. 25.50x (ISBN 0-405-12308-6). Ayer Co Pubs.

--Managerial Innovation at General Motors: An Original Anthology. LC 79-7524. (History of Management Thought & Practice Ser.). 1980. lib. bdg. 16.00x (ISBN 0-405-12309-4). Ayer Co Pubs.

--Precursors of Modern Management: An Original Anthology. LC 79-7527. (History of Management Thought & Practice Ser.). 1980. lib. bdg. 28.50x (ISBN 0-405-12311-6). Ayer Co Pubs.

--The Railroads: Pioneers in Modern Management, an Original Anthology. LC 79-7528. (History of Management Thought & Practice Ser.). 1980. lib. bdg. 28.50x (ISBN 0-405-12312-4). Ayer Co Pubs.

Chandler, Alfred D., ed. see Arnold, Horace L.

Chandler, Alfred D., ed. see Austin, Bertram & Lloyd, W. Francis.

Chandler, Alfred D., ed. see Berriman, A. E., et al.

Chandler, Alfred D., ed. see Cadbury, Edward.

Chandler, Alfred D., ed. see Carlson, Sune.

Chandler, Alfred D., ed. see Carney, Edward M., et al.

Chandler, Alfred D., ed. see Casson, Herbert N.

Chandler, Alfred D., ed. see Church, A. Hamilton.

Chandler, Alfred D., ed. see Davis, Ralph C.

Chandler, Alfred D., ed. see Devinat, Paul.

Chandler, Alfred D., ed. see Diemer, Hugo.

Chandler, Alfred D., ed. see Elbourne, Edward T.

Chandler, Alfred D., ed. see Emerson, Harrington.

Chandler, Alfred D., ed. see Kirkman, Marshall M.

Chandler, Alfred D., ed. see Laurence, Edward.

Chandler, Alfred D., ed. see Lee, John.

Chandler, Alfred D., jt. ed. see Lee, John.

Chandler, Alfred D., ed. see McKinsey, James O.

Chandler, Alfred D., ed. see Rowntree, B. Seebohm.

Chandler, Alfred D., ed. see Schell, Erwin H.

Chandler, Alfred D., ed. see Sheldon, Oliver.

Chandler, Alfred D., ed. see Tead, Ordway & Metcalfe, Henry C.

Chandler, Alfred D., ed. see Urwick, Lyndall.

Chandler, Alfred D., Jr. Henry Varnum Poor: Business Editor, Analyst, & Reformer. Bruchey, Stuart, ed. LC 80-1297. (Railroads Ser.). 1981. Repr. of 1956 ed. lib. bdg. 35.00x (ISBN 0-405-13767-2). Ayer Co Pubs.

--Strategy & Structure: Chapters in the History of the American Industrial Enterprise. 1962. pap. 8.95x (ISBN 0-262-53009-0). MIT Pr.

--The Visible Hand: The Managerial Revolution in American Business. 1977. 27.50x (ISBN 0-674-94051-2, Belknap Pr); pap. 9.95 (ISBN 0-674-94052-0). Harvard U Pr.

Chandler, Alfred D., Jr. & Daems, Herman. Managerial Hierarchies: Comparative Perspectives on the Rise of the Modern Industrial Enterprise. (Harvard Studies in Business History: No. 32). 256p. 1983. pap. text ed. 7.95X (ISBN 0-674-54741-1). Harvard U Pr.

Chandler, Alfred D., Jr. & Salsbury, Stephen. Pierre S. Dupont & the Making of the Modern Corporation. LC 78-123920. (Illus.). 1971. 20.00i (ISBN 0-06-010701-4, HarpT). Har-Row.

Chandler, Alfred D., Jr., ed. The Papers of Dwight David Eisenhower: The War Years, 5 Vols. LC 65-27672. (Illus., Sold as set only). 1970. Set. 95.00x (ISBN 0-8018-1078-7). Johns Hopkins.

Chandler, Alfred D., Jr. & Bruchey, Stuart, eds. The Railroads: The Nation's First Big Business Sources & Readings. LC 80-1298. (Railroads Ser.). 1981. Repr. of 1965 ed. lib. bdg. 20.00x (ISBN 0-405-13768-0). Ayer Co Pubs.

Chandler, Alfred D., Jr & Bruchley, Stuart, eds. Giant Enterprise: Ford, General Motors, & the Automobile Industry. LC 80-18483. (Multinational Corporations Ser.). 1980. Repr. of 1964 ed. lib. bdg. 28.50x (ISBN 0-405-13349-9). Ayer Co Pubs.

Chandler, Alfred D., Jr. & Daems, Herman, eds. Managerial Hierarchies: Comparative Perspectives on the Rise of Modern Industrial Enterprise. (Harvard Studies in Business History: No. 32). (Illus.). 1980. text ed. 16.50x (ISBN 0-674-54740-3). Harvard U Pr.

Chandler, Alfred N. Land Titles Origins. Bruchey, Stuart, ed. LC 78-56712. (Management of Public Lands in the U. S. Ser.). 1979. Repr. of 1945 ed. lib. bdg. 38.00x (ISBN 0-405-11324-2). Ayer Co Pubs.

Chandler, Alice. A Dream of Order: The Medieval Ideal in Nineteenth-Century English Literature. LC 69-10413. pap. 72.50 (ISBN 0-317-29140-8, 2025016). Bks Demand UMI.

Chandler, Allison. When Oklahoma Took the Trolley. Sebree, Mac, ed. LC 79-92539. (Special Ser.: No. 71). 1980. 21.95 (ISBN 0-916374-35-1). Interurban.

Chandler, Arthur & Pope, Wayne. Stereo Views. LC 78-11761. 32p. (Orig.). 1978. pap. 7.95 (ISBN 0-8431-4096-8, 96-5). Troubador Pr.

Chandler, Arthur, ed. see Hayakawa, S. I.

Chandler, Arthur B. Old Tales of San Francisco. LC 77-78491. (History Ser.). (Illus.). 1977. pap. text ed. 8.95 (ISBN 0-8403-1746-8). Kendall-Hunt.

Chandler, Asa C. & Read, C. P. Introduction to Parasitology: With Special References to the Parasites of Man. 10th ed. LC 61-5670. 822p. 1961. 45.45x (ISBN 0-471-14487-8). Wiley.

Chandler, Authur. The Aesthetics of Piet Mondrian. LC 72-7934. 67p. 1972. pap. text ed. 9.95x (ISBN 0-8422-0266-8). Irvington.

Chandler, B. & Magnus, W. History of Combinatorial Group Theory: A Case Study of the History of Ideas. (Studies in the History of Mathematics & Physical Sciences: Vol. 9). (Illus.). 234p. 1982. 52.00 (ISBN 0-387-90749-1). Springer-Verlag.

Chandler, B., jt. auth. see Baumslag, C. B.

Chandler, B., ed. see Magnus, W.

Chandler, B. V. see Mrak, E. M. & Stewart, G. F.

Chandler, Barbara. How to Cope at Home. 160p. 1981. 30.00x (ISBN 0-7063-5918-6, Pub. by Ward Lock Ed England). State Mutual Bk.

Chandler, Betty. The Make-a-Pattern Coloring Book. (Orig.). 1977. pap. 2.95 (ISBN 0-8431-0235-7). Price Stern.

--Quilting Coloring Book. 1976. pap. 2.95 (ISBN 0-8431-0228-4). Price Stern.

Chandler, Betty J. The Mysteries of Swift Creek. 1983. 8.95 (ISBN 0-533-05629-2). Vantage.

Chandler, Beverly J. Poetry...A Way of Seeing. 1984. 5.95 (ISBN 0-533-05920-8). Vantage.

Chandler, Billy J. The Bandit King: Lampiao of Brazil. LC 77-99275. 284p. 1978. 17.50x (ISBN 0-89096-050-X); pap. 8.95 (ISBN 0-89096-194-8). Tex A&M Univ Pr.

--The Feitosas & the Sertao Dos Inhamuns: The History of a Family & a Community in Northeast Brazil, 1700-1930. LC 74-178988. (University of Florida Latin American Monographs: No. 10). 1972. 7.50 (ISBN 0-8130-0348-2). U Presses Fla.

Chandler, Bob. Violent Sundays. (Orig.). 1984. pap. 8.95 (ISBN 0-671-47460-X, Fireside). S&S.

Chandler, Bob, et al. The Unofficial NFL Players Handbook. (Illus., Orig.). 1984. pap. 5.95 (ISBN 0-671-47615-7, Wallaby). S&S.

Chandler, Bruce, ed. see Andrewes, William & Atwood, Seth.

Chandler, Bruce, ed. see Turner, Anthony.

Chandler, Bryn. Ambition. (Love & Life Ser.). 176p. (Orig.). 1983. pap. 1.75 (ISBN 0-345-31217-1). Ballantine.

Chandler, C., ed. see Durey, Peter.

Chandler, Cathleen, jt. auth. see Landers, Jonathan M.

Chandler, Charles D. & Lahm, Frank P. How Our Army Grew Wings. Kohn, Richard H., ed. LC 78-22377. (American Military Experience Ser.). (Illus.). 1979. Repr. of 1943 ed. lib. bdg. 27.50x (ISBN 0-405-11854-6). Ayer Co Pubs.

Chandler, Charles L., et al. Philadelphia: Port of History 1609-1837. (Illus.). 82p. 1976. pap. 3.25 (ISBN 0-913346-02-0). Phila Maritime Mus.

Chandler, Charlotte. The Ultimate Seduction. LC 83-14149. 384p. 1984. 16.95 (ISBN 0-385-18953-2). Doubleday.

Chandler, Craig C. & Cheney, Phillip. Fire in Forestry: Forest Fire Management & Organization, Vol. II. LC 83-5088. 298p. 1983. 42.50x (ISBN 0-471-87447-7, Wiley-Interscience). Wiley.

Chandler, Craig C., et al. Fire in Forestry: Forest Fire Behavior & Effects, Vol. I. LC 83-5088. 450p. 1983. 49.95x (ISBN 0-471-87442-6, Wiley-Interscience). Wiley.

Chandler, D. C., ed. see Tacitus.

Chandler, D. L. One Hundred Tons of Gold. 1980. pap. 2.25 (ISBN 0-440-16687-X). Dell.

Chandler, D. S., jt. auth. see Burkholder, Mark A.

Chandler, Daniel. Young Learners & the Microcomputer. 128p. 1984. 34.00x (ISBN 0-335-10579-3, Pub. by Open Univ Pr); pap. 13.00x (ISBN 0-335-10578-5, Pub. by Open Univ Pr). Taylor & Francis.

Chandler, Daniel R. The Rhetorical Tradition, Principles & Practice. 1978. pap. text ed. 9.95 (ISBN 0-8403-1934-7). Kendall-Hunt.

Chandler, David. The Campaigns of Napoleon: The Mind & Method of History's Greatest Soldier. 1182p. 1973. 55.00 (ISBN 0-02-523660-1). Macmillan.

--Dialing for Data: A Consumer's How-To Handbook on Computer Communications. LC 84-42659. (Illus.). 256p. 1984. pap. 9.95 (ISBN 0-394-72774-6). Random.

--Dictionary of the Napoleonic Wars. (Illus.). 1979. 40.00 (ISBN 0-02-523670-9). Macmillan.

--Kelly. LC 81-71684. 320p. 1982. 14.95 (ISBN 0-87795-395-3). Arbor Hse.

--The Masters Connection. LC 80-70213. 384p. 1981. 12.95 (ISBN 0-87795-302-3). Arbor Hse.

--The Middleman. LC 80-66504. 1981. 12.95 (ISBN 0-87795-279-5). Arbor Hse.

--The Middleman. 368p. 1982. pap. 2.75 (ISBN 0-345-30024-6). Ballantine.

Chandler, David, jt. ed. see Chandler, Susan.

Chandler, David G. Atlas of Military Strategy. (Illus.). 1980. Repr. 29.95 (ISBN 0-02-905750-7). Free Pr.

--Sedgemoor Sixteen Eighty-Five: An Account & an Anthology. 240p. 1985. 29.95 (ISBN 0-312-70918-8). St Martin.

Chandler, David L. Health & Slavery in Colonial Columbia. Bruchey, Stuart, ed. LC 80-2799. (Dissertations in European Economic History II). (Illus.). 1981. lib. bdg. 31.00x (ISBN 0-405-13983-7). Ayer Co Pubs.

Chandler, David P. A History of Cambodia. LC 83-1391. 237p. 1983. lib. bdg. 26.50x (ISBN 0-86531-578-7). Westview.

--The Land & People of Cambodia. LC 72-2270. (Portraits of the Nation Ser). (Illus.). 160p. (gr. 6 up). 1972. 11.49i (ISBN 0-397-31321-7). Lipp Jr Bks.

Chandler, David P. & Kiernan, Ben, eds. Revolution & Its Aftermath in Kampuchea: Eight Essays. LC 83-50326. (Monograph Ser.: No. 25). 319p. 1983. pap. 14.00x (ISBN 0-938692-05-4). Yale U SE Asia.

Chandler, Douglas R. Pilgrimage of Faith: A Centennial History of Wesley Theological Seminary 1882-1982. Goen, C. C., ed. LC 84-1415. 312p. 1984. 19.95 (ISBN 0-932020-27-5). Seven Locks Pr.

Chandler, E. M. Educating Adolescent Girls. (Unwin Education Books Ser.). 240p. (Orig.). 1980. text ed. 27.50x (ISBN 0-04-370096-9); pap. text ed. 10.50x (ISBN 0-04-370097-7). Allen Unwin.

Chandler, E. Ted & Bloomfield, Robert L. The Foremost Physician, the Farseeing Physician. LC 83-82069. 1983. 9.75 (ISBN 0-9612242-0-7). Harbinger Med Pr NC.

Chandler, Edmund. Pater on Style. LC 74-3038. 1958. lib. bdg. 12.50 (ISBN 0-8414-3556-1). Folcroft.

Chandler, Edna W. Cowboy Andy. LC 59-4447. (Illus.). (gr. 1-2). 1959. PLB 6.99 (ISBN 0-394-90008-1). Beginner.

--Five Cent, Five Cent (Liberia) LC 67-17414. (Illus.). (gr. 1-3). 1967. PLB 9.50 (ISBN 0-8075-2463-8). A Whitman.

Chandler, Elizabeth L. A Study of the Source of the Tales & Romances Written by Nathaniel Hawthorne. LC 75-9569. Repr. of 1926 ed. lib. bdg. 15.00 (ISBN 0-8414-3645-2). Folcroft.

--A Study of the Sources of the Tales & Romances Written by Nathaniel Hawthorne Before 1853. 1978. Repr. of 1926 ed. lib. bdg. 15.00 (ISBN 0-8495-0832-0). Arden Lib.

Chandler, Elizabeth M. Poetical Works of Elizabeth Margaret Chandler. facs. ed. LC 71-83930. (Black Heritage Library Collection Ser). 1836. 12.25 (ISBN 0-8369-8534-6). Ayer Co Pubs.

Chandler, Ernest. Awnings & Tents. 1912. 65.00 (ISBN 0-318-01554-4, 21040). Indus Fabrics.

Chandler, F. W. Color Atlas & Textbook of the Histopathology of Mycotic Diseases. 1980. 99.95 (ISBN 0-8151-1637-3). Year Bk Med.

--Romances of Roguery: The Picaresque Novel in Spain. 1977. lib. bdg. 59.95 (ISBN 0-8490-2540-0). Gordon Pr.

Chandler, Frank W. Aspects of Modern Drama. 1975. Repr. of 1914 ed. 30.00 (ISBN 0-8274-4110-X). R West.

--The Literature of Roguery, 2 vols. 1977. Repr. of 1907 ed. lib. bdg. 85.00 set (ISBN 0-8495-0707-3). Arden Lib.

--Literature of Roguery, 2 vols. in 1. 1966. Repr. of 1907 ed. 35.50 (ISBN 0-8337-0526-1). B Franklin.

--Modern Continental Playwrights. 1975. Repr. of 1931 ed. 40.00 (ISBN 0-8274-4111-8). R West.

--Romances of Roguery: An Episode in the History of the Novel. 1961. Repr. of 1899 ed. 29.00 (ISBN 0-8337-0527-X). B Franklin.

Chandler, G. How to Find Out. 5th rev. ed. 1982. text ed. 16.50 (ISBN 0-08-027433-1). Pergamon.

--How to Find Out about the Novel. 5th ed. 1982. 16.50 (ISBN 0-08-027433-1). Pergamon.

Chandler, George. International & National Library & Information Services: A Review of Recent Developments. (Recent Advances in Library & Information Services: Vol. 2). (Illus.). 230p. 1982. 22.00 (ISBN 0-08-025793-3). Pergamon.

--Libraries, Documentation & Bibliography in the U. S. S. R. Nineteen Seventeen to Nineteen Seventy-One. LC 72-84273. (International Bibliographical & Library Ser). 1973. 36.50 (ISBN 0-12-785105-4). Acad Pr.

--Libraries in the East: An International & Comparative Study. (International Bibliographical & Library Ser.). 214p. 1971. 37.50 (ISBN 0-12-785104-6). Acad Pr.

Chandler, George F., et al. The Policeman's Art: As Taught in the New York State School for Police. LC 70-156009. Repr. of 1922 ed. 15.00 (ISBN 0-404-09172-5). AMS Pr.

Chandler, H. W. A Practical Introduction to Greek Accentuation. rev. 2nd ed. (College Classical Ser.). xxxiii, 292p. 1981. Repr. of 1881 ed. lib. bdg. 30.00x (ISBN 0-89241-112-0). Caratzas.

Chandler, Harry E. How to Write What. 1978. 16.00 (ISBN 0-87170-001-8). ASM.

Chandler, Harry E., ed. Technical Writer's Handbook. 1983. 44.00 (ISBN 0-87170-151-0). ASM.

Chandler, J. A. Representation in Virginia. 1973. pap. 9.00 (ISBN 0-384-08462-1). Johnson Repr.

Chandler, James K. Wordsworth's Second Nature: A Study of the Poetry & Politics. LC 84-5979. 352p. 1984. lib. bdg. 30.00x (ISBN 0-226-10080-4); pap. text ed. 14.95x (ISBN 0-226-10081-2). U of Chicago Pr.

Chandler, Jean. The Poky Little Puppy & the Patchwork Blanket. (Big Golden Story Bks). (Illus.). 24p. (ps-1). 1983. 3.50 (ISBN 0-307-11418-X, 10387, Golden Bks). Western Pub.

Chandler, John & Cockle, Paul. Techniques of Scenario Planning. (Illus.). 192p. 1982. 35.00 (ISBN 0-07-084570-0). McGraw.

Chandler, John W., jt. ed. see O'Connor, G. Richard.

Chandler, Julian A. The History of Suffrage in Virginia. LC 78-63881. (Johns Hopkins University. Studies in the Social Sciences. Nineteenth Ser. 1901: 6-7). Repr. of 1901 ed. 13.00 (ISBN 0-404-61136-2). AMS Pr.

--Representation in Virginia. LC 78-63850. (Johns Hopkins University. Studies in the Social Sciences. Fourteenth Ser. 1896: 6-7). Repr. of 1896 ed. 11.50 (ISBN 0-404-61107-9). AMS Pr.

Chandler, K. A. Marine & Offshore Corrosion. 2nd ed. 432p. 1985. text ed. 79.95 (ISBN 0-408-01175-0). Butterworth.

Chandler, Kathleen. Les Belles Lettres. (Illus.). 160p. 1981. 7.95 (ISBN 0-89962-204-6). Todd & Honeywell.

Chandler, Keith. Kett's Rebellion & Other Poems. 64p. 1982. pap. text ed. 7.50x (ISBN 0-85635-277-2, 80112, Pub. by Carcanet New Pr England). Humanities.

Chandler, Lana J. Invitation to DOS-JCL for Application Programmers. (Illus.). 120p. 1985. pap. text ed. 12.00 (ISBN 0-89433-271-6). Petrocelli.

--Invitation to DOS JCL for Application Programmers. (Illus.). 120p. 1985. pap. 12.00 (ISBN 0-89433-271-6). Van Nos Reinhold.

Chandler, Laurel. Boundless Love. (Rapture Romance Ser.: No. 59). 1984. pap. 1.95 (ISBN 0-451-12811-7, Sig). NAL.

--Heart's Victory. (Rapture Romance Ser.: No. 30). 1983. pap. 1.95 (ISBN 0-451-12511-8, Sig). NAL.

--Treasure of Love. (Rapture Romance Ser.: No. 15). 1983. pap. 1.95 (ISBN 0-451-12379-4, Sig). NAL.

Chandler, Lester. Inflation in the United States 1940-1948. (Fdr & the Era of the New Deal). 1976. Repr. of 1951 ed. lib. bdg. 39.50 (ISBN 0-306-70804-3). Da Capo.

Chandler, Lester V. America's Greatest Depression, Nineteen Twenty-Nineto Nineteen Forty-One. LC 79-108407. 1970. pap. text ed. 16.75 scp (ISBN 0-06-041229-1, HarpC). Har-Row.

--Benjamin Strong: Central Banker. Wilkins, Mira, ed. LC 78-3903. (International Finance Ser.). 1978. Repr. of 1958 ed. lib. bdg. 42.00x (ISBN 0-405-11208-4). Ayer Co Pubs.

Chandler, Lester V., jt. auth. see Goldfeld, Stephen M.

Chandler, Linda S. David Asks, "Why?". LC 80-70519. (gr. 1-6). 1981. 5.95 (ISBN 0-8054-4266-9, 4242-66). Broadman.

--Hello, My Church. (gr. k-3). 1980. 5.95 (ISBN 0-8054-4259-6). Broadman.

--Uncle Ike. LC 80-70520. (gr. 1-6). 1981. 5.95 (ISBN 0-8054-4264-2, 4242-64). Broadman.

--When I Talk to God. LC 84-4967. (Illus.). (gr. k-3). 1984. 5.95 (ISBN 0-8054-4291-X, 4242-91). Broadman.

Chandler, Louis A. Children under Stress: Understanding Emotional Adjustment Reactions. (Illus.). 126p. 1982. 18.75x (ISBN 0-398-04617-4). C C Thomas.

--Children under Stress: Understanding Emotional Adjustment Reactions. 2nd ed. 128p. 1985. 18.75x (ISBN 0-398-05169-0). C C Thomas.

Chandler, M., ed. Tournament Chess, Vol. 2. (Illus.). 128p. 1982. pap. 19.95 (ISBN 0-08-026891-9). Pergamon.

--Tournament Chess, Vol. 12. 215p. 1984. pap. 19.95 (ISBN 0-08-029758-7). Pergamon.

--Tournament Chess, Vol. 14. 178p. 1984. pap. 28.75 (ISBN 0-08-029760-9). Pergamon.

--Tournament Chess, Vol. 15. 188p. 1985. pap. 28.75 (ISBN 0-08-029761-7). Pergamon.

--Tournament Chess, Vol. 16. (Illus.). 176p. 1985. pap. 28.75 (ISBN 0-08-029762-5, Pub. by P P L). Pergamon.

Chandler, M. & Miles, A., eds. Tournament Chess. (Tournament Chess Ser.: Vol. 5). 176p. 1982. pap. 19.95 (ISBN 0-08-029720-X). Pergamon.

--Tournament Chess, Vol. 3. (Illus.). 170p. 1982. pap. 19.95 (ISBN 0-08-026892-7). Pergamon.

--Tournament Chess, Vol. 4. 150p. 1982. 19.95 (ISBN 0-08-026893-5). Pergamon.

--Tournament Chess, Vol. 6. 176p. 1983. pap. 19.95 (ISBN 0-08-029721-8). Pergamon.

--Tournament Chess, Vol. 7. (Illus.). 143p. 1983. pap. 19.95 (ISBN 0-08-029736-6). Pergamon.

--Tournament Chess, Vol. 8. (Illus.). 200p. 1983. pap. 19.95 (ISBN 0-08-029737-4). Pergamon.

--Tournament Chess, Vol. 9. (Illus.). 176p. 1983. pap. 19.95 (ISBN 0-08-029742-0, 62). Pergamon.

--Tournament Chess, Vol. 10. 166p. 1983. pap. 19.95 (ISBN 0-08-029743-9). Pergamon.

Chandler, M., ed. see Varnusz, E.

Chandler, M. E. Upper Eocene Flora of Hordle, Pts. 1-2. 1925-26. Set. 20.00 (ISBN 0-384-08455-9). Johnson Repr.

Chandler, Maggie. Seek Ye First: Song of Solomon. 128p. 1979. pap. 2.50 (ISBN 0-89114-089-1). Baptist Pub Hse.

Chandler, Margaret K. Management Rights & Union Interests. LC 78-6226. (Illus.). 1978. Repr. of 1964 ed. lib. bdg. 55.00x (ISBN 0-313-20495-0, CHMA). Greenwood.

Chandler, Marsha A., jt. ed. see Atkinson, Michael M.

Chandler, Melbourne C. Of Garry Owen in Glory: The History of the Seventh U. S. Cavalry Regiment. (Illus.). 1960. 50.00 (ISBN 0-682-40021-1). Exposition Pr FL.

Chandler, Michael. Stepfathering. 3.50 (ISBN 0-318-04449-8). Pudding.

Chandler, Michael, jt. auth. see Mettling, Stephen R.

Chandler, Murray. Sicilian 2c3. (Algebraic Chess Openings Ser.). (Illus.). 96p. 1981. pap. 13.95 (ISBN 0-7134-1933-4, Pub. by Batsford England). David & Charles.

Chandler, P. G. Some Methods of Teaching in Six Representative Teachers Colleges of the United States. LC 77-176634. (Columbia University. Teachers College. Contributions to Education: No. 425). Repr. of 1930 ed. 22.50 (ISBN 0-404-55425-3). AMS Pr.

Chandler, P. J., jt. auth. see Stubbs, A. E.

Chandler, Peleg W. American Criminal Trials, 2 vols. LC 71-113576. Repr. of 1844 ed. Set. 42.50 (ISBN 0-404-01445-3). AMS Pr.

--American Criminal Trials, 2 Vols. facs. ed. LC 77-109618. (Select Bibliographies Reprint Ser). 1844. Set. 60.50 (ISBN 0-8369-5227-8). Ayer Co Pubs.

Chandler, Peter. Bucks. 272p. (Orig.). 1980. pap. 2.50 (ISBN 0-380-75218-2, 75218). Avon.

Chandler, Ralph & Plano, Jack C. The Public Administration Dictionary. LC 81-12945. 406p. 1982. write for info. (ISBN 0-471-09121-9); pap. text ed. 19.95 (ISBN 0-471-09119-7). Wiley.

Chandler, Ralph C. The Moral Dimensions of Public Policy. 1982. 6.50 (ISBN 0-932826-17-2). New Issues MI.

Chandler, Ralph C., et al. The Constitutional Law Dictionary, Vol. 1: Individual Rights. LC 84-12320. (Clio Dictionaries in Political Science Ser.: No. 8). 507p. 1985. lib. bdg. 47.50 (ISBN 0-87436-031-5); pap. 24.50 (ISBN 0-87436-366-7). ABC-Clio.

Chandler, Ralph Clark, jt. ed. see Frederickson, H. George.

Chandler, Raymond. The Big Sleep. (YA) 1976. pap. 2.95 (ISBN 0-394-72631-6, Vin). Random.

--The Big Sleep: A Film Adaptation Directed by Howard Hawks. Garrett, George, et al, eds. LC 71-135273. (Film Scripts Ser.). 1983. pap. 12.95x (ISBN 0-89197-677-9). Irvington.

--The Blue Dahlia: A Screenplay. LC 75-44121. (Screenplay Library). 162p. (Orig.). 1976. 12.95x (ISBN 0-8093-0758-8). S Ill U Pr.

--Chandler Before Marlowe: Raymond Chandler's Early Prose & Poetry 1908-1912. 2nd ed. Bruccoli, Matthew J., ed. LC 72-13403. xviii, 110p. 1973. 12.95 (ISBN 0-87249-305-9). U of SC Pr.

--Farewell, My Lovely. (YA) 1976. pap. 3.95 (ISBN 0-394-72138-1, Vin). Random.

--The High Window. (YA) 1976. pap. 3.95 (ISBN 0-394-72141-1, Vin). Random.

--The Lady in the Lake. (YA) 1976. pap. 3.95 (ISBN 0-394-72145-4, Vin). Random.

--The Little Sister. 1985. pap. 2.95 (ISBN 0-345-32217-7). Ballantine.

--The Long Goodbye. 1977. pap. 2.25 (ISBN 0-345-28859-9). Ballantine.

--The Notebooks of Raymond Chandler. MacShane, Frank, ed. Incl. English Summer: A Gothic Romance. LC 76-3322. (Illus.). 150p. 1976. 10.00 (ISBN 0-912946-33-4). Ecco Pr.

--Pickup on Noon Street. 1977. pap. 2.25 (ISBN 0-345-28861-0). Ballantine.

--Playback. 1977. pap. 2.95 (ISBN 0-345-32226-6). Ballantine.

--The Raymond Chandler Omnibus. LC 79-92498. 1980. 8.95 (ISBN 0-394-60492-X). Modern Lib.

--Raymond Chandler Speaking. fascimile ed. Gardiner, Dorothy & Sorley, Kathrine, eds. LC 76-146855. (Select Bibliographies Reprint Ser.). 1972. Repr. of 1962 ed. 20.00 (ISBN 0-8369-5622-2). Ayer Co Pubs.

--Raymond Chandler's Unknown Thriller: The Screenplay of Playback. 1985. 15.95 (ISBN 0-89296-128-7). Mysterious Pr.

--The Science Fiction Stories. 16.95 (ISBN 0-88411-421-X, Pub. by Aeonian Pr). Amereon Ltd.

--Simple Art of Murder. 1977. pap. 2.25 (ISBN 0-345-28860-2). Ballantine.

--Trouble Is My Business. pap. 2.50 (ISBN 0-345-32021-2). Ballantine.

Chandler, Richard E. & Schwartz, Kessel. New History of Spanish Literature. LC 61-15756. (Illus.). xiii, 696p. 1961. text ed. 37.50x (ISBN 0-8071-0343-8). La State U Pr.

Chandler, Richard E. & Schwartz, Kessel, eds. New Anthology of Spanish Literature, 2 Vols. LC 67-18263. 1967. Vol. 1; x, 380. text ed. 27.50x (ISBN 0-8071-0344-6); Vol. 2; x, 506. text ed. 32.50x (ISBN 0-8071-0345-4). La State U Pr.

Chandler, Robert, tr. The Magic Ring & Other Russian Folktales. 112p. (gr. 3 up). 1979. pap. 3.95 (ISBN 0-571-13006-2). Faber & Faber.

Chandler, Robert, tr. see Afanasyev, Alexander.

Chandler, Robert F., Jr. Rice in the Tropics: A Guide to Development of National Programs. (IADS Development-Oriented Literature Ser.). 1979. lib. bdg. 24.50x (ISBN 0-89158-361-0). Westview.

Chandler, Robert W. War of Ideas: The U. S. Propaganda Compaign in Vietnam. LC 80-24127. (Special Studies in National Defense & Security Ser.). 320p. 1981. softcover 26.50x (ISBN 0-86531-082-3). Westview.

Chandler, S. B. Manzoni. 139p. 1974. 14.00x (ISBN 0-85224-247-6, Pub. by Edinburgh U Pr Scotland). Columbia U Pr.

Chandler, Stanley B. & Molinaro, J. A., eds. The World of Dante: Six Studies in Language & Thought. LC 66-7811. 1966. pap. 35.80 (ISBN 0-317-09697-4, 2020466). Bks Demand UMI.

Chandler, Susan & Chandler, David, eds. Favourite Stories from Cambodia. (Favourite Stories Ser.). 1978. pap. text ed. 2.50x (ISBN 0-686-60357-5, 00309). Heinemann Ed.

Chandler, T. J. Selected Bibliography on Urban Climate. 383p. (Orig.). 1970. pap. 35.00 (ISBN 0-685-04924-8, W90, WMO). Unipub.

--Urban Climatology & Its Relevance to Urban Design. (Technical Note Ser.: No. 149). (Illus.). 61p. 1976. pap. 15.00 (ISBN 0-685-68977-8, W198, WMO). Unipub.

Chandler, Ted, jt. auth. see Bloomfield, Robert.

Chandler, Ted, jt. auth. see Bloomfield, Robert L.

Chandler, Ted E. How to Have Good Health. LC 81-68045. 1982. 7.95 (ISBN 0-8054-5298-2). Broadman.

Chandler, Tertius. Approaches to Sex. 2nd ed. 12p. 1984. 2.00. Chandler Tertius.

--Chandler's Half-Encyclopedia. 2nd, rev. ed. (Illus.). 1670p. 1983. 200.00 (ISBN 0-9603872-2-6). Gutenberg.

--Godly Kings & Early Ethics. rev. ed. (Illus.). 220p. 1981. 24.00 (ISBN 0-9603872-4-2). Gutenberg.

--Remote Kingdoms. rev. ed. (Illus.). 111p. 1981. pap. 14.00 (ISBN 0-9603872-5-0). Gutenberg.

--The Tax We Need. 100p. (Orig.). 1980. pap. 5.00 (ISBN 0-9603872-3-4). Gutenberg.

--The Tax We Need. 2nd ed. 100p. 1984. pap. 5.00 (ISBN 0-9603872-3-4). Gutenberg.

Chandler, Tertius & Fox, Gerald. Three Thousand Years of Urban Growth. LC 72-84378. (Studies in Population Ser). 1974. 85.00 (ISBN 0-12-785109-7). Acad Pr.

Chandler, W. U., jt. auth. see Gibbons, John H.

Chandler, Walter M. The Trial of Jesus from a Lawyer's Standpoint, 2 vols. LC 83-82312. 1983. Repr. of 1925 ed. 115.00 set (ISBN 0-89941-294-7). W S Hein.

Chandler, William. Improving World Health: A Least Cost Strategy. (Worldwatch Institute Papers: No. 59). 66p. 1984. pap. 2.95 (ISBN 0-916468-59-3, WW59, WW). Unipub.

Chandler, William F. Carotid Artery Injuries. LC 81-71908. (Illus.). 192p. 1982. 22.50 (ISBN 0-87993-174-4). Futura Pub.

Chandler, William J. The Science of History: A Cybernetic Approach. (Studies in Cybernetics: Vol. 7). 160p. 1984. text ed. 37.00 (ISBN 2-88124-012-7). Gordon.

Chandler, William U. Energy Productivity: Key to Environmental Protection & Economic Progress. (Worldwatch Papers). 1985. pap. 4.00 (ISBN 0-916468-63-1). Worldwatch Inst.
--Investing in Children. (Worldwatch Papers). 1985. pap. 4.00 (ISBN 0-916468-64-X). Worldwatch Inst.
--Least-Cost Health Strategy. (Worldwatch Papers). 1984. pap. 4.00 (ISBN 0-916468-58-5). Worldwatch Inst.
--Materials Recycling: The Virtue of Necessity. LC 83-51109. (Worldwatch Papers). 1983. pap. 2.00 (ISBN 0-916468-55-0). Worldwatch Inst.
--Materials Recycling: The Virtue of Necessity. (Worldwatch Institute Papers: No. 56). 52p. 1984. pap. 2.95 (ISBN 0-916468-55-0, WW56, WW). Unipub.
--Myth of TVA: Conservation & Development in the Tennessee Valley, 1933-1983. LC 83-21333. 264p. 1984. prof. ref. 25.00x (ISBN 0-88410-976-3). Ballinger Pub.
Chandler, Zelphs E. Analysis of the Stylistic Technique of Addison, Johnson, Hazlitt & Pater. 1928. lib. bdg. 10.00 (ISBN 0-8414-3633-9). Folcroft.
Chandless, William. Visit to Salt Lake. LC 76-134391. Repr. of 1857 ed. 24.50 (ISBN 0-404-08434-6). AMS Pr.
Chandley, A. C., jt. auth. see Bond, D. J.
Chandmal, Asit. One Thousand Moons: Krishnamurti at Eighty-Five. (Illus.). 128p. 1985. 25.00 (ISBN 0-8109-1209-0). Abrams.
Chandoha, Walter, photos by. Puppies & Kittens. (Teddy Board Bks.). (Illus.). (ps). 1983. 3.50 (ISBN 0-448-40874-0, G&D). Putnam Pub Group.
Chandola, Anoop. Folk Drumming in the Himalayas. LC 76-23549. (Illus.). 1977. 29.50 (ISBN 0-404-15403-4). AMS Pr.
--Situation to Sentence: An Evolutionary Method for Descriptive Linguistics. LC 78-7125. 1978. 29.50 (ISBN 0-404-16038-7). AMS Pr.
--A Systematic Translation of Hindi-Urdū into English. LC 79-127886. 365p. 1970. pap. 12.50x (ISBN 0-8165-0289-7). U of Ariz Pr.
Chandon, Jean-Louis. A Comparative Study of Media Exposure Models. LC 84-46067. 631p. 1985. lib. bdg. 60.00 (ISBN 0-8240-6761-4). Garland Pub.
Chandonnet, Ann F. Ptarmigan Valley. LC 79-84634. (Lightning Tree Contemporary Poets Ser.: No. 5). 1980. 12.95 (ISBN 0-89016-054-6); pap. 4.95 (ISBN 0-89016-053-8). Lightning Tree.
Chandor, Anthony. Diccionario de Computadores. 402p. (Span.). 1975. leather 28.50 (ISBN 84-335-6411-0, S-31859). French & Eur.
--The Facts on File Dictionary of Micro Computers. 1981. 14.95 (ISBN 0-87196-597-6). Facts on File.
--The Penguin Dictionary of Microprocessors. 192p. 1981. pap. 5.95 (ISBN 0-14-051100-8). Penguin.
Chandor, Anthony, ed. Dictionary of Computers. (Reference Ser.). (Orig.). 1970. pap. 5.95 (ISBN 0-14-051039-7). Penguin.
Chandos, John. Boys Together: English Public Schools 1800-1864. LC 84-40192. (Illus.). 400p. 1984. 29.95x (ISBN 0-300-03215-3). Yale U Pr.
Chandra, Bipan. Communalism in Modern India. 363p. 1984. pap. text ed. 15.95x (ISBN 0-7069-2655-2, Pub. by Vikas India); text ed. 40.00x (ISBN 0-7069-2655-2). Advent NY.
--Nationalism & Colonialism in Modern India. 408p. 1979. 35.00x (ISBN 0-686-78885-0, Pub. by Orient Longman India). State Mutual Bk.
--Nationalism & Colonialism in Modern India. 408p. 1981. text ed. 32.50x (ISBN 0-86131-194-9, Pub. by Orient Longman Ltd India). Apt Bks.
Chandra, Bipan, ed. The Indian Left: Critical Appraisals. 1983. text ed. 45.00x (ISBN 0-7069-2103-8, Pub. by Vikas India). Advent NY.
Chandra, G. S. Sharat. The Ghost of Meaning. 1978. pap. 4.95 (ISBN 0-917652-11-8). Confluence Pr.
Chandra, Girish & Gupta, V. K. Ichneumonologia Orientalis, Pt. VII: The Tribes Lissonotini & Banchini (Hym: Ichneumonidae) (Oriental Insects Monograph: No. 7). 1977. 45.00x (ISBN 0-318-01585-4). Oriental Insects.
Chandra, Harish. Collected Papers. Varadarajan, V. S., ed. (Illus.). 2400p. 1984. 160.00 (ISBN 0-387-90782-3). Springer-Verlag.
Chandra, J. & Flaherty, J. E., eds. Computational Aspects of Penetration Mechanics. (Lecture Notes in Engineering: Vol. 3). 221p. 1983. pap. 19.00 (ISBN 0-387-12634-1). Springer-Verlag.
Chandra, J. & Scott, A. C., eds. Coupled Nonlinear Oscillators: Proceedings of the Joint U. S. Army-Center for Nonlinear Studies Workshop, Los Alamos, New Mexico, 21-23 July, 1981. (North-Holland Mathematics Studies: No. 80). 124p. 1983. 36.25 (ISBN 0-444-86677-9, North Holland). Elsevier.
Chandra, Jagdish, compiled by. Bibliography of Indian Art, History & Archaeology: Dr. Anand K. Coomanaswamy Memorial Volume, Vol. 1. 1978. text ed. 66.00x (ISBN 0-391-01072-7). Humanities.
Chandra, Jagdish, ed. Chaos in Nonlinear Dynamical Systems. LC 84-52603. viii, 191p. 1984. text ed. 25.00 (ISBN 0-89871-052-9). Soc Indus Appl Math.
Chandra, Kananur V. Black Student's Concern in a Black College. LC 75-36570. 1976. pap. 9.00 perfect bdg. softcover (ISBN 0-88247-375-1). R & E Pubs.
--Racial Discrimination in Canada: Asian Minorities. LC 73-76006. lib. bdg. 10.00 (ISBN 0-88247-208-9). R & E Pubs.
Chandra, Moti. World of Courtesans. 1974. 15.00x (ISBN 0-7069-0082-0). Intl Bk Dist.
Chandra, P., jt. auth. see Ramaiah, L. S.
Chandra, P., ed. Antiviral Mechanisms in the Control of Neoplasia. LC 78-10779. (NATO ASI Series A, Life Sciences: Vol. 20). 771p. 1979. 85.00x (ISBN 0-306-40063-4, Plenum Pr). Plenum Pub.
Chandra, Prakash. International Politics. 1980. text ed. 15.00x (ISBN 0-7069-0773-6, Pub by Vikas India). Advent NY.
Chandra, Prakash P., ed. Biochemical & Biological Markers of Neoplastic Transformations. (NATO ASI Series A, Life Sciences: Vol. 57). 650p. 1983. 89.50x (ISBN 0-306-41240-3, Plenum Press). Plenum Pub.
Chandra, Pramod. On the Study of Indian Art. (Illus.). 136p. 1983. text ed. 12.95x (ISBN 0-674-63762-3). Harvard U Pr.
--The Sculpture of India, 1300 BC-AD 3000. (Illus.). 224p. 1985. 60.00 (ISBN 0-674-79590-3). Harvard U Pr.
--The Scuplture of India, Three Thousand B.C. to Thirteen Hundred A.D. LC 85-4832. (Illus.). 224p. 1985. 20.00 (ISBN 0-89468-082-X). Natl Gallery Art.
--Studies in Indian Temple Architecture. LC 75-904089. 1975. 40.00x (ISBN 0-88386-649-8). South Asia Bks.
Chandra, R. K. & Newberne, P. M. Nutrition, Immunity & Infection: Mechanisms of Interaction. LC 77-21209. (Illus.). 262p. 1977. 29.50x (ISBN 0-306-31058-9, Plenum Pr). Plenum Pub.
Chandra, R. K., ed. Critical Reviews in Tropical Medicine, Vol. 1. 412p. 1982. 49.50X (ISBN 0-306-40959-3, Plenum Pr). Plenum Pub.
--Critical Reviews in Tropical Medicine, Vol. 2. 269p. 1984. 45.00x (ISBN 0-306-41561-5, Plenum Pr). Plenum Pub.
--Food Intolerance. 224p. 1984. 29.50 (ISBN 0-444-00743-1, Biomedical Pr). Elsevier.
--The Liver & Biliary Tract in Infants & Children. (Illus.). 1979. text ed. 59.50 (ISBN 0-443-01456-6). Churchill.
--Nutrition, Immunity & Illness in the Elderly: Proceedings of An International Conference on Nutrition, Immunity & Illness in the Elderly, St. John's, Newfoundland, Canada, July 9-11, 1984. 400p. 1985. 45.00 (ISBN 0-08-032404-5, Pub. by Aberdeen Scotland). Pergamon.
--Progress in Food & Nutrition Science. (Illus.). 198p. 1984. pap. 84.00 (ISBN 0-08-030928-3). Pergamon.
Chandra, Ram. Road to Freedom: Revealing Sidelights. 362p. 1980. 29.95x (ISBN 0-940500-21-3); lib. bdg. 29.95x (ISBN 0-686-92327-8). Asia Bk Corp.
Chandra, Ramesh. Introductory Physics of Nuclear Medicine. 2nd ed. LC 81-17149. (Illus.). 237p. 1982. text ed. 17.50 (ISBN 0-8121-0826-4). Lea & Febiger.
Chandra, Ranjit K., ed. Trace Elements in Nutrition of Children. (Nestle Nutrition Workshop Ser.: Vol. 8). 336p. 1985. text ed. 28.50 (ISBN 0-88167-117-7). Raven.
Chandra, S. Superionic Solids: Principles & Applications. 404p. 1981. 74.50 (ISBN 0-444-86039-8, North-Holland). Elsevier.
Chandra, S., ed. Edible Aroids. (Illus.). 1984. 34.95x (ISBN 0-19-859486-0). Oxford U Pr.
Chandra, Satish. Regionalism & National Integration. 1976. 12.50x (ISBN 0-88386-870-9). South Asia Bks.
Chandra, Satish & Masterman, L., eds. Curricula & Syllabi in Hydrology. 2nd ed. (Technical Papers in Hydrology: No. 22). (Illus.). 111p. 1983. pap. text ed. 12.25 (ISBN 92-3-102106-0, U1310, UNESCO). Unipub.
Chandra, Subrato see Marier, Donald & Stoiaken, Larry.
Chandra, Suresh. Photoelectrochemical Solar Cells. (Electrocomponent Science Monographs: Vol. 5). 245p. 1985. text ed. 59.00 (ISBN 2-88124-014-3). Gordon.
Chandra, T. P., jt. auth. see Ramaiah, L. S.
Chandra Das, S. Tibetan-English Dictionary: With Sanskrit Synonyms. Sanberg, Graham & Heyde, A. William, eds. 1389p. (Tibetan & Eng.). 1976. Repr. 37.50 (ISBN 0-89581-177-4). Asian Human Pr.
Chandralekha. The Hindu Temple. 200p. 1982. 49.00x (ISBN 0-686-94078-4, Pub. by Garlandfold England). State Mutual Bk.
Chandras, Kananur V. Arab, Armenian, Syrian, Lebanese, East Indian, Pakistani & Bangla Deshi Americans: A Study Guide & Source Book. LC 77-81032. 1977. soft bdg. 8.00 (ISBN 0-88247-475-8). R & E Pubs.
--Four Thousand Years of Indian Education: A Short History of the Hindu, Buddhist & Moslem Periods. LC 77-81034. 1977. soft bdg. 11.95 (ISBN 0-88247-474-X). R & E Pubs.
Chandras, Kananur V., ed. Racial Discrimination Against Neither-White-nor-Black American Minorities. LC 77-91409. 1978. soft cover 12.00 (ISBN 0-88247-497-9). R & E Pubs.
Chandrasekaran, B. & Radicchi, S., eds. Computer Program Testing. 362p. 1981. 42.75 (ISBN 0-444-86292-7, North-Holland). Elsevier.
Chandrasekaran, C. & Hermalin, A. I., eds. Measuring the Effect of Family Planning Programs on Fertility. 570p. 1976. 45.00 (ISBN 0-685-90711-2, ORD5, ORDINA). Unipub.
Chandrasekaran, S. K., ed. Controlled Release Systems. LC 81-8019. (AICHE Symposium Ser.: Vol. 77). 85p. 1981. pap. 22.00 (ISBN 0-8169-0202-X, S-206); pap. 12.00 members (ISBN 0-686-47543-7). Am Inst Chem Eng.
Chandrasekhar, S. Abortion in a Crowded World: The Problem of Abortion with Special Reference to India. LC 73-19750. (John Danz Lecture Ser.). 150p. 1974. 17.50x (ISBN 0-295-95317-9). U of Wash Pr.
--Eddington: The Most Distinguished Astrophysicist of His Time. 64p. 1984. 12.50 (ISBN 0-521-25746-8). Cambridge U Pr.
--Hydrodynamic & Hydromagnetic Stability. (Illus.). 704p. pap. 11.95 (ISBN 0-486-64071-X). Dover.
--Infant Mortality, Population Growth & Family Planning in India. LC 78-170290. (Illus.). 399p. 1972. 27.50 (ISBN 0-8078-1185-8). U of NC Pr.
--Liquid Crystals. LC 75-32913. (Cambridge Monographs in Physics). (Illus.). 1977. 90.00 (ISBN 0-521-21149-2). Cambridge U Pr.
--Liquid Crystals. (Cambridge Monographs in Physics). (Illus.). 352p. 1980. pap. 29.95 (ISBN 0-521-29841-5). Cambridge U Pr.
--The Mathematical Theory of Black Holes. (International Series of Monographs on Physics). (Illus.). 1982. 110.00x (ISBN 0-19-851291-0). Oxford U Pr.
--Plasma Physics. LC 60-7234. (Midway Reprint Ser.). (Illus.). x, 218p. 1975. pap. text ed. 8.00x (ISBN 0-226-10085-5). U of Chicago Pr.
Chandrasekhar, S., ed. From India to America: A Brief History of Immigration, Admission & Assimilation. LC 82-60824. 111p. 1982. 25.00 (ISBN 0-9609080-0-5); pap. 10.00. Population Review.
Chandrasekhar, Sripati. Dirty Filthy Book: The Writings of Charles Knowlton & Annie Besant on Birth Control & Reproductive Physiology & an Account of the Bradlaugh-Pesant Trial. LC 80-15570. 1981. 19.95 (ISBN 0-520-04168-2). U of Cal Pr.
Chandrasekhar, Sripati, ed. Asia's Population Problems: With a Discussion of Population & Immigration in Australia. LC 76-57691. (Illus.). 1977. Repr. of 1967 ed. lib. bdg. 19.75x (ISBN 0-8371-9468-7, CHAPP). Greenwood.
Chandrasekhar, Subrahmanyan. An Introduction to the Study of Stellar Structure. 1939. pap. 8.95 (ISBN 0-486-60413-6). Dover.
--Radiative Transfer. (Illus.). 1960. pap. 7.95 (ISBN 0-486-60590-6). Dover.
Chandrasekharan, K. Arithmetical Functions. LC 72-102384. (Die Grundlehren der Mathematischen Wissenschaften: Vol. 167). (Illus.). 1971. 39.00 (ISBN 0-387-05114-7). Springer-Verlag.
--Elliptic Functions. (Grundlehren der Mathematischen Wissenschaften: Vol. 281). (Illus.). 190p. 1985. 48.00 (ISBN 0-387-15295-4). Springer Verlag.
--Introduction to Analytic Number Theory. LC 68-21990. (Die Grundlehren der Mathematischen Wissenschaften: Vol. 14). (Illus.). 1968. 21.00 (ISBN 0-387-04141-9). Springer-Verlag.
Chandrasekharan, K., jt. auth. see Bochner, S.
Chandrasekharan, K. R. Bhabani Bhattacharya. (Indian Writers Ser.). 1976. 8.50 (ISBN 0-89253-505-9). Ind-US Inc.
Chandris, Eugenia. Venus Syndrome: A Four-Step Plan for Improving the Bottom-Heavy Figure. LC 84-10108. (Illus.). 304p. 1985. 15.95 (ISBN 0-385-19253-3). Doubleday.
Chandurkar, P. J. Plant Anatomy. 256p. 1974. 40.00x (ISBN 0-686-84462-9, Pub. by Oxford & I B H India). State Mutual Bk.
Chandy, K. & Yeh, Raymond T., eds. Current Trends in Programming Methodology: Software Modeling, Vol. 3. (Illus.). 1978. ref. 34.95 (ISBN 0-13-195727-9). P-H.
Chandy, Mani K., jt. auth. see Sauer, Charles.
Chaneles, Sol, ed. Counseling Juvenile Offenders in Institutional Settings. (Journal of Offender Counseling Services & Rehabilitation Ser.: Vol. 6, No. 3). 85p. 1983. pap. text ed. 8.95 (ISBN 0-86656-170-6, B170). Haworth Pr.
--Current Trends in Correctional Education, Vol. 7, Nos. 3-4. LC 83-18542. (Journal of Offender Counseling, Services & Rehabilitation: Vol. 7. nos. 3-4). 117p. 1983. text ed. 17.95 (ISBN 0-86656-268-0). Haworth Pr.
--Gender Issues, Sex Offenses & Criminal Justice: Current Trends. LC 84-15830. (Journal of Offender Counseling, Services, & Rehabilitation Ser.: Vol. 9, Nos. 1 & 2). 170p. 1984. text ed. 19.95 (ISBN 0-86656-357-1). Haworth Pr.
--Prisons & Prisoners: Historical Documents. (Journal of Offender Counseling, Services & Rehabiliation Ser.: Vol. 10, Nos. 1-2). 312p. 1985. text ed. write for info. (ISBN 0-86656-464-0). Haworth Pr.
--Strategies of Intervention with Public Offenders. LC 82-15383. (Journal of Offender Counseling, Services & Rehabilitation Ser.: Vol. 6, Nos. 1-2). 137p. 1982. pap. text ed. 11.95 (ISBN 0-86656-171-4, B171). Haworth Pr.
Chaney & Putnam, eds. Electronic Properties Research Literature Retrieval Guide 1972-1976, 4 vols. LC 79-16082. 1374p. 1979. Set. 375.00x (ISBN 0-306-68010-6, IFI Plenum). Plenum Pub.
Chaney, jt. ed. see Demars.
Chaney, Charles. Church Planting in America at the End of the Twentieth Century. 128p. 1982. pap. 6.95 (ISBN 0-8423-0279-4). Tyndale.
Chaney, Charles & Skee, Stanley. Plaster Mold & Model Making. LC 80-21932. 144p. 1981. Repr. of 1973 ed. text ed. 14.00 (ISBN 0-89874-282-X). Krieger.
Chaney, Charles L. Birth of Missions in America. LC 75-26500. 352p. 1976. pap. 7.95 (ISBN 0-87808-146-1). William Carey Lib.
Chaney, Charles L. & Lewis, Ron S. Design for Church Growth. LC 77-87364. 1978. pap. 6.95 (ISBN 0-8054-6218-X). Broadman.
--Manual for Design for Church Growth. 1978. pap. text ed. 2.50 (ISBN 0-8054-6219-8). Broadman.
Chaney, David. Fictions & Ceremonies: The Ethnography of Popular Narratives. LC 78-31437. 1979. 25.00 (ISBN 0-312-28814-X). St Martin.
Chaney, Earlyne. The Masters & Astara. 2nd ed. (Illus.). 100p. 1982. pap. 8.95 (ISBN 0-918936-13-6). Astara.
Chaney, Earlyne & Messick, William L. Kundalini & the Third Eye. Chaney, Sita, ed. LC 80-67635. (Illus.). 127p. 1982. pap. 12.95 (ISBN 0-918936-08-X). Astara.
Chaney, Earlyne C. Revelations of Things to Come. (Illus.), 156p. 1982. pap. 13.95 (ISBN 0-918936-12-8). Astara.
--Secrets from Mt. Shasta. 70p. 1953. pap. 7.95 (ISBN 0-918936-10-1). Astara.
--Shining Moments of a Mystic. LC 76-24187. 56p. 1976. pap. 3.95 (ISBN 0-918936-19-5). Astara.
Chaney, Elsa M. Supermadre: Women in Politics in Latin America. LC 79-620012. (Latin American Monographs: No. 50). 222p. 1979. text ed. 17.50x (ISBN 0-292-77554-7). U of Tex Pr.
Chaney, Elsa M., jt. auth. see Bunster, Ximena.
Chaney, Elsa M., jt. auth. see Sutton, Constance R.
Chaney, Harriet S., jt. auth. see Beare, Patricia.
Chaney, J. F. & Ramdas, V., eds. Thermophysical Properties Research Literature Retrieval Guide 1900-1980, Vol. 5: Oxide Mixtures & Minerals. LC 81-15776. 414p. 1982. 85.00x (ISBN 0-306-67225-1, Plenum Pr). Plenum Pub.
--Thermophysical Properties Research Literature Retrieval Guide 1900-1980, Vol. 4: Alloys, Intermetallic Compounds & Ceramics. LC 81-15776. 736p. 1982. 125.00x (ISBN 0-306-67224-3, Plenum Pr). Plenum Pub.
--Thermophysical Properties Research Literature Retrieval Guide 1900-1980, Vol. 7: Coatings, Systems, Composites, Foods, Animal & Vegetable Products. LC 81-15776. 642p. 1982. 110.00x (ISBN 0-306-67227-8, Plenum Pr); Set of 7 Vols. 750.00 (ISBN 0-686-97458-1). Plenum Pub.
--Thermophysical Properties Research Literature Retrieval Guide 1900-1980, Vol. 6: Mixtures & Solutions. LC 81-155776. 498p. 1982. 95.00x (ISBN 0-306-67226-X, Plenum Pr). Plenum Pub.
--Thermophysical Properties Research Literature Retrieval Guide 1900-1980, Vol. 2: Inorganic Compounds. LC 81-15776. 1094p. 1982. 195.00x (ISBN 0-306-67222-7, Plenum Pr). Plenum Pub.
--Thermophysical Properties Research Literature Retrieval Guide 1900-1980, Vol. 3: Organic Compounds & Polymeric Materials. 2nd ed. LC 81-15776. 630p. 1982. 115.00x (ISBN 0-306-67223-5, Plenum Pr). Plenum Pub.
--Thermophysical Properties Research Literature Retrieval Guide 1900-1980, Vol. 1: Elements. LC 81-15776. 804p. 1982. 135.00x (ISBN 0-306-67221-9, Plenum Pr). Plenum Pub.
Chaney, Katherine & Shaw, Don. Pathfinder: A Backpacker's Guide. (Illus.). 128p. (YA) (gr. 11 up). 1980. pap. 6.95 (ISBN 0-87670-060-1). Athletic Inst.
Chaney, Margaret S., et al. Nutrition. 9th ed. LC 78-69546. (Illus.). 1979. text ed. 31.95 (ISBN 0-395-25448-5). HM.
Chaney, Norman. Theodore Roethke: The Poetics of Wonder. LC 81-40571. 130p. (Orig.). 1982. lib. bdg. 22.00 (ISBN 0-8191-2013-8); pap. text ed. 9.25 (ISBN 0-8191-2014-6). U Pr of Amer.
Chaney, Ralph W. & Sanborn, Ethel I. Goshen Flora of West Central Oregon. Repr. 19.00 (ISBN 0-384-08461-3). Johnson Repr.
Chaney, Robert. Mysticism: The Journey Within. LC 79-52959. 1979. softcover 12.50 (ISBN 0-918936-06-3). Astara.
Chaney, Robert, jt. auth. see Pevarnik, Carrie.
Chaney, Robert G. The Essenes & Their Ancient Mysteries. (Adventures in Esoteric Learning Ser.). 1968. pap. 4.25 (ISBN 0-918936-14-4). Astara.
--Reincarnation: Cycle of Opportunity. LC 84-72387. (Adventures in Esoteric Learning Ser.). (Illus.). 56p. 1984. pap. 4.25 (ISBN 0-918936-13-6). Astara.
--Think on New Levels. (Adventures in Esoteric Learning Ser.). 56p. 1963. pap. 4.25 (ISBN 0-918936-16-0). Astara.
--Transmutation. (Adventures in Esoteric Learning Ser.). 56p. 1969. pap. 4.25 (ISBN 0-918936-17-9). Astara.

--Unfolding the Third Eye. (Adventures in Esoteric Learning Ser.). 48p. 1970. pap. 4.25 (ISBN 0-918936-18-7). Astara.

Chaney, Sita, ed. see Chaney, Earlyne & Messick, William L.

Chaney, Victor. Passing Through. LC 85-50097. 74p. 1985. 5.95 (ISBN 0-938232-34-7). Winston-Derek.

Chaney, Warren H. & Beech, Thomas R. The Union Epidemic: A Prescription for Supervisors. LC 76-24132. 180p. 1977. 33.00 (ISBN 0-912862-28-9). Aspen Systems.

Chang. Chinese Cooking: Quick & Easy. 4.95x (ISBN 0-685-70742-3). Wehman.

--Tumors of the Central Nervous System. LC 81-17125. (Illus.). 264p. 1982. 57.50 (ISBN 0-89352-137-X). Masson Pub.

Chang, jt. auth. see Godfrey.

Chang & Hudson, eds. Methods & Models for Predicting Fatigue Crack Growth under Random Loading - STP 748. 140p. 1981. 16.50 (ISBN 0-8031-0715-3, 04-748000-30). ASTM.

Chang, A. I. The Tao of Architecture. 1981. 14.50x (ISBN 0-691-03963-1); pap. 5.95x (ISBN 0-691-00330-0). Princeton U Pr.

Chang, Arnold. Painting in the People's Republic of China: The Politics of Style. (Westview Replica Edition Ser.). 1980. 19.00x (ISBN 0-89158-676-8). Westview.

Chang, C. C. Buddhist Teaching of Totality. LC 70-136965. 1971. 24.50x (ISBN 0-271-01179-3); pap. 12.50x (ISBN 0-271-01142-4). Pa St U Pr.

Chang, C. C. & Keisler, H. J. Model Theory. 2nd ed. (Studies in Logic & the Foundations of Mathematics Ser.: Vol. 73). 552p. 1977. 76.50 (ISBN 0-7204-2273-6, North-Holland); pap. 36.25 (ISBN 0-7204-0692-7). Elsevier.

Chang, C. C., ed. see Catholic University of America, Washington, D.C., June 11-14, 1963.

Chang, C. M., ed. see ASME-ASLE Lubrication Conference, Washington, DC, Oct. 1982.

Chang, C. Nora, jt. ed. see Barnett, Gene.

Chang, C. S. The Japanese Auto Industry & the U.S. Market. LC 81-11901. 224p. 1981. 34.95 (ISBN 0-03-059733-1). Praeger.

Chang, C. W. Increasing Food Production Through Education, Research & Extension. (Freedom from Hunger Campaign Basic Studies: No. 9). 78p. (Orig., 2nd Printing 1965). 1962. pap. 5.25 (ISBN 92-5-101637-2, F240, FAO). Unipub.

Chang, Carsun. The Development of Neo-Confucian Thought. LC 77-8338. 1977. Repr. of 1957 ed. lib. bdg. 26.25x (ISBN 0-8371-9693-0, CHDN). Greenwood.

--The Development of Neo-Confucian Thought, Vol. 1. 1957. pap. 9.95x (ISBN 0-8084-0105-X); 12.95x (ISBN 0-8084-0104-1). New Coll U Pr.

Chang, Charlotte M., jt. ed. see Livingston, G. E.

Chang, Chih-Tung. China's Only Hope: An Appeal by Her Greatest Viceroy with the Sanction of the Present Emperor, Kwang Su. LC 74-10099. (China Studies: from Confusius to Mao Ser). (Illus.). 151p. 1975. Repr. of 1900 ed. 17.60 (ISBN 0-88355-164-0). Hyperion Conn.

Chang, Chin-Liang. Introduction to Artificial Intelligence Techniques. LC 85-60670. 182p. (Orig.). 1985. pap. 18.00 (ISBN 0-9614742-0-3). JMA Pr.

Chang, Chin-Liang & Lee, Richard C. Symbolic Logic & Mechanical Theorem Proving. (Computer Science & Applied Mathematics Ser). 1973. 65.00 (ISBN 0-12-170350-9). Acad Pr.

Chang, Ching-sheng. Sex Histories: China's First Modern Treatise on Sex Education. 3rd ed. Levy, Howard S., tr. (Orig.). 1970. pap. 10.00 (ISBN 0-910878-03-X). Oriental Bk Store.

Chang, Ching-Yu, ed. Davis, Brody & Associates, Architects. (Stylos: Architecture International Ser.: No. 3). (Illus.). 1979. pap. 18.50 (ISBN 0-89860-031-6). Eastview.

--Landscape Architecture. (Stylos: Architecture International Ser.: No. 2). (Illus.). 1979. pap. 18.50 (ISBN 0-89860-030-8). Eastview.

--Phenomenal Architecture: Cesar Pelli. (Stylos: Architecture International Ser.: No. 1). (Illus.). 1979. pap. 18.50 (ISBN 0-89860-029-4). Eastview.

Chang, Chung-Fu. The Anglo-Japanese Alliance. LC 78-64282. (Johns Hopkins University. Studies in the Social Sciences. Extra Volumes-New Ser.: 12). Repr. of 1931 ed. 26.00 (ISBN 0-404-61382-9). AMS Pr.

Chang, Chung-Li. Chinese Gentry: Studies on Their Role in 19th-Century Chinese Society. LC 55-6738. (Washington Paperbacks on Russia & Asia: No. 4). (Illus.). 272p. 1967. 20.00x (ISBN 0-295-73743-3). U of Wash Pr.

--The Income of the Chinese Gentry. LC 81-6471. (University of Washington Publications on Asia Ser.). xvii, 369p. 1981. Repr. of 1962 ed. lib. bdg. 35.00x (ISBN 0-313-23106-0, CHIC). Greenwood.

Chang, Chung-Li, jt. auth. see Michael, Franz.

Chang, Constance D. Chinese Cooking. (Quick & Easy Ser.). (Illus.). 60p. (Orig.). 1969. pap. 3.95 (ISBN 4-07-973719-X, Pub. by Shufunmato Co Ltd Japan). C E Tuttle.

--Chinese Cooking at Home. (Illus.). 60p. 1977. pap. 4.95 (ISBN 4-07-972418-7, Pub. by Shufunotomo Co Ltd Japan). C E Tuttle.

--Chinese Cooking Lessons. (Illus.). 122p. 1976. 9.95 (ISBN 4-07-972341-5, Pub. by Shufunmoto Co Ltd Japan). C E Tuttle.

--The Chinese Menu Cookbook. (Illus.). 64p. 1980. 7.95 (ISBN 4-07-973470-0, Pub. by Shufunotomo Co. Ltd Japan). C E Tuttle.

--The Japanese Menu Cookbook. (Illus.). 69p. 1975. 7.95 (ISBN 4-07-972275-3, Pub. by Shufunmoto Co Ltd Japan). C E Tuttle.

Chang, Dae H. Introduction to Criminal Justice: Theory & Application. (Orig.). 1979. pap. text ed. 16.95 (ISBN 0-8403-2102-3). Kendall-Hunt.

Chang, Dae H., jt. ed. see Iacovetta, Ronald G.

Chang, Dae H., jt. ed. see Zastrow, Charles H.

Chang, David, tr. see Morgan, G. Campbell.

Chang, David W. Zhou Enlai & Deng Xiaping in the Chinese Leadership Succession Crisis. LC 83-16863. 410p. (Orig.). 1984. lib. bdg. 28.50 (ISBN 0-8191-3586-0); pap. text ed. 16.75 (ISBN 0-8191-3587-9). U Pr of Amer.

Chang, Diana. What Matisse Is After. (Poetry Ser.). (Illus.). 60p. (Orig.). 1985. pap. 4.00 (ISBN 0-936556-12-9). Contact Two.

Chang, Donald, jt. auth. see Mitchell, John D.

Chang, Donald C., et al, eds. Structure & Function of Excitable Cells. 516p. 1983. 65.00x (ISBN 0-306-41338-8, Plenum Pr). Plenum Pub.

Chang, Dorothy K. A Guide of Understanding & Teaching of Mexican-American Adolescents. LC 73-78064. pap. 10.00 (ISBN 0-88247-220-8). R & E Pubs.

Chang, Ducksoo. British Methods of Industrial Peace. LC 68-58556. (Columbia University Studies in the Social Sciences: No. 425). Repr. of 1936 ed. 24.50 (ISBN 0-404-51425-1). AMS Pr.

Chang, Edward C., tr. see Cleland, Nona.

Chang, Fa-Hwa. Applied Strength of Materials. 459p. 1986. text ed. price not set (ISBN 0-02-322320-0). Macmillan.

Chang, Florence C. Believe It or Not: An Anthology of Ancient Tales Retold. LC 80-68258. (Chinese Can Be Fun Bks.: Level 5). (Illus.). 80p. (gr. 10-12). 1980. pap. 5.75x (wkbk. incl.) (ISBN 0-936620-02-1). Ginkgo Hut.

--China Is Farther Than the Sun? A Beginning Chinese-English Reader. LC 80-68256. (Chinese Can Be Fun Bks.: Level 2). (Illus.). 51p. (gr. 3-4). 1980. pap. 5.00x (wkbk. incl.) (ISBN 0-936620-00-5). Ginkgo Hut.

--Chinese-Can-Be-Fun-Workbooks for Textbooks: Levels 2, 4, 5. (Chinese-Can Be-Fun-Textbooks). 44p. 1981. pap. 2.00 ea. (ISBN 0-936620-02-1). Ginkgo Hut.

--Maomao & Mimi. LC 81-80784. (Chinese Can Be Fun Bks.: Level 3). (Illus.). 80p. (Orig.). (gr. 5-6). 1981. pap. 3.90x (ISBN 0-936620-05-6). Ginkgo Hut.

--Puppy's Tail. (Chinese Can Be Fun Bks.: Level 1). (Illus.). 72p. (Orig.). (gr. 1-2). 1981. pap. 3.90x (ISBN 0-936620-06-4). Ginkgo Hut.

--With Sound & Color: An Intermediate Chinese-English Reader. LC 80-68257. (Chinese Can Be Fun Bks.: Level 4). (Illus.). 71p. (Orig.). (gr. 7-9). 1980. pap. 5.50x (wkbk. incl.) (ISBN 0-936620-01-3). Ginkgo Hut.

Chang, Garma C. Teachings of Tibetan Yoga. 128p. 1974. pap. 3.45 (ISBN 0-8065-0460-9). Citadel Pr.

Chang, Garma C., ed. A Treasury of Mahayana Sutras: Selections from the Maharatnakuta Sutra. Buddhist Association of the United States, tr. from Chinese. LC 82-42776. (Institute for Advanced Study of World Religions (IASWR) Ser.). 512p. 1983. 26.75x (ISBN 0-271-00341-3). Pa St U Pr.

Chang, Garma C., tr. from Tibetan. The Hundred Thousand Songs of Milarepa, 2 Vols. LC 76-55120. 1977. pap. 14.95 ea.; Vol. 1, 356p. (ISBN 0-87773-095-4, 73346-0); Vol. 2, 374p. (ISBN 0-87773-096-2, 72996-X). Shambhala Pubns.

Chang, Ginger. Guide to Vancouver's Chinese Restaurants. (Illus.). 136p. (Orig.). 1985. pap. 7.95 (ISBN 0-88839-995-2). Hancock House.

Chang, H. Allegory & Courtesy in Spenser. 1955. lib. bdg. 10.00 (ISBN 0-8414-3351-8). Folcroft.

--Magnetic Bubble Memory Technology. (Electrical Engineering & Electronics Ser.: Vol. 6). 1978. 35.00 (ISBN 0-8247-6795-0). Dekker.

Chang, H. C., ed. Chinese Literature: Popular Fiction & Drama. 466p. 1982. pap. 15.00x (ISBN 0-231-05367-3). Columbia U Pr.

Chang, H. C., ed. & tr. Chinese Literature: Tales of the Supernatural. (Chinese Literature in Translation Ser.). 169p. 1983. 21.00x (ISBN 0-231-05794-6). Columbia U Pr.

Chang, H. C., tr. from Chinese. Chinese Literature: Nature Poetry, Vol. 2. LC 73-79265. (Chinese Literature Ser.). 124p. 1977. 14.00x (ISBN 0-231-04288-4). Columbia U Pr.

Chang, H. M., et al, eds. Advances in Chinese Medicinal Materials Research: Proceedings of the International Symposium, Hong Kong, June 12-14, 1984. 600p. 1984. 80.00x (ISBN 9971-966-71-9, Pub. by World Sci Singapore). Taylor & Francis.

Chang, Hao. Liang Ch'i-Ch'ao & Intellectual Transition in China, 1890-1907. LC 75-162635. (East Asian Ser: No. 64). 1971. 20.00x (ISBN 0-674-53009-8). Harvard U Pr.

Chang, Herbert Y., et al. Fault Diagnosis of Digital Systems. LC 74-6455. 174p. 1974. Repr. of 1970 ed. 10.95 (ISBN 0-88275-174-3). Krieger.

Chang, Hsin. Allegory & Courtesy in Spenser. LC 75-30924. (English Literature Ser., No. 33). 1975. lib. bdg. 43.95x (ISBN 0-8383-2100-3). Haskell.

Chang, Hsin-Chang. Allegory & Courtesy in Spencer. 1978. Repr. of 1955 ed. lib. bdg. 30.00 (ISBN 0-8495-0840-1). Arden Lib.

Chang, Hsu, ed. Magnetic Bubble Technology: Integrated Circuit Magnetics for Digital Storage & Processing. LC 73-87653. 712p. 1975. 47.80 (ISBN 0-87942-034-0, PC00521). Inst Electrical.

Chang, Huan-Yang & Over, Ira Earl. Selected Numerical Methods & Computer Programs for Chemical Engineers. 235p. (Orig.). 1980. pap. text ed. 11.95 (ISBN 0-88408-131-1). Sterling Swift.

Chang, James W. A Field Guide to the Birds of Taiwan (Formosa) (Illus.). 336p. 1981. 38.00x (ISBN 0-686-34578-9). IR Pubns.

Chang, John B., ed. Vascular Surgery. LC 85-2319. 275p. 1985. text ed. 48.95 (ISBN 0-89335-232-2). SP Med & Sci Bks.

Chang, Jolan. The Tao of Love & Sex: The Ancient Chinese Way to Ecstasy. 1977. pap. 8.50 (ISBN 0-525-47453-6, 0826-240). Dutton.

--The Tao of the Loving Couple: True Liberation Through the Tao. (Illus.). 129p. 1983. 15.95 (ISBN 0-525-24183-3, 01549-460); pap. 8.95 (ISBN 0-525-48042-0, 0869-260). Dutton.

Chang, Julius see Alder, B., et al.

Chang, K. C. Art, Myth, & Ritual: The Path to Political Authority in Ancient China. (Illus.). 160p. 1983. text ed. 18.50x (ISBN 0-674-04807-5). Harvard U Pr.

--Early Chinese Civilization: Anthropological Perspectives. (Harvard-Yenching Institute Monograph Ser.). (Illus.). 252p. 1976. 16.50x (ISBN 0-674-21999-6). Harvard U Pr.

Chang, K. C., ed. Food in Chinese Culture: Anthropological & Historical Perspectives. LC 75-43312. (Illus.). 448p. 1981. 41.00 (ISBN 0-300-01938-6); pap. 11.95x (ISBN 0-300-02759-1, Y-402). Yale U Pr.

Chang, K. C., et al, trs. see Wang, Zhongshu.

Chang, K. W. & Howes, F. A. Nonlinear Singular Perturbation Phenomena: Theory & Applications. (Applied Mathematical Sciences Ser.: Vol. 56). (Illus.). viii, 180p. 1984. pap. 18.80 (ISBN 0-387-96066-X). Springer-Verlag.

Chang, Kang-I S. The Evolution of Chinese Tz'u Poetry: From Late T'ang to Northern Sung. LC 79-3195. (Illus.). 1980. 26.00 (ISBN 0-691-06425-3). Princeton U Pr.

Chang, Kathleen. The Iron Moonhunter: Bilingual in Chinese & English. LC 77-73783. (Fifth World Tales Ser.). (Illus.). (gr. k-6). 1978. pap. 4.95 (ISBN 0-89239-011-5, Imprenta de Libros Infantiles). Childrens Book Pr.

Chang, King-yuh. A Perspectives on Development in Mainland China. (Replica Edition Ser.). 510p. 1985. pap. 35.00x (ISBN 0-86531-858-1). Westview.

Chang, Kuo Sin. Mao Tse-Tung & His China. LC 79-112635. (Orig.). 1978. pap. text ed. 10.95x (ISBN 0-686-71778-3, 00125). Heinemann Ed.

Chang, Kwang-Chih. The Archaeology of Ancient China. 3rd rev. & enlarged ed. LC 77-23212. (Illus.). 1977. 45.00x (ISBN 0-300-02144-5); pap. 14.95x (ISBN 0-300-02145-3). Yale U Pr.

--Fengpitou, Tapenkeng & the Prehistory of Taiwan. LC 69-11698. (Publications in Anthropology: No. 73). 1969. pap. 15.00 (ISBN 0-913516-06-6). Yale U Anthro.

--Shang Civilization. LC 79-19107. (Illus.). 1980. 42.00x (ISBN 0-300-02428-2); pap. 11.95x (ISBN 0-300-02885-7, Y-435). Yale U Pr.

Chang, Leroy L. & Giessen, B. C., eds. Synthetic Modulated Structures. (Materials Science & Technology Ser.). Date not set. 87.00 (ISBN 0-12-170470-X). Acad Pr.

Chang, Leroy L. & Ploog, Klaus, eds. Molecular Beam Epitaxy & Heterostructures. 1985. lib. bdg. 90.00 (ISBN 90-247-3118-6, Pub. by Martinus Nijloff Netherlands). Kluwer Academic.

Chang, Lit-Sen. Transcendental Meditation. 1978. pap. 2.95 (ISBN 0-87552-133-9). Presby & Reformed.

--True Gospel vs. Social Activism. 1976. pap. 0.60 (ISBN 0-87552-134-7). Presby & Reformed.

Chang, Louis W. A Color Atlas & Manual for Applied Histochemistry. (Illus.). 126p. 1979. photocopy ed. spiral 17.50x (ISBN 0-398-03914-3). C C Thomas.

Chang, Lucia S. & Most, Kenneth S. The Perceived Usefulness of Financial Statements for Investors' Decisions. LC 84-25788. xiv, 160p. 1985. pap. 15.00 (ISBN 0-8130-0752-6). U Presses Fla.

Chang, Luke T. China Boundary Treaties & Frontier Disputes. LC 82-3483. 256p. 1982. 45.00 (ISBN 0-379-20733-8). Oceana.

Chang, M. S., jt. auth. see Chang, R.

Chang, Margaret S., jt. auth. see Chang, Raymond.

Chang, Maria H., jt. auth. see Gregor, A. J.

Chang, Maria H., jt. auth. see Gregor, A. James.

Chang, N. P., ed. Five Decades of Weak Interactions, Vol. 294. (Annals of the New York Academy of Sciences Ser.). 102p. 1977. 12.00x (ISBN 0-89072-040-1). NY Acad Sci.

Chang, Ning-San. Image Analysis & Image Database Management. Stone, Harold S., ed. LC 81-10406. (Computer Science: Artificial Intelligence Ser.: No. 9). 154p. 1981. 34.95 (ISBN 0-8357-1217-6). UMI Res Pr.

Chang, Pao-Min. Beijing, Hanoi & the Overseas Chinese. (China Research Monographs: No. 24). 1982. pap. 8.00x (ISBN 0-912966-50-5). IEAS.

Chang, Parris H. Elite Conflict in the Post-Mao China. rev. ed. (Occasional Papers--Reprints Series in Contemporary Asian Studies: No. 2-1983 (55)). 45p. 1983. pap. text ed. 2.50 (ISBN 0-942182-54-5). U MD Law.

--Power & Policy in China. 2nd, enl. ed. LC 78-50773. (Illus.). 1978. 24.95x (ISBN 0-271-00543-2); pap. text ed. 12.50x (ISBN 0-271-00544-0). Pa St U Pr.

Chang, Paul see Aisner, Joseph.

Chang, Paul K. Control of Flow Separation: Energy Conservation, Operational Efficiency & Safety. (McGraw-Hill Series in Thermal & Fluids Engineering). (Illus.). 1976. text ed. 65.00x (ISBN 0-07-010513-8). McGraw.

--Recent Development in Flow Separation. LC 83-72431. (Illus.). 300p. 1983. write for info. (ISBN 0-9612410-6-3). P K Chang.

Chang, P'Eng-Ch'Un. Education for Modernization in China: A Search for Criteria of Curriculum Construction in View of the Transition in National Life, with Special Reference to Secondary Education. LC 70-176635. (Columbia University. Teachers College. Contributions to Education: No. 137). Repr. of 1923 ed. 22.50 (ISBN 0-404-55137-8). AMS Pr.

Chang, Peter, ed. Readings in Black Aged. 212p. 1977. text ed. 29.50x (ISBN 0-8422-0556-X); pap. text ed. 8.95x (ISBN 0-8422-5251-7). Irvington.

Chang, R. & Chang, M. S. Speaking of Chinese. 2nd ed. Crystal, David, ed. (Language Library). 198p. 1980. 24.95x (ISBN 0-233-97176-9). Basil Blackwell.

Chang, R. P. & Abeles, B., eds. Plasma Synthesis & Etching of Electronic Materials, Vol. 38. LC 85-3085. 1985. text ed. 43.00 (ISBN 0-931837-03-0). Materials Res.

Chang, Raymond. Basic Principles of Spectroscopy. LC 77-10971. 314p. 1978. Repr. of 1971 ed. lib. bdg. 21.50 (ISBN 0-88275-613-3). Krieger.

--Chemistry. 2nd ed. 832p. 1985. text ed. 35.00 (ISBN 0-394-32983-X, RanC); wkbk. 11.95 (ISBN 0-394-33475-2); solutions manual 9.95 (ISBN 0-394-33538-4). Random.

--Chinese Petroleum: An Annotated Bibliography. 1982. lib. bdg. 36.50 (ISBN 0-8161-8333-3, Hall Reference). G K Hall.

--Introduction to Chemistry. 1981. text ed. 35.00x (ISBN 0-394-32983-X, RanC); wkbk. 11.95 (ISBN 0-394-33475-2). Random.

--Physical Chemistry with Applications to Biological Systems. 2nd ed. (Illus.). 1981. text ed. 29.95 (ISBN 0-02-321040-0). Macmillan.

Chang, Raymond & Chang, Margaret S. Speaking of Chinese. (Illus.). 1978. 12.95 (ISBN 0-393-04503-X). Norton.

--Speaking of Chinese. (Illus.). 208p. 1983. pap. 4.95 (ISBN 0-393-30061-7). Norton.

Chang, Richard. Read Chinese, Bk. 2. rev. ed. 7.95 (ISBN 0-88710-066-X); tapes avail. (ISBN 0-88710-067-8). Far Eastern Pubns.

Chang, Richard, jt. auth. see Wang, Fred.

Chang, Richard C., jt. auth. see Smith, Frank C.

Chang, Richard F., ed. Under the Eaves of Shanghai: Shanghai Wuyansya, an Annotated Chinese Play. 1974. 5.50 (ISBN 0-88710-122-4). Far Eastern Pubns.

Chang, Richard F. & McDonald, William L. Modern Chinese Poetry. 6.50 (ISBN 0-88710-049-X). Far Eastern Pubns.

Chang, Richard K. & Furtak, Thomas E., eds. Surface Enhanced Raman Scattering. LC 81-22739. 450p. 1982. text ed. 55.00x (ISBN 0-306-40907-0, Plenum Pr). Plenum Pub.

Chang, Richard T. Historians & Meiji Statesmen. LC 78-631066. (University of Florida Social Sciences Monographs: No. 41). (Illus.). 1970. pap. 3.50 (ISBN 0-8130-0307-5). U Presses Fla.

--The Justice of the Western Consular Courts in Nineteenth Century Japan. LC 83-12573. (Contributions in Intercultural & Comparative Studies: No. 10). (Illus.). xiv, 183p. 1984. 35.00 (ISBN 0-313-24103-1, CJW/). Greenwood.

Chang, Roy, jt. auth. see Li, Tze-Chung.

Chang, S. Chinese-English Dictionary of Physical Terms. 405p. (Eng. & Ger.). 1969. pap. 75.00 (ISBN 0-686-56601-7, M-7322, Pub. by Harrassowitz). French & Eur.

Chang, S. H. Spelling Bee Speller, 3 vols. LC 81-90754. (Orig.). (gr. 4-8). 1984. Set. pap. 19.95 (ISBN 0-942462-22-X). Hondale.

--The Spelling Bee Speller: The Final Rounds, Vol. 3. LC 81-90754. (The Spelling Bee Speller Ser.). 240p. (Orig.). (gr. 4-8). 1984. pap. 7.95 (ISBN 0-942462-03-3). Hondale.

--The Spelling Bee Speller: The First Round, Vol. 1. LC 81-90754. (The Spelling Bee Speller Ser.). 240p. (Orig.). (gr. 4-8). 1984. pap. 7.95 (ISBN 0-942462-01-7). Hondale.

--The Spelling Bee Speller: The Middle Rounds, Vol. 2. LC 81-90754. (The Spelling Bee Speller Ser.). 240p. (Orig.). (gr. 4-8). 1984. pap. 7.95 (ISBN 0-942462-02-5). Hondale.

Chang, S. H., jt. auth. see Pincus, Alexis G.

Chang, S. K. & Fu, K. S., eds. Pictorial Information Systems. (Lecture Notes in Computer Science: Vol. 80). 441p. 1980. pap. 28.00 (ISBN 0-387-09757-0). Springer-Verlag.

Chang, S. K., jt. ed. see Wang, Paul P.

Chang, S. L. Fundamentals Handbook of Electrical & Computer Engineering, 3 Vols. 1983. 189.95 (ISBN 0-471-89690-X). Wiley.
--Multiple Diffraction of X-Rays in Crystals. (Springer Series in Solid State Sciences: Vol. 50). (Illus.). 320p. 1984. 49.50 (ISBN 0-387-12955-3). Springer-Verlag.
Chang, S. T. & Hayes, W. A., eds. The Biology & Cultivation of Edible Mushrooms. LC 77-6591. 1978. 79.50 (ISBN 0-12-168050-9). Acad Pr.
Chang, Semoon. Practitioners' Guide to Econometrics. (Illus.). 190p. (Orig.). 1984. pap. text ed. 11.50 (ISBN 0-8191-3693-X). U Pr of Amer.
Chang, Sheldon S. L. Fundamentals Handbook of Electrical & Computer Engineering: Communications, Control, Devices & Systems, Vol. 2. LC 82-4872. 737p. 1983. 74.95x (ISBN 0-471-86213-4). Wiley.
--Fundamentals Handbook of Electrical & Computer Engineering: Vol. 1: Circuits, Fields, & Electronics. LC 82-4872. 707p. 1982. 74.95x (ISBN 0-471-86215-0, Pub. by Wiley-Interscience). Wiley.
--Fundamentals Handbook of Electrical & Computer Engineering: Vol. 3: Computer Hardware, Software & Applications. LC 82-4872. 507p. 1982. 71.50 (ISBN 0-471-86214-2, Pub. by Wiley-Interscience). Wiley.
Chang, Shi-Kuo, ed. Management & Office Information Systems. 490p. 1984. 59.50x (ISBN 0-306-41447-3, Plenum Pr). Plenum Pub.
Chang, Shiang-hua. Sleepless Green Green Grass & Sixty-Eight Other Poems. Smith, Stephan L., tr. from Chinese. (Illus.). 151p. 1982. 7.95 (ISBN 0-917056-15-9, Pub. by C & T). Cheng & Tsui.
Chang, Shung-Huei, jt. ed. see Pincus, Alexis G.
Chang, Sonia. Echocardiography: Techniques & Interpretation. 2nd. ed. LC 81-2200. (Illus.). 362p. 1981. text ed. 22.50 (ISBN 0-8121-0784-5). Lea & Febiger.
Chang, Stephen T. The Complete Book of Acupuncture. LC 75-28762. (Illus.). 256p. 1976. pap. 8.95 (ISBN 0-89087-124-8). Celestial Arts.
--The Great Tao. (Illus.). 464p. 1985. 26.00 (ISBN 0-942196-01-5). Tao Pub.
--The Tao of Sexology. (Illus.). 240p. 1985. 17.00 (ISBN 0-942196-03-1). Tao Pub.
Chang, Stephen T. & Miller, Richard C. The Book of Internal Exercises. LC 78-18320. (Illus., Orig.). 1978. casebound 12.95 (ISBN 0-89407-068-1). Strawberry Hill.
Chang, Sung-Un. Korean Newspaper Readings. 4.95 (ISBN 0-88710-042-2). Far Eastern Pubns.
Chang, Sung-Un & Martin, Samuel E. Readings in Contemporary Korean. 4.95 (ISBN 0-88710-075-9). Far Eastern Pubns.
Chang, Sunny, jt. auth. see Bennett, Frances.
Chang, Sunny, jt. auth. see Bennett, Frances C.
Chang, T. M. & Crombag, H. F. Distance Learning: On the Design of an Open University. 1982. 30.00 (ISBN 0-89838-096-0). Kluwer Nijhoff.
Chang, T. M., ed. Artificial Kidney, Artificial Liver, & Artificial Cells. LC 77-18738. 324p. 1978. 45.00x (ISBN 0-306-31125-9, Plenum Pr). Plenum Pub.
--Biomedical Applications of Immobilized Enzymes & Proteins, 2 vols. Incl. Vol. 1. 448p. 1977. 49.50x (ISBN 0-306-34311-8); Vol. 2. LC 76-56231. 379p. 1977. 49.50x (ISBN 0-306-34312-6). (Illus., Plenum Pr). Plenum Pub.
Chang, T. M., jt. ed. see Bonomini, V.
Chang, T. M., ed. see Meeting on Hemoperfusion, Kidney & Liver Supports & Detoxification, Haifa, Aug 25-26, 1979.
Chang, T. S., ed. Principles, Techniques & Applications in Microsurgery. Leung, P. C., tr. 850p. 1985. 114.00 (ISBN 0-317-30930-7). Taylor & Francis.
Chang, T. Y. & Krempl, F., eds. Inelastic Behavior of Pressure Vessel & Piping Components, PVP-PB-028. (Pressure Vessel & Piping Division Ser.: Bk. No. G00136). 1978. 20.00 (ISBN 0-685-37568-4). ASME.
Chang, Thomas M. Artificial Cells. (Illus.). 224p. 1972. photocopy ed. 25.50x (ISBN 0-398-02257-7). C C Thomas.
Chang, Tse Chun. Cyclical Movements in the Balance of Payments. LC 85-12539. (Illus.). x, 224p. 1985. Repr. of 1951 ed. lib. bdg. 45.00x (ISBN 0-313-24947-4, CHCM). Greenwood.
Chang, Wallace H. & Petry, Judith J. The Breast: An Atlas of Reconstruction. (Illus.). 456p. 1983. lib. bdg. 77.00 (ISBN 0-683-01668-7). Williams & Wilkins.
Chang, Wonona W., et al. Encyclopedia of Chinese Food & Cooking. LC 78-93402. (Illus.). 1973. 8.98 (ISBN 0-517-50661-0). Crown.
Chang, Y. A. & Smith, J. F. Calculation of Phase Diagrams & Thermochemistry of Alloy Phases. 286p. 30.00 (ISBN 0-89520-356-1); members 18.00 (ISBN 0-317-37185-1); student members 10.00 (ISBN 0-317-37186-X). Metal Soc.
Chang, Y. A., ed. see TMS-AIME Fall Meeting, Milwaukee, 1979.
Chang, Y. Austin & Ahmand, Nazeer. Thermodynamic Data on Metal Carbonates & Related Oxides. (Technology of Metallurgy Ser.). 235p. 1982. 30.00 (ISBN 0-89520-451-7); members 20.00 (ISBN 0-317-37181-9); student members 10.00 (ISBN 0-317-37182-7). Metal Soc.
Chang, Y. N. & Campo-Flores, Filemon. Business Policy & Strategy: Text & Cases. 1980. text ed. 28.20x (ISBN 0-673-16073-4). Scott F.
Chang, Yi-Ting. The Interpretation of Treaties by Judicial Tribunals. LC 68-58557. (Columbia University Studies in the Social Studies Ser.: No. 389). Repr. of 1933 ed. 17.50 (ISBN 0-404-51389-1). AMS Pr.
Chang, Yu-Chuan. Wang Shou-Jen As a Statesman. (Studies in Chinese History & Civilization). 517p. 1977. Repr. of 1940 ed. 21.00 (ISBN 0-89093-094-5). U Pubns Amer.
Chang, Yu-Hung & Chu, Kwo-Ray, trs. Miao & Yao Linguistic Studies: Selected Articles in Chinese. Purnell, Herbert C., ed. (Linguistics Ser.: Vol. 7). 282p. 1972. pap. text ed. 4.00 (ISBN 0-87727-088-0, DP 88). Cornell SE Asia.
Chang, Yu-Kon, et al, trs. from Chinese. Civil Code of the Republic of China. Hsia, Ching-Lin. (Studies in Chinese Government & Law). 400p. 1977. Repr. of 1930 ed. 26.50 (ISBN 0-89093-055-4). U Pubns Amer.
Chang Cheng-Chi. The Practice of Zen. LC 78-618. 1978. Repr. of 1959 ed. lib. bdg. 29.75x (ISBN 0-313-20264-8, CHPZ). Greenwood.
Chang Ch'ien-Ch'ang. Children's Songs from the Hakka of Mei Hsien. (Folklore Series of National Sun Yat-Sen University: No. 26). (Chinese.). 16.00x (ISBN 0-89986-094-X). Oriental Bk Store.
Chang Ch'Ing-Chiu. A Collection of Folksongs of the Po Tribe in Yun-Nan. (National Peking University & Chinese Assn. for Folklore, Folklore & Folkliterature Ser.: No. 44). (Chinese.). 16.00x (ISBN 0-89986-136-9). Oriental Bk Store.
Chang Chung-Yuan. Creativity & Taoism. (Illus.). 1970. pap. 5.95x (ISBN 0-06-131968-6, TB1968, Torch). Har-Row.
Chang Chung-Yuan, ed. The Original Teachings of Ch'an Buddhism. LC 82-48003. (Grove Press Eastern Philosophy & Religion Ser.). 320p. 1982. pap. 9.95 (ISBN 0-394-62417-3, E813, Ever). Grove.
Chang Dae Han. Multiphase Flow in Polymer Processing. LC 80-70598. 1981. 67.50 (ISBN 0-12-322460-8). Acad Pr.
Change Institute. University of Maryland. Frontiers in Librarianship: Proceedings of Change Institute 1969. Wasserman, Paul, ed. LC 78-149958. (Contributions in Librarianship & Information Science: No. 2). 1972. lib. bdg. 35.00 (ISBN 0-8371-5823-0, WPC/). Greenwood.
Changeux, Jean-Pierre. Neuronal Man: The Biology of Mind. Garey, Laurence, tr. LC 84-42970. (Illus.). 384p. 1985. 19.95 (ISBN 0-394-53692-4). Pantheon.
Changeux, Jean-Pierre, et al. The Harvey Lectures. (Serial Publication: No. 75). 1981. 65.00 (ISBN 0-12-312075-6). Acad Pr.
Changeuz, J., et al, eds. Molecular & Cellular Interactions Underlying Higher Brain Function: Proceedings of the 9th Meeting of the International Neurobiology Society, Abbaye Royale de Fontevraud, France September 1-4, 1981. (Progress in Brain Research Ser.: No. 58). xvi, 484p. 1983. 95.75 (ISBN 0-444-80432-3, I-025-83, Biomedical Pr). Elsevier.
Chang-Fee Lee. Financial Analysis & Planning: A Book of Readings. LC 82-72275. 780p. (Orig.). 1983. pap. text ed. 17.95 (ISBN 0-201-04449-8). Addison-Wesley.
Chang-guk, Yi, et al, trs. see Chong-in, So, et al.
Chang Hsiao-Ch'ao. Four Jest Books. (National Peking University & Chinese Assn. for Folklore & Folkliterature Ser.: No. 113 &114). (Chinese.). 28.00x (ISBN 0-89986-191-1). Oriental Bk Store.
Chang Hsi-Ch'eng. Problems of Divorce: A Special Issue of the Ladies Journal. (National Peking University & Chinese Assn. for Folklore, Folklore & Folkliterature Ser.: No. 125). (Chinese.). 16.00x (ISBN 0-89986-200-4). Oriental Bk Store.
Chang Hsing-Chou. Studies on Ningpo Customs. (National Peking University & Chinese Assn. for Folklore, Folklore & Folkliterature Ser.: No. 109). (Chinese.). 16.00x (ISBN 0-89986-187-3). Oriental Bk Store.
Chang Huo-Jan. Tales About the Stupid Son-in-Law. Lin Lan, ed. (Tales from the Orient Ser.: No. 26). (Chinese.). 15.00x (ISBN 0-89986-250-0). Oriental Bk Store.
Changing Times Education Service Editors. Consumer Law. rev. ed. LC 81-7720. (Illus.). 144p. 1982. pap. text ed. 5.95 (ISBN 0-88436-804-1, 30263). EMC.
--Housing. rev. ed. LC 81-400. (Illus.). 144p. 1982. pap. text ed. 5.95 (ISBN 0-88436-798-3, 30264). EMC.
--Insurance. rev. ed. LC 81-7857. (Illus.). 144p. 1982. pap. text ed. 5.95 (ISBN 0-88436-813-0, 30265). EMC.
--Marketplace. rev. ed. LC 81-4686. (Illus.). 56p. 1982. pap. text ed. 3.25 (ISBN 0-88436-801-7, 30262). EMC.
--Money Management. rev. ed. LC 81-7859. (Illus.). 64p. 1982. pap. text ed. 4.25 (ISBN 0-88436-810-6, 30261). EMC.
--Saving & Investing. rev. ed. LC 81-7860. (Illus.). 112p. 1982. pap. text ed. 4.95 (ISBN 0-88436-807-6, 30266). EMC.
Chang Kia-ngau, pseud. China's Struggle for Railroad Development. LC 74-34331. (China in the 20th Century Ser). (Illus.). vii, 340p. 1975. Repr. of 1943 ed. lib. bdg. 39.50 (ISBN 0-306-70689-X). Da Capo.
Chang K'uang. Tales About the Stupid Daughter-in-Law. Lin Lan, ed. (Tales from the Orient Ser.: No. 27). (Chinese.). 15.00x (ISBN 0-89986-251-9). Oriental Bk Store.
Chang Kuo-t'ao. The Rise of the Chinese Communist Party, 1928-1938: Volume Two of the Autobiography of Chang Kuo-t'ao. 1972. 35.00x (ISBN 0-7006-0088-4). U Pr of KS.
Chang Nan-Chuang. Ho Tien, Folkliterature with Proverbs. (National Peking University & Chinese Assn. for Folklore, Folklore & Folkliterature Ser.: No. 8). (Chinese.). 16.00x (ISBN 0-89986-108-3). Oriental Bk Store.
Chang Pei-Kang. Agriculture & Industrialization. LC 69-13854. Repr. of 1949 ed. lib. bdg. 15.00x (ISBN 0-8371-1057-2, CHAI). Greenwood.
Chang-Rodriguez, Raquel & Yates, Donald A., eds. Homage to Irving A. Leonard: Essays on Hispanic Art, History, & Literature. LC 77-72628. (Illus.). pap. 57.80 (ISBN 0-317-10539-6, 2050373). Bks Demand UMI.
Chang-Rodriquez, E., jt. auth. see Juilland, Alphonse.
Changshou, Zhang, jt. auth. see Zhimm, An.
Chang Shu-Ting. The Chinese Mushroom (Volvariella volvacea) Morphology, Cytology, Genetics, Nutrition, & Cultivation. (Illus.). 118p. 1972. 12.50x (ISBN 0-295-95743-3, Pub by Chinese Univ Hong Kong). U of Wash Pr.
Chang-sop, Son, et al. A Respite & Other Korean Short Stories. Korean National Commission for UNESCO, ed. Chong-un, Kim, et al, trs. from Korean. (Modern Korean Short Stories Ser.: No. 6). vii, 169p. 1983. 20.00 (ISBN 0-89209-207-6). Pace Intl Res.
Chang Tien-Tse. Sino-Portuguese Trade from 1514 to 1644: A Synthesis of Portuguese & Chinese Sources. LC 78-38052. Repr. of 1934 ed. 10.00 (ISBN 0-404-56906-4). AMS Pr.
Chang Ti Shang, ed. Microsurgery in China. 800p. 1984. write for info. (Pub. by World Sci Singapore). Taylor & Francis.
Chang Ven, Chen, et al, eds. see Hue, Huang S.
Chang Wen-Ch'eng. The Dwelling of Playful Goddesses. Levy, Howard S., tr. 18.00 (ISBN 0-686-38451-2). Oriental Bk Store.
Chang Ya-Hsiung. Love-Songs of Northwest China. (National Peking University & Chinese Assn. for Folklore, Folklore & Folkliterature Ser.: No. 94). (Chinese.). 16.00x (ISBN 0-89986-174-1). Oriental Bk Store.
Chang-Yen, Chen, ed. see Huei, Huang S.
Chanin, Harry. From Generation to Generation. LC 83-72656. 191p. 1984. pap. 9.95 (ISBN 0-937444-09-X). Caislan Pr.
Chanin, Leah F. Reference Guide to Georgia Legal History & Legal Research. 177p. 1980. 20.00 (ISBN 0-87215-315-0); 1983 supplement 7.50 (ISBN 0-87215-711-3). Michie Co.
Chanin, Myra. Jewish Penicillin: Mother Wonderful's Profusely Illustrated Guide to the Proper Preparation of Chicken Soup. LC 84-42925. (Illus.). 48p. 7.95 (ISBN 0-317-05410-4); 12-copy prepack 47.70 (ISBN 0-317-05411-2). One Hund One Prods.
Chanin, Robert H., jt. auth. see Wollett, Donald H.
Chankin, Donald O. Anonymity & Death: The Fiction of B. Traven. LC 75-1376. 160p. 1975. 18.95x (ISBN 0-271-01190-4). Pa St U Pr.
Chankong & Haimes. Multiobjective Decision Making Theory & Methodology. (Systems Science & Engineering Ser.: Vol. 8). 406p. 1983. 47.25 (ISBN 0-444-00710-5, North-Holland). Elsevier.
Chankong, V., jt. ed. see Haimes, Y. Y.
Chanler, Julie. His Messengers Went Forth. facs. ed. LC 77-148209. (Biography Index Reprint Ser.). (Illus.). 1948. 13.00 (ISBN 0-8369-8056-5). Ayer Co Pubs.
Chanler, William A. Through Jungle & Desert, Travels in E. Africa. 1896. 59.00x (ISBN 0-403-00438-1). Scholarly.
Chanlett, Emil T. Environmental Protection. 2nd ed. (Environmental Engineering Ser.). 1979. text ed. 45.00 (ISBN 0-07-010531-6). McGraw.
Chanley, Matoira H., jt. ed. see Smith, Walter L.
Ch'an Master Yung Chia. The Song of Enlightenment. Tripitaka Master Hua, commentary by. Buddhist Text Translation Society, et al, trs. from Chinese. (Illus.). 84p. (Orig.). 1983. pap. 5.00 (ISBN 0-917512-20-0). Buddhist Text.
Channa, V. C. Caste: Identity & Continuity. 1979. text ed. 11.00x (ISBN 0-391-01871-X). Humanities.
Channan, Krishan K. The Lure of Politics. 68p. 1980. 6.00 (ISBN 0-682-49641-3). Exposition Pr FL.
Channell, Paul J., ed. see AIP Conference Proceedings No. 90. Los Alamos, 1982.
Channell, Shila R. Manual IV Therapy Procedures. 2nd ed. 200p. 1985. pap. 12.95 (ISBN 0-87489-370-4). Med Economics.
Channels Magazine Editors, jt. auth. see Brown, Les.
Channels, Noreen. Social Science Methods in the Legal Process. 250p. 1984. 24.50 (ISBN 0-86598-013-6). Biblio Dist.
Channels, Noreen L. Social Science Methods in the Legal Process. LC 84-11527. (Illus.). 286p. 1985. 39.95x (ISBN 0-86598-013-6). Rowman & Allanheld.
Channels, Vera G. Experiences in Interpersonal Relationships. 335p. 1975. pap. text ed. 4.95 (ISBN 0-8134-1703-1, 1703); teacher's manual 0.50 (ISBN 0-8134-1708-2, 1708). Interstate.
Channels, Vera G. & Kupsinel, Penelope K. Career Education in Home Economics. LC 73-77545. (Illus.). 238p. 1973. pap. text ed. 4.95x (ISBN 0-8134-1573-X, 1573). Interstate.
Channels, Vera G., jt. auth. see Kupsinel, Penelope E.
Channer, Burley, tr. see Richter, Gottfried.
Channer, C. C. & Waller, M. Lacemaking Point Ground. (Illus.). 60p. 1984. 6.95 (ISBN 0-85219-612-1, Pub. by Batsford England). David & Charles.
Channing, C. P., jt. auth. see Fujii, T.
Channing, C. P., jt. ed. see Franchimont, P.
Channing, C. P., et al, eds. Ovarian Follicular & Corpus Luteum Function. LC 79-48. (Advances in Experimental Medicine & Biology Ser.: Vol. 112). 824p. 1979. 95.00x (ISBN 0-306-40149-5, Plenum Pr). Plenum Pub.
Channing, Cornelia C. & Segal, Sheldon J., eds. Intraovarian Control Mechanisms. (Advances in Experimental Medicine & Biology Ser.: Vol. 147). 402p. 1982. 55.00x (ISBN 0-306-41030-3, Plenum Pr). Plenum Pub.
Channing, E. Narragansett Planters: A Study of Causes. 1973. pap. 9.00 (ISBN 0-384-08464-8). Johnson Repr.
--Town & County Government in the English Colonies of North America. 1973. pap. 9.00 (ISBN 0-384-08463-X). Johnson Repr.
Channing, Edward. A History of the United States, 6 vols. 1976. Repr. of 1932 ed. lib. bdg. 172.50x set (ISBN 0-374-91414-1). Octagon.
--Jeffersonian System: Eighteen Hundred One to Eighteen Hundred Eleven. LC 67-30020. 1968. Repr. of 1906 ed. 22.50 (ISBN 0-8154-0049-7). Cooper Sq.
--The Narragansett Planters: A Study of Causes. LC 78-63760. (Johns Hopkins University. Studies in the Social Sciences. Fourth Ser. 1886: 3). Repr. of 1886 ed. 11.50 (ISBN 0-404-61028-5). AMS Pr.
--Town & Country Government in the English Colonies of North America. LC 78-63749. (Johns Hopkins University. Studies in the Social Sciences. Second Ser. 1884: 10). Repr. of 1884 ed. 11.50 (ISBN 0-404-61018-8). AMS Pr.
Channing, Edward & Coolidge, Archibald C. The Barrington-Bernard Correspondence, & Illustrative Matter, 1760-1770. LC 75-109612. (Era of the American Revolution Ser). 1970. Repr. of 1912 ed. lib. bdg. 39.50 (ISBN 0-306-71909-6). Da Capo.
Channing, Edward T. Lectures Read to the Seniors in Harvard College. Anderson, Dorothy I. & Braden, Waldo W., eds. LC 68-25559. (Landmarks in Rhetoric & Public Address Ser). 377p. 1968. 12.50x (ISBN 0-8093-0308-6). S Ill U Pr.
Channing, Eva, tr. see Pestalozzi, Johann H.
Channing, Mark. White Python: Adventure & Mystery in Tibet. Reginald, R. & Melville, Douglas, eds. LC 77-84208. (Lost Race & Adult Fantasy Ser.). 1978. Repr. of 1934 ed. lib. bdg. 26.50x (ISBN 0-405-10964-4). Ayer Co Pubs.
Channing, S. Confederate Ordeal. LC 83-17988. (Civil War Ser.). (gr. 7 up). 1983. lib. bdg. 19.94 (ISBN 0-8094-4729-0, Pub. by Time-Life). Silver.
Channing, Steven A. Crisis of Fear: Secession in South Carolina. (Illus.). 320p. 1974. pap. 6.95 (ISBN 0-393-00730-8, Norton Lib). Norton.
--The Encyclopedia of Kentucky. (The Encyclopedia of the U. S. Ser.). (Illus.). 500p. 1985. Repr. lib. bdg. 79.00x (ISBN 0-403-09981-1). Somerset Pub.
--Kentucky. (The States & the Nation Ser.). (Illus.). 1977. 14.95 (ISBN 0-393-05654-6, Co-Pub by AASLH). Norton.
Channing, William. Character & Writings of John Milton. 1826. lib. bdg. 8.50 (ISBN 0-8414-3465-4). Folcroft.
Channing, William E. The Character & Writings of John Milton. 1978. Repr. lib. bdg. 10.00 (ISBN 0-8495-0837-1). Arden Lib.
--Collected Poems, 1817-1901. Harding, Walter, ed. LC 67-21749. 1967. 100.00x (ISBN 0-8201-1009-4). Schol Facsimiles.
--Discourses on War. LC 77-149545. (Library of War & Peace; Relig. & Ethical Positions on War). 1972. lib. bdg. 46.00 (ISBN 0-8240-0508-2). Garland Pub.
--Discourses on War. 59.95 (ISBN 0-8490-0051-3). Gordon Pr.
--Discourses on War. LC 71-137531. (Peace Movement in America Ser). lxi, 229p. 1972. Repr. of 1903 ed. lib. bdg. 18.95x (ISBN 0-89198-059-8). Ozer.
--Emancipation. LC 75-82181. (Anti-Slavery Crusade in America Ser). 1969. Repr. of 1840 ed. 9.00 (ISBN 0-405-00619-5). Ayer Co Pubs.
--Poems. LC 72-4955. (The Romantic Tradition in American Literature Ser.). 162p. 1972. Repr. of 1843 ed. 20.00 (ISBN 0-405-04627-8). Ayer Co Pubs.
--Poems of Sixty-Five Years. Sanborn, F. B., ed. LC 72-4956. (The Romantic Tradition in American Literature Ser.). 232p. 1972. Repr. of 1902 ed. 25.50 (ISBN 0-405-04628-6). Ayer Co Pubs.

--Remarks on the Character & Writings of John Milton. 3rd ed. LC 72-966. Repr. of 1828 ed. 12.50 (ISBN 0-404-01448-8). AMS Pr.

--Self-Culture. LC 74-89163. (American Education: Its Men, Institutions & Ideas, Ser. 1). 1969. Repr. of 1838 ed. 11.00 (ISBN 0-405-01401-5). Ayer Co Pubs.

--Slavery. LC 71-82180. (Anti-Slavery Crusade in America Ser). 1969. Repr. of 1836 ed. 11.50 (ISBN 0-405-00620-9). Ayer Co Pubs.

--Slavery & Emancipation. LC 68-55928. Repr. of 1841 ed. cancelled (ISBN 0-8371-0347-9). Greenwood.

--Thoreau, Poet-Naturalist. new & enl. ed. Sanborn, F. B., ed. LC 65-27095. (Illus.). 1902. 15.00x (ISBN 0-8196-0173-X). Biblo.

--Thoreau the Poet-Naturalist: With Memorial Verses. LC 80-2680. Repr. of 1873 ed. 37.50 (ISBN 0-404-19073-1). AMS Pr.

--Works of William Ellery Channing, 2 vols. in 1. LC 70-114815. (Research & Source Works Ser.: No. 626). 1971. Repr. of 1882 ed. lib. bdg. 46.50 (ISBN 0-8337-0530-X). B Franklin.

Channock, Martin. Britain, Rhodesia & South Africa, 1900-1945: The Unconsummated Union. (Illus.). 289p. 1977. 29.50x (ISBN 0-7146-6001-9, F Cass Co). Biblio Dist.

Channon, D. F., jt. ed. see Stopford, J. M.

Channon, Derek F. Bank Strategic Management & Marketing: Text & Cases. 550p. 1984. text ed. 45.00 (ISBN 0-471-90383-3). Wiley.

--The Service Industries: Strategy, Structure & Financial Performance. 336p. 1978. text ed. 53.75x (ISBN 0-8419-5032-6). Holmes & Meier.

--The Strategy & Structure of British Enterprise. LC 72-94362. 248p. 1973. 16.95 (ISBN 0-87584-101-5). Harvard Busn.

Channon, Derek F. & Jalland, Michael. Multinational Strategic Planning. 1979. 35.00 (ISBN 0-8144-5575-1). AMACOM.

Chanock, Martin. Law, Custom, & Social Order: The Colonial Experience in Malawi & Zambia. LC 84-23207. (African Studies: No. 45). 1985. 42.50 (ISBN 0-521-30137-8). Cambridge U Pr.

Chanock, Robert & Lerner, Richard. Modern Approaches to Vaccines: Molecular & Chemical Basis of Virulence & Immunogenicity. LC 83-73176. (Illus.). 475p. 1984. 57.00x (ISBN 0-87969-165-4). Cold Spring Harbor.

Chanover, Alice, jt. auth. see Chanover, Hyman.

Chanover, Hyman. Haggadah for the School. (Illus.). 1964. pap. 2.25x (ISBN 0-8381-0175-5). United Syn Bk.

Chanover, Hyman & Chanover, Alice. Pesah Is Coming. (Holiday Series of Picture Story Books). (Illus.). (gr. k-2). 1956. 5.95 (ISBN 0-8381-0713-3, 10-713). United Syn Bk.

--Pesah Is Here. (Holiday Series of Picture Story Books). (Illus.). (gr. k-2). 1956. 5.95 (ISBN 0-8381-0714-1). United Syn Bk.

Chanover, Hyman & Zusman, Evelyn. A Book of Prayer for Junior Congregations: Sabbath & Festivals. 256p. (Eng. & Heb.). (gr. 4-7). 4.50x (ISBN 0-8381-0174-7, 10-174). United Syn Bk.

Chanover, Hyman, adapted by. Service for the High Holy Days Adapted for Youth. new ed. LC 72-2058. 192p. (gr. 8up). 1972. pap. 3.95x (ISBN 0-87441-123-8). Behrman.

Chanover, Hyman, ed. see Rossel, Seymour.

Chan-Palay, V. Cerebellar Dentate Nucleus: With Applications to the Terrestrinal Planets & Meteorites. LC 76-46462. 1977. 132.00 (ISBN 0-387-07958-0). Springer-Verlag.

Chan-Palay, V., jt. auth. see Palay, S. L.

Chan-Palay, Victoria & Palay, Sanford L. Coexistence of Neuroactive Substances in Neurons. LC 83-14694. (Neurosciences Ser.: I-584). 1075p. 1984. 89.95 (ISBN 0-471-89503-2, Pub. by Wiley-Interscience). Wiley.

Chan-Palay, Victoria, jt. auth. see Conference, Bethesda, Md, June, 1981.

Chan Sin-wai, tr. see T'an Ssu-t'ung.

Chansky, Norman M. Untapped Good: The Rehabilitation of School Dropouts. (Illus.). 288p. 1966. 24.50x (ISBN 0-398-00302-5). C C Thomas.

Chant, Barry. Straight Talk About Sex. (Illus.). (gr. 10-12). 1977. pap. 2.95 (ISBN 0-88368-078-5). Whitaker Hse.

Chant, Chris. Armed Forces of the United Kingdom. LC 80-66428. (Illus.). 80p. 1980. 14.95 (ISBN 0-7153-8024-9). David & Charles.

--Jetliner: From Takeoff to Touchdown. LC 82-81164. (Inside Story Ser.). (Illus.). 40p. 1982. PLB 9.90 (ISBN 0-531-03461-5). Watts.

Chant, Chris, ed. Military Aircraft of the World. (Concise Guide Ser.). (Illus.). 224p. 1981. pap. 9.95 (ISBN 0-600-34966-7, Pub. by Hamlyn Pub England). Presidio Pr.

Chant, Christopher. Bell UH-1. (Super Profile Ser.). (Illus.). 56p. 1985. 9.95 (ISBN 0-85429-437-6, Pub. by G T Foulis Ltd). Interbook.

--Grumman F8F Bearcat. (Super Profile Ser.). (Illus.). 56p. 1985. 9.95 (ISBN 0-85429-447-3, Pub. by G T Foulis Ltd). Interbook.

Chant, Christopher, jt. auth. see Hogg, Ian.

Chant, Colin & Fauvel, John. Darwin to Einstein: Historical Studies in Science & Belief. (Illus.). 352p. 1981. text ed. 27.00x (ISBN 0-582-49156-8). Longman.

Chant, Joy. The Grey Mane of Morning. 1977. 12.50 (ISBN 0-04-823137-1). Allen Unwin.

--The High Kings. (Illus.). 248p. 1983. pap. 24.95 (ISBN 0-553-05045-1). Bantam.

Chant, Peter D., et al. Griffin, Williams, & Larson's Advanced Accounting. Canadian Edition. 1983. 38.95x (ISBN 0-256-02395-6). Irwin.

Chant, Roy H. Spanish Tiger. 196p. 1984. 17.95 (ISBN 0-88254-883-2). Hippocrene Bks.

Chant, S. R., jt. ed. see Heywood, V. H.

Chantal, tr. see Du Gard, Rene C.

Chantelou, Paul F. De see De Chantelou, Paul F.

Chantelou, Paul F. de see De Chantelou, Paul F.

Chantico-QED. Disaster Recovery: Contingency Planning & Program Evaluation. LC 85-60177. (The Chantico Technical Management Ser.). (Illus.). 230p. (Orig.). 1985. pap. 29.50 (ISBN 0-89435-152-4, CP 1524). QED Info Sci.

--Management Evaluation of Software Packages. LC 85-60181. (The Chantico Technical Management Ser.). (Illus.). 150p. (Orig.). 1985. pap. 29.50 (ISBN 0-89435-155-9, CP 1559). QED Info Sci.

--Reviewing the Operation of Small Computer Systems. LC 85-60180. (The Chantico Technical Management Ser.). (Illus.). 166p. (Orig.). 1985. pap. 29.50 (ISBN 0-89435-153-2, CP 1532). QED Info Sci.

--Security Evaluation for Small Computer Systems. LC 85-60178. (The Chantico Technical Management Ser.). (Illus.). 159p. (Orig.). 1985. 29.50 (ISBN 0-89435-154-0, CP 1540). QED Info Sci.

--Strategic & Operational Planning for Information System. LC 85-60179. (The Chantico Technical Management Ser.). (Illus.). 200p. (Orig.). Date not set. pap. 29.50 (ISBN 0-89435-151-6, CP 1516). QED Info Sci.

Chantigny, J. A. De see De Chantigny, J. A.

Chantikian, Kosrof. Imaginations & Self-Discoveries: Poems 1971-73. (Illus.). 52p. (Orig.). 1974. pap. 15.00 signed (ISBN 0-916426-00-9). KOSMOS.

--Prophecies & Transformations. LC 75-35012. (Modern Poets Ser.). 88p. (Orig.). 1978. pap. 5.95 (ISBN 0-916426-01-7). KOSMOS.

Chantikian, Kosrof, ed. Octavio Paz: Homage to the Poet. LC 80-82167. 248p. (Orig.). 1981. text ed. 20.00x (ISBN 0-916426-03-3); pap. 7.95 (ISBN 0-916426-04-1). KOSMOS.

Chantikian, Kosrof, ed. see Alberti, Rafael.

Chantiles, Vilma L. The Food of Greece. 384p. 1985. pap. 10.95 (ISBN 0-396-08613-6). Dodd.

--The New York Ethnic Food Market Guide & Cookbook. (Illus.). 416p. 1984. pap. 14.95 (ISBN 0-396-08282-3). Dodd.

Chantler, A. Programming Techniques & Practice. 250p. 1981. pap. 22.95 (ISBN 0-471-89422-2). Wiley.

Chantler, Alan. Programming Techniques & Practice. 250p. 1981. pap. 24.50x (ISBN 0-85012-338-0). Intl Pubns Serv.

Chantler, Clyde. The Ghana Story. 216p. 1971. 12.00x (ISBN 0-8464-0452-4). Beekman Pubs.

Chantler, Eric N. & Elder, James B., eds. Mucus in Health & Disease II. LC 82-424. (Advances in Experimental Mental Medicine & Biology Ser.: Vol. 144). 458p. 1982. 59.50x (ISBN 0-306-40906-2, Plenum Pr). Plenum Pub.

Chan-Toon. Nature & Value of Jurisprudence. 2nd ed. xxiv, 187p. 1982. Repr. of 1889 ed. lib. bdg. 22.50x (ISBN 0-8377-0436-7). Rothman.

Chantre, Jean-Claude. Les Considerations Religieuses et Esthetiques D'un "Sturmer und Dranger". (European University Studies: No.1, Vol. 507). 650p. (Fr.). 1982. 62.10 (ISBN 3-261-04989-8). P Lang Pubs.

Chantry, Art, ed. Instant Litter. (Illus.). 112p. (Orig.). 1985. pap. 10.00 (ISBN 0-941104-15-X). Real Comet.

Chantry, G. W. Modern Aspects of Microwave Spectroscopy. LC 78-73876. 1980. 95.00 (ISBN 0-12-168150-5). Acad Pr.

--Submillimetre Spectroscopy. 1972. 66.50 (ISBN 0-12-170550-1). Acad Pr.

Chantry, G. W. & Bolton, B., eds. Dielectric Phenomena: Proceedings Institution of Electrical Engineers Special Issue, Part A, Vol. 128, No. 3, 1981. 79p. 1981. 31.00 (ISBN 0-317-34279-7). Inst Elect Eng.

Chantry, George W. Long-Wave Optics, Vol. 1. 1984. 60.00 (ISBN 0-12-168101-7). Acad Pr.

--Long-Wave Optics, Vol. 2. 1984. 55.00 (ISBN 0-12-168102-5). Acad Pr.

Chantry, Walter. Signs of the Apostles. 1979. pap. 3.95 (ISBN 0-85151-175-9). Banner of Truth.

--Today's Gospel. 1980. pap. 2.95 (ISBN 0-85151-027-2). Banner of Truth.

Chantry, Walter J. God's Righteous Kingdom. 151p. (Orig.). 1980. pap. 3.95 (ISBN 0-85151-310-7). Banner of Truth.

--Shadow of the Cross: Studies in Self-denial. 79p. (Orig.). 1981. pap. 2.95 (ISBN 0-85151-331-X). Banner of Truth.

Chantz, N. E. Just Pick a Murricane? (Oleander Language & Literature Ser.: Vol. 3). 1.25 (ISBN 0-902675-11-7). Oleander Pr.

Chanute, Octave. Progress in Flying Machines. 12.50 (ISBN 0-916494-00-4, Pub. by Lorenz & Herwig). Aviation.

--Progress in Flying Machines. 1976. Repr. 12.50 (ISBN 0-916494-00-4). Lorenz & Herweg.

Chan-Yap, Gloria, jt. auth. see Pascasio, Emy M.

Chao & Woyczynski. Probability Theory & Harmonic Analysis. (Pure & Applied Mathematics Ser.). 320p. 1986. price not set (ISBN 0-8247-7473-6). Dekker.

Chao, Arnold, jt. ed. see Wei, Lin.

Chao, Buwei Y. How to Cook & Eat in Chinese. 320p. 1972. pap. 3.95 (ISBN 0-394-71703-1, V703, Vin). Random.

Chao, Chum K. & Weakland, John. Secret Techniques of Wing Chun, Vol. 2. 1984. 27.00x (ISBN 0-901764-49-3, Pub. by P H Crompton Ltd UK). State Mutual Bk.

Chao, Denise W. Le Style du Journal d'un Cure de Campagne de Georges Bernanos. LC 80-67223. 120p. (Fr.). 1981. lib. bdg. 19.00 (ISBN 0-8191-1644-0). U Pr of Amer.

Chao, Evelina. Gates of Grace. 384p. 1985. 15.50 (ISBN 0-446-51303-2). Warner Bks.

Chao, J. A. & Woyczynski, W. A., eds. Martingale Theory in Harmonic Analysis & Banach Spaces, Cleveland, Ohio 1981: Proceedings. (Lecture Notes in Mathematics: Vol. 939). 225p. 1982. pap. 14.00 (ISBN 0-387-11569-2). Springer-Verlag.

Chao, John, jt. auth. see Jee, Bil.

Chao, John, jt. auth. see Tao, Sil l.

Chao, K. C. & Greenkorn, R. A. Thermodynamics of Fluids: An Introduction to Equilibrium Theory. (Chemical Processing & Engineering Ser.: Vol. 4). 1975. soft cover 65.00 (ISBN 0-8247-7035-8). Dekker.

Chao, K. C. & Robinson, Robert, eds. Equations of State in Engineering & Research. LC 79-23696. (Advances in Chemistry Ser.: No. 182). 1979. 59.95 (ISBN 0-8412-0500-0). Am Chemical.

Chao, Kang. Agricultural Production in Communist China, Nineteen Forty-Nine to Nineteen Sixty-Five. LC 70-121766. (Illus.). 374p. 1970. 30.00x (ISBN 0-299-05770-4). U of Wis Pr.

--Capital Formation in Mainland China, 1952-1965. LC 72-85526. 1974. 37.50x (ISBN 0-520-02304-8). U of Cal Pr.

--The Development of Cotton Textile Production in China. (East Asia Monographs: No. 74). 1977. 22.50x (ISBN 0-674-20021-7). Harvard U Pr.

--The Economic Development of Manchuria: The Rise of a Frontier Economy. (Michigan Monographs in Chinese Studies: No. 43). (Orig.). 1983. pap. 7.00 (ISBN 0-89264-043-X). U of Mich Ctr Chinese.

Chao, Kuo-Chun. Agrarian Policies of Mainland China: A Documentary Study, 1949-56. LC 57-3362. (East Asian Monographs Ser: No. 4). 1957. pap. 12.50x (ISBN 0-674-01150-3). Harvard U Pr.

--Economic Planning & Organization in Mainland China: A Documentary Study, 1949-1957, 2 Vols. LC 59-4569. (East Asian Monographs Ser: No. 7). 1959. pap. 11.00x ea.; Vol. 1. pap. (ISBN 0-674-22900-2); Vol. 2. pap. (ISBN 0-674-22901-0). Harvard U Pr.

Chao, L. Statistics: Methods & Analyses. 2nd ed. 1974. text ed. 34.95 (ISBN 0-07-010525-1). McGraw.

Chao, Lincoln L. Statistics for Management. 2nd ed. (Illus.). 752p. 1983. text ed. 28.75 (ISBN 0-89426-039-1); study guide 10.00 (ISBN 0-89426-040-5); Solutions Manual avail. (ISBN 0-89426-041-3). Scientific Pr.

Chao, Lorna, tr. see Morgan, G. Campbell.

Chao, Lorna, tr. see Sanders, J. Oswald.

Chao, Lorna Y., tr. see Dunn, Ronald.

Chao, Lorna Y., tr. see Flynn, Leslie B.

Chao, Lorna Y., tr. see Shelly, Bruce L.

Chao, Mei-Po. The Yellow Bell: A Brief Sketch of the History of Chinese Music. lib. bdg. 79.95 (ISBN 0-87968-135-7). Krishna Pr.

Chao, Paul. Chinese Kinship. 220p. 1983. 30.00x (ISBN 0-7103-0020-4). Routledge & Kegan.

--Women Under Communism: Family in Russia & China. LC 77-89932. 231p. 1977. lib. bdg. 27.95x (ISBN 0-930390-01-6); pap. text ed. 14.95x (ISBN 0-930390-00-8). Gen Hall.

Chao, Richard L., jt. auth. see Oppenheimer, Steven B.

Chao, Samuel, tr. see Sanders, J. Oswald.

Chao, Yuen R. Mandarin Primer: An Intensive Course in Spoken Chinese. LC 48-8224. (Illus.). 1948. 20.00x (ISBN 0-674-54800-0). Harvard U Pr.

Chao, Yuen R. & Yang, Lien-Sheng. Concise Dictionary of Spoken Chinese. LC 47-5464. (Harvard-Yenching Institute Publications Ser). 1947. 20.00x (ISBN 0-674-15800-8). Harvard U Pr.

Chao, Yuen Ren. A Grammar of Spoken Chinese. LC 65-10576. 1968. 52.50x (ISBN 0-520-00219-9). U of Cal Pr.

Chao, Yuen-Ren. Language & Symbolic Systems. (Orig.). 1968. 37.50 (ISBN 0-521-04616-5); pap. 14.95 (ISBN 0-521-09457-7, 457). Cambridge U Pr.

Chao Ching-Sheng. Essays on Folk Tales. (Folklore Series of National Sun Yat-Sen University: No. 12). (Chinese.). 16.00x (ISBN 0-89986-082-6). Oriental Bk Staff.

Chao Kuo-Chun. Agrarian Policy of the Chinese Communist Party, Nineteen Twenty-One to Nineteen Fifty-Nine. LC 77-14587. 1977. Repr. of 1960 ed. lib. bdg. 31.25x (ISBN 0-8371-9861-5, CHAP). Greenwood.

Chao Pu-Wei. Autobiography of a Chinese Woman, Buwei Yang Chao. Chao Yuen-Ren, tr. LC 72-100225. Repr. of 1947 ed. lib. bdg. 22.50x (ISBN 0-8371-3712-8, CHCW). Greenwood.

Chao Yuen-Ren. Cantonese Primer. LC 73-90482. Repr. of 1947 ed. lib. bdg. 18.75x (ISBN 0-8371-2263-5, CHCP). Greenwood.

Chao Yuen-Ren, tr. see Chao Pu-Wei.

Chapa, Evey & Andrade, Sally. La Mujer Chicana. 68p. 1976. pap. 16.00 (ISBN 0-931738-07-5). Info Systems.

Chapanis, Alfred R. E. Research Techniques in Human Engineering. LC 59-10765. pap. 82.00 (ISBN 0-317-10928-6, 2002276). Bks Demand UMI.

Chapanis, Alphonse. Man-Machine Engineering. LC 65-15099. (Behavioral Science in Industry Ser). (Orig.). 1966. pap. text ed. 7.25 pub net (ISBN 0-8185-0306-8). Brooks-Cole.

Chapanis, Alphonse, ed. Ethnic Variables in Human Factors Engineering. LC 74-24393. 310p. 1975. 27.50x (ISBN 0-8018-1668-8). Johns Hopkins.

Chapchal, G. Reconstruction Surgery & Traumatology, Vol. 14. (Illus.). 200p. 1974. 21.00 (ISBN 3-8055-1563-4). S Karger.

Chapchal, G., ed. Fractures in Children. (Reconstruction Surgery & Traumatology Ser.: Vol. 17). (Illus.). x, 182p. 1979. 33.75 (ISBN 3-8055-3013-7). S Karger.

--Reconstruction Surgery & Traumatology, Vol. 12. 1971. 41.75 (ISBN 3-8055-1183-3). S Karger.

--Reconstruction Surgery & Traumatology, Vol. 13. Incl. Scoliosis; Traumatology; Operative Treatment of Cerebral Palsy. (Illus.). 1972. 41.75 (ISBN 3-8055-1385-2). S Karger.

--Reconstruction Surgery & Traumatology, Vol. 15. 1976. 29.50 (ISBN 3-8055-2250-9). S Karger.

--Reconstruction Surgery & Traumatology, Vol. 16. (Illus.). 1977. 24.75 (ISBN 3-8055-2696-2). S Karger.

Chapchal, George. Fractures in Children. (Illus.). 259p. 1983. 39.95 (ISBN 0-86577-004-2). Thieme-Stratton.

Chapchal, George, ed. Injuries of the Ligaments & Their Repair: Hand-Knee-Foot. LC 77-76624. (Illus.). 252p. 1977. 36.00 (ISBN 0-88416-133-1). PSG Pub Co.

Chapdelaine, Perry A., Sr. The Laughing Terran. 176p. 1977. 7.50 (ISBN 0-317-01161-8). Authors Co-op.

--Spork of the Ayor. 208p. 1978. 7.50. Authors Co-op.

Chapdelaine, Perry A., Sr., et al, eds. John W. Campbell & L. Ron Hubbard. 1981. pap. Authors Co-Op.

Chapekar, Nalinee M. Ancient India & Greece. 1977. 10.00x (ISBN 0-686-22657-7). Intl Bk Dist.

Chapel, Charles E. The Gun Collector's Handbook of Value. 1984. pap. 11.95 (ISBN 0-399-50906-2, Perigee). Putnam Pub Group.

--The Gun Collector's Handbook of Values. 14th ed. (Illus.). 504p. 1983. 19.95 (ISBN 0-698-11240-7, Coward). Putnam Pub Group.

Chapel, Jeannie. Victorian Taste: The Complete Catalogue of Paintings at the Royal Hollaway College. (Illus.). 144p. 1983. pap. 25.00 (ISBN 0-8390-0302-1). Abner Schram Ltd.

Chapel, Yves, ed. Administrative Management for Development: A Reader. 220p. (Co-published with the International Institute of Administrative Sciences, Brussels). 1977. pap. 13.25 (ISBN 92-3-101176-6, U800, UNESCO). Unipub.

Chapell, Alan, ed. Sailboat Buyers' (Illus.). 376p. 1984. pap. 12.95 (ISBN 0-9611342-0-8). Sea Shore Pubn.

Chapelle, Howard I. The American Fishing Schooners: 1825-1935. (Illus.). 1973. 32.95 (ISBN 0-393-03123-3). Norton.

--American Small Sailing Craft. (Illus.). 1951. 26.95 (ISBN 0-393-03143-8). Norton.

--Boatbuilding. (Illus.). 1941. 25.95 (ISBN 0-393-03113-6). Norton.

--The Search for Speed under Sail, 1700-1855. (Illus.). 1984. 50.00 (ISBN 0-393-03127-6). Norton.

--Yacht Designing & Planning. rev. ed. (Illus.). 1971. 25.00 (ISBN 0-393-03169-1). Norton.

Chapelle, Howard I. & Polland, Leon D. The Constellation Question. LC 77-609565. (Smithsonian Studies in History & Technology Ser.: No. 5). (Illus.). pap. 42.30 (ISBN 0-317-09469-6, 2004204). Bks Demand UMI.

Chapelle, Howard I., jt. auth. see Adney, Edwin T.

Chapeville, F. & Haenni, A. O., eds. Chemical Recognition in Biology. (Molecular Biology, Biochemistry & Biophysics: Vol. 32). (Illus.). 430p. 1980. 64.00 (ISBN 0-387-10205-1). Springer-Verlag.

Chapey, Roberta. Language Intervention Strategies in Adult Aphasia. (Illus.). 384p. 1981. 37.00 (ISBN 0-683-01511-7, 1511-7). Williams & Wilkins.

Chapian, Marie. Free to Be Thin. LC 79-15656. (Illus.). 192p. 1979. pap. 5.95 (ISBN 0-87123-560-9, 210560); study guide (No. 1) by Neva Coyle 64 pgs. 2.50 (ISBN 0-87123-163-8, 210163). Bethany Hse.

--Fun to Be Fit. (Illus.). 224p. 1982. pap. 10.95 (ISBN 0-8007-1317-6). Revell.

--Growing Closer: How to Win Friends & Create Loving Relationships. 192p. 1985. 9.95 (ISBN 0-8007-1445-8). Revell.

--Love & Be Loved. 192p. 1983. pap. 6.95 (ISBN 0-8007-5092-6, Power Bks). Revell.
--Of Whom the World Was Not Worthy. LC 78-769. (Illus.). 256p. 1978. pap. 5.95 (ISBN 0-87123-250-2, 210417). Bethany Hse.
--Staying Happy in an Unhappy World. 160p. 1984. 8.95 (ISBN 0-8007-1217-X). Revell.
Chapian, Marie & Sadler, Robert. Help Me Remember...Help Me Forget. (Illus.). 236p. 1981. pap. 3.95 (ISBN 0-87123-203-0, 200203). Bethany Hse.
Chapian, Marie, jt. auth. see Backus, William.
Chapian, Marie, jt. auth. see Coyle, Neva.
Chapian, Marie, jt. auth. see Netherton, Tom.
Chapian, Marie, jt. auth. see Sadler, Robert.
Chapin & Hassett. Credit & Collection Principles & Practice. 7th ed. 1960. text ed. 40.95 (ISBN 0-07-010538-3). McGraw.
Chapin, Alice. Building Your Child's Faith. 144p. (Orig.). 1983. pap. 5.95 (ISBN 0-86605-115-5). Campus Crusade.
--Four Hundred Creative Ways to Say I Love You. 2nd ed. 96p. 1985. 2.50 (ISBN 0-8423-0919-5). Tyndale.
Chapin, Anna A. Greenwich Village. Repr. of 1917 ed. 20.00 (ISBN 0-8482-3568-1). Norwood Edns.
--The Heart of Music: The Story of the Violin. facsimile ed. LC 77-169753. (Select Bibliographies Reprint Ser.). Repr. of 1906 ed. 21.00 (ISBN 0-8369-5973-6). Ayer Co Pubs.
Chapin, Anna Alice. The Story of the Rhinegold: Der Ring Des Nibelungen. 138p. 1980. Repr. of 1897 ed. lib. bdg. 25.00 (ISBN 0-89760-119-X). Telegraph Bks.
Chapin, Bradley. American Law of Treason: Revolutionary & Early National Origins. LC 64-11053. (University of Washington Publications in History). 182p. 1964. 20.00x (ISBN 0-295-73705-0, UWPH). U of Wash Pr.
--Criminal Justice in Colonial America, 1606-1660. LC 82-2753. 224p. 1983. 18.00x (ISBN 0-8203-0624-X). U of Ga Pr.
--Early America. LC 83-8276. 302p. lib. bdg. 16.95x (ISBN 0-89198-129-2); pap. text ed. 9.95x (ISBN 0-89198-130-6). Ozer.
Chapin, Brenda. Guide to the Recommended Country Inns of New York, New Jersey, Pennsylvania, Delaware, Maryland, Virginia, Washington D.C., & West Virginia. LC 84-27903. (Guide to the Recommended Country Inns Ser.). (Illus.). 300p. (Orig.). 1985. pap. 8.95 (ISBN 0-87106-864-8). Globe Pequot.
Chapin, C. E. & Elston, W. E., eds. Ash Flow Tuffs. LC 79-53022. (Special Paper: No. 180). (Illus.). 1979. pap. 38.00 (ISBN 0-8137-2180-6). Geol Soc.
Chapin, Charles E. Charles E. Chapin's Story. (Amer. Newspapermen Ser.: 1790-1933). 334p. 1978. Repr. of 1920 ed. 17.50x (ISBN 0-8464-0028-6). Beekman Pubs.
Chapin, Charles V. A Report on State Public Health Work, Based on a Survey of State Boards of Health. Rosenkrantz, Barbara G., ed. LC 76-25657. (Public Health in America Ser.). (Illus.). 1977. Repr. of 1915 ed. lib. bdg. 20.00x (ISBN 0-405-09807-3). Ayer Co Pubs.
Chapin, Chester F. Personification in Eighteenth-Century English Poetry. 1967. lib. bdg. 18.50x (ISBN 0-374-91425-7). Octagon.
Chapin, Edwin H. Humanity in the City. LC 73-11901. (Metropolitan America Ser.). 254p. 1974. Repr. 19.00 (ISBN 0-405-05389-4). Ayer Co Pubs.
Chapin, F. Stuart. Education & the Mores. LC 68-56649. (Columbia University. Studies in the Social Sciences: No. 110). Repr. of 1911 ed. 12.50 (ISBN 0-404-51110-4). AMS Pr.
--Field Work & Social Research. Coser, Lewis A. & Powell, Walter W., eds. LC 79-6987. (Perennial Works in Sociology Ser.). (Illus.). 1979. Repr. of 1920 ed. lib. bdg. 19.00x (ISBN 0-405-12087-7). Ayer Co Pubs.
--An Introduction to the Study of Social Evolution: The Prehistoric Period. 1917. 17.50 (ISBN 0-8482-3572-X). Norwood Edns.
Chapin, F. Stuart & Queen, Stuart A. Research Memorandum on Social Work in the Depression. LC 73-162849. (Studies in the Social Aspects of the Depression). 1971. Repr. of 1937 ed. 17.00 (ISBN 0-405-00852-X). Ayer Co Pubs.
Chapin, F. Stuart, Jr. Human Activity Patterns in the City: Things People Do in Time & in Space. LC 74-5364. (Wiley Urban Research Ser.). Repr. of 1974 ed. 76.50 (ISBN 0-8357-9908-5, 2015175). Bks Demand UMI.
Chapin, F. Stuart, Jr. & Kaiser, Edward J. Urban Land Use Planning. 3rd ed. LC 64-18666. (Illus.). 672p. 1979. 22.50x (ISBN 0-252-00580-5); wkbk 6.95 (ISBN 0-252-00791-3). U of Ill Pr.
Chapin, F. Stuart, Jr. & Weiss, Shirley F., eds. Urban Growth Dynamics: In a Regional Cluster of Cities. LC 76-54709. 496p. 1977. Repr. of 1962 ed. 24.50 (ISBN 0-88275-486-6). Krieger.
Chapin, Francis S. Experimental Designs in Sociological Research. LC 73-16867. (Illus.). 297p. 1974. Repr. of 1955 ed. lib. bdg. 20.00x (ISBN 0-8371-7239-X, CHSO). Greenwood.
Chapin, Frederick H. The Land of the Cliff-Dwellers. LC 74-7945. Repr. of 1892 ed. 23.50 (ISBN 0-404-11832-1). AMS Pr.
Chapin, Henry. A Celebration: Collected Poems. 1974. 5.95 (ISBN 0-87233-030-3). Bauhan.
--The Constant God. LC 78-10965. 1979. pap. 4.95 (ISBN 0-87233-046-X). Bauhan.
--A Countdown at Eighty: An American Perspective. LC 77-4360. (Illus.). 1977. pap. 4.95 (ISBN 0-87233-041-9). Bauhan.
--The Haunt of Time Chosen Poems: Old & New. LC 81-8103. 1981. pap. 6.95 (ISBN 0-87233-056-7). Bauhan.
--To the End of West. 1970. pap. 3.95 (ISBN 0-87233-017-6). Bauhan.
Chapin, Isolde & Mock, Richard. New Faces in Public Places: Volunteers in Humanities. 60p. 1979. pap. 3.95 (ISBN 0-318-17176-7, C42). Natl Ctr Cit Involv.
Chapin, Isolde, jt. auth. see Allen, Kerry K.
Chapin, Isolde, et al, eds. A Writer's Guide to Washington. LC 83-50044. 192p. (Orig.). 1983. pap. 7.95 (ISBN 0-912521-00-7). Wash In Writers.
Chapin, J. & Messick, R. California: People of a Region. 4th ed. (Our Nation, Our World Ser.). 288p. 1984. text ed. 18.48 (ISBN 0-07-010561-8). McGraw.
Chapin, John C. A Census of United States Plate Blocks 1851-1882. (Illus.). 116p. 19.50x (ISBN 0-912574-35-6); pap. 12.50x (ISBN 0-912574-36-4). Collectors.
Chapin, June R. & Felton, Randall G. Chronicles of Time: A World History. (Illus.). 768p. (gr. 10). 1983. 23.00 (ISBN 0-07-001112-5). McGraw.
Chapin, Kim. Dogwood Afternoons. 288p. 1985. 13.95 (ISBN 0-374-14316-1). FS&G.
Chapin, Ned. Three-Sixty-Three-Seventy Programming in Assembly Language. 1973. text ed. 44.50 (ISBN 0-07-010552-9). McGraw.
Chapin, Robert C. Standard of Living Among Workingmen's Families in New York City. LC 72-137159. (Poverty U.S.A. Historical Record Ser). 1971. Repr. of 1909 ed. 32.00 (ISBN 0-405-03097-5). Ayer Co Pubs.
Chapin, Russell. Uniform Rules of Criminal Procedure for All Courts. 66p. 1983. pap. 4.95 (ISBN 0-8447-3530-2). Am Enterprise.
Chapin-Park, Sue, jt. auth. see Park, William R.
Chapiro, A., jt. ed. see Duplan, J. F.
Chapla, John D. Forty Second Virginia Infantry. (The Virginia Regimental Histories Ser.). (Illus.). 147p. 1983. 16.45 (ISBN 0-930919-04-1). H E Howard.
Chaplain, Tim. Shadow Catcher. 224p. (Orig.). 1985. pap. 2.50 (ISBN 0-345-32340-8). Ballantine.
Chaplais, Pierre. Essays in Medieval Diplomacy & Administration. (No. 2). 496p. 1981. 50.00 (ISBN 0-9506882-2-3). Hambledon Press.
Chaplan, Marie, jt. auth. see Backus, William.
Chaplenko, Natalia. Ukrainian Culinary Glossary. LC 80-54687. 113p. 1980. pap. 6.00 (ISBN 0-317-36114-7). UNWLA.
--Ukrainian Women's Bibliography Beyond the Borders of Ukraine. 54p. 1974. pap. 2.00 (ISBN 0-317-36115-5). UNWLA.
Chaplin, A. The Romance of Language. 1920. 12.50 (ISBN 0-8274-3302-6). R West.
Chaplin, A. H. A Hundred Years of Cataloging at the British Museum. 300p. 1985. text ed. write for info. (ISBN 0-566-03434-4). Gower Pub Co.
Chaplin, Annabel. The Bright Light of Death. 1977. pap. 4.95 (ISBN 0-87516-230-4). De Vorss.
Chaplin, Arnold. The Illness & Death of Napoleon Bonaparte: A Medical Criticism. 1977. lib. bdg. 59.95 (ISBN 0-8490-2033-6). Gordon Pr.
--Medicine in England During the Reign of George III. LC 75-23695. Repr. of 1919 ed. 15.50 (ISBN 0-404-13244-8). AMS Pr.
Chaplin, Charles. My Early Years. (Illus.). 164p. 1984. 12.95 (ISBN 0-370-30230-3). Merrimack Pub Cir.
Chaplin, Charles C. Fishwatcher's Guide to West Atlantic Coral Reefs. rev. ed. LC 72-9309. (Illus.). 64p. 1979. plastic bdg. 8.95 (ISBN 0-915180-08-1); pap. 4.95 (ISBN 0-915180-09-X). Harrowood Bks.
Chaplin, David. Peruvian Industrial Labor Force. 1967. 33.00x (ISBN 0-691-09324-5). Princeton U Pr.
Chaplin, David, ed. Peruvian Nationalism: A Corporatist Revolution. LC 73-85099. (Third World Ser.). 600p. 1976. 19.95x (ISBN 0-87855-077-1); pap. 6.95x (ISBN 0-87855-573-0). Transaction Bks.
Chaplin, Dorothea. Mythological Bonds Between East & West. 1976. lib. bdg. 59.95 (ISBN 0-8490-2325-4). Gordon Pr.
Chaplin, George & Paige, Glenn D., eds. Hawaii Two Thousand: Continuing Experiment in Anticipatory Democracy. 500p. 1973. 14.95 (ISBN 0-8248-0252-7). UH Pr.
Chaplin, Gillian, jt. auth. see Mitchell, David.
Chaplin, H., ed. The Organization of the Library Profession. 2nd ed. (IFLA Publication Ser.: No. 6). 132p. 1976. lib. bdg. 12.00 (ISBN 3-7940-4309-X). K G Saur.
Chaplin, Hamako & Martin, Samuel. Advanced Japanese Conversation. 1976. 8.95 (ISBN 0-88710-000-7); tapes avail. (ISBN 0-88710-127-5). Far Eastern Pubns.
Chaplin, Hamako I., jt. auth. see Jorden, Eleanor H.
Chaplin, Heman W. Five Hundred Dollars & Other Stories of New England Life. facsimile ed. LC 79-106260. (Short Story Index Reprint Ser.). 1887. 18.00 (ISBN 0-8369-3297-8). Ayer Co Pubs.
Chaplin, Hugh, Jr. Immune Hemolytic Anemias. (Methods in Hematology Ser.: Vol. 12). (Illus.). 266p. 1985. text ed. 35.00 (ISBN 0-443-08320-7). Churchill.
Chaplin, J. P. Dictionary of Psychology. 608p. 1975. pap. 3.50 (ISBN 0-440-31926-9, LE). Dell.
--Dictionary of Psychology. 3rd rev. ed. 1985. pap. 5.95 (ISBN 0-440-31925-0, LE). Dell.
Chaplin, J. P. & Krawiec, T. Systems & Theories of Psychology. 4th ed. LC 78-21930. 1979. text ed. 32.95 (ISBN 0-03-020271-X, HoltC). HR&W.
Chaplin, J. P., jt. auth. see Young, P. T.
Chaplin, Jack W. Metal Manufacturing Technology. (gr. 10 up). 1976. text ed. 19.96 (ISBN 0-87345-132-5). McKnight.
Chaplin, James P. & Demers, Aline. Primer of Neurology & Neurophysiology. LC 78-6680. 272p. 1984. pap. 20.50 (ISBN 0-471-03027-9). Krieger.
Chaplin, Jane D. Out of the Wilderness. facsimile ed. LC 74-38644. (Black Heritage Library Collection). Repr. of 1869 ed. 20.25 (ISBN 0-8369-9002-1). Ayer Co Pubs.
Chaplin, Jeremiah. The Riches of Bunyan: Selected from His Works, for the American Tract Society. 488p. 1983. Repr. of 1850 ed. lib. bdg. 50.00 (ISBN 0-8495-0870-3). Arden Lib.
Chaplin, L. Tarin, jt. auth. see Blom, Lynne A.
Chaplin, Mary. Gardening for the Physically Handicapped & Elderly. 1978. 12.95 (ISBN 0-7134-1081-7, Pub. by Batsford England). David & Charles.
Chaplin, Miriam T. Reading Comes to College. 1978. 8.95 (ISBN 0-317-17270-0). Banner Pr AL.
Chaplin, Patrice. The Unforgotten. 1984. 14.95 (ISBN 0-517-55284-1, Harmony). Crown.
Chaplin, Ralph. Centralia Conspiracy. facsimile ed. (Shorey Historical Ser.). 84p. pap. 8.95 (ISBN 0-8466-0183-4, SJS183). Shorey.
--The Centralia Conspiracy. 85p. 1973. Repr. of 1920 ed. lib. bdg. 25.95 (ISBN 0-88286-097-6). C H Kerr.
--The General Strike. 1982. pap. 1.00 (ISBN 0-686-46446-X). Indus Workers World.
--Wobbly. LC 70-166089. (Civil Liberties in American History Ser). 1972. Repr. of 1948 ed. lib. bdg. 49.50 (ISBN 0-306-70212-6). Da Capo.
Chaplin, Ralph, et al. Centralia Case: Three Views of the Armistice Day Tragedy at Centralia, Washington, November 11, 1919. LC 77-160845. (Civil Liberties in American History Ser). 1971. Repr. of 1924 ed. lib. bdg. 35.00 (ISBN 0-306-70211-8). Da Capo.
Chaplin, Stephen. How to Pick Winners of a Baseball Game. pap. 2.95 (ISBN 0-685-38434-9). Wehman.
Chaplin, Steve. Bettor's Guide to Harness Racing. 1977. 15.00 (ISBN 0-686-65434-X). Landau.
Chaplin, Stewart. Suspension of the Power of Alienation, & Postponement of Vesting, Under the Laws of New York, Michigan, Minnesota & Wisconsin. xxxix, 370p. 1981. Repr. of 1891 ed. lib. bdg. 30.00x (ISBN 0-8377-0428-6). Rothman.
Chapman. Medical Dictionary for the Non-Professional. 1984. pap. 5.95 (ISBN 0-8120-2247-5). Barron.
--Superbikes. (Young Engineer Books). (gr. 4-6). 1979. (Usborne-Hayes); PLB 12.95 (ISBN 0-88110-014-5). EDC.
Chapman & Rutland. Book of Speed. (Young Engineer Bks.). (gr. 4-6). 1978. 12.95 (ISBN 0-86020-183-X, Usborne-Hayes). EDC.
Chapman, jt. auth. see Oliver.
Chapman, jt. ed. see Haugen.
Chapman, et al. Introduction & Methodology to the Study of Police Assaults in the South Central United States. (Criminal Justice Policy & Administration Research Ser: No. 1). 30p. 1974. pap. 1.00 (ISBN 0-686-20784-X). Univ OK Gov Res.
--Management of the Neurogenic Bowel & Bladder. (Illus.). 189p. 1979. pap. text ed. 5.95x (ISBN 0-934670-00-5). Eterna Pr.
Chapman, jt. ed. see Milligan.
Chapman, A. & Gale, A. Psychology & People. (Psychology for Professional Groups Ser.). 528p. 1982. text ed. 28.25x (ISBN 0-333-33145-1, Pub. by Macmillan England); pap. text ed. 13.50x (ISBN 0-333-33147-8). Humanities.
Chapman, A. B., jt. auth. see Shillington, Violet M.
Chapman, A. B., ed. General & Quantitative Genetics. (World Animal Science Ser.: No. 4A). 300p. 1985. 92.75 (ISBN 0-444-42203-X). Elsevier.
Chapman, A. C. Small Business Opportunities. 348p. 1985. 28.50 (ISBN 0-317-19977-3). Porter.
Chapman, A. H. The Games Children Play. 408p. 1978. pap. 1.95 (ISBN 0-425-03982-X, Medallion). Berkley Pub.
Chapman, A. H. & Chapman, Miriam. Harry Stack Sullivan's Concept of Personality Development & Psychiatric Illness. LC 80-13866. 224p. 1980. 22.50 (ISBN 0-87630-236-3). Brunner-Mazel.
Chapman, A. J. & Jones, D. M., eds. Models of Man. 430p. 1981. pap. 19.95x (ISBN 0-901715-12-3). L Erlbaum Assocs.
Chapman, A. J., jt. ed. see Crozier, W. R.
Chapman, A. L. Capital Transfer Tax. 4th ed. 1982. 95.00x (ISBN 0-85459-019-6, Pub. by Tolley Pub England). State Mutual Bk.
Chapman, A. L., ed. Tolley's Company Law. 1982. 75.00x (ISBN 0-85459-069-2, Pub. by Tolley Pub England). State Mutual Bk.
--Tolley's Tax Planning, 1984. 1984. 190.00x (ISBN 0-85459-047-1, Pub. by Tolley Pub England). State Mutual Bk.
Chapman, A. R. Biology of Seaweeds. (Illus.). 160p. 1979. pap. text ed. 15.00 (ISBN 0-8391-1340-4). Univ Park.
Chapman, Abraham, ed. Black Voices: An Anthology of Afro-American Literature. 1968. pap. 4.95 (ISBN 0-451-62205-7, ME2205, Ment). NAL.
--Jewish-American Literature: An Anthology. 727p. pap. 2.25 (ISBN 0-686-95132-8). ADL.
--New Black Voices. pap. 4.95 (ISBN 0-451-62292-8, ME2292, Ment). NAL.
Chapman, Al. Coloring Book of New Mexico Santos. Ortega, Pedro R., tr. 32p. (Span. & Eng.). (gr. 1-8). 1982. pap. 3.00 (ISBN 0-913270-19-9). Sunstone Pr.
Chapman, Alan J. Heat Transfer. 4th ed. (Illus.). 620p. 1984. text ed. write for info. (ISBN 0-02-321470-8). Macmillan.
Chapman, Alexandra, jt. auth. see Oakes, George W.
Chapman, Anne. Drama & Power in a Hunting Society: The Selk'nam of Tierra del Fuego. LC 82-4286. (Illus.). 240p. 1982. 44.50 (ISBN 0-521-23884-6). Cambridge U Pr.
Chapman, Anne, ed. Feminist Resources for Schools & Colleges: A Guide to Curricular Materials. 3rd ed. 225p. 1985. pap. 12.95 (ISBN 0-935312-35-8). Feminist Pr.
Chapman, Annie B., jt. auth. see Hart, Albert B.
Chapman, Antony J., jt. auth. see Gale, Anthony.
Chapman, Antony J., jt. auth. see McGhee, Paul E.
Chapman, Antony J., jt. ed. see Jones, Dylan M.
Chapman, Antony J., et al. Pedestrian Accidents. 250p. 1982. 59.95 (ISBN 0-471-10057-9, Pub. by Wiley-Interscience). Wiley.
Chapman, Arthur. The Pony Express: The Reader of Romantic Adventure in Business. LC 70-164522. (Illus.). 320p. 1971. Repr. of 1932 ed. 23.50 (ISBN 0-8154-0391-7). Cooper Sq.
Chapman, Arthur G. & Wray, Robert D. Christmas Trees for Pleasure & Profit. 3rd ed. (Illus.). 1979. 12.95 (ISBN 0-8135-0872-X). Rutgers U Pr.
--Christmas Trees for Pleasure & Profit. rev. ed. 220p. 1984. pap. text ed. 14.95 (ISBN 0-8135-1074-0). Rutgers U Pr.
Chapman, B. & Potter, A. M., eds. WJMM-Political Questions: Essays in Honour of W. J. M. Mackenzie. 294p. 1974. 24.00 (ISBN 0-7190-0594-9, Pub. by Manchester Univ Pr). Longwood Pub Group.
Chapman, B. R., jt. ed. see Martin, R. E.
Chapman, Benjamin. Card-Guide to New Testament Exegesis. 2.95 (ISBN 0-8010-2396-3). Baker Bk.
--Card-Guide to New Testament Greek. 1.95 (ISBN 0-8010-2388-2). Baker Bk.
--Greek New Testament Insert. 1.95 (ISBN 0-8010-2405-6). Baker Bk.
--New Testament Greek Notebook. 1976. looseleaf 19.95 (ISBN 0-8010-2389-0). Baker Bk.
--New Testament: Greek Notebook Exegesis Filler. 1.00 (ISBN 0-8010-2425-0). Baker Bk.
Chapman, Berlin & Webster Springs High School. Education in Central West Virginia, 1910-1975. 1974. 10.50 (ISBN 0-87012-160-X). McClain.
Chapman, Berlin B. Federal Management & Disposition of the Lands of Oklahoma Territory, 1866-1907. Bruchey, Stuart, ed. LC 78-56717. (Management of Public Lands in the U. S. Ser.). (Illus.). 1979. lib. bdg. 28.50x (ISBN 0-405-11325-0). Ayer Co Pubs.
--Four Principles That Portray the Pattern of All History. 1979. 3.00 (ISBN 0-87012-339-4). McClain.
Chapman, Betsy & Bookman, Barbara. Closet Full of Clothes & Something to Wear. (Illus.). 40p. (Orig.). 1984. pap. 4.95 (ISBN 0-9613544-8-8). Chapman & Bkman.
Chapman, Blanche A. Marriages of Isle of Wight County, Virginia, 1628-1800. LC 75-29198. 124p. 1982. Repr. of 1933 ed. 12.50 (ISBN 0-8063-0710-2). Genealog Pub.
--Wills & Administrations of Elizabeth City County, Virginia, 1688-1800. LC 80-68127. 198p. 1980. Repr. of 1941 ed. 15.00 (ISBN 0-8063-0909-1). Genealog Pub.
--Wills & Administrations of Southampton County, Virginia, 1749-1800. LC 80-68126. 208p. 1980. Repr. of 1947 ed. 15.00 (ISBN 0-8063-0907-5). Genealog Pub.
Chapman, Brian. Glow Discharge Processes: Sputtering & Plasma Etching. LC 80-17047. 406p. 1980. 48.95x (ISBN 0-471-07828-X, Pub. by Wiley-Interscience). Wiley.
--Introduction to French Local Government. LC 78-19030. (Illus.). 1978. Repr. of 1953 ed. lib. bdg. 22.25x (ISBN 0-313-20538-8, CHIF). Greenwood.
--Introduction to French Local Government. LC 78-59010. (Illus.). 1979. Repr. of 1953 ed. 18.50 (ISBN 0-88355-685-5). Hyperion Conn.
--The Profession of Government: The Public Service in Europe. LC 80-17162. 352p. 1980. Repr. of 1959 ed. lib. bdg. 32.50x (ISBN 0-313-22588-5, CHPG). Greenwood.
Chapman, Brian, jt. auth. see Chapman, Mike.
Chapman, Bruce, jt. auth. see Bayles, Michael D.

Chapman, C. Keeler & Traister, John E. Homes for the Nineteen-Eighties: An Energy & Construction Design Aid. LC 82-5929. (Illus.). 256p. (Orig.). 1982. pap. 17.95 (ISBN 0-8306-1425-7, 1425). TAB Bks.

Chapman, Carl B. & Reinmiller, Elinor C. The Physiology of Physical Stress: A Selective Bibliography, 1500-1964. LC 74-15565. 400p. 1974. text ed. 22.50x (ISBN 0-674-66670-4). Harvard U Pr.

Chapman, Carl H. The Archaeology of Missouri, Vol. II. LC 73-92242. 336p. 1980. text ed. 27.00x (ISBN 0-8262-0284-5). U of Mo Pr.

--Archaeology of Missouri, Vol. I. LC 73-92242. 320p. 1975. 26.00x (ISBN 0-8262-0160-1). U of Mo Pr.

Chapman, Carl H. & Chapman, Eleanor F. Indians and Archaelology of Missouri. rev. ed. LC 83-3596. (Illus.). 176p. 1983. pap. 9.95 (ISBN 0-8262-0401-5). U of Mo Pr.

--Indians & Archaeology of Missouri. rev. ed. LC 64-64127. (Missouri Handbook Ser.). (Illus.). 1983. pap. 4.00x (ISBN 0-8262-0589-5). U of Mo Pr.

Chapman, Carl H., jt. auth. see Howard, James H.

Chapman, Carl H., ed. see Adams, Lee M.

Chapman, Carl H., ed. see Hamilton, Henry, et al.

Chapman, Carl H., ed. see Hamilton, Henry W.

Chapman, Carl H., ed. see Hamilton, Henry W. & Willoughby, Charles C.

Chapman, Carl H., ed. see Healan, Dan M.

Chapman, Carl H., ed. see Hopgood, James F.

Chapman, Carl H., ed. see Klippel, Walter E.

Chapman, Carl H., ed. see Marshall, Richard A.

Chapman, Carl H., ed. see Nichols, George W., et al.

Chapman, Carl H., ed. see Perino, Gregory.

Chapman, Carl H., ed. see Ross, Harold M.

Chapman, Carl H., ed. see Shippee, J. M.

Chapman, Carl H., ed. see Turner, Richard.

Chapman, Carleton A. Geology of Acadia National Park. LC 73-107079. (Illus.). 1970. 12.95 (ISBN 0-87638-012-7); pap. 5.95 (ISBN 0-85699-010-8). Chatham Pr.

Chapman, Carleton B. Physicians, Law & Ethics. 200p. 1984. 27.00x (ISBN 0-8147-1392-0, H842130); pap. 12.50x (ISBN 0-8147-1393-9). NYU Pr.

Chapman, Carleton B., ed. Physiology of Muscular Exercise. (AHA Monograph Ser.: Vol. 15). pap. text ed. cancelled (ISBN 0-87493-010-3, 73-010A). Am Heart.

Chapman, Carol. Herbie's Troubles. LC 80-21848. (Illus.). (ps-1). 1981. 9.95 (ISBN 0-525-31645-0, 0966-290). Dutton.

--Ig Lives in a Cave. LC 78-12831. (Illus.). (ps-3). 1979. 7.95 (ISBN 0-525-32534-4, Smart Cat). Dutton.

--The Tale of Meshka the Kvetch. LC 80-11225. (Illus.). 32p. (gr. k-3). 1980. 8.95 (ISBN 0-525-40745-6). Dutton.

Chapman, Carolyn K. Inspirational Poems to Touch the Heart. Date not set. 5.95. Carlton.

Chapman, Charles E. History of California: The Spanish Period. LC 74-144942. (Illus.). 1971. Repr. of 1921 ed. 69.00x (ISBN 0-403-03600-3). Scholarly.

--A History of Spain Founded on the Historia de Espana Y de La Civilizacion Espanola of Rapael Altamira. 559p. 1983. Repr. of 1938 ed. lib. bdg. 75.00 (ISBN 0-89987-137-2). Darby Bks.

--History of the Cuban Republic. LC 75-96177. 1970. Repr. of 1927 ed. lib. bdg. 49.00x (ISBN 0-374-91444-3). Octagon.

--A History of the Cuban Republic: A Study in Hispanic American Politics. 1976. lib. bdg. 59.95 (ISBN 0-8490-1993-1). Gordon Pr.

Chapman, Charles F. & Maloney, E. S. Chapman Piloting, Seamanship & Small Boat Handling. 55th ed. 640p. 1981. 19.95 (ISBN 0-87851-809-6); deluxe ed. 24.95 (ISBN 0-87851-810-X). Hearst Bks.

--Chapman's Piloting, Seamanship & Small Boat Handling. 56th rev. ed. (Illus.). 624p. 1983. FPT 23.95 (ISBN 0-87851-814-2, Pub. by Hearst Bks); deluxe ed. 33.95 FPT (ISBN 0-87851-815-0). Morrow.

Chapman, Charles F., jt. auth. see Lynch, Barbara S.

Chapman, Charlotte G. Milocca: A Sicilian Village. 256p. 1971. text ed. 15.50x (ISBN 0-87073-764-3). Schenkman Bks Inc.

Chapman, Christine M. Medical Nursing. 9th ed. (Illus.). 384p. 1977. pap. 9.50 (ISBN 0-7216-0820-5, Pub. by Bailliere-Tindall). Saunders.

--Sociology for Nurses. 2nd ed. (Illus.). 210p. 1982. pap. 8.50 (ISBN 0-7216-0900-7, Pub. by Bailliere-Tindall). Saunders.

Chapman, Christopher. The Right Side of the Hedge. LC 77-89372. 1977. 8.95 (ISBN 0-7153-7342-0). David & Charles.

Chapman, Claire. Teaching Squash. 1977. pap. 13.50x (ISBN 0-7135-1951-7, SpS). Sportshelf.

Chapman, Clark R. Planets of Rock & Ice: From Mercury to the Moons of Saturn. (Illus.). 256p. 1982. 13.95 (ISBN 0-684-17484-7, ScribT). Scribner.

Chapman, Clark R. & Cruikshank, Dale P., eds. Observing the Moon, Planets, & Comets, 2 vols. LC 83-11556. (Orig.). 1985. Set. pap. text ed. 46.00 (ISBN 0-89490-098-6). Enslow Pubs.

Chapman, Colin. The Case for Christianity. 320p. 30.00x (ISBN 0-686-45617-3, Pub. by Lion Pub England). State Mutual Bk.

--The Case for Christianity. (Illus.). 313p. 1984. pap. 12.95 (ISBN 0-8028-1984-2). Eerdmans.

Chapman, Coolidge O. An Index of Names in Pearl, Purity, Patience & Gawain. LC 77-29259. 1978. Repr. of 1951 ed. lib. bdg. 18.75x (ISBN 0-313-20213-3, CHIN). Greenwood.

Chapman, D. Biological Membranes, 3 vols. Vol. 1 1968. o.s.i 70.00 (ISBN 0-12-168540-3); Vol. 2 1973. 60.00 (ISBN 0-12-168542-X); Vol. 3 1976. 60.00 (ISBN 0-12-168544-6). Acad Pr.

--Biological Membranes, Vol. 4. 1982. 70.00 (ISBN 0-12-168545-4). Acad Pr.

--Biological Membranes: Trigger Processes in Cell Biology, Vol. 5. (Biological Membranes Ser.). 1985. 75.00 (ISBN 0-12-168546-2). Acad Pr.

Chapman, D., ed. Biomembrane Structure & Function. (Topics in Molecular & Structural Biology Ser.: Vol. 4). 414p. 1984. 71.20x (ISBN 0-89573-208-4). VCH Pubs.

Chapman, D. G. & Gallucci, V. F., eds. Quantitative Population Dynamics. (Statistical Ecology Ser.). 290p. 1981. 30.00 (ISBN 0-89974-010-3). Intl Co-Op.

Chapman, D. J., jt. auth. see Chapman, V. J.

Chapman, D. J., jt. auth. see Round, F. E.

Chapman, D. J., jt. ed. see Round, F. E.

Chapman, D. S., tr. see Buntebarth, G.

Chapman, Daniel K., jt. ed. see Morse, Ronald A.

Chapman, Danny. Circus Buffoon. 238p. (Orig.). 1983. pap. 6.00 (ISBN 0-9611172-0-6). S K Chapman.

Chapman, David, jt. auth. see Visser, John.

Chapman, David J., jt. ed. see Ragan, Mark A.

Chapman, David W., ed. Improving College Information for Prospective Students. 128p. 1980. pap. 14.50 (ISBN 0-89964-162-8). Coun Adv & Supp Ed.

--Improving College Information for Prospective Students. 128p. 10.50 (ISBN 0-89964-162-8). Coun Adv & Supp Ed.

Chapman, David W., et al. Hazardous Wastes & the Consumer Connection: A Guide for Educators & Citizens Concerned with the Role of Consumers in the Generation of Hazardous Wastes. (Hazardous Chemicals Education Project Ser.). 36p. (Orig.). 1984. pap. write for info.; pap. text ed. write for info. Sci Citizens.

Chapman, Desmond, intro. by. Daisy Princess of Pless (Herself) 529p. 1982. Repr. of 1928 ed. lib. bdg. 50.00 (ISBN 0-89987-166-6). Darby Bks.

Chapman, Donald & Chapman, Norma. Fallow Deer. (Illus.). 1979. 39.00x (ISBN 0-900963-50-6, Pub. by Terence Dalton England). State Mutual Bk.

Chapman, Duane. Energy Resources & Energy Corporations. LC 82-74022. (Illus.). 368p. 1983. 19.95x (ISBN 0-8014-1305-2). Cornell U Pr.

Chapman, E., jt. auth. see Uvarov, B. P.

Chapman, E. F. Notable Indian Women of the Nineteenth Century. 139p. 1984. text ed. 20.00x (ISBN 0-86590-392-1, Inter India Pubns Delhi). Apt Bks.

Chapman, Edgar L. The Magic Labyrinth of Philip Jose Farmer. LC 81-21603. (The Milford Series-Popular Writers of Today: Vol. 38). 96p. 1984. lib. bdg. 12.95x (ISBN 0-89370-158-0); pap. text ed. 4.95x (ISBN 0-89370-258-7). Borgo Pr.

Chapman, Edward A., et al. Library Systems Analysis Guidelines. LC 75-109391. pap. 46.00 (ISBN 0-317-10516-7, 2013055). Bks Demand UMI.

Chapman, Edward M. English Literature in Account with Religion. 1977. lib. bdg. 59.95 (ISBN 0-8490-1775-0). Gordon Pr.

--New England Village Life. LC 72-143643. 1971. Repr. of 1937 ed. 40.00x (ISBN 0-8103-3699-5). Gale.

Chapman, Eleanor F., jt. auth. see Chapman, Carl H.

Chapman, Elisabeth. My Wayward Parent: A Book About Irvin S. Cobb. LC 71-156182. (Illus.). 1971. Repr. of 1945 ed. lib. bdg. 18.75x (ISBN 0-8371-6125-8, CHWP). Greenwood.

Chapman, Elizabeth K. Visually Handicapped Children & Young People. (Special Needs in Education Ser.). 1978. 16.95x (ISBN 0-7100-8878-7). Routledge & Kegan.

Chapman, Elizabeth R. A Companion to "In Memoriam". 1978. Repr. of 1901 ed. lib. bdg. 10.00 (ISBN 0-8495-0841-X). Arden Lib.

--A Companion to "In Memoriam". 1973. lib. bdg. 12.50 (ISBN 0-8414-1150-6). Folcroft.

Chapman, Elwood. College Survival: Find Yourself, Find a Career. 2nd ed. 192p. 1981. pap. text ed. 9.95 (ISBN 0-574-20615-9, 13-3615). SRA.

--Comfort Zones: A Practical Guide for Retirement Planning. 320p. Date not set. pap. 12.95 (ISBN 0-317-19901-3). Crisp Pubns.

--Dynamic Retailing. 416p. 1981. pap. text ed. 21.95 (ISBN 0-574-20610-8, 13-3610); instr's. guide avail. (ISBN 0-574-20611-6, 13-3611). SRA.

Chapman, Elwood N. Career Search. LC 75-35758. (Illus.). 200p. 1976. pap. text ed. 9.95 (ISBN 0-574-20005-3, 13-3005); instr's guide avail. (ISBN 0-574-20006-1, 13-3006). SRA.

--Comfort Zones: A Practical Guide for Retirement Planning. (Illus.). 320p. 1985. pap. 12.95 (ISBN 0-931961-00-9). Crisp Pubns.

--The Fifty Minute Sales Training Program. (Illus.). 64p. (Orig.). 1985. pap. 4.95 (ISBN 0-931961-02-5). Crisp Pubns.

--The Fifty Minute Supervisor. (Illus.). 64p. (Orig.). 1985. pap. 4.95 (ISBN 0-931961-03-3). Crisp Pubns.

--From Campus to Career Success. LC 78-9085. 304p. 1978. pap. text ed. 9.95 (ISBN 0-574-20580-2, 13-3580); instr's guide avail. (ISBN 0-574-20581-0, 13-3581). SRA.

--Put More Leadership into Your Style. 144p. 1984. pap. text ed. 11.95 (ISBN 0-574-20710-4, 13-3710); tchr's. ed. o.p. 1.95 (ISBN 0-574-20711-2, 13-3711). SRA.

--Supervisor's Survival Kit. 3rd ed. 224p. 1982. pap. text ed. 12.95 (ISBN 0-574-20635-3, 13-3635); instr. guide avail. (ISBN 0-574-20636-1, 13-3636); self-paced exercise guide 5.95 (ISBN 0-574-20637-X, 13-3637); self-paced guide - hospitality industry 5.95 (13-3638); self-paced guide - supermarket industry 5.95 (13-3639); self-paced guide - health care industry 5.95 (13-3567). SRA.

--Your Attitude Is Changing. 1966. pap. text ed. 10.95 (ISBN 0-574-15300-4, 15-0300 TEXT). SRA.

--Your Attitude Is Showing. 4th ed. 224p. 1983. text ed. 11.95 (ISBN 0-574-20680-9, 13-3680); leader's guide avail. (ISBN 0-574-20681-7, 13-3681); self-paced exercise guide 5.95 (ISBN 0-574-20683-3, 13-3683). SRA.

Chapman, Emalee. Fast Italian Meals. LC 83-6255. (Illus.). 168p. 1983. pap. 7.95 (ISBN 0-89286-210-6). One Hund One Prods.

--Fifteen-Minute Meals: Fresh, Fantastic & Nutritious Recipes. LC 81-9567. (Illus.). 168p. (Orig.). 1981. pap. 7.95 (ISBN 0-89286-192-4). One Hund One Prods.

Chapman, Ernest T., jt. auth. see Wanklyn, J. Alfred.

Chapman, Eugenia & Major, Jill C. Clean Your House & Everything in It. (Illus.). 160p. 1982. pap. 6.95 (ISBN 0-399-50765-5, G&D). Putnam Pub Group.

--More Clean Your House & Everything in It. 160p. 1985. pap. 7.95 (ISBN 0-399-51095-8, Perigee). Putnam Pub Group.

Chapman, F. Solar Plasma, Geomagnetism & Aurora. (Documents on Modern Physics Ser.). (Illus.). 150p. 1964. 44.25 (ISBN 0-677-00130-4). Gordon.

Chapman, F., ed. see France, Anatole.

Chapman, F. B. Flute Technique. 4th ed. 1973. pap. 8.75 (ISBN 0-19-318609-8). Oxford U Pr.

Chapman, F. S., jt. auth. see Holland, F. A.

Chapman, F. Spencer. Lhasa the Holy City. facsimile ed. LC 75-37875. (Select Bibliographies Reprint Ser). Repr. of 1940 ed. 32.00 (ISBN 0-8369-6712-7). Ayer Co Pubs.

Chapman, Frank. The Spell of Hungry Wolf. 47p. 1975. pap. 2.50 (ISBN 0-913270-42-3). Sunstone Pr.

Chapman, Frank E., Jr., jt. ed. see Berlowitz, Marvin J.

Chapman, Frank M. Essays in South American Ornithogeography: Original Anthology. Sterling, Keir B., ed. LC 77-81087. (Biologists & Their World Ser.). (Illus.). 1978. lib. bdg. 59.50x (ISBN 0-405-10663-7). Ayer Co Pubs.

--The Handbook of Birds, 2 vols. (Illus.). 367p. 1985. Repr. of 1898 ed. Set. 177.45 (ISBN 0-89901-211-6). Found Class Reprints.

--The Warblers of North America. (Illus.). 13.25 (ISBN 0-8446-1838-1). Peter Smith.

Chapman, Frank T. The Germanization of Europe: The Peace-War Prospects for the World. (Illus.). 146p. 1981. 63.45x (ISBN 0-930008-72-3). Inst Econ Pol.

Chapman, Frederic. The Works of Anatole France in An English Translation, 34 Vols. 1983. Repr. of 1909 ed. lib. bdg. 800.00 set (ISBN 0-89987-280-8). Darby Bks.

Chapman, Frederic, ed. Novels & Short Stories of Anatole France, 19 vols. 1980. Set. lib. bdg. 425.00 (ISBN 0-8495-0790-1). Arden Lib.

Chapman, Frederic, tr. see France, Anatole.

Chapman, Frederik H. Architectura Navalis Mercatoria: Facsimile of the Classic Eighteenth Century Treatise on Shipbuilding. 152p. 75.00 (ISBN 0-229-97491-0). Sheridan.

Chapman, G., tr. see Hesoid.

Chapman, G. P. & Tarawall, S. A., eds. Systems for Cytogenetic Analysis in Vicia faba L. (Advances in Agricultural Biotechnology). 1984. lib. bdg. 38.00 (ISBN 90-247-3089-9, Pub. by Martinus Nijhoff Netherlands). Kluwer Academic.

Chapman, G. w. & Allen, T. G. Establishment Techniques for Forest Plantations. 2nd ed. (Forestry Papers: No. 8). 190p. (Eng., Fr. & Span., Orig. Ed. 1978). 1981. pap. 13.75 (ISBN 92-5-100535-4, F1491, FAO). Unipub.

Chapman, Gary. Now That You Are Single Again. 80p. 1985. wkbk. 3.95 (ISBN 0-89840-087-2). Heres Life.

--Toward a Growing Marriage. LC 79-21376. 1979. pap. 4.95 (ISBN 0-8024-8787-4). Moody.

Chapman, Gary & Bryant, Steven, eds. Melodic Index to Haydn's Instrumental Music: A Thematic Locator for the Hoboken Thematisch-Bibliographisches Werkverzeichnis, Vols. I & II. (Thematic Catalogue Ser.: No. 8). 100p. 1981. lib. bdg. 28.00 (ISBN 0-918728-19-3). Pendragon NY.

Chapman, Gary D. Hope for the Separated. LC 81-18667. 160p. 1982. pap. 4.95 (ISBN 0-8024-3616-1). Moody.

Chapman, Geoffrey. Book of Gospels. (Illus.). 672p. 1985. 95.00 (ISBN 0-225-66351-1). Winston Pr.

--Lectionary, 3 vols. 3500p. 1985. Vol. 1: The Proper of the Seasons, Sundays in Ordinary Time. 60.00 (ISBN 0-225-66350-3). Vol. 2: Weekdays in Ordinary Time, Proper of Saints, Commons. Vol. 3: Rituals Celebrations, Masses for Various Needs & Occasions, Votive Masses, Masses for the Dead. Winston Pr.

Chapman, George. All Fools. Manley, Frank, ed. LC 68-10664. (Regents Renaissance Drama Ser). xx, 103p. 1968. pap. 2.75x (ISBN 0-8032-5256-0, BB 229, Bison). U of Nebr Pr.

--The Blind Begger of Alexandria. LC 82-45794. (Malone Society Reprint Ser.: No. 64). Repr. of 1928 ed. 40.00 (ISBN 0-404-63064-2). AMS Pr.

--Bussy d'Ambois. Lordi, Robert J., ed. LC 64-11358. (Regents Renaissance Drama Ser). xxxii, 128p. 1964. 13.95x (ISBN 0-8032-0256-3); pap. 3.25x (ISBN 0-8032-5257-9, BB 205, Bison). U of Nebr Pr.

--Bussy d'Ambois. Brooke, Nicholas, ed. (The Revels Plays Ser.). 169p. 1964. 24.00 (ISBN 0-7190-1505-7, Pub. by Manchester Univ Pr); pap. 5.00 1979 (ISBN 0-7190-1616-9). Longwood Pub Group.

--The Gentleman Usher. Smith, John H., ed. LC 69-12399. (Regents Renaissance Drama Ser). xxxiv, 149p. 1970. 15.95x (ISBN 0-8032-0285-7); pap. 3.95x (ISBN 0-8032-5286-2, BB 232, Bison). U of Nebr Pr.

--George Chapman: Selected Poems. Wain, Eirian, ed. (Fyfield Ser.). 1978. pap. 5.75x (ISBN 0-85635-242-X, Pub. by Carcanet New Pr England). Humanities.

--An Humorous Day's Mirth. LC 82-45688. (Malone Society Reprint Ser.: No. 85). Repr. of 1599 ed. 40.00 (ISBN 0-404-63085-5). AMS Pr.

--The Plays of George Chapman: The Comedies. Holaday, Allan, ed. LC 69-11044. 594p. 1970. 39.95x (ISBN 0-252-78423-5). U of Ill Pr.

--The Widow's Tears. Smeak, Ethel M., ed. LC 65-24305. (Regents Renaissance Drama Ser). xxvi, 119p. 1966. 12.50x (ISBN 0-8032-0257-1); pap. 3.50x (ISBN 0-8032-5258-7, BB 217, Bison). U of Nebr Pr.

--The Widow's Tears. Yamada, Akihiro, ed. (The Revels Plays Ser.). 152p. 1975. 23.50 (ISBN 0-7190-1510-3, Pub. by Manchester Univ Pr). Longwood Pub Group.

Chapman, George see Harrier, Richard C.

Chapman, George, jt. auth. see Marlowe, Christopher.

Chapman, George, tr. see Homer.

Chapman, George, et al. Bussy d'Ambois. Evans, Maurice, ed. (New Mermaid Ser.). 1976. pap. 2.95x (ISBN 0-393-90001-0). Norton.

--Eastward Ho! Petter, C. G., ed. (New Mermaid Ser.). 1976. pap. 3.95x (ISBN 0-393-90002-9). Norton.

--Eastward Ho. Van Fossen, R. W., et al, eds. LC 79-83851. (Revels Plays Ser.). 1979. text ed. 20.00x (ISBN 0-8018-2252-1). Johns Hopkins.

Chapman, Gerald W. Edmund Burke: The Practical Imagination. LC 67-17305. 1967. 20.00x (ISBN 0-674-23750-1). Harvard U Pr.

Chapman, Graham. A Liar's Autobiography, Vol. VI. 240p. 1981. 13.95 (ISBN 0-416-00901-8, NO. 0240). Methuen Inc.

Chapman, Graham P. Human & Environmental Systems: A Geographer's Appraisal. 1978. 67.00 (ISBN 0-12-168650-7). Acad Pr.

Chapman, Guy. Beckford. 1937. lib. bdg. 30.00 (ISBN 0-8414-3448-4). Folcroft.

--A Bibliography of William Beckford of Fonthill. 1973. lib. bdg. 25.00 (ISBN 0-8414-1812-8). Folcroft.

--The Dreyfus Case: A Reassessment. LC 78-31754. (Illus.). 1979. Repr. of 1956 ed. lib. bdg. 26.25x (ISBN 0-313-20980-4, CHDC). Greenwood.

Chapman, H. John. Studies on the Early Papacy. LC 76-118517. 1971. Repr. of 1928 ed. 21.00x (ISBN 0-8046-1139-4, Pub. by Kennikat). Assoc Faculty Pr.

Chapman, Harmon M. Sensations & Phenomenology. LC 66-22443. pap. 43.30 (ISBN 0-317-08107-1, 2050043). Bks Demand UMI.

Chapman, Harold C., ed. Biological Control of Mosquitoes. (Illus., Orig.). 1985. pap. write for info. (ISBN 0-9606210-2-4). Am Mosquito.

--Biological Control of Mosquitoes. (Bulletin: No. 6). 218p. 1985. write for info. Am Mosquito.

Chapman, Harry, jt. auth. see Chapman, Jane.

Chapman, Harvey W. see Robinson, Fred C.

Chapman, Helen E. Paul Brewster & Son. facs. ed. LC 79-85681. (American Fiction Reprint Ser). 1875. 17.00 (ISBN 0-8369-7010-1). Ayer Co Pubs.

Chapman, Herbert O. Chinese Revolution, Nineteen Twenty-Six to Nineteen Twenty-Seven: A Record of the Period Under Communist Control As Seen from the Nationalist Capital. LC 75-39022. (China Studies: from Confucius to Mao Ser.). (Illus.). xvii, 310p. 1977. Repr. of 1928 ed. lib. bdg. 25.85 (ISBN 0-88355-379-1). Hyperion-Conn.

Chapman, Hester. Four Fine Gentlemen. LC 77-20589. (Illus.). 301p. 1978. 21.95x (ISBN 0-8032-1401-4). U of Nebr Pr.

Chapman, Hester W. Great Villiers: A Study of George Villiers, 2nd Duke of Buckingham, 1628-1687. 1949. Repr. 25.00 (ISBN 0-8274-2448-5). R West.

--Mary Second: Queen of England. LC 75-17197. 1976. Repr. of 1953 ed. lib. bdg. 19.50x (ISBN 0-8371-8302-2, CHMQ). Greenwood.

Chapman, Hester W. & Romanovsky Pavlovsky. Diversion. 1977. Repr. of 1946 ed. lib. bdg. 10.00 (ISBN 0-8495-0701-4). Arden Lib.

Chapman, Homer D. & Pratt, Parker F. Methods of Analysis for Soils, Plants, & Waters. 2nd ed. 310p. 1982. pap. text ed. 8.00x (ISBN 0-931876-55-9, 4034). Ag & Nat Res.

Chapman, I. M., tr. see Buntebarth, G.

Chapman, Isaac. The History of Wyoming Valley in Pennsylvania. 1975. Repr. 10.00 (ISBN 0-686-20872-2). Polyanthos.

Chapman, J. Maxims of Ali. pap. 2.00 (ISBN 0-686-18316-9). Kazi Pubns.

Chapman, J. B. Dr. Schuessler's Biochemistry. 1973. 6.95x (ISBN 0-7225-0639-2). Thorsons Pubs.

Chapman, J. B. & Perry, Edward L. The Biochemic Handbook. Orig. Title: Biochemic Theory & Practice. 1976. pap. 1.50 (ISBN 0-89378-051-0). Formur Intl.

Chapman, J. C., et al. Principles of Education. Cubberley, Ellwood P., ed. 645p. 1980. Repr. of 1924 ed. lib. bdg. 25.00 (ISBN 0-8495-0851-7). Arden Lib.

Chapman, J. Carol, ed. see De Montaigne, Michel.

Chapman, J. Dudley. Feminine Mind & Body. 1968. pap. 2.25 (ISBN 0-8065-0150-2, C273). Citadel Pr.

--The Sexual Equation. LC 77-75256. (Illus.). 1977. 16.95 (ISBN 0-8022-2201-3). Philos Lib.

Chapman, J. M. & Ayrey, G. The Use of Radioactive Isotopes in the Life Sciences. (Illus.). 148p. 1981. text ed. 28.50x (ISBN 0-04-570011-7); pap. text ed. 9.95x (ISBN 0-04-570012-5). Allen Unwin.

Chapman, J. M., jt. auth. see Edelman, J.

Chapman, J. R. Computers in Mass Spectrometry. 1978. 49.50 (ISBN 0-12-168750-3). Acad Pr.

--Practical Organic Mass Spectrometry. 29.95 (ISBN 0-471-90696-4). Wiley.

Chapman, J. W. & Drifte, R., eds. Japan's Quest for Comprehensive Security: Defense, Diplomacy & Dependence. LC 81-48263. 272p. 1983. 25.00x (ISBN 0-312-44070-7). St Martin.

Chapman, J. W., Jr. State Tax Commissions in the United States. 1973. Repr. of 1897 ed. 13.00 (ISBN 0-384-08507-5). Johnson Repr.

Chapman, James C. Individual Differences in Ability & Improvement & Their Correlations. LC 74-176636. (Columbia University. Teachers College. Contributions to Education: No. 63). Repr. of 1914 ed. 22.50 (ISBN 0-404-55063-0). AMS Pr.

Chapman, James W. & Boersma, Frederic J. Affective Correlates of Learning Disabilities. (Modern Approaches to the Diagnosis & Instruction of Multihandicapped Children Ser.: Vol. 15). 108p. 1980. text ed. 17.50 (ISBN 90-265-0341-5, Pub. by Swets & Zeitlinger Netherlands). Hogrefe Intl.

Chapman, James W., Jr. State Tax Commissions in the United States. LC 78-63860. (Johns Hopkins University. Studies in the Social Sciences. Fifteenth Ser. 1897: 10-11). Repr. of 1897 ed. 11.50 (ISBN 0-404-61116-8). AMS Pr.

Chapman, Jane & Chapman, Harry. Psychology of Health Care: A Humanistic Perspective. LC 82-21873. 250p. 1983. pap. text ed. 14.50 pub net (ISBN 0-534-01291-4). Brooks-Cole.

Chapman, Jane R. Economic Realities & Female Crime: Program Choices & Economic Rehabilitation. LC 79-3785. 240p. 1980. 26.50x (ISBN 0-669-03515-7). Lexington Bks.

Chapman, Jane R., ed. Economic Independence for Women: The Foundation for Equal Rights. LC 75-11129. (Sage Yearbooks in Women's Policy Studies: Vol. 1). 285p. 1976. 28.00 (ISBN 0-8039-0444-4); pap. 14.00 (ISBN 0-8039-0517-3). Sage.

Chapman, Jane R. & Gates, Margaret, eds. The Victimization of Women. LC 77-93701. (Sage Yearbooks in Women's Policy Studies: Vol. 3). 282p. 1978. 28.00 (ISBN 0-8039-0923-3); pap. 14.00 (ISBN 0-8039-0924-1). Sage.

--Women into Wives: The Legal & Economic Impact of Marriage. LC 76-47070. (Sage Yearbooks in Women's Policy Studies: Vol. 2). 320p. 1977. 14.00 (ISBN 0-8039-0700-1). Sage.

Chapman, Jean. Haunts & Taunts. (Teacher Resource Collections Ser.). (Illus.). 190p. 1983. 19.95 (ISBN 0-516-08959-5). Childrens.

--Moon Eyes. Lacis, Astra, tr. LC 79-22088. (Illus.). (gr. k-3). 1980. 8.95 (ISBN 0-07-010648-7). McGraw.

--Pancakes & Painted Eggs. (Teacher Resource Collections Ser.). (Illus.). 1982. PLB 19.95 (ISBN 0-516-08951-X). Childrens.

--The Sugar-Plum Christmas Book. (Teacher Resource Collections Ser.). (Illus.). 190p. 1982. lib. bdg. 19.95 (ISBN 0-516-08952-8). Childrens.

--Velvet Paws & Whiskers. (Teacher Resource Collections Ser.). (Illus.). 168p. 1982. lib. bdg. 19.95 (ISBN 0-516-08953-6). Childrens.

Chapman, Jean, ed. see McDonald, Lucile.

Chapman, Jefferson. The Icehouse Bottom Site. (Illus.). 146p. 1975. pap. 7.95 (ISBN 0-87049-179-2, Pub. by U of TN Dept of Anthropology). U of Tenn Pr.

Chapman, Jeffrey I. Proposition Thirteen & Land Use: A Case Study of Fiscal Limits in California. LC 79-3749. 1981. 27.50x (ISBN 0-669-03471-1). Lexington Bks.

Chapman, John. Adult English One. (Illus.). 1978. pap. 12.50 (ISBN 0-13-008821-8). P-H.

--Adult English Three. 1978. pap. 12.50 (ISBN 0-13-008862-5). P-H.

--Adult English Two. (Illus.). 1978. pap. 12.50 (ISBN 0-13-008839-0). P-H.

--Know & Tell the Gospel. LC 84-63149. 196p. 1985. pap. 5.95 (ISBN 0-89109-534-9). NavPress.

--Reading Development & Cohesion. x, 147p. 1983. pap. text ed. 7.50x (ISBN 0-435-10161-7). Heinemann Ed.

--Saint Benedict & the Sixth Century. LC 79-109719. 239p. 1972. Repr. of 1929 ed. lib. bdg. 15.00x (ISBN 0-8371-4209-1, CHSB). Greenwood.

--Tell It to Sweeney: The Informal History of the New York Daily News. LC 77-8991. (Illus.). 1977. Repr. of 1961 ed. lib. bdg. 27.50x (ISBN 0-8371-9724-4, CHTS). Greenwood.

--Welcome to English. (gr. 3-6). 1978. tchr's manual, 1-3 7.50 (ISBN 0-88345-355-X, 18495). Regents Pub.

--Welcome to English: Let's Begin. (Welcome to English Ser.). (Illus.). 48p. 1980. pap. 3.25 (ISBN 0-88345-422-X, 18480); tchr's manual 4.50 (ISBN 0-88345-423-8, 18493); tchr's. manual 4-5 7.50 (ISBN 0-88345-368-1, 18499). Regents Pub.

Chapman, John, ed. The Best Plays of 1947-1948. LC 75-19860. (The Best Plays Series). 1976. 25.00x (ISBN 0-405-09176-1). Ayer Co Pubs.

--Best Plays of 1948-1949. LC 75-19860. (Best Plays Ser). 1976. 25.00x (ISBN 0-405-07657-6). Ayer Co Pubs.

--The Best Plays of 1950-1951. LC 75-19860. (The Best Plays Series). 1976. 25.00x (ISBN 0-405-09178-8). Ayer Co Pubs.

--The Best Plays of 1951-1952. LC 75-19860. (The Best Plays Series). 1976. 27.50x (ISBN 0-405-07658-4). Ayer Co Pubs.

--Burns Mantle Best Plays of Nineteen Forty-Nine to Nineteen Fifty. LC 75-19860. (The Best Plays Series). 1976. 27.50x (ISBN 0-405-09177-X). Ayer Co Pubs.

Chapman, John & Sherwood, Garrison P., eds. The Best Plays of 1894-1899. facsimile ed. LC 73-5663. (Play Anthology Reprint Ser.). Repr. of 1955 ed. 16.75 (ISBN 0-8369-8249-5). Ayer Co Pubs.

Chapman, John, et al. Talk It Over: Discussion Topics for Intermediate Students. (English As a Second Language Bk.). (Illus.). 1978. pap. text ed. 3.95x (ISBN 0-582-79719-5); cassettes 10.50x (ISBN 0-582-79720-9). Longman.

Chapman, John A. Hamlet. 1932. lib. bdg. 10.00 (ISBN 0-8414-3494-8). Folcroft.

--History of Edgefield County from the Earliest Settlements to 1897. LC 80-17884. 521p. 1980. Repr. of 1897 ed. 30.00 (ISBN 0-87152-338-8). Reprint.

--History of Edgefield County, South Carolina. LC 75-44665. 521p. 1979. Repr. of 1897 ed. 30.00 (ISBN 0-89308-004-7). Southern Hist Pr.

--Papers on Shelley, Wordsworth & Others. facs. ed. LC 67-23191. (Essay Index Reprint Ser). 1929. 14.00 (ISBN 0-8369-0288-2). Ayer Co Pubs.

--Papers on Shelley, Wordsworth & Others. 1929. lib. bdg. 12.50 (ISBN 0-8414-3558-8). Folcroft.

--Wordsworth & Literary Criticism. LC 76-30784. 1977. Repr. of 1932 ed. lib. bdg. 8.50 (ISBN 0-8414-3463-8). Folcroft.

Chapman, John A., jt. auth. see O'Neall, John B.

Chapman, John B. Horace & His Poetry. LC 70-120975. (Poetry & Life Ser.). Repr. of 1913 ed. 7.25 (ISBN 0-404-52505-9). AMS Pr.

Chapman, John D. & Sherman, John C., eds. Oxford Regional Economic Atlases: The United States & Canada. 2nd ed. (Illus.). 1975. pap. 14.95x (ISBN 0-19-894308-3). Oxford U Pr.

Chapman, John F., jt. ed. see Bursk, Edward C.

Chapman, John J. Causes & Consequences. 59.95 (ISBN 0-87968-821-1). Gordon Pr.

--Emerson & Other Essays. LC 75-108126. 1970. Repr. of 1899 ed. 19.50 (ISBN 0-404-00619-1). AMS Pr.

--Emerson & Other Essays. 59.95 (ISBN 0-8490-0105-6). Gordon Pr.

--Glance Toward Shakespeare. facsimile ed. LC 70-109643. (Select Bibliographies Reprint Ser). 1922. 14.00 (ISBN 0-8369-5252-9). Ayer Co Pubs.

--Glance Toward Shakespeare. 1973. Repr. of 1922 ed. 8.50 (ISBN 0-8274-1496-X). R West.

--Learning, & Other Essays. facs. ed. LC 68-16918. (Essay Index Reprint Ser). 1910. 17.00 (ISBN 0-8369-0290-4). Ayer Co Pubs.

--Letters & Religion. 1977. Repr. 29.00x (ISBN 0-403-07361-8). Scholarly.

--Memories & Milestones. facs. ed. LC 70-152161. (Essay Index Reprint Ser). 1915. 18.00 (ISBN 0-8369-2183-6). Ayer Co Pubs.

--Practical Agitation. LC 1581. (American Studies). 1970. Repr. of 1900 ed. 14.00 (ISBN 0-384-08505-9). Johnson Repr.

--Selected Writings. LC 83-45729. Repr. of 1957 ed. 29.50 (ISBN 0-404-20054-0). AMS Pr.

--William Lloyd Garrison. (American Newspapermen 1790-1933 Ser.). 1974. Repr. 17.50x (ISBN 0-8464-0027-8). Beekman Pubs.

Chapman, John J., ed. The Political Nursery: 1897-1901, Vols. 1-4. LC 75-309. (The Radical Tradition in America Ser). 1975. Repr. of 1897 ed. Set. 25.00 (ISBN 0-88355-213-2). Hyperion Conn.

Chapman, John Jay. The Collected Works of John Jay Chapman, 12 vols. Bernstein, Melvin H., ed. (Illus.). 4350p. 1970. 265.00x set (ISBN 0-87730-003-8). M&S Pr.

--William Lloyd Garrison. 1913. 15.00 (ISBN 0-8414-3016-0). Folcroft.

Chapman, John M. & Westerfield, Ray B. Branch Banking: Its Historical & Theoretical Position in America & Abroad. Bruchey, Stuart, ed. LC 80-1140. (The Rise of Commercial Banking Ser.). 1981. Repr. of 1940 ed. lib. bdg. 39.00x (ISBN 0-405-13640-4). Ayer Co Pubs.

Chapman, John M. & Shay, Robert P., eds. The Consumer Finance Industry: Its Costs & Regulations. LC 67-21693. (Illus.). pap. 38.60 (ISBN 0-317-09347-9, 2015323). Bks Demand UMI.

Chapman, John S. The Anonymous Mycobacteria in Human Disease. (Illus.). 184p. 1960. photocopy ed. 18.75x (ISBN 0-398-00303-3). C C Thomas.

--The Atypical Mycobacteria & Human Mycobacteriosis. LC 77-1824. (Current Topics in Infectious Diseases Ser.). (Illus.). 216p. 1977. 32.50x (ISBN 0-306-30997-1, Plenum Pr). Plenum Pub.

--Byron & the Honourable Augusta Leigh. LC 74-29714. pap. 76.50 (ISBN 0-317-29586-1, 2021987). Bks Demand UMI.

Chapman, John W. Rousseau: Totalitarian or Liberal. LC 68-54260. (Columbia University Studies in the Social Sciences Ser.: No. 589). Repr. of 1956 ed. 16.50 (ISBN 0-404-51589-4). AMS Pr.

--Ten'a Texts & Tales from Anvik, Alaska...with Vocabulary by Pliny Earle Goddard. LC 73-3541. (American Ethnological Society. Publications: No. 6). Repr. of 1914 ed. 30.00 (ISBN 0-404-58156-0). AMS Pr.

Chapman, John W., jt. auth. see Pennock, J. Roland.

Chapman, John W., ed. The Western University on Trial. LC 82-20120. 256p. 1983. text ed. 24.50x (ISBN 0-520-04940-3). U of Cal Pr.

Chapman, John W., jt. ed. see Pennock, J. R.

Chapman, John W., jt. ed. see Pennock, J. Roland.

Chapman, John W., jt. ed. see Penrock, J. Roland.

Chapman, Joseph A. & Pursley, Duane. Worldwide Furbearer Conference Proceedings, 3-11 August 1980, Frostburg, Maryland, 3 Vols. 2056p. 1983. 60.00 set (WFC100, Worldwide Furbearer Con). Unipub.

Chapman, Joseph A. & Feldhamer, George A., eds. Wild Mammals of North America: Biology, Management, & Economics. LC 81-8209. 1184p. 1982. text ed. 55.00x (ISBN 0-8018-2353-6). Johns Hopkins.

Chapman, K. G., tr. see Vesaas, T.

Chapman, Karen, tr. see Dadie, Bernard.

Chapman, Kate & Stewart, Dorothy. Adobe Notes. (Illus.). 44p. 1977. 1.75 (ISBN 0-941270-10-6). Ancient City Pr.

Chapman, Keith. People, Pattern & Processes: An Introduction to Human Geography. LC 79-18917. 334p. 1979. 63.95x (ISBN 0-470-26719-4). Halsted Pr.

Chapman, Kenneth, jt. auth. see Haugen, Einar.

Chapman, Kenneth C. Tarjei Vesaas. LC 78-110715. (World Authors Ser.). 1970. lib. bdg. 15.95 (ISBN 0-8057-2948-8). Irvington.

Chapman, Kenneth G., tr. see Thordarson, Thorbergur.

Chapman, Kenneth M. The Pottery of Santo Domingo Pueblo: A Detailed Study of Its Decoration. LC 77-81985. (School of American Research). (Illus.). 192p. 1977. Repr. of 1938 ed. 29.95x (ISBN 0-8263-0460-5). U of NM Pr.

Chapman, L. R. The Process of Learning Mathematics. LC 71-178683. 405p. 1972. pap. text ed. 23.00 (ISBN 0-08-017357-8). Pergamon.

Chapman, Laura. A Change of Heart. 1977. pap. 1.50 (ISBN 0-380-00977-3, 32540). Avon.

--Discover Art, Bks. 1-3. (Illus.). (gr. 1-6). 1985. Bk. 1. text ed. 13.25 (ISBN 0-87192-153-7); Bk. 2. text ed. 13.25 (ISBN 0-87192-154-5); Bk. 3. text ed. 13.25 (ISBN 0-87192-155-3); Bk. 1. tchr's. ed. 14.95 (ISBN 0-87192-159-6); Bk. 2. tchr's. ed. 14.95 (ISBN 0-87192-160-X); Bk. 3. tchr's. ed. 14.95 (ISBN 0-87192-161-8). Davis Mass.

--Discover Art, Bks. 4-6. (Illus.). (gr. 1-6). 1985. Bk. 4. text ed. 13.25 (ISBN 0-87192-156-1); Bk. 5. text ed. 13.25 (ISBN 0-87192-157-X); Bk. 6. text ed. 13.25 (ISBN 0-87192-158-8); Bk. 4. tchr's. ed. 14.95 (ISBN 0-317-19614-6); Bk. 5. tchr's. ed. 14.95 (ISBN 0-87192-163-4); Bk. 6. tchr's. ed. 14.95 (ISBN 0-87192-164-2). Davis Mass.

--Patricia Renick: Triceracopter. Meyer, Ruth K., ed. (Illus.). pap. 6.50 (ISBN 0-917562-06-2). Contemp Arts.

Chapman, Laura H. Approaches to Art in Education. 444p. 1978. text ed. 24.95 (ISBN 0-15-502896-0, HC). HarBraceJ.

--Instant Art, Instant Culture: The Unspoken Policy for American Schools. 1982. text ed. 15.95x (ISBN 0-8077-2722-9). Tchrs Coll.

Chapman, Leslie. Waste Away. 224p. 1982. 17.95 (ISBN 0-7011-2629-9, Pub. by Chatto & Windus). Merrimack Pub Cir.

Chapman, Linda L., et al. Louis H. Sullivan Architectural Ornament Collection: Southern Illinois University at Edwardsville. LC 81-51083. (Illus.). 79p. (Orig.). 1981. pap. 10.00 (ISBN 0-89062-136-5, Pub by Southern Illinois Univ Edwardsville). Pub Ctr Cult Res.

Chapman, Liz. How to Catalogue: A Practical Handbook Using Library of Congress. 96p. 1983. 16.50 (ISBN 0-85157-369-X, Pub. by Bingley England). Shoe String.

Chapman, M. A. & Lewis, M. H. An Introduction to the Freshwater Crustacea of New Zealand. (Illus.). 261p. 1983. 19.95x (ISBN 0-00-216905-3, Pub. by W Collins New Zealand). Intl Spec Bk.

Chapman, M, Winslow. Seen from Space. 1972. 4.00 (ISBN 0-685-02640-X). Golden Quill.

--Temples. 1979. 6.00 (ISBN 0-8233-0303-9). Golden Quill.

Chapman, Malcolm. The Gaelic Vision in Scottish Culture. 1979. 21.50x (ISBN 0-7735-0506-7). McGill-Queens U Pr.

Chapman, Margaret. Directing the Work of Others. (Illus.). 20p. 1972. pap. 0.35 (ISBN 0-88441-023-4, 19-981-010); pap. 2.00 package of 10. GS.

--When Steak Was a Shilling a Pound. 72p. 1981. 21.00x (ISBN 0-906379-02-4, Pub. by Jupiter England). State Mutual Bk.

Chapman, Margaret, jt. auth. see Neumann, Phyllis.

Chapman, Maria. Right & Wrong in Massachusetts. LC 70-90110. Repr. of 1839 ed. 17.50x (ISBN 0-8371-2024-1, CHW&). Greenwood.

Chapman, Maria W., compiled by. Songs of the Free. facsimile ed. LC 71-170693. (Black Heritage Library Collection). Repr. of 1836 ed. 17.50 (ISBN 0-8369-8883-3). Ayer Co Pubs.

Chapman, Marie. Fun with Bible Geography. LC 80-65055. (Teaching Aid Ser.). 65p. 1980. plastic spiral 5.95 (ISBN 0-89636-044-X). Accent Bks.

Chapman, Marie M. Puppet Animals Tell Bible Stories. LC 77-75134. (Illus.). 1977. tchr's ed. spiral bdg. 4.95 (ISBN 0-916406-74-1). Accent Bks.

Chapman, Marvey. Marmac Guide to Los Angeles. Smith, Susan H., ed. (Marmac Guide Ser.). (Illus.). 336p. (Orig.). 1983. pap. 8.95 (ISBN 0-939944-14-6). Marmac Pub.

Chapman, Maybelle K. Great Britain & the Bagdad Railway. LC 48-8011. (Studies in History: No. 31). 1948. pap. 8.40 (ISBN 0-87391-001-X). Smith Coll.

Chapman, Michael S., jt. auth. see Gardner, James F.

Chapman, Mike. A History of Wrestling in Iowa: From Gotch to Gable. LC 80-28728. (Illus.). 376p. 1981. 17.50 (ISBN 0-87414-017-X); pap. 9.95 (ISBN 0-87414-018-8). U of Iowa Pr.

--The Toughest Men in Sport. LC 83-80730. (Illus.). 192p. (Orig.). 1984. pap. 10.95 (ISBN 0-88011-187-9). Leisure Pr.

Chapman, Mike & Chapman, Brian. Evy & the Hawks: The Golden Years of Hawkeye Football. LC 83-80728. (Illus.). 288p. (Orig.). 1983. pap. 12.95 (ISBN 0-88011-186-0). Leisure Pr.

Chapman, Miriam, jt. auth. see Chapman, A. H.

Chapman, Murray & Prothero, Mansell, eds. Circulation in Population Movement: Substance & Concepts from the Melanesian Case. (Illus.). 480p. 1985. 59.00x (ISBN 0-7102-0451-5). Routledge & Kegan.

Chapman, Murray, jt. ed. see Prothero, Mansell.

Chapman, N. B. & Shorter, J., eds. Advances in Linear Free-Energy Relationships. LC 78-161305. 448p. 1972. 65.00x (ISBN 0-306-30566-6, Plenum Pr). Plenum Pub.

--Correlation Analysis in Chemistry: Recent Advances. LC 78-1081. (Illus.). 560p. 1978. 79.50x (ISBN 0-306-31068-6, Plenum Pr). Plenum Pub.

Chapman, Norma, jt. auth. see Chapman, Donald.

Chapman, O. L., ed. Organic Photochemistry, Vol. 1. 1967. 69.75 (ISBN 0-8247-1095-9). Dekker.

--Organic Photochemistry, Vol. 3. 320p. 1973. 69.75 (ISBN 0-8247-1096-7). Dekker.

Chapman, Orville L. Organic Syntheses, Vol. 60. LC 21-17747. (Organic Syntheses Ser.). 156p. 1981. 26.50 (ISBN 0-471-09359-9, Pub. by Wiley-Interscience). Wiley.

Chapman, P. A. An Anthology of Seventeenth Century French Literature. Princeton University Department of Modern Languages Staff, compiled by. 404p. 1981. Repr. of 1927 ed. lib. bdg. 50.00 (ISBN 0-89984-116-3). Century Bookbindery.

--An Anthology of Seventeenth Century French Literature. 1927. 25.00 (ISBN 0-686-17673-1). Quaker City.

Chapman, P. F. & Roberts, F. Metal Resources & Energy. (Monographs on Materials). 238p. 1983. text ed. 49.95 (ISBN 0-408-10801-0); pap. text ed. 19.95 (ISBN 0-408-10802-9). Butterworth.

Chapman, P. H. Concepts in Pediatric Neurosurgery. (Concepts in Pediatric Neurosurgery: Vol. 6). (Illus.). viii, 242p. 1985. 74.50 (ISBN 3-8055-4136-8). S Karger.

Chapman, Paul. Unmet Needs & the Delivery of Care. 110p. 1979. pap. text ed. 9.75x (ISBN 0-7199-0962-7, Pub. by Bedford England). Brookfield Pub Co.

Chapman, Paul H. The Norse Discovery of America. LC 80-82715. 120p. 1981. lib. bdg. 10.95 (ISBN 0-914032-02-X); pap. 7.95 (ISBN 0-686-77506-6). One Candle.

Chapman, Peter & Martin, Margaret. An Illustrated Guide to Cacti & Succulents. LC 83-83423. (Illustrated Gardening Guides Ser.). (Illus.). 160p. 1984. 9.95 (ISBN 0-668-06194-4, 6194-4). Arco.

Chapman, Peter, ed. see Boyes, G. T.

Chapman, Peter S. & Kirch, P. V. Archaeological Excavations at Seven Sites, Southeast Maui, Hawaiian Islands. (Departmental Report: 79-1). 40p. 1979. pap. 5.00 (ISBN 0-910240-86-8). Bishop Mus.

Chapman, Phil. Electricity. (Young Scientist Ser.). (gr. 5-9). 1976. (Usborne-Hayes); PLB 12.95 (ISBN 0-88110-006-4); pap. 4.95 (ISBN 0-86020-078-7). EDC.

Chapman, R., ed. Essays & Studies, 1984. 103p. 1984. text ed. 20.50x (ISBN 0-391-03059-0, Pub. by John Murray England). Humanities.

Chapman, R. E. Geology & Water: An Introduction to Fluid Mechanics for Geologists. 1982. 44.50 (ISBN 90-247-2455-4, Pub. by Martinus Nijhoff Netherlands). Kluwer Academic.

--Petroleum Geology. (Developments in Petroleum Science Ser.: Vol. 16). 416p. 1983. 44.25 (ISBN 0-444-42165-3, I-424-83). Elsevier.

--Petroleum Geology: A Concise Study. LC 72-97426. 310p. 1976. pap. 30.00 (ISBN 0-444-41432-0). Elsevier.

Chapman, R. F. Biology of Locusts. (Studies in biology: No. 71). 72p. 1978. pap. text ed. 8.95 (ISBN 0-7131-2619-1). E Arnold.

--The Insects: Structure & Function. 3rd ed. (Illus.). 992p. 1982. text ed. 37.50x (ISBN 0-674-45487-1). Harvard U Pr.

--A Laboratory Study of Roosting Behavior in Hoppers of the African Migratory Locust (Locusta Migratoria Migratorioides R & F) 1955. 35.00x (ISBN 0-85135-007-0, Pub. by Centre Overseas Research). State Mutual Bk.

Chapman, R. J. & Wood, Michael. Australian Local Government: The Federal Dimension. 208p. 1984. text ed. 30.00x (ISBN 0-86861-183-2). Allen Unwin.

Chapman, R. J., jt. auth. see Oliver, E. C.

Chapman, R. W. Five Letters from Jane Austen to Her Niece Fanny Knight. 1924. lib. bdg. 8.50 (ISBN 0-8414-2970-7). Folcroft.

--Johnson, Boswell, & Mrs. Piozzi: A Supressed Passage Restored. 1973. lib. bdg. 8.50 (ISBN 0-8414-3569-3). Folcroft.

Chapman, R. W., ed. Johnsonian Bibliography: A Supplement to Courtney. Bd. with Bibliographic Reflections of a Biologist. Cole, J. F., ed; The First Edition of Herbert's Temple. Hutchinson, F. E., ed. (Oxford Bibliographic Society Ser.: Vol. 3, Pt. 3). pap. 13.00 (ISBN 0-317-16504-6). Kraus Repr.

--The Letters of Samuel Johnson with Mrs. Thrale's Genuine Letters to Him. (Illus.). 1984. Vol. I, 34.50x (ISBN 0-19-818536-7); Vol. II, 34.50x (ISBN 0-19-818537-5); Vol. III, 34.50x (ISBN 0-19-818538-3). Oxford U Pr.

Chapman, R. W., ed. see Austen, Jane.

Chapman, R. W., ed. see Boswell, James.

Chapman, Rachael L. The U. S. A. Men & Machines, Vol. 3. (gr. 7 up). 1968. pap. 3.75 (ISBN 0-88345-242-1, 18437). Regents Pub.

Chapman, Raymond. The Language of English Literature. 160p. 1982. pap. text ed. 11.95 (ISBN 0-7131-6371-2). E Arnold.

--Linguistics & Literature: An Introduction to Literary Stylistics. (Quality Paperback Ser.: No. 267). 119p. 1973. pap. 3.95 (ISBN 0-8226-0267-9). Littlefield.

--Short Way to Better English. pap. 7.50x (ISBN 0-392-04585-0, SpS). Sportshelf.

--The Treatment of Sounds in Language & Literature. Crystal, David, ed. (Language Library). 272p. 1984. 29.95x (ISBN 0-631-13657-6). Basil Blackwell.

Chapman, Renate. Dark Moon. 1983. 8.95 (ISBN 0-317-17593-9, Avalon). Bouregy.

--Fool's Paradise. 1984. 8.95 (ISBN 0-8034-8453-4, Avalon). Bouregy.

--The Haunted Heart. 1983. 8.95 (ISBN 0-8034-8329-5, Avalon). Bouregy.

--House of Shadows. 1982. 8.95 (ISBN 0-686-84750-4, Avalon). Bouregy.

--Love's Secret Plan. 1984. 8.95 (ISBN 0-8034-8422-4, Avalon). Bouregy.

--Milmorra House. (YA) 1978. 8.95 (ISBN 0-685-53391-3, Avalon). Bouregy.

--Mystic Island. (YA) 1980. 8.95 (ISBN 0-686-59793-1, Avalon). Bouregy.

--Waters Dark & Deep. 1982. 8.95 (ISBN 0-686-84191-3, Avalon). Bouregy.

Chapman, Richard A. Leadership in the British Civil Service. 224p. 1984. 28.00 (ISBN 0-7099-3402-5, Pub. by Croom Helm Ltd). Longwood Pub Group.

Chapman, Richard M., jt. auth. see Broaker, Frank.

Chapman, Richard N. Contours of Public Policy, 1939-1945. Freidel, Frank, ed. LC 80-8460. (Modern American History Ser.). 319p. 1982. lib. bdg. 43.00 (ISBN 0-8240-4851-2). Garland Pub.

Chapman, Rick, ed. see Baba, Meher.

Chapman, Robert. Pilot Fatigue: A Deadly Coverup. (Illus.). 240p. 1982. 10.95 (ISBN 0-682-49900-5). Exposition Pr FL.

Chapman, Robert & Coxe, Louis O. Billy Budd. (Mermaid Dramabook Ser.). 90p. 1962. pap. 4.95 (ISBN 0-8090-1204-9). Hill & Wang.

Chapman, Robert, ed. see Clarke, David L.

Chapman, Robert, et al, eds. The Archaeology of Death. LC 80-41751. (New Directions in Archaeology Ser.). (Illus.). 200p. 1981. 34.50 (ISBN 0-521-23775-0). Cambridge U Pr.

Chapman, Robert D. Discovering Astronomy. LC 77-16024. (Illus.). 518p. 1978. text ed. 34.95 (ISBN 0-7167-0034-4); pap. text ed. 20.95 (ISBN 0-7167-0033-6); instructors' guide avail. W H Freeman.

Chapman, Robert D. & Brandt, John C. The Comet Book. (Illus.). 176p. 1984. pap. write for info. (ISBN 0-86720-029-4). Jones & Bartlett.

Chapman, Robert D., jt. auth. see Brandt, John C.

Chapman, Robert L. Roget's International Thesaurus. 4th ed. LC 84-47562. 1318p. (Orig.). 1984. pap. 8.61i (ISBN 0-06-091169-7, CN 1169, CN). Har-Row.

Chapman, Robert W. Johnsonian & Other Essays & Reviews. LC 78-158502. Repr. of 1953 ed. 29.00x (ISBN 0-403-01297-X). Scholarly.

--Johnsoniana & Other Essays & Reviews. 1973. Repr. of 1953 ed. 18.50 (ISBN 0-8274-1343-2). R West.

--Portrait of a Scholar, & Other Essays Written in Macedonia, 1916-1918. facs. ed. LC 68-29197. (Essay Index Reprint Ser). 1968. Repr. of 1920 ed. 15.00 (ISBN 0-8369-0291-2). Ayer Co Pubs.

Chapman, Robin. The Duchess's Diary. LC 84-25880. 128p. 1985. 18.95 (ISBN 0-571-13441-6); pap. 6.95 (ISBN 0-571-13442-4). Faber & Faber.

Chapman, Robin S. The Interpretation of Deviant Sentences in English. LC 73-87531. (Janua Linguarum, Ser. Minor: No. 189). (Illus.). 95p. 1974. pap. text ed. 10.80x (ISBN 90-2793-112-7). Mouton.

Chapman, Roger. No Time on Our Side. (Illus.). 163p. pap. 9.95 (ISBN 0-88826-059-8). Superior Pub.

Chapman, Roger, jt. auth. see Landon, Robbins H.

Chapman, Ronald F. Leonard Wood & Leprosy in the Philippines: The Culion Leper Colony, 1921-1927. LC 80-6301. (Illus.). 238p. (Orig.). 1982. lib. bdg. 24.75 (ISBN 0-8191-1976-8); pap. text ed. 12.25 (ISBN 0-8191-1977-6). U Pr of Amer.

Chapman, Royal N. Animal Ecology: Special Reference to Insects. Egerton, Frank N., 3rd, ed. LC 77-74208. (History of Ecology Ser.). 1978. Repr. of 1932 ed. lib. bdg. 36.50x (ISBN 0-405-10379-4). Ayer Co Pubs.

Chapman, Ruth. Fingerprints. (gr. 3-6). 1981. 6.95 (ISBN 0-86653-045-2, GA 274). Good Apple.

Chapman, S. & Cowling, T. G. Mathematical Theory of Non-Uniform Gases. 3rd ed. LC 70-77285. (Illus.). 1970. 54.50 (ISBN 0-521-07577-7). Cambridge U Pr.

Chapman, S. & Lindzen, R. S. Atmospheric Tides, Thermal & Gravitational. 210p. 1970. 57.75 (ISBN 0-677-61810-7). Gordon.

--Atmospheric Tides: Thermal & Gravitational. 200p. 1970. 23.70 (ISBN 90-277-0113-X, Pub. by Reidel Holland). Kluwer Academic.

Chapman, S. D. Stanton & Staveley: A Business History. (Illus.). 240p. (Orig.). 1981. 22.50 (ISBN 0-85941-172-9). Woodhead-Faulkner.

Chapman, S. D. & Chassagne, S. European Textile Printers in the Eighteenth Century: A Study of Peel & Oberkampf. (Pasold Studies in Textile History). (Illus.). xiii, 257p. 1981. text ed. 45.00x (ISBN 0-435-32170-6). Gower Pub Co.

Chapman, S. J. Electric Machinery Fundamentals. 672p. 1984. 32.50 (ISBN 0-07-010662-2). McGraw.

--Political Economy. 1979. Repr. of 1912 ed. lib. bdg. 20.00 (ISBN 0-8495-0936-X). Arden Lib.

Chapman, Samuel. The Postage Stamps of Mexico, 1856-1868. LC 75-40501. (Illus.). 1976. Repr. 35.00x (ISBN 0-88000-079-1). Quarterman.

Chapman, Samuel G. Police Dogs in America. (Criminal Justice Policy & Administration Research Ser.). 75p. 1979. 5.00 (ISBN 0-686-32070-0). Univ OK Gov Res.

--Police Patrol Readings. 2nd. ed. (Illus.). 788p. 1972. 50.75x (ISBN 0-398-00304-1). C C Thomas.

Chapman, Samuel G. & Peck, Gail. Dogs in Police Work in Oklahoma. 1978. 4.00 (ISBN 0-686-00896-0). Univ OK Gov Res.

Chapman, Samuel G., et al. A Descriptive Profile of the Assault Incident. (Criminal Justice Policy & Administration Research Ser.: No. 3). 1974. pap. 4.50 (ISBN 0-686-18640-0). Univ OK Gov Res.

Chapman, Stanley. The Rise of Merchant Banking. (Illus.). 240p. 1984. text ed. 27.50x (ISBN 0-04-332094-5). Allen Unwin.

Chapman, Stanley, jt. ed. see Brena, Steven.

Chapman, Stanley D. The Cotton Industry in the Industrial Revolution. (Studies in Economic & Social History). 1972. pap. text ed. 6.00x (ISBN 0-333-13584-9). Humanities.

Chapman, Stephen & Nakielny, Richard. A Guide to Radiological Procedures. 1981. pap. text ed. 17.95x (ISBN 0-7216-0712-8, Bailliere-Tindall). Saunders.

Chapman, Stephen, ed. see Bishop, Douglas D.

Chapman, Stephen R. & Carter, Lark P. Crop Production: Principles & Practices. LC 75-40318. (Illus.). 566p. 1976. text ed. 31.95 (ISBN 0-7167-0581-8). W H Freeman.

Chapman, Sue, jt. auth. see Harris, Mollie.

Chapman, Susan. Breaking the Stranglehold. (Illus.). 28p. (Orig.). 1978. 2.00 (ISBN 0-931482-00-3). Word Merchant Pr.

--Conversations with Dracaena. (Illus.). 32p. (Orig.). 1982. saddlestitched 6.00 (ISBN 0-931482-01-1). Word Merchant Pr.

--The Get Along Gang & the Crybaby. (The Get Along Gang Ser.). (Illus.). 32p. (Orig.). (ps-2). 1984. pap. 1.50 (ISBN 0-590-33278-3). Scholastic Inc.

Chapman, Suzanne E. Early American Design Motifs. 1983. 13.25 (ISBN 0-8446-5958-4). Peter Smith.

--Historic Floral & Animal Designs for Embroiderers & Craftsmen. LC 77-75740. (Pictorial Archive Ser.). (Illus.). 1978. pap. 3.50 (ISBN 0-486-23526-2). Dover.

--Historic Floral & Animal Designs for Embroiderers & Craftsmen. 14.00 (ISBN 0-8446-5564-3). Peter Smith.

Chapman, Suzanne E., ed. Early American Design Motifs. LC 73-86040. (Illus.). 160p. 1974. 7.95 (ISBN 0-486-23084-8); pap. 5.95 (ISBN 0-486-22985-8). Dover.

Chapman, Sydney J. Lancaster Cotton Industry. LC 68-55503. Repr. of 1904 ed. 29.50x (ISBN 0-678-00896-5). Kelley.

Chapman, T. Time: A Philosophical Analysis. 1982. 29.50 (ISBN 90-277-1465-7, Pub. by Reidel Holland). Kluwer Academic.

Chapman, T. A. Controlled Simple Homotopy Theory & Applications. (Lecture Notes in Mathematics: Vol. 1009). 94p. 1983. pap. 10.00 (ISBN 0-387-12338-5). Springer-Verlag.

--Lectures on Hilbert Cube Manifolds. LC 76-48316. (Conference Board of the Mathematical Sciences Ser.: No. 28). 1982. pap. 15.00 (ISBN 0-8218-1678-0, CBMS28). Am Math.

Chapman, Thomas A. Approximation Results in Topological Manifolds. LC 81-12791. (Memoirs of the American Mathematical Society: No. 251). 65p. 1981. pap. 9.00 (ISBN 0-8218-2251-9). Am Math.

Chapman, Tom. Aunt Zona's Web: Life of Arizona Hughes, a Pioneer Teacher. rev. ed. (Illus.). 1979. 5.00 (ISBN 0-686-27735-X). Puddingstone.

Chapman, Tom, jt. auth. see Petigura, Erika.

Chapman, V. J. Coastal Vegetation. 2nd ed. 1976. pap. text ed. 18.75 (ISBN 0-08-019687-X). Pergamon.

--Mangrove Vegetation. 1976. 52.50 (ISBN 3-7682-0926-1). Lubrecht & Cramer.

--Salt Marshes & Salt Deserts of the World. 2nd ed. 1974. 52.50 (ISBN 3-7682-0927-X). Lubrecht & Cramer.

Chapman, V. J. & Chapman, D. J. The Algae. 2nd ed. 500p. 1975. 29.95 (ISBN 0-312-01715-4). St Martin.

--Seaweeds & Their Uses. 1980. 49.95x (ISBN 0-412-15740-3, NO. 6362, Pub. by Chapman & Hall England). Methuen Inc.

Chapman, V. J., ed. The Marine Algae of New Zealand: Phaeophyceae, Vol.2. 1961. pap. 14.00 (ISBN 3-7682-0077-9). Lubrecht & Cramer.

Chapman, Valentine J., ed. Wet Coastal Ecosystems. LC 77-342. (Ecosystems of the World Ser.: Vol. 1). 428p. 1977. 81.00 (ISBN 0-444-41560-2). Elsevier.

Chapman, Vera. Blaedud the Birdman. 1980. pap. 1.95 (ISBN 0-380-45070-4, 45070). Avon.

--King Arthur's Daughter. 1978. pap. 1.75 (ISBN 0-380-01958-2, 38398). Avon.

--The King's Damsel. 1978. pap. 1.50 (ISBN 0-380-01916-7, 37606). Avon.

--Miranty & the Alchemist. (Illus.). 96p. (Orig.). (gr. 4-7). 1983. pap. 2.25 (ISBN 0-380-79269-9, 79269-9, Camelot). Avon.

Chapman, W. William Shakespeare & Robert Greene: The Evidence. LC 73-18209. (Studies in Shakespeare, No. 24). 1974. lib. bdg. 49.95x (ISBN 0-8383-1731-6). Haskell.

Chapman, W. A. Workshop Technology, Pt. 1. 5th ed. (Illus.). 1976. pap. 22.95x (ISBN 0-7131-3269-8). Intl Ideas.

--Workshop Technology, Pt. 2. 4th ed. (Illus.). 1972. 22.95x (ISBN 0-7131-3272-8). Intl Ideas.

--Workshop Technology, Part 3. 3rd. ed. (Illus.). 675p. 1975. pap. 29.95x (ISBN 0-7131-3351-1). Intl Ideas.

Chapman, William E. Roots of Character Education: An Exploration of the American Heritage from the Decade of the 1920s. LC 77-84299. 1977. pap. 2.95 (ISBN 0-915744-08-2). Character Res.

Chapnick, jt. auth. see Waite.

Chapon, A., jt. auth. see Aldman, B.

Chapon, Francois & Rouault, Isabelle. Rouault's Complete Graphic Work, 2 Vols. (Illus.). 714p. 1978. Vol. 1, 340p. 225.00 (ISBN 0-915346-86-9). Vol. 2, 374p. A Wofsy Fine Arts.

Chapot, V., jt. auth. see Cagnat, R.

Chapot, Victor. The Roman World. 449p. 1980. Repr. of 1928 ed. lib. bdg. 50.00 (ISBN 0-89760-118-1). Telegraph Bks.

Chapoy, L. L., ed. Recent Advances in Liquid Crystalline Polymers: Proceedings of the European Science Foundation Sixth Polymer Workshop, Lyngby, Denmark, 12-14 September 1983. (Illus.). 352p. 1985. 60.00 (ISBN 0-85334-313-6, Pub. by Elsevier Applied Sci England). Elsevier.

Chappat, Djenane. Diccionario de la Limpieza. 234p. (Span.). 1970. pap. 3.50 (ISBN 84-206-1282-0, S-12249). French & Eur.

Chappe, D'Auteroche. Journey into Siberia, Made by Order of the King of France. LC 77-115518. (Russia Observed Ser). Repr. of 1770 ed. 24.50 (ISBN 0-405-03074-6). Ayer Co Pubs.

Chappe, Eli. Winning Government Contracts: A Complete 27 Step Guide for Small Businesses. LC 83-22954. 266p. 1984. Repr. 69.95 (ISBN 0-13-960998-9, Busn). P-H.

Chappe d'Auteroche, Jean. A Voyage to California to Observe the Transit of Venus. 120p. 1984. Repr. of 1788 ed. 32.00x (ISBN 0-85546-174-8, Pub. by Richmond Pub England). State Mutual Bk.

Chappel, Alan. Sailboat Buyer's Guide. 384p. 1984. pap. 12.95 (ISBN 0-9611342-0-8). Sea Shore Pubn.

Chappel, Allen H., tr. see Aichinger, Ilse.

Chappel, Bernice M. In the Palm of the Mitten: A Memory Book of the Early 1900's. LC 81-82290. (Illus.). 300p. (Orig.). 1981. pap. 7.95 (ISBN 0-9606400-0-2). Great Lakes Bks.

--Independent Language Arts Activities: Seatwork for the Primary Grades. 2nd ed. LC 66-26670. 1973. pap. 4.95 (ISBN 0-8224-4215-9). Pitman Learning.

--Listening & Learning: Practical Activities for Developing Listening Skills. (gr. k-3). 1973. pap. 7.50 (ISBN 0-8224-4306-6). Pitman Learning.

--A Time for Learning: A Self-Instructional Handbook for Parents & Teachers of Young Children. 144p. 1974. pap. text ed. 5.00x (ISBN 0-89039-059-2). Ann Arbor FL.

Chappel, James. The Potter's Complete Book of Clay & Glazes. 448p. 1977. 27.50 (ISBN 0-8230-4202-2). Watson-Guptill.

Chappelear, Claude S. Health Subject Matter in Natural Sciences. LC 78-176637. (Columbia University. Teachers College. Contributions to Education: No. 341). Repr. of 1929 ed. 22.50 (ISBN 0-404-55341-9). AMS Pr.

Chappelear, George W., jt. auth. see Kaylor, Peter C.

Chappell, A. F. The Enigma of Rabelais: An Essay in Interpretation. Repr. of 1924 ed. lib. bdg. 15.00 (ISBN 0-8414-3412-3). Folcroft.

Chappell, Annette J. Skiing Is for Me. LC 78-12411. (The Sports for Me Bks). (Illus.). (gr. 5 up). 1978. PLB 7.95 (ISBN 0-8225-1082-0). Lerner Pubns.

Chappell, Annette Jo, jt. auth. see Dickmeyer, Lowell A.

Chappell, Clovis G. The Best of C. G. Chappell. (Best Ser.). 240p. 1984. pap. 5.95 (ISBN 0-8010-2500-1). Baker Bk.

--Chappell's Special Day Sermons. (Pocket Pulpit Library Ser.). 204p. 1983. pap. 4.50 (ISBN 0-8010-2383-1). Baker Bk.

--Faces About the Cross. (Glovis Chappell Library). pap. 3.95 (ISBN 0-8010-2364-5). Baker Bk.

--Feminine Faces. (Pocket Pulpit Library). 1978. pap. 3.95 (ISBN 0-8010-2355-6). Baker Bk.

--The Sermon on the Mount. (Pulpit Libarary Ser). 1979. pap. 4.95 (ISBN 0-8010-2363-7). Baker Bk.

--Sermons on Biblical Characters. (Pocket Pulpit Lib.). 192p. 1981. pap. 3.95 (ISBN 0-8010-2330-0). Baker Bk.

--The Seven Words: The Words of Jesus on the Cross Reveal the Heart of the Christian Faith. (Pocket Pulpit Library). 80p. 1976. pap. 2.95 (ISBN 0-8010-2387-4). Baker Bk.

Chappell, D. J. An Economic History of England. 320p. 1980. pap. 15.95x (ISBN 0-7121-0587-5). Trans-Atlantic.

Chappell, David. Report Writing for Architects. 128p. 1984. 26.50 (ISBN 0-89397-189-8). Nichols Pub.

Chappell, David W., ed. see Chegwan.

Chappell, David W., jt. ed. see Saso, Michael.

Chappell, Dick, tr. see Shlyapnikov, Alexander.

Chappell, Duncan, et al, eds. Forcible Rape: The Crime, the Victim & the Offender. LC 77-3377. 393p. 1977. 36.00x (ISBN 0-231-03839-9); pap. 16.00x (ISBN 0-231-04641-3). Columbia U Pr.

Chappell, Fred. Bloodfire: Poems. LC 78-13578. 1978. 13.95x (ISBN 0-8071-0451-5); pap. 4.95 (ISBN 0-8071-0452-3). La State U Pr.

--Castle Tzingal. 46p. 1984. text ed. 13.95x (ISBN 0-8071-1190-2); pap. 6.95 (ISBN 0-8071-1203-8). La State U Pr.

--Earthsleep: A Poem. LC 80-13622. 64p. 1980. pap. 4.95 (ISBN 0-8071-0698-4). La State U Pr.

--I Am One of You Forever. LC 84-23335. 192p. 1985. 14.95 (ISBN 0-8071-1216-X). La State U Pr.

--Midquest: A Poem. LC 81-847470. 1981. 12.95 (ISBN 0-8071-0877-4). La State U Pr.

--Moments of Light. LC 80-81219. 195p. 1980. 12.95 (ISBN 0-917990-05-6). Volcano Pr.

--Source. 64p. 1985. text ed. 13.95 (ISBN 0-8071-1276-3); pap. 6.95 (ISBN 0-8071-1277-1). La State U Pr.

--Wind Mountain: Poems. LC 79-12332. 1979. text ed. 13.95x (ISBN 0-8071-0566-X); pap. 4.95 (ISBN 0-8071-0567-8). La State U Pr.

--World Between the Eyes: Poems. LC 73-152706. 1971. 9.95 (ISBN 0-8071-0942-8). La State U Pr.

Chappell, Fred A. Bibliography of H. G. Wells with a Prologue Introducing Mr. Wells to the Future. 1924. lib. bdg. 20.00 (ISBN 0-8414-3475-1). Folcroft.

Chappell, Gordon. Summer Helmets of the U.S. Army, 1875-1910. 2nd ed. (Illus.). 34p. 1976. pap. 2.00 (ISBN 0-943398-05-3). Wyoming State Archives.

Chappell, Helen. All Things in Their Season. (Orig.). 1983. pap. 3.95 (ISBN 0-440-10057-7). Dell.

Chappell, J. B. The Energetics of Mitochondria. rev. ed. Head, J. J., ed. LC 77-70873. (Carolina Biology Readers Ser.). (Illus.). 32p. (gr. 10 up). 1979. pap. 2.00 (ISBN 0-89278-219-6, 45-9619). Carolina Biological.

Chappell, James D. COBOL Demand Processing Manual. 80p. 1981. pap. text ed. 6.95 (ISBN 0-8403-2376-X). Kendall-Hunt.

Chappell, M. N. & Hooper, C. E. Radio Audience Measurement. 246p. 1980. Repr. lib. bdg. 20.00 (ISBN 0-89984-104-X). Century Bookbindery.

Chappell, Michael, jt. auth. see Thompson, Leroy.

Chappell, Mollie. Romantic Widow. 1979. pap. 1.75 (ISBN 0-449-50013-6, Coventry). Fawcett.

Chappell, Pat. The Hot One: Chevrolet, Nineteen Fifty-Five to Nineteen Fifty-Seven. 3rd ed. LC 77-21298. (Illus.). 228p. 1981. 23.95 (ISBN 0-9606148-0-X). Dragonwyck Pub.

Chappell, Paul. Dr. S. S. Wesley 1810-1876: Portrait of a Victorian Musician. (Illus.). 220p. 1977. pap. text ed. 13.50 (ISBN 0-85597-198-3). Attic Pr.

Chappell, R. T. & Read, W. L. Business Communications. 4th ed. 232p. (Orig.). 1979. pap. text ed. 18.50x (ISBN 0-7121-0272-8, Pub. by Macdonald & Evans England). Trans-Atlantic.

--Business Communications. 5th ed. 216p. 1984. 18.50x (ISBN 0-7121-2403-9). Trans-Atlantic.

Chappell, Sally K. & Van Zanten, Ann. Barry Byrne & John Lloyd Wright: Architecture & Design. LC 82-71372. (Illus.). 72p. 1982. pap. 9.95 (ISBN 0-913820-11-3). Chicago Hist.

Chappell, V. C., ed. Hume: A Collection of Critical Essays. 1968. 18.95 (ISBN 0-268-00124-3). U of Notre Dame Pr.

--Hume: A Collection of Critical Essays. 429p. 1974. pap. 9.95x (ISBN 0-268-00560-5). U of Notre Dame Pr.

--The Philosophy of Mind. 1982. pap. 3.95 (ISBN 0-486-24212-9). Dover.

Chappell, W. & Ebsworth, J. W., eds. Roxburghe Ballads, 8 Vols. Repr. of 1899 ed. Set. 570.00 (ISBN 0-404-50840-5); 71.25 ea. AMS Pr.

Chappell, W. Reid. The Shropshire of Mary Webb. 1930. Repr. 20.00 (ISBN 0-8274-3410-3). R West.

Chappell, Warren. The Living Alphabet. LC 75-5884. (Illus.). 64p. 1980. pap. 4.95 (ISBN 0-8139-0873-6). U Pr of Va.

--A Short History of the Printed Word. LC 79-90409. (Nonpareil Bks.). (Illus.). 288p. 1980. pap. 9.95 (ISBN 0-87923-312-5). Godine.

--A Short History of the Printed Word. 17.00 (ISBN 0-405-13093-7). Ayer Co Pubs.

Chappell, Warren & Cusick, Rick. The Proverbial Bestiary. (Illus.). 64p. 1983. 10.95 (ISBN 0-931474-12-4). TBW Bks.

Chappell, Warren, ed. The Nutcracker: Based on the Alexandre Dumas pere Version of the Story by E. T. A. Hoffmann. LC 80-15576. (Illus.). 40p. (gr. k-6). 1980. pap. 5.95 (ISBN 0-8052-0660-4). Schocken.

Chappell, Warren, adapted by. & illu see Perrault, Charles.

Chappell, Willard & Peterson, Kathy. Molybdenum in the Environment, Vol. 2: The Geochemistry, Cycling, & Industrial Uses of Molybdenum. 1977. 79.75 (ISBN 0-8247-6495-1). Dekker.

Chappell, William, ed. Well, Dearie! The Letters of Edward Burra. 224p. 59.00x (ISBN 0-86092-076-3, Pub. by Fraser Bks). State Mutual Bk.

Chappell, William L., jt. auth. see Barton, Charles R.

Chappell, Williard R. & Paterson, Kathy K. Molybdenum in the Environment, Vol. 1: The Biology of Molybdenum. 1976. 79.75 (ISBN 0-8247-6405-6). Dekker.

Chappert, J. & Grynszpan, R. I., eds. Muons & Pions in Materials Research: Proceedings of the Muon Spin Research School, Aussois, France, May 16-20, 1983. 400p. 1984. 46.50 (ISBN 0-444-86900-X, North-Holland). Elsevier.

Chapple, Beryl. Dogs, Dogs, Dogs: The Best of Beryl Chapple's Paintings. LC 83-51828. (Illus.). 1984. 12.95f (ISBN 0-500-01333-0). Thames Hudson.

Chapple, Christopher, ed. The Bhagavad Gita. rev. ed. Sargeant, Winthrop, tr. from Sanskrit. (Cultural Perspectives Ser.). 777p. 1984. 39.50x (ISBN 0-87395-831-4); pap. 10.95 (ISBN 0-87395-830-6). State U NY Pr.

--Samkhya-Yoga: Proceedings of the IASWR Conference, 1981. 181p. 1983. pap. text ed. 10.00 (ISBN 0-915078-04-X). Inst Adv Stud Wld.

Chapple, Eliot D. The Biological Foundations of Individuality & Culture. LC 79-23284. 388p. (Orig.). 1980. lib. bdg. 19.50 (ISBN 0-89874-041-X). Krieger.

--Rehabilitation: Dynamics of Change (An Anthropological View) LC 79-10094. 138p. 1979. pap. text ed. 6.50 (ISBN 0-88275-774-1). Krieger.

Chapple, Eliot D. & Coon, Carlton S. Principles of Anthropology. 2nd. ed. LC 77-9616. 768p. 1978. 37.50 (ISBN 0-88275-583-8). Krieger.

Chapple, Gerald & Schulte, Hans H., eds. The Turn of the Century German Literature & Art, 1890-1915. (Modern German Studies: Vol. 5). (Illus.). 564p. 1983. 65.00x (ISBN 3-416-01588-6, Pub. by Bouvier Verlag W Germany). Benjamins North Am.

Chapple, Gerald, et al, trs. see Zimmer, Heinrich.

Chapple, J. A. & Sharps, J. G. Elizabeth Gaskell: A Portrait in Letters. (Illus.). 168p. 1983. (Pub. by Manchester Univ Pr); pap. 8.00 (ISBN 0-7190-0985-5). Longwood Pub Group.

Chapple, John A., ed. see Gaskell, Elizabeth C.

Chapple, Jonathan, jt. auth. see Porter, James.

Chapple, Judy. Your Horse: A Step-by-Step Guide to Horse Ownership. LC 84-47789. (Illus.). 192p. (gr. 8 up). 1984. 15.00 (ISBN 0-88266-358-5); pap. 9.95 (ISBN 0-88266-353-4). Garden Way Pub.

Chapple, M. A-Level Physics: Electricity & Semiconductors, Vol.3. 2nd ed. (Illus.). 288p. (Orig.). 1980. pap. text ed. 14.95x (ISBN 0-7121-0158-6). Trans-Atlantic.

--A Level Physics: Mechanics & Heat, Vol. 1. 2nd ed. (Illus.). 336p. (Orig.). 1979. pap. text ed. 14.95x (ISBN 0-7121-0154-3, Pub. by Macdonald & Evans England). Trans-Atlantic.

--A Level Physics: Wave Motion-Sound & Light, Vol. 2. 2nd ed. (Illus.). 240p. (Orig.). 1979. pap. text ed. 14.95x (ISBN 0-7121-0155-1, Pub. by Macdonald & Evans England). Trans-Atlantic.

Chapple, P. J., jt. ed. see Stinebring, W.

Chapple, Richard. A Dostoevsky Dictionary. 512p. 1983. 35.00 (ISBN 0-88233-727-0). Ardis Pubs.

Chapple, Richard L. Soviet Satire of the Twenties. LC 79-23575. (University of Florida Humanities Monographs: No. 47). ix, 172p. (Orig.). 1980. pap. 7.25 (ISBN 0-8130-0643-0). U Presses Fla.

Chapple, Steve. Outlaws in Babylon. 229p. (Orig.). 1984. pap. 6.95 (ISBN 0-671-46417-5, Long Shadow Bks). PB.

Chapple, Steve, jt. auth. see Garofalo, Reebee.

Chapppel, Bernice M. Bittersweet Trail: An American Saga of the 1800's. LC 84-80978. (Illus.). 480p. 1985. 15.95 (ISBN 0-9606400-1-0); pap. 8.95 (ISBN 0-9606400-2-9). Great Lakes Bks.

Chapra, S. C. & Canale, R. P. Numerical Methods for Engineering with Personal Computer Applications. 400p. 1985. 34.95 (ISBN 0-07-010664-9). McGraw.

Chapra, Steven, jt. auth. see Reckhow, Kenneth H.

Chapuis, Alfred. History of the Musical Box & of Mechanical Music. Fitch, Howard M. & Fitch, Helen F., eds. Roesch, Joseph E., tr. from Fr. LC 80-12449. (Illus.). xvi, 304p. 1980. 27.50 (ISBN 0-915000-01-6). Musical Box Soc.

Chapuis, Auguste see Rameau, Jean Philippe.

Chapuis, R. J. One Hundred Years of Telephone Switching (1878-1978) Part 1, Manual & Electromechanical Switching, 1878-1960s. (Studies in Telecommunications: Vol. 1). 464p. 1982. 95.00 (ISBN 0-444-86289-7, North Holland). Elsevier.

Chapuisat, X., et al, eds. Theory. (Topics in Current Chemistry Ser: Vol. 68). 1976. 34.00 (ISBN 0-387-07932-7). Springer-Verlag.

Chaput, Donald. Francois X. Aubry. (Illus.). 1975. 15.50 (ISBN 0-87062-110-6). A H Clark.

Chaput, Linda, ed. see Teyler.

Chaput, Marcel. Why I Am a Separatist. Taylor, Robert, tr. from Fr. LC 75-9634. 101p. 1975. Repr. of 1962 ed. lib. bdg. 15.00x (ISBN 0-8371-8107-0, CHWI). Greenwood.

Chapygin, Aleksei P. Stepan Razin. Paul, Cedar, tr. from Rus. LC 72-14051. (Soviet Literature in English Translation Ser). 480p. 1973. Repr. of 1946 ed. 27.50 (ISBN 0-88355-002-4). Hyperion Conn.

Char, Devron H. Immunology of Uveitis & Ocular Tumors. (Current Ophthalmology Monographs). 144p. 1978. 37.00 (ISBN 0-8089-1147-3, 790822). Grune.

--Thyroid Eye Disease. 225p. 1985. 58.00 (ISBN 0-683-01519-2). Williams & Wilkins.

Char, John K. Holistic Dentistry, Vol. 2. (Illus.). 1980. lib. bdg. 95.00 (ISBN 0-686-29720-2). Nutri-Kinetic.

Char, Rene. L' Age Cassant. 64p. 1965. 55.00 (ISBN 0-686-54147-2). French & Eur.

--Aromates Chasseurs. 52p. 1976. 9.95 (ISBN 0-686-54148-0). French & Eur.

--Arriere-Histoire du Poeme Pulverise. (Illus.). 64p. 1972. 15.00 (ISBN 0-686-54149-9). French & Eur.

--Chants de la Balandrane: Poemes. 80p. 1977. 9.95 (ISBN 0-686-54150-2). French & Eur.

--Claire: Theatre de Verdure. 112p. 1949. 4.95 (ISBN 0-686-54151-0). French & Eur.

--Commune Presence. 328p. 1964. 12.95 (ISBN 0-686-54152-9). French & Eur.

--Dans la Pluie Giboyeuse. 44p. 1968. 3.95 (ISBN 0-686-54153-7). French & Eur.

--Fureur et Mystere. 264p. 1949. 6.95 (ISBN 0-686-54156-1). French & Eur.

--L' Inclemence Lointaine. (Illus.). 30.00 (ISBN 0-686-54157-X). French & Eur.

--Le Marteau Sans Maitre: Avec: Le Moulin Premier (1927-1935) 128p. 12.50 (ISBN 0-686-54158-8). French & Eur.

--Les Matinaux. 156p. 1950. 4.95 (ISBN 0-686-54159-6). French & Eur.

--Les Matinaux: Avec: La Parole en Archipel. 218p. 1969. 4.95 (ISBN 0-686-54160-X). French & Eur.

--Le Monde de l'Art n'est pas le Morde du Pardon. (Illus.). 132p. 1974. 300.00 (ISBN 0-686-54161-8). French & Eur.

--No Siege Is Absolute. Wright, Franz, tr. from Fr. LC 82-84378. (Lost Roads Ser.: No.24). 55p. (Orig., Fr. & Eng.). 1983. pap. 5.95 (ISBN 0-918786-25-8). Lost Roads.

--La Nuit Talismanique. (Illus.). 102p. 1972. 39.95 (ISBN 0-686-54163-4). French & Eur.

--La Parole en Archipel. 168p. 1962. 3.95 (ISBN 0-686-54164-2). French & Eur.

--Picasso Sous les Ventes Etesiens. 10p. 1973. 7.95 (ISBN 0-686-54166-9). French & Eur.

--Poemes et Prose Choisis. 320p. 1957. 6.95 (ISBN 0-686-54167-7). French & Eur.

--Recherche de la Base et du Sommet. 192p. 1977. 3.95 (ISBN 0-686-54168-5). French & Eur.

--Retour Amont. 96p. 1966. 4.95 (ISBN 0-686-54169-3). French & Eur.

--Se Rencontrer Paysage Avec Joseph Sema. 20p. 1974. 7.95 (ISBN 0-686-54170-7). French & Eur.

--Sur la Poesie. 35p. 1974. 8.95 (ISBN 0-686-54171-5). French & Eur.

Char, Rene & Eluard, Paul. Deux Poemes. (Illus.). 15p. 1960. 15.00 (ISBN 0-686-54154-5). French & Eur.

Char, Rene & Feld, Charles. Picasso, Dessins. 256p. 1969. 65.00 (ISBN 0-686-54165-0). French & Eur.

Char, Rene & Heidigger, Martin. L' Endurance de la Pensee: Pour Saleur Jean Beaufret. 360p. 1968. 10.95 (ISBN 0-686-54155-3). French & Eur.

Char, S. V. Readings in the Constitutional History of India. 1983. 53.00x (ISBN 0-19-561264-7). Oxford U Pr.

Char, Tin-Yuke & Char, Wai J. Chinese Historic Sites & Pioneer Families of the Island of Hawaii. LC 83-9294. (Illus.). 247p. 1983. pap. text ed. 20.00x (ISBN 0-8248-0863-0). UH Pr.

Char, Tin-Yuke, ed. The Sandalwood Mountains: Readings & Stories of the Early Chinese in Hawaii. LC 74-76375. 374p. 1975. 14.95 (ISBN 0-8248-0305-1). UH Pr.

Char, Wai J., jt. auth. see Char, Tin-Yuke.

Characklis. Biofilms: Formation & Consequences. (Environmental & Applied Microbiology Ser.). 1986. price not set (ISBN 0-471-82663-4). Wiley.

Character Research Project Staff, jt. auth. see Ligon, Ernest M.

Charak, Sukhdev S., et al. Encyclopedia of Indian History & Culture, Vol. 1. 550p. 1981. text ed. 40.50x (ISBN 0-391-02535-X, Pub. by UBS India). Humanities.

Charak, Sukhdev Singh. History & Culture of Himalayan States of the Jammu Kingdom, Vol. V, Pt. II. 421p. 1981. text ed. 37.25x (ISBN 0-391-02232-6, Pub. by UBS India). Humanities.

Charalambous, George. Analysis of Foods & Beverages: Modern Techniques. LC 83-11783. (Food Science & Technology Ser.). 1984. 82.00 (ISBN 0-12-169160-8). Acad Pr.

Charalambous, George, ed. Analysis & Control of Less-Desirable Flavors in Foods & Beverages. 1980. 35.00 (ISBN 0-12-169065-2). Acad Pr.

--Analysis of Foods & Beverages: Headspace Techniques. 1978. 49.50 (ISBN 0-12-169050-4). Acad Pr.

--Liquid Chromatographic Analysis of Food & Beverages, 2 vols. LC 78-27595. 1979. Vol. 1. 35.00 (ISBN 0-12-169001-6); Vol. 2. 50.00 (ISBN 0-12-169002-4). Acad Pr.

Charalambous, George & Inglett, George, eds. Chemistry of Foods & Beverages: Recent Developments. LC 82-4043. 1982. 37.50 (ISBN 0-12-169080-6). Acad Pr.

Charalambous, George & Inglett, George E., eds. Flavor of Foods & Beverages: Chemistry & Technology. 1978. 51.00 (ISBN 0-12-169060-1). Acad Pr.

Charalambous, George & Inglett, George, eds. Instrumental Analysis of Foods: Recent Progress, 2 vols. LC 83-11756. (Symposia). Vol. 1, 1983. 42.00 (ISBN 0-12-168901-8); Vol. 2, 1984. 55.00 (ISBN 0-12-168902-6). Acad Pr.

--The Quality of Foods & Beverages: Chemistry & Technology, 2 vols, Vols. 1 & 2. LC 81-7912. 1981. Vol. 1. 40.00 (ISBN 0-12-169101-2); Vol. 2. 36.00 (ISBN 0-12-169102-0). Acad Pr.

Charalambous, George & Katz, Ira, eds. Phenolic, Sulfur, & Nitrogen Compounds in Food Flavors. LC 76-16544. (ACS Symposium Ser: No. 26). 1976. 23.95 (ISBN 0-8412-0330-X). Am Chemical.

Charalambous, George, jt. ed. see Inglett, G. E.

Charap, Stanley H., jt. auth. see Chikazumi, Sushin.

Charash, Leon I., et al. Psychosocial Aspects of Muscular Dystrophy & Allied Diseases: Commitment to Life, Health & Function. (Illus.). 332p. 1983. 29.75x (ISBN 0-398-04811-8). C C Thomas.

Charash, Leon I., et al, eds. Muscular Dystrophy & Allied Diseases: Impact on Patients, Family & Staff. (Current Thanatology Ser.). 100p. 1985. pap. 13.95 (ISBN 0-930194-38-1). Ctr Thanatology.

Charatsis, E. G., ed. Proceedings of the Econometric Society European Meeting, 1979: Papers in Memory of Stefan Valavanis. (Contributions to Economic Analysis Ser.: Vol. 138). 444p. 1982. 106.50 (ISBN 0-444-86184-X, North-Holland). Elsevier.

Charbeneau, Gerald T., et al, eds. Principles & Practice of Operative Dentistry. 2nd ed. LC 80-21029. (Illus.). 474p. 1981. text ed. 32.50 (ISBN 0-8121-0775-6). Lea & Febiger.

Charbon, Marie. Vocal Music from Fifteen Twelve to Sixteen Fifty, Vol. 2: Of the Hague Municipal Museum Catalogue of the Music Library. Von Gleich, C. C., ed. LC 73-18245. (Music Ser.). 1974. Repr. lib. bdg. 37.50 (ISBN 0-306-77222-1). Da Capo.

Charbon, Marie H. Historical & Theoretical Works to 1800: Vol 1 of the Hague Municipal Museum Catalog of the Music Library. LC 76-84485. (Music Ser). 1923-1925. 32.50 (ISBN 0-306-77221-3). Da Capo.

Charboneau, Joe, et al. Super Joe: The Life & Legend of Joe Charboneau. LC 80-6169. 256p. 1981. 12.95 (ISBN 0-8128-2806-2). Stein & Day.

Charbonnaud, Roger. Idees Economiques de Voltaire. LC 76-126403. (Fr). 1970. Repr. lib. bdg. 22.50 (ISBN 0-8337-0533-4). B Franklin.

Charbonneau, Gary. Index to Aerospace Historian: Cumulative Index by Author, Title, & Subject 1954-1973. 106p. 1974. pap. text ed. 12.00x (ISBN 0-89126-011-0). MA-AH Pub.

Charbonneau, Gerard & Seguin, Hubert. Workbook in Everyday French, 2 bks. rev. ed. 213p. (gr. 9-11). 1971. Bk. 1. pap. text ed. 5.45 (ISBN 0-88345-167-0, 17479); Bk. 2. pap. text ed. 5.45 (ISBN 0-88345-168-9, 17480); answer key 2.95 (ISBN 0-685-38985-5, 18131). Regents Pub.

Charbonneau, Harvey C. & Webster, Gordon L. Industrial Quality Control. (Illus.). 1978. ref. 27.95 (ISBN 0-13-464255-4). P-H.

Charbonneau, Louis, ed. see Fisher, William W.

Charbonneau, Rene, ed. see International Congress of Phonetic Sciences, 7th, Montreal, 1971.

Charbonneau, Rene, jt. ed. see Rigault, Andre.

Charchat, Isaac. A Constant Reminder. LC 84-51586. 460p. 1984. 20.00 (ISBN 0-88400-109-1). Shengold.

Charcot, Jean. The Voyage of the Pourquoi Pas? in the Antarctic: The Journal of the Second French South Polar Expedition, 1908-1910. (Illus.). vi, 315p. 1978. Repr. of 1911 ed. 30.00 (ISBN 0-208-01644-9, Archon). Shoe String.

Charcot, Jean M. Clinical Lectures on Senile & Chronic Diseases. Kastenbaum, Robert, ed. Tuke, William S., tr. LC 78-22189. (Aging & Old Age Ser.). 1979. Repr. of 1881 ed. lib. bdg. 23.00x (ISBN 0-405-11807-4). Ayer Co Pubs.

--Oeuvres completes: de J. M. Charcot, 9 vols. LC 70-169463. Repr. of 1894 ed. Set. 290.00 (ISBN 0-404-10000-7); 32.50 ea. AMS Pr.

Chard, Chester S. Northeast Asia in Prehistory. LC 73-2040. (Illus.). 232p. 1974. 18.50x (ISBN 0-299-06430-1). U of Wis Pr.

Chard, T. An Introduction to Radioimmunoassay & Related Techniques. 2nd, rev. & enl. ed. (Laboratory Techniques in Biochemistry & Molecular Biology Ser.: Vol. 6, Pt. 2). 284p. 1982. 72.25 (ISBN 0-444-80420-X, Biomedical Pr); pap. 27.75 (ISBN 0-444-80424-2). Elsevier.

Chard, T. & Klopper, A. I. Placental Function Tests. (Illus.). 96p. 1982. pap. 25.90 (ISBN 0-387-11529-3). Springer-Verlag.

Chard, T. & Lilford, R. Basic Sciences for Obstetrics & Gynaecology. (Illus.). 225p. 1983. 20.00 (ISBN 0-387-12529-9). Springer-Verlag.

Chard, T. see Work, T. S. & Work, E.

Chard, T., jt. ed. see Klopper, A. I.

Chard, Tim & Richards, Martin. Benefits & Hazards of the New Obstetrics. (Clinics in Developmental Medicine Ser.: Vol. 64). 169p. 1977. text ed. 29.00 (ISBN 0-433-05481-6, Pub. by Spastics Intl England). Lippincott.

Chardans, J. L. & Vega, Vicente. Diccionario Ilustrado de Trucos. 700p. (Span.). 1970. leatherette 24.75 (ISBN 84-252-0206-X, S-14532). French & Eur.

Chardenon, Ludo. In Praise of Wild Herbs: Remedies & Recipes From Old Provence. Kienull, Susan & Frederick, John, trs. from Fr. LC 83-24069. (Illus.). 112p. 1984. pap. 7.95 (ISBN 0-88496-208-3). Capra Pr.

Chardiet. Herself the Elf's Autumn. 1985. 2.95 (ISBN 0-590-32916-2). Scholastic Inc.

Chardiet, Bernice. The Carrot-Top Mystery. (Who Did It Sticker Mysteries Ser.). (Illus.). 16p. (Orig.). (ps-2). 1985. pap. 2.95 (ISBN 0-590-33426-3). Scholastic Inc.

--Juan Bobo & the Pig: A Puerto Rican Folktale Retold. LC 73-81783. (Illus.). 32p. (gr. k-3). 1973. 5.95 (ISBN 0-8027-6155-0); PLB 5.85 (ISBN 0-8027-6156-9). Walker & Co.

Chardin, John. Sir John Chardin's Travels in Persia. LC 76-181928. (BCL Ser.: No. I). Repr. of 1927 ed. 24.50 (ISBN 0-404-01449-6). AMS Pr.

Chardin, Pierre Teilhard De see Teilhard De Chardin, Pierre.

Chardin, Teilhard de see De Chardin, Teilhard.

Chardon, Carlos A. Estudios Sobre el Libertador Simon Bolivar. 3.10 (ISBN 0-8477-0824-1); pap. 2.50 (ISBN 0-8477-0825-X). U of PR Pr.

Chardon, Henri. Noveaux Documents sur la vie de Moliere. Incl. Vol. 2. Noveaux documents sur les comediens de campagne, la vie de Moliere et le theatre de college dans le Maine. (Research & Source Works Ser). 728p. (Fr.). 1972. Repr. of 1905 ed. lib. bdg. 20.00 (ISBN 0-8337-0536-9). B Franklin.

Charell, Ralph. Great New Way to Make Money. 1979. pap. 1.95 (ISBN 0-8128-7009-3). Stein & Day.

--How to Get the Upper Hand. 1979. pap. 2.25 (ISBN 0-380-42796-6, 42796-6). Avon.
--How to Make Things Go Your Way. 192p. 1981. pap. 5.95 (ISBN 0-346-12518-9). Cornerstone.
--Satisfaction Guaranteed: The Ultimate Guide to Consumer Self-Defense. 1985. 14.95 (ISBN 0-671-49804-5, Linden Pr). S&S.

Charents, Eghishe. Across Two Worlds: The Selected Prose of Eghishe Charents. Margossian, Marzbed & Antreassian, Jack, trs. from Armenian. 180p. (Orig.). 1985. pap. 10.00 (ISBN 0-935102-17-5). Ashod Pr.
--Land of Fire: Selected Poems. Hovanessian, Diana Der & Margossian, Marzbed, eds. 228p. 1985. 25.00 (ISBN 0-88233-922-2). Ardis Pubs.

Charernbhak, Wichit. Chicago School Architects & Their Critics. Foster, Stephen, ed. LC 83-24299. (Architecture & Urban Design Ser.: No. 1). 228p. 1984. 39.95 (ISBN 0-8357-1537-X). UMI Res Pr.

Charette, Bev & Macari, Mario, Jr. Star Rangers Meet the Solar Robot. LC 84-50624. (Fantasy Forest Adventures Ser.). 80p. (gr. 2-5). 1984. pap. 1.95 (ISBN 0-394-72783-5, Pub. by BYR). Random.

Charette, Beverly. Deluxe Story of Easter for Children. (Illus.). 48p. (gr. k-6). 1985. 5.95 (ISBN 0-8249-8076-X). Ideals.

Charette, Beverly, ed. see Lawson, Susan.

Charette, Beverly, ed. see Moore, Roger E.

Charette, Jean J. An Introduction to the Theory of Molecular Structure. LC 66-22648. pap. 50.00 (ISBN 0-317-08508-5, 2007249). Bks Demand UMI.

Chargaff, Erwin. Heraclitean Fire: Sketches from a Life before Nature. LC 77-95216. 252p. 1978. 14.00x (ISBN 0-87470-029-9). Rockefeller.

Chargaff, Erwin & Davidson, J. N., eds. The Nucleic Acids: Chemistry & Biology, 3 vols. Vol. 1 1955. 83.50 (ISBN 0-12-169201-9); Vol. 2 1955. 82.00 (ISBN 0-12-169202-7); Vol. 3 1960. 82.00 (ISBN 0-12-169203-5). Acad Pr.

Chargar, William & Nunes, Morris A. The Property Maintenance Logbook. LC 84-17818. 612p. 1985. 39.95 (ISBN 0-13-731134-6, Busn). P-H.

Chari, M. V. & Silvester, P., eds. Finite Elements in Electrical & Magnetic Field Problems. LC 79-1037. (Wiley Series in Numerical Methods in Engineering). 219p. 1980. 53.95 (ISBN 0-471-27578-6, Pub. by Wiley-Interscience). Wiley.

Chari, S. M. Advaita & Visistadvaita. 2nd ed. 1976. 8.95 (ISBN 0-8426-0886-9). Orient Bk Dist.
--Advaita & Visistadvaita: A Study Based on Vedanta Desika's Satudasani. 2nd ed. 1976. 10.00 (ISBN 0-8426-0886-9). Verry.

Chari, V. K. Whitman in the Light of Vedantic Mysticism: An Interpretation. Landmark ed. LC 64-19853. (Landmark Ed Ser.). xvi, 176p. 1976. 15.95x (ISBN 0-8032-0014-5). U of Nebr Pr.

Charig, A. J. & Krebs, B. Theodontia. (Encyclopedia of Paleoherpetology Ser.: Pt. 13). (Illus.). 137p. 1976. lib. bdg. 54.20x (ISBN 3-437-30184-5). Lubrecht & Cramer.

Charig, Alan. A New Look at Dinosaurs. (Illus.). 1979. 12.50 (ISBN 0-8317-6354-X, Mayflower Bks). Smith Pubs.
--A New Look at the Dinosaurs. (Illus.). 160p. 1983. 15.95 (ISBN 0-87196-139-3). Facts on File.

Charing, Douglas. The Jewish World. LC 83-50693. (Religions of the World Ser.). 48p. 1983. PLB 13.72 (ISBN 0-382-06720-7); 9.25 (ISBN 0-382-06930-7). Silver.

Charite, Raymond C. La see La Charite, Raymond C.

Charite, Raymond C. la see La Charite, Raymond C.

Charite, Virginia A. La see La Charite, Virginia A.

Chariton, Igumen. The Art of Prayer. Kadloubovsky, Palmer, tr. 288p. 1966. 26.95 (ISBN 0-571-06899-5). Faber & Faber.

Charitonuk, Katherine E. Book of Prayers. LC 84-91336. 189p. 1985. 8.95 (ISBN 0-533-06433-3). Vantage.

Charitos, Minas, jt. auth. see Livadeas, Themistocles.

Charity Organisation Society. The Epileptic & Crippled Child & Adult. Phillips, William R. & Rosenberg, Janet, eds. LC 79-6899. (Physically Handicapped in Society Ser.). 1980. Repr. of 1893 ed. lib. bdg. 17.00x (ISBN 0-405-13109-7). Ayer Co Pubs.

Charity, Ralph La see La Charity, Ralph.

Charke, Charlotte C. Narrative of the Life of Mrs. Charlotte Charke. LC 70-81365. (Illus.). 1969. Repr. of 1755 ed. 45.00x (ISBN 0-8201-1065-5). Schol Facsimiles.

Charland, Thomas C. Cost & Schedule Control Techniques Handbook. (Illus.). 104p. 1982. 79.95 (ISBN 0-9610754-0-6). T C Charland.

Charland, William A., Jr. Decide to Live. LC 79-9563. 156p. 1979. pap. 6.95 (ISBN 0-664-24277-4). Westminster.

Charlebois, Robert, et al. Saints for Kids by Kids. 80p. 1984. pap. 2.95 (ISBN 0-89243-223-3). Liguori Pubns.

Charlemagne. The Merry Pilgrimage: How Charlemagne Went on a Pilgrimage to Jerusalem in Order to See Whether Hugo of Constantinople Was a Handsomer Man Than He. Sherwood, Merriam, tr. LC 78-63455. (Illus.). Repr. of 1927 ed. 16.00 (ISBN 0-404-16377-7). AMS Pr.

Charles. The Cocktail Year: Three Hundred Sixty-Five Happy Hours. 120p. 1985. 12.95 (ISBN 0-668-06396-3); pap. 8.95 (ISBN 0-668-06400-5). Arco.
--Josquin Resource Manual. 1983. lib. bdg. 40.00 (ISBN 0-8240-9387-9). Garland Pub.
--Timex-Sinclair BASIC. 1983. 12.95 (ISBN 0-317-02380-2, 1065). Hayden.

Charles, Amy, ed. see Herbert, George.

Charles, Amy M. A Life of George Herbert. LC 77-3116. (Illus.). 232p. 1977. 25.00x (ISBN 0-8014-1014-2). Cornell U Pr.

Charles, Amy M., ed. see Knevet, Ralph.

Charles, Andre. Halley's Syndrome: A Tale. 180p. (Orig.). 1985. pap. price not set (ISBN 0-9611870-1-8). Neo Med Pub.

Charles, B. G., ed. Calender of Records of the Borough of Haverfordwest, 1539-1660. (History & Law Ser.). 274p. 1967. text ed. 21.50x (ISBN 0-7083-0002-2, Pub. by Univ of Wales Pr England). Humanities.

Charles, Barbara. Fun with Knitted Toys. (Learning with Fun). 64p. (gr. 2-5). 1980. 8.95 (ISBN 0-7182-0094-2, Pub. by Kaye & Ward). David & Charles.

Charles, Bernard H. Pottery & Porcelain: A Glossary of Terms. (Illus.). 320p. 1983. pap. 8.95 (ISBN 0-88254-278-8). Hippocrene Bks.

Charles, Bob. Lefthanded Golf with Bob Charles. (Illus.). 1965. 9.95 (ISBN 0-13-527200-9); pap. 5.95. P-H.

Charles, C. M. Building Classroom Discipline: From Models to Practice. 2nd ed. 256p. 1984. pap. text ed. 13.95x (ISBN 0-582-28532-1). Longman.
--Elementary Classroom Management: A Handbook for Excellence in Teaching. Akers, Lane, ed. LC 82-13973. (Illus.). 452p. (Orig.). 1983. pap. text ed. 15.45x (ISBN 0-582-28349-3). Longman.
--Individualizing Instruction. 2nd ed. LC 79-26645. (Illus.). 284p. 1980. pap. 15.95 (ISBN 0-8016-0974-7). Mosby.
--Teacher's Petit Piaget. LC 74-83219. 1974. pap. 4.95 (ISBN 0-8224-6780-1). Pitman Learning.

Charles, C. M. & Malian, Ida. The Special Student: Practical Help for the Classroom Teacher. LC 80-13053. (Illus.). 246p. 1980. pap. text ed. 15.95 (ISBN 0-8016-1132-6). Mosby.

Charles, Carol M., et al. Schooling, Teaching & Learning: American Education. LC 77-13496. (Illus.). 466p. 1978. text ed. 23.95 (ISBN 0-8016-0966-6). Mosby.

Charles, Carole. The Boston Tea Party. LC 75-33156. (Stories of the Revolution Ser.). (Illus.). (gr. 2-6). 1975. PLB 5.95 (ISBN 0-913778-18-4). Childs World.
--General George at Yorktown. LC 75-33158. (Stories of the Revolution Ser.). (Illus.). (gr. 2-6). 1975. PLB 5.95 (ISBN 0-913778-23-0). Childs World.
--John Paul Jones, Victory at Sea. LC 75-33157. (Stories of the Revolution Ser.). (Illus.). (gr. 2-6). 1975. PLB 5.95 (ISBN 0-913778-21-4). Childs World.
--Martha Helps the Rebel. LC 75-33126. (Stories of the Revolution). (Illus.). (gr. 2-6). 1975. PLB 5.95 (ISBN 0-913778-22-2). Childs World.
--Paul Revere & the Minutemen. LC 75-33204. (Stories of the Revolution Ser.). (Illus.). (gr. 2-6). 1975. PLB 5.95 (ISBN 0-913778-19-2). Childs World.
--Survival at Valley Forge. LC 75-33159. (Stories of the Revolution Ser.). (Illus.). (gr. 2-6). 1975. PLB 5.95 (ISBN 0-913778-20-6). Childs World.

Charles, Cecil. Rudyard Kipling, His Life & Works. 1978. Repr. of 1911 ed. lib. bdg. 17.50 (ISBN 0-8495-0838-X). Arden Lib.
--Rudyard Kipling: His Life & Works. 1973. lib. bdg. 10.00 (ISBN 0-8414-0903-X). Folcroft.

Charles, Cheryl. Science & Society: Knowing, Teaching, Learning. Charles, Cheryl & Samples, Bob, eds. LC 78-70847. (National Council for the Social Studies, Bulletin: 57). pap. 24.00 (ISBN 0-317-20135-2, 2023190). Bks Demand UMI.

Charles, Cheryl & Samples, Bob, eds. Science & Society: Knowing, Teaching, Learning. LC 78-70847. (Bulletin Ser.: No. 57). 1978. pap. 6.95 (ISBN 0-87986-021-9, 498-15274). Nat Coun Soc Studies.

Charles, Conn A. Liar's Dice. 320p. 1985. pap. 3.50 (ISBN 0-8125-0128-4). Tor Bks.

Charles, David. Aristotle's Philosophy of Action. LC 83-73068. 300p. 1984. 39.50x (ISBN 0-8014-1708-2). Cornell U Pr.
--Infections in Obstetrics & Gynecology. LC 79-67789. (Major Problems in Obstetrics & Gynecology Ser.: Vol. 12). (Illus.). 440p. 1980. text ed. 39.00 (ISBN 0-7216-2492-8). Saunders.
--Self-Assessment of Current Knowledge in Obstetrics & Gynecology. 4th ed. 1984. pap. text ed. 23.00 (ISBN 0-87488-265-6). Med Exam.

Charles, David & Finland, Maxwell, eds. Obstetric & Perinatal Infections. LC 79-170731. (Illus.). Repr. of 1973 ed. 120.00 (ISBN 0-8357-9412-1, 2014530). Bks Demand UMI.

Charles, Donald. Calico Cat at School. LC 81-6096. (Calico Cat Story Bks.). (Illus.). 32p. (ps-3). 1981. 10.35 (ISBN 0-516-03445-6); pap. 2.95 (ISBN 0-516-43445-4). Childrens.
--Calico Cat at the Zoo. LC 80-25380. (Calico Cat Storybooks). (Illus.). 32p. (gr. 3). 1981. PLB 10.35 (ISBN 0-516-03443-X); pap. 2.95 (ISBN 0-516-43443-8). Childrens.
--Calico Cat Looks Around. LC 75-12947. (Calico Cat Story Bks.). (Illus.). 32p. (ps-3). 1975. PLB 10.35 (ISBN 0-516-03436-7); pap. 2.95 (ISBN 0-516-43436-5). Childrens.
--Calico Cat Meets Bookworm. LC 78-6557. (Calico Cat Story Bks.). (Illus.). 32p. (gr. 3). 1978. PLB 10.35 (ISBN 0-516-03441-3); pap. 2.95 (ISBN 0-516-43441-1). Childrens.
--Calico Cat's Exercise Book. LC 82-9640. (Calico Cat's Storybooks). (Illus.). (ps-3). 1982. PLB 10.35 (ISBN 0-516-03457-X); pap. 2.95 (ISBN 0-516-43457-8). Childrens.
--Calico Cat's Rainbow. LC 75-12948. (Calico Cat Story Bks.). (Illus.). 32p. (ps-3). 1975. PLB 10.35 (ISBN 0-516-03437-5); pap. 2.95 (ISBN 0-516-43437-3). Childrens.
--Calico Cat's Year. LC 83-23160. (Calico Cat Ser.). (Illus.). 32p. (ps-3). 1984. lib. bdg. 10.35 (ISBN 0-516-03461-8); pap. 2.95 (ISBN 0-516-43461-6). Childrens.
--Count on Calico Cat. LC 74-8007. (Calico Cat Story Bks.). (Illus.). 32p. (ps-3). 1974. PLB 10.35 (ISBN 0-516-03435-9); pap. 2.95 (ISBN 0-516-43435-7). Childrens.
--Fat Fat Calico Cat. LC 77-7154. (Calico Cat Story Bks.). (Illus.). 32p. (gr. 3). 1977. PLB 10.35 (ISBN 0-516-03456-1); pap. 2.95 (ISBN 0-516-43456-X). Childrens.
--The Jolly Pancake. LC 79-13304. (Illus.). 32p. (gr. k-3). 1979. PLB 10.35 (ISBN 0-516-03513-4). Childrens.
--Letters from Calico Cat. LC 74-8181. (Calico Cat Story Bks.). (Illus.). 32p. (ps-3). 1974. PLB 10.35 (ISBN 0-516-03519-3); pap. 2.95 (ISBN 0-516-43519-1). Childrens.
--Shaggy Dog's Animal Alphabet. LC 78-12904. (Illus.). 32p. (ps-3). 1979. PLB 10.35 (ISBN 0-516-03674-2). Childrens.
--Shaggy Dog's Halloween. LC 84-5901. (Easy Reading Bks.). (Illus.). 32p. (ps-3). 1984. lib. bdg. 10.35 (ISBN 0-516-03575-4); pap. text ed. 2.95 (ISBN 0-516-43575-2). Childrens.
--Shaggy Dog's Tall Tale. LC 79-26493. (Illus.). 32p. (ps-3). 1980. PLB 10.35 (ISBN 0-516-03616-5). Childrens.
--Time to Rhyme with Calico Cat. LC 77-20994. (Calico Cat Story Bks.). (Illus.). 32p. (ps-3). 1978. PLB 10.35 (ISBN 0-516-03629-7); pap. 2.95 (ISBN 0-516-43629-5). Childrens.

Charles, E. Some Dickens Women. 59.95 (ISBN 0-8490-1076-4). Gordon Pr.
--Some Dickens Women. 1973. 25.00 (ISBN 0-8274-1109-X). R West.

Charles, Edgar D. & Kronenfeld, Jennie J., eds. Social & Economic Impacts of Coronary Artery Disease. LC 79-1554. 160p. 1980. 25.00x (ISBN 0-669-02912-2). Lexington Bks.

Charles, Edna K. Christina Rossetti: Critical Perspectives, 1862-1982. LC 84-40392. (Illus.). 192p. 1985. 24.50 (ISBN 0-941664-06-6). Susquehanna U.

Charles, Elizabeth. The Bertram Family. Wolff, Robert L., ed. LC 75-494. (Victorian Fiction Ser.). 1975. Repr. of 1876 ed. lib. bdg. 73.00 (ISBN 0-8240-1570-3). Garland Pub.
--Chronicles of the Schonberg-Cotta Family, 2 vols. in 1. LC 79-8251. Repr. of 1864 ed. 44.50 (ISBN 0-404-61818-9). AMS Pr.

Charles, Elizabeth R. Luther: By Those Who Knew Him. 1983. pap. 5.95 (ISBN 0-8024-0314-X). Moody.
--Three Martyrs of the Nineteenth Century. LC 73-77196. Repr. of 1886 ed. 19.75 (ISBN 0-8371-1296-6, CHM&). Greenwood.

Charles, F. W. B. The Conservation of Timber Buildings. LC 84-12984. (Illus.). 256p. 1984. 72.50 (ISBN 0-09-145090-X, Pub. by Hutchinson Educ). Longwood Pub Group.

Charles First. Charles First 101, King of Great Britain: Letters of King Charles First to Queen Henrietta Maria. 1856. 19.00 (ISBN 0-384-08515-6). Johnson Repr.

Charles First, King of Great Britain. Charles First, in 1646: Letters of King Charles First to Queen Henrietta Maria. Bruce, John, ed. LC 17-1236. (Camden Society, London. Publications. First Ser.: No. 63). Repr. of 1856 ed. 19.00 (ISBN 0-404-50163-X). AMS Pr.

Charles, Fred, jt. auth. see Miller, Clyde R.

Charles, Freda. The Mystery of Missing Challah. 40p. (ps). 1981. pap. 5.95 (ISBN 0-8246-0264-1). Jonathan David.

Charles, G. J., jt. auth. see Patsavos, L. J.

Charles, Gordon. Pigeon River Country: The Big Wild. (Illus.). 104p. 1985. pap. 7.95 (ISBN 0-8028-7050-3). Eerdmans.

Charles Hall Page & Assocs., ed. see Foundation for San Francisco's Architectural Heritage.

Charles, Howard H. Alcohol & the Bible. LC 66-10970. 40p. 1981. pap. 1.50 (ISBN 0-8361-1941-X). Herald Hse.

Charles, J. A. & Crane, F. A. Selection & Use of Engineering Materials. (Illus.). 328p. 1984. text ed. 49.95 (ISBN 0-408-10858-4); pap. text ed. 29.95 (ISBN 0-408-10859-2). Butterworth.

Charles, J. Norman & Charles, Sharon. Heaven on Earth, Family Style. LC 80-84230. (Orig.). 1980. pap. 4.95 (ISBN 0-88270-495-8, Pub. by Logos). Bridge Pub.

Charles, Jean C. The Missing Boy & the Escapee, Pt. 2. LC 83-70229. 50p. 1984. pap. 3.50 (ISBN 0-9610796-8-1). Adelphi Pr.

Charles, John, jt. auth. see Yates, Miles.

Charles, St. John W. Educational Achievement in Relation to Intelligence. (Harvard Studies in Education: Vol. 15). 1930. 19.00 (ISBN 0-384-52975-5). Johnson Repr.

Charles, Joseph. Origins of the American Party System. 12.50 (ISBN 0-8446-1840-3). Peter Smith.

Charles, Joseph J. Basic Training for Compucolor Computers. LC 80-65071. (Illus.). viii, 192p. 1980. pap. 14.95 (ISBN 0-9607080-0-6). J Charles Pub.
--Timex-Sinclair BASIC. 192p. pap. 9.95 (2102). Hayden.

Charles, K. J. Total Development: Essays Toward an Integration of Marxian & Gandhian Perspectives. 1983. text ed. 30.00x (ISBN 0-7069-2075-9, Pub. by Vikas India). Advent NY.

Charles, M. E., jt. ed. see McGrath, H. G.

Charles, Marie. Claimed by Rapture. (Second Chance at Love Ser.: No. 145). 192p. 1983. pap. 1.95 (ISBN 0-515-07233-8). Jove Pubns.

Charles, Marie. Scenes from the Heart. (Second Chance at Love Ser.: No. 107). 192p. 1983. pap. 1.75 (ISBN 0-515-06871-3). Jove Pubns.

Charles, Mickey, jt. auth. see Neibart, Wally.

Charles, Milene. The Soviet Union & Africa: The History of the Involvement. LC 80-67227. 250p. 1980. lib. bdg. 22.50 (ISBN 0-8191-1255-0); pap. text ed. 11.25 (ISBN 0-8191-1256-9). U Pr of Amer.

Charles, Nicholas. Visitation of the County of Huntingdon. 1849. 19.00 (ISBN 0-384-08525-3). Johnson Repr.
--Visitation of the County of Huntingdon, Under the Authority of William Camden. Ellis, Henry, ed. LC 17-1223. (Camden Society, London. Publications, First Ser.: No. 43). Repr. of 1849 ed. 19.00 (ISBN 0-404-50143-5). AMS Pr.

Charles, Pavel. Open Quantum Systems & Feynman Integrals. 376p. 1984. 64.00 (ISBN 90-277-1678-1, Pub. by Reidel Holland). Kluwer Academic.

Charles, Pierre. Prayer for All Times. Waterfield, Robin, tr. from Fr. 157p. 1983. pap. 5.95 (ISBN 0-87061-090-2). Chr Classics.

Charles, R. H. Lectures on the Apocalypse. (British Academy, London, Schweich Lectures on Biblical Archaeology Series, 1919). pap. 19.00 (ISBN 0-317-15765-5). Kraus Repr.

Charles, R. H., ed. & The Book of Enoch: Or One Enoch. 2nd ed. 331p. pap. 10.95 (ISBN 0-88697-009-1). Life Science.

Charles, R. H., ed. The Book of Jubilees: The Little Genesis. 1984. Repr. of 1902 ed. 39.00x (ISBN 0-403-08996-4, Regency). Scholarly.
--The Book of the Secrets of Enoch. 100p. pap. 7.95 (ISBN 0-88697-010-5). Life Science.
--The Ethiopic Version of the Book of Enoch. LC 79-8595. Repr. of 1906 ed. 37.50 (ISBN 0-404-18448-0). AMS Pr.

Charles, R. H., intro. by. The Apoclypse of Baruch. 1976. Repr. of 1896 ed. 39.00x (ISBN 0-685-71069-6, Regency). Scholarly.

Charles, R. H., et al. Apocrypha & Pseudepigrapha of the Old Testament, 2 Vols. Vol. 1. 69.00x (ISBN 0-19-826155-1); Vol. 2. 69.00x (ISBN 0-19-826152-7). Oxford U Pr.

Charles River Associates, Inc & International Trade Administration, U. S Department of Commerce. Advanced Ceramics Technology: An Overview. LC 85-71512. 228p. (Orig.). 1985. pap. 44.50x Two Monographs (ISBN 0-318-04693-8, BT019). No. 1, Technological & Economic Assessment of Advanced Ceramic Materials. No. 2, Competitive Assessment of the U. S. Advanced Ceramics Industry. Business Technology Bks.

Charles River Associates Incorporated, et al. Advanced Ceramic Materials: Technological & Economic Assessment. LC 85-4978. (Illus.). 651p. 1985. 64.00 (ISBN 0-8155-1037-3). Noyes.

Charles, Robert. The Comet. Orig. Title: Night World. 352p. 1985. pap. 3.50 (ISBN 0-8125-0141-1). Tor Bks.

Charles, Robert H. A Critical History of the Doctrine of a Future Life, in Israel, in Judaism, & in Christianity. LC 79-8600. Repr. of 1899 ed. 38.50 (ISBN 0-404-18455-3). AMS Pr.

Charles, Rodger. Social Teaching of Vatican II: Its Origin & Development. Catholic Social Ethics-an Historical & Comparative Study. LC 81-83567. 569p. 1982. 30.00 (ISBN 0-89870-013-2). Ignatius Pr.

Charles, St. Narcotics Menace. 3.00 (ISBN 0-87505-229-0). Borden.

Charles, Sara C. & Kennedy, Eugene. Defendant: A Psychiatrist on Trial for Medical Malpractice. 224p. 1985. 16.30x (ISBN 0-02-905910-0). Free Pr.

Charles Scribner's Sons Editorial Staff, ed. Stories by American Authors, 10 vols in 5. 1972. Repr. of 1884 ed. lib. bdg. 100.00 set (ISBN 0-685-36668-5); Vols. 1-2. (ISBN 0-8422-8142-8); Vols. 3-4. (ISBN 0-8422-8143-6); Vols 5-6. (ISBN 0-8422-8144-4); Vols 7-8. (ISBN 0-8290-1658-9); Vols. 9-10. (ISBN 0-8422-8146-0); lib. bdg. 25.00 ea., 5 individual vols. Irvington.

--Stories by English Authors, 10 vols in 5. 1972. Repr. of 1896 ed. Set. lib. bdg. 100.00 (ISBN 0-8290-1414-4); Vols. 1-2. 25.00 (ISBN 0-8422-8147-9); Vols 3-4. 25.00 (ISBN 0-8422-8148-7); Vols. 5-6. 25.00 (ISBN 0-8422-8149-5); Vols.-7-8. 25.00 (ISBN 0-8422-8150-9); Vols. 9-10. 25.00 (ISBN 0-8422-8151-7). Irvington.

--Stories by Foreign Authors, 10 vols in 5. 1972. Repr. of 1896 ed. lib. bdg. 125.00 set (ISBN 0-685-36671-5); Vols 1-2. Fr. (ISBN 0-8422-8152-5); Vols 3-4. Fr. - Ger. (ISBN 0-8422-8153-3); Vols 5-6. Ger. - It. (ISBN 0-8422-8154-1); Vols. 7-8. Rus.-Scand. (ISBN 0-8422-8155-X); Vols. 9-10. Span. & Polish (ISBN 0-8422-8156-8); lib. bdg. 30.00 ea., 5 individual vols. Irvington.

Charles, Searle F. Minister of Relief: Harry Hopkins & the Depression. LC 74-2585. (Illus.). 286p. 1974. Repr. of 1963 ed. lib. bdg. 22.50x (ISBN 0-8371-7407-4, CHMR). Greenwood.

Charles, Sharon, jt. auth. see Charles, J. Norman.

Charles, Sydney R. Handbook of Music & Music Literature: In Sets & Series. LC 71-143502. 1972. 24.95 (ISBN 0-02-905400-1). Free Pr.

Charles, Sylvia. Women in the Word. LC 84-72958. 1985. pap. 3.50 (ISBN 0-88270-579-2). Bridge Pub.

Charles, Thomas W. & Stiner, Frederic M., Jr. Your Name Company: Accounting Practice Set for the Computer. 144p. 1985. pap. write for info. (ISBN 0-534-04506-5). Kent Pub Co.

Charles, V. & Hartung, Adelina. Wisconsin Map Studies Program: Activity Manual. Irvine, J. L., ed. (Illus.). 82p. (gr. 4). 1981. Duplication Masters 49.00 (ISBN 0-943068-04-5); Teacher's Guide 5.00 (ISBN 0-943068-03-7). Graphic learning.

Charles, Vera K. Introduction to Mushroom Hunting. LC 73-85355. (Illus.). 1974. Repr. of 1931 ed. 2.50 (ISBN 0-486-20667-X). Dover.

--Introduction to Mushroom Hunting. (Illus.). 12.25 (ISBN 0-8446-5015-3). Peter Smith.

Charles, Vic. Sport Karate. 1984. 27.00x (ISBN 0-901764-63-9, Pub. by P H Crompton Ltd UK). State Mutual Bk.

Charles, Victorin. Diccionario Atomico. 296p. (Span.). 1962. 14.95 (ISBN 0-686-56708-0, S-33057). French & Eur.

Charles-Dominique, P. & Martin, R. D. Behavior & Ecology of Nocturnal Prosimians: Field Studies in Gabon & Madagascar. (Advances in Ethology Ser.: Vol. 9). (Illus.). 91p. (Orig.). 1972. pap. text ed. 23.50 (ISBN 3-489-64536-7). Parey Sci Pubs.

Charles-Dominique, P., et al. Nocturnal Malagasy Primates: Ecology, Physiology & Behavior. LC 89-6799. (Communication & Behavior: an Interdisciplinary Ser.). 1980. 39.50 (ISBN 0-12-169350-3). Acad Pr.

Charles-Dominique, Pierre. Ecology & Behavior of Nocturnal Primates. Martin, R. D., tr. LC 77-1227. (Illus.). 277p. 1977. 30.00x (ISBN 0-231-04362-7). Columbia U Pr.

Charles-Edwards, D., ed. Physiological Determinants of Crop Growth. 1983. 37.00 (ISBN 0-12-169360-0). Acad Pr.

Charles-Edwards, D. A. The Mathematics of Photosynthesis & Productivity. LC 81-66387. (Experimental Botany Ser.). 1982. 29.50 (ISBN 0-12-170580-3). Acad Pr.

Charles Louis De Bourbon. Bibliotheque liturgique, 2 vols. in 1. Ales, Anatole, ed. LC 72-130592. (Fr). 1970. Repr. of 1898 ed. lib. bdg. 40.50 (ISBN 0-8337-0036-7). B Franklin.

Charles-Picard, Gilbert, ed. Larousse Encyclopedia of Archaeology. Ward, Anne, tr. LC 83-80485. (Illus.). 432p. 1983. 24.95 (ISBN 0-88332-316-8, 8052). Larousse.

Charles-Roux, Edmonde. Chanel & Her World. Wheeler, Dan, tr. from Fr. (Illus.). 202p. 1981. 50.00 (ISBN 0-86565-011-X). Vendome.

--Chanel & Her World. LC 81-10366. (Illus.). 356p. 1982. pap. 17.95 (ISBN 0-86565-024-1). Vendome.

Charleston Free Library. Index to Wills of Charleston County, South Carolina, 1671-1868. LC 73-16329. 324p. 1974. Repr. of 1950 ed. 17.50 (ISBN 0-8063-0591-6). Genealog Pub.

Charleston Mercury & New York Times. The Civil War Extra: From the Pages of the Charleston Mercury & the New York Times. new ed. Moehring, Eugene & Keylin, Arleen, eds. LC 75-20220. 310p. 1975. 12.98 (ISBN 0-405-06662-7). Ayer Co Pubs.

Charleston, R. J. English Glass & the Glass Used in England, circa 400-1940. Wakefield, Hugh, ed. (English Decorative Arts Ser.). (Illus.). 216p. 1984. 40.00x (ISBN 0-04-748003-3). Allen Unwin.

Charleston, R. J., jt. auth. see Cook, R. M.

Charleston, R. J., et al. Glass & Enamels. (The Waddesdon Catalogues Ser.). (Illus.). 496p. 1985. text ed. 75.00 (ISBN 0-7078-0066-8, Pub. by P Wilson Pubs). Sotheby Pubns.

Charleston, Robert. Masterpieces of Glass: A World History from the Corning Museum of Glass. (Illus.). 1980. 40.00 (ISBN 0-8109-1753-X). Abrams.

Charleston, Robert J. Islamic Pottery. LC 78-55079. (Masterpieces of Western & Near Eastern Ceramics: Vol. IV). (Illus.). 1980. 250.00 (ISBN 0-87011-345-3). Kodansha.

Charleston, Robert J., jt. auth. see Scheurleer, Lunsingh.

Charleston, Robert J., ed. see Boston, David M.

Charleston, Robert J., ed. see Cook, R. M. & Charleston, R. J.

Charleston, Robert J., ed. see Fourest, Henri-Pierre.

Charleston, Robert J., ed. see Hennessy, Basil J.

Charleston, Robert J., ed. see Liverani, Giuseppe.

Charleston, Robert J., ed. see Reinheckel, Gunter.

Charlesworth, A. S. & Fletcher, J. R. Systematic Analog Computer Programming. 2nd ed. 1975. 19.50x (ISBN 0-8464-0905-4). Beekman Pubs.

Charlesworth, Andrew. Social Portrait in a Rural Society. (Historical Geography Research Ser.). 1980. pap. 3.50x (ISBN 0-686-27387-7, Pub. by GEO Abstracts England). State Mutual Bk.

Charlesworth, Andrew, ed. An Atlas of Rural Protest in Britain, 1549-1900. LC 82-8362. (Illus.). 224p. 1982. 27.50x (ISBN 0-8122-7853-4). U of Pa Pr.

Charlesworth, Arthur R. Paradise Found. LC 72-91109. 1973. 7.50 (ISBN 0-8022-2104-1). Philos Lib.

Charlesworth, B. Evolution in Age-Structured Populations. LC 79-8909. (Cambridge Studies in Mathematical Biology: No. 1). 250p. 1980. 49.50 (ISBN 0-521-23045-4); pap. 16.95 (ISBN 0-521-29786-9). Cambridge U Pr.

Charlesworth, B., tr. see Jacquard, A.

Charlesworth, Chris. A-Z of Rock Guitarists. (Illus.). 128p. 1983. 16.95 (ISBN 0-86276-081-X); pap. 10.95 (ISBN 0-86276-080-1). Proteus Pub NY.

--Cat Stevens. (Illus.). 128p. 1984. 17.95 (ISBN 0-86276-063-1); pap. 10.95 (ISBN 0-86276-062-3). Proteus Pub NY.

--David Bowie: Profile. (Illus.). 96p. (Orig.). 1985. pap. 10.95 (ISBN 0-906071-67-4). Proteus Pub NY.

--Pete Townshend. (Illus.). 176p. 1984. 18.95 (ISBN 0-86276-246-4); pap. 10.95 (ISBN 0-86276-245-6). Proteus Pub NY.

--Rock Heritage: The Sixties. (Illus.). 160p. 1984. 20.95 (ISBN 0-86276-132-8); pap. 12.95 (ISBN 0-86276-131-X). Proteus Pub NY.

Charlesworth, D., tr. see Jacquard, A.

Charlesworth, Edward A. & Nathan, Ronald G. Stress Management: A Comprehensive Guide to Wellness. LC 84-45060. 292p. 1984. 17.95 (ISBN 0-689-11503-2). Atheneum.

--Stress Management: A Comprehensive Guide to Wellness. 432p. 1985. pap. 4.95 (ISBN 0-345-32734-9). Ballantine.

Charlesworth, Edward A., jt. auth. see Nathan, Ronald G.

Charlesworth, James. The History of the Rechabites, Vol. 1: The Greek Recension. LC 82-3370. (SBL Texts & Translations). 1982. pap. 9.50 (ISBN 0-89130-567-X, 060217). Scholars Pr GA.

Charlesworth, James C. America's Changing Role as a World Leader. Lambert, Richard D., ed. LC 76-85466. (Annals Ser.: 384). 1969. 15.00 (ISBN 0-87761-118-1); pap. 7.95 (ISBN 0-87761-117-3). Am Acad Pol Soc Sci.

--The Future of the Western Alliance. LC 74-10657. 145p. 1974. Repr. of 1957 ed. lib. bdg. 15.00x (ISBN 0-8371-7647-6, CHWA). Greenwood.

--Governmental Administration. LC 70-38127. (Illus.). 713p. 1972. Repr. of 1951 ed. lib. bdg. 32.50x (ISBN 0-8371-6324-2, CHGO). Greenwood.

Charlesworth, James C., ed. Changing American People: Are We Deteriorating or Improving? LC 68-27641. (Annals of the American Academy of Political & Social Science: No. 378). 1968. 15.00 (ISBN 0-87761-109-2); pap. 7.95 (ISBN 0-87761-108-4). Am Acad Pol Soc Sci.

--Contemporary Political Analysis. LC 67-14374. (Orig.). 1967. pap. text ed. 16.95 (ISBN 0-02-905470-2). Free Pr.

--Design for Political Science: Scope, Objectives, & Methods. facs. ed. LC 74-117766. (Essay Index Reprint Ser). 1966. 19.00 (ISBN 0-8369-1789-8). Ayer Co Pubs.

Charlesworth, James C. & Lambert, Richard D., eds. New American Posture Toward Asia. LC 72-120283. (Annals of the American Academy of Political & Social Science Ser.: No. 390). 1970. 15.00 (ISBN 0-87761-128-9); pap. 7.95 (ISBN 0-87761-127-0). Am Acad Pol Soc Sci.

Charlesworth, James H. The New Discoveries in St. Catherine's Monastery: A Preliminary Report on the Manuscripts. Freedman, David N., intro. by. LC 81-10992. (American Schools of Oriental Research Monographs: No. 3). (Illus.). 45p. (Orig.). 1982. pap. text ed. 6.00x (ISBN 0-89757-403-6, Am Sch Orient Res). Eisenbrauns.

--The Odes of Solomon. LC 77-21285. (SBL Texts & Translations). 192p. 1983. pap. 8.95 (ISBN 0-89130-202-6, 06 02 13). Scholars Pr GA.

--The Pseudepigrapha & Modern Research, with a Supplement. LC 76-25921. (Society Biblical Literature Septuagint & Cognate Studies). 344p. 1981. pap. 12.75 (ISBN 0-89130-440-1, 06 0707S). Scholars Pr GA.

--Pseudepigrapha Prolegomena. (Society for New Testament Studies Monographs). 240p. Date not set. 34.50 (ISBN 0-521-30190-4). Cambridge U Pr.

Charlesworth, James H., ed. Old Testament Pseudepigrapha, 2 vols. 1056p. 1986. slipcased set 80.00 (ISBN 0-385-19491-9). Doubleday.

--Old Testament Pseudepigrapha: Expansions of the Old Testament & Legends, Wisdom & Philosophical Literature, Prayers, Psalms & Odes, Fragments of Lost Judeo-Hellenistic Words, Vol. II. 1056p. 1985. 35.00 (ISBN 0-385-18813-7). Doubleday.

--Old Testament Pseudepigrapha, Vol. I: Apocalyptic Literature & Testaments. LC 80-2443. 1056p. 1983. 35.00 (ISBN 0-385-09630-5). Doubleday.

Charlesworth, John & Brown, Tony. Tom Sawyer: A Play. 1976. pap. text ed. 4.00x (ISBN 0-435-23169-3). Heinemann Ed.

Charlesworth, Kate. Exotic Species. 96p. (Orig.). 1984. pap. 3.95 (ISBN 0-907040-38-1, Pub. by GMP England). Alyson Pubns.

Charlesworth, M. J., tr. St. Anselm's Proslogion. LC 78-63300. 1979. text ed. 17.95x (ISBN 0-268-01696-8); pap. text ed. 6.95x (ISBN 0-268-01697-6). U of Notre Dame Pr.

Charlesworth, M. P. The Heritage of Early Britain. (Illus.). 1979. lib. bdg. 30.00 (ISBN 0-8495-0946-7). Arden Lib.

--Lost Province of the Worth of Britain. 89p. 1949. text ed. 3.25x (ISBN 0-7083-0065-0, Pub. by Univ of Wales Pr England). Humanities.

--Trade Routes & Commerce of the Roman Empire. LC 74-77865. 320p. 1975. Repr. 15.00 (ISBN 0-89005-063-5). Ares.

Charlesworth, M. P., tr. see Parvan, Vasile.

Charlesworth, Martin P. Five Men: Character Studies from the Roman Empire. facsimile ed. LC 67-30202. (Essay Index Reprint Ser.: Martin Classical Lectures, Vol. 6). Repr. of 1936 ed. 15.00 (ISBN 0-8369-0292-0). Ayer Co Pubs.

Charlesworth, Max. The Existentialists & Jean-Paul Sartre. 1976. 19.95 (ISBN 0-312-27580-3). St Martin.

Charlesworth, Max, et al, eds. Religion in Aboriginal Australia: An Anthology. LC 83-23437. (Illus.). 458p. 1984. text ed. 35.00x (ISBN 0-7022-1754-9). U of Queensland Pr.

Charlesworth, Neil. British Rule & Indian Economy Eighteen Hundred to Nineteen Fourteen. (Studies in Economic & Social History). 91p. 1982. pap. text ed. 6.75x (ISBN 0-333-27966-2, Pub. by Macmillan England). Humanities.

--Peasants & Imperial Rule: Agriculture & Agrarian Society in the Bombay Presidency, 1850-1935. (South Asian Studies: No. 32). 320p. 1985. 49.50 (ISBN 0-521-23206-6). Cambridge U Pr.

Charlesworth, R. & Radeloff, D. J. Experiences in Math for Young Children. LC 77-80039. 1978. pap. text ed. 12.40 (ISBN 0-8273-1660-7); instructor's guide 4.20 (ISBN 0-8273-1661-5). Delmar.

Charlesworth, Rosalind. Understanding Child Development. LC 81-66763. (Child Care Ser.). (Illus.). 246p. (Orig.). 1983. text ed. 18.00 (ISBN 0-8273-1855-3); instructor's guide 4.20 (ISBN 0-8273-1856-1). Delmar.

Charlesworth, Sarah, et al. Aperture 100: The Edge of Illusion. Date not set. price not set. Aperture.

Charlesworth, William. One Year of Haiku. (Illus.). 1978. pap. 1.00 (ISBN 0-685-41948-7). Nodin Pr.

Charleton, H. B., ed. see Marlowe, Christopher.

Charleton, Walter. The Immorality of the Human Soul, Demonstrated by the Light of Nature: In Two Dialogues. LC 83-46043. (Scientific AWakeningin the Restoration Ser.: No. 2). (Illus.). 224p. 1985. Repr. of 1657 ed. 87.50 (ISBN 0-404-63302-1). AMS Pr.

--Physiologia Epicuro-Gassendo-Charltoniana; or, a Fabrick of Science Natural Upon the Hypothesis of Atoms. 1967. Repr. of 1654 ed. 50.00 (ISBN 0-384-08535-0). Johnson Repr.

Charlevoix, F. X. De see De Charlevoix, F. X.

Charlevoix, Pierre, et al. Charlevoix's Louisiana: Selections from the History & the Journal. O'Neill, Charles E., ed. LC 77-3343. (Louisiana Bicentennial Reprint Ser.). (Illus.). xliv, 257p. 1977. 20.00x (ISBN 0-8071-0250-4). La State U Pr.

Charley, Helen. Food Science. 2nd ed. LC 81-11366. 564p. 1982. 29.00 (ISBN 0-471-06206-5); text ed. 26.95 (ISBN 0-471-06160-3). Wiley.

--Food Study Manual. 3rd ed. LC 79-75636. (Illus.). 275p. (Orig.). 1971. 26.95 (ISBN 0-471-06160-3). Wiley.

Charley, Julian. Cincuenta Palabras Claves de la Biblia. Diaz, Jorge E. & Diaz, Myriam, trs. from Eng. Orig. Title: Fifty Key Words-The Bible. (Illus.). 80p. (Span.). Date not set. pap. price not set (ISBN 0-311-04029-2). Casa Bautista.

Charlick, Robert B. Animation Rurale Revisited: Participatory Techniques for Improving Agriculture & Social Services in 5 Francophone Countries. (Special Series on Animation Rurale: No. 1). 243p. (Orig.). 1984. pap. text ed. 10.00 (ISBN 0-86731-041-3). RDC Ctr Intl Stud.

Charlick, Robert B., et al. Animation Rurale & Rural Development: The Experience of Upper Volta. (Special Series on Animation Rurale: No. 3). 133p. (Orig.). 1983. pap. text ed. 6.65 (ISBN 0-86731-042-X). RDC Ctr Intl Stud.

Charlier, Jean-Michel, jt. auth. see Giruad, Jean.

Charlier, Rodger H. & Karpeck, John J. The World Around Us: A Book of Readings. 253p. 1970. pap. text ed. 8.95x (ISBN 0-8290-1087-4). Irvington.

Charlier, Roger H. Non-Living Ocean Resources. 1979. pap. 5.00 (ISBN 0-686-27713-9). Maple Mont.

--Tidal Energy. 1982. 31.00 (ISBN 0-442-24425-8). Van Nos Reinhold.

Charlier, Roger H. & Gordon, Bernard L. Ocean Resources: An Introduction to Economic Oceanography. LC 78-61393. (Illus.). 1978. pap. text ed. 11.00 (ISBN 0-8191-0599-6). U Pr of Amer.

Charlip, Remy. I Love You. 1981. pap. 1.50 (ISBN 0-380-53090-2, 53090-2). Avon.

--It Looks Like Snow. 1982. pap. 3.45 (ISBN 0-688-01542-5). Greenwillow.

Charlot. Electroanalytical Methods. 1958. 11.50 (ISBN 0-444-40105-9). Elsevier.

Charlot, G. Colorimetric Determination of Elements. 449p. 1964. 64.00 (ISBN 0-444-40104-0). Elsevier.

Charlot, Jean. Art from the Mayans to Disney. facsimile ed. LC 78-99623. (Essay Index Reprint Ser.). 1939. 24.50 (ISBN 0-8369-1399-X). Ayer Co Pubs.

--An Artist on Art: Collected Essays of Jean Charlot, 2 Vols. LC 77-120323. (Illus.). 1972. Set. box 40.00 (ISBN 0-87022-118-3). UH Pr.

--The Mexican Mural Renaissance Nineteen Twenty to Nineteen Twenty-Five. LC 79-83880. (Illus.). 1979. Repr. of 1962 ed. lib. bdg. 35.00 (ISBN 0-87817-251-3). Hacker.

--The Mexican Mural Renaissance 1920-1925. LC 62-8238. (Illus.). pap. 96.50 (ISBN 0-317-10023-8, 2005384). Bks Demand UMI.

Charlot, Martin. Sunnyside Up. LC 73-173473. (Illus.). (gr. 1-7). 1972. 5.95 (ISBN 0-89610-020-0). Island Herit.

Charlotte, C. S. A Sheaf of Songs from a Family Garden. 1985. write for info. Crambruck.

Charlotte, Elisabeth. A Woman's Life in the Court of the Sun King: Letters of Liselotte von der Pfalz, 1652-1722. Forster, Elborg, tr. LC 84-5718. (Illus.). 352p. 1984. 25.00 (ISBN 0-8018-3159-8). Johns Hopkins.

Charlotte, Emily & Bronte, Anne. The Penguin Bronte Sisters. 1072p. 1984. pap. 7.95 (ISBN 0-14-009015-0). Penguin.

Charlotte Hall-Meier, jt. ed. see Brawner, Charles O.

Charlotte-Georgi & Fate, Terry. Fund-Raising, Grants, & Foundations. 175p. 1985. lib. bdg. 27.50 (ISBN 0-87287-441-9). Libs Unl.

Charlsey, Simon. Culture & Sericulture: Social Anthropology & Development in a South Indian Livestock Industry. (Studies in Anthropology). 1982. 35.00 (ISBN 0-12-169380-5). Acad Pr.

Charlton, ed. see Aristotle.

Charlton, Andrew. The Charlton Method for the Recorder: A Manual for the Advanced Recorder Player. LC 81-1172. 192p. (Orig.). 1982. pap. text ed. 24.95x (ISBN 0-8262-0345-0). U of Mo Pr.

Charlton, Andrew & DeVries, John. Jazz & Commercial Arranging, 2 vols. 1982. Vol. I, 208p. pap. 22.95 (ISBN 0-13-509869-6); Vol. II, 176p. 22.95 (ISBN 0-13-509893-9). P-H.

Charlton, Bill, jt. auth. see Bentley, John.

Charlton, C. A. The Urological System. 2nd ed. (Penguin Library of Nursing Ser.). (Illus.). 1983. pap. text ed. 6.75 (ISBN 0-443-02606-8). Churchill.

Charlton, D. G., ed. France: Companion to French Studies. (Illus.). 1979. 45.00x (ISBN 0-416-72300-4, NO.2042); pap. 19.95 (ISBN 0-416-72310-1, NO.3832). Methuen Inc.

--The French Romantics, Vols. 1 & 2. (Illus.). 1984. Vol. 1, 224p. 44.50 (ISBN 0-521-24413-7); Vol. 1. pap. 15.95 (ISBN 0-521-28673-5); Vol. 2, 240p. 44.50 (ISBN 0-521-25971-1); Vol. 2. pap. 15.95 (ISBN 0-521-27779-5). Cambridge U Pr.

Charlton, D. G., jt. ed. see Potts, D. C.

Charlton, David, ed. Etienne-Nicolas Mehul, Three Symphonies (3,4,5) (The Symphony 1720-1840 Series D: Vol. 8). 1982. lib. bdg. 90.00 (ISBN 0-8240-3812-6). Garland Pub.

Charlton, Don. Growing & Showing Roses. (Growing & Showing Ser.). (Illus.). 68p. 1984. 9.95 (ISBN 0-7153-8576-3). David & Charles.

Charlton, Donald. New Images of the Natural in France: A Study in European Cultural History, 1750-1800. 264p. 1985. 49.50 (ISBN 0-521-24940-6); pap. 13.95 (ISBN 0-521-27090-1). Cambridge U Pr.

Charlton, Donald G. Positivist Thought in France During the Second Empire: 1852-1870. LC 76-44305. 1976. Repr. of 1959 ed. lib. bdg. 20.25x (ISBN 0-8371-9076-2, CHPT). Greenwood.

Charlton, E. Harper, jt. auth. see Hennick, Louis.

Charlton, E. Harper, jt. auth. see Hennick, Louis G.

Charlton, Elizabeth. Jeremy & the Ghost. LC 78-72120. (Illus.). (gr. k-3). 1979. 6.75 (ISBN 0-89799-118-4); pap. 3.50 (ISBN 0-89799-019-6). Dandelion Pr.

--Terrible Tyrannosaurus. LC 80-26318. (Illus.). 32p. (ps-3). 1982. 5.95 (ISBN 0-525-66724-5). Dandelion Pr.

--Things I See. LC 78-72122. (Illus.). (ps). 1979. 3.50 (ISBN 0-89799-138-9); pap. 1.50 (ISBN 0-89799-008-0). Dandelion Pr.

Charlton, F. G., jt. auth. see Farraday, R. V.

Charlton, G., et al. Bogglers: Twenty-Two Smart Games (2k to 16k) in Timex-Sinclair BASIC. 224p. 1983. pap. 9.95 (ISBN 0-07-023959-2, BYTE Bks). McGraw.

Charron, Jean D. The Wisdom of Pierre Charron: An Original & Orthodox Code of Morality. LC 78-12595. (Illus.). 1979. Repr. of 1961 ed. lib. bdg. 19.75x (ISBN 0-313-21064-0, CHWO). Greenwood.

Charron, Pierre. Of Wisdome, 3 bks. LC 79-171739. (English Experience Ser.: No. 315). 1971. Repr. of 1612 ed. 72.00 (ISBN 90-221-0315-3). Walter J Johnson.

Charrow, Veda & Erhardt, Myra. Clear & Effective Legal Writing. LC 84-80740. 1985. text ed. price not set (ISBN 0-316-13771-5). Little.

Charry, Dana. Mental Health Skills for Clergy. 160p. 1981. 10.95 (ISBN 0-8170-0886-1). Judson.

Charry, Elias & Segal, Abraham. The Eternal People. (Illus.). 448p. (gr. 9-11). 7.50x (ISBN 0-8381-0206-9, 10-206). United Syn Bk.

Charry, Lawrence B. Comprehension Crosswords, 10 bks. Incl. Bk. 1. (gr. 3) (ISBN 0-89061-175-0, 101); Bk. 2. (gr. 4) (ISBN 0-89061-176-9, 102); Bk. 3. (gr. 5) (ISBN 0-89061-177-7, 103); Bk. 4. (gr. 6) (ISBN 0-89061-178-5, 104); Bk. 5. (gr. 7) (ISBN 0-89061-179-3, 105); Bk. 6. (gr. 8) (ISBN 0-89061-180-7, 106); Bk. 7. (gr. 9) (ISBN 0-89061-181-5, 107); Bk. 8. (gr. 10) (ISBN 0-89061-182-3, 108); Bk. 9. (gr. 11) (ISBN 0-89061-183-1, 109); Bk. 10. (gr. 12) (ISBN 0-89061-184-X, 110). (24p ea.). (gr. 3-12). 1979. pap. 12.00x ea. spirit masters. Jamestown Pubs.

Charry, Myrna, jt. auth. see Bateman, Kitty.

Charschan, Sidney S. Lasers in Industry. 650p. 1984. text ed. 62.00 (ISBN 0-912035-24-2). Laser Inst.

Charter, Angus, jt. auth. see Boden, Clive.

Charter, Jan & Fackre, Gabriel. Youth Ministry: The Gospel & the People. 1979. pap. 5.95 (ISBN 0-8170-0829-2). Judson.

Charter, K. W., ed. see Proceedings of the Institute of Petroleum & Stephens, R. W.

Charter, P. Marking & Assessment in English. (Teaching English Ser.). 1985. cancelled (ISBN 0-416-33180-7, NO. 3866); pap. cancelled (ISBN 0-416-33190-4, NO. 3867). Methuen Inc.

Charteris, A. H. When the Scot Smiles. lib. bdg. 17.50 (ISBN 0-8495-0702-2). Arden Lib.

--When the Scot Smiles. Repr. of 1932 ed. 17.50 (ISBN 0-8274-4150-9). R West.

Charteris, Evan. John Sargent. LC 71-174842. (Illus.). Repr. of 1927 ed. 33.00 (ISBN 0-405-08350-5, Blom Pubns). Ayer Co Pubs.

--The Life & Letters of Sir Edmund Gosse. LC 72-2097. (English Literature Ser., No. 33). 1972. Repr. of 1931 ed. lib. bdg. 66.95x (ISBN 0-8383-1456-2). Haskell.

--The Life & Letters of Sir Edmund Gosse. 1973. Repr. of 1931 ed. 30.00 (ISBN 0-8274-1582-6). R West.

Charteris, Evan E. John Sargent: With Reproductions from His Paintings & Drawings. LC 70-164163. (Illus.). xii, 308p. 1972. Repr. of 1927 ed. 42.00x (ISBN 0-8103-3946-3). Gale.

Charteris, Henry, jt. auth. see Robertson, George.

Charteris, Leslie. Alias the Saint. (Saint Ser.). 160p. 1980. pap. 1.95 (ISBN 0-441-01350-3, Pub. by Charter Bks). Ace Bks.

--Angels of Doom. (The Saint Ser.). (Illus.). 320p. 1982. pap. 2.50 (ISBN 0-441-74875-9, Pub. by Charter Bks). Ace Bks.

--The Avenging Saint. (Saint Ser.). 256p. 1979. pap. 1.95 (ISBN 0-441-03655-4, Pub. by Charter Bks). Ace Bks.

--The Avenging Saint. 13.95 (ISBN 0-88411-267-5, Pub. by Aeonian Pr). Amereon Ltd.

--Call for the Saint. (The Saint Ser.). 224p. 1981. pap. 2.25 (ISBN 0-441-09151-2, Pub. by Charter Bks). Ace Bks.

--Daredevil. (The Saint Ser.). 1976. Repr. of 1929 ed. lib. bdg. 18.95 (ISBN 0-89190-383-6, Pub. by River City Pr). Amereon Ltd.

--Featuring the Saint. 1980. pap. 1.95 (ISBN 0-441-23155-1, Pub. by Charter Bks). Ace Bks.

--Follow the Saint. (The Saint Ser.). (Illus.). 288p. 1982. pap. 2.50 (ISBN 0-441-24211-1, Pub. by Charter Bks). Ace Bks.

--Follow the Saint. 1976. Repr. of 1938 ed. lib. bdg. 16.95x (ISBN 0-89190-382-8, Pub. by River City Pr). Amereon Ltd.

--Getaway. 1975. Repr. of 1933 ed. lib. bdg. 17.95x (ISBN 0-89190-388-7, Pub. by River City Pr). Amereon Ltd.

--Holy Terror. facsimile ed. LC 72-106261. (Short Story Index Reprint Ser.). 1932. 18.00 (ISBN 0-8369-3298-6). Ayer Co Pubs.

--Prelude for War. (The Saint Ser.). 294p. 1982. pap. 2.95 (ISBN 0-441-67714-2, Pub. by Charter Bks). Ace Bks.

--The Saint & Mr. Teal. (The Saint Ser.). 176p. 1981. pap. 2.25 (ISBN 0-441-74911-9, Pub. by Charter Bks). Ace Bks.

--The Saint & the Happy Highwayman. (The Saint Ser.). 224p. 1981. pap. 2.50 (ISBN 0-441-74891-0, Pub. by Charter Bks). Ace Bks.

--The Saint & the Templar Treasure. LC 78-22154. (Crime Club Ser.). 1979. 9.95 (ISBN 0-385-15097-0). Doubleday.

--The Saint & the Templar Treasure. 13.95 (ISBN 0-88411-266-7, Pub. by Aeonian Pr). Amereon Ltd.

--The Saint Bids Diamonds. 256p. 1982. 20.00x (ISBN 0-7278-0639-4, Pub. by Severn Hse). State Mutual Bk.

--The Saint Goes On. 1982. pap. 2.50 (ISBN 0-441-74882-1, Pub. by Charter Bks). Ace Bks.

--The Saint Goes West. 200p. 1982. pap. 2.50 (ISBN 0-441-74883-X, Pub. by Charter Bks). Ace Bks.

--The Saint Goes West. 11.95 (ISBN 0-89190-391-7, Pub. by Am Repr). Amereon Ltd.

--The Saint in Europe. (Saint Ser.). 144p. 1981. pap. 2.50 (ISBN 0-441-74886-4). Ace Bks.

--The Saint in Europe. 1975. Repr. of 1953 ed. lib. bdg. 13.95 (ISBN 0-89190-387-9, Pub. by River City Pr). Amereon Ltd.

--The Saint in London. 192p. 1982. 20.00x (ISBN 0-7278-0468-5, Pub. by Severn Hse). State Mutual Bk.

--The Saint in Miami. (Saint Ser.). 1981. pap. 2.50 (ISBN 0-441-75352-3). Ace Bks.

--The Saint Intervenes. 1976. Repr. of 1934 ed. lib. bdg. 16.95 (ISBN 0-89190-384-4, Pub. by River City Pr). Amereon Ltd.

--The Saint Meets His Match. 14.95 (ISBN 0-89190-343-7, Pub. by Am Repr). Amereon Ltd.

--The Saint on Guard. 1975. Repr. of 1944 ed. lib. bdg. 15.95 (ISBN 0-89190-386-0, Pub. by River City Pr). Amereon Ltd.

--The Saint on Guard. 192p. 1982. 20.00x (Pub. by Severn Hse). State Mutual Bk.

--The Saint Overboard. 1976. Repr. of 1936 ed. lib. bdg. 17.95 (ISBN 0-89190-381-X, Pub. by River City Pr). Amereon Ltd.

--The Saint Plays with Fire. 192p. 1982. 20.00x (ISBN 0-7278-0537-1, Pub. by Severn Hse). State Mutual Bk.

--The Saint Sees It Through. 1975. Repr. of 1946 ed. lib. bdg. 16.95 (ISBN 0-89190-389-5, Pub. by River City Pr). Amereon Ltd.

--The Saint Sees it Through. 256p. 1982. 20.00x (ISBN 0-7278-0600-9, Pub. by Severn Hse). State Mutual Bk.

--The Saint Steps in. 1976. Repr. of 1943 ed. lib. bdg. 14.95 (ISBN 0-89190-385-2, Pub. by River City Pr). Amereon Ltd.

--The Saint Steps In. 192p. 1982. 20.00x (ISBN 0-7278-0474-X, Pub. by Severn Hse). State Mutual Bk.

--The Saint vs. Scotland Yard. 1975. Repr. of 1932 ed. lib. bdg. 14.95x (ISBN 0-89190-390-9, Pub. by River City Pr). Amereon Ltd.

--The Saint's Sporting Chance. 15.95 (ISBN 0-89190-344-5, Pub. by Am Repr). Amereon Ltd.

Charteris, Richard. Alphonso Ferrabosco the Elder, 1543-1588: A Thematic Catalogue of His Music & a Biographical Calendar. (Thematic Catalogue Ser.: No. 11). (Illus.). 190p. 1984. lib. bdg. 32.00x (ISBN 0-918728-44-4). Pendragon NY.

--John Coprario: A Thematic Catalogue of His Music. (Thematic Catalogue Ser.: No. 3). 1977. lib. bdg. 24.00 (ISBN 0-918728-05-3). Pendragon NY.

Charters. The Roots of the Blues. 15.00 (ISBN 0-7145-2705-X). M Boyars.

Charters, A. Accessibility of Resources for Educators of Adults. (MS Ser.: No. 9). 1977. 3.50 (ISBN 0-686-63885-9, MSS 9). Syracuse U Cont Ed.

--Aids to Access: Resources for Educators of Adults. (MS Ser.). 1978. 4.25 (ISBN 0-686-52208-7, MSS 1). Syracuse U Cont Ed.

--Continuing Education for Educators of Adults: The Roles of Research. (MS Ser.). 1977. 4.00 (ISBN 0-686-52213-3, MSS 6). Syracuse U Cont Ed.

--Hill & the Valley: The Story of University College at Syracuse University Through 1964. LC 77-18954. (Occasional Papers: No. 27). 1972. pap. text ed. 2.25 (ISBN 0-87060-050-8, OCP 27). Syracuse U Cont Ed.

--Professional Development of Educators of Adults. (MS Ser,). (Sp.). 1977. 3.50 (ISBN 0-686-52209-5, MSS 2). Syracuse U Cont Ed.

--Report on the Nineteen Sixty-Nine Galaxy Conference of Adult Education Organizations. (Landmark Ser.: No. 1). 1971. pap. text ed. 2.00 (ISBN 0-87060-005-2, LNH 1). Syracuse U Cont Ed.

Charters, A. & Hilton, R. Who We Are: What Some Educators Say About Their Characteristics, Competencies & Roles. (MS Ser.). 1977. 5.00 (ISBN 0-686-52212-5, MSS 5). Syracuse U Cont Ed.

Charters, A. & Holmwood, D. Periodicals, Newsletters & Indexes in E. S. Bird Library & Clearinghouse of Resources for Educators of Adults. (MS Ser.: No. 8). 1978. 3.50 (ISBN 0-686-63883-2, MSS 8). Syracuse U Cont Ed.

Charters, A., compiled by. Abstracts of Theses & Dissertations in Adult Education, Syracuse University. 1979. 4.50 (ISBN 0-686-65496-X, MSS 11). Syracuse U Cont Ed.

--Adult & Continuing Education Collections: A Descriptive List of Manuscript Holdings in Syracuse University Libraries. 1977. 5.00 (ISBN 0-686-50189-6, MSS 16). Syracuse U Cont Ed.

--Audio Tapes: E. S. Bird Library. 1976. 3.75 (ISBN 0-686-63886-7, MSS 22). Syracuse U Cont Ed.

--Omnibus Series: E. S. Byrd Library. 1976. 4.65 (ISBN 0-686-50190-X, MSS 24). Syracuse U Cont Ed.

--The Paul Hoy Helms Library in Liberal Adult Education. 1973. 4.55 (ISBN 0-686-50191-8, MSS 20). Syracuse U Cont Ed.

Charters, A. N. Real Estate Tax Exemption for Continuing Education. LC 76-189508. (Occasional Paper Ser.: No. 26). 1972. pap. 2.00 (ISBN 0-87060-049-4, OCP 26). Syracuse U Cont Ed.

Charters, Alexander N. Adult Education Activity of Selected International Organizations. 1971. 5.00 (ISBN 0-87060-076-1, WPT 4). Syracuse U Cont Ed.

--Adult Education Master's Theses & Doctoral Dissertations on Microfilm in Syracuse University Libraries. 1977. pap. 5.00 (ISBN 0-685-87565-2, MSS 17). Syracuse U Cont Ed.

--Adult Education Sound & Video Recordings E. S. Bird Library. 1982. 8.00 (ISBN 0-87060-031-1, MSS 23). Syracuse U Cont Ed.

--Dessarollo Professional De Educadores De Alultos. 1977. 4.00 (ISBN 0-87060-077-X, MSS 3). Syracuse U Cont Ed.

--The International Handbook of Resources for the Educators of Adults. 1977. 20.00 (ISBN 0-685-87564-4, MSS 18). Syracuse U Cont Ed.

--Omnibus Series: E. S. Bird Library. 1976. 4.50 (ISBN 0-317-18233-1, MSS 21). Syracuse U Cont Ed.

--Publications in Continuing Education. (MS Ser.: No. 12). 1980. 4.50 (ISBN 0-686-64687-8, MSS 12). Syracuse U Cont Ed.

--Toward the Educative Society. LC 74-149023. (Notes & Essays No. 67). 1971. pap. 2.50 (ISBN 0-87060-039-7, NES 67). Syracuse U Cont Ed.

Charters, Alexander N. & Goodman, Edward. Acquisition List Pamphlet File. rev. ed. (E. S. Bird Library). 1983. 8.00 (ISBN 0-87060-073-7, MSS 13). Syracuse U Cont Ed.

Charters, Alexander N. & Gschwender, Edward. Adult Education Periodicals & Newsletters in Bird Library. 1983. 8.00 (ISBN 0-87060-037-0, MSS 29). Syracuse U Cont Ed.

Charters, Alexander N., ed. Publications in Continuing Education. 1983. 8.00 (ISBN 0-87060-038-9, MSS 26). Syracuse U Cont Ed.

Charters, Alexander N. & Rivera, William M., eds. International Seminar on Publications in Continuing Education. LC 76-39028. (Notes & Essays Ser. No. 72). 112p. (Orig.). 1972. pap. 3.00 (ISBN 0-87060-048-6, NES 72). Syracuse U Cont Ed.

Charters, Alexander N., et al. Comparing Adult Education Worldwide. LC 80-8911. (Higher Education Ser.). 1981. text ed. 19.95x (ISBN 0-87589-494-1). Jossey-Bass.

Charters, Alexanders N. & Holmwood, Donald. Professional Development for Educators of Adults: A Bibliography. 1977. 8.00 (ISBN 0-87060-078-8, CRE 3). Syracuse U Cont Ed.

Charters, Ann. Jack Kerouac. 2nd rev. ed. LC 75-30147. (Phoenix Bibliographies Ser.). (Illus.). 1975. 10.00 (ISBN 0-916228-06-1). Phoenix Bk Shop.

--Nobody, The Story of Bert Williams. (Roots of Jazz Ser.). (Illus.). 157p. 1983. Repr. of 1970 ed. lib. bdg. 19.50 (ISBN 0-306-76190-4). Da Capo.

--Olson, Melville: A Study in Affinity. (Illus.). 1968. 5.00 (ISBN 0-685-19074-9); pap. 2.50 (ISBN 0-685-19075-7). Oyez.

Charters, Ann & Charters, Samuel. I Love: The Story of Vladimir Mayakovsky & Lili Brik. 432p. 1979. 17.50 (ISBN 0-374-17406-7). FS&G.

Charters, Ann, ed. The Beats, 2 Vols. (Dictionary of Literary Biography Ser.: Vol. 16). 400p. 1983. 170.00x (ISBN 0-8103-1148-8). Gale.

--The Story & Its Writer: An Introduction to Short Fiction. LC 82-62584. 1200p. 1983. pap. text ed. 16.95 (ISBN 0-312-76251-8); instr's. manual avail. St. Martin.

Charters, Ann, compiled by see Ginsberg, Allen.

Charters, Margaret. Consumer Education Programming in Continuing Education. LC 72-13366. (Occasional Papers, No. 34). 36p. (Orig.). 1973. pap. 2.00 (ISBN 0-87060-057-5, OCP 34). Syracuse U Cont Ed.

Charters, Samuel. From a Swedish Notebook. 1973. 5.00 (ISBN 0-685-36814-9); pap. 2.50 (ISBN 0-685-36815-7). Oyez.

--In Lagos, Ereko Street, Nine p.m. 1976. saddlestitched in wrappers 1.50 (ISBN 0-685-79011-8). Oyez.

--Jelly Roll Morton's Last Night at the Jungle Inn: An Imaginary Memoir. (Illus.). 160p. 1984. 12.95 (ISBN 0-7145-2805-6, Dist. by Scribner). M Boyars.

--The Legacy of the Blues: Art & Lives of Twelve Great Bluesmen. LC 76-51809. (Roots of Jazz Ser.). (Illus.). 1977. 22.50 (ISBN 0-306-70847-7); pap. 6.95 (ISBN 0-306-80054-3). Da Capo.

--Mr. Jabi & Mr. Smythe. LC 82-12818. 192p. 1983. 12.95 (ISBN 0-7145-2779-3, Dist. by Scribner). M Boyars.

--Of Those Who Died. 1980. pap. 3.00 (ISBN 0-317-17645-5). Oyez.

--Some Poems - Poets. 1971. 5.95 (ISBN 0-685-04674-5); pap. 2.95 (ISBN 0-685-04675-3). Oyez.

Charters, Samuel, jt. auth. see Charters, Ann.

Charters, Samuel B. The Country Blues. LC 75-14122. (The Roots of Jazz Ser.). (Illus.). 288p. 1975. lib. bdg. 25.00 (ISBN 0-306-70678-4); pap. 6.95 (ISBN 0-306-80014-4). Da Capo.

--Jazz: New Orleans 1885-1963. (Roots of Jazz Ser.). 173p. 1983. Repr. of 1963 ed. lib. bdg. 19.50 (ISBN 0-306-76189-0). Da Capo.

Charters, Samuel B. & Kunstadt, Leonard. Jazz: A History of the New York Scene. (Roots of Jazz Ser.). 1981. lib. bdg. 35.00 (ISBN 0-306-76055-X); pap. 9.95 (ISBN 0-306-80225-2). Da Capo.

Charters, W. W. Curriculum Construction. LC 74-165713. (American Education, Ser. 2). 1972. Repr. of 1923 ed. 30.00 (ISBN 0-405-03702-3). Ayer Co Pubs.

--Methods of Teaching. (Educational Ser.). 1909. Repr. 10.00 (ISBN 0-8482-3584-3). Norwood Edns.

--Motion Pictures & Youth: A Summary. LC 73-124025. (Literature of Cinema Ser.: Payne Fund Studies of Motion Pictures & Social Values). Repr. of 1933 ed. 8.00 (ISBN 0-405-01642-5). Ayer Co Pubs.

Charters, W. W., jt. ed. see Schmuck, Patricia.

Chartham, Robert. The Sensuous Couple. 2nd ed. 192p. 1981. pap. 2.50 (ISBN 0-345-29543-9); 12 copy counter display 30.00 (ISBN 0-686-96670-8). Ballantine.

Chartier & Langlais. L' Anglais Chez Soi: C-Course. (Pergamon Institute of English Courses Ser.). (Illus.). 160p. 1984. kit 25.45 (ISBN 0-08-025308-3); pap. 7.95 (ISBN 0-08-025309-1). Pergamon.

Chartier, Alain. Fifteenth-Century English Translations of Alain Chartier's "le Traite de l'Esperance" & "le Quadrilogue Invectif". Blayney, Margaret S., ed. (Early English Text Society Ser.). (Illus.). 1980. 26.50x (ISBN 0-19-722283-8). Oxford U Pr.

Chartier, Armand. Litterature historique populaire franco-americaine. 108p. (Fr.). 1981. pap. text ed. 3.00 (ISBN 0-911409-40-8). Natl Mat Dev.

Chartier, Emile A. see Alain, pseud.

Chartier, Emile-Auguste see Alain, pseud.

Chartier, Gary D. Tulip the Toad. (gr. 1-3). 1983. 4.95 (ISBN 0-8062-2159-3). Carlton.

Chartier, J. P. & Culhane, T. L' Anglais Chez Soi: A Self Study Course for Near Beginners. (Institute of English Courses Ser.). (Illus.). 160p. 1984. Set. 25.45 (ISBN 0-317-12561-3); pap. 7.95 (ISBN 0-08-025309-1). Pergamon.

Chartier, Jan. Developing Leadership in the Teaching Church. 112p. 1985. pap. 7.95 (ISBN 0-8170-1067-X). Judson.

Chartier, Jan, jt. auth. see Chartier, Myron.

Chartier, Myron & Chartier, Jan. Trusting Together in God. LC 83-73132. (Illus.). 172p. (Orig.). 1984. pap. 6.95 (ISBN 0-87029-193-9, 20285-3). Abbey.

Chartier, Myron R. Preaching As Communication: An Interpersonal Perspective. LC 80-21304. (Abingdon Preacher Library). 128p. (Orig.). 1981. pap. 5.95 (ISBN 0-687-33826-3). Abingdon.

Chartier, P. & Palz, W., eds. Energy from Biomass. x, 220p. 1981. 28.00 (ISBN 90-277-1348-0, Pub. by Reidel Holland). Kluwer Academic.

Chartier, P., jt. ed. see Palz, W.

Chartier, Sandra. Time for Bed, Sleepyheads. LC 82-82565. (Golden Storytime Bk.). (Illus.). 24p. 1983. 1.95 (ISBN 0-307-11964-5, 11964, Golden Bks). Western Pub.

Chartism & Chartists. Joneg. 1975. 25.00. St Martin.

Chartists, jt. auth. see Chartism.

Chartkoff, Joseph L. & Chartkoff, Kerry K. The Archaeology of California. LC 82-60182. (Illus.). 480p. 1984. 32.50x (ISBN 0-8047-1157-7). Stanford U Pr.

Chartkoff, Kerry K., jt. auth. see Chartkoff, Joseph L.

Chartock, Roselle & Spencer, Jack. The Holocaust Years: Society on Trial. 244p. Repr. 2.95 (ISBN 0-686-95069-0). ADL.

Charton, Balthazar, jt. auth. see Capitaine, Jean L.

Charton, M. & Motoc, I., eds. Steric Effects in Drug Design. (Topics in Current Chemistry Ser.: Vol. 114). (Illus.). 172p. 1983. 35.00 (ISBN 0-387-12398-9). Springer-Verlag.

Charton, Nancy, ed. The Ciskei: Economics & Politics of Dependence in a South African Homeland. 256p. 1980. 32.50 (ISBN 0-7099-0332-4, Pub. by Croom Helm Ltd). Longwood Pub Group.

Chartrand, G., ed. see Conference On Graph Theory - Western Michigan University - Kalamazoo - 1968.

Chartrand, Gary. Introductory Graph Theory. (Popular Science Ser.). 320p. 1985. pap. 5.95 (ISBN 0-486-24775-9). Dover.

Chartrand, Gary, et al, eds. The Theory & Application of Graphs: Fourth International Conference, Western Michigan Univ., May 6-9, 1980. Chartrand, Gary, et al. LC 80-27978. 611p. 1981. 53.50x (ISBN 0-471-08473-5, Pub. by Wiley-Interscience). Wiley.

Chartrand, Marilyn J. & Williams, Constance D., eds. Educational Software Directory: A Subject Guide to Microcomputer Software. 1982. pap. text ed. 27.50 (ISBN 0-87287-352-8). Libs Unl.

Chartrand, Mark R. Skyguide. LC 81-70086. (A Golden Field Guide Ser.). (Illus.). 280p. 1982. pap. 7.95 (ISBN 0-307-13667-1, Golden Pr). Western Pub.

Chartrand, P., ed. see Bacon, F., et al.

Chartrand, P., ed. see Fortin, A., et al.

Chartrand, Rene, jt. auth. see Summers, Jack L.

Chartrand, Robert L. Computers & Political Campaigning. LC 72-75713. 1972. 5.00 (ISBN 0-87671-178-6). Chartrand.

Chartrand, Robert L. & Morentz, James W. Information Technology Serving Society. (Illus.). 1979. 42.00 (ISBN 0-08-021979-9). Pergamon.

Chartrand, Robert L., ed. Computers in the Service of Society. LC 73-112401. 256p. 1972. 32.00 (ISBN 0-08-016332-7). Pergamon.

Chartrand, Robert Lee & Morentz, James W., Jr., eds. Information Technology Serving Society. 1979. 25.00 (ISBN 0-08-021979-9). Chartrand.

Chartres, J. A. Internal Trade in England 1500-1700. (Studies in Economic & Social History). 1977. pap. text ed. 5.25x (ISBN 0-333-18358-4). Humanities.

Charubel, pseud. The Degrees of the Zodiac Symbolised: Symbolic Meaning for Each Degree. updated ed. Sepharial, tr. from Sp. 1985. pap. 3.50 (ISBN 0-933646-01-1). Aries Pr.

Charudattan, R. & Walker, H. Lynn. Biological Control of Weeds with Plant Pathogens. LC 82-1879. 293p. 1982. 45.50x (ISBN 0-471-08598-7, Pub. by Wiley-Interscience). Wiley.

Charushin, Y. How They Live. 16p. 1977. pap. 0.99 (ISBN 0-8285-1164-0, Pub. by Progress Pubs USSR). Imported Pubns.

--My Animal Book. 72p. 1980. 7.45 (ISBN 0-8285-1842-4, Pub. by Progress Pubs USSR). Imported Pubns.

Charvat, J., et al. Review of the Nature & Uses of Examinations in Medical Education. (Public Health Papers Ser: No. 36). 74p. 1968. pap. 4.00 (ISBN 92-4-130036-1, 548). World Health.

Charvat, William. The Profession of Authorship in America, 1800-1870: The Papers of William Charvat. Bruccoli, Matthew J., ed. LC 68-18107. (Illus.). 358p. 1968. 7.00 (ISBN 0-8142-0039-7). Ohio St U Pr.

Charvat, William & Kraus, Michael. William Hickling Prescott. 1979. Repr. of 1943 ed. lib. bdg. 35.00 (ISBN 0-8482-7562-4). Norwood Edns.

--William Hickling Prescott: Representative Selections, with Introduction, Bibliography & Notes. 466p. 1983. Repr. of 1943 ed. lib. bdg. 50.00 (ISBN 0-89987-144-5). Darby Bks.

--William Hickling Prescott: Representative Selections with Introduction, Bibliography & Notes. 466p. 1983. lib. bdg. 50.00 (ISBN 0-8495-0962-9). Arden Lib.

Charvat, William, et al, eds. see Hawthorne, Nathaniel.

Charvet, John. A Critique of Freedom & Equality. (Cambridge Studies in the History & Theory of Politics). 224p. 1982. 44.50 (ISBN 0-521-23727-0). Cambridge U Pr.

--Feminism. (Modern Ideologies Ser.). 168p. 1982. text ed. 15.00x (ISBN 0-460-10255-9, BKA 04799, Pub. by J M Dent England); pap. text ed. 7.95x (ISBN 0-460-11255-4, BKA04800, Pub. by J M Dent England). Biblio Dist.

--The Social Problems in the Philosophy of Rousseau. LC 73-88311. (Cambridge Studies in the History & Theory of Politics). pap. 39.50 (ISBN 0-317-26041-3, 2024436). Bks Demand UMI.

Charvet, P. E., tr. see Baudelaire, Charles.

Charvet, Patrice, tr. see Potter, Beatrix.

Charwood, Godfrey R. Abraham Lincoln. LC 83-45730. Repr. of 1916 ed. 49.50 (ISBN 0-404-20056-7). AMS Pr.

Chary, Pauline De see Von Klarwill, Victor.

Charyn, Jerome. The Catfish Man: A Conjured Life. 320p. 1981. pap. 3.50 (ISBN 0-380-56168-9, 56168, Bard). Avon.

--Darlin' Bill. LC 85-70635. 304p. 1985. pap. 8.95 (ISBN 0-917657-40-3, Pub. by Primus Lib Contemp). D I Fine.

--Darlin' Bill: A Love Story of the Wild West. 304p. 1982. pap. 3.50 (ISBN 0-380-57745-3, 57745-3, Bard). Avon.

--The Education of Patrick Silver. 208p. 1981. pap. 2.75 (ISBN 0-380-01698-2, 53603-X, Bard). Avon.

--Marilyn the Wild. 208p. 1981. pap. 2.95 (ISBN 0-380-00964-1, 54536, Bard). Avon.

--Panna Maria: Which in English Means "Virgin Mary". LC 81-66960. 320p. 1982. 17.50 (ISBN 0-87795-328-7); pap. 9.50 (ISBN 0-87795-408-9). Arbor Hse.

--Pinocchio's Nose. 1983. 15.95 (ISBN 0-87795-438-0). Arbor Hse.

--Secret of Isaac. 240p. 1980. pap. 2.75 (ISBN 0-380-47126-4, 47126, Bard). Avon.

--The Seventh Babe. LC 78-73866. 1979. 9.95 (ISBN 0-87795-220-5). Arbor Hse.

--The Seventh Babe. 352p. 1980. pap. 2.95 (ISBN 0-380-51540-7, 51540, Bard). Avon.

--War Cries over Avenue C. LC 84-73516. 352p. 1985. 17.95 (ISBN 0-917657-30-6). D I Fine.

Charyulu. Homones & Cancer. 1979. 32.50 (ISBN 0-8151-1644-6). Year Bk Med.

--Selected Topics of Cancer: Current Concepts. 1979. 29.95 (ISBN 0-8151-1643-8). Year Bk Med.

Chas. Winthrope & Sons Staff. Nineteen Eighty-Three Bradford Book of Collector's Plates. (Illus.). 352p. 1985. pap. 14.50 (ISBN 0-9611012-0-2). Wallace-Homestead.

Chasan, Daniel J. The Fall of the House of WPPSS. Brewster, David, ed. 128p. (Orig.). 1985. pap. 9.95 (ISBN 0-912365-05-6). Sasquatch Pub.

--Up for Grabs: Inquiries into Who Wants What. LC 77-23881. 134p. 1977. 9.95 (ISBN 0-914842-18-8); pap. 5.95 (ISBN 0-914842-17-X). Madrona Pubs.

--The Water Link: A History of Puget Sound As a Resource. (Puget Sound Bks). (Illus.). 192p. 1981. pap. 8.95 (ISBN 0-295-95782-4, Pub. by Washington Sea Grant). U of Wash Pr.

Chase & Ducat. Chase & Ducat Constitutional Interpretation, Cases-Essays-Materials. 2nd ed. LC 79-14772. 1490p. 1979. text ed. 25.95 (ISBN 0-8299-2052-8); supplement avail. (ISBN 0-314-69638-5). West Pub.

Chase & John. A Guide for the Elementary Social Studies Teacher. 3rd ed. 1985. 21.43 (ISBN 0-205-05938-4, 235938). Allyn.

Chase, Agnes. First Book of Grasses: The Structure of Grasses Explained for Beginners. 3rd ed. LC 76-48919. (Illus.). 127p. 1977. text ed. 8.95x (ISBN 0-87474-307-9). Smithsonian.

Chase, Agnes, ed. see Smithsonian Institution, Washington, D. C.

Chase, Alexander J. Next Case. 128p. 1985. 8.95 (ISBN 0-89962-461-8). Todd & Honeywell.

Chase, Allan. The Legacy of Malthus: The Social Costs of the New Scientific Racism. LC 79-22799. 732p. 1980. pap. 12.50x (ISBN 0-252-00790-5). U of Ill Pr.

--Magic Shots: A Human & Scientific Account of the Long & Continuing Struggle to Eradicate Infectious Diseases by Vaccination. LC 82-12505. 600p. 1982. 19.95 (ISBN 0-688-00787-2). Morrow.

--The Truth about STD: The Old Ones-Herpes & Other New Ones-the Primary Causes-the Available Cures. LC 82-20855. 188p. 1983. 11.95 (ISBN 0-688-01896-3). Morrow.

--The Truth about STD: The Old Ones-Herpes & Other New Ones-the Primary Causes-the Available Cures. LC 82-21446. 188p. 1983. pap. 5.70 (ISBN 0-688-01835-1, Quill). Morrow.

Chase, Allen. Falange: The Axis Secret Army in the Americas. LC 78-63659. (Studies in Fascism: Ideology & Practice). Repr. of 1943 ed. 32.00 (ISBN 0-404-16919-8). AMS Pr.

--The Legacy of Malthus: The Social Costs of the New Scientific Racism. 1977. 20.00 (ISBN 0-394-48045-7). Knopf.

Chase, Alston H. A New Introduction to Latin. (gr. 9). text ed. 7.00x (ISBN 0-88334-001-1). Ind Sch Pr.

Chase, Alston H. & Phillips, Henry, Jr. New Introduction to Greek. 3rd, rev. & enl ed. LC 61-13748. (Illus.). 1961. 15.00 (ISBN 0-674-61600-6). Harvard U Pr.

Chase, Alston H. & Phillips, Henry, Jr., eds. New Greek Reader. LC 54-12234. (Illus.). (gr. 10 up). Repr. of 1954 ed. 91.20 (ISBN 0-8357-9169-6, 2016728). Bks Demand UMI.

Chase, Andrew, ed. The Use & Processing of Renewable Resources: Chemical Engineering Challenge of the Future. LC 81-12682. (AIChE Symposium: Vol. 77). 141p. 1981. pap. 32.00 (ISBN 0-8169-0205-4, S-207); pap. 17.00 members (ISBN 0-686-47542-9). Am Inst Chem Eng.

Chase, Arlen F. & Rice, Prudence M., eds. The Lowland Maya Postclassic. (Illus.). 328p. 1985. text ed. 27.50x (ISBN 0-292-74643-1). U of Tex Pr.

Chase, Bernard L. Look from Within. 40p. (Orig.). 1982. pap. 2.25 (ISBN 0-943512-00-X, 164H). Linwood Pub.

Chase Brass & Copper Co. Evaluation of Clears for Protection of Copper-Base Alloys. 131p. 1966. 19.60 (ISBN 0-317-34523-0, 16). Intl Copper.

Chase, C. B. Sherwood Anderson. LC 72-3565. (Studies in Fiction, No. 34). 1972. Repr. of 1927 ed. lib. bdg. 29.95x (ISBN 0-8383-1543-7). Haskell.

Chase, Carroll. The Three-Cent Stamp of the United States, 1851-1857 Issue. LC 75-18277. (Illus.). 384p. 1976. Repr. 30.00x (ISBN 0-88000-070-8). Quarterman.

Chase, Carroll & Cabeen, Richard M. The First Hundred Years of United States Territorial Postmarks Seventeen Eighty-Seven to Eighteen Eighty-Seven. LC 79-67393. 341p. 1980. Repr. of 1950 ed. lib. bdg. 35.00x (ISBN 0-88000-112-7). Quarterman.

Chase, Catherine. An Alphabet Book. LC 78-72095. (Illus.). (gr. k). 1979. 6.75 (ISBN 0-89799-087-0); pap. 3.50 (ISBN 0-89799-000-5). Dandelion Pr.

--Baby Mouse Goes Searching. LC 81-2243. (Illus.). 32p. (ps-3). 1982. 6.75 (ISBN 0-525-66742-3). Dandelion Pr.

--Baby Mouse Learns His ABC's. LC 78-72096. (Illus.). (ps). 1979. 6.75 (ISBN 0-89799-089-7); pap. 1.50 (ISBN 0-89799-001-3). Dandelion Pr.

--Duncan McTavish in Switzerland. LC 78-64488. (Illus.). (gr. k-3). 1978. 3.50 (ISBN 0-89799-101-X); pap. 1.50 (ISBN 0-89799-010-2). Dandelion Pr.

--Feet. LC 78-72105. (First Reader Ser.). (Illus.). (gr. k-3). 1979. 3.50 (ISBN 0-89799-104-4); pap. 1.50 (ISBN 0-89799-020-X). Dandelion Pr.

--Hot & Cold. LC 78-72101. (First Reader Ser.). (Illus.). (gr. k-3). 1979. 6.75 (ISBN 0-89799-110-9); pap. 3.50 (ISBN 0-89799-021-8). Dandelion Pr.

--The Miracles at Cana. LC 78-64117. (Illus.). (gr. k-5). 1979. 3.50 (ISBN 0-89799-124-9); pap. 1.50 (ISBN 0-89799-033-1). Dandelion Pr.

--The Mouse in My House. LC 78-72103. (First Reader Ser.). (Illus.). (gr. k-3). 1979. 3.50 (ISBN 0-89799-126-5); pap. 1.50 (ISBN 0-89799-024-2). Dandelion Pr.

--My Balloon. LC 78-72102. (First Reader Ser.). (Illus.). (gr. k-3). 1979. 3.50 (ISBN 0-89799-127-3); pap. 1.50 (ISBN 0-89799-022-6). Dandelion Pr.

--The Nightingale & the Fool. LC 78-72915. (Illus.). (gr. 1-4). 1979. 3.50 (ISBN 0-89799-129-X); pap. 1.50 (ISBN 0-89799-059-5). Dandelion Pr.

--Noah's Ark. LC 78-64415. (Illus.). (gr. k-5). 1979. 3.50 (ISBN 0-89799-130-3); pap. 1.50 (ISBN 0-89799-031-5). Dandelion Pr.

--Pete, the Wet Pet. LC 81-2203. (Illus.). 32p. (ps-3). 1982. 6.75 (ISBN 0-525-66746-6). Dandelion Pr.

--See the Fly Fly. LC 78-72104. (First Reader Ser.). (Illus.). (gr. k-3). 1979. 6.75 (ISBN 0-89799-133-8); pap. 3.50 (ISBN 0-89799-023-4). Dandelion Pr.

Chase, Catherine, ed. The Birth of Moses. LC 78-73540. (Illus.). (gr. k-5). Date not set. 6.00 (ISBN 0-89799-151-6); pap. price not set (ISBN 0-89799-069-2). Dandelion Pr.

Chase, Chris, jt. auth. see Ford, Betty.

Chase, Chris, jt. auth. see Russell, Rosalind.

Chase, Claire, jt. auth. see Zager, Masha.

Chase, Cleveland B. Sherwood Anderson. 1978. Repr. of 1927 ed. lib. bdg. 15.00 (ISBN 0-8495-0821-5). Arden Lib.

--Sherwood Anderson. 1927. lib. bdg. 15.00 (ISBN 0-8414-3352-6). Folcroft.

--The Young Voltaire. 253p. 1980. Repr. of 1926 ed. lib. bdg. 35.00 (ISBN 0-8495-0799-5). Arden Lib.

--The Young Voltaire. facsimile ed. LC 79-160962. (Select Bibliographies Reprint Ser). Repr. of 1926 ed. 22.00 (ISBN 0-8369-5830-6). Ayer Co Pubs.

Chase, Clinton I. Elementary Statistical Procedures. 3rd ed. 416p. 1984. text ed. 26.95 (ISBN 0-07-010677-0). McGraw.

--Measurement for Educational Evaluation. 2nd ed. LC 77-79456. (Illus.). 1978. text ed. 23.75 (ISBN 0-201-01019-4); student study guide 7.55 (ISBN 0-201-01029-1); instr's. manual 4.10 (ISBN 0-201-01006-2). Addison-Wesley.

Chase, Cochran, et al. Solving Marketing Problems with VisiCalc on Apple II, IIe Computers. 300p. (Orig.). 1984. pap. 29.95 incl. disc (ISBN 0-8019-7422-4). Chilton.

--Solving Marketing Problems with VisiCalc on the IBM PC. 300p. (Orig.). 1984. pap. 29.95 incl. disc (ISBN 0-8019-7542-5). Chilton.

Chase, Cohrane & Barasch, Kenneth. Solving Marketing Problems with VisiCalc. LC 83-45392. 300p. (Orig.). 1984. pap. 14.95 (ISBN 0-8019-7423-2). Chilton.

Chase, Cora G. Earthen Pots & a Stone Wall. (Illus.). 48p. 1982. pap. 5.95 (ISBN 0-933992-21-1). Coffee Break.

--Unto the Least Seattle Ryther Center. 152p. pap. 5.95 (ISBN 0-8466-0283-0, S283). Shorey.

--The Weed Eaters Cook Book. rev., 2nd ed. (Illus.). 66p. 1981. pap. 5.95 (ISBN 0-933992-18-1). Coffee Break.

Chase, D. P. The Nicomachean Ethics of Aristotle. 1911. 10.00 (ISBN 0-8274-3037-X). R West.

Chase, Deborah. Dying at Home with Hospice. 1985. 15.95 (ISBN 0-8016-0959-3). Mosby.

--The Extend Your Life Diet. 1983. pap. 2.95 (ISBN 0-671-46536-8). PB.

--The Medically-Based No-Nonsense Beauty Book. LC 74-7728. 352p. 1974. 17.50 (ISBN 0-394-48049-X). Knopf.

Chase, Don. People of the Valley: The Concow Maidu. ltd. ed. (Illus.). 1973. velo-bind ltd. 3.50 (ISBN 0-918634-35-0); pap. 3.00 ltd. D M Chase.

--A Road Past His Door: Gasquet. (Illus.). 1973. velo-bind 2.50 (ISBN 0-918634-30-X); pap. 2.25 (ISBN 0-918634-37-7). D M Chase.

--They Came This Way: The Humboldt Valley, Highroad to the Gold Rush. ltd. ed. (Illus.). 1973. velo-bind 3.50 (ISBN 0-918634-31-8); pap. 3.00 limited ed. (ISBN 0-918634-33-4). D M Chase.

Chase, Don & Helms, Marjory. Pack Saddles & Rolling Wheels: A Century of Travel & Transportation in N. W. California & South Oregon. (Illus.). 1959. pap. 3.00 (ISBN 0-918634-28-8). D M Chase.

Chase, Don M. Basket Maker Artists. (Illus.). 1977. pap. 2.50 (ISBN 0-918634-34-2). D M Chase.

--He Opened the West: Jedediah Strong Smith. (Illus.). 40p. 1958. pap. 2.50 (ISBN 0-918634-26-1). D M Chase.

Chase, Don M., jt. auth. see Church, Patrick.

Chase, Doris. They Pushed Back the Forest: A Century in Del Norte Country, Cal. (Illus.). 1959. pap. 3.00 (ISBN 0-918634-33-4). D M Chase.

Chase, Ed. Plymouth Beach: Protective Barrier of Plymouth Harbor. (Pilgrim Society Notes Ser.: No. 22). 1.00 (ISBN 0-940628-32-5). Pilgrim Hall.

Chase, Edith N. Twigs from My Tree. LC 83-22408. 79p. (Orig.). 1984. pap. 5.95 (ISBN 0-87233-074-5). Bauhan.

Chase, Edward L. Big Book of Horses. (Illus.). (gr. 4-6). 1964. (G&D); PLB 2.99 (ISBN 0-448-03692-4). Putnam Pub Group.

Chase, Elaine. Double Occupancy. (Candlelight Ecstasy Ser.: No. 56). (Orig.). 1982. pap. 1.95 (ISBN 0-440-11732-1). Dell.

--Rules of the Game. (Orig.). 1980. pap. 1.25 (ISBN 0-440-17340-X). Dell.

Chase, Elaine R. Best Laid Plans. (Finding Mr. Right Ser.). 224p. 1983. pap. 2.75 (ISBN 0-380-82743-3, 82743-3). Avon.

--Designing Woman. (Candlelight Ecstasy Ser.: No. 72). (Orig.). 1982. pap. 1.95 (ISBN 0-440-12091-8). Dell.

--A Dream Come True. (Candlelight Ecstasy Ser.: No. 43). (Orig.). 1982. pap. 1.75 (ISBN 0-440-11697-X). Dell.

--No Easy Way Out. (Candlelight Ecstasy Ser.: No. 100). (Orig.). 1982. pap. 1.95 (ISBN 0-440-16119-3). Dell.

--Special Delivery. (Candlelight Ecstasy Ser.: No. 226). (Orig.). 1984. pap. 1.95 (ISBN 0-440-18164-X). Dell.

--Video Vixen. (Candlelight Ecstasy Ser.: No. 162). 192p. (Orig.). 1983. pap. 1.95 (ISBN 0-440-19584-5). Dell.

Chase, Elise, compiled by. Healing Faith: An Annotated Bibliography of Christian Self-Help Books. LC 85-929. (Bibliographies & Indexes in Religious Studies: No. 3). xxxiv, 192p. 1985. lib. bdg. 29.95 (ISBN 0-313-24014-0, DHF/). Greenwood.

Chase, Elizabeth, ed. Pioneer Churches of Florida. LC 77-72276. (Illus.). 74p. 1977. pap. 10.39 (ISBN 0-913122-11-4). Mickler Hse.

Chase, Elizabeth, et al, eds. see Moore, Michael & Arno, Michael.

Chase, Ellen. Beginnings of the American Revolution, 3 Vols. LC 77-120871. (American Bicentennial Ser). 1970. Repr. of 1910 ed. Set. 92.50x (ISBN 0-8046-1264-1, Pub. by Kennikat). Assoc Faculty Pr.

Chase, Emily. Best Friends Forever. (The Girls of Canby Hall Ser.: No. 6). 192p. (Orig.). (gr. 7-12). 1984. pap. 1.95 (ISBN 0-590-33238-4). Scholastic Inc.

--The Big Crush. (The Girls of Canby Hall Ser.: No. 8). 192p. (Orig.). (gr. 7-12). 1985. pap. 1.95 (ISBN 0-590-33249-X). Scholastic Inc.

--Boy Trouble. (The Girls of Canby Hall: No. 9). 176p. (Orig.). (gr. 6 up). 1985. pap. 1.95 (ISBN 0-590-33399-2). Scholastic Inc.

--Dinner Menus With Wine. Jacobs, Marjorie K. & Bannerman, Elizabeth, eds. (Wine Cookbook Ser.). (Illus.). 128p. pap. 6.95 (ISBN 0-932664-30-X). Wine Appreciation.

--Four Is a Crowd. (The Girls of Canby Hall Ser.: No. 7). 160p. (Orig.). (gr. 6 up). 1984. pap. 1.95 (ISBN 0-590-33248-1). Scholastic Inc.

--Here Come the Boys. (The Girls of Canby Hall Ser.: No. 13). 176p. (YA) (gr. 7 up). 1985. pap. 1.95 (ISBN 0-590-33685-1). Scholastic Inc.

--Keeping Secrets. (The Girls of Canby Hall Ser.: No. 4). 176p. (Orig.). (gr. 7 up). 1984. pap. 1.95 (ISBN 0-590-32892-1). Scholastic Inc.

--Make Me a Star. (The Girls of Canby Hall Ser.: No. 10). 176p. (Orig.). (gr. 6 up). 1985. pap. 1.95 (ISBN 0-590-33400-X). Scholastic Inc.

--Our Roommate Is Missing. (Girls of Canby Hall Ser.: No. 2). 192p. (Orig.). (gr. 7 up). 1984. pap. 1.95 (ISBN 0-590-32850-6). Scholastic Inc.

--Our Roommate Is Missing. (The Girls of Canby Hall Ser.: No. 2). 208p. (Orig.). (gr. 7 up). 1986. pap. 2.25 (ISBN 0-590-40079-7). Scholastic Inc.

--Roommates. (Girls of Canby Hall Ser.: No. 1). 224p. (Orig.). (gr. 7 up). 1984. pap. 1.95 (ISBN 0-590-32843-3). Scholastic Inc.

--Roommates. (The Girls of Canby Hall Ser.: No. 1). 224p. (Orig.). (gr. 7 up). 1986. pap. 2.25 (ISBN 0-590-40078-9). Scholastic Inc.

--Summer Blues. (The Girls of Canby Hall Ser.: No. 5). 192p. (Orig.). (gr. 7 up). 1984. pap. 1.95 (ISBN 0-590-33237-6). Scholastic Inc.

--Three of a Kind. (Girls of Canby Hall Ser.: No. 16). (Illus.). 176p. (Orig.). (gr. 6 up). 1985. pap. 1.95 (ISBN 0-590-33706-8). Scholastic Inc.

--To Tell The Truth. (The Girls of Canby Hall Ser.: No. 15). 176p. (Orig.). (gr. 7 up). 1985. pap. 1.95 (ISBN 0-590-33759-9). Scholastic Inc.

--What's A Girl to Do? (The Girls of Canby Hall Ser.: No. 14). 176p. (Orig.). (gr. 7 up). 1985. pap. 1.95 (ISBN 0-590-33707-6). Scholastic Inc.

--Who's the New Girl? (Girls of Canby Hall Ser.: No. 12). 176p. (Orig.). (YA) (gr. 7 up). 1985. pap. 1.95 (ISBN 0-590-33472-7). Scholastic Inc.

--Wine Cookbook of Dinner Menus. (Illus.). 1978. 4.95 (ISBN 0-932664-04-0). Wine Appreciation.

--With Friends Like That. (The Girls of Canby Hall Ser.: No. 11). 192p. (Orig.). (gr. 7 up). 1985. pap. 1.95 (ISBN 0-590-33401-8). Scholastic Inc.

--You're No Friend of Mine. (The Girls of Canby Hall Ser.). 192p. (Orig.). (gr. 7 up). 1984. pap. 1.95 (ISBN 0-590-32889-1). Scholastic Inc.

Chase, Emma L., ed. see Chivers, Thomas Holley.

Chase, Ernest D. Romance of Greeting Cards: An Historical Account of the Origin, Evolution, & Development. LC 76-159914. (Tower Bks.). (Illus.). 1971. Repr. of 1926 ed. 51.00x (ISBN 0-8103-3903-X). Gale.

Chase, Evelyn H. Mountain Climber: George B. Bayley, 1840-1894. LC 80-23877. (Illus.). 1981. 12.95 (ISBN 0-87015-235-1). Pacific Bks.

Chase, Ezra B. Teachings of Patriots & Statesmen. LC 79-75549. Repr. of 1860 ed. cancelled (ISBN 0-8371-1015-7, Pub. by Negro U Pr). Greenwood.

--Teachings of Patriots & Statesmen: Or, the 'Founders of the Republic' on Slavery. facs. ed. LC 72-83941. (Black Heritage Library Collection Ser). 1860. 20.50 (ISBN 0-8369-8535-4). Ayer Co Pubs.

Chase, Francis S. Education Faces New Demands. LC 56-12940. (Horace Mann Lecture Ser., 1956). Repr. of 1956 ed. 20.00 (ISBN 0-8357-9754-6, 2017874). Bks Demand UMI.

Chase, Frederic H. Lemuel Shaw, Chief Justice of the Supreme Court of Massachusetts, 1830-1860. 15.50 (ISBN 0-8369-7104-3, 7938). Ayer Co Pubs.

Chase, G. H. The Shield Devices of the Greeks in Art & Literature. (Illus.). 1978. Repr. of 1902 ed. 20.00 (ISBN 0-89005-260-3). Ares.

Chase, Gary A., jt. auth. see Murphy, Edmond A.

Chase, George H. A History of Sculpture. LC 72-138015. (Illus.). 582p. 1972. Repr. of 1925 ed. lib. bdg. 23.25x (ISBN 0-8371-5681-5, CHHS). Greenwood.

Chase, George W. History of Haverhill, Massachusetts. LC 83-61980. (Illus.). 1983. Repr. of 1861 ed. 45.00 (ISBN 0-89725-040-0). NE History.

Chase, Gilbert. America's Music, from the Pilgrims to the Present. 2nd rev. ed. LC 80-28027. (Illus.). xxi, 759p. 1981. Repr. of 1966 ed. lib. bdg. 45.00x (ISBN 0-313-22391-2, CHAM). Greenwood.

Chase, Gilbert & Budwig, Andrew. Manuel De Falla. LC 84-48406. 150p. 1985. lib. bdg. 20.00 (ISBN 0-317-29332-X). Garland Pub.

Chase, Gilbert, ed. American Composer Speaks: A Historical Anthology, 1770-1965. LC 66-11661. x, 318p. 1966. 27.50x (ISBN 0-8071-0347-0). La State U Pr.

--Guide to the Music of Latin America. 2nd rev. & enl. ed. LC 70-18910. (BCL Ser.: No. II). Repr. of 1962 ed. 22.50 (ISBN 0-404-08306-4). AMS Pr.

Chase, Glen. Busted. (Cherry Delight Ser: No. 16). 1974. pap. 1.25 (ISBN 0-685-51409-9, LB214ZK, Leisure Bks). Dorchester Pub Co.

--Cherry Delight up Your Ante. 1976. pap. 1.25 (ISBN 0-685-72568-5, LB407, Leisure Bks). Dorchester Pub Co.

--Crack Shot. 1976. pap. 1.25 (ISBN 0-685-72569-3, LB400ZK, Leisure Bks). Dorchester Pub Co.

--The Devil to Pay. (Cherry Delight Ser.). 1977. pap. 1.50 (ISBN 0-8439-0473-9, Leisure Bks). Dorchester Pub Co.

--Gemas Fatales. Ibero, Jairo, tr. from Eng. (Pimienta Collection, Cereza Delicias Ser: No. 8). Orig. Title: Hot Rocks. (Illus., Span.). 1976. pap. 1.25 (ISBN 0-88473-249-5). Fiesta Pub.

--Greek Fire. (Cherry Delight Ser.). 1977. pap. 1.50 (ISBN 0-8439-0462-3, Leisure Bks). Dorchester Pub Co.

--Hang Loose. (Cherry Delight Ser.: No. 18). 1974. pap. 1.25 (ISBN 0-685-47977-3, LB233ZK, Leisure Bks). Dorchester Pub Co.

--I'm Cherry, Fly Me. 1976. pap. 1.25 (ISBN 0-685-69160-8, LB368ZK, Leisure Bks). Dorchester Pub Co.

--In a Bind. (Cherry Delight Ser: No. 19). (Orig.). 1975. pap. 1.25 (ISBN 0-685-52171-0, LB242ZK, Leisure Bks). Dorchester Pub Co.

--Lights! Action! Murder! (Cherry Delight Ser.). (Orig.). 1975. pap. 1.25 (ISBN 0-685-53127-9, LB274ZK, Leisure Bks). Dorchester Pub Co.

--Made in Japan. (Cherry Delight Ser.). 1976. pap. 1.25 (LB423ZK, Leisure Bks). Dorchester Pub Co.

--The Man Who Was God. (Cherry Delight Ser.). 1978. pap. 1.50 (ISBN 0-8439-0517-4, Leisure Bks). Dorchester Pub Co.

--Mexican Standoff. (Cherry Delight Ser: No. 21). (Orig.). 1975. pap. 1.25 (ISBN 0-685-52941-X, LB260ZK, Leisure Bks). Dorchester Pub Co.

--The Moorland Monster. (Cherry Delight Ser.). 1977. pap. 1.50 (ISBN 0-8439-0489-5, Leisure Bks). Dorchester Pub Co.

--Roman Candle. (Cherry Delight Ser.). (Orig.). 1975. pap. 1.25 (ISBN 0-685-54127-4, LB2932K, Leisure Bks). Dorchester Pub Co.

--Sube Tu Apuesta. new ed. De Torres, Jacinto, tr. from Eng. (Pimienta Collection, Cereza Delicias: No. 4). 160p. (Span.). 1974. pap. 1.00 (ISBN 0-88473-220-7). Fiesta Pub.

--Tiradora Infalible. new ed. De Torres, Jacinto, tr. from Eng. (Pimienta Collection Ser.: Cereza Delicias: No. 5). Orig. Title: Crack Shot. 160p. (Span.). 1975. pap. 1.00 (ISBN 0-88473-228-2). Fiesta Pub.

--Up Your Ante. (Cherry Delight Ser.: No. 4). 1975. pap. 1.25 (ISBN 0-685-46896-8, LB4072K, Leisure Bks). Dorchester Pub Co.

--What a Way to Go. (Cherry Delight Ser.: No. 15). 1974. pap. 1.25 (ISBN 0-685-47978-1, LB208ZK, Leisure Bks). Dorchester Pub Co.

--Where the Action Is. (Cherry Delight Ser.). 1977. pap. 1.50 (ISBN 0-8439-0495-X, Leisure Bks). Dorchester Pub Co.

--Yo Soy Cereza, Vuela Conmigo. new ed. De Torres, J., tr. from Eng. (Pimienta Collection, Cereza Delicias Ser: No. 6). 160p. (Span.). 1975. pap. 1.25 (ISBN 0-88473-236-3). Fiesta Pub.

Chase, Glenn. Sexo, Dinero y Balas. new ed. Cesto, Danilo, tr. from Eng. (Cereza Delicias: No.7). Orig. Title: Chuck You Farley! (Illus.). 160p. (Span.). 1975. pap. 1.25 (ISBN 0-88473-241-X). Fiesta Pub.

Chase, Gordon & Reveal, Betsy. How to Manage in the Public Sector. 150p. 1983. pap. text ed. 11.95 (ISBN 0-394-34943-1, RanC). Random.

Chase, Grafton D. & Rabinowitz, Joseph L. Principles of Radioisotope Methodology. 3rd ed. LC 66-19903. 1967. text ed. 37.95x (ISBN 0-8087-0308-0). Burgess.

Chase, H., ed. see Corwin, E. S.

Chase, Harold, et al, eds. Biographical Dictionary of the Federal Judiciary. LC 76-18787. (Illus.). 256p. 1976. 90.00x (ISBN 0-8103-1125-9). Gale.

Chase, Harold W., jt. auth. see Ducat, Craig R.

Chase, Harold W., ed. see Corwin, Edward S.

Chase, Harry E. Eden in Winter. LC 78-71941. 1978. write for info. (ISBN 0-9601662-2-X). C Schneider.

--Gold I have Given Away. LC 82-62610. 1982. write for info (ISBN 0-9601662-3-8). C Schneider.

Chase, Helen M., jt. auth. see Chase, William D.

Chase, Heman. Beginning at Williams Monument. LC 81-3605. (Illus.). 72p. 1981. pap. 4.95 (ISBN 0-87233-060-5). Bauhan.

Chase, Henry. North & the South Being a Statistical View of the Condition of the Free & the Slave States. LC 75-107504. Repr. of 1857 ed. 15.00x (ISBN 0-8371-3775-6, CHN&, Pub. by Negro U Pr). Greenwood.

Chase, Henry & Sanbourn, Charles W. The North & South: A Statistical View of the Conditions of the Free & Slave States. LC 75-116280. 191p. 1972. Repr. of 1857 ed. 13.00x (ISBN 0-403-00437-3). Scholarly.

Chase, Ilka. New York Twenty Two. LC 73-112322. 308p. Repr. of 1951 ed. lib. bdg. 19.75x (ISBN 0-8371-4710-7, CHNY). Greenwood.

Chase, Jackson H. Cryptic Masonry. Repr. of 1981 ed. s.p. soft cover 4.75 (ISBN 0-88053-014-6). Macoy Pub.

Chase, James H. You Have Yourself a Deal. 1984. pap. 2.95 (ISBN 0-8027-3098-1). Walker & Co.

Chase, Janet. Daughters of Change: Growing up Female in America. 1981. 11.95 (ISBN 0-316-13820-7). Little.

Chase, Joan. During the Reign of the Queen of Persia. LC 82-48680. 224p. 1983. 13.41i (ISBN 0-06-015136-6, HarpT). Har-Row.

--During the Reign of the Queen of Persia. (General Ser.). 390p. 1983. lib. bdg. 16.95 (ISBN 0-8161-3611-4, Large Print Bks). G K Hall.

--During the Reign of the Queen of Persia. 256p. 1984. pap. 3.50 (ISBN 0-345-31525-1). Ballantine.

Chase, Joan A., jt. auth. see Ames, Louise B.

Chase, Joan B. Retrolental Fibroplasia & Autistic Symptomatology: An Investigation Into Some Relationships Among Neonatal, Environmental, Developmental & Affective Variables in Blind Prematures. 215p. 1968. pap. 3.00 (ISBN 0-89128-050-2, PCR050). Am Foun Blind.

Chase, John. Exterior Decoration: Hollywood's Inside-Out Houses. Gebhard, David, ed. LC 82-9268. (California Architecture & Architects Ser.: No. 2). (Illus.). 128p. 1982. pap. 19.95 (ISBN 0-912158-88-3). Hennessey.

--Frenchmen, Desire, Good Children & Other New Orleans Streets. LC 49-48566. 268p. 1982. 12.95 (ISBN 0-88289-384-X). Pelican.

--Frenchmen, Desire, Good Children: And Other Streets of New Orleans. 3rd ed. 1979. pap. 5.95 (ISBN 0-02-030980-5, Collier). Macmillan.

--Louisiana Purchase: America's Best Buy. 4.95 (ISBN 0-911116-24-9); pap. 1.50 (ISBN 0-911116-68-0). Pelican.

--The Sidewalk Companion to Santa Cruz Architecture. rev. ed. Gant, Michael S., ed. LC 79-64876. (Illus.). 367p. (Orig.). 1979. pap. 9.95 (ISBN 0-934136-00-9). Western Tanager.

Chase, John C. & Chamberlain, George W. Seven Generations of the Descendants of Aquila & Thomas Chase. LC 83-60849. (Illus.). 650p. 1983. Repr. of 1928 ed. 35.00 (ISBN 0-89725-038-9). NE History.

Chase, Justine. Document of a Child. LC 79-24192. 1981. 7.95 (ISBN 0-87233-052-4). Bauhan.

Chase, Karen. Eros & Psyche: The Representation of Personality in Charlotte Bronte, Charles Dickens, & George Eliot. 213p. 1984. pap. 9.95 (ISBN 0-416-36520-5, NO. 4015); 27.00 (ISBN 0-416-36510-8, NO. 4014). Methuen Inc.

Chase, Katherin. Navajo Painting, Vol. 54, No. 1. 32p. 1982. pap. 4.00 (ISBN 0-686-46249-1). Mus Northern Ariz.

Chase, L. Poe & His Poetry. lib. bdg. 17.50 (ISBN 0-8414-3453-0). Folcroft.

Chase, Larry. The Other Side of the Report Card: A How-to-Do-It Program for Affective Education. LC 74-10233. 264p. 1975. pap. 12.95 (ISBN 0-673-16408-X). Scott F.

Chase, Lawrence, et al. Practicing Management: A Guide to Accompany Tansik, Chase, & Aquilano's Management: a Life Cycle Approach. 1980. pap. 9.50x (ISBN 0-256-02354-9). Irwin.

Chase, Leslie, jt. ed. see Rosenau, Fred S.

Chase, Leslie R. & Henderson, Faye, eds. Information Sources, 1985. 1984. 59.75 (ISBN 0-317-16325-6). Info Indus.

Chase, Leslie R. & Landeis, Robert, eds. Annual High Technology Marketing Seminar, 3rd: Proceedings. 1985. pap. 59.95 (ISBN 0-942774-21-3). Info Indus.

Chase, Leslie R. & Landers, Robert, eds. Artificial Intelligence: Reality or Fantasy? 1984. 59.95 (ISBN 0-942774-19-1). Info Indus.

Chase, Leslie R. & Tuttle, Patti, eds. Information Sources, 1986. 1985. pap. price not set (ISBN 0-942774-22-1). Info Indus.

Chase, Leslie R., jt. ed. see Rosenau, Fred S.

Chase, Lewis. Poe & His Poetry. LC 75-38649. (Studies in Poe, No. 23). 1976. Repr. of 1924 ed. lib. bdg. 34.95x (ISBN 0-8383-2112-7). Haskell.

--A Sense of Values. LC 79-92431. 1980. 7.50 (ISBN 0-8022-2362-1). Philos Lib.

Chase, Lewis N. Poe & His Poetry. LC 72-120973. (Poetry & Life Ser.). Repr. of 1913 ed. 7.25 (ISBN 0-404-52506-7). AMS Pr.

Chase, Lucien B. English Serfdom & American Slavery. LC 68-58052. Repr. of 1854 ed. 22.50x (ISBN 0-8371-0348-7, CHE&, Pub. by Negro U Pr). Greenwood.

--English Serfdom & American Slavery: Or, Ourselves As Others See Us. facs. ed. LC 77-83929. (Black Heritage Library Collection Ser). 1854. 15.50 (ISBN 0-8369-8536-2). Ayer Co Pubs.

Chase Manhattan Bank. The Cashier. (Illus.). 96p. (gr. 10-12). 1975. pap. 9.84 wktext (ISBN 0-07-010690-8). McGraw.

Chase, Margaret. Never Too Late. LC 83-71143. (Illus.). 224p. 1983. 14.95 (ISBN 0-912429-00-3). Ausonia Pr.

Chase, Marian T, jt. auth. see Chase, Stuart.

Chase, Mary. The Wicked Pigeon Ladies in the Garden. 13.50 (ISBN 0-8446-6192-9). Peter Smith.

Chase, Mary E. Bible & the Common Reader. rev. ed. 1962. pap. 2.95 (ISBN 0-02-084390-9, Collier). Macmillan.

--A Goodly Fellowship. LC 83-45731. Repr. of 1939 ed. 29.50 (ISBN 0-404-20057-5). AMS Pr.

--Lovely Ambition. 1960. 5.95 (ISBN 0-393-08477-9). Norton.

--The Lovely Ambition. 288p. 1985. pap. 5.95 (ISBN 0-393-30234-2). Norton.

Chase, Mary E. & Macgregor, Margaret E., eds. Writing of Informal Essays. facsimile ed. LC 79-93326. (Essay Index Reprint Ser.). 1928. 26.50 (ISBN 0-8369-1556-9). Ayer Co Pubs.

Chase, Merrill W., jt. ed. see Williams, Curtis A.

Chase, Michael & Weitzman, Eliott, eds. Sleep Disorders: Basic & Clinical Research. (Advances in Sleep Research: Vol. 8). (Illus.). 604p. 1983. text ed. 85.00 (ISBN 0-89335-166-0). SP Med & Sci Bks.

Chase, Mildred L. Housekeeping Management for Health Care Facilities. rev. ed. LC 78-23436. 1978. pap. 11.00 (ISBN 0-87125-045-4). Cath Health.

Chase, Mildred P. Just Being at the Piano. LC 84-71666. 118p. 1985. pap. 6.95 (ISBN 0-916870-94-4). Creative Arts Bk.

Chase, Myrna. Elie Halevy: An Intellectual Biography. LC 79-24314. 1980. 26.00x (ISBN 0-231-04856-4). Columbia U Pr.

Chase, Naomi F. A Child Is Being Beaten: Violence Against Children, an American Tragedy. LC 76-25577. (McGraw-Hill Paperbacks). 1976. pap. 5.95 (ISBN 0-07-010685-1). McGraw.

--Listening for Water. LC 80-80070. 60p. 1980. 8.95 (ISBN 0-915822-04-0); pap. 2.95 (ISBN 0-915822-05-9); microfiche 0.95 (ISBN 0-915822-06-7). Archival Pr.

Chase, Ned, ed. see Ketwig, John.

Chase, Ned, ed. see North, James.

Chase, Nicholas. Locksley. LC 83-9644. 288p. 1983. 12.95 (ISBN 0-312-49428-9, Pub. by Marek). St Martin.

--Locksley. (Penguin Fiction Ser.). 320p. 1985. pap. 3.95 (ISBN 0-14-006939-9). Penguin.

Chase, Oscar G. Teacher's Guide to Civil Litigation in New York. LC 85-103805. (Cases & Materials). write for info. Amer Bar Assn.

Chase, Otto L. November Violets. 1973. 4.00 (ISBN 0-8233-0190-7). Golden Quill.

Chase, Philip N. & Parrott, Linda J., eds. Psychological Aspects of Language. 276p. 1985. 29.50x (ISBN 0-398-05155-0). C C Thomas.

Chase, Ray E., tr. see Rocker, Rudolf.

Chase, Richard. American Folk Tales & Songs. 1971. pap. 3.95 (ISBN 0-486-22692-1). Dover.

--American Folk Tales & Songs. (Illus.). 14.25 (ISBN 0-8446-0057-1). Peter Smith.

--The American Novel & Its Tradition. LC 78-3457. 1978. Repr. of 1957 ed. 12.50x (ISBN 0-87752-209-X). Gordian.

--The American Novel & Its Tradition. LC 79-3702: 288p. 1980. pap. 6.95x (ISBN 0-8018-2303-X). Johns Hopkins.

--Grandfather Tales. (Illus.). 240p. (gr. 4-6). 1948. 13.95 (ISBN 0-395-06692-1). HM.

--Jack Tales. (Illus.). 202p. (gr. 4-6). 1943. 10.95 (ISBN 0-395-06694-8). HM.

--Singing Games & Playparty Games. (Illus.). 63p. (gr. 1-4). 1949. pap. 2.25 (ISBN 0-486-21785-X). Dover.

--Singing Games & Playparty Games. (Illus.). 12.50 (ISBN 0-8446-4721-7). Peter Smith.

Chase, Richard, ed. Melville: A Collection of Critical Essays. (Orig.). 1962. 12.95 (ISBN 0-13-574293-5, Spec). P-H.

--Old Songs & Singing Games. LC 72-85499. (Illus.). 64p. 1973. pap. 2.00 (ISBN 0-486-22879-7). Dover.

Chase, Richard, ed. see Crane, Stephen.

Chase, Richard, ed. see Harris, Joel C.

Chase, Richard A., et al, eds. Your Baby: The First Wondrous Year. (Illus.). 416p. 1984. 12.95 (ISBN 0-02-075810-3). Macmillan.

Chase, Richard B. & Aquilano, Nicholas J. Production & Operations Management: A Life Cycle Approach. 3rd ed. 1981. 32.95x (ISBN 0-256-02525-8). Irwin.

Chase, Richard V. The Democratic Vista. LC 72-12325. 180p. 1973. Repr. of 1958 ed. lib. bdg. 22.50x (ISBN 0-8371-6732-9, CHDV). Greenwood.

--Emily Dickinson. LC 70-136058. (Illus.). 1971. Repr. of 1951 ed. lib. bdg. 35.00x (ISBN 0-8371-5208-9, CHD). Greenwood.

Chase, Robert A. Atlas of Hand Surgery, Vol. 1. LC 72-97907. (Illus.). 438p. 1973. text ed. 60.00 (ISBN 0-7216-2495-2). Saunders.

--Atlas of Hand Surgery, Vol. 2. (Illus.). 496p. 1984. 85.00 (ISBN 0-7216-2497-9). Saunders.

Chase, Roland F., jt. auth. see Harper, Elizabeth J.

Chase, S. U., et al. Galois Theory & Cohomology of Commutative Rings. LC 52-42839. (Memoirs: No. 52). 79p. 1978. pap. 9.00 (ISBN 0-8218-1252-1, MEMO-52). Am Math.

Chase, Salmon P. Diary & Correspondence of Salmon P. Chase. LC 74-75301. (Law, Politics, & History Ser). 1971. Repr. of 1903 ed. lib. bdg. 59.50 (ISBN 0-306-71264-4). Da Capo.

--Inside Lincoln's Cabinet. Donald, David, ed. Repr. of 1954 ed. 28.00 (ISBN 0-527-16200-0). Kraus Repr.

--Reclamation of Fugitives from Service. facs. ed. LC 77-138334. (Black Heritage Library Collection Ser). 1847. 11.25 (ISBN 0-8369-8726-8). Ayer Co Pubs.

Chase, Salmon P., jt. auth. see Cleveland, Charles D.

Chase, Samuel. Trial of Samuel Chase, an Associate Justice of the Supreme Court Impeached by the House of Representatives, 2 vols. LC 69-11324. (Law, Politics, & History Ser). 1970. Repr. of 1805 ed. Set. lib. bdg. 79.50 (ISBN 0-306-71181-8). Da Capo.

Chase, Samuel B., Jr., ed. Problems in Public Expenditure Analysis: Papers Presented at a Conference of Experts: Sept. 15-16 1966. LC 67-30589. (Brookings Institution Studies of Government Finance). pap. 70.80 (ISBN 0-317-20786-5, 2125369). Bks Demand UMI.

Chase, Stella & Whitbread, Jane. Daughters: From Infancy to Independence. 1979. pap. 4.95 (ISBN 0-452-25219-9, Z5219, Plume). NAL.

Chase, Stuart. American Credos. LC 75-8835. 216p. 1975. Repr. of 1962 ed. lib. bdg. 15.00x (ISBN 0-8371-8108-9, CHAC). Greenwood.

--The Economy of Abundance. facsimile ed. LC 79-37876. (Select Bibliographies Reprint Ser). Repr. of 1934 ed. 21.00 (ISBN 0-8369-6713-5). Ayer Co Pubs.

--Economy of Abundance. LC 75-137934. (Economic Thought, History & Challenge Ser). 1971. Repr. of 1934 ed. 23.50x (ISBN 0-8046-1439-3, Pub. by Kennikat). Assoc Faculty Pr.

--Government in Business. LC 71-136849. 296p. 1971. Repr. of 1935 ed. lib. bdg. 15.50x (ISBN 0-8371-5283-6, CHGB). Greenwood.

--Mexico: A Study of Two Americans. 1931. 30.00 (ISBN 0-8482-3585-1). Norwood Edns.

--The Most Probable World. LC 81-2037. xii, 239p. 1981. Repr. of 1968 ed. lib. bdg. 25.00x (ISBN 0-313-22971-6, CHMP). Greenwood.

--Rich Land, Poor Land. LC 70-92612. (Illus.). Repr. of 1936 ed. 26.50 (ISBN 0-404-01478-X). AMS Pr.

--Roads to Agreement: Successful Methods in the Science of Human Relations. LC 71-109287. Repr. of 1951 ed. lib. bdg. 22.50x (ISBN 0-8371-3830-2, CHRA). Greenwood.

--Some Things Worth Knowing. facsimile ed. LC 76-90622. (Essay Index Reprint Ser.). 1958. 21.50 (ISBN 0-8369-1557-7). Ayer Co Pubs.

--The Tyranny of Words. LC 38-27108. 1959. pap. 7.95 (ISBN 0-15-692394-7, Harv). HarBraceJ.

Chase, Stuart & Brunner, Edmund de S. The Proper Study of Mankind. rev. ed. LC 78-87. 1978. Repr. of 1963 ed. lib. bdg. 29.50x (ISBN 0-313-20261-3, CHPS). Greenwood.

Chase, Stuart & Chase, Marian T. Power of Words. LC 54-5980. 1954. 9.95 (ISBN 0-15-173487-9). HarBraceJ.

Chase, Stuart, et al, eds. see American Trade Union Delegation to the Soviet Union.

Chase, Thomas N., jt. ed. see Friedhoff, Arnold J.

Chase, Thornton. In Galilee. Facsimile reprint ed. (Illus.). 98p. 1985. Repr. of 1908 ed. 7.95 (ISBN 0-933770-38-3). Kalimat.

Chase, Virginia. Speaking of Maine: A Selection from the Writings of Virginia Chase. Shea, Margaret, ed. (Illus.). 128p. (Orig.). 1983. pap. 8.95 (ISBN 0-89272-170-7). Down East.

Chase, W. Corwin. Tepee Fires. (Illus.). 126p. (Orig.). 1981. pap. 14.95 (ISBN 0-933992-17-3). Coffee Break.

Chase, W. Howard. Issue Management: Origins of the Future. LC 83-83079. (Illus.). 170p. 1984. 24.95 (ISBN 0-913869-01-5). Issue Action Pubns.

Chase, W. Howard, ed. see Gollner, Andrew B.

Chase, W. Parker. New York Nineteen Thirty-Two: The Wonder City. (Illus.). 304p. 1983. 18.95 (ISBN 0-9608788-3-1); pap. 9.95 (ISBN 0-9608788-2-3). NY Bound.

Chase, Warren. The Fugitive Wife. LC 78-22162. (Free Love in America). Repr. of 1861 ed. 19.50 (ISBN 0-404-60959-0). AMS Pr.

--The Life-Line of the Lone One. LC 72-2950. Repr. of 1865 ed. 24.00 (ISBN 0-404-10715-X). AMS Pr.

Chase, William C. The American Law School & the Rise of Administrative Government. LC 81-69816. 192p. 1982. text ed. 19.95x (ISBN 0-299-09100-7). U of Wis Pr.

Chase, William D. Chases Calendar of Annual Events: Special Days, Weeks, & Months in 1979. LC 57-14540. (Illus.). 1978. lib. bdg. 12.95 (ISBN 0-913082-24-4); pap. 7.95 (ISBN 0-913082-25-2). Apple Tree.

--Chases' Calendar of Annual Events: Special Days, Weeks & Months in 1980. rev. ed. LC 57-14540. (Illus., Orig.). 1979. lib. bdg. 14.95 (ISBN 0-913082-27-9); pap. 9.95 (ISBN 0-913082-26-0). Apple Tree.

--Chases Calendar of Annual Events: Special Days, Weeks, & Months in 1978. (Illus.). 1977. pap. 7.95 (ISBN 0-913082-23-6). Apple Tree.

Chase, William D. & Chase, Helen M. Chase's Annual Events: Special Days, Weeks & Months in 1985. (Illus.). 224p. (Orig.). 1984. pap. 14.95 (ISBN 0-8092-5398-4). Contemp Bks.

--Chase's Annual Events: Special Days, Weeks, & Months in 1986. (Illus.). 224p. (Orig.). 1985. pap. 14.95 (ISBN 0-8092-5142-6). Contemp Bks.

--Chases' Calendar of Annual Events: Special Days, Weeks & Months in 1982. rev. ed. (Illus.). 176p. (Orig.). 1981. pap. 12.95 (ISBN 0-913082-29-5). Apple Tree.

--Chase's Calendar of Annual Events: Special Days, Weeks & Months in 1981. rev. ed. (Illus., Orig.). 1980. pap. 12.95 (ISBN 0-913082-28-7). Apple Tree.

--Chases' Calendar of Annual Events: Special Days, Weeks & Months in 1983. rev. ed. (Illus.). 180p. (Orig.). 1982. pap. 12.95 (ISBN 0-913082-30-9). Apple Tree.

Chase, William G., ed. see Carnegie Symposium on Cognition, Eighth Annual.

Chase, Wilton P. Management of System Engineering. LC 83-18746. 1984. Repr. of 1974 ed. lib. bdg. 26.50 (ISBN 0-89874-682-5). Krieger.

Chase-Dunn, Christopher, jt. auth. see Bornschier, Volker.

Chase-Dunn, Christopher K. Socialist States in the World-System. (Sage Focus Editions: Vol. 58). 320p. 1982. 28.00 (ISBN 0-8039-1878-X); pap. 14.00 (ISBN 0-8039-1879-8). Sage.

Chasek, Judith, jt. auth. see Nagle, Robert.

Chasen, S. H. & Dow, J. W. The Guide for the Evaluation & Implementation of Cad-Cam Systems. 2nd ed. (Illus.). 461p. 1983. text ed. 250.00 (ISBN 0-938800-01-9). Cad Cam.

Chasen, Sylvan H. Geometric Principles & Procedures for Computer Graphic Applications. LC 78-7998. (Illus.). 1978. 37.50 (ISBN 0-13-352559-7). P-H.

Chase-Riboud, Barbara. Sally Hemings. 416p. 1980. pap. 3.50 (ISBN 0-380-48686-5, 60075). Avon.

--Sally Hemings. 1979. 12.95 (ISBN 0-670-61605-2). Viking.

Chasin, Barbara, jt. auth. see Franke, Richard.

Chasin, Helen. Coming Close & Other Poems. LC 75-21576. (Yale Ser. of Younger Poets: No. 63). Repr. of 1968 ed. 18.00 (ISBN 0-404-53863-0). AMS Pr.

Chasin, Joseph, ed. Straight Talk about Attitude Research. LC 81-22916. (Proceedings Ser.). (Illus., Orig.). 1982. pap. text ed. 11.00 (ISBN 0-87757-156-2). Am Mktg.

Chasin, M. Computer Connections on a Budget. 224p. 1985. 12.95 (ISBN 0-07-010667-3). McGraw.

Chasin, Mark. Assembly Language: Programming for the Atari Computer. (A BYTE Book). 1984. pap. 15.95 (ISBN 0-07-010679-7). Mcgraw.

Chasins, Abram. Leopold Stokowski: A Profile. (Quality Paperbacks Ser.). (Illus.). 313p. 1981. pap. 8.95 (ISBN 0-306-80146-9). Da Capo.

--Speaking of Pianists. 3rd ed. (Quality Paperback Ser.). x, 330p. 1982. pap. 9.95 (ISBN 0-306-80168-X). Da Capo.

Chasis, David A. Plastic Piping Systems. LC 75-45420. 216p. 1976. 25.00. Krieger.

Chasis, Herbert & Goldring, William, eds. Homer William Smith, Sc. D. His Scientific & Literary Achievements. LC 65-10765. pap. 58.60 (ISBN 0-8357-9478-4, 2010289). Bks Demand UMI.

Chaska. The Nursing Profession. (Illus.). 1977. pap. text ed. 28.00 (ISBN 0-07-010695-9). McGraw.

Chaska, N. The Nursing Profession: A Time to Speak. (Illus.). 944p. (Orig.). 1983. 28.00 (ISBN 0-07-010696-7). McGraw.

Chasler, Charles N. The Newborn Skull: Atlas of the Normal & Abnormal Newborn & Infant Skull with Emphasis on Fetal Radiology. LC 76-9681. 228p. 1972. 25.00 (ISBN 0-87527-028-X). Green.

Chasles, Emile. Comedie en France au Seizieme Siecle. LC 71-168279. (Theatre & Drama Ser.: No. 21). (Fr). 1971. Repr. of 1862 ed. 19.00 (ISBN 0-8337-0546-6). B Franklin.

Chasman, Herbert. Who Gets the Business? A Guide to Passing on a Closely Held Business Interest. LC 83-80632. 200p. 1983. 14.95 (ISBN 0-910580-73-1). Farnswth Pub.

Chasman, Herbert, jt. auth. see White, Edwin H.

Chasnoff, Robert & Muniz, Peter. Consultation: A Training Program. 18p. 1980. pap. text ed. 4.50 (ISBN 0-943300-02-9). LABS.

--Managing Human Resources: A Practical Guide. 63p. 1981. pap. text ed. 9.25 (ISBN 0-943300-00-2). LABS.

Chasnoff, Robert, jt. auth. see Muniz, Peter.

Chassagne, S., jt. auth. see Chapman, S. D.

Chassan, J. B. Research Design in Clinical Psychology & Psychiatry. 2nd, enl. & rev. ed. LC 78-23548. 492p. 1979. 19.50x (ISBN 0-470-26577-9). Halsted Pr.

--Research Design in Clinical Psychology & Psychiatry. 496p. 1982. text ed. 19.50x (ISBN 0-8290-1009-2); pap. text ed. 14.50x (ISBN 0-8290-1035-1). Irvington.

Chassant, Alphonse A. Dictionnaire des Abbreviations Latines et Francaises Usitees dans les Inscriptions Lapidaires et Metalliques, les Manuscrits et les Chartes de Moyen Age. 5th ed. LC 73-3365. (Illus., Fr.). 1973. Repr. of 1884 ed. lib. bdg. 22.50 (ISBN 0-8337-0547-4). B Franklin.

Chassany, Jean-Philippe. Dictionnaire de Meteorologie Populaire. 416p. (Fr.). 1970. 35.00 (ISBN 0-686-56945-8, M-6067). French & Eur.

Chassard, Jean & Weil, Gonthier. Dictionnaire des Oeuvres et des Themes de la Litterature Allemande. (Fr.). 1973. pap. 8.95 (ISBN 0-686-56853-2, M-6631). French & Eur.

Chasse, Paul. Les Arts et la litterature chez la Franco-Americains de la Nouvelle-Angleterre. 46666p. (Fr.). (gr. 9-10). 1977. pap. text ed. 1.25 (ISBN 0-911409-10-6). Natl Mat Dev.

Chasseaud, L. F., jt. auth. see Bridges, J. W.

Chasseaud, L. F., jt. ed. see Bridges, J. W.

Chasseguet-Smirgel, Janine. Creativity & Perversion. 172p. 1984. 22.50 (ISBN 0-393-01938-1). Norton.

--The Ego Ideal: A Psychoanalytic Essay on the Malady of the Ideal. 271p. 1985. 24.95 (ISBN 0-393-01971-3). Norton.

Chassin, Charles L. Les Elections et les cahiers de Paris en 1789, 4 vols. LC 76-38039. Repr. of 1889 ed. Set. 280.00 (ISBN 0-404-52590-3); 70.00 ea.; Vol. 1. (ISBN 0-404-52591-1); Vol. 2. (ISBN 0-404-52592-X); Vol. 3. (ISBN 0-404-52593-8); Vol. 4. (ISBN 0-404-52594-6). AMS Pr.

--Les Volontaires nationaux pendant la Revolution, 3 vols. LC 70-38040. Repr. of 1906 ed. Set. 210.00 (ISBN 0-404-52600-4); 70.00 ea.; Vol. 1. (ISBN 0-404-52601-2); Vol. 2. (ISBN 0-404-52602-0); Vol. 3. (ISBN 0-404-52603-9). AMS Pr.

Chassin, J. L. Operative Strategy in General Surgery: A Text an Atlas, Vol. 1. (Illus.). 384p. 1980. 86.00 (ISBN 0-387-90452-2). Springer-Verlag.

--Operative Strategy in General Surgery, Vol. 2. (Illus.). 655p. 1984. 98.00 (ISBN 0-387-90984-2). Springer-Verlag.

Chast, Roz. Parallel Universe: An Assortment of Cartoons. LC 84-47563. (Illus.). 128p. (Orig.). 1984. pap. 7.64i (ISBN 0-06-091177-8, CN 1177, CN). Har-Row.

Chastain, James G., tr. see Stadelmann, Rudolph.

Chastain, Joel W., Jr., ed. U. S. Research Reactors. AEC Technical Information Center. 78p. 1957. pap. 11.50 (ISBN 0-87079-380-2, TID-7013); microfiche 4.50 (ISBN 0-87079-483-3, TID-7013). DOE.

Chastain, Josephine K. Word Pictures. 108p. 1983. 7.00 (ISBN 0-682-49950-1). Exposition Pr FL.

Chastain, K. Relatos Simbolicos: Reading for Skill Development & Communication. 1983. 12.95 (ISBN 0-8384-1181-9). Heinle & Heinle.

Chastain, Kenneth. Developing Second Language Skills: Theory to Practice. 2nd ed. 1976. 22.95 (ISBN 0-395-31008-3). HM.

--Spanish Grammar in Review: Patterns for Communication. pap. 20.95 (ISBN 0-395-30966-2). HM.

--Vamos: Bienvenidos al Mundo Hispanico. 576p. 1985. text ed. 26.95 (ISBN 0-8384-1277-7); instr's. ed. avail. (ISBN 0-8384-1280-7); wkbk. 11.95 (ISBN 0-8384-1279-3); tapes 125.00 (ISBN 0-8384-1281-5). Heinle & Heinle.

Chastain, Madye L. Emmy Keeps a Promise. LC 56-9200. (Illus.). (gr. 4-6). 1966. pap. 0.75 (ISBN 0-15-628776-5, AVB21, VoyB). HarBraceJ.

Chastain, Thomas. Nightscape. 1983. pap. 2.95 (ISBN 0-451-12505-3, Sig). NAL.

--Who Killed the Robins Family? & Where & When & Why & How Did They Die? LC 83-61371. 156p. 1983. 9.95 (ISBN 0-688-02524-2). Morrow.

Chastain, Thomas & Adler, Bill. The Revenge of the Robins Family. 1985. pap. 3.50 (ISBN 0-446-32533-3). Warner Bks.

Chastain, Thomas, jt. auth. see Adler, Bill.

Chasteen, Edgar R. Runner. LC 79-53673. (Illus.). 177p. 1980. 12.95 (ISBN 0-934864-00-4). Amity Bks MO.

Chasteen, Joseph E. Essentials of Clinical Dental Assisting. 2nd. ed. LC 80-372. (Illus.). 1980. 25.95 (ISBN 0-8016-0976-3). Mosby.

Chasteen, Lanny & Flaherty, Richard. Intermediate Accounting. 1984. text ed. 37.00 (ISBN 0-394-32535-4, RanC); Student Guide, Vol. 1. 10.95 (ISBN 0-394-33750-6); Student Guide, Vol. 2. 10.95 (ISBN 0-394-33751-4); Working Papers. 9.95 (ISBN 0-394-33749-2); Practice Set. 7.95 (ISBN 0-394-33748-4); Computer Practice Set for Apple. write for info. (ISBN 0-394-33915-0); Computer Practice Set for IBM Personal Computer. 15.00; Computer Practice Set for Mainframe. 10.00 (ISBN 0-394-33920-7); Vol. 2, 448pgs. working papers 9.95 (ISBN 0-394-34078-7). Random.

Chastek, Winifred K. Keyboard Skills: Sight Reading, Transposition, Harmonization, Improvisation. 1967. write for info. (ISBN 0-534-00666-3). Wadsworth Pub.

Chastel, Andre. Art de France, Vol. 1. (Illus., Orig.). 1961. pap. 25.00x (ISBN 0-8150-0909-7). Wittenborn.

--A Chronicle of Italian Renaissance Painting. Murray, Linda & Murray, Peter, trs. LC 83-73211. (Illus.). 256p. 1984. 99.50x (ISBN 0-8014-1524-1). Cornell U Pr.

--The Sack of Rome, 1527. Archer, Beth, tr. LC 82-47587. (Illus.). 1983. 42.50x (ISBN 0-691-09947-2). Princeton U Pr.

Chastel, Andre & Grayson, Cecil. The Renaissance: Essays in Interpretation. 336p. 1982. 42.00 (ISBN 0-416-31130-X, NO. 3770). Methuen Inc.

Chastel, Andre, intro. by. The Vatican Frescoes of Michelangelo, 2 vols. Rosenthal, Raymond, tr. from Fr. LC 80-66646. (Illus.). 528p. 1980. ltd. ed. 7500.00 (ISBN 0-89659-158-1). Abbeville Pr.

Chastellux, Francois J. Essay on Public Happiness, 2 Vols. LC 67-29497. 1969. Repr. of 1774 ed. Set. 75.00x (ISBN 0-678-00557-5). Kelley.

Chastellux, Francois J. De see De Chastellux, Francois J.

Chastenet, Jacques. Godoy: Master of Spain. Huntington, J. F., tr. LC 70-153205. 1971. Repr. of 1953 ed. 21.00x (ISBN 0-8046-1515-2, Pub. by Kennikat). Assoc Faculty Pr.

Chastin, Thomas, jt. auth. see Adler, Bill.

Chaston, A. Norton. Electrical Machinery. 1985. text ed. 32.95 (ISBN 0-8359-1580-8). Reston.

Chaston, Gloria, jt. auth. see Jaussi, Laureen.

Chaston, I. R., intro. by. Asian Mining '81. 311p. (Orig.). pap. text ed. 100.00x (ISBN 0-900488-61-1). IMM North Am.

Chaston, Ian. Business Management in Fisheries & Aquaculture. (Illus.). 128p. 1985. pap. 18.00 (ISBN 0-85238-132-8, FN109, FNB). Unipub.

--Marketing in Fisheries & Aquaculture. 143p. (Orig.). 1984. pap. 19.95x (ISBN 0-85238-129-8, Pub. by Fishing News Bks NK). State Mutual Bk.

--Marketing in Fisheries & Aquaculture. 143p. 1983. pap. 14.95 (ISBN 0-85238-129-8, FN102, FNB). Unipub.

Chaszar, Edward. Decision in Vienna. 1978. 10.00 (ISBN 0-87934-018-5). Danubian.

Chatagnier, Louis J., et al. Images de la France contemporaine. (Illus.). 211p. 1965. text ed. 5.00x (ISBN 0-8354-2079-5); tchrs' key 1.00 (ISBN 0-8354-2080-9). Intl Film.

Chatalbash, Ron. Dr. Blackfoot's Carnival Extraordinaire. LC 81-85126. (Illus.). 32p. (gr. 2-5). 1982. 10.95 (ISBN 0-87923-426-1). Godine.

--A Perfect Day for the Movies. LC 82-48702. (Illus.). 32p. (gr. 3 up). 1983. 11.95 (ISBN 0-87923-463-6). Godine.

Chatani, Masahiro. Pop-Up Origamic Architecture. (Illus.). 87p. (Orig.). 1985. pap. 7.95 (ISBN 0-87040-656-6). Japan Pubns USA.

Chateau, B. & Lapillone, B. Energy Demand: Facts & Trends. (Topics in Energy Ser.). (Illus.). 280p. 1982. 41.00 (ISBN 0-387-81675-5). Springer-Verlag.

Chateaubriand, Francois R. Chateaubriand's Travels in America. Switzer, Richard, ed. & tr. LC 68-55043. (Illus.). 248p. 1969. 22.00x (ISBN 0-8131-1178-1). U Pr of Ky.

Chateaubriand, Francois R. De see De Chateaubriand, Francois R.

Chateaubriand, Francois-Rene de. Atala & Rene. Putter, Irving, tr. 1952. pap. 5.95x (ISBN 0-520-00223-7, CAMPUS8). U of Cal Pr.

Chateaubriand, Rene de. Atala: Edition Critique. 208p. 1952. 12.50 (ISBN 0-686-54360-2). French & Eur.

--Le Genie Du Christianisme, 2 vols. Reboul, Pierre, ed. 512p. 1966. 3.95 ea. French & Eur.

--Incidences. 100p. 1947. 2.50 (ISBN 0-686-54364-5). French & Eur.

--Lettres a Madame Recamier. 576p. 1951. 6.95 (ISBN 0-686-54366-1). French & Eur.

--Lettres et Manuscripts (Illustre) Nombres Lettres Inedites de Chateaubriand a Benjamin Constant, a Armand Carrel, au Sculpteur Emoyne, Vol. 19. (Illus.). 96p. 1976. 35.00 (ISBN 0-686-54367-X). French & Eur.

--Lettres Inedites et Manuscripts: Bulletins de la Societe Chateaubriand, Vol. 15. (Illus.). 96p. 1972. 35.00 (ISBN 0-686-54368-8). French & Eur.

--Maximes et Pensees. 4.95 (ISBN 0-686-54369-6). French & Eur.

--Memoires de Ma Vie. 141p. 1976. 19.50 (ISBN 0-686-54371-8). French & Eur.

--Memoires d'Outre-Tombe: Texte de l'Edition Originale, 1849, 3 vols. 1973. 4.50 ea. French & Eur.

--Napoleon. 1969. 7.95 (ISBN 0-686-54372-6). French & Eur.

--Oeuvres Completes: Paris, 1826-1831, 27 vols. facsimile ed. 50.00 ea. French & Eur.

--Promenades Romaines. 20p. 1963. 99.50 (ISBN 0-686-54373-4). French & Eur.

--Rene. 128p. 1970. 2.95 (ISBN 0-686-54374-2). French & Eur.

Chateaubriand, Rene de & Giraud, Victor. Amour et Vieillesse: Avec: Etude sur Chateau Briand Romanesque et Amoreaux. 43p. 1922. 50.00 (ISBN 0-686-54359-9). French & Eur.

Chateaubriand, Rene de & Guyard, Marius Francois. Vie de Rance. 3.95 (ISBN 0-686-54375-0). French & Eur.

Chateaubriand, Rene de & Letessier, Fernand. Atala: Avec: Rene, Le Dernier Abencerage. 512p. 1958. 10.95 (ISBN 0-686-54361-0). French & Eur.

Chateaubriand, Rene de & Mourot, Jean. Itineraire De Paris a Jerusalem. 448p. 1968. 3.50 (ISBN 0-686-54365-3). French & Eur.

Chateaubriand, Rene de & Roy, Claude. Memoires. 576p. 1964. 3.95 (ISBN 0-686-54370-X). French & Eur.

Chateaubriand, Rene De see De Chateaubriand, Rene.

Chateaubriand, Rene de see De Chateaubriand, Rene.

Chateaubriand, Rene De see De Chateaubriand, Rene.

Chateaubriand, Rene de, et al. Correspondance Generale: 1789-1807, Vol. 1. 682p. 1977. 59.95 (ISBN 0-686-54363-7). French & Eur.

--Les Aventures Du Dernier Abencerage. 139p. 1926. 37.50 (ISBN 0-686-54362-9). French & Eur.

Chateaubriand, Viscount de see De Chateaubriand, Viscount.

Chatelain, Agnes, jt. ed. see Cimino, Louis.

Chatelain, Alfred V. Ancient Europe in the Vision of the Rarest Available Steel Engravings. (Illus.). 99p. Repr. of 1887 ed. 227.75 (ISBN 0-89901-112-8). Found Class Reprints.

Chatelain, C., jt. auth. see Kuess, R.

Chatelain, Emile L. Introduction a la lecture des notes tironiennes. (Illus.). 1964. Repr. of 1900 ed. 24.50 (ISBN 0-8337-0549-0). B Franklin.

Chatelain, Heli, ed. Folk Tales of Angola: Fifty Tales. LC 69-19354. (Illus., Ki-Mbundu & Eng). Repr. of 1894 ed. cancelled (ISBN 0-8371-0895-0, CHF&, Pub. by Negro U Pr). Greenwood.

Chatelain, Heli, tr. Folk-Tales of Angola. LC 9-697. (AFS.M.). Repr. 25.00 (ISBN 0-527-01053-7). Kraus Repr.

Chatelain, Henri L. Recherches sur le vers francais au quinzieme siecle: rimes, metres et strophes. LC 79-149950. (Research & Source Works Ser.: No. 725). 1971. Repr. of 1908 ed. lib. bdg. 26.50 (ISBN 0-8337-0550-4). B Franklin.

Chatelaine, Kenneth L. Harry Stack Sullivan: The Formative Years. LC 80-6251. 577p. (Orig.). 1981. pap. text ed. 21.00 (ISBN 0-8191-1553-3); lib. bdg. 34.00 (ISBN 0-8191-1552-5). U Pr of Amer.

Chatelet, Francois, et al. La Revolution Sans Modele. (Archontes Ser: No. 6). 188p. (Fr.). 1975. pap. text ed. 25.00x (ISBN 90-2797-615-5). Mouton.

Chatelin, Francoise. Spectral Approximation of Linear Operators. (Computer Science & Applied Mathematics Ser.). 1983. 69.50 (ISBN 0-12-170620-6). Acad Pr.

Chater. The Oil Industry & Microbial Ecosystems. 260p. 1978. 65.95 (ISBN 0-471-25627-7, Pub. by John Wiley & Sons England). Heyden.

Chater, A. G., tr. see Ibsen, Henrik.

Chater, A. G., tr. see Undset, S.

Chater, A. G., tr. see Undset, Sigrid.

Chater, A. G., tr. see Valentin, Hugo.

Chater, Arthur G., tr. see Nansen, Fridtjof.

Chater, Elizabeth. Angela. (Coventry Romance Ser.: No. 167). 224p. 1982. pap. 1.50 (ISBN 0-449-50268-6, Coventry). Fawcett.

--A Delicate Situation. (Coventry Romance Ser.: No. 191). 192p. 1982. pap. 1.50 (ISBN 0-449-50294-5, Coventry). Fawcett.

--The Earl & the Emigree. 192p. (Orig.). 1985. pap. 2.25 (ISBN 0-449-20542-8, Crest). Fawcett.

--The Elsingham Portrait. (Orig.). 1980. pap. 1.75 (ISBN 0-449-50018-7, Coventry). Fawcett.

--Gallant Lady. 288p. 1981. pap. 1.50 (ISBN 0-449-50217-1, GM). Fawcett.

--The Gamester. (Orig.). 1980. pap. 1.75 (ISBN 0-449-50047-0, Coventry). Fawcett.

--The King's Doll. 176p. 1984. pap. 2.25 (ISBN 0-449-20084-1, Crest). Fawcett.

--Milord's Liegewoman. (Coventry Romance Ser.: No. 176). 224p. 1982. pap. 1.50 (ISBN 0-449-50277-5, Coventry). Fawcett.

--The Random Gentleman. 224p. 1981. pap. 1.95 (ISBN 0-449-50210-4, Crest). Fawcett.

--The Runaway Debutante. 176p. 1985. pap. 2.50 (ISBN 0-449-20747-1, Crest). Fawcett.

Chater, Hara H. & Williams, A. O. An Enumeration of the Flowering Plants of Nepal: Vol. 3, Dicotyledons. (Illus.). 226p. 1982. pap. text ed. 66.00x (ISBN 0-565-00854-4). Sabbot-Natural Hist Bks.

Chater, James. Luca Marenzio & the Italian Madrigal, 1577-1593, 2 vols. Fortune, Nigel, ed. LC 81-13095. (British Studies in Musicology: No. 4). 518p. 1981. Set. 79.95 (ISBN 0-8357-1242-7). Vol. 1, 274 pgs (ISBN 0-8357-1255-9). Vol. 2, 244 pgs (ISBN 0-8357-1256-7). UMI Res Pr.

Chater, K., et al, eds. Genetic Rearrangement: Proceedings of the John Innes Symposium, 5th, 1982. LC 83-4680. 300p. 1983. text ed. 45.00x (ISBN 0-87893-086-8); pap. text ed. 27.50x (ISBN 0-87893-087-6). Sinauer Assoc.

Chater, R., et al, eds. Incomes Policy. 1981. 37.50x (ISBN 0-19-877145-2). Oxford U Pr.

Chater, S. Understanding Research in Nursing. (Offset Pub.: No. 14). (Also avail. in French). 1975. pap. 2.40 (ISBN 92-4-170014-9). World Health.

Chaterji, Bijan R. Indian Cultural Influences in Cambodia. LC 77-87486. Repr. of 1928 ed. 28.00 (ISBN 0-404-16799-3). AMS Pr.

Chatfield, C. Analysis of Time Series: An Introduction. 3rd ed. 286p. 1984. pap. text ed. 16.95 (ISBN 0-412-26030-1, NO.9011, Pub. by Chapman & Hall). Methuen Inc.

--Statistics for Technology: A Course in Applied Statistics. 3rd ed. 1983. pap. 12.95 (ISBN 0-412-25340-2, NO. 6845, Pub. by Chapman & Hall). Methuen Inc.
--Teutonic Antiquities: Historical & Geographical Sketches of Roman & Barbarian History. LC 77-6984. 1977. Repr. of 1828 ed. lib. bdg. 30.00 (ISBN 0-89341-210-4). Longwood Pub Group.
Chatfield, C. & Collins, A. J. Introduction to Multivariate Analysis. 1980. 19.95x (ISBN 0-412-16030-7, NO.6397, Pub. by Chapman & Hall). Methuen Inc.
Chatfield, Charles. Devere Allen & a Radical Approach to War. LC 75-147691. (Library of War & Peace; Documentary Anthologies). 1976. lib. bdg. 46.00 (ISBN 0-8240-0447-7). Garland Pub.
--For Peace & Justice: Pacifism in America 1914-1941. LC 70-142143. pap. 116.00 (ISBN 0-317-28045-7, 2025558). Bks Demand UMI.
--Kirby Page & the Social Gospel: Pacifist & Socialist Aspects. LC 70-147695. (Library of War & Peace: Documentary Anthologies). 1976. lib. bdg. 46.00 (ISBN 0-8240-0451-5). Garland Pub.
Chatfield, Charles, jt. auth. see Gara, Larra.
Chatfield, Charles, ed. Peace Movements in America. LC 72-94294. 1973. pap. 3.95 (ISBN 0-8052-0386-9). Schocken.
Chatfield, Charles, ed. see Cook, Blanche.
Chatfield, Charles, ed. see Dix, Otto.
Chatfield, Douglas, jt. auth. see Lawlis, G. Frank.
Chatfield, Hale. Little Fictions, Loving Lies. LC 81-2813. (Illus.). 60p. 1981. 30.00 (ISBN 0-916906-34-5); pap. 15.95 (ISBN 0-916906-35-3). Konglomerati.
--Possesions. (Cleveland Poets Ser.: No. 36). 34p. (Orig.). 1984. pap. 4.00 (ISBN 0-914946-39-0). Cleveland St Univ Poetry Ctr.
--Water Colors. LC 78-11143. 1979. cloth 20.00 (ISBN 0-916906-11-6); signed ed. 50.00 (ISBN 0-916906-12-4); pap. 12.00 (ISBN 0-916906-10-8). Konglomerati.
--What Color Are Your Eyes? (WNJ Ser.: No. 9). 1977. signed ed. o.p. 20.00 (ISBN 0-686-61913-7); 10.00 (ISBN 0-686-61914-5); pap. 6.00 (ISBN 0-686-61915-3). Juniper Pr WI.
Chatfield, Mark. Churches the Victorians Forgot. (Illus.). 1979. 15.00 (ISBN 0-903485-76-1, Pub. by Moorland Pub Co England). Eastview.
--English Church Monuments. 224p. 1983. text ed. 36.45x (ISBN 0-86127-012-6, Pub. by Avebury England); pap. text ed. 20.45x (ISBN 0-86127-013-4, Pub. by Avebury England). Humanities.
Chatfield, Michael. A History of Accounting Thought. rev. ed. LC 76-49566. 322p. 1977. 20.50 (ISBN 0-88275-929-9); pap. 12.50 (ISBN 0-88275-469-6). Krieger.
Chatfield, Michael & Nielson, Denis P. Cost Accounting. 1172p. 1983. text ed. 32.95 (ISBN 0-15-514140-6, HC); solution manual avail. (ISBN 0-15-514142-2); study guide avail. HarBraceJ.
Chatfield, Michael & Brief, Richard P., eds. The English View of Accountants Duties & Responsibilities: 1881-1902. LC 77-87312. (Development of Contemporary Accounting Thought Ser.). 1978. lib. bdg. 22.00x (ISBN 0-405-10925-3). Ayer Co Pubs.
Chatfield-Taylor, H. C. Moliere: A Biography. 1973. Repr. of 1907 ed. 50.00 (ISBN 0-8274-1498-6). R West.
Chatfield-Taylor, Joan. Picnics. LC 79-64872. (Illus.). 1980. pap. 5.95 (ISBN 0-394-73760-1, Dist. by Random). Taylor & NG.
Chatham, Bill. Journey to Nazgar's Fortress: A Robo Force Adventure. LC 84-62071. (Robo Force Mini-Storybooks). (Illus.). 32p. (ps-3). 1985. pap. 1.25 (ISBN 0-394-87175-8, BYR). Random.
Chatham House Study Group, jt. auth. see Royal Institute of Internatinal Affairs.
Chatham, James R. & McClendon, Carmen C. Dissertations in Hispanic Languages & Literatures: An Index of Dissertations Completed in the United States & Canada, Vol. 2, 1967-1977. LC 70-80093. 176p. 1981. 20.00x (ISBN 0-8131-1415-2). U Pr of Ky.
Chatham, James R. & Ruiz-Fornells, Enrique. Dissertations in Hispanic Languages & Literatures: An Index of Dissertations Completed in the United States & Canada, Vol. 1, 1876-1966. LC 70-80093. 136p. 1970. 16.00x (ISBN 0-8131-1183-8). U Pr of Ky.
Chatham, Joe. Eternal Security Obtained After Completing a Faithful Course. 1978. pap. 1.50 (ISBN 0-934942-05-6). White Wing Pub.
Chatham, Margaret & Knapp, Barbara. Patient Education Handbook. LC 81-17027. (Illus.). 192p. 1981. pap. text ed. 12.95 (ISBN 0-89303-055-4). Brady Comm.
Chatham, Patricia M. Treatment of the Borderline Personality. LC 84-20425. 544p. 1985. 40.00 (ISBN 0-87668-754-0). Aronson.
Chatham, Robert. Classical Orders of Architecture. LC 85-43080. (Illus.). 144p. 1985. pap. 17.50 (ISBN 0-8478-0671-5). Rizzoli Intl.
Chatham, Russell. Striped Bass on the Fly: A Guide to California Waters. LC 77-71001. (A California Living Book). (Illus.). 1977. pap. 4.50 (ISBN 0-89395-000-9). Cal Living Bks.
Chathasaigh, Maire Ni, ed. see Woods, Sylvia.
Chatman, Seymour. Antonioni, or, the Surface of the World. LC 85-1025. 384p. 1985. 35.00 (ISBN 0-520-05205-6); pap. 12.95 (ISBN 0-520-05341-9, CAL 782). U of Cal Pr.
--Story & Discourse: Narrative Structure in Fiction & Film. 288p. 1978. 29.95x (ISBN 0-8014-1131-9); pap. 7.95x (ISBN 0-8014-9186-X). Cornell U Pr.
--Theory of Meter. (Janua Linguarum, Ser. Minor: No. 36). (Orig.). 1964. pap. text ed. 19.20x (ISBN 0-686-22469-8). Mouton.
Chatman, Seymour, ed. & frwd. by see Columbia University. English Institute. Annual Publications.
Chatman, Seymour, et al, eds. A Semiotic Landscape-Panorama Semiotique. (Approaches to Semiotics Ser.: No. 29). (Fr.). 1979. text ed. 100.00x (ISBN 90-279-7928-6). Mouton.
Chatman, Urella, et al, eds. see Lynch, L. Riddick.
Chatov, Robert. Corporate Financial Reporting: Public or Private Control? LC 74-15368. 1975. 17.95 (ISBN 0-02-905410-9). Free Pr.
Chatrath, M. S., jt. auth. see Swithi, G. R.
Chatt, J., et al, eds. New Trends in the Chemistry of Nitrogen Fixation. 1980. 60.00 (ISBN 0-12-169450-X). Acad Pr.
Chatt, Orville K. Design Is Where You Find It. LC 79-146932. (Illus.). 124p. 1972. 8.95 (ISBN 0-8138-0415-9). Iowa St U Pr.
Chattalas, Angelos M. Pearls of Wisdom. Date not set. 9.50 (ISBN 0-8062-2507-6). Carlton.
Chattapadhyaya. Muhammad, the Prophet of Islam. 1981. 1.25 (ISBN 0-686-97878-1). Kazi Pubns.
Chattaway, Deborah, tr. see Potter, Beatrix.
Chatten, Elizabeth N. Samuel Foote. (English Authors Ser.). 1980. lib. bdg. 14.50 (ISBN 0-8057-6779-7, Twayne). G K Hall.
Chatten, Leslie G., ed. Pharmaceutical Chemistry: Theory & Application, Vol. 1. Incl. Vol. 2. Instrumental Techniques. pap. 160.00 (ISBN 0-317-28673-0). LC 66-11286. pap. 130.00 (ISBN 0-317-28672-2, 2055063). Bks Demand UMI.
Chattergy, R., jt. auth. see Pooch, U.
Chattergy, Rahul & Pooch, Udo W. Top-Down, Modular Programming in FORTRAN with WATFIV. 217p. (Orig.). 1980. pap. 16.95 (ISBN 0-316-13826-6). Little.
Chattergy, Rahul, jt. auth. see Pooch, Udo W.
Chatterjee. Monoclonal Antibodies. 1985. 50.00 (ISBN 0-88416-511-6). PSG Pub Co.
Chatterjee, A. K. Yogacara Idealism. 2nd rev. ed. 1976. 14.00 (ISBN 0-8426-0742-0). Orient Bk Dist.
Chatterjee, A. N. Sri Krsna Caitanya: A Historical Study of Gaudiya Vaisnavism. 1985. 22.00x (ISBN 0-8364-1321-0, Pub. by Assoc Bks India). South Asia Bks.
Chatterjee, Asim K. Comprehensive History of Jainism, 1000 AD to 1600 AD, Vol. II. 1984. 28.50x (ISBN 0-8364-1123-4, Pub. by Mukhopadhyay India). South Asia Bks.
Chatterjee, B., jt. ed. see Roy, A. K.
Chatterjee, B. K. Theory & Design of Concrete Shells. 256p. 1971. 69.50 (ISBN 0-677-61740-2). Gordon.
Chatterjee, B. N. How Viable is an One Acre Farm? 1983. 4.50x (ISBN 0-8364-0929-9, Pub. by Pearl Pub). South Asia Bks.
Chatterjee, Bhabatosh. John Keats: His Mind & Work. 504p. 1981. 60.00x (ISBN 0-86125-129-6, Pub. by Orient Longman India). State Mutual Bk.
Chatterjee, Dwarka N. Storm Over the Congo. 224p. 1980. text ed. 22.50x (ISBN 0-7069-0996-8, Vikas India). Advent NY.
Chatterjee, Enakshi, jt. auth. see Chatterjee, Santimay.
Chatterjee, Enakshi, tr. see Gangopadhyay, Sunil.
Chatterjee, K., et al. Drug Treatment of Heart Failure. 207p. 1983. write for info. (ISBN 0-911741-04-6). Advanced Thera Comm.
Chatterjee, Lata & Nijkamp, Peter. Urban & Regional Policy Analysis In Developing Coutries. 270p. 1983. text ed. 37.95x (ISBN 0-566-00623-5). Gower Pub Co.
--Urban Problems & Economic Development. (NATO Advanced Study, Behavioral & Social Sciences Ser.: No. 6). 359p. 1981. 40.00 (ISBN 90-286-2661-1). Sijthoff & Noordhoff.
Chatterjee, Lata, jt. auth. see Lakshmanan, T. R.
Chatterjee, M. The Religious Spectrum. 193p. 1984. text ed. 25.50x (ISBN 0-391-03152-X, Pub. by Allied Pubs India). Humanities.
Chatterjee, Maiti. Rice Production Technology Manual. 139p. 1981. 19.00x (ISBN 0-686-76661-X, Pub. by Oxford & IBH India). State Mutual Bk.
Chatterjee, Margaret. At the Homeopath's. (Writers Workshop Greenbird Ser.). 87p. 1975. 12.00 (ISBN 0-88253-504-8). Ind-US Inc.
--Gandhi's Religious Thought. LC 83-5841. 224p. 1984. text ed. 19.95x (ISBN 0-268-01009-9, 85-10091). U of Notre Dame Pr.
--The Language of Philosophy. 152p. 1981. 26.00 (ISBN 90-247-2372-8, Pub. by Martinus Nijhoff Netherlands). Kluwer Academic.
--The Sandalwood Tree. 4.80 (ISBN 0-89253-457-5); flexible cloth 4.00 (ISBN 0-89253-458-3). Ind-US Inc.
--The Spring & the Spectacle. 4.80 (ISBN 0-89253-555-5); flexible cloth 4.00 (ISBN 0-89253-556-3). Ind-US Inc.
--Towards the Sun. (Writers Workshop Redbird Ser.). 1975. 8.00 (ISBN 0-88253-664-8); pap. text ed. 3.00 (ISBN 0-88253-663-X). Ind-US Inc.
Chatterjee, Margaret, ed. Contemporary Indian Philosophy, Series Two. (Muirhead Library of Philosophy). 323p. 1974. text ed. 20.50x (ISBN 0-391-00347-X). Humanities.
Chatterjee, P. K. & Wetherall, P. J. Winding Engine Calculations for the Mining. 1982. 36.00 (ISBN 0-419-12650-3, NO. 6693, Pub. by E & FN Spon). Methuen Inc.
Chatterjee, P. K., ed. Absorbency: Textile Science & Technology, Vol. 7. 334p. 1985. 85.25 (ISBN 0-444-42377-X). Elsevier.
Chatterjee, Partha. Bengal, Nineteen Twenty to Forty-Seven: The Land Question. 1985. 18.50x (ISBN 0-8364-1305-9, Pub. by KP Bagchi India). South Asia Bks.
Chatterjee, Pranab. Taste of a Rain Forest. (Redbird Bk.). 1976. lib. bdg. 10.00 (ISBN 0-89253-121-5); flexible bdg. 4.80 (ISBN 0-89253-137-1). Ind-US Inc.
Chatterjee, R. K. India's Land Border Problems & Challenges. 1978. 17.50 (ISBN 0-89684-547-8). Orient Bk Dist.
Chatterjee, Ranjit, jt. ed. see Nicholson, Colin.
Chatterjee, Romir. Rural Energy Planning in Developing Countries. Meier, Peter M., ed. (Energy Management Training Program Ser.). 200p. 1985. pap. 20.00x (ISBN 0-86531-761-5). Westview.
Chatterjee, S. K. Legal Aspects of International Drug Control. 612p. 1981. 117.00 (ISBN 90-286-2091-5). Sijthoff & Noordhoff.
--Legal Aspects of International Drug Control. 612p. 1981. lib. bdg. 124.00 (ISBN 90-247-2556-9, Pub. by Martinus Nijhoff Netherlands). Kluwer Academic.
Chatterjee, S. K., ed. The Cultural Heritage of England, Vol. 5. 60.00x (ISBN 0-686-75617-7, Pub. by Ramakrishna Vedanta England). State Mutual Bk.
Chatterjee, S. K., jt. auth. see Ray, Amal.
Chatterjee, S. N., et al. Manual of Renal Transplantation. 1979. 39.50 (ISBN 0-387-90337-2). Springer-Verlag.
Chatterjee, S. P. Elements of Economic Geography. 128p. 1981. 35.00x (ISBN 0-86131-091-8, Pub. by Orient Longman India). State Mutual Bk.
--An Introductory Regional Geography. 170p. 1981. 29.00x (ISBN 0-86125-704-9, Pub. by Orient Longman India). State Mutual Bk.
--An Introductory Regional Geography: India. 64p. 1981. 29.00x (ISBN 0-86125-620-4, Pub. by Orient Longman India). State Mutual Bk.
--Junior College Geography, Vol. II. (Illus.). 132p. 1983. pap. 5.95x (ISBN 0-86131-090-X). Apt Bks.
--Junior College Geography, Vol. 1. (Illus.). 268p. 1977. pap. text ed. 8.95x (ISBN 0-86125-446-5). Apt Bks.
Chatterjee, Samprit & Price, Bertram. Regression Analysis by Example. LC 77-24510. (Probability & Mathematical Statistics Ser.: Applied Probability Section). 228p. 1977. 31.95 (ISBN 0-471-01521-0, Pub. by Wiley-Interscience). Wiley.
Chatterjee, Santimay. Collected Works of Meghnad Saha, Vol. 1. 591p. text ed. 55.00x (ISBN 0-86131-348-8, Pub. by Orient Longman Ltd India). Apt Bks.
Chatterjee, Santimay & Chatterjee, Enakshi. Satyendra Nath Bose. (National Biography Ser.). 1979. pap. 4.25 (ISBN 0-89744-196-6). Auromere.
Chatterjee, Satya N., ed. Organ Transplantation. LC 81-21862. (Illus.). 640p. 1982. text ed. 60.50 (ISBN 0-7236-7008-0). PSG Pub Co.
--Renal Transplantation. 295p. 1980. 38.50 (ISBN 0-89004-308-6). Raven.
Chatterjee, Sisir. Aldous Huxley. 1955. lib. bdg. 12.50 (ISBN 0-8414-3483-2). Folcroft.
--James Joyce: A Study in Technique. 104p. 1981. 29.00x (ISBN 0-86125-128-8, Pub. by Orient Longman India). State Mutual Bk.
--Novel As a Modern Epic. 1955. lib. bdg. 8.50 (ISBN 0-8414-3565-0). Folcroft.
Chatterjee, Sukhen. Design of Modern Steel Bridges. 300p. 1986. 50.00x (ISBN 0-246-11718-4, Pub. by Granada England). Sheridan.
Chatterjee, Sunjeeb C. Bengal Ryots. Banerjee, A. C., ed. 1977. 9.00x (ISBN 0-8364-0015-1). South Asia Bks.
Chatterjee, Surendra N. Tripura: A Profile. (Illus.). xii, 67p. 1984. text ed. 22.50x (ISBN 0-86590-327-1, Pub. by Inter-India Pubns N Delhi). Apt Bks.
Chatterjee, Vera. All This Is Ended: The Life & Times of Her Highness Begum Sumroo. 1979. 12.00x (ISBN 0-7069-0719-1, Pub. by Vikas India). Advent NY.
Chatterjee, Visvanath, ed. Sir Philip Sidney: An Apology for Poetry. 96p. 1975. pap. 3.95x (ISBN 0-86125-617-4, Pub. by Orient Longman India). Apt Bks.
Chatterji, Bhola. Indo-British Cultural Confrontation: Gooroodas Banerjee & His Times. 1979. 11.00x (ISBN 0-8364-0037-2). South Asia Bks.
Chatterji, J. C. Wisdom of the Vedas. LC 80-51550. 100p. 1980. pap. 3.95 (ISBN 0-8356-0538-8, Quest). Theos Pub Hse.
Chatterji, M., ed. Space Location & Regional Development. 240p. 1976. pap. 18.95x (ISBN 0-85086-054-7, 2943, Pub. by Pion England). Methuen Inc.
Chatterji, M. & Rompuy, P. Van, eds. Energy, Regional Science & Public Policy. 1976. pap. 20.00 (ISBN 0-387-07692-1). Springer-Verlag.
Chatterji, Manas. Health Care Cost-Containment Policy: An Econometric Study. 1983. lib. bdg. 69.50 (ISBN 0-89838-119-3). Kluwer Nijhoff.
--Management & Regional Science for Economic Development. 1982. lib. bdg. 30.00 (ISBN 0-89838-108-8). Kluwer-Nijhoff.
Chatterji, Manas, ed. Energy & Environment in the Developing Countries. LC 80-42143. 357p. 1981. 58.95x (ISBN 0-471-27993-5, Pub. by Wiley-Interscience). Wiley.
Chatterji, Manas, et al, eds. Spatial, Environmental, & Resource Policy in the Developing Countries. LC 83-16448. 448p. 1984. text ed. 41.95x (ISBN 0-566-00650-2). Gower Pub Co.
Chatterji, Mohini M. Viveka-Chudamani or the Crest Jewel of Wisdom. 3.50 (ISBN 0-8356-7091-0). Theos Pub Hse.
Chatterji, Rakhahari. Working Class & the Natonalist Movement in India: The Critical Years. 1985. 14.50x (ISBN 0-8364-1371-7, Pub. by South Asia Pubs). South Asia Bks.
Chatterji, Reena. Impact of Raja Rammohun Roy Education in India. 1984. 16.00x (ISBN 0-8364-1101-3, Pub. by S Chand India). South Asia Bks.
Chatterji, Ruby. Existentialism in American Literature. 176p. 1983. text ed. 12.50x (ISBN 0-391-02890-1). Humanities.
Chatterji, S. & Fenyoe, I., eds. Jahrbuch Ueberblicke Mathematik: Mathematical Surveys, Vol. 16, 1983. 200p. (Ger. & Eng.). 1983. text ed. 19.95 (ISBN 3-411-01650-7). Birkhauser.
Chatterji, Suniti K., ed. Some Aspects of Indo-Iranian Literary & Cultural Traditions. (Illus.). 1977. 36.00x (ISBN 0-686-22674-7). Intl Bk Dist.
Chatterji, Sunjti K. Selected Writings, Vol. I. 1978. text ed. 25.00x (ISBN 0-7069-0533-4, RS 85, Pub. by Vikas India). Advent NY.
Chatters, A. W. & Hajarnavis, C. R. Rings with Chain Conditions. LC 80-19315. (Research Notes in Mathematics Ser.: No. 44). 198p. (Orig.). 1980. pap. text ed. 23.95 (ISBN 0-273-08446-1). Pitman Pub MA.
Chatters, C. H. & Hillhouse, A. M. Local Government Debt Administration. 1977. lib. bdg. 59.95 (ISBN 0-8490-2178-2). Gordon Pr.
Chatterton, Betty J. Grandma's Down-Home Recipes. LC 77-85849. (Illus.). 1978. 6.95 (ISBN 0-930574-02-8); pap. 4.95 (ISBN 0-930574-01-X). Chatterton Pr.
Chatterton, Brigadier G. Wings of Pegasus. (Airborne Ser.: No. 14). (Illus.). 282p. 1982. 18.95 (ISBN 0-89839-060-5). Battery Pr.
Chatterton, E. K. Sailing Ships: The Story of Their Development from the Earliest Times to the Present Day. 1977. lib. bdg. 75.00 (ISBN 0-8490-2554-0). Gordon Pr.
Chatterton, E. Keble. King's Cutters & Smugglers, 1700-1855. LC 79-173106. (Illus.). Repr. of 1912 ed. 22.00 (ISBN 0-405-08351-3, Blom Pubns). Ayer Co Pubs.
--Q-Ships & Their Story. LC 79-6105. (Navies & Men Ser.). (Illus.). 1980. Repr. of 1972 ed. lib. bdg. 28.50x (ISBN 0-405-13034-1). Ayer Co Pubs.
--Whalers & Whaling: The Story of the Whaling Ships up to the Present Day. LC 79-178626. (Illus.). 248p. 1975. Repr. of 1925 ed. 40.00x (ISBN 0-8103-4028-3). Gale.
Chatterton, Edward K. English Seamen & the Colonization of America. facsimile ed. LC 74-37332. (Select Bibliographies Reprint Ser.). (Illus.). Repr. of 1930 ed. 26.50 (ISBN 0-8369-6679-1). Ayer Co Pubs.
Chatterton, Howard A. A Pocket Guide to Maryland's Chesapeake Bay. (Illus.). 48p. (Orig.). 1984. pap. 4.95 (ISBN 0-933852-46-0). Nautical & Aviation.
Chatterton, Keble. Sailing Ships & Their Story. LC 68-54240. (Illus.). 1968. Repr. of 1923 ed. 20.00 (ISBN 0-87266-004-4). Argosy.
Chatterton, Louise. Just the Right Age. (First Love Ser.). 186p. (YA) 1984. pap. 1.95 (ISBN 0-671-53392-4). PB.
Chatterton, M., jt. ed. see Nevill, A. M.
Chatterton, M., jt. ed. see Neville, A. M.
Chatterton, Mark. The Saab: The Innovator. (Illus.). 192p. 1980. 22.50 (ISBN 0-7153-7945-3). David & Charles.
Chatterton, Pauline. Scandinavian Knitting Designs. LC 76-27879. (Encore Edition). (Illus.). 272p. 1977. 5.95 (ISBN 0-684-16538-4, ScribT); pap. 14.95 (ISBN 0-684-17420-0). Scribner.
Chatterton, Robert T., jt. auth. see Zaneveld, L. J.
Chatterton, Roland H. Methods of Lesson Observing by Preservice Student-Teachers; a Comparative Study. LC 72-178801. (Columbia University. Teachers College. Contributions to Education: No. 834). Repr. of 1941 ed. 22.50 (ISBN 0-404-55834-8). AMS Pr.
Chatterton, Thomas. Poetical Works of Thomas Chatterton, 2 Vols. Skeat, W. W., ed. LC 68-59008. (BCL Ser.: No. I). Repr. of 1875 ed. Set. 75.00 (ISBN 0-404-01484-4). AMS Pr.
--The Rowley Poems. 17.50 (ISBN 0-8369-7105-1, 7939). Ayer Co Pubs.

--Works of Thomas Chatterton, 3 Vols. Southey, Robert & Cottle, Joseph, eds. LC 71-80892. 1968. Repr. of 1803 ed. Set. 125.00 (ISBN 0-404-01540-9). Vol. 1 (ISBN 0-404-01541-7). Vol. 2 (ISBN 0-404-01542-5). Vol. 3 (ISBN 0-404-01543-3). AMS Pr.

Chatterton, Wayne. Vardis Fisher: The Frontier & Regional Works. LC 72-619585. (Western Writers Ser: No. 1). (Illus.). 51p. (Orig.). 1972. pap. 2.00x (ISBN 0-88430-000-5). Boise St Univ.

Chatterton-Hill, Georges. Philosophy of Nietzsche: An Exposition & Appreciation. LC 70-152409. (Studies in German Literature, No. 13). 1971. Repr. of 1914 ed. lib. bdg. 53.95x (ISBN 0-8383-1232-2). Haskell.

--The Sociological Value of Christianity. LC 83-45605. Date not set. Repr. of 1912 ed. 36.00 (ISBN 0-404-19873-2). AMS Pr.

Chatto, Beth. The Damp Garden. 224p. 1982. 40.00x (ISBN 0-460-04551-2, Pub. by J M Dent). State Mutual Bk.

--The Damp Garden. (Illus.). 336p. 1982. 19.95x (ISBN 0-460-04551-2, Pub. by J M Dent England). Biblio Dist.

--The Dry Garden. 190p. 1978. 30.00x (ISBN 0-460-04317-X, Pub. by J M Dent England). State Mutual Bk.

--The Dry Garden. (Illus.). 190p. 1983. pap. 9.95x (ISBN 0-460-02222-9, Pub. by J M Dent England). Biblio Dist.

Chatto, James. The Seducer's Cookbook. LC 81-68499. (Illus.). 64p. 1982. 9.95 (ISBN 0-7153-8201-2). David & Charles.

Chatto, William A. Treatise on Wood Engraving, Historical & Practical. LC 69-16477. (Illus.). 1969. Repr. of 1861 ed. 65.00x (ISBN 0-8103-3531-X). Gale.

Chatton, E. Les Peridiniens Parasites. 1975. Repr. lib. bdg. 63.00x (ISBN 3-87429-100-6). Lubrecht & Cramer.

Chattopadhaya, Kamaladevi. Carpets & Floor Coverings of India. 2nd, rev. ed. (Illus.). viii, 71p. 1981. text ed. 35.00x (ISBN 0-86590-049-3, Pub. by Taraporevala India). Apt Bks.

Chattopadhya, A. Why Have I Accepted Islam? pap. 1.75 (ISBN 0-686-18476-9). Kazi Pubns.

Chattopadhyay, Kamaladevi. Tribalism in India. (Illus.). 1978. text ed. 18.25x (ISBN 0-7069-0652-7). Humanities.

Chattopadhyay, S. B. Principles & Procedures of Plant Protection. 480p. 1980. 69.00x (ISBN 0-686-84466-1, Oxford & I B H India). State Mutual Bk.

Chattopadhyaya, Alaka. Atisa & Tibet: Life & Works of Dimpakara Srijnana in Relation to the History & Religion of Tibet. 563p. 1981. Repr. 25.00 (ISBN 0-89581-123-5). Asian Human Pr.

Chattopadhyaya, Alalca, tr. see Taranatha, Lama.

Chattopadhyaya, Alaska, ed. see Das, S. C.

Chattopadhyaya, D. P., ed. Indian Studies: Past & Present, 1959-1960, Vol 1. 1960. 40.00 (ISBN 0-88065-031-1, Pub. by Messers Today & Tomorrows Printers & Publishers India). Scholarly Pubns.

--Indian Studies: Past & Present, 1960-1961, Vol. 2. 723p. 1961. 40.00 (ISBN 0-88065-032-X, Pub. by Messers Today & Tomorrows Printers & Publishers India). Scholarly Pubns.

--Indian Studies: Past & Present, 1962-1963, Vol. 4. 508p. 1963. 40.00 (ISBN 0-88065-034-6, Pub. by Messers Today & Tomorrows Printers & Publishers India). Scholarly Pubns.

--Indian Studies: Past & Present, 1963-1964, Vol. 5. 376p. 1964. 40.00 (ISBN 0-88065-035-4, Pub. by Messers Today & Tomorrows Printers & Publishers India). Scholarly Pubns.

--Indian Studies: Past & Present, 1964-1965, Vol. 6. 466p. 1965. 40.00 (ISBN 0-88065-036-2, Pub. by Messers Today & Tomorrows Printers & Publishers India). Scholarly Pubns.

--Indian Studies: Past & Present, 1965-1966, Vol. 7. 454p. 1966. 40.00 (ISBN 0-88065-037-0, Pub. by Messers Today & Tomorrows Printers & Publishers India). Scholarly Pubns.

--Indian Studies: Past & Present, 1966-1967, Vol. 8. 401p. 1967. 40.00 (ISBN 0-88065-038-9, Pub. by Messers Today & Tomorrows Printers & Publishers India). Scholarly Pubns.

--Indian Studies: Past & Present, 1967-1968, Vol. 9. 398p. 1968. 40.00 (ISBN 0-88065-039-7, Pub. by Messers Today & Tomorrows Printers & Publishers Indiadia). Scholarly Pubns.

--Indian Studies: Past & Present, 1968-1969, Vol. 10. 383p. 1969. 40.00 (ISBN 0-88065-040-0, Pub. by Messers Today & Tomorrows Printers & Publishers India). Scholarly Pubns.

--Indian Studies: Past & Present, 1969-1970, Vol. 11. 430p. 1970. 40.00 (ISBN 0-88065-041-9, Pub. by Messers Today & Tomorrows Printers & Publishers India). Scholarly Pubns.

--Studies in the History of Indian Philosophy, 3 vols. 1981. text ed. 39.75x (ISBN 0-391-01805-1). Humanities.

Chattopadhyaya, Debiprasad. Marxism & Indology. 273p. 1982. Repr. of 1981 ed. text ed. 20.00x (ISBN 0-391-02512-0). Humanities.

--Science & Society in Ancient India. (Philosophical Currents Ser.: No. 22). 1978. text ed. 34.75x (ISBN 90-6032-098-0). Humanities.

Chattopadhyaya, Kamaladevi. Indian Woman's Battle. 1983. 10.00x (ISBN 0-8364-0948-5, Pub. by Abhinav). South Asia Bks.

Chattopadhyaya, S. Early History of North India. 3rd rev. ed. 1976. 8.95 (ISBN 0-89684-197-9). Orient Bk Dist.

Chattopadhyaya, Saratchandra. Chandranath. 101p. 1969. pap. 2.50 (ISBN 0-88253-027-5). Ind-US Inc.

--Shrikant. 168p. 1969. pap. 2.50 (ISBN 0-88253-028-3). Ind-US Inc.

Chattopadhyaya, Sisir. The Technique of the Modern English Novel. 1978. Repr. of 1957 ed. lib. bdg. 30.00 (ISBN 0-8495-0843-6). Arden Lib.

--Technique of the Modern English Novel. 1959. lib. bdg. 20.00 (ISBN 0-8414-3604-5). Folcroft.

Chattopadhyaya, Sudhakar. Reflections on the Tantras. 1978. 8.50 (ISBN 0-89684-028-X, Pub. by Motilal Banarsidass India). Orient Bk Dist.

--Reflections on the Tantras. 1979. 8.25x (ISBN 0-89684-028-X). South Asia Bks.

Chattopadhyaya, Tapan. The Story of LalBazar. 1983. 16.50x (ISBN 0-8364-0959-0, Pub by Mukhopadhyay India). South Asia Bks.

Chattopadyaya, S. Some Early Dynasties of South India. 1974. 9.95 (ISBN 0-89684-320-3). Orient Bk Dist.

Chattoraj, D. K. & Birdi, K. S. Adsorption & the Gibbs Surface Excess. 441p. 1984. 59.50x (ISBN 0-306-41334-5, Plenum Pr). Plenum Pub.

Chattpadhyaya, D. P., ed. Indian Studies: Past & Present, 1961-1962, Vol. 3. 658p. 1962. 40.00 (ISBN 0-88065-033-8, Pub. by Messers Today & Tomorrows Printers & Publishers India). Scholarly Pubns.

Chatty, Dawn. From Camel to Truck: The Bedouin in the Modern World. 1985. 14.50 (ISBN 0-317-28892-X). Vantage.

Chaturshreni, Ved V. Indo-US Relations. 388p. 1980. 24.95 (ISBN 0-940500-08-6, Pub. by National Delhi India). Asia Bk Corp.

Chaturvedi, D. N., jt. ed. see Jain, P. C.

Chaturvedi, H. R. Bureaucracy & Local Community: Dynamics of Rural Deveolpment, India. 1977. 9.50x (ISBN 0-88386-990-X). South Asia Bks.

Chaturvedi, Mahendra & Bhola, Nath T. A Practical Hindi-English Dictionary. 700p. (Hindi & Eng.). 1974. 14.00x (ISBN 0-88386-380-4). South Asia Bks.

Chatwin, Bruce. On the Black Hill. 256p. 1983. 14.75 (ISBN 0-670-52492-1). Viking.

--On the Black Hill. 256p. 1984. pap. 5.95 (ISBN 0-14-006896-1). Penguin.

--The Viceroy of Ouidah. pap. 5.15 (ISBN 0-686-36917-3). Summit Bks.

Chatwin, Bruce, jt. auth. see Hodgkin, Howard.

Chatwin, Bruce, jt. auth. see Mapplethorpe, Robert.

Chatzidakis, Manolis. Benaki Museum. Cicellis, Kay, tr. from Gr. (Greek Museums Ser.). (Illus.). 48p. 1975. pap. 7.50 (ISBN 0-89241-015-9). Caratzas.

--Byzantine Museum. Jonas, Brian De, tr. from Gr. (Greek Museums Ser.). (Illus.). 44p. 1975. pap. 9.50 (ISBN 0-89241-014-0). Caratzas.

--Etudes sur la Peinture Postbyzantine. 430p. 1976. 70.00x (ISBN 0-902089-96-X, Pub. by Variorum). State Mutual Bk.

--The Icons of Patmos: Problems in Byzantine & Metabyzantine Painting. (Illus.). 205p. 1981. text ed. 90.00 (ISBN 0-89241-106-6, Nat'l Bank of Greece). Caratzas.

--Mystras. (Athenon Illustrated Guides Ser.). (Illus.). 124p. 1984. pap. 12.95 (ISBN 0-88332-343-5, 8254, Pub. by Ekdotike Athenon Greece). Larousse.

Chau, A. S. & Afghan, B. K. Analysis of Pesticides in Water, Vol. 3. 264p. 1982. 76.50 (ISBN 0-8493-5212-6). CRC Pr.

Chau, Heng, jt. auth. see Sure, Heng.

Chau, Ling-Lie, ed. Flavor Mixing in Weak Interactions. (Ettore Majorana International Science Ser.: Vol. 20-Physical Sciences). 816p. 1985. 120.00x (ISBN 0-306-41895-9, Plenum Pr). Plenum Pub.

Chau, S. Y., ed. Analysis of Pesticides in Water, Significance, Principles, Techniques, & Chemistry: Significance, Principles, Techniques, & Chemistry, Vol. I. Afghan, B. K. 216p. 1982. 71.50 (ISBN 0-8493-5210-X). CRC Pr.

Chau, Ta N. Demographic Aspects of Educational Planning. (Fundamentals of Educational Planning: No. 9). (Illus.). 80p. (Orig., 2nd Printing 1980). 1969. pap. 6.00 (ISBN 92-803-1028-3, U153, UNESCO, IIEP). Unipub.

--Population Growth & Costs of Education in Developing Countries. (Illus.). 313p. (Orig.). 1972. pap. 14.50 (ISBN 92-803-1049-6, U470, UNESCO). Unipub.

Chau, Ta Ngoc, jt. auth. see Carron, Gabriel.

Chau, Ta Ngoc, jt. ed. see Carron, Gabriel.

Chaube, S. P. Adolescent Psychology. 200p. 1983. text ed. 20.00x (ISBN 0-7069-2138-0, Pub. by Vikas India). Advent NY.

Chaubey, N. P., jt. ed. see Rangarao, B. V.

Chaucer. Troilus & Criseyde. 1983. 35.00x (ISBN 0-900000-55-4, Pub. by Centaur Pr). State Mutual Bk.

Chaucer, Geoffrey. Cambridge Library: MS GG. 4.27, 3 Vols. Parkes, Malcolm & Beadle, Richard, eds. 1984. 550.00x (ISBN 0-317-04071-5). Pilgrim Bks OK.

--Canon's Yeoman's Tale. Hussey, M., et al, eds. (Selected Tales from Chaucer). 1965. text ed. 5.95x (ISBN 0-521-04623-8). Cambridge U Pr.

--The Canterbury Tales. Hieatt, A. Kent & Hieatt, Constance, eds. Hieatt, A. Kent & Hieatt, Constance, trs. from Eng. (Bantam Classics Ser.). 421p. (gr. 9-12). 1981. pap. 2.95 (ISBN 0-553-21082-3). Bantam.

--Canterbury Tales. 1976. 12.95x (ISBN 0-460-10307-5, Evman); pap. 3.95x (ISBN 0-460-01307-6, Evman). Biblio Dist.

--Canterbury Tales, 3 Vols. Wright, Thomas, ed. Repr. of 1851 ed. 32.00 ea. (ISBN 0-384-08565-2). Johnson Repr.

--Canterbury Tales. Coghill, Nevill, tr. (Classics Ser.). (Orig.). (YA) (gr. 9 up). 1951. pap. 2.95 (ISBN 0-14-044022-4). Penguin.

--The Canterbury Tales. LC 80-22141. (Raintree Short Classics). (Illus.). 48p. (gr. 4 up). 1981. PLB 15.15 (ISBN 0-8172-1666-9). Raintree Pubs.

--Canterbury Tales. Wright, David, tr. 1965. pap. 4.95 (ISBN 0-394-70293-X, Vin). Random.

--The Canterbury Tales. Stewart, Diana, adapted by. LC 80-22141. (Raintree Short Classics Ser.). (Illus.). 48p. (gr. 4-12). 1983. pap. 9.27 (ISBN 0-8172-2007-0). Raintree Pubs.

--The Canterbury Tales: A Facsimile & Transcription of the Hengwrt Manuscript with Variants from the Ellesmere Manuscript. Ruggiers, Paul G., ed. LC 77-18611. (Illus.). 1078p. 1979. 145.00x (ISBN 0-8061-1416-9). U of Okla Pr.

--Canterbury Tales: A Selection. Howard, Donald R. & Dean, James M., eds. 1969. pap. 2.95 (ISBN 0-451-51514-5, CE1514, Sig Classics). NAL.

--The Canterbury Tales: An Illustrated Selection. Coghill, Nevil, tr. (Large Format Ser). (Illus.). 1977. pap. 12.95 (ISBN 0-14-004452-3). Penguin.

--Canterbury Tales of Chaucer, 5 Vols. Tyrwhitt, Thomas, ed. LC 74-39160. Repr. of 1778 ed. Set. 162.50 (ISBN 0-404-01550-6); 32.50 ea. Vol. 1 (ISBN 0-404-01551-4). Vol. 2 (ISBN 0-404-01552-2). Vol. 3 (ISBN 0-404-01553-0). Vol. 4 (ISBN 0-404-01554-9). Vol. 5 (ISBN 0-404-01555-7). AMS Pr.

--Canterbury Tales of Chaucer. Lumiansky, R. M., tr. (Illus.). pap. 3.95 (ISBN 0-671-54061-0). WSP.

--Canterbury Tales of Geoffrey Chaucer. abr. ed. Cook, Daniel, ed. LC 61-9496. pap. 2.95 (ISBN 0-385-09869-3, Anch). Doubleday.

--Canterbury Tales, Prologue: Complete Study Edition. Lamb, Sidney, ed. (Illus., Orig.). pap. 3.95 (ISBN 0-8220-1404-1). Cliffs.

--Canterbury Tales (Selected) An Interlinear Translation. Hopper, Vincent F., ed. LC 70-99791. 1970. pap. text ed. 6.95 (ISBN 0-8120-0039-0). Barron.

--Chanticleer & the Fox. LC 58-10449. (Illus.). 40p. (ps-3). 1982. 10.53 (ISBN 0-690-18561-8); PLB 11.89 (ISBN 0-690-18562-6); pap. 3.80i (ISBN 0-690-04318-X). Crowell Jr Bks.

--Chaucer's Troilus & Cresyde. Stanley-Wrench, Margaret, tr. 1965. 10.00x (ISBN 0-87556-051-2). Saifer.

--Chaucer's Troylus & Crysede. LC 76-23188. 1976. Repr. of 1873 ed. lib. bdg. 50.00 (ISBN 0-8414-7338-2). Folcroft.

--Clerk's Prologue & Tale. Winny, J., ed. (Selected Tales from Chaucer). 1966. text ed. 5.95x (ISBN 0-521-04632-7). Cambridge U Pr.

--The Complete Poetry & Prose of Geoffrey Chaucer. Fisher, John H., ed. LC 76-44011. 1977. text ed. 39.00 (ISBN 0-03-080273-3, HoltC). HR&W.

--Complete Works. Skeat, Walter W., ed. (Oxford Standard Authors). 1933. 35.00 (ISBN 0-19-254119-6). Oxford U Pr.

--Complete Works, 7 Vols. 2nd ed. Skeat, Walter W., ed. 1894-1900. 195.00x set (ISBN 0-19-811314-5). Oxford U Pr.

--Franklin's Prologue & Tale. Spearing, A. C., ed. (Selected Tales from Chaucer). text ed. 5.95x (ISBN 0-521-04624-6). Cambridge U Pr.

--The Franklin's Tale. Hodgson, Phyllis, ed. 160p. 1980. pap. 8.95 (ISBN 0-485-61007-8, Pub. by Athlone Pr Ltd). Longwood Pub Group.

--The Friar's Summoner's & Pardoner's Tales. Havely, N. R., ed. LC 75-19090. (London Medieval & Renaissance Ser.). 164p. 16.50x (ISBN 0-8419-0220-8); pap. 9.00x (ISBN 0-8419-0224-0). Holmes & Meier.

--The General Prologue, the Canon's Yeoman's Prologue & Tale. Schmidt, A. V., ed. LC 75-17975. (London Medieval & Renaissance Ser.). 175p. 1975. 16.50x (ISBN 0-8419-0219-4); pap. 9.00x (ISBN 0-8419-0223-2). Holmes & Meier.

--General Prologue to the Canterbury Tales. Winny, J., ed. (Selected Tales from Chaucer). 1965. text ed. 5.95x (ISBN 0-521-04629-7). Cambridge U Pr.

--The General Prologue to the Canterbury Tales. Hodgson, Phyllis, ed. 220p. 1969. pap. 8.95 (ISBN 0-485-61006-X, Pub. by Athlone Pr Ltd). Longwood Pub Group.

--Introduction to Chaucer. Hussey, Maurice, et al, eds. (Selected Tales from Chaucer). (Orig.). 1965. 29.95 (ISBN 0-521-05353-6); pap. 10.95x (ISBN 0-521-09286-8). Cambridge U Pr.

--Knight's Tale. Spearing, A. C., ed. (Selected Tales from Chaucer). 1966. text ed. 7.95x (ISBN 0-521-04633-5). Cambridge U Pr.

--Love Visions. Stone, Brian, tr. (Penguin Classics Ser.). 256p. 1983. pap. 4.95 (ISBN 0-14-044408-4). Penguin.

--Merchant's Prologue & Tale. Hussey, M., ed. (Selected Tales from Chaucer). 1966. text ed. 5.95x (ISBN 0-521-04631-9). Cambridge U Pr.

--Miller's Prologue & Tale. Winny, J., ed. LC 76-132283. (Selected Tales from Chaucer). 1970. text ed. 5.95x (ISBN 0-521-08033-9). Cambridge U Pr.

--The Miller's Tale. (Illus.). 1973. pap. 3.95 (ISBN 0-88388-022-9). Bellerophon Bks.

--The Miller's Tale. Ross, Thomas W., ed. LC 81-40286. (A Variorum Edition of the Works of Geoffrey Chaucer: Vol. II, Pt. 3). 304p. 1983. 38.50x (ISBN 0-8061-1785-0). U of Okla Pr.

--Nun's Priest's Prologue & Tale. Hussey, M., ed. (Selected Tales from Chaucer). 1966. text ed. 5.95x (ISBN 0-521-04626-2). Cambridge U Pr.

--The Nun's Priest's Tale. Pearsall, Derek, ed. LC 83-5760. (The Variorum Chaucer Ser.: Vol. II, Pt. 9). 300p. 1984. 42.50x (ISBN 0-8061-1779-6). U of Okla Pr.

--Pardoner's Prologue & Tale. Spearing, A. C., ed. (Selected Tales from Chaucer). 1966. text ed. 5.95x (ISBN 0-521-04627-0). Cambridge U Pr.

--The Parlement of Foulys. new ed. Brewer, D. S., ed. (Old & Middle English Texts). 1976. pap. 10.95x (ISBN 0-06-491190-X). B&N Imports.

--Poetical Works of Geoffrey Chaucer, 6 Vols. Nicolas, Harris, ed. LC 72-971. Repr. of 1845 ed. Set. 210.00 (ISBN 0-404-01560-3); 35.00 ea. AMS Pr.

--The Poetical Works of Geoffrey Chaucer: The Minor Poems, Troilus & Criseyde, the Canterbury Tales, the Legend of Good Women, the Parlement of Foules & Lydgate's Temple of Glass, 3 Vols. 1980. 550.00 (ISBN 0-85991-070-9). Pilgrim Bks OK.

--The Portable Chaucer. rev. ed. Morrison, Theodore, ed. LC 75-2224. (Viking Portable Library: P 81). 1977. pap. 7.95 (ISBN 0-14-015081-1). Penguin.

--The Prioress' Prologue & Tale. Winny, J., ed. LC 74-19531. (Selected Tales from Chaucer Ser.). 64p. 1974. pap. text ed. 5.95 (ISBN 0-521-20744-4). Cambridge U Pr.

--The Reeve's Prologue & Tale. Spearing, A. C., et al, eds. LC 78-19695. (Selected Tales from Chaucer Ser.). 1979. limp bdg. 5.95x (ISBN 0-521-22211-7). Cambridge U Pr.

--The Tales of Canterbury: Complete. Pratt, Robert A., ed. LC 72-9380. (Illus.). 587p. 1974. text ed. 26.50 (ISBN 0-395-14052-8). HM.

--Troilus & Cressida in Modern English Verse. Krapp, George P., tr. 1957. pap. 3.95 (ISBN 0-394-70142-9, Vin, V142). Random.

--Troilus & Criseyde. 1974. 9.95x (ISBN 0-460-10992-8, Evman); pap. 6.95x (ISBN 0-460-11992-3, Evman). Biblio Dist.

--Troilus & Criseyde. Coghill, Nevill, tr. (Classics Ser). 1971. pap. 3.95 (ISBN 0-14-044239-1). Penguin.

--Troilus & Criseyde. Windeatt, Barry A., ed. 1983. pap. text ed. 90.00x (ISBN 0-582-49072-3). Longman.

--Troilus & Criseyde (Abridged) Brewer, D. S. & Brewer, L. E., eds. 1977. pap. 5.95x (ISBN 0-7100-6642-2). Routledge & Kegan.

--Wife of Bath's Prologue & Tale. Winny, J., ed. (Selected Tales from Chaucer). 1966. text ed. 5.95x (ISBN 0-521-04630-0). Cambridge U Pr.

--The Wife of Bath's Prologue & Tale & the Clerk's Prologue & Tale. Cigman, Gloria, ed. LC 75-17976. (London Medieval & Renaissance Ser.). 94p. 1976. text ed. 16.50x (ISBN 0-8419-0225-9); pap. 9.00x (ISBN 0-8419-0226-7). Holmes & Meier.

--Wife of Bath's Tale- Complete Study Edition. Lamb, Sidney, ed. (Illus., Orig.). pap. 3.95 (ISBN 0-8220-1408-4). Cliffs.

--The Workes: Fifteen Thirty-Two. 1969. 120.00 (ISBN 0-317-12637-7). Scolar.

--Works of Geoffrey Chaucer. Pollard, Alfred W., ed. LC 73-399393. (Select Bibliographies Reprint Ser.). 1972. Repr. of 1898 ed. 33.00 (ISBN 0-8369-9903-7). Ayer Co Pubs.

--Works of Geoffrey Chaucer. 2nd ed. Robinson, F. N., ed. (New Cambridge Editions). xliv, 1002p. 1957. text ed. 29.95 (ISBN 0-395-05568-7). HM.

Chaucer, Geoffrey see Swan, D. K.

Chaucer, Geoffrey, jt. ed. see Baker, Donald C.

Chaucer, Geoffrey, jt. ed. see Morgan, Gerald.

Chaucer, Geoffrey, tr. see Boethius, Anicius.

Chaucer Society. Chaucer Society Publications, 46 Vols. 1868-1912. Set. 1900.00 (ISBN 0-384-08590-3). Johnson Repr.

Chaucz, Angelico. La Conquistadora: The Autobiography of an Ancient Statue. rev. ed. LC 81-14473. 96p. 1984. pap. 6.95 (ISBN 0-86534-041-2). Sunstone Pr.

Chaudenson, Robert. Textes Creoles Anciens (La Reunion & Ile Maurice) Comparison et Essai d'Analyse, Vol. 1. (Kreokische Bibliothek Ser.). 280p. (Orig.). 1981. pap. text ed. 18.00x (ISBN 3-87118-483-7, Pub. by Helmut Buske Verlag Hamburg). Benjamins North Am.

Chaudhari, R. V., jt. auth. see Ramachandran, P. A.

Chaudhary, Anju, jt. auth. see Martin, L. John.

Chaudhary, H. K. Elementary Principles of Plant Breeding. 1981. 35.00x (ISBN 0-686-76634-2, Pub. by Oxford & IBH India). State Mutual Bk.

Chaudhri, A. R. Substance of Muhammahan Law. 1970. 3.85x (ISBN 0-87902-157-8). Orientalia.
Chaudhri, D. P. & Dasgupta, Ajit K. Agriculture & the Development Process: A Study of Punjab. LC 84-27507. 216p. 1985. 34.50 (ISBN 0-7099-3408-4, Pub. by Croom Helm Ltd). Longwood Pub Group.
Chaudhri, D. P., jt. ed. see Lea, David A.
Chaudhri, S. A., jt. auth. see Garner, R. J.
Chaudhri, Sandhya. Gandhi & the Partition of India. 244p. 1984. text ed. 25.00x (ISBN 0-86590-334-4, Pub. by Sterling Pubs India). Apt Bks.
Chaudhry, M. H. & Yevjevich, V. Closed-Conduit Flow. LC 81-51337. 1981. 35.00 (ISBN 0-918334-41-1). WRP.
Chaudhry, M. L. & Templeton, J. G. A First Course in Bulk Queues. LC 82-21764. 372p. 1983. 53.50x (ISBN 0-471-86260-6, Pub. by Wiley-Interscience). Wiley.
Chaudhry, Mokhtar, tr. see Amanuddin, Syed.
Chaudhry, Shadid A. People's Democratic Republic of Yemen: A Review of Economic & Social Development. vi, 169p. 1979. pap. 15.00 (ISBN 0-686-36126-1, RC-7903). World Bank.
Chaudhuri, Amal. Classical Mechanics. (Illus.). 1984. 18.95x (ISBN 0-19-561343-0). Oxford U Pr.
Chaudhuri, Buddhadeb. The Barkreshwar Temple. 117p. 1981. text ed. 14.25x (ISBN 0-391-02380-2, Pub. by Concept India). Humanities.
Chaudhuri, Buddhadeb, ed. Tribal Development: Problems & Prospects in India. 400p. 1982. text ed. 29.00x (ISBN 0-391-02643-7, Pub. by Concept India). Humanities.
Chaudhuri, Dulal. Goddess Durga: The Great Mother. 1985. 7.50x (ISBN 0-8364-1289-3, Pub. by Mrimol). South Asia Bks.
Chaudhuri, Haridas. Being, Evolution & Immortality. rev. ed. LC 74-4821. Orig. Title: Philosophy of Integralism. 224p. 1974. pap. 6.95 (ISBN 0-8356-0449-7, Quest). Theos Pub Hse.
--Evolution of Integral Consciousness. LC 77-4219. 1977. pap. 3.75 (ISBN 0-8356-0494-2, Quest). Theos Pub Hse.
--Integral Philosophy of Sri Aurobindo. Spiegelberg, Frederic, ed. 350p. 1980. 10.00 (ISBN 0-89744-992-4, Pub. by Cultural Integration). Auromere.
--Integral Yoga. LC 73-17170. 1981. pap. 4.95 (ISBN 0-8356-0444-6, Quest). Theos Pub Hse.
--Integral Yoga: The Concept of Harmonious & Creative Living. 160p. 1981. pap. 6.95 (ISBN 0-04-149031-2). Allen Unwin.
--Mastering the Problems of Living. new ed. LC 75-4172. 222p. 1975. pap. 2.75 (ISBN 0-8356-0463-2, Quest). Theos Pub Hse.
--Philosophy of Integralism. 184p. (Orig.). pap. 3.50 (ISBN 0-686-64766-1, Pub. by Sri). Auromere.
Chaudhuri, Haridas & Frank, Leonard R. Mahatma Gandhi. (Orig.). 1969. pap. 1.50 (ISBN 0-89744-993-2, Pub. by Cultural Integration). Auromere.
Chaudhuri, J. B., jt. auth. see Natha, Prana.
Chaudhuri, J. N. An Autobiography. 1978. 16.50x (ISBN 0-7069-0655-1, Pub. by Vikas India). Advent NY.
Chaudhuri, K. N. English East India Company: Study of the Early Joint-Stock Company, 1600-1640. 245p. 1965. 32.50x (ISBN 0-7146-1286-3, F Cass Co). Biblio Dist.
--English East India Company: The Study of an Early Jointstock Company 1600-1640. LC 66-88. 1965. 30.00x (ISBN 0-678-05037-6). Kelley.
--Trade & Civilisation in the Indian Ocean: An Economic History from the Rise of Islam to 1750. (Illus.). 256p. 1985. 42.50 (ISBN 0-521-24226-6); pap. 16.95 (ISBN 0-521-28542-9). Cambridge U Pr.
--The Trading World of Asia & the English East India Company, 1660-1760. LC 77-77745. (Illus.). 1978. 107.50 (ISBN 0-521-21716-4). Cambridge U Pr.
Chaudhuri, K. N. & Dewey, Clive J., eds. Economy & Society: Essays in Indian Economic & Social History. (Illus.). 1979. 19.95x (ISBN 0-19-561073-3). Oxford U Pr.
Chaudhuri, Kalyan. Genocide in Bangladesh. 1972. 14.50x (ISBN 0-8046-8807-9, Pub. by Kennikat). Assoc Faculty Pr.
Chaudhuri, Nirad C. Hinduism: A Religion to Live by. 1979. 27.50x (ISBN 0-19-520112-4, GB 612); pap. 9.95 (ISBN 0-19-520221-X). Oxford U Pr.
Chaudhuri, Pramit. The Indian Economy: Poverty & Development. LC 77-88457. 1979. 26.00x (ISBN 0-312-41378-5). St Martin.
--Readings in Indian Agricultural Development. LC 72-191003. pap. 48.00 (ISBN 0-317-20062-3, 2023324). Bks Demand UMI.
Chaudhuri, R. H. Social Aspects of Fertility in India. 200p. 1982. 40.00x (ISBN 0-686-94060-1, Pub. by Garlandfold England). State Mutual Bk.
Chaudhuri, Sukanta. The Glass King & Other Poems. (Writers Workshop Redbird Book Ser.). 32p. 1975. pap. text ed. 3.00 (ISBN 0-88253-547-1). Ind-US Inc.
--Infirm Glory: Shakespeare & the Renaissance Image of Man. 1981. 42.00x (ISBN 0-19-812801-0). Oxford U Pr.
--Poems. 8.00 (ISBN 0-89253-500-8); flexible cloth 4.00 (ISBN 0-89253-501-6). Ind-US Inc.
Chaudhuri, Tapan & Chaudhuri, Tukin, eds. Differential Diagnosis in Nuclear Medicine. (Illus.). 400p. Date not set. text ed. price not set (ISBN 0-397-50502-7, Lippincott Medical). Lippincott.
Chaudhuri, Tukin, jt. ed. see Chaudhuri, Tapan.
Chaudhury, B. D., jt. auth. see Singh, B. K.
Chaudhury, Bani R. Folk Tales of Rajasthan. LC 72-906833. (Folk Tales of India Ser.: No. 9). 120p. 1972. 3.75x (ISBN 0-89684-389-0). Orient Bk Dist.
Chaudhury, Jackie & Agley, Lyn. Simple Data Processing: A Practical Introduction to Business Information Technology. (Illus.). 60p. 1983. pap. 12.95x (ISBN 0-317-02460-4). Intl Ideas.
Chaudhury, P. C. Sri Lanka. (Lands & Peoples of the World Ser.). 150p. 1985. text ed. 15.00x (ISBN 0-86590-732-3, Pub. by Sterling Pubs India). APT Bks.
Chaudhury, P. Roy. Folk Tales of India, 21 vols. (Illus.). 1975. Set. 73.50 (ISBN 0-86578-007-2). Ind-US Inc.
Chaudhury, R. R., ed. Pharmacology of Estrogens. (International Encyclopedia of Pharmacology & Therapeutics: Section. 106). (Illus.). 180p. 1981. 55.00 (ISBN 0-08-026869-2). Pergamon.
Chaudhury, Sukomal. Analytical Study of the Abhidharmakosa. 1983. 18.00x (ISBN 0-8364-1017-3, Pub. by Mukhopadyaya). South Asia Bks.
Chaudier, Louann. Leading Consultants in Computer Software. 2nd ed. 290p. (Orig.). 1984. pap. 67.00 (ISBN 0-943692-08-3). Res Pubns VA.
Chauffurin, L. Petit Dictionnaire bilingue Larousse, francais-anglais et English-French. (Adonis). (Fr. & Eng.). plastic bdg. 6.25 (ISBN 0-685-14032-6, 3768). Larousse.
Chauhan, Eklavya, jt. auth. see Desh Bandhu.
Chauhan, Ela, jt. auth. see Harris, Helen.
Chauhan, Manhar & Venning, Sue, illus. Jim Henson's Muppet Show Pop-Up Book. LC 82-60285. (Pop-Up Bks.). (Illus.). 12p. (gr. 1 up). 1984. 9.95 (ISBN 0-394-85512-4, BYR). Random.
Chauhan, S. S. Advanced Educational Psychology. 7th ed. 487p. 1984. pap. text ed. 20.00x (ISBN 0-7069-2519-X, Pub. by Vikas India). Advent NY.
--Innovations in Teaching-Learning Process. 1980. text ed. 13.95x (ISBN 0-7069-0779-5, Pub. by Vikas India). Advent NY.
--Principles & Techniques of Guidance. 300p. 1982. (Pub. by Vikas India); pap. text ed. 15.95 (ISBN 0-7069-2084-8). Advent NY.
Chauliaguet, Charles, et al. Solar Energy in Buildings. LC 8-27031. 174p. 1979. 42.95 (ISBN 0-471-27570-0, Pub. by Wiley-Interscience). Wiley.
Chaum, David, ed. Advances in Cryptology: Proceedings of Crypto 83. 408p. 1984. 55.00x (ISBN 0-306-41637-9, Plenum Pr). Plenum Pub.
Chaumont Guitry, Guy de. Lettres d'Indochine. LC 79-179177. (South & Southeast Asia Studies). Repr. of 1951 ed. 16.00 (ISBN 0-404-54807-5). AMS Pr.
Chauncey, Charles F. County Funding of the Arts in New York State. 1975. pap. 2.00x (ISBN 0-89062-033-4, Pub. by NYSCA). Pub Ctr Cult Res.
Chauncey, Marlin R. The Educational & Occupational Preferences of College Seniors: Their Significance for College Achievement. LC 75-176639. (Columbia University. Teachers College. Contributions to Education: No. 533). Repr. of 1932 ed. 22.50 (ISBN 0-404-55533-0). AMS Pr.
Chauncy, Charles. Mystery Hid from All Ages & Generations. LC 70-83414. (Religion in American, Ser. 1). 1969. Repr. of 1784 ed. 23.50 (ISBN 0-405-00235-1). Ayer Co Pubs.
Chaundler, Christine. The Book of Superstitions. pap. 2.45 (ISBN 0-8065-0302-5). Citadel Pr.
Chaundler, Thomas. Liber Apologeticus de omni statu humanae naturae (1460) Shoukri, Doris E., ed. 1974. write for info. Renaissance Soc Am.
Chaundy, Leslie. Bibliography of the First Editions of the Works of Robert Bontine Cunninghame Graham. 1924. lib. bdg. 10.00 (ISBN 0-8414-3018-7). Folcroft.
Chaundy, Theodore W., et al. The Printing of Mathematics: Aids for Authors & Editions & Rules for Compositors & Readers at the University Press, Oxford. pap. 29.80 (ISBN 0-317-10261-3, 2051896). Bks Demand UMI.
Chaunu, P. European Expansion in the Later Middle Ages. LC 78-5809. (Europe in the Middle Ages: Selected Studies: Vol. 10). 326p. 1979. 59.75 (ISBN 0-444-85132-1, North Holland). Elsevier.
Chau Phan Thien. Vietnamese Communism: A Research Bibliography. LC 75-16961. 359p. 1975. lib. bdg. 45.00 (ISBN 0-8371-7950-5, CVC/). Greenwood.
Chaussinand-Nogaret, Guy. The French Nobility in the Eighteenth Century: From Feudalism to Enlightenment. Doyle, William, tr. 197p. 37.50 (ISBN 0-521-25623-2); pap. 10.95 (ISBN 0-521-27590-3). Cambridge U Pr.
--Une Histoire Des Elites, 1700-1848. (Recueil De Textes Presentes et Commentes Par le Savoir Historique Ser.: No. 6). 1975. pap. 16.80x (ISBN 90-2797-872-7). Mouton.
Chaussy, C., et al. Extracorporeal Shock Wave Lithotripsy. (Illus.). viii, 112p. 1982. pap. 26.50 (ISBN 3-8055-3620-8). S Karger.
Chaussy, Charles, et al. Beruehrungsfreie Nierensteinzertruemmerung durch extrakorporal erzeugte, fokussierte Stosswellen. (Beitraege zur Urologie: Vol. 2). vi, 94p. 1980. pap. 21.50 (ISBN 3-8055-1901-X). S Karger.
Chautard, Jean-Baptiste. The Soul of the Apostolate. 1977. pap. 6.00 (ISBN 0-89555-031-8). TAN Bks Pubs.
Chautauqua Literary & Scientific Circle. Studies in European Literature: A Series of Studies (Montaigne, Hugo, Balzac, Goethe, Ibsen) 302p. 1985. Repr. of 1908 ed. lib. bdg. 40.00 (ISBN 0-8414-4100-6). Folcroft.
Chauvenet, Beatrice. Hewett & Friends: A Biography of Santa Fe's Vibrant Era. 240p. 1983. 14.95 (ISBN 0-89013-136-8). Museum NM Pr.
--John Gaw Meem: Pioneer in Historic Preservation. LC 84-27295. (Illus.). 128p. 1984. 13.95 (ISBN 0-89013-151-1). Museum NM Pr.
Chauvicourt, J. & Chauvicourt, S. Fanorona: The National Game of Madagascar. Fox, Leonard, tr. from Fr. (Illus.). ix, 44p. 1984. pap. 3.75 (ISBN 0-932329-00-4). Intl Fanorona.
Chauvicourt, S., jt. auth. see Chauvicourt, J.
Chauvin, Remy. Ethology-the Biological Study of Animal Behavior. Diamanti, Joyce, tr. from Fr. LC 76-46818. 245p. (Orig.). 1977. 32.50 (ISBN 0-8236-1770-X). Intl Univs Pr.
--Parapsychology: When the Irrational Rejoins Science. Banham, Katharine M., tr. LC 84-43225. 220p. (Fre.). 1985. lib. bdg. 18.95 (ISBN 0-89950-145-1). McFarland & Co.
Chauvire, Yvette, jt. auth. see LeMaitre, Jerome.
Chavan, K. K. Maratha Murals: Late Medieval Painting of the Deccan: 1650-1850 A.D. (Illus.). 122p. 1983. text ed. 30.00x (ISBN 0-86590-126-0). Apt Bks.
Chavan, R. S. An Approach to International Law. 1983. text ed. 27.50x (ISBN 0-86590-160-0, Pub. by Sterling India). Apt Bks.
Chavan, Sunanda P. The Fair Voice: A Study of Indian Women Poets in English. 137p. 1984. text ed. 20.00x (ISBN 0-86590-591-6, Pub. by Sterling Pubs India). Apt Bks.
Chavanne, J., et al. Die Literatur Uber Die Polar Regionen der Erde Bis 1875. (Ger.). 1978. pap. text ed. 19.25x (ISBN 90-6041-007-6). Humanities.
Chavanne, Josef. Sahara: Oder, Von Oase Zu Oase. (Illus.). 1879. 50.00 (ISBN 0-384-08595-4). Johnson Repr.
Chavannes, Albert. Future Commonwealth, or What Samuel Balcom Saw in Socioland. LC 71-154433. (Utopian Literature Ser). 1971. Repr. of 1892 ed. 14.00 (ISBN 0-405-03516-0). Ayer Co Pubs.
Chavarria, Jesus. Jose Carlos Mariategui & the Rise of Modern Peru, 1890-1930. LC 78-21426. 1979. 14.95x (ISBN 0-8263-0507-5). U of NM Pr.
Chavasse, Antoine, ed. Le Sacramentaire Dans le Groupe Dit "Gelasiens du Ville Siecle", 2 Vols. (Fr.). Date not set. pap. text ed. 70.50 (ISBN 90-247-3173-9, Pub. by Martnus Nijhoff Netherlands). Kluwer Academic.
Chave, Anna. Mark Rothko: His Subject Matter. (Illus.). 128p. 1985. cancelled (ISBN 0-943828-65-1). Karz-Cohl Pub.
Chave, Edith H., jt. auth. see Hobson, Edmund.
Chavel, C. B., tr. The Commandments of Maimonides, 2 vols. 305p. 1967. 35.00 (ISBN 0-900689-71-4); pap. 25.00. Soncino Pr NY.
--The Disputation at Barcelona. 48p. 1983. pap. 2.95 (ISBN 0-88328-025-6). Shilo Pub Hse.
--The Gate of Reward. 144p. 1983. pap. 4.95 (ISBN 0-88328-024-8). Shilo Pub Hse.
--The Law of the Eternal is Perfect. 128p. 1983. pap. 4.95 (ISBN 0-88328-023-X). Shilo Pub Hse.
Chavel, Charles B. Encyclopedia of Torah Thoughts. Orig. Title: Rabeinu Bachya Ben Asher "Kad Hakemach". 734p. 1980. 19.50 (ISBN 0-88328-016-7); pap. 14.50 (ISBN 0-88328-017-5). Shilo Pub Hse.
--Ramban: His Life & Teachings. LC 63-1543. pap. 3.95 (ISBN 0-87306-037-7). Feldheim.
--Ramban (Nachmanides) Commentary on the Torah, 5 vols. 2575p. 1971. 84.75 set (ISBN 0-686-86743-2); Vol. I, Book Of Genesis. 16.95 ea. (ISBN 0-88328-006-X). Vol. II, Book Of Exodus (ISBN 0-88328-007-8). Vol. III, Book Of Leviticus (ISBN 0-88328-008-6). Vol. IV, Book Of Numbers (ISBN 0-88328-009-4). Vol. V, Book Of Deuteronomy (ISBN 0-88328-010-8). Shilo Pub Hse.
--Ramban (Nachmanides) Writings & Discourses, 2 vols. 768p. 1978. Set. slipcase 33.00 (ISBN 0-88328-013-2). Shilo Pub Hse.
Chavel, I. & Farkas, H. M., eds. Differential Geometry & Complex Analysis. (Illus.). 225p. 1985. 32.00 (ISBN 0-387-13543-X). Springer-Verlag.
Chavel, Isaac. Eigenvalues in Riemannian Geometry: Monograph. (Pure & Applied Mathematics Ser.). 1984. 62.00 (ISBN 0-12-170640-0). Acad Pr.
Chavers-Wright, Madrue. The Guarantee: P. W. Chavers; Banker, Entrepreneur, Philanthropist in Chicago's Black Belt of the Twenties. Messmer, Sara E., ed. LC 85-51854. (Illus.). 425p. (Orig.). 1985. 25.00 (ISBN 0-931505-03-8); pap. 14.95 (ISBN 0-931505-02-X). Wright Armstead.
--The Guarantee: P. W. Chavers; Banker, Entrepreneur, Philanthropist in Chicago's Black Belt of the Twenties. (Biography Ser.). 283p. 1985. 25.00 (ISBN 0-918233-00-3); pap. 14.95 (ISBN 0-918233-01-1). MBPI.
Chaves, Doris, et al, trs. see Williams, Letty.
Chaves, Eduardo & Jelly, Frederick M., eds. God: Tradition & Modernity. (God Ser.). (Orig.). Date not set. text ed. price not set (ISBN 0-913757-30-6, Pub. by New Era Bks); pap. text ed. price not set (ISBN 0-913757-31-4, Pub. by New Era Bks). Paragon Hse.
Chaves, Jonathan. Mei Yao-Ch'en & the Development of Early Sung Poetry. LC 75-40299. (Studies in Oriental Culture). 254p. 1976. 24.00x (ISBN 0-231-03965-4). Columbia U Pr.
Chaves, Jonathan, tr. from Chines see Yang Wan-Li.
Chaves, Jonathan, tr. see Yuan Hung-Tao.
Chavez, Angelico. Coronado's Friars: The Franciscans in the Coronado Expedition. (Monograph Ser.). (Illus.). 1968. 10.00 (ISBN 0-88382-058-7). AAFH.
--From an Altar Screen, el Retablo: Tales from New Mexico. facs. ed. LC 72-85690. (Short Story Index Reprint Ser). 1957. 12.00 (ISBN 0-8369-3031-2). Ayer Co Pubs.
--Muy Macho, He Said: Padre Gallegos, New Mexico's First Congressman. 1985. 15.00 (ISBN 0-88307-669-1). Gannon.
--New Mexico Triptych. LC 75-31416. 84p. 1976. lib. bdg. 9.50x (ISBN 0-88307-520-2). Gannon.
--Origins of New Mexico Families in the Spanish Colonial Period. LC 75-13387. 360p. 1982. lib. bdg. 35.00x (ISBN 0-88307-514-8). Gannon.
Chavez, Angelico, ed. The Oroz Codex, or Relation of the Description of the Holy Gospel Province in New Spain, & the Lives of the Founders & Other Note-Worthy Men of Said Province Composed by Fray Pedro Oroz: 1584-1586. (Documentary Ser.). 1972. 25.00 (ISBN 0-88382-011-0). AAFH.
Chavez, Angelico, jt. ed. see Adams, Eleanor B.
Chavez, Carlos. Musical Thought. LC 60-15236. (Charles Norton Lectures Ser.: 1958-1959). (Illus.). pap. 33.50 (ISBN 0-317-10111-0, 2006416). Bks Demand UMI.
--Toward a New Music: Music & Electricity. Weinstock, Herbert, tr. from Span. LC 74-28308. (Music Reprint Ser.). (Illus.). 180p. 1975. Repr. of 1937 ed. lib. bdg. 25.00 (ISBN 0-306-70719-5). Da Capo.
Chavez, Denise. The Last of the Menu Girls. LC 84-72304. 160p. (Orig.). 1985. pap. write for info. (ISBN 0-934770-46-8). Arte Publico.
Chavez, Fray A. But Time & Chance: The Biography of Padre Martinez of Taos. LC 81-27. 176p. 1981. 35.00x (ISBN 0-913270-96-2); pap. 11.95 (ISBN 0-913270-95-4). Sunstone Pr.
--La Conquistadora: The Autobiography of an Ancient Statue. LC 81-14413. (Illus.). 1983. pap. 6.95 (ISBN 0-913270-43-1). Sunstone Pr.
--Song of Francis. LC 73-75205. (Illus.). 64p. 1973. 6.50 (ISBN 0-87358-105-9). Northland.
Chavez, John R. The Lost Land: The Chicano Image of the Southwest. LC 84-11950. 208p. 1984. 19.95x (ISBN 0-8263-0749-3); pap. 9.95 (ISBN 0-8263-0750-7). U of NM Pr.
Chavez, Jose. Santa Maria de Guadalupe. (Span.). 1963. pap. 1.00 (ISBN 0-8198-6825-6). Dghtrs St Paul.
Chavez, Juana. Mother Deer & Her Spotted Fawns. (Illus.). 14p. (Orig.). (ps-7). 1981. pap. 3.75 (ISBN 0-915347-10-5). Pueblo Acoma Pr.
Chavez, Moises. Hebreo Biblico Juego de Dos Tomos, 2 vols. (Span., Vol. I - 568 pgs., Vol. II - 240 pgs.). 1984. Set. pap. 28.95 (ISBN 0-311-42070-2, Edit Mundo). Casa Bautista.
--Modelo de Oratoria. 144p. (Orig., Span.). 1979. pap. 3.50 (ISBN 0-89922-141-6). Edit Caribe.
Chavez, Rick & Nieder, Lois. Teaching Tennis. LC 81-71259. (Sport Teaching Ser.). 150p. (Orig.). 1982. pap. text ed. 8.95x (ISBN 0-8087-4803-3). Burgess.
Chavez-Irvin, Dixie L. & O'Malley, Thomas. Secrets of Service (How to Make Money in the Restaurant Business) 1978. pap. 10.95x (ISBN 0-931976-01-4). Inst Pr.
Chavignerie, Emile B. De La see De La Chavignerie, Emile B. & Auvray, Louis.
Chavigny, Camille de see De Chavigny, Camille.
Chavin, Remy & Muckenstrum-Chavin, Bernadette. Behaviorial Complexities. LC 79-20944. xiv, 257p. 25.00 (ISBN 0-8236-0495-0, BN#00495). Intl Univs Pr.
Chavira, Juan A., jt. auth. see Trotter, Robert T., 2nd.
Chavis, Benjamin F., Jr. Psalms from Prison. 192p. 1983. 10.95 (ISBN 0-8298-0661-X); pap. 7.95 (ISBN 0-8298-0666-0). Pilgrim NY.
Chavis, Lee D., ed. see Legal Researcher.
Chavis, Richard M., ed. see Krohel, Gregory, et al.
Chavkin, Samuel. The Mind Stealers: Psychosurgery & Mind Control. 1978. 8.95 (ISBN 0-395-26381-6). HM.
--The Mind Stealers: Psychosurgery & Mind Control. new ed. 240p. (Orig.). 1980. pap. 5.95 (ISBN 0-88208-119-5). Lawrence Hill.
--Murder of Chile. (Illus.). 288p. 1982. 13.95 (ISBN 0-89696-137-0, An Everest House Book). Dodd.

--Storm over Chile: The Junta under Siege. Rev. ed. 1985. pap. 8.95 (ISBN 0-88208-175-6). Lawrence Hill.

Chavkin, Wendy, ed. Double Exposure: Women's Health Hazards on the Job & at Home. LC 83-42525. (New Feminist Library Ser.). 288p. 1984. 26.00 (ISBN 0-85345-632-1); pap. 10.00 (ISBN 0-85345-633-X). Monthly Rev.

Chavrukov, Georgy. Bulgarian Monasteries: Monuments of History, Culture & Art. 1981. 80.00x (ISBN 0-569-08507-1, Pub. by Collet's). State Mutual Bk.

Chawla, H. M., jt. auth. see Sharma, K. K.

Chawla, K. K., jt. auth. see Meyers, Marc A.

Chawla, Sudershan & SarDesai, D. R., eds. Changing Patterns of Security & Stability in Asia. LC 79-22977. 272p. 1980. 39.95x (ISBN 0-03-052416-4); pap. 14.95x (ISBN 0-03-052411-3). Praeger.

Chawla, Veena, jt. auth. see Tyer, Janaki.

Chay, John, jt. ed. see Kwak, Tai-Hwan.

Chaya, Ruth K. & Miller, Joan M. More BASIC Programming for the Classroom & Home Teacher (IBM PC, IBM PCjr, Commodore, Apple, Macintosh) 262p. (Orig.). 1985. pap. text ed. 17.95X (ISBN 0-8077-2780-6). Tchrs Coll.

Chaya, Ruth K., jt. auth. see Miller, Joan M.

Chayanov, A. Journey of My Brother Alexsey to the Land of Peasant Utopia. 2nd ed. Poliak, Gregory, ed. Poluchina, V., tr. (Illus., Orig., Russian.). 1982. pap. 8.50 (ISBN 0-940294-00-1). Silver Age Pub.

Chayefsky, Paddy. Altered States. LC 77-11542. 1978. 12.45i (ISBN 0-06-010727-8, HarpT). Har-Row.

Chayen & Chayen, Bitensky. Cytochemical Bioassays: Techniques & Applications. (Basic & Clinical Endocrinology Ser.). 424p. 1983. 65.00 (ISBN 0-8247-7001-3). Dekker.

Chayen, Bitensky. Investigative Microtechniques in Medicine & Biology, Vol. 1. 416p. 1984. 75.00 (ISBN 0-8247-7139-7). Dekker.

Chayen, Bitensky, jt. auth. see Chayen.

Chayen, J. The Cytochemical Bioassay of Polypeptide Hormones. (Monographs on Endocrinology: Vol. 17). (Illus.). 230p. 1980. 51.00 (ISBN 0-387-10040-7). Springer-Verlag.

Chayen, Joseph, et al. Practical Histochemistry. LC 72-8596. 271p. 1973. 42.95 (ISBN 0-471-14950-0, Pub. by Wiley-Interscience). Wiley.

Chayes. International Legal Process (1968, 3 vols. 1985. Set. text ed. 31.00 (ISBN 0-316-13829-0); Volume 1. text ed. 15.00 (ISBN 0-316-13830-4); Volume 2. text ed. 15.00 (ISBN 0-316-13831-2); Documents Volume. text ed. 9.95 (ISBN 0-316-13832-0). Little.

Chayes, Abraham & Lewis, W. Bennett, eds. International Arrangements for Nuclear Fuel Reprocessing. LC 76-52961. 280p. 1976. prof ref 27.50 (ISBN 0-88410-052-9). Ballinger Pub.

Chayes, Abram. The Cuban Missile Crisis. (International Crisis & the Role of Law Ser.). 1974. pap. text ed. 5.95x (ISBN 0-19-825320-6). Oxford U Pr.

--An Imperial Judiciary: Fact or Myth? 42p. 1978. 3.75 (ISBN 0-8447-2145-X). Am Enterprise.

Chayes, Abram, et al. Vietnam Settlement: Why 1973 Not 1969? 1973. 15.25 (ISBN 0-8447-2038-0). Am Enterprise.

Chayes, Felix. Ratio Correlation: A Manual for Students of Petrology & Geochemistry. LC 71-146110. 1971. text ed. 7.00x (ISBN 0-226-10218-1); pap. text ed. 3.00x (ISBN 0-226-10220-3). U of Chicago Pr.

Chayet, Neil. Looking at the Law. 448p. 1981. 14.95 (ISBN 0-8317-5623-3, Rutledge Pr). Smith Pubs.

Chayevsky, Paddy see Cerf, Bennett.

Chaykin C. P. A. Review & Lakin, Leonard. Business Law. LC 84-248737. 426p. 1984. 30.00 (ISBN 0-8403-3415-X). Kendall-Hunt.

Chaykin, Lenore. Perks for the Average Shareholder. 200p. (Orig.). 1984. pap. 8.95 cancelled (ISBN 0-930369-08-4). Invest Info.

Chaykin, Sterling. Biochemistry Laboratory Techniques. LC 76-52458. (Illus.). 178p. 1977. Repr. of 1966 ed. lib. bdg. 11.50 (ISBN 0-88275-517-X). Krieger.

Chayton, H. J., ed. see Ferrero, Guglielmo.

Chayton, H. J., tr. see Ferrero, Guglielmo.

Chaytor, A. H. Letters to a Salmon Fisher's Sons. 316p. 1984. pap. 12.95 (ISBN 0-233-97604-3, Pub. by A Deutsch England). David & Charles.

Chaytor, A. H., ed. see Maitland, F. W.

Chaytor, H. J. Savaric De Mavleon. 1939. 20.00 (ISBN 0-8274-3326-3). R West.

Chaytor, H. J., tr. see Becker, C. H.

Chaytor, H. J., tr. see Ferrero, Guglielmo.

Chaytor, Henry J. From Script to Print. LC 74-16460. 1974. Repr. of 1966 ed. lib. bdg. 20.00 (ISBN 0-685-51256-8). Folcroft.

--History of Aragon & Catalonia. LC 73-92610. (BCL Ser.: No. II). (Illus.). 1969. Repr. of 1933 ed. 18.50 (ISBN 0-404-01479-8). AMS Pr.

--Troubadors. LC 74-102836. 1970. Repr. of 1912 ed. 19.00x (ISBN 0-8046-0751-6, Pub by Kennikat). Assoc Faculty Pr.

--The Troubadours of Dante: Being Selections from the Works of the Provencal Poets Quoted by Dante, with Introduction, Notes, Concise Grammar & Glossary. LC 79-178520. Repr. of 1902 ed. 27.50 (ISBN 0-404-56533-6). AMS Pr.

Chazal, Malcolm De see De Chazal, Malcolm.

Chazan, Barry. Contemporary Approaches to Moral Education: An Analysis of Alternative Theories. 176p. 1985. pap. text ed. 14.95x (ISBN 0-8077-2765-2). Tchrs Coll.

--Language of Jewish Education. LC 77-21638. 1978. 10.00 (ISBN 0-87677-147-9). Hartmore.

Chazan, Barry, ed. Studies in Jewish Education, Vol. 1. 239p. 1983. pap. text ed. 25.50x (Pub. by Magnes Israel). Humanities.

Chazan, Barry I. & Soltis, Jonas F., eds. Moral Education. LC 72-89127. Repr. of 1973 ed. 51.00 (ISBN 0-8357-9603-5, 2017764). Bks Demand UMI.

Chazan, M., et al. Helping Young Children with Behavior Difficulties. LC 83-80750. 320p. 1983. 18.00 (ISBN 0-8391-1914-3). Pro Ed.

Chazan, Maurice & Laing, Alice F. The Early Years. 128p. 1982. 32.00x (ISBN 0-335-10050-3, Pub. by Open Univ Pr); pap. 13.00x (ISBN 0-335-10052-X). Taylor & Francis.

Chazan, Maurice, ed. International Research in Early Childhood Education. 228p. 1978. 17.00 (ISBN 0-85633-143-0, Pub. by NFER Nelson UK). Taylor & Francis.

Chazan, Maurice, et al. Some of Our Children: The Discovery, Care & Education of Under-Fives with Special Needs. 272p. 1980. 35.00x (ISBN 0-7291-0197-5, Pub. by Open Bks England). State Mutual Bk.

Chazan, Naomi, jt. auth. see Pellow, Deborah.

Chazan, Naomi H. An Anatomy of Ghanaian Politics: Managing Political Recession, 1969-1982. LC 83-1405. (Special Study on Africa). 429p. 1982. softcover 29.00x (ISBN 0-86531-439-X). Westview.

Chazan, Robert. Church, State & Jew in the Middle Ages. new ed. Kozodoy, Neal, ed. LC 78-27221. (Library of Jewish Studies). 1979. pap. text ed. 9.95x (ISBN 0-87441-302-8). Behrman.

--Medieval Jewry in Northern France: A Poltical & Social History. LC 73-8129. (Johns Hopkins University Studies in Historical & Political Science: 91st; 2). pap. 63.00 (ISBN 0-317-20643-5, 2024132). Bks Demand UMI.

Chazan, Robert & Raphael, Marc L., eds. Modern Jewish History: A Source Reader. LC 74-9131. 395p. 1974. pap. text ed. 9.95x (ISBN 0-8052-0462-8). Schocken.

Chazanof, William. Joseph Ellicott & the Holland Land Company: The Opening of Western New York. 1979. pap. 9.95 (ISBN 0-8156-0161-1). Syracuse U Pr.

--Welch's Grape Juice. 1979. pap. 9.95x (ISBN 0-8156-2211-2). Syracuse U Pr.

Chazarain, J. Fourier Integral Operators & Partial Differential Equations. (Lecture Notes in Mmathematics: Vol. 459). 372p. 1975. pap. 21.00 (ISBN 0-387-07180-6). Springer-Verlag.

Chazarain, J. & Piriou, A. Introduction to the Theory of Linear Partial Differential Equations. (Studies in Mathematics & Its Applications: Vol. 14). 560p. 1982. 74.50 (ISBN 0-444-86452-0, North Holland). Elsevier.

Chaze, Elliott. Goodbye, Goliath. 192p. 1983. 11.95 (ISBN 0-684-17844-3, ScribT). Scribner.

--Little David: A Crime Novel. 192p. 1985. 12.95 (ISBN 0-684-18286-6, ScribT). Scribner.

--Mr. Yesterday. 184p. 1984. 12.95 (ISBN 0-684-18115-0, ScribT). Scribner.

Chazel, Francois. La Theorie Analytique de le Societe dans l'Oeuvre de Talcott Parsons Societe, Mouvements Sociaux et Ideologies. (Premiere Serie Etudes: No. 16). 1974. pap. 14.00x (ISBN 90-2797-306-7). Mouton.

Chazel, Francois, et al, eds. L' Analyse des Processus Sociaux. (Methods De la Sociologie: No. 3). (Illus.). 1970. pap. 14.00x (ISBN 90-2796-297-9). Mouton.

Chazov, E. & Saks, V., eds. Advances in Myocardiology, Vol. 4. 625p. 1982. 69.50 (ISBN 0-306-40877-5, Plenum Med Bk). Plenum Pub.

Chazov, E. & Smirnov, V., eds. Advances in Myocardiology, Vol. 3. 640p. 1982. 69.50 (ISBN 0-306-40876-7, Plenum Med Bk). Plenum Pub.

Chazov, E. I. Anticoagulants & Fibrinolytics. 1980. 44.50 (ISBN 0-8151-1649-7). Year Bk Med.

Chazov, E. I., ed. Cardiology in the U. S. S. R. 223p. 1982. pap. 8.95 (ISBN 0-8285-2748-2, Pub. by Mir Pubs USSR). Imported Pubns.

Chazov, E. I. & Smirnov, V. N., eds. Vessel Wall in Athero & Thrombogenesis: Studies in the U. S. S. R. (Illus.). 224p. 1982. pap. 56.90 (ISBN 0-387-11384-3). Springer-Verlag.

Chazov, E. I., et al, eds. Cardiology: An International Perspective. Proceedings of the Ninth World Congress of Cardiology Held in Moscow, USSR, June 20-26, 1982. 1422p. 1984. 195.00x (ISBN 0-306-41709-X, Plenum Pr). Plenum Pub.

Chazov, Y., et al. Nuclear War: The Medical & Biological Consequences. 239p. 1984. pap. 3.95 (ISBN 0-8285-2834-9, Pub. by Novosti Pr USSR). Imported Pubns.

Che, Wai-Kin. The Modern Chinese Family. LC 77-91415. 1979. perfect bdg. 11.00 (ISBN 0-88247-554-1). R & E Pubs.

Cheadle, J. A. A Donkey's Life: A Story for Children. LC 80-123421. iii, 88p. (Orig.). (gr. 2-6). 1979. pap. 3.50 (ISBN 0-9604244-0-7). Heahstan Pr.

Cheadle, John R. Basic Greek Vocabulary. (Gr.). 1969. text ed. 7.95 (ISBN 0-312-06790-9). St Martin.

Cheadle, Russell F., jt. auth. see Leventhal, Ruth.

Cheales, Alan B. Proverbial Folk-Lore. 1978. Repr. of 1875 ed. lib. bdg. 27.50 (ISBN 0-8495-0834-7). Arden Lib.

--Proverbial Folk-Lore. LC 76-56174. 1976. Repr. of 1875 ed. lib. bdg. 20.00 (ISBN 0-8414-3598-7). Folcroft.

Cheape, Charles W. Family Firm to Modern Multinational: Norton Company, a New England Enterprise. (Harvard Studies in Business History: No. 36). (Illus.). 426p. 1985. text ed. 25.00x (ISBN 0-674-29261-8). Harvard U Pr.

--Moving the Masses: Urban Public Transit in New York, Boston, & Philadelphia, 1880 to 1912. LC 79-15875. (Harvard Studies in Business History: No. 31). (Illus.). 1980. text ed. 18.50x (ISBN 0-674-58827-4). Harvard U Pr.

Cheasebro, Margaret. Puppet Scripts by the Month. 1985. pap. 4.95 (ISBN 0-8054-7524-9). Broadman.

Cheatham, Annie & Powell, Mary C. This Way Daybreak Comes: Womens Values & the Future. 1986. lib. bdg. 34.95 (ISBN 0-86571-070-8); pap. 12.95 (ISBN 0-86571-069-4). New Soc Pubs.

Cheatham, Dan. That You Might Have Life. 1979. pap. 5.25 (ISBN 0-89536-355-0). CSS of Ohio.

Cheatham, K. Follis. The Best Way Out. LC 81-47528. 168p. 1982. 9.95 (ISBN 0-15-206741-8, HJ). HarBraceJ.

--Bring Home the Ghost. LC 80-7981. 325p. (gr. 7 up). 1980. 8.95 (ISBN 0-15-212485-3, HJ). HarBraceJ.

Cheatham, Margaret. Peter Tuttle & the Great Mr. Paddy. LC 82-90586. 150p. 1983. 7.95 (ISBN 0-533-05505-9). Vantage.

Cheatham, Robert W. & Merrit, Robert G., Jr. California Real Estate Forms & Commentaries. (Marxist Regimes Ser.). 730p. 1984. 85.00 (ISBN 0-317-14888-5, Law & Business). HarBraceJ.

Cheatham, T. Richard & Erickson, Keith. The Police Officer's Guide to Better Communication. (PROCOM Ser.). 1983. pap. 9.95 (ISBN 0-673-15556-0). Scott F.

Cheatham, Val R. Cartooning for Kids Who Draw & Kids Who Don't Draw. (Illus.). (gr. 4-12). 1976. 2.95 (ISBN 0-914634-34-8). DOK Pubs.

--Christmas in Oz. 1983. pap. 4.95 (ISBN 0-686-39595-6). Eldridge Pub.

--Skits & Spoofs for Young Actors. (gr. 7-12). 1977. 10.95 (ISBN 0-8238-0220-5). Plays.

Cheatum, Billye A. Golf. 2nd ed. LC 74-6680. (Physical Activities Ser.). (Illus.). 117p. 1975. pap. text ed. 9.95 (ISBN 0-7216-2501-0); instr's manual 3.95 (ISBN 0-03-057216-9). SCP.

Cheatum, Billye A., jt. auth. see Ebert, Frances H.

Cheatwood, Derral. The Human Image: Sociology & Photography. 60p. 1976. pap. 5.00 (ISBN 0-87855-637-0). Transaction Bks.

Cheatwood, Kiarri T. Valley of the Anointers. LC 78-70230. 73p. 1979. pap. 4.00x perf. bound (ISBN 0-916418-19-7). Lotus.

Cheatwood, Kiarri T-H. Elegies for Patrice. LC 83-82771. 36p. 1984. pap. 3.00x (ISBN 0-916418-51-0). Lotus.

--Psalms of Redemption. LC 82-83855. 53p. 1983. pap. 4.00x perf. bnd. (ISBN 0-916418-41-3). Lotus.

Cheavens, Frank. Dandelion & Devil-Horse. 96p. 1974. 4.95 (ISBN 0-918954-13-4). Baylor Univ Pr.

Cheborateu, A. see Wiin-Nielsen, A.

Chebotarev, ed. see I.A.U. Symposium, No. 45, Leningrad, U.S.S.R., August 4-11, 1970.

Chebotarevskaia, Anastasiia, compiled by. O Fedore Sologube: Kritika, Stat'i i Zametki. 356p. 1983. 35.00 (ISBN 0-88233-849-8). Ardis Pubs.

Chebotayev, V. P., jt. auth. see Letokhov, V. S.

Chebyshev, Pafnuti L. Oeuvres: Collected Papers, 2 Vols. LC 61-17956. (Fr). 99.50 set (ISBN 0-8284-0157-8). Chelsea Pub.

--Theorie der Congruenzen. 2nd ed. LC 71-113123. xvii, 366p. (Ger.). 1972. text ed. 17.50 (ISBN 0-8284-0254-X). Chelsea Pub.

Checchi, Vincent, et al. Honduras: A Problem in Economic Development. LC 76-49911. 1977. Repr. of 1958 ed. lib. bdg. 22.50x (ISBN 0-8371-9393-1, CHHO). Greenwood.

Chechland, S. G. The Upas Tree- & After. 160p. 1982. 50.00x (ISBN 0-85261-168-4, Pub. by U of Glasgow Pr Scotland). State Mutual Bk.

Chechva & Vadym. Tiurmy, Tabory I Zaslannia. 150p. 1981. 10.00 (ISBN 0-686-73808-X). Slavia Lib.

Checinski, Michael. Poland: Communism, Nationalism, Anti-Semitism. 320p. 1982. text ed. 22.95x (ISBN 0-918294-18-5). Karz-Cohl Pub.

Check, William A., jt. auth. see Fettner, Ann G.

Checkland, O. & Lamb, M. Health Care As Social History: The Glasgow Case. (Illus.). 308p. 1982. 38.00 (ISBN 0-08-028444-2, R130). Pergamon.

Checkland, Olive. Philanthropy in Victorian Scotland. (Illus.). 1980. text ed. 52.50x (ISBN 0-85976-041-3). Humanities.

Checkland, Olive, jt. auth. see Checkland, Sydney.

Checkland, P. B. Systems Thinking, Systems Practice. LC 80-41381. 330p. 1981. 39.95 (ISBN 0-471-27911-0, Pub. by Wiley-Interscience). Wiley.

Checkland, Sydney. British Public Policy Seventeen Seventy-Six to Nineteen Thirty-Nine: An Economic & Social Perspective. LC 82-9552. 432p. 59.50 (ISBN 0-521-24596-6). Cambridge U Pr.

--British Public Policy, Seventeen Seventy-Six to Nineteen Thirty-Nine: An Economic, Social & Political Perspective. 440p. Date not set. pap. price not set (ISBN 0-521-27086-3). Cambridge U Pr.

Checkland, Sydney & Checkland, Olive. Industry & Ethos: Scotland Eighteen Thirty-Two to Nineteen Fourteen. (New History of Scotland Ser.). 192p. 1984. pap. text ed. 14.95 (ISBN 0-7131-6317-8). E Arnold.

Checkley, T. Finance for Farming: A Guide for the Lending Banker. 1982. 40.00x (ISBN 0-317-20363-0, Pub. by Inst Bankers UK). State Mutual Bk.

Checkover, V., jt. auth. see Averbakh, Y.

Checkoway, Barry, ed. Citizens & Health Care: Participation & Planning for Social Change. (Pergamon Policy Studies on Social Policy). (Illus.). 328p. 1981. 36.00 (ISBN 0-08-027192-8). Pergamon.

Checroun, Natalie. Pull up a Chair. LC 67-15704. (People & Their Useful Things Ser.). (Illus.). (gr. 5-10). 1967. PLB 3.95g (ISBN 0-8225-0265-8). Lerner Pubns.

Chedid, Andree. From Sleep Unbound. Spencer, Sharon, tr. from Fr. LC 82-22459. xvi, 141p. 1983. 18.95 (ISBN 0-8040-0399-8, 82-75430, Swallow); pap. 8.95 (ISBN 0-8040-0837-X, 82-76099, Swallow). Ohio U Pr.

--The Show-Man. Londre, Felicia, tr. from Fr. (Ubu Repertory Theater Publications Ser.: No. 8). 120p. (Orig.). 1984. pap. text ed. 6.25 (ISBN 0-913745-07-3, Dist. by Publishing Center for Cultural Resources). Ubu Repertory.

Chedid, L., ed. Immunostimulation. (Illus.). 236p. 1980. 26.00 (ISBN 0-387-10354-6). Springer-Verlag.

Chee, Anthony N. C. Anatomy & Physiology. A Dynamic Approach. 2nd ed. (Illus.). 287p. (Orig.). 1981. pap. text ed. 15.95x (ISBN 0-89641-064-1). American Pr.

Chee, Chan H. A Sensation of Independence: Singapore's David Marshall. (Illus.). 320p. 1985. pap. 18.95 (ISBN 0-19-582607-8). Oxford U Pr.

Chee, Siew N. Developmental Challenge in Malaysia. LC 69-104443. (Papers in International Studies: Southeast Asia Ser.: No. 3). pap. 20.00 (ISBN 0-317-09525-0, 2004377). Bks Demand UMI.

Chee, Stephen. Rural Local Government & Rural Development in Malaysia. (Special Series on Rural Local Government: No. 9). 112p. (Orig.). 1974. pap. text ed. 3.50 (ISBN 0-86731-095-2). RDC Ctr Intl Stud.

Cheeger, J. & Ebin, D. G. Comparison Theorems in Riemannian Geometry. LC 74-83725. (Mathematical Library: Vol. 9). 174p. 1975. 47.00 (ISBN 0-444-10764-9, North-Holland). Elsevier.

Cheek. Drawing Hands. (Grosset Art Instruction Ser.: Vol. 15). pap. 3.95 (ISBN 0-399-51035-4, G&D). Putnam Pub Group.

Cheek, David B. & LeCron, Leslie M. Clinical Hypnotherapy. LC 68-16304. 256p. 1968. 37.00 (ISBN 0-8089-0097-8, 790825). Grune.

Cheek, Donald B., ed. Human Growth: Body Composition, Cell Growth, Energy & Intelligence. LC 67-25087. (Illus.). Repr. of 1968 ed. 160.00 (ISBN 0-8357-9405-9, 2014531). Bks Demand UMI.

Cheek, Earl H., Jr. & Cheek, Martha C. Reading Instruction Through Content Teaching. 1983. text ed. 22.95 (ISBN 0-675-20026-1). Additional supplements may be obtained from publisher. Merrill.

Cheek, Earl H., Jr. & Collins, Martha D. Strategies for Reading Success. 256p. 1985. pap. text ed. 9.95 (ISBN 0-675-20227-2). Additional supplements may be obtained from publishers. Merrill.

Cheek, Earl H., Jr., jt. auth. see Collins-Cheek, Martha.

Cheek, Frances E. Stress Management for Correctional Officers & Their Families. Howard, Roberta L., et al, eds. (Illus.). 120p. 1984. pap. 10.00 (ISBN 0-942974-63-8). Am Correctional.

Cheek, G. Manufacturing Processes: Woods. 1975. 7.20 (ISBN 0-13-555656-2); pap. text ed. 8.84 (ISBN 0-13-555649-X). P-H.

Cheek, Helen N., et al, eds. Diagnostic & Prescriptive Mathematics: Issues, Ideas, & Insights. LC 84-60179. (Illus.). 88p. 1984. pap. 7.50x (ISBN 0-940466-09-0). Research Council.

Cheek, Logan. Zero-Base Budgeting Comes of Age. (Illus.). 1979. pap. 8.95 (ISBN 0-8144-7516-7). AMACOM.

Cheek, Logan M. Zero-Base Budgeting Comes of Age: What It Is & What It Takes to Make It Work. LC 77-4362. pap. 82.00 (ISBN 0-317-26733-7, 2023526). Bks Demand UMI.

Cheek, Logan M., jt. auth. see Austin, L. Allan.

Cheek, Martha C., jt. auth. see Cheek, Earl H., Jr.

Cheek, Philip & Pointon, Mair. History of the Sauk County Rifleman: Known As Company A, Sixth Wisconsin Veteran Volunteer Infantry, 1861-65. 240p. 1984. Repr. of 1909 ed. 26.50X (ISBN 0-913419-12-5). Butternut Pr.

Cheek, Roland. Montana's Bob Marshall Wilderness. (Illus.). 80p. 1982. 20.00 (ISBN 0-918981-00-X); pap. 8.95 (ISBN 0-918981-01-8). Skyline Pub.

Cheeke, Peter R. & Shull, L. R. Natural Toxicants in Feeds & Poisonous Plants. (Illus., Orig.). 1985. deluxe ed. 69.50 (ISBN 0-87055-482-4). AVI.

Cheeke, Peter R., et al. Rabbit Production. 5th ed. 250p. 1982. 12.50 (ISBN 0-8134-2222-1). Interstate.

Cheeks, James E. How to Compensate Executives. 3rd ed. LC 82-71349. 312p. 1982. 19.95 (ISBN 0-87094-341-3). Dow Jones-Irwin.

Cheema, G. Shabbir. Decentralization & Rural Development: The Case Study of Qi-Yi People's Commune in China. (Working Papers Ser.: No. 83-4). 36p. 1983. pap. text ed. 6.00 (ISBN 0-317-00885-4, CRD158, UNCRD). Unipub.

Cheema, G. Shabbir, ed. Reaching the Urban Poor: Project Implementation in Developing Countries. (Special Studies Ser.). 1985. pap. 22.50 (ISBN 0-8133-7129-5). Westview.

Cheema, G. Shabbir & Hosaka, Mitsuhiko, eds. Administration of Regional & Local Development: Studies on Coordination. 335p. 1982. pap. 25.00 (CRD151, UNCRD). Unipub.

Cheema, G. Shabbir & Rondinelli, Dennis A., eds. Decentralization & Developement: Policy Implementation in Developing Countries. 320p. 1983. 27.95 (ISBN 0-8039-1988-3). Sage.

Cheema, M. A., jt. ed. see Ghani, M. A.

Cheeney, R. F. Statistical Methods in Geology: For Field & Lab Decisions. (Illus.). 192p. 1983. text ed. 25.00x (ISBN 0-04-550029-0); pap. text ed. 11.95x (ISBN 0-04-550030-4). Allen Unwin.

Cheeseman, C. L. & Mitson, R. B., eds. Telemetric Studies of Vertebrates. (Symposia of the Zoological Society of London Ser.: No. 49). 1982. 59.00 (ISBN 0-12-613349-2). Acad Pr.

Cheeseman, G. W., jt. ed. see Bird, C. W.

Cheeseman, Henry R. The Legal & Regulatory Environment of Business. 800p. 1985. text ed. write for info. (ISBN 0-02-322260-3); solutions manual 8.00 (ISBN 0-02-322240-9). Macmillan.

Cheeseman, Peter, ed. Fight for Shelton Bar. 1981. pap. 6.95 (ISBN 0-413-38040-8, NO. 6469). Methuen Inc.

Cheesman, E. F., jt. auth. see Cole, Christopher.

Cheesman, G. L. Auxilia of the Roman Imperial Army. 1975. pap. 7.50 (ISBN 0-89005-096-1). Ares.

Cheesman, John, et al. The Grace of God in the Gospel. 1976. pap. 3.45 (ISBN 0-85151-153-8). Banner of Truth.

Cheesman, P. L. & Watts, P. E. Positive Behavior Management: A Manual for Teachers. 140p. 1985. 23.50 (ISBN 0-89397-227-4); pap. 14.50 (ISBN 0-89397-228-2). Nichols Pub.

Cheesman, Paul R. The World of the Book of Mormon. LC 84-80485. 216p. 1984. 11.95 (ISBN 0-88290-239-3). Horizon Utah.

Cheesman, Paul R. & Hutchins, Barbara W. Pathways to the Past. LC 83-83236. 210p. 1984. 7.95 (ISBN 0-88290-236-9). Horizon Utah.

Cheesman, Paul R., ed. see Porter, Larry.

Cheesman, R. E. Lake Tana & the Blue Nile: Abyssinian Quest. (Illus.). 400p. 1967. Repr. of 1936 ed. 42.50x (ISBN 0-7146-1641-9, BHA-01641, F Cass Co). Biblio Dist.

Cheesman, Willard. Kansas Night Wind. LC 84-91298. 80p. 1985. 6.95 (ISBN 0-533-06390-6). Vantage.

Chee Soo. The Tao of Long Life: The Chinese Art of Ch'ang Ming. 176p. 1983. pap. 7.95 (ISBN 0-85030-320-6). Newcastle Pub.

--Taoist Yoga: The Chinese Art of K'ai Men. 160p. 1983. pap. 7.95 (ISBN 0-85030-332-X). Newcastle Pub.

Cheetham, Erika. The Further Prophecies of Nostradamus Nineteen Eighty five & Beyond: 1985 & Beyond. 256p. (Orig.). 1985. pap. 6.95 (ISBN 0-399-51121-0, Perigee). Putnam Pub Group.

Cheetham, Erika, ed. The Prophecies of Nostradamus. 1975. pap. 6.95 (ISBN 0-399-50345-5, Perigee). Putnam Pub Group.

Cheetham, Erika, ed. & tr. The Prophecies of Nostradamus: The Man Who Saw Tomorrow. 448p. 1982. pap. 3.95 (ISBN 0-425-05772-0). Berkley Pub.

Cheetham, Francis. English Medieval Alabasters: With a Catalogue of the Collection in the Victoria & Albert Museum. (Illus.). 360p. 1984. 150.00 (ISBN 0-7148-8014-0, Pub. by Salem Hse Ltd). Merrimack Pub Cir.

Cheetham, Juliet, ed. Social Work & Ethnicity. (National Institute & Social Services Library: No. 43). 256p. 1982. text ed. 28.50x (ISBN 0-04-362050-7); pap. text ed. 12.95x (ISBN 0-04-362051-5). Allen Unwin.

--Social Work & Ethnicity. 1982. 30.00x (ISBN 0-317-05807-X, Pub. by Natl Inst Social Work). State Mutual Bk.

Cheetham, Loney & Prescott. Social & Community Work in a Multiracial Society. 340p. 1982. text ed. 26.50 (ISBN 0-06-318197-5, Pub. by Har-Row Ltd England); pap. text ed. 15.50 (ISBN 0-06-318198-3, Pub. by Har-Row Ltd England). Har-Row.

Cheetham, Nicholas. Mediaeval Greece. LC 80-13559. 352p. 1981. 36.00x (ISBN 0-300-02421-5). Yale U Pr.

Cheetham, Nicolas. Keepers of the Keys: A History of the Popes from St. Peter to John Paul II. LC 82-16950. (Illus.). 352p. 1983. 19.95 (ISBN 0-684-17863-X, ScribT). Scribner.

Cheetham, Samuel, jt. ed. see Smith, William.

Cheever, Daniel S., jt. auth. see Esman, Milton J.

Cheever, George B. The American Common-Place Book of Poetry. LC 74-15734. (Popular Culture in America Ser.). 406p. 1975. Repr. of 1831 ed. 32.00x (ISBN 0-405-06369-5). Ayer Co Pubs.

--God Against Slavery. facs. ed. LC 76-78995. (Black Heritage Library Collection Ser). 1857. 13.00 (ISBN 0-8369-8537-0). Ayer Co Pubs.

--God Against Slavery & the Freedom & Duty of the Pulpit to Rebuke It, As a Sin Against God. LC 79-82182. (Anti-Slavery Crusade in America Ser). 1969. Repr. of 1857 ed. 13.00 (ISBN 0-405-00621-7). Ayer Co Pubs.

--God Against Slavery, & the Freedom & Duty of the Pulpit to Rebuke It, As a Sin Against God. LC 70-97360. Repr. of 1857 ed. 19.75x (ISBN 0-8371-2446-8, CHQ&, Pub. by Negro U Pr). Greenwood.

--Guilt of Slavery & the Crime of Slaveholding. LC 69-16586. Repr. of 1860 ed. cancelled (ISBN 0-8371-1380-6, CHG&, Pub. by Negro U Pr). Greenwood.

--The Prose Writers of America: A Collection of Eloquent & Interesting Extracts from the Writings of American Authors. 1979. Repr. of 1853 ed. lib. bdg. 40.00 (ISBN 0-8495-0939-4). Arden Lib.

--The Prose Writers of America: A Collection of Eloquent & Interesting Extracts from the Writings of American Authors. 468p. 1982. Repr. of 1853 ed. lib. bdg. 75.00 (ISBN 0-89987-132-1). Darby Bks.

Cheever, John. Bullet Park. 1980. pap. 2.75 (ISBN 0-345-28590-5). Ballantine.

--Bullet Park. 1969. 13.95 (ISBN 0-394-41819-0). Knopf.

--The Enormous Radio. (Classic Short Stories). 32p. 1983. PLB 8.95 (ISBN 0-87191-959-1). Creative Ed.

--Falconer. 1978. pap. 2.75 (ISBN 0-345-28589-1). Ballantine.

--Falconer. 1977. 13.95 (ISBN 0-394-41071-8). Knopf.

--Oh What a Paradise It Seems. 1982. 10.00 (ISBN 0-394-51334-7). Knopf.

--Oh What A Paradise It Seems. (General Ser.). 1982. lib. bdg. 13.95 (ISBN 0-8161-3423-5, Large Print Bks). G K Hall.

--Oh What a Paradise It Seems. 112p. 1983. pap. 2.50 (ISBN 0-345-30883-2). Ballantine.

--Some People, Places, & Things That Will Not Appear in My Next Novel. LC 79-116947. (Short Story Index Reprint Ser). 1961. 15.00 (ISBN 0-8369-3449-0). Ayer Co Pubs.

--The Stories of John Cheever. 1980. pap. 3.50 (ISBN 0-345-28436-4). Ballantine.

--The Stories of John Cheever. LC 78-106. 1978. 20.00 (ISBN 0-394-50087-3). Knopf.

--The Stories of John Cheever. LC 81-40192. 704p. 1981. pap. 7.95 (ISBN 0-394-74799-2, Vin). Random.

--The Wapshot Scandal. 224p. 1983. pap. 2.95 (ISBN 0-345-29409-2). Ballantine.

Cheever, Mary. The Need for Chocolate: And Other Poems. LC 80-5390. 96p. 1980. 12.50 (ISBN 0-8128-2728-7). Stein & Day.

Cheever, Raymond C., ed. Accent on Living Reprint Series, No. 1. 26p. 1975. pap. text ed. 1.95 (ISBN 0-915708-01-9). Cheever Pub.

--Home Operated Business Opportunities for the Disabled. (Illus.). 1977. pap. 4.50 (ISBN 0-915708-04-3). Cheever Pub.

--Laugh with Accent. 2nd ed. (Illus.). 96p. 1984. pap. 4.95 (ISBN 0-915708-16-7). Cheever Pub.

Cheever, Raymond C. & Elmer, Charles D., eds. Bowel Management: A Manual of Ideas & Techniques. 32p. 1975. pap. 3.50 (ISBN 0-915708-02-7). Cheever Pub.

Cheever, Raymond C., ed. see Gregory, Martha F.

Cheever, Susan. The Cage. 1982. 11.95 (ISBN 0-395-32111-5). HM.

--The Cage. 1983. pap. 2.50 (ISBN 0-449-20339-5, Crest). Fawcett.

--A Handsome Man. 224p. 1982. pap. 2.50 (ISBN 0-449-24570-5, Crest). Fawcett.

--Home Before Dark. 1985. pap. 4.50 (ISBN 0-671-60370-1). PB.

--Home Before Dark: A Biographical Memoir of John Cheever. LC 84-9057. 1984. 15.95 (ISBN 0-395-35297-5). HM.

--Looking for Work. 256p. 1981. pap. 2.50 (ISBN 0-449-24389-3, Crest). Fawcett.

Cheevers, Joe & Kluft, Neil. Dirt & Trail Guide for Southern California. 150p. Date not set. price not set. Master Link.

Chef Cosmo Appleduck. Chef's Secrets. 8.95 (ISBN 0-911505-05-9). Lifecraft.

--Kitchen Fun Cookbook, Vol. 1. 13.95 (ISBN 0-911505-13-X). Lifecraft.

--My Cookbook: Do-It-Yourself Cookbook. (Kitchen Fun). 75p. 1982. 6.95 (ISBN 0-911505-06-7). Lifecraft.

Chef, R., ed. Real Time Ultrasound in Perinatal Medicine. (Contributions to Gynecology & Obstetrics: Vol. 6). (Illus.). 1979. pap. 33.75 (ISBN 3-8055-2976-7). S Karger.

Chefdor, Monique. Blaise Cendrars. (World Authors Ser.). 1980. 14.50 (ISBN 0-8057-6413-5, Twayne). G K Hall.

Chefdor, Monique, et al, eds. Modernism: Challenges & Perspectives. LC 84-21932. (Illus.). 296p. 1985. 20.95x (ISBN 0-252-01207-0). U of Ill Pr.

Cheffers, John T. & Evual, Thomas. Introduction to Physical Education: Concepts of Human Movement. (Illus.). 1978. text ed. 28.95 (ISBN 0-13-493031-2). P-H.

Chegodayev, A. Bockwell Kent. 1976. 25.00x (ISBN 0-317-14225-9, Pub. by Collet's). State Mutual Bk.

Che Guevara see also Guevara, Ernesto.

Chegwan. T'ien-t'ai Buddhism: An Outline of the Fourfold Teachings. Chappell, David W. & Ichishima, Masao, eds. 191p. 1984. text ed. 25.00x (ISBN 0-8248-0953-X). UH Pr.

Cheifetz, et al. Logic & Set Theory: With an Introduction to Computer Programming. 2nd ed. LC 76-126359. 1983. 19.75x (ISBN 0-916060-05-5). Math Alternatives.

Cheifetz, Philip, ed. see DeSanto, et al.

Cheigh, Jhoong S., et al. Manual of Clinical Nephrology. Stenzel, Kurt H. & Rubin, Albert L., eds. 470p. 1981. 65.00 (ISBN 90-247-2397-3, Pub. by Martinus Nijhoff Netherlands). Kluwer Academic.

Cheilik, Michael. Ancient History: From Its Beginnings to the Fall of Rome. LC 79-76467. (Orig.). 1969. pap. 5.00 (ISBN 0-06-460001-7, CO 1, COS). B&N NY.

Chein, Orin. Moufang Loops of Small Order. LC 77-25155. (Memoirs Ser.: No. 197). 131p. 1978. pap. 14.00 (ISBN 0-8218-2197-0, MEMO197). Am Math.

Chein, Orin, jt. auth. see Averbach, Bonnie.

Chein-Pai Han, jt. auth. see Bancroft.

Cheiro. Cheiro's Book of Numbers. LC 64-11269. (Illus., Orig.). 1964. pap. 2.50 (ISBN 0-668-01170-X, 1169). Arco.

--Cheiro's Language of the Hand. LC 62-16458. (Illus.). 1968. pap. 1.95 (ISBN 0-668-01780-5). Arco.

--Cheiro's Palmistry for All. LC 64-14518. (Illus., Orig.). 1968. pap. 2.25 (ISBN 0-668-01194-7). Arco.

--Cheiro's World Predictions. 240p. 1981. pap. 12.00 (ISBN 0-89540-088-X, SB-088). Sun Pub.

Cheiro, pseud. Mysteries & Romances of the World's Greatest Occultists. 1972. 7.95 (ISBN 0-8216-0121-0). Univ Bks.

Chejne, A. Succession to the Rule in Islam. 1960. 4.60x (ISBN 0-87902-158-6). Orientalia.

Chejne, A. G. Ibn Hazm. 24.95 (ISBN 0-686-83558-1); pap. 15.95. Kazi Pubns.

Chejne, Anver. Ibn Hazm al Undalasi. 320p. (Orig.). 1982. 24.95x (ISBN 0-935782-03-6); pap. 15.95x (ISBN 0-935782-04-4). Kazi Pubns.

Chejne, Anwar. Succession to the Rule in Muslim. 154p. (Orig.). 1981. pap. 4.50 (ISBN 0-88004-001-7). Sunwise Turn.

Chejne, Anwar G. Islam & the West: The Moriscos. LC 82-703. 368p. 1983. 44.50x (ISBN 0-87395-603-6); pap. 17.95x (ISBN 0-87395-606-0). State U NY Pr.

--Muslim Spain: Its History & Culture. LC 73-87254. (Illus.). 616p. 1974. 29.50x (ISBN 0-8166-0688-9). U of Minn Pr.

Chek-Chart. Car & Light Truck Diesel Engine Service Manual. (Automotive Service Ser.). 128p. (gr. 12). 1983. pap. text ed. 9.95x (ISBN 0-88098-016-8); 3.50x (ISBN 0-88098-046-X). H M Gousha.

--Complete Automotive Service Library. (Automotive Service Ser.). (Illus.). 665p. (gr. 12). 1983. pap. text ed. 52.55 (ISBN 0-88098-053-2). H M Gousha.

Chek-Chart, ed. Automotive Preview 1985. (Illus.). 16p. 1984. pap. text ed. 2.25x (ISBN 0-88098-025-7). H M Gousha.

Chek-Chart Engineers. Auto Mechanics Refresher Course. wkbk. 42.00 (ISBN 0-88098-078-8). H M Gousha.

Chek Chart Staff. Car Care Guide, 1985. Fennema, Roger L., ed. (Illus.). 432p. 1985. pap. 39.75x wkbk. (ISBN 0-88098-058-3). H M Gousha.

--Car Service Manual. rev. ed. Fennema, Roger & Phelps, Jennifer, eds. (Apprentice Mechanics Ser.). (Illus.). 144p. 1984. pap. 9.15x wkbk. (ISBN 0-88098-051-6); quiz 3.45x (ISBN 0-317-18170-X). H M Gousha.

Chek-Chart Staff. Master Lubrication Handbook, 1985. (Illus.). 1000p. wkbk. 90.00 (ISBN 0-88098-059-1); Supplement 85.45 (ISBN 0-88098-075-3). H M Gousha.

Che Kan Leong. Children with Specific Reading Disability. (Modern Approaches to the Diagnosis & Instruction of Multi-Handicapped Children Ser.). 160p. Date not set. text ed. price not set (Pub. by Swets & Zeitlinger Netherlands). Hogrefe Intl.

Cheke, Marcus. Carlota Joaquina, Queen of Portugal. facsimile ed. LC 70-94266. (Select Bibliographies Reprint Ser). 1947. 19.00 (ISBN 0-8369-5040-2). Ayer Co Pubs.

--Dictator of Portugal: A Life of the Marquis of Pombal, 1699-1782. facsimile ed. LC 74-94267. (Select Bibliographies Reprint Ser). 1938. 24.25 (ISBN 0-8369-5041-0). Ayer Co Pubs.

Chekhanin, E. The Soviet Political System Under Developed Socialism. 1978. 14.95x (ISBN 0-8464-0874-0). Beekman Pubs.

Chekhov. Tales of Chekhov, 13 vols. 1983. Set. pap. 8.50. Vol.1 (ISBN 0-88001-038-X). Vol.2 (ISBN 0-88001-039-8). Ecco Pr.

Chekhov, A. P. Cherry Orchard. Hitchcock, D. R, ed. (Library of Russian Classics). 130p. pap. text ed. 9.95 (ISBN 0-904679-13-6). Basil Blackwell.

--Lady with the Dog. Waddington, Patrick, ed. (Library of Russian Classics). (Illus.). 80p. pap. text ed. 9.95x (ISBN 0-631-14391-2). Basil Blackwell.

--Uncle Vania. Magarshak, David, ed. (Library of Russian Classics). 104p. pap. text ed. 9.95x (ISBN 0-631-14389-0). Basil Blackwell.

--The Wedding. Murphy, A. B, ed. (Library of Russian Classics). 68p. pap. text ed. 9.95x (ISBN 0-900186-48-8). Basil Blackwell.

Chekhov, Anton. Anton Chekhov: Four Plays. Magarshack, David, tr. from Rus. Incl. Seagull; Uncle Vanya; Three Sisters; Cherry Orchard. (Mermaid Dramabook Ser.). 256p. (Orig.). 1969. pap. 7.95 (ISBN 0-8090-0743-6). Hill & Wang.

--Anton Chekhov's Plays. Bristow, Eugene K., ed. (Norton Critical Edition Ser.). pap. 7.95x, 1977 (ISBN 0-393-09163-5). Norton.

--Anton Chekhov's Short Stories. Matlaw, Ralph E., ed. Garnett, Constance, et al, trs. (Critical Edition). 1979. pap. text ed. 6.95x (ISBN 0-393-09002-7). Norton.

--Anton Tchehov: Literary & Theatrical Reminiscences. Koteliansky, S. S., tr. LC 65-16231. 1927. 20.00 (ISBN 0-685-06946-X, Pub. by Blom). Ayer Co Pubs.

--Bear. (Adapted from the Libretta by Paul Dehn & William Walton). 1967. 4.75 (ISBN 0-19-338442-6). Oxford U Pr.

--Best Plays. Young, Stark, tr. LC 56-8837. 6.95 (ISBN 0-394-60459-8). Modern Lib.

--Best Plays. Young, Stark, tr. LC 56-8837. 1966. pap. 3.95 (Mod LibC). Modern Lib.

--The Bishop & Other Stories. Garnett, Constance, tr. from Rus. (The Tales of Chekhov Ser.). 302p. 1985. pap. 8.50 (ISBN 0-88001-054-1). Ecco Pr.

--The Brute & Other Farces: Seven Short Plays. Bentley, Eric, ed. Hoffman, Theodore, tr. from Rus. 128p. 1985. 14.95 (ISBN 0-87910-224-1); pap. 5.95 (ISBN 0-87910-223-3). Limelight Edns.

--Chekhov Five Major Plays. Hingley, Ronald, tr. from Russian. (Bantam Classics Ser.). 368p. 1982. pap. 2.95 (ISBN 0-553-21211-7). Bantam.

--Chekhov: Selected Stories. Dunnigan, Ann, tr. pap. 2.95 (ISBN 0-451-51847-0, CE1847, Sig Classics). NAL.

--Chekhov: The Early Stories 1883-88. Miles, Patrick & Pitcher, Harvey, trs. (Illus.). 224p. 1983. 14.95 (ISBN 0-02-524620-8). Macmillan.

--Chekhov: The Early Stories: 1883-88. Miles, Patrick & Pitcher, Harvey, trs. 204p. 1984. pap. 5.95 (ISBN 0-02-049390-8, Collier). Macmillan.

--Chekhov, the Major Plays: Ivanov, Sea Gull, Uncle Vanya, Three Sisters, Cherry Orchard. Dunnigan, Ann, tr. 1964. pap. 2.95 (ISBN 0-451-51767-9, CL1767, Sig Classics). NAL.

--Cherry Orchard. 1965. pap. 0.95 (ISBN 0-380-01093-3, 36848, Bard). Avon.

--The Cherry Orchard. Frayn, Michael, tr. from Rus. 67p. 1978. pap. 6.95 (ISBN 0-413-39340-2, NO.2989). Methuen Inc.

--Cherry Orchard. Gielgud, John, ed. (Orig.). 1963. pap. 3.50x (ISBN 0-87830-510-6). Theatre Arts.

--The Chorus Girl & Other Stories. Garnett, Constance, tr. from Rus. (The Tales of Chekhov Ser.). 301p. 1985. pap. 8.50 (ISBN 0-88001-055-X). Ecco Pr.

--A Day in the Country. Redpath, Ann, ed. (Classic Short Stories Ser.). (Illus.). 32p. (gr. 7 up). 1985. PLB 8.95 (ISBN 0-88682-004-9). Creative Ed.

--The Duel & Other Stories. Wilks, Ronald, tr. 256p. 1984. pap. 4.95 (ISBN 0-14-044415-7). Penguin.

--A Father. Goldberg, Isaac, ed. Long, R. E., tr. (International Pocket Library). pap. 3.00 (ISBN 0-8283-1450-0). Branden Pub Co.

--Five Major Plays. Hingley, Ronald, tr. Incl. The Cherry Orchard; Ivanov; The Seagull; Three Sisters; Uncle Vanya. 1977. pap. 4.95 (ISBN 0-19-502250-5, GB 466). Oxford U Pr.

--Image of Chekhov: Forty Stories in the Order in Which They Were Written. Payne, Robert, ed. 1963. 15.00 (ISBN 0-394-43009-3). Knopf.

--The Island: A Journey to Sakhalin. Terpak, Luba & Terpak, Michael, trs. from Russian. LC 76-56795. (Illus.). 1977. Repr. of 1967 ed. lib. bdg. 26.50x (ISBN 0-8371-9430-X, CHTI). Greenwood.

--Kiss & Other Stories. 1982. pap. 3.95 (ISBN 0-14-044336-3). Penguin.

--Lady with Lapdog & Other Stories. Magarshack, David, tr. (Classics Ser.). (Orig.). 1964. pap. 3.95 (ISBN 0-14-044143-3). Penguin.

--The Lady with the Dog & Other Stories. Garnett, Constance, tr. from Rus. LC 84-6121. (The Tales of Chekhov Ser.: Vol. 3). 300p. 1984. pap. 8.50 (ISBN 0-88001-050-9). Ecco Pr.

--Late-Blooming Flowers & Other Stories. 272p. 1984. pap. 8.95 (ISBN 0-88184-029-7). Carroll & Graf.

--The Letters of Anton Chekhov. Yarmolinsky, Avrahm, ed. 480p. 1973. 20.00 (ISBN 0-670-42596-6). Viking.

--Letters of Anton Tchehov to Olga Knipper. Garnett, Constance, tr. LC 65-16232. 1925. 24.00 (ISBN 0-405-08354-8, Blom Pubns). Ayer Co Pubs.

--Letters on the Short Story. 59.95 (ISBN 0-8490-0513-2). Gordon Pr.

--Letters on the Short Story, the Drama & Other Literary Topics. Friedland, Louis S., ed. 346p. 1982. Repr. of 1924 ed. lib. bdg. 35.00 (ISBN 0-89987-141-0). Darby Bks.

--Life & Letters of Anton Chekhov. Koteliansky, S. S. & Tomlinson, Phillip, trs. LC 65-16230. (Illus.). 1925. 26.50 (ISBN 0-405-08355-6, Pub. by Blom). Ayer Co Pubs.

--Oeuvres: Recits (1887-1892, Vol. 2. 1032p. 33.95 (ISBN 0-686-56580-0). French & Eur.

--Oeuvres: Recits (1892-1903, Vol. 3. 1048p. 33.95 (ISBN 0-686-56581-9). French & Eur.

--The Oxford Chekhov. Hingley, Ronald, ed. & tr. Incl. Vol. 1. Short Plays. 1968. 34.95x (ISBN 0-19-211349-6); Vol. 2. Platonov, Ivanov, the Seagull. 1967. 34.95x (ISBN 0-19-211347-X); Vol. 5. Stories, 1889-1891. 1970. 34.95x (ISBN 0-19-211353-4); Vol. 6. Stories, 1892-1893. 1971. 34.95x (ISBN 0-19-211363-1); Vol. 8. Stories, 1895-1897. 1965. 34.95x (ISBN 0-19-211340-2). Oxford U Pr.

--The Oxford Chekhov, Vol. 3: Uncle Vanya, Three Sisters, The Cherry Orchard, the Wood-Demon. Hingley, Ronald, tr. 1964. 34.95x (ISBN 0-19-211339-9). Oxford U Pr.

--The Oxford Chekhov, Vol. 4: Stories, 1888-1889. Hingley, Ronald, tr. 1980. 39.50x (ISBN 0-19-211389-5). Oxford U Pr.

--Oxford Chekhov, Vol. 7: Stories 1893-1895. Hingley, Ronald, ed. (Oxford Chekhov Ser.). 1978. 34.95x (ISBN 0-19-211388-7). Oxford U Pr.

--The Oxford Chekhov, Vol. 9: Stories 1898 - 1904. Hingley, Ronald, ed. 1975. 34.95x (ISBN 0-19-211383-6). Oxford U Pr.

--The Party & Other Stories. Garnett, Constance, tr. from Rus. LC 84-6122. (The Tales of Chekhov Ser.: Vol. 4). 300p. 1984. pap. 8.50 (ISBN 0-88001-051-7). Ecco Pr.

--Plays. Fen, Elisaveta, tr. Incl. Ivanov; Seagull; Uncle Vanya; Three Sisters; Cherry Orchard; Bear; The Marriage Proposal; Jubilee. (Classics Ser.). 1959. pap. 3.95 (ISBN 0-14-044096-8). Penguin.

--The Portable Chekhov. Yarmolinsky, Avrahm, ed. (Viking Portable Library: P 35). 1977. pap. 7.95 (ISBN 0-14-015035-8). Penguin.

--The Russian Master & Other Stories. Hingley, Ronald, tr. from Rus. (World's Classics Ser.). 1984. pap. 3.95 (ISBN 0-19-281680-2). Oxford U Pr.

--Sea Gull. Eisemann, Fred & Murphy, Oliver F., trs. Bd. with Tragedian in Spite of Himself. (Orig.). pap. 3.00 (ISBN 0-8283-1454-3). Branden Pub Co.

--The Selected Letters of Anton Chekhov. Hellman, Lillian, ed. Lederer, Sidonie K., tr. from Rus. 366p. 1955. 16.95 (ISBN 0-374-25800-7); pap. 7.95, 1984 (ISBN 0-374-51838-6). FS&G.

--Selected Works, 2 vols. 485p. 1979. Set. 13.50 (ISBN 0-8285-1931-5, Pub. by Progress Pubs USSR). Imported Pubns.

--Seven Short Novels. Makanowitzky, Barbara, tr. from Rus. 1971. pap. 8.95 (ISBN 0-393-00552-6, Norton Lib). Norton.

--Seven Short Stories. Hingley, Ronald, tr. from Rus. & intro. by. (Oxford Paperbacks Ser). 1974. 6.95x (ISBN 0-19-281159-2). Oxford U Pr.

--Sinner from Toledo & Other Stories. Hinchliffe, Arnold, tr. LC 70-147269. 168p. 1972. 14.50 (ISBN 0-8386-7890-4). Fairleigh Dickinson.

--Three Sisters. Frayn, Michael, tr. (Theatre Classics Ser.). 1983. pap. 6.95 (ISBN 0-413-52450-7, NO.3940). Methuen Inc.

--Vishnevi Saad: The Cherry Orchard. 175p. (Rus.). 1946. text ed. 20.00 (ISBN 0-8236-0720-8). Intl Univs Pr.

--Ward Six & Other Short Novels. Dunnigan, Ann, tr. (Orig.). 1965. pap. 3.95 (ISBN 0-451-51895-0, Sig Classics). NAL.

--The Wife & Other Stories. Garnett, Constance, tr. from Rus. (The Tales of Chekhov Ser.). 200p. 1985. pap. 8.50 (ISBN 0-88001-052-5). Ecco Pr.

--Wild Honey. Frayn, Michael, tr. 1984. pap. 6.95 (ISBN 0-413-55160-1, 9045, Pub. by Eyre Methuen, England). Methuen Inc.

--The Witch & Other Stories. Garnett, Constance, tr. from Rus. (The Tales of Chekhov Ser.). 200p. 1985. pap. 8.50 (ISBN 0-88001-053-3). Ecco Pr.

Chekhov, Anton see Caputi, Anthony.

Chekhov, Anton see Goldberg, Isaac.

Chekhov, Anton see Laurel Editions Editors.

Chekhov, Anton see Weiss, Samuel A.

Chekhov, Anton P. Anton Tchehov's Letters on the Short Story, the Drama, & Other Literary Topics. Friedland, Louis S., ed. LC 64-14695. 1965. 26.50 (ISBN 0-405-08352-1, Blom Pubns). Ayer Co Pubs.

--Best Known Works, Vol. 1. LC 72-5899. (Short Story Index Reprint Ser). Repr. of 1929 ed. 32.75 (ISBN 0-8369-4198-5). Ayer Co Pubs.

--Black Monk, & Other Stories. Long, R. E., tr. LC 79-121527. (Short Story Index Reprint Ser). 1903. 17.00 (ISBN 0-8369-3483-0). Ayer Co Pubs.

--Grasshopper, & Other Stories. facsimile ed. Chamot, A. E., tr. from Rus. LC 72-37538. (Short Story Index Reprint Ser). Repr. of 1926 ed. 16.00 (ISBN 0-8369-4097-0). Ayer Co Pubs.

--The Kiss, & Other Stories. facsimile ed. Long, R. E., tr. LC 76-37539. (Short Story Index Reprint Ser.). Repr. of 1915 ed. 20.00 (ISBN 0-8369-4098-9). Ayer Co Pubs.

--My Life, & Other Stories. facsimile ed. Koteliansky, S. S. & Cannan, Gilbert, trs. LC 77-169544. (Short Story Index Reprint Ser.). Repr. of 1920 ed. 16.00 (ISBN 0-8369-4005-9). Ayer Co Pubs.

--Nine Humorous Tales. facsimile ed. LC 76-106262. (Short Story Index Reprint Ser.). 1918. 13.00 (ISBN 0-8369-3299-4). Ayer Co Pubs.

--Rothschild's Fiddle, & Other Stories. LC 72-121528. (Short Story Index Reprint Ser). 1917. 16.00 (ISBN 0-8369-3484-9). Ayer Co Pubs.

--Russian Silhouettes. facs. ed. Fell, Marian, tr. LC 72-142260. (Short Story Index Reprint Ser). 1915. 21.00 (ISBN 0-8369-3744-9). Ayer Co Pubs.

--Steppe & Other Stories. facsimile ed. Kaye, Adeline L., tr. LC 70-106263. (Short Story Index Reprint Ser.). 1915. 16.00 (ISBN 0-8369-3300-1). Ayer Co Pubs.

--Three Sisters. Davidson, J. M. C., ed. (Library of Russian Classics). 120p. Date not set. pap. text ed. 9.95x (ISBN 0-900186-46-1). Basil Blackwell.

--Three Stories. Le Fleming, L. S., ed. (Library of Russian Classics). 146p. pap. text ed. 9.95x (ISBN 0-900186-09-7). Basil Blackwell.

--Uncle Vanya: Scenes from Country Life in Four Acts. LC 75-75974. (Minnesota Drama Editions Ser.: 5). pap. 23.00 (ISBN 0-317-27952-1, 2055849). Bks Demand UMI.

Chekhov, Michael. Lessons for the Professional Actor. Hurst du Prey, Deirdre, ed. (Orig.). 1985. 19.95 (ISBN 0-317-18493-8); pap. 8.95 (ISBN 0-317-18494-6). Performing Arts.

--To the Actor. LC 52-11680. (Illus.). 1953. 12.45i (ISBN 0-06-010755-3, HarpT). Har-Row.

--To the Director & Playwright. Leonard, Charles, compiled by. (Illus.). 1977. Repr. of 1963 ed. lib. bdg. 27.50x (ISBN 0-8371-9615-9, CHTD). Greenwood.

--To the Director & Playwright. Leonard, Charles, ed. LC 84-9676. (Illus.). 340p. 1984. pap. 9.95 (ISBN 0-87910-018-4). Limelight Edns.

Chekhov, Micheal. To the Actor. (Illus.). 208p. 1985. pap. 5.72i (ISBN 0-06-463707-7, EH 707). B&N NY.

Chekhover, V., jt. auth. see Averbakh, Yuri.

Chekki, D. A. Sociology of Contemporary India. 1978. 12.50x (ISBN 0-8364-0245-6). South Asia Bks.

Chekki, Dan A., ed. Community Development: Theory & Method of Planned Change. LC 79-907884. xiv, 258p. 1980. text ed. 27.50x (ISBN 0-7069-0819-8, Pub. by Vikas India). Advent NY.

--Participatory Democracy in Action: International Profiles of Community Development. xvi, 306p. 1980. text ed. 27.50x (ISBN 0-7069-0923-2, Pub. by Vikas India). Advent NY.

Chekki, Dan A., ed. see Fritz, Jan M.

Chekki, Danesh A. The Social System & Culture of Modern India: A Research Bibliography. LC 74-19226. (Reference Library of Social Science: No. 1). 873p. 1974. lib. bdg. 103.00 (ISBN 0-8240-1056-6). Garland Pub.

Chekov, A. Kashtanka. 61p. 2.95 (ISBN 0-8285-1171-3, Pub. by Progress Pubs USSR). Imported Pubns.

Chekov, Anton. The Plays of Anton Chekov. 17.95 (ISBN 0-89190-432-8, Pub. by Am Repr). Amereon Ltd.

--Three Sisters. Wilson, Lanford, tr. 1984. pap. 3.35x (ISBN 0-317-17221-2). Dramatists Play.

Chekrezi, Constantine A. Albania, Past & Present. LC 75-135798. (Eastern Europe Collection Ser). 1970-71. Repr. of 1919 ed. 16.00 (ISBN 0-405-02740-0). Ayer Co Pubs.

Cheldelin, Larry V. Your Baby's Secret World: Four Phases for Effective Parenting (A Professional & Practical Guide) Brown, J., ed. (Illus., Orig.). 1983. pap. 4.95 (ISBN 0-8283-1850-6). Branden Pub Co.

Chelebi, Ewliya. Turkish Instruments of Music in the Seventeenth Century. Farmer, Henry G., ed. LC 76-42034. 1977. Repr. of 1937 ed. lib. bdg. 12.50 (ISBN 0-89341-068-3). Longwood Pub Group.

Chelf, Carl P. Congress in the American System. LC 77-1084. 272p. 1978. text ed. 22.95x (ISBN 0-88229-210-2); pap. 10.95x (ISBN 0-88229-517-9). Nelson-Hall.

--Public Policymaking in America: Difficult Choices, Limited Solutions. 1981. text ed. 21.70x (ISBN 0-673-16276-1). Scott F.

Cheli, R. & Molinari, F. Drug Induced Gastric Lesions. (Illus.). 91p. 1981. text ed. 23.00 (ISBN 88-212-0778-1, Pub. by Piccin Italy). J K Burgess.

Cheli, R. & Schelotto, G. Psychological Involvement in Digestive Endoscopy. (Illus.). 85p. 1981. pap. text ed. 4.50 (ISBN 88-212-0893-1, Pub. by Piccin Italy). J K Burgess.

Chelin, Jean. The Hands of Fate. LC 84-90014. 57p. 1985. 7.95 (ISBN 0-317-17448-7). Vantage.

Chelius, Carl R. & Frentz, Henry J., eds. Basic Meterology Exercise Manual. (Illus.). 1984. 11.95 (ISBN 0-8403-3340-4). Kendall-Hunt.

Chelius, James R. Workplace Safety & Health. 1977. pap. 4.25 (ISBN 0-8447-3274-5). Am Enterprise.

Chelkowski, A. Dielectric Physics. (Studies in Physical & Theoretical Chemistry: Vol. 9). 396p. 1980. 74.50 (ISBN 0-444-99766-0). Elsevier.

Chelkowski, Peter J. Mirror of the Invisible World: Tales from the Khamseh of Nizami. LC 75-28305. (Illus.). 128p. 1975. 15.00 (ISBN 0-87099-142-6). Metro Mus Art.

Chell, Elizabeth. Participation & Organization: A Social Psychological Approach. 320p. 1985. 22.00 (ISBN 0-8052-3950-2). Schocken.

Chell, G. G., ed. Developments in Fracture Mechanics, Vols. 1 & 2. Vol. 1, 1979. 52.00 (ISBN 0-85334-858-8, Pub. by Elsevier Applied Sci England); Vol. 2, 1981. 57.50 (ISBN 0-85334-973-8, Pub. by Elsevier Applied Sci England). Elsevier.

Chellappa, Rama & Sawchuk, Alexander. Tutorial: Digital Image Processing & Analysis, 2 vols. Incl. Vol. 2. Digital Image Analysis. 66.00 (ISBN 0-8186-0666-5); prepub. 32.95 (ISBN 0-317-31786-5); Vol. 1. Digital Image Processing. Set. 132.00 (ISBN 0-317-31784-9); prepub. 72.00 (ISBN 0-317-31785-7). IEEE Comp Soc.

Chellas, Brian F. Modal Logic. LC 76-47197. 1980. 57.50 (ISBN 0-521-22476-4); pap. 16.95x (ISBN 0-521-29515-7). Cambridge U Pr.

Chellis, Marcia. Living with the Kennedys: The Joan Kennedy Story. 320p. 1985. 17.95 (ISBN 0-671-50152-6). S&S.

Chellis, Robert D., et al, eds. Congregate Housing for Older People: A Solution for the 1980's. LC 81-47983. 240p. 1982. 27.50x (ISBN 0-669-05210-8). Lexington Bks.

Chelminski, Rudolph. The French at Table. (Illus.). 276p. 1985. 15.95 (ISBN 0-688-04459-X). Morrow.

Chelminski, Rudolph, jt. auth. see Ruo-Wang, Bao.

Chelune, Gordon J., jt. ed. see McReynolds, Paul.

Chelune, Gordon J., et al. Self-Disclosure: Origins, Patterns, & Implications of Openness in Interpersonal Relationships. LC 79-88766. (Social & Behavioral Science Ser.). 1979. text ed. 35.00x (ISBN 0-87589-433-X). Jossey-Bass.

Chelvam, Reginald T. Einstein Was Wrong: Or the Scroll Theory of Cosmology & of Matter. LC 82-71689. (Illus.). 268p. (Orig.). 1982. pap. 19.95 (ISBN 0-943796-00-8). Penso Pubns.

Chem Systems International Ltd. Reducing Pollution from Selected Energy Transformation Sources. 230p. 1976. 21.00x (ISBN 0-86010-036-7, Pub. by Graham & Trotman England). State Mutual Bk.

Chemerinsky, Erwin, et al. The Complete Handbook of Issues on World Resources. 1975. pap. text ed. 4.00 (ISBN 0-8442-5216-6). Natl Textbk.

Chemers, Martin M., jt. auth. see Altman, Irwin.

Chemers, Martin M., jt. auth. see Fiedler, Fred E.

Chemey, David R., ed. see Cheney, David R. & Hunt, Leigh.

Chemezie, Amuzie. Black Culture: Theory & Practice. 136p. (Orig.). 1984. pap. 9.50x (ISBN 0-933144-01-6). Keeble Pr.

Chemi, James M., et al. The Yucatan Affair: The Works of Raoul Ch. De Thuin, Philatelic Counterfeiter. (Illus.). 523p. Repr. 20.00 (ISBN 0-318-12929-9). Am Philatelic Society.

Chemical & Allied Products Industry Training Board, ed. Instrument Manual: A Training Guide For Instrument Personnel. (Illus.). 650p. 1983. pap. 175.00x spiral bdg. (ISBN 0-89563-062-1). Intl Ideas.

Chemical & Petroleum Industries Instrumentation Symposium. Instrumentation in the Chemical & Petroleum Industries: Proceedings of the 20th Chemical & Petroleum Industries Instrumentation Symposium, Vol. 15. LC 64-7505. 124p. 1979. pap. text ed. 19.00x (ISBN 0-87664-432-9). Instru Soc.

--Instrumentation in the Chemical & Petroleum Industries, Vol. 16: Proceedings of the 21st Chemical & Petroleum Industries Instrumentation Symposium. LC 64-7505. 196p. 1980. pap. text ed. 36.00x (ISBN 0-87664-469-8). Instru Soc.

Chemical Engineering Magazine. Calculator Programs for Chemical Engineers, Vol. 1. (Chemical Engineering Ser.). 304p. 1981. 34.95 (ISBN 0-07-010793-9). McGraw.

--Calculator Programs for Chemical Engineers, Vol 2. 300p. 1984. 37.50 (ISBN 0-07-010849-8). McGraw.

--Fluid Movers: Pumps, Compressors, Fans & Blowers. (Chemical Engineering Bks.). (Illus.). 384p. 1980. 39.50 (ISBN 0-07-010769-6). McGraw.

--Industrial Waste Water & Solid Waste Engineering. LC 80-12608. 376p. 1980. pap. 37.50 (ISBN 0-07-010694-0). McGraw.

--Microcomputer Programs for Chemical Engineers. Deutsch, David J., ed. LC 83-6386. 320p. 1984. 39.95 (ISBN 0-07-010852-8). McGraw.

--Modern Cost Engineering Methods & Data. 1979. 49.50 (ISBN 0-07-010733-5). McGraw.

--Modern Cost Engineering: Methods & Data, Vol. II. 2nd ed. 320p. 1984. 47.00 (ISBN 0-07-010851-X). McGraw.

--Physical Properties. 1977. 54.50 (ISBN 0-07-010715-7). McGraw.

--Process Energy Conservation: Methods & Technology. (Illus.). 300p. 1982. 39.95 (ISBN 0-07-010697-5). McGraw.

--Process Heat Exchange. (Chemical Engineering Book Ser.). (Illus.). 624p. 1980. 47.50 (ISBN 0-07-010742-4). McGraw.

--Process Piping Systems. Deutsch, David J., ed. LC 80-13774. (Chemical Engineering Ser.). 484p. 1980. 46.95 (ISBN 0-07-010706-8). McGraw.

--Process Technology & Flowsheets. LC 79-12117. (Chemical Engineering Bks). 384p. 1980. 35.00 (ISBN 0-07-010741-6). McGraw.

--Process Technology & Flowsheets, Vol. 2. LC 83-12117. 360p. 1983. 36.95 (ISBN 0-07-024388-3). McGraw.

--Safe & Efficient Plant Operation & Maintenance. LC 80-14762. (Chemical Engineering Ser.). 400p. 1980. 37.50 (ISBN 0-07-010707-6). McGraw.

--Selecting Materials for Process Equipment. (Chemical Engineering Ser.). 280p. 1980. 35.00 (ISBN 0-07-010692-4). McGraw.

--Separation Techniques I: Liquid-Liquid Systems. (Chemical Engineering Book). 384p. 1980. 39.50 (ISBN 0-07-010711-4). McGraw.

--Separation Techniques II: Gas-Liquid-Solid Systems. (Chemical Engineering Book). 400p. 1980. 35.00 (ISBN 0-07-010717-3). McGraw.

--Skills Vital to Successful Managers. 1979. 33.50 (ISBN 0-07-010737-8). McGraw.

--Solids Handling. McNaughton, Kenneth, ed. (Illus.). 263p. 1981. 32.50 (ISBN 0-07-010781-5). McGraw.

--Synfuels Engineering. (Illus.). 300p. 1982. 45.00 (ISBN 0-07-010698-3). McGraw.

Chemical Engineering Magazine, jt. auth. see Kraus, Milton N.

Chemical Engineering Magazine Staff, jt. auth. see Pulsafeeder, Inc.

Chemical Engineering Progress, ed. see American Institute of Chemical Engineers National Meeting, Philadelphia June 8-12, 1980.

Chemical Manufacturers Association. Risk Management of Existing Chemicals. LC 84-80974. (Illus.). 192p. 1984. pap. 28.00 (ISBN 0-86587-065-9). Gov Insts.

Chemitz, Martin. Ministry, Word, & Sacraments: An Enchiridion. Poellot, Luther, tr. 1981. pap. 16.95 (ISBN 0-570-03295-4, 15-2730). Concordia.

Chemnitz, Martin. Examination of the Council of Trent. Kramer, Fred, tr. from Lat. LC 79-143693. 1971. 25.95 (ISBN 0-570-03213-X, 15-2113). Concordia.

--Examination of the Council of Trent: Part II. 1979. 25.95 (ISBN 0-570-03272-5, 15-2717). Concordia.

--Two Natures in Christ. Preus, J. A., tr. LC 74-115465. Orig. Title: De Duabus Naturis in Christo. 1970. 22.95 (ISBN 0-570-03210-5, 15-2109). Concordia.

Chemsak, John A. & Linsky, E. G. Checklist of Cerambycidae: The Longhorned Beetles. (Checklist of the Beetle of Canada United States, Mexico, Central America & the West Indies Ser.). 138p. (Orig.). 1982. pap. text ed. 18.00x (ISBN 0-937548-04-9). Plexus Pub.

Chemsak, John A. & Linsley, E. G. Checklist of the Beetles of North & Central America & the West Indies: The Longhorned Beetles, Vol. 7. 138p. 1982. pap. 18.00x (ISBN 0-937548-04-9). Flora & Fauna.

Chemsoft Inc. Staff. CHEMCALC (TM) 6: Heat Exchanger Design (Shell & Tube) (CHEMCALC (TM) Software for Chemical Engineers Ser.). 80p. 1985. incl. floppy disk 995.00x (ISBN 0-87201-090-2). Gulf Pub.

--CHEMCALC (TM) 7: Physical Properties Databank. (CHEMCALC (TM) Software for Chemical Engineers Ser.). 40p. 1985. incl. floppy disk 495.00x (ISBN 0-87201-093-7). Gulf Pub.

Chen. Advanced BASIC for the Vax. 1986. price not set (ISBN 0-471-82632-4). Wiley.

--One Dimensional Digital Signal Processing. (Electrical Engineering & Electronics Ser.: Vol. 9). 1979. 39.75 (ISBN 0-8247-6877-9). Dekker.

--Passive & Active Filters: Theory & Implementation. 1986. price not set (ISBN 0-471-82352-X). Wiley.

Chen, Andrew C., jt. auth. see Cooper, Sol E.

Chen, Anita. Children of Mao: Personality Development & Political Activism in the Red Guard Generation. LC 84-21944. 256p. 1985. pap. 19.95x (ISBN 0-295-96212-7). U of Wash Pr.

Chen, Annie. The What & How of Chinese Painting. (Illus.). 200p. 1978. 10.95 (ISBN 0-917056-81-7, Pub. by Art Bk Taiwan). Cheng & Tsui.

Chen, Bang-Yen. Total Mean Curvature & Submanifold of Finite Type. (Lecture Notes on Pure Mathematics: Vol. 1). 200p. 1984. 26.00x (ISBN 9971-966-02-6, Pub. by World Sci Singapore); pap. 14.00x (ISBN 9971-966-03-4, Pub. by World Sci Singapore). Taylor & Francis.

Chen, C. H. Nonlinear Maxium Entropy Spectral Analysis Methods for Signal Recognition. LC 82-8630. (Pattern Recognition & Image Processing Research Studies). 170p. 1982. 34.95 (ISBN 0-471-10497-3, Pub by Res Stud Pr). Wiley.

--Seismic Signal Analysis & Discrimination. (Methods in Geochemistry & Geophysics: Vol. 17). 196p. 1983. 53.25 (ISBN 0-444-42136-X). Elsevier.

Chen, C. H., ed. Digital Waveform Processing & Recognition. 224p. 1982. 68.00 (ISBN 0-8493-5777-2). CRC Pr.

--Pattern Recognition & Artificial Intelligence: Proceedings of a Joint Workshop held at Hyannis, Mass., June 1976. 1976. 68.50 (ISBN 0-12-170950-7). Acad Pr.

--Pattern Recognition & Signal Processing, No. 29. (NATO Advanced Study Institute Ser.). 666p. 1978. 46.00x (ISBN 90-286-0978-4). Sijthoff & Noordhoff.

--Seismic Signal Analysis & Discrimination III. (Methods in Geochemistry & Geophysics Ser.: Vol. 22). 170p. 1985. Repr. 46.50 (ISBN 0-444-42430-X). Elsevier.

Chen, C. J. Vertical Turbulent Buoyant Jets: A Review of Experimental Data. (Heat & Mass Transfer: Vol. 4). (Illus.). 94p. 1979. 33.00 (ISBN 0-08-024772-5). Pergamon.

Chen, C. S., ed. Rural People's Communes in Lien-Chiang. Ridley, Charles P., tr. LC 69-20277. (Publications Ser.: No. 83). (Illus.). 1969. 11.95x (ISBN 0-8179-1831-0). Hoover Inst Pr.

Chen, C. T. Analysis & Synthesis of Linear Control Systems. 1978. 25.50x (ISBN 0-9604338-0-5). Pond Woods.

--Linear System Theory & Design. LC 83-128918. 662p. 1984. text ed. 42.95 (ISBN 0-03-060289-0, HoltC). HR&W.

Chen, C. V. & Keesee, Allen. Commercial, Business & Trade Laws: Taiwan. 1983. looseleaf 125.00 (ISBN 0-379-22004-0). Oceana.

Chen, Carson. Active Filter Design. 144p. pap. 11.95 (0959). Hayden.

Chen, Charlie C., ed. Experimental Verification of Process Models. 1983. 61.00 (ISBN 0-87170-133-2). ASM.

Chen, Chen, et al. Everything You Want to Know About Chinese Cooking. 1983. 21.95 (ISBN 0-8120-5361-3). Barron.

Chen, Chi. Watercolors, Drawings, Sketches. (Illus.). 1983. pap. 30.00 (ISBN 0-8038-8103-7). Hastings.

Ch'En, Chi-Yun. Hsun Yueh & the Mind of Late Han China: A Translation of the Shen-Chien by Chi-Yun Ch'en. LC 79-3196. (Princeton Library of Asian Translations). 1980. 24.00 (ISBN 0-691-05295-6). Princeton U Pr.

Chen, Chih-Wen. Magnetism & Metallurgy of Soft Magnetic Materials. 574p. 1986. pap. 12.50 (ISBN 0-486-64997-0). Dover.

Chen, Ching-Chih. Applications of Operations Research Models to Libraries: A Case Study in the Use of Monographs in the Francis A. Countway Library of Medicine, Harvard University. LC 75-28210. 192p. 1976. 32.50x (ISBN 0-262-03056-X). MIT Pr.

--Library Management Without Bias. Stueart, Robert D., ed. LC 80-82482. (Foundations in Library & Information Sciences Ser.: Vol. 13). 300p. (Orig.). 1981. 37.50 (ISBN 0-89232-163-6). Jai Pr.

--Zero-Base Budgeting in Library Management: A Manual for Librarians. (Neal-Schuman Professional Books). 292p. 1980. lib. bdg. 35.00x (ISBN 0-912700-18-1). Oryx Pr.

Chen, Ching-chih & Bressler, Stacey E. Microcomputers in Libraries. (Applications in Information Management & Technology Ser.). (Illus.). 259p. (Orig.). 1982. pap. text ed. 27.95 (ISBN 0-918212-61-8). Neal-Schuman.

Chen, Ching-Chih & De Young, Barbara. Integrating Micro-Based IBMs Libraries. 107p. pap. 14.95 (ISBN 0-931555-10-8). Microuse Info.

Chen, Ching-Chih & Hernon, Peter. Numeric Databases. LC 83-25761. 320p. 1984. pap. 35.00 (ISBN 0-89391-247-6). Ablex Pub.

Chen, Ching-Chih, ed. Scientific & Technical Information Sources. 1977. 50.00x (ISBN 0-262-03062-4). MIT Pr.

Chen, Ching-Chin & De Young, Barbara. The dBASE Workbook for Librarians. 69p. pap. 9.95 (ISBN 0-931555-11-6). Microuse Info.

Chen, D. Y., jt. ed. see Baliga, B. J.

Chen, David, jt. auth. see Adams, Raymond.

Chen, E. W., ed. Magnetism & Metallurgy of Soft Magnetic Materials. 1978. 81.50 (ISBN 0-7204-0706-0, North Holland). Elsevier.

Chen, Edward K. Hyper-Growth in Asian Economies. LC 79-13399. (Illus.). 180p. 1979. text ed. 49.50x (ISBN 0-8419-0527-4). Holmes & Meier.

--Multinational Corporations, Technology & Employment. LC 81-18353. 1983. 32.50 (ISBN 0-312-55255-6). St Martin.

Chen, F. H. Foundations on Expansive Soils. (Developments in Geotechnical Engineering Ser.: Vol. 12). 208p. 1976. 59.75 (ISBN 0-444-41393-6). Elsevier.

Chen, Fan Y. Mechanics & Design of Cam Mechanisms. LC 81-11927. (Illus.). 523p. 1982. 77.00 (ISBN 0-08-028049-8, A115). Pergamon.

Chen, Francis F. Introduction to Plasma Physics. LC 74-9632. (Illus.). 330p. 1974. 21.50x (ISBN 0-306-30755-3, Plenum Pr). Plenum Pub.

--Introduction to Plasma Physics & Controlled Fusion: Vol. 1: Plasma Physics. 2nd ed. 400p. 1984. 24.50x (ISBN 0-306-41332-9, Plenum Pr). Plenum Pub.

Chen, Frederick T., ed. China Policy & National Security. 250p. 1984. lib. bdg. 35.00 (ISBN 0-941320-17-0). Transnatl Pubs.

Chen, H. Recursive Estimation & Control for Stochastic Systems. (Probability & Mathematical Statistics Ser.). 378p. 1985. 39.95 (ISBN 0-471-81566-7). Wiley.

Chen, H. S. Space Remote Sensing System: An Introduction. Date not set. price not set (ISBN 0-12-170880-2). Acad Pr.

Chen, Han-Seng A. Industrial Capital & Chinese Peasants: A Study of the Livelihood of Chinese Tobacco Cultivators. Myers, Ramon H., ed. 48.00 (ISBN 0-8240-4266-2). Garland Pub.

Chen, Hollis C. Theory of Electromagnetic Waves: A Coordinate Free Approach. (McGraw-Hill Series in Electrical Engineering). (Illus.). 464p. 1983. text ed. 46.00 (ISBN 0-07-010688-6). McGraw.

Ch'En, Hsi-En see Chen, Theodore H., pseud.

Chen, Hsuan-Shan. The Comparative Coachability of Certain Types of Intelligence Tests. (Columbia University. Teachers College. Contributions to Education: No. 338). Repr. of 1928 ed. 22.50 (ISBN 0-404-55338-9). AMS Pr.

Chen, Huan-Chang. The Economic Principles of Confucius & His School, 2 vols. lib. bdg. 250.00 set (ISBN 0-87968-080-6). Krishna Pr.

Chen, Hung-Shan, et al. The Seeds & Other Stories. 193p. 1972. 5.95 (ISBN 0-917056-42-6, Pub. by Foreign Lang Pr China). Cheng & Tsui.

Chen, I. Hsuan. Chinese Community in New York, Nineteen Twenty to Nineteen Forty: Thesis. LC 74-76755. 1974. Repr. of 1942 ed. soft bdg. 12.00 (ISBN 0-88247-287-9). R & E Pubs.

Chen, J. C. & Bankoff, S. G., eds. Nonequilibrium Interfacial Transport Processes. 1979. 18.00 (ISBN 0-686-59664-1, I00124). ASME.

Chen, Jack. The Chinese of America. LC 80-7749. 288p. 1982. pap. 8.61i (ISBN 0-06-250139-9, CN 4037, HarpR). Har-Row.

--New Earth. LC 72-75332. (Illus.). 271p. 1972. 8.95x (ISBN 0-8093-0584-4). S Ill U Pr.

Chen, James C. Cain Sugar Handbook: Manual for Cane Sugar Manufacturers & Their Chemists. 11th ed. 1134p. 1985. 110.00x (ISBN 0-471-86650-4, Pub. by Wiley-Interscience). Wiley.

Chen, James C., jt. auth. see Meade, George P.

Chen, Janey. Practical English-Chinese Pronouncing Dictionary. LC 78-77122. (Eng. & Chinese.). 1970. 22.50 (ISBN 0-8048-0663-2). C E Tuttle.

Ch'en, Jerome. China & the West: Society & Culture 1815-1937. LC 79-2704. (Illus.). 488p. 1980. 25.00x (ISBN 0-253-12032-2). Ind U Pr.

Chen, Jerome. State Economic Policies of the Ch'ing Government: 1840-1895. LC 78-24797. (The Modern Chinese Economy Ser.: Vol. 2). 250p. 1980. lib. bdg. 33.00 (ISBN 0-8240-4251-4). Garland Pub.

Ch'en, Jerome. Yuan Shih-k'ai. 2nd ed. LC 76-153815. 1972. 20.00x (ISBN 0-8047-0789-8). Stanford U Pr.

Chen, Jo-hsi. Execution of Mayor Yin & Other Stories from the Great Proletarian Cultural Revolution. Ing, Nancy & Goldblatt, Howard, trs. LC 78-1956. (Midland Bks: Chinese Literature in Translation Ser: No. 231). 248p. 1978. 15.95x (ISBN 0-253-12475-1); pap. 6.95x (ISBN 0-253-20231-0). Ind U Pr.

Chen, John C. & Bishop, A. A., eds. Liquid-Metal Heat Transfer & Fluid Dynamics: Presented at the Annual Winter Meeting of ASME, New York, N. Y., November 30, 1970. LC 76-141816. pap. 46.30 (ISBN 0-317-09992-2). Bks Demand UMI.

Chen, Joyce. Joyce Chen Cook Book. LC 82-49008. (Illus.). 224p. 1983. pap. 7.12i (ISBN 0-06-464060-4, BN 4060). B&N NY.

Chen, K. Tai-Chi Ch'uan: Its Effects & Practical Application. 1979. pap. 5.95 (ISBN 0-87877-043-7). Newcastle Pub.

Chen, K. & Uppal, J. India & China. LC 71-142355. 1971. 15.95 (ISBN 0-02-905420-6). Free Pr.

Chen, K. C. & McGarrah, Robert E. Productivity Management: Test & Cases. 564p. 1982. text ed. 33.95x (ISBN 0-03-048901-6); instr's manual 20.95 (ISBN 0-03-052231-5). Dryden Pr.

Chen, Kan, ed. Technology & Social Institutions. LC 74-77658. 1974. 20.75 (ISBN 0-87942-035-9, PC00315). Inst Electrical.

Ch'en, Kenneth. Buddhism in China: A Historical Survey. (Studies in History of Religion: Vol. 1). 1974. pap. 12.50x (ISBN 0-691-00015-8). Princeton U Pr.

Ch'en, Kenneth K. Buddhism: The Light of Asia. LC 67-30496. 1968. pap. text ed. 5.95 (ISBN 0-8120-0272-5). Barron.

Chen, King C. Vietnam & China, Nineteen Thirty-Eight to Nineteen Fifty-Four. LC 78-83684. 1969. 42.00x (ISBN 0-691-03078-2). Princeton U Pr.

Chen, King C., ed. China & the Three Worlds: A Foreign Policy Reader. LC 78-51973. 400p. 1979. 25.00 (ISBN 0-87332-134-0); pap. 12.95 (ISBN 0-87332-118-9). M E Sharpe.

Chen, Kuan-I. World Population Growth & Living Standards. 8.95x (ISBN 0-317-18410-5). New Coll U Pr.

Chen, Kuan Y. Chinese Education: Old & New, Radical & Reformed. (TWEC World Education Monograph Ser.). 24p. 1980. 1.50. Thut World Ed Ctr.

Ch'en, Kung-Po. Communist Movement in China. 1966. lib. bdg. 19.00x (ISBN 0-374-91464-8). Octagon.

Chen, L. H. Y., et al, eds. Proceedings of the International Mathematics Conference, Singapore, 1981. (Mathematics Studies: Vol. 74). 202p. 1983. 38.50 (ISBN 0-444-86510-1, North-Holland). Elsevier.

Chen, L. T., ed. see Sun Yat-sen.

Chen, Lai Nam. Images of Southeast Asia in Children's Fiction. (Illus.). 144p. 1981. 8.50x (ISBN 9971-69-042-X, 82-93938, Pub. by Singapore U Pr). Ohio U Pr.

Chen, Lincoln C. & Scrimshaw, Nevin S., eds. Diarrhea & Malnutrition: Interactions, Mechanisms, & Interventions. 384p. 1983. 39.50x (ISBN 0-306-41046-X, Plenum Pr). Plenum Pub.

Chen, Lincoln C., jt. ed. see Mosley, Henry W.

Chen, Lincoln C., jt. ed. see Mosley, W. Henry.

Chen, Lung-Fong. State Succession Relating to Unequal Treaties. xiii, 324p. 1974. 25.00 (ISBN 0-208-01433-0, Archon). Shoe String.

Chen, Lydia & Echo Books. Chinese Knotting. Wu, Linda & Yao Meng-chia, eds. (Echo Craft Bks.). (Illus.). 116p. 1982. 19.95 (ISBN 0-8048-1389-2). C E Tuttle.

Chen, M. M., et al, eds. Transport Phenomena in Materials Processing. (HTD Ser.: Vol. 10). 124p. 1983. pap. text ed. 30.00 (ISBN 0-317-02657-7, H00283). ASME.

Chen, Marth A. A Quiet Revolution: Women in Transition in Rural Bangladesh. 256p. 1983. 24.95 (ISBN 0-87073-452-0); pap. 15.95 (ISBN 0-87073-453-9). Schenkman Bks Inc.

Chen, Milton & Paisley, William, eds. Children & Microcomputers. 1985. 29.00 (ISBN 0-8039-2446-1); pap. 14.95 (ISBN 0-8039-2447-X). Sage.

Chen, Ning H. Process Reactor Design. 512p. 1983. scp 41.73 (ISBN 0-205-07903-2, 327903). Allyn.

Chen, P. Problems Among Nations. 1969. pap. text ed. 7.95x (ISBN 0-8290-1173-0). Irvington.

Chen, P., ed. see CISM (International Center for Mechanical Sciences), Dept for Mechanics of Rigid Bodies.

Chen, P. P., ed. Entity-Relationship Approach to Information Modeling & Analysis: Proceedings of the Second International Conference on Entity-Relationship Approach, Washington, D. C., Oct. 12-14, 1981. 602p. 1984. 55.00 (ISBN 0-444-86747-3, I-492-83, North Holland). Elsevier.

Chen, P. S. Biochemical Aspects of Insect Development. (Monographs in Developmental Biology: Vol. 3). (Illus.). 1971. 30.75 (ISBN 3-8055-1265-1). S Karger.

Chen, P. Y., ed. Flow-Induced Vibration Design Guidelines. (PVP Ser.: Vol. 52). 143p. 1981. 30.00 (ISBN 0-686-34512-6, H00188). ASME.

Chen, Pah I., jt. auth. see Holbrook, Edward L.

Ch'En, Paul H. Chinese Legal Tradition Under the Mongols: The Code of 1291 As Reconstructed. LC 78-70283. (Studies in East Asian Law, Harvard University). 1979. 28.00x (ISBN 0-691-09237-0). Princeton U Pr.

--The Formation of the Early Meiji Legal Order: The Japanese Code of 1871 & Its Chinese Foundation. (London Oriental Ser.: Vol. 35). 1981. 32.50x (ISBN 0-19-713601-X). Oxford U Pr.

Chen, Peter. The Entity-Relationship Approach to Logical Data Base Design. Curtice, Robert M., ed. (Data Base Monograph Ser.: No. 6). 1977. pap. text ed. 15.00 (ISBN 0-89435-020-X). QED Info Sci.

Chen, Peter P., jt. auth. see Chu, Wesley W.

Chen, Peter S., jt. auth. see Chen, Thomas S.

Chen, Peter S., jt. auth. see Kuo, Eddie C.

Chen, Peter S., ed. Singapore: Development Policies & Trends. (Illus.). 1983. 47.50x (ISBN 0-19-582514-4). Oxford U Pr.

Chen, Peter S. & Fawcett, James T., eds. Public Policy & Population Change in Singapore. LC 79-21096. 275p. (Orig.). 1979. pap. text ed. 6.95 (ISBN 0-87834-034-3). Population Coun.

Chen, Peter W. Chinese-Americans View Their Mental Health. LC 77-81019. 1977. soft bdg. 11.00 (ISBN 0-88247-476-6). R & E Pubs.

Chen, Philip S. Chemistry: Inorganic, Organic & Biological. 2nd ed. (College Outline Ser.). 288p. 1980. pap. 6.50 (ISBN 0-06-460182-X, CO 182, COS). B&N NY.

--Soybeans for Health & a Longer Life. rev. ed. LC 73-83947. (Pivot Fact Book). 224p. 1974. pap. 1.50 (ISBN 0-87983-061-1). Keats.

Chen, Ping, jt. auth. see Matsunaga, Spark M.

Chen, R. F. & Edelhoch, H., eds. Biochemical Fluorescence: Concepts, Vol. 1. 424p. 1975. 75.00 (ISBN 0-8247-6222-3). Dekker.

--Biochemical Fluorescence: Concepts, Vol. 2. 336p. 1976. 75.00 (ISBN 0-8247-6223-1). Dekker.

Chen, Reuven & Kirsh, D. Y. The Analysis of Thermally Stimulated Processes. 1981. 66.00 (ISBN 0-08-022930-1). Pergamon.

Chen, Robert S. & Boulding, Elise. Social Science Research & Climate Change. 1983. lib. bdg. 43.50 (ISBN 90-277-1490-8, Pub. by Reidel Holland). Kluwer Academic.

Chen, Ronald. Foreign Medical Graduates in Psychiatry: Issues & Problems. LC 79-17189. 443p. 1981. 34.95 (ISBN 0-87705-485-1). Human Sci Pr.

Chen, Ruth T., tr. see Demarest, Bruce A.

Chen, Ruth T., tr. see Nee, Watchman.

Chen, Ruth T., tr. see Spurgeon, Charles.

Chen, Ruth T., tr. see Strauss, Richard L.

Chen, S. H., et al, trs. see K'ung, Shang-Jen.

Chen, S. S. & Paidoussis, M. P., eds. Flow-Induced Vibration of Circular Cylindrical Structures 1982. (PVP Ser.: Vol. 63). 223p. 1982. 44.00 (H00220). ASME.

Chen, Samuel S. The Theory & Practice of International Organization. 2nd ed. 133p. 1974. text ed. 29.75x (ISBN 0-8422-5139-1); pap. text ed. 9.75x (ISBN 0-8422-0362-1). Irvington.

Chen, Shao-Kwan. System of Taxation in China in the Tsing Dynasty, 1644-1911. LC 79-120215. (Columbia University Studies in the Social Sciences: No. 143). 1970. Repr. of 1914 ed. 12.50 (ISBN 0-404-51143-0). AMS Pr.

Chen, Shao Y. Yung Wing: The First Chinese Student in the United States. (Connecticut Educational History Ser.). 1984. 1.50 (ISBN 0-317-12719-5). I N Thut World Educ Ctr.

Chen, Shoei-Sheng, ed. see National Congress on Pressure Vessel & Piping (3rd: 1979: San Francisco).

Chen, Shu-Jen, jt. auth. see Sawatzky, Jasper J.

Chen, Sow-Hsin & Yip, Sidney, eds. Spectroscopy in Biology & Chemistry: Neutron, X-Ray, Laser. 1974. 55.00 (ISBN 0-12-170850-0). Acad Pr.

Chen, Sow-Hsin, et al, eds. Scattering Techniques Applied to Supramolecular & Non-Equilibrium Systems. LC 81-13767. (NATO ASI Series B, Physics: Vol. 73). 942p. 1981. text ed. 125.00x (ISBN 0-306-40828-7, Plenum Pr). Plenum Pub.

Chen, Stephen. Missouri in the Federal System. LC 80-54752. (Illus.). 234p. (Orig.). 1981. lib. bdg. 25.50 (ISBN 0-8191-1720-X); pap. text ed. 13.00 (ISBN 0-8191-1721-8). U Pr of Amer.

Chen, Stephen C. Missouri in the Federal System. 2nd ed. LC 82-24834. (Illus.). 238p. 1983. pap. text ed. 11.50 (ISBN 0-8191-3037-0). U Pr of Amer.

Chen, Susan W., tr. see Feng Jicai.

Chen, T. P. Aquaculture Practices in Taiwan. 1978. 30.00x (ISBN 0-685-63392-6). State Mutual Bk.

--Aquaculture Practices in Taiwan. (Illus.). 176p. 21.50 (ISBN 0-85238-080-1, FN2, FNB). Unipub.

Chen, T. T., ed. Research in Protozoology, Vol. 4. 1972. 76.00 (ISBN 0-08-016437-4). Pergamon.

Ch'En, Ta. Emigrant Communities in South China: A Study of Overseas Migration & Its Influence on Standards of Living & Social Change. LC 75-30052. (Institute of Pacific Relations). Repr. of 1940 ed. 27.50 (ISBN 0-404-59515-4). AMS Pr.

Chen, Ta. Population in Modern China. 1973. lib. bdg. 14.50x (ISBN 0-374-91467-2). Octagon.

Chen, Ta-Chuan, jt. auth. see Nichols, Paul L.

Chen, Theodore H., pseud. Thought Reform of the Chinese Intellectuals. LC 78-2821. 247p. 1980. Repr. of 1960 ed. 23.00 (ISBN 0-8305-0001-4). Hyperion Conn.

Chen, Thomas S. & Chen, Peter S. Understanding the Liver: A History. LC 83-22631. (Contributions in Medical History Ser.: No. 14). (Illus.). xiii, 293p. 1984. lib. bdg. 45.00 (ISBN 0-313-23472-8, CLV/). Greenwood.

Chen, Tony, illus. Wild Animals. LC 80-53105. (Board Bks.). (Illus.). 14p. (ps). 1981. boards 3.50 (ISBN 0-394-84748-2). Random.

Chen, Virginia, compiled by. The Economic Conditions of East & Southeast Asia: A Bibliography of English-Language Material, 1965 to 1977. LC 78-57762. 840p. 1978. lib. bdg. 75.00 (ISBN 0-313-20565-5, CEC/). Greenwood.

Chen, W. F. Plasticity in Reinforced Concrete. (Illus.). 576p. 1982. text ed. 46.95 (ISBN 0-07-010687-8). McGraw.

Chen, W. F. & Han, D. J. Tubular Members in Offshore Structures. (Surveys in Structural Engineering & Structural Mechanics Ser.). 1985. text ed. 34.95 (ISBN 0-273-08581-6). Pitman Pub MA.

Chen, W. F. & Lewis, A. D., eds. Recent Advances in Engineering Mechanics & Their Impact on Civil Engineering Practice, 2 Vols. 1378p. 1983. pap. 106.00x (ISBN 0-87262-358-0). Am Soc Civil Eng.

Chen, W. F. & Ting, E. C., eds. Fracture in Concrete. LC 80-69656. 114p. 1980. pap. 12.00x (ISBN 0-87262-259-2). Am Soc Civil Eng.

Chen, W. K. Applied Graph Theory: Graphs & Electrical Networks. 2nd rev. ed. (North-Holland Ser. in Applied Mathematics & Mechanics: Vol. 13). 1976. (North-Holland); pap. text ed. 47.00 (ISBN 0-7204-2835-1). Elsevier.

Chen, Wai-Fah. Limit Analysis & Soil Plasticity. LC 74-84058. (Developments in Geotechnical Engineering: Vol. 7). 638p. 1975. 140.50 (ISBN 0-444-41249-2). Elsevier.

Chen, Wai-Fah & Saleeb, Atef F. Constitutive Equations for Engineering Materials: Elasticity & Modeling, Vol. 1. LC 81-16433. 580p. 1982. 78.95x (ISBN 0-471-09149-9, Pub. by Wiley-Interscience). Wiley.

Chen, Y. K. Tai-Chi Ch'uan: Its Effects & Practical Applications. LC 80-19810. 184p. 1980. Repr. of 1979 ed. lib. bdg. 15.95x (ISBN 0-89370-643-4). Borgo Pr.

Chen, Yu-shih. Realism & Allegory in the Early Fiction of Mao Tun. LC 84-48486. (Studies in Chinese Literature & Society). 272p. 1986. 24.95 (ISBN 0-253-34950-8). Ind U Pr.

Chen, Yuan-Tsun. The Dragon's Village. 1981. pap. 5.95 (ISBN 0-14-005811-7). Penguin.

Chen, Yung-Ping. Background Paper on Income for the Nineteen Seventy-One White House Conference on Aging. 1971. 3.00 (ISBN 0-89215-054-8). U Cal LA Indus Rel.

--Social Security in a Changing Society: An Introduction to Programs, Concepts, & Issues. 2nd ed. LC 83-73241. (Illus.). 200p. (Orig.). 1980. pap. text ed. 14.00 (ISBN 0-937094-00-5). McCahan Found.

Chen, Z. W., et al. Microsurgery. (Illus.). 510p. 1982. 135.00 (ISBN 0-387-11281-2). Springer-Verlag.

Chenault, Alice A. Nutrition & Health. 1984. pap. text ed. 25.95 (ISBN 0-03-047561-9). HR&W.

Chenault, Joann & Burnford, J. F. Human Services Professional Development: Future Directions. 1978. text ed. 22.95 (ISBN 0-07-010732-7). McGraw.

Chenault, Steve. Re'lize Whut Ahm Talkin' 'Bout. softcover 7.95 (ISBN 0-912216-24-7). Angel Pr.

Chenault, V. Michele. Clinical Chemistry Lab Manual for the Medical Technology Student. 1979. pap. text ed. 10.95x (ISBN 0-89917-014-5). TIS Inc.

Chen Chang-Yen, ed. see Huei, Huang Su.

Chen Chang-Yen, tr. see Huang Su Huei.

Chen Chi. Heaven & Water. (Illus.). 80p. 1983. signed 60.00 (ISBN 0-9604652-2-7); deluxe ed. 200.00 (ISBN 0-317-03540-1). Chen Chi Studio.

Chen Chih-Mai. Parliamentary Opinion of Delegated Legislation. LC 70-76628. (Columbia University Studies in the Social Sciences: No. 394). Repr. of 1933 ed. 15.00 (ISBN 0-404-51394-8). AMS Pr.

Chene, Brent de see De Chene, Brent.

Chenel, Laura & Siegfried, Linda. Chevre! The Goat Cheese Cookbook. LC 83-62381. (Illus.). 119p. (Orig.). 1983. pap. 9.95 (ISBN 0-914015-00-1, 0-671-55801-3, Pub. by Peaks Pike Publishing Co.). Aris Bks Harris.

Chenery, Hollis. Industrialization & Growth - The Experience of Large Countries. (Working Paper: No. 539). 38p. 1982. pap. 3.00 (ISBN 0-8213-0097-0). World Bank.

Chenery, Hollis & Keesing, Donald B. The Changing Composition of Developing Country Exports. (Working Paper: No. 314). 51p. 1979. 3.00 (ISBN 0-686-36205-5, WP-0314). World Bank.

Chenery, Hollis, et al. Redistribution with Growth: An Approach to Policy. 1974. pap. 9.95x (ISBN 0-19-920070-X). Oxford U Pr.

--Patterns of Development 1950-1970. (World Bank Research Publications Ser). (Illus.). 1975. 19.95x (ISBN 0-19-920075-0); pap. 8.95x (ISBN 0-19-920076-9). Oxford U Pr.

Chenery, Hollis B. Structural Change & Development Policy. (World Bank Research Publications Ser.). (Illus.). 1979. 34.50x (ISBN 0-19-520094-2); pap. 12.95x (ISBN 0-19-520095-0). Oxford U Pr.

--Studies in Developmental Planning. LC 70-143227. (Economic Studies: No. 136). 1971. 27.50x (ISBN 0-674-84725-3). Harvard U Pr.

Chenery, Janet. Toad Hunt. LC 66-18653. (Science I Can Read Bk.). (Illus.). 64p. (gr. k-3). 1967. 9.89i (ISBN 0-06-021262-4); PLB 8.89 (ISBN 0-06-021263-2). HarpJ.

Chenery, Janet D. Pickles & Jake. (Puffin Story Bks). (Illus.). (gr. 1 up). 1977. pap. 2.95 (ISBN 0-14-030964-0, Puffin). Penguin.

Chenery, William H. Fourteenth Regiment Rhode Island Heavy Artillery, Colored in the War to Preserve the Union, 1861-1865. LC 77-82049. Repr. of 1898 ed. cancelled (ISBN 0-8371-1565-5, CFR&, Pub. by Negro U Pr). Greenwood.

Chenery, William L. Freedom of the Press. LC 77-14294. 1978. Repr. of 1955 ed. lib. bdg. 27.50x (ISBN 0-8371-9835-6, CHFP). Greenwood.

--Industry & Human Welfare. Stein, Leon, ed. LC 77-70487. (Work Ser.). 1977. Repr. of 1922 ed. lib. bdg. 20.00x (ISBN 0-405-10159-7). Ayer Co Pubs.

Chenery, William L. & Merrit, Ella A., eds. Standards of Child Welfare: A Report of the Children's Bureau Conferences, May & June, 1919. LC 74-1672. (Children & Youth Ser.: Vol. 6). 464p. 1974. Repr. of 1919 ed. 33.00x (ISBN 0-405-05952-3). Ayer Co Pubs.

Chenetier, Marc. Richard Brautigan. LC 82-20880. (Contemporary Writers Ser.). 96p. 1983. pap. 4.75 (ISBN 0-416-32960-8, NO. 3751). Methuen Inc.

Chenetier, Marc, ed. see Lindsay, Vachel.

Chenevert, M., et al. HP-41CV Applied Drilling Engineering Manual. LC 82-20983. 152p. (Orig.). 1983. 29.95x (ISBN 0-87201-355-3); Bar Code Supplement pap. 48p. 49.95x (ISBN 0-87201-356-1). Gulf Pub.

Chenevert, Martin & Braunlin, Walter A. PETROCALC (TM) 2: Drilling Engineering. LC 83-18562. (PETROCALC (TM) Software for Petroleum Engineers Ser.). 1984. incl. disk 250.00x (ISBN 0-87201-728-1). Gulf Pub.

Chenevert, Martin & Roye, J. PIPECALC (TM) 1: Practical Pipeline Hydraulics. LC 84-9007. (Microcomputer Software for Pipeline Engineers Ser.). 1984. incl. disk 295.00x (ISBN 0-87201-741-9). Gulf Pub.

Chenevert, Martin, jt. auth. see Sinclair, Richard.

Chenevert, Martin E. & Hollo, Reuven. TI-Fifty-Nine Drilling Engineering Manual. LC 81-1110. 249p. 1981. 65.95 (ISBN 0-87814-161-8). Pennwell Bks.

Chenevert, Melodie. STAT: Special Techiques in Assertiveness Training for Women in the Health Professions. 2nd ed. LC 82-22857. (Illus.). 121p. 1983. text ed. 11.95 (ISBN 0-8016-1135-0). Mosby.

Cheney. The Amazon. (First Books). (Illus.). 72p. lib. bdg. 8.90 (ISBN 0-531-04818-7). Watts.

Cheney, Anne. Lorraine Hansberry. (United States Authors Ser.: No. 430). 1984. lib. bdg. 13.95 (ISBN 0-8057-7365-7, Twayne). G K Hall.

--Millay in Greenwich Village. LC 74-23424. (Illus.). 176p. 1975. 11.95 (ISBN 0-8173-7161-3). U of Ala Pr.

Cheney, Brainard. This Is Adam. 1958. 7.95 (ISBN 0-8392-1116-3). Astor-Honor.

Cheney, C. E., ed. Handbook of Dates for Students of British History. (Royal Historical Society Ser.). 182p. 1981. Repr. of 1945 ed. 7.75 (ISBN 0-318-04210-X, BAB 01343, Pub. by Boydell & Brewer). Biblio Dist.

Cheney, C. R. From Becket to Langton: English Church Government between 1170 & 1213. 1956. 19.00 (ISBN 0-7190-0064-5, Pub. by Manchester Univ Pr). Longwood Pub Group.

--Medieval Texts & Studies. 1973. 45.00x (ISBN 0-19-822399-4). Oxford U Pr.

Cheney, C. R., ed. Handbook of Dates for Students of British History. (Royal Historical Society Ser.). 164p. 1970. Repr. of 1945 ed. 7.75x (ISBN 0-8476-1343-7). Rowman.

--Handbook of Dates For Students of History. (RHS Guides & Handbooks: No. 4). 164p. 1970. Repr. 7.50 (ISBN 0-901050-10-5, Pub. by Boydell & Brewer). Longwood Pub Group.

Cheney, C. R. & Jones, Bridgette A., eds. English Episcopal Acta: Canterbury, 1193-1205, 2 vols, Vols. II & III. (Episcopal Acta). 1984. Set. 77.00x (ISBN 0-19-726022-5). Oxford U Pr.

Cheney, Christopher R. The English Church & Its Law Twelfth to Fourteenth Centuries: Fifteen Studies in English 1931-1981. 312p. 1982. 75.00x (ISBN 0-86078-108-9, Pub. by Variorum England). State Mutual Bk.

--Episcopal Visitation of Monasteries in the Thirteenth Century. 2nd, rev. ed. xxxi, 192p. 1983. lib. bdg. 19.50x (ISBN 0-87991-638-9). Porcupine Pr.

--The Papacy & England, 12th-14th Centuries, Historical & Legal Studies: Centuries, Historical & Legal Studies. 346p. 1982. 75.00x (ISBN 0-86078-099-6, Pub. by Variorum England). State Mutual Bk.

Cheney, Cora. Alaska: Indians, Eskimos, Russians, & the Rest. LC 79-6638. (Illus.). (gr. 5 up). 1980. 7.95 (ISBN 0-396-07792-7). Dodd.

--The Christmas Tree Hessian. 151p. (gr. 4-6). 1976. pap. 3.95 (ISBN 0-914378-10-4). Countryman.

--Vermont: The State with the Storybook Past. 2nd ed. LC 76-13804. (Illus.). 256p. (gr. 3-6). 1981. pap. 10.95 (ISBN 0-8289-0440-5). Greene.

Cheney Cowles Memorial Museum of the Eastern Washington State Historical Society. Cornhusk Bags of the Plateau Indians. LC 76-9025. 1976. 4 color fiches 30.00 (ISBN 0-226-68987-5, Chicago Visual Lib). U of Chicago Pr.

Cheney, Daniel P. & Mumford, Thomas M., Jr. Shellfish & Seaweed Harvests of Puget Sound. (A Puget Sound Bk.). (Illus.). 144p. (Orig.). 1984. pap. 8.95 (ISBN 0-295-95990-8, Pub. by Wash Sea Grant). U of Wash Pr.

Cheney, David M. Son of Minos. LC 64-25838. (gr. 7). 10.00x (ISBN 0-8196-0142-X). Biblo.

Cheney, David R. & Hunt, Leigh. Musical Evenings: Or Selections, Vocal & Instrumental. Chemey, David R., ed. LC 64-12876. 68p. 1964. 6.00x (ISBN 0-8262-0033-8). U of Mo Pr.

Cheney, David R., ed. Broad's Critical Essays in Moral Philosophy. (Muirhead Library of Philosophy). 1971. text ed. 18.00x (ISBN 0-391-00178-7). Humanities.

Cheney, Donna B. Thoughts for Living. LC 78-52641. (Illus.). 1978. pap. 3.50 (ISBN 0-9602708-0-9). D B Cheney.

--Thoughts of Being Human. (Illus.). 140p. (Orig.). 1984. 5.50 (ISBN 0-87527-332-7). Green.

--Thoughts on Being Human. LC 83-82480. (Illus.). 140p. 1984. pap. 5.50 (ISBN 0-9602708-1-7). D B Cheney.

Cheney, E. W., ed. Approximation Theory III. LC 80-19723. 1980. 74.50 (ISBN 0-12-171050-5). Acad Pr.

Cheney, Ednah D. Louisa May Alcott. LC 80-24025. (American Men & Women of Letters Ser.). 410p. 1981. pap. 5.95 (ISBN 0-87754-162-0). Chelsea Hse.

Cheney, Frances N. & Williams, Wiley J. Fundamental Reference Sources. 2nd ed. x, 351p. 1980. 15.00x (ISBN 0-8389-0308-8). ALA.

Cheney, Frances N., ed. see Tate, Allen.

Cheney, Glenn A. El Salvador: Country in Crisis. (Impact Bks.). (Illus.). 96p. (gr. 7 up). 1982. PLB 9.90 (ISBN 0-531-04423-8). Watts.

--Mineral Resources. (Natural Resoures Ser.: No. 1). (Illus.). 72p. (gr. 4 up). 1985. lib. bdg. 9.40 (ISBN 0-531-04915-9). Watts.

--Mohandas Gandhi. (Impact Biography Ser.). (Illus.). 128p. (gr. 7 up). 1983. PLB 9.90 (ISBN 0-531-04600-1). Watts.

--Responsibility. (American Values First Bk.). (Illus.). 72p. (gr. 7-9). 1985. PLB 9.40 (ISBN 0-531-10045-6). Watts.

--Television in American Society. (Impact Ser.). 96p. (gr. 7 up). 1983. PLB 9.90 (ISBN 0-531-04402-5). Watts.

Cheney, Glenn Alan. Revolution in Central America. (Impact Ser.). (Illus.). 96p. (gr. 7up). lib. bdg. 9.90 (ISBN 0-531-04761-X). Watts.

Cheney, Jean E., jt. auth. see Cheney, Robert S.

Cheney, Johnston M. The Life of Christ in Stereo. Ellisen, Stanley A., ed. LC 84-8280. 275p. 1984. pap. 6.95 (ISBN 0-88070-068-8). Multnomah.

Cheney, Joyce, ed. Lesbian Land. (Illus.). 200p. 1985. pap. 15.00 (ISBN 0-318-12064-X). Word Weavers.

Cheney, Joyce, et al, eds. All Our Lives: A Women's Songbook. (Illus.). 1976. pap. 6.50 (ISBN 0-88447-008-3). Diana Pr.

Cheney, Judy. The New Civil War Book. (Illus.). 64p. 1983. pap. text ed. 2.00 (ISBN 0-936672-16-1). Aerial Photo.

Cheney, L. J. The World of Man: Prose Passages Chiefly from the Works of the Great Historians, Classical & English. 1979. Repr. of 1933 ed. lib. bdg. 30.00 (ISBN 0-8492-3966-4). R West.

--The World of Man: Prose Passages from the Works of the Great Historians, Classical & English. 1933. 15.00 (ISBN 0-686-17674-X). Quaker City.

Cheney, Liana. The Paintings of the Casa Vasari. Freedberg, S. J., ed. (Outstanding Dissertations in Fine Arts Ser.). (Illus.). 675p. 1985. Repr. of 1978 ed. 65.00 (ISBN 0-8240-6852-1). Garland Pub.

--Quattrocento Neoplatonism & Medici Humanism in Botticelli's Mythological Paintings. (Illus.). 154p. (Orig.). 1985. lib. bdg. 22.50 (ISBN 0-8191-4663-3); pap. text ed. 11.00 (ISBN 0-8191-4664-1). U Pr of Amer.

Cheney, Lynne V., jt. auth. see Cheney, Richard B.

Cheney, Margaret. Tesla: Man out of Time. (Illus.). 320p. 1981. 16.95 (ISBN 0-13-906859-7). P-H.

--Tesla: Man out of Time. (Illus.). 336p. 1983. pap. 4.95 (ISBN 0-440-39077-X, LE). Dell.

Cheney, Mary A. Life & Letters of Horace Bushnell. LC 74-83415. (Religion in America, Ser. 1). 1969. Repr. of 1880 ed. 23.50 (ISBN 0-405-00236-X). Ayer Co Pubs.

Cheney, Mary G. Roger, Bishop of Worcestor Eleven Sixty Four to Eleven Seventy Nine: An English Bishop of the Age of Becket. (Oxford Historical Monographs). (Illus.). 1980. 63.00x (ISBN 0-19-821879-6). Oxford U Pr.

Cheney, Phillip, jt. auth. see Chandler, Craig C.

Cheney, Ray E. Equipment Specifications for High Schools, Their Use & Imporvement: A New Aproach. LC 73-176641. (Columbia University. Teachers College. Contributions to Education: No. 612). Repr. of 1934 ed. 22.50 (ISBN 0-404-55612-4). AMS Pr.

Cheney, Richard B. & Cheney, Lynne V. Kings of the Hill: Power & Personality in the House of Representatives. (Illus.). 224p. 1983. 14.95 (ISBN 0-8264-0230-5). Crossroad NY.

Cheney, Robert. Tunnel Rats. 400p. 1984. pap. 19.95 (ISBN 0-913783-00-5). Mariana Books.

Cheney, Robert, ed. see Naismith, James.

Cheney, Robert B. Basketball: Sixty-Five Programmed Principles. new ed. (Educational-Athletic Principles Ser). (Illus.). 84p. (Orig., Prog. Bk.). 1972. pap. 1.35 (ISBN 0-912934-02-6). Bear.

--Soccer: Forty-Two Programmed Principles. 3rd ed. (Educational Athletic Principles Ser.). (Illus.). 1976. pap. 1.95 (ISBN 0-912934-01-8). Bear.

Cheney, Robert S. & Cheney, Jean E. Coping: Survival in a Computerized Society. 1984. 19.95 (ISBN 0-89433-232-5). Petrocelli.

--Coping: Survival in a Computerized Society. (Illus.). 250p. 1984. pap. 19.95. Van Nos Reinhold.

Cheney, Roberta, jt. auth. see Mygatt, Emmie.

Cheney, Roberta C. The Big Missouri Winter Count. LC 79-15790. (Illus.). 63p. 1979. 9.95 (ISBN 0-87961-082-4); pap. text ed. 3.95 (ISBN 0-87961-081-6). Naturegraph.

--Names on the Face of Montana. 320p. (Orig.). 1983. pap. 9.95 (ISBN 0-87842-150-5). Mountain Pr.

Cheney, Ruth G., ed. The Christian Education Catalog. 192p. (Orig.). 1981. pap. 10.95 (ISBN 0-8164-2328-8, Pub. by Seabury). Winston Pr.

Cheney, S. Art Theater. rev. enl. ed. Repr. of 1925 ed. 17.00 (ISBN 0-527-16300-7). Kraus Repr.

--Open-Air Theatre. Repr. of 1918 ed. 23.00 (ISBN 0-527-16310-4). Kraus Repr.

Cheney, Sheldon. Expressionism in Art. new ed. LC 79-131276. (Illus.). 1962. 10.95x (ISBN 0-87140-530-X). Liveright.

--New Movement in the Theatre. LC 70-88532. 22.00 (ISBN 0-405-08356-4, Blom Pubns). Ayer Co Pubs.

--New Movement in the Theatre. LC 70-95089. Repr. of 1914 ed. lib. bdg. 24.75x (ISBN 0-8371-3081-6, CHNT). Greenwood.

--New World Architecture. LC 72-100513. (BCL Ser.: No. II). (Illus.). Repr. of 1930 ed. 28.50 (ISBN 0-404-01487-9). AMS Pr.

--Stage Decoration. LC 66-29421. (Illus.). 1967. Repr. of 1928 ed. 20.00 (ISBN 0-405-08357-2, Blom Pubns). Ayer Co Pubs.

Cheney, Shelton. The Evolution, Tradition & Progress of the Impressionist Movement Throughout the World, 2 Vols. (Illus.). 450p. 1985. Repr. of 1934 ed. 227.55 set (ISBN 0-317-17783-4). Found Class Reprints.

Cheney, Simeon P. The American Singing Book. (Earlier American Music Ser.: No. 17). (Illus.). 1980. Repr. of 1879 ed. lib. bdg. 32.50 (ISBN 0-306-77322-8). Da Capo.

Cheney, Theodore A. Day of Fate. 288p. (Orig.). 1981. pap. 2.50 (ISBN 0-441-13908-6, Pub. by Charter Bks). Ace Bks.

--Getting the Words Right: How to Revise, Edit, & Rewrite. LC 83-16661. 215p. 1983. 13.95 (ISBN 0-89879-114-6). Writers Digest.

Cheney, Thomas E., ed. Mormon Songs from the Rocky Mountains: A Compilation of Mormon Folksong. 224p. 1981. pap. 9.95 (ISBN 0-87480-196-6). U of Utah Pr.

Cheney, Vance. What It Is That Heals. 1980. 18.50x (ISBN 0-686-64693-2, Pub. by Daniel Co England). State Mutual Bk.

Cheney, Ward. Introduction to Approximation Theory. 2nd ed. LC 81-6208. x, 260p. 1980. text ed. 14.95 (ISBN 0-8284-0317-1). Chelsea Pub.

Cheney, Ward & Kincaid, David. Numerical Mathematics & Computing. 2nd ed. LC 84-27420. (Mathematics Ser.). 512p. 1985. text ed. 25.25 pub net (ISBN 0-534-04356-9). Brooks-Cole.

Cheney, Ward E. & Kincaid, David. Numerical Mathematics & Computing. 2nd ed. 400p. 1984. write for info. solutions manual. Wadsworth Pub.

Cheney, William. H. Dickon Arkwright's Digest of a Journey Lately Undergone. viii, 20p. 1977. Repr. of 1960 ed. cloth 10.00 (ISBN 0-317-11647-9). Dawsons.

Cheney, Winifred G. Cooking for Company. LC 84-60290. (Illus.). 272p. 1985. 17.26i (ISBN 0-8487-0632-3). Oxmoor Hse.

Cheney-Coker, S. Graveyard Also Has Teeth. (African Writers Ser.). (Orig.). 1980. pap. text ed. 6.50x (ISBN 0-435-90221-0). Heinemann Ed.

Cheney-Coker, Syl. Concerto for an Exile. (African Writers Ser.). 1973. pap. text ed. 3.50x (ISBN 0-435-90126-5). Heinemann Ed.

Cheney-Rose, Lynne. Child of the Washed World. (Herland Ser.: No. 5). 30p. (Orig.). 1984. pap. 4.00 (ISBN 0-934996-25-3). Am Stud Pr.

Chenfeld, Mimi B. Teaching Language Arts Creatively. (Illus.). 359p. 1978. pap. text ed. 13.95 (ISBN 0-15-588807-2, HC). HarBraceJ.

Chenfield, Mimi B. Creative Activities for Young Children. 299p. 1983. pap. text ed. 20.95 (ISBN 0-15-515795-7, HC). HarbraceJ.

Cheng & Smith. Tai Chi. 16.95x (ISBN 0-685-22124-5). Wehman.

Cheng, jt. auth. see Bulla.

Cheng, Bin. The Law of International Air Transport. LC 61-18387. (Library of World Affairs). 726p. 1977. Repr. 75.00 (ISBN 0-379-00697-9). Oceana.

Cheng, Charles W. Teacher Unions & the Power Structure. LC 81-82467. (Fastback Ser.: No. 165). 50p. 1981. pap. 0.75 (ISBN 0-87367-165-1). Phi Delta Kappa.

Cheng, Chia-Jui. Basic Documents on International Trade Law. LC 85-8804. Date not set. price not set (ISBN 9-02-473168-2, Pub. by Martinus Nilhoff Netherlands). Kluwer Academic.

Cheng, Chin-Chuan. A Synchronic Phonology of Mandarin Chinese. LC 72-88180. (Monographs on Linguistic Analysis Ser: No. 4). 81p. (Orig.). 1973. pap. text ed. 11.60x (ISBN 90-2792-407-4). Mouton.

Cheng, Chu-Yuan. China's Economic Development: Growth & Structural Change. LC 81-11671. (Illus.). 536p. (Orig.). 1981. 38.00x (ISBN 0-89158-788-8); pap. 16.50x (ISBN 0-89158-892-2). Westview.

--The Demand & Supply of Primary Energy in Mainland China. (Mainland China Economic Ser.: No. 3). (Illus.). 186p. 1985. pap. text ed. 22.00x (ISBN 0-295-96206-2). U of Wash Pr.

Cheng, Chung-Ying. Tai Chen's Inquiry into Goodness. LC 70-113573. 187p. 1971. 12.00x (ISBN 0-8248-0093-1, Eastwest Ctr). UH Pr.

Cheng, Chung-ying, ed. Philosophical Aspects of the Mind-Body Problem. 226p. 1975. text ed. 16.00x (ISBN 0-8248-0342-6). UH Pr.

Cheng, D. C. A Comparison of Fourteen Commercial Viscometers & Home-Made Instruments, 1978. 1981. 85.00x (ISBN 0-686-97047-0, Pub. by W Spring England). State Mutual Bk.

--A Study Into the Possiblity of Scale-Up in Thixotropic Pipe-Flow, 1979. 1981. 45.00x (ISBN 0-686-97142-6, Pub. by W Spring England). State Mutual Bk.

Cheng, D. G. Analysis of Linear Systems. 1959. 29.95 (ISBN 0-201-01020-8). Addison-Wesley.

Cheng, D. K. Field & Wave Electromagnetics. 640p. 1983. text ed. 39.95 (ISBN 0-201-01239-1). Addison-Wesley.

Cheng, David, jt. auth. see O'Neill, Gerald K.

Cheng, DeWitt. Low Life: Drawings & Paintings by DeWitt Cheng. LC 82-91177. (Illus.). 64p. (Orig.). 1983. pap. 11.95 (ISBN 0-9610974-0-X). Telamon.

Cheng, Eva. The Elder Chinese. LC 77-83484. (Elder Minority Ser.). 1978. 3.50 (ISBN 0-916304-35-3). SDSU Press.

Cheng, F. T., tr. from Chinese. The Chinese Supreme Court Decisions: Relating to General Principles of Civil Law, Obligations & Commercial Law. 229p. 1979. Repr. of 1923 ed. 22.50 (ISBN 0-89093-065-1). U Pubns Amer.

--Judgements of the High Prize Court of the Republic of China. vi, 146p. 1983. Repr. of 1919 ed. lib. bdg. 24.00x (ISBN 0-8377-0449-9). Rothman.

Cheng, F. Y., jt. auth. see Tuma, J. J.

Cheng, Fa-Hwa. Statics & Strength of Materials. 500p. Date not set. text ed. price not set (ISBN 0-02-322300-6). Macmillan.

Cheng, Francois. Chinese Poetic Writing: With an Anthology of Tang Poetry. Riggs, Donald A. & Seaton, Jerome P., trs. from Chinese. LC 81-48382. (Studies in Chinese Literature & Society Midland Books: No.284). 246p. 1983. 25.00x (ISBN 0-253-31358-9); pap. 12.95x (ISBN 0-253-20284-1). Ind U Pr.
Cheng, H. L. Nagarjuna's Twelve Gate Treatise. 1982. 36.95 (ISBN 90-277-1380-4, Pub. by Reidel Holland). Kluwer Academic.
Cheng, H. S. & Keer, L. M., eds. Solid Contact & Lubrication. (AMD: Vol. 39). 248p. 1980. 30.00 (ISBN 0-686-69861-4, G00172). ASME.
Cheng, H. S., jt. ed. see Rohde, S. M.
Cheng, Henry, jt. auth. see Bishop, Errett.
Cheng, Herbert S., jt. ed. see Kennedy, Francis E.
Cheng, Hou-Tien. The Chinese New Year. LC 76-8229. (Illus.). (gr. k-3). 1976. reinforced bdg. 7.95 (ISBN 0-03-017511-9). HR&W.
Cheng, Hsueh-li. Empty Logic: Madhyamika Buddhism from Chinese Sources. LC 83-13246. 220p. 1984. 17.95 (ISBN 0-8022-2442-3). Philos Lib.
Cheng, J. Chester, ed. Politics of the Chinese Red Army. LC 65-28426. (Publications Ser.: No. 42). 776p. 1966. 35.00x (ISBN 0-8179-1421-8). Hoover Inst Pr.
Cheng, J. Chester, tr. Documents of Dissent: Chinese Political Thought Since Mao. (Publication Ser.: No. 230). 120p. (Orig.). 1980. pap. 7.95x (ISBN 0-8179-7302-8). Hoover Inst Pr.
Cheng, Joseph. Chong Woo Kwan Chun. 1984. 27.00 (ISBN 0-901764-40-X, Pub. by P H Crompton Ltd UK). State Mutual Bk.
Cheng, Joseph Y. Hong Kong: In Search of a Future. 1985. pap. 13.95 (ISBN 0-19-583747-9). Oxford U Pr.
Cheng, Julia C. Chinese Home Cooking. LC 79-174217. (Illus.). 1981. pap. 8.25 (ISBN 0-87011-439-5). Kodansha.
Cheng, K. L. & Ueno, Keihei. CRC Handbook of Organic Analytical Reagents. 544p. 1982. 78.00 (ISBN 0-8493-0771-6). CRC Pr.
Cheng, Lorraine, ed. see New York Academy of Sciences, Feb 20-22, 1980.
Cheng, Lucie & Bonacich, Edna, eds. Labor Immigration under Capitalism: Asian Workers in the United States Before World War II. LC 82-21765. (Illus.). 635p. 1984. lib. bdg. 38.50x (ISBN 0-520-04829-6). U of Cal Pr.
Cheng, Lucie, et al. Linking Our lives: Chinese American Women of Los Angeles. LC 84-72431. (Illus.). xvii, 122p. (Orig.). 1984. pap. 9.95 (ISBN 0-930377-00-1). Chinese Hist CA.
Cheng, Lucie, et al, eds. Women in China: Bibliography of Available English Language Materials. LC 84-81228. (China Research Monograph (Special) Ser.). 100p. (Orig.). 1984. pap. 12.00x (ISBN 0-912966-72-6). IEAS.
Cheng, Man-Ch'ing & Smith, Robert W. T'ai-Chi-the Supreme Ultimate Exercise for Health, Sport, & Self-Defense. LC 67-23009. (Illus.). 1967. 16.95 (ISBN 0-8048-0560-1). C E Tuttle.
Cheng, Peter. A Chronology of the People's Republic of China from Oct. 1, 1949. 347p. 1972. 10.00x (ISBN 0-87471-099-5). Rowman.
Cheng, Peter, ed. China. (World Bibliographical Ser.: No. 35). 371p. 1984. lib. bdg. 55.00 (ISBN 0-903450-81-X). ABC-Clio.
Cheng, Peter P. A Chronology of the People's Republic of China from October 1, 1949. LC 70-184667. (Quality Paperbacks Ser.: No. 250). 347p. (Orig.). 1972. pap. 2.95 (ISBN 0-8226-0250-4). Littlefield.
Cheng, Philip C. Accounting & Fiananncing for Motor Carriers. LC 83-48661. 448p. 1984. 45.00x (ISBN 0-669-07340-7). Lexington Bks.
--Accounting & Finance in Mass Transit. LC 80-70920. (Illus.). 336p. 1982. text ed. 52.50x (ISBN 0-86598-035-7). Allanheld.
Cheng, Phillip C. Financial Management in the Shipping Industry. LC 79-15869. 377p. 1979. 27.50x (ISBN 0-87033-249-X). Cornell Maritime.
--Steamship Accounting. LC 70-80637. 192p. 1969. 11.00x (ISBN 0-87033-117-5). Cornell Maritime.
Cheng, Rose & Morris, Michele. Chinese Cookery. LC 81-80800. 192p. 1981. pap. 9.95 (ISBN 0-89586-088-0). H P Bks.
Cheng, Sally, jt. auth. see Feuerwerker, Albert.
Cheng, Seymour C. Schemes for the Federation of the British Empire. LC 68-59048. (Columbia University Studies in the Social Sciences: No. 335). Repr. of 1931 ed. 24.50 (ISBN 0-404-51335-2). AMS Pr.
Cheng, T., jt. ed. see Bulla, L.
Cheng, T. K. Archaeological Studies in Szechwan. 1957. 59.50 (ISBN 0-521-04635-1). Cambridge U Pr.
Cheng, Ta-Pei & Li, Ling-Fong. Gauge Theory of Elementary Particle Physics. (Illus.). 1984. 39.00x (ISBN 0-19-851956-7); pap. 29.00 (ISBN 0-19-851961-3). Oxford U Pr.
Cheng, Te-k'un. Studies in Chinese Art. LC 83-50019. (Illus.). 350p. 1983. 39.50x (ISBN 0-295-96053-1). U of Wash Pr.
Cheng, Thomas, ed. Current Topics in Comparative Pathobiology, 2 vols. 1971-73. Vol. 1. 70.00 (ISBN 0-12-153401-4); Vol. 2. 80.00 (ISBN 0-12-153402-2). Acad Pr.
Cheng, Thomas C. General Parasitology. 1973. text ed. 32.00i (ISBN 0-12-170750-4). Acad Pr.
Cheng, Thomas C., ed. Invertebrate Blood: Cells & Serum Factors. (Comparative Pathobiology Ser.: Vol. 6). 204p. 1984. 45.00x (ISBN 0-306-41674-3, Plenum Pr). Plenum Pub.
--Molluscicides in Schistosomiasis Control. 1974. 45.00 (ISBN 0-12-170740-7). Acad Pr.
--Pathogens of Invertebrates: Application in Biological Control & Transmission Mechanisms. (Comparative Pathobiology Ser.: Vol. 7). 268p. 1984. 49.50x (ISBN 0-306-41700-6, Plenum Pr). Plenum Pub.
--Structure of Membranes & Receptors. (Comparative Pathobiology Ser.: Vol. 5). 296p. 1984. 49.50x (ISBN 0-306-41503-8, Plenum Pr). Plenum Pub.
Cheng, T'ien-Hsi. China Moulded by Confucius. LC 73-869. (China Studies: from Confucius to Mao Ser.). (Illus.). 264p. 1973. Repr. of 1947 ed. 21.50 (ISBN 0-88355-064-4). Hyperion Conn.
Cheng, Vincent J. Shakespeare & Joyce: A Study of Finnegans Wake. LC 82-42781. 256p. 1983. 26.75x (ISBN 0-271-00342-1). Pa St U Pr.
Cheng, Ying-Wan. Postal Communication in China & Its Modernization, 1860-1896. LC 70-120316. (East Asian Monographs Ser: No. 34). (Illus.). xii, 150p. 1970. pap. 11.00x (ISBN 0-674-69320-5). Harvard U Pr.
Cheng, Yung-Chi, et al, eds. The Development of Target-Oriented Anticancer Drugs. (Progress in Cancer Research & Therapy Ser.: Vol. 28). 262p. 1983. text ed. 47.50 (ISBN 0-89004-161-X). Raven.
Cheng'an, Jiang, tr. see Shufen, Li.
Cheng'en, Wu. Journey to the West, Bk. 1. Jenner, W. J. F., tr. from Chinese. (Illus.). 575p. 1982. 15.95 (ISBN 0-8351-1003-6). China Bks.
Cheng Few, Lee. Financial Analysis & Planning: Theory & Application. LC 84-317. 1985. text ed. 35.95 (ISBN 0-201-04475-7). Addison-Wesley.
Cheng Man-Ching. Master Cheng's Thirteen Chapters on T'ai-Chi Ch'uan. 3rd ed. Wile, Douglas, tr. from Chinese. (Illus.). 72p. (Orig.). 1982. pap. 8.95 (ISBN 0-912059-00-1). Sweet Ch'i Pr.
--T'ai Chi Ch'uan: A Simplified Method of Calisthenics for Health. Tseng, Beauson, tr. from Chinese. (Illus.). 160p. (Orig.). 1981. pap. 8.95 (ISBN 0-913028-85-1). North Atlantic.
Cheng Te-k'un. Studies in Chinese Archaeology. (Illus.). 160p. 1982. 33.00x (ISBN 0-295-95912-6, Pub. by Chinese Univ Hong Kong). U of Wash Pr.
Ch'Eng T'Ien-Fang. A History of Sino-Russian Relations. LC 72-14084. 389p. 1973. Repr. of 1957 ed. lib. bdg. 39.75x (ISBN 0-8371-6751-5, CHSR). Greenwood.
Cheng Wang. The Kuomintang: A Sociological Study of Demoralization. Myers, Ramon H., ed. LC 80-8824. (China During the Interregnum 1911-1949, the Economy & Society Ser.). 179p. 1982. lib. bdg. 24.00 (ISBN 0-8240-4679-X). Garland Pub.
Cheng-Yih, W. & H. Y. Hou, eds. The Vegetation of China, Vol. 1. 1983. 95.50 (ISBN 0-677-31080-3). Gordon.
Cheng Yu-K'Uei. Foreign Trade & Industrial Development of China: An Historical & Integrated Analysis Through 1948. LC 77-26190. (Illus.). 1978. Repr. of 1956 ed. lib. bdg. 22.00x (ISBN 0-313-20062-9, CHFO). Greenwood.
Ch'en Hai-Hung. Cartoons About the Tales of the Snake Bridegroom. (National Peking University & Chinese Assn. for Folklore, Folklore & Folkliterature Ser.: No. 117). (Chinese.). 16.00x (ISBN 0-89986-194-6). Oriental Bk Store.
Chenhall, Robert H., et al. The Organizational Context of Management Accounting. LC 81-844. (Finance & Accounting Ser.). 398p. (Orig.). 1981. pap. text ed. 24.95 (ISBN 0-273-01644-X). Pitman Pub MA.
Chen Han-sheng. Landlord & Peasant in China: A Study of the Agrarian Crisis in South China. LC 73-866. (China Studies: from Confucius to Mao Ser). (Illus.). xvii, 144p. 1973. Repr. of 1936 ed. 17.50 (ISBN 0-88355-062-8). Hyperion Conn.
Ch'En Hsi-Ju, et al. Twenty Papers on Statistics & Probability. LC 61-9803. (Selected Translations in Mathematical Statistics & Probability Ser.: Vol. 12). 1973. 46.00 (ISBN 0-8218-1462-1, STAPRO-12). Am Math.
Chenier, Andre. Oeuvres Completes. 35.95 (ISBN 0-685-11442-2). French & Eur.
Chenier, Blanche. Lady of Fortune. (Orig.). 1980. pap. 1.75 (ISBN 0-449-50028-4, Coventry). Fawcett.
--Love in Exile. (Orig.). 1980. pap. 1.75 (ISBN 0-449-50046-2, Coventry). Fawcett.
Chenier, Louis De see De Chenier, Louis.
Chenieux-Gendron, Jacqueline, jt. auth. see Bonnet, Marguerite.
Ch'en Kou-Chun. Studies in Marriage & Funerals of Taiwan Aborigines. (Asian Folklore & Social Life Monograph: No. 4). (Chinese.). 1970. 14.00 (ISBN 0-89986-007-9). Oriental Bk Store.
--Studies on the Society of Aborigines in Kweichow, China. (Asian Folklore & Social Life Monograph: No. 46). 400p. (Chinese.). 1973. 20.00 (ISBN 0-89986-044-3). Oriental Bk Store.
Chenn, Lynn P. Burns: Therapy & Psychology with Subject Analysis & Research Bibliography. LC 84-45661. 150p. 1984. 29.95 (ISBN 0-88164-208-8); pap. 21.95 (ISBN 0-88164-209-6). ABBE Pubs Assn.
Chennakesavan, Sarasvati. Concepts of Indian Philosophy. lib. bdg. cancelled (ISBN 0-685-63872-3, Orient Longman); text ed. cancelled (ISBN 0-685-63873-1). South Asia Bks.
--Concepts of Mind in Indian Philosophy. 1980. 14.00x (ISBN 0-8364-0638-9). South Asia Bks.
Chennakesvan, Sarasvati. A Critical Study of Hinduism. 1980. 12.50x (ISBN 0-8364-0614-1). South Asia Bks.
Chennus, Ptolemaeus. Philosoph und Grammatiker Ptolemaeus Chennos. Repr. 12.00 (ISBN 0-384-48135-3). Johnson Repr.
Chenoweth, H. H., jt. auth. see Jensen, A.
Chenoweth, Harry, jt. auth. see Jensen, Alfred.
Chenoweth, Harry H., jt. auth. see Jensen, Alfred E.
Chenoweth, J. M. & Impagliazzo, M., eds. Fouling in Heat Exchange Equipment. 105p. 1981. 20.00 (ISBN 0-686-34494-4, G00206). ASME.
Chenoweth, J. M., et al, eds. Advances in Enhanced Heat Transfer. 168p. 1979. 24.00 (ISBN 0-686-59659-5, I00122). ASME.
Chenoweth, Linda. God's People: Nursery Leader's Guide. 64p. 1981. 2.95 (ISBN 0-686-74751-8). Westminster.
--God's People Share. Duckert, Mary, ed. 64p. 1981. nursery ldrs. guide 3.95 (ISBN 0-664-24337-1); pap. 1.55 students' book (ISBN 0-664-24336-3); resource Packet 8.95 (ISBN 0-664-24338-X). Westminster.
Chenoweth, Mary, ed. see Lawrence, D. H.
Chenoweth, Maynard B., ed. Modern Inhalation Anesthetics. LC 76-156998. (Handbook of Experimental Pharmacology: Vol. 30). (Illus.). 1972. 129.80 (ISBN 0-387-05135-X). Springer-Verlag.
Chenoweth, Patricia & Chenoweth, Thomas. How to Raise & Train a Lhasa Apso. (Orig.). pap. 2.95 (ISBN 0-87666-334-X, DS-1097). TFH Pubns.
Chenoweth, Richard & Strand, Mark. AC-SU: A History of the North Dakota Agricultural College & North Dakota State University in Photographs. LC 84-61566. (Illus.). 196p. 1985. price not set (ISBN 0-911042-30-X). N Dak Inst.
Chenoweth, Thomas, jt. auth. see Chenoweth, Patricia.
Chenoweth, Vida. Melodic Perception & Analysis: A Manual on Ethnic Melody. 132p. 1972. pap. 6.00x (ISBN 0-88312-841-1); microfiche (2) 2.86x (ISBN 0-88312-356-8). Summer Inst Ling.
--The Usarufas & Their Music. (Museum of Anthropology Publications: No. 5). 258p. 1979. 14.95x (ISBN 0-88312-154-9); microfiche 3.00x (ISBN 0-88312-242-1). Summer Inst Ling.
Chenowith, H., jt. auth. see Jensen, A. C.
Chen Shao-teh. Etude Sur le Marche Monetaire de Changhai. Myers, Ramon H., ed. LC 80-8834. (China During the Interregnum 1911-1949, The Economy & Society Ser.). 494p. 1982. lib. bdg. 55.00 (ISBN 0-8240-4693-5). Garland Pub.
Ch'en Szu-Shu. The People of T'eng-Hsien, Kuangsi. (National Peking University & Chinese Assn. for Folklore, Folklore & Folkliterature Ser.: No. 107). (Chinese.). 16.00x (ISBN 0-89986-185-7). Oriental Bk Store.
Chen-Tau, Wu. Studies on the Tea in Modern Taiwan. (Asian Folklore & Social Life Ser.: Vol. 94). 1977. 17.00 (ISBN 0-89986-326-4). Oriental Bk Store.
Chen-Tung, Chang, et al. The Case of Singapore. (Culture & Fertility Ser.). 95p. (Orig.). 1980. pap. text ed. 13.00x (ISBN 9971-902-16-8, Pub. by Inst Southeast Asian Stud). Gower Pub Co.
Chenu, M. D. Nature, Man, & Society in the Twelfth Century: Essays on New Theological Perspectives in the Latin West. Taylor, Jeromr & Little, Lester K., eds. Taylor, Jerome & Little, Lester K., trs. LC 68-15574. (Midway Reprint Ser.). xxii, 362p. 1968. pap. 16.00x (ISBN 0-226-10256-4). U of Chicago Pr.
Chen Wai-Fah & Atsuta, Toshio. Theory of Beam Columns, Vol. 2: Space Behavior & Design. 1977. text ed. 78.00x (ISBN 0-07-010759-9). McGraw.
Chen Wai-Kai. Active Network Feedback Amplifier Theory. LC 79-16997. (Illus.). 550p. 1980. text ed. 48.00 (ISBN 0-07-010779-3). McGraw.
Cheny, David, jt. auth. see Sanders, Steven.
Ch'en Ying-chen. Exiles at Home: Stories by Ch'en Ying-chen. Miller, Lucien, tr. from Chinese. (Michigan Monographs in Chinese Studies: No. 57). 150p. (Orig.). 1985. text ed. 15.00 (ISBN 0-89264-067-7); pap. text ed. 8.00 (ISBN 0-89264-068-5). U of Mich Ctr Chinese.
Chen Yuan-Chu. Songs of Tai-Shan Kwangtung. (Folklore Series of National Sun Yat-Sen University: No. 25). (Chinese.). 16.00x (ISBN 0-89986-093-1). Oriental Bk Store.
Cheo, Peter K. Fiber Optics: Devices & Systems. (Illus.). 256p. 1985. text ed. 32.95 (ISBN 0-13-314204-3). P-H.
Cheok, Cheong Kee & Lean, Lim Lin. Demographic Impact on Socio-Economic Development. LC 81-71612. (Development Studies Centre Monograph: No. 29). 129p. (Orig.). 1982. pap. text ed. 10.00 (ISBN 0-909150-69-9, 1224). Australia N U P.
Cheong, Kee Cheok & D'Silva, Emmanuel H. Prices, Terms of Trade, & the Role of Government in Pakistan's Agriculture. LC 84-7273. (World Bank Staff Working Papers: No. 643). 70p. 1984. 5.00 (ISBN 0-8213-0361-9). World Bank.
Cheong, V. E. & Hirschheim, R. A. Local Area Networks: Issues, Products & Developments. LC 82-23778. (Wiley Series in Computing). 190p. 1983. 29.95x (ISBN 0-471-90134-2, 1-320, Wiley-Interscience). Wiley.
Cheong, W. E. Mandarins & Merchants: A China Agency of the Early Nineteenth Century. (Scandinavian Inst. of Asian Studies, Monographs: No. 26). (Illus.). 1977. pap. text ed. 13.50x (ISBN 0-7007-0094-3). Humanities.
Cheong Cheng Leong & Draeger, Donn F. Phoenix-Eye Fist: A Shaolin Fighting Art of South China. LC 77-23373. (Illus.). 1977. pap. 8.95 (ISBN 0-8348-0127-2). Weatherhill.
Chepesiuk, Ronald & Shankman, Arnold, eds. American Indian Archival Material: A Guide to Holdings in the Southeast. LC 82-15447. xiii, 323p. 1982. lib. bdg. 45.00 (ISBN 0-313-23731-X, CAI/). Greenwood.
Cheradame, H., jt. auth. see Gandini, A.
Cheraksin & Ringsdorf. Predictive Medicine. 1972. 5.95x (ISBN 0-87983-150-2). Cancer Control Soc.
Cheraskin, E. Psychodietetics. 1976. pap. 3.50 (ISBN 0-553-24568-6). Bantam.
Cheraskin, E. & Ringsdof, W. Psycho-Dietetics. 2.95x (ISBN 0-553-02125-7). Cancer Control Soc.
Cheraskin, E. & Ringsdorf, W. Diet & Disease. 7.95x (ISBN 0-87983-143-X). Cancer Control Soc.
Cheraskin, E. & Ringsdorf, W. M., Jr. Predictive Medicine. LC 77-73617. (Illus.). 1977. pap. 5.95 (ISBN 0-87983-150-2). Keats.
Cheraskin, E., et al. Diet & Disease. LC 76-58773. (Illus.). 1977. pap. 7.95 (ISBN 0-87983-143-X). Keats.
Cheraskin, Emanuel, et al. The Vitamin C Connection. 336p. 1984. pap. 3.95 (ISBN 0-553-24434-5). Bantam.
Cherbonneau, Auguste. Arabic-French Dictionary, 2 vols. (Arabic & Fr.). Set. 30.00x (ISBN 0-86685-103-8). Intl Bk Ctr.
Cherches, Peter, jt. auth. see Acker, Kathy.
Cherdron, Harald, jt. auth. see Braun, Dietrich.
Cherdyntsev, Viktor. Abundance of Chemical Elements. LC 61-11892. pap. 78.50 (ISBN 0-317-26166-5, 2024087). Bks Demand UMI.
Chereck, Mary. Poems. (Nebraska Review Chapbook Ser.: No. 3). 8p. (Orig.). 1980. pap. 1.00 (ISBN 0-937796-02-6). Nebraska Review.
Cherel, Albert O. Aleman Sin Esfuerzo. 11.95 (ISBN 0-685-10984-4); records 65.00 (ISBN 0-685-10985-2); of 3 cassettes 65.00 set (ISBN 0-685-10986-0). French & Eur.
--Alemao Sem Custo. 11.95 (ISBN 0-685-10987-9); records 65.00 (ISBN 0-685-10988-7); of 3 cassettes 65.00 set (ISBN 0-685-10989-5). French & Eur.
--Allemand sans Peine. 11.95 (ISBN 0-685-10990-9). French & Eur.
--Anglais Sans Peine. 11.95 (ISBN 0-685-11001-X); record sets for both texts 65.00 ea.; of 3 cassettes 65.00 set (ISBN 0-685-11003-6). French & Eur.
--Duits Zonder Moeite. 11.95 (ISBN 0-685-11150-4). French & Eur.
--Engels Zonder Moeite. 11.95 (ISBN 0-685-11162-8). French & Eur.
--Englisch Ohne Muhe. 9.95 (ISBN 0-685-11163-6). French & Eur.
--Espagnol Sans Peine. 11.95 (ISBN 0-685-11166-0). French & Eur.
--Frances Sem Custo. 9.95 (ISBN 0-685-11200-4). French & Eur.
--Frances Sin Esfuerzo. 11.95 (ISBN 0-685-11201-2). French & Eur.
--Francese Senza Sforzo. 9.95 (ISBN 0-685-11202-0). French & Eur.
--Francuski Bez Muke. (Assimil Textbks). 11.95 (ISBN 0-685-11203-9). French & Eur.
--Frans Zonder Moeite. 11.95 (ISBN 0-685-11204-7). French & Eur.
--Franzoesisch Ohne Muhe. 9.95 (ISBN 0-685-11205-5). French & Eur.
--French Without Toil. 11.95 (ISBN 0-685-11209-8); records 75.00 (ISBN 0-686-66422-1); 75.00, 3 sets cassette (ISBN 0-686-66423-X). French & Eur.
--German Without Toil. 11.95 (ISBN 0-685-11213-6). French & Eur.
--Grec Sans Peine. 9.95 (ISBN 0-685-11224-1). French & Eur.
--Ingles Sem Custo. 9.95 (ISBN 0-685-11249-7). French & Eur.
--Ingles Sin Esfuerzo. 11.95 (ISBN 0-685-11250-0). French & Eur.
--Inglese Senze Sforzo. 9.95 (ISBN 0-685-11251-9). French & Eur.
--Italiaans Zonder Moeite. 16.95 (ISBN 0-685-11262-4). French & Eur.
--Italian Without Toil. 9.95 (ISBN 0-685-11263-2). French & Eur.
--Italien Sans Peine. 9.95 (ISBN 0-685-11264-0). French & Eur.
--Italienisch Ohne Muhe. 9.95 (ISBN 0-685-11265-9). French & Eur.
--Latin Sans Peine. 9.95 (ISBN 0-685-11288-8). French & Eur.
--Neerlandais Sans Peine. 10.95 (ISBN 0-685-11415-5). French & Eur.
--Nemacki Bez Muke. 11.95 (ISBN 0-685-11417-1). French & Eur.
--Niederlandisch Ohne Muhe. 9.95 (ISBN 0-685-11422-8). French & Eur.

--Portugais Sans Peine. 9.95 (ISBN 0-685-11505-4). French & Eur.

--Portugiesisch Ohne Muhe. 9.95 (ISBN 0-685-11507-0). French & Eur.

--Russe Sans Peine. 9.95 (ISBN 0-685-11550-X). French & Eur.

--Spaans Zonder Moeite. 11.95 (ISBN 0-685-11570-4). French & Eur.

--Spagnolo Senza Sforzo. 9.95 (ISBN 0-685-11571-2). French & Eur.

--Spanisch Ohne Muhe. 9.95 (ISBN 0-685-11573-9). French & Eur.

--Spanish Without Toil. 9.95 (ISBN 0-685-11574-7). French & Eur.

--Tedesco Senza Sforzo. 9.95 (ISBN 0-685-11582-8). French & Eur.

Cherellia, George. All about Hitting the Sweet Spot. 1976. pap. text ed. 4.80x (ISBN 0-87563-105-3). Stipes.

Cheremisinoff. Guide for Industrial Noise Control. 190p. 1982. softcover 29.95 (ISBN 0-250-40536-9). Butterworth.

--Process Level Instrumentation & Control. (Engineering Measurement & Instrumentation Ser.: Vol. 2). 256p. 1981. 45.00 (ISBN 0-8247-1212-9). Dekker.

Cheremisinoff, et al. Alternative Sources of Energy Transportation: Biomass Overview, No. 48, Mar.-Apr. 81. Marier, Donald, et al, eds. 60p. (Orig.). 1981. pap. 3.50 (ISBN 0-917328-38-8). ASEI.

Cheremisinoff, Nicholas. Applied Fluid Flow Measurement. (Engineering Measurement & Instumentation: Vol. 1). 1979. 45.00 (ISBN 0-8247-6871-X). Dekker.

Cheremisinoff, Nicholas P. Fluid Flow Pocket Handbook. LC 83-22619. 330p. 1984. Flexi-bound 21.95x (ISBN 0-87201-707-9). Gulf Pub.

--Heat Transfer Pocket Handbook. LC 84-654. (Illus.). 240p. 1984. flex-bound 24.95x (ISBN 0-87201-379-0). Gulf Pub.

--Pocket Handbook for Solid-Liquid Separations. LC 84-8970. 160p. 1984. 21.95x (ISBN 0-87201-830-X). Gulf Pub.

Cheremisinoff, Nicholas P. & Azbel, David S. Fluid Mechanics & Unit Operations. LC 82-48638. (Illus.). 1100p. 1983. 79.95 (ISBN 0-250-40541-5). Butterworth.

Cheremisinoff, Nicholas P. & Cheremisinoff, Paul N. Cooling Towers: Selection, Design, Practice. LC 81-65711. 1981. text ed. 59.95 (ISBN 0-250-40407-9). Butterworth.

--Hydrodynamics of Gas-Solids Fluidization. LC 83-18555. 1000p. 1984. 89.95x (ISBN 0-87201-352-9). Gulf Pub.

Cheremisinoff, Nicholas P., ed. Encyclopedia of Fluid Mechanics, Vol. 1: Flow Phenomena & Measurement. LC 85-9742. (Illus.). 1500p. 1985. 149.95x (ISBN 0-87201-513-0). Gulf Pub.

--Encyclopedia of Fluid Mechanics, Vol. 2: Dynamics of Single-Fluid Flows & Mixing. LC 85-9742. (Illus.). 1500p. 1985. 149.95x (ISBN 0-87201-514-9). Gulf Pub.

--Encyclopedia of Fluid Mechanics, Vol. 3: Gas-Liquid Flows. (Illus.). 1600p. 1985. 149.95x (ISBN 0-87201-515-7). Gulf Pub.

--Handbook of Heat & Mass Transfer, Vol. 1: Heat Transfer Operations. LC 84-25338. (Illus.). 1350p. 1985. 149.95x (ISBN 0-87201-411-8). Gulf Pub.

--Handbook of Heat & Mass Transfer, Vol. 2: Mass Transfer & Reactor Design. LC 84-25338. (Illus.). 1400p. 1985. 149.95x (ISBN 0-87201-412-6). Gulf Pub.

Cheremisinoff, Nicholas P. & Azbel, David S., eds. Liquid Filtration. LC 82-46063. (Illus.). 400p. 1983. 59.95 (ISBN 0-250-40600-4). Butterworth.

Cheremisinoff, Nicholas P. & Cheremisinoff, Paul N., eds. Unit Conversions & Formulas Manual. LC 79-55140. (Illus.). 1980. pap. 9.95 (ISBN 0-250-40331-5). Butterworth.

Cheremisinoff, Nicholas P. & Gupta, Ramesh, eds. Handbook of Fluids in Motion. LC 82-70706. (Illus.). 1200p. 1983. 79.95 (ISBN 0-250-40458-3). Butterworth.

Cheremisinoff, Nicholas P., et al. Flare Gas Systems Pocket Handbook. LC 85-12665. (Illus.). 100p. 1985. flexi-bound 18.95x (ISBN 0-87201-310-3). Gulf Pub.

Cheremisinoff, P., jt. ed. see Dickerson, W.

Cheremisinoff, P. H., et al. Woodwastes Utilization & Disposal. LC 76-16931. (Illus.). 1976. pap. 9.95x (ISBN 0-87762-211-6). Technomic.

Cheremisinoff, Paul & Young, Richard, eds. Air Pollution Control & Design Handbook, Pt. 1. (Pollution Engineering & Technology Ser.: Vol. 2). 1977. 85.00 (ISBN 0-8247-6444-7). Dekker.

Cheremisinoff, Paul N. Management of Hazardous Occupational Environments: Analysis Revised. LC 84-51008. 202p. 1984. pap. 24.95 (ISBN 0-317-17391-X). Technomic.

Cheremisinoff, Paul N. & Ellerbusch, Fred. Resource Conservation & Recovery Act. LC 79-66748. 69p. 1979. pap. 9.95 (ISBN 0-87762-276-0). Technomic.

Cheremisinoff, Paul N. & Young, Richard A. Pollution Engineering Practice Handbook. LC 74-14427. 1975. 59.95 (ISBN 0-250-40075-8). Butterworth.

Cheremisinoff, Paul N., jt. auth. see Bhatia, Mahesh V.

Cheremisinoff, Paul N., jt. auth. see Cheremisinoff, Nicholas P.

Cheremisinoff, Paul N., jt. auth. see DePol, Dennis R.

Cheremisinoff, Paul N., jt. auth. see Teresinski, Michael F.

Cheremisinoff, Paul N., jt. auth. see Tripodi, Raymond A.

Cheremisinoff, Paul N. & Young, Richard C., eds. Air Pollution Control & Design Handbook, Pt. 2. (Pollution Engineering & Technology Ser.: Vol. 2). 1977. 75.00 (ISBN 0-8247-6448-X). Dekker.

Cheremisinoff, Paul N., jt. ed. see Bhatia, M. V.

Cheremisinoff, Paul N., jt. ed. see Bhatia, Mahesh V.

Cheremisinoff, Paul N., jt. ed. see Cheremisinoff, Nicholas P.

Cheremisinoff, Paul N., et al. Groundwater-Leachate - Modeling-Monitoring-Sampling. LC 84-51875. 146p. 1984. pap. 24.50 (ISBN 0-87762-376-7). Technomic.

--Leachate from Hazardous Wastes Sites. LC 83-50748. 92p. 1983. 18.00 (ISBN 0-87762-334-1). Technomic.

Cheren, Stanley, ed. Psychosomatic Medicine: Theory, Physiology, & Practice. (Stress & Health Ser.: No. 1-2). 1000p. 1985. Set. text ed. 60.00 (ISBN 0-8236-5725-6); text ed. write for info. (ISBN 0-8236-5726-4). Intl Univs Pr.

Cherene, L. J., Jr. Set Valued Dynamical Systems & Economic Flow. (Lecture Notes in Economics & Mathematical Systems: Vol. 158). 1978. pap. 12.00 (ISBN 0-387-08847-4). Springer-Verlag.

Cherepanov, A. I. As Military Advisor in China. 333p. 1982. 8.70 (ISBN 0-8285-2290-1, Pub. by Progress Pubs USSR). Imported Pubns.

Cherepanov, C. P. Mechanics of Brittle Fracture. 1980. 150.00 (ISBN 0-07-010739-4). McGraw.

Cherepanov, Y. Las Travesuras De Pepito. (Illus.). 14p. (Span.). 1976. pap. 0.99 (ISBN 0-8285-1308-2, Pub. by Progress Pubs USSR). Imported Pubns.

--Watch Your Step. 140p. 1979. pap. 4.95 (ISBN 0-8285-1589-1, Pub. by Progress Pubs USSR). Imported Pubns.

Cherepov, George, jt. auth. see Blake, Wendon.

Cherep-Spriridovich, Count. The Secret World Government: Or, the Hidden Hand of the Unrevealed in History. 1977. lib. bdg. 69.95 (ISBN 0-8490-2586-9). Gordon Pr.

Cheret, Jules & Broido, Lucy. Posters of Jules Cheret. (Illus.). 128p. (Orig.). 1980. pap. 8.95 (ISBN 0-486-24010-X). Dover.

--The Posters of Jules Cheret. (Illus.). 19.00 (ISBN 0-8446-5742-5). Peter Smith.

Cherevik, E. ABC of Planning. 247p. 1982. 6.45 (ISBN 0-8285-2472-6, Pub. by Progress Pubs USSR). Imported Pubns.

Cherfas, Jeremy. Man-Made Life: An Overview of the Science, Technology & Commerce of Genetic Engineering. 279p. 1983. 15.45 (ISBN 0-394-52926-X). Pantheon.

Cherfas, Jeremy & Gribbin, John. The Redundant Male: Is Sex Irrelevant in the Modern World? LC 84-42971. 208p. 15.95 (ISBN 0-394-53030-6); pap. 7.95 (ISBN 0-394-74005-X). Pantheon.

Cherfas, Jeremy, jt. auth. see Gribbin, John.

Cherfas, Jeremy & Lewin, Roger, eds. Not Work Alone: A Cross-Cultural View of Activities Superfluous to Survival. LC 79-3805. (Illus.). 255p. 1980. 25.00 (ISBN 0-8039-1394-X). Sage.

Cherico, Daniel J. & Margolis, Otto S. Thanatology Course Outlines, Vol. 2. 16.50 (ISBN 0-405-12514-3). Ayer Co Pubs.

Cherico, Daniel J., jt. auth. see Margolis, Otto S.

Cherim, Stanley M., jt. auth. see Masterton, William.

Cherimisinoff & Moresi. Benzene: Basic & Hazardous Properties. (Pollution Engineering & Technology Ser.: Vol. 9). 1979. 49.75 (ISBN 0-8247-6860-4). Dekker.

Cherimisinoff, et al. Biomass: Applications, Technology & Production, Vol. 5. (Energy Power & Environment Ser.). 232p. 1980. 45.00 (ISBN 0-8247-6933-3). Dekker.

Cherimisinoff, Paul N. & Morresi, Angelo. Energy from Solid Wastes. (Pollution Engineering & Technology Ser.: Vol. 1). 1976. 85.00 (ISBN 0-8247-6454-4). Dekker.

Cherin, Allen H. An Introduction to Optical Fibers. (McGraw-Hill Series in Electrical Engineering). (Illus.). 336p. 1982. text ed. 44.00 (ISBN 0-07-010703-3). McGraw.

Cherington, Charles R. The Regulation of Railroad Abandonments. Bruchey, Stuart, ed. LC 80-1299. (Railroads Ser.). (Illus.). 1981. Repr. of 1948 ed. lib. bdg. 25.00x (ISBN 0-405-13769-9). Ayer Co Pubs.

Cherington, Paul T. Advertising As a Business Force: A Compilation of Experience Records. LC 75-39238. (Getting & Spending: the Consumer's Dilemma). (Illus.). 1976. Repr. of 1913 ed. 26.50x (ISBN 0-405-08015-8). Ayer Co Pubs.

--The Consumer Looks at Advertising. LC 84-46043. 210p. 1985. lib. bdg. 30.00 (ISBN 0-8240-6737-1). Garland Pub.

Cheriton, David R. Thoth System: Multi-Process Structuring & Probability. (Operating & Programming Systems Ser.: Vol. 8). 191p. 1982. 47.00 (ISBN 0-444-00701-6, North-Holland). Elsevier.

Cherkas, Selma. Dining with Celebrities. LC 66-16265. 1966. 6.50 (ISBN 0-8048-0139-8). C E Tuttle.

Cherkasky, Paul. The Rochester Diet. LC 82-83773. 288p. 1983. 14.95 (ISBN 0-8119-0488-1). Fell.

Cherkin, Arthur, et al, eds. Physiology & Cell Biology of Aging. LC 77-94148. (Aging Ser.: Vol. 8). 245p. 1979. text ed. 37.50 (ISBN 0-89004-283-7). Raven.

Cherkis, Laurence D., et al. Collier Real Estate Transactions & the Bankruptcy Code. LC 84-70341. 1984. 80.00. Bender.

Cherkovski, Neeli. Clear Wind. LC 84-70518. 65p. (Orig.). 1984. pap. 6.95 (ISBN 0-932238-21-1, Pub. by Avant Bks.). Slawson Comm.

--The Waters Re-Born. 1975. pap. 2.50 (ISBN 0-88031-017-0). Invisible-Red Hill.

Cherlin, Andrew. Marriage, Divorce, Remarriage. 160p. 1983. pap. 4.95 (ISBN 0-674-55081-1). Harvard U Pr.

Cherlin, Andrew & Celebuski, Carin. Are Jewish Families Different? 12p. 1982. pap. 1.00 (ISBN 0-686-91970-X). Am Jewish Comm.

Cherlin, Andrew J. Marriage, Divorce, Remarriage. LC 81-2901. (Social Trends in the United States Ser.). (Illus.). 160p. 1981. text ed. 14.00x (ISBN 0-674-55080-3). Harvard U Pr.

Cherlin, G. Model Theoretic Algebra Selected Topics. LC 76-15388. (Lecture Notes in Mathematics: Vol. 521). 1976. pap. 16.00 (ISBN 0-387-07696-4). Springer-Verlag.

Cherm, S. S., ed. Seminar on Nonlinear Partial, & Differential Equations. (Mathematical Sciences Research Institute Publications: Vol. 2). (Illus.). 373p. 1984. 24.00 (ISBN 0-387-96079-1). Springer-Verlag.

Chermak, A. Czech-English, English-Czech Dictionary. (Czech. & Eng.). 29.50 (ISBN 0-87557-012-7, 012-7). Saphrograph.

--English-Czech, Czech-English Dictionary. (Eng. & Czech.). 29.50 (ISBN 0-87557-012-7). Saphrograph.

Chermak, Gail D. Handbook of Audiological Rehabilitation. (Illus.). 468p. 1981. 34.75x (ISBN 0-398-04170-9). C C Thomas.

Chermayeff, Ivan. Tomato & Other Colors. (ps-3). 1981. 12.95 (ISBN 0-13-924753-X). P-H.

Chermayeff, Serge. Design & the Public Good: Selected Writings of Serge Chermayeff, 1930 to 1980. Plunz, Richard, ed. (Illus.). 336p. 1982. 37.50 (ISBN 0-262-16088-9). MIT Pr.

Chermayeff, Serge & Alexander, Christopher. Community & Privacy: Toward a New Architecture of Humanism. LC 63-10704. 1963. pap. 2.50 (ISBN 0-385-03476-8, Anch). Doubleday.

Chermet, J. & Bigot, J. M. Venography of the Inferior Vena Cava & Its Branches. Wackanheim, A., tr. from Fr. (Illus.). 280p. 1980. 116.90 (ISBN 0-387-09905-0). Springer-Verlag.

Chermet, Jacques. Atlas of Phlebography of the Lower Limbs. 256p. 1982. 69.50 (ISBN 90-247-2525-9, Pub. by Martinus Nijhoff Netherlands). Kluwer Academic.

Chermisinoff, Nicholas P. Fluid Flow: Pumps, Pipes & Channels. LC 81-68034. (Illus.). 702p. 1981. 45.00 (ISBN 0-250-40432-X). Butterworth.

Chern, Kenneth S. Dilemma in China: America's Policy Debate Nineteen Forty-Five. 277p. 1980. 19.50 (ISBN 0-208-01829-8, Archon). Shoe String.

Chern, Margaret B. New Complete Newfoundland. 2nd ed. LC 75-18266. (Complete Breed Book Ser.). (Illus.). 288p. 1985. 15.95 (ISBN 0-87605-217-0). Howell Bk.

Chern, S. S. Complex Manifolds Without Potential Theory. (Universitext Ser.). 1979. 18.00 (ISBN 0-387-90422-0). Springer-Verlag.

--Differential Geometry & Differential Equations: Proceedings of the 1980 Conference in Beijing, The People's Republic of China. 652p. 1982. 341.25 (ISBN 0-677-31120-6). Gordon.

--Selected Papers. (Illus.). 1978. 36.00 (ISBN 0-387-90339-9). Springer-Verlag.

Chern, S. S., ed. see Symposium in Pure Mathematics, - Stanford, Calif., 1973.

Chern, S. S., et al, eds. see Symposium in Pure Mathematics - San Diego - 1966.

Chernaik, Warren L. The Poet's Time: Politics & Religion in the Work of Andrew Marvell. LC 82-4395. 250p. 1983. 37.50 (ISBN 0-521-24773-X). Cambridge U Pr.

Cherne, J. The Learning Disabled Child in Your Church School. LC 12-2818. (09). 1983. pap. 3.25 (ISBN 0-570-03883-9). Concordia.

Cherne, Jacqueline. This Encircling Chain. Lando, Gail, ed. (Illus.). 60p. (Orig.). 1985. pap. text ed. 4.95 (ISBN 0-931323-04-5). Mini World Pubns.

Chernecky, Cynthia & Ramsey, Patricia W. Critical Nursing Care of the Client with Cancer. 320p. 1984. pap. 19.95 (ISBN 0-8385-1243-7). ACC.

Chernenko, K. U. Speeches & Writings: Leaders of the World. LC 84-1116. 1984. 25.00 (ISBN 0-08-031825-8). Pergamon.

Chernenko, Konstantin. Selected Speeches & Writings. (Illus.). 250p. 1982. 30.00 (ISBN 0-08-025848-4). Pergamon.

Chernenko, Konstantin U. Human Rights in Soviet Society. LC 81-6948. 144p. (Orig.). 1981. pap. 2.95 (ISBN 0-7178-0588-3). Intl Pubs Co.

Cherner, Anne. The Surveyor's Hand. LC 81-70100. 80p. (Orig.). 1981. pap. 10.00 (ISBN 0-9607302-0-6). Compton Pr.

Chernev, Irving. Capablanca's Best Chess Endings: 60 Complete Games. (Illus.). 288p. 1982. pap. 4.95 (ISBN 0-486-24249-8). Dover.

--The Chess Companion. 1973. pap. 9.95 (ISBN 0-671-21651-1, Fireside). S&S.

--Combinations: The Heart of Chess. (Illus.). 1966. pap. 4.50 (ISBN 0-486-21744-2). Dover.

--Logical Chess: Move by Move. pap. 6.95 (ISBN 0-671-21135-8, Fireside). S&S.

--The One Thousand Best Short Games of Chess. 1963. pap. 7.95 (ISBN 0-671-53801-2, Fireside). S&S.

--Practical Chess Endings. LC 69-15362. (Illus.). 1969. pap. 4.00 (ISBN 0-486-22208-X). Dover.

--Winning Chess Traps. 1946. pap. 6.95 (ISBN 0-679-14037-9, Tartan). McKay.

--Wonders & Curiosities of Chess. LC 73-76884. 224p. (Orig.). 1974. pap. 5.95 (ISBN 0-486-23007-4). Dover.

Chernev, Irving & Harkness, Kenneth. Invitation to Chess. (Fireside); pap. 5.95 (ISBN 0-671-21270-2, Fireside). S&S.

Chernev, Irving & Reinfeld, Fred. Fireside Book of Chess. 1966. pap. 8.95 (ISBN 0-671-21221-4, Fireside). S&S.

Chernev, Irving, jt. auth. see Marshall, Frank J.

Cherney, Brian. Harry Somers. LC 75-15845. (Canadian Composers Ser.). (Illus.). 1975. 22.50x (ISBN 0-8020-5325-4). U of Toronto Pr.

Cherniack, H. D. & Schneider, Jerry B. A New Approach to the Delineation of Hospital Service Areas. (Discussion Paper Ser.: No. 16). 1967. pap. 5.75 (ISBN 0-686-32185-5). Regional Sci Res Inst.

Cherniack, Louis, jt. auth. see Cherniack, Reuben M.

Cherniack, Reuben M. Current Therapy in Respiratory Medicine 1984-1985. 360p. 1984. casebound 44.00 (ISBN 0-317-01501-X, D1174-1). Mosby.

--Pulmonary Function Testing. LC 77-75533. (Illus.). 1977. pap. text ed. 12.50 (ISBN 0-7216-2528-2). Saunders.

Cherniack, Reuben M. & Cherniack, Louis. Respiration in Health & Disease. 3rd ed. (Illus.). 480p. 1983. 22.95 (ISBN 0-7216-2527-4). Saunders.

Cherniak, Laurence. The Great Books of Cannabis: Researching the Pleasures of the High Society, Vol. I. (The Great Books of Cannabis: Bk. II). (Illus.). 208p. (Orig.). 1983. 29.95 (ISBN 0-911093-03-6); pap. text ed. 19.95 (ISBN 0-911093-02-8). Cherniak-Damele.

--The Great Books of Hashish, Vol. I, Bk. I. LC 79-17557. (Illus.). 176p. 1979. pap. 14.95 (ISBN 0-915904-41-1). And-Or Pr.

Cherniak, Samuel, tr. see Hyppolite, Jean.

Cherniavsky, O. F., jt. auth. see Gokhfeld, D. A.

Chernichovsky, Dov & Meesook, Oey Astra. Regional Aspects of Family Planning & Fertility Behavior in Indonesia. (Working Paper: No. 462). 62p. 1981. 3.00 (ISBN 0-686-36192-X, WP-0462). World Bank.

Chernick, Victor, jt. ed. see Kendig, Edwin L., Jr.

Chernicoff. Mac Revealed: Programming with the Macintosh Toolbox. 256p. 1984. 19.95 (ISBN 0-317-06578-5, 6551). Hayden.

--Macintosh Pascal. Date not set. price not set. Hayden.

--Macintosh Revealed: Programming the Macintosh Toolbox. Date not set. 29.95 (ISBN 0-8104-6551-5). Hayden.

Chernicoff, S. MacPascal. (Mac Library). 256p. 1984. 19.95 (ISBN 0-317-05880-0, 6553). Hayden.

Chernicott. Macintosh Revealed: Programming with the Macintosh Toolbox. (Mac Library). 256p. 1984. 19.95 (ISBN 0-317-05879-7). Hayden.

Chernik, Barbara E. Introduction to Library Services for Library Technicians. LC 81-15663. (Illus.). 187p. 1982. text ed. 28.00 (ISBN 0-87287-275-0); 20.00 (ISBN 0-87287-282-3). Libs Unl.

--Procedures for Library Media Technical Assistants. LC 83-7070. 296p. 1983. lib. bdg. 25.00x (ISBN 0-8389-0384-3). ALA.

Chernikov, G. The Crisis of Capitalism & the Condition of the Working People. 252p. 1980. 7.45 (ISBN 0-8285-1775-4, Pub. by Progress Pubs USSR). Imported Pubns.

Chernin, Dennis K. & Manteuffel, Gregory. Health: A Holistic Approach. LC 84-40270. (Illus.). 285p. (Orig.). 1984. pap. 7.50 (ISBN 0-8356-0590-6, Quest). Theos Pub Hse.

Chernin, Kim. The Hungry Self: Women, Eating, & Identity. LC 84-40416. 224p. 1985. 15.95 (ISBN 0-8129-1146-6). Times Bks.

--In My Mother's House. LC 82-19514. 307p. (gr. 7 up). 1983. 14.95 (ISBN 0-89919-167-3). Ticknor & Fields.

--In My Mother's House: A Daughter's Story. LC 84-47564. 320p. 1984. pap. 5.72 (ISBN 0-06-091170-0, CN 1170, CN). Har-Row.

--The Obsession. LC 81-47224. 224p. 1982. pap. 4.76i (ISBN 0-06-090967-6, CN 967, CN). Har-Row.

--The Obsession: Reflections on the Tyranny of Slenderness. LC 81-47224. 192p. 1981. 12.98i (ISBN 0-06-014884-5, HarpT). Har-Row.

Cherniss, Cary. Professional Burnout in Human Services Organizations. LC 80-12136. 318p. 1980. 34.95 (ISBN 0-03-056912-5). Praeger.

--Staff Burnout: Job Stress in the Human Services. LC 80-19408. (Sage Studies in Community Mental Health: Vol. 2). (Illus.). 200p. 1980. 25.00 (ISBN 0-8039-1338-9); pap. 12.50 (ISBN 0-8039-1339-7). Sage.

Cherniss, Harold. Aristotle's Criticism of Presocratic Philosophy. 1964. lib. bdg. 32.50x (ISBN 0-88254-836-0). Octagon.

--The Riddle of the Early Academy. LC 78-66594. (Ancient Philosophy Ser.). 111p. 1982. lib. bdg. 18.00 (ISBN 0-8240-9604-5). Garland Pub.

--Selected Papers. Taran, Leonardo, ed. (Illus.). 1977. text ed. 80.50x (ISBN 90-04-05235-6). Humanities.

Cherniss, Harold F. Aristotle's Criticism of Plato & the Academy, Vol. 1. LC 62-13831. 1962. Repr. of 1944 ed. 23.00x (ISBN 0-8462-0152-6). Russell.

--Platonism of Gregory of Nyssa. 1971. Repr. of 1930 ed. lib. bdg. 18.50 (ISBN 0-8337-0556-3). B Franklin.

Cherniss, Michael D. Ingeld & Christ: Heroic Conceptions & Values in Old English Christian Poetry. (Studies in English Literature: No. 74). 267p. 1972. text ed. 29.60x (ISBN 90-2792-335-3). Mouton.

Chernoff, H. see Dantzig, G. B., et al.

Chernoff, Herman. Sequential Analysis & Optimal Design. (CBMS-NSF Regional Conference Ser.: No. 8). (Illus.). v, 119p. (Orig.). 1972. pap. text ed. 12.00 (ISBN 0-89871-006-5). Soc Indus-Appl Math.

Chernoff, Hyman M. Workbook in Clinical Electrocardiography: Problems for Self-Assessment. 162p. 1972. pap. 18.50 (ISBN 0-686-65358-0). Krieger.

Chernoff, John M. African Rhythm & African Sensibility: Aesthetics & Social Action in African Musical Idioms. LC 79-189. xviii, 262p. 1981. 10.95x (ISBN 0-226-10345-5, Phoen); cassette tape 15.00 (ISBN 0-686-86803-X, 10346-3). U of Chicago Pr.

--African Rhythm & African Sensibility. LC 79-189. 1980. 20.00x (ISBN 0-226-10344-7). U of Chicago Pr.

Chernoff, Maxine. New Faces of Nineteen Fifty-two. LC 84-25214. 57p. (Orig.). 1985. pap. 6.00 (ISBN 0-87886-124-6). Ithaca Hse.

--Utopia TV Store. LC 79-14606. 1979. pap. 3.00 (ISBN 0-916328-13-9). Yellow Pr.

Chernoff, P. R. & Marsden, J. E. Properties of Infinite Dimensional Hamiltonian Systems. LC 74-22373. (Lecture Notes in Mathematics Ser.: Vol. 425). iv, 160p. 1974. pap. 14.00 (ISBN 0-387-07011-7). Springer-Verlag.

Chernoff, Paul R. Product Formulas, Nonlinear Semigroups & Addition of Unbounded Operators. LC 73-22235. (Memoirs: No. 140). 140p. 1974. pap. 11.00 (ISBN 0-8218-1840-6, MEMO-140). Am Math.

Chernogorova, V. Enigmas Del Micromundo. 317p. (Span.). 1977. pap. 3.45 (ISBN 0-8285-1694-4, Pub. by Mir Pubs USSR). Imported Pubns.

Chernok, Norma. Your Future in Medical Assisting. LC 67-10176. (Careers in Depth Ser.). (gr. 7 up). 1982. lib. bdg. 7.97 (ISBN 0-8239-0351-6). Rosen Group.

Chernok, Norma B. Your Future in Medical Assisting. rev. ed. 1982. 8.97 (ISBN 0-8239-0359-1). Rosen Group.

Chernousov, M. Soviet Ambassador Reports Back. 167p. 1983. pap. 3.95 (ISBN 0-8285-2539-0, Pub. by Progress Pubs USSR). Imported Pubns.

Chernov, A. & Bessrebrennikov, N. Fundamentals of Heat Engineering & Hydraulics. Troitsky, A., tr. from Rus. (Illus.). 407p. 1969. 17.00x (ISBN 0-8464-0437-0). Beekman Pubs.

Chernov, A. A. Modern Crystallography III. (Series in Solid State Sciences: Vol. 36). (Illus.). 530p. 1984. 59.50 (ISBN 0-387-11516-1). Springer-Verlag.

Chernov, A. A., ed. Growth of Crystals, Vol. 12. Bradley, J. E., tr. from Russ. (Illus.). 400p. 1984. 65.00 (ISBN 0-306-18112-6, Plenum Pr.). Plenum Pub.

Chernov, A. A. & Mueller-Krumbhar, H., eds. Modern Theory of Crystal Growth I. (Chrystals - Growth, Properties, & Applications: Vol. 9). (Illus.). 146p. 1983. 40.00 (ISBN 0-387-12161-7). Springer-Verlag.

Chernov, A. A. see Shubnikov, A. V. & Sheftal, N. N.

Chernov, V. A. Moscow: A Short Guide. 220p. 1977. 6.45 (ISBN 0-8285-0537-3, Pub. by Progress Pubs USSR). Imported Pubns.

Chernov, Yu I. The Living Tundra. Love, Doris, tr. (Studies in Polar Research). (Illus.). 200p. 1985. 49.50 (ISBN 0-521-25393-4). Cambridge U Pr.

Chernova, G. P., jt. auth. see Tomashov, N. D.

Chernova-Kolbasina, Olga. Reminiscences of the Russian Revolution. LC 74-10076. (Russian Studies: Perspectives on the Revolution Ser). 287p. 1975. Repr. of 1936 ed. 22.00 (ISBN 0-88355-184-5). Hyperion Conn.

Chernow, Barbara A. Robert Morris: Land Speculator 1790-1801. LC 77-14762. (Dissertations in American Economic History Ser.). 1978. 27.50 (ISBN 0-405-11029-4). Ayer Co Pubs.

Chernow, Bart, jt. ed. see Geelhoed, Glenn.

Chernow, Burt. The Drawings of Milton Avery. LC 83-9245. (Illus.). 131p. 1984. 17.95 (ISBN 0-8008-2298-6); pap. 11.95 (ISBN 0-8008-2299-4). Taplinger.

--Gabor Peterdi: Paintings. LC 82-50989. (Illus.). 120p. 1983. 29.95 (ISBN 0-8008-3121-7). Taplinger.

--Lester Johnson: The Kaleidoscopic Crowd. LC 74-34550. (Illus.). 72p. 1975. 12.00 (ISBN 0-685-56529-7, Dist. by David Anderson Gallery). D Anderson.

Chernow, Carol, jt. auth. see Chernow, Fred.

Chernow, Carol, jt. auth. see Chernow, Fred B.

Chernow, Fred. Business Mathematics Simplified & Self-Taught. LC 82-1713. 144p. 1982. pap. 4.95 (ISBN 0-668-05390-9, 5390). Arco.

Chernow, Fred & Chernow, Carol. School Administrator's September-June Almanac of Events, Activities & Procedures. 1977. 18.50x (ISBN 0-13-792242-6, Parker). P-H.

Chernow, Fred, et al, eds. Ion Implantation in Semiconductors 1976. Brice, David K. LC 77-2980. 754p. 1977. 95.00x (ISBN 0-306-36256-2, Plenum Pr). Plenum Pub.

Chernow, Fred B. & Chernow, Carol. Careers for the Community College Graduate. LC 81-702. 192p. 1981. lib. bdg. 11.95 (ISBN 0-668-05089-6); pap. 6.95 (ISBN 0-668-05091-8). Arco.

--Classroom Discipline & Control: One Hundred & One Practical Techniques. LC 80-21700. 204p. 1981. 16.95 (ISBN 0-13-136283-6, Parker). P-H.

Chernow, Fred B., et al. Reading Exercises on Spanish Americans: Puerto Ricans, Cubans & Latin Americans. (Illus.). 64p. (gr. 4 up). 1973. pap. 1.25 (ISBN 0-8454-2103-4); tchr's ed. incl. (ISBN 0-685-31674-2); thirty posters 10.50 (ISBN 0-8454-2104-2). Continental Pr.

Cherns, A. B., intro. by. Social Science Organization & Policy, First Series: Belgium, Chile, Egypt, Hungary, Nigeria & Sri Lanka. (New Babylon Studies in the Social Sciences: No. 17). 1974. pap. text ed. 16.00x (ISBN 90-2797-290-7). Mouton.

--Social Science Organization & Policy: First Ser.: Belgium, Chile, Egypt, Hungary, Nigeria, Sri Lanka. 352p. (Orig., Co-published with Mouton, The Hague). 1974. pap. 21.00 (ISBN 92-3-101084-0, U614, UNESCO). Unipub.

Cherns, Albert & Shelhav, Moshe. Communities in Crisis. 1985. text ed. price not set (ISBN 0-566-00816-5). Gower Pub Co.

Cherns, Albert, ed. Quality of Working Life & the Kibbutz Experience. 287p. 1980. lib. bdg. 32.50 (ISBN 0-8482-3550-9). Norwood Edns.

Cherns, Albert, intro. by see Shoham, S. Giora.

Cherns, Albert B., jt. ed. see Davis, Louis E.

Chernuchin, Michael, ed. Vonnegut Talks! 1977. pap. text ed. write for info (ISBN 0-918524-04-0). Pylon.

Chernukh, A. M., ed. Regulation of the Capacitance Vessel. 1978. 46.00 (ISBN 0-9960009-1-7, Pub. by Akademiai Kaido Hungary). Heyden.

Chernukhin, A. E. English-Russian Polytechnical Dictionary. (Eng. & Rus.). 97.00 (ISBN 0-08-021936-5). Pergamon.

--English-Russian Polytechnical Dictionary. 647p. 1976. 20.50 (ISBN 0-8285-0595-0, Pub. by Rus Lang Pubs USSR). Imported Pubns.

Chernukhin, A. E., ed. English-Russian Polytechnical Dictionary. 688p. (Eng. & Rus.). 1979. 70.00x (ISBN 0-569-08580-2, Pub. by Collets). State Mutual Bk.

Cherny, G. G., ed. see CISM (International Center for Mechanical Sciences).

Cherny, Robert W. Populism, Progressivism, & the Transformation of Nebraska Politics; 1885-1915. LC 80-11151. (Illus.). xviii, 227p. 1981. 19.95x (ISBN 0-8032-1407-3). U of Nebr Pr.

--A Righteous Cause: The Life of William Jennings Bryan. Handlin, Oscar, ed. LC 84-19434. 256p. 1985. 15.95. Little.

--A Righteous Cause: The Life of William Jennings Bryan. (Library of American Biography). 1984. pap. text ed. 6.95 (ISBN 0-316-13856-8). Little.

Cherny, Robert W. & Issel, William. San Francisco. Hundley, Norris, Jr. & Schutz, John A., eds. LC 81-67253. (Golden State Ser.). (Illus.). 120p. 1981. pap. text ed. 6.95x (ISBN 0-87835-120-5). Boyd & Fraser.

Chernyavsky, V., ed. CIA in the Dock. 176p. 1983. 6.95 (ISBN 0-8285-2686-9, Pub. by Progress Pubs USSR). Imported Pubns.

Chernyi, G. G. Introduction to Hypersonic Flow. Probstein, Ronald F., ed. 1961. 59.50 (ISBN 0-12-170650-8). Acad Pr.

Chernyonok, Mikhail. Losing Bet: An Anton Birukov Mystery. Bouis, Antonia W., tr. LC 83-18965. 240p. 1984. 14.95 (ISBN 0-385-27853-5, Dial). Doubleday.

Chernyshevskii, Nikolai G. Selected Philosophical Essays. LC 79-2896. 610p. 1981. Repr. of 1953 ed. 45.00 (ISBN 0-8305-0064-2). Hyperion Conn.

Chernyshevsky, N. What Is to be Done? 485p. 1983. 11.95 (ISBN 0-8285-2556-0, Pub. by Raduga Pubs USSR). Imported Pubns.

Chernyshevsky, Nikolai. What Is to Be Done? Feuer, K., ed. & tr. from Rus. 482p. 1985. pap. 6.95 (ISBN 0-317-31562-5). Ardis Pubs.

Cheron, T., tr. see Donski, A. V., et al.

Cheronis, Nicholas & Entrikin, John B. Identification of Organic Compounds: A Student's Text Using Semimicro Techniques. LC 62-21450. pap. 122.30 (ISBN 0-317-26179-7, 2025183). Bks Demand UMI.

Cheronis, Nicholas D. & Entrikin, John B. Identification of Organic Compounds: A Students Text Using Semimicro Techniques. 1963. 55.00 (ISBN 0-470-15279-6, Pub. by Wiley-Interscience). Wiley.

Cheronis, Nicholas D., et al. Semimicro Qualitative Organic Analysis: The Systematic Identification of Organic Compounds. 3rd ed. LC 80-461. 1072p. 1983. Repr. of 1965 ed. lib. bdg. 62.50 (ISBN 0-89874-124-6). Krieger.

Cherow, Evelyn. Hearing-Impaired Children & Youth with Development Disabilities: An Interdisciplinary Foundation for Service. Matkin, Noel D. & Trybus, Raymond J., eds. LC 85-4356. 416p. 1985. 29.95 (ISBN 0-913580-97-X). Gallaudet Coll.

Cherpack, Clifton. Logos in Mythos: Ideas & Early French Narrative. LC 83-80663. (Monographs: No. 46). 212p. 1983. pap. 15.00x (ISBN 0-917058-46-1). French Forum.

Cherpin, Jean. Cezanne's Graphic Work. 128p. (Orig.). 1972. pap. 40.00 (ISBN 0-915346-87-7). A Wofsy Fine Arts.

Cherrier, Francois. Fascinating Experiments in Physics. Egan, E. W., tr. LC 78-57789. (Illus.). 96p. (gr. 7 up). 1978. 14.95 (ISBN 0-8069-3104-3); PLB 17.79 (ISBN 0-8069-3105-1). Sterling.

Cherrington, jt. auth. see Jensen.

Cherrington, B. E. Gaseous Electronics & Gas Lasers. 1979. text ed. 57.00 (ISBN 0-08-020622-0). Pergamon.

Cherrington, Ben M. Methods of Education in International Attitudes. LC 77-176642. (Columbia University. Teachers College. Contributions to Education: No. 595). Repr. of 1934 ed. 22.50 (ISBN 0-404-55595-0). AMS Pr.

Cherrington, David J. Personnel Management: Human Resource Management. 720p. 1983. text ed. write for info. (ISBN 0-697-08085-4); instrs' manual avail. (ISBN 0-697-08093-5); study guide avail. (ISBN 0-697-08094-3). Wm C Brown.

--The Work Ethic: Working Values & Values That Work. LC 80-65871. pap. 75.50 (ISBN 0-317-26705-1, 2023512). Bks Demand UMI.

Cherrington, Ernest H. Evolution of Prohibition in the United States of America: A Chronological History of the Liquor Problem & the Temperance Reform in the United States from the Earliest Settlements to the Consummation of National Prohibition. LC 69-14916. (Criminology, Law Enforcement, & Social Problems Ser.: No. 40). 1969. Repr. of 1920 ed. 13.50x (ISBN 0-87585-040-5). Patterson Smith.

--Exploring the Moon Through Binoculars & Small Telescopes. (Illus.). 224p. 1983. pap. 10.95 (ISBN 0-486-24491-1). Dover.

Cherrington, Homer V. The Investor & the Securities Act. LC 78-173651. (FDR & the Era of the New Deal Ser.). 266p. 1973. Repr. of 1942 ed. lib. bdg. 27.50 (ISBN 0-306-70371-8). Da Capo.

Cherrington, J. Owen. Accounting Basics. LC 80-24923. 431p. 1981. text ed. write for info. (ISBN 0-534-00902-6); wkbk. 9.95x (ISBN 0-534-00903-4). Kent Pub Co.

Cherrington, J. Owen, et al. Cost & Managerial Accounting. 912p. 1984. text ed. write for info. (ISBN 0-697-08231-8); instr's. manual avail. (ISBN 0-697-00251-9); wkbk. avail. (ISBN 0-697-00244-6); transparencies avail. (ISBN 0-697-00287-X); solutions manual avail. (ISBN 0-697-00357-4). Wm C Brown.

Cherrington, John. A Farming Year. (Illus.). 136p. 1984. 24.00 (ISBN 0-340-28209-6, Pub. by Hodder & Stoughton UK). David & Charles.

Cherry. Plating Waste Treatment. LC 81-68033. 324p. 1982. 59.95 (ISBN 0-250-40417-6). Butterworth.

Cherry, Annie, ed. see Brown, Shiron L.

Cherry, B. W. Polymer Surfaces. LC 80-40013. (Cambridge Solid State Science Ser.). (Illus.). 150p. 1981. 42.50 (ISBN 0-521-23082-9); pap. 17.95 (ISBN 0-521-29792-3). Cambridge U Pr.

Cherry, Bridget & Pevsner, Nikolaus. London One: The Cities of London & Westminster. (An Allen Lane Bk.). 20.00 (ISBN 0-14-071012-4). Viking.

--London One: The Cities of London & Westminster. 756p. 1984. 20.00 (ISBN 0-14-071012-4). Allen Lane.

--London Two: South. (An Allen Lane Book). 20.00 (ISBN 0-14-071047-7). Viking.

--London Two: South. 812p. 1984. 20.00 (ISBN 0-14-071047-7). Allen Lane.

Cherry, C. God's New Israel: Religious Interpretations of American Destiny. 1971. pap. 24.95 (ISBN 0-13-357335-4). P-H.

Cherry, C. J. Chanur's Venture. 320p. 1985. pap. 2.95 (ISBN 0-87997-989-5). DAW Bks.

Cherry, Caroline L. The Most Unvaluedst Purchase: Women in the Plays of Thomas Middleton. (Salzburg Studies in English Literature, Jacobean Drama Studies: No. 34). 114p. 1973. pap. text ed. 25.50x (ISBN 0-391-01342-4). Humanities.

Cherry, Clare. Creative Art for the Developing Child: A Teacher's Handbook for Early Childhood Education. LC 72-81202. 1972. pap. 8.95 (ISBN 0-8224-1630-1). Pitman Learning.

--Creative Movement for the Developing Child: A Nursery School Handbook for Non-Musicians. rev. ed. LC 79-125140. 1971. pap. 5.95 (ISBN 0-8224-1660-3). Pitman Learning.

--Creative Play for the Developing Child. LC 75-16950. 1976. pap. 11.95 (ISBN 0-8224-1632-8). Pitman Learning.

--Nursery School Bulletin Boards. 1973. pap. 4.95 (ISBN 0-8224-4786-X). Pitman Learning.

--Parent, Please Don't Sit on Your Kids: Alternatives to Punitive Discipline. LC 82-81981. 1982. pap. 8.95 (ISBN 0-8224-5474-2). Pitman Learning.

--Think of Something Quiet. LC 80-82981. (Early Childhood Library). 1981. pap. 7.95 (ISBN 0-8224-6949-9). Pitman Learning.

Cherry, Clare, et al. Nursery School & Day Care Center Management Guide. rev ed. 1978. looseleaf bdg. o.p. 22.50 (ISBN 0-8224-4791-6); pap. 19.95 (ISBN 0-8224-4792-4). Pitman Learning.

Cherry, Colin. The Age of Access: Information Technology & Social Revolution. Edmondson, William, ed. (New Information Technology Ser.). 176p. 1985. 29.00 (ISBN 0-7099-3458-0, Pub. by Croom Helm Ltd). Longwood Pub Group.

--On Human Communication: A Review, a Survey & a Criticism. 3rd ed. 1978. pap. 9.95x (ISBN 0-262-53038-4). MIT Pr.

Cherry, Colin, ed. Pragmatic Aspects of Human Communication. LC 73-91427. (Theory & Decision Library: No. 4). 176p. 1974. lib. bdg. 31.50 (ISBN 90-277-0432-5, Pub. by Reidel Holland); pap. 21.00 (ISBN 90-277-0520-8, Pub. by Reidel Holland). Kluwer Academic.

Cherry, Conrad. Nature & Religious Imagination: From Edwards to Bushnell. LC 79-7374. 256p. 1980. 13.95 (ISBN 0-8006-0550-0, 1-550). Fortress.

Cherry, Conrad, ed. Horace Bushnell: Sermons. (Sources of American Spirituality Ser.). 256p. (Orig.). 1985. 14.95 (ISBN 0-8091-0362-1). Paulist Pr.

Cherry, Conrad, ed. see Wyllie, Robert W.

Cherry, Conrad, et al. Jonathan Edwards: His Life & Influence. Angoff, Charles, ed. LC 74-4516. (Leverton Lecture Series II). 65p. 1975. 9.50 (ISBN 0-8386-1571-6). Fairleigh Dickinson.

Cherry, David. Preparing Artwork for Reproduction. 1976. 19.95 (ISBN 0-7134-3097-4, Pub. by Batsford England). David & Charles.

Cherry, Don. Grapes: Les Raining De La Victorie. (Fr.). 1984. pap. 4.50 (ISBN 0-380-68163-3, 68163). Avon.

Cherry, Don & Fischler, Stan. Grapes: A Vintage View of Hockey. 218p. 1983. 15.95 (ISBN 0-13-363499-X). P-H.

--Grapes: A Vintage View of Hockey. 1983. pap. 3.50 (ISBN 0-380-65177-7, 65177). Avon.

Cherry, Eloise H. The Complete Chesapeake Bay Retriever. LC 80-25037. (Complete Breed Book). (Illus.). 288p. 1985. 15.95 (ISBN 0-87605-074-7). Howell Bk.

Cherry, G., jt. auth. see Brecher, J.

Cherry, G., ed. Pioneers in British Planning. (Illus.). 272p. 1981. pap. text ed. 18.80x (ISBN 0-85139-566-X, Pub. by Architectural Pr England). Humanities.

Cherry, G. E., jt. auth. see Burton, Thomas L.

Cherry, George. Parallel Programming in ANSI Standard Ada. 1984. text ed. 21.95 (ISBN 0-8359-5434-X). Reston.

--Pascal Programming Structures for Motorola Microprocessors. 1981. text ed. 24.95 (ISBN 0-8359-5465-X); pap. text ed. 16.95 (ISBN 0-8359-5471-4). Reston.

Cherry, George, jt. auth. see Brecher, Jerry.

Cherry, George, jt. auth. see Cortesi, David.

Cherry, George L. Convention Parliament, 1689: A Biographical Study of Its Members. LC 65-24394. 218p. 1966. text ed. 27.00x (ISBN 0-8290-0163-8). Irvington.

Cherry, George W. Pascal Programming Structures: An Introduction to Systematic Programming. (Illus.). 336p. 1980. text ed. 20.95 O.P. (ISBN 0-8359-5463-3); pap. text ed. 18.95 (ISBN 0-8359-5462-5). Reston.

Cherry, Gordon E., ed. Shaping an Urban World: Planning in the Twentieth Century. LC 80-17276. 1980. 30.00 (ISBN 0-312-71618-4). St Martin.

Cherry, James D., jt. auth. see Feigin, Ralph D.

Cherry, Joe H. Molecular Biology of Plants: A Text Manual. (A Molecular Biology Ser.). 204p. 1973. 29.50x (ISBN 0-231-03642-6). Columbia U Pr.

Cherry, Joetta & Tomlin, Gwynne. Disco Dancing. LC 79-51213. (Illus.). (gr. 2 up). 1979. PLB 3.79 (ISBN 0-448-13613-9, G&D). Putnam Pub Group.

Cherry, John A., jt. auth. see Freeze, R. Allan.

Cherry, John P., ed. Food Protein Deterioration: Mechanisms & Functionality. LC 82-20739. (ACS Symposium Ser.: No. 206). 444p. 1982. lib. bdg. 49.95x (ISBN 0-8412-0751-8). Am Chemical.

--Protein Functionality in Foods. LC 81-97. (ACS Symposium Ser.: No. 147). 1981. 44.95 (ISBN 0-8412-0605-8). Am Chemical.

Cherry, Kelly. Conversion. (Story Ser.: No. 8). (Illus.). 52p. 1979. signed 8.00 (ISBN 0-914232-29-0); pap. 2.50 (ISBN 0-914232-28-2). McPherson & Co.

--In the Wink of an Eye. 320p. 1983. 15.95 (ISBN 0-15-144656-3). HarBraceJ.

--The Lost Traveller's Dream. 227p. 1984. 13.95 (ISBN 0-15-153567-1). HarBraceJ.

--Relativity: A Point of View. LC 76-45643. x, 59p. 1977. 13.95x (ISBN 0-8071-0276-8); pap. 4.95 (ISBN 0-8071-0277-6). La State U Pr.

Cherry, Kelly, et al. Secrets. MacArthur, Mary, ed. 1979. pap. 3.50 (ISBN 0-916300-18-8). Gallimaufry.

Cherry, M. L. & Lande, K., eds. Solar Neutrinos & Neutrino Astronomy. LC 84-63143. (Conference Proceedings Ser.: No. 126). 320p. 1985. lib. bdg. 44.25 (ISBN 0-88318-325-0). Am Inst Physics.

Cherry, Marlin O. Botany Laboratory Workbook. 4th ed. (Illus.). 140p. 1982. pap. text ed. 6.95x (ISBN 0-89641-077-3). American Pr.

--Zoology Laboratory Workbook. 4th ed. 152p. 1982. pap. text ed. 6.95x (ISBN 0-89641-108-7). American Pr.

Cherry, R. C., et al, eds. Materials of Construction of Fluid Machinery & Their Relationship to Design & Performance. 104p. 1981. 24.00 (ISBN 0-686-34499-5, H00208). ASME.

Cherry, R. L., ed. see Saxton, Dean & Saxton, Lucille.

Cherry, Raymond. General Plastics: Projects & Procedures. rev. ed. (Illus.). (gr. 10-12). 1967. text ed. 16.64 (ISBN 0-87345-162-7). McKnight.

--Leathercrafting: Procedures & Projects. LC 79-83885. (Illus.). 1979. pap. 7.28 (ISBN 0-87345-153-8, B81925). McKnight.

Cherry, Robert D. Macroeconomics. LC 79-3130. (Economics Ser.). 1980. text ed. 25.95 (ISBN 0-201-00911-0). Addison-Wesley.

Cherry, Sheldon. Understanding Pregnancy & Childbirth. rev. ed. 192p. 1984. pap. 3.95 (ISBN 0-553-23934-1). Bantam.

Cherry, Sheldon H. Rovinsky & Guttmacher's Medical Surgical & Gynecologic Complications of Pregnancy. 3rd ed. 1056p. 1985. 98.00 (ISBN 0-683-01670-9). Williams & Wilkins.

--Understanding Pregnancy & Childbirth. rev. ed. LC 82-17800. 272p. 1983. 11.95 (ISBN 0-672-52758-8). Bobbs.

Cherry, Susan S., ed. Video Involvement for Libraries: A Current Awareness Package for Professionals. LC 81-2337. 84p. 1981. pap. 6.00x (ISBN 0-8389-0323-1). ALA.

Cherry, William. Economic Geography. 1975. text ed. write for info. (ISBN 0-88429-008-5). Collegiate Pub.

Cherryh, C. J. Angel with the Sword. 1985. 15.50 (ISBN 0-8099-0001-7). DAW Bks.

--Brothers of Earth. (Science Fiction Ser). 1976. pap. 2.95 (ISBN 0-87997-869-4, UE1869). DAW Bks.

--Cuckoo's Egg. 1985. 17.00 (ISBN 0-932096-34-4). Phantasia Pr.

--Cuckoo's Egg. 319p. 1985. pap. 3.50 (ISBN 0-88677-083-1). DAW Bks.

--Downbelow Station. (Science Fiction Ser.). 1983. pap. 3.50 (ISBN 0-87997-987-9). Daw Bks.

--The Dreamstone. 1983. pap. 2.95 (ISBN 0-88677-013-0). DAW Bks.

--The Faded Sun: Kesrith. (Science Fiction Ser). (Orig.). 1978. pap. 3.50 (ISBN 0-87997-960-7, UE1960). DAW Bks.

--The Faded Sun: Kutath. (Science Fiction Ser.). (Orig.). 1980. pap. 2.75 (ISBN 0-87997-856-2). DAW Bks.

--The Faded Sun: Shon'jir. (Science Fiction Ser.). 1979. pap. 2.95 (ISBN 0-87997-889-9). DAW Bks.

--Fires of Azeroth. (Science Fiction Ser.). 1984. pap. 2.50 (ISBN 0-87997-925-9). DAW Bks.

--Forty Thousand in Gehenna. 1984. pap. 3.50 (ISBN 0-87997-952-6). DAW Bks.

--Gate of Ivrel. (Science Fiction Ser.). 1976. pap. 2.50 (ISBN 0-87997-956-9, UE1615). DAW Bks.

--Hestia. (Daw Science Fiction Ser.). (Orig.). 1979. pap. 2.25 (ISBN 0-87997-680-2). Daw Bks.

--Hunter of Worlds. (Science Fiction Ser.). (Orig.). 1977. pap. 2.95 (ISBN 0-87997-872-4). DAW Bks.

--The Kif Strike Back. 1985. 17.00 (ISBN 0-932096-35-2). Phantasia Pr.

--Merchanter's Luck. 208p. 1982. pap. 2.95 (ISBN 0-87997-745-0). DAW Bks.

--The Pride of Chanur. 1982. pap. 2.95 (ISBN 0-87997-694-2, UE1694). DAW Bks.

--Serpent's Reach. (Science Fiction Ser.). 1985. pap. 3.50 (ISBN 0-88677-088-2). DAW Bks.

--Sunfall. 1983. pap. 2.50 (ISBN 0-87997-881-3, UE1881). DAW Bks.

--The Tree of Swords & Jewels. 1983. pap. 2.95 (ISBN 0-87997-850-3). DAW Bks.

--Voyager in Night. 224p. 1984. pap. 2.95 (ISBN 0-87997-920-8). DAW Bks.

--Wave Without a Shore. (Science Fiction Ser.). 176p. 1981. pap. 2.50 (ISBN 0-87997-957-7). DAW Bks.

--Well of Shiuan. (Science Fiction Ser.). (Orig.). 1978. pap. 2.95 (ISBN 0-87997-986-0). DAW Bks.

Cherryh, C. J., tr. see Walther, Daniel.

Cherryholmes, C. & Manson, G. Our Communities. (Illus.). (gr. 3). text ed. 14.00 (ISBN 0-07-011983-X). McGraw.

Cherryholmes, Lynn. Learning about People. (Illus.). (gr. 2). 1979. tchr's. ed. 12.88 (ISBN 0-07-011982-1). McGraw.

Chertijin, V., et al. America Latina: Nacionalismo, Democracia y Revolucion. 188p. (Span.). 1978. pap. 4.95 (ISBN 0-8285-1675-8, Pub. by Progress Pubs USSR). Imported Pubns.

Chertkov, Aleksandr D. Opisanie Voiny Velikago Kniazia Sviatoslava Igorevicha Protiv Bolgar I Grekov V 967-971 Godakh. (Rus.). 1972. 30.00 (ISBN 0-918884-24-1). Slavia Lib.

Chertkov, Vladimir. Short Biography of William Lloyd Garrison. LC 78-111569. Repr. of 1904 ed. 17.50x (ISBN 0-8371-4590-2, CLG&). Greenwood.

Chertkov, Vladimir G. The Last Days of Tolstoy. Duddington, Nathalie A., tr. from Rus. LC 73-9663. (Illus.). 180p. 1973. 21.00 (ISBN 0-527-16500-X). Kraus Repr.

Chertoff, Mordecai, jt. ed. see Alexander, Yona.

Chertoff, Mordecai S., jt. ed. see Curtis, Michael.

Chertoff, Mordecai S., jt. ed. see Leftwich, Joseph.

Chertoff, Mordechai, ed. Zionism: A Basic Reader. 1976. 1.00 (ISBN 0-685-82601-5). Herzl Pr.

Chertok, Barbara L., et al. IBM PC & XT Owner's Manual: A Practical Guide to Operations. LC 83-15576. 224p. 1983. pap. 14.95 (ISBN 0-89303-531-9). Brady Comm.

Chertok, L., ed. see International Congress of Psychosomatic Medicine, 4th, Paris, Sept. 1970.

Chertok, Leon. Sense & Nonsense in Psychotherapy: The Challenge of Hypnosis. LC 80-41755. (Illus.). 260p. 1981. 40.00 (ISBN 0-08-026793-9); pap. 19.75 (ISBN 0-08-026813-7). Pergamon.

Chertok, Semen. Poslednyaya lyubov' Maykovskogo. LC 83-173. (Illus., Orig., Rus.). 1983. pap. 7.00 (ISBN 0-938920-31-6). Hermitage.

Chertow, Bruce S., et al. Patient Management Problems: Exercises in Decision Making & Problem Solving. 333p. 1979. pap. 35.00 (ISBN 0-8385-7769-5). ACC.

Chertow, D., jt. auth. see Whipple, J.

Chertow, Doris, ed. Agenda for Comparative Studies in Adult Education. 1972. 3.00 (ISBN 0-87060-052-4, OCP 29). Syracuse U Cont Ed.

Chertow, Doris S., jt. ed. see Reagen, Michael V.

Cherubim, Dieter, ed. Sprachwandel: Reader Zur diachronischen Sprachwissenschaft. (Grundlagen der Kommunikation). x, 362p. 1979. pap. 14.40x (ISBN 3-11-004330-0). De Gruyter.

Cherubini, Isabella, tr. see Roncaglia, Alessandro.

Cherubini, Maria L. Demophoon. Gossett, Philip & Rosen, Charles, eds. LC 76-49213. (Early Romantic Opera Ser.: Vol. 32). 1979. lib. bdg. 90.00 (ISBN 0-8240-2931-3). Garland Pub.

--Les Deux Journees. Gossett, Phillip & Rosen, Charles, eds. LC 76-49214. (Early Romantic Opera Ser.: No. 35). 1980. lib. bdg. 99.00 (ISBN 0-8240-2934-8). Garland Pub.

--Eliza Ou le Voyage Aux Glaciers Du Mont S. Bernard. Gossett, Philip & Rosen, Charles, eds. LC 76-49216. (Early Romantic Opera Ser.). 1979. lib. bdg. 99.00 (ISBN 0-8240-2933-X). Garland Pub.

--Lodoiska. Gossett, Philip & Rosen, Charles, eds. LC 76-49217. (Early Romantic Opera Ser.: Vol. 33). 1979. lib. bdg. 99.00 (ISBN 0-8240-2932-1). Garland Pub.

Cherulnik, Paul D. Behavioral Research: Assessing the Validity of Research Findings in Psychology. 371p. 1983. text ed. 20.50 scp (ISBN 0-06-041258-5, HarpC). Har-Row.

Chervel, ed. see Saint Simon, L.

Chervin, Ronda. Victory over Death. LC 85-8213. (Orig.). 1985. pap. 4.00 (ISBN 0-932506-43-7). St Bedes Pubns.

Chervin, Ronda & Neill, Mary. The Woman's Tale: A Journal of Inner Exploration. 160p. (Orig.). 1980. pap. 7.95 (ISBN 0-8164-2016-5, Pub. by Seabury). Winston Pr.

Chervokas, John. Pinstripe Prayers: Or How to Talk to God While Pursuing Mammon. 48p. (Orig.). 1984. pap. 2.95 (ISBN 0-86683-874-0, 7457, Seabury). Winston Pr.

Chervokas, John V. How to Keep God Alive From Nine to Five. LC 85-12879. 120p. 1986. 11.95 (ISBN 0-385-23327-2). Doubleday.

Cherwitz, Richard A. & Hikins, James W. Communication & Knowledge. (Rhetoric-Communication Ser.). 200p. 1985. text ed. 17.95x (ISBN 0-87249-465-9). U of SC Pr.

Chesanow, Neil. Europe for One: A Complete Guide for Solo Travelers. LC 82-9850. 362p. 1982. pap. 8.25 (ISBN 0-525-93227-5, 0801-240). Dutton.

--The World-Class Executive: How to Do Business Like a Pro Anywhere on the Globe. LC 84-43106. 320p. 1985. 16.95 (ISBN 0-89256-258-7). Rawson Assocs.

Chesapeake Research Consortium, ed. Background Papers on Chesapeake Bay in Research & Related Matters. pap. 2.00 (ISBN 0-943676-14-2). MD Sea Grant Col.

Chesbro, George. The Beasts of Valhalla. LC 84-20354. 352p. 1985. 15.95 (ISBN 0-689-11516-4). Atheneum.

--Turn Loose the Dragon. 320p. 1982. pap. 2.95 (ISBN 0-345-29029-1). Ballantine.

Chesbro, George C. An Affair of Sorcerers. 352p. 1982. 20.00x (ISBN 0-7278-0647-5, Pub. by Severn Hse). State Mutual Bk.

--City of Whispering Stone. 224p. 1982. 20.00x (ISBN 0-7278-0733-1, Pub. by Severn Hse). State Mutual Bk.

--Shadow of a Broken Man. 240p. 1982. 20.00x (ISBN 0-7278-0702-1, Pub. by Severn Hse). State Mutual Bk.

Chesbro, Paul L. & Crosby, Chester A. Osterville, a Walk Through the Past, Five Hundred Photos, Eighteen Sixty to Nineteen Thirty. (Illus.). 1979. 30.00x (ISBN 0-88492-026-7). W S Sullwold.

Chescoe, Dawn & Goodhew, Peter. The Operation of the Transmission Electron Microscope. (Royal Microscopical Society Handbooks Ser.). (Illus.). 1984. pap. 7.95x (ISBN 0-19-856402-3). Oxford U Pr.

Chesebro & Hamsher. MODCOM: Orientations to Public Communication. Applbaum, Ronald & Hart, Roderick, eds. 1984. pap. text ed. 2.25 (ISBN 0-574-22513-7, 13-5513). SRA.

Chesebro, Doreen, jt. auth. see Badasch, Shirley.

Chesebro, James W., ed. Gayspeak: Gay Male & Lesbian Communication. LC 82-355. 384p. 1981. 17.95 (ISBN 0-8298-0472-2); pap. 9.95 (ISBN 0-8298-0456-0). Pilgrim NY.

Chesham, Sallie. One Hand upon Another. (Illus.). 160p. (Orig.). 1978. pap. 1.50 (ISBN 0-89216-016-0). Salvation Army.

--Peace Like a River. 1981. pap. 5.95 (ISBN 0-86544-014-X). Salvation Army.

--Preaching Ladies. (Illus.). 179p. (Orig.). 1983. pap. 3.50 (ISBN 0-89216-045-4). Salvation Army.

--Wind Chimes. 1983. 4.95 (ISBN 0-86544-021-2). Salvation Army.

Chesher, Richard H. The Systematics of Sympatric Species in West Indian Spatangoids: A Revision of the Genera Brissopsis, Plethotaenia, Paleopneustes, & Saviniaster. LC 68-30264. (Studies in Tropical Oceanography Ser: No. 7). 1968. 12.00x (ISBN 0-87024-088-9). U Miami Marine.

Cheshire, D. F. Music Hall in Britain. LC 74-2581. (Illus.). 112p. 1974. 18.00 (ISBN 0-8386-1563-5). Fairleigh Dickinson.

Cheshire, David. The Book of Movie Photography. LC 79-2128. (Illus.). 1979. 22.50 (ISBN 0-394-50787-8). Knopf.

Cheshire, Jenny. Variation in an English Dialect: A Sociolinguistic Study. LC 82-4189. (Cambridge Studies in Linguistics: No. 37). (Illus.). 150p. 1982. 34.50 (ISBN 0-521-23802-1). Cambridge U Pr.

Cheshire, M. V. Nature & Origin of Carbohydrates in Soils. LC 79-40898. 1980. 48.00 (ISBN 0-12-171250-8). Acad Pr.

Cheshire, Neil M. The Nature of Psychodynamic Interpretation. LC 75-1391. pap. 60.30 (ISBN 0-317-30311-2, 2024798). Bks Demand UMI.

Cheshire, P. C., jt. auth. see Bowers, J. K.

Chesire, Leone, et al. Computing Diagrams for the Tetrachoric Correlation Coefficient. 58p. 1968. pap. text ed. 10.00 (ISBN 0-317-11974-5, Pub. by William James). Psychometric.

Cheska, Alyce, jt. auth. see Blanchard, Kendall.

Cheska, Alyce T. Play As Context. (Illus., Orig.). 1981. pap. text ed. 14.95 (ISBN 0-918438-66-7). Leisure Pr.

Cheskin, Louis. Color for Profit. (Illus.). 1951. 6.95x (ISBN 0-87140-964-X). Liveright.

Cheslen, Emily K. Employment in Massachusetts. 239p. 1984. looseleaf 37.50 (ISBN 0-88063-041-8). Butterworth Legal Pubs.

Chesler, Bernice. Bed & Breakfast in the Northeast: From Maine to Washington, D. C., 300 Selected B&B's. LC 38-48194. (Illus.). 512p. (Orig.). 1983. pap. 9.95 (ISBN 0-87106-917-2). Globe Pequot.

--In & Out of Boston, with Children. 2nd ed. (Illus.). (gr. 4 up). 1969. pap. 7.50 (ISBN 0-517-52184-9). Barre.

--In & Out of Boston With (or Without) Children. 4th ed. LC 81-86605. (Illus.). 352p. 1982. pap. 10.95 (ISBN 0-87106-968-7). Globe Pequot.

Chesler, Bernice & Kaye, Evelyn. The Family Guide to Cape Cod. (Illus.). 320p. 1976. pap. 6.95 (ISBN 0-517-52096-6). Barre.

Chesler, Elliot. Schire's Clinical Cardiology. 4th ed. (Illus.). 320p. 1981. pap. text ed. 36.00 (ISBN 0-7236-0600-5). PSG Pub Co.

Chesler, Evan R. The Russian Jewry Reader. 147p. pap. 2.45 (ISBN 0-686-95145-X). ADL.

Chesler, Mark A. & Cave, William. A Sociology of Education. (Illus.). 1981. text ed. write for info. (ISBN 0-02-322150-X). Macmillan.

Chesler, Mark A., et al. Making Desegregation Work. (Sage Human Services Guides Ser.: Vol. 23). 160p. 1981. 9.95 (ISBN 0-8039-1725-2). Sage.

Chesler, Phyllis. Mothers on Trial: The Battle for Children & Custody. 1985. 19.95 (ISBN 0-07-010701-7). McGraw.

--With Child. 1981. pap. 2.95 (ISBN 0-425-04834-9). Berkley Pub.

--With Child: A Diary of Motherhood. LC 79-7081. 1979. 12.45i (ISBN 0-690-01835-5). T Y Crowell.

--Women & Madness. 1973. pap. 4.95 (ISBN 0-380-01627-3, 65672-8, Discus). Avon.

Chesler, Phyllis & Goodman, Emily J. Women, Money, & Power. LC 75-25922. 256p. 1976. 8.95 (ISBN 0-688-02990-6). Morrow.

Chesley, Alan B., illus. Cabin Cars of the Pennsylvania & Long Island Railroads. LC 82-81756. (Caboose Data Bk.: No. 2). (Illus.). 64p. 1982. pap. 12.98 (ISBN 0-934088-08-X). NJ Intl Inc.

--Pennsylvania Railroad Heavyweight Passenger Equipment: Plan & Photo Book. LC 83-63343. (Illus.). 120p. 1984. 19.95 (ISBN 0-934088-11-X). NJ Intl Inc.

Chesley, Robert. Stray Dog Story. (Gay Play Script Ser.). (Illus.). 112p. (Orig.). 1984. pap. 6.95 (ISBN 0-935672-11-7). JH Pr.

Cheslock, Louis, ed. see Mencken, H. L.

Cheslow, Melvyn. A Road Pricing & Transit Improvement Program in Berkeley, California: A Preliminary Analysis. 73p. 1978. pap. 6.00x (ISBN 0-87766-233-9, 22300). Urban Inst.

Chesman, Andrea. Pickles & Relishes: One Hundred Fifty Recipes, Apple to Zucchini. LC 83-1460. (Illus.). 160p. (Orig.). 1983. pap. 5.95 (ISBN 0-88266-321-6). Garden Way Pub.

--Salsas! (Illus.). 128p. (Orig.). 1985. 16.95 (ISBN 0-89594-179-1); pap. 6.95 (ISBN 0-89594-180-5). Crossing Pr.

--Summer in a Jar: Making Pickles, Jams & More. Williamson, Susan, ed. 160p. 1985. pap. 7.95 (ISBN 0-913589-14-4). Williamson Pub Co.

Chesman, Andrea, ed. see Ballantyne, Janet.

Chesman, Andrea, ed. see Shelton, Jay.

Chesman, Andrea, ed. see Vivian, John.

Chesmond, C. J. Control Systems Technology. 480p. 1984. pap. text ed. 29.95 (ISBN 0-7131-3508-5). E Arnold.

Chesne, Joseph du see Du Chesne, Joseph.

Chesneau, Roger. Aircraft Carriers of the World: 1914 to the Present. (Illus.). 256p. 1984. 27.95 (ISBN 0-87021-902-2). Naval Inst Pr.

Chesneaux, Jean. China: The People's Republic, 1949-1976. Auster, Paul & Davis, Lydia, trs. from Fr. LC 78-51797. 1979. pap. 5.95 (ISBN 0-394-73623-0). Pantheon.

--Chinese Labor Movement, 1919-1927. Wright, H. M., tr. 1968. 35.00x (ISBN 0-8047-0644-1). Stanford U Pr.

--Secret Societies in China: In the Nineteenth & Twentieth Centuries. Nettle, Gillian, tr. LC 76-124425. 1972. 7.95x (ISBN 0-472-08207-8). U of Mich Pr.

Chesneaux, Jean, ed. Popular Movements & Secret Societies in China, 1840-1950. LC 70-153816. 342p. 1972. 27.50x (ISBN 0-8047-0790-1). Stanford U Pr.

Chesneaux, Jean, et al. China from the Opium Wars to the Nineteen Hundred Eleven Revolution. Destenay, Anne, tr. from Fr. LC 76-9570. 1977. pap. 9.95 (ISBN 0-394-70934-9). Pantheon.

--China from the Nineteen Eleven Revolution to Liberation. Auster, Paul & Davis, Lydia, trs. LC 77-76494. 1978. pap. 8.95 (ISBN 0-394-73332-0). Pantheon.

Chesnel De La Charbouclais, L. P. Dictionnaire de Geologie... et Dictionnaire de Chronologie Universelle par M. Champagnac, Vol. 50. Migne, J. P., ed. (Encyclopedie Theologique Ser.). 728p. (Fr.). Repr. of 1849 ed. lib. bdg. 192.50x (ISBN 0-89241-253-4). Caratzas.

--Dictionnaire de la Sagesse Populaire. Migne, J. P., ed. (Troisieme et Derniere Encyclopedie Theologique Ser.: Vol. 11). 626p. (Fr.). Repr. of 1855 ed. lib. bdg. 81.00x (ISBN 0-89241-295-X). Caratzas.

--Dictionnaire de Technologie, 2 vols. Migne, J. P., ed. (Troisieme et Derniere Encyclopedie Theologique Ser.: Vols. 28-29). 1306p. (Fr.). Repr. of 1858 ed. lib. bdg. 166.50x (ISBN 0-89241-308-5). Caratzas.

--Dictionnaire des Merveilles et Curiosites de Nature et De Art. Migne, J. P., ed. (Nouvelle Encyclopedie Theologique Ser.: Vol. 44). 634p. (Fr.). Repr. of 1853 ed. lib. bdg. 81.00x (ISBN 0-89241-283-6). Caratzas.

--Dictionnaire des Superstitions, Erreurs, Prejuges et Traditions Populaires. Migne, J. P., ed. (Troisieme et Derniere Encyclopedie Theologique Ser.: Vol. 20). 680p. (Fr.). Repr. of 1856 ed. lib. bdg. 86.50x (ISBN 0-89241-303-4). Caratzas.

Chesney, Alan M. The Johns Hopkins Hospital & the Johns Hopkins University School of Medicine: A Chronicle, 2 vols. Incl. Vol. 1. 1867-1893. 318p. 1943; Vol. 2. 1893-1905. 499p. 1958. 35.00x (ISBN 0-8018-0113-3); Vol. 3. 1905-1914. 350p. 1963. 30.00x (ISBN 0-8018-0114-1). Johns Hopkins.

Chesney, Allen, ed. Chattanooga Album: Thirty-Two Historic Postcards. LC 82-17330. (Illus.). 16p. 1983. pap. 3.95 (ISBN 0-87049-381-7). U of Tenn Pr.

Chesney, D. Noreen & Chesney, Muriel O. Radiographic Anatomy of the Chest & Abdomen: A Student's Handbook. (Blackwell Scientific Pubns.). (Illus.). 1976. 19.50 (ISBN 0-8016-1034-6). Mosby.

Chesney, Elizabeth A. The Countervoyage of Rabelais & Ariosto: A Comparative Reading of Two Renaissance Mock Epics. LC 81-5410. 240p. 1982. 22.00 (ISBN 0-8223-0456-2). Duke.

Chesney, Francis R. Expedition for the Survey of the Rivers Euphrates - Tigris, Carried Out by Order of the British Government in the Years 1835-1837. Incl. Geographical & Historical Notices of the Regions Situated Between the Rivers Nile & Indus. LC 68-55182. 1968. Repr. of 1850 ed. Set. 2 Vols. lib. bdg. 63.50x (ISBN 0-8371-3796-9, CHET). Greenwood.

Chesney, Margaret A. & Rosenman, Ray H., eds. Anger & Hostility in Cardiovascular & Behavioral Disorders. LC 84-25348. (Health Psychology & Behavioral Medicine Ser.). (Illus.). 294p. 1985. 39.95 (ISBN 0-89116-393-X). Hemisphere Pub.

Chesney, Marion. Constant Companion. 224p. 1980. pap. 1.75 (ISBN 0-449-50114-0, Coventry). Fawcett.

--Daphne. (The Six Sisters Ser.: Vol. 4). 192p. 1984. 10.95 (ISBN 0-312-18221-X). St Martin.
--Daphne. 176p. 1986. pap. 2.50 (ISBN 0-449-20583-5, Crest). Fawcett.
--Deidre & Desire. 208p. 1985. pap. 2.50 (ISBN 0-449-20582-7, Crest). Fawcett.
--Deirdre & Desire. (Six Sisters Ser.: Vol. 3). 192p. 1984. 10.95 (ISBN 0-312-19136-7). St Martin.
--Deirdre & Desire. (Nightingale Paperbacks (Large Print) Ser.). 1985. pap. 10.95 (ISBN 0-317-19808-4). G K Hall.
--Diana the Huntress. (Six Sisters Ser.: Vol. 5). 192p. 1985. 12.95 (ISBN 0-312-19937-6). St Martin.
--Duke's Diamonds. 160p. (Orig.). 1983. pap. 2.25 (ISBN 0-449-20085-X, Crest). Fawcett.
--The Education of Miss Paterson. 1985. pap. text ed. 2.50 (ISBN 0-451-14005-2, Sig). NAL.
--The Flirt. 208p. (Orig.). 1985. pap. 2.50 (ISBN 0-449-20531-2, Crest). Fawcett.
--Frederica in Fashion. 176p. 1985. 11.95 (ISBN 0-312-30363-7). St Martin.
--The French Affair. 176p. (Orig.). 1984. pap. 2.25 (ISBN 0-449-20119-8, CRest). Fawcett.
--Lady Margery's Intrigue. 224p. 1980. pap. 1.75 (ISBN 0-449-50053-5, Coventry). Fawcett.
--Love & Lady Lovelace. 192p. (Orig.). 1982. pap. 1.50 (ISBN 0-449-50314-3, Coventry). Fawcett.
--Minerva. 192p. 1984. pap. 2.25 (ISBN 0-449-20580-0, Crest). Fawcett.
--Minerva. (Nightingale Large Print Ser.). 1985. pap. text ed. 10.95 (ISBN 0-8161-3745-5, Large Print Bks). G K Hall.
--Minerva: Being the First of the Six Sisters. 192p. 1983. 10.95 (ISBN 0-312-53360-8). St Martin.
--My Lords, Ladies & Marjorie. 224p. 1981. pap. 1.50 (ISBN 0-449-50216-3, Crest). Fawcett.
--The Original Miss Honeyford. 1985. pap. 2.50 (ISBN 0-451-13566-0, Sig). NAL.
--The Poor Relation. 1984. pap. 2.95 (ISBN 0-451-12818-4, Sig). NAL.
--Quadrille. 224p. 1981. pap. 1.95 (ISBN 0-449-50174-4, Coventry). Fawcett.
--Regency Gold. 1980. pap. 1.75 (ISBN 0-449-50002-0, Coventry). Fawcett.
--Sweet Masquerade. 176p. (Orig.). 1984. pap. 2.25 (ISBN 0-449-20120-1, Crest). Fawcett.
--The Taming of Annabelle. 208p. 1983. 10.95 (ISBN 0-312-78489-9). St Martin.
--The Taming of Annabelle. 192p. 1985. pap. 2.25 (ISBN 0-449-20581-9, Crest). Fawcett.
--The Taming of Annabelle. (Nightingale Ser.). 1985. pap. 10.95 (ISBN 0-8161-3823-0, Large Print Bks). G K Hall.
--The Westerby Inheritance. 352p. (Orig.). 1982. pap. 3.50 (ISBN 0-523-41276-2). Pinnacle Bks.
--The Westerby Sisters. 384p. (Orig.). 1983. pap. 3.50 (ISBN 0-523-41277-0). Pinnacle Bks.
Chesney, Muriel O., jt. auth. see Chesney, D. Noreen.
Chesney, W. Inhuman Medical Experiments on Humans & Pets. 1966. 1.25x (ISBN 0-686-32627-X). Cancer Control Soc.
Chesnoff, Richard Z. Philippines. canase ed. (Illus.). 128p. 1981. 25.00 (ISBN 0-8109-1475-1). Abrams.
--The Philippines. LC 77-99197. (Illus.). 288p. 1978. 125.00 (ISBN 0-8109-1458-1). Abrams.
Chesnut, D. B. Finite Groups & Quantum Theory. LC 81-19351. 270p. 1982. Repr. of 1974 ed. lib. bdg. 26.50 (ISBN 0-89874-468-7). Krieger.
Chesnut, Glenn F. The First Christian Histories: Eusebius Socrates, Sozomen, Theodoret, & Evagrius. 2nd, rev. ed. 304p. 1985. 23.95x (ISBN 0-86554-164-7, MUP/H154). Mercer Univ Pr.
--Images of Christ: An Introduction to Christology. 160p. (Orig.). 1984. pap. 8.95 (ISBN 0-86683-875-9, 7918, Pub. by Seabury). Winston Pr.
Chesnut, Mary B. A Diary from Dixie. Williams, Ben A., ed. 608p. 1980. 25.00x (ISBN 0-674-20290-2); pap. 8.95 (ISBN 0-674-20291-0). Harvard U Pr.
--A Diary from Dixie. Martin, Isabella & Avary, Myrta L., eds. (Illus.). 16.50 (ISBN 0-8446-1109-3). Peter Smith.
Chesnut, V. K. Thirty Poisonous Plants of North America. (Illus.). 36p. 1976. pap. 1.95 (ISBN 0-8466-6051-2). Shorey.
Chesnutt, Charles W. Colonel's Dream. facs. ed. LC 73-83928. (Black Heritage Library Collection Ser). 1905. 18.00 (ISBN 0-8369-8538-9). Ayer Co Pubs.
--Colonel's Dream. LC 77-100261. Repr. of 1905 ed. 22.50x (ISBN 0-8371-2857-9, CCD, Pub. by Negro U Pr). Greenwood.
--The Colonel's Dream. LC 68-57517. (Muckrakers Ser.). Repr. of 1905 ed. lib. bdg. 15.00 (ISBN 0-8398-0257-9). Irvington.
--Colonel's Dream. pap. 2.95 (ISBN 0-685-16781-X, N255P). Mnemosyne.
--The Conjure Woman. 1977. Repr. 29.00x (ISBN 0-403-07386-3). Scholarly.
--Conjure Woman. 1969. pap. 8.50 (ISBN 0-472-06156-9, 156, AA). U of Mich Pr.
--Frederick Douglass. LC 72-19028. 1971. Repr. of 1899 ed. 15.00 (ISBN 0-384-08630-6). Johnson Repr.
--Marrow of Tradition. LC 72-1564. Repr. of 1901 ed. 10.00 (ISBN 0-404-00014-2). AMS Pr.
--Marrow of Tradition. facs. ed. LC 70-83927. (Black Heritage Library Collection Ser). 1901. 14.00 (ISBN 0-8369-8539-7). Ayer Co Pubs.
--Marrow of Tradition. LC 69-18585. (American Negro: His History & Literature Ser., No. 2). 1969. Repr. of 1901 ed. 14.00 (ISBN 0-405-01855-X). Ayer Co Pubs.
--The Marrow of Tradition. LC 74-78571. (Muckrakers Ser.). lib. bdg. 13.00 (ISBN 0-8398-0260-9); pap. 6.95x (ISBN 0-89197-836-4). Irvington.
--The Marrow of Tradition. 1969. 9.95x (ISBN 0-472-09147-6); pap. 8.95 (ISBN 0-472-06147-X). U of Mich Pr.
--Wife of His Youth & Other Stories. (Illus.). 1968. pap. 8.95 (ISBN 0-472-06134-8, 134, AA). U of Mich Pr.
Chesnutt, David, ed. see Laurens, Henry.
Chesnutt, David R., ed. see Laurens, Henry.
Chesnutt, David R., et al, eds. see Laurens, Henry.
Chesnutt, Helen M. Charles Waddell Chesnutt: Pioneer of the Color Line. ix, 324p. 1952. 14.95 (ISBN 0-8078-0621-8). U of NC Pr.
Chesnutt, Margaret. Studies in Short Stories of William Carleton. (Gothenborg Studies in English: No. 34). 1976. pap. text ed. 21.50x (ISBN 91-7346-027-3). Humanities.
Chesnutt, N. P. Southern Union. LC 79-87779. 1979. 14.00 (ISBN 0-930208-07-2). Mangan Bks.
Chess & Thomas. Annual Progress in Child Psychiatry & Child Development, 1983. 35.00 (ISBN 0-317-04097-9). Brunner-Mazel.
Chess, Alexander, jt. ed. see Chess, Stella.
Chess, David M. Programming in IBM PC DOS Pascal. (Illus.). 240p. 1985. pap. text ed. 16.95 (ISBN 0-13-730292-4). P-H.
Chess, Stella. An Introduction to Child Psychiatry. 2nd ed. LC 69-15085. 272p. 1969. 37.00 (ISBN 0-8089-0098-6, 790830). Grune.
Chess, Stella & Hassibi, Mahin. Principles & Practice of Child Psychiatry. LC 78-1604. (Illus.). 512p. 1978. 32.50x (ISBN 0-306-31131-3, Plenum Pr). Plenum Pub.
Chess, Stella & Thomas, Alexander. Origins & Evolution of Behavior Disorders: From Infancy to Early Adult Life. LC 84-14227. 320p. 1984. 30.00 (ISBN 0-87630-368-8). Brunner-Mazel.
Chess, Stella, jt. auth. see Thomas, Alexander.
Chess, Stella & Chess, Alexander, eds. Annual Progress in Child Psychiatry & Child Development, 1984. LC 68-23452. 514p. 1984. 35.00 (ISBN 0-87630-375-0). Brunner-Mazel.
Chess, Stella & Thomas, Alexander, eds. Annual Progress in Child Psychiatry & Child Development, 12 vols. Incl. Vol. 1. 1968; Vol. 2. 1969; Vol. 3. 1970; Vol. 4. 1971. (ISBN 0-87630-004-2); Vol. 5. 1972; Vol. 6. 1973; Vol. 7. 1974; Vol. 8. 1975 (ISBN 0-87630-107-3); Vol. 9. 1976; Vol. 10. 1977; Vol. 11. 1978 (ISBN 0-87630-180-4); Vol. 12. 1979 (ISBN 0-87630-216-9). LC 68-23452. (Illus.). Vols. 2-4 & 6-12. 30.00 ea. Brunner-Mazel.
--Annual Progress in Child Psychiatry & Child Development. LC 66-4030. 600p. 1980. 35.00. Brunner-Mazel.
--Annual Progress in Child Psychiatry & Child Development, 1981. 688p. 1981. 35.00 (ISBN 0-87630-284-3). Brunner-Mazel.
--Annual Progress in Child Psychiatry & Child Development, 1982. LC 68-23452. 600p. 1982. 35.00 (ISBN 0-87630-317-3). Brunner-Mazel.
--Annual Progress in Child Psychiatry & Child Development, 1983. LC 68-23452. 560p. 1983. 35.00 (ISBN 0-87630-343-2). Brunner-Mazel.
--Annual Progress in Child Psychiatry & Child Development 1985. 500p. 1985. 35.00 (ISBN 0-87630-402-1). Brunner-Mazel.
Chess, Stella, et al. Your Child Is a Person: A Psychological Approach to Parenthood Without Guilt. 224p. 1977. pap. 3.95 (ISBN 0-14-004439-6). Penguin.
Chess, Victoria. Alfred's Alphabet Walk. LC 79-1185. (Illus.). (gr. k-3). 1979. 11.75 (ISBN 0-688-80223-0); PLB 11.88 (ISBN 0-688-84223-2). Greenwillow.
--Catcards. (Illus.). 24p. 1982. pap. 4.95 (ISBN 0-02-042290-3, Collier); 12-copy prepack 59.40 (ISBN 0-02-042300-4, Collier). Macmillan.
--Catcards & Catcards for Christmas. Bd. with Catcards (ISBN 0-02-042290-3); Catcards for Christmas (ISBN 0-02-042240-7). 24p. 1982. pap. 4.95x ea. Macmillan.
--Catcards for Christmas: A Purrfectly Wonderful Collection of Christmas Cards. (Illus.). 24p. 1982. pap. 4.95 (ISBN 0-02-042240-7, Pub. by Collier). Macmillan.
--Poor Esme. LC 82-2924. (Illus.). 32p. (ps-3). 1982. Reinforced bdg. 12.95 (ISBN 0-8234-0455-2). Holiday.
Chess Visions, Inc. Staff, compiled by. Minor Piece Endgames: Yuri Averbakh Endgames Cassettes. (Illus.). 60p. 1982. 21.90 (ISBN 0-939786-03-6). Chess Visions.
Chess Visions, Inc. Staff, ed. Rook & Minor Pieces: Yuri Averbakh Endgame Cassettes. (Illus.). 56p. 1982. 21.90 (ISBN 0-939786-04-4). Chess Visions.
Chesse, Bruce K. Puppets from Polyfoam: Sponge-Es. (gr. 3 up). 1975. pap. 3.95 (ISBN 0-915786-00-1). Early Stages.
--Titeres De "Polyfoam". Esponjaditos. Olsen, Dorothy, et al, trs. from Eng. Orig. Title: Puppets from Polyfoam: Spongee-Es. (Illus.). 36p. (Span.). 1976. pap. 3.95 (ISBN 0-915786-01-X). Early Stages.
Chesse, Bruce K., jt. ed. see Sims, Judy.
Chessell. Photo DX, 4 vols. 1985. 10.95 ea. Vol. 1 (ISBN 0-8151-1653-5). Vol. 2 (ISBN 0-8151-1654-3). Vol. 3 (ISBN 0-8151-1655-1). Vol. 4 (ISBN 0-8151-1656-X). Year Bk Med.
Chesseman, G. W. & Cookson, R. F. Condensed Pyrazines, Vol. 35. 835p. 1979. 275.95 (ISBN 0-471-38204-3, Pub. by Wiley-Interscience). Wiley.
Chesser, Barbara J. & Gray, Ava A. Marriage: Creating a Partnership, an Experiential Approach to the Study of Marriage & the Family. 2nd ed. (Orig.). 1979. pap. text ed. 19.95 (ISBN 0-8403-2101-5). Kendall-Hunt.
Chesser, Edward S., jt. auth. see Meyer, Victor C.
Chesser, Eustace. Do You Want to Stop Smoking? 128p. 1976. Cornerstone.
Chessex, Jacques. A Father's Love. 1977. pap. 1.25 (ISBN 0-8439-0429-1, Leisure Bks). Dorchester Pub Co.
Chesshire, Gustave. Analysis of Construction Techniques Used in the Building of Colonial Homes Prior to 1700. (Illus.). 134p. 1982. 145.75 (ISBN 0-86650-017-0). Gloucester Art.
Chesshire, Howard J. Shenanigan. LC 75-5226. (Illus.). pap. 2.75 (ISBN 0-9603226-0-4). Mandala Bks.
Chessick, Richard. Intensive Psychotherapy of the Borderline Patient. LC 76-22867. 303p. 1977. 25.00x (ISBN 0-87668-254-9, 25494). Aronson.
--The Psychology of the Self & the Therapy of Narcissism. 300p. 1985. 30.00 (ISBN 0-87668-903-9). Aronson.
--Why Psychotherapists Fail. LC 84-45108. 203p. 1983. 20.00x (ISBN 0-87668-700-1). Aronson.
Chessick, Richard D. A Brief Introduction to the Genius of Nietzsche. LC 83-10305. 160p. (Orig.). 1983. lib. bdg. 23.25 (ISBN 0-8191-3336-1); pap. text ed. 11.00 (ISBN 0-8191-3337-X). U Pr of Amer.
--Freud Teaches Psychotherapy. LC 79-84334. (Illus.). 352p. 1980. 25.00 (ISBN 0-915144-63-8). Hackett Pub.
--Great Ideas in Psychotherapy. LC 76-22868. 1977. 30.00x (ISBN 0-87668-256-5, 256-50). Aronson.
--How Psychotherapy Heals: The Process of Intensive Psychotherapy. LC 77-91953. 1969. 15.00x (ISBN 0-87668-023-6). Aronson.
--Technique & Practice of Intensive Psychotherapy. LC 84-45001. 375p. 1983. 25.00x (ISBN 0-87668-657-9). Aronson.
Chessmore, Roy A. Profitable Pasture Management. LC 78-70056. 1979. 14.50 (ISBN 0-8134-2056-3, 2056). Interstate.
Chesson, Lela, jt. auth. see Pattillo, Carol.
Chesson, Michael B. Richmond After the War, Eighteen Sixty-Five to Eighteen Ninety. LC 80-25833. (Illus.). 1981. pap. 12.50 (ISBN 0-88490-086-X). VA State Lib.
Chesson, W. H., jt. auth. see Villiers, Brougham.
Chesswas, J. D. Methodologies of Educational Planning for Developing Countries, 2 vols. 1968. Set. pap. 11.00 (ISBN 92-803-1033-X, U379, UNESCO). Unipub.
Chestang, Leon W., jt. ed. see Cafferty, Pastora S.
Chester, A. N., jt. ed. see Martellucci, S.
Chester, Alan, ed. see Shakespeare, William.
Chester, Alden. Legal & Judicial History of New York, 3 vols. LC 83-82570. 1983. Repr. of 1911 ed. Set. 95.00 (ISBN 0-89941-297-1). W S Hein.
Chester, Allan G. Hugh Latimer, Apostle to the English. 1978. Repr. of 1954 ed. lib. bdg. 20.00x (ISBN 0-374-91492-3). Octagon.
Chester, Allan G., ed. see Latimer, Hugh.
Chester, Andrew, tr. see Schweizer, Edward.
Chester, Arthur N., jt. ed. see Martellucci, S.
Chester, Carol. Hawaiian Islands. (Illus.). 176p. 1984. 17.50 (ISBN 0-88254-892-1). Hippocrene Bks.
Chester, Carole. California & the Golden West. LC 82-61197. (Pocket Guide Ser.). (Illus.). 1983. pap. 4.95 (ISBN 0-528-84894-1). Rand.
--Florida. (Illus.). 176p. 1982. 21.00 (ISBN 0-7134-3807-X, Pub. by Batsford England). David & Charles.
--Germany. LC 79-89186. (Pocket Guide Ser.). (Illus., Orig.). 1980. pap. 4.95 (ISBN 0-528-84287-0). Rand.
--New York. 1977. 19.95 (ISBN 0-7134-0183-4, Pub. by Batsford England). David & Charles.
Chester, D. K., et al. Mount Etna: The Anatomy of a Volcano. (Illus.). 406p. 1985. text ed. 42.50x (ISBN 0-8047-1308-1). Stanford U Pr.
Chester, D. N. The Organization of British Central Government, 1914-64. Willson, F. M., ed. 521p. 1968. 49.00 (ISBN 0-686-45744-7, Pub. by Pubns Clerk Royal England). State Mutual Bk.
Chester, D. N. & Bowring, Nona. Questions in Parliament. LC 74-9164. 335p. 1974. Repr. of 1962 ed. lib. bdg. 19.75x (ISBN 0-8371-7614-X, CHQP). Greenwood.
Chester, D. N. & Wilson, F. M. The Organization of British Central Government 1914-64. 512p. 1968. 50.00x (ISBN 0-686-96572-8, Pub by Royal Inst Pub Admin England). State Mutual bk.
Chester, Daniel N., ed. Lessons of the British War Economy. LC 70-157956. 260p. 1972. Repr. of 1951 ed. lib. bdg. 22.50x (ISBN 0-8371-6175-4, CHWE). Greenwood.
Chester, Deborah. French Slippers. 320p. 1982. pap. 3.50 (ISBN 0-440-12757-2). Dell.
--Heart's Desire. 1983. pap. 2.50 (ISBN 0-380-84798-1, 84798). Avon.
--A Love So Wild. 1981. pap. 2.50 (ISBN 0-345-28773-8). Ballantine.
--Royal Intrigue. (Candlelight Regency Ser.: No. 712). (Orig.). 1982. pap. 2.25 (ISBN 0-440-17065-6). Dell.
Chester, Edward W. A Guide to Political Platforms. 373p. 1977. 25.00 (ISBN 0-208-01609-0, Archon). Shoe String.
--Issues & Responses in State Political Experience. LC 68-19377. (Quality Paperback Ser.: No. 95). 199p. (Orig.). 1968. pap. 2.25 (ISBN 0-8226-0095-1). Littlefield.
--Sectionalism, Politics & American Diplomacy. LC 74-30418. 362p. 1975. 20.00 (ISBN 0-8108-0787-4). Scarecrow.
--The United States & Six Atlantic Outposts: The Military & Economic Considerations. (National University Publications, American Studies Ser.). 1980. 24.50x (ISBN 0-8046-9236-X, Pub by Kennikat). Assoc Faculty Pr.
--United States Oil Policy & Diplomacy: A Twentieth Century Overview. LC 82-9379. (Contributions in Economics & Economic History Ser.: No. 52). (Illus.). 384p. 1983. lib. bdg. 35.00 (ISBN 0-313-23174-5, CUO/). Greenwood.
Chester, Eng. Diocese. Child-Marriages, Divorces, & Ratifications Etc. 1561-66. Furnivall, F. J., ed. (EETS, OS Ser.: No. 108). Repr. of 1897 ed. 25.00 (ISBN 0-527-00112-0). Kraus Repr.
Chester, Eric T. Socialists & the Ballot Box: An Historical Analysis. LC 85-6475. 192p. 1985. 28.95 (ISBN 0-03-004142-2). Praeger.
Chester, George R. The Jingo. Reginald, R. & Melville, Douglas, eds. LC 77-84210. (Lost Race & Adult Fantasy Ser.). (Illus.). 1978. Repr. of 1912 ed. lib. bdg. 35.50x (ISBN 0-405-10965-2). Ayer Co Pubs.
Chester, Giraud, et al. Television & Radio. 5th ed. (Illus.). 1978. ref. ed. 30.95 (ISBN 0-13-902981-8). P-H.
Chester, Helen. Cocktails. (Illus.). 80p. 1983. pap. 4.95 (ISBN 0-312-14634-5). St Martin.
Chester, Laura. Proud & Ashamed. 1977. 5.00 (ISBN 0-87922-128-3). Christopher's Bks.
--Watermark. 1978. signed 10.00 (ISBN 0-685-90011-8); pap. 4.00 (ISBN 0-685-90012-6). Figures.
Chester, Laura & Barba, Sharon, eds. Rising Tides: Twentieth Century American Women Poets. (Orig.). 1973. pap. 1.95 (ISBN 0-671-48753-1). WSP.
Chester, Margaret. Linsang. 1983. 4.95 (ISBN 0-533-05594-6). Vantage.
Chester, Michael. Particles: An Introduction to Particle Physics. LC 77-12352. (Illus.). 154p. (gr. 7 up). 1978. 10.95 (ISBN 0-02-718240-1, 71824). Macmillan.
--Particles: An Introduction to Particle Physics. 1980. pap. 2.50 (ISBN 0-451-61899-8, ME1899, Ment). NAL.
--Robots: Facts Behind the Fiction. LC 83-61237. (Illus.). 96p. (gr. 5-9). 1983. 9.95 (ISBN 0-02-718220-7). Macmillan.
Chester, Norman. The English Administrative System, Seventeen Eighty to Eighteen Seventy. 1981. 72.00x (ISBN 0-19-822643-5). Oxford U Pr.
Chester, R., jt. auth. see Riley, J. P.
Chester, R., ed. Divorce in Europe. 1977. pap. text ed. 23.00 (ISBN 90-207-0652-7, Pub. by Martinus Nijhoff Netherlands). Kluwer Academic.
Chester, R. & Peel, J., eds. Equalities & Inequalities in Family Life. 1978. 37.00 (ISBN 0-12-171650-3). Acad Pr.
Chester, R., jt. ed. see Riley, J. P.
Chester, R., jt. ed. see Roberts, D. F.
Chester, R., et al, eds. Changing Patterns of Child Bearing & Child Rearing. (Eugenic Society Symposium Ser.). 1982. 37.00 (ISBN 0-12-171660-0). Acad Pr.
Chester, R. J. Hypnotism in East & West: Twenty Hypnotic Methods. 1982. pap. 6.95 (ISBN 0-900860-98-7, Pub. by Octagon Pr England). Ins Study Human.
Chester, Roberta. Light Years. Hunting, Constance, ed. 96p. 1983. pap. 5.95 (ISBN 0-913006-29-7). Puckerbrush.
Chester, Ronald. Inheritance, Wealth, & Society. LC 81-48082. 256p. 1982. 22.50x (ISBN 0-253-33009-2). Ind U Pr.
--Unequal Access: Women Lawyers in a Changing America. 144p. 1984. 24.95 (ISBN 0-89789-052-3). Bergin & Garvey.
Chester, Samuel B. Anomalies of the English Law. 287p. 1980. Repr. of 1911 ed. lib. bdg. 22.50x (ISBN 0-8377-0426-X). Rothman.
Chester, W. Mechanics. (Illus.). 1980. text ed. 50.00x (ISBN 0-04-510058-6); pap. text ed. 24.95x (ISBN 0-04-510059-4). Allen Unwin.
Chester, William L. Kioga of the Wilderness. (Science Fiction Ser.). 1976. pap. 2.95 (ISBN 0-87997-847-3, UE1847). DAW Bks.

Chesterfield, Fourth Earl of & Bellerophn Books Editors. The Book of Good Manners. (Illus., Orig.). pap. 3.50 (ISBN 0-88388-102-0). Bellerophon Bks.

Chesterfield, Lord. Letters to His Son & Others. 334p. 1984. pap. 5.95x (ISBN 0-460-11823-4, DEL-05075, Pub. by Evman England). Biblio Dist.

--Letters Written by Lord Chesterfield to His Son, 2 vols. 1912. Set. 65.00 (ISBN 0-8274-2857-X). R West.

--Some Unpublished Letters of Lord Chesterfield. 1937. 25.00 (ISBN 0-8274-3465-0). R West.

--The Wit & Wisdom of the Earl of Chesterfield: Being Selections from the Miscellaneous Writings in Prose & Verse. Ernst-Browning, W., ed. 1875. 25.00 (ISBN 0-8274-3726-9). R West.

Chesterfield, Mona. To Love & to Nourish: A Cookery Book for Brides. 624p. 1973. 10.00 (ISBN 0-8048-1089-3). C E Tuttle.

Chesterfield, Ray, jt. auth. see Ruddle, Kenneth.

Chester-Jones, I. & Henderson, I. W., eds. General, Comparative & Clinical Endocrinology of the Adrenal Cortex, Vol. 1. 1976. 79.50 (ISBN 0-12-171501-9). Acad Pr.

--General, Comparative & Clinical Endocrinology of the Adrenal Cortex, 2 vols, Vols. 2 & 3. Vol. 2, 1978. 95.00 (ISBN 0-12-171502-7); Vol. 3, 1981. 97.50 (ISBN 0-12-171503-5). Acad Pr.

Chesterman, A., tr. see Karlsson, Fred.

Chesterman, Charles W., jt. auth. see Audubon Society.

Chesterman, Michael. Charities, Trusts & Social Welfare. (Law in Context Ser.). xxxii, 490p. 1979. 42.50x (ISBN 0-297-77590-1, Pub. by Weidenfeld & Nicolson). Rothman.

Chesteron, G. K. The New Jerusalem. 304p. Date not set. Repr. of 1984 ed. lib. bdg. 65.00 (ISBN 0-89760-182-3). Telegraph Bks.

Chesters, G. Some Functions of Sound-Repetition in 'Les Fleurs du Mal' (Occasional Papers in Modern Languages: No. 11). 91p. 1975. pap. text ed. 6.75x (ISBN 0-85958-403-8, Pub. by U Hull England). Humanities.

Chesters, G., jt. auth. see Broome, P.

Chesters, Gordon, jt. auth. see Novotny, Vladimir.

Chesters, J. H. Refractories for Iron & Steelmaking. 502p. 1974. text ed. 30.00x (ISBN 0-900497-89-0, Metals Soc). Brookfield Pub Co.

--Refractories: Production & Properties. 562p. (Orig.). 1973. pap. text ed. 50.00x (ISBN 0-900497-84-X, Metals Soc). Brookfield Pub Co.

Chesterton, A. Creed of a Facist Revolutionary. 1982. lib. bdg. 59.95 (ISBN 0-87700-345-9). Revisionist Pr.

Chesterton, A. K. Menace of the Money Power. 1982. lib. bdg. 69.95 (ISBN 0-87700-369-6). Revisionist Pr.

--The New Unhappy Lords. 255p. (Orig.). 1970. pap. 4.50x (ISBN 0-911038-83-3, Christian Book Club of America). Noontide.

Chesterton, D. Coastal Cargo Ships. pap. 4.00x (ISBN 0-392-09088-0, SpS). Sportshelf.

Chesterton, G. K. All Is Grist: A Book of Essays. 1971. Repr. of 1932 ed. 15.00x (ISBN 0-403-00902-2). Scholarly.

--All Things Considered. LC 70-84060. 1969. 12.95 (ISBN 0-8023-1225-X). Dufour.

--All Things Considered. 1978. Repr. of 1915 ed. lib. bdg. 20.00 (ISBN 0-8414-0893-9). Folcroft.

--Appreciations & Criticism of the Works of Charles Dickens. LC 68-766. (Studies in Fiction, No. 34). 1969. Repr. of 1928 ed. lib. bdg. 39.95x (ISBN 0-8383-0524-5). Haskell.

--Appreciations & Criticisms of the Works of Charles Dickens. LC 74-18247. 1974. Repr. of 1911 ed. lib. bdg. 27.50 (ISBN 0-8414-3547-2). Folcroft.

--Appreciations & Criticisms of the Works of Charles Dickens. 1978. 30.00 (ISBN 0-8492-4007-7). R West.

--As I Was Saying. 1973. lib. bdg. 20.00 (ISBN 0-8414-3020-9). Folcroft.

--Autobiography. 1978. Repr. of 1936 ed. lib. bdg. 30.00 (ISBN 0-8495-0716-2). Arden Lib.

--The Ball & the Cross. 384p. 1985. pap. 6.95 (ISBN 0-85115-236-8, Pub. by Boydell England). Academy Chi Pubs.

--Basic Chesterton. 1984. pap. 14.95 (ISBN 0-87243-130-4). Templegate.

--The Book of Father Brown. Repr. lib. bdg. 17.95x (ISBN 0-89190-576-6, Pub. by River City Pr). Amereon Ltd.

--Chaucer. 1973. lib. bdg. 30.00 (ISBN 0-8414-3021-7). Folcroft.

--The Collected Poems of G. K. Chesterton. LC 80-16874. 1980. pap. 5.95 (ISBN 0-396-07896-6). Dodd.

--The Complete Father Brown. 1982. pap. 8.95 (ISBN 0-14-005977-6). Penguin.

--Do We Agree? 1928. lib. bdg. 10.00 (ISBN 0-8414-3021-7). Folcroft.

--Do We Agree: A Debate. LC 65-15899. (Studies in Irish Literature, No. 16). 1969. Repr. of 1928 ed. lib. bdg. 39.95x (ISBN 0-8383-0525-3). Haskell.

--The Everlasting Man. 320p. 1981. Repr. of 1925 ed. lib. bdg. 25.00 (ISBN 0-8495-0855-X). Arden Lib.

--The Everlasting Man. 344p. 1981. Repr. of 1926 ed. lib. bdg. 20.00 (ISBN 0-89984-115-5). Century Bookbindery.

--The Everlasting Man. 280p. 1974. pap. 4.50 (ISBN 0-385-07198-1, Im). Doubleday.

--The Everlasting Man. LC 72-11233. 344p. 1974. Repr. of 1925 ed. lib. bdg. 21.75x (ISBN 0-8371-6636-5, CEVM). Greenwood.

--The Father Brown Omnibus. 1983. 14.95 (ISBN 0-396-08159-2). Dodd.

--The Father Brown Stories. 718p. 1982. Repr. of 1929 ed. lib. bdg. 45.00 (ISBN 0-8495-0867-3). Arden Lib.

--G. F. Watts. 1979. Repr. lib. bdg. 25.00 (ISBN 0-8492-4019-0). R West.

--The G. K. Chesterton Calendar: A Quotation from the Works of G. K. Chesterton for Every Day in the Year. 75.00 (ISBN 0-87968-325-2). Gordon Pr.

--G. K. Chesterton: The Spirit of Christmas. Smith, Marie, ed. 96p. 1985. 11.95 (ISBN 0-396-08712-4). Dodd.

--George Bernard Shaw. 1978. Repr. of 1961 ed. lib. bdg. 30.00 (ISBN 0-8414-1876-4). Folcroft.

--George Bernard Shaw. 296p. Repr. of 1909 ed. lib. bdg. 50.00 (ISBN 0-89760-186-6). Telegraph Bks.

--Handful of Authors. Collins, Dorothy, ed. Repr. of 1953 ed. 15.00 (ISBN 0-527-16600-6). Kraus Repr.

--The Incredulity of Father Brown. 1975. pap. 3.50 (ISBN 0-14-001069-6). Penguin.

--The Incredulity of Father Brown. (Nightingale Ser.). 1984. lib. bdg. 11.95 (ISBN 0-8161-3732-3, Large Print Bks); pap. 9.95 (ISBN 0-8161-3680-7). G K Hall.

--The Incredulity of Father Brown. 13.95 (ISBN 0-89190-339-9, Pub. by Am Repr). Amereon Ltd.

--The Innocence of Father Brown. 1975. pap. 3.50 (ISBN 0-14-000765-2). Penguin.

--The Innocence of Father Brown. 16.95 (ISBN 0-89190-338-0, Pub. by Am Repr). Amereon Ltd.

--The Innocence of the Father Brown. LC 75-44963. (Crime Fiction Ser.). 1976. Repr. of 1911 ed. lib. bdg. 21.00 (ISBN 0-8240-2359-5). Garland Pub.

--The Man Who Was Thursday. Repr. lib. bdg. 17.95x (ISBN 0-89190-577-4, Pub. by River City Pr). Amereon Ltd.

--Miscellany of Men. LC 74-84061. (G. K. Chesterton Reprint Ser). 1969. 12.95 (ISBN 0-8023-1224-1). Dufour.

--Miscellany of Men. 1973. lib. bdg. 25.00 (ISBN 0-8414-3023-3). Folcroft.

--A Miscellany of Men. LC 75-144945. 1972. Repr. of 1927 ed. 20.00x (ISBN 0-403-00903-0). Scholarly.

--Napoleon of Notting Hill. LC 77-99307. 228p. 1978. pap. 3.45 (ISBN 0-8091-2096-8). Paulist Pr.

--The New Jerusalem. 1976. lib. bdg. 59.95 (ISBN 0-8490-2339-4). Gordon Pr.

--Orthodoxy. 160p. 1973. pap. 3.50 (ISBN 0-385-01536-4, Im). Doubleday.

--Robert Browning. 1973. Repr. of 1904 ed. 20.00 (ISBN 0-8274-1497-8). R West.

--Robert Louis Stevenson. 1978. Repr. of 1928 ed. lib. bdg. 25.00 (ISBN 0-8414-0077-6). Folcroft.

--St. Francis of Assisi. 1979. Repr. lib. bdg. 25.00 (ISBN 0-8495-0933-5). Arden Lib.

--Saint Francis of Assisi. LC 57-1230. 1957. pap. 2.95 (ISBN 0-385-02900-4, Im). Doubleday.

--Saint Thomas Aquinas. 200p. 1974. pap. 3.50 (ISBN 0-385-09002-1, Im). Doubleday.

--The Scandal of Father Brown. (Crime Monthly Ser.). 1982. pap. 3.50 (ISBN 0-14-004739-5). Penguin.

--The Secret of Father Brown. 1975. pap. 3.50 (ISBN 0-14-003807-8). Penguin.

--The Secret of Father Brown. 13.95 (ISBN 0-89190-337-2, Pub. by Am Repr). Amereon Ltd.

--A Short History of England. 241p. 1983. Repr. of 1964 ed. lib. bdg. 35.00 (ISBN 0-8495-0978-5). Arden Lib.

--The Spirit of Christmas: Stories, Poems, Essays. 96p. 1985. 8.95 (ISBN 0-317-30922-6). Dodd.

--Sword of Wood. 1928. lib. bdg. 15.00 (ISBN 0-8414-0902-1). Folcroft.

--Thomas Carlyle. LC 73-9601. (Studies in Thos. Carlyle, No. 53). 1973. Repr. lib. bdg. 37.95x (ISBN 0-8383-1705-7). Haskell.

--Tremendous Trifles. 1927. 25.00 (ISBN 0-8414-9128-3). Folcroft.

--Uses of Diversity. 1973. 25.00 (ISBN 0-8274-0086-1). R West.

--What I Saw in America. 2nd ed. LC 68-16226. (American Scene Ser). 1968. Repr. of 1922 ed. 37.50 (ISBN 0-306-71009-9). Da Capo.

--What's Wrong with the World. 293p. 1984. Repr. of 1910 ed. lib. bdg. 40.00 (ISBN 0-89760-171-8). Telegraph Bks.

--William Blake. 1973. Repr. of 1910 ed. 25.00 (ISBN 0-8274-0715-7). R West.

--William Blake. 210p. Repr. of 1984 ed. lib. bdg. 45.00 (ISBN 0-89760-185-8). Telegraph Bks.

--The Wisdom of Father Brown. 1975. pap. 3.50 (ISBN 0-14-003118-9). Penguin.

--The Wisdom of Father Brown. 14.95 (ISBN 0-89190-336-4, Pub. by Am Repr). Amereon Ltd.

--Wit & Wisdom of G. K. Chesterton. 233p. 1980. Repr. of 1911 ed. lib. bdg. 30.00 (ISBN 0-8414-9990-X). Folcroft.

Chesterton, G. K. & Garnett, Richard. Tennyson. Repr. of 1903 ed. lib. bdg. 10.00 (ISBN 0-8414-1028-3). Folcroft.

Chesterton, G. K. & Kitton, F. G. Charles Dickens. 1973. lib. bdg. 17.50 (ISBN 0-8414-0978-1). Folcroft.

Chesterton, G. K. & Melville, Lewis. Thackeray. LC 72-12906. 1973. lib. bdg. 10.00 (ISBN 0-8414-1025-9). Folcroft.

Chesterton, G. K. & More, Thomas. Orthodoxy. (Books to Live Ser.). 1985. Repr. of 1908 ed. 10.95 (ISBN 0-88347-184-1). Thomas More.

Chesterton, G. K. & Williams, J. E. Thomas Carlyle. 1973. lib. bdg. 10.00 (ISBN 0-8414-0981-1). Folcroft.

Chesterton, G. K., jt. auth. see Meynell, Alice.

Chesterton, G. K., intro. by. A Century of Detective Stories. 1979. Repr. lib. bdg. 35.00 (ISBN 0-8495-0947-5). Arden Lib.

Chesterton, G. K., et al. Twelve Modern Apostles & Their Creeds. facs. ed. LC 68-16982. (Essay Index Reprint Ser). 1926. 17.00 (ISBN 0-8369-0955-0). Ayer Co Pubs.

Chesterton, George L. Revelations of Prison Life with an Enquiry into Prison Discipline & Secretary Punishments, 2 vols. LC 83-49323. (Crime & Punishment in England, 1850-1922 Ser.). 641p. 1984. Set. lib. bdg. 80.00 (ISBN 0-8240-6206-X). Garland Pub.

Chesterton, Gilberrt K. Sidelights on New London & Newer New York. 1981. Repr. lib. bdg. 29.00x (ISBN 0-403-00551-5). Scholarly.

Chesterton, Gilbert K. All I Survey. facs. ed. LC 67-26723. (Essay Index Reprint Ser). 1933. 20.00 (ISBN 0-8369-0293-9). Ayer Co Pubs.

--All Is Grist: A Book of Essays. facs. ed. LC 67-22058. (Essay Index Reprint Ser). 1932. 17.00 (ISBN 0-8369-0294-7). Ayer Co Pubs.

--All Things Considered. facsimile ed. LC 74-156629. (Essay Index Reprint Ser). Repr. of 1908 ed. 19.00 (ISBN 0-8369-2275-1). Ayer Co Pubs.

--As I Was Saying. facsimile ed. LC 67-22085. (Essay Index Reprint Ser). 1936. 17.00 (ISBN 0-8369-0295-5). Ayer Co Pubs.

--The Ball & the Cross. 1979. Repr. lib. bdg. 25.00 (ISBN 0-8492-4020-4). R West.

--The Ballad of the White Horse. Totten, John, et al, eds. (Illus., Orig.). 1950. pap. text ed. 12.95 (ISBN 0-910334-21-8). Cath Authors.

--Chaucer. LC 69-13856. Repr. of 1956 ed. lib. bdg. 22.50x (ISBN 0-8371-2237-6, CHCH). Greenwood.

--Come to Think of It. facs. ed. LC 73-142614. (Essay Index Reprint Ser). 1931. 18.00 (ISBN 0-8369-2042-2). Ayer Co Pubs.

--Defendant. LC 70-177955. (Essay Index Reprint Ser.). Repr. of 1901 ed. 12.25 (ISBN 0-8369-2841-5). Ayer Co Pubs.

--Do We Agree? 1978. Repr. of 1928 ed. lib. bdg. 10.00 (ISBN 0-8495-0741-3). Arden Lib.

--End of the Armistice. facs. ed. LC 78-117767. (Essay Index Reprint Ser.). 1940. 17.00 (ISBN 0-8369-1644-1). Ayer Co Pubs.

--Five Types. facs. ed. LC 79-86741. (Essay Index Reprint Ser). 1911. 12.25 (ISBN 0-8369-1125-3). Ayer Co Pubs.

--G. K. C. As M. C. Being a Collection of Thirty-Seven Introductions. facs. ed. LC 77-23193. (Essay Index Reprint Ser). 1929. 16.00 (ISBN 0-8369-0297-1). Ayer Co Pubs.

--Generally Speaking. facs. ed. LC 68-14898. (Essay Index Reprint Ser). 1929. 19.00 (ISBN 0-8369-0296-3). Ayer Co Pubs.

--George Bernard Shaw. 1978. Repr. of 1914 ed. lib. bdg. 25.00 (ISBN 0-8495-0729-4). Arden Lib.

--Heretics. facs. ed. LC 75-128220. (Essay Index Reprint Ser). 1905. 19.00 (ISBN 0-8369-1869-X). Ayer Co Pubs.

--Leo Tolstoy. Garnett, Edward, ed. LC 77-470. 1977. lib. bdg. 12.50 (ISBN 0-8414-3446-8). Folcroft.

--Lunacy & Letters. Collins, Dorothy, ed. LC 72-4607. (Essay Index Reprint Ser.). Repr. of 1958 ed. 15.00 (ISBN 0-8369-2937-3). Ayer Co Pubs.

--Man Who Was Chesterton. facs. ed. LC 79-128221. (Essay Index Reprint Ser). 1937. 42.00 (ISBN 0-8369-1908-4). Ayer Co Pubs.

--Miscellany of Men. facsimile ed. LC 73-90624. (Essay Index Reprint Ser). 1912. 21.00 (ISBN 0-8369-1281-0). Ayer Co Pubs.

--Orthodoxy. 297p. 1980. Repr. lib. bdg. 25.00 (ISBN 0-89987-125-9). Darby Bks.

--Orthodoxy. LC 74-2837. 299p. 1974. Repr. of 1909 ed. lib. bdg. 22.50x (ISBN 0-8371-7438-4, CHOR). Greenwood.

--Sidelights of New London & Newer York, & Other Essays. facs. ed. LC 68-8447. (Essay Index Reprint Ser). 1968. Repr. of 1932 ed. 16.00 (ISBN 0-8369-0298-X). Ayer Co Pubs.

--Tennyson. 1977. Repr. 17.00 (ISBN 0-403-07393-6). Scholarly.

--Thomas Carlyle. 40p. 1980. Repr. of 1902 ed. lib. bdg. 10.00 (ISBN 0-8495-0398-1). Arden Lib.

--Twelve Types. LC 75-30017. Repr. of 1906 ed. 18.00 (ISBN 0-404-14022-X). AMS Pr.

--Utopia of Usurers, & Other Essays. facs. ed. LC 67-26724. (Essay Index Reprint Ser). 1917. 15.00 (ISBN 0-8369-0299-8). Ayer Co Pubs.

--Varied Types. facs. ed. LC 68-16919. (Essay Index Reprint Ser). 1903. 17.00 (ISBN 0-8369-0300-5). Ayer Co Pubs.

--William Blake. LC 76-7995. 1976. Repr. of 1910 ed. lib. bdg. 17.50 (ISBN 0-8414-3383-6). Folcroft.

Chesterton, Keith. A Guide to the London Countryway. 2nd ed. 280p. 1981. 25.00x (ISBN 0-686-81496-7, Pub. by Constable Pubs). State Mutual Bk.

Chestnut, H., et al, eds. Supplemental Ways for Improving International Stability: Proceedings of the IFAC Workshop, Laxenburg, Austria, 13-15, September, 1983. (An IFAC Publication Ser.). 304p. 1984. 75.00 (ISBN 0-08-031631-X). Pergamon.

Chestnut, Harold. Systems Engineering Methods. LC 67-17336. (Wiley Ser. on Systems Engineering & Analysis). pap. 101.00 (ISBN 0-317-08335-X, 2051601). Bks Demand UMI.

--Systems Engineering Tools. LC 65-19484. (Wiley Series on Systems Engineering & Analysis). (Illus.). pap. 160.00 (ISBN 0-317-08334-1, 2055158). Bks Demand UMI.

Chestnut, Lauraine G., jt. auth. see Rowe, Robert D.

Chestnut, Lauraine G., jt. ed. see Rowe, Robert D.

Chestnut, Mary B., jt. ed. see Woodward, C. Vann.

Chestnut, Robert W., jt. auth. see Jacoby, Jacob.

Chestnutt, Charles W. Conjure Woman. 1978. Repr. of 1899 ed. lib. bdg. 35.00 (ISBN 0-8495-0756-1). Arden Lib.

Cheston, Molly. It's Your Life: A Personal & Social Course. 1982. 25.00x (ISBN 0-08-025614-7, Pub. by A Wheaton). State Mutual Bk.

Cheston, Stephen T. & Loeffke, Bernard, eds. Aspects of Soviet Policy Toward Latin America. LC 74-7328. 147p. 1974. 19.50x (ISBN 0-8422-5183-9); pap. text ed. 9.50x (ISBN 0-8422-0411-3). Irvington.

Chetanananda. Songs from the Center of the Well. rev. ed. 96p. 1985. pap. 6.95 (ISBN 0-915801-03-5). Rudra Pr.

Chetanananda, tr. see Avadhuta.

Chetanananda, Swami. Swami Adbhutananda: Teachings & Reminiscences. LC 80-50962. (Illus.). 175p. 1980. pap. 6.95 (ISBN 0-916356-59-0). Vedanta Soc St Louis.

Chetanananda, Swami, jt. auth. see Hatengdi, M. U.

Chetanananda, Swami, compiled by see Vivekananda, Swami.

Chetel, Mitchel. Music Reading & Piano Playing Simplified. LC 83-14806. 138p. 1983. pap. text ed. 12.25 (ISBN 0-8191-3501-1). U Pr of Amer.

Chetham, Charles. Nineteenth & Twentieth Century Paintings from the Collection of the Smith College Museum of Art. (Illus.). 1969. pap. 5.00 (ISBN 0-685-39815-3). Am Fed Arts.

--The Role of Vincent Van Gogh's Copies in the Development of His Art. LC 75-23788. (Outstanding Dissertations in the Fine Arts - 19th Century). (Illus.). 1976. lib. bdg. 50.00 (ISBN 0-8240-1984-9). Garland Pub.

Chetin, Helen. Angel Island Prisoner. Harvey, Catherine, tr. LC 82-51170. (Illus., Chinese-English.). (gr. 3 up). 1982. 7.00. New Seed.

--Frances Ann Speaks Out: My Father Raped Me. 2nd ed. (Illus.). 20p. (gr. 6 up). 1981. pap. 2.50 (ISBN 0-938678-05-1). New Seed.

--How Far Is Berkeley? LC 77-76435. 122p. (gr. 4-7). 1977. 6.95 (ISBN 0-15-236750-0, HJ). HarBraceJ.

Chetkin, Len. Guess Who's Jewish (You'll Never Guess) Friedman, Robert S., ed. (Illus.). 176p. (Orig.). 1985. pap. 6.95 (ISBN 0-89865-403-3). Donning Co.

Chetkovich, Carol A., jt. ed. see Radl, Shirley L.

Chetta, Holly. Poems Toward the Twenty-First Century. LC 84-90189. 58p. 1985. 6.95 (ISBN 0-533-06246-2). Vantage.

Chettle, Henry. Englandes Mourning Garment Worne Here by Plaine Shepheardes, in Memorie of Their Mistresse Elizabeth. LC 73-6112. (English Experience Ser.: No. 579). 50p. 1973. Repr. of 1603 ed. 5.00 (ISBN 90-221-0579-2). Walter J Johnson.

--Hoffman. LC 78-133645. (Tudor Facsimile Texts. Old English Plays: No. 138). Repr. of 1913 ed. 49.50 (ISBN 0-404-53438-4). AMS Pr.

--Kind-Heart's Dream. Bd. with The Mirror of Monsters. Rankins, William. Repr. of 1587 ed. Repr. of 1592 ed. 25.00 (ISBN 0-384-08684-5). Johnson Repr.

--Piers Plainnes Seauen Yeres Prentship. LC 80-2476. Repr. of 1595 ed. 32.50 (ISBN 0-404-19108-8). AMS Pr.

Chettle, Henry, jt. auth. see Day, John.

Chettle, Henry, jt. auth. see Munday, Anthony.

Chettle, Henry see Rankins, William.

Chettle, Henry, et al. Patient Grissil. LC 78-133653. (Tudor Facsimile Texts. Old English Plays: No. 101). Repr. of 1911 ed. 49.50 (ISBN 0-404-53401-5). AMS Pr.

Chetwin, Grace. On All Hallows' Eve. LC 84-4391. 160p. (gr. 6 up). 1984. 10.25 (ISBN 0-688-03012-2). Lothrop.

--Out of the Dark World. 160p. (gr. 6 up). 1985. 10.25 (ISBN 0-688-04272-4). Lothrop.

Chetwood, William R. The Voyages, Dangerous Adventures & Imminent Escapes of Captain Richard Falconer. LC 77-170543. (Foundations of the Novel Ser.: Vol. 32). 1973. lib. bdg. 61.00 (ISBN 0-8240-0544-9). Garland Pub.

--The Voyages, Travels & Adventures of William Owen Gwin Vaughan, Esq, Pt. 2. LC 76-170591. (Foundations of the Novel Ser.: Vol. 62). 1972. lib. bdg. 61.00 (ISBN 0-8240-0574-0). Garland Pub.

Chetwynd, Jane & Hartnett, Oonagh, eds. The Sex-Role System: Psychological & Sociological Perspectives. (Orig.). 1978. pap. 8.95x (ISBN 0-7100-8722-5). Routledge & Kegan.

Chetwynd, Tom. A Dictionary for Dreamers. LC 73-163190. pap. 63.80 (ISBN 0-317-10393-8, 2012170). Bks Demand UMI.

Chetwynd-Hayes, R. And Love Survived. 1979. pap. 2.25 (ISBN 0-89083-531-4). Zebra.

--Dominique. 1979. pap. 1.50 (ISBN 0-505-51345-5, Pub. by Tower Bks). Dorchester Pub Co.

Chety, Sida. Research on Thailand in the Philippines: An Annotated Bibliography of Theses, Dissertations, & Investigation Papers. LC 77-152541. (Cornell University, Southeast Asia Program, Data Paper: No. 107). pap. 25.00 (ISBN 0-317-29630-2, 2021849). Bks Demand UMI.

Cheung, F., jt. auth. see Martin, A.

Cheung, Peter, et al, eds. Theory, Design, & Biomedical Application of Solid State Chemical Sensors. (Uniscience Ser.). 320p. 1978. 84.00 (ISBN 0-8493-5375-0). CRC Pr.

Cheung, Steven. The Myth of Social Cost. LC 80-26083. (Cato Papers: No. 16). 74p. 1980. pap. 5.00x (ISBN 0-932790-21-6). Cato Inst.

Cheung, Steven N. The Myth of the Social Cost. (Institute of Economic Affairs Ser.: Hobart Paper 82). 1979. pap. 5.95 technical (ISBN 0-255-36112-2). Transatlantic.

--Theory of Share Tenancy. LC 70-80862. 1969. 17.00x (ISBN 0-226-10358-7). U of Chicago Pr.

--Will China Go Capitalist? (Institute of Economic Affairs, Hobart Papers Ser.: No. 94). pap. 5.95 technical (ISBN 0-255-36152-1). Transatlantic.

Cheung, W. Stephen & Levien, Frederic H. Microwaves Made Simple: Principles & Applications. 1985. text ed. 55.00 (ISBN 0-89006-173-4). Artech Hse.

Cheung, Wai Y., ed. Calcium & Cell Function, Vol. 4. (Molecular Biology Ser.). 1983. 70.00 (ISBN 0-12-171404-7). Acad Pr.

Cheung, Wai Yiu. Calcium & Cell Function, Vol. 3. (Molecular Biology Ser.). 432p. 1983. 64.00 (ISBN 0-12-171403-9). Acad Pr.

Cheung, Wai Yiu, ed. Calcium & Cell Function, Vol. 5. (Molecular Biology Ser.). 1984. 49.00 (ISBN 0-12-171405-5). Acad Pr.

--Calcium & Cell Function: Vol. 1, Calmodulin. LC 80-985. (Molecular Biology Ser.). 1980. 60.00 (ISBN 0-12-171401-2). Acad Pr.

Cheung, William. Kung Fu Butterfly Swords. Lee, Mike, ed. LC 84-62297. (Ser. 438). 224p. (Orig.). 1985. pap. 7.95 (ISBN 0-89750-125-X). Ohara Pubns.

--Wing Chun Bil Jee: The Deadly Art of Thrusting Fingers. (Illus.). 160p. (Orig.). 1983. pap. 8.95 (ISBN 0-86568-045-0, 214). Unique Pubns.

Cheung, Y. K. & Yeo, M. F. A Practical Introduction to Finite Element Analysis. LC 79-4262. (Civil Engineering Ser.). 180p. 1979. text ed. 29.95 (ISBN 0-273-01083-2). Pitman Pub MA.

Cheuse, Alan. The Bohemians: The Story of John Reed & His Friends. 1982. 12.95 (ISBN 0-918222-32-X); pap. 7.95 (ISBN 0-918222-60-5). Apple Wood.

--Candace & Other Stories. 104p. 1980. 9.50 (ISBN 0-918222-18-4); pap. 4.50 (ISBN 0-918222-19-2). Apple-Wood.

--The Grandmothers Club. 1985. 15.95 (ISBN 0-918222-67-2). Apple Wood.

Cheuse, Alan & Koffler, Richard, eds. The Rarer Action: Essays in Honor of Francis Fergusson. LC 70-127050. 1970. 35.00x (ISBN 0-8135-0670-0). Rutgers U Pr.

Cheu Thao, tr. English-Hmong Phrasebook with Useful Wordlist. (Illus.). 124p. 1981. pap. 5.00x (ISBN 0-15-599276-7, BB-50). Ctr Appl Ling.

Chevalier, ed. see Pascal, Blaise.

Chevalier Au Barisel. Conte du Barril. Bates, Robert C., ed. LC 72-1640. (Yale Romanic Studies: No. 4). Repr. of 1932 ed. 34.00 (ISBN 0-404-53204-7). AMS Pr.

Chevalier, C. Ulysse. Repertoire Des Sources Historiques Du Moyen Age: Bio-Bibliographie, 2 vols. 2nd ed. 1905-07. Set. 275.00 (ISBN 0-527-16700-2). Kraus Repr.

Chevalier, Charles. Nouvelles Instructions Sur L'usage De Daguerreotype et Melanges Photographiques, 2 vols. in 1. Bunnell, Peter C. & Sobieszek, Robert A., eds. LC 76-23036. (Sources of Modern Photography Ser.). (Illus.). 1979. Repr. of 1844 ed. lib. bdg. 21.00x (ISBN 0-405-09599-6). Ayer Co Pubs.

Chevalier, Christa. The Little Bear Who Forgot. Tucker, Kathleen, ed. LC 83-26083. (Just for Fun Bks.). (Illus.). 32p. (ps-3). 1984. PLB 10.75 (ISBN 0-8075-4571-6). A Whitman.

--Little Green Pumpkins. Tucker, Cathy, ed. LC 81-12999. (Just for Fun Bks.). (Illus.). 32p. (ps-1). 1982. PLB 10.75 (ISBN 0-8075-4593-7). A Whitman.

--Spence & the Sleepytime Monster. Tucker, Kathleen, ed. LC 83-25988. (Just for Fun Bks.). (Illus.). 32p. (ps-1). 1984. PLB 10.25 (ISBN 0-8075-7574-7). A Whitman.

--Spence Isn't Spence Anymore. Levine, Abby, ed. (Illus.). 32p. (ps-1). 1985. 10.25 (ISBN 0-8075-7565-8). A Whitman.

--Spence Makes Circles. Tucker, Kathy, ed. LC 82-11017. (Just-For-Fun Bks). (Illus.). 32p. (ps-1). 1982. 10.25 (ISBN 0-8075-7570-4). A Whitman.

Chevalier, Cyr U. Repertoire des Sources Historiques du Moyen Age: Topo Bibliographie, 1894-1903, 2 vols. (Fr.). 225.00 (ISBN 0-527-16710-X). Kraus Repr.

Chevalier, Denys. Maillol. (QLP Art Ser). (Illus.). 1970. 9.95 (ISBN 0-517-02688-0). Crown.

--Paul Klee. (Quality-Low-Price Art Ser.). 1983. 9.95 (ISBN 0-517-50302-6). Crown.

--Picasso: Blue & Rose Periods. (Q L P Art Ser.). (Illus.). 1969. 9.95 (ISBN 0-517-00904-8). Crown.

Chevalier, Francois. Land & Society in Colonial Mexico: The Great Hacienda. Eustis, Alvin, tr. Simpson, Lesley B., ed. & frwd. by. 1963. 34.00x (ISBN 0-520-00229-6); pap. 8.95 (ISBN 0-520-04653-6). U of Cal Pr.

Chevalier, Haakon, tr. see Fanon, Frantz.

Chevalier, Haakon M., tr. see Malraux, Andre.

Chevalier, Jacques. Civilization & the Stolen Gift: Capital, Kin, & Cult in Eastern Peru. 484p. 1982. 49.50x (ISBN 0-8020-5520-6). U of Toronto Pr.

--Henri Bergson. Clare, Lilian A., tr. LC 70-93774. (BCL Ser.: No. I). (Fr). 1969. Repr. of 1928 ed. 17.00 (ISBN 0-404-01488-7). AMS Pr.

--Henri Bergson. facsimile ed. LC 78-107797. (Select Bibliographies Reprint Ser.). 1928. 25.50 (ISBN 0-8369-5179-4). Ayer Co Pubs.

Chevalier, Jean & Gheerbrant, Alain. Dictionnaire des Symboles, 4 vols. 416p. (Fr.). 1973. Set. pap. 22.50 (ISBN 0-686-56946-6, M-6068). French & Eur.

Chevalier, Jean C., et al, eds. see Zwanenburg, Wiecher.

Chevalier, Jean-Marie. The New Oil Stakes. Rock, Ian, tr. from Fr. 187p. 1973, text ed. 14.75x (ISBN 0-8464-1182-2). Beekman Pubs.

Chevalier, L. Laboring Classes & Dangerous Classes in Paris During the First Half of the 19th Century. Jellinek, F., tr. 1981. pap. 12.95 (ISBN 0-691-00783-7). Princeton U Pr.

Chevalier, Michael. Society, Manners & Politics in the United States: Letters on North America. Ward, John W., ed. Bradford, T. G., tr. 11.50 (ISBN 0-8446-1111-5). Peter Smith.

Chevalier, Michel. On the Probable Fall in the Value of Gold. Cobden, Richard, ed. LC 68-28619. Repr. of 1859 ed. lib. bdg. 22.50x (ISBN 0-8371-0045-3, CHPF). Greenwood.

--Society, Manners & Politics in the United States. LC 66-21661. Repr. of 1839 ed. 37.50x (ISBN 0-678-00195-2). Kelley.

--Society, Manners & Politics in the United States: Being a Series of Letters on North America. 1969. Repr. of 1839 ed. 20.50 (ISBN 0-8337-0560-1). B Franklin.

Chevalier, Steven A. Thoughts. 57p. 1984. 3.50 (ISBN 0-89697-200-3). Intl Univ Pr.

Chevalier, Ulysse. Repertoire Des Sources Historiques Du Moyen Age: Topo-Bibliographie, 2 Vols. 2nd ed. 1894-1903. Set. 225.00 (ISBN 0-527-16710-X). Kraus Repr.

Chevalier De Latocnaye. A Frenchman's Walk Through Ireland 1796-1797. Stevenson, John, tr. from Fr. (Tour of Ireland Ser.). 304p. 1984. Repr. of 1917 ed. 11.95 (ISBN 0-85640-308-3, Pub. by Blackstaff Pr). Longwood Pub Group.

Chevalier-Skolnikoff, Suzanne. The Ontogeny of Communication in the Stumptail Macaque. (Contributions to Primatology: Vol. 2). (Illus.). 174p. 1974. 31.50 (ISBN 3-8055-1647-9). S Karger.

Chevalley, Abel. The Modern English Novel. LC 72-3283. (Studies in Fiction, No. 34). 1972. Repr. of 1925 ed. lib. bdg. 49.95x (ISBN 0-8383-1530-5). Haskell.

Chevalley, C., ed. Methode et Philosophie en Physique Fondamentale Aujourd'Hui. 104p. 1984. pap. 18.00 (ISBN 0-08-031846-0). Pergamon.

Chevalley, Claude. Fundamental Concepts of Algebra. (Pure and Applied Mathematics Ser.: Vol. 7). 1957. 49.50 (ISBN 0-12-172050-0). Acad Pr.

--Theory of Lie Groups. (Mathematical Ser.: Vol. 8). 1946. 24.50x (ISBN 0-691-08052-6). Princeton U Pr.

Chevalley, Claude C. Introduction to the Theory of Algebraic Functions of One Variable. LC 51-4714. (Mathematical Surveys Ser.: No. 6). 188p. 1979. pap. 25.00 (ISBN 0-8218-1506-7, SURV-6). Am Math.

Chevalley, Sylvie, jt. auth. see Bassan, Fernande.

Chevallier, F., ed. Biodynamics & Indicators. 236p. 1977. 37.25 (ISBN 0-677-30440-4). Gordon.

--Biodynamique et Indicateurs: Cours et Documents de Biologie. 226p. (Fr.). 1972. 57.75 (ISBN 0-677-50440-3). Gordon.

Chevallier, J. Cando Medical et Pharmaceutique. 2nd ed. 996p. (Fr.). 1974. 79.95 (ISBN 0-686-56947-4, M-6069). French & Eur.

--Precis De Terminologie Medicale. 2nd ed. 208p. (Fr.). 1977. 19.95 (ISBN 0-686-56948-2, M-6070). French & Eur.

Chevallier, P., et al. L' Enseignement Francais de la Revolution a Nos Jours: Publications De L'universite Des Sciences Sociales De Grenoble-Collection Du Centre De Recherche D'histoire Economique, Sociale et Instututionnelle, 2 tomes. Incl. Tome I. (No. 1). 1968. pap. 14.00x (ISBN 90-2796-364-9); Tome II. Documents. (No. 3). 1971. pap. 21.60x (ISBN 90-2796-932-9). (Serie Histoire Institutionelle). pap. Mouton.

Chevallier, Pierre, ed. La Scolarisation En France Depuis un Siecle: Colloque Tenu a Grenoble En Mai 1968. (Publications De L'universite Des Sciences Sociales De Grenoble, Collection Du Centre De Recherche D'histoire Economique, Sociale et Institutionnelle, Serie Histoire Institutionelle: No. 5). (Illus.). 1974. pap. 14.00x (ISBN 90-2797-307-5). Mouton.

Chevallier, Raymond. Roman Roads. LC 74-82845. 1976. 55.00x (ISBN 0-520-02834-1). U of Cal Pr.

Cheve, C. F. Dictionnaire des Apologistes Involontaires, 2 vols. Migne, J. P., ed. (Nouvelle Encyclopedie Theologique Ser.: Vols. 38-39). 1494p. (Fr.). Repr. of 1853 ed. lib. bdg. 189.50x (ISBN 0-89241-279-8). Caratzas.

--Dictionnaire des Bienfaits et Beautes du Christianisme. Migne, J. P., ed. (Troisieme et Derniere Encyclopedie Theologique Ser.: Vol. 9). 732p. (Fr.). Repr. of 1856 ed. lib. bdg. 95.00x (ISBN 0-89241-293-3). Caratzas.

--Dictionnaire des Conversions. Migne, J. P., ed. (Nouvelle Encyclopedie Theologique Ser.: Vol. 33). 836p. (Fr.). Repr. of 1852 ed. lib. bdg. 106.00x (ISBN 0-89241-275-5). Caratzas.

--Dictionnaire des Papes ou Histoire Complete des tous les Souvenirs Pontifes. Migne, J. P., ed. (Troisieme et Derniere Encyclopedie Theologique Ser.: Vol. 32). 706p. (Fr.). Repr. of 1857 ed. lib. bdg. 90.00x (ISBN 0-89241-311-5). Caratzas.

Chevedden, Paul E. The Photographic Heritage of the Middle East: An Exhibition of Early Photographs of Egypt, Palestine, Syria, Turkey, Greece, & Iran, 1849-1893. (Occasional Papers on the Near East: Vol. 1, Fascicle 3). (Illus.). 40p. (Orig.). 1981. pap. text ed. 7.00x (ISBN 0-89003-096-0). Undena Pubns.

Chevelier, Pierre. Subterranean Climbers: Twelve Years in the World's Deepest Chasm. Hatt, E. M., tr. LC 75-34044. (Illus.). 223p. 1975. 10.50 (ISBN 0-914264-14-1); pap. 5.95 (ISBN 0-914264-15-X). Cave Bks MO.

Cheveres, Gloria. Love Me, Love Me Not. 1983. 6.95 (ISBN 0-8062-2256-5). Carlton.

Chevigny, Bell G. The Woman & the Myth: Margaret Fuller's Life & Writings. LC 76-19030. (Midland Bks.: No. 243). 528p. 1976. 20.00x (ISBN 0-253-16574-1); pap. 8.95x (ISBN 0-253-20243-4). Ind U Pr.

Chevigny, Bell G., ed. Woman & the Myth: Margaret Fuller's Life & Writings. 500p. (Orig.). 1977. pap. 8.95 (ISBN 0-912670-43-6). Feminist Pr.

Chevigny, Hector. Lord of Alaska. LC 51-4156. 1970. 8.95 (ISBN 0-8323-0055-1); pap. 6.50 (ISBN 0-8323-0406-9). Binford.

--Lost Empire: The Life of Nikolai Rezanov. LC 58-11484. 1965. pap. 5.95 (ISBN 0-8323-0345-3). Binford.

--Russian America: The Great Alaskan Venture 1741-1867. LC 65-12027. 1979. pap. 7.95 (ISBN 0-8323-0320-8). Binford.

Chevigny, Hector & Braverman, Sydell. Adjustment of the Blind. 1950. 49.50x (ISBN 0-685-89731-1). Elliots Bks.

Cheville, N. F. Cytopathology in Viral Diseases. Melnick, J. L., ed. (Monographs in Virology: Vol. 10). (Illus.). xii, 236p. 1975. 54.25 (ISBN 3-8055-2203-7). S Karger.

Cheville, Norman F. Cell Pathology. 2nd ed. (Illus.). 682p. 1983. text ed. 58.50x (ISBN 0-8138-0310-1). Iowa St U Pr.

Cheville, Roy A. Scriptures from Ancient America. LC 64-12944. 1964. pap. 10.00 (ISBN 0-8309-0252-X). Herald Hse.

Cheviot, A. Proverbs, Proverbial Expressions & Popular Rhymes of Scotland. 59.95 (ISBN 0-8490-0911-1). Gordon Pr.

Cheviot, Andrew, ed. Proverbs, Proverbial Expressions, & Popular Rhymes of Scotland. LC 68-23144. 1969. Repr. of 1896 ed. 40.00x (ISBN 0-8103-3198-5). Gale.

Chevli & Farmer. Tits & Clits, No. 3. (Women's Humor Ser.). (Illus.). 1977. 1.25 (ISBN 0-918440-04-1). Nanny Goat.

--Tits & Clits, No. 1. (Women's Humor Ser.). (Illus.). 1972. 1.25 (ISBN 0-918440-00-9). Nanny Goat.

Chevli, jt. auth. see Farmer.

Chevrette, John M., jt. auth. see Colfer, George R.

Chevreul, M. E. The Principles of Harmony & Contrast of Colors. 1967. pap. 19.95 (ISBN 0-442-21212-7). Van Nos Reinhold.

Chevrier, Jean-Francois, jt. auth. see Hers, Francois.

Chevrillon, Andre. Three Studies in English Literature, Kipling, Galsworthy & Shakespeare. LC 67-27585. Repr. of 1923 ed. 19.50x (ISBN 0-8046-0077-5, Pub by Kennikat). Assoc Faculty Pr.

Chevrolet Motor Co. Chevrolet Passenger Car Shop Manual: 1949-54. Post, Dan R., ed. LC 78-68380. 512p. 1978. 28.95 (ISBN 0-911160-24-8); pap. 21.95 (ISBN 0-911160-25-6). Post-Era.

Chevrot, Georges. On the Third Day. 208p. 1961. 5.95 (ISBN 0-933932-10-3); pap. 2.95 (ISBN 0-933932-11-1). Scepter Pubs.

--Simon Peter. 223p. 1980. pap. 4.95 (ISBN 0-933932-43-X). Scepter Pubs.

Chevy Chase Manuscripts Staff, ed. see Johnson, Hubert R.

Chew, Alexander L. The Lollipop Test: A Diagnostic Screening Test for School Readiness. 14p. pap. 19.95 (ISBN 0-89334-028-6). Humanics Ltd.

Chew, Allen F. An Atlas of Russian History: Eleven Centuries of Changing Borders. 1967. pap. text ed. 10.95x (ISBN 0-300-01445-7). Yale U Pr.

Chew, Benjamin. Sketch of the Politics, Relations & Statistics of the Western World. LC 77-128427. Repr. of 1827 ed. 19.50 (ISBN 0-404-01489-5). AMS Pr.

Chew, Charles & Schlawin, Sheila. To Teach Writing Right. St. Clair, Robert N., ed. (Language & Literacy Ser.). (Orig.). 1983. pap. 14.95 (ISBN 0-88499-604-2). Inst Mod Lang.

Chew, Charles R., ed. Computers in the English Classroom: Promises & Pitfalls. 148p. 1984. pap. text ed. 5.00 (ISBN 0-930348-11-7). NY St Eng Coun.

Chew, Charles R. & Schlawin, Sheila A., eds. Written Composition: Process, Product, Program. 165p. 1983. pap. text ed. 5.00 (ISBN 0-930348-09-5). NY St Eng Coun.

Chew, Doris N. Ada Nield Chew: The Life & Writings of a Working Woman. 256p. 1983. pap. 8.95 (ISBN 0-86068-294-3, Pub. by Virago Pr). Merrimack Pub Cir.

Chew, G. see Dal Cin, Mario, et al.

Chew, Helena & Weinbaum, Martin. The London Eyre of Twelve Forty-Four. 1970. 50.00x (ISBN 0-686-96614-7, Pub by London Rec Soc England). State Mutual Bk.

Chew, Helena M. The English Ecclesiastical Tenants-in-Chief & Knight Service, Especially in the Thirteenth & Fourteenth Centuries. LC 80-2310. Repr. of 1932 ed. 37.50 (ISBN 0-404-18558-4). AMS Pr.

--London Possessory Assizes: A Calendar. 1965. 50.00x (ISBN 0-686-96618-X, Pub by London Rec Soc England). State Mutual Bk.

Chew, Helena M. & Kellaway, William, eds. London Assize of Nuisance, 1301-1431: A Calendar. 1973. 50.00x (ISBN 0-686-36878-9, Pub by London Rec Soc England). State Mutual Bk.

Chew, J. C. & Bawkoff, S. G., eds. Interfacial Transport Phenomena. (Bound Conference Volumes in Heat Transfer Ser.: Vol. 23). 109p. 1983. pap. text ed. 24.00 (ISBN 0-317-02628-3, H00269). ASME.

Chew, John J., Jr. Transformational Analysis of Modern Colloquial Japanese. (Janua Linguarum Ser. Practica: No. 56). 1974. pap. text ed. 23.20x (ISBN 90-2792-597-6). Mouton.

Chew, Paul, jt. auth. see Freiberger, Stephen.

Chew, Paul A., ed. Southwestern Pennsylvania Painters, 1800-1945. LC 81-52933. (Illus.). 178p. (Orig.). 1983. pap. 12.95 (ISBN 0-931241-17-0). Westmoreland.

Chew, Ruth. Earthstar Magic. (Illus.). (gr. 2-6). 1979. 7.95 (ISBN 0-8038-1955-2). Hastings.

--Magic Cave. (Illus.). (gr. 2-6). 1978. 7.95g (ISBN 0-8038-4711-4). Hastings.

--The Magic Coin. (Illus.). 128p. (Orig.). (gr. 3-5). 1983. pap. 1.95 (ISBN 0-590-32640-6). Scholastic Inc.

--No Such Thing As a Witch. (gr. 2 up). 1980. 7.95 (ISBN 0-8038-5073-5). Hastings.

--No Such Thing As a Witch. (Illus.). (gr. 4-6). 1972. pap. 1.95 (ISBN 0-590-09261-8). Scholastic Inc.

--Second Hand Magic. (Illus.). 128p. (Orig.). 1981. pap. 1.95 (ISBN 0-590-31387-8). Scholastic Inc.

--Secondhand Magic. LC 81-3822. 128p. (gr. 3-7). 1981. 7.95 (ISBN 0-8234-0430-7). Holiday.

--Summer Magic. (gr. k-3). 1977. pap. 1.95 (ISBN 0-590-10421-7). Scholastic Inc.

--Trapped in Time. (Illus.). 128p. (Orig.). (gr. 2-3). 1986. pap. 2.25 (ISBN 0-590-33813-7, Lucky Star). Scholastic Inc.

--The Trouble with Magic. (Illus.). 112p. (gr. 2-5). 1985. pap. 2.25 (ISBN 0-590-33606-1, Lucky Star). Scholastic Inc.

--The Wishing Tree. new ed. 144p. (gr. 7-12). 1980. 8.95 (ISBN 0-8038-8099-5). Hastings.

--The Witch at the Window. (Illus.). 128p. (Orig.). (gr. 2-4). 1985. pap. 2.25 (ISBN 0-590-33225-2, Lucky Star). Scholastic Inc.

--Witch in the House. (gr. 2-4). 1976. 7.95g (ISBN 0-8038-8080-4). Hastings.

--Witch in the House. (Illus.). (gr. 2-3). 1976. pap. 1.95 (ISBN 0-590-00093-4). Scholastic Inc.

--The Witch's Buttons. (Illus.). 128p. (gr. 2-6). 1974. PLB 7.95 (ISBN 0-8038-8071-5). Hastings.

--The Witch's Garden. (Illus.). (gr. 2-6). 1979. 7.95g (ISBN 0-8038-8093-6). Hastings.

Chew, S. C. Thomas Hardy: Poet & Novelist. 59.95 (ISBN 0-8490-1200-7). Gordon Pr.

Chew, Samuel C. Byron in England: His Fame & After-Fame. LC 79-115233. (Illus.). 420p. 1972. Repr. of 1924 ed. 9.00x (ISBN 0-403-00475-6). Scholarly.

--The Crescent & the Rose: Islam & England During the Renaissance. 59.95 (ISBN 0-87968-962-5). Gordon Pr.

--Crescent & the Rose: Islam & England During the Renaissance. 1965. lib. bdg. 37.50x (ISBN 0-374-91501-6). Octagon.
--Dramas of Lord Byron: A Critical Study. LC 70-131665. 1970. Repr. of 1915 ed. 8.00 (ISBN 0-403-00552-3). Scholarly.
--Swinburne. Repr. of 1931 ed. 30.00 (ISBN 0-8274-4332-3). R West.
--Swinburne. (Illus.). viii, 335p. 1966. Repr. of 1929 ed. 22.00 (ISBN 0-208-00557-9, Archon). Shoe String.

Chew, Teresa, jt. auth. see Jue, Daniel N.

Chew Kang, Lee. Orchids. (Illus.). 1979. 15.00 (ISBN 0-89860-032-4). Eastview.

Chewning. Business Ethics in a Changing Culture. LC 82-74194. pap. 13.95 (ISBN 0-8359-0566-7). Reston.

Chewning, Betty. Staff Manual for Teaching Patients about Hypertension. LC 82-8745. (Illus.). 372p. 1982. 3-ring binder 47.50 (ISBN 0-87258-400-3, AHA-070122). AHPI.

Chewning, Emily B. Emergency First Aid for Children. LC 83-25828. (Kid Care Ser.). (Illus.). 64p. 1984. pap. 3.95 (ISBN 0-201-10812-7). Addison-Wesley.

Chewoweth, J., ed. Flow Induced Heat Exchanger Tube Vibration-1980, HTD-Vol.9. 72p. 1980. 16.00 (ISBN 0-317-33520-0, G00182); 8.00 (ISBN 0-317-33521-9). ASME.

Chey, William Y., ed. Functional Disorders of the Digestive Tract. 368p. 1983. text ed. 54.50 (ISBN 0-89004-859-2). Raven.

Cheyenne. Posing Techniques for Photographers & Models. (Illus.). 160p. 1983. 24.95 (ISBN 0-8174-4525-0, Amphoto). Watson-Guptill.

Cheyette, Frederic, ed. Lordship & Community in Medieval Europe. LC 75-12657. 448p. 1975. Repr. of 1968 ed. 19.50 (ISBN 0-88275-283-9). Krieger.

Cheyfitz, Eric. The Trans-Parent: Sexual Politics in the Language of Emerson. LC 80-25750. 224p. 1981. text ed. 18.00x (ISBN 0-8018-2450-8). Johns Hopkins.

Cheyne, Charles H. An Elementary Treatise in the Planetary Theory. Cohen, I. Bernard, ed. LC 80-2117. (Development of Science Ser.). (Illus.). 1981. lib. bdg. 15.00x (ISBN 0-686-73597-8). Ayer Co Pubs.
--An Elementary Treatise on the Planetary Theory. 15.00 (ISBN 0-405-13837-7). Ayer Co Pubs.

Cheyne, George. The English Malady. LC 76-49853. (History of Psychology Ser.). 1976. Repr. of 1733 ed. 50.00x (ISBN 0-8201-1281-X). Schol Facsimiles.
--An Essay of Health & Long Life. Kastenbaum, Robert, ed. LC 78-22191. (Aging & Old Age Ser.). 1979. Repr. of 1724 ed. lib. bdg. 21.00x (ISBN 0-405-11808-2). Ayer Co Pubs.

Cheyne, T. K. & Black, J. S., eds. Encyclopedia Biblica, 4 vols. 1977. lib. bdg. 425.95 (ISBN 0-8490-1764-5). Gordon Pr.

Cheyne, W. M., jt. ed. see Clark, M. M.

Cheyney, Arnold. The Poetry Corner. 1982. pap. 11.95 (ISBN 0-673-16461-6). Scott F.
--The Writing Corner. LC 78-16075. (Illus.). 1978. pap. 12.95 (ISBN 0-673-16155-2). Scott F.

Cheyney, Arnold & Capone, Donald. The Map Corner. 1983. pap. 12.95 (ISBN 0-673-16615-5). Scott F.

Cheyney, Arnold B. The Spelling Corner. 1984. pap. 8.95 (ISBN 0-673-15960-4). Scott F.
--Teaching Children of Different Cultures in the Classroom: A Language Approach. (Elementary Education Ser.). 1976. pap. text ed. 14.50 (ISBN 0-675-08622-1). Merrill.
--Teaching Reading Skills Through the Newspaper. 2nd ed. LC 84-10884. (Reading Aids Ser.). 1984. 4.50 (ISBN 0-87207-210-X). Intl Reading.

Cheyney, Arnold B., ed. The Ripe Harvest: Educating Migrant Children. LC 73-158927. 256p. 1972. 11.95x (ISBN 0-87024-206-7). U of Miami Pr.

Cheyney, E. P. Law in History, & Other Essays. 1977. lib. bdg. 59.95 (ISBN 0-8490-2134-0). Gordon Pr.

Cheyney, Edward P. European Background of American History 1390-1600. 11.25 (ISBN 0-8446-1851-9). Peter Smith.
--A History of England from the Defeat of the Armada to the Death of Elizabeth, 2 vols. Set. 26.00 (ISBN 0-8446-1112-3). Peter Smith.
--History of the University of Pennsylvania: 1740-1940. Metzger, Walter P., ed. LC 76-55192. (The Academic Profession Ser.). 1977. Repr. of 1940 ed. lib. bdg. 35.50x (ISBN 0-405-10020-5). Ayer Co Pubs.
--Industrial & Social History of England. 1909. 25.00 (ISBN 0-8482-3570-3). Norwood Edns.
--Introduction to the Industrial & Social History of England. rev. ed. LC 79-92609. (BCL Ser.: No. I). (Illus.). Repr. of 1920 ed. 21.50 (ISBN 0-404-01524-7). AMS Pr.
--Reading in English History Drawn from the Original Sources. 1908. 25.00 (ISBN 0-8482-3594-0). Norwood Edns.
--A Short History of England. 750p. 1981. Repr. of 1904 ed. lib. bdg. 75.00 (ISBN 0-8495-0860-6). Arden Lib.
--A Short History of England. 1904. 40.00 (ISBN 0-685-43753-1). Norwood Edns.
--Social Changes in England in the Sixteenth-Century As Reflected in Contemporary Literature. LC 76-168055. (Illus.). Repr. of 1895 ed. 12.50 (ISBN 0-404-01523-9). AMS Pr.

Chezet, Jean-Paul de, tr. see Larbaud, Valery.

Chhabra, G. S. Advanced Study in the History of Modern India, 3 vols. 2nd, rev. ed. 1984. Set. text ed. 100.00x (ISBN 0-86590-589-4, Pub. by Sterling Pubs India). Vol. 1, 403 pp. Vol. 2, 652 pp. Vol. 3, 245 pp. Apt Bks.

Chheda, H. R., jt. auth. see Crowder, L. V.

Chhibber, Harbans L. The Geology of Burma. LC 77-87011. Repr. of 1934 ed. 38.50 (ISBN 0-404-16803-5). AMS Pr.
--The Physiography of Burma. LC 72-179178. (Illus.). Repr. of 1933 ed. 17.50 (ISBN 0-404-54808-3). AMS Pr.

Chi Ch'ao-Ting. Key Economic Areas in Chinese History. LC 70-104612. (Illus.). Repr. of 1936 ed. 22.50 (ISBN 0-678-00594-X). Kelley.

Chi, Chen. Chen Chi Watercolors, Drawings, Sketches. (Illus.). 108p. 1980. 30.00 (ISBN 0-9604652-0-0). Chen Chi Studio.

Chi, Hsi-Sheng. Nationalist China at War: Military Defeats & Political Collapse, 1937-45. (Michigan Studies on China Ser.). 1982. text ed. 20.00x (ISBN 0-472-10018-1). U of Mich Pr.

Ch'i, Hsi-sheng. Warlord Politics in China, 1916-1928. LC 75-7482. xiv, 282p. 1976. 22.50x (ISBN 0-8047-0894-0). Stanford U Pr.

Chi, Joseph. CADSES: Computer Aided Design of Scientific & Engineering Systems. 268p. (Orig.). 1984. pap. text ed. 24.95 (ISBN 0-930945-01-8). HCP Systems.

Chi, Keon. State Futures Commissions. Purcell, L. Edward, ed. (Orig.). pap. 12.00 (ISBN 0-87292-039-9). Coun State Govts.

Chi, M. T., ed. Trends in Memory Development Research. (Contributions to Human Development: Vol. 9). (Illus.). xii, 128p. 1983. pap. 21.00 (ISBN 3-8055-3661-5). S Karger.

Chi, Madeleine. China Diplomacy, Nineteen Fourteen to Nineteen Eighteen. LC 77-82302. (East Asian Monographs Ser: No. 31). 1970. pap. 11.00x (ISBN 0-674-11825-1). Harvard U Pr.

Chi, Michelene T., ed. Trends in Memory Development. 174p. 1983. pap. 29.50. Transaction Bks.

Chi, Pang-Yuan, et al, eds. An Anthology of Contemporary Chinese Literature: Taiwan: 1949-1974, Poems & Essays, Vol. 1. LC 75-42791. 580p. 1976. 20.00x (ISBN 0-295-95502-3, Pub. by Natl Inst Comp Taiwan); pap. 12.50x (ISBN 0-295-95628-3); 2 Vol. Set 40.00x. U of Wash Pr.
--An Anthology of Contemporary Chinese Literature: Taiwan: 1949-1974, Short Stories, Vol. 2. LC 75-42791. 484p. 1976. 20.00x (ISBN 0-295-95503-1, Pub. by Natl Inst Comp Taiwan); pap. 12.50x (ISBN 0-295-95629-1); Set. 40.00x. U of Wash Pr.

Chi, Wen-shun. Ideological Conflicts in Modern China: Democracy & Authoritarianism. 430p. 1985. 29.95 (ISBN 0-88738-054-9). Transaction Bks.

Chia, Bhikshuni Heng, tr. from Chinese. Flower Adornment Sutra, Chapter 24: Praises in the Tushita Heaven. (Illus.). 130p. (Orig.). 1982. pap. 5.00 (ISBN 0-917512-39-1). Buddhist Text.

Chia, C. Y. Nonlinear Analysis of Plates. (Illus.). 448p. 1980. text ed. 78.00 (ISBN 0-07-010746-7). McGraw.

Chia, F. & Rice, M. E., eds. Settlement & Metamorphosis of Marine Invertebrate Larvae: Proceedings of a Symposium Held at Toronto, Canada, Dec. 27-28, 1977. 290p. 1979. 45.50 (ISBN 0-444-00277-4, Biomedical Pr). Elsevier.

Chia, L. S. & MacAndrews, C. Southeast Asian Seas: Frontiers for Development. 1982. 36.50 (ISBN 0-07-099247-9). McGraw.

Chia, L. S., jt. auth. see MacAndrews, C.

Chia, Mantak. Taoist Secrets of Love: Cultivating Male Sexual Energy. 1984. pap. 12.50 (ISBN 0-943358-19-1). Aurora Press.

Chia-Ao, see Chang Kia-ngau, pseud.

Chiamos, Mary, et al. Zoom. (Illus., Orig.). (gr. k-3). 1973. pap. 7.50 (ISBN 0-918932-46-7). Activity Resources.

Chiampi, Luke. Rebuild My Church. LC 72-87090. 105p. 1972. pap. 0.95 (ISBN 0-8199-0502-X). Franciscan Herald.

Chiandussi, L., ed. see International Symposium on: HBsAg Containing Immune Complexes: Renal & Other Extra-Hepatic Manifestations: Italy, Sept. 1979, et al.

Chiang. Time for a New Direction. 208p. 1984. pap. text ed. 9.95 (ISBN 0-8403-3432-X). Kendall-Hunt.

Chiang, Chin L. Introduction to Stochastic Processes, & Their Applications. LC 74-14821. 544p. 1980. 39.50 (ISBN 0-88275-200-6). Krieger.
--Life Table & Its Applications. LC 82-20331. 336p. 1984. 32.50 (ISBN 0-89874-570-5). Krieger.

Chiang, Gregory K., jt. ed. see Seybolt, Peter J.

Chiang, H. S., jt. auth. see Peng, Syd.

Chiang, Hai D., jt. ed. see Ooi, Jin-Bee.

Chiang, Hai H. Electronics for Nuclear Instrumentation, Theory & Applications. LC 82-8974. 670p. 1985. lib. bdg. 54.50 (ISBN 0-89874-483-0). Krieger.

Chiang Kai-Shek. Collected Wartime Messages of Generalissimo Chiang Kai-Shek 1937 to 1945, 2 Vols. in 1. LC 46-7008. 1969. Repr. of 1946 ed. 56.00 (ISBN 0-527-16800-9). Kraus Repr.
--Resistance & Reconstruction. facsimile ed. LC 71-111819. (Essay Index Reprint Ser.). 1943. 24.50 (ISBN 0-8369-1597-6). Ayer Co Pubs.

Chiang, Monlin. Tides from the West, a Chinese Autobiography. LC 75-37249. Repr. of 1947 ed. 25.50 (ISBN 0-404-14490-X). AMS Pr.
--Tides from the West: A Chinese Autobiography. 1947. 23.50x (ISBN 0-686-83825-4). Elliots Bks.

Chiang, Pei-Heng. Non-Governmental Organizations at the United Nations: Identity, Role, & Function. LC 81-8685. 368p. 1981. 41.95 (ISBN 0-03-058632-1). Praeger.

Chiang, Win-Shin S. Guide to Louisiana Legal Research. 1985. pap. text ed. write for info. (ISBN 0-409-25090-2). Butterworth TX.

Chiang, Win-Shin S., jt. auth. see Dickson, Lance E.

Chiang Yee. The Chinese Eye: An Interpretation of Chinese Painting. (Midland Bks.: No. 62). (Illus.). 264p. 1964. pap. 5.95x (ISBN 0-253-20062-8). Ind U Pr.
--Silent Traveller in Boston. (Illus.). 1959. 7.50 (ISBN 0-393-08474-4). Norton.
--Silent Traveller in San Francisco. (Illus.). 1964. 12.50 (ISBN 0-393-08422-1). Norton.

Chiang Hsiao-Mei. Stories from Taiwan. (National Peking University & Chinese Assn. for Folklore, Folklore & Folkliterature Ser.: No. 118-120). (Chinese.). 45.00x (ISBN 0-89986-195-4). Oriental Bk Store.

Chiang Kai-Shek. China's Destiny. LC 76-24849. 260p. 1976. Repr. of 1947 ed. lib. bdg. 32.50 (ISBN 0-306-70821-3). Da Capo.
--China's Destiny. Chung-Hui, Wang, tr. from Chinese. LC 84-22503. xii, 260p. 1985. Repr. of 1947 ed. lib. bdg. 35.00x (ISBN 0-313-24676-9, CHCD). Greenwood.

Chiang K'ang-Hsin. The Snake Bridegroom. Lin Lan, ed. (Tales from the Orient Ser.: No. 11). (Chinese.). 15.00x (ISBN 0-89986-235-7). Oriental Bk Store.

Chiang Ker Chiu. Cantonese for Beginners, 2 vols. 5.00x (ISBN 0-686-00846-4). Colton Bk.

Chiang Ker-Chiu. Chinese Idioms. 5.00x (ISBN 0-686-00847-2). Colton Bk.
--Mandarin Made Easy, 3 Vols. Set. 8.50x (ISBN 0-686-00873-1). Colton Bk.
--Practical English-Cantonese Dictionary. (Eng. & Cantonese.). 25.00x (ISBN 0-686-00881-2). Colton Bk.

Chiang Yee. China Revisited. (Illus.). 1977. 9.95 (ISBN 0-393-08791-3). Norton.
--Chinese Calligraphy: An Introduction to Its Aesthetic & Technique. 3rd ed. LC 72-75400. (Illus.). 272p. 1973. 16.50x (ISBN 0-674-12225-9); pap. 8.95 (ISBN 0-674-12226-7). Harvard U Pr.
--The Silent Traveller in Japan. (Illus.). 1972. 15.00 (ISBN 0-393-08642-9). Norton.
--The Silent Traveller in San Francisco. (Illus.). 384p. 1981. pap. 6.95 (ISBN 0-393-00064-8). Norton.

Chianis, Sotirios. Folk Songs of Mantneia, Greece. (University of California Publications, Folklore Studies Ser.: No. 15). (Illus.). pap. 45.80 (ISBN 0-317-09980-9, 2011356). Bks Demand UMI.

Chiao, T. T. & Schuster, D. M., eds. Failure Modes in Composites III. LC 76-23498. pap. 81.50 (ISBN 0-317-08667-7, 2012650). Bks Demand UMI.

Ch'Iao-Mu, Hu. Thirty Years of the Communist Party of China: An Outline History. LC 73-877. (China Studies: from Confucius to Mao Ser.). (Illus.). 95p. 1973. Repr. of 1951 ed. 13.50 (ISBN 0-88355-071-7). Hyperion Conn.

Chiao Wan-Hsuan. Devolution in Great Britain. LC 76-78010. (Columbia University Studies in the Social Sciences: No. 272). Repr. of 1926 ed. 22.50 (ISBN 0-404-51272-0). AMS Pr.

Chiapetta, Eugene L., jt. auth. see Collette, Alfred T.

Chiapetta, Vincent J., jt. auth. see Greulach, Victor A.

Chiappa, Joseph A & Forish, Joseph J. The VD Book. LC 77-84938. 1977. 13.95 (ISBN 0-03-018796-6, HoltC); pap. 9.95 prof. ed. (ISBN 0-03-018341-3). HR&W.

Chiappa, Joseph A. & Forish, Joseph J. VD Book: For People Who Care about Themselves & Others. LC 76-17596. (Illus.). 145p. 1977. pap. 3.95 (ISBN 0-8290-0287-1). Irvington.

Chiappa, Keith H. Evoked Potentials in Clinical Medicine. (Illus.). 352p. 1983. text ed. 39.50 (ISBN 0-89004-777-4). Raven.

Chiappa, S., et al. Endolymphatic Radiotherapy in Malignant Lymphomas. LC 78-148260. (Recent Results in Cancer Research Ser.: Vol. 37). (Illus.). 1971. 31.00 (ISBN 0-387-05330-1). Springer-Verlag.

Chiappelli, Fredi, ed. First Images of America: The Impact of the New World. LC 75-7191. 1976. 180.00x (ISBN 0-520-03010-9). U of Cal Pr.

Chiapuris, John P. The Ait Ayash of the High Molouuya Plain: Rural Social Organization in Morocco. (Anthropological Papers Ser.: No. 69). 1980. pap. 6.00x (ISBN 0-932206-83-2). U Mich Mus Anthro.

Chiapusso, Jan. Bach's World. LC 79-20813. (Illus.). 1980. Repr. of 1968 ed. lib. bdg. 45.00x (ISBN 0-313-22139-1, CHBW). Greenwood.

Chiara, jt. auth. see Piero.

Chiara, Edith D. see Uhlin, Donald H. & De Chiara, Edith.

Chiara, G. Di see Di Chiara, G. & Gessa, G. L.

Chiara, Joseph De see De Chiara, Joseph.

Chiara, Joseph De see De Chiara, Joseph & Callender, John.

Chiara, Joy de see De Chiara, Joy.

Chiara, M. L., ed. Italian Studies in the Philosophy of Science. Fawcett, Carolyn, tr. (Boston Studies in the Philosophy of Science: No. 47). 525p. 1980. lib. bdg. 73.50 (ISBN 90-277-0735-9, Pub. by Reidel Holland); pap. 34.00 (ISBN 90-277-1073-2, Pub. by Reidel Holland). Kluwer Academic.

Chiaramonte, Giovanni. The Story of Photography: An Illustrated History. Piero, W. S., tr. LC 83-70829. (Illus.). 126p. 1983. 17.50 (ISBN 0-89381-122-X). Aperture.

Chiarappa, L., jt. auth. see Hewitt, William B.

Chiarelli, A. B. Taxonomic Atlas of Living Primates. 1972. 67.50 (ISBN 0-12-172550-2). Acad Pr.

Chiarelli, A. B., ed. Perspectives in Primate Biology. LC 74-10968. (Advances in Behavioral Biology Ser.: Vol. 9). 333p. 1974. 45.00x (ISBN 0-306-37909-0, Plenum Pr). Plenum Pub.

Chiarelli, A. B. & Corruscini, R. S., eds. Advanced Views in Primate Biology: Proceedings. (Proceedings in Life Sciences Ser.). (Illus.). 266p. 1982. 48.00 (ISBN 0-387-11092-5). Springer-Verlag.
--Primate Behavior & Sociobiology: Selected Papers - Proceedings, Pt. B. (Proceedings in Life Sciences Ser.). (Illus.). 230p. 1981. 36.00 (ISBN 0-387-11024-0). Springer-Verlag.
--Primate Evolutionary Biology: Selected Papers - Proceedings, Pt. A. (Illus.). 150p. 1981. 29.00 (ISBN 0-387-11023-2). Springer-Verlag.

Chiarelli, A. B., jt. ed. see Ciochon, Russell L.

Chiarelli, Alessandra, ed. Giovanni Maria Bononcini (1642-1678), Guiseppe Colombi (1635-1694), Domenico Gabrielli (1651-1690), & Giovanni Maria Bononcini (Angelo) (1678-1735) (The Italian Cantata in the Seventeenth Century Ser.). 250p. 1985. 60.00 (ISBN 0-8240-8888-3). Garland Pub.

Chiarelli, Brunetto, et al, eds. Comparative Karyology of Primates. (World Anthropology Ser.). text ed. 26.40x (ISBN 9-0279-7840-9). Mouton.

Chiarelli, Luigi see Dent, Anthony.

Chiarello, Gail D. Bhangra Dance: Poems, Nineteen Sixty-Seven to Nineteen Seventy. pap. 2.00 (ISBN 0-685-04665-6). Oyez.

Chiarenza, Carl. Aaron Siskind: Pleasures & Terrors. 1982. 60.00 (ISBN 0-8212-1522-1). NYGS.

Chiarenza, G. A. & Pakakostopoulos, D., eds. Clinical Application of Cerebral Evoked Potentials in Pediatric Medicine: Proceedings of the International Conference, Milan, Italy, January 14-16, 1982. (International Congress Ser.: No. 595). 416p. 1982. 63.50 (ISBN 0-444-90278-3, Excerpta Medica). Elsevier.

Chiarenza, G. A. & Papakostopoulos, D., eds. Clinical Application of Cerebral Evoked Potentias in Pediatric Medicine: Proceedings of the International Conference, Milan, Italy, January 14-16, 1982. (International Congress Ser.: No. 595). xviii, 416p. 1982. 63.50 (ISBN 0-444-90278-3, Excerpta Medica). Elsevier.

Chiarenza, Loretta & Burkart, John, eds. Human Biology. 2nd ed. 316p. 1984. pap. text ed. 16.95 (ISBN 0-89529-134-7). Avery Pub.

Chiari, Joseph. Art & Knowledge. LC 76-57236. 1977. 11.00x (ISBN 0-87752-208-1). Gordian.
--Christopher Columbus: A Play. LC 78-23741. 1979. 8.50 (ISBN 0-87752-216-2). Gordian.
--Collected Poems. LC 77-26826. 1978. 10.00x (ISBN 0-87752-213-8). Gordian.
--Contemporary French Poetry. facs. ed. LC 68-20289. (Essay Index Reprint Ser). 1952. 15.00 (ISBN 0-8369-0301-3). Ayer Co Pubs.
--Contemporary French Theatre: The Flight from Naturalism. LC 76-128187. 1970. Repr. of 1958 ed. text ed. 12.50x (ISBN 0-87752-126-3). Gordian.
--Impressions of People & Literature: On Scottish Life & Literature. 1973. 20.00 (ISBN 0-8274-1532-X). R West.
--Landmarks of Contemporary Drama. LC 76-148616. 1971. Repr. of 1965 ed. text ed. 12.50x (ISBN 0-87752-144-1). Gordian.
--Lights in the Distance. LC 72-148615. 1971. text ed. 5.00x (ISBN 0-87752-148-4). Gordian.
--The Necessity of Being. LC 73-3338. 168p. 1973. 10.00x (ISBN 0-87752-167-0). Gordian.
--Poetic Drama of Paul Claudel. LC 71-90365. 1969. Repr. of 1954 ed. text ed. 12.50x (ISBN 0-87752-018-6). Gordian.
--Realism & Imagination. LC 74-131248. 1970. Repr. of 1960 ed. text ed. 12.50x (ISBN 0-87752-019-4). Gordian.
--Reflections on Life & Death. LC 77-4054. 1977. 9.00x (ISBN 0-87752-212-X). Gordian.
--Symbolisme from Poe to Mallarme: The Growth of a Myth. LC 76-114096. 1970. Repr. of 1956 ed. text ed. 12.50x (ISBN 0-87752-020-8). Gordian.
--T. S. Eliot: A Memoir. (Illus.). 1982. 12.00 (ISBN 0-905289-33-1). Small Pr Dist.
--T. S. Eliot: Poet & Dramatist. LC 79-158. 1979. Repr. of 1972 ed. 12.00x (ISBN 0-87752-218-9). Gordian.

--The Time of the Rising Sea. LC 74-29585. 52p. 1975. 5.00x (ISBN 0-87752-195-6). Gordian.

--Twentieth Century French Thought: From Bergson to Levi-Strauss. LC 75-1574. 210p. 1975. 14.00x (ISBN 0-87752-185-9). Gordian.

Chiari, Joseph, ed. Harrap Anthology of French Poetry. LC 70-131247. 1970. Repr. of 1958 ed. text ed. 15.00x (ISBN 0-87752-017-8). Gordian.

Chiarkas. Alabama Criminal Trial Practice. incl. latest pocket part supplement 55.95 (ISBN 0-686-90120-7); separate pocket part supplement, 1983 27.95 (ISBN 0-686-90121-5). Harrison Co GA.

--Alabama Criminal Trial Practice Forms. incl. latest pocket part supplement 59.95; separate pocket part supplement, 1983 (for use in 1984) 29.95. Harrison Co GA.

Chiarkas, et al. Criminal Offenses & Defenses in Alabama. 42.95 (ISBN 0-686-90114-2). Harrison Co GA.

Chiaro, Mario A. Del see Del Chiaro, Mario A.

Chiaromonte, Nicola. The Paradox of History: Stendahl, Tolstoy, Pasternak & Others. rev. ed. LC 84-28102. 168p. 1985. pap. text ed. 13.95 (ISBN 0-8122-1210-X). U of Pa Pr.

--The Worm of Consciousness & Other Essays. Ferrone, J. & Willen, D., eds. LC 76-29695. 1977. 3.95 (ISBN 0-15-698370-2, Harv). HarBraceJ.

Chia-Shun, Yih, ed. Advances in Applied Mechanics, Vol. 22. (Serial Publication Ser.). 1982. 65.00 (ISBN 0-12-002022-X). Acad Pr.

Chia-Shun Yih. Stratified Flows. LC 79-24817. 1980. 39.50 (ISBN 0-12-771050-7). Acad Pr.

Chia-Shun Yih, ed. Advances in Applied Mechanics, Vol. 19. LC 48-8503. 1979. 65.00 (ISBN 0-12-002019-X). Acad Pr.

Chia Shun Yih, ed. Advances in Applied Mechanics, Vol. 21. (Serial Publication Ser.). 1981. 59.50 (ISBN 0-12-002021-1). Acad Pr.

Chiasson, Elias, jt. auth. see Warren, Eugene.

Chiasson, Robert B. Laboratory Anatomy of the Perch. 3rd ed. (Laboratory Anatomy Ser.). 80p. 1980. wire coil write for info. (ISBN 0-697-04638-9). Wm C Brown.

--Laboratory Anatomy of the Pigeon. 3rd ed. (Laboratory Anatomy Ser.). 96p. 1984. write for info. wire coil (ISBN 0-697-04927-2). Wm C Brown.

--Laboratory Anatomy of the White Rat. 4th ed. (Laboratory Anatomy Ser.). 112p. 1980. wire coil write for info. (ISBN 0-697-04644-3). Wm C Brown.

Chiasson, Robert B. & Booth, Ernest S. Laboratory Anatomy of the Cat. 7th ed. (Laboratory Anatomy Ser.). 112p. 1982. wire coil write for info. (ISBN 0-697-04722-9). Wm C Brown.

Chiasson, Robert B., jt. auth. see Ashley, Laurence M.

Chiasson, Robert B., jt. auth. see McLaughlin, Charles A.

Chia-Sun Yih see Von Mises, Richard & Von Karman, Theodore.

Chiat, Marilyn. Handbook of Synagogue Architecture. LC 81-9419. (Brown Judiac Studies). 1982. pap. 20.00 (ISBN 0-89130-524-6, 14-00-29). Scholars Pr GA.

Chia-Yu Wang. Loves & Lives of Chinese Emperors. 246p. 1980. 8.95 (ISBN 0-89955-179-3, Pub. by Mei Ya China); pap. 5.95 (ISBN 0-89955-199-8, Pub. by Mei Ya China). Intl Spec Bk.

Chiazze, Leonard, Jr. & Lundin, Frank E., eds. Methods & Issues in Occupational & Environmental Epidemiology. LC 82-72346. (Illus.). 225p. 1983. 49.95 (ISBN 0-250-40576-8). Butterworth.

Chiba, H., et al, eds. Food Science & Technology: Proceedings of the 5th International Congress. LC 79-20898. (Developments in Food Science Ser.: Vol. 2). 448p. 1980. 106.50 (ISBN 0-444-99770-9). Elsevier.

Chiba, Reiko. Hiroshige's Tokaido in Prints & Poetry. LC 57-11672. (Illus.). 10.50 (ISBN 0-8048-0246-7). C E Tuttle.

--Japanese Screens in Miniature. LC 60-9285. 1960. brocade case 19.50 (ISBN 0-8048-0317-X). C E Tuttle.

--Making of a Japanese Print. LC 59-14277. (Illus.). 1960. brocade 6.95 (ISBN 0-8048-0393-5). C E Tuttle.

--Painted Fans of Japan: Fifteen Noh Drama Masterpieces. LC 62-20775. (Illus., Fr., Or Eng). 1962. 15.50 (ISBN 0-8048-0468-0). C E Tuttle.

--Sesshu's Long Scroll: A Zen Landscape Journey. LC 54-14085. (Illus.). 1959. 14.50 (ISBN 0-8048-0677-2). C E Tuttle.

--Seven Lucky Gods of Japan. LC 65-25467. (Illus.). 1966. 10.95 (ISBN 0-8048-0521-0). C E Tuttle.

Chiba, Reiko, ed. Copybook for Japanese Ink Painting. LC 64-14192. (Illus.). 1964. bds. 9.50 (ISBN 0-8048-0124-X). C E Tuttle.

--Down the Emperor's Road with Hiroshige. LC 65-18959. (Illus.). 1965. 10.50 (ISBN 0-8048-0143-6). C E Tuttle.

--Japanese Fortune Calendar. LC 54-14085. (Illus.). 1965. 9.50 (ISBN 0-8048-0300-5). C E Tuttle.

Chibata, Ichiro, ed. Immobilized Enzymes: Research & Development. LC 78-13266. 284p. 1978. 53.95x (ISBN 0-470-26531-0). Halsted Pr.

Chibata, Ichiro & Fukui, Saburo, eds. Enzyme Engineering, Vol. 6. LC 74-13768. 560p. 1982. 69.50x (ISBN 0-306-41121-0, Plenum Pr). Plenum Pub.

Chibata, Ichiro & Wingard, Lemuel B., Jr., eds. Applied Biochemistry & Bioengineering: Vol. 4: Immobilized Cells. (Serial Publication). 1983. 65.00 (ISBN 0-12-041104-0). Acad Pr.

Chibbett, D. G. The History of Japanese Printing & Book Illustration. LC 76-9362. (Illus.). 264p. 1977. 65.00 (ISBN 0-87011-288-0). Kodansha.

Chibbett, David, tr. see Kato, Shuichi.

Chibbett, David G., tr. see Doppo, Kunikida.

Chibisova, O. I. & Kozar, L. A., eds. English-Russian Biological Dictionary. 3rd ed. LC 78-40145. 1980. text ed. 145.00 (ISBN 0-08-023163-2). Pergamon.

Chibnall, Albert C. Protein Metabolism in the Plant. 1939. 39.50x (ISBN 0-685-69795-9); pap. 19.50x (ISBN 0-685-69796-7). Elliots Bks.

Chibnall, Bernard. The Organisation of Media. 80p. 1976. 11.50 (ISBN 0-208-01525-6, Linnet). Shoe String.

Chibnall, Majorie. The World of Orderic Vitalis. (Illus.). 1984. 29.95x (ISBN 0-19-821937-7). Oxford U Pr.

Chibnall, Majorie, ed. & tr. see Vitalis, Orderic.

Chibnall, Marjorie, ed. Charters & Custumals of the Abbey of Holy Trinity, Caen. (Records of Social & Economic History Ser.). (Illus.). 1982. 37.50x (ISBN 0-19-726009-8). Oxford U Pr.

--The Ecclesiastical History of Orderic Vitalis, Vol. 1. (Oxford Medieval Texts Ser.). (Illus.). 1981. 98.00x (ISBN 0-19-822243-2). Oxford U Pr.

Chibnall, Marjorie, ed. & tr. see Vitalis, Orderic.

Chi-Bonnardel, Regine Van see Van Chi-Bonnardel, Regine.

Chibucos, Thomas R., ed. Toward Broader Conceptualization of Child Mistreatment. LC 80-82468. (Special Issue of Infant Mental Health Journal: Vol. 1, No. 4). 73p. 1980. pap. 9.95 (ISBN 0-89885-052-5). Human Sci Pr.

Chibwe, E. C. Afro-Arab Relations in the New World Order. LC 77-90935. 1978. 25.00 (ISBN 0-312-01063-X). St Martin.

Chicago Board of Education. Gold Level Comprehension Book. 2nd ed. (Chicago Mastery Learning Reading Ser.). 229p. (gr. 6). 1982. 3.75 (ISBN 0-88106-038-0, 6110). Mastery Ed.

--Purple Level Student Book. (Vocabulary Learning Strategies Ser.). (Orig.). (gr. 7). 1984. wkbk. 3.75 (ISBN 0-88106-087-9, 7130). Mastery Ed.

--Purple Level Teacher Manual. (Vocabulary Learning Strategies Ser.). (Orig.). (gr. 7). 1984. tchr's. ed. 12.00 (ISBN 0-88106-088-7, 7230). Mastery Ed.

--Red Level Teacher: Word Attack & Study Skills. 2nd ed. (Chicago Mastery Learning Reading Ser.). 643p. (gr. 1). 1982. 20.00 (ISBN 0-88106-009-7, 1220). Mastery Ed.

--Red Level Word Attack & Study Skills. 2nd ed. (Chicago Mastery Learning Reading Ser.: Bk. 1). 199p. (gr. 1). 1982. 2.00 (ISBN 0-88106-007-0, 1121). Mastery Ed.

--Silver Level Student Book. (Vocabulary Learning Strategies Ser.). (Orig.). (gr. 8). 1984. wkbk. 3.75 (ISBN 0-88106-089-5, 8130). Mastery Ed.

--Silver Level Teacher Manual. (Vocabulary Learning Strategies Ser.). (Orig.). (gr. 8). 1984. tchr's. ed. 12.00 (ISBN 0-88106-090-9, 8230). Mastery Ed.

Chicago Civil Service Commission. Chicago Police Investigations: Three Reports. LC 76-154557. (The Police in America Ser.). 1971. Repr. of 1898 ed. 11.00 (ISBN 0-405-03365-6). Ayer Co Pubs.

Chicago Commission On Race Relations Editors. Negro in Chicago: A Study of Race Relations & a Race Riot. LC 68-28990. (American Negro: His History & Literature Ser., No. 1). 1968. Repr. of 1922 ed. 21.00 (ISBN 0-405-01807-X). Ayer Co Pubs.

Chicago Community Trust. Reports Comprising the Survey of the Cook County Jail. facsimile ed. LC 73-3818. (Criminal Justice in America Ser.). (Illus.). 1974. Repr. of 1923 ed. 24.50x (ISBN 0-405-06139-0). Ayer Co Pubs.

Chicago Council on Foreign Relations. American Public Opinion & U. S. Foreign Policy, 1982. 2nd ed. LC 84-81558. 1984. write for info. codebook (ISBN 0-89138-896-6). ICPSR.

Chicago Cutlery. Cooking with Style. 148p. 1984. 8.95 (ISBN 0-914091-44-1). Chicago Review.

--Cooking with Style. (Illus.). 144p. 1984. 8.95 (ISBN 0-914091-44-1). BH & GB.

Chicago Dietetic Association & South Suburban Dietetic Association. Manual of Clinical Dietetics. LC 80-53899. 1981. text ed. 25.00 (ISBN 0-7216-2537-1); physician's guide 29.95 (ISBN 0-7216-2539-8). Saunders.

Chicago Fact Book Consortium. Local Community Fact Book: Chicago Metropolitan Area. (Illus.). 468p. 1984. 25.00 (ISBN 0-914091-60-3); pap. 17.50 (ISBN 0-914091-61-1). Chicago Review.

Chicago Historical Society Staff & Darling, Sharon S. Decorative & Architectural Arts in Chicago, 1871-1933. LC 81-16253. (Chicago Visual Library Ser.: No. 39). (Illus.). 84p. 1982. text-fiche 65.00 (ISBN 0-226-68884-4). U of Chicago Pr.

Chicago Institute for Psychanalysis, ed. see Fleming, Joan & Benedek, Therese.

Chicago Institute for Psychoanalysis, ed. see Mahony, Patrick.

Chicago Institute for Psychoanalysis. Annual of Psychoanalysis, Vol. 9. 1981. 30.00 (ISBN 0-8236-0370-9). Intl Univs Pr.

--Annual of Psychoanalysis, Vol. 10. 1982. 30.00 (ISBN 0-8236-0371-7). Intl Univs Pr.

Chicago Institute for Psychoanalysis Staff, ed. Annual of Psychoanalysis, 1974, Vol. 2. LC 72-91376. (Illus.). x, 420p. 1975. text ed. 30.00X (ISBN 0-8236-0362-8). Intl Univs Pr.

--Annual of Psychoanalysis, 1975, Vol. 3. LC 72-91376. viii, 441p. 1976. text ed. 30.00X (ISBN 0-8236-0363-6). Intl Univs Pr.

--Annual of Psychoanalysis, 1976, Vol. 4. LC 72-91376. (Illus.). xi, 508p. 1977. text ed. 30.00X (ISBN 0-8236-0364-4). Intl Univs Pr.

--Annual of Psychoanalysis, 1977, Vol. 5. LC 72-91376. (Illus.). ix, 443p. 1978. text ed. 30.00X (ISBN 0-8236-0366-0). Intl Univs Pr.

--Annual of Psychoanalysis, 1978, Vol. 6. LC 72-91376. (Illus.). x, 489p. 1979. text ed. 30.00X (ISBN 0-8236-0367-9). Intl Univs Pr.

--Annual of Psychoanalysis, 1979, Vol. 7. LC 72-91376. (Illus.). x, 416p. 1980. text ed. 30.00X (ISBN 0-8236-0368-7). Intl Univs Pr.

--Annual of Psychoanalysis, 1980, Vol. 8. LC 72-91376. (Illus.). xiii, 359p. 1981. text ed. 30.00X (ISBN 0-8236-0369-5). Intl Univs Pr.

--Annual of Psychoanalysis, 1983, Vol. 11. LC 72-91376. xii, 365p. 1984. text ed. 30.00X (ISBN 0-8236-0372-5). Intl Univs Pr.

Chicago Jewish Vocational Services. Goal Attainment Scaling in Rehabilitation. White, Buffy, ed. 52p. (Orig.). 1976. pap. 4.75x (ISBN 0-916671-27-5). Material Dev.

Chicago, Judy. Birth Project. LC 84-18783. (Illus.). 232p. 1985. 35.00 (ISBN 0-385-18709-2, Anchor Pr); pap. 17.95 (ISBN 0-385-18710-6, Anchor Pr). Doubleday.

--The Complete Dinner Party: The Dinner Party & Embroidering Our Heritage, 2 vols. (Illus.). 544p. 1981. pap. 28.90 boxed set (ISBN 0-385-17311-3, Anch). Doubleday.

--The Dinner Party. LC 78-69653. 1979. 24.95 (ISBN 0-385-14566-7, Anchor Pr); pap. 15.95 (ISBN 0-385-14567-5, Anchor Pr). Doubleday.

--Through the Flower: My Struggle As a Woman Artist. rev. and updated ed. LC 81-43748. (Illus.). 216p. 1982. pap. 8.95 (ISBN 0-385-18084-5, Anch). Doubleday.

Chicago, Judy & Hill, Susan. Embroidering Our Heritage: The Dinner Party Needlework. LC 79-6645. (Illus.). 288p. 1980. 34.95 (ISBN 0-385-14568-3, Anchor Pr); pap. 15.95 (ISBN 0-385-14569-1, Anchor Pr). Doubleday.

Chicago Metropolitan Board YMCA. Volunteer Management. Broadway, Beth, ed. (Resource Ser.: 4 Bklts.). 105p. 1981. pap. 16.00x (ISBN 0-88035-001-6). YMCA USA.

Chicago Museum of Science & Industry Staff. A Guide to 150 Years of Chicago Architecture. (Illus.). 144p. 1985. 17.95 (ISBN 0-914091-83-2); pap. 9.95 (ISBN 0-914091-81-6). Chicago Review.

Chicago Tribune. Century of Tribune Editorials. facsimile ed. LC 72-93327. (Essay Index Reprint Ser.). 1947. 17.00 (ISBN 0-8369-1558-5). Ayer Co Pubs.

Chicago Tribune Staff. Chicago Tribune Chicagoland Map, 1983-1984. 1983. Repr. 195.00 (ISBN 0-686-40853-5). Chicago Trib.

Chicago University. English Studies, 5 Vols. Repr. of 1909 ed. Set. 127.50 (ISBN 0-404-50260-1). AMS Pr.

--Germanic Studies, 3 Vols. Repr. of 1897 ed. Set. 54.00 (ISBN 0-404-50270-9). AMS Pr.

--Linguistic Studies in Germanic, 5 vols. Repr. of 1920 ed. Set. 105.00 (ISBN 0-404-50280-6). AMS Pr.

--Selected Bibliography of the Philippines, Topically Arranged & Annotated. LC 72-9605. 138p. 1973. Repr. of 1956 ed. lib. bdg. 18.75x (ISBN 0-8371-6591-1, SBPH). Greenwood.

Chicago University Department Of Mathematics. Contributions to the Calculus of Variations, 1930-41, 4 Vols. Bliss, G. A., ed. 1933-42. Set. 190.00 (ISBN 0-384-08750-7); 50.00 ea. Johnson Repr.

Chicago University - Graduate Library School. Education for Librarianship. facs. ed. LC 71-117776. (Essay Index Reprint Ser). 1949. 21.50 (ISBN 0-8369-1701-4). Ayer Co Pubs.

Chicano Periodical Indexing Project, et al, eds. Chicano Periodical Index (ChPI) A Comprehensive Subject, Author, & Title Index for 1982-83. (Chicano Studies Library Publications). 660p. 1985. lib. bdg. 75.00x (ISBN 0-918520-10-X). UC Chicano.

Chi Chen. Chen Chi Watercolors, Drawings, Sketches: Deluxe Edition. (Illus.). 108p. 1980. deluxe ed. 100.00 leather bound (ISBN 0-9604652-1-9). Chen Chi Studio.

Chichester, A. Lee, ed. see Moore, Jack S.

Chichester, C. O., ed. Advances in Food Research, Vol. 27. (Serial Publication Ser.). 1981. 60.00 (ISBN 0-12-016427-2). Acad Pr.

--Advances in Food Research, Vol. 28. 403p. 1982. 60.00 (ISBN 0-12-016428-0). Acad Pr.

Chichester, C. O. & Graham, H. D., eds. Microbial Aspects of Fishery Products. 1973. 50.00 (ISBN 0-12-172740-8). Acad Pr.

Chichester, C. O., et al, eds. Advances in Food Research, Vol. 26. LC 48-7808. 1980. 55.00 (ISBN 0-12-016426-4). Acad Pr.

--Advances in Food Research, Vol. 25. 1979. 60.00 (ISBN 0-12-016425-6). Acad Pr.

Chichester, C. O., et al see Mrak, E. M., et al.

Chichester, Francis. Solo to Sydney. 224p. 1982. 30.00x (ISBN 0-85177-254-4, Pub. by Conway Maritime England). State Mutual Bk.

Chichester, Francis C. Ride on the Wind. Gilbert, James, ed. LC 79-7236. (Flight: Its First Seventy-Five Years Ser.). (Illus.). 1979. Repr. of 1937 ed. lib. bdg. 24.50x (ISBN 0-405-12152-0). Ayer Co Pubs.

Chichester, Sir Francis. Solo to Sydney. LC 81-48449. (Illus.). 208p. 1982. 13.95 (ISBN 0-8128-2865-8). Stein & Day.

Chichester, Michael & Wilkinson, John. The Uncertain Ally. 264p. 1982. text ed. 38.00x (ISBN 0-566-00534-4). Gower Pub Co.

Chichester, O. see Mrak, E. M. & Stewart, G. F.

Chichetto, James. Stones: A Litnay. (Illus.). 20p. 1980. pap. 4.00 (ISBN 0-939622-06-8). Four Zoas Night.

Chichinadze, A. V., ed. Polymers in Friction Assemblies of Machines & Devices: A Handbook. xii, 280p. 1984. 68.50 (ISBN 0-89864-010-5). Allerton Pr.

Chick, Edson. Dances of Death: Wedekind, Brecht, Durrenmatt & the Satiric Tradition. LC 83-70286. (Studies in German Literature, Linguistics, & Culture: Vol. 19). (Illus.). 181p. 1983. 15.95x (ISBN 0-938100-24-6). Camden Hse.

Chick, Jack T. The Big Betrayal, Vol. 2. (Sword Ser.). (Illus.). 64p. (Orig.). 1981. pap. 1.65 (ISBN 0-937958-08-5). Chick Pubns.

--Cortinas de Humo. (Illus., Orig., Span.). 1984. pap. 2.50 (ISBN 0-937958-20-4). Chick Pubns.

--King of Kings. (Sword Ser.: Vol. 1). (Illus.). 64p. (Orig.). 1980. pap. 1.65 (ISBN 0-937958-07-7). Chick Pubns.

--The Last Call. (Illus.). 64p. (Orig.). 1963. pap. 1.95 (ISBN 0-937958-06-9). Chick Pubns.

--The Next Step. (Illus.). 64p. (Orig.). 1978. pap. 1.95 (ISBN 0-937958-04-2). Chick Pubns.

--El Proximo Paso. (Illus.). 64p. (Orig., Span.). 1983. pap. 1.95 (ISBN 0-937958-15-8). Chick Pubns.

--Smokescreens. (Illus.). 93p. 1982. pap. 2.50 (ISBN 0-937958-14-X). Chick Pubns.

--La Ultima Llamada. (Illus.). 64p. (Orig., Span.). 1972. pap. 1.95 (ISBN 0-937958-02-6). Chick Pubns.

Chick, W. L., ed. see Conference Hoechst, 5th, Kitzbuhel, 5-9 Oct. 1976.

Chicken, John C. Hazard Control Policy in Britain. LC 75-12900. 204p. 1975. text ed. 32.00 (ISBN 0-08-019739-6). Pergamon.

Chickering, Arthur W. Commuting Versus Resident Students: Overcoming the Educational Inequities of Living Off Campus. LC 74-6737. (Higher Education Ser.). 144p. 1974. 17.95x (ISBN 0-87589-231-0). Jossey-Bass.

--Education & Identity. LC 70-75938. (Higher Education Ser.). 1969. 18.95x (ISBN 0-87589-035-0). Jossey-Bass.

--Experience & Learning: An Introduction to Experiential Learning. LC 77-72980. 89p. 1977. pap. 5.95 (ISBN 0-915390-10-8, Pub. by Change Mag). Transaction Pubs.

Chickering, Arthur W., et al. The Modern American College: Responding to the New Realities of Diverse Students & a Changing Society. LC 80-8010. (Higher Education Ser.). 1981. text ed. 35.00x (ISBN 0-87589-466-6). Jossey-Bass.

--Developing the College Curriculum: A Handbook for Faculty & Administrators. Quehl, Gary H. & Gee, Marguerite, eds. LC 77-90328. 1977. pap. text ed. 10.00 (ISBN 0-937012-04-1). Coun Indep Colleges.

Chickering, Carol R. Flowers of Guatemala. LC 72-9278. (Illus.). 180p. 1973. 19.95 (ISBN 0-8061-1081-3); pap. 11.95 (ISBN 0-8061-1368-5). U of Okla Pr.

Chickering, Elenita C. Arthur J. Stone: Handwrought Silver, 1901-1937. LC 81-68101. (Illus.). 24p. (Orig.). 25.00 (ISBN 0-934552-37-1). Boston Athenaeum.

Chickering, Howell D., Jr., ed. Beowulf: A Dual Language Edition. LC 75-21250. (Anchor Literary Library). 1977. pap. 9.95 (ISBN 0-385-06213-3, Anch). Doubleday.

Chickering, Jesse. Immigration into the United States. LC 70-145473. (The American Immigration Library). 94p. 1971. Repr. of 1848 ed. lib. bdg. 8.95x (ISBN 0-89198-006-7). Ozer.

Chickering, K., ed. Pipeline Engineering Symposium. 96p. 1983. pap. text ed. 24.00 (ISBN 0-317-02640-2, I00157). ASME.

Chickering, Lawrence. Readings in Public Policy. 338p. (Orig.). 1984. pap. 9.95 (ISBN 0-917616-66-9). ICS Pr.

Chickering, Robert B. & Hartman, Susan. How to Register a Copyright & Protect Your Creative Work. 192p. 1981. 12.95 (ISBN 0-684-16705-0, ScribT). Scribner.

Chickering, Roger. Imperial Germany & a World Without War: The Peace Movement & German Society, 1892-1914. LC 75-29883. 550p. 1975. 48.00 (ISBN 0-691-05228-X); pap. 20.00 LPE (ISBN 0-691-10036-5). Princeton U Pr.

Chickering, William H. Within the Sound of These Waves: The Story of the Kings of Hawaii Island, Containing a Full Account of the Death of Captain Cook, Together with the Hawaiian Adventures of George Vancouver & Sundry Other Mariners. LC 70-138584. (Illus.). 1971. Repr. of 1941 ed. lib. bdg. 24.75x (ISBN 0-8371-5783-8, CHSW). Greenwood.

Chicoine, David, jt. ed. see Walzer, Norman.

Chicoine, David L. & Walzer, Norman. Governmental Structure & Local Public Finance. LC 84-11874. 1985. text ed. 27.50 (ISBN 0-89946-187-5). Oelgeschlager.

Chicoine, Rene, jt. auth. see Mather, Edith.

Chicoine, Rene, tr. see McLaren, Norman.

Chicorel, Marietta. Chicorel Abstracts to Reading & Learning Disabilities, 1976 Annual. (Chicorel Index Ser.). 500p. 1976. text ed. 125.00x ca. (ISBN 0-934598-15-0); Vol. 19. text ed. Am Lib Pub Co.

--Chicorel Index to Abstracting & Indexing, 2 vols, Vols. 11 & 11a. 2nd. ed. (Chicorel Index Ser.). 1978. text ed. 250.00x set (ISBN 0-934598-20-7). Vol. 11 (ISBN 0-934598-03-7). Vol. 11A (ISBN 0-934598-04-5). Am Lib Pub Co.

Chicorel, Marietta, ed. Chicorel Abstracts to Reading & Learning Disabilities, Periodicals, 1980 Annual, Vol.19. Annual Edition. (Illus.). 380p. 1982. 125.00x (ISBN 0-934598-80-0). Am Lib Pub Co.

--Chicorel Abstracts to Reading and Learning Disabilities: 1977 Annual, Vol. 19. (Index Ser.). 1977. text ed. 125.00x (ISBN 0-934598-17-7). Am Lib Pub Co.

--Chicorel Bibliography to Books on Music & Musicians, Vol. 10. LC 74-161012. (Chicorel Index Ser). 500p. 1974. 125.00x (ISBN 0-934598-18-5). Am Lib Pub Co.

Chicorel, Marietta, ed. & intro. by. Chicorel Bibliography to the Performing Arts, Vol. 3A. LC 71-106198. (Chicorel Index Ser.). 498p. 1972. text ed. 125.00x (ISBN 0-934598-19-3). Am Lib Pub Co.

Chicorel, Marietta, ed. Chicorel Index to Biographies, Vols. 15 & 15A. LC 74-175082. 900p. 1974. Set. 250.00x (ISBN 0-934598-21-5). Am Lib Pub Co.

--Chicorel Index to Environment & Ecology, 2 vols. LC 75-306805. (Index Ser.). 1000p. 1974. Set. 250.00 (ISBN 0-934598-21-5). Vol. 16 (ISBN 0-934598-25-8). Vol. 16A (ISBN 0-934598-26-6). Am Lib Pub Co.

--Chicorel Index to Film Literature, Vols. 22 & 22A. LC 75-22340. (Index Ser.). 1975. Set. 250.00 (ISBN 0-934598-29-0). Am Lib Pub Co.

--Chicorel Index to Learning Disorders, 2 vols. LC 75-9713. (Index Ser.). 1000p. 1975. Set. 250.00x (ISBN 0-934598-32-0). Vol. 18 (ISBN 0-934598-30-4). Vol. 18A (ISBN 0-934598-31-2). Am Lib Pub Co.

--Chicorel Index to Literary Criticism: U.S., Canada, Vol. 23. (Index Ser.). 1979. text ed. 125.00x (ISBN 0-934598-14-2). Am Lib Pub Co.

--Chicorel Index to Mental Health Book Reviews, 1974 Annual, Vol. 26. 322p. 1982. 125.00x (ISBN 0-934598-81-9). Am Lib Pub Co.

--Chicorel Index to Mental Health Book Reviews, 1975 Annual, Vol. 26. 287p. 1982. 125.00x (ISBN 0-934598-82-7). Am Lib Pub Co.

--Chicorel Index to Parapsychology & Occult. (Index Ser.: Vol. 24). 1978. text ed. 125.00x (ISBN 0-934598-33-9). Am Lib Pub Co.

--Chicorel Index to Poetry & Poets: Literature, Vols. 20 & 20A. LC 75-40039. (Index Ser.). 1000p. 1976. 250.00x set (ISBN 0-934598-37-1). Am Lib Pub Co.

--Chicorel Index to Poetry in Anthologies & Collections in Print, Vols. 5, 5a, 5b, 5c. 1898p. 1974. Set. 500.00x (ISBN 0-934598-42-8). Am Lib Pub Co.

--Chicorel Index to Poetry in Anthologies & Collections: Retrospective, Vols. 6, 6A, 6B, 6C. 1975. 500.00 set (ISBN 0-934598-47-9). Am Lib Pub Co.

--Chicorel Index to Poetry in Collections on Discs & Tapes, Vol. 4. LC 71-106198. 443p. 1972. 125.00x (ISBN 0-934598-48-7). Am Lib Pub Co.

--Chicorel Index to Poetry Nineteen Seventy-Five - Nineteen Seventy-Seven, 2 vols. 2nd. ed. (Chicorel Index Ser.). 1979. Set. text ed. 250.00 (ISBN 0-934598-13-4). Vol. 5 (ISBN 0-934598-11-8). Vol. 5A (ISBN 0-934598-12-6). Am Lib Pub Co.

--Chicorel Index to Reading & Learning Disabilities: An Annotated Guide, 1976, Vol. 14A. annual ed. (Chicorel Index Ser.). 1976. 125.00x (ISBN 0-934598-49-5). Am Lib Pub Co.

--Chicorel Index to Reading & Learning Disabilities: Books, 1977 Annual, Vol. 14A. LC 76-14381. (Index Ser). 1977. text ed. 125.00x (ISBN 0-934598-50-9). Am Lib Pub Co.

--Chicorel Index to Reading Disabilities: An Annotated Guide, Vol. 14. 500p. 1974. 125.00x (ISBN 0-934598-51-7). Am Lib Pub Co.

--Chicorel Index to Short Stories in Anthologies & Collections, 4 vols, Vols. 12, 12a, 12b, 12c. 1974. Set. 500.00 (ISBN 0-934598-56-8). Am Lib Pub Co.

--Chicorel Index to Short Stories: 1977 Edition, 2 vols. 2nd. ed. (Index Ser). 1977. Set. text ed. 250.00 (ISBN 0-934598-05-3). Vol. 12 (ISBN 0-934598-06-1). Vol. 12A (ISBN 0-934598-07-X). Am Lib Pub Co.

--Chicorel Index to the Crafts: Ceramics, Leather, Wood, Vol. 13B. 1977. 125.00x (ISBN 0-934598-58-4). Am Lib Pub Co.

--Chicorel Index to the Crafts: Education, Recreation, & Therapy, Vol. 13C. 1975. 125.00x (ISBN 0-934598-60-6). Am Lib Pub Co.

--Chicorel Index to the Crafts: Glass, Enamel, Metal, Vol. 13A. 1975. 125.00x (ISBN 0-934598-59-2). Am Lib Pub Co.

--Chicorel Index to the Crafts: Needlework, Crochet to Tie Dye, Vol. 13. LC 74-195924. 500p. 1974. 125.00x (ISBN 0-934598-57-6). Am Lib Pub Co.

--Chicorel Index to the Spoken Arts on: Discs, Tapes & Cassettes, Vol. 7B. LC 71-106198. 500p. 1974. 125.00x (ISBN 0-934598-61-4). Am Lib Pub Co.

Chicorel, Marietta, ed. & intro. by. Chicorel Index to the Spoken Arts on Discs, Tapes, & Cassettes, Vol 7. 500p. 1973. 125.00x (ISBN 0-934598-62-2). Am Lib Pub Co.

Chicorel, Marietta, ed. Chicorel Index to Urban Planning & Environmental Design, 2 vols. LC 75-30637. (Index Ser.). 1000p. 1975. Set. 250.00 (ISBN 0-934598-65-7). Vol. 17 (ISBN 0-934598-64-9). Vol. 17A. Am Lib Pub Co.

--Chicorel Index to Video Tapes & Cassettes, Vol. 27. 1978. 125.00x (ISBN 0-934598-66-5). Am Lib Pub Co.

--Chicorel Theater Index to Drama Literature, Vol. 21. (Index Ser.). 500p. 1975. 125.00x (ISBN 0-934598-67-3). Am Lib Pub Co.

--Chicorel Theater Index to Plays for Young People, Vol. 9. 500p. 1974. 125.00x (ISBN 0-934598-34-7). Am Lib Pub Co.

--Chicorel Theater Index to Plays in Anthologies & Collections: 1970-1976, Vol. 25. LC 76-54172. (Chicorel Index Ser). 1976. text ed. 125.00x (ISBN 0-934598-68-1). Am Lib Pub Co.

--Chicorel Theater Index to Plays in Anthologies, Periodicals, Discs & Tapes, Vol. 1. LC 71-106198. 1970. 125.00x (ISBN 0-934598-69-X). Am Lib Pub Co.

--Chicorel Theater Index to Plays in Anthologies, Periodicals, Discs & Tapes, Vol. 2. LC 71-106198. 1971. 125.00x (ISBN 0-934598-70-3). Am Lib Pub Co.

--Chicorel Theater Index to Plays in Anthologies, Periodicals, Discs & Tapes, Vol. 3. LC 71-106198. 1972. 125.00x (ISBN 0-934598-71-1). Am Lib Pub Co.

--Chicorel Theater Index to Plays in Anthologies, Periodicals, Discs & Tapes, Vol. 8. LC 71-106198. 1973. 125.00x (ISBN 0-934598-72-X). Am Lib Pub Co.

Chicoteau, Christine. Chere Rose: A Biography of Rosalie de Constant (1758-1834) (European University Studies: Ser. 13, Vol. 65). 370p. 1980. pap. 31.85 (ISBN 3-261-04751-8). P Lang Pubs.

Chidakel, Susan. Starting & Operating a Playgroup for Profit. LC 75-44029. 47p. 1985. pap. 3.95 (ISBN 0-87576-055-4). Pilot Bks.

Chidamian. Camellias & Common Sense. pap. 2.00 (ISBN 0-87505-277-0). Borden.

Chidamian, Claude. The Book of Cacti & Other Succulents. (Illus.). 260p. 1984. pap. 13.95 (ISBN 0-917304-90-X). Timber.

Chiddick, D. & Spedding, A., eds. Land Management: New Directions. 488p. 1984. 49.95 (ISBN 0-419-13080-2, 6901, Pub. by E & FN Spon England). Methuen Inc.

Chidester, Ann. The Long Year. LC 74-26097. (Labor Movement in Fiction & Non-Fiction). Repr. of 1946 ed. 25.00 (ISBN 0-404-58411-X). AMS Pr.

Chidiac, Emile. Ambiguities in Law. 120p. 1984. 19.95 (ISBN 0-89697-064-7). Intl Univ Pr.

Chidley, John. Discovering Book Collecting. (Discovering Ser.: No. 267). (Illus.). 80p. (Orig.). 1983. pap. 3.95 (ISBN 0-85263-588-5, Pub. by Shire Pubns England). Seven Hills Bks.

Chidsey, Donald B. Captain Crossbones. (Illus.). 240p. Date not set. pap. 2.50 (ISBN 0-441-09131-8, Pub. by Charter Bks). Ace Bks.

Chiechi, Carolyn P., jt. auth. see Smith, William H.

Chief Justice Earl Warren Conference on Advocacy in the United States & Roscoe Pound-American Trial Lawyers Foundation Staff. Ethics & Government: Final Report. LC 82-62513. (Illus.). 158p. 1982. write for info. Assn Trial Lawyers.

Chiefari, Janet. Introducing the Drum & Bugle Corps. LC 82-45379. (Illus.). 128p. (gr. 5 up). 1982. 10.95 (ISBN 0-396-08088-X). Dodd.

--Kids Are Baby Goats. LC 83-25342. (Illus.). 60p. (gr. 2-5). 1984. PLB 9.95 (ISBN 0-396-08316-1). Dodd.

--Logging Machines in the Forest. (Illus.). 64p. (gr. 2-5). 1985. 10.95 (ISBN 0-396-08564-4). Dodd.

Chiefari, Janet & Wightman, Nancy. Better Synchronized Swimming for Girls. (Better Sports Ser.). (Illus.). 64p. (gr. 4-9). 1981. PLB 8.95 (ISBN 0-396-07995-4). Dodd.

Chieger, Bob. Voices of Baseball: Quatations on the Summer Game. 1984. pap. 2.95 (ISBN 0-451-12821-4, Sig). NAL.

--Voices of Baseball: Quotations on the Summer Game. LC 82-73027. 288p. (Orig.). 1983. pap. 8.95 (ISBN 0-689-70646-4). Atheneum.

--Was It Good for You, Too? Quotations on Love & Sex. LC 83-45061. 256p. 1983. pap. 8.95 (ISBN 0-689-70650-2). Atheneum.

Chieger, Bob & Sullivan, Pat. Inside Golf: Quotations on the Royal & Ancient Game. LC 84-45615. 256p. 1985. pap. 9.95 (ISBN 0-689-11546-6). Atheneum.

Chiel, Arthur A., ed. Perspectives on Jews & Judaism: Essays in Honor of Wolfe Kelman. 25.00x (ISBN 0-87068-683-6). Ktav.

Chiel, Kinneret. Complete Book of Hanukah. (Illus.). (gr. 6-8). pap. 6.95x (ISBN 0-87068-367-5). Ktav.

Chiel, Samuel. Living Courageously. 1984. 15.00 (ISBN 0-88125-046-5). Ktav.

Chielens, Edward E. The Literary Journal in America, 1900-1950: A Guide to Information Sources. LC 74-11534. (American Literature, English Literatures, & World Literature in English Information Guide Ser.: Vol. 16). 1977. 60.00x (ISBN 0-8103-1240-9). Gale.

Chielens, Edward E., ed. The Literary Journal in America to 1900: A Guide to Information Sources. LC 74-11533. (American Literature, English Literature & World Literatures in English Information Guide Ser.: Vol. 3). 228p. 1975. 58.00x (ISBN 0-8103-1239-5). Gale.

Chiellini, E. & Giusti, P., eds. Polymers in Medicine: Biomedical & Pharmacological Applications. 425p. 1983. 57.50x (ISBN 0-306-41360-4, Plenum Pr). Plenum Pub.

Chiellini, E., et al. Initiators - Poly-Reactions - Optical Activity. (Advances in Polymer Science, Fortschritte der Hochpolymerenforschung: Vol. 62). (Illus.). 190p. 1984. 39.00 (ISBN 0-387-13232-5). Springer-Verlag.

Chien. Novel Drug Delivery Systems. (Drugs & the Pharmaceutical Sciences Ser.). 584p. 1982. 65.00 (ISBN 0-8247-1831-3). Dekker.

--Using BASIC for Business: Apple IIe. (Illus.). 250p. 1985. pap. text ed. write for info. (ISBN 0-8087-6402-0). Burgess.

--Using BASIC for Business: IBM-PC. 250p. 1985. pap. text ed. write for info. (ISBN 0-8087-6403-9). Burgess.

Chien, C. L. & Westgate, C. R., eds. The Hall Effect & Its Applications. LC 80-18566. 560p. 1980. 79.50x (ISBN 0-306-40556-3, Plenum Pr). Plenum Pub.

Chien, Chao. Programming the IBM Personal Computer: Assembly Language. 1984. 17.95 (ISBN 0-03-070442-1). HR&W.

--TRS-80 Assembly Language. 1984. 17.95 (ISBN 0-03-070441-3). HR&W.

Chien, Chao C. Advanced Business BASIC for Microcomputers. Fetter, Robert B. & McMillan, Claude, eds. LC 84-81736. (Irwin Series in Information & Decision Sciences). (Illus.). 343p. 1985. pap. text ed. 21.95x (ISBN 0-256-03175-4). Irwin.

Ch'ien, Edward T. Chiao Hung & the Restructuring of Neo-Confucianism in the Late Ming. (Neo-Confucian Studuies). 328p. 1985. 27.50 (ISBN 0-231-06022-X). Columbia U Pr.

Chien, Frederick F. The Opening of Korea: A Study of Chinese Diplomacy, 1876-1885. LC 67-30793. pap. 95.30 (ISBN 0-317-08138-1, 2010210). Bks Demand UMI.

Chien, James C. Polyacetylene: Chemistry, Physics, & Material Science. LC 83-7237. 1984. 89.00 (ISBN 0-12-172460-3). Acad Pr.

Chien, Po-Tsan. Concise History of China. 1976. lib. bdg. 59.95 (ISBN 0-8490-1661-4). Gordon Pr.

Chien, Robert I., ed. Issues in Pharmaceutical Economics. LC 78-19726. 1979. 25.00x (ISBN 0-669-02729-4). Lexington Bks.

Chien, Robert T., jt. auth. see Kim, Wan-hui.

Ch'ien, Tuan-sheng. The Government & Politics of China. LC 50-8563. pap. 136.50 (ISBN 0-317-08617-0, 2006005). Bks Demand UMI.

Chien, Y. T. Interactive Pattern Recognition. (Electrical Engineering & Electronics Ser.: Vol. 3). 1978. 55.00 (ISBN 0-8247-6631-8). Dekker.

Chien, Y. W. Transnasal Systemic Medications: Fundamentals, Developmental Concepts & Biomedical Assessment. 1985. 53.75 (ISBN 0-444-42460-1). Elsevier.

Chien, Yi-Tzuu, jt. auth. see Booth, Taylor L.

Ch'ien Chung-shu. Fortress Besieged. Kelly, Jeanne & Mao, Nathan K., trs. LC 78-24846. (Chinese Literature in Translation Ser.). 416p. 1980. 17.50x (ISBN 0-253-16518-0). Ind U Pr.

Ch'ien Nan-Yang. A History of Riddles. (Folklore Series of National Sun Yat-Sen University: No. 27). (Chinese.). 16.00x (ISBN 0-89986-095-8). Oriental Bk Store.

Chiera, E. Lists of Personal Names from the Temple School of Nippur: A Syllabary of Personal Names. (Publications of the Babylonian Section: Vol. 11-1). (Illus.). 88p. 1916. soft bound 10.50x (ISBN 0-686-11923-1). Univ Mus of U PA.

--Lists of Personal Names from the Temple School of Nippur: Lists of Akkadian Personal Names. (Publications of the Babylonian Section: Vol. 11-2). (Illus.). 85p. 1916. soft bound 10.50x (ISBN 0-686-11924-X). Univ Mus of U PA.

--Old Babylonian Contracts. (Publications of the Babylonian Section: Vol. 8-2). (Illus.). 115p. 1922. bound 10.50xsoft (ISBN 0-686-11922-3). Univ Mus of U PA.

Chiera, Edward. Lists of Personal Names from the Temple School of Niopur: Lists of Sumerian Personal Names. LC 17-5006. (University of Pennsylvania, University Museum, Publications of the Babylonian Section: Vol. 11, No. 3). pap. 34.00 (ISBN 0-317-28537-8, 2052027). Bks Demand UMI.

--They Wrote on Clay: The Babylonian Tablets Speak Today. Cameron, George G., ed. LC 38-27631. (Illus.). 1938. 11.00x (ISBN 0-226-10424-9). U of Chicago Pr.

--They Wrote on Clay: The Babylonian Tablets Speak Today. Cameron, George G., ed. LC 38-27631. (Illus.). 1956. pap. 3.50 (ISBN 0-226-10425-7, P2, Phoen). U of Chicago Pr.

Chierichetti, David, jt. auth. see Schapiro, Steve.

Chiesa, Bruno. The Emergence of Hebrew Biblical Pointing, Vol. 1. (Judentum v. Umwelt Ser.: Vol. 1). 92p. 1979. pap. 17.70 (ISBN 3-8204-6419-0). P Lang Pubs.

Chiesi, Harry L., et al. Processes of Acquisition in Individuals with High & Low Baseball Knowledge: The First Inning. 63p. 1977. 1.50 (ISBN 0-318-14727-0). Learn Res Dev.

Chiffriller, T. F., Jr. Successful Restaurant Operation. 290p. 1982. 26.95 (ISBN 0-8436-2221-0). Van Nos Reinhold.

Chigier, N. A. Progress in Energy & Combustion Science, Vol. 4. 224p. 1980. 125.00 (ISBN 0-08-024257-X). Pergamon.

Chigier, N. A., jt. auth. see Beer, J. M.

Chigier, N. A., ed. Energy & Combustion Science: Selected Papers from Progress in Energy & Combustion Science. LC 79-40860. (Illus.). 1979. 48.00 (ISBN 0-08-024781-4); pap. 15.75 (ISBN 0-08-024780-6). Pergamon.

--Progress in Energy & Combustion Science, Vol. 6. (Illus.). 388p. 1981. 130.00 (ISBN 0-08-027153-7). Pergamon.

--Progress in Energy & Combustion Science, Vol. 6, Pt. 2. 102p. 1980. pap. 27.00 (ISBN 0-08-026059-4). Pergamon.

--Progress in Energy & Combustion Science, Vol. 7. (Illus.). 316p. 1982. 145.00 (ISBN 0-08-029124-4). Pergamon.

--Progress in Energy & Combustion Science, Vol. 8. 354p. 1983. 144.00 (ISBN 0-08-031041-9). Pergamon.

--Progress in Energy & Combustion Science, Vol. 9. (Illus.). 378p. 1984. 144.00 (ISBN 0-08-031727-8). Pergamon.

Chigier, Norman A. Energy, Combustion & Environment. (Illus.). 689p. 1981. text ed. 55.00 (ISBN 0-07-010766-1). McGraw.

Chigier, Norman A., ed. Progress in Energy & Combustion Science, Vols. 1-2. Incl. Vol. 1, Pt. 1. pap. 15.50 (ISBN 0-08-019931-3); Vol. 1, Pts. 2-3. pap. 25.00 (ISBN 0-08-021023-6); Vol. 1, Pt. 4. pap. 22.00 (ISBN 0-08-021041-4); Vol. 1, Complete. Pollution Formation & Destruction in Flames. 97.50 (ISBN 0-08-020307-8); Vol. 2, Pt. 1. pap. 14.00 (ISBN 0-08-021211-5); Vol. 2, Pt. 2. pap. 14.00 (ISBN 0-08-021213-1); Vol. 2, Pt. 3. pap. 12.50 (ISBN 0-08-021215-8); Vol. 2, Pt. 4. 97.50 (ISBN 0-08-021217-4); Vol. 2 Complete, 1978. 50.00 (ISBN 0-08-021219-0). LC 75-24822. 1976-78. pap. write for info. Pergamon.

Chigier, Norman A. & Stern, Edward A., eds. Collective Phenomena & the Applications of Physics to Other Fields of Science. 491p. 1976. pap. text ed. 25.00x (ISBN 0-916088-01-4). Brain Res.

Chignell, A. H. Retinal Detachment Surgery. (Illus.). 1980. 40.00 (ISBN 0-387-09475-X). Springer-Verlag.

Chignell, Colin F., ed. Methods in Pharmacology: Physical Methods, Vol. 2. 511p. 1972. 59.50x (ISBN 0-306-50072-8, Plenum Pr). Plenum Pub.

Chigounis, Evans. Secret Lives. LC 74-185195. (Wesleyan Poetry Program: Vol. 60). 80p. (Orig.). 1972. 15.00x (ISBN 0-8195-2060-8); pap. 6.95 (ISBN 0-8195-1060-2). Wesleyan U Pr.

Ch'ih, Bhikshuni Heng & Nicholson, Upasika T., trs. from Chinese. Human Roots: Buddhist Stories for Young Readers, Vol. I. (Illus.). 95p. (Orig.). (gr. 6-12). 1982. pap. 5.00 (ISBN 0-88139-500-5). Buddhist Text.

Ch'ih, Bhikshuni Heng, et al, trs. from Chinese. Dharma Flower Sutra, Vol. X. 150p. (Orig.). pap. 7.50 (ISBN 0-917512-34-0). Buddhist Text.

Chih, Yu-Ju. A Primer of Newspaper Chinese. rev. ed. 8.95 (ISBN 0-88710-056-2); tapes avail. (ISBN 0-88710-057-0). Far Eastern Pubns.

Chi Ha, Kim. The Middle Hour: Selected Poems of Kim Chi Ha. McCann, David R., tr. from Korean. 100p. 1980. 9.50 (ISBN 0-930576-36-5). E M Coleman Ent.

Chihabi. Agriculture, Forestry, & Allied Terminology Dictionary: English-Arabic with Arabic Glossary. Khatib, A., ed. (Eng. & Arabic.). 1978. 40.00x (ISBN 0-86685-072-4). Intl Bk Ctr.

Chihal, Jane. Premenstrual Syndrome. LC 84-71600. 1985. 7.95 (ISBN 0-917634-15-2). Creative Infomatics.

Chihara, H., ed. see International Conference on Thermal Analysis.

Chihara, T. S. An Introduction to Orthogonal Polynomials. (Mathematics & Its Applications Ser.). 262p. 1978. 65.95 (ISBN 0-677-04150-0). Gordon.

Chih Ma, Nancy. Chinese Cooking for Two. new ed. Kovaks, Grace Chu, tr. (Illus.). 1980. 12.95 (ISBN 0-8120-5267-6). Barron.

Chih-Mai, Ch'En. Chinese Calligraphers & Their Art. 1966. 41.00x (ISBN 0-522-83559-7, Pub. by Melbourne U Pr). Intl Spec Bk.

Chih-Nung. Legends & Riddles of Fu-Chien. (National Peking University & Chinese Assn. for Folklore, Folklore & Folkliterature Ser.: No. 138). (Chinese.). 16.00x (ISBN 0-89986-212-8). Oriental Bk Store.

Chijioke, F. A. Ancient Africa. LC 75-80850. (Illus.). 48p. (gr. 5-8). 1969. pap. 3.95x (ISBN 0-8419-0013-2, Africana). Holmes & Meier.

Chikamatsu, Shigenori. Stories from a Tearoom Window. Mori, Toshiko, ed. Mori, Kozaburo, tr. from Japanese. LC 82-80013. Orig. Title: Chaso Kanawa. (Illus.). 192p. 1982. 12.95 (ISBN 0-8048-1385-X). C E Tuttle.

Chikan, A. Economics & Management of Inventories, 2 pts. (Studies in Production & Engineering Economics: Vol. 2). 1982. Set. 159.75 (ISBN 0-444-99718-0); Pt. A. 55.50 (ISBN 0-444-99720-2); Pt. B. 110.75 (ISBN 0-444-99719-9, I-330-81). Elsevier.

--New Results in Inventory Research. (Studies in Production & Engineering Economics: Vol. 3). 1984. 146.50 (ISBN 0-444-99609-5). Elsevier.

Chikashige, M. Oriental Alchemy. LC 74-77742. 1974. pap. 1.95 (ISBN 0-87728-260-9). Weiser.

Chikashige, Masumi. Alchemy & Other Chemical Achievements of the Ancient Orient. LC 79-8602. Repr. of 1936 ed. 27.50 (ISBN 0-404-18456-1). AMS Pr.

Chikazumi, S., jt. ed. see Miura, N.

Chikazumi, Sushin & Charap, Stanley H. Physics of Magnetism. LC 78-2315. 566p. 1978. Repr. of 1964 ed. lib. bdg. 37.50 (ISBN 0-88275-662-1). Krieger.

Chi-keung, Leung, jt. ed. see Ngok, Lee.

Chikishev, A. G. Plant Indicators of Soil, Rocks & Subsurface Waters. LC 65-15596. 210p. 1965. 37.50x (ISBN 0-306-10730-9, Consultants). Plenum Pub.

Chikishev, A. G., ed. Landscape Indicators. LC 72-88886. (Illus.). 165p. 1973. 35.00x (ISBN 0-306-10875-5, Consultants). Plenum Pub.

Chikota, Richard A., ed. see Journal Of Urban Law Editors.

Chiland, Colette, jt. auth. see Anthony, E. James.

Chiland, Colette, ed. Long-Term Treatments of Psychotic States. LC 76-46582. 696p. 1977. text ed. 44.95 (ISBN 0-87705-252-2). Human Sci Pr.

Chilcoat, Beth & Chilcoat, David. A Taste of Columbus II. (Illus.). 128p. (Orig.). 1982. pap. 8.95 (ISBN 0-9608710-1-2). Corban Prods.

Chilcoat, David, jt. auth. see Chilcoat, Beth.

Chilcot, Thomas. Two Suites for Harpsichord. Beechey, Gwilym, ed. LC 72-626211. (Penn State Music Series, No. 22). pap. 4.00 (ISBN 0-271-09122-3). Pa St U Pr.

Chilcote, Ann. The Other Half of the Egg. LC 84-80297. 80p. 1985. 11.95 (ISBN 0-89016-081-3); pap. 3.95 (ISBN 0-89016-080-5). Lightning Tree.

Chilcote, Ronald H. The Press in Latin America, Spain & Portugal. 48p. 1963. pap. 1.00 (ISBN 0-912098-02-3). Cal Inst Intl St.

--Revolution & Structural Change in Latin America, 2 Vols. LC 68-28100. (Bibliographical Ser.: No. 40). 1970. Set. 40.00x (ISBN 0-8179-2401-9). Hoover Inst Pr.

--Theories of Comparative Politics: The Search for a Paradigm. LC 80-19762. 480p. (Orig.). 1981. pap. 15.50x (ISBN 0-89158-971-6). Westview.

Chilcote, Ronald H. & Edelstein, Joel. Latin America: Capitalist & Socialist Perspectives of Development & Underdevelopment. (Latin American Perspectives Ser.). 250p. 1985. 32.00x (ISBN 0-8133-0238-2); pap. text ed. 13.95x (ISBN 0-8133-0239-0). Westview.

Chilcote, Ronald H., ed. Brazil & Its Radical Left: An Annotated Bibliography on the Communist Movement & the Rise of Marxism, 1922-1972. LC 80-12617. 1981. lib. bdg. 65.00 (ISBN 0-527-16821-1). Kraus Intl.

--Cuba, Nineteen Fifty-Three to Nineteen Seventy-Eight: A Bibliographic Guide to the Literature, 3 Vols. 1986. lib. bdg. price not set (ISBN 0-527-16824-6). Kraus Intl.

--Dependency & Marxism: Toward a Resolution of the Debate. LC 82-11056. (Latin American Perpsective Ser.: No. 1). 179p. 1982. 21.00x (ISBN 0-86531-457-8); pap. text ed. 10.50x (ISBN 0-86531-458-6). Westview.

Chilcote, Ronald H. & Edelstein, Joel C., eds. Latin America: The Struggle with Dependency & Beyond. 800p. 1974. pap. 15.25 (ISBN 0-87073-069-X). Schenkman Bks Inc.

Chilcote, Ronald H. & Johnson, Dale L., eds. Theories of Development: Mode of Production or Dependency? (Class, State & Development Ser.: Vol. 2). (Illus.). 272p. 1983. 25.00 (ISBN 0-8039-1925-5); pap. 12.50 (ISBN 0-8039-1926-3). Sage.

Chilcote, Ronald H., compiled by. Emerging Nationalism in Portuguese Africa: A Bibliography of Documentary Ephemera Through 1965. LC 71-155299. (Bibliographical Ser.: No. 39). 114p. 1969. 9.95x (ISBN 0-8179-2391-8); pap. 5.95 (ISBN 0-8179-2392-6). Hoover Inst Pr.

--Emerging Nationalism in Portuguese Africa: Documents. LC 71-155299. (Publications Ser.: No. 97). (Illus.). 646p. 1972. 25.00x (ISBN 0-8179-1971-6). Hoover Inst Pr.

Chilcote, Russell Q. Quest for Meaning. pap. 1.25x (ISBN 0-8358-0262-0). Upper Room.

--Sharad: Camel Driver for the Kings. 1978. pap. 1.75x (ISBN 0-8358-0379-1). Upper Room.

Child. Organization. 2nd ed. 1984. (Pub. by Har-Row Ltd England); pap. text ed. 12.50 (ISBN 0-06-318275-0, Pub. by Har-Row Ltd England). Har-Row.

Child, jt. auth. see Bellamy.

Child, Arthur H. Interpretation: A General Theory. LC 65-64890. (University of California Publications in Philosophy Ser.: Vol. 36). pap. 37.50 (ISBN 0-317-10192-7, 2021179). Bks Demand UMI.

Child, C. Allan, jt. auth. see Nakamura, Koichiro.

Child, Charles M. Senescence & Rejuvenescence. Kastenbaum, Robert, ed. LC 78-22192. (Aging & Old Age Ser.). (Illus.). 1979. Repr. of 1915 ed. lib. bdg. 34.50x (ISBN 0-405-11809-0). Ayer Co Pubs.

Child, Charles M., et al. Unconscious, a Symposium. facs. ed. LC 67-22125. (Essay Index Reprint Ser). 1928. 17.00 (ISBN 0-8369-0957-7). Ayer Co Pubs.

Child, Clarence G. Palatal Diphthongization of Stem Vowels in the Old English Dialects. 1978. Repr. of 1903 ed. lib. bdg. 20.00 (ISBN 0-8495-0839-8). Arden Lib.

--Palatal Diphthongization of Stem Vowels in the Old English Dialects. LC 73-12892. 1903. lib. bdg. 25.00 (ISBN 0-8414-3392-5). Folcroft.

--Selections from Chaucer: Including His Earlier & Later Verse & an Example of His Prose. LC 74-16296. 74. Repr. of 1912 ed. lib. bdg. 20.00 (ISBN 0-8414-3578-2). Folcroft.

Child, Clarence G., ed. see Udall, Nicholas.

Child, Clifton J. German-Americans in Politics, 1914-1917. LC 70-129394. (American Immigration Collection, Ser. 2). (Illus.). 1970. Repr. of 1939 ed. 12.50 (ISBN 0-405-00549-0). Ayer Co Pubs.

Child, Daphne, ed. Portrait of a Pioneer: The Letters of Sidney Turner from South Africa. (Illus.). 144p. 1982. 19.95x (ISBN 0-86954-095-5, Pub. by Macmillan S Africa). Intl Spec Bk.

--The Zulu War Journal of Henry Harford, C.B. 88p. 1980. 12.50 (ISBN 0-208-01858-1, Archon). Shoe String.

Child, David L. Despotism of Freedom: Or, Tyranny & Cruelty of American Republican Slavemasters. facs. ed. LC 76-149865. (Black Heritage Library Collection Ser). 1833. 11.50 (ISBN 0-8369-8747-0). Ayer Co Pubs.

Child, Francis J. Child Memorial Volume. LC 73-11352. 1896. lib. bdg. 45.00 (ISBN 0-8414-3378-X). Folcroft.

--English & Scottish Popular Ballads, Vol. I. Set. 72.00 (ISBN 0-8446-1852-7); 15.00. Peter Smith.

--Letters on Scottish Ballads from Professor Francis J. Child to W. W. Aberdeen. LC 77-24106. 1977. Repr. of 1930 ed. lib. bdg. 10.00 (ISBN 0-8414-1808-X). Folcroft.

Child, Francis J. & Lowell, James R. The Scholar-Friends: Letters of Francis James Child & James Russell Lowell. Cottrell, G. W., Jr. & De Wolfe Howe, M. A., eds. LC 79-104223. (Illus.). 84p. Repr. of 1952 ed. lib. bdg. 18.75x (ISBN 0-8371-3333-5, CHSF). Greenwood.

Child, Frank C. Theory & Practice of Exchange in Germany. Wilkins, Mira, ed. LC 78-3904. (International Finance Ser.). 1978. Repr. of 1958 ed. lib. bdg. 23.50x (ISBN 0-405-11209-2). Ayer Co Pubs.

Child, Frank S. Colonial Parson of New England. LC 74-19532. 1974. Repr. of 1896 ed. 35.00x (ISBN 0-8103-3667-7). Gale.

Child, Gilbert W. Church & State Under the Tudors. LC 72-183695. 452p. 1974. Repr. of 1890 ed. lib. bdg. 29.50 (ISBN 0-8337-4041-5). B Franklin.

Child, H. Thomas Hardy. LC 72-3631. (Studies in Thomas Hardy, No. 14). 1972. Repr. of 1916 ed. lib. bdg. 35.95x (ISBN 0-8383-1584-4). Haskell.

Child, Harold. Essays & Reflections: Jonson, De La Mare, Leigh Hunt, Trollope, Stevenson, Shakespeare, John Fletcher, Thomas Dekker, William Congreve, J. M. Barrie. Roberts, S. C., ed. LC 78-7791. 1948. Repr. 25.00 (ISBN 0-8414-0052-0). Folcroft.

--Thomas Hardy. LC 78-8740. 1916. lib. bdg. 12.50 (ISBN 0-8414-3366-6). Folcroft.

Child, Harold, ed. see Hudson, Derek.

Child, Harold H. Shakespearian Production of John Philip Kemble. 1973. Repr. of 1935 ed. 10.00 (ISBN 0-8274-1499-4). R West.

Child, Heather. Calligraphy Today. (Illus.). 1979. pap. 7.95 (ISBN 0-8008-1186-0, Pentalic). Taplinger.

--Heraldic Design: A Handbook for Students. LC 66-31918. (Illus.). 180p. 1982. Repr. of 1966 ed. 18.50 (ISBN 0-8063-0071-X). Genealog Pub.

Child, Heather, ed. see Johnston, Edward.

Child, Irvin L., jt. auth. see Whiting, John W.

Child, J. Business Enterprise in Modern Industrial Society. 1970. pap. text ed. 2.45x (ISBN 0-02-972630-1). Macmillan.

Child, J. M., ed. see Barrow, Isaac.

Child, Jack. Geopolitics & Conflict in South America: Quarrels Among Neighbors. LC 84-18326. 208p. 1985. 34.95 (ISBN 0-03-001453-0). Praeger.

Child, Jack, ed. see International Peace Academy Conference.

Child, James E., ed. Nuclear War: The Moral Dimension. 160p. (Orig.). 1985. 16.95 (ISBN 0-912051-04-3, Dist. by Transaction Bks); pap. 8.95 (ISBN 0-912051-05-1). Soc Phil Pol.

Child, James W. Nuclear War: The Moral Dimension. 160p. 1985. 16.95 (ISBN 0-912051-04-3); pap. 8.95 (ISBN 0-912051-05-1). Transaction Bks.

Child, John. Australian Alpine Life. (Periwinkle Colour Ser.). (Illus.). (gr. 9 up). 1969. pap. 8.50x (ISBN 0-392-01184-0, ABC). Sportshelf.

--Australian Spider. pap. 8.50x (ISBN 0-392-07647-0, SpS). Sportshelf.

--Organization: A Guide to Problems & Practice. 2nd ed. 309p. 1984. pap. text ed. 16.50 scp (ISBN 0-06-041254-2, HarpC). Har-Row.

Child, John & Partridge, Bruce. Lost Managers: Supervisors in Industry & Society. LC 81-17979. (Management & Industrial Relations Ser.: No. 1). (Illus.). 1982. 34.50 (ISBN 0-521-23356-9); pap. 11.95 (ISBN 0-521-29931-4). Cambridge U Pr.

Child, John, jt. ed. see Finan, John J.

Child, Josiah. New Discourse of Trade: Fifth Edition-1751. 1981. write for info. (ISBN 0-08-027646-6, HE 041); microfiche 12.50 (ISBN 0-686-79353-6). Pergamon.

Child, Julia. The French Chef Cookbook. 1979. pap. 4.50 (ISBN 0-553-24789-1). Bantam.

--French Chef Cookbook. (Illus.). 1968. 15.50 (ISBN 0-394-40135-2). Knopf.

--From Julia Child's Kitchen. LC 75-8248. 1982. pap. 12.95 (ISBN 0-394-71027-4). Knopf.

--From Julia Child's Kitchen. 1975. 20.00 (ISBN 0-394-48071-6). Knopf.

--Julia Child & Company. LC 78-54922. (Illus.). 1978. 17.95 (ISBN 0-394-50200-0). Knopf.

--Julia Child & More Company. LC 79-2226. (Illus.). 1979. 17.95 (ISBN 0-394-50710-X); pap. 12.95 (ISBN 0-394-73806-3). Knopf.

Child, Julia & Yntema, E. S. Julia Child & Company. 1984. pap. 4.95 (ISBN 0-317-05207-1). Ballantine.

Child, Julia, et al. Mastering the Art of French Cooking, 2 vols. 2nd ed. (Illus.). Vol. 1. 22.50 (ISBN 0-394-53399-2); Vol. 2. 22.50 (ISBN 0-394-40152-2); Set. boxed 45.00 (ISBN 0-394-40178-6). Knopf.

--Mastering the Art of French Cooking. rev. ed. LC 83-48113. 1983. Vol. 1. pap. 12.95 (ISBN 0-394-72178-0); Vol. 2. pap. 12.95 (ISBN 0-394-72177-2); Boxed set. 25.95 (ISBN 0-394-72114-4). Knopf.

Child, L. Maria, ed. see Brent, Linda.

Child, L. Maria, ed. see Jacobs, Harriet B.

Child, Lincoln, ed. Dark Banquet: A Feast of Ghost Stories. 304p. 1985. 15.95 (ISBN 0-312-18233-3). St Martin.

--Dark Company: The Ten Greatest Ghost Stories. 356p. 1983. 12.95 (ISBN 0-312-18231-7). St Martin.

--Dark Company: The Ten Greatest Ghost Stories. 356p. 1984. pap. 6.95 (ISBN 0-312-18232-5). St Martin.

Child, Lydia. The Mother's Book. LC 73-169377. (Family in America Ser). 184p. 1972. Repr. of 1831 ed. 12.00 (ISBN 0-405-03854-2). Ayer Co Pubs.

Child, Lydia M. The American Frugal Housewife. (Illus.). 130p. 1971. Repr. 5.95 (ISBN 0-88215-022-7). Ohio St U Lib.

--The American Frugal Housewife. 132p. 1985. 7.95 (ISBN 0-918222-73-7). Apple Wood.

--The American Frugal Housewife. Date not set. 7.95 (ISBN 0-918222-73-7). Arbor Hse.

--Appeal in Favor of That Class of Americans Called Africans. LC 68-28988. (American Negro: His History & Literature, Ser. No. 1). 1968. Repr. of 1836 ed. 10.00 (ISBN 0-405-01808-8). Ayer Co Pubs.

--Freedmen's Book. LC 68-28989. (American Negro: His History & Literature Ser., No. 1). (Illus.). 1968. Repr. of 1865 ed. 13.00 (ISBN 0-405-01809-6). Ayer Co Pubs.

--History of the Condition of Women in Various Ages & Nations. 59.95 (ISBN 0-8490-0350-4). Gordon Pr.

--Hobomok: A Tale of Early Times. 1972. Repr. of 1824 ed. 16.50 (ISBN 0-8422-8185-1). Irvington.

--Isaac T. Hopper: A True Life. LC 79-88998. Repr. of 1854 ed. 22.00x (ISBN 0-8371-1737-2, CHH&, Pub. by Negro U Pr). Greenwood.

--Letters from New York. facs. 3rd ed. LC 79-137726. (American Fiction Reprint Ser). 1845. 19.00 (ISBN 0-8369-7025-X). Ayer Co Pubs.

--Letters of Lydia Maria Child. LC 73-165169. Repr. of 1883 ed. 10.00 (ISBN 0-404-00141-6). AMS Pr.

--Letters of Lydia Maria Child. LC 72-82183. (Anti-Slavery Crusade in America Ser). 1969. Repr. of 1883 ed. 12.00 (ISBN 0-405-00622-5). Ayer Co Pubs.

--Letters of Lydia Maria Child. LC 73-92740. Repr. of 1883 ed. 22.50x (ISBN 0-8371-2189-2, CHL&, Pub. by Negro U Pr). Greenwood.

--Lydia Maria Child: Selected Letters, 1817-1880. Meltzer, Milton & Holland, Patricia G., eds. LC 82-8464. (New England Writer's Ser.). 608p. 1982. lib. bdg. 35.00x (ISBN 0-87023-332-7). U of Mass Pr.

--Over the River & Through the Wood. LC 74-79700. (Illus.). 32p. (ps-3). 1974. 8.95 (ISBN 0-698-20301-1, Coward). Putnam Pub Group.

--Over the River & Through the Wood. (Illus.). (gr. k-3). 1975. pap. 1.95 (ISBN 0-590-09937-X). Scholastic Inc.

--Philothea: A Romance. facs. ed. LC 72-85682. (American Fiction Reprint Ser). Orig. Title: Philothea: A Grecian Romance. 1836. 17.00 (ISBN 0-8369-7011-X). Ayer Co Pubs.

--The Rebels; or Boston Before the Revolution. LC 78-64069. Repr. of 1825 ed. 37.50 (ISBN 0-404-17058-7). AMS Pr.

--Right Way the Safe Way Proved by Emancipation in the British West Indies, & Elsewhere. LC 76-82184. (Anti-Slavery Crusade in America Ser). 1969. Repr. of 1860 ed. 9.50 (ISBN 0-405-00623-3). Ayer Co Pubs.

--Right Way the Safe Way, Proved by Emancipation in the British West Indies & Elsewhere. LC 74-97419. Repr. of 1862 ed. 15.00x (ISBN 0-8371-2712-2, CHU&). Greenwood.

--Romance of the Republic. facs. ed. LC 76-83926. (Black Heritage Library Collection Ser). 1867. 18.00 (ISBN 0-8369-8540-0). Ayer Co Pubs.

Child, Lydia M., ed. see Jacobs, Harriet B.

Child, M. S. Molecular Collision Theory. 1974. 56.00 (ISBN 0-12-172650-9). Acad Pr.

Child, M. S., ed. see NATO Advanced Study Institute, Cambridge, England, September, 1979.

Child, Mark. Discovering Church Architecture. (Discovering Ser.: No. 214). (Illus., Orig.). 1984. pap. 3.50 (ISBN 0-85263-328-9, Pub. by Shire Pubns England). Seven Hills Bks.

--Discovering Churchyards. (Discovering Ser.: No. 268). (Illus.). 80p. 1983. pap. 3.50 (ISBN 0-85263-603-2, Pub. by Shire Pubns England). Seven Hills Bks.

--English Church Architecture. (Illus.). 120p. 1981. (Pub. by Batsford England); pap. 12.95 (ISBN 0-7134-3763-4). David & Charles.

--Wiltshire. (Shire County Guide Ser.: No. 5). (Illus.). 56p. (Orig.). 1984. pap. 4.95 (ISBN 0-85263-685-7, Pub. by Shire Pubns England). Seven Hills Bks.

Child, Nellise. If I Come Home. LC 74-29041. (The Labor Movement Fiction & Non-Fiction Ser.). Repr. of 1943 ed. 23.00 (ISBN 0-404-58522-1). AMS Pr.

Child, Peter. The Craftsman Woodturner. (Illus.). 256p. (Orig.). 1984. pap. 12.95 (ISBN 0-8069-7882-1). Sterling.

Child, Richard W. Battling the Criminal. 1979. Repr. of 1925 ed. lib. bdg. 25.00 (ISBN 0-8492-3854-4). R West.

Child, Ruth C. The Aesthetic of Walter Pater. 1978. Repr. of 1940 ed. lib. bdg. 20.00 (ISBN 0-8495-0749-9). Arden Lib.

--Aesthetic of Walter Pater. LC 74-3152. 1972. lib. bdg. 20.00 (ISBN 0-8414-3600-2). Folcroft.

--Aesthetic of Walter Pater. LC 76-96153. 1970. Repr. of 1940 ed. lib. bdg. 17.00x (ISBN 0-374-91520-2). Octagon.

Child Study Association. Brothers & Sisters Are Like That: Stories to Read Yourself. LC 78-158703. (Illus.). (gr. 1-4). 1971. Crowell Jr Bks.

Child Study Association of America see Child Study Association Of America-Children'S Book Committee.

Child Study Association of America Children's Book Committee see Child Study Association Of America-Children'S Book Committee.

Child Study Association of America-Children's Book Committee see Child Study Association Of America-Children'S Book Committee.

Child Study Association Of America. Behavior: The Unspoken Language of Children. rev. ed. LC 67-31324. 1967. pap. 0.75 (ISBN 0-87183-050-7). Child Study.

--Content for Training in Project ENABLE. LC 67-30071. 1967. pap. 2.65 (ISBN 0-87183-195-3). Child Study.

--Courage to Adventure: Stories of Boys & Girls Growing up with America. LC 75-29159. (Illus.). (gr. 2-6). 1976. 10.53i (ISBN 0-690-01035-4). Crowell Jr Bks.

--Pets & More Pets. LC 69-11825. (Illus.). (gr. 1-5). 1969. Crowell Jr Bks.

--Read-To-Me Storybook. LC 47-31488. (Illus.). (ps-1). 1947. 10.53i (ISBN 0-690-68832-6). Crowell Jr Bks.

--Round About the City: Stories You Can Read to Yourself. LC 66-10055. (Illus.). (gr. k-5). 1966. 11.95 (ISBN 0-690-71317-7); PLB 8.79 (ISBN 0-690-71318-5). Crowell Jr Bks.

--Sex Education: Recommended Reading. 1969. pap. 0.50 (ISBN 0-87183-243-7). Child Study.

--What to Tell Your Child about Sex. LC 84-45134. 97p. 1983. Repr. 15.00x (ISBN 0-87668-708-7). Aronson.

Child Study Association of America & Twins Mother's Club of Bergen County. And Then There Were Two. rev. ed. LC 73-110754. 1973. pap. 1.50 (ISBN 0-87183-090-6). Child Study.

Child Study Association Of America Conference, 43rd. Children of Poverty - Children of Affluence: Proceedings. LC 66-17843. (Orig.). 1967. pap. 2.45 (ISBN 0-87183-325-5, 737). Child Study.

Child Study Association Of America-Children'S Book Committee. Children's Books of the Year 1968. Incl. 1971. Child Study Association of America Children's Book Committee. 1972. 0.75 (ISBN 0-87183-173-2); 1968. Child Study Association of America-Children's Book Committee. LC 67-14889. (Orig.). 1969. pap. 0.75 (ISBN 0-87183-170-8); 1969. Children's Book Committee-Child Study Association of America. LC 67-14889. (Children's Boos of the Year Ser.). (Orig.). 1970. pap. 0.75 (ISBN 0-87183-171-6); 1970. Children's Book Committee-Child Study Association of America. LC 67-14889. 1971. pap. 0.75 (ISBN 0-87183-172-4); 1972. Child Study Association of America. LC 67-14889. 1973. 1.00 (ISBN 0-685-41668-2); 1973. Child Study Association of America. LC 67-14889. 1974. 3.00 (ISBN 0-685-41669-0); 1975. Child Study Association of America. Children's Book Committee. LC 75-43432. 1976. 2.50 (ISBN 0-87183-177-5); 1976. Children's Book Committee of CSAA Wel-Met Inc. (Children's Books of the Year Ser.). 1977. pap. 1.50 (ISBN 0-87183-178-3). LC 67-14889. (Orig.). 1969. pap. 0.75 (ISBN 0-87183-170-8). Child Study.

Child Study Association Of America Conference - 1968. Function of Rebellion: Is Youth Creating New Family Values: Proceedings. LC 67-14887. 1969. pap. 2.45 (ISBN 0-87183-330-1). Child Study.

Child Study Association Of America Conference - 1963. Future of the American Family: Proceedings. 1963. pap. 1.00 (ISBN 0-87183-300-X). Child Study.

Child Study Association of America Conference 1965. Preparing Our Children to Live in a World of Diversity by Strengthening Their Sense of Identity & Each Child an Individual. LC 66-17843. 1966. pap. 2.00 (ISBN 0-87183-315-8). Child Study.

Child Study Association Of America Conference - 1966. Sex Education & the New Morality: A Search for a Meaningful Social Ethic: Proceedings. LC 67-14887. 1967. pap. 1.95 (ISBN 0-87183-320-4). Child Study.

Child Study Children's Association, ed. Friends Are Like That! Stories to Read to Yourself. LC 78-22513. (Illus.). (gr. 3-6). 1979. 11.49 (ISBN 0-690-03979-4); PLB 11.89 (ISBN 0-690-03980-8). Crowell Jr Bks.

Child Welfare League of America. Maternal Deprivation. LC 61-18462. pap. 20.00 (ISBN 0-317-10514-0, 2003668). Bks Demand UMI.

Child Welfare League of America, Committee on Standards. Child Welfare League of America Standards for Unmarried. LC 52-4649. 1971. pap. 7.50 (ISBN 0-87868-093-4, UM-13). Child Welfare.

Child, William H. History of the Town of Cornish New Hampshire with Genealogical Record, 1763-1910, 2 vols. in 1. LC 75-28084. (Illus.). 879p. 1975. Repr. of 1911 ed. 25.00 (ISBN 0-87152-213-6). Reprint.

Child, William S. Legal Revolution of 1902. LC 75-154434. (Utopian Literature Ser). 1971. Repr. of 1898 ed. 24.50 (ISBN 0-405-03517-9). Ayer Co Pubs.

Childbirth Association of Tulsa, Inc. Our Baby....Our Birth. 2nd ed. Shimer, Ellie, et al, eds. (Avery's Childbirth Education Ser.). (Illus.). 128p. 1981. pap. text ed. 5.95 (ISBN 0-89529-148-7). Avery Pub.

Childbirth Education Association of Greater Philadelphia, Inc. Counseling the Nursing Mother. (Childbirth Reference Ser.). 528p. 1983. loose leaf 26.95 (ISBN 0-89529-206-8). Avery Pub.

Childbirth Education Association of Jacksonville, Fla., Inc & Brinkley, Ginny. Your Child's First Journey: A Guide to Prepared Birth from Pregnancy to Parenthood. (Avery's Childbirth Education Ser.). (Illus.). 256p. (Orig.). 1982. pap. 9.95 (ISBN 0-89529-150-9). Avery Pub.

Childe, Henry L. Everyman's Guide to Concrete Work. LC 71-487900. pap. 42.50 (ISBN 0-317-27787-1, 2025238). Bks Demand UMI.

Childe, T., tr. see Huygens, Christiaan.

Childe, V. Gordon. Man Makes Himself. 1983. pap. 7.95 (ISBN 0-452-00624-4, Mer). NAL.

--New Light on the Most Ancient East. 4th ed. (Library Ser). (Illus.). 1969. pap. 4.95x (ISBN 0-393-00469-4, Norton Lib). Norton.

--Prehistoric Communities of the British Isles. LC 72-82207. (Illus.). Repr. of 1940 ed. 26.50 (ISBN 0-405-08358-0, Blom Pubns). Ayer Co Pubs.

--Prehistoric Migrations in Europe. 1976. lib. bdg. 69.95 (ISBN 0-8490-2467-6). Gordon Pr.

--What Happened in History. (Peregrine Ser.). 304p. 1985. pap. 5.95 (ISBN 0-14-055157-3). Penguin.

Childe, V. Gordon, tr. see Moret, A. & Davy, G.

Childe, Vera G. Progress & Archaeology. LC 70-114499. 1971. Repr. of 1944 ed. lib. bdg. 22.50x (ISBN 0-8371-4779-4, CHPA). Greenwood.

Childe, Vere G. The Danube in Prehistory. LC 75-41055. (BCL Ser.: No. I). Repr. of 1929 ed. 40.00 (ISBN 0-404-14520-5). AMS Pr.

--Prehistoric Communities of the British Isles. 2nd ed. LC 76-114498. (Illus.). 1971. Repr. of 1947 ed. lib. bdg. 17.50x (ISBN 0-8371-4732-8, CHPC). Greenwood.

--Society & Knowledge. LC 72-10690. 131p. 1973. Repr. of 1956 ed. lib. bdg. 15.00x (ISBN 0-8371-6620-9, CHSK). Greenwood.

Childe, Vere G., et al. Skara Brae: A Pictish Village in Orkney. LC 77-86427. Repr. of 1931 ed. 24.50 (ISBN 0-404-16633-4). AMS Pr.

Childe, Wilfred R. Dream English: A Fantastical Romance. 1978. Repr. of 1917 ed. lib. bdg. 20.00 (ISBN 0-8492-3964-8). R West.

Childerhose, R. J. & Trim, Marj. Pacific Salmon & Steelhead Trout. LC 78-65830. (Illus.). 166p. 1979. pap. 16.95 (ISBN 0-295-95866-9). U of Wash Pr.

Childers, Cleta M. Tabitha. 1964. pap. 0.45 (ISBN 0-87148-825-6). Pathway Pr.

Childers, D. G., ed. Modern Spectrum Analysis. LC 78-55097. 1978. 41.55 (ISBN 0-87942-107-X, PC01040). Inst Electrical.

Childers, Donald G. & Durling, Allen E. Digital Filtering & Signal Processing. LC 75-8776. (Illus.). 539p. 1975. text ed. 38.95 (ISBN 0-8299-0056-X). West Pub.

Childers, Donald G., jt. auth. see Perry, Nathan W., Jr.

Childers, Erskine. Military Rule in Ireland. 59.95 (ISBN 0-8490-0637-6). Gordon Pr.

--The Riddle of the Sands. 1976. Repr. of 1913 ed. lib. bdg. 16.95 (ISBN 0-89190-240-6, Pub. by River City Pr). Amereon Ltd.

--The Riddle of the Sands. 352p. 1976. pap. 4.50 (ISBN 0-486-23280-8). Dover.

--The Riddle of the Sands. (Crime Ser.). 1978. pap. 3.95 (ISBN 0-14-000905-1). Penguin.

--The Riddle of the Sands. 358p. 1981. 39.00x (ISBN 0-686-78991-1, Pub. by Bowker & Bertram Ltd). State Mutual Bk.

Childers, J. Wesley. Motif-Index of the Cuentos of Juan Timoneda. Dorson, Richard M., ed. LC 80-791. (Folklore of the World Ser.). 1980. Repr. of 1948 ed. lib. bdg. 14.00x (ISBN 0-405-13330-8). Ayer Co Pubs.

Childers, James S. War Eagles. Gray, James A., ed. 369p. Repr. 20.00 (ISBN 0-941624-71-4). Eagle Pub.

Childers, James W. Tales from Spanish Picaresque Novels: A Motif-Index. LC 77-8780. 1977. 29.50x (ISBN 0-87395-188-3). State U NY Pr.

Childers, John V. The Lazy Way to Buy Real Estate. 1985. 15.95 (ISBN 0-910019-33-9). Invest Tax Pubn.

Childers, N. F., jt. ed. see Eck, Paul.

Childers, Norman B. Modern Fruit Science. 9th ed. (Illus.). 600p. 1983. 40.00 (ISBN 0-317-03711-0); pap. 35.00 (ISBN 0-317-03712-9). Horticult Pubns.

Childers, Norman F. & Zutter, Hans. Modern Fruit Science Lab Manual. 250p. 1975. pap. 8.75 (ISBN 0-317-03713-7). Horticult Pubns.

Childers, Norman F., ed. Strawberries: Cultivars to Marketing. (Illus.). 550p. 1981. 24.90 (ISBN 0-317-03715-3). Horticult Pubns.

Childers, Norman F., jt. ed. see Eck, Paul.

Childers, Norman F., jt. ed. see Zwet, Tom Van Der.

Childers, Peter G., jt. auth. see Schank, Roger C.

Childers, Thomas. Information & Referral: Libraries & Information Science. LC 83-21492. (Libraries & Information Science Ser.). 384p. (Orig.). 1984. text ed. 39.50. Ablex Pub.

--The Nazi Voter: The Social Foundations of Fascism in Germany, 1919-1933. LC 83-5924. (Illus.). xvi, 367p. 1984. 32.00 (ISBN 0-8078-1570-5). U of NC Pr.

Children of the Kazoo School. Windows. 60p. 1980. pap. 5.00 (ISBN 0-89062-137-3). Pub Ctr Cult Res.

Children's Aid Society. Children's Aid Society Annual Reports, Nos. 1-10, February, 1854-February, 1863. LC 72-137191. (Poverty U. S. A. Historical Record Ser). 1971. Repr. of 1854 ed. 47.50 (ISBN 0-405-03135-1). Ayer Co Pubs.

--New York Street Kids. (Illus.). 11.75 (ISBN 0-8446-5743-3). Peter Smith.

Children's Allowance Conference, 1967. Children's Allowance & the Economic Welfare of Children: The Report of a Conference. facsimile ed. Burns, Eveline M., ed. LC 74-1695. (Children & Youth Ser.). 208p. 1974. Repr. of 1968 ed. 20.00x (ISBN 0-405-05971-X). Ayer Co Pubs.

Children's Book Committee. Children's Books of the Year 1976. 1977. pap. 2.90 (ISBN 0-87183-178-3). Jewish Bd Family.

Children's Book Committee see Child Study Association Of America-Children'S Book Committee.

Children's Book Committee-Child Study Association of America see Child Study Association Of America-Children'S Book Committee.

Children's Book Committee-Child Study Association of America. Reading with Your Child Through Age Five. rev. ed. LC 71-177477. 1976. pap. 1.50 (ISBN 0-685-23774-5). Child Study.

Children's Book Committee of CSAA Wel-Met Inc. see Child Study Association Of America-Children'S Book Committee.

Childrens Book International Symposium, 1st, Boston Public Library, 1975. Childrens Books International I: Proceedings. 1976. 7.50 (ISBN 0-685-72172-8). Boston Public Lib.

Children's Creative Response to Conflict Program, ed. Friendly Classroom for a Small Planet. 100p. 7.95 (ISBN 0-317-34153-7). Fellowship of Recon.

Children's Defense Fund. Children & the Federal Budget. 40p. (Orig.). 1981. pap. 2.50 (ISBN 0-938008-14-5). Children's Defense.

--Children in Adult Jails. LC 76-55873. 77p. (Orig.). 1976. pap. 4.40 (ISBN 0-938008-24-2). Children's Defense.

--Children Out of School in America. LC 74-20229. 366p. (Orig.). 1974. pap. 5.50 (ISBN 0-938008-25-0). Children's Defense.

--Children Without Health Care. 32p. (Orig.). 1981. pap. 2.20 (ISBN 0-938008-26-9). Children's Defense.

--Children Without Homes: An Examination of Public Responsibility to Children in Out-of-Home Care. LC 78-74230. 282p. (Orig.). 1978. pap. 5.50 (ISBN 0-938008-21-8). Children's Defense.

--A Corporate Reader: Work & Family Life in the 1980's. LC 83-70745. 160p. 1983. pap. 7.50 (ISBN 0-938008-04-8). Children's Defense.

Children's Defense Fund, et al. Adolescent Pregnancy Child Watch Manual. 177p. (Orig.). 1984. pap. 9.50 (ISBN 0-938008-36-6). Children's Defense.

Children's Defense Fund Staff. American Children in Poverty. 96p. (Orig.). 1984. pap. 9.95 (ISBN 0-938008-32-3, 0-938008-32-3). Children's Defense.

--The Child Care Handbook: Needs, Programs, & Possibilities. LC 81-71944. 116p. (Orig.). 1982. pap. 7.50 (ISBN 0-938008-15-3). Children's Defense.

--A Children's Defense Budget: An Analysis of the President's FY 1985 Budget & Children. rev. ed. (A Children's Defense Budget Ser.: No. 4). 280p. (Orig.). 1984. pap. 12.95 (ISBN 0-938008-30-7). Children's Defense.

--Employed Parents & Their Children: A Data Book. LC 81-71942. 78p. (Orig.). 1982. pap. 8.00 (ISBN 0-938008-08-0). Children's Defense.

--For the Welfare of Children. 40p. (Orig.). 1978. pap. 2.50 (ISBN 0-938008-17-X). Children's Defense.

--Give More Children a Head Start: It Pays. LC 83-70226. 27p. (Orig.). 1983. pap. 3.50 (ISBN 0-938008-03-X). Children's Defense.

--How to Help Handicapped Children Get an Education: A Success Story. 28p. (Orig.). 1981. pap. 2.20 (ISBN 0-938008-18-8). Children's Defense.

--It's Time to Stand Up for Your Children: A Parent's Guide to Child Advocacy. 48p. (Orig.). 1982. pap. 2.50 (ISBN 0-938008-19-6). Children's Defense.

--Lobbying & Political Activity for Nonprofits: What You Can (& Can't) Do Under Federal Law. LC 83-70227. 15p. (Orig.). 1983. pap. 3.50 (ISBN 0-938008-02-1). Children's Defense.

--Paying Children's Health Bills: Some Dos & Don'ts in Tight Fiscal Times. LC 81-71943. 64p. (Orig.). 1982. pap. 3.00 (ISBN 0-938008-10-2). Children's Defense.

--Your School Records. Rev. ed. 12p. (YA) (gr. 9-12). 1981. pap. 1.10 (ISBN 0-938008-16-1). Children's Defense.

Children's Defense Fund Staff & Educational Law Center, Inc. Staff. Ninety Four-One Forty Two & Five Hundred Four: Numbers That Add Up to Educational Rights for Handicapped Children. 2nd, rev. ed. 50p. 1984. pap. 4.75 (ISBN 0-938008-34-X). Children's Defense.

Children's Defense Fund Staff, et al. EPSDT: Does It Spell Health Care for Poor Children. LC 77-80325. 304p. (Orig.). 1977. pap. 5.50 (ISBN 0-938008-23-4). Children's Defense.

--In Celebration of Children: An Interfaith Religious Action Kit. LC 83-71460. 90p. (Orig.). (gr. 12 up). 1983. pap. 6.50 (ISBN 0-938008-07-2). Children's Defense.

--School Suspensions: Are They Helping Children? LC 75-26436. 257p. 1975. pap. 5.50 (ISBN 0-938008-12-9). Children's Defense.

Children's Hospital, Boston, Department of Medicine Staff. Manual of Pediatric Therapeutics. Graef, John W. & Cone, Thomas E., Jr., eds. (The Spiral Manual Ser.). 1984. spiral 17.95 (ISBN 0-316-13907-6). Little.

Children's Hospital Medical Center, Boston. Manual of Pediatric Therapeutics. 2nd ed. Graef, John W. & Cone, Thomas E., Jr., eds. 450p. 1980. 17.95 (ISBN 0-316-13911-4). Little.

Children's Rights Workshop, ed. see Leeson, Robert.

Children's Rights Workshop Staff, ed. Sexism in Children's Books. (Papers on Children's Literature). (Illus.). 64p. (Orig.). 1981. pap. 1.95 (ISBN 0-904613-22-4). Writers & Readers.

Children's Television Workshop Staff, jt. auth. see Stein, Sara B.

Children's TV Workshop, ed. Sesame Street Book of Shapes. (Illus.). (gr. k-2). 1971. pap. 0.75 (ISBN 0-451-04500-9, Q4500, Sig). NAL.

Childress, Alice. A Hero Ain't Nothin' but a Sandwich. 100p. (gr. 5-9). 1973. 8.95 (ISBN 0-698-20278-3, Coward). Putnam Pub Group.

--A Hero Ain't Nothin but a Sandwich. 128p. (YA) 1982. pap. 2.50 (ISBN 0-380-00132-2, 69824-2, Flare). Avon.

--Rainbow Jordan. (Illus.). (gr. 7 up). 1981. 9.95 (ISBN 0-698-20531-6, Coward). Putnam Pub Group.

--Rainbow Jordan. 128p. 1982. pap. 2.50 (ISBN 0-380-58974-5, 69828-5, Flare). Avon.

--A Short Walk. 336p. 1981. pap. 3.95 (ISBN 0-380-54239-0, 64790-7, Bard). Avon.

Childress, David H. A Hitchhiker's Guide to Africa & Arabia. (Illus.). 304p. 1984. pap. 8.95 (ISBN 0-914091-42-5). Chicago Review.

Childress, Harvey. Expanding Outlines of the New Testament Books. 5.95 (ISBN 0-89137-536-8). Quality Pubns.

--My Triumphant Life. 1978. pap. 2.25 (ISBN 0-88027-087-X). Firm Foun Pub.

--My Wonderful Salvation. 1978. pap. 1.75 (ISBN 0-88027-088-8). Firm Foun Pub.

Childress, Harvey A. The Lord's Own Church. 1980. pap. 2.25 (ISBN 0-88027-086-1). Firm Foun Pub.

Childress, James F. Civil Disobedience & Political Obligation: A Study in Christian Social Ethics. LC 75-158137. (Yale Publication in Religion Ser.: No. 16). pap. 66.50 (ISBN 0-317-09428-9, 2021988). Bks Demand UMI.

--Moral Responsibility in Conflicts: Essays on Nonviolence, War, & Conscience. LC 82-15197. 224p. 1982. text ed. 22.50x (ISBN 0-8071-1019-1). La State U Pr.

--Priorities in Biomedical Ethics. LC 81-3. 144p. 1981. pap. 8.95 (ISBN 0-664-24368-1). Westminster.

--Who Should Decide? Paternalism in Health Care. 1982. text ed. 24.95x (ISBN 0-19-503127-X). Oxford U Pr.

Childress, James F., jt. auth. see Beauchamp, Tom L.

Childress, Mark. A World Made of Fire. LC 84-47902. 283p. 1984. 14.95 (ISBN 0-394-53634-7). Knopf.

--A World Made of Fire. 272p. 1985. pap. 3.95 (ISBN 0-345-32466-8). Ballantine.

Childress, R. L. Fundamentals of Finite Mathematics. (Illus.). 1976. ref. ed. 27.95. P-H.

Childress, Robert L. Calculus for Business & Economics. 2nd ed. LC 77-2855. (Illus.). 1978. text ed. 27.95 (ISBN 0-13-111534-0). P-H.

--Mathematics for Managerial Decisions. LC 73-17352. (Illus.). 656p. 1974. ref. ed. 29.95 (ISBN 0-13-562231-X). P-H.

Childress, Stephen. Mechanics of Swimming & Flying. LC 80-23364. (Cambridge Studies in Mathematical Biology: No. 2). (Illus.). 170p. 1981. 39.50 (ISBN 0-521-23613-4); pap. 16.95 (ISBN 0-521-28071-0). Cambridge U Pr.

Childress, William. Lobo. LC 75-188839. 64p. 1972. 8.95 (ISBN 0-87929-012-9). Barlenmir.

Childs, et al see Turetzky.

Childs, Alan W. & Melton, Gary B., eds. Rural Psychology. 458p. 1983. 39.50x (ISBN 0-306-41045-1, Plenum Pr). Plenum Pub.

Childs, B., et al, eds. Codes for Boundary-Value Problems in Ordinary Differential Equations. (Lecture Notes in Computer Science: Vol. 76). 388p. 1979. pap. 22.00 (ISBN 0-387-09554-3). Springer-Verlag.

Childs, B. J. & Ptacnik, D. J. Emergency Ambulance Driving. (Illus.). 288p. 1985. pap. text ed. 16.95 (ISBN 0-89303-427-4). Brady Comm.

Childs, Barney, jt. ed. see Schwartz, Elliot.

Childs, Brevard S. The Book of Exodus: A Critical, Theological Commentary. LC 73-23120. (Old Testament Library). 686p. 1974. 26.50 (ISBN 0-664-20985-8). Westminster.

--Introduction to the Old Testament As Scripture. LC 78-14665. 688p. 1979. 29.95 (ISBN 0-8006-0532-2, 1-532). Fortress.

--The New Testament As Canon: An Introduction. LC 84-21169. 640p. 1985. 22.95 (ISBN 0-8006-0739-2, 1-739). Fortress.

--Old Testament Books for Pastor and Teacher. LC 76-52457. 120p. 1977. pap. 4.95 (ISBN 0-664-24120-4). Westminster.

Childs, Corinne. Yasmina's Daughter. 1981. pap. 2.50 (ISBN 0-8439-0838-6, Leisure Bks). Dorchester Pub Co.

--Yasmina's Daughter. 320p. 1984. pap. 3.25 (ISBN 0-8439-2125-0, Leisure Bks). Dorchester Pub Co.

Childs, David. Britain Since Nineteen Forty-Five: A Political History. LC 79-8507. 1980. 27.50 (ISBN 0-312-09880-4). St Martin.

--Britain Since Nineteen Forty-Five: A Political History. 320p. 1984. pap. 12.95x (ISBN 0-416-36480-2, NO. 4058). Methuen Inc.

--The GDR: Moscow's German Ally. 192p. 1983. text ed. 27.50x (ISBN 0-04-354029-5); pap. text ed. 14.50x (ISBN 0-04-354030-9). Allen Unwin.

--Germany since Nineteen Eighteen. LC 80-5321. 1980. 25.00 (ISBN 0-312-32628-9). St Martin.

Childs, David & Johnson, Jeffrey. West Germany: Politics & Society. 1981. 26.00 (ISBN 0-312-86300-4). St Martin.

Childs, David, ed. The Changing Face of Western Communism. LC 79-25754. 286p. 1980. 25.00 (ISBN 0-312-12951-3). St Martin.

--Honecker's Germany. (Illus.). 200p. 1985. text ed. 25.00x (ISBN 0-04-354031-7). Allen Unwin.

Childs, Frances W. French Refugee Life in the United States, 1790-1800: An American Chapter of the French Revolution. LC 78-15085. (Perspectives in American History Ser.: No. 47). (Illus.). Repr. of 1940 ed. lib. bdg. 19.50x (ISBN 0-87991-371-1). Porcupine Pr.

Childs, Frank H. Where & How to Find the Law. LC 85-60261. (Legal Bibliographic & Research Reprint Ser.: Vol. 4). vi, 119p. 1985. Repr. of 1929 ed. lib. bdg. 28.50 (ISBN 0-89941-397-8). W S Hein.

Childs, George W. Recollections. 1890. 25.00 (ISBN 0-932062-31-8). Sharon Hill.

--Recollections: Shakespeare, Milton. 1973. Repr. of 1890 ed. 20.00 (ISBN 0-8274-1531-1). R West.

Childs, Harwood L. Labor & Capital in National Politics. LC 73-19137. (Politics & People Ser.). (Illus.). 290p. 1974. Repr. 20.00x (ISBN 0-405-05862-4). Ayer Co Pubs.

--Reference Guide to the Study of Public Opinion. LC 73-12777. Repr. of 1934 ed. 40.00x (ISBN 0-8103-3704-5). Gale.

Childs, Harwood L., ed. Propaganda & Dictatorship: A Collection of Papers. LC 72-4659. (International Propaganda & Communications Ser.). 153p. 1972. Repr. of 1936 ed. 11.00 (ISBN 0-405-04742-8). Ayer Co Pubs.

Childs, Harwood L. & Whitton, John B., eds. Propaganda by Short Wave. Bd. with The War on the Short Waves. Rigby, Charles A. Repr. of 1944 ed. LC 72-4660. (International Propaganda & Communications Ser.). (Illus.). 365p. 1972. Repr. of 1942 ed. 24.00 (ISBN 0-405-04743-6). Ayer Co Pubs.

Childs, Harwood L., tr. see Brennecke, Fritz.

Childs, J. F., ed. see International Organization of Citrus Virologists - 4th Conference.

Childs, J. Rives. Foreign Service Farewell. LC 71-76185. (Illus.). 208p. 1969. 12.95x (ISBN 0-8139-0261-4). U Pr of Va.

Childs, James B., ed. Government Document Bibliography in the United States & Elsewhere. 3rd ed. 1942. 12.00 (ISBN 0-384-08785-X). Johnson Repr.

Childs, James J. Numerical Control Part Programming. LC 73-9766. (Illus.). 340p. 1973. 24.95 (ISBN 0-8311-1099-6). Indus Pr.

--Principles of Numerical Control. 3rd ed. LC 81-20296. (Illus.). 316p. 1982. 24.95 (ISBN 0-8311-1135-6). Indus Pr.

Childs, John. Armies & Warfare in Europe, 1648-1789. 208p. 1983. text ed. 27.50x (ISBN 0-8419-0820-6). Holmes & Meier.

--The Army, James II & the Glorious Revolution. 1981. 27.50 (ISBN 0-312-04949-8). St Martin.

Childs, John F. Corporate Finance & Capital Management for the Chief Executive Officer & Directors. 160p. 1979. 29.95 (ISBN 0-13-174003-2). P-H.

Childs, John L. Education & Morals: An Experimentalist Philosophy of Education. LC 72-165734. (American Education, Ser. 2). 1972. Repr. of 1950 ed. 19.00 (ISBN 0-405-03603-5). Ayer Co Pubs.

--Education & the Philosophy of Experimentalism. LC 76-165735. (American Education, Ser. 2). 1972. Repr. of 1931 ed. 18.00 (ISBN 0-405-03604-3). Ayer Co Pubs.

--Education & the Philosophy of Experimentalism. 264p. 1980. Repr. of 1931 ed. lib. bdg. 25.00 (ISBN 0-89760-115-7). Telegraph Bks.

Childs, L. N. A Concrete Introduction to Higher Algebra. LC 78-21870. (Undergraduate Texts in Mathematics). (Illus.). 340p. 1979. 24.00 (ISBN 0-387-90333-X). Springer-Verlag.

Childs, Linda T. Somber Shadows. 12.50 (ISBN 0-8062-2488-6). Carlton.

Childs, Marjorie. Fabric of the ERA: Congressional Intent. (Illus.). 144p. 1982. 10.00 (ISBN 0-682-49864-5). Exposition Pr FL.

Childs, Marleta. North Louisiana Census Reports: Vol. 1, 1830 & 1840, Parishes of Union, Claiborne, Caldwell, Catahoula & Ouachita. 1975. 15.00 (ISBN 0-686-20886-2). Polyanthos.

Childs, Marleta & Ross, John. North Louisiana Census Reports. Incl. Vol. II. 1830 & 1840, Parishes of Caddo, Claiborne, & Natchitoches; Vol. III. 1850 & 1860, Union Parish. 1977. 20.00 (ISBN 0-686-20579-0). Polyanthos.

Childs, Marquis. The Farmer Takes a Hand: The Electric Power Revolution in Rural America. LC 73-19736. (Fdr & the Era of the New Deal Ser.). (Illus.). 256p. 1974. Repr. of 1952 ed. lib. bdg. 35.00 (ISBN 0-306-70478-1). Da Capo.

Childs, Marquis & Engel, Paul. This Is Iowa. Andrews, Clarence A., ed. LC 82-61137. (Illus.). 320p. 1982. board 14.95 (ISBN 0-934582-05-X). Midwest Heritage.

--This Is Iowa. Andrews, Clarence A., ed. LC 82-61137. (Illus.). 320p. 1982. lib. bdg. 14.95 (ISBN 0-934582-04-1). Midwest Heritage.

Childs, Marquis W. Sweden: the Middle Way on Trial. LC 79-24714. 188p. 04/1980 20.00x (ISBN 0-300-02443-6); pap. 7.95x 02/1984 (ISBN 0-300-03181-5, Y 483). Yale U Pr.

--This Is Democracy: Collective Bargaining in Scandinavia. 1938. 39.50x (ISBN 0-685-89790-7). Elliots Bks.

--Yesterday, Today & Tomorrow: The Farmer Takes a Hand. rev. ed. LC 52-5629. 178p. 1980. pap. 2.25 (ISBN 0-686-28113-6). Natl Rural.

Childs, Marquis W. & Cater, Douglass. Ethics in a Business Society. LC 73-7073. 191p. 1973. Repr. of 1954 ed. lib. bdg. 15.00x (ISBN 0-8371-6905-4, CHBS). Greenwood.

Childs, Nathan B. Leader of the Pack. (Illus.). 125p. (Orig.). 1985. pap. text ed. 10.00 (ISBN 0-318-04697-0). Childs Pub.

Childs, Phyllis. Color Me. 35p. (ps-k). 1985. wkbk. 2.95 (ISBN 0-931749-03-4). Childs Play.

--The Language Ladder, Bk. I. 76p. (ps-k). 1985. wkbk. 6.50 (ISBN 0-931749-01-8). Childs Play.

--Speak Up. 78p. (ps-k). 1985. wkbk. 6.50 (ISBN 0-931749-00-X). Childs Play.

Childs, Phyllis, et al. First Book of Numbers. 55p. (ps-k). 1985. wkbk. 4.95 (ISBN 0-931749-02-6). Childs Play.

Childs, St. Julien R. Malaria & Colonization in the Carolina Low Country, 1526-1696. LC 78-64178. (Johns Hopkins University. Studies in the Social Sciences. Fifty-Eighth Ser. 1940: 1). Repr. of 1940 ed. 25.50 (ISBN 0-404-61286-5). AMS Pr.

Childs, Wendy R. Anglo-Castilian Trade in the Later Middle Ages. (Illus.). 264p. 1978. 23.50x (ISBN 0-8476-6071-0). Rowman.

Childs, Williams A. The City Reliefs of Lycia. LC 78-51169. (Monographs in Art & Archaeology: No. 42). (Illus.). 1978. 45.00x (ISBN 0-691-03554-7). Princeton U Pr.

Childs World Editors. How Do You Feel? LC 73-4745. (Illus.). (ps-2). 1973. 7.45 (ISBN 0-913778-01-X). Childs World.

Childs World Editors, ed. Glad or Sad: How Do You Feel? rev. ed. LC 79-12152. (Illus.). (ps-3). 1979. PLB 5.95 (ISBN 0-89565-072-X). Childs World.

Childs-Gowell, Elaine. Reparenting Schizophrenics. LC 78-66873. (Illus.). 1979. 12.95 (ISBN 0-8158-0372-9). Chris Mass.

Chiles, Fran. Parties, Parties. LC 83-18572. (Illus.). 120p. 1984. 19.95x (ISBN 0-87201-656-0). Gulf Pub.

Chiles, Frances. Octavio Paz: The Mythic Dimension. LC 83-49095. (American University Studies II (Romance Languages & Literature): Vol. 6). 190p. 1985. text ed. 24.50 (ISBN 0-8204-0079-3). P Lang Pubs.

Chiles, John. Teenage Depression & Drugs. (Encyclopedia of Psychoactive Drugs Ser.). (Illus.). 1985. PLB 15.95x (ISBN 0-87754-771-8). Chelsea Hse.

Chiles, L. B., et al, eds. Lift (Elevator) Erection. (Engineering Craftsmen: No. J26). (Illus.). 1978. spiral bdg. 39.95x (ISBN 0-85083-414-7). Intl Ideas.

--Lift (Elevator) Practice. (Engineering Craftsmen Ser.: No. J5). (Illus.). 203p. 1979. spiral bdg. 49.95x (ISBN 0-85083-458-9). Intl Ideas.

--Lift (Elevator) Servicing & Maintenance. (Engineering Craftsmen: No. J25). (Illus.). 1974. spiral bdg. 39.95x (ISBN 0-85083-236-5). Intl Ideas.

Chiles, Paul N. The Puerto Rican Press Reaction to the United States, 1888-1898. LC 74-14225. (The Puerto Rican Experience Ser.). 124p. 1975. Repr. 11.00x (ISBN 0-405-06215-X). Ayer Co Pubs.

Chiles, Robert E. Scriptural Christianity: A Call to John Wesley's Disciples. 160p. 1984. pap. 5.95 (ISBN 0-310-45781-5). Zondervan.

--Theological Transition in American Methodism, 1790-1935. LC 83-16666. 238p. 1983. pap. text ed. 11.00 (ISBN 0-8191-3551-8). U Pr of Amer.

Chiles, Robert E., jt. ed. see Burtner, Robert W.

Chiles, Webb. The Ocean Waits. LC 81-14014. (Illus.). 1984. 18.95 (ISBN 0-393-03286-8). Norton.

--The Open Boat - Across the Pacific. (Illus.). 224p. 1982. 16.95 (ISBN 0-393-03268-X). Norton.

--The Open Boat II: The East. (Illus.). 18.95. Norton.

Chilimidos, R. S. Auto Theft Investigation. LC 79-155290. 1971. 14.00x (ISBN 0-910874-18-2). Legal Bk Co.

Chilingar, G. V., jt. ed. see Larsen, G.

Chilingarian, G. V. & Vorabutr, P. Drilling & Drilling Fluids. (Developments in Petroleum Science Ser.: Vol. 11). xx, 802p. 1983. pap. 49.50 (ISBN 0-444-42177-7). Elsevier.

Chilingarian, G. V., jt. auth. see Rieke, H. H.

Chilingarian, G. V., jt. auth. see Yen, T. F.

Chilingarian, G. V. & Wolf, K., eds. Compaction of Coarse-Grained Sediments, 2 pts. LC 73-85220. 550p. 1975-77. Pt. 1. 104.25 (ISBN 0-444-41152-6); Pt. 2. 117.00 (ISBN 0-444-41361-8). Elsevier.

Chilingarian, G. V. & Yen, T. F., eds. Bitumens, Asphalts & Tar Sands. (Developments in Petroleum Science Ser.: Vol. 7). 332p. 1978. 91.50 (ISBN 0-444-41619-6). Elsevier.

Chill, Abraham. The Minhagim: The Customs & Ceremonies of Judaism, Their Origins & Rationale. 2nd corrected ed. LC 78-62153. (Illus.). 339p. 1980. 14.95 (ISBN 0-87203-076-8); pap. 10.95 (ISBN 0-87203-077-6). Hermon.

--Mitzvot: The Commandments & Their Rationale. LC 74-14055. 544p. 1974. cancelled (ISBN 0-8197-0376-1). Bloch.

Chilla, R., ed. Sialadenosis & Sialadenitis. (Advances in Oto-Rhino-Laryngology: Vol. 26). (Illus.). viii, 252p. 1981. 67.25 (ISBN 3-8055-1669-X). S Karger.

Chillingarian, G. V. Drilling & Drilling Fluids. (Development in Petroleum Science Ser.: Vol. 11). 1981. 119.25 (ISBN 0-444-41867-9). Elsevier.

Chillingworth, D., ed. see Symposium on Differential Equations & Dynamical Systems, Warwickshire, 1968.

Chillingworth, H. R. Complex Variables. LC 72-86178. 280p. 1973. pap. text ed. 21.00 (ISBN 0-08-016939-2). Pergamon.

Chillingworth, William. Works of William Chillingworth, 3 Vols. Repr. of 1838 ed. Set. lib. bdg. 95.00 (ISBN 0-404-01570-0). Vol. 1 (ISBN 0-404-01571-9). Vol. 3 (ISBN 0-404-01572-7). Vol. 4 (ISBN 0-404-01573-5). AMS Pr.

Chilman, Catherine S. Adolescent Sexuality in a Changing American Society: Social & Psychological Perspectives for the Human Service Professions. LC 82-20185. (Personality Processes Ser.). 334p. 1983. 31.95 (ISBN 0-471-09162-6, Pub. by Wiley-Interscience). Wiley.

Chilnick, Lawrence D., ed. see Morris, Lois B., et al.

Chilo, et al. Life Threatening Emergencies in the Dental Office. 1984. 29.50 (ISBN 88-299-0264-0). Ishiyaku Euro.

Chilson, Kathleen G., ed. see Verdon, Timothy.

Chilson, Kathryn E., ed. see Jarrell, Howard R.

Chilson, Richard. Creed for a Young Catholic. LC 80-2073. 128p. 1981. pap. 2.75 (ISBN 0-385-17436-5, Im). Doubleday.

--Faith of Catholics: An Introduction. rev. ed. LC 72-81229. 320p. 1975. pap. 3.95 (ISBN 0-8091-1873-4, Deus). Paulist Pr.

--Way to Christianity: The Pilgrim. 1980. pap. 8.95 (ISBN 0-03-053426-7). Winston Pr.

Chilson, Richard W. Full Christianity: A Catholic Response to Fundamental Questions. 144p. (Orig.). 1985. pap. 3.95 (ISBN 0-8091-2669-9). Paulist Pr.

--A Lenten Pilgrimage-Dying & Rising in the Lord: A Manual for Ministry in the Lenten Catechumenate. (Orig.). 1984. pap. 7.95 (ISBN 0-8091-2589-7); handbook 3.95 (ISBN 0-8091-2569-2). Paulist Pr.

Chilstrom, Herbert W. Hebrews: A New & Better Way. LC 83-5600. 80p. 1984. pap. 3.95 (ISBN 0-8006-1717-7, 1-1717). Fortress.

Chilstrom-Meixner, Esther. The Red Ribbons: The Journeys of Armegott Printz. 256p. 1982. 12.00 (ISBN 0-8059-2813-8). Dorrance.

Chiltern, Crispin, jt. ed. see Aubrey, Paul.

Chilton. Chilton's Easy Car Care. 3rd ed. LC 78-7152. 1985. text ed. 14.95 (ISBN 0-8019-7554-9); pap. 12.95 (ISBN 0-8019-7553-0). Chilton.

--Chilton's Repair & Tune-Up Guide: Ford Bronco, 1983, Vol. II. LC 83-70993. 224p. (Orig.). 1984. pap. 11.95 (ISBN 0-8019-7408-9). Chilton.

--Chilton's Repair & Tune-up Guide for Ford-Mercury FWD 1982-1985. 240p. 1985. pap. 11.95 (ISBN 0-8019-7544-1). Chilton.

--Chilton's Repair & Tune Up Guide: Mustang & Cougar, 1965-83. LC 83-70992. 252p. (Orig.). 1983. pap. 11.95 (ISBN 0-8019-7405-4). Chilton.

--Plymouth Car: How to Fix. 1954. 3.95x (ISBN 0-685-21976-3). Wehman.

Chilton, Arthur B. & Shultis, Kenneth. Principles of Radiation Shielding. (Illus.). 464p. 1984. 42.95 (ISBN 0-13-709907-X). P-H.

Chilton Automotive Editorial Staff. Chilton's Auto Repair Manual 1985. LC 76-648878. 1344p. 1984. 20.95 (ISBN 0-8019-7470-4); 21.75 (ISBN 0-8019-7471-2); pap. cancelled. Chilton.

--Chilton's Guide to Fuel Injection & Carburetors. LC 83-45323. 256p. 1985. pap. 16.95 (ISBN 0-8019-7488-7). Chilton.

--Chilton's Spanish Auto Repair Manual 1979-83. LC 76-648878. 1296p. (Span.). 1984. 22.95 (ISBN 0-8019-7476-3). Chilton.

--Chilton's Truck & Van Repair Manual 1975-1982. (Illus.). 20.95 (ISBN 0-8019-7150-0). Chilton.

--Subaru 1970-84: RTUG. LC 83-45314. 312p. 1984. pap. 11.95 (ISBN 0-8019-7479-8). Chilton.

Chilton, Bruce, ed. The Kingdom of God in the Teaching of Jesus. LC 83-20569. (Issues in Religion & Theology Ser.). 192p. 1984. pap. 6.95 (ISBN 0-8006-1769-X, 1-769). Fortress.

Chilton, Bruce D. A Galilean Rabbi & His Bible: Jesus' Use of the Interpreted Scripture of His Time. (Good News Studies Ser.: Vol. 8). 7.95 (ISBN 0-89453-374-6). M Glazier.

--The Glory of Israel: The Theology & Provenience of the Isaiah Targum. (JSOT Supplement Ser.: No. 23). ix, 178p. 1984. text ed. 28.00x (ISBN 0-905774-46-9, Pub. by JSOT Pr England); pap. text ed. 18.50 (ISBN 0-905774-47-7, Pub. by JSOT Pr England). Eisenbrauns.

Chilton, C. H., jt. auth. see Perry, Robert H.

Chilton, Carl S. Successful Small Client Accounting Practice. 224p. 1976. 34.95 (ISBN 0-13-872556-X); pap. 9.95 (ISBN 0-13-872549-7). P-H.

Chilton, Carl S., Jr. The Successful Professional Client Accounting Practice. LC 82-15143. 217p. 1983. 39.95 (ISBN 0-13-868208-9, Busn). P-H.

Chilton, Charles, et al. Oh What a Lovely War. (Illus.). 109p. 1967. pap. 6.95 (ISBN 0-413-30210-5, NO. 3009). Methuen Inc.

Chilton, Craig. The Coin-Flip Fleece: How to Make All Your Dreams Come True. (Illus.). 50p. (Orig.). 1982. pap. 12.95 (ISBN 0-933638-05-1). Xanadu Ent.

--H Two: Unlimited Energy Forever. (Illus., Orig.). 1982. pap. 3.95 (ISBN 0-933638-04-3). Xanadu Ent.

--How to Get Paid Thirty Thousand Dollars a Year to Travel Without Selling Anything. LC 79-63095. (The Xanadu System). (Illus., Orig.). 1979. pap. 19.95 (ISBN 0-933638-01-9). Xanadu Ent.

--How to Get Paid Two Hundred Dollars a Day to Travel This Summer Without Selling Anything: The Xanadu System. (Orig.). 1979. pap. 2.95 (ISBN 0-933638-02-7). Xanadu Ent.

--The Xanadu System. LC 79-63095. (Illus., Orig.). 1979. pap. 19.95 (ISBN 0-933638-03-5). Xanadu Ent.

Chilton, David. Paradise Restored: A Biblical Theology of Dominion. LC 84-62186. 318p. 1984. 14.95 (ISBN 0-930462-04-1). Am Bur Eco Res.

--Productive Christians in An Age of Guilt Manipulators. 3rd ed. 480p. 1985. pap. 9.95 (ISBN 0-930464-04-4). Inst Christian.

Chilton, Eleanor Carroll & Agar, Herbert. The Garment of Praise. 1929. Repr. 30.00 (ISBN 0-8274-2391-8). R West.

Chilton, J. S., jt. auth. see Stamets, Paul.

Chilton, John. Billie's Blues: The Story of Billie Holiday, 1933-1959. LC 75-8837. pap. 1.95 (ISBN 0-8128-7004-2). Stein & Day.

--Teach Yourself Jazz. 1979. pap. 3.95 (ISBN 0-679-12225-7). McKay.

--Who's Who of Jazz. 4th ed. (Roots of Jazz Ser.). (Illus.). 362p. 1985. 25.00 (ISBN 0-306-76271-4); pap. 11.95 (ISBN 0-306-80243-0). Da Capo.

Chilton, Lance, et al. New Mexico: A New Guide to the Colorful State. LC 83-27351. (Illus.). 416p. 1984. pap. 17.50 (ISBN 0-8263-0733-7). U of NM Pr.

Chilton, Neal, ed. Design & Analysis in Dental & Oral Research. 2nd ed. LC 82-591. 460p. 1982. 49.95x (ISBN 0-03-056157-4). Praeger.

Chilton, Patricia, jt. ed. see Howorth, Jolyon.

Chilton, Paul, ed. Language & the Nuclear Arms Debate: Nukespeak Today. (Open Linguistics Ser.). 200p. 1985. 20.00 (ISBN 0-86187-464-1, Pub. by Frances Pinter). Longwood Pub Group.

Chilton, Paul A., tr. see De Navarre, Marguerite.

Chilton, Richard L. The Great American Baseball Lineup Quiz Book. LC 83-45528. 288p. 1984. pap. 9.95 (ISBN 0-689-70673-1). Atheneum.

Chilton Staff. Chilton's Auto Repair Manual (CARM) 1980-87. LC 76-648878. 1416p. 1986. 21.95 (ISBN 0-8019-7670-7); slipcase 22.70 (ISBN 0-8019-7671-5). Chilton.

--Chilton's Auto Service Manual: 1983-87. LC 82-72944. 1824p. 1986. pap. 46.00 (ISBN 0-8019-7690-1). Chilton.

--Chilton's Emission Control Manual 1986-87 Domestic Cars: 1986-87 Domestic Cars, Motor-Age Professional Mechanics Edition (Supplement) LC 85-47954. 336p. 1986. pap. 30.00 (ISBN 0-8019-7693-6). Chilton.

--Chilton's Emission Control Manual 1986-87 Import Cars: 1986-87 Import Cars, Motor-Age Professional Mechanics Edition (Supplement) LC 85-47953. 336p. 1986. pap. 30.00 (ISBN 0-8019-7694-4). Chilton.

--Chilton's Illustrated Diagnostic Manual. LC 85-47988. 1986. pap. 30.00 (ISBN 0-8019-7689-8). Chilton.

--Chilton's Import Car Repair Manual: 1980-87. LC 80-68280. 1488p. 1986. 21.95 (ISBN 0-8019-7672-3); slipcase 22.70 (ISBN 0-8019-7673-1). Chilton.

--Chilton's Import Car Repair Manual 1979-86: 1979-86 Motor-Age Professional Mechanics Edition. LC 82-72910. 1848p. 1986. 46.00 (ISBN 0-8019-7638-3). Chilton.

--Chilton's Motorcycle & ATV Repair Manual: 1945-85. LC 85-47957. 1456p. 1986. 27.95 (ISBN 0-8019-7635-9); slipcase 28.70 (ISBN 0-8019-7636-7). Chilton.

--Chilton's Parts & Labor Guide: 1983-87, Motor-Age Professional Mechanic's Edition. LC 82-72943. 1688p. 1986. 48.00 (ISBN 0-8019-7691-X). Chilton.

--Chilton's Repair & Tune-up Guide: Cadillac 1967-86. LC 85-47984. 314p. (Orig.). 1986. pap. 12.50 (ISBN 0-8019-7684-7). Chilton.

--Chilton's Repair & Tune-up Guide: Chevy-GMC Pickups & Suburban 1970-86. LC 85-47966. 312p. (Orig.). 1986. pap. 12.50 (ISBN 0-8019-7665-0). Chilton.

--Chilton's Repair & Tune-up Guide: Chevrolet Mid-Size 1964-86. LC 85-47968. 336p. (Orig.). 1986. pap. 12.50 (ISBN 0-8019-7677-4). Chilton.

--Chilton's Repair & Tune-up Guide: Chevrolet Nova 1985. LC 85-47959. 188p. (Orig.). 1986. pap. 12.50 (ISBN 0-8019-7658-8). Chilton.

--Chilton's Repair & Tune-up Guide: Chevette-Pontiac T1000 1976-86. LC 85-47967. 256p. (Orig.). 1986. pap. 12.50 (ISBN 0-8019-7666-9). Chilton.

--Chilton's Repair & Tune-up Guide: Datsun-Nissan F-10, 310 & Stanza 1970-85. LC 85-47961. 256p. (Orig.). 1986. pap. 12.50 (ISBN 0-8019-7660-X). Chilton.

--Chilton's Repair & Tune-up Guide: Datsun-Nissan Z & ZX 1970-86. LC 85-47965. 256p. (Orig.). 1986. pap. 12.50 (ISBN 0-8019-7664-2). Chilton.

--Chilton's Repair & Tune-up Guide: Datsun-Nissan 1200, 210, Sentra & Pulsar 1970-86. LC 85-47969. 264p. (Orig.). 1986. pap. 12.50 (ISBN 0-8019-7679-0). Chilton.

--Chilton's Repair & Tune-up Guide: Datsun-Nissan 200SX, 510, 610, 710, 810 Maxima 1973-1986. LC 85-47980. 336p. (Orig.). 1986. pap. 12.50 (ISBN 0-8019-7680-4). Chilton.

--Chilton's Repair & Tune-up Guide: Dodge-Plymouth Trucks 1967-86. LC 85-47983. 288p. (Orig.). 1986. pap. 12.50 (ISBN 0-8019-7683-9). Chilton.

--Chilton's Repair & Tune-up Guide: Dodge-Plymouth Vans 1967-86. LC 85-47986. 336p. (Orig.). 1986. pap. 12.50 (ISBN 0-8019-7686-3). Chilton.

--Chilton's Repair & Tune-up Guide: Ford Pickups 1965-86. LC 85-47964. 356p. (Orig.). 1986. pap. 12.50 (ISBN 0-8019-7662-6). Chilton.

--Chilton's Repair & Tune-up Guide: Ford Vans 1961-86. LC 85-47964. 356p. (Orig.). 1986. pap. 12.50 (ISBN 0-8019-7663-4). Chilton.

--Chilton's Repair & Tune-up Guide: GM N-Body 1985-86 Buick, Somerset, Olds Calais & Pontiac Grand Am. LC 85-47958. 224p. (Orig.). 1986. pap. 12.50 (ISBN 0-8019-7657-X). Chilton.

--Chilton's Repair & Tune-up Guide: Honda 1973-86. LC 85-47978. 304p. (Orig.). 1986. pap. 12.50 (ISBN 0-8019-7676-6). Chilton.

--Chilton's Repair & Tune-up Guide: Jeep CJ 1945-85. LC 85-47977. 388p. (Orig.). 1986. pap. 12.50 (ISBN 0-8019-7675-8). Chilton.

--Chilton's Repair & Tune-up Guide: Mazda Pickup 1971-86. LC 85-47960. 312p. (Orig.). 1986. pap. 12.50 (ISBN 0-8019-7659-6). Chilton.

--Chilton's Repair & Tune-up Guide: Omni, Horizon, Rampage 1978-86. LC 85-47985. 256p. (Orig.). 1986. pap. 12.50 (ISBN 0-8019-7685-5). Chilton.

--Chilton's Repair & Tune-up Guide: Outboard Motors 0-65 HP 1975-85. LC 85-47974. 512p. (Orig.). 1986. pap. 16.95 (ISBN 0-8019-7630-8). Chilton.

--Chilton's Repair & Tune-up Guide: Outboard Motors 70 HP & Above 1975-1985. LC 85-47975. 512p. (Orig.). 1986. pap. 16.95 (ISBN 0-8019-7631-6). Chilton.

--Chilton's Repair & Tune-up Guide: Subaru 1970-86. LC 85-47979. 304p. (Orig.). 1986. pap. 12.50 (ISBN 0-8019-7678-2). Chilton.

--Chilton's Repair & Tune-up Guide: Toyota Trucks 1970-86. LC 85-47962. 288p. (Orig.). 1986. pap. 12.50 (ISBN 0-8019-7661-8). Chilton.

--Chilton's Repair & Tune-up Manual: Corvette 1963-83. LC 85-47981. 264p. (Orig.). 1986. pap. 12.50 (ISBN 0-8019-7681-2). Chilton.

--Chilton's Service Bay Handbook: 1980-87. LC 85-47989. 148p. 1986. pap. 5.00 (ISBN 0-8019-7692-8). Chilton.

--Chilton's Truck & Van Repair Manual: 1979-86. LC 81-70221. 1344p. 1986. 21.95 (ISBN 0-8019-7655-3); slipcase 22.70 (ISBN 0-8019-7656-1). Chilton.

--Chilton's Truck & Van Repair Manual: 1980-86 Motor-Age Professional Mechanics Edition. LC 82-71518. 1848p. 1986. 47.50 (ISBN 0-8019-7688-X). Chilton.

--Chilton's Wiring Diagram Manual 1984-86 Import Cars: 1984-86 IMport Cars, Motor-Age Professional Mechanics Edition. LC 85-47955. 1088p. 1986. pap. 59.00 (ISBN 0-8019-7642-1). Chilton.

--Chilton's Wiring Diagram Manual: 1985-86 Domestic Cars, Motor-Age Professional Mechanics Edition. 1512p. 1986. pap. 47.00 (ISBN 0-8019-7641-3). Chilton.

--Corvette: 1984-86. LC 85-47982. 224p. (Orig.). 1986. pap. 12.50 (ISBN 0-8019-7682-0). Chilton.

--General Motors Diagnosis & Repair (GMDR) LC 85-47972. (Orig.). 1986. pap. price not set (ISBN 0-8019-7669-3). Chilton.

--Guide to Appliance Repair. LC 85-47987. 624p. (Orig.). 1986. pap. 16.95 (ISBN 0-8019-7687-1). Chilton.

--Guide to Auto Body Repair & Painting. LC 85-47970. 304p. (Orig.). 1986. pap. 16.95 (ISBN 0-8019-7667-7). Chilton.

--Guide to Diagnosis & Repair of GM Cars & Trucks 1970-85. (Orig.). 1986. pap. 16.95 (ISBN 0-8019-7668-5). Chilton.

--Guide to Emission Diagnosis, Tune-up & Alignment: 1975-78. LC 85-47973. 544p. (Orig.). 1986. pap. 16.95 (ISBN 0-8019-7701-0). Chilton.

--Toyota Corona, Cressida, Crown, Mark II, Camry, Van: 1970-86. LC 85-47976. 312p. (Orig.). 1986. pap. 12.50 (ISBN 0-8019-7674-X). Chilton.

Chilton, Stuart, ed. Selected Readings in Education Adminstration. 141p. 1970. pap. text ed. 9.95x (ISBN 0-8290-1094-7). Irvington.

Chilton, Thomas. Strong Water: Nitric Acid, Its Sources, Methods of Manufacture, & Uses. 1968. 16.50x (ISBN 0-262-03023-3). MIT Pr.

Chilton's Automotive Editorial Staff. Chilton's Motor Age Professional Transmission Manual. 1980. 65.00x (ISBN 0-8019-6927-1). Chilton.

--AMC, Nineteen Seventy to Nineteen Eighty-Two. 1982. pap. 11.95 (ISBN 0-8019-7199-3). Chilton.

--Auto Heating & Air Conditioning Manual 1982-1985. LC 84-45460. (Motor Age Professional Mechanics Ser.). 1148p. 1985. 36.00 (ISBN 0-8019-7594-8). Chilton.

--Automotive Service Manual 1982-86. LC 82-72944. (Motor Age Professional Mechanics Ser.). 1632p. 1985. 39.00 (ISBN 0-8019-7597-2). Chilton.

--Buick Century-Regal 1975-85. LC 84-45479. 256p. (Orig.). 1985. pap. 11.95 (ISBN 0-8019-7570-0). Chilton.

--Buick-Olds-Pontiac 1975-85. LC 84-45490. 320p. (Orig.). 1985. pap. 11.95 (ISBN 0-8019-7560-3). Chilton.

--Cadillac Nineteen Sixty-Seven to Nineteen Eighty Four: RTUG. LC 83-45304. 288p. 1984. pap. 11.95 (ISBN 0-8019-7462-3). Chilton.

--Camaro, 1967-1981. (Illus.). 1981. pap. 11.95 (ISBN 0-8019-7045-8). Chilton.

--Camaro, 1982-1985. LC 84-45480. 208p. (Orig.). 1985. pap. 11.95 (ISBN 0-8019-7569-7). Chilton.

--Cavalier: Cimarron, J-2000, 1982. (Illus.). 1981. pap. 11.95 (ISBN 0-8019-7059-8). Chilton.

--Chevette-T-1000, 1976-1982. 1982. pap. 11.95 (ISBN 0-8019-7162-4). Chilton.

--Chevette T-1000 1976-84. LC 83-45300. 212p. 1984. pap. 11.95 (ISBN 0-8019-7457-7). Chilton.

--Chevrolet-GMC Pick-Ups 1970-82: RTUG. LC 83-45311. 352p. 1984. pap. 11.95 (ISBN 0-8019-7468-2). Chilton.

--Chevrolet GMC Pick-Ups 1970-84: RTUG - Includes Suburban. LC 83-45306. 312p. 1984. pap. 11.95 (ISBN 0-8019-7464-X). Chilton.

--Chevrolet-GMC Vans, 1967-1982. 1982. pap. 11.95 (ISBN 0-8019-7169-1). Chilton.

--Chevrolet-GMC Vans 1967-84: RTUG. LC 83-45322. 248p. 1985. pap. 11.95 (ISBN 0-8019-7487-9). Chilton.

--Chevrolet Mid-Size 1964-84. LC 83-45299. 304p. 1984. pap. 11.95 (ISBN 0-8019-7456-9). Chilton.

--Chevrolet: Nineteen Sixty-Eight to Nineteen Eighty-One. (Illus.). 1981. pap. 11.95 (ISBN 0-8019-7135-7). Chilton.

--Chevrolet, Nineteen Sixty-Eight to Nineteen Seventy-Nine. LC 78-20251. (Chilton's Repair & Tune-Up Guides). (Illus.). 1979. pap. text ed. 11.95 (ISBN 0-8019-6839-9, 6839). Chilton.

--Chevrolet 1968-85. LC 84-45467. 272p. (Orig.). 1985. pap. 11.95 (ISBN 0-8019-7588-3). Chilton.

--Chevy S-10 Blazer, S-15 Jimmy 1982-85. LC 84-45482. 224p. (Orig.). 1985. pap. 11.95 (ISBN 0-8019-7568-9). Chilton.

--Chevy S-10, GMC S15 Pick Up 1982-85. LC 84-45486. 224p. (Orig.). 1985. pap. 11.95 (ISBN 0-8019-7564-6). Chilton.

--Chevy Two & Nova, Nineteen Sixty-Two to Nineteen Seventy-Nine. LC 78-20253. (Chilton's Repair & Tune-up Guides). (Illus.). 1979. pap. 11.95 (ISBN 0-8019-6841-0, 6841). Chilton.

--Chilton's Auto Repair Manual, 1940-1953 Ed. LC 54-17274. (Illus.). 1971. Repr. of 1953 ed. 22.95 (ISBN 0-8019-5631-5). Chilton.

--Chilton's Auto Repair Manual, 1954-1963 Ed. LC 54-17274. (Illus.). 1971. 22.95 (ISBN 0-8019-5652-8). Chilton.

--Chilton's Auto Repair Manual, 1964-1971. LC 54-17274. (Illus.). 1536p. 1974. 22.95 (ISBN 0-8019-5974-8). Chilton.

--Chilton's Auto Repair Manual 1979-86. LC 76-648878. 1344p. 1985. shrink 21.95 (ISBN 0-8019-7575-1); hollow 22.75 (ISBN 0-8019-7574-3). Chilton.

--Chilton's Auto Repair Manual, 1980. LC 76-648878. (Chilton's Do-It Yourself Repair Manuals). (Illus.). 1979. 15.95. Chilton.

--Chilton's Auto Service Manual 1979-84. LC 82-72944. (Motor-Age Professional Mechanics Edition Ser.). 1824p. 1983. 33.00 (ISBN 0-8019-7348-1). Chilton.

--Chilton's Auto Service Manual 1979-85. LC 83-45331. (Motor Age Professional Mechanics Edition Ser.). 1632p. 1985. text ed. 36.00 (ISBN 0-8019-7495-X). Chilton.

--Chilton's Automatic Transmission Service Manual: 1980-84. LC 83-45327. 1536p. 1984. pap. 54.00 (ISBN 0-8019-7390-2). Chilton.

--Chilton's B.E.S.T. Service Manual: Brakes, Exhaust, Suspension & Steering Tune Up. LC 83-70521. (Motor Age Professional Mechanics Edition Ser.). 480p. 1983. pap. 17.00 (ISBN 0-8019-7398-8). Chilton.

--Chilton's Datsun Pick-Ups: 1970-1979 Repair & Tune-up Guide. LC 78-20245. (Repair & Tune-up Guides Ser.). 1979. pap. 11.95 (ISBN 0-8019-6816-X). Chilton.

--Chilton's Diesel Engine Service Manual 1978-84. LC 83-45326. (Motor Age Professional Mechanics Edition). 1216p. 1984. text ed. 37.50 (ISBN 0-8019-7444-5). Chilton.

--Chilton's Easy Car Care Study Guide. LC 83-70015. 64p. (gr. 12). 1984. pap. 6.60 (ISBN 0-8019-7380-5). Chilton.

--Chilton's Emission Diagnostic Manual: Import Cars 1983-84. LC 83-45334. (Motor Age Professional Mechanics Edition Ser.). 480p. 1984. pap. 20.00 (ISBN 0-8019-7491-7). Chilton.

--Chilton's Emission Diagnostic Manual 1983-84. LC 83-45333. (Motor Age Professional Mechanics Edition Ser.). 480p. 1984. pap. 20.00 (ISBN 0-8019-7497-6). Chilton.

--Chilton's Farm & Utility Tractor Repair Manual 6 to 30 PTO Horsepower. (Illus.). 1981. 22.95 (ISBN 0-8019-7057-1). Chilton.

--Chilton's GM Diagnosis & Repair Manual. LC 83-70014. 624p. 1983. pap. 17.95 (ISBN 0-8019-7374-0). Chilton.

--Chilton's Guide to Auto Body Repair & Painting. LC 83-70543. 197p. 1983. pap. 11.95 (ISBN 0-8019-7378-3). Chilton.

--Chilton's Guide to Auto Electronic Accessories: Sound, Safety & Security. LC 82-72906. 224p. 1983. pap. 11.95 (ISBN 0-8019-7322-8). Chilton.

--Chilton's Guide to Auto Tune-Up & Troubleshooting. LC 83-70544. 220p. 1983. pap. 11.95 (ISBN 0-8019-7376-7). Chilton.

--Chilton's Guide to Diesel Cars & Trucks. LC 82-72915. 216p. 1983. pap. 11.95 (ISBN 0-8019-7377-5). Chilton.

--Chilton's Guide to Small Engine Repair 6-20HP. LC 82-72908. 304p. 1983. 12.95 (ISBN 0-8019-7333-3); pap. 11.95 (ISBN 0-8019-7334-1). Chilton.

--Chilton's Guide to Small Engine Repair: Up to Six Horse Power. LC 82-72907. 350p. 1983. 12.95 (ISBN 0-8019-7319-8); pap. 11.95 (ISBN 0-8019-7320-1). Chilton.

--Chilton's Guide to Small Engine Repair: Up to Twenty Horse Power. LC 83-70013. 250p. 1983. pap. 11.95 (ISBN 0-8019-7379-1). Chilton.

--Chilton's Guide to Turbocharged Cars & Trucks. LC 83-45309. 248p. 1984. pap. 11.95 (ISBN 0-8019-7397-X). Chilton.

--Chilton's Illustrated Diagnostic Manual. LC 83-70019. (Motor-Age Professional Mechanics Edition Ser.). 624p. 1983. pap. 20.00 (ISBN 0-8019-7375-9). Chilton.

--Chilton's Import Auto Parts & Labor Guide 1976-83. LC 82-72911. (Motor-Age Professional Mechanics Edition Ser.). 1488p. 1983. 34.00 (ISBN 0-8019-7351-1). Chilton.

--Chilton's Import Auto Repair Manual 1977-84. LC 78-20243. 1488p. 1983. 20.95 (ISBN 0-8019-7328-7). Chilton.

--Chilton's Import Auto Service Manual 1976-83. LC 82-72910. (Motor-Age Professional Mechanics Edition Ser.). 1920p. 1983. 33.00 (ISBN 0-8019-7350-3). Chilton.

Chilton's Automotive Editorial Staff, ed. Chilton's Import Car Repair Manual, 1975-81. LC 78-20243. (Illus.). 1536p. 1981. 19.95 (ISBN 0-8019-7029-6). Chilton.

Chilton's Automotive Editorial Staff. Chilton's Import Car Repair Manual 1979-86. LC 78-20243. 1464p. 1985. shrink 21.95 (ISBN 0-8019-7577-8); hollow 22.75 (ISBN 0-8019-7578-6). Chilton.

--Chilton's Import Car Repair Manual 1985. LC 78-20243. 1468p. 1984. 20.95 (ISBN 0-8019-7473-9); 21.75 (ISBN 0-8019-7474-7); pap. cancelled. Chilton.

--Chilton's Import Car Wiring Diagram Manual 1978-84. LC 83-70545. (Motor-Age Professional Mechanics Edition Ser.). 1000p. 1983. pap. 49.00 (ISBN 0-8019-7389-9). Chilton.

--Chilton's Labor Guide & Parts Manual 1979-85. LC 83-45332. (Motor Age Professional Mechanics Edition Ser.). 1632p. 1985. text ed. 38.00 (ISBN 0-8019-7496-8). Chilton.

--Chilton's Light Truck & Van Wiring Diagram Manual 1980-98: Moter-Age Professional Mechanic's Edition. LC 85-47806. 1200p. 1985. pap. 49.00 (ISBN 0-8019-7634-0). Chilton.

--Chilton's Mechanics Handbook, 2 vols. Incl. Vol. 1. Emission Diagnosis, Tune-Up, Allignment. pap.; Vol. 2. Engine Rebuilding, Engine Repair, Engine Theory (ISBN 0-8019-7006-7). pap.. (Illus.). 1980. 16.95 ea.; pap. 14.95 ea. Chilton.

--Chilton's Mechanics Handbook: Emission, Tune-Up & Vacuum Diagrams, Vol. 7. LC 82-72909. 544p. 1983. pap. 14.95 (ISBN 0-8019-7324-4). Chilton.

--Chilton's Mechanics's Handbook, Vol. 4: Automatic Transmission Repair. (Illus.). 1981. pap. 14.95 (ISBN 0-8019-7060-1). Chilton.

--Chilton's Mercedes-Benz: 1974-1979, Repair & Tune-up Guide. LC 78-22141. (Repair & Tune-up Guides Ser.). (Illus.). 1979. pap. 11.95 (ISBN 0-8019-6809-7). Chilton.

--Chilton's Motor Professional Automotive Service Manual 1981. LC 54-17274. (Illus.). 1980. 26.00 (ISBN 0-8019-6976-X). Chilton.

--Chilton's Motor Professional Labor Guide & Parts Manual 1981. LC 78-66360. (Illus.). 1980. 29.00 (ISBN 0-8019-7005-9). Chilton.

--Chilton's Motorcycle Owner's Handbook. (Illus.). 1979. pap. 9.95 (ISBN 0-8019-6867-4, 795). Chilton.

--Chilton's Motorcycle Troubleshooting Guide. 2nd ed. LC 77-121. 1977. pap. 11.95 (ISBN 0-8019-6587-X, 6587). Chilton.

--Chilton's Mustang II: 1974-1978, Repair & Tune-up Guide. LC 78-22143. (Repair & Tune-up Guides Ser.). (Illus.). 1979. pap. 11.95 (ISBN 0-8019-6812-7). Chilton.

--Chilton's Parts & Labor Guide 1978-84. LC 82-72943. (Motor-Age Professional Mechanics Edition Ser.). 1568p. 1984. 34.00 (ISBN 0-8019-7347-3). Chilton.

--Chilton's Professional Import Labor Guide & Parts Manual, 1981. (Illus.). 1981. 29.00 (ISBN 0-8019-6998-0). Chilton.

--Chilton's Professional Labor Guide & Parts Manual, 1981. (Illus.). 1981. 29.00 (ISBN 0-8019-7005-9). Chilton.

--Chilton's Professional Mechanics Reference Guide. LC 82-72913. 128p. 1983. pap. 5.00 (ISBN 0-8019-7349-X). Chilton.

--Chilton's Professional Wiring Diagrams Manual: American Cars 1979 to 1981. (Illus.). 1981. pap. 34.00 (ISBN 0-8019-7020-2). Chilton.

--Chilton's Repair & Tune-Up Guide: Blazer-Jimmy 1983. LC 83-70018. 224p. 1983. pap. 11.95 (ISBN 0-8019-7383-X). Chilton.

--Chilton's Repair & Tune-Up Guide: BMW 1970-82. LC 82-72937. 272p. 1983. pap. 11.95 (ISBN 0-8019-7315-5). Chilton.

--Chilton's Repair & Tune-Up Guide: Buick Century-Regal 1975-83. LC 82-72929. 224p. 1983. pap. 11.95 (ISBN 0-8019-7307-4). Chilton.

--Chilton's Repair & Tune-Up Guide: Buick-Olds-Pontiac Full Size 1975-83. LC 82-72930. 308p. 1983. pap. 11.95 (ISBN 0-8019-7308-2). Chilton.

--Chilton's Repair & Tune-Up Guide: Camaro 1982-83. LC 82-72939. 217p. 1983. pap. 11.95 (ISBN 0-8019-7317-1). Chilton.

--Chilton's Repair & Tune-Up Guide: Champ-Arrow-Sapporo 1978-83. LC 82-72939. 224p. 1983. pap. 11.95 (ISBN 0-8019-7344-9). Chilton.

--Chilton's Repair & Tune-Up Guide: Chevrolet-GMC S-10, S-15 1982-83. LC 82-72932. 224p. 1983. pap. 11.95 (ISBN 0-8019-7310-4). Chilton.

--Chilton's Repair & Tune-Up Guide: Chevrolet 1968-83. LC 82-72935. 288p. 1983. pap. 11.95 (ISBN 0-8019-7313-9). Chilton.

--Chilton's Repair & Tune-Up Guide: Colt-Challenger 1971-83. LC 82-72925. 224p. 1983. pap. 11.95 (ISBN 0-8019-7343-0). Chilton.

--Chilton's Repair & Tune-Up Guide: Corvette 1963-84. LC 83-45315. 288p. 1984. pap. 11.95 (ISBN 0-8019-7480-1). Chilton.

--Chilton's Repair & Tune-Up Guide: Firebird 1982-83. LC 82-72927. 217p. 1983. pap. 11.95 (ISBN 0-8019-7345-7). Chilton.

--Chilton's Repair & Tune-up Guide for Audi, 1970-1973. (Illus.). 190p. 1973. pap. 11.95 (ISBN 0-8019-5902-0). Chilton.

--Chilton's Repair & Tune-up Guide for Barracuda & Challenger: 1965-1972. LC 72-7036. (Illus.). 128p. 1972. pap. 11.95 (ISBN 0-8019-5807-5). Chilton.

--Chilton's Repair & Tune-up Guide: For Blazer-Jimmy, 1969-1977. LC 76-53144. (Chilton's Repair & Tune up Guides). 1977. pap. 11.95 (ISBN 0-8019-6558-6). Chilton.

--Chilton's Repair & Tune-up Guide: Ford Bronco 1966-83. LC 82-72919. 288p. 1983. pap. 11.95 (ISBN 0-8019-7337-6). Chilton.

--Chilton's Repair & Tune-up Guide for Chevrolet 1968-1977. LC 76-57317. (Chilton's Repair & Tune-up Guides). (Illus., Orig.). 1977. pap. 11.95 (ISBN 0-8019-6615-9, 6615). Chilton.

Chilton's Automotive Editorial Staff, ed. Chilton's Repair & Tune-up Guide for Colt, 1971-1976. (Illus.). 1976. pap. 11.95 (ISBN 0-8019-6475-X). Chilton.

Chilton's Automotive Editorial Staff. Chilton's Repair & Tune-Up Guide: Ford Courier 1972-82. LC 82-72923. 232p. 1983. pap. 11.95 (ISBN 0-8019-7341-4). Chilton.

--Chilton's Repair & Tune-up Guide for Cutlass-442, 1970-1977. LC 77-89117. (Chilton's Repair & Tune-up Guides). (Illus., Orig.). 1978. pap. 11.95 (ISBN 0-8019-6597-7, 6597). Chilton.

--Chilton's Repair & Tune-up Guide for Dodge Dart & Demon, 1968-1976. (Illus.). 190p. 1976. pap. 11.95 (ISBN 0-8019-6324-9). Chilton.

--Chilton's Repair & Tune-up Guide for Datson Pick-Ups, 1970-1975. LC 75-22134. (Illus.). 180p. 1975. pap. 11.95 (ISBN 0-8019-6333-8). Chilton.

--Chilton's Repair & Tune-up Guide for Dodge 1968-1977. LC 77-71635. (Chilton's Repair & Tune-up Guides Ser.). (Illus.). 1977. pap. 11.95 (ISBN 0-8019-6554-3). Chilton.

--Chilton's Repair & Tune-up Guide for Datsun: 1961-1972. LC 72-188664. (Illus.). 1972. pap. 11.95 (ISBN 0-8019-5790-7). Chilton.

--Chilton's Repair & Tune-up Guide for Datsun 240-260-280z, 1970-1977. LC 77-85345. (Chilton's Repair & Tune-up Guides). (Illus., Orig.). 1977. pap. 11.95 (ISBN 0-8019-6638-8, 6638). Chilton.

--Chilton's Repair & Tune-up Guide for Fairlane & Torino, 1962-1975. (Illus.). 250p. 1975. pap. 11.95 (ISBN 0-8019-6320-6). Chilton.

--Chilton's Repair & Tune-up Guide for Ford Courier 1972-78. (Repair & Tune-up Guides Ser.). (Illus.). pap. 11.95 (ISBN 0-8019-6723-6). Chilton.

--Chilton's Repair & Tune-up Guide for Ford Vans 1966-1977. LC 76-57320. (Chilton's Repair & Tune-up Guides). (Illus., Orig.). 1977. pap. 11.95 (ISBN 0-8019-6585-3, 6585). Chilton.

--Chilton's Repair & Tune-Up Guide for Honda 350-550, 1972-1977. LC 77-89115. (Chilton's Repair & Tune-up Guides). (Illus., Orig.). 1977. pap. 10.95 (ISBN 0-8019-6603-5, 6603). Chilton.

--Chilton's Repair & Tune-up Guide for Maverick & Comet 1970-1977. LC 77-75991. (Chilton's Repair & Tune-up Guides). (Illus., Orig.). 1977. pap. 11.95 (ISBN 0-8019-6634-5, 6634). Chilton.

--Chilton's Repair & Tune-up Guide for Mercedes-Benz: 1961-1970. LC 70-131236. (Illus.). 1970. pap. 11.95 (ISBN 0-8019-6065-7). Chilton.

--Chilton's Repair & Tune-up Guide for Mercedes Benz 2, 1968-1973. (Illus.). 224p. 1974. pap. 11.95 (ISBN 0-8019-5907-1). Chilton.

--Chilton's Repair & Tune-up Guide for Mazda 1971-78. (Repair & Tune-up Guides Ser.). (Illus.). 1978. pap. 11.95 (ISBN 0-8019-6746-5). Chilton.

--Chilton's Repair & Tune-Up Guide: Ford-Mercury 1968-83. LC 82-72940. 288p. 1983. pap. 11.95 (ISBN 0-8019-7318-X). Chilton.

--Chilton's Repair & Tune-up Guide for Road Runner, Satellite, Belvedere, GTX, 1968-1973. LC 73-4347. (Illus.). 224p. 1973. pap. 11.95 (ISBN 0-8019-5821-0). Chilton.

--Chilton's Repair & Tune-up Guide for Rabbit-Scirocco 1975-1978. (Repair & Tune-up Guides Ser.). (Illus.). 1978. pap. 11.95 (ISBN 0-8019-6736-8). Chilton.
--Chilton's Repair & Tune-up Guide: Ford Ranger 1983. LC 82-72920. 240p. 1983. pap. 11.95 (ISBN 0-8019-7338-4). Chilton.
--Chilton's Repair & Tune-up Guide for Tempest, GTO & Le Mans, 1968-1973. LC 73-10219. (Illus.). 190p. 1973. pap. 11.95 (ISBN 0-8019-5905-5). Chilton.
--Chilton's Repair & Tune-up Guide for Triumph 2, 1969-1973. LC 73-18387. (Illus.). 224p. 1974. pap. 11.95 (ISBN 0-8019-5910-1). Chilton.
--Chilton's Repair & Tune-up Guide for Valiant & Duster, 1968-1976. (Illus.). 190p. 1975. pap. 10.95 (ISBN 0-8019-6326-5). Chilton.
--Chilton's Repair & Tune-up Guide for Volkswagen: 1949-1971. LC 74-154691. (Illus.). 212p. 1971. pap. 11.95 (ISBN 0-8019-5796-6). Chilton.
--Chilton's Repair & Tune-Up Guide: GM A-Body (Front Wheel Drive) 1982-83. LC 82-72931. 177p. 1983. pap. 11.95 (ISBN 0-8019-7309-0). Chilton.
--Chilton's Repair & Tune-Up Guide: GM X-Body 1980-83. LC 82-72917. 256p. 1983. pap. 11.95 (ISBN 0-8019-7335-X). Chilton.
--Chilton's Repair & Tune-Up Guide: Granada-Monarch 1975-83. LC 82-72933. 260p. 1983. pap. 11.95 (ISBN 0-8019-7311-2). Chilton.
--Chilton's Repair & Tune-up Guide: Pontiac Mid-Size 1974-83. LC 82-72928. 288p. 1983. pap. 11.95 (ISBN 0-8019-7346-5). Chilton.
--Chilton's Repair & Tune-up Guide: Toyota Corona, Crown, Cressida, Mark II, Camry 1970-84. LC 88-70268. 288p. 1984. pap. 11.95 (ISBN 0-8019-7342-2). Chilton.
--Chilton's Repair & Tune-Up Guide: Toyota Corolla, Carina Tercel, Starlet 1970-83. LC 82-72938. 240p. 1983. pap. 11.95 (ISBN 0-8019-7316-3). Chilton.
--Chilton's Repair & Tune-Up Guide: Toyota Celica-Supra 1971-83. LC 82-72936. 328p. 1983. pap. 11.95 (ISBN 0-8019-7314-7). Chilton.
--Chilton's Repair & Tune-up Guide: Toyota Truck 1970-83. LC 82-72918. 288p. 1983. pap. 11.95 (ISBN 0-8019-7336-8). Chilton.
--Chilton's Repair & Tune-Up Guide: Volvo 1970-83. LC 82-72922. 304p. 1983. pap. 11.95 (ISBN 0-8019-7340-6). Chilton.
--Chilton's Repair & Tune up Guide: VW Front Wheel Drive 1974-83. LC 82-72921. 288p. 1982. pap. 11.95 (ISBN 0-8019-7339-2). Chilton.
--Chilton's Service Bay Handbook 1977-84. LC 83-45330. (Motor Age Professional Mechanics Edition Ser.). 148p. 1984. pap. 5.00 (ISBN 0-8019-7494-1). Chilton.
--Chilton's Small Engine Repair Activity Guide. LC 83-70016. 64p. 1985. pap. 6.60 (ISBN 0-8019-7381-3). Chilton.
--Chilton's Small Engines: Repair & Tune-up Guide. 2nd ed. LC 78-21829. (Repair & Tune-up Guides Ser.). (Illus.). 1979. pap. 11.95 (ISBN 0-8019-6811-9). Chilton.
--Chilton's Spanish Language Edition of Chilton's Easy Car Care. 2nd ed. (Illus.). 1983. 12.95 (ISBN 0-8019-7085-7). Chilton.
--Chilton's Spanish Language Edition of Chevrolet 1968 to 1979 Repair & Tune-up Guide. (Illus.). 1981. 11.95 (ISBN 0-8019-7082-2). Chilton.
--Chilton's Spanish Language Edition of Datsun 1973 to 1980 Repair & Tune-up Guide. (Illus.). 1981. 11.95 (ISBN 0-8019-7083-0). Chilton.
--Chilton's Spanish Language Edition of Ford 1968 to 1979 Repair & Tune-up Guide. (Illus.). 304p. 1981. 11.95 (ISBN 0-8019-7084-9). Chilton.
--Chilton's Spanish Language Edition of Volkswagen 1970 to 1979 Repair Tune-up Guide. (Illus.). 1981. 11.95 (ISBN 0-8019-7081-4). Chilton.
--Chilton's Truck & Van Repair Manual 1977-84. LC 77-16756. 1464p. 1984. sw 20.75 (ISBN 0-8019-7357-0); hw o.p. 21.75. Chilton.
--Chilton's Truck & Van Service Manual 1978-84. LC 82-71518. (Motor Age Professional Mechanics Edition). 1632p. 1984. text ed. 37.50 (ISBN 0-8019-7358-9). Chilton.
--Chilton's Wiring Diagram Manual: Domestic Cars 1982-84. LC 83-45329. (Motor Age Professional Mechanics Edition). 1200p. 1984. text ed. 37.00 (ISBN 0-8019-7493-3). Chilton.
--Chrysler K-Car Nineteen Eighty-One to Nineteen Eighty-Five. LC 84-45488. 224p. (Orig.). 1985. pap. 11.95 (ISBN 0-8019-7562-X). Chilton.
--Colt-Challenger-Vista, 1971-85. LC 84-45471. 256p. (Orig.). 1985. pap. 11.95 (ISBN 0-8019-7584-0). Chilton.
--Cutlass 1970-85. LC 84-45464. 296p. (Orig.). 1985. pap. 11.95 (ISBN 0-8019-7591-3). Chilton.
--Datsun F-Ten, Three Ten, & Nissan Stanza, Nineteen Seventy-Seven to Nineteen Eighty-Two. 1982. pap. 11.95 (ISBN 0-8019-7196-9). Chilton.
--Datsun Pick-Ups, 1970 to 1981. (Illus.). 1981. pap. 11.95 (ISBN 0-8019-7050-4). Chilton.
--Datsun Pick-Ups 1970-84. LC 84-45483. 272p. (Orig.). 1985. pap. 11.95 (ISBN 0-8019-7567-0). Chilton.
--Datsun Two Ten & Twelve Hundred, Nineteen Seventy-Three to Nineteen Eighty-Two. 1982. pap. 11.95 (ISBN 0-8019-7197-7). Chilton.
--Datsun Z & ZX, Nineteen Seventy to Nineteen Eighty-Two. 1982. pap. 11.95 (ISBN 0-8019-7172-1). Chilton.
--Datsun Z & ZX 1970-84: RTUG. LC 83-45308. 224p. 1984. pap. 11.95 (ISBN 0-8019-7466-6). Chilton.
--Datsun 1200, 210 & Nissan Sentra 1973-84: RTUG. LC 83-45325. 112p. 1984. pap. 11.95 (ISBN 0-8019-7490-9). Chilton.
--Datsun 200 SX, 510, 610, 710, 810, 1973-84: RTUG. LC 83-45313. 212p. 1984. pap. 11.95 (ISBN 0-8019-7478-X). Chilton.
--Dodge - Plymouth Vans 1967-84: RTUG. LC 83-45307. 264p. 1984. pap. 11.95 (ISBN 0-8019-7465-8). Chilton.
--Dodge Caravan 1984: RTUG (New Dodge FWD Van) LC 83-45317. 192p. 1984. pap. 11.95 (ISBN 0-8019-7482-8). Chilton.
--Dodge Colt & Challenger Nineteen Seventy-one to Nineteen Eighty-One. LC 80-70346. (Illus.). 242p. 1980. pap. 11.95 (ISBN 0-8019-7037-7). Chilton.
--Dodge D-50-Plymouth Arrow Pickups, 1979 to 1981. (Illus.). 1981. pap. 11.95 (ISBN 0-8019-7032-6). Chilton.
--Dodge-Plymouth Vans, Nineteen Sixty-Seven to Nineteen Eighty-Two. 1982. pap. 11.95 (ISBN 0-8019-7168-3). Chilton.
--Dodge Trucks Nineteen Sixty-Seven through Eighty-Four: RTUG - Includes Pick-Ups, Ramcharger, Trailduster. LC 83-45302. 288p. 1984. pap. 11.95 (ISBN 0-8019-7459-3). Chilton.
--Eighty-Five Test Eighty-Five. 1982. 8.95 (ISBN 0-8019-7278-7). Chilton.
--Escort & Lynx, 1981 to 1982. (Illus.). 1981. pap. 11.95 (ISBN 0-8019-7055-5). Chilton.
--Firebird, Ninteen Sixty-Seven to Nineteen Eighty-One. (Illus.). 1981. pap. 11.95 (ISBN 0-8019-7046-6). Chilton.
--Firebird 1982-85. LC 84-45474. 208p. (Orig.). 1985. pap. 12.50 (ISBN 0-8019-7582-4). Chilton.
--Ford Courier 1972-1980. (Illus.). 1980. pap. 11.95 (ISBN 0-8019-6983-2). Chilton.
--Ford Fiesta, 1978 to 1980. LC 78-20258. (Chilton's Repair & Tune-up Guides). (Illus.). 1979. pap. 11.95 (ISBN 0-8019-6846-1, 6846). Chilton.
--Ford Mercury Mid-Size: 1971-1985. LC 84-45484. 392p. (Orig.). 1985. pap. 11.95 (ISBN 0-8019-7566-2). Chilton.
--Ford Mercury: 1968-1985. LC 84-45476. 288p. (Orig.). 1985. pap. 11.95 (ISBN 0-8019-7573-5). Chilton.
--Ford Pick-Ups: 1965-1982 RTUG. Span. ed. LC 83-45312. 362p. 1984. pap. 11.95 (ISBN 0-8019-7469-0). Chilton.
--Ford Pick-Ups 1965-84: RTUG. LC 83-45303. 312p. 1984. pap. 11.95 (ISBN 0-8019-7461-5). Chilton.
--Ford Vans, Nineteen Sixty-One to Nineteen Eighty-Two. 1982. pap. 11.95 (ISBN 0-8019-7171-3). Chilton.
--Ford Vans 1961-84. LC 83-45301. 308p. 1984. pap. 11.95 (ISBN 0-8019-7458-5). Chilton.
--GM A-Body 1982-85. LC 84-45469. 224p. (Orig.). 1985. pap. 11.95 (ISBN 0-8019-7586-7). Chilton.
--GM C-Body 1985. LC 84-45468. 196p. (Orig.). 1985. pap. 12.50 (ISBN 0-8019-7587-5). Chilton.
--GM J-Car 1982-85. LC 84-45485. 256p. (Orig.). 1985. pap. 11.95 (ISBN 0-8019-7565-4). Chilton.
--GM X-Body, 1980 to 1981. (Illus.). 1981. pap. 11.95 (ISBN 0-8019-7049-0). Chilton.
--GM X-Body 1980-85. LC 84-45462. 240p. (Orig.). 1985. pap. 11.95 (ISBN 0-8019-7592-1). Chilton.
--Honda, 1973-1980. (Illus.). 1980. pap. 11.95 (ISBN 0-8019-6980-8). Chilton.
--Honda 1973-84: RTUG. LC 83-45324. 224p. 1984. pap. 11.95 (ISBN 0-8019-7489-5). Chilton.
--Honda 750 1969-1980. (Illus.). 1980. pap. 10.95 (ISBN 0-8019-6968-9). Chilton.
--Import Automotive Parts & Labor Guide 1975-85. LC 82-72911. (Motor Age Professional Mechanics Ser.). 1428p. 1985. 38.00 (ISBN 0-8019-7596-4). Chilton.
--Import Automotive Service Manual 1977-1985. LC 82-72910. (Professional Mechanics Ser.). 1848p. 1985. 36.00 (ISBN 0-8019-7595-6). Chilton.
--Jeep CJ 1945-1984: RTUG. LC 83-45320. 312p. 1984. pap. 11.95 (ISBN 0-8019-7484-4). Chilton.
--Labor Guide & Parts Manual 1980-86. LC 83-45332. (Motor Age Professional Mechanics Ser.). 1632p. 1985. 41.00 (ISBN 0-8019-7598-0). Chilton.
--Laser-Daytona 1984-85. LC 84-45487. 240p. (Orig.). 1985. pap. 11.95 (ISBN 0-8019-7563-8). Chilton.
--Mazda, 1971-84: RTUG. LC 83-45321. 248p. 1985. pap. 11.95 (ISBN 0-8019-7486-0). Chilton.
--Mechanics Handbook: Air Conditioning, Vol. 9. LC 84-45472. 384p. (Orig.). 1985. pap. 14.95 (ISBN 0-8019-7580-8). Chilton.
--Mechanics Handbook: New Electronic Engine Control, Vol. 8. LC 84-45481. 816p. (Orig.). 1985. pap. 16.95 (ISBN 0-8019-7535-2). Chilton.
--Mechanics' Handbook, Vol. 5: Brakes-Steering-Suspension. 1983. pap. 14.95 (ISBN 0-8019-7205-1). Chilton.
--Mercedes Benz Nineteen Seventy-Four to Nineteen Eighty-Four: RTUG. LC 83-45305. 224p. 1984. pap. 11.95 (ISBN 0-8019-7463-1). Chilton.
--Mitsubishi Cordia, Tredia & Starion 1983-85. LC 84-45473. 256p. (Orig.). 1985. pap. 12.50 (ISBN 0-8019-7583-2). Chilton.
--Motor Age Service Bay Handbook for Mechanics. LC 84-45461. 144p. 1985. pap. 5.00 (ISBN 0-8019-7599-9). Chilton.
--Mustang Capri, Nineteen Seventy-Nine to Nineteen Eighty-Five. LC 84-45470. 272p. (Orig.). 1985. pap. 11.95 (ISBN 0-8019-7585-9). Chilton.
--Omni & Horizon, Nineteen Seventy-Eight to Nineteen Eighty. LC 78-20257. (Chilton's Repair & Tune-Up Guides Ser.). (Illus.). 1979. pap. 11.95 (ISBN 0-8019-6845-3, 6845). Chilton.
--Omni-Horizon 1978-84: RTUG. LC 83-45319. 224p. 1984. pap. 11.95 (ISBN 0-8019-7485-2). Chilton.
--Plymouth Champ-Arrow-& Sapporo, 1977 to 1981. LC 80-70347. (Illus.). 208p. 1981. pap. 11.95 (ISBN 0-8019-7041-5). Chilton.
--Pontiac Fiero: 1984-85. LC 84-45478. 224p. (Orig.). 1985. pap. 11.95 (ISBN 0-8019-7571-9). Chilton.
--Porsche Nine Twenty-Four & Nine Twenty-Eight, 1977-1981. (Illus.). 1981. pap. 11.95 (ISBN 0-8019-7048-2). Chilton.
--Rabbit Scirocio, 1974-1980. (Illus.). 1980. pap. 11.95 (ISBN 0-8019-6962-X). Chilton.
--Renault 1975-85. LC 84-45489. 224p. (Orig.). 1985. pap. 11.95 (ISBN 0-8019-7561-1). Chilton.
--Saab 900 1976-85. LC 84-45477. 272p. (Orig.). 1985. pap. 11.95 (ISBN 0-8019-7572-7). Chilton.
--Snowmobiles, Nineteen Sixty-Nine to Nineteen Eighty. (Illus.). 1981. pap. 11.95 (ISBN 0-8019-6978-6). Chilton.
--Toyota Celica & Supra 1971-84. LC 84-45465. 288p. (Orig.). 1985. pap. 12.50 (ISBN 0-8019-7590-5). Chilton.
--Toyota Corolla, Carina, Tercel & Starlet 1970-84. LC 84-45466. 304p. (Orig.). 1985. pap. 12.50 (ISBN 0-8019-7589-1). Chilton.
--Toyota 1970-79: RTUG. Span. ed. LC 83-45310. 248p. 1984. pap. 12.50 (ISBN 0-8019-7467-4). Chilton.
--Truck & Van Repair Manual 1977-84. LC 77-16756. 1468p. 1984. pap. 20.95 (ISBN 0-8019-7357-0). Chilton.
--Volkswagen, 1970-81. LC 78-20249. (Chilton's Repair & Tune-up Guides Ser.). (Illus.). 1979. pap. 11.95 (ISBN 0-8019-6837-2). Chilton.
--VW Front Wheel Drive 1974-85. LC 84-45463. 256p. (Orig.). 1985. pap. 11.95 (ISBN 0-8019-7593-X). Chilton.
--Yamaha XS360-400 1976-1980. (Illus.). 1981. pap. 10.95 (ISBN 0-8019-6969-7). Chilton.
--Yamaha 650, 1970-79. (Chilton's Repair & Tune-Up Guides). (Illus.). 1979. pap. 10.95 (ISBN 0-8019-6895-X, 6895). Chilton.
--Zephyr 1978-1980. (Illus.). 1980. pap. 11.95 (ISBN 0-8019-6965-4). Chilton.
Chilton'sAutomotive Editorial Staff, ed. Chilton's Mechanics' Handbook: Automobile Sheet Metal Repair, Vol. III. (Illus.). 300p. 1981. pap. 14.95 (ISBN 0-8019-7034-2). Chilton.
Chilver, A. H., jt. auth. see Case, John.
Chilver, G. E. A Historical Commentary on Tacitus' Histories I & II. (Illus.). 1979. text ed. 47.50x (ISBN 0-19-814830-5). Oxford U Pr.
Chilver, G. E. & Townend, G. B. A Historical Commentary on Tacitus' Histories IV & V. 128p. 1985. 24.95x (ISBN 0-19-814852-6). Oxford U Pr.
Chilver, Guy E. Cisalpine Gaul: Social & Economic History from 49 B.C. to the Death of Trajan. LC 75-7308. (Roman History Ser.). (Illus.). 1975. Repr. 21.00x (ISBN 0-405-07190-6). Ayer Co Pubs.
Chilver, J. W. People, Communication & Organisation: A Case Study Approach. (Illus.). 224p. 1984. 24.00 (ISBN 0-08-030838-4); pap. 12.00 (ISBN 0-08-030839-2). Pergamon.
Chilver, P. & Gould, G. Learning & Language in the Classroom: Discussive Talking & Writing Across the Curriculum. 110p. 1982. 22.00 (ISBN 0-08-026777-7). Pergamon.
Chilver, Peter. Teaching Improvised Drama. 1978. 17.95 (ISBN 0-7134-1036-1, Pub. by Batsford England). David & Charles.
Chilvers, Donald & Shewell, Paul. Receivership Manual. 2nd ed. 1982. 110.00x (ISBN 0-85459-070-6, Pub. by Tolley Pub England). State Mutual Bk.
Chilvers, Lloyd & Foster, Robin. The International Sugar Market: Prospects for the 1980s. (EIU Special Report: No. 106). pap. 30.00 (ISBN 0-317-20534-X, 2022840). Bks Demand UMI.
Chilvers, Timothy, tr. see Schlegel, H. & Verster De Wulverhorst, J. A.
Chimenti, Dale E., jt. ed. see Thompson, D. O.
Chimenti, Dale E., jt. ed. see Thompson, Donald O.
Chimenti, Elisa. Tales & Legends of Morocco. Benamy, Arnon, tr. (Illus.). (gr. 5 up). 1965. 6.95 (ISBN 0-8392-3049-4). Astor-Honor.
Chimenti, Francesca. The Web of Allyngrood. LC 76-56276. 1977. 10.95 (ISBN 0-385-12740-5, BFYR). Doubleday.
Chimery, Michael. Garden Birds. (Illus.). 112p. 1983. 19.95 (ISBN 0-396-08170-3). Dodd.
Chimienti, Teresa, ed. see Schmitt, Conrad J.
Ch'i Ming. Tales About Hsu Wen-Ch'ang. Lin Lan, ed. (Tales from the Orient Ser.: No. 28). (Chinese.). 15.00x (ISBN 0-89986-252-7, Pub. by E Langstaff). Oriental Bk Store.
Chimnoy, Sri. The Golden Boat, 20 vols. (Illus.). 50p. (Orig.). 1974. pap. 3.00 ea. Aum Pubns.
--Obedience or Oneness. 54p. (Orig.). 1977. pap. 2.00 (ISBN 0-88497-374-3). Aum Pubns.
Chimombo, Steve. The Rainmaker. (Malawian Writers Ser.: No. 4). 51p. (Orig.). (gr. 9-12). 1978. pap. 5.00x (ISBN 0-686-63965-0). Three Continents.
Chi-mun, So, et al, trs. see Kyong-ae, Kang, et al.
Chin, A. F., jt. auth. see Jones, L.
Chin, Audrey & Peterson, Mark A. Deep Pockets, Empty Pockets: Who Wins in Cook County Jury Trials. LC 85-9517. Date not set. price not set (ISBN 0-8330-0651-7). Rand Corp.
Chin, Chen-An & Song, Pill-Soon. Reactivity Indices for Biomolecules. (Graduate Studies: No. 24). (Illus.). 176p. 1981. 33.00 (ISBN 0-89672-093-4); pap. 20.00 (ISBN 0-89672-092-6). Tex Tech Pr.
Chin, D. & Staples, M. Hop Gar Kung Fu. 1976. 5.50x (ISBN 0-685-83526-X). Wehman.
Chin, David & Staples, Michael. Hop Gar Kung Fu. LC 80-107762. (Illus.). 94p. 1976. pap. 4.50 (ISBN 0-86568-005-1). Unique Pubns.
Chin, Der-Tau, jt. ed. see Alkire, Richard.
Chin, Edwin, Jr., jt. auth. see Shrewsbury, Marvin M.
Chin, F. Automation & Robots: A Selected Bibliography of Books. (Public Administration Ser.: Bibliography P-969). 19p. 1982. 3.00 (P-969). Vance Biblios.
Chin, Felix. Cable Television: A Comprehensive Bibliography. LC 78-1526. 300p. 1978. 85.00x (ISBN 0-306-65172-6, Plenum Pr). Plenum Pub.
--Cable Television: A Selected Bibliography. (Public Administration Ser.: P 5). 1978. pap. 6.00 (ISBN 0-88066-001-5). Vance Biblios.
--The Davis-Bacon Act: A Selected Bibliography. LC 81-158284. (Public Administration Ser. - Bibliography). Date not set. price not set. Vance Biblios.
--Regulatory Reform of Telecommunications: A Selected Bibliography. (Public Administration Ser.: Bibliography P-521). 50p. 1980. pap. 5.50 (ISBN 0-88066-074-0). Vance Biblios.
Chin, Frank. The Chickencoop Chinaman & The Year of the Dragon: Two Plays. LC 81-985. (Illus.). 172p. 1981. 22.50x (ISBN 0-295-95830-8); pap. 9.95x (ISBN 0-295-95833-2). U of Wash Pr.
Chin, Frank, et al, eds. The Big AIIIEEEEE. 600p. 1985. 21.95 (ISBN 0-88258-108-2). Howard U Pr.
Chin, G. Y., ed. Advances in Power Technology. 1982. 80.00 (ISBN 0-87170-142-1). ASM.
Chin, John M. The Sarawak Cheese. (Illus.). 1981. 21.95x (ISBN 0-19-580470-8). Oxford U Pr.
Chin, Kin Wah. The Defence of Malaysia & Singapore: The Transformation of a Security System 1957-1971. LC 82-4330. (International Studies). 200p. 1983. 42.50 (ISBN 0-521-24325-4). Cambridge U Pr.
Chin, Leeann. Betty Crocker's Chinese Cookbook. LC 80-6044. (Illus.). 96p. 1981. 8.95 (ISBN 0-394-51881-0). Random.
Chin, Pa. Family. LC 72-79433. 360p. 1972. pap. 5.50 (ISBN 0-385-05787-3, Anch). Doubleday.
Chin, Richard, jt. auth. see Ribner, Susan.
Chin, Rockwood. Management, Industry & Trade in Cotton Textiles. 1965. 10.95x (ISBN 0-8084-0207-2). New Coll U Pr.
Chin, S. L. & Lambropoulos, Peter. Multiphoton Ionization of Atoms: Quantum Electronics; Principles & Applications. LC 83-98663. 1984. 59.50 (ISBN 0-12-172780-7). Acad Pr.
China Art Publishing Company, ed. see Quan, Yang, et al.
China Building Industry. Ancient Chinese Architecture. (Illus.). 1982. 79.50 (ISBN 0-917056-35-3, Pub. by China Build Joint). Cheng & Tsui.
China Building Industry Staff. Classical Chinese Gardens. 69.50 (ISBN 0-917056-37-X, Pub. by China Build Joint). Cheng & Tsui.
China Educational Commission. Christian Education in China: A Study. LC 75-36223. Repr. of 1922 ed. 34.50 (ISBN 0-404-14474-8). AMS Pr.
China Foundation. Bulletins of the Social Research Department: China During the Interregnum 1911-1949. Myers, Ramon H., ed. LC 80-8877. (The Economy & Society Ser.). 231p. 1982. lib. bdg. 36.00 (ISBN 0-8240-4686-2). Garland Pub.
China Handbook Editorial Committee. Culture. (Illus.). 141p. (Orig.). 1982. pap. 3.95 (ISBN 0-8351-0991-7). China Bks.
China Handbook Editorial Committee, ed. Economy. Gengkang, Hu, et al, trs. from Chinese. (China Handbook Ser.). (Illus.). 425p. (Orig.). 1984. pap. 6.95 (ISBN 0-8351-0987-9). China Bks.
China Handbook Editorial Committee. Education & Science. Yicheng, Zhou, tr. (China Handbook Ser.). (Illus.). 243p. 1983. pap. 5.50 (ISBN 0-8351-0988-7). China Bks.
--Geography. Liangxing, Liang, tr. (China Handbook Ser.). (Illus.). 260p. (Orig.). 1983. pap. 5.95 (ISBN 0-8351-0984-4). China Bks.
--History. Li, Dun J., tr. (China Handbook Ser.). (Illus.). 189p. 1982. pap. 5.95 (ISBN 0-8351-0985-2). China Bks.

China Handbook Editorial Committee, ed. Literature & the Arts. (China Handbook Ser.). (Illus.). 217p. (Orig.). 1983. pap. 4.95 (ISBN 0-8351-0989-5). China Bks.

--Politics. Zengming, Huang & Ji, Zhou, trs. from Chinese. (China Handbook Ser.). (Illus.). 209p. (Orig.). 1985. pap. 4.95 (ISBN 0-8351-0986-0). China Bks.

China Handbook Editorial Committee. Tourism. Huang, Youyi, tr. (China Handbook Ser.). (Illus.). 149p. (Orig.). 1984. pap. 4.95 (ISBN 0-8351-1188-1). China Bks.

China Institute of International Affairs. China & the United Nations. LC 74-6706. (National Studies on International Organization Ser). 285p. 1975. Repr. of 1959 ed. lib. bdg. 22.50x (ISBN 0-8371-7542-9, CIUN). Greenwood.

China International Famine Relief Commission. Herr Raiffeisen Among Chinese Farmers. LC 78-74320. (The Modern Chinese Economy Ser.: Vol. 22). 140p. 1980. lib. bdg. 20.00 (ISBN 0-8240-4270-0). Garland Pub.

China Ministry of Information & Tong, Hollington K., eds. China Handbook, Nineteen Thirty-Seven to Nineteen Forty-Five: A Comprehensive Survey of Major Developments in China. rev. enl. ed. (China in the 20th Century Ser). (Illus.). xvi, 862p. 1975. Repr. of 1947 ed. lib. bdg. 95.00 (ISBN 0-306-70701-2). Da Capo.

China National Stamp Corp. Staff. Postage Stamp Catalog of PRC (1949-1980) (Illus.). 132p. (Orig.). 1982. pap. 15.00 (ISBN 0-8351-1033-8). China Bks.

China National Stamp Corporation. Postage Stamp Catalogue of the People's Republic of China, 1949-1980. 132p. (Orig.). 1983. pap. 15.00 (ISBN 0-88727-020-4, Pub. by People's Posts CC). Cheng & Tsui.

China (People's Republic of China), 1949- Tai Piao Ta Hui. Second Session of the Second National People's Congress of the People's Republic of China: Documents. LC 79-38053. (China: Classic & Contemporary Works in Reprint Ser.). Repr. of 1960 ed. 14.50 (ISBN 0-404-56907-2). AMS Pr.

China Pictorial, ed. China in Pictures. (Illus.). 96p. (Orig.). 1984. pap. 7.95 (ISBN 0-8351-1405-8). China Bks.

China Pictorial, "The People's Republic of China" Editorial Staff. Chinese Cuisine: From the Master Chefs of China. (Illus.). 256p. 1983. 29.95i (ISBN 0-316-54994-0). Little.

China Publications Centre. The Constitution of the People's Republic of China. LC 83-13222. 99p. 1983. 7.10 (ISBN 0-08-030818-X); pap. 3.50 (ISBN 0-08-030817-1). Pergamon.

China Sports & New World Press, ed. Traditional Chinese Fitness Exercises. (China Spotlight Ser.). (Illus.). 135p. (Orig.). 1984. pap. 3.95 (ISBN 0-8351-1407-4). China Bks.

China Sports Editorial Board, ed. Wushu among Chinese Moslems. (China Sports Ser.). (Illus.). 184p. (Orig.). 1984. pap. 4.95 (ISBN 0-8351-1539-9). China Bks.

China Sports, Peking Staff. Health Exercises from China. 63p. 5.75 (ISBN 0-317-31557-9). Chans Corp.

Chinard, G. Volney et L'Amerique D'appres Des Documents Inedits et Sa Correspondance Avec Jefferson. 1973. Repr. of 1923 ed. 19.00 (ISBN 0-384-08797-3). Johnson Repr.

Chinard, Gilbert. Benjamin Franklin on the Art of Eating. (APS Benjamin Franklin Ser). 70p. 1980. Repr. 5.00 (ISBN 0-317-33120-5, APS-10). Am Philos.

--Honest John Adams. 12.00 (ISBN 0-8446-1854-3). Peter Smith.

--Jefferson et les Ideologues. Mayer, J. P., ed. LC 78-67341. (European Political Thought Ser.). (Fr.). 1979. Repr. of 1925 ed. lib. bdg. 21.00x (ISBN 0-405-11685-3). Ayer Co Pubs.

--Thomas Jefferson: The Apostle of Americanism. 1957. pap. 7.95 (ISBN 0-472-06013-9, 13, AA). U of Mich Pr.

Chinard, Gilbert, ed. Treaties of Seventeen Seventy-Eight & Allied Documents. LC 73-181911. (BCL Ser.: No. I). Repr. of 1928 ed. 15.00 (ISBN 0-404-52421-4). AMS Pr.

Chinas, Beverly. The Isthmus Zapotecs: Women's Roles in Cultural Context. (Illus.). 122p. 1983. pap. text ed. 6.95x (ISBN 0-88133-053-1). Waveland Pr.

Chinbnall, Marjorie, et al, eds. Anselm Studies: An Occasional Journal. 273p. (Orig.). 1983. lib. bdg. 35.00x (ISBN 0-527-03662-5). Kraus Intl.

Chinchilla, Anastasio. Anales Historicos De la Medicina En General y Biografico-Bibliograficos De la Espanola En Particular, 4 vols. (Sources of Science Ser.: No. 8). (Span.). 1967. Repr. of 1846 ed. Set. 280.00 (ISBN 0-384-08850-3). Johnson Repr.

Chin-Chiu, Lee. Essential Biology. LC 73-13537. 1973. pap. text ed. 6.00x (ISBN 0-8422-0353-2). Irvington.

Chinen, Jon J. Great Mahele: Hawaii's Land Division of 1848. LC 57-14473. 44p. (Orig.). 1958. pap. text ed. 3.95x (ISBN 0-87022-125-6). UH Pr.

Chinery. A Field Guide to the Insects of Britain & Northern Europe. 24.95 (ISBN 0-00-219216-0, Collins Pub England). Greene.

Chinery, Michael, ed. Dictionary of Animals. LC 84-716. (Illus.). 380p. (gr. 7 up). 1984. 17.95 (ISBN 0-668-06155-3, 6155-3). Arco.

Chinese Academy of Science, jt. auth. see Institute of National Science.

Chinese Academy of Social Sciences, Institute of Literature, ed. Stories About Not Being Afraid of Ghosts. 2nd ed. Yang, Gladys & Hsien-Yi, Yang, trs. from Chinese. 1979. pap. 2.95 (ISBN 0-8351-0608-X). China Bks.

Chinese Art Appraisers Association. Concepts in Dating Chinese Paintings. LC 78-60305. (Publication date to be announced). 24.00 (ISBN 0-930940-06-7); pap. 14.00 (ISBN 0-930940-07-5). Chinese Art App.

Chinese Association of Automation, ed. Recent Developments in Control Theory & Its Applications: Proceedings of Bilateral Meeting on Control Systems. 1006p. 1982. 132.00 (ISBN 0-677-31040-4). Gordon.

Chinese Eastern Railroad Printing Office. North Manchuria & the Chinese Eastern Railway. Myers, Ramon H., ed. LC 80-8832. (China During the Interregnum 1911-1949, The Economy & Society Ser.). 454p. 1982. lib. bdg. 73.00 (ISBN 0-8240-4688-9). Garland Pub.

Chinese-English Translation Assistance Group, ed. Chinese Dictionaries: An Extensive Bibliography of Dictionaries in Chinese & Other Languages. LC 82-923. xvi, 448p. (Chinese & Eng.). 1982. lib. bdg. 49.95 (ISBN 0-313-23505-8, MDC/). Greenwood.

Chinese Handbook Editorial Committee, ed. Life & Life Styles. Zhucai, Chen, tr. from Chinese. (China Handbook Ser.). (Illus.). 261p. 1985. pap. 4.95 (ISBN 0-8351-0992-5). China Bks.

Chinese Mechanical Engineering Society & Chinese Society of Theoretical & Applied Mechanics, eds. Finite Element Methods: Proceedings of the 1981 Symposium, Hefei, People's Republic of China. 486p. 1982. 92.50 (ISBN 0-677-31020-X). Gordon.

Chinese People's Institute of Foreign Affairs. China Supports the Arab People's Struggle for National Independence: A Selection of Important Documents. LC 75-38060. Repr. of 1958 ed. 12.50 (ISBN 0-404-56916-1). AMS Pr.

Chinese Society of International Law, ed. Selected Articles from Chinese Yearbook of International Law. 308p. (Orig.). 1983. pap. 6.95 (ISBN 0-8351-1279-9). China Bks.

Chinese Society of Theoretical & Applied Mechanics, jt. ed. see Chinese Mechanical Engineering Society.

Chinese, U. S. Symposium on Systems Analysis & Gray, Paul. Proceedings. LC 83-1210. (Wiley Series on Systems Engineering & Analysis). 349p. 1983. 74.50 (ISBN 0-471-89585-7, Pub. by Wiley-Interscience). Wiley.

Ching, Chauncey. Simple Computing: What Computers Can Do for You. LC 84-33. (Orig.). 1984. pap. 9.95 (ISBN 0-915805-00-6). Total Concepts.

Ching, Eugene & Ching, Nora. Two Hundred One Chinese Verbs: Compounds & Phrases for Everyday Usage. LC 77-8811. 1977. pap. text ed. 10.95 (ISBN 0-8120-0674-7). Barron.

Ching, Francis D. Architecture: Space, Form & Order. 350p. 1979. 22.50 (ISBN 0-442-21534-7); pap. 14.95 (ISBN 0-442-21535-5). Van Nos Reinhold.

--Building Construction Illustrated. 1975. 21.95 (ISBN 0-442-21533-9). Van Nos Reinhold.

Ching, Francis D. & Miller, Dale E. Home Renovation. 350p. 1983. 21.95 (ISBN 0-442-21591-6); pap. 14.95 (ISBN 0-442-21592-4). Van Nos Reinhold.

Ching, Frank. Architectural Graphics. 2nd ed. (Illus.). 192p. 1985. 25.00 (ISBN 0-442-21862-1); pap. 14.95 (ISBN 0-442-21864-8). Van Nos Reinhold.

--Building Construction Illustrated. (Illus.). 320p. 1984. 21.95 (ISBN 0-317-19529-8); pap. 14.95 (ISBN 0-317-19530-1). Van Nos Reinhold.

Ching, Heng, tr. see Hua, Husan.

Ching, Hih Chen. MicroUse Directory: Software. 440p. (Orig.). 1984. pap. 99.50 (ISBN 0-931555-01-9). MicroUse Info.

Ching, Julia. Confucianism & Christianity. LC 77-75962. 234p. 1978. 16.95x (ISBN 0-87011-303-8). Kodansha.

--To Acquire Wisdom: The Way of Wang Yang-Ming. LC 75-20038. (Studies in Oriental Culture). 373p. 1976. 31.50x (ISBN 0-231-03938-7). Columbia U Pr.

Ching, Lee S. Cook Malaysian. (Golden Asia Cookbks.). (Illus.). 146p. 1984. pap. 12.95. Hippocrene Bks.

Ching, Marvin K., et al, eds. Linguistic Perspectives on Literature. 1980. pap. 10.95x (ISBN 0-7100-0383-8). Routledge & Kegan.

Ching, Mary. Chinese Garden Music. (Readers Theatre Ser.). (Illus.). 40p. (Orig.). 1982. pap. text ed. 30.00 package of 6 scripts only (ISBN 0-912484-22-5). Joseph Nichols.

Ching, Nora, jt. auth. see Ching, Eugene.

Chingari, et al. Renewable Energy Systems Market & Analysis in Italy, Spain & Greece. 220p. 1981. pap. 39.50x (ISBN 0-89934-147-0, I071). Solar Energy Info.

Ching-Chih Chen. Health Sciences Information Sources. 808p. 1981. 75.00x (ISBN 0-262-03074-8). MIT Pr.

Ching-Chih Chen, ed. Quantitative Measurement & Dynamic Library Service. (Neal-Schuman Professional Bk.). 290p. 1978. lib. bdg. 29.95x (ISBN 0-912700-17-3). Oryx Pr.

Chingen. Miraculous Tales of the Lotus Sutra from Ancient Japan: The Dainihonkoku Hokekyokenki of Priest Chingen. Dykstra, Yohiko K., tr. 169p. (Japanese.). 1984. text ed. 25.00x (ISBN 0-8248-0967-X, Pub by Kansai Univ). UH Pr.

Chinggaltai. A Grammar of Mongol Language. Rev. ed. LC 77-985065. pap. 44.30 (ISBN 0-317-10162-5, 2019600). Bks Demand UMI.

Ching-hih Chen & Hernon, Peter. Information Seeking: Assessing & Anticipating User Needs. 222p. 1982. 27.00 (ISBN 0-918212-50-2). Neal-Schuman.

Ching-hih Chen & Schweizer, Susanna. Online Bibliographic Searching: Learning Manual. 244p. 1981. 24.95 (ISBN 0-918212-59-6). Neal-Schuman.

Ching-liang, Na. Chinese Jades: Archaic & Modern. 176p. 1980. 70.00x (ISBN 0-85331-401-2, Pub. by Lund Humphries England). State Mutual Bk.

Chingos, Peter T. & Cronquist, Neil R. Financial Considerations of Executive Compensation & Retirement Plans: Accounting, Actuary, Tax & Plan Design. LC 83-26076. (Wiley-Ronald Series in Professional Accounting & Business: 1-560). 236p. 1984. 32.95x (ISBN 0-471-87489-2, Pub. by Ronald Pr). Wiley.

Ching-Shan. Diary of His Excellency Ching-Shan: Being a Chinese Account of the Boxer Trouble. Duyvendak, Jan J., tr. from Chinese. (Studies in Chinese History & Civilization). 134p. 1977. Repr. of 1924 ed. 14.50 (ISBN 0-89093-074-0). U Pubns Amer.

Ch'ing Shui. Stories About Poor Scholar. Lin Lan, ed. (Tales from the Orient Ser.: No. 20). (Chinese.). 15.00x (ISBN 0-89986-244-6). Oriental Bk Store.

Ching-Shui. The Sun & the Moon. (National Peking University &Chinese Assn. for Folklore, Folklore & Folkliterature Ser.: No. 54). (Chinese.). 16.00x (ISBN 0-89986-145-8). Oriental Bk Store.

Ch'ing Shui. Tales of the Dragon's Daughter. (Folklore Series of National Sun Yat-Sen University: No. 7). (Chinese.). 16.00x (ISBN 0-89986-077-X). Oriental Bk Store.

Ching Ti, tr. see Shen Ts'Ung-Wen.

Ching Wen. More Tales About Other Wise Men. Lin Lan, ed. (Tales from the Orient Ser.: No. 29). (Chinese.). 30.00x (ISBN 0-89986-253-5). Oriental Bk Store.

Ching-Yao Hsieh, jt. auth. see Aschheim, Joseph.

Ching Yee, Janice. The Fast Gourmet from Hawaii. (Illus.). (gr. 10 up). 1977. 14.95 (ISBN 0-931420-06-7). Pi Pr.

--God's Busiest Angels. (Illus.). (gr. k-6). 1975. 2.00. Pi Pr.

--God's Meekest Angels. (Illus.). (gr. k-6). 1981. pap. 2.00. Pi Pr.

--God's Naughtiest Angels. (Illus.). (gr. k-6). 1974. 1.75 (ISBN 0-931420-08-3); pap. 1.05 (ISBN 0-685-88635-2). Pi Pr.

--God's Purest Angels. (Illus.). (gr. k-6). 1976. 2.00. Pi Pr.

--Success Is a Good Word. (gr. 9 up). 1979. 5.00 (ISBN 0-931420-22-9). Pi Pr.

--This Gift I Present of Poetry from Hawaii. 3rd ed. (Poetry Gift Ser.). (Illus.). 54p. (gr. 8 up). 1980. pap. 5.00 (ISBN 0-931420-01-6). Pi Pr.

Ching Yee, Janice see AHI.

Ching Yee, Janice see Yee, Janice C.

Chin Hao. Stories About Ghosts. Lin Lan, ed. (Tales from the Orient Ser.: No. 14). (Chinese.). 15.00x (ISBN 0-89986-238-1). Oriental Bk Store.

Chiniquy, Charles. Fifty Years in the "Church" of Rome. abr. ed. 366p. 1985. pap. 7.95 (ISBN 0-937958-21-2). Chick Pubns.

--The Priest, the Woman, & the Confessional. 144p. 1979. pap. 4.50 (ISBN 0-937958-03-4). Chick Pubns.

Chinitz, Benjamin, ed. Central City Economic Development. LC 78-67847. 1979. text ed. 25.00 (ISBN 0-89011-524-9). Abt Bks.

--Central City Economic Development. 212p. 1984. Repr. of 1979 ed. lib. bdg. 25.00 (ISBN 0-8191-4112-7). U Pr of Amer.

--City & Suburb. LC 76-1850. 181p. 1976. Repr. of 1965 ed. lib. bdg. 15.50x (ISBN 0-8371-8679-X, CHCS). Greenwood.

Chinitz, Jacob, ed. see Adler, Morris.

Chinitz, M. Paul. Logic Design of Computers: An Introduction. LC 81-50566. 416p. 1981. pap. 15.95 (ISBN 0-672-21800-3, 21800). Sams.

Chinloy, Peter. Labor Productivity. (Illus.). 160p. 1981. text ed. 25.00 (ISBN 0-89011-561-3). Abt Bks.

--Labor Productivity. 160p. 1981. 29.95x (ISBN 0-89011-561-3). Ballinger Pub.

Chinloy, Peter, jt. auth. see Goldberg, Michael A.

Chinmaya, Swami Prem, ed. see Rajneesh, Bhagwan S.

Chinmaya, Swami Prem, ed. see Rajneesh, Bhagwan Shree.

Chinmoy. India & Her Miracle Feast-Come & Enjoy Yourself, 5 pts. Incl. Pt. 1. Traditional Indian Stories About Troilanga Swami. (ISBN 0-88497-354-9); Pt. 2. Traditional Indian Stories About Shayama Charan Lahiri. (ISBN 0-88497-355-7); Pt. 3. Traditional Indian Stories About Shayama Charan Lahiri. (ISBN 0-88497-356-5); Pt. 4. Traditional Indian Stories About Bhaskarananda. (ISBN 0-88497-357-3); Pt. 5. Traditional Indian Stories About Devadas Maharaj. (ISBN 0-88497-358-1). (Orig.). 1977. pap. 1.00 ea. Aum Pubns.

Chinmoy, Sri. Aspiration & Gods Hour. 63p. (Orig.). 1977. pap. 2.00 (ISBN 0-88497-397-2). Aum Pubns.

--Aspiration-Glow & Dedication-Flow, 2 pts. (Orig.). 1977. Pt. 1, 60p. pap. text ed. 2.00 (ISBN 0-88497-386-7); Pt. 2, 70p. pap. 2.00 (ISBN 0-686-68529-6). Aum Pubns.

--Astrology, the Supernatural & the Beyond. LC 74-75131. 123p. (Orig.). 1974. pap. 3.00 (ISBN 0-88497-037-X). Aum Pubns.

--Beauty-Drops. 51p. (Orig.). 1975. pap. 2.00 (ISBN 0-88497-224-0). Aum Pubns.

--Colour Kingdom. (Illus.). 105p. (Orig.). 1974. pap. 5.00 (ISBN 0-685-41609-7). Aum Pubns.

--Creation & Perfection. 49p. (Orig.). 1976. pap. 2.00 (ISBN 0-88497-320-4). Aum Pubns.

--Death & Reincarnation: Eternity's Voyage. LC 74-81308. (Illus.). 143p. (Orig.). 1974. pap. 3.00 (ISBN 0-88497-038-8). Aum Pubns.

--Dedication-Drops. 50p. (Orig.). 1976. pap. 2.00 (ISBN 0-88497-267-4). Aum Pubns.

--Dreams That Fly. 50p. (Orig.). 1976. pap. 2.00 (ISBN 0-88497-228-3). Aum Pubns.

--Ego & Self-Complacency. 54p. (Orig.). 1977. pap. 2.00 (ISBN 0-88497-381-6). Aum Pubns.

--Einstein: Scientist-Sage: Brother of Atom-Universe. 1979. pap. 4.95 (ISBN 0-88497-461-8). Aum Pubns.

--Everest-Aspiration. 1979. pap. 2.95 (ISBN 0-88497-460-X). Aum Pubns.

--Father's Day: Father with His European Children. 54p. (Orig.). 1976. pap. 2.00 (ISBN 0-88497-297-6). Aum Pubns.

--Fifty Freedom-Boats to One Golden Shore, Pt. 1. 93p. (Orig.). 1974. pap. 3.00 (ISBN 0-88497-087-6). Aum Pubns.

--Fifty Freedom-Boats to One Golden Shore, Pt. 2. 108p. 1974. pap. 3.00 (ISBN 0-88497-101-5). Aum Pubns.

--Fifty Freedom-Boats to One Golden Shore, Pt. 3. 94p. 1974. pap. 3.00 (ISBN 0-88497-071-X). Aum Pubns.

--Fifty Freedom-Boats to One Golden Shore, Pt. 4. 112p. (Orig.). 1974. pap. text ed. 3.00 (ISBN 0-88497-073-6). Aum Pubns.

--Flame Waves: Questions Answered at the United Nations, Pts. 6-11. Incl. Pt. 6. 49p (ISBN 0-88497-325-5); Pt. 7. 49p (ISBN 0-88497-326-3); Pt. 8. 52p (ISBN 0-88497-327-1); Pt. 9. 52p (ISBN 0-88497-451-0); Pt. 10. 50p (ISBN 0-88497-452-9); Pt. 11. 57p (ISBN 0-88497-453-7). (Orig.). 1976-79. pap. 2.00 ea. Aum Pubns.

--Four Intimate Friends: Insincerity, Impurity, Doubt & Self-Indulgence. 59p. (Orig.). 1977. pap. 2.00 (ISBN 0-88497-382-4). Aum Pubns.

--The Garden of Love-Light, Vols 1 & 2. Chinmoy, Sri, tr. from Bengali. (Illus., Orig.). 1973. pap. 2.00 ea.; pap. write for info. (ISBN 0-88497-031-0); pap. write for info. (ISBN 0-88497-032-9); Vol. 1 & 2. pap. write for info. (ISBN 0-88497-030-2). Aum Pubns.

--Giving & Becoming. 50p. (Orig.). 1975. pap. 2.00 (ISBN 0-88497-122-8). Aum Pubns.

--God, Avatars & Yogis. (Orig.). 1977. pap. 2.00 (ISBN 0-88497-369-7). Aum Pubns.

--God's Orchestra. (Illus.). 108p. (Orig.). 1979. pap. 2.00 (ISBN 0-685-39935-4). Aum Pubns.

--God's Vision Promise. 50p. (Orig.). pap. 2.00 (ISBN 0-88497-125-2). Aum Pubns.

--Gratitude-Sky & Ingratitude-Sea. 61p. (Orig.). 1974. pap. 2.00 (ISBN 0-88497-098-1). Aum Pubns.

--Great Indian Meals: Divinely Delicious & Supremely Nourishing, 4 pts. Incl. Pt. 1. 54p (ISBN 0-88497-462-6); Pt. 2. 67p (ISBN 0-88497-463-4); Pt. 3. 68p (ISBN 0-88497-464-2); Pt. 4. 58p (ISBN 0-88497-465-0). 1979. pap. 2.00 ea. Aum Pubns.

--Great Masters & the Cosmic Gods. 61p. (Orig.). 1977. pap. 2.00 (ISBN 0-88497-395-6). Aum Pubns.

--I Need Only God. 50p. (Orig.). 1975. pap. 2.00 (ISBN 0-88497-133-3). Aum Pubns.

--Immortality's Dance. 50p. (Orig.). 1974. pap. 2.00 (ISBN 0-88497-132-5). Aum Pubns.

--The Inner Journey. 52p. (Orig.). 1977. pap. 2.00 (ISBN 0-88497-377-8). Aum Pubns.

--Inner Progress & Satisfaction-Life. 54p. (Orig.). 1977. pap. 2.00 (ISBN 0-88497-373-5). Aum Pubns.

--Inspiration-Garden & Aspiration-Leaves. 58p. (Orig.). 1977. pap. 2.00 (ISBN 0-88497-379-4). Aum Pubns.

--The Jewel of Humility. (Illus.). 56p. (Orig.). 1980. pap. 2.00 (ISBN 0-88497-493-6). Aum Pubns.

--Justice-Light & Satisfaction-Delight. (Soulful Questions & Fruitful Answers on Law & Justice). 41p. (Orig.). 1977. pap. 2.00 (ISBN 0-88497-338-7). Aum Pubns.

--Kennedy: The Universal Heart. 30p. 1973. pap. 1.00 (ISBN 0-88497-033-7). Aum Pubns.
--Light-Delight-Journeys. 67p. (Orig.). 1975. pap. 2.00 (ISBN 0-88497-102-3). Aum Pubns.
--Light of the Beyond. (Teachings of an Illumined Master). 221p. (Orig.). 1980. pap. 4.95 (ISBN 0-88497-481-2). Aum Pubns.
--Lord, Receive This Little Undying Cry. 50p. (Orig.). 1975. pap. 2.00. Aum Pubns.
--A Lost Friend. 53p. (Orig.). 1976. pap. 2.00 (ISBN 0-88497-268-2). Aum Pubns.
--The Master's Inner Life. 68p. (Orig.). 1977. pap. 2.00 (ISBN 0-88497-393-X). Aum Pubns.
--Meditation: Man-Perfection in God-Satisfaction. (Illus.). 1979. pap. 4.95 (ISBN 0-88497-444-8). Aum Pubns.
--My Life-Tree. 50p. (Orig.). 1975. pap. 2.00 (ISBN 0-88497-221-6). Aum Pubns.
--My Maple Tree. 121p. (Orig.). 1974. pap. 3.00 (ISBN 0-685-41607-0). Aum Pubns.
--My Salutation to Japan. 65p. 1973. 2.00 (ISBN 0-88497-034-5). Aum Pubns.
--O My Pilot Beloved. 54p. (Orig.). 1980. pap. 2.00 (ISBN 0-88497-502-9). Aum Pubns.
--Obedience. (A Supreme Virtue). 61p. (Orig.). 1977. pap. 2.00 (ISBN 0-88497-368-9). Aum Pubns.
--One Lives, One Dies. 81p. 1974. pap. 2.00 (ISBN 0-88497-072-8). Aum Pubns.
--Opportunity & Self-Transcendance. 64p. (Orig.). 1977. pap. 2.00 (ISBN 0-88497-375-1). Aum Pubns.
--Perfection & Transcendence. 60p. (Orig.). 1977. pap. 2.00 (ISBN 0-88497-372-7). Aum Pubns.
--Perfection in the Head World. 55p. (Orig.). 1980. pap. 2.00 (ISBN 0-88497-492-8). Aum Pubns.
--Perseverence & Aspiration. 54p. (Orig.). 1976. pap. 2.00 (ISBN 0-88497-333-6). Aum Pubns.
--Secrets of the Inner World. (Illus.). 54p. (Orig.). 1980. pap. 2.00 (ISBN 0-88497-499-5). Aum Pubns.
--The Seeker's Mind: Talks Delivered at the United Nations. 1979. pap. 3.00 (ISBN 0-88497-449-9). Aum Pubns.
--The Significance of a Smile. 52p. (Orig.). 1977. pap. 2.00 (ISBN 0-88497-367-0). Aum Pubns.
--The Silence of Death. (Illus.). 46p. (Orig.). 1973. pap. 2.00 (ISBN 0-88497-035-3). Aum Pubns.
--Something, Somehow, Somewhere, Someday. 70p. (Orig.). 1973. pap. 2.00 (ISBN 0-88497-025-6). Aum Pubns.
--Soul-Education for the Family-World. 89p. (Orig.). 1977. pap. 3.00 (ISBN 0-88497-390-5). Aum Pubns.
--A Soulful Tribute to the Secretary-General: The Pilot Supreme of the United Nations. (Illus.). 1978. pap. 4.95 (ISBN 0-88497-443-X). Aum Pubns.
--The Souls Evolution. 63p. (Orig.). 1977. pap. 2.00 (ISBN 0-88497-396-4). Aum Pubns.
--Sri Chinmoy Primer. 122p. (Orig.). 1974. pap. 2.00 (ISBN 0-88497-084-1). Aum Pubns.
--Sri Chinmoy Speaks, 10 pts. Incl. Pt. 1. 55p (ISBN 0-88497-282-8); Pt. 2. 58p (ISBN 0-88497-285-2); Pt. 3. 65p (ISBN 0-88497-286-0); Pt. 4. 62p (ISBN 0-88497-288-7); Pt. 5. 56p (ISBN 0-88497-289-5); Pt. 6. 57p (ISBN 0-88497-290-9); Pt. 7. 58p (ISBN 0-88497-294-1); Pt. 8. 56p (ISBN 0-88497-295-X); Pt. 9. 51p (ISBN 0-88497-296-8); Pt. 10. 62p (ISBN 0-88497-335-2). 1976-77. pap. 2.00 ea. Aum Pubns.
--Supreme - His Four Children. LC 72-188849. 1973. pap. 3.00 (ISBN 0-8303-0121-6). Fleet.
--This Is God's Home. 50p. (Orig.). pap. 2.00 (ISBN 0-88497-233-X). Aum Pubns.
--Transformation of the Ego. 52p. (Orig.). 1977. pap. 2.00 (ISBN 0-88497-371-9). Aum Pubns.
--A Twentieth-Century Seeker. 62p. (Orig.). 1977. pap. 2.00 (ISBN 0-88497-385-9). Aum Pubns.
--Union & Oneness. 50p. (Orig.). 1976. pap. 2.00 (ISBN 0-88497-266-6). Aum Pubns.
--Union Vision. (Talks Delivered at the United Nations). 102p. (Orig.). 1977. pap. 3.00. Aum Pubns.
--Wisdom-Waves in New York, 2 pts. (Orig.). 1979. pap. 2.00 ea. Pt. 1, 53p (ISBN 0-88497-487-1). Pt. 2, 50p (ISBN 0-88497-488-X). Aum Pubns.
--Yoga & Spiritual Life. rev. ed. LC 74-81309. 160p. 1974. pap. 3.00 (ISBN 0-88497-040-X). Aum Pubns.
--A Yogi's Justice, an Avatar's Justice & God's Justice. 63p. (Orig.). 1974. pap. 2.00 (ISBN 0-88497-149-X). Aum Pubns.

Chinn, Edward. The Wonder of Words: One Hundred Words & Phrases Shaping How Christians Think & Live. (Orig.). 1985. pap. 4.50 (ISBN 0-89536-737-8). CSS of Ohio.

Chinn, Gary. The Garrett Wade Book of Woodworking Tools. LC 79-7082. (Illus.). 1980. 19.18i (ISBN 0-690-01840-1). T Y Crowell.

Chinn, Jeff. Manipulating Soviet Population Resources. LC 77-11683. 163p. 1978. text ed. 34.50x (ISBN 0-8419-0345-X). Holmes & Meier.

Chinn, L. J., et al. Chemistry & Biochemistry of Steroids. (Illus.). 1969. text ed. 12.00x (ISBN 0-87672-003-3). Geron-X.

Chinn, Peggy L. & Jacobs, Maeona K. Theory & Nursing: A Systematic Approach. LC 82-7912. (Illus.). 222p. 1983. pap. text ed. 15.95 (ISBN 0-8016-0961-5). Mosby.

Chinn, Peggy L., jt. auth. see Wheeler, Charlene E.

Chinn, Peggy L., ed. Advances in Nursing Theory Development. LC 82-13945. 299p. 1983. 31.00 (ISBN 0-89443-842-5). Aspen Systems.

Chinn, Peggy L., jt. ed. see Brown, Barbara J.

Chinn, Philip C., jt. auth. see Kamp, Susan H.

Chinn, Philip C., et al. Mental Retardation: A Life Cycle Approach. 2nd ed. LC 78-31835. 492p. 1979. text ed. 22.95 (ISBN 0-8016-0968-2). Mosby.

Chinn, Phillip C., ed. Education of Culturally & Linguistically Exceptional Children. 85p. 1984. 8.00 (ISBN 0-86586-152-8); 6.80. Coun Exc Child.

Chinn, W. G. & Steenrod, N. E. First Concepts of Topology. LC 66-20367. (New Mathematical Library: No. 18). 160p. 1975. pap. 10.00 (ISBN 0-88385-618-2). Math Assn.

Chinn, William G., jt. auth. see Blakeslee, David W.

Chinn, William G., jt. auth. see Davis, Philip J.

Chinn, William G., et al. Arithmetic & Calculators: How to Deal with Arithmetic in the Calculator Age. LC 77-11111. (Illus.). 488p. 1978. pap. text ed. 17.95 (ISBN 0-7167-0015-8). W H Freeman.

Chinnery, John D. & Mingqui, Cui. Corresponding English & Chinese Proverbs & Phrases. 258p. 1984. pap. 3.95 (ISBN 0-8351-0951-8). China Bks.

Chinnery, Victor. Oak Furniture, the British Tradition. (Illus.). 580p. 1979. 69.50 (ISBN 0-902028-61-8). Antique Collect.
--Oak Furniture, the British Tradition. (Illus.). 1979. 69.50 (ISBN 0-902028-61-8). Apollo.

Chinnici, Joseph P. The English Catholic Enlightenment: John Lingard & the Cisalpine Movement, 1780 to 1850. LC 79-20250. (Illus.). xiv, 262p. 1980. 24.95x (ISBN 0-915762-10-2). Patmos Pr.

Chinnici, Joseph P., ed. Devotion to the Holy Spirit in American Catholicism. (Sources of American Spirituality Ser.). 256p. 1985. pap. 12.95 (ISBN 0-8091-0366-4). Paulist Pr.

Chinnov, Igor. Avtograph, Stikhy. 104p. (Orig., Rus.). 1984. pap. 9.00 (ISBN 0-914265-03-2). New Eng Pub MA.

Chino, Yuko, ed. The Door to Heaven. 1980. 12.50 (ISBN 4-915502-04-X, C0090, Pub. by Jlhi-to-Al). Jl Pub Co.
--Under the Light of Heaven. 14.95 (ISBN 4-915502-04-X, C0094, Pub. by Jlhi-to-Al); pap. 7.95 (ISBN 4-915502-04-X, C0094). JL Pub Co.
--The Witness of the Kingdom of Heaven. 1981. 14.95 (ISBN 0-318-00416-X, C 0091, Pub. by Jlhi-to-Al). Jl Pub Co.

Chino, Yuko & Kyoto Group, eds. Sermes: The Poems of the Angels. 1984. pap. 7.50 (ISBN 4-915502-04-X, C0100, Pub. by Jlhi-to-Al) Jl Pub Co.

Chinook, Nipi. The Ski Bum's Guide to Mountain Wildlife. LC 78-67640. (Illus.). 1978. pap. 3.25 (ISBN 0-9602038-0-X). Bowery Pub.

Chinoy, Ely. Sociological Perspective. 2nd rev. & enl. ed. 11.75 (ISBN 0-8446-1855-1). Peter Smith.

Chinoy, Ely & Hewitt, John. Sociological Perspectives: Basic Concepts & Their Applications. 3rd ed. 1974. pap. text ed. 7.50x (ISBN 0-394-31869-2, RanC). Random.

Chinoy, Ely, ed. The Urban Future. (Controversy Ser). 200p. 1973. 11.95x (ISBN 0-88311-200-0); pap. 5.95x (ISBN 0-88311-201-9). Lieber-Atherton.

Chinoy, Helen K. Reunion: A Self-Portrait of the Group Theatre. (Illus.). 112p. 1983. pap. text ed. 7.50 (ISBN 0-8191-3531-3, Co-pub. by Am Theat Assn). U Pr of Amer.

Chinoy, Helen K. & Jenkins, Linda W. Women in American Theatre. Michelman, Herber, ed. (Illus.). 384p. 1981. Outlet 4.98 (ISBN 0-517-53729-X, Michelman Books). Crown.

Chinoy, Helen K., ed. Reunion: A Self Portrait of the Group Theatre (1976) 77p. Repr. 4.00x (ISBN 0-940528-11-8). Am Theatre Assoc.

Chinoy, Helen K., jt. ed. see Cole, Toby.

Chinoy, Helen Krich, jt. auth. see Cole, Toby.

Chinoy, Michael. China: People-Questions. (People & Systems Ser). (Orig.). 1975. pap. 1.75 (ISBN 0-377-00032-9). Friend Pr.

Chinoy, Michael, et al, eds. U. S. A. Packet on "People & Systems". (People & Systems Ser). (Orig.). 1975. pap. 6.95 (ISBN 0-377-00038-8). Friend Pr.

Chinoy, N. J., ed. The Role of Ascorbic Acid in Growth, Differentiation & Metabolism of Plants. (Advances in Agricultural Biotechnology Ser.). 1984. lib. bdg. 46.50 (ISBN 90-247-2908-4, Pub. by Martinus Nijhoff Netherlands). Kluwer-Academic.

Chinoy, Rustam, jt. ed. see Witherell, Peter.

Chin-Sheng, Chou. An Economic History of China. Kaplan, Edward H., tr. from Chinese. LC 74-620032. (Program in East Asian Studies Occasional Papers Ser: No. 7). Orig. Title: Chung-Kuo Ching-Chi Shih. (Illus.). 250p. 1974. pap. 6.60 (ISBN 0-914584-07-3). West Wash Univ.

Chinsky, J. M., jt. auth. see Allen, G. J.

Chintamani, Sir Shirroavoore Y. Indian Politics Since the Mutiny: Being an Account of the Development of Public Life & Political Institutions of Prominent Local Political Personalities. LC 79-4911. 1981. Repr. of 1947 ed. 19.50 (ISBN 0-88355-961-7). Hyperion Conn.

Chinul. The Korean Approach to Zen: The Collected Works of Chinul. Buswell, Robert E., Jr., tr. LC 82-23873. 484p. 1983. text ed. 29.95x (ISBN 0-8248-0785-5). UH Pr.

Chinweizu. Energy Crisis & Other Poems. LC 77-90075. 1978. 9.95 (ISBN 0-88357-062-9); pap. 4.50 (ISBN 0-88357-063-7). NOK Pubs.
--The West & the Rest of Us: White Predators, Black Slavers & the African Elite. 544p. 1978. text ed. 21.95x (ISBN 0-88357-015-7); pap. 9.95 (ISBN 0-88357-016-5). Nok Pubs.

Chinweizu, et al. Toward the Decolonization of African Literature, Vol. I. LC 82-23357. 320p. 1982. 14.95 (ISBN 0-88258-122-8); pap. 7.95 (ISBN 0-88258-123-6). Howard U Pr.
--Towards the Decolonization of African Literature: African Fiction & Poetry & Their Critics. 320p. 1985. pap. 19.95s (ISBN 0-7103-0123-5, Kegan Paul International). Routledge & Kegan.

Chin-W Kim, ed. Papers in Korean Linguistics. 1979. pap. text ed. 6.75 (ISBN 0-917496-11-6). Hornbeam Pr.

Chiodi, Pietro. Sartre & Marxism. Soper, Kate, tr. from It. (European Philosophy & the Human Sciences Ser.). 1976. text ed. 30.50x (ISBN 0-391-00590-1); pap. text ed. 11.00x (ISBN 0-391-00886-2). Humanities.

Chiodini, P. G. & Liuzzi, A. The Regulation of Growth Hormone Secretion, Vol. 1. Horrobin, D. F., ed. (Annual Research Reviews Ser.). 1979. 24.00 (ISBN 0-88831-050-1). Eden Pr.

Chioffi, Nancy & Mead, Gretchen. Keeping the Harvest. rev. ed. LC 80-19577. (Illus.). 208p. 1980. pap. text ed. 7.95 (ISBN 0-88266-247-3). Garden Way Pub.

Chiogioji. Industrial Energy Conservation. (Energy, Power & Environment Ser.: Vol. 4). 1979. 89.75 (ISBN 0-8247-6809-4). Dekker.

Chiogioji, Oura. Energy Conservation in Commercial & Residential Buildings. (Clinical & Biochemical Analysis Ser.). 536p. 1982. 69.75 (ISBN 0-8247-1874-7). Dekker.

Chiosi, C. & Stalio, R., eds. Effects of Mass Loss on Stellar Evolution. 375p. 1981. 73.50 (ISBN 90-277-1292-1, Pub. by Reidel Holland). Kluwer Academic.

Chiosi, Cesare & Renzini, Alvio, eds. Stellar Nucleosynthesis. 1984. lib. bdg. 55.00 (ISBN 90-277-1729-X, Pub. by Reidel Holland). Kluwer Academic.

Chiozza Money, L. C. Riches & Poverty. LC 79-56955. (The English Working Class Ser.). 358p. 1980. lib. bdg. 40.00 (ISBN 0-8240-0109-5). Garland Pub.

Chipa, A. K. Beauty & Wisdom of the Holy Qur'an. 1971. 2.50x (ISBN 0-87902-159-4). Orientalia.

Chipasula, Frank. O Earth, Wait for Me. (Staffrider Ser.: No. 22). 88p. 1984. pap. 9.95 (ISBN 0-86975-258-8, Pub. by Ravan Pr). Ohio U Pr.

Chipasula, Frank, ed. When My Brothers Come Home: Poems from Central & Southern Africa. 320p. 1985. 30.00x (ISBN 0-8195-5092-2); pap. 14.95 (ISBN 0-8195-6089-8). Wesleyan U Pr.

Chipeta, Chinyamata. Economics of Indigenous Labor. 1982. 9.95 (ISBN 0-533-04995-4). Vantage.
--Indigenous Economics: A Cultural Approach. (Illus.). 280p. 1981. 12.50x (ISBN 0-682-49657-X). Exposition Pr FL.

Chipiez, Charles, jt. auth. see Perrot, Charles.

Chipiez, Charles, jt. auth. see Perrot, Georges.

Chiplin, Brian & Sloane, Peter. Tackling Discrimination at the Workplace: An Analysis of Sex Discrimination in Britain. LC 82-4384. (Management & Industrial Relations Ser.: No. 2). (Illus.). 190p. 1983. pap. 32.50 (ISBN 0-521-24565-6). Cambridge U Pr.

Chiplin, Brian & Sloane, Peter J. Sex Discrimination in the Labour Market. 1976. text ed. 21.50x (ISBN 0-8419-5018-0). Holmes & Meier.

Chiplin, Brian & Sturgess, Brian. Economics of Advertising. 157p. 1983. cancelled (ISBN 0-03-910315-3, Pub. by Holt-Saunders England). Transaction Bks.

Chipman, Clark, ed. Emergency Department Orthopaedics. LC 82-8768. 200p. 1982. 34.00 (ISBN 0-89443-803-4). Aspen Systems.

Chipman, Donald, jt. ed. see Peden, Creighton.

Chipman, George, jt. auth. see Chipman, Jeane.

Chipman, Harold H. Children's Construction of the English Pronominal System. (Studies in Psychology: No. 7). (Illus.). 138p. (Orig.). 1980. pap. text ed. 19.50 (ISBN 3-456-80747-3, Pub. by Hans Huber Switzerland). J K Burgess.

Chipman, J. S. & Kindleberger, C. P., eds. Flexible Exchange Rates & the Balance of Payments: Essays in Memory of Egon Sohmen. (Studies in International Economics: Vol. 7). 368p. 1981. 59.75 (ISBN 0-444-86045-2, North-Holland). Elsevier.

Chipman, Jeane & Chipman, George. Games! Games! Games! LC 83-18993. 1983. 7.95 (ISBN 0-87747-983-6). Deseret Bk.

Chipman, John S. The Theory of Inter-Sectoral Money Flows & Income Formation. LC 78-64212. (Johns Hopkins University. Studies in the Social Sciences. Sixty-Eighth Ser. 1950: 2). 160p. 1982. Repr. of 1851 ed. 24.50 (ISBN 0-404-61317-9). AMS Pr.

Chipman, Kathe, jt. ed. see Parry, Pamela J.

Chipman, Nathaniel. Principles of Government: A Treatise on Free Institutions. LC 76-99478. (American Constitutional & Legal History Ser.). 1970. Repr. of 1833 ed. 39.50 (ISBN 0-306-71851-0). Da Capo.
--Principles of Government, a Treatise on Free Institutions, Including the Constitution of the U. S. 1969. 20.50 (ISBN 0-8337-0562-8). B Franklin.

Chipman, R., jt. ed. see Jasentuliyana, N.

Chipman, R. A. Transmission Lines. (Schaum Outline Ser.). 1968. pap. 9.95 (ISBN 0-07-010747-5). McGraw.

Chipman, Susan F., et al, eds. Women & Mathematics: Balancing the Equation. 400p. 1985. text ed. 39.95 (ISBN 0-89859-369-7). L Erlbaum Assocs.

Chipot, M. Variational Inequalities & Flow in Porous Media. (Applied Mathematical Sciences Ser.: Vol. 52). (Illus.). 120p. 1984. pap. 16.00 (ISBN 0-387-96002-3). Springer-Verlag.

Chipp, Herschel B. Theories of Modern Art: A Source Book by Artists & Critics. (California Studies in the History of Art: No. XI). (Illus.). 680p. 1968. pap. 10.95x (ISBN 0-520-01450-2, CAMPUS 289). U of Cal Pr.

Chipp, Herschel B., et al. Theories of Modern Art: A Source Book by Artists. (Cal Ser.: No. 168). (Illus.). 680p. 1984. pap. 12.95 (ISBN 0-520-05256-0). U of Cal Pr.

Chipp, Sylvia A. & Green, Justin J., eds. Asian Women in Transition. LC 79-20517. (Illus.). 256p. 1980. text ed. 24.95x (ISBN 0-271-00251-4); pap. text ed. 12.50x (ISBN 0-271-00257-3). Pa St U Pr.

Chippendale, G. M. Eucalypts of the Western Australian Goldfields. 1982. 30.00x (ISBN 0-686-97915-X, Pub. by CSIRO Australia). State Mutual Bk.

Chippendale, Thomas. Gentleman & Cabinet-Maker's Director. 3rd ed. (Illus.). 1966. pap. 8.95 (ISBN 0-486-21601-2). Dover.
--Gentleman & Cabinet-Makers Director. 3rd ed. (Illus.). 18.00 (ISBN 0-8446-1856-X). Peter Smith.

Chippindale, Christopher. Stonehenge Complete: Archaeology, History, Heritage. LC 83-70803. (Illus.). 300p. 1983. 29.50 (ISBN 0-8014-1639-6). Cornell U Pr.

Chippindale, Warren & Defliese, Philip L., eds. Current Value Accounting: A Practical Guide for Business. LC 77-21422. 1977. 21.95 (ISBN 0-8144-5459-3). AMACOM.
--Current Value Accounting: A Practical Guide for Business. LC 77-21422. pap. 48.00 (ISBN 0-317-26722-1, 2023522). Bks Demand UMI.

Chippindall, W. H. History of the Parish of Tunstall. 1940. 16.00 (ISBN 0-384-08875-9). Johnson Repr.
--History of the Township of Ireby. 1935. 16.00 (ISBN 0-384-08885-6). Johnson Repr.
--History of Whittington. 1938. 24.00 (ISBN 0-384-08895-3). Johnson Repr.
--Sixteenth Century Survey & Year's Account of the Estates of Hornby Castles, Lancashire. 1939. 16.00 (ISBN 0-384-08905-4). Johnson Repr.

Chipps, Genie, jt. auth. see Jessup, Claudia.

Chiranky, Gary, ed. see Colletti, Anthony B.

Chiras, Daniel D. Environmental Science: A Framework for Decision Making. 1985. text ed. 33.95 (ISBN 0-8053-2255-8). Benjamin-Cummings.

Chiras, J., jt. auth. see Merland, J. J.

Chirban, John T., ed. Marriage & the Family Medicine, Psychology & Religion: New Directions, New Integrations. (Series on Medicine, Psychology & Religion). (Illus.). 94p. (Orig.). 1983. pap. text ed. 4.95 (ISBN 0-916586-63-4). Holy Cross Orthodox.

Chirelstein, Marvin A. Federal Income Taxation: A Law Student Guide to the Leading Cases & Concepts. 3rd ed. LC 82-4990. (University Textbook Ser.). 348p. 1982. pap. text ed. 13.50 (ISBN 0-88277-059-4). Foundation Pr.
--Federal Income Taxation: A Law Student's Guide to the Leading Cases & Concepts. 4th ed. (University Textbook Ser.). 1985. pap. text ed. write for info. (ISBN 0-88277-236-8). Foundation Pr.

Chirelstein, Marvin A., jt. auth. see Brudney, Victor.

Chirenje, D. Chief Kgama & His Times. Rex Collings Ltd., ed. 30.00x (ISBN 0-86036-062-8, Pub. by R Collings UK). State Mutual Bk.

Chirenje, J. Mutero. Chief Kgama & His Times Eighteen Thirty-Five to Nineteen Twenty-Three: The Story of a Southern African Ruler. 140p. 1978. 12.75x (ISBN 0-8476-1892-7). Rowman.
--A History of Northern Botswana 1850-1910. LC 74-194. (Illus.). 316p. 1976. 27.50 (ISBN 0-8386-1537-6). Fairleigh Dickinson.

Chirgotis, William G. Encyclopedia of Architect-Designed Homes. Theuerkauf, Bruce H., ed. (Illus.). 312p. 1985. lib. bdg. 25.00 (ISBN 0-933133-00-6). Nat Home Planning.
--One Hundred & Fifty Home Plans: Ranch Style, Single Story. Auer, Marilyn M., ed. LC 81-67295. 160p. 1981. 19.95 (ISBN 0-932944-47-7); pap. 6.95 (ISBN 0-932944-48-5). Creative Homeowner.
--One Hundred & Seventy-Five Multi-Level Home Plans for Today's Living. Lurie, Anne, ed. LC 79-54251. (Illus.). 1979. 19.95 (ISBN 0-932944-05-1); pap. 6.95 (ISBN 0-932944-04-3). Creative Homeowner.
--One Hundred Eighty Affordable Home Plans. Jenny, Betsy, ed. LC 84-73196. (Illus.). 176p. (Orig.). 1985. 19.95 (ISBN 0-932944-79-5); pap. 6.95 (ISBN 0-932944-74-4). Creative Homeowner.
--Two Hundred Fifty Home Plans. LC 78-65787. (Illus.). 240p. 1980. pap. 7.95 (ISBN 0-932944-70-1). Creative Homeowner.

--Two Hundred Fifty Home Plans for Today's Living. Birnbaum, Allan R. & Drate, Stanley, eds. LC 78-65787. (Illus.). 240p. 1979. 19.95 (ISBN 0-932944-03-5). Creative Homeowner.

--Two Hundred Fifty Home Plans for Today's Living. rev. ed. LC 78-65787. (Illus.). 240p. 1983. pap. 7.95 (ISBN 0-932944-70-1). Creative Homeowner.

Chirgwin, B. & Plumpton, C. A. Course of Mathematics for Engineers & Scientists. 2nd ed. 1984. 18.00 (ISBN 0-08-021678-1); Vol. 2, 1972. 18.25 (ISBN 0-08-015970-2); Vol. 3, 1978. 15.00 (ISBN 0-08-023042-3). Pergamon.

--Elementary Classical Hydrodynamics. 1968. 23.00 (ISBN 0-08-012406-2); pap. 11.75 (ISBN 0-08-012405-4). Pergamon.

Chirgwin, B., et al. Elementary Electromagnetic Theory, 3 vols. Incl. Vol. 1. Steady Electric Fields & Currents. 1971. pap. 9.00 (ISBN 0-08-016080-8); Vol. 2. Magnetic Fields, Special Relativity & Potential Theory. 1972. pap. 9.00 (ISBN 0-08-016600-8); Vol. 3. Maxwell's Equations & Their Consequences. 1973. pap. 10.00 (ISBN 0-08-017121-4). pap. write for info. Pergamon.

Chirgwin, John F. & Oldfield, Phyllis. The Library Assistant's Manual. 2nd, rev. ed. 137p. 1983. 14.00 (ISBN 0-85157-350-9, Pub. by Bingley England). Shoe String.

Chirich, Nancy. The Graphics Connection. (Illus.). 272p. (Orig.). 1985. pap. 11.95 (ISBN 0-912761-04-0). Ed-it Prods.

--Life with Wine: A Self-Portrait of the Wine Business in the Napa & Sonoma Valleys Plus 100 Recipes That Go with the Product. LC 83-16556. (Illus.). 192p. (Orig.). 1984. pap. 7.95 (ISBN 0-912761-00-8). Ed-it Prods.

--Savoring Plain Old Charleston. Stengel, Gretchen, ed. (Illus.). 144p. (Orig.). 1985. pap. 9.95 (ISBN 0-912761-01-6). Ed-it Prods.

--Yugocooks. Radulovic, Danilo, ed. (Illus.). 208p. (Orig.). 1985. pap. 9.95 (ISBN 0-912761-05-9). Ed-it Prods.

Chirich, Nancy, ed. The Ethnic Chef. (Illus.). 256p. (Orig.). 1985. pap. 9.95 (ISBN 0-912761-03-2). Ed-it Prods.

Chirichigno, F. Norma. Clave Para Identificar los Peces Del Peru. (Institut del Mar del Peru Ser.: Informe 44). (Illus.). 388p. (Span.). 1978. pap. text ed. 49.00x (ISBN 3-87429-131-6). Lubrecht & Cramer.

Chirichigno, G. C., jt. auth. see Archer, Gleason L.

Chirico, Giorgio De see De Chirico, Giorgio.

Chirico, Peter. Infallibility: The Crossroads of Doctrine. (Theology & Life Ser.: Vol. 1). pap. 9.95 (ISBN 0-89453-296-0). M Glazier.

Chirife, Jorge, jt. ed. see Iglesias, Hector A.

Chirigos, Michael A., ed. Control of Neoplasia by Modulation of the Immune System. LC 76-5665. (Progress in Cancer Research & Therapy Ser.: Vol. 2). 619p. 1977. 57.00 (ISBN 0-89004-125-3). Raven.

--Immune Modulation & Control of Neoplasia by Adjuvant Therapy. LC 76-5665. (Progress in Cancer Research & Therapy: Vol. 7). 519p. 1978. 70.00 (ISBN 0-89004-220-9). Raven.

Chirigos, Michael A., et al, eds. Mediation of Cellular Immunity in Cancer by Immune Modifiers. (Progress in Cancer Research & Therapy Ser.: Vol. 19). 288p. 1981. text ed. 45.50 (ISBN 0-89004-628-X). Raven.

Chirikjian, J. C., ed. Restriction Endonucleases. (Gene Amplification & Analysis Ser.: Vol. 1). 246p. 1981. 61.00 (ISBN 0-444-00610-9, Biomedical Pr). Elsevier.

Chirikjian, J. C. & Papas, T. S., eds. Structural Analysis of Nucleic Acids. (Gene Amplification & Analysis Ser.: Vol. 2). 554p. 1981. 108.50 (ISBN 0-444-00636-2, Biomedical Pr). Elsevier.

Chirinian, Helene. Getting to Know Computers. (Growing Up With Computers Ser.). (Illus.). 48p. 1984. pap. 3.95 (ISBN 0-86582-203-4, EN79310). Enrich.

--Instant Activities for the Apple. (Growing Up With Computers Ser.). (Illus.). 48p. 1984. pap. 3.95 (ISBN 0-86582-205-0, EN79313). Enrich.

--Instant Activities for the Commodore 64. (Growing Up with Computers Ser.). (Illus.). 48p. 1984. pap. 3.95 (ISBN 0-317-05531-3, EN79314). Enrich.

--Learning about Computers. (Growing Up with Computers Ser.). (Illus.). 48p. 1984. pap. 3.95 (ISBN 0-86582-204-2, EN79311). Enrich.

Chirino, Alfonso. The Texts & Concordances of Escorial Manuscript: Menor dano de la Medicina. Ardemagni, Enrica J., ed. Richards, Ruth M. & Solomon, Michael R. (Medieval Spanish Medical Texts Ser.: No. 2). 11p. incl. 11 microfiches 1984 10.00x (ISBN 0-942260-41-4). Hispanic Seminary.

Chirkin, V. Y. & Yudin, Y. A. A Socialist Oriented State: Instrument of Revolutionary Change. (Problems of Developing Countries Ser). 1978. 4.95 (ISBN 0-8285-3333-4, Pub. by Progress Pubs USSR). Imported Pubns.

Chirlian. Analysis & Design of Integrated Circuits, Vol. 1: Devices. 1982. pap. text ed. 23.50 (ISBN 0-06-318213-0, Pub. by Har-Row Ltd England). Har-Row.

--Analysis & Design of Integrated Circuits, Vol. 2: Digital. 1982. pap. text ed. 15.50 (ISBN 0-06-318215-7, Pub. by Har-Row Ltd England). Har-Row.

--Analysis & Design of Integrated Circuits, Vol. 3: Analogue. 1982. pap. text ed. 15.50 (ISBN 0-06-318214-9, Pub. by Har-Row Ltd England). Har-Row.

Chirlian, Barbara. Simply dBASE II. (Illus.). 300p. 1984. pap. 9.95 (ISBN 0-88056-138-6). Dilithium Pr.

--Simply VisiCalc. 158p. 1983. pap. 12.95 (ISBN 0-88056-130-0). Dilithium Pr.

Chirlian, Barbara S. Simply Multiplan. 225p. 1984. pap. 9.95 (ISBN 0-88056-333-8). Dilithium Pr.

--Simply VisiCalc. (Illus.). 100p. 1984. pap. 9.95 (ISBN 0-88056-130-0). Dilithium Pr.

Chirlian, Paul. Fundamentals of Electrical Engineering Analysis. 750p. 1984. text ed. 34.95. Matrix Pub.

--Introduction to Ada. Morrice, Nancy, ed. LC 84-15456. 300p. 1985. pap. 19.95 (ISBN 0-916460-42-8). Matrix Pub.

--Introduction to Modula 2. (Illus.). 288p. 1984. pap. 19.95. Dilithium Pr.

--Introduction to Modula 2. Morrice, Nancy, ed. 288p. 1985. pap. 19.95 (ISBN 0-916460-41-X). Matrix Pub.

Chirlian, Paul M. Analysis & Design of Digital Circuits & Computer Systems. (Illus.). 662p. 1976. 29.95 (ISBN 0-916460-03-7). Matrix Pub.

--Analysis & Design of Integrated Electronic Circuits. (Illus.). 1072p. 1981. text ed. 38.75 scp (ISBN 0-06-041266-6, HarpC); solutions's manual avail. (ISBN 0-06-361176-7). Har-Row.

--Basic Network Theory. LC 68-25648. (Electrical & Electronic Eng. Ser). (Illus.). 1968. 48.00 (ISBN 0-07-010788-2). McGraw.

--Beginning BASIC. LC 77-15576. 1978. pap. 14.95 (ISBN 0-918398-06-1). Dilithium Pr.

--Beginning FORTH. rev. ed. 220p. (Orig.). 1983. pap. 16.95 (ISBN 0-916460-36-3). Matrix Pub.

--Beginning FORTH. 220p. 16.95. Dilithium Pr.

--Beginning FORTH. LC 84-8915. (Illus.). 256p. 1985. 24.95 (ISBN 0-8306-0822-2, 1822); pap. write for info. TAB Bks.

--Digital Circuits with Microprocessor Applications. 432p. 1981. text ed. 26.95 (ISBN 0-916460-32-0). Matrix Pub.

--Fundamentals of Electrical Engineering Analysis. 650p. 1984. 34.95. Dilithium Pr.

--Introduction to Ada. 224p. 1984. pap. 19.95 (ISBN 0-916460-42-8). Dilithium Pr.

--Introduction to C. 300p. 1984. pap. 16.95 (ISBN 0-916460-37-1). Dilithium Pr.

--Introduction to Modula 2. 19.95 (ISBN 0-317-26565-2). Merl Miller Assoc.

--Introduction to Structured FORTRAN. (Illus.). 480p. 1979. pap. 16.95 (ISBN 0-916460-07-X). Matrix Pub.

--Microsoft FORTRAN. LC 80-70797. 325p. 1981. pap. 15.95 (ISBN 0-918398-46-0). Dilithium Pr.

--Pascal. 224p. 1980. pap. 12.95 (ISBN 0-916460-28-2). Matrix Pub.

Chiro, Giovanni Di see Di Chiro, Giovanni, et al.

Chiro, Giovoanni Di see Di Chiro, Giovanni.

Chirogos, jt. auth. see Fenichel.

Chirol, Valentine. India. LC 72-2561. (Select Bibliographies Reprint Ser.). 1972. Repr. of 1926 ed. 22.00 (ISBN 0-8369-6851-4). Ayer Co Pubs.

Chirol, Yves, et al. Delinquance Juvenile et Developpement Socio-Economique. (Publication Du Centre De Europeen De Coordination De Recherche et De Documentation En Sciences Sociales: No. 6). (Illus.). pap. 25.20x (ISBN 90-2797-882-4). Mouton.

Chironis, Nicholas P. Mechanisms, Linkages, & Mechanical Controls. 1965. 57.75 (ISBN 0-07-010775-0). McGraw.

Chironna, Mark. The Elisha Principle. 54p. (Orig.). 1985. pap. 2.95 (ISBN 0-938612-11-5). Revival Press.

Chirot, D., tr. see Stahl, Henri.

Chirot, Daniel. Social Change in the Twentieth-Century. 1977. pap. text ed. 15.95 (ISBN 0-15-581420-6, HC). HarBraceJ.

Chirot, Daniel, ed. Social Changes in a Peripheral Society: The Creation of a Balkan Colony. 1976. 34.50 (ISBN 0-12-173150-2). Acad Pr.

Chirot, H. C., tr. see Stahl, Henri.

Chirovsky, Nicholas & Mott, Vincent. Philosophical Foundations of Economic Doctrines. 3rd ed. 1981. pap. 5.95 (ISBN 0-912598-20-4). Florham.

Chirovsky, Nicholas L. A History of the Russian Empire, Vol. 1. LC 72-78164. (Illus.). 440p. 1973. 15.00 (ISBN 0-8022-2091-6). Philos Lib.

--An Introduction to Ukrainian History, Vol. 1. LC 79-84848. 350p. 1981. 19.95 (ISBN 0-8022-2248-X). Philos Lib.

--An Introduction to Ukrainian History, Vol. III: Nineteenth & Twentieth Century Ukraine, 3 Vols. LC 79-84848. (Illus.). 1985. 30.00 (ISBN 0-8022-2481-4). Philos Lib.

--An Introduction to Ukrainian History, Vol. II: The Lithuanian-Rus' Commonwealth, the Polish Domination & the Cossack-Hetman State. LC 82-12255. (Illus.). 399p. 1984. 25.00 (ISBN 0-8022-2407-5). Philos Lib.

Chirri, Mohamad J. The Brother of the Prophet Mohammad, Vol. II. LC 79-127838. 400p. 1982. 15.00 (ISBN 0-942778-00-6). Islamic Ctr.

Chisari, Francis V., ed. Advances in Hepatitis Research. LC 83-25633. (Illus.). 315p. 1984. 69.50 (ISBN 0-89352-218-X). Masson Pub.

Chisenhall, Fred, jt. auth. see McKee, Margaret.

Chisholm. Living in Prehistoric Times. 1983. 6.95 (ISBN 0-86020-624-6, 310011); pap. 2.95 (ISBN 0-86020-623-8, 310012); lib. bdg. 11.95 (ISBN 0-88110-104-4). EDC.

--Our Earth: Let's Find Out About. (gr. 2-5). 1982. 6.95 (ISBN 0-86020-583-5, Usborne-Hayes); lib. bdg. 11.95 (ISBN 0-88110-016-1); pap. 2.95 (ISBN 0-86020-582-7). EDC.

Chisholm & Williams. Scientific Foundations of Urology. 2nd ed. 1983. 135.00 (ISBN 0-8151-9345-9). Year Bk Med.

Chisholm, jt. auth. see Hawsby.

Chisholm, A. A., jt. auth. see Shaw, J.

Chisholm, A. H. First Kuwait Oil Concession: Record of the Negotiations, 1911-1934. 272p. 1975. 37.50x (ISBN 0-7146-3002-0, F Cass Co). Biblio Dist.

Chisholm, A. H., jt. auth. see Snow, David.

Chisholm, Alan R. Towards Herodiade: A Literary Genealogy. LC 77-10255. Repr. of 1934 ed. 22.50 (ISBN 0-404-16310-6). AMS Pr.

Chisholm, Alec H. Bird Wonders of Australia. (Illus.). 1958. 5.00 (ISBN 0-87013-033-1). Mich St U Pr.

Chisholm, Alex & Chisholm, Sarah. Emotions: Can You Trust Them? Leader's Guide. 48p. 1984. pap. 3.95 (ISBN 0-8307-0992-4, 6101926). Regal.

Chisholm, Anne. Nancy Cunard: A Biography. 544p. 1981. pap. 6.95 (ISBN 0-14-005572-X). Penguin.

Chisholm, Anthony H. & Tyers, Rodney, eds. Food Security in Asia & the Pacific Rim: Perspectives & Policy Issues. LC 81-48396. (Illus.). 384p. 1982. 32.50x (ISBN 0-669-05356-2). Lexington Bks.

Chisholm, C. D., ed. Group Theoretical Techniques in Quantum Chemistry. 1976. 49.50 (ISBN 0-12-172950-8). Acad Pr.

Chisholm, Clarence E. & Stewart, Alva W. Regulatory Reform since Nineteen Seventy-Seven: A Bibliographic Overview. (Public Administration Ser.: Bibliography P 1619). 1985. pap. 2.00 (ISBN 0-89028-289-7). Vance Biblios.

Chisholm, Craig M. & Chisholm, Ella. Hawaiian Hiking Trails. rev. 5th ed. LC 85-80148. (Illus.). 152p. 1985. pap. 9.95 (ISBN 0-9612630-0-8). Fernglen Pr.

Chisholm, D., ed. Developments in Heat Exchanger Technology, Vol. 1. (Illus.). 294p. 1980. 64.75 (ISBN 0-85334-913-4, Pub. by Elsevier Applied Sci England). Elsevier.

Chisholm, David. Goethe's Knittelvers: A Prosodic Analysis. (Abhandlungen zur Kunst-, Musik- und Literaturwissenschaft: Vol. 185). iv, 213p. (Orig.). 1975. pap. 20.00x (ISBN 3-416-01084-1, Pub. by Bouvier Verlag W Germany). Benjamins North Am.

Chisholm, Ella, jt. auth. see Chisholm, Craig M.

Chisholm, Emily, tr. see Thurian, Max.

Chisholm, Francis P. Introductory Lectures on General Semantics. 1971. Repr. of 1944 ed. 5.00x (ISBN 0-910780-05-6). Inst Gen Seman.

Chisholm, Gloria. Andrea. LC 83-71614. 160p. (Orig.). 1983. pap. 2.95 (ISBN 0-87123-297-9). Bethany Hse.

--Encourage One Another. 168p. 1985. 9.95 (ISBN 0-8499-0472-2, 0472-2). Word Bks.

Chisholm, H., tr. see Deutsch, Lev G.

Chisholm, J. Biology. (Basic Guides Ser.). 48p. (gr. 3-6). 1984. 8.95 (ISBN 0-86020-708-0); PLB 12.95 (ISBN 0-88110-166-4); pap. 5.95 (ISBN 0-86020-707-2). EDC.

--Book of Science. (Basic Guides Ser.). 48p. (gr. 3-6). 1984. 12.95 (ISBN 0-86020-721-8). EDC.

Chisholm, J. S. Vectors in Three-Dimensional Space. LC 77-82492. (Illus.). 1978. 69.50 (ISBN 0-521-21832-2); pap. 18.95 (ISBN 0-521-29289-1). Cambridge U Pr.

Chisholm, J. S. & Morris, R. M. Mathematical Methods in Physics. 2nd, rev. ed. 720p. 1983. 51.00 (ISBN 0-444-86621-3, North Holland). Elsevier.

Chisholm, Jack M. My Life's Venture in Prayer. (Prayer in My Life Ser.: Ser. II). 1974. pap. 1.25x (ISBN 0-8358-0316-3). Upper Room.

Chisholm, James. South Pass, 1868: James Chisholm's Journal of the Wyoming Gold Rush. Homsher, Lola M., ed. LC 60-12692. (Pioneer Heritage Ser: Vol. 3). (Illus.). vi, 250p. 1960. pap. 6.50 (ISBN 0-8032-5824-0, BB 606, Bison). U of Nebr Pr.

Chisholm, James S. Navajo Infancy: An Ethological Study of Child Development. LC 83-12258. (Biological Foundations of Human Behavior Ser.). 267p. 1983. text ed. 29.95x (ISBN 0-202-01169-0). Aldine Pub.

Chisholm, Jan. Living in Roman Times. 24p. (gr. 3-6). 1982. 6.95 (ISBN 0-86020-620-3, 310021); pap. 2.95 (ISBN 0-86020-619-X, 310022); lib. bdg. 11.95 (ISBN 0-88110-105-2). EDC.

Chisholm, Jane. First Book to History. 72p. 1983. 10.95 (ISBN 0-86020-625-4, 21151). EDC.

Chisholm, Kitty see Ferguson, John.

Chisholm, L. J. Units of Weight & Measure: International (Metric) & U. S. Customary. LC 74-20726. (Illus.). 256p. 1975. Repr. of 1967 ed. 40.00x (ISBN 0-8103-4163-8). Gale.

Chisholm, Leslie L. The Economic Ability of the States to Finance Public Schools. LC 70-176643. (Columbia University. Teachers College. Contributions to Education: No. 669). Repr. of 1936 ed. 22.50 (ISBN 0-404-55669-8). AMS Pr.

Chisholm, Louey, ed. The Golden Staircase: Poems & Verses for Children. LC 79-51973. (Granger Poetry Library). (Illus.). (gr. 3-8). 1980. Repr. of 1906 ed. 23.50x (ISBN 0-89609-182-1). Granger Bk.

Chisholm, Lovey, ed. The Golden Staircase: Poems & Verses for Children. facsimile ed. LC 71-37011. (Granger Index Reprint Ser.). 22.00 (ISBN 0-8369-6310-5). Ayer Co Pubs.

Chisholm, M. & Manners, G., eds. Spatial Policy Problems of the British Economy. LC 70-160090. (Illus.). 1971. 39.50 (ISBN 0-521-08235-8). Cambridge U Pr.

Chisholm, Malcolm, ed. Reactivity of Metal-Metal Bonds. LC 81-361. (ACS Symposium Ser.: No. 155). 1981. 41.95 (ISBN 0-8412-0624-4). Am Chemical.

Chisholm, Malcolm H., ed. Inorganic Chemistry: Toward the Twenty-First Century. LC 82-24505. (ACS Symposium Ser.: No. 211). 566p. 1983. lib. bdg. 59.95x (ISBN 0-8412-0763-1). Am Chemical.

Chisholm, Michael. Modern World Development: A Geographical Perspective. LC 82-11404. (Illus.). 216p. 1982. text ed. 28.50x (ISBN 0-389-20320-3, 07160); pap. text ed. 14.50x (ISBN 0-389-20321-1, 07161). B&N Imports.

--The Taurus Method. 2nd ed. 1985. 75.00 (ISBN 0-318-04661-X). Windsor.

Chisholm, R. & Haller, R., eds. Die Philosophie Franz Brentanos: Beitrage Zur Brentano-Konferenz Graz 4-8, September 1977. (Grazer Philosophische Studien: No. 5). 1978. pap. text ed. 29.50x (ISBN 90-6203-692-9). Humanities.

Chisholm, R., tr. see Brentano, Franz.

Chisholm, Richard. Meet Me in Istanbul. (Heinemann Guided Readers). (Orig.). 1979. pap. text ed. 2.00x (ISBN 0-435-27060-5). Heinemann Ed.

--Scottish Adventure. (Heinemann Guided Readers Ser.). 1977. pap. text ed. 2.00x (ISBN 0-435-27044-3). Heinemann Ed.

Chisholm, Roderick. The First Person: An Essay on Reference & Intentionality. LC 80-24910. 144p. 1982. pap. 10.95x (ISBN 0-8166-1075-4). U of Minn Pr.

--The First Person: An Essay on Reference & Intentionality. LC 80-24910. 192p. 1981. 22.50x (ISBN 0-8166-1045-2). U of Minn Pr.

--Theory of Knowledge. 2nd ed. (Foundations of Philosophy Ser.). 1977. pap. text ed. 13.95 (ISBN 0-13-914150-2). P-H.

Chisholm, Roderick, tr. see Brentano, Franz.

Chisholm, Roderick M. The Foundations of Knowing. LC 81-19707. 256p. 1982. pap. 10.95x (ISBN 0-8166-1104-1). U of Minn Pr.

--Perceiving: A Philosophical Study. LC 74-7639. (Contemporary Philosophy Ser.). 214p. 1957. 22.50x (ISBN 0-8014-0077-5). Cornell U Pr.

--Person & Object: A Metaphysical Study. LC 75-29952. (The Paul Carus Lecture Ser.). 230p. 1976. 19.95 (ISBN 0-87548-341-0). Open Court.

--The Problem of the Criterion (Nineteen Seventy-Three Aquinas Lecture) gold stamped titles 7.95 (ISBN 0-87462-138-0). Marquette.

Chisholm, Roderick M., ed. Realism & the Background of Phenomenology. vii, 308p. 1981. lib. bdg. 24.00x (ISBN 0-917930-34-7); pap. text ed. 8.50x (ISBN 0-917930-14-2). Ridgeview.

--The Vocation of Man: Fichte. 1956. pap. text ed. write for info. (ISBN 0-02-322530-0). Macmillan.

Chisholm, Roger & McCarty, Marilu. Principles of Economics. 2nd ed. 1981. text ed. 29.30x (ISBN 0-673-15492-0). Scott F.

--Principles of Macroeconomics. 2nd ed. 1981. pap. text ed. 18.60x (ISBN 0-673-15493-9). Scott F.

--Principles of Microeconomics. 2nd ed. 1981. pap. text ed. 18.60x (ISBN 0-673-15402-5). Scott F.

Chisholm, Sarah, jt. auth. see Chisholm, Alex.

Chisholm, Stuart. The Independence of Chile. 1976. lib. bdg. 59.95 (ISBN 0-8490-2047-6). Gordon Pr.

Chisholm, William, et al, eds. Interrogativity: A Colloquium in the Grammar, Typology & Pragmatics of Questions in Seven Diverse Languages, Cleveland, Ohio, October 5th, 1981 to May 3rd, 1982. (Typological Studies in Language: 4). 302p. 1984. 37.00x (ISBN 0-915027-02-X); pap. 22.00 (ISBN 0-915027-03-8). Benjamins North Am.

Chishom, J. & Lynnington, M. Chemistry. (Basic Guides Ser.). (Illus.). 48p. (gr. 6 up). 1983. 8.95 (ISBN 0-86020-710-2); lib. bdg. 12.95 (ISBN 0-88110-151-6); pap. 5.95 (ISBN 0-86020-709-9). EDC.

Chisick, Harvey. The Limits of Reform in the Enlightenment: Attitudes Toward the Education of the Lower Classes in Eighteenth Century France. LC 80-7512. 296p. 1981. 34.00 (ISBN 0-691-05305-7). Princeton U Pr.

Chislett, William. George Meredith: A Study & an Appraisal. LC 68-905. (Studies in Fiction, No. 34). 1969. Repr. of 1925 ed. lib. bdg. 48.95x (ISBN 0-8383-0526-1). Haskell.

--Moderns & Near-Moderns. LC 76-57978. 1977. lib. bdg. 27.50 (ISBN 0-8414-3434-4). Folcroft.

--Moderns & Near-Moderns: Essays on Henry James, Stockton, Shaw & Others. facs. ed. LC 67-30180. (Essay Index Reprint Ser). 1928. 16.00 (ISBN 0-8369-0302-1). Ayer Co Pubs.

Chislett, William, Jr. Classical Influence in English Literature. LC 74-8491. 1918. lib. bdg. 25.00 (ISBN 0-8414-3503-0). Folcroft.

Chisman, Forrest & Pifer, Alan, eds. Report of the Committee on Economic Security of 1935. LC 85-60612. 304p. 1985. 35.00 (ISBN 0-933597-02-9); pap. 9.95 (ISBN 0-933597-03-7). Natl Conf Soc Welfare.

Chisman, Forrest P. Attitude Psychology & the Study of Public Opinion. LC 76-10345. (Illus.). 1977. 24.95x (ISBN 0-271-01227-7). Pa St U Pr.

Chisnall, Heather, ed. Learning from Work & Community Experience. 208p. 1983. 24.00x (ISBN 0-7005-0620-9, Pub. by NFER Nelson UK). Taylor & Francis.

Chisnall, Peter M. Marketing Research: Analysis & Measurement. 2nd ed. (Illus.). 384p. 1982. 37.50 (ISBN 0-07-084559-X). McGraw.

Chisolm, J. J. Manual of Confederate Military Surgeons. 600p. 1983. 40.00 (ISBN 0-89029-068-7). Pr of Morningside.

Chisolm, J. J. & O'Hara, D. M. Lead Absorption in Children: Management, Clinical & Environmental Aspects. LC 81-16306. (Illus.). 240p. 1982. 32.50 (ISBN 0-8067-0331-8). Urban & S.

Chisolm, J. J., Jr., et al, eds. Diagnosis & Treatment of Lead Poisoning. 213p. 1976. text ed. 37.50x (ISBN 0-8422-7262-3). Irvington.

Chisolm, Jane & Johnson, Mary. Introduction to Chemistry. (Illus.). 48p. (gr. 5-8). 1983. 8.95 (ISBN 0-86020-710-2, Usborne-Hayes); PLB 12.95 (ISBN 0-88110-151-6, Usborne-Hayes); pap. 3.95 (ISBN 0-86020-709-9, Usborne-Hayes). EDC.

Chisolm, Kitty & Ferguson, John. Rome: The Augustan Age: A Source Book. (Illus.). 1981. text ed. 59.00x (ISBN 0-19-872108-0); pap. text ed. 29.95x (ISBN 0-19-872109-9). Oxford U Pr.

Chisolm, Lawrence W. Fenollossa: The Far East & American Culture. LC 76-22680. (Yale Publications in American Studies Ser: No. 8). (Illus.). 297p. 1976. Repr. of 1963 ed. lib. bdg. 24.75x (ISBN 0-8371-8975-6, CHFE). Greenwood.

Chisolm, Roderick M. Brentano & Meinong Studies. (Studien zur Oesterreichischen Philosophie: Band III). 124p. 1982. pap. text ed. 12.00x (ISBN 0-391-02347-0). Humanities.

Chissell, Joan. Brahms. (The Great Composer Ser.). (Illus.). 104p. 1977. 8.95 (ISBN 0-571-10791-5). Faber & Faber.

--Clara Schumann: A Dedicated Spirit; A Study of Her Life & Work. LC 83-50182. (Illus.). 200p. 1983. 19.95 (ISBN 0-8008-1624-2, Crescendo). Taplinger.

--Schumann. Rev. ed. (The Master Musicians Ser.). (Illus.). 268p. 1977. text ed. 13.50x (ISBN 0-460-03170-8, BKA 03021, Pub. by J M Dent England). Biblio Dist.

--Schumann Piano Music. LC 72-550. (BBC Guide Ser.). (Illus.). 72p. (Orig.). 1972. pap. 4.95 (ISBN 0-295-95252-0). U of Wash Pr.

Chissick, S. S. & Derricott, R. Asbestos(Properties of Materials, Safety & Environmental Factors) Properties, Applications & Hazards, Vol.2. 672p. 1983. 84.95 (ISBN 0-471-10489-2). Wiley.

--Occupational Health & Safety Management: Property of Materials: Safety & Environmental Factors. LC 79-41218. 705p. 1981. 106.95 (ISBN 0-471-27646-4, Pub. by Wiley-Interscience). Wiley.

Chissick, S. S., jt. auth. see Michaels, L.

Chissick, S. S., jt. ed. see Price, W. C.

Chissick, Seymour, jt. auth. see Derricott, Robert.

Chissick, Seymour S., jt. auth. see Derricott, R.

Chissin, Chaim. A Palestine Diary. 1976. 10.00 (ISBN 0-685-82598-1). Herzl Pr.

Chissov, et al. Atlas on Oncological Surgery. Date not set. price not set (BN#00435). Intl Univs Pr.

Chistayakova, Tatyana, tr. see Rudakova, Ye. & Kandinsky, A. I.

Chisum. Patents, 6 vols. 1983. Updates avail. looseleaf 400.00 (#525); looseleaf 1983 208.50; looseleaf 1984 291.00. Bender.

Chiswick, Barry, ed. Gateway: U. S. Immigration Issues & Policies. 476p. 1982. 22.95 (ISBN 0-8447-2221-9); pap. 12.95 (ISBN 0-8447-2220-0). Am Enterprise.

Chiswick, Barry, jt. auth. see Cafferty, P.

Chiswick, Barry R. The Employment of Immigrants in the United States. 37p. 1982. 2.95 (ISBN 0-8447-3501-9). Am Enterprise.

--Income Inequality: Regional Analyses Within a Human Capital Framework. (Studies in Human Behavior & Social Institutions: No. 4). 228p. 1974. 15.00 (ISBN 0-87014-264-X, Dist. by Columbia U Pr). Natl Bur Econ Res.

Chiswick, Barry R. & Chiswick, Stephen J. Statistics & Econometrics. (Illus.). 280p. 1975. pap. 21.00 (ISBN 0-8391-0694-7). Univ Park.

Chiswick, Barry R. & O'Neill, June, eds. Human Resources & Income Distribution. (Illus.). 1977. pap. 5.95x (ISBN 0-393-09131-7). Norton.

Chiswick, D., et al. Prosecution of the Mentally Disturbed: Dilemmas of Identification & Discretion. 192p. 1984. 24.00 (ISBN 0-08-028481-7). Pergamon.

Chiswick, Malcolm L. Neonatal Medicine. (Illus.). 1978. text ed. 10.50x (ISBN 0-906141-01-X, Pub. by Update Pubns England). Kluwer Academic.

Chiswick, Stephen J., jt. auth. see Chiswick, Barry R.

Chiszar, David & Smith, Rozella. Fifty Years of Herpetology Publications of Hobart M. Smith. 90p. 1982. pap. text ed. 4.00x (ISBN 0-910914-17-6). J Johnson.

Chitale, A. R., jt. auth. see Jussawalla, D. J.

Chitale, V. P. Project Viability in Inflationary Conditions. 144p. 1980. text ed. 17.95x (ISBN 0-7069-1132-6, Pub. by Vikas India). Advent NY.

--Risk Capital for Industry, India. 1984. 12.50x (ISBN 0-8364-1176-5, Pub. by Allied India). South Asia Bks.

Chitayat, Gideon. Trade Union Mergers & Labor Conglomerates. LC 79-2966. (Praeger Special Studies Ser.). 240p. 1979. 38.95 (ISBN 0-03-051326-X). Praeger.

Chiteji, Frank M. The Development & Socio-Economic Impact of Transportation in Tanzania Eighteen Eighty-Four - Present. LC 80-5092. 151p. 1980. pap. text ed. 9.75 (ISBN 0-8191-1041-8). U Pr of Amer.

Chitham, E. & Winnifrith, T. Bronte Facts & Bronte Problems. 176p. 1983. text ed. 30.50x (ISBN 0-333-30698-8, Pub. by Macmillan). Humanities.

Chitham, Edward. The Brontes' Irish Background. 176p. 1985. 25.00 (ISBN 0-312-10598-3). St Martin.

--The Poems of Anne Bronte: A New Text & Commentary. 217p. 1979. 21.50x (ISBN 0-8476-6100-8). Rowman.

Chitham, Robert. Measured Drawings for Architects. (Illus.). 128p. 1980. 28.50x (ISBN 0-85139-391-8); pap. 17.50x (ISBN 0-85139-392-6). Nichols Pub.

Chitlangou, pseud. Chitlangou, Son of a Chief. LC 74-140805. (Illus.). 208p. 1972. Repr. of 1950 ed. text ed. cancelled (ISBN 0-8371-5839-7, CCH&, Pub. by Negro U Pr). Greenwood.

Chitnis, Sima. A Long Way to Go: Report on a Survey of Scheduled Caste High School & College Students in 15 States of India. 350p. 1981. 39.95x (ISBN 0-8364-0759-8, Pub. by Allied India). South Asia Bks.

Chitnis, Suma & Altbach, Philip. The Indian Academic Profession. 1979. 13.00x (ISBN 0-8364-0561-7, Pub. by Macmillan India). South Asia Bks.

Chittenden, F. J. & Synge, P. M., eds. Dictionary of Gardening: A Practical & Scientific Encyclopedia of Horticulture, 4 Vols. 2nd ed. 1956. 275.00x (ISBN 0-19-869106-8). Oxford U Pr.

Chittenden, Gertrude. Experimental Study in Measuring & Modifying Assertive Behavior in Young Children. (SRCD M Ser.: Vol. 7, No. 1). 1942. pap. 16.00 (ISBN 0-527-01522-9). Kraus Repr.

Chittenden, Hiram M. American Fur Trade in the Far West, 2 vols. LC 73-21914. (Illus.). Repr. of 1935 ed. Set. lib. bdg. 75.00x (ISBN 0-678-01035-8). Kelley.

--Early Steamboat Navigation on the Missouri River. Repr. 15.00 (ISBN 0-87018-009-6). Ross.

Chittenden, Hiram Martin. H. M. Chittenden: A Western Epic. Le Roy, Bruce, ed. LC 61-64226. (Illus.). 136p. (Ed. limited to 1000 copies). 1961. 10.00 (ISBN 0-917048-17-2); deluxe ed. 25.00 (ISBN 0-686-96919-7). Wash St Hist Soc.

Chittenden, L. E. Personal Reminiscences, Eighteen Forty to Eighteen Ninety. facsimile ed. LC 72-37302. (Black Heritage Library Collection). Repr. of 1893 ed. 26.25 (ISBN 0-8369-8939-2). Ayer Co Pubs.

--Report of the Debates & Proceedings of the Peace Convention Held in Washington, D.C., Feb. 1861. LC 70-158578. 626p. 1971. Repr. of 1864 ed. lib. bdg. 79.50 (ISBN 0-306-70190-1). Da Capo.

Chittenden, Margaret. Merrymaking in Great Britain. LC 73-12822. (Around the World Holidays Ser.). (Illus.). 96p. (gr. 4-7). 1974. PLB 7.98 (ISBN 0-8116-4952-0). Garrard.

--The Mystery of the Missing Pony. LC 79-19084. (Mystery Ser.). (Illus.). (gr. 3). 1980. PLB 7.68 (ISBN 0-8116-6411-2). Garrard.

Chittenden, Russel H. History of the Sheffield Scientific School of Yale, 2 vols. 1928. 150.00x (ISBN 0-685-69797-5). Elliots Bks.

Chittendon, Hiram M. The Yellowstone National Park. LC 64-11334. (Illus.). 208p. 1964. pap. 6.95 (ISBN 0-8061-0937-8). U of Okla Pr.

Chittick, Donald E. The Controversy: Roots of the Creation-Evolution Conflict. LC 84-22670. (Critical Concern Ser.). 1984. 12.95 (ISBN 0-88070-019-X). Multnomah.

Chittick, H. Neville & Rotberg, Robert I., eds. East Africa & the Orient: Cultural Syntheses in Pre-Colonial Times. LC 73-89568. 350p. 1975. text ed. 45.00x (ISBN 0-8419-0142-2, Africana). Holmes & Meier.

Chittick, Victor L. Thomas Chandler Haliburton, "Sam Slick". LC 24-29336. Repr. of 1924 ed. 20.00 (ISBN 0-404-01525-5). AMS Pr.

Chittick, William & Wilson, Peter, trs. Fakhruddin Iraqi: Divine Flashes. 1982. 11.95 (ISBN 0-8091-0329-X); pap. 7.95 (ISBN 0-8091-2372-X). Paulist Pr.

Chittick, William, tr. see Nurbakhsh, Javad.

Chittick, William, tr. see Tabatabai, Muhammad.

Chittick, William C. The Sufi Path of Love: The Spiritual Teachings of Rumi. LC 82-19511. (SUNY Series in Islam). 400p. 1983. 44.50x (ISBN 0-87395-723-7); pap. 12.95x (ISBN 0-87395-724-5). State U NY Pr.

Chittick, William C., tr. see Al-Abidin, Zayn.

Chittick, William C., tr. see Muhammad.

Chittick, William C., tr. see Talib, Ali I.

Chittister, Joan. Women, Ministry, & the Church. LC 82-62418. 1983. pap. 5.95 (ISBN 0-8091-2528-5). Paulist Pr.

Chittister, Joan & Kownacki, Mary L. Psalm Journal. LC 85-50308. 104p. (Orig.). 1985. pap. 6.95 (ISBN 0-934134-28-6). Leaven Pr.

Chittister, Joan, et al. Midwives of the Future: American Sisters Tell Their Story. Ware, Ann P., ed. LC 84-82554. 237p. (Orig.). 1984. pap. 8.95 (ISBN 0-934134-11-1). Leaven Pr.

Chittister, Joan D. & Marty, Martin E. Faith & Ferment: An Interdisciplinary Study of Christian Beliefs & Practices. Bilheimer, Robert S., ed. 352p. 1983. pap. 14.95 (ISBN 0-8146-1289-X). Liturgical Pr.

Chittum, Ida. The Cat's Pajamas. LC 80-10579. (Illus.). 48p. (ps-3). 1980. 5.95 (ISBN 0-686-86560-X); PLB 5.95 (ISBN 0-686-91529-1). Parents.

--The Ghost Boy of el Toro. (Illus.). 176p. 1982. pap. 1.95 (ISBN 0-448-16927-4, Pub. by Tempo). Ace Bks.

--The Ghost Boy of el Toro. LC 78-1079. 1978. 8.00 (ISBN 0-8309-0201-5). Ind Pr MO.

Chitty, Cordelia, jt. auth. see Hinde, Thomas.

Chitty, Derwas J. The Desert a City. 222p. 1977. pap. 7.95 (ISBN 0-913836-45-1). St Vladimirs.

Chitty, Susan, ed. see White, Antonia.

Chitwood, B. Introduction to Nematology. (Illus.). 344p. 1975. pap. text ed. 35.00 (ISBN 0-8391-0697-1). Univ Park.

Chitwood, Deb. The Magic Ring. LC 82-62432. (Illus.). 32p. (ps-3). 1983. 9.95 (ISBN 0-942044-01-0). Polestar.

Chitwood, Oliver P. Justice in Colonial Virginia. LC 78-63909. (Johns Hopkins University. Studies in the Social Sciences. Twenty-Third Ser. 1905: 7-8). Repr. of 1905 ed. 12.00 (ISBN 0-404-61161-3). AMS Pr.

--Justice in Colonial Virginia. LC 72-87557. (American Constitutional & Legal History Ser). 1971. Repr. of 1905 ed. lib. bdg. 19.50 (ISBN 0-306-71388-8). Da Capo.

--Richard Henry Lee: Statesman of the Revolution. (Illus.). 1967. 7.00 (ISBN 0-685-30817-0). McClain.

Chitwood, Terry. How to Defend Yourself Without Even Trying. (Illus.). 96p. 1981. pap. 6.95 (ISBN 0-942044-00-2). Polestar.

--Meeting Force with Silence. (Illus.). 82p. (Orig.). 1985. pap. 6.95 (ISBN 0-942044-03-7). Polestar.

Chiu, Arthur, jt. ed. see Ishizaki, Hatsuo.

Ch'iu, Chang-Wei. Speaker of the House of Representatives Since 1896. LC 68-58558. (Columbia University Studies in the Social Sciences: No. 297). Repr. of 1928 ed. 24.50 (ISBN 0-404-51297-6). AMS Pr.

Chiu, Hong-Yee & Muriel, Amador, eds. Stellar Evolution. 827p. 1972. 55.00x (ISBN 0-262-12058-5). MIT Pr.

Chiu, Hungdah. Agreements of the People's Republic of China: A Calendar of Events, 1966-1980. LC 81-8686. 350p. 1981. 41.95x (ISBN 0-03-059443-X). Praeger.

--China & the Taiwan Issue. LC 79-14270. (Praeger Special Studies). 310p. 1979. 42.95x (ISBN 0-03-048911-3). Praeger.

--Chinese Law & Justice: Trends over Three Decades. (Occasional Papers - Reprints Series in Contemporary Asian Studies: No. 7-1982 (52)). 34p. (Orig.). 1982. pap. text ed. 2.00 (ISBN 0-942182-51-0). U MD Law.

--Chinese Yearbook of International Law & Affairs, 1983, Vol. 3. LC 82-645664. 350p. 1984. 12.00 (ISBN 0-942182-95-2). Occasional Papers.

--Chinese Yearbook of International Law & Affairs, 1984, Vol. 4. LC 82-645664. 400p. 1985. 12.00 (ISBN 0-942182-96-0). Occasional Papers.

--People's Republic of China & the Law of Treaties. LC 72-173411. (Studies in East Asian Law: No. 5). 1972. 14.00x (ISBN 0-674-66175-3). Harvard U Pr.

Chiu, Hungdah & Downen, Robert. Multi-System Nations & International Law, the International Status of Germany, Korea & China. LC 81-85785. (Occasional Papers Reprints Series in Contemporary Asian Studies, No. 8-1981). 203p. (Orig.). 1982. pap. text ed. 5.00 (ISBN 0-942182-44-8). Occasional Papers.

Chiu, Hungdah, jt. auth. see Cohen, Jerome A.

Chiu, Hungdah, jt. auth. see Leng, Shao-Chaun.

Chiu, Hungdah, ed. Chinese Yearbook of International Law & Affairs, 1981, Vol. I. (Chinese Yearbook of International Law & Affairs Ser.). 392p. 1982. pap. 12.00 (ISBN 0-942182-93-6). Occasional Papers.

--Socialist Legalism: Reform & Continuity in Post-Mao People's Republic of China. (Occasional Papers-Reprints Series in Contemporary Asian Studies: No. 1). 35p. (Orig.). 1982. pap. text ed. 2.00 (ISBN 0-942182-45-6). Occasional Papers.

Chiu, Hungdah & Leng, Shao-chuan, eds. China: Seventy Years after the 1911 Hsin-hai Revolution. LC 84-7217. 589p. 1985. text ed. 20.00x (ISBN 0-8139-1027-7). U Pr of Va.

Chiu, Hungdah, jt. ed. see Leng, Snao-Chuan.

Chiu, Kwong Ki see Kwong Ki Chaou.

Chiu, Lee C., jt. auth. see Yiu-Chiu, Victoria S.

Chiu, Milton M. The Tao of Chinese Religion. (Illus.). 432p. (Orig.). 1985. lib. bdg. 26.50 (ISBN 0-8191-4263-8); pap. text ed. 17.25 (ISBN 0-8191-4264-6). U Pr of Amer.

Chiu, Ray C. Myocardial Protection in Regional & Global Ischemia, Vol. 1. (Annual Research Reviews). 177p. 1981. 26.00 (ISBN 0-88831-097-8). Eden Pr.

Chiu, Shui-Chen, jt. auth. see Townes, Henry.

Chiu, Tony. Realm Seven. 288p. (Orig.). 1984. pap. 3.50 (ISBN 0-553-23847-7). Bantam.

Chiu, Y. & Mullish, H. Crunchers: Twenty-One Games for the Timex-Sinclair 1000 (2k) (McGraw-Hill VTX Ser.). 144p. 1983. pap. 8.95 (ISBN 0-07-010831-5, BYTE Bks). McGraw.

--Munchers: Twenty-Five Simple Games for the Texas Instruments 99-2 Basic Computer. (Illus.). 160p. 1984. pap. 9.95 (ISBN 0-07-010839-0, BYTE Bks). Mcgraw.

Chiu, Yin & Tucker, Michael. The Commodore 64 Home Financial Planner. 192p. (Orig.). 1984. pap. 9.95 (ISBN 0-916688-75-5, 75-5). Creative Comp.

Ch'iu Chun. Alternate Love Songs. (Folklore Series of National Sun Yat-Sen University: No. 31). (Chinese.). 16.00x (ISBN 0-89986-099-0). Oriental Bk Store.

Chiu Hone-Yee. Neutrino Astrophysics. (Documents on Modern Physics Ser.). 116p. 1965. 31.25 (ISBN 0-677-01110-5). Gordon.

Chiu Hone-Yee, et al. Stellar Astronomy, 2 Vols. 756p. 1969. Vol. 1,388. 119.25 (ISBN 0-677-13790-7); Vol. 2,368. 93.75 (ISBN 0-677-13800-8); Set. 183.75 (ISBN 0-677-12980-7). Gordon.

Chiu Hone-Yeel & Muriel, Amador. Galactic Astronomy, Vols. 1 & 2. 1970. Vol. 1,344p. 93.75 (ISBN 0-677-13750-8); Vol. 2,310p. 80.95 (ISBN 0-677-13760-5); Set, 654p. 157.25 (ISBN 0-677-13770-2). Gordon.

Chiumello, G. & Laron, Z., eds. Recent Progress in Pediatric Endocrinology. 1978. 55.00 (ISBN 0-12-173250-9). Acad Pr.

Chiumello, Giuseppe & Sperling, Mark, eds. Recent Progress in Pediatric Endocrinology. (Serono Symposia Publications from Raven Press Ser.: Vol. 4). (Illus.). 392p. 1983. text ed. 84.00 (ISBN 0-89004-869-X). Raven.

Chiurdoglu, G., ed. Conformational Analysis: Scope & Present Limitations. (Organic Chemistry Ser.: Vol. 21). 1971. 67.50 (ISBN 0-12-173050-6). Acad Pr.

Chiva, I. & Rambaud, P., eds. Les Etudes Rurales En France: Tendances & Organisation De la Recherche Service D'echange D'informations Scientifiques. (Serie B: Guides & Repertoires: No. 3). 1973. pap. 21.60x (ISBN 90-2797-161-7). Mouton.

Chivers, D. J., et al. The Siamang in Malaya: A Field Study of a Primate in Tropical Rain Forest. Hofer, H. & Schultz, A. H., eds. (Contributions to Primatology: Vol. 4). (Illus.). 250p. 1974. 73.25 (ISBN 3-8055-1668-1). S Karger.

Chivers, David, jt. ed. see Preuschoft, Holger.

Chivers, David C., ed. Recent Advances in Primatology, Vols. 1-4. Vol. 1, 1978. 85.50 (ISBN 0-12-173301-7); Vol. 2, 1978. 56.00 (ISBN 0-12-173302-5); Vol. 3, 1978. 66.50 (ISBN 0-12-173303-3); Vol. 4, 1978. 44.00 (ISBN 0-12-173304-1). Acad Pr.

Chivers, David J., ed. Malayan Forest Primates: Ten Years' Study in a Tropical Rain Forest. LC 80-25181. 388p. 1980. 49.50x (ISBN 0-306-40626-8, Plenum Pr). Plenum Pub.

Chivers, David J., et al, eds. Food Acquisition & Processing in Primates. 574p. 1984. 85.00x (ISBN 0-306-41701-4, Plenum Pr). Plenum Pub.

Chivers, G. R. Introduction to Parliamentary Democracy. LC 74-19741. 1973. 26.00 (ISBN 0-8420-1783-6). Scholarly Res Inc.

Chivers, Ian D. & Clark, Malcolm W. Interactive FORTRAN Seventy-Seven: A Hands on Approach. (Computers & Their Applications Ser.). 231p. 1984. text ed. 29.95x (ISBN 0-470-20101-0). Halsted Pr.

Chivers, Keith. The Shire Horse. (Illus.). 36.00 (ISBN 0-85131-245-4, BL176, Dist. by Miller). J A Allen.

Chivers, Keith, jt. auth. see Rayner, Nick.

Chivers, Thomas H. Conrad & Eudora. LC 78-18338. 1978. Repr. of 1834 ed. 30.00x (ISBN 0-8201-1315-8). Schol Facsimiles.

--Eonchs of Ruby: A Gift of Love. LC 72-4957. (The Romantic Tradition in American Literature Ser.). 172p. 1972. Repr. of 1851 ed. 18.00 (ISBN 0-405-04629-4). Ayer Co Pubs.

--Nacoochee. LC 77-24233. 1977. Repr. of 1837 ed. 35.00x (ISBN 0-8201-1295-X). Schol Facsimilies.

--Path of Sorrow (1832), Eonchs of Ruby (1851), Memoralia (1849), Virginalia (1853), Sons of Usna (1858, 5 vols. in 1. LC 79-22103. 1979. 80.00x (ISBN 0-8201-1340-9). Schol Facsimiles.

--Search After Truth (1848), the Lost Pleiad (1845) & Atlanta (1853) LC 76-18173. 1976. Repr. of 1853 ed. lib. bdg. 35.00x (ISBN 0-8201-1269-0). Schol Facsimiles.

--Unpublished Plays of Thomas Holley Chivers. LC 79-29747. 75.00x (ISBN 0-8201-1350-6). Schol Facsimiles.

--Virginalia; or, Songs of My Summer Nights: A Gift of Love for the Beautiful. LC 72-4958. (The Romantic Tradition in American Literature Ser.). 136p. 1972. Repr. of 1853 ed. 16.00 (ISBN 0-405-04630-8). Ayer Co Pubs.

Chivers, Thomas Holley. The Complete Works of Thomas Holley Chivers, Vol. 1. Chase, Emma L. & Parks, Lois F., eds. LC 57-8677. pap. 84.00 (ISBN 0-317-20638-9, 2024129). Bks Demand UMI.

Chivian, Eric, ed. see International Physicians for the Prevention of Nuclear War, et al.

Chivian, Suzanna, ed. see International Physicians for the Prevention of Nuclear War, et al.

Chivington, Paul K., jt. auth. see Keyes, Elizabeth.

Chi Wen-Shun, ed. Chinese-English Dictionary of Contemporary Usage. (Chinese & Eng.). 1977. 30.00x (ISBN 0-520-02655-1). U of Cal Pr.

--Readings in Chinese Communist Ideology. LC 67-11201. 1968. 38.50x (ISBN 0-520-00232-6). U of Cal Pr.

Chi-Ying Chen. Fool in the Reeds. 302p. 1980. 10.45 (ISBN 0-89955-143-2, Pub. by Mei Ya China). Intl Spec Bk.

Chi-Yu Ho see DeFrancis, John.

Chizikova, Z. A. Research on Spectroscopy & Luminescence: Pt. 4, Radioluminescene Yield of Organic Substances. LC 62-12860. (P. N. Lebedev Physics Institute Ser.: Vol. 15). 50p. 1962. 22.50x (ISBN 0-306-17044-2, Consultants). Plenum Pub.

Chkhikvadze, Victor. State, Democracy & Legality in the U. S. S. R. 371p. 1975. 13.95x (ISBN 0-8464-0883-X). Beekman Pubs.

Chlad, Dorothy. Animals Can be Special Friends. 1985. 2.95 (ISBN 0-516-41978-1). Childrens.

--Bicycles Are Fun to Ride. LC 83-23234. (Safety Town Ser.). (Illus.). 32p. (ps-2). 1984. lib. bdg. 10.60 (ISBN 0-516-01975-9); pap. 2.95 (ISBN 0-516-41975-7). Childrens.

--Matches, Lighters, & Firecrackers Are not Toys. LC 81-18125. (Safety Town Bks.). (Illus.). (gr. k-3). 1982. PLB 10.60 (ISBN 0-516-01982-1); pap. 2.95 (ISBN 0-516-41982-X). Childrens.

--Poisons Make You Sick. LC 83-24029. (Safety Town Ser.). (Illus.). 32p. (ps-2). 1984. lib. bdg. 10.60 (ISBN 0-516-01976-7); pap. 2.95 (ISBN 0-516-41976-5). Childrens.

--Stop, Look, & Listen for Trains. LC 83-7213. (Safety Town Ser.). (Illus.). 32p. (ps-2). 1983. lib. bdg. 10.60 (ISBN 0-516-01988-0); pap. 2.95 (ISBN 0-516-41988-9). Childrens.

--Strangers. LC 81-18109. (Safety Town Bks.). (Illus.). (gr. k-3). 1982. PLB 10.60 (ISBN 0-516-01984-8); pap. 2.95 (ISBN 0-516-41984-6). Childrens.

--When I Cross the Street. LC 81-18108. (Safety Town Bks.). (Illus.). (gr. k-3). 1982. PLB 10.60 (ISBN 0-516-01985-6); pap. 2.95 (ISBN 0-516-41985-4). Childrens.

--When I Ride in a Car. LC 83-7382. (Safety Town Ser.). (Illus.). 32p. (ps-2). 1983. lib. bdg. 10.60 (ISBN 0-516-01987-2); pap. 2.95 (ISBN 0-516-41987-0). Childrens.

--When There Is a Fire-Go Outside. (Safety Town Bks.). (Illus.). (gr. k-3). 1982. PLB 10.60 (ISBN 0-516-01986-4); pap. 2.95 (ISBN 0-516-41986-2). Childrens.

Chlamtac, Imrich, jt. auth. see Franta, W. R.

Chlapowski, F., jt. auth. see PreTest Service, Inc.

Chlapowski, Francis J. Appleton's Review for National Boards, Pt. I. 448p. 1984. pap. 29.95 (ISBN 0-8385-0204-0). ACC.

Chlorine Institute. Properties of Chlorine in SI Units. LC 81-67483. (Illus.). 64p. 1981. pap. text ed. 23.00x (ISBN 0-940230-02-X). Chlorine Inst.

Chloros, A. G. European Family Law. 1978. pap. 53.00 (ISBN 90-268-0899-2, Pub. by Kluwer Law Netherlands). Kluwer Academic.

Chmaj, Betty E., et al. Image, Myth & Beyond, Pt. 1; American Women, Pt. 2; American Studies, Pt. 3, 3 pts. 1972. Know Inc.

Chmel, Joseph, ed. Urkunde, Briefe und Actenstuecke Zur Geschichte der Habsburgischen Fuersten K. Ladislaus Posth: Erzherzog Albrecht Vi, & Herzog Siegmund Von Oesterreich. (Ger). Repr. of 1850 ed. 62.00 (ISBN 0-384-08898-8). Johnson Repr.

--Urkunden Zur Geschichte Von Oesterreich, Steiermark, Kaernten, Krain, Goerz, Triest, Istrien, Tirol Aus Den Jahren 1246-1300. (Ger). Repr. of 1849 ed. 23.00 (ISBN 0-384-08897-X). Johnson Repr.

Chmielarz, Sharon. Different Arrangements. LC 82-61650. (Minnesota Voices Project Ser.: No. 10). (Illus.). 103p. 1982. pap. 3.00 (ISBN 0-89823-042-X). New Rivers Pr.

Chmielewski, Edward. The Polish Question in the Russian State Duma. LC 77-100411. pap. 49.00 (ISBN 0-317-29722-8, 2022213). Bks Demand UMI.

Chmielewski, Edward V. Tribune of the Slavophiles: Konstantin Aksakov. LC 62-63051. (University of Florida Social Sciences Monographs: No. 12). 1961. pap. 3.50 (ISBN 0-8130-0047-5). U Presses Fla.

Chmura, Louis J., jt. auth. see Ledgard, Henry F.

Chmura, Louis J., Jr., jt. auth. see Ledgard, Henry F.

Cho, Cheng & Dudding, Burton. Pediatric Infectious Diseases. (Medical Outline Ser.). 1978. pap. 30.00 (ISBN 0-87488-659-7). Med Exam.

Cho, Chin-Kuei. An Introduction to Software Quality Control. LC 80-15244. (Business Data Processing Ser.). 445p. 1980. 48.50 (ISBN 0-471-04704-X, Pub. by Wiley-Interscience). Wiley.

Cho, Chun H. Computer Based Energy Management Systems: Technology & Applications (Monograph) (Energy Science & Engineering Ser.). 1984. 45.00 (ISBN 0-12-173380-7). Acad Pr.

--Efficient Allocation of Steam. Gyftopoulos, Elias P. & Cohen, Karen C., eds. (Industrial Energy-Conservation Manuals: No. 16). (Illus.). 40p. 1982. loose-leaf 20.00x (ISBN 0-262-03085-3). MIT Pr.

--Measurement & Control of Liquid Level: An Independent Learning Module of the Instrument Society of America. LC 82-48156. 288p. 1982. text ed. 39.95x (ISBN 0-87664-625-9). Instru Soc.

Cho, Emily. Looking, Working, Living Terrific 24 Hours a Day. 160p. 1983. pap. 6.95 (ISBN 0-345-30938-3). Ballantine.

Cho, Emily & Lueders, Hermine. Looking, Working, Living Terrific Twenty-Four Hours a Day. (Illus.). 160p. 1982. 13.95 (ISBN 0-399-12745-3, Putnam). Putnam Pub Group.

Cho, Gene J. Melodic, Dyadic & Harmonic Singing: Graded Exercises. 64p. 1983. pap. text ed. 6.95 (ISBN 0-8403-2991-1, 40299101). Kendall-Hunt.

--Melody Harmonization at the Keyboard. 96p. 1983. pap. text ed. 7.95 (ISBN 0-8403-2911-3). Kendall-Hunt.

Cho, H. R., jt. auth. see Iribarne, J. V.

Cho, Hee I. Complete Martial Artist, 3 vols. (Illus.). 967p. (Orig.). 1981. Vols. 1 & 3. 27.95 ea.; Vols. 1 & 2. pap. 19.95 ea. Unique Pubns.

--Complete Taekwondo Hyung, 3 vols. (Illus.). 205p. (Orig.). 1984. pap. 12.95 ea. Unique Pubns.

--Man of Contrasts. (Illus.). 224p. (Orig.). 1977. pap. 14.95 (ISBN 0-317-27208-X). Unique Pubns.

Cho, K., ed. Excitons. (Topics in Current Physics Ser.: Vol. 14). (Illus.). 1979. 43.00 (ISBN 0-387-09567-5). Springer-Verlag.

Cho, Lee-Jay, ed. Introduction to Cencuses of Asia & the Pacific, 1970-1974. LC 76-7232. 209p. 1976. pap. text ed. 8.00x (ISBN 0-8248-0468-6, Eastwest Ctr). UH Pr.

Cho, Lee-Jay & Hearn, Robert L., eds. Censuses of Asia & the Pacific: 1980 Round. 404p. 1985. 15.00 (ISBN 0-86638-052-3). E W Center HI.

Cho, Lee-Jay & Kobayashi, Kazumasa, eds. Fertility Transition of East Asian Populations. (Monographs of the Center for Southeast Asian Studies, Kyoto University). 306p. 1979. text ed. 20.00x (ISBN 0-8248-0648-4); pap. text ed. 13.00x (ISBN 0-8248-0649-2). UH Pr.

Cho, Lee-Jay, et al. Population Growth of Indonesia: An Analysis of Fertility & Mortality Based on the 1971 Population Census. 135p. 1980. text ed. 16.00x (ISBN 0-8248-0691-3, Pub. by Ctr Southeast Asian Studies Kyoto Univ Japan); pap. text ed. 10.00x (ISBN 0-8248-0696-4). UH Pr.

Cho, Paul Y. The Fourth Dimension. LC 79-65588. 1979. pap. 4.95 (ISBN 0-88270-380-3, Pub. by Logos). Bridge Pub.

--The Leap of Faith. 120p. 1984. pap. 2.95 (ISBN 0-88270-574-1). Bridge Pub.

--Solving Life's Problems. LC 80-82787. (Orig.). 1980. pap. 4.95 (ISBN 0-88270-450-8, Pub. by Logos). Bridge Pub.

Cho, Paul Y. & Hostetler, Harold. Successful Home Cell Groups. LC 81-80025. 1981. pap. 4.95 (ISBN 0-88270-513-X, Pub. by Logos). Bridge Pub.

Cho, Paul Y. & Manzano, R. Whitney. The Fourth Dimension, Vol. 2. LC 79-65588. 183p. 1983. pap. 4.95 (ISBN 0-88270-561-X). Bridge Pub.

--Prayer: Key to Revival. 224p. 1984. 8.95 (ISBN 0-8499-0453-6, 0453-6). Word Bks.

Cho, S. H. Korean Karate. 25.50x (ISBN 0-685-22014-1). Wehman.

Cho, Sihak H. Better Karate for Boys. LC 71-124421. (gr. 3 up). 1970. PLB 8.95 (ISBN 0-396-06568-6); pap. 2.95 (ISBN 0-396-08477-X). Dodd.

--Korean Karate: Free Fighting Techniques. LC 68-18608. (Illus.). 1968. 25.50 (ISBN 0-8048-0350-1). C E Tuttle.

--Self-Defense Karate. LC 71-84824. (Illus.). 1969. 7.95 (ISBN 0-87396-005-X); pap. 3.95 (ISBN 0-87396-006-8). Stravon.

Cho, Z. H., jt. ed. see Nalcioglu, O.

Choat, Curt & Haynes, J. H. Yamaha XZ 550 Vision V-Twins '82. pap. 10.50 (ISBN 0-85696-821-8, 821). Haynes Pubns.

Choat, Ernest. Children's Acquisition of Mathematics. 132p. 1978. 12.00x (ISBN 0-85633-154-6, Pub. by NFER Nelson UK). Taylor & Francis.

--Mathematics & the Primary School Curriculum. 128p. 1980. 15.00x (ISBN 0-85633-206-2, Pub. by NFER Nelson UK). Taylor & Francis.

Choate, Albert G. The Core of Creation: An Investigation into the Fundamentals of Reality & the Foundation of Existence. LC 82-80727. (Illus.). 128p. 1982. pap. 7.50 (ISBN 0-943108-00-4). Syzygy.

Choate, Curt. Toyota Celica Supra '79 - '81. 177p. 1983. pap. 12.95 (ISBN 0-85696-680-0, NO. 680). Haynes Pubns.

Choate, Curt & Haynes, J. H. Honda Hawk 400 Twins '78-'81. pap. 10.50 (ISBN 0-85696-701-7, 701). Haynes Pubns.

Choate, Curt, jt. auth. see Haynes, J. H.

Choate, Curt, jt. auth. see Meek, Martyn.

Choate, Ernest A. The Dictionary of American Bird Names. Rev. ed. 240p. 1985. 17.95 (ISBN 0-87645-121-0, Pub. by Gambit); pap. 9.95 (ISBN 0-87645-117-2). Harvard Common Pr.

Choate, F. The Indian Fairy Book: From the Original Legends. 1977. lib. bdg. 59.95 (ISBN 0-8490-2053-0). Gordon Pr.

Choate, Jerry R. Systematics & Zoogeography of Middle American Shrews of the Genus Cryptotis. (Museum Ser.: Vol. 19, No. 3). 123p. 1970. 6.25 (ISBN 0-317-04961-5). U of KS Mus Nat Hist.

Choate, Joseph H. American Addresses. facsimile ed. LC 76-93328. (Essay Index Reprint Ser.). 1911. 24.50 (ISBN 0-8369-1400-7). Ayer Co Pubs.

--Ralph Waldo Emerson. 1978. Repr. of 1903 ed. lib. bdg. 8.50 (ISBN 0-8495-0818-5). Arden Lib.

--Ralph Waldo Emerson. LC 73-4034. 1973. lib. bdg. 7.50 (ISBN 0-8414-1831-4). Folcroft.

--Two Hague Conferences. (Reprints in Government & Political Science Ser). 1970. Repr. of 1913 ed. 13.00 (ISBN 0-384-08915-1). Johnson Repr.

--Two Hague Conferences. LC 13-4133. 1969. Repr. of 1913 ed. 11.00 (ISBN 0-527-16850-5). Kraus Repr.

Choate, Joyce S., jt. auth. see Rakes, Thomas A.

Choate, Judith. The Great American Pie Book. LC 83-51247. (Illus.). 144p. (Orig.). 1984. pap. 8.95 (ISBN 0-89909-030-3). Yankee Bks.

Choate, Judith, jt. auth. see Bergman, Abraham.

Choate, Julian E., Jr., jt. auth. see Frantz, Joe B.

Choate, Pat & Walter, Susan. America in Ruins: The Decaying Infrastructure. LC 82-20963. (Duke Press Policy Studies). 115p. 1983. pap. 9.75 (ISBN 0-8223-0554-2). Duke.

--Thinking Strategically: A Primer for Public Leaders. 103p. 1984. 7.95 (ISBN 0-934842-19-1). Coun State Plan.

Choate, Pat & Walter, Susan M. America in Ruins: Beyond the Public Works Pork Barrel. LC 81-66253. 100p. (Orig.). 1981. pap. 9.95 (ISBN 0-934842-25-6). Coun State Plan.

Choate, Pat, jt. auth. see Schwartz, Gail G.

Choate, R., ed. A Guide to Sources of Information on the Arts in Australia. (Guides to Australian Information Sources Ser.). 120p. 1983. pap. 11.95 (ISBN 0-08-029835-4). Pergamon.

Choate, Robert, jt. auth. see Rossi, Nick.

Choate, Robert A. & Francis, William H. Patent Law, Cases & Materials Also Including Trade Secrets - Copyrights - Trademaks. 2nd ed. LC 80-27863. (American Casebook Ser.). 1110p. 1981. text ed. 28.95 (ISBN 0-8299-2124-9). West Pub.

Choate, Robert A., ed. Documentary Report of the Tanglewood Symposium. LC 68-57058. 160p. (Orig.). 1968. pap. 12.50 (ISBN 0-940796-02-3, 1011). Music Ed Natl.

Choate, Rufus. Works of Rufus Choate, 2 Vols. Brown, Samuel G., ed. LC 72-70. Repr. of 1862 ed. Set. 82.00 (ISBN 0-404-01526-3). AMS Pr.

Choate, Sharr. Creative Casting. (Arts & Crafts Ser). (Illus.). 1966. 14.95 (ISBN 0-517-02445-4). Crown.

Choate, Sharr & De May, Bonnie C. Creative Gold & Silversmithing: Jewelry, Decorative Metalcraft. (Arts & Crafts Ser). (Illus.). 1970. pap. 8.95 (ISBN 0-517-52413-9). Crown.

Choay, Francoise. Modern City: Planning in the Nineteenth Century. LC 77-90408. (Planning & Cities Ser). (Illus.). 1969. 7.95 (ISBN 0-8076-0516-6); pap. 7.95 (ISBN 0-8076-0520-4). Braziller.

Choca, James. Manual for Clinical Psychology Practicums. LC 80-18731. 172p. 1980. pap. 12.50 (ISBN 0-87630-240-1). Brunner-Mazel.

Chocano, Jose S. Spirit of the Andes. Underwood, E. W., tr. 1977. lib. bdg. 59.95 (ISBN 0-8490-2660-1). Gordon Pr.

Chochem, Corinne & Roth, Muriel. Palestine Dances: Folk Dances of Palestine. LC 77-26081. (Illus.). 1978. Repr. of 1941 ed. lib. bdg. 15.00x (ISBN 0-313-20176-5, CHPD). Greenwood.

Chock, Eric, ed. Talk Story: An Anthology of Hawaii's Local Writers. 1978. pap. 3.95 (ISBN 0-932136-03-6). Petronium Pr.

Chock, Eric & Lum, Darrell, eds. The Best of Bamboo Ridge. 200p. 1986. pap. 7.00 (ISBN 0-910043-07-8). Bamboo Ridge Pr.

Chock, Judy & Miner, Margaret. Birth. LC 77-2603. (Illus.). 1978. 15.34i (ISBN 0-690-01434-1). T Y Crowell.

Choco, John & Choco, Ronalyn. Britain & Ireland on Your Own. LC 81-71884. (Illus.). 224p. 1982. 7.95 (ISBN 0-939596-01-6). Country Rd.

Choco, Ronalyn, jt. auth. see Choco, John.

Choda, Kelly. Speed Reading Self Taught: A Blank Book. 64p. (Orig.). 1983. pap. 1.50 (ISBN 0-86541-023-2). Filter.

--Thirty Pound Rails. LC 57-17961. (Wild & Woolly West Ser., No. 1). (Illus., Orig.). 1956. 8.00 (ISBN 0-910584-90-7); pap. 1.50 (ISBN 0-910584-01-X). Filter.

--The West on Wood: Antique Wood Engravings of the Old West, 8 vols. Incl. Vol. 1. Southwestern Indians (ISBN 0-86541-015-1); Vol. 2. Plains Indians (ISBN 0-86541-016-X); Vol. 3. Scenic Mountains (ISBN 0-86541-017-8); Vol. 4. Scenic Southwest (ISBN 0-86541-018-6); Vol. 5. Railroads (ISBN 0-86541-019-4); Vol. 6. Mining Camps & Miners (ISBN 0-86541-020-8); Vol. 7. Ancient Pueblos Ruins (ISBN 0-86541-021-6); Vol. 8. National Parks (ISBN 0-86541-022-4). (Illus.). 1983. Set. pap. 12.00 (ISBN 0-86541-014-3); pap. 1.50 ea. Filter.

--Your Hypochondria Gives Me Migraine: A Collection of Nasty Little Posters. (Illus.). 48p. 1981. pap. 1.50 (ISBN 0-86541-007-0). Filter.

Chodakowska, Elzbieta, tr. see Pomorski, Stanislaw.

Chodat, R. & Fischer, W. La Vegetation du Paraguay: Resultats Scientifiques d'une Mission Botanquie au Paraguay. Repr. of 1977 ed. 42.00 (ISBN 3-7682-1106-1). Lubrecht & Cramer.

Choderlos De Laclos, P. Oeuvres Completes. Allen, ed. (Bibl. De la Pleiade). 1943. lea. 41.50 (ISBN 0-685-11443-0). French & Eur.

Choderlos de Laclos, Pierre-Ambroise F. Les Liaisons Dangereuses. (Coll. Prestige). 1958. 29.95 (ISBN 0-685-11294-2). French & Eur.

--Liaisons Dangereuses. Le Hir, ed. (Class Garnier). pap. 13.95 (ISBN 0-685-34037-6). French & Eur.

--Les Liaisons Dangereuses. (Coll. GF). pap. 4.50 (ISBN 0-685-34038-4). French & Eur.

Chodes, John. Corbitt: The Story of Ted Corbitt, Long Distance Runner. LC 73-76246. (Illus.). 1974. 4.50 (ISBN 0-911520-45-7). Tafnews.

Chodkowski, Dick, jt. auth. see Levine, Laura.

Chodoff, Paul, jt. ed. see Bloch, Sidney.

Chodoff, Peter, jt. ed. see Siegel, John H.

Chodorov, Edward see Freedley, George.

Chodorov, Frank. Income Tax: The Root of All Evil. rev. ed. 1959. 10.00 (ISBN 0-8159-5809-9). Devin.

--Out of Step: An Autobiography. 1962. 6.95 (ISBN 0-8159-6408-0). Devin.

Chodorow, M., et al, eds. see Gutfreund, H., et al.

Chodorow, Nancy. The Reproduction of Mothering: Psychoanalysis & the Sociology of Gender. 263p. 1978. 22.00x (ISBN 0-520-03133-4, CAL 424); pap. 7.95x (ISBN 0-520-03892-4). U of Cal Pr.

Chodorow, Stanley. Christian Political Theory & Church Politics in the Mid-Twelfth Century: The Ecclesiology of Gratian's Decretum. LC 71-138512. (UCLA Center for Medieval & Renaissance Studies). 1972. 44.00x (ISBN 0-520-01850-8). U of Cal Pr.

Chodorow, Stanley & Stearns, Peter. The Other Side of Western Civilization: Readings in Everyday Life, 2 vols. 3rd. ed. 1984. pap. 12.95 vol. I, The Ancient World to the Reformation, 378 pp (ISBN 0-15-567651-2, HC); pap. 12.95 vol. II, The 16th Cent. to the Present, 402 pp (ISBN 0-15-567652-0). HarBraceJ.

Chodorow, Stanley, jt. auth. see Hoyt, Robert S.

Chodos, A., et al, eds. Lewes Workshop on Solitons in Nuclear & Elementary Particle Physics: Proceedings of the Workshop Held at Delaware University, June 1984. 320p. 1984. 40.00x (ISBN 9971-966-89-1, Pub. by World Sci Singapore). Taylor & Francis.

--Proceedings of the Lewes Workshop on Solutions in Nuclear & Elementary Particle Physics, Yale University, June 1984. 320p. 1985. 40.00x (ISBN 9971-966-89-1, Pub. by World Sci Singapore). Taylor & Francis.

Chodzko, A. B. Fairy Tales of the Slav Peasants & Herdsmen. Repr. of 1896 ed. 24.00 (ISBN 0-527-16900-5). Kraus Repr.

Chodzko, Alexander B., compiled by. Specimens of the Popular Poetry of Persia: As Found in the Adventures & Improvisations of Kurroglu, the Bandit-Minstrel of Northern Persia. LC 74-153024. (Research & Source Works Ser.: No. 672). 1971. Repr. of 1842 ed. lib. bdg. 32.00 (ISBN 0-8337-0563-6). B Franklin.

Choe, Boum Jone & Lambertini, Adrain. Global Energy Prospects. (Working Paper: No. 489). 50p. 1981. 5.00 (ISBN 0-686-36153-9, WP-0489). World Bank.

Choe, Boum-Jung. A Model of World Energy Markets & OPEC Pricing. 186p. 5.00 (ISBN 0-318-02816-6, WP0633). World Bank.

Choe Ching Young. The Rule of the Taewon'gun, 1864-1873: Restoration in Yi Korea. LC 73-183975. (East Asian Monographs Ser: No. 45). 1972. pap. 11.00x (ISBN 0-674-78030-2). Harvard U Pr.

Choffray, Jean-Marie & Lilien, Gary L. Market Planning for New Industrial Products. LC 80-11347. (Ronald Series on Marketing Management). 294p. 1980. 39.95 (ISBN 0-471-04918-2, Pub. by Ronald Pr). Wiley.

Choguill, Charles L. Spatial Planning for Urban Development in Bangladesh. (Working Papers Ser.: No. 82-3). 27p. 1982. pap. 6.00 (ISBN 0-686-95384-3, CRD135, UNCRD). Unipub.

Chohan, et al. Economics: Syllabus. 1974. pap. text ed. 7.45 (ISBN 0-89420-028-3, 112050); cassette recordings 223.15 (ISBN 0-89420-142-5, 112000). Natl Book.

Choh Hao Li, ed. Hormonal Proteins & Peptides: Gonadotropic Hormones, Vol. XI. LC 82-22770. 1983. 47.50 (ISBN 0-12-447211-7). Acad Pr.

--Hormonal Proteins & Peptides: Prolactin, Vol. 8. LC 80-11061. 1980. 44.00 (ISBN 0-12-447208-7). Acad Pr.

--Hormonal Proteins & Peptides: Techniques in Protein Chemistry, Vol. 9. LC 80-11061. (Hormonal Proteins & Peptides Ser.). 1980. 49.50 (ISBN 0-12-447209-5). Acad Pr.

Choi, C. Y. Chinese Migration & Settlement in Australia. (Illus.). 144p. 1975. 23.00x (ISBN 0-424-06810-9, Pub. by Sydney U Pr). Intl Spec Bk.

Choi, Frederick D. Multinational Accounting: A Research Framework for the Eighties. LC 81-16448. (Research for Business Decisions Ser.: No. 46). 260p. 1981. 39.95 (ISBN 0-8357-1267-2). UMI Res Pr.

Choi, Frederick D. & Mueller, Gerhard. International Accounting. (Illus.). 416p. 1984. text ed. 30.95 (ISBN 0-13-470931-4). P-H.

Choi, Frederick D. & Mueller, Gerhard G. Frontiers of International Accounting: An Anthology. Farmer, Richard, ed. LC 85-5865. (Research for Business Decisions Ser.: No. 77). 314p. 1985. pap. text ed. 44.95 (ISBN 0-8357-1660-0); 24.95 (ISBN 0-8357-1688-0). UMI Res Pr.

Choi, Frederick D., jt. auth. see Mueller, Gerhard G.

Choi, H., jt. auth. see Rohsenow, Warren M.

Choi, Jai. Out-of-Pocket Cost & Acquisition of Prescribed Medicines, U.S., 1973. Brown, Arlett, ed. (Ser 10: No. 108). 1977. pap. text ed. 1.75 (ISBN 0-8406-0091-7). Natl Ctr Health Stats.

Choi, Jongmoo J. International Trade & Transmission of Inflation: Survey of the Literature, Theory & the Japanese Experience. LC 85-720. (Illus.). 170p. (Orig.). 1985. lib. bdg. 22.50 (ISBN 0-8191-4574-2); pap. text ed. 11.00 (ISBN 0-8191-4575-0). U Pr of Amer.

Choi, Kwang. Theories of Comparative Economic Growth. (Illus.). 298p. 1983. pap. text ed. 19.95x (ISBN 0-8138-1771-4). Iowa St U Pr.

Choi, Noah C. & Grillo, Hermes C., eds. Thoracic Oncology. (Illus.). 384p. 1983. text ed. 48.00 (ISBN 0-89004-434-1, 494). Raven.

Choi, Sung C. Introductory Applied Statistics in Science. (Illus.). 1978. ref. ed. 26.95 (ISBN 0-13-501619-3). P-H.

Choi, Sunu. National Museum of Korea, Seoul. LC 80-82645. (Oriental Ceramic Ser.: Vol. 2). (Illus.). 180p. 1982. 68.00 (ISBN 0-87011-441-7). Kodansha.

Choi, Thomas & Greenberg, Jay N., eds. Social Science Approaches to Health Services Research. LC 82-23225. 350p. 1983. text ed. 28.00x (ISBN 0-914904-83-3). Health Admin Pr.

Choi, Woonsang. Commercial, Business & Trade Laws: Japan, Release 1. 1985. looseleaf 125.00 (ISBN 0-379-23108-5). Oceana.

--Commercial, Business & Trade Laws: Republic of Korea (South Korea) 1984. looseleaf 125.00 (ISBN 0-379-22016-4); Set. 250.00. Oceana.

--Fall of the Hermit Kingdom. LC 66-11939. 192p. 1967. 10.00 (ISBN 0-379-00277-9). Oceana.

--Korea: A Chronology & Fact Book. (World Chronology Ser.). 1983. lib. bdg. 8.50 (ISBN 0-379-16319-5). Oceana.

Choi, Ying-Pik, et al. The Multi-Fibre Arrangement in Theory & Practice. LC 85-3459. 154p. 1985. 18.00 (ISBN 0-86187-552-4). Longwood Pub Group.

Choi, Yvonne, et al. The Multi-Fibre Arrangement in Theory & Practice. LC 85-3459. 150p. 1984. 18.00 (ISBN 0-86187-552-4). F Pinter Pubs.

Choiseul, Etienne F. Memoire Historique sur la Negociation de la France & de l'Angleterre Depuis le 26 Mars 1761 Jusqu'au 20 Septembre de la Meme Annee Avec les Pieces Justificatives (Paris, 1761) (Canadiana Avant 1861: No. 8). 1966. 14.00x (ISBN 90-2796-327-4). Mouton.

Choiseul, Etienne F., ed. Memoire Historique sur la Negociation de la France et de l'Angleterre. 1761. 15.00 (ISBN 0-384-08930-5). Johnson Repr.

Chojnacki, Stanislaw, jt. auth. see Langmuir, Elizabeth C.

Cho Joong Ok. Home Style Korean Cooking in Pictures. LC 80-84417. (Illus., Orig.). 1981. pap. 10.50 (ISBN 0-87040-497-0). Japan Pubns USA.

Chokai, M. Sherlock Holmes & the Jewel & Other Short Plays. (Sangam English Supplementary Readers Ser.). 169p. (gr. 6). 1983. pap. 3.95x (ISBN 0-86131-330-5). Apt Bks.

Choksi, Armeane, et al. The Planning of Investment Programs in the Fertilizer Industry. LC 78-8436. (World Bank Ser: No. 2). 352p. 1980. text ed. 28.50x (ISBN 0-8018-2138-X); pap. text ed. 15.00x (ISBN 0-8018-2153-3). Johns Hopkins.

Choksi, Armeane M. State Intervention in the Industrialization of Developing Countries: Selected Issues. (Working Paper: No. 341). xx, 193p. 1979. 5.00 (ISBN 0-686-36188-1, WP-0341). World Bank.

Choksi, Mithan, jt. auth. see Gedge, E. C.

Choksy, Lois. Kodaly Context. 1981. 23.95 (ISBN 0-13-516674-8); pap. 18.95 (ISBN 0-13-516666-7). P-H.

--The Kodaly Method: Comprehensive Music Education from Infant to Adult. LC 73-18316. (Illus.). 224p. 1974. O.P. 21.95 (ISBN 0-13-516765-5); pap. 18.95 (ISBN 0-13-516757-4). P-H.

Choksy, Lois, et al. Teaching Music in Twentieth-Century America. (Illus.). 400p. 1985. text ed. 21.95 (ISBN 0-13-892662-X). P-H.

Choksy, Nasli H. see Gamkrelidze, R. V.

Cholakian, Rouben. Deflection - Reflection in the Lyric Poetry of Charles D'Orleans. 1985. 25.00 (ISBN 0-916379-21-3). Scripta.

Cholden, Louis S. A Psychiatrist Works with Blindness. 1958. pap. 7.00 (ISBN 0-89128-032-4, PPP032). Am Foun Blind.

Choldin, H. M. Cities & Suburbs: An Introduction to Urban Sociology. 512p. 1984. 25.95 (ISBN 0-07-010816-1). McGraw.

Choldin, Harvey M., jt. ed. see Micklin, Michael.

Choldin, Marianna T., ed. Access to Resources in the Eighties: Proceedings of the First International Conference of Slavic Librarians & Information Specialists. LC 82-60216. (Russica Bibliography Ser. No. 2). (Orig.). 1982. pap. 7.50 (ISBN 0-686-97604-5). Russica Pubs.

Choldin, Marinna T. A Fence Around the Empire: Russian Censorship of Western Ideas under the Tsars. LC 85-4557. (Policy Studies Ser.). (Illus.). 312p. 1985. 42.50 (ISBN 0-8223-0625-5). Duke.

Chole, Richard A. Color Atlas of Ear Disease. 80p. 1982. 49.00 (ISBN 0-8385-1177-5). ACC.

Cholerton, Judy. Hints on Tap Dancing. pap. 3.50x (ISBN 0-392-09690-0, SpS). Sportshelf.

--Modern Musical Enchainments. pap. 4.00x (ISBN 0-392-09723-0, SpS). Sportshelf.

Cholewinski, F. M. Hankel Convolution Complex Inversion Theory. LC 52-42839. (Memoirs: No. 58). 67p. 1965. pap. 9.00 (ISBN 0-8218-1258-0, MEMO-58). Am Math.

Chollet, Deborah J., jt. auth. see Employee Benefit Research Institute Staff.

Chollet, Roland, jt. auth. see Balzac, Honore De.

Cholmeley, Katharine. Margery Kempe, Genius & Mystic. LC 78-7811. 1978. Repr. of 1947 ed. lib. bdg. 17.50 (ISBN 0-8414-0296-5). Folcroft.

Cholmondeley, Mary. Moth & Rust & Other Stories. facsimile ed. LC 71-101794. (Short Story Index Reprint Ser.). 1902. 18.00 (ISBN 0-8369-3182-3). Ayer Co Pubs.

--Romance of His Life, & Other Romances. facsimile ed. LC 70-37540. (Short Story Index Reprint Ser.). Repr. of 1921 ed. 17.00 (ISBN 0-8369-4099-7). Ayer Co Pubs.

Cholmondely, Mary see Besant, Walter.

Cholnoky, B. J. Die Oekologie der Diatomeen in Binnengewaessern. (Illus.). 1968. 52.50 (ISBN 3-7682-5421-6). Lubrecht & Cramer.

Cholnoky, B. J., ed. Diatomaceae I. 1966. 42.00 (ISBN 3-7682-5421-6). Lubrecht & Cramer.

Cholnoky, B. J., jt. ed. see Gerloff, J.

Cholst, Sheldon. The Psychology of the Artist. LC 91-7319. 1978. pap. 9.95 (ISBN 0-931174-00-7). Beau Rivage.

Cholvis, F. Diccionario de Contabilidad. 469p. (Span.). 1977. 65.00 (ISBN 0-686-92515-7, S-33738). French & Eur.

Choma, John. Electrical Networks: Theory & Analysis. LC 84-15319. 752p. 1985. 52.50 (ISBN 0-471-08528-6, Pub. by Wiley-Interscience). Wiley.

Chomenko, Alex G. Atlas for Maxillofacial Pantomographic Interpretation. (Illus.). 328p. 1985. pap. text ed. 72.00x (ISBN 0-86715-126-9). Quint Pub Co.

Chomer, S., tr. see Bliokh, P. V., et al.

Chomet, S., tr. see Koltun, M. M.

Chomet, S., tr. see Smolyakov, A. V. & Tkachenko, V. M.

Chomiak, Martha & Rosenthal, Bernice. A Revolution of the Spirit: Crisis of Value in Russia, Eighteen-Ninety to Nineteen-Eighteen. Schwarz, Marian, tr. 360p. 1982. 27.00 (ISBN 0-89250-062-X). Orient Res Partners.

Chomicki, William P. Your Secret to Vibrant Good Health. 1984. 4.95 (ISBN 0-8062-1802-9). Carlton.

Chomin, Nakae. A Discourse by Three Drunkards on Government. Tsukui, Nobuko, tr. from Japanese. 136p. (Orig.). 1984. pap. 12.50 (ISBN 0-8348-0192-2, Pub. by John Weatherhill Inc Tokyo). C E Tuttle.

Chommie, J. G. El Derecho De los Estados Unidos: 3 Vols. (Orig., Span.). 1963. Set. pap. 24.00 (ISBN 0-379-00396-1); pap. 8.00 ea. Oceana.

Chompff, A. J. & Newman, S., eds. Polymer Networks: Structure & Mechanical Properties. LC 73-163286. 493p. 1971. 69.50 (ISBN 0-306-30544-5, Plenum Pr). Plenum Pub.

Chomsky, Carol S. The Acquisition of Syntax in Children from 5 to 10. 1970. pap. 7.95x (ISBN 0-262-53020-1). MIT Pr.

Chomsky, Noam. Aspects of the Theory of Syntax. 1965. 22.00x (ISBN 0-262-03011-X); pap. 6.95x (ISBN 0-262-53007-4). MIT Pr.

--Cartesian Linguistics: A Chapter in the History of Rationalist Thought. LC 83-6936. 132p. 1983. pap. text ed. 7.50 (ISBN 0-8191-3092-3). U Pr of Amer.

--Current Issues in Linguistic Theory. (Janua Linguarum, Ser. Minor: No. 38). (Orig.). 1964. pap. text ed. 22.00x (ISBN 90-2790-700-5). Mouton.

--The Fateful Triangle: The United States, Israel & the Palestinians. LC 83-61480. 492p. 1983. 25.00 (ISBN 0-89608-188-5); pap. 10.00 (ISBN 0-89608-187-7). South End Pr.

--Language & Mind. enl. ed. 194p. 1972. pap. text ed. 12.95 (ISBN 0-15-549257-8, HC). HarBraceJ.

--Language: Its Nature, Origins, & Use. Anshen, Ruth N., ed. (Convergence Ser.). 192p. 1985. pap. 9.95 (ISBN 0-03-005552-0). Praeger.

--Lectures on Government & Binding. 384p. 1981. 30.00x (ISBN 90-70176-28-9); pap. 20.00x (ISBN 90-70176-13-0). Foris Pubns.

--The Logical Structure of Linguistic Theory. LC 75-26985. (Illus.). 573p. 1975. 45.00x (ISBN 0-306-30760-X, Plenum Pr). Plenum Pub.

--The Logical Structure of Linguistic Theory. LC 84-16211. 592p. 1985. pap. text ed. 17.50x (ISBN 0-226-10436-2). U of Chicago Pr.

--Modular Approaches to the Study of the Mind. (SDSU Distinguished Research Lecture Ser.). 120p. 1983. 14.50x (ISBN 0-916304-56-6); pap. 6.50x (ISBN 0-916304-55-8). SDSU Press.

--Morphophonemics of Modern Hebrew. Hankamer, Jorge, ed. LC 78-66579. (Outstanding Dissertations in Linguistics Ser.). 1985. 15.00 (ISBN 0-8240-9688-6). Garland Pub.

--Problems of Knowledge & Freedom: The Russell Lectures. 1972. pap. 2.95 (ISBN 0-394-71815-1, V815, Vin). Random.

--Rules & Representations. LC 79-26145. (Woodbridge Lectures Ser.: No. 11). 1980. 25.00x (ISBN 0-231-04826-2); pap. 13.00x (ISBN 0-231-04827-0). Columbia U Pr.

--Some Concepts & Consequences of the Theory of Government & Binding. (Linguistic Inquiry Monographs). 96p. 1982. 20.00x (ISBN 0-262-03090-X); pap. text ed. 7.95x (ISBN 0-262-53042-2). MIT Pr.

--Strukturen der Syntax. (Janua Linguarum, Series Minor: No. 182). 1973. pap. 10.00x (ISBN 90-2792-490-2). Mouton.

--Studies on Semantics in Generative Grammar. LC 74-189711. (Janua Linguarum, Ser. Minor: No. 107). 207p. (Orig.). 1972. pap. text ed. 12.80x (ISBN 90-2797-964-2). Mouton.

--Syntactic Structures. (Janua Linguarum Ser. Minor: No. 4). 1978. 6.00 (ISBN 90-279-3385-5). Mouton.

--Topics in the Theory of Generative Grammar. (Janua Linguarum, Ser. Minor: No. 56). (Orig.). 1978. pap. text ed. 8.00x (ISBN 90-279-3122-4). Mouton.

--Towards a New Cold War: Essays on the Current Crisis & How We Got There. LC 81-47190. 537p. 1982. 20.00 (ISBN 0-394-51873-X); pap. 8.95 (ISBN 0-394-74944-8). Pantheon.

Chomsky, Noam & Halle, Morris. The Sound Pattern of English. LC 67-23446. 1968. text ed. 30.50 scp (ISBN 0-06-041276-3, HarpC). Har-Row.

Chomsky, Noam & Herman, Edward S. After the Cataclysm: Postwar Indocchina & the Reconstruction of Imperial Ideology, Vol. 2. LC 79-64138. (Political Economy of Human Rights Ser.). 393p. 1979. 15.00 (ISBN 0-89608-101-X); pap. 7.50 (ISBN 0-89608-100-1). South End Pr.

--The Washington Connection & Third World Facism, Vol. I. LC 79-64085. (Political Economy of Human Rights Ser.). 441p. 1979. 15.00 (ISBN 0-89608-091-9); pap. 10.00 (ISBN 0-89608-090-0). South End Pr.

Chomsky, Noam & Miller, George A. Analyse Formelle Des Langues Naturelles. (Mathematiques et Sciences De L'homme: No. 8). 1971. pap. text ed. 9.60 (ISBN 90-2796-796-2). Mouton.

Chomsky, William. Hebrew: The Eternal Language. LC 57-8140. 322p. 1975. 5.95 (ISBN 0-8276-0077-1, 384). Jewish Pubns.

Chonchuenchob, Pradit, et al. Hanging Culture of the Green Mussel in Thailand (Mytilus Smaragdinus Chemnitz) (Illus.). 1983. pap. 2.00 (ISBN 0-89955-383-4, Pub. by ICLARM Philippines). Intl Spec Bk.

Chong, C. T. Techniques of Admissible Recursion Theory. (Lecture Notes in Mathematics Ser.: Vol. 1106). ix, 214p. 1984. pap. 11.00 (ISBN 0-387-13902-8). Springer-Verlag.

Chong, C. T. & Wicks, M. J., eds. Southeast Asian Conference on Logic: Proceedings of the Logic Conference Singapore, 1981. (Studies in Logic & the Foundations of Mathematics: No. 111). xiv, 210p. 1983. 38.50 (ISBN 0-444-86706-6, I-250-83, North-Holland). Elsevier.

Chong, Jun. Kicking Strategy: The Art of Korean Sparring. LC 82-83443. (Illus.). 99p. (Orig.). 1983. pap. 6.95 (ISBN 0-86568-037-X, 351). Unique Pubns.

Chong, K. C., et al. Inputs as Related to Output in Milkfish Production in the Philippines. (ICLARM Technical Reports Ser.: No. 3). (Illus.). 82p. (Orig.). 1982. pap. 10.00x (ISBN 0-89955-421-0, Pub. by ICLARM Philippines). Intl Spec Bk.

--Milkfish Production Dualism in the Philippines: A Multi-Disciplinary Perspective on Continous Low Yields & Constraints to Aquaculture Development. (ICLARM Technical Reports Ser.: No. 15). (Illus.). 70p. (Orig.). 1984. pap. 10.50 (ISBN 0-317-17296-4, Pub. by ICLARM Philippines). Intl Spec Bk.

Chong, K. P. & Ward-Smith, J., eds. Mechanics of Oil Shale. 603p. 1984. 112.50 (ISBN 0-85334-273-3, Pub. by Elsevier Applied Sci England). Elsevier.

Chong, Kee Chai & Smith, Ian R. Economics of the Philippine Milkfish Resource System. 66p. 1982. pap. 11.75 (ISBN 92-808-0346-8, TUNU182, UNU). Unipub.

Chong, Key R. Americans & Chinese Reform & Revolution, 1898-1922: The Role of Private Citizens in Diplomacy. 322p. (Orig.). 1984. lib. bdg. 24.75 (ISBN 0-8191-4032-5); pap. text ed. 14.50 (ISBN 0-8191-4033-3). U Pr of Amer.

Chong, Lu-Sheng, jt. tr. see Young, Judy.

Chong-Bun Yap, jt. auth. see Brumlik, Joel.

Chong-hui, Choe. The Cry of the Harp & Other Korean Short Stories. Korean National Commission for UNESCO, ed. Poitras, Genell, tr. from Korean. (The Best Korean Short Stories Ser.: No. 2). xiii, 207p. 1983. 20.00 (ISBN 0-89209-213-0). Pace Intl Res.

Chong-in, So, et al. The Cruel City & Other Korean Short Stories. Korean National Commission for UNESCO, ed. Chang-guk, Yi, et al, trs. from Korean. (The Best Korean Short Stories Ser.: No. 1). xviii, 210p. 1983. 20.00 (ISBN 0-89209-212-2). Pace Intl Res.

Chong-Ki, Kim, jt. auth. see Won-Yong, Kim.

Chong-Sik Lee, ed. & tr. from Korean. Materials on Korean Communism, 1945-1947. LC 77-80003. (Occasional Papers: No. 7). 268p. 1977. pap. 6.00x (ISBN 0-917536-11-8). Ctr Korean U HI at Manoa.

Chong Sun Kim. Reverend Sun Myung Moon. LC 78-52115. 1978. pap. text ed. 9.25 (ISBN 0-8191-0494-9). U Pr of Amer.

Chong Sun Kim, ed. see Kim, Chi-ha.

Chong-un, Kim, et al, trs. see Chang-sop, Son, et al.

Chong-un, Kim, et al, trs. see Hwi, Sonu & In-hun, Choe.

Chong-un, Kim, et al, trs. see Sun-won, Hwang & Pom-son, Yi.

Chong-Wha, Chung, ed. Modern Korean Short Stories. (Writing in Asia Ser.). (Orig.). 1981. pap. text ed. 9.00x (ISBN 0-686-79035-9, 00256). Heinemann Ed.

Chonko, Lawrence B. & Enis, Ben M. Selling & Sales Management: A Bibliography. LC 80-11270. (Bibliography Ser.). 74p. 1980. pap. 6.00 (ISBN 0-87757-137-6). Am Mktg.

Chope, R. P. The Dialect of Hartland, Devonshire. (English Dialect Society Publications Ser.: No. 65). pap. 16.00 (ISBN 0-317-15989-5). Kraus Repr.

Choper, Jesse, et al. The Supreme Court: Trends & Developments 1978-1979. Tribe, Laurence & Kamisar, Yale, eds. LC 79-93039. 370p. 1979. 30.00 (ISBN 0-686-31601-0). Natl Prac Inst.

Choper, Jesse, et al, eds. The Supreme Court: Trends & Developments 1979-1980. 322p. 1981. 30.00 (ISBN 0-686-31602-9). Natl Prac Inst.

Choper, Jesse H. Judicial Review & the National Political Process: A Functional Reconsideration of the Role of the Supreme Court. LC 79-21135. 1980. lib. bdg. 35.00x (ISBN 0-226-10443-5). U of Chicago Pr.

--Judicial Review & the National Political Process: A Functional Reconsideration of the Role of the Supreme Court. LC 79-21135. 494p. 1983. pap. 11.95x (ISBN 0-226-10444-3). U of Chicago Pr.

Chopin. Henri Chopin. (Pub. by Ceolfrith Pr England). Intl Spec Bk.

Chopin, Frederic. Complete Ballades, Impromptus & Sonatas: The Paderewski Edition. Bronarski, L. & Turczynski, J., eds. 240p. 1981. pap. 7.95 (ISBN 0-486-24164-5). Dover.

--Complete Preludes & Etudes for Solo Piano. Paderewski, Ignacy J., ed. 224p. 1980. pap. 7.50 (ISBN 0-486-24052-5). Dover.

--Nocturnes & Polonaises. (Music Ser.). 272p. 1984. pap. 8.95 (ISBN 0-486-24564-0). Dover.

--Waltzes & Scherzos, Vols. IX, XII, V. (Music Scores Ser.). (Illus.). 208p. 1983. pap. 6.95 (ISBN 0-486-24316-8). Dover.

--Waltzes for Piano. (Carl Fischer Music Library: No. 309). 80p. 1902. pap. 6.00 (ISBN 0-8258-0103-6, L 193). Fischer Inc NY.

Chopin, Frederick. Chopin's Letters. Opienski, Henry K., ed. Voynich, E. L., tr. LC 79-163798. 424p. 1972. 45.00x (ISBN 0-8443-0020-9); pap. 15.00x (ISBN 0-8443-0090-X). Vienna Hse.

Chopin, K. Awakening & Other Stories. Leary, L., ed. LC 79-103399. (Rinehart Editions Ser.). 1970. pap. text ed. 11.95 (ISBN 0-03-078395-X, HoltC). HR&W.

Chopin, Kate. At Fault. (Reprints Ser.). 200p. 1985. pap. 4.95 (ISBN 0-9614285-1-1). Green St Pr.

--The Awakening. 1972. pap. 2.95 (ISBN 0-380-00245-0, 60180-X, Bard). Avon.

--The Awakening. 3.95 (ISBN 0-686-85783-6, Pub. by Quartet England). Charles River Bks.

--The Awakening. 1974. 69.95 (ISBN 0-87968-395-3). Gordon Pr.

--The Awakening. new ed. Culley, Margaret, ed. (Critical Edition Ser.). 256p. 1977. pap. price not set; pap. text ed. 4.95x (ISBN 0-393-09172-4). Norton.

--Awakening & Other Stories. 18.75 (ISBN 0-8446-0544-1). Peter Smith.

--The Awakening & Other Stories. Bayn, Nina, ed. (Modern Library College Editions Ser.). 354p. 1981. pap. text ed. 3.95 (ISBN 0-394-32667-9, RanC). Random.

--The Awakening & Selected Short Stories. (Bantam Classics Ser.). 224p. (Orig.). (gr. 9-12). 1981. pap. 2.95 (ISBN 0-553-21194-3). Bantam.

--The Awakening & Selected Stories. Baym, Nina, ed. 1981. pap. 3.95 (ISBN 0-394-32667-9, Mod LibC). Modern Lib.

--The Awakening & Selected Stories. (Penguin American Library). 320p. 1984. pap. 3.95 (ISBN 0-14-039022-7). Penguin.

--The Awakening & Selected Stories. Date not set. pap. 8.95 (ISBN 0-394-60508-X, Vin). Random.

--Bayou Folk. 1974. lib. bdg. 69.95 (ISBN 0-87968-712-6). Gordon Pr.

--Collected Works, 4 vols. Incl. At Fault. 1890. Repr. 25.00 (ISBN 0-403-04558-4); Bayou Folk. 1894. Repr. 25.00 (ISBN 0-403-04559-2); A Night at Acadie. 25.00 (ISBN 0-403-04560-6). LC 72-78673. 1890-99. Set. 95.00 (ISBN 0-403-03454-X). Somerset Pub.

--Complete Works of Kate Chopin, 2 Vols. Seyersted, Per, ed. LC 73-80043. 1032p. 1969. 60.00x (ISBN 0-8071-0849-9). La State U Pr.
--A Night in Acadie. 69.95 (ISBN 0-8490-0734-8). Gordon Pr.
--A Night in Acadie. 1972. Repr. of 1897 ed. lib. bdg. 23.00 (ISBN 0-8422-8025-1). Irvington.
--Portraits. 4.95 (ISBN 0-7043-3844-0, Pub. by Quartet England). Charles River Bks.
Choppin. Evaluation in Education: An Experiment in Rural Primary Schools in Malaysia, Vol. 4, No. 2. (Illus.). 121p. 1980. 20.00 (ISBN 0-08-027138-3). Pergamon.
Choppin, B. H., ed. Evaluation in Education, Vol. 4, No. 3. LC 77-81507. (Illus.). 93p. 1981. pap. 23.00 (ISBN 0-08-027134-0). Pergamon.
Choppin, B. H. & Postlethwaite, T. N., eds. Evaluation in Education, Vol. 3. (Reviews in Educational Evaluation Ser.). 250p. 1980. 62.00 (ISBN 0-08-026066-7). Pergamon.
--Evaluation in Education, Vol. 6. (An International Review Ser.). (Illus.). 386p. 72.00 (ISBN 0-08-031493-7). Pergamon.
--Evaluation in Education: Four Complete. (Illus.). 370p. 1981. 69.00 (ISBN 0-08-028404-3). Pergamon.
Choppin, Bruce, jt. auth. see Dean, Judy.
Choppin, G. & Ryberg, J., eds. Nuclear Chemistry: Theory & Applications. (Illus.). 1980. text ed. 105.00 (ISBN 0-08-023826-2); pap. text ed. 32.00 (ISBN 0-08-023823-8). Pergamon.
Choppin, Gregory R., jt. ed. see Carnall, William T.
Choppin, P. W. & Douglas, R. G. Hospital Practice: Status Report on Influenza. LC 77-81508. (Illus.). 1977. pap. text ed. 2.50 (ISBN 0-913800-08-2). HP Pub Co.
Chopra, A. K. India's Policy on Disarmament. 356p. 1984. text ed. 28.00x (ISBN 0-391-03326-3, Pub. by ABC Pub Hse India). Humanities.
Chopra, Anil K. Dynamics of Structures: A Primer. 120p. 1982. 10.00 (ISBN 0-9605004-4-8). Earthquake Eng.
Chopra, Deepak. Creating Health: The Psychophysiological Connection. 1984. 12.95 (ISBN 0-533-06007-9). Vantage.
Chopra, H. S., jt. ed. see Lall, K. B.
Chopra, I. J. Triiodothyronines in Health & Disease. (Monographs in Endocrinology: Vol. 18). (Illus.). 160p. 1981. 48.00 (ISBN 0-387-10400-3). Springer-Verlag.
Chopra, Kasturi L. Thin Film Phenomena. LC 78-12782. 864p. 1979. Repr. of 1969 ed. 48.00 (ISBN 0-88275-746-6). Krieger.
Chopra, Kasturi L. & Das, Sunhit R. Thin Film Solar Cells. 599p. 1983. 85.00x (ISBN 0-306-41141-5, Plenum Pr). Plenum Pub.
Chopra, Kuldip R. Technical Guideline for Sorghum & Millet: Seed Production. 110p. 1982. pap. text ed. 8.75 (ISBN 92-5-101259-8, F2377, FAO). Unipub.
Chopra, M. G. & Kumar, Ram. FORTRAN IV Programming. 248p. 1981. pap. 15.00x (ISBN 0-7069-1535-6, Pub. by Vikas India). Advent NY.
Chopra, Maharaj K. India & the Indian Ocean: New Horizons. 280p. 1982. text ed. 15.50x (ISBN 0-391-02770-0). Humanities.
Chopra, O. P. Tax Ethics, Unaccounted Income-Some Tax Reforms: Or Black Money-the Norm of the Day. (Illus.). vi, 119p. 1985. text ed. 32.50x (ISBN 0-86590-602-5, Pub. by B R Pub Corp Delhi). Apt Bks.
Chopra, P. N. Ladakh. 109p. 1980. 14.95 (ISBN 0-940500-14-0, Pub. by S Chand India). Asia Bk Corp.
--Sikkim. 114p. 1979. 14.95x (ISBN 0-940500-65-5). Asia Bk Corp.
Chopra, P. N., jt. auth. see Majumdar, R. C.
Chopra, P. N., ed. Contributions of Buddhism to World Civilization & Culture. 408p. 1983. text ed. 32.75x (ISBN 0-391-02904-5, Pub. by S Chand India). Humanities.
--Religions & Communities of India. 316p. 1982. text ed. 32.75x (ISBN 0-391-02748-4). Humanities.
--Religions & Communities of India. 1982. 59.00x (ISBN 0-85692-081-9, Pub. by E-W Pubns England). State Mutual Bk.
Chopra, P. N., et al. History of South India, 3 vols. 852p. 1981. 100.00x (ISBN 0-686-78920-2, Pub. by Chand & Co India). State Mutual Bk.
Chopra, Pran. India's Second Liberation. (Illus.). 1973. 7.50 (ISBN 0-7069-0259-9). Intl Bk Dist.
--India's Second Liberation. 1974. 25.00x (ISBN 0-262-03048-9). MIT Pr.
--Uncertain India: A Political Profile of Two Decades of Freedom. 1969. 30.00x (ISBN 0-262-03030-6). MIT Pr.
Chopra, Pran, ed. Contemporary Pakistan: New Aims & Images. 184p. 1983. text ed. 18.95x (ISBN 0-7069-2052-X, Pub. by Vikas India). Advent NY.
Chopra, R. N. Evolution of Food Policy in India. 1981. 30.00x (ISBN 0-8364-0724-5, Pub. by Macmillan India). South Asia Bks.
Chopra, Raj K. Making a Bad Situation Good. 1984. 10.95 (ISBN 0-8407-5406-X). Nelson.
Chopra, Ravi, jt. auth. see Morehouse, Ward.
Chopra, S. N. India: An Area Study. 237p. 1977. 26.00x (ISBN 0-7069-0494-X, Pub. by Vikas India). Advent NY.
Chopra, S. R., ed. Early Man in North-West India. 1979. 10.00x (ISBN 0-8364-0451-3). South Asia Bks.
Chopra, Surendra, jt. ed. see Wallace, Paul.
Chopra, V. D. India & the Socialist World. 1984. write for info. (Pub. by Allied India). South Asia Bks.
Chopra, V. D., et al. Agony of Punjab. 1985. 19.00x (ISBN 0-8364-1315-6, Pub. by Patriot). South Asia Bks.
Choquet, Gustav. Topology. (Pure & Applied Mathematics Ser.: Vol. 19). 1966. 65.00 (ISBN 0-12-173450-1). Acad Pr.
Choquet, Gustave. Lectures on Analysis, 3 vols. Marsden, J., et al, eds. Incl. Vol. 1. Integration & Topological Vector Spaces. pap. 30.95 (ISBN 0-8053-6955-4); Vol. 2. Representation Theory. pap. 30.95 (ISBN 0-8053-6957-0); Vol. 3. Infinite Dimensional Measures & Problem Solutions. 24.95 (ISBN 0-8053-6959-7). (Math Lecture Notes Ser.: Nos. 24, 25, & 26). 1969. pap. Benjamin-Cummings.
--What Is Modern Mathematics. 46p. 1963. pap. 2.75 (ISBN 0-685-46930-1). Ed Solutions.
Choquet-Bruhat, Y., et al. Analysis, Manifolds & Physics. rev. ed. 630p. 1982. 29.50 (ISBN 0-444-86017-7, North-Holland). Elsevier.
Choquette, Diane, compiled by. New Religious Movements in the United States & Canada: A Critical Assessment & Annotated Bibliography. LC 85-9964. (Bibliographies & Indexes in Religious Studies Ser.: No. 5). 254p. 1985. lib. bdg. 39.95 (ISBN 0-313-23772-7, CRM/). Greenwood.
Choquette, P. W., jt. auth. see Roehl, P. O.
Chorafas, D. Interactive Message Services: Planning, Designing & Implementing Videotex. 352p. 1984. 32.95 (ISBN 0-07-010850-1). McGraw.
Chorafas, D. N. Fourth & Fifth Generation Programming Languages, Vol. 1: Integrated Software, Database Languages & Expert Systems. 288p. 1986. price not set (ISBN 0-07-010864-1). McGraw.
--Management Workstations for Greater Productivity. 256p. 1986. 24.95 (ISBN 0-07-010859-5). McGraw.
Chorafas, Dimitris. Computer Networks for Distributed Information Systems. 1980. 24.00 (ISBN 0-89433-105-1). Petrocelli.
--Data Communications for Distributed Information Systems. (Illus.). 300p. text ed. 24.00 (ISBN 0-89433-108-6). Petrocelli.
--Interactive Videotex. (Illus.). 300p. 1981. text ed. 21.95 (ISBN 0-89433-127-2). Petrocelli.
Chorafas, Dimitris N. Computer in der Medizin. (IS-Informations-Systeme). (Illus.). 127p. 1973. 20.00x (ISBN 3-11-004031-X). De Gruyter.
--Databases for Networks & Minicomputers. (Illus.). 250p. 1982. 25.00 (ISBN 0-89433-136-1). Petrocelli.
--Databases Management Systems for Distributed Computer & Networks. (Illus.). 240p. 1983. 24.95 (ISBN 0-89433-184-1). Petrocelli.
--Designing & Implementing Local Area Networks. (Illus.). 256p. 1984. 35.95 (ISBN 0-07-010819-6). McGraw.
--Handbook of Data Communication & Computer Networks. (Illus.). 600p. 1985. text ed. 59.95 (ISBN 0-89433-244-9). Petrocelli.
--Information Systems in Financial Institutions: A Guide to Strategic Planning Based on the Japanese Experience. (Illus.). 208p. 1983. wire 59.95 (ISBN 0-13-464669-X). P-H.
--Interactive Workstation: Software & Hardware. (Illus.). 272p. 1985. text ed. 27.95 (ISBN 0-89433-258-9). Petrocelli.
--Money: Bank of the Eighties. (Illus.). 256p. 1981. 27.50 (ISBN 0-89433-182-5). Petrocelli.
--Office Automation: The Productivity Challenge. (Illus.). 304p. 1982. text ed. 36.95 (ISBN 0-13-631028-1). P-H.
--Personal Computers & Data Communications. LC 84-19972. 400p. 1985. pap. text ed. 19.95 (ISBN 0-88175-052-2). Computer Sci.
--Telephony: Today & Tomorrow. (Illus.). 272p. 1984. pap. text ed. 23.95 (ISBN 0-13-902700-9). P-H.
Chorafas, Dimitrius N. Control Systems Functions & Programming Approaches, 2 Vols. (Mathematics in Science & Engineering: Vol. 27A & B). 1966. Vol. A. 76.00 (ISBN 0-12-174061-7); Vol. B. 63.00 (ISBN 0-12-174062-5). Acad Pr.
Chorafas, Dirmitris N. The Software Handbook. (Illus.). 500p. 1984. reference 49.95 (ISBN 0-89433-248-1). Petrocelli.
Chorafas, Dmitris N. Interactive Workstations: Software & Hardware. (Illus.). 272p. 1985. 27.95 (ISBN 0-89433-258-9). Van Nos Reinhold.
Chorao, Kay. The Baby's Bedtime Book. LC 84-6067. (Illus.). 64p. (ps). 1984. 11.95 (ISBN 0-525-44149-2, 01160-350). Dutton.
--The Baby's Lap Book. (Illus.). (ps-k). 1977. 9.95 (ISBN 0-525-26100-1, 0966-290). Dutton.
--The Baby's Story Book. Durrell, Ann, ed. LC 84-26005. (Illus.). 64p. (ps-1). 1985. 11.95 (ISBN 0-525-44200-6). Dutton.
--Ida Makes a Movie. LC 73-20147. (Illus.). 48p. (ps-3). 1974. 5.95 (ISBN 0-395-28782-0, Clarion). HM.
--Kate's Box. LC 82-2403. (Illus.). 24p. (ps). 1982. 3.95 (ISBN 0-525-44010-0, 0383-120). Dutton.
--Kate's Car. LC 82-2393. (Illus.). 24p. (ps). 1982. 3.95 (ISBN 0-525-44011-9, 0383-120). Dutton.
--Kate's Quilt. LC 82-2395. (Illus.). 24p. (ps). 1982. 3.95 (ISBN 0-525-44012-7, 0383-120). Dutton.
--Kate's Snowman. LC 82-2407. (Illus.). 24p. (ps). 1982. 3.95 (ISBN 0-525-44013-5, 0383-120). Dutton.
--Lemon Moon. LC 83-220. (Illus.). 32p. (gr. k-3). 1983. reinforced bdg 8.95 (ISBN 0-8234-0490-0). Holiday.
--Magic Eye for Ida. LC 72-85337. (Illus.). 48p. (ps-3). 1973. 6.95 (ISBN 0-395-28783-9, Clarion). HM.
--Molly's Moe. LC 76-3526. (Illus.). 32p. (ps-3). 1979. 7.50 (ISBN 0-395-28784-7, Clarion). HM.
--Oink & Pearl. LC 80-8439. (I Can Read Bk.). (Illus.). 64p. (gr. k-3). 1981. 8.64i (ISBN 0-06-021272-1); PLB 9.89g (ISBN 0-06-021273-X). HarpJ.
Choraqui, Andre. A Man Alone. 284p. 1970. 12.95x (ISBN 0-87855-180-8). Transaction Bks.
Chorba, Ronald W., jt. auth. see Bommer, Michael R.
Chorell, Walentin see Friis, Erik J., et al.
Chorin, A. J. & Marsden, J. E. A Mathematical Introduction to Fluid Mechanics. (Universitexts Ser.). (Illus.). 1979. pap. 22.00 (ISBN 0-387-90406-9). Springer-Verlag.
Chorin, Alexandre J. Lectures on Turbulence Theory. LC 75-11033. (Mathematics Lecture Ser., No. 5). 160p. 1975. pap. text ed. 12.00 (ISBN 0-914098-14-4). Publish or Perish.
Chorley, Henry F. Modern German Music: Recollections & Criticisms, 2 vols. LC 79-110994. (Music Reprint Ser.). 1973. Repr. of 1854 ed. 75.00 (ISBN 0-306-71911-8). Da Capo.
--Music & Manners in France & Germany, 3 Vols. 1983. Repr. of 1844 ed. Set. lib. bdg. 89.50 (ISBN 0-306-76217-X). Da Capo.
--Thirty Years' Musical Recollections. LC 77-183330. 436p. 1972. Repr. of 1926 ed. 40.00x (ISBN 0-8443-0026-8). Vienna Hse.
--Thirty Years' Musical Recollections. Newman, Ernest, ed. LC 77-183330. 411p. Date not set. Repr. of 1926 ed. 75.00. Vienna Hse.
--Thirty Years' Musical Recollections, 2 vols. (Music Reprint Ser.). 1983. Repr. of 1862 ed. Set. lib. bdg. 59.50 (ISBN 0-306-76216-1); Vol. I: 312 pp. lib. bdg. Vol. II: 323 pp. lib. bdg. Da Capo.
Chorley, R. J. & Haggett, P. Socio-Economic Models in Geography. 468p. 1968. pap. 12.95x (ISBN 0-416-29630-0, NO.2137). Methuen Inc.
Chorley, R. J., jt. auth. see Barry, Roger G.
Chorley, R. J., jt. auth. see Bennett, R. J.
Chorley, R. J., et al. History of the Study of Landforms; or, the Development of Geomorphology, Vol. 2: The Life & Work of William Morris Davis. 874p. 1973. 75.00x (ISBN 0-416-26890-0, NO. 2139). Methuen Inc.
Chorley, Richard J., ed. Integrated Models in Geography. Haggett, Peter. 1969. pap. 12.50x (ISBN 0-416-29840-0, NO. 2132). Methuen Inc.
--Introduction to Fluvial Processes. (Illus.). 1971. pap. 14.95x (ISBN 0-416-68820-9, NO. 2133). Methuen Inc.
--Introduction to Geographical Hydrology. (Illus.). 1971. pap. 12.95 (ISBN 0-416-68830-6, NO.2134). Methuen Inc.
--Introduction to Physical Hydrology. 1971. pap. 12.95 (ISBN 0-416-68810-1, NO.2135). Methuen Inc.
--Water, Earth & Man. 1969. 58.00x (ISBN 0-416-12030-X, NO. 2138). Methuen Inc.
Chorley, Richard J. & Haggett, Peter, eds. Models in Geography. 1967. 82.00x (ISBN 0-416-29020-5, NO. 2136). Methuen Inc.
Chorley, Richard J., et al. Geomorphology. (Orig.). 1985. pap. text ed. 30.00 (ISBN 0-416-32590-4, 9361). Methuen Inc.
Chorlton, Frank. Textbook of Dynamics. 2nd ed. (Mathematics & Its Applications Ser.). 271p. 1983. 51.95x (ISBN 0-470-27407-7); pap. 32.95x (ISBN 0-470-27408-5). Halsted Pr.
Chorlton, W. Cloud Dwellers of the Himalayas: The Bhotia. (Peoples of the Wild Ser.). 1982. 15.94 (ISBN 0-7054-0705-5, Pub. by Time-Life). Silver.
Chorlton, Windsor. Ice Ages. LC 82-16765. (Planet Earth Ser.). (gr. 7 up). 1983. lib. bdg. 19.94 (ISBN 0-8094-4329-5, Pub. by Time-Life). Silver.
Chormack, D. & Dowsett, B. O. Troilboom: An Assessment of Design Concept & General Reliability, 1977. 1981. 35.00x (ISBN 0-686-97155-8, Pub. by W Spring England). State Mutual Bk.
Choron, Jacques. Death & Western Thought. LC 62-17575. 320p. 1973. pap. 7.95 (ISBN 0-02-064710-7, Collier). Macmillan.
Choron, Sandra. The Big Book of Kids' Lists. (Illus.). 288p. (Orig.). 1985. pap. 8.95 (ISBN 0-345-32189-8). World Almanac.
--The Big Books of Kids' Lists. 288p. 1985. pap. 8.95 (ISBN 0-317-18437-7). World Almanac.
Choron, Sandra, jt. auth. see Malca, Edward.
Choroszewski, Walter. New Jersey: A Scenic Discovery. (Scenic Discovery Ser.). (Illus.). 120p. 1984. 27.50 (ISBN 0-89909-049-4). Foremost Pubs.
Chorover, Stephan. From Genesis to Genocide: The Meaning of Human Nature & the Power of Behavior Control. 256p. 1979. pap. 8.95x (ISBN 0-262-53039-2). MIT Pr.
Chorpenning, Charlotte B. Abe Lincoln: New Salem Days. (Children's Theatre Playscript Ser.). 1954. pap. 2.25x (ISBN 0-88020-006-5). Coach Hse.
--The Adventures of Tom Sawyer. (Children's Theatre Playscript Ser.). 1956. pap. 2.25x (ISBN 0-88020-008-1). Coach Hse.
--Alice in Wonderland. rev. ed. (Children's Theatre Playscript Ser.). 1959. pap. 2.25x (ISBN 0-88020-018-9). Coach Hse.
--Hansel & Gretel. (Children's Theatre Playscript Ser.). 1956. pap. 2.25x (ISBN 0-88020-029-4). Coach Hse.
--Lincoln's Secret Messenger: Boy Detective to a President. (Children's Theatre Playscript Ser.). 1955. pap. 2.25x (ISBN 0-88020-036-7). Coach Hse.
--Radio Rescue. (Children's Theatre Playscript Ser.). 1970. pap. 2.00x (ISBN 0-88020-046-4). Coach Hse.
--Rip Van Winkle. (Children's Theatre Playscript Ser.). 1954. pap. 2.25x (ISBN 0-88020-050-2). Coach Hse.
Chorpenning, Charlotte B. & Nicholson, Anne. Three Plays of Adventure. 1972. 5.00x (ISBN 0-85343-504-9). Coach Hse.
Chorpenning, Charlotte B., jt. auth. see Nicholson, Anne.
Chorzempa, Rosemary A. Design Your Own Coat of Arms: An Introduction to Heraldry. 48p. (Orig.). 1986. pap. 2.95 (ISBN 0-486-24993-X). Dover.
--My Family Tree Workbook: Genealogy for Beginners. 64p. 1982. pap. 2.25 (ISBN 0-486-24229-3). Dover.
Chose, T. K., et al, eds. Downstream Processing. (Advances in Biochemical Engineering-Biotechnology: Vol. 26). (Illus.). 209p. 1983. 37.50 (ISBN 0-387-12096-3). Springer-Verlag.
Chotas, James, jt. auth. see Sturm, James L.
Chothia, J. Forging a Language. LC 78-73239. (Illus.). 1980. 34.50 (ISBN 0-521-22569-8). Cambridge U Pr.
Chothia, Jean. Forging a Language: A Study of the Plays of Eugene O'Neill. LC 78-73239. (Illus.). 243p. 1982. pap. 14.95 (ISBN 0-521-28523-2). Cambridge U Pr.
Chotiner, Barbara A. Khrushchev's Party Reform: Coalition Building & Institutional Innovation. LC 83-10733. (Contributions in Political Science Ser.: No. 106). (Illus.). 328p. 1984. lib. bdg. 35.00 (ISBN 0-313-23730-1, CH0/). Greenwood.
Chotiner, Renee D. Marriage & the Supreme Court: A Study of the Judicial Attitudes & Woman's Legal Status. LC 73-10873. (Law & Women Ser.). 32p. 1974. pap. 2.00 (ISBN 0-87999-003-1). Today News.
Chotzen, Theodor M. Recherches sur la poesie de Dafydd ab Gwilym, barde gallois du XIVe siecle. LC 78-72622. (Celtic Language & Literature: Goidelic & Brythonic). Repr. of 1927 ed. 42.50 (ISBN 0-404-17546-5). AMS Pr.
Chotzinoff, Samuel. Eroica: A Novel Based on the Life of Ludwig Von Beethoven. LC 72-1021. Repr. of 1930 ed. 23.00 (ISBN 0-404-01529-8). AMS Pr.
--A Lost Paradise: Early Reminiscences. facsimile ed. LC 74-27970. (Modern Jewish Experience Ser.). 1975. Repr. of 1955 ed. 31.00x (ISBN 0-405-06700-3). Ayer Co Pubs.
--Toscanini: An Intimate Portrait. LC 76-7576. (Music Reprint Ser.). 1976. Repr. of 1956 ed. lib. bdg. 25.00 (ISBN 0-306-70777-2). Da Capo.
Chotzner, J. Hebrew Humour & Other Essays. 1977. Repr. of 1905 ed. lib. bdg. 25.00 (ISBN 0-8495-0703-0). Arden Lib.
--Hebrew Humour & Other Essays. 1979. Repr. of 1905 ed. lib. bdg. 20.00 (ISBN 0-8414-9985-3). Folcroft.
--Hebrew Humour & Other Essays. Repr. of 1905 ed. 25.00 (ISBN 0-8274-4151-7). R West.
Chou, C. P. D., jt. auth. see Lundin, C. D.
Chou, Calvin. The Hollow Line in Dating Chinese Porcelains. LC 77-87445. (Illus.). 1978. l.t.d. ed. 20.00 (ISBN 0-930940-03-2); pap. 12.00 (ISBN 0-930940-00-8). Chinese Art App.
Chou, Eric. Mao Tse-Tung: The Man & the Myth. LC 80-22758. 304p. 1982. 19.95 (ISBN 0-8128-2769-4). Stein & Day.
Chou, George. Microcomputer Programming in BASIC: With Business Applications. 2nd ed. 298p. 1984. pap. text ed. 17.50 (ISBN 0-06-041298-4, HarpC). Har Row.
Chou, George T. The dBASE III Handbook. LC 85-60691. (Orig.). 1985. pap. 19.95 (ISBN 0-88022-159-3, 178). Que Corp.
Chou, Hsiang-Kuang. A History of Chinese Buddhism. LC 78-72396. Repr. of 1956 ed. 29.50 (ISBN 0-404-17255-5). AMS Pr.
Chou, Hung-hsiang. Oracle Bone Collections in the United States. LC 74-34551. (Publications, Occasional Papers, Archaeology: Vol. 10). 1976. pap. 24.00x (ISBN 0-520-09534-0). U of Cal Pr.
Chou, Ju-hsi. The Hua-Yu-Lu & Tao-Chi's Theory of Painting. (Occasional Paper; Arizona State Univ., Center for Asian Studies: No. 9). 49p. 1977. pap. text ed. 6.00 (ISBN 0-939252-05-8). ASU Ctr Asian.
Chou, Marilyn, et al. World Food Prospects & Agriculture Potential. LC 76-24346. 336p. 1977. text ed. 42.95 (ISBN 0-275-23770-2). Praeger.
Chou, Marylin & Harmon, David P., Jr. Critical Food Issues of the Nineteen Eighties. LC 79-14718. (Pergamon Policy Studies). (Illus.). 1979. 52.00 (ISBN 0-08-024611-7); pap. 9.95 (ISBN 0-08-024639-7). Pergamon.

Chou, Min-chih. Hu Shih & Intellectual Choice in Modern China. (Studies on China). 320p. 1984. text ed. 28.00x (ISBN 0-472-10039-4). U of Mich Pr.

Chou, Peter, tr. see Spurgeon, Charles.

Chou, Shelley N. & Seljeskog, Edward L., eds. Spinal Deformities & Neurological Dysfunction. LC 76-5665. (Seminars in Neurological Surgery). 300p. 1978. 48.50 (ISBN 0-89004-183-0). Raven.

Chou, Shu-Jen. Ah Q, & Others: Selected Stories of Lusin. facsimile ed. Wang, Chi-Chen, tr. LC 70-150542. (Short Story Index Reprint Ser.). Repr. of 1941 ed. 17.00 (ISBN 0-8369-3839-9). Ayer Co Pubs.

Chou, Shu-jen see Lu Hsun, pseud.

Chou Shun-Hsin. The Chinese Inflation, Nineteen Thirty-Seven to Nineteen Forty-Nine. LC 62-18260. (Studies of the East Asian Institute). 1963. 31.50x (ISBN 0-231-02565-3). Columbia U Pr.

Chou, T. W., jt. auth. see Vinson, J. R.

Chou, Te-Chaun. Electrocardiography in Clinical Practice. 2nd ed. LC 79-838. 1985. price not set (ISBN 0-8089-1772-2). Grune.

Chou, Te-Chuan. Electrocardiography in Clinical Practice. 624p. 1979. 49.50 (ISBN 0-8089-1138-4, 790837). Grune.

Chou, Te-Chuan, et al. Clinical Vectorcardiography. 2nd ed. LC 74-3202. (Illus.). 480p. 1974. 64.50 (ISBN 0-8089-0838-3, 790835). Grune.

Chou, Wushow. Computer Communications: Systems & Applications, Vol. II. (Illus.). 496p. 1983. text ed. 41.95 (ISBN 0-13-165050-5). P-H.

Chou, Wushow, ed. Computer Communications, Vol. I: Principles. (Illus.). 496p. 1982. text ed. 41.95 (ISBN 0-13-165043-2). P-H.

Chou, Ya-Lun. Probability & Statistics for Decision-Making. 1982. Repr. of 1972 ed. text ed. cancelled (ISBN 0-8290-0599-4). Irvington.

Chou, Ya-Lun & Bauer, Bertrand. Modern Business Statistics. 576p. 1983. text ed. 26.00 (ISBN 0-394-32802-7, Ran B). Random.

Chou Ch'i-Ming. Essays on Folklore & Folk Literature. (National Peking University & Chinese Assn. for Folklore, Folklore & Folk Literature Ser.: No. 63). (Chinese.). 16.00x (ISBN 0-89986-153-9). Oriental Bk Store.

Chou Ching-Wen. Ten Years of Storm: The True Story of the Communist Regime in China. Ming Lai, tr. LC 72-12632. 323p. 1973. Repr. of 1960 ed. lib. bdg. 17.50x (ISBN 0-8371-6685-3, CHTY). Greenwood.

Chouchkov, C. N. Cutaneous Receptors. (Advances in Anatomy, Embryology & Cell Biology Ser.: Vol. 54, Part 5). (Illus.). 1978. pap. 22.00 (ISBN 0-387-08826-1). Springer-Verlag.

Choucri, Nazli. Energy & Development in Latin America: Perspectives for Public Policy. LC 81-47741. 240p. 1982. 28.50x (ISBN 0-669-04799-6). Lexington Bks.

--International Energy Futures: Petroleum Prices, Power & Payments. (Illus.). 250p. 1981. 40.00x (ISBN 0-262-03075-6). MIT Pr.

Choucri, Nazli & North, Robert. Nations in Conflict: National Growth & International Violence. LC 74-23453. (Illus.). 356p. 1975. text ed. 33.95 (ISBN 0-7167-0773-X). W H Freeman.

Choucri, Nazli, ed. Multidisciplinary Perspectives on Population & Conflict. LC 84-2641. 240p. 1984. text ed. 30.00x (ISBN 0-8156-2314-3); pap. text ed. 13.95x (ISBN 0-8156-2315-1). Syracuse U Pr.

Choucri, Nazli & Robinson, Thomas W., eds. Forecasting in International Relations: Theory, Methods, Problems, Prospects. LC 78-19169. (Illus.). 468p. 1978. text ed. 47.95 (ISBN 0-7167-0059-X). W H Freeman.

Choudhary, B. The Elements of Complex Analysis. LC 83-12820. 262p. 1983. 19.95x (ISBN 0-470-27492-1). Halsted Pr.

Choudhary, Bani R. Stories from Panchatantra. (Illus.). (gr. 3-10). 1979. 7.25 (ISBN 0-89744-136-2). Auromere.

--The Story of Krishna. (Illus.). (gr. 3-10). 1979. 7.25 (ISBN 0-89744-134-6). Auromere.

--The Story of Ramayan. (Illus.). (gr. 3-10). 1979. 7.50 (ISBN 0-89744-133-8). Auromere.

Choudhary, G., ed. Chemical Hazards in the Workplace: Measurement & Control. LC 81-130. (ACS Symposium Ser.: No. 149). 1981. 54.95 (ISBN 0-8412-0608-2). Am Chemical.

Choudhary, G. & Keith, L. H., eds. Chlorinated Dioxins & Dibenzofurane. 1983. text ed. 42.50 (ISBN 0-250-40604-7). Butterworth.

Choudhary, K. P. Modern Indian Mysticism. 1981. 17.00x (ISBN 0-8364-0744-X, Pub. by Motilal Banarsidass). South Asia Bks.

Choudhary, Valmik, ed. Dr. Rajendra Prasad: Correspondence & Select Documents, Vol. 1. 1984. 24.00x (ISBN 0-8364-1179-X, Pub. by Allied India). South Asia Bks.

Choudhry, G. G. & Hutzinger, O. Mechanistic Aspects of the Thermal Formation of Halogenated Organic Compounds Including Polychlorinated Dibenzo-p-Dioxins. LC 83-1640. (Current Topics in Environmental & Toxicological Chemistry Ser.: Vol. 4). (Illus.). 210p. 1983. 39.00 (ISBN 0-677-06130-7). Gordon.

Choudhry, Ghulam G. Humic Substances: Structural, Photophysical, Photochemical & Free Radial Aspects & Interactions with Environmental Chemistry. (Current Topics in Environmental & Toxicological Chemistry Ser.: Vol. 7). 180p. 1984. 44.00 (ISBN 0-677-06440-3). Gordon.

Choudhuri, A. D. The Face of Illusion in American Drama. 1980. text ed. 13.50x (ISBN 0-391-01728-4). Humanities.

Choudhuri, Subir R., ed. see Elliot, Madge.

Choudhury, Bikram & Reynolds, Bonnie J. Bikram's Beginning Yoga Class. new ed. LC 76-29218. (Illus.). 224p. 1977. pap. 9.95 (ISBN 0-87477-082-3). J P Tarcher.

Choudhury, Golam. Chinese Perception of the New World. 1978. pap. text ed. 9.50 (ISBN 0-8191-0527-9). U Pr of Amer.

Choudhury, Golam W. China in World Affairs: The Foreign Policy of the PRC since 1970. (Special Studies on China & East Asia). 310p. (Orig.). 1982. 30.00x (ISBN 0-89158-937-6); pap. 13.50x (ISBN 0-86531-329-6). Westview.

Choudhury, Masudul A. An Islamic Social Welfare Function. Quinlan, Hamid, ed. LC 82-74125. (Illus.). 66p. 1983. pap. 3.50 (ISBN 0-89259-041-6). Am Trust Pubns.

Choudhury, N. D. Historical Archaelogy of Central Assam: From Earliest Times to 12th Century A. D. (Illus.). 287p. 1985. text ed. 100.00x (ISBN 0-86590-712-9, Pub. by B R Pub Corp India). Apt Bks.

Choudhury, Rabindra N., tr. see Tagore, Rabindranath.

Choudhury, Sadananda. Economic History of Colonialism. 1979. text ed. 14.75x (ISBN 0-391-01852-3). Humanities.

Chouemi, M. & Pellat, C. H. Al-Kamil Dictionnaire Arabe-Francais-Anglais. 64p. (Arabic, Fr. & Eng.). 1981. write for info. (M-9286). French & Eur.

Chouemi, Moustafa, jt. auth. see Blachere, Regis.

Chough, Sung K. Marine Geology of Korean Seas. (Illus.). 157p. 1983. text ed. 36.00 (ISBN 0-934634-61-0). Intl Human Res.

Chou Hui-Ying. Folksongs from the Northwest. (National Peking University & Chinese Assn. for Folklore, Folklore & Folkliterature Ser.: No. 112). (Chinese.). 16.00x (ISBN 0-89986-190-3). Oriental Bk Store.

Chouinard, A., jt. ed. see Davy, F. B.

Chouinard, A., jt. ed. see Losos, G.

Chouinard, Yvon. Climbing Ice. LC 77-19137. (Illus.). 192p. 1978. 19.95 (ISBN 0-87156-207-3); pap. 16.95 (ISBN 0-87156-208-1). Sierra.

Choukas-Bradley, Melanie & Alexander, Polly. City of Trees: Trees of the World, the Complete Botanical & Historical Guide to the Trees of Washington, D.C. LC 81-17553. (Illus.). 283p. 1981. 24.95 (ISBN 0-87491-440-X). Acropolis.

Choukri, Mohamed. Jean Genet in Tangier. LC 73-86613. 1974. 5.95 (ISBN 0-912946-08-3). Ecco Pr.

--Jean Genet in Tangier. Bowles, Paul, tr. from Arabic. LC 73-86613. (Illus.). 76p. (Orig.). 1975. pap. 2.95 (ISBN 0-912946-09-1). Ecco Pr.

Choundhry, G. G., et al, eds. The Natural Environment & the Biogeochemical Cycles. (The Handbook of Environmental Chemistry Ser.: Vol. I, Pt. C). (Illus.). 250p. 1984. 48.00 (ISBN 0-387-13226-0). Springer-Verlag.

Chouquet, Gustave. Histoire De la Musique Dramatique En France Depuis Ses Origines Jusqu'a Nos Jours. LC 80-2265. Repr. of 1873 ed. 45.00 (ISBN 0-404-18818-4). AMS Pr.

Chouraqui, Andre. Letter to an Arab Friend. Gugli, William V., tr. LC 72-77573. 284p. 1973. 17.50x (ISBN 0-87023-108-1). U of Mass Pr.

--A Man in Three Worlds. Kilmer, Kenton, tr. from Fr. LC 84-15338. (Illus.). 246p. (Orig.). 1985. lib. bdg. 22.50 (ISBN 0-8191-4242-5); pap. text ed. 10.75 (ISBN 0-8191-4243-3). U Pr of Amer.

--The People & the Faith of the Bible. Gugli, William V., tr. LC 74-21237. 224p. 1975. 15.00x (ISBN 0-87023-172-3). U of Mass Pr.

Chou Shu-Jen. Ah Q, & Others: Selected Stories of Lusin. Wang, Chi-Chen, tr. from Chinese. LC 75-143310. 1971. Repr. of 1941 ed. lib. bdg. 24.75x (ISBN 0-8371-5965-2, CHAQ). Greenwood.

Chou Tso-Jen. Stories About Birds. Lin Lan, ed. (Tales from the Orient Ser.: No. 15). (Chinese.). 15.00x (ISBN 0-89986-239-X). Oriental Bk Store.

Choux, M., ed. Shunts & Problems in Shunts. (Monographs in Neural Sciences: Vol. 8). (Illus.). x, 230p. 1982. pap. 49.00 (ISBN 3-8055-2465-X). S Karger.

Cho Van Tran, tr. English-Chinese Phrasebook with Useful Worldlist (for Cantonese Speakers) (Illus.). 146p. 1981. pap. 5.00x (ISBN 0-15-599279-1, BB-70). Ctr Appl Ling.

Chow, Brian G. The Liquid Metal Fast Breeder Reactor: An Economic Analysis. LC 75-39899. 1975. pap. 4.25 (ISBN 0-8447-3192-7). Am Enterprise.

Chow, Brian G., rev. by see Walker, Westbrook A.

Chow, Chuen-Yen, jt. auth. see Kuethe, Arnold M.

Chow, David & Spangler, Richard. Kung Fu, History, Philosophy, & Techniques. LC 73-14043. (Illus.). 220p. 1980. pap. 11.50 (ISBN 0-86568-011-6). Unique Pubns.

Chow, Dolly. Chow: Secrets of Chinese Cooking. pap. 3.95 (ISBN 0-8048-1073-7). C E Tuttle.

Chow, G. C. & Corsi, P. Evaluating the Reliability of Macro-Economic Models. 315p. 1982. 57.95 (ISBN 0-471-10150-8). Wiley.

Chow, Gregory. The Chinese Economy. 308p. 1984. text ed. 25.50 scp (ISBN 0-06-041255-0, HarpC). Har-Row.

Chow, Gregory C. Analysis & Control of Dynamic Economic Systems. LC 74-22433. (Probability & Mathematical Statistics Ser). 316p. 1975. 44.95x (ISBN 0-471-15616-7, Pub. by Wiley-Interscience). Wiley.

--Econometric Analysis by Control Methods. LC 81-571. (Wiley Series in Probability & Mathematical Statistics). 320p. 1981. 46.95 (ISBN 0-471-08706-8, Pub. by Wiley-Interscience). Wiley.

--Econometrics. (Illus.). 416p. 1983. text ed. 29.95 (ISBN 0-07-010847-1). McGraw.

Chow, J. H., ed. Time-Scale Modeling of Dynamic Networks with Applications to Power Systems. (Lecture Notes in Control & Information Sciences Ser.: Vol. 46). 218p. 1982. pap. 14.00 (ISBN 0-387-12106-4). Springer-Verlag.

Chow, J. K., ed. Industrial Pollution Control. 198p. 1983. pap. text ed. 40.00 (ISBN 0-317-02626-7, I00156). ASME.

Chow, Marian. To Be a Mother & Other Poems. 1984. 5.95 (ISBN 0-8062-2273-5). Carlton.

Chow, Marilyn P., et al. Handbook of Pediatric Primary Care. 2nd ed. LC 83-26038. 1304p. 1984. 37.95 (ISBN 0-471-86944-9, Pub by Wiley Med). Wiley.

Chow, Norman, jt. auth. see Edwards, LaVell.

Chow, P. L., et al, eds. Multiple Scattering & Waves in Random Media. 286p. 1981. 42.75 (ISBN 0-444-86280-3, North-Holland). Elsevier.

Chow, S. Y. General Theory of Lie Algebra, 2 vols. 942p. 1978. Set. 119.25 (ISBN 0-677-03890-9). Gordon.

Chow, Shui-Nee & Hale, Jack. Methods of Bifurcation Theory. (Grundlehren der Mathematischen Wissenschaften Ser.: Vol. 251). (Illus.). 512p. 1982. 55.00 (ISBN 0-387-90664-9). Springer-Verlag.

Chow, T. S. Software Quality Assurance: A Practical Approach. 1984. write for info. IEEE Comp Soc.

Chow, Ven Te, ed. Advances in Hydroscience, Vol. 13. 393p. 1982. 77.00 (ISBN 0-12-021813-5). Acad Pr.

Chow, Willard T. The Reemergence of an Inner City: The Pivot of Chinese Settlement in the East Bay Region of the San Francisco Bay Area. LC 77-75492. 1977. 14.00 (ISBN 0-88247-457-X). R & E Pubs.

Chow, William. Cost Reduction in Product Design. 1978. 32.50x (ISBN 0-442-21540-1). Van Nos Reinhold.

Chow, Woo F. Principles of Tunnel Diode Circuits. LC 64-20080. 387p. 1964. text ed. 24.50 (ISBN 0-471-15615-9, Pub. by Wiley). Krieger.

Chow, Y. Modern Abstract Algebra, 2 vols. 782p. 1976. Set. 113.50 (ISBN 0-677-03880-1). Gordon.

Chow, Y. S. & Teicher, H. Probability Theory: Independence, Interchangeability, Martingales. 1978. 36.00 (ISBN 0-387-90331-3). Springer-Verlag.

Chowan College Creative Writing Group & North Carolina Writers Conference. Strange Things Happen. Harris, Bernice K., ed. 1971. 7.50 (ISBN 0-930230-24-8). Johnson NC.

Chow Chen-Ho. Customs of Su-Chow. Bd. with Legends from Northern Chiang-Su. Hsiao Han. (Folklore Series of National Sun Yat-Sen University: No. 14). (Chinese.). 15.00x (ISBN 0-89986-066-4). Oriental Bk Store.

Chowder, Ken. Blackbird Days. LC 79-1704. 256p. 1980. 11.49i (ISBN 0-06-011496-7, HarpT). Har-Row.

--Delicate Geometry. LC 81-48052. 352p. 1982. 12.45i (ISBN 0-06-014973-6, HarpT). Har-Row.

--Jadis. LC 84-48145. 224p. 1985. 14.37 (ISBN 0-06-015388-1, HarpT). Har Row.

Chowdhary, Savitri. Indian Cooking. 2nd ed. 1976. pap. 3.50 (ISBN 0-89253-070-7). Ind-US Inc.

--Indian Cooking. 194p. 1954. 9.95 (ISBN 0-233-95522-4). Andre Deutsch.

--Indian Cooking. 194p. 1954. 9.95 (ISBN 0-233-95522-4, Pub. by A Deutsch England). David & Charles.

Chowdhry, Kamla, ed. see Sarabhai, Vikram A.

Chowdhury, Anwarullah. Agrarian Social Relations & Rural Development in Bangladesh. LC 81-19062. (Illus.). 122p. 1983. text ed. 28.95x (ISBN 0-86598-077-2). Allanheld.

Chowdhury, N. N., jt. auth. see Rao, K. Bhasker.

Chowdhury, Prem. Punjab Politics: The Role of Sir Chhotu Ram. 336p. 1984. text ed. 40.00x (ISBN 0-7069-2473-8, Pub. by Vikas India). Advent NY.

Chowdhury, R. H. Social Aspects of Fertility. 247p. 1982. text ed. 27.50x (ISBN 0-7069-1211-X, Pub by Vikas India). Advent NY.

Chowdhury, R. N. Slope Analysis. (Developments in Geotechnical Engineering Ser.: Vol. 22). 422p. 1978. 83.00 (ISBN 0-444-41724-9). Elsevier.

Chowdhury, Subrata R., jt. ed. see Hossain, Kamal.

Chowdhury, Tushar K. & Weiss, A. Kurt, eds. Concanavalin A. LC 75-4528. (Advances in Experimental Medicine & Biology Ser.: Vol. 55). 373p. 1975. 49.50x (ISBN 0-306-39055-8, Plenum Pr). Plenum Pub.

Chowla, S. Riemann Hypothesis & Hilberts Tenth Problem. (Mathematics & Its Applications Ser.). 134p. 1965. 44.25 (ISBN 0-677-00140-1). Gordon.

Chowning, Larry S. Barcat Skipper: Tales of a Tangier Island Waterman. LC 82-74135. 160p. 1983. 11.95 (ISBN 0-87033-300-3). Tidewater.

Chow Tse-Tsung. May Fourth Movement: Intellectual Revolution in Modern China. LC 60-10034. (East Asian Ser.: No. 6). 1960. 30.00x (ISBN 0-674-55750-6); pap. 9.95x (ISBN 0-674-76450-1). Harvard U Pr.

Chow Tun Yi. The Book of Universality: A Supplement to the Book of Changes. Hsu, F. G., tr. from Chinese. 70p. 1979. pap. 2.00 (ISBN 0-89071-242-5). Matagiri.

Chow Ven-Te. Handbook of Applied Hydrology: A Compendium of Water Resources Technology. 1964. 83.95 (ISBN 0-07-010774-2). McGraw.

--Open-Channel Hydraulics. (Civil Engineering Ser). 1959. 49.00 (ISBN 0-07-010776-9). McGraw.

Chow Ven Te, ed. Advances in Hydroscience, 12 vols. Incl. Vol. 1. 1964. 87.50 (ISBN 0-12-021801-1); Vol. 2. 1966. 87.50 (ISBN 0-12-021802-X); Vol. 3. 1967. 87.50 (ISBN 0-12-021803-8); Vol. 4. 1968. 87.50 (ISBN 0-12-021804-6); Vol. 5. 1969. 87.50 (ISBN 0-12-021805-4); Vol. 6. 1970. 87.50 (ISBN 0-12-021806-2); Vol. 7. 1971. 87.50 (ISBN 0-12-021807-0); Vol. 8. 1972. 87.50 (ISBN 0-12-021808-9); Vol. 9. 1973. 87.50 (ISBN 0-12-021809-7); Vol. 10. 1975. 90.00 (ISBN 0-12-021810-0); Vol. 11. 1978. 90.00 (ISBN 0-12-021811-9); lib. bdg. 120.00 o.p (ISBN 0-12-021876-3); Vol. 12. 1981. 80.00 (ISBN 0-12-021812-7). Acad Pr.

Choy, Bong-Yon. Koreans in America. LC 79-9791. 376p. 1979. 24.95x (ISBN 0-88229-352-4). Nelson-Hall.

Choy, Bong-youn. A History of the Korean Reunification Movement: Its Issues & Prospects. LC 84-61844. 353p. (Orig.). 1984. pap. text ed. 15.95 (ISBN 0-930433-00-9). Res Comm Korean.

--Korea: A History. LC 73-147180. (Illus.). 1971. 21.50 (ISBN 0-8048-0249-1). C E Tuttle.

Choy, Dexter, jt. auth. see Gee, Choy Y.

Choy, Leona. Andrew Murray: Apostle of Abiding Love. 1978. 7.95 (ISBN 0-87508-368-4); pap. 5.95 (ISBN 0-87508-367-6). Chr Lit.

Choy, Leona, jt. auth. see Carter, Evelyn.

Choy, Leona, jt. auth. see Murray, Andrew.

Choy, Penelope & McCormick, James. Basic Grammar & Usage. 2nd, alt. ed. 255p. 1985. pap. text ed. 12.95 (ISBN 0-15-504932-1, HC); instr's. manual avail. (ISBN 0-15-504934-8). HarBraceJ.

Choy, Penelope & McCormick, James R. Basic Grammar & Usage. 2nd ed. 248p. 1983. pap. text ed. 12.95 (ISBN 0-15-504930-5, HC); instr's. manual avail. (ISBN 0-15-504931-3). HarbraceJ.

Choy, Rita M. Read & Understand Chinese: A Guide to the Usage of Chinese Characters. 368p. (Chinese.). 1985. pap. text ed. 10.95 (ISBN 0-941340-10-4). China West.

Choy, Rita Mei-Wah see Mei-Wah Choy, Rita.

Choyke, jt. auth. see Picraux.

Choyke, Arthur, jt. ed. see Choyke, Phyllis F.

Choyke, Phyllis F. & Choyke, Arthur, eds. Gallery Series: Poets, 5 bks. Incl. Bk. 1. In Retrospect, J. M. Murphy. Kirkland, Wallace, photos by. pap. 1.25 (ISBN 0-933908-00-8); Bk. 2. Poems of the Inner World. Laughlin, Clarence J., photos by. pap. 1.50 (ISBN 0-933908-01-6); Bk. 3. Levitations & Observations. Abercrombie, Gertrude, et al, illus. pap. 1.75 (ISBN 0-933908-02-4); Bk. 4. I Am Talking About Revolution. Thecla, Julia, et al, illus. pap. 2.00 (ISBN 0-933908-03-2); Bk. 5. To an Aging Nation (with Occult Overtones) Burrows, Peggy, et al, illus. pap. 2.25 (ISBN 0-933908-04-0). (Illus.). 1967-77. Set. pap. 8.75 (ISBN 0-933908-05-9). Harper Sq Pr.

Cho-Yun Hsu. Ancient China in Transition: An Analysis of Social Mobility, 722-222 B. C. LC 65-13110. (Illus.). 1965. 20.00x (ISBN 0-8047-0223-3); pap. 6.95 (ISBN 0-8047-0224-1, SP85). Stanford U Pr.

Chr, Great Master Lyan, et al, eds. Essentials of the Shramanera Vinaya & Rules of Deportment: A General Explanation. Buddhist Text Translation Society, tr. from Chinese. (Illus.). 112p. (Orig., Eng.). 1975. pap. 5.00 (ISBN 0-917512-04-9). Buddhist Text.

Chraibi, Driss. The Butts. Harter, Hugh, tr. from Fr. 124p. 1983. 15.00 (ISBN 0-89410-324-5); pap. 8.00 (ISBN 0-89410-325-3). Three Continents.

--Heirs to the Past. (African Writers Ser.). 1972. pap. text ed. 5.50x (ISBN 0-435-90079-X). Heinemann Ed.

--Mother Comes of Age. Harter, Hugh, tr. from Fr. LC 81-51655. 121p. 1984. 15.00 (ISBN 0-89410-322-9); pap. 8.00 (ISBN 0-89410-323-7). Three Continents.

Chrakian, E. B., tr. see Issahakian, Avedick.

Chretien. Perceval: Or, the Story of the Holy Grail. 260p. 1983. 30.00 (ISBN 0-08-026296-1). Pergamon.

--The Pleuara in Health & Disease. (Lung Biology in Health & Disease Ser.). 904p. 1986. price not set (ISBN 0-8247-7380-2). Dekker.

Chretien de Troyes. Le Chevalier au Lion. 240p. 1970. 7.95 (ISBN 0-686-54376-9). French & Eur.

--Business Policy: Text & Cases. 5th ed. 1982. 31.50 (ISBN 0-256-02626-2). Irwin.

Christensen, Carl. Index Filicum. 1973. 92.75 (ISBN 3-87429-048-4). Lubrecht & Cramer.

--Index Filicum: Supplementum, Vols. 1, 2 & 3. 1973. 59.50 (ISBN 3-87429-049-2). Lubrecht & Cramer.

Christensen, Carl C. Art & the Reformation in Germany. (Studies in the Reformation Ser.: Vol.2). (Illus.). 269p. 1981. 18.95x (ISBN 0-8214-0388-5, 82-82816, Co-Pub by Wayne State U Pr). Ohio U Pr.

--Art & the Reformation in Germany. American Society for Reformation Research, ed. LC 79-16006. (Studies in the Reformation: Vol. 2). 228p. 1979. 18.95x (ISBN 0-8143-1634-4, Co-Published by Ohio Univ Pr). Wayne St U Pr.

Christensen, Carol W., compiled by. Guide to Religion-Based Organizations of Attorneys. (Tarlton Law Library Legal Bibliography Ser.: No. 19). 33p. 1979. 15.00 (ISBN 0-935630-01-5). U of Tex Tarlton Law Lib.

Christensen, Chris, jt. auth. see Calhoun, Fred.

Christensen, Chuck & Christensen, Winnie. Acts 1-12: God Moves in the Early Church. rev. ed. (Fisherman Bible Study Guide Ser.). 68p. 1979. saddle stitch 2.95 (ISBN 0-87788-007-7). Shaw Pubs.

--Acts 13-28: God Moves in a Pagan World. rev. ed. (Fisherman Bible Study Guide Ser.). 65p. 1979. saddle stitch 2.95 (ISBN 0-87788-008-5). Shaw Pubs.

--How to Listen When God Speaks. LC 78-73294. 79p. 1979. pap. 2.95 (ISBN 0-87788-355-6). Shaw Pubs.

--James: Faith in Action. LC 75-33442. (Fisherman Bible Studyguide Ser.). 55p. 1975. saddle-stitched 2.95 (ISBN 0-87788-421-8). Shaw Pubs.

--Mark: God in Action. LC 72-88935. (Fisherman Bible Studyguide Ser.). 94p. 1972. saddle-stitched 2.95 (ISBN 0-87788-309-2). Shaw Pubs.

Christensen, Clay B. & Wolfe, David E. Vistas Hispanicas: Introduccion a la Lengua y la Cultura. 2nd ed. 26.95 (ISBN 0-395-30972-7); instr's. manual 1.25 (ISBN 0-395-30974-3); student wkbk. & lab manual 10.50 (ISBN 0-395-30973-5); Tapes (cassette) 150.00 (ISBN 0-395-30975-1). HM.

Christensen, Clyde M. Edible Mushrooms. 2nd, rev. ed. (Illus.). 136p. 1981. 12.95 (ISBN 0-8166-1049-5); pap. 6.95 (ISBN 0-8166-1050-9). U of Minn Pr.

--The Molds & Man: An Introduction to the Fungi. 3rd ed. LC 65-17718. pap. 77.50 (ISBN 0-317-27948-3, 2055850). Bks Demand UMI.

--Molds, Mushrooms, & Mycotoxins. LC 74-21808. (Illus.). 292p. 1975. 15.95x (ISBN 0-8166-0743-5). U of Minn Pr.

Christensen, Clyde M. & Kaufmann, Henry H. Grain Storage: The Role of Fungi in Quality Loss. LC 70-76174. (Illus.). 1969. 10.95x (ISBN 0-8166-0518-1). U of Minn Pr.

Christensen, Conway B., ed. Programmer's Handbook to the Apple II. rev. ed. (Illus.). 108p. 1983. pap. 12.95 (ISBN 0-913249-01-7); looseleaf bdr. ed. o.p. 29.95 (ISBN 0-913249-00-9). Comp Stations.

Christensen, Culley K. The Adam-God Maze. 333p. 1982. 14.95 (ISBN 0-9608134-0-3). Indep Pubs.

Christensen, D., ed. Yearbook for Traditional Music. Orig. Title: International Folk Music Council Journal. 200p. (Eng., Fr., & Ger.). 22.00 (ISBN 0-318-14547-2). Intl Coun Trad.

Christensen, D. & Schramm, A. Reyes, eds. Working Papers of the Twenty-Third Conference. 163p. (Eng., Fr. & Ger.). 1975. 7.00 (ISBN 0-318-17461-8). Intl Coun Trad.

Christensen, Darrel E., et al, eds. Contemporary German Philosophy, Vol. 1. 320p. 1982. 22.50x (ISBN 0-271-00336-7). Pa St U Pr.

--Contemporary German Philosophy, Vol. 2. 320p. 1982. 22.50x (ISBN 0-271-00352-9). Pa St U Pr.

--Contemporary German Philosophy, Vol. 4. 336p. 1985. text ed. 22.50x (ISBN 0-271-00381-2). Pa St U Pr.

--Contemporary German Philosophy: Volume 3. (Contemporary German Philosophy Ser.). 1984. text ed. 22.50x (ISBN 0-271-00365-0). Pa St U Pr.

Christensen, David. Slot Machines: A Pictorial Review. LC 76-22637. (Illus.). 1977. Repr. of 1972 ed. 14.95 (ISBN 0-911572-13-9). Vestal.

Christensen, Deb. The Beginner's Guide to the 1541 Disk Drive. (Illus.). 250p. 1984. 14.95 (ISBN 0-8359-0455-5). Reston.

Christensen, Deborah. My Baha'i Book. (Sunflower Bks. for Young Children: Bk. 1). (Illus., Orig.). (ps-2). 1980. pap. 2.95 (ISBN 0-87743-141-8, 353-001). Baha'i.

Christensen, Devon, jt. auth. see Benson, Pagnar.

Christensen, Donald, jt. auth. see Fiday, David.

Christensen, Doris, jt. auth. see Feeney, Stephanie.

Christensen, Douglas D. Planning & Evaluating Student Activity Programs. 1978. pap. 4.00 (ISBN 0-88210-085-8). Natl Assn Principals.

Christensen, Edith A., ed. Approved Methods of the American Association of Cereal Chemists. 8th ed. LC 82-46081. 1200p. 1983. text ed. 140.00 member; text ed. 190.00 non member (ISBN 0-913250-31-7). Am Assn Cereal Chem.

Christensen, Edward, jt. ed. see MacKenzie, Ossian.

Christensen, Edward L. & Bell, R. Dermont. Century Twenty-One Shorthand: Theory & Practice. (gr. 9-12). 1974. text ed. 7.94 (ISBN 0-538-18100-1, R10). SW Pub.

Christensen, Edwin R., jt. ed. see Lambert, Michael J.

Christensen, Eleanor I. The Art of Haiti. LC 71-37807. (Illus.). 1975. 20.00 (ISBN 0-87982-006-3). Art Alliance.

Christensen, Eli H., jt. auth. see Acosta-Belen, Edna.

Christensen, Erwin. Early American Wood Carving. pap. 4.50 (ISBN 0-486-21840-6). Dover.

--Early American Woodcarving. (Illus.). 11.25 (ISBN 0-8446-4722-5). Peter Smith.

Christensen, Fern, jt. ed. see Prud'Homme, Luclie.

Christensen, Francis & Christensen, Bonniejean. A New Rhetoric. 256p. 1976. pap. text ed. 14.00 scp (ISBN 0-06-041282-8, HarpC); instructor's manual avail. (ISBN 0-06-361172-4). Har-Row.

--Notes Toward a New Rhetoric: Nine Essays for Teachers. 2nd ed. 1978. pap. text ed. 10.50 scp (ISBN 0-06-041263-1, HarpC). Har-Row.

Christensen, Francis, et al. The Sentence & the Paragraph. 76p. 1966. pap. 4.50 (ISBN 0-8141-4329-6). NCTE.

Christensen, G. S., jt. auth. see El-Hawary, M. E.

Christensen, Gary L. & Practising Law Institute. Cable Television in a New Era. LC 83-61003. (Patents, Copyrights, Trademarks, & Literary Property Course Handbook Ser.: No. 158). (Illus.). 424p. 1983. 35.00. PLI.

Christensen, George C., jt. auth. see Evans, Howard E.

Christensen, H., jt. ed. see Prakash, Braham.

Christensen, Harold T. & Johnsen, Kathryn P. Marriage & the Family. 3rd ed. LC 71-155205. pap. 138.50 (ISBN 0-317-09385-1, 2012476). Bks Demand UMI.

Christensen, Howard B. Statistics: Step-by-Step. LC 76-10903. (Illus.). 1977. text ed. 28.50 (ISBN 0-395-24527-3); instr's. manual with solutions 3.50 (ISBN 0-395-24528-1). HM.

Christensen, Inger. The Meaning of Metafiction. 200p. 1981. pap. 18.00x (ISBN 0-8200-5697-9). Universitet.

Christensen, J. A. Young Writer. LC 74-88375. (Illus.). (gr. 8-12). 1970. text ed. 12.95x (ISBN 0-87015-180-0). Pacific Bks.

Christensen, J. Ippolito & Ashner, S. Shapiro. Needlepoint & Bargello Stitchery. LC 80-51926. (Illus.). 96p. 1980. pap. 5.95 (ISBN 0-8069-8932-7). Sterling.

Christensen, J. Ippolito, jt. auth. see Weeks, Linda S.

Christensen, J. P. Topology & Borel Structure. (Mathematical Studies: Vol. 10). 133p. 1974. pap. 42.75 (ISBN 0-444-10608-1, North-Holland). Elsevier.

Christensen, J. P., jt. auth. see Berg, C.

Christensen, Jack F., jt. ed. see Kaufman, John E.

Christensen, James E. & Fisher, Jamer E. Analytic Philosophy of Education as a Sub-Discipline of Educology: An Introduction to Its Techniques & Application. LC 79-66235. 1979. pap. text ed. 10.50 (ISBN 0-8191-0802-2). U Pr of Amer.

Christensen, James J., jt. ed. see Izatt, Reed M.

Christensen, James J., et al. Handbook of Heats of Mixing. 1586p. 1982. 159.95 (ISBN 0-471-07960-X). Wiley.

Christensen, James L. Before Saying "I Do". 160p. 1983. pap. 4.95 (ISBN 0-8007-5128-0, Power Bks). Revell.

--Communion Reflections & Prayers. Lambert, Herbert, ed. 64p. (Orig.). 1985. pap. 4.95 (ISBN 0-8272-0446-9). CBP.

--Contemporary Worship Services. LC 75-137445. Repr. of 1971 ed. 64.00 (ISBN 0-8357-9517-9, 2011444). Bks Demand UMI.

--The Minister's Marriage Handbook. rev. ed. 160p. 1974. Repr. 10.95 (ISBN 0-8007-1424-5). Revell.

Christensen, James M., ed. Gastrointestinal Motility. 543p. 1980. 69.00 (ISBN 0-89004-503-8, 566). Raven.

Christensen, James R. Field Guide to the Butterflies of the Pacific Northwest. LC 80-52967. (GEM Bks. - Natural History). (Illus.). 200p. (Orig.). 1981. pap. 16.95. U Pr of Idaho.

Christensen, James R. & Larrison, Earl J. Mammals of the Pacific Northwest. LC 82-60054. (Illus.). 166p. 1982. 17.95 (ISBN 0-89301-085-5). U Pr of Idaho.

Christensen, Jane, jt. auth. see Committee on the Junior High & Middle School Booklist.

Christensen, Jerome. Coleridge's Blessed Machine of Language. LC 81-66644. 286p. 1981. 24.50x (ISBN 0-8014-1405-9). Cornell U Pr.

Christensen, Jo I. The Needlepoint Scraps Book: What to Do with Your Needlepoint Leftovers. (Illus.). 178p. 1982. 19.95 (ISBN 0-13-611020-7); pap. 9.95 (ISBN 0-13-611012-6). P-H.

--Teach Yourself Needlepoint. LC 78-838. (Creative Handcrafts Ser.). (Illus.). 1978. (Spec); pap. 10.95 (ISBN 0-13-888016-6, Spec). P-H.

Christensen, Jo Ippolito. The Needlepoint Book: 303 Stitches with Patterns & Projects. (Illus.). 384p. 1976. 19.95 (ISBN 0-13-610980-2, Spec); pap. 11.95 (ISBN 0-13-610972-1). P-H.

Christensen, Joe J. To Grow in Spirit. 81p. 1983. 6.95 (ISBN 0-87747-968-2). Deseret Bk.

Christensen, Joe J. & Christensen, Barbara K. Making Your Home a Missionary Training Center. 140p. 1985. 6.95 (ISBN 0-87747-589-X). Deseret Bk.

Christensen, John B. & Telford, Ira. Synopsis of Gross Anatomy With Clinical Correlations. 4th ed. (Illus.). 400p. 1982. pap. text ed. 21.50 (ISBN 0-06-140632-5, 14-06321, Harper Medical). Lippincott.

Christensen, John W. Energy, Resources & Environment. 224p. 1981. pap. text ed. 12.95 (ISBN 0-8403-2473-1); lab manual 6.95 (ISBN 0-8403-2575-4). Kendall-Hunt.

Christensen, K. K., et al, eds. Neonatal Group B Streptococcal Infections. (Antibiotics & Chemotherapy: Vol. 35). (Illus.). x, 350p. 1985. 105.25 (ISBN 3-8055-3953-3). S Karger.

Christensen, Karen, jt. auth. see Christensen, Roger.

Christensen, Kathleen. Social Impacts of Land Development: An Initial Approach for Estimating Impacts on Neighborhood Usages & Perceptions. (Land Development Impact Ser.). 144p. 1976. pap. 6.00x (ISBN 0-87766-171-5, 15700). Urban Inst.

Christensen, Kenneth E., jt. auth. see Wilson, Paul W.

Christensen, L. P., et al. Grapevine Nutrition & Fertilization in the San Joaquin Valley. 1978. pap. 5.00 (ISBN 0-931876-25-7, 4087). Ag & Nat Res.

Christensen, Larry B. Experimental Methodology. 3rd ed. 1984. text ed. 26.27 (ISBN 0-205-08244-0, 798244); lab manual 7.50 (798246). Allyn.

Christensen, Leon. Christensen's Collection. 4.00 (ISBN 0-8283-1268-0). Branden Pub Co.

Christensen, Leon N. The Little Book: Why I Am a Mormon. 1976. 12.00 (ISBN 0-8283-1606-6). Branden Pub Co.

Christensen, Lilian L. Chocolate & Coffee Cookbook. 192p. 1984. Repr. of 1968 ed. pap. 5.95 large print ed. (ISBN 0-8027-2453-1). Walker & Co.

Christensen, Lilian L. & Smith, Carol S. Appetizers & Canapes Cookbook. 192p. 1984. pap. 5.95 large print ed. (ISBN 0-8027-2448-5). Walker & Co.

--Brunch Cookbook. 192p. 1984. pap. 5.95 large print ed. (ISBN 0-8027-2449-3). Walker & Co.

--Canned Fish Cookbook. 192p. 1984. pap. 5.95 large print ed. (ISBN 0-8027-2450-7). Walker & Co.

--Chicken & Egg Cookbook. 192p. 1984. pap. 5.95 large print ed. (ISBN 0-8027-2451-5). Walker & Co.

--Chill & Serve Cookbook. 192p. 1984. pap. 5.95 large print ed. (ISBN 0-8027-2452-3). Walker & Co.

--Christmas Cookbook. 192p. 1984. pap. 5.95 large print ed. (ISBN 0-8027-2455-8). Walker & Co.

--Emergency Cookbook. 192p. 1984. pap. 5.95 large print ed. (ISBN 0-8027-2456-6). Walker & Co.

--Getting Married Cookbook. 192p. 1984. pap. 5.95 large print ed. (ISBN 0-8027-2457-4). Walker & Co.

--Homemade Gift Cookbook. 1984. pap. 5.95 large print ed. (ISBN 0-8027-2458-2). Walker & Co.

--One-Pot Cookbook. 192p. 1984. pap. 5.95 large print ed. (ISBN 0-8027-2459-0). Walker & Co.

--Outdoor Cookbook. 192p. 1984. pap. 5.95 large print ed. (ISBN 0-8027-2460-4). Walker & Co.

--Pasta, Rice & Potato Cookbook. 192p. 1984. pap. 5.95 large print ed. (ISBN 0-8027-2461-2). Walker & Co.

--Quick Meats Cookbook. 192p. 1984. pap. 5.95 large print ed. (ISBN 0-8027-2462-0). Walker & Co.

--Shellfish Cookbook. 192p. 1984. pap. 5.95 large print ed. (ISBN 0-8027-2463-9). Walker & Co.

--Soups & Salads Cookbook. 192p. 1984. pap. 5.95 large print ed. (ISBN 0-8027-2464-7). Walker & Co.

Christensen, M. N., jt. auth. see Gilbert, C. M.

Christensen, Mark & Stauth, Cameron. The Sweeps: A Year in the Life of a Television Network. LC 84-9021. (Illus.). 432p. 1984. 15.95 (ISBN 0-688-03912-X). Morrow.

Christensen, Mark J. Computing for Calculus. 240p. 1981. pap. 7.75 (ISBN 0-12-304365-4). Acad Pr.

Christensen, Mary L. Basic Laboratory Procedures in Diagnostic Virology. (Illus.). 128p. 1977. spiral 15.75x (ISBN 0-398-03617-9). C C Thomas.

--Microbiology for Nursing & Allied Health Students. (Illus.). 624p. 1982. 39.50x (ISBN 0-398-04176-8). C C Thomas.

Christensen, Nadia, tr. see Rifbjerg, Klaus.

Christensen, Nadia, tr. see Thorup, Kirsten.

Christensen, Niels J., et al, eds. Adrenergic Physiology & Pathophysiology. (Alfred Benzon Symposium Ser.: Vol. 23). 1986. text ed. price not set (ISBN 0-88167-149-5). Raven.

Christensen, Olive. Concise Needlecraft. 1982. 20.00x (ISBN 0-08-018306-9, Pub. by A Wheaton). State Mutual Bk.

Christensen, Oscar C. & Schramski, Thomas G., eds. Adlerian Family Counseling. LC 83-80003. (Illus.). 400p. (Orig.). 1983. pap. text ed. 14.95x (ISBN 0-932796-16-8). Ed Media Corp.

Christensen, Paul. Charles Olson: Call Him Ishmael. 261p. 1979. text ed. 15.00x (ISBN 0-292-71046-1). U of Tex Pr.

--Signs of the Whelming. pap. 5.00 (ISBN 0-318-04290-8). Latitudes Pr.

Christensen, Paula J., jt. auth. see Griffith, Janet W.

Christensen, R. Computer Implementation of Entropy Minimax. (Entropy Minimax Sourcebook Ser.: Vol. III). x, 254p. 1980. 32.95 (ISBN 0-938876-05-8). Entropy Ltd.

--Foundations of Inductive Reasoning. (Entropy Minimax Sourcebook Ser.: Vol. VII). xii, 363p. 1964. 34.95 (ISBN 0-938876-00-7). Entropy Ltd.

--General Description of Entropy Minimax. (Entropy Minimax Sourcebook Ser.: Vol. I). 692p. 1981. text ed. 39.50 (ISBN 0-938876-06-6). Entropy Ltd.

--Mathematical Analysis of Bluffing in Poker. 60p. Date not set. 9.50 (ISBN 0-686-28920-X). Entropy Ltd.

--Multivariate Statistical Modeling. (Entropy Minimax Source Ser.: Vol. V). (Illus.). x, 724p. 1983. lib. bdg. 49.95 (ISBN 0-938876-14-7). Entropy Ltd.

--Philosophical Origins of Entropy Minimax. (Entropy Minimax Sourcebook Ser.: Vol. II). x, 218p. 1980. 29.95 (ISBN 0-938876-04-X). Entropy Ltd.

--Statistical Distributions Software Sourcebook. (Entropy Minimax Sourcebook Ser.: Vol. IX). 1985. lib. bdg. 149.00 (ISBN 0-938876-20-1). Entropy Ltd.

--Thermal Mechanical Behavior of UO2 Nuclear Fuel: Electrothermal Analysis, Vol. II. x, 122p. 1978. 19.50 (ISBN 0-938876-10-4). Entropy Ltd.

--Thermal Mechanical Behavior of UO2 Nuclear Fuel: Multi-Cycle Test Description, Vol. IV. xii, 329p. 1978. 49.50 (ISBN 0-938876-12-0). Entropy Ltd.

--Thermal Mechanical Behavior of UO2 Nuclear Fuel: Single Cycle Test Data Discriptions, Vol. III. xii, 321p. 1978. 46.50 (ISBN 0-938876-11-2). Entropy Ltd.

Christensen, R., ed. Applications of Entropy Minimax. (Entropy Minimax Sourcebook Ser.: Vol. IV). xxii, 787p. 1981. 59.50 (ISBN 0-938876-07-4). Entropy Ltd.

--Thermal Mechanical Behavior of UO2 Nuclear Fuel, Vol. I-IV. Set. 130.00 (ISBN 0-938876-13-9). Entropy Ltd.

Christensen, R., et al. Futuristic Community Development: East Central Florida Crime Impact 1974-1984. xxii, 390p. 1973. pap. 15.00 (ISBN 0-686-28750-9, 04-80-04). Entropy Ltd.

Christensen, R. M. Theory of Viscoelasticity: An Introduction. 2nd ed. 357p. 1982. 49.50 (ISBN 0-12-174252-0). Acad Pr.

Christensen, Raymond P. Efficient Use of Food Resources in the United States. LC 75-26300. (World Food Supply Ser). (Illus.). 1976. Repr. of 1948 ed. 12.00x (ISBN 0-405-07772-6). Ayer Co Pubs.

Christensen, Richard D. Motorcycles in Magazines, Eighteen Ninety-Five to Nineteen Eighty-Three. LC 84-22119. 350p. 1984. 19.50 (ISBN 0-8108-1756-X). Scarecrow.

Christensen, Richard M. Mechanics of Composite Materials. LC 79-14093. 348p. 1979. 54.95x (ISBN 0-471-05167-5, Pub. by Wiley-Interscience). Wiley.

Christensen, Roger & Christensen, Karen. The Ultimate Movie, TV & Rock Directory. 496p. 1984. 35.00 (ISBN 0-9608038-1-5). Cardiff.

Christensen, Roland C. Management Succesion in Small & Growing Enterpises. Bruchey, Stuart & Carosso, Vincent P., eds. LC 78-18957. (Small Business Enterprise in America Ser.). 1979. Repr. of 1953 ed. lib. bdg. 17.00x (ISBN 0-405-11516-4). Ayer Co Pubs.

Christensen, Ronald. Belief & Behavior. (Entropy Minimax Sourcebook Ser.: Vol. VI). xii, 379p. 1982. 37.95 (ISBN 0-938876-16-3). Entropy Ltd.

--Data Distributions. (Entropy Minimax Sourcebook Ser.: Vol. VIII). (Illus.). x, 299p. 1984. lib. bdg. 36.95 (ISBN 0-938876-17-1). Entropy Ltd.

--The Death of Plato, the Aftermath. vii, 120p. 1983. lib. bdg. 8.95 (ISBN 0-938876-18-X). Entropy Ltd.

--Order & Time. (Entropy Minimax Sourcebook: Vol. 10). (Illus.). x, 134p. 1984. lib. bdg. 19.95 (ISBN 0-938876-19-8). Entropy Ltd.

Christensen, Rudolph P. Gothic & Renaissance Architecture in Great Britain. (The Art Library of the Great Masters of the World). (Illus.). 183p. 1982. Repr. of 1922 ed. 117.15 (ISBN 0-89901-073-3). Found Class Reprints.

Christensen, S., jt. auth. see Lambert, Carroll.

Christensen, S. M. Quantum Theory of Gravity. 500p. 1984. 54.00 (ISBN 0-9960042-1-1, Pub. by A Hilger England). Heyden.

Christensen, Stanley G. Lamb's Questions & Answers on the Marine Diesel Engine. 7th. ed. 466p. 1978. text ed. 29.75x (ISBN 0-85264-248-2). Lubrecht & Cramer.

Christensen, Terri & Gomez, Dolores. Easy Way to Weekend Riches. LC 82-19228. (Illus.). 96p. (Orig.). 1983. pap. 9.95 (ISBN 0-910927-00-6). Ter Bear.

Christensen, Terry, jt. auth. see Trounstine, Philip J.

Christensen, Terry, et al. The California Connection: Politics in the Golden State. 1984. 11.95 (ISBN 0-316-13901-7). Little.

Christensen, Thomas, tr. see Cortazar, Julio.

Christensen, Thomas P. A History of the Danes in Iowa. Scott, Franklyn D., ed. LC 78-15212. (Scandinavians in America Ser.). 1979. Repr. of 1952 ed. lib. bdg. 21.00x (ISBN 0-405-11634-9). Ayer Co Pubs.

Christensen, Val J., jt. auth. see Heasley, Victor L.

Christensen, W. N., jt. auth. see King-Farlow, J.

Christensen, Walter K. Upper Cretaceous Belemnites from the Kristianstad Area. (Fossils & Strata: No. 7). 1975. pap. text ed. 15.00x (ISBN 8-200-09374-3, Dist. by Columbia U Pr). Universitet.

Christensen, William W. & Stearns, Eugene I. Microcomputers in Health Care Management. 270p. 1984. 34.00 (ISBN 0-89443-596-5). Aspen Systems.

Christensen, Winnie. Women Who Achieved for God. (Fisherman Bible Studyguide). 80p. 1984. pap. 2.95 (ISBN 0-87788-937-6). Shaw Pubs.

--Women Who Believed God. (Fisherman Bible Studyguide Ser.). 77p. 1983. saddle-stiched 2.95 (ISBN 0-87788-936-8). Shaw Pubs.

Christensen, Winnie, jt. auth. see Christensen, Chuck.

Christenson, Andrew L. & Parry, William J. Excavations on Black Mesa, 1983: A Descriptive Report. (Research Paper: No. 46). Date not set. price not set. (ISBN 0-88104-024-X). Center Archaeo.

Christenson, Andrew L., jt. auth. see Earle, Timothy K.

Christenson, Boyd & Hanson, Nancy E. Boyd Christenson Interviews. (Illus.). 224p. 1983. 15.95 (ISBN 0-911007-00-8); pap. 9.95 (ISBN 0-911007-01-6). Prairie Hse.

Christenson, Carroll L. Economic Redevelopment in Bituminous Coal: The Special Case of Technological Advance in United States Coal Mines, 1930-1960. LC 62-8178. (Wertheim Publications in Industrial Relations Ser). (Illus.). 1962. 20.00x (ISBN 0-674-23000-0). Harvard U Pr.

Christenson, Charles & Voxman, William. Aspects of Topology. (Textbooks & Monographs in Pure & Applied Maths: Vol.39). 1977. 29.75 (ISBN 0-8247-6331-9). Dekker.

Christenson, Charles J., jt. auth. see Bower, Joseph L.

Christenson, Charles O., tr. see Reidemeister, Kurt.

Christenson, Charles O., tr. see Gramain, Andre.

Christenson, Christina & Johnson, Thomas W. Supervising. 336p. 1982. 30.95 (ISBN 0-201-03431-X); Instrs' Manual 11.95 (ISBN 0-201-03432-8). Addison-Wesley.

Christenson, Cornelia V. Kinsey: A Biography. LC 72-154897. (Illus.). 1971. pap. 48.10 (ISBN 0-317-08006-7, 2055215). Bks Demand UMI.

Christenson, Evelyn. Cambiame, Senor! 224p. 1980. 2.95 (ISBN 0-88113-035-4). Edit Betania.

--Gaining Through Losing. LC 80-51630. 180p. 1981. 5.95 (ISBN 0-88207-795-3); pap. 5.95 (ISBN 0-88207-344-3). Victor Bks.

--Lord, Change Me. LC 77-81219. 192p. 1977. pap. 4.95 (ISBN 0-88207-756-2). Victor Bks.

--Perder Para Ganar. 1983. 3.25 (ISBN 0-88113-243-8). Edit Betania.

Christenson, Evelyn & Blake, Viola. What Happens When Women Pray. 144p. 1975. pap. 4.95 (ISBN 0-88207-715-5). Victor Bks.

Christenson, Gordon A., ed. see University Of Oklahoma Executive Planning Committee.

Christenson, James A. & Robinson, Jerry W., Jr. Community Development in America. 246p. 1980. text ed. 9.95x (ISBN 0-8138-1475-8). Iowa St U Pr.

Christenson, James A., jt. auth. see Warner, Paul D.

Christenson, Kathy. Apples, Bunnies & Bears. (Illus.). 28p. 1984. pap. 4.95 (ISBN 0-9605904-8-X). Hot Off Pr.

Christenson, Kenneth L. Draw Me a World? 1982. 6.95 (ISBN 0-533-05390-0). Vantage.

Christenson, Larry. Back to Square One. LC 79-16413. 144p. 1979. pap. 3.95 (ISBN 0-87123-025-9, 210025). Bethany Hse.

--Christ & His Church. (Trinity Bible Ser.). 160p. 1973. pap. 4.95 spiral wkbk. (ISBN 0-87123-550-1, 240550). Bethany Hse.

--The Covenant. (Trinity Bible Ser.). 144p. 1973. pap. 4.95 spiral wkbk. (ISBN 0-87123-551-X, 240551). Bethany Hse.

--La Familia Cristiana. 238p. 1972. 3.75 (ISBN 0-88113-080-X). Edit Betania.

--Family Pocket Promise Book. LC 83-72175. 128p. (Orig.). 1983. pap. 2.95 (ISBN 0-87123-303-7). Bethany Hse.

--Gift of Tongues. 1963. pap. 0.95 (ISBN 0-87123-184-0, 260184). Bethany Hse.

--Hacia Donde Va la Familia? 32p. 1978. 1.35 (ISBN 0-88113-110-5). Edit Betania.

--How to Have a Daily Quiet Time. 16p. 1979. saddle stitch 0.99 (ISBN 0-87123-235-9, 200235). Bethany Hse.

--The Kingdom. (Trinity Bible Ser.). 160p. 1972. pap. 4.95x (ISBN 0-87123-548-X, 240548). Bethany Hse.

--La Mente Renovada. 128p. 1975. 2.25 (ISBN 0-88113-199-7). Edit Betania.

--La Pareja Cristiana. 1982. 3.25 (ISBN 0-88113-314-0). Edit Betania.

--Speaking in Tongues. LC 97-5595. 1968. pap. 3.50 (ISBN 0-87123-518-8, 200518). Bethany Hse.

--Trinity Teacher Training Workshop Booklet. (Trinity Bible Ser.). 80p. (gr. 4-6). 1975. pap. 2.95 (ISBN 0-87123-552-8, 240552). Bethany Hse.

--The Wonderful Way That Babies Are Made. LC 82-12813. 48p. (Orig.). (ps up). 1982. 7.95 (ISBN 0-87123-627-3, 230627). Bethany Hse.

Christenson, Larry & Christenson, Nordis. The Christian Couple. LC 77-24085. 1977. pap. 4.95 (ISBN 0-87123-051-8); study guide 1.50 (ISBN 0-87123-046-1, 210046). Bethany Hse.

Christenson, Mark & Stauth, Cameron. The Sweeps: Behind the Scenes in Network TV. LC 85-6130. (Illus.). 416p. 1985. pap. 7.95 (ISBN 0-553-34223-1). Bantam.

Christenson, Nordis, jt. auth. see Christenson, Larry.

Christenson, Reo M. American Politics: Understanding What Counts. (Illus.). 341p. 1980. pap. text ed. 15.95 scp (ISBN 0-06-041259-3, HarpC). Har-Row.

--The Brannan Plan: Farm Politics & Policy. LC 74-10728. 207p. 1974. Repr. of 1959 ed. lib. bdg. 15.00x (ISBN 0-8371-7650-6, CHBP). Greenwood.

--Challenge & Decision: Political Issues of Our Time. 6th ed. 223p. 1982. pap. text ed. 10.50 scp (ISBN 0-06-041257-7, HarpC). Har-Row.

--Heresies Right & Left: Some Political Assumptions Reexamined. LC 83-5848. 196p. 1983. pap. text ed. 9.75 (ISBN 0-8191-3086-9). U Pr of Amer.

Christenson, Reo M., et al. Ideologies & Modern Politics. 3rd ed. 260p. 1981. pap. 12.25 scp (ISBN 0-06-041273-9, HarpC). Har-Row.

Christenson, Ronald S. Political Trials: Gordian Knots in the Law. 252p. (Orig.). 1985. 29.95 (ISBN 0-88738-076-X). Transaction Bks.

Christenson, Toni & Feia, Marian R. The Tree Book: Teaching Responsible Enviromental Education, Vol. 1. (Illus.). 78p. (Orig.). 1981. tchr's ed. 6.95 (ISBN 0-686-36286-1). Creative Curriculum.

Christesen, Barbara. The Magic & Meaning of Voodoo. LC 77-12781. (Myth, Magic & Superstition Ser.). (Illus.). (gr. 4-5). 1977. PLB 14.25 (ISBN 0-8172-1030-X). Raintree Pubs.

--Myths of the Orient. LC 77-22199. (Myth, Magic & Superstition). (Illus.). (gr. 4-5). 1977. PLB 14.25 (ISBN 0-8172-1043-1). Raintree Pubs.

--Prehistoric Animals in the Modern World. LC 83-60116. (Strange but True Ser.). 1984. 10.00 (ISBN 0-382-06682-0). Silver.

Christeson, R. P. The Old Time Fiddler's Repertory: 245 Traditional Tunes. LC 73-80036. 1973. pap. 15.95 (ISBN 0-8262-0439-2). U of Mo Pr.

Christeson, R. P., ed. The Old-Time Fiddler's Repertory: Two Hundred Forty-Five Traditional Tunes. 224p. 1984. pap. 15.95 (ISBN 0-8262-0439-2); 2-record album 14.95 (ISBN 0-8262-0199-7); 24.95 (ISBN 0-8262-0440-6). U of Mo Pr.

Christgau, John. Enemies: World War II Alien Internment. (Illus.). 187p. 1985. 25.00 (ISBN 0-8138-0558-9). Iowa St U Pr.

--Spoon. LC 77-22081. (Richard Seaver Bk). 1978. 10.95 (ISBN 0-670-66455-3). Viking.

Christian, Anne H. The Search for Holmes, Robson, Hind, Steele & Graham Families of Cumberland & Northumberland, England. (Illus.). 184p. 1985. 17.95 (ISBN 0-9613723-0-3). Search CA.

Christian, Anthony J. Management, Machines & Methods in Civil Engineering. LC 81-2434. (Construction Management & Engineering Ser.). 360p. 1981. 45.95x (ISBN 0-471-06334-7, Pub. by Wiley-Interscience). Wiley.

Christian, Barbara. Black Feminist Criticism: Perspectives on Black Women Writers. LC 84-22805. (Athene Ser.). 350p. 1985. 29.95 (ISBN 0-08-031956-4); pap. 13.50 (ISBN 0-08-031955-6). Pergamon.

--Black Women Novelists: The Development of a Tradition, 1892-1976. LC 79-8953. (Contributions in Afro-American & African Studies: No. 52). xiv, 275p. 1980. lib. bdg. 29.95 (ISBN 0-313-20750-X, CBW/). Greenwood.

--Creative Escapes. LC 80-65477. 1980. pap. 6.95 (ISBN 0-8224-1631-X). Pitman Learning.

Christian Brothers. New Irish Grammar. 152p. (Orig.). 1980. pap. text ed. 6.50 (ISBN 0-7144-0315-6, Pub. by C J Fallon Ireland). Irish Bk Ctr.

Christian, C. D., jt. ed. see Reid, Duncan E.

Christian, C. Donald, jt. auth. see Zuspan, Frederick P.

Christian, C. W. Friedrich Schleiermacher. 157p. 1984. pap. text ed. 7.95 (ISBN 0-8499-3005-7, 3005-7). Word Bks.

Christian, Catherine. The Pendragon. 1984. pap. cancelled (ISBN 0-446-32193-1). Warner Bks.

Christian Center. Bible Birthday Book. 1983. 5.95t (ISBN 0-911346-06-6). Christianica.

Christian, Charles. Brief Treatise on the Police of the City of New York. LC 76-112548. (Rise of Urban America). 1970. Repr. of 1812 ed. 14.00 (ISBN 0-405-02442-8). Ayer Co Pubs.

Christian, Charles M. & Harper, Robert A. Modern Metropolitan Systems. 504p. 1982. text ed. 26.95 (ISBN 0-675-09892-0). Merrill.

Christian College Coalition. A Guide to Christian Colleges 1984-85. rev. ed. 160p. 1984. pap. 12.95 (ISBN 0-8028-0010-6). Eerdmans.

Christian, D. G., jt. auth. see Smith, R. E.

Christian, Diane. Wide-Ons. LC 81-8979. 64p. 1981. 9.00 (ISBN 0-912184-00-0); pap. 4.00 (ISBN 0-912184-01-9). Synergistic Pr.

Christian, Diane, jt. auth. see Jackson, Bruce.

Christian, Donna. Language Arts & Dialect Differences. (Dialects & Educational Equity Ser.: No. 5). 23p. 1979. pap. 2.75x (ISBN 0-15-599046-2). Ctr Appl Ling.

Christian, Donna & Wolfram, Walt. Exploring Dialects. (Dialects & Educational Equity Ser.: No. 2). 20p. 1979. pap. 2.75x (ISBN 0-15-599047-0). Ctr Appl Ling.

Christian, Donna, jt. auth. see Wolfram, Walt.

Christian, Edmund B. A Short History of Solicitors. xiv, 255p. 1983. Repr. of 1896 ed. lib. bdg. 25.00x (ISBN 0-8377-0448-0). Rothman.

Christian, Erich. LC-Filters: Design, Testing, & Manufacturing. LC 82-13425. (Filters: Design, Manufacturing & Applications Ser.). 242p. 1983. 29.95x (ISBN 0-471-09053-0, Pub. by Wiley Interscience). Wiley.

Christian, Ernest S., Jr. State Taxation of Foreign Source Income. LC 81-70922. 1982. 5.00 (ISBN 0-910586-44-6). Finan Exec.

Christian, Esther. Family Enrichment: A Manual for Promoting Family Togetherness. Sorenson, Don L., ed. LC 82-70356. 160p. 1982. pap. text ed. 5.95x (ISBN 0-932796-12-5). Ed Media Corp.

Christian, F. W. Caroline Islands: Travel in the Sea of the Little Lands. (Illus.). 412p. 1967. Repr. of 1899 ed. 32.50x (ISBN 0-7146-1123-9, BHA-01123, F Cass Co). Biblio Dist.

--Vocabulary of the Mangaian Language. (BMB Ser.). (Mangaian.). pap. 8.00 (ISBN 0-527-02114-8). Kraus Repr.

Christian, Frederick W. Eastern Pacific Lands: Tahiti & the Marquesas Islands. LC 75-35185. (Illus.). Repr. of 1910 ed. 28.00 (ISBN 0-404-14212-5). AMS Pr.

Christian, Gary D. Analytical Chemistry. 3rd ed. LC 79-19692. 643p. 1980. text ed. 38.50x (ISBN 0-471-05181-0); solution manual 11.50 (ISBN 0-471-06377-0). Wiley.

Christian, Gary D. & Feldman, Fredric J. Atomic Absorption Spectroscopy: Applications in Agriculture, Biology & Medicine. LC 78-23204. 512p. 1979. Repr. of 1970 ed. lib. bdg. 30.50 (ISBN 0-88275-797-0). Krieger.

Christian, Harry, ed. The Sociology of Journalism & the Press. (Sociological Review Monograph: No. 29). 396p. 1980. 35.00x (ISBN 0-8476-3798-0); pap. 18.95x (ISBN 0-8476-3257-1). Rowman.

Christian, Henry A., ed. Louis Adamic: A Checklist. LC 76-634011. (Serif Ser.: No. 20). 211p. 1971. 13.00x (ISBN 0-87338-115-7). Kent St U Pr.

Christian, J. H., jt. auth. see Troller, John A.

Christian, J. W. Theory of Transformations in Metals & Alloys., Part 1: Equilibrium & General Kinetic Theory. 2nd ed. LC 74-22470. 564p. 1975. text ed. 67.00 (ISBN 0-08-018031-0). Pergamon.

Christian, J. W. & Haasen, P., eds. Progress in Materials Science, Vol. 26. (Illus.). 420p. 1982. 130.00 (ISBN 0-08-029122-8). Pergamon.

--Progress in Materials Science, Vol. 27. (Illus.). 460p. 1983. 130.00 (ISBN 0-08-030029-4). Pergamon.

Christian, J. W., et al. Progress in Materials Science, Vol. 25. 110.00x (ISBN 0-08-029096-5). Pergamon.

Christian, J. W., et al, eds. Materials Science Progress: Supplement to Progress in Materials Science. (Illus.). 330p. 1981. 55.00 (ISBN 0-08-027147-2). Pergamon.

--Progress in Material Science, Vol. 24. (Illus.). 346p. 1980. 105.00 (ISBN 0-08-027107-3). Pergamon.

Christian, James L. Extra-Terrestrial Intelligence: The First Encounter. 1976. pap. 6.00 (ISBN 0-87980-350-9). Wilshire.

Christian, James L., ed. Extraterrestrial Intelligence: The First Encounter. LC 76-25328. (Science & the Paranormal Ser.). 303p. 1976. 17.95 (ISBN 0-87975-063-4); pap. 9.95 (ISBN 0-87975-064-2). Prometheus Bks.

Christian, Janet L. & Greger, Janet L. Nutrition for Living. 1985. text ed. 24.95 (ISBN 0-8053-2000-8); instr's guide 5.95 (ISBN 0-8053-2001-6); study guide by Bernice Stewart 10.95 (ISBN 0-8053-2002-4); transparencies 50.00 (ISBN 0-8053-2003-2); instr's. guide 5.95 (ISBN 0-8053-2001-6); 10.95 (ISBN 0-8053-2002-4). Benjamin-Cummings.

Christian, Jeffrey M. & Reibsamen, Gary G. World Guide to Battery Powered Road Transportation. (Illus.). 352p. 1980. 59.50 (ISBN 0-07-010790-4). McGraw.

Christian, John. The Oxford Union Murals. LC 79-23664. (Chicago Visual Library: CVL 33). (Illus.). 84p. 1981. incl. fiche 24.00 (ISBN 0-226-68922-0). U of Chicago Pr.

Christian, K. R., et al. Simulation of Grazing Systems. 121p. 1978. pap. 14.50 (ISBN 0-686-93181-5, PDC106, Pudoc). Unipub.

Christian, Kaare. The UNIX Operating System. LC 82-24811. 318p. 1983. text ed. 28.95 (ISBN 0-471-87542-2); pap. 21.95 (ISBN 0-471-89052-9). Wiley.

Christian Life. America's Great Revivals. 1970. pap. 2.50 (ISBN 0-87123-003-8). Bethany Hse.

Christian, M. Blount. CB Convoy Caper. (The Goosehill Gang Series: No. 2). (gr. 2-5). 1981. pap. 1.10 (ISBN 0-570-07352-9, 39-1042). Concordia.

Christian, Marcus B. Negro Ironworkers in Louisiana. LC 72-85953. (Illus.). 64p. (Orig.). 1972. pap. 4.95 (ISBN 0-911116-74-5). Pelican.

Christian, Mary. Breaking Through Barriers: Workers with Disabilities. (Illus.). 60p. pap. text ed. 8.95 (ISBN 0-916855-00-7). New Jersey.

Christian, Mary B. Anna & the Strangers. LC 81-243. 32p. (gr. 1-3). 1981. 6.50g (ISBN 0-687-01529-4). Abingdon.

--April Fool. LC 81-3782. (Ready-to-Read Ser.). (Illus.). 48p. (gr. 1-4). 1981. 8.95 (ISBN 0-02-718280-0). Macmillan.

--Christmas Reflections. 1980. pap. 3.95 (ISBN 0-570-03494-9, 56-1711). Concordia.

--Dead Man in Catfish Bay. Tucker, Kathleen, ed. LC 84-19616. (High-Low Mysteries Ser.). (Illus.). 128p. (gr. 4-9). 1985. 8.95 (ISBN 0-8075-1522-1). A Whitman.

--Deadline for Danger. Tucker, Kathy, ed. LC 82-17470. (High-Low Mysteries Ser.). (Illus.). 128p. (gr. 4-9). 1982. PLB 8.95 (ISBN 0-8075-1518-3). A Whitman.

--The Disappearing Dues. (Goosehill Gang Ser.). (Illus.). 32p. (gr. 1-4). 1976. pap. 1.10 (ISBN 0-570-03607-0, 39-1032). Concordia.

--The Doggone Mystery. Fay, Ann, ed. LC 80-10448. (A First Read-Alone Mystery Bk.). (Illus.). (gr. 1-3). 1980. PLB 7.75 (ISBN 0-8075-1656-2). A Whitman.

--The Firebug Mystery. Tucker, Kathleen, ed. LC 81-11493. (High-Low Mysteries Ser.). (Illus.). 128p. (gr. 4-9). 1981. PLB 8.95 (ISBN 0-8075-2444-1). A Whitman.

--Go West, Swamp Monsters. LC 84-12686. (Easy-to-Read Bks.). (Illus.). 48p. (ps-3). 1985. 8.95 (ISBN 0-8037-0091-1); PLB 8.89 (ISBN 0-8037-0144-6). Dial Bks Young.

--The Goosehill Gang Cookbook. (Goosehill Gang Ser.: No. 3). (Illus.). (gr. 1-4). 1978. pap. 1.10 (ISBN 0-570-07361-8, 39-1053). Concordia.

--The Goosehill Gang Craft Book. (Goosehill Gang Ser.: No. 3). (Illus.). (gr. 1-4). 1978. pap. 1.10 (ISBN 0-570-07362-6, 39-1054). Concordia.

--Grandfathers: God's Gift to Children. 1982. pap. 2.75 (ISBN 0-570-04069-8, 56-1372). Concordia.

--Grandmothers: God's Gift to Children. 1982. pap. 2.75 (ISBN 0-570-04068-X, 56-1371). Concordia.

--The Green Thumb Thief. Fay, Ann, ed. LC 81-23989. (First Read-Alone Mystery Ser.). (Illus.). 32p. (gr. 1-3). 1982. PLB 7.75 (ISBN 0-8075-3040-9). A Whitman.

--Growin' Pains. LC 85-42796. (Illus.). 180p. (gr. 5-9). 1985. 10.95 (ISBN 0-02-718490-0). Macmillan.

--Just Once. (Sundown Fiction Ser.). 48p. 1982. 2.00 (ISBN 0-88336-750-5). New Readers.

--The Lucky Man. LC 79-11024. (Ready-to-Read Ser.). (Illus.). 64p. (gr. 1-4). 1979. 7.95 (ISBN 0-02-718270-3, 71827). Macmillan.

--Microcomputers. Schroeder, Howard, ed. LC 83-7876. (Technology (How Things Are Made) Ser.). (Illus.). 48p. (gr. 4 up). 1983. PLB 8.95 (ISBN 0-89686-239-9). Crestwood Hse.

--The Mysterious Case Case. Amper, Julie, ed. LC 85-6948. (Determined Detectives Ser.). (Illus.). 64p. (gr. 2-6). 1985. 9.95 (ISBN 0-525-44217-0). Dutton.

--Mystery at Camp Triumph. (High-Low Mystery Ser.). (Illus.). 128p. (gr. 4-9). 1985. 8.95 (ISBN 0-8075-5366-2). A Whitman.

--The Mystery of the Double, Double Cross. Tucker, Kathleen, ed. LC 82-2575. (High-Low Mysteries Ser.). (Illus.). 128p. (gr. 5-10). 1982. PLB 8.95 (ISBN 0-8075-5374-3). A Whitman.

--Sebastian (Super Sleuth) & the Bone to Pick Mystery. LC 83-5406. (Sebastian Super Sleuth Mystery Ser.). (Illus.). 64p. (gr. 2-5). 1983. SBE 7.95 (ISBN 0-02-718440-4). Macmillan.

--Sebastian (Super Sleuth) & the Crummy Yummies Caper. LC 82-20861. (Sebastian (Super Sleuth) Mystery Ser.). (Illus.). 64p. (gr. 2-5). 1983. SBE 7.95 (ISBN 0-02-718430-7). Macmillan.

--Sebastian (Super Sleuth) & the Hair of the Dog Mystery. LC 82-10066. (Sebastian Super Sleuth Mystery Ser.). (Illus.). 64p. (gr. 2-5). 6.95 (ISBN 0-02-718260-6). Macmillan.

--Sebastian (Super Sleuth) & the Secret of the Skewered Skier. LC 83-19569. (Sebastian Super Sleuth Mystery Ser.). (Illus.). 64p. (gr. 2-6). 1984. SBE 8.95 (ISBN 0-02-718450-1). Macmillan.

--Sebastian (SuperSleuth) & the Clumsy Cowboy. LC 84-21758. (Illus.). 64p. (gr. 2-6). 1985. 9.95 (ISBN 0-02-718480-3). Macmillan.

--Sebastian (SuperSleuth) & the Crummy Yummies Caper. 64p. (gr. 6 up). 1985. pap. 2.25 (ISBN 0-553-15293-9). Bantam.

--Sebastian (SuperSleuth) & the Hair of the Dog Mystery. (Illus.). 64p. (gr. 3-7). 1984. pap. 2.25 (ISBN 0-553-15260-2, Skylark). Bantam.

--Sebastian (SuperSleuth) & the Santa Claus Caper. LC 84-4424. (Illus.). 64p. (gr. 2-6). 1984. 8.95 (ISBN 0-02-718460-9). Macmillan.

--Swamp Monsters. LC 82-1574. (Easy-to-Read Bk.). (Illus.). 56p. (ps-3). 1983. PLB 8.89 (ISBN 0-8037-7616-0); pap. 3.95 (ISBN 0-8037-7614-4, 0383-120). Dial Bks Young.

--The Toady & Dr. Miracle. LC 84-21278. (Illus.). 56p. (gr. 1-4). 1985. PLB 9.95 (ISBN 0-02-718470-6). Macmillan.

--Two-Ton Secret. Fay, Ann, ed. LC 81-346. (First Read-Alone Mysteries Ser.). (Illus.). 32p. (gr. 1-3). 1981. PLB 7.75 (ISBN 0-8075-8165-8). A Whitman.

--The Undercover Kids & the Museum Mystery. Fay, Ann, ed. LC 83-16682. (First Read-Alone Mysteries Ser.). (Illus.). 32p. (gr. 1-3). 1983. PLB 7.75 (ISBN 0-8075-8302-2). A Whitman.

Christian, Mary B. & Van Woerkom, Dorothy. Bible Heroes, Kings & Prophets. (gr. 3-8). 1982. pap. 3.75 (ISBN 0-570-04066-3, 56-1718). Concordia.

Christian, Mary Blount. J. J. Leggett, Secret Agent. (Illus.). (gr. 1-3). 1978. PLB 10.88 (ISBN 0-688-51864-8). Lothrop.

Christian, Nancy K. Education in the Eighties: Vocational Education. 120p. 1982. 15.95 (ISBN 0-8106-3168-7); pap. 9.95 (ISBN 0-8106-3167-9). NEA.

Christian, Paul. The Revolution in Real Estate: Extraordinary Listing & Selling Techniques That Dramatically Boost Income. 1982. 100.00 (ISBN 0-13-780619-1). Exec Reports.

Christian, Paula. Amanda. LC 81-50052. 144p. 1981. pap. 7.50 (ISBN 0-931328-07-1). Timely Bks.

--Another Kind of Love. LC 79-92584. 144p. 1980. pap. 7.50 (ISBN 0-931328-06-3). Timely Bks.

--The Cruise. LC 82-60183. 224p. (Orig.). 1982. pap. 8.95 (ISBN 0-931328-09-8). Timely Bks.

--Edge of Twilight. LC 78-54182. 160p. 1978. pap. 7.50 (ISBN 0-931328-00-4). Timely Bks.

--Love Is Where You Find It. LC 78-68727. 168p. 1979. pap. 7.50 (ISBN 0-931328-05-5). Timely Bks.

--The Other Side of Desire. LC 81-50051. 160p. 1981. pap. 7.50 (ISBN 0-931328-08-X). Timely Bks.

--This Side of Love. LC 78-54181. 144p. 1978. pap. 7.50 (ISBN 0-931328-01-2). Timely Bks.

Christian, Portia, ed. Agricultural Enterprises Management in an Urban-Industrial Society: A Guide to Information Sources. LC 76-27856. (Management Information Guide Ser.: No. 34). 1978. 60.00x (ISBN 0-8103-0834-7). Gale.

Christian, Portia & Hicks, Richard, eds. Ethics in Business Conduct: A Guide to Information Sources. LC 77-127411. (Management Information Guides Ser.: No. 21). 1970. 60.00x (ISBN 0-8103-0821-5). Gale.

Christian Publications, Inc., ed. Fifty-Two Visual Ideas for Opening Assemblies, 3 vols. 2.25 ea. Vol. 1 (ISBN 0-87509-271-3). Vol. 2 (ISBN 0-87509-272-1). Vol. 3 (ISBN 0-87509-273-X). Chr Pubns.

Christian, Quentin A. The Beanbag Curriculum. 160p. pap. text ed. 9.95x (ISBN 0-89582-121-4). Morton Pub.

--The Beanbag Curriculum: A Homemade Approach to Physical Activity for Children. rev., 3rd ed. (Illus.). 160p. 1983. pap. text ed. 9.95x (ISBN 0-88136-003-1). Jostens.

Christian, R., jt. auth. see Wiener, R.

Christian, R. F., jt. auth. see Borras, F. M.

Christian, R. F., ed. & tr. see Tolstoy, Leo.

Christian, Reginald F. Tolstoy: A Critical Introduction. LC 69-19373. 1970. pap. 14.95 (ISBN 0-521-09585-9, 585). Cambridge U Pr.

Christian, Robert R. Introduction to Logic & Sets. 2nd ed. LC 65-14567. (Blaisdell Books in the Pure & Applied Sciences). pap. 32.00 (ISBN 0-317-08549-2, 2055126). Bks Demand UMI.

Christian, Roy. Vanishing Britain. 1977. 8.95 (ISBN 0-7153-7346-3). David & Charles.

Christian, S. D. & Zuckerman, J. J. Energy & the Chemical Sciences. 34.00 (ISBN 0-08-022094-0). Pergamon.

Christian, S. Rickly. Alive! Daily Devotions for Young People. 192p. 1983. pap. 7.95 (ISBN 0-310-47121-4). Zondervan.

--The Woodland Hills Tragedy. LC 85-70474. 192p. (Orig.). 1985. pap. 6.95 (ISBN 0-89107-360-4, Crossway Bks). Good News.

Christian Science Monitor. Man's Great Future. facsimile condensed ed. Canham, Erwin D., ed. LC 71-37866. (Essay Index Reprint Ser). Repr. of 1959 ed. 18.00 (ISBN 0-8369-2585-8). Ayer Co Pubs.

Christian Science Monitor, jt. auth. see Ladies Home Journal.

Christian, Sheldon. Maine Writers' Conference Chapbook, No. 13. 1971. pap. 2.00 (ISBN 0-917638-06-9). Pejepscot.

--The Road Again Taken: Select Poems. LC 77-78820. (Illus.). 1978. 6.95 (ISBN 0-917638-13-1). Pejepscot.

Christian, Sheldon, ed. Maine Writers' Conference Chapbook, No. 11. 1969. pap. 2.00 (ISBN 0-917638-04-2). Pejepscot.

--Maine Writers' Conference Chapbook, No. 12. 1970. pap. 2.00 (ISBN 0-917638-05-0). Pejepscot.

--Maine Writers' Conference Chapbook, No. 14. 1972. pap. 2.00 (ISBN 0-917638-07-7). Pejepscot.

--Maine Writers' Conference Chapbook, No. 15. 1973. pap. 2.00 (ISBN 0-917638-08-5). Pejepscot.

--Maine Writers' Conference Chapbook, No. 16. 1974. pap. 2.00 (ISBN 0-917638-09-3). Pejepscot.

--Maine Writers' Conference Chapbook, No. 17. 1975. pap. 2.00 (ISBN 0-917638-10-7). Pejepscot.

--Maine Writers' Conference Chapbook, No. 18. 1976. pap. 2.00 (ISBN 0-917638-11-5). Pejepscot.

--The Maine Writers' Conference Chapbook, No. 19. 1977. soft cover 2.00 (ISBN 0-917638-12-3). Pejepscot.

--Maine Writers' Conference Chapbook, No. 20. 1978. pap. 2.00 (ISBN 0-917638-14-X). Pejepscot.

--Maine Writers' Conference Chapbook, No. 21. 1979. pap. 2.00 (ISBN 0-917638-15-8). Pejepscot.

Christian, Shirley. Nicaragua: Revolution in the Family. LC 84-45754. 335p. 1985. 19.95 (ISBN 0-394-53575-8). Random.

Christian, Timothy J. & Robb, James C. Employee-Employer Rights in Alberta. 2nd ed. 95p. 1984. 6.95 (ISBN 0-88908-232-4). Self Counsel Pr.

Christian, U. Selberg's Zeta-, L-, & Eisensteinseries. (Lecture Notes in Mathematics: Vol. 1030). 196p. 1983. pap. 13.00 (ISBN 0-387-12701-1). Springer Verlag.

Christian, Virgil L., Jr., jt. ed. see Marshall, Ray.

Christian, W., jt. auth. see Luce, S.

Christian, W., jt. auth. see Tsuboi, T.

Christian, W. P., et al. Schedule-Induced Behavior, Vol. 1. 1977. 14.40 (ISBN 0-904406-52-0). Eden Pr.

Christian, Walter P., jt. auth. see Luce, Stephen C.

Christian, Walter P., et al, eds. Programming Effective Human Services: Strategies for Institutional Change & Client Transition. 538p. 1984. 45.00x (ISBN 0-306-41526-7, Plenum Pr). Plenum Pub.

Christian, William, ed. The Idea File of Harold Adam Innis. 1980. pap. 9.95 (ISBN 0-8020-6382-9). U of Toronto Pr.

Christian, William A. Divided Island: Faction & Unity on Saint Pierre. LC 69-12720. (Illus.). 1969. 15.00x (ISBN 0-674-21285-1). Harvard U Pr.

--An Interpretation of Whitehead's Metaphysics. LC 77-5619. 1977. Repr. of 1959 ed. lib. bdg. 35.00x (ISBN 0-8371-9638-8, CHIW). Greenwood.

--Marah. facsimile ed. LC 76-39079. (Black Heritage Library Collection). Repr. of 1903 ed. 22.50 (ISBN 0-8369-9017-X). Ayer Co Pubs.

Christian, William A., Jr. Apparitions in Late Medieval & Renaissance Spain. LC 80-8541. (Illus.). 304p. 1981. 32.00x (ISBN 0-691-05326-X). Princeton U Pr.

--Local Religion in Sixteenth-Century Spain. LC 80-7513. 296p. 1981. 26.50 (ISBN 0-691-05306-5). Princeton U Pr.

--Person & God in a Spanish Valley. LC 72-7697. (Studies in Social Discontinuity). 210p. 1972. 36.00 (ISBN 0-12-785119-4). Acad Pr.

Christian Writers Inst. The Successful Writers & Editors Guidebook Market Guide, 1983-1984 with Update. LC 83-71425. 1982. 5.95 (ISBN 0-88419-186-9). Creation Hse.

Christian Writers Institute. Successful Writers & Editors Guidebook Market Guide: 1985-86. 1985. pap. 6.95 (ISBN 0-88419-186-9). Creation Hse.

Christian Writers Institute, ed. The Successful Writers & Editors Guidebook. LC 76-62692. 1977. 10.95 (ISBN 0-88419-014-5). Creation Hse.

Christian Writers Institute Staff. How to Prepare Your Manuscript for Publication. 1983. 5.95 (ISBN 0-88419-190-7). Creation Hse.

Christiani, Adolph. The Principles of Expression in Pianoforte Playing. LC 74-1348. (Music Reprint Ser.). 303p. 1974. Repr. of 1886 ed. lib. bdg. 29.50 (ISBN 0-306-70623-7). Da Capo.

Christiani, Dounia B., ed. see Ibsen, Henrik.

Christiani, Leon. Evidence of Satan in the Modern World. 1975. pap. 1.50 (ISBN 0-380-00413-5, 25122). Avon.

--St. Francis of Assisi. LC 74-79802. 1975. 4.95 (ISBN 0-8198-0494-0). Dghtrs St Paul.

Christiani, Sigyn. Samuel Johnson Als Kritiker Im Lichte Von Pseudoklassizismus und Romantik. 1931. 12.00 (ISBN 0-384-08955-0). Johnson Repr.

Christianica Center. Christianica. LC 74-13005. (Illus.). 1975. 5.50 (ISBN 0-911346-02-3). Christianica.

--Scriptural Rosary. LC 64-66463. (Illus.). 1961. 4.95 (ISBN 0-911346-01-5). Christianica.

Christianica Ctr. Rosario Biblico. (Illus.). 1980. 5.50 (ISBN 0-911346-04-X). Christianica.

Christiano, David & Young, Lisa. Human Rights Organizations & Periodicals Directory. 5th ed. Date not set. 22.00 (ISBN 0-317-12586-9); pap. 9.95 (ISBN 0-317-12587-7). Meiklejohn Civ Lib.

Christiano, David, jt. ed. see Ginger, Ann Fagan.

Christians, Charles J. Aberdeen Angus Bloodlines. LC 60-63767. 140p. 1958. 5.00 (ISBN 0-911042-03-2). N Dak Inst.

Christians, Clifford, et al. Media Ethics: Cases & Moral Reasoning. LC 82-7761. (Annenberg Communication Ser.). (Illus.). 320p. 1983. 24.95x (ISBN 0-582-28447-3); pap. text ed. 16.95x (ISBN 0-582-28371-X). Longman.

Christians, Clifford G. & Covert, Catherine L. Teaching Ethics in Journalism Education. LC 80-10426. (The Teaching of Ethics Ser.). 71p. 1980. pap. 4.00 (ISBN 0-916558-08-8). Hastings Ctr Inst Soc.

Christians, Clifford G. & Van Hook, Jay M., eds. Jacques Ellul: Interpretive Essays. LC 80-12342. 352p. 1981. 24.95 (ISBN 0-252-00812-X); pap. 8.95x (ISBN 0-252-00890-1). U of Ill Pr.

Christiansen, Bjorn. Attitudes Toward Foreign Affairs as a Function of Personality. LC 72-14085. (Illus.). 283p. 1974. Repr. of 1959 ed. lib. bdg. 18.75x (ISBN 0-8371-6754-X, CHFA). Greenwood.

--Thus Speaks the Body: Attempts Toward a Personology from the Point of View of Respiration & Postures. LC 72-342. (Body Movement Ser.: Perspectives in Research). 246p. 1972. Repr. of 1963 ed. 22.00 (ISBN 0-405-03141-6). Ayer Co Pubs.

Christiansen, Donald, jt. auth. see Fink, Donald G.

Christiansen, Eric. The Northern Crusades: The Baltic & the Catholic Frontier, 1100-1525. (Illus.). xxii, 265p. 1981. 25.00x (ISBN 0-8166-0994-2); pap. 10.95x (ISBN 0-8166-1018-5). U of Minn Pr.

Christiansen, F. B. & Fenchel, T. M. Theories of Populations in Biological Communities. LC 76-49871. (Ecological Studies: Vol. 20). 1977. 39.00 (ISBN 3-540-08010-4). Springer-Verlag.

Christiansen, F. B. & Fenchel, T. M., eds. Measuring Selection in Natural Populations. LC 77-11040. (Lecture Notes in Biomathematics: Vol. 19). 1977. pap. text ed. 28.00 (ISBN 0-387-08435-5). Springer-Verlag.

Christiansen, Fred B., jt. auth. see Feldman, Marc.

Christiansen, Greg, jt. auth. see Haveman, Robert H.

Christiansen, Harley D. Basic Background for Test Interpretation. (Illus.). 96p. (Orig.). 1981. pap. text ed. 9.95 (ISBN 0-915456-04-4). P Juul Pr.

--Casebook of Test Interpretation in Counseling. (Illus.). 96p. (Orig.). 1985. pap. text ed. 9.95 (ISBN 0-915456-05-2). P Juul Pr.

--Key Readings in Testing. 96p. (Orig.). 1985. pap. text ed. 9.95 (ISBN 0-915456-06-0). P Juul Pr.

--Self Relaxation: Comfort in Times of Tension. (Illus.). 96p. (Orig.). 1981. pap. 9.95 (ISBN 0-915456-02-8). P Juul Pr.

--Testing in Counseling, Uses & Misuses. (Illus.). 96p. (Orig.). 1981. pap. text ed. 9.95 (ISBN 0-915456-03-6); pap. text ed. 9.95 velo. binding (ISBN 0-915456-07-9). P Juul Pr.

Christiansen, Harley D. & Vergata, Marie L. Study Power: Better Study Skills-Greater Success in College. Turk, Laraine, ed. LC 75-5919. 1975. 9.95 (ISBN 0-915456-01-X); pap. 6.95 (ISBN 0-915456-00-1). P Juul Pr.

Christiansen, Heinz C. Fritz Reuter Gedenkschrift. (Amsterdamer Publikationen Zur Sprache und Literature Ser.: No. 18). (Illus.). 1976. pap. text ed. 20.50x (ISBN 90-6203-468-3). Humanities.

Christiansen, J. Reproduction in the Dog & Cat. (Illus.). 225p. Date not set. pap. price not set (Pub. by Bailliere-Tindall). Saunders.

Christiansen, J., ed. Hyperfine Interactions of Radioactive Nuclei. (Topics in Current Physics: Vol. 31). (Illus.). 366p. 1983. 38.00 (ISBN 0-387-12110-2). Springer-Verlag.

Christiansen, J. R., et al. Disaster Preparedness: A Family Protection Handbook. 1985. 13.95. Horizon Utah.

Christiansen, James. Educational & Psychological Problems of Abused Children. LC 79-93303. 125p. 1980. 11.95 (ISBN 0-86548-003-6). R & E Pubs.

Christiansen, Karl O., jt. auth. see Hurwitz, Stephan.

Christiansen, Keith. Gentile Da Fabriano. LC 80-70584. (Illus.). 300p. 1981. 85.00x (ISBN 0-8014-1360-5). Cornell U Pr.

Christiansen, Keith, jt. auth. see Gregori, Mina.

Christiansen, Kenneth & Bellinger, Peter. The Collembola of North America, North of the Rio Grande: A Taxonomic. (Illus.). 1322p. 1981. 35.00 (ISBN 0-686-34383-2). Grinnell Coll.

Christiansen, Larry. Nineteen Eighty-One U. S. Championship. (Illus.). 132p. 1981. pap. text ed. 5.00 (ISBN 0-931462-14-2). Chess Ent Inc.

--The U. S. Championship, 1983. (U. S. Tournament Ser.). (Illus.). 135p. (Orig.). 1984. pap. 6.50 (ISBN 0-931462-28-2). Chess Ent Inc.

Christiansen, Larry A. Business Law: A Study Outline. 64p. 1981. pap. text ed. 6.50 saddle stitched (ISBN 0-8403-2390-5). Kendall-Hunt.

Christiansen, Larry K. & Strate, James W. Attitude Development for Retail Management. (Gregg-McGraw-Hill Marketing Ser.). (Illus.). 256p. 1981. wkbk. 9.90 (ISBN 0-07-010820-X). McGraw.

Christiansen, M. N. & Lewis, Charles F., eds. Breeding Plants for Less Favorable Environments. LC 81-10346. 459p. 1982. 57.50 (ISBN 0-471-04483-0, Pub. by Wiley-Interscience). Wiley.

Christiansen, Michael. Strumming, Finger-Picking, Playing the Melody: A Beginning Guitar Method for Group, Individual, or Self-Instruction. 112p. 1980. pap. text ed. 10.95 (ISBN 0-8403-2247-X). Kendall-Hunt.

Christiansen, Monty L. Park Planning Handbook: Fundamentals of Physical Planning for Parks & Recreation Areas. LC 77-51844. 413p. 1977. text ed. 41.45 (ISBN 0-471-15619-1). Wiley.

--Vandalism Control Management in Parks & Recreation. (New Directions in Leisure Ser.). (Illus.). 128p. (Orig.). 1983. pap. 9.95 (ISBN 0-910251-06-1). Venture Pub PA.

Christiansen, Nels W. The Relation of Supervision & Other Factors to Certain Phases of Musical Achievement in the Rural Schools of Utah. LC 79-176699. (Columbia University. Teachers College. Contributions to Education: No. 934). Repr. of 1948 ed. 22.50 (ISBN 0-404-55934-4). AMS Pr.

Christiansen, Pauline G. From Inside Out: Writing from Subjective to Objective. (Orig.). 1978. pap. text ed. 11.95 (ISBN 0-316-14068-6); tchrs' manual avail. (ISBN 0-316-14069-4). Little.

Christiansen, R. Regional Railway History of the Railways of Great Britain, Vol. 13: Thames & Severn. LC 80-68696. (Illus.). 224p. 1981. 23.00 (ISBN 0-7153-8004-4). David & Charles.

Christiansen, Reidar T. The Migratory Legends: List of Types with a Systematic Catalogue of the Norwegian Variants. Dorsen, Richard M., ed. LC 77-70585. (International Folklore Ser.). 1977. Repr. of 1958 ed. lib. bdg. 22.00x (ISBN 0-405-10087-6). Ayer Co Pubs.

Christiansen, Reidar T., ed. Folktales of Norway. Iversen, Pat S., tr. LC 64-15830. (Folktales of the World Ser). 1964. 12.00x (ISBN 0-226-10509-1); pap. 9.00 (ISBN 0-226-10510-5, FW5). U of Chicago Pr.

Christiansen, Reider T. Studies in Irish & Scandinavian Folktales. Dorson, Richard M., ed. LC 80-741. (Folklore of the World Ser.). 1980. Repr. of 1959 ed. lib. bdg. 26.50x (ISBN 0-405-13307-3). Ayer Co Pubs.

Christiansen, Rex. Forgotten Railways: North & Mid Wales. LC 75-31317. (Forgotten Railways Ser.). (Illus.). 144p. 1976. 14.95 (ISBN 0-7153-7059-6). David & Charles.

--Forgotten Railways: North & Mid Wales. (Illus.). 168p. 1984. 18.95 (ISBN 0-946537-05-4). David & Charles.

--Forgotten Railways: West Midlands. (Forgotten Railways of Great Britain Ser.). (Illus.). 192p. 1985. 19.95 (ISBN 0-946537-01-1). David & Charles.

--A Regional History of the Railways of Great Britain: Vol. 7: The West Midlands. 2nd ed. (Illus.). 305p. 1983. 23.50 (ISBN 0-946537-00-3). David & Charles.

Christiansen, Sigurd. Chaff Before the Wind. Anderson, Isaac, tr. LC 73-22750. 319p. 1974. Repr. of 1934 ed. lib. bdg. 24.75x (ISBN 0-8371-7349-3, CHCB). Greenwood.

--Two Living & One Dead. Bjorkman, Edwin, tr. from Norwegian. LC 73-22751. 288p. 1975. Repr. of 1932 ed. lib. bdg. 19.75x (ISBN 0-8371-7348-5, CHTL). Greenwood.

Christiansen, W. N. & Hogbom, J. A. Radiotelescopes. 2nd ed. (Monographs in Physics). (Illus.). 250p. 1985. 59.50 (ISBN 0-521-26209-7). Cambridge U Pr.

Christiansen, Wayne & Kaitchuck, Ron. Investigations in Observational Astronomy. 1978. coil bdg. 9.95 (ISBN 0-88252-054-7). Paladin Hse.

Christianson, Arne. The Future Is Now. 1983. 8.95 (ISBN 0-533-05552-0). Vantage.

Christianson, Betsy P. Interview Research. (Illus.). 32p. (gr. 3-9). 1983. pap. 3.95 Tchr Enrichment Bk (ISBN 0-88047-016-X, 8220). DOK Pubs.

Christianson, Birgitte, jt. auth. see Christianson, John.

Christianson, Gale E. In the Presence of the Creator: Issac Newton & His Times. LC 83-49211. 608p. 1984. 27.50 (ISBN 0-02-905190-8). Free Pr.

--This Wild Abyss: The Story of the Men Who Made Modern Astronomy. LC 77-81428. (Illus.). 1979. pap. text ed. 9.95 (ISBN 0-02-905660-8). Free Pr.

--This Wild Abyss: The Story of the Men Who Made Modern Astronomy. LC 77-81428. (Illus.). 1978. 14.95 (ISBN 0-02-905380-3). Free Pr.

--This Wild Abyss: The Story of the Men Who Made Modern Astronomy. 1979. pap. 9.95x (ISBN 0-317-30517-4). Free Pr.

Christianson, Helen M. Bodily Rhythmic Movements of Young Children in Relation to Rhythm in Music. LC 74-176644. (Columbia University. Teachers College. Contributions to Education: No. 736). Repr. of 1938 ed. 22.50 (ISBN 0-404-55736-8). AMS Pr.

Christianson, John & Christianson, Birgitte. The Dream of America Series, 7 vols. Incl. Europe & the Flight to America; America Fever; The Westward Journey; They Came to America; Shattered Dreams-Joe Hill; Portal to America-New York City; Ireland in Flight. (Illus.). (gr. 4-12). Set. PLB 69.95 (ISBN 0-317-31004-6). Creative Ed.

Christianson, Jon B. & Smith, Kenneth R. Current Strategies for Containing Health Care Expenditures. 156p. Date not set. text ed. price not set (ISBN 0-89335-233-0). SP Med & Sci Bks.

Christianson, Jon B., jt. auth. see Marmor, Theodore R.

Christianson, M. E., jt. auth. see Gray, J. S.

Christianson, Scott, et al, eds. Index to Minorities & Criminal Justice: An Index to Periodicals & Books Relating to Minorities & Criminal Justice in the United States. 1981 Cumulative Edition. 288p. 1981. lib. bdg. 85.00 (ISBN 0-940826-00-3). Ctr Minorities.

Christianson, Victoria, jt. auth. see Laumark, Eleanor.

Christiansson, Carl. Soil Erosion & Sedimentation in Semi-Arid Tanzania: Studies of Environmental Change & Ecological Imbalance. 208p. 1983. pap. text ed. 24.50x (ISBN 0-8419-9743-8, Africana). Holmes & Meier.

Christie, A. B. Infectious Diseases: Epidemiology & Clinical Practice. 3rd ed. (Illus.). 1981. text ed. 98.00 (ISBN 0-443-02263-1). Churchill.

Christie, A. D. Ultrasound & Infertility. 179p. (Orig.). 1981. pap. text ed. 29.95x (ISBN 0-86238-017-0, Pub. by Chartwell-Bratt England). Brookfield Pub Co.

Christie, Agahta. The Mysterious Affair at Styles. 15.95 (ISBN 0-88411-385-X, Pub. by Aeonian Pr). Amereon Ltd.

Christie, Agatha. The A. B. C. Murders. 256p. 1985. 12.95 (ISBN 0-396-08698-5). Dodd.

--ABC Murders. 240p. 1985. pap. 3.50 (ISBN 0-671-60063-X). PB.

--And Then There Were None. 218p. 1985. 12.95 (ISBN 0-396-08572-5). Dodd.

--Appointment with Death. 224p. 1984. pap. 2.95 (ISBN 0-425-06775-0). Berkley Pub.

--At Bertram's Hotel. rev. ed. 1984. pap. 3.50 (ISBN 0-671-54385-7). PB.
--The Big Four. 1982. pap. 2.95 (ISBN 0-440-10562-5). Dell.
--The Big Four. 224p. 1984. pap. 2.95 (ISBN 0-425-06776-9). Berkley Pub.
--The Body in the Library. 1983. pap. 2.95 (ISBN 0-671-46496-5). PB.
--The Body in the Library. 240p. 1985. 12.95 (ISBN 0-396-08699-3). Dodd.
--The Boomerang Clue. 240p. 1984. pap. 2.95 (ISBN 0-425-06777-7). Berkley Pub.
--By the Pricking of My Thumbs. 1985. pap. 3.50 (ISBN 0-671-54208-7). PB.
--Cards on the Table. 240p. 1984. pap. 2.95 (ISBN 0-425-06778-5). Berkley Pub.
--A Caribbean Mystery. (Greenway Edition). 1979. 9.95 (ISBN 0-396-07768-4). Dodd.
--A Caribbean Mystery. 1982. pap. 2.95 (ISBN 0-671-46920-7). PB.
--A Caribbean Mystery. 1985. pap. 3.50 (ISBN 0-671-55523-5). PB.
--Cat Among the Pigeons. 1985. pap. 3.50 (ISBN 0-671-55700-9). PB.
--Clocks. 1983. pap. 2.95 (ISBN 0-671-47296-8). PB.
--Come Tell Me How You Live. 1983. pap. 2.95 (ISBN 0-671-49162-8). PB.
--Crooked House. 1984. pap. 3.50 (ISBN 0-671-54321-0). PB.
--Curtain. 1983. pap. 2.95 (ISBN 0-671-47985-7). PB.
--Curtain. 16.95 (ISBN 0-88411-386-8, Pub. by Aeonian Pr). Amereon Ltd.
--Dead Man's Folly. 1984. pap. 3.50 (ISBN 0-671-54318-0). PB.
--Dead Man's Mirror. 240p. 1985. pap. 2.95 (ISBN 0-425-06779-3). Berkley Pub.
--Death Comes As the End. LC 82-73252. (Greenway Edition). 1982. 9.95 (ISBN 0-396-08109-6). Dodd.
--Death Comes As the End. 1984. pap. 3.50 (ISBN 0-671-54319-9). PB.
--Death in the Air. 240p. 1984. pap. 2.95 (ISBN 0-425-06780-7). Berkley Pub.
--Death on the Nile. 288p. 1981. pap. 2.95 (ISBN 0-553-23776-4). Bantam.
--Death on the Nile. 340p. 1985. 12.95 (ISBN 0-396-08573-3). Dodd.
--Destination Unknown. (Greenway Edition Ser.). 1978. 9.95 (ISBN 0-396-07514-2). Dodd.
--Double Sin & Other Stories. 224p. 1984. pap. 2.95 (ISBN 0-425-06781-5). Berkley Pub.
--Easy to Kill. 1984. pap. 3.50 (ISBN 0-671-44723-8). PB.
--Elephants Can Remember. (Greenway Edition). 1979. 9.95 (ISBN 0-396-07769-2). Dodd.
--Elephants Can Remember. (General Ser.). 1973. Repr. lib. bdg. 9.95 (ISBN 0-8161-6086-4, Large Print Bks). G K Hall.
--Elephants Can Remember. 224p. 1985. pap. 2.95 (ISBN 0-425-06782-3). Berkley Pub.
--Endless Night. 1985. pap. 3.50 (ISBN 0-671-60427-9). PB.
--Endless Night. 224p. 1985. 12.95 (ISBN 0-396-08700-0). Dodd.
--Evil under the Sun. 224p. 1983. pap. 2.95 (ISBN 0-671-47427-8). PB.
--Evil under the Sun. 240p. 1985. 12.95 (ISBN 0-396-08701-9). Dodd.
--Evil under the Sun. 1985. pap. 3.50 (ISBN 0-671-60174-1). PB.
--The Four-Fifty from Paddington. LC 82-73250. (Greenway Edition). 1982. 9.95 (ISBN 0-396-08110-X). Dodd.
--Funerals Are Fatal. 1985. pap. 3.50 (ISBN 0-671-55695-9). PB.
--Gaints' Bread. LC 72-97688. 1982. pap. 5.95 (ISBN 0-87795-387-2). Arbor Hse.
--The Golden Ball & Other Stories. 240p. 1984. pap. 2.95 (ISBN 0-425-06783-1). Berkley Pub.
--Halloween Party. 1984. pap. 3.50 (ISBN 0-671-54203-6). PB.
--Hercule Poirot's Casebook: Fifty Stories. 1984. 18.95 (ISBN 0-396-08417-6). Dodd.
--Hercule Poirot's Early Cases. 15.95 (ISBN 0-88411-388-4, Pub. by Aeonian Pr). Amereon Ltd.
--Hickory Dickory Death. 224p. 1983. pap. 2.95 (ISBN 0-671-49166-0). PB.
--Holiday for Murder. 176p. 1980. pap. 2.95 (ISBN 0-553-24144-3). Bantam.
--The Hollow. 240p. 1984. pap. 2.95 (ISBN 0-425-06784-X). Berkley Pub.
--The Labors of Hercules. 1982. pap. 2.95 (ISBN 0-440-14620-8). Dell.
--The Labours of Hercules. (Greenway Edition). 1967. 9.95 (ISBN 0-396-05578-8). Dodd.
--The Man in the Brown Suit. 224p. 1981. pap. 2.95 (ISBN 0-440-15230-5). Dell.
--The Man in the Brown Suit. 240p. 1984. pap. 2.95 (ISBN 0-425-06786-6). Berkley Pub.
--The Mirror Crack'd. 224p. 1985. pap. 3.50 (ISBN 0-671-55701-7). PB.
--Miss Marple, the Complete Short Stories: The Collected Short Stories. 320p. 1985. 14.95 (ISBN 0-396-08747-7). Dodd.
--Mister Parker Pyne, Detective. 224p. 1981. pap. 2.50 (ISBN 0-440-15888-5). Dell.
--Mr. Parker Pyne, Detective. 208p. 1984. pap. 2.95 (ISBN 0-425-06788-2). Berkley Pub.
--The Mousetrap & Other Plays. 720p. 1981. pap. 4.50 (ISBN 0-553-24627-5). Bantam.
--The Mousetrap & Other Plays. 1978. 12.95 (ISBN 0-396-07631-9). Dodd.
--The Moving Finger. 192p. 1982. pap. 2.95 (ISBN 0-440-15861-3). Dell.
--The Moving Finger. 208p. 1985. pap. 2.95 (ISBN 0-425-06787-4). Berkley Pub.
--Mrs. McGinty's Dead. 240p. 1985. pap. 3.50 (ISBN 0-671-83440-1). PB.
--Murder at Hazelmoor. 192p. 1979. pap. 2.95 (ISBN 0-440-15940-7). Dell.
--The Murder at Hazelmoor. 240p. 1984. pap. 2.95 (ISBN 0-425-06789-0). Berkley Pub.
--The Murder at the Vicarage. 224p. 1982. pap. 2.95 (ISBN 0-440-15946-6). Dell.
--The Murder at the Vicarage. 240p. 1984. pap. 2.95 (ISBN 0-425-06790-4). Berkley Pub.
--Murder in Mesopotamia. 192p. 1982. pap. 2.95 (ISBN 0-440-15982-2). Dell.
--Murder in Mesopotamia. 240p. 1984. pap. 2.95 (ISBN 0-425-06791-2). Berkley Pub.
--Murder in Retrospect. 192p. 1981. pap. 2.95 (ISBN 0-440-16030-8). Dell.
--Murder in Retrospect. 224p. 1985. pap. 2.95 (ISBN 0-425-06792-0). Berkley Pub.
--Murder in Three Acts. 224p. 1984. pap. 2.95 (ISBN 0-425-06793-9). Berkley Pub.
--Murder Is Announced. 1982. pap. 2.95 (ISBN 0-671-45934-1). PB.
--Murder Is Announced. 1985. pap. 3.50 (ISBN 0-671-55267-8). PB.
--A Murder Is Announced. 224p. 1985. 12.95 (ISBN 0-396-08702-7). Dodd.
--Murder Is Easy. (Greenway Edition of Agatha Christie Ser.). 1981. 9.95 (ISBN 0-396-08016-2). Dodd.
--The Murder of Roger Ackroyd. (Greenway Edition). 9.95 (ISBN 0-396-05580-X). Dodd.
--The Murder of Roger Ackroyd. (A Hercule Poirot Murder Mystery Ser.). 256p. 1983. pap. 2.95 (ISBN 0-671-49856-8). PB.
--The Murder of Roger Ackroyd. 276p. 1985. 12.95 (ISBN 0-396-08574-1). Dodd.
--Murder on the Links. 1983. pap. 2.95 (ISBN 0-440-16102-9). Dell.
--Murder on the Links. 240p. 1984. pap. 2.95 (ISBN 0-425-06794-7). Berkley Pub.
--Murder on the Orient Express. 256p. 1985. pap. 3.50 (ISBN 0-671-52368-6). PB.
--Murder on the Orient Express. 263p. 1985. 12.95 (ISBN 0-396-08575-X). Dodd.
--Murder with Mirrors. 1982. pap. 2.95 (ISBN 0-671-46537-6). PB.
--Murder with Mirrors. 192p. 1985. 9.95 (ISBN 0-553-35027-7). Bantam.
--The Mysterious Affair at Styles. 192p. 1981. pap. text ed. 2.95 (ISBN 0-553-24093-5). Bantam.
--The Mysterious Affair at Styles. 240p. 1985. 12.95 (ISBN 0-396-08703-5). Dodd.
--The Mysterious Mr. Quin. 256p. 1984. pap. 2.95 (ISBN 0-425-06795-5). Berkley Pub.
--The Mysterious Mr. Quinn. 1982. pap. 2.95 (ISBN 0-440-16246-7). Dell.
--The Mystery of the Blue Train. 1982. pap. 2.95 (ISBN 0-671-45961-9). PB.
--N or M? 192p. 1981. pap. 2.95 (ISBN 0-440-16254-8). Dell.
--N or M? 208p. 1985. pap. 2.95 (ISBN 0-425-06796-3). Berkley Pub.
--Nemesis. 1984. pap. 3.50 (ISBN 0-671-54206-0). PB.
--Ordeal by Innocence. 1985. pap. 3.50 (ISBN 0-671-54209-5). PB.
--Ordeal by Innocence. 256p. 1985. 12.95 (ISBN 0-396-08704-3). Dodd.
--An Overdose of Death. 1982. pap. 2.95 (ISBN 0-440-16780-9). Dell.
--The Pale Horse. 224p. 1985. pap. 3.50 (ISBN 0-671-54207-9). PB.
--The Pale Horse. 256p. 1985. 12.95 (ISBN 0-396-08705-1). Dodd.
--Partners in Crime. 240p. 1984. pap. 2.95 (ISBN 0-425-07662-8). Berkley Pub.
--Passenger to Frankfurt. 1983. pap. 2.95 (ISBN 0-671-47346-8). PB.
--Passenger to Frankfurt. 15.95 (ISBN 0-88411-384-1, Pub. by Aeonian Pr). Amereon Ltd.
--The Patriotic Murders. 240p. 1985. pap. 2.95 (ISBN 0-425-06797-1). Berkley Pub.
--Peril at End House. 1982. pap. 2.95 (ISBN 0-671-46538-4). PB.
--Peril at End House. 224p. 1985. 12.95 (ISBN 0-396-08706-X). Dodd.
--A Pocket Full of Rye. LC 81-67345. (The Greenway Edition). 1981. 9.95 (ISBN 0-396-08019-7). Dodd.
--Pocket Full of Rye. 1985. pap. 3.50 (ISBN 0-671-55796-3). PB.
--Poirot Investigates. 208p. 1982. pap. 2.95 (ISBN 0-553-23908-2). Bantam.
--Poirot Loses a Client. 224p. 1982. pap. 2.95 (ISBN 0-440-16984-4). Dell.
--Poirot Loses a Client. 256p. 1985. pap. 2.95 (ISBN 0-425-06799-8). Berkley Pub.
--Postern of Fate. 288p. 1980. pap. 3.50 (ISBN 0-553-25493-6). Bantam.
--Postern of Fate. 1985. pap. 10.95 (ISBN 0-8161-3123-6, Large Print Bks). G K Hall.
--The Regatta Mystery. 1983. pap. 2.95 (ISBN 0-440-17336-1). Dell.
--The Regatta Mystery & Other Stories. 208p. 1984. pap. 2.95 (ISBN 0-425-06800-5). Berkley Pub.
--The Regetta Mystery & Other Stories. 208p. 1985. pap. 2.95 (ISBN 0-425-07998-8). Berkley Pub.
--Remembered Death. 1984. pap. 3.50 (ISBN 0-671-54320-2). PB.
--Sad Cypress. 224p. 1982. pap. 2.95 (ISBN 0-440-17552-6). Dell.
--Sad Cypress. LC 82-73251. (Greenwood Edition). 1982. 9.95 (ISBN 0-396-08112-6). Dodd.
--Sad Cypress. 240p. 1985. pap. 2.95 (ISBN 0-425-06801-3). Berkley Pub.
--The Secret Adversary. 224p. 1981. pap. 2.95 (ISBN 0-553-24035-8). Bantam.
--The Secret of Chimneys. 224p. 1981. pap. 2.95 (ISBN 0-440-17708-1). Dell.
--The Secret of Chimneys. 256p. 1984. pap. 2.95 (ISBN 0-425-06802-1). Berkley Pub.
--The Seven Dials Mystery. 224p. 1980. pap. 2.95 (ISBN 0-553-23905-8). Bantam.
--Sleeping Murder. 224p. 1981. pap. 2.95 (ISBN 0-553-23753-5). Bantam.
--Sleeping Murder. 15.95 (ISBN 0-88411-387-6, Pub. by Aeonian Pr). Amereon Ltd.
--So Many Steps to Death. 1982. pap. 2.75 (ISBN 0-671-46151-6). PB.
--Surprise Surprise. 1979. pap. 2.95 (ISBN 0-440-18389-8). Dell.
--Ten Little Indians. 176p. 1983. pap. 3.95 (ISBN 0-671-49949-1). PB.
--There Is a Tide. 240p. 1984. pap. 2.95 (ISBN 0-425-06803-X). Berkley Pub.
--They Came to Baghdad. 1977. pap. 2.95 (ISBN 0-440-18700-1). Dell.
--They Came to Baghdad. (Greenway Edition). 1969. 9.95 (ISBN 0-396-06066-8). Dodd.
--They Came to Baghdad. 240p. 1984. pap. 2.95 (ISBN 0-425-06804-8). Berkley Pub.
--Third Girl. 1984. pap. 3.50 (ISBN 0-671-54212-5). PB.
--Thirteen at Dinner. 240p. 1982. pap. 2.95 (ISBN 0-440-18742-7). Dell.
--Thirteen at Dinner. 240p. 1984. pap. 2.95 (ISBN 0-425-06805-6). Berkley Pub.
--Thirteen for Luck. 1980. pap. 2.95 (ISBN 0-440-18753-2). Dell.
--Three Blind Mice & Other Stories. 1980. pap. 2.95 (ISBN 0-440-15867-2). Dell.
--Three Blind Mice & Other Stories. 224p. 1985. pap. 2.95 (ISBN 0-425-06806-4). Berkley Pub.
--Three Blind Mice & Other Stories. 240p. 1985. 12.95 (ISBN 0-396-08707-8). Dodd.
--Towards Zero. 1982. pap. 2.95 (ISBN 0-671-47049-3). PB.
--The Tuesday Club Murders. 224p. 1984. pap. 2.95 (ISBN 0-425-06807-2). Berkley Pub.
--The Underdog & Other Stories. 192p. 1978. pap. 2.50 (ISBN 0-440-19228-5). Dell.
--The Underdog & Other Stories. 224p. 1985. pap. 2.95 (ISBN 0-425-06808-0). Berkley Pub.

Christie, Agatha, pseud. The Westmacott-Christie Reader: Six Novels by Agatha Christie Writing under the Name Mary Westmacott. 1983. 25.00 (ISBN 0-87795-494-1). Arbor Hse.

Christie, Agatha. What Mrs. McGillicuddy Saw. 1985. pap. 3.50 (ISBN 0-671-55645-2). PB.
--What Mrs. McGuillicuddy Saw. 1983. pap. 2.95 (ISBN 0-671-49454-6). PB.
--Why Didn't They Ask Evans. 224p. 1981. pap. 2.95 (ISBN 0-440-10704-0). Dell.
--Why Didn't They Ask Evans? (Greenway Edition). 1981. 9.95 (ISBN 0-396-05778-0). Dodd.
--Witness for the Prosecution. 1983. pap. 2.95 (ISBN 0-440-19619-1). Dell.
--The Witness for the Prosecution. 240p. 1984. pap. 2.95 (ISBN 0-425-06809-9). Berkley Pub.
--The Witness for the Prosecution. 297p. 1985. 12.95 (ISBN 0-396-08576-8). Dodd.

Christie, Agatha see Westmacott, Mary, pseud.

Christie, Agatha, et al. The Scoop & Behind the Screen. Berkeley, Anthony & Dane, Clemence, eds. LC 83-47845. (Cornelia & Michael Bessie Ser.). 175p. 1983. 13.41i (ISBN 0-06-039030-1, HarpT). Har-Row.
--The Scoop. Bd. with Behind the Screen. 208p. 1984. pap. 2.95 (ISBN 0-441-75505-4, Pub. by Charter Bks). Ace Bks.

Christie, Alice M., ed. see Perez, Bernard.

Christie, Andrew & Heuler, Karen. I Wasn't Kidding: How to Commit Suicide So They'll Never Forget. 96p. 1984. pap. 3.95 (ISBN 0-345-31510-3). Ballantine.

Christie, Anna & Daton, Liz. In the Pink: The Raving Beauties. (Illus.). 128p. 1985. pap. 4.95 (ISBN 0-7043-3920-X). Merrimack Pub Cir.

Christie, Anne. First Act. 256p. 1984. 13.95 (ISBN 0-312-29216-3). St Martin.

Christie, Anthony. Chinese Mythology. LC 85-5975. (The Library of the World's Myths & Legends). (Illus.). 144p. 1985. 17.95 (ISBN 0-87226-015-1). P Bedrick Bks.

Christie, Archibald H. Pattern Design: An Introduction to the Study of Formal Ornament. 2nd ed. 1969. pap. 5.95 (ISBN 0-486-22221-7). Dover.

Christie, B., jt. auth. see Ashton, M.

Christie, Bert, jt. auth. see Tomes, Dwight.

Christie, Bruce. Face to File Communication: A Psychological Approach to Information Systems. LC 80-41686. (Wiley Series in Information Processing). 306p. 1981. 45.95x (ISBN 0-471-27939-0, Pub. by Wiley Series in Information Processing). Assn Inform & Image Mgmt.
--Human Factors of Information Technology in the Office. LC 84-20903. (Information Processing Ser.). 1985. 26.95 (ISBN 0-471-90631-X). Wiley.

Christie, G. A., jt. ed. see Briggs, M. H.

Christie, George A., jt. auth. see Fisher, Richard B.

Christie, George C. Law, Norms & Authority. 227p. 1982. 29.50x (ISBN 0-7156-1593-9). Sheridan.
--The Law of Torts Cases & Materials. LC 83-3642. (American Casebook Ser.). 1213p. 1983. text ed. 25.95 (ISBN 0-314-69804-3). West Pub.
--Text & Readings on Jurisprudence: The Philosophy of Law. 1056p. 1973. write for info. West Pub.

Christie, George N. & Bracuti, Albert E. Credit Management. LC 81-66837. 700p. 1981. text ed. 45.00 (ISBN 0-939050-00-5). Credit Res Found.

Christie, Grace. Embroidery & Tapestry Weaving. LC 78-21371. (Illus.). 1979. pap. 9.95 (ISBN 0-8008-2401-6, Pentalic). Taplinger.
--Samplers & Stitches. (Illus.). 192p. 1985. pap. 11.95 (ISBN 0-7134-4796-6, Pub. by Batsford England). David & Charles.

Christie, Herbert, jt. auth. see Turvey, Ralph.

Christie, Howard E. Beyond the Distant Shore. 152p. 1985. 9.95 (ISBN 0-8059-2981-9). Dorrance.

Christie, Ian R. Crisis of Empire: Great Britain & the American Colonies 1754-1783. (Foundations of Modern History Ser). 1966. pap. 4.95x (ISBN 0-393-09650-5, NortonC). Norton.
--Stress & Stability in Late Eighteenth-Century Britain: Reflections on the British Avoidance of Revolution. 250p. 1984. 34.50x (ISBN 0-19-820064-1). Oxford U Pr.
--Wars & Revolutions: Britain, 1760-1815. (New History of England Ser.). (Illus.). 384p. 1982. text ed. 25.00x (ISBN 0-674-94760-6). Harvard U Pr.
--Wars & Revolutions: Britain, 1760-1815. (New History of England Ser.). 368p. 1985. pap. text ed. 8.95x (ISBN 0-674-94761-4). Harvard U Pr.

Christie, Ian R., jt. auth. see Brown, Lucy M.

Christie, Irene. Birds: A Guide to a Mixed Collection. Denham, Ken, ed. (Illus.). 144p. 1985. 13.95 (ISBN 0-948075-00-7). Howell Bk.

Christie, J. Edward. Steel Steeds Christie: A Memoir of J. Walter Christie. (Illus.). 86p. 1985. pap. text ed. 16.00x (ISBN 0-89745-059-0). Sunflower U Pr.

Christie, J. Elmer, jt. ed. see Budke, George H.

Christie, Jean. Morris Llewellyn Cooke: Progressive Engineer. Burke, Robert E. & Freidel, Frank, eds. (Modern American Histoy Ser.). 73.00 (ISBN 0-8240-5653-1). Garland Pub.

Christie, John A. Thoreau As World Traveler. LC 65-24586. (Illus.). 358p. 1966. 30.00x (ISBN 0-231-02833-4). Columbia U Pr.
--Thoreau As World Traveler. (Illus.). 358p. 1965. 7.50 (ISBN 0-318-12736-9). Am Geographical.

Christie, John D., ed. see Virgil.

Christie, Keith. Jumping Cholla: Genesis of a Bronze Sculpture. LC 78-51848. (Illus.). 80p. 1981. pap. 16.95 (ISBN 0-87358-292-6); ltd. ed. 1200.00 (ISBN 0-87358-290-X). Northland.

Christie, L. John, jt. auth. see Christie, Linda G.

Christie, Les. Dating & Waiting: A Chrisitan View of Love, Sex, & Dating. LC 83-1232. (Illus.). 80p. (Orig.). 1983. pap. 2.95 (ISBN 0-87239-643-6, 39972). Standard Pub.
--Getting a Grip on Time Management. 64p. 1984. pap. 4.95 (ISBN 0-88207-192-0). Victor Bks.

Christie, Linda G. Human Resources: A Hidden Profit Center. 168p. 1983. 14.95 (ISBN 0-13-445874-5); pap. 7.95 (ISBN 0-13-445866-4). P-H.
--Managing Today & Tomorrow With On-Line Information. 275p. 1985. 25.00 (ISBN 0-87094-666-8). Dow Jones-Irwin.
--The Simon & Schuster Guide to Peripherals. 288p. 1985. pap. 12.95 (ISBN 0-671-50628-5, Pub. by Computer Bks). S&S.

Christie, Linda G. & Bullard, Gary. Understanding & Using dBASE III: A Guide for Business & Professional Users. 224p. 1985. pap. 14.95 (ISBN 0-13-937087-0). P-H.

Christie, Linda G. & Bullard, Gary J. Almost Free Computer Stuff for Kids. 1984. 9.95 (ISBN 0-452-25561-9, PLume). NAL.

Christie, Linda G. & Christie, L. John. The Encyclopedia of Microcomputer Terminology: A Sourcebook for Business & Professional People. LC 84-2055. 320p. 1984. 19.95 (ISBN 0-13-276098-3); pap. 9.95 (ISBN 0-13-276080-0). P-H.

Christie, Linda G. & Curry, Jesse W., Jr. The ABC's of Microcomputers: A Computer Literacy Primer. (Illus.). 218p. 1983. 15.95 (ISBN 0-13-000620-3, Spec); pap. 7.95 (ISBN 0-13-000612-2). P-H.

Christie, M. F. Aborigines in Colonial Victoria, Eighteen Thirty-Five to Eighteen-Sixty. (Illus.). 1980. 33.00x (ISBN 0-424-00066-0, Pub. by Sydney U Pr). Intl Spec Bk.

Christie, Maralyn, jt. auth. see Brown, Barrie J.

Christie, Margaret J. & Mellett, Peter. Foundations of Psychosomatics. LC 80-42011. 428p. 1981. 44.95x (ISBN 0-471-27855-6, Pub. by Wiley-Interscience). Wiley.

Christie, Margaret J., jt. auth. see Venables, Peter H.

Christie, Mary. Be a Sport: Level 1. McConcohie, Jean, ed. 64p. 1984. pap. text ed. 2.25 (ISBN 0-88345-494-7, 20747). Regents Pub.
Christie, Nils. Limits to Pain. 96p. 1981. pap. 10.00x (ISBN 82-00-05528-0). Universitet.
Christie, O. F. Johnson, the Essayist: His Opinions of Men, Morals & Manners. LC 68-688. (Studies in Scandinavian Life & Literature, No. 18). 1969. Repr. of 1924 ed. lib. bdg. 39.95x (ISBN 0-8383-0527-X). Haskell.
Christie, Octavius F. Dickens & His Age. LC 74-11342. 240p. 1974. Repr. of 1939 ed. 12.00x (ISBN 0-87753-058-0). Phaeton.
Christie, Renfrew. Electricity, Industry & Class in South Africa. 161p. 1984. 34.50x (ISBN 0-87395-854-3); pap. 12.95x (ISBN 0-87395-855-1). State U NY Pr.
Christie, Richard & Jahoda, Marie, eds. Studies in the Scope & Method of "The Authoritarian Personality". LC 81-584. (Continuities in Social Research Ser.). 279p. 1981. Repr. of 1954 ed. lib. bdg. 25.00x (ISBN 0-313-22444-7, CHSS). Greenwood.
Christie, Richard, et al. Studies in Machiavellianism. (Social Psychology Ser). 1970. 60.00 (ISBN 0-12-174450-7). Acad Pr.
Christie, Richard C. Etienne Dolet the Martyr of the Renaissance, 1508-1546: A Biography. 21.75 (ISBN 0-8369-6999-5, 7876). Ayer Co Pubs.
Christie, Richard C., ed. see Copley, Thomas.
Christie, Stuart. The Christie File. LC 80-83542. (Illus.). 384p. (Orig.). 1980. pap. 9.95 (ISBN 0-935150-01-3). Partisan Pr.
--Christie File. (Illus.). 370p. (Orig.). 1980. pap. 2.50 (ISBN 0-904564-37-1). Left Bank.
Christie, Tom & Holmes, Deb. Thumbs Up. (gr. 5-12). 1978. 11.95 (ISBN 0-916456-34-X, GA88). Good Apple.
Christie, W. J. A Study of Freshwater Fishery Regulation Based on North American Experience. (Fisheries Technical Papers: No. 180). 53p. 1978. pap. 7.50 (ISBN 92-5-100579-6, F1464, FAO). Unipub.
Christie, W. W. Lipid Analysis. 2nd ed. 1973. text ed. 55.00 (ISBN 0-08-023791-6). Pergamon.
--Lipid Analysis: Isolation, Separation, Identification & Structural Analysis of Lipids. 2nd ed. LC 82-491. (Illus.). 220p. 1982. 55.00 (ISBN 0-08-023791-6); 19.75 (ISBN 0-08-023792-4). Pergamon.
Christie, W. W., ed. Lipid Metabolism in Ruminant Animals. (Illus.). 464p. 1981. 77.00 (ISBN 0-08-023789-4). Pergamon.
Christie, William D., ed. Letters Addressed from London to Sir Joseph Williamson While Plenipotentiary at the Congress of Cologne in the Years 1673 & 1674, 2 Vols. Repr. of 1874 ed. 54.00 (ISBN 0-384-08959-3). Johnson Repr.
Christie, William M., Jr. Preface to a Neo-Firthian Linguistics. LC 80-21016. (Edward Sapir Monograph Series in Language, Culture, & Cognition: No. 7). viii, 70p. (Orig.). 1980. pap. 6.00x (ISBN 0-933104-11-1). Jupiter Pr.
--A Stratificational View of Linguistic Change. LC 79-115787. (Edward Sapir Monograph Ser. in Language, Culture & Cognition: No. 4). viii, 71p. (Orig.). 1977. pap. 5.00x (ISBN 0-933104-04-9). Jupiter Pr.
Christienn, jt. auth. see Kennett.
Christienne, Charles & Lissarrague, Pierre. A History of French Military Aviation. Kianka, Frances, tr. from Fr. LC 85-600032. (Illus.). 400p. 1985. 39.95 (ISBN 0-87474-310-9, CHHF). Smithsonian.
Christiernin, P. N. The Swedish Bullionist Controversy: P. N. Christiernin's Lectures on the High Price of Foreign Exchange in Sweden. Eagly, Robert V., ed. LC 74-161990. (American Philosophical Society Memoirs Ser.: Vol. 87). pap. 32.30 (ISBN 0-317-27884-3, 2025137). Bks Demand UMI.
Christie-Seely, Janet. Working with the Family in Primary Care: A Systems Approach to Health & Illness. 576p. 1983. 27.95 (ISBN 0-03-063899-2). Praeger.
Christin, Pierre & Mezieres, Jean-Claude. Ambassador of the Shadows. (Valerian Ser.). (Illus.). 48p. pap. 4.95 (ISBN 2-205-06949-7). Dargaud Pub.
--Heroes of the Equinox. (Valerian Ser.). (Illus.). 48p. pap. 4.95 (ISBN 2-205-06575-0). Dargaud Pub.
--Welcome on Alfloflo. (Valerian Ser.). (Illus.). 48p. pap. 4.95 (ISBN 2-205-06951-9). Dargaud Pub.
--World Without Stars. (Valerian Ser.). (Illus.). 48p. pap. 4.95 (ISBN 2-205-06573-4). Dargaud Pub.
Christina, Frank & Christina, Teresa. Billy Jack. 1973. pap. 1.25 (ISBN 0-380-01062-3, 26351). Avon.
Christina, Teresa, jt. auth. see Christina, Frank.
Christine, Lois. The Secret Life of Numbers. 208p. (Orig.). 1984. pap. 8.00 postponed (ISBN 0-936878-06-1). Lorian Pr.
Christison, M. A. & Bassano, S., eds. Look Who's Talking: A Guide to the Development of Successful Conversational Groups. (Language Teaching Methodology Ser.). (Illus.). 128p. 1982. pap. 6.95 (ISBN 0-08-029445-6). Pergamon.
Christison, Mary A., jt. auth. see Bassano, Sharron.
Christison, Mary Ann. English Through Poetry. 130p. (gr. 3-6). 1982. pap. text ed. 7.95x (ISBN 0-88084-002-1). Alemany Pr.
Christison, Mary Ann & Bassano, Sharron. Look Who's Talking: Language Acquisition Activities. (Illus.). 1981. pap. text ed. 7.95x (ISBN 0-88084-004-8). Alemany Pr.
Christison, Robert. Treatise on Poisons in Relation to Medical Jurisprudence, Physiology & the Practice of Physic. LC 79-156011. Repr. of 1845 ed. 45.00 (ISBN 0-404-09111-3). AMS Pr.
Christ-Janer, Albert. Eliel Saarinen: Finnish-American Architect & Educator. 2nd rev. ed. LC 79-832. 1980. Repr. of 1948 ed. lib. bdg. 32.50x (ISBN 0-226-10464-8). U of Chicago Pr.
--Eliel Saarinen: Finnish-American Architect & Educator. rev. ed. LC 79-832. (Illus.). 190p. 1985. pap. 17.95 (ISBN 0-226-10465-6). U of Chicago Pr.
Christ-Janer, Albert, et al, eds. American Hymns Old & New: Notes on the Hymns & Biographies of the Authors & Composers, 2 vols. LC 79-4630. (Illus.). 1454p. 1980. 60.00 (ISBN 0-231-05148-4). Columbia U Pr.
Christlieb, A. Richard see Marble, Alexander, et al.
Christman, Catherine, jt. auth. see Christman, Ernest H.
Christman, Donald A., jt. auth. see Holtje, Bert F.
Christman, Elizabeth. Flesh & Spirit. 1980. pap. 2.25 (ISBN 0-380-52142-3, 52142). Avon.
Christman, Ernest H. Prescription for Reading: Teach Them Phonics. LC 83-70696. (Illus.). 290p. (Orig.). 1983. 22.95 (ISBN 0-912329-01-7); pap. 15.95 (ISBN 0-912329-00-9). Tutorial Press.
Christman, Ernest H. & Christman, Catherine. Darby's Stable: Cartoons & Stories Level Two, Progressive Phonics. LC 84-50859. (Illus.). 88p. (Orig.). (gr. k-12). 1984. pap. 7.50 (ISBN 0-912329-04-1). Tutorial Press.
Christman, Ernst H. Primer on Refraction. (Illus.). 128p. 1972. photocopy ed. 16.75x (ISBN 0-398-02258-5). C C Thomas.
Christman, Florence. The Romance of Balboa Park. 4th ed. (Illus.). 136p. 1985. pap. 9.50 (ISBN 0-918740-03-7). San Diego Hist.
Christman, Henry. Tin Horns & Calico, a Decisive Period in the Emergence of Democracy. 1978. pap. 4.95 (ISBN 0-685-61130-2). Hope Farm.
Christman, Henry M. Mahout. LC 81-53008. (Illus.). 114p. (Orig.). 1982. pap. 5.95 (ISBN 0-8356-0555-8, Quest). Theos Pub Hse.
Christman, Henry M., ed. Indira Gandhi Speaks on Democracy, Socialism & Third World Non-Alignment. LC 72-6611. 160p. 1975. 8.95 (ISBN 0-8008-4180-8). Taplinger.
Christman, Henry M., ed. & intro. by. Kingfish to America: "Share Our Wealth". Selected Senatorial Papers of Huey P. Long. 176p. 1985. 14.95 (ISBN 0-8052-3998-7). Schocken.
Christman, Henry M., ed. Walt Whitman's New York. LC 74-39704. (Select Bibliographies Reprint Ser). 1972. Repr. of 1963 ed. 15.00 (ISBN 0-8369-9933-9). Ayer Co Pubs.
Christman, Henry M., ed. see Altgeld, John P.
Christman, Henry M., ed. see Nation Magazine.
Christman, Henry M., ed. see Warren, Earl.
Christman, J. R. Physics Problems for Programmable Calculators. Incl. Wave Mechanics, Optics & Modern Physics. 609p. 1982 (ISBN 0-471-86062-X); Mechanics & Electromagnetism. 299p. 1981 (ISBN 0-471-08212-0). pap. 15.95 (ISBN 0-317-31547-1). Wiley.
Christman, Luther & Counte, Michael A. Hospital Organization & Health Care Delivery. (Behavioral Science for Health Care Professionals Ser.). 128p. 1981. lib. bdg. 17.00x (ISBN 0-86531-006-8); pap. 8.50x (ISBN 0-86531-007-6). Westview.
Christman, Luther, jt. auth. see Counte, Michael A.
Christman, Margaret C. S. Fifty American Faces from the Collection of the National Portrait Gallery. LC 78-3526. (Illus.). 1978. 35.00 (ISBN 0-87474-312-5). Smithsonian.
Christman, R., et al. The Natural Environment: Wastes & Control. LC 74-18363. pap. 64.00 (ISBN 0-317-10968-5, 2007755). Bks Demand UMI.
Christman, Raymond J. Sensory Experience. 2nd ed. LC 78-15276. 1979. text ed. 23.50 scp (ISBN 0-06-041284-4, HarpC). Har-Row.
Christman, Ronald & Schibilla, Linda. Lessons on Doctrine: For Youth (Teacher) 48p. (Orig.). 1982. pap. 1.95 (ISBN 0-87239-604-5, 3376). Standard Pub.
--Lessons on Doctrine: For Youth (Workbook) (Illus.). 64p. (Orig.). (gr. 6 up). 1982. pap. 3.50 (ISBN 0-87239-603-7, 3377). Standard Pub.
Christman, Russell F. & Gjessing, Egil, eds. Aquatic & Terrestrial Humic Materials. LC 82-71526. (Illus.). 538p. 1982. 49.95 (ISBN 0-250-40550-4). Butterworth.
Christman, Rutch C., ed. see American Association For The Advancement Of Science.
Christman-Rothlein, Liz, jt. auth. see Caballero, Jane.
Christman-Rothlein, Liz, jt. auth. see Forgan, Henry.
Christmas, F. E. The Parson in English Literature: A Galaxy of Clerical Figures Gathered from the Writers of Six Centuries. Repr. of 1950 ed. 20.00 (ISBN 0-686-19851-4). Ridgeway Bks.
Christmas, Joyce. Dark Tide. 256p. 1983. pap. 2.95 (ISBN 0-380-83667-X, 83667). Avon.
Christmas, Liz, jt. auth. see Dalby, Gill.
Christmas, Liz, jt. auth. see Vellacott, Audrey.
Christmas, Rachel J. & Christmas, Walter. Fielding's Bermuda & the Bahamas. (Illus.). 224p. (Orig.). 1984. pap. 7.70 (ISBN 0-688-02433-5, Pub. by Fielding). Morrow.
--Fielding's Bermuda & the Bahamas, 1985. (Illus.). 256p. 1984. 7.95 (ISBN 0-688-03965-0). Fielding Travel Bks.
--Fielding's Bermuda & the Bahamas, 1986. rev. ed. (Illus.). 256p. (Orig.). 1985. pap. 7.95 (ISBN 0-688-04463-8). Fielding Travel Bks.
Christmas Seal League of South Western Pennsylvania. Self Help: Your Strategy for Living with COPD. 1984. 3.95 (ISBN 0-915950-64-2). Bull Pub.
Christmas, Walter, jt. auth. see Christmas, Rachel J.
Christner, Barbara, jt. auth. see Hershberger, Mary.
Christner, D. W. Epitaph for Emily. (Mystery Puzzler Ser.: No. 13). (Illus., Orig.). 1979. pap. 1.95 (ISBN 0-89083-433-4). Zebra.
Christo, Carlos A. Libanio Against Principalities & Powers: Letters from a Brazilian Jail. Drury, John, tr. from Italian. LC 76-43030. Orig. Title: Dai Sotteranei Della Storia. 1977. 8.95 (ISBN 0-88344-007-5); pap. 4.95 (ISBN 0-88344-008-3). Orbis Bks.
Christodoulou, G. N. The Delusional Misidentification Syndromes. (Bibliotheca Psychiatrica: No. 164). (Illus.). viii, 150p. 1986. 41.75 (ISBN 3-8055-4213-5). S Karger.
Christodoulou, G. N., ed. Aspects of Preventive Psychiatry. (Bibliotheca Psychiatrica: No. 160). (Illus.). viii, 116p. 1981. soft cover 27.75 (ISBN 3-8055-1218-X). S Karger.
Christofalo, Vincent J., jt. ed. see Rothblat, George H.
Christofano. Wild about Pasta & Pizza. (Wild about Ser.). 1985. pap. 5.95 (ISBN 0-8120-2912-7). Barron.
Christofer, Barbara, illus. Embroidered Samplers Full-Color Iron-on Transfer Patterns. (Transfer Patterns for Embroidery & Other Crafts Ser.). 36p. 1984. pap. 2.25 (ISBN 0-486-24664-7). Dover.
Christofer, Michael. The Lady & the Clarinet. 102p. 1985. pap. 3.35x (ISBN 0-317-18646-9). Dramatists Play.
Christoff, Nicholas B. Saturday Night, Sunday Morning: Singles & the Church. LC 77-7841. 160p. 1980. pap. 4.95 (ISBN 0-06-061381-5, RD 341, HarpR). Har-Row.
Christoff, Peter K. An Introduction to Nineteenth Century Russian Slavophilism: A Study in Ideas, Vol. 2. (Slavistic Printings & Reprintings Ser). 1972. text ed. 44.00x (ISBN 90-2792-297-7). Mouton.
--K. S. Askakov, a Study in Ideas: An Introduction to Nineteenth Century Russian Slavophilism. LC 81-47117. (Vol. III). (Illus.). 480p. 1982. 42.00 (ISBN 0-691-05334-0). Princeton U Pr.
Christoffel, Doris & Perry, Annabelle. Acrylics: A First Step. (Illus.). 68p. (Orig.). pap. 6.95 (ISBN 0-917119-14-2, 45-1032). Priscillas Pubns.
Christoffel, R. Zwingli or the Rise of the Reformation in Switzerland. 1977. lib. bdg. 59.95 (ISBN 0-8490-2859-0). Gordon Pr.
Christoffel, R. J., et al, eds. see Bolton Conference, 5th.
Christoffel, Tom. Health & the Law: A Handbook for Health Professionals. 464p. 1982. text ed. 29.95 (ISBN 0-02-905370-6). Free Pr.
Christoffel von Grimmelshausen, Hans J. The Singular Life Story of Heedless Hopalong. Hiller, Robert L. & Osborne, John C., trs. LC 81-10446. 160p. 1981. 12.95 (ISBN 0-8143-1688-3). Wayne St U Pr.
Christoffers, Adele. A Word Directory: Spelling-Division. 1957. 5.50 (ISBN 0-682-40023-8). Exposition Pr FL.
Christoffers, Henry, tr. see Boltyanskii, Vladimir G. & Gokhberg, Izrail T.
Christoffersen, Per, jt. auth. see Poulsen, Hemming.
Christoffersen, Ralph E., ed. Algorithms for Chemical Computations. LC 77-5030. (ACS Symposium Ser.: No. 46). 1977. 24.95 (ISBN 0-8412-0371-7). Am Chemical.
Christoffersen, Ralph E. & Olson, Edward C., eds. Computer-Assisted Drug Design. LC 79-21038. (ACS Symposium Ser.: No. 112). 1979. 59.95 (ISBN 0-8412-0521-3). Am Chemical.
Christofides, Nicos, et al, eds. Combinatorial Optimization. LC 78-11131. 425p. 1979. 84.95 (ISBN 0-471-99749-8, Pub. by Wiley-Interscience). Wiley.
Christofordidis, A. John. Atlas of Cross-Sectional Anatomy. Date not set. price not set (ISBN 0-7216-1278-4). Saunders.
Christol, Carl Q. The Modern International Law of Outer Space. (Pergamon Policy Studies on International Politics). (Illus.). 945p. 1982. 94.00 (ISBN 0-08-029367-0, K130). Pergamon.
Christopeit, N., jt. ed. see Kohlmann, M.
Christoph, Florence, jt. auth. see Christoph, Peter.
Christoph, Florence, jt. ed. see Christoph, Peter.
Christoph, H. J. Diseases of Dogs. 2nd ed. LC 71-163386. 279p. 1980. text ed. 28.00 (ISBN 0-08-025940-5). Pergamon.
Christoph, James B. Capital Punishment & British Politics. LC 62-12639. Repr. of 1962 ed. 38.00 (ISBN 0-8357-9644-2, 2015752). Bks Demand UMI.
Christoph, Peter & Christoph, Florence. New York Historical Manuscripts: English: Books of General Entries of the Colony of New York, 1674-1688. LC 79-92327. 473p. 1982. 30.00 (ISBN 0-8063-0991-1). Genealog Pub.
Christoph, Peter & Christoph, Florence, eds. New York Historical Manuscripts: English Books of General Entries of the Colony of New York, 1664-1673. LC 79-92327. 602p. 1982. 35.00 (ISBN 0-8063-0990-3). Genealog Pub.
--New York Historical Manuscripts: English: Records of the Court of Assizes for the Colony of New York, 1665-1682. LC 79-92327. 322p. 1983. 25.00 (ISBN 0-8063-1048-0). Genealog Pub.
Christoph, Peter R., ed. New York Historical Manuscripts: English: Administrative Papers of Governors Richard Nicolls & Francis Lovelace, 1664-1673, Vol. 22. LC 79-92327. 261p. 1980. 18.50 (ISBN 0-8063-0880-X). Genealog Pub.
Christoph, R. Peter. New York Historical Manuscripts: Dutch, Kingston Papers, 2 vols. Scott, Kenneth & Stryker-Rodda, Kenn, eds. Versteeg, Dingman, tr. LC 75-5971. (Illus.). 849p. 1976. Set. 40.00 (ISBN 0-8063-0720-X). Genealog Pub.
Christoph, S. G. Collision Theory & Statistical Theory of Chemical Reactions. (Lectures Notes in Chemistry: Vol. 18). (Illus.). 322p. 1980. pap. 32.00 (ISBN 0-387-10012-1). Springer-Verlag.
Christoph, Siegfried R. Wolfram Vom Eschenbach's Couples. (Amsterdamer Publikationen Zur Sprache und Literatur: Vol. 44). 250p. 1981. pap. text ed. 29.00x (ISBN 90-6203-573-6, Pub. by Rodopi Holland). Humanities.
Christophe, Henri. Henri Christophe & Thomas Clarkson, a Correspondence. Griggs, Earl L. & Praton, Clifford H., eds. LC 68-23281. (Illus.). 1968. Repr. of 1952 ed. lib. bdg. 16.25x (ISBN 0-8371-0091-7, CHCC). Greenwood.
Christophe, Jules, jt. auth. see Cerfberr, Anatole.
Christophensen, Scavenius & Kirkeby, Willie, eds. Norwegian-English Dictionary, Vol. II. 4th ed. 1983. 22.00x (ISBN 8-2573-0006-3, N482). Vanous.
Christopher. An Attitude of Giving: Notes & Other Things. 1974. pap. 1.00 (ISBN 0-686-09900-1). FAS Pubs.
--An Attitude of Giving: Notes & Other Things. 2nd ed. (Illus.). 1978. pap. 1.00 (ISBN 0-916940-02-0). World Light.
--A Good Feeling. 1978. pap. 1.00 (ISBN 0-916940-03-9). World Light.
--Our New Age: Words for the People. 1st ed. LC 77-72309. (Illus., Orig.). 1977. pap. 2.95 (ISBN 0-916940-01-2). World Light.
--Scott. new ed. (Orig.). 1978. pap. 3.95 (ISBN 0-87243-078-2). Templegate.
Christopher, A. J. Colonial Africa. 240p. 1984. 28.50x (ISBN 0-389-20452-8, 08013). B&N Imports.
--South Africa. LC 81-8254. (The World's Landscapes Ser.). (Illus.). 256p. (Orig.). 1982. pap. text ed. 15.95x (ISBN 0-582-49001-4). Longman.
--Southern Africa. (Studies in Historical Geography Ser.). (Illus.). 294p. 1976. 22.50 (ISBN 0-208-01620-1, Archon). Shoe String.
Christopher, Barbara. Audubon's Birds Iron-on Transfer Patterns. (Illus.). 1979. pap. 2.95 (ISBN 0-486-23767-2). Dover.
--Fruit & Vegetable Iron-On Transfer Patterns. (Dover Needlework Ser.). (Illus.). 1977. pap. 2.25 (ISBN 0-486-23556-4). Dover.
Christopher, Beth. Love for the Taking. (Finding Mr. Right Ser.). 208p. 1983. pap. 2.75 (ISBN 0-380-83311-5, 83311-5). Avon.
Christopher, Bob & Christopher, Ellen. America's Favorite Restaurants & Inns. 7th, rev. ed. LC 79-2034. 1019p. (Orig.). 1980. pap. 8.95 (ISBN 0-688-08550-4). Morrow.
--Christopher's America on Fifteen to Twenty-Five Dollars a Night: Northwest States. 80p. (Orig.). 1983. pap. 4.95 (ISBN 0-930570-06-5). Travel Discover.
--Christopher's America on Fifteen to Twenty-Five Dollars a Night Dining & Lodging Guide: Southwest States. 80p. (Orig.). 1983. pap. 4.95 (ISBN 0-930570-05-7). Travel Discover.
--Christopher's America on Fifteen to Twenty-Five Dollars a Night: Mid-West States. 80p. (Orig.). 1983. pap. 4.95 (ISBN 0-930570-04-9). Travel Discover.
--Christopher's America on Fifteen to Twenty-Five Dollars a Night Dining & Lodging Guide: Southern States. 80p. (Orig.). 1983. pap. 4.95 (ISBN 0-930570-03-0). Travel Discover.
--Christopher's America on Fifteen to Twenty-Five Dollars a Night Dining & Lodging Guide: Northeast States. 80p. (Orig.). 1983. pap. 4.95 (ISBN 0-930570-02-2). Travel Discover.
--Christopher's Bed & Breakfast Guide to U. S. & Canada. 80p. (Orig.). 1983. pap. 4.95 (ISBN 0-930570-07-3). Travel Discover.
Christopher, Catherine. Complete Book of Doll Making & Collecting. 2nd rev. ed. LC 76-102176. 1970. pap. 4.95 (ISBN 0-486-22066-4). Dover.
--The Complete Book of Doll Making & Collecting. 2nd & rev. ed. (Illus.). 14.75 (ISBN 0-8446-0058-X). Peter Smith.
Christopher, David. The Samaritan Scheme. (Orig.). 1978. pap. 2.25 (ISBN 0-89083-413-X). Zebra.

Christopher, David L. Winning at the Track. LC 83-81134. (Illus.). 144p. (Orig.). 1983. pap. 9.95 (ISBN 0-89709-044-6). Liberty Pub.
Christopher, Dean A. Manual Communication. LC 75-38884. (Illus.). 544p. 1976. pap. 20.00 (ISBN 0-936104-63-5). Pro Ed.
Christopher, E. P., rev. by see Bailey, Liberty H.
Christopher, Edward E. Behavioral Theory for Managers. 1977. pap. text ed. 12.25 (ISBN 0-8191-0352-7). U Pr of Amer.
Christopher, Edward E., jt. auth. see Christopher, Rachelle G.
Christopher, Ellen, jt. auth. see Christopher, Bob.
Christopher, Ellen, jt. auth. see Christopher, Robert.
Christopher, Frederick J. Basketry. (Illus.). 1952. pap. 2.50 (ISBN 0-486-20677-7). Dover.
Christopher, George, Jr. Jesus of Nazareth: The Man, the Myth, the Enigma. 50p. 1984. 4.95 (ISBN 0-89697-176-7). Intl Univ Pr.
Christopher, Georgia B. Milton & the Science of the Saints. LC 81-47911. 240p. 1982. 25.00 (ISBN 0-691-06508-X). Princeton U Pr.
Christopher, J. The School of Natural Healing. 630p. 40.00 (ISBN 0-318-15686-5). Natl Health Fed.
Christopher, J. R. & Ostling, Joan K. C. S. Lewis: An Annotated Checklist. LC 73-76556. (Serif Ser.: No. 30). 402p. 1974. 20.00x (ISBN 0-87338-138-6). Kent St U Pr.
Christopher, James W. Conflict in the Far East: American Diplomacy in China from 1928-1933. LC 77-111736. (American Imperialism: Viewpoints of United States Foreign Policy, 1898-1941). 1970. Repr. of 1950 ed. 20.00 (ISBN 0-405-02007-4). Ayer Co Pubs.
Christopher, John. Beyond the Burning Lands. LC 78-152288. 180p. (gr. 5-9). 1974. 9.95x (ISBN 0-02-718420-X, 04238, Collier); pap. 2.75 (ISBN 0-02-042380-2). Macmillan.
--Career Mathematics. (Illus.). 352p. 1986. pap. text ed. 23.95 (ISBN 0-13-114943-1). P-H.
--City of Gold & Lead. LC 67-21245. 224p. (gr. 5-9). 1967. 10.95 (ISBN 0-02-718380-7); pap. 3.95 (ISBN 0-02-042700-X). Macmillan.
--The Death of Grass. (Alpha Books). (Orig.). 1979. pap. text ed. 2.95x (ISBN 0-19-424232-3). Oxford U Pr.
--Empty World. (gr. 7-9). 1978. 10.95 (ISBN 0-525-29250-0). Dutton.
--Fireball. LC 80-22094. (gr. 5-7). 1981. 11.95 (ISBN 0-525-29738-3, 01160-350). Dutton.
--Fireball. 160p. 1984. pap. 2.25 (ISBN 0-441-23845-9). Ace Bks.
--Guardians. LC 78-99118. 192p. (gr. 5-9). 1972. pap. 1.95 (ISBN 0-02-042680-1, Collier). Macmillan.
--Introductory Technical Mathematics. (Illus.). 448p. 1982. 26.95 (ISBN 0-13-501635-5). P-H.
--Lotus Caves. LC 74-78074. 160p. (gr. 5-9). 1971. pap. 3.95 (ISBN 0-02-042690-9, Collier). Macmillan.
--New Found Land. LC 82-18354. 160p. (gr. 5-9). 1983. 9.95 (ISBN 0-525-44049-6, 0966-290). Dutton.
--Pool of Fire. LC 68-23062. 178p. (gr. 5-7). 1968. 10.95 (ISBN 0-02-718350-5). Macmillan.
--Pool of Fire. (gr. 5 up). 1970. pap. 2.95 (ISBN 0-02-042720-4, Collier). Macmillan.
--Prince in Waiting. LC 70-119838. 192p. (gr. 5-9). 1974. pap. 2.75 (ISBN 0-02-042400-0, 04240, Collier). Macmillan.
--The Prince in Waiting. 1984. 13.50 (ISBN 0-8446-6157-0). Peter Smith.
--The Sword of the Spirit. 1984. 13.50 (ISBN 0-8446-6158-9). Peter Smith.
--The Sword of the Spirits. LC 74-20762. (gr. 5-9). 1976. pap. 2.75 (ISBN 0-02-042640-2, 04264, Collier). Macmillan.
--The Sword of the Spirits Trilogy, 3 bks. Incl. Beyond the Burning Lands; The Prince in Waiting; The Sword of the Spirits. (gr. 6 up). 1980. Boxed Set. pap. 7.95. Macmillan.
--The Tripods Trilogy, 3 bks. Incl. The White Mountains; the City of Gold & Lead; The Pool of Fire. (gr. 6 up). 1980. Boxed Set. pap. write for info. (Collier). Macmillan.
--White Mountains. (gr. 5 up). 1970. pap. 3.95 (ISBN 0-02-042710-7, Collier). Macmillan.
--The White Moutains. LC 67-10362. 192p. (gr. 5-9). 1967. 11.95 (ISBN 0-02-718360-2); pap. 3.95x (ISBN 0-02-042710-7). Macmillan.
--Wild Jack. LC 74-6428. 160p. (gr. 5-9). 1974. 9.95 (ISBN 0-02-718300-9, 71830). Macmillan.
--The World in Winter. (Alpha Bks.). (Orig.). 1979. pap. text ed. 2.95x (ISBN 0-19-424238-2). Oxford U Pr.
Christopher, John B. The Islamic Tradition. (Major Traditions in World Civilization Ser.). 1972. pap. text ed. 10.95 scp (ISBN 0-06-041283-6, HarpC). Har-Row.
Christopher, John B., et al. Civilization in the West, Pt. 2. 4th ed. (Illus.). 512p. 1981. pap. text ed. 20.95 (ISBN 0-13-134932-5). P-H.
Christopher, John B., jt. auth. see Brinton, Crane.
Christopher, John R. The Cold Sheet: Treatment & Aids for the Common Cold. 1.25 (ISBN 0-89557-033-5). Bi World Indus.
Christopher, Joseph P., tr. see Augustine, St.
Christopher, Kenneth. Damien & the Island of Sickness: A Story About Damien. new ed. (Stories About Christian Heroes Ser.). (Illus.). (gr. 1-3). 1979. pap. 1.95 (ISBN 0-86683-768-X). Winston Pr.
--The Merry Missionary: A Story About Philip Neri. (Stories About Christian Heroes Ser.). (Illus.). 32p. (gr. 6-9). pap. 1.95 (ISBN 0-03-056876-5). Winston Pr.
--Ten Catholics: Lives to Remember. (Nazareth Bks). 120p. 1983. pap. 3.95 (ISBN 0-86683-715-9). Winston Pr.
Christopher, Mark S., jt. auth. see Newman, Steven L.
Christopher, Martin. Logistics & the National Economy. 1981. 95.00x (ISBN 0-86176-073-5, Pub. by MCB Pubns). State Mutual Bk.
--Production of Professional Information Services. 1978. 29.95x (ISBN 0-905440-35-8, Pub. by MCB Pubns). State Mutual Bk.
--The Strategy of Distribution Management. LC 84-18214. (Illus.). x, 192p. 1985. lib. bdg. 35.00 (ISBN 0-89930-114-2, CSD/, Quorum). Greenwood.
--Total Distribution: A Framework for Analysis, Costing & Control. 188p. 1971. 17.95x (ISBN 0-8464-1145-8). Beekman Pubs.
Christopher, Martin & Gattorna, John. Controlling the Distribution Function. 1977. 90.00x (ISBN 0-903763-77-X, Pub. by MCB Pubns). State Mutual Bk.
Christopher, Martin & Ray, David. Costing in Distribution: Problems & Procedures. 1977. 59.00x (ISBN 0-903763-76-1, Pub. by MCB Pubns). State Mutual Bk.
Christopher, Martin & Schary, Philip. Customer Service. 1980. 90.00 (ISBN 0-86176-000-X, Pub. by MCB Pubns). State Mutual Bk.
Christopher, Martin, jt. auth. see Midgley, David.
Christopher, Martin, jt. auth. see Schary, Philip.
Christopher, Martin, jt. ed. see Wentworth, Felix.
Christopher, Martin, et al. Effective Marketing Management. 200p. 1980. text ed. 37.25x (ISBN 0-566-02237-0). Gower Pub Co.
--Customer Service & Distribution Strategy. LC 79-24121. 191p. 1980. 41.95x (ISBN 0-470-26890-5). Halsted Pr.
--Effective Distribution Management. 1978. 90.00x (ISBN 0-903763-78-8, Pub. by MCB Pubns). State Mutual Bk.
--Introduction to Marketing. 1978. 95.00x (ISBN 0-905440-80-3, Pub. by MCB Pubns). State Mutual Bk.
Christopher, Matt. Baseball Pals. (Illus.). (gr. 4-6). 1956. 7.95 (ISBN 0-316-13950-5). Little.
--Catch That Pass! LC 77-77442. (Illus.). (gr. 4-6). 1969. 8.95 (ISBN 0-316-13932-7). Little.
--Catcher with a Glass Arm. (Illus.). (gr. 4-6). 1964. 8.95 (ISBN 0-316-13931-9); pap. 3.70i (ISBN 0-316-13985-8). Little.
--Dirt Bike Racer. LC 79-745. (gr. 4-6). 1979. 11.45i (ISBN 0-316-13977-7). Little.
--Dirt Bike Runaway. LC 83-13538. (Illus.). 160p. (gr. 4-6). 1983. 11.45i (ISBN 0-316-13956-4). Little.
--The Dog That Called the Signals. LC 82-15234. (Illus.). 48p. (gr. 3-5). 1982. PLB 8.95 (ISBN 0-316-13980-7). Little.
--The Dog That Stole Football Plays. (Illus.). 48p. (gr. 3-5). 1980. 7.95 (ISBN 0-316-13978-5). Little.
--Drag Strip Racer. 180p. (gr. 4-6). 1982. 8.95g (ISBN 0-316-13904-1). Little.
--Earthquake. 128p. (gr. 4-6). 1975. 7.95 (ISBN 0-316-13968-8). Little.
--Face-off. (Illus.). 160p. (gr. 4-6). 1972. 7.95 (ISBN 0-316-13917-3). Little.
--Favor for a Ghost. LC 83-14493. (Illus.). 108p. (gr. 3-6). 1983. 10.95 (ISBN 0-664-32708-7). Westminster.
--Football Fugitive. (Illus.). 128p. (gr. 4-6). 1976. 7.95 (ISBN 0-316-13971-8). Little.
--The Fox Steals Home. LC 78-17526. (Illus.). (gr. 4-6). 1978. 8.95 (ISBN 0-316-13976-9). Little.
--The Fox Steals Home. (Illus.). 192p. (gr. 4-6). 1985. pap. 3.95 (ISBN 0-316-13986-6). Little.
--Glue Fingers. (Illus.). 48p. (gr. 1-3). 1975. 7.95 (ISBN 0-316-13939-4). Little.
--The Great Quarterback Switch. LC 83-25628. (Illus.). (gr. 4-6). 1984. 10.45i (ISBN 0-316-13903-3). Little.
--Ice Magic. (Illus.). (gr. 4-6). 1973. 8.95 (ISBN 0-316-13958-0). Little.
--Jackrabbit Goalie. LC 78-5438. (Illus.). (gr. 1-3). 1978. 8.95 (ISBN 0-316-13975-0). Little.
--Jinx Glove. (Illus.). 48p. (gr. 1-3). 1974. 7.95 (ISBN 0-316-13965-3). Little.
--Johnny No Hit. LC 77-5488. (Illus.). (gr. 1-3). 1977. 8.95 (ISBN 0-316-13974-2). Little.
--Kid Who Only Hit Homers. (gr. 4-6). 1972. 12.45i (ISBN 0-316-13918-1). Little.
--Look Who's Playing First Base. LC 74-129907. (Illus.). (gr. 4-6). 1971. 9.95 (ISBN 0-316-13933-5). Little.
--No Arm in Left Field. (Illus.). 160p. (gr. 4-6). 1974. 8.95 (ISBN 0-316-13964-5). Little.
--Power Play. (Illus.). (gr. 1-3). 1976. 7.95 (ISBN 0-316-14015-5). Little.
--The Return of the Headless Horseman. LC 81-21936. (Illus.). 96p. (gr. 3-5). 1982. 8.95 (ISBN 0-664-32690-0). Westminster.
--Run, Billy, Run. 156p. (gr. 3-6). 1980. 8.95 (ISBN 0-316-14020-1). Little.
--Shortstop from Tokyo. LC 72-97141. (Illus.). (gr. 4-6). 1970. 7.95 (ISBN 0-316-13951-3). Little.
--Soccer Halfback. (Illus.). (gr. 4-6). 1978. 10.45i (ISBN 0-316-13946-7). Little.
--Soccer Halfback. (Illus.). 182p. (gr. 4-6). 1984. pap. 3.95 (ISBN 0-316-13981-5, Pub. by Atlantic Monthly Pr). Little.
--Stranded. (Illus.). 176p. (gr. 4-6). 1974. 8.70i (ISBN 0-316-13935-1). Little.
--Supercharged Infield. (Illus.). (gr. 4-6). 1985. 12.95 (ISBN 0-316-13983-1). Little.
--Tight End. 128p. (gr. 3 up). 1981. 9.70 (ISBN 0-316-14017-1). Little.
--Touchdown for Tommy. (Illus.). (gr. 4-6). 1959. 8.95 (ISBN 0-316-13938-6). Little.
--Touchdown for Tommy. (Illus.). 145p. (gr. 4-6). 1984. pap. 3.95 (ISBN 0-316-13982-3, Pub. by Atlantic Monthly Pr). Little.
--The Twenty-One Mile Swim. LC 79-15197. (gr. 3-7). 1979. 8.95g (ISBN 0-316-13979-3). Little.
--The Year Mom Won the Pennant. LC 68-11110. (Illus.). (gr. 4-6). 1968. 7.95 (ISBN 0-316-13954-8). Little.
Christopher, Maurine. America's Black Congressman. LC 76-8943. (Apollo Eds.). (Illus.). 288p. 1975. pap. 3.95i (ISBN 0-8152-0376-4, A-376). T Y Crowell.
Christopher, Milbourne. Houdini: A Pictorial Life. (Illus.). 1976. 16.30i (ISBN 0-690-01152-0). T Y Crowell.
--Houdini: The Untold Story. (Illus.). 378p. Repr. of 1969 ed. lib. bdg. 18.95x (ISBN 0-89190-981-8, Pub. by River City Pr). Amereon Ltd.
--The Illustrated History of Magic. LC 73-10390. (Illus.). 452p. 1973. 14.95i (ISBN 0-690-43165-1). T Y Crowell.
--Mediums, Mystics & the Occult. LC 74-26812. (Illus.). 288p. 1975. 9.95i (ISBN 0-690-00476-1, TYC-T). T Y Crowell.
--Milbourne Christopher's Magic Book. (Illus.). 216p. 1985. pap. 5.72i (ISBN 0-06-463708-5, EH 708). B&N NY.
--Panorama of Magic. (Illus., Orig.). 1962. pap. 6.95 (ISBN 0-486-20774-9). Dover.
--Search for the Soul. LC 78-3298. 1979. 12.45i (ISBN 0-690-01760-X). T Y Crowell.
Christopher, Nicholas. On Tour with Rita. LC 81-17209. 1982. 11.95 (ISBN 0-394-51921-3); pap. 6.95 (ISBN 0-394-74998-7). Knopf.
Christopher, Noreen. Enjoy Santa Clara Valley: A Guide of Places to go & Things to Do. 3rd ed. (Illus.). 134p. (Orig.). 1980. pap. 5.95 (ISBN 0-9606134-0-4). A N C Ent.
Christopher, Rachelle G. & Christopher, Edward E. Job Enrichment: How Far Have We Come? LC 79-8992. 1979. pap. text ed. 9.50 (ISBN 0-8191-0857-X). U Pr of Amer.
Christopher, Robert. The Japanese Mind: The Goliath Explained. 352p. 1983. 16.95 (ISBN 0-671-44947-8, Linden Pr). S&S.
Christopher, Robert & Christopher, Ellen. America's Favorite Restaurants & Inns: From Budget to Luxury. 1024p. 1980. pap. 11.95 (ISBN 0-930570-01-4). Travel Discover.
Christopher, Robert C. The Japanese Mind. 320p. 1984. pap. 7.95 (ISBN 0-449-90120-3, Columbine). Fawcett.
--The Japanese Mind. 320p. 1984. pap. 7.95 (ISBN 0-317-07487-3). Ballantine.
Christopher Street Editors, ed. Aphrodisiac: Fiction from Christopher Street. 324p. 1982. pap. 7.95 (ISBN 0-399-50603-9, Perigee). Putnam Pub Group.
Christopher Street Magazine. And God Bless Uncle Harry & His Roommate Jack Who We Are Not Supposed to Talk About. 1979. pap. 2.95 (ISBN 0-380-01897-7, 37291-6). Avon.
Christopher, Warren, et al. American Hostages in Iran: The Conduct of a Crisis. LC 84-19592. (A Council on Foreign Relations Bk.). 448p. 1985. pap. 25.00 (ISBN 0-300-03233-1). Yale U Pr.
Christopher, William F. Management for the Nineteen Eighties. 1979. pap. 6.95 (ISBN 0-13-549154-1, Spec). P-H.
--Management for the Nineteen Eighties. rev. ed. LC 79-55061. pap. 75.80 (ISBN 0-317-27305-1, 2023529). Bks Demand UMI.
Christophers, A. An Index to Nineteenth Century British Educational Biography. 1965. 30.00x (ISBN 0-900008-06-7, Pub. by U of London England). State Mutual Bk.
Christophers, E. & Goos, M., eds. Lymphoproliferate Disease of the Skin. (Illus.). 296p. 1982. pap. 49.00 (ISBN 0-387-11222-7). Springer-Verlag.
Christophers, Richard A. George Abbot, Archbishop of Canterbury, 1562-1633: A Bibliography. LC 65-27845. pap. 59.00 (ISBN 0-317-10344-X, 2016440). Bks Demand UMI.
Christophers, S. Diptera: Diptera, Family Culicidae, Tribe Anophelini, Vol. 3. (Fauna of British India Ser.). (Illus.). vi, 372p. 1977. Repr. of 1933 ed. 30.00 (ISBN 0-88065-042-7, Pub. by Messers Today & Tomorrows Printers & Publishers India). Scholarly Pubns.
--Diptera: Family Culicidae, Tribe Anophelini, Vol. 4. (Fauna of British India Ser.). 1977. Repr. of 1933 ed. 30.00 (ISBN 0-88065-043-5, Pub. by Today & Tomorrows Printers & Publishers India). Scholarly Pubns.
Christophersen, E. Flowering Plants of Samoa, 2 Vols. (BMB). Repr. of 1938 ed. 46.00 set (ISBN 0-686-57457-5); Vol. 1. 31.00 (ISBN 0-527-02234-9); Vol. 2. 15.00 (ISBN 0-527-02262-4). Kraus Repr.
--Vegetation of Pacific Equatorial Islands. (BMB Ser.). Repr. of 1927 ed. 14.00 (ISBN 0-527-02147-4). Kraus Repr.
Christophersen, E. & Caum, E. L. Vascular Plants of the Leeward Island, Hawaii. Repr. of 1931 ed. 11.00 (ISBN 0-527-02187-3). Kraus Repr.
Christophersen, Edward R. The Baby Owner's Manual: What to Expect & How to Survive the First 30 Days. (Illus.). 49p. (Orig.). 1984. pap. 6.00 (ISBN 0-930851-00-5). Overland Pr.
--Little People. rev. ed. LC 79-112461. 170p. 1982. pap. 11.00 (ISBN 0-89079-032-9). Pro Ed.
--Little People: Guidelines for Common Sense Child Rearing. 2nd ed. (Illus.). 166p. 1984. pap. 10.50 (ISBN 0-930851-01-3). Overland Pr.
Christophersen, Hans O. Bibliographical Introduction to the Study of John Locke. LC 68-56598. (Bibliography & Reference Ser: No. 11). 1969. Repr. of 1930 ed. 18.50 (ISBN 0-8337-0565-2). B Franklin.
Christophersen, Merrill G. Biography of an Island: General C. C. Pinckney's Sea Island Plantation. LC 76-18611. (Illus.). 1976. pap. 10.00 (ISBN 0-87423-020-9, 012). Westburg.
--Furwick Poems. LC 77-81225. (Illus.). 1977. pap. 5.00 (ISBN 0-685-54383-8). Westburg.
Christophersen, Merrill G. & Leon, Adolfo. Cidean Ballads, Ballads About the Great Spanish Hero, El Cid. LC 74-24580. (Comparative Literature Studies Ser). 180p. pap. 10.00 (ISBN 0-87423-012-8). Westburg.
Christopherson. Life Geosystems: A Physical Geography. 1983. pap. text ed. write for info. (ISBN 0-471-08650-9). Wiley.
Christopherson, John. An Exhortation to All Menne to Take Hede & Beware of Rebellion. LC 73-6113. (English Experience Ser.: No. 580). 504p. 1973. Repr. of 1554 ed. 29.00 (ISBN 90-221-0580-6). Walter J Johnson.
Christopherson, Paul, tr. see Bang, Herman.
Christopherson, Ragnar, tr. see Madsen, Stephan T.
Christopherson, Roger. The Love Experience. Hirst, Sheri, ed. 124p. (Orig.). 1984. pap. 5.95 (ISBN 0-914597-01-9). Juno-West.
Christopherson, Victor A., et al. Rehabilitation Nursing: Perspectives & Applications. (Illus.). 512p. (Orig.). 1973. 28.00 (ISBN 0-07-010815-3). McGraw.
Christopherson, W. M., jt. auth. see Riotton, G.
Christopherson, William, jt. auth. see Riotton, C.
Christophorou, L. G. Atomic & Molecular Radiation Physics. LC 72-129159. (Wiley Monographs in Chemical Physics). pap. 160.00 (ISBN 0-317-29345-1, 2023999). Bks Demand UMI.
--Electron Molecule Interactions & Their Applications. LC 83-7648. 1984. Vol. 1. 80.00 (ISBN 0-12-174401-9); Vol. 2. 85.00 (ISBN 0-12-174402-7). Acad Pr.
Christophorou, L. G., ed. Gaseous Dielectrics III: Proceedings of the Third International Symposium on Gaseous Dielectrics, Knoxville, Tennessee, USA, March 7-11, 1982. LC 82-9825. (Illus.). 600p. 1982. 105.00 (ISBN 0-08-029381-6, A110). Pergamon.
Christophorou, L. G. & Pace, M. O., eds. Gaseous Dielectrics: Proceedings of the Fourth International Symposium on Gaseous Dielectrics, Knoxville, Tennessee, U. S. A., April 29-May 3, 1984, No. IV. LC 84-18997. (Illus.). 624p. Date not set. 105.00 (ISBN 0-08-031570-4). Pergamon.
Christophorou, Loucas G., ed. Electron & Ion Swarms: Proceedings of the Second International Swarm Seminar. (Illus.). 279p. 1981. 25.00 (ISBN 0-08-028084-6). Pergamon.
--Gaseous Dielectrics II: Proceedings of the Second International Symposium on Gaseous Dielectrics, Knoxville, Tenn., U.S.A., March 9-13, 1980. 506p. 1980. 30.00 (ISBN 0-08-025978-2). Pergamon.
Christophory, Jules, jt. ed. see Hury, Carlo.
Christophus, Mike, jt. auth. see Kenyon, Mel.
Christopoulos, George A. & Bastias, John C., eds. The Archaic Period, Eleven Hundred to Four Hundred Seventy-Nine B C. Sherrard, Philip, tr. LC 75-27171. (History of the Hellenic World Ser.: Vol. 2). (Illus.). 620p. 1975. 56.50 (ISBN 0-271-01214-5). Pa St U Pr.
--Prehistory & Protohistory to Eleven Hundred B.C. Sherrard, Philip, tr. LC 75-18610. (History of the Hellenic World Ser.: Vol. 1). (Illus.). 420p. 1975. 56.50 (ISBN 0-271-01199-8). Pa St U Pr.
Christos, Edith. Alcohol Drinking: Medical Subject Analysis & Research Index with Bibliography. LC 83-71648. 140p. 1983. 29.95 (ISBN 0-88164-010-7); pap. 21.95 (ISBN 0-88164-011-5). ABBE Pubs Assn.
Christos, Edith Marie, et al. Science, Medicine & Psychology of Automobiles: Subject Analysis & Research Guide. LC 83-45545. 140p. 1984. 29.95 (ISBN 0-88164-112-X); pap. 21.95 (ISBN 0-88164-113-8). ABBE Pubs Assn.

Christos, George. Criminal & Non-Criminal Homicide: Medical Guidebook for Research & Reference. LC 84-45217. 150p. 1985. 29.95 (ISBN 0-88164-176-6); pap. 21.95 (ISBN 0-88164-177-4). ABBE Pubs Assn.

Christou, Chrysanthos. Greek Painting, Eighteen Thirty-Two to Nineteen Twenty-Two. (Illus.). 212p. 1983. lib. bdg. 90.00 (ISBN 0-89241-379-4). Caratzas.

Christout, Marie-Francoise. Merveilleux et le Theatre Du Silence En France a Partir Du Dix-Sept Siecle. 1965. text ed. 32.20x (ISBN 90-2796-385-1). Mouton.

Christovale, Cindy. Personal Development for Christian Women. 80p. (Orig.). 1983. pap. 2.95 (ISBN 0-88144-018-3, CPS-018). Christian Pub.

Christovich, Mary L., ed. see Wilson, Samuel, Jr. & Lemann, Bernard.

Christovich, Mary L., et al. New Orleans Architecture: Esplanade Ridge, Vol. 5. LC 72-172272. (New Orleans Architecture Ser.). (Illus.). 172p. 1977. 27.50 (ISBN 0-88289-151-0). Pelican.

--New Orleans Architecture, The American Sector, Vol. 2. LC 72-172272. (New Orleans Architecture Ser.). (Illus.). 244p. 1972. 27.50 (ISBN 0-911116-80-X). Pelican.

Christovich, Mary Louise, jt. auth. see Toledano, Roulhac B.

Christy, Albert. Numeral Philosophy. 82p. 1983. pap. 5.50 (ISBN 0-89540-141-X, SB-141). Sun Pub.

Christy, Ann. From the Torrid Past. (Second Chance at Love Ser.: No. 49). (Orig.). 1982. pap. 1.75 (ISBN 0-515-06540-4). Jove Pubns.

--Mystique. (Second Chance at Love Ser.: No. 223). 192p. 1984. pap. 1.95 (ISBN 0-515-08118-3). Jove Pubns.

Christy, Arthur. Orient in American Transcendentalism: A Study of Emerson, Thoreau & Alcott. 1963. lib. bdg. 26.00x (ISBN 0-374-91539-3). Octagon.

Christy, Arthur, ed. Asian Legacy & American Life, Essays. LC 68-9541. (Illus.). 1968. Repr. of 1945 ed. lib. bdg. 19.00x (ISBN 0-8371-0046-1, CHAL). Greenwood.

Christy, Arthur, ed. see Langlois.

Christy, Arthur E. & Wells, Henry W., eds. World Literature. facs. ed. LC 77-149100. (Granger Index Reprint Ser). 1947. 58.00 (ISBN 0-8369-6225-7). Ayer Co Pubs.

Christy, Craig. Uniformitarianism in Linguistics. (Studies in the History of Linguistics: 31). 139p. 1983. 20.00x (ISBN 90-272-4513-4). Benjamins North Am.

Christy, David. Cotton Is King. 2nd ed. LC 70-136634. Repr. of 1856 ed. 35.00x (ISBN 0-678-00807-8). Kelley.

--Ethiopia: Her Gloom & Glory. LC 73-75550. Repr. of 1857 ed. 19.75x (ISBN 0-8371-1016-5, CHR&, Pub. by Negro U Pr). Greenwood.

--Pulpit Politics. 3rd ed. LC 77-77197. Repr. of 1862 ed. 27.00x (ISBN 0-8371-1284-2, CPP&). Greenwood.

Christy, Dennis T. Elementary Functions. (Illus.). 1978. text ed. 23.50 scp (ISBN 0-06-041297-6, HarpC); avail. answers to even number excercises (ISBN 0-06-361191-0). Har-Row.

--Essentials of Precalculus Mathematics. 2nd ed. 598p. 1981. text ed. 25.50 scp (ISBN 0-06-041303-4, HarpC); answers to even-numbered exercises avail. (ISBN 0-06-361192-9). Har-Row.

Christy, F. T., Jr., ed. Law of the Sea: Problems of Conflict & Management of Fisheries in Southeast Asia. (Illus.). 68p. 1983. pap. text ed. 12.00 (ISBN 0-89955-387-7, Pub. by ICLARM Philippines). Intl Spec Bk.

Christy, Francis T., jt. auth. see Potter, Neal.

Christy, Francis T., Jr. Summary Report of the ICLARM-ISEAS Workshop on Law of the Sea: Problems of Conflict & Management of Fisheries in Southeast Asia. (ICLARM Conference Proceedings Ser.: No. 3). (Illus.). 11p. (Orig.). 1980. pap. 5.00 (ISBN 0-89955-422-9, Pub. by ICLARM Philippines). Intl Spec Bk.

--Territorial Use Rights in Marine Fisheries: Definitions & Conditions. (Fisheries Technical Papers: No. 227). 16p. (Eng., Fr. & Span.). 1982. pap. 7.50 (ISBN 92-5-101269-5, F2371, FAO). Unipub.

Christy, G. A. & Clendenin, J. C. Introduction to Investments. 8th ed. (Finance Ser.). 784p. 1982. 31.95x (ISBN 0-07-010833-1). McGraw.

Christy, George A. & Roden, Foster. Finance: Environment & Decisions. 3rd ed. 445p. 1981. text ed. 24.75 scp (ISBN 0-06-041302-6, HarpC); instructors manual avail. (ISBN 0-06-361193-7). Har-Row.

Christy, Howard A., ed. see Palmer, Richard F. & Butler, Karl D.

Christy, Howard C. The American Girl. LC 76-4778. 1976. lib. bdg. 39.50 (ISBN 0-306-70854-X); pap. 8.95 (ISBN 0-306-80042-X). Da Capo.

Christy, Howard C. & Betts, Ethel F., illus. The Complete Works of James Whitcomb Riley, 10 Vol. set. 1983. Repr. of 1916 ed. Set. lib. bdg. 300.00 (ISBN 0-8495-4578-1). Arden Lib.

Christy, James. The Puppet Ministry. 1978. 2.50 (ISBN 0-8341-0532-2). Beacon Hill.

Christy, Jim. The Price of Power: A Biography of Charles Eugene Bedaux. LC 84-10290. 356p. 1985. 21.95 (ISBN 0-385-18909-5). Doubleday.

Christy, Joe. Aircraft Construction, Repair & Inspection. (Illus.). 240p. 1984. pap. 13.50 (ISBN 0-8306-2377-9, 2377). TAB Bks.

--American Air Power: The First Seventy-Five Years. (Illus.). 208p. 1982. 21.95 (ISBN 0-8306-2327-2, 2327). TAB Bks.

--Build Your Own Low-Cost Hangar. (Illus.). 126p. (Orig.). 1983. pap. 9.25 (ISBN 0-8306-2357-4, 2357). TAB Bks.

--The Complete Guide to Single-Engine Beechcrafts. 2nd ed. (Illus.). 1979. 7.95 (ISBN 0-8306-9791-8); pap. 4.95 o.p (ISBN 0-8306-2258-6, 2258). TAB Bks.

--The Complete Guide to Single-Engine Cessnas. 3rd ed. (Illus.). 1979. 10.95 (ISBN 0-8306-9800-0); pap. 7.95 (ISBN 0-8306-2268-3, 2268). TAB Bks.

--Engines for Homebuilt Aircraft & Ultralights. (Illus.). 112p. 1984. pap. 8.95 (ISBN 0-8306-2347-7, 2347). TAB Bks.

--High Adventure: The First Seventy-Five Years of Civil Aviation. LC 84-16453. (Illus.). 234p. (Orig.). 1984. pap. 16.95 (ISBN 0-8306-2387-6, 2387). TAB Bks.

--How to Install & Finish Synthetic Aircraft Fabrics. (Modern Aviation Ser.). (Illus.). 1979. 8.95 (ISBN 0-8306-9828-0); pap. 4.95 (ISBN 0-8306-2252-7, 2252). TAB Bks.

--Illustrated Handbook of Aviation & Aerospace Facts. (Illus.). 720p. (Orig.). 1984. pap. 29.50 (ISBN 0-8306-2397-3, 2397). TAB Bks.

--Lightplane Owner's Maintenance Guide. (Modern Aircraft Ser.). 1978. pap. 4.95 (ISBN 0-8306-2244-6, 2244). TAB Bks.

--Low-Cost Private Flying. (Modern Aviation Ser.). (Illus.). 160p. (Orig.). 1980. 9.95 (ISBN 0-8306-9930-9); pap. 4.95 (ISBN 0-8306-2298-5, 2298). TAB Bks.

--Maintenance-Overhaul Guide to Lycoming Aircraft Engines. (Modern Aviation Ser.). (Illus.). 128p. 1980. 9.95 (ISBN 0-8306-9733-0, 2277). TAB Bks.

--The Private Pilot's Handy Reference Guide. (Illus.). 224p. 1980. 14.95 (ISBN 0-8306-9663-6, 2325); pap. 11.95 (ISBN 0-8306-2325-6, 2325). TAB Bks.

--Racing Planes & Pilots. (Illus.). 208p. 1982. pap. 8.95 (ISBN 0-8306-2322-1, 2322). TAB Bks.

--Refinishing Metal Aircraft. (Modern Aircraft Ser.). (Illus.). 128p. (Orig.). 1980. pap. 4.95 (ISBN 0-8306-2291-8, 2291). TAB Bks.

--Ultralight Flying for the Private Pilot. (Illus.). 192p. 1985. pap. 12.95 (ISBN 0-8306-2382-5, 2382). TAB Bks.

Christy, Joe & Johnson, Clay. Your Pilot's License. 3rd ed. (Illus.). 160p. 1983. pap. 9.95 (ISBN 0-8306-2367-1, 2367). TAB Bks.

Christy, Joe, jt. auth. see Ethell, Jeff.

Christy, Joe, jt. auth. see Holding, Vera.

Christy, John & Friedman, David. Racing Cobra: A Definitive Illustrated History. (Illus.). 208p. 1982. 24.95 (ISBN 0-85045-457-3, Pub. by Osprey England). Motorbooks Intl.

Christy, John & Ludvigsen, Karl. The Complete MG Guide Model by Model. 2nd ed. (Illus.). 1979. pap. 4.95 (ISBN 0-8306-2056-7, 2056). TAB Bks.

Christy, Lawrence C. Legislative Principles of Soil Conservation. (Soils Bulletins: No. 15). 73p. (2nd Printing 1977). 1971. pap. 7.50 (ISBN 92-5-100257-6, F1157, FAO). Unipub.

Christy, Margaret P. Charcoal Portraits. (Illus.). 1978. pap. 4.95x (ISBN 0-918342-07-4). Cambric.

Christy, Marian. Invasion of Privacy: Notes from a Celebrity Journalist. LC 84-10999. 1984. 14.95 (ISBN 0-201-10336-2). Addison-Wesley.

Christy, Miller, ed. The Voyage of Captain Luke Foxe of Hull & Captain Thomas James of Bristol, in Search of a Northwest Passage, in 1631-32. (Hakluyt Society. Publications: Nos. 88-89). (Illus.). 1966. Repr. of 1894 ed. 63.00 (ISBN 0-8337-0568-7). B Franklin.

Christy, Robert. Proverbs, Maxims & Phrases of All Ages: Classified Subjectively & Arranged Alphabetically, 2 vols. in one. 1977. Repr. of 1888 ed. lib. bdg. 100.00 (ISBN 0-8482-0476-X). Norwood Edns.

Christy, Ron & Jones, Billy M. The Complete Information Bank for Entrepreneurs & Small Business Managers. LC 81-70750. (Illus.). 300p. 19.50 (ISBN 0-941958-00-0, Wichita Ctr Entrep SBM). WSU Hist Resources.

Christy, Teresa E. Cornerstone for Nursing Education: A History of the Division of Nursing Education at Teachers College, Columbia University, 1899-1947. LC 79-96868. pap. write for info. (2052126). Bks Demand UMI.

Christy, Thomas, jt. auth. see Leonard, C. Henri.

Christy, Van A. Expressive Singing, Vol. 1. 3rd ed. 256p. 1974. plastic comb write for info. (ISBN 0-697-03649-9). Wm C Brown.

--Expressive Singing, Vol. 2. 3rd ed. 432p. 1975. plastic comb write for info. (ISBN 0-697-03650-2). Wm C Brown.

--Expressive Singing: Song Anthology: Vol. I - High Voice, Medium Voice, Low Voice. 2nd ed. 224p. 1982. Vol. I high voice. write for info. wire coil bdg. (ISBN 0-697-03524-7); Vol. I medium voice. write for info. wire coil bdg. (ISBN 0-697-03523-9); Vol. I low voice. write for info. wire coil bdg. (ISBN 0-697-03522-0). Wm C Brown.

--Expressive Singing: Song Anthology: Vol. II - High Voice, Medium Voice, Low Voice. 2nd ed. 240p. 1982. Vol. II high voice. write for info. wire coil (ISBN 0-697-03532-8); Vol. II medium voice. write for info. wire coil (ISBN 0-697-03531-X); Vol. II low voice. write for info. wire coil (ISBN 0-697-03530-1). Wm C Brown.

--Foundations in Singing: A Basic Text in the Fundamentals of Teaching & Song Interpretation - Medium-High Voice Edition. 272p. 1981. write for info. plastic comb bind. (ISBN 0-697-03483-6). Wm C Brown.

--Foundations in Singing: Med-Low Voice. 4th ed. 272p. 1982. write for info. plastic comb. bdg. (ISBN 0-697-03639-1). Wm C Brown.

Christy, Van Ambrose. Evaluation of Choral Music. LC 75-176698. (Columbia University. Teachers College. Contributions to Education: No. 885). Repr. of 1948 ed. 22.50 (ISBN 0-404-55885-2). AMS Pr.

Chriswell, John. How to Get By on Ten Thousand Dollars a Day! 2nd, rev. ed. 155p. (Orig.). pap. write for info. (ISBN 0-915451-00-X). New Start Pubns.

Chriswell, M. Irving. Within My Sacred Lodge. (Illus.). 20p. 1981. pap. 2.50 (ISBN 0-88053-006-5). Macoy Pub.

Chritton, Michael, photos by. Cyclist's Training Diary. rev. ed. (Illus.). 192p. 1985. 7.95 (ISBN 0-941950-08-5). Velo-News.

Chrodegang, Saint The Old English Version of the Enlarged Rule of Chrodegang. (EETS, OS Ser.: No. 150). Repr. of 1916 ed. 10.00 (ISBN 0-527-00146-5). Kraus Repr.

Chroman, Eleanor. The Potter's Primer. 1974. pap. 5.95 (ISBN 0-8015-5959-6, Hawthorn). Dutton.

--Songs That Children Sing. new ed. LC 79-93961. (Orig.). (gr. k-6). 1970. pap. 5.95 (ISBN 0-8256-0011-1, Oak). Music Sales.

Chronic, Halka. Pages of Stone: Geology of Western National Parks & Monuments. (Rocky Mountains & Western Great Plains Ser.: Vol. 1). (Illus.). 192p. (Orig.). 1984. pap. 14.95 (ISBN 0-89886-095-4). Mountaineers.

--Roadside Geology of Arizona. 320p. 1983. pap. 9.95 (ISBN 0-87842-147-5). Mountain Pr.

--Roadside Geology of Colorado: Roadside Geology Ser. LC 79-11148. (Illus.). 322p. 1980. pap. 9.95 (ISBN 0-87842-105-X). Mountain Pr.

--Time, Rocks & the Rockies: The Geology of Rocky Mountain National Park. (Roadside Geology Ser.). (Illus.). 200p. (Orig.). 1984. pap. 7.95 (ISBN 0-87842-172-6). Mountain Pr.

Chronicle Guidance Publications. Chronicle Guide for Transfers. rev. ed. 170p. 1983. pap. 12.00 (ISBN 0-912578-57-2). Chron Guide.

--Occupational Profiles. rev. ed. LC 75-6566. 183p. 1981. pap. 14.65 (ISBN 0-912578-22-X). Chron Guide.

Chronicle Staff. C-LECT Professional Manual. 12p. (Orig.). 1983. write for info. (ISBN 0-912578-59-9). Chron Guide.

--C-LECT User Guide. (Orig.). 1983. pap. text ed. write for info. (ISBN 0-912578-60-2). Chron Guide.

Chronicles of England. The Brut: Part II. (EETS, OS Ser.: No. 136). Repr. of 1908 ed. 50.00 (ISBN 0-527-00134-1). Kraus Repr.

Chronicon Aulae Regiae. Die Koenigsaaler Geschichts-Quellen Mit Den Zusaetzen & Die Fortsetzung Des Domherrn Franz Von Prag. 628p. Repr. of 1875 ed. 62.00 (ISBN 0-384-08980-1). Johnson Repr.

Chronicon Petroburgense. Nunc Primum Typis Mandatum, Curante Thoma Stapleton. (Camden Society, London. Publications. First Ser.: No. 47). Repr. of 1849 ed. 24.00 (ISBN 0-404-50147-8). AMS Pr.

Chronis, Valerie. Valerie. pap. 3.00 (ISBN 0-938078-11-9). Anhinga Pr.

Chronister, R. B. & De France, J. F., eds. The Neurobiology of the Nucleus Accumbens. (Illus.). 380p. (Orig.). 1981. pap. 39.95 (ISBN 0-940090-00-7). Haer Inst.

Chronister, Richard, jt. ed. see Kraehenbuehl, David.

Chroust & Muhlbacher, eds. Firmware Microprogramming & Restructurable Hardware. 310p. 1980. 42.75 (ISBN 0-444-86056-8, North-Holland). Elsevier.

Chroust, Anton-Hermann. Aristotle, New Light on His Life & Some of His Lost Works, 2 vols. Incl. Vol. 1. Some Novel Interpretations of the Man & His Life. 448p (ISBN 0-268-00517-6); Vol. 2. Observations on Some of Aristotle's Lost Works. 495p (ISBN 0-268-00518-4). LC 73-8892. 1973. text ed. 30.00. U of Notre Dame Pr.

--The Rise of the Legal Profession in America, 2 Vols. 1965. boxed set 45.00x (ISBN 0-8061-0654-9). U of Okla Pr.

Chroust, Anton-Hermann, ed. Aristotle: Protrepticus, A Reconstruction. 1964. pap. 2.95x (ISBN 0-268-00013-1). U of Notre Dame Pr.

Chruchman, Charles W. Prediction & Optimal Decision: Philosophical Issues of a Science Values. LC 82-6264. (International Management Ser.). xvi, 394p. 1982. Repr. lib. bdg. 39.75x (ISBN 0-313-23418-3, CHUP). Greenwood.

Chruden, Herbert J. & Sherman, Arthur W., Jr. Managing Human Resources. 1984. text ed. 22.45 (ISBN 0-538-07820-0, G82). SW Pub.

Chruden, Herbert J. & Sherman, Arthur W. Readings in Human Resources Management. 1984. text ed. 11.95 (ISBN 0-538-07880-4, G88). SW Pub.

Chruscie, T. L. & Chrusciel, M. Selected Bibliography on Detection of Dependence-Producing Drugs in Body Fluids. (Offset Pub.: No. 17). (Also avail. in France). 1975. pap. 6.00 (ISBN 92-4-052004-X). World Health.

Chrusciel, M., jt. auth. see Chruscie, T. L.

Chrysander, F. Melius, ed. see Handel, George.

Chrysler Corporation. Glossary of Automotive Terminology: French-English English-French. 230p. (Fr. & Eng.). 1977. 18.00 (ISBN 0-89883-195-4, SP-423). Soc Auto Engineers.

--Glossary of Automotive Terminology: Spanish-English English-Spanish. 380p. (Span. & Eng.). 1978. 22.00 (ISBN 0-89883-208-X, SP-436). Soc Auto Engineers.

Chrysler Learning, Inc. Weldtech Series in Welding: Basic Gas Metal-Arc Welding. (Illus.). 128p. 1983. pap. text ed. 10.95 (ISBN 0-13-948075-7). P-H.

--Weldtech Series in Welding: Basic Shielded Metal-Arc Welding. 128p. 1983. pap. 10.95 (ISBN 0-13-948083-8). P-H.

--Weldtech Series in Welding: Oxyacetylene Welding, Cutting, & Brazing. (Illus.). 80p. 1983. pap. 10.95 (ISBN 0-13-948091-9). P-H.

Chrysostom, John. Discourses Against Judaizing Christains. (Fathers of the Church Ser.: Vol. 68). 286p. 1979. 29.95x (ISBN 0-8132-0068-7). Cath U Pr.

--On the Incomprehensible Nature of God. Harkins, Paul W., tr. from Greek. LC 83-1984. (Fathers of the Church Ser.: No. 72). 357p. 1984. 29.95x (ISBN 0-8132-0072-5). Cath U Pr.

--St. John Chrysostom on the Priesthood. 160p. 1977. pap. 3.95 (ISBN 0-913836-38-9). St Vladimirs.

Chrysostom, St. John. Duties of Parents & Children to One Another. pap. 0.25 (ISBN 0-686-17310-4). Eastern Orthodox.

Chrysostomos, Archimandrite. The Ancient Fathers of the Church: Translated Narratives from the Evertinos on Passions & Perfection in Christ. (Illus.). 118p. 1980. 7.95 (ISBN 0-916586-77-4); pap. 4.95 (ISBN 0-686-69869-X). Hellenic Coll Pr.

--Orthodox Liturgical Vesture: An Historical Treatment. 76p. 1981. 6.95 (ISBN 0-916586-43-X); pap. 3.95 (ISBN 0-916586-44-8). Holy Cross Orthodox.

--Orthodoxy & Papism. Williams, Theodore M., ed. LC 82-73693. 70p. 1982. pap. 4.50 (ISBN 0-911165-00-2). Ctr Trad Orthodox.

Chrysostomos, Archimandrite & Ambrosios, Hieromonk. Obedience. Young, Alexey & Derugin, Vladimir, eds. (Themes in Orthodox Patristic Psychology Ser.: Vol. 2). 90p. (Orig.). 1984. text ed. write for info. (ISBN 0-916586-88-X); pap. text ed. write for info. (ISBN 0-916586-31-6). Holy Cross Orthodox.

Chrysostomos, Archimandrite & Auxentios, Hieromonk. Scripture & Tradition. 96p. 1984. pap. 5.00 (ISBN 0-911165-04-5). Ctr Trad Orthodox.

Chrysostomos, Archimandrite & Williams, Theodore. Humility, Vol. 1. LC 82-74509. (Themes in Orthodox Patristic Psychology Ser.). 90p. (Orig.). 1983. pap. text ed. 4.50 (ISBN 0-911165-01-0); pap. write for info. (ISBN 0-911165-02-9). Ctr Trad Orthodox.

Chrysostomos, Archimandrite, tr. see Cavarnos, Constantine.

Chrysostomos, Archimandrite, et al. The Old Calendar Orthodox Church of Greece. 116p. 1985. pap. 4.50 (ISBN 0-911165-05-3). Ctr Trad Orthodox.

Chrysovitsiotis, I. Greek-English, English-Greek Commercial Economics & Related Fields Dictionary. 2nd rev ed. (Gr. & Eng.). 45.00 (ISBN 0-685-79112-2). Heinman.

Chryssafis, G. A Textual & Stylistic Commentary on Theocritus' Idyll Twenty Five. (London Studies in Classical Philology Ser.: Vol. I). 289p. 1981. pap. text ed. 52.00x (ISBN 90-70265-21-4, Pub. by Gieben Holland). Humanities.

Chryssis, George. High Frequency Switching Power Supplies: Theory & Design. 224p. 1984. 35.00 (ISBN 0-07-010949-4). McGraw.

Chryssostomidis, C., jt. ed. see Dyer, Ira.

Chryssostomidis, Chryssostomos & Connor, Jerome J., eds. Behaviour of Off-Shore Structures: Proceedings of the Third International Conference, 2 Vols. LC 82-11749. (Illus.). 1622p. 1982. Set. text ed. 179.00 (ISBN 0-89116-343-3). Hemisphere Pub.

Chrystal, George. Textbook of Algebra, 2 Vols. 7th ed. LC 64-21987. (gr. 9-12). text ed. 15.95 ea. (ISBN 0-8284-0084-9). Chelsea Pub.

Chrystal, K. A. Controversies in Macroeconomics. 2nd ed. 181p. 1983. text ed. 21.50x (ISBN 0-86003-053-9, Pub. by Philip Allan England); pap. text ed. 11.00x (ISBN 0-86003-147-0). Humanities.

Chrystal, K. Alec, jt. auth. see Alt, James E.

Chrystal, William G. A Father's Mantle: The Legacy of Gustav Niebuhr. LC 81-21108. 160p. (Orig.). 1982. pap. 7.95 (ISBN 0-8298-0494-3). Pilgrim NY.

Chrystal, William G., ed. Young Reinhold Niebuhr: The Early Writings - 1911 to 1931. rev. ed. 256p. 1982. pap. 8.95 (ISBN 0-8298-0607-5). Pilgrim NY.

Chrystal-Smith, G. Estimating for Alterations & Repairs. 128p. 1982. 29.00x (ISBN 0-7198-2545-8, Pub. by Northwood Bks). State Mutual Bk.

Chrystie, Frances N. Pets. rev. 3rd ed. (Illus.). (gr. 4 up). 1974. 14.45i (ISBN 0-316-14051-1). Little.

Chrystie, Thomas L. & Fabozzi, Frank J., eds. Left Hand Financing: An Emerging Field of Techniques in Corporate Finance. LC 82-72366. 1982. 30.00 (ISBN 0-87094-342-1). Dow Jones-Irwin.

Chrzanowski, Gerard, jt. ed. see Arieti, Silvano.

Chu. Biochemical Markers for Cancer. (Clinical & Biochemical Analysis Ser.: Vol. 11). 400p. 1982. 65.00 (ISBN 0-8247-1535-7). Dekker.

Chu, et al. Acupuncture Manual. 1979. 29.75 (ISBN 0-8247-6798-5). Dekker.

Chu, Alfian, ed. Satellite Television in Indonesia. Chu, Godwin C. vi, 211p. (Orig.). 1981. pap. 6.00 (ISBN 0-86638-002-7). E W Center HI.

Chu, Alfred E., jt. auth. see Triebel, Walter A.

Chu, Arthur & Chu, Grace. Oriental Cloisonne & Other Enamels: A Guide to Collecting & Repairing. (Illus.). 256p. 1975. 12.95 (ISBN 0-517-52352-3). Crown.

Chu, Benjamin. Laser Light Scattering. 1974. 75.00 (ISBN 0-12-174550-3). Acad Pr.

Chu, C. W. & Woolam, J. A., eds. High Pressure & Low-Temperature Physics. LC 78-7290. 614p. 1978. 89.50x (ISBN 0-306-40014-6, Plenum Pr). Plenum Pub.

Chu, Charles. China's Picasso, Ch'i Pai-Shih: His Life & Works. 4.75 (ISBN 0-88710-010-4); tapes avail. (ISBN 0-88710-011-2). Far Eastern Pubns.

--A Sketch of Chinese Geography (in Characters) 5.25 (ISBN 0-88710-089-9); tapes avail. (ISBN 0-88710-090-2). Far Eastern Pubns.

Chu, Charles, annotations by. Contemporary Chinese Writings. 5.95 (ISBN 0-88710-021-X). Far Eastern Pubns.

Chu, Chauncey C. A Reference Grammar of Mandarin Chinese for English Speakers. LC 83-48754. (American University Studies VI: Vol. 2). 291p. 1983. pap. text ed. 29.00 (ISBN 0-8204-0042-4). P Lang Pubs.

Chu, Chin. Tariff Problem in China. LC 68-56650. (Columbia University Studies in the Social Sciences: No. 169). 17.50 (ISBN 0-404-51169-4). AMS Pr.

Chu, D., ed. Modal Testing & Model Refinement. 164p. 1983. pap. text ed. 34.00 (ISBN 0-317-02633-X, H00274). ASME.

Chu, D. K., jt. ed. see Wong, K. A.

Chu, David S., ed. Sociology & Society in Contemporary China, 1979-1983: A Special Issue of Chinese Sociology & Anthrology. 224p. 1984. pap. 12.95 (ISBN 0-87332-278-9). M E Sharpe.

Chu, Don-Chean. Chairman Mao: Education of the Proletariat. 1980. 19.95 (ISBN 0-8022-2236-6). Philos Lib.

--Patterns of Education for the Developing Nations: Tao's Work in China 1917-1946. LC 66-5481. xi, 177p. 1966. 2.00 (ISBN 0-913973-11-4); pap. 1.00 (ISBN 0-913973-07-6). Inst Sino-Amer.

--Philosophic Foundations of American Education. LC 70-150045. 392p. 1971. pap. 7.00 (ISBN 0-913973-08-4). Inst Sino-Amer.

--The Story of China. 156p. 1968. pap. write for info. (ISBN 0-913973-09-2). Inst Sino-Amer.

Chu, Donald. Dimensions of Sport Studies. LC 81-16425. 299p. 1982. text ed. 23.45 (ISBN 0-471-08576-6). Wiley.

Chu, Donald, jt. auth. see Krepton, Dorie.

Chu, Donald, et al, eds. Sport in Higher Education. 1985. text ed. 24.95x (ISBN 0-87322-000-5, BCHU0000). Human Kinetics.

Chu, E. & Generoso, W., eds. Mutation, Cancer, & Malformation. (Environmental Science Research Ser.: Vol. 31). 855p. 1984. 97.50x (ISBN 0-306-41820-7, Plenum Press). Plenum Pub.

Chu, Ernest, jt. auth. see Russell, Doug.

Chu, Franklin D. & Trotter, Sharland. The Madness Establishment: Ralph Nader's Study Group Report on the National Institute of Mental Health. LC 73-83701. 232p. 1974. 12.95 (ISBN 0-670-44734-X, Grossman). Viking.

Chu, Franklin D. see Simmonds, Kenneth R.

Chu, Franklin D., jt. auth. see Nee, Owen D.

Chu, Godwin. Radical Change Through Communication in Mao's China. LC 77-3874. 350p. 1977. text ed. 17.50x (ISBN 0-8248-0515-1, Eastwest Ctr). UH Pr.

Chu, Godwin C. & Schramm, Wilbur. Learning from Television: What the Research Says. 116p. 1979. pap. 6.00 (ISBN 0-686-77626-7, Pub Telecomm). NAEB.

Chu, Godwin C. see Chu, Alfian.

Chu, Godwin C., ed. Popular Media in China: Shaping New Cultural Patterns. LC 78-13282. 273p. 1978. text ed. 14.00x (ISBN 0-8248-0622-0, Eastwest Ctr). UH Pr.

Chu, Godwin C. & Hsu, Francis L., eds. China's New Social Fabric. 1983. pap. 16.95x (ISBN 0-7103-0050-6). Routledge & Kegan.

--Moving a Mountain: Cultural Change in China. LC 79-22037. (Illus.). 455p. 1979. text ed. 22.00x (ISBN 0-8248-0667-0, Eastwest Ctr). UH Pr.

Chu, Godwin C., et al, eds. Institutional Exploration in Communication Technology. (Communications Monographs: No. 4). 184p. 1978. pap. text ed. 6.00x (ISBN 0-8248-0664-6, Eastwest Ctr). UH Pr.

Chu, Grace, jt. auth. see Chu, Arthur.

Chu, Grace, jt. auth. see Chue, Arthur.

Chu, Grace, ed. see Namba, Ayako.

Chu, Grace Z. The Pleasures of Chinese Cooking. (Illus.). 239p. 1975. pap. 3.95 (ISBN 0-671-22181-7, Fireside). S&S.

Chu, H. F. How to Know the Immature Insects. 2nd ed. (Pictured Key Nature Ser.). 240p. 1983. wire coil write for info. (ISBN 0-697-04806-3); Wm C Brown.

Chu, Hsiu-Feng, et al. English-Chinese Chinese-English Dictionary of Business Terms. 476p. (Orig.). 1973. pap. 8.95 (ISBN 0-917056-85-X, Pub. by Chih-Wen Pub Co China). Cheng & Tsui.

Chu, J. & Cafritz, E. The Music Video Guide. (Illus.). 352p. 1985. pap. price not set (ISBN 0-07-010865-X). McGraw.

Chu, Jennings P. Chinese Students in America: Qualities Associated with Their Success. LC 78-176645. (Columbia University. Teachers College. Contributions to Education: No. 127). Repr. of 1922 ed. 22.50 (ISBN 0-404-55127-0). AMS Pr.

Chu, John W. Selections from the New Testament in Chinese. 6.00 (ISBN 0-88710-083-X); tapes avail. (ISBN 0-88710-084-8). Far Eastern Pubns.

Chu, Jonathan M. Neighbors, Friends, or Madmen: The Puritan Adjustment to Quakerism in Seventeenth-Century Massachusetts Bay. LC 84-29035. (Contributions to the Study of Religion Ser.: No. 14). 192p. 1985. lib. bdg. 27.95 (ISBN 0-313-24809-5, CNE/). Greenwood.

Chu, Kwo-Ray, jt. tr. see Chang, Yu-Hung.

Chu, Lawrence C. Chef Chu's Distinctive Cuisine of China. LC 83-47846. (Illus.). 224p. 1983. 21.63i (ISBN 0-06-181158-0, HarpT). Har-Row.

Chu, Limin. The Images of China & the Chinese in the Overland Monthly, 1868-1875, 1883-1935. LC 74-76753. 1974. Repr. of 1965 ed. soft bdg. 14.00 (ISBN 0-88247-255-0). R & E Pubs.

Chu, Louis. Eat a Bowl of Tea. LC 78-21209. 250p. 1979. pap. 8.95 (ISBN 0-295-95607-0). U of Wash Pr.

Chu, Paul E. Life Before Birth, Life on Earth, Life after Death. 4.95 (ISBN 0-931610-02-8); pap. 2.95 (ISBN 0-931610-01-X). World View Pr.

Chu, Po. Tracks in the Snowy Forests. 3rd ed. Shapiro, Sidney, et al, trs. from Chinese. (Illus.). 559p. 1978. pap. 7.95 (ISBN 0-917056-72-8, Pub. by Foreign Lang Pr China). Cheng & Tsui.

Chu, R. C., jt. auth. see Seely, John H.

Chu, Raymond W. & Saywell, William G. Career Patterns in the Ch'ing Dynasty: The Office of the Governor-General. (Michigan Monographs in Chinese Studies: No. 51). 225p. 1985. 15.00t (ISBN 0-89264-055-3); pap. 8.00t (ISBN 0-89264-056-1). U of Mich Ctr Chinese.

Chu, Show-chih Rai. Chinese for the English-Speaking Student: An Approach Through English Grammar, Vol. 1. LC 72-87136. 330p. 1973. 11.95 (ISBN 0-913973-00-9); pap. 9.95 (ISBN 0-913973-01-7); tapes 14.95 (ISBN 0-913973-02-5). Inst Sino-Amer.

--Chinese for the English-Speaking Student: An Approach Through English Grammar, Vol. 2. 424p. 1976. 12.95 (ISBN 0-913973-10-6); pap. 10.95 (ISBN 0-913973-03-3); tapes 19.95 (ISBN 0-913973-04-1). Inst Sino-Amer.

Chu, T. K., jt. auth. see Klemens, P. G.

Chu, T. K., ed. see AIP Conference, Princeton, 1970.

Ch'u, T'ung-tsu. Han Social Structure. Dull, Jack L., ed. LC 69-14206. (Han Dynasty China Ser.: Vol. 1). 570p. 1972. 30.00x (ISBN 0-295-95068-4). U of Wash Pr.

Chu, W. K., jt. auth. see Sherrill, W. A.

Chu, W. K., tr. see Sherril, W. A.

Chu, Wei-Kan, et al. Backscattering Spectroscopy. 1978. 65.00 (ISBN 0-12-173850-7). Acad Pr.

Chu, Wen-Djang. Moslem Rebellion in Northwest China, 1862-1878. (Central Asiatic Studies: No. 5). 1966. pap. text ed. 31.20x (ISBN 90-2790-017-5). Mouton.

Chu, Wen-Kaung, jt. auth. see Melyan, Gary G.

Chu, Wen Kuan. Tao & Longevity: Mind Body Transformation. LC 82-60164. 192p. (Orig.). 1984. pap. 7.95 (ISBN 0-87728-542-X). Weiser.

Chu, Wesley W. & Chen, Peter P. Centralized & Distributed Data Base Systems. (Tutorial Texts Ser.). 662p. 1979. 32.00 (ISBN 0-8186-0261-9, Q261). IEEE Comp Soc.

Chu, Wesley W., ed. Advances in Computer Communications & Networking. LC 79-55305. (Illus.). 1979. pap. 49.00x (ISBN 0-89006-049-5). Artech Hse.

Chu, Yaohan. High-Level Language Computer Architecture. 1975. 74.50 (ISBN 0-12-174150-8). Acad Pr.

--Software Blueprint & Examples. LC 81-48268. (Computer Science Ser.). (Illus.). 544p. 1982. 40.00x (ISBN 0-669-05329-5). Lexington Bks.

Chua, J. E. & Ling, S. C. The Management of Business. 2nd ed. 1983. 10.00 (ISBN 0-07-099205-3). McGraw.

Chua, Jose. Bok Pai Kung Fu. Date not set. pap. 5.95 (ISBN 0-86635-018-7). Koinonia Prods.

--The Eagle Claw of Choi Lay Fut. Date not set. pap. 5.95 (ISBN 0-86635-020-9). Koinonia Prods.

--Go Cho Kuen Kung Fu. Date not set. pap. 5.95 (ISBN 0-86635-017-9). Koinonia Prods.

--The Locking Hand of Praying Mantis. Date not set. pap. 5.95 (ISBN 0-86635-019-5). Koinonia Prods.

Chua, L. & Lin, P. Computer-Aided Analysis of Electronic Circuits: Algorithms & Computational Techniques. 1975. 41.95 (ISBN 0-13-165415-2). P-H.

Chua, Leon O. Introduction to Nonlinear Network Theory, 3 vols. LC 78-9734. 1978. Repr. of 1969 ed. Set. lib. bdg. 59.50 (ISBN 0-686-86256-2). Vol. 1, Foundations of Nonlinear Network Theory, 315 P (ISBN 0-88275-588-9). Vol. 2, Resistive Nonlinear Networks, 480 P (ISBN 0-88275-865-9). Vol. 3, Dynamic Nonlinear Networks, 438 P (ISBN 0-88275-866-7). Krieger.

Chua, Rebecca. The Newspaper Editor & Other Stories. (Writing in Asia Ser.). vi, 180p. (Orig.). 1982. pap. text ed. 5.50x (ISBN 9-971-64031-7, 00266). Heinemann Ed.

Chuan, Han-Sheng & Kraus, Richard A. Mid-Ch'ing Rice Markets & Trade: An Essay in Price History. LC 74-24937. (East Asian Monographs Ser: No. 54). 185p. (Orig.). 1975. pap. text ed. 11.00x (ISBN 0-674-57340-4). Harvard U Pr.

Chuan, Helen, ed. Medical-Surgical Nursing: Pretest Self-Assessment & Review. Allman, Margaret. LC 78-50598. (PreTest Self-Assessment & Review). (Illus.). 1978. pap. 13.95 (ISBN 0-07-051567-0). McGraw-Pretest.

Chuan, Tan Hoch. The Magic of Tan Hoch Chuan. 1977. 7.50 (ISBN 0-915926-21-0). Magic Ltd.

Chuan, Victor L. California Debt Collection Manual. LC 77-91934. 858p. 1978. 65.00 (ISBN 0-88124-053-2, BU-32220). Cal Cont Ed Bar.

Chuan, Victor L. & California Continuing Education of the Bar. California Breach of Contract Remedies: A Basic Guide for General Practitioners. LC 79-54861. ix, 235p. 1980. 50.00 (ISBN 0-88124-070-2). Cal Cont Ed Bar.

Chuang, Hain C. The Little Red Book & Current Chinese Language. LC 68-66865. (Studies in Chinese Communist Terminology Ser.: No. 13). pap. 20.00 (ISBN 0-317-09288-X, 2003418). Bks Demand UMI.

Chuang Hsin-Cheng. Evening Chats at Yenshan; or, the Case of Teng T'o. (Current Chinese Language Project: No. 14). 46p. 1970. pap. 2.00x (ISBN 0-912966-01-7). IEAS.

Chuang, S. H., ed. Animal Life & Nature in Singapore. 316p. 1973. 20.00x (ISBN 0-8214-0496-2, 82-93326, Pub. by Singapore U Pr). Ohio U Pr.

Chuang, Shen-lun. Investigation of Impact of Rigid & Elastic Bodies with Water. LC 70-139810. 124p. 1970. 25.00 (ISBN 0-403-04489-8). Scholarly.

Chuang, Y. H., et al. The Bangladesh Fertilizer Sector. McCune, D. L., intro. by. (Technical Bulletin Ser.: No. T-11). (Illus.). 61p. (Orig.). 1978. pap. 4.00 (ISBN 0-88090-010-5). Intl Fertilizer.

Chuang, Yao H. Fuentes de Informacion sobre el Mercado Internacional de Fertilizantes. Ralph McElroy Company, tr. (Reference Manual Ser.: RS-2). 51p. (Orig., Span.). 1980. pap. text ed. 4.00 (ISBN 0-88090-031-8). Intl Fertilizer.

--International Fertilizer Market Information Sources. Roth, B. N., ed. (IFDC Reference Manual Ser.: R-4). 55p. (Orig.). 1984. pap. text ed. 4.00 (ISBN 0-88090-049-0). Intl Fertilizer.

Chuang Tsu. Chuang Tsu - Inner Chapters. Gia-Fu Feng, ed. English, Jane, tr. (Giant Ser.). pap. 10.95 (ISBN 0-394-71990-5, V-990, Vin). Random.

Chuang Tzu. Chuang Tzu: Basic Writings. Watson, Burton, tr. from Chinese. LC 64-21079. (Oriental Classics Ser.). 148p. 1964. pap. 8.50x (ISBN 0-231-08606-7). Columbia U Pr.

--Chuang Tzu: Mystic, Moralist, & Social Reformer. 2nd rev. ed. Giles, Herbert A., tr. LC 70-38059. (BCL Ser.: No. II). Repr. of 1926 ed. 34.50 (ISBN 0-404-56915-3). AMS Pr.

--The Complete Works of Chuang Tzu. Watson, Burton, tr. LC 68-19000. (Translations from the Oriental Classics & Records of Civilization Ser.). 397p. 1968. 32.00x (ISBN 0-231-03147-5). Columbia U Pr.

Ch'Uan-K'Ai Leung, Kenneth, jt. auth. see Klein, Jeffery A.

Chuaqui, R. B. Axiomatic Set Theory of Classes: Impredicative Theories of Classes. (Mathematics Studies: Vol. 51). 388p. 1981. 59.75 (ISBN 0-444-86178-5, North-Holland). Elsevier.

Chuaqui, Rolando. Analysis, Geometry & Probability. (Lecture Notes in Pure & Applied Mathematics Ser.). 352p. 1985. 65.00 (ISBN 0-8247-7419-1). Dekker.

Chubak, Sadeq. Sadeq Chubak: An Anthology. Bagley, F. R., ed. LC 81-17970. (Modern Persian Literature Ser.). 1983. 35.00x (ISBN 0-88206-048-1). Caravan Bks.

Chubb, Basil. The Government & Politics of Ireland. 2nd ed. LC 81-50785. 416p. 1982. 35.00x (ISBN 0-8047-1115-1). Stanford U Pr.

Chubb, Bruce. Computers in Model Railroading. Hayden, Bob, ed. (Illus., Orig.). 1985. pap. price not set (ISBN 0-89024-077-9). Kalmbach.

Chubb, Bruce A. How to Operate Your Model Railroad. LC 77-74095. 1977. pap. 13.95 (ISBN 0-89024-528-2). Kalmbach.

Chubb, Edwin W. Masters of English Literature. facs. ed. LC 67-23194. (Essay Index Reprint Ser.). 1914. 19.50 (ISBN 0-8369-0303-X). Ayer Co Pubs.

--Sketches of Great Painters. facs. ed. LC 68-55843. (Essay Index Reprint Ser). 1915. 20.00 (ISBN 0-8369-0304-8). Ayer Co Pubs.

--Stories of Authors, British & American. facs. ed. LC 68-54338. (Essay Index Reprint Ser). 1926. 21.50 (ISBN 0-8369-0305-6). Ayer Co Pubs.

Chubb, Holly R., jt. auth. see Chubb, Michael.

Chubb, J. Faith Possesses Understanding: A Suggestion for a New Direction in Rational Theology. 200p. 1983. text ed. 16.25x (ISBN 0-391-02756-5, Pub. by Concept India). Humanities.

Chubb, John E. Interest Groups & the Bureaucracy: The Politics of Energy. LC 82-60106. xiv, 319p. 1983. 29.50x (ISBN 0-8047-1158-5). Stanford U Pr.

Chubb, John E. & Peterson, Paul E., eds. The New Direction in American Politics. 250p. 1985. 26.95 (ISBN 0-8157-1406-8); pap. 9.95 (ISBN 0-8157-1405-X). Brookings.

Chubb, Judith. Patronage, Power & Poverty in Southern Italy: A Tale of Two Cities. LC 82-1325. (Cambridge Studies in Modern Political Economies). (Illus.). 320p. 1983. 42.50 (ISBN 0-521-23637-1). Cambridge U Pr.

Chubb, L. J. Geology of Galapagos, Cocos & Easter Islands. (BMB Ser.). Repr. of 1933 ed. 11.00 (ISBN 0-527-02216-0). Kraus Repr.

--Geology of the Marquesas Islands. (BMB Ser.). Repr. of 1930 ed. 12.00 (ISBN 0-527-02174-1). Kraus Repr.

Chubb, Michael & Chubb, Holly R. One Third of Our Time? An Introduction to Recreation Behavior & Resources. LC 80-25131. 742p. 1981. text ed. 36.45 (ISBN 0-471-15637-X). Wiley.

Chubb, Thomas. Comparative Excellence & Obligation of Moral & Positive Duties, 1731. Wellek, Rene, ed. LC 75-11205. (British Philosophers & Theologians of the 17th & 18th Centuries Ser.). 1978. lib. bdg. 51.00 (ISBN 0-8240-1760-9). Garland Pub.

Chubb, Thomas C. The Life of Giovanni Boccaccio. 1979. Repr. of 1930 ed. lib. bdg. 40.00 (ISBN 0-8492-3967-2). R West.

--White God & Other Poems. LC 76-144712. (Yale Ser. of Younger Poets: No. 5). Repr. of 1920 ed. 11.00 (ISBN 0-404-53805-3). AMS Pr.

--The White God & Other Poems. 1920. pap. 9.50x (ISBN 0-686-51325-8). Elliots Bks.

Chubb, Thomas C., tr. Sonnets of a Handsome & Well-Mannered Rogue: Translations from Cecco Angiolieri of Siena. LC 73-114193. xii, 81p. 1970. 13.00 (ISBN 0-208-01034-3, Archon). Shoe String.

Chubin, Barry. The Feet of a Snake. 1984. 14.95 (ISBN 0-87795-571-9). Arbor Hse.

Chubin, Daryl, ed. Interdisciplinarity. Date not set. price not set. Lomond.

Chubin, Daryl E. Sociology of Sciences: An Annotated Bibliography on Invisible Colleges, 1972-1981. LC 82-48773. 216p. 1983. lib. bdg. 33.00 (ISBN 0-8240-9223-6). Garland Pub.

Chubin, Daryl E., jt. auth. see Studer, Kenneth E.

Chubin, Shahram, ed. Domestic Political Factors. LC 81-572. (Security in the Persian Gulf Ser.: Vol. 1). 104p. 1981. pap. text ed. 12.50x (ISBN 0-86598-044-6). Allanheld.

--The Role of Outside Powers. LC 80-28314. (Security in the Persian Gulf Ser.: Vol. 4). 180p. 1982. pap. 12.50x (ISBN 0-86598-047-0). Allanheld.

Ch'u Chai & Chai, Winberg. Confucianism. LC 73-3977. 1974. pap. text ed. 5.50 (ISBN 0-8120-0303-9). Barron.

Chu-Chang, Mae, ed. Asian-Pacific-American Perspectives in Bilingual Education. LC 82-10764. (Bilingual Education Ser.). 1983. pap. text ed. 17.95x (ISBN 0-8077-2723-7). Tchrs Coll.

Chu Ch'eng. Notes on Products of the Eastern Hills of Lake Tungting. (National Peking University & Chinese Assn. for Folklore, Folklore & Folkliterature Ser.: No. 130). (Chinese.). 16.00x (ISBN 0-89986-204-7). Oriental Bk Store.

Chu-Chi, W. English-Chinese Dictionary of Physical Terms. 218p. (Eng. & Chinese.). 1973. leatherette 25.00 (ISBN 0-686-92350-2, M-9258). French & Eur.

Chu Chien-Fan. Studies in Chinese Proverbs. (Asian Folklore & Social Life Monograph: No. 5). (Chinese.). 1972. 14.00 (ISBN 0-89986-008-7). Oriental Bk Store.

Chudacoff, Edward, jt. auth. see Berry, Wallace.

Chudacoff, Howard P. The Evolution of American Urban Society. 2nd ed. (Illus.). 256p. 1981. pap. text ed. 19.95 (ISBN 0-13-293605-4). P-H.

Chudakhov, Grigori. Pioneers of Soviet Photography: 1917-1942. LC 83-50103. (Illus.). 1983. 40.00f (ISBN 0-500-54095-0). Thames Hudson.

Chudakov, A. P. Chekhov's Poetics. Cruise, Edwina & Dragt, Donald, trs. from Rus. 1983. 32.50 (ISBN 0-88233-780-7); pap. 7.50 cancelled (ISBN 0-88233-781-5). Ardis Pubs.

Chudinov, S. M., jt. auth. see Brandt, N. B.

Chu Djang, tr. see Yang Chiang.

Chudnovsky, D. V. & Chudnovsky, G. V. The Riemann Problem: Complete Integrability & Arithmetic Applications Proceedings. (Lecture Notes In Mathematics: Vol. 925). 373p. 1982. pap. 22.00 (ISBN 0-387-11483-1). Springer-Verlag.

Chudnovsky, D. V., et al. Number Theory: A Seminar held at the Graduate School & University Center of the City University of N.Y. 1982. (Lecture Notes in Mathematics Ser.: Vol. 1052). v, 309p. 1984. 18.00 (ISBN 0-387-12909-X). Springer-Verlag.

Chudnovsky, Daniel, et al. Capital Goods Production in the Third World: An Economic Study of Technology Acquisition. LC 83-11059. 236p. 1984. 27.50 (ISBN 0-312-11927-5). St Martin.

Chudnovsky, G. V. Contributions to the Theory of Transcendental Numbers. LC 83-15728. (Mathematical Surveys Monographs Ser.: No. 19). 450p. 1984. 80.00 (ISBN 0-8218-1500-8). Am Math.

Chudnovsky, G. V., jt. auth. see Chudnovsky, D. V.

Chudoba, Bohdan. Spain & the Empire: 1519-1643. LC 71-84177. 1969. Repr. of 1952 ed. lib. bdg. 23.00x (ISBN 0-374-91559-8). Octagon.

Chudoba, F. Short History of Czech Literature. 1924. 22.00 (ISBN 0-527-17000-3). Kraus Repr.

Chudodeyev, Y. V., et al. Soviet Volunteers in China, Nineteen Twenty-Five to Nineteen Forty-Five. 320p. 1980. 8.95 (ISBN 0-8285-1932-3, Pub. by Progress Pubs USSR). Imported Pubns.

Chudy, Harry T. The Complete Guide to Automotive Refinishing. (Illus.). 464p. 1982. reference 24.95 (ISBN 0-13-160440-6). P-H.

Chue, Arthur & Chu, Grace. Oriental Antiques & Collectibles, a Guide. (Illus.). 288p. 1973. 10.95 (ISBN 0-517-50098-1). Crown.

Chuen-Yen, Chow. An Introduction to Computational Fluid Mechanics. Rev. ed. (Illus.). 400p. 1983. Repr. text ed. 35.00 (ISBN 0-9612302-0-7). Seminole Pub Co.

Chugh, Y. P., intro. by. State-of-the-Art of Ground Control in Longwall Mining & Mining Subsidence. LC 82-71991. (Illus.). 271p. (Orig.). 1982. pap. text ed. 38.00x (ISBN 0-89520-400-2, 400-2). Soc Mining Eng.

Chugh, Yoginder P., ed. Ground Control in Room & Pillar Mining. LC 82-74112. (Illus.). 157p. 1983. 22.00 (ISBN 0-89520-407-X). Soc Mining Eng.

Chu Hsi. The Philosophy of Human Nature. Bruce, J. Percy, tr. LC 73-38057. (BCL Ser.: No. II). Repr. of 1922 ed. 27.50 (ISBN 0-404-56913-7). AMS Pr.

Chui, C. K., et al, eds. Approximation Theory IV: Symposium. 1984. 55.00 (ISBN 0-12-174580-5). Acad Pr.

Chui, Charles K., jt. auth. see Allen, G. D.

Chuikov, V. The End of the Third Reich. 273p. 1978. 6.95 (ISBN 0-8285-0453-9, Pub. by Progress Pubs USSR). Imported Pubns.

Chuilleanain, Eilean N. The Second Voyage. 1977. pap. 4.25 (ISBN 0-916390-05-5). Wake Forest.

Chuilleanain, Eilean N., ed. & intro. by see Riain, Noirin N., et al.

Chu-Jeng Chiu, Ray. Myocardial Protection in Regional & Global Ischemia, Vol. 2. Horrobin, D. F., ed. (Annual Research Reviews Ser.). 296p. 1984. 44.00 (ISBN 0-88831-121-4). Eden Pr.

Chujoy, Anatole. The New York City Ballet. (Series in Dance Ser.). (Illus.). xxviii, 382p. 1981. Repr. of 1953 ed. lib. bdg. 35.00 (ISBN 0-306-76035-5). Da Capo.

Chujoy, Anatole, et al, trs. see Vaganova, Agrippina.

Chukayne, Edward C., jt. auth. see Bush, Lee O.

Chukerman, Amy & Marks, Mitchell, eds. Proceedings: Papers from the 19th Regional Meeting. LC 76-27943. 407p. 1983. pap. 8.00 (ISBN 0-914203-19-3). Chicago Ling.

Chu-Kia Wang & Salmon, Charles G. Introductory Structural Analysis. (Illus.). 656p. 1983. 37.95 (ISBN 0-13-501569-3). P-H.

Chukovski, Kornei. Viva el Agua y el Jabon. (Illus.). 18p. (Span.). 1974. pap. 1.49 (ISBN 0-8285-1309-0, Pub. by Progress Pubs USSR). Imported Pubns.

Chukovsky, K. Aymeduele. (Illus.). 30p. (Span.). 1975. pap. 1.49 (ISBN 0-8285-1280-9, Pub. by Progress Pubs USSR). Imported Pubns.

--Cock-the-Roach. 18p. 1981. pap. 1.60 (ISBN 0-8285-2217-0, Pub. by Progress Pubs USSR). Imported Pubns.

--Doctor Powderpill. 16p. 1978. pap. 1.99 (ISBN 0-8285-1131-4, Pub. by Progress Pubs USSR). Imported Pubns.

--The Muddle. 8p. 1976. pap. 0.99 (ISBN 0-8285-1209-4, Pub. by Progress Pubs USSR). Imported Pubns.

--Stolen Sun. 18p. 1983. pap. 3.95 (ISBN 0-8285-2953-1, Pub. by Malysh Pubs USSR). Imported Pubns.

--Telephone. 1982. pap. 4.00 (ISBN 0-8285-2245-6, Pub. by Malysh Pubs USSR). Imported Pubns.

--The Wonder Tales. 50p. 1973. 2.95 (ISBN 0-8285-1276-0, Pub. by Progress Pubs USSR). Imported Pubns.

Chukovsky, Kornei. Alexander Blok As Man & Poet. Burgin & O'Connor, trs. from Rus. 1982. 22.00 (ISBN 0-88233-491-3). Ardis Pubs.

--Alexander Blok As Man & Poet. Burgin, Diana, ed. O'Connor, Katherine, tr. LC 82-1809. 1982. 22.00 (ISBN 0-88233-485-9). Ardis Pubs.

--The Art of Translation: Kornei Chukovsky's "A High Art". Leighton, Lauren G., ed. LC 83-6457. 328p. 1984. 19.95x (ISBN 0-87049-405-8). U of Tenn Pr.

--Chekhov, the Man. LC 74-6384. (Studies in Russian Literature & Life, No. 100). 1974. lib. bdg. 49.95x (ISBN 0-8383-1867-3). Haskell.

--From Two to Five. Morton, Miriam, ed. & tr. LC 63-19028. (YA) (gr. 7 up). 1963. pap. 5.95 (ISBN 0-520-00238-5, CAL119). U of Cal Pr.

--The Poet & the Hangman: Nekrasov & Muravyov. Rotsel, R. W., tr. from Russian. (Ardis Essay Ser.: No. 5). 1977. 10.00 (ISBN 0-88233-217-1); pap. 2.95 (ISBN 0-88233-218-X). Ardis Pubs.

--Poet I Palach (Nekrasov I Murav'ev) (Rus.). 1976. 10.00 (ISBN 0-88233-258-9); pap. 3.00 (ISBN 0-88233-259-7). Ardis Pubs.

Chuks-Orji, Ogonna. Names from Africa. 1972. pap. 8.95 (ISBN 0-87485-046-0). Johnson Chi.

Chukumba, Stephen U. The Big Powers Against Ethiopia. 1977. pap. text ed. 20.50 (ISBN 0-8191-0230-X). U Pr of Amer.

Chukuocha, Bessie. Accounting Methods for Non-Profit Organizations. 1981. 6.95 (ISBN 0-8062-1650-6). Carlton.

Chul Myung, Hyo see Myung, Hyo C.

Chuman, Frank. Bamboo People. 386p. 1976. pap. 9.25 (ISBN 0-89163-013-9). Japanese Am Citizens.

Chumbley, Lee C. Ophthalmology in Internal Medicine. (Illus.). 288p. 1981. 34.00 (ISBN 0-7216-2578-9). Saunders.

Chun, Bong D., et al. Traditional Korean Legal Attitudes. (Korean Research Monographs: No. 2). 101p. 1980. pap. 8.00x (ISBN 0-912966-30-0). IEAS.

Chun, Ki-Taek, et al. Measures for Psychological Assessment: A Guide to 3,000 Original Sources & Their Applications. LC 74-620127. 688p. 1975. 30.00x (ISBN 0-87944-168-2). Inst Soc Res.

Chun, Patrick. Cardiopulmonary Technology Examination Review Book, Vol. 1. 2nd ed. 1980. pap. 16.00 (ISBN 0-87488-473-X). Med Exam.

--Textbook Study Guide: Cardiology. 1984. pap. text ed. write for info. (ISBN 0-87488-742-9). Med Exam.

Chun, Patrick K. MERB: Cardiovascular Diseases, Vol. 28. 2nd ed. 1984. pap. text ed. write for info. (ISBN 0-87488-209-5). Med Exam.

Chun, R. Moo Duk Kwan. 9.50x (ISBN 0-685-63769-7). Wehman.

Chun, Richard. Advancing in Tae Kwon Do. LC 82-47519. (Illus.). 352p. 1983. 34.62i (ISBN 0-06-015029-7, HarpT). Har-Row.

--Moo Duk Kwan, Vol. II. LC 81-186107. (Series 422). (Illus.). 256p. (Orig.). 1983. pap. 9.95 (ISBN 0-89750-085-7, 422). Ohara Pubns.

--Moo Duk Kwan Tae Kwon Do, Korean Art of Self-Defense. Johnson, Gilbert & Adachi, Geraldine, eds. LC 75-3784. (Ser. 120). (Illus.). 1975. pap. text ed. 9.50 (ISBN 0-89750-015-6). Ohara Pubns.

--Tae Kwon-Do. 39.95x (ISBN 0-685-70709-1). Wehman.

--Tae Kwon Do: The Korean Martial Art & National Sport. LC 74-1799. (Illus.). 544p. 1976. 38.41i (ISBN 0-06-010779-0, HarpT). Har-Row.

Chunder, M. Nelson. I Hate You! An Angry Man's Guide to Revenge. (Illus.). 182p. 1983. 12.95 (ISBN 0-87364-278-3). Paladin Pr.

--Mad As Hell: A Master Tome of Revengemanship. 168p. (Orig.). 1984. 12.95 (ISBN 0-87364-295-3). Paladin Pr.

Chung. Fundamentals of Electrocardiography. (Illus.). 352p. 1984. pap. text ed. 25.00 (ISBN 0-8391-1872-4, 19143). Univ Park.

--Manual of Artificial Cardiac Pacing. (Illus.). 176p. 1983. 25.00 (ISBN 0-8391-1877-5, 19151). Univ Park.

--Office Electrocardiography. (Illus.). 384p. 1984. 30.00 (ISBN 0-8391-1878-3, 19178). Univ Park.

Chung, C. S. Practical Organic Chemistry. (Orig.). 1973. pap. text ed. 3.95x (ISBN 0-686-71781-3, 00127). Heinemann Ed.

Chung, Catherine, ed. Directory of Periodicals Online: Indexed, Absracted & Full Text, Vol. 1: News, Law & Business. 524p. 1985. pap. 90.00 (ISBN 0-932929-00-1). Fed Doc Retrieval.

--Directory of Periodicals Online: Indexed, Abstracted & Full-Text, Vol. 2: Medicine & Social Science, Vol. 2. 1986. pap. price not set (ISBN 0-932929-01-X). Fed Doc Retrieval.

Chung, Chin O. Pyongyang Between Peking & Moscow: North Korea's Involvement in the Sino-Soviet Dispute, 1958-1975. LC 76-44261. 240p. 1978. 17.95 (ISBN 0-8173-4728-3). U of Ala Pr.

Chung, Chin S. & Steinhoff, Patricia G. The Effects of Induced Abortion on Subsequent Reproductive Function & Pregnancy Outcome: Hawaii. LC 83-11536. (Paper Series of the East-West Population Institute: No. 86). xii, 144p. 1983. pap. text ed. 3.00 (ISBN 0-86638-046-9). E W Center HI.

Chung, Chin S., jt. ed. see Morton, Newton E.

Chung, Chong-Wook. Maoism & Development: The Politics of Industrial Management in China. (The Institute of Social Sciences International Studies Ser.: No. 1). 219p. 1980. text ed. 18.00x (ISBN 0-8248-0939-4). UH Pr.

Chung, David. Anesthesia in Patients with Ischemic Heart Disease. (Current Topics in Anesthesia Ser.: No. 6). 192p. 1982. text ed. 34.50 (ISBN 0-7131-4407-6). E Arnold.

Chung, David C. & Lamb, Arthur M. Essentials of Anesthesiology. (A Volume in the Saunders Blue Book Ser.). (Illus.). 256p. 1983. pap. 15.95 spiral bound (ISBN 0-7216-1042-0). Saunders.

Chung, E. K. Ambulatory Electrocardiography: Holter Monitor Electrocardiography. (Illus.). 1979. 34.00 (ISBN 0-387-90360-7). Springer-Verlag.

--Cardiovascular Emergencies: Current Therapy. (Illus.). x, 250p. 1985. 72.00 (ISBN 3-8055-3679-8). S Karger.

--Complex Arrhythmias: Self Assessment. (Illus.). xii, 308p. 1985. 35.00 (ISBN 3-8055-3639-9). S Karger.

Chung, Edward K. Artificial Cardiac Pacing. 2nd ed. (Illus.). 342p. 1983. lib. bdg. 51.00 (ISBN 0-683-01572-9). Williams & Wilkins.

--A Clinical Manual of Cardiovascular Medicine. 797p. 1983. pap. 22.50x (ISBN 0-8385-1138-4). ACC.

--Electrocardiography: Practical Applications with Vectorial Principles. 3rd ed. (Illus.). 784p. 1985. 75.00 (ISBN 0-8385-2167-3). ACC.

--Manual of Cardiac Arrhythmias. (Illus.). 350p. 1985. text ed. write for info. (ISBN 0-914316-44-3). Yorke Med.

--One Heart...One Life: A Healthy Heart Handbook. (Illus.). 379p. 1982. 18.95 (ISBN 0-13-634642-1); pap. 8.95 (ISBN 0-13-634634-0). P-H.

--Quick Reference to Cardiovascular Diseases. 2nd ed. (Illus.). 672p. 1982. text ed. 39.50 (ISBN 0-397-50482-9, 65-06232, Lippincott Medical). Lippincott.

Chung, Edward K. & Chung, Lisa S. Introduction to Clinical Cardiology. (Karger Continuing Education Series: Vol. 4). (Illus.). xiv, 546p. 1983. 41.75 (ISBN 3-8055-2997-X). S Karger.

Chung, Edward K., ed. Cardiac Emergency Care. 3rd ed. LC 84-27844. (Illus.). 415p. 1985. text ed. write for info. (ISBN 0-8121-0978-3). Lea & Febiger.

--Non-Invasive Cardiac Diagnosis. LC 75-38915. (Illus.). 319p. 1976. text ed. 18.00 (ISBN 0-8121-0541-9). Lea & Febiger.

Chung, Henry. Henry Chung's Hunan Style Chinese Cookbook. (Illus.). 1978. 12.95 (ISBN 0-517-53325-1, Harmony). Crown.

--Oriental Policy of the United States. LC 70-111737. (American Imperialism: Viewpoints of United States Foreign Policy, 1898-1941). 1970. Repr. of 1919 ed. 20.00 (ISBN 0-405-02008-2). Ayer Co Pubs.

Chung, J. S., ed. Offshore Mechanics-Artic Engineering-Deepsea Systems Symposium, First: Proceedings, 2 Vols, Vol. 2. 289p. 1982. 45.00 (I00148). ASME.

Chung, J. S. & Lunardini, V. J., eds. Offshore Mechanics & Arctic Engineering Symposium, 2nd International: Proceedings. 812p. 1983. pap. text ed. 100.00 (ISBN 0-317-02642-9, I00156). ASME.

Chung, K. L. Elementary Probability Theory with Stochastic Processes. (Undergraduate Texts in Mathematics Ser.). (Illus.). 1979. 19.80 (ISBN 0-387-90362-3). Springer-Verlag.

--Lectures from Markov Processes to Brownian Motion. (Grundlehren der Mathematischen Wissenschaften). (Illus.). 256p. 1982. 39.50 (ISBN 0-387-90618-5). Springer-Verlag.

--Lectures on Boundary Theory for Markov Chains. (Annals of Mathematics Studies: No. 65). 1970. 15.50 (ISBN 0-691-08075-5). Princeton U Pr.

Chung, K. L. & Williams, Ruth. An Introduction to Stochastic Integration. (Progress in Probability & Statistics Ser.: Vol. 4). 217p. 1983. text ed. 19.95 (ISBN 0-8176-3117-8). Birkhauser.

Chung, Kae H. & Megginson, Leon C. Organizational Behavior: Developing Managerial Skills. 560p. 1981. text ed. 23.50 scp (ISBN 0-06-041299-2, HarpC); instructor's manual avail. (ISBN 0-06-361217-8). Har-Row.

Chung, Kae H., ed. Academy of Management 1981: Proceedings. 1981. 12.00 (ISBN 0-915350-20-3). Acad of Mgmt.

--Academy of Management 1982: Proceedings. 12.00 (ISBN 0-686-97952-4). Acad of Mgmt.

Chung, Kai L. A Course in Probability Theory. 2nd ed. (Probability & Mathematical Statistics: A Series of Monographs & Textbooks). 1974. 25.00i (ISBN 0-12-174650-X). Acad Pr.

Chung Kai Lai. Markov Chains with Stationary Transition Probabilities. 2nd ed. (Die Grundlehren der Mathematischen Wissenschaten: Vol. 104). 1967. 44.00 (ISBN 0-387-03822-1). Springer-Verlag.

Chung, Lisa S., jt. auth. see Chung, Edward K.

Chung, Norman H., jt. auth. see Rogers, David.

Chung, S. U. & Lindenbaum, S. J., eds. Experimental Meson Spectroscopy 1980: Sixth International Conference, Brookhaven. LC 80-71123. (AIP Conference Proceedings: No. 67). 608p. 1981. lib. bdg. 37.50 (ISBN 0-88318-166-5). Am Inst Physics.

Chung, Sandra. Case Marking & Grammatical Relations in Polynesian. LC 78-56993. 415p. 1978. text ed. 22.50x (ISBN 0-292-71051-8). U of Tex Pr.

Chung, Stanley M., ed. Hip Disorders in Infants & Children. LC 81-1549. (Illus.). 396p. 1981. text ed. 40.00 (ISBN 0-8121-0706-3). Lea & Febiger.

Chung, Sun-ai. Flower Arrangement of Korea: Its Beauty & Spirit. LC 84-80496. (Illus.). 111p. 1984. 19.50x (ISBN 0-930878-36-1). Hollym Intl.

Chung, T. J. & Karr, Gerald R. Development in Theoretical & Applied Mechanics, Vol. XI. 638p. 1982. 50.00 (ISBN 0-942166-00-0). U AL Dept Mech Eng.

Chung, Wah Nan. The Art of Chinese Gardens. (Illus.). 254p. 1983. 40.00 (ISBN 0-295-96086-8). U of Wash Pr.

Chung, William K., jt. auth. see Denison, Edward F.

Chung Yung. The Conduct of Life; or, the Universal Order of Confucius. lib. bdg. 79.95 (ISBN 0-87968-497-6). Krishna Pr.

Chungara, Domatila De see De Chungara, Domitila B. & Viezzer, Moema.

Chung Ching-Wen. Essays on Folk Literature. (Folklore Series of National Sun Yat-Sen University: No. 3). (Chinese.). 16.00x (ISBN 0-89986-073-7). Oriental Bk Store.

--Essays on Folk Literature. (National Peking University & Chinese Assn. for Folklore, Folklore & Folk Literature Ser.: No. 16). (Chinese.). 16.00x (ISBN 0-89986-116-4). Oriental Bk Store.

--Folksongs of the Tanka of Canton. (National Peking University & Chinese Assn. for Folklore, Folklore & Folkliterature Ser.: No. 3). (Chinese.). 16.00x (ISBN 0-89986-103-2). Oriental Bk Store.

--The Golden Frog. Lin Lan, ed. (Tales from the Orient Ser.: No. 6). (Chinese.). 14.00x (ISBN 0-89986-230-6). Oriental Bk Store.

--Legends About Relics & Living Things. Lin Lan, ed. (Tales from the Orient Ser.: No. 5). (Chinese.). 15.00x (ISBN 0-89986-229-2). Oriental Bk Store.

--Myths & Legends in the Ch'u Tz'u. (Folklore Series of National Sun Yat-Sen University: No. 11). (Chinese.). 16.00x (ISBN 0-89986-081-8). Oriental Bk Store.

--Stories About Clever Women. Lin Lan, ed. (Tales from the Orient Ser.: No. 25). (Chinese.). 15.00x (ISBN 0-89986-249-7). Oriental Bk Store.

--Tribal Love-Songs from Canton. (Folklore Series of National Sun Yat-Sen University: No. 16). (Chinese.). 16.00x (ISBN 0-89986-085-0). Oriental Bk Store.

Chung Chong-wha, ed. Modern Far Eastern Stories. (Writing in Asia Ser.). 1978. pap. text ed. 7.50x (ISBN 0-686-60446-6, 00205). Heinemann Ed.

Chungen, Liu, ed. Mount Lushan. (Famous Chinese Mountains Ser.). (Illus.). 119p. 1983. pap. 7.95 (ISBN 0-8351-1065-6). China Bks.

Chung-Hui, Wang, tr. see Chiang Kai-Shek.

Chung-hyun, Kim, jt. auth. see Kichang, Kim.

Chung-Kuo Kung Chan Tang. Proceedings of the National Congress of the Communist of China, 8th, 3 vols. LC 79-38061. Repr. of 1956 ed. Set. 67.50 (ISBN 0-404-56917-X). AMS Pr.

Chung Kuo-Lou. Stories About Scholars. Lin Lan, ed. (Tales from the Orient Ser.: No. 22). (Chinese.). 15.00x (ISBN 0-89986-246-2). Oriental Bk Store.

Chung-Liang Huang, Al, jt. auth. see Watts, Alan.

Chung-Lin, Yu, illus. The Flowers & Birds Paintings. (Illus.). 219p. 1978. pap. 35.00 (ISBN 0-917056-27-2, Pub. by Art Bk Taiwan). Cheng & Tsui.

Chung Ling, jt. tr. see Rexroth, Kenneth.

Chung-shil, Shim. Korean Recipes. (Illus.). 80p. (Orig.). 1984. pap. 10.00 (ISBN 0-8048-1479-1, Pub. by Seoul Intl Publishing House). C E Tuttle.

Chung-Yuan, Chang. Original Teachings of Cha'an Buddhism. pap. 9.95 (ISBN 0-394-62417-3, V-333, Vin). Random.

Chun-hu Chang, tr. see Lu Yu.

Chun-Ie, Fang, jt. auth. see Editorial Committee Staff.

Chun Koh, Hesung, ed. Korean & Japanese Women: An Analytic Bibliographical Guide. LC 81-80305. (Illus.). 912p. 1982. lib. bdg. 75.00 (ISBN 0-313-23387-X, KJW). Greenwood.

Chunn, Calvin E. Not by Bread Alone. (Illus.). 86p. (Orig.). 1981. pap. 5.00 (ISBN 0-9606828-1-3). SDWA.

Chunn, Jay, II, et al, eds. Mental Health & People of Color: Curriculum Development & Change. LC 83-295. (Illus.). 688p. 1982. 27.50 (ISBN 0-88258-097-3). Howard U Pr.

Chun-shu Chang. Premodern China: A Bibliographical Introduction. (Michigan Monographs in Chinese Studies: No. 11). 183p. 1971. pap. 6.00 (ISBN 0-89264-011-1). U of Mich Ctr Chinese.

Chupack, Henry. Roger Williams. (United States Authors Ser.). 14.50 (ISBN 0-8057-0808-1, Twayne). G K Hall.

Chupco, Lee & Coachman, Ward. Creek (Muscogee) New Testament Concordance. 167p. 1982. spiral bdg. 12.50x (ISBN 0-940392-10-0). Indian U Pr OK.

Chupp, Charles S. & Sherf, Arden F. Vegetable Diseases & Their Control. (Illus.). 693p. 1960. 37.50x (ISBN 0-471-06807-1, Pub. by Wiley-Interscience). Wiley.

Chupp, E. L. Gamma-Ray Astronomy: Nuclear Transition Region. LC 76-21711. (Geophysics & Astrophysics Monographs: No. 14). 1976. lib. bdg. 55.00 (ISBN 90-277-0695-6, Pub. by Reidel Holland); pap. 26.00 (ISBN 90-277-0696-4, Pub. by Reidel Holland). Kluwer Academic.

Chupungco, Anscar J. Cultural Adaptation of the Liturgy. 117p. (Orig.). 1982. pap. 4.95 (ISBN 0-8091-2452-1). Paulist Pr.

Churacek, Jaroslov, ed. see Gasparic, Jiri.

Churba, Joseph. The American Retreat: The Reagan Foreign & Defense Policy. 260p. 1984. 18.95 (ISBN 0-89526-604-0). Regnery-Gateway.

Church & Schatz. Office Systems & Careers: A Resource for Administrative Assistants. 780p. 1981. text ed. 30.00 (ISBN 0-205-07134-1, 087134-6). Allyn.

Church, A. Hamilton. The Proper Distribution of Expense Burden. Chandler, Alfred D., ed. LC 79-7538. (History of Management Thought & Practice Ser.). 1980. Repr. of 1908 ed. lib. bdg. 12.00x (ISBN 0-405-12323-X). Ayer Co Pubs.

Church Administration Department. Illustrating the Gospel of Matthew. LC 81-68044. 1982. pap. 5.25 (ISBN 0-8054-2243-9). Broadman.

Church, Albert. Taxation of Nonrenewable Resources. LC 80-8784. (Illus.). 352p. 1981. 36.00 (ISBN 0-669-04367-2). Lexington Bks.

Church, Albert M. Conflicts over Resource Ownership: The Use of Public Policy by Private Interests. LC 82-47942. (Lincoln Institute of Land Policy Bk.). 256p. 1982. 27.50x (ISBN 0-669-05712-6). Lexington Bks.

Church, Albert M. & Gustafson, Robert H. Statistics & Computers in the Appraisal Process. 160p. 1976. pap. 15.00 (ISBN 0-88329-006-5). Intl Assess.

Church, Albert M., ed. Non-Renewable Resource Taxation in the Western States. (Monograph: No. 77-2). 1977. pap. text ed. 10.00 (ISBN 0-686-20037-3). Lincoln Inst Land.

Church, Alexander H. Production Factors in Cost Accounting & Works Management. LC 75-18461. (History of Accounting Ser.). (Illus.). 1976. Repr. of 1910 ed. 16.00x (ISBN 0-405-07545-6). Ayer Co Pubs.

--The Science & Practice of Management. LC 77-17901. (Management History Ser.: No. 24). 555p. Repr. of 1914 ed. 32.50 (ISBN 0-87960-037-3). Hive Pub.

Church, Alfred C. The Laureate's Country. 1891. Repr. 50.00 (ISBN 0-8274-2805-7). R West.

Church, Alfred J. Callias: A Tale of the Fall of Athens. Repr. of 1891 ed. 15.00 (ISBN 0-686-20087-X). Quality Lib.

--Callias: A Tale of the Fall of Athens. 1891. 10.00 (ISBN 0-8274-3939-3). R West.

--Lucius, Adventures of a Roman Boy. LC 60-16706. (gr. 7-11). 10.00x (ISBN 0-8196-0108-X). Biblo.

--Memories of Men & Books. 1973. Repr. of 1908 ed. 20.00 (ISBN 0-8274-1539-7). R West.

--Roman Life in the Days of Cicero. LC 61-24994. (gr. 7-11). 12.00x (ISBN 0-8196-0105-5). Biblo.

--Stories from the Greek Comedians Aristophanes, Philemon, Piphilus, Menander, Apollodorus. 1893. 17.50 (ISBN 0-8274-3940-7). R West.

--Stories from the Greek Tragedians. 1883. 17.50 (ISBN 0-8274-3941-5). R West.

--Stories of the Magicians. Repr. of 1887 ed. 25.00 (ISBN 0-89987-109-7). Darby Bks.

--The Story of Early Britain. 375p. 1980. Repr. lib. bdg. 30.00 (ISBN 0-8495-0788-X). Arden Lib.

--The Story of the Persian War: From Herodotus. 1979. Repr. of 1881 ed. lib. bdg. 20.00 (ISBN 0-8482-7577-2). Norwood Edns.

Church, Alfred J. & Gilman, Arthur. Carthage: Or, the Empire of Africa. facsimile ed. LC 72-165620. (Select Bibliographies Reprint Ser). Repr. of 1886 ed. 27.50 (ISBN 0-8369-5927-2). Ayer Co Pubs.

Church, Alfred S. Early Britain. LC 73-16020. 1889. lib. bdg. 20.00 (ISBN 0-8414-3498-0). Folcroft.

Church, Alonzo. Calculi of Lambda Conversion. (Annals of Math). 1941. pap. 10.00 (ISBN 0-527-02722-7). Kraus Repr.

--Introduction to Mathematical Logic. (Mathematical Ser.: Vol. 17). 1956. 40.00 (ISBN 0-691-07984-6). Princeton U Pr.

--Introduction to Mathematical Logic, Pt. 1. (Annals of Math). 1944. 12.00 (ISBN 0-527-02729-4). Kraus Repr.

Church, Archibald G. East Africa, a New Dominion: A Crucial Experiment in Tropical Development & Its Significance to the British Empire. LC 79-137229. Repr. of 1927 ed. cancelled (ISBN 0-8371-3646-6, CND&, Pub. by Negro U Pr). Greenwood.

Church, Austin H. Centrifugal Pumps & Blowers. (Illus.). 320p. 1972. Repr. of 1944 ed. text ed. 20.50 (ISBN 0-88275-008-9). Krieger.

--Mechanical Vibrations. 2nd ed. LC 63-14755. Repr. of 1963 ed. 85.90 (ISBN 0-8357-9933-6, 2013179). Bks Demand UMI.

Church, Benjamin. The History of King Philip's War. LC 72-78674. 1867. 19.00 (ISBN 0-403-01937-0). Somerset Pub.

Church, Benjamin, jt. auth. see Walker, Jeffrey B.

Church, Carol B. Billie Jean King: Queen of the Courts. Bender, David L. & Mc Cuen, Gary E., eds. (Focus on Famous Women Ser.). (Illus.). (gr. 3-9). 1976. 8.95 (ISBN 0-912616-41-5); read-along cassette 9.95 (ISBN 0-89908-240-8). Greenhaven.

--Carol Burnett: Star of Comedy. Bender, David L. & Mc Cuen, Gary E., eds. (Focus on Famous Women Ser.). (Illus.). (gr. 3-9). 1976. 8.95 (ISBN 0-912616-42-3); read-along cassette 9.95 (ISBN 0-89908-241-6). Greenhaven.

--Dorothy Day: Friend of the Poor. Bender, David L. & Mc Cuen, Gary E., eds. (Focus on Famous Women Ser.). (Illus.). (gr. 3-9). 1976. 8.95 (ISBN 0-912616-45-8); read-along cassette 9.95 (ISBN 0-89908-244-0). Greenhaven.

--Indira Gandhi: Rose of India. Bender, David L. & McCuen, Gary E., eds. (Focus on Famous Women Ser.). (gr. 3-9). 1976. 8.95 (ISBN 0-912616-43-1); read-along cassette 9.95 (ISBN 0-89908-242-4). Greenhaven.

--Margaret Mead: Student of the Global Village. Bender, David L. & McCuen, Gary E., eds. (Focus on Famous Women Ser.). (Illus.). (gr. 3-9). 1976. 8.95 (ISBN 0-912616-46-6); read-along cassette 9.95 (ISBN 0-89908-245-9). Greenhaven.

--Rose Kennedy: No Time for Tears. Bender, David L. & Mc Cuen, Gary E., eds. (Focus on Famous Women Ser.). (Illus.). (gr. 3-9). 1976. 8.95 (ISBN 0-912616-44-X); read-along cassette 9.95 (ISBN 0-89908-243-2). Greenhaven.

Church, Clive. Europe in Eighteen Thirty. 224p. 1983. text ed. 22.50x (ISBN 0-04-940067-3). Allen Unwin.

Church, Clive, ed. Practice & Perspective in Validation. 180p. 1983. 20.00 (ISBN 0-900868-94-5). Taylor & Francis.

Church, Clive H. Revolution & Red Tape: The French Ministerial Bureaucracy, 1770-1850. (Illus.). 1981. 64.00x (ISBN 0-19-822562-8). Oxford U Pr.

Church, Connie, jt. auth. see Jackson, Gerald.

Church, Connie, jt. auth. see Struna, Monika.

Church, D. C. Digestive Physiology & Nutrition of Ruminants: Digestive Physiology, Vol. 1. 1976. text ed. 22.00x (ISBN 0-9601586-4-2). O & B Bks.

Church, D. C. & Pond, W. G. Basic Animal Nutrition & Feeding. 2nd ed. 403p. 1982. pap. 21.95 (ISBN 0-471-87514-7). Wiley.

Church, D. C., ed. Digestive Physiology & Nutrition of Ruminants: Nutrition, Vol. 2. 2nd ed. 1979. text ed. 27.50x (ISBN 0-9601586-5-0). O & B Bks.

Church, D. C., et al. Livestock Feeds & Feeding. 1977. 18.00 (ISBN 0-9601586-1-8). O & B Bks.

--Livestock Feeds & Feeding. Church, D. C., ed. LC 83-90118. (Illus.). 549p. 1984. text ed. 28.00x (ISBN 0-9601586-8-5); pap. text ed. 21.00x (ISBN 0-9601586-9-3). O & B Bks.

Church, E. D. Catalog of Books Relating to the Discovery & Early History of North & South America, 5 vols. Cole, G. W., compiled by. Set. 120.00 (ISBN 0-8446-1113-1). Peter Smith.

Church, Earl & Quinn, Alfred O. Elements of Photogrammetry. rev. ed. (Illus.). 1948. 8.95x (ISBN 0-8156-2002-0). Syracuse U Pr.

Church, Ellen C. Learning Things: Games That Make Learning Fun for Children 3-8 Years Old. LC 81-82033. (ps-3). 1982. pap. 10.95 (ISBN 0-8224-4268-X). Pitman Learning.

Church, F. Forrester. Father & Son: A Personal Biography of Senator Frank Church Of Idaho by His Son. LC 85-42558. (Illus.). 256p. 1985. 17.79i (ISBN 0-06-039046-8, C&M Bessie Bks). Harper Row.

Church, F. J. Phaedo Church Plato. 1951. pap. text ed. write for info. (ISBN 0-02-322400-2). Macmillan.

Church, F. J. & Cummings, Robert D. Plato: Euthyphro, Apology, Crito. 1956. pap. text ed. write for info. (ISBN 0-02-322410-X). Macmillan.

Church, F. J., tr. see Plato.

Church, Fermor & Church, Peggy P. When Los Alamos Was a Ranch School. LC 74-78849. (Illus.). 64p. (Orig.). 1974. pap. 3.95 (ISBN 0-317-14839-7). Los Alamos Hist Soc.

Church, Frederic C., Jr. Avoiding Surprises: 8 Steps to an Efficient, Low-Cost Corporate Risk Management & Insurance Program. LC 81-71318. (Illus.). 286p. 1982. 19.95 (ISBN 0-9607398-0-7). Boston Risk Magmt.

Church, Gale E. Mr. Snowman & a Speical Christmas. 5.95 (ISBN 0-8062-2377-4). Carlton.

Church, George E. Aborigines of South America. 1977. lib. bdg. 59.95 (ISBN 0-8490-1374-7). Gordon Pr.

Church, Gilbert, ed. see Steiner, Rudolf.

Church, Gilbert, et al, eds. see Steiner, Rudolf.

Church, Gordon, ed. see Talley, Jo E.

Church, Helen N., jt. auth. see Pennington, Jean A.

Church, Herbert, Jr. British & American Poetry. (gr. 9-11). 1970. pap. text ed. 5.25x (ISBN 0-88334-027-5). Ind Sch Pr.

Church, Horace K. Excavation Handbook. 1981. 63.50 (ISBN 0-07-010840-4). McGraw.

Church, J. E. Quest for the Highest: A Diary of the East African Revival. 280p. 1981. pap. text ed. 10.95 (ISBN 0-85364-328-8). Attic Pr.

Church, J. M., jt. auth. see Simonds, H. R.

Church, J. W. Deep in Piney Woods. facsimile ed. LC 70-39080. (Black Heritage Library Collection Ser.). Repr. of 1910 ed. 20.75 (ISBN 0-8369-9018-8). Ayer Co Pubs.

Church, James C. Practical Plumbing Design Guide. LC 78-18823. (Illus.). 1979. 37.50 (ISBN 0-07-010832-3). McGraw.

Church, Jeremiah. Journal of Travels. Aurand, A. Monroe, Jr., ed. 1933. Repr. of 1845 ed. 15.00x (ISBN 0-686-17389-9). R S Barnes.

Church, John, jt. auth. see Louden, Louise.

Church, John I. Hoosier College Poet. 48p. (Orig.). 1984. pap. 4.95 (ISBN 0-916127-00-1). Friendly VA.

Church, Joseph. Understanding Your Child from Birth to Three. 1982. pap. 2.95 (ISBN 0-671-45763-2). PB.

Church, Joseph, jt. auth. see Stone, L. Joseph.

Church, Joseph, ed. Three Babies: Biographies of Cognitive Development. LC 78-14252. 1978. Repr. lib. bdg. 32.50x (ISBN 0-313-21029-2, CHTB). Greenwood.

Church, Leslie F. Oglethorpe: A Study of Philanthropy in England & Georgia. LC 33-9419. 1932. 15.00x (ISBN 0-8401-0391-3). A R Allenson.

Church, Leslie F., ed. see Henry, Matthew.

Church, Margaret. Beginning Cross-Country Skiing. LC 79-14636. (Sports for Everyone Ser.). (Illus.). 48p. (gr. 3 up). 1979. PLB 10.60 (ISBN 0-516-04371-4); pap. 2.95 (ISBN 0-516-44371-2). Childrens.

--Structure & Theme: Don Quixote to James Joyce. LC 83-2292. 219p. 1983. 15.00 (ISBN 0-8142-0348-5). Ohio St U Pr.

Church, Mary C., ed. Life & Letters of Dean Church. 428p. 1981. Repr. of 1897 ed. lib. bdg. 45.00 (ISBN 0-8495-0859-2). Arden Lib.

Church Music Committee, ed. Festival Anthems. pap. 2.95 (ISBN 0-87747-351-X). Deseret Bk.

Church, Nancy S. Future Opportunities in Franchising: A Realistic Appraisal. LC 79-18545. 47p. 1979. pap. 3.50 (ISBN 0-87576-086-4). Pilot Bks.

--Tips for Waiters & Waitresses. LC 84-1692. (Illus.). 40p. (Orig.). 1984. pap. 3.50 (ISBN 0-87576-109-7). Pilot Bks.

Church, Norm. KeepTrack File Manager for Personal Computers. 100p. 1984. pap. 9.95 (ISBN 0-88056-128-9); incl. disk 29.95 (ISBN 0-88056-185-8); incl. cassette 29.95 (ISBN 0-88056-192-0). Dilithium Pr.

Church, Norm & Schneider, Bruce. KeepTrack Reporter. 100p. 1984. Commodore 64 or VIC 20. pap. 9.95 (ISBN 0-88056-142-4); Commodore 64 or VIC 20. incl. cassette 39.95 (ISBN 0-88056-197-1); incl. disk 39.95 (ISBN 0-88056-196-3). Dilithium Pr.

Church, Norm, jt. auth. see Caba, Sid.

Church, O. Station KBOE. 3rd ed. 240p. 1984. 5.64 (ISBN 0-07-010837-4). McGraw.

Church of Christ. Forty-Seven Leading Thinkers. What Lack We Yet? Thomas, J. D., ed. LC 74-170920. 319p. 1974. 13.95 (ISBN 0-89112-027-0). Bibl Res Pr.

Church of England. Articles to Be Inquired of, in the First Metropoliticall Visitation of the Most Reverend Father, Richarde...Archbishop of Canterbury. LC 74-28851. (English Experience Ser.: No. 732). 1975. Repr. of 1605 ed. 3.50 (ISBN 90-221-0732-9). Walter J Johnson.

--A Booke of Certaine Canons, Concernynge Some Parte of the Discipline of the Churche of England. LC 70-26475. (English Experience Ser.: No. 312). 1971. Repr. of 1571 ed. 7.00 (ISBN 9-0221-0312-9). Walter J Johnson.

--Certaine Sermons or Homilies Appointed to Be Read in the Churches in the Time of Elizabeth 1st, 1547-1571, 2 vols. in 1. LC 68-17016. 1968. Repr. of 1623 ed. 50.00x (ISBN 0-8201-1008-6). Schol Facsimiles.

--The Durham Book: Being the First Draft of the Revision of the Book of Common Prayer in 1661. Cuming, G. J., ed. LC 79-12674. 1979. Repr. of 1961 ed. lib. bdg. 32.50x (ISBN 0-313-21481-6, CEBC). Greenwood.

--A Parte of a Register, Contayninge Sundrie Memorable Matters, Written by Diuers Godly & Learned in Our Time, Which Stande for the Reformation of Our Church. LC 72-5981. (English Experience Ser.: No. 509). 1973. Repr. of 1593 ed. 67.00 (ISBN 90-221-0509-1). Walter J Johnson.

Church of God Editorial Department, ed. Manual for Editors & Writers. 1976. pap. 4.95 (ISBN 0-87148-568-0). Pathway Pr.

Church of Scienthology Information Service. The Indispensability of Scientology Press, Vol. 1, Pt. 5. 1976. pap. 2.60 (ISBN 0-915598-10-8). Church of Scient Info.

Church of Scientology Information Service. The Indispensability of Scientology, 1 vol. in 4 pts. Incl. 1975. Pt. 1. pap. (ISBN 0-915598-04-3); 1976. Pt. 2. pap. (ISBN 0-915598-05-1); 1975. Pt. 3. pap. (ISBN 0-915598-06-X); 1975. Pt. 4. pap. (ISBN 0-915598-07-8). pap. 2.60 ea. Church of Scient Info.

Church of Scientology Information Service & Hubbard, L. Ron. Success with Scientology. 112p. 1976. pap. 8.00 (ISBN 0-915598-01-9). Church of Scient Info.

Church of Scotland. The First & Second Books of Discipline: Together with Some Acts of the General Assemblies. LC 77-7433. (English Experience Ser.: No. 893). 1977. Repr. of 1621 ed. lib. bdg. 6.00 (ISBN 90-221-0893-7). Walter J Johnson.

--Register of Ministers, Exhorters & Readers & of Their Stipends. LC 71-174310. (Maitland Club, Glasgow. Publications: No. 5). Repr. of 1830 ed. 15.00 (ISBN 0-404-52929-1). AMS Pr.

Church of Scotland Committee on Public Worship & Aids to Devotion. The Book of Common Order. 1979. 8.95x (ISBN 0-7152-0391-6); leather 14.00 (ISBN 0-686-75148-5). Outlook.

Church of Scotland - Committee on Public Worship & Aids to Devotion. New Ways to Worship. 1980. pap. 4.95x (ISBN 0-7152-0454-8). Outlook.

--Prayers for Contemporary Worship. 1977. pap. 4.95x (ISBN 0-7152-0351-7). Outlook.

--Prayers for Sunday Services. 1980. pap. 6.95x (ISBN 0-7152-0456-4). Outlook.

Church of Scotland - General Assembly - Committee On Public Worship And Aids To Devotion. Prayers for the Christian Year. 2nd ed. 1952. 10.95x (ISBN 0-19-145602-0). Oxford U Pr.

Church of Scotland, The Woman's Guild. Let's Choose Our Worship: Prayers for Women's Meetings. 1980. pap. 1.65 (ISBN 0-7152-0461-0). Outlook.

Church of South India. Book of Common Worship. 1963. 7.95x (ISBN 0-19-149906-4). Oxford U Pr.

Church, Olive. Office Dynamics Company: An Office Services & Temporary Help Agency Practice Set. 250p. 1981. pap. text ed. 10.36 (ISBN 0-205-07136-8, EDP 087136); tchr's ed. avail. (ISBN 0-205-07361-1). Allyn.

--Shadow Mountain Lodge, Typing Practice Set. (Illus.). (gr. 9-12). 1977. pap. 9.52 (ISBN 0-07-010835-8). McGraw.

Church, Olive D. Small Business Management & Entrepreneurship. 544p. 1984. 24.95 (ISBN 0-574-20715-5, 13-3715); instr's guide avail. (ISBN 0-574-20716-3, 13-3716). SRA.

--Stanley Junction. pap. text ed. 6.95 (ISBN 0-574-20717-1, 13-3717); write for info tchr's. ed (ISBN 0-317-00610-X, 13-3718). SRA.

Church, Patrick & Chase, Don M. Jedediah Strong Smith. (Illus.). 53p. (Orig.). 1976. pap. 3.00x limited ed. (ISBN 0-918634-36-9). D M Chase.

Church, Peggy P. Birds of Daybreak. LC 84-82440. 1985. pap. 6.95 (ISBN 0-88307-664-0). Gannon.

--House at Otowi Bridge: The Story of Edith Warner & Los Alamos. LC 60-13408. (Zia Bks.). (Illus.). 149p. 1973. pap. 6.95 (ISBN 0-8263-0281-5). U of NM Pr.

--Peggy Pond Church, New & Selected Poems. 3rd ed. Trusky, Tom, ed. LC 75-29917. (Modern & Contemporary Western Poets). 80p. (Orig.). 1976. pap. 3.00 (ISBN 0-916272-02-8). Ahsahta Pr.

--The Ripened Fields: 15 Sonnets of a Marriage. 1978. pap. 3.95 (ISBN 0-89016-043-0). Lightning Tree.

Church, Peggy P., jt. auth. see Church, Fermor.

Church, R. A. The Great Victorian Boom. (Studies in Economic & Social History). 1975. pap. text ed. 6.00x (ISBN 0-333-14350-7). Humanities.

Church, R. E., jt. auth. see Sneddon, I. B.

Church, R. J. Some Geographical Aspects of Western African Development. LC 72-634680. (Papers in International Studies: Africa Ser.: No. 10). (Illus.). 1971. pap. 3.50x (ISBN 0-89680-043-1, 82-91619, Ohio U Ctr Intl). Ohio U Pr.

Church, R. J., et al. Advanced Geography of Northern & Western Europe. 1968. 18.95 (ISBN 0-7175-0873-0). Dufour.

--Africa & the Islands. 4th ed. LC 77-3459. 542p. 1977. pap. text ed. 19.95x (ISBN 0-470-99085-6). Halsted Pr.

Church, R. W. The Beginning of the Middle Ages. 1977. lib. bdg. 59.95 (ISBN 0-8490-1484-0). Gordon Pr.

--The Beginning of the Middle Ages. 1978. Repr. of 1892 ed. lib. bdg. 20.00 (ISBN 0-8492-3977-X). R West.

--An Essay on Critical Appreciation. 1973. Repr. of 1938 ed. 20.00 (ISBN 0-8274-1538-9). R West.

--Miscellaneous Essays. 1973. Repr. of 1888 ed. 10.00 (ISBN 0-8274-1534-6). R West.

--Occasional Papers, 2 vols. 1973. Repr. of 1897 ed. 20.00 set (ISBN 0-8274-1533-8). R West.

--The Oxford Movement: Twelve Years 1833-1845. 1979. Repr. of 1891 ed. lib. bdg. 35.00 (ISBN 0-8482-7569-1). Norwood Edns.

Church, Ralph W. Hume's Theory of the Understanding. LC 79-55608. 238p. 1980. Repr. of 1935 ed. lib. bdg. 22.50x (ISBN 0-313-20651-1, CHHU). Greenwood.

--Study in the Philosophy of Malebranche. LC 74-102564. 1970. Repr. of 1931 ed. 28.50x (ISBN 0-8046-0724-9, Pub. by Kennikat). Assoc Faculty Pr.

Church, Randolph W., intro. by. Virginia Legislative Petitions: Bibliography, Calendar, & Abstracts from Original Sources, 6 May 1776-21 June 1782. 508p. 1984. 35.00 (ISBN 0-88490-114-9). Va State Lib.

Church, Richard. The Collected Poems of Richard Church. LC 75-41058. Repr. of 1948 ed. 23.50 (ISBN 0-404-14522-1). AMS Pr.

--Eight for Immortality. facs. ed. LC 70-90623. (Essay Index Reprint Ser). 1941. 17.00 (ISBN 0-8369-1204-7). Ayer Co Pubs.

--Eight for Immortality. LC 74-3176. 1941. lib. bdg. 15.00 (ISBN 0-8414-3602-9). Folcroft.

--John Keats: An Introduction & Selection. 1948. Repr. 20.00 (ISBN 0-8274-2623-2). R West.

--London in Color. (Illus.). 160p. 1980. 19.95 (ISBN 0-7134-0020-X, Pub. by Batsford England). David & Charles.

--Mary Shelley. 1978. Repr. of 1928 ed. lib. bdg. 17.50 (ISBN 0-8495-0743-X). Arden Lib.

--Mary Shelley. LC 72-193688. 1928. lib. bdg. 17.50 (ISBN 0-8414-3027-6). Folcroft.

--Mary Shelley. 10.75 (ISBN 0-8369-6925-1, 7806). Ayer Co Pubs.

Church, Richard W. Bacon. Morley, John, ed. LC 68-58371. Repr. of 1902 ed. 12.50 (ISBN 0-404-51704-8). AMS Pr.

--Bacon. LC 73-11039. 1973. lib. bdg. 17.50 (ISBN 0-8414-3404-2). Folcroft.

--Dante & Other Essays. 1893. lib. bdg. 17.50 (ISBN 0-8414-3028-4). Folcroft.

--Dante & Other Essays. LC 76-86002. 1969. Repr. of 1888 ed. 21.00x (ISBN 0-8046-0606-4, Pub. by Kennikat). Assoc Faculty Pr.

--Spenser. Morley, John, ed. LC 68-58372. (English Men of Letters). Repr. of 1887 ed. lib. bdg. 12.50 (ISBN 0-404-51703-X). AMS Pr.

--Spenser. 1973. lib. bdg. 15.00 (ISBN 0-8414-3029-2). Folcroft.

Church, Robert L. Education in the United States: An Interpretive History. LC 75-22764. 1976. text ed. 18.95 (ISBN 0-02-905490-7). Free Pr.

Church, Ronald J. Modern Colonization. LC 78-14111. 1980. Repr. of 1951 ed. 18.75 (ISBN 0-88355-835-1). Hyperion Conn.

Church, Roy. Herbert Austin: The British Motor Car Industry to 1941. (Europa Library of Business Biography: No. 4). (Illus.). 233p. 1979. 30.00x (ISBN 0-905118-29-4). Intl Pubns Serv.

Church, Roy, ed. Dynamics of Victorian Business: Problems & Perspectives to the 1870's. (Illus.). 280p. 1980. text ed. 37.50x (ISBN 0-04-330300-5). Allen Unwin.

Church, Roy A. Economic & Social Change in a Midland Town: Victorian Nottingham, 1815-1900. (Illus.). 409p. 1966. 30.00x (ISBN 0-7146-1290-1, F Cass Co). Biblio Dist.

--Kendricks in Hardware: A Family Business 1791-1966. LC 72-77875. (Illus.). 1969. 24.95x (ISBN 0-678-05524-6). Kelley.

Church, Russell M., jt. ed. see Boe, Erling E.

Church, Ruth E. Wines of the Midwest. LC 77-83753. (Illus.). vii, 248p. 1982. cloth 21.95 (ISBN 0-8040-0779-9, 82-75828, Pub by Swallow); pap. 9.95 (ISBN 0-8040-0426-9, 82-75836, Pub by Swallow). Ohio U Pr.

Church, Thomas, et al. Gardens Are for People. 2nd ed. (Illus.). 256p. 1983. 41.95 (ISBN 0-07-010844-7). McGraw.

Church, Thomas M., ed. Marine Chemistry in the Coastal Environment. (ACS Symposium Ser.: No. 18). 1979. pap. 34.95 (ISBN 0-8412-0531-0). Am Chemical.

Church, Virginia W., ed. International Short Stories. LC 72-5902. (Short Story Reprint Ser.). Repr. of 1934 ed. 25.00 (ISBN 0-8369-4199-3). Ayer Co Pubs.

Church, W. H. Gods in the Making: And Other Writings. (Illus.). 216p. (Orig.). 1983. pap. text ed. 6.95 (ISBN 0-87604-148-9). ARE Pr.

--Many Happy Returns: The Lives of Edgar Cayce. LC 84-47717. 256p. 1984. 14.37 (ISBN 0-06-250150-X, HarpR). Har-Row.

Church, William C. Ulysses S. Grant & the Period of National Preservation & Reconstruction. LC 73-14437. (Heroes of the Nation Ser.). Repr. of 1897 ed. 49.50 (ISBN 0-404-58255-9). AMS Pr.

Church, William F. Constitutional Thought in Sixteenth Century France. LC 77-86273. 1969. Repr. of 1941 ed. lib. bdg. 26.00x (ISBN 0-374-91596-2). Octagon.

--Louis the Fourteenth in Historical Thought. (Historical Controversies Ser.). 128p. 1976. pap. text ed. 2.95x (ISBN 0-393-09211-9). Norton.

--Richelieu & Reason of State. LC 76-181518. 582p. 1972. 49.00x (ISBN 0-691-05199-2). Princeton U Pr.

Church, William F., ed. Greatness of Louis the Fourteenth. 2nd ed. (Problems in European Civilization Ser.). 1972. pap. text ed. 5.95 (ISBN 0-669-82016-4). Heath.

--The Impact of Absolutism in France: National Experience Under Richelieu, Mazarin, & Louis XIV. LC 68-31294. (Major Issues in History Ser.). pap. 51.30 (ISBN 0-317-09321-5, 2012573). Bks Demand UMI.

--Influence of the Enlightenment on the French Revolution. 2nd ed. (Problems in European Civilization Ser). 1974. pap. text ed. 5.95 (ISBN 0-669-82024-5). Heath.

Churcher, Barbara. Physical Education for Teaching. (Unwin Education Books). 1973. pap. text ed. 8.95x (ISBN 0-04-371024-7). Allen Unwin.

Churches Alive. There Is Help for Your Church. LC 81-65669. 40p. (Orig.). 1981. pap. text ed. 0.95 (ISBN 0-934396-14-0). Churches Alive.

Churches Alive Inc. Communicating. LC 79-52133. (Love One Another Bible Study). (Illus.). 1979. wkbk. 2.50 (ISBN 0-934396-06-X). Churches Alive.

--Contributing. LC 79-52132. (Love One Another Bible Study Ser.). (Illus.). 1979. wkbk. 2.50 (ISBN 0-934396-05-1). Churches Alive.

--Forgiving. LC 79-52128. (Love One Another Bible Study). (Illus.). 1979. wkbk. 2.50 (ISBN 0-934396-01-9). Churches Alive.

Churches Alive, Inc. Growing by Discipling Pastor's Handbook. rev. ed. (Illus.). 150p. 1980. pap. text ed. 12.00 (ISBN 0-934396-09-4). Churches Alive.

--Growth Group Leader's Guide. rev. ed. LC 80-52536. (Illus.). 110p. 1980. pap. 11.00 (ISBN 0-934396-10-8). Churches Alive.

Churches Alive Inc. Growth Group Member's Notebook. LC 80-52536. (Illus.). 105p. (Orig.). 1980. pap. text ed. 6.00 (ISBN 0-934396-11-6). Churches Alive.

--Maintaining Unity. LC 79-52134. (Love One Another Bible Study). (Illus.). 1979. wkbk. 2.50 (ISBN 0-934396-07-8). Churches Alive.

--Submitting. LC 79-52131. (Love One Another Bible Study). (Illus.). 1979. wkbk. 2.50 (ISBN 0-934396-04-3). Churches Alive.

Churches Alive, Inc. Staff. Esteeming. LC 79-52130. (Love One Another Bible Study Ser.). (Illus.). 1979. wkbk. 2.50 (ISBN 0-317-27076-1). Churches Alive.

Churches Alive Inc. Staff. Understanding. LC 79-52129. (Love One Another Bible Study). (Illus.). 1979. wkbk. 2.50 (ISBN 0-934396-02-7). Churches Alive.

Churches Alive Staff. Caring. rev. ed. LC 81-66927. 60p. 1981. pap. text ed. 3.95 (ISBN 0-934396-23-X). Churches Alive.

--God's Family Bible Study. LC 82-72563. 112p. 1983. pap. text ed. 3.75 (ISBN 0-934396-34-5). Churches Alive.

--God's Family Leader's Guide Edition. LC 82-72564. 135p. 1983. pap. text ed. 5.00 (ISBN 0-934396-35-3). Churches Alive.

--Going up! rev. ed. 82p. 1980. pap. text ed. 5.00 (ISBN 0-934396-26-4). Churches Alive.

--Love One Another Leader's Guide. LC 79-52128. (Love One Another Ser.). (Illus.). 85p. (Orig.). 1981. pap. text ed. 5.00 (ISBN 0-934396-13-2). Churches Alive.

--Visitation Evangelism Leader's Guide. rev. ed. LC 84-73068. (Illus.). 112p. 1985. pap. text ed. 20.00 (ISBN 0-934396-40-X). Churches Alive.

--Visitation Evangelism Member's Notebook. rev. ed. (Illus.). 80p. 1985. pap. text ed. 9.00 (ISBN 0-934396-39-6). Churches Alive.

Churches Alive Staff, ed. Growing as a Disciple Conference Notebook. rev. ed. 85p. 1983. pap. write for info. (ISBN 0-934396-37-X). Churches Alive.

Churchhouse, Robert F., jt. ed. see Ledermann, Walter.

Churchill, Allen. Park Row. LC 73-14193. 344p. 1973. Repr. of 1958 ed. lib. bdg. 24.75x (ISBN 0-8371-7146-6, CHPR). Greenwood.

Churchill, Anthony, et al. Road User Charges in Central America. LC 70-187219. (World Bank Staff Occasional Papers Ser: No. 15). 192p. 1972. pap. 6.00x (ISBN 0-8018-1334-4). Johns Hopkins.

Churchill, Anthony A. Shelter. 39p. 1980. pap. 3.00 (ISBN 0-686-39677-4). World Bank.

Churchill, Awnsham & Churchill, John. A Collection of Voyages & Travels, Published in England in Eight Volumes: 1752 Edition. 1981. write for info. (ISBN 0-08-027647-4, HE 073); microfiche 530.00 (ISBN 0-686-79340-4). Pergamon.

Churchill, Bob & Davies, Granville. Modern Airweapon Shooting. (Illus.). 188p. 1981. 19.95 (ISBN 0-7153-8123-7). David & Charles.

Churchill, Bruce, jt. auth. see Jordan, Larry E.

Churchill, Caroline N. Active Footsteps. Baxter, Annette K., ed. LC 79-8781. (Signal Lives Ser.). (Illus.). 1980. Repr. of 1909 ed. lib. bdg. 27.50x (ISBN 0-405-12830-4). Ayer Co Pubs.

Churchill, Caryl. Churchill: Plays One. 400p. 1985. pap. 5.95 (ISBN 0-413-56670-6, 9499). Methuen Inc.

--Cloud Nine. 56p. (Orig.). 1981. pap. 3.95 (ISBN 0-86104-216-6). Pluto Pr.

--Cloud Nine. 122p. 1984. pap. 5.50 (ISBN 0-416-00951-4, NO. 4016). Methuen Inc.

--Fen. 28p. 1983. pap. 4.95 (ISBN 0-413-52990-8, NO. 3903). Methuen Inc.

--Light Shining in Buckinghamshire. 64p. (Orig.). 1982. pap. 4.95 (ISBN 0-904383-74-1). Pluto Pr.

--Softcops. 28p. 1984. pap. 4.95 (ISBN 0-413-54910-0, NO. 4106). Methuen Inc.

--Top Girls. 56p. 1984. pap. 5.50 (ISBN 0-413-55480-5, NO. 9145). Methuen Inc.

--Traps, Traps. 52p. (Orig.). 1981. pap. 5.95 (ISBN 0-904383-75-X, NO. 4122). Pluto Pr.

Churchill, Charles. Poetical Works. Grant, Douglas, ed. 1956. 54.00x (ISBN 0-19-811316-1). Oxford U Pr.

Churchill, Charles, ed. The City of Beirut: A Socio-Economic Survey. 78p. 1954. pap. 12.95x (ISBN 0-8156-6023-5, Am U Beirut). Syracuse U Pr.

Churchill, Charles H. The Druzes & the Maronites Under the Turkish Rule from 1840 to 1860. LC 73-6273. (The Middle East Ser.). Repr. of 1862 ed. 20.00 (ISBN 0-405-05329-0). Ayer Co Pubs.

--Mount Lebanon: A Ten Years' Residence, from 1842 to 1852, 3 vols. LC 77-87615. Repr. of 1853 ed. Set. 87.50 (ISBN 0-404-16440-4). AMS Pr.

Churchill, Charles W. Fortunes Are for the Few Letters of a Forty-Niner. Smith, Duane A. & Weber, David J., eds. LC 77-76134. (Illus.). 136p. 1977. 12.50 (ISBN 0-918740-00-2). San Diego Hist.

--The Italians of Newark. LC 74-17922. (Italian American Experience Ser). (Illus.). 220p. 1975. 20.00x (ISBN 0-405-06395-4). Ayer Co Pubs.

Churchill, Charles W., ed. see Lutfiyya, Abdulla H.

Churchill College, Cambridge England. Human Factors in Telecommunications International Symposium, 8th. 1977. 75.00 (ISBN 0-686-37980-2). Info Gatekeepers.

Churchill, Creighton. The World of Wine. (Illus.). 384p. 1980. pap. 7.95 (ISBN 0-02-009460-4, Collier). Macmillan.

Churchill, Don W. Language of Autistic Children. LC 78-18860. 139p. 1978. 14.95x (ISBN 0-470-26417-9). Halsted Pr.

Churchill, Don W., et al. Infantile Autism: Proceedings. (Illus.). 360p. 1971. 30.50x (ISBN 0-398-00307-6). C C Thomas.

Churchill, E. Richard. Colorado Quiz Bag. 1978. 2.00 (ISBN 0-913488-04-6). Timberline Bks.

--Doc Holliday, Bat Masterson, Wyatt Earp: Their Colorado Careers. 1978. 2.00 (ISBN 0-913488-05-4). Timberline Bks.

--The McCartys. 1978. 2.00 (ISBN 0-913488-02-X). Timberline Bks.

Churchill, E. Richard & Churchill, Linda R. Enriched Social Studies Teaching. LC 72-97017. 1973. pap. 5.95 (ISBN 0-8224-2705-2). Pitman Learning.

Churchill, E. Richard, jt. auth. see Blair, Edward.

Churchill, Edwin A. Maine Communities & the War for Independence. 1976. study guide 2.95x (ISBN 0-913764-08-6). Maine St Mus.

--Simple Forms & Vivid Colors: Maine Painted Furniture, 1800-1850. LC 83-61807. (Illus.). 116p. 1983. 25.95 (ISBN 0-913764-15-9); pap. 17.95 (ISBN 0-913764-16-7). Maine St Mus.

Churchill, George B. The Originality of William Wycherley in Schelling Anniversary Papers. 1923. 40.00 (ISBN 0-8274-3079-5). R West.

--Richard the Third up to Shakespeare. 55.00 (ISBN 0-384-09040-0); pap. 50.00 (ISBN 0-685-02232-3). Johnson Repr.

--Richard the Third up to Shakespeare. 548p. 1976. Repr. of 1900 ed. 22.50x (ISBN 0-87471-773-6). Rowman.

Churchill, Gilbert A. Marketing Research. 3rd ed. 704p. 1983. text ed. 35.95x (ISBN 0-03-060608-X); instr's. manual 20.00 (ISBN 0-03-060609-8). Dryden Pr.

Churchill, Gilbert A., Jr., et al. Sales Force Management: Planning, Implementation & Control. 1981. 27.95x (ISBN 0-256-02531-2). Irwin.

Churchill, Henry S. City Is the People. 1962. pap. 1.95x (ISBN 0-393-00174-1, Norton Lib). Norton.

Churchill, J., jt. auth. see Witcomb, John.

Churchill, J. J. The Reminiscences of Lady Randolph Churchill. Repr. of 1908 ed. 23.00 (ISBN 0-527-17100-X). Kraus Repr.

Churchill, J. W., ed. see Harlow, Louis K.

Churchill, Jacqueline C., jt. auth. see Fromstein, Roberta H.

Churchill, James, jt. auth. see Hardy, Judith.

Churchill, James E. The Backyard Building Book. LC 76-17609. (Illus.). 192p. 1976. pap. 6.95 (ISBN 0-8117-2105-1). Stackpole.

--The Backyard Building Book II. LC 78-17947. 192p. 1978. pap. 6.95 (ISBN 0-8117-2128-0). Stackpole.

--The Big Backyard Building Book. (Illus.). 224p. 1983. 19.95 (ISBN 0-8117-0278-2); pap. 14.95 (ISBN 0-8117-2184-1). Stackpole.

--The Complete Book of Tanning Skins & Furs. 224p. 1983. 14.95 (ISBN 0-8117-1719-4). Stackpole.

--The Homesteader's Handbook. 1975. pap. 2.95 (ISBN 0-394-71346-X). Random.

Churchill, James S., tr. see Husserl, Edmund.

Churchill, James S., tr. see Plessner, Helmuth.

Churchill, Jeremy. Honda MB-MT50 '80-'82. pap. 10.50 (ISBN 0-85696-731-9, 731). Haynes Pubns.

Churchill, John, jt. auth. see Churchill, Awnsham.

Churchill, John G. What the Bible Tells Me. 1976. pap. 1.50 (ISBN 0-8341-0412-1). Beacon Hill.

Churchill, Kenneth. Italy & English Literature: Seventeen Sixty-Four to Nineteen Thirty. LC 79-55524. 230p. 1980. text ed. 29.50x (ISBN 0-06-491130-6, 06397). B&N Imports.

Churchill, Linda E., jt. auth. see Churchill, Richard E.

Churchill, Linda R., jt. auth. see Churchill, E. Richard.

Churchill, Marilyn K., jt. auth. see Jacobson, Patricia O.

Churchill, Peter. Riding from A to Z: A Practical Manual of Horsemanship. LC 77-88451. (Illus.). 1978. 9.95 (ISBN 0-8008-6796-3). Taplinger.

Churchill, R. C. Bibliography of Dickensian Criticism, Eighteen Thirty-Six to Nineteen Seventy-Four. LC 75-5119. (Reference Library of the Humanities: No. 12). 300p. 1975. lib. bdg. 48.00 (ISBN 0-8240-1083-3). Garland Pub.

--He Served Human Liberty. An Essay on the Genius of Swift. LC 74-3019. 1946. lib. bdg. 12.50 (ISBN 0-8414-3572-3). Folcroft.

Churchill, R. H. Speeches Eighteen Eighty to Eighteen Eighty-Eight, 2 vols. Repr. of 1889 ed. Set. 44.00 (ISBN 0-527-17110-7). Kraus Repr.

Churchill, R. R. & Lowe, A. V. The Law of the Sea. LC 83-12019. 320p. 1984. 25.00 (ISBN 0-7190-0936-7, Pub. by Manchester Univ Pr). Longwood Pub Group.

Churchill, R. V., ed. see Symposium in Applied Mathematics, Ann Arbor, 1949.

Churchill, Randolph S. Winston S. Churchill, 3 vols. Incl. Vol. 1. Youth, 1874-1900. 1966. 40.00 (ISBN 0-395-07530-0); Vol. 2. Young Statesman, 1901-1914. 1967. 40.00 (ISBN 0-395-07526-2); companion vol. II, pt. 1. 1901-1907 15.00 (ISBN 0-395-07525-4); companion vol. II, pt. 2.1907-1911 15.00 (ISBN 0-395-07524-6); companion vol. II, pt. 3. 1911-1914 40.00 (ISBN 0-395-07523-8); companion vol. 1, pt. 1&2. 80.00 (ISBN 0-395-07527-0); companion vol. 2, pt. 1&2&3. 45.00 (ISBN 0-395-07522-X). HM.

Churchill, Randolph S., ed. see Churchill, Winston L.

Churchill, Reginald C. English Literature of the Nineteenth Century. facs. ed. LC 75-140351. (Select Bibliographies Reprint Ser.). 1951. 16.00 (ISBN 0-8369-5594-3). Ayer Co Pubs.

--He Served Human Liberty. 1978. lib. bdg. 10.00 (ISBN 0-8495-0738-3). Arden Lib.

Churchill, Richard. Devilish Bets to Trick Your Friends. LC 84-24114. (Illus.). 128p. (gr. 4 up). 1985. 7.95 (ISBN 0-8069-4706-3); lib. bdg. 9.99 (ISBN 0-8069-4707-1); pap. 3.50 (ISBN 0-8069-7968-2). Sterling.

--I Bet I Can-I Bet You Can't. LC 82-50551. (Illus.). 128p. (gr. 3 up). 1982. 8.95 (ISBN 0-8069-4664-4); PLB 10.99 (ISBN 0-8069-4665-2). Sterling.

--The Six-Million-Dollar Cucumber. 96p. 1977. pap. 1.25 (ISBN 0-440-97973-0, LFL). Dell.

Churchill, Richard E. & Churchill, Linda E. The Bionic Banana. 96p. (gr. 3 up). pap. 1.50 (ISBN 0-440-97973-0, LFL). Dell.

Churchill, Robin & Nordquist, Myron, eds. New Directions in the Law of the Sea: Documents, 11 vols. LC 72-12713. 1973-1981. Vol. 3. lib. bdg. 35.00 (ISBN 0-379-00496-8); Vols. 1, 2, & 4-11. lib. bdg. 45.00 ea. (ISBN 0-379-00029-6); Set. lib. bdg. 485.00. Oceana.

Churchill, Rogers P. The Anglo-Russian Convention of Nineteen Seven. LC 72-73. (Select Bibliographies Reprint Ser). 1972. Repr. of 1939 ed. 18.75 (ISBN 0-8369-9956-8). Ayer Co Pubs.

--The Anglo-Russian Convention of 1907. 1939. 15.00x (ISBN 0-686-17413-5). R S Barnes.

Churchill, Ruel V. Operational Mathematics. 3rd ed. 1971. text ed. 40.95 (ISBN 0-07-010870-6). McGraw.

Churchill, Ruel V. & Brown, James W. Complex Variables & Applications. 4th ed. (Illus.). 416p. 1984. text ed. 40.95 (ISBN 0-07-010873-0). McGraw.

--Fourier Series & Boundary Value Problems. 3rd ed. 1978. text ed. 40.95 (ISBN 0-07-010843-9). McGraw.

Churchill, Sallie R., et al, eds. No Child Is Unadoptable: A Reader on Adoption of Children with Special Needs. LC 78-26357. (Sage Human Service Guides: Vol. 8). 173p. 1979. pap. 9.95 (ISBN 0-8039-1215-3). Sage.

Churchill, Sam. Big Sam. LC 65-13975. (Illus.). 1979. pap. 2.25 (ISBN 0-89174-034-1). Comstock Edns.

Churchill, Sarah J., ed. see Marlborough, Sarah J.

Churchill, Stuart W. The Interpretation & Use of Rate Data: The Rate Concept. rev. ed. LC 78-23365. (Illus.). 510p. 1982. pap. text ed. 32.50 (ISBN 0-89116-234-8); solution manual 5.95 (ISBN 0-89116-260-7). Hemisphere Pub.

Churchill, Thomas. Centralia Dead March. LC 79-9146. 214p. 1980. pap. 9.95 (ISBN 0-915306-17-4). Curbstone.

Churchill, Ward, ed. Marxism & Native Americans. 250p. 1984. 20.00 (ISBN 0-89608-178-8); pap. 7.50 (ISBN 0-89608-177-X). South End Pr.

Churchill, William. Beach-la-Mar, the Jargon or Trade Speech of the Western Pacific. LC 75-32806. Repr. of 1911 ed. 14.00 (ISBN 0-404-14110-2). AMS Pr.

--Easter Island: The Rapanui Speech & the Peopling of Southeast Polynesia. LC 75-34642. Repr. of 1912 ed. 29.00 (ISBN 0-404-14214-1). AMS Pr.

--The Polynesian Wanderings. LC 75-35186. Repr. of 1911 ed. 45.00 (ISBN 0-404-14215-X). AMS Pr.

--Sissano, Movements of Migration Within & Through Melanesia. LC 16-23055. (Carnegie Institution of Washington Publications: No. 244). (Illus.). pap. 22.30 (ISBN 0-317-10107-2, 2015706). Bks Demand UMI.

--Weather Words of Polynesia. LC 8-11468. (AAA. M.: No. 7). 1907. 11.00 (ISBN 0-527-00506-1). Kraus Repr.

Churchill, Winston. Coniston. LC 72-96877. (Illus.). 543p. Repr. of 1906 ed. lib. bdg. 27.00 (ISBN 0-8398-0264-1). Irvington.

--Coniston. (Illus.). 543p. 1981. Repr. of 1906 ed. lib. bdg. 30.00 (ISBN 0-89760-157-2). Telegraph Bks.

--The Crisis. 1901. lib. bdg. 30.00 (ISBN 0-8414-3033-0). Folcroft.

--The Crisis. (Illus.). 522p. 1981. Repr. of 1901 ed. lib. bdg. 37.50 (ISBN 0-89760-156-4). Telegraph Bks.

--The Crisis. 432p. 1984. Repr. lib. bdg. 19.95x (ISBN 0-89966-510-1). Buccaneer Bks.

--The Crossing. (Illus.). 598p. 1981. Repr. of 1903 ed. lib. bdg. 35.00 (ISBN 0-89760-158-0). Telegraph Bks.

--A History of the English Speaking Peoples: Vol. III-The Age of Revolution. 416p. 1983. pap. 8.95 (ISBN 0-396-08273-4). Dodd.

--The Inside of the Cup. 513p. 1981. Repr. of 1913 ed. lib. bdg. 37.50 (ISBN 0-89760-160-2). Telegraph Bks.

--Marlborough & His Times. Abr. ed. (Illus.). 1200p. 1982. 40.00 (ISBN 0-684-17674-2, ScribT). Scribner.

--Mr. Crewe's Career. 1908. lib. bdg. 20.00 (ISBN 0-8414-3034-9). Folcroft.

--Mr. Crewe's Career. LC 68-59351. (The Muckrakers Ser.). (Illus.). Repr. of 1908 ed. lib. bdg. 13.50 (ISBN 0-8398-0266-8). Irvington.

--Mr. Crewe's Career. 498p. 1981. Repr. of 1908 ed. lib. bdg. 30.00 (ISBN 0-89760-161-0). Telegraph Bks.

--A Modern Chronicle. 1910. lib. bdg. 20.00 (ISBN 0-8414-3035-7). Folcroft.

--Richard Carvel. 1899. lib. bdg. 30.00 (ISBN 0-8414-3036-5). Folcroft.
--Richard Carvel. 538p. 1981. Repr. of 1899 ed. lib. bdg. 30.00 (ISBN 0-89760-159-9). Telegraph Bks.
--Savrola. 15.95 (ISBN 0-88411-074-5, Pub. by Aeonian Pr). Amereon Ltd.
--Step by Step, Nineteen Thirty-Six to Nineteen Thirty-Nine. facsimile ed. LC 72-156631. (Essay Index Reprint Ser). Repr. of 1939 ed. 19.00 (ISBN 0-8369-2310-3). Ayer Co Pubs.
Churchill, Winston J. Running in Place. LC 72-92832. 212p. 1973. 5.95 (ISBN 0-8076-0662-6). Braziller.
Churchill, Winston L. The Sinews of Peace, Post-War Speeches. Churchill, Randolph S., ed. LC 83-45733. Repr. of 1949 ed. 30.00 (ISBN 0-404-20059-1). AMS Pr.
Churchill, Winston S. Amid These Storms: Thoughts & Adventures. LC 72-5698. (Essay Index Reprint Ser). 1972. Repr. of 1932 ed. 18.00 (ISBN 0-8369-2985-3). Ayer Co Pubs.
--Defending the West. 1981. 40.00x (ISBN 0-85117-210-5, Pub. by M Temple Smith). State Mutual Bk.
--End of the Beginning: War Speeches. LC 72-4588. (Essay Index Reprint Ser.). Repr. of 1945 ed. 19.00 (ISBN 0-8369-2939-X). Ayer Co Pubs.
--For Free Trade. LC 76-26306. 1977. Repr. of 1906 ed. 17.50 (ISBN 0-917684-06-0); lib. bdg. 16.00 (ISBN 0-685-87406-0). Churchilliana.
--George Bernard Shaw in Great Contemporaries. Repr. of 1942 ed. 25.00 (ISBN 0-8274-3850-8). R West.
--Great Contemporaries. facsimile ed. LC 79-156630. (Essay Index Reprint Ser). Repr. of 1937 ed. 23.00 (ISBN 0-8369-2309-X). Ayer Co Pubs.
--Great Contemporaries. LC 73-77128. (Illus.). 1976. pap. 4.95 (ISBN 0-226-10631-4, P692, Phoen). U of Chicago Pr.
--A History of the English Speaking Peoples, 4 Vols. 1983. Set. 35.00 (ISBN 0-396-08275-0). Dodd.
--A History of the English Speaking Peoples: Vol. I-The Birth of Britain. 544p. 1983. pap. 8.95 (ISBN 0-396-08271-8). Dodd.
--A History of the English Speaking Peoples: Vol. IV-The Great Democracies. 416p. 1983. pap. 8.95 (ISBN 0-396-08274-2). Dodd.
--A History of the English Speaking Peoples: Vol. II-The New World. 446p. 1983. pap. 8.95 (ISBN 0-396-08272-6). Dodd.
--The Island Race. (Illus.). 320p. 1985. 24.95 (ISBN 0-396-08750-7). Dodd.
--Liberalism & the Social Problem. LC 72-3299. (British History Ser., No. 30). 1972. Repr. of 1909 ed. lib. bdg. 53.95x (ISBN 0-8383-1528-3). Haskell.
--Mr. Brodrick's Army. LC 76-26305. 1977. Repr. of 1903 ed. 17.50 (ISBN 0-917684-03-6); lib. bdg. 16.00 (ISBN 0-685-87405-2). Churchilliana.
--My Early Life: A Roving Commission. (Illus.). 1930. lib. rep. ed. 17.50 (ISBN 0-684-15154-5, ScribT). Scribner.
--The Second World War, 6 vols. Incl. The Gathering Storm. 1948. 19.95 (ISBN 0-395-07537-8); Their Finest Hour. 1949. 19.95 (ISBN 0-395-07536-X); The Grand Alliance. 1950. 19.95 (ISBN 0-395-07538-6); The Hinge of Fate. 1960. 19.95 (ISBN 0-395-07539-4); Closing the Ring. 1951. 19.95 (ISBN 0-395-07535-1); Triumph & Tragedy. 1953. 19.95 (ISBN 0-395-07540-8). 22.95 ea.; Set. 134.70 (ISBN 0-395-07541-6). HM.
--The Second World War: Chartwell Edition, 6 Vols. 1983. 300.00 set (ISBN 0-395-34929-X). HM.
--Unrelenting Struggle: War Speeches. facsimile ed. Eade, Charles, compiled by. LC 78-167325. (Essay Index Reprint Ser). Repr. of 1942 ed. 20.00 (ISBN 0-8369-2450-9). Ayer Co Pubs.
--While England Slept: A Survey of World Affairs 1932-1938. 415p. 1982. Repr. of 1938 ed. lib. bdg. 22.00 (ISBN 0-8290-0804-7). Irvington.
--While England Slept: A Survey of World Affairs 1932-8. facsimile ed. LC 76-165621. (Select Bibliographies Reprint Ser). Repr. of 1938 ed. 23.00 (ISBN 0-8369-5928-0). Ayer Co Pubs.
Churchill, Winston S. & Glubb, John. Great Issues 71: A Forum on Important Questions Facing the American Public. 1972. 5.95x (ISBN 0-686-70487-8). Troy State Univ.
Churchill, Winton, jt. auth. see Albrecht, Karl.
Churchill-Davidson, H. C., ed. Wylie & Churchill-Davidson: A Practice of Anesthesia. 4th ed. (Illus.). 1542p. 1978. 25.00 (ISBN 0-7216-2577-0). Saunders.
Churchill-Taylor, Samuel E. Tea & Sects. 64p. (Orig.). 1975. pap. 3.95x (ISBN 0-938758-01-2). MTM Pub Co.
Churchland, P. M. Scientific Realism & the Plasticity of Mind. LC 78-73240. (Cambridge Studies in Philosophy). (Illus.). 1979. 29.95 (ISBN 0-521-22632-5). Cambridge U Pr.
Churchland, Paul M. Matter & Consciousness: A Contemporary Introduction to the Philosophy of Mind. LC 83-1339. (Illus.). 172p. (Orig.). 1984. text ed. 22.50x (ISBN 0-262-03103-5); pap. text ed. 8.95x (ISBN 0-262-53050-3). MIT Pr.
Churchland, Paul M. & Hooker, Clifford A., eds. Images of Science: Essays on Realism & Empiricism, with a Reply from Bas C. Van Fraassen. LC 85-1128. (Illus.). 352p. 1985. lib. bdg. 50.00x (ISBN 0-226-10653-5); pap. text ed. 19.95x (ISBN 0-226-10654-3). U of Chicago Pr.
Churchman & Mason, eds. World Modeling: A Dialogue, Vol. 2. (TIMS Studies in the Management Sciences). 179p. 24.50 (ISBN 0-318-14464-6). Inst Mgmt Sci.
Churchman, C. W. & Mason, R. O., eds. World Modeling: A Dialogue. (North-Holland - TIMS Studies in the Management Sciences: Vol. 2). 164p. 1976. pap. 32.50 (ISBN 0-7204-0388-X, North-Holland). Elsevier.
Churchman, C. West. Design of Inquiring Systems, Basic Concepts in Systems Analysis. LC 72-174810. 1972. 18.50x (ISBN 0-465-01608-1). Basic.
--The Systems Approach. rev. & updated ed. (YA) (gr. 7-12). 1983. pap. 3.95 (ISBN 0-440-38407-9, LE). Dell.
--The Systems Approach & Its Enemies. LC 78-19937. 1979. 15.95x (ISBN 0-465-08342-0). Basic.
--Thought & Wisdom. (Systems Inquiry Ser.). 150p. 1982. pap. text ed. 9.95x (ISBN 0-914105-03-5). Intersystems Pubns.
Churchman, C. West & Smith, Spencer. Natural Resource Administration: Introducing a New Methodology for Management Development. (Special Study in Natural Resources & Energy Management Ser.). 180p. 1984. pap. 20.00x (ISBN 0-86531-709-7). Westview.
Churchman, P. H. & Peers, E. A. A Survey of the Influence of Sir Walter Scott in Spain. LC 73-9842. 1922. lib. bdg. 7.50 (ISBN 0-8414-1848-9). Folcroft.
Churchman, Phillip H. A First Book in French. (Illus.). 1935. text ed. 3.00x (ISBN 0-911090-05-3). Pacific Bk Supply.
Churchouse, Jack. Glamour Ships of the Union Steam Ship Company. (Illus.). 104p. 26.95 (ISBN 0-908582-41-2, Pub. by Salem Hse Ltd). Merrimack Pub Cir.
Churchward, Albert. The Signs & Symbols of Primordial Man. LC 75-104257. 1978. Repr. of 1913 ed. lib. bdg. 50.50x (ISBN 0-8371-3908-2, CHPM). Greenwood.
Churchward, Clerk M. Rotuman Grammar & Dictionary. LC 75-32808. Repr. of 1940 ed. 30.75 (ISBN 0-404-14112-9). AMS Pr.
Churchward, L. G. Australia & America: 1788-1972. 290p. 1981. 16.95 (ISBN 0-909188-03-3, Alternative Publishing Cooperative Ltd). Lawrence Hill.
--Contemporary Soviet Government. 2nd ed. 385p. 1975. text ed. 24.95 (ISBN 0-444-19518-1). Elsevier.
Churchyard, T., tr. see Meteren, Emanuel van.
Churchyard, Thomas. A Lamentable & Pitifull Description of the Wofull Warres in Flaunders. LC 76-57372. (English Experience Ser.: No. 790). 1977. Repr. of 1578 ed. lib. bdg. 8.00 (ISBN 90-221-0790-6). Walter J Johnson.
--Worthiness of Wales. 1966. Repr. of 1587 ed. 54.00 (ISBN 0-8337-0570-9). B Franklin.
Churg, Jacob, et al. Renal Disease-Classification & Atlas of Glomerular Diseases. LC 81-13444. (Illus.). 372p. 1982. text ed. 63.00 (ISBN 0-89640-066-2). Igaku-Shoin.
Churgin, Bathia. Giovanni Battista Sammartini's "Sonate a tre Stromenti:" Six Notturnos for String Trio, Op. 7. LC 80-12339. (Early Musical Masterworks Ser.). 81p. 1981. 20.00x (ISBN 0-8078-1446-6). U of NC Pr.
Churgin, Bathia, jt. ed. see Jenkins, Newell.
Churgin, Jonah R. The New Woman & the Old Academe: Sexism & Higher Education. LC 77-91470. 1979. 7.95 (ISBN 0-87212-076-7). Libra.
Churgin, Pinchas & Smolar, Leivy. Studies in Targum Jonathan to the Prophets. 59.50x (ISBN 0-87068-109-5). Ktav.
Churgin, Pinkos. Targum Jonathan to the Prophets. LC 78-63558. (Yale Oriental Ser. Researches: No. 14). Repr. of 1927 ed. 32.50 (ISBN 0-404-60284-3). AMS Pr.
Churma, Donald G. Arguments from External Evidence in Phonology. (Outstanding Dissertations in Linguistics Ser.). 123p. 1985. 25.00 (ISBN 0-8240-5422-9). Garland Pub.
Churms, Shirley C. CRC Handbook of Chromatography, Carbohydrates, Vol. I. 288p. 1982. 58.00 (ISBN 0-8493-3061-0). CRC Pr.
Churne, William, jt. auth. see Paget, Francis E.
Chusack, Margaret. The Christmas Carol Sampler. (Illus.) (gr. 4-6). 10.95 (ISBN 0-15-217752-3, HJ). HarBraceJ.
Chused, Richard H. A Modern Approach to Property: Cases, Notes, Materials. LC 78-5110. (American Casebook Ser.). 1069p. 1978. text ed. 26.95 (ISBN 0-8299-2004-8). West Pub.
Chusid, E. Leslie, ed. The Selective & Comprehensive Testing of Adult Pulmonary Function. LC 82-84736. (Illus.). 360p. 1983. monograph 44.50 (ISBN 0-87993-195-7). Futura Pub.
Chusid, Joseph G. Correlative Neuroanatomy & Functional Neurology. 19th ed. LC 85-50602. (Illus.). 513p. 1985. lexotone cover 19.50 (ISBN 0-87041-014-8). Lange.
Chusid, Martin. A Catalogue of Verdi's Operas. (Music Indexes & Bibliographies: No. 5). 1974. pap. 17.00 (ISBN 0-913574-05-8). Eur-Am Music.
Chusid, Martin, ed. see Schubert, Franz.
Chusid, Martin, ed. see Verdi, Giuseppe.
Chusid, Martin, jt. ed. see Weaver, William.
Chusmir, Leonard H. & Durand, Douglas E. Pink-Collar Management: The Complete Guide to Managing Women at Work. 1984. cancelled (ISBN 0-672-52806-1). Bobbs.
Chuta, E., jt. auth. see Allal, M.
Chuta, E., ed. see International Labour Office Staff.
Chuta, Enyinna & Liedholm, Carl. Employment & Growth in Small-Scale Industry: Empirical Evidence & Policy Assessment from Sierra Leone. 256p. 1985. 29.95 (ISBN 0-312-24458-4). St Martin.
Chuta, Enyinna & Sethuraman, S. V., eds. Rural Small-Scale Industries & Employment in Africa & Asia: A Review of Programmes & Policies. 159p. 1984. pap. text ed. 14.25 (ISBN 92-2-103513-1, ILO274, ILO). Unipub.
Chute, Carlton F. Modern Ideas for Administrative Assistants to the Mayor in Large American Cities. 63p. 1971. 1.00 (ISBN 0-318-15808-6). Citizens Forum Gov.
Chute, Carolyn. The Beans of Egypt, Maine. LC 84-8840. 228p. 1985. 15.95 (ISBN 0-89919-314-5); pap. 7.95 (ISBN 0-89919-362-5). Ticknor & Fields.
--The Beans of Egypt, Maine. 15.95 (ISBN 0-89919-314-5); pap. 7.95 (ISBN 0-89919-362-5). HM.
Chute, Carolyn, et al. Inside Vacationland: New Fiction from the Real Maine. Melnicove, Mark, ed. LC 85-7074. 192p. (Orig.). 1985. pap. 8.95 (ISBN 0-937966-18-5). Dog Ear.
Chute, George M. & Chute, Robert D. Electronics in Industry. 5th ed. (Illus.). 1979. text ed. 34.00 (ISBN 0-07-010934-6). McGraw.
Chute, Marchette. Introduction to Shakespeare. (gr. 7 up). 1951. 12.95 (ISBN 0-525-32587-5, 01258-370). Dutton.
--Shakespeare of London. 1957. pap. 8.95 (ISBN 0-525-47001-8, 0869-290). Dutton.
--Stories from Shakespeare. (YA) 1971. pap. 3.50 (ISBN 0-451-62183-2, ME2183, Ment). NAL.
--Two Gentle Men: The Lives of George Herbert & Robert Herrick. 1959. 6.95 (ISBN 0-525-22528-5). Dutton.
Chute, Patricia. Eva's Music. LC 82-45934. (Illus.). 288p. 1984. 14.95 (ISBN 0-385-18133-7). Doubleday.
Chute, Phillip B. American Independent Business: Formation, Operations & Philosophy for the 1980's. (Illus., Orig.). 1985. pap. text ed. write for info. (ISBN 0-930981-00-6). Chute Corp.
Chute, Robert D., jt. auth. see Chute, George M.
Chute, William J. Damn Yankee: The First Career of Frederick A. P. Barnard. (National University Pubns. Ser. in American Studies). 1978. 19.50x (ISBN 0-8046-9177-0, Pub. by Kennikat). Assoc Faculty Pr.
Chu T'ien-Min. Children's Songs from Sixteen Provinces. (National Peking University & Chinese Assn. for Folklore, Folklore & Folkliterature Ser.: No. 134). (Chinese.). 16.00x (ISBN 0-89986-208-X). Oriental Bk Store.
Chuto, J. R. The James Clarence Mangan Bibliography. 1982. 95.00x (ISBN 0-905473-48-5, Pub. by Wolfhound Pr Ireland). State Mutual Bk.
Ch'u Tung-Tsu. Law & Society in Traditional China. LC 79-1602. 1981. Repr. of 1961 ed. 25.00 (ISBN 0-88355-905-6). Hyperion Conn.
Ch'u T'ung-tsu. Local Government in China under the Ch'ing. LC 62-11396. (East Asian Ser: No. 9). 1962. 22.50x (ISBN 0-674-53675-4). Harvard U Pr.
Chuun, Calvin E. Not for Bread Alone. (Illus.). 64p. 1981. 3.00 (ISBN 0-318-16568-6). Soc Descend Wash Army.
Chu Yen. Description of Chinese Pottery & Porcelain. LC 77-38058. Repr. of 1910 ed. 12.50 (ISBN 0-404-56914-5). AMS Pr.
Chu-yuan Cheng. China's Allocation of Fixed Capital Investment, 1952-1957. (Michigan Monographs in Chinese Studies: No. 17). (Illus.). 115p. 1974. pap. 1.50 (ISBN 0-89264-017-0). U of Mich Ctr Chinese.
Chuzeville, Jean, ed. see Vigny, Alfred de.
Chvala, M., et al. The Horse Flies of Europe (Tabanidae) 1972. 125.00x (ISBN 0-317-07096-7, Pub. by EW Classey UK). State Mutual Bk.
Chvalovsky, Vaclav & Bellama, J. M., eds. Carbon-Functional Organosilicon Compounds. (Modern Inorganic Chemistry Ser.). 318p. 1984. 45.00x (ISBN 0-306-41671-9, Plenum Pr). Plenum Pub.
Chvany, Catherine V., jt. auth. see Brecht, Richard D.
Chvany, Catherine V. & Brecht, Richard D., eds. Morphosyntax in Slavic. (Illus.). v, 316p. (Orig.). 1981. pap. 14.95 (ISBN 0-89357-070-2). Slavica.
Chvatal, V. Linear Programming. LC 82-21132. (Illus.). 744p. 1983. text ed. 49.95 (ISBN 0-7167-1195-8); pap. 26.95 (ISBN 0-7167-1587-2). W H Freeman.
Chvatal, V., jt. ed. see Berge, C.
Chvatal, Vasek. Solutions Manual for Linear Programming. 119p. 1984. write for info (ISBN 0-7167-1678-X). W H Freeman.
Chvidchenko, Ivan, jt. auth. see CNES.
Chwast, Seymour. The Left-Handed Designer. (Illus.). 144p. 1985. 35.00 (ISBN 0-8109-1289-9). Abrams.
--Sweetheart & Others. 1975. pap. 2.25 (ISBN 0-380-00351-1, 23572-2). Avon.
--Tall City, Wide Country: A Book to Read Forward & Backward. (Illus.). 32p. (ps-k). 1983. 7.95 (ISBN 0-670-69236-0). Viking.
Chwast, Seymour & Schickele, Peter. Happy Birthday Bach. (Illus.). 144p. 1985. 12.95 (ISBN 0-385-19912-0, Dolp). Doubleday.
Chwast, Seymour & Heller, Steven, eds. The Art of New York. (Illus.). 192p. 1983. 49.50 (ISBN 0-8109-1809-9). Abrams.
Chwast, Seymour, illus. Bushy Bride: Norwegian Fairy Tale. (Collection of Fairy Tales Ser.). 32p. 1983. 7.95 (ISBN 0-87191-952-4). Creative Ed.
Chwast, Seymour, jt. auth. see Bruckner, J. R.
Chwast, Seymour, jt. ed. see Heller, Steven.
Chwat, Jacques, ed. see Marlowe, Christopher.
Chwolsohn, D. Die Ssabier und der Ssabismus, 2 Vols. 1856. 85.00 (ISBN 0-384-09053-2). Johnson Repr.
Chwolson, D. A. Hebrew Grave Inscriptions from the Crimea & Corpus of Hebrew in Scriptions. 1978. lib. bdg. 44.95 (ISBN 0-87700-294-0). Revisionist Pr.
Chyet, Stanley F. Lopez of Newport: Colonial American Merchant Prince. LC 78-93898. 240p. 1970. 11.95x (ISBN 0-8143-1407-4). Wayne St U Pr.
Chyet, Stanley F., jt. auth. see Herscher, Uri D.
Chyet, Stanley F., jt. ed. see Gutmann, Joseph.
Chyet, Stanley F., jt. tr. see Bargad, Warren.
Chylinska, Teresa. Szymanowski. Jordan, A. T., tr. (Library of Polish Studies: Vol. 1). (Illus.). 1973. text ed. 9.00 (ISBN 0-917004-04-3). Kosciuszko.
Chynn, K. Y. & Finby, N. Manual of Cranial Computerized Tomography. (Illus.). vi, 106p. 1982. 84.25 (ISBN 3-8055-3432-9). S Karger.
Chynoweth, A. G., ed. see American Physical Society Conference, New York City, Feb. 2-5, 1976.
Chynoweth, Alan G., jt. ed. see Miller, Stewart E.
Chytil, M. Mathematical Foundations of Computer Science 1981. Gruska, J., ed. (Lecture Notes in Computer Science Ser.: Vol. 118). 589p. 1981. pap. 31.50 (ISBN 0-387-10856-4). Springer-Verlag.
Chytil, M. P., et al. Mathematical Foundations of Computer Science 1984: Praha, Czechoslovakia, September 3-8, 1984. (Lecture Notes in Computer Science Ser.: Vol. 176). xi, 581p. pap. 28.00 (ISBN 0-387-13372-0). Springer-Verlag.
Chyzhevskyi, Dmytro. History of Russian Literature from the Eleventh Century to the End of the Baroque. LC 79-3074. (Illus.). 451p. 1981. Repr. of 1960 ed. 38.50 (ISBN 0-8305-0067-7). Hyperion Conn.
Chyzowych, Walt. The World Cup. (Illus.). 200p. 1984. 15.95 (ISBN 0-89651-900-7); pap. 8.95 (ISBN 0-89651-905-8). Icarus.
Chyzowych, Walter. The Official Soccer Book of the United States Soccer Federation. LC 78-7100. (Illus.). 256p. 1978. 14.95 (ISBN 0-528-81008-1); pap. 8.95 (ISBN 0-528-88125-6). Rand.
CIA. Rote Kapelle. Kesaris, Paul, ed. 1979. 29.50 (ISBN 0-89093-203-4). U Pubns Amer.
Ciabotti, Patricia. Gaming It up with Shakespeare. Smith, Linda H., ed. 1980. pap. 4.95 (ISBN 0-936386-09-6). Creative Learning.
Ciabotti, Patricia A. & Crocker, Herbert L. Career Awareness Day: A Prescription for Creating Job Awareness in Elementary & Intermediate School Students. 1981. pap. 7.95 (ISBN 0-936386-15-0). Creative Learning.
Ciaburri, William. Suburban Lyrics. 1980. 6.95 (ISBN 0-89962-014-0). Todd & Honeywell.
Ciaccio, David J. Site Sections & Details: A Reference Guide to Site Construction Details. LC 84-5095. (Illus.). 128p. 1984. o. p. 22.50 (ISBN 0-442-21617-3); pap. 14.95 (ISBN 0-442-23522-4). Van Nos Reinhold.
Ciaccio, Leoanrd L., ed. Water & Water Pollution Handbook, Vol. 3. 1972. 95.00 (ISBN 0-8247-1117-3). Dekker.
--Water & Water Pollution Handbook, Vol. 4. 548p. 1973. 95.00 (ISBN 0-8247-1118-1). Dekker.
Ciaccio, Leonard L., ed. Water & Water Pollution Handbook, Vol. 1. 1971. 95.00 (ISBN 0-8247-1104-1). Dekker.
--Water & Water Pollution Handbook, Vol. 2. 400p. 1971. 95.00 (ISBN 0-8247-1116-5). Dekker.
Cialdella, Gary & Bartley, Lynwood, eds. The Stuart Avenue Project. (Illus.). 16p. (Orig.). pap. 2.00 (ISBN 0-933742-02-9). Kalamazoo Inst Arts.
Cialdini, Robert. Influence: The New Psychology of Modern Persuasion. rev. ed. LC 84-24791. (Illus.). 304p. 1985. pap. 7.95 (ISBN 0-688-04107-8, Quill). Morrow.
Cialdini, Robert B. Influence. 1985. pap. text ed. 9.95 (ISBN 0-673-15514-5). Scott F.
--Influence: How & Why People Agree to Do Things. LC 83-21963. 290p. 1984. 15.95 (ISBN 0-688-01560-3). Morrow.
Ciampi, C. Artificial Intelligence & Legal Information Systems. 476p. 1982. 57.50 (ISBN 0-444-86414-8, I-187-82, North-Holland). Elsevier.
Ciampi, C. & Martino, A. A. Artificial Intelligence & Legal Information. 1984. 108.50 (ISBN 0-444-86413-X). Elsevier.
Ciampi, Elgin, jt. auth. see Boyle, Robert H.
Ciampi, Luke. Watering the Seed. 1977. 5.95 (ISBN 0-685-71934-0). Franciscan Herald.
Cianciolo, Patricia. Picture Books for Children. 2nd ed. LC 80-39958. 254p. 1981. pap. 15.00x (ISBN 0-8389-0315-0). ALA.
Cianciolo, Pauline, jt. ed. see Laybonrne, Kit.

Ciancutti, Arthur R. The View from the Gurney Up: Dealing with People in Crisis & Emergency. LC 83-51731. 111p. 1984. pap. 14.00 (ISBN 0-87762-338-4). Technomic.

Cianflone, Ralph. This Could Be Your Life. 128p. 1980. 7.95 (ISBN 0-89962-039-6). Todd & Honeywell.

Cianfrani, Theodore. A Short History of Obstetrics & Gynecology. (Illus.). 466p. 1960. photocopy ed. 44.00x (ISBN 0-398-00308-4). C C Thomas.

Ciani, Alfred J., ed. Motivating Reluctant Readers. 112p. (Orig.). 1981. pap. text ed. 6.00 (ISBN 0-87207-530-3, 530). Intl Reading.

Ciano, Galeazzo. The Ciano Diaries, Nineteen Thirty-Nine to Nineteen Forty-Three: The Complete, Unabridged Diaries of Count Galeazzo Ciano, Italian Minister for Foreign Affairs, 1936-1943. Gibson, Hugh, ed. LC 83-1703. xxxi, 584p. Repr. of 1946 ed. lib. bdg. write for info. (ISBN 0-313-23959-2, CIDI). Greenwood.

--Ciano's Diplomatic Papers. Muggeridge, Malcolm, ed. Head, Stuart, tr. LC 83-45734. Date not set. Repr. of 1948 ed. 41.50 (ISBN 0-404-20060-5, DG575). AMS Pr.

Ciaramataro, Andrew J. Beat the IRS (Legally) 1983 Edition for Your 1982 Returns. (Orig.). 1982. pap. 3.95 (ISBN 0-425-05550-7). Berkley Pub.

Ciaramella, J. P., jt. auth. see LeMaraic, A. L.

Ciaramella, J. P., jt. ed. see LeMaraic, A. L.

Ciaramitaro, Barbara. Help for Depressed Mothers. Meyer, Linda, ed. LC 81-70362. 155p. 1982. 12.95 (ISBN 0-9603516-4-7); pap. 7.95 (ISBN 0-686-80938-6). C Franklin Pr.

Ciarcia, S. Ciarcia's Circuit Cellar, 3 Vols. 128p. 1979. Vol. I. pap. 14.95 (ISBN 0-07-010960-5, BYTE Bks); Vol. II. pap. 18.95 (ISBN 0-07-010963-X); Vol. III. pap. 18.95 (ISBN 0-07-010965-6). Mcgraw.

Ciarcia, S., jt. auth. see Dahmke, Mark.

Ciarcia, Steve. Build Your Own Z80 Computer. 473p. 1980. (BYTE Bks); pap. 19.95 (ISBN 0-07-010962-1). McGraw.

--Ciarcia's Circuit Cellar, Vol. IV. (BYTE Bks.). (Illus.). 1984. pap. 18.95 (ISBN 0-07-010966-4). McGraw.

Ciardelli, F. & Giusti, P. Structural Order in Polymers: International Symposium on Macromolecules, Florence, Italy, 7-12 September 1980. (IUPAC Symposium Ser.). (Illus.). 260p. 1981. 77.00 (ISBN 0-08-025296-6). Pergamon.

Ciardelli, I., jt. ed. see Lenz, R. W.

Ciardi, J. E., jt. ed. see Doyle, R. J.

Ciardi, John. Birds of Pompeii. 80p. 1985. 9.95 (ISBN 0-938626-44-2); pap. 5.95 (ISBN 0-938626-45-0). U of Ark Pr.

--A Browser's Dictionary. LC 79-1658. 464p. 1980. 17.26i (ISBN 0-06-010766-9, HarpT). Har-Row.

--Doodle Soup. LC 85-814. (Illus.). 64p. (gr. 2-5). 1985. 11.95 (ISBN 0-395-38395-1). HM.

--Fast & Slow: Poems for Advanced Children of Beginning Parents. LC 74-22405. (Illus.). 68p. (gr. k-3). 1974. 6.95 (ISBN 0-395-20282-5); pap. 1.95 (ISBN 0-395-26680-7). HM.

--For Instance. 1979. pap. 4.95 (ISBN 0-393-00939-4). Norton.

--I Met a Man. (Illus.). (gr. 2-4). 1961. PLB 8.95 (ISBN 0-395-18018-X). HM.

--A Second Browser's Dictionary: Native's Guide to the Unknown American Language. LC 82-48658. 420p. 1983. 16.30i (ISBN 0-06-015125-0, HarpT). Har-Row.

--Selected Poems. LC 83-24254. 222p. 1984. 21.00 (ISBN 0-938626-29-9); pap. 8.95 (ISBN 0-938626-30-2). U of Ark Pr.

--This Strangest Everything. 1966. 8.95 (ISBN 0-8135-0526-7). Rutgers U Pr.

--You Read to Me, I'll Read to You. LC 62-16296. (Illus.). (gr. k-6). 1961. 9.57i (ISBN 0-397-30645-8); PLB 9.89 (ISBN 0-397-30646-6). Lipp Jr Bks.

Ciardi, John & Williams, Miller. How Does a Poem Mean. 2nd ed. LC 74-11592. 432p. 1975. 18.95 (ISBN 0-395-18605-6). HM.

Ciardi, John, jt. auth. see Asimov, Isaac.

Ciardi, John, jt. auth. see Roberts, Joseph B., Jr.

Ciardi, John, tr. Purgatorio by Dante. 1971. pap. 3.50 (ISBN 0-451-62206-5, ME2206, Ment). NAL.

Ciardi, John, tr. see Alighiere, Dante.

Ciardi, John, tr. see Dante Alighieri.

Ciarlet, P. G. The Finite Element Method for Elliptic Problems. (Studies in Mathematics & Its Applications: Vol. 4). 530p. 1978. 85.00 (ISBN 0-444-85028-7, North-Holland); pap. 36.25 (ISBN 0-444-86016-9). Elsevier.

--Lectures on Three-Dimensional Elasticity. (Tata Institute Lectures on Mathematics). 160p. 1983. pap. 7.90 (ISBN 0-387-12331-8). Springer-Verlag.

--Topics in Mathematical Elasticity. (Studies in Mechanical Engineering). 1984. write for info. (North-Holland). Elsevier.

Ciarlet, P. G. & Roseau, M., eds. Trends & Applications of Pure Mathematics to Mechanics: Invited & Contributed Papers Presented at a Symposium at Ecole Polytechnique, Palaiseau, France, Nov. 28-Dec. 2 1983. (Lecture Notes in Physics: Vol. 195). (Fr. & Eng.). 1984. pap. 23.50 (ISBN 0-387-12916-2). Springer Verlag.

Ciarlo, Hector O. El Camino de Occidente: Introduccion a las Humanidades. LC 82-7003. 258p. (Orig., Span.). 1984. pap. 5.00 (ISBN 0-8477-3504-4). U of PR Pr.

--Critica de la Razon Poetica. 170p. (Orig.). 1982. pap. 3.50x (ISBN 0-8477-2824-2). U of PR Pr.

--El Escritor y su Obra: Al encuentro de Concha Melendez y otros ensayos. LC 82-6894. 138p. (Orig., Span.). 1982. pap. 3.50 (ISBN 0-8477-3509-5). U of PR Pr.

Ciarlo, James A., ed. Utilizing Evaluation: Concepts & Measurement Techniques. (Research Progress Series in Evaluation: Vol. 6). 152p. 1981. pap. 9.95 (ISBN 0-8039-1522-5); 20.00 (ISBN 0-8039-1521-7). Sage.

Ciarlone, Alfred E., jt. auth. see Gangerosa, Louis P.

Ciatti, Mario, jt. auth. see Martin, Genevieve A.

Ciavolella, M., tr. see Caro, Annibal.

Ciba. Human Lens in Relation to Cataract. (Ciba Symposium Ser.: No. 19). 1974. 29.00 (ISBN 0-444-15016-1). Elsevier.

--Major Mental Handicap: Methods & Costs of Prevention. (Ciba Symposium Ser.: No. 59). 1978. 29.00 (ISBN 0-444-90033-0). Elsevier.

--Metabolic Activities of the Lung. (Ciba Symposia Ser.: No. 78). 1981. 71.50 (ISBN 0-444-90159-0). Elsevier.

--Phosphorous & the Environment: Its Chemistry & Biochemistry. (Ciba Symposium Ser.: No. 57). 1978. 41.00 (ISBN 0-444-90031-4). Elsevier.

--Respiratory Tract Mucus. (Ciba Symposium Ser.: No. 54). 1978. 46.00 (ISBN 0-444-90016-0). Elsevier.

Ciba Foundation. Acute Diarrhoea in Childhood. LC 76-13875. (Ciba Foundation Symposium, New Ser.: 42). pap. 96.30 (ISBN 0-317-29785-6, 2022170). Bks Demand UMI.

--Aromatic Amino Acids in the Brain. LC 73-91643. (Ciba Foundation Symposium: New Ser.: No. 22). pap. 101.50 (ISBN 0-317-29189-0, 2022152). Bks Demand UMI.

--Atherogenesis: Initiating Factors. LC 73-76974. (Ciba Foundation Symposium: New Ser.: No. 12). pap. 74.00 (ISBN 0-317-28304-9, 2022143). Bks Demand UMI.

--Biochemistry & Pharmacology of Platelets. (Ciba Foundation Symposium: New Ser.: No. 35). pap. 90.00 (ISBN 0-317-29173-4, 2022163). Bks Demand UMI.

--Biological Roles of Copper. LC 80-23396. (Ciba Foundation Symposium, New Ser.: 79). pap. 87.80 (ISBN 0-317-29742-2, 2022198). Bks Demand UMI.

--Blood Cells & Vessel Walls: Functional Interractions. (Ciba Symposium Ser.: No. 71). 1980. 47.00 (ISBN 0-444-90112-4). Elsevier.

--Blood Cells & Vessel Walls: Functional Interactions. LC 79-26528. (Ciba Foundation Symposium, New Ser.: 71). pap. 92.30 (ISBN 0-317-29758-9, 2022190). Bks Demand UMI.

--Breast-Feeding & the Mother. LC 76-44816. (Ciba Foundation SYmposium, New Ser.: No. 45). pap. 72.00 (ISBN 0-317-29780-5, 2022173). Bks Demand UMI.

--Carbon-Fluorine Compounds: Chemistry, Biochemistry & Biological Activities. LC 72-76005. (Ciba Foundation Symposium Ser.: No. 2). pap. 106.30 (ISBN 0-317-28328-6, 2022135). Bks Demand UMI.

--Cell Patterning. LC 78-304197. (Ciba Foundation Symposium: New Ser.: No. 29). pap. 91.00 (ISBN 0-317-29180-7, 2022157). Bks Demand UMI.

--Cerebral Vascular Smooth Muscle & Its Control. LC 77-28855. (Ciba Foundation Symposium, New Ser.: 56). pap. 102.00 (ISBN 0-317-29773-2, 2022181). Bks Demand UMI.

--Child Sexual Abuse Within the Family. 176p. 1985. 28.00 (ISBN 0-422-79280-2, 9325, Pub. by Tavistock England); pap. 12.95x (9326, Pub. by Tavistock England). Methuen Inc.

--Civilization & Science in Conflict or Collaboration? LC 77-188826. (Ciba Foundation Symposium - New Ser.: No. 1). pap. 59.30 (ISBN 0-317-28331-6, 2022134). Bks Demand UMI.

--Congenital Disorders of Erythropoiesis. (Ciba Foundation Symposium: New Ser.: No. 37). pap. 104.00 (ISBN 0-317-29170-X, 2022165). Bks Demand UMI.

--Corneal Graft Failure. LC 73-82445. (Ciba Foundation Symposium: New Ser.: No. 15). pap. 92.80 (ISBN 0-317-28298-0, 2022146). Bks Demand UMI.

--Development of Mammalian Absorptive Processes. (Ciba Symposium Ser.: Vol. 70). 1980. 47.75 (ISBN 0-444-90101-9). Elsevier.

--Development of Mammalian Absorptive Processes. LC 79-20804. (Ciba Foundation Symposium, New Ser.: 70). pap. 87.50 (ISBN 0-317-29760-0, 2022189). Bks Demand UMI.

--Drug Concentrations in Neuropsychiatry. LC 80-11309. (Ciba Foundation Symposium, New Ser.: 74). pap. 68.50 (ISBN 0-317-29752-X, 2022193). Bks Demand UMI.

--Embryogenesis in Mammals. LC 76-7009. (Ciba Foundation Symposium, New Ser.: 40). pap. 79.00 (ISBN 0-317-29788-0, 2022168). Bks Demand UMI.

--Energy Transformation in Biological Systems. LC 76-350357. (Ciba Foundation Symposium: New Ser.: No. 31). pap. 106.50 (ISBN 0-317-29178-5, 2022159). Bks Demand UMI.

--Environmental Chemicals, Enzyme Function & Human Disease. LC 80-18000. (Ciba Foundation Symposium, New Ser.: 76). pap. 97.50 (ISBN 0-317-29748-1, 2022195). Bks Demand UMI.

--Enzyme Defects & Immune Dysfunction. LC 79-17092. (Ciba Foundation Symposium, New Ser.: No. 68). pap. 74.80 (ISBN 0-317-29762-7, 2022188). Bks Demand UMI.

--The Fetus & Independent Life: Ciba Foundation Symposium '86. 320p. 1981. 120.00x (ISBN 0-272-79650-6, Pub. by Pitman Bks England). State Mutual Bk.

--The Freezing of Mammalian Embryos. LC 77-10122. (Ciba Foundation Symposium, New Ser.: 52). pap. 85.00 (ISBN 0-317-29775-9, 2022177). Bks Demand UMI.

--The Future As an Academic Discipline. LC 76-363694. (Ciba Foundation Symposium: New Ser.: No. 36). pap. 60.00 (ISBN 0-317-29171-8, 2022164). Bks Demand UMI.

--The Future of Philanthropic Foundations. LC 75-398199. (Ciba Foundation Symposium: New Ser.: No. 30). pap. 62.00 (ISBN 0-317-29179-3, 2022158). Bks Demand UMI.

--Haemopoietic Stem Cells. LC 73-76975. (Ciba Foundation Symposium: New Ser.: No. 13). pap. 88.80 (ISBN 0-317-28301-4, 2022144). Bks Demand UMI.

--Hard Tissue Growth, Repair & Remineralization. LC 72-97287. (Ciba Foundation Symposium: New Ser.: No. 11). pap. 116.50 (ISBN 0-317-28305-7, 2022142). Bks Demand UMI.

--Health & Disease in Tribal Societies. LC 77-9478. (Ciba Foundation Symposium, New Ser.: 49). pap. 88.00 (ISBN 0-317-29778-3, 2022175). Bks Demand UMI.

--Health & Industrial Growth. LC 76-370643. (Ciba Foundation Symposium: New Ser.: No. 32). pap. 68.80 (ISBN 0-317-29177-7, 2022160). Bks Demand UMI.

--Health Care in a Changing Setting: The UK Experience. LC 76-15417. (Ciba Foundation Symposium, New Ser.: 43). pap. 49.00 (ISBN 0-317-29783-X, 2022171). Bks Demand UMI.

--The Human Lens: In Relations to Cataract. LC 73-85703. (Ciba Foundation Symposium: New Ser.: No. 19). pap. 84.00 (ISBN 0-317-28288-3, 2022150). Bks Demand UMI.

--Immunopotentiation. LC 73-84990. (Ciba Foundation Symposium: New Ser.: No. 18). pap. 91.30 (ISBN 0-317-28290-5, 2022149). Bks Demand UMI.

--Iron Metabolism. LC 77-24153. (Ciba Foundation Symposium, New Ser.: 51). pap. 100.30 (ISBN 0-317-29777-5, 2022176). Bks Demand UMI.

--Law & Ethics of A. I. D. & Embryo Transfer. LC 73-80904. (Ciba Foundation Symposium: New Ser.: No. 17). pap. 29.50 (ISBN 0-317-28291-3, 2022148). Bks Demand UMI.

--Locomotion of Tissue Cells. LC 73-80386. (Ciba Foundation Symposium: New Ser.: No. 14). pap. 97.30 (ISBN 0-317-28300-6, 2022145). Bks Demand UMI.

--Lung Liquids. LC 76-870. (Ciba Foundation Symposium, New Ser.: 38). pap. 85.00 (ISBN 0-317-29790-2, 2022166). Bks Demand UMI.

--Major Mental Handicap: Methods & Costs of Prevention. LC 78-15495. (Ciba Foundation Symposium, New Ser.: 59). pap. 58.50 (ISBN 0-317-29768-6, 2022183). Bks Demand UMI.

--Medical Care of Prisoners & Detainees. LC 73-82148. (Ciba Foundation Symposium: New Ser.: No. 16). pap. 61.50 (ISBN 0-317-28294-8, 2022147). Bks Demand UMI.

--Medical Research Systems in Europe: A Joint Wellcome Trust-Ciba Foundation Symposium. LC 73-86342. (Ciba Foundation Symposium: New Ser.: No. 21). pap. 85.80 (ISBN 0-317-29190-4, 2022151). Bks Demand UMI.

--Metabolic Activities of the Lung. LC 80-20318. (Ciba Foundation Symposium, New Ser.: 78). pap. 102.80 (ISBN 0-317-29743-0, 2022197). Bks Demand UMI.

--Molecular Interactions & Activity in Proteins. LC 78-14500. (Ciba Foundation Symposium, New Ser.: 60). pap. 71.80 (ISBN 0-317-29766-X, 2022184). Bks Demand UMI.

--Monoamine Oxidase & Its Inhibition. LC 76-10396. (Ciba Foundation Symposium, New Ser.: 39). pap. 106.80 (2022167). Bks Demand UMI.

--Ontogeny of Acquired Immunity. LC 72-81001. (Ciba Foundation Symposium Ser.: No. 5). pap. 73.30 (ISBN 0-317-28322-7, 2022137). Bks Demand UMI.

--Outcome of Severe Damage to the Central Nervous System. LC 76-361019. (Ciba Foundation Symposium: New Ser.: No. 34). pap. 91.00 (ISBN 0-317-29174-2, 2022162). Bks Demand UMI.

--Parasites in the Immunized Host: Mechanisms of Survival. LC 75-311586. (Ciba Foundation Symposium: New Ser.: No. 25). pap. 72.00 (ISBN 0-317-29185-8, 2022154). Bks Demand UMI.

--Pathogenic Mycoplasmas. LC 72-88563. (Ciba Foundation Symposium Ser.: No. 6). pap. 103.50 (ISBN 0-317-28318-9, 2022138). Bks Demand UMI.

--Peptide Transport in Bacteria & Mammalian Cut. LC 72-76006. (Ciba Foundation Symposium Ser.: No. 4). pap. 42.50 (ISBN 0-317-28325-1, 2022136). Bks Demand UMI.

--Perinatal Infections. (Ciba Symposia Ser.: No. 77). 1980. 56.25 (ISBN 0-444-90158-2). Elsevier.

--Perinatal Infections. LC 80-23631. (Ciba Foundation Symposium, New Ser.: 77). pap. 76.00 (ISBN 0-317-29745-7, 2022196). Bks Demand UMI.

--Phosphorus in the Environment: Its Chemistry & Biochemsitry. LC 78-4289. (Ciba Foundation Symposium, New Ser.: 57). pap. 82.50 (ISBN 0-317-29771-6, 2022182). Bks Demand UMI.

--The Physiological Basis of Starling's Law of the Heart. LC 74-77177. (Ciba Foundation Symposium: New Ser.: No. 24). pap. 77.00 (ISBN 0-317-29186-6, 2022153). Bks Demand UMI.

--Physiology, Emotion & Psychosomatic Illness. LC 72-93253. (Ciba Foundation Symposium: New Ser.: No. 8). pap. 107.50 (ISBN 0-317-28312-X, 2022140). Bks Demand UMI.

--The Poisoned Patient: The Role of the Laboratory. LC 75-317672. (Ciba Foundation Symposium: New Ser.: No. 26). pap. 83.30 (ISBN 0-317-29183-1, 2022155). Bks Demand UMI.

--Polymerization in Biological Systems. LC 72-86558. (Ciba Foundation Symposium: New Ser.: No. 13). pap. 80.50 (ISBN 0-317-28314-6, 2022139). Bks Demand UMI.

--Protein Degradation in Health & Disease. (Ciba Symposium Ser.: No. 75). 1980. 76.75 (ISBN 0-444-90148-5). Elsevier.

--Protein Degradation in Health & Disease. LC 80-15308. (Ciba Foundation Symposium, New Ser.: 75). pap. 107.00 (ISBN 0-317-29749-X, 2022194). Bks Demand UMI.

--Protein Turnover. LC 72-96519. (Ciba Foundation Symposium: New Ser.: No. 9). pap. 81.80 (ISBN 0-317-28310-3, 2022141). Bks Demand UMI.

--Purine & Pyrimidine Metabolism. LC 76-52420. (Ciba Foundation Symposium, New Ser.: 48). pap. 95.30 (ISBN 0-317-29779-1, 2022174). Bks Demand UMI.

--Research & Medical Practice: Their Interaction. LC 76-24846. (Ciba Foundation Symposium, New Ser.: 44). pap. 57.00 (ISBN 0-317-29782-1, 2022172). Bks Demand UMI.

--Respiratory Tract Mucus. LC 77-16019. (Ciba Foundation Symposium, New Ser.: 54). pap. 85.50 (ISBN 0-317-29774-0, 2022179). Bks Demand UMI.

--Sex, Hormones & Behaviour. (CIBA Foundation Symposium: No. 62). 1979. 47.00 (ISBN 0-444-90045-4). Elsevier.

--Sex, Hormones & Behaviour. (Ciba Foundation Symposium, New Ser.: 62). pap. 97.50 (ISBN 0-317-29765-1, 2022185). Bks Demand UMI.

--The Structure & Function of Chromatin. LC 76-357416. (Ciba Foundation Symposium: New Ser.: No. 28). pap. 94.50 (ISBN 0-317-29182-3, 2022156). Bks Demand UMI.

--Submolecular Biology & Cancer. LC 79-10949. (Ciba Foundation Ser.: No. 67). 360p. 1979. 48.50 (ISBN 0-444-90078-0, Excerpta Medica). Elsevier.

--Submolecular Biology & Cancer. LC 79-14324. (Ciba Foundation Symposium, New Ser.: 67). pap. 90.00 (ISBN 0-317-29763-5, 2022187). Bks Demand UMI.

--Sulphur in Biology. (Ciba Symposium Ser.: Vol. 72). 1980. 55.75 (ISBN 0-444-90108-6). Elsevier.

--Sulphur in Biology. LC 79-24939. (Ciba Foundation Symposium, New Ser.: 72). pap. 81.00 (ISBN 0-317-29756-2, 2022191). Bks Demand UMI.

--Trends in Enzyme Histochemistry & Cytochemistry. (Ciba Symposium Ser.: No. 73). 1980. 58.50 (ISBN 0-444-90135-3). Elsevier.

--Trends in Enzyme Histochemistry & Cytochemistry. LC 80-11757. (Ciba Foundation Symposium, New Ser.: 73). pap. 80.50 (ISBN 0-317-29754-6, 2022192). Bks Demand UMI.

Ciba Foundation, ed. Acute Diarrhea in Childhood. (Ciba Foundation Symposium: No. 42). 1976. 42.75 (ISBN 90-219-4047-7, Excerpta Medica). Elsevier.

--Outcome of Severe Damage to the Central Nervous System. (CIBA Foundation Symposium Ser.: No. 34). 340p. 1976. 36.25 (ISBN 0-444-15182-6, Excerpta Medica). Elsevier.

--Polypeptide Hormones: Molecular & Cellular Aspects. (CIBA Foundation Symposium Ser.: No. 41). 1976. 44.00 (ISBN 0-444-15207-5, Excerpta Medica). Elsevier.

Ciba Foundation Staff. Aromatic Amino Acids in the Brain: Proceedings. (Ciba Foundation Symposium: No. 22). 1974. 34.00 (ISBN 90-219-4023-X, Excerpta Medica). Elsevier.

--Further Perspectives in Organic Chemistry. (Ciba Foundation Symposium: New Ser. 53). pap. 55.00 (ISBN 0-317-08911-0, 2022178). Bks Demand UMI.

--Parent-Infant Interaction. (Ciba Symposium Ser.: No. 33). 1975. 33.00 (ISBN 0-444-15181-8). Elsevier.

--Parent-Infant Interaction. LC 77-676760. (Ciba Foundation, Symposium Ser.: No. 33). 1975. pap. 84.00 (ISBN 0-317-08142-X, 2022161). Bks Demand UMI.

--Polypeptide Hormones: Molecular & Cellular Aspects. LC 76-2666. (Ciba Foundation Symposium, New Ser.: 41). pap. 100.00 (ISBN 0-317-29787-2, 2022169). Bks Demand UMI.

CIBA Foundation Symposium. Biological Roles of Copper. (Ciba Symposium Ser.: No. 79). 1981. 61.50 (ISBN 0-444-90177-9). Elsevier.

Ciba Founndation. The Poisoned Patient: The Role of the Laboratory. (Ciba Symposium Ser.: No. 26). 335p. 1974. 37.00 (ISBN 0-444-15144-3, Excerpta Medica). Elsevier.

Cibbarelli, Pamela & Kazlauskas, Edward, eds. Directory of Information Management Software for Libraries, Information Centers, Record Centers, 1985-1986. 239p. 1985. pap. 49.00 (ISBN 0-913203-14-9). Pacific Info.

Cibber, Colley. Apology for the Life of Colley Cibber. 1976. 12.95x (ISBN 0-460-00668-1, Evman). Biblio Dist.

--Apology for the Life of Colley Cibber Written by Himself, 2 Vols. rev. ed. Lowe, R. W., ed. LC 25-7679. Repr. of 1889 ed. 75.00 (ISBN 0-404-01544-1). AMS Pr.

--The Careless Husband. Appleton, William W., ed. LC 66-15482. (Regents Restoration Drama Ser). xvi, 135p. 1966. 12.50x (ISBN 0-8032-0352-7); pap. 3.95x (ISBN 0-8032-5352-4, BB 257, Bison). U of Nebr Pr.

--Colley Cibber, 2 vols. 400p. 1982. Repr. lib. bdg. 65.00 (ISBN 0-89760-164-5). Telegraph Bks.

--Dramatic Works, 5 vols. Baker, D. E., ed. Repr. of 1777 ed. Set. 187.50 (ISBN 0-404-01590-5); 37.50 ea. Vol. 1 (ISBN 0-404-01591-3). Vol. 2 (ISBN 0-404-01592-1). Vol. 3 (ISBN 0-404-01593-X). Vol. 4 (ISBN 0-404-01594-8). Vol. 5 (ISBN 0-404-01595-6). AMS Pr.

--The Plays of Colley Cibber, 2 vols. Hayley, Rodney, ed. LC 78-66634. (Eighteenth Century English Drama Ser.). 1980. Set. lib. bdg. 145.00 (ISBN 0-8240-3582-8). Garland Pub.

Cibber, Colley, jt. auth. see Vanbrugh, John.

Cibber, Susanna, jt. auth. see Cibber, Tehophilus.

Cibber, Tehophilus & Cibber, Susanna. The Plays of Tehophilus & Susanna Cibber. Mann, David, ed. (Eighteen Century English Drama Ser.). 1981. lib. bdg. 73.00 (ISBN 0-8240-3583-6). Garland Pub.

Cibber, Theophilus. Lives of the Poets of Great Britain & Ireland, to the Time of Dean Swift, 5 Vols. 1968. Repr. of 1753 ed. Set. 152.00x (ISBN 3-4870-2038-6). Adlers Foreign Bks.

Cibils, Luis A. Electronic Fetal-Material Monitoring: Antepartum-Intrapartum. (Illus.). 510p. 1981. text ed. 62.50 (ISBN 0-88416-192-7). PSG Pub Co.

--Gynecologic Laparoscopy: Diagnostic & Operatory. LC 75-9554. (Current Concepts in Obstetrics & Gynecology Ser.). pap. 46.30 (ISBN 0-317-28175-5, 2014532). Bks Demand UMI.

Cibinic, jt. auth. see Nash.

Cibinic, John, jt. auth. see Nash, Ralph C.

Ciboski, Kenneth N., jt. ed. see Kozak, David C.

Cibrowski, Lee, jt. auth. see Slater, Shirley.

Cibula, Adam B. Biological Science Laboratory Guide, Vol. 1. 1976. pap. text ed. 7.95 (ISBN 0-8403-1049-8). Kendall-Hunt.

--Biological Science Laboratory Guide: Preliminary Edition, Vol. 2. 1977. pap. text ed. 7.95 (ISBN 0-8403-1844-8). Kendall-Hunt.

--Biological Sciences Laboratory Guide, Volume 3. 1977. pap. text ed. 5.95 (ISBN 0-8403-1732-8). Kendall-Hunt.

Cibula, William G. An Ecological & Taxonomic Study of Selected Higher Fungi in Northeastern Ohio. 1974. 4.00 (ISBN 0-86727-075-6). Ohio Bio Survey.

Cibulka, James G. & O'Brien, Timothy J. Inner City Private Elementary Schools: A Study. 225p. 1982. pap. 11.95 (ISBN 0-87462-463-0). Marquette.

Cibulskis, Margaret M. Essentials of Pharmacology. 240p. 1982. pap. text ed. 12.50 (ISBN 0-397-54334-4, Lippincott Medical). Lippincott.

Cicalese, Michael. Emergency Response Directory for Hazardous Materials Accidents. LC 83-63323. 251p. 1984. pap. text ed. 34.00 (ISBN 0-930500-01-6). Odin Pr.

Cicchelli, Terry & Ashby-Davis, Claire. Teaching Exceptional Children & Youth in the Regular Classroom. 368p. (Orig.). 1985. text ed. 29.95x (ISBN 0-8156-2341-0); pap. text ed. 12.95 (ISBN 0-8156-2342-9). Syracuse U Pr.

Cicchetti, Charles J & Gillen, William J. The Marginal Cost & Pricing of Electricity: An Applied Approach. LC 77-2312. 1977. prof ref 30.00x (ISBN 0-88410-612-8). Ballinger Pub.

Cicchetti, Dante & Hesse, Petra, eds. Emotional Development. LC 80-84258. (Child Development Ser.: No. 16). 1982. 8.95x (ISBN 0-87589-876-9). Jossey-Bass.

Cicciarella, Charles F. The Sport of Skin Diving. (Illus.). 68p. (Orig.). 1982. pap. text ed. 3.95x (ISBN 0-89641-100-1). American Pr.

--Water Polo. 108p. 1981. pap. text ed. 3.95x (ISBN 0-89641-066-8). American Pr.

Cicciarella, Gloria. Mama's Italian Cooking. 1985. 8.95 (ISBN 0-533-06596-8). Vantage.

Cicco, Philip Di see Krutza, William J. & Dicicco, Philip P.

Cicco, Philip P. Di see Krutza, William J. & DiCicco, Philip P.

Ciccoritti, Linda C., jt. auth. see Harvey, Dodd L.

Cicellis, Kay, tr. see Andronikos, Manolis.

Cicellis, Kay, tr. see Chatzidakis, Manolis.

Cicellis, Kay, tr. see Karageorghis, Vassos.

Cicellis, Kay, tr. see Lorenzatos, Zissimos.

Cicero. Ad C. Herennium, De Ratione Dicendi: Rhetorica Ad Herennium. (Loeb Classical Library: No. 403). 12.50x (ISBN 0-674-99444-2). Harvard U Pr.

--Brutus. Bd. with Orator. (Loeb Classical Library: No. 342). (Lat. & Eng.). 12.50x (ISBN 0-674-99377-2). Harvard U Pr.

--Cicero in His Letters. Tyrrell, Robert Y., ed. (College Classical Ser.). 448p. pap. text ed. 12.50x (ISBN 0-89241-347-6). Caratzas.

--Cicero: Pro Archia. Nall, G. H., ed. (Elementary Classics Ser.). (Latin). 1969. Repr. of 1901 ed. 10.95 (ISBN 0-312-13685-4). St Martin.

--Cicero's Selected Orations. annotated ed. 232p. 1961. 2.00 (ISBN 0-685-27927-8). Landau.

--Correspondence of M. Tullius Cicero, 7 Vols. Tyrell, R. Y. & Purser, L. C., eds. Repr. Set. 350.00x (ISBN 3-4870-2445-4). Adlers Foreign Bks.

--De Finibus. (Loeb Classical Library: No. 40). 1914. 12.50x (ISBN 0-674-99044-7). Harvard U Pr.

--De Inventione. Warmington, E. H., ed. Bd. with De Optimo Genere Oratorum; Topica. (Loeb Classical Library: No. 386). (Lat. & Eng.). 12.50x (ISBN 0-674-99425-6). Harvard U Pr.

--De Natura Deorum. Bd. with Academica 1-2. (Loeb Classical Library: No. 268). 12.50x (ISBN 0-674-99296-2). Harvard U Pr.

--De Officiis. (Loeb Classical Library: No. 30). 1930. 12.50x (ISBN 0-674-99033-1). Harvard U Pr.

--De Oratore, Bk 3, Vol. 4. Bd. with De Fato; Paradoxa Stoicorum; De Partitione Oratoria. (Loeb Classical Library: No. 349). 12.50x (ISBN 0-674-99384-5). Harvard U Pr.

--De Oratore, Bks 1 & 2, Vol. 3. (Loeb Classical Library: No. 348). 12.50x (ISBN 0-674-99383-7). Harvard U Pr.

--De Re Publica. Bd. with De Legibus. (Loeb Classical Library: No. 213). (Lat. & Eng.). 12.50x (ISBN 0-674-99235-0). Harvard U Pr.

--De Senectute. Bd. with De Amicitia; De Divinatione. (Loeb Classical Library: No. 154). (Lat. & Eng.). 12.50x (ISBN 0-674-99170-2). Harvard U Pr.

--Epistulae, 3 vols. in 4 pts. Incl. Vol. 1. Ad Familiares. 2nd ed. Purser, L. C., ed. 1982. 19.95x (ISBN 0-19-814660-4); Vol. 2, Pt. 1. Ad Atticum, Bks. 1-8. Watt, W. S., ed. 1965. 19.95x (ISBN 0-19-814645-0); Vol. 2, Pt. 2. Ad Atticum, Bks. 9-16. Bailey, D. Shackleton, ed. 1961. 17.50x (ISBN 0-19-814641-8); Vol. 3. Ad Quintum Fratrem, Ad M. Brutum, Fragmenta Epistularum, Commentariolum Petitionis, Pseudo-Ciceronis Epistula Ad Octavianum. Watt, William S., ed. 1958. 18.95x (ISBN 0-19-814614-0). (Oxford Classical Texts Ser). Oxford U Pr.

--Epistulae Ad Familiares: 47-43 B.C, Vol. 2. Bailey, D. R., ed. LC 76-11079. (Classical Texts & Commentaries Ser.: No. 17). 1977. 87.50 (ISBN 0-521-21152-2). Cambridge U Pr.

--Epistulae Ad Familiares: 62-47 B.C, Vol. 1. Bailey, D. R., ed. LC 76-11079. (Classical Texts & Commentaries Ser.: No. 16). 1977. 85.00 (ISBN 0-521-21151-4). Cambridge U Pr.

--Epistulae Ad Quintum Fratrem et M. Brutum. Bailey, D. R., ed. (Cambridge Classical Texts & Commentaries Ser.: No. 22). 300p. 1981. 54.50 (ISBN 0-521-23053-5). Cambridge U Pr.

--In Catilinam, 1-4. Bd. with Pro Murena; Pro Sulla; Pro Flacco. (Loeb Classical Library: No. 324). (Lat. & Eng.). 12.50x (ISBN 0-674-99358-6). Harvard U Pr.

--In L. Calpurnium Pisonem. Nisbet, R. G., ed. (Lat). 1961. 17.95x (ISBN 0-19-814427-X). Oxford U Pr.

--Letters to Atticus, 3 Vols. (Loeb Classical Library: No. 7, 8, 97). 12.50x ea. Bks. 1-6 (ISBN 0-674-99008-0). Bks. 7-11 (ISBN 0-674-99009-9). Bks. 12-16 (ISBN 0-674-99108-7). Harvard U Pr.

--Letters to His Brother Quintus. Bd. with Letters to Brutus; Handbook of Electioneering; Letter to Octavian. (Loeb Classical Library: No. 462). 12.50x (ISBN 0-674-99509-0). Harvard U Pr.

--Letters to His Friends, 3 Vols. (Loeb Classical Library: No. 205, 216, 230). 1927-29. 12.50x ea. Bks. 1-6 (ISBN 0-674-99225-3). Bks. 7-12 (ISBN 0-674-99238-5). Bks. 13-16 (ISBN 0-674-99253-9). Harvard U Pr.

--M. Tulli Ciceronis Ad M Brutum Orator. Connor, W. R. & Sandys, John E., eds. LC 78-67148. (Latin Texts & Commentaries Ser.). (Latin & Eng.). 1979. Repr. of 1885 ed. lib. bdg. 25.50x (ISBN 0-405-11616-0). Ayer Co Pubs.

--M. Tulli Ciceronis De Diinatione, 2 vols. in one. Connor, W. R., ed. LC 78-67146. (Latin Texts & Commentaries Ser.). (Latin & Eng.). 1979. Repr. of 1923 ed. lib. bdg. 44.00x (ISBN 0-405-11614-4). Ayer Co Pubs.

--M. Tulli Ciceronis De Domo Sua Ad Pontifices Oratio. Connor, W. R. & Nisbert, Robert G., eds. LC 78-67143. (Latin Texts & Commentaries Ser.). (Latin & Eng.). 1979. Repr. of 1939 ed. lib. bdg. 21.00x (ISBN 0-405-11612-8). Ayer Co Pubs.

--M. Tulli Ciceronis De Natura Deorum, 2 vols. Connor, W. R., ed. LC 78-67145. (Latin Texts & Commentaries Ser.). 1979. Repr. of 1958 ed. Set. lib. bdg. 86.00x (ISBN 0-405-11613-6). Ayer Co Pubs.

--M. Tulli Ciceronis De Oratore, 3 vols. in one. Connor, W. R., ed. LC 78-67162. (Latin Texts & Commentaries Ser.). (Latin & Eng.). 1979. Repr. of 1892 ed. lib. bdg. 51.50x (ISBN 0-405-11624-1). Ayer Co Pubs.

--M. Tulli Ciceronis De Provinciis Consularibus Oratio Ad Senatum. Connor, W. R., ed. LC 78-67125. (Latin Texts & Commentaries Ser.). (Latin & Eng.). 1979. Repr. lib. bdg. 12.00x (ISBN 0-405-11596-2). Ayer Co Pubs.

--M. Tulli Ciceronis Tusculanarum Disputationum Libra Quinque, 2 vols. in one. Connor, W. R., ed. LC 78-67129. (Latin Texts & Commentaries Ser.). (Lat. & Eng.). 1979. Repr. of 1934 ed. lib. bdg. 46.00x (ISBN 0-405-11599-7). Ayer Co Pubs.

--Murder at Larinum. Grose-Hodge, Humfrey, ed. (Latin). 1932. text ed. 5.95 (ISBN 0-521-04648-3). Cambridge U Pr.

--Murder Trials. Grant, Michael, tr. (Classics Ser.). 368p. (Orig.). 1975. pap. 5.95 (ISBN 0-14-044288-X). Penguin.

--Nature of the Gods. McGregor, Horace C., tr. (Classics Ser.). 280p. (Orig.). 1972. pap. 5.95 (ISBN 0-14-044265-0). Penguin.

--Offices & Select Letters. Cockman, Thomas, tr. Incl. Laelius, on Friendship; & Cato, on Old Age & Selected Letters. Melmouth, W., tr. 1953. 12.95x (ISBN 0-460-00345-3, Evman). Biblio Dist.

--On the Commonwealth. Sabine, George H & Smith, Stanley B, trs. LC 50-11678. 1929. pap. 8.40 scp (ISBN 0-672-60309-8). Bobbs.

--On the Good Life. (Classics Ser.). 1971. pap. 4.95 (ISBN 0-14-044244-8). Penguin.

--Orationes, 6 vols. Incl. Vol. 1. Pro Sex. Roscio, De Imperio, Cn. Pompei, Pro Cluentio, in Catilinam, Pro Murena, Pro Caelio. Clark, A. C., ed. 1905. 14.95x (ISBN 0-19-814605-1); Vol. 2. Pro Milone, Pro Marcello, Pro Ligario, Pro Rege Deiotaro, Philip Picae, 1-14. 2nd ed. Clark, A. C., ed. 1918. 14.95x (ISBN 0-19-814606-X); Vol. 3. Divinatio in Q. Caecilium, in C. Verrem. 2nd ed. Peterson, William, ed. 1917. 24.00x (ISBN 0-19-814607-8); Vol. 4. Pro P. Quincto, Pro Q. Roscio Comoedo, Pro A. Caecina, De Lege Agraria Contra Rullum, Pro C. Rabirio Perduellionis Reo, Pro L. Flacco, In L. Pisonem, Pro C. Rabirio Postumo. Clark, A. C., ed. 1909. 17.50x (ISBN 0-19-814608-6); Vol. 5. Cum Senatui Gratias Egit, Cum Populo Gratias Egit, De Domo Sua, De Haruspicium Responso, Pro Sestio, in Vatinium, De Provinciis Consularibus, Pro Balbo. Peterson, William, ed. 1911. 17.50x (ISBN 0-19-814609-4); Vol. 6. Pro Tullio, Pro Fonteio, Pro Sulla, Pro Archia, Pro Plancio. Pro Scauro. Clark, A. C. 1911. 13.95x (ISBN 0-19-814610-8). (Oxford Classical Texts Ser). Oxford U Pr.

--Philippics. (Loeb Classical Library: No. 189). 1926. 12.50x (ISBN 0-674-99208-3). Harvard U Pr.

--Pro Archia. Bd. with Post Redifum in Senatu; Post Redifum Ad Quirites; De Domo Sua; De Haruspicum Responsis; Pro Cn. Plancio. (Loeb Classical Library: No. 158). (Lat. & Eng.). 12.50x (ISBN 0-674-99174-5). Harvard U Pr.

--Pro Caelio. Bd. with De Provinciis Consularibus; Pro Balbo. (Loeb Classical Library: No. 447). 12.50x (ISBN 0-674-99492-2). Harvard U Pr.

--Pro Lege Manilia. Bd. with Pro Caecina; Pro Cluentio; Pro Rabirio Perduellionis Reo. (Loeb Classical Library: No. 198). (Lat. & Eng.). 12.50x (ISBN 0-674-99218-0). Harvard U Pr.

--Pro M. Caelio Oratio. 3rd ed. Austin, R. G., ed. 1960. 11.95x (ISBN 0-19-814401-6). Oxford U Pr.

--Pro Milone. Bd. with In Prisonen; Pro Sauro; Pro Fonteio; Pro Rabirio Postumo; Pro Marcello; Pro Ligario; Pro Rege Deiotaro. (Loeb Classical Library: No. 252). 12.50x (ISBN 0-674-99278-4). Harvard U Pr.

--Pro Quinctio. Bd. with Pro Roscio Amerino; Pro Roscio Comoedo; Three Speeches on the Agrarian Law Against Rullus. (Loeb Classical Library: No. 240). (Lat. & Eng.). 12.50x (ISBN 0-674-99265-2). Harvard U Pr.

--Pro Sestio. Bd. with In Vatinium. (Loeb Classical Library: No. 309). 12.50x (ISBN 0-674-99341-1). Harvard U Pr.

--Re Publica Librorum sex quae Manserunt. 183p. 1985. Repr. of 1915 ed. 15.00 (ISBN 0-89005-455-X). Ares.

--Rhetorica, 2 vols. Wilkins, A. S., ed. Incl. Vol. 1. Libros De Oratore Tres. 1903. 18.95x (ISBN 0-19-814615-9); Vol. 2. Brutus, Orator, De Optimo Genere Oratorum, Partitiones Oratoriae, Topica. 1935. 18.95x (ISBN 0-19-814616-7). (Oxford Classical Texts Ser). Oxford U Pr.

--Select Letters. Bailey, D. R., ed. LC 78-67430. (Cambridge Greek & Latin Classics). 250p. 1980. 44.50 (ISBN 0-521-22492-6); pap. 16.95x (ISBN 0-521-29524-6). Cambridge U Pr.

--Select Letters, 2 vols. How, W. W., ed. Vol. 1. 1925 Text. 16.95x (ISBN 0-19-814403-2); Vol. 2. 1926 Notes. 24.00x (ISBN 0-19-814404-0). Oxford U Pr.

--Selected Political Speeches. Grant, Michael, tr. (Classics Ser). 1977. pap. 4.95 (ISBN 0-14-044214-6). Penguin.

--Thirty-Five Letters of Cicero. Stockton, David, ed. 1969. pap. 7.95x (ISBN 0-19-912005-6). Oxford U Pr.

--Trisculan Disputations, Bk. 1. Douglas, A. E., ed. 24.00x (ISBN 0-86516-097-X); pap. 12.00x (ISBN 0-86516-072-4). Bolchazy Carducci.

--Tusculan Disputations. (Loeb Classical Library: No. 141). 1927. 12.50x (ISBN 0-674-99156-7). Harvard U Pr.

--Tusculanarum Disputationum I-V. 190p. (Latin.). 1985. 15.00 (ISBN 0-89005-462-2). Ares.

--Verrine Orations, 2 Vols. (Loeb Classical Library: No. 221, 293). 1935. Pt. 1. 12.50x (ISBN 0-674-99243-1); Pt. 2. 7.00x (ISBN 0-674-99323-3). Harvard U Pr.

Cicero, M. T. On Old Age & on Friendship. Copley, Frank O., tr. 1971. pap. 4.50 (ISBN 0-472-06178-X, 178, AA). U of Mich Pr.

Cicero, Marcus. Cicero's Brutus: Or, History of Famous Orators. Jones, Ernest, tr. LC 72-158313. Repr. of 1776 ed. 39.50 (ISBN 0-404-54106-2). AMS Pr.

Cicero, Marcus T. Cato Major. Kastenbaum, Robert, ed. LC 78-22193. (Aging & Old Age Ser.). 1979. Repr. of 1744 ed. lib. bdg. 14.00x (ISBN 0-405-11810-4). Ayer Co Pubs.

--De Senectute: De Amicicia. LC 77-6867. (English Experience Ser.: No. 861). 1977. Repr. of 1481 ed. lib. bdg. 25.00 (ISBN 90-221-0861-9). Walter J Johnson.

--The Four Cicero's Orations Against Catiline in Both Latin & English. (Illus.). 139p. 1984. Repr. of 1885 ed. 98.75 (ISBN 0-89901-156-X). Found Class Reprints.

--Selected Works. Grant, Michael, tr. Incl. Against Verres; Twenty Three Letters; Second Phillipic Against Anthony; On Duties; An Old Age. (Classics Ser.). (Orig.). (gr. 9 up). 1960. pap. 4.95 (ISBN 0-14-044099-2). Penguin.

Ciceron, Marco Tulio. Las Leyes. bilingual ed. (Biblioteca De Cultura Basica Ser.). 1.85 (ISBN 0-8477-0702-4). U of PR Pr.

Cichanowski, Gerald W. Macro Eleven Programming & PDP Eleven Organization. LC 82-11498. 248p. 1982. pap. text ed. 12.95x (ISBN 0-910554-38-2). Engineering.

Cichetti, Barbara, jt. auth. see Willson, Peggy.

Cichocki, K., ed. see IFAC-IFORS-IIASA Workshop, Bielsko-Biala, Poland, June 1977.

Cicholas, Shirley T. The Long Recess. LC 82-24389. 223p. 1985. 10.95 (ISBN 0-87949-235-X). Ashley Bks.

Cichy, F. C. & Schenck, H. V. Corrosion of Steel & Aluminum Scuba Tanks. (Technical Report Ser.: No. 62). 20p. 1978. 2.00 (ISBN 0-938412-05-1, P769). URI MAS.

Cichy, Helen J. Defrosting of Minnesota. LC 77-86170. 1977. 12.50 (ISBN 0-9601852-0-8); pap. 7.00 (ISBN 0-9601852-1-6). H J Cichy.

Cichy, Ronald, jt. auth. see Minor, L. J.

Cichy, Ronald F. Sanitation Management: Strategies for Success. Bogart, Margo, ed. 1984. 34.95 (ISBN 0-86612-018-1). Educ Inst Am Hotel.

Cicirelli, Victor G. Helping Elderly Parents: The Role of Adult Children. LC 81-10880. 199p. 1981. 24.95 (ISBN 0-86569-080-4). Auburn Hse.

Cicogna, Emmanuele A. Saggio di Bibliografia Veneziana, 2 vols. Bd. with Bibliografia Veneziana, 2 vols in 1. Sorarzo, Girolamo. Repr. of 1885 ed. 58.50 (ISBN 0-685-23105-4). 1965. Repr. of 1847 ed. Set. 105.50 (ISBN 0-8337-0574-1). B Franklin.

Cicourel, A., jt. ed. see Knorr-Cetina, K.

Cicourel, Aaron V. Cognitive Sociology. LC 73-18771. 1973. pap. text ed. 9.95 (ISBN 0-02-905450-8). Free Pr.

--Method & Measurement in Sociology. LC 64-16970. 1964. 22.95 (ISBN 0-02-905480-X). Free Pr.

--Theory & Method in a Study of Argentine Fertility. LC 73-14985. 212p. 1974. lib. bdg. 16.00 (ISBN 0-471-15793-7). Krieger.

Cicourel, Aaron V., et al. Language Use & School Performance. 1974. 40.00 (ISBN 0-12-174950-9). Acad Pr.

Cid Campeador. Cronica Del Famoso Caualllero Cid Ruy Diez Campeador. facsimile ed. 1512. 27.00 (ISBN 0-527-17400-9). Kraus Repr.

--Cronica Del Muy Esforcado y Inuencible Caualllero el Cid Ruy Diaz Campeador Delas Espanas. facsimile ed. 1903. 15.00 (ISBN 0-527-17410-6). Kraus Repr.

--Poem of the Cid. Huntington, Archer M., tr. LC 42-50955. Repr. of 1942 ed. 18.00 (ISBN 0-527-17420-3). Kraus Repr.

Cie, jt. auth. see Gumuchian.

Ciechalski, Joseph C., jt. auth. see Locke, Don C.

Ciechanowicz, Z. J., jt. ed. see Wichmann, Brian A.

Ciechanowska, Paola. Le Pur-Sang Francais. (Illus.). 18.35 (ISBN 0-85131-003-6, Dist. by Sporting Book Center). J A Allen.

Ciegler, jt. auth. see Bennett.

Ciekot, Jerald & Miriam-Therese. Hunger on Spaceship Earth Simulation Game. pap. 1.50 (ISBN 0-686-95393-2). Am Fr Serv Comm.

Cienciala, Anna & Komarnicki, Titus. From Versailles to Locarno: Keys to Polish Foreign Policy, 1919-1925. (Illus.). 384p. 1984. 29.95x (ISBN 0-7006-0247-X). U Pr of KS.

Cienciala, Anna see International Congress of Slavists, 7th, 1973.

Cienkus, Robert, jt. auth. see Manoni, Mary H.

Cieplak, Tadeusz N., ed. Poland Since Nineteen Fifty-Six: Readings & Essays on Polish Government & Politics. LC 79-125262. 482p. 1972. text ed. 34.50x (ISBN 0-8290-0193-X); pap. text ed. 16.50x (ISBN 0-8290-0374-6). Irvington.

Cierjacks, S., ed. Neutron Sources: For Applied & Pure Nuclear Research. (Neutron Physics & Nuclear Data in Science & Technology Ser.: Vol. 2). 370p. 1982. 72.00 (ISBN 0-08-029351-4). Pergamon.

Ciesielski, Z. Approximation & Function Spaces: Proceedings of the International Conference in Gdansk, Aug. 1979. 898p. 1982. 117.00 (ISBN 0-444-86143-2, North-Holland). Elsevier.

Ciesielski, Z., ed. see Mathematical Institute of the Polish Academy of Sciences & Institute of Mathematics of the Adam Mickiewicz University, Poznan, Aug. 22-26, 1972.

Ciesla, William M., intro. by. Color Aerial Photography in the Pl Sc & Related Fields: Seventh Biennial Workshop. 255p. 1979. pap. 12.00 (7.00 member) (ISBN 0-937294-11-X). ASP & RS.

Cieslewicz, W. J., tr. see Makogon, Yuri F.

Cieslik, Jurgen & Cieslik, Marianne. German Doll Encyclopedia. (Illus.). 362p. 1985. 49.95 (ISBN 0-87588-238-2). Hobby Hse.

--Lehmann Toys. (Illus.). 220p. 24.95 (ISBN 0-904568-40-7, Pub. by New Cavendish England). Schiffer.

Cieslik, Marianne, jt. auth. see Cieslik, Jurgen.

Cieszkowski, August. Selected Writings of August Cieszkowski. Liebich, Andre, ed. LC 77-94371. (Studies in the History & Theory of Politics). 1979. 32.50 (ISBN 0-521-21986-8). Cambridge U Pr.

Cieza de Leon, Pedro D. The War of Chupas (Civil Wars of Peru) Markham, Clements, ed. (Hakluyt Society Works Ser.: Vol. 2, Vol. 42). (Illus.). Repr. of 1917 ed. 42.00 (ISBN 0-317-16774-X). Kraus Repr.

--The War of the Salinas (Civil Wars of Peru) Markham, Clements, ed. (Hakluyt Society Works Ser.: No. 2, Vol. 54). Repr. of 1923 ed. 32.00 (ISBN 0-317-16775-8). Kraus Repr.

Cieza De Leon, Pedro De see De Cieza De Leon, Pedro.

Cifar. Libro Del Cauallero Zifar: El Libro Del Cauallero De Dios. Wagner, C. P., ed. Repr. of 1929 ed. 48.00 (ISBN 0-527-17500-5). Kraus Repr.

Cifelli, Edward M. David Humphreys. (United States Authors Ser.). 1982. lib. bdg. 15.95 (ISBN 0-8057-7363-0, Twayne). G K Hall.

Cifelli, Edward M., jt. auth. see Zulauf, Sander.

Cifelli, Edward M., jt. auth. see Zulauf, Sander W.

Ciferri, A. & Krigbaum, W. R., eds. Polymer Liquid Crystals. 394p. 1982. 62.50 (ISBN 0-12-174680-1). Acad Pr.

Ciferri, A. & Ward, I. M., eds. Ultra-High Modulus Polymers. (Illus.). 362p. 1979. 63.00 (ISBN 0-85334-800-6, Pub. by Elsevier Applied Sci England). Elsevier.

Cifuentes Delatte, L., et al, eds. see Renal Stone Research Symposium, Madrid, Sept. 1972.

Cigan, J. M., jt. ed. see Cotterill, C. H.

Cigan, T. S., ed. see World Symposium at the AIME Annual Meeting, Las Vegas, 1980.

Cigar, Norman, ed. Muhammad Al-Qadiris Nashr Al Mathani: The Chronicles. (Fontes Historiae Africanae Ser.). (Illus.). 1981. 49.95x (ISBN 0-19-725994-4). Oxford U Pr.

Ciger-Hronsky, Jozef. Jozef Mak. Cincura, Andrew, tr. from Slovak. (Slovak Literature & Language Ser.: No. 1). (Illus.). 232p. (Eng.). 1985. 12.95 (ISBN 0-89357-129-6). Slavica.

Cigler, et al. Banach Modules & Functors on Categories of Banach Spaces. (Lecture Notes in Pure & Applied Mathematics Ser.: Vol. 46). 1979. 55.00 (ISBN 0-8247-6867-1). Dekker.

Cigler, Allan & Loomis, Burdett. Interest Group Politics. LC 82-22208. 373p. 1983. pap. 12.50 (ISBN 0-87187-247-1). Congr Quarterly.

Cigman, Gloria, ed. see Chaucer, Geoffrey.

Cigno, A., jt. auth. see Day, R. H.

Cihak, Mary K. & Heron, Barbara J. Games Children Should Play: Sequential Lessons for Teaching Communication Skills in Grades K-6. 1980. pap. 12.95 (ISBN 0-673-16370-9). Scott F.

Cihal, V. Intergranular Corrosion of Steels & Alloys. (Materials Science Monographs: Vol. 18). 1984. 96.25 (ISBN 0-444-99644-3, I-035-84). Elsevier.

Cihar, Jiri, jt. auth. see Zahradnik, Jiri.

Cihlar, Many. Misticos en Oracion. AMORC Staff, tr. from Eng. 59p. (Orig., Span.). 1982. pap. 7.00 (ISBN 0-912057-82-3, GS-509). AMORC.

Cihlar, Many, compiled by. Mystics at Prayer. 19th ed. LC 36-17108. 1982. 11.00 (ISBN 0-912057-08-4, G-509). AMORC.

Ciholas, Karin. Gide's Art of the Fugue: A Thematic Study of "Les Faux-Monnayeurs". (Studies in the Romance Languages & Literatures: No. 153). 125p. 1974. pap. 10.50x (ISBN 0-8078-9153-3). U of NC Pr.

Cihui, Y. Dongwuxue. English-Chinese Biology Dictionary. 477p. (Eng. & Chinese.). 1975. 25.00 (ISBN 0-686-92343-X, M-9277). French & Eur.

Cikorsky, Nicolai & Quick, Michael. George Inness. LC 84-48410. (Illus.). 216p. 1985. 38.46 (ISBN 0-06-430710-7, Icon Edns). Har-Row.

Cikovsky, Nicolai & Robinson, William, eds. Paintings from the C. R. Smith Collection. LC 73-171236. (Illus.). 1970. pap. 6.00 (ISBN 0-87959-030-0). U of Tex H Ransom Ctr.

Cikovsky, Nicolai, Jr. The Life & Work of George Inness. LC 76-23605. (Outstanding Dissertations in the Fine Arts - American). (Illus.). 1977. Repr. of 1965 ed. lib. bdg. 85.00 (ISBN 0-8240-2679-9). Garland Pub.

Cikovsky, Nicolai, Jr. & Quick, Michael. George Inness. (Illus.). 216p. (Orig.). 1985. pap. 24.95 (ISBN 0-87587-124-0, Co-Pub. by Har-Row). LA Co Art Mus.

Cikovsky, Nicolai, Jr., ed. Lectures on the Affinity of Painting with the Other Fine Arts by Samuel F. B. Morse. LC 82-13551. (Illus.). 144p. 1983. text ed. 20.00 (ISBN 0-8262-0389-2). U of Mo Pr.

Cilag-Chemie, ed. Toxikologische, endokrinologische und klinische Aspekte bei der Pruefung eines neuen Neuroleptikums. Ein wissenschaftliches Gespraech. (Intern. Pharmacopsychiatry: Vol. 13, Suppl. 1). (Illus.). 1978. pap. 12.50 (ISBN 3-8055-2931-7). S Karger.

Cilento, G., jt. ed. see Adam, Waldemar.

Cilento, Lady P. You Don't Have to Be Sick, 4 bks. in 1. 336p. 1984. pap. 3.50 (ISBN 0-87983-403-X). Keats.

Cilento, Raphael W. Causes of Depopulation in the Western Islands of the Territory of New Guinea. LC 75-32809. Repr. of 1928 ed. 16.00 (ISBN 0-404-14113-7). AMS Pr.

--Tropical Diseases in Australasia, a Handbook. LC 75-32810. (Illus.). Repr. of 1940 ed. 30.50 (ISBN 0-404-14114-5). AMS Pr.

Cilento, V., ed. see Marien, Bert.

Ciliberti, Anthony. Bank Internal Auditing Manual. 1984. 175.00 (ISBN 0-88712-132-2). Warren.

Ciliberto, C. & Ghione, F., eds. Algebraic Geometry: Open Problems. (Lecture Notes in Mathematics Ser.: Vol. 997). 411p. 1983. pap. 22.00 (ISBN 0-387-12320-2). Springer-Verlag.

Ciliga, Ante. Russian Enigma. Renier, F. G. & Cliff, Anne, trs. (Ink Link ser.). 582p. (Russian.). 1980. 22.95 (ISBN 0-906133-22-X); pap. 11.95 (ISBN 0-906133-23-8). Pluto Pr.

--The Russian Enigma. Fernier, Fernand G., et al, trs. from Fr. 573p. 1979. 22.95 (ISBN 0-906133-22-X, Pub. by Ink Links Ltd.); pap. 11.95 (ISBN 0-906133-23-8). Longwood Pub Group.

Ciliga, Anton. The Russian Enigma. Renier, Fernand G. & Cliff, Anne, trs. from Rus. LC 73-836. (Russian Studies: Perspectives on the Revolution Ser.). xi, 304p. 1973. Repr. of 1940 ed. 25.85 (ISBN 0-88355-032-6). Hyperion Conn.

Cilingiroglu, Ayhan. Manufacture of Heavy Electrical Equipment in Developing Countries. LC 76-89962. (World Bank Staff Occasional Papers Ser: No. 9). (Illus.). 135p. 1969. pap. 5.50x (ISBN 0-8018-1097-3). Johns Hopkins.

Ciliotta, Claire, jt. auth. see Livingston, Carole.

Cilleuls, Alfred Des see Des Cilleuls, Alfred.

Cillie, Francois S. Centralization or Decentralization? A Study in Educational Adaptation. LC 71-176646. (Columbia University. Teachers College. Contributions to Education: No. 789). Repr. of 1940 ed. 22.50 (ISBN 0-404-55789-9). AMS Pr.

Cilliers, J. K. Counter-Insurgency in Rhodesia. LC 84-45702. 266p. 1985. 29.00 (ISBN 0-7099-3412-2, Pub. by Croom Helm Ltd). Longwood Pub Group.

Cilliota, Jeannine, tr. see Hirai, Kiyoshi.

Cilmore, William J. Psychohistorical Inquiry: A Comprehensive Bibliography. LC 82-49165. (Reference Library of Social Science). 400p. 1983. lib. bdg. 53.00 (ISBN 0-8240-9167-1). Garland Pub.

Cimasoni, G. Crevicular Fluid Updated. (Monographs in Oral Science: Vol. 12). (Illus.). viii, 152p. 1983. 49.50 (ISBN 3-8055-3705-0). S Karger.

Cimasoni, G., jt. ed. see Lehner, T.

Cimasoni, Geneve. The Crevicular Fluid. (Monographs in Oral Science: Vol. 3). 121p. 1974. 24.00 (ISBN 3-8055-1699-1). S Karger.

Cimbala, Stephen J., ed. National Security Strategy: Choices & Limits. (Foreign Policy Issues: A Foreign Policy Research Institute Ser.). 384p. 1984. 34.95 (ISBN 0-03-069657-7). Praeger.

Cimbolic, jt. auth. see Corry.

Cimbolic, Peter, jt. auth. see Hipple, John.

Cimbuna, Al, jt. auth. see Avery, Constance.

Ciment, Michel. Conversations with Losey. 320p. 1985. 39.95 (ISBN 0-416-40470-7, 9601); pap. 16.95 (ISBN 0-416-40120-1, 9602). Methuen Inc.

--Kazan on Kazan. LC 73-11978. (Cinema One Ser). (Illus.). 176p. 1974. 10.00 (ISBN 0-670-41187-6). Viking.

--Kubrick. Adair, Gilbert, tr. from Fr. LC 82-6224. (Illus.). 240p. 1983. 25.00 (ISBN 0-03-061687-5); pap. 16.95 (ISBN 0-03-063949-2). HR&W.

Ciminero, Anthony R., jt. auth. see Lahey, Benjamin B.

Ciminero, Anthony R., et al, eds. Handbook of Behavioral Assessment. LC 76-54170. (Personality Processes Ser). 721p. 1977. 57.95 (ISBN 0-471-15797-X, Pub. by Wiley-Interscience). Wiley.

Ciminillo, Lewis, jt. auth. see Ban, John.

Cimino, Harry, jt. auth. see Repplier, Agnes.

Cimino, Louis & Chatelain, Agnes, eds. Directory of Practicing Anthropologists. 1981. pap. 6.00 (ISBN 0-686-36594-1). Am Anthro Assn.

Cimino, Moyra. A Servant of the Stuarts. 1982. 32.00x (ISBN 0-7223-1557-0, Pub. by Stockwell). State Mutual Bk.

Cimmino, Marion, jt. auth. see Edwards, Gabrielle.

Cimmino, Marion, jt. auth. see Edwards, Gabrielle I.

Cimmora, Clemente. Rockefeller & His Times. 1974. lib. bdg. 59.95 (ISBN 0-8490-0967-7). Gordon Pr.

Cimorell-Strong, Jacqueline M. Language Facilitation: A Cognitive Approach. LC 83-1075. 224p. 1983. spiral 19.00 (ISBN 0-8391-1799-X). Pro-Ed.

Cimprich, John. Slavery's End in Tennessee, 1861-1865. LC 84-16200. (Illus.). 224p. 1985. 27.50 (ISBN 0-8173-0257-3). U of Ala Pr.

Cin, Mario Dal see Dal Cin, Mario, et al.

Cina, Susan & Caro, Francis G. Supporting Families Who Care for Severly Disabled Children at Home: A Public Policy Perspective. 74p. (Orig.). 1984. pap. 5.00 (ISBN 0-88156-038-3). Comm Serv Soc Ny.

Cinader, Bernard, ed. Immunology of Receptors. (Immunology Ser.: Vol. 6). 544p. 1977. 79.75 (ISBN 0-8247-6674-1). Dekker.

Cinader, Bernhard. Regulation of the Antibody Response. 2nd ed. (Illus.). 417p. 1971. photocopy ed. 34.00x (ISBN 0-398-00309-2). C C Thomas.

Cinard, Judith E. see National Geographic Society.

Cinca, Sylvia. Night of the Rising Dead. LC 85-71313. 125p. (Orig.). 1985. pap. 8.95 (ISBN 0-931494-61-3). Brunswick Pub.

Cincerelli, Sr. Carol J. Opening Five: Art for Grade Five. LC 79-3013. 192p. (gr. 5). 1980. pap. text ed. 8.95 (ISBN 0-934902-10-0). Learn Concepts OH.

--Opening Four: Art for Grade Four. LC 79-3013. 192p. (gr. 4). 1979. pap. text ed. 8.95 (ISBN 0-934902-05-4). Learn Concepts OH.

--Opening One: Art for Grade One. LC 79-3013. 174p. (gr. 1). 1979. pap. text ed. 8.95 (ISBN 0-934902-07-0). Learn Concepts OH.

--Opening Six: Art for Grade Six. LC 79-3013. 192p. (gr. 6). 1980. pap. text ed. 8.95 (ISBN 0-934902-11-9). Learn Concepts OH.

--Opening Three: Art for Grade Three. LC 79-3013. 195p. (gr. 3). 1980. pap. text ed. 8.95 (ISBN 0-934902-09-7). Learn Concepts OH.

--Opening-Two: Art for Grade Two. LC 79-3013. (gr. 2). 1979. pap. text ed. 8.95 (ISBN 0-934902-06-2). Learn Concepts OH.

--Opening VII: Art for Grade Seven. LC 79-3013. 192p. (gr. 7). 1980. pap. text ed. 8.95 (ISBN 0-934902-12-7). Learn Concepts OH.

--Opening VIII: Art for Grade Eight. LC 79-3013. 192p. (gr. 8). 1979. pap. text ed. 8.95 (ISBN 0-934902-13-5). Learn Concepts OH.

Cincinati Art Museum. Art of the First Americans. (Illus.). 104p. 1976. pap. 15.00 (ISBN 0-295-96108-2). U of Wash Pr.

Cincinnato, Paul D. & Tursi, Joseph A. Italian Two & Three Years. (It.). (gr. 9-12). 1978. pap. text ed. 7.92 (ISBN 0-87720-594-9). AMSCO Sch.

Cincinnatus. Self-Destruction: The Disintergration & Decay of the U. S. Army During the Vietnam Era. (Illus.). 1981. 15.95 (ISBN 0-393-01346-4). Norton.

--War! War! War! rev. ed. Mullins, Eustace, frwd. by. 291p. 1984. pap. 6.00 (ISBN 0-89562-100-2). Sons Lib.

Cincura, Andrew, tr. see Ciger-Hronsky, Jozef.

Cindro, N., ed. Nuclear Molecular Phenomena: Proceedings of the International Conference on Resonances in Heavy Ion Reactions, Yuogslavia-1977. 1978. 66.00 (ISBN 0-444-85116-X, North-Holland). Elsevier.

Cindro, N., et al, eds. Dynamics of Heavy-Ion Collisions: Proceedings of Adriatic Europhysics Conference on the Dynamics of Heavy-Ion Collisions, 3rd, Hvar Croatia, Yugoslavia, May 25-30, 1981. 382p. 1982. 68.00 (ISBN 0-444-86332-X, North-Holland). Elsevier.

Cindro, N., et al, eds. see Europhysics Study Conference, Plitvice Lakes, Yugoslavia, 1972.

Cinel, Dino. From Italy to San Francisco: The Immigrant Experience. LC 80-53224. (Illus.). 360p. 1982. 25.00x (ISBN 0-8047-1117-8). Stanford U Pr.

Cinelli, Ferdinand H., et al, eds. Etruscans: Bulletin of the Etruscan Foundation, Vol: 1. LC 76-88799. 56p. 1970. pap. text ed. 2.95x (ISBN 0-8143-1423-6). Wayne St U Pr.

Cinema Commission Of Inquiry. Cinema: Its Present Position & Future Possibilities. LC 78-124002. (Literature of Cinema Ser). Repr. of 1917 ed. 20.00 (ISBN 0-405-01608-5). Ayer Co Pubs.

Cini, M. Introduction a la Mecanique des Particules. (Cours & Documents de Mathematiques & de Physique Ser.). 364p. (Fr.). 1972. 93.75 (ISBN 0-677-50380-6). Gordon.

Cinlar, E. Introduction to Stochastic Processes. (Illus.). 448p. 1975. ref. ed. 32.95 (ISBN 0-13-498089-1). P-H.

Cinlar, E., et al. Seminar on Stochastic Processes, 1982. (Progress in Probability & Statistics Ser.: Vol. 5). 310p. 1983. text ed. 24.95 (ISBN 0-8176-3131-3). Birkhauser.

Cinlar, E., et al, eds. Seminar on Stochastic Processes, 1981. (Progress in Probability & Statistics: Vol. 1). 248p. 1982. text ed. 17.50 (ISBN 0-8176-3072-4). Birkhauser.

--Seminar in Stochastic Processes: 1983. (Progress in Probability & Statistics Ser.: Vol. 7). 290p. 1985. text ed. 34.95x (ISBN 0-8176-3293-X). Birkhauser.

Cinnamon, Allan, ed. International Tax Planner's Manual. 547p. 1984. 75.00 (ISBN 0-317-30624-3, 3707). Commerce.

Cinnamon, Kenneth & Farson, Dave. Cults & Cons: The Exploitation of the Emotional Growth Consumer. LC 79-1174. 128p. 1979. 16.95x (ISBN 0-88229-456-3). Nelson-Hall.

Cinnamon, Kenneth, jt. auth. see Silverman, William.

Cinnamon, Kenneth M., jt. auth. see Armstrong, Terry R.

Cinnamon, Kenneth M., jt. auth. see Morris, Kenneth T.

Cinnamon, Kenneth M. & Matulef, Norman J., eds. Assessment & Interviewing. LC 79-56024. (Applied Skills Training Ser.: Vol. 4). 215p. looseleaf binder 79.95 (ISBN 0-89889-003-9). Univ Assocs.

--Creative Problem Solving. LC 79-52727. (Applied Skills Training Ser.: Vol. 2). 155p. 1979. looseleaf binder 79.95 (ISBN 0-89889-001-2). Univ Assocs.

--Effective Supervision. LC 79-51177. (Applied Skills Training Ser.: Vol. 1). 134p. 1979. looseleaf binder 79.95 (ISBN 0-89889-000-4). Univ Assocs.

--Human Relations Development. LC 79-52728. (Applied Skills Training Ser.: Vol. 3). 156p. 1979. looseleaf 79.95 (ISBN 0-89889-002-0). Univ Assocs.

Cinnamon, Pamela A. & Swanson, Marilyn A. Everything About Exchange Values for Foods. LC 81-53064. 60p. 1981. 3.50 (ISBN 0-89301-083-9). U Pr of Idaho.

Cinotti, Alfonse A. Handbook of Ophthalmologic Emergencies. 3rd ed. 1984. pap. text ed. write for info. (ISBN 0-87488-532-9). Med Exam.

Cinqualbre, J., jt. ed. see Bollack, C.

Cinque, Marianne V. Bottom Zero. 32p. 1984. 6.95 (ISBN 0-89962-376-X). Todd & Honeywell.

Cinquin, Emmanuelle. To Share With God's Poor: Sister among the Outcasts. LC 83-47735. (Illus.). 458p. 1983. pap. 5.72 (ISBN 0-06-061392-0, RD-485, HarpR). Har-Row.

Cinquino, J., tr. see Francesconi, Mario.

Cintas, Pierre F; see Born, Warren C.

Cinti, Decio, ed. Dizionario dei Sinonimi e dei Contrari. 585p. (Ital.). 1984. 24.00x (ISBN 0-913298-75-1). S F Vanni.

Cintron, Ralph. Maria, Maria, Look! 1982. 1.50 (ISBN 0-942582-04-7). Erie St Pr.

Ciobanu, A. Cooling Technology in the Food Industry. 1976. 41.00 (ISBN 0-9961000-1-6, Pub. by Abacus England). Heyden.

Ciocco, A. Hearing of School Children. (SRCD M Ser.). 1941. pap. 15.00 (ISBN 0-527-01519-9). Kraus Repr.

Ciochon & Fleagle. Primate Evolutionary Biology. 1985. text ed. 19.95 (ISBN 0-8053-2240-X). Benjamin-Cummings.

Ciochon, Russell L. & Chiarelli, A. B., eds. Evolutionary Biology of the New World Monkeys & Continental Drift. LC 80-16063. (Advances in Primatology Ser.). 560p. 1981. 59.50x (ISBN 0-306-40487-7, Plenum Pr). Plenum Pub.

Ciochon, Russell L. & Corruccini, Robert S., eds. New Interpretations of Ape & Human Ancestry. (Advances In Primatology Ser.). 850p. 1983. 95.00 (ISBN 0-306-41072-9, Plenum Pr). Plenum Pub.

Cioffari, Angelina G., jt. auth. see Cioffari, Vincenzo.

Cioffari, Bernard & Edmonds, Dean. Experiments in College Physics. 7th ed. 1983. pap. text ed. 17.95x (ISBN 0-669-04492-X). Heath.

Cioffari, Vincenzo. Beginning Italian. 3rd ed. 1979. text ed. 20.95x (ISBN 0-669-00580-0); wkbk. & lab manual 9.95x (ISBN 0-669-00581-9); tapes-reels 70.00 (ISBN 0-669-00582-7); cassettes 25.00 (ISBN 0-669-00583-5). Heath.

--Italian Review Grammar & Composition. 3rd ed. (Illus.). 1969. text ed. 17.95x (ISBN 0-669-47290-5). Heath.

--Spoken Italian. LC 75-15151. (Spoken Language Ser.). 220p. (Prog. Bk.). 1976. pap. 10.00x (ISBN 0-87950-130-8). cassettes six dual track 60.00x (ISBN 0-87950-135-9); cassettes with course-bk. 65.00x (ISBN 0-87950-136-7). Spoken Lang Serv.

Cioffari, Vincenzo & Cioffari, Angelina G. Graded Italian Render: Seconda Tappa. 2nd ed. 208p. 1984. pap. text ed. 8.95 (ISBN 0-669-06325-8). Heath.

Cioffari, Vincenzo & Gonzalez, Emilio. Repaso Pratico y Cultural. 4th ed. 1977. text ed. 20.95x (ISBN 0-669-96461-1); wkbk. 8.95 (ISBN 0-669-96479-4); 6 cassette set 30.00 (ISBN 0-669-00333-6); 6 reel set 40.00 (ISBN 0-669-97782-9). Heath.

Cioffari, Vincenzo, ed. & tr. see Da Pisa, Guido.

Cioffari, Vincenzo, et al. Graded Italian Reader: Prima Tappa. 2nd ed. 1979. pap. text ed. 8.95 (ISBN 0-669-01955-0). Heath.

Cioffi, F., jt. ed. see Borger, R.

Cioffi, Frank. Formula Fiction? An Anatomy of American Science Fiction, 1930-1940. LC 82-6112. (Contributions to the Study of Science Fiction & Fantasy Ser.: No. 3). xi, 181p. 1982. lib. bdg. 27.50 (ISBN 0-313-23326-8, CIF/). Greenwood.

Cioffi, Luigi A., et al, eds. Body Weight Regulatory System: Normal & Disturbed Mechanisms. 398p. 1981. text ed. 57.00 (ISBN 0-89004-659-X). Raven.

Cioffi-Revilla, Claudio A. Mathematical Models in International Relations: A Bibliography. LC 79-25527. (IRSS Technical Papers: No. 4). 152p. (Orig.). 1979. pap. text ed. 7.00 (ISBN 0-89143-088-1). U NC Inst Res Soc Sci.

Ciompi, L., jt. auth. see Mueller, C H.

CIOMS Round Table Conference, Geneva, 1970. Training of Research Workers in the Medical Sciences: Proceedings. 186p. 1972. pap. 9.60 (ISBN 92-4-156040-1, 566). World Health.

Cioni, Maria L. Women & Law in Elizabethan England with Particular Reference to the Court of Chancery. LC 84-45998. 311p. 1985. lib. bdg. 30.00 (ISBN 0-8240-6678-2). Garland Pub.

Cioni, Ray & Cioni, Sally. The Babe & the Lamb: A Droodles Christmas Adventure. (The Droodles Bks.). 8.95 (ISBN 0-89191-635-0, 56358). Cook.

--The Droodles Storybook of Proverbs. (gr. k-5). 8.95 (ISBN 0-89191-472-2, 54726). Cook.

--The Droodles Ten Commandments Storybook. (Droodles Adventure Ser.). (Illus.). 64p. (gr. 1-5). 1983. text ed. 8.95 (ISBN 0-89191-636-9). Cook.

Cioni, Sally, jt. auth. see Cioni, Ray.

Cioppa, Anne L., jt. ed. see McIntire, Sue N.

Cioran, E. M. Drawn & Quartered. Howard, Richard, tr. from Fr. LC 81-2872. 192p. 1983. 17.95 (ISBN 0-394-51811-X); pap. 9.95 (ISBN 0-394-17841-6). Seaver Bks.

--The Trouble with Being Born. Howard, Richard, tr. from Fr. LC 81-51526. Orig. Title: L' Inconvenient d'etre Ne. 208p. 1981. pap. 5.95 (ISBN 0-394-17847-5). Seaver Bks.

Cioran, S. D., tr. see Dostoyevsky, Fyodor.

Cioran, Sam, tr. see Sologub, Fyodor.

Cioran, Samuel, tr. see Orlova, Raisa.

Cioran, Samuel, tr. see Saltykov-Shchedrin.

Cioran, Samuel, tr. see Shaginyan, Marietta.

Cioran, Samuel, tr. see Sologub, Fyodor.

Cioranesco. Bibliographie de la Litterature Francaise Du XVIIe Siecle, 3 Vols. Tome 1, A-C. 49.95 (ISBN 0-685-11047-8); Tome 2, D-M. 59.95 (ISBN 0-685-11048-6); Tome 3, N-Z. Tables. 54.95 (ISBN 0-685-11049-4). French & Eur.

--Bibliographie de la Litterature Francaise du 18eme Siecle, 3 tomes. Tome 1, A-D. 59.95 (ISBN 0-686-52227-3); Tome 2, E-Q. 54.95 (ISBN 0-686-52228-1); Tome 3, R-Z. 54.95 (ISBN 0-686-52229-X). French & Eur.

Cioranescu, A. Bibliographie de la litterature francaise du 18e siecle, 3 vols. 2266p. Pt. 1. 29.90x (ISBN 0-685-99776-6); Pt. 2. 32.70x (ISBN 0-686-66719-0); Pt. 3. 32.70x (ISBN 0-686-66720-4). Adlers Foreign Bks.

Cioranescu, Alexandre. Bibliographie de la litterature francaise du 17e siecle, 3 Vols. 1965-67. Pt. 1. 29.90x (ISBN 0-685-99752-9); Pt. 2. 36.00x (ISBN 0-685-99753-7); Pt. 3. 32.70x (ISBN 0-685-99754-5). Adlers Foreign Bks.

--Ion Barbu. (World Authors Ser.). 1981. lib. bdg. 16.95 (ISBN 0-8057-6432-1, Twayne). G K Hall.

--Vasile Alecsandri. LC 79-169637. (World Authors Ser.). 1973. lib. bdg. 15.95 (ISBN 0-8057-2020-0). Irvington.

Cios. Management & Growth Proceedings. 463p. 1969. 123.75 (ISBN 0-677-61575-2). Gordon.

--Management & the World of Tomorrow: Key Issues for Management in Economic Growth, Technological Change & Human Welfare. 450p. 1981. text ed. 40.25x (ISBN 0-566-02239-7). Gower Pub Co.

Ciosek, Karen, jt. auth. see Donnelly, Thomas R.

CIP Group, ed. The Munich Project CIP. (Lecture Notes in Computer Science Ser.: Vol. 183). (Illus.). xi, 275p. 1985. pap. 16.60 (ISBN 0-387-15187-7). Springer-Verlag.

Cipel, Louis. Radiology of the Acute Abdomen in the Newborn: A Self-Teaching Manual. 336p. 1978. 68.50 (ISBN 0-8089-1071-X, 790842). Grune.

Ciplijauskaite, Birute, et. see Gongora, Luis De.

Cipolla, C. M. Public Health & the Medical Profession in Renaissance Italy. LC 25-22984. (Illus.). 1976. 27.50 (ISBN 0-521-20959-5). Cambridge U Pr.

Cipolla, Carlo M. Before the Industrial Revolution: European Economy & Society, 1000-1700. 2nd, rev. ed. (Illus.). 1980. 16.95 (ISBN 0-393-01343-X); pap. text ed. 8.95x (ISBN 0-393-95115-4). Norton.

--Clocks & Culture, 1300-1700. (Illus.). 1978. pap. 5.95 (ISBN 0-393-00866-5, N866, Norton Lib). Norton.

--Faith, Reason & the Plague in Seventeenth-Century Tuscany. Kittel, Muriel, tr. from Ital. LC 79-2479. (Illus.). 140p. 1980. 17.50x (ISBN 0-8014-1230-7). Cornell U Pr.

--Faith, Reason, & the Plague in Seventeenth-Century Tuscany. 128p. 1981. pap. 4.95 (ISBN 0-393-00045-1). Norton.

--Fighting the Plague in Seventeenth-Century Italy. (Curti Lecture Ser.). 162p. 1980. 20.00x (ISBN 0-299-08340-3); pap. 7.95x (ISBN 0-299-08344-6). U of Wis Pr.

--Guns, Sails & Empire. 1985. Repr. price not set (ISBN 0-89745-071-X). Sunflower U Pr.

--The Monetary Policy of Fourteenth Century Florence. 100p. 1983. 16.95x (ISBN 0-520-04606-4). U of Cal Pr.

--Money, Prices & Civilization in the Mediterranean World. LC 67-18440. (Illus.). 1967. cloth 7.00x (ISBN 0-87752-021-6); pap. 4.75x (ISBN 0-686-86000-4). Gordian.

Cipolla, Carlo M., ed. The Economic History of World Population. 7th ed. (Illus.). 155p. 1978. text ed. 26.50x (ISBN 0-06-491138-1, 06398). B&N Imports.

--The Fontana Economic History of Europe: Contemporary Economies. LC 75-26207. (Fontana Economic History of Europe Ser.: Vol. 6 Pt. 2). (Illus.). 404p. 1977. Repr. of 1976 ed. text ed. 26.50x (ISBN 0-06-492184-0, 06475). B&N Imports.

--The Fontana Economic History of Europe: The Emergence of Industrial Societies. LC 75-26027. (Fontana Economic History of Europe Ser: Vol. 4, Pt. 2). (Illus.). 479p. 1976. text ed. 26.50x (ISBN 0-06-492180-8, 06471). B&N Imports.

--The Fontana Economic History of Europe: The Industrial Revolution, 1700-1914. LC 75-26027. (Fontana Economic History of Europe: Vol. 3). 624p. 1976. text ed. 22.50x (ISBN 0-06-492178-6, 06469). B&N Imports.

--The Fontana Economic History of Europe: The Middle Ages. LC 75-26027. (Fontana Ser.: Vol. 1). (Illus.). 389p. 1976. text ed. 26.50x (ISBN 0-06-492176-X, 06467). B&N Imports.

--The Fontana Economic History of Europe: The Twentieth Century. LC 75-26207. (Fontana Ser.: Vol. 5, Pt. 1). (Illus.). 402p. 1977. Repr. of 1976 ed. text ed. 26.50x (ISBN 0-06-492181-6, 06472). B&N Imports.

--The Fontana Economic History of Europe: The 16th & 17th Centuries. LC 75-26207. (Fontana Economic History of Europe Ser: Vol. 2). (Illus.). 640p. 1977. Repr. of 1974 ed. text ed. 23.50x (ISBN 0-06-492177-8, 06468). B&N Imports.

Cipolla, Wilma. Catalog of the Works of Arthur William Foote, Eighteen Fifty-Three to Nineteen Thirty-Seven. LC 79-92139. (Bibliographies in American Music: No. 6). 1980. 17.50 (ISBN 0-89990-000-3). Info Coord.

Cipollaro, Anthony C. & Crossland, Paul M. X-Rays & Radium in the Treatment of Diseases of the Skin. LC 66-23240. (Illus.). Repr. of 1967 ed. 160.00 (ISBN 0-8357-9425-3, 2014533). Bks Demand UMI.

Cipparone, Salvatore. From Dusk to Dawn. 4.95 (ISBN 0-686-20574-X). Ivory Scroll.

--From the Fountain of Life. 4.95 (ISBN 0-686-20576-6). Ivory Scroll.

--Sayings of the Hour. 4.95 (ISBN 0-686-20575-8). Ivory Scroll.

--Sorrow, Grief & God. 4.95 (ISBN 0-686-20577-4). Ivory Scroll.

--Yet I Weep, Yet I Joy. 4.95 (ISBN 0-686-20578-2). Ivory Scroll.

Cippico, A., et al, eds. Dante: Essays in Commemoration, 1321-1921. facs. ed. LC 68-16923. (Essay Index Reprint Ser). 1921. 18.00 (ISBN 0-8369-0360-9). Ayer Co Pubs.

Cipra, Barry. Mistakes & How to Find Them Before the Teacher. 70p. 1983. pap. text ed. 4.95 (ISBN 0-8176-3083-X). Birkhauser.

Cipriani, Anita A., ed. see American Association of Teachers of French.

Cipriano, Anthony J., jt. auth. see Numeroff, William J.

Cipriano, Joseph. Photographic Manual of Regional Orthopaedic Tests. 200p. 1985. lib. bdg. 24.95 (ISBN 0-683-01700-4). Williams & Wilkins.

Cipriano, Margaret M. Sunflowers & Hollyhocks. 1983. 5.95 (ISBN 0-8062-2154-2). Carlton.

Cipriano, Robert, ed. Special Olympics. (Special Education Ser.). (Illus., Orig.). 1980. pap. 16.00 (ISBN 0-89568-111-0). Spec Learn Corp.

Ciranna, Alfonso. Giacomo Manzu: Catalogue of the Graphic Work. 295p. (Ital.). 125.00 (ISBN 0-915346-48-6). A Wofsy Fine Arts.

Circle Books. Aspect Finder. 2.25 (ISBN 0-318-01817-9). Am Fed Astrologers.

Circle Fine Art. Circle Fine Art: Editions Catalog. LC 80-54149. (Orig.). 1980. pap. write for info. (ISBN 0-932240-01-1). Circle Fine Art.

Ciria, Alberto. Parties & Power in Modern Argentina, 1930-1946. Astiz, Carlos A. & McCarthy, Mary F., trs. LC 70-129642. 1974. 44.50x (ISBN 0-87395-079-8). State U NY Pr.

Ciriani, Tito A., et al, eds. Mathematical Models for Surface Water Hydrology: Proceedings of the Workshop Held at the IBM Scientific Center, Pisa Italy. LC 76-13457. 423p. 1977. 109.95x (ISBN 0-471-99400-6, Pub. by Wiley-Interscience). Wiley.

Ciriello, Janet, jt. auth. see Schave, Barbara.

Cirillo, Bob & Ahearn, Kevin. Dry Faces. (Illus.). 1978. pap. 6.00 (ISBN 0-910158-37-1). Art Dir.

Cirillo, Dennis & Rubenstein, Mark. The Complete Book of Cosmetic Facial Surgery: A Step-by-Step Guide to the Physical & Psychological Process. LC 84-1397. (Illus.). 176p. 1984. 16.95 (ISBN 0-671-47743-9). S&S.

Cirillo, Dennis P., jt. auth. see Rubinstein, Mark.

Cirillo, Joan. The Westchester Book. LC 76-6456. (Illus.). 1976. 12.95; pap. 6.95 (ISBN 0-8128-1922-5). Stein & Day.

Cirillo, R. The Economics of Vilfredo Pareto. 148p. 1979. 28.50x (ISBN 0-7146-3108-6, F Cass Co). Biblio Dist.

Cirincione-Coles, Kathryn, ed. The Future of Education: Policy Issues & Challenges. LC 81-1528. (Sage Focus Editions Ser.: Vol. 28). 274p. 1981. 28.00 (ISBN 0-8039-1538-1); pap. 14.00 (ISBN 0-8039-1539-X). Sage.

Cirino, Andre. In the Womb of the Cave. 366p. 1981. 14.00 (ISBN 0-933402-26-0); pap. 9.00 (ISBN 0-933402-25-2). Charisma Pr.

Cirino, Andre & Rogers, Francine. Teens Encounter Christ. LC 77-88321. (Illus., Orig.). 1978. pap. 2.25 (ISBN 0-8189-1156-5, 156, Pub. by Alba Bks). Alba.

Cirino, Antonio, jt. auth. see Rose, Augustus F.

Cirino, Linda D., jt. auth. see Arbeiter, Jean.

Cirino, Tony. U. S. Soccer vs. the World. 200p. (Orig.). 1983. pap. 6.95 (ISBN 0-910641-00-5). Damon Pr.

Cirker, Blanche. The Book of Kells: Selected Plates in Full Color. (Fine Art, History of Art Ser.). (Illus.). 32p. 1982. pap. 4.50 (ISBN 0-486-24345-1). Dover.

Cirker, Blanche, jt. auth. see Cirker, Hayward.

Cirker, Blanche, ed. Needlework Alphabets & Designs. pap. 2.95 (ISBN 0-486-23159-3). Dover.

Cirker, Blanche, ed. see Bewick, Thomas.

Cirker, Blanche, jt. ed. see Cirker, Hayward.

Cirker, Hayward & Cirker, Blanche. Dictionary of American Portraits. Dover Editorial Staff, ed. 1967. 65.00 (ISBN 0-486-21823-6). Dover.

--Golden Age of the Poster. 1971. pap. 6.95 (ISBN 0-486-22753-7). Dover.

--Monograms & Alphabetic Devices. (Illus., Orig.). 1970. pap. 6.95 (ISBN 0-486-22330-2). Dover.

--Monograms & Alphabetic Devices. (Illus.). 16.75 (ISBN 0-8446-0546-8). Peter Smith.

Cirker, Hayward, jt. auth. see Appelbaum, Stanley.

Cirker, Hayward, ed. Thirty Two Picture Postcards of Old New York. (Illus.). 16p. (Orig.). 1976. pap. 2.50 (ISBN 0-486-23287-5). Dover.

Cirker, Hayward & Cirker, Blanche, eds. The Golden Age of the Poster. (Illus.). 15.25 (ISBN 0-8446-0059-8). Peter Smith.

--Masterpieces of the Poster from the Belle Epoque: 48 Full-Color Plates from "Les Maitres de L'Affiche". (Fine Art Ser.). 48p. 1984. pap. 5.95 (ISBN 0-486-24549-7). Dover.

--Twenty-Four Art Nouveau Postcards in Full Colors: From Classic Posters. (Illus.). 12p. (Orig.). 1983. pap. 2.95 (ISBN 0-486-24389-3). Dover.

Cirker, Haywood, ed. Italian Master Drawings from the Uffizi. (Fine Art Ser.). (Illus.). 96p. (Orig.). 1983. pap. 5.95 (ISBN 0-486-24467-9). Dover.

Cirkinian, Loraine V. The Vicissitudes of Life. 1984. 7.95 (ISBN 0-8062-2413-4). Carlton.

Cirlot, J. Diccionario de Simbolos. (Span.). pap. 32.95 (ISBN 84-335-7016-1, S-12244). French & Eur.

Cirlot, J. E. A Dictionary of Symbols. 2nd ed. (Illus.). 544p. 1972. 22.50 (ISBN 0-8022-2083-5). Philos Lib.

Cirlot, Juan-Eduardo. Diccionario Universal del Arte y los Artistas, 9 vols. 2794p. (Span.). 1969. Set. leatherette 229.50 (ISBN 0-686-57347-1, S-12283). French & Eur.

Cirner, Randall & Cirner, Therese. Ten Weeks to a Better Marriage. 132p. (Orig.). 1985. pap. 7.95 (ISBN 0-89283-237-1). Servant.

Cirner, Randall J., jt. auth. see Scanlan, Michael.

Cirner, Therese. The Facts About Your Feelings: What Every Christian Woman Should Know. 142p. 1982. pap. 4.95 (ISBN 0-89283-103-0). Servant.

Cirner, Therese, jt. auth. see Cirner, Randall.

Cirou, Joseph, et al. The Johannine Hymnal. LC 75-14542. (Melody ed). 1970. 3.95 (ISBN 0-915866-00-5). Am Cath Pr.

Cirovic, Michael M. Basic Electronics. 2nd ed. (Illus.). 1979. text ed. 30.00 (ISBN 0-8359-0370-2); solutions manual avail. (ISBN 0-8359-0371-0). Reston.

--Integrated Circuits: A User's Handbook. 2nd ed. (Illus.). 1982. text ed. 23.95 (ISBN 0-8359-3095-5). Reston.

Cirre, Jose F. & Cirre, Manuela M. Espana y los Espanoles. 2nd ed. LC 80-23274. 190p. 1981. text ed. 15.95 (ISBN 0-03-058051-X, HoltC). HR&W.

Cirre, Manuela M., jt. auth. see Cirre, Jose F.

Cirtautas, Arista M., compiled by. Nicholas Poppe: A Bibliography of Publications from 1924-1977. (Parerga Ser.: No. 4). 62p. 1978. pap. 3.75x (ISBN 0-295-95601-1). U of Wash Pr.

Cisco, Jay G. Historic Sumner County Tennessee. (Illus.). 1971. Repr. of 1909 ed. 25.00 (ISBN 0-918450-04-7). C Elder.

Cise, Jerrold G. Van see Van Cise, Jerrold G.

Cise, Philip S. Van see Van Cise, Philip S.

Cisek, James & George, Anthea. Deciding for Yourself. 240p. 1985. instrs.' manual 3 ring binder incl. cassettes 49.95 (ISBN 0-932723-00-4). Life Skills.

--Deciding for Yourself Youth Manual. (Illus.). 60p. (Orig.). 1985. pap. 5.95 (ISBN 0-9604510-1-3). Life Skills.

--Finding Solutions: How to Get "IDEAL" Answers to Problems & Decisions. rev. ed. (Illus.). 60p. 1985. pap. 4.95 (ISBN 0-9604510-8-0). Life Skills.

--Life Skills: Teaching Attitudes & Behaviors for Success in Life. 280p. 1985. instrs. manual incl. wkbk. & cassettes 59.95 (ISBN 0-9604510-9-9). Life Skills.

--Loosening Up: Getting Rid of Those Uptight Feelings. (Illus.). 40p. 1985. pap. 4.25x (ISBN 0-9604510-7-2). Life Skills.

Cisin, Fred & Parvin, Jack. How to Keep Your Honda Car Alive: A Manual of Step by Step Procedures for the Compleat Idiot. (Illus.). 272p. (Orig.). 1983. 14.00 (ISBN 0-912528-25-7). John Muir.

Cisin, I. H., jt. auth. see Cahgalan, D.

Ciske, Karen L. & Mayer, Gloria G., eds. Primary Nursing. LC 79-90370. 103p. 1980. pap. text ed. 17.95 (ISBN 0-913654-60-4). Aspen Systems.

CISM (International Center for Mechanical Sciences), Dept. of Automation & Information, Academy of Sciences, Warsaw, 1971. Algebraic Methods in Pattern Recognition. Kulikowsky, J., ed. (CISM Pubns. Ser.: No. 85). (Illus.). 82p. 1973. pap. 12.40 (ISBN 0-387-81128-1). Springer-Verlag.

CISM (International Center for Mechanical Sciences), Dept. for General Mechanics, Technical Univ. of Vienna, 1971. Approximate Analysis of Stochastic Processes in Mechanics. Zeman, J. L., ed. (CISM Pubns. Ser.: No. 95). (Illus.). iv, 157p. 1973. pap. 16.40 (ISBN 0-387-81131-1). Springer-Verlag.

CISM (International Center for Mechanical Sciences), Dept. of Automation & Information, 1970. Channel Coding Theory. Csiszar, I., ed. (CISM Pubns. Ser.: No. 29). 79p. 1974. pap. 12.40 (ISBN 0-387-81089-7). Springer-Verlag.

CISM (International Center for Mechanical Sciences), Dept. of Automation & Information, University of Trieste, 1971. Coding for Markov Sources. Longo, G., ed. (CISM Pubns. Ser.: No. 110). (Illus.). 99p. 1973. pap. 13.90 (ISBN 0-387-81154-0). Springer-Verlag.

CISM (International Center for Mechanical Sciences) Dept. of Automation & Information. Combinatorial Search Problems. Katona, G., ed. (CISM Pubns. Ser: No. 145). 57p. 1973. pap. 8.60 (ISBN 0-387-81169-9). Springer-Verlag.

CISM (International Center for Mechanical Sciences), Dept. for General Mechanics, 1972, et al. Computer Aided Automatic Design. Bona, C., et al, eds. (CISM International Centre for Mechanical Science: No. 155). (Illus.). 35p. 1975. pap. 7.10 (ISBN 0-387-81205-9). Springer-Verlag.

CISM (International Center for Mechanical Sciences), Dept. of Automation & Information, University of Trieste, 1969 & Marzollo, A. Controllability & Optimization. (CISM Pubns. Ser.: No. 17). 80p. 1973. pap. 12.40 (ISBN 0-387-81123-0). Springer-Verlag.

CISM (International Center for Mechanical Sciences), Dept. of Automation & Information, Univ of Geneva, 1971. Controlled & Conditioned Invariance. Basile, G., ed. (CISM Pubns. Ser.: No. 109). (Illus.). 51p. 1973. pap. 7.50 (ISBN 0-387-81132-X). Springer-Verlag.

CISM (International Center for Mechanical Sciences), Dept. for Mechanics of Deformable Bodies. Creep Transition in Cylinders. Seth, B. R., ed. (CISM Pubns. Ser.: No. 149). 29p. 1973. pap. 5.90 (ISBN 0-387-81170-2). Springer-Verlag.

CISM (International Center for Mechanical Sciences), Dept. for General Mechanics, 1970. Critical Speeds of Gyroscopes. Schweitzer, G., ed. (CISM Pubns. Ser.: No. 55). (Illus.). 95p. 1973. pap. 13.50 (ISBN 0-387-81150-8). Springer-Verlag.

CISM (International Center for Mechanical Sciences), Dept. of Experimental Methods in Mechanics, 1971. Dynamic Positioning of Vessels at Sea. Pinkster, J., ed. (CISM International Centre for Mechanical Sciences Ser.: No. 105). (Illus.). 36p. 1974. pap. 6.70 (ISBN 0-387-81221-0). Springer-Verlag.

CISM (International Center for Mechanical Sciences) Dept. of General Mechanics, Dubrovnik, 1971. Dynamics of Flexible Spacecraft. Likins, P. W., et al, eds. (CISM International Centre for Mechanical Sciences Ser.: No. 103). (Illus.). 158p. 1974. pap. 17.40 (ISBN 0-387-81199-0). Springer-Verlag.

CISM (International Center for Mechanical Sciences), Dept. of Mechanics of Solids, 1971. Entropy, Absolute Temperature & Coldness in Thermodynamics Boundary Conditions in Porous Material. Muller, I., ed. (CISM Pubns. Ser.: No. 76). (Illus.). 53p. 1973. pap. text ed. 8.20 (ISBN 0-387-81126-5). Springer-Verlag.

CISM (International Center for Mechanical Sciences) Examples to Extremum & Variational Principles in Mechanics. Besdo, D., ed. (CISM International Centre for Mechanical Sciences Ser.: No. 65). (Illus.). 236p. 1974. pap. 23.80 (ISBN 0-387-81230-X). Springer-Verlag.

CISM (International Center for Mechanical Sciences), Dept. for General Mechanics, Technical Univ. of Brunswick, 1970. Extremum & Variational Principles in Mechanics. Lippmann, H., ed. (CISM Pubns. Ser.: No. 54). (Illus.). ii, 239p. 1972. pap. 33.10 (ISBN 0-387-81115-X). Springer-Verlag.

CISM (International Center for Mechanical Sciences), Dept. of Mechanics of Solids. Field Equations for Thermoelastic Bodies with Uniform Symmetry - Acceleration Waves in Thermoelastic Bodies. Wang, C. C., ed. (CISM Pubns. Ser.: No. 112). 41p. 1973. pap. 6.70 (ISBN 0-387-81180-X). Springer-Verlag.

CISM (International Center for Mechanical Sciences), Dept. of Hydro & Gasdynamics, Technical Univ. of Turin, 1970. Fluid Dynamics of Jet Amplifiers. Romiti, A., ed. (CISM Pubns. Ser.: No. 66). (Illus.). 1973. pap. 12.60 (ISBN 0-387-81152-4). Springer-Verlag.

CISM (International Center for Mechanical Sciences) Fluidic Applications. Belforte, G., ed. (CISM Intl. Centre for Mechanical Sciences, Courses & Lectures Ser.: No. 60). (Illus.). 156p. 1974. pap. 16.90 (ISBN 0-387-81220-2). Springer-Verlag.

--Fluidic Sensors & Some Large Scale Devices. Jacobs, B. E., ed. (CISM Intl. Centre for Mechanical Sciences, Courses & Lectures: No. 52). (Illus.). 41p. 1974. pap. 6.70 (ISBN 0-387-81228-8). Springer-Verlag.

CISM (International Center for Mechanical Sciences Ser. Foundations of the Mathematical Theory of Structures. Oliveira, E. De Arantes, ed. (CISM Pubs. Ser: No. 121). (Illus.). 223p. 1976. pap. 26.00 (ISBN 0-387-81312-8). Springer-Verlag.

CISM (International Center for Mechanical Sciences), Dept. for General Mechanics, Vienna, 1970. Gas-Lubricated Bearings of Gyroscopes. Heinrich, G., ed. (CISM Pubns. Ser.: No. 43). (Illus.). 57p. 1973. pap. 10.00 (ISBN 0-387-81147-8). Springer-Verlag.

CISM (International Center for Mechanical Sciences), Dept. for General Mechanics, 1973. The General & Restricted Problems of Three Bodies. Szebehely, V., ed. (CISM International Centre for Mechanical Sciences Ser.: No. 170). (Illus.). 53p. 1974. pap. 6.20 (ISBN 0-387-81264-4). Springer-Verlag.

CISM (International Center for Mechanical Sciences), Dept. of Automation & Information, 1970. General Theory of Noiseless Channels. Katona, G., ed. (CISM International Center for Mechanical Sciences Ser.: No. 31). 69p. 1975. pap. 12.40 (ISBN 0-387-81167-2). Springer-Verlag.

CISM (International Center for Mechanical Sciences) Gyrodynamics. Magnus, K., ed. (CISM Intl. Centre for Mechanical Science, Courses & Lectures Ser.: No. 53). (Illus.). x, 280p. 1974. pap. 15.40 (ISBN 0-387-81229-6). Springer-Verlag.

CISM (International Center for Mechanical Sciences), Dept. of Automation & Information. Information Transmission with Symbols of Different Cost. Csiszar, I., ed. (CISM Pubns. Ser.: No. 136). 36p. 1973. pap. 5.40 (ISBN 0-387-81136-2). Springer-Verlag.

CISM (International Center for Mechanical Sciences) Introduction to Gasdynamics of Explosions. Oppenheim, A. K., ed. (CISM Pubns. Ser.: No. 48). (Illus.). 220p. 1972. pap. 23.80 (ISBN 0-387-81083-8). Springer-Verlag.

CISM (International Center for Mechanical Sciences), Dept. of Automation & Information, Denmark, 1971. An Introduction to the Design of Pattern Recognition Devices. Becker, P. W., ed. (CISM Pubns. Ser.: No. 83). (Illus.). 188p. 1973. pap. 19.00 (ISBN 0-387-81153-2). Springer-Verlag.

CISM (International Center for Mechanical Sciences) Irreversible Thermodynamics of Continuous Media: Internal Variable Theory. Valanis, K. C., ed. (CISM Pubns. Ser: No. 77). (Illus.). 172p. 1973. pap. 17.10 (ISBN 0-387-81127-3). Springer-Verlag.

--Laser Cinematography of Explosions. Oppenheim, A. K. & Kamel, M. M., eds. (CISM Pubns. Ser.: No. 100). (Illus.). 226p. 1974. pap. 26.60 (ISBN 0-387-81179-6). Springer-Verlag.

--Lectures on Radiating Gasdynamics: General Equations & Boundary Conditions. Ferrari, C., ed. (CISM Pubns. Ser.: No. 146). (Illus.). 83p. 1975. pap. 12.40 (ISBN 0-387-81204-0). Springer-Verlag.

--Lectures on the Theory of Exothermic Flows Behind Shock Waves. Cherny, G. G., ed. (CISM Intl. Centre for Mechanical Sciences, Courses & Lectures Ser.: No. 36). (Illus.). 143p. 1974. pap. 18.90 (ISBN 3-211-81168-0). Springer-Verlag.

CISM (International Center for Mechanical Sciences), Dept. of Mechanics of Solids, 1972. The Linear Theory of Thermoelasticity. Sneddon, I. N., ed. (CISM International Center for Mechanical Sciences Ser.: No. 119). (Illus.). 197p. 1974. pap. 16.30 (ISBN 0-387-81257-1). Springer-Verlag.

CISM (International Center for Mechanical Sciences), Dept. of Mechanics of Solids, Vienna, 1972. Magneto-Thermoelasticity. Parkus, H., ed. (CISM Pubns. Ser.: No. 118). 61p. 1973. pap. 9.80 (ISBN 0-387-81134-6). Springer-Verlag.

CISM (International Center for Mechanical Sciences), Dept. of Automation & Information. Mathematical Structure of Finite Random Cybernetic Systems. Quiasu, S., ed. (CISM Pubns. Ser.: No. 86). (Illus.). 215p. 1974. pap. 21.00 (ISBN 0-387-81174-5). Springer-Verlag.

CISM (International Center for Mechanical Sciences), Dept. of Mechanics of Solids, 1972. Matrix Analysis of Discrete Elastic Systems. Kardestuncer, H., ed. (CISM International Centre for Mechanical Sciences Ser.: No. 179). (Illus.). 47p. 1975. pap. 5.80 (ISBN 0-387-81235-0). Springer-Verlag.

CISM (International Center for Mechanical Sciences) Dept. of Mechanics & Solids, 1972. Micropolar Elasticity. Olszak, W. & Nowacki, W., eds. (CISM International Centre for Mechanical Sciences Ser.: No. 151). (Illus.). vii, 168p. 1974. pap. 15.70 (ISBN 0-387-81262-8). Springer-Verlag.

CISM (International Center for Mechanical Sciences) Nonlinear Thermoelasticity. Stojanovic, R., ed. (CISM Pubns. Ser.: No. 120). 85p. 1974. pap. 12.40 (ISBN 0-387-81200-8). Springer-Verlag.

CISM (International Center for Mechanical Sciences)-IFTOMM Symposium, 1st, 1973. On Theory & Practice of Robots & Manipulators: Proceedings. (CISM International Centre for Mechanical Sciences Ser.: No. 201). (Illus.). 668p. 1974. pap. 53.10 (ISBN 0-387-81252-0). Springer-Verlag.

CISM (International Center for Mechanical Sciences), Dept. for General Mechanics, 1971. Optical Filtering. Parkus, H., ed. (CISM Pubns. Ser.: No. 94). (Illus.). 59p. 1973. pap. 10.70 (ISBN 0-387-81130-3). Springer-Verlag.

CISM (International Center for Mechanical Sciences), Dept. of Automation & Information, 1972. Periodic Optimization, 2 vols. Marzollo, A., ed. (CISM Pubns. Ser.: No. 135). (Illus.). 532p. 1973. Set. pap. 50.70 (ISBN 0-387-81135-4). Springer-Verlag.

CISM (International Center for Mechanical Sciences), Dept. for Mechanics of Deformable Bodies, 1970. Photoelasticity in Theory & Practice. Brcic, V., ed. (CISM International Center for Mechanical Sciences Ser.: No. 59). (Illus.). 242p. 1975. pap. 23.30 (ISBN 0-387-81081-1). Springer-Verlag.

CISM (International Center for Mechanical Sciences) Physiological Fluid Mechanics. Lighthill, J., ed. (CISM Pubns. Ser.: No. 111). 59p. 1973. pap. 9.80 (ISBN 0-387-81133-8). Springer Verlag.

--Polorization Gradient in Elastic Dielectric. Mindlin, R. D., ed. (CISM Pubns. Ser.: No. 24). (Illus.). 55p. 1973. pap. 10.40 (ISBN 0-387-81087-0). Springer-Verlag.

CISM (International Center for Mechanical Sciences), Dept of Automation & Information. Quantitative-Qualitative Measure of Information. Longo, G., ed. (CISM Pubns. Ser.: No. 138). (Illus.). 51p. 1973. pap. 8.80 (ISBN 0-387-81182-6). Springer-Verlag.

CISM (International Center for Mechanical Sciences), Dept. for Mechanics of Deformable Bodies, Univ. of Vienna, 1970. Radiation Damage. Schmid, E. & Lintner, K., eds. Incl. Behavior of Insonated Metals. (CISM Pubns. Ser.: No. 64). (Illus.). 88p. 1973. pap. 10.60 (ISBN 0-387-81124-9). Springer-Verlag.

CISM (International Center for Mechanical Sciences) Random Processes in Mechanical Sciences. Parkus, H., ed. (CISM Pubns. Ser.: No. 9). (Illus.). vi, 169p. 1973. pap. 19.80 (ISBN 0-387-81086-2). Springer-Verlag.

CISM (International Center for Mechanical Sciences), Dept. of Mechanics of Solids. Random Theory of Deformation of Structured Media: Thermodynamics of Deformation in Structured Media. Axelrad, D. R. & Provan, J. W., eds. (CISM Pubns. Ser.: No. 71). (Illus.). 57p. 1973. pap. 9.50 (ISBN 0-387-81175-3). Springer-Verlag.

CISM (International Center for Mechanical Sciences. Random Vibrations. Robson, et al, eds. (CISM Pubns. Ser.: No. 115). (Illus.). 219p. 1974. pap. 20.50 (ISBN 0-387-81223-7). Springer-Verlag.

CISM (International Center for Mechanical Sciences), Dept for Mechanics of Deformable Bodies, Univ. of Belgrade, 1970. Recent Developments in the Theory of Polar Continua. (CISM Pubns. Ser.: No. 27). 345p. 1973. pap. 32.50 (ISBN 0-387-81144-3). Springer-Verlag.

CISM (International Center for Mechanical Sciences), Dept for General Mechanics, Dubrovnik, 1971. Rotational Dynamics of Orbiting Gyrostats: Proceedings. Roberson, R., et al, eds. (CISM Pubns. Ser.: No. 102). (Illus.). 208p. 1974. pap. 23.10 (ISBN 0-387-81198-2). Springer-Verlag.

CISM (International Center for Mechanical Sciences), Dept. of Automation & Informations, 1969. Selected Topics in Information Theory. Longo, G., ed. (CISM International Center for Mechanical Sciences Ser.: No. 18). (Illus.). 111p. 1974. pap. 15.70 (ISBN 0-387-81166-4). Springer-Verlag.

CISM (International Center for Mechanical Sciences), Dept. of Hydro & Gas Dynamics, 1970. Shock Waves in Real Gases. Bazhenova, T. V., ed. (CISM International Center for Mechanical Sciences Ser.: No. 37). (Illus.). 78p. 1974. pap. 12.40 (ISBN 3-211-81219-9). Springer-Verlag.

CISM (International Center for Mechanical Sciences), Dept. of Automation & Information. Source Coding Theory. Longo, G., ed. (CISM Pubns. Ser.: No. 32). (Illus.). 83p. 1973. pap. 12.40 (ISBN 0-387-81090-0). Springer-Verlag.

CISM (International Center for Mechanical Sciences), Dept. for General Mechanics, 1970. Special Problems in Gyrodynamics. Muller, P. C., ed. (CISM Pubns. Ser.: No. 63). (Illus.). 96p. 1973. pap. 14.20 (ISBN 0-387-81085-4). Springer-Verlag.

CISM (International Center for Mechanical Sciences) Statistical Continuum Mechanics. Kroener, E., ed. (CISM Pubns. Ser.: No. 92). (Illus.). 157p. 1974. pap. 16.40 (ISBN 0-387-81129-X). Springer-Verlag.

--Structural Dynamics Heat Conduction. De Veubeke, B. F., et al, eds. (CISM Pubns. Ser.: No. 126). (Illus.). 256p. 1974. pap. 25.60 (ISBN 0-387-81201-6). Springer-Verlag.

--A Survey of Algebraic Coding Theory. Berlekamp, E. R., ed. (CISM Pubns. Ser.: No. 28). (Illus.). 75p. 1973. pap. 12.40 (ISBN 0-387-81088-9). Springer-Verlag.

CISM (International Center for Mechanical Sciences), Dept. of Automation & Information, 1972. Theory of Bilinear Dynamical Systems. Isidori, A., et al, eds. (CISM Pubns. Ser.: No. 158). (Illus.). 69p. 1974. pap. 10.70 (ISBN 0-387-81206-7). Springer-Verlag.

CISM (International Center for Mechanical Sciences), Dept. for Mechanics of Deformable Bodies, 1970. Theory of Couple-Stresses in Bodies with Constrained Rotations. Sokolowski, M., ed. (CISM International Centre for Mechanical Sciences Ser.: No. 26). (Illus.). 143p. 1974. pap. 14.90 (ISBN 0-387-81143-5). Springer-Verlag.

--Theory of Popular Elasticity: Proceedings. Nowacki, W., ed. (CISM Pubns. Ser.: No. 25). (Illus.). 286p. 1974. pap. 27.20 (ISBN 0-387-81078-1). Springer-Verlag.

CISM (International Center for Mechanical Sciences), Dept for Mechanics of Rigid Bodies. Thermodynamic Effects in Wave Propogation. Chen, P., ed. (CISM Pubns. Ser.: No. 72). 33p. 1973. pap. 7.70 (ISBN 0-387-81176-1). Springer-Verlag.

CISM (International Center for Mechanical Sciences), Dept. of Mechanics of Solids. Thermodynamics in Contemporary Dynamics. Glansdorff, P., ed. (CISM Pubns. Ser.: No. 74). (Illus.). 120p. 1973. pap. 14.80 (ISBN 0-387-81177-X). Springer-Verlag.

--Thermodynamics of Materials with Memory. Coleman, B. D., ed. (CISM Pubns. Ser.: No. 73). iii, 47p. 1973. pap. 8.90 (ISBN 0-387-81125-7). Springer Verlag.

CISM (International Center for Mechanical Sciences), Dept. of Mechanics of Solids, 1971. The Tragicomedy of Classical Thermodynamics. Truesdell, C. A., ed. (CISM Pubns. Ser.: No. 70). (Illus.). 41p. 1973. pap. 9.50 (ISBN 0-387-81114-1). Springer-Verlag.

CISM (International Center for Mechanical Sciences), Dept. for Mechanics of Deformable Bodies, Technical Univ. of Vienna, 1970. Variational Principles in Thermo- & Magneto-Elasticity. Parkus, H., ed. (CISM Pubns. Ser.: No. 58). 47p. 1973. pap. 9.50 (ISBN 0-387-81080-3). Springer-Verlag.

Cismaru, Alfred. Marivaux & Moliere: A Comparison. 139p. 1977. 12.95 (ISBN 0-89672-055-1). Tex Tech Pr.

Cisneros, Antonio. At Night the Cats. Ahern, Maureen & Tipton, David, trs. from Span. LC 85-60358. 250p. (Eng. & Span.). 1985. 14.95 (ISBN 0-87376-044-1). Red Dust.

Cisneros, Henry G. The Entrepreneurial City. 280p. 1986. 24.95 (ISBN 0-88730-054-5). Ballinger Pub.

Cisneros, Jose. Faces of the Borderlands. (Southwestern Studies: No. 52). 1977. 3.00 (ISBN 0-87404-111-2). Tex Western.

--Riders Across the Centuries. 248p. 1984. 36.00 (ISBN 0-87404-089-2). Tex Western.

Cisneros, Sandra. The House on Mango Street. LC 82-72278. 80p. 1983. 7.50 (ISBN 0-934770-20-4). Arte Publico.

Cisse, Y., jt. auth. see Dieterlen, G.

Cissell, Helen, et al. Mathematics of Finance. 6th ed. 1982. 28.95 (ISBN 0-395-31692-8); instr's manual 2.50 (ISBN 0-395-31693-6). HM.

Cissell, James C. Federal Criminal Trials. 935p. 1983. 50.00 (ISBN 0-87215-615-X). Michie Co.

Cissley, Charles H. Management Science in Life Companies. LC 75-32898. (FLMI Insurance Education Program Ser.). 1975. pap. text ed. 6.00 (ISBN 0-915322-15-3). LOMA.

--Systems & Data Processing in Insurance Companies. rev. ed. LC 82-80670. (FLMI Insurance Education Program Ser.). 287p. 1982. text ed. 12.00 (ISBN 0-915322-55-2); pap. 5.00 wkbk. (ISBN 0-915322-56-0); student guide avail. LOMA.

Cist, Charles. Cincinnati Miscellany, or Antiquities of the West: Pioneer History & General & Local Statistics Compiled from the Western General Advertiser, 2 Vols. in 1. LC 72-146381. (First American Frontier Ser). 1971. Repr. of 1845 ed. 40.00 (ISBN 0-405-02832-6). Ayer Co Pubs.

Cistercian Abbey of las Huelgas, Burgos, Spain. El Codex Musical de las Huelgas, 3 vols. LC 71-178510. (Publications del Departament de Musica, Biblioteca de Catalunya: No. 6). (Illus.). Repr. of 1931 ed. Set. 235.00 (ISBN 0-404-56504-2). AMS Pr.

Ciszek, Walter J. & Flaherty, Daniel. He Leadeth Me. LC 73-79654. 240p. 1975. pap. 3.95 (ISBN 0-385-02805-9, Im). Doubleday.

Ciszek, Walter J. & Flaherty, Daniel L. With God in Russia. pap. 4.50 (ISBN 0-385-03954-9, Im). Doubleday.

Cita, M. B., jt. ed. see Schlanger, S. O.

Citino, David. The Appassionata Poems. 47p. (Orig.). 1983. pap. 4.50 (ISBN 0-914946-35-8). Cleveland St Univ Poetry Ctr.

--Last Rites & Other Poems. LC 80-14993. 105p. 1980. 13.50 (ISBN 0-8142-0314-0). Ohio St U Pr.

Citizens' Association Of New York. Report of the Council of Hygiene & Public Health of the Citizens' Association of New York Upon the Sanitary Condition of the City. LC 77-112532. (Rise of Urban America). (Illus.). 1970. Repr. of 1866 ed. 46.50 (ISBN 0-405-02443-6). Ayer Co Pubs.

Citizens' Commission on Civil Rights Staff. A Decent Home: A Report on the Continuing Failure of the Federal Government to Provide Equal Housing Opportunity. 1983. write for info. CU Law Natl.

--There Is No Liberty... A Report on Congressional Efforts to Curb the Federal Courts & to Undermine the Brown Decision. 1984. write for info. CU Law Natl.

Citizen's Committee for New York City & Community Service Society. Funding Neighborhood Programs. LC 84-167344. 1980. pap. 3.50 (ISBN 0-318-00901-3). Comm Serv Soc NY.

Citizens' Police Committee. Chicago Police Problems. LC 69-16230. (Criminology, Law Enforcement, & Social Problems Ser.: No. 89). 1969. Repr. of 1931 ed. 12.00x (ISBN 0-87585-089-8). Patterson Smith.

Citizens Policy Center. Our Future at Stake: A Teenager's Guide to Stopping the Nuclear Arms Race. 68p. 1984. lib. bdg. 19.95 (ISBN 0-86571-055-4); pap. 6.95 (ISBN 0-86571-054-6). New Soc Pubs.

Citizens Research & Investigation Committee & Tackwood, Louis. The Glass House Tapes. Freed, Donald, ed. 1973. pap. 1.75 (ISBN 0-380-01215-4, 14555). Avon.

Citizen's Scholarship Foundation of America, ed. see Johnson, Marlys C. & Thompson, Linda J.

Citizenship Education Study & Meier, Arnold R. Curriculum for Citizenship: A Total School Approach. LC 78-92298. Repr. of 1952 ed. lib. bdg. 15.00x (ISBN 0-8371-2448-4, CUFC). Greenwood.

Citrenbaum, Charles, et al. Modern Clinical Hypnosis for Habit Control. 1985. 18.50 (ISBN 0-393-70003-8). Norton.

Citrin, Anthony. Victims All: A Teaching Guide for Child Abuse & Neglect Prevention. LC 83-83314. 160p. (Orig.). 1985. pap. text ed. cancelled (ISBN 0-918452-57-0). Learning Pubns.

Citrin, Jack. United Nations Peacekeeping Activities: A Case Study in Organizational Task Expansion. (Monograph Series in World Affairs: Vol. 3 1965-66 Ser., Bk. 1). 85p. (Orig.). 1965. 3.95 (ISBN 0-87940-007-2). Monograph Series.

Citrin, Jack & Elkins, David J. Political Disaffection among British University Students: Concepts, Measurement, & Causes. LC 75-620051. (Research Ser.: No. 23). 80p. 1975. pap. 2.00x (ISBN 0-87725-123-1). U of Cal Intl St.

Citrin, Jack, jt. auth. see Sears, David O.

Citrine, W. M. Men & Work: An Autobiography. LC 75-36094. (Illus.). 1976. Repr. of 1964 ed. lib. bdg. 24.00x (ISBN 0-8371-8613-7, CIMW). Greenwood.

Citroen. Valse Zilvermerken in Nederland. Date not set. 21.50 (ISBN 0-686-94103-9). Elsevier.

Citroen, K. A. Amsterdam Silversmiths & Their Marks. (Studies in Silver Ser.: Vol. 1). 352p. 1975. 153.25 (ISBN 0-444-10730-4, North-Holland). Elsevier.

Citron, ed. see De Balzac, Honore.

Citron, Anne M., jt. auth. see Trousseau, Marie M.

Citron, Casper. John V. Lindsay. LC 65-26494. (Illus.). 1965. 7.50 (ISBN 0-8303-0045-7). Fleet.

Citron, Marcia. The Letters of Fanny Mendelssohn Hensel to Felix Mendelssohn. 600p. (Ger.). 1985. lib. bdg. 64.00 (ISBN 0-918728-52-5). Pendragon NY.

Citron, Minna. From the Eighty Years of Minna Citron. (Illus., Orig.). 1976. pap. 6.95x (ISBN 0-8150-0836-8). Wittenborn.

Citron, Pierre, jt. auth. see Balzac, Honore De.

Citron, Pierre, jt. auth. see Balzac, Honore de.

Citron, Samuel J. Dramatics for Creative Teaching. (Illus.). 1961. 9.50x (ISBN 0-8381-0212-3). United Syn Bk.

Citron, Stephen. Songwriting: A Complete Guide to the Craft. LC 85-11515. (Illus.). 320p. 1985. 17.95 (ISBN 0-688-04466-2). Morrow.

Cits. Technological Value of the Sugar Beet. 1968. 32.00 (ISBN 0-444-40112-1). Elsevier.

City Art Musuem, St. Louis. Max Beckmann, Nineteen Eighty-Four: Retrospective Exhibition Organized by City Art Musuem of St. Louis. LC 83-45798. 55.00 (ISBN 0-404-20225-X, ND588). AMS Pr.

City Literary Institute Of London. Tradition & Experiment in Present-Day Literature. facs. ed. LC 68-20290. (Essay Index Reprint Ser). 1968. Repr. of 1929 ed. 15.00 (ISBN 0-8369-0307-2). Ayer Co Pubs.

City of Los Angeles, City Attorney's Office. Los Angeles Municipal Code, 5 vols. 4th rev. ed. 3300p. 1979. Set. looseleaf 375.00 (ISBN 0-911110-33-X); current 1984 revision incl. (ISBN 0-685-26720-2). Parker & Son.

Ciuba, Edward J. Who Do You Say That I Am? An Adult Inquiry into the First Three Gospels. LC 74-10808. 155p. 1974. pap. 5.95 (ISBN 0-8189-0295-7). Alba.

Ciucci, Giorgio, et al. The American City: From the Civil War to the New Deal. La Penta, Barbara L., tr. from Italian. (Illus.). 580p. 1979. pap. text ed. 17.50 (ISBN 0-262-53044-9). MIT Pr.

Ciuffreda, A. R., ed. Evaluation of Materials in Process Equipment After Long Term Service in the Petroleum Industry: MPC-12. 64p. 1980. 8.00 (ISBN 0-317-33506-5, I00126); members 4.00 (ISBN 0-317-33507-3). ASME.

Ciuffreda, Kenneth J., jt. ed. see Schor, Clifton M.

Ciulionis, M. K. Sonataos in Fugos. 1980. 32.00x (ISBN 0-317-14318-2, Pub. by Collet's). State Mutual Bk.

Ciulla, A. J., ed. see Akel, Abdullatif A.

Ciulla, Andrew J. Papa Was a Riot. LC 83-61413. (Illus.). 212p. 1983. pap. 5.95 (ISBN 0-913791-00-8). Rubicon Bks.

Ciupik, Larry A. The Universe. LC 77-27567. (Read About Science). (Illus.). (gr. k-3). 1978. PLB 14.25 (ISBN 0-8393-0089-1). Raintree Pubs.

--The Universe. LC 77-27567. (Read about Science Ser.). (Illus.). 48p. (gr. 2-5). 1983. pap. 9.27g (ISBN 0-8393-0304-1). Raintree Pubs.

Ciupik, Larry A. & Seevers, James A. Space Machines. LC 78-26991. (Machine World). (Illus.). (gr. 2-4). 1979. PLB 14.65 (ISBN 0-8172-1325-2). Raintree Pubs.

Civan, Mortimer M. Epithelial Ions & Transport: Application of Biophysical Techniques. (Membrane Transport in Life Sciencies Ser.). 204p. 1983. 64.50 (ISBN 0-471-04869-0, Pub. by Wiley-Interscience). Wiley.

Civardi. Clues & Suspects. (Good Detective Guides Ser.). (gr. 2-5). 1979. 6.95 (ISBN 0-86020-226-7, Usborne-Hayes); PLB 11.95 (ISBN 0-88110-039-0); pap. 2.95 (ISBN 0-86020-229-1). EDC.

Civardi & Kilpatrick. How Animals Live. (Animal World Ser.). (gr. 4-6). 1981. 8.95 (ISBN 0-86020-057-4, Usborne-Hayes); PLB 12.95 (ISBN 0-88110-081-1); pap. 5.95 (ISBN 0-86020-196-1). EDC.

Civardi, Anne. Picture Word Finder in German. (Picture Word Bk.). 48p. (gr. k-3). 1984. 10.95 (ISBN 0-86020-771-4). EDC.

--Picture Word Finders in English. (Picture Word Finders Bk.). 48p. (gr. k-3). 1984. 10.95 (ISBN 0-86020-767-6). EDC.

Civen, Janice D. Illuminations. (Illus.). 128p. 1984. 15.95 (ISBN 0-396-08176-2). Dodd.

Civetta, Joseph M. Intensive Care Therapeutics. (Illus.). 422p. 1980. pap. 24.95 (ISBN 0-8385-4305-7). ACC.

Civetta, L., et al. Physical Volcanology. (Developments in Solid Earth Geophysics Ser.: Vol. 6). 333p. 1974. 87.25 (ISBN 0-444-41141-0). Elsevier.

Civic Federation of Chicago, Chicago Conference on Trusts, Sept. 1899. Chicago Conference on Trusts: Speeches, Debates, Resolutions, List of the Delegates, Committees, Etc. LC 73-1996. (Big Business; Economic Power in a Free Society Ser.). Repr. of 1900 ed. 38.50 (ISBN 0-405-05078-X). Ayer Co Pubs.

Civica Biblioteca Berio (Berio Civic Library). Genoa. Catalogo della Raccolta Colombiana (Catalog of the Columbus Collection) 1963. lib. bdg. 78.00 (ISBN 0-8161-0637-1, Hall Library). G K Hall.

Civikly, Jean M. Contexts of Communication. LC 80-19274. 333p. 1981. pap. text ed. 15.95 (ISBN 0-03-053536-0, HoltC). HR&W.

Civil Aeronautics Authority. Airports Survey. LC 77-74965. (American Federalism Ser.). (Illus.). 1978. Repr. of 1939 ed. lib. bdg. 20.00x (ISBN 0-405-10507-X). Ayer Co Pubs.

Civil Aviation Authority, ed. Aircraft Noise & Sleep Disturbance: A Description of the Noise Measurement & Analysis Programme for the Main Phase of the Study. 1980. 35.00x (ISBN 0-686-79160-6, Pub. by Civil Aviation England). State Mutual Bk.

--World Airline Accident Summary, 1981-1984, 4 vols. 1981. 170.00x ea. (Pub. by Civil Aviation England). State Mutual Bk.

Civil Engineering Society, jt. auth. see Building Industry.

Civil Rights Congress. We Charge Genocide: The Historic Petition to the United Nations for Relief from a Crime of the United States Government Against the Negro People. Patterson, William L., ed. LC 76-140208. pap. 64.00 (ISBN 0-317-28065-1, 2025547). Bks Demand UMI.

Civitello, Andrew M., Jr. Construction Operations Manual of Policies & Procedures. LC 82-16156. 300p. 1983. looseleaf bdg. 69.95x (ISBN 0-13-168773-5, Busn). P-H.

Civitello, Andrew M., Jr., jt. auth. see Iannone, Anthony L.

Civrieux, Marc de see De Civrieux, Marc.

Cixous, Helene. Angst. Levy, Jo, tr. from Fr. 180p. (Orig.). 1985. pap. 7.95 (ISBN 0-7145-3905-8). Riverrun NY.

--The Exile of James Joyce. Purcell, Sally, tr. from Fr. 1980. 35.00 (ISBN 0-7145-3507-9). Riverrun NY.

Cizauskas, Albert C. The Changing Nature of Export Finance & Its Implications for Developing Countries. (Working Paper: No. 409). 43p. 1980. pap. 3.00 (ISBN 0-686-39738-X, WP-0409). World Bank.

Cizevska, Tatjana. Glossary of the Igor Tale. (S P R Ser: No. 53). 1966. text ed. 46.00x (ISBN 90-2790-198-8). Mouton.

Cizevskij, Dimitrij. History of Russian Literature. 3rd. ed. (Slavistic Printings & Reprintings Ser: No. 12). 1971. text ed. 26.00x (ISBN 90-2791-917-8). Mouton.

Cizevskij, Dmitrij. Comparative History of Slavic Literatures. Porter, Richard N. & Rice, Martin P., trs. from Ger. LC 74-124115. Orig. Title: Vergleichende Geschichte der Slavischen Literaturen. 1971. 12.95x (ISBN 0-8265-1159-7). Vanderbilt U Pr.

--History of Nineteenth-Century Russian Literature, Vol. 1: The Romantic Period. Zenkovsky, Serge A., ed. Porter, Richard N., tr. from Russian. (Vanderbilt University Press Bks.). 236p. 1974. pap. 7.95 (ISBN 0-8265-1188-0). U of Ill Pr.

--History of Nineteenth-Century Russian Literature, Vol. 2: The Realistic Period. Zenkovsky, Serge A., ed. Porter, Richard N., tr. from Russian. (Vanderbilt University Press Bks.). 218p. 1974. pap. 7.95 (ISBN 0-8265-1190-2). U of Ill Pr.

--History of Nineteenth-Century Russian Literature, 2 vols. Zenkovsky, Serge A., ed. Porter, Richard N., tr. from Ger. Incl. Vol. 2. The Realistic Period. 218p. 1974. o.p. 15.00x ea.; pap. 7.95x ea.; Vol. 1. pap. (ISBN 0-8265-1188-0); Vol. 2. pap. (ISBN 0-8265-1190-2). Vanderbilt U Pr.

Cizik, Richard. The High Cost of Indifference. LC 84-15957. 1984. pap. 6.95 (ISBN 0-8307-1000-0, 5418377). Regal.

Cjosaeter, J. & Kawaguchi, K. A Review of the World Resources of Mesopelagic Fish. (Fisheries Technical Papers: No. 193). 156p. 1980. pap. 11.50 (ISBN 92-5-100924-4, F2074, FAO). Unipub.

Claasen, M., jt. auth. see Fruehmorgen, P.

Claasen, P. Plecoptera Nymphs of America. 210p. 1931. 21.75x (ISBN 0-398-05132-1). C C Thomas.

Claassen, E. M., ed. see Paris-Dauphine Conference on Money & International Monetary Problems, 5th, 1981.

Claassen, Lynda C. Finder's Guide to Prints & Drawings in the Smithsonian Institution. LC 81-607070. (Finder's Guides Ser.: Vol. 1). (Illus.). 210p. 1981. text ed. 19.95x (ISBN 0-87474-316-8); pap. text ed. 9.95x (ISBN 0-87474-317-6). Smithsonian.

Clabaugh, Gary K. Thunder on the Right: The Protestant Fundamentalists. LC 74-9551. 283p. 1974. 19.95x (ISBN 0-88229-108-4). Nelson-Hall.

Clabault, James M. & Block, Michael K. Sherman Act Indictments: 1955-1980, 2 vols. LC 81-71098. 1000p. 1981. Set. deluxe ed. 135.00 (ISBN 0-87945-038-X). Fed Legal Pubn.

Clabault, James M. & Burton, John F., Jr. Sherman Act Indictments, 1955-1965: A Legal & Economic Analysis. 504p. 1966. 25.00 (ISBN 0-87945-000-2). Fed Legal Pubn.

Clabburn, Pamela. Patchwork. (Shire Album Ser.: No. 101). (Illus.). 32p. (Orig.). 1983. pap. 2.95 (ISBN 0-85263-631-8, Pub. by Shire Pubns England). Seven Hills Bks.

--Patchwork. 3.00 (ISBN 0-913714-62-3). Legacy Bks.

--Samplers. (Album Ser.: No. 30). (Illus.). 32p. 1983. pap. 2.95 (ISBN 0-85263-407-2, Pub. by Shire Pubns Eng). Seven Hills Bks.

Clabby, D. A., jt. auth. see Attwell, Arthur A.

Clabby, J. The History of the RAVC, 1919-1961. (Illus.). 16.95 (ISBN 0-85131-082-6, NL51, Dist. by Miller). J A Allen.

--History of the Royal Army Veterinary Corps. 1919-1961. (Illus.). 244p. 1963. 22.50x (ISBN 0-87556-053-9). Saifer.

Clabby, John, et al. Teach Your Child Decision Making for Everyday Living. LC 85-101232. (Illus.). 336p. 1986. 15.95 (ISBN 0-385-19389-0). Doubleday.

Clabes, Judith G., ed. New Guardians of the Press: Selected Profiles of America's Women Newspaper Editors. LC 83-71282. 140p. 1983. 18.95x (ISBN 0-89730-106-4). R J Berg & Co.

Clack, ed. Black Literature Resources. (Library & Information Science: Vol.16). 224p. 1975. 45.00 (ISBN 0-8247-6307-6). Dekker.

Clack, Alice & Leitch, Carol. Amusements Developing Algebra Skills, Vol. 1 & 2. 1975. pap. 7.95ea. (ISBN 0-686-57841-4). Vol. 1 (ISBN 0-910974-76-4). Vol. 2 (ISBN 0-910974-77-2) (ISBN 0-686-57842-2). Midwest Pubns.

--Mathamerica, Vols 1 & 2. 1975. pap. 4.95 ea. Vol. 1 (ISBN 0-910974-80-2); Vol. 2 (ISBN 0-910974-81-0). Midwest Pubns.

Clack, Doris H., ed. The Making of a Code: The Issues Underlying AACR2. LC 80-17496. 264p. 1980. pap. 15.00x (ISBN 0-8389-0309-6). ALA.

Clack, R. James, jt. auth. see Conyne, Robert K.

Clack, Robert W. Celestial Symphonies: A History of Chinese Music. 1975. lib. bdg. 69.95 (ISBN 0-87968-447-X). Gordon Pr.

--The Herd Boy & the Weaver Maid: A Definitive Anthology of Chinese Love Songs & Poetry. 1975. lib. bdg. 69.95 (ISBN 0-87968-461-5). Gordon Pr.

--Millenniums of Moonbeams: A Definitive History & Anthology of Chinese Poetry, 3 vols. 995p. 1975. Set. lib. bdg. 300.00 (ISBN 0-87968-445-3). Gordon Pr.

--The Soul of Yamato: A History & Anthology of Japanese Poetry, 2 vols. 1975. Set. lib. bdg. 250.00 (ISBN 0-87968-446-1). Gordon Pr.

Claeraut, David. Liberation from Loneliness. LC 83-51426. 224p. 1984. 6.95 (ISBN 0-8423-2157-8). Tyndale.

Claerbaut, David. Black Jargon in White America. LC 72-77176. pap. 22.30 (ISBN 0-317-09489-0, 2012858). Bks Demand UMI.

--Urban Ministry. 224p. 1984. pap. 7.95 (ISBN 0-310-45961-3). Zondervan.

Claerbaut, David, ed. New Directions in Ethnic Studies: Minorities in America. LC 80-69327. 115p. 1981. perfect bdg. 9.95 (ISBN 0-86548-025-7). R & E Pubs.

Claerbaut, David P. Black Student Alienation: A Study. LC 77-90351. 1978. pap. 10.00 perfect bdg. (ISBN 0-88247-508-8). R & E Pubs.

Claerbout, Jon F. Fundamentals of Geophysical Data Processing. (Illus.). 274p. 1985. pap. text ed. 39.95x (ISBN 0-86542-305-9). Blackwell Pubns.

--Imaging the Earth's Interior. (Illus.). 412p. 1985. pap. text ed. 39.95x (ISBN 0-86542-304-0). Blackwell Pubns.

Claes, Frank. Waldo County: The Way It Was. (Illus.). 224p. 1985. pap. write for info. (ISBN 0-89272-176-6). Down East.

Claes, Frans M. A Bibliography of Netherlandic Dictionaries: Dutch-Flemish. 1980. lib. bdg. 55.00 (ISBN 3-601-00048-2). Kraus Intl.

Claes, Frans M, compiled by. A Bibliography of Netherlandic (Dutch, Flemish) Dictionaries. xvi, 314p. 1980. 68.00x (ISBN 3-262-02024-9). Benjamins North Am.

Claes, Lutz, jt. ed. see Burri, Caius.

Claesges. Edmund Husserls Theorie der Raumkonstition. (Phaenomenologica Ser: No. 19). 1964. lib. bdg. 18.50 (ISBN 90-247-0251-8, Pub. by Martinus Nijhoff Netherlands). Kluwer Academic.

Claesges & Held. Perspektiven Transzendentalphanomelogischer Forschung. (Phaenomenologica Ser: No. 49). 1972. lib. bdg. 37.00 (ISBN 90-247-1313-7, Pub. by Martinus Nijhoff Netherlands). Kluwer Academic.

Claeson, Eva, tr. see Ekstrom, Margareta.

Claessen, Henri J. & Skalnik, Peter, eds. The Early State. (New Babylon Ser.: No. 32). 1976. 48.40x (ISBN 90-279-7904-9). Mouton.

--The Study of the State. (New Babylon Studies in the Social Sciences Ser.: No.35). 535p. 1981. 42.00 (ISBN 90-279-3348-0). Mouton.

Claessen, Henri J., et al, eds. Development & Decline: The Evolution of Sociopolitical Organization. 384p. 1985. 34.95 (ISBN 0-89789-075-2). Bergin & Garvey.

Claessen, Henry J., jt. ed. see Seaton, S. Lee.

Claessens, Charon, jt. auth. see Bricklin, Mark.

Claessens, Sharon. Healthy Cooking: The Best, the Healthiest Recipes Selected from Cuisines Around the World. Keough, Carol, ed. (Illus.). 176p. 1985. pap. 9.95 (ISBN 0-87857-559-6). Rodale Pr Inc.

--Prevention Total Health System Prevention Healthy Cooking. (The Prevention Total Health System Ser.). (Illus.). 176p. 1984. 14.95 (ISBN 0-87857-466-2, 051690). Rodale Pr Inc.

--The Twenty-Minute Natural Foods Cookbook: Over 300 Kitchen-Tested Recipes. (Illus.). 1982. 14.95 (ISBN 0-87857-375-5). Rodale Pr Inc.

Claessens, Sharon & Rodale Food Center Staff. The Lose Weight Naturally Cookbook. Tkac, Debra, ed. (Illus.). 400p. 1985. 21.95 (ISBN 0-87857-539-1). Rodale Pr Inc.

Claesson, Bent H. Boy-Girl-Man-Woman. Hauch, Christine, tr. (Illus.). 160p. 1982. 12.00 (ISBN 0-7145-0759-8, Dist by Scribner). M Boyars.

Claflin, Edward B. & Heil, John A. Programming Adam: Home Applications in the BASIC Language. 320p. 1984. pap. 14.95 (ISBN 0-88693-034-0). Banbury Bks.

Claflin, Mary B. Personal Recollections of John G. Whittier. 1893. Repr. 17.50 (ISBN 0-8492-9981-0). R West.

Claflin, Stephen T., Jr. A Radical Proposal for Full Use of Free Speech. LC 79-84849. 120p. 1979. 9.95 (ISBN 0-8022-2246-3). Philos Lib.

Claflin, W. H. Stalling's Island Mound, Columbia County, Georgia. (HU PMP). 1931. 14.50 (ISBN 0-527-01232-7). Kraus Repr.

Claflin, William E. Collecting, Culturing, & Caring for Living Materials: A Guide for the Teacher, Student & Hobbyist. LC 80-69329. 110p. 1981. perfect bdg. 8.50 (ISBN 0-86548-026-5). R & E Pubs.

Clagett, Cricket, jt. auth. see Bennett, Vivo.

Clagett, Helen L. A Guide to the Law & Legal Literature of Bolivia. 1977. lib. bdg. 75.00 (ISBN 0-8490-1918-4). Gordon Pr.

--A Guide to the Law & Legal Literature of Paraguay. 1977. 75.00 (ISBN 0-8490-1919-2). Gordon Pr.

--A Guide to the Law & Legal Literature of Urug. 1977. lib. bdg. 75.00 (ISBN 0-8490-1920-6). Gordon Pr.

--A Guide to the Law & Legal Literature of Argentina. 1977. lib. bdg. 75.00 (ISBN 0-8490-1921-4). Gordon Pr.

--A Guide to the Law & Legal Literature of the Mexican States. 1977. 75.00 (ISBN 0-8490-1922-2). Gordon Pr.

Clagett, Helen L., jt. auth. see Vance, John T.

Clagett, John Y. Christian Conscience. LC 84-9824. 1984. pap. 3.95 (ISBN 0-87227-097-1). Reg Baptist.

Clagett, Marshall. Archimedes in the Middle Ages, Vol. IV. LC 62-7218. (Memoirs: Vol. 137). 1980. 30.00 (ISBN 0-87169-137-X). Am Philos.

--Archimedes in the Middle Ages. 667p. 1984. 50.00 (ISBN 0-87169-157-4). Am Philos.

--Archimedes in the Middle Ages, Vol. 1. Arabo-Latin Tradition. LC 62-7218. (Medieval Science Pubns., No. 6). (Illus.). Repr. of 1964 ed. 120.00 (ISBN 0-8357-9771-6, 2012629). Bks Demand UMI.

--Archimedes in the Middle Ages, Vol. 5: Quasi-Archimedean Geometry in the Thirteenth Century, Vol. 157. LC 62-7218. (Memoirs Ser.). 1984. 50.00 (ISBN 0-87169-157-4). Am Philos.

--Giovanni Marliani & Late Medieval Physics. LC 70-181929. (Columbia University Studies in the Social Sciences: No. 483). Repr. of 1941 ed. 12.50 (ISBN 0-404-51483-9). AMS Pr.

--Greek Science in Antiquity. facs. ed. LC 77-142615. (Essay Index Reprint Ser.). 1955. 17.00 (ISBN 0-8369-2150-X). Ayer Co Pubs.

--Studies in Medieval Physics & Mathematics. 366p. 1980. 75.00x (ISBN 0-86078-048-1, Pub. by Variorum England). State Mutual Bk.

Clagett, Marshall, ed. Archimedes in the Middle Ages: The Fate of the Medieval Archimedes, Vol. III. LC 76-9435. (Memoirs Ser.: Vol. 125). (Illus.). 1978. 75.00 (ISBN 0-87169-125-6). Am Philos.

--Archimedes in the Middle Ages: The Translations from the Greek by William of Moerbeke, 2 vols, Vol. 2. LC 76-9435. (Memoirs Ser.: Vol. 117). (Illus.). 1976. Set. 40.00 (ISBN 0-87169-117-5). Am Philos.

--Critical Problems in the History of Science. LC 59-5304. pap. 108.20 (ISBN 0-8357-9773-2, 2015357). Bks Demand UMI.

Clagett, Marshall, tr. Nicole Oresme & the Medieval Geometry of Qualities & Motions. (Medieval Science Pubns., No. 12). (Illus.). 728p. 1968. 50.00x (ISBN 0-299-04880-2). U of Wis Pr.

Clagett, Marshall, et al, eds. see University of Wisconsin, Division of Humanities.

Clagett, Patricia D., jt. ed. see Baughman, Susan S.

Clagg, Sam. Cam Henderson Story. 1981. 14.95 (ISBN 0-87012-431-5). McClain.

--West Virginia Historical Almanac. 1975. 6.95 (ISBN 0-87012-231-2). McClain.

Claggett, Marshall. Greek Science in Antiquity. 1963. pap. 2.50 (ISBN 0-02-091880-1, Collier). Macmillan.

Claghorn, Charles E. Biographical Dictionary of Jazz. 377p. 1983. 25.00 (ISBN 0-13-077966-0, Busn). P-H.

Claghorn, Gene. Women Composers & Hymnists: A Concise Biographical Dictionary. LC 83-20429. 288p. 1984. 22.50 (ISBN 0-8108-1680-6). Scarecrow.

Claghorn, K. H; see Bernard, William S.

Claghorn, Kate. Immigrant's Day in Court. LC 69-18765. (American Immigration Collection Ser., No. 1). Repr. of 1923 ed. 22.50 (ISBN 0-405-00513-X). Ayer Co Pubs.

Clague, Christopher, jt. auth. see Betancourt, Roger.

Clague, Ewan. Statistics & Economic Policy. 39p. 1966. 2.00 (ISBN 0-89215-049-1). U Cal LA Indus Rel.

Clague, Ewan & Kramer, Leo. Manpower Policies & Programs: A Review, 1935-75. 93p. 1976. pap. 4.95 (ISBN 0-911558-03-9). W E Upjohn.

Clague, Ewan, jt. ed. see Kramer, Leo.

Clague, Maryhelen. Beside the Still Waters. 560p. 1984. pap. 3.95 (ISBN 0-425-06273-2). Berkley Pub.

--Moment of the Rose. 448p. (Orig.). 1983. pap. 2.95 (ISBN 0-449-12444-4, GM). Fawcett.

Clague, Mayhelen. Cole's Landing. 240p. 1985. pap. 2.95 (ISBN 0-449-12642-0, GM). Fawcett.

Clahsen, Harald. Spracherwerb in der Kindheit. (Language Development Ser.: No. 4). 180p. (Orig., German.). 1982. pap. 20.00x (ISBN 3-87808-548-6). Benjamins North Am.

Clahsen, Harold, et al. Deutsch als Zweitsprache Der Spracherwerb Auslandischer Arbeiter. (Language Development (LD) Ser.: No. 3). 383p. (Ger.). 1982. 43.00x (ISBN 3-87808-253-3); pap. 25.00 (ISBN 3-87808-544-3). Benjamins North Am.

Claiborn, Charles D., jt. auth. see Strong, Stanley R.

Claiborn, William, jt. ed. see Evans, Dorothy.

Claiborn, William, jt. ed. see Specter, Gerald.

Claiborn, William L., et al. Working with Police Agencies: The Inter-relations Between Law Enforcers & the Behavioral Scientist. Sprafkin, Robert, ed. LC 75-17450. (Continuing Series in Community-Clinical Psychology: Vol. III). 200p. 1976. text ed. 24.95 (ISBN 0-87705-224-7). Human Sci Pr.

Claiborn, William L., jt. ed. see Cohen, Lawrence.

Claiborne, Craig. Cooking with Herbs & Spices. LC 82-48224. (Illus.). 400p. 1984. pap. 9.57i (ISBN 0-06-090998-6, CN 998, CN). Har-Row.

--Cooking with Herbs & Spices. LC 83-48224. 400p. 1984. 18.22 (ISBN 0-06-015251-6, HarpT). Har-Row.

--Craig Claiborne's: A Feast Made for Laughter. LC 81-43437. (Illus.). 432p. 1982. 17.95 (ISBN 0-385-15700-2). Doubleday.

--Craig Claiborne's Gourmet Diet. 1981. pap. 2.95 (ISBN 0-345-29579-X). Ballantine.

--Craig Claiborne's Kitchen Primer. LC 68-23951. (Illus.). (YA) 1969. 12.95 (ISBN 0-394-42071-3); pap. 3.95 (ISBN 0-394-71854-2). Knopf.

--Craig Claiborne's Memorable Meals: Menus, Memories & Recipes from over Twenty Years of Entertaining. (Illus.). 224p. 1985. 25.00 (ISBN 0-525-24352-6). Dutton.

--Craig Claiborne's The New York Times Food Encyclopedia. LC 85-40272. (Illus.). 640p. 1985. 24.95 (ISBN 0-8129-1271-3). Times Bks.

--A Feast Made for Laughter. (Illus.). 432p. 1983. pap. 7.95 (ISBN 0-03-064007-5, Owl Bks.). HR&W.

--New York Times Cook Book. (Illus.). 1961. 18.22 (ISBN 0-06-010790-1, HarpT). Har-Row.

--The New York Times Cook Book. Incl. The New York Times Menu Cook Book. (Illus.). 1975. boxed set 29.95i (ISBN 0-06-010775-8, HarpT). Har-Row.

--New York Times International Cookbook. LC 70-156514. (Illus.). 1971. 23.99 (ISBN 0-06-010788-X, HarpT). Har-Row.

--New York Times Menu Cook Book. (Illus.). 1966. 17.95i (ISBN 0-06-010791-X, HarpT). Har-Row.

Claiborne, Craig & Franey, Pierre. Cooking with Craig Claiborne & Pierre Franey. LC 83-45038. 512p. 1983. 17.95 (ISBN 0-8129-1078-8). Times Bks.

--Cooking with Craig Claiborne & Pierre Franey. 1985. pap. 9.95 (ISBN 0-449-90130-0, Columbine). Fawcett.

--Craig Claiborne's Gourmet Diet. 288p. 1980. 16.95 (ISBN 0-8129-0914-3). Times Bks.

--Craig Claiborne's New New York Times Cookbook. LC 79-51428. (Illus.). 1979. 19.95 (ISBN 0-8129-0835-X, Dist. by Har-Row). Times Bks.

--Veal Cookery. LC 78-2123. (Illus.). 1978. 14.37i (ISBN 0-06-010773-1, HarpT). Har-Row.

Claiborne, Craig & Lee, Virginia. The Chinese Cookbook. LC 82-48827. (Illus.). 476p. (Orig.). 1983. pap. 9.95 (ISBN 0-06-464063-9, BN 4063). B&N NY.

Claiborne, J. F. Life & Times of General Sam Dale: The Mississippi Partisan. LC 75-46532. (Illus.). 234p. 1976. Repr. of 1860 ed. 12.50 (ISBN 0-87152-214-4). Reprint.

Claiborne, John F. Mississippi As a Province, Territory & State. LC 78-2291. 1978. 25.00 (ISBN 0-87152-264-0). Reprint.

Claiborne, Mary, jt. auth. see Rierson, Judy.

Claiborne, Nathaniel H. Notes on the War in the South: With Biographical Sketches of the Lives of Montgomery, Jackson, Sevier, Late Governor Claiborne & Others. LC 76-146382. (First American Frontier Ser). 1971. Repr. of 1819 ed. 17.00 (ISBN 0-405-02833-4). Ayer Co Pubs.

Claiborne, Robert. God or Beast: Evolution & Human Nature. (Illus.). 1974. 7.95 (ISBN 0-393-06399-2). Norton.

Claiborne, Robert, jt. ed. see Weissmann, Gerald.

Claiborne, William C. Official Letter Books, 1801 to 1816, 6 Vols. Rowland, Dunbar, ed. LC 72-980. Repr. of 1917 ed. Set. 195.00 (ISBN 0-404-01600-6); 32.50 ea. AMS Pr.

Clain. Demonstrations of Physical Signs. 17th ed. 1986. price not set (ISBN 0-7236-0827-X). PSG Pub Co.

--Demonstrations of Physical Signs on Clinical Surgery. 16th ed. 624p. 1980. 37.00 (ISBN 0-7236-0518-1). PSG Pub Co.

--Self-Assessment Q & A for Physical Signs. 2nd ed. 1986. price not set. PSG Pub Co.

--Self Assessment Questions & Answers on Clinical Surgery. 240p. 1980. pap. 13.00 (ISBN 0-7236-0546-7). PSG Pub Co.

Clain-Stefanelli, E. E. Russian Gold Coins. 1962. 5.00 (ISBN 0-685-51560-5, Pub by Spink & Son England). S J Durst.

Clain-Stefanelli, Elvira. Numismatic Biography. 2nd ed. 1848p. 1985. 75.00 (ISBN 0-87341-082-3). Krause Pubns.

Clain-Stefanelli, Elvira E. Numismatic Bibliography. 1848p. 1984. lib. bdg. 100.00 (ISBN 3-598-07507-3). K G Saur.

Clain-Steffanelli, Elvira. Numismatic Bibliography. 1848p. 1985. 75.00 (ISBN 0-8069-0274-4). Sterling.

Clair, Barry St. see St. Clair, Barry.

Clair, Bernard & Daniels, Anthony. Consultation with a Divorce Lawyer: Everything You Must Know to Protect Your Rights. 224p. 1982. pap. 9.95 (ISBN 0-671-44192-2, Fireside). S&S.

Clair, Bernard E. & Daniele, R. Anthony. Love Pact: A Layman's Complete Guide to Legal Living Together Agreements. LC 79-6158. 224p. (Orig.). 1980. pap. 6.95 (ISBN 0-394-17652-9, E753, Ever). Grove.

Clair, Bevan. Run Roadrunner. LC 80-82912. 1980. pap. 1.25 (ISBN 0-686-30719-4). B A Scott.

Clair, Charles Le see Le Clair, Charles.

Clair, Colin. Dictionnaire des Herbes et des Epices. 259p. (Fr.). 1963. pap. 6.95 (ISBN 0-686-56842-7, M-6621). French & Eur.

--Early Printing in Malta. (Spread of Printing Ser.: No. 2). (Illus.). 1969. pap. 9.75 (ISBN 0-8390-0017-0). Abner Schram Ltd.

Clair, Colin, ed. see Benedikz, Benedickt S.

Clair, Colin, ed. see Borchardt, D. H.

Clair, Colin, ed. see De Graaf, H. J.

Clair, Colin, ed. see Macmillan, Fiona.

Clair, Colin, ed. see Oldendow, Knud.

Clair, Colin, ed. see Rhodes, Dennis E.

Clair, Colin, ed. see Smith, Anne H.

Clair, Colin, ed. see Tousaint, Auguste.

Clair, Daphne. Depuis Toujours. (Harlequin Romantique Ser.). 192p. 1983. pap. 1.95 (ISBN 0-373-41192-8). Harlequin Bks.

--The Loving Trap. (Harlequin Presents Ser.). 192p. 1982. pap. 1.75 (ISBN 0-373-10506-1). Harlequin Bks.

--Pacific Pretence. (Harlequin Romance Ser.). 1982. pap. 1.75 (ISBN 0-373-02516-5). Harlequin Bks.

--Promise to Pay. (Harlequin Presents Ser.). 192p. 1982. pap. 1.75 (ISBN 0-373-10481-2). Harlequin Bks.

--La Verite Tout Simplement. (Collection Harlequin Ser.). 192p. 1984. pap. 1.95 (ISBN 0-373-49385-1). Harlequin Bks.

Clair, Elizabeth St. see St. Clair, Elizabeth.

Clair, Frederic F. Ultimate Defense: A Practical Plan to Prevent Man's Self-Destruction. LC 59-6490. 1959. 3.00 (ISBN 0-8048-0606-3). C E Tuttle.

Clair, Joy St. see St. Clair, Joy.

Clair, Nancy. The Grammmar Handbook Part One: Elementary-Intermediate ESL. Clark, Raymond C., ed. LC 84-11548. (InterplayESL Ser.). (Illus.). 176p. (Orig.). 1984. pap. text ed. 6.00x (ISBN 0-86647-004-2). Pro Lingua.

Clair, Oswald St see St. Clair, Oswald.

Clair, R. N. St. see Giles, Howard & St. Clair, R. N.

Clair, Rene. A Nous la Liberte; Entre'acte. (Lorrimer Classic Screenplay Ser.). (Illus.). 10.95 (ISBN 0-8044-2122-6); pap. 6.95 (ISBN 0-8044-6080-9). Ungar.

Clair, Rene see Otten, Anna.

Clair, Robert C. Le see James, William & Flournoy, Theodore.

Clair, Robert C. Le see Le Clair, Robert C.

Clair, Robert St. see St. Clair, Robert.

Clair, Wilcox, jt. auth. see Shepherd, William G.

Clair, William, jt. auth. see Abshire, Richard.

Clairborne, Robert. Our Marvelous Native Tongue: The Life & Times of the English Language. LC 82-40363. 339p. 1983. 18.95 (ISBN 0-8129-1038-9). Times Bks.

Claire, Anne. Andro, Star of Bethlehem. Mahany, Patricia, ed. LC 82-62727. (Happy Day Bks.). (Illus.). 24p. (ps-2). 1983. pap. 1.39 (ISBN 0-87239-631-2, 3551). Standard Pub.

--Andro, the Star of Bethlehem. LC 81-50997. (Illus.). 32p. (Orig.). (gr. k-6). 1981. pap. 1.95 (ISBN 0-87239-472-7, 2870). Standard Pub.

Claire, Elizabeth. A Foreign Student's Guide to Dangerous English. (Illus.). 91p. (Orig.). 1983. pap. 6.95 (ISBN 0-937630-00-4). Eardley Pubns.

--What's So Funny? A Foreign Student's Introduction to American Humor. (Illus.). 160p. 1984. pap. 7.95 (ISBN 0-937630-01-2). Eardley Pubns.

Claire, Evelyn. Storm Remembered. LC 84-4198. (Starlight Romance Ser.). 192p. 1984. 11.95 (ISBN 0-385-19581-8). Doubleday.

Claire, Hilary, jt. auth. see Salmon, Phillida.

Claire, Marie, jt. auth. see Wrage, William.

Claire, Roma, ed. Modern American Verse. 1978. Repr. of 1918 ed. lib. bdg. 20.00 (ISBN 0-8482-7557-8). Norwood Edns.

Claire, Rosine. French Vegetarian Cosmetics. LC 78-50439. (Illus., Orig.). 1979. pap. 5.95 (ISBN 0-89407-016-9). Strawberry Hill.

Claire, William, ed. see Van Doren, Mark.

Claire, William F., ed. Publishing in the West: Alan Swallow. LC 73-89794. 1974. 10.00 (ISBN 0-89016-003-1). Lightning Tree.

Claire Zellerbach Saroni Tumor Institute & Rosenbaum, Ernest H. Can You Prevent Cancer? Realistic Guidelines for Developing Cancer-Preventive Life Habits. LC 83-11387. (Illus.). 352p. 1984. pap. 11.95 (ISBN 0-8016-4198-5, 4198-5). Mosby.

Clairmont, Christoph W. Excavations at Salona, Yugoslavia. LC 75-29768. (Illus.). 300p. 1976. 36.00 (ISBN 0-8155-5040-5, NP). Noyes.

--The Glass Vessels: Final Report IV, Part V. LC 43-2669. 20.00 (ISBN 0-685-71743-7). J J Augustin.

Clairmont, Claire. The Journals of Claire Clairmont. Stocking, Marion K. & Stocking, David M., eds. LC 68-17634. (Illus.). 1968. 35.00x (ISBN 0-674-48500-9). Harvard U Pr.

Clairmont, Elva, jt. auth. see Hamill, Dorothy.

Clairmont, George B. & Sokoloff, Kiril. Street Smart Investing: A Price-Value Approach to Stock Market Profits. Date not set. pap. 5.95 (ISBN 0-394-72424-0, Vin). Random.

--Street Smart Investment: A Price & Value Approach to Stock Market Profits. LC 82-4282. 182p. 1983. 16.95 (ISBN 0-394-52338-5). Random.

Clairmont, Ingrid & Clairmont, Leonard. Blood in the Furrows: A Historical Novel. (Illus.). 1979. 12.00 (ISBN 0-682-49504-2, Banner). Exposition Pr FL.

Clairmont, Leonard. Tahitian-English, English Tahitian Dictionary. (Tahitian & Eng.). 22.50 (ISBN 0-87559-053-5). Shalom.

Clairmont, Leonard, jt. auth. see Clairmont, Ingrid.

Clairmont, R. A Commentary on Seneca's Apocolocyntosis Divi Clavdii. (Illus.). 135p. 1980. 15.00 (ISBN 0-89005-342-1). Ares.

Clairmonte, Frederick & Cavanagh, John. The World in their Web: The Dynamics of Textile Multinationals. 290p. 1982. 33.00x (ISBN 0-905762-95-9, Pub. by Zed Pr England). Biblio Dist.

Clairmonte, Frederick F., jt. auth. see Cavanagh, John.

Clairmonte, Glenn. Truth to Tell. LC 78-66006. 1979. 4.95 (ISBN 0-87159-155-3). Unity School.

Clairon, Hippolyte. Memoirs of Hippolyte Clairon, 2 Vols. in 1. LC 79-82821. 1800. 25.00 (ISBN 0-405-08359-9, Blom Pubns). Ayer Co Pubs.

Claiss, jt. auth. see Tertian.

Claman, Henry N., ed. see New York Academy of Sciences Annals of, October 19-21, 1981.

Claman, Priscilla H. & Claman, Victor N. Sixty-Plus in Massachusetts: The Guide to Benefits, Bargains, & Better Living for People Over 60. (Illus.). 80p. (Orig.). 1981. pap. 5.95 (ISBN 0-939532-00-X). Ctr Info Sharing.

Claman, Victor N., jt. auth. see Claman, Priscilla H.

Clammer, John. Anthropology & Political Economy: Theoretical & Asian Perspectives. 224p. 1985. 27.50 (ISBN 0-312-04345-7). St Martin.

Clammer, John R. Straits Chinese Society: Studies in the Sociology of the Baba Communities of Malaysia & Singapore. 1981. 18.00x (ISBN 9971-69-009-8, 82-93664, Pub. by Singapore U Pr); pap. 8.95x (ISBN 9971-69-015-2, 82-93680, Pub. by Singapore U Pr). Ohio U Pr.

Clamp, Hugh. Shorter Forms of Building Contract. 200p. 1984. cancelled (ISBN 0-246-11964-0, Pub. by Granada England). Sheridan.

Clampett, Frederick W. Luther Burbank, Our Beloved Infidel, His Religion of Humanity. LC 73-109720. (Illus.). 144p. Repr. of 1926 ed. lib. bdg. 15.00x (ISBN 0-8371-4210-5, CLLB). Greenwood.

Clampitt, Amy. The Kingfisher. LC 82-47963. (Poetry Ser.: No. 9). 150p. 1983. 15.95 (ISBN 0-394-52840-9); pap. 10.95 (ISBN 0-394-71251-X). Knopf.

--What the Light Was Like. Quinn, Alice, ed. LC 84-48652. (Poetry Ser.: No. 18). 111p. 1985. 14.95 (ISBN 0-394-54318-1); pap. 8.95 (ISBN 0-394-72937-4). Knopf.

Clance, Pauline R. The Imposter Phenomenon: Overcoming the Fear That Haunts Your Success. LC 85-60596. 224p. 1985. 14.95 (ISBN 0-931948-77-0). Peachtree Pubs.

Clancey, K. Seminormal Operators. (Lecture Notes in Mathematics: Vol. 742). 1979. pap. 13.00 (ISBN 0-387-09547-0). Springer-Verlag.

Clanchy, M. T. England & Its Rulers Ten Sixty-Six to Twelve Seventy-Two: Foreign Lordship & National Identity. LC 83-11950. 320p. 1983. 27.50x (ISBN 0-389-20423-4, 07309). B&N Imports.

--From Memory to Written Record in England, 1066-1307. (Illus.). 1979. text ed. 22.50x (ISBN 0-674-32510-9). Harvard U Pr.

Clanchy, M. T., ed. see Gillingham, John.

Clancy, Bill. Jesus: The Ultimate E.T. Howard, Dick, ed. 40p. (Orig.). 1983. pap. 1.75 (ISBN 0-912573-00-7). Believers Faith.

Clancy, Charles J. English Romantic Drama. LC 77-21840. 1977. lib. bdg. 27.50 (ISBN 0-8414-1838-1). Folcroft.

--Lava, Hock & Soda-Water: Byron's Don Juan. (Salzburg Studies in English Literature, Romantic Reassessment: No. 41). 1974. pap. text ed. 25.50x (ISBN 0-391-01344-0). Humanities.

--A Selected Bibliography of English Romantic Drama. 1978. Repr. of 1976 ed. lib. bdg. 15.00 (ISBN 0-8492-3938-9). R West.

Clancy, Charles J., jt. auth. see Hogg, James.

Clancy, Dell. I Searched for the Wondrous. pap. 1.00 (ISBN 0-87516-011-5). De Vorss.

Clancy, Herbert J. Presidential Election of Eighteen Eighty. LC 58-12311. (Jesuit Studies). 1958. 4.00 (ISBN 0-8294-0012-5). Loyola.

Clancy, Joanne D. A Way Out from In. 1971. 6.65 (ISBN 0-940058-00-6). Clancy Pubns.

Clancy, John. The John Clancy Baking Book. 1975. pap. 3.95 (ISBN 0-445-08327-1). Clancys Kitchen.

--John Clancy's Christmas Cookbook. (Illus.). 1982. 17.50 (ISBN 0-87851-207-1). Hearst Bks.

--Site Surveying & Leveling. 256p. 1981. pap. text ed. 11.95 (ISBN 0-7131-3439-9). E Arnold.

Clancy, Joseph P., tr. see Horace.

Clancy, Judith. The Ecotopian Sketchbook. 48p. 1981. pap. 4.25 (ISBN 0-9604320-2-7). Synergistic Pr.

--Last Look at the Old Met. LC 79-103983. (Illus.). 54p. 1969. bds. 5.95 (ISBN 0-912184-02-7). Synergistic Pr.

Clancy, Judith & Fisher, M. F. Not a Station but a Place. LC 79-20885. (Illus.). 72p. 1979. bds. 9.95 (ISBN 0-912184-03-5); pap. 5.95 (ISBN 0-912184-02-7). Synergistic Pr.

Clancy, Laurence J. Aerodynamics. LC 73-15266. 610p. 1975. text ed. 34.95x (ISBN 0-470-15837-9). Halsted Pr.

Clancy, Laurie. The Novels of Vladimir Nabokov. LC 83-3355. 180p. 1985. 18.95 (ISBN 0-312-57970-5). St Martin.

--Xavier Herbert. (World Authors Ser.). 1981. lib. bdg. 16.95 (ISBN 0-8057-6394-5, Twayne). G K Hall.

Clancy, Lillian S. Alameda County Public Schools: How Are They Doing? (1984) (How Are They Doing Ser.). 80p. (Orig.). 1984. pap. 11.95 (ISBN 0-939580-08-X). Sindowilf Ltd.

--Bay Area Counties Public Schools: How Are They Doing? 1985. (California Public Schools Ser.: Vol. 5). 360p. 1984. pap. 23.95 (ISBN 0-939580-23-3). Sindowilf Ltd.

--Bay Area Public Schools: How Are They Doing? (1984) (How Are They Doing Ser.). 330p. (Orig.). 1984. pap. 17.95 (ISBN 0-939580-05-5). Sindowilf Ltd.

--Central California Counties Public Schools: How Are They Doing? 1985. (California Public Schools: How are They Doing? 1985 Ser.: Vol. 4). 390p. 1984. pap. 23.95 (ISBN 0-939580-22-5). Sindowilf Ltd.

--Contra Costa County Public Schools: How Are They Doing? 312p. (Orig.). 1981. pap. 9.95 (ISBN 0-939580-00-4). Sindowilf Ltd.

--Contra Costa County Public Schools: How Are They Doing? (1984) (How Are They Doing Ser.). 65p. (Orig.). 1984. pap. 8.95 (ISBN 0-939580-04-7). Sindowilf Ltd.

--Contra Costa County Public Schools: How Are They Doing? 1985. (California Public Schools Ser.). 61p. (Orig.). 1984. pap. 12.95 (ISBN 0-939580-26-8). Sindowilf Ltd.

--Los Angeles County Public Schools: How Are They Doing? (1984) (How Are They Doing Ser.). 360p. 1984. pap. 17.95 (ISBN 0-939580-12-8). Sindowilf Ltd.

--Los Angeles County Public Schools: How Are They Doing? 1985. (California Public Schools: How Are They Doing? 1985 Ser.: Vol. 2). 420p. (Orig.). 1984. pap. 23.95 (ISBN 0-939580-20-9). Sindowilf Ltd.

--Northern California Public Schools: How Are They Doing? (1984) (How Are They Doing Ser.). 1200p. (Orig.). 1984. pap. 40.00 (ISBN 0-939580-07-1). Sindowilf Ltd.

--Northern Central California Counties Public Schools: How Are They Doing? 1985, Vol. 6. (California Public Schools Ser.). 307p. (Orig.). 1984. pap. 23.95 (ISBN 0-939580-24-1). Sindowilf Ltd.

--Orange County Public Schools: How Are They Doing? (1984) (How Are They Doing Ser.). 120p. (Orig.). 1984. pap. 13.95 (ISBN 0-939580-13-6). Sindowilf Ltd.

--Sacramento, El Dorado, Placer & Yolo Counties Public Schools: How Are They Doing? (1984) (How Are They Doing Ser.). 145p. (Orig.). 1984. pap. 13.95 (ISBN 0-939580-11-X). Sindowilf Ltd.

--San Bernardino County Public Schools: How Are They Doing? (1984) (How Are THey Doing Ser.). 90p. 1984. pap. 13.95 (ISBN 0-939580-14-4). Sindowilf Ltd.

--San Diego County Public Schools: How Are They Doing? (1984) (How Are They Doing Ser.). 125p. (Orig.). 1984. pap. 13.95 (ISBN 0-939580-15-2). Sindowilf Ltd.

--San Francisco & North Bay Counties Public Schools: How Are They Doing? (1984) (How Are They Doing Ser.). 160p. (Orig.). 1984. pap. 13.95 (ISBN 0-939580-09-8). Sindowilf Ltd.

--San Mateo, Santa Clara & Santa Cruz Counties Public Schools: How Are They Doing? (1984) (How Are They Doing Ser.). 180p. (Orig.). 1984. pap. 13.95 (ISBN 0-939580-10-1). Sindowilf Ltd.

--Santa Barbara & Ventura Counties Public Schools: How Are They Doing? (1984) (How Are They Doing Ser.). 100p. (Orig.). pap. 13.95 (ISBN 0-939580-16-0). Sindowilf Ltd.

--South Central California Counties Public Schools: How Are They Doing? 1985. (California Public Schools: How Are They Doing?: Vol. 3). 415p. (Orig.). 1984. pap. 23.95 (ISBN 0-939580-21-7). Sindowilf Ltd.

--Southern California Counties Public Schools: How Are They Doing? (California Public Schools: How Are They Doing? 1985 Ser.: Vol. 1). 370p. (Orig.). 1984. pap. 23.95 (ISBN 0-939580-19-5). Sindowilf Ltd.

--Southern California Public Schools: How Are They Doing? (1984) (How Are They Doing Ser.). 1185p. (Orig.). 1984. pap. 40.00 (ISBN 0-939580-06-3). Sindowilf Ltd.

--The Top One Hundred: How Are They Doing? 1985. (California Public Schools Ser.). 75p. (Orig.). 1984. pap. 5.95 (ISBN 0-939580-27-6). Sindowilf Ltd.

--Upper Northern California Counties Public Schools: How Are They Doing? 1985, Vol. 7. (California Public Schools Ser.). 325p. (Orig.). 1984. pap. 23.95 (ISBN 0-939580-25-X). Sindowilf Ltd.

Clancy, Michael, jt. auth. see Cooper, Doug.

Clancy, Paul R. Just a Country Lawyer: A Biography of Senator Sam Ervin. LC 73-16528. (Illus.). pap. 58.90 (ISBN 0-8357-9221-8, 2055214). Bks Demand UMI.

Clancy, Peter L. Nineteen Improving Schools & Why Their "Formula for Success". (Illus.). 206p. (Orig.). 1982. pap. text ed. 7.95 (ISBN 0-911467-00-9). Educ Leadership.

Clancy, Robert. A Seed Was Sown. (Illus.). 124p. 1964. pap. 1.00 (ISBN 0-911312-41-2). Schalkenbach.

Clancy, Roger. Ships, Ports & Pilots: A History of the Piloting Profession. LC 84-42600. (Illus.). 223p. 1984. lib. bdg. 16.95x (ISBN 0-89950-125-7). McFarland & Co.

Clancy, Thomas H. The Conversational Word of God: A Commentary on the Doctrine of St. Ignatius of Loyola Concerning Spiritual Conversation, with Four Early Jesuit Texts. Ganss, George E., frwd. by. LC 78-51343. (Study Aids on Jesuit Topics: No. 8 in Ser. IV). 83p. 1978. 5.00 (ISBN 0-912422-33-5); pap. 2.50 smyth sewn (ISBN 0-912422-34-3). Inst Jesuit.

--English Catholic Books, 1641-1700. LC 74-704. 158p. 1974. pap. 8.00 (ISBN 0-8294-0231-4). Loyola.

--An Introduction to Jesuit Life: The Constitutions & History Through 435 Years. Ganss, George E., ed. LC 75-46080. (Study Aids on Jesuit Topics Ser.: No. 3). 422p. 1976. 12.00 (ISBN 0-912422-15-7); pap. 5.50 (ISBN 0-912422-12-2). Inst Jesuit.

--Papist Pamphleteers. LC 64-14078. (Jesuit Studies). 1964. 4.95 (ISBN 0-8294-0013-3). Loyola.

Clancy, Tom. The Hunt for Red October. 416p. 1984. 14.95 (ISBN 0-87021-285-0). Naval Inst Pr.

--The Hunt for Red October. 480p. 1985. pap. 4.50 (ISBN 0-425-08383-7). Berkley Pub.

Clanton, A. L. The Pentecostal Home: Study Guide. 80p. (Orig.). 1978. pap. 1.00 (ISBN 0-912315-43-1). Word Aflame.

Clanton, A. L., ed. Through the Bible Study Series, 7 vol. set. 2688p. 1982. text ed. 54.95 per set (ISBN 0-912315-51-2). Word Aflame.

--Through the Bible Study Series, Vol. VII. 384p. 1982. text ed. 6.95 (ISBN 0-912315-58-X). Word Aflame.

--Through the Bible Study Series, Vol. VI. 384p. 1981. text ed. 6.95 (ISBN 0-912315-57-1). Word Aflame.

--Through the Bible Study Series, Vol. V. 384p. 1981. text ed. 6.95 (ISBN 0-912315-56-3). Word Aflame.

--Through the Bible Study Series, Vol. IV. 384p. 1981. text ed. 6.95 (ISBN 0-912315-55-5). Word Aflame.

--Through the Bible Study Series, Vol. III. 384p. 1981. text ed. 6.95 (ISBN 0-912315-54-7). Word Aflame.

--Through the Bible Study Series, Vol. 1. 384p. 1981. text ed. 6.95 (ISBN 0-912315-52-0). Word Aflame.

Clanton, Arthur L. United We Stand. (Illus.). 207p. 1970. pap. 5.95 (ISBN 0-912315-42-3). Word Aflame.

Clanton, Arthur L., ed. see Willoughby, David.

Clanton, Bruce. Family Adventures. LC 80-51060. (ps-6). 1980. pap. 4.95 (ISBN 0-89390-018-4). Resource Pubns.

--In Season & Out. LC 80-54272. 80p. 1981. pap. 7.95 (ISBN 0-89390-025-7). Resource Pubns.

Clanton, Charles, ed. see Chambers, Catherine.

Clanton, Charles, ed. see Freeman, Nona.

Clanton, Charles, ed. see Thompson, Mollie.

Clanton, Gordon & Smith, Lynn G., eds. Jealousy. 1976. (Spec); pap. text ed. 4.95 (ISBN 0-13-509356-2). P-H.

Clap, Roger. Memoirs of Roger Clap: Collections of the Dorchester Antiquarian & Historical Society, No. 1. facsimile ed. LC 73-150176. (Select Bibliographies Reprint Ser.). 1972. Repr. of 1843 ed. 12.00 (ISBN 0-8369-5689-3). Ayer Co Pubs.

Claparede, Edouard. Experimental Pedagogy & the Psychology of the Child. Louch, Mary & Holman, Henry, trs. from Fr. LC 74-21404. (Classics in Child Development Ser). 344p. 1975. Repr. 27.00x (ISBN 0-405-06457-8). Ayer Co Pubs.

Clapesattle, Helen. Dr. Webb of Colorado Springs. 1984. 19.50 (ISBN 0-87081-050-2). Colo Assoc.

--Doctors Mayo. 1980. pap. 3.95 (ISBN 0-671-42696-6). PB.

--Doctors Mayo. 2nd ed. (Illus.). 1954. 19.50 (ISBN 0-8166-0029-5). U of Minn Pr.

Clapham, Adam & Constable, Robin. As Nature Intended: A Pictorial Historial of the Nudists. 144p. 1982. 18.95x (ISBN 0-434-98026-9, Pub. by Heinemann England); pap. 12.95 (ISBN 0-434-98034-X). Elysium.

Clapham, Alfred W., jt. auth. see Reddan, Minnie.

Clapham, Arthur R. Flora of the British Isles. 2nd ed. 1269p. 1985. pap. 39.50 (ISBN 0-521-31519-0). Cambridge U Pr.

Clapham, Arthur R., ed. The IBP Survey of Conservation Sites: An Experimental Study. LC 79-50233. (International Biological Programme Ser.: No. 24). (Illus.). 500p. 1980. 62.50 (ISBN 0-521-22697-X). Cambridge U Pr.

Clapham, Arthur R., et al. Excursion Flora of the British Isles. 3rd ed. LC 79-51679. 600p. 1981. 32.50 (ISBN 0-521-23290-2). Cambridge U Pr.

--Flora of the British Isles Illustrations, 4 vols. Incl. Vol. 1. Pteridophyta to Papilionaceae. 144p (ISBN 0-521-26962-8); Vol. 2. Rosaceae to Polemoniaceae. 128p (ISBN 0-521-26963-6); Vol. 3. Boraginaceae to Compositae. 124p (ISBN 0-521-26964-4); Vol. 4. Monocotyledons. 128p (ISBN 0-521-26965-2). pap. 17.95 ea. Cambridge U Pr.

Clapham, C. Liberia and Sierra Leone. LC 75-32447. (African Studies: No.20). (Illus.). 160p. 1976. 29.95 (ISBN 0-521-21095-X). Cambridge U Pr.

Clapham, Christopher. Private Patronage & Public Power: Political Clientelism in the Modern State. LC 81-16753. 1982. 25.00 (ISBN 0-312-64717-4). St Martin.

--Third World Politics: An Introduction. 256p. 1985. 25.00x (ISBN 0-299-10330-7); pap. text ed. 12.50x (ISBN 0-299-10334-X). U of Wis Pr.

Clapham, Christopher, et al, eds. The Political Dilemmas of Military Regimes. LC 84-18414. 294p. 1985. 28.50x (ISBN 0-389-20533-8, 08095). B&N Imports.

Clapham, Frances, ed. see Towson, W. D.

Clapham, John. Dvorak. (Illus.). 1979. 19.95x (ISBN 0-393-01204-2). Norton.

--The Historie of Great Britannie - from the Romans First Entrance, Untill the Raigne of Egbert, the West-Saxon Prince. LC 74-28837. (English Experience Ser.: No. 719). 1975. Repr. of 1606 ed. 22.00 (ISBN 90-221-0719-1). Walter J Johnson.

--Smetana. (The Master Musicians Ser.). (Illus.). 171p. 1972. 13.50x (ISBN 0-460-03133-3, Pub. by J. M. Dent England). Biblio Dist.

Clapham, John H. A Concise Economic History of Britain, from the Earliest Times to 1750. LC 75-41059. (BCL Ser.: No. II). 1976. Repr. of 1949 ed. 25.00 (ISBN 0-404-14654-6). AMS Pr.

--Economic Development of France & Germany 1815-1914. 4th ed. 1935. pap. 21.95 (ISBN 0-521-09150-0, 150). Cambridge U Pr.

Clapham, Ronald. Small & Medium Enterprises in Southeast Asia. 152p. 1985. pap. text ed. 18.50x (ISBN 9-971902-99-0, Pub. by Inst Southeast Asian Stud). Gower Pub Co.

Clapham, Sidney. Fuchsias for House & Garden. LC 82-8401. (Illus.). 152p. 1982. text ed. 15.00x (ISBN 0-87663-404-8). Universe.

Clapham, V. M., ed. see International Conference on Solid State Nuclear Track Detectors, 11th, Bristol, UK, Sept. 1981.

Clapham, W. B., Jr. Human Ecosystems. 1981. pap. write for info. (ISBN 0-02-322510-6). Macmillan.

--Natural Ecosystems. 2nd ed. 256p. 1983. pap. write for info. (ISBN 0-02-322520-3). Macmillan.

Clapin, S. A New Dictionary of Americanisms. 59.95 (ISBN 0-8490-0721-6). Gordon Pr.

Clapin, Sylva. Dictionnaire Canadien-Francais. 394p. (Canadian & Fr.). 1974. 17.50 (ISBN 0-686-56809-5, M-6587). French & Eur.

Clapin, Sylvia. New Dictionary of Americanisms. LC 68-17985. 1968. Repr. of 1902 ed. 42.00x (ISBN 0-8103-3244-2). Gale.

Clapp, Allen L. NESC Handbook: Development & Application of the American National Standard National Electrical Safety Code. (Grounding Rules, General Rules, & Parts Ser.: No. 1-3). 430p. 1984. text ed. 22.00x (ISBN 0-471-80783-4, Pub. by Wiley-Interscience). Wiley.

Clapp, B. W., ed. Documents in English Economic History, Vol. 2: England Since 1760. 544p. 1976. 40.00x (ISBN 0-8476-6085-0). Rowman.

Clapp, Brian W. John Owens, Manchester Merchant. LC 67-31834. 1967. 25.00x (ISBN 0-678-06755-4). Kelley.

Clapp, Charles L. The Congressman: His Work As He Sees It. LC 79-28559. xi, 452p. 1980. Repr. of 1963 ed. lib. bdg. 32.50x (ISBN 0-313-22296-7, CLCG). Greenwood.

Clapp, Doug. Doug Clapp's Jazz Book. 1985. pap. 17.95 (ISBN 0-673-18266-5). Scott F.

--Macintosh! Complete. 1984. pap. 19.95 (ISBN 0-88701-009-1). Softalk Pub.

Clapp, Edwin J. Economic Aspects of the War. 1915. 49.50x (ISBN 0-685-69798-3). Elliots Bks.

Clapp, Elsie R. Community Schools in Action. LC 78-165714. (American Education, Ser. 2). 1972. Repr. of 1939 ed. 26.50 (ISBN 0-405-03703-1). Ayer Co Pubs.

Clapp, Fredrick M. Jacopo Carrucci da Pontormo: His Life & Work. (Illus.). 355p. 1972. Repr. 50.00 (ISBN 0-8390-9047-1). Abner Schram Ltd.

Clapp, Henry. The Pioneer: Or, Leaves from an Editor's Portfolio. 1969. Repr. of 1846 ed. 19.00 (ISBN 0-384-09195-4). Johnson Repr.

Clapp, Henry A. Reminiscences of a Dramatic Critic. 1975. Repr. of 1902 ed. 12.25 (ISBN 0-8274-4112-6). R West.

--Reminiscences of a Dramatic Critic: With an Essay on the Art of Henry Irving. LC 72-5536. (Select Bibliographies Reprint Ser). 1972. Repr. of 1902 ed. 21.00 (ISBN 0-8369-6902-2). Ayer Co Pubs.

Clapp, James A. The City: A Dictionary of Quotable Thought on Cities & Urban Life. LC 83-19006. 288p. 1984. text ed. 30.00 (ISBN 0-88285-095-4). Ctr Urban Pol Res.

--New Towns: An Emphasis on the American Enterprise, No. 982. 1976. 10.00 (ISBN 0-686-20387-9). CPL Biblios.

Clapp, Jeremy, jt. ed. see Langan, John.

Clapp, John, jt. auth. see Mitchell, Daniel J.

Clapp, John B. Players of the Present, 3 vols in 1. LC 77-130100. (Dunlap Society Publications Ser: Nos. 9, 11, 13). 1970. Repr. of 1901 ed. lib. bdg. 34.00 (ISBN 0-8337-0577-6). B Franklin.

Clapp, John B. & Edgett, Edwin F. Players of the Present, 3 Vols. in 1. LC 72-91897. 1899-1901. 21.50 (ISBN 0-405-08360-2, Blom Pubns). Ayer Co Pubs.

--Plays of the Present. LC 73-83498. 1902. 22.00 (ISBN 0-405-08361-0, Blom Pubns). Ayer Co Pubs.

Clapp, John M., jt. auth. see Case, Frederick E.

Clapp, John T. A Journal of Travels to & from California. 100p. Date not set. price not set (ISBN 0-87770-164-4). Ye Galleon.

Clapp, Joy & Stevens, Paul C. Geography of Colorado. pap. 4.00x (ISBN 0-933472-34-X). Johnson Bks.

Clapp, Margaret A., ed. Modern University. vii, 115p. 1968. Repr. of 1950 ed. 15.00 (ISBN 0-208-00355-X, Archon). Shoe String.

Clapp, Ouida H., ed. Classroom Practices in Teaching English, 1975-1976: On Righting Writing. LC 75-26121. 121p. 1975. pap. 4.50 (ISBN 0-8141-0685-4); pap. 3.50 members. NCTE.

Clapp, Patricia. Constance: A Story of Early Plymouth. LC 68-14064. (gr. 7-12). 1968. PLB 11.88 (ISBN 0-688-51127-9). Lothrop.

--Jane-Emily. 160p. (gr. 5 up). 1973. pap. 2.25 (ISBN 0-440-94185-7, LFL). Dell.

--Jane-Emily. LC 69-14326. (gr. 5-6). 1969. PLB 11.88 (ISBN 0-688-51019-1). Lothrop.

--Witches' Children. LC 81-13678. 160p. (gr. 6 up). 1982. 11.75 (ISBN 0-688-00890-9). Lothrop.

Clapp, Priscilla & Halperin, Morton H., eds. United States-Japanese Relations: The 1970's. LC 74-80441. 256p. 1974. text ed. 16.50x (ISBN 0-674-92571-8). Harvard U Pr.

Clapp, Steve. Christian Education As Evangelism. 154p. (Orig.). 1982. pap. 9.00 (ISBN 0-914527-11-8). C-Four Res.

--Ministerial Competency Report. (Practice of Ministry Ser.). 123p. (Orig.). 1982. pap. 8.00 (ISBN 0-914527-10-X). C-Four Res.

--Retreat Guide I. 20p. (Orig.). 1981. pap. 2.00 (ISBN 0-914527-04-5). C-Four Res.

--Retreat Guide II. (The C-4 Journals). 29p. (Orig.). 1982. pap. 2.00 (ISBN 0-914527-13-4). C-Four Res.

--Sermons on Shalom. 79p. (Orig.). 1982. pap. 8.00 (ISBN 0-914527-37-1). C-Four Res.

--Shalom: Hope for the World. 178p. (Orig.). 1982. pap. 8.00 (ISBN 0-914527-35-5). C-Four Res.

--Teenage Sexuality: A Crisis & an Opportunity for the Church. (Youth Sexuality Ser.). 82p. (Orig.). 1981. pap. 7.00 (ISBN 0-914527-06-1). C-Four Res.

Clapp, Steve & Cook, Jerry O. Youth Workers' Handbook. 280p. 1981. pap. 11.00 (ISBN 0-914527-05-3). C-Four Res.

Clapp, Steve & Mauck, Sue I. A Primer for Angry Christians. 138p. (Orig.). 1981. pap. 6.00 (ISBN 0-914527-09-6). C-Four Res.

--Repairing Christian Lifestyles. 2nd ed. (Repairing Christian Lifestyles Ser.). 174p. (YA) (gr. 7-12). 1983. pap. 6.00 (ISBN 0-914527-26-6); pap. 5.00 leader's guide (ISBN 0-914527-27-4). C-Four Res.

--Through the Bible, Vol. I. (C-Four Youth Bible Materials Ser.). 138p. (Orig.). 1982. pap. 10.00 (ISBN 0-914527-15-0). C-Four Res.

Clapp, Steve, jt. auth. see Conn, Robert.

Clapp, Steve, jt. auth. see Davis, Dennis M.

Clapp, Steve, ed. Devotional Journal I. (The C-4 Journals Ser.). 63p. (Orig.). (YA) (gr. 7-12). 1979. pap. 6.00 (ISBN 0-914527-03-7). C-Four Res.

Clapp, Steve, frwd. by. Mid-Winter Festivals: Anthology of Stories, Traditions & Poems. (Family Reading Ser.). 211p. (Orig.). 1983. pap. 10.00 (ISBN 0-914527-01-0). C-Four Res.

Clapp, Steve, ed. Prayer & the Christian Life: C-4 Devotional Journal II. (The C-4 Journals Ser.). 126p. (Orig.). 1982. pap. 6.00 (ISBN 0-317-11522-7). C-Four Res.

Clapp, Steve, et al. A Christian View of Youth & Sexuality. (Youth Sexuality Ser.). 140p. (Orig.). 1981. pap. 7.00 (ISBN 0-914527-07-X). C-Four Res.

--A Christian View of Youth & Sexuality Adult Guide. (Youth Sexuality Ser.). 67p. (Orig.). 1981. pap. 5.00 (ISBN 0-914527-08-8). C-Four Res.

--Youth Experiential Annual Resource 1. 122p. (Orig.). 1981. pap. 10.00 (ISBN 0-914527-42-8). C-Four Res.

Clapp, Theodore. Autobiographical Sketches & Recollections: During a 35 Years Residence in New Orleans. LC 77-38346. (Select Bibliographies Reprint Ser.). Repr. of 1857 ed. 23.50 (ISBN 0-8369-6763-1). Ayer Co Pubs.

Clapp, Tom. Dracula. rev. ed. 1985. pap. text ed. 5.00 (ISBN 0-88734-202-7). Players Pr.

--The Open Boat. 1985. pap. text ed. 5.00 (ISBN 0-88734-200-0). Players Pr.

Clapp, William W. Record of the Boston Stage. LC 68-58197. 1968. Repr. of 1853 ed. 33.00 (ISBN 0-405-08362-9, Blom Pubns). Ayer Co Pubs.

--Record of the Boston Stage. LC 69-13861. Repr. of 1853 ed. lib. bdg. 22.50x (ISBN 0-8371-0350-9, CLBS). Greenwood.

--A Record of the Boston Stage. (Miscellany of the Theatre Ser). 1969. Repr. of 1853 ed. 30.00 (ISBN 0-384-09205-5). Johnson Repr.

--Record of the Boston Stage. LC 11-19303. 1853. 12.00 (ISBN 0-403-00473-X). Scholarly.

Clappe, Arthur A. The Wind-Band & Its Instruments. LC 76-22327. (Illus.). 1976. Repr. of 1911 ed. lib. bdg. 25.00 (ISBN 0-89341-011-X). Longwood Pub Group.

Clappe, Louise. Shirley Letters. LC 77-141468. (Illus.). 224p. 1970. pap. 5.95 (ISBN 0-87905-004-7, Peregrine Smith). Gibbs M Smith.

Clapper, Raymond. Racketeering in Washington: An Account of the Grafting in Small & Great Things by Our Senators & Members of the House of Representatives & Executives in Public Departments. LC 73-19138. (Politics & People Ser.). 356p. 1974. Repr. 24.50x (ISBN 0-405-05863-2). Ayer Co Pubs.

--Watching the World. (FDR & the Era of the New Deal Ser.). 1975. Repr. of 1944 ed. 45.00 (ISBN 0-306-70730-6). Da Capo.

Clapper, Ronald. The Development of "Walden". A Genetic Text. LC 80-2503. 1981. 75.00 (ISBN 0-404-19051-0). AMS Pr.

Clapperton, C. M. see Bowen, D. Q.

Clapperton, Chalmers, ed. Scotland: A New Study. (Illus.). 344p. 1983. 27.50 (ISBN 0-7153-8084-2). David & Charles.

--Scotland: A New Study. (Illus.). 344p. 1985. pap. 16.95 (ISBN 0-7153-8489-9). David & Charles.

Clapperton, H. Journal of a Second Expedition into the Interior of Africa from the Bight of Benin to Soccatoo. 355p. 1966. Repr. of 1829 ed. 45.00x (ISBN 0-7146-1798-9, F Cass Co). Biblio Dist.

Clapsadle, Mark & Aemmer, Gail. Community Helpers Fun Book. (Stick-Out-Your-Neck Ser.). (Illus.). 32p. (ps-2). 1984. pap. 1.25 (ISBN 0-88724-061-5, CD-8050). Carson-Dellos.

Clapton, Diana. Lou Reed. 1983. pap. 9.95 (ISBN 0-86276-055-0); 15.95 (ISBN 0-86276-056-9). Proteus Pub NY.

Clapton, M. J. Aikido. 1984. 20.00 (ISBN 0-901764-22-1, Pub. by P H Crompton Ltd UK). State Mutual Bk.

Clar, C. Raymond. Out of the River Mist. 3rd ed. (Illus.). 135p. 1984. pap. 6.95 (ISBN 0-9613635-0-9). C R Clar.

Clar, E. Polycyclic Hydrocarbons, 2 Vols. 1964. Vol. 1. 79.50 (ISBN 0-12-174701-8); Vol. 2. 79.50 (ISBN 0-12-174702-6). Acad Pr.

Clar, Erich J. The Aromatic Sextet. LC 72-616. pap. 34.50 (ISBN 0-317-29344-3, 2023998). Bks Demand UMI.

Clar, Lawrence & Hart, James. Calculus with Analytic Geometry for the Technologies. (Ser. in Technological Mathematics). (Illus.). 1980. text ed. 24.95 (ISBN 0-13-111856-0). P-H.

--Mathematics for the Technologies with Calculus. (P-H Series in Technical Mathematics). (Illus.). 1978. ref. ed. 29.95 (ISBN 0-13-562553-X). P-H.

Clar, Lawrence M. & Hart, James A. Mathematics for Business & Consumers. (Illus.). 1980. text ed. write for info. (ISBN 0-02-322540-8). Macmillan.

--Mathematics for the Technologies. (Illus.). 1978. text ed. 27.95 (ISBN 0-13-565200-6). P-H.

Clar, Raymond C. Quarterdecks & Spanish Grants. (Illus.). 156p. 1984. pap. 15.00 (ISBN 0-910845-23-9, 909). Landmark Ent.

Clara, Louise P. & Nelson, B. P. Solving Writing Problems: A Self-Paced Workbook. LC 78-11147. 1979. pap. text ed. 14.95 (ISBN 0-03-042986-2, HoltC); instrs' manual 19.95 (ISBN 0-03-044906-5). HR&W.

Clara, M. & Herschel, K. Atlas of the Normal Microscopic Anatomy of Man. (Illus., Eng., Ger., Rus., & Span.). 1973. 156.00x (ISBN 0-685-39789-0). Adlers Foreign Bks.

Clarac see De La Fontaine, Jean.

Clarac see Proust, Marcel.

Clarac, F., jt. ed. see Bush, B. M.

Clarac, Pierre De see De Clarac, Pierre.

Claraso, N. Vademecum del Arquitecto de Jardines. 256p. (Span.). 1977. pap. 12.50 (ISBN 84-252-0428-3, S-35347). French & Eur.

Claraso, V. Diccionario Humoristico. 297p. (Span.). 1966. 26.95 (ISBN 0-686-92238-7, S-37662). French & Eur.

Clarc, Michel. Les Meteques Atheniens. Vlastos, Gregory, ed. LC 78-15862. (Morals & Law in Ancient Greece Ser.). 1979. Repr. of 1893 ed. lib. bdg. 34.50x (ISBN 0-405-11533-4). Ayer Co Pubs.

Clardy, Andrea, ed. Gordon Gammack: Columns from Three Wars. 1979. 10.95 (ISBN 0-8138-0130-3). Iowa St U Pr.

Clardy, Andrea F. Dusty Was My Friend. 32p. 1984. 10.95 (ISBN 0-89885-141-6). Human Sci Pr.

--A Sense of Place: Small Communitites Near Ithaca, New York. (Illus.). 96p. 1982. pap. 9.95 (ISBN 0-935526-09-9). McBooks Pr.

Clardy, Andrea F., ed. Ithaca: A Book of Photographs. LC 80-26849. (Illus.). 96p. (Orig.). 1980. pap. 9.95 (ISBN 0-935526-03-X). McBooks Pr.

Clare, A., jt. auth. see Williams, P.

Clare, A. W. & Corney, R. H., eds. Social Work & Primary Health Care. 1983. 39.00 (ISBN 0-12-174740-9). Acad Pr.

Clare, A. W. & Lader, M., eds. Psychiatry & General Practice. 1982. 32.50 (ISBN 0-12-174720-4). Acad Pr.

Clare, Andrea M., ed. see Dickens, Charles.

Clare, Andrea M., ed. see Verne, Jules.

Clare, Anthony. In the Psychiatrist's Chair. 192p. 1985. 16.95 (ISBN 0-7011-2793-7, Pub. by Chatto & Windus-Hogarth Pr); pap. 7.95 (ISBN 0-7011-2837-2). Merrimack Pub Cir.

--Psychiatry in Dissent: Controversial Issues in Thought & Practice. LC 78-16835. (Illus.). 464p. 1979. 20.00 (ISBN 0-915980-92-4). ISHI PA.

Clare, Anthony & Thompson, Sally. Let's Talk about Me. 248p. 1981. 40.00x (ISBN 0-563-17761-6, Pub. by BBC Pubns). State Mutual Bk.

Clare, C. P. & Loucopoulos, P. Data Processing: Current Theories & Practices. 1983. 16.00 (ISBN 0-9961005-6-3, Pub. by Abacus England). Heyden.
--Fundamentals of Systems Analysis. 1984. 25.00 (ISBN 0-9901004-4-8, Pub. by Abacus England). Heyden.
Clare, Dollie. The Tantalizing Disclosures of a Welsh Girl. LC 77-87938. (Illus.). 1978. 8.50 (ISBN 0-8022-2218-8). Philos Lib.
Clare, Frances. Wow God. 189p. pap. 4.95 (ISBN 0-89221-131-8). New Leaf.
Clare, Francis. Your Move, God. LC 82-81212. 144p. 1982. pap. 4.95 (ISBN 0-89221-102-4). New Leaf.
Clare, Frederick. They Blew Our Weather. (Illus.). 192p. 1982. 20.00 (ISBN 0-682-49824-6). Exposition Pr FL.
Clare, George. ABC of the Foreign Exchanges. Wilkins, Mira, ed. LC 78-3905. (International Finance Ser.). (Illus.). 1978. Repr. of 1895 ed. lib. bdg. 17.00x (ISBN 0-405-11210-6). Ayer Co Pubs.
--Last Waltz in Vienna: The Rise & Destruction of a Family, 1842-1942. 1982. 16.45 (ISBN 0-03-060406-0). HR&W.
--The Last Waltz in Vienna: The Rise & Destruction of a Family, 1842-1942. 1983. pap. 3.95 (ISBN 0-380-64709-5, 64709, Discus). Avon.
Clare, J. N. & Sinclair, M. A., eds. Search & the Human Observer. (Illus.). 198p. 1979. pap. 25.00x (ISBN 0-85066-193-5). Taylor & Francis.
Clare, James S. Winchester College. 1982. 50.00x (ISBN 0-686-98443-9, Pub. by Cave Pubns England). State Mutual Bk.
Clare, John. Clare's Countryside. (Illus.). 1981. 19.95 (ISBN 0-434-98013-7, Pub. by W Heinemann Ltd). David & Charles.
--John Clare's Autobiographical Writings. Robinson, Eric, ed. (Illus.). 1983. 15.95 (ISBN 0-19-211774-2). Oxford U Pr.
--John Clare's Birds. Robinsson, Eric & Fitter, Richard, eds. (Illus.). 1982. 16.50x (ISBN 0-19-212977-5). Oxford U Pr.
--The Journals, Essays, & the Journey from Essex. Tibble, Anne, ed. 139p. 1980. text ed. 19.45x (ISBN 0-85635-344-2, Pub. by Carcanet New Pr England). Humanities.
--The Later Poems of John Clare, 1837-1864, Vols. I & II. Robinson, Eric, et al, eds. (Oxford English Texts Ser.). (Illus.). 1984. Set. 155.00x (ISBN 0-19-811874-0). Oxford U Pr.
--The Rural Muse. 184p. 1982. text ed. 13.00x (ISBN 0-85635-397-3, 80449, Pub. by Carcanet New Pr England). Humanities.
--Selected Poems. Tibble, J. W., ed. 1965. 12.85x (ISBN 0-460-00563-4, Evman); pap. 4.95x (ISBN 0-460-01563-X, Evman). Biblio Dist.
--Selected Poems & Prose of John Clare. Robinson, Eric & Summerfield, Geoffrey, eds. (Illus.). 1967. pap. 9.95 (ISBN 0-19-281232-7). Oxford U Pr.
--The Shepherd's Calendar. Robinson, Eric & Summerfield, Geoffrey, eds. (Oxford Paperbacks Ser). 1973. 15.95x (ISBN 0-19-211249-X, OPB308); pap. 8.95x (ISBN 0-19-281142-8). Oxford U Pr.
Clare, Josephine. Deutschland & Other Places. 52p. (Orig.). 1974. pap. 3.00 (ISBN 0-913028-22-3). North Atlantic.
--Mammatocumulus. LC 76-58627. (Poetry Ser.). 1977. pap. 4.50 (ISBN 0-685-75802-8). Ocotillo.
Clare, Lilian, tr. see Levy-Bruhl, Lucien.
Clare, Lilian A., tr. see Chevalier, Jacques.
Clare, Lilian A., tr. see Levy-Bruhl, Lucien.
Clare, Lillian A., tr. see Levy-Bruhl, Lucien.
Clare, M. V., Sr., tr. see Eugene, P. M.
Clare, Maurice. A Day with Charles Dickens. 10.00 (ISBN 0-8274-2147-8). R West.
--A Day with Charles Kingsley. Repr. 10.00 (ISBN 0-8274-2148-6). R West.
--A Day with George Eliot. 10.00 (ISBN 0-8274-2149-4). R West.
--A Day with Ralph Waldo Emerson. LC 78-12781. 1978. Repr. lib. bdg. 15.00 (ISBN 0-8414-9980-2). Folcroft.
--A Day with Robert Louis Stevenson. Repr. 10.00 (ISBN 0-8274-2152-4). R West.
--A Day with Robert Louis Stevenson. 55p. 1981. Repr. of 1980 ed. lib. bdg. 17.50 (ISBN 0-89760-162-9). Telegraph Bks.
--A Day with Thomas Carlyle. 10.00 (ISBN 0-8274-2153-2). R West.
--A Day with William Makepeace Thackeray. 10.00 (ISBN 0-8274-2154-0). R West.
Clare, Morris. Quantitative Approaches in Business Studies. (M&E Higher Business Education Ser.). (Illus.). 400p. 1983. text ed. 30.00x (ISBN 0-7121-1706-7, Macdonald & Evans); pap. text ed. 16.50x (ISBN 0-7121-1705-9). Sheridan.
Clare, Norman. Billiards & Snooker Bygones. (Shire Album Ser.: No. 136). (Illus.). 32p. (Orig.). 1985. pap. 3.50 (ISBN 0-85263-730-6, Pub. by Shire Pubns England). Seven Hills Bks.
Clare, Shannon. The Queen's Rival. 1978. pap. 1.95 (ISBN 0-8439-0590-5, Leisure Bks). Dorchester Pub Co.
--Sweet Temptation. (Superromances). 384p. 1982. pap. 2.50 (ISBN 0-373-70043-1, Pub. by Worldwide). Harlequin Bks.
Clarebout, David, ed. Ethnic Group Adjustment in America. new ed. 1980. lib. bdg. 9.95 (ISBN 0-915574-19-5). Soc Sci & Soc Res.
Claremon, Neil. Borderland. 1976. pap. 1.75 (ISBN 0-380-00679-0, 29736). Avon.
Claremont, C. A. Intelligence & Mental Growth. 1928. 12.50 (ISBN 0-932062-30-X). Sharon Hill.
Claremont, Chris & McLeod, Bob. The New Mutants. (Marvel Graphic Novel: No. 4). 4.95 (ISBN 0-939766-20-5). Marvel Comics.
Claremont, Chris & Simonson, Walter. Marvel & DC Present: The Uncanny X-Men & the New Teen Titans. 160p. (Orig.). 1983. pap. cancelled (ISBN 0-446-30529-4). Warner Bks.
Claremont, Christopher & Anderson, Brent E. The X-Men. (Marvel Graphic Novel: No. 5). 5.95 (ISBN 0-939766-20-5). Marvel Comics.
Claremont, Claude A., tr. see Montessori, Maria.
Claremont, Lewis De see De Claremont, Lewis.
Claremont De Castillejo, Irene. Knowing Woman: A Feminine Psychology. LC 72-80470. 1973. 8.00 (ISBN 0-913430-01-3). C G Jung Foun.
--Knowing Woman: Feminine Psychology. 192p. 1974. pap. 5.72i (ISBN 0-06-090349-X, CN349, CN). Har-Row.
Clarence-Smith, Gervase. The Third Portuguese Empire, 1825-1975. LC 84-9701. 246p. 1985. 29.50 (ISBN 0-7190-1719-X, Pub. by Manchester Univ Pr). Longwood Pub Group.
Clarence-Smith, W. G. Slaves, Peasants, & Capitalists in Southern Angola: Eighteen Forty to Nineteen Twenty-Six. LC 78-67805. (African Studies: No. 27). (Illus.). 1979. 27.95 (ISBN 0-521-22406-3). Cambridge U Pr.
Clarenden, Edward & Hyde, Earlay. Selections from "The History of the Rebellion" & "The Life by Himself". Huehns, G., intro. by. 1978. 13.95x (ISBN 0-19-215852-X). Oxford U Pr.
Clarendon, Colin & Strock, Sylvia. Clarendon Guide to Kansas City Restaurants. (Illus.). 195p. (Orig.). pap. 7.50 (ISBN 0-9609028-0-5). C & S Ent.
Clarendon, Cyrus. The Tragic Dilemma of the Swiss Banks, Authorities & People. (Illus.). 1979. deluxe ed. 67.50x (ISBN 0-930008-23-5). Inst Econ Pol.
Clarendon, Lorrain. The Twenty-Five Reproductions in Full Colours of the Greatest Paintings of the World with Critical Commentaries. (Illus.). 120p. 1983. 79.85x (ISBN 0-86650-088-X). Gloucester Art.
Clarendon Pr. Cartographic Dept. Staff. Oxford Economic Atlas of the World. 4th ed. (Illus.). 1972. 39.95x (ISBN 0-19-894106-4); pap. 14.95x (ISBN 0-19-894107-2). Oxford U Pr.
Clarendon Press - Cartographic Department. Oxford Home Atlas of the World. 3rd ed. 1960. 10.95x (ISBN 0-19-891103-3). Oxford U Pr.
Clarens, Carlos. Crime Movies. (Illus.). 1980. pap. 9.95 (ISBN 0-393-00940-8). Norton.
Clareson, Thomas. SF: the Other Side of Realism. 370p. 14.95 (ISBN 0-87972-022-0); pap. 8.95 (ISBN 0-87972-023-9). Bowling Green Univ.
Clareson, Thomas & Wymer, Thomas. Voices for the Future: Essays on Major Science Fiction Writers, Vol. 3. LC 76-10939. 1983. 19.95 (ISBN 0-87972-251-7); pap. 8.95 (ISBN 0-87972-252-5). Bowling Green Univ.
Clareson, Thomas D. Many Futures, Many Worlds: Theme & Form in Science Fiction. LC 76-42448. 300p. 1977. 8.00x (ISBN 0-87338-199-8). Kent St U Pr.
--Reader's Guide to Robert Silverberg. Schlobin, Roger C., ed. LC 83-542. (Starmont Reader's Guides to Contemporary Science Fiction & Fantasy Authors Ser.: Vol. 18). (Illus., Orig.). 1983. 13.95x (ISBN 0-916732-48-7); pap. text ed. 5.95x (ISBN 0-916732-47-9). Starmont Hse.
--Robert Silverberg. LC 83-15623. (Starmont Reader's Guides Ser.: No. 18). 96p. 1983. Repr. lib. bdg. 13.95x (ISBN 0-89370-021-5). Borgo Pr.
--Robert Silverberg: A Primary & Secondary Bibliography. 336p. 1983. lib. bdg. 50.00 (ISBN 0-8161-8118-7, Hall Reference). G K Hall.
--Science Fiction Criticism: An Annotated Checklist. LC 71-181084. (Serif Ser.: No. 23). 238p. 1972. 13.00x (ISBN 0-87338-123-8). Kent St U Pr.
--Science Fiction in America, Eighteen Seventies-Nineteen Thirties: An Annotated Bibliography of Primary Sources. LC 84-8934. (Bibliographies & Indexes in American Literature Ser.: No. 1). xiii, 305p. 1984. lib. bdg. 35.00 (ISBN 0-313-23169-9, CSF/). Greenwood.
--Some Kind of Paradise: The Emergence of American Science Fiction. LC 84-29060. (Contribution to the Study of Science Fiction & Fantasy: No. 16). 288p. 1985. lib. bdg. 29.95 (ISBN 0-313-23167-2, CSK/). Greenwood.
--Voices for the Future: Essays on Major Science Fiction Writers. 1976. 13.95 (ISBN 0-87972-119-7); pap. 7.95 (ISBN 0-87972-120-0). Bowling Green Univ.
--Voices for the Future: Essays on Major Science Fiction Writers, Vol. 2. LC 78-61202. 1979. 13.95 (ISBN 0-87972-135-9); pap. 7.95 (ISBN 0-87972-136-7). Bowling Green Univ.
Claret. Melissa Mouse. 28p. 5.95 (ISBN 0-8120-5623-X). Barron.
Claret, Maria. The Chocolate Rabbit. 28p. 1985. 5.95 (ISBN 0-8120-5624-8). Barron.
Claretie, Jules. The Crime of the Boulevard. Kingsbury, Carlton A., tr. LC 75-32739. (Literature of Mystery & Detection). 1976. Repr. of 1897 ed. 19.00x (ISBN 0-405-07867-6). Ayer Co Pubs.
Clarey, Elizabeth M. & Dixson, Robert J. Pronunciation Exercises in English. (gr. 9 up). 1963. pap. text ed. 3.95 (ISBN 0-88345-135-2, 17418); cassettes 25.00 (ISBN 0-686-86692-4). Regents Pub.
Clarey, M. Elizabeth & Dixson, Robert J. Curso Practico de Pronunciacion del Ingles. Andujar, Julio I., ed. (gr. 10 up). 1967. pap. text ed. 4.50 (ISBN 0-88345-039-9, 17377); with cassettes 25.00 (ISBN 0-685-04773-3, 40105). Regents Pub.
Clarfield, Gerard H. Timothy Pickering & the American Republic. LC 79-24326. 1980. 26.95x (ISBN 0-8229-3414-0). U of Pittsburgh Pr.
Clarfield, Gerard H. & Wiecek, William M. Nuclear America: Military & Civilan Power in the United States, 1940-1980. LC 84-47565. 528p. 1985. pap. 10.95 (ISBN 0-06-091244-8, PL 1244, PL). Har-Row.
--Nuclear America: Military & Civilian Nuclear Power in the United States, 1940-1980. LC 84-47565. (Illus.). 528p. 1984. 19.18 (ISBN 0-06-015336-9, HarpT). Har-Row.
Clarida, Glen, jt. auth. see Stringer, James.
Claridge, G. Cyril. Wild Bush Tribes of Tropical Africa. LC 74-90111. (Illus.). Repr. of 1922 ed. 25.00x (ISBN 0-8371-2029-2, CLB&). Greenwood.
Claridge, Gordon S., et al. Personality Differences & Biological Variations: A Study of Twins. LC 72-10132. 1973. text ed. 33.00 (ISBN 0-08-017124-9). Pergamon.
Claridge, Mary. Margaret Clitherow: 1556-1586. LC 66-19228. xii, 196p. 1966. 20.00 (ISBN 0-8232-0695-5). Fordham.
Claridge, W. W. History of Gold Coast & Ashanti, 2 vols. 2nd ed. 1964. 95.00x (ISBN 0-7146-1642-7, F Cass Co). Biblio Dist.
Clarie, Thomas C. Occult Bibliography: An Annotated List of Books Published in English, 1971 Through 1975. LC 78-17156. 482p. 1978. 28.50 (ISBN 0-8108-1152-9). Scarecrow.
--Occult-Paranormal Bibliography: An Annotated List of Books Published in English, 1976-1981. LC 83-20319. 579p. 1984. 35.00 (ISBN 0-8108-1674-1). Scarecrow.
Claringbloud, M. H., jt. ed. see Schadee, H.
Clarins, Dana. Guilty Parties. 1985. pap. 3.50 (ISBN 0-317-19533-6). Bantam.
--Woman in the Window. 304p. (Orig.). 1984. pap. 3.50 (ISBN 0-553-24257-1). Bantam.
Clariodus. Clariodus: A Metrical Romance. Irving, David, ed. LC 72-1035. (Maitland Club, Glasgow. Publications: No. 9). Repr. of 1830 ed. 22.00 (ISBN 0-404-52937-2). AMS Pr.
Clarizio, Harvey F. Toward Positive Classroom Discipline. 3rd ed. LC 79-22392. 246p. 1980. pap. text ed. 18.95 (ISBN 0-471-05960-9). Wiley.
Clarizio, Harvey F. & Craig, Robert C. Contemporary Issues in Educational Psychology. 4th ed. Mehrens, William A., ed. 350p. 1981. pap. text ed. 20.00 (ISBN 0-205-07331-X, 247331). Allyn.
Clarizio, Harvey F. & McCoy, George F. Behavior Disorders in Children. 3rd ed. 724p. 1983. text ed. 28.95 scp (ISBN 0-06-041304-2, HarpC); instr's. manual avail. (ISBN 0-06-361270-4). Har-Row.
Clark. Advances in Infared & Raman Spectroscopy, Vol. 9. 1982. 124.95 (ISBN 0-471-26215-3). Wiley.
--Advances in Infrared & Raman Spectroscopy, Vol. 8. 1981. 130.95 (ISBN 0-471-25640-4, Pub. by Wiley Heyden). Wiley.
--Asthma. 2nd ed. 1984. 44.95 (ISBN 0-8151-1756-6). Year Bk Med.
--Clinical Investigation of Respiratory Disease. 1982. 52.50 (ISBN 0-8151-1756-6). Year Bk Med.
--Instructions to Christian Converts. pap. 1.95 (ISBN 0-686-12883-4). Schmul Pub Co.
--Lighthouse Boy. 1976. pap. 3.75 (ISBN 0-89272-043-3). Down East.
--Social Therapy in Psychiatry. 2nd ed. 1981. pap. text ed. 8.25 (ISBN 0-686-29678-8). Churchill.
--Year Book of Cancer, 1984. 1984. 44.95 (ISBN 0-8151-1792-2). Year Bk Med.
Clark & Clark. Settlements Law & Strategies, Clark & Clarks. (The Lawin Ga. Ser.). 132p. 1981. incl. latest pocket part supplement 24.95 (ISBN 0-317-14680-7); separate pocket part supplement, 1982 14.95. Harrison Co GA.
Clark & LaBarre. Advanced Structured BASIC. 1985. text ed. 11.95 (ISBN 0-538-10870-3, J87). SW Pub.
Clark & Lambrecht. Information Processing: Concepts, Principles & Procedures. 3rd ed. 1985. text ed. 14.95 (ISBN 0-538-10540-2, J54). SW Pub.
Clark & Matko. Soviet Economic Facts: 1917-1981. LC 81-23299. 200p. 1983. 25.00x (ISBN 0-312-74758-6). St Martin.
Clark & Starr. Secondary & Middle School Teaching Methods. 5th ed. 973p. 1986. text ed. write for info. (ISBN 0-02-322600-5). Macmillan.
Clark & White. Computer Confidence: A Challenge for Today. 1986. text ed. price not set (ISBN 0-538-10010-9, J01). SW Pub.
Clark, jt. auth. see MacLeod.
Clark, jt. auth. see Turner.
Clark, jt. auth. see Warren.
Clark, ed. The Arts & Crafts Movement in America, 1876-1916. pap. 17.50 (ISBN 0-691-03884-8). Princeton U Pr.
Clark, jt. ed. see Hahn.
Clark, et al. Holt General Mathematics. 1982. text ed. 17.72 (ISBN 0-03-058911-8, HoltE); tchr's ed. 24.92 (ISBN 0-03-058912-6); testmasters avail. (ISBN 0-03-058913-4); skillmasters avail. (ISBN 0-03-058914-2). HR&W.
Clark, A. Cosmic Mysteries of the Universe. 1974. pap. 3.45 (ISBN 0-13-179192-3, Reward). P-H.
Clark, A., ed. see Godstow Nunnery.
Clark, A. C. see Cicero.
Clark, A. C., et al. From the Orange Mailbox: Notes from a Few Country Acres. LC 85-45024. (Illus.). 224p. 1985. 14.95 (ISBN 0-88448-033-X); pap. 8.95 (ISBN 0-88448-034-8). Harpswell Pr.
Clark, A. F., ed. Advances in Cryogenic Engineering, Vol. 30. 1020p. 1984. 95.00x (ISBN 0-306-41704-9, Plenum Pr). Plenum Pub.
Clark, A. F. & Reed, R. P., eds. Advances in Cryogenic Engineering, Vol. 26. LC 57-35598. 717p. 1981. 89.50x (ISBN 0-306-40531-8, Plenum Pr). Plenum Pub.
Clark, A. F., jt. ed. see Reed, R. P.
Clark, A. F., et al, eds. Nonmetallic Materials & Composites at Low Temperatures One. LC 78-26576. (Cryogenic Materials Ser.). 456p. 1979. 69.50x (ISBN 0-306-40077-4, Plenum Pr). Plenum Pub.
Clark, A. H. Ophiuroidea of the Hawaiian Islands. (BMB Ser.). Repr. of 1949 ed. 19.00 (ISBN 0-527-02303-5). Kraus Repr.
Clark, A. J. General Pharmacology. LC 75-105699. (Handbook of Experimental Pharmacology: Vol. 4). (Illus.). 1970. Repr. of 1937 ed. 50.80 (ISBN 0-387-04845-6). Springer-Verlag.
Clark, A. M. & Courtman-Stock, J. The Echinoderms of Southern Africa. (Illus.). 1976. 55.00x (ISBN 0-565-00776-9, Pub. by Brit Mus Nat Hist). Sabbot-Natural Hist Bks.
Clark, A. M. see Gibson, S. & Gibson, M. A.
Clark, A. P. Principles of Digital Data Transmission. 2nd ed. LC 83-6710. 1983. 26.95x (ISBN 0-470-27458-1). Halsted Pr.
Clark, Admont G. They Built Clipper Ships in Their Back Yard. 32p. 1963. pap. 1.95 (ISBN 0-940160-00-5). Parnassus Imprints.
Clark, Al. The Film Yearbook 1983. (Illus.). 192p. (Orig.). 1983. pap. 12.95 (ISBN 0-394-62465-3, E853, Ever). Grove.
--The Film Yearbook, 1985. LC 83-644931. (Illus.). 192p. 1984. pap. 12.95 (ISBN 0-394-62321-5, Ever). Grove.
--Raymond Chandler in Hollywood. (Illus.). 160p. 1983. 17.95 (ISBN 0-86276-110-7); pap. 11.95 (ISBN 0-86276-109-3). Proteus Pub NY.
Clark, Al, ed. The Film Year Book 1984. (Illus.). 192p. 1983. 12.95 (ISBN 0-394-62488-2, E 867, Ever). Grove.
--The Film Yearbook 1986. (Illus.). 192p. 1985. 24.95 (ISBN 0-312-28934-0); pap. 13.95 (ISBN 0-312-28935-9). St Martin.
--The Rock Yearbook, 1984. 240p. 1983. 14.95 (ISBN 0-312-68786-9). St Martin.
--The Rock Yearbook 1985. (Illus.). 224p. 1985. 24.95 (ISBN 0-312-68788-5); pap. 13.95 (ISBN 0-312-68787-7). St Martin.
Clark, Alan. Barbarossa: The Russian-German Conflict, 1941-1945. LC 85-502. (Illus.). 528p. 1985. pap. 12.95 (ISBN 0-688-04268-6, Quill). Morrow.
Clark, Alan & Ashford, David. Comic Art of Roy Wilson. (Illus.). 128p. 1983. 17.50 (ISBN 0-88254-828-X, Pub. by Midas England). Hippocrene Bks.
Clark, Alan F., jt. ed. see Suenaga, Masaki.
Clark, Albert C. Prose Rhythm in English. LC 74-7411. 1913. lib. bdg. 7.50 (ISBN 0-8414-3589-8). Folcroft.
Clark, Alex W. Through a Glass Clearly. 159p. 1981. 30.00x (ISBN 0-901482-28-5, Pub. by Golden Eagle England). State Mutual Bk.
Clark, Alexander F. Boileau & the French Classical Critics in England, 1660-1830. LC 75-147841. (Revue de litterature comparee bibliotheque: Vol. 19). 1971. Repr. of 1925 ed. lib. bdg. 29.00 (ISBN 0-8337-4046-6). B Franklin.
Clark, Alexander, ed. Schoolday Dialogues. facsimile ed. LC 72-103085. (Granger Index Reprint Ser). 1897. 17.00 (ISBN 0-8369-6100-5). Ayer Co Pubs.
--Standard Dialogues. facsimile ed. LC 77-109137. (Granger Index Reprint Ser). 1898. 15.00 (ISBN 0-8369-6121-8). Ayer Co Pubs.
Clark, Alfred. The Chemisorptive Bond: Basic Concepts. (Physical Chemistry: A Series of Monographs, Vol. 32). 1974. 57.50 (ISBN 0-12-175440-5). Acad Pr.
--Theory of Adsorption & Catalysis. (Physical Chemistry Ser.: Vol. 18). 1970. 78.00 (ISBN 0-12-175450-2). Acad Pr.
Clark, Alfred T., jt. auth. see Schachter, Norman.
Clark, Alfred T., Jr., jt. auth. see Schachter, Norman.
Clark, Alfred W., ed. Experimenting with Organizational Life: The Action Research Approach. LC 75-45035. (Illus.). 270p. 1976. 29.50x (ISBN 0-306-30879-7, Plenum Pr). Plenum Pub.
Clark, Alice. Working Life of Women in the Seventeenth Century. 328p. 1968. Repr. of 1919 ed. 29.50x (ISBN 0-7146-1291-X, BHA-01291, F Cass Co). Biblio Dist.
--Working Life of Women in the Seventeenth Century. LC 67-31558. Repr. of 1919 ed. 27.50x (ISBN 0-678-05039-2). Kelley.

--Working Life of Women in the Seventeenth Century. 368p. 1982. pap. 9.95 (ISBN 0-7100-9045-5). Routledge & Kegan.

Clark, Alice & Leitch, Carol. Math Amusements in Developing Skills, Vol. 1. (Illus.). (gr. 4-9). pap. 6.95 (ISBN 0-910974-68-3); 57 duplicating masters o.p. 13.95 (ISBN 0-685-40576-1). Midwest Pubns.

Clark, Alice S. Managing Curriculum Materials in the Academic Library. LC 81-16574. 227p. 1982. 15.00 (ISBN 0-8108-1482-X). Scarecrow.

Clark, Alice S., jt. ed. see Hoadley, Irene B.

Clark, Allan. Elements of Abstract Algebra. 205p. 1984. pap. 6.00 (ISBN 0-486-64725-0). Dover.

Clark, Amalia R. Special Mexican Dishes. pap. 6.95x (ISBN 0-89741-010-6). Roadrunner Tech.

Clark, Andrew. Elizabethan Domestic Drama: A Survey of the Origins, Antecedents, & Nature of the Domestic Play in England, 1500-1640, 2 vols. (Salzburg Studies in English Literature, Jacobean Drama Studies: Vol. 49). 455p. (Orig.). 1975. Set. pap. text ed. 50.75x (ISBN 0-391-01345-9). Humanities.

Clark, Andrew H. Acadia: The Geography of Early Nova Scotia to 1760. (Illus.). 470p. 1968. 30.00x (ISBN 0-299-05080-7). U of Wis Pr.

--Invasion of New Zealand by People, Plants & Animals: The South Island. LC 71-100249. Repr. of 1949 ed. lib. bdg. 20.50x (ISBN 0-8371-2982-6, CLIN). Greenwood.

--Three Centuries & the Island: A Historical Geography of Settlement & Agriculture in Prince Edward Island, Cananda. LC 59-2157. pap. 75.00 (ISBN 0-317-27978-5, 2055817). Bks Demand UMI.

Clark, Ann L. & Mandell, Steven L. A Short Course in PL-I PL-C. (Series in Data Processing & Information Systems). 1978. pap. text ed. 15.95 (ISBN 0-8299-0219-8); instrs.' manual avail. (ISBN 0-8299-0465-4). West Pub.

Clark, Ann L., ed. Culture & Childrearing. LC 80-19481. (Illus.). 248p. 1981. 24.00x (ISBN 0-8036-1836-0). Davis Co.

Clark, Ann L., et al. Childbearing: A Nursing Perspective. 2nd ed. LC 78-24575. (Illus.). 1052p. 1979. text ed. 23.00x (ISBN 0-8036-1831-X). Davis Co.

Clark, Ann N. In the Land of Small Dragon. LC 78-26233. (Illus.). (gr. k-3). 1979. 11.50 (ISBN 0-670-39697-4). Viking.

--Secret of the Andes. (Puffin Story Ser). (gr. 3-7). 1976. pap. 3.50 (ISBN 0-14-030926-8, Puffin). Penguin.

--Secret of the Andes. (Illus.). (gr. 4-8). 1952. 13.95 (ISBN 0-670-62975-8). Viking.

--To Stand Against the Wind. LC 78-5966. (gr. 3-7). 1978. 11.50 (ISBN 0-670-71773-8). Viking.

Clark, Anna K., jt. ed. see Murray, Janet H.

Clark, Anne. Australian Adventure: Letters from an Ambassador's Wife. (Illus.). 246p. 1969. 16.95x (ISBN 0-292-70001-6). U of Tex Pr.

--Lewis Carroll: A Biography. LC 79-64116. (Illus.). 1979. 12.95 (ISBN 0-8052-3722-4). Schocken.

--The Real Alice. (Illus.). 256p. 1982. 17.95 (ISBN 0-8128-2870-4). Stein & Day.

Clark, Anne B., jt. auth. see Klein, Donald.

Clark, Annie M. The Alcotts in Harvard. LC 78-8815. 1902. 10.00 (ISBN 0-8414-0881-5). Folcroft.

Clark, Anthony M. Studies in Roman Eighteenth-Century Painting. Bowron, Edgar P., ed. (Art History Ser.: Vol. IV). (Illus.). 320p. 1981. 75.00 (ISBN 0-916276-10-4). Decatur Hse.

Clark, Anthony M. & Brown, Edgar P. Pompeo Batoni: A Complete Catalogue of His Paintings & Drawings. 416p. 1985. 125.00x (ISBN 0-8147-1397-1). NYU Pr.

Clark, Anthony M. Catalogue of European Paintings in the Minneapolis Institute of Arts. LC 77-129877. (Illus.). 1970. 15.00 (ISBN 0-912964-03-0). Minneapolis Inst Arts.

Clark, Arben O., jt. auth. see Strong, Kline D.

Clark, Arnold M., et al. Aging in Insects. (Aging Ser.). 201p. 1976. text ed. 24.50x (ISBN 0-8422-7269-0). Irvington.

Clark, Arthur. Autobiography, Its Genesis & Phases. LC 76-40066. 1935. lib. bdg. 10.00 (ISBN 0-8414-3481-6). Folcroft.

Clark, Arthur C. Two Thousand Ten: Odyssey Two. 1984. pap. 3.95 (ISBN 0-345-30306-7, Del Rey). Ballantine.

Clark, Arthur M. Murder Under Trust: A Topical Macbeth & other Jacobean Matters. 208p. 1982. 17.50x (ISBN 0-7073-0312-5, Pub. by Scottish Academic Pr Scotland). Columbia U Pr.

--The Realistic Revolt in Modern Poetry. LC 74-32221. Repr. of 1822 ed. lib. bdg. 10.00 (ISBN 0-8414-3617-7). Folcroft.

--Realistic Revolt in Modern Poetry. (Studies in Comparative Literature, No. 35). 1970. pap. 27.95x (ISBN 0-8383-0087-1). Haskell.

--Studies in Literary Modes. LC 76-58436. 1946. lib. bdg. 20.00 (ISBN 0-8414-3428-X). Folcroft.

Clark, Mrs. Arthur, ed. Bayou Cuisine. 438p. 1970. 9.95 (ISBN 0-686-15358-8). Bayou Cuisine.

Clark, Asa A., et al, eds. The Defense Reform Debate: Issues & Analysis. LC 83-49196. 392p. 1984. 30.00x (ISBN 0-8018-3205-5); pap. 12.95x (ISBN 0-8018-3206-3). Johns Hopkins.

Clark, Aubert J. The Movement for International Copyright in Nineteenth Century America. LC 73-9209. 215p. 1973. Repr. of 1960 ed. lib. bdg. 15.00x (ISBN 0-8371-6980-1, CLIC). Greenwood.

Clark, Audrey N., jt. auth. see Stamp, Dudley.

Clark, Austen. Psychological Models & Neural Mechanisms: An Examination of Reductionism in Psychology. (CLLP Ser.). (Illus.). 1980. text ed. 29.95x (ISBN 0-19-824422-3). Oxford U Pr.

Clark, Axel. Christopher Brennan. 358p. 1980. 38.50x (ISBN 0-522-84182-1, Pub. by Melbourne Univ Pr Australia). Intl Spec Bk.

Clark, B. The Past, Present, & Future in Prose & Poetry. LC 72-947. Repr. of 1867 ed. 16.25 (ISBN 0-404-00015-0). AMS Pr.

Clark, B. D. & Gleave, M. B., eds. Social Patterns in Cities. (The Special Publication of the Institute of British Geographers Ser.: No. 5). 1980. 27.00 (ISBN 0-12-175580-0). Acad Pr.

Clark, B. F. The Genetic Code & Protein Biosynthesis. 2nd ed. (Studies in Biology: No. 83). 80p. 1984. pap. text ed. 8.95 (ISBN 0-7131-2887-9). E Arnold.

Clark, B. H. How to Produce Amateur Plays. 144p. 1980. Repr. of 1916 ed. lib. bdg. 25.00 (ISBN 0-89984-102-3). Century Bookbindery.

--Maxwell Anderson, the Man & His Plays. pap. 10.00 (ISBN 0-527-17620-6). Kraus Repr.

Clark, B. H., ed. Masterpieces of Modern Spanish Drama. Repr. of 1928 ed. 17.00 (ISBN 0-527-17600-1). Kraus Repr.

Clark, Badger. Sun & Saddle Leather. Reissue ed. 190p. 9.95 (ISBN 0-318-02288-5). Westerners Intl.

Clark, Barbara. Growing up Gifted. 544p. 1983. pap. text ed. 24.95 (ISBN 0-675-20060-1). Merrill.

--Pieces. 72p. 1985. pap. 6.95 (ISBN 0-9612296-3-2). Williams Com.

Clark, Barbara L. Nine-Square. 88p. 1980. 5.00 (ISBN 0-8059-2690-9). Dorrance.

Clark, Barbara R. Reflections. Davis, Ruby & Gerstung, Estella, eds. Clark, Carl R. & Williams, Cecil J. 72p. (Orig.). (gr. 4-12). 1982. pap. 4.95 (ISBN 0-686-37922-5). Williams Com.

Clark, Barkley. The Law of Bank Deposits, Collections & Credit Cards: Cumulative Supplementation. 2nd ed. 1981. 64.00 (ISBN 0-88262-547-0). Warren.

--The Law of Secured Transactions Under the Uniform Commercial Code: Annual Supplement. LC 80-50775. 1981. 64.00 (ISBN 0-88262-383-4). Warren.

Clark, Barkley & Smith, Christopher. Law of Product Warranties. 1984. 77.00 (ISBN 0-88712-098-9). Warren.

Clark, Baron, jt. auth. see Clark, Kenneth M.

Clark, Barrett H. Blush of Shame: A Few Considerations on Verbal Obscenity in the Theatre. 1932. pap. 1.50 (ISBN 0-910664-01-3). Gotham.

--British & American Drama of Today. LC 76-155635. (BCL Ser.: No. I). 1971. Repr. of 1921 ed. 23.50 (ISBN 0-404-01547-6). AMS Pr.

--European Theories of the Drama. rev. ed. Popkin, Henry, ed. (YA) (gr. 9 up). 1965. 19.95 (ISBN 0-517-50539-8). Crown.

--Great Short Biographies of Modern Times, the Seventeenth, Eighteenth, & Nineteenth Centuries. 1406p. 1982. Repr. of 1928 ed. lib. bdg. 65.00 (ISBN 0-89987-136-4). Darby Bks.

--Great Short Biographies of the World: A Collection of Short Biographies. 1979. Repr. of 1929 ed. lib. bdg. 40.00 (ISBN 0-8492-4037-9). R West.

--An Hour of American Drama. 159p. Date not set. Repr. of 1930 ed. lib. bdg. 25.00 (ISBN 0-89760-183-1). Telegraph Bks.

--Intimate Portraits. LC 77-93059. (Essay & General Literature Index Reprint Ser). 1970. Repr. of 1951 ed. 21.00x (ISBN 0-8046-0672-2, Pub. by Kennikat). Assoc Faculty Pr.

--Maxwell Anderson: The Man & His Plays. LC 74-7388. 1933. lib. bdg. 17.00 (ISBN 0-8414-3585-5). Folcroft.

--Paul Green. LC 74-1164. (Studies in Drama, No. 39). 1974. lib. bdg. 29.95x (ISBN 0-8383-2016-3). Haskell.

--A Study of the Modern Drama. 527p. 1982. Repr. of 1925 ed. lib. bdg. 48.50 (ISBN 0-89984-117-1). Century Bookbindery.

Clark, Barrett H., ed. World Drama, Vol. 1: Ancient Greece, Rome, India, China, Japan, Medieval Europe, England. pap. 8.95 (ISBN 0-486-20057-4). Dover.

--World Drama, Vol. 2: Italy, Spain, France, Germany, Denmark, Russia, Norway. 1933. pap. 9.95 (ISBN 0-486-20059-0). Dover.

Clark, Barrett H. & Lieber, Maxim, eds. Great Short Stories of the World. 1978. Repr. of 1926 ed. lib. bdg. 50.00 (ISBN 0-8482-3520-7). Norwood Edns.

Clark, Barrett H., jt. ed. see Sanborn, Ralph.

Clark, Ben T. Russian. 3rd ed. 668p. 1983. text ed. 23.95 scp (ISBN 0-06-041296-8, HarpC); instr's. mamual avail. (ISBN 0-06-361250-X); scp cassette tapes 229.00 (ISBN 0-06-047441-6). Har-Row.

Clark, Bernadine, ed. The Writer's Resource Guide. 2nd ed. 480p. 1983. 16.95 (ISBN 0-89879-102-2). Writers Digest.

Clark, Bettie. A Ham for All Seasons. LC 85-61032. (Illus.). 128p. (Orig.). 1985. pap. text ed. 7.95 (ISBN 0-933050-27-5). New Eng Pr VT.

Clark, Beverly L. Talking about Writing: A Guide for Tutor & Teacher Conferences. (Illus.). 192p. 1985. pap. text ed. 9.95x (ISBN 0-472-08062-8). U of Mich Pr.

Clark, Beverly L., jt. auth. see Friedman, Melvin J.

Clark, Blanche H. The Tennessee Yeomen, 1840-1860. LC 76-154662. xxiii, 200p. 1971. Repr. of 1942 ed. lib. bdg. 18.50x (ISBN 0-374-91669-1). Octagon.

Clark Boardman Publishing. Clark Boardman's Security Law Series. 1250.00 (ISBN 0-686-89384-0). Boardman.

Clark, Boden. The Work of Katherine Kurtz: An Annotated Bibliography & Guide. (Bibliographies of Modern Authors: No. 7). 50p. 1985. lib. bdg. 19.95x (ISBN 0-89370-386-9); pap. text ed. 9.95x (ISBN 0-89370-486-5). Borgo Pr.

Clark, Bori S., ed. Trinidad Women Speak. 71p. (Orig.). 1981. pap. text ed. 10.00x (ISBN 0-914369-00-8). Libros Latinos.

Clark, Brian. Whose Life Is It Anyway? 160p. 1980. pap. 2.95 (ISBN 0-380-52407-4, 64808-3, Bard). Avon.

Clark, Brian D., et al. Perspectives on Environmental Impact Assessment. 1984. lib. bdg. 69.00 (ISBN 90-277-1753-2, Pub. by Reidel Holland). Kluwer Academic.

Clark, Brian F. C. & Petersen, Hans Uffe, eds. Gene Expression: The Translational Step & Its Control. (Alfred Benzon Symposium Ser.: Vol. 19). 528p. 1984. text ed. 54.50 (ISBN 0-317-19787-8). Raven.

Clark, Bruce. Deathstalk. 1981. pap. 1.75 (ISBN 0-8439-0897-1, Pub. by Nordon Pubns). Dorchester Pub Co.

--Deathstalk. 192p. 1985. pap. 2.50 (ISBN 0-8439-2231-1, Leisure Bks). Dorchester Pub Co.

Clark, Bruce & Smith, Dennis A. An Introduction to Pharmacokinetics. (Illus.). 64p. 1981. pap. text ed. 7.25 (ISBN 0-632-00743-5, B 1083-4). Mosby.

Clark, Bryant R. Rains in Meadow Valley. 1979. 8.50 (ISBN 0-682-49329-5). Exposition Pr FL.

Clark, Buddy & Davis, Craig. Alone, Unarmed, but Safe! An Illustrated Guide to Judo Defense. (Illus.). 128p. 1981. 8.00 (ISBN 0-682-49712-6); pap. 5.00 (ISBN 0-682-49711-8). Exposition Pr FL.

Clark, Burton R. Academic Power in Italy: Bureaucracy & Oligarchy in National University System. LC 77-4010. (Illus.). 1977. lib. bdg. 15.00x (ISBN 0-226-10847-3). U of Chicago Pr.

--Adult Education in Transition: A Study of Institutional Insecurity. Zuckerman, Harriet & Merton, Robert K., eds. LC 79-8982. (Dissertations on Sociology). 1980. lib. bdg. 16.00x (ISBN 0-405-12957-2). Ayer Co Pubs.

--The Higher Education System: Academic Organization in Cross-National Perspective. LC 82-13521. 1983. text ed. 27.50x (ISBN 0-520-04841-5). U of Cal Pr.

Clark, Burton R., ed. Perspectives on Higher Education: Eight Disciplinary & Comparative Views. LC 83-24342. 350p. 1984. text ed. 28.50x (ISBN 0-520-05151-3). U of Cal pr.

Clark, C. Decoying the Yanks. LC 83-9138. (Civil War Ser.). (gr. 7 up). 1984. lib. bdg. 19.94 (ISBN 0-8094-4725-8, Pub. by Time-Life). Silver.

--Dickens' London. 59.95 (ISBN 0-8490-0029-7). Gordon Pr.

--Shakespeare & Psychology. (Studies in Shakespeare: No. 24). 1981. lib. bdg. 48.95x (ISBN 0-8383-2143-7). Haskell.

--Shakespeare & the Supernatural. LC 72-92957. (Studies in Shakespeare, No. 24). 1970. Repr. of 1931 ed. lib. bdg. 49.95x (ISBN 0-8383-0966-6). Haskell.

--The Shakespeare Key. 59.95 (ISBN 0-8490-1036-5). Gordon Pr.

Clark, C., jt. auth. see Clark, M. Cowden.

Clark, C. E., jt. ed. see Bruccoli, Matthew J.

Clark, C. E. Frazer, ed. Nathaniel Hawthorne Journal. Incl. 1973. 25.00 (ISBN 0-910972-50-8); 1974. 25.00 (ISBN 0-910972-39-7); 1976. 25.00 (ISBN 0-910972-60-5). Bruccoli.

Clark, C. E. Frazer, Jr., ed. Hawthorne at Auction 1894-1971. LC 70-38939. (A Bruccoli Clark Book, Authors at Auction Ser.). 490p. 1972. 44.00x (ISBN 0-8103-0919-X). Gale.

Clark, C. E. Frazer, Jr., jt. ed. see Bruccoli, Matthew J.

Clark, C. E., Jr., ed. Nathaniel Hawthorne Journal, Nineteen Seventy-Seven. (Illus.). 1980. 64.00x (ISBN 0-8103-0926-2, Bruccoli Clark Bk.). Gale.

Clark, C. E., Jr. & Bruccoli, Matthew J., eds. Pages: The World of Books, Writers & Writing, Vol. 1. LC 76-20369. (Illus.). 1976. 34.00x (ISBN 0-8103-0925-4). Gale.

Clark, C. E., Jr., jt. ed. see Bruccoli, Matthew J.

Clark, C. Frazer, Jr. Nathaniel Hawthorne: A Descriptive Bibliography. LC 76-50885. (Pittsburgh Series in Bibliography). 1978. 60.00x (ISBN 0-8229-3343-8). U of Pittsburgh Pr.

Clark, C. Frazer, Jr., ed. Nathaniel Hawthorne Journal Nineteen Seventy-Eight. (Bruccoli Clark Bk.). (Illus.). 400p. 1984. 64.00x (ISBN 0-8103-0929-7). Gale.

Clark, C. R. Florida Trade Tokens. (Illus.). 1980. 25.00 (ISBN 0-912317-04-3). World Exo.

Clark, C. Scott, jt. auth. see Avio, K. L.

Clark, C. W. Bioeconomic Modelling & Fisheries Management. 352p. 1985. 47.95 (ISBN 0-471-87394-2). Wiley.

Clark, C. Wells, ed. see Bigl, Joseph H., et al.

Clark, Cal & Farlow, Robert L. Comparative Patterns of Foreign Policy & Trade: The Communist Balkans & Politics. LC 76-9078. (Studies in East European & Soviet Planning, Development & Trade: No. 23). (Illus.). 1976. pap. 6.00 (ISBN 0-89249-016-0). Intl Development.

Clark, Campbell. Raiders of the Lost Ark: A Novelization Adapted from the Screenplay by Lawrence Kasden. 192p. 1981. 6.95 (ISBN 0-345-28480-1); pap. 2.50 (ISBN 0-345-29490-4). Ballantine.

Clark, Candace, jt. ed. see Robboy, Howard.

Clark, Carl D. & Essary, Loris. Semi-Constructs of the Secretaire De Registre. 1980. pap. 2.00 (ISBN 0-918406-07-2). Future Pr.

Clark, Carl R. see Clark, Barbara R.

Clark, Carol. American Impressionist & Realist Paintings & Drawings from the William Marshall Fuller Collection. LC 78-54779. (Illus.). 56p. 1978. pap. 8.95 (ISBN 0-88360-029-3). Amon Carter.

--Charles M. Russell. pap. 12.50 (ISBN 0-88360-046-3, Dist. by Univ. of Texas Pr.). Amon Carter.

--Thomas Moran: Watercolors of the American West. LC 80-13459. (Illus.). 192p. 1980. 25.00 (ISBN 0-292-75059-5). U of Tex Pr.

Clark, Carol, jt. auth. see Kownacki, Mary L.

Clark, Carol, jt. auth. see Kownacki, Mary Lou.

Clark, Carol, ed. Charles M. Russell. (Illus.). 1984. 12.50 (ISBN 0-88360-046-3). Amon Carter.

--A Legacy Remembered: The Relief Society Magazine. (Illus.). 1982. 6.95 (ISBN 0-87747-926-7). Deseret Bk.

Clark, Carol L. A Citizen's Directory: Who to Contact to Get Things Done. 320p. 1984. pap. 8.95 (ISBN 0-87196-849-5). Facts on File.

--The Red Tape Cutter's Handbook: A Working Tool for Dealing with Bureaucracies. 328p. 1982. 17.95x (ISBN 0-87196-389-2). Facts on File.

Clark, Carol R., jt. auth. see Schallert, William F.

Clark, Carolyn & Shea, Carole A. Management in Nursing. (Illus.). 1979. text ed. 29.00 (ISBN 0-07-011135-9). McGraw.

Clark, Carolyn C. Assertive Skills for Nurses. LC 78-53071. 236p. 1978. pap. text ed. 24.00 (ISBN 0-913654-46-9). Aspen Systems.

--Classroom Skills for Nurse Educators. LC 78-4486. (Teaching of Nursing Ser.: Vol. 4). 1978. pap. 18.95 (ISBN 0-8261-2431-3). Springer Pub.

--Enhancing Wellness. 1981. text ed. 29.95 (ISBN 0-8261-2950-1); pap. text ed. 18.95 (ISBN 0-8261-2951-X). Springer Pub.

--The Nurse As Continuing Educator. LC 79-18283. (Teaching of Nursing Ser.: Vol. 6). 1979. pap. text ed. 19.95 (ISBN 0-8261-2791-6). Springer Pub.

--The Nurse As Group Leader. LC 77-7778. (Teaching of Nursing Ser.: Vol. 3). 1977. 14.95 (ISBN 0-8261-2331-7). Springer Pub.

Clark, Catherine H. & Widutis, Florence, eds. Books for New Age Children & Youth. (ps-9). 1977. pap. 2.95 (ISBN 0-930296-00-1). Beautiful Day.

Clark, Cecil. Tales of B. C. Provincial Police. (Illus.). 184p. 9.95 (ISBN 0-88826-029-6). Superior Pub.

Clark, Cecily, jt. auth. see Fell, Christine.

Clark, Cecily, tr. see Bourcier, Georges.

Clark, Champ. Flood. (Planet Earth Ser.). 1982. 14.95 (ISBN 0-8094-4308-2). Time-Life.

--Gettysburg. LC 85-1046. (Civil War Ser.). 1985. lib. bdg. 19.94 (ISBN 0-8094-4757-6, Pub. by Time-Life). Silver.

--My Quarter Century of American Politics, 2 Vols in 1. LC 20-4643. 1969. Repr. of 1920 ed. 44.00 (ISBN 0-527-17640-0). Kraus Repr.

Clark, Charles. Publishing Agreements: A Book of Precedents. 176p. 1980. text ed. 19.50x (ISBN 0-04-655015-1). Allen Unwin.

Clark, Charles A. Directory of Scholarships. 250p. pap. 15.00x (ISBN 0-686-31596-0). Adv Accept.

Clark, Charles A., III & Clark, Patricia Z. Financial Aid for Student Athletes. rev ed. 180p. (gr. 10-12). 1984. pap. text ed. 7.00X (ISBN 0-317-14167-8). AAP Pub.

Clark, Charles B. When Hot Springs Was a Pup. (Illus.). 1976. pap. 7.95x (ISBN 0-917624-25-4). Lame Johnny.

Clark, Charles E. The Eastern Frontier: The Settlement of Northern New England, 1610-1763. LC 82-40477. (Illus.). 464p. 1983. pap. 15.00x (ISBN 0-87451-252-2). U Pr of New Eng.

--Maine: A History. (State & the Nation Ser.). (Illus.). 1977. 14.95 (ISBN 0-393-05653-8, Co-Pub by AASLH). Norton.

--My Fifty Years in the Navy. (Classics of Naval Literature Ser.). (Illus.). 416p. 1984. Repr. of 1917 ed. 16.95 (ISBN 0-87021-401-2). Naval Inst Pr.

Clark, Charles E. & Eastman, Charles W. The Portsmouth Project: A Documentary View of Portsmouth, 1740-1760. LC 74-18701. (Illus.). 100p. 1974. pap. 10.00x (ISBN 0-912274-46-8). NH Pub Co.

Clark, Charles G. Color Atlas of Upper Gastrointestinal Surgery. 200p. (Orig.). 1983. 110.00 (ISBN 0-87489-358-5). Med Economics.

Clark, Charles H. Out of the Hurly-Burly; or, Life in an Odd Corner. LC 70-158228. (Illus.). Repr. of 1874 ed. 34.50 (ISBN 0-404-00295-1). AMS Pr.

--Random Shots. facsimile ed. LC 70-164557. (American Fiction Reprint Ser). Repr. of 1879 ed. 24.50 (ISBN 0-8369-7033-0). Ayer Co Pubs.

Clark, Charles L., ed. A Guide to Theories of Economic Development: Cross-National Tests. LC 82-82662. (Theoretical Information Control Guides Ser.). 329p. (Orig.). 1982. 60.00 (ISBN 0-87536-734-8). HRAFP.

Clark, Charles M. History of Australia, Vol. I. 1971. 28.50x (ISBN 0-522-84008-6, Pub. by Melbourne U Pr Australia); pap. 17.50 (ISBN 0-522-84165-1, Pub. by Melbourne U Pr Australia). Intl Spec Bk.

--History of Australia, Vol. II. LC 63-5969. (Illus.). 1975. 28.50x (ISBN 0-522-83821-9, Pub. by Melbourne U Pr Australia); pap. 17.50x (ISBN 0-522-84166-X, Pub. by Melbourne U Pr Australia). Intl Spec Bk.

--History of Australia, Vol. IV. 1977. 28.50x (ISBN 0-522-84147-3, Pub. by Melbourne U Pr Australia); pap. 17.50x (ISBN 0-522-84144-9, Pub. by Melborne U Pr Australia). Intl Spec Bk.

--A History of Australia: The Beginning of Australian Civilization, Vol. III. 1973. 28.50x (ISBN 0-522-84054-X, Pub. by Melbourne U Pr Australia); pap. 17.50x (ISBN 0-522-84154-6, Pub. by Melbourne U Pr Australia). Intl Spec Bk.

Clark, Charles T. & Jordan, Eleanor W. Introduction to Business & Economic Statistics. 7th ed. 1985. 21.95 (ISBN 0-538-13260-4, M26). SW Pub.

Clark, Charles T. & Schkade, Lawrence L. Statistical Analysis for Administrative Decisions. 1983. text ed. 26.50 (ISBN 0-538-13280-9, M28). SW Pub.

Clark, Charles U. United Roumania. LC 79-135799. (Eastern Europe Collection Ser). 1970. Repr. of 1932 ed. 25.50 (ISBN 0-405-02741-9). Ayer Co Pubs.

Clark, Charlie, III. Sexual Geometry. Sanfilippo, Rose E., ed. LC 82-91125. 112p. 1983. 8.95 (ISBN 0-9609808-0-6). New Pen Pub Co.

Clark, Charlotte & Davies, Cornelia Oakes. Standard Rebus Glossary. 95p. 1974. pap. text ed. 7.25 (ISBN 0-913476-41-2). Am Guidance.

Clark, Charlotte, jt. auth. see Woodcock, Richard.

Clark, Charlotte, jt. auth. see Woodstock, Richard.

Clark, Chloe, jt. auth. see Brewer, Henry.

Clark, Chris & Rush, Sheila. How to Get Along with Black People: A Handbook for White Folks & Some Black Folks Too. LC 73-162960. 156p. 1971. 8.95 (ISBN 0-89388-018-3); pap. 5.95. Okpaku Communications.

Clark, Chris L. & Asquith, Stewart. Social Work & Social Philosophy: A Guide for Practice. 160p. 1985. 22.95x (ISBN 0-7102-0610-0); pap. 12.95x (ISBN 0-7100-9630-5). Routledge & Kegan.

Clark, Christine L. The Make-It-Yourself Shoe Book. 1977. pap. 5.95 (ISBN 0-394-73303-7). Knopf.

Clark, Clara E. A Tangram Diary. (Illus.). 64p. (Orig.). (gr. 3-6). 1980. pap. 6.95 (ISBN 0-934734-05-4). Construct Educ.

Clark, Clara E. & Sternberg, Betty J. Math in Stride, Bk. 1. (Illus.). 166p. (Orig.). (gr. k-2). 1980. pap. 5.95 (ISBN 0-934734-06-2); tchr's. manual 19.95 (ISBN 0-934734-12-7). Construct Educ.

--Math in Stride, Bk. 2. (Illus.). 203p. (Orig.). (gr. 1-3). 1980. pap. 6.50 (ISBN 0-934734-07-0); tchr's. manual 19.95 (ISBN 0-934734-13-5). Construct Educ.

--Math in Stride, Bk. 3. (Illus.). 219p. (Orig.). (gr. 2-4). 1980. pap. 6.95 (ISBN 0-934734-08-9). Construct Educ.

Clark, Clifford E., Jr. Henry Ward Beecher: Spokesman for a Middle-Class America. LC 78-1721. 288p. 1978. 22.50x (ISBN 0-252-00608-9). U of Ill Pr.

Clark, Colette, ed. Home at Grasmere: Extracts from the Journal of Dorothy Wordsworth & from the Poems of William Wordsworth. (English Library). 1979. pap. 4.95 (ISBN 0-14-043136-5). Penguin.

Clark, Colin. Conditions of Economic Progress. LC 82-48297. (The World Economy Ser.). 735p. 1982. lib. bdg. 88.00 (ISBN 0-8240-5352-4). Garland Pub.

--Elementary Mathematical Analysis. 2nd ed. LC 81-4759. 256p. 1981. text ed. write for info. (ISBN 0-534-98018-X). Wadsworth Pub.

--The Myth of Over-Population. 133p. 1975. pap. 3.50 (ISBN 0-912414-26-X). Lumen Christi.

--National Income & Outlay. 304p. 1965. Repr. 30.00x (ISBN 0-7146-1216-2, F Cass Co). Biblio Dist.

--National Income Nineteen Twenty-Four to Nineteen Thirty-One. LC 67-33571. Repr. of 1932 ed. 25.00x (ISBN 0-678-05161-5). Kelley.

--National Income, 1924-1931. 180p. 1965. Repr. 30.00x (ISBN 0-7146-1215-4, F Cass Co). Biblio Dist.

--Population. 30p. 1974. pap. 0.50 (ISBN 0-912414-19-7). Lumen Christi.

--Regional & Urban Location. LC 81-21510. 1982. 32.50x (ISBN 0-312-66903-8). St Martin.

Clark, Colin G., ed. see Jones, George T.

Clark, Colin W. Mathematical Bioeconomics: The Optimal Management of Renewable Resources. LC 76-16473. (Pure & Applied Mathematics Ser.). 352p. 1976. 39.95x (ISBN 0-471-15856-9, Pub. by Wiley-Interscience). Wiley.

Clark, Connie, jt. auth. see Hayward, Mary.

Clark, Cumberland. Astronomy in the Poets. LC 72-191653. lib. bdg. 17.50 (ISBN 0-8414-3038-1). Folcroft.

--Charles Dickens & Clarkson Stanfield. 1918. lib. bdg. 10.00 (ISBN 0-8414-3522-7). Folcroft.

--Charles Dickens & the Begging-Letter Writer. LC 72-3492. (Studies in Dickens, No. 52). 1972. Repr. of 1923 ed. lib. bdg. 22.95x (ISBN 0-8383-1532-1). Haskell.

--Charles Dickens & the Yorkshire Schools: With His Letter to Mrs. Hall. 1978. Repr. of 1918 ed. lib. bdg. 10.00 (ISBN 0-8495-0902-5). Arden Lib.

--Charles Dickens & the Yorkshire Schools, with His Letter to Mrs. Hall. LC 75-20086. 1975. Repr. of 1918 ed. lib. bdg. 15.00 (ISBN 0-8414-3627-4). Folcroft.

--Dickens' London. LC 74-12164. 1974. Repr. of 1923 ed. lib. bdg. 18.50 (ISBN 0-8414-3521-9). Folcroft.

--Dickens' London. LC 73-9522. (Studies in Dickens, No. 52). 1973. Repr. of 1923 ed. lib. bdg. 29.95x (ISBN 0-8383-1714-6). Haskell.

--The Dogs in Dickens. LC 73-9642. (Studies in Dickens, No. 52). 1973. Repr. of 1926 ed. lib. bdg. 40.95x (ISBN 0-8383-1713-8). Haskell.

--The Eternal Shakespeare. 1978. Repr. of 1930 ed. lib. bdg. 30.00 (ISBN 0-8495-0757-X). Arden Lib.

--Shakespeare & Costume. LC 78-17589. 1937. lib. bdg. 32.50 (ISBN 0-8414-0897-1). Folcroft.

--Shakespeare & Costume. 1979. Repr. of 1937 ed. lib. bdg. 35.00 (ISBN 0-8482-7570-5). Norwood Edns.

--Shakespeare & Dickens. LC 73-9794. (Studies in Dickens, No. 52). 1973. Repr. of 1918 ed. lib. bdg. 29.95x (ISBN 0-8383-1703-0). Haskell.

--Shakespeare & National Character. LC 76-181002. (Studies in Shakespeare, No. 24). 308p. 1972. Repr. of 1932 ed. lib. bdg. 49.95x (ISBN 0-8383-1371-X). Haskell.

--Shakespeare & Psychology. LC 76-10781. 1936. lib. bdg. 27.00 (ISBN 0-8414-3499-9). Folcroft.

--Shakespeare & Science. LC 79-92956. (Studies in Shakespeare, No. 24). 1970. Repr. of 1929 ed. lib. bdg. 39.95x (ISBN 0-8383-0965-8). Haskell.

--Shakespeare & the Supernatural. LC 72-186985. 1931. lib. bdg. 37.50 (ISBN 0-8414-0341-4). Folcroft.

--Shakespeare & the Supernatural. 346p. Repr. of 1931 ed. 29.00 (ISBN 0-403-04266-6). Somerset Pub.

--The Story of a Great Friendship: Charles Dickens & Clarkson Stanfield. 1978. Repr. of 1918 ed. lib. bdg. 10.00 (ISBN 0-8495-0736-7). Arden Lib.

--The Story of a Great Friendship: Charles Dickens & Clarkson Stanfield. LC 73-18187. Repr. of 1918 ed. lib. bdg. 8.50 (ISBN 0-8414-3522-7). Folcroft.

--A Study of Hamlet. LC 77-6817. 1926. lib. bdg. 22.50 (ISBN 0-8414-1801-2). Folcroft.

--A Study of Macbeth. LC 77-10885. 1977. Repr. lib. bdg. 27.50 (ISBN 0-8414-1839-X). Folcroft.

--A Study of Shakespeare's Henry VIII. LC 78-7503. 1978. Repr. of 1931 ed. lib. bdg. 27.50 (ISBN 0-8414-0059-8). Folcroft.

--A Study of the Merchant of Venice. LC 76-22473. 1927. lib. bdg. 30.00 (ISBN 0-8414-3629-0). Folcroft.

Clark, Cynthia, jt. auth. see Schneller, Sibyl.

Clark, Cynthia & Chadwick, Donnacompiled by. Clinically Adapted Instruments for the Multiply Handicapped: A Sourcebook. rev. ed. (Illus.). 1980. 14.50 (ISBN 0-918812-13-5). MMB Music.

Clark, Cyril D., tr. see Su Shih.

Clark, D. Help, Hospitals & the Handicapped. 126p. 1984. pap. text ed. 23.50x (ISBN 0-08-030402-8, Pub. by Aberdeen U Scotland); pap. text ed. 13.00x (ISBN 0-08-030377-3, Pub. by Aberdeen U Scotland). Humanities.

Clark, D. & Unwin, K. Information Services in Rural Areas: Prospects for Telecommunications Access. 122p. 1980. 25.00x (ISBN 0-86094-058-6, Pub. by GEO Abstracts England). State Mutual Bk.

Clark, D. C. Bartending Made Simple. (Illus.). 65p. (Orig.). spiral bound 4.50 (ISBN 0-940144-00-X). Self-Motiv Careers.

Clark, D. Cecil. Using Instructional Objectives in Teaching. 168p. 1972. pap. 8.25x (ISBN 0-673-07620-2). Scott F.

Clark, D. H. & Stephenson, F. R., eds. Historical Supernovae. LC 76-44364. 1977. text ed. 31.00 (ISBN 0-08-020914-9); pap. text ed. 13.00 (ISBN 0-08-021639-0). Pergamon.

Clark, D. J. & Mundhenk, N. Translator's Handbook on the Books of Obadiah & Micah. LC 82-8481. (Helps for Translators Ser.). 208p. 1982. pap. 3.30x (ISBN 0-8267-0129-9, 08567). Am Bible.

Clark, D. M., jt. auth. see Krauss, P. H.

Clark, D. P. & Ashall, C. Field Studies on the Australian Plague in the Channel Country of Queensland. 1969. 40.00x (ISBN 0-85135-047-X, Pub. by Centre Overseas Research). State Mutual Bk.

Clark, D. S., jt. auth. see Kushner, H. J.

Clark, D. W., ed. see Finley, James B.

Clark, Dana. Classroom Notes for Fundamentals of Computer Science. 256p. 1981. pap. text ed. 8.95 (ISBN 0-8403-2395-6). Kendall-Hunt.

Clark, Daniel. Proofs of the Corruption of Gen. James Wilkinson & of His Connexion with Aaron Burr, with a Full Refutation of His Slanderous Allegations in Relation to the Character of the Principle Witness Against Him. LC 70-146383. (First American Frontier Ser.). 1971. Repr. of 1809 ed. 23.50 (ISBN 0-405-02834-2). Ayer Co Pubs.

--Proofs of the Corruption of General James Wilkinson, & of His Connexion with Aaron Burr. facs. ed. LC 70-117868. (Select Bibliographies Reprint Ser). 1809. 24.50 (ISBN 0-8369-5321-5). Ayer Co Pubs.

Clark, David. Between Pulpit & Pew: Folk Religion in a North Yorkshire Fishing Village. LC 81-18166. (Illus.). 216p. 1982. 32.50 (ISBN 0-521-24071-9). Cambridge U Pr.

--Plane & Geodetic Surveying for Engineers, 2 vols. 6th rev. ed. Incl. Vol. 1. Plane Surveying. xvii, 693p. 35.00 (ISBN 0-8044-4148-0); Vol. 2. Higher Surveying. xv, 582p. (Appendix on Mechanical Computing by L. J. Comrie). 35.00 (ISBN 0-8044-4149-9). Ungar.

--Post-Industrial America: A Geographic Perspective. 192p. (Orig.). 1985. text ed. 29.95x (ISBN 0-416-38250-9, 9308); pap. text ed. 11.95x (ISBN 0-416-38260-6, 9307). Methuen Inc.

--The Quest for SS433. 224p. 1985. 15.95 (ISBN 0-670-80388-X). Viking.

--Urban Geography: An Introductory Guide. 256p. 1983. text ed. 24.00x (ISBN 0-8018-2965-8); pap. text ed. 8.95x (ISBN 0-8018-2966-6). Johns Hopkins.

Clark, David, jt. auth. see Burgoyne, Jacqueline.

Clark, David A. The Giant Joke Book. LC 80-2242. (Doubleday Fatback Ser.). (Illus.). 408p. (Orig.). (gr. 6-8). 1981. pap. 4.95 (ISBN 0-385-14721-X, BFYR). Doubleday.

Clark, David E., et al. Corrosion of Glass. LC 79-50921. 75p. 1979. 24.95 (ISBN 0-911993-18-5). Ashlee Pub Co.

Clark, David G., et al, eds. Mass Media & the Law. LC 76-115653. 478p. 1970. 29.50 (ISBN 0-471-15851-8, Pub. by Wiley). Krieger.

Clark, David H. Superstars: How Stellar Explosions Shape the Destiny of Our Universes. (Illus.). 224p. 1984. 17.95. McGraw.

Clark, David H., jt. auth. see Stephenson, F. Richard.

Clark, David L. Brockden Brown & the Rights of Women. LC 73-542. 1912. lib. bdg. 10.00 (ISBN 0-8414-1546-3). Folcroft.

--Charles Brockden Brown: Pioneer Voice of America. LC 75-181909. (BCL Ser.). Repr. of 1952 ed. 22.50 (ISBN 0-404-01548-4). AMS Pr.

--L. A. on Foot. (Illus.). 1985. pap. 4.95 (ISBN 0-913290-03-3). Camaro Pub.

--Stratigraphy & Glacial-Marine Sediments of the Amerasian Basin, Central Artic Ocean. LC 80-65270. (Geological Society of America Ser.: No. 181). pap. 23.80 (ISBN 0-317-27883-5, 2025453). Bks Demand UMI.

Clark, David L., ed. Conodont Biofacies & Provincialism. (Special Paper Ser.: No. 196). (Illus.). 1984. 36.00 (ISBN 0-8137-2196-2). Geol Soc.

--Shelley's Prose. LC 54-6517. 1954. 17.50 (ISBN 0-8263-0015-4). Lib Soc Sci.

Clark, David L., et al. Stratigraphy & Glacial-Marine Sediments of the Amerasian Basin,Central Arctic Ocean. LC 80-65270. (Special Paper: No. 181). (Illus., Orig.). 1980. pap. 13.00 (ISBN 0-8137-2181-4). Geol Soc.

Clark, David R. Computers for Image-Making. (Audio-Visual Media for Education & Research Ser.: Vol. 2). (Illus.). 166p. 1980. 34.00 (ISBN 0-08-024058-5); pap. 17.00 (ISBN 0-08-024059-3). Pergamon.

--Critical Essays on Hart Crane. (Critical Essays on American Literature Ser.). 1982. lib. bdg. 30.00 (ISBN 0-8161-8380-5, Twayne). G K Hall.

--That Black Day: The Manuscripts of 'Crazy Jane on the Day of Judgement' (New Years Papers Ser.: No. XVIII). (Illus.). 56p. 1980. pap. text ed. 12.25x (ISBN 0-85105-355-6, Dolmen Pr). Humanities.

--Yeats at Songs & Choruses. LC 81-16096. (Illus.). 308p. 1983. lib. bdg. 30.00x (ISBN 0-87023-358-0). U of Mass Pr.

Clark, David R., et al. Druid Craft: The Writing of "The Shadowy Waters". LC 74-103474. 376p. 1971. 25.00x (ISBN 0-87023-068-9). U of Mass Pr.

Clark, David S., jt. auth. see Merryman, John H.

Clark, David S., jt. auth. see Sharpe, Anthony N.

Clark, David S., compiled by. Index to Maps of the American Revolution in Books & Periodicals. LC 74-7543. (Illus., Orig.). 1974. lib. bdg. 35.00 (ISBN 0-8371-7582-8, DAR/). Greenwood.

Clark, David T. & Feast, W. J., eds. Polymer Surfaces. LC 77-17426. (Illus.). pap. 114.30 (ISBN 0-317-09334-7, 2022101). Bks Demand UMI.

Clark, Deborah B. & Bradford, Debra. Pressure Cycled Ventilators. (Illus.). 208p. 1984. text ed. 24.95 (ISBN 0-13-699090-8); pap. text ed. 19.95 (ISBN 0-13-699082-7). P-H.

Clark, Dennis. The Irish in Philadelphia: Ten Generations of Urban Experience. LC 72-95884. 264p. 1974. 29.95 (ISBN 0-87722-057-3). Temple U Pr.

--The Irish in Philadelphia: Ten Generations of Urban Experience. 246p. 1982. pap. 9.95x (ISBN 0-87722-227-4). Temple U Pr.

--The Irish Relations: Trials of an Immigrant Tradition. LC 81-65293. 356p. 1982. 24.50 (ISBN 0-8386-3083-9). Fairleigh Dickinson.

Clark, Dennis E. Jesus Christ, His Life & Teaching. 324p. pap. 4.95 (ISBN 0-89191-117-0, 23341). Cook.

Clark, Dennis J. Irish Blood: Northern Ireland and the American Conscience. LC 76-21808. (National University Publications Series in American Studies). 1977. 11.00x (ISBN 0-8046-9163-0, Pub. by Kennikat). Assoc Faculty Pr.

Clark, Dennis J., ed. Philadelphia: Seventeen Seventy-Six to Two Thousand Seventy-Six, a Three Hundred Year View. (Interdisciplinary Urban Ser.). 130p. 1975. 13.95x (ISBN 0-8046-9141-X, Pub. by Kennikat). Assoc Faculty Pr.

Clark, Diana, ed. see Smith, Franci & Coleman, Susan.

Clark, Diane. Diane Clark's Microwave Cookbook: Gourmet Meals with Fast, Easy, Preparation. Schrader, C., ed. 256p. 1981. 15.50 (ISBN 0-8015-2023-1, 01505-450, Hawthorn). Dutton.

Clark, Diane, jt. auth. see Odom, Mildred.

Clark, Don. Loving Someone Gay. 1978. pap. 4.50 (ISBN 0-451-13742-6, AE2945, Sig). NAL.

Clark, Don & Kadis, Asya. Humanistic Teaching. LC 70-173877. 190p. 1971. pap. text ed. 9.95 (ISBN 0-675-09626-X). Merrill.

Clark, Donald B. Alexander Pope. (English Authors Ser.). 1966. lib. bdg. 15.95 (ISBN 0-8057-1452-9, Twayne). G K Hall.

--Way to Live. 1978. pap. 7.95 (ISBN 0-8403-1915-0). Kendall Hunt.

Clark, Donald C., jt. auth. see Georgiades, William D.

Clark, Donald C., jt. ed. see Thornburg, Hershel D.

Clark, Donald L. John Milton at St. Paul's School: A Study of Ancient Rhetoric in English Renaissance Education. x, 269p. 1964. Repr. of 1948 ed. 19.50 (ISBN 0-208-00148-4, Archon). Shoe String.

--Rhetoric in Greco-Roman Education. LC 77-21723. 1977. Repr. of 1957 ed. lib. bdg. 55.00x (ISBN 0-8371-9790-2, CLRH). Greenwood.

Clark, Donald R., Jr. Ecological Study of the Worm Snake Carphophis Vermis (Kennicott) (Museum Ser.: Vol. 19, No. 2). 110p. 1970. pap. 5.75 (ISBN 0-686-79836-8). U of KS Mus Nat Hist.

Clark, Donald T. & Gottfried, Bert A., eds. University Dictionary of Business & Finance. (Apollo Eds.). 1972. pap. 4.95i (ISBN 0-8152-0143-5, A143). T Y Crowell.

Clark, Donna. Christ People. LC 80-81940. (Illus.). 160p. (Orig.). 1980. pap. 5.95 (ISBN 0-9604636-0-7). New World Cup CA.

Clark, Donna, jt. ed. see Clark, Keith.

Clark, Dora M. Rise of the British Treasury: Colonial Administration in the 18th Century. x, 249p. 1969. Repr. of 1960 ed. 20.00 (ISBN 0-208-00788-1, Archon). Shoe String.

Clark, Dorothy. Shepherd's Pie. (Julia MacRae Blackbird Bks.). (Illus.). 48p. (gr. k-3). 1983. 5.95 (ISBN 0-531-04577-3, MacRae). Watts.

Clark, Dorothy, jt. auth. see Clark, Michael.

Clark, Doug. They Saw the Second Coming: An Explosive Novel About the End of the World! LC 78-71427. 1979. pap. 4.95 (ISBN 0-89081-190-3). Harvest Hse.

Clark, Douglas. Dead Letter: A Masters & Green Mystery. LC 84-48586. 224p. 1985. pap. 3.37i (ISBN 0-317-15865-1, P753, PL). Har-Row.

--Dread & Water. LC 83-48336. 160p. 1984. pap. 2.84i (ISBN 0-06-080688-5, P688, PL). Har-Row.

--The Gimmel Flask. (Murder Ink Ser.: No. 41). (Orig.). 1982. pap. 2.25 (ISBN 0-440-13160-X). Dell.

--Golden Rain. (Murder Ink Ser.: No. 47). 224p. 1982. pap. 2.50 (ISBN 0-440-12932-X). Dell.

--Heberden's Seat. LC 84-47664. 192p. 1985. pap. 3.37i (ISBN 0-06-080724-5, P724, PL). Har-Row.

--The Longest Pleasure. LC 83-48335. 192p. 1984. pap. 2.84 (ISBN 0-06-080689-3, P689, PL). Har-Row.

--The Monday Theory. LC 84-48146. 208p. 1984. pap. 3.37 (ISBN 0-06-080737-7, PL). Har-Row.

--Poacher's Bag. LC 82-48810. 176p. 1983. pap. 2.84i (ISBN 0-06-080643-5, P 643, PL). Har-Row.

--Roast Eggs. LC 82-48811. 176p. 1983. pap. 2.84i (ISBN 0-06-080644-3, P 644, PL). Har-Row.

--Shelf Life. LC 83-47581. 176p. 1983. pap. 2.84i (ISBN 0-06-080675-3, P675, PL). Har-Row.

--Sick to Death. LC 83-47582. 176p. 1983. pap. 2.84i (ISBN 0-06-080676-1, P676, PL). Har-Row.

--Table D'Hote. LC 84-47665. 208p. 1985. pap. 3.37i (ISBN 0-06-080723-7, P723, PL). Har-Row.

--Vicious Circle: A Masters & Green Mystery. LC 85-42559. 208p. 1985. pap. 3.37i (ISBN 0-06-080778-4, P 778, PL). Har-Row.

Clark, Douglas A. Aerospace Historian: Cumulative Index by Author, Book Review, Title & Subject 1974-1983. 122p. 1985. pap. text ed. 17.50 (ISBN 0-89126-124-9). MA-AH Pub.

Clark, Douglas L. Preventing Crime in Small Business. Ramey, Emmett, ed. (Successful Business Library). 220p. 1984. 3-ring binder 32.95 (ISBN 0-916378-42-X, Oasis Pr). PSI Res.

--Starting a Successful Business on the West Coast. 208p. Date not set. pap. 12.95 (ISBN 0-317-30527-1, 9513, Pub. by Intl Self-Counsel Pr). TAB Bks.
--Starting a Successul Business on the West Coast. 194p. (Orig.). 1982. pap. 12.95 (ISBN 0-88908-910-8). Self Counsel Pr.
Clark, Duncan L. Public Policy & Political Institutions: Defense & Foreign Policy. LC 85-12705. Date not set. price not set (ISBN 0-89232-374-4). Jai Pr.
Clark, Duncan W. & Macmahon, Brian, eds. Preventive & Community Medicine. 2nd ed. 1981. 32.50 (ISBN 0-316-14596-3). Little.
Clark, Dymphna, jt. ed. see Sack, Peter.
Clark, Dymphna, jt. ed. see Sack, Peter G.
Clark, E. C. An Analysis of Criminal Liability. xii, 115p. 1983. Repr. of 1880 ed. lib. bdg. 20.00x (ISBN 0-8377-0446-4). Rothman.
--Practical Jurisprudence: A Comment on Austin. xii, 403p. 1980. Repr. of 1883 ed. lib. bdg. 30.00x (ISBN 0-8377-0427-8). Rothman.
Clark, E. Culpepper. Francis Warrington Dawson & the Politics of Restoration: South Carolina, Eighteen Seventy-Four to Eighteen Eighty-Nine. LC 79-27884. (Illus.). 256p. 1980. 19.95 (ISBN 0-8173-0039-2). U of Ala Pr.
Clark, E. F. & De Winter, Francis, eds. The Control of Solar Energy Systems for Heating & Cooling. (International Solar Energy Society, American Section, Workshops Ser.). 1978. pap. text ed. 36.00x (ISBN 0-89553-017-1). Am Solar Energy.
Clark, Ed. A New Beginning. 135p. 1980. 5.95 (ISBN 0-89803-047-1). Green Hill.
Clark, Edie, ed. The Forgotten Arts, Bk. 4. LC 75-10770. (Forgotten Arts Ser.). (Illus.). 64p. (Orig.). 1979. pap. 4.95 (ISBN 0-911658-95-5). Yankee Bks.
Clark, Edith. My Mother Who Fathered Me: A Study of the Family in the Selected Communities in Jamaica. 1976. pap. text ed. 9.95x (ISBN 0-04-573010-5). Allen Unwin.
Clark, Edna M. Ohio Art & Artists. LC 74-13860. xvi, 509p. 1975. Repr. of 1932 ed. 65.00x (ISBN 0-8103-4058-5). Gale.
Clark, Edward W., jt. ed. see Vaughan, Alden T.
Clark, Edwin C. History of Roman Private Law, 3 vols in 4. Incl. Vol. 1. Source. 168p; Vol. 2. Jurisprudence, 2 vols. 1234p; Vol. 3. Regal. 634p. LC 64-13392. 2036p. 1906. 50.00x set (ISBN 0-8196-0146-2). Biblo.
Clark, Edwin H., II, et al. Eroding Soils: The Off-Farm Impacts. LC 85-9619. (Illus.). 252p. (Orig.). 1985. pap. 15.00 (ISBN 0-89164-086-X). Conservation Foun.
Clark, Eleanor. The Bitter Box. LC 76-11510. (BCL Ser.: No. II). Repr. of 1946 ed. 23.50 (ISBN 0-404-15279-1). AMS Pr.
--Eyes, Etc. 1979. pap. 1.95 (ISBN 0-671-82516-X). PB.
--The Oysters of Locmariaquer. LC 77-82670. (Illus.). 1978. pap. 3.95 (ISBN 0-226-10763-9, P752, Phoen). U of Chicago Pr.
--Plate Collecting: A Guide to a Fascinating Hobby. (Illus.). 1977. 17.95 (ISBN 0-8065-0478-1). Citadel Pr.
--Rome & a Villa. enl. ed. LC 74-5979. 384p. 1982. pap. 8.95 (ISBN 0-689-70630-8, 1). Atheneum.
--Tamrart: Thirteen Days in the Sahara. LC 84-51414. (Illus.). 120p. 1984. 15.00 (ISBN 0-913773-15-8). S Wright.
Clark, Elias, jt. auth. see Bittker, Boris.
Clark, Elias, et al. Gratuitous Transfers, Wills Interstate Succession, Trusts, Gifts & Future Interests. 3rd ed. (American Casebook Ser.). 1075p. 1985. text ed. write for info. West Pub.
Clark, Elizabeth & Hatch, Diane. The Golden Bough, the Oaken Cross: AAR Texts & Translations Ser. LC 81-5081. 1981. pap. text ed. 15.95 (ISBN 0-89130-482-7, 010205). Scholars Pr GA.
Clark, Elizabeth & Richardson, Herbert W., eds. Women & Religion: Readings in the Western Tradition from Aeschylus to Mary Daly. LC 76-9975. 1976. pap. 9.57 (ISBN 0-06-061398-X, RD-178, HarpR). Har-Row.
Clark, Elizabeth A. Clement's Use of Aristotle: The Aristotelian Contribution of Clement of Alexandria's Refutation of Gnosticism. LC 77-93913. (Texts & Studies in Religion: Vol. 1). vii, 192p. 1981. Repr. of 1977 ed. text ed. 49.95x (ISBN 0-88946-984-9). E Mellen.
--Jerome, Chrysostom & Friends: Essays & Translations. LC 82-20829. (Studies in Women & Religion: Vol. 2). xi, 270p. 1983. Repr. of 1979 ed. 49.95x (ISBN 0-88946-541-X). E Mellen.
--The Life of Melania the Younger: Introduction, Translation & Commentary. LC 84-20635. (Studies in Women & Religion: Vol. 14). 305p. 1985. 49.95x (ISBN 0-88946-535-5). E Mellen.
--Women in the Early Church. (Message of the Fathers of the Church Ser.: Vol. 13). 15.00 (ISBN 0-89453-353-3); pap. 9.95 (ISBN 0-89453-332-0). M Glazier.
Clark, Elizabeth A. see Shore, Sally R.
Clark, Elizabeth F. & De Winter, Francis, eds. Use of Solar Energy for the Cooling of Buildings. (International Solar Energy Society, American Section, Workshop Ser.). 1978. pap. text ed. 36.00x (ISBN 0-89553-012-0). Am Solar Energy.
Clark, Ella. Guardian Spirit Quest. (Indian Culture Ser.). (gr. 5-12). 1974. pap. 1.95 (ISBN 0-89992-045-4). Coun India Ed.
Clark, Ella, ed. In the Beginning. (gr. 5 up). 1977. 1.95 (ISBN 0-89992-055-1). Coun India Ed.
Clark, Ella E. Indian Legends from the Northern Rockies. (Civilization of the American Indian Ser.: No. 82). (Illus.). 416p. 1977. Repr. of 1966 ed. 17.95 (ISBN 0-8061-0701-4). U of Okla Pr.
--Indian Legends of the Pacific Northwest. (Illus.). (YA) (gr. 9-12). 1953. pap. 5.95 (ISBN 0-520-00243-1, CAL18). U of Cal Pr.
Clark, Ella E. & Edmonds, Margot. Sacagawea of the Lewis & Clark Expedition. LC 78-65466. 1980. 10.95 (ISBN 0-520-03822-3). U of Cal Pr.
--Sacagawea of the Lewis & Clark Expedition. (Illus.). 179p. 1983. pap. 5.95 (ISBN 0-520-05060-6). U of Cal Pr.
Clark, Ellery H., Jr. Boston Red Sox: Seventy-Fifth Anniversary History, 1901-1975. LC 75-17066. 1975. 7.50 (ISBN 0-682-48317-6, Banner). Exposition Pr FL.
--Red Sox Fever. LC 79-88276. 1979. 9.95 (ISBN 0-682-49397-X, Banner). Exposition Pr FL.
--Red Sox Forever. 1977. 7.50 (ISBN 0-682-48867-4, Banner). Exposition Pr FL.
Clark, Elmer T. The Small Sects in America. 11.75 (ISBN 0-8446-1862-4). Peter Smith.
Clark, Elmer T., et al, eds. see Asbury, Francis.
Clark, Emery, illus. Recipes & Reminiscences of New Orleans. (Illus.). 237p. (Orig.). 1971. pap. 6.95 (ISBN 0-9604718-0-4). Old Ursuline.
Clark, Emily. Ingenue among the Lions: The Letters of Emily Clark to Joseph Hergesheimer. Langford, Gerald, ed. 245p. 1965. 13.50x (ISBN 0-292-73274-0). U of Tex Pr.
--Stuffed Peacocks. facsimile ed. LC 75-110181. (Short Story Index Reprint Ser.). 1927. 18.00 (ISBN 0-8369-3332-X). Ayer Co Pubs.
Clark, Eric. China Run. 288p. 1985. 15.95 (ISBN 0-316-14491-6). Little.
Clark, Ernest. Fatal Run. 240p. 1985. pap. 3.50 (ISBN 0-440-11783-6). Dell.
Clark, Erskine. Wrestlin Jacob: A Portrait of Religion in the Old South. LC 78-52453. 1979. pap. 1.99 (ISBN 0-8042-1089-6). John Knox.
Clark, Eunice, tr. see De La Fontaine, Jean & Calder, Alexander.
Clark, Eunice N. Clarks from Pennsylvania & Allied Families from Early 1700s to 1984. (Illus.). 429p. 1984. 35.00x (ISBN 0-9614199-0-3). E N Clark.
Clark, Eva T. Hidden Allusions in Shakespeare's Plays: A Study of the Early Court Revels & Personalities of the Times. 3rd rev. ed. Miller, Ruth L., ed. LC 74-5443. (Illus.). 1974. 32.50x (ISBN 0-8046-1878-X, Pub. by Kennikat). Assoc Faculty Pr.
--Man Who Was Shakespeare. LC 75-113577. Repr. of 1937 ed. 24.00 (ISBN 0-404-01549-2). AMS Pr.
Clark, Evans. Financing the Consumer. LC 75-39239. (Getting & Spending: the Consumer's Dilemma). (Illus.). 1976. Repr. of 1933 ed. 29.00x (ISBN 0-405-08016-6). Ayer Co Pubs.
Clark, Eve V., jt. auth. see Clark, Herbert H.
Clark, Ewen M. & Forbes, J. A. Evaluating Primary Care: Some Experiments in Quality Measurement in an Academic Unit of Primary Medical Care. (Illus.). 235p. 1979. 21.25 (ISBN 0-85664-856-6, Pub. by Croom Helm Ltd). Longwood Pub Group.
Clark, F. Arthur. How to Beat Lonelines. LC 81-68725. 165p. (Orig.). 1981. pap. 9.95 (ISBN 0-941030-05-9). C&G Pub.
Clark, F. E. Corrosion & Encrustation in Water Wells. (Irrigation & Drainage Papers: No. 34). 108p. 1980. pap. 7.50 (ISBN 92-5-100933-3, F2080, FAO). Unipub.
Clark, Fay M. You Will Take It with You. 135p. 1976. pap. 4.95 (ISBN 0-686-12934-2). Hiawatha Pub.
Clark, Felton G. The Control of State-Supported Teacher-Training Programs for Negroes. LC 75-176647. (Columbia University. Teachers College. Contributions to Education: No. 605). Repr. of 1934 ed. 22.50 (ISBN 0-404-55605-1). AMS Pr.
Clark, Ferdinand L. Growing Old in a Mechanized World. Stein, Leon, ed. LC 79-8663. (Growing Old Ser.). (Illus.). 1980. Repr. of 1969 ed. lib. bdg. 14.00x (ISBN 0-405-12780-4). Ayer Co Pubs.
Clark, Fiona. Hats. (Illus.). 96p. 1982. text ed. 13.95x (ISBN 0-7134-3774-X). Drama Bk.
Clark, Floyd B. The Constitutional Doctrines of Justice Harlan. LC 78-63945. (Johns Hopkins University. Studies in the Social Sciences. Thirty-Third Ser. 1915: 4). Repr. of 1915 ed. 14.50 (ISBN 0-404-61202-4). AMS Pr.
--The Constitutional Doctrines of Justice Harlan. LC 74-87560. (Law, Politics & History Ser). 1969. Repr. of 1915 ed. lib. bdg. 29.50 (ISBN 0-306-71391-8). Da Capo.
Clark, Frances. ABC Papers. 32p. (gr. k-6). 1947. pap. text ed. 7.95 (ISBN 0-87487-198-0). Birch Tree Gr.
--Look & Listen, Pt. A. (Frances Clark Library for Piano Students). 48p. (Orig.). (gr. k-6). 1962. pap. text ed. 6.75 (ISBN 0-87487-176-X). Birch Tree Gr.
--Look & Listen, Pt. B. (Frances Clark Library for Piano Students). 48p. (Orig.). (gr. k-12). 1962. pap. text ed. 7.95 (ISBN 0-87487-177-8). Birch Tree Gr.
--Look & Listen, Pt. C. (Frances Clark Library for Piano Students). 48p. (Orig.). (gr. k-12). 1962. pap. text ed. 7.95 (ISBN 0-87487-178-6). Birch Tree Gr.
--Look & Listen, Pt. D. (Frances Clark Library for Piano Students). 48p. (Orig.). (gr. k-12). 1962. pap. text ed. 7.95 (ISBN 0-87487-179-4). Birch Tree Gr.
Clark, Frances & Goss, Louise. Keyboard Musician for the Adult Beginner. 208p. (Orig.). 1980. pap. text ed. 24.95 (ISBN 0-87487-103-4). Birch Tree Gr.
--The Music Tree, 3 pts. Incl. Pt A. 9.95 (ISBN 0-87487-121-2); Pt B. 9.95 (ISBN 0-87487-122-0); Pt C. 9.95 (ISBN 0-87487-123-9). (Frances Clark Library for Piano Students). 1973. Birch Tree Gr.
--The Music Tree: Time to Begin. (Frances Clark Library for Piano Students). 1973. pap. text ed. 9.95 (ISBN 0-87487-120-4). Birch Tree Gr.
--Playtime: Supplementary Music, 3 parts. Incl. Pt A. 5.95 (ISBN 0-87487-137-9); Pt B. 5.95 (ISBN 0-87487-138-7); Pt C. 5.95 (ISBN 0-87487-139-5). (Frances Clark Library for Piano Students). 1976. Birch Tree Gr.
--Teaching the Music Tree: A Handbook for Teachers. (Frances Clark Library for Piano Students). 1973. pap. text ed. 5.95 (ISBN 0-87487-124-7). Birch Tree Gr.
Clark, Frances & Goss, Louise. Write & Play Time, Pt. A. (Frances Clark Library for Piano Students). 64p. (Orig.). (gr. k-6). 1973. pap. text ed. 9.95 (ISBN 0-87487-196-4). Birch Tree Gr.
Clark, Frances & Goss, Louise, eds. Contemporary Piano Literature. Incl. Bk 1. 1961. pap. text ed. 5.95 (ISBN 0-87487-107-7); Bk 2. 1955. pap. text ed. 5.95 (ISBN 0-87487-108-5); Bks 3 & 4. 1957. pap. text ed. 9.95 (ISBN 0-87487-109-3); Bks 5 & 6. pap. text ed. 9.95 (ISBN 0-87487-110-7). (Frances Clark Library for Piano Students Ser.). (Illus.). pap. text ed. Birch Tree Gr.
--Piano Literature of the 17th, 18th, & 19th Centuries. Incl. Bk. 1. 1964. pap. text ed. 5.95 (ISBN 0-87487-125-5); Bk. 2. (Illus.). 1954. pap. text ed. 5.95 (ISBN 0-87487-126-3); Bks. 3, 4a & 4b. (Illus.). 1957. pap. text ed. 9.95 (ISBN 0-87487-127-1); Bks. 5a & 6a. (Illus.). 1974. pap. text ed. 7.95 (ISBN 0-87487-128-X); Bk. 5b. (Illus.). 1957. pap. text ed. 7.95 (ISBN 0-87487-129-8); Bk. 6b. (Illus.). 1956. pap. text ed. 9.95 (ISBN 0-87487-130-1). (Frances Clark Library for Piano Students). pap. text ed. Birch Tree Gr.
--Piano Technic, 6 bks. Incl. Bk. 1. 1954. pap. text ed. 7.95 (ISBN 0-87487-131-X); Bk. 2. 1955. pap. text ed. 7.95 (ISBN 0-87487-132-8); Bk. 3. 1955. pap. text ed. 7.95 (ISBN 0-87487-133-6); Bk. 4. 1960. pap. text ed. 7.95 (ISBN 0-87487-134-4); Bk. 5. 1960. pap. text ed. 7.95 (ISBN 0-87487-135-2); Bk. 6. 1960. pap. text ed. 7.95 (ISBN 0-87487-136-0). (Frances Clark Library for Piano Students). pap. text ed. Birch Tree Gr.
Clark, Frances, ed. see George, Jon.
Clark, Frances, ed. see Kraehenbuehl, David.
Clark, Frances, ed. see Kraehenbuehl, David, et al.
Clark, Frances, et al. Pencil Play, Pts. C & D. (Francis Clark Library for Piano Students). 40p. (Orig.). (gr. k-6). 1962. pap. text ed. 7.95 (ISBN 0-87487-185-9). Birch Tree Gr.
Clark, Francis, ed. see George, Jon & Kraehenbuehl, David.
Clark, Francis, et al. Pencil Play, Pts. A & B. (Frances Clark Library for Piano Students). 56p. (Orig.). (gr. k-6). 1958. pap. text ed. 8.95 (ISBN 0-87487-184-0). Birch Tree Gr.
Clark, Francis E. New Way Around an Old World. LC 70-115519. (Russia Observed, Series I). 1970. Repr. of 1901 ed. 20.00 (ISBN 0-405-03014-2). Ayer Co Pubs.
--Our Italian Fellow Citizens in Their Old Homes & Their New. LC 74-17923. (Italian American Experience Ser). (Illus.). 260p. 1975. Repr. 19.00x (ISBN 0-405-06396-2). Ayer Co Pubs.
Clark, Francis I. The Position of Women in Contemporary France. LC 79-5210. 250p. 1981. Repr. of 1937 ed. 21.50 (ISBN 0-8305-0101-0). Hyperion Conn.
Clark, Frank. Mathematics for Data Processing. 2nd ed. 1982. text ed. 23.95 (ISBN 0-8359-4263-5); instr's. manual avail. (ISBN 0-8359-4264-3). Reston.
Clark, Frank M. Insulating Materials for Design & Engineering Practice. LC 62-17460. pap. 160.00 (ISBN 0-317-10029-7, 2051339). Bks Demand UMI.
Clark, Frank P. Special Effects in Motion Picture: Some Methods for Producing Mechanical Special Effects. (Illus.). 238p. 7.50 (ISBN 0-318-16592-9). Soc Motion Pic & TV Engrs.
--Special Effects in Motion Pictures. (Illus.). 238p. 1982. pap. text ed. 20.00 (ISBN 0-940690-00-4). Soc Motion Pic & TV Engrs.
Clark, Frank P., ed. Technologies in the Laboratory Handling of Motion Picture & Other Long Films. (Illus.). 223p. 1971. 1.00 (ISBN 0-318-16593-7). Soc Motion Pic & TV Engrs.
Clark, Frank W., et al. The Pursuit of Competence in Social Work: Contemporary Issues in the Definition, Assessment, & Improvement of Effectiveness in the Human Services. LC 79-83570. (Social & Behavioral Science Ser.). (Illus.). 1979. text ed. 27.95x (ISBN 0-87589-404-6). Jossey-Bass.
Clark, Fred E. Principles of Marketing. Assael, Henry, ed. LC 78-255. (Century of Marketing Ser.). 1978. Repr. of 1922 ed. lib. bdg. 46.50x (ISBN 0-405-11158-4). Ayer Co Pubs.
Clark, Fred M. Objective Methods for Testing Authenticity & the Study of Ten Doubtful "Comedias" Attributed to Lope de Vega. (Studies in the Romance Languages & Literatures: No. 106). 186p. 1971. pap. 9.50x (ISBN 0-8078-9106-1). U of NC Pr.
Clark, Frederick L. & Pirie, Norman W., eds. Four Thousand Million Mouths. facs. ed. LC 71-117768. (Essay Index Reprint Ser). 1951. 19.00 (ISBN 0-8369-1746-4). Ayer Co Pubs.
Clark, Frederick R., jt. auth. see Nosow, Sigmund.
Clark, G. Housing & Planning in the Countryside. (Geography & Public Policy Research Studies). 159p. 1982. 64.95 (ISBN 0-471-10212-1). Wiley.
Clark, G., jt. auth. see Fletcher, A.
Clark, G. C., jt. ed. see Punt, W.
Clark, G. Kitson. The Critical Historian. Winks, Robin W., ed. Bd. with Guide for Research Students Working on Historical Subjects. LC 83-49175. (History & Historiography Ser.). 267p. 1985. lib. bdg. 25.00 (ISBN 0-8240-6354-6). Garland Pub.
--Making of Victorian England. LC 62-51827. 1967. pap. text ed. 6.95x (ISBN 0-689-70049-0, 104). Atheneum.
--Peel & Conservative Party. 2nd ed. (Illus.). 544p. 1964. 30.00x (ISBN 0-7146-1462-9, F Cass Co). Biblio Dist.
Clark, G. M. Structure of Non-Molecular Solids: A Coordinated Polyhedron Approach. (Illus.). 365p. 1972. 50.00 (ISBN 0-85334-544-9, Pub. by Elsevier Applied Sci England). Elsevier.
Clark, G. Thomas. Winter Twigs of Arkansas: A Field Guide to Deciduous Woody Plants. LC 81-50399. (Illus.). 93p. (Orig.). 1981. pap. 9.95 (ISBN 0-914546-35-X). Rose Pub.
Clark, Gail. Bachelor's Fare. (Orig.). 1981. pap. 1.95 (ISBN 0-671-41276-0). PB.
--The Baroness of Bow Street. 1980. pap. 1.75 (ISBN 0-671-83391-X). PB.
--Dulcie Bligh. 1979. pap. 1.95 (ISBN 0-671-82251-9). PB.
--The Right Honorable Viscount. (Orig.). 1981. pap. 1.95 (ISBN 0-671-41275-2). PB.
Clark, Garth. American Potters: The Work of Twenty Modern Masters. (Illus.). 144p. 1981. 26.50 (ISBN 0-8230-0213-6). Watson-Guptill.
--Michael Cardew. LC 76-9358. (Illus.). 228p. 1976. 27.95 (ISBN 0-87011-277-5). Kodansha.
Clark, Garth R. & Hughto, Margie. A Century of Ceramics in the United States 1879-1979. (Illus.). 1979. pap. 12.95 (ISBN 0-525-47574-5, 01257-380). Dutton.
Clark, Gary. Computers & Young Minds. (Illus.). 1984. pap. 9.95 (ISBN 0-88190-372-8, BO372). Datamost.
Clark, Gary S., jt. auth. see Bray, Grady P.
Clark, Gene E. Let's Talk about You. 109p. 1982. pap. 3.50 (ISBN 0-87516-478-1). De Vorss.
Clark, Geoffrey. What the Moon Said. (Illus.). 128p. 1983. 11.95 (ISBN 0-931704-11-1); pap. 3.95 (ISBN 0-931704-10-3). Story Pr.
Clark, Geoffrey, ed. see Galoppi-Stevens, Nanja, et al.
Clark, Geoffrey A. The Asturian of Cantabria: Early Holocene Hunter-Gatherers in Northern Spain. LC 83-1052. (Anthropological Papers Ser.: No. 41). 171p. 1983. pap. 18.95x monograph (ISBN 0-8165-0800-3). U of Ariz Pr.
Clark, George. Early Modern Europe: From About 1450 to About 1720. 2nd ed. 1966. pap. 4.95x (ISBN 0-19-888004-9). Oxford U Pr.
--War & Society in the Seventeenth Century. LC 85-12551. viii, 157p. 1985. Repr. of 1958 ed. lib. bdg. 35.00 (ISBN 0-313-24948-2, CWSO). Greenwood.
Clark, George & Clark, Margaret P. Primer in Neurological Staining Procedures. (Illus.). 84p. 1971. 12.75x (ISBN 0-398-02176-7). C C Thomas.
Clark, George & Kasten, Frederick H. History of Staining. 3rd ed. (Illus.). 301p. 1983. lib. bdg. 31.00 (ISBN 0-683-01705-5). Williams & Wilkins.
Clark, George, jt. ed. see Barker, Ernest.
Clark, George A., Jr., jt. ed. see Brush, Alan H.
Clark, George B. Basic Properties of Ammonium Nitrate Fuel Oil Explosives (ANFO) Raese, Jon W., ed. LC 81-38436. (Colorado School of Mines Quarterly Ser.: Vol. 76, No. 1). (Illus.). 32p. 1981. pap. text ed. 10.00 (ISBN 0-686-46975-5). Colo Sch Mines.
--Geotechnical Centrifuges for Model Studies & Physical Property Testing of Rock & Rock Structures. Raese, Jon W., ed. LC 81-21614. (Colorado School of Mines Quarterly Ser.: Vol. 76, No. 4). (Illus.). 63p. 1982. pap. text ed. 12.00 (ISBN 0-686-79746-9). Colo Sch Mines.
--Industrial High Explosives: Composition & Calculations for Engineers. Raese, Jon W., ed. LC 80-18063. (CSM Quarterly Ser.: Vol. 75, No. 1). (Illus.). 47p. (Orig.). 1980. pap. 8.00 (ISBN 0-686-63161-7). Colo Sch Mines.

--Principles of Rock Drilling & Bit Wear, Pt. 1. Raese, Jon W., ed. LC 82-1148. (Colorado School of Mines Quarterly Ser.: Vol. 77, No. 1). (Illus.). 118p. 1982. 12.00. Colo Sch Mines.
--Principles of Rock Drilling & Bit Wear, Pt. 2. rev. ed. Raese, Jon W., ed. LC 82-1148. (Colorado School of Mines Quarterly Ser.: Vol. 77 No. 2). (Illus.). 42p. 1982. pap. text ed. 10.00 (ISBN 0-686-79748-5). Colo Sch Mines.
Clark, George C., Jr. & Cain, J. Bibb. Error-Correction Coding for Digital Communications. LC 81-1630. (Applications of Communications Theory Ser.). 436p. 1981. 45.00x (ISBN 0-306-40615-2, Plenum Pr). Plenum Pub.
Clark, George N. English History: A Survey. 1971. 35.00x (ISBN 0-19-822339-0). Oxford U Pr.
--Later Stuarts, Sixteen Sixty to Seventeen Fourteen. 2nd ed. (Oxford History of England Ser.). 1955. 42.00x (ISBN 0-19-821702-1). Oxford U Pr.
--The Seventeenth Century. 2nd ed. LC 80-27737. (Illus.). xix, 378p. 1981. Repr. of 1947 ed. lib. bdg. 39.25x (ISBN 0-313-22765-9, CLSC). Greenwood.
Clark, George R. Col. George Rogers Clark's Sketch of His Campaign in the Illinois in 1778-9 with an Introduction by Hon. Henry Pirtle. LC 73-146384. (First American Frontier Ser). 1971. Repr. of 1869 ed. 17.00 (ISBN 0-405-02835-0). Ayer Co Pubs.
--History of the U. S. Navy. lib. bdg. 75.00 (ISBN 0-8490-2008-5). Gordon Pr.
--Papers, Seventeen Seventy-One to Seventeen Eighty-Four, 2 Vols. James, James A., ed. LC 72-444. Repr. of 1926 ed. Set. 130.00 (ISBN 0-404-01556-5). AMS Pr.
Clark, Gertrude M., tr. see Kant, Immanuel.
Clark, Gilbert & Zimmerman, Enid. Art Design: Communicating Visually. (Illus.). 1978. text ed. 19.70x (ISBN 0-912242-16-7); tchr's. manual 4.70x (ISBN 0-685-62932-5). Art Educ.
Clark, Gilbert A. & Zimmerman, Enid D. Educating Artistically Talented Students. LC 84-16368. (Illus.). 216p. 1984. text ed. 20.00x (ISBN 0-8156-2320-8). Syracuse U Pr.
Clark, Gilbert J. Life Sketches of Eminent Lawyers, American, English & Canadian, to Which Is Added Thoughts, Facts & Facetiae, 2 Vols. (Illus.). 1983. Repr. of 1895 ed. Vol. I, xi, 368p. lib. bdg. 75.00x set (ISBN 0-8377-0447-2). Vol. 2, xi, 384p. Rothman.
Clark, Glen, jt. ed. see Solberg, William K.
Clark, Glenn. Beatitudes of Married Life. pap. 0.20 (ISBN 0-910924-02-3). Macalester.
--Come Follow Me. 4.95 (ISBN 0-910924-04-X). Macalester.
--Divine Plan. pap. 0.50 (ISBN 0-910924-05-8). Macalester.
--Fishers of Men. pap. 1.95 (ISBN 0-910924-62-7). Macalester.
--From Crime to Christ. pap. 2.50 (ISBN 0-910924-61-9). Macalester.
--God's Voice in the Folklore. 4.95 (ISBN 0-910924-06-6). Macalester.
--Holy Spirit. pap. 0.50 (ISBN 0-910924-07-4). Macalester.
--I Will Lift Up Mine Eyes. 1937. pap. 7.64 (ISBN 0-06-061393-9, RP518, HarpR). Har-Row.
--I Will Lift up Mine Eyes. LC 77-7830. (Illus.). 208p. 1984. pap. 7.64 (ISBN 0-06-061394-7, RD 518, HarpR). Har-Row.
--Living Prayer. 1980. pap. 0.50 (ISBN 0-910924-88-0). Macalester.
--Lord's Prayer. pap. 0.50 (ISBN 0-910924-08-2). Macalester.
--Man Who Talks with the Flowers. pap. 0.95 (ISBN 0-910924-09-0). Macalester.
--Man Who Tapped Secrets of the Universe. pap. 2.25 (ISBN 0-910924-10-4). Macalester.
--Man's Reach. 1977. Repr. of 1949 ed. 4.50 (ISBN 0-910924-82-1). Macalester.
--Song of Souls of Men. pap. 0.95 (ISBN 0-910924-14-7). Macalester.
--Thought Farthest Out. pap. 0.95 (ISBN 0-910924-16-3). Macalester.
--Three Mysteries of Jesus. 1978. 0.95 (ISBN 0-910924-85-6). Macalester.
--Under the Shelter of His Wings. pap. 0.20 (ISBN 0-910924-50-3). Macalester.
--Water of Life. 1979. pap. 5.95 (ISBN 0-910924-86-4). Macalester.
--What Would Jesus Do? pap. 7.95 (ISBN 0-910924-20-1). Macalester.
Clark, Glenn T., jt. auth. see Solberg, William K.
Clark, Gordon H. Biblical Predestination. 1969. pap. 4.95 (ISBN 0-87552-137-1). Presby & Reformed.
--A Christian View of Men & Things. (Twin Brooks Ser.). 325p. 1981. pap. 8.95 (ISBN 0-8010-2466-8). Baker Bk.
--Concept of Biblical Authority. 1979. 0.75 (ISBN 0-87552-143-6). Presby & Reformed.
--Dewey. (Modern Thinkers Ser.). 1960. pap. 2.00 (ISBN 0-87552-582-2). Presby & Reformed.
--First & Second Peter. 1980. pap. 5.95 (ISBN 0-87552-167-3). Presby & Reformed.
--James. (Modern Thinkers Ser.). 1963. pap. 2.00 (ISBN 0-87552-584-9). Presby & Reformed.
--Language & Theology. 1979. 4.95 (ISBN 0-87552-141-X). Presby & Reformed.
--Thales to Dewey. (Twin Brooks Ser.). pap. 9.95 (ISBN 0-8010-2446-3). Baker Bk.
Clark, Gordon H., ed. Selections from Hellenistic Philosophy. LC 40-31306. 1964. pap. text ed. 9.95x (ISBN 0-89197-396-6). Irvington.
Clark, Gordon L. Interregional Migration, National Policy & Social Justice. LC 83-3170. 224p. 1983. text ed. 34.95x (ISBN 0-86598-124-8). Rowman & Allanheld.
--Judges & the Cities: Interpreting Local Autonomy. LC 85-1018. (Illus.). 248p. 1985. 25.00x (ISBN 0-226-10753-1). U of Chicago Pr.
Clark, Gordon L. & Dear, Michael. State Apparatus: The Structures & Language of Legitimacy. 256p. 1984. text ed. 29.95x (ISBN 0-04-320159-8); pap. text ed. 11.95 (ISBN 0-04-320160-1). Allen Unwin.
Clark, Grahame. Aspects of Prehistory. LC 73-94989. 1970. 28.50x (ISBN 0-520-01584-3). U of Cal Pr.
--The Earlier Stone Age Settlement of Scandanavia. LC 73-94358. (Illus.). 304p. 1975. 57.50 (ISBN 0-521-20446-1). Cambridge U Pr.
--The Identity of Man. (Illus.). 224p. 1983. 17.95x (ISBN 0-416-33550-0, N0. 3773). Methuen Inc.
--Prehistoric England. 1979. Repr. of 1940 ed. lib. bdg. 30.00 (ISBN 0-8495-0948-3). Arden Lib.
--Symbols of Excellence: Precious Materials As Expressions of Status. 150p. Date not set. price not set (ISBN 0-521-30264-1). Cambridge U Pr.
Clark, Grenville. World Peace through World Law: Two Alternative Plans. 3rd ed. LC 66-21198. pap. 147.30 (ISBN 0-317-09601-X, 2003006). Bks Demand UMI.
Clark, Grenville & Sohn, Louis. Introduction to World Peace Through World Law. (Modern Classics of Peace Ser). 112p. 1984. pap. 4.95 (ISBN 0-912018-18-6). World Without War.
Clark, Grover. Economic Rivalries in China. 1932. 49.50x (ISBN 0-685-69799-1). Elliots Bks.
--The Great Wall Crumbles. facsimile ed. LC 70-175694. (Select Bibliographies Reprint Ser). Repr. of 1935 ed. 32.00 (ISBN 0-8369-6609-0). Ayer Co Pubs.
Clark, H. A First Course in Quantum Mechanics. rev. ed. 1982. 12.95 (ISBN 0-442-30173-1). Van Nos Reinhold.
Clark, H., tr. see Favre, Jules.
Clark, H. B. & Spencer, Richard M. Callaghan's Michigan Civil Practice Forms, Vols. 1-10. LC 67-23959. Date not set. 550.00. Callaghan.
Clark, H. H. & Foerster, Norman. Lowell. 498p. 1980. Repr. lib. bdg. 40.00 (ISBN 0-89987-108-9). Darby Bks.
Clark, Halsey. Deepwater Showdown. (Submarine Ser.: No. 2). 320p. (Orig.). 1983. pap. 3.25 (ISBN 0-440-01840-4, Emerald). Dell.
--Depths of Danger. (Periscope Ser.: No. 3). (Orig.). 1983. pap. 3.25 (ISBN 0-440-01888-9). Dell.
--Grand Finale. (Periscope Ser.: No. 4). 352p. (Orig.). 1983. pap. 3.95 (ISBN 0-440-03127-3, Emerald). Dell.
--Supersub. (Periscope Ser.: No. 5). 320p. (Orig.). 1983. pap. 3.25 (ISBN 0-440-08403-2, Emerald). Dell.
Clark, Harold. The New Creationism. LC 79-22250. (Horizon Ser.). 1980. pap. 9.95 (ISBN 0-8127-0247-6). Review & Herald.
Clark, Harold B. Callaghan's Illinois Civil Practice Forms: 1954-1983, 10 vols. LC 54-11368. 1983. Set. 525.00 (ISBN 0-317-12059-X); Suppl., 1982. 55.00; Suppl., 1983. 65.00. Callaghan.
Clark, Harold B. & Spencer, M. Callaghan's Michigan Civil Practice Forms: 1968-1983, 10 vols. LC 67-23959. 1983. Set. 550.00 (ISBN 0-317-12072-7). Callaghan.
Clark, Harold F. The Cost of Government & the Support of Education: An Intensive Study of New York State with Results Applicable Over the Entire Country. LC 79-17668. (Columbia University. Teachers College. Contributions to Education: No. 145). Repr. of 1924 ed. 22.50 (ISBN 0-404-55145-9). AMS Pr.
--Economic Theory & Correct Occupational Distribution. Stein, Leon, ed. LC 77-70488. (Work Ser.). 1977. Repr. of 1931 ed. lib. bdg. 19.00x (ISBN 0-405-10160-0). Ayer Co Pubs.
Clark, Harold W. Fossils, Flood & Fire. (Illus.). 1968. 8.95 (ISBN 0-911080-16-3). Outdoor Pict.
Clark, Harry. A Venture in History: The Production, Publication, & Sale of the Works of Hubert Howe Bancroft. LC 72-173900. 1973. pap. 35.00x (ISBN 0-520-09417-4). U of Cal Pr.
Clark, Harry H. Thomas Paine. 436p. 1980. Repr. lib. bdg. 35.00 (ISBN 0-8495-0794-4). Arden Lib.
Clark, Harry H., compiled by. American Literature: Poe Through Garland. LC 77-137641. (Goldentree Bibliographies in Language & Literature Ser.). (Orig.). 1971. 15.95x (ISBN 0-88295-509-8); pap. 6.95x (ISBN 0-88295-508-X). Harlan Davidson.
Clark, Harry H., ed. Poems of Freneau. 425p. 1983. Repr. of 1929 ed. lib. bdg. 50.00 (ISBN 0-89760-168-8). Telegraph Bks.
Clark, Harry H., jt. ed. see Wilson, GayA.
Clark, Hazel. Fibres to Fabrics: Techniques & Projects for Hanspinners. (Illus.). 144p. 1985. 19.95 (ISBN 0-7134-4616-1, Pub. by Batsford England). David & Charles.
--Textile Printing. (Shire Album Ser.: No. 135). (Orig.). 1985. pap. 3.50 (ISBN 0-85263-729-2, Pub. by Shire Pubns England). Seven Hills Bks.
Clark, Henry. The Church & Residential Desegregation. 1965. 11.95x (ISBN 0-8084-0076-2). New Coll U Pr.
--The Irony of American Morality. 1972. 10.95x (ISBN 0-8084-0036-3); pap. 7.95x (ISBN 0-8084-0037-1). New Coll U Pr.
Clark, Henry B. Practical Oral Surgery. LC 65-19426. pap. 95.60 (ISBN 0-317-28180-1, 2014534). Bks Demand UMI.
Clark, Henry B., ed. see Linnell, Robert.
Clark, Henry B., II. Freedom of Religion in America: Historical Roots, Philosophical Concepts, Contemporary Problems. 143p. 1982. pap. 6.95 (ISBN 0-87855-925-6). Transaction Bks.
Clark, Henry W. History of Alaska. facsimile ed. LC 72-37877. (Select Bibliographies Reprint Ser). Repr. of 1930 ed. 23.50 (ISBN 0-8369-6714-3). Ayer Co Pubs.
Clark, Herbert. Characteristic Studies of the Cornet. (Illus.). 64p. 1915. pap. 7.00 (ISBN 0-8258-0250-4, 0-2281). Fischer Inc NY.
Clark, Herbert H. Semantics & Comprehension. (Janua Linguarum, Series Minor: No. 187). 148p. 1976. pap. text ed. 15.60x (ISBN 90-2793-384-7). Mouton.
Clark, Herbert H. & Clark, Eve V. Psychology & Language: An Introduction to Psycholinguistics. (Illus.). 608p. 1977. text ed. 29.95 (ISBN 0-15-572815-6, HC). HarBraceJ.
Clark, Homer H. Domestic Relations. (Hornbook Ser.). 754p. 1968. 20.95 (ISBN 0-317-00020-9). West Pub.
Clark, Homer H., Jr. Domestic Relations Cases & Problems. 3rd ed. LC 80-19763. (American Casebook Ser.). 1153p. 1980. text ed. 27.95 (ISBN 0-8299-2104-4); tchrs.' manual avail. (ISBN 0-314-63411-8). West Pub.
Clark, Howard. Making Non-Violent Revolution. 30p. 1981. lib. bdg. 12.95 (ISBN 0-88286-142-5); pap. 2.50 (ISBN 0-88286-117-4). C H kerr.
Clark, Howard, ed. Twentieth Century Interpretations of the Odyssey. 131p. 1983. pap. 4.95 (ISBN 0-13-934844-1). P-H.
Clark, Hubert L. Catalogue of the Recent Sea-Urchins (Echinoidea) in the Collection of the British Museum (Natural History) (Illus.). xxviii, 250p. 1925. 25.00x (ISBN 0-565-00165-5, Pub. by British Mus Nat Hist England). Sabbot-Natural Hist Bks.
Clark, Hyla. The Tin Can Book. (Art Bks). (Illus., Orig.). 1977. pap. 6.95 (ISBN 0-451-79965-8, G9965, Sig). NAL.
Clark, I. C. Limited Nuclear War. 1982. 25.00 (ISBN 0-691-07644-8). Princeton U Pr.
Clark, I. E. Christmas Dream. (Illus.). 21p. (Director's Production Script). 1970. pap. 5.00 (ISBN 0-88680-026-9). I E Clark.
--Gammer Gurton's Needle. (Illus.). 40p. (Director's Production Script). 1965. pap. 6.50 (ISBN 0-88680-065-X). I E Clark.
--Gammer Gurton's Needle in Three Acts. (Illus.). 67p. (Director's Production Script). 1970. pap. 7.50 (ISBN 0-88680-067-6). I E Clark.
--Hansel & Gretel. (Illus.). 38p. 1970. pap. 2.00 (ISBN 0-88680-075-7); royalty 35.00 (ISBN 0-317-03602-5). I E Clark.
--Hansel & Gretel. (Illus.). 58p. (Director's Production Script). 1970. pap. 7.50 (ISBN 0-88680-076-5). I E Clark.
--I Hate War. (Illus.). 26p. (Director's Production Script). 1970. pap. 5.00 (ISBN 0-88680-087-0). I E Clark.
--It's a Dungaree World. 77p. (Piano-Vocal Score, Music by Kit Carter, Lyrics by I. E. Clark & Kit Carter). 1974. pap. 10.00 (ISBN 0-88680-098-6). I E Clark.
--Pandora & the Magic Box. (Illus.). 20p. (Director's Production Script). 1968. pap. 5.00 (ISBN 0-88680-148-6). I E Clark.
--Ragweed Cowboy Joe. (Illus.). 24p. 1974. pap. 1.75 (ISBN 0-88680-159-1); royalty 25.00 (ISBN 0-317-03600-9). I E Clark.
--Ragweed Cowboy Joe. (Director's Production Script Ser.). (Illus.). 44p. 1974. pap. 6.50 (ISBN 0-88680-160-5). I E Clark.
--The Saga of Sagebrush Sal. (Illus.). 20p. 1972. pap. 1.75 (ISBN 0-88680-167-2); royalty 25.00 (ISBN 0-317-03597-5). I E Clark.
--Saga of Sagebrush Sal. (Illus.). 38p. (Director's Production Script). 1972. pap. 6.50 (ISBN 0-88680-168-0). I E Clark.
--The Shaky Tale of Dr. Jakey. (Illus.). 40p. 1984. pap. 2.00 (ISBN 0-88680-228-8). I E Clark.
--Stagecrafters' Handbook. 2nd ed. (Illus.). 56p. 1977. pap. 4.00 (ISBN 0-88680-182-6). I E Clark.
--Twelve Dancing Princesses. 40p. 1969. pap. 2.00 (ISBN 0-88680-197-4); royalty 35.00 (ISBN 0-317-03614-9). I E Clark.
--Twelve Dancing Princesses. (Illus.). 53p. (Director's Production Script Ser.). 1969. pap. 7.50 (ISBN 0-88680-198-2). I E Clark.
Clark, I. E. & Carter, Kit. It's a Dungaree World. (Illus.). 40p. 1974. pap. 2.50 (ISBN 0-88680-097-8); royalty 50.00 (ISBN 0-317-03622-X). I E Clark.
--It's a Dungaree World. (Illus.). 67p. (Director's Production Script). 1974. pap. 10.00 (ISBN 0-88680-099-4). I E Clark.
Clark, I. E., tr. see Sachs, Hans.
Clark, Ian. Nuclear Past, Nuclear Present: Hiroshima, Nagasaki, & Contemporary Strategy. (A Westview Special Study Ser.). 120p. 1985. softcover 15.00x (ISBN 0-8133-7049-3). Westview.
--Reform & Resistance in the International Order. LC 79-54017. 1980. 29.50 (ISBN 0-521-22998-7); pap. 11.95 (ISBN 0-521-29763-X). Cambridge U Pr.
Clark, Ian, jt. ed. see Bowman, Larry W.
Clark, Ira. Christ Revealed: The History of the Neotypological Lyric in the English Renaissance. LC 82-2696. (University of Florida Humanities Monographs: No. 51). xiv, 218p. 1982. pap. 15.00x (ISBN 0-8130-0712-7). U Presses Fla.
Clark, Isobel. Practical Geostatistics. (Illus.). 129p. 1979. 24.00 (ISBN 0-85334-843-X, Pub. by Elsevier Applied Sci England). Elsevier.
Clark, J. The Care of Books. 1976. lib. bdg. 59.95 (ISBN 0-8490-1572-3). Gordon Pr.
--Handbook for Office Workers. 3rd ed. 1982. 13.95 (ISBN 0-442-21494-4). Van Nos Reinhold.
Clark, J., jt. auth. see Downing, D.
Clark, J., et al. Thin Seam Coal Mining Technology. LC 82-7968. (Energy Tech. Rev. 80). (Illus.). 385p. 1983. 36.00 (ISBN 0-8155-0909-X). Noyes.
Clark, J. A. Environmental Aspects of Housing for Animal Production. 1981. text ed. 130.00 (ISBN 0-408-10688-3). Butterworth.
Clark, J. A., jt. ed. see Cena, K.
Clark, J. A., jt. ed. see Cooper, C. A.
Clark, J. Anthony, jt. auth. see American Prepaid Legal Services Institute Staff.
Clark, J. B., jt. ed. see Comins, N. R.
Clark, J. B., jt. auth. see Lancaster, John H.
Clark, J. Bunker. Transposition in Seventeenth Century English Organ Accompaniments & the Transposing Organ. LC 72-96873. (Detroit Monographs in Musicology: No. 4). 1974. 5.00 (ISBN 0-911772-56-1). Info Coord.
Clark, J. C. The Dynamics of Change: The Crisis of the 1750s & English Party Systems. LC 81-9999. (Cambridge Studies in the History & Theory of Politics). 600p. 1982. 80.00 (ISBN 0-521-23830-7). Cambridge U Pr.
Clark, J. Desmond. Excavations at Star Carr: An Early Mesolithic Site at Seamer Near Scarborough, Yorkshire. LC 75-172830. (Illus.). 226p. 1971. 87.50 (ISBN 0-521-08394-X). Cambridge U Pr.
--Kalambo Falls Prehistoric Site, 2 vols. LC 68-25084. (Illus.). 1973. Vol. 2. 150.00 (ISBN 0-521-20009-1). Cambridge U Pr.
Clark, J. Desmond & Brandt, Steven A., eds. From Hunters to Farmers: The Causes & Consequences of Food Production in Africa. LC 82-20004. (Illus.). 344p. 1984. lib. bdg. 55.00x (ISBN 0-520-04574-2). U of Cal Pr.
Clark, J. Desmond, jt. ed. see Bishop, Walter W.
Clark, J. G. Audiology for the School Speech-Language Clinician. (Illus.). 208p. 1980. 14.75x (ISBN 0-398-04004-4). C C Thomas.
--Mesolithic Prelude: The Paleolithic-Neolithic Transition in Europe & the Near East. 122p. 1980. 16.00x (ISBN 0-85224-365-0, Pub. by Edinburgh U Pr Scotland). Columbia U Pr.
Clark, J. H. & Peck, E. J. Female Sex Steroids: Receptors & Function. (Monographs on Endocrinology: Vol. 14). (Illus.). 1979. 50.00 (ISBN 0-387-09375-3). Springer-Verlag.
Clark, J. H. & Benforado, J., eds. Wetlands of Bottomland Hardwood Forests: Proceedings at Lake Lanier, Georgia, June 1-5, 1980. (Developments in Agricultural & Managed-Forest Ecology Ser.: Vol. 11). 402p. 1981. 95.75 (ISBN 0-444-42020-7). Elsevier.
Clark, J. H., jt. ed. see Leavitt, W. W.
Clark, J. H., jt. ed. see Roy, A. K.
Clark, J. H., et al, eds. Hormone & Antihormone, Action at the Target Cell. (Dahlem Workshop Reports Ser.: L.S.R.R. No.3). 228p. 1976. pap. 26.50x (ISBN 0-89573-087-1). VCH Pubs.
Clark, J. Kent. Goodwin Wharton. 1985. 24.95x (ISBN 0-19-212234-7). Oxford U Pr.
Clark, J. L., jt. auth. see Cracknell, A. P.
Clark, J. R. Essentials of Economics: Study Guide. 2nd ed. 1985. text ed. 8.00i (ISBN 0-12-311037-8). Acad Pr.
--Gwartney's Essentials of Economics: Instructor's Manual & Test Bank. 2nd ed. 1985. text ed. 10.00i (ISBN 0-12-311036-X). Acad Pr.
Clark, J. R., ed. Chemistry & Physics of Minerals. (Transactions of the American Crystallographic Association Ser.: Vol. 15). 120p. 1979. pap. 15.00 (ISBN 0-686-60385-0). Polycrystal Bk Serv.
Clark, J. Reuben, Jr. Why the King James Version. LC 79-15008. (Classics in Mormon Literature Ser.). 535p. 1979. 7.95 (ISBN 0-87747-773-6). Deseret Bk.
Clark, J. S. & De Corso, S. M., eds. Stationary Gas Turbine Alternative Fuels - STP 809. LC 82-73767. 360p. 1983. 43.00 (ISBN 0-8031-0199-6, 04-809000-13). ASTM.
Clark, J. W., ed. see Cervantes.
Clark, J. Willis. Old Friends at Cambridge & Elsewhere. 1973. Repr. of 1900 ed. 30.00 (ISBN 0-8274-1535-4). R West.
Clark, James. Cars. LC 80-17876. (A Look Inside). (Illus.). 48p. (gr. 4-12). 1981. PLB 15.52 (ISBN 0-8172-1405-4). Raintree Pubs.
--Cars. LC 80-17876. (A Look Inside Ser.). (Illus.). 48p. (gr. 4-12). 1985. pap. 9.27 (ISBN 0-8172-1428-3). Raintree Pubs.

Clark, James, jt. auth. see Halbouty, Michel.
Clark, James A., ed. see Halbouty, Michel T.
Clark, James C. Faded Glory: Presidents Out of Power. LC 84-18327. 176p. 1985. 32.95 (ISBN 0-03-002569-9); pap. 9.95 (ISBN 0-03-002572-9). Praeger.
--Last Train South: The Flight of the Confederate Government from Richmond. LC 84-42610. (Illus.). 192p. 1984. lib. bdg. 17.95x (ISBN 0-89950-115-X). McFarland & Co.
--The Story of "Eight Deer" in Codex Columbino. Young, Karl, ed. (Fourth Sun Ser.). (Illus.). lib. bdg. cancelled (ISBN 0-932282-34-2); pap. cancelled (ISBN 0-932282-33-4). Caledonia Pr.
Clark, James D. Pulp Technology & Treatment for Paper. rev. ed. (Illus.). 880p. 1985. price not set (ISBN 0-87930-164-3). Miller Freeman.
Clark, James d'A. Pulp Technology & Treatment for Paper. LC 78-59149. (A Pulp & Paper Book). (Illus.). 752p. 1978. 75.00 (ISBN 0-87930-066-3). Miller Freeman.
Clark, James E. & Hertz, Karl V., eds. Major Topics of School Business Management in the Mid 1980's. 1984. 7.95 (ISBN 0-317-17735-4). Assn Sch Busn.
Clark, James F. & Drum, William O. Structured BASIC. 1983. 13.70 (ISBN 0-538-10800-2, J80). SW Pub.
Clark, James F., jt. auth. see Bux, William.
Clark, James H. Take Aim, Vol. I. (Illus.). 400p. 1981. pap. 19.95 (ISBN 0-916460-29-0). Matrix Pub.
Clark, James I. Shortcut to Peril. LC 79-22151. (Quest, Adventure, Survival). (Illus.). (gr. 4-9). 1982. pap. 9.27 (ISBN 0-8172-2070-4). Raintree Pubs.
--Shortcut to Peril. LC 79-22151. (Quest, Adventure, Survival). (Illus.). (gr. 4-8). 1980. PLB 14.25 (ISBN 0-8172-1570-0). Raintree Pubs.
--Steel Coffin at Forty Fathoms. LC 79-21052. (Quest, Adventure, Survival). (Illus.). (gr. 4-8). 1980. PLB 14.25 (ISBN 0-8172-1567-0). Raintree Pubs.
--Steel Coffin at Forty Fathoms. LC 79-21052. (Quest, Adventure, Survival). (Illus.). 46p. (gr. 4-9). 1982. pap. 9.27 (ISBN 0-8172-2071-2). Raintree Pubs.
--Three Years on the Ocean. LC 79-21873. (Quest, Adventure, Survival). (Illus.). 46p. (gr. 4-9). 1982. pap. 9.27 (ISBN 0-8172-2072-0). Raintree Pubs.
--Three Years on the Ocean. LC 79-21873. (Quest, Adventure, Survival). (Illus.). (gr. 4-8). 1980. PLB 14.25 (ISBN 0-8172-1572-7). Raintree Pubs.
--Video Games. LC 84-9790. (A Look Inside Ser.). (Illus.). 48p. (gr. 4-12). 1984. PLB 15.52 (ISBN 0-8172-1410-0). Raintree Pubs.
--Video Games. LC 84-9790. (A Look Inside Ser.). (Illus.). 48p. (gr. 4-12). 1985. pap. 9.27 (ISBN 0-8172-1436-4). Raintree Pubs.
Clark, James I. & Remini, Robert O. Freedom Frontiers: The Story of the American People. 1975. 13.95 (ISBN 0-02-640660-8, 64066); tchr's manual 3.48 (ISBN 0-02-640670-5, 64067). Macmillan.
Clark, James I., jt. auth. see Ryan, Frank L.
Clark, James I., ed. see Swiger, Elinor P.
Clark, James J., jt. ed. see Woodward, Robert H.
Clark, James L. Operation Swordfish. 1983. 11.95 (ISBN 0-533-05441-9). Vantage.
Clark, James L. & Clark, Lyn R. How Four: A Handbook for Office Workers. write for info. Wadsworth Pub.
--How-4: A Handbook for Office Workers. 4th ed. LC 84-23366. 336p. 1984. pap. text ed. write for info. (ISBN 0-534-04542-1). Kent Pub Co.
--Universal Transcription. LC 84-23328. 224p. 1985. pap. write for info. (ISBN 0-534-04530-8). Kent Pub Co.
Clark, James M. Great German Mystics: Eckhart, Tauler & Suso. LC 73-81493. 1970. Repr. of 1949 ed. 15.00x (ISBN 0-8462-1351-6). Russell.
--Teachers & Politics in France: A Pressure Group Study of the Federation de l'Education Nationale. LC 67-13494. 1967. 12.00x (ISBN 0-8156-2103-5). Syracuse U Pr.
--The Vocabulary of Anglo-Irish. LC 73-12699. (Eng. & Irish.). 1917. lib. bdg. 16.50 (ISBN 0-8414-3394-1). Folcroft.
Clark, James M., tr. see Echkart, Meister, et al.
Clark, james T. The Concept of Self-Examination. LC 83-90852. 60p. 1984. 7.95 (ISBN 0-533-05860-0). Vantage.
Clark, James W., ed. see Loose Leaf Reference Services.
Clark, Jan R. Reservoir of Power. 1981. 25.00x (ISBN 0-686-78923-7, Pub. by Pickering & Inglis Scotland). State Mutual Bk.
Clark, Jane E., jt. auth. see Kelso, J. A.
Clark, Jane P. Deportation of Aliens from the United States to Europe. LC 79-76633. (Columbia University Studies in the Social Sciences: No. 351). Repr. of 1931 ed. 12.50 (ISBN 0-404-51351-4). AMS Pr.
--Deportation of Aliens from the United States to Europe. LC 69-18766. (American Immigration Collection Ser., No. 1). 1969. Repr. of 1931 ed. 20.00 (ISBN 0-405-00514-8). Ayer Co Pubs.
Clark, Janet W. Geer Hill School: A History of the Smallest One Room School in Connecticut. (Connecticut Educational History Ser.). 23p. 1983. 1.50 (ISBN 0-317-12718-7). I N Thut World Educ Ctr.
Clark, Jean. The Marriage Bed. LC 82-13134. 320p. 1983. 16.95 (ISBN 0-399-12746-1, Putnam). Putnam Pub Group.
--Untie the Winds. 1978. pap. 2.25 (ISBN 0-89083-393-1). Zebra.
Clark, Jeff. San Francisco: Dream City. Campe-Aguilar, Patricia, ed. (Illus.). 48p. (Orig.). 1984. pap. 12.00 (ISBN 0-931290-88-0). Alchemy Bks.
Clark, Jeff, jt. auth. see Downing, Douglas.
Clark, Jeffrey, jt. auth. see Evans, G. Edward.
Clark, Jeffrey T., jt. auth. see Kelly, Marion.
Clark, Jeffrey T. & Kirch, Patrick V., eds. Archaeological Investigations of the Mudlane-Waimea Kawaihae Road Corridor, Island of Hawaii. LC 83-70203. (Departmental Report: No. 83-1). 532p. 1983. pap. 15.00 (ISBN 0-686-47626-3). Bishop Mus.
Clark, Jerome, jt. auth. see Rogo, D. Scott.
Clark, Jerry E. The Shawnee. LC 77-73700. (Kentucky Bicentennial Bookshelf Ser). (Illus.). 112p. 1977. 6.95 (ISBN 0-8131-0233-2). U Pr of Ky.
Clark, Jewell T., compiled by. A Guide to Church Records in the Archives Branch, Virginia State Library. x, 271p. (Orig.). 1981. pap. 5.00 (ISBN 0-88490-105-X). VA State Lib.
Clark, Jim, jt. auth. see Beck, Ken.
Clark, Joan. Thomasina & the Trout Tree. LC 72-179431. (Illus.). 40p. (gr. 2 up). 1971. 9.95 (ISBN 0-88776-018-X). Tundra Bks.
Clark, Joe. Tennessee Hill Folk. LC 72-2880. (Illus.). 96p. 1972. 10.95 (ISBN 0-8265-1183-X). Vanderbilt U Pr.
Clark, Joe, photos by. Tennessee Hill Folk. (Vanderbilt University Press Bks.). (Illus.). 96p. 1972. 10.95 (ISBN 0-8265-1183-X). U of Ill Pr.
Clark, John. Basic Process Industries, Vol. 2. LC 84-10125. (Technological Trends & Employment Ser.). 228p. 1984. text ed. 31.50 (ISBN 0-566-00709-6). Gower Pub Co.
--Businesses Today: Successes & Failures. 1979. pap. text ed. 5.95x (ISBN 0-394-32334-3, RanC). Random.
--History of Epic Poetry: Post-Virgilian. LC 65-15876. (Studies in Poetry, No. 38). 1969. Repr. lib. bdg. 39.95x (ISBN 0-8383-0528-8). Haskell.
Clark, John, jt. auth. see Cooper, Charles.
Clark, John, jt. auth. see Ringold, Paul L.
Clark, John, tr. from Lat. The Military Institutions of the Romans. Phillips, Thomas R., ed. LC 83-45853. 1944. 24.50 (ISBN 0-404-20275-6, U101). AMS Pr.
Clark, John, tr. see Kawai, Toyoaki.
Clark, John, tr. see Vegetius Renatus, Flavia.
Clark, John, et al. Small Seaports: Revitalization Through Conserving Heritage Resources. LC 79-67736. (Illus.). 64p. (Orig.). 1979. pap. 6.50 (ISBN 0-89164-059-2). Conservation Foun.
Clark, John A. How to Save Time & Taxes in Handling Estates. 2nd ed. (How to Save Time & Taxes Ser.). 1964. Updates avail. 80.00 (203); looseleaf 1983 77.00; looseleaf 1984 38.50. Bender.
Clark, John B. Distribution of Wealth. LC 65-19641. Repr. of 1899 ed. 35.00x (ISBN 0-678-00078-6). Kelley.
--Essentials of Economic Theory. LC 68-8972. Repr. of 1907 ed. 45.00x (ISBN 0-678-00425-0). Kelley.
--Philosophy of Wealth. 2nd ed. LC 67-25955. Repr. of 1887 ed. 25.00x (ISBN 0-678-00275-4). Kelley.
Clark, John B. & Clark, John M. Control of Trusts. LC 70-108000. Repr. of 1914 ed. lib. bdg. 25.00x (ISBN 0-678-00606-7). Kelley.
Clark, John B., jt. ed. see Speich, Gilbert R.
Clark, John D. The Federal Trust Policy. LC 78-64285. (Johns Hopkins University. Studies in the Social Sciences. Extra Volumes: 15). 312p. 1982. Repr. of 1931 ed. 26.00 (ISBN 0-404-61385-3). AMS Pr.
--The Prehistoric Cultures of the Horn of Africa. LC 70-159173. xix, 385p. 1971. Repr. of 1954 ed. lib. bdg. 29.00x (ISBN 0-374-91657-8). Octagon.
--The Prehistory of Africa. LC 84-676. (Illus.). 302p. 1984. Repr. of 1970 ed. lib. bdg. 37.50x (ISBN 0-313-24214-3, CPAF). Greenwood.
--Stone Age Cultures of Northern Rhodesia, with Particular Reference to the Cultural & Climatic Succession in the Zambezi Valley & Its Tributaries. LC 78-111570. (Illus.). Repr. of 1950 ed. 21.50x (ISBN 0-8371-4595-3, CNR&, Pub. by Negro U Pr). Greenwood.
Clark, John E. Structural Concrete Cost Estimating. 256p. 1983. 34.50 (ISBN 0-07-011163-4). McGraw.
Clark, John G. The Grain Trade in the Old Northwest. LC 80-18227. (Illus.). xi, 324p. 1980. Repr. of 1966 ed. lib. bdg. 32.50x (ISBN 0-313-22419-6, CLGT). Greenwood.
--The Mesolithic Age in Britain. LC 76-44704. Repr. of 1932 ed. 24.00 (ISBN 0-404-15914-1). AMS Pr.
--Mesolithic Settlement of Northern Europe. LC 75-95090. Repr. of 1936 ed. lib. bdg. 18.50 (ISBN 0-8371-2579-0, CLMS). Greenwood.
--New Orleans, 1718-1812: An Economic History. LC 77-119115. (Illus.). xii, 396p. 1970. 35.00x (ISBN 0-8071-0346-2). La State U Pr.
--La Rochelle & the Atlantic Economy During the Eighteenth Century. LC 80-29275. (Illus.). 304p. 1981. text ed. 28.50x (ISBN 0-8018-2529-6). Johns Hopkins.
--Science Project Puzzlers: Starter Ideas for the Curious. Stone, Harris. (Illus.). 61p. (gr. 7 up). 1981. pap. 4.95 (ISBN 0-13-795450-6, Pub. by Treehouse). P-H.
Clark, John G. & Yanick, Paul, Jr. Tinnitus & Its Management: A Clinical Text for Audiologists. (Illus.). 206p. 1984. 24.75x (ISBN 0-398-05043-0). C C Thomas.
Clark, John G., et al. Three Generations in Twentieth Century America: Family, Community & Nation. rev. ed. 1982. pap. 23.00x (ISBN 0-256-02449-9). Dorsey.
Clark, John Grahame Douglas. World Prehistory in New Perspective. 3rd ed. LC 76-51318. (Illus.). 1977. 67.50 (ISBN 0-521-21506-4); pap. 19.95 (ISBN 0-521-29178-X). Cambridge U Pr.
Clark, John H., jt. auth. see Cohen, John.
Clark, John J. & Clark, Margaret T. A Statistics Primer for Managers: How to Ask the Right Questions About Forecasting, Control & Investment. (Illus.). 272p. 19.95 (ISBN 0-02-905800-7). Macmillan.
--A Statistics Primer for Managers: How to Read a Statistical Report or a Computer Printout & Get the Right Answer. (Illus.). 258p. 1983. 19.95 (ISBN 0-02-905800-7). Free Pr.
Clark, John J., jt. auth. see Elgers, Pieter T.
Clark, John J., et al. Capital Budgeting: Planning & Control of Capital Expenditures. 2nd ed. (Illus.). 656p. 1984. 34.95 (ISBN 0-13-114348-4). P-H.
Clark, John M. Competition As a Dynamic Process. LC 79-26651. xvii, 501p. 1980. Repr. of 1961 ed. lib. bdg. 42.50x (ISBN 0-313-22300-9, CLCD). Greenwood.
--Costs of the World War to the American People. LC 68-55507. Repr. of 1931 ed. 27.50x (ISBN 0-678-00662-8). Kelley.
--Economic Institutions & Human Welfare. LC 77-27310. 1978. Repr. of 1957 ed. lib. bdg. 22.50x (ISBN 0-313-20184-6, CLEI). Greenwood.
--Economics of Planning Public Works. LC 65-19647. Repr. of 1935 ed. 22.50x (ISBN 0-678-00099-9). Kelley.
--Emergency & High Speed Driving Techniques. LC 76-1675. pap. 35.50 (ISBN 0-317-26817-1, 2024311). Bks Demand UMI.
--Preface to Social Economics. LC 67-28453. Repr. of 1936 ed. 37.50x (ISBN 0-678-00333-5). Kelley.
--Private Monopolies & the Trust Problem in the United States. (Illus.). 147p. 1984. 117.45 (ISBN 0-86654-130-6). Inst Econ Finan.
--Social Control of Business. 2nd ed. LC 68-55508. Repr. of 1939 ed. 39.50x (ISBN 0-678-00526-5). Kelley.
--Standards of Reasonableness in Local Freight Discriminations. LC 68-56651. (Columbia University. Studies in the Social Sciences: No. 97). Repr. of 1910 ed. 16.50 (ISBN 0-404-51097-3). AMS Pr.
--Strategic Factors in Business Cycles. Repr. of 1934 ed. 25.00x (ISBN 0-678-00016-6). Kelley.
--Studies in the Economics of Overhead Costs. (Midway Reprint). 1981. pap. 27.00x (ISBN 0-226-10851-1). U of Chicago Pr.
Clark, John M., jt. auth. see Clark, John B.
Clark, John M., jt. auth. see Ward, Alfred D.
Clark, John M., Jr. & Switzer, Robert L. Experimental Biochemistry. 2nd ed. (Illus.). 335p. 1977. lab. manual 17.95 (ISBN 0-7167-0179-0). W H Freeman.
Clark, John P. America, Their America. LC 79-80851. 224p. 1969. pap. 9.50x (ISBN 0-8419-0012-4, Africana). Holmes & Meier.
--Casualties, Poems Nineteen Sixty-Six to Nineteen Sixty-Eight. LC 73-113090. 63p. 1970. 9.50x (ISBN 0-8419-0096-5, Africana); pap. 6.00x (ISBN 0-8419-0041-8, Africana). Holmes & Meier.
--The Example of Shakespeare. 1971. 11.95 (ISBN 0-8101-0340-0); pap. 5.95 (ISBN 0-8101-0341-9). Northwestern U Pr.
--Max Stirner's Egoism. 111p. (Orig.). pap. 4.00 (ISBN 0-900384-14-X). Left Bank.
--The Philosophical Anarchism of William Godwin. LC 76-24291. 1977. 38.50x (ISBN 0-691-07217-5). Princeton U Pr.
Clark, John P., jt. auth. see Hollinger, Richard C.
Clark, John R. The Beaches of Maui County. LC 80-13857. (Illus.). 172p. 1980. pap. 9.95 (ISBN 0-8248-0694-8). UH Pr.
--The Beaches of O'Ahu. LC 77-8244. (Illus.). 210p. (Orig.). 1977. pap. 5.95 (ISBN 0-8248-0510-0). UH Pr.
--Beaches of the Big Island. (Illus.). 204p. 1985. pap. 12.95 (ISBN 0-8248-0976-9). UH Pr.
--Coastal Ecosystem Management. LC 81-18650. 940p. 1983. Repr. of 1977 ed. lib. bdg. 59.50 (ISBN 0-89874-456-3). Krieger.
--Commentary on Agreements for Engineering Services & Contract Documents. 62p. 1981. 10.00 (ISBN 0-686-48322-7). Am Consul Eng.
--The Great Living System. 1984. pap. 7.95 (ISBN 0-933840-24-1). Unitarian Univ.
Clark, John S. & Odell, John P. Study of English & American Writers: A Laboratory Method. LC 72-1070. Repr. of 1916 ed. 34.50 (ISBN 0-404-01559-X). AMS Pr.
Clark, John W. The Care of Books: An Essay on the Development of Libraries & Their Fittings, from the Earliest Times to the End of the 18th Century. 442p. 1980. 50.00x (ISBN 0-902089-78-1, Pub. by Variorum England). State Mutual Bk.
Clark, John W., jt. auth. see Partridge, Eric.
Clark, John W., et al. Water Supply & Pollution Control. 3rd ed. 661p. 1977. text ed. 38.75 scp (ISBN 0-7002-2495-5, HarpC); scp solution manual 4.50 (ISBN 0-7002-2496-3). Har-Row.
Clark, Johnnie M. Guns Up! 368p. (Orig.). 1984. pap. 3.50 (ISBN 0-345-31507-3). Ballantine.
Clark, Jon & Hoffer, Jeffrey A. Physical Data Base Record Design. (The Data Base Monograph Ser.: No. 7). (Illus.). 1979. pap. 15.00 (ISBN 0-89435-008-0). QED Info Sci.
Clark, Jon, et al. Trade Unions, National Politics & Economic Management. 132p. 1980. 36.00x (ISBN 0-905492-24-2, Pub. by Anglo-german Found England). State Mutual Bk.
Clark, Jon D. Data Base Selection, Design, & Administration. LC 80-607121. 250p. 1980. 37.95x (ISBN 0-03-055891-3). Praeger.
Clark, Jon D. & Reisman, Arnold. Computer System Selection: An Intergrated Approach. LC 80-21496. 236p. 1981. 37.95x (ISBN 0-03-057888-4). Praeger.
Clark, Joseph G. Lights & Shadows of Sailor Life. facsimile ed. LC 70-169754. (Select Bibliographies Reprint Ser). Repr. of 1847 ed. 22.00 (ISBN 0-8369-5974-4). Ayer Co Pubs.
Clark, Joseph S. Congress, the Sapless Branch. LC 74-1778. 268p. 1976. Repr. of 1964 ed. lib. bdg. 18.50x (ISBN 0-8371-7398-1, CLCO). Greenwood.
Clark, Joseph S., et al. The Senate Establishment. LC 83-26395. 138p. 1984. Repr. of 1963 ed. lib. bdg. 25.00x (ISBN 0-313-24285-2, CLSE). Greenwood.
Clark, Joshua V. Onondaga, or, Reminiscences of Earlier & Later Times, Being a Series of Historical Sketches Relative to Onondaga.., 2 vols. LC 73-12561. (Illus.). 796p. 1973. Repr. of 1849 ed. Set. 29.00 ea. (ISBN 0-527-17665-6). Kraus Repr.
Clark, Julia B., et al. Pharmacological Basis of Nursing Practice. LC 81-14192. (Illus.). 692p. 1982. pap. text ed. 29.95 (ISBN 0-8016-4061-X). Mosby.
Clark, Julia H., jt. ed. see Reynolds, Cecil R.
Clark, June & Hiller, Renate B. Community Care. 2nd ed. 160p. 1980. 8.95 (ISBN 0-471-25641-2, Pub. by Wiley Heyden). Wiley.
Clark, June & Henderson, Jill, eds. Community Health. LC 82-22038. (Illus.). 317p. 1983. pap. text ed. 24.00 (ISBN 0-443-02000-0). Churchill.
Clark, K. & Tarnbund, S. A. Logic Programming. 1982. 37.50 (ISBN 0-12-175520-7). Acad Pr.
Clark, Kate. Chile: Reality & Prospects of Popular Unity. 142p. 1972. pap. 8.95x (ISBN 0-8464-0245-9). Beekman Pubs.
--White Butterflies & Other Stories. facsimile ed. LC 75-103505. (Short Story Index Reprint Ser). 1900. 18.00 (ISBN 0-8369-3247-1). Ayer Co Pubs.
Clark, Kate M. Maori Tales & Legends. LC 78-67696. (The Folktale). Repr. of 1896 ed. 14.00 (ISBN 0-404-16067-0). AMS Pr.
Clark, Katerina. The Soviet Novel: History As Ritual. LC 80-18758. (Chicago Original Paperback). 1981. U of Chicago Pr.
--The Soviet Novel: History As Ritual. LC 80-18758. 1985. pap. 11.95 (ISBN 0-317-27258-6). U of Chicago Pr.
Clark, Katerina & Holquist, Michael. Mikhail Bakhtin. (Illus.). 416p. 1985. 25.00 (ISBN 0-674-57416-8, Belknap Pr). Harvard U Pr.
Clark, Kathy. Another Sunny Day. (Candlelight Ecstasy Ser.: No. 306). (Orig.). 1985. pap. 1.95 (ISBN 0-440-10202-2). Dell.
--Golden Days. (Candlelight Ecstasy Ser.: No. 378). (Orig.). 1985. pap. 2.25 (ISBN 0-440-13170-7). Dell.
--A Private Affair. (Candlelight Ecstasy Ser.: No. 356). 1985. pap. 2.25 (ISBN 0-440-17101-6). Dell.
Clark, Keith. An Experience of Celibacy. LC 81-69747. (Illus.). 176p. (Orig.). 1982. pap. 4.95 (ISBN 0-87793-240-9). Ave Maria.
--International Communications, the American Attitude. LC 68-58559. (Columbia University Studies in the Social Sciences: No. 340). Repr. of 1931 ed. 21.00 (ISBN 0-404-51340-9). AMS Pr.
--Make Space, Make Symbols. LC 78-73826. (Illus.). 112p. 1979. pap. 2.45 (ISBN 0-87793-173-9). Ave Maria.
Clark, Keith & Clark, Donna, eds. Daring Donald McKay: Or Last War Trail of the Modocs. LC 74-184573. (Illus.). 1971. pap. 2.95 (ISBN 0-87595-032-9). Oreg Hist Soc.
Clark, Keith L. & McCabe, Frank. Micro-Prolog: Programming in Logic. 1984. pap. 16.95 (ISBN 0-13-581264-X). P-H.
Clark, Kenneth. Another Part of the Wood: A Self-Portrait. LC 74-15816. (Illus.). 300p. 1975. 14.95i (ISBN 0-06-010783-9, HarpT). Har-Row.
--The Art of Humanism. LC 82-48689. (Illus.). 192p. 1983. 19.23i (ISBN 0-06-430861-8, Icon Edns). Har-Row.
--Civilisation: A Personal View. LC 75-97174. (Illus.). 416p. 1970. 28.80i (ISBN 0-06-010800-2, CN 787, HarpT). Har-Row.

--The Drawings by Sandro Botticelli for Dante's Divine Comedy: After the Originals in the Berlin Museums & the Vatican. LC 76-5990. (Illus.). 192p. 1976. 55.00i (ISBN 0-06-010777-4, HarpT). Har-Row.
--The Gothic Revival: An Essay in the History of Taste. LC 73-21308. (Icon Editions). (Illus.). 248p. 1974. pap. 6.95xi (ISBN 0-06-430048-X, IN-48, HarpT). Har-Row.
--An Introduction to Rembrandt. LC 77-3745. (Illus.). 160p. 1979. (Econ Edns); pap. 8.95i (ISBN 0-06-430092-7, IN 92). Har-Row.
--Landscape into Art. rev. & enl. ed. (Icon Editions). (Illus.). 1979. pap. 12.95 (ISBN 0-06-430088-9, IN-88, HarpT). Har-Row.
--Landscape into Art. rev. & enl. ed. LC 75-23876. (Illus.). 320p. 1976. 19.95i (ISBN 0-06-010781-2, HarpT). Har-Row.
--Leonardo Da Vinci. 256p. 1976. pap. 4.95 (ISBN 0-14-020430-X, Pelican). Penguin.
--Moments of Vision: & Other Essays. LC 81-47225. 192p. 1982. 14.37i (ISBN 0-06-014885-3, HarpT). Har-Row.
--The Other Half: A Self-Portrait. LC 77-82356. (Illus.). 1978. 13.95i (ISBN 0-06-010774-X, HarpT). Har-Row.
--Piero Della Francesca. 2nd ed. LC 81-66150. (Cornell-Phaidon Bks.). (Illus.). 239p. 1981. 85.00x (ISBN 0-8014-1423-7). Cornell U Pr.
--Rembrandt & the Italian Renaissance. LC 66-13550. (Illus.). 1966. 45.00x (ISBN 0-8147-0080-2). NYU Pr.
--The Romantic Rebellion: Romantic Versus Classic Art. LC 72-9751. (Illus.). 320p. (YA) 1974. 25.00i (ISBN 0-06-010802-9, HarpT). Har-Row.
--What Is a Masterpiece? (Illus.). 1981. pap. 3.95 (ISBN 0-500-27206-9). Thames Hudson.
--What Is a Masterpiece? 1983. 13.00 (ISBN 0-8446-5991-6). Peter Smith.
Clark, Kenneth, ed. Ruskin Today. 350p. 1983. pap. 5.95 (ISBN 0-14-006326-9). Penguin.
Clark, Kenneth B. Dark Ghetto: Dilemmas of Social Power. pap. 6.95xi (ISBN 0-06-131317-3, TB1317, Torch). Har-Row.
--King, Malcolm, Baldwin: Three Interviews. (Illus.). viii, 60p. 1985. pap. 9.95 (ISBN 0-8195-6090-1); 16.00x (ISBN 0-8195-5110-4). Wesleyan U Pr.
--Pathos of Power. 188p. 1975. pap. 5.95x (ISBN 0-06-131857-4, TB1857, Torch). Har-Row.
--Prejudice & Your Child. xxi, 252p. 1986. pap. 10.95 (ISBN 0-8195-6155-X). Wesleyan U Pr.
Clark, Kenneth B. & Franklin, John Hope. The Nineteen Eighties: Prologue & Prospect. 22p. (Orig.). 1981. pap. 2.95 (ISBN 0-941410-20-X). Jt Ctr Pol Studies.
Clark, Kenneth L. Civilisation. LC 75-97174. (Illus.). 1970. pap. 11.49 (ISBN 0-06-090787-8, CN). Har-Row.
Clark, Kenneth M. The Artist Grows Old. LC 72-898082. (Rede Lecture, 1970 Ser.). (Illus.). pap. 20.00 (ISBN 0-317-10528-0, 2051371). Bks Demand UMI.
--The Nude: A Study in Ideal Form. (Bollingen Series, No. 35: A. W. Mellon Lectures in the Fine Arts, Vol. 2). (Illus.). 458p. 1972. 70.00x (ISBN 0-691-09792-5); pap. 14.95x (ISBN 0-691-01788-3). Princeton U Pr.
Clark, Kenneth M. & Clark, Baron. Landscape Painting. LC 83-45735. Repr. of 1950 ed. 57.50 (ISBN 0-404-20061-3). AMS Pr.
Clark, Kim B., jt. auth. see Abernathey, William J.
Clark, Kim B., jt. auth. see Abernathy, William J.
Clark, Kim B., et al, eds. The Uneasy Alliance: Managing the Productivity - Technology Dilemma. 480p. 1985. 32.95 (ISBN 0-87584-172-4). Harvard Busn.
Clark, L. A., jt. ed. see Cope, R. J.
Clark, L. D. Civil War Recollections of James Lemuel Clark. LC 84-40138. (Essays on the American West Sponsored by the Elma Dill Russell Spencer Foundation Ser.: No. 7). 120p. 1984. 12.50 (ISBN 0-89096-205-7). Tex A&M Univ Pr.
--The Fifth Wind. 128p. 1981. 15.00 (ISBN 0-933188-18-8); pap. 6.95 (ISBN 0-933188-17-X). Blue Moon Pr.
--Is This Naomi & Other Stories: A Cycle of Rural Life. (Fiction Ser.). (Illus., Orig.). 1979. pap. 4.95 (ISBN 0-933188-11-0). Blue Moon Pr.
--The Minoan Distance: The Symbolism of Travel in D. H. Lawrence. LC 80-18844. 428p. 1980. pap. 14.95x (ISBN 0-8165-0712-0). U of Ariz Pr.
Clark, L. H., jt. auth. see Ruttenber, E. M.
Clark, L. H., jt. ed. see Ruttenber, E. M.
Clark, L. J. Surface Crystallography: An Introduction to Low Energy Electron Diffraction. 1985. 49.95 (ISBN 0-471-90513-5). Wiley.
Clark, L. R., et al. The Ecology of Insect Populations in Theory & Practice. 1974. pap. 11.95 (ISBN 0-412-21170-X, NO.6059, Pub. by Chapman & Hall). Methuen Inc.
Clark, L. Roy & Locke, Sam. How to Survive Your Doctor's Care. Straubing, Harold E., ed. (Illus.). 80p. 1981. pap. 4.95 (ISBN 0-87786-005-X). Gold Penny.
Clark, Laura V. A Study of the Relationship Between the Vocational Home Economics Teacher Training Curricula of a Group of Women's Colleges & Expected Responsibilities of Beginning Teachers. LC 72-176649. (Columbia University. Teachers College. Contributions to Education: No. 586). Repr. of 1933 ed. 22.50 (ISBN 0-404-55586-1). AMS Pr.
Clark, LaVerne H. The Deadly Swarm & Other Stories. LC 85-61099. (Illus.). 136p. (Orig.). 1985. pap. 5.00 (ISBN 0-9605008-2-0). Hermes Hse.
--Focus One Hundred One. LC 78-57156. (Illus.). 1979. pap. text ed. 7.95 (ISBN 0-918606-03-9). Heidelberg Graph.
--They Sang for Horses: The Impact of the Horse on Navajo & Apache Folklore. LC 66-18527. (Illus.). 225p. 1966. pap. 14.95 (ISBN 0-8165-0810-0). U of Ariz Pr.
Clark, LaVerne H. & MacArthur, Mary. The Face of Poetry. 2nd ed. LC 79-17351. (Illus.). 1979. pap. text ed. 8.95 (ISBN 0-918606-04-7); Focus 101 7.95 (ISBN 0-918606-03-9). Heidelberg Graph.
Clark, Lawerence S., jt. auth. see Schroeder, Betty L.
Clark, Lawrence. Sayula Popoluca Verb Derivation. (Language Data, Amerindian Ser.: No. 8). 80p. (Orig.). 1983. pap. 8.50 (ISBN 0-88312-616-8); microfiche 1.93 (ISBN 0-88312-508-0). Summer Inst Ling.
Clark, Lawrence & Clark, Nancy. Vocabulario Popoluca de Sayula. (Vocabularios Indigenas Ser.: No. 4). 165p. (Span.). 1960. pap. 3.00x (ISBN 0-88312-663-X); microfiche 2.25 (ISBN 0-88312-365-7). Summer Inst Ling.
Clark, Lawrence P. Designs for Evaluating Social Programs. (Learning Packages in the Policy Sciences Ser.: No. 11). 44p. 1979. pap. text ed. 3.00x (ISBN 0-936826-00-2). Pol Stud Assocs.
--Introduction to Surveys & Interviews. (Learning Packages in the Policy Sciences Ser.: No. 12). (Illus.). 56p. 1978. pap. text ed. 3.00x (ISBN 0-936826-01-0). Pol Stud Assocs.
Clark, Leon E. Through African Eyes: From Tribe to Town - Problems of Adjustment, Vol. 2. (Illus.). 125p. (YA) (gr. 9-12). 1981. pap. 5.95x (ISBN 0-938960-08-3). CITE.
--Through African Eyes: Nation-Building - Tanzania & the World, Vol. 6. (Illus.). 160p. (YA) (gr. 9-12). 1981. pap. 5.95x (ISBN 0-938960-12-1). CITE.
--Through African Eyes: The Colonial Experience - An Inside View, Vol. 4. (Illus.). 135p. (YA) (gr. 9-12). 1981. pap. 5.95x (ISBN 0-938960-10-5). CITE.
--Through African Eyes: The Rise of Nationalism - Freedom Regained, Vol. 5. (Illus.). 141p. (YA) (gr. 9-12). 1981. pap. 5.95x (ISBN 0-938960-11-3). CITE.
Clark, Leon E., ed. see Johnson, Donald J. & Johnson, Jean E.
Clark, Leon E., ed. see Minear, Richard H.
Clark, Leon E., ed. see Pearson, Robert P.
Clark, Leon E., ed. see Seybolt, Peter J.
Clark, Leonard. Alfred Williams: His Life & Work. LC 69-13754. (Illus.). Repr. of 1945 ed. 25.00x (ISBN 0-678-05512-2). Kelley.
--The Hearing Heart. 1973. 5.00 (ISBN 0-685-40892-2, Pub. by Enitharmon Pr); pap. 3.50 (ISBN 0-685-40893-0); signed, limited 12.50 (ISBN 0-685-40894-9). Small Pr Dist.
--Walking with Trees, Poems. 1970. pap. 4.50 (ISBN 0-685-01019-8, Pub. by Enitharmon Pr). Small Pr Dist.
Clark, Leonard & Blunden, Edmund. A Tribute to Walter De La Mare. 1974. wrappers, 225 copies 6.00 (ISBN 0-685-46798-8, Pub. by Enitharmon Pr). Small Pr Dist.
Clark, Leonard H. & Klein, Raymond L. The American Secondary School Curriculum. 2nd ed. (Illus.). 544p. 1972. text ed. write for info. (ISBN 0-02-322580-7, 32258). Macmillan.
Clark, Leonard H. & Starr, Irving S. Secondary School Teaching Methods. 4th ed. (Illus.). 512p. 1981. text ed. write for info. (ISBN 0-02-322650-1, 322650). Macmillan.
Clark, Leonard H., jt. auth. see Callahan, Joseph F.
Clark, Leslie F., jt. auth. see Graesser, Arthur C.
Clark, Leta W. How to Open Your Own Shop or Gallery. (Handbook Ser.). 1980. pap. 5.95 (ISBN 0-14-046409-3). Penguin.
Clark, Lewis J. Wild Flowers of Marsh & Waterway. (Lewis Clark's Field Guides: E.T.T.A.). 1974. pap. 4.95 (ISBN 0-88826-052-0). Superior Pub.
--Wild Flowers of the Arid Flatlands. (Lewis Clark's Field Guides). 1975. pap. 4.95 (ISBN 0-88826-054-7). Superior Pub.
--Wild Flowers of the Pacific Northwest: From Alaska to Northern California. Trelawny, John G., ed. (Illus.). 1976. 55.95 (ISBN 0-686-67594-0). Superior Pub.
--Wild Flowers of the Pacific Northwest from Alaska to Northern California. Trelawny, John G., ed. (Illus.). 616p. 1976. Repr. of 1976 ed. 40.00 (ISBN 0-295-96079-5). U of Wash Pr.
--Wild Flowers of the Sea Coast. (Lewis Clark's Field Guides). 1974. pap. 4.95 (ISBN 0-88826-053-9). Superior Pub.
Clark, Lewis J. & Trelawny, John G., eds. Wildflowers of Marsh & Waterway in the Pacific Northwest. (Illus.). 64p. 1976. pap. 4.95 (ISBN 0-295-96091-4). U of Wash Pr.
--Wildflowers of the Arid Flatlands in the Pacific Northwest. (Illus.). 80p. 1976. pap. 4.95 (ISBN 0-295-96093-0). U of Wash Pr.
--Wildflowers of the Field & Slope in the Pacific Northwest. (Illus.). 64p. 1976. pap. 4.95 (ISBN 0-295-96125-2). U of Wash Pr.
--Wildflowers of the Forest & Woodland in the Pacific Northwest. (Illus.). 64p. 1976. pap. 4.95 (ISBN 0-295-96099-X). U of Wash Pr.
--Wildflowers of the Mountains. (Illus.). 64p. 1976. pap. 4.95 (ISBN 0-295-96098-1). U of Wash Pr.
--Wildflowers of the Sea Coast in the Pacific Northwest. (Illus.). 64p. 1976. pap. 4.95 (ISBN 0-295-96092-2). U of Wash Pr.
Clark, Lincoln H. & Assael, Henry, eds. Consumer Behavior. LC 78-294. (Century of Marketing Ser.). (Illus.). 1978. Repr. of 1958 ed. lib. bdg. 38.50x (ISBN 0-405-11166-5). Ayer Co Pubs.
Clark, Linda. Are You Radioactive? LC 73-76155. 128p. 1973. pap. 5.95 (ISBN 0-8159-5013-6). Devin.
--Be Slim & Healthy. (Spanish ed.). 1980. pap. 5.95 (ISBN 0-87983-187-1). Keats.
--Be Slim & Healthy. LC 72-83520. (Pivot Original Health Book). 192p. (Orig.). 1972. pap. 1.95 (ISBN 0-87983-025-5). Keats.
--Beauty Questions & Answers. 1981. pap. 8.95x (Regent House). B of A.
--The Best of Linda Clark. LC 77-352686. (Orig.). 1976. pap. 4.50 (ISBN 0-87983-062-X). Keats.
--The Best of Linda Clark, Vol. 2. LC 77-352686. Date not set. pap. 6.95 (ISBN 0-87983-249-5). Keats.
--Color Therapy. LC 74-75389. 1975. 9.95 (ISBN 0-8159-5206-6). Devin.
--Color Therapy. 1981. pap. 2.75 (ISBN 0-671-44508-1). PB.
--Face Improvement Through Exercise & Nutrition. LC 72-97919. (Pivot Original Health Bk.). (Illus.). 96p. 1973. pap. 2.25 (ISBN 0-87983-034-4). Keats.
--Get Well Naturally. LC 65-18927. 1968. pap. 2.95 (ISBN 0-668-01762-7). Arco.
--Get Well Naturally. 5.95x (ISBN 0-686-29889-6); pap. 2.95x (ISBN 0-668-01762-7). Cancer Control Soc.
--Get Well Naturally. 1974. Repr. of 1965 ed. 11.95 (ISBN 0-8159-5605-3). Devin.
--Go-Caution-Stop Carbohydrate Computer. (Pivot Health Book Ser.). 48p. (YA) 1973. pap. 1.95 (ISBN 0-87983-056-5). Keats.
--Handbook of Natural Remedies. pap. 3.50x (ISBN 0-671-42382-7). Cancer Control Soc.
--Handbook of Natural Remedies for Common Ailments. LC 75-13349. 292p. 1976. 14.95 (ISBN 0-8159-5710-6). Devin.
--The Health & Beauty Book for Pets: A Nutritional Guide. LC 79-11545. (Illus., Orig.). 1980. pap. 5.95 (ISBN 0-89407-028-2). Strawberry Hill.
--Help Yourself to Health. 2nd, rev. ed. 268p. 1985. pap. 9.95 (ISBN 0-8159-5722-X). Devin.
--How to Improve Your Health. LC 78-61329. 1979. 8.95 (ISBN 0-87983-181-2); pap. 4.95 (ISBN 0-87983-180-4). Keats.
--Know Your Nutrition. rev. ed. LC 80-84437. 275p. 1981. pap. 4.95 (ISBN 0-87983-247-9). Keats.
--Know Your Nutrition. LC 80-84437. 276p. 1984. pap. 3.50 (ISBN 0-87983-401-3). Keats.
--Light on Your Health Problems. LC 72-83522. (Pivot Original Health Book). 240p. 1972. pap. 1.50 (ISBN 0-87983-026-3). Keats.
--Linda Clark's Cookbook. LC 77-8716. (Illus., Orig.). 1977. pap. 4.95 (ISBN 0-89407-009-6). Strawberry Hill.
--Mantegase Delgado Y Sano. Orig. Title: Be Slim & Healthy. (Orig., Span.). 1980. pap. 5.95 (ISBN 0-87983-187-1). Keats.
--Rejuvenation. 1978. 12.95 (ISBN 0-8159-6718-7). Devin.
--Rejuvenation. 201p. 10.00 (ISBN 0-318-15684-9). Natl Health Fed.
--Sepa Como Alimentarse. Orig. Title: Know Your Nutrition. (Orig., Span.). 1980. pap. 5.95 (ISBN 0-87983-174-X). Keats.
--Stay Young Longer. 3.50x (ISBN 0-8158-0177-7). Cancer Control Soc.
--What's in It for You: Natural. 1981. pap. 4.95x (ISBN 0-317-06945-4, Regent House). B of A.
Clark, Linda & Martine, Yvonne. Health, Youth & Beauty Through Color Breathing. LC 75-28754. 160p. 1976. pap. 4.95 (ISBN 0-89087-113-2). Celestial Arts.
Clark, Linda & Ronan, Marian. Image Breaking - Image Building: A Handbook for Creative Worship. LC 80-28896. 144p. (Orig.). 1981. pap. 7.95 (ISBN 0-8298-0407-2). Pilgrim NY.
Clark, Linda, et al. Your Natural Beauty Sampler. LC 77-92810. 1978. pap. 1.95 (ISBN 0-87983-168-5). Keats.
Clark, Linda A. Secrets of Health & Beauty: How to Make Yourself Over. 1969. 9.95 (ISBN 0-8159-6807-8). Devin.
Clark, Linda L. Schooling the Daughters of Marianne: Textbooks & the Socialization of Girls in Modern French Primary Schools. (European Social History Ser.). 226p. 1984. 34.50x (ISBN 0-87395-787-3); pap. 12.95x (ISBN 0-87395-786-5). State U NY Pr.
--Social Darwinism in France. LC 82-21795. xi, 261p. 1984. text ed. 28.75 (ISBN 0-8173-0149-6). U of Ala Pr.
Clark, Lorenne & Lange, Lynda, eds. The Sexism of Social & Political Theory: Women & Reproduction from Plato to Nietzsche. LC 79-17862. 1979. o. p. 20.00x (ISBN 0-8020-5459-5); pap. 8.95 (ISBN 0-8020-6375-6). U of Toronto Pr.
Clark, Lorenzoni. Applied Cost Engineering. 2nd, rev. & exp. ed. (Cost Engineering Ser.). 288p. 1985. 32.50 (ISBN 0-8247-7264-4). Dekker.
Clark, Louis E., jt. auth. see Treadway, F. H., Jr.
Clark, Louis H. The Complete Guide for the Manufacturer's Rep: How to Get & Hold Key Accounts. 264p. 1975. 26.50 (ISBN 0-07-011160-X). McGraw.
Clark, Lyn R., jt. auth. see Clark, James L.
Clark, M. Amazing Circulatory System. LC 76-24995. (Tech. Monograph: No. 5). 66p. 1976. 5.95 (ISBN 0-89051-024-5). Master Bks.
--Peter Porcupine in America: Career of William Cobbett 1792-1800. LC 73-16217. 1973. lib. bdg. 25.00 (ISBN 0-8414-3512-X). Folcroft.
Clark, M. Cowden & Clark, C. Recollections of Writers. 364p. 1969. 22.00x (ISBN 0-8464-0785-X). Beekman Pubs.
Clark, M. D., ed. see Kuhlman, Raymond H.
Clark, M. Douglas. Managing the Troubled Employee. LC 79-91188. (Illus.). 77p. 1979. Incl. transparency masters. 69.50 (ISBN 0-88061-009-3). Inst Pub GA.
--Risk Control for Churches. LC 81-86316. (Illus.). 1981. 3-ring binder 39.50 (ISBN 0-88061-007-7). Inst Pub GA.
Clark, M. Douglas & Germain, George L. Supervisory Safety Promotion. (Illus.). 1978. Incl. transparency masters. 3-ring binder 49.50 (ISBN 0-88061-020-4). Inst Pub GA.
Clark, M. Gardner. The Development of China's Steel Industry & Soviet Technical Aid. LC 72-619194. 168p. 1973. pap. 7.00 (ISBN 0-87546-292-8); special hard bdg. 11.00 (ISBN 0-87546-293-6). ILR Pr.
Clark, M. J. Politics & the Media: Film & Television for the Political Scientist & Historian. (Audio-Visual Media Education & Research: Vol. 1). 1979. o. p. 30.00 (ISBN 0-08-022483-0); pap. 15.50 (ISBN 0-08-022484-9). Pergamon.
Clark, M. M. & Cheyne, W. M., eds. Studies in Pre-School Education. (SCRE Ser.: No. 70). 292p. 1979. text ed. 20.50x (ISBN 0-901116-68-8, Pub. by Scottish Coun Res Uk). Humanities.
Clark, M. R. Organized Labor in Mexico. 1976. lib. bdg. 59.95 (ISBN 0-8490-2381-5). Gordon Pr.
Clark, Sr. M. Ursula. Cult of Enthusiasm in French Romanticism. LC 70-94179. (Catholic University of America. Studies in Romance Languages & Literatures: No. 37). Repr. of 1950 ed. 25.00 (ISBN 0-404-50337-3). AMS Pr.
Clark, Macdonald. Maurice Maeterlinck Poet & Philosopher. 1916. Repr. 30.00 (ISBN 0-8274-2694-1). R West.
Clark, Magnus. Nudism in Australia. McAdam, N. & Newhouse, C., eds. (Illus.). 364p. (Orig.). 1984. pap. 19.95 (ISBN 0-910550-53-0). Elysium.
Clark, Malcolm. Invitations to Thinking: A Philosophical Workbook. 208p. 1981. pap. text ed. 12.95 (ISBN 0-8403-2431-6). Kendall-Hunt.
Clark, Malcolm, Jr. & Porter, Kenneth W. War on the Webfoot Saloon & Other Tales of Feminine Adventures. (Illus.). 54p. 1969. pap. 2.95 (ISBN 0-87595-023-X). Oreg Hist Soc.
Clark, Malcolm, Jr., intro. by see Deady, Matthew P.
Clark, Malcolm W., jt. auth. see Chivers, Ian D.
Clark, Manning. Occasional Writings & Speeches. 269p. pap. 8.95x (ISBN 0-00-635723-7, Pub. by W Collins Australia). Intl Spec Bk.
Clark, Marcus. For the Term of His Natural Life. Bowker, R. M., ed. 460p. 1981. 39.00x (ISBN 0-686-79247-5, Pub. by Bowker & Bentram UK). State Mutual Bk.
Clark, Marden J. & Cox, Soren F. About Language. 2nd ed. 733p. 1975. pap. text ed. write for info. (ISBN 0-02-322620-X, Pub. by Scribner). Macmillan.
Clark, Marden J., et al. About Language: Contexts for College Writing. 2nd ed. LC 74-13382. 1975. pap. text ed. 13.95x (ISBN 0-684-14098-5, ScribT). Scribner.
Clark, Margaret. Barney in Space. (Illus.). 160p. (gr. 4 up). 1981. PLB 7.95 (ISBN 0-396-08001-4). Dodd.
--Young Fluent Readers. 1976. pap. text ed. 10.00x (ISBN 0-435-80220-8). Heinemann Ed.
Clark, Margaret & Anderson, Barbara G. Culture & Aging. Stein, Leon, ed. LC 79-8827. (Growing Old Ser.). (Illus.). 1980. Repr. of 1967 ed. lib. bdg. 44.00x (ISBN 0-405-12781-2). Ayer Co Pubs.
--Culture & Aging: An Anthropological Study of Older Americans. (Illus.). 496p. 1967. 44.50x (ISBN 0-398-00312-2). C C Thomas.
Clark, Margaret G. Barney & the UFO. LC 79-52046. (Illus.). (gr. 4 up). 1979. 7.95 (ISBN 0-396-07711-0). Dodd.
--Barney on Mars. (Illus.). (gr. 5 up). 1983. 8.95 (ISBN 0-396-08222-X). Dodd.
--Benjamin Banneker: Astronomer & Scientist. LC 74-131055. (Americans All Ser.). (Illus.). (gr. 3-6). 1971. PLB 7.98 (ISBN 0-8116-4564-9). Garrard.
--The Boy from the UFO. 160p. (gr. 3-7). 1981. pap. 1.95 (ISBN 0-590-31594-3). Scholastic Inc.
--The Boy from the UFO Returns. (Illus.). 160p. (gr. 3-6). 1983. pap. 1.95 (ISBN 0-590-32509-4). Scholastic Inc.

--Freedom Crossing. 192p. (Orig.). (gr. 3-7). 1980. pap. 1.95 (ISBN 0-590-31299-5). Scholastic Inc.
--The Latchkey Mystery. 128p. (gr. 4 up). 1985. 10.95 (ISBN 0-396-08639-X). Dodd.
--The Mystery in the Flooded Museum. LC 77-16860. (Illus.). (gr. 5 up). 1978. 7.95 (ISBN 0-396-07550-9). Dodd.
--Their Eyes on the Stars: Four Black Writers. LC 73-3499. (Toward Freedom Ser.). (Illus.). (gr. 5-9). 1973. PLB 4.47 (ISBN 0-8116-4804-4). Garrard.
--Who Stole Kathy Young? LC 80-1013. (gr. 5 up). 1980. 7.95 (ISBN 0-396-07888-5). Dodd.
--Who Stole Kathy Young? (Cat's Eye Mysteries Ser.). 192p. (gr. 3-6). 1983. pap. 1.95 (ISBN 0-590-32165-X). Scholastic Inc.
Clark, Margaret M. Reading Difficulties in Schools. LC 80-670036. (Orig.). 1980. pap. text ed. 10.00x (ISBN 0-435-80221-6). Heinemann Ed.
Clark, Margaret P., jt. auth. see Clark, George.
Clark, Margaret S. & Fiske, Susan T. Affect & Cognition: The Seventeenth Annual Carnegie Symposium on Cognition. (Ongoing Ser.). 368p. 1982. text ed. 36.00x (ISBN 0-89859-212-7). L Erlbaum Assocs.
Clark, Margaret T., jt. auth. see Clark, John J.
Clark, Marguerite, jt. auth. see Holcomb, Brent.
Clark, Marjorie R. A History of the French Labor Movement, 1910-1928. 1930. 15.00 (ISBN 0-384-09215-2). Johnson Repr.
Clark, Mark W. From the Danube to the Yalu. LC 72-12495. (Illus.). 369p. 1973. Repr. of 1954 ed. lib. bdg. 23.00x (ISBN 0-8371-6742-6, CLDY). Greenwood.
Clark, Marlyn E. Optimal Design in Cardiovascular Fluid Mechanics: Our Amazing Circulatory System. LC 76-24995. (ICR Technical Monograph No. 5). (Illus.). 1976. pap. 5.95. Master Bks.
Clark, Martin. Antonio Gramsci & the Revolution That Failed. LC 76-49754. 1977. 31.00x (ISBN 0-300-02077-5). Yale U Pr.
--Modern Italy Eighteen Seventy-One to Nineteen Eighty-Two. (Longman History of Italy Ser.). (Illus.). 448p. 1984. text ed. 35.00 (ISBN 0-582-48361-1); pap. text ed. 19.95 (ISBN 0-582-48362-X). Longman.
Clark, Martin, jt. auth. see Morris, Henry M.
Clark, Martin E. Choosing Your Career: The Christian's Decision Manual. 1981. pap. 3.95 (ISBN 0-87552-205-X). Presby & Reformed.
--Choosing Your Career: The Christian's Decision Manual. 120p. (Orig.). 1983. pap. 3.95 (ISBN 0-8010-2483-8). Baker Bk.
Clark, Marty, ed. see Ellison, Harlan.
Clark, Marvin H., Jr. Pinnell & Talifson: Last of the Great Brown Bear Men. (Illus.). 224p. 1980. 19.95 (ISBN 0-937708-00-3). Great Northwest.
--Pinnell & Talifson: Last of the Great Brown Bear Men. (Illus.). 224p. 1985. pap. 12.95 (ISBN 0-937708-03-8). Great Northwest.
--Track of the Kodiak. (Illus.). 224p. 1984. 19.95 (ISBN 0-937708-01-1). Great Northwest.
Clark, Mary. Stop that Witch! LC 85-51048. (Crimson Crystal Adventures Ser.). (Illus.). 160p. (gr. 4-6). 1985. pap. 2.95 (ISBN 0-394-74241-9). Random.
Clark, Mary, jt. auth. see Hudson, M. E.
Clark, Mary, ed. The Whole Literature Catalogue: American Writing in the 1980s-Where to Find It & How to Get It. (Illus.). 120p. (Orig.). 1983. pap. 7.95x (ISBN 0-686-88904-5). Public Pr.
Clark, Mary Cowden see Cowden-Clark, Mary.
Clark, Mary E. Contemporary Biology. 2nd ed. 1979. text ed. 32.95 (ISBN 0-7216-2598-3, CBS C). SCP.
--Peter Porcupine in America: The Career of William Cobbett. (American Newspapermen 1790-1933 Ser.). v, 193p. 1974. Repr. of 1939 ed. 11.00x (ISBN 0-8464-0026-X). Beekman Pubs.
--Peter Porcupine in America: The Career of William Cobbett, 1792-1800. 1978. Repr. of 1937 ed. lib. bdg. 25.00 (ISBN 0-8495-0830-4). Arden Lib.
Clark, Mary F. Hiding, Hurting, Healing. 176p. (Orig.). 1985. pap. 6.95 (ISBN 0-310-30551-9, Pub. by Zondervan Bks). Zondervan.
Clark, Mary H. The Cradle Will Fall. 432p. 1981. pap. 3.95 (ISBN 0-440-11545-0). Dell.
--A Cry in the Night. (General Ser.). 1983. lib. bdg. 15.95 (ISBN 0-8161-3482-0, Large Print Bks). G K Hall.
--A Cry in the Night. 320p. 1983. pap. 3.95 (ISBN 0-440-11065-3). Dell.
--Stillwatch. 1984. 14.95 (ISBN 0-671-46952-5). S&S.
--Stillwatch. (General Ser.). 1985. lib. bdg. 15.95 (ISBN 0-8161-3694-7, Large Print Bks). G K Hall.
--A Stranger Is Watching. 288p. 1979. pap. 3.95 (ISBN 0-440-18127-5). Dell.
--Where Are the Children? 256p. (YA) (gr. 7 up). pap. 3.95 (ISBN 0-440-19593-4). Dell.
--Where Are the Children. (General Ser.). 330p. 1983. lib. bdg. 13.95 (ISBN 0-8161-3511-8, Large Print Bks). G K Hall.
Clark, Mary Jo. Community Nursing: Health Care for Today & Tomorrow. 1984. text ed. 24.95 (ISBN 0-8359-0842-9); instr's manual avail. (ISBN 0-8359-0843-7). Reston.
Clark, Mary L. Dinosaurs. LC 81-7750. (The New True Books). (Illus.). 48p. (gr. k-4). 1981. PLB 10.60 (ISBN 0-516-01612-1); pap. 3.95 (ISBN 0-516-41612-X). Childrens.
Clark, Mary T., jt. auth. see Casey, Helen.
Clark, Mary T., ed. An Aquinas Reader. LC 72-76709. pap. 6.95 (ISBN 0-385-02505-X, Im). Doubleday.
Clark, Mary T., tr. see Augustine of Hippo.
Clark, Mason A., ed. The Healing Wisdom of Doctor P. P. Quimby. LC 82-24232. (Illus.). 128p. (Orig.). 1982. pap. text ed. 8.95 (ISBN 0-931400-02-3). Frontal Lobe.
Clark, Mavis T. If the Earth Falls In. LC 75-4781. 176p. (gr. 6 up). 1975. 6.95 (ISBN 0-395-28900-9, Clarion). HM.
Clark, Melanie B. A Treasury of Poetry. 1981. 4.50 (ISBN 0-8062-1687-5). Carlton.
Clark, Melville & Hansen, K. F. Numerical Methods of Reactor Analysis. (Nuclear Science & Technology: Vol. 3). 1964. 68.50 (ISBN 0-12-175350-6). Acad Pr.
Clark, Merrian E. Ford's Deck Plan Guide. 7th, rev. ed. LC 74-27649. 1982. 50.00 (ISBN 0-916486-58-3). M Clark.
--Ford's Freighter Travel Guide. 63rd rev. ed. LC 54-3845. (Illus.). 144p. 1984. pap. 7.50 (ISBN 0-916486-26-5). Fords Travel.
--Ford's Freighter Travel Guide: 1984-85. rev. ed. LC 54-3845. (Illus.). 144p. 1984. pap. 7.50 (ISBN 0-317-13129-X). Fords Travel.
--Ford's International Cruise Guide. 41st rev. ed. LC 75-27925. (Illus.). 160p. 1984. pap. 8.95 (ISBN 0-916486-27-3). Fords Travel.
--Ford's International Cruise Guide: 1984. rev., 42nd ed. LC 75-27925. (Illus.). 160p. 1984. pap. 8.95 (ISBN 0-317-13128-1). Fords Travel.
--Ford's International Cruise Guide: 1984-85. rev., 43rd ed. LC 75-27925. (Illus.). 160p. 1984. pap. 8.95 (ISBN 0-317-13127-3). Fords Travel.
Clark, Michael. Jacques Lacan: An Annotated Bibliography. LC 84-45394. 400p. 1985. lib. bdg. 54.00 (ISBN 0-8240-8848-4). Garland Pub.
Clark, Michael & Clark, Dorothy. Sexual Joy in Marriage. (Illus.). 256p. (Orig.). 1980. pap. 7.95 (ISBN 0-523-41137-5). Pinnacle Bks.
Clark, Michael, jt. auth. see Small, John.
Clark, Michael D. Coherent Variety: The Idea of Diversity in British & American Conservative Thought. LC 82-9228. (Contributions in Political Science Ser.: No. 86). viii, 228p. 1983. lib. bdg. 35.00 (ISBN 0-313-23284-9, CCV/). Greenwood.
--Worldly Theologians: The Persistence of Religion in Nineteenth Century American Thought. LC 80-5840. 328p. (Orig.). 1982. lib. bdg. 26.25 (ISBN 0-8191-1778-1); pap. text ed. 14.25 (ISBN 0-8191-1779-X). U Pr of Amer.
Clark, Michael P. Michel Foucault: An Annotated Bibliography Took Kit for A New Age. Cain, William, ed. LC 82-48474. (Modern Critics & Critical Schools Ser.). 600p. 1983. lib. bdg. 66.00 (ISBN 0-8240-9253-8). Garland Pub.
Clark, Miles. Glenn Clark: His Life & Writings. LC 75-6877. Repr. of 1975 ed. 30.40 (ISBN 0-8357-9008-8, 2016361). Bks Demand UMI.
Clark, Millard W. Supplement to Trends in Nonprofit Organizations Law, 1979: No. B228. 25p. 1979. pap. 5.00 (ISBN 0-317-30152-6). Am Law Inst.
Clark, Monika T. Just Ducky Dining. 101p. (Orig.). 1984. pap. 10.95 (ISBN 0-9613068-1-5). M T C Pub Co.
--The Poet's Kitchen: A Collector's Work of Original, Creative Entertaining - It's About Time. 152p. (Orig.). 1984. pap. 16.95 (ISBN 0-9613068-0-7). M T C Pub Co.
Clark, Murtie J. Colonial Soldiers of the South, 1732-1774. LC 83-81076. 1246p. 1983. 50.00 (ISBN 0-8063-1036-7). Genealog Pub.
--Loyalists in the Southern Campaign of the Revolutionary War: Official Rolls of Loyalists Recruited from North & South Carolina, Georgia, Florida, Mississippi, & Louisiana, Vol. 1. LC 80-84321. 635p. 1981. 30.00 (ISBN 0-8063-0924-5). Genealog Pub.
--Loyalists in the Southern Campaign of the Revolutionary War: Official Rolls of Loyalists Recruited from Maryland, Pennsylvania, Virginia, & Those Recruited from Other Colonies, Vol. 2. LC 80-84321. 687p. 1981. 30.00 (ISBN 0-8063-0941-5). Genealog Pub.
--Loyalists in the Southern Campaign of the Revolutionary War: Official Rolls of Loyalists Recruited from the Middle Atlantic Colonies, with Lists of Refugees from Other Colonies, Vol. 3. LC 80-84321. 484p. 1981. 25.00 (ISBN 0-8063-0952-0). Genealog Pub.
Clark, N. & Peters, M. Scorable Self-Care Evaluation (SSCE) LC 82-61594. 64p. 1983. pap. 16.50 (ISBN 0-943432-24-3). Slack Inc.
Clark, N. F., et al, eds. Electronic Equipment Wiring & Assembling: Part Two. (Engineering Craftsmen: No. G25). (Illus.). 1969. spiral bdg. 47.50x (ISBN 0-89563-004-4). Trans-Atlantic.
Clark, Nancy. Littleton: A Pictorial History. Friedman, Donna R., ed. LC 80-39601. (Illus.). 208p. 1981. pap. 12.95 cancelled (ISBN 0-89865-112-3). Donning Co.
Clark, Nancy, jt. auth. see Clark, Lawrence.
Clark, Nancy, ed. see Lodo, Venerable L.
Clark, Nancy, ed. see Lodo, Venerable Larma.
Clark, Nancy, et al. Ventilation: A Practical Guide. LC 84-12680. (Illus.). 128p. (Orig.). 1984. pap. text ed. 7.50 (ISBN 0-918875-00-5). Ctr Occupational Hazards.
Clark, Nancy H. How to Cut Kids' Hair. LC 83-25837. (Kid Care Ser.). (Illus.). 64p. 1984. pap. 3.95 (ISBN 0-201-10811-9). Addison-Wesley.
Clark, Naomi. Burglaries & Celebrations. 1977. 6.95 (ISBN 0-685-80001-6); sewn in wrappers 2.95 (ISBN 0-685-80002-4). Oyez.
Clark, Neal. Eastern Birds of Prey: A Guide to the Private Lives of Eastern Raptors. LC 83-4775. (Illus.). 160p. 1983. pap. 7.95 (ISBN 0-89621-073-1). Thorndike Pr.
Clark, Neil. Campfires & Cattle Trails. LC 70-109537. 1970. pap. 2.95 (ISBN 0-87004-195-9). Caxton.
Clark, Neil, et al. Unfinished Business: The Theory & Practice of Personal Process Work in Training. LC 84-8134. 200p. 1984. text ed. 35.50x (ISBN 0-566-02514-0). Gower Pub Co.
Clark, Neil M., jt. auth. see Thorp, N. Howard.
Clark, Nelson. Perceptives in Electronic Technology: Application to Occupational Therapy. LC 85-61755. (Current Practice Ser.). 150p. 1985. pap. text ed. 14.50 (ISBN 0-943432-49-9). Slack Inc.
Clark, Nicolette, jt. auth. see Gibbs, Gloria.
Clark, Noel. The Millionaire Sourcebook. 1971. 10.00 (ISBN 0-685-27198-6). Claitors.
Clark, Norma L. Fanny. 1980. pap. 1.75 (ISBN 0-449-50030-6, Coventry). Fawcett.
--Kitty Quinn. 320p. (Orig.). 1984. pap. 3.50 (ISBN 0-449-20310-7, Crest). Fawcett.
--Lady Jane. 224p. 1982. 11.95 (ISBN 0-8027-0699-1). Walker & Co.
--Mallory. 1978. pap. 1.75 (ISBN 0-449-23608-0, Crest). Fawcett.
--Marriage Mart. 1984. pap. 2.25 (ISBN 0-451-12816-8, Sig). NAL.
--Megan. 1979. pap. 1.75 (ISBN 0-449-50005-5, Coventry). Fawcett.
--The Perfect Match. 224p. 1983. pap. 2.25 (ISBN 0-451-12483-9, Sig). NAL.
--The Tynedale Daughters. LC 80-54482. 192p. 1981. 9.95 (ISBN 0-8027-0676-2). Walker & Co.
--The Tynedale Daughters. (Coventry Romance Ser.: No. 183). 224p. 1982. pap. 1.50 (ISBN 0-449-50285-6, Coventry). Fawcett.
--Zandra. 224p. (Orig.). 1980. pap. 1.75 (ISBN 0-449-50075-6, Coventry). Fawcett.
Clark, Norma Lee. The Impulsive Miss Pymbroke. 1984. pap. 2.50 (ISBN 0-451-13273-4, Sig). NAL.
Clark, Norman. Deliver Us from Evil: An Interpretation of American Prohibition. (Norton Essays in American History Ser.). 1976. pap. 6.95x (ISBN 0-393-09170-8). Norton.
Clark, Norman H. Mill Town: A Social History of Everett, Washington, from Its Earliest Beginnings on the Shores of Puget Sound to the Tragic & Infamous Event Known As the Everett Massacre. LC 75-117726. (Washington Paperback Ser.: No. 63). (Illus.). 277p. 1970. 15.95x (ISBN 0-295-95079-X); pap. 8.95 (ISBN 0-295-95241-5). U of Wash Pr.
--Washington. (States & the Nation Ser). (Illus.). 1976. 14.95 (ISBN 0-393-05587-6, Co-Pub by AASLH). Norton.
Clark, Norman L., ed. see Gaudet, Patricia K.
Clark, Oliver. Never Catch Colds Again. 64p. 1979. pap. 6.95x (ISBN 0-8464-1035-4). Beekman Pubs.
--Never Catch Colds Again. 1980. 15.00x (ISBN 0-85032-162-X, Pub. by Daniel Co England). State Mutual Bk.
--Never Catch Colds Again. 102p. 1983. 9.95 (ISBN 0-13-611590-X); pap. 4.95 (ISBN 0-13-611582-9). P-H.
Clark, Ovilene. Heirloom of Memories. 1983. 8.50 (ISBN 0-8062-2137-2). Carlton.
Clark, P. A. & Slack, P. A. English Towns in Transition Fifteen Hundred to Seventeen Hundred. (Opus 78). (Illus.). 1976. pap. 7.95x (ISBN 0-19-289060-3). Oxford U Pr.
Clark, P. M. & Kricka, L. J. Medical Consequences of Alcohol Abuse. LC 80-41993. (Chemical Science Ser.). 282p. 1980. 115.95x (ISBN 0-470-27076-4). Halsted Pr.
Clark, P. M., jt. auth. see Kricka, L. J.
Clark, Pamela I., jt. auth. see Glasser, Stephen P.
Clark, Patricia Z., jt. auth. see Clark, Charles A., III.
Clark, Patrick. Sports Firsts. 320p. 1981. 14.95 (ISBN 0-87196-302-7). Facts on File.
Clark, Paul F. The Miners' Fight for Democracy: Arnold Miller & the Reform of the United Mine Workers. LC 81-2011. (Cornell Studies in Industrial & Labor Relations: No. 21). (Illus.). 194p. 1981. 16.95 (ISBN 0-87546-086-0); pap. 9.95 (ISBN 0-87546-087-9). ILR Pr.
--University of Wisconsin Medical School: A Chronicle, 1848-1948. (Illus.). 286p. 1967. 19.95x (ISBN 0-299-04350-9). U of Wis Pr.
Clark, Paul O. Gulliver Dictionary. LC 75-100739. (Studies in Comparative Literature, No. 35). 1970. pap. 11.95x (ISBN 0-8383-0015-4). Haskell.
Clark, Paul R. High Seas, High Adventure. LC 83-50649. 264p. 1983. 12.95 (ISBN 0-318-01076-3); pap. 7.95 (ISBN 0-318-01077-1). Stonegate Pub.
Clark, Peggy, et al. Isozymes: Biochemical & Genetic Studies. LC 73-10223. 242p. 1973. text ed. 27.50x (ISBN 0-8422-7126-0). Irvington.
Clark, Perceval. Index to Trevelyan's Life & Letters of Lord Macaulay. LC 73-11257. 1881. lib. bdg. 15.00 (ISBN 0-8414-3408-5). Folcroft.
Clark, Pete Alan. The English Alehouse: A Social History, 1200-1830. 384p. 1983. pap. 19.95 (ISBN 0-582-50835-5). Longman.
Clark, Peter. Black Brigade of Cincinnati: Being a Report of Its Labors & a Muster-Roll of Its Members: Together with Various Orders, Speeches, Etc. Relating to It. LC 73-92227. (American Negro: His History & Literature, Ser. No. 3). 1970. Repr. of 1864 ed. 11.00 (ISBN 0-405-01917-3). Ayer Co Pubs.
--The English Alehouse: A Social History. 1983. pap. 45.00x (ISBN 0-317-20315-0, Pub. by Pinhorns UK). State Mutual Bk.
--Henry Hallam. (English Authors Ser.). 1982. lib. bdg. 16.95 (ISBN 0-8057-6818-1, Twayne). G K Hall.
--O'Neill's Plays Notes. (Orig.). 1966. pap. 3.95 (ISBN 0-8220-0910-2). Cliffs.
Clark, Peter & Landfield, Judy. Natural Energy Workbook Two. rev. & expanded ed. (Illus.). 1976. pap. text ed. 3.95 (ISBN 0-917198-01-8). Visual Purple.
Clark, Peter, ed. Country Towns in Preindustrial England. (Themes in Urban History Ser.). 1982. 30.00 (ISBN 0-312-17033-5). St Martin.
--The European Crisis of the Fifteen Nineties: Essays in Comparative History. 352p. 1985. text ed. 37.50x (ISBN 0-04-940074-6). Allen Unwin.
--The Transformation of English Provincial Towns, 1600-1800. LC 85-4253. (Illus.). 359p. 1984. 33.00 (ISBN 0-09-154610-9, Pub. by Hutchinson Educ); pap. 13.95 (ISBN 0-09-154611-7). Longwood Pub Group.
Clark, Peter, et al, eds. English Commonwealth Fifteen Forty-Seven to Sixteen Forty: Essays in Politics & Society. LC 78-32060. (Illus.). 272p. 1979. text ed. 33.50x (ISBN 0-06-491171-3, 06399). B&N Imports.
Clark, Peter A. Action Research & Organizational Change. 1973. text ed. 9.80 (ISBN 0-06-318001-4, IntlDept); pap. text ed. 4.20 (ISBN 0-06-318004-9, IntlDept). Har-Row.
Clark, Phil. A Flower Lover's Guide to Mexico. (Illus.). 128p. 1978. pap. 7.00 (ISBN 0-912434-06-6). Ocelot Pr.
Clark, Philip. The Dark River. Barzun, J. & Taylor, W. H., eds. LC 81-47335. (Crime Fiction 1950-1975 Ser.). 191p. 1982. lib. bdg. 18.00 (ISBN 0-8240-4978-0). Garland Pub.
--Tyrants of the Twentieth Century. LC 81-86279. (In Profile Ser.). PLB 12.68 (ISBN 0-382-06633-2). Silver.
Clark, Philip, ed. see Evans, Jeremy.
Clark, Philip M. Microcomputer Spreadsheet Models for Libraries: Preparing Documents, Budgets, & Statistical Reports. LC 84-20470. 134p. 1985. pap. text ed. 24.95x (ISBN 0-8389-0403-3). ALA.
Clark, Phillip G., jt. ed. see Callahan, Daniel.
Clark, Phyllis E., jt. auth. see Lehrman, Robert.
Clark, R. Chemistry of Titanium & Vanadium. 1968. 70.29 (ISBN 0-444-40679-4). Elsevier.
--Golf: A Royal & Ancient Game. (Illus.). 1976. Repr. 25.00x (ISBN 0-7158-1116-9). Charles River Bks.
Clark, R., jt. auth. see Son, Duk S.
Clark, R., jt. auth. see Zimmerman, L.
Clark, R. see Kalven, H., Jr.
Clark, R. B. The Waters of Britain. 1985. 39.95x (ISBN 0-19-828492-6). Oxford U Pr.
Clark, R. B., intro. by. The Long-Term Effects of Oil Pollution on Marine Populations, Communities & Ecosystems: Proceedings. (RSL Philosophies. Transactions Series B, Vol. 297: No. 1087). (Illus.). 260p. 1982. text ed. 80.00x (ISBN 0-85403-188-X). Scholium Intl.
Clark, R. B., jt. ed. see Heywood, V. H.
Clark, R. Bradbury. California Corporation Laws: Supplemented 1984, 6 vols. 4th ed. LC 63-47230. 450.00 (ISBN 0-911110-00-3). Parker & Son.
Clark, R. D. Australian Renewable Energy Resources Index, Nos. 1-3. (Microfiche only). 1978. 9.00 (C052, CSIRO). Unipub.
Clark, R. H. An Historical Survey of Selected Great Western Stations, Layouts & Illustrations, Vol. 3. 200p. 45.00x (ISBN 0-86093-111-0, Pub. by ORPC Ltd UK). State Mutual Bk.
Clark, R. H., jt. auth. see Bruce, J. P.
Clark, R. H., jt. auth. see Mayneord, W. V.
Clark, R. J. & Hester, R. E. Advances In Infrared & Raman Spectroscopy, Vol. 10. 454p. 1983. 118.00 (ISBN 0-471-26216-1, Pub. by Wiley Heyden). Wiley.
Clark, R. J., jt. auth. see Quigley, Hugh.
Clark, R. J. & Hester, R. E., eds. Advances in Infrared & Raman Spectroscopy, 5 vols. Vol. 1. 1975 ed. 96.95 (ISBN 0-471-25631-5, Pub. by Wiley Heyden); Vol. 2. 1976 ed. 96.95 (ISBN 0-471-25632-3); Vol. 3. 1977 ed. o.p. 89.95 (ISBN 0-471-25633-1); Vol. 4. 1978 ed. o.p. 121.95 (ISBN 0-471-25634-X). Wiley.
--Advances in Infrared & Raman Spectroscopy, Vol. 5. 404p. 1978. casebound 130.95 (ISBN 0-471-25636-6, Pub. by Wiley Heyden). Wiley.
--Advances in Infrared & Raman Spectroscopy, Vol. 6. (Advances in Infrared & Raman Spectroscopy Ser.). 355p. 1979. 130.95 (ISBN 0-471-25637-4, Pub. by Wiley Heyden). Wiley.
--Advances in Infrared & Raman Spectroscopy, Vol. 7. (Advances in Infrared & Raman Spectroscopy Ser.). 400p. 1980. 129.95 (ISBN 0-471-25639-0, Pub. by Wiley Heyden). Wiley.
--Advances in Infrared & Raman Spectroscopy, Vol. 12. price not set (ISBN 0-471-90674-3). Wiley.

Clark, R. J. H. & Hester, R. E. Advances in Infrared & Raman Spectroscopy, Vol. 11. 383p. 1984. 98.00x (ISBN 0-471-26267-6, Pub. by Wiley Heyden). Wiley.

Clark, R. L. & Rushforth, S. R. Diatom Studies of the Headwaters of Henrys Fork of the Snake River, Island Park, Idaho, USA. (Bibliotheca Phycologica Ser.: No. 33). 1977. pap. text ed. 17.50x (ISBN 3-7682-1149-5). Lubrecht & Cramer.

Clark, R. L. & Spengler, J. J. The Economics of Individual & Population Aging. LC 79-19495. (Cambridge Surveys of Economic Literature Ser.). (Illus.). 1980. 34.50 (ISBN 0-521-22883-2); pap. 12.95 (ISBN 0-521-29702-8). Cambridge U Pr.

Clark, R. T., tr. see Ritter, Gerhard.

Clark, R. Theodore, Jr. Coping with Mediation, Fact Finding, & Forms of Arbitration. (Public Employee Relations Library Ser.: No. 42). pap. 10.00 (ISBN 0-87373-142-5). Intl Personnel Mgmt.

Clark, R. Theodore, Jr. & Zemm, Sandra P. Drafting the Public Sector Labor Agreement. (Public Employee Relations Library: No. 56). 92p. 1977. pap. 12.00 non-members (ISBN 0-686-81160-7); pap. 10.00 members. Intl Personnel Mgmt.

Clark, Ralph D. Case Studies in Echocardiography: A Diagnostic Workbook. LC 76-1212. (Illus.). 1977. pap. 25.00 (ISBN 0-7216-2594-0). Saunders.

Clark, Ramsey, jt. auth. see Ervin, Sam J., Jr.

Clark, Ramsey, ed. Crime & Justice. LC 74-7581. (Great Contemporary Issues). (Illus.). 1974. 35.00 (ISBN 0-405-04167-5, Co Pub by New York Times). Ayer Co Pubs.

Clark, Randolph L., ed. Year Book of Cancer, 1981. 1981. 44.95 (ISBN 0-8151-1789-2). Year Bk Med.

--Year Book of Cancer 1983. 1983. 44.95 (ISBN 0-8151-1791-4). Year Bk Med.

Clark, Randolph L., et al, eds. Year Book of Cancer, 1982. (Illus.). 575p. 1982. 44.95 (ISBN 0-8151-1790-6). Year Bk Med.

Clark, Randy & Koehler, Stephen. The UCSD Pascal Handbook. (Software Ser.). (Illus.). 384p. 1982. text ed. 24.95 (ISBN 0-13-935544-8); pap. text ed. 18.95 (ISBN 0-13-935536-7). P-H.

Clark, Raymond C. Language Teaching Techniques. LC 80-84109. (Pro Lingua Language Resource Handbook Ser.: No. 1). (Illus.). 128p. (Orig.). 1980. pap. 6.50x (ISBN 0-86647-000-X). Pro Lingua.

--Potluck: Exploring American Foods & Meals. (Vocabureader Workbook Ser.: No. 2). (Illus.). 128p. (Orig.). 1985. text ed. 6.00x (ISBN 0-86647-012-3). Pro Lingua.

Clark, Raymond C. & Brown, Ruthanne. Index Card Games for ESL. LC 82-9786. (Supplementary Materials Handbook Ser.: No. 1). (Illus.). 80p. (Orig.). 1982. pap. 6.00x (ISBN 0-86647-002-6). Pro Lingua.

Clark, Raymond C., jt. auth. see Jerald, Michael.

Clark, Raymond C., ed. see Burrows, Arthur A.

Clark, Raymond C., ed. see Clair, Nancy.

Clark, Raymond C., ed. see Gaston, Jan.

Clark, Raymond C., jt. ed. see Miller, John N.

Clark, Raymond C., et al. The ESL Miscellany: An Inventory of American English for Teachers & Students. LC 81-8581. (Pro Lingua Language Resource Handbook Ser.: No. 2). (Illus.). 284p. (Orig.). 1981. pap. 12.50x (ISBN 0-86647-001-8). Pro Lingua.

Clark, Raymond H. Handbook of Printed Circuit Manufacturing. 1984. 49.50 (ISBN 0-442-21610-6). Van Nos Reinhold.

Clark, Raymond J. Catabasis: Vergil & the Wisdom Tradition. 1979. pap. text ed. 34.75x (ISBN 9-0603-2104-9). Humanities.

Clark, Rebecca. The Rainbow Connection. LC 82-84590. 192p. 1983. 4.95 (ISBN 0-87159-136-7). Unity School.

Clark, Reginald M. Family Life & School Achievement: Why Poor Black Children Succeed or Fail. LC 83-3481. (Illus.). 232p. 1983. lib. bdg. 22.50x (ISBN 0-226-10769-8). U of Chicago Pr.

--Family Life & School Achievement: Why Poor Black Children Succeed or Fail. LC 83-3481. xiv, 250p. 1984. pap. 7.95x (ISBN 0-226-10770-1). U of Chicago Pr.

Clark, Richard & Pinchuck, Tony. Medicine for Beginners. 1984. 14.95 (ISBN 0-86316-006-9); pap. 4.95 (ISBN 0-86316-007-7). Writers & Readers.

Clark, Richard C. Technological Terrorism. 1980. 10.00 (ISBN 0-8159-6915-5). Devin.

Clark, Richard C. see Gillespie, John.

Clark, Richard E., jt. auth. see Shipley, Reginald A.

Clark, Richard L. What's Your Position? Nautical Whimsey. (Illus.). 60p. (Orig.). 1980. pap. 5.95 (ISBN 0-936374-00-4). Bartco.

Clark, Richard L., jt. auth. see Bookstein, Joseph J.

Clark, Robert. History & Myth in American Fiction, 1823-1852. LC 83-40161. 224p. 1984. 22.95 (ISBN 0-312-37407-0). St Martin.

--The Role of Private Pensions in Maintaining Living Standards in Retirement. LC 77-87188. 64p. 1977. 3.50 (ISBN 0-89068-041-8). Natl Planning.

Clark, Robert, jt. auth. see Kreps, Juanita.

Clark, Robert, jt. auth. see Minium, Edward W.

Clark, Robert, jt. auth. see Zuck, Roy B.

Clark, Robert, ed. see Cooper, James F.

Clark, Robert A. Mental Illness in Perspective. 101p. (Orig.). 1973. 3.75 (ISBN 0-910286-34-5); pap. 2.95 (ISBN 0-910286-29-9). Boxwood.

--Six Talks on Jung's Psychology. (Orig.). 1953. pap. 4.50 (ISBN 0-910286-07-8). Boxwood.

Clark, Robert A., jt. auth. see Elkinton, Russell J.

Clark, Robert B. Dynamics in Metazoan Evolution: The Origin of the Coelom & Segments. 1964. 45.00x (ISBN 0-19-854353-0). Oxford U Pr.

Clark, Robert C. Beginnings of Texas, Sixteen Eighty-Four to Seventeen Eighteen. LC 76-11795. (Perspectives in American History Ser., No. 25). (Illus.). 104p. 1976. Repr. of 1907 ed. lib. bdg. 15.00x (ISBN 0-87991-349-5). Porcupine Pr.

Clark, Robert D., ed. Australian Renewable Energy Resources Index: Issue No. 1. 1979. pap. 7.00x (ISBN 0-686-24273-4, Pub. by CSIRO). Intl Spec Bk.

Clark, Robert E. Teaching Preschoolers with Confidence. 48p. 1983. pap. 2.95 (ISBN 0-910566-37-2); seminar planbook 2.95 (ISBN 0-910566-38-0). Evang Tchr.

Clark, Robert E., jt. auth. see Brubaker, J. Omar.

Clark, Robert E., ed. Waters & Water Rights: 1978 Supplements for Vols. 1, 2, & 4-7. 1978. pap. text ed. 60.00x (ISBN 0-87473-187-9). A Smith Co.

Clark, Robert E. see Clark, Thomas C.

Clark, Robert Emmet, ed. Waters & Water Rights, 7 vols. 1969-84. Set. text ed. 245.00x (ISBN 0-87473-029-5); 1978 suppls. for vols. 1, 2, 4-7& 1985 suppl. for vol. 3 incl. A Smith Co.

Clark, Robert G. Programming in Ada: A First Course. 350p. 1985. 39.50 (ISBN 0-521-25728-X); pap. 17.95 (ISBN 0-521-27675-6). Cambridge U Pr.

Clark, Robert J., jt. auth. see Duk Song Son.

Clark, Robert L. Cost-Effective Pension Planning. (Work in America Institute Studies in Productivity: No. 20). 42p. 1982. pap. 35.00 (ISBN 0-08-029501-0, L120). Pergamon.

--Cost Effective Pension Planning, Vol. 20. (Studies in Productivity - Highlights of the Literature). (Orig.). pap. 35.00 (ISBN 0-89361-030-5). Work in Amer.

Clark, Robert L. & Barker, David T. Reversing the Trend Toward Early Retirement. 1981. pap. 4.25 (ISBN 0-8447-3433-0). Am Enterprise.

Clark, Robert L., ed. Retirement Policy in an Aging Society. LC 79-56502. (Illus.). 230p. 1980. 21.00 (ISBN 0-8223-0441-4). Duke.

Clark, Robert L., et al. Inflation & the Economic Well-Being of the Elderly. LC 84-7863. 1984. text ed. 18.50x (ISBN 0-8018-3218-7). Johns Hopkins.

Clark, Robert L., Jr., jt. auth. see Cranfill, Thomas M.

Clark, Robert P. The Basque Insurgents: ETA, 1952-1980. LC 83-40259. (Illus.). 400p. 1984. text ed. 29.50x (ISBN 0-299-09650-5). U of Wis Pr.

--The Basques: The Franco Years & Beyond. LC 79-24926. (Basque Bk.). xvii, 434p. 1980. 17.50 (ISBN 0-87417-057-5). U of Nev Pr.

--Power & Policy in the Third World. 2nd ed. LC 81-19705. 168p. 1982. pap. text ed. 15.95x (ISBN 0-471-09008-5). Wiley.

Clark, Robert P., jt. auth. see White, Louise G.

Clark, Robert S. The Criminal Justice System: An Analytical Approach. 1981. pap. text ed. 26.95 (ISBN 0-205-07358-1, 8273588); tchr's guide free (ISBN 0-205-07359-X, 8273596). Allyn.

--Fundamentals of Criminal Justice Research. (Illus.). 1977. 23.50x (ISBN 0-669-01005-7). Lexington Bks.

--Planning for Justice: The Problems of Justice with Specific Approaches to the Issues. LC 83-18135. 168p. 1984. pap. 14.75x (ISBN 0-398-04952-1). C C Thomas.

Clark, Roberta. Mari's Caress. 1983. pap. 3.50 (ISBN 0-8217-1250-0). Zebra.

--Why. LC 83-7306. (Question Bks). (Illus.). 32p. (gr. k-2). 1983. 10.35 (ISBN 0-516-06594-7); pap. 2.95 (ISBN 0-516-46594-5). Childrens.

Clark, Rodney. The Japanese Company. 1979. 36.00x (ISBN 0-300-02310-3); pap. 9.95x (ISBN 0-300-02646-3). Yale U Pr.

Clark, Roger. Precedents in Architecture. 1984. pap. 19.95 (ISBN 0-442-21668-8). Van Nos Reinhold.

Clark, Roger E. Executive SuperCalc for the Osborne I. LC 84-6275. 1245p. 1984. pap. 12.95 (ISBN 0-201-10241-2). Addison-Wesley.

--Executive VisiCalc for the Apple Computer. LC 82-11663. (Microcomputer Bks.-Executive). 192p. 1982. pap. 14.95 (ISBN 0-201-10242-0). Addison-Wesley.

--Executive VisiCalc for the IBM Personal Computer. 192p. 1983. pap. 12.95 (ISBN 0-201-10243-9). Addison-Wesley.

Clark, Ron. Color Computer Graphics. (Illus.). 128p. 1983. 9.95 (ISBN 0-86668-012-8). ARCsoft.

--The Color Computer Songbook. (Illus.). 96p. 1983. 7.95 (ISBN 0-86668-011-X). ARCsoft.

--Fifty-Five Color Computer Programs for the Home, School & Office. 128p. (Orig.). 1982. pap. 9.95 (ISBN 0-86668-005-5). ARCsoft.

--Fifty-five More Color Computer Programs for the Home, School & Office. (Illus.). 112p. (Orig.). 1982. pap. 9.95 (ISBN 0-86668-008-X). ARCsoft.

--One Hundred One Color Computer Programming Tips & Tricks. 128p. (Orig.). 1982. pap. 7.95 (ISBN 0-86668-007-1). ARCsoft.

--TRS-80 Color Computer Program Writing Workbook. 96p. pap. 4.95 (ISBN 0-86668-816-1). ARCsoft.

Clark, Ron, ed. My Buttons Are Blue & Other Love Poems from the Digital Heart of an Electronic Computer. (Illus.). 96p. 1983. 4.95 (ISBN 0-86668-013-6). ARCsoft.

Clark, Ronald. Instructions to Young Ramblers. (gr. 9 up). 14.50x (ISBN 0-392-03517-0, SpS). Sportshelf.

--J. B. S. The Life & Work of J. B. S. Haldane. (Illus., Orig.). 1984. pap. 7.95 (ISBN 0-19-281430-3). Oxford U Pr.

--Works of Man. 1985. 25.00 (ISBN 0-670-80483-5). Viking.

Clark, Ronald D. & Amai, Robert L. Chemistry: The Science & the Scene. LC 74-22969. 356p. 1975. 21.50 (ISBN 0-471-15857-7). Krieger.

Clark, Ronald W. Balmoral: Queen Victoria's Highland Home. (Illus.). 144p. 1981. 10.98 (ISBN 0-500-25078-2). Thames Hudson.

--Benjamin Franklin: A Biography. LC 82-40115. (Illus.). 480p. 1983. 22.95 (ISBN 0-394-50222-1). Random.

--Einstein: The Life & Times. (Illus.). 896p. 1972. pap. 5.95 (ISBN 0-380-01159-X, 63636-0, Discus). Avon.

--Einstein: The Life & Times: An Illustrated Biography. (Illus.). 368p. 1984. 28.50 (ISBN 0-8109-0875-1). Abrams.

--Freud: The Man & the Cause-a Biography. LC 79-4756. (Illus.). 1980. 19.95 (ISBN 0-394-40983-3). Random.

--The Greatest Power on Earth: The International Race for Supremacy. LC 80-7899. (Illus.). 352p. 1981. 14.37i (ISBN 0-06-014846-2, HarpT). Har-Row.

--Role of the Bomber. (Illus.). 160p. 14.95 (ISBN 0-690-01720-0). Presidio Pr.

--The Survival of Charles Darwin: A Biography of a Man & an Idea. LC 84-42507. (Illus.). 544p. 1985. 19.45 (ISBN 0-394-52134-X). Random.

--War Winners. (Illus.). 154p. 1980. 14.95 (ISBN 0-283-98503-8, Pub. by Sidgwick & Jackson England). Presidio Pr.

Clark, Rosalind. Enter Any Door. LC 77-86734. 1977. 5.50 (ISBN 0-8233-0269-5). Golden Quill.

Clark, Rosalind L. Oregon Style: Architecture from 1840-1950. Meidell, Pamela S., ed. LC 83-11108. (Photographic History of Architecture in the West Ser.: Vol. 1). (Illus.). 238p. 1983. 29.95 (ISBN 0-943226-00-7); pap. 19.95 (ISBN 0-943226-01-5). Prof Bk Ctr Inc.

Clark, Ross D. & Stainer, Joan R., eds. Medical & Genetic Aspects of Purebred Dogs. LC 83-80248. (Illus.). 584p. 29.50x (ISBN 0-935078-24-X). Veterinary Med.

Clark, Roy, jt. auth. see Edholm, Otto.

Clark, Roy P., ed. Best Newspaper Writing, 1983: Winners of the American Society of Newspaper Editors Competition. LC 80-646604. (Illus.). 185p. 1983. pap. 6.95 (ISBN 0-935742-08-5). Mod Media Inst.

--Best Newspaper Writing, 1984: Winners of the American Society of Newspaper Editors Competition. LC 80-646604. (Illus.). 263p. 1984. pap. 6.95 (ISBN 0-935742-09-3). Mod Media Inst.

Clark, Rufus W. African Slave Trade. facs. ed. LC 70-133151. (Black Heritage Library Collection). 1860. 10.75 (ISBN 0-8369-8706-3). Ayer Co Pubs.

Clark, Ruth. Strangers & Sojourners at Port Royal. 1972. lib. bdg. 26.00x (ISBN 0-374-91664-0). Octagon.

Clark, Ruth A. Persuasive Messages. 288p. 1983. pap. text ed. 16.50 (ISBN 0-06-041306-9, HarpC). Har-Row.

Clark, Ruth M., jt. auth. see Vaughn, Gwenyth R.

Clark, S. H. & Campbell, W. The Federal Reserve Monster. 1979. lib. bdg. 59.95 (ISBN 0-8490-2914-7). Gordon Pr.

Clark, S. H., ed. Handbook of Best Readings. LC 72-5593. (Granger Index Reprint Ser.). 1972. Repr. of 1902 ed. 29.00 (ISBN 0-8369-6382-2). Ayer Co Pubs.

Clark, S. K. & Dodge, R. N. A Handbook for the Rolling Resistance of Pneumatic Tires. (Illus.). 78p. 1979. 12.00 (ISBN 0-938654-26-8, TIRES). Indus Dev Inst Sci.

Clark, Sally & Perschetz, Lois. Making Space: How to Get the Space You Need Out of the Space You Have. 24.95 (ISBN 0-517-54716-3). Crown.

Clark, Sam. Designing & Building Your Own House Your Own Way. 1978. pap. 11.95 (ISBN 0-395-26685-8). HM.

--The Motion-Minded Kitchen: Step-by-Step Prodecures for Designing & Building the Kitchen You Want with the Space & Money You Have. (Illus.). 1983. 19.95 (ISBN 0-395-32197-2); pap. 9.95 (ISBN 0-395-34930-3). HM.

Clark, Sam L., ed. see Ranson, Stephen W.

Clark, Samuel. Social Origins of the Irish Land War. LC 79-83980. (Rural Social Structure & Collective Action in 19th Century Ireland). 1979. 40.00x (ISBN 0-691-05272-7); pap. 16.50x LPE (ISBN 0-691-10068-3). Princeton U Pr.

Clark, Samuel & Donnelly, James S., Jr., eds. Irish Peasants: Violence & Political Unrest, 1780-1914. LC 83-1289. 416p. 1983. text ed. 35.00x (ISBN 0-299-09370-0). U of Wis Pr.

Clark, Samuel, ed. see Love, John.

Clark, Samuel D. Movements of Political Protest in Canada, 1640-1840. LC 60-29. (Social Credit in Alberta Ser.: 9). pap. 132.00 (ISBN 0-317-28762-1, 2055462). Bks Demand UMI.

--The Social Development of Canada. LC 75-41060. Repr. of 1942 ed. 29.50 (ISBN 0-404-14655-4). AMS Pr.

--The Suburban Society. LC 66-1140. pap. 60.80 (ISBN 0-317-07767-8, 2019193). Bks Demand UMI.

Clark, Sandra. Elizabethan Pamphleteers: Popular Moralistic Pamphlets, 1580-1640. LC 81-72064. (Illus.). 320p. 1982. 32.50 (ISBN 0-8386-3173-8). Fairleigh Dickinson.

--Moonlight Enough. (Harlequin Romances Ser.). 192p. 1983. pap. 1.75 (ISBN 0-373-02533-5). Harlequin Bks.

--Stormy Weather. (Harlequin Romances Ser.). 192p. 1983. pap. 1.75 (ISBN 0-373-02569-6). Harlequin Bks.

--The Wolf Man. (Harlequin Presents Ser.). 192p. 1982. pap. 1.75 (ISBN 0-373-10514-2). Harlequin Bks.

Clark, Sara. The Capitols of Texas: A Visual History. new ed. (Illus.). 130p. 1975. 15.00 (ISBN 0-88426-046-1). Encino Pr.

Clark, Sara, jt. auth. see Wittliff, William.

Clark, Sara B. Centrist. 1981. 6.50 (ISBN 0-8062-1577-1). Carlton.

Clark, Sarah. From Grammar to Paragraphs. 306p. 1981. pap. text ed. 10.95 (ISBN 0-394-32560-5, RanC). Random.

Clark, Scott, jt. auth. see Blaine, Vera.

Clark, Shirley M., jt. auth. see Lewis, Darrell R.

Clark, Stephen, jt. auth. see Beckerman, Wilfred.

Clark, Stephen & Kane, Randall, eds. Arrow Street Guide of the Capitol District. 1973. 1.95 (ISBN 0-913450-19-7). Arrow Pub.

Clark, Stephen B. Man & Woman in Christ: An Examination of the Roles of Men & Women in Light of Scripture & the Social Sciences. 754p. (Orig.). 1980. 24.95 (ISBN 0-89283-084-0). Servant.

Clark, Stephen B., ed. Patterns of Christian Community. 98p. (Orig.). 1984. pap. 4.95 (ISBN 0-89283-186-3). Servant.

Clark, Stephen R. Aristotle's Man: Speculations upon Aristotelian Anthropology. 1983. pap. 12.95x (ISBN 0-19-824715-X). Oxford U Pr.

--From Athens to Jerusalem: The Love of Wisdom & the Love God. 1984. 24.95x (ISBN 0-19-824698-6); pap. 9.95x (ISBN 0-19-824697-8). Oxford U Pr.

--The Moral Status of Animals. 240p. 1984. pap. 7.95x (ISBN 0-19-283040-6). Oxford U Pr.

--The Nature of the Beast: Are Animals Moral? 1984. 14.95 (ISBN 0-19-219130-6); pap. 6.95 (ISBN 0-19-283041-4). Oxford U Pr.

Clark, Steve. Illustrated Basketball Dictionary for Young People. (Illus.). (gr. 4 up). 1978. pap. 2.50 (ISBN 0-13-450940-4, Pub. by Treehouse). P-H.

Clark, Steve, jt. ed. see Barnes, Jack.

Clark, Steve B. Baptized in the Spirit & Spiritual Gifts. 1967. pap. 2.95 (ISBN 0-89283-033-6). Servant.

--Growing in Faith. (Living As a Christian Ser.). 1972. pap. 2.25 (ISBN 0-89283-004-2). Servant.

--Knowing God's Will. (Living As a Christian Ser.). 1974. pap. 2.50 (ISBN 0-89283-005-0). Servant.

Clark, Susan L. & Wasserman, Julian N. The Poetics of Conversion: Number Symbolism & Alchemy in Gottfried's "Tristan". (Utah Studies in Literature & Linguistics: Vol. 7). 168p. 1977. pap. 20.90 (ISBN 3-261-02085-7). P Lang Pubs.

Clark, Sydney P. Structure of the Earth. (Foundations of Earth Science Ser). 1971. pap. text ed. 15.95 (ISBN 0-13-854646-0). P-H.

Clark, T. A Handbook of Computational Chemistry: A Practical Guide to Chemical Structure & Energy Calculations. 304p. 1985. 35.00 (ISBN 0-471-88211-9). Wiley.

Clark, T. & Jaffe, D. Toward a Radical Therapy. (Social Changes Ser.). 296p. 1973. 42.95 (ISBN 0-677-04730-4). Gordon.

Clark, T. & Rees, J. Practical Management of Asthma. (Practical Problems in Medicine Ser.). (Illus.). 174p. 1985. lib. bdg. 45.00 (ISBN 0-906348-74-9, Pub. by Martin Dunitz Ltd UK). VCH Pubs.

Clark, T. J. The Absolute Bourgeois: Artists & Politics in France, 1848-1851. LC 81-82044. (Illus.). 224p. (Orig.). 1982. 32.00x (ISBN 0-691-03981-X); pap. 10.95 (ISBN 0-691-00338-6). Princeton U Pr.

--Image of the People: Gustave Courbet & the 1848 Revolution. LC 81-82045. (Illus.). 208p. (Orig.). 1982. 32.00 (ISBN 0-691-03980-1); pap. 9.95 (ISBN 0-691-00339-4). Princeton U Pr.

--The Organization of Hospital Clinical Work. 92p. 1979. 15.00x (ISBN 0-686-87380-7, Pub. by Kings Fund). State Mutual Bk.

--The Painting of Modern Life: Paris in the Art of Manet & His Followers. LC 84-47509. (Illus.). 338p. 1985. 25.00 (ISBN 0-394-49580-2). Knopf.

--Steroids in Asthma: A Reappraisal in the Light of Inhalation Therapy. (Illus.). 236p. 1983. 48.00 (ISBN 0-683-11204-X). Williams & Wilkins.

Clark, T. J. see Mygind, N.

Clark, T. J. & Cochrane, G. W., eds. Brochodilator Therapy: The Basis of Asthma & Chronic Obstructive Airways Disease Management. (Illus.). 240p. 1984. 62.00 (ISBN 0-683-11203-1). Williams & Wilkins.

Clark, T. W., ed. The Novel in India: Its Birth & Development. LC 70-119719. 1970. 33.00x (ISBN 0-520-01725-0). U of Cal Pr.

Clark, Taylor, jt. auth. see Bannon, Lois.

Clark, Ted. The Oppression of Youth. 9.00 (ISBN 0-8446-5169-9). Peter Smith.

Clark, Ted, et al. Outreach Family Therapy. LC 81-66756. 432p. 1982. 25.00 (ISBN 0-87668-482-7). Aronson.

Clark, Terry & Ferguson, Lorna. City Money: Political Processes, Fiscal Strain, & Retrenchment. 384p. 1983. 40.00x (ISBN 0-231-05688-5); pap. 16.00x (ISBN 0-231-05689-3). Columbia U Pr.

Clark, Terry C., ed. see Tarde, Gabriel.

Clark, Terry N. Prophets & Patrons: The French University & the Emergence of the Social Sciences. LC 72-93947. (Illus.). 311p. 1973. 18.50x (ISBN 0-674-71580-2). Harvard U Pr.

--Research in Urban Policy, Vol. 1. 47.50 (ISBN 0-89232-325-6). Jai Pr.

--Urban Policy Analysis: Directions for Future Research. (Urban Affairs Annual Reviews: Vol. 21). 400p. 1981. 28.00 (ISBN 0-8039-1627-2); pap. 14.00 (ISBN 0-8039-1628-0). Sage.

Clark, Terry N., jt. auth. see Ben-David, Joseph.

Clark, Terry N., jt. auth. see Leif, Irving P.

Clark, Terry N., ed. Comparative Community Politics. LC 72-98030. 415p. 1974. 19.95x (ISBN 0-470-15858-1). Halsted Pr.

Clark, Terry N., et al. Financial Handbook for Mayors & City Managers. (Illus.). 240p. 1985. 34.50 (ISBN 0-442-21775-7). Van Nos Reinhold.

Clark, Theodore G., jt. auth. see Stephenson, Richard M.

Clark, Thom B., jt. auth. see Reeves, Charles A.

Clark, Thomas, jt. auth. see McNichols, Charles.

Clark, Thomas A. Blacks in Suburbs. LC 79-12171. 1979. pap. text ed. 17.50 (ISBN 0-88285-061-X). Ctr Urban Pol Res.

--Some Particulars. 1971. pap. 5.00 (ISBN 0-912330-12-0, Dist. by Inland Bk). Jargon Soc.

--Ways Through Bracken. 1980. signed ltd. ed. 20.00x (ISBN 0-912330-44-9); pap. 7.50 (ISBN 0-686-96760-7). Jargon Soc.

Clark, Thomas Arkle. Nathaniel Hawthorne: Selections from His Writings. 1900. Repr. 10.00 (ISBN 0-8274-3011-6). R West.

Clark, Thomas B. Omai: First Polynesian Ambassador to England. 1969. Repr. of 1940 ed. text ed. 12.00x (ISBN 0-87022-140-X). UH Pr.

Clark, Thomas C. Poems for Life: Quotable Verse. 370p. 1980. Repr. of 1941 ed. lib. bdg. 30.00 (ISBN 0-8492-4044-1). R West.

--Poems of Justice. 306p. 1980. Repr. lib. bdg. 30.00 (ISBN 0-89987-109-7). Darby Bks.

Clark, Thomas C. & Gillespie, Esther A. Quotable Poems: An Anthology of Modern Verse. 1979. Repr. of 1928 ed. lib. bdg. 20.00 (ISBN 0-8495-0781-2). Arden Lib.

Clark, Thomas C., ed. Master of Men. fascimile ed. LC 72-116396. (Granger Index Reprint Ser.). 1930. 15.00 (ISBN 0-8369-6137-4). Ayer Co Pubs.

--Poems for Daily Needs. LC 36-23888. (Granger Poetry Library). 1976. Repr. of 1936 ed. 21.50x (ISBN 0-89609-012-4). Granger Bk.

Clark, Thomas C. & Garrison, Winfred E., eds. One Hundred Poems of Peace: An Anthology. facsimile ed. LC 75-160902. (Granger Index Reprint Ser.). Repr. of 1934 ed. 12.00 (ISBN 0-8369-6265-6). Ayer Co Pubs.

Clark, Thomas C. & Gillespie, Esther A., eds. New Patriotism. facsimile ed. LC 73-108581. (Granger Index Reprint Ser). 1927. 12.00 (ISBN 0-8369-6109-9). Ayer Co Pubs.

Clark, Thomas C. & Clark, Robert E.compiled by. Poems for the Great Days. LC 72-11861. (Granger Index Reprint Ser). 1973. Repr. of 1948 ed. 20.00 (ISBN 0-8369-6401-2). Ayer Co Pubs.

Clark, Thomas C. & Gillespie, Esthercompiled by. One Thousand Quotable Poems: An Anthology of Modern Verse, 2 vols. in 1. LC 72-11995. (Granger Index Reprint Ser.). 1973. Repr. of 1937 ed. 47.00 (ISBN 0-8369-6400-4). Ayer Co Pubs.

Clark, Thomas D. Agrarian Kentucky. LC 77-73703. (Kentucky Bicentennial Bookshelf Ser.). (Illus.). 152p. 1977. 6.95 (ISBN 0-8131-0237-5). U Pr of Ky.

--The Greening of the South: The Recovery of Land & Forest. LC 84-17301. (New Perspectives on the South Ser.). (Illus.). 208p. 1984. 20.00x (ISBN 0-8131-0305-3). U Pr of KY.

--Historic Maps of Kentucky. LC 79-4003. (Illus.). 96p. 1979. 28.00 (ISBN 0-8131-0097-6). U Pr of Ky.

--Indiana University: Midwestern Pioneer, 3 vols. Incl. Vol. 1. The Early Years. (Illus.). 392p. 1970. 20.00x (ISBN 0-253-14170-2); Vol. 2. In Mid-Passage. (Illus.). 448p. 1973. 20.00x (ISBN 0-253-32995-7); Vol. 3. Years of Fulfillment. 704p. 1977. 20.00x (ISBN 0-253-32996-5). LC 74-126207. (Illus.). Set. 50.00x (ISBN 0-253-32997-3). Ind U Pr.

--The Rampaging Frontier. LC 75-17477. 350p. 1976. Repr. of 1939 ed. lib. bdg. 15.00x (ISBN 0-8371-8313-8, CLRF). Greenwood.

--The Southern Country Editor. 1964. 11.25 (ISBN 0-8446-1115-8). Peter Smith.

Clark, Thomas D. & Kirwan, Albert D. The South Since Appomattox: A Century of Regional Change. LC 80-24023. (Illus.). vii, 438p. 1980. Repr. of 1967 ed. lib. bdg. 42.50x (ISBN 0-313-22698-9, CLSS). Greenwood.

Clark, Thomas D., ed. Indiana University: Midwestern Pioneer, Historical Documents Since 1816, Vol. 4. LC 74-126207. 704p. 1977. 15.00x (ISBN 0-253-37501-0). Ind U Pr.

--Travels in the Old South: A Bibliography. 1st ed. LC 56-8016. (American Exploration & Travels Ser.: No. 19). Vol. 1. pap. 85.80 (ISBN 0-317-10655-4, 2016201); Vol. 2. pap. 75.50 (ISBN 0-317-10656-2); Vol. 3. pap. 104.30 (ISBN 0-317-10657-0). Bks Demand UMI.

Clark, Thomas D., intro. by see Gray, Charles G.

Clark, Thomas L. A Guide for the Church Usher. LC 83-26211. 1984. pap. 4.95 (ISBN 0-8054-3517-4). Broadman.

Clark, Thomas L., ed. Marietta, Ohio: The Continuing Erosion of a Speech Island. (Publication of the American Dialect Society Ser.: No. 57). 64p. 1972. pap. text ed. 5.85 (ISBN 0-8173-0657-9, Am Dialect Soc). U of Ala Pr.

Clark, Thomas L., jt. ed. see Taulbee, Earl S.

Clark, Thomas L., et al. Needed Research in American English. (Publication of the American Dialect Society Ser.: No. 71). iv, 76p. (Orig.). 1984. pap. 5.30 (ISBN 0-8173-0238-7). U of Ala Pr.

Clark, Timothy B., et al. Reforming Regulation. 1980. 13.25 (ISBN 0-8447-2189-1); pap. 7.25 (ISBN 0-8447-2188-3). Am Enterprise.

Clark, Timothy W. Ecology & Ethology of the White-Tailed Prairie Dog (Cynomys Lecurus) 97p. 1978. 8.75 (ISBN 0-89326-009-6). Milwaukee Pub Mus.

Clark, Tom. At Malibu. 1975. 7.00 (ISBN 0-686-11115-X); pap. 3.50 (ISBN 0-686-11116-8). Kulchur Foun.

--Blue. (Illus.). 80p. (Orig.). 1974. pap. 3.00 (ISBN 0-87685-183-9). Black Sparrow.

--The Border. (Morning Coffee Chapbook Ser.). (Illus.). 24p. (Orig.). 1985. pap. 7.50 (ISBN 0-918273-06-4). Coffee Hse.

--Fan Poems. (Illus.). 1976. pap. 3.00 (ISBN 0-913028-45-2). North Atlantic.

--Gutenberg: An Account. 1985. price not set (ISBN 0-931460-29-8). Bieler.

--How I Broke In & Six Modern Masters. (Illus.). 1977. wrappers 3.00 (ISBN 0-939180-06-5). Tombouctou.

--Jack Kerouac. 1984. pap. 10.95 (ISBN 0-15-645662-1, Harv). HarBraceJ.

--The Last Gas Station & Other Stories. 200p. 1980. 14.00 (ISBN 0-87685-457-9); signed ed. 20.00 (ISBN 0-87685-458-7); pap. 6.00 (ISBN 0-87685-456-0). Black Sparrow.

--Late Returns: A Personal Memoir of Ted Berrigan. 88p. 1985. pap. 7.00 (ISBN 0-939180-35-9); 25.00 (ISBN 0-939180-29-4). Tombouctou.

--Nine Songs. 16p. 12.50 (ISBN 0-918824-25-7). Turkey Pr.

--One Last Round for the Shuffler. 160p. 1978. 12.95 (ISBN 0-916562-21-2); pap. 4.95 (ISBN 0-916562-20-4). Truck Pr.

--Paradise Resisted: Selected Poems 1978-1984. 150p. 1984. 14.00 (ISBN 0-87685-612-1); signed ed. 25.00 (ISBN 0-87685-613-X); pap. 8.50 (ISBN 0-87685-611-3). Black Sparrow.

--Property. (Tadbooks). (Illus.). 16p. pap. 4.00 (ISBN 0-89807-117-8); 15.00 (ISBN 0-89807-122-4). Illuminati.

--Under the Fortune Palms. 72p. 1982. 40.00x (ISBN 0-918824-38-9). Turkey Pr.

--When Things Get Tough on Easy Street: Selected Poems 1963-1978. 180p. (Orig.). 1978. pap. 6.00 (ISBN 0-87685-348-3). Black Sparrow.

--Who Is Sylvia? LC 79-19070. 1979. 19.95 (ISBN 0-912652-54-3); pap. 6.95 (ISBN 0-912652-53-5); signed & numbered ed. 29.95x (ISBN 0-912652-55-1). Blue Wind.

Clark, Tom C., ed. see U. S. Department of Justice.

Clark, Truman R. Puerto Rico & the United States, 1917-1933. LC 74-26019. (Pitt Latin American Ser.). pap. 63.50 (ISBN 0-317-26631-4, 2025433). Bks Demand UMI.

Clark, Ursula D. Home in Singapore. 8.75 (ISBN 0-8062-2427-4). Carlton.

Clark, V. A., tr. see Von Nageli, Carl.

Clark, Vernon M., intro. by see Howard, Robert E.

Clark, Victor S. History of Manufacturers in the U. S., from 1607-1928, 3 vols. (Illus.). Set. 60.00 (ISBN 0-8446-1116-6). Peter Smith.

--Labour Movement in Australasia: A Study in Social Democracy. LC 77-122222. (Research & Source Ser.: No. 506). 1970. Repr. of 1906 ed. lib. bdg. 23.50 (ISBN 0-8337-0583-0). B Franklin.

Clark, Victor S., et al. Puerto Rico & Its Problems. LC 74-14226. (The Puerto Rican Experience Ser). (Illus.). 748p. 1975. Repr. 56.50x (ISBN 0-405-06216-8). Ayer Co Pubs.

Clark, Virginia, jt. auth. see Afifi, Abdelmonem.

Clark, Virginia A., jt. auth. see Afifi, Abdelmonem.

Clark, Virginia A., jt. auth. see Dunn, Olive J.

Clark, Virginia A., jt. auth. see Gross, Alan J.

Clark, Virginia P., et al, eds. Language: Introductory Readings. 4th ed. LC 84-51144. 672p. 1985. pap. text ed. 15.95 (ISBN 0-312-46797-4). St Martin.

Clark, Vivian. God's Remedy for Depression. (Direction Bks.). (Orig.). 1980. pap. 3.50 (ISBN 0-8010-2444-7). Baker Bk.

Clark, Vynomma. So You're a Woman. LC 70-180790. 4.95 (ISBN 0-89112-050-5). Bibl Res Pr.

Clark, W. A. & Moore, Eric G. Population Mobility & Residential Change. (Studies in Geography: No. 25). 1978. pap. 6.95 (ISBN 0-8101-0523-3). Northwestern U Pr.

Clark, W. A., jt. auth. see Blair, William A.

Clark, W. A., jt. auth. see Nelson, Howard J.

Clark, W. A. V. & Moore, Eric G., eds. Residential Mobility & Public Policy. LC 80-12624. (Urban Affairs Annual Reviews: Vol. 19). (Illus.). 320p. 1980. 28.00 (ISBN 0-8039-1447-4); pap. 14.00 (ISBN 0-8039-1448-2). Sage.

Clark, W. E. The Fossil Evidence for Human Evolution: An Introduction to the Study of Paleoanthropology. 3rd rev. ed. Campbell, Bernard G., ed. LC 78-529. (Illus.). 1979. 16.00x (ISBN 0-226-10937-2); pap. 4.95x (ISBN 0-226-10938-0, P502, Phoen). U of Chicago Pr.

--History of the Primates. 5th ed. (Illus.). 1966. pap. 1.25 (ISBN 0-226-10936-4, P227, Phoen). U of Chicago Pr.

Clark, W. Edmund. Socialist Development & Public Investment in Tanzania, Nineteen Sixty-Four to Nineteen Seventy-Three. LC 77-8180. 1978. 35.00x (ISBN 0-8020-5376-9). U of Toronto Pr.

Clark, W. H. & Adams, T. S., eds. Advances in Invertebrate Reproduction. (Developments in Endocrinology Ser.: Vol. 11). 400p. 1981. 68.50 (ISBN 0-444-00594-3, Biomedical Pr). Elsevier.

Clark, W. Hartley. The Politics of the Common Market. LC 75-3987. 180p. 1975. Repr. of 1967 ed. lib. bdg. 15.00x (ISBN 0-8371-7456-2, CLCM). Greenwood.

Clark, W. Kemp, jt. auth. see Neuwelt, Edward A.

Clark, W. P. The Indian Sign Language. LC 81-16420. viii, 443p. 1982. 26.95x (ISBN 0-8032-1414-6); pap. 8.50 (ISBN 0-8032-6309-0, BB 792, Bison). U of Nebr Pr.

Clark, W. V. The Track of the Cat. 18.95 (ISBN 0-88411-389-2, Pub. by Aeonian Pr). Amereon Ltd.

Clark, Wallace H., et al, eds. Human Malignant Melanoma. (Clinical Oncology Monographs). 528p. 1979. 59.00 (ISBN 0-8089-1110-4, 790850). Grune.

Clark, Walter. The Papers of Walter Clark, 2 vols. Brooks, Aubrey J. & Lefler, Hugh T., eds. Incl. Vol. 1. xv, 607p. 1948 (ISBN 0-8078-0526-2); Vol. 2. vii, 608p. 1950 (ISBN 0-8078-0591-2). 27.50x ea. U of NC Pr.

Clark, Walter, ed. Histories of the Several Regiments & Battalions from North Carolina in the Great War 1861-65, 5 vols. (Illus.). 3982p. 1982. Repr. of 1901 ed. 250.00x (ISBN 0-916107-11-6). Broadfoot.

Clark, Walter, ed. see North Carolina General Assembly.

Clark, Walter E. Josiah Tucker, Economist: A Study in the History of Economics. LC 77-76670. (Columbia University. Studies in the Social Sciences: No. 49). Repr. of 1903 ed. 21.50 (ISBN 0-404-51049-3). AMS Pr.

Clark, Walter E., jt. auth. see Jenks, Jeremiah W.

Clark, Walter H., et al. Religious Experience: Its Nature & Function in the Human Psyche. (Illus.). 168p. 1973. 11.75x (ISBN 0-398-02550-9). C C Thomas.

Clark, Walter J. How to Use New Testament Greek Study Aids. 256p. 1984. pap. 6.95 (ISBN 0-87213-079-7). Loizeaux.

Clark, Walter V. Ox Bow Incident. (YA) (RL 10). 1943. pap. 2.95 (ISBN 0-451-51892-6, CE1497, Sig Classics). NAL.

--Ox-Bow Incident. 9.50 (ISBN 0-8446-0060-1). Peter Smith.

--The Track of the Cat. LC 80-22458. 344p. 1981. 25.50x (ISBN 0-8032-1412-X); pap. 5.95 (ISBN 0-8032-6307-4, BB 734, Bison). U of Nebr Pr.

Clark, Walter Van Tilbuer see Van Tilbuer Clark, Walter.

Clark, Walter Van Tilburg see Van Tilburg Clark, Walter.

Clark, Warren E. Traffic Management & Collision Investigation. (Illus.). 320p. 1982. 28.95 (ISBN 0-13-926162-1). P-H.

Clark, Wayne C. God Is My Strength. 1977. pap. 1.25 (ISBN 0-8170-0763-6); pap. 5.95 per dozen (ISBN 0-686-77289-X). Judson.

--The Meaning of Church Membership. pap. 3.95 (ISBN 0-8170-0103-4). Judson.

Clark, Wayne N., jt. auth. see Brown, Sanford M.

Clark, Wick see Frost, David.

Clark, Wilfrid E. Early Forerunners of Man. LC 76-44705. Repr. of 1934 ed. 29.50 (ISBN 0-404-15915-X). AMS Pr.

Clark, William. Cataclysm: The North-South Conflict of 1987. LC 85-2549. 327p. 1985. 15.95 (ISBN 0-312-12362-0). St Martin.

--Sing Peace to Cedar River. Brunelle, Jim, ed. (Illus.). 240p. 1983. pap. 10.95 (ISBN 0-930096-41-X). G Gannett.

Clark, William, jt. auth. see Lewis, Meriwether.

Clark, William, jt. auth. see Pelham, Anabel.

Clark, William, ed. Modelling Housing Market Search. LC 82-872. 256p. 1982. 30.00x (ISBN 0-312-53536-8). St Martin.

Clark, William, ed. see Shane, Harold G.

Clark, William A., Jr. Library of William Andrews Clark, Jr., Cruikshank & Dickens 1921-23. (English Literary Reference Ser). 1969. Repr. of 1923 ed. 16.00 (ISBN 0-384-09225-X). Johnson Repr.

Clark, William B. Ben Franklin's Privateers: A Naval Epic of the American Revolution. LC 74-90485. Repr. of 1956 ed. lib. bdg. 15.00x (ISBN 0-8371-2262-7, CLFP). Greenwood.

--Critical Essays on Robert Penn Warren. (Critical Essays on American Literature Ser.). 1981. 29.00 (ISBN 0-8161-8424-0, Twayne). G K Hall.

--Lambert Wickes: Sea Raider & Diplomat-the Story of a Naval Captain of the Revolution. 1932. 59.50x (ISBN 0-685-69800-9). Elliots Bks.

Clark, William C. Carbon Dioxide Review, 1982. (Illus.). 1982. pap. 45.00x (ISBN 0-19-855368-4). Oxford U Pr.

Clark, William C., jt. auth. see Johnston, Bruce F.

Clark, William D. Conducting Technique. LC 78-66123. 1979. pap. text ed. 11.25 (ISBN 0-8191-0684-4). U Pr of Amer.

--Death Valley: The Story Behind the Scenery. rev. ed. LC 79-91050. (Illus.). 1980. 8.95 (ISBN 0-916122-37-9); pap. 3.75 (ISBN 0-916122-12-3). KC Pubns.

Clark, William E. Fire Fighting Principles & Practices. (Illus.). 1974. 22.95 (ISBN 0-686-12259-3). Fire Eng.

Clark, William G., ed. see Shakespeare, William.

Clark, William H. Farms & Farmers. facsimile ed. LC 75-99625. (Essay Index Reprint Ser.). 1945. 32.00 (ISBN 0-8369-1560-7). Ayer Co Pubs.

--Ships & Sailors: The Story of Our Merchant Marine. LC 74-22736. (Illus.). Repr. of 1938 ed. 21.00 (ISBN 0-404-58488-8). AMS Pr.

Clark, William J. Great American Sculptures. LC 75-28869. (Art Experience in Late 19th Century America Ser.: Vol. 5). (Illus.). 1976. Repr. of 1878 ed. lib. bdg. 53.00 (ISBN 0-8240-2229-7). Garland Pub.

Clark, William M., ed. Model Dialogues. facsimile ed. LC 70-109138. (Granger Index Reprint Ser). 1897. 14.00 (ISBN 0-8369-6122-6). Ayer Co Pubs.

--Sterling Dialogues. facsimile ed. LC 76-103086. (Granger Index Reprint Ser). 1898. 17.00 (ISBN 0-8369-6101-3). Ayer Co Pubs.

Clark, William N. see Hovey, Alvah.

Clark, William R. The Experimental Foundations of Modern Immunology. 2nd ed. LC 80-13565. 453p. 1983. text ed. 36.50x (ISBN 0-471-86534-6). Wiley.

--Savanarola, His Life & Times. LC 83-45654. Date not set. Repr. of 1890 ed. 34.50 (ISBN 0-404-19804-X). AMS Pr.

Clark, William R. & Golstein, Pierre, eds. Mechanisms of Cell-Mediated Cytotoxicity. LC 82-5312. (Advances in Experimental Medicine & Biology: Vol. 146). 610p. 1982. 79.50x (ISBN 0-306-41012-5, Plenum Pr). Plenum Pub.

Clark, William R., ed. & tr. see Hefele, Karl J.

Clark, William S. The Early Irish Stage, the Beginnings to 1720. LC 73-9262. (Illus.). 227p. 1973. Repr. of 1955 ed. lib. bdg. 22.50x (ISBN 0-8371-7004-4, CLIS). Greenwood.

Clark, William S., jt. auth. see Lefranc, Maurice N., Jr.

Clark, Wilson & Page, Jake. Energy, Vulnerability, & War: Alternatives for America. 1981. 12.95 (ISBN 0-393-01468-1); pap. 5.95 (ISBN 0-393-00059-1). Norton.

Clark, Yoko, et al. California Murals. (Lancaster-Miller Art Ser.). (Illus.). 1980. 8.95 (ISBN 0-89581-016-6). Asian Human Pr.

Clark, Zenas R. The Recognition of Merit in Superintendents' Reports to the Public. LC 77-176650. (Columbia University. Teachers College. Contributions to Education: No. 471). Repr. of 1931 ed. 22.50 (ISBN 0-404-55471-7). AMS Pr.

Clarke. Aspects of the Hague Rules. 1976. pap. 45.00 (ISBN 90-247-1806-6, Pub. by Martinus Nijhoff Netherlands). Kluwer Academic.

Clarke & Prins. Contemporary Systems Analysis & Design. write for info. (ISBN 0-534-04233-3). Wadsworth Pub.

Clarke & Stewart. Children Development Through Adolescence. 2nd ed. 1986. price not set (ISBN 0-471-82461-5). Wiley.

Clarke & Wilson. Foam Floation: Theory & Application. 480p. 1983. 69.75 (ISBN 0-8247-1775-9). Dekker.

Clarke, A., jt. ed. see Morris, G. J.

Clarke, A. B. & Disney, R. L. Probability & Random Processes for Engineers & Scientists. 1970. 45.45 (ISBN 0-471-15980-8). Wiley.

Clarke, A. Bruce & Disney, Ralph L. Probability & Random Processes: A First Course with Applications. (Probability & Mathematical Statistics Ser.). 324p. 1985. 32.95 (ISBN 0-471-08535-9). Wiley.

Clarke, A. D., jt. ed. see Clarke, Ann M.

Clarke, A. F. Contact. LC 83-7743. 160p. 1984. 14.95 (ISBN 0-8052-3879-4). Schocken.

Clarke, A. Mason. A Biographical Dictionary of Fiddlers Including Performers on the Violon, Cello & Double Bass. LC 79-166225. 360p. 1895. Repr. 39.00x (ISBN 0-403-01352-6). Scholarly.

--The Violin & Old Violin Makers. 1976. lib. bdg. 29.00 (ISBN 0-403-03813-8). Scholarly.

Clarke, A. W. Jasper Tristram. LC 82-49093. (Degeneration & Regeneration Ser.). 351p. 1984. lib. bdg. 45.00 (ISBN 0-317-11903-6). Garland Pub.

Clarke, Adam. Clarke's Commentary, 3 vols. Incl. Vol. 1. Genesis-Esther (ISBN 0-687-09119-5); Vol. 2. Job-Malachi (ISBN 0-687-09120-9); Vol. 3. Matthew-Revelation (ISBN 0-687-09121-7). 1977. Set. 95.00 (ISBN 0-687-09118-7); 34.50 ea. Abingdon.

Clarke, Adam, ed. Adam Clarke's Commentary on the Entire Bible. 29.95 (ISBN 0-8010-2321-1). Baker Bk.

Clarke, Alan. The Magic of Barry Manilow. (Illus.). 32p. 1981. pap. 3.95 (ISBN 0-86276-009-7). Proteus Pub NY.

Clarke, Alfred C., jt. auth. see Curry, Timothy J.

Clarke, Allan L. From the Beginning to the End. LC 81-90239. (Illus.). 259p. 1983. 10.95 (ISBN 0-533-05119-3). Vantage.

Clarke, Amanda. Finding Out about Victorian Schools. (Finding Out About Ser.). (Illus.). 72p. (gr. 7-12). 1983. 12.50 (ISBN 0-7134-3667-0, Pub. by Batsford England). David & Charles.

--Growing up in Ancient Britain. (Growing up Ser.). (Illus.). 72p. (gr. 6 up). 1981. 14.95 (ISBN 0-7134-3557-7, Pub. by Batsford England). David & Charles.

--Growing up in Elizabethan Times. LC 79-56439. (Growing up Ser.). (Illus.). 72p. (gr. 7 up). 1980. text ed. 14.95 (ISBN 0-7134-3364-7, Pub. by Batsford England). David & Charles.

--Growing up in Puritan Times. LC 79-56452. (Growing up Ser.). (Illus.). 72p. (gr. 7 up). 1980. text ed. 14.95 (ISBN 0-7134-3366-3, Pub. by Batsford England). David & Charles.

Clarke, Ann M. & Clarke, A. D., eds. Early Experience: Myth & Evidence. LC 76-21992. 1979. pap. text ed. 13.95 (ISBN 0-02-905690-X). Free Pr.

--Mental Deficiency: The Changing Outlook. 3rd ed. LC 75-6314. 1975. 25.00 (ISBN 0-02-905620-9). Free Pr.

Clarke, Anna. Last Judgment. LC 84-13598. (Crime Club Ser.). 192p. 1985. 11.95 (ISBN 0-385-19666-0). Doubleday.

--The Poisoned Web. 182p. 1982. 10.95 (ISBN 0-312-61992-8). St Martin.

--Soon She Must Die. LC 83-11497. (Crime Club Ser.). 192p. 1983. 11.95 (ISBN 0-385-19106-5). Doubleday.

--Soon She Must Die. (Nightingale Paperbacks Ser.). 1984. pap. 9.95 (ISBN 0-8161-3703-X, Large Print Bks). G K Hall.

Clarke, Anna P. Canine Clinic: The Veterinarian's Handbook to the Diagnosis & Treatment of Your Dog's Health Problems. (Illus.). 336p. 1984. 19.95 (ISBN 0-02-525860-5). Macmillan.

Clarke, Anthony S. Succeeding with Confidence: An Introductory Guide. 288p. 1986. pap. 9.95 (ISBN 0-934397-17-1). Seton Pr.

Clarke, Arthur. The Sentinel. 1983. pap. 6.95 (ISBN 0-425-06183-3). Berkley Pub.

--Song of Songs. pap. 4.00 (ISBN 0-937396-39-7). Walterick Pubs.

--The Tribe Alasmidontini: Unioidae Anodontinae. LC 80-23747. (Smithsonian Contributions to Zoology Ser.: No. 326). pap. 20.00 (ISBN 0-317-26683-7, 2025112). Bks Demand UMI.

Clarke, Arthur A., tr. see Gauss, Karl F.

Clarke, Arthur C. Ascent to Orbit: A Scientific Autobiography. LC 83-26039. 226p. 1984. text ed. 21.50 (ISBN 0-471-87910-X). Wiley.

--Challenge of the Spaceship. 1980. pap. 2.50 (ISBN 0-671-82139-3). PB.

--Childhood's End. LC 53-10419. 1980. pap. 2.50 (ISBN 0-345-29730-X, Del Rey). Ballantine.

--Childhood's End. 240p. 1981. pap. 5.95 (ISBN 0-345-29467-X, Del Rey). Ballantine.

--Childhood's End. LC 53-10419. 1963. 14.95 (ISBN 0-15-117205-6). HarBraceJ.

--Childhood's End. 14.95 (ISBN 0-8488-0157-1, Pub. by Amereon Hse). Amereon Ltd.

--A Choice of Futures. 272p. 1984. pap. 3.50 (ISBN 0-317-14137-6, Del Rey). Ballantine.

--The City & the Stars. 192p. (RL 7). 1973. pap. 2.95 (ISBN 0-451-13315-3, Sig). NAL.

--The Deep Range. 1974. pap. 2.50 (ISBN 0-451-12361-1, AE2361, Sig). NAL.

--Dolphin Island. 192p. 1983. pap. 2.50 (ISBN 0-425-07143-X, Medallion). Berkley Pub.

--The Exploration of Space. rev. ed. (gr. 10-12). 1979. pap. 2.50 (ISBN 0-671-82140-7). PB.

--Fall of Moondust. 224p. (YA) 1974. pap. 2.50 (ISBN 0-451-12367-0, Sig). NAL.

--The Fountains of Paradise. 320p. 1980. pap. 2.50 (ISBN 0-345-25356-6, Del Rey). Ballantine.

--The Fountains of Paradise. (Reader's Request Ser.). 1980. lib. bdg. 15.95 (ISBN 0-8161-3039-6, Large Print Bks). G K Hall.

--Glidepath. 208p. 1973. pap. 2.75 (ISBN 0-451-12706-4, AE2706, Sig). NAL.

--The Gods Themselves. 288p. 1984. pap. 2.95 (ISBN 0-345-31831-5, Del Rey). Ballantine.

--I Remember Babylon & Other Stories. 240p. Repr. lib. bdg. 13.85x (ISBN 0-89190-955-9, Pub. by River City Pr). Amereon Ltd.

--Imperial Earth. (Reader's Request Ser.). 1980. lib. bdg. 16.95 (ISBN 0-8161-3037-X, Large Print Bks). G K Hall.

--Interplanetary Flight. 192p. 1985. pap. 2.95 (ISBN 0-425-06448-4). Berkley Pub.

--Islands in the Sky. 1979. lib. bdg. 11.95 (ISBN 0-8398-2516-1, Gregg). G K Hall.

--Islands in the Sky. pap. 2.25 (ISBN 0-451-12697-1, AE2697, Sig). NAL.

--Lost Worlds of 2001. (RL 7). pap. 2.95 (ISBN 0-451-12536-3, AE2536, Sig). NAL.

--Nineteen Eighty-Four: Spring: A Choice of Futures. LC 83-15643. 272p. 1984. 14.95 (ISBN 0-345-31357-7, Del Rey). Ballantine.

--The Other Side of the Sky: Stories of the Future. 160p. 1985. pap. 2.95 (ISBN 0-451-14018-4, Sig). NAL.

--The Possessed & Other Stories. 188p. Repr. lib. bdg. 12.05x (ISBN 0-89190-956-7, Pub. by River City Pr). Amereon Ltd.

--Prelude to Space. 192p. 1976. pap. 2.25 (ISBN 0-345-30579-5). Ballantine.

--Profiles of the Future. 304p. (Orig.). 1985. pap. 3.50 (ISBN 0-446-32107-9). Warner Bks.

--The Promise of Space. 336p. 1985. pap. 3.50 (ISBN 0-425-07565-6) (ISBN 0-317-13693-3). Berkley Pub.

--Reach for Tomorrow. (Science Fiction Ser.). (Orig.). 1975. pap. 1.50 (ISBN 0-345-25819-3). Ballantine.

--Rendezvous with Rama. 1984. pap. 2.95 (ISBN 0-345-31560-X). Ballantine.

--Rendezvous with Rama. (Reader's Request Ser.). 1980. lib. bdg. 15.95 (ISBN 0-8161-3038-8, Large Print Bks). G K Hall.

--Report on Planet Three & Other Speculations. LC 74-156515. 1972. 9.95i (ISBN 0-06-010793-6, HarpT). Har-Row.

--Report on Planet Three & Other Speculations. 1982. pap. 2.50 (ISBN 0-451-11573-2, Sig). NAL.

--Report on Planet Three & Other Speculations. 256p. 1985. pap. 3.50 (ISBN 0-425-07592-3). Berkley Pub.

--The Sands of Mars. (RL 7). pap. 2.50 (ISBN 0-451-12312-3, AE2312, Sig). NAL.

--Spring, 1984: A Choice of Futures. 272p. 1984. pap. 3.50 (ISBN 0-345-31358-5). Fawcett.

--Tales from the White Hart. 1981. pap. 2.25 (ISBN 0-345-29880-2). Ballantine.

--Tales from the White Heart. 10.95 (ISBN 0-89190-249-X, Pub. by Am Repr). Amereon Ltd.

--Tales of Ten Worlds. (RL 7). 1973. pap. 2.95 (ISBN 0-451-13233-5, AE3233, Sig). NAL.

--Two Thousand & One: A Space Odyssey. 1972. pap. 3.50 (ISBN 0-451-13469-9, Sig). NAL.

--Two Thousand & Ten: Odyssey Two. 320p. 1982. 14.95 (ISBN 0-345-30305-9, Del Rey). Ballantine.

--Voice Across the Sea. rev. ed. LC 74-15817. (Illus.). 228p. (YA) 1975. 10.00i (ISBN 0-06-010782-0, HarpT). Har-Row.

--Voices from the Sky. (gr. 11 up). 1980. pap. 2.50 (ISBN 0-671-82141-5). PB.

--The Wind from the Sun: Stories of the Space Age. LC 77-182325. 1972. 6.50 (ISBN 0-15-196810-1). HarBraceJ.

--The Wind from the Sun: Stories of the Space Age. 176p. (RL 7). 1973. pap. 1.95 (ISBN 0-451-11475-2, AJ1475, Sig). NAL.

Clarke, Arthur C. & Hyams, Peter. The Odyssey File. 224p. (Orig.). 1985. pap. 3.95 (ISBN 0-345-32108-1). Fawcett.

Clarke, Arthur C. & Proctor, George, eds. The Science Fiction Hall of Fame, Vol. 3: The Nebula Winners. 688p. 1982. pap. 3.95 (ISBN 0-380-79335-0, 79335-0). Avon.

Clarke, Arthur G. Analytical Studies in the Psalms. LC 79-2518. 1979. 12.95 (ISBN 0-8254-2322-8). Kregel.

Clarke, Arthur H. The Freshwater Molluscs of Canada. (Illus.). 416p. 1982. lib. bdg. 39.95x (ISBN 0-660-00022-9, 56350-2, Pub. by Natl Mus Canada). U of Chicago Pr.

Clarke, Asia. The Elder & the Younger Booth. 14.25 (ISBN 0-8369-7144-2, 7977). Ayer Co Pubs.

--Unlocked Book: A Memoir of John Wilkes Booth by His Sister. LC 74-88533. (Illus.). 1938. 22.00 (ISBN 0-405-08363-7, Blom Pubns). Ayer Co Pubs.

Clarke, Athur C. Profiles of the Future: An Inquiry into the Limits of the Possible. rev. ed. 1984. 15.95 (ISBN 0-03-069783-2). HR&W.

Clarke, Audrey, ed. see Stamp, Dudley.

Clarke, Austin. Celtic Twilight & the Nineties. 1970. 12.95 (ISBN 0-85105-010-7). Dufour.

--The Collected Poems of Austin Clarke. LC 75-41061. (BCL Ser.: No. II). Repr. of 1936 ed. 24.50 (ISBN 0-404-14523-X). AMS Pr.

--Echo at Coole & Other Poems. LC 68-26020. 1968. 12.95 (ISBN 0-8023-1155-5). Dufour.

--The Frenzy of Sweeney. (Dolmen Editions Ser.: No. XXIX). 1980. text ed. 26.50x (ISBN 0-85105-349-1, Dolmen Pr). Humanities.

--Liberty Lane: A Ballad Play of Dublin in Two Acts with a Prologue by Austin Clarke. (Dolmen Editions: No. XXVII). 1978. text ed. 22.75x (ISBN 0-85105-324-6, Dolmen Pr). Humanities.

--Poetry in Modern Ireland. 1978. Repr. of 1951 ed. lib. bdg. 15.00 (ISBN 0-8495-0904-1). Arden Lib.

--Poetry in Modern Ireland. LC 74-12114. 1973. lib. bdg. 12.00 (ISBN 0-8414-3363-1). Folcroft.

--The Selected Poetry of Austin Clarke. Kinsella, Thomas, ed. 207p. 1976. 13.50 (ISBN 0-916390-04-7). Wake Forest.

--The Singing Men at Cashel. 320p. 1980. pap. text ed. 16.25x (ISBN 0-85105-354-8, Dolmen Pr). Humanities.

--The Third Kiss. (Dolmen Editions: No. XxIV). 1976. text ed. 20.00x (ISBN 0-85105-292-4, Dolmen Pr). Humanities.

Clarke, B. Mental Disorder in Earlier Britain: Exploratory Studies. 335p. 1975. text ed. 38.25x (ISBN 0-7083-0562-8, Pub. by Univ of Wales Pr England). Humanities.

Clarke, B. & Shov, S B. Forest Fire Control. (Forestry & Forest Products Studies: No. 5). 110p. (3rd Printing 1978). 1953. pap. 8.00 (ISBN 92-5-100488-9, F1443, FAO). Unipub.

Clarke, B. M., jt. auth. see Crocetti, Gino.

Clarke, Basil. The Building of the Eighteenth Century Church. LC 66-37309. (Illus.). 1963. text ed. 20.00x (ISBN 0-8401-0404-9). A R Allenson.

Clarke, Basil, ed. Chinese Science & the West. 1984. 30.00x (ISBN 0-686-45585-1, Pub. by Nile & Mackenzie Ltd England). State Mutual Bk.

Clarke, Basil F. Church Builders of the Nineteenth Century. LC 69-10849. (Illus.). Repr. of 1938 ed. 19.50x (ISBN 0-678-05513-0). Kelley.

Clarke, Betty. Saleswomanship. 1980. pap. 3.95 (ISBN 0-346-12392-5). Cornerstone.

Clarke, Bill. The Illustrated Buyer's Guide to Used Airplanes. (Illus.). 288p. 1985. pap. 15.95 (ISBN 0-8306-2372-8, 2372). TAB Bks.

Clarke, Bob, jt. auth. see De Bartolo, Dick.

Clarke, Bob, jt. auth. see Jacobs, Frank.

Clarke, Bob, jt. auth. see Koch, Tom.

Clarke, Bob C. & Garner, Philippe. Obsession. (Illus.). 160p. 1982. 29.50 (ISBN 0-7043-2298-6, Pub. by Quartet Bks). Merrimack Pub Cir.

--Obsession. (Illus.). 160p. 1984. pap. 17.95 (ISBN 0-7043-3472-0, Pub. by Quartet Bks). Merrimack Pub Cir.

Clarke, Boden. Jeffrey M. Elliot, Boswell of Modern America. LC 84-12305. (Borgo Bioviews Ser.: No. 12). 96p. (Orig.). 1986. lib. bdg. 19.95x (ISBN 0-89370-347-8); pap. text ed. 9.95x (ISBN 0-89370-447-4). Borgo Pr.

--Lords Temporal & Lords Spiritual. LC 80-10979. (Stokvis Studies in Historical Chronology & Thought: No. 1). 160p. 1985. lib. bdg. 19.95x (ISBN 0-89370-800-3); pap. 9.95x (ISBN 0-89370-900-X). Borgo Pr.

--The Work of Jeffrey M. Elliot: An Annotated Bibliography & Guide. LC 84-21745. (Bibliographies of Modern Authors Ser.: No. 2). 64p. 1984. lib. bdg. 19.95x (ISBN 0-89370-381-8); pap. text ed. 9.95x (ISBN 0-89370-481-4). Borgo Pr.

Clarke, Boden & Burgess, Mary W. Eastern Churches Review: An Index to Volumes One Through Ten, 1966-1978. LC 80-2550. (Borgo Reference Library: Vol. 6). 96p. 1985. lib. bdg. 19.95x (ISBN 0-89370-812-7); pap. text ed. 9.95x (ISBN 0-89370-912-3). Borgo Pr.

Clarke, Bowman & Long, Eugene T., eds. God & Temporality. (God Ser.). 200p. (Orig.). 1984. text ed. 17.95 (ISBN 0-913757-11-X, Pub. by New Era Bks); pap. text ed. 12.95 (ISBN 0-913757-10-1, Pub. by New Era Bks). Paragon Hse.

Clarke, Bowman L. Language & Natural Theology. (Janua Linguarum, Ser. Minor: No. 47). (Orig.). 1966. pap. text ed. 18.00 (ISBN 90-2790-580-0). Mouton.

Clarke, Brenna K. The Emergence of the Irish Peasant Play at the Abbey Theatre. Beckerman, Bernard, ed. LC 82-4757. (Theater & Dramatic Studies: No. 12). 236p. 1982. 39.95 (ISBN 0-8357-1293-1). UMI Res Pr.

Clarke, Brenna K. & Ferrar, Harold. The Dublin Drama League. (Irish Theatre Ser.: No. 9). 1979. pap. text ed. 5.75x (ISBN 0-85105-316-5, Dolmen Pr). Humanities.

Clarke, Brian. Architectural Stained Glass. LC 79-211. (Illus.). 1979. 42.00 (ISBN 0-07-011264-9). McGraw.

Clarke, Brian & Goddard, John. The Trout & the Fly: A New Approach. 192p. 1984. pap. 17.95 (ISBN 0-8329-0318-3, Pub. by Winchester Pr). New Century.

Clarke, Brian, jt. auth. see Reger, Janet.

Clarke, C. Elementary General Relativity. 131p. 1980. pap. 25.95x (ISBN 0-470-26930-8). Halsted Pr.

Clarke, C. B. Compositae Indicae. (Lat.). 1978. Repr. of 1876 ed. 56.25x (ISBN 0-89955-257-9, Pub. by Intl Bk Dist). Intl Spec Bk.

Clarke, C. G., jt. auth. see Dickenson, J. P.

Clarke, C. P. Church History from Nero to Constantine. 1977. lib. bdg. 59.95 (ISBN 0-8490-1626-6). Gordon Pr.

Clarke, Carl D. Illustration, Its Technique & Application to the Sciences. 2nd ed. (Illus.). 258p. 1949. 25.00 (ISBN 0-685-25473-9). Standard Arts.

--Metal Casting of Sculpture & Ornament. 2nd ed. (Illus.). 250p. 1985. 25.00 (ISBN 0-685-50214-7). Standard Arts.

--Molding & Casting: Its Technique & Application. 3rd ed. (Illus.). 380p. 1972. 25.00 (ISBN 0-685-25470-4). Standard Arts.

--Pictures, Their Preservation & Restoration. (Illus.). 250p. 1959. 25.00 (ISBN 0-685-25472-0). Standard Arts.

--Prosthetics: Methods of Producing Facial & Body Restorations. (Illus.). 336p. 1965. 25.00 (ISBN 0-685-25471-2). Standard Arts.

Clarke, Catherine. Red Horse. (Illus.). 26p. (Orig.). 1981. pap. 2.50 (ISBN 0-914278-33-9). Copper Beech.

Clarke, Charles, jt. auth. see Bonington, Chris.

Clarke, Charles B. A Review of the Ferns of Northern India: With an Index of the Species & 36 Plates. (Illus.). 1978. Repr. of 1880 ed. 62.50x (ISBN 0-89955-303-6, Pub. by Intl Bk Dist). Intl Spec Bk.

Clarke, Charles C. Moliere-Characters. LC 75-35806. 1975. Repr. of 1865 ed. lib. bdg. 33.00 (ISBN 0-8414-3399-2). Folcroft.

--Shakespeare-Characters. LC 72-961. Repr. of 1863 ed. 22.50 (ISBN 0-404-01567-0). AMS Pr.

Clarke, Charles G., ed. American Cinematographer Manual. 5th ed. 628p. 1980. 25.00 (ISBN 0-935578-01-3); flexbound 18.95. Am Soc Cine.

Clarke, Charlotte. A Narrative on the Life of Mrs. Charlotte Clarke, Daughter of Colley Cibber. 223p. 1982. Repr. of 1755 ed. lib. bdg. 30.00 (ISBN 0-8495-0879-7). Arden Lib.

Clarke, Charlotte B. Edible & Useful Plants of California. LC 76-14317. (Natural History Guide Ser). (Illus.). 1978. 14.95 (ISBN 0-520-03261-6); pap. 5.95 (ISBN 0-520-03267-5). U of Cal Pr.

Clarke, Charlotte L., jt. auth. see Farlie, Barbara L.

Clarke, Chas & Cowden, Mary. Recollections of Writers. 24.00x (ISBN 0-87556-542-5). Saifer.

Clarke, Christina. Cook with Tofu. 224p. (Orig.). 1985. pap. 3.25 (ISBN 0-380-89721-0). Avon.

Clarke, Christopher M. China's Provinces: An Organizational & Statistical Guide. 462p. 1982. pap. text ed. 235.00x (ISBN 0-8103-2037-1, Pub. by Natl Coun US-China). Gale.

Clarke, Clara & Mahone, Stella. Coping Alone: How to Be a Successful Single Parent. (Arlen House Ser.). 160p. pap. 5.95 (ISBN 0-905223-25-X, Dist. by Scribner). M Boyars.

Clarke, Claudia, tr. see Moog, Helmut.

Clarke, Clorinda. The American Revolution, Seventeen Seventy-Five to Seventeen Eighty-Three. Reeves, Marjorie, ed. (Then & There Ser.). (Illus.). 100p. (Orig.). (gr. 7-12). 1964. pap. text ed. 3.40x (ISBN 0-582-20398-8). Longman.

Clarke, Colin & Ley, David, eds. Geography & Ethnic Pluralism. 320p. 1984. text ed. 30.00 (ISBN 0-04-309107-5); pap. text ed. 14.95 (ISBN 0-04-309108-3). Allen Unwin.

Clarke, Colin C. Romantic Paradox: An Essay on the Poetry of Wordsworth. LC 78-10859. 1979. Repr. of 1963 ed. lib. bdg. 22.50x (ISBN 0-313-20758-5, CLPA). Greenwood.

Clarke, Colin G. Kingston, Jamaica: Urban Growth & Social Change, 1692-1962. (Illus.). 1976. 52.50x (ISBN 0-520-02025-1). U of Cal Pr.

Clarke, Colin G. & Hodgkiss, Alan G. Jamaica in Maps. LC 74-84659. (Graphic Perspectives of Developing Countries Ser.). (Illus.). 125p. 1975. text ed. 35.00x (ISBN 0-8419-0175-9, Africana). Holmes & Meier.

--Sierra Leone in Maps. (Graphic Perspectives of Developing Countries Ser.). 120p. 1972. 34.50x (ISBN 0-8419-0070-1). Holmes & Meier.

Clarke, Cyril, tr. see Cortot, Alfred.

Clarke, Cyril A. & McConnell, Richard B. Prevention of Rh-Hemolytic Disease. (Illus.). 136p. 1972. 19.50x (ISBN 0-398-02259-3). C C Thomas.

Clarke, D., jt. auth. see Roy, A. E.

Clarke, D. A. A London Bibliography of Social Sciences, Ninth Supplement: 1974, Vol. 32. 461p. 1975. 64.00 (ISBN 0-7201-0524-2). Mansell.

--London Bibliography of Social Sciences, Tenth Supplement: 1975, Vol. 33. 418p. 1976. 64.00 (ISBN 0-7201-0634-6). Mansell.

--A London Bibliography of the Social Sciences: Eleventh Suppliment, 1976, Vol. 34. LC 31-9970. 458p. 1977. lib. bdg. 64.00 (ISBN 0-7201-0721-0). Mansell.

--A London Bibliography of the Social Sciences: Eighth Supplement, 1972-1973, Vols. 29-31. 1768p. 1975. 191.00x (ISBN 0-7201-0454-8). Mansell.

Clarke, D. A., ed. A London Bibliography of the Social Sciences: Eighteenth Supplement, 1983, Vol. 41. 896p. 1984. 100.00 (ISBN 0-7201-1649-X). Mansell.

--London Bibliography of the Social Sciences: Fourteenth Supplement, 1979, Vol. 37. 400p. 1980. lib. bdg. 80.00 (ISBN 0-7201-1594-9). Mansell.

--A London Bibliography of the Social Sciences, Twelfth Supplement, 1977, Vol. 35. 402p. 1978. lib. bdg. 48.00x (ISBN 0-7201-0829-2). Mansell.

--London Bibliography of the Social Sciences: Thirteenth Supplement, 1978, Vol. 36. 416p. 1979. lib. bdg. 69.00 (ISBN 0-7201-0929-9). Mansell.

Clarke, D. A., et al. Foundations of Analysis: With An Introduction to Logic & Set Theory. LC 73-136217. (Century Mathematics Ser.). (Illus., Orig.). 1971. text ed. 19.95x (ISBN 0-89197-171-8). Irvington.

Clarke, D. B. & Barnes, A. D. Intensive Care for Nurses. 3rd ed. (Illus.). 176p. 1981. pap. text ed. 18.95 (ISBN 0-632-00696-X, B-1150-4). Mosby.

Clarke, D. D. Language & Action: A Generative Account of Interaction Sequences. (International Series in Experimental Social Psychology: Vol. 7). (Illus.). 392p. 1983. 40.00 (ISBN 0-08-026090-X). Pergamon.

Clarke, D. H. An Evolution of Singlehanders. 224p. 1982. 30.00x (ISBN 0-540-07145-5, Pub. by Stanford Maritime England). State Mutual Bk.

Clarke, D. S., Jr. Deductive Logic: An Introduction to Evaluation Technique & Logical Theory. LC 73-10459. 255p. 1973. pap. 7.95x (ISBN 0-8093-0657-3). S Ill U Pr.

--Practical Inferences. (International Library of Philosophy). 192p. 1985. 32.50x (ISBN 0-7102-0415-9). Routledge & Kegan.

Clarke, D. V. & O'Connor, Anne, eds. From the Stone Age to the Forty-Five: Studies in Scottish Material Culture Presented to R. B. K. Stevenson, Former Keeper, National Museum of Antiquities of Scotland. 1983. text ed. 57.50x (ISBN 0-85976-046-4, Pub. by John Donald). Humanities.

Clarke, David, jt. auth. see Roy, Archie E.

Clarke, David, ed. Spatial Archaeology. 1977. 50.00 (ISBN 0-12-175750-1). Acad Pr.

Clarke, David D. & Crossland, Jill. Action Systems: An Introduction to the Analysis of Complex Behavior. 160p. 1985. 27.00 (ISBN 0-416-36120-X, 4175); pap. 11.95 (ISBN 0-416-36130-7, 4176). Methuen Inc.

Clarke, David E., jt. auth. see Bridgman, Jon.

Clarke, David H. Exercise Physiology. LC 75-9735. 1975. 26.95 (ISBN 0-13-294967-9). P-H.

Clarke, David H. & Clarke, H. Harrison. Research Processes in Physical Education. 2nd ed. (Illus.). 528p. 1984. pap. 27.95 (ISBN 0-13-774513-3). P-H.

Clarke, David H. & Eckert, Helen M., eds. The Limits of Human Performance. (American Academy of Physical Education Papers: No. 18). 144p. 1985. pap. text ed. 12.00x (ISBN 0-931250-99-4, BCLA0099). Human Kinetics.

Clarke, David L. Analytical Archaeology. 2nd ed. Chapman, Robert, ed. LC 78-16957. 526p. 1978. 42.00x (ISBN 0-231-04630-8); pap. 17.00x (ISBN 0-231-04631-6). Columbia U Pr.

Clarke, David L., ed. Analytical Archaeologist: Collected Papers of David L. Clarke. (Studies in Archaeology). 1979. 49.00 (ISBN 0-12-175760-9). Acad Pr.

--Models in Archaeology. 1972. 89.00x (ISBN 0-416-16540-0, NO. 2144). Methuen Inc.

Clarke, David S. An Argument in Favor of Sharpshooting. (Illus.). 176p. 1984. 19.95 (ISBN 0-88192-004-5). Timber.

Clarke, David S., ed. see De Mauni, Roger.

Clarke, David W. William Shakespeare. LC 70-179330. (Illus.). Repr. of 1950 ed. 12.50 (ISBN 0-404-01568-9). AMS Pr.

Clarke, Desmond. Dublin. 1977. 17.95 (ISBN 0-7134-0146-X, Pub. by Batsford England). David & Charles.

Clarke, Desmond, jt. auth. see Meenan, James.

Clarke, Desmond M. Descartes' Philosophy of Science. LC 82-82082. 224p. 1982. text ed. 22.50x (ISBN 0-271-00325-1). Pa St U Pr.

Clarke, Desmond M., ed. Morality & the Law. 130p. 1983. pap. 5.95 (ISBN 0-85342-669-4, Pub. by Mercier Pr Ireland). Irish Bks Media.

Clarke, Donald. Enciclopedia De los Inventos. 2nd ed. 128p. (Espn.). 1978. 25.50 (ISBN 84-7091-134-1, S-50483). French & Eur.

--How It Works: The Illustrated Science & Invention Encyclopedia. 3rd ed. (Illus.). 3440p. 1983. lib. bdg. 324.95x (ISBN 0-686-39381-3). M Cavendish Corp.

Clarke, Dorothy C. Allegory, Decalogue, & Deadly Sins in La Celestina. LC 68-65019. 136p. 1983. Repr. of 1968 ed. lib. bdg. 19.95x (ISBN 0-89370-760-0). Borgo Pr.

--Juan De Mena's "Laberinto de Fortuna". Classic Epic & Mester de Clerecia. LC 73-89015. (Romance Monographs: No. 5). 1973. 12.00x (ISBN 84-399-1732-5); pap. 9.00x (ISBN 0-686-17914-5). Romance.

Clarke, Dorothy J. Terre Haute: Wabash River City. (Illus.). 112p. 1983. 19.95 (ISBN 0-89781-089-9). Windsor Pubns Inc.

Clarke, Doug, ed. see Ring, Leonard.

Clarke, Douglas A. Hierarchies of Predicates of Finite Types. LC 52-42839. (Memoirs: No. 51). 95p. 1964. pap. 9.00 (ISBN 0-8218-1251-3, MEMO-51). Am Math.

Clarke, Duncan L. Politics of Arms Control: The Role & Effectiveness of the U. S. Arms Control & Disarmament Agency. LC 79-1955. 1979. 22.95 (ISBN 0-02-905700-0). Free Pr.

--The Politics of Arms Control: The Role & Effectiveness of the US Arms Control & Disarmament Agency. 232p. 1979. 14.35 (ISBN 0-317-33393-3). Arms Control.

Clarke, Duncan L., jt. ed. see Brauch, Hans G.

Clarke, E. & Kozen, D., eds. Logics of Program: Workshop, Carnegie-Mellon University, Pittsburgh, Pa., June 6-8, 1983. (Lecture Notes in Computer Science: Vol. 164). vi, 528p. 1984. pap. 25.50 (ISBN 0-387-12896-4). Springer-Verlag.

Clarke, E. D. Elements of Practical Geology. 4th ed. 1967. 11.75x (ISBN 0-85564-028-6, Pub by U of W Austral Pr). Intl Spec Bk.

Clarke, E. G. Targum Pseudo-Jonathan of the Pentateuch. 1983. 150.00x (ISBN 0-88125-015-5). Ktav.

--The Wisdom of Solomon. (Cambridge Bible Commentary on the New English Bible, Old Testament Ser.). 148p. 1973. 18.95 (ISBN 0-521-08635-3); pap. 8.95 (ISBN 0-521-09756-8). Cambridge U Pr.

Clarke, E. Y. Illustrated History of Atlanta. LC 70-11145. (Illus.). 210p. 1971. Repr. of 1877 ed. 8.50 (ISBN 0-87797-015-7). Cherokee.

Clarke, Edward. Benjamin Disraeli: The Romance of a Great Career 1804-1881. 1973. Repr. of 1926 ed. 30.00 (ISBN 0-8274-0088-8). R West.

--Sex in Education; or, a Fair Chance for the Girls. LC 74-180566. (Medicine & Society in America Ser.). 190p. 1972. Repr. of 1873 ed. 14.00 (ISBN 0-405-03943-3). Ayer Co Pubs.

Clarke, Edward, jt. auth. see Walker-Smith, Derek.

Clarke, Edward D. Travels to Russia, Tartary & Turkey. LC 75-115520. (Russia Observed, Series I). 1970. Repr. of 1811 ed. 32.00 (ISBN 0-405-03015-0). Ayer Co Pubs.

Clarke, Edward H. Century of American Medicine, 1776-1876. LC 77-168275. (Research & Source Works Ser.: No. 843). 1971. Repr. of 1876 ed. lib. bdg. 23.50 (ISBN 0-8337-0584-9). B Franklin.

--Demand Revelation & the Provision of Public Goods. LC 79-25743. 264p. 1980. prof ref 32.50 (ISBN 0-88410-686-1). Ballinger Pub.

Clarke, Edwin. Modern Methods in the History of Medicine. (Illus.). 389p. 1971. 65.00 (ISBN 0-485-11121-7, Pub. by Athlone Pr Ltd). Longwood Pub Group.

Clarke, Edwin & O'Malley, C. D. The Human Brain & Spinal Cord: A Historical Study Illustrated By Writings from Antiquity to the Twentieth Century. LC 68-11275. pap. 160.00 (ISBN 0-317-30005-9, 2051865). Bks Demand UMI.

Clarke, Edwin, ed. & tr. see Neuberger, Max.

Clarke, Edwin L. American Men of Letters: Their Nature & Nurture. LC 76-76714. (Columbia University Studies in the Social Sciences: No. 168). Repr. of 1916 ed. 8.50 (ISBN 0-404-51168-6). AMS Pr.

--American Men of Letters: Their Nature & Nurture. 1916. 10.00 (ISBN 0-8274-1853-1). R West.

Clarke, Elissa. Stopping Sexual Harassment: A Handbook. 2nd. ed. 60p. 1982. pap. 2.50 (ISBN 0-914093-02-9). Labor Ed & Res.

Clarke, Eliza. Handel. LC 70-158201. (Studies in Music, No. 42). 1971. Repr. of 1885 ed. lib. bdg. 48.95x (ISBN 0-8383-1250-0). Haskell.

Clarke, Elizabeth D., et al. The Joy of Service. (Illus.). 1979. 5.95 (ISBN 0-686-26879-2). YWCA.

Clarke, Elton. Options. 384p. (Orig.). 1985. pap. 3.75 (ISBN 0-8439-2268-0, Leisure Bks). Dorchester Pub Co.

Clarke, Emerson. Guide to Technical Literature Production. 1960. pap. 10.00 (ISBN 0-686-00899-5). T W Pubs.

--Personal Security for Senior Citizens. 1975. pap. 3.00x (ISBN 0-918384-00-1). Personal Security.

Clarke, F. H. Optimization & Nonsmooth Analysis. (Canadian Mathematical Society Ser.). 308p. 1983. 37.50 (ISBN 0-471-87504-X). Wiley.

Clarke, F. L. The Tangled Web of Price Variation Accounting: The Development of Ideas Underlying Professional Prescriptions in Six Counties. LC 82-82485. (Accountancy in Transition Ser.). 466p. 1982. lib. bdg. 61.00 (ISBN 0-8240-5300-1). Garland Pub.

Clarke, F. P. & Nahm, M. C. Philosophical Essays in the Honor of Edgar Arthur Singer Jr. LC 78-80394. (Essay Index Reprint Ser). 1942. 23.75 (ISBN 0-8369-1062-1). Ayer Co Pubs.

Clarke, F. R. Healey Willan: Life & Music. 312p. 1983. 40.00x (ISBN 0-8020-5549-4). U of Toronto Pr.

Clarke, F. W., ed. The Comedy of George A. Green. LC 82-45759. (Malone Society Reprint Ser.: No. 26). Repr. of 1911 ed. 40.00 (ISBN 0-404-63026-X). AMS Pr.

Clarke, Frances E. Poetry's Plea for Animals. 1977. Repr. of 1927 ed. 30.00 (ISBN 0-89984-163-5). Century Bookbindery.

Clarke, Francis E. Poetry's Plea for Animals. 1927. 20.00 (ISBN 0-686-17675-8). Quaker City.

Clarke, Francis G. The Land of Contrarieties: British Attitudes to the Australian Colonies, 1828-1855. 1977. 16.00x (ISBN 0-522-84112-0, Pub. by Melbourne U Pr Australia). Intl Spec Bk.

Clarke, Frank, tr. see Kasemann, Ernst.

Clarke, Frank H. Calculator Programming for Chemistry & the Life Sciences. LC 81-15046. 1981. 33.00 (ISBN 0-12-175320-4). Acad Pr.

Clarke, Frank H. & Henkel, James G., eds. Molecular Graphics on the Apple Microcomputer. Date not set. 129.50 (ISBN 0-12-175780-3). Acad Pr.

Clarke, Frank H., jt. ed. see Henkel, James G.

Clarke, Frank J., jt. auth. see Rupnow, Roger F.

Clarke, G. Selected Poems. 112p. 1985. pap. text ed. 8.45x (ISBN 0-85635-594-1, Pub. by Carcanet New Pr England). Humanities.

Clarke, G. C., jt. auth. see Punt, W.

Clarke, G. C., jt. ed. see Punt, W.

Clarke, G. C. S. & Duckett, J. G., eds. Bryophyte Systematics, No. 14. LC 79-40897. (Systematics Association Special Ser.). 1980. 95.00 (ISBN 0-12-175050-7). Acad Pr.

Clarke, G. M. & Cooke, D. A Basic Course in Statistics. LC 78-10749. 368p. 1978. pap. text ed. 29.95x (ISBN 0-470-26527-2). Halsted Pr.

--A Basic Course in Statistics. 2nd ed. 440p. 1984. text ed. 19.95 (ISBN 0-7131-3496-8). E Arnold.

Clarke, G. W., tr. see Lawler, Thomas C. & Burghart, Johannes.

Clarke, Garry E. Essays on American Music. LC 76-52606. (Contributions in American History Ser.: No. 62). (Illus.). 1977. lib. bdg. 27.50 (ISBN 0-8371-9484-9, CAM/). Greenwood.

Clarke, Geoffrey M. Statistics & Experimental Design. 2nd ed. 200p. 1980. pap. text ed. 19.95 (ISBN 0-7131-2797-X). E Arnold.

Clarke, Gerald. Capote: A Biography. 1986. price not set. S&S.

Clarke, Gerald E. Airling.... & Other Poems. 1977. 5.00 (ISBN 0-8233-0256-3). Golden Quill.

--McGregor School. 1980. 5.50 (ISBN 0-8233-0310-1). Golden Quill.

Clarke, Giles. Pre-Roman & Roman Winchester, Part 2: The Roman Cemetary at Lankhills. Biddle, Msartin, contrib. by. (Winchester Studies). (Illus.). 1979. text ed. 105.00x (ISBN 0-19-813177-1). Oxford U Pr.

Clarke, Graehme W., tr. The Letters of St. Cyprian, Vol. 1. (Ancient Christian Writers Ser.: No. 43). 416p. 1983. 24.95 (ISBN 0-8091-0341-9). Paulist Pr.

Clarke, Graeme W., tr. The Letters of St. Cyprian, Vol. 2. (Ancient Christian Writers Ser.: No. 44). 352p. 1983. 22.95 (ISBN 0-8091-0342-7). Paulist Pr.

Clarke, H. Browning's England. 59.95 (ISBN 0-87968-797-5). Gordon Pr.

Clarke, H., et al. Political Choice in Canada. 1979. text ed. 24.95 (ISBN 0-07-082783-4). McGraw.

Clarke, H. B. Spanish Literature: A Handbook with Index. 1977. lib. bdg. 59.95 (ISBN 0-8490-2651-2). Gordon Pr.

Clarke, H. Butler. Spanish Literature. LC 77-103220. 1970. Repr. of 1893 ed. 21.00x (ISBN 0-8046-0857-1, Pub. by Kennikat). Assoc FAculty Pr.

Clarke, H. C. Menu Terminology. 1969. pap. 7.95 (ISBN 0-08-006525-2). Pergamon.

Clarke, H. D. & Hamamura, Motoko. Colloquial Japanese. (Colloquial Ser.). (Orig.). 1981. pap. 9.95 (ISBN 0-7100-0595-4). Routledge & Kegan.

Clarke, H. Edwards. The Greyhound. rev., 7th ed. 222p. 1980. text ed. 24.95x (ISBN 0-09-141410-5, SpS). Sportshelf.

Clarke, H. Harrison. Application of Measurement to Health & Physical Education. 5th ed. (Illus.). 464p. 1976. 26.95 (ISBN 0-13-039024-0). P-H.

Clarke, H. Harrison, jt. auth. see Clarke, David H.

Clarke, H. T. A Handbook of Organic Analysis: Qualitative & Quantitative. 5th ed. Haynes, B., ed. LC 74-83479. 320p. 1975. pap. 20.50x (ISBN 0-8448-0662-5). Crane-Russak Co.

Clarke, H. W., tr. see Dessemontet, Francois.

Clarke, Hans T., ed. Chemistry of Penicillin. 1949. 95.00x (ISBN 0-691-07922-6). Princeton U Pr.

Clarke, Harold. Growing Berries & Grapes at Home. 384p. 1976. pap. 4.50 (ISBN 0-486-23274-3). Dover.

--The Splendour of Ireland. (Illus.). 64p. 1982. 15.95 (ISBN 0-900346-36-1, Pub. by Salem House). Merrimack Pub Cir.

--The Splendour of Ireland. (Illus.). 64p. 1976. 14.95 (ISBN 0-900346-36-1, Pub. by Eason & Son Ireland). Irish Bk Ctr.

Clarke, Harold, et al. Canadian National Election Study, 1974. 1977. codebook write for info. (ISBN 0-89138-156-2). ICPSR.

Clarke, Harold D., jt. ed. see Kornberg, Allan.

Clarke, Heather F., jt. auth. see Robinson, Geoffrey C.

Clarke, Helen. The Professional Training of the Hospital Dietician. LC 70-176651. (Columbia University. Teachers College. Contributions to Education: No. 602). Repr. of 1934 ed. 22.50 (ISBN 0-404-55602-7). AMS Pr.

--Vikings. (Civilization Library). (Illus.). (gr. 5 up). 1979. PLB 9.40 s&l (ISBN 0-531-03412-7, Gloucester Press). Watts.

--Vikings. (Civilization Library Ser.). 32p. (gr. 4 up). 1984. lib. bdg. 9.40 (ISBN 0-531-03481-X, Gloucester Pr). Watts.

Clarke, Helen A. Browning & His Century. LC 73-18248. (Studies in Browning, No. 4). 1974. lib. bdg. 59.95x (ISBN 0-8383-1734-0). Haskell.

--Browning's Italy. LC 72-3566. (Studies in Browning, No. 4). (Illus.). 1972. Repr. of 1907 ed. lib. bdg. 59.95x (ISBN 0-8383-1546-1). Haskell.

--Longfellow's Country. 1978. Repr. of 1909 ed. lib. bdg. 40.00 (ISBN 0-8495-0733-2). Arden Lib.

--Longfellow's Country. 1979. Repr. of 1909 ed. lib. bdg. 35.00 (ISBN 0-8492-4030-1). R West.

--The Poet's New England. 1911. Repr. 30.00 (ISBN 0-8274-3165-1). R West.

Clarke, Helen A., ed. see Browning, Elizabeth Barrett.

Clarke, Helen Archibald. Hawthorne's Country. LC 73-12227. 1910. lib. bdg. 42.50 (ISBN 0-8414-3390-9). Folcroft.

Clarke, Helen I. Social Legislation. 2nd ed. LC 57-6100. 1957. 28.00x (ISBN 0-8290-1656-2); pap. text ed. 6.95x (ISBN 0-8290-1657-0). Irvington.

Clarke, Henry B. The Cid Campeador & the Waning of the Crescent in the West. LC 73-14438. (Heroes of the Nation Ser.). (Illus.). Repr. of 1897 ed. 30.00 (ISBN 0-404-58256-7). AMS Pr.

--Modern Spain. LC 70-90098. (BCL Ser.: No. II). Repr. of 1906 ed. 32.50 (ISBN 0-404-01569-7). AMS Pr.

--Spanish Literature: A Handbook. 1980. lib. bdg. 64.50 (ISBN 0-8490-3194-X). Gordon Pr.

Clarke, Herbert L. Elementary Studies for the Trumpet. (Illus.). 53p. 1936. pap. 6.50 (ISBN 0-8258-0234-2, 0-2279). Fischer Inc NY.

--Technical Studies for the Cornet. 53p. 1934. pap. 6.50 (ISBN 0-8258-0158-3, 02280). Fischer Inc NY.

Clarke, Herman F. John Coney, Silversmith: 1655-1722. LC 71-87562. (Architecture & Decorative Art Ser.: Vol. 38). (Illus.). lx, 104p. 1971. Repr. of 1932 ed. lib. bdg. 32.50 (ISBN 0-306-71393-4). Da Capo.

Clarke, Herman F. & Foote, Henry W. Jeremiah Dummer: Colonial Craftsman & Merchant 1645-1718. LC 75-87563. (Architecture & Decorative Art Ser). (Illus.). 1970. Repr. of 1935 ed. 29.50 (ISBN 0-306-71394-2). Da Capo.

Clarke, Hockley. Bird Watching for Everyone. 128p. 1980. 29.00x (ISBN 0-905418-30-1, Pub. by Gresham England). State Mutual Bk.

Clarke, Howard. Homer's Readers: A Historical Introduction to the Iliad & the Odyssey. LC 78-66824. 328p. 1980. 26.50 (ISBN 0-87413-150-2). U Delaware Pr.

Clarke, Howard B., tr. see Duby, Georges.

Clarke, Hugh A. Pronouncing Dictionary of Musical Terms, Giving the Meaning Derivation & Pronunciation of Italian, German, French & Other Words. 1977. Repr. 15.00 (ISBN 0-403-07492-4). Scholarly.

Clarke, Hugh V. Last Stop Nagasaki! (Illus.). 152p. 1985. 18.50x (ISBN 0-86861-412-2). Allen Unwin.

Clarke, I. Shelley & Byron. LC 74-118006. (English Literature Ser., No. 33). 1970. Repr. of 1934 ed. lib. bdg. 49.95x (ISBN 0-8383-1062-1). Haskell.

Clarke, I. F., ed. Tale of the Future: From the Beginning to the Present Day. 3rd ed. 374p. 1978. pap. 15.00x (ISBN 0-8389-3225-8). ALA.

Clarke, I. F., jt. ed. see Butt, J.

Clarke, Ian M. The Spatial Organization of Multinational Corporations. 288p. 1985. 35.00x (ISBN 0-312-75028-5). St Martin.

Clarke, Ida C. American Women & the World War. LC 74-75233. (The United States in World War 1 Ser.). xix, 545p. 1974. Repr. of 1918 ed. lib. bdg. 25.95x (ISBN 0-89198-096-2). Ozer.

Clarke, Isabel C. Elizabeth Barrett Browning. 1973. Repr. of 1929 ed. 20.00 (ISBN 0-8274-1712-8). R West.

--Elizabeth Barrett Browning: A Portrait. LC 73-103075. 1970. Repr. of 1929 ed. 24.50x (ISBN 0-8046-0812-1, Pub. by Kennikat). Assoc Faculty Pr.

--Katherine Mansfield: A Biography. 1978. Repr. of 1944 ed. lib. bdg. 15.00 (ISBN 0-8495-0803-7). Arden Lib.

--Katherine Mansfield: A Biography. LC 74-7387. 1944. lib. bdg. 10.00 (ISBN 0-8414-3579-0). Folcroft.

--Maria Edgeworth: Her Family & Friends. 1978. Repr. of 1949 ed. lib. bdg. 25.00 (ISBN 0-8495-0905-X). Arden Lib.

--Maria Edgeworth: Her Family & Friends. LC 72-10250. 1973. lib. bdg. 15.00 (ISBN 0-8414-0691-X). Folcroft.

--Six Portraits. facs. ed. LC 67-26725. (Essay Index Reprint Ser). 1935. 20.00 (ISBN 0-8369-0309-9). Ayer Co Pubs.

Clarke, J. Advances in Radar Techniques. (Electromagnetic Waves Ser.: No. 20). 1985. 72.00 (ISBN 0-86341-021-9). Inst Electrical.

Clarke, J., et al, eds. Working Class Culture: Studies in History & Theories. 1980. 26.00x (ISBN 0-312-88978-X). St Martin.

Clarke, J. A., ed. see Mixing, Second European Conference.

Clarke, J. C. Agoraphobia: A Clinical & Personal Account. (Illus.). 202p. 1985. 23.50 (ISBN 0-08-029866-4, Pub. by P P A); pap. 13.00 (ISBN 0-08-029846-X). Pergamon.

Clarke, J. Christopher & Jackson, Arthur. Hypnosis & Behavior Therapy: The Treatment of Anxiety & Phobias. (Behavior Therapy Behavioral Medicine Ser.: Vol. 11). 384p. 1983. text ed. 26.95 (ISBN 0-8261-3450-5). Springer Pub.

Clarke, J. Harold. Getting Started with Rhododendrons & Azaleas. LC 82-16995. (Illus.). 268p. 1982. pap. 14.95 (ISBN 0-917304-30-6). Timber.

--Growing Berries & Grapes at Home. (Illus.). 14.50 (ISBN 0-8446-5474-4). Peter Smith.

Clarke, J. I. Population Geography. 2nd ed. LC 70-183339. 187p. 1972. pap. text ed. 8.50 (ISBN 0-08-016854-X). Pergamon.

--Population Geography & Developing Countries. 1972. 21.00 (ISBN 0-08-016445-5); pap. 10.50 (ISBN 0-08-016446-3). Pergamon.

Clarke, J. I. & Bowen-Jones, H. Change & Development in the Middle East: Essays in Honour of W. B. Fisher. 1981. 45.00x (ISBN 0-416-71080-8, NO.6504). Methuen Inc.

Clarke, J. I. & Fisher, W. B. Populations of the Middle East & North Africa: A Geographical Approach. LC 72-80410. 432p. 1972. text ed. 44.50x (ISBN 0-8419-0125-2). Holmes & Meier.

Clarke, J. I. & Pinchemel, P. Human Geography in France & Britain. 77p. 1976. 20.00x (ISBN 0-900296-39-9, Pub. by Social Sci Res). State Mutual Bk.

Clarke, J. I., ed. Geography & Population: Approaches & Applications. LC 83-22028. (Pergamon Oxford Geographics Ser.). (Illus.). 264p. 1984. 32.00 (ISBN 0-08-028781-6); pap. 11.50 (ISBN 0-08-028780-8). Pergamon.

Clarke, J. I., et al. An Advanced Geography of Africa. 530p. Date not set. 18.95 (ISBN 0-7175-0600-2). Dufour.

Clarke, J. R., ed. Oxford Reviews of Reproductive Biology, Vol. 6. (Illus.). 356p. 1984. text ed. 79.00x (ISBN 0-19-857539-4). Oxford U Pr.

Clarke, Jack. Gabriel Naude, Sixteen Hundred to Sixteen Fifty three. 183p. 1970. 17.50 (ISBN 0-208-00971-X, Archon). Shoe String.

Clarke, Jack A. Research Materials in the Social Sciences. 2nd ed. LC 67-25948. pap. 20.00 (ISBN 0-317-27035-4, 2023629). Bks Demand UMI.

Clarke, Jack A., ed. Research Materials in the Social Sciences. 2nd ed. 64p. 1967. pap. 5.95x (ISBN 0-299-01923-3). U of Wis Pr.

Clarke, Jack A., ed. see Conference on Book Publishing in Wisconsin, May 6, 1977, et al.

Clarke, Jack A., ed. see Conference on Periodical Publishing in Wisconsin, May 11-12, 1978, et al.

Clarke, Jack A. see Prakken, Sarah L.

Clarke, James, jt. auth. see Coulson, David.

Clarke, James F. Anti-Slavery Days: A Sketch of the Struggle Which Ended in the Abolition of Slavery in the United States. LC 72-1050. Repr. of 1883 ed. 9.00 (ISBN 0-404-00252-8). AMS Pr.

--Anti Slavery Days: A Sketch of the Struggle Which Ended in the Abolition of Slavery in the United States. LC 70-106869. Repr. of 1883 ed. 17.50x (ISBN 0-8371-3286-X, CSL&, Pub. by Negro U Pr). Greenwood.

--Bible Societies, American Missionaries & the National Revival of Bulgaria. LC 71-135841. (Eastern Europe Collection Ser). 1970. 20.00 (ISBN 0-405-02783-4). Ayer Co Pubs.

--James Freeman Clarke: Autobiography, Diary & Correspondence. Hale, Edward E., ed. LC 68-55876. Repr. of 1891 ed. cancelled (ISBN 0-8371-0351-7, CLC&, Pub. by Negro U Pr). Greenwood.

--Nineteenth Century Questions. facsimile ed. LC 71-37527. (Essay Index Reprint Ser). Repr. of 1897 ed. 21.50 (ISBN 0-8369-2539-4). Ayer Co Pubs.

Clarke, James M. The Life & Adventures of John Muir. new ed. LC 79-64178. (Illus.). 1979. 14.95 (ISBN 0-932238-01-7, Pub. by Avant Bks). Slawson Comm.

--The Life & Adventures of John Muir. LC 79-64178. (Sierra Club Paperback Library Ser.). (Illus.). 338p. 1980. pap. 7.95 (ISBN 0-87156-241-3). Sierra.

Clarke, James W. American Assassins: The Darker Side of Politics. LC 81-47912. (Illus.). 332p. 1984. 25.00 (ISBN 0-691-07637-5); pap. 8.95 (ISBN 0-691-02221-6). Princeton U Pr.

Clarke, Janet R., jt. auth. see Scott, Kenneth.

Clarke, Jean. Self-Esteem: A Family Affair. pap. 6.95 (ISBN 0-86683-615-2). NACAC.

Clarke, Jean I. Self-Esteem: A Family Affair. 280p. 1980. pap. 8.95 (ISBN 0-86683-615-2). Winston Pr.

--Self Esteem: A Family Affair Leader Guide. 280p. 1981. pap. 14.95 (ISBN 0-03-059064-7, AY8948). Winston Pr.

--Who, Me Lead A Group? 128p. (Orig.). 1983. pap. 3.95 (ISBN 0-86683-724-8, AY8284). Winston Pr.

Clarke, Jeanne N. & McCool, Daniel. Staking Out the Terrain: An Analysis of Agency Power among Our Natural Heritage Protectors. (Environmental Public Policy Ser.). 224p. 1985. lib. bdg. 34.50 (ISBN 0-88706-020-X); pap. text ed. 10.95 (ISBN 0-88706-021-8). State U NY Pr.

Clarke, Jennie T. Songs of the South. 1977. Repr. of 1896 ed. 20.00 (ISBN 0-89984-164-3). Century Bookbindery.

--Songs of the South. 1896. 25.00 (ISBN 0-686-17676-6). Quaker City.

Clarke, Jennifer. In Our Grandmothers' Footsteps: A Walking Tour of London. LC 85-47598. 176p. (Orig.). 1985. pap. 7.95 (ISBN 0-689-11623-3). Atheneum.

Clarke, Jenny, ed. see Internal & External Protection of Pipes, 2nd International Conference.

Clarke, John. Demonstration of Some of the Principal Sections of Sir Isaac Newton's Principles of Natural Philosophy. 1972. Repr. of 1730 ed. 28.00 (ISBN 0-384-09226-8). Johnson Repr.

--Introduction to the Fernandian Tongue. facsimile ed. LC 73-161257. (Black Heritage Library Collection). Repr. of 1848 ed. 11.50 (ISBN 0-8369-8531-1). Ayer Co Pubs.

--The Price of Progress: Cobbett's England, Seventeen Eighty to Eighteen Thirty-Five. 1979. 19.95 (ISBN 0-8464-0098-7). Beekman Pubs.

--The Price of Progress: Cobbett's England Seventeen Eighty to Eighteen Thirty-Five. 224p. 1980. text ed. 18.75x (ISBN 0-246-10604-2). Humanities.

--Resource Based Learning for Higher & Continuing Education. LC 81-6718. (New Pattern of Learning Ser.). 211p. 1982. 34.95x (ISBN 0-470-27248-1). Halsted Pr.

--The Virgin Seducer. Bd. with The Batchelor-Keeper; A Voyage to Cacklagallinia. Brunt, Samuel; An Account of the State of Learning in the Empire of Lilliput. (Foundations of the Novel Ser.: Vol. 49). 1972. lib. bdg. 61.00 (ISBN 0-8240-0561-9). Garland Pub.

Clarke, John & Critcher, Chas. The Devil Makes Work: Leisure in Capitalist Britain. LC 85-8457. 224p. 1985. 24.95x (ISBN 0-252-01259-3). U of Ill Pr.

Clarke, John & McLoughlin, William G. Colonial Baptists: Massachusetts & Rhode Island. original anthology ed. Gaustad, Edwin S., ed. LC 79-52586. (The Baptist Tradition Ser.). 1980. lib. bdg. 17.00x (ISBN 0-405-12453-8). Ayer Co Pubs.

Clarke, John & Wittes, Simon. Clarke Reading Self-Assessment Survey. (gr. 10-12). 1978. pap. 4.00x (ISBN 0-87879-207-4); pap. 25.00 pkg. of 10 (ISBN 0-87879-207-4). Acad Therapy.

Clarke, John, tr. Saint Therese of Lisieux General Correspondence: Vol. I, 1877-1890. LC 81-6474. 700p. (Orig.). 1982. pap. 9.95x (ISBN 0-9600876-9-9). ICS Pubns.

Clarke, John, tr. from Fr. St. Therese of Lisieux: Her Last Conversations. LC 76-27207. (Illus.). 1977. pap. 6.95x (ISBN 0-9600876-3-X). ICS Pubns.

--Story of a Soul: The Autobiography of St. Therese of Lisieux. LC 76-43620. 1976. pap. 6.95x (ISBN 0-9600876-4-8). ICS Pubns.

Clarke, John A., ed. Laie Bible: A Poem of the Fourteenth Century. LC 24-4800. (Columbia University. Studies in Romance Philology & Literature: No. 35). Repr. of 1923 ed. 16.00 (ISBN 0-404-50635-6). AMS Pr.

Clarke, John H. Clinical Repertory. 346p. 1979. text ed. 24.95x (ISBN 0-8464-1000-1). Beekman Pubs.

--Clinical Repertory. 1980. 25.00x (ISBN 0-85032-179-4, Pub. by Daniel Co England). State Mutual Bk.

--A Clinical Repertory to the Dictionary of Materia Medica. 1979. 15.95x (ISBN 0-85032-061-5, Pub. by C. W. Daniels). Formur Intl.

--A Dictionary of Practical Materia Medica. 1980. 125.00x (ISBN 0-85032-139-5, Pub. by Daniel Co England). State Mutual Bk.

--From Copernicus to William Blake. 1978. Repr. of 1928 ed. lib. bdg. 10.00 (ISBN 0-8495-0903-3). Arden Lib.

--From Copernicus to William Blake. LC 74-7391. 1928. lib. bdg. 10.00 (ISBN 0-8414-3583-9). Folcroft.

--God of Shelley & Blake. LC 73-12459. 1973. lib. bdg. 10.00 (ISBN 0-8414-3425-5). Folcroft.

--God of Shelley & Blake. (English Literature Ser., No. 33). 1970. Repr. of 1930 ed. lib. bdg. 22.95x (ISBN 0-8383-0342-0). Haskell.

--The Prescriber. 11th ed. 382p. 1972. 11.95x (ISBN 0-8464-1041-9). Beekman Pubs.

--The Prescriber. 1972. 8.95x (ISBN 0-85032-088-7, Pub. by C. W. Daniels). Formur Intl.

--The Prescriber. 1980. 20.00x (ISBN 0-85032-050-X, Pub. by Daniel Co England). State Mutual Bk.

--William Blake on the Lord's Prayer: 1757-1827. LC 70-95421. (Studies in Blake, No. 3). 1971. Repr. of 1927 ed. lib. bdg. 48.95x (ISBN 0-8383-0967-4). Haskell.

Clarke, John H., ed. American Negro Short Stories. 355p. 1966. pap. 10.95 (ISBN 0-8090-2530-2, Am Century); pap. 6.95 (ISBN 0-8090-0080-6). Hill & Wang.

--Marcus Garvey & the Vision of Africa. 1974. pap. 5.95 (ISBN 0-394-71888-7, Vin). Random.

Clarke, John I. & Kosinski, Leszek A. Redistribution of Population in Africa. xii, 212p. 1982. text ed. 58.00x (ISBN 0-435-95030-4); pap. text ed. 20.00x (ISBN 0-435-95031-2). Heinemann Ed.

Clarke, John I., et al, eds. Population & Development: Projects in Africa. 336p. Date not set. price not set. (ISBN 0-521-30527-6). Cambridge U Pr.

Clarke, John J. A History of Local Government of the United Kingdom. LC 77-23552. 1977. Repr. of 1955 ed. lib. bdg. 23.50x (ISBN 0-8371-9701-5, CLLG). Greenwood.

Clarke, John J. & Bailey, Henry J., III. Bank Deposits & Collections. 4th ed. 285p. 1972. pap. 11.00 (ISBN 0-317-30888-2, B378). Am Law Inst.

Clarke, John L., ed. Educational Development: A Select Bibliography. 180p. 1981. 33.50 (ISBN 0-89397-092-1). Nichols Pub.

Clarke, John M. James Hall of Albany: Geologist & Palaeontologist, 1811-1898. Albritton, Claude C., ed. LC 77-6511. (History of Geology Ser.). (Illus.). Repr. of 1923 ed. lib. bdg. 46.50x (ISBN 0-405-10435-9). Ayer Co Pubs.

--Organic Dependence & Disease: Their Origin & Significance. 1921. 39.50x (ISBN 0-686-51283-9). Elliots Bks.

Clarke, John R. Surgical Judgement Using Decision Sciences. LC 83-24594. (Surgical Science Ser.: Vol. III). 124p. 1984. 25.95 (ISBN 0-03-070666-1). Praeger.

Clarke, John S. Teach Yourself Chemistry. 1979. pap. text ed. 5.95 (ISBN 0-679-12055-6). McKay.

Clarke, K. W., jt. auth. see Hall, L. W.

Clarke, Katherine A., tr. see Giono, Jean.

Clarke, Kenneth & Clarke, Mary. The Harvest & the Reapers: Oral Traditions of Kentucky. LC 74-7872. (Kentucky Bicentennial Bookshelf Ser.). 112p. 1974. 6.95 (ISBN 0-8131-0201-4). U Pr of Ky.

Clarke, Kenneth & Kohn, Ira. Kentucky's Age of Wood. LC 76-4432. (Kentucky Bicentennial Bookshelf Ser.). (Illus.). 88p. 1976. 6.95 (ISBN 0-8131-0225-1). U Pr of Ky.

Clarke, Kenneth K. & Hess, Donald T. Communication Circuits: Analysis & Design. LC 78-125610. (Engineering Ser). 1971. text ed. 38.95 (ISBN 0-201-01040-2). Addison-Wesley.

Clarke, Kenneth L., jt. auth. see Bala, Nicholas C.

Clarke, Lewis G. Narratives of the Sufferings of Lewis & Milton Clarke, Sons of a Soldier of the Revolution. LC 73-82186. (Anti-Slavery Crusade in America Ser). 1969. Repr. of 1846 ed. 14.00 (ISBN 0-405-00624-1). Ayer Co Pubs.

Clarke, Liam. Domiciliary Services for the Elderly. 190p. 1984. 23.00 (ISBN 0-7099-0756-7, Pub. by Croom Helm Ltd). Longwood Pub Group.

Clarke, Louise. Can't Read, Can't Write, Can't Talk Too Good Either: How to Recognize & Overcome Dyslexia in Your Child. 1974. pap. 3.95 (ISBN 0-14-003767-5). Penguin.

Clarke, Loyal & Davidson, R. Manual for Process Engineering Calculations. 2nd ed. (Chemical Engineering Ser). 39.50 (ISBN 0-07-011249-5). McGraw.

Clarke, Lynda, jt. auth. see Anderson, Elizabeth M.

Clarke, M. Practical Nursing. 13th ed. (Illus.). 416p. 1983. pap. 7.95 (ISBN 0-7216-0932-5, Pub. by Bailliere-Tindall). Saunders.

Clarke, M., ed. Shipbuilding Contracts. 1982. 45.00 (ISBN 0-907432-25-5). Lloyds London Pr.

Clarke, M. J., et al. Copper, Molybdenum, & Vanadium in Biological Systems: Structure & Bonding, Vol. 53. (Illus.). 166p. 1983. 39.50 (ISBN 0-387-12042-4). Springer-Verlag.

Clarke, M. J., et al, eds. Inorganic Chemistry. (Structure & Bonding Ser.: Vol. 46). (Illus.). 190p. 1981. 44.00 (ISBN 0-387-10655-3). Springer-Verlag.

--Solar Energy Materials. (Structure & Bondigg Ser.: Vol. 49). (Illus.). 182p. 1982. 44.00 (ISBN 0-387-11084-4). Springer-Verlag.

--Structure vs. Special Properties. (Structure & Bonding Ser.: Vol. 52). (Illus.). 204p. 1982. 50.00 (ISBN 0-387-11781-4). Springer-Verlag.

--Topics in Inorganic & Physical Chemistry. (Structure & Bonding Ser.: Vol. 50). (Illus.). 178p. 1982. 46.00 (ISBN 0-387-11454-8). Springer-Verlag.

Clarke, M. L. Bangor Cathedral. 125p. 1969. text ed. 3.25x (ISBN 0-900768-23-1, Pub. by Univ of Wales Pr England). Humanities.

--The Noblest Roman: Marcus Brutus & His Reputation. LC 80-69178. (Aspects of Greek & Roman Life Ser.). 157p. 1981. 27.50x (ISBN 0-8014-1393-1). Cornell U Pr.

--Richard Porson: A Biographical Essay. 1978. Repr. of 1937 ed. lib. bdg. 20.00 (ISBN 0-8495-0828-2). Arden Lib.

Clarke, M. L., tr. see Von Bode, Wilhelm.

Clarke, M. P. Parliamentary Privilege in the American Colonies. LC 76-166322. (American Constitutional & Legal History Ser.). 304p. 1971. Repr. of 1943 ed. lib. bdg. 35.00 (ISBN 0-306-70237-1). Da Capo.

Clarke, M. R. Advances in Computer Chess II. 142p. 1980. 16.00x (ISBN 0-85224-377-4, Pub. by Edinburgh U Pr Scotland). Columbia U Pr.

Clarke, M. R., ed. see International Conference on Advances in Computer Chess, London, UK, April 1981.

Clarke, M. W. David G. Burnett, First President of Texas. LC 77-79108. (Illus.). limited ed. 85.00 (ISBN 0-685-13270-6). Jenkins.

Clarke, Magnus. The Nuclear Destruction of Britain. (Illus.). 290p. 1982. 25.00 (ISBN 0-7099-0458-4, Pub. by Croom Helm Ltd). Longwood Pub Group.

Clarke, Malcolm R., jt. ed. see Trueman, E. R.

Clarke, Marcus. His Natural Life. Murray-Smith, Stephen, ed. (English Library). 928p. 1985. pap. 6.95 (ISBN 0-14-043051-2). Penguin.

Clarke, Marilee M. Arizona Civil Remedies. LC 84-132863. 1982. write for info. Az St Bar.

Clarke, Martin, ed. Planning & Analytic Methods in Health Care Systems. (Pion London Papers in Regional Science Ser.: No. 13). 220p. 1984. pap. 15.00x (ISBN 0-85086-108-X, NO. 5073). Methuen Inc.

Clarke, Martin L. Roman Mind: Studies in the History of Thought from Cicero to Marcus Aurelius. 1968. pap. 6.95 (ISBN 0-393-00452-X, Norton Lib). Norton.

Clarke, Mary. The Sadler's Wells Ballet: A History & an Appreciation. LC 77-563. (Series in Dance Ser.). 1977. Repr. of 1955 ed. lib. bdg. 29.50 (ISBN 0-306-70863-9). Da Capo.

Clarke, Mary & Crisp, Clement. Ballet: An Illustrated History. LC 73-84141. (Illus.). 1973. pap. 8.95x (ISBN 0-87663-977-5). Universe.

--Understanding Ballet. (Illus.). 1976. (Dist. by Crown); pap. 1.00 (ISBN 0-517-52649-2). Crown.

Clarke, Mary, jt. auth. see Clarke, Kenneth.

Clarke, Mary, jt. auth. see Crisp, Clement.

Clarke, Mary, et al. How to Enjoy Ballet. Bragg, Melvyn, ed. (How to Enjoy Ser.). (Illus.). 206p. 1984. 15.00 (ISBN 0-86188-147-8, Pub. by Salem Hse Ltd). Merrimack Pub Cir.

Clarke, Mary C. Complete Concordance to Shakespeare. rev. ed. LC 72-1029. Repr. of 1881 ed. lib. bdg. 47.50 (ISBN 0-404-01574-3). AMS Pr.

--The Girlhood of Shakespeare's Heroines, 3 vols. LC 72-1011. Repr. of 1852 ed. Set. 125.00 (ISBN 0-404-01610-3). AMS Pr.

--My Long Life: An Autobiographic Sketch. LC 12-31352. 1969. Repr. of 1896 ed. 25.00x (ISBN 0-403-00105-6). Scholarly.

--World-Noted Women. (Women Ser.). 1858. 50.00 (ISBN 0-8482-7587-X). Norwood Edns.

Clarke, Mary W. Chief Bowles & the Texas Cherokees. LC 72-160490. (The Civilization of the American Indian Ser.). pap. 47.80 (ISBN 0-317-28340-5, 2016202). Bks Demand UMI.

--John Chisum: Jinglebob King of the Pecus. (Illus.). 160p. 1985. 11.95 (ISBN 0-89015-465-1). Eakin Pubns.

--Kentucky Quilts & Their Makers. LC 79-1502. (Illus.). 136p. 1982. Repr. of 1976 ed. 12.00 (ISBN 0-8131-0096-8). U Pr of Ky.

--The Slaughter Ranches & their Makers. (Illus.). 12.95 (ISBN 0-686-70086-4). Jenkins.

--Thomas J. Rusk: Soldier, Statesman, Jurist. LC 79-157043. (Illus.). 1971. 9.50 (ISBN 0-685-00320-5). Jenkins.

Clarke, Mary W., jt. ed. see Lemaster, J. R.

Clarke, Maude V. Fourteenth Century Studies. facs. ed. Sutherland, L. G. & McKisack, M., eds. LC 67-30181. (Essay Index Reprint Ser). 1937. 20.50 (ISBN 0-8369-0310-2). Ayer Co Pubs.

Clarke, Michael. The Tempting Prospect: Social History of English Watercolours. 160p. 1981. 40.00x (ISBN 0-7141-8016-5, Pub. by Brit Mus Pubns England). State Mutual Bk.

Clarke, Michael, jt. auth. see Smith, Steve.

Clarke, Michael, ed. Corruption: Causes, Consequences & Control. LC 83-9712. 250p. 1984. 25.00 (ISBN 0-312-17007-6). St Martin.

Clarke, Michael & Mowlam, Marjorie, eds. Debate on Disarmament. 192p. (Orig.). 1982. pap. 8.95x (ISBN 0-7100-9269-5). Routledge & Kegan.

Clarke, Michael & Penny, Nicholas, eds. The Arrogant Connoisseur: Richard Payne Knight 1751-1824. (Illus.). 208p. 1982. 45.00 (ISBN 0-7190-0871-9, Pub. by Manchester Univ Pr). Longwood Pub Group.

Clarke, Michael G., jt. ed. see Drucker, Henry M.

Clarke, Myra L., et al. Veterinary Toxicology. 2nd ed. 336p. 1981. 51.00 (ISBN 0-7216-0785-3, Pub. by Bailliere-Tindall). Saunders.

Clarke, Nancy. Party Dances. pap. 4.50x (ISBN 0-392-09799-0, SpS). Sportshelf.

--Party Dances. (Ballroom Dance Ser.). 1985. lib. bdg. 60.00 (ISBN 0-87700-827-2). Revisionist Pr.

Clarke, Nicholas, ed. see Brosnac, Donald.

Clarke, Nina H. History of the Nineteenth-Century Black Churches in Maryland & Washington, D. C. LC 82-90248. 319p. 1983. 12.95 (ISBN 0-533-05366-8). Vantage.

Clarke, Nita. Timothy & the Blanket Fairy. (gr. k-6). 1981. 6.95 (ISBN 0-933184-06-9); pap. 4.95 (ISBN 0-933184-16-6). Flame Intl.

Clarke, Nita & Evans, Phil. London for Beginners. (Beginners Ser.). (Illus.). 176p. (Orig.). 1985. pap. 5.95 (ISBN 0-86316-078-5). Writers & Readers.

Clarke, Norman E., Sr., ed. Warfare along the Mississippi. (Illus.). 153p. 1961. 7.50 (ISBN 0-317-18876-3, Pub. by Clarke Hist Collect Central MI Univ). Hardscrabble Bks.

Clarke, Oliver F., tr. see Berdyaev, Nicholas.

Clarke, Oz. Essential Wine Book. 1985. 19.95 (ISBN 0-670-80731-1). Viking.

Clarke, P. F. Lancashire & the New Liberalism. (Illus.). 1971. 57.50 (ISBN 0-521-08075-4). Cambridge U Pr.

Clarke, P. H., jt. auth. see Hoyle, Russel D.

Clarke, P. H., ed. & tr. see Smyslov, V. V.

Clarke, P. H., ed. see Suetin, A. S.

Clarke, Patricia, ed. Paul of Venice: Logica Magna, Pt. 1, Fascicule 7. (Classical & Medieval Logic Texts Ser.). 1982. 135.00x (ISBN 0-19-726003-9). Oxford U Pr.

Clarke, Patti. Creative Jewelry. LC 77-90127. 1978. 13.95 (ISBN 0-8008-1995-0). Taplinger.

Clarke, Penny. Growing up During the Industrial Revolution. LC 79-56472. (Growing up Ser.). (Illus.). 72p. (gr. 7 up). 1980. text ed. 14.95 (ISBN 0-7134-3370-1, Pub. by Batsford England). David & Charles.

Clarke, Peter. A Free Church in a Free Society: The Ecclesiology of John England Bishop of Charleston, 1820-1842. 561p. 1983. (Pub. by John England Stud Inc); pap. 15.95x (ISBN 0-87921-073-7). Attic Pr.

--The Gift of Gab. 144p. (Orig.). 1983. pap. 5.00 (ISBN 0-9612162-0-4). P Clarke.

--Liberals & Social Democrats. LC 78-6970. 1978. 44.50 (ISBN 0-521-22171-4); Dec. 1981. pap. 15.95 (ISBN 0-521-28651-4). Cambridge U Pr.

--West Africa & Islam. 280p. 1982. pap. text ed. 19.95 (ISBN 0-7131-8029-3). E Arnold.

Clarke, Peter & Evans, Susan H. Covering Campaigns: Journalism in Congressional Elections. LC 82-60738. 168p. 1983. 17.50x (ISBN 0-8047-1159-3). Stanford U Pr.

Clarke, Peter, ed. New Models for Communication Research. LC 72-98031. (Sage Annual Reviews of Communication Research Ser.: Vol. 2). 320p. 1973. 25.00 (ISBN 0-8039-0201-8); pap. 12.50 (ISBN 0-8039-0812-1). Sage.

Clarke, Peter, jt. ed. see Evans, Susan H.

Clarke, Peter, jt. ed. see Kline, F. Gerald.

Clarke, Peter B., jt. auth. see Wilkinson, C. W.

Clarke, Peyton N. Old King William Homes & Families: An Account of Some of the Old Homesteads & Families of King William County, Virginia, from Its Earliest Settlement. LC 64-21422. (Illus.). 211p. 1976. Repr. of 1897 ed. 15.00 (ISBN 0-8063-7956-1). Genealog Pub.

Clarke, Phillip. The Dark River. LC 84-48587. 256p. 1985. pap. 3.37i (ISBN 0-06-080759-8, P759, PL). Har-Row.

--Flight into Darkness. LC 84-48588. 224p. 1985. pap. 3.37 (ISBN 0-06-080760-1, P760, PL). Har-Row.

Clarke, Prescott & Gregory, J. S., eds. Western Reports on the Taiping: A Selection of Documents. LC 81-68942. 484p. 1982. text ed. 25.00x (ISBN 0-8248-0807-X); pap. text ed. 15.95x (ISBN 0-8248-0809-6). UH Pr.

Clarke, Prescott, jt. ed. see King, Frank H.

Clarke, R., jt. auth. see Bookstaber, R.

Clarke, R. & Bauchop, T., eds. Microbial Ecology of the Gut. 1978. 69.50 (ISBN 0-12-175550-9). Acad Pr.

Clarke, R. Floyd. The Science of Law & Lawmaking: Being an Introduction to Law, a General View of Its Forms & Substance, & a Discussion of the Question of Codification. xvi, 473p. 1982. Repr. of 1898 ed. lib. bdg. 37.50x (ISBN 0-8377-0437-5). Rothman.

Clarke, R. H. College Statistics. 1969. pap. 18.95x (ISBN 0-17-741010-8). Intl Ideas.

Clarke, R. H. & Brown, John. Diffraction Theory & Antennas. LC 80-40388. (Ser. in Electrical & Electronic Engineering). 292p. 1980. 101.95x (ISBN 0-470-27003-9). Halsted Pr.

Clarke, R. J. Transform Coding of Images. (Microelectronics & Signal Processing Ser.). Date not set. price not set (ISBN 0-12-175730-7). Acad Pr.

Clarke, R. M. AC Cobra, 1962-1969. (Brooklands Bks.). (Illus.). 100p. (Orig.). 1980. pap. 11.95 (ISBN 0-906589-78-9, Pub. by Brooklands Bks England). Motorbooks Intl.

--Alfa Romeo Spider 1966-1981. (Illus.). 100p. 1982. pap. 11.95 (ISBN 0-907073-56-5, Pub. by Brooklands Bks England). Motorbooks Intl.

--American Motors Muscle Cars 1966-1970. (Illus.). 100p. 1982. pap. 11.95 (ISBN 0-907073-58-1, Pub. by Brooklands Bks England). Motorbooks Intl.

--Austin Healey One Hundred & Three Thousand Collection, No. 1. (Brooklands Bks.). (Illus.). 70p. (Orig.). 1982. pap. 8.95 (ISBN 0-907073-51-4, Pub. by Brooklands Bks England). Motorbooks Intl.

--Austin-Healy 3000 1959-1967. (Brookland Bks.). (Illus.). 100p. 1979. pap. text ed. 11.95 (ISBN 0-906589-64-9, Pub. by Brooklands Bks England). Motorbooks Intl.

--BMW 1600 Collection. (Brooklands Bks: No. 1). (Illus.). 70p. (Orig.). 1981. pap. 8.95 (ISBN 0-907073-27-1, Pub. by Brooklands Bks England). Motorbooks Intl.

--BMW 2002 Collection. (Brooklands Bks: No. 1). (Illus.). 70p. (Orig.). 1981. pap. 8.95 (ISBN 0-907073-28-X, Pub. by Brooklands Bks England). Motorbooks Intl.

--Cadillac in the Sixties Collection, No. 1. (Brooklands Bks.). (Illus.). 70p. 1982. pap. 8.95 (ISBN 0-907073-53-0, Pub. by Brooklands Bks England). Motorbooks Intl.

--Camaro Muscle Cars, 1966-1972. (Illus.). 100p. 1982. pap. 11.95 (ISBN 0-907073-65-4, Pub. by Brooklands Bks England). Motorbooks Intl.

--Camaro, 1966-1970. (Brooklands Bks.). (Illus.). 100p. (Orig.). 1980. pap. 11.95 (ISBN 0-906589-82-7, Pub. by Brooklands Bks England). Motorbooks Intl.

--Chevrolet Muscle Cars, 1966-1971. (Illus.). 100p. 1982. pap. 11.95 (ISBN 0-907073-61-1, Pub. by Brooklands Bks England). Motorbooks Intl.

--De Tomaso Collection, No. 1. (Illus.). 70p. pap. 8.95 (ISBN 0-686-44135-4, Pub. by Brooklands Bks England). Motorbooks Intl.

--Ferrari Cars: 1962-1966. (Brooklands Bks.). (Illus.). 100p. 1979. pap. 11.95 (ISBN 0-906589-57-6, Pub. by Brooklands Bks England). Motorbooks Intl.

--Ferrari Cars, 1966 to 1969. (Brooklands Bks.). (Illus., Orig.). 1979. pap. 11.95 (ISBN 0-906589-59-2, Pub. by Enthusiast Pubns. England). Motorbooks Intl.

--Ferrari Cars, 1973-1977. (Brooklands Bks.). (Illus.). 100p. (Orig.). 1981. pap. 11.95 (ISBN 0-907073-03-4, Pub. by Booklands Bks England). Motorbooks Intl.

--Ferrari Cars: 1977-1981. (Brooklands Bks.). (Illus.). 100p. (Orig.). 1981. pap. 11.95 (ISBN 0-686-75135-3, Pub. by Brooklands Bks England). Motorbooks Intl.

--Ferrari: Collection No. 1. (Illus.). 70p. (Orig.). 1980. pap. 8.95 (ISBN 0-907073-10-7, Brooklands Bks). Motorbooks Intl.

--Ford GT40 1964-1978. (Brooklands Bks.). (Illus.). 70p. (Orig.). 1981. pap. 8.95 (ISBN 0-907073-14-X, Pub. by Brooklands Bks England). Motorbooks Intl.

--Ford Mustang: Nineteen Sixty-Four to Nineteen Sixty-Seven. (Brooklands Bks.). (Illus.). 100p. (Orig.). 1979. pap. 11.95 (ISBN 0-906589-70-3, Pub. by Brooklands Bks England). Motorbooks Intl.

--Ford Mustang Nineteen Sixty-Seven to Nineteen Seventy-Three. (Brooklands Bks.). (Illus.). 100p. (Orig.). 1981. pap. 2.95 (ISBN 0-907073-29-8, Pub. by Brooklands Bks England). Motorbooks Intl.

--Jaguar E-Type, 1961-1966. (Brookland Bks). (Illus.). 1978. pap. 11.95 (ISBN 0-906589-26-6, Pub. by Enthusiast Pubns. England). Motorbooks Intl.

--Jaguar E-Type, 1966-1971. (Brooklands Bks.). (Illus.). 100p. 1979. pap. 11.95 (ISBN 0-906589-58-4). Motorbooks Intl.

--Jaguar E Type, 1971-1975. (Brooklands Bks). (Illus.). 100p. (Orig.). 1979. pap. 11.95 (ISBN 0-906589-77-0, Pub. by Brooklands Bks England). Motorbooks Intl.

--Jaguar XJ6, 1968-1972. (Brooklands Bks.). (Illus., Orig.). 1981. pap. 11.95 (ISBN 0-907073-04-2, Pub. by Brooklands Bks England). Motorbooks Intl.

--Jaguar XJ6, 1973-1980. (Brooklands Bks.). (Illus.). 100p. (Orig.). 1981. pap. 11.95 (ISBN 0-907073-05-0, Pub. by Brooklands Bks England). Motorbooks Intl.

--Jaguar XKE: Collection No.1. (Illus.). 70p. (Orig.). 1980. pap. 8.95 (ISBN 0-907073-08-5, Brooklands Bks). Motorbooks Intl.

--Jeep Collection, No. 1. (Illus.). 70p. (Orig.). 1982. pap. 8.95 (ISBN 0-907073-54-9, Pub. by Brooklands Bks. England). Motorbooks Intl.

--Jensen-Healey 1972-1976. (Brooklands Bks). (Illus.). 100p. (Orig.). 1981. pap. 11.95 (ISBN 0-906589-89-4, Pub. by Brooklands Bks England). Motorbooks Intl.

--Jensen Interceptor 1966-1976. (Brooklands Bks.). (Illus.). 100p. (Orig.). 1981. pap. 11.95 (ISBN 0-686-30670-8, Pub. by Brooklands Bks England). Motorbooks Intl.

--Lamborghini Cars, 1964-1970. (Brooklands Bks.). (Illus., Orig.). 1979. pap. 11.95 (ISBN 0-906589-74-6, Pub. by Brooklands Bks England). Motorbooks Intl.

--Lamborghini Cars, 1970-1975. (Brooklands Bks.). (Illus.). 100p. (Orig.). 1980. pap. 11.95 (ISBN 0-906589-95-9, Pub. by Brooklands Bks England). Motorbooks Intl.

--Lamborghini Countach Collection, No. 1. (Illus.). 70p. 1982. pap. 8.95 (ISBN 0-907073-64-6, Pub. by Brooklands Bks England). Motorbooks Intl.

--Lotus Elan Collection, No. 2. (Brooklands Bks.). (Illus.). 70p. 1982. pap. 8.95 (ISBN 0-907073-68-9, Pub. by Brooklands Bks England). Motorbooks Intl.

--Lotus Elite & Eclat 1974-1981. (Illus.). 100p. (Orig.). 1982. pap. 11.95 (ISBN 0-907073-41-7, Pub. by Brooklands Bks England). Motorbooks Intl.

--Lotus Elite, 1957-1964. (Brooklands Bks.). (Illus.). 100p. 1982. pap. 11.95 (ISBN 0-907073-66-2, Pub. by Brooklands Bks England). Motorbooks Intl.

--Lotus Esprit Nineteen Seventy-Five to Nineteen Eighty-One. (Brooklands Bks.). (Illus.). 100p. 1982. pap. 11.95 (ISBN 0-907073-42-5, Pub. by Brooklands Bks England). Motorbooks Intl.

--Lotus Europa Collection, No. 1. (Brooklands Bks.). (Illus.). 70p. (Orig.). 1982. pap. 8.95 (ISBN 0-907073-49-2, Pub. by Brooklands Bks England). Motorbooks Intl.

--Lotus Seven Collection, No. 1. (Brooklands Bks.). (Illus.). 70p. 1982. pap. 8.95 (ISBN 0-907073-50-6, Pub. by Brooklands Bks England). Motorbooks Intl.

--Lotus Seven 1957-1980. (Brooklands Bks.). (Illus.). 100p. (Orig.). 1981. pap. 11.95 (ISBN 0-907073-13-1, Pub. by Brooklands Bks England). Motorbooks Intl.

--Maserati 1965-1970. (Brooklands Bks.). (Illus.). 100p. (Orig.). 1981. pap. 11.95 (ISBN 0-906589-98-3, Pub. by Brooklands Bks England). Motorbooks Intl.

--Maserati 1970-1975. (Brooklands Bks.). (Illus.). 100p. (Orig.). 1981. pap. 11.95 (ISBN 0-906589-99-1, Pub. by Brooklands Bks England). Motorbooks Intl.

--Mercedes-Benz Cars, Nineteen Forty-Nine to Nineteen Sixty-One. (Brooklands Bks.). (Illus.). 1979. pap. 11.95 (ISBN 0-906589-27-4, Pub. by Enthusiast Pubns. England). Motorbooks Intl.

--MG MGA 1955-1962. (Brooklands Bks.). (Illus.). 100p. (Orig.). 1981. pap. 11.95 (ISBN 0-906589-97-5, Pub. by Brooklands Bks England). Motorbooks Intl.

--MG MGB 1970-1980. (Brooklands Bks.). (Illus.). 100p. (Orig.). 1981. pap. 11.95 (ISBN 0-906589-90-8, Pub. by Brooklands Bks England). Motorbooks Intl.

--Morris Minor 1948-1970. (Brooklands Bks.). (Illus.). 100p. (Orig.). 1981. pap. 11.95 (ISBN 0-906589-83-5, Pub. by Brooklands Bks England). Motorbooks Intl.

--Muscle Cars Compared 1966-1970. (Brooklands Bks). (Illus.). 100p. 1982. pap. 11.95 (ISBN 0-907073-62-X, Pub. by Brooklands Bks England). Motorbooks Intl.

--Opel GT 1968-1973. (Illus.). 100p. 1982. pap. 11.95 (ISBN 0-907073-63-8, Pub. by Brooklands Bks England). Motorbooks Intl.

--Pantera, Nineteen Seventy to Nineteen Seventy-Three. (Brooklands Bks.). (Illus., Orig.). 1979. pap. 8.95 (ISBN 0-906589-75-4, Pub. by Brooklands Bks England). Motorbooks Intl.

--Pontiac Firebird, 1967 to 1973. (Brooklands Bks.). (Illus.). 100p. (Orig.). 1981. pap. 11.95 (ISBN 0-907073-30-1, Pub. by Brooklands Bks England). Motorbooks Intl.

--Pontiac GTO: 1964-1970. (Illus.). 100p. (Orig.). 1980. pap. 11.95 (ISBN 0-907073-02-6, Brooklands Bks). Motorbooks Intl.

--Porsche Cars 1960-1964. (Brooklands Bks.). (Illus.). 100p. (Orig.). pap. 11.95 (ISBN 0-906589-45-2, Pub. by Brooklands Bks England). Motorbooks Intl.

--Porsche Nine Twenty-Eight Collection, No. 1. (Illus.). 70p. (Orig.). 1981. pap. 8.95 (ISBN 0-907073-33-6, Pub. by Booklands Bks England). Motorbooks Intl.

--Porsche Turbo: Collection No. 1. (Illus.). 70p. (Orig.). 1980. pap. 8.95 (ISBN 0-907073-09-3, Brooklands Bks). Motorbooks Intl.

--Porsche 911 Collection, No. 2. (Brooklands Bks.). (Illus.). 70p. (Orig.). 1982. pap. 8.95 (ISBN 0-907073-44-1, Pub. by Brooklands Bks England). Motorbooks Intl.

--Porsche 911: Collection No. 1. (Illus.). 70p. (Orig.). 1980. pap. 8.95 (ISBN 0-907073-12-3, Pub. by Brooklands Bks England). Motorbooks Intl.

--Porsche 914: 1969-1975. (Brooklands Bks.). (Illus.). 100p. (Orig.). 1980. 11.95 (ISBN 0-906589-84-3). Motorbooks Intl.

--Porsche 924: 1975 to 1981. (Brooklands Bks.). (Illus.). 100p. (Orig.). 1982. pap. 11.95 (ISBN 0-907073-43-3, Pub. by Brooklands Bks England). Motorbooks Intl.

--Rolls-Royce Silver Shadow Nineteen Sixty-Five to Nineteen Eighty. (Brooklands Bks.). (Illus.). 100p. (Orig.). 1982. pap. 11.95 (ISBN 0-907073-45-X, Pub. by Brooklands Bks England). Motorbooks Intl.

--Sunbeam Alpine & Tiger, 1959-1967. (Brooklands Bks.). (Illus., Orig.). 1979. pap. 11.95 (ISBN 0-906589-57-6, Pub. by Brooklands Bks England). Motorbooks Intl.

--Triumph Spitfire 1962-1980. (Brooklands Bks.). (Illus.). 100p. (Orig.). 1981. pap. 11.95 (ISBN 0-907073-25-5, Pub. by Brooklands Bks England). Motorbooks Intl.

--Triumph Stag Nineteen Seventy to Nineteen Eighty. (Brooklands Bks.). (Illus.). 100p. (Orig.). 1981. pap. 11.95 (ISBN 0-907073-26-3, Pub. by Brooklands Bks England). Motorbooks Intl.

--TVR: Nineteen Sixty to Nineteen Eighty. (Illus.). 100p. 1981. 11.95 (ISBN 0-907073-20-4, Pub. by Brooklands Bks England). Motorbooks Intl.

--Volvo Eighteen Hundred: Nineteen Sixty to Nineteen Seventy-Three. (Illus.). 100p. 1981. 11.95 (ISBN 0-907073-15-8, Pub. by Brooklands Bks England). Motorbooks Intl.

--VW Beetle, Nineteen Fifty-Six to Nineteen Seventy-Seven. (Brooklands Bks.). (Illus.). 100p. (Orig.). 1981. pap. 11.95 (ISBN 0-907073-18-2, Pub. by Brooklands Bks England). Motorbooks, Intl.

--VW Karmann-Ghia Collection, No. 1. (Brooklands Bks.). (Illus.). 70p. 1981. pap. 8.95 (ISBN 0-907073-35-2). Motorbooks Intl.

Clarke, R. M., ed. Buick Muscle 1965-1970. 100p. 1984. pap. 11.95 (ISBN 0-946489-41-6, Pub. by Brookland Bks England). Motorbooks intl.

--Lotus Elan 1962-1973. (Brooklands Bks.). (Illus.). 100p. (Orig.). 1980. pap. 11.95 (ISBN 0-906589-60-6). Motorbooks Intl.

--Pantera & Mangusta, Nineteen Sixty-Nine to Nineteen Seventy-Four. (Illus.). 70p. (Orig.). 1980. pap. 8.95 (ISBN 0-907073-00-X). Motorbooks Intl.

Clarke, R. V. & Hough, J. M., eds. The Effectiveness of Policing. 184p. 1980. 22.00x (ISBN 0-566-00297-3, 03295-6, Pub by Gower Pub Co England). Lexington Bks.

Clarke, Ralph E. Be Safe, Girl. 1975. pap. 3.00x (ISBN 0-918384-01-X). Personal Security.

Clarke, Rebecca. Sonata for Viola (or Violincello) & Piano. (Women Composers Ser.: No.20). 65p. 1985. Repr. of 1921 ed. lib. bdg. 26.50 (ISBN 0-306-76251-X). Da Capo.

--Trio for Piano, Violin & Cello. LC 80-20960. (Women Composer Ser.: No. 5). (Illus.). 64p. 1980. Repr. of 1928 ed. 26.50 (ISBN 0-306-76053-3). Da Capo.

Clarke, Rena, tr. see Cortot, Alfred.

Clarke, Richard. Anglo-American Collaboration in War & Peace 1942-1949. Cairncross, Alec, ed. 1982. 29.95x (ISBN 0-19-828439-X). Oxford U Pr.

--The Copperdust Hills. 1983. 11.95 (ISBN 0-8027-4018-9). Walker & Co.

Clarke, Richard, tr. see Sengtsan.

Clarke, Richard F., ed. Cardinal Lavigerie & the African Slave Trade. LC 74-77199. Repr. of 1889 ed. 25.00x (ISBN 0-8371-1283-4, CCL&, Pub. by Negro U Pr). Greenwood.

Clarke, Richard H., ed. Triplet State ODMR Spectroscopy: Techniques & Applications to Biophysical Systems. LC 81-10486. 566p. 1982. 67.95x (ISBN 0-471-07988-X, Pub. by Wiley-Interscience). Wiley.

Clarke, Richard S. You Only Have One Life--Give It Your Best Shot: Five Steps to Health, Wealth, Happiness. 1979. 8.99 (ISBN 0-682-49280-9, Banner). Exposition Pr FL.

Clarke, Robert C. Marijuana Botany: An Advanced Study; the Propagation & Breeding of Distinctive Cannabis. LC 81-2478. (Illus.). 200p. 1981. pap. 10.95 (ISBN 0-915904-45-4). And-Or Pr.

Clarke, Robert L., ed. Afro-American History: Sources for Research. LC 80-19197. (National Archives Conference Ser.: Vol. 13). 1981. 17.50 (ISBN 0-88258-018-3). Howard U Pr.

Clarke, Robin. Building for Self-Sufficiency. LC 76-5093. (Illus.). 302p. 1977. pap. 5.95 (ISBN 0-87663-945-7). Universe.

--Science & Technology in World Development. 208p. 1985. 19.95x (ISBN 0-19-219195-0); pap. 7.95x (ISBN 0-19-289176-6). Oxford U Pr.

Clarke, Robin & Palmer, Judi. The Human Environment: Action or Disaster? An Account of the Public Hearing Held in London, June 1982. Lamb, Robert, ed. (Illus.). vi, 74p. 1983. pap. text ed. 7.50 (ISBN 0-907567-65-7, TYP150, TYP). Unipub.

Clarke, Robin, ed. More than Enough: An Optimistic Assessment of World Energy. (Sextant Ser.: No. 1). 182p. 1982. pap. 18.00 (ISBN 92-3-101986-4, U1206, UNESCO). Unipub.

--Notes for the Future: An Alternative History of the Past Decade. LC 75-37295. 232p. 1976. 10.00x (ISBN 0-87663-255-X); pap. 4.50x (ISBN 0-87663-929-5). Universe.

Clarke, Roger, jt. auth. see Hart, P. E.

Clarke, Roger A., tr. see Leptin, Gert & Melzer, Manfred.

Clarke, Ronald. Brough Superior: The Rolls Royce of Motorcycles. 3rd ed. (Illus.). 192p. 12.95 (ISBN 0-85429-454-6, F454). Haynes Pubns.

Clarke, Ronald & Hope, Tim. Coping with Burglary: Research Perspectives on Policy. LC 84-3970. (International Series in Social Welfare). Date not set. price not set (ISBN 0-89838-151-7). Kluwer-Nijhoff.

Clarke, Ronald V. & Cornish, Derek B., eds. Crime Control in Britain: A Review of Policy Research. (Critical Issues in Criminal Justice Ser.). 269p. 1983. 39.50x (ISBN 0-87395-737-7). State U NY Pr.

Clarke, Rosy. Japanese Antique Furniture: A Guide to Evaluating & Restoring. LC 82-21916. (Illus.). 168p. (Orig.). 1983. pap. 14.95 (ISBN 0-8348-0178-7). Weatherhill.

Clarke, Samuel. The Works, 4 vols. LC 75-11207. (British Philosophers & Theologians of the 17th & 18th Century Ser.: Vol. 12). 3274p. 1976. Repr. of 1742 ed. Set. lib. bdg. 204.00 (ISBN 0-8240-1762-5). Garland Pub.

Clarke, Samuel R. Among the Tribes in South-West China. LC 77-87073. Repr. of 1911 ed. 25.00 (ISBN 0-404-16804-3). AMS Pr.

Clarke, Sebastian. Jah Music: The Evolution of the Popular Jamaican Music. (Illus.). 216p. (Orig.). 1980. pap. text ed. 12.50x (ISBN 0-435-82140-7). Heinemann Ed.

--Sun Song. (Heritage Ser). 1973. pap. 2.50x (ISBN 0-685-42540-1). Broadside.

Clarke, Sidney W. The Annals of Conjuring. LC 85-90373. (Illus.). 377p. 1985. text ed. 45.00 (ISBN 0-916638-34-0). Meyerbooks.

Clarke, Simon. Foundations of Structuralism: A Critique of Levi-Strauss & the Structuralist Movement. 272p. 1981. 29.50x (ISBN 0-389-20115-4). B&N Imports.

--Marx, Marginalism & Modern Sociology. (Contemporary Social Theory Ser.). 272p. 1982. text ed. 28.00x (ISBN 0-333-29252-9, Pub. by Macmillan England); pap. text ed. 12.45x (ISBN 0-333-29253-7). Humanities.

Clarke, Simon, et al. One Dimensional Marxism: Althusser & the Politics of Culture. LC 80-40595. 256p. 1980. text ed. 17.00x (ISBN 0-8052-8066-9, Pub. by Allison & Busby England); pap. 7.95 (ISBN 0-8052-8065-0, Pub. by Allison & Busby England). Schocken.

Clarke, Stephan. The Lord Peter Wimsey Companion. 1985. 49.95 (ISBN 0-89296-125-2). Mysterious Pr.

Clarke, Stephen. The Lord Peter Wimsey Companion. (Illus.). 49.95 (ISBN 0-89296-125-2). FS&G.

Clarke, Stephen F., jt. auth. see Schroff, Kersi B.

Clarke, Stephen V. The Reconstruction of the International Monetary System: The Attempts of 1922 & 1933. LC 73-9360. (Princeton Studies in International Finance Ser.: No. 33). pap. 20.00 (ISBN 0-317-28836-9, 2017823). Bks Demand UMI.

Clarke, Steve. The Who: In Their Own Words. (Illus.). 128p. 1982. pap. 6.95 (ISBN 0-399-41006-6). Delilah Bks.

Clarke, Steve, compiled by. The Who in Their Own Words. (Illus.). 1982. pap. 6.95 (ISBN 0-399-41006-6, Perigee). Putnam Pub Group.

Clarke, Stevens H. Law of Probation & Parole in North Carolina. 131p. 1979. 6.50 (ISBN 0-686-39460-7). U of NC Inst Gov.

--Service of North Carolina Prison & Jail Sentences: Parole Eligibility, Good Time, & Gain Time. LC 84-621823. Date not set. price not set. U of NC Inst Gov.

Clarke, Stevens H., et al. North Carolina Crimes: A Guidebook for Law Enforcement Officers. 360p. 1980. 6.50 (ISBN 0-686-39462-3). U of NC Inst Gov.

--The Effectiveness of Bail Systems: An Analysis of Failure to Appear in Court & Rearrest while on Bail. (Illus.). 37p. 1976. pap. 3.00 (ISBN 0-318-00251-5). U of NC Inst Gov.

--Felony Prosecution & Sentencing in North Carolina. 118p. 1982. 5.00 (ISBN 0-686-39420-8). U of NC Inst Gov.

Clarke, Stewart W. & Pavia, Demetri, eds. Aerosols & the Lung: Clinical & Experimental Aspects. (Illus.). 288p. 1984. text ed. 79.95 (ISBN 0-407-00265-0). Butterworth.

Clarke, Susan E. & Obler, Jeffrey L., eds. Urban Ethnic Conflict: A Comparative Perspective. LC 77-686. (Comparative Urban Studies Monograph: No.3). 257p. 1976. pap. text ed. 5.50 (ISBN 0-89143-046-6). U NC Inst Res Soc Sci.

Clarke, T. E. Murder at Buckingham Palace. (Fingerprint Mystery Ser.). 192p. 1983. pap. 5.95 (ISBN 0-312-55282-3). St Martin.

Clarke, T. S. & Corlett, E. N. The Ergonomics of Workspaces & Machines: A Design Manual. LC 84-242. (Illus.). 100p. 1984. pap. 31.00x (ISBN 0-85066-246-X). Taylor & Francis.

Clarke, Terence. The Englewood Readings. (The American Dust Ser.: No.5). 64p. 1976. 6.95 (ISBN 0-913218-30-8); pap. 2.50 (ISBN 0-913218-29-4). Dustbooks.

Clarke, Theodore H., ed. Yearbook of Podiatric Medicine & Surgery 1981. (Illus.). 512p. 1981. 49.00 (ISBN 0-87993-129-9). Futura Pub.

--Yearbook of Podiatry: 1978-79. (Illus.). 320p. 1979. 31.50 (ISBN 0-87993-099-3). Futura Pub.

Clarke, Thomas, et al. The American Railway: Its Constructon, Development, Management, & Appliances. LC 74-189048. (Illus.). Repr. of 1889 ed. 25.00 (ISBN 0-405-08364-5, Blom Pubns). Ayer Co Pubs.

Clarke, Thomas A., et al. Biology of Plankton. 206p. 1972. text ed. 29.00x (ISBN 0-8422-7016-7). Irvington.

Clarke, Thomas E., ed. Above Every Name: The Lordship of Christ & Social Systems. LC 80-82082. (Woodstock Studies). 312p. (Orig.). 1980. pap. 7.95 (ISBN 0-8091-2338-X). Paulist Pr.

Clarke, Thomas J. People & Their Religions, Part One. (Literacy Volunteers of America Readers Ser.). 48p. (Orig.). 1983. pap. 2.46 (ISBN 0-8428-9609-0). Cambridge Bk.

--People & Their Religions, Part Two. (Literacy Volunteers of America Readers Ser.). 48p. (Orig.). 1983. pap. 2.46 (ISBN 0-8428-9610-4). Cambridge Bk.

Clarke, Thursten. Evaluating Written Copy-Techniques for High-Tech Managers. 82p. Date not set. 19.95 (ISBN 0-935506-29-2). Carnegie Pr.

Clarke, Thurston. Thirteen O'Clock: A Novel about George Orwell & 1984. LC 83-25306. 277p. 1984. 14.95 (ISBN 0-385-19211-8). Doubleday.

Clarke, Thurston, jt. auth. see Werbell, Frederick E.

Clarke, Thurston, jt. auth. see Werbell, Frederick kE.

Clarke, Tisha, jt. auth. see Barnes, Bonnie M.

Clarke, Tom. My Northcliffe Diary. 1977. Repr. of 1931 ed. lib. bdg. 12.00 (ISBN 0-686-19820-4). Havertown Bks.

--My Northcliffe Diary. 1978. Repr. of 1931 ed. lib. bdg. 15.00 (ISBN 0-8495-0731-6). Arden Lib.

Clarke, Tom & Clements, Laurie, eds. Trade Unions under Capitalism. 1978. text ed. 25.25x (ISBN 0-391-00728-9). Humanities.

Clarke, W. Walt Whitman. LC 77-130249. (Studies in Whitman, No. 28). 1970. Repr. of 1906 ed. lib. bdg. 29.95x (ISBN 0-8383-1139-3). Haskell.

Clarke, W. E. Reminiscences of Robert Louis Stevenson. 1978. Repr. of 1908 ed. lib. bdg. 8.50 (ISBN 0-8495-0910-6). Arden Lib.

--Reminiscences of Robert Louis Stevenson. LC 73-561. 1973. lib. bdg. 9.50 (ISBN 0-8414-1552-8). Folcroft.

Clarke, W. G., ed. see Prehistoric Society of East Anglia.

Clarke, W. J., et al, eds. Biochemistry. (Structure & Bonding Ser.: Vol. 48). (Illus.). 140p. 1982. 31.00 (ISBN 0-387-10986-2). Springer-Verlag.

--Myeloproliferative Disorders of Animals & Man: Proceedings. LC 70-605836. (AEC Symposium Ser.). 765p. 1970. pap. 27.25 (ISBN 0-87079-280-6, CONF-680529); microfiche 4.50 (ISBN 0-87079-281-4, CONF-680259). DOE.

Clarke, W. K., tr. & intro. by see Basilius.

Clarke, W. M. How the City Works: An Introduction. (How the City Works Ser.). (Illus.). 96p. 1985. pap. 8.50 (ISBN 0-08-039235-0). Pergamon.

--Private Enterprise in Developing Countries. 1969. pap. 4.60 (ISBN 0-08-012142-X). Pergamon.

Clarke, W. M., ed. How the City Works: The Professions. (How the City Works Ser.). 1983. 13.50 (ISBN 0-08-039149-4). Pergamon.

Clarke, Wilbert. The Moral Degeneration of the American Female. (Illus.). 1978. deluxe ed. 43.45 (ISBN 0-930582-09-8). Gloucester Art.

Clarke, William. Clarke Papers, 4 Vols. Firth, C. H., ed. 105.00 (ISBN 0-384-09232-2); 27.00 ea. Johnson Repr.

--Walt Whitman. 1906. Repr. 8.75 (ISBN 0-8274-3907-5). R West.

Clarke, William C. Place & People: An Ecology of a New Guinean Community. LC 78-126764. (Illus.). 1971. 42.50x (ISBN 0-520-01791-9). U of Cal Pr.

Clarke, William H. An Outline of the Structure of the Pipe Organ. (Illus.). 1977. pap. text ed. 10.00x (ISBN 0-913746-09-6). Organ Lit.

Clarke, William M. Inside the City. rev. ed. 304p. 1983. pap. text ed. 12.95x (ISBN 0-04-332091-0). Allen Unwin.

Clarke, William N. Immortality. 1920. 29.50x (ISBN 0-686-83578-6). Elliots Bks.

Clarke, Winifred. George Bernard Shaw. LC 74-7377. 1949. lib. bdg. 10.00 (ISBN 0-8414-3587-1). Folcroft.

--George Bernard Shaw: An Appreciation & Interpretation. 1978. Repr. of 1948 ed. lib. bdg. 10.00 (ISBN 0-8495-0829-0). Arden Lib.

Clarke-Stewart, Alison. Daycare. (The Developing Child Ser.). (Illus.). 160p. 1982. text ed. 9.95x (ISBN 0-674-19403-9); pap. 4.95 (ISBN 0-674-19404-7). Harvard U Pr.

Clarke-Stewart, Alison & Koch, Joanne B. Children: Development Through Adolescence. LC 82-21763. 536p. 1983. text ed. 29.95 (ISBN 0-471-03069-4); tchrs. manual avail. (ISBN 0-471-87302-0); sol avail. (ISBN 0-471-87197-4); pap. 9.95 study guide (ISBN 0-471-87303-9). Wiley.

Clarke-Stewart, Alison, jt. auth. see Fein, Greta G.

Clarke-Stewart, Alison, et al. Child Development: A Topical Approach. 821p. 1985. 26.95 (ISBN 0-471-81347-8); student study guide avail. (ISBN 0-471-81662-0). Wiley.

Clarke-Stewart, K. Alison, jt. ed. see Glick, Joseph.

Clarkin, William. Mathew Carey: A Bibliography of His Publications 1785-1824. LC 82-48280. (Humanities Ser.). 316p. 1984. lib. bdg. 60.00 (ISBN 0-8240-9248-1). Garland Pub.

Clarking, J. J. The Art of Betting Horses & Winning Consistently. 32p. 1985. pap. 5.95 (ISBN 0-934650-08-X). Sunnyside.

Clark-Kennedy, A. E. Man, Medicine, & Morality. 214p. 1969. 17.50 (ISBN 0-208-00972-8, Archon). Shoe String.

Clark-Langager, Sarah. Order & Engima American Art Between the Two Wars. (Illus.). 95p. pap. 15.00 (ISBN 0-915895-02-1). Munson Williams.

--Sculpture Space Recent Trends. (Illus.). 48p. pap. 5.00 (ISBN 0-915895-01-3). Munson Williams.

Clark-Monks, C. & Parker, J. M. Stones & Cord in Glass. 208p. 95.00x (ISBN 0-686-79278-5, Pub. by Soc Glass Tech England). State Mutual Bk.

Clarkson, Albert. Toward Effective Strategic Analysis: New Applications of Information Technology. LC 81-69202. (Special Studies in National Security & Defense Policy). 179p. 1981. lib. bdg. 25.00x (ISBN 0-86531-243-5). Westview.

Clarkson, Atelia & Cross, Gilbert B. World Folktales: A Scribner Resource Collection. LC 79-20921. 480p. 1984. 27.50 (ISBN 0-684-16290-3, ScribT); pap. 14.95 (ISBN 0-684-17763-3). Scribner.

Clarkson, Charles E. A Rose of Old Virginia: A Romance of the Old South & the War Between the States. 59p. 1927. 6.00 (ISBN 0-937130-11-7). Burke's Bk Store.

Clarkson, Charles T. & Richardson, J. Hall. Police! LC 83-49237. (Crime & Punishment in England, 1850-1922 Ser.). 380p. 1984. lib. bdg. 45.00 (ISBN 0-8240-6216-7). Garland Pub.

Clarkson College of Technology. Polymeric Ligands Selective for Copper (II) 324p. 1978. free (233). Intl Copper.

--Stable Colloidal Dispersions of Copper. 73p. 1972. 10.95 (ISBN 0-317-34547-8, 174). Intl Copper.

Clarkson, D. Ion Transport & Cell Structure in Plants. LC 74-7132. 350p. 1974. text ed. 42.95x (ISBN 0-470-15985-5). Halsted Pr.

Clarkson, D., jt. ed. see Torrey, John G.

Clarkson, E. Margaret. Susie's Babies. (Illus.). (gr. 3-6). 1960. pap. 3.95 (ISBN 0-8028-4005-1). Eerdmans.

Clarkson, E. N. Invertebrate Palaeontology & Evolution. (Illus.). 1979. text ed. 40.00x (ISBN 0-04-560007-4); pap. text ed. 19.95x (ISBN 0-04-560008-2). Allen Unwin.

Clarkson, Ellen. Six Acts on a Flying Trapeze. (Illus.). 160p. 1986. pap. text ed. 9.95 (ISBN 0-13-811308-4). P H.

Clarkson, Ewan. The Wake of the Storm. LC 83-21177. (Illus.). 224p. 1983. 12.95 (ISBN 0-312-85452-8). St Martin.

Clarkson, G. P. & Elliott, B. J. Managing Money & Finance. 3rd ed. Johnson, Alan, ed. 278p. 1983. text ed. 28.00x (ISBN 0-566-02402-0). Gower Pub Co.

Clarkson, Grosvenor B. Industrial America in the World War: The Strategy Behind the Line, 1917-1918. LC 74-75234. (The United States in World War 1 Ser). (Illus.). xxiii, 573p. 1974. Repr. of 1923 ed. lib. bdg. 28.95x (ISBN 0-89198-097-0). Ozer.

Clarkson, Henry. The Yachtsman's A-Z. (Illus.). 160p. 1983. 10.50 (ISBN 0-7153-7561-X). David & Charles.

Clarkson, Iain, jt. auth. see Ureland, P. Sture.

Clarkson, J. Dunsmore. Labour & Nationalism in Ireland. LC 78-12024. (Columbia University Studies in the Social Sciences: No. 266). Repr. of 1925 ed. 31.50 (ISBN 0-404-51266-6). AMS Pr.

Clarkson, James. The Elastic Analysis of Flat Grillages: With Particular Reference to Ship Structures. LC 65-16200. (Cambridge Engineering Ser.). pap. 35.80 (ISBN 0-317-08721-5, 2050786). Bks Demand UMI.

Clarkson, James D. The Cultural Ecology of a Chinese Village: Cameron Highlands, Malaysia. LC 67-28490. (Research Papers Ser.: No. 114). 174p. 1968. pap. 10.00 (ISBN 0-89065-022-5). U Chicago Dept Geog.

Clarkson, Jessie D., ed. see American Historical Assn.

Clarkson, John F., et al, eds. see St. Mary's College, Kansas, Jesuit Fathers.

Clarkson, Kenneth, et al, eds. Federal Trade Commission since 1970: Economic Regulation & Bureaucratic Behavior. (Illus.). 448p. 1981. 47.50 (ISBN 0-521-23378-X). Cambridge U Pr.

Clarkson, Kenneth W. Catalog of Research Issues for Understanding National Economic Plannimg. LC 76-1551. 1976. pap. 15.00 (ISBN 0-916770-01-X). Law & Econ U Miami.

--Food Stamps & Nutrition. LC 75-4377. 1975. pap. 4.25 (ISBN 0-8447-3155-2). Am Enterprise.

--Intangible Capital & Rates of Return. 1977. pap. 4.25 (ISBN 0-8447-3235-4). Am Enterprise.

Clarkson, Kenneth W. & Martin, Donald L. Economics of Nonproprietary Organizations, No. 1. Zerbe, Richard O., Jr., ed. (Research in Law & Economics Supplement Ser.: N. 1). 288p. 34.50 (ISBN 0-89232-132-6). Jai Pr.

Clarkson, Kenneth W. & Meiners, Roger E. Inflated Unemployment Statistics: The Effects of Welfare Work Registration Requirements. LC 77-74738. 1977. pap. 2.50 (ISBN 0-916770-04-4). Law & Econ U Miami.

Clarkson, Kenneth W. & Miller, Roger L. Industrial Organization. (Illus.). 576p. 1981. 31.95 (ISBN 0-07-042036-X). McGraw.

Clarkson, Kenneth W., et al. West's Business Law: Alternate UCC Comprehensive Edition. 880p. 1981. text ed. 26.95 (ISBN 0-8299-0366-6). West Pub.

--Alternate Test Items to Accompany West's Business Law: Alternate UCC Comprehensive Edition. 1980. write for info. (ISBN 0-8299-0526-X). West Pub.

Clarkson, Kenneth W., jt. auth. see Hoel, Arline A.

Clarkson, L. A., jt. ed. see Goldstrom, J. M.

Clarkson, Margaret. Destined for Glory: The Meaning of Suffering. 144p. 1983. pap. 4.95 (ISBN 0-8028-1953-2). Eerdmans.

--Grace Grows Best in Winter. 208p. 1985. Repr. 10.95 (ISBN 0-8028-3616-X). Eerdmans.

--So You're Single. LC 78-53012. 167p. 1978. pap. 5.95 (ISBN 0-87788-772-1). Shaw Pubs.

--So You're Single. rev. ed. 167p. 1984. pap. 5.95 (ISBN 0-87788-772-1). Shaw Pubs.

Clarkson, Mary C., compiled by. Mainstreaming the Exceptional Child: A Bibliography. LC 81-84656. (Checklists in the Humanities & Education Ser.). 225p. 1982. 25.00 (ISBN 0-911536-92-2); pap. 15.00 (ISBN 0-939980-02-9). Trinity U Pr.

Clarkson, Paul S. & Warren, Clyde T. Law of Property in Shakespeare & the Elizabethan Drama. LC 68-9790. 1968. Repr. of 1942 ed. 12.50x (ISBN 0-87752-022-4). Gordian.

Clarkson, Quentin D. Handbook of Field Botany. LC 61-13273. (Illus.). 1961. pap. 2.00 (ISBN 0-8323-0350-X). Binford.

Clarkson, Richard J., jt. auth. see Adams, Gilbert T., Jr.

Clarkson, Rosetta E. The Golden Age of Herbs & Herbalists. (Illus.). 352p. 1972. pap. 5.95 (ISBN 0-486-22869-X). Dover.

--The Golden Age of Herbs & Herbalists. Orig. Title: Green Enchantment. (Illus.). 11.25 (ISBN 0-8446-4623-7). Peter Smith.

Clarkson, Roy B. Tumult on the Mountains: Lumbering in West Virginia,1770-1920. 1964. 18.00 (ISBN 0-87012-004-2). McClain.

Clarkson, Roy B., et al. Forest Wildlife Plants of the Monangahela National Forest. 1980. pap. 7.95x (ISBN 0-910286-82-5). Boxwood.

Clarkson, Thomas. Essay on the Impolicy of the African Slave Trade, 2 Pts. facs. ed. LC 71-154074. (Black Heritage Library Collection Ser.). 1788. 15.25 (ISBN 0-8369-8785-3). Ayer Co Pubs.

--Essay on the Slavery & Commerce of the Human Species. facs. ed. LC 73-93417. (Black Heritage Library Collection Ser). 1786. 15.50 (ISBN 0-8369-8542-7). Ayer Co Pubs.

--Essay on the Slavery & Commerce of the Human Species, Particularly the African. LC 72-8360. Repr. of 1788 ed. 12.50 (ISBN 0-404-00253-6). AMS Pr.

--History of the Rise, Progress & Accomplishment of the Abolition of the African Slave-Trade by the British Parliament, 2 vols. 1968. Repr. of 1808 ed. 95.00x set (ISBN 0-7146-1889-6, F Cass Co). Biblio Dist.

Clarkson, Thomas, ed. see Wilberforce, W. & Wilberforce, S.

Clarkson, Thomas B., jt. ed. see Wagner, William D.

Clarkson, Thomas W., jt. auth. see Miller, Morton W.

Clarkson, Tom W., et al, eds. Reproductive & Developmental Toxicity of Metals. 850p. 1983. 115.00x (ISBN 0-306-41396-5, Plenum Pr). Plenum Pub.

Claro. Catcher in the Rye (Salinger) (Book Notes Ser.). 1984. pap. 2.50 (ISBN 0-8120-3407-4). Barron.

--Huckleberry Finn (Twain) (Book Notes). 1984. pap. 2.50 (ISBN 0-8120-3420-1). Barron.

Claro, F., ed. Nonlinear Phenomena in Physics. (Springer Proceedings in Physics: Vol. 3). (Illus.). ix, 441p. 1985. 35.00 (ISBN 0-387-15273-3). Springer-Verlag.

Claro, Joe. Condorman. (Illus.). 131p. (Orig.). (gr. 7-12). 1981. pap. 1.95 (ISBN 0-590-32022-X). Scholastic Inc.

--Herbie Goes Bananas. (Illus.). 96p. (gr. 3-7). 1980. pap. 1.95 (ISBN 0-590-31609-5). Scholastic Inc.

--Snowball Express. (gr. 3-5). 1980. pap. 1.50 (ISBN 0-590-30359-7). Scholastic Inc.

Clarricoats, P. J. Progress in Optical Communication, Vol. 2. (IEE Reprint Ser.: No. 4). 344p. 1982. pap. 60.00 (ISBN 0-906048-84-2, RE004, Pub. by Peregrinus England). Inst Elect Eng.

Clarricoats, P. J., ed. Optical-Fibre Waveguides. (IEE Reprint Ser.: No. 1). 335p. 1975. pap. 32.00 (ISBN 0-901223-76-X, RE001, Pub. by Peregrinus England). Inst Elect Eng.

--Progress in Optical Communication, 1978-79. 1980. pap. 50.00 (ISBN 0-906048-32-X). Inst Elect Eng.

Clarricoats, P. J. B., ed. Optical-Fibre Waveguides. 335p. 1975. Repr. 32.00 (ISBN 0-901223-76-X, RE001). Inst Elect Eng.

Clarson-Leach, Robert. Berlioz: His Life & Times. (Composer - Life & Times Ser.). (Illus.). 124p. 1984. 16.95x (ISBN 0-88254-666-X). Hippocrene Bks.

Clary, Chanda, jt. auth. see Brown, Donald A.

Clary, Jack. Career in Sports. (Illus.). 192p. (Orig.). 1982. pap. 8.95 (ISBN 0-8092-5849-8). Contemp Bks.

Clary, James. Ladies of the Lakes. LC 81-620035. 192p. 1981. 24.95 (ISBN 0-941912-01-9). Mich Nat Res.

Clary, John J., et al, eds. Formaldehyde: Toxicology-Epidemiology-Mechanisms. (Illus.). 296p. 1983. 45.00 (ISBN 0-8247-7025-0). Dekker.

Clary, Linda, jt. auth. see Collins, Ann.

Clary, Raymond. The Making of Golden Gate Park: The Early Years, 1865-1906. LC 79-51159. (Illus.). 224p. 1980. 25.00 (ISBN 0-89395-024-6); pap. 10.95 (ISBN 0-89395-025-4). Cal Living Bks.

Clary, Raymond H. The Making of Golden Gate Park: The Early Years, 1865-1906. 192p. 1985. 18.95 (ISBN 0-917583-03-5); pap. 12.95 (ISBN 0-917583-02-7). Don't Call Frisco.

Clary, Thomas C., et al. Transactional Analysis: Improving Communications. 1974. pap. 24.90 (ISBN 0-685-73198-7); pap. 21.50 for 2 or more (ISBN 0-685-73199-5); pap. 24.90 french ed. (ISBN 0-89401-102-2); pap. 0.50 leader guide (ISBN 0-685-73200-2). Didactic Syst.

Clary, Wayne. OS Debugging for the COBOL Programmer. LC 80-84122. (Illus.). 312p. (Orig.). 1981. pap. 20.00 (ISBN 0-911625-10-0). M Murach & Assoc.

--OS JCL. LC 80-82867. (Illus.). 330p. 1980. pap. 22.50 (ISBN 0-911625-08-9). M Murach & Assoc.

Clarys, J. Swimming II. (Intl. Series on Sport Sciences: Vol. 2). 352p. 1975. text ed. 27.00 (ISBN 0-8391-0817-6). Univ Park.

Clarysse, A., et al. Cancer Chemotherapy. (Recent Results in Cancer Research Ser: Vol. 53). 1976. 59.00 (ISBN 0-387-07573-9). Springer-Verlag.

Clasby, Miriam. Community Perspectives on the Role of the School in the Community. (IRE Reports: No. 3). 1981. pap. 2.75. Inst Responsive.

Clasen, Karl H. Der Meister der schoenen Madonnen: Herkunft, Entfaltung und Umkreis. 474p. 1973. 94.00x (ISBN 3-11-003944-3). De Gruyter.

Clasen, Souphronius, ed. Henrici De Werla, O. F. M. Opera Omnia: Tractatus De Immaculata Conceptione Beatae Mariae Virginis. (Text Ser). 1955. 6.00 (ISBN 0-686-11555-4). Franciscan Inst.

Clasing, Henry. The Dow Jones-Irwin Guide to Put & Call Options. rev. ed. LC 77-85775. 1978. 24.95 (ISBN 0-87094-148-8). Dow Jones-Irwin.

Clasing, Henry K., Jr., jt. auth. see Rudd, Andrew.

Clason, Carla & Moreno, Carlos. Puppets & the Theater, No. 12. (Technical Notes Ser.). 29p. (Orig.). 1975. pap. 1.00 ea. Eng (ISBN 0-932288-26-X). Span (ISBN 0-932288-27-8). Ctr Intl Ed U of MA.

Clason, Carla, jt. auth. see Gunter, Jock.

Clason, Carla, tr. see Evans, David & Hoxeng, James.

Clason, Carla, tr. see Gunter, Jock.

Clason, Carla, tr. see Hoxeng, James, et al.

Clason, Carla, tr. see Hoxeng, James.

Clason, Carla, tr. see Smith, William A.

Clason, George S. Richest Man in Babylon. 1955. 10.25 (ISBN 0-8015-6360-7, 0996-290, Hawthorn); pap. 5.95 (ISBN 0-8015-6366-6, 0578-170, Hawthorn). Dutton.

Clason, Robert G., jt. ed. see Bidwell, James K.

Clason, W. Elsevier's Dictionary of Chemical Engineering, 2 Vols. (Eng., Fr., Span., Ital., Dutch, & Ger.). 1969. Set. 170.25 (ISBN 0-444-40736-7); Vol. 1. 98.00 (ISBN 0-444-40714-6); Vol. 2. 98.00 (ISBN 0-444-40715-4). Elsevier.

--Elsevier's Dictionary of Television & Video Recording. LC 74-77577. 608p. (Eng., Ger., Fr., Span., Ital. & Dutch.). 1975. 125.75 (ISBN 0-444-41224-7). Elsevier.

--Elsevier's Dictionary of Tools & Ironware. 298p. (Eng., Fr., Span., Ital., Dutch & Ger.). 1982. 74.50 (ISBN 0-444-42085-1, I-263-82). Elsevier.

Clason, W. & Salem, S. Dictionary of Library Science Information & Documentation. rev. ed. 708p. (Eng., Fr., Span., Ital., Dutch, Ger., & Arabic.). 1977. 108.50 (ISBN 0-444-41475-4). Elsevier.

Clason, W. E. Elsevier's Dictionary of Cinema, Sound & Music. 948p. (Eng., Fr., Span., Ital., Dutch, & Ger., Polyglot). 1956. 127.75 (ISBN 0-444-40117-2). Elsevier.

--Elsevier's Dictionary of Computers, Automatic Control & Data Processing. 2nd ed. 474p. (Eng., Fr., Span., & Ital., Polyglot). 1971. 98.00 (ISBN 0-444-40928-9). Elsevier.

--Elsevier's Dictionary of Electronics & Waveguides. 2nd ed. 833p. (Eng., Fr., Span., Ital., Dutch & Ger., Polyglot). 1965. 119.25 (ISBN 0-444-40119-9). Elsevier.

--Elsevier's Dictionary of General Physics. 859p. (Eng., Fr., Span., Ital., Dutch & Ger., Polyglot). 1962. 123.50 (ISBN 0-444-40122-9). Elsevier.

--Elsevier's Dictionary of Measurement & Control. 886p. (Eng., Fr., Span., Ital., Ger. & Dutch.). 1977. 136.25 (ISBN 0-444-41582-3). Elsevier.

--Elsevier's Dictionary of Metallurgy & Metal Working. 848p. (Eng., Fr., Span., Ital., Dutch & Ger.). 1978. 136.25 (ISBN 0-444-41695-1). Elsevier.

--Elsevier's Dictionary of Nuclear Science & Technology. 2nd rev. ed. 787p. (Eng., Fr., Span., Ital., Dutch & Ger.). 1970. 132.00 (ISBN 0-444-40810-X). Elsevier.

--Elsevier's Electrotechnical Dictionary. 731p. (Eng., Fr., Span., Ital., Dutch & Ger.). 1965. 125.75 (ISBN 0-444-40118-0). Elsevier.

--Elsevier's Telecommunication Dictionary. 2nd rev. ed. 604p. (Eng., Fr., Ital., Span., Dutch & Ger.). 1976. 125.75 (ISBN 0-444-41394-4). Elsevier.

Clason, W. E., jt. auth. see De Vries, L.

Clasper, James W. & Dellenbach, Carolyn M. Guide to the Holdings of the American Jewish Archives. 1980. 20.00x (ISBN 0-87820-007-X). Ktav.

Clasper, Paul. Eastern Paths & the Christian Way. LC 80-13730. 128p. (Orig.). 1980. pap. 5.95 (ISBN 0-88344-100-4). Orbis Bks.

--Theological Ferment: Personal Reflections. 226p. (Orig.). 1982. pap. 6.75x (ISBN 0-686-37687-0, Pub. by New Day Philippines). Cellar.

Clasper, Paul D. The Yogi, the Commissar & the Third World Church. 92p. (Orig.). 1982. pap. 5.75 (ISBN 0-686-37580-7, Pub. by New Day Philippines). Cellar.

Class, Edward C. Prescription & Election in Elementary-School Teacher-Training Curricula in State Teachers Colleges. LC 74-176652. (Columbia University. Teachers College. Contributions to Education: No. 480). Repr. of 1931 ed. 22.50 (ISBN 0-404-55480-6). AMS Pr.

Class, Gary. Love Is the Revolution & Other Poems. 40p. (Orig.). 1982. pap. 2.50 (ISBN 0-943530-01-6). Pro Libris Pr.

--Three Days with Johnny Two-Suits. 56p. (Orig.). 1981. pap. 1.95 (ISBN 0-943530-00-8). Pro Libris Pr.

--Workshirts & Silk Suits. 4.00 (ISBN 0-318-11914-5). Great Raven Pr.

Class of 1926 Memorial Committee. Sampler from the Class of 1926 Memorial Collection of Illustrated Books Published in New England, 1769-1869. LC 77-125188. (Illus.). 36p. 1970. 10.00x (ISBN 0-87451-995-0); pap. 5.00x (ISBN 0-87451-994-2). U Pr of New Eng.

Classe, A., jt. auth. see Busnel, R. G.

Classe, Andre. The Rhythm of English Prose. 1978. Repr. of 1939 ed. lib. bdg. 20.00 (ISBN 0-8495-0900-9). Arden Lib.

--The Rhythm of English Prose. LC 73-12136. 1939. lib. bdg. 25.00 (ISBN 0-8414-3416-6). Folcroft.

Classen, E. Lectures on Style & Composition. 1973. Repr. of 1917 ed. 15.00 (ISBN 0-8274-1528-1). R West.

Classen, E., ed. see Backman, Eugene L.

Classen, E., tr. see Bjerre, Andreas.

Classen, E., tr. see Wicksell, Knut.

Classen, Ernest. Outlines of the History of the English Language. LC 79-95091. Repr. of 1919 ed. lib. bdg. 18.75x (ISBN 0-8371-2547-2, CLEL). Greenwood.

Classen, M., et al, eds. Nonsurgical Biliary Drainage. (Illus.). 150p. 1984. 25.00 (ISBN 0-387-11786-5). Springer-Verlag.

Classical Art Galleries Editors. A Collection of Reproductions in Full Colors of Some of the Greatest Paintings in American Galleries. (Illus.). 91p. 1985. 97.50 (ISBN 0-86650-137-1). Gloucester Art.

Classical Music Magazine. British Music Yearbook, 1984. 656p. 1984. text ed. 29.95 (ISBN 0-02-870180-1). Schirmer Bks.

Claster, Jill N. The Medieval Experience, Three Hundred to Fourteen Hundred. (Illus.). 352p. 1982. 35.00x (ISBN 0-8147-1384-X); pap. 16.00x (ISBN 0-8147-1381-5). NYU Pr.

Claster, Jill N., ed. Athenian Democracy: Triumph or Travesty? LC 78-7828. (European Problem Studies). 128p. 1978. pap. text ed. 5.95 (ISBN 0-88275-581-1). Krieger.

Clatanoff, Robert M. Adjusting for Terms of Financing: A Bibliography. (Bibliographic Ser.). 8p. 1982. pap. 5.00 (ISBN 0-88329-115-0). Intl Assess.

--Computer Assisted Appraisal & Assessment Systems: An Annotated Bibliography, Supplement I. (Bibliographic Ser.: No. 2-I). 57p. 1983. pap. 14.00 (ISBN 0-88329-148-7). Intl Assess.

--Government Assessing Manuals: A Checklist. (Bibliographic Ser.). 1982. pap. 8.00 (ISBN 0-88329-117-7). Intl Assess.

--Property Tax & National Income in the U.S., 1929 to 1980. (Research & Information Ser.). 85p. 1982. 14.50 (ISBN 0-88329-042-1). Intl Assess.

--Real Property Time Shares: An Appraisal Guide & Bibliography. (Bibliographic Ser.). 1982. pap. 5.00 (ISBN 0-88329-116-9). Intl Assess.

--Valuation & Property Taxation of Forests, Orchards, & Trees: A Bibliography. (Bibliographic Ser.: No. 4). 77p. 1982. pap. 14.00 (ISBN 0-88329-118-5). Intl Assess.

--Valuation & Property Taxation of Nonrenewable Resources: An Annotated Bibliography. (CPL Bibliographies Ser.: No. 99). 53p. 1983. 8.00 (ISBN 0-86602-099-3). Coun Plan Librarians.

--Valuation of Commercial Sales Property: A Classified Annotated Bibliography. LC 84-29005. (Bibliographic Ser.: No. 10). 57p. 1985. 14.00 (ISBN 0-88329-137-1). Intl Assess.

--Valuation of Commercial Services Property: A Classified Annotated Bibliography. (Bibliographic Ser.: No. 9). 101p. 1985. 18.00 (ISBN 0-88329-136-3). Intl Assess.

--Valuation of Utility & Transportation Property: A Classified Annotated Bibliography. (Bibliographic Ser.: No. 5). 52p. 1983. pap. 13.50 (ISBN 0-88329-147-9). Intl Assess.

Clatanoff, Robert M., ed. Ad Valorem Assessment of Telecommunications Property: A Bibliography, Directory & Resource Guide. (CPL Bibliographies Ser: No. 83). 32p. 1982. 8.00 (ISBN 0-86602-083-7). Coun Plan Librarians.

Claton, Rose, ed. see Kirby, Edward.

Clatonoff, Robert M. Ad Valorem Assessment of Telecommunications Property. (Research & Information Ser.: No.2). 103p. 1981. 16.50 (ISBN 0-88329-049-9). Intl Assess.

Claud, Howard. Coleridge's Idealism: A Study of Its Relationship to Kant & to the Cambridge Platonists. 1978. Repr. of 1924 ed. lib. bdg. 15.00 (ISBN 0-8495-2312-5). Arden Lib.

Claude, Inis L. National Minorities: An International Problem. LC 78-90486. Repr. of 1955 ed. lib. bdg. 15.00x (ISBN 0-8371-2283-X, CLMN). Greenwood.

Claude, Inis L., Jr. Power & International Relations. 1962. text ed. 17.00 (ISBN 0-394-30133-1, RanC). Random.

--Swords into Plowshares: The Problems & Progress of International Organization. 4th ed. 1971. text ed. 19.00 (ISBN 0-394-34053-1, RanC). Random.

Claude, Richard. The Supreme Court & the Electoral Process. LC 70-94885. pap. 78.50 (ISBN 0-317-07954-9, 2015687). Bks Demand UMI.

Claude, Richard P., ed. Comparative Human Rights. LC 76-7043. pap. 81.20 (ISBN 0-317-07752-X, 2009034). Bks Demand UMI.

Claudel, B., jt. auth. see Prettre, M.

Claudel, Calvin A. Louisiana Creole Poems. LC 82-80025. (Illus.). 50p. (Orig.). 1982. pap. 3.50 (ISBN 0-942544-00-5). Negative Capability Pr.

Claudel, Paul. Annonce Faite a Marie: Theatre. (Coll. Soleil). 1959. 11.50 (ISBN 0-685-11006-0); pap. 3.95 (ISBN 0-686-66413-2). French & Eur.

--Les Aventures de Sophie. 1937. pap. 4.95 (ISBN 0-686-51960-4). French & Eur.

--The Book of Christopher Columbus: A Lyrical Drama in Two Parts. 1930. 49.50x (ISBN 0-686-51348-7). Elliots Bks.

--Breviaire Poetique. pap. 3.95 (ISBN 0-686-51961-2). French & Eur.

--Cent Phrases pour Eventails. pap. 5.95 (ISBN 0-686-50141-1). French & Eur.

--Le Chemin de la Croix. pap. 11.95 (ISBN 0-686-51962-0). French & Eur.

--Les Choephores et les Eumerides d'Eschyle. 1952. pap. 3.95 (ISBN 0-686-50142-X). French & Eur.

--Cinq Grandes Odes: Processional Pour Saluer le Siecle Nouveau la Cantate a Trois Voix. (Coll. Poesie). 1966. pap. 4.95 (ISBN 0-685-11085-0). French & Eur.

--Claudel on the Theatre. Petit, Jacques & Kempf, Jean-Pierre, eds. Trollope, Christine, tr. LC 76-121683. (Illus.). 1972. 10.00x (ISBN 0-87024-158-3). U of Miami Pr.

--Connaissance de l'est. pap. 3.95 (ISBN 0-686-51963-9). French & Eur.

--Contacts et Circumstances. 1940. pap. 4.95 (ISBN 0-686-51964-7). French & Eur.

--Conversations dans le Coir-et-Cher. 1935. pap. 7.95 (ISBN 0-686-51965-5). French & Eur.

--Corona Benignitatis Anni Dei. 1916. pap. 3.95 (ISBN 0-686-51966-3). French & Eur.

--Correspondance avec Andre Gide: 1899-1926. 1949. pap. 7.95 (ISBN 0-686-51967-1). French & Eur.

--Correspondance avec Andre Suares: 1904-1938. 1951. pap. 5.95 (ISBN 0-686-51968-X). French & Eur.

--Correspondance avec Francis Jammes et Gabriel Frizeau: 1897-1938. 1952. pap. 7.95 (ISBN 0-686-51969-8). French & Eur.

--Discours et Remerciements. 1947. pap. 3.95 (ISBN 0-686-51970-1). French & Eur.

--L' Echange. pap. 3.95 (ISBN 0-686-50144-6). French & Eur.

--L' Eloge du Daphine. 1965. 125.00 (ISBN 0-686-50145-4). French & Eur.

--L' Epee et le Miroir. 1939. pap. 4.95 (ISBN 0-686-50146-2). French & Eur.

--L' Evangile d'Isale. 1951. pap. 5.95 (ISBN 0-686-51971-X). French & Eur.

--Eye Listens. Pell, Elsie, tr. LC 76-86003. (Essay & General Literature Index Reprint Ser). 1969. Repr. of 1950 ed. 23.00x (ISBN 0-8046-0549-1, Pub. by Kennikat). Assoc Faculty Pr.

--Feuilles de Saints. 208p. 1925. 4.95 (ISBN 0-686-54390-4). French & Eur.

--Figures et Paraboles. 264p. 1936. 4.95 (ISBN 0-686-54391-2). French & Eur.

--L' Histoire de Tobie et de Sara. 128p. 1942. 4.95 (ISBN 0-686-54392-0). French & Eur.

--Introduction au Livre de Ruth. 1953. 3.95 (ISBN 0-686-54393-9). French & Eur.

--Je Crois en Dieu. 432p. 1961. 8.95 (ISBN 0-686-54394-7). French & Eur.

--Jeanne d'Arc Au Bucher. 94p. 1939. 3.95 (ISBN 0-686-54395-5). French & Eur.

--La Jeune Fille Violaine. 170p. 1926. 5.95 (ISBN 0-686-54396-3). French & Eur.

--Journal, 2 tomes. Vrillon & Petit, eds. (Bibliotheque de la Pleiade). Set. 80.45 (ISBN 0-685-37275-8). French & Eur.

--La Legende de Prakhriti: Ossements. Le Bestiaire Spirituel. 216p. 1972. 25.00 (ISBN 0-686-54398-X). French & Eur.

--Le Livre de Christophe Colomb. 252p. 1932. 6.95 (ISBN 0-686-54399-8). French & Eur.

--Memoires Improvises. 384p. 1969. 4.50 (ISBN 0-686-54400-5). French & Eur.

--Mes Idees sur le Theatre. (Illus.). 256p. 1966. 8.95 (ISBN 0-686-54401-3). French & Eur.

--La Messe la-bas. 132p. 1919. 3.95 (ISBN 0-686-54402-1). French & Eur.

--Au Milieu des Vitraux de l'Apocalypse. 1966. pap. 12.50 (ISBN 0-686-50143-8). French & Eur.

--Le Monde de Vezelay. (Illus.). 200p. 27.50 (ISBN 0-686-54403-X). French & Eur.

--L' Oeil Ecoute. (Illus.). 272p. 1946. 27.50 (ISBN 0-686-54404-8). French & Eur.

--Oeuvre Poetique, 2 vols. Fumet, ed. 1957. 87.95 (ISBN 0-685-11432-5). French & Eur.

--L' Oiseau Noir Dans le Soleil Levant. 248p. 1929. 3.95 (ISBN 0-686-54405-6). French & Eur.

--L' Orestie. 256p. 1961. 3.95 (ISBN 0-686-54406-4). French & Eur.

--Otage: Theatre. (Coll. Soleil). 1962. 13.95 (ISBN 0-685-11472-4). French & Eur.

--Pages de Prose. 428p. 1944. 14.95 (ISBN 0-686-54407-2). French & Eur.

--Le Pain Dur: Avec: Le Pere Humilie, L'Otage. (Folio 170). 1972. 3.95 (ISBN 0-686-54408-0). French & Eur.

--Pain Dur: Theatre. (Coll. Soleil). 1918. 11.50 (ISBN 0-685-11474-0). French & Eur.

--Partage de Midi. 252p. 1949. 7.95 (ISBN 0-686-54409-9). French & Eur.

--Paul Claudel Interroge L'Apocalypse. 384p. 1952. 6.95 (ISBN 0-686-54411-0). French & Eur.

--Paul Claudel Interroge le Cantique Des Cantiques. 540p. 1954. 8.95 (ISBN 0-686-54412-9). French & Eur.

--La Peinture Hollandaise Etautres Crits sur l'Art. (Illus.). 192p. 1966. 3.95 (ISBN 0-686-54413-7). French & Eur.

--Le Pere Humile. 194p. 1920. 10.95 (ISBN 0-686-54414-5); pap. 3.95 (ISBN 0-686-54415-3). French & Eur.

--La Perle Noire. 250p. 1947. 4.95 (ISBN 0-686-54416-1). French & Eur.

--Poemes et Paroles Durant la Guerre De Trente Ans. 216p. 1945. 3.95 (ISBN 0-686-54417-X). French & Eur.

--Poesies. 192p. 1970. 3.95 (ISBN 0-686-54418-8). French & Eur.

--Le Poete et le Shamisen: Avec: Le Poete et le Vase d'Encens, Jules ou l'Homme-aux-deux-cravates. 368p. 1970. 30.00 (ISBN 0-686-54419-6). French & Eur.

--Un Poete Regarde la Croix. 290p. 1938. 4.95 (ISBN 0-686-54420-X). French & Eur.

--Poetic Art. LC 73-86004. 1969. Repr. of 1948 ed. 19.00x (ISBN 0-8046-0607-2, Pub. by Kennikat). Assoc Faculty Pr.

--Portage de Midi. 160p. (Folio 245). 1972. 3.95 (ISBN 0-686-54410-2). French & Eur.

--La Porte Ouverte: Lettres Inedites. Avec: Du Guerard, France. Images de Paul Claudel, Itineraire. 67p. 1970. 25.00 (ISBN 0-686-54421-8). French & Eur.

--Positions et Propositions, 2 vols. 1928. Vol. 1. pap. 4.95 (ISBN 0-686-54422-6); Vol. 2. pap. 5.95 (ISBN 0-686-54423-4). French & Eur.

--Presence et Prophetie. 320p. 1958. 4.95 (ISBN 0-686-54424-2). French & Eur.

--Prose. Petit & Galperine, eds. (Bibliotheque De la Pleiade). 1965. 33.95 (ISBN 0-685-11455-4). French & Eur.

--Protee. 1972. 3.95 (ISBN 0-686-54425-0). French & Eur.

--Psaumes. 280p. 1966. 12.95 (ISBN 0-686-54426-9). French & Eur.

--Qui Ne Souffre Pas... Reflexions sur le Probleme Social. 160p. 1958. 3.95 (ISBN 0-686-54427-7). French & Eur.

--Reflexions Sur la Poesie. 192p. 1963. 3.95 (ISBN 0-686-54428-5). French & Eur.

--Le Repos Du Septieme Jour. 1973. 14.95 (ISBN 0-686-54429-3). French & Eur.

--Richard Wagner: Reverie d'un Poete Francais. 180p. 22.50 (ISBN 0-686-54430-7). French & Eur.

--La Rose et le Rosaire. 272p. 1947. 4.95 (ISBN 0-686-54431-5). French & Eur.

--La Sagesse ou La Parabole du Festin. 1939. 2.50 (ISBN 0-686-54432-3). French & Eur.

--Sainte Agnes et Poemes Inedits. (Illus.). 60.00 (ISBN 0-686-54433-1). French & Eur.

--Seigneur Apprenez-Nous a Prier. 128p. 1943. 2.95 (ISBN 0-686-54434-X). French & Eur.

--Les Sept Psaumes de la Penitence. 1945. 3.95 (ISBN 0-686-54435-8). French & Eur.

--Le Soulier de satin. (Documentation thematique). (Illus.). 159p. (Fr.). 1975. pap. 2.95 (ISBN 0-685-54487-7, 173). Larousse.

--Soulier De Satin: Theatre. (Coll. Soleil). 1963. 15.90 (ISBN 0-685-11568-2). French & Eur.

--Sous le Signe du Dragon. 232p. 1958. 3.95 (ISBN 0-686-54436-6). French & Eur.

--Le Symbolisme de la Salette. 64p. 1952. 2.95 (ISBN 0-686-54437-4). French & Eur.

--Tete d'Or. 326p. 1959. 14.95 (ISBN 0-686-54438-2); pap. 3.95 (ISBN 0-686-54439-0). French & Eur.

--Theatre, 2 Vols. Madaule, ed. (Bibliotheque De la Pleiade). 1948-1966. Set. 81.45 (ISBN 0-685-11589-5). French & Eur.

--Toi, qui es-tu? 1936. 2.95 (ISBN 0-686-54440-4). French & Eur.

--Trois Figures Saintes. 148p. 1953. 3.95 (ISBN 0-686-54441-2). French & Eur.

--La Ville. 1967. 19.95 (ISBN 0-686-54442-0); pap. 3.95 (ISBN 0-686-54443-9). French & Eur.

--Visages Radieux. 144p. 1947. 2.95 (ISBN 0-686-54444-7). French & Eur.

--Une Voix sur Israel. 46p. 1950. 2.95 (ISBN 0-686-54445-5). French & Eur.

--Ways & Crossways. facs. ed. O'Conner, Fr. J., tr. LC 67-28732. (Essay Index Reprint Ser.). 1933. 20.00 (ISBN 0-8369-0313-7). Ayer Co Pubs.

--Ways & Crossways. LC 68-15820. 1968. Repr. of 1933 ed. 19.50x (ISBN 0-8046-0079-1, Pub. by Kennikat). Assoc Faculty Pr.

Claudel, Paul & Petit, Jacques. La Jeune Fille Violaine: Premiere et Seconde Versions, Pieces en 4 Actes. 259p. 1977. 27.50 (ISBN 0-686-54397-1). French & Eur.

Clauder, Amelia C. American Commerce As Affected by the Wars of the French Revolution & Napoleon. LC 68-55509. Repr. of 1932 ed. 27.50x (ISBN 0-678-00905-8). Kelley.

Claudian. Poems, 2 Vols. (Loeb Classical Library: No. 135, 136). 12.50x ea. Vol. 1 (ISBN 0-674-99150-8). Vol. 2 (ISBN 0-674-99151-6). Harvard U Pr.

Claudianus Mamertus. Opera. Engelbrecht, A., ed. (Corpus Scriptorum Ecclesiasticorum Latinorum Ser: Vol. 11). 1885. 50.00 (ISBN 0-384-09245-4). Johnson Repr.

Claudin, Fernando. The Communist Movement: From Comintern to Cominform, 2 vols. Pearce, Brian, tr. from Fr. LC 74-25015. 739p. 1976. Set. 27.00 (ISBN 0-85345-366-7). Monthly Rev.

--Communist Movement: From Comintern to Cominform, 2 vols. Pearce, Brian, tr. from Fr. LC 74-25015. (Eng.). 1977. Set. pap. 11.90. Monthly Rev.

Claudin-Urondo, Carmen. Lenine & la Revolution Culturelle. (Archontes Ser: No. 4). 119p. (Fr.). 1975. pap. text ed. 14.00x (ISBN 90-2797-625-2). Mouton.

Claudon, Michael, ed. World Debt Crisis: International Lending on Trial. 288p. 1985. prof. ref. 29.95x (ISBN 0-88730-052-9). Ballinger Pub.

Claudon, Michael P. & Cornwall, Richard. Incomes Policy for the United States: New Approaches. 240p. 1980. lib. bdg. 18.00 (ISBN 0-89838-048-0, Pub. by Martinus Nijhoff Netherlands). Kluwer Academic.

Claudy, Carl H., ed. Foreign Countries: A Gateway to the Interpretation & Development of Certain Symbols of Freemasonry. 1971. Repr. of 1925 ed. text ed. 6.00 (ISBN 0-88053-039-1, M-88). Macoy Pub.

Claugher, D. Scanning Nature. LC 83-5155. 116p. 1983. 24.95 (ISBN 0-521-25705-0); pap. 10.95 (ISBN 0-521-27664-0). Cambridge U Pr.

Claus, A., jt. auth. see Kottmeyer, W.

Claus, Audrey, jt. auth. see Kottmeyer, William.

Claus, H. R., jt. auth. see Brady, G. S.

Claus, Heinrich. Die Wagogo: Ethnographische Skizze Eines Ostafricanischen Bantustammes. 1911. 10.00 (ISBN 0-384-09255-1). Johnson Repr.

Claus, Horst. The Theatre Director Otto Brahm. Beckerman, Bernard, ed. LC 81-15951. (Theater & Dramatic Studies: No. 10). 164p. 1981. 39.95 (ISBN 0-8357-1266-4). UMI Res Pr.

Claus, Karen E. & Bailey, June T. Living with Stress & Promoting Well Being: A Handbook for Nurses. LC 80-14605. (Illus.). 1980. pap. text ed. 15.95 (ISBN 0-8016-1148-2). Mosby.

Claus, Karen E. & Claus, R. J. The On-Premise Signs Industry: Present Status & Future Potential. 1974. pap. 4.00 (ISBN 0-685-51829-9). Signs of Times.

Claus, Karen E., jt. auth. see Bailey, June T.

Claus, R. J. Some Policy Considerations for Sign Legislation. 1973. pap. 3.00 (ISBN 0-911380-31-0). Signs of Times.

Claus, R. J., jt. auth. see Claus, Karen E.

Claus, V., ed. Graph-Grammars & Their Application to Computer Science & Biology: Proceedings, International Workshop, Bad Honnef, October 30-November 3, 1978. (Lecture Notes in Computer Science: Vol. 73). 1979. pap. 26.00 (ISBN 0-387-09525-X). Springer-Verlag.

Clausager, Anders D. Porsche. 224p. 1983. 29.95 (ISBN 0-312-63170-7). St Martin.

Clause, Frank, jt. auth. see McBride, Patty.

Clausen, Aage R. How Congressmen Decide: A Policy Focus. 192p. 1973. text ed. 16.95 (ISBN 0-312-39480-2); pap. text ed. 8.95 (ISBN 0-312-39445-4). St Martin.

Clausen, Andy. Austin, Texas. 1981. lib. bdg. 20.00 (ISBN 0-916908-33-X); pap. 3.50 (ISBN 0-916908-16-X). Place Herons.

--Extreme Unction. 1974. saddle stich bdg 5.00 (ISBN 0-915214-05-9). Litmus.

Clausen, C. A. & Lovoll, Odd S. A Chronicler of Immigrant Life: Svein Nilsson's Articles in Billed-Magazin, 1868-1870. (Travel & Description Ser.). (Illus.). 171p. 1982. 12.00 (ISBN 0-87732-067-5). Norwegian-Am Hist Assn.

Clausen, Carl J., jt. auth. see Burgess, Robert F.

Clausen, Carol, jt. ed. see Waserman, Manfred.

Clausen, Chris A., III & Mattson, Guy C. Principles of Industrial Chemistry. LC 78-9450. 412p. 1978. 45.00 (ISBN 0-471-02774-X, Pub. by Wiley-Interscience). Wiley.

Clausen, Christopher. The Place of Poetry: Two Centuries of an Art in Crisis. LC 80-5172. 160p. 1981. 15.00x (ISBN 0-8131-1429-2). U Pr of Ky.

Clausen, Edwin & Bermingham, Jack. Chinese & African Professionals in California: A Case Study of Equality & Opportunity in the United States. LC 80-67233. 134p. (Orig.). 1982. lib. bdg. 21.75 (ISBN 0-8191-2075-8); pap. text ed. 9.25 (ISBN 0-8191-2076-6). U Pr of Amer.

--Pluralism, Racism & Public Policy: The Search for Equality. (University Bks.). 1981. lib. bdg. 21.00 (ISBN 0-8161-9041-0, Univ Bks). G K Hall.

Clausen, Gale, ed. Serve with Love. (Illus.). 416p. 1982. plastic spine 9.95 (ISBN 0-943980-02-X). AIGA Pubns.

Clausen, H. & Tipsen, E. Farm Animals in Color. (Illus.). 1970. 9.95 (ISBN 0-7137-0539-6, Pub by Blandford Pr England). Sterling.

Clausen, J., et al, eds. Laboratory Techniques in Biochemistry & Molecular Biology: Vol. 1, Pt. 3, Immunochemical Techniques for the Indentification & Estimation of Macromolecules. 2nd. rev. ed. 1981. 78.75 (ISBN 0-444-80245-2, Biomedical Pr); pap. 28.50 (ISBN 0-444-80244-4). Elsevier.

Clausen, Jack L. & Zimet, Irwin, eds. Pulmonary Function Testing. LC 82-3968. (Continuing Medical Education Ser.). 1982. 47.50 (ISBN 0-12-788125-5). Acad Pr.

Clausen, Jan. Duration. 1983. pap. 5.00 (ISBN 0-914610-36-8). Hanging Loose.

--Mother, Sister, Daughter, Lover: A Collection of Short Stories Dealing with Woman's Relations to Woman. LC 80-16386. (The Feminist Ser.). 136p. (Orig.). 1980. 15.95 (ISBN 0-89594-034-5); pap. 6.95 (ISBN 0-89594-033-7). Crossing Pr.

--A Movement of Poets: Thoughts on Poetry & Feminism. 1982. pap. 3.25 (ISBN 0-9602284-1-1). Long Haul.

--Sinking-Stealing: A Novel. LC 85-4158. (Feminist Ser.). 280p. (Orig.). 1985. 16.95 (ISBN 0-89594-160-0); pap. 8.95 (ISBN 0-89594-159-7). Crossing Pr.

--Waking at the Bottom of the Dark. LC 78-71983. 1979. pap. 3.00 (ISBN 0-9602284-0-3). Long Haul.

Clausen, Jens, et al. Plant Evolution Through Amphiploidy & Autoploidy, with Examples from the Madiinae. (Experimental Studies on the Nature of Species: Vol. 2). (Illus.). 564p. 1945. pap. 7.25 (ISBN 0-87279-575-6). Carnegie Inst.

--Effect of Varied Environments on Western North American Plants. (Experimental Studies on the Nature of Species, Vol. 1). (Illus.). 459p. 1940. pap. 16.50 (ISBN 0-87279-530-6, 520). Carnegie Inst.

Clausen, John A. Sociology of the Life Course. (Illus.). 192p. 1986. pap. text ed. 14.95 (ISBN 0-13-821349-6). P-H.

Clausen, Joy, et al. Maternity Nursing Today. 2nd ed. (Illus.). 1976. text ed. 36.00 (ISBN 0-07-011284-3). McGraw.

Clausen, Muriel C. Menopause: Vitamins & You. 105p. (Orig.). 1980. pap. 4.75 (ISBN 0-9603664-1-5). M C Clausen.

--Premenopause. 53p. 1979. pap. 6.25 (ISBN 0-9603664-0-7). M C Clausen.

Clausen, Robert H. Martin Luther Speaks to Our Day. 1975. 2.75 (ISBN 0-317-04063-4). CSS of Ohio.

--Snake. 1971. pap. 2.75 (ISBN 0-89536-219-8). CSS of Ohio.

--What's Happening Out There in the Dark Tonight? (Orig.). 1977. pap. 6.50 (ISBN 0-89536-264-3). CSS of Ohio.

Clausen, Robert T., ed. Sedum of North America North of the Mexican Plateau. LC 75-6084. (Illus.). 784p. 1975. 95.00x (ISBN 0-8014-0950-0). Comstock.

Clausen, Sophronius. St. Anthony: Doctor of the Gospel. Brady, Ignatius, tr. from Ger. LC 61-11200. Orig. Title: Antonius. 140p. pap. 2.50 (ISBN 0-8199-0458-9). Franciscan Herald.

Clausen, W. V., jt. ed. see Kenney, E. J.

Clausen, W. V., ed. see Persius & Juvenal.

Clausen, W. V., et al, eds. see Virgil.

Clausen, Wendell, ed. Harvard Studies in Classical Philology, Vol. 86. (Illus.). 296p. 1982. text ed. 30.00x (ISBN 0-674-37933-0). Harvard U Pr.

Clauser, H., jt. auth. see Brady, G. S.

Clauser, H., ed. Progress in Assessing Technological Innovation, Vol. 1. 103p. 1975. text ed. 7.95x (ISBN 0-87762-169-1). Technomic.

Clauser, H. R. Diccionario De Materiales y Procesos De Ingenieria. 820p. (Span.). 1970. 98.00 (ISBN 84-335-6404-8, S-50067). French & Eur.

--Encyclopedia Handbook of Materials, Parts & Finishes. new rev. ed. LC 75-43010. 1976. 29.00 (ISBN 0-87762-189-6). Technomic.

Clauser, Henry. Industrial & Manufacturing Materials. (Illus.). 416p. 1975. text ed. 34.25 (ISBN 0-07-011285-1). McGraw.

Clauser, Suzanne. A Girl Named Sooner. (YA) 1975. pap. 2.50 (ISBN 0-380-00216-7, 69047-0). Avon.

Clauser, Suzanne S., jt. auth. see Thomas, Deborah.

Clausewitz, Carl Von. On War. Howard, Michael & Paret, Peter, eds. LC 75-30190. 1976. 31.00x (ISBN 0-691-05657-9). Princeton U Pr.

Clausewitz, Carl Von see Von Clausewitz, Carl.

Clausewitz, Karl Von. The Campaign of Eighteen Twelve in Russia. LC 79-84266. (Illus.). 1977. Repr. of 1843 ed. lib. bdg. 45.00x (ISBN 0-8371-5004-3, CLCA). Greenwood.

Clausewitz, Karl Von see Von Clausewitz, Karl.

Clausing, Gerhard & Mueller, Klaus I. An Individualized Instruction Program in Basic German. 2nd ed. 1975. pap. text ed. 5.95x (ISBN 0-394-32434-X). Random.

--An Individualized Instruction Program in Basic German. 3rd ed. 1980. pap. text ed. 5.95x (ISBN 0-394-32434-X, RanC). Random.

Clausing, Roth. Roman Colonate: The Theories of Its Origin. LC 70-78011. (Columbia University Studies in the Social Sciences: No. 260). 1969. Repr. of 1925 ed. 27.50 (ISBN 0-404-51260-7). AMS Pr.

Clauson, Gerard. An Etymological Dictionary of Pre-Thirteenth Century Turkish. (Turkish.). 1972. 160.00x (ISBN 0-19-864112-5). Oxford U Pr.

Clauss, Francis J. Solid Lubricants & Self-Lubricating Solids. 1972. 61.50 (ISBN 0-12-176150-9). Acad Pr.

Clauss, J., ed. MASH: The First Five Years. pap. 5.95 (ISBN 0-88411-197-0, Pub. by Aeonian Pr). Amereon Ltd.

--P. G. Thodehouse Checklist. 5.95 (ISBN 0-89190-843-9, Pub. by Am Repr). Amereon Ltd.

--Timeless Children's Tales from Around the World. 1st ed. (Illus.). 1976. lib. bdg. 16.95x (ISBN 0-88411-992-0, Pub. by Aeonian Pr). Amereon Ltd.

Clauss, J., intro. by see Aesop.

Clauss, J. E. John D. MacDonald: A Checklist. pap. 10.95 (ISBN 0-88411-799-5, Pub. by Aeonian Pr). Amereon Ltd.

--Louis L'Amour Checklist. pap. 10.95 (ISBN 0-88411-244-6, Pub. by Aeonian Pr). Amereon Ltd.

Clauss, J. E., ed. see Grey, Zane.

Clauss, J. E., ed. see Hill, Grace L.

Clauss, J. Ed. The Star Trek Guide. 1976. pap. 5.95x (ISBN 0-88411-079-6, Pub. by Aeonian Pr). Amereon Ltd.

Clauss, Jed. Zane Grey: A Checklist. pap. 5.95 (ISBN 0-89190-768-8, Pub. by River City Pr). Amereon Ltd.

Claussen, B., jt. auth. see Borchling, C.

Claussen, C. & Lochner, B. Dynamic Computed Tomography. Dougherty, F. C., tr. from Ger. (Illus.). 175p. 1985. 21.00 (ISBN 0-387-13435-2). Springer-Verlag.

Claussen, Claus F. & Desa, Joe V. Clinical Study of Human Equilibrium by Electonystagmography & Allied Tests. (Illus.). xiii, 437p. 1980. text ed. 50.00x (ISBN 0-86590-002-7). Apt Bks.

Claussen, Claus-Frenz. Differential Diagnosis of Vertigo: Equilibrium in Patients & Research. (Proceedings of the 6th Scientific Meeting of the NES, Turku-Finland, 1979). 617p. 1980. 48.00 (ISBN 3-11-008298-5). De Gruyter.

Claussen, E. Neal, ed. see Lawson, John.

Claussen, Evelyn B., jt. auth. see Claussen, Martin P.

Claussen, Martin P. Standardization of Air Material, Nineteen Thirty-Nine - Nineteen Forty-Four: Controls, Policies, Procedures. (USAF Historical Studies: No. 67). 81p. 1951. pap. text ed. 10.00x (ISBN 0-317-20158-1). MA-AH Pub.

Claussen, Martin P. & Claussen, Evelyn B. The Voice of Christian & Jewish Dissenters in America: U. S. Internal Revenue Service Hearings, December 1978. xv, 591p. 1982. pap. 25.00. Piedmont.

Claussen, N., jt. ed. see Heuer, A. H.

Claussen, Russell, ed. The Church's Growing Edge: Single Adults. 1981. pap. 4.95 (ISBN 0-8298-0429-3). Pilgrim NY.

Claus-Walker, Jacqueline, jt. auth. see Halstead, Lauro S.

Clautice, Edward W. A Little Nonsense. LC 84-91697. (Illus.). 168p. (Orig.). 1985. pap. 8.50 (ISBN 0-9614359-0-9). Clautice Pubs.

Claux, Mary du see Du Claux, Mary.

Claval, P, jt. ed. see Johnston, R. J.

Clavel, Maurice, jt. auth. see Sollers, Philippe.

Clavel, Pierre. Opposition Planning in Wales & Appalachia. LC 82-10322. 251p. 1983. text ed. 29.95 (ISBN 0-87722-276-2). Temple U Pr.

Clavel, Pierre & Goldsmith, William W., eds. Urban & Regional Planning in an Age of Austerity. LC 79-21416. (Policy Studies in Urban Affairs). 402p. 1980. 46.00 (ISBN 0-08-025539-6); pap. 8.75 (ISBN 0-08-025540-X). Pergamon.

Clavell, James. The Children's Story. 1981. 7.95 (ISBN 0-385-28135-8). Delacorte.

--The Children's Story. 96p. 1982. pap. 1.95 (ISBN 0-440-31227-2, LE); tchr's guide by Lou Stanek 0.50. Dell.

--King Rat. 352p. (gr. 9 up). 1982. pap. 3.95 (ISBN 0-440-14546-5). Dell.

--King Rat. 384p. 1983. 17.95 (ISBN 0-385-29211-2). Delacorte.

--Noble House. 1200p. 1981. 22.95 (ISBN 0-385-28737-2). Delacorte.

--Noble House. 1800p. 1982. pap. 6.95 (ISBN 0-440-16483-4). Dell.

--Shogun. 1983. 21.95 (ISBN 0-385-29224-4). Delacorte.

--Shogun: A Novel of Japan. 1216p. (YA) (gr. 11 up). 1982. pap. 5.50 (ISBN 0-440-17800-2). Dell.

--Tai-Pan. 736p. (YA) (gr. 11 up). 1982. pap. 4.25 (ISBN 0-440-18462-2). Dell.

--Tai-Pan. 1983. 19.95 (ISBN 0-385-29218-X). Delacorte.

Clavell, James, frwd. by. The Making of James Clavell's Shogun. (Illus.). 1980. pap. 8.95 (ISBN 0-440-55709-7). Dell.

Clavell, James, ed. see Sun Tzu.

Clavell, John. The Soddered Citizen. LC 82-45683. (Malone Society Reprint Ser.: No. 80). Repr. of 1935 ed. 40.00 (ISBN 0-404-63080-4). AMS Pr.

Claveloux, Nicole, jt. auth. see Sand, Georges.

Claver, Francisco F. The Stones Will Cry Out: Grassroots Pastorals. LC 78-4235. 196p. (Orig.). 1978. pap. 7.95 (ISBN 0-88344-471-2). Orbis Bks.

Claverie, Jean, jt. auth. see Price, Mathew.

Clavers, Mary, jt. auth. see Kirkland, Caroline M.

Clavert, A., jt. ed. see Bollack, C.

Clavert, A., jt. ed. see Bollack, C. G.

Clavert, C., jt. auth. see Henderson, Bernard.

Claviere, Maude la & Rene de, Marie Alphonse. The Women of the Renaissance. 510p. 1980. Repr. of 1905 ed. lib. bdg. 57.50 (ISBN 0-8482-5077-X). Norwood Edns.

Claviez, Wolfram. Seemaennisches Woerterbuch. (Ger.). 1973. 38.50 (ISBN 3-7688-0166-7, M-7620, Pub. by Delius, Klaving & Co.). French & Eur.

Clavigero, Francesco S. The History of Mexico, 2 vols. Feldman, Burton & Richardson, Robert D., eds. LC 78-60908. (Myth & Romanticism Ser.: Vol. 7). (Illus.). 1979. Set. lib. bdg. 160.00 (ISBN 0-8240-3556-9). Garland Pub.

Clavigero, Francisco J. History of Lower California. Gray, A. A., ed. Lake, Sara E., tr. from Italian. LC 79-150156. 1971. Repr. of 1937 ed. lib. bdg. 69.50x (ISBN 0-910950-03-2). Ransom Dist Co.

Clavijo, Uva A. Entresemaforos: Poemas Escritos En Ruta. LC 80-68479. (Coleccion Espejo de Paciencia). 89p. (Orig., Span.). 1981. pap. 5.95 (ISBN 0-89729-275-8). Ediciones.

Clawson, Aileen. Bender Visual Motor Gestalt Test for Children: A Manual. (Illus.). 92p. 1962. pap. 15.75x (ISBN 0-87424-035-2). Western Psych.

Clawson, D. Kay, jt. auth. see Iversen, Larry D.

Clawson, Dan. Bureaucracy & the Labor Process: The Transformation of U. S. Industry, 1860-1920. LC 79-3885. 284p. 1982. pap. 7.50 (ISBN 0-85345-543-0). Monthly Rev.

Clawson, George. Trapping & Tracking. LC 82-62598. (Illus.). 1977. 14.95 (ISBN 0-8329-1980-2, Pub. by Winchester Pr). New Century.

Clawson, James G. & Ward, David D. An MBA's Guide to Self-Assessment & Career Development. (Illus.). 368p. 1986. pap. 12.95 (ISBN 0-13-566811-5). P-H.

Clawson, James G., et al. Self-Assessment & Career Development. 2nd ed. (Illus.). 512p. 1985. pap. text ed. 24.95 (ISBN 0-13-803107-X). P-H.

Clawson, M. & Landsberg, H. H. Desalting Seawater. 286p. 1972. 57.75 (ISBN 0-677-02710-9). Gordon.

Clawson, Marion. America's Land & Its Uses. LC 70-167985. (Resources for the Future Ser.). (Illus.). 166p. 1972. pap. 5.00x (ISBN 0-8018-1330-1). Johns Hopkins.

--America's Land & Its Uses. 178p. 1972. pap. 5.00 (ISBN 0-8018-1330-1). Resources Future.

--Decision Making in Timber Production, Harvest, & Marketing. LC 77-84930. (Resources for the Future Research Papers Ser.: No. R-4). pap. 32.30 (ISBN 0-317-29715-5, 2019816). Bks Demand UMI.

--The Economics of National Forest Management. 128p. 1976. Working Paper. 4.50 (ISBN 0-8018-1889-3). Resources Future.

--The Economics of U. S. Nonindustrial Private Forests. LC 79-2196. 436p. 1979. pap. 12.95 (ISBN 0-8018-2282-3). Resources Future.

--Economics of U. S. Nonindustrial Private Forests in the United States. LC 79-2196. (Resources for the Future Ser.). 436p. 1979. pap. 12.95x (ISBN 0-8018-2282-3). Johns Hopkins.

--The Federal Lands Revisited. LC 83-42904. 208p. 1983. 25.00x (ISBN 0-8018-3097-4); pap. 8.95x (ISBN 0-8018-3098-2). Johns Hopkins.

--The Federal Lands Revisited. 1983. lib. bdg. 25.00 (ISBN 0-8018-3097-4); pap. text ed. 8.95 (ISBN 0-8018-3098-2). Resources Future.

--Federal Lands since Nineteen Fifty-Six: Recent Trends in Use & Management. LC 67-16034. (Resources for the Future Ser.). 128p. (Orig.). 1967. pap. 4.00x (ISBN 0-8018-0120-6). Johns Hopkins.

--The Federal Lands Since Nineteen Fifty Six: Recent Trends in Use & Management. 128p. 1967. pap. 4.00 (ISBN 0-8018-0120-6). Resources Future.

--Forests for Whom & for What? LC 74-24399. (Resources for the Future Ser). (Illus.). 192p. 1975. pap. 5.00x (ISBN 0-8018-1751-X). Johns Hopkins.

--Forests for Whom & for What? 194p. 1975. pap. 5.00 (ISBN 0-8018-1751-X). Resources Future.

--The Land System of the United States: An Introduction to the History & Practice of Land Use & Land Tenure. LC 68-10250. (Illus.). x, 145p. 1968. 12.95x (ISBN 0-8032-0016-1). U of Nebr Pr.

--Man, Land & the Forest Environment. LC 76-45999. (Geo. S. Long Publication Ser.). (Illus.). 86p. 1977. 12.50x (ISBN 0-295-95540-6). U of Wash Pr.

--New Deal Planning: The National Resources Planning Board. LC 80-8777. 376p. 1981. 32.50x (ISBN 0-8018-2595-4). Johns Hopkins.

--Policy Directions for U. S. Agriculture: Long-Range Choices in Farming & Rural Living. LC 68-16163. pap. 104.00 (ISBN 0-317-09637-0, 2020958). Bks Demand UMI.

--Suburban Land Conversion in the United States: An Economic & Governmental Process. LC 70-149239. (Resources for the Future Ser). (Illus.). Repr. of 1971 ed. 106.00 (ISBN 0-8357-9287-0, 2017571). Bks Demand UMI.

--Uncle Sam's Acres. LC 74-106685. Repr. of 1951 ed. lib. bdg. 19.00x (ISBN 0-8371-3356-4, CLSA). Greenwood.

--The Western Range Livestock Industry. Bruchey, Stuart, ed. LC 78-56713. (Management of Public Land Law in the U. S. Ser.). (Illus.). 1979. Repr. of 1950 ed. lib. bdg. 28.50x (ISBN 0-405-11326-9). Ayer Co Pubs.

Clawson, Marion & Hall, Peter. Planning & Urban Growth: An Anglo-American Comparison. LC 72-12364. (Resources for the Future Ser.). (Illus.). 312p. 1973. 26.95x (ISBN 0-8018-1496-0). Johns Hopkins.

--Planning & Urban Growth: An Anglo-American Comparison. 312p. 1973. 26.95 (ISBN 0-8018-1496-0). Resources Future.

Clawson, Marion & Held, Burnell. The Federal Lands: Their Use & Management. LC 57-12121. (Illus.). xxii, 501p. 1965. pap. 5.95x (ISBN 0-8032-5034-7, BB 318, Bison). U of Nebr Pr.

Clawson, Marion & Held, R. Burnell. Land for the Future. LC 60-9917. pap. 148.00 (ISBN 0-317-09633-8, 2020956). Bks Demand UMI.

Clawson, Marion & Knetsch, Jack L. Economics of Outdoor Recreation. LC 66-16040. (Resources for the Future Ser). 348p. 1967. pap. 9.50x (ISBN 0-8018-1302-6). Johns Hopkins.

--Economics of Outdoor Recreation. 348p. 1977. pap. 9.50 (ISBN 0-8018-1302-6). Resources Future.

Clawson, Marion, jt. auth. see Montgomery, Mary.

Clawson, Marion, ed. Modernizing Urban Land Policy: Papers Presented at an RFF Forum Held in Washington, D. C., 1972. LC 72-12365. pap. 64.00 (ISBN 0-317-26456-7, 2023792). Bks Demand UMI.

--Natural Resources & International Development. LC 77-86392. (Resources for the Future, Inc. Publications). Repr. of 1964 ed. 32.50 (ISBN 0-404-60330-0). AMS Pr.

Clawson, Marion, ed. see Forum on Forest Policy for the Future.

Clawson, Patrick, jt. auth. see Laibman, David.

Clawson, Robert W., jt. auth. see Kaplan, Lawrence S.

Clawson, Robert W., ed. East-West Rivalry in the Third World: Security Issues & Regional Perspectives. 424p. 1985. price not set (ISBN 0-8420-2236-8). Scholarly Res Inc.

Clawson, Robert W. & Kaplan, Lawrence S., eds. The Warsaw Pact: Political Purpose & Military Means. LC 81-86387. 300p. 1982. lib. bdg. 30.00 (ISBN 0-8420-2198-1); pap. text ed. 11.95 (ISBN 0-8420-2199-X). Scholarly Res Inc.

Clawson, Robert W., jt. ed. see Kaplan, Lawrence S.

Clawson, Virginia. The Family Symphony. LC 84-17524. 1984. 7.95 (ISBN 0-8054-5661-9). Broadman.

Claxon, Guy. Live & Learn. 1984. pap. text ed. 11.50 (ISBN 0-06-318277-7). Har-Row.

Claxton, Guy, ed. Cognitive Psychology: New Directions. (International Library of Psychology). 1980. 35.00x (ISBN 0-7100-0485-0); pap. 17.50x (ISBN 0-7100-0486-9). Routledge & Kegan.

Claxton, John D., et al, eds. Consumers & Energy Conservation: International Perspectives on Research & Policy Options. LC 81-10626. 318p. 1981. 42.95x (ISBN 0-03-059659-9). Praeger.

Claxton, William J. A Book of Nature Poetry. 1978. Repr. of 1912 ed. lib. bdg. 20.00 (ISBN 0-8495-0767-7). Arden Lib.

Claxton Stevens, C., jt. auth. see Whittington, St.

Clay, A. M., jt. ed. see Greenidge, A. H.

Clay, A. T. Documents from the Temple Archives of Nippur Dated in the Reigns of Cassite Rulers with Incomplete Dates. (Publications of the Babylonian Section, Ser. A: Vol. 15). (Illus.). xii, 68p. 1906. soft bound 12.00x (ISBN 0-686-11914-2). Univ Mus of U PA.

--Legal & Commercial Transactions Dated in the Assyrian, Neo-Babylonian & Persian Periods, Chiefly from Nippur. (Publications of the Babylonian Section, Ser. A: Vol 8, No. 1). (Illus.). x, 85p. 1908. soft bound 12.00x (ISBN 0-686-11913-4). Univ Mus of U PA.

Clay, A. T., jt. auth. see Hilprecht, Hermann.

Clay, A. T., ed. Babylonian Records in the Library of J. Pierpont Morgan, Vols. 1-4. (The Yale Babylonian Collecton Ser.). Repr. of 1923 ed. Set. 122.00 (ISBN 0-404-60120-0). AMS Pr.

Clay, Albert T. Babylonian Business Transactions of the First Millenium B.C. LC 78-63516. (Babylonian Records in the Library of J. Pierpont Morgan: No. I). 27.50 (ISBN 0-404-60121-9). AMS Pr.

--Business Documents of Murashu Sons of Nippur: Dated in the Reign of Darius II (424-404 B. C.) LC 8-33650. (University of Pennsylvania, Babylonian Expedition, Series A: Cuneiform Texts: Vol. 10). pap. 51.80 (ISBN 0-317-28571-8, 2052021). Bks Demand UMI.

--Business Documents of Murashu Sons of Nippur Dated in the Reign of Darius II. LC 13-1107. (University of Pennsylvania, The Museum, Publications of the Babylonian Section: Vol. 2, No. 1). pap. 45.00 (ISBN 0-317-29796-1, 2052016). Bks Demand UMI.

--Documents from the Temple Archives of Nippur Dated in the Reigns of Cassite Rulers (Complete Dates) LC 8-33649. (University of Pennsylvania, Babylonian Expedition, Series A: Cuneiform Texts: Vol. 14). pap. 47.00 (ISBN 0-317-29792-9, 2052017). Bks Demand UMI.

--Documents from the Temple Arhcives of Nippur Dated in the Reigns of Cassite Rulers. LC 13-1106. (University of Pennsylvania, The Museum, Pulications of the Babyllonian Section: Vol. 2, No. 2). pap. 27.00 (ISBN 0-317-28572-6, 2052022). Bks Demand UMI.

--The Empire of the Amorites. LC 78-63550. (Yale Oriental Ser. Researches: No. 6). Repr. of 1919 ed. 30.00 (ISBN 0-404-60276-2). AMS Pr.

--Empire of the Amorites. (Yale Oriental Researches Ser.: No. VI). 1919. 28.50x (ISBN 0-685-69801-7). Elliots Bks.

--Epics, Hymns, Omens & Other Texts. LC 78-63519. (Babylonian Records in the Library of J. Pierpont Morgan: 4). Repr. of 1923 ed. 30.00 (ISBN 0-404-60124-3). AMS Pr.

--A Hebrew Deluge Story in Cuneiform. LC 78-63549. (Yale Oriental Ser. Researches: No. 5, Pt. 3). Repr. of 1922 ed. 20.00 (ISBN 0-404-60275-4). AMS Pr.

--Hebrew Deluge Story in Cuneiform. (Yale Oriental Researches Ser.: No. V, Pt. III). 1922. 19.50x (ISBN 0-685-69802-5). Elliots Bks.

--Legal Documents from Erech, Dated in the Seleucid Era (312-65 B.C.) LC 78-63517. (Babylonian Records in the Library of J. Pierpont Morgan: 2). Repr. of 1913 ed. 34.50 (ISBN 0-404-60122-7). AMS Pr.

--Letters & Transactions from Cappadocia. LC 78-63523. (Babylonian Inscriptions in the Collection of James B. Nies: 4). Repr. of 1927 ed. 30.00 (ISBN 0-404-60134-0). AMS Pr.

--Miscellaneous Inscriptions in the Yale Babylonian Collection. LC 78-63530. (Yale Oriental Series: Babylonian Texts: No. 1). (Illus.). 232p. Repr. of 1915 ed. 42.00 (ISBN 0-404-60251-7). AMS Pr.

--Neo-Babylonian Letters from Erech. LC 78-63532. (Yale Oriental Series: Babylonian Texts: No. 3). (Illus.). 184p. Repr. of 1920 ed. 35.00 (ISBN 0-404-60253-3). AMS Pr.

--Neo-Babylonian Letters From Erech. 1920. 22.50x (ISBN 0-686-83634-0). Elliots Bks.

--The Origin of Biblical Tradition. LC 78-63556. (Yale Oriental Ser. Researches: No. 12). Repr. of 1923 ed. 37.50 (ISBN 0-404-60282-7). AMS Pr.

--Personal Names from Cuneiform Inscriptions of the Cassite Period. LC 78-63543. (Yale Oriental Ser. Researches: No. I). Repr. of 1912 ed. 37.50 (ISBN 0-404-60271-1). AMS Pr.

Clay, Albert T. see Grice, Ettalene M.

Clay, Anthony, jt. auth. see Marchington, John.

Clay, Brenda J. Pinikindu: Maternal Nurture, Paternal Substance. LC 76-8083. (Illus.). 1977. lib. bdg. 14.00x (ISBN 0-226-10943-7). U of Chicago Pr.

Clay, C. H. & Kovari, J., eds. Inland Aquaculture Engineering: Lectures Presented at the ADCP Inter-regional Training Course in Inland Aquaculture Engineering, Budapest, 6 June - 3 September 1983. 591p. 1985. pap. 23.80 (ISBN 92-5-102168-6, F2729, FAO). Unipub.

Clay, Cassius M. Life of Cassius Marcellus Clay. LC 75-89028. Repr. of 1886 ed 19.75x (ISBN 0-8371-1907-3, CLL&, Pub. by Negro U Pr). Greenwood.

--Writings of Cassius Marcellus Clay: Including Speeches & Addresses. Greeley, Horace, ed. LC 70-82185. (Anti-Slavery Crusade in America Ser). 1969. Repr. of 1848 ed. 24.50 (ISBN 0-405-00634-9). Ayer Co Pubs.

--Writings of Cassius Marcellus Clay, Including Speeches & Addresses. Greeley, Horace, ed. & pref. by. LC 75-90130. Repr. of 1848 ed. 19.75x (ISBN 0-8371-1993-6, CLW&). Greenwood.

Clay, Catherine L. Escape from Eden: A Novel. LC 77-77112. 232p. 1981. 10.50 (ISBN 0-86533-005-0). Bk Pools.

Clay, Charles & Wheble, Bernard. Modern Merchant Banking: A Guide to the Workings of the Accepting Houses of the City of London & Their Services to Industry & Commerce. 2nd ed. LC 83-14777. 150p. 1983. 19.75 (ISBN 0-85941-216-4). Woodhead-Faulkner.

Clay, Charlotte N. The Role of Anxiety in English Tragedy, 1580-1642. (Salzburg Studies in English Literature, Jacobean Drama Studies: No. 23). 1974. pap. text ed. 25.50x (ISBN 0-391-01343-2). Humanities.

Clay, Clarence S. & Medwin, Herman. Acoustical Oceanography: Principles & Applications. LC 77-1133. (Ocean Engineering Ser.). 544p. 1977. text ed. 59.95x (ISBN 0-471-16041-5, Pub. by Wiley-Interscience). Wiley.

Clay, Diskin. Lucretius & Epicurus. LC 83-45142. 384p. 1983. 39.50x (ISBN 0-8014-1559-4). Cornell U Pr.

Clay, Diskin, tr. see Sophocles.

Clay, E. J. & Schaffer, B. B. Room for Manoeuvre. LC 84-5631. 210p. 1984. 27.50 (ISBN 0-8386-3243-2). Fairleigh Dickinson.

Clay, E. Jefferson. Aces Wild. Bd. with Badge for Brazos. 1980. pap. 2.25 (ISBN 0-505-51470-2, Pub. by Tower BKs). Dorchester Pub Co.

--Adios, Bandido! Bd. with Desparados on the Loose. 1980. pap. 2.25 (ISBN 0-505-51459-1, Pub. by Tower Bks). Dorchester Pub Co.

Clay, Edith. Lady Blessington at Naples. 1979. 12.50 (ISBN 0-241-89975-3, Pub. by Hamish Hamilton England). David & Charles.

Clay, Edward, et al. Food Policy Issues in Low-Income Countries. (Working Paper: No. 473). vii, 115p. 1981. pap. 5.00 (ISBN 0-686-39742-8, WP-0473). World Bank.

Clay, Floyd M. Coozan Dudley LeBlanc: From Huey Long to Hadacol. LC 73-14609. (Illus.). 264p. 1974. 15.00 (ISBN 0-911116-69-9). Pelican.

Clay, Grady. Alleys: A Hidden Resource. 59p. 1978. pap. 8.00 (ISBN 0-318-13110-2). Am Plan Assn.

--Close-up: How to Read the American City. LC 79-26307. (Illus.). 1980. pap. 9.95 (ISBN 0-226-10945-3, P863, Phoen). U of Chicago Pr.

--Close-Up: How to Read the American City. 192p. pap. 6.95 (ISBN 0-318-12948-5). Am Plan Assn.

Clay, Henry. Lord Norman. Wilkins, Mira, ed. LC 78-3906. (International Finance Ser.). (Illus.). 1978. Repr. of 1957 ed. lib. bdg. 43.00x (ISBN 0-405-11211-4). Ayer Co Pubs.

--The Papers of Henry Clay, Vol. 2. Hopkins, James F. & Hargreaves, Mary W. M., eds. LC 59-13605. pap. 160.00 (ISBN 0-317-26735-3, 2024359). Bks Demand UMI.

--Private Correspondence of Henry Clay. facsimile ed. Colton, Calvin, ed. LC 78-169756. (Select Bibliographies Reprint Ser). Repr. of 1855 ed. 35.50 (ISBN 0-8369-5976-0). Ayer Co Pubs.

Clay, Henry & Mallory, Daniel. The Life & Speeches of the Hon. Henry Clay. 47.00 (ISBN 0-8369-6983-9, 7861). Ayer Co Pubs.

Clay, Henry, II. The Papers of Henry Clay, 8 vols. Hopkins, James F. & Hargreaves, Mary W., eds. Incl. Vol. 1. The Rising Statesman, 1797-1814. 1060p. 1959 (ISBN 0-8131-0051-8); Vol. 2. The Rising Statesman, 1815-1820. 952p. 1961 (ISBN 0-8131-0052-6); Vol. 3. Presidential Candidate, 1821-1824. 944p. 1963 (ISBN 0-8131-0053-4); Vol. 4. Secretary of State, 1825. 1004p. 1972 (ISBN 0-8131-0054-2); Vol. 5. Secretary of State, 1826. 1104p. 1973 (ISBN 0-8131-0055-0); Vol. 6. Secretary of State, 1827. 1456p. 1981 (ISBN 0-8131-0056-9); Vol. 7. Secretary of State, 1828-1829. 792p, 1982 (ISBN 0-8131-0057-7); Vol. 8. Candidate, Compromiser, Whig, March 5, 1829 to December31, 1836. 1984 (ISBN 0-8131-0058-5). LC 59-13605. 40.00x ea. U Pr of Ky.

Clay, Horace F. & Hubbard, James C. Tropical Shrubs. LC 77-7363. (Hawaii Garden Ser: No. 2). (Illus.). 312p. 1977. 40.00 (ISBN 0-8248-0466-X). UH Pr.

Clay, J. Randolph, tr. see Casati, Gaetano.

Clay, Jack, jt. auth. see Anderson, Ken.

Clay, James W., et al, eds. North Carolina Atlas: Portrait of a Changing Southern State. LC 75-6984. xi, 331p. 1975. 8.95 (ISBN 0-8078-1244-7). U of NC Pr.

Clay, Jean. Romanticism. Wheeler, Dan, tr. from Fr. (Illus.). 320p. 1981. 60.00 (ISBN 0-86565-012-8). Vendome.

Clay, Jenny S. The Wrath of Athena: Gods & Men in the Odyssey. LC 83-2996. 240p. 1983. 27.50x (ISBN 0-691-06574-8). Princeton U Pr.

Clay, Katherine, ed. Microcomputers in Education: A Handbook of Resources. LC 82-12596. 80p. 1982. pap. 27.50 (ISBN 0-89774-064-5). Oryx Pr.

Clay, Lucius D. Decision in Germany. LC 72-110045. Repr. of 1950 ed. lib. bdg. 22.50x (ISBN 0-8371-4427-2, CLDG). Greenwood.

Clay, Marie. Stones: Concepts About Print Test. (Orig.). 1980. pap. text ed. 2.50x (ISBN 0-86863-268-6, 00556). Heinemann Ed.

Clay, Marie, jt. auth. see Butler, Dorothy.

Clay, Marie M. Early Detection of Reading Difficulties. 2nd ed. 1980. pap. text ed. 10.00x (ISBN 0-86863-253-8, 00557). Heinemann Ed.

--Observing Young Readers: Selected Papers. LC 82-12047. 256p. 1982. text ed. 15.00x (ISBN 0-435-08200-0); pap. text ed. 10.00x (ISBN 0-435-08208-6). Heinemann Ed.

--Reading: The Patterning of Complex Behaviour. 2nd ed. 1980. pap. text ed. 11.50x (ISBN 0-86863-251-1, 00558). Heinemann Ed.

--Sand: The Concepts about Print Test. 1972. pap. text ed. 2.50x (ISBN 0-435-80237-2). Heinemann Ed.

--What Did I Write? LC 79-17088. 1975. pap. text ed. 6.00x (ISBN 0-435-01120-0). Heinemann Ed.

Clay, Marie M., et al. Record of Oral Language & Biks & Gutches. (Illus.). 91p. (Orig.). 1983. pap. text ed. 7.50x (ISBN 0-86863-269-4, 00571). Heinemann Ed.

Clay, N. L. The Narrative Art in Verse. 1973. lib. bdg. 10.00 (ISBN 0-8414-3041-1). Folcroft.

Clay, N. L., ed. see Austen, Jane.

Clay, N. L., ed. see Bronte, Emily.

Clay, N. L., ed. see Conrad, Joseph.

Clay, N. L., ed. see Dickens, Charles.

Clay, N. L., ed. see Eliot, George.

Clay, N. L., ed. see Swift, Jonathan.

Clay, Patrick. Firebolt. (Sargeant Hawk Ser.: No. 5). 240p. (Orig.). 1982. pap. 2.25 (ISBN 0-8439-1169-7, Leisure Bks). Dorchester Pub Co.

--The Return of Sgt. Hawk. (Sgt. Hawk Ser.: No. 2). 1980. pap. 1.95 (ISBN 0-8439-0845-9, Pub. by Nordon Pubns). Dorchester Pub Co.

--Sgt. Hawk. 1979. pap. 1.75 (ISBN 0-8439-0640-5, Leisure Bks). Dorchester Pub Co.

Clay, Phillip L. Neighborhood Renewal: Trends & Strategies. LC 78-14153. 1979. 19.00 (ISBN 0-669-02681-6). Lexington Bks.

--Neighbourhood Renewal. 128p. 1979. 14.00 (ISBN 0-318-13119-6); 13.00 (ISBN 0-318-13120-X). Am Plan Assn.

Clay, Phillip L. & Hollister, Robert M., eds. Neighborhood Policy & Planning. (The Politics of Planning Ser.). 240p. 1983. 26.00 (ISBN 0-669-06302-9); pap. 11.00 (ISBN 0-669-06936-1). Lexington Bks.

Clay, Phyllis L. Single Parents & the Public Schools. 77p. 1981. pap. 4.25x (ISBN 0-934460-15-9). NCCE.

Clay, R. M. Mediaeval Hospitals of England. 357p. 1966. 30.00x (ISBN 0-7146-1292-8, F Cass Co). Biblio Dist.

Clay, Reginald S. & Court, T. H. The History of the Microscope. (Illus.). 60.00 (ISBN 0-87556-605-7). Saifer.

Clay, Reginald S. & Court, Thomas H. The History of the Microscope. LC 77-6994. 1977. Repr. of 1932 ed. lib. bdg. 30.00 (ISBN 0-89341-143-4). Longwood Pub Group.

Clay, Richard. Nonlinear Networks & Systems. LC 76-127660. (Illus.). pap. 74.00 (ISBN 0-317-09121-2, 2010179). Bks Demand UMI.

Clay, Robin. Teach Yourself Backgammon. (Teach Yourself Ser.). (Illus.). 1978. pap. 3.95 (ISBN 0-679-10241-8). McKay.

Clay, Rotha M. Hermits & Anchorites of England. LC 68-21759. (Illus.). 1968. Repr. of 1914 ed. 40.00x (ISBN 0-8103-3424-0). Gale.

Clay, Sampson. The Present Day Rock Garden. LC 76-1833. (Illus.). 1976. Repr. of 1937 ed. 25.00 (ISBN 0-913728-09-8). Theophrastus.

Clay, Susan & Brooks, JoeAnn. Software Primer: Computer Accounting. Harper, Larry D., ed. LC 83-82214. (Software Primer Ser.). 180p. 1984. binder cancelled (ISBN 0-913871-04-4). JNZ.

Clay, Thomas. Briefe, Easie & Necessary Tables for the Valuation of Leases. LC 76-57373. (English Experience Ser.: No. 791). 1977. Repr. of 1622 ed. lib. bdg. 8.00 (ISBN 90-221-0791-4). Walter J Johnson.

Clay, Vidals. Women: Menopause & Middle Age. 1977. perfect bdg. 5.00 (ISBN 0-912786-37-X). Know Inc.

Clay, Walter L. Our Convict System. LC 83-49252. (Crime & Punishment in England, 1850-1922 Ser.). 223p. 1984. lib. bdg. 30.00 (ISBN 0-8240-6207-8). Garland Pub.

--Prison Chaplin: Memoirs of the Rev. John Clay with Selections from His Reports & Correspondence & a Sketch of Prison Discipline in England. LC 69-16232. (Criminology, Law Enforcement, & Social Problems Ser.: No. 90). (Index added). 1969. Repr. of 1861 ed. 25.00 (ISBN 0-87585-090-1). Patterson Smith.

Clay, William C., Jr. The Dow Jones-Irwin Guide to Estate Planning. 6th ed. LC 84-71303. 166p. postponed 14.95 (ISBN 0-87094-571-8). Dow Jones-Irwin.

Clay, William C., Jr., jt. auth. see Martin, Gerald D.

Clay, William L., Sr. To Kill or Not to Kill: Thoughts on Capital Punishment. (Great Issues of the Day Ser.: No. 4). 144p. 1985. lib. bdg. 16.95x (ISBN 0-89370-331-1); pap. text ed. 8.95x (ISBN 0-89370-431-8). Borgo Pr.

Claybrook, Billy G. File Management Techniques. 247p. 1983. text ed. 28.95 (ISBN 0-471-04596-9). Assn Inform & Image Mgmt.

--File Management Techniques. 247p. 1983. 28.95 (ISBN 0-471-04596-9). Wiley.

Claybrook, Joan & Public Citizen Staff. Retreat from Safety: Reagan's Attack on America's Health. 1984. pap. 8.95 (ISBN 0-394-72244-2). Pantheon.

Clayburn, Barbara B. Prairie Stationmaster: The Story of One Man's Railroading Career in Nebraska 1917-1963. LC 78-78305. (Illus.). 128p. 1979. 6.50 (ISBN 0-8187-0034-3). Harlo Pr.

Claycomb. Arkansas Corporations: Formation with Forms. incl. latest pocket part supplement 39.95 (ISBN 0-686-90146-0); separate pocket part supplement, 1982 7.45 (ISBN 0-686-90147-9). Harrison Co GA.

Claycomb, Mary. Brain Research & Learning. pap. 20.00 (ISBN 0-317-30392-9, 2024754). Bks Demand UMI.

Claycombe, W. Wayne, jt. auth. see Sullivan, William F.

Claycombe, William W. & Sullivan, William G. Foundations of Mathematical Programming. (Illus.). 304p. 1975. 24.95 (ISBN 0-87909-282-3). Reston.

Clayden, P. W. The Early Life of Samuel Rogers. 1977. Repr. lib. bdg. 30.00 (ISBN 0-8492-3820-X). R West.

--The Early Life of Samuel Rogers. 461p. 1983. Repr. of 1887 ed. lib. bdg. 50.00 (ISBN 0-8495-0960-2). Arden Lib.

--England Under Lord Beaconfield. 550p. 1984. Repr. of 1880 ed. 49.00x (ISBN 0-85546-165-9, Pub. by Richmond Pub England). State Mutual Bk.

Claydon, Graham. Time with God: How to Improve Your Daily Devotions. 48p. (Orig.). 1982. mass market 1.95 (ISBN 0-310-45202-3). Zondervan.

Claydon, L., ed. Rousseau. 1969. pap. text ed. 1.95x (ISBN 0-02-972580-1). Macmillan.

Claydon, Leslie, et al. Curriculum & Culture: Schooling in a Pluralist Society. LC 77-78551. 1978. pap. text ed. 8.95x (ISBN 0-86861-032-1). Allen Unwin.

Clayes, Stanley A. Drama & Discussion. 2nd ed. (Illus.). 1978. pap. text ed. 19.95 (ISBN 0-13-219030-3). P-H.

Clayman. Dukes of Hazzard. (TV & Movie Tie-ins Ser.). (Illus.). 32p. (gr. 4-12). 1985. 7.95 (ISBN 0-317-31171-9). Creative Ed.

Clayman, Henry. The Surgeon's Guide to Intraocular Lens Implantation. LC 84-50461. 176p. 1985. text ed. 49.50 (ISBN 0-943432-26-X). Slack Inc.

Clayman, Henry M., et al. Intraocular Lens Implantation: Techniques & Complications. LC 82-8267. (Illus.). 300p. 1983. text ed. 64.95 (ISBN 0-8016-1080-X). Mosby.

Claypole, William & Robottom, John. Caribbean Story, Bks. 1 & 2. (Longman Caribbean Ser.). (Illus., Orig.). 1981. Bk. 1, Foundations. pap. text ed. 7.95x (ISBN 0-582-76534-X); Bk. 2, The Inheritors. pap. text ed. 7.95x (ISBN 0-582-76533-1). Longman.

Claypool, Bob. Saturday Night at Gilley's. (Illus.). 1980. write for info. Delilah Bks.

Claypool, Gavin, ed. see Pournelle, Jerry.

Claypool, Jane. Alcohol & You. LC 80-25660. (Impact Bks.). (Illus.). 1981. 9.90 (ISBN 0-531-04259-6). Watts.

--Food Trips & Traps. (Single Titles Ser.). 96p. (YA) (gr. 7 up). lib. bdg. 8.90 (ISBN 0-531-04664-8). Watts.

--How to Get a Good Job. (Triumph Bks.). (Illus.). 96p. (gr. 7 up). 1982. PLB 8.90 (ISBN 0-531-04493-9). Watts.

--Jasmine Finds Love. LC 82-13633. (A Hiway-Floweromance Bk.: A High Interest-Low Reading Level Book). 80p. (gr. 7-10). 1982. 8.95 (ISBN 0-664-32699-4). Westminster.

--A Love For Violet. LC 82-10980. (A Hiway-Floweromance Bk.: A High Interest-Low Reading Level Book). 76p. (gr. 7-10). 1982. 8.95 (ISBN 0-664-32697-8). Westminster.

--Manufacturing. (First Bks.). (Illus.). 72p. 1984. lib. bdg. 8.90 (ISBN 0-531-04825-X). Watts.

--Unemployment. (Impact Ser.). 96p. (gr. 7 up). 1983. PLB 9.90 (ISBN 0-531-04586-2). Watts.

--Why Do Some People Get Fat? (Creative's Little Question Books). (Illus.). 32p. (gr. 3-4). 1982. lib. bdg. 6.95 (ISBN 0-87191-898-6). Creative Ed.

--The Worker in America. (Issues in American History Ser.). 128p. (gr. 7 up). 1984. PLB 9.90 (ISBN 0-531-04929-9). Watts.

Claypool, John. Glad Reunion. 144p. 1985. 8.95 (ISBN 0-8499-0469-2, 0469-2). Word Bks.

--The Light Within You: Looking at Life Through New Eyes. 1983. 9.95 (ISBN 0-8499-0273-8). Word Bks.

Claypool, John R. Opening Blind Eyes. Raines, Robert A., ed. 128p. 1983. 10.95 (ISBN 0-687-29213-1). Abingdon.

--The Preaching Event. 1980. 6.95 (ISBN 0-8499-0131-6). Word Bks.

--Tracks of a Fellow Struggler. LC 73-91553. 1976. pap. 5.95 Gift Edition (ISBN 0-8499-0324-6). Word Bks.

Claypoole, James. James Claypoole's Letter Book: London & Philadelphia, 1681-1684. Balderston, Marion, ed. LC 66-25063. 256p. 1967. 10.00 (ISBN 0-87328-027-X). Huntington Lib.

Claypool-Miner, Jane. A Day at a Time. (Crisis Ser.). (gr. 7-12). 1982. pap. 4.64 (ISBN 0-8224-1651-4). Pitman Learning.

--Miracle of Time. (Crisis Ser.). (gr. 7-12). 1982. pap. 4.64 (ISBN 0-8224-1652-2). Pitman Learning.

--Mountain Fear. (Crisis Ser.). (gr. 7-12). 1982. pap. 4.64 (ISBN 0-8224-1653-0). Pitman Learning.

--New Beginning. (Crisis Ser.). (gr. 7-12). 1982. pap. 4.64 (ISBN 0-8224-1654-9). Pitman Learning.

--She's My Sister. (Crisis Ser.). (gr. 7-12). 1982. pap. 4.64 (ISBN 0-8224-1655-7). Pitman Learning.

--Split Decision. (Crisis Ser.). (gr. 7-12). 1982. pap. 4.64 (ISBN 0-8224-1656-5); 25.44 (ISBN 0-8224-1650-6). Pitman Learning.

Clayre, Alasdair. The Heart of the Dragon. (Illus.). 304p. 1985. 29.95 (ISBN 0-395-35336-X). HM.

Clayre, Alasdair, ed. Nature & Industrialization. (Illus.). 1977. pap. 10.95x (ISBN 0-19-871097-6). Oxford U Pr.

--The Political Economy of the Third Sector: Co-Operation & Participation. 1980. 29.95x (ISBN 0-19-877137-1); 15.95x (ISBN 0-19-877138-X). Oxford U Pr.

Clayson, Rodman R. Egypt's Ancient Heritage. 3rd ed. LC 78-146589. 1977. 12.50 (ISBN 0-912057-25-4, G634). AMORC.

Clayton. No Second Class Christians. LC 76-8558. pap. 1.25 (ISBN 0-8054-5240-0). Broadman.

Clayton, Aileen. The Enemy is Listening. (Ballantine Espionage Intelligence Library: No. 22). 416p. 1982. pap. 3.95 (ISBN 0-345-30250-8). Ballantine.

Clayton, Alfred S. Emergent Mind & Education: A Study of George H. Mead's Bio-Social Behaviorism from an Educational Point of View. LC 70-176694. (Columbia University. Teachhers College. Contributions to Education: No. 867). Repr. of 1943 ed. 22.50 (ISBN 0-404-55867-4). AMS Pr.

Clayton, Anthony. Communication for New Loyalties: African Soldiers' Songs. LC 78-17653. (Papers in International Studies: Africa Ser.: No. 34). (Illus.). 1978. pap. 6.00x (ISBN 0-89680-069-5, 82-91858, Ohio U Ctr Intl). Ohio U Pr.

--Communication for New Loyalties: African Soldier's Songs. (Papers in International Studies: Africa Ser.: No. 34). pap. 20.00 (ISBN 0-317-09667-2, 2007851). Bks Demand UMI.

--The Zanzibar Revolution & Its Aftermath. (Illus.). 1981. 22.50 (ISBN 0-208-01925-1, Archon). Shoe String.

Clayton, Anthony & Savage, Donald C. Government & Labour in Kenya, 1895-1963. 480p. 1974. 38.50x (ISBN 0-7146-3025-X, F Cass Co). Biblio Dist.

Clayton, B. R. & Bishop, R. E. Mechanics of Marine Vehicles. LC 82-81291. 598p. 1982. 55.50x (ISBN 0-87201-897-0). Gulf Pub.

Clayton, Barbara & Whitley, Kathleen. Exploring Coastal Massachusetts. (Illus.). 1983. pap. 14.95 (ISBN 0-396-08131-2). Dodd.

--Exploring Coastal New England: Gloucester to Kennebunkport. LC 79-624. (Illus.). 1979. pap. 9.95 (ISBN 0-396-07698-X). Dodd.

--Guide to New Bedford. (Illus.). 192p. pap. 4.95 (ISBN 0-87106-035-3). Globe Pequot.

Clayton, Bernard. The Breads of France. LC 77-94452. (Illus.). 1978. pap. 8.95 (ISBN 0-672-52693-X). Bobbs.

Clayton, Bernard, Jr. The Complete Book of Breads. 1974. 18.95 (ISBN 0-671-21548-5). S&S.

--The Complete Book of Pastry: Sweet & Savory. (Illus.). 1981. 17.95 (ISBN 0-671-24276-8). S&S.

--The Complete Book of Pastry: Sweet & Savory. (Illus.). 416p. 1984. pap. 9.95 (ISBN 0-671-53074-7, Fireside). S&S.

--The Complete Book of Soups & Stews. (Illus.). 416p. 1984. 17.95 (ISBN 0-671-43863-8). S&S.

Clayton, Bob. Outstanding Black Collegians, 1982. 100p. 1982. 54.95 (ISBN 0-686-36273-X). Ebonics.

Clayton, Bruce. Fallout Survival: A Guide to Radiological Defense. (Illus.). 180p. (Orig.). 1984. pap. 12.00 (ISBN 0-87364-280-5). Paladin Pr.

--Forgotten Prophet: The Life of Randolph Bourne. LC 84-5748. 275p. 1984. text ed. 25.00x (ISBN 0-8071-1169-4). La State U Pr.

--Life after Doomsday. (Illus.). 200p. 1980. 19.95 (ISBN 0-87364-175-2). Paladin Pr.

--Survival Books, Nineteen Eighty-One. LC 81-80117. (Illus.). 180p. (Orig.). 1981. pap. 14.95 (ISBN 0-939216-00-0). Media West.

--Thinking about Survival. (Illus.). 144p. (Orig.). 1984. pap. 10.00 (ISBN 0-87364-293-7). Paladin Pr.

Clayton, Bruce, jt. auth. see Clayton, Mary Ellen.

Clayton, Bruce D. Life after Doomsday: A Survivalist Guide to Nuclear War & Other Disasters. (Illus.). 192p. 1981. pap. 8.95 (ISBN 0-385-27148-4, Dial). Doubleday.

--Mosby's Handbook of Pharmacology in Nursing. 3rd ed. (Illus.). 560p. 1984. pap. text ed. 14.95 (ISBN 0-8016-4243-4). Mosby.

Clayton, Bruce D., jt. auth. see Ryan, Sheila A.

Clayton, Bruce D., jt. auth. see Squire, Jessie.

Clayton, C. Sing a Song of Gladness. (Arch Bk.). (Illus.). 32p. (gr. k-4). 1974. pap. 0.99 (ISBN 0-570-06087-7, 59-1302). Concordia.

Clayton, C. G., ed. Modern Developments in Flow Measurement: Proceedings of the International Conference Held at Harwell, 21st-23rd September, 1971. LC 73-173002. (PPL Conference Publication Ser.: No. 10). (Illus.). pap. 103.80 (ISBN 0-317-09262-6, 2011896). Bks Demand UMI.

--Nuclear Geophysics: Selected Papers on Applications of Nuclear Techniques in Minerals Exploration, Mining & Process Control. (Illus.). 500p. 1983. 60.00 (ISBN 0-08-029158-9, 82-24570). Pergamon.

Clayton, C. R. & Preece, C. M., eds. Corrosion of Metal Processed by Directed Energy Beams: Proceedings TMS-AIME Fall Meeting, Louisville, KY, 1981. (Illus.). 163p. 36.00 (ISBN 0-89520-393-6); members 24.00 (ISBN 0-317-36300-X); student 12.00 (ISBN 0-317-36301-8). ASM.

Clayton, C. R., ed. see TMS-AIME Fall Meeting, Louisville, Kentucky, Oct. 14-15, 1981.

Clayton, Candyce. At the Barre. Perlman, James, ed. LC 77-89854. (Orig.). 1977. pap. 2.50 (ISBN 0-930100-00-X). Holy Cow.

Clayton, Charles C. Little Mack: Joseph B. McCullagh of the St. Louis Globe Democrat. LC 75-76186. (New Horizons in Journalism Ser.). (Illus.). 344p. 1969. 8.95x (ISBN 0-8093-0399-X). S Ill U Pr.

Clayton, Christopher, et al. Site Investigation: A Handbook for Engineers. LC 81-21973. 448p. 1982. 54.95x (ISBN 0-470-27328-3). Halsted Pr.

Clayton, Dean. One Hundred One Typewriting Time Writings with Selected Drills. (gr. 9-12). 1980. text ed. 5.45 (ISBN 0-538-20180-0, T18). SW Pub.

--T-Shirt Factory: A Typewriting Simulation. (YA) (gr. 9-12). 1982. text ed. 3.95 wkbk. (ISBN 0-538-11700-1, K70). SW Pub.

Clayton, Dean & Fries, Albert C. Timed Writings about Careers. 3rd ed. 1985. pap. 5.35 (ISBN 0-538-20790-6, T79). SW Pub.

Clayton, Derek. Running to the Top. LC 79-64297. (Illus.). 160p. 1980. pap. 5.95 (ISBN 0-89037-212-8). Anderson World.

Clayton, Donald D. Principles of Stellar Evolution & Nucleosynthesis. LC 83-5106. (Illus.). xii, 612p. 1984. 37.00x (ISBN 0-226-10952-6); pap. 17.00x (ISBN 0-226-10953-4). U of Chicago Pr.

Clayton, E. & Petry, F. Monitoring Systems for Agricultural & Rural Development Projects, 2 vols. (Economic & Social Development Papers: No. 12). 269p. (Eng. & Fr., 2nd Printing 1983). 1981. pap. 17.50 (ISBN 92-5-101071-4, F2195, FAO); pap. 16.50 (ISBN 9-2510-1358-6). Unipub.

Clayton, Ed. Martin Luther King: The Peaceful Warrior. (gr. 4-6). 1969. pap. 1.75 (ISBN 0-671-42686-9). Archway.

Clayton, Edward R., jt. auth. see Moore, Laurence.

Clayton, Edward T. Negro Politician. 1964. 4.95 (ISBN 0-87485-008-8). Johnson Chi.

Clayton, Ellen. English Female Artists, 2 vols. 1976. lib. bdg. 250.00 (ISBN 0-8490-1774-2). Gordon Pr.

Clayton, Ellen C. Queens of Song: Being Memoirs of Some of the Most Celebrated Female Vocalists. facsimile ed. LC 77-38713. (Essay Index Reprint Ser). Repr. of 1865 ed. 30.00 (ISBN 0-8369-2640-4). Ayer Co Pubs.

Clayton, F. E., jt. auth. see Clayton, G. D.

Clayton, Florence, jt. auth. see Clayton, George D.

Clayton, Florence E., jt. auth. see Clayton, George D.

Clayton, Florence E. see Clayton, George D.

Clayton, Florence E., jt. ed. see Clayton, George D.

Clayton, G. Operational Amplifiers. 2nd ed. 1979. text ed. 39.95 (ISBN 0-408-00370-7). Butterworth.

Clayton, G. B. Data Converters. 238p. 1982. 29.95x (ISBN 0-470-27321-6). Halsted Pr.

Clayton, G. D. & Clayton, F. E. Pattys Industrial Hygiene & Toxicology, 4 vols. 3rd ed. 937p. 1981. 85.00 (ISBN 0-471-08431-X). Wiley.

Clayton, Gary E. & Spivey, Christopher B. The Time Value of Money: Worked & Solved Problems. LC 77-11332. (Illus.). 160p. 1978. pap. text ed. 13.95x (ISBN 0-7216-2602-5). Dryden Pr.

Clayton, George D. & Clayton, Florence E. Patty's Industrial Hygiene & Toxicology: General Principles, Vol. 1. 3rd rev. ed. LC 77-17515. 1978. 148.00 (ISBN 0-471-16046-6, Pub. by Wiley-Interscience). Wiley.

--Patty's Industrial Hygiene & Toxicology, Vol. 2C. 3rd. rev. ed. 1296p. 1982. 127.00 (ISBN 0-471-09258-4, Pub. by Wiley-Interscience). Wiley.

Clayton, George D. & Clayton, Florence. Patty's Industrial Hygiene & Toxicology: Toxicology, Vol. IIA. 3rd rev. ed. LC 77-17515. 1420p. 1981. 140.00 (ISBN 0-471-16042-3, Pub. by Wiley Interscience). Wiley.

Clayton, George D., ed. Patty's Industrial Hygiene & Toxicology: Vol. 2, Toxicology, 3 Pts. 3rd ed. Clayton, Florence E. 3300p. Pt. A. 125.00 (ISBN 0-317-36217-8, Pub. by Wiley-Interscience); Pt. B. 90.00 (ISBN 0-317-36218-6); Pt. C. 115.00 (ISBN 0-317-36219-4). Am Indus Hygiene.

Clayton, George D. & Clayton, Florence E., eds. Patty's Industrial Hygiene & Toxicology, 5 pts. 3rd ed. 1983. Set. 515.00 (ISBN 0-471-87350-0). Wiley.

Clayton, George T. The Site Plan for Architectural Working Drawings. (Illus.). 42p. 1973. pap. text ed. 3.00X (ISBN 0-87563-252-1). Stipes.

Clayton, Giles. Approved Order of Martiall Dicipline, with Every Particular Offycer His Offyce & Dutie. LC 73-6114. (English Experience Ser.: No. 581). 84p. 1973. Repr. of 1591 ed. 9.50 (ISBN 90-221-0581-4). Walter J Johnson.

Clayton, Hazel, et al. A Poet Black. Knight, Leon, ed. 66p. 1982. pap. 3.50 (ISBN 0-940248-11-5). Guild Pr.

--Being Black. LC 81-82051. (Illus.). 60p. (Orig.). 1981. pap. 3.50 (ISBN 0-940248-04-2). Guild Pr.

Clayton, Hugh. Royal Faces: Nine Hundred Years of British Monarchy. LC 82-80980. (Illus.). 1982. 14.95 (ISBN 0-500-01287-3). Thames Hudson.

Clayton, Irene, jt. auth. see Schmottlach, Neil.

Clayton, J. Introduction to Statistics: A Linguistic Approach. 2nd ed. 1984. 6.25 (ISBN 0-931021-00-6). Hurd Comm.

--Irsud. (Science Fiction Ser.). (Orig.). 1981. pap. 2.50 (ISBN 0-87997-839-2, UE 1839). DAW Bks.

Clayton, J. P., jt. auth. see Sykes, S. W.

Clayton, James E., ed. see Barth, Alan.

Clayton, James L. Does Defense Beggar Welfare: Myths vs. Realities. 71p. 1979. pap. text ed. 3.95 (ISBN 0-87855-802-0). Transaction Bks.

--On the Brink: Defense, Deficits & Welfare Spending. LC 83-23052. (Orig.). 1984. 8.95 (ISBN 0-915071-01-0). Ramapo Pr.

Clayton, Jo. A Bait of Dreams: A Five-Summer Quest. 408p. 1985. pap. 3.50 (ISBN 0-88677-001-7). DAW Bks.

--Changer's Moon. (Duel of Sorcery Ser.: No. 3). 1985. pap. 3.50 (ISBN 0-88677-065-3). DAW Bks.

--Diadem from the Stars. (Science Fiction Ser.). 1977. pap. 2.50 (ISBN 0-87997-977-1, UE1520). DAW Bks.

--Ghosthunt. 192p. 1983. pap. 2.75 (ISBN 0-88677-015-7). DAW Bks.

--Lamarchos. (Science Fiction Ser.). 1981. pap. 2.50 (ISBN 0-87997-971-2, UE1627). DAW Bks.

--Maeve: A Novel of the Diadem. (Science Fiction Ser.). 1979. pap. 2.25 (ISBN 0-87997-760-4, UE1760). DAW Bks.

--Moongather. 240p. 1985. pap. 3.50 (ISBN 0-88677-072-6). DAW Bks.

--Moonscatter. 304p. 1985. pap. 3.50 (ISBN 0-88677-071-8). Daw Bks.

--The Nowhere Hunt. 1981. pap. 2.50 (ISBN 0-87997-874-0). DAW Bks.

--Snarls of Ibex. Date not set. pap. 2.95 (ISBN 0-87997-974-7). DAW Bks.

--Star Hunters. (Science Fiction Ser.). 1980. pap. 2.75 (ISBN 0-88677-014-9). DAW Bks.

Clayton, John. Reverend John Clayton: A Parson with a Scientific Mind. Berkeley, Edmund & Berkeley, Dorothy S., eds. LC 65-23459. (Virginia Historical Document: No. 6). (Illus.). 1965. 15.00x (ISBN 0-8139-0067-0). U Pr of Va.

Clayton, John J. Bodies of the Rich. LC 83-4873. (Illinois Short Fiction Ser.). 144p. 1984. pap. 11.95 (ISBN 0-252-01097-3). U of Ill Pr.

--The Heath Introduction to Fiction. 2nd ed. 820p. 1983. pap. text ed. 7.95 (ISBN 0-669-06444-0). Heath.

--Saul Bellow: In Defense of Man. 2nd ed. LC 78-19554. 352p. 1979. 20.00x (ISBN 0-253-14995-9). Ind U Pr.

Clayton, John L., ed. Heath Introduction to Fiction. 1977. pap. text ed. 6.95 (ISBN 0-669-99986-5). Heath.

Clayton, John P. The Concept of Correlation: Paul Tillich & the Possibility of a Mediating Theology. (Theologische Bibliothek Topelmann: No. 37). 427p. 1979. text ed. 33.60x (ISBN 3-11007-914-3). De Gruyter.

Clayton, Joseph D. The Ruger Number One Rifle. Amber, John T., ed. (Know Your Gun Ser.: No. 2). (Illus.). 212p. 1982. 39.95 (ISBN 0-941540-06-5). Blacksmith Corp.

Clayton, Joyce A., jt. auth. see Clayton, Robert D.

Clayton, Keith. An Introduction to Statistics for Psychology & Education. (No. 309). 448p. 1984. 22.95 (ISBN 0-675-20154-3); Additional supplements may be obtained from publisher. student guide 9.95 (ISBN 0-675-20258-2). Merrill.

Clayton, Keith, jt. auth. see Straw, Allan.

Clayton, Lawrence A. The Bolivarian Nations. (The World of Latin America Ser.). (Illus.). 102p. 1984. pap. text ed. 5.95 (ISBN 0-88273-603-5). Forum Pr IL.

--Caulkers & Carpenters in a New World: The Shipyards of Colonial Guayaquil. LC 80-11547. (Papers in International Studies: Latin America: No. 8). (Orig.). 1980. pap. 15.00x (ISBN 0-89680-103-9, 82-92591, Ohio U Ctr Intl). Ohio U Pr.

--Grace: W. R. Grace & Co., Eighteen Fifty to Nineteen Thirty. LC 85-14856. (Illus.). 400p. 1985. 22.50 (ISBN 0-915463-25-3, Dist. by Kampmann). Jameson Bks.

Clayton, Lawrence A. & Badger, R. Reid. Alabama & the Borderlands: From Prehistory to Statehood. LC 83-17957. (Illus.). 240p. 1985. 27.50 (ISBN 0-8173-0208-5). U of Ala Pr.

Clayton, Lloyd. Simple Guide to Medicinal Herbs. 1981. pap. 8.95x (ISBN 0-317-07279-X, Regent House). B of A.

Clayton, M. The Collector's Dictionary of the Silver & Gold of Great Britain & North America. 2nd ed. (Illus.). 1985. 89.50 (ISBN 0-907462-57-X). Antique Collect.

Clayton, Mary Ellen & Clayton, Bruce. Urban Alert! Emergency Survival for City Dwellers. (Illus.). 192p. 1982. 14.95 (ISBN 0-87364-246-5). Paladin Pr.

Clayton, Merle. Union Station Massacre. 1977. pap. 1.50 (ISBN 0-8439-0430-5, Leisure Bks). Dorchester Pub Co.

Clayton, Michael. Cutting the Cost of Energy: A Practical Guide for the Householder. LC 80-67579. (Illus.). 160p. 1981. 14.95 (ISBN 0-7153-7927-5). David & Charles.

--A Hunting We Will Go. write for info (ISBN 0-85131-178-4, NL51, Dist. by Miller). J A Allen.

--Jeep. (Illus.). 128p. 1982. 21.00 (ISBN 0-7153-8066-4). David & Charles.

Clayton, Michael F. & Scott, Preston T. Juvenile Justice in Virginia. xiv, 345p. 1982. 30.00 (ISBN 0-87215-584-6). Michie Co.

Clayton, Nanalee. Young Living. rev. ed. (Illus.). (gr. 7-8). 1983. text ed. 16.88 (ISBN 0-02-666440-2); tchr's. guide 11.20 (ISBN 0-02-666450-X); student ed. 5.32 (ISBN 0-02-666460-7). Bennett IL.

Clayton, P. The Filtration Efficiency of a Range of Filter Media for Sub-Micrometre Aerosols, 1978. 1981. 50.00x (ISBN 0-686-97079-6, Pub. by W Spring England). State Mutual Bk.

Clayton, P. & Wallin, S. C. An Environmental Study of an Activated Carbon Plant, 1978. 1981. 60.00x (ISBN 0-686-97068-3, Pub. by W Green England). State Mutual Bk.

Clayton, P., jt. auth. see Bailey, D. L.

Clayton, P., et al. An Investigation of the Lead Emissions from a Lead Works & Their Effect on Ambient Lead Concentrations, 1977. 1982. 50.00x (ISBN 0-686-97095-0, Pub. by W Spring England). State Mutual Bk.

Clayton, P. M. & Tiller, K. G. A Chemical Method for the Determination of the Heavy Metal Content of Soils in Environmental Studies. 1980. 20.00x (ISBN 0-643-00341-X, Pub. by CSJRO Australia). State Mutual Bk.

Clayton, Paula J. & Barrett, James E., eds. Treatment of Depression: Old Controversies & New Approaches. (American Psychopathological Association Ser.). 352p. 1983. text ed. 64.00 (ISBN 0-89004-745-6). Raven.

Clayton, Peter & Gammond, Peter. Fourteen Miles on a Clear Night. LC 78-5685. (Illus.). 1978. Repr. of 1966 ed. lib. bdg. 22.50x (ISBN 0-313-20475-6, CLFM). Greenwood.

Clayton, Peter, jt. auth. see Gammond, Peter.

Clayton, Peter, ed. A Companion to Roman Britain. 188p. 1980. 40.00x (ISBN 0-7148-2031-8, Pub. by Phaidon Pr). State Mutual Bk.

Clayton, Peter A., rev. by see Lurker, Manfred.

Clayton, Philip T., jt. auth. see Smolin, Pauline.

Clayton, Powell. Aftermath of the Civil War, in Arkansas. LC 79-89029. Repr. of 1915 ed. 25.00x (ISBN 0-8371-1820-4, CLA&, Pub. by Negro U Pr). Greenwood.

Clayton, R. B. see Colowick, Sidney P. & Kaplan, Nathan O.

Clayton, R. F. Monitoring of Radioactive Contamination on Surfaces. (Technical Reports Ser.: No. 120). (Illus.). 33p. (Orig.). 1970. pap. 7.50 (ISBN 92-0-125570-5, IDC120, IAEA). Unipub.

Clayton, R. K. Photosynthesis: Physical Mechanisms & Chemical Patterns. LC 79-27543. (IUPAB Biophysics Ser.: No. 4). 295p. 1981. 49.50 (ISBN 0-521-22300-8); pap. 16.95 (ISBN 0-521-29443-6). Cambridge U Pr.

Clayton, R. K. & Sistrom, W. R., eds. The Photosynthetic Bacteria. LC 78-2835. (Illus.). 968p. 1978. 115.00x (ISBN 0-306-31133-X, Plenum Pr). Plenum Pub.

Clayton, R. M. & Haywood, J., eds. Problems of Normal & Genetically Abnormal Retinas. 1983. 44.00 (ISBN 0-12-176180-0). Acad Pr.

Clayton, R. M. & Truman, D. E., eds. Stability & Switching in Cellular Differentiation. (Advances in Experimental Medicine & Biology: Vol. 158). 496p. 1982. 62.50x (ISBN 0-306-41181-4, Plenum Pr). Plenum Pub.

Clayton, R. R. & Preece, C. M., eds. Corrosion of Metals Processed by Directed Energy Beams. 163p. 1981. 36.00 (ISBN 0-89520-393-6); members 24.00 (ISBN 0-317-37204-1); student members 12.00 (ISBN 0-317-37205-X). Metal Soc.

Clayton, Richard R. Family Marriage & Social Change. 2nd ed. 1979. text ed. 23.95 (ISBN 0-669-01957-7); instr's manual 1.95 (ISBN 0-669-01956-9). Heath.

Clayton, Robert D. & Clayton, Joyce A. Concepts & Careers in Physical Education. 3rd ed. 174p. 1982. pap. text ed. 12.95x (ISBN 0-8087-2972-1). Burgess.

Clayton, Robert D., jt. auth. see Torney, John A., Jr.

Clayton, Sheryl H. Black Men Role Models of Greater St. Louis. 1983. 16.95 (ISBN 0-9607958-2-0); pap. 10.95 (ISBN 0-9607958-3-9). Essai Seay Pubns.

Clayton, Sheryl H., ed. Black Women Role Models of Greater St. Louis. LC 81-71873. 381p. (Orig.). (gr. 6 up). 1982. 14.95 (ISBN 0-9607958-0-4). Essai Seay Pubns.

Clayton, Stanley & Lewis, T. L. Gynecology by Ten Teachers. 13th ed. 396p. 1981. pap. text ed. 19.50 (ISBN 0-7131-4394-0). E Arnold.

Clayton, Stanley & Newton, John R. A Pocket Gynaecology. 10th ed. (Illus.). 1983. pap. text ed. 8.50 (ISBN 0-443-02402-2). Churchill.
--A Pocket Obstetrics. 10th ed. (Illus.). 1983. pap. text ed. 8.50 (ISBN 0-443-02401-4). Churchill.
Clayton, Thomas. The Cavalier Poets. (Standard Authors Ser.). 1978. pap. text ed. 6.95x (ISBN 0-19-281204-1). Oxford U Pr.
Clayton, Thomas H. Close to the Land: The Way We Lived in North Carolina, 1820-1870. Nathans, Sydney, ed. LC 82-20143. (The Way We Lived in North Carolina Ser.). (Illus.). viii, 98p. (gr. 8-12). 1983. 11.95 (ISBN 0-8078-1551-9); pap. 6.95 (ISBN 0-8078-4103-X). U of NC Pr.
Clayton, Victoria V. White & Black Under the Old Regime. facs. ed. LC 70-119928. (Select Bibliographies Reprint Ser). 1899. 18.00 (ISBN 0-8369-5371-1). Ayer Co Pubs.
Clayton, Vista. The Phantom Caravan or Abd el Kader, Emir of Algeria (1808-1883) LC 75-10617. 1975. 15.00 (ISBN 0-682-48263-3, University). Exposition Pr FL.
Clayton, W. E. Humidity Factors Affecting Storage & Handling of Fertilizers. Roth, B. N. & Frederick, E. D., eds. (Paper Ser.). (Illus., Orig.). 1984. pap. 4.00 (ISBN 0-88090-050-4). Intl Fertilizer.
--Review of the Fertilizer Distribution & Handling System in Bangladesh. (IFDC Miscellaneous Publication Ser. A-2). 1981. 10.00 (ISBN 0-686-95959-0). Intl Fertilizer.
Clayton, W. W. History of Davidson County, Tennessee. (Illus.). 1971. Repr. of 1880 ed. 85.00 (ISBN 0-918450-03-9). C Elder.
--History of Onondaga County, New York, Sixteen Fifteen to Eighteen Seventy-Eight. (Illus.). 430p. 1980. Repr. of 1878 ed. 27.50x (ISBN 0-931308-03-8). Molly Yes.
Clayton, William. The Latter-Day Saints' Emigrants' Guide. Kimball, Stanley B. & Allen, James B., eds. LC 83-2473. (Illus.). vi, 111p. 1983. 12.95 (ISBN 0-935284-27-3); pap. 8.95 (ISBN 0-935284-36-2). Patrice Pr.
--The Latter-Day Saints' Emigrants Guide: Being A Table of Distances Showing All the Springs, Creeks, Hills, Mountains, Camping Places, & All Other Notable Places from Council Bluffs to the Valley of the Great Salt Lake. 24p. 1973. pap. 3.95 (ISBN 0-87770-040-0). Ye Galleon.
--Selected Papers of William Clayton. Dobney, Frederick J., ed. LC 70-164565. pap. 80.00 (ISBN 0-317-19877-7, 2023093). Bks Demand UMI.
--William Clayton's Journal: A Daily Record of the Journey of the Original Company of Mormon Pioneers from Nauveo, Illinois, to the Valley of the Great Salt Lake. LC 72-9435. (The Far Western Frontier Ser.). 380p. 1973. Repr. of 1921 ed. 26.50 (ISBN 0-405-04965-X). Ayer Co Pubs.
Clayton, William R. Matter & Spirit. LC 80-81694. 136p. 1981. 8.75 (ISBN 0-8022-2368-0). Philos Lib.
Cleaf, David W. van see Brooks, Douglas M. & Van Cleaf, David W.
Cleage, Albert B., Jr. Black Messiah. LC 68-9370. 1969. pap. 5.95 (ISBN 0-8362-0014-4). Andrews McMeel Parker.
Cleaning Consultant Services, Inc. The Comprehensive Custodial Training Manual. 1980. 46.00x (ISBN 0-9601054-1-7). Cleaning Consul.
Clear, Celia. Royal Children. (Illus.). 1984. 12.95 (ISBN 0-517-55361-9). Crown.
--Royal Children Eighteen Forty to Nineteen Eighty: From Queen Victoria to Queen Elizabeth II. LC 81-5289. (Illus.). 166p. 1981. 12.95 (ISBN 0-8128-2826-7). Stein & Day.
Clear, Michael. Dialectic Empiricism. 1983. 6.95 (ISBN 0-8062-2022-8). Carlton.
Clear, Todd R. & O'Leary, Vincent. Controlling the Offenders in the Community: Reforming the Community Supervision Function. LC 81-47444. 208p. 1982. 31.00 (ISBN 0-669-04633-7). Lexington Bks.
Clear, Todd R., jt. auth. see Hewitt, John D.
Clear, Val. Making Money with Birds. (Illus.). 192p. 1981. 12.95 (ISBN 0-87666-825-2, H-1031). TFH Pubns.
Clear, Val & Greenberg, Martin H., eds. Marriage & the Family Through Science Fiction. LC 75-38023. 400p. 1976. pap. text ed. 10.95 (ISBN 0-312-51590-1). St Martin.
Cleare, John. World Guide to Mountains & Mountaineering. LC 78-25727. (Illus.). 1979. 19.95 (ISBN 0-8317-9546-8, Mayflower Bks). Smith Pubs.
Clearfield, A. Inorganic Ion Exchange Materials. 304p. 1982. 84.50 (ISBN 0-8493-5930-9). CRC Pr.
Clearfield, Andrew M. These Fragments I Have Shored: Collage & Montage in Early Modernist Poetry. Litz, Walton, ed. LC 84-57. (Studies in Modern Literature: No. 36). 162p. 1984. 34.95 (ISBN 0-8357-1539-6). UMI Res Pr.
Clearfield, Harris R. & Dinoso, Vicente P., eds. Gastrointestinal Emergencies: Thirty-Fourth Hahnemann Symposium. LC 75-37629. (34th). (Illus.). 336p. 1976. 63.00 (ISBN 0-8089-0713-1, 790860). Grune.
Clearly, Beverly. The Luckiest Girl. 224p. (gr. 6-9). pap. 2.25 (ISBN 0-440-94899-1, LFL). Dell.
Clearly, James. Prosecuting the Shoplifter: The Dual Legal Aspects. LC 85-11342. Date not set. price not set (ISBN 0-409-95116-1). Butterworth TX.
Clearman, Brian. Transportation Markings: A Study in Communication. LC 80-6184. (Illus.). 489p. (Orig.). 1981. lib. bdg. 30.25 (ISBN 0-8191-1653-X); pap. text ed. 18.50 (ISBN 0-8191-1654-8). U Pr of Amer.
--Transportation Markings: A Study in Communication, Vol. II, Pt. E. LC 80-6184. (International Traffic Control Devices Ser.). (Illus.). 269p. (Orig.). 1984. pap. 9.95 (ISBN 0-918941-00-8). Mt Angel Abbey.
Clearman, Mary. Lambing Out & Other Stories. LC 77-274. (Breakthrough Bks). 107p. 1977. 8.95 (ISBN 0-8262-0227-6). U of Mo Pr.
Clearwater, Bonnie. Mark Rothko: Works on Paper. LC 83-22843. (Illus.). 144p. 1984. 35.00 (ISBN 0-933920-53-9); pap. 17.50 for museum distribution only (ISBN 0-933920-54-7). Hudson Hills.
--Mark Rothko: Works on Paper. LC 83-22843. (Illus.). 144p. 1984. 35.00 (ISBN 0-933920-53-9). Viking.
Cleary & Graham. Handbook of Illinois Evidence: 1983 Supplement. 18.50 (ISBN 0-316-14724-9). Little.
Cleary, A. A. Men Homeward. 54p. 1980. pap. 9.95x (ISBN 0-904461-35-1, Pub. by Ceolfrith Pr England). Intl Spec Bk.
Cleary, Alan. Instrumentation for Psychology. LC 77-1250. pap. 85.80 (ISBN 0-317-26137-1, 2024276). Bks Demand UMI.
Cleary, Beverly. Beezus & Ramona. 160p. (gr. 4-6). 1979. pap. 2.95 (ISBN 0-440-40665-X, YB). Dell.
--Beezus & Ramona. (Illus.). (gr. 3-7). 1955. PLB 10.88 (ISBN 0-688-31076-1); pap. 10.75 (ISBN 0-688-21076-7). Morrow.
--Cutting up with Ramona! (Illus.). 24p. (gr. 1-5). 1983. pap. 3.50 (ISBN 0-440-41627-2, YB). Dell.
--Dear Mr. Henshaw. LC 83-5372. (Illus.). 144p. (gr. 4-6). 1983. 10.25 (ISBN 0-688-02405-X); PLB 10.88 (ISBN 0-688-02406-8). Morrow.
--Dear Mr. Henshaw. (Illus.). 144p. (gr. k-6). 1984. pap. 2.50 (ISBN 0-440-41794-5, YB). Dell.
--Ellen Tebbits. 160p. (gr. 4-6). 1979. pap. 2.50 (ISBN 0-440-42299-X, YB). Dell.
--Ellen Tebbits. (Illus.). (gr. 3-7). 1951. 10.75 (ISBN 0-688-21264-6); PLB 10.88 (ISBN 0-688-31264-0). Morrow.
--Emily's Runaway Imagination. 224p. (gr. k-6). 1980. pap. 2.75 (ISBN 0-440-42215-9, YB). Dell.
--Emily's Runaway Imagination. (Illus.). (gr. 3-7). 1961. 11.95 (ISBN 0-688-21267-0); PLB 11.47 (ISBN 0-688-31267-5). Morrow.
--Fifteen. 192p. (gr. 6-9). 1980. pap. 2.25 (ISBN 0-440-92559-2, LFL). Dell.
--Fifteen. (Illus.). (gr. 6-9). 1956. 11.75 (ISBN 0-688-21285-9); PLB 11.28 (ISBN 0-688-31285-3). Morrow.
--Henry & Beezus. (Illus.). (gr. 3-7). 1952. 11.25 (ISBN 0-688-21383-9); PLB 10.88 (ISBN 0-688-31383-3). Morrow.
--Henry & Beezus. (Illus.). 196p. (gr. 3-7). pap. 2.50 (ISBN 0-440-43295-2, YB). Dell.
--Henry & Ribsy. 196p. (gr. 3 up). 1979. pap. 2.50 (ISBN 0-440-43296-0, YB). Dell.
--Henry & Ribsy. (Illus.). (gr. 3-7). 1954. 11.25 (ISBN 0-688-21382-0); PLB 10.88 (ISBN 0-688-31382-5). Morrow.
--Henry & the Clubhouse. (Illus.). (gr. 3-7). 1962. 10.75 (ISBN 0-688-21381-2); PLB 10.88 (ISBN 0-688-31381-7). Morrow.
--Henry & the Clubhouse. (Illus.). 196p. (gr. 3-7). pap. 2.95 (ISBN 0-440-43305-3, YB). Dell.
--Henry & the Paper Route. 196p. (gr. k-6). 1980. pap. 2.95 (ISBN 0-440-43298-7, YB). Dell.
--Henry & the Paper Route. (Illus.). (gr. 3-7). 1957. 11.25 (ISBN 0-688-21380-4); PLB 10.88 (ISBN 0-688-31380-9). Morrow.
--Henry Huggins. 160p. (gr. 4-6). 1979. pap. 2.50 (ISBN 0-440-43551-X, YB). Dell.
--Henry Huggins. (Illus.). (gr. 3-7). 1950. 10.75 (ISBN 0-688-21385-5); PLB 10.88 (ISBN 0-688-31385-X). Morrow.
--Henry Huggins. Palacios, Argentina, tr. (Spanish Translation.). (gr. 3-7). 1983. 10.25 (ISBN 0-688-02014-3). Morrow.
--Hullabaloo ABC. LC 60-9710. (Illus.). (gr. k-2). 1960. 6.95 (ISBN 0-87466-048-3, Pub. by Parnassus). HM.
--Jean & Johnny. 224p. (gr. 6-9). pap. 2.25 (ISBN 0-440-94358-2, LE). Dell.
--Jean & Johnny. (Illus.). (gr. 6-9). 1959. 11.75 (ISBN 0-688-21740-0); PLB 11.28 (ISBN 0-688-31740-5). Morrow.
--Leave it to Beaver. 11.95 (ISBN 0-88411-248-9, Pub. by Aeonian Pr). Amereon Ltd.
--The Luckiest Girl. (gr. 7 up). 1958. PLB 12.39 (ISBN 0-688-31741-3). Morrow.
--Lucky Chuck. LC 83-13386. 40p. (gr. k-3). 1984. 10.25 (ISBN 0-688-02736-9); PLB 10.88 (ISBN 0-688-02738-5). Morrow.
--Mitch & Amy. 224p. (gr. k-6). 1980. pap. 2.75 (ISBN 0-440-45411-5, YB). Dell.
--Mitch & Amy. (Illus.). (gr. 3-7). 1967. 11.25 (ISBN 0-688-21688-9); PLB 10.88 (ISBN 0-688-31688-3). Morrow.
--The Mouse & the Motorcycle. 160p. (gr. k-6). 1980. pap. 2.50 (ISBN 0-440-46075-1, YB). Dell.
--The Mouse & the Motorcycle. (Illus.). (gr. 2-6). 1965. 11.25 (ISBN 0-688-21698-6); PLB 11.88 (ISBN 0-688-31698-0). Morrow.
--Otis Spofford. 192p. (gr. k-6). 1980. pap. 2.95 (ISBN 0-440-46651-2, YB). Dell.
--Otis Spofford. (Illus.). (gr. 3-7). 1953. 11.25 (ISBN 0-688-21720-6); PLB 10.88 (ISBN 0-688-31720-0). Morrow.
--Ralph S. Mouse. LC 82-3516. (Illus.). 160p. (gr. 4-6). 1982. 10.25 (ISBN 0-688-01452-6); lib. bdg. 10.88 (ISBN 0-688-01455-0). Morrow.
--Ralph S. Mouse. (Illus.). 144p. (gr. 2-6). pap. 2.95 (ISBN 0-440-47582-1, YB). Dell.
--Ramona & Her Father. LC 77-1614. (gr. 3-7). 1977. 10.75 (ISBN 0-688-22114-9); PLB 10.88 (ISBN 0-688-32114-3). Morrow.
--Ramona & Her Father. (Illus.). 196p. (gr. 3-7). pap. 2.95 (ISBN 0-440-47241-5, YB). Dell.
--Ramona & Her Friends. pap. 9.00 (ISBN 0-440-47222-9). Dell.
--Ramona & Her Mother. 208p. (gr. k-6). 1980. pap. 2.50 (ISBN 0-440-47243-1, YB). Dell.
--Ramona & Her Mother. LC 79-10323. (Illus.). 192p. (gr. 4-6). 1979. 10.95 (ISBN 0-688-22195-5); PLB 10.88 (ISBN 0-688-32195-X). Morrow.
--Ramona, Forever. LC 84-704. (Illus.). 192p. (gr. 3-7). 1984. 9.25 (ISBN 0-688-03785-2, Morrow Junior Books); PLB 8.59 (ISBN 0-688-03786-0). Morrow.
--Ramona, Forever. (gr. k-6). 1985. pap. 2.95 (ISBN 0-440-47210-5, YB). Dell.
--Ramona Quimby, Age Eight. LC 80-28425. (Illus.). 192p. (gr. 4-6). 1981. 10.25 (ISBN 0-688-00477-6); PLB 10.88 (ISBN 0-688-00478-4). Morrow.
--Ramona Quimby, Age Eight. (Illus.). 192p. (gr. 3-7). 1982. pap. 2.95 (ISBN 0-440-47350-0, YB). Dell.
--The Ramona Quimby Diary. (Illus.). 160p. (gr. 3-7). 1984. pap. 7.95 (ISBN 0-688-03883-2, Morrow Junior Books). Morrow.
--Ramona the Brave. LC 74-164968. (Illus.). 192p. (gr. 3-7). 1975. 11.25 (ISBN 0-688-22015-0); PLB 10.88 (ISBN 0-688-32015-5). Morrow.
--Ramona the Brave. (Illus.). 192p. (gr. k-6). 1984. pap. 2.50 (ISBN 0-440-47351-9, YB). Dell.
--Ramona the Pest. 192p. (gr. 4-7). 1982. pap. 2.50 (ISBN 0-440-47209-1, YB). Dell.
--Ramona the Pest. (Illus.). (gr. 3-7). 1968. 10.75 (ISBN 0-688-21721-4); PLB 10.88 (ISBN 0-688-31721-9). Morrow.
--Ramona the Pest. Palacios, Argentina, tr. LC 83-23805. 208p. (Spanish.). (gr. 3-7). 1984. 9.50 (ISBN 0-688-02783-0). Morrow.
--The Real Hole. (Illus.). 32p. (ps-2). 1986. 10.25 (ISBN 0-688-05850-7); PLB 10.88 (ISBN 0-688-05851-5). Morrow.
--Ribsy. 192p. (gr. 3-7). 1982. pap. 2.95 (ISBN 0-440-47456-6, YB). Dell.
--Ribsy. (Illus.). (gr. 3-7). 1964. 10.75 (ISBN 0-688-21662-5); PLB 10.88 (ISBN 0-688-31662-X). Morrow.
--Runaway Ralph. 176p. (gr. k-6). 1981. pap. 2.50 (ISBN 0-440-47519-8, YB). Dell.
--Runaway Ralph. (Illus.). (gr. 3-7). 1970. 10.95 (ISBN 0-688-21701-X); PLB 10.88 (ISBN 0-688-31701-4). Morrow.
--Sister of the Bride. 128p. (gr. 6-9). 1981. pap. 2.50 (ISBN 0-440-94358-2, LE). Dell.
--Sister of the Bride. (Illus.). (gr. 7 up). 1963. PLB 12.88 (ISBN 0-688-31742-1). Morrow.
--Socks. 160p. (gr. k-6). 1980. pap. 2.95 (ISBN 0-440-48256-9, YB). Dell.
--Socks. LC 72-10298. (Illus.). 192p. (gr. 3-7). 1973. 10.75 (ISBN 0-688-20067-2); PLB 10.88 (ISBN 0-688-30067-7). Morrow.
--Two Dog Biscuits. (Illus.). (ps-1). 1961. PLB 10.88 (ISBN 0-688-31656-5). Morrow.
--Two Dog Biscuits. (Illus.). 32p. (ps-2). 1986. 10.25 (ISBN 0-688-05847-7); PLB 10.88 (ISBN 0-688-05848-5). Morrow.
Cleary, Bill, jt. auth. see Stern, David.
Cleary, Christopher, tr. see Hui, Ta.
Cleary, David P. Great American Brands: The Success Formulas That Made Them Famous. (Illus.). 300p. 1981. text ed. 17.50 (ISBN 0-87005-338-8). Fairchild.
Cleary, Denis & Maher, Frank. The Hook. 160p. 1982. 20.00x (ISBN 0-7278-0634-3, Pub. by Severn Hse). State Mutual Bk.
--Sahara Strike. 160p. 1982. 20.00x (ISBN 0-7278-0654-8, Pub. by Severn Hse). State Mutual Bk.
Cleary, Donna M., ed. Thinking Thursdays: Language Arts in the Reading Lab. 1978. pap. text ed. 4.00 (ISBN 0-87207-223-1). Intl Reading.
Cleary, Edward. McCormick on Evidence. 3rd, Lawyer's Ed. ed. LC 83-26694. (Hornbook Ser.). 1372p. 1984. text ed. 41.95 (ISBN 0-314-77626-5). West Pub.
--McCormick on Evidence, 3rd, student ed. LC 83-26695. (Hornbook Ser.). 1156p. 1984. text ed. 25.95 (ISBN 0-314-77625-7). West Pub.
--The ORANSCO Story: Water Quality Management in the Ohio Valley under an Interstate Compact. LC 67-16036. pap. 87.80 (ISBN 0-317-19885-8, 2023087). Bks Demand UMI.
Cleary, Edward J. The ORSANCO Story: Water Quality Management in the Ohio Valley under an Interstate Compact. LC 67-16036. pap. 66.40 (ISBN 0-317-11233-3, 2016036). Bks Demand UMI.
Cleary, Edward J. & Gearin, Kathleen R. Ramsey County Juvenile Court Bench Book. 1982. looseleaf 29.00 (ISBN 0-86678-044-0). Butterworth MN.
Cleary, Edward L. Crisis & Change: The Church in Latin America Today. LC 84-16478. 208p. (Orig.). 1985. pap. 11.95 (ISBN 0-88344-149-7). Orbis Bks.
Cleary, Edward W. & Strong, John W. Evidence, Cases Materials, Problems. 3rd ed. LC 81-10426. (American Casebook Ser.). 1143p. 1981. text ed. 27.95 (ISBN 0-314-59847-2). West Pub.
Cleary, Eileen M., ed. Nursing Eighty-Four Career Directory, Vol. 6, No. 1. (Illus.). 400p. (Orig.). 1984. pap. 10.00 (ISBN 0-916730-84-0). Springhouse Corp.
Cleary, Florence D. Blueprints for Better Reading. 2nd ed. 1972. 20.00 (ISBN 0-8242-0406-9). Wilson.
--Discovering Books & Libraries: A Handbook for Student in the Middle & Upper Grades. 2nd ed. LC 76-55368. 216p. 1977. pap. 8.00 (ISBN 0-8242-0594-4). Wilson.
Cleary, J. B. & Lacombe, J. M. English Style Skill Builders: A Self-Improvement Program for Transcribers & Typists. 1980. text ed. 13.44 (ISBN 0-07-011305-X). McGraw.
Cleary, James, tr. see White, Carol.
Cleary, James P. & Levenbach, Hans. The Professional Forecaster: The Forecasting Process Through Data Analysis. (Quantitative Methods for Managers Ser.). (Illus.). 402p. 1982. text ed. 31.50 (ISBN 0-534-97960-2). Lifetime Learn.
--The Professional Forecaster: The Forecasting Process Through Data Analysis. 402p. 1982. 31.50 (ISBN 0-534-97960-2). Van Nos Reinhold.
Cleary, James P., jt. auth. see Levenbach, Hans.
Cleary, James W. & Haberman, Frederick W. Rhetoric & Public Address: A Bibliography, 1947-1961. LC 64-7959. pap. 126.50 (ISBN 0-317-10231-1, 2021132). Bks Demand UMI.
Cleary, James W., ed. see Bulwer, John.
Cleary, Jon. The Faraway Drums. LC 81-14091. 320p. 1982. 13.50 (ISBN 0-688-00790-2). Morrow.
--The Golden Sabre. LC 80-26827. 300p. 1981. 12.95 (ISBN 0-688-00415-6). Morrow.
--High Road to China. 320p. 1983. pap. 2.95 (ISBN 0-446-31178-2). Warner Bks.
--Spearfield's Daughter. LC 82-14542. 567p. 1983. Repr. 15.95 (ISBN 0-688-01736-3). Morrow.
--The Sundowners. LC 67-14015. 382p. 1984. pap. 7.95 (ISBN 0-684-13364-4, ScribT). Scribner.
--The Sundowners. 20.95 (ISBN 0-88411-467-8, Pub. by Aeonian Pr). Amereon Ltd.
Cleary, Joseph & Gleason, Joseph. Arithmetic: A Problem Solving Approach. (Illus.). 550p. 1985. pap. text ed. 23.95 (ISBN 0-314-78011-4). West Pub.
Cleary, Maureen D. The Bible, You, & Your Students. 1977. pap. 3.95 (ISBN 0-8407-5622-4). Nelson.
Cleary, Michael J. & Amsden, Robert T. A Data Analysis Handbook Using the SPSS System. (Illus., Orig.). 1979. pap. 9.95x (ISBN 0-89894-015-X). Advocate Pub Group.
Cleary, Patrick. The Church & Usury. 1979. lib. bdg. 59.95 (ISBN 0-8490-2884-1). Gordon Pr.
Cleary, Patti, ed. see Lander, Jack.
Cleary, Robert E., ed. The Role of Government in the United States-Practice & Theory: A Report of a Conference at the College of Public & International Affairs of the American University, Washington, D. C.. March 2-3. 1984. 250p. (Orig.). 1985. lib. bdg. 22.75 (ISBN 0-8191-4798-2); pap. text ed. 11.75 (ISBN 0-8191-4799-0). U Pr of Amer.
Cleary, T. A. & McCandless, S. A. Summary of Score Changes (in Other Tests) 1977. 2.00 (ISBN 0-87447-088-9, 251710). College Bd.
Cleary, Thomas. Entry into the Inconceivable: An Introduction to Hua-yen Buddhism. LC 83-3613. 227p. 1983. text ed. 16.95x (ISBN 0-8248-0824-X). UH Pr.
--Henry Fielding: Political Writer. 368p. 1984. text ed. 32.75x (ISBN 0-88920-131-5, Pub. by Wilfrid U Pr). Humanities.
--Timeless Spring: A Soto Zen Anthology. LC 79-26677. 176p. 1980. 7.95 (ISBN 0-8348-0148-5). Weatherhill.
Cleary, Thomas, ed. The Original Face: An Anthology of Rinzai Zen. LC 77-91354. 1978. pap. 4.95 (ISBN 0-394-17038-5, E707, Ever). Grove.
Cleary, Thomas, tr. The Book of Serenity. 464p. 1985. 24.95 (ISBN 0-89281-072-6); pap. 14.95 (ISBN 0-89281-074-2). Inner Tradit.
--The Flower Ornament Scripture: A Translation of the Avatamsaka Sutra, Vol. 1. LC 83-2370. 703p. 1984. 35.00 (ISBN 0-87773-767-3, 53690-8). Shambhala Pubns.
--Sayings & Doings of Pai-Chang. LC 78-21228. (Zen Writings Ser.: Vol. 6). 1979. pap. 5.95 (ISBN 0-916820-10-6). Center Pubns.
Cleary, Vincent J. & Wells, Theodore W., eds. The Pervigilium Veneris: A Late Latin Poem of Love & Springtime. 46p. (Lat.). (gr. 10-12). 1981. pap. text ed. 3.50x (ISBN 0-88334-151-4). Ind Sch Pr.
Cleasby, Richard & Vigfusson, Gudbrand, eds. Icelandic-English Dictionary. 2nd ed. (Icelandic & Eng.). 1957. 135.00x (ISBN 0-19-863103-0). Oxford U Pr.

Cleather, Alice L. The Ring of the Nibelung. LC 77-18100. 1977. Repr. of 1924 ed. lib. bdg. 25.00 (ISBN 0-8414-1844-6). Folcroft.

Cleaton, Allen, jt. auth. see Cleaton, Irene.

Cleaton, Irene & Cleaton, Allen. Books & Battles: American Literature, 1920-1930. LC 73-124269. (Illus.). 1970. Repr. of 1937 ed. lib. bdg. 21.50 (ISBN 0-8154-0339-9). Cooper Sq.

Cleaton-Jones, Peter. Essential Medicine for Dental Practice. 96p. 1971. 15.75X (ISBN 0-398-02260-7). C C Thomas.

Cleator, P. E. Letters from Baltimore: The Mencken-Cleator Correspondence. LC 78-75176. 280p. 1982. 32.50 (ISBN 0-8386-3075-8). Fairleigh Dickinson.

Cleave, Charles Van see Van Cleave, Charles & AEC Technical Information Center.

Cleave, Janice P. van see Van Cleave, Janice P.

Cleave, Richard. The Student Map Manual: Historical Geography of the Bible Lands. Monson, J., et al, eds. 168p. 1980. 29.95 (ISBN 0-310-42980-3). Zondervan.

Cleave, Shirley. Managing the Sport Club Program: From Theory to Practice. Zeigler, Earle F., ed. (Stipes Monograph Series on Sport & Physical Education Management). 49p. 1984. pap. text ed. 3.20X (ISBN 0-87563-244-0). Stipes.

Cleave, Shirley, et al. And So to School. 224p. 1982. 16.00x (ISBN 0-85633-245-3, Pub. by NFER Nelson UK). Taylor & Francis.

Cleave, T. On the Causation of Varicose Veins. 1981. pap. 4.95x (ISBN 0-317-07275-7, Regent House). B of A.

Cleave, T. L. The Saccharine Disease: Sugar & Its Role in Disease. 5.70 ea. Hypoglycemia Foun.

--Saccharine Disease: The Master Disease of Our Time. LC 75-15456. 224p. 1975. 7.95 (ISBN 0-87983-116-2); pap. 4.95 (ISBN 0-87983-117-0). Keats.

Cleave, William R. Van see Van Cleave, William R. & Thompson, Scott W.

Cleave Alexander, Michael Van see Van Cleave Alexander, Michael.

Cleaveland, A. & Craven, J. Universals of Culture. 72p. 5.00 (ISBN 0-318-14215-5, GPH 103). Global Perspectives.

Cleaveland, Agnes M. No Life for a Lady. LC 77-6825. (Illus.). viii, 356p. 1977. pap. 7.50 (ISBN 0-8032-5868-2, BB 652, Bison). U of Nebr Pr.

Cleaveland, Alice A., jt. auth. see Reeve, Frank.

Cleaveland, Elizabeth W. A Study of Tindale's Genesis: Compared with the Genesis of Coverdale & of the Authorized Version. (Yale Studies in English Ser.: No. 43). xliii, 258p. 1972. Repr. of 1911 ed. 21.00 (ISBN 0-208-01126-9, Archon). Shoe String.

Cleaveland, Henry W., et al. Village & Farm Cottages. (Library of Victorian Culture). (Illus.). 1976. pap. text ed. 9.00 (ISBN 0-89257-008-3). Am Life Foun.

Cleaveland, John & Hutchinson, G. S. The Banking System of the State of New York. Bruchey, Stuart, ed. LC 80-1181. (The Rise of Commercial Banking Ser.). 1981. Repr. of 1864 ed. lib. bdg. 35.00x (ISBN 0-405-13642-0). Ayer Co Pubs.

Cleaveland, Nehemiah. Greenwood Cemetery: A History. 59.95 (ISBN 0-8490-0265-6). Gordon Pr.

Cleaveland, Parker. An Elementary Treatise on Mineralogy & Geology. Albritton, Claude C., Jr., ed. LC 77-6513. (History of Geology Ser.). (Illus.). 1978. Repr. of 1816 ed. lib. bdg. 53.00 (ISBN 0-405-10436-7). Ayer Co Pubs.

Cleaver. Pennsylvania Probate & Estate Administration. incl. latest pocket part supplement 39.95 (ISBN 0-686-90966-6); separate pocket part supplement, 1984(for use in 1985 11.95. Harrison Co GA.

Cleaver, A. H., jt. auth. see Hatton, T.

Cleaver, Betty & Taylor, William. Involving the School Library Media Specialist in Curriculum Development. LC 82-22759. (School Media Centers: Focus on Trends & Issues: No. 8). viii, 70p. 1983. pap. text ed. 7.00x (ISBN 0-8389-3280-0). ALA.

Cleaver, Bill & Cleaver, Vera. Grover. LC 69-12001. (Illus.). (gr. 4-6). 1970. 12.02 (ISBN 0-397-31118-4). Har-Row.

Cleaver, Bill, jt. auth. see Cleaver, Vera.

Cleaver, C., jt. ed. see Baker, J.

Cleaver, Charles G. Japanese & Americans: Cultural Parallels & Paradoxes. 1976. 12.75x (ISBN 0-8166-0761-3). U of Minn Pr.

Cleaver, Claire M. Step into Sales: Six Weeks to Successful Direct Selling from Your Home. (Illus.). 256p. 1983. 8.95 (ISBN 0-380-65391-5, 65391). Avon.

Cleaver, Dale G. Art: An Introduction. 4th ed. (Illus.). 469p. 1985. pap. text ed. 21.95 (ISBN 0-15-503433-2, HC). HarBraceJ.

Cleaver, David S., jt. auth. see Hsiao, James C.

Cleaver, Diane. The Literary Agent & the Writer: A Professional Guide. 1984. pap. 10.00 (ISBN 0-87116-135-4). Writer.

Cleaver, Eldridge. Soul on Ice. 224p. 1968. 11.95 (ISBN 0-07-011307-6). McGraw.

Cleaver, Elizabeth. ABC. LC 84-11137. (Illus.). 48p. (gr. 1-5). 1985. 5.95 (ISBN 0-689-31072-2). Atheneum.

--The Enchanted Caribou. LC 85-7465. (Illus.). 32p. (gr. 4). 1985. 9.95 (ISBN 0-689-31170-2). Atheneum.

Cleaver, Elizabeth, retold by. & illus. Petrouchka. LC 79-14436. (Illus.). 32p. (ps-4). 1980. 12.95 (ISBN 0-689-30704-7). Atheneum.

Cleaver, Harry. Reading CAPITAL Politically. 219p. 1979. text ed. 14.95x (ISBN 0-292-77014-6); pap. 7.95x (ISBN 0-292-77015-4). U of Tex Pr.

Cleaver, Harry, tr. see Negri, Antonio.

Cleaver, James. A History of Graphic Art. (Illus.). 1977. Repr. of 1963 ed. 32.00x (ISBN 0-7158-1209-2). Charles River Bks.

--History of Graphic Art. LC 73-95115. Repr. of 1963 ed. lib. bdg. 24.00x (ISBN 0-8371-2522-7, CLGA). Greenwood.

Cleaver, Kevin M. Economic & Social Analysis of Projects & of Price Policy: The Morocco Fourth Agricultural Credit Project. (Working Paper: No. 369). 59p. 1980. 3.00 (ISBN 0-686-36084-2, WP-0369). World Bank.

--Economic & Social Analysis of Projects & of Price Policy: The Morocco Fourth Agricultural Credit Project. (Working Paper: No. 369). 59p. 1980. pap. 3.00 (ISBN 0-686-39650-2, WP-0369). World Bank.

Cleaver, Vera. Hazel Rye. LC 85-42741. (Trophy Bk.). 192p. (gr. 5-7). 1985. pap. 2.84i (ISBN 0-06-440156-1, Trophy). HarpJ.

--Me Too. LC 85-42745. (Trophy Bk.). 160p. (gr. 5-7). 1985. pap. 2.84i (ISBN 0-06-440161-8, Trophy). HarpJ.

--Sugar Blue. LC 83-19910. (Illus.). 160p. (gr. 5 up). 1984. 12.00 (ISBN 0-688-02720-2). Lothrop.

--Sweetly Sings the Donkey. LC 85-40098. 160p. (gr. 5-9). 1985. 12.50i (ISBN 0-397-32156-2); PLB 11.89g (ISBN 0-397-32157-0). Lipp Jr Bks.

Cleaver, Vera & Cleaver, Bill. Dust of the Earth. LC 75-18939. 160p. (gr. 7 up). 1975. 12.02i (ISBN 0-397-31650-X). Lipp Jr Bks.

--Ellen Grae & Lady Ellen Grae. (RL 4). 1978. pap. 1.95 (ISBN 0-451-09832-3, J9832, Sig). NAL.

--Grover. (RL 5). 1975. pap. 1.95 (ISBN 0-451-13216-5, AE3216, Sig). NAL.

--Hazel Rye. LC 81-48603. 160p. (gr. 5-7). 1983. 12.02i (ISBN 0-397-31951-7); PLB 12.89g (ISBN 0-397-31952-5). Lipp Jr Bks.

--I Would Rather Be a Turnip. (RL 5). 1976. pap. 2.25 (ISBN 0-451-12353-0, Sig). NAL.

--The Kissimmee Kid. LC 80-29262. 160p. (gr. 5 up). 1981. 11.25 (ISBN 0-688-41992-5); PLB 11.88 (ISBN 0-688-51992-X). Lothrop.

--Lady Ellen Grae. LC 68-10981. (Illus.). (gr. 4-6). 1968. PLB 11.89 (ISBN 0-397-30938-4). Lipp Jr Bks.

--A Little Destiny. LC 79-10322. (gr. 5 up). 1979. 11.25 (ISBN 0-688-41904-6); PLB 11.88 (ISBN 0-688-51904-0). Lothrop.

--Me Too. 160p. (gr. 7-9). 1973. 11.49i (ISBN 0-397-31485-X). Lipp Jr Bks.

--Mock Revolt. LC 75-151467. 160p. (gr. 6 up). 1971. PLB 11.89 (ISBN 0-397-31238-5); pap. 1.95 (ISBN 0-397-31237-7). Lipp Jr Bks.

--Queen of Hearts. LC 77-18252. 158p. (gr. 5-7). 1978. 10.95 (ISBN 0-397-31771-9). Lipp Jr Bks.

--Trial Valley. LC 76-54303. 1977. 10.95i (ISBN 0-397-31722-0). Lipp Jr Bks.

--Where the Lilies Bloom. LC 75-82402. (Illus.). (gr. 4-9). 1969. 11.49i (ISBN 0-397-31111-7). Lipp Jr Bks.

--Where the Lilies Bloom. 1974. pap. 1.95 (ISBN 0-451-12292-5, AJ2292, Sig). NAL.

Cleaver, Vera, jt. auth. see Cleaver, Bill.

Cleaves. Meade of Gettysburg. 1980. 17.50 (ISBN 0-89029-052-0). Pr of Morningside.

Cleaves, A. B., jt. auth. see Schultz, John R.

Cleaves, Anne, jt. ed. see Horn, Robert E.

Cleaves, Bennett & Cameron, Charles. Control Your Blood Pressure Without Drugs. LC 83-45022. 15.95 (ISBN 0-385-18927-3). Doubleday.

Cleaves, Cheryl & Hobbs, Margie. Basic Mathematics for Trades & Technologies. (Illus.). 640p. 1983. text ed. 25.95 (ISBN 0-13-063032-2). P-H.

Cleaves, Cheryl S., et al. Mathematics of the Business World. LC 78-18635. (Illus.). 1979. pap. text ed. 19.95 (ISBN 0-201-02773-9); instr's. manual 3.50 (ISBN 0-201-02774-7). Addison-Wesley.

Cleaves, Francis W., ed. & tr. from Mongolian. The Secret History of the Mongols. (Harvard-Yenching Institute Ser.). 344p. 1982. text ed. 22.50x (ISBN 0-674-79670-5). Harvard U Pr.

Cleaves, Francis W., jt. ed. see Mostaert, Antoine.

Cleaves, Francis W., ed. see Rasipungsuy.

Cleaves, Francis W., ed. see Secen, Sayang.

Cleaves, Francis W., tr. see Kahn, Paul.

Cleaves, Freeman. Rock of Chickamauga, the Life of General George H. Thomas. LC 73-8253. (Illus.). 328p. 1974. Repr. of 1948 ed. lib. bdg. 27.50x (ISBN 0-8371-6973-9, CLRC). Greenwood.

Cleaves, Margaret M. Midnight Surrender. (Orig.). 1980. pap. 1.50 (ISBN 0-440-15023-X). Dell.

Cleaves, Peter S. Bureaucratic Politics & Administration in Chile. LC 73-76111. 1974. 40.00x (ISBN 0-520-02448-6). U of Cal Pr.

--Developmental Processes in Chilean Local Government. (Politics of Modernization Ser.: No. 8). 1969. pap. 1.50x (ISBN 0-87725-208-4). U of Cal Intl St.

Cleaves, Peter S. & Scurrah, Martin J. Agriculture, Bureaucracy & Military Government in Peru. (Illus.). 336p. 1980. 34.95x (ISBN 0-8014-1300-1). Cornell U Pr.

Clebert, Jean Paul. Dictionnaire du Symbolisme Animal. 455p. (Fr.). 1974. pap. 29.95 (ISBN 0-686-56877-X, M-581). French & Eur.

Clebsch, Alfred. Theorie De L'elasticite Des Corps Solides. 1883. 60.00 (ISBN 0-384-09285-3). Johnson Repr.

Clebsch, Rudolph F., tr. Vorlesungen Ueber Geometrie Mit Besonderer Benutzung der Vortrage Von Clebsch, 2 Vols. in 3 Pts. (Bibliotheca Mathematica Teubneriana Ser. 43-44). (Ger). 1969. Repr. Set. 140.00 (ISBN 0-384-09295-0). Johnson Repr.

Clebsch, William. Christianity in European History. 1979. pap. 7.95x (ISBN 0-19-502472-9). Oxford U Pr.

Clebsch, William & Jaekle, Charles. Pastoral Care in Historical Perspective. LC 84-451130. 344p. 1983. Repr. of 1975 ed. 30.00x (ISBN 0-87668-717-6). Aronson.

Clebsch, William A. American Religious Thought: A History. LC 73-82911. xii, 212p. 1985. pap. text ed. 10.00x (ISBN 0-226-10962-3). U of Chicago Pr.

--England's Earliest Protestants, 1520-1535. LC 80-15226. (Yale Publications in Religion: No. 11). xvi, 358p. 1980. Repr. of 1964 ed. lib. bdg. 32.50x (ISBN 0-313-22420-X, CLEE). Greenwood.

--From Sacred to Profane America: The Role of Religion in American History. LC 81-9142. (Classics & Reprints Series of the American Academy of Religion & Scholars Press). 1981. 9.95 (ISBN 0-89130-517-3, 01 05 02). Scholars Pr GA.

Clebsch, William A., ed. see Donne, John.

Clebsch, William A., ed. see Jastrow, Morris, Jr.

Clecak, Peter. America's Quest for the Ideal Self: Dissent & Fulfillment in the 60s & 70s. 1983. 27.50 (ISBN 0-19-503226-8); pap. 8.95 (ISBN 0-19-503544-5). Oxford U Pr.

--Radical Paradoxes: Dilemmas of the American Left, 1945-1970. LC 73-4072. 1973. text ed. 18.50x (ISBN 0-06-010819-3). Irvington.

Cleckley, Franklin D. Handbook on Evidence for West Virginia Lawyers. 1978. 40.00, with 1983 suppl (ISBN 0-87215-202-2); 1983 suppl 15.00 (ISBN 0-87215-625-7). Michie Co.

--Handbook on West Virginia Criminal Procedure, 2 vols. 1985. Set. 90.00 (ISBN 0-87215-846-2). Michie Co.

Cleckley, Hervey M., jt. auth. see Thigpen, Corbett.

Clede, Bill. Police Handgun Manual: How to Get Street-Smart Survival Habits. Fish, Chet, ed. (Illus.). 128p. 1985. 11.95 (ISBN 0-8117-1275-3). Stackpole.

Cleef, A. M. The Vegetation of the Paramos of the Colombian Cordillera Oriental. (Dissertationes Botanicae Ser.: Vol. 61). (Illus.). 320p. 1981. text ed. 21.00x (ISBN 3-7682-1302-1). Lubrecht & Cramer.

Cleef, A. Van see Van Cleef, A.

Cleef, Eugene Van see Van Cleef, Eugene.

Cleef, Monique Von see Von Cleef, Monique & Waterman, William.

Cleefe, Mark Van see Van Cleefe, Mark.

Cleeland, Caryn L., jt. auth. see Castelli, Louis.

Cleemput, W. M. Van see Van Cleemput, W. M.

Cleere, Henry, ed. Approaches to the Archaeological Heritage: A Comparative Study of World Cultural Resource Management Systems. (New Directions in Archaeology Ser.). (Illus.). 160p. 1984. 39.50 (ISBN 0-521-24305-X). Cambridge U Pr.

Cleere, Henry, jt. ed. see Taylor, Joan Du Plat.

Cleese, John, jt. auth. see Skynner, Robin.

Cleeton, Claud E. Strategies for the Options Trader. LC 78-11230. 172p. 1979. 42.95 (ISBN 0-471-04973-5, Pub. by Wiley-Interscience). Wiley.

Cleeve, Brian. Hester. 1982. pap. 2.95 (ISBN 0-425-04754-7). Berkley Pub.

--Nineteen Thirty-Eight: A World Vanishing. 160p. 1982. 40.00x (ISBN 0-907675-08-5, Pub. by Buchan & Enright England). State Mutual Bk.

--A View of the Irish. 204p. 1985. 12.95 (ISBN 0-907675-17-4, Pub. by Salem Hse Ltd). Merrimack Pub Cir.

Cleeve, Brian, jt. auth. see Brady, Anne.

Cleeve, Martin. Screwcutting in the Lathe. (Workshop Practice Ser.: No. 3). (Illus.). 128p. 1985. pap. 9.95 (ISBN 0-85242-838-3, Pub. by Argus). Aztex.

Cleeve, Roger. Daughters of Jerusalem. 1986. Repr. of 1985 ed. 15.95 (ISBN 0-917561-02-3). Adler & Adler.

--The Last Long Journey. LC 83-18172. (Phoenix Fiction Ser.). 272p. 1984. pap. 7.95 (ISBN 0-226-10990-9). U of Chicago Pr.

Cleevely, R. J. World Palaeontological Collections. 450p. 1982. 100.00x (ISBN 0-7201-1655-4). Mansell.

Clegg, jt. auth. see Thompson.

Clegg, Charles, jt. auth. see Beebe, Lucius.

Clegg, Chris W., jt. ed. see Kelly, John E.

Clegg, E. J. & Garlick, J. P., eds. Disease & Urbanization. (Symposia of the Society for the Study of Human Biology: Vol. 20). 1980. text ed. 22.75x (ISBN 0-85066-190-0). Humanities.

Clegg, Edward. Race & Politics: Partnership in the Federation of Rhodesia & Nyasaland. LC 75-3731. 280p. 1975. Repr. of 1960 ed. lib. bdg. 22.50 (ISBN 0-8371-8061-9, CLRPO). Greenwood.

Clegg, Holly Berkowitz & Jarrett, Beverly. From a Louisiana Kitchen. LC 82-62564. (Illus.). 256p. 1983. pap. 9.95 (ISBN 0-9610888-0-X). Wimmer Bks.

Clegg, Hugh A. A History of British Trade Unions since 1889: 1911-1933, Vol. II. 800p. 1985. 67.00x (ISBN 0-19-828298-2). Oxford U Pr.

Clegg, Hugh A., et al. History of British Trade Unions since 1889 Vol. 1: 1889-1910. 1964. 59.00x (ISBN 0-19-828229-X). Oxford U Pr.

--Trade Union Officers: A Study of Full-Time Officers, Branch Secretaries & Shop Stewards in British Trade Unions. LC 61-65475. 1961. 16.50x (ISBN 0-674-89970-9). Harvard U Pr.

Clegg, Hugh G. The Reparative Motif in Child & Adult Therapy. LC 84-2901. (Illus.). 226p. 1984. 25.00 (ISBN 0-87668-704-4). Aronson.

Clegg, I. E., tr. see Pirenne, Henri.

Clegg, Ian. Workers' Self-Management in Algeria. (Illus.). 256p. 1971. 8.95 (ISBN 0-85345-200-8). Monthly Rev.

Clegg, J. B., jt. auth. see Weatherall, D. J.

Clegg, James S., jt. ed. see Crowe, John H.

Clegg, Jerry S. The Structure of Plato's Philosophy. LC 75-31467. 207p. 1978. 20.00 (ISBN 0-8387-1878-7). Bucknell U Pr.

Clegg, Joan. Dictionary of Social Services: Policy & Practice. 3rd ed. 148p. 1980. 15.00x (ISBN 0-7199-1039-0). Intl Pubns Serv.

--Dictionary of Social Services: Policy & Practice. 147p. 1977. text ed. 14.50x (ISBN 0-7199-0932-5, Pub. by Bedford England). Brookfield Pub Co.

Clegg, John. Guide to Ponds & Streams. 1985. 12.95 (ISBN 0-946284-61-X, Pub. by Crowood Pr). Longwood Pub Group.

Clegg, John, ed. see White, Gilbert.

Clegg, Michael. Tax Records of Portage, Summit & Portions of Medina Cos., 1808-1820. 10.00 (ISBN 0-318-04653-9). OH Genealogical.

Clegg, Michael T, jt. auth. see Fristrom, James W.

Clegg, Peter & Watkins, Derry. The Complete Greenhouse Book: Building & Using Greenhouses from Cold Frames to Solar Structures. LC 78-24572. (Illus.). 288p. 1978. pap. 10.95 (ISBN 0-88266-141-8). Garden Way Pub.

Clegg, Peter, jt. auth. see Wolfe, Ralph.

Clegg, Reed K. Probation & Parole: Principles & Practices. 196p. 1979. pap. 24.50x spiral (ISBN 0-398-03036-7). C C Thomas.

Clegg, Richard & Thompson, William A. Modern Sports Officiating: A Practical Guide. 2nd ed. 256p. 1979. pap. text ed. write for info. (ISBN 0-697-07165-0). Wm C Brown.

--Modern Sports Officiating: A Practical Guide. 3rd ed. 288p. 1985. pap. write for info. (ISBN 0-697-00464-3). Wm C Brown.

Clegg, Stewart & Dunkerley, David. Organization, Class & Control. 1980. 40.00x (ISBN 0-7100-0421-4); pap. 20.00x (ISBN 0-7100-0435-4). Routledge & Kegan.

Clegg, W. Paul & Styring, John S. British Nationalized Shipping 1947-1968. LC 68-26163. 1968. 24.95x (ISBN 0-678-05587-4). Kelley.

Clegg, W. Paul, ed. Ships Annual, 1967. 7.50 (ISBN 0-392-09060-0, SpS). Sportshelf.

Cleghorn, Paul L. The Hilina Pali Petroglyph Cave, Hawai'i Island: A Report on Preliminary Archaeological Investigations. (Departmental Report: No. 80-1). 32p. 1980. pap. 4.00 (ISBN 0-910240-88-4). Bishop Mus.

--The Hilina Pali Petroglyph Cave, Hawaii Island: A Report on Preliminary Archaeological Excavations in Kahana Valley Oahu, 1972. 48p. write for info. Bishop Mus.

Cleghorn, Sarah N. Threescore. Baxter, Annette K., ed. LC 79-8783. (Signal Lives Ser.). (Illus.). 1980. Repr. of 1936 ed. lib. bdg. 34.50x (ISBN 0-405-12831-2). Ayer Co Pubs.

Cleghorn, Spencer. Kabbalistic Discoveries into Hebrew & Aegyptian Mysteries, 2 Vols. (Illus.). 121p. 1983. 177.75 (ISBN 0-89920-057-5). Am Inst Psych.

Cleghorn, William, jt. auth. see Keddie, James.

Cleir, Piaras V. De see De Cleir, Piaras V.

Cleland & King. Project Management Handbook. 752p. 1983. 44.50 (ISBN 0-442-23878-9). Van Nos Reinhold.

Cleland, Charles. Mental Retardation: A Developmental Approach. (Spec. Educ. Ser.). 1978. ref. ed. 28.95x (ISBN 0-13-576504-8). P-H.

Cleland, Charles C. The Profoundly Mentally Retarded. LC 79-1258. 1979. text ed. 19.95 (ISBN 0-13-729566-9). P-H.

Cleland, Charles C. & Swartz, Jon D. Exceptionalities Through the Life Span: An Introduction. 1982. text ed. write for info. (ISBN 0-02-322860-1). Macmillan.

--Mental Retardation-Approaches to Institutional Change. LC 69-19945. 288p. 1969. 56.00 (ISBN 0-8089-0100-1, 790865). Grune.

Cleland, Craig J., jt. auth. see Wilson, Robert M.

Cleland, D. I. & King, W. R. Systems Analysis & Project Management. 3rd ed. (Illus.). 512p. 1983. 31.95 (ISBN 0-07-011311-4). McGraw.

Cleland, David I. Matrix Management Systems Handbook. 768p. 1983. 52.50 (ISBN 0-442-21448-0). Van Nos Reinhold.
--The Origin & Development of a Philosophy of Long-Range Planning in American Business. LC 75-41751. (Companies & Men: Business Enterprises in America). (Illus.). 1976. 32.00x (ISBN 0-405-08068-9). Ayer Co Pubs.
Cleland, David I. & King, William R. Management: A Systems Approach. (Management Ser.). (Illus.). 456p. 1972. text ed. 31.95 (ISBN 0-07-011314-9). McGraw.
Cleland, David I. & Kocaoglu, Dundar F. Engineering Management. (Industrial Engineering & Management Science Ser.). (Illus.). 528p. 1981. text ed. 42.00 (ISBN 0-07-011316-5). McGraw.
Cleland, Herdman F. Our Prehistoric Ancestors. 1979. Repr. of 1929 ed. lib. bdg. 50.00 (ISBN 0-8495-0922-X). Arden Lib.
Cleland, James. The Institution of a Young Noble Man. LC 47-12445. 1979. Repr. of 1607 ed. 55.00x (ISBN 0-8201-1216-X). Schol Facsimiles.
Cleland, John. Fanny Hill. 256p. 1982. pap. 2.95 (ISBN 0-440-05555-5). Dell.
--The Illustrated Fanny Hill: Memoirs of a Women of Pleasure. LC 77-92115. (Illus.). 1978. o. p. 14.95 (ISBN 0-913568-27-9); ultra ed. 19.95 (ISBN 0-913568-26-0). Avant-Garde.
--Memoirs of a Woman of Pleasure. Sabor, Peter, ed. (WC-P Ser.). 256p. 1985. pap. 3.95 (ISBN 0-19-281634-9). Oxford U Pr.
--Memoirs of Fanny Hill. pap. 2.25 (ISBN 0-451-09634-7, E9634, Sig). NAL.
Cleland, John & Hobcraft, John. Reproductive Change in Developing Countries. (Illus.). 320p. 1985. 24.95x (ISBN 0-19-828465-9). Oxford U Pr.
Cleland, John & Stirling, Bob. The Amatory Experiences of a Surgeon - The Town Bull. 192p. 1984. pap. 3.95 (ISBN 0-446-30794-7). Warner Bks.
Cleland, Lucille H. Trails & Trials of the Pioneers of the Olympic Peninsula. 312p. pap. 14.95 (ISBN 0-8466-0302-0, S-302). Shorey.
Cleland, Max. Strong at the Broken Places. 160p. 1980. PLB 6.95 (ISBN 0-310-60450-8, Pub by Chosen Bks). Zondervan.
Cleland, Nona, ed. Knocking at the Gate of Life & Other Healing Exercises from China: Official Manual of the People's Republic of China. Chang, Edward C., tr. (Illus.). 288p. 1985. 17.95 (ISBN 0-87857-581-2); pap. 10.95 (ISBN 0-87857-582-0). Rodale Pr Inc.
Cleland, R. The Mexican Yearbook. 1976. lib. bdg. 59.95 (ISBN 0-8490-2240-1). Gordon Pr.
--One Hundred Years of the Monroe Doctrine. 1976. lib. bdg. 59.95 (ISBN 0-8490-2376-9). Gordon Pr.
Cleland, Robert. A History of California: The American Period. LC 75-3483. (Illus.). 512p. 1975. Repr. of 1930 ed. lib. bdg. 27.25x (ISBN 0-8371-8155-0, CLHC). Greenwood.
Cleland, Robert G. California in Our Time, Nineteen Hundred to Nineteen Forty. 1947. 20.00 (ISBN 0-8495-0856-8). Arden Lib.
--The Irvine Ranch. 3rd ed. LC 62-18134. (Illus.). 167p. 1984. pap. 7.50 (ISBN 0-87328-067-9). Huntington Lib.
--This Reckless Breed of Men: The Trappers & Fur Traders of the Southwest. LC 75-46376. 1976. pap. 8.95 (ISBN 0-8263-0415-X). U of NM Pr.
Cleland, Robert G. & Putnam, Frank B. Isaias W. Hellman & the Farmers & Merchants Bank. LC 65-12230. (Huntington Library Classics). (Illus.). 136p. 1980. pap. 4.00 (ISBN 0-87328-018-0). Huntington Lib.
Cleland, Robert G. & Brooks, Juanita, eds. A Mormon Chronicle: The Diaries of John D. Lee, 1848-1876, 2 vols. (Illus.). xxxii, 824p. 1983. Repr. of 1955 ed. Set. 39.95 (ISBN 0-87480-230-X). U of Utah Pr.
Cleland, William, et al. Medical & Surgical Cardiology. (Illus.). 1168p. 1969. 29.75 (ISBN 0-8016-1089-3, Blackwell). Mosby.
Clellan, Doug, jt. auth. see Geddes, Robert.
Clelland, Doug, ed. Berlin: An Architectural History-An Architectural Design Profile. (Illus.). 88p. 1984. pap. 14.95 (ISBN 0-312-07614-2). St Martin.
Clelland, Richard C., et al. Basic Statistics with Business Applications. LC 72-8057. (Probability & Mathematical Statistics: Applied Probability & Statistics Section). (Illus.). pap. 120.00 (ISBN 0-8357-9843-7, 2055099). Bks Demand UMI.
Clelland, Richard W. Civil Rights for the Handicapped. 1978. pap. 4.95 (ISBN 0-686-12213-5, 021-00327). Am Assn Sch Admin.
Clelland, Richard W., jt. auth. see Barbacovi, Don R.
Clem, Alan I. Precinct Returns for Major Elections in South Dakota, 1968. 1969. write for info. U of SD Gov Res Bur.
Clem, Alan L. Characteristics of South Dakota County Officers. 1962. write for info. U of SD Gov Res Bur.
--Cooling the Coffee in the Saucer: Bicameralism & the Legislative Product. 1978. write for info. U of SD Gov Res Bur.
--Election in South Dakota, 1966. 1967. write for info. U of SD Gov Res Bur.
--Election in South Dakota, 1970. 1971. write for info. U of SD Gov Res Bur.
--Election in South Dakota, 1974. 1975. write for info. U of SD Gov Res Bur.
--Election in South Dakota, 1976. 1976. write for info. U of SD Gov Res Bur.
--Election in South Dakota, 1978. 1979. write for info. U of SD Gov Res Bur.
--The Geography of South Dakota's Presidential Vote from Hoover to Nixon: A Note on Eleven Maps. 1971. write for info. U of SD Gov Res Bur.
--Ideology in State Legislative Decision-Making. 1974. write for info. U of SD Gov Res Bur.
--Measuring Legislative Committee Performance. 1975. write for info. U of SD Gov Res Bur.
--Money & Schools: Campaign Strategy in School Bond Elections. 1964. write for info. U of SD Gov Res Bur.
--The Nineteen-Eighty Election in South Dakota: End of an Era. 1981. write for info. U of SD Gov Res Bur.
--The Nineteen Eighty-Two Election in South Dakota. 1983. write for info. U of SD Gov Res Bur.
--The Nineteen Sixty-Four Election: Has South Dakota Become a Two-Party State? 1965. write for info. U of SD Gov Res Bur.
--Political Attitudes & Preferences of South Dakotans in the 1968 Presidential Election. 1972. write for info. U of SD Gov Res Bur.
--Precinct-Level Voting Returns for Major Races in the 1972 Primary Election in South Dakota. 1972. write for info. U of SD Gov Res Bur.
--Precinct-Level Voting Returns for Major Races in the 1974 Primary Election in South Dakota. 1975. write for info. U of SD Gov Res Bur.
--Precinct Returns for Major Elections in South Dakota, 1972. 1973. write for info. U of SD Gov Res Bur.
--Precinct Returns for the Nineteen Seventy-Four General Election in South Dakota. 1975. write for info. U of SD Gov Res Bur.
--Precinct Returns for the Nineteen Seventy-Six General Election in South Dakota. write for info. U of SD Gov Res Bur.
--Precinct Voting. 1964. write for info. U of SD Gov Res Bur.
--Presidential Politics in South Dakota. 1967. write for info. U of SD Gov Res Bur.
--Reconstruction of County Representation. 1968. write for info. U of SD Gov Res Bur.
--Roll Call Voting Behavior in the South Dakota Legislature. 1966. write for info. U of SD Gov Res Bur.
--South Dakota's Congressional Staffs. 1981. write for info. U of SD Gov Res Bur.
--Spirit Mound Township Revisited: A Rural View of the 1972 Campaign. 1973. write for info. U of SD Gov Res Bur.
--The Submerging Republican Majority: The 1972 Election in South Dakota. 1973. write for info. U of SD Gov Res Bur.
--Tenure in the Courthouse. 1973. write for info. U of SD Gov Res Bur.
--Voting Behavior in the South Dakota Legislature: An Exploratory Investigation into Divisible Roll Calls. 1966. write for info. U of SD Gov Res Bur.
--West River Voting Patterns. 1965. write for info. U of SD Gov Res Bur.
Clem, Alan L. & Farber, William. Multi-Member Districting & Minorities. 1978. write for info. U of SD Gov Res Bur.
Clem, Alan L. & Meyer, Kenneth. Another Look at the Effects of Divisive Party Primaries: The South Dakota Experience, 1946 to 1974. 1975. write for info. U of SD Gov Res Bur.
Clem, Alan L. & Platt, George M. A Bibliography of South Dakota Government & Politics. 1965. write for info. U of SD Gov Res Bur.
Clem, Alan L. & Rumbolz, James M. Law Enforcement: The South Dakota Experience. (Illus.). 310p. 1982. 18.50 (ISBN 0-9608456-0-7). SD Peace Officers.
Clem, Alan L., ed. Contemporary Approaches to State Constitutional Revision. 1970. 1.00 (ISBN 0-686-31878-1). U of SD Gov Res Bur.
Clem, Orlie M. Detailed Factors in Latin Prognosis. LC 78-176653. (Columbia University. Teachers College. Contributions to Education Ser.: No. 144). Repr. of 1924 ed. 22.50 (ISBN 0-404-55144-0). AMS Pr.
Clem, Ralph S., et al, eds. No Room for Man: Population & the Future Through Science-Fiction. (Quality Paperback Ser.: No. 346). 247p. 1979. pap. 4.95 (ISBN 0-8226-0346-2). Littlefield.
--No Room for Man: Population & the Future Through Science Fiction. 247p. 1979. 11.50x (ISBN 0-8476-6181-4). Rowman.
Cleman, Wolfgang, ed. see Shakespeare, William.
Clemeau, Carol. The Ariadne Clue. (Nightingale Ser.). 253p. 1983. pap. 9.95 (ISBN 0-8161-3539-8, Large Print Bks). G K Hall.
--The Ariadne Clue. 176p. 1983. pap. 2.50 (ISBN 0-345-30736-4). Ballantine.
Clemen & Eigsti. Comprehensive Family & Community Health Nursing. (Illus.). 544p. 1981. text ed. 34.95 (ISBN 0-07-011324-6). McGraw.
Clemen, Carl. Religionsgeschichtliche Erklaerung des Neuen Testamentes: Die Abhaengigkeit des aeltesten Christentums von nichtjuedischen Religionen und philosophischen Systemen. 440p. 1973. Repr. of 1924 ed. text ed. 59.20x (ISBN 3-11-002412-8). De Gruyter.
Clemen, Carl C., et al. Religions of the World. facs. ed. LC 69-17570. (Essay Index Reprint Ser). 1931. 35.50 (ISBN 0-8369-0011-1). Ayer Co Pubs.
Clemen, D. D. Primitive Christianity & Its Non-Jewish Sources. 1977. lib. bdg. 59.95 (ISBN 0-8490-2472-2). Gordon Pr.
Clemen, Otto, ed. see Luther, Martin.
Clemen, Otto see Luther, Martin.
Clemen, Rudolf A. The American Livestock & Meat Industry. abr. ed. (Illus.). 1923. 35.00 (ISBN 0-384-09305-1). Johnson Repr.
Clemen, Wolfgang. Chaucer's Early Poetry. (Methuen Library Reprints). 1980. 39.95 (ISBN 0-416-74370-6, NO.6360). Methuen Inc.
--English Tragedy Before Shakespeare. 1980. 42.00x (ISBN 0-416-74380-3, NO.2976). Methuen Inc.
--Der Junge Chaucer. 1938. pap. 20.00 (ISBN 0-384-09315-9). Johnson Repr.
--Shakespeare's Dramatic Art. (Methuen Library Reprints). 1981. 45.00x (ISBN 0-416-30580-6, NO. 2218). Methuen Inc.
--Shakespeare's Soliloquies. LC 76-58367. 1977. Repr. of 1964 ed. lib. bdg. 8.50 (ISBN 0-8414-3440-9). Folcroft.
Clemen, Wolfgang H. The Development of Shakespeare's Imagery. 2nd ed. 237p. 1977. 37.00x (ISBN 0-416-85740-X, NO.2764); pap. 14.95x (ISBN 0-416-85730-2, NO.2765). Methuen Inc.
Clemence, B. J., jt. auth. see Bowen, Bob.
Clemence, Richard, jt. auth. see Stout, Ruth.
Clemence, Richard V. & Doody, Francis S. Schumpeterian System. LC 65-25862. Repr. of 1950 ed. 17.50x (ISBN 0-678-00136-7). Kelley.
Clemenceau, Georges. American Reconstruction, Eighteen Sixty-Five to Eighteen Seventy. 2nd ed. LC 68-16229. (American Scene Ser). 1969. Repr. of 1928 ed. 35.00 (ISBN 0-306-71010-2). Da Capo.
Clemenceau, Georges E. Surprises of Life. facs. ed. Hall, Grace, tr. LC 77-132113. (Short Story Index Reprint Ser). 1920. 18.00 (ISBN 0-8369-3670-1). Ayer Co Pubs.
Clemencon, H., ed. see Symposium Lausanne, Switzerland Aug. 16 to 20 1976.
Clemens, C. Herbert. A Scrapbook of Complex Curve Theory. LC 80-20214. (The University Series in Mathematics). 200p. 1980. 29.50x (ISBN 0-306-40536-9, Plenum Pr). Plenum Pub.
Clemens, Clara. My Father, Mark Twain. LC 74-6024. (BCL Ser.: No. I). (Illus.). Repr. of 1931 ed. 28.50 (ISBN 0-404-11544-6). AMS Pr.
--My Husband Gabrilowitsch. (Music Reprint Ser.). 1979. Repr. of 1938 ed. 32.50 (ISBN 0-306-79563-9). Da Capo.
Clemens, Cyril. A Chat with Robert Frost. LC 7-860. 1977. lib. bdg. 10.00 (ISBN 0-8414-3567-7). Folcroft.
--A Chat with Rudyard Kipling. 1943. lib. bdg. 10.00 (ISBN 0-8414-3042-X). Folcroft.
--Chesterton As Seen by His Contemporaries. 1973. 69.95 (ISBN 0-87968-027-X). Gordon Pr.
--Chesterton As Seen by His Contemporaries. LC 76-92958. (English Biography Ser., No. 31). 1969. Repr. of 1938 ed. lib. bdg. 48.95x (ISBN 0-8383-0968-2). Haskell.
--Clemens,Cyril. 1978. Repr. of 1937 ed. lib. bdg. 17.50 (ISBN 0-8482-3549-5). Norwood Edns.
--An Evening with A. E. Housman. LC 77-3670. 1937. lib. bdg. 10.00 (ISBN 0-8414-3594-4). Folcroft.
--Josh Billings: Yankee Humorist. LC 76-25855. 1932. lib. bdg. 27.50 (ISBN 0-8414-3491-3). Folcroft.
--Lytton Strachey. LC 73-15585. 1942. lib. bdg. 10.00 (ISBN 0-8414-3476-X). Folcroft.
--Mark Twain & Harry S. Truman. 1978. Repr. of 1950 ed. lib. bdg. 8.50 (ISBN 0-8495-0901-7). Arden Lib.
--Mark Twain & Harry S. Truman. LC 73-18198. 1950. lib. bdg. 10.00 (ISBN 0-8414-3526-X). Folcroft.
--Mark Twain Wit & Wisdom. LC 77-21955. 1977. lib. bdg. 30.00 (ISBN 0-8414-1819-5). Folcroft.
--My Chat with Thomas Hardy. LC 77-1147. 1944. lib. bdg. 10.00 (ISBN 0-8414-3592-8). Folcroft.
--My Cousin Mark Twain. 1978. Repr. of 1939 ed. lib. bdg. 20.00 (ISBN 0-8495-0827-4). Arden Lib.
--My Cousin Mark Twain. LC 74-10995. 1939. 30.00 (ISBN 0-8414-3601-0). Folcroft.
--My Cousin, Mark Twain. LC 74-16297. (American Literature Ser., No. 49). 1974. lib. bdg. 46.95x (ISBN 0-8383-1744-8). Haskell.
--Young Sam Clemens. LC 76-49929. 1977. lib. bdg. 30.00 (ISBN 0-8414-3473-5). Folcroft.
Clemens, Cyril, ed. see Truman, Harry S.
Clemens, Dale P. Advanced Custom Rod Building. LC 82-62340. (Illus.). 1978. 21.95 (ISBN 0-8329-2587-X, Pub. by Winchester Pr). New Century.
--Fiberglass Rod Making. LC 83-62349. 1974. 17.95 (ISBN 0-8329-1360-X, Pub. by Winchester Pr). New Century.
--Fiberglass Rod Making. (Illus.). 212p. pap. 8.95 (ISBN 0-88317-042-6). Stoeger Pub Co.
Clemens, David A. The Cutting Edge, Vol. 2. LC 79-52420. (Steps to Maturity Ser.). 1975. student's manual 15.95x (ISBN 0-86508-003-8); tchr's. manual 17.95x (ISBN 0-86508-004-6). BCM Inc.
--God Encountered, Vol. 1. LC 79-52420. (Steps to Maturity Ser.). 1973. tchrs'. manual 17.95x (ISBN 0-86508-002-X); student's manual 15.95x (ISBN 0-86508-001-1); visuals packett 4.95x (ISBN 0-86508-007-0). BCM Inc.
--Living, Vol. 3. LC 79-55503. (Steps to Maturity Ser.). 1980. tchr's. manual 17.95x (ISBN 0-86508-006-2); students' manual 15.95x (ISBN 0-86508-005-4). BCM Inc.
Clemens, Frances & Tully, Robert, eds. Recreation & the Local Church. LC 57-18412. pap. 47.80 (ISBN 0-317-28391-X, 2022409). Bks Demand UMI.
Clemens, Gus. Christmas at Fort Concho. (Illus.). 32p. (Orig.). 1984. pap. 3.00 (ISBN 0-938036-06-8). Mulberry Ave Bks.
--The Concho Country: A History of the Concho River Region of West Texas. LC 80-83291. (Illus.). 232p. 1981. 25.00 (ISBN 0-938036-01-7); collector's ltd. ed. 50.00 (ISBN 0-938036-03-3); deluxe ed. 100.00 (ISBN 0-938036-00-9). Mulberry Ave Bks.
--Legacy: The Story of the Permian Basin Region of West Texas & Southeast New Mexico. (Illus.). 256p. 1983. 25.95 (ISBN 0-938036-04-1). Mulberry Ave Bks.
Clemens, J. H. Balance Sheets & the Lending Banker. 5th ed. LC 78-670081. 1977. 17.50x (ISBN 0-905118-15-4). Intl Pubns Serv.
Clemens, James A., et al. Non-Sexual Hormonal Influences on the Electrophysiology of the Brain. LC 74-6074. (Biology of Sex Ser.). 188p. 1974. text ed. 24.50x (ISBN 0-8422-7223-2). Irvington.
Clemens, John. Polls, Politics & Populism. 208p. 1983. text ed. 35.50x (ISBN 0-566-00602-2). Gower Pub Co.
Clemens, Lois G. Woman Liberated. LC 79-141830. 176p. 1975. pap. 1.75 (ISBN 0-87983-111-1). Keats.
Clemens, Michael J. Gene Expression, Vol. I. (Biochemistry of Cellular Regulation Ser.). 1980. 84.50 (ISBN 0-8493-5454-4). CRC Pr.
Clemens, Paul, ed. see Gawain, Elizabeth.
Clemens, Paul G. The Atlantic Economy & Colonial Maryland's Eastern Shore: From Tobacco to Grain. LC 79-26181. (Illus.). 256p. 1980. 24.95x (ISBN 0-8014-1251-X). Cornell U Pr.
Clemens, S. L. Mark Twain's Autobiography & First Romance. LC 74-128410. (American Biography Ser., No. 32). 1970. Repr. of 1871 ed. lib. bdg. 29.95x (ISBN 0-8383-1152-0). Haskell.
Clemens, Samuel. The Adventures of Huckleberry Finn. (Illus.). 352p. 1984. 11.95 (ISBN 0-396-08253-X). Dodd.
--Editorial Wild Oats. LC 77-125685. (American Journalists Ser). 1970. Repr. of 1905 ed. 17.50 (ISBN 0-405-01662-X). Ayer Co Pubs.
--Huckleberry Finn. (Tempo Classic Ser.). (gr. 4 up). 1979. pap. 1.50 (ISBN 0-448-17108-2, Pub. by Tempo). Ace Bks.
--Huckleberry Finn. Farr, Naunerle, ed. LC 73-75468. (Now Age Illustrated Ser.). (Illus.). 64p. (Orig.). (gr. 5-10). 1973. 5.00 (ISBN 0-88301-207-3); pap. 1.95 (ISBN 0-88301-098-4). Pendulum Pr.
--Is Shakespeare Dead? 1919. 20.00 (ISBN 0-8274-2591-0). R West.
Clemens, Samuel, pseud. The Man That Corrupted Hadleyburg: A Classic Story of Satire. (Classic Short Stories Ser.). (Illus.). (gr. 4 up). PLB 8.95 (ISBN 0-317-30956-0). Creative Ed.
Clemens, Samuel. Mark Twain's Notebook. 1973. 35.00 (ISBN 0-8274-1403-X). R West.
--Tom Sawyer. new ed. Shapiro, Irwin, ed. LC 73-75465. (Now Age Illustrated Ser.). (Illus.). 64p. (Orig.). (gr. 5-10). 1973. 5.00 (ISBN 0-88301-220-0); pap. 1.95 (ISBN 0-88301-103-4); student activity bk. 1.25 (ISBN 0-88301-179-4). Pendulum Pr.
Clemens, Samuel see Sr. Teresa Agnes.
Clemens, Samuel see Twain, Mark, pseud.
Clemens, Samuel L. Adventures of Huckleberry Finn. 2nd ed. Bradley, Sculley & Beatty, Richmond C., eds. LC 76-30648. (Critical Editions). 1977. 19.95 (ISBN 0-393-04454-8); pap. 5.95x (ISBN 0-393-09146-5). Norton.
--The Adventures of Tom Sawyer. (Illus.). 352p. 1984. 11.95 (ISBN 0-396-08254-8). Dodd.
--The American Claimant. 1981. Repr. lib. bdg. 39.00x (ISBN 0-403-00103-X). Scholarly.
--The Celebrated Jumping Frog of Calaveras County. LC 75-91075. (The American Humorist Ser.). Repr. of 1867 ed. lib. bdg. 27.00 (ISBN 0-8398-0267-6). Irvington.
--A Connecticut Yankee in King Arthur's Court. Ensor, Allison E., ed. (Norton Critical Editions Ser.). (Illus.). 450p. 1982. 24.95 (ISBN 0-393-01378-2); pap. text ed. 6.95x (ISBN 0-393-95137-5). Norton.
--A Connecticut Yankee in King Arthur's Court. (Illus.). 512p. 1985. 12.95 (ISBN 0-396-08686-1). Dodd.
--Contributions to the Galaxy: 1868-1871. LC 61-5053. 1977. lib. bdg. 30.00x (ISBN 0-8201-1254-2). Schol Facsimiles.
--The Curious Republic of Gondour. LC 74-10998. Repr. of 1919 ed. lib. bdg. 25.00 (ISBN 0-8414-3603-7). Folcroft.
--Curious Republic of Gondour. LC 74-3396. (Mark Twain Ser. No. 76). 1974. lib. bdg. 39.95x (ISBN 0-8383-2070-8). Haskell.

--How to Tell a Story. 1981. Repr. lib. bdg. 39.00x (ISBN 0-403-00103-X). Scholarly.

--Letters from the Sandwich Islands. LC 72-2113. (American Literature Ser., No. 49). 1972. Repr. of 1938 ed. lib. bdg. 49.95x (ISBN 0-8383-1471-6). Haskell.

--The Love Letters of Mark Twain. Wecter, Dixon, ed. LC 76-20557. (Illus.). 374p. 1976. Repr. of 1949 ed. lib. bdg. 27.50x (ISBN 0-8371-8995-0, WELL). Greenwood.

--The Man That Corrupted Hadleyburg. 1981. Repr. lib. bdg. 49.00x (ISBN 0-403-00103-X). Scholarly.

--Mark Twain-Howells Letters: The Correspondence of Samuel L. Clemens & William D. Howells, 1872-1910, 2 vols. Smith, Henry N. & Gibson, William M., eds. LC 60-5397. 1960. 55.00x set (ISBN 0-674-54900-7, Belknap Pr). Harvard U Pr.

--Mark Twain's Letters, 2 vols. LC 74-6025. (BCL Ser.: No. II). Repr. of 1917 ed. Set. 85.00 (ISBN 0-404-11545-4). AMS Pr.

--Mark Twain's Letters to Mary. Leary, Lewis, ed. LC 61-7714. 138p. 1963. pap. 10.00x (ISBN 0-231-08545-1). Columbia U Pr.

--Mark Twain's Notebook. LC 72-77127. 1972. Repr. of 1935 ed. lib. bdg. 27.50 (ISBN 0-8154-0418-2). Cooper Sq.

--Mark Twain's San Francisco. Taper, Bernard, ed. LC 77-19241. Repr. of 1963 ed. lib. bdg. 24.75x (ISBN 0-313-20254-0, CLMT). Greenwood.

--Mark Twain's Speeches. Howells, William Dean, ed. 1910. 45.00 (ISBN 0-8274-2677-1). R West.

--Mark Twain's Works: 1899-1907, 25 vols. deluxe ed. Set. 450.00 (ISBN 0-8274-2678-X). R West.

--One Million Pound Bank-Note & Other New Stories. LC 76-121529. (Short Story Index Reprint Ser). 1893. 16.00 (ISBN 0-8369-3485-7). Ayer Co Pubs.

--Personal Recollections of Joan of Arc by the Sieur Louis De Conte. LC 80-23663. (Illus.). xiv, 461p. 1980. Repr. of 1906 ed. lib. bdg. 60.50x (ISBN 0-313-22373-4, CLPR). Greenwood.

--Pudd'nhead Wilson & Those Extraordinary Twins. Berger, Sidney E., ed. (Norton Critical Edition Ser.). (Illus.). 1981. 22.50 (ISBN 0-393-01337-5); pap. text ed. 6.95x (ISBN 0-393-95027-1). Norton.

--Sketches: New & Old. 1981. Repr. lib. bdg. 49.00x (ISBN 0-403-00103-X). Scholarly.

--Stolen White Elephant, Etc. LC 70-121530. (Short Story Index Reprint Ser). 1882. 17.00 (ISBN 0-8369-3486-5). Ayer Co Pubs.

--What Is Man? And Other Essays. LC 71-167326. (Essay Index Reprint Ser.). Repr. of 1917 ed. 23.00 (ISBN 0-8369-2762-1). Ayer Co Pubs.

--The Writings of Mark Twain, 25 vols. Incl. Vols. 1 & 2. The Innocents Abroad, Pts. 1 & 2. Set. 75.00 (ISBN 0-686-66711-5); (ISBN 0-403-02325-4); (ISBN 0-403-02326-2); Vols. 3 & 4. The Gilded Age, Pts. 1 & 2. Set. 75.00 (ISBN 0-686-66712-3); (ISBN 0-403-02327-0); (ISBN 0-403-02328-9); Vols. 5 & 6. A Tramp Abroad, Pts. 1 & 2. Set. 50.00x (ISBN 0-686-66713-1); (ISBN 0-403-02329-7); (ISBN 0-403-02330-0); Vols. 7 & 8. Following the Equator, Pts. 1 & 2. Set. 75.00x (ISBN 0-686-66714-X); (ISBN 0-403-02331-9); (ISBN 0-403-02332-7); Vols. 9 & 10. Roughing It, Pts. 1 & 2. Set. 75.00x (ISBN 0-686-66715-8); (ISBN 0-403-02333-5); (ISBN 0-403-02334-3); Vol. 11. Life on the Mississippi. 69.00x (ISBN 0-403-02341-6); Vol. 12. Adventures of Tom Sawyer. 39.00x (ISBN 0-403-02342-4); Vol. 13. Huckleberry Finn. 39.00x (ISBN 0-403-02335-1); Vol. 14. Pudd'nhead Wilson. 39.00x (ISBN 0-403-02336-X); Vol. 15. The Prince & the Pauper. 39.00x (ISBN 0-403-02337-8); Vol. 16. A Connecticut Yankee in King Arthur's Court. 39.00x (ISBN 0-403-02338-6); Vols. 17 & 18. Joan of Arc, Pts. 1 & 2. Set. 75.00x (ISBN 0-685-27293-1); (ISBN 0-403-02240-1); (ISBN 0-403-02239-8); Vol. 19. A Connecticut Yankee in King Arthur's Court. 39.00x (ISBN 0-685-27294-X); Vol. 20. Tom Sawyer Abroad. 39.00x (ISBN 0-403-02343-2); Vol. 24. The Thirty Thousand Bequest. 39.00x (ISBN 0-403-02348-3); Vol. 25. Christian Science. 39.00x (ISBN 0-403-02349-1). LC 79-7769. 1869-1909. Set. 1495.00 (ISBN 0-403-03736-0). Scholarly.

Clemens, Samuel L. see Fried, M. B.

Clemens, Samuel L., jt. auth. see Harte, Bret.

Clemens, Samuel L. see Twain, Mark, pseud.

Clemens, Samuel L. see Twain, Mark.

Clemens, Samuel Langhorne. Republican Letters. LC 77-787. 1977. Repr. of 1941 ed. lib. bdg. 20.00 (ISBN 0-8414-3417-4). Folcroft.

Clemens, Siegfried M., tr. see Bleuler, Manfred.

Clemens, Susie. Green Paisley. 33p. 1976. pap. 3.50x (ISBN 0-942256-01-8). Flower Pr.

Clemens, Susy. Papa: An Intimate Biography of Mark Twain by His Daughter Susy, Age 13. Neider, Charles, ed. LC 85-6782. (Illus.). 192p. 1985. 15.95 (ISBN 0-385-23245-4). Doubleday.

Clemens, Sydney G. The Sun's Not Broken, A Cloud's Just in the Way: On Child Centered Teaching. 137p. (Orig.). 1984. pap. 8.95 (ISBN 0-87659-109-8, 10001). Gryphon Hse.

Clemens, Virginia P. Behind the Filmmaking Scene. LC 82-1926. (Illus.). 156p. (gr. 6-10). 1982. 12.95 (ISBN 0-664-32691-9). Westminster.

--A Horse in Your Backyard? LC 77-7394. (Illus.). 154p. (gr. 7-10). 1977. 8.50 (ISBN 0-664-32616-1). Westminster.

--SuperAnimals & Their Unusual Careers. LC 79-10932. (Illus.). 192p. (gr. 4-7). 1979. 9.95 (ISBN 0-664-32649-8). Westminster.

--The Team Behind Your Favorite Record. LC 80-15999. (Illus.). 94p. 1980. 8.95 (ISBN 0-664-32668-4). Westminster.

Clemens, Walter C., Jr., compiled by. Soviet Disarmament Policy, 1917-1963: An Annotated Bibliography of Soviet-Western Sources. LC 65-12623. (Bibliographical Ser.: No. 22). 1965. pap. 6.95x (ISBN 0-8179-2222-9). Hoover Inst Pr.

Clemens, Will M. A Ken of Kipling: Being a Biographical Sketch of Rudyard Kipling, with an Appreciation and Some Anecdotes. 1899. Repr. 15.00 (ISBN 0-8274-2648-8). R West.

--Mark Twain: His Life & Work. LC 75-11841. 1894. lib. bdg. 30.00 (ISBN 0-8414-3643-6). Folcroft.

Clemens, William A., Jr. Records of the Fossil Mammal Sinclairella, Family Apatemyidae, from the Chadronian & Orellan. (Museum Ser.: Vol. 14, No. 17). 9p. 1964. pap. 1.25 (ISBN 0-317-04964-X). U of KS Mus Nat Hist.

Clemens, William M. American Marriage Records Before 1699. LC 67-30754. 259p. 1984. Repr. of 1926 ed. 12.50 (ISBN 0-8063-0075-2). Genealog Pub.

--North & South Carolina Marriage Records from the Earliest Colonial Days to the Civil War. LC 73-1942. 295p. 1981. Repr. of 1927 ed. 15.00 (ISBN 0-8063-0555-X). Genealog Pub.

Clemensen, Jessie. Mountainside Reflections. (Illus.). 64p. 1980. 5.95 (ISBN 0-89962-022-1). Todd & Honeywell.

--Study Outlines in Physics; Construction & Experimental Evaluation. LC 71-176654. (Columbia University. Teachers College. Contributions to Education: No. 553). Repr. of 1933 ed. 22.50 (ISBN 0-404-55553-5). AMS Pr.

Clemenson, Heather. English Country Houses & Landed Estates. LC 82-3298. (Illus.). 256p. 1982. 30.00x (ISBN 0-312-25414-8). St Martin.

Clemen-Stone, S. A. & Eigsti, D. G. Comphrensive Family & Community Health Nursing. 2nd ed. 800p. 1986. price not set (ISBN 0-07-011325-4). McGraw.

Clement, Alexis. Basic Russian Through Conversation. 1960. pap. text ed. 3.25 (ISBN 0-940630-12-5, T-7183(WRS-212)). Playette Corp.

Clement, Arthur J. Pentecost or Pretense. 1981. pap. 7.95 (ISBN 0-8100-0118-7, 12N1718). Northwest Pub.

Clement, Catherine. The Lives & Legends of Jacques Lacan. Goldhammer, Arthur, tr. from Fr. LC 83-4283. 232p. 1983. 24.00x (ISBN 0-231-05568-4); pap. 12.00 (ISBN 0-231-05569-2). Columbia U Pr.

Clement, Charles. Gericault: Etude Biographique et Critique, averc le Catalogue Raisonne de l'Oeuvre du Maitre. rev ed. LC 73-83834. (Graphic Art Ser.). (Illus.). 550p. (Fr.). 1974. Repr. of 1879 ed. lib. bdg. 75.00 (ISBN 0-306-70643-1). Da Capo.

--Limit Bid! Limit Bid! 200p. 1984. 13.95 (ISBN 0-915463-01-6, Dist. by Kampmann). Jameson Bks.

Clement, Charles B. The Fairy Godmother. 192p. 1986. pap. 3.50 (ISBN 0-446-32649-6). Warner Bks.

--The Fairy Godmother: A Novel. 1981. 8.95 (ISBN 0-89803-035-8, Dist. by Kampmann). Green Hill.

Clement, Clara. A Handbook of Legendary & Mythological Art. 59.95 (ISBN 0-8490-0279-6). Gordon Pr.

Clement, Clara E. Constantinople. 1977. lib. bdg. 59.95 (ISBN 0-8490-1668-1). Gordon Pr.

--Handbook of Legendary & Mythological Art. LC 68-26616. (Illus.). 1969. Repr. of 1881 ed. 45.00x (ISBN 0-8103-3175-6). Gale.

--Saints in Art. LC 77-89303. 1976. Repr. of 1899 ed. 46.00x (ISBN 0-8103-3030-X). Gale.

--Women in the Fine Arts: From the Seventh Century B. C. to the Twentieth Century A. D. (Illus.). 395p. 1977. Repr. of 1904 ed. 18.50 (ISBN 0-87928-079-4). Corner Hse.

Clement, Clare E. & Hutton, Laurence. Artists of the Nineteenth Century & Their Work. LC 70-88820. (Art Histories Collection Ser). Repr. of 1894 ed. 24.00 (ISBN 0-405-02222-0). Ayer Co Pubs.

Clement, David D., tr. see Zehme, Friedrich W.

Clement, F. A., jt. auth. see Thomason, Calvin C.

Clement, Felix & Larousse, Pierre. Dictionnaire Des Operas, 2 Vols. LC 69-15617. (Music Reprint Ser). (Fr.). 1969. Repr. of 1905 ed. Set. 110.00 (ISBN 0-306-71197-4). Da Capo.

Clement, Francois. The Birth of an Island. 1977. pap. 1.75 (ISBN 0-380-00952-8, 32284). Avon.

Clement, Frederic. Transformations: Frederic Clement. LC 85-70658. (Illus.). 56p. (gr. 1 up). 1985. pap. 14.95 (ISBN 0-88138-028-8, Star & Elephant Bks.). Green Tiger Pr.

Clement, George H. The ABC's of the Prophetical Scriptures. pap. 2.25 (ISBN 0-685-61832-3). Reiner.

Clement, Hal. Close to Critical. 192p. (Orig.). 1975. pap. 1.95 (ISBN 0-345-29168-9). Ballantine.

--Cycle of Fire. 192p. 1981. pap. 2.25 (ISBN 0-345-29172-7, Del Rey). Ballantine.

--Iceworld. (Del Rey Bks). 1977. pap. 2.50 (ISBN 0-345-31621-5). Ballantine.

--Left of Africa. (Lost Manuscripts Ser.). 160p. 1976. 12.95 (ISBN 0-936414-01-4). Manuscript Pr.

--Mission of Gravity. 1984. pap. 2.75 (ISBN 0-345-31622-3, Del Rey). Ballantine.

--The Nitrogen Fix. 288p. 1982. pap. 2.95 (ISBN 0-441-58118-8). Ace Bks.

--Through the Eye of a Needle. (Del Rey Bks). 1979. pap. 1.95 (ISBN 0-345-28410-0). Ballantine.

Clement, Henry. The Clairvoyant. 224p. (Orig.). 1984. pap. 2.50 (ISBN 0-523-41920-1). Pinnacle Bks.

--The Franky Doyle Story. (Prisoner: Cell Block H Ser.: No.2). 224p. (Orig.). 1981. pap. 2.25 (ISBN 0-523-41175-8). Pinnacle Bks.

Clement, J., jt. auth. see De Montalembert, M. R.

Clement, J., ed. Noble Deeds of American Women. 480p. 1975. Repr. of 1856 ed. 18.50 (ISBN 0-87928-061-1). Corner Hse.

Clement, Jacqueline P. Sex Bias in School Leadership. LC 75-3712. 1975. 2.70 (ISBN 0-912008-10-5). Integrated Ed Assoc.

Clement, Jan P. see Suver, James D. & Kahn, Charles N., III.

Clement, Jane T. The Sparrow. Hutteria Society of Brothers, ed. LC 68-21133. 1978. pap. 4.95 (ISBN 0-87486-009-1). Plough.

Clement, Janequin see Janequin, Clement, et al.

Clement, Jean-Luc, jt. ed. see Howse, P. E.

Clement, Jean-Michel. Dictionnaire des Industries Alimentaires. 361p. (Fr.). 1978. 32.50 (ISBN 0-686-56949-0, M-6071). French & Eur.

Clement, Jesse, ed. Noble Deeds of American Women: With Biographical Sketches of Some of the More Prominent. LC 74-3935. (Women in America Ser). (Illus.). 482p. 1974. Repr. of 1851 ed. 38.50x (ISBN 0-405-06082-3). Ayer Co Pubs.

Clement, John, jt. auth. see Atkinson, Phillip S.

Clement, John, jt. ed. see Lochhead, Jack.

Clement, Lee, ed. & intro. by see Young, Andrew J.

Clement, M., ed. Correspondence & the Minutes of the S.P.C.K. Relating to Wales. (History & Law Ser.). 369p. 1952. text ed. 27.75x (ISBN 0-7083-0109-6, Pub. by Univ of Wales Pr England). Humanities.

Clement, M. A. Transmission. 52p. 7.00 (ISBN 0-317-06288-3). Telephony.

Clement, Mary, ed. Correspondence & Records of the S.P.G. Relating to Wales 1701-1750. 102p. 1973. text ed. 13.00x (ISBN 0-7083-0519-9, Pub. by Univ of Wales Pr England). Humanities.

Clement, Nemours H. Influence of the Arthurian Romance on the Five Books of Rabelais. LC 71-91346. 1970. 9.00x (ISBN 0-87753-008-4). Phaeton.

--Romanticism in France. (MLA Rev. Fund Ser.). 1938. 41.00 (ISBN 0-527-17800-4). Kraus Repr.

Clement, Olivier. The Spirit of Solzhenitsyn. Burns, Paul, tr. Fawcett, Sarah, ed. LC 76-40371. 235p. 1977. Repr. of 1976 ed. text ed. 22.50x (ISBN 0-06-491212-4). B&N Imports.

Clement, Paul A., jt. auth. see Packard, Pamela M.

Clement, Paul W., jt. ed. see Tweedie, Donald F.

Clement, Pierre. Histoire du systeme protecteur en France depuis le ministere de Colbert jusqu'a la revolution de 1848. (Research & Source Works Ser.: No. 205). 1968. Repr. of 1854 ed. 29.00 (ISBN 0-8337-0590-3). B Franklin.

--Hypnosis & Power Learning. 135p. 1979. pap. 7.95 (ISBN 0-930298-02-0). Westwood Pub Co.

Clement, Preston R. & Johnson, Walter C. Electrical Engineering Science. LC 82-14796. 602p. 1982. Repr. of 1960 ed. lib. bdg. 35.50 (ISBN 0-89874-442-3). Krieger.

Clement, Priscilla F. Welfare & the Poor in the Nineteenth-Century City: Philadelphia, 1800-1854. LC 83-49357. (Illus.). 224p. 1985. 27.50 (ISBN 0-8386-3216-5). Fairleigh Dickinson.

Clement, Russell T., compiled by. Mormons in the Pacific: A Bibliography. 1981. 12.95 (ISBN 0-939154-17-X); pap. 7.95 (ISBN 0-939154-18-8). Inst Polynesian.

Clement, Russell T., jt. ed. see Craig, Robert D.

Clemente, Carlo C. Di see Prochaska, James O. & DiClemente, Carlo C.

Clemente, Carmine D. Anatomy. A Regional Atlas of the Human Body. 2nd ed. LC 80-28394. (Illus.). 395p. 1981. text ed. 36.00 (ISBN 0-8067-0322-9). Urban & S.

Clemente, Carmine D., ed. Gray's Anatomy of the Human Body. 30th ed. LC 84-5741. (Illus.). 1676p. 1984. 68.50 (ISBN 0-8121-0644-X). Lea & Febiger.

Clemente, Carmine D. & Purpura, Dominick P., eds. Sleep & the Maturing Nervous System. (Illus.). 1972. 65.50 (ISBN 0-12-176250-5). Acad Pr.

Clemente, Elizabeth M. de see Van Ness, Bethann & De Clemente, Elizabeth M.

Clemente, Frank & Lambert, Richard D., eds. The New Rural America. LC 76-27028. (Annals Ser.: No. 429). 1977. 15.00 (ISBN 0-87761-208-0); pap. 7.95 (ISBN 0-87761-209-9). Am Acad Pol Soc Sci.

Clemente, Jose E., ed. Martin Fierro, un Siglo. limited ed. (Illus., Span., Special centennial vol., vols. no. 500-1000 only, for sale). 1972. 50.00 (ISBN 0-935738-03-7). US Comm Unicef.

Clemente, Vince & Everett, Graham, eds. Paumanok Rising: An Anthology of Eastern Long Island Aesthetics. LC 81-50937. (Illus.). 216p. (Orig.). 1981. pap. 7.50 (ISBN 0-935252-27-4). Street Pr.

Clementel, E. & Villi, C. Direct Interactions & Nuclear Reaction Mechanisms. 1238p. 1963. 264.75 (ISBN 0-677-10070-1). Gordon.

Clementes, Julia. The Flower Arranger's Bedside Book. (Illus.). 80p. 1982. 12.50 (Pub. by Batsford England). David & Charles.

Clementi, E. Computational Aspects for Large Chemical Systems. (Lecture Notes in Chemistry: Vol. 19). (Illus.). 184p. 1980. pap. 21.00 (ISBN 0-387-10014-8). Springer-Verlag.

--Determination of Liquid Water Structure, Coordination Numbers for Ions & Solvation for Biological Molecules. (Lecture Notes in Chemistry: Vol. 2). 1976. soft cover 13.00 (ISBN 0-387-07870-3). Springer-Verlag.

--Selected Topics in Molecular Physics. (Illus.). 1972. 40.00x (ISBN 3-527-25388-2). VCH Pubs.

Clementi, Enrico & Sarma, Ramaswamy, eds. Structure & Dynamics of Nucleic Acids & Proteins. (Illus.). 600p. 1983. text ed. 49.00 (ISBN 0-940030-04-7). Adenine Pr.

Clementi, F., ed. see International Symposium on Cell Biology & Cytopharmacology, First.

Clementi, Muzio. Collected Works, 13 vols in 5. LC 70-75299. (Music Reprint Ser). 1973. 69.50 ea.; Set. 325.00 (ISBN 0-306-77260-4); fascicle of flute & violin pts. 18.50 (ISBN 0-306-77267-1); fascicle of cello pts. 18.50 (ISBN 0-306-77268-X). Da Capo.

--Complete Works for Piano Solo, Vol. 2. LC 84-756297. (The London Pianoforte School 1770-1860 Ser.). 200p. 1984. lib. bdg. 60.00 (ISBN 0-8240-6151-9). Garland Pub.

--Complete Works for Piano Solo, Vol. 3. (The London Pianoforte School 1770-1860 Ser.). 250p. 1984. lib. bdg. 60.00 (ISBN 0-8240-6152-7). Garland Pub.

--Complete Works for Piano Students, Vol. 4. Temperley, Nicholas, ed. (The London Pianoforte School 1770-1860 Ser.). 225p. 1985. lib. bdg. 60.00 (ISBN 0-317-14486-3). Garland Pub.

--Gradus Ad Parnassum. (Music Reprint Ser.: 1979). 1980. Repr. of 1826 ed. lib. bdg. 49.50 (ISBN 0-306-79570-1). Da Capo.

--Gradus ad Parnassum: Twenty-Nine Selected Studies for Piano. (Carl Fischer Music Library: No. 388). 76p. 1983. pap. 6.00 (ISBN 0-8258-0119-2, L 388). Fischer Inc NY.

--Introduction to the Art of Playing on the Pianoforte. LC 70-125067. 1974. Repr. of 1801 ed. lib. bdg. 25.00 (ISBN 0-306-70004-2). Da Capo.

Clement Of Alexandria. Christ the Educator. LC 66-20313. (Fathers of the Church Ser.: Vol. 23). 309p. 1954. 16.95x (ISBN 0-8132-0023-7). Cath U Pr.

--Exhortation to the Greeks, the Rich Man's Salvation, to the Newly Baptized. (Loeb Classical Library: No. 92). 12.00x (ISBN 0-674-99103-6). Harvard U Pr.

Clements, Abigail. The Sea-Harrower. (Orig.). 1980. pap. 2.25 (ISBN 0-449-14326-0, GM). Fawcett.

Clements, Alan. Principles of Computer Hardware. (Illus.). 450p. 1985. 32.50 (ISBN 0-19-853704-2); pap. 16.95 (ISBN 0-19-853703-4). Oxford U Pr.

Clements, Arthur F. Tudor Translations. 1978. Repr. of 1940 ed. lib. bdg. 20.00 (ISBN 0-8495-0831-2). Arden Lib.

Clements, Arthur L., ed. see Donne, John.

Clements, Barbara E. Bolshevik Feminist: The Life of Aleksandra Kollontai. LC 78-3240. (Illus.). 384p. 1979. 20.00x (ISBN 0-253-31209-4). Ind U Pr.

Clements, Barthe. Sixth Grade Can Really Kill You. LC 85-40382. 144p. (gr. 4-6). 1985. 11.95 (ISBN 0-670-80656-0, Viking Kestrel). Viking.

Clements, Barthe de see De Clements, Barthe.

Clements, Bruce. Anywhere Else but Here. LC 80-11345. 208p. (gr. 7 up). 1980. 10.95 (ISBN 0-374-30371-1). FS&G.

--Anywhere Else but Here. 160p. (gr. 7 up). 1982. pap. 1.95 (ISBN 0-440-90247-9, LFL). Dell.

--Coming About. LC 83-47841. 92p. (gr. 5 up). 1984. 11.95 (ISBN 0-374-31457-8). FS&G.

--From Ice Set Free: The Story of Otto Kiep. LC 70-184703. 224p. (gr. 7 up). 1972. 5.50 (ISBN 0-374-32468-9). FS&G.

--I Tell a Lie Every So Often. LC 73-22356. 149p. (gr. 7 up). 1974. 9.95 (ISBN 0-374-33619-9); pap. 3.45 (ISBN 0-374-43539-1). FS&G.

--Prison Window, Jerusalem Blue. LC 77-10081. 256p. (gr. 7 up). 1977. 10.95 (ISBN 0-374-36126-6). FS&G.

Clements, Bruce & Clements, Hanna. Coming Home to a Place You've Never Been Before. LC 75-26716. 192p. (gr. 7 up). 1975. 6.95 (ISBN 0-374-31530-2). FS&G.

Clements, Charles. Witness to War: An American Doctor in El Salvador. 288p. 1984. 15.95 (ISBN 0-553-05064-8). Bantam.

Clements, Claire B. & Clements, Robert D. Art & Mainstreaming: Art Instruction for Exceptional Children in Regular School Classes. (Illus.). 186p. 1984. pap. 17.50x (ISBN 0-398-04891-6). C C Thomas.

Clements, Colin, jt. auth. see Ryerson, Florence.

Clements, Colin C. Plays for Pagans. LC 77-94337. (One-Act Plays in Reprint Ser.). 1978. Repr. of 1924 ed. 18.75x (ISBN 0-8486-2035-6). Core Collection.

Clements, Colin C., ed. Sea Plays. LC 79-50022. (One-Act Plays in Reprint Ser.). (Illus.). 1980. Repr. of 1925 ed. 23.50x (ISBN 0-8486-2046-1). Core Collection.

Clements, Colleen D. Medical Genetics Casebook: A Clinical Introduction to Medical Ethics Systems Theory. LC 81-8220. (Contemporary Issues in Biomedicine, Ethics, & Society Ser.). 256p. 1982. 29.50 (ISBN 0-89603-033-4). Humana.

Clements, Colleen D., jt. auth. see Teichler-Zallen, Doris.

Clements, D. J. & Anderson, B. D. Singular Optimal Control: The Linear-Quadratic Problem. (Lecture Notes in Control & Information Science: Vol. 5). 1978. pap. 12.00 (ISBN 0-387-08694-3). Springer-Verlag.

Clements, David L. Boundary Value Problems Governed by Second Order Elliptic Systems. LC 80-20820. (Monographs & Studies: No. 12). 176p. 1981. text ed. 58.95 (ISBN 0-273-08502-6). Pitman Pub MA.

--An Introduction to Mathematical Models in Economic Dynamics. LC 83-23078. 175p. 1984. 18.95x (ISBN 0-936428-07-4). Polygonal Pub.

Clements, Dorothy J. Heard from Heaven. (Orig.). 1985. pap. 5.00 (ISBN 0-915541-06-8). Star Bks Inc.

Clements, Douglas, jt. auth. see Reidesel, C. Alan.

Clements, Douglas H. Computers in Early & Primary Education. (Illus.). 352p. 1985. text ed. 17.95 (ISBN 0-13-164013-5). P-H.

Clements, E. Introduction to the Study of Indian Music. LC 77-75213. 1977. Repr. of 1913 ed. lib. bdg. 20.00 (ISBN 0-89341-113-2). Longwood Pub Group.

Clements, E. S., jt. auth. see Clements, F. E.

Clements, F. A. Oman: The Reborn Land. 181p. 1980. text ed. 27.00x (ISBN 0-582-78300-3). Longman.

Clements, F. E. & Clements, E. S. Rocky Mountain Flowers: An Illustrated Guide for Plant-Lovers & Plant-Users. 3rd ed. (Illus.). 1963. 17.95x (ISBN 0-02-842970-2). Hafner.

Clements, Frank. The Emergence of Arab Nationalism. LC 76-5160. 1976. 25.00 (ISBN 0-8420-2096-9). Scholarly Res Inc.

--T. E. Lawrence: A Reader's Guide. 208p. 1973. 17.50 (ISBN 0-208-01313-X, Archon). Shoe String.

Clements, Frank A. Kuwait. (World Bibliographical Ser.: No. 56). 195p. 1985. lib. bdg. 30.00 (ISBN 0-903450-99-2, Pub. by Clio Press England). ABC-Clio.

--Oman. (World Bibliographical Ser.: No. 29). 216p. 1981. lib. bdg. 32.50 (ISBN 0-903450-43-7). ABC-Clio.

--Saudi Arabia. (World Bibliographical Ser.: No. 5). 197p. 1979. 25.25 (ISBN 0-903450-15-1). ABC-Clio.

--United Arab Emirates. (World Bibliographical Ser.: No. 43). 164p. 1983. lib. bdg. 26.00 (ISBN 0-903450-74-7). ABC-Clio.

Clements, Frederic E. Plant Competition: An Analysis of Community Functions. Egerton, Frank N., ed. LC 77-74209. (History of Ecology Ser.). (Illus.). 1978. Repr. of 1929 ed. lib. bdg. 37.50x (ISBN 0-405-10380-8). Ayer Co Pubs.

--Plant Succession & Indicators: A Definitive Edition of Plant Succession & Plant Indicators. (Illus.). 1973. Repr. 23.95x (ISBN 0-02-843020-4). Hafner.

--Research Methods in Ecology. Egerton, Frank, 3rd, ed. LC 77-74210. (History of Ecology Ser.). (Illus.). 1977. Repr. of 1905 ed. lib. bdg. 30.00x (ISBN 0-405-10381-6). Ayer Co Pubs.

Clements, Frederic E., jt. auth. see Pound, Roscoe.

Clements, George N. & Keyser, Samuel J. CV Phonology: A Generative Theory of the Syllable. (Linguistic Inquiry Monograph Ser.: No. 9). (Illus.). 192p. (Orig.). 1983. text ed. 30.00x (ISBN 0-262-03098-5); pap. text ed. 15.00x (ISBN 0-262-53047-3). MIT Pr.

Clements, George N., jt. auth. see Halle, Morris.

Clements, Hanna, jt. auth. see Clements, Bruce.

Clements, Harold M., Sr. Mechanization of Agriculture in Brazil: A Sociological Study of Minas Gerais. LC 76-93194. (University of Florida Latin American Monographs: No. 7). (Illus.). 1969. 7.50 (ISBN 0-8130-0281-8). U Presses Fla.

Clements, Harry. Diets to Help Kidney Disorders. 1981. pap. 4.95x (ISBN 0-317-06968-3, Regent House). B of A.

--Diets to Help Prostate Troubles. 1981. pap. 4.95x (ISBN 0-317-07296-X, Regent House). B of A.

--Self-Help Arthritis. 1981. pap. 4.95x (ISBN 0-317-07284-6, Regent House). B of A.

--Self Help-Banish Backache. 1981. pap. 4.95x (ISBN 0-317-07285-4, Regent House). B of A.

--Self Help-Colitis. 1981. pap. 4.95x (ISBN 0-317-07286-2, Regent House). B of A.

--Self Help-Headache & Migraine. 1982. pap. 4.95x (ISBN 0-317-07315-X, Regent House). B of A.

--Self Help-Hernia. 1982. pap. 4.95x (ISBN 0-317-07314-1, Regent House). B of A.

--Self Help-Painful Joints. 1981. pap. 4.95x (ISBN 0-317-07312-5, Regent House). B of A.

--Self Help-Prostate Troubles. pap. 4.95x (ISBN 0-317-07309-5, Regent House). B of A.

--Self Help-Shingles & Cold Sores. 1979. pap. 4.95x (ISBN 0-317-07310-9, Regent House). B of A.

--Self Help-Skin Trouble. 1981. pap. 4.95x (ISBN 0-317-07281-1, Regent House). B of A.

Clements, Harry F. Sugarcane Crop Logging & Crop Control: Principles & Practices. LC 79-9894. (Illus.). 540p. 1980. text ed. 40.00x (ISBN 0-8248-0508-9). UH Pr.

Clements, Imelda W. & Buchanan, Diane E. Family Therapy: A Nursing Perspective. LC 81-13129. 356p. 1982. 20.95x (ISBN 0-471-08146-9, Pub. by Wiley Med). Wiley.

Clements, Imelda W. & Roberts, Florence B. Family Health: A Theoretical Approach to Nursing Care. LC 81-13129. 492p. 1983. 17.50 (ISBN 0-471-08536-7, Pub. by Wiley Med). Wiley.

Clements, J., jt. auth. see Hromadka, T. V., II.

Clements, James. Birds of the World: A Checklist. 600p. 1981. 24.95 (ISBN 0-87196-556-9). Facts on File.

Clements, James P., jt. auth. see Hodge, Bartow.

Clements, Judge. Tudor Translations: An Anthology. LC 74-7478. 1940. lib. bdg. 17.50 (ISBN 0-8414-3577-4). Folcroft.

Clements, Julia. The Art of Arranging a Flower. (Illus.). 112p. 1981. 15.95 (ISBN 0-8027-0688-6). Walker & Co.

--Flower Arrangements: Month by Month, Step by Step. (Illus.). 109p. 1984. pap. 7.95 (ISBN 0-7134-4720-6, Pub. by Batsford England). David & Charles.

--Flowers in Praise: Church Flower Arrangements & Festivals. LC 79-57312. (Illus.). 96p. 1980. 16.95 (ISBN 0-7134-3328-0, Pub. by Batsford England). David & Charles.

--Julia Clements' Book of Rose Arrangements. LC 84-3003. (Illus.). 128p. 1984. 16.95 (ISBN 0-668-06212-6, 6212-6). Arco.

--Julia Clement's Flower Arrangements. 1976. pap. 5.50 (ISBN 0-7134-3246-2, Pub. by Batsford England). David & Charles.

Clements, Keith. Henry Lamb: His Life & Works. 224p. 1984. 40.00x (ISBN 0-905459-55-5, Pub. by Redcliffe Pr Ltd). State Mutual Bk.

Clements, Kendrick A. William Jennings Bryan: Missionary Isolationist. LC 82-8342. (Illus.). 232p. 1983. text ed. 19.95x (ISBN 0-87049-364-7). U of Tenn Pr.

Clements, Kendrick A., ed. James F. Byrnes & the Origins of the Cold War. LC 81-70435. (Illus.). 127p. 1982. 13.95 (ISBN 0-89089-225-3). Carolina Acad Pr.

Clements, Kenneth W. The Trade Balance in Monetary General Equilibrium. LC 79-52688. (Outstanding Dissertations in Economics Ser.). 1984. lib. bdg. 23.00 (ISBN 0-8240-4151-8). Garland Pub.

Clements, Laurie, jt. ed. see Clarke, Tom.

Clements, Marcelle. Dog Is Us: And Other Observations. 360p. 1985. 17.95 (ISBN 0-670-80839-3). Viking.

Clements, Patricia. Baudelaire & the English Tradition. (Illus.). 448p. 1985. text ed. 33.50x (ISBN 0-691-06649-3). Princeton U Pr.

Clements, Patricia & Grindle, Juliet, eds. The Poetry of Thomas Hardy. (Critical Studies Ser.). 194p. 1980. 28.50x (ISBN 0-389-20057-3). B&N Imports.

Clements, Patricia & Grundy, Isobel, eds. Virginia Woolf: New Critical Essays. LC 83-6374. (Critical Studies). 224p. 1983. text ed. 28.50x (ISBN 0-389-20375-0). B&N Imports.

Clements, Paul. The Improvised Play: The Work of Mike Leigh. (A Theatrefile Ser.). 96p. 1983. pap. 7.95 (ISBN 0-413-50440-9, NO. 3943). Methuen Inc.

Clements, Paul H. Boxer Rebellion. LC 79-15870. (Columbia University Studies in the Social Sciences: No. 160). Repr. of 1915 ed. 12.50 (ISBN 0-404-51160-0). AMS Pr.

Clements, R. E. Isaiah & the Deliverance of Jerusalem. (Journal for the Study of the Old Testament, Supplement Ser.: No. 13). 1980. text ed. 18.95x (ISBN 0-905774-23-X, Pub. by JSOT Pr England). Eisenbrauns.

--New Century Bible Commentary on Isaiah 1-39. rev. ed. 320p. 1980. pap. 8.95 (ISBN 0-8028-1841-2). Eerdmans.

--Prophecy & Tradition. LC 74-3713. 96p. 1975. pap. 2.75 (ISBN 0-8042-0110-2). John Knox.

Clements, R. E., ed. Exodus: Cambridge Bible Commentary on the New English Bible. (Old Testament Ser.). 1972. 32.50 (ISBN 0-521-08218-8); pap. 10.95 (ISBN 0-521-09656-1). Cambridge U Pr.

Clements, R. J. & Cameron, D. G. Collecting & Testing Tropical Forage Plants. 162p. 1980. pap. 12.75 (ISBN 0-643-00389-4, C061, CSIRO). Unipub.

Clements, R. J. & Cameron, D. G., eds. Collecting & Testing Tropical Forage Plants. 154p. 1981. 35.00x (ISBN 0-643-00389-4, Pub. by CSIRO Australia). State Mutual Bk.

--Collecting & Testing Tropical Forage Plants. 154p. 1981. 20.00x (ISBN 0-686-78035-3, Pub. by CSIRO Australia). State Mutual Bk.

--Collecting & Testing Tropical Forage Plants. 1982. pap. 10.00x (ISBN 0-643-00389-4, Pub. by CSIRO). Intl Spec Bk.

Clements, R. W., jt. auth. see Tetreault, W. F.

Clements, Robert D., jt. auth. see Clements, Claire B.

Clements, Robert J. Comparative Literature as Academic Discipline: A Statement of Principles, Praxis, Standards. LC 77-91123. xxii, 342p. 1978. 35.00x (ISBN 0-87352-375-X, T200); pap. 14.50x (ISBN 0-87352-376-8, T201). Modern Lang.

--Critical Theory & Practice of the Pleiade. LC 68-16770. 1969. Repr. lib. bdg. 21.50x (ISBN 0-374-91691-8). Octagon.

--The Peregrine Muse: Studies in Comparative Renaissance Literature. rev. ed. (Studies in the Romance Languages & Literatures: No. 82). 214p. 1969. pap. 11.00x (ISBN 0-8078-9082-0). U of NC Pr.

Clements, Robert J. & Gibaldi, Joseph. The Anatomy of the Novella: The European Tale Collection from Boccaccio & Chaucer to Cervantes. LC 76-52548. 1977. 30.00x (ISBN 0-8147-1369-6); pap. 13.50x (ISBN 0-8147-1370-X). NYU Pr.

Clements, Robert J., ed. Michelangelo: A Self-Portrait. LC 68-31495. (Illus.). pap. 59.30 (ISBN 0-317-10353-9, 2009062). Bks Demand UMI.

Clements, Robert W., jt. auth. see Tetreault, Wilfred F.

Clements, Ronald, ed. see Grayston, Kenneth.

Clements, Ronald, et al, eds. see Clines, D. J.

Clements, Ronald E. Abraham & David: Genesis 15 & Its Meaning for Israelite Tradition. LC 67-8569. (Studies in Biblical Theology, 2nd Ser.: No. 5). 1967. pap. 10.00x (ISBN 0-8401-3055-4). A R Allenson.

--In Spirit & in Truth: Insights from Biblical Prayers. 264p. Date not set. pap. 9.95 (ISBN 0-8042-0071-8). John Knox.

--One Hundred Years of Old Testament Interpretation. LC 76-23236. 160p. 1976. pap. 7.95 (ISBN 0-664-24747-4). Westminster.

Clements, Ronald E., ed. see Hyatt, J. P.

Clements, Ronald E., ed. see Mayes, A. D.

Clements, Ronald E., ed. see Rowley, H. H.

Clements, Ronald E., ed. see Wevers, John W.

Clements, Ronald E., ed. see Whybray, R. N.

Clements, Sallee, jt. auth. see Bagwell, Marilyn.

Clements, Simon, jt. ed. see Bright, Laurence.

Clements, Tad S. Science & Man: The Philosophy of Scientifc Humanism. (American Lecture Philosophy). 168p. 1968. 14.75x (ISBN 0-398-00316-5). C C Thomas.

Clements, Thomas. Geological Story of Death Valley. (Illus.). 64p. 1977. wrappers 3.95 (ISBN 0-936932-03-1). Death Valley Fortyniners.

Clements, W. & Berlo, R. The Scientific Report: A Guide for Authors. Society for Technical Communication, ed. 52p. (Orig.). pap. text ed. 15.00x (ISBN 0-914548-39-5). Soc Tech Comm.

Clements, W. & Waite, R. G. Guide for Beginning Technical Editors. Society for Technical Communication, ed. 54p. 1983. pap. text ed. 15.00x (ISBN 0-914548-40-9). Soc Tech Comm.

Clements, William M. Care & Counseling of the Aging. Clinebell, Howard J. & Stone, Howard W., eds. LC 78-54547. (Creative Pastoral Care & Counseling Ser). 96p. 1979. pap. 4.50 (ISBN 0-8006-0561-6, 1-561). Fortress.

Clements, William M. & Malpezzi, Frances M. Native American Folklore, 1879-1979: An Annotated Bibliography. LC 83-6672. xxiv, 247p. 1984. text ed. 34.95x (ISBN 0-8040-0831-0, 82-76032, Swallow). Ohio U Pr.

Clements, William M., jt. auth. see Ball, Larry D.

Clements, William M., ed. Ministry with the Aging: Designs-Challenges-Foundations. LC 80-7739. 1983. pap. 8.61i (ISBN 0-06-061497-8, RD/452, HarpR). Har-Row.

--Native American Folklore in Nineteenth Century Periodicals. 250p. 1985. text ed. 21.95x (ISBN 0-8040-0872-8, Pub. by Swallow). Ohio U Pr.

Clements, Wilma H. Canny wi' the Sugar: A Collection of Poems. Westburg, Mildred W., ed. (Illus.). 88p. 1984. pap. 10.00 (ISBN 0-317-17840-7). Westburg.

Clements, Zacharie J. & Burrell, Leon F. I Want to Make It: A Primer for Minority Students & Others Who Want to be Successful in College. LC 82-50564. 125p. (Orig.). (gr. 7-12). 1983. pap. 5.95 (ISBN 0-88247-686-6). R & E Pubs.

Clements, Zacharie J. & Hawhes, Richard R. Mastermind: Excercises in Critical Thinking. (gr. 4-6). 1985. pap. 6.95 (ISBN 0-673-16653-8). Scott F.

Clementson. On Systems. (Information Technology Ser.). 1984. 25.00 (ISBN 0-9901003-3-2, Pub. by Abacus England). Heyden.

Clemeny, Hal. Ice World. 1981. pap. 2.25 (ISBN 0-345-30082-3, Del Rey). Ballantine.

Clemes, Harris & Bean, Reynold. Self-Esteem: The Key to Your Child's Well-Being. 1982. pap. 3.50 (ISBN 0-8217-1096-6). Zebra.

Clemes, Harris, jt. auth. see Bean, Reynold.

Cleminshaw, Clarence H. Beginner's Guide to the Skies. LC 76-28317. 1977. 14.37 (ISBN 0-690-01214-4). T Y Crowell.

Cleminson, Ronald W., et al, eds. Guidelines & Competencies for Elementary Science Education. 93p. 1974. pap. text ed. 9.95x (ISBN 0-8422-0446-6). Irvington.

Clemmensen, Jane. Nonionizing Radiation: A Case for Federal Standards. (Illus.). 1984. pap. 7.50 (ISBN 0-911302-51-4). San Francisco Pr.

Clemmer, Richard B., jt. auth. see Schreiber, Arthur F.

Clemmer, Richard O. Continuities of Hopi Culture Change. 1978. pap. 9.50 (ISBN 0-916552-15-2). Acoma Bks.

Clemmer, Richard O., jt. auth. see Jorgensen, Joseph G.

Clemmesen, J., et al, eds. see Symposium on Comparative Leukemia Research, 7th International, Copenhagen, October, 1975.

Clemmow, P. C. An Introduction to Electromagnetic Theory. LC 73-77174. (Illus.). 320p. 1973. pap. 18.95 (ISBN 0-521-09815-7). Cambridge U Pr.

Clemo, Jack. Wilding Graft. 304p. 1983. pap. 7.50 (ISBN 0-907746-17-9, Pub. by A Mott Ltd). Longwood Pub Group.

Clemoes, Peter & Hughes, Kathleen, eds. England Before the Conquest. LC 76-154508. (Illus.). 1971. 59.50 (ISBN 0-521-08191-2). Cambridge U Pr.

Clemoes, Peter see Malone, Kemp & Schibsbye, Knud.

Clemons, Neil L., jt. auth. see Heinzen, Richard H.

Clemow, Joyce E., tr. see De Cayeux, Andre.

Clemson, D. Organizational Cybernetics. 1984. 25.00 (ISBN 0-9961005-9-8, Pub. by Abacus England). Heyden.

Clemson Extension Home Economics Staff, jt. ed. see South Carolina Extension Homemakers Council.

Clench, W. J. Cyclophoridae & Pupinidae of Caroline, Fijian, & Samoan Islands. (BMB Ser.). pap. 10.00 (ISBN 0-527-02304-3). Kraus Repr.

Clench, William J. & Turner, Ruth D. New Names Introduced by H. A. Pilsbry in the Mollusca & Crustacea. (Special Publication: No. 4). 218p. (Orig.). 1962. pap. 10.00 (ISBN 0-910006-32-6). Acad Nat Sci Phila.

Clendenen, Clarence, jt. auth. see Duignan, Peter.

Clendenen, Clarence, et al. Americans in Africa, Eighteen Sixty-Five to Nineteen Hundred. LC 66-14462. (Studies Ser.: No. 17). 1966. pap. 4.95x (ISBN 0-8179-3172-4); 7.95 (ISBN 0-8179-3171-6). Hoover Inst Pr.

Clendenen, Lois R. Lines by Lois. 1984. pap. 4.95 (ISBN 0-916573-13-3). D R Benbow.

Clendenin, jt. auth. see Mannaioni.

Clendenin, J. C., jt. auth. see Christy, G. A.

Clendenin, William R. History of Music. (Quality Paperback Ser.: No. 272). (Illus.). 464p. 1974. pap. 6.95 (ISBN 0-8226-0272-5). Littlefield.

Clendening, Corinne P. & Davies, Ruth A. Challenging the Gifted. LC 82-20777. (Serving Special Populations Ser.). 1983. 39.95 (ISBN 0-8352-1682-9). Bowker.

--Creating Programs for the Gifted. (Illus.). 500p. 1980. 29.95 (ISBN 0-8352-1265-3). Bowker.

Clendening, Logan. Source Book of Medical History. 1942. pap. 10.95 (ISBN 0-486-20621-1). Dover.

Clendening, Logan, ed. Source Book of Medical History. 15.50 (ISBN 0-8446-1871-3). Peter Smith.

Clendenning, Anna M. Darling Beast. 40p. 1985. 5.95 (ISBN 0-8059-2985-1). Dorrance.

Clendenning, Anne. Hello, Busdriver. 1984. 10.95 (ISBN 0-533-06030-3). Vantage.

Clendenning, John. The Life & Thought of Josiah Royce. LC 85-40364. 400p. 1985. text ed. 27.50x (ISBN 0-299-10310-2). U of Wis Pr.

Clendenning, John, ed. see Royce, Josiah.

Clendenning, P. H. & Bartlett, R. Eighteenth Century Russia: A Select Bibliography of Works Published Since 1955. (Russian Bibliography Ser.: No. 3). (Illus.). 260p. 1981. 30.00 (ISBN 0-89250-110-3). Orient Res Partners.

Clendenning, Sheila T. Emily Dickinson: A Bibliography, 1850-1966. LC 67-65585. (Serif Ser.: No. 3). 175p. 1969. 10.00x (ISBN 0-87338-016-9). Kent St U Pr.

Cleobury, F. H. From Clerk to Cleric. 64p. 1977. pap. 3.00 (ISBN 0-227-67825-7). Attic Pr.

--Liberal Christian Orthodoxy. 164p. 1963. 15.95 (ISBN 0-227-67668-8). Attic Pr.

--Return to Natural Theology. 246p. 1967. 17.95 (ISBN 0-227-67722-6). Attic Pr.

Cleophas, Sr. M. Little Apple Tree's Wish. (Illus.). 1.75 (ISBN 0-8198-0079-1). Dghtrs St Paul.

Clephane, Irene, jt. auth. see Bott, Alan.

Clepper, Henry, jt. auth. see Randall, C.

Clepper, Henry, ed. Careers in Conservation: Opportunities in Natural Resource Management. 2nd ed. LC 78-21917. 1979. 42.00x (ISBN 0-471-05163-2, Pub. by Ronald Pr). Wiley.

--Leaders of American Conservation. LC 75-155206. Repr. of 1971 ed. 69.40 (ISBN 0-8357-9921-2, 2012429). Bks Demand UMI.

Clepper, Henry, ed. see Carlton, Frank.

Clepper, Henry, ed. see Carlton, Frank E.

Clepper, Henry, jt. ed. see Stroud, Richard H.

Clepper, Henry, ed. see Stroud, Richard H.

Clepper, Henry, jt. ed. see Stroud, Richard H.

Clepper, Henry E. Professional Forestry in the United States. LC 70-171107. pap. 66.40 (ISBN 0-317-29882-8, 2015737). Bks Demand UMI.

Clerc, Andre D. see Chitlangou, pseud.

Clerc, Charles & Leiter, Louis. Seven Contemporary Short Novels. 3rd ed. 1982. pap. text ed. 14.70x (ISBN 0-673-15569-2). Scott F.

Clerc, Charles & Leiter, Louis H. Seven Contemporary Short Novels. 2nd ed. 1975. pap. 14.70x (ISBN 0-673-07971-6). Scott F.

Clerc, Charles, ed. Approaches to "Gravity's Rainbow". 315p. 1983. 25.00 (ISBN 0-8142-0337-X). Ohio St U Pr.

Clerc, J. T., et al. Structural Analysis of Organic Compounds by Combined Application of Spectroscopic Methods. (Studies in Analytical Chemistry: Vol. 1). 288p. 1982. 61.75 (ISBN 0-444-99748-2). Elsevier.

Clercq, Chretien Le see Le Clercq, Chretien.

Clercq, E. de see De Clercq, E. & Walker, R. T.

Clercq, Guido De see Steenbergen, Jacques & De Clercq, Guido.

Clercq, H. De see De Clercq, H., et al.

Clercx, Suzanne. La Baroque et la Musique: Essai d'Esthetique Musicale. (Publications de la Societe Belge de Musicologie: Serie 2, tome 1). (Illus.). 243p. (Orig., Fr.). 1948. pap. 9.50 (ISBN 0-934082-15-4, Pub. by Editions de la Lib Belgium). Theodore Front.

Clercx, Suzanne. Le Baroque et la musique: Essai d'esthetique musicale. LC 76-43910. Repr. of 1948 ed. 24.50 (ISBN 0-404-60153-7). AMS Pr.

--Gretry: 1741-1813. LC 76-43911. (Music & Theatre in France in the 17th & 18th Centuries). (Fr.). Repr. of 1944 ed. 19.00 (ISBN 0-404-60154-5). AMS Pr.

Clere, Jules. Hommes de la Commune: Biographie Complete de Tous ses Membres. LC 72-1005. Repr. of 1871 ed. 17.50 (ISBN 0-404-07119-8). AMS Pr.

Clergue, Gerard, jt. auth. see Liotet, Serge.

Clergue, Lucien. Nude Workshop. LC 82-70177. (Illus.). 112p. 1982. 40.00 (ISBN 0-670-51824-7, Studio). Viking.

--Practical Nude Photography. (Practical Ser.). (Illus.). 1984. 29.95 (ISBN 0-240-51202-2). Focal Pr.

Clerin, Rose M. Taxation Planning for Middle East Operations. 1978. pap. 19.00 (ISBN 90-200-0515-4, Pub. by Kluwer Law Netherlands). Kluwer Academic.

Clerk, E. M. Fable & Song in Italy. LC 74-9812. 1899. 32.50 (ISBN 0-8414-3509-X). Folcroft.

Clerk, John. Etchings, Chiefly of Views in Scotland. LC 72-1019. (Bannatyne Club, Edinburgh. Publications: No. 8). Repr. of 1825 ed. 57.50 (ISBN 0-404-52719-1). AMS Pr.

--Series of Etchings: Chiefly of Views in Scotland. Laing, David, ed. LC 72-963. (Bannatyne Club, Edinburgh. Publications: No. 98). Repr. of 1855 ed. 85.00 (ISBN 0-404-52854-6). AMS Pr.

Clerk, William. An Epitome of Certaine Late Aspersions Cast at Civilians. LC 79-84095. (English Experience Ser.: No.915). 56p. 1979. Repr. of 1631 ed. lib. bdg. 7.00 (ISBN 90-221-0915-1). Walter J Johnson.

Clerke, Agnes M. A Popular History of Astronomy in the Nineteenth Century. LC 70-166614. 1908. Repr. 39.00 (ISBN 0-403-01492-1). Scholarly.

Clerman, Robert J., jt. auth. see Joglekar, Rajani.

Clermont, Kevin M. Civil Procedure. LC 82-2742. (Black Letter Ser.). 308p. 1982. pap. text ed. 13.95 (ISBN 0-314-65090-3). West Pub.

--Federal Rules of Civil Procedure-1984. 456p. 1984. pap. text ed. 10.50 (ISBN 0-88277-183-3). Foundation Pr.

Clermont, Shana. Memphis. (Orig.). 1981. pap. 2.95 (ISBN 0-89083-807-0). Zebra.

--Natchez. (Orig.). 1981. pap. 3.50 (ISBN 0-89083-891-7). Zebra.

Cleron, Jean P. Saudi Arabia Two Thousand: A Strategy for Growth. LC 77-9238. 1978. 26.00x (ISBN 0-312-69978-6). St Martin.

Clery, Val. Conran's the Solo Chef. 144p. 1981. 5.95 (ISBN 0-8317-7907-1, Rutledge Pr). Smith Pubs.

Cleton, F. J & Simons, J. W., eds. Genetic Origins of Tumor Cells. (Developments in Oncology Ser.: Vol. 1). xv, 125p. 1980. lib. bdg. 26.00 (ISBN 90-247-2272-1, Pub. by Martinus Nijhoff Netherlands). Kluwer Academic.

Cleugh, James. The Marquis & the Chevalier: A Study in the Psychology of Sex As Illustrated by the Lives & Personalities of the Marquis De Sade, 1740-1814 & the Chevalier Von Sacher-Masoch, 1836-1905. LC 70-142317. (Illus.). 295p. 1972. Repr. of 1952 ed. lib. bdg. 19.25x (ISBN 0-8371-5920-2, CLMC). Greenwood.

--Prelude to Parnassus: Scenes from the Life of Alexander Sergeyvich Pushkin 1799-1847. 1973. Repr. of 1936 ed. 20.00 (ISBN 0-8274-1775-6). R West.

Cleugh, James, tr. see Flaceliere, Robert.

Cleugh, James, tr. see Gasset, Jose Ortega Y.

Cleugh, James, tr. see Jungk, Robert.

Cleugh, James, tr. see Vega, Garcilaso De La.

Cleugh, James, tr. see Wendt, Herbert.

Cleugh, M. F. Teaching the Slow Learner in the Special School. 10.00 (ISBN 0-8022-0265-9). Philos Lib.

Cleve, Harry Van see McCracken, Harold & Van Cleve, Harry.

Cleve, John. The Crusader: Books 3 & 4, The Accursed Tower & The Passionate Princess. LC 80-1000. 384p. (Orig.). 1981. pap. 4.95 (ISBN 0-394-17736-3, B-441, BC). Grove.

--The Crusader No. 2: The Passionate Princess. 1974. pap. 1.50 (ISBN 0-685-47911-0, D6039 314, BC). Grove.

--The Crusader No. 3: Julanar the Lioness. 1975. pap. 1.50 (ISBN 0-685-56547-5, D4731, BC). Grove.

--The Crusader No. 4: My Lady Queen. 1975. pap. 1.50 (ISBN 0-685-56548-3, D5749, Dist. by Dell). Grove.

--Santana Enslaved. LC 81-85828. (Spaceways Ser.: No. 4). 224p. (Orig.). 1982. pap. 2.50 (ISBN 0-86721-111-3). Playboy Pbks.

--Spaceways, No. 13: Jonuta Rising. 224p. 1983. pap. 2.50 (ISBN 0-425-06405-0). Berkley Pub.

--Spaceways, No. 14: Assignment Hellhole. 224p. 1983. pap. 2.50 (ISBN 0-425-06407-7). Berkley Pub.

--Spaceways, No. 15: Starship Sapphire. 224p. 1984. pap. 2.50 (ISBN 0-425-06539-1). Berkley Pub.

--Spaceways, No. 18: Race Across the Stars. 224p. 1984. pap. 2.95 (ISBN 0-425-07024-7). Berkley Pub.

--Spaceways No. 19: King of the Slavers. 224p. 1985. pap. 2.95 (ISBN 0-425-07134-0). Berkley Pub.

--Spaceways, No. 3: Escape from Macho. 223p. 1983. pap. 2.50 (ISBN 0-425-05957-X). Berkley Pub.

--Spaceways, No. 9: In Quest of Qalara. 224p. 1983. pap. 2.50 (ISBN 0-425-06456-5). Berkley Pub.

Cleve, John, ed. Lady Beth. (Victorian Library). 224p. 1984. pap. 3.95 (ISBN 0-394-62328-2, B-512, BC). Grove.

Cleve, John Van see Van Cleve, John W.

Cleve, P. T. Synopsis of the Naviculoid Diatoms. (Illus.). 1965. Repr. of 1895 ed. 41.85 (ISBN 90-6123-034-9). Lubrecht & Cramer.

Cleve, P. T. & Grunow, A. Beitraege zur Kenntnis der arctischen Diatomeen. 1976. pap. text ed. 17.15 (ISBN 3-87429-101-4). Lubrecht & Cramer.

Cleve, Spike Van see Van Cleve, Spike.

Cleve-Euler, A. Die Diatomeen von Schweden und Finnland, 5 pts. (Kungl. Sv. Vetenskapsak Handl Ser.). (Illus.). 1968. pap. 122.50 (ISBN 3-7682-0550-9). Lubrecht & Cramer.

Cleveland, A., ed. see R. S. Means Co. Staff.

Cleveland, Ana D., jt. auth. see Cleveland, Donald B.

Cleveland, Anne T. It's Better with Your Shoes Off. (Illus.). 1958. pap. 3.75 (ISBN 0-8048-1197-0). C E Tuttle.

Cleveland, Bernard F. Master Teaching Techniques. rev. ed. LC 83-73524. (Illus.). 218p. 1984. pap. 12.50 (ISBN 0-9608678-1-3). Connecting Link.

Cleveland, Bess A. California Mission Recipes. LC 65-16741. (Illus.). 142p. 1984. pap. 8.25 (ISBN 0-8048-0078-2). C E Tuttle.

Cleveland, Catherine. The True Story of Kaspar Hauser. 1976. lib. bdg. 59.95 (ISBN 0-8490-2774-8). Gordon Pr.

Cleveland, Catherine C. The Great Revival in the West, 1797-1805. 11.25 (ISBN 0-8446-1117-4). Peter Smith.

Cleveland, Charles. A Compendium of English Literature, Chronologically Arranged, from Sir John Mandville to William Cowper. 1973. Repr. of 1848 ed. 25.00 (ISBN 0-8274-1530-3). R West.

Cleveland, Charles, jt. auth. see Zender, Bob.

Cleveland, Charles D. Compendium of American Literature. 3rd ed. LC 75-122645. 1971. Repr. of 1859 ed. 55.00x (ISBN 0-8046-1293-5, Pub. by Kennikat). Assoc Faculty Pr.

--Complete Concordance to the Poetical Works of John Milton. LC 76-57784. 1867. lib. bdg. 38.50 (ISBN 0-8414-3459-X). Folcroft.

Cleveland, Charles D. & Chase, Salmon P. Anti-Slavery Addresses of Eighteen Forty-Four & Eighteen Forty-Five. LC 79-97420. Repr. of 1867 ed. 17.50x (ISBN 0-8371-2716-5, CLD&, Pub. by Negro U Pr). Greenwood.

Cleveland Consulting Associates, jt. auth. see Ernst & Whinney.

Cleveland, David. The April Rabbits. (Illus.). 32p. (gr. k-3). 1980. pap. 1.50 (ISBN 0-590-05727-8). Scholastic Inc.

--The Frog on Robert's Head. (Illus.). (gr. 1-4). 1981. 8.95 (ISBN 0-698-20512-X, Coward). Putnam Pub Group.

Cleveland, Donald B. & Cleveland, Ana D. Introduction to Indexing & Abstracting. 209p. 1983. lib. bdg. 19.50 (ISBN 0-87287-346-3). Libs Unl.

Cleveland, E. E. The Exodus. Wheeler, Gerald, ed. 1985. write for info. (ISBN 0-8280-0299-1). Review & Herald.

--The Gates Shall Not. (Horizon Ser.). 96p. 1980. pap. 5.95 (ISBN 0-8127-0325-1). Review & Herald.

--Milk & Honey. Wheeler, Gerald, ed. 1985. write for info. (ISBN 0-8280-0301-7). Review & Herald.

--One More River. Wheeler, Gerald, ed. 1985. write for info. (ISBN 0-8280-0300-9). Review & Herald.

Cleveland Foundation. Criminal Justice in Cleveland. Pound, Roscoe & Frankfurter, Felix, eds. LC 68-55769. (Criminology, Law Enforcement, & Social Problems Ser.: No. 8). (Illus.). 1968. Repr. of 1922 ed. 30.00x (ISBN 0-87585-008-1). Patterson Smith.

Cleveland, Frederick A. Chapters Municipal Administration & Accounting. Brief, Richard P., ed. LC 80-1479. (Dimensions of Accounting Theory & Practice Ser.). 1981. Repr. of 1909 ed. lib. bdg. 40.00x (ISBN 0-405-13509-2). Ayer Co Pubs.

Cleveland, Frederick A. & Powell, Fred W. Railroad Promotion & Capitalization in the United States. Bruchey, Stuart, ed. LC 80-1698. (Railroads Ser.). 1981. Repr. of 1909 ed. lib. bdg. 35.00x (ISBN 0-405-13770-2). Ayer Co Pubs.

Cleveland, Grover. Presidential Problems. facsimile ed. LC 78-152978. (Select Bibliographies Reprint Ser.). Repr. of 1904 ed. 20.00 (ISBN 0-8369-5730-X). Ayer Co Pubs.

--Writings & Speeches of Grover Cleveland. Parker, G. F., ed. 1892. 32.00 (ISBN 0-527-17900-0). Kraus Repr.

Cleveland, Harlan. The Future Executive: A Guide for Tomorrow's Managers. LC 79-138715. 128p. 1972. 14.37i (ISBN 0-06-010817-7, HarpT). Har-Row.

--The Knowledge Executive: Leadership in an Information Society. 1985. 18.95 (ISBN 0-525-24338-0, 01840-550X, Pub. by Truman Talley Bk). Dutton.

--Seven Everyday Collisions in American Higher Education. (Occasional Paper of ICED). 1974. pap. 1.00 (ISBN 0-89192-154-0). Interbk Inc.

--The Third Try at World Order. 3.95 (ISBN 0-686-25998-X). Aspen Inst Human.

--Toward a Strategy for the Management of Peace: U. S. Foreign Policy in the 1980's. 1983. write for info. U of SD Gov Res Bur.

--Triple Collision of Modernization. 17p. 1979. pap. 1.50 (ISBN 0-89940-000-0). LBJ Sch Pub Aff.

Cleveland, Harlan & Wilson, T., Jr. Humangrowth: An Essay on Growth, Values & the Quality of Life. 3.00 (ISBN 0-686-26001-5). Aspen Inst Human.

Cleveland, Harlan, ed. Energy Futures of Developing Countries: The Neglected Victims of the Energy Crisis. LC 80-10702. 104p. 1980. 33.95x (ISBN 0-03-058669-0). Praeger.

--The Management of Sustainable Growth. LC 80-24162. (Pergamon Policy Studies on International Development). 386p. 1981. 44.00 (ISBN 0-08-027171-5). Pergamon.

Cleveland, Harlan, ed. see McKay, Robert B.

Cleveland, Harlan, et al. After Afghanistan: The Long Haul. (Atlantic Council Policy Papers). 71p. 1980. 6.00 (ISBN 0-317-33689-4). Atlantic Council US.

--The Overseas Americans. Bruchey, Stuart, ed. LC 80-558. (Multinational Corporations Ser.). 1980. Repr. of 1960 ed. lib. bdg. 33.50x (ISBN 0-405-13354-5). Ayer Co Pubs.

Cleveland, Harlan, jt. auth. see Wolf, Joseph J.

Cleveland, Harland. World Affairs Don't Have to Be Boring. 1960. 2.50 (ISBN 0-87060-085-0, PUC 11). Syracuse U Cont Ed.

Cleveland, Harold Van B. & Brittain, W. Bruce. The Great Inflation: A Monetarist View. LC 76-41068. 72p. 1976. 3.50 (ISBN 0-89068-003-5). Natl Planning.

Cleveland, Harold Van B. & Huertas, Thomas F. Citibank, Eighteen Twelve to Nineteen Seventy. (Harvard Studies in Business History: No. 37). (Illus.). 512p. 1985. text ed. 25.00x (ISBN 0-674-13175-4). Harvard U Pr.

Cleveland High School Writing Class. The Duwamish Diary. (Shorey Historical Ser.). 132p. pap. 7.95 (ISBN 0-8466-0308-X, S308). Shorey.

Cleveland, James O., jt. auth. see Peterson, Raymond M.

Cleveland, Jefferson, jt. ed. see Nix, Verolga.

Cleveland, Jess M. The Chemistry of Plutonium. LC 78-60617. (ANS Monograph). (Illus.). 1979. Repr. of 1970 ed. 49.00x (ISBN 0-89448-013-8, 300014). Am Nuclear Soc.

Cleveland, John F., jt. auth. see Greeley, Horace.

Cleveland, Josephine. Easy-to-Do Publicity Ideas for Classrooms & Libraries. new ed. (Illus., Orig.). 1971. 3.95 (ISBN 0-914208-00-4); pap. 2.95 (ISBN 0-914208-01-2). Longhorn Pr.

Cleveland, L. David. Harvard Square Restaurants & a Guidebook of History. (Illus.). 150p. (Orig.). 1983. pap. text ed. 4.95 (ISBN 0-938534-00-9). Soup to Nuts.

Cleveland, Michael G. Age Discrimination in Employment: A Guide to the Law. 1979. pap. 5.95 (ISBN 0-917386-86-8). Exec Ent Inc.

Cleveland Museum of Art. Indian Art from the George P. Bickford Collection. LC 74-29377. (Illus.). pap. 33.00 (ISBN 0-317-10489-6, 2014497). Bks Demand UMI.

Cleveland Musuem of Art. Catalogue of an Exhibition of the Art of Lithography. LC 83-45736. Date not set. Repr. 57.50 (ISBN 0-404-20062-1). AMS Pr.

Cleveland Public Library - John G. White Department. Catalog of the Chess Collection, Including Checkers, 2 Vols. (Ser. Seventy). 1964. Set. 151.00 (ISBN 0-8161-0681-9, Hall Library). G K Hall.

Cleveland, Ray L. An Ancient South Arabian Necropolis: Objects from the Second Campaign 1951 in the Timna Cemetery. (American Foundation for the Study of Man: Vol. 4). (Illus.). 202p. 1965. 40.00x (ISBN 0-8018-0129-X). Johns Hopkins.

Cleveland, Reginald M. Your German Shepherd. LC 66-22306. (Your Dog Book Ser). (Illus.). 1966. pap. 4.95 (ISBN 0-87714-009-X). Denlingers.

Cleveland, Richard J. Voyages & Commercial Enterprises of the Sons of New England. 1969. Repr. of 1857 ed. 24.00 (ISBN 0-8337-0592-X). B Franklin.

Cleveland, Rose E. George Eliot's Poetry: And Other Studies. LC 74-4275. (Essay Index Reprint Ser.). Repr. of 1885 ed. 16.75 (ISBN 0-518-10176-2). Ayer Co Pubs.

Cleveland, Sidney E., jt. auth. see Fisher, Seymour.

Cleveland Symposium on Macromolecules, 1st, Case Western Reserve Univ., Oct. 1976. Proceedings. Walton, A. G., ed. 310p. 1977. 64.00 (ISBN 0-444-41561-0). Elsevier.

Cleveland, William A. Britannica Atlas. 1984. 79.00 (ISBN 0-85229-415-8). Ency Brit Ed.

Cleveland, William C., jt. auth. see Delivanis, Demetre J.

Cleveland, William L. Islam Against the West: Shakib Arslan & the Campaign for Islamic Nationalism. (Center for Middle Eastern Studies, Modern Middle East Ser.: No. 10). (Illus.). 240p. 1985. 19.95 (ISBN 0-292-77594-6). U of Tex Pr.

--Islam against the West: Shakib Arslan & the Campaign for Islamic Nationalism. (Modern Middle East Ser.: No. 10). (Illus.). 246p. 1985. 19.95 (ISBN 0-292-77594-6). U of Tex Pr.

--Making of an Arab Nationalist: Ottomanism & Arabism in the Life & Thought of Sati' Al-Husri. LC 78-155961. 1972. 23.50 (ISBN 0-691-03088-X). Princeton U Pr.

Cleveland, William S. The Elements of Graphing Data. 350p. write for info. (ISBN 0-534-03729-1); pap. write for info (ISBN 0-534-03730-5). Wadsworth Pub.

Cleveland, William S., ed. see Becker, Richard A., et al.

Cleveland, William S., ed. see Tukey, John W.

Cleveland, William S., jt. auth. see Chambers, John M.

Cleven, Andrew N., tr. see Parra-Perez, Caracciolo.

Cleven, Harry T., tr. see Jervell, Jacob.

Clevenger & Hill. History of the Bible Church. 1973. pap. 1.50 (ISBN 0-88428-006-3, 171). Parchment Pr.

Clevenger & Hill, eds. Bible Characters. 1973. pap. 1.50 (ISBN 0-88428-008-X, 161). Parchment Pr.

--Bible Doctrine. 1973. pap. 1.50 (ISBN 0-88428-002-0, 131). Parchment Pr.

--Bible Geography. 1973. pap. 1.50 (ISBN 0-88428-003-9, 111). Parchment Pr.

--Jesus of the Bible. 1973. pap. 1.50 (ISBN 0-88428-007-1, 101). Parchment Pr.

--Wisdom Books of the Bible. 1973. pap. 1.50 (ISBN 0-88428-001-2, 121). Parchment Pr.

Clevenger, Ernest. The Art of Greeting & Seating. 1983. pap. 0.95 (ISBN 0-88428-024-1, 305). Parchment Pr.

Clevenger, Ernest A., Jr. The Art of Greeting & Seating: The Church Usher's Guide. (Illus.). 16p. 1983. pap. 0.95 (ISBN 0-88428-000-4). Parchment Pr.

--Bible Characters. (Bible Drill Flash Cards Flipbook Ser.). (gr. 3 up). 1982. pap. 4.25 (ISBN 0-88428-018-7). Parchment Pr.

--The Church. (Bible Drill Flash Card Flipbook Ser.). 104p. (gr. 3 up). 1983. pap. 4.25 (ISBN 0-88428-016-0). Parchment Pr.

--A Pocket Bible Ready Reference for Personal Workers. (Bible Ready Reference Ser.). 24p. (Orig.). 1982. pap. 0.50 (ISBN 0-88428-011-X). Parchment Pr.

Clevenger, Ernest A., Jr. & Clevenger, Glenda W. Comprehensive Topical & Textual Lesson Commentary Index: 1922-1982. 4th ed. 114p. 1981. pap. text ed. 6.95 (ISBN 0-88428-019-5). Parchment Pr.

Clevenger, Ernest, Jr. A Beginning Course in Church Leadership Training for Men. (Illus.). 42p. 1975. 3.25 (ISBN 0-88428-036-5). Parchment Pr.

--Directory Alabama Churches of Christ, 1976. (Illus.). 1976. pap. 2.00 (ISBN 0-88428-039-X). Parchment Pr.

--General Bible Knowledge Bible Drill: Flash Cards Flipbook. (Bible Drill Flash Cards Flipbook Ser.). 104p. (gr. 3 up). 1983. pap. 4.25 (ISBN 0-88428-017-9). Parchment Pr.

--Parchment Notes on the New Testament. (Parchment Notes). (Illus.). 1976. pap. 6.95 (ISBN 0-88428-040-3, 040-3). Parchment Pr.

Clevenger, Ernest, Jr. & Hill, Samuel G. Bible Evidences. (Bible Centered Studies). (Illus.). 73p. (Orig.). 1973. pap. 1.50 (ISBN 0-88428-009-8). Parchment Pr.

Clevenger, Ernest, Jr., ed. Bible Survey. 1973. pap. 1.50 (ISBN 0-88428-005-5, 141). Parchment Pr.

Clevenger, Glenda W., jt. auth. see Clevenger, Ernest A., Jr.

Clevenger, Norma K., ed. see Beserra, Sarah S. & Franklin, Sterling C.

Clevenger, Shobal V. A Treatise on the Method of Government Surveying. 1978. pap. 8.50 (ISBN 0-686-25541-0). CARBEN Survey.

Clevenot, Michel. Materialist Approaches to the Bible. Nottingham, William, tr. LC 84-14711. 160p. (Orig.). 1985. pap. 8.95 (ISBN 0-88344-343-0). Orbis Bks.

Clever. Argon: Gas Solubilities. (IUPAC Solubility Data Ser.: Vol. 4). (Illus.). 348p. 1980. 100.00 (ISBN 0-08-022353-2). Pergamon.

--Helium & Neon. 1979. 100.00 (ISBN 0-08-022351-6). Pergamon.

--Krypton, Xenon, & Radon: Gas Solubilities. (Solubility Data Ser.: Vol. 2). 1979. 100.00 (ISBN 0-08-022352-4). Pergamon.

Clever, A. S. Methane. 100.01 (ISBN 0-08-029200-3). Pergamon.

Cleverdon, Catherine L. The Woman Suffrage Movement in Canada: The Start of Liberation. LC 73-82587. (Social History of Canada Ser.). 1974. pap. 9.95 (ISBN 0-8020-6218-0). U of Toronto Pr.

Cleverdon, Dorothy, et al. Play in a Hospital: Why & How. (Illus.). 54p. (Orig.). 1971. pap. 2.00x (ISBN 0-686-01102-3); pap. text ed. 1.50x (ISBN 0-936426-08-X). Play Schs.

Cleverdon, Dorthy & Rosenzweig, Louis E. A Work Play Program for the Trainable Mentally Deficient. pap. 1.00 (ISBN 0-936426-02-0). Play Schs.

Cleverdon, Douglas. The Growth of Milkwood. LC 79-75384. 1969. 8.50 (ISBN 0-8112-0260-7). New Directions.

Cleverdon, Robert & Edwards, Anthony. International Tourism to 1990. (Economist Intelligence Unit Ser.). (Illus.). 256p. 1982. 25.00 (ISBN 0-89011-582-6). Abt Bks.

Cleverdon, Robert, jt. auth. see Edwards, Anthony.

Cleverley, Graham. The Fleet Street Disaster: British National Newspapers As a Case Study in Mismanagement. LC 76-25733. (Communication & Society: Vol. 7). 175p. 1976. 29.95 (ISBN 0-8039-9989-5, Co-Pub with Constable). Sage.

Cleverley, John. The Schooling of China. (Illus.). 320p. 1985. text ed. 27.50x (ISBN 0-86861-533-1); pap. text ed. 13.50x (ISBN 0-86861-525-0). Allen Unwin.

Cleverley, John & Phillips, D. C. From Locke to Spock. (Second Century in Australian Education Ser.: No. 14). 1976. pap. 8.00x (ISBN 0-522-84104-X, Pub. by Melbourne U Pr Australia). Intl Spec Bk.

Cleverley, John F. The First Generation: The School & Society in Early Australia. LC 72-166084. 168p. 1971. (Pub. by Sydney U Pr); pap. 16.00x (ISBN 0-424-06250-X, Pub. by Sydney U Pr). Intl Spec Bk.

Cleverley, William O. Essentials of Hospital Finance. LC 78-7447. 225p. 1978. text ed. 26.50 (ISBN 0-89443-035-1). Aspen Systems.

--Financial Management of Health Care Facilities. LC 76-4034. 376p. 1976. 37.50 (ISBN 0-912862-20-3). Aspen Systems.

--Handbook of Health Care Accounting & Finance, 2 vols. LC 82-6784. 1385p. 1982. text ed. 150.00 set (ISBN 0-89443-364-4). Aspen Systems.

Cleverly, John F. & Wescombe, Christabel. Papua New Guinea: Guide to Sources in Education. LC 79-670399. 1979. pap. 22.00x (ISBN 0-424-00043-1, Pub. by Sydney U Pr). Intl Spec Bk.

Cleves, William, et al, trs. see Fuchs, Josef.

Clevett, Kenneth J. Handbook of Process Stream Analysis. LC 73-14416. (Ser. in Analytical Chemistry). (Illus.). 470p. 1973. 74.95x (ISBN 0-470-16048-9). Halsted Pr.

Clevin, Jorgen. Pete & Johnny to the Rescue. LC 74-4926. (Illus.). 64p. (ps-k). 1974. Random.

Clew, J. R., jt. auth. see Burgess, R. W.

Clew, Jeff. British Racing Motorcycles. 183p. 16.95 (ISBN 0-85429-161-X, F161). Haynes Pubns.

--BSA A7 & A10 Twins '47 - '54. (Owners Workshop Manuals Ser.: No. 121). 1979. 10.50 (ISBN 0-85696-121-3, Pub. by J H Haynes England). Haynes Pubns.

--Bultaco Competition Bikes '72-'75. new ed. (Owners Workshop Manuals Ser.: No. 219). 1979. 10.50 (ISBN 0-85696-219-8, Pub. by J H Haynes England). Haynes Pubns.

--The Douglas Motorcycle: 'The Best Twin' 250p. 19.95 (ISBN 0-85429-299-3, F299). Haynes Pubns.

--Francis Beart: A Single Purpose. (Illus.). 205p. 14.95 (ISBN 0-85429-236-5, F236). Haynes Pubns.

--Harley Davidson Owners Workshop Manual: Sportster '70 Thru '76. (Owners Workshop Manuals Ser.: No. 250). 1979. 10.50 (ISBN 0-85696-250-3, Pub. by J H Haynes England). Haynes Pubns.

--Harry Weslake: Lucky All My Life. (Illus.). 165p. 16.95 (ISBN 0-85429-254-3, F254). Haynes Pubns.

--Honda Owner's Workshop Manual: Fifty Ohv & Ohc '62 Thru '71. (Owners Workshop Manuals Ser.: No. 114). 1979. 10.50 (ISBN 0-85696-114-0, Pub. by J H Haynes England). Haynes Pubns.

--Honda Owner's Workshop Manual: Sixty-Five, Seventy, Ninety & '64-72. (Owners Workshop Manuals Ser.: No. 116). 1979. 10.50 (ISBN 0-85696-116-7, Pub. by J H Haynes England). Haynes Pubns.

--Honda XL250 & 350 Trail Bikes '72 - '75. (Owners Workshop Manuals Ser.: No. 209). 1979. 10.50 (ISBN 0-85696-209-0, Pub. by J H Haynes England). Haynes Pubns.

--Honda 125, 160, 175, 200 & CD175 Twins '70 - '78: One Twenty-Five to Two Hundred Twins '64-78. (Owners Workshop Manuals Ser.: No. 067). 1979. 10.50 (ISBN 0-900550-67-8, 067, Pub. by J H Haynes England). Haynes Pubns.

--Honda 250 Elsinore '73 - '75. (Owners Workshop Manuals Ser.: No. 217). 1979. 10.50 (ISBN 0-85696-217-1, Pub. by J H Haynes England). Haynes Pubns.

--Honda 50 '63 -'70. (Owners Workshop Manual Ser.). 12.95 (ISBN 0-85696-114-0, 114). Haynes Pubns.

--Honda 65, 70 & 90 '65-'67. (Owners Workshop Manual Ser.). 10.50 (ISBN 0-85696-116-7, 116). Haynes Pubns.

--Honda 750 sohc Fours '70 - '79. (Owners Workshop Manuals Ser.: No. 131). 1979. 10.50 (ISBN 0-85696-521-9, Pub. by J H Haynes England). Haynes Pubns.

--J. A. P. The Vintage Years. (Illus.). 240p. 1985. 17.95 (ISBN 0-85429-458-9, Pub. by G T Foulis Ltd). Interbook.

--Norton Commando '68 - '77. new ed. (Owners Workshop Manuals Ser.: No. 125). 1979. 10.50 (ISBN 0-85696-125-6, Pub. by J H Haynes England). Haynes Pubns.

--The Restoration of Vintage & Thoroughbred Motorcycles. (Illus.). 200p. 15.95 (ISBN 0-85429-185-7, F185). Haynes Pubns.

--Sammy Miller: The Will to Win. 165p. 12.95 (ISBN 0-85429-219-5, F219). Haynes Pubns.

--The Scott Motorcycle: The Yowling Two-Stroke. 239p. 19.95 (ISBN 0-85429-164-4, F164). Haynes Pubns.

--Suzuki. (Illus.). 235p. 17.95 (ISBN 0-317-30509-3, F243). Haynes Pubns.

--Suzuki 250 & 350 Twins '69 - '78. new ed. (Owners Workshop Manuals Ser.: No. 120). 1979. 10.50 (ISBN 0-85696-120-5, Pub. by J H Haynes England). Haynes Pubns.

--Triumph Pre-Unit Twins '47 - '60. (Owners Workshop Manuals Ser.: No. 251). 1979. 10.50 (ISBN 0-85696-251-1, Pub. by J H Haynes England). Haynes Pubns.

--Velocette Singles '53 - '70. new ed. (Owners Workshop Manuals Ser.: No. 186). 1979. 10.50 (ISBN 0-85696-186-8, Pub. by J H Haynes England). Haynes Pubns.

--Vespa Scooters '64 - '79. new ed. (Owners Workshop Manuals Ser.: No. 126). 1979. 10.50 (ISBN 0-85696-126-4, Pub. by J H Haynes England). Haynes Pubns.

--Yamaha 250 & 350 Twins '70 - '79. (Owners Workshop Manuals Ser.: No. 040). 1980. 10.50 (ISBN 0-85696-505-7, Pub. by J H Haynes England). Haynes Pubns.

--Yamaha 500 Twin '73 - '79. new ed. (Owners Workshop Manuals Ser.: No. 308). 1980. 10.50 (ISBN 0-85696-308-9, Pub. by J H Haynes England). Haynes Pubns.

Clew, Jeff & Rogers, Chris. Puch Maxi Mopeds '69 - '80. (Owners Workshop Manuals Ser.: No. 107). 1979. 10.50 (ISBN 0-85696-582-0, Pub. by J H Haynes England). Haynes Pubns.

--Triumph 650 & 750 4-valve Twins '63 - '83. (Owners Workshop Manuals Ser.: No. 122). 1981. 10.50 (ISBN 0-85696-579-0, Pub. by J H Haynes England). Haynes Pubns.

Clew, Kenneth R. The Kennet & Avon Canal. (Illus.). 240p. 1985. 22.50. David & Charles.

Clewell, Andre F. Guide to the Vascular Plants of the Florida Panhandle. LC 84-29126. (Illus.). 608p. 1985. 30.00 (ISBN 0-8130-0779-8). U Presses Fla.

Clewell, David. Room to Breathe. LC 76-42865. 1976. pap. 5.00 (ISBN 0-915316-29-3); signed ltd. ed. o.p. 15.00x (ISBN 0-915316-30-7). Pentagram.

Clewes, Dorothy. Missing from Home. LC 78-52826. (gr. 7 up). 1978. 6.95 (ISBN 0-15-254882-3, HJ). HarBraceJ.

Clewett, John & Critical Mass Energy Project Staff. Nuclear Power Safety Report, 1983. 1983. pap. 5.00 (ISBN 0-937188-22-0). Pub Citizen Inc.

Clewlow, C. William, Jr. & Whitley, David S., eds. The Archaeology of Oak Park, Ventura County, California: Vol. III. (Monographs: No. XI). (Illus.). 186p. (Orig.). 1979. pap. 8.00x (ISBN 0-917956-08-7). UCLA Arch.

Clewlow, C. William, Jr., et al, eds. Archaeological Investigations at the Ring Brothers Site Complex, Thousand Oaks, California. (Monographs: No. XIII). (Illus.). 156p. 1979. pap. 10.00x (ISBN 0-917956-13-3). UCLA Arch.

Clewlow, Carol. Hong Kong Macau & Canton. (Lonely Planet Travel Guides Ser.). 192p. 1982. pap. 6.95 (ISBN 0-908086-20-2, Pub. by Lonely Planet Australia). Hippocrene Bks.

Clewlow, William C., Jr., jt. auth. see Wells, Helen F.

Clews, F. H. Heavy Clay Technology. 2nd ed. 1969. 44.00 (ISBN 0-12-176350-1). Acad Pr.

Clews, G. & Leonard, R. Technology & Production. (Industrial Studies). 192p. 1985. text ed. 25.25x (ISBN 0-86003-527-1, Pub. by Philip Alan). Humanities.

Clews, Henry. Fifty Years in Wall Street. LC 73-2948. (Big Business; Economic Power in a Free Society Ser.). Repr. of 1908 ed. 60.00 (ISBN 0-405-05079-8). Ayer Co Pubs.

--The Intimate Story of One of the Most Daring Speculators in Wall Street & of His Most Remarkable Exploits: Daniel Drew, 2 vols. (Illus.). 227p. 1984. Set. 189.85x (ISBN 0-86654-119-5). Inst Econ Finan.

--Wall Street Point of View. LC 68-28620. (Illus.). 1968. Repr. of 1900 ed. lib. bdg. 15.00x (ISBN 0-8371-0048-8, CLWS). Greenwood.

Clews, Roderick, ed. A Textbook of Insurance Broking. 209p. (Orig.). 1980. 18.00 (ISBN 0-85941-121-4). Woodhead-Faulkner.

Clews, Vince, jt. auth. see Reiff, Tana.

Cleyre, Voltairine De see De Cleyre, Voltairine.

Cleyre, Voltairne de see De Cleyre, Voltairine.

Clezy. Modification of the Mother-Child Interchange. LC 78-23352. (Illus.). 176p. 1979. 12.00 (ISBN 0-8391-1319-6). Pro Ed.

Cliatt, Mary J. & Shaw, Jean M. Junk Treasures: A Sourcebook for Using Recycled Materials with Children. (Illus.). 256p. 1981. pap. text ed. 15.95 (ISBN 0-13-512608-8). P-H.

Cliatt, Mary Jo P., jt. auth. see Shaw, Jean M.

Clibborn, Edward B., ed. American Illustration, No. 2. 1985. 37.50 (ISBN 0-8109-1812-9). Abrams.

--European Illustration: 1983. 1985. 45.00 (ISBN 0-8109-0868-9). Abrams.

--European Photography: 1983-84. 1985. 45.00 (ISBN 0-8109-0870-0). Abrams.

Clibborn, Edward B. see Booth-Clibborn, Edward.

Click, J. W. & Baird, Russell N. Magazine Editing & Production. 3rd ed. 352p. 1982. pap. text ed. write for info (ISBN 0-697-04352-5). Wm C Brown.

Click, Marilyn J. & Ueberle, Jerrie K. L Correction Contracts. 1981. text ed. 5.75x (ISBN 0-8134-2197-7). Interstate.

--LISP Correction Program. 1972 ed. pap. text ed. 5.75x (ISBN 0-8134-1451-2, 1451). Interstate.

--R Reinforcement Contracts. 1981. text ed. 5.75x (ISBN 0-8134-2198-5). Interstate.

Click, Phyllis. Administration of Schools for Young Children. 2nd ed. LC 79-55285. (Early Childhood Education Ser.). 244p. 1981. pap. text ed. 13.80 (ISBN 0-8273-1575-9); instr's. guide 4.20 (ISBN 0-8273-1576-7). Delmar.

Clidero, Robert & Sharpe, Kenneth. Construction Wiring. (Electrical Trades Ser.). (Illus.). 1982. Repr. text ed. 17.80 (ISBN 0-8273-2134-1). Delmar.

Clidero, Robert K. & Sharpe, Kenneth H. Applied Electrical Systems for Construction. 1982. 21.95 (ISBN 0-442-21660-2). Van Nos Reinhold.

Clief, Ron Van see Van Clief, Ron.

Clief, Ron van see Van Clief, Ron.

Clief, Sylvia, jt. auth. see Heide, Florence P.

Clief, Sylvia Van see Heide, Florence P. & Van Clief, Sylvia.

Cliff, A. D. & Ord, J. K. Spatial Autocorrelation. (Monographs in Spatial & Environmental Analysis). (Illus.). 178p. 1974. 17.95x (ISBN 0-85086-036-9, MNO.2954, Pub. by Pion England). Methuen Inc.

--Spatial Processes: Models & Applications. 1980. 30.00x (ISBN 0-85086-081-4, NO.2225, Pub. by Pion). Methuen Inc.

Cliff, A. D., et al. Elements of Spatial Structure. LC 74-12973. (Geographical Studies Ser.: No. 6). (Illus.). 206p. 1974. 44.50 (ISBN 0-521-20689-8). Cambridge U Pr.

--Spatial Diffusion: An Historical Geography of Epidemics in an Island Community. (Cambridge Geographical Studies: No. 14). (Illus.). 244p. 1981. 49.50 (ISBN 0-521-22840-9). Cambridge U Pr.

Cliff, Anne, tr. see Ciliga, Anton.

Cliff, Anne, tr. see Ciliga, Ante.

Cliff, Freda & Cliff, Philip. A Diary for Teachers of Young Children. pap. 1.95x (ISBN 0-8192-4036-2). Morehouse.

Cliff, K. S., jt. auth. see Waters, W. E.

Cliff, Kenneth S. Accidents: Causes, Prevention & Services. LC 84-9567. 301p. 1984. 28.00 (ISBN 0-7099-0792-3, Pub. by Croom Helm Ltd). Longwood Pub Group.

Cliff, Michelle. ABENG: A Novel. (Crossing Press Feminist Ser.). 180p. 1984. 16.95 (ISBN 0-89594-140-6); pap. 6.95 (ISBN 0-89594-139-2). Crossing Pr.

--The Land of Look Behind: Prose & Poetry. 112p. (Orig.). 1985. 13.95 (ISBN 0-932379-09-5); pap. 6.95 (ISBN 0-932379-08-7). Firebrand Bks.

Cliff, Michelle, ed. see Smith, Lillian.

Cliff, Philip, jt. auth. see Cliff, Freda.

Cliff, Stafford, jt. auth. see Slesin, Suzanne.

Cliff, Tony. State Capitalism in Russia. 309p. 1974. pap. 5.95 (ISBN 0-902818-51-1). Pluto Pr.

Cliffe, et al. Government & Rural Development in East Africa: Essays on Political Penetration. (Development of Societies Ser: No. 2). 1977. pap. 26.00 (ISBN 90-247-1884-8, Pub. by Martinus Nijhoff Netherlands). Kluwer Academic.

Cliffe, A. E. Let Go & Let God. 1951. pap. 4.95 (ISBN 0-13-531509-3). P-H.

Cliffe, Albert E. Lessons in Successful Living. 142p. 1982. pap. 4.95 (ISBN 0-13-530824-0). P-H.

Cliffe, J. T. The Puritan Gentry: The Great Puritan Families of Early Stuart England. 300p. 1984. 25.00x (ISBN 0-7102-0007-2). Routledge & Kegan.

Cliffe, R. Woodworking Principles & Practices. (Illus.). 1981. 20.95 (ISBN 0-8269-4820-0). Am Technical.

Cliffe, Roger W. Table Saw Techniques. LC 84-8676. (Illus.). 352p. 1985. cancelled (ISBN 0-8069-5540-6); pap. 14.95 (ISBN 0-8069-7912-7). Sterling.

Clifford, Eth. The Remembering Box. (Illus.). 64p. (gr. 2-5). 1985. 12.95 (ISBN 0-395-38476-1). HM.

Clifford. Microphones. 2nd ed. (Illus.). 264p. 1982. 14.95 (ISBN 0-8306-0097-3); pap. 10.25 (ISBN 0-8306-1475-3, 1475). TAB Bks.

Clifford & Clifford. Computer Mathematics Handbook. 15.95x (ISBN 0-205-04311-9, 2043114). Allyn.

Clifford, jt. auth. see Morris.

Clifford, A. A. Multivariate Error Analysis: A Handbook of Error Propagation & Calculation in Many-Parameter Systems. (Illus.). ix, 112p. 1973. 24.00 (ISBN 0-85334-566-X, Pub. by Elsevier Applied Sci England). Elsevier.

Clifford, A. H. & Preston, G. B. Algebraic Theory of Semigroups, 2 Vols. LC 61-15686. (Mathematical Surveys Ser.: Vol. 7). 1977. Repr. of 1961 ed. Vol. 1, 224p. with corrections 27.00 (ISBN 0-8218-0271-2, SURV-7-1); Vol. 2, 352p. with corrections 35.00 (ISBN 0-8218-0272-0, SURV-7.2). Am Math.

Clifford, A. Jerome. Independence of the Federal Reserve System. LC 63-7862. 1965. 25.00x (ISBN 0-8122-7355-9). U of Pa Pr.

Clifford, Alan. The Middle Ages. Yapp, Malcolm, et al, eds. (World History Ser.). (Illus.). (gr. 10). 1980. lib. bdg. 6.95 (ISBN 0-89908-028-6); pap. text ed. 2.45 (ISBN 0-89908-003-0). Greenhaven.

Clifford, Alejandro, tr. see Ten Boom, Corrie.

Clifford, Anne, jt. ed. see Katz, Bill.

Clifford, Brian & Bull, Ray. The Psychology of Person Identification. 1978. 29.95x (ISBN 0-7100-8867-1). Routledge & Kegan.

Clifford, Brian C., jt. auth. see Jones, D. Gareth.

Clifford, Brian R., jt. auth. see Lloyd-Bostock, Sally M.

Clifford, C. R., ed. Lace Dictionary: Including Historic & Commercial Terms, Technical Terms, Native & Foreign. (Illus.). 156p. 1981. Repr. of 1913 ed. 35.00x (ISBN 0-8103-4311-8). Gale.

Clifford, Craig E. In the Deep Heart's Core: Reflections on Life, Letters, & Texas. LC 85-40040. (Tarleton State University Southwestern Studies in the Humanities: No. 1). 168p. 1985. 12.95 (ISBN 0-89096-233-2). Tex A&M Univ Pr.

Clifford, David. The Two Jerusalems in Prophecy. LC 78-14922. (Illus.). 1978. pap. 3.50 (ISBN 0-87213-081-9). Loizeaux.

Clifford, Denis. Plan Your Estate: Wills, Probate Avoidance, Trusts & Taxes. 5th ed. Warner, Ralph, ed. LC 80-117753. (Illus.). 246p. 1985. pap. 15.95 (ISBN 0-87337-008-2). Nolo Pr.

--Power of Attorney. LC 85-61925. (Illus.). 200p. 1985. 14.95 (ISBN 0-917316-95-9). Nolo Pr.

Clifford, Denis & Warner, Ralph. The Partnership Book. 2nd ed. (Illus.). 221p. 1984. pap. 17.95 (ISBN 0-917316-91-6). Nolo Pr.

Clifford, Denis, jt. auth. see Curry, Hayden.

Clifford, Denis, jt. auth. see Pladsen, Carol.

Clifford, Denis, jt. auth. see Simons, Jim.

Clifford, Donald K., Jr. & Cavanagh, Richard E. The Winning Performance. LC 85-47651. 320p. 1985. 17.95 (ISBN 0-553-05103-2). Bantam.

Clifford, E., jt. auth. see Hampton, C. W.

Clifford, Eth. The Curse of the Moonraker. LC 77-24431. 192p. (gr. 5-9). 1977. 6.95 (ISBN 0-395-25837-5). HM.

--The Dastardly Murder of Dirty Pete. (Illus.). 128p. (gr. 2-5). 1981. 11.95 (ISBN 0-395-31671-5). HM.

--Harvey's Horrible Snake Disaster. LC 83-27299. 128p. (gr. 3-6). 1984. 10.95 (ISBN 0-395-35378-5, 5-83913). HM.

--Help! I'm a Prisoner in the Library. (Illus.). 112p. (gr. 2-5). 1979. 8.95 (ISBN 0-395-28478-3). HM.

--Help! I'm A Prisoner in the Library. 96p. (gr. 4-6). 1985. pap. 2.25 (ISBN 0-590-33481-6, Apple Paperbacks). Scholastic Inc.

--Just Tell Me When We're Dead! LC 83-10865. (Illus.). 144p. (gr. 2-5). 1983. 8.95 (ISBN 0-395-33071-8). HM.

--Just Tell Me When We're Dead! 144p. (gr. 4-6). 1985. pap. 2.25 (ISBN 0-590-33663-0, Apple Paperbacks). Scholastic Inc.

--The Killer Swan. (gr. 5-8). 1980. 6.95 (ISBN 0-395-29742-7). HM.

--The Remembering Box. 1985. 12.95 (ISBN 0-317-31617-6). HM.

--The Rocking Chair Rebellion. (gr. 5-9). 1978. 8.95 (ISBN 0-395-27163-0). HM.

--The Strange Reincarnations of Hendrik Verloom. (gr. 3-6). 1982. 8.95 (ISBN 0-395-32433-5); 8.70. HM.

--The Wild One. LC 74-8899. (Illus.). 208p. (gr. 5-9). 1974. 5.95 (ISBN 0-395-19491-1). HM.

Clifford, F. S. Romance of Perfume. 1977. lib. bdg. 59.95 (ISBN 0-8490-2536-2). Gordon Pr.

Clifford, Francis. Amigo, Amigo. 195p. 1985. pap. 4.95 (ISBN 0-89733-136-2). Academy Chi Pubs.

--The Blind Side. 243p. 1985. pap. 4.95 (ISBN 0-89733-170-2). Academy Chi Pubs.

--The Naked Runner. 192p. 1984. pap. 4.95 (ISBN 0-89733-119-2). Academy Chi Pubs.

Clifford, Frederick. A History of Private Bill Legislation, 2 vols. 1968. 85.00x (ISBN 0-7156-1563-7, F Cass Co). Biblio Dist.

Clifford, George. Heating, Ventilating & Air Conditioning. 1984. text ed. 39.95 (ISBN 0-8359-2812-8); sol. manual avail. (ISBN 0-8359-2813-6). Reston.

Clifford, Geraldine J. Edward L. Thorndike: The Sane Positivist. (Illus.). 134p. 1984. pap. 15.00x (ISBN 0-8195-6092-8). Wesleyan U Pr.

Clifford, H. T. & Constantine, J. Ferns, Fern Allies & Conifers of Australia. (Illus.). 150p. 1980. text ed. 29.95x (ISBN 0-7022-1447-7). U of Queensland Pr.

Clifford, H. T. & Ludlow, Gwen. Keys to the Families & Genera of Queensland. 2nd ed. (Flowering Plants (Magnoliophyta)). (Illus.). 1979. pap. 19.95x (ISBN 0-7022-1225-3). U of Queensland Pr.

Clifford, H. T. & Specht, R. L. The Vegetation of North Stradbroke Island. (Illus.). 1979. pap. 12.95x (ISBN 0-7022-1267-9). U of Queensland Pr.

Clifford, H. T. & Stephenson, W. An Introduction to Numerical Classification: Primarily for Biologists. 1975. 41.00 (ISBN 0-12-176750-7). Acad Pr.

Clifford, H. T. & Watson, L. Identifying Grasses: Data, Methods & Illustrations. 1977. text ed. 35.00x (ISBN 0-7022-1312-8). U of Queensland Pr.

Clifford, H. T., jt. auth. see Dahlgren, R. M.

Clifford, Harold B. The Boothbay Region, Nineteen Hundred Six to Nineteen Sixty. LC 61-14423. (Illus.). 368p. 1982. Repr. of 1961 ed. 15.95 (ISBN 0-87027-204-7). Cumberland Pr.
Clifford, Howard. Doing the White Pass. LC 82-62466. (Illus.). 96p. (Orig.). 1983. pap. 4.25 (ISBN 0-911803-04-1). Sourdough.
--Rails North: The Story of the Railroads of Alaska & the Yukon. (Illus.). 176p. 1981. 22.95 (ISBN 0-87564-536-4). Superior Pub.
--The Skagway Story. LC 75-13918. (Illus.). 167p. 1975. pap. 5.95 (ISBN 0-88240-046-0). Alaska Northwest.
--Western Rail Guide. (Illus.). 168p. 1983. pap. 9.95 (ISBN 0-87564-540-2). Superior Pub.
Clifford, Hugh C. Further Side of Silence. facsimile ed. LC 79-110182. (Short Story Index Reprint Ser.). 1927. 24.50 (ISBN 0-8369-3333-8). Ayer Co Pubs.
--In a Corner of Asia. facsimile ed. LC 77-106265. (Short Story Index Reprint Ser.). 1926. 17.00 (ISBN 0-8369-3302-8). Ayer Co Pubs.
--In Days That Are Dead. facsimile ed. LC 77-113651. (Short Story Index Reprint Ser.). 1926. 19.00 (ISBN 0-8369-3380-X). Ayer Co Pubs.
--Studies in Brown Humanity Being Scrawls & Smudges in Sepia, White & Yellow. text ed. 16.00 (ISBN 0-8369-9240-7, 9094). Ayer Co Pubs.
Clifford, J. G., jt. auth. see Paterson, Thomas G.
Clifford, J. L. & Landa, L., eds. Pope & His Contemporaries: Essays Presented to George Sherburn. 1978. Repr. of 1949 ed. lib. bdg. 24.00x (ISBN 0-374-91700-0). Octagon.
Clifford, J. L., ed. see Smollett, Tobias.
Clifford, James. Person & Myth: Maurice Leenhardt in the Melanesian World. LC 81-4509. (Illus.). 320p. 1982. 29.50x (ISBN 0-520-04247-6). U of Cal Pr.
Clifford, James, jt. auth. see Ariav, Gadi.
Clifford, James L. Dictionary Johnson. 384p. 1981. pap. 6.95 (ISBN 0-07-011379-3). McGraw.
--Young Sam Johnson. (McGraw-Hill Paperbacks Ser.). (Illus.). 400p. 1981. pap. 6.95 (ISBN 0-07-011381-5). McGraw.
Clifford, James L. & Greene, Donald J. Samuel Johnson: A Survey & Bibliography of Critical Studies. LC 74-109940. 1970. 15.00x (ISBN 0-8166-0572-6). U of Minn Pr.
Clifford, James L., ed. Eighteenth Century English Literature: Modern Essays in Criticism. (Orig.). 1959. pap. 6.95 (ISBN 0-19-500682-8, GB). Oxford U Pr.
Clifford, James L. & Landa, Louis A., eds. Pope & His Contemporaries. LC 83-45420. Repr. of 1949 ed. 32.00 (ISBN 0-404-20063-X). AMS Pr.
Clifford, James L., ed. see Smollett, Tobias.
Clifford, Jane. A House in the Cotswolds: A Laura Ashley Decoration Book. 1984. pap. 4.50 (ISBN 0-517-55334-1, Harmony). Crown.
Clifford, Jerrold R. Basic Woodworking & Carpentry...with Projects. (Illus.). 252p. 1980. pap. 6.95 (ISBN 0-8306-1058-6, 1058). TAB Bks.
Clifford, Joan. Capability Brown. (Lifelines Ser.: No. 33). 1983. pap. 3.50 (ISBN 0-85263-274-6, Pub. by Shire Pubns Eng). Seven Hills Bks.
Clifford, John. Educational Theatre Management. 1972. text ed. 9.00 (ISBN 0-8442-5121-6). Natl Textbk.
Clifford, John & Waterhouse, Robert. Sentence Combining & Flexibility. 224p. 1983. pap. text ed. write for info. (ISBN 0-02-322920-9). Macmillan.
--Sentence Combining: Shaping Ideas for Better Style. 224p. (Orig.). 1983. pap. text ed. 10.83 scp (ISBN 0-672-61605-X); scp instr's. guide 3.67 (ISBN 0-672-61604-1). Bobbs.
Clifford, John & Yanni, Robert. Modern American Prose: A Reader for Writers. 416p. 1982. pap. text ed. 13.00 (ISBN 0-394-32896-5, RanC). Random.
Clifford, John, jt. auth. see Grierson, Herbert.
Clifford, John, jt. auth. see Veit, Richard.
Clifford, John E. Tense & Tense Logic. (Janua Linguarum, Ser. Minor: No. 215). 173p. (Orig.). 1975. pap. text ed. 18.40x (ISBN 90-2793-453-3). Mouton.
Clifford, John G. The Citizen Soldiers: The Plattsburg Training Camp Movement, 1913-1920. LC 71-183350. 336p. 1972. 25.00x (ISBN 0-8131-1262-1). U Pr of Ky.
Clifford, Joseph A. Administrative Law. 30p. 1963. pap. 1.50 (ISBN 0-87526-001-2). Gould.
Clifford, Kay. A Temporary Affair. (Harlequin Romances Ser.). 192p. 1982. pap. 1.50 (ISBN 0-373-02505-X). Harlequin Bks.
Clifford, Laurie. Ride the Blue Bazoo. LC 83-15959. (What If Ser.). (gr. 4-9). 1983. pap. 2.25 (ISBN 0-8307-0901-0, 5900062). Regal.
Clifford, Laurie B. Accept the Royal Challenge. LC 84-4776. (What If...Bks.). 136p. (gr. 5-9). 1984. pap. text ed. 2.50 (ISBN 0-8307-0940-1, 5900102). Regal.
--Before the Dawn Wind Rises. 182p. (Orig.). 1985. pap. 6.95 (ISBN 0-317-19333-3, 5418539). Regal.
--Evergreen Castles. (No. 1). 1983. pap. 3.50 (ISBN 0-8423-0779-6). Tyndale.
--Follow the Lone Cry. LC 83-15960. (What If Ser.). 136p. (gr. 5-9). 1983. pap. 2.25 (ISBN 0-8307-0913-4, 5900074). Regal.
--The Peppermint Gang & Frog Heaven. (Peppermint Gang Ser.). 160p. (gr. 8-12). 3.50 (ISBN 0-8423-0935-7). Tyndale.
--The Peppermint Gang & the Million Dollar Night, No. 3. 207p. (gr. 5-7). 1983. pap. 3.50 (ISBN 0-8423-4284-2). Tyndale.
--The Secret of the Golden Crosses, No. 2. 1983. pap. 3.50 (ISBN 0-8423-5854-4). Tyndale.
--Sneak Behind Enemy Lines. LC 84-1995. (What If...Bks.). (gr. 5-9). 1984. pap. text ed. 2.50 (ISBN 0-8307-0939-8, 5900094). Regal.
--Some Strange Joy. LC 83-24797. (Orig.). 1984. pap. 5.95 (ISBN 0-8307-0930-4, 5418152). Regal.
Clifford, Lucy. Eve's Lover, & Other Stories. LC 70-128724. (Short Story Index Reprint Ser). 1924. 17.00 (ISBN 0-8369-3615-9). Ayer Co Pubs.
--Last Touches, & Other Stories. facsimile ed. LC 76-150470. (Short Story Index Reprint Ser.). Repr. of 1892 ed. 18.00 (ISBN 0-8369-3810-0). Ayer Co Pubs.
Clifford, M. N. & Willson, K. C., eds. Coffee: Botany, Biochemistry & Production of Beans & Beverage. 1985. lib. bdg. 55.00 (ISBN 0-87055-491-3). AVI.
Clifford, Margaret A. & Drummond, Ann E. Radiographic Techniques Related to Pathology. 2nd ed. 88p. 1977. pap. text ed. 10.50 (ISBN 7236-0679-X). PSG Pub Co.
Clifford, Margaret M. Activities & Readings in Learning & Development. LC 80-84892. (Illus.). 256p. 1981. pap. text ed. 12.95 (ISBN 0-395-29924-1); FRAME-the ed syke game 3.50 (ISBN 0-395-29926-8). HM.
--Practicing Educational Psychology. (Illus.). 752p. 1981. text ed. 26.95 (ISBN 0-395-29921-7); pap. text ed. 25.95 (ISBN 0-395-29922-5); instr's manual 1.50 (ISBN 0-395-29923-3); test bank 3.50 (ISBN 0-395-29925-X). HM.
Clifford, Martin. Complete Guide to Car Audio. LC 80-50560. 256p. 1981. pap. 9.95 (ISBN 0-672-21820-8). Sams.
--The Complete Guide to High Fidelity. LC 82-50014. 15.95 (ISBN 0-672-21892-5). Sams.
--The Complete Guide to Satellite TV. (Illus.). 256p. 1984. 17.95 (ISBN 0-8306-0685-8, 1685); pap. 11.95 (ISBN 0-8306-1685-3). TAB Bks.
--The Complete Guide to Security. LC 82-50656. 336p. 1982. pap. 13.95 (ISBN 0-672-21955-7). Sams.
--The Complete Guide to Video. LC 83-60165. 342p. 1983. pap. text ed. 15.95 (ISBN 0-672-21912-3). Sams.
--Master Handbook of Electronic Tables & Formulas. 4th ed. LC 84-8529. (Illus.). 392p. 1984. pap. 13.95 (ISBN 0-8306-1625-X, 1625). TAB Bks.
--Your Telephone: Operation, Selection & Installation. LC 83-50377. 336p. 1983. pap. 13.95 (ISBN 0-672-22065-2, 22065). Sams.
Clifford, Mary E., et al, eds. News Dictionary 1976. LC 65-17649. 1977. lib. bdg. 14.95 (ISBN 0-87196-103-2). Facts on File.
Clifford, Mary L. Land & People of Afghanistan. rev. ed. LC 72-13178. (Portraits of the Nations Ser). (Illus.). (gr. 5-10). 1977. PLB 10.89 (ISBN 0-397-31685-2). Lipp Jr Bks.
--The Land & People of Sierra Leone. LC 73-20317. (Portraits of the Nations Ser.). (Illus.). 160p. (gr. 7 up). 1974. 10.53i (ISBN 0-397-31490-6). Lipp Jr Bks.
Clifford, Mary Louise & Jensen, Lynn A. Court Case Management Information Systems Manual: With Model Data Elements, Reporting Forms, & Management Reports. LC 83-17382. (Illus.). 327p. 1983. pap. text ed. 15.00 (ISBN 0-89656-071-6, R-082). Natl Ctr St Courts.
Clifford, Michael. The dBASE Book of Business Applications. (Illus.). 256p. 1984. pap. 19.95 (ISBN 0-8359-1242-6). Reston.
Clifford, Michael J., jt. auth. see Linzey, Donald W.
Clifford, Mike. The Harmony Illustrated Encyclopedia of Rock. 4th ed. (Illus.). 1984. (Harmony); pap. 11.95 (ISBN 0-517-55262-0). Crown.
Clifford, Nicholas. Retreat from China: British Policy in the Far East, 1937-1941. (China in the 20th Century Ser.). 1976. Repr. of 1967 ed. lib. bdg. 27.50 (ISBN 0-306-70757-8). Da Capo.
Clifford, Nicholas R. Shanghai, Nineteen Twenty-five: Urban Nationalism & the Defense of Foreign Privilege. LC 79-14469. (Michigan Monographs in Chinese Studies: No. 37). (Orig.). 1979. pap. text ed. 6.00 (ISBN 0-89264-037-5). U of Mich Ctr Chinese.
Clifford, Peter. Art & Science of Motor Cycle Road Racing. (Illus.). 260p. 1982. 16.95 (ISBN 0-905138-24-4, Pub. by Hazelton England). Motorbooks Intl.
Clifford, Peter, ed. Motocourse, 1982-1983. (Illus.). 192p. 1983. 17.95 (ISBN 0-905138-22-8, Pub. by Hazelton England). Motorbooks Intl.
Clifford, Philip G. Nathan Clifford, Democrat (1803-1881) (Illus.). 356p. 1922. 7.50x (ISBN 0-686-05089-4). O'Brien.
Clifford, Richard. Deuteronomy, with Excursus on Covenant & Law. (Old Testament Message Ser.: Vol. 4). 1982. 12.95 (ISBN 0-89453-404-1); pap. 7.95 (ISBN 0-89453-239-1). M Glazier.
Clifford, Richard J. The Cosmic Mountain in Canaan & the Old Testament. LC 71-188968. (Semitic Monographs: No. 4). (Illus.). 221p. 1972. 18.50x (ISBN 0-674-17425-9). Harvard U Pr.
--Fair-Spoken & Persuading: An Interpretation of Second Isaiah. (Theological Inquiries Ser.). (Orig.). 1984. pap. 8.95. Paulist Pr.
Clifford, Richard J. & Rockwell, Hays H. Holy Week. Achtemeier, Elizabeth, ed. LC 79-7377. (Proclamation 2, Ser. C). 1980. pap. 3.50 (ISBN 0-8006-4088-8, 1-4088). Fortress.
Clifford, Richard M., jt. auth. see Harms, Thelma.
Clifford, Sandy. The Roquefort Gang. (Illus.). (gr. 2-6). 1981. 7.95 (ISBN 0-395-29521-1). HM.
Clifford, Susan B., jt. auth. see Anderson, Pauline.
Clifford, T. N. & Gass, I. G., eds. African Magmatism & Tectonics. (Illus.). 1970. 40.95x (ISBN 0-02-842990-7). Hafner.
Clifford, Terry. Tibetan Buddhist Medicine & Psychiatry: The Diamond Healing. LC 82-61872. 288p. 1984. 15.95 (ISBN 0-87728-528-4). Weiser.
Clifford, Tom N. Review of African Granulites & Related Rocks. LC 74-84196. (Geological Society of America Ser.: No. 156). pap. 20.00 (ISBN 0-317-28368-5, 2025471). Bks Demand UMI.
Clifford, Vladimir H. The Symbolic Paintings by G. Segantini. (The Art Library of the Great Masters of the World). (Illus.). 109p. 1983. 81.65x (ISBN 0-86650-084-7). Gloucester Art.
Clifford, William, jt. auth. see Freuchen, Dagmar.
Clifford, William & Milton, Daniel, eds. Treasury of Modern Asian Stories. pap. 2.95 (ISBN 0-452-25052-8, Z5052, Plume). NAL.
Clifford, William G. Books in Bottles: The Curious in Literature. LC 70-78125. 194p. 1971. Repr. of 1926 ed. 35.00x (ISBN 0-8103-3791-6). Gale.
Clifford, William K. Lectures & Essays. write for info. (ISBN 0-685-50585-5). Chelsea Pub.
--Mathematical Papers. LC 67-28488. 1968. Repr. 35.00 (ISBN 0-8284-0210-8). Chelsea Pub.
Clifford Rose, F., ed. Migraine. (Illus.). xii, 356p. 1985. 74.50 (ISBN 3-8055-4039-6). S Karger.
Cliff's Notes Editors. Canterbury Tales Notes. (Orig.). 1964. pap. 3.25 (ISBN 0-8220-0292-2). Cliffs.
Cliff's Notes Staff. Moby Dick Notes. (Orig.). 1966. pap. 2.95 (ISBN 0-8220-0852-1). Cliffs.
Clift, Charles, III & Greer, Archie, eds. Broadcast Programming, the Current Perspective. 7th ed. LC 81-40728. 260p. (Orig.). 1981. pap. text ed. 9.75 (ISBN 0-8191-1894-X). U Pr of Amer.
Clift, Dominique. Quebec Nationalism in Crisis. Orig. Title: Le Declin du Nationalisme au Quebec. 162p. 1982. 20.00x (ISBN 0-7735-0381-1); pap. 7.95 (ISBN 0-7735-0383-8). McGill Queen's U Pr.
Clift, Dominique, jt. auth. see Arnopoulos, Sheila M.
Clift, G. Glenn. Kentucky Marriages, 1797-1865. LC 66-27027. 258p. 1983. Repr. of 1940 ed. 15.00 (ISBN 0-8063-0076-0). Genealog Pub.
--Second Census of Kentucky: 1800. LC 66-19191. 333p. 1982. Repr. of 1954 ed. 18.50 (ISBN 0-8063-0077-9). Genealog Pub.
Clift, G. Glenn, ed. see Butler, Mann.
Clift, Garrett G. The Cornstalk Militia of Kentucky (1792-1811) 248p. 1982. Repr. of 1957 ed. 25.00 (ISBN 0-89308-318-6). Southern Hist Pr.
Clift, Glen G. Kentucky Obituaries, 1787-1854. LC 76-57789. 254p. 1984. Repr. of 1941 ed. 15.00 (ISBN 0-8063-0758-7). Genealog Pub.
Clift, J. C. & Imrie, B. W. Assessing Students, Appraising Teaching. LC 80-23135. (New Patterns of Learning Ser.). 176p. 1981. 34.95x (ISBN 0-470-27098-5). Halsted Pr.
Clift, Jean, jt. auth. see Clift, Wallace.
Clift, Philip, et al. The Aims, Role & Deployment of Staff in the Nursery. 224p. 1980. 18.00x (ISBN 0-85633-197-X, Pub. by NFER Nelson UK). Taylor & Francis.
Clift, Roland, et al. Bubbles, Drops & Particles. LC 77-6592. 1978. 58.50 (ISBN 0-12-176950-X). Acad Pr.
Clift, Virgil A., jt. auth. see Low, W. Augustus.
Clift, Virgil A., jt. auth. see Moseley, H. Jewel.
Clift, Wallace & Clift, Jean. Symbols of Transformation in Dreams. 144p. 1984. pap. 13.95 (ISBN 0-8245-0653-7). Crossroad NY.
Clift, Wallace B. Jung & Christianity: The Challenge of Reconciliation. LC 81-17395. 192p. 1983. pap. 8.95 (ISBN 0-8245-0552-2). Crossroad NY.
Clift, William. Tim Bunker Paper, or Yankee Farming. facs. ed. LC 72-137727. (American Fiction Reprint Ser). 1868. 20.00 (ISBN 0-8369-7026-8). Ayer Co Pubs.
Clifton, A. Kay, jt. auth. see Lee, Dorothy E.
Clifton, Barbara. KET Adult Math Series Computer. Webb, Sidney, ed. (Adult Math Ser.). 40p. 1984. tchrs. guide 3.50 (ISBN 0-910475-28-8). KET.
Clifton, Barbara, ed. see Gnam, Rene.
Clifton, Barbara, ed. see Shapero, Albert.
Clifton, Barbara, et al. Using Your Computer. Webb, Sidney L., ed. (Business of Better Writing Ser.). 34p. 1984. write for info. wkbk. (ISBN 0-910475-21-0). KET.
Clifton, Barbarba, ed. see Garinger, Alan K.
Clifton, C. E., et al, eds. Annual Review of Microbiology, Vol. 26. LC 49-432. (Illus.). 1972. text ed. 20.00 (ISBN 0-8243-1126-4). Annual Reviews.
Clifton, Chas. Ghost Tales of Cripple Creek. (Illus.). 30p. (Orig.). 1983. pap. 2.95 (ISBN 0-936564-24-5). Little London.
Clifton, Chester V., jt. auth. see Stoughton, Cecil.
Clifton, Claire. Edible Flowers. (Illus.). 96p. 1984. 10.95 (ISBN 0-07-011382-3). McGraw.
Clifton, David S., Jr. & Fyffe, David E. Project Feasibility Analysis: A Guide to Profitable New Ventures. LC 76-51321. 340p. 1977. text ed. 59.95 (ISBN 0-471-01611-X, Pub. by Wiley-Interscience). Wiley.
Clifton, E. & Grimaux. Nouveau Dictionnaire Anglais-Francais. (Eng. & Fr.). 1914. 100.00 (ISBN 0-686-17758-4). Ridgeway Bks.
Clifton, Fred. Darl. (Illus.). 104p. (gr. 2-6). 1973. 5.95 (ISBN 0-89388-098-1). Okpaku Communications.
Clifton, H. D. Choosing & Using Computers: Assessing Data Processing Requirements for Smaller Companies. 1975. 22.00x (ISBN 0-8464-0247-5). Beekman Pubs.
Clifton, Jack. The Eye of the Artist. LC 81-896. 1973. pap. 14.95 (ISBN 0-89134-034-3). North Light Pub.
Clifton, James A. The Pokagons, Sixteen Eighty-Three to Nineteen Eighty-Three: Catholic Potawatomi Indians of the St. Joseph River Valley. (Illus.). 182p. (Orig.). 1985. lib. bdg. 22.75 (ISBN 0-8191-4282-4, Pub. by Potawatomi Indian Not); pap. text ed. 11.50 (ISBN 0-8191-4283-2, Pub. by Potawatomi Indian Not). U Pr of Amer.
--The Prairie People: Continuity & Change in Potawatomi Indian Culture, 1665-1965. LC 76-51774. 1977. 25.00x (ISBN 0-7006-0155-4). U Pr of KS.
Clifton, James A., retold by. Star Woman & Other Shawnee Tales. 94p. (Orig.). 1984. lib. bdg. 17.75 (ISBN 0-8191-3712-X); pap. text ed. 6.25 (ISBN 0-8191-3713-8). U Pr of Amer.
Clifton, James M., ed. Life & Labor on Argyle Island: Letter & Documents of a Savannah River Rice Plantation, 1833-1867. LC 77-85735. 365p. 1978. 22.50x (ISBN 0-8139-0951-1). U Pr of Va.
Clifton, Lucille. The Boy Who Didn't Believe in Spring. (Illus.). (gr. 3-4). 1978. 8.25 (ISBN 0-525-27145-7, 0801-240); pap. 1.95 (ISBN 0-525-45038-6, Anytime Bks). Dutton.
--Everett Anderson's 1-2-3. LC 76-25866. (Illus.). (gr. k-3). 1977. reinforced bdg. 6.95 (ISBN 0-03-017441-4). HR&W.
--The Lucky Stone. LC 78-72862. (Illus.). 64p. (gr. 4-6). 1979. PLB 9.95 (ISBN 0-385-28600-7). Delacorte.
--El Nino Que No Creia En la Primavera: Spanish Edition of The Boy Who Didn't Believe in Spring. Ada, Alma F., tr. (gr. k-3). 1976. 6.95 (ISBN 0-525-29170-9). Dutton.
--Sonora Beautiful. LC 81-2094. (Illus.). 24p. (gr. 5 up). 1981. 8.95 (ISBN 0-525-39680-2, 0869-260, Skinny Book). Dutton.
--The Times They Used to Be. LC 73-21859. (Illus.). 64p. (gr. 3-7). 1974. reinforced bdg. 4.95 (ISBN 0-03-012171-X). HR&W.
--Two-Headed Woman. LC 80-5379. 72p. 1980. lib. bdg. 8.00x (ISBN 0-87023-309-2); pap. 4.50 (ISBN 0-87023-310-6). U of Mass Pr.
Clifton, Lucille & Di Grazia, Thomas. My Friend Jacob. LC 79-19168. 32p. (gr. k-2). 1980. 9.95 (ISBN 0-525-35487-5, 0966-290). Dutton.
Clifton, Lucille, et al. Everett Anderson's Goodbye. (Illus.). 32p. (ps-1). 1983. 9.95 (ISBN 0-03-063518-7). HR&W.
Clifton, Merritt. A Baseball Classic. 1978. pap. 3.00 (ISBN 0-686-00579-1). Samisdat.
--Baseball Stories for Boys & Girls. 20p. 1982. pap. 1.50 (ISBN 0-686-37933-0). Samisdat.
--Betrayal. 1980. 2.50 (ISBN 0-686-26981-0). Samisdat.
--Disorganized Baseball: History of Quebec Provincial League, 1920-1969. 36p. 1983. pap. 6.00 (ISBN 0-686-89393-X). Samisdat.
--Freedom Comes from Human Beings. 80p. (Orig.). 1980. pap. 4.00 (ISBN 0-686-28738-X). Samisdat.
--From an Age of Cars. 23p. (Orig.). 1980. pap. 2.50 (ISBN 0-938566-03-2). Adastra Pr.
--Help! For Small Press People. 40p. 1985. pap. 5.00 (ISBN 0-317-16911-4). Samisdat.
--Japanese Baseball Makes the Big Leagues. 20p. 1985. pap. 1.50 (ISBN 0-317-16915-7). Samisdat.
--Learning Disabilities: What the Publicity Doesn't Tell. 24p. 1982. pap. 3.00 (ISBN 0-686-37937-3). Samisdat.
--On Small Press As Class Struggle. 1976. pap. 1.00 (ISBN 0-686-20630-4). Samisdat.
--Relative Baseball. 1979. 5.00 (ISBN 0-686-00580-5). Samisdat.
--The Samisdat Method: A Guide to Do-It-Yourself Offset Printing. 1978. pap. 2.00 (ISBN 0-686-12106-6). Samisdat.
--Three of a Kind. 20p. 1979. pap. 1.00 (ISBN 0-686-27927-1). Samisdat.
--Two from Armageddon. (Illus.). 20p. 1976. pap. 1.00 (ISBN 0-686-20756-4). Samisdat.
--Vindictment. 1977. pap. 1.00 (ISBN 0-686-23159-7). Samisdat.
Clifton, Merritt & Palmer, Pete. Relative Baseball II. 80p. 1985. 5.00 (ISBN 0-317-19196-9). Samisdat.
Clifton, Merritt & Powers, Jack. The White Man Problem. 12p. 1985. 1.00 (ISBN 0-317-19193-4). Samisdat.
Clifton, Merritt, ed. see Payack, Paul J.

Clifton, Merritt, et al, eds. Those Who Were There: Eyewitness Accounts of the War in Southeast Asia, 1956-1975, & Aftermath; Annotated Bibliography of Books, Articles, & Topic-Related Magazines, Covering Writings Both Factual & Imaginative. LC 83-25434. (American Dust Ser.: No. 15). 297p. 1984. 12.95 (ISBN 0-913218-97-9). Dustbooks.
Clifton, N. Roy. The Figure in Film. LC 80-54539. 580p. 1982. 49.50 (ISBN 0-87413-189-8). U Delaware Pr.
Clifton, R. H. Principles of Planned Maintenance. 1974. pap. 22.50x (ISBN 0-7131-3317-1). Intl Ideas.
Clifton, Robert B. Murder by Mail: And Other Postal Investigations. LC 79-51377. (Illus.). 240p. 1979. 7.95 (ISBN 0-8059-2649-6). Dorrance.
Clifton, Robert T. Barbs, Prongs, Points, Prickers, & Stickers: Complete & Illustrated Catalogue of Antique Barbed Wire. LC 78-88140. (Illus.). 1970. pap. 12.95 (ISBN 0-8061-0876-2). U of Okla Pr.
Clifton, Robin. The Last Popular Rebellion: The Western Rising of 1685. LC 84-40230. 308p. 1984. 27.50 (ISBN 0-312-47123-8). St Martin.
Clifton, RoMichelle. The Pillory Poetics. 3rd rev. ed. 24p. 1979. pap. 1.00 (ISBN 0-686-27505-5). Samisdat.
Clifton, Thomas. Music as Heard: A Study in Applied Phenomenology. LC 82-10944. (Illus.). 336p. 1983. text ed. 36.00x (ISBN 0-300-02091-0). Yale U Pr.
Clifton, Tony & Leroy, Catherine. God Cried. 29.95 (ISBN 0-318-01966-3, Pub. by Quartet Bks). Merrimack Pub Cir.
Clifton, Violet. The Book of Talbot. 439p. 1981. Repr. of 1933 ed. lib. bdg. 25.00 (ISBN 0-89987-114-3). Darby Bks.
--The Book of Talbot. 1933. 20.00 (ISBN 0-932062-29-6). Sharon Hill.
Clifton, Williams. March from "Symphonic Suite" for Orchestra: Score. pap. 39.80 (ISBN 0-317-09827-6, 2002893). Bks Demand UMI.
Clifton-Taylor, Alec. The Cathedrals of England. (Illus.). 1980. pap. 8.95 (ISBN 0-500-20062-9). Thames Hudson.
--English Parish Churches As Works of Art. 1974. 22.50 (ISBN 0-7134-2776-0, Pub. by Batsford England). David & Charles.
--The Pattern of English Building. 2nd ed. 466p. 1972. pap. 21.95 (ISBN 0-571-09526-7). Faber & Faber.
--Six English Towns. 176p. 1978. 35.00x (ISBN 0-563-17397-1, Pub. by BBC Pubns). State Mutual Bk.
Clifton-Taylor, Alec & Ireson, A. S. English Stone Building. 224p. 1983. 27.50 (ISBN 0-575-03214-6, Gollancz England). David & Charles.
Clifton-Taylor, Alec, jt. auth. see Brunskill, Ronald.
Clignet, Remi. The Africanization of the Labor Market: Educational & Occupational Segmentations in the Camerouns. LC 75-13145. 1976. 35.00x (ISBN 0-520-03019-2). U of Cal Pr.
--Liberty & Equality in the Educational Process. LC 74-9737. 418p. 1974. 25.00 (ISBN 0-471-16057-1, Pub. by Wiley). Krieger.
--Many Wives, Many Powers: Authority & Power in Polygynous Families. LC 75-89821. pap. 76.00 (ISBN 0-8357-9464-4, 2010258). Bks Demand UMI.
--The Structure of Artistic Revolutions. LC 84-25625. 344p. 1985. text ed. 30.00 (ISBN 0-8122-7978-6). U of Pa Pr.
Clignet, Remi & Foster, P. Fortunate Few: A Study of Secondary Schools & Students in the Ivory Coast. (Northwestern University African Studies Ser.: No. 18). 1966. 15.95 (ISBN 0-8101-0064-9). Northwestern U Pr.
Cliinchy, Everett R., Jr. Equality of Opportunity for Latin-Americans in Texas. LC 73-14199. (The Mexican American Ser.). 224p. 1974. 22.00x (ISBN 0-405-05673-7). Ayer Co Pubs.
Climatic Impact Committee. Environmental Impact of Stratospheric Flight. 1975. pap. 12.00 (ISBN 0-309-02346-7). Natl Acad Pr.
Climenson, Emily J. Elizabeth Montagu: The Queen of the Bluestockings, 2 vols. 1906. Repr. Set. 85.00 (ISBN 0-8274-2239-3). R West.
Climer, James H., et al, eds. Public Utilities in a Changing Society. (Michigan Business Papers: No. 49). 1968. pap. 2.00 (ISBN 0-87712-098-6). U Mich Busn Div Res.
Climer, Jerry. How to Raise a Cat When Nobody's Home. (Illus.). 150p. 1983. pap. 7.95 (ISBN 0-911793-01-1). Penny Dreadful Pubs.
--How to Raise a Dog When Nobody's Home. (Illus.). 156p. (Orig.). 1983. pap. 7.95 (ISBN 0-911793-00-3). Penny Dreadful Pubs.
Climo, Lindee. Chester's Barn. (Illus.). (gr. 1 up). 1982. 13.95 (ISBN 0-88776-132-1); pap. 7.95 (ISBN 0-88776-155-0). Tundra Bks.
Climo, Shirley. Cobweb Christmas. LC 81-43879. (Illus.). 32p. (ps-3). 1982. 11.06 (ISBN 0-690-04215-9); PLB 11.89 (ISBN 0-690-04216-7). Crowell Jr Bks.
--Gopher, Tanker, & the Admiral. LC 83-45240. (Illus.). 128p. (gr. 2-6). 1984. 10.53i (ISBN 0-690-04382-1); PLB 10.89g (ISBN 0-690-04383-X). Crowell Jr Bks.
--Piskies, Spriggans, & Other Magical Beings: Tales from the Droll-Teller. LC 79-7839. (Illus.). 128p. (gr. 4-7). 1981. 9.57i (ISBN 0-690-04063-6); PLB 10.89 (ISBN 0-690-04064-4). Crowell Jr Bks.
Climo, Shirley & Zimmer, Dirk. Someone Saw a Spider: Spider Facts & Folktales. LC 85-45340. (Illus.). 128p. (gr. 4-7). 1985. 11.06i (ISBN 0-690-04435-6); PLB 11.89g (ISBN 0-690-04436-4). Crowell Jr Bks.
Clinard, Helen. Winning Ways to Succeed with People. LC 84-22473. (Illus.). 272p. 1985. 21.95x (ISBN 0-87201-686-2). Gulf Pub.
Clinard, Linda M. The Reading Triangle. 1985. pap. 7.95 (ISBN 0-8224-5815-2). Pitman Learning.
Clinard, Marshall B. Anomie & Deviant Behavior: A Discussion & Critique. LC 64-20314. (Illus.). 1964. pap. text ed. 5.95 (ISBN 0-02-905550-4). Free Pr.
--Black Market: A Study of White Collar Crime. LC 69-16233. (Criminology, Law Enforcement, & Social Problems Ser.: No. 87). 1969. 17.00 (ISBN 0-87585-087-1); pap. 7.50x (ISBN 0-87585-912-7). Patterson Smith.
Clinard, Marshall B. & Abbott, Daniel J. Crime in Developing Countries: A Comparative Perspective. LC 3-4031. 319p. 1973. 39.50 (ISBN 0-471-16060-1, Pub. by Wiley-Interscience). Wiley.
Clinard, Marshall B. & Meier, Robert F. Sociology of Deviant Behavior. 5th ed. LC 78-10495. 1979. text ed. 27.95x (ISBN 0-03-045026-8, HoltC); instr's. manual 20.00 (ISBN 0-03-045031-4). HR&W.
Clinard, Marshall B. & Yeager, Peter C. Corporate Crime. LC 80-2156. 1983. pap. 8.95 (ISBN 0-02-905880-5); text ed. 17.95 (ISBN 0-02-905710-8). Free Pr.
Clinard, Marshall Barron. Corporate Ethics & Crime. LC 83-3105. 1983. 25.00 (ISBN 0-8039-1972-7). Sage.
Clinard, Turner N. Responding to God: The Life of Stewardship. LC 79-24762. 118p. 1980. pap. 6.95 (ISBN 0-664-24292-8). Westminster.
Clinch, George. Handbook of English Antiquities for the Collector & Student. LC 77-94552. 1979. Repr. of 1905 ed. lib. bdg. 40.00 (ISBN 0-89341-220-1). Longwood Pub Group.
--Old English Churches: Their Architecture, Furniture, Decorations & Monuments. 1977. lib. bdg. 59.95 (ISBN 0-8490-2368-8). Gordon Pr.
--Old English Churches: Their Architecture, Furniture, Decoration & Monuments. LC 77-94552. 1978. Repr. of 1900 ed. lib. bdg. 30.00 (ISBN 0-89341-221-X). Longwood Pub Group.
Clinch, Minty. Burt Lancaster. LC 84-40625. 192p. 1985. 15.95 (ISBN 0-8128-3016-4). Stein & Day.
--James Cagney: The Story of His Film Career. (Illus.). 128p. 1982. 16.95 (ISBN 0-86276-061-5); pap. 10.95 (ISBN 0-86276-060-7). Proteus Pub NY.
Clinch, Nicholas. A Walk in the Sky: Climbing Hidden Peak. (Illus.). 232p. 1982. 18.95 (ISBN 0-89886-042-3). Mountaineers.
Clinch, Simon & Peters, Stephen. Programming with RT-11, Vol. 1: Program Development Facilities. (Illus.). 200p. 1984. pap. 28.00 (ISBN 0-932376-32-0, EY-00022-DP). Digital Pr.
--Tailoring RT-11: System Management & Programming Facilities. (Illus.). 220p. 1984. pap. 36.00 (ISBN 0-932376-34-7, EY-00024-DP). Digital Pr.
Clinchy, Everett. The World We Want to Live in. 1942. 20.00 (ISBN 0-8482-7588-8). Norwood Edns.
Cline & McHaffie. The People's Guide, 1874: Directory of Henry Co., Indiana. 398p. 1979. 22.00 (ISBN 0-686-27818-6). Bookmark.
Cline, et al. Prescriptions for Good Eating. 304p. (Orig.). 1984. pap. 11.95 (ISBN 0-9613679-0-3). Greenville County Med.
Cline, Barbara L., rev. by see Bolton, Sarah K.
Cline, Ben E. An Introduction to Automated Data Acquisitions. 294p. 1984. 29.95 (ISBN 0-89433-192-2). Petrocelli.
--An Introduction to Automated Data Acquisition. (Illus.). 294p. 1984. 29.95 (ISBN 0-89433-192-2). Van Nos Reinhold.
--Microprogramming Concepts & Techniques. (Illus.). 240p. 1981. 20.00 (ISBN 0-89433-133-7). Petrocelli.
Cline, C. Byron, Shelley & Their Pisan Circle. 1952. Repr. 25.00 (ISBN 0-8274-1991-0). R West.
Cline, C. L. The Fate of Cassandra: The Newspaper War of 1821-22 & Sir Walter Scott. LC 72-5780. (Quarterly Ser). 1971. 5.95 (ISBN 0-87959-069-6). U of Tex H Ransom Ctr.
Cline, C. L., ed. The Owl & the Rossettis: Letters of Charles A. Howell & Dante Gabriel, Christina, & William Michael Rossetti. LC 77-88468. 1978. 28.50x (ISBN 0-271-00530-0). Pa St U Pr.
--Rinehart Book of Short Stories. LC 57-9640. (Rinehart Editions). 1952. pap. text ed. 12.95 (ISBN 0-03-008165-3, HoltC). HR&W.
Cline, C. L., ed. see Meredith, George.
Cline, C. Terry. Missing Persons. 288p. 1983. pap. 2.95 (ISBN 0-449-20015-9, Crest). Fawcett.
Cline, C. Terry, Jr. The Attorney Conspiracy. LC 82-72059. 375p. 1983. 15.50 (ISBN 0-87795-371-6). Arbor Hse.
--Cross Current. 1980. pap. 2.50 (ISBN 0-449-24289-7, Crest). Fawcett.
--Damon. 320p. 1978. pap. 2.25 (ISBN 0-449-22702-2, Crest). Fawcett.
--Death Knell. 1978. pap. 2.25 (ISBN 0-449-23639-0, Crest). Fawcett.
--Missing Persons. LC 80-70215. 320p. 1981. 12.95 (ISBN 0-87795-304-X). Arbor Hse.
--Missing Persons. 1983. pap. 2.95 (ISBN 0-686-43229-0). Ballantine.
--Prey. 304p. 1985. 14.95 (ISBN 0-453-00480-6). NAL.
Cline, Catherine A. E. D. Morel Eighteen Seventy-Three to Nineteen Twenty-Four: The Strategies of Protest. 192p. 1980. 21.95 (ISBN 0-85640-213-3, Pub. by Blackstaff Pr). Longwood Pub Group.
--Recruits to Labour: The British Labour Party, 1914-1931. LC 63-13888. 1963. 14.95x (ISBN 0-8156-2046-2). Syracuse U Pr.
Cline, Charles. Crossing the Ohio. 1976. 6.00 (ISBN 0-8233-0237-7). Golden Quill.
--Questions for the Snow. 1979. 5.00 (ISBN 0-8233-0304-7). Golden Quill.
Cline, D. B. & Mills, F. E., eds. The Unification of Elementary Forces & Gauge Theories: Proceedings. 792p. 1980. lib. bdg. 57.75 (ISBN 0-906346-00-2). Harwood Academic.
Cline, Dallas. Homemade Instruments. LC 76-8073. 1976. pap. 5.95 (ISBN 0-8256-0186-X, Oak). Music Sales.
Cline, Dallas & Tornborg, Pat. How to Play Nearly Everything. 64p. 1982. pap. 3.95 (ISBN 0-8256-9539-2, Putnam). Putnam Pub Group.
Cline, David, jt. auth. see Barger, Vernon.
Cline, David, et al. Dictionary of Visual Science. 3rd ed. LC 78-14640. 736p. 1980. 40.00 (ISBN 0-8019-6778-3). Chilton.
Cline, Don & Pitzer, Sara. Buying & Selling Antiques. LC 85-61478. 200p. (Orig.). 1986. 19.95 (ISBN 0-88266-407-7, Pub. by Storey Pub); pap. 11.95 (ISBN 0-88266-406-9). Storey Comm Inc.
Cline, Dorothy I. New Mexico's Nineteen-Ten Constitution: A 19th Century Product. 96p. (Orig.). Date not set. pap. 7.95 (ISBN 0-89016-086-4). Lightning Tree.
Cline, Gloria G. Exploring the Great Basin. LC 83-22871. xviii, 254p. 1984. Repr. of 1963 ed. lib. bdg. 35.00x (ISBN 0-313-24241-0, CLEX). Greenwood.
Cline, H. E., jt. ed. see Lemkey, F. D.
Cline, Howard F. Mexico: Revolution to Evolution, 1940 to 1960. 3rd ed. LC 81-3819. (Illus.). xiv, 375p. 1981. Repr. of 1971 ed. lib. bdg. 29.75x (ISBN 0-313-22993-7, CLME). Greenwood.
--U. S. & Mexico. LC 52-12258. 1963. pap. text ed. 4.95x (ISBN 0-689-70050-4, 40). Atheneum.
Cline, Howard F. see Wauchope, Robert.
Cline, Howard F., et al see Wauchope, Robert.
Cline, Hugh F. & Sinnott, Loraine T. Building Library Collections: Policies & Practices in Academic Libraries. LC 80-8602. (Illus.). 192p. 1981. 21.50 (ISBN 0-669-04321-4). Lexington Bks.
--The Electronic Library: Automation in Academic Libraries. LC 81-47871. 208p. 1983. 20.00 (ISBN 0-669-05113-6). Lexington Bks.
Cline, Hugh F., et al, eds. The Electronic Schoolhouse. 148p. 1985. text ed. 16.50 (ISBN 0-89859-649-1). L Erlbaum Assocs.
Cline, L., et al. Practical Law. LC 78-21522. 1978. text ed. 8.64 (ISBN 0-03-044146-3, HoltE); pap. 8.64 tchrs guide (ISBN 0-03-044151-X). HR&W.
Cline, Leonard. The Dark Chamber. 288p. 1983. pap. 2.95 (ISBN 0-523-41879-5). Pinnacle Bks.
Cline, Leonard, tr. see Raucat, Thomas.
Cline, Lora L. Just Before Sunset. rev. ed. LC 84-80632. (Illus.). 162p. 1984. pap. 11.95 (ISBN 0-9613425-0-1). J & L Ent.
Cline, Marjorie W., et al, eds. Scholar's Guide to Intelligence Literature: Bibliography of the Russell J. Bowen Collection. 1983. 40.00 (ISBN 0-89093-540-8, Pub. by National Intelligence Study Center). U Pubns Amer.
Cline, Martin, ed. Leukocyte Function. (Methods in Hematology: Vol. 3). (Illus.). 224p. 1981. text ed. 36.00 (ISBN 0-686-28872-6). Churchill.
Cline, Martin J. The White Cell. LC 74-25998. (Commonwealth Fund Publications Ser). (Illus.). 608p. 1975. text ed. 40.00x (ISBN 0-674-95142-5). Harvard U Pr.
Cline, Martin J. & Haskell, Charles M. Cancer Chemotherapy. 3rd ed. (Illus.). 397p. 1980. text ed. 35.95 (ISBN 0-7216-2609-2). Saunders.
Cline, Paul. Fools, Clowns, & Jesters. LC 84-144859. (Illus.). 58p. 1983. pap. 12.95 (ISBN 0-914676-88-1, Star & Elephant Bks.). Green Tiger Pr.
Cline, Paul C. & Fleming, Daniel B., Jr. By the Good People of Virginia: Our Commonwealth's Government. (Virginia Government Textbook Ser.). (Illus.). 1983. 6.00 (ISBN 0-318-01330-4). VA Chamber Com.
Cline, R. M. & Hays, J. D., eds. Investigation of Late Quaternary Paleoceanography & Paleoclimatology. LC 75-40899. (Memoir: No. 145). (Illus.). 1976. 30.00 (ISBN 0-8137-1145-2). Geol Soc.
Cline, Randall E. Elements of the Theory of Generalized Inverses of Matrices. (UMAP Modules). 94p. 1979. pap. text ed. 6.95x (ISBN 0-8176-3013-9). Birkhauser.
Cline, Ray. Secrets, Spies & Scholars. 1986. pap. 24.95 (ISBN 0-89568-502-7). Spec Learn Corp.
Cline, Ray S. The CIA: The Reality vs. Myth. LC 81-12857. 351p. 1981. 12.50 (ISBN 0-87491-527-9); pap. 8.95. Acropolis.
--U. S. Power in a World of Conflict, Vol. II. LC 80-415. (Significant Issues Ser.: No. 7). 53p. 1980. 5.95 (ISBN 0-89206-021-2). CSI Studies.
--World Power Assessment: A Calculus of Strategic Drift. new ed. LC 75-21986. (Illus.). 250p. 1975. pap. text ed. 4.95 (ISBN 0-89206-000-X). CSI Studies.
--World Power Trends & U. S. Foreign Policy for the 1980s. LC 79-26790. (Illus.). 228p. 1980. pap. 11.50x (ISBN 0-89158-790-X). Westview.
Cline, Ray S. & Alexander, Yonah. Terrorism: The Soviet Connection. LC 83-23162. 165p. 1984. pap. 9.75x (ISBN 0-8448-1471-7). Crane-Russak Co.
Cline, Ray S., jt. auth. see Block, Herbert.
Cline, Ray S., et al. Main Trends in World Power: Political Impact of Strategic Weapons. 1978. pap. text ed. 2.95 (ISBN 0-89206-004-2). CSI Studies.
Cline, Ray S., et al, eds. Southeast Asia: Problems & Prospects a Conference Report. 125p. (Orig.). 1985. pap. 10.00 (ISBN 0-318-12024-0). World Power Prog.
Cline, Robert F. The Tattooed Innocent & the Raunchy Grandmother: An Adult Fairy Tale, Quite Grim. LC 81-69430. 192p. (Orig.). 1983. pap. 7.95 (ISBN 0-9607082-0-0). Argos House.
Cline, Rodney. Pioneer Leaders & Early Institutions in Louisiana Education. 1969. 12.50 (ISBN 0-87511-018-5). Claitors.
Cline, Ruth H., tr. see De Troyes, Chretien.
Cline, Ruth K. & McBride, William G. A Guide to Literature for Young Adults: Backgound, Selection, & Use. 1983. pap. text ed. 10.80x (ISBN 0-673-16030-0). Scott F.
Cline, Starr. A Practical Guide to Independent Study: Instructional Manuals for Students & Teachers. 75p. 12.00 (ISBN 0-89824-041-7). Trillium Pr.
--Teaching for Talent. (Illus.). 56p. (Orig.). (gr. k-6). 1984. 5.95 (ISBN 0-88047-040-2, 8406). DOK Pubs.
Cline, Thomas L. Critical Opinion in the Eighteenth Century. LC 76-58463. 1923. lib. bdg. 10.00 (ISBN 0-8414-3442-5). Folcroft.
Cline, Victor, et al. Between Ring & Temple: A Marriage Handbook for Engaged L. D. S. Couples. LC 81-80348. 1981. 7.95 (ISBN 0-913420-87-5). Olympus Pub Co.
Cline, Victor B. How to Make Your Child a Winner: Ten Keys to Rearing Successful Children. 320p. 1980. 14.95 (ISBN 0-8027-0658-4); pap. 10.95 (ISBN 0-8027-7165-3). Walker & Co.
Cline, Walter B. Notes on the People of Siwah & el Garah in the Libyan Desert. LC 76-44706. Repr. of 1936 ed. 24.50 (ISBN 0-404-15916-8). AMS Pr.
Cline, William. Policy Alternatives for a New International Economic Order. LC 79-87553. 410p. 1979. 17.95 (ISBN 0-03-049471-0); pap. 17.95 (ISBN 0-03-049466-4). Praeger.
Cline, William C. In the Nick of Time: Motion Picture Sound Serials. LC 83-22231. (Illus.). 293p. 1984. lib. bdg. 19.95x (ISBN 0-89950-101-X). McFarland & Co.
Cline, William P., jt. auth. see Bergsten, C. Fred.
Cline, William R. Another Multi-Fiber Arrangement? (Policy Analyses in International Economics Ser.). 64p. (Orig.). 1985. pap. 10.00x (ISBN 0-88132-025-0). MIT (ISBN 0-262-53054-6, CLIAP). Inst Intl Eco.
--Exports of Manufactures from Developing Countries. 229p. 1984. 26.95 (ISBN 0-8157-1464-5); pap. 9.95 (ISBN 0-8157-1463-7). Brookings.
--International Debt & Stability of the World Economy. 1983. pap. 6.00x. MIT Pr.
--An International Debt & the Stability of the World Economy. LC 83-12888. (Policy Analyses in International Economics Ser.: No. 4). 141p. (Orig.). 1983. pap. 10.00x (ISBN 0-88132-010-2). MIT (CLIIP). Inst Intl Eco.
--International Debt: Systemic Risk & Policy Response. LC 83-26518. 336p. (Orig.). 1984. 30.00x (ISBN 0-88132-015-3). MIT (ISBN 0-262-03100-0, CLIIH). Inst Intl Eco.
--International Monetary Reform & the Developing Countries. 1976. 22.95 (ISBN 0-8157-1476-9); pap. 8.95 (ISBN 0-8157-1475-0). Brookings.
--International Trade in Automobiles: Liberalization or Further Restraint? (Policy Analyses in International Economics Ser.). 64p. (Orig.). 1986. pap. 10.00x (ISBN 0-88132-022-6). MIT (ISBN 0-262-53052-X, CLINP). Inst Intl Eco.
--Reciprocity: A New Approach to World Trade Policy? LC 82-15678. (Policy Analyses in International Economics Ser.: No. 2). 41p. (Orig.). 1982. pap. 8.00 (ISBN 0-88132-001-3). MIT (CLIPP). Inst Intl Eco.
--Toward Cartelization of World Steel Trade? (Policy Analyses in International Economics Ser.). 64p. (Orig.). 1986. pap. 10.00x (ISBN 0-88132-023-4, CLITP). Inst Intl Eco.
--Trade Controls in Three Industries: The Automobile, Steel & Textile Cases. 250p. (Orig.). 1986. cancelled (ISBN 0-88132-027-7). MIT (ISBN 0-262-03107-8, CLICH). Inst Intl Eco.
Cline, William R. & Weintraub, Sidney. Economic Stabilization in Developing Countries. LC 80-70079. 514p. 1981. 32.95 (ISBN 0-8157-1466-1); pap. 15.95 (ISBN 0-8157-1465-3). Brookings.
Cline, William R., jt. auth. see Bergsten, C. Fred.
Cline, William R., jt. auth. see Berry, Albert R.

Cline, William R., ed. Policy Alternatives for a New International Economic Order: An Economic Analysis. LC 79-87553. 410p. 1979. pap. 7.95 (ISBN 0-03-049466-4). Overseas Dev Council.
--Trade Policy in the Nineteen Eighties. LC 83-4310. 810p. (Orig.). 1984. pap. 20.00x (ISBN 0-262-53060-0); MIT. 35.00 (ISBN 0-262-03099-3, CLIPP). Inst Intl Eco.
Cline, William R. & Delgado, Enrique, eds. Economic Integration in Central America. LC 78-60708. 1978. 31.95 (ISBN 0-8157-1470-X). Brookings.
Cline, William R., et al. Trade Negotiations in the Tokyo Round: A Quantitative Assessment. 1978. 18.95 (ISBN 0-8157-1472-6). Brookings.
--World Inflation & the Developing Countries. 266p. 1981. 22.95 (ISBN 0-8157-1468-8); pap. 8.95 (ISBN 0-8157-1467-X). Brookings.
Clineball, Howard J., ed. see Clinebell, Charlotte H.
Clinebell, Charlotte H. Counseling for Liberation. Clineball, Howard J. & Stone, Howard W., eds. LC 75-36447. (Creative Pastoral Care & Counseling Ser). 96p. (Orig.). 1976. pap. 4.50 (ISBN 0-8006-0555-1, 1-555). Fortress.
--Meet Me in the Middle: On Becoming Human Together. LC 72-11353. 160p. 1973. pap. 2.95i (ISBN 0-06-061502-8, RD 193, HarpR). Har-Row.
Clinebell, Charlotte H. & Clinebell, Howard J., Jr. Intimate Marriage. LC 72-109062. 1970. 13.41i (ISBN 0-06-061499-4, HarpR). Har-Row.
Clinebell, Howard. Basic Types of Pastoral Care & Counseling. 464p. 1984. 17.95 (ISBN 0-687-02492-7). Abingdon.
--Contemporary Growth Therapies. LC 80-24368. 304p. 1981. 11.95 (ISBN 0-687-09502-6). Abingdon.
Clinebell, Howard J. Growth Counseling for Marriage Enrichment: Pre-Marriage & the Early Years. Stone, Howard W., ed. LC 74-26335. (Creative Pastoral Care & Counseling Ser.). 96p. 1975. pap. 3.95 (1-551). Fortress.
--Growth Counseling for Mid-Years Couples. Stone, Howard W., ed. LC 76-7863. (Creative Pastoral Care & Counseling Ser.). 1977. pap. 4.50 (ISBN 0-8006-0558-6, 1-558). Fortress.
Clinebell, Howard J., ed. see Augsburger, David W.
Clinebell, Howard J., ed. see Clements, William M.
Clinebell, Howard J., ed. see Cobb, John B., Jr.
Clinebell, Howard J., ed. see Colston, Lowell G.
Clinebell, Howard J., ed. see Irwin, Paul B.
Clinebell, Howard J., ed. see Leas, Speed & Kittlaus, Paul.
Clinebell, Howard J., ed. see Pattison, E. Mansell.
Clinebell, Howard J., ed. see Stone, Howard W.
Clinebell, Howard J., Jr. Understanding & Counseling the Alcoholic. rev. ed. LC 56-10143. 1968. 10.95 (ISBN 0-687-42803-3). Abingdon.
Clinebell, Howard J., Jr., jt. auth. see Clinebell, Charlotte H.
Clinefelter, Dennis & Clinefelter, Terry. Premarital Planning. 1982. pap. 5.00 (ISBN 0-8309-0356-9). Herald Hse.
Clinefelter, Terry, jt. auth. see Clinefelter, Dennis.
Cline Love, L. J. & Eastwood, Delyle, eds. Advances in Luminesince Spectroscopy - STP 863. LC 84-74320. (Illus.). 129p. 1985. pap. text ed. 26.00 (ISBN 0-8031-0412-X, 04-863000-39). ASTM.
Clines, D. J. Ezra, Nehemiah, Esther. Clements, Ronald, et al, eds. (New Century Bible Commentary Ser.). 384p. 1984. pap. 8.95 (ISBN 0-8028-0017-3). Eerdmans.
Clines, D. J. & Gunn, D. M. Art & Meaning: Rhetoric in Biblical Literature. (Journal for the Study of the Old Testament, Supplement Ser.: No. 19). viii, 266p. 1982. text ed. 25.00x (ISBN 0-905774-38-8, Pub. by JSOT Pr England); pap. text ed. 13.95x (ISBN 0-905774-39-6). Eisenbrauns.
Clines, David J. The Esther Scroll: Its Genesis, Growth, & Meaning. (JSOT Supplement Ser.: No. 30). 260p. 1984. text ed. 29.50x (ISBN 0-905774-66-3, Pub. by JSOT Pr England); pap. text ed. 13.50x (ISBN 0-905774-67-1, Pub. by JSOT Pr England). Eisenbrauns.
--I, He, We & They: A Literary Approach to Isaiah Fifty-Three. (JSOT Supplement Ser.: No. 1). 65p. 1976. pap. text ed. 4.95x (ISBN 0-905774-00-0, Pub. by JSOT Pr England). Eisenbrauns.
--The Theme of the Pentateuch. (Journal for the Study of the Old Testament Supplement Ser.: No. 10). 152p. 1978. text ed. 22.95x (ISBN 0-905774-14-0, Pub. by JSOT Pr England); pap. text ed. 10.95x (ISBN 0-905774-15-9, Pub. by JSOT Pr England). Eisenbrauns.
Clines, David J., jt. auth. see Sawyer, John F.
Clinevell, Howard J., ed. see Oates, Wayne E.
Clingan, T., ed. Law of the Sea: State Practice in Zones of Special Jurisdiction. 1982. 28.50 (ISBN 0-911189-02-5). Law Sea Inst.
Clinic on Library Applications of Data Processing Proceedings, 1976. The Economics of Library Automation. Divilbiss, J. L., ed. LC 77-75153. 163p. 1977. 8.00x (ISBN 0-87845-046-7). U of Ill Lib Info Sci.
Clinic on Library Applications of Data Processing, 1968. Proceedings. Carroll, Dewey E., ed. LC 65-1841. 235p. 1969. 7.00x (ISBN 0-87845-017-3). U of Ill Lib Info Sci.
Clinic on Library Applications of Data Processing, 1969. Proceedings. Carroll, Dewey E., ed. LC 65-1841. 149p. 1970. 7.00x (ISBN 0-87845-018-1). U of Ill Lib Info Sci.
Clinical Research Centre Symposium, Sept. 1981, 2nd, et al. Advances in the Treatment of Inborn Errors of Metabolism: Proceedings. 384p. 1982. 53.95x (ISBN 0-471-10123-0, Pub. by Wiley Med). Wiley.
Clinical Research Institute of Montreal Symposium. Hypertension Nineteen Seventy-Two: Proceedings. Genest, J. & Koiw, E., eds. (Illus.). 635p. 1972. pap. 64.90 (ISBN 0-387-05755-2). Springer-Verlag.
Clinkard, C. E. The Uses of Juices. pap. 2.50 canceled (ISBN 0-87904-039-4). Lust.
Clinkscale, Edward, ed. Les OEuvres Completes d'Antoine de Fevin. (Gesamtausgaben - Collected Works Ser.: Vol. XI, No. 1). xvi, 134p. (Eng. & Ger.). 1980. lib. bdg. 55.00 (ISBN 0-912024-68-2). Inst Mediaeval.
Clinkscale, Edward & Brook, Claire, eds. A Musical Offering: Essays in Honor of Martin Bernstein. (Festschrift Ser.: No. 1). lib. bdg. 32.00 (ISBN 0-918728-03-7). Pendragon NY.
Clinkscales, C. C., III, ed. see Kubek, Anthony.
Clinkscales, C. C., III, ed. see Lucas, Warren J.
Clinkscales, John D. Kyle's Story: Friday Never Came. 1981. 9.95 (ISBN 0-533-04951-2). Vantage.
Clinkscales, John G. On the Old Plantation Reminiscences of His Childhood. LC 77-91255. Repr. of 1916 ed. 15.00x (ISBN 0-8371-2063-2, CLO&, Pub. by Negro U Pr). Greenwood.
Clint, Florence. Pennsylvania Area Key. 149p. 1976. 12.00 (ISBN 0-686-38096-7). Keyline Pubs.
Clint, Florence & Fay, Loren V. New York State Area Key. 208p. 1979. pap. 12.00 (ISBN 0-686-27873-9). Keyline Pubs.
Clinton, Alan. The Post Office Worker: A Trade Union & Social History. (Illus.). 304p. 1984. text ed. 50.00x (ISBN 0-04-331086-9). Allen Unwin.
--Printed Ephemera: Collection, Organization, Access. 125p. 1981. 15.00 (ISBN 0-85157-337-1, Pub. by Bingley England). Shoe String.
--The Trade Union Rank & File: Trades Councils in Britain, 1900-1940. 262p. 1977. 21.50x (ISBN 0-87471-982-8). Rowman.
Clinton, Catherine. The Other Civil War: American Women in the Nineteenth Century. Foner, Eric, ed. (American Century Ser.). 1984. 17.95 (ISBN 0-8090-7460-5); pap. 7.25 (ISBN 0-8090-0156-X). Hill & Wang.
--The Plantation Mistress: Woman's World in the Old South. 1984. pap. 7.95 (ISBN 0-394-72253-1). Pantheon.
--The Plantation Mistress: Woman's World in the Old South, 1780-1835. LC 82-3549. 368p. 1983. 19.45 (ISBN 0-394-51686-9). Pantheon.
Clinton, Charles A. Local Success & Federal Failure: A Study of Community Development & Educational Change in the Rural South. LC 79-55667. 1979. text ed. 20.00 (ISBN 0-89011-538-9). Abt Bks.
--Local Success & Federal Failure: A Study of Community Development & Educational Change in the Rural South. 208p. 1984. Repr. of 1979 ed. lib. bdg. 22.50 (ISBN 0-8191-4066-X). U Pr of Amer.
Clinton, D. The Conquistador Dog Texts. 1976. signed ed. 10.00 (ISBN 0-685-73651-2); pap. 3.00 (ISBN 0-686-67569-X). New Rivers Pr.
Clinton, D. & Maclean, Crystal. New BkMk Poets. LC 81-670229. 1977. 2.50 (ISBN 0-933532-22-9). BkMk.
Clinton, Daniel J. Gomez, Tyrant of the Andes. LC 70-97833. Repr. of 1936 ed. lib. bdg. 16.25x (ISBN 0-8371-2698-3, CLG). Greenwood.
Clinton, Dewitt, jt. auth. see Literary & Philosophical Society of New York, May, 1814.
Clinton, Elizabeth. The Countesse of Lincolnes Nurserie. LC 74-28838. (English Experience Ser.: No. 720). 1975. Repr. of 1622 ed. 3.50 (ISBN 90-221-0720-5). Walter J Johnson.
Clinton, F. G. The Tin Cop. 240p. 1983. pap. 2.50 (ISBN 0-523-41923-6). Pinnacle Bks.
Clinton, George. Memoirs of the Life & Writings of Lord Byron, 3 vols. LC 75-28482. 1975. Repr. of 1827 ed. lib. bdg. 125.00 (ISBN 0-8414-3379-8). Folcroft.
--Public Papers of George Clinton, 10 Vols. Hastings, Hugh & Holden, J. A., eds. LC 72-968. Repr. of 1914 ed. Set. 700.00 (ISBN 0-404-01620-0); 70.00 ea. AMS Pr.
Clinton, George, ed. see Doyle, Michael.
Clinton, Henry F. Fasti Hellenici: The Civil & Literary Chronology of Greece Through the Death of Augustus, 3 Vols. 1965. Repr. of 1834 ed. Set. 137.00 (ISBN 0-8337-0599-7). B Franklin.
--Fasti Romani: The Civil & Literary Chronology of Rome & Constantinople from the Death of Augustus to the Death of Justin the 2nd, 2 Vols. 1965. Repr. of 1850 ed. Set. 105.50 (ISBN 0-8337-0602-0). B Franklin.
Clinton, Iris. Friend of Chiefs, Robert Moffat. (Stories of Faith & Fame). 1975. pap. 2.50 (ISBN 0-87508-608-X). Chr Lit.
--Young Man in a Hurry (William Carey) 1961. pap. 2.50 (ISBN 0-87508-630-6). Chr Lit.
Clinton, J. V. The Rescue of Charlie Kalu. (Heinemann Secondary Readers Ser.). 1971. pap. text ed. 3.00x (ISBN 0-435-92502-4). Heinemann Ed.
Clinton, Jerome W. The Divan of Manuchihri Damghani: A Critical Study. LC 72-87873. (Studies in Middle Eastern Literatures: No. 1). 1972. pap. 15.00x (ISBN 0-88297-001-1). Bibliotheca.
Clinton, Kevin. The Sacred Officials of the Eleusinian Mysteries. LC 73-79573. (Transaction Ser.: Vol. 64, Pt. 3). (Illus.). 1974. pap. 12.00 (ISBN 0-87169-643-6). Am Philos.
Clinton, Richard H. The Great American Novel. 210p. (Orig.). 1981. pap. 3.95x (ISBN 0-9605338-1-8). Blue Lagoon.
Clinton, Robert, jt. auth. see Price, Monroe E.
Clinton, Ronald F. How to Prevent Burnout & Achieve Personal Well-Being. LC 80-81868. 71p. 4.95 (ISBN 0-686-28066-0). Human Potential.
Clinton-Baddeley, V. C. Death's Bright Dart. (Murder Ink Ser.: No. 45). 1982. pap. 2.25 (ISBN 0-440-11944-8). Dell.
--To Study a Long Silence. 1984. pap. 2.84 (ISBN 0-06-080690-7). Har-Row.
Clinton-Baddley, V. C. No Case for the Police. (A Murder Ink Mystery Ser.: No. 35). 1982. pap. 2.25 (ISBN 0-440-16424-9). Dell.
Clinton-Tullie, Verna, jt. auth. see Begay, Shirley M.
Clio Press Ltd. Photography. (Modern Art Bibliographical Ser.: No. 2). 284p. 1982. lib. bdg. 62.00 (ISBN 0-903450-59-3). ABC-Clio.
Clipman, William. Dog Light. LC 81-875. (Wesleyan Poetry Program Ser.: Vol. 102). 1981. 15.00x (ISBN 0-8195-2102-7); pap. 6.95 (ISBN 0-8195-1102-1). Wesleyan U Pr.
Clipper, Lawrence, jt. auth. see Ackerley, Chris.
Clipper, Paul. The Best of Last Over. (Illus.). 128p. (Orig.). 1985. pap. 5.95 (ISBN 0-931517-00-1). Windemede Pub.
Clippinger, Dorinda. Word Processing Input. 1983. pap. text ed. 15.95 (ISBN 0-8359-8802-3). Reston.
Clippinger, John H., Jr. Meaning & Discourse: A Computer Model of Psychoanalytic Speech & Cognition. LC 77-4779. 256p. 1978. text ed. 24.50x (ISBN 0-8018-1943-1). Johns Hopkins.
Clipson, Colin W. & Wehrer, Joseph J. Planning for Cardiac Care: A Guide to the Planning & Design of Cardiac Care Facilities. LC 73-83855. (Illus.). 420p. 1973. text ed. 25.00x (ISBN 0-914904-03-5). Health Admin Pr.
Clise, Michele. My Circle of Bears. LC 84-149174. (Orig.). 1981. pap. 9.95 (ISBN 0-914676-65-2, Star & Elephant Bks.). Green Tiger Pr.
Clise, Michele D. Ophelia's World: Or the Memoirs of a Parisian Shop Girl. (Illus.). 1984. 12.95 (ISBN 0-517-55048-2, C N Potter Bks). Crown.
Clissold & Tweddell. Brown's Nautical Star Chart. pap. 5.50x (ISBN 0-85174-435-4). Sheridan.
Clissold, Peter. Basic Seamanship. 1981. 20.00x (ISBN 0-85174-368-4, Pub. by Nautical England). State Mutual Bk.
--Basic Seamanship. 6th ed. 353p. 1975. pap. 11.50x (ISBN 0-85174-255-6). Sheridan.
Clissold, Stephen. DJILAS: The Progress of a Revolutionary. LC 83-4906. 352p. 1983. text ed. 27.50x (ISBN 0-87663-431-5). Universe.
--St. Teresa of Avila. 288p. (Orig.). 1982. pap. 8.95 (ISBN 0-8164-2621-X, Pub. by Seabury). Winston Pr.
--The Wisdom of the Spanish Mystics. (Wisdom Bks.). 8.00 (ISBN 0-8112-0663-7, NDP442); pap. 4.95 (ISBN 0-8112-0664-5). New Directions.
Clissold, Stephen, compiled by. The Wisdom of St. Francis & His Companions. LC 78-27504. (Wisdom Books). 1979. pap. 4.95 (ISBN 0-8112-0721-8, NDP477). New Directions.
Clissold, Stephen, ed. Yugoslavia & the Soviet Union 1939-1973: A Documentary Survey. (Royal Institute of International Affairs Ser). 1975. 32.50x (ISBN 0-19-218315-X). Oxford U Pr.
Clissold, Stephen, et al, eds. Short History of Yugoslavia. LC 66-20181. (Illus.). 1968. pap. 15.95 (ISBN 0-521-09531-X). Cambridge U Pr.
Clive, Alan. State of War: Michigan in World War II. LC 79-10213. (Illus.). 1979. text ed. 15.00 (ISBN 0-472-10001-7). U of Mich Pr.
Clive, Mrs. Caroline A. Paul Ferroll: A Tale. LC 79-8256. Repr. of 1855 ed. 44.50 (ISBN 0-404-61821-9). AMS Pr.
--Year After Year: A Tale. LC 79-8252. Repr. of 1858 ed. 44.50 (ISBN 0-404-61822-7). AMS Pr.
Clive, Geoffrey. Philosophy of Nietzsche. 1984. pap. 4.95 (ISBN 0-452-00699-6, Mer). NAL.
--The Romantic Enlightenment. LC 72-8238. 219p. 1973. Repr. of 1960 ed. lib. bdg. 16.00x (ISBN 0-8371-6544-X, CLRE). Greenwood.
Clive, H. P., ed. see De Navarre, Marguerite.
Clive, H. P., tr. see Taille, Jean.
Clive, John, jt. auth. see Gilman, J. D.
Clive, John, ed. see Bolingbroke.
Clive, John, ed. see Buckle, Henry T.
CLive, John, ed. see Carlyle, Thomas.
Clive, John, ed. see Macaulay, Thomas B.
Clive, John, ed. see Mittelberger, Gottlieb.
Clive, Williams S. & Prioh, John G., eds. Firm Foundation of God Standeth Sure. 1984. 14.94 (ISBN 0-317-16698-0). Firm Foun Pub.
Cloak, F. T., Jr. A Natural Order of Cultural Adoption & Loss in Trinidad. (Working Papers in Methodology Ser.: No. 1). 177p. 1967. pap. text ed. 4.00 - (ISBN 0-89143-025-3). U NC Inst Res Soc Sci.
Cloar, Carroll. Hostile Butterflies & Other Paintings. LC 77-7549. (Illus.). 216p. 1980. Repr. of 1977 ed. 39.95 (ISBN 0-87870-040-4). Memphis St Univ.
Clock, Herbert & Boetzel, Eric. The Light in the Sky. Reginald, R. & Melville, Douglas, eds. LC 77-84211. (Lost Race & Adult Fantasy Ser.). 1978. Repr. of 1929 ed. lib. bdg. 26.50x (ISBN 0-405-10966-0). Ayer Co Pubs.
Clocksin, W. F. & Mellish, C. S. Programming in Prolog. 279p. 1982. pap. 16.95 (ISBN 0-387-11046-1). Springer-Verlag.
--Programming in Prolog. 2nd ed. xv, 297p. 1984. pap. 17.95 (ISBN 0-387-15011-0). Springer-Verlag.
Clodd, Edward. The Childhood of the World: A Simple Account of Man's Origin & Early History. 1979. Repr. of 1914 ed. lib. bdg. 25.00 (ISBN 0-8492-4035-2). R West.
--Concerning a Pilgrimage to the Grave of Edward Fitzgerald. 1902. 10.00 (ISBN 0-8274-2088-9). R West.
--Magic in Names & in Other Things. LC 67-23906. 248p. 1968. Repr. of 1920 ed. 30.00x (ISBN 0-8103-3024-5). Gale.
--Magic in Names & Other Things. 59.95 (ISBN 0-8490-0577-9). Gordon Pr.
--Memories: Meredith, Gissing, Samuel Butler. 1973. Repr. of 1916 ed. 25.00 (ISBN 0-8274-1529-X). R West.
--Myths & Dreams. LC 70-159918. 264p. 1971. Repr. of 1891 ed. 40.00x (ISBN 0-8103-3776-2). Gale.
--Pioneers of Evolution: From Thales to Huxley; with an Intermediate Chapter on the Causes of Arrest of the Movement. facsimile ed. LC 74-37470. (Essay Index Reprint Ser). Repr. of 1897 ed. 19.00 (ISBN 0-8369-2540-8). Ayer Co Pubs.
--The Story of Creation: A Plain Account of Evolution. 1979. Repr. of 1894 ed. lib. bdg. 20.00 (ISBN 0-8492-4033-6). R West.
--The Story of "Primitive" Man. 1979. Repr. of 1904 ed. lib. bdg. 20.00 (ISBN 0-8482-7578-0). Norwood Edns.
--The Story of "Primitive" Man. 1979. Repr. of 1910 ed. lib. bdg. 20.00 (ISBN 0-8492-4032-8). R West.
--The Story of the Alphabet. 1979. Repr. of 1904 ed. lib. bdg. 25.00 (ISBN 0-8492-4034-4). R West.
--Thomas Henry Huxley. LC 75-30018. Repr. of 1902 ed. 14.50 (ISBN 0-404-14023-8). AMS Pr.
--Thomas Henry Huxley. LC 74-2491. 1902. lib. bdg. 15.00 (ISBN 0-685-45595-5). Folcroft.
--Tom Tit Tot. LC 67-23907. 264p. 1968. Repr. of 1898 ed. 35.00x (ISBN 0-8103-3459-3). Gale.
Clode, Drew, et al. Consumers & Welfare. 160p. 1986. text ed. write for info. (ISBN 0-566-05009-9). Gower Pub Co.
Clodfelter, Cherie, et al. Why Not the Best? NCPA Task Force on Education - Certification of Texas Teachers. (Task Force on Education Ser.). Date not set. price not set (ISBN 0-943802-10-5). Natl Ctr Pol.
Clodfelter, Frank. Fogg & Steam. LC 78-15604. (Illus.). 1978. 75.00 (ISBN 0-87108-522-4). Pruett.
Cloe, John H. & Monaghan, Michael. Top Cover for America: The Air Force in Alaska, 1920-1983. LC 84-60821. (Illus.). 272p. 1984. pap. 13.95 (ISBN 0-933126-47-6). Pictorial Hist.
Cloete, G. D., ed. A Moment of Truth: The Confession of the Dutch Reformed Mission Church, 1982. 176p. (Orig.). 1984. pap. 10.95x (ISBN 0-8028-0011-4). Eerdmans.
Cloete, Stuart. Rags of Glory. 1973. pap. 1.50 (ISBN 0-380-01516-1, 15792). Avon.
Clogan, P. M., ed. Medievalia et Humanistica, Vols. 1-7. Incl. Vol. 1. LC 75-32451. 251p. 1976. (ISBN 0-521-21032-1); Vol. 2. Medieval & Renaissance Studies in Review. LC 75-32452. 223p. (ISBN 0-521-21033-X); Vol. 3. Social Dimension in Medieval & Renaissance Studies. LC 75-32453. 328p; Vol. 6. LC 75-16872. 1979 (ISBN 0-521-20999-4); Vol. 7. Studies in Medieval & Renaissance Culture: Medieval Poetics. LC 76-12914. 1977. (ISBN 0-521-21331-2); Vol. 8. Studies in Medieval & Renaissance Culture Transformation & Continuity. LC 75-32451. 1978 (ISBN 0-521-21783-0); Vol. 9. LC 75-32451. 1979 (ISBN 0-521-22446-2). 37.50 ea.; Vols. 8-9. 39.50 ea. Cambridge U Pr.
Clogan, Paul M. Medieval Poetics. LC 75-32451. (Medievalia et Humanistica: New Ser., No. 7). pap. 55.30 (ISBN 0-317-26029-4, 2024433). Bks Demand UMI.
Clogan, Paul M., ed. Medievalia et Humanistica, Vol. 11. (New Studies in Medieval & Renaissance Culture). 318p. 1982. text ed. 33.95x (ISBN 0-8476-7105-4). Rowman.
--Medievalia et Humanistica: Studies in Medieval & Renaissance Culture. (New Ser.: No. 10). 264p. 1981. 29.95x (ISBN 0-8476-6944-0). Rowman.
--Medievalia et Humanistica: Studies in Medieval & Renaissance Culture. LC 47-36424. (Studies in Byzantine & Western Studies: No. 12). 264p. 1984. text ed. 42.50x (ISBN 0-8476-7209-3). Rowman & Allanheld.
--Medievalia et Humanistica: Studies in Medieval & Renaissance Culture. (New Ser.: No. 13). 200p. 1985. 46.50x (ISBN 0-8476-7210-7). Rowman.
Clogg, Clifford C. Measuring Underemployment: Demographic Indicators for the United States. LC 79-22916. (Studies in Population). 1979. 37.50 (ISBN 0-12-176560-1). Acad Pr.

Clogg, Mary Jo & Clogg, Richard. Greece. Collison, Robert L., ed. (World Bibliographical Ser.: No. 17). 224p. 1980. 34.50 (ISBN 0-903450-30-5). ABC Clio.

Clogg, R. A Short History of Modern Greece. LC 78-72083. (Illus.). 1979. 44.50 (ISBN 0-521-22479-9); pap. 13.95 (ISBN 0-521-29517-3). Cambridge U Pr.

Clogg, Richard, jt. auth. see Clogg, Mary Jo.

Clogg, Richard, ed. Balkan Society in the Age of Greek Independence. (Studies in Russian & East European History). 260p. 1981. 29.00x (ISBN 0-389-20024-7). B&N Imports.

--Greece in the Nineteen Eighties. LC 82-10243. 250p. 1983. 27.50 (ISBN 0-312-34714-6). St Martin.

--The Struggle for Greek Independence: Essays to Mark the 150th Anniversary of the Greek War of Independence. 224p. 1973. 20.00 (ISBN 0-208-01303-2, Archon). Shoe String.

Cloherty, John P. & Stark, Ann B., eds. Manual of Neonatal Care. (Spiral Manual Ser.). 1980. 17.95 (ISBN 0-316-14749-4). Little.

Cloke, Marjane & Wallace, Robert. The Modern Business Letter Writer's Manual. LC 69-12209. 216p. 1969. pap. 4.95 (ISBN 0-385-06952-9, Dolp). Doubleday.

Cloke, Paul J. An Introduction to Rural Settlement Planning. 450p. 1983. pap. 19.95 (ISBN 0-416-73800-1, NO. 3834). Methuen Inc.

Cloke, Paul J. & Park, Chris C. Rural Resource Management. LC 84-22858. 496p. 1985. 40.00 (ISBN 0-312-69602-7). St Martin.

Cloke, Rene. Chickweed. 4.50 (ISBN 0-392-16655-0, SpS). Sportshelf.

Cloke, Richard. Earth Ovum. LC 82-71685. 124p. (Orig.). 1982. pap. 3.50 (ISBN 0-686-91614-X). Cerulean Pr.

--Earth Ovum. LC 82-71685. 1982. pap. 3.25 (Cerulean Pr). Kent Pubns.

--Jerry the Put. LC 78-57812. 1978. pap. 4.95 (ISBN 0-917458-06-0). Kent Pubns.

--Liberty Boys & Belles. LC 80-84878. 1982. pap. text ed. 4.25 (ISBN 0-917458-07-9, Pub. by Cerulean Pr). Kent Pubns.

--Mister Pistol-John. LC 76-23360. 1976. pap. 4.75 (ISBN 0-917458-01-X). Kent Pubns.

--My Pal Al. LC 77-81442. 1978. pap. 5.25 (ISBN 0-917458-05-2). Kent Pubns.

--Vector-Lee. LC 76-56063. 1977. pap. 5.25 (ISBN 0-917458-03-6). Kent Pubns.

--Yvar, Prince of Rus. LC 80-80543. (Illus.). pap. 8.75 (ISBN 0-917458-08-7, Pub. by Cerulean Pr). Kent Pubns.

Clokey, Joseph W. & Kirk, Hazel J. Childe Jesus: A Christmas Cantata for Mixed Voices. pap. 20.00 (ISBN 0-317-09646-X, 2017838). Bks Demand UMI.

Clokey, Richard M. William H. Ashley: Enterprise & Politics in the Trans-Mississippi West. LC 78-21396. (Illus.). 320p. 1980. 22.95 (ISBN 0-8061-1525-4). U of Okla Pr.

Clokie, Hugh M. & Robinson, J. William. Royal Commissions of Inquiry: The Significance of Investigation in British Politics. LC 70-86274. 1969. Repr. of 1937 ed. lib. bdg. 17.00x (ISBN 0-374-91710-8). Octagon.

Cloney, Gordon J., jt. auth. see Yochelson, John N.

Cloney, Will, frwd. by see Bergin, Thomas G.

Clonts, Howard A., jt. ed. see Molnar, Joseph J.

Clontz, Ralph C., Jr. Fair Credit Reporting Manual: Annual Cumulative Supplement. 2nd ed. 1977. 72.00 (ISBN 0-88262-134-3). Warren.

--Truth-in-Lending Manual: Cumulative Supplementation, 2 vols. 5th ed. 1982. Set. 96.00 (ISBN 0-88262-757-0). Warren.

Clontz, Ralph C., Jr. & Tarlow, Eric K. Equal Credit Opportunity Manual: Cumulative Supplementation. 3rd. ed. 1979. 78.00 (ISBN 0-88262-321-4, 79-65646). Warren.

Cloonan, James B. Handbook of Investment Terminology. (American Association of Individual Investor's Library of Financial Planning). 208p. 1985. 14.95 (ISBN 0-930369-09-2). Invest Info.

Cloonan, William. Michel Tournier. (World Author Ser.). 1985. lib. bdg. 19.95 (ISBN 0-8057-6595-6, Twayne). G K Hall.

Cloonan, William J. Racine's Theatre: The Politics of Love. LC 77-8683. (Romance Monographs, Inc: No. 28). 1978. 15.00x (ISBN 84-399-7422-1). Romance.

Cloonen, F. Blake, jt. auth. see Hall, Robert D., Jr.

Cloos, Ernst. Microtectonics along the Western Edge of the Blue Ridge, Maryland, & Virginia. LC 77-156828. (Johns Hopkins University Studies in Geology Ser.: No. 20). pap. 65.30 (ISBN 0-317-29738-4, 2015688). Bks Demand UMI.

Cloots, Anacharsis, pseud. Oeuvres, 3 Vols. 1980. lib. bdg. 165.00 (ISBN 3-601-00188-8). Kraus Intl.

Cloots, Jean-Baptiste. Republique Universelle, ou Adresse aux Tyrannicides. LC 72-147425. (Library of War & Peace; Proposals for Peace, a History). lib. bdg. 46.00 (ISBN 0-8240-0217-2). Garland Pub.

Cloots, Jean Baptiste see Cloots, Anacharsis, pseud.

Clopinel, J., jt. auth. see Lorris, Guillaume de.

Clopper, Edward N. Child Labor in City Streets. LC 74-22737. (Labor Movement in Fiction & Non-Fiction). Repr. of 1912 ed. 17.50 (ISBN 0-404-58489-6). AMS Pr.

--Child Labor in City Streets. LC 74-1677. (Children & Youth Ser.: Vol. 2). 294p. 1974. Repr. of 1912 ed. 25.50x (ISBN 0-405-05956-6). Ayer Co Pubs.

Clopper, Jonas. Fragments of the History of Bawlfredonia. LC 79-91076. (The American Humorists Ser.). 1979. Repr. of 1819 ed. lib. bdg. 27.75 (ISBN 0-8398-0268-4). Irvington.

Clopper, Lawrence M., ed. Chester. LC 79-16420. (Records of Early English Drama Ser.). 1979. 50.00x (ISBN 0-8020-5460-9). U of Toronto Pr.

Clopton, Beverly B. Her Honor the Judge. (Illus.). 262p. 1980. 15.95x (ISBN 0-8138-0565-1). Iowa St U Pr.

Clopton, Nancy. Caring for Your Child with Spina Bifida. (Illus.). 210p. 1981. pap. text ed. 5.95 (ISBN 0-934670-04-8). Eterna Pr.

Clopton, Robert W., tr. see Dewey, John.

Clor, Harry M. Obscenity & Public Morality: Censorship in a Liberal Society. LC 69-16772. 1985. text ed. 16.00x (ISBN 0-226-11035-4, Midway Reprint). U of Chicago Pr.

Clorfene, Richard, jt. auth. see Margolis, Jack S.

Clos, J. Tournyal Du see Tournyal Du Clos, J.

Close. Manual of Life Insurance. 318p. 1969. 12.00. Anderson Pub Co.

--Manual of Multiple Line Insurance. 1984. 21.50. Anderson Pub Co.

Close, A. The Romantic Approach to Don Quixote. LC 76-57097. 1978. 52.50 (ISBN 0-521-21490-4). Cambridge U Pr.

Close, Angela, jt. ed. see Wendorf, Fred.

Close, Angela E., jt. auth. see Wendorf, Fred.

Close, Angela E., jt. ed. see Wendorf, Fred.

Close, Ann, ed. see Leithauser, Brad.

Close, Ann, ed. see Sagan, Eli.

Close, Arthur & Curtis, Jody, eds. National Directory of Corporate Public Affairs, 1985. 3rd ed. LC 83-1412. 491p. 1984. pap. 50.00 (ISBN 0-910416-51-6). Columbia Bks.

Close, Arthur C., ed. National Directory of Corporate Public Affairs, 1983. 378p. 1983. pap. 45.00 (ISBN 0-910416-38-9). Columbia Bks.

--National Directory of Corporate Public Affairs, 1986. 4th ed. 500p. 1985. pap. 55.00 (ISBN 0-910416-56-7). Columbia Bks.

Close, Arthur C. & Colgate, Craig, Jr., eds. Washington Representatives, 1980. 4th ed. LC 76-21152. 1980. pap. 30.00x (ISBN 0-910416-33-8). Columbia Bks.

Close, Arthur C. & Curtis, Jody, eds. Washington Representatives, 1985. 9th ed. LC 76-21152. 650p. 1985. pap. 45.00 (ISBN 0-910416-54-0). Columbia Bks.

Close, Arthur C. & Evans, Laurie A., eds. Washington Representatives, 1982. 6th annual ed. LC 76-21152. 583p. 1982. pap. 35.00 (ISBN 0-910416-40-0). Columbia Bks.

Close, Arthur C. & Freedman, Stephany J., eds. National Directory of Corporate Public Affairs, 1984. 2nd ed. 429p. 1983. pap. 50.00 (ISBN 0-910416-46-X). Columbia Bks.

--Washington Representatives, 1983. 7th ed. LC 76-21152. 611p. 1983. pap. 40.00 (ISBN 0-910416-42-7). Columbia Bks.

Close, Arthur C., jt. ed. see Colgate, Craig, Jr.

Close, Arthur C., et al, eds. Washington Representatives, 1984. 8th ed. LC 76-21152. 605p. 1984. pap. 40.00 (ISBN 0-910416-49-4). Columbia Bks.

Close, Burt E. How to Create Super Slide Shows. LC 84-5102. 233p. 1984. pap. 10.95 (ISBN 0-89879-133-2). Writers Digest.

Close, Charles M. Analysis of Linear Circuits. 716p. 1966. text ed. 36.95 (ISBN 0-15-502610-0, HC); solutions manual avail. (ISBN 0-15-502611-9, HC). HarBraceJ.

Close, Charles M. & Frederick, Dean K. Modeling & Analysis of Dynamic Systems. LC 77-74421. (Illus.). 1978. text ed. 41.50 (ISBN 0-395-25040-4). HM.

Close, D. H. & Bridge, C. R., eds. Revolution: The History of an Idea. LC 84-28372. 224p. 1985. 23.50x (ISBN 0-389-20560-5). B&N Imports.

Close, Darwin B. Multiple-Line Insurance. 2nd ed. 696p. 1985. pap. text ed. 25.00 (ISBN 0-87084-144-0). Anderson Pub Co.

Close, David. Pottery Designs. (Illus.). 72p. 1984. 14.95 (ISBN 0-7134-0297-0, Pub. by Batsford England). David & Charles.

Close, Edward R. The Book of Atma. LC 77-87461. 1978. 6.95 (ISBN 0-87212-077-5). Libra.

Close, F. E. Introduction to Quarks & Partons. LC 78-54530. 1979. 55.00 (ISBN 0-12-175150-3); pap. 29.00, 1980 (ISBN 0-12-175152-X). Acad Pr.

Close, F. Perry. History of Hartford Streets. facsimile ed. 125p. 1969. pap. 2.50x (ISBN 0-940748-24-X). Conn Hist Soc.

Close, J. R. Motor Function in the Lower Extremity: Analyses by Electronic Instrumentation. (Illus.). 176p. 1964. photocopy ed. 18.75x (ISBN 0-398-00317-3). C C Thomas.

Close, J. Robert. Functional Anatomy of the Extremities: Some Electronic & Kinematic Methods of Study. (Illus.). 268p. 1973. photocopy ed. 34.50x (ISBN 0-398-02525-8). C C Thomas.

Close, Jim, jt. auth. see Cassidy, Pat.

Close, John J., et al. Team Teaching Experiments. 156p. 1974. 12.00x (ISBN 0-85633-045-0, Pub. by NFER Nelson UK). Taylor & Francis.

Close, K. J. & Yarwood, J. Experimental Electronics for Students. 280p. 1979. 16.95x (ISBN 0-412-14760-2, NO. 6060, Pub. by Chapman & Hall England). Methuen Inc.

--Introduction to Semiconductors. 1971. pap. text ed. 10.00x (ISBN 0-435-68081-1). Heinemann Ed.

Close, Kenneth. AppleWorks with Advanced Applications: Calc, File, Write & GRAPH. (Micropower Ser.). 208p. 1985. deluxe ed. 24.95 incl. diskette (ISBN 0-697-00805-3); pap. 13.95 (ISBN 0-697-00804-5). Wm C Brown.

Close, Kenneth S., jt. auth. see Hite, Eugene.

Close, Pat, ed. see Dunning, Al.

Close, Paul & Collins, Rosemary, eds. Family & Economy in Modern Society. 242p. 1985. 26.00 (ISBN 0-333-37437-1, Pub. by Salem Acad). Merrimack Pub Cir.

Close, Paul D. Sound Control & Thermal Insulation of Buildings. LC 65-28400. 510p. 1966. 31.50 (ISBN 0-442-35058-9). Krieger.

Close, R. A. English As a Foreign Language. 3rd ed. 224p. (Orig.). 1981. pap. text ed. 8.95x (ISBN 0-04-425025-8). Allen Unwin.

Close, Reg A. A Reference Grammar for Students of English. (English As a Second Language Bk.). (Illus.). 342p. 1975. pap. text ed. 10.75 (ISBN 0-582-52277-3). Longman.

Close, Richard W. Practical Swimming Officiating. 5th ed. LC 77-154622. 1979. pap. 4.00 (ISBN 0-9602982-0-7). Dolphin Aquatics.

Close, Robert. Europe Without Defense? Forty-Eight Hours That Could Change the Face of the World. LC 79-4693. (Pergamon Policy Studies). (Illus.). 1979. 24.00 (ISBN 0-08-023108-X). Pergamon.

--Time for Action. (Brassey Books). 170p. 1983. 24.50 (ISBN 0-08-028344-6); pap. 14.50 (ISBN 0-08-028345-4). Pergamon.

Close, Sylvia. Sex During Pregnancy & after Childbirth. 144p. 1985. pap. 7.95 (ISBN 0-7225-0929-4). Newcastle Pub.

--The Toddler & the New Baby. 128p. 1980. pap. 7.95 (ISBN 0-7100-0523-7). Routledge & Kegan.

Close Up Foundation. Perspectives. rev. ed. Bandy, Patricia & Fritsche, Joellen, eds. LC 78-640988. 278p. (Orig.). 1985. pap. text ed. 9.00 (ISBN 0-932765-00-9). Close Up Foun.

Close, Virginia L. Essex Institute Historical Collections Index: 1950-1969, Vol. 5. LC 76-18417. 1977. 45.00 (ISBN 0-88389-067-4). Essex Inst.

Closen, Michael L. Agency, Employment, & Partnership Law: Contemporary Cases & Materials. 1984. 35.00 (ISBN 0-86678-321-0). Butterworth MN.

Closser, Lynne, ed. see John, Da Free.

Closson, Ernest. History of the Piano. LC 76-181124. 168p. 1947. Repr. 39.00x (ISBN 0-403-01523-5). Scholarly.

Closson, Ernest, ed. see Gretry, Andre E.

Closson, Ernest, tr. see Strauss, Richard.

Closson, Kay. Reaching in Silence. (Contemporary Poets Ser.: No. 2). 56p. (Orig.). 1983. pap. 3.95 (ISBN 0-916982-27-0, RL227). Realities.

Closson, Marietta, jt. auth. see Closson, Robert.

Closson, Robert & Closson, Marietta. Thirty Perry County, Pa. Cemeteries. 348p. (Orig.). perfect bdg. 36.00 (ISBN 0-318-03865-X). Closson Pr.

Closter, Susan V. Joyce Cary & Lawrence Durrell: A Reference Guide. (Reference Guides in Literature Ser.). 1985. lib. bdg. 48.00 (ISBN 0-8161-8627-8). G K Hall.

Closurdo, Janette S., ed. Library Management: Papers from the Management Workshops, Vol. 1. pap. 25.30 (ISBN 0-317-10347-4, 2017281). Bks Demand UMI.

Clot, J., ed. see International Symposium, Montpellier, March 1974.

Clotfelter, Cecil F. & Clotfelter, Mary L., eds. Camping & Backpacking: A Guide to Information Sources. LC 79-84659. (Sports, Games, & Pastimes Information Guide Ser.: Vol. 2). 344p. 1978. 60.00x (ISBN 0-8103-1437-1). Gale.

Clotfelter, Charles T. Federal Tax Policy & Charitable Giving. LC 84-16336. (National Bureau of Economic Research-Monograph Ser.). 264p. 1985. lib. bdg. 39.00x (ISBN 0-226-11048-6). U of Chicago Pr.

Clotfelter, Charles T. & Salamon, Lester M. The Federal Government & the Nonprofit Sector: The Impact of the 1981 Tax Act on Individual Charitable Giving. LC 82-113321. cancelled. Urban Inst.

Clotfelter, James & Prysby, Charles. Political Choices: A Study of Election & Voters. LC 79-26838. 186p. 1980. pap. text ed. 9.95 (ISBN 0-275-85780-8, HoltC). HR&W.

Clotfelter, James, jt. auth. see Naylor, Thomas H.

Clotfelter, Mary L., jt. ed. see Clotfelter, Cecil F.

Clothey, Fred & Long, J. Bruce, eds. Experiencing Siva: Encounters with a Hindu Diety. 1983. 24.00x (ISBN 0-8364-1041-6). South Asia Bks.

Clothey, Fred W. The Many Faces of Murukan: The History & Meaning of a South Indian God. (Religion & Society Ser.: No. 6). 1978. text ed. 27.60x (ISBN 90-2797-632-5). Mouton.

--Rhythm & Intent: Ritual Studies from South India. 1984. 15.00x (ISBN 0-8364-1219-2, Pub. by Blackie & Sons). South Asia Bks.

Clothier, Peter. Aspley Guise. 1970. wrappers 2.00 (ISBN 0-88031-002-2). Invisible-Red Hill.

--Chiaroscuro: A Mystery. 272p. 1985. 14.95 (ISBN 0-312-13178-X). St Martin.

--Parapoems. 1974. pap. 3.95 (ISBN 0-8180-1570-5). Horizon.

Clouard. Alexandre Dumas. 12.95 (ISBN 0-685-34895-4). French & Eur.

Clouard, Henri & Leggewie, Robert, eds. Anthologie de la Litterature Francaise, 2 vols. 2nd ed. 860p. 1975. Vol. 1. pap. text ed. 19.95x (ISBN 0-19-501877-X); Vol. 2. pap. text ed. 19.95x (ISBN 0-19-501878-8). Oxford U Pr.

Cloud, Carey C. Cloud Nine: The Dreamer & the Realist. (Illus.). 154p. 1983. 16.95 (ISBN 0-686-38768-6). Cloudcrest.

Cloud, D., et al. Coggins Auto Supply: Practice Set One to Accompany College Accounting Procedures, Chapters 1-26. 1985. pap. price not set (ISBN 0-471-80892-X). Wiley.

Cloud, Deborah A., ed. Market & Economic Feasibility Studies: Guidelines for Continuing Care Retirement Communities. LC 84-72540. (Orig.). 1984. pap. text ed. 4.50x (ISBN 0-943774-20-9, 20-9). Am Assn Homes.

--Obtaining Capital for Housing & Services for the Elderly. LC 84-72541. (Orig.). 1984. pap. text ed. 6.50x (ISBN 0-943774-19-5, 19-5). Am Assn Homes.

Cloud, Deborah A., ed. see American Assn. of Homes for the Aging Staff.

Cloud, Douglas. College Accounting Procedures: A Competency Based Approach, Chapters 1-11. LC 84-13040. 424p. 1984. 15.95 (ISBN 0-471-88774-9). Wiley.

--College Accounting Procedures: A Competency Based Approach, Chapters 1-15. LC 84-13038. 562p. 1984. 18.95 (ISBN 0-471-88896-X). Wiley.

--College Accounting Procedures: A Competency Based Approach, Chapters 1-26. LC 84-13039. 941p. 1985. 24.95 (ISBN 0-471-88894-3). Wiley.

Cloud, Douglas, et al. Donamy Manufacturing Corporation: A Practice Set for a Manufacturing Firm to Accompany College Accounting Procedures - Chapters 1-26. 1985. pap. price not set (ISBN 0-471-82226-4). Wiley.

--College Accounting Procedures: Best Sound Music Center - Practice Set 2 (Chapters 1-26) 1985. pap. price not set (ISBN 0-471-80893-8). Wiley.

--College Accounting Procedures: Study Guide & Working Papers (Chapters 1-11) 324p. 1985. pap. 9.95 (ISBN 0-471-88592-4). Wiley.

--College Accounting Procedures: Study Guide & Working Papers (Chapters 16-26) 228p. 1985. pap. 8.95 (ISBN 0-471-88591-6). Wiley.

--College Accounting Procedures: Study Guide & Working Papers (Chapters 1-15) 400p. 1985. pap. 10.95 (ISBN 0-471-88593-2). Wiley.

Cloud, Flyin' Thunda. A Small Pain. LC 84-50315. 36p. 1985. pap. 8.00 (ISBN 0-934172-11-0). Wim Pubns.

Cloud, Jess. Touch & Die. 240p. 1981. pap. 2.25 (ISBN 0-8439-0987-0, Leisure Bks). Dorchester Pub Co.

Cloud, Jonathan, tr. see Gorz, Andre.

Cloud, Josie, jt. ed. see Emery, Sarah.

Cloud, Josie H., jt. ed. see Emery, Sarah.

Cloud, Kate, et al. Watermelons Not War! A Support Book for Parenting in the Nuclear Age. 175p. 1984. lib. bdg. 24.95 (ISBN 0-86571-033-3); pap. 9.95 (ISBN 0-86571-032-5). New Soc Pubs.

Cloud, Mory. From Pine to Wave. 1976. 5.00 (ISBN 0-8233-0251-2). Golden Quill.

Cloud, Peter B. Elderberry Flute Song: Contemporary Coyote Tales. LC 82-4965. (Illus.). 142p. 1982. 16.95 (ISBN 0-89594-070-1); pap. 7.95 (ISBN 0-89594-069-8). Crossing Pr.

--The Paranoid Foothills. (Illus., Orig.). 1981. pap. 2.50 (ISBN 0-942396-29-4). Blackberry ME.

Cloud, Preston. Cosmos, Earth & Man: A Short History of the Universe. LC 78-2666. (Illus.). 1978. 31.00x (ISBN 0-300-02146-1); pap. 10.95 (ISBN 0-300-02594-7). Yale U Pr.

Cloud, R. L., jt. ed. see Bohm, G. J.

Cloudsley, Anne. Women of Omdurman: Life, Love & the Cult of Virginity. LC 83-40625. 181p. 1985. 22.50 (ISBN 0-312-88755-8). St Martin.

Cloudsley-Thompson, J. L. Animal Conflict & Adaptation. LC 65-26318. (Illus.). 1965. 13.95 (ISBN 0-8023-1026-5). Dufour.

--Animal Twilight, Man & Game in Eastern Africa. (Illus.). 1967. 13.95 (ISBN 0-85429-062-1). Dufour.

--Dietary Adaptions in Animals. 76p. 1976. 39.00x (ISBN 0-686-96990-1, Pub. by Meadowfield Pr England). State Mutual Bk.

--The Ecology of Oases. 49p. 1974. 39.00x (ISBN 0-900541-71-7, Pub. by Meadowfield Pr England). State Mutual Bk.

--Evolutionary Trends in the Mating of Arthropoda. 92p. 1976. 39.00x (ISBN 0-900541-82-2, Pub. by Meadowfield Pr England). State Mutual Bk.

--Form & Function in Animals. 92p. 1979. 39.00x (ISBN 0-900541-90-3, Pub. by Meadowfield Pr England). State Mutual Bk.

--The Temperature & Water Relations of Reptiles. 166p. 1971. 39.00x (ISBN 0-900541-28-8, Pub. by Meadowfield Pr England). State Mutual Bk.

--Tooth & Claw: Defensive Strategies in the Animal World. (Illus.). 252p. 1980. 22.50 (ISBN 0-460-04360-9, Pub. by J. M. Dent England). Biblio Dist.

--The Water & Temperature Relations of Woodlice. 90p. 1977. 39.00x (ISBN 0-900541-85-7, Pub. by Meadowfield Pr England). State Mutual Bk.

Cloudsley-Thompson, John. Crocodiles & Alligators. LC 79-19556. (Animals of the World). (Illus.). (gr. 4-8). 1980. PLB 15.95 (ISBN 0-8172-1084-9). Raintree Pubs.

Cloudsley-Thompson, John, et al. Nightwatch: The Natural World from Dusk to Dawn. (Illus.). 1983. 24.95 (ISBN 0-87196-271-3). Facts on File.

Clouet, Doris H., ed. Narcotic Drugs: Biochemical Pharmacology. LC 76-128503. 528p. 1971. 55.00x (ISBN 0-306-30495-3, Plenum Pr). Plenum Pub.

Clouette, Bruce & Roth, Matthew. Bristol, Connecticut: A Bicentennial History, 1785-1985. LC 84-22807. (Illus.). 336p. 1984. 22.00 (ISBN 0-914659-09-X). Phoenix Pub.

Clough. Amours De Voyage. Scott, Patrick, ed. 1974. 14.95x (ISBN 0-7022-0847-7); pap. 8.95x (ISBN 0-7022-0841-8). U of Queensland Pr.

Clough, Arthur H. The Bothie: The Text of 1848. Scott, Patrick, ed. (Victorian Texts: No. 4). 1977. 10.95x (ISBN 0-7022-1153-2); pap. 6.25x (ISBN 0-7022-1163-X). U of Queensland Pr.

--Poems & Prose Remains of Arthur Hugh Clough with a Selection from His Letters & Memoirs 2 Vols. LC 77-107167. 1970. Repr. of 1869 ed. Set. 69.00x (ISBN 0-403-00202-8). Scholarly.

--The Poems of Arthur Hugh Clough. 2nd ed. Mulhauser, F. L., ed. (Oxford English Texts Ser). 1974. 79.00x (ISBN 0-19-811898-8). Oxford U Pr.

--Selections from the Poems of Arthur Hugh Clough. 1977. Repr. of 1894 ed. lib. bdg. 10.00 (ISBN 0-8482-0498-0). Norwood Edns.

Clough, B. F., ed. Mangrove Ecosystems in Australia. LC 81-68098. 302p. 1982. text ed. 15.00 (ISBN 0-7081-1170-X, 1222). Australia N U P.

Clough, B. W. The Crystal Crown. 208p. 1984. pap. 2.75 (ISBN 0-87997-922-4). DAW Bks.

--The Dragon of Mishbill. 1985. pap. 2.95 (ISBN 0-88677-078-5). DAW Bks.

Clough, Bonnie M., jt. auth. see Clough, Dick B.

Clough, Carmen P. Spanish in the Fields: Practical Spanish for Ranchers, Farmers Vintners. LC 83-62192. 256p. 1983. 19.95 (ISBN 0-914330-59-4). Panorama West.

Clough, Cecil H. The Duchy of Urbino in the Renaissance. 390p. 1981. 70.00x (ISBN 0-86078-075-9, Pub. by Variorum). State Mutual Bk.

Clough, Cecil H., ed. see Myers, A. R.

Clough, Charles W. & Secrest, William B., Jr. Fresno County the Pioneer Years: From the Beginnings to 1900, Vol. 1. Temple, Bobbye S., ed. LC 84-61577. (Illus.). 372p. 1984. 29.95 (ISBN 0-914330-70-5). Panorama West.

Clough, D. J. & Morley, L. W., eds. Earth Observation Systems for Resource Management & Environmental Control. LC 77-13989. (NATO Conference Series II, Systems Science: Vol. 4). 487p. 1977. 69.50x (ISBN 0-306-32844-5, Plenum Pr). Plenum Pub.

Clough, Dick B. & Clough, Bonnie M. A Handbook of Effective Techniques for Teacher Aides. (Illus.). 200p. 1978. 11.75x (ISBN 0-398-03809-0). C C Thomas.

--Utilizing Teacher Aides in the Classroom. 160p. 1978. 13.50x (ISBN 0-398-03741-8). C C Thomas.

Clough, Donald. Decisions in Public & Private Sectors: Theories, Practices, & Processes. (Illus.). 448p. 1984. text ed. 27.95 (ISBN 0-13-198226-5). P-H.

Clough, E. R. A Study of Mary Wollstonecraft & the Rights of Woman. 1972. 59.95 (ISBN 0-8490-1154-X). Gordon Pr.

Clough, Elizabeth E., et al. Assessing Pupils: Policy, Practice & Innovation. 192p. 1984. 15.00 (ISBN 0-7005-0664-0). Taylor & Francis.

Clough, Emma R. A Study of Mary Wollstonecraft & the Rights of Woman. LC 74-9555. 1898. lib. bdg. 30.00 (ISBN 0-8414-3364-X). Folcroft.

Clough, Eric & Quarmby, Jacqueline, eds. A Public Library Service for Ethnic Minorities in Great Britain. LC 78-13622. (Illus.). 1978. lib. bdg. 35.00x (ISBN 0-313-21201-5, CPL/). Greenwood.

Clough, Francis F., ed. World's Encyclopedia of Recorded Music, 3 vols. LC 71-100214. Repr. of 1966 ed. Set. lib. bdg. 103.50x (ISBN 0-8371-3003-4, CLRM). Greenwood.

Clough, Frank C. William Allen White of Emporia. LC 73-100149. Repr. of 1941 ed. lib. bdg. 18.75x (ISBN 0-8371-3910-4, CLWA). Greenwood.

Clough, John & Conley, Joyce. Basic Harmonic Progressions. (Orig.). 1984. pap. text ed. 11.95x (ISBN 0-393-95372-6). Norton.

--Scales, Intervals, Keys, Triads, Rhythm & Meter. rev. ed. 1983. 14.95x (ISBN 0-393-95189-8). Norton.

Clough, John D., jt. ed. see Krakauer, Randall S.

Clough, Michael. A Transatlantic Symposium: Where Is South Africa Headed? (II) (Seven Springs Reports). 48p. 1980. pap. 3.00 (ISBN 0-943006-12-0). Seven Springs.

Clough, Michael, jt. auth. see Kitchen, Helen.

Clough, Michael, ed. Changing Realities in Southern Africa: Implications for American Policy. LC 82-12124. (Research Ser.: No. 47). x, 320p. 1982. pap. 12.50x (ISBN 0-87725-147-9). U of Cal Intl St.

Clough, Monica. The Field of Thistles: Kings & Queens of Scotland. 128p. 1982. 59.00x (ISBN 0-904265-96-X, Pub. by Macdonald Pub UK). State Mutual Bk.

Clough, R. & Penzien, J. Dynamics of Structures. (Illus.). 672p. 1975. text ed. 48.00 (ISBN 0-07-011392-0). McGraw.

Clough, Ralph N. Deterrence & Defense in Korea: The Role of U. S. Forces. (Studies in Defense Policy). 1976. pap. 6.95 (ISBN 0-8157-1481-5). Brookings.

--East Asia & U. S. Security. 1975. 22.95 (ISBN 0-8157-1480-7); pap. 8.95 (ISBN 0-8157-1479-3). Brookings.

--Island China. LC 78-9483. (Twentieth Century Fund Study). 1978. 17.50x (ISBN 0-674-46875-9). Harvard U Pr.

Clough, Ralph N., et al. The United States, China & Arms Control. LC 75-15650. pap. 41.30 (ISBN 0-317-20793-8, 2125370). Bks Demand UMI.

Clough, Richard H. Construction Contracting. 4th ed. LC 81-7449. 502p. 1981. 33.95 (ISBN 0-471-08657-6, Pub. by Wiley-Interscience). Wiley.

Clough, Richard H. & Sears, Glenn A. Construction Project Management. 2nd ed. LC 78-25855. 341p. 1979. 41.95 (ISBN 0-471-04895-X, Pub. by Wiley-Interscience). Wiley.

Clough, Roger. Old Age Homes. (National Institute Social Services Library Ser.: No. 42). 224p. 1981. text ed. 28.50x (ISBN 0-04-362043-4). Allen Unwin.

--Old Age Homes. 1981. 32.00x (ISBN 0-317-05813-4, Pub. by Natl Inst Social Work). State Mutual Bk.

Clough, Rosa. Futurism: The Story of a Modern Art Movement, a New Appraisal. LC 71-90487. Repr. of 1961 ed. lib. bdg. 25.00x (ISBN 0-8371-2166-3, CLFU). Greenwood.

Clough, S. B., et al. European History in a World Perspective, 2 vols. 3rd ed. Incl. Vol. 1. 848p. study guide 7.95 (ISBN 0-669-93120-9); Vol. 2. 800p. pap. text ed. 16.95 (ISBN 0-669-85530-8); study guide 7.95x (ISBN 0-669-93153-5). 1975. Heath.

--European History in a World Perspective, 3 vols. Incl. Vol. 1. 544p. pap. text ed. 14.95x (ISBN 0-669-85548-0); Vol. 2. 544p; Vol. 3. 648p. 1975. pap. Heath.

Clough, Shepard B. Basic Values of Western Civilization. LC 84-27971. xi, 132p. 1985. Repr. of 1960 ed. lib. bdg. 29.75 (ISBN 0-313-24735-8, CLBV). Greenwood.

--European Economic History. 3rd ed. Orig. Title: The Economic Development of Western Civilization. (Illus.). 640p. 1975. text ed. 47.00 (ISBN 0-07-011393-9). McGraw.

--The Life I've Lived. LC 80-5503. 297p. 1981. lib. bdg. 24.75 (ISBN 0-8191-1116-3); pap. text ed. 13.00 (ISBN 0-8191-1117-1). U Pr of Amer.

--The Rise & Fall of Civilization: An Inquiry into the Relationship Between Economic Development & Civilization. LC 77-25973. (Illus.). 1978. Repr. of 1951 ed. lib. bdg. 23.00x (ISBN 0-313-20092-0, CLRI). Greenwood.

Clough, T. H., ed. Sylloge of Coins of the British Isles: Vol. 26, Museums of East Anglia. 1980. 99.00x (ISBN 0-19-725991-X). Oxford U Pr.

Clough, T. H. & Cummins, W. A., eds. Stone Axe Studies: Archaeological, Petrological, Experimental & Ethnographic. (CBA Research Report Ser.: No. 23). 137p. 1979. pap. text ed. 35.50 (ISBN 0-900312-63-7, Pub. by Coun Brit Archaeology). Humanities.

Clough, W. R., ed. Reactive Metals: Proceedings of the 3rd Reactive Metals Conference, Buffalo, 1958. LC 59-14889. (Metallurgical Society Conference: Vol. 2). pap. 156.30 (ISBN 0-317-10823-9, 2000665). Bks Demand UMI.

Clough, Wilson, tr. see Moraze, Charles.

Clough, Wilson O. The Science of Grammar. 1942. 17.50 (ISBN 0-8274-3337-9). R West.

Clough, Wilson O., tr. see Durye, Pierre.

Clough, Wilson O., tr. see Simonin, Louis L.

Clougher, N., tr. see Pissarro, Camille.

Clough-Smith, J. H. An Introduction to Spherical Trigonometry. 1981. 50.00x (ISBN 0-85174-320-X, Pub. by Nautical England). State Mutual Bk.

Clouscard, Michel. L' Etre & le Code: Le Proces De Production D'un Ensemble Precapitaliste. 1972. pap. 38.50x (ISBN 90-2797-010-6). Mouton.

Clouse, B. The Student Writer: Editor & Critic. 416p. 1986. pap. 14.95 (ISBN 0-07-011410-2). McGraw.

Clouse, Barbara F. Writing: From Inner World to Outer World. (Illus.). 368p. 1983. pap. text ed. 14.95 (ISBN 0-07-011407-2). McGraw.

Clouse, Bonnidell. Moral Development. 1985. pap. 13.95 (ISBN 0-8010-2507-9). Baker Bk.

Clouse, Jerry A., jt. auth. see Myers, Forrest D.

Clouse, Melvin E. Clinical Lymphography. LC 76-50804. 234p. (Orig.). Repr. of 1977 ed. 44.00 (ISBN 0-683-01883-3). Krieger.

--Clinical Lymphography. 2nd ed. (Illus.). 620p. 1985. 55.00 (ISBN 0-683-16512-7, 1651-2). Williams & Wilkins.

Clouse, Robert. Church in an Age of Orthodoxy & Enlightenment. 1980. pap. 4.95 (ISBN 0-570-06273-X, 12-2746). Concordia.

Clouse, Robert, et al. Church in History Series, 6 bks. 1980. pap. 26.95 set (ISBN 0-570-06277-2, 12-2780). Concordia.

Clouse, Robert G. The Meaning of the Millennium. 212p. 1978. pap. 5.95 (ISBN 0-88469-099-7). BMH Bks.

--Wealth & Poverty: Four Christian Views of Economics. LC 84-3808. 240p. (Orig.). 1984. pap. 5.95 (ISBN 0-87784-347-3). Inter-Varsity.

Clouse, Robert G. & Pierard, Richard V. Streams of Civilization: The Modern World to the Nuclear Age, Vol. 2. LC 78-17811. (Illus.). (gr. 7-12). 1980. text ed. 14.95x (ISBN 0-915134-45-4); Tchrs Guide. pap. 3.95x (ISBN 0-915134-47-0). Mott Media.

--Streams of Civilization, Vol. II: The Modern World to the Nuclear Age. LC 78-17811. 1979. text ed. 14.95x (ISBN 0-89051-051-2, Co-Pub by Mott Media); tchr's guide 3.95x (ISBN 0-915134-47-0). Master Bks.

Clouse, Robert G., ed. The Meaning of the Millennium: Four Views. 1977. pap. 6.95 (ISBN 0-87784-794-0). Inter-Varsity.

--War: Four Christian Views. LC 81-1020. 220p. 1981. pap. 6.95 (ISBN 0-87784-801-7). Inter Varsity.

Clouse, Robert G., ed. see Hoyt, Herman A., et al.

Clouse, Robert G., et al, eds. Protest & Politics: Christianity & Contemporary Affairs. 277p. 1968. 7.50 (ISBN 0-87921-000-1). Attic Pr.

Clouser, John W. & Fisher, David. The Most Wanted Man in America. LC 74-26961. 228p. 1975. pap. 1.95 (ISBN 0-8128-2115-7). Stein & Day.

Clouser, Joseph L. Keller Plan for Self-Paced Study Using Masterton & Slowinski's Chemical Principles. pap. text ed. cancelled (ISBN 0-8290-0633-8). Irvington.

Clouser, K. Danner. Teaching Bioethics: Strategies, Problems & Resources. LC 80-10492. (The Teaching of Ethics Ser.: Vol. IV). 77p. 1980. pap. 4.00 (ISBN 0-916558-07-X). Hastings Ctr Inst Soc.

Clouser, R. L. Federal Executive Branch Expenditures in the United States with Reference to Florida, Fiscal Years 1970, 1975, 1980. LC 82-622722. (Economic Information Report; 155). write for info. Amer Bar Assn.

Clouston, A. E. The Dangerous Skies. Gilbert, James, ed. LC 79-7240. (Flight: Its First Seventy-Five Years Ser.). (Illus.). 1979. Repr. of 1954 ed. 17.00x (ISBN 0-405-12155-5). Ayer Co Pubs.

Clouston, Brian. Landscape Design with Plants. 1984. pap. 25.00 (ISBN 0-442-21581-9). Van Nos Reinhold.

Clouston, Brian & Stansfield, Kathy, eds. After the Elm. (Illus.). 186p. 1980. text ed. 24.50x (ISBN 0-8419-6107-7). Holmes & Meier.

--Trees in Towns: Maintenance & Management. (Illus.). 182p. 1981. 28.50 (ISBN 0-85139-658-5). Nichols Pub.

Clouston, Kate W. The Chippendale Period in English Furniture. (Illus.). 1976. Repr. 25.00x (ISBN 0-7158-1127-4). Charles River Bks.

Clouston, R. S. English Furniture & Furniture Makers of the Eighteenth Century. (Illus.). 1977. Repr. of 1906 ed. 29.00 (ISBN 0-686-57965-8). Charles River Bks.

Clouston, W. A. Literary Coincidences: A Bookstall Bargain. LC 73-11482. 1973. lib. bdg. 22.50 (ISBN 0-8414-3386-0). Folcroft.

Clouston, W A., jt. auth. see Saxby, Jessie M.

Clouston, W. A., jt. ed. see Furnivall, F. J.

Clouston, William A. Book of Noodles: Stories of Simpletons. LC 67-24351. 288p. 1969. Repr. of 1888 ed. 35.00x (ISBN 0-8103-3519-0). Gale.

--Flowers from a Persian Garden & Other Papers. Dorsen, Richard M., ed. LC 77-70584. (International Ser.). Repr. of 1890 ed. lib. bdg. 29.00x (ISBN 0-405-10088-4). Ayer Co Pubs.

--A Group of Eastern Romances & Stories, from the Persian, Tamil & Urdu. LC 77-26116. 1977. Repr. of 1889 ed. lib. bdg. 67.50 (ISBN 0-685-87254-8). Folcroft.

--Popular Tales & Fictions, Their Migrations & Transformations, 2 Vols. LC 67-23920. 512p. 1968. Repr. of 1887 ed. Set. 95.00x (ISBN 0-8103-3460-7). Gale.

Clout, H. The Regional Problem in Western Europe. LC 75-7216. (Topics in Geography Ser.). (Illus.). 64p. 1976. 16.95 (ISBN 0-521-20909-9); pap. text ed. 7.95 (ISBN 0-521-09997-8). Cambridge U Pr.

--A Rural Policy for the EEC? (EEC Ser.). 227p. 1984. text ed. 25.00 (ISBN 0-416-34540-9, 9104); pap. text ed. 11.50 (ISBN 0-416-34550-6, 9105). Methuen Inc.

Clout, H., et al. Western Europe: Geographical Perspectives. (Illus.). 1984. pap. text ed. 17.95 (ISBN 0-318-02989-8). Longman.

Clout, H. C. Themes in the Historical Geography of France. 1977. 79.00 (ISBN 0-12-175850-8). Acad Pr.

Clout, H. D. Changing London. 1981. 20.00x (ISBN 0-7231-0762-9, Pub. by Univ Tutorial England). State Mutual Bk.

Clout, Hugh. Agriculture in France on the Eve of the Railway Age. (Illus.). 239p. 1980. 28.50x (ISBN 0-389-20017-4). B&N Imports.

--The Land of France, 1815-1914. (London Research Series in Geography: No. 1). 176p. 1982. text ed. 24.95x (ISBN 0-04-911003-9). Allen Unwin.

Clout, Hugh D. The Geography of Post-War France: A Social & Economic Approach. 180p. 1972. pap. text ed. 11.00 (ISBN 0-08-016766-7). Pergamon.

--Regional Development in Western Europe. 2nd ed. LC 80-40852. 417p. 1981. 53.95x (ISBN 0-471-27846-7, Pub. by Wiley-Interscience); pap. 24.95 (ISBN 0-471-27845-9, Pub. by Wiley-Interscience). Wiley.

--Rural Geography. 1972. 21.00 (ISBN 0-08-017041-2); pap. 9.95 (ISBN 0-08-017042-0). Pergamon.

Clout, Hugh D. & Dennis, Richard J. Social Geography of Great Britain: An Introduction. (Pergamon Oxford Geographies). 1980. 36.00 (ISBN 0-08-021802-4); pap. 14.50 (ISBN 0-08-021801-6). Pergamon.

Cloutier, Anne Marie, jt. auth. see Leopold, Allison K.

Cloutier, David. My Grandfather's House: Tlingit Songs of Death & Sorrow. LC 80-15499. (Illus.). 40p. (Orig.). 1980. pap. 3.00 (ISBN 0-914974-26-2). Holmgangers.

--Soft Lightnings. (Illus.). 54p. 1982. pap. 4.50 (ISBN 0-914278-35-5). Copper Beech.

--Spirit Spirit: Shaman Songs. rev. enl. ed. (Illus.). 100p. 1980. pap. 4.50 (ISBN 0-914278-30-4). Copper Beech.

--Tongue & Thunder. (Illus.). 64p. (Orig.). 1980. pap. 4.50 (ISBN 0-914278-32-0). Copper Beech.

Cloutier, David, tr. see Esteban, Claude.

Cloutier, David, tr. see Laude, Jean.

Cloutier, James. The Alpine Tavern: Photographs of a Social Gathering Place. LC 77-77899. (Illus.). 1977. pap. 9.95x (ISBN 0-918966-00-0). Image West.

--The Great Texas Joke Book. LC 81-84158. (Illus.). 128p. 1981. pap. 9.95 (ISBN 0-918966-08-6). Image West.

--Hugh Wetshoe's Oregon Coloring Book. (Illus.). 48p. (gr. 4-12). 1981. pap. 3.95 (ISBN 0-918966-07-8). Image West.

--Orygone IV; If This Is July & It's Raining, This Must Be Oregon. LC 78-71301. (Illus., Orig.). 1978. pap. 4.95 (ISBN 0-918966-03-5). Image West.

--Orygone, Too or, a Nice Place to Visit but You Wouldn't Want to Get Stuck There. LC 80-83718. (Illus.). 160p. (Orig.). 1980. pap. 4.95 (ISBN 0-918966-05-1). Image West.

--This Day in Oregon. LC 80-83719. (Illus.). 128p. 1981. pap. 6.95 (ISBN 0-918966-06-X). Image West.

Cloutier, Pierre, tr. see Ferron, Jacques.

Cloutier, Roger J., et al, eds. Medical Radionuclides: Radiation Dose & Effects, Proceedings. LC 70-606556. (AEC Symposium Ser.). 528p. 1970. pap. 21.25 (ISBN 0-87079-269-5, CONF-691212); microfiche 4.50 (ISBN 0-87079-270-9, CONF-691212). DOE.

Clouzet, Maryse. Sigmund Freud: A New Appraisal. LC 72-9606. 141p. 1974. Repr. of 1963 ed. lib. bdg. 18.75x (ISBN 0-8371-6593-8, CLSF). Greenwood.

Clouzot, Henri & Morris, Frances. Painted & Printed Fabrics: The History of the Manufactory at Jouy & Other Ateliers in France, 1760-1815 by Henri Clouzot: Notes on the History of Cotton Printing Especially in England & America by Frances Morris. LC 70-168418. (Metropolitan Museum of Art Publications in Reprint). (Illus.). 222p. 1972. Repr. of 1927 ed. 31.00 (ISBN 0-405-02256-5). Ayer Co Pubs.

Clover, Anne. Homeopathy: A Patient's Guide. (Orig.). 1984. pap. 4.95 (ISBN 0-7225-0892-1). Thorsons Pubs.

Clover, Carol J. The Medieval Saga. LC 81-17432. 224p. 1982. 22.50x (ISBN 0-8014-1447-4). Cornell U Pr.

Clover, Carol J. & Londow, John, eds. Old Norse-Icelandic Literature: A Critical Guide. LC 85-47697. (Islandica Ser.). 376p. 1985. text ed. 29.95x (ISBN 0-8014-1755-4). Cornell U Pr.

Clover, Helen, ed. see Lanfranc.

Clover, Vernon T. & Balsley, Howard L. Business Research Methods. 3rd ed. LC 83-1689. (Management Ser.). 450p. 1984. 33.95 (ISBN 0-471-84155-2, Pub. by Grid); text ed. 28.95. Wiley.

Cloverdale Press Staff, ed. see Cone, E. Paul.

Clovis, Albert I., et al, eds. Consumer Protection: A Symposium. LC 72-6757. 1972. Repr. of 1968 ed. lib. bdg. 19.50 (ISBN 0-306-70524-9). Da Capo.

Clovis, Albert L., jt. auth. see Nordstrom, Robert J.

Clovis California Adult School. LifeSchool Beginning Classroom Modules: Life Skills Literacy, 4 binders. Incl. Binder 1. Consumer Economics (ISBN 0-8224-4350-3); Binder 2. Health (ISBN 0-8224-4351-1); Binder 3. Government & Law: Community Resources (ISBN 0-8224-4352-X); Binder 4. Occupational Knowledge: Interpersonal Relations (ISBN 0-8224-4353-8). (gr. 9-12). 1981. looseleaf binders instructional modules with duplicatable handouts 106.00 ea. (ISBN 0-8224-4354-6); comp. set 384.00. Pitman Learning.

Clow, Archibald & Clow, Nan L. Chemical Revolution. facs. ed. (Essay Index Reprint Ser). 1952. 42.00 (ISBN 0-8369-1909-2). Ayer Co Pubs.

Clow, C. A. & MacDonald, R. D. Punched-Card Data Processing System. 2nd ed. 1975. 9.00 (ISBN 0-07-011424-2). McGraw.

Clow, David. Understanding Cities. LC 82-84486. (Development Component Ser.). (Illus.). 63p. (Orig.). 1982. pap. 10.00 (ISBN 0-87420-617-0, D25). Urban Land.

Clow, Duane J. & Urquhart, Scott N. Mathmatics in Biology: Calculus & Related Topics. (Illus.). 726p. 1984. pap. text ed. 25.95 (ISBN 0-912675-06-3). Ardsley.

Clow, Nan L., jt. auth. see Clow, Archibald.

Clow, W. Bible Reader's Encyclopedia & Concordance. (Illus.). 9.95 (ISBN 0-529-05899-5, RT1). World Bible.

Cloward, Richard, jt. auth. see Piven, Frances F.

Cloward, Richard A., jt. auth. see Piven, Frances F.

Clowdus, B., tr. see Otto, P. & Ewe, K.

Clower, Jerry. Let the Hammer Down. 1979. pap. 1.95 (ISBN 0-671-82626-3). PB.

Clower, Robert W., et al. Growth Without Development: An Economic Survey of Liberia. (Northwestern University African Studies Ser.: No. 16). 1966. 18.95x (ISBN 0-8101-0065-7). Northwestern U Pr.

Clowers, Don. The Power of God's Character. 230p. (Orig.). 1983. pap. text ed. 5.50 (ISBN 0-914307-14-2). Word Faith.

Clowers, Myles L. & Letendre, Lorin. Understanding American Politics Through Fiction. 2nd ed. 1977. pap. text ed. 20.95 (ISBN 0-07-011450-1). McGraw.

Clowers, Myles L. & Mori, Stephen. Understanding Sociology Through Fiction. LC 76-9108. 1976. pap. text ed. 19.95 (ISBN 0-07-011452-8). McGraw.

Clowers, Myles L., jt. auth. see Beck, Warren A.

Clowers, Norman L. Patrolman Patterns, Problems, & Procedures. 308p. 1971. 29.75x (ISBN 0-398-00318-1). C C Thomas.

Clowes, Florence. Polish Americans in Pittsfield, Massachussetts. 144p. 1975. pap. 5.50 (ISBN 0-317-36719-6). Kosciuszko.

Clowes, Kenneth W. The Impact of Computers on Managers. Dickson, Gary, ed. LC 82-4879. (Management Information Systems Ser.: No. 2). 206p. 1982. 39.95 (ISBN 0-8357-1337-7). UMI Res Pr.

Clowes, Royston. The Structure of Life. (Illus.). 11.25 (ISBN 0-8446-1873-X). Peter Smith.

Clowes, William. A Guide to Printing, an Introduction for Print Buyers. LC 73-717. (Illus.). 134p. 1973. Repr. of 1963 ed. lib. bdg. 24.75x (ISBN 0-8371-6786-8, CLGP). Greenwood.

--A Profitable & Necessarie Booke of Observations. LC 73-171740. (English Experience Ser.: No. 366). 1971. Repr. of 1596 ed. 33.50 (ISBN 90-221-0366-8). Walter J Johnson.

--A Right Fruteful Treatise for the Artificial Cure of Struma. LC 72-25835. (English Experience Ser.: No. 238). 68p. 1970. Repr. of 1602 ed. 9.50 (ISBN 90-221-0238-6). Walter J Johnson.

--A Short & Profitable Treatise Touching the Cure of the Morbus Gallicus by Unctions. LC 75-38166. (English Experience Ser.: No. 443). 118p. 1972. Repr. of 1579 ed. 16.00 (ISBN 90-221-0443-5). Walter J Johnson.

Clowes, William L. Black America: A Study of the Ex-Slave - His Late Master. LC 78-109322. Repr. of 1891 ed. 19.75x (ISBN 0-8371-3588-5, CBA&, Pub. by Negro U Pr). Greenwood.

Clowes, William L., ed. Royal Navy: A History from the Earliest Times, 7 vols. Repr. of 1903 ed. Set. 290.00 (ISBN 0-404-01640-5); 41.50 ea. AMS Pr.

Clowney, Deborah, jt. auth. see Weininger, Jay.

Clowney, Edmund. Called to the Ministry. 1976. pap. 3.50 (ISBN 0-87552-144-4). Presby & Reformed.

Clowney, Edmund P. Christian Meditation. 1979. pap. 2.50 (ISBN 0-934532-06-0). Presby & Reformed.

--Preaching & Biblical Theology. 1956. pap. 3.75 (ISBN 0-87552-145-2). Presby & Reformed.

Clowney, Paul & Clowney, Tessa. Exploring Churches. LC 82-210857. pap. 23.50 (ISBN 0-317-30134-9, 2025317). Bks Demand UMI.

Clowney, Tessa, jt. auth. see Clowney, Paul.

Clowse, Barbara B., ed. Brainpower for the Cold War: The Sputnik Crisis & National Defense Education Act of 1958. LC 81-1477. (Contributions to the Study of Education Ser.: No. 3). x, 225p. 1981. lib. bdg. 29.95 (ISBN 0-313-22813-2, CCW). Greenwood.

Clowse, Converse. Economic Beginnings in Colonial South Carolina, 1670-1730. LC 78-120578. (Tricentennial Studies: No. 3). xiv, 284p. 1971. 19.95x (ISBN 0-87249-186-2). U of SC Pr.

Clowse, Converse D. Measuring Charleston's Overseas Commerce, 1717-1767: Statistics from the Port's Naval Lists. LC 81-40640. (Illus.). 170p. (Orig.). 1982. lib. bdg. 25.00 (ISBN 0-8191-2055-3); pap. text ed. 11.75 (ISBN 0-8191-2056-1). U Pr of Amer.

Cloyd, Betty S. Glory Beyond All Comparison. LC 81-52216. 1981. pap. 4.50x (ISBN 0-8358-0423-2). Upper Room.

Cloyd, Jerald W. Drugs & Information Control: The Role of Men & Manipulation in the Control of Drug Trafficking. LC 81-6675. (Contributions in Legal Studies Ser.: No. 23). xi, 195p. 1982. lib. bdg. 29.95 (ISBN 0-313-22178-2, CDS). Greenwood.

Cloyes, Shirley A., jt. auth. see Soelle, Dorothee.

CLSA Staff. Annual Convention Proceedings, 45th: 1983. 354p. 1984. pap. 7.00 (ISBN 0-943616-22-0). Canon Law Soc.

Club Jules Gonin Meeting, 8th, Miami, 1972, et al. Limitations & Prospects for Retinal Surgery: Proceedings. (Modern Problems in Ophthalmology: Vol. 12). (Illus.). 1974. 74.50 (ISBN 3-8055-1629-0). S Karger.

Club Managers Association & Duncan, Horace G. Club Management Operations. 320p. (Orig.). 1982. text ed. 22.95 (ISBN 0-8403-2826-5). Kendall-Hunt.

Clubb, Bruce E. U. S. Foreign Trade Law. write for info. Little.

Clubb, Jerome, et al. Partisan Realignment: Voters, Parties, & Government in American History. LC 80-16474. (Sage Library of Social Research: Vol. 108). 320p. 1980. 28.00 (ISBN 0-8039-1445-8); pap. 14.00 (ISBN 0-8039-1446-6). Sage.

Clubb, Jerome M. Ecological Data in Comparative Research: Report on a First International Data Confrontation Seminar. (Reports & Papers in the Social Sciences: No. 25). 37p. 1970. pap. 5.00 (ISBN 92-3-100845-5, U174, UNESCO). Unipub.

Clubb, Jerome M., et al. Analyzing Electoral History: A Guide to the Study of American Voting Behavior. (Sage Focus Editions: Vol. 33). 320p. 1981. 28.00 (ISBN 0-8039-1673-6); pap. 14.00 (ISBN 0-8039-1674-4). Sage.

Clubb, Louise G. Giambattista Della Porta: Dramatist. 1965. 40.00 (ISBN 0-691-06051-7). Princeton U Pr.

Clubb, Louise G., tr. see Della Porta, Giambattista.

Clubb, Merrel D., ed. Christ & Satan: An Old English Poem. (Yale Studies in English Ser.: No. 70). lx, 175p. 1972. Repr. of 1925 ed. 18.50 (ISBN 0-208-01127-7, Archon). Shoe String.

Clubb, O. Edmund. China & Russia: "The Great Game". LC 72-155362. (Studies of the East Asian Institute). (Illus.). 578p. 1970. 37.00x (ISBN 0-231-02740-0); pap. 16.00x (ISBN 0-231-08305-X). Columbia U Pr.

--Communism in China As Reported from Hankow in 1932. LC 68-56634. (Illus.). 123p. 1968. 21.00x (ISBN 0-231-03209-9). Columbia U Pr.

--Twentieth Century China. 3rd ed. 559p. 1978. 37.00x (ISBN 0-231-04518-2); pap. 16.00x (ISBN 0-231-04519-0). Columbia U Pr.

--The Witness & I. LC 74-11385. 314p. 1975. 24.00x (ISBN 0-231-03859-3). Columbia U Pr.

Clubb, Oliver. KAL Flight 007: The Hidden Story. LC 84-62522. 160p. 1985. 15.95 (ISBN 0-932966-59-4). Permanent Pr.

Clubb, William G., ed. & tr. see Corneille, Pierre.

Clubbe, John. Victorian Forerunner: The Later Career of Thomas Hood. LC 68-28520. Repr. of 1968 ed. 52.30 (ISBN 0-8357-9120-3, 2017893). Bks Demand UMI.

Clubbe, John & Lovell, Ernest J., Jr. English Romanticism: The Grounds of Belief. LC 82-22586. 195p. 1983. 22.50 (ISBN 0-87580-092-0). N Ill U Pr.

Clubbe, John, ed. Carlyle & His Contemporaries: Essays in Honor of Charles Richard Sanders. LC 74-31830. xvii, 371p. 1976. 22.75 (ISBN 0-8223-0340-X). Duke.

Clubbe, John, ed. see Froude, James A.

Clubbe, John B. Two Reminiscences of Thomas Carlyle. LC 73-81497. xiv, 145p. 1974. 12.75 (ISBN 0-8223-0307-8). Duke.

Clube, Victor & Napier, Bill. The Cosmic Serpent: A Catastrophist View of Earth History. LC 81-19699. (Illus.). 299p. 1982. 20.00x (ISBN 0-87663-379-3). Universe.

Clubley, Sally. Trading in Oil Futures. 180p. 1985. 28.50 (ISBN 0-89397-220-7). Nichols Pub.

Clubualt & Burton. Sherman Act Indictments, 1955-1965: Cumulative Statistical Supplement. 146p. 1968. pap. 5.95 (ISBN 0-87945-001-0). Fed Legal Pubn.

Cluchey, David P. & Seitzinger, Michael D. Maine Criminal Practice, No. 1. 800p. 1985. post binder 85.00 (ISBN 0-89442-054-2). Tower Pub Co.

Cluck, Nancy. Literature & Music. LC 81-1070. 1981. 9.95 (ISBN 0-8425-1943-2). Brigham.

Clues, Andrew & Jack, David. Soccer for Players & Coaches. (Illus.). 176p. 1980. 16.95 (ISBN 0-13-815274-8, Spec); pap. 7.95 (ISBN 0-13-815266-7). P-H.

Cluett, Robert. Prose Style & Critical Reading. LC 75-40035. (Illus.). 1976. text ed. 17.95x (ISBN 0-8077-2491-2). Tchrs Coll.

Cluff, Anthony T., jt. auth. see Arrington, Leonard J.

Cluff, Buster R. The Riot War. LC 76-13240. 1977. 12.95 (ISBN 0-87949-073-X). Ashley Bks.

Cluff, E. Dale. Microforms. Duane, James E., ed. LC 80-21457. (The Instructional Media Library: Vol. 7). (Illus.). 104p. 1981. 19.95 (ISBN 0-87778-167-2). Educ Tech Pubns.

Cluff, E. F., ed. The Computer User, No. 6. (Computer State of the Art Report Ser.: 11-6). 400p. 1983. 445.00 (ISBN 0-08-028577-5). Pergamon.

Cluff, L. E., jt. auth. see Petrie, J. C.

Cluff, Leighton E. & Caranasos, George J. Clinical Problems with Drugs. LC 74-24512. (Major Problems in Internal Medicine Ser.: Vol. 5). pap. 79.50 (ISBN 0-317-08699-5, 2016656). Bks Demand UMI.

Cluff, Leila L. Anatomy & Physiology Clarified for Effective Learning. 2nd ed. Printing Inc. Art Staff, tr. LC 82-81215. (Illus.). 300p. (Orig.). 1982. pap. 8.95 (ISBN 0-89829-114-3). Health Ed Aids.

Clugston, Donald L. All That Money & No Cash. (Illus.). 128p. 1981. 7.50 (ISBN 0-682-49678-2). Exposition Pr FL.

Clugston, George A. A Looking Glasse for London & England by Thomas Lodge & Robert Greene: A Critical Edition. Orgel, Stephen, ed. LC 79-3098. (Renaissance Drama Second Ser.). 300p. 1980. lib. bdg. 36.00 (ISBN 0-8240-4482-7). Garland Pub.

Clukey, Lee P. UNIX & XENIX Demystified. LC 85-2658. (Illus.). 250p. 1985. 21.95 (ISBN 0-8306-0874-5, 1874); pap. 16.95 (ISBN 0-8306-1874-0). TAB Bks.

Cluley, Elizabeth M. see Miller, Walter J. & Morse-Cluley, Elizabeth.

Cluley, J. C. Interfacing to Microprocessors. 160p. 1983. 26.50 (ISBN 0-07-011409-9). McGraw.

--Minicomputer & Microprocessor Interfacing. 2nd ed. LC 82-8003. (Computer Systems Engineering Ser.). 272p. 1982. 27.50x (ISBN 0-8448-1400-8). Crane-Russak Co.

--Minicomputer & Microprocessor Interfacing. 280p. 1982. 95.00x (ISBN 0-7131-3474-7, Pub. by E Arnold). State Mutual Bk.

--Programming for Minicomputers. LC 77-83270. (Computer Systems Engineering Ser.). 288p. 1978. 19.50x (ISBN 0-8448-1259-5). Crane-Russak Co.

Cluley, John C. Computer Interfacing & On-Line Operation. LC 74-16952. (Computer Systems Engineering Ser.). (Illus.). 181p. 1975. 19.50x (ISBN 0-8448-0567-X). Crane-Russak Co.

Clulow, C. F. To Have & to Hold: Marriage, the First Baby, & Preparing Couples for Parenthood. 168p. 1982. 16.50 (ISBN 0-08-028470-1); pap. 9.50 (ISBN 0-08-028471-X). Pergamon.

Clum, Franklin D. Inebriety: Its Causes, Its Results, Its Remedy. Grob, Gerald N., ed. LC 80-1217. (Addiction in America Ser.). 1981. Repr. of 1888 ed. lib. bdg. 20.00x (ISBN 0-405-13573-4). Ayer Co Pubs.

Clum, J. A., ed. see AIME 114th Annual Meeting, New York, Feb. 1985.

Clum, W. Apache Agent: The Story of John P. Clum. 1977. lib. bdg. 59.95 (ISBN 0-8490-1441-7). Gordon Pr.

Clum, Woodworth. Apache Agent: The Story of John P. Clum. LC 77-14135. (Illus.). xvi, 297p. 1978. pap. 5.95 (ISBN 0-8032-5886-0, BB 654, Bison). U of Nebr Pr.

Clumpner, Mick. Nez Perce Legend. (Orig.). 1983. pap. 2.95 (ISBN 0-440-06330-2, Banbury). Dell.

--Outlaws' Gold. 224p. (Orig.). 1981. pap. 1.95 (ISBN 0-89083-712-0). Zebra.

Clumpner, Mike. The Broncbuster. 220p. (Orig.). 1980. pap. 1.95 (ISBN 0-89083-671-X). Zebra.

Clunas, Craig. Chinese Export Watercolours. (Illus.). 128p. (Orig.). 1984. pap. 18.95 (ISBN 0-905209-61-3, Pub. by Victoria & Albert Mus UK). Faber & Faber.

Clune, Anne, ed. Poetry & Prose of Ireland: Readings in Anglo-Irish Literature, 3 vols. 1200p. 1985. cancelled (ISBN 0-906187-21-4, Pub. by Univ Pr of Ireland); pap. cancelled (ISBN 0-906187-22-2). Longwood Pub Group.

Clune, Anne, et al, eds. Anglo-Irish Literature: A Cultural History, 3 vols. 1104p. 1985. cancelled (ISBN 0-906187-17-6, Pub. by Univ Pr of Ireland); cancelled (ISBN 0-906187-18-4); cancelled (ISBN 0-906187-19-2); cancelled (ISBN 0-906187-20-6). Longwood Pub Group.

Clunie, J. G. & Hayman, W. K., eds. Symposium on Complex Analysis. LC 73-92787. (London Mathematical Society Lecture Note Ser.: No. 12). 200p. 1974. 24.95 (ISBN 0-521-20452-6). Cambridge U Pr.

Clunie, J. G., jt. ed. see Brannan, D. A.

Clunies, Louise, et al. The Right Balance: Provision for Slow Learners in Secondary Schools. 192p. 1983. 11.00x (ISBN 0-7005-0555-5, Pub by NFER Nelson UK). Taylor & Francis.

Clunies Ross, Anthony I., jt. auth. see Garnaut, Ross.

Clunn, Harold. The Face of London. 1978. lib. bdg. 40.00 (ISBN 0-8482-7552-7). Norwood Edns.

Clunn, Patricia A., ed. see Payne, Dorris B.

Cluotier, David, tr. see Hafiz of Shiraz.

Clurman, David. The Business Condominium: A New Form of Business Property Ownership. LC 73-10089. (Real Estate for Professional Practitioners Ser.). 185p. 1973. 42.95x (ISBN 0-471-16129-2). Wiley.

Clurman, David & Hebard, Edna L. Condominiums & Cooperatives. LC 73-106012. (Real Estate for Professional Practitioners Ser.). 1970. 49.95 (ISBN 0-471-16130-6, Pub. by Wiley-Interscience). Wiley.

Clurman, David, et al. Condominiums & Cooperatives. 2nd ed. LC 84-3643. (Real Estate for Professional Practitioners: 1-242). 350p. 1984. text ed. 29.95 (ISBN 0-471-89197-5). Wiley.

Clurman, Harold. The Fervent Years: The Group Theatre & the Thirties. (Quality Paperbacks Ser.). (Illus.). 352p. 1983. pap. 9.95 (ISBN 0-306-80186-8). Da Capo.

--On Directing. 308p. 1972. 13.95 (ISBN 0-02-526410-9). Macmillan.

--On Directing. (Illus.). 336p. 1974. pap. 8.95 (ISBN 0-02-013350-2, Collier). Macmillan.

Clurman, Harold, ed. Famous American Plays of the Nineteen Sixties. 400p. (Orig.). 1972. pap. 5.95 (ISBN 0-440-32609-5, LE). Dell.

--Famous American Plays of the Nineteen Thirties. Incl. Awake & Sing. Odets, Clifford; End of Summer. Behrman, Samuel N; Idiot's Delight. Sherwood, Robert F; Of Mice & Men. Steinbeck, John; Time of Your Life. Saroyan, William. (American Drama Ser.). 480p. 1959. pap. 4.95 (ISBN 0-440-32478-5, LE). Dell.

--Nine Plays of the Modern Theater: Waiting for Godot; The Visit; Tango; The Caucasian Chalk Circle; The Balcony; Rhinoceros; American Buffalo; The Birthday Party; Rosencrantz & Guildenstein are Dead. LC 79-52121. 896p. 1981. pap. 11.95 (ISBN 0-394-17411-9, E773, Ever). Grove.

Clurman, Harold, ed. see Miller, Arthur.

Clusius, Carolus. Plant & Floral Woodcuts for Designers & Craftsmen. Menten, Theodore, ed. LC 74-77539. (Illus.). 192p. 1974. pap. 6.00 (ISBN 0-486-20722-6). Dover.

--Plant & Floral Woodcuts for Designers & Craftsmen: 419 Illustrations from the Renaissance Herbal of Clusius. 11.25 (ISBN 0-8446-5170-2). Peter Smith.

Cluster, Dick & Rutter, Nancy. Shrinking Dollars, Vanishing Jobs: Why the Economy Isn't Working for You. LC 79-53756. 1980. 14.50x (ISBN 0-8070-3200-X); pap. 6.95 (ISBN 0-8070-3201-8, BP-599). Beacon Pr.

Cluster, Dick, ed. They Should Have Served That Cup of Coffee. LC 78-68476. (Illus.). 270p. 1979. 15.00 (ISBN 0-89608-083-8); pap. 8.50 (ISBN 0-89608-082-X). South End Pr.

Clute, P. D. The Legal Aspects of Prisons & Jails. 248p. 1980. 25.75x (ISBN 0-398-04005-2). C C Thomas.

Clute, Robin & Andersen, Juel. Juel Andersen's Tempeh Primer. (Illus.). 58p. (Orig.). 1983. pap. 3.95 (ISBN 0-916870-59-6). Creative Arts Bk.

Clute, Robin & Andersen, Sigrid. Carob Primer. (Illus.). 64p. pap. 3.95 (ISBN 0-916870-59-6). Creative Arts Bk.

--Juel Andersen's Carob Primer. 56p. (Orig.). 1983. pap. 3.95 (ISBN 0-916870-60-X). Creative Arts Bk.

--Tempeh Primer. 2nd ed. (Illus.). 64p. pap. 3.95 (ISBN 0-916870-59-6). Creative Arts Bk.

Clute, Willard N. The Fern-Collector's Guide. (Shorey Lost Arts Ser.). (Illus.). 52p. pap. 3.95 (ISBN 0-8466-6026-1, U26). Shorey.

Clutesi, George. Potlatch. 188p. 1969. pap. 2.95 (ISBN 0-88826-046-6). Superior Pub.

--Son of Raven. (Illus.). 1967. pap. 2.95 (ISBN 0-88826-060-1). Superior Pub.

Clutter, Jerome L. & Fortson, James C. Timber Management: A Quantitative Approach. LC 82-25611. 333p. 1983. 32.50 (ISBN 0-471-02961-0). Wiley.

Clutter, Mary E., ed. Dormancy & Developmental Arrest: Experimental Analysis in Plants & Animals. 1978. 50.50 (ISBN 0-12-177050-8). Acad Pr.

Clutterbuck, Charlie & Lang, Tim. More Than We Can Chew: The Crazy World of Food & Farming. 128p. (Orig.). 1983. pap. 3.75 (ISBN 0-86104-501-7). Pluto Pr.

Clutterbuck, David. How to Be a Good Corporate Citizen. 254p. 1982. 35.00 (ISBN 0-07-084560-3). McGraw.

Clutterbuck, David & Hill, Roy. The Re-Making of Work: Changing Work Patterns & How to Capitalize on Them. 240p. 1981. 29.00x (ISBN 0-86216-044-8, Pub. by Marston Bk Serv). State Mutual Bk.

Clutterbuck, David, jt. auth. see Goldsmith, Walter.

Clutterbuck, David, ed. New Patterns of Work. LC 85-1960. 136p. 1985. 25.00 (ISBN 0-312-56842-8). St Martin.

Clutterbuck, Richard. Conflict & Violence in Singapore & Malaysia 1945-1983. 412p. 1984. 24.00x (ISBN 0-8133-0168-8). Westview.

--Guerrillas & Terrorists. LC 80-83219. 125p. 1980. 12.95x (ISBN 0-8214-0590-X, 82-83798); pap. 7.00x (ISBN 0-8214-0592-6, 82-83806). Ohio U Pr.

--Industrial Conflict & Democracy: The Last Chance. 250p. 1984. 29.50x (ISBN 0-8448-1479-2). Crane-Russak Co.

--Kidnap & Ransom: The Response. 192p. 1978. pap. 7.95 (ISBN 0-571-11327-3). Faber & Faber.

Clutton, Cecil & Daniels, George. Watches: A Complete History of the Technical & Decorative Development of the Watch. 3rd rev. & enlarg. ed. (Illus.). 312p. 1979. 95.00 (ISBN 0-85667-058-8, Pub by Sotheby Pubns England). Biblio Dist.

Clutton, Cecil, jt. ed. see Daniels, George.

Clutton-Brock, A. Shakespeare's Hamlet. LC 73-6586. 1973. lib. bdg. 10.00 (ISBN 0-8414-3362-3). Folcroft.

--Shakespeare's "Hamlet". LC 76-52923. (Studies in Shakespeare, No. 24). 1977. Repr. of 1922 ed. lib. bdg. 39.95x (ISBN 0-8383-2133-X). Haskell.

--William Morris: His Work & Influence. 1978. Repr. of 1914 ed. lib. bdg. 20.00 (ISBN 0-8495-0849-5). Arden Lib.

--William Morris: His Work & Influence. 1978. Repr. of 1919 ed. lib. bdg. 20.00 (ISBN 0-8492-3900-1). R West.

Clutton-Brock, A., et al. Necessity of Art. LC 78-93366. (Essay Index Reprint Ser.). 1924. 17.00 (ISBN 0-8369-1364-7). Ayer Co Pubs.

Clutton-Brock, Alan. Blake. 1973. lib. bdg. 10.75 (ISBN 0-8414-3044-6). Folcroft.
--Blake. LC 77-119438. (Studies in Blake, No. 3). 1970. Repr. of 1933 ed. lib. bdg. 45.95x (ISBN 0-8383-1055-9). Haskell.
Clutton-Brock, Alan F., jt. ed. see Marvin, Francis S.
Clutton-Brock, Arthur. Essays on Art. facs. ed. LC 68-22906. (Essay Index Reprint Ser). 1919. 14.00 (ISBN 0-8369-0314-5). Ayer Co Pubs.
--Essays on Books. facs. ed. LC 68-29198. (Essay Index Reprint Ser). 1968. Repr. of 1920 ed. 15.00 (ISBN 0-8369-0316-1). Ayer Co Pubs.
--Essays on Life. facs. ed. LC 75-121455. (Essay Index Reprint Ser). 1925. 17.00 (ISBN 0-8369-1702-2). Ayer Co Pubs.
--Essays on Literature & Life. facs. ed. LC 68-54339. (Essay Index Reprint Ser). 1927. 17.00 (ISBN 0-8369-0317-X). Ayer Co Pubs.
--Essays on Religion. facs. ed. LC 79-84302. (Essay Index Reprint Ser). 1926. 14.50 (ISBN 0-8369-1078-8). Ayer Co Pubs.
--More Essays on Books. facs. ed. LC 68-57313. (Essay Index Reprint Ser). 1921. 15.00 (ISBN 0-8369-0315-3). Ayer Co Pubs.
--More Essays on Religion. facsimile ed. LC 76-156632. (Essay Index Reprint Ser). Repr. of 1928 ed. 18.00 (ISBN 0-8369-2349-9). Ayer Co Pubs.
--Shelley the Man & the Poet. 16.25 (ISBN 0-8369-7106-X, 7940). Ayer Co Pubs.
Clutton-Brock, Juliet. Domesticated Animals from Early Times. (Illus.). 210p. 1981. 24.95 (ISBN 0-292-71532-3). U of Tex Pr.
Clutton-Brock, T. H. & Guinness, F. E. Red Deer: Behavior & Ecology of Two Sexes. LC 81-22025. (Wildlife Behavior & Ecology (WBE)). (Illus.). 1982. lib. bdg. 40.00x (ISBN 0-226-11056-7); pap. 14.00x (ISBN 0-226-11057-5). U of Chicago Pr.
Clutton-Brock, T. H., ed. Primate Ecology: Studies of Feeding & Ranging Behavior in Lemurs, Monkeys & Apes. 1977. 75.00 (ISBN 0-12-176850-3). Acad Pr.
Clutton Brock, Tim & Ball, Martim. Rhum: The Natural History of an Island. 160p. 1986. 25.00x (ISBN 0-85224-513-0, Pub. by Edinburgh U Pr Scotland). Columbia U Pr.
Cluysenaar, Anne & Hewat, Sybil. Double Helix. 180p. 1982. pap. text ed. 13.00x (ISBN 0-85635-428-7, 51083, Pub. by Carcanet New Pr England). Humanities.
Cluysenaer, O. J. & VanTongeren, J. H. Malabsorption in Coeliac Sprue. 1977. lib. bdg. 47.50 (ISBN 90-247-2000-1, Pub. by Martinus Nijhoff Netherlands). Kluwer Academic.
Clyde, Ahmad. Cheng Ho's Voyage. LC 81-66951. (Children's Book Ser.). (Illus.). 32p. (Orig.). (gr. 3-7). 1981. pap. 1.35 (ISBN 0-89259-021-1). Am Trust Pubns.
Clyde, Arlene, compiled by. International Cookbook. (Orig.). 1979. pap. 4.95 (ISBN 0-89367-035-9). Light & Life.
Clyde, James E. Construction Inspection: A Field Guide to Practice. 2nd ed. LC 83-6977. (Practical Construction Guides Ser.: I-344). 416p. 1983. 44.95x (ISBN 0-471-88861-3, Pub. by Wiley-Interscience). Wiley.
Clyde, John S. Computerized Career Information & Guidance Systems. 61p. 1979. 4.50 (ISBN 0-318-15430-7, IN 178). Natl Ctr Res Voc Ed.
Clyde, Norman. Close-ups of the High Sierra. rev. ed. (Illus.). 1966. wrappers 3.50 (ISBN 0-910856-11-7). La Siesta.
--El Picacho Del Diablo: The Conquest of Lower California's Highest Peak, 1932 & 1937. Robinson, John W., ed. (Baja California Travels Ser.: No. 36). (Illus.). 95p. 1975. 18.00 (ISBN 0-87093-236-5). Dawsons.
Clyde, Paul H. Japan's Pacific Mandate. LC 67-27586. Repr. of 1935 ed. 19.50x (ISBN 0-8046-0081-3, Pub. by Kennikat). Assoc Faculty Pr.
Clyde, Paul H. & Beers, Burton F. Far East: A History of Western Impacts & Eastern Responses (1830-1975) 6th ed. (Illus.). 576p. 1976. 33.95 (ISBN 0-13-302968-9). P-H.
Clyde, William M. Struggle for the Freedom of the Press from Caxton to Cromwell. LC 70-122223. (Research & Source Works: No. 479). 1970. Repr. of 1934 ed. lib. bdg. 23.50 (ISBN 0-8337-0606-3). B Franklin.
Clydesdale, F. M. & Francis, F. J. Food, Nutrition & Health. (Illus.). 1985. text ed. write for info. (ISBN 0-87055-507-3); text ed. 22.00 pre-pub. AVI.
Clydesdale, F. M., jt. auth. see Francis, F. J.
Clydesdale, Fergus. Food Science & Nutrition: Current Issues & Answers. (Illus.). 1979. ref. 22.95. P-H.
Clydesdale, Fergus M. & Francis, Frederick J. Human Ecological Issues: A Reader. 320p. (Orig.). 1980. pap. text ed. 9.95 (ISBN 0-8403-2197-X). Kendall-Hunt.
Clydesdale, Fergus M. & Wiemer, Kathryn L., eds. Iron Fortification of Foods. (Food Science & Technology Ser.). 1985. 36.50 (ISBN 0-12-177060-5). Acad Pr.
Clydesdale, Fergus S. & Francis, F. J. Food, Nutrition & You. (Illus.). 1977. lib. bdg. 17.95 (ISBN 0-13-323048-1); pap. text ed. 16.95 (ISBN 0-13-323030-9). P-H.

Clygout, Sanivar H. Homosexuality: Medical Subject Analysis & Research Guide with Bibliography. LC 83-45538. 156p. 1985. 29.95 (ISBN 0-88164-090-5); pap. 21.95 (ISBN 0-88164-091-3). ABBE Pubs Assn.
Clyman, James. Journal of a Mountain Man. Hasselstrom, Linda M., ed. (Classics of the Fur Trade Ser.). 308p. 1984. 24.95 (ISBN 0-87842-181-5); pap. 9.95 (ISBN 0-87842-182-3). Mountain Pr.
Clyman, Toby, tr. see Bitsilli, Peter.
Clyman, Toby W., ed. A Chekhov Companion. LC 84-29024. (Illus.). 384p. 1985. lib. bdg. 45.00 (ISBN 0-313-23423-X, CHC/). Greenwood.
Clymer, Eleanor. Chipmunk in the Forest. LC 65-15908. (Illus.). 64p. (gr. 2-5). 1965. pap. 0.95 (ISBN 0-689-70311-2, A-14, Aladdin). Atheneum.
--The Get-Away Car. (gr. 4-7). 1978. 8.95 (ISBN 0-525-30470-3). Dutton.
--Harry, the Wild West Horse. LC 63-10375. (Illus.). 64p. (gr. 2-5). 1963. pap. 1.95 (ISBN 0-689-70303-1, A-7, Aladdin). Atheneum.
--Horatio. (Illus.). (ps-3). 1974. pap. 1.25 (ISBN 0-689-70403-8, A-33, Aladdin). Atheneum.
--Horatio Goes to the Country. LC 78-5137. (Illus.). 64p. (ps-3). 1978. 7.95 (ISBN 0-689-30649-0). Atheneum.
--Horatio Solves a Mystery. LC 79-22590. (Illus.). 64p. (ps-3). 1980. 9.95 (ISBN 0-689-30734-9). Atheneum.
--Horatio's Birthday. LC 76-89. (Illus.). 64p. (gr. k-4). 1976. 6.95 (ISBN 0-689-30520-6). Atheneum.
--The Horse in the Attic. LC 83-6377. (Illus.). 70p. (gr. 5-7). 1983. 9.95 (ISBN 0-02-719040-4). Bradbury Pr.
--The Horse in the Attic. (gr. k-6). 1985. pap. 2.50 (ISBN 0-440-43798-9, YB). Dell.
--Leave Horatio Alone. LC 74-75557. (Illus.). 64p. (ps-3). 1974. 6.95 (ISBN 0-689-30405-6). Atheneum.
--My Mother Is the Smartest Woman in the World. LC 82-1685. (Illus.). 96p. (gr. 3-7). 1982. 8.95 (ISBN 0-689-30916-3). Atheneum.
--A Search for Two Bad Mice. LC 80-12789. (Illus.). 80p. (gr. 2-5). 1980. 9.95 (ISBN 0-689-30771-3). Atheneum.
Clymer, Emerson M. A Reason for Being. 116p. 1971. 6.95 (ISBN 0-932785-42-5). Philos Pub.
Clymer, Emerson M., et al, eds. see Randolph, Paschal B.
Clymer, Floyd. Album of Historical Steam Traction Engines. 160p. 10.00 (ISBN 0-318-14827-7, S121). Midwest Old Settlers.
--Floyd Clymer's Album of Historical Steam Traction Engines & Threshing Equipment. (Illus.). 160p. pap. 9.95 (ISBN 0-317-11542-1). Diamond Farm Bk.
Clymer Publications. Bultaco Service Repair Handbook: 125-370cc, Through 1977. (Illus.). pap. 13.95 (ISBN 0-89287-174-1, M303). Clymer Pubns.
--Corvette V-Eight, Nineteen Fifty-Five to Nineteen Sixty-Two: Complete Owner's Handbook. (Illus.). pap. 7.95 (ISBN 0-89287-082-6, A141). Clymer Pubns.
--Ford Fairmont and Mercury Zephyr, 1978-1983: Shop Manual. Jorgensen, Eric, ed. (Illus., Orig.). 12.95 (ISBN 0-89287-307-8, A174). Clymer Pubns.
--Harley-Davidson Service-Repair Handbook: Sportster Series, 1959-1984. Robinson, Jeff, ed. (Illus.). pap. 13.95 (ISBN 0-89287-126-1, M419). Clymer Pubns.
--Honda Service-Repair Handbook: CB 750SOHC Fours, 1969-1978. Jorgensen, Eric, ed. (Illus.). pap. 13.95 (ISBN 0-89287-167-9, M341). Clymer Pubns.
--Jeep Service, Repair Handbook: Covers Willy-Overland Model MB & Ford Model GPW. (Illus.). pap. 7.95 (ISBN 0-89287-250-0, A162). Clymer Pubns.
--Mustang II Service Repair Handbook All Models, 1974-1978. (Illus., Orig.). pap. text ed. 12.95 (ISBN 0-89287-119-9, A169). Clymer Pubns.
--Porsche Owners Handbook & Service Manual: Covers All Porsche Models up to 356c. (Illus.). pap. 7.95 (ISBN 0-89287-251-9, A181). Clymer Pubns.
--Suzuki: 380-750cc Triples, 1972-1977 Service, Repair, Maintenance. (Illus.). 1977. pap. 13.95 (ISBN 0-89287-285-3, M368). Clymer Pubns.
--Yamaha Service Repair Handbook: 80-175cc Piston Port Singles, 1968-1976. (Illus.). pap. text ed. 13.95 (ISBN 0-89287-235-7, M410). Clymer Pubns.
--Yamaha: 250-400cc Piston Port Singles, 1968-76, Service, Repair, Performance. 3rd ed. Jorgensen, Eric, ed. (Illus.). pap. 13.95 (ISBN 0-89287-276-4, M415). Clymer Pubns.
--Yamaha: 250-400cc, 2-Stroke Twins 1965-1979, Service, Repair, Performance. 3rd ed. Jorgensen, Eric, ed. (Illus.). pap. 13.95 (ISBN 0-89287-283-7, M401). Clymer Pubns.
Clymer Publications, ed. Sunbeam Owners Handbook of Maintenance & Repair. (Illus.). pap. 8.95 (ISBN 0-89287-253-5, A189). Clymer Pubns.
--Triumph Spitfire Owner's Handbook: 1962-1970. (Illus.). 1971. pap. 8.95 (ISBN 0-89287-254-3, A215). Clymer Pubns.
Clymer Publications, ed. see Bell, Doug.

Clymer, R. S. Las Esenanzas Hermeticas. 1962. pap. 2.75 (ISBN 0-686-10444-7). Philos Pub.
Clymer, R. Swimburne. The Living Christ: Church of Illumination. 58p. 1979. pap. 2.95 (ISBN 0-932785-27-1). Philos Pub.
Clymer, R. Swinborne. The Rosicrucian Fraternity in America, 2 vols. 1935. 75.00 (ISBN 0-686-10446-3). Philos Pub.
Clymer, R. Swinburne. Book of Rosicruciae, 3 Vols. 1948. Set. 27.00 (ISBN 0-686-00809-X). Philos Pub.
--The Book of Rosicruciae, Vol. I. 286p. 1946. 9.95 (ISBN 0-932785-03-4). Philos Pub.
--The Book of Rosicruciae, Vol. II. 279p. 1947. 9.95 (ISBN 0-932785-04-2). Philos Pub.
--The Book of Rosicruciae, Vol. III. 304p. 1949. 9.95 (ISBN 0-932785-05-0). Philos Pub.
--Ciencia del Alma. Aparis, Fina, tr. 272p. (Orig., Span.). 1967. pap. 6.95 (ISBN 0-932785-51-4). Philos Pub.
--Compendium of Occult Laws. 311p. 1966. 9.95 (ISBN 0-932785-08-5). Philos Pub.
--Cultura Prenatal: Coma Crear el Hijo Perfecto por la Influencia Prenatal. Aparis, Fina, tr. 173p. (Orig., Span.). 1950. pap. 4.95 (ISBN 0-932785-53-0). Philos Pub.
--Diet: A Key to Health. 1966. 4.95 (ISBN 0-686-05800-3). Philos Pub.
--La Filosofia del Fuego. Morel, Hector V., tr. 190p. (Orig., Span.). 1980. pap. 5.95 (ISBN 0-932785-54-9). Philos Pub.
--Fraternitas Rosae Crucis. 1929. 9.95 (ISBN 0-932785-11-5). Philos Pub.
--The Great Work, 4 vols. Incl. Its Neophytes. 1964. 7.95 (ISBN 0-932785-15-8); Council of Three. 1963. 7.95 (ISBN 0-932785-14-X); Coming Masters. 1962. 7.95 (ISBN 0-932785-13-1); Spiritual Initiation. 1961. 7.95 (ISBN 0-932785-12-3). Set. 28.95. Philos Pub.
--Hidden Teachings of the Initiate Masters. 1957. 4.95 (ISBN 0-686-00811-1). Philos Pub.
--Initiates & the People, 1928-1932, 5 vols. 1933. Repr. Set. 37.95 (ISBN 0-686-15595-5). Vol. I, 204 pp (ISBN 0-932785-18-2). Vol. II, 208 pp (ISBN 0-932785-19-0). Vol. III, 200 pp (ISBN 0-932785-20-4). Vol. IV, 192 pp (ISBN 0-932785-21-2). Vol. V, 207 pp (ISBN 0-932785-22-0). Philos Pub.
--Interpretation of St. John. 266p. 1953. 9.95 (ISBN 0-932785-23-9). Philos Pub.
--La Ley Divina: La Senda Hacia la Maestria. (Orig., Span.). 1972. pap. 6.95 (ISBN 0-932785-55-7). Philos Pub.
--Manual of the Church of Illumination. 100p. 1952. 5.95 (ISBN 0-932785-28-X). Philos Pub.
--Master Initiate & the Maid. 1956. 7.95 (ISBN 0-686-00816-2). Philos Pub.
--Mastership: The Divine Law. 256p. 1949. 7.95 (ISBN 0-932785-30-1). Philos Pub.
--El Misterio del Sexo y la Regeneracion de la Raza. 2nd ed. Morel, Hector V., tr. 229p. (Span.). 1978. pap. 6.95 (ISBN 0-932785-56-5). Philos Pub.
--Los Misterios De Osiris. 2nd ed. 278p. (Orig.). 1978. pap. 6.95 (ISBN 0-932785-57-3). Philos Pub.
--Mysteries of Osiris: Egyptian Initiation. 287p. 1951. 8.95 (ISBN 0-932785-31-X). Philos Pub.
--Mystery of Sex: Race Regeneration. 273p. 1950. 7.95 (ISBN 0-932785-32-8). Philos Pub.
--Mysticism of Masonry. 1924. 4.95 (ISBN 0-686-00820-0). Philos Pub.
--Nature's Healing Agents. 5th new & rev. ed. 1973. 6.95 (ISBN 0-686-05880-1). Philos Pub.
--Nature's Healing Agents. 5th ed. 278p. 1985. text ed. 14.95 (ISBN 0-916638-11-1). Meyerbooks.
--Philosophic Initiation: Soul Conciousness. 268p. 1955. 8.95 (ISBN 0-932785-37-9). Philos Pub.
--The Philosophy of Fire. 5th ed. 285p. 1964. 7.95 (ISBN 0-932785-38-7). Philos Pub.
--Philosophy of Immortality. 208p. 1960. 6.95 (ISBN 0-932785-39-5). Philos Pub.
--Prenatal Culture: How to Create the Perfect Baby. 144p. 1950. 4.95 (ISBN 0-932785-50-6). Philos Pub.
--The Rosy Cross: Its Teachings. 287p. 1965. 7.95 (ISBN 0-932785-43-3). Philos Pub.
--Science of Spiritual Alchemy. 235p. 1959. 9.95 (ISBN 0-932785-44-1). Philos Pub.
--Science of the Soul. 1944. 4.95 (ISBN 0-686-00828-6). Philos Pub.
--Sons of God. 1925. 5.95 (ISBN 0-686-00829-4). Philos Pub.
--Soul Consciousness. 1955. 6.95 (ISBN 0-686-00830-8). Philos Pub.
--The Teachings of the Masters. 256p. 1952. 8.95 (ISBN 0-932785-46-8). Philos Pub.
--The Way to Life & Immortality. 244p. 1948. 7.95 (ISBN 0-932785-48-4). Philos Pub.
Clymer, R. Swinburne & Lippard, George. Cristification: And la Hermanidad de la Rosa Cruz. 2nd ed. Bucheli, J. E., tr. 206p. (Span.). 1980. pap. 6.95 (ISBN 0-932785-52-2). Philos Pub.
Clymer, R. Swinburne, jt. auth. see Betiero, J. T.
Clymer, R. Swinburne, jt. auth. see McDaniel, Ivan G.
Clymer, R. Swinburne, ed. see Phelon, William & Phelon, Mira M.
Clymer, R. Swinburne, ed. see Randolph, Paschal B.
Clymer, R. Swineburn & Morey, Grace K. Mystic Americanism or the Spiritual Heritage of America Revealed. 328p. 1975. 7.95 (ISBN 0-932785-33-6). Philos Pub.

Clymer, Reuben S. Alchemy & the Alchemists, 3 vols. LC 79-8603. Repr. of 1907 ed. Set. 105.00 (ISBN 0-404-18457-X). AMS Pr.
Clymer, Swinburne R. The Age of Treason. 396p. 1959. 3.95 (ISBN 0-916285-34-0); pap. 3.95 (ISBN 0-916285-35-9). Humanitarian.
--Your Health & Sanity in the Age of Treason. 294p. 1958. 3.95 (ISBN 0-916285-32-4); pap. 3.95 (ISBN 0-916285-33-2). Humanitarian.
Clymer, Ted & Miles, Miska. Horse & The Bad Morning. LC 81-12660. (Illus.). 32p. (ps-2). 1982. 8.95 (ISBN 0-525-45103-X, 0869-260, Unicorn Bk). Dutton.
Clymer, Theodore W. & Barrett, Thomas C. Clymer-Barrett Readiness Test: Form A - Additional Manual. rev. ed. pap. 3.00 (ISBN 0-930687-02-7). Chapman Brook.
--Clymer-Barrett Readiness Test: Form A Package. rev. ed. 1983. pap. 14.50 (ISBN 0-930687-01-9). Chapman Brook.
--Clymer-Barrett Readiness Test: Form A-Additional Test Booklets. rev. ed. 1983. pap. 7.50 (ISBN 0-930687-04-3). Chapman Brook.
--Clymer-Barrett Readiness Test: Form B Package. rev. ed. 1983. pap. 14.50 (ISBN 0-930687-11-6). Chapman Brook.
--Clymer-Barrett Readiness Test: Form B-Specimen Set. rev. ed. 1983. pap. 3.00 (ISBN 0-930687-13-2). Chapman Brook.
--Clymer-Barrett Readiness Test: Form B-Additional Manual. rev. ed. 1983. pap. 2.00 (ISBN 0-930687-12-4). Chapman Brook.
--Clymer-Barrett Readiness Test: Forms A & B-Specimen Set. rev. ed. 1983. pap. 4.50 (ISBN 0-930687-05-1). Chapman Brook.
--Clymer-Barrett Readiness Test, Specimen Set Form A: Specimen Set-Form A. rev. ed. 1983. pap. 3.00 (ISBN 0-930687-03-5). Chapman Brook.
--Clymer-Barrett Reading Readiness Test, Form B Additional Test Booklets: Form B-Additional Test Booklets. rev. ed. 1983. pap. 7.50 (ISBN 0-930687-14-0). Chapman Brook.
Clymer, W. B. Selections from the Writings of Walter Savage Landor. 1979. Repr. of 1898 ed. lib. bdg. 20.00 (ISBN 0-8492-4038-7). R West.
Clymer, William B. James Fenimore Cooper. LC 68-24933. (American Biography Ser., No. 32). 1969. Repr. of 1900 ed. lib. bdg. 49.95 (ISBN 0-8383-0925-9). Haskell.
Clyne, Densey. The Garden Jungle. 184p. 1980. 27.95 (ISBN 0-00-216411-6, Pub. by W Collins Australia). Intl Spec Bk.
Clyne, Douglas G. A Concise Textbook for Midwives. 5th ed. (Illus.). 528p. 1980. pap. 19.95 (ISBN 0-571-18018-3). Faber & Faber.
Clyne, Jim, ed. Exquisite Creatures. LC 84-60617. 96p. 1984. 22.50 (ISBN 0-688-02496-3). Morrow.
Clyne, M. A., jt. ed. see Fontijn, A.
Clyne, Michael G. Language & Society in the German Speaking Countries: A Sociolinguistic Perspective. LC 83-23981. 225p. 1984. 32.50 (ISBN 0-521-25759-X); pap. 9.95 (ISBN 0-521-27697-7). Cambridge U Pr.
Clyne, Norval. The Romantic Scottish Ballads & the Lady Wardlaw Heresy. LC 77-27936. 1859. 10.00 (ISBN 0-8414-0567-0). Folcroft.
--The Romantic Scottish Ballads & the Lady Wardlaw Heresy. LC 74-13040. 1974. Repr. of 1859 ed. lib. bdg. 15.00 (ISBN 0-88305-119-2). Norwood Edns.
Clyne, Patricia E. Caves for Kids. LC 78-31634. 1980. pap. 8.95 (ISBN 0-912526-24-6). Lib Res.
--The Corduroy Road. (Illus.). 1984. 15.25 (ISBN 0-8446-6163-5). Peter Smith.
--The Curse of the Camp Grey Owl. LC 80-2783. 176p. (gr. 5 up). 1981. PLB 7.95 (ISBN 0-396-07922-9). Dodd.
--Patriots in Petticoats. LC 75-38361. (Illus.). 128p. (gr. 5 up). 1976. 8.95 (ISBN 0-396-07292-5). Dodd.
Clyne, Paul R., et al, eds. The Elements: Proceedings Papers from the Parasession on Linguistic Units & Levels. LC 79-53852. 481p. 1979. pap. 8.00 (ISBN 0-914203-12-6). Chicago Ling.
--Proceedings: Papers from the 15th Regional Meeting. LC 76-27943. 403p. 1979. pap. 8.00 (ISBN 0-914203-11-8). Chicago Ling.
Clynes, Manfred, ed. Music, Mind, & Brain: The Neuropsychology of Music. LC 82-546. 444p. 1982. 39.50x (ISBN 0-306-40908-9, Plenum Pr). Plenum Pub.
Clytus, John & Rieker, Jane. Black Man in Red Cuba. LC 76-107984. 1970. 7.95x (ISBN 0-87024-142-7). U of Miami Pr.
CNES. Solar Cells. (Illus.). 690p. 1971. 163.25 (ISBN 0-677-50450-0). Gordon.
CNES & Chvidchenko, Ivan. Large Space Programs Management. (Illus.). 364p. 1971. 93.75 (ISBN 0-677-50670-8). Gordon.
C'Ng, Victor D'V. The Eye of a Flame. 1982. 6.95 (ISBN 0-533-05077-4). Vantage.
Cnossen, S., ed. Comparative Tax Studies: Essays in Honor of Richard Goode. (Contributions to Economic Analysis Ser.: Vol. 144). 450p. 1983. 76.75 (ISBN 0-444-86421-0, I-339-82, North Holland). Elsevier.
CNRS. New Physical, Mechanical & Chemical Properties of Very High Purity Iron. 438p. 119.25 (ISBN 0-677-30730-6). Gordon.

CNRS Colloquium, Paris, June 21-22, 1972. Investigation & Stimulation of Immunity in Cancer Patients: Proceedings. Mathe, G. & Weiner, R., eds. LC 74-1816. (Recent Results in Cancer Research: Vol. 47). (Illus.). ix, 501p. 1974. 58.00 (ISBN 0-387-06771-X). Springer-Verlag.

CNRS Staff. Fundamental Physics & Astrophysics. 176p. Date not set. 55.00 (ISBN 0-677-30860-4). Gordon.

Co, Francesco Dal see Dal Co, Francesco.

Co, Francesco Dal see Tafuri, Manfredo & Dal Co, Francesco.

Co, Francesco Dal see Dal Co, Francesco & Mazzariol, Giuseppe.

Co, Frqncesco Dal see Dal Co, Francesco.

Co No Ciofalo & Kahn, Frederick E., eds. Breakfast & Brunch Cookbook. (Preparing Food the Healthy Way Ser.). (Illus.). 144p. (Orig.). 1984. pap. 4.95 (ISBN 0-941476-03-0). Nautilus Comm Inc.

Co-op Information Consortium, 1983. Finding Co-ops: A Resource Guide & Directory. 288p. 1983. 15.95 (ISBN 0-318-17919-9, G18B). NASCO.

Co-Operative Central Exchange. The Co-Operative Pyramid Builder: Published in the Interest of the Consumer's Cooperative Movement, 3 vols. facsimile ed. McCurry, Dan C. & Rubenstein, Richard E., eds. LC 74-30626. (American Farmers & the Rise of Agribusiness Ser.). (Illus.). 1975. Repr. of 1931 ed. Set. 114.00x (ISBN 0-405-06824-7); Vol. 1. 37.50x (ISBN 0-405-06825-5); Vol. 2. 49.00x (ISBN 0-405-06826-3); Vol. 3. 27.50x (ISBN 0-686-67166-X). Ayer Co Pubs.

Co-operative Union of Canada, jt. auth. see MacPherson, Ian.

Coachman, Lawrence K., et al. Bering Strait: The Regional Physical Oceanography. LC 75-40881. (Illus.). 186p. 1976. 35.00x (ISBN 0-295-95442-6). U of Wash Pr.

Coachman, Ward, jt. auth. see Chupco, Lee.

Coad, F. Roy. A History of the Brethren Movement: Its Origins, Its Worldwide Development, & Its Significance for the Present Day. rev. ed. 336p. 1976. pap. 9.50 (ISBN 0-85364-164-1). Attic Pr.

Coad, Jonathan. Historic Architecture of the Royal Navy: An Introduction. (Illus.). 160p. 1983. 32.00 (ISBN 0-575-03277-4, Pub. by Gollancz England). David & Charles.

Coad, Malcolm, tr. see Skarmeta, Antonio.

Coad, Oral S. American Stage. 1929. 22.50x (ISBN 0-686-37861-X). Elliots Bks.

Coad, Oral S. see Gabriel, Ralph H.

Coad, Rhonda, jt. auth. see Lane, Lois.

Coad, William J. Energy Engineering & Management for Building Systems. 320p. 1981. text ed. 36.95 (ISBN 0-442-25467-9). Van Nos Reinhold.

Coady, Mary-Francis. Steve Podborski. (Picture Life Ser.). (Illus.). 48p. (gr. k-3). 1983. PLB 9.90 (ISBN 0-531-04599-4). Watts.

Coaker, T. H. Advances in Applied Biology, 2 vols. (Serial Publication Ser.). 1983. Vol. 8. 55.00 (ISBN 0-12-040908-9); Vol. 9. 65.00 (ISBN 0-12-040909-7). Acad Pr.

--Advances in Applied Biology, Vol. 5. LC 76-1065. (Serial Publication Ser.). 1980. 75.00 (ISBN 0-12-040905-4). Acad Pr.

Coaker, T. H., ed. Advances in Applied Biology, Vol. 6. LC 76-1065. (Serial Publication Ser.). 332p. 1981. 65.00 (ISBN 0-12-040906-2). Acad Pr.

--Advances in Applied Biology, Vol. 7. (Serial Publication Ser.). 1983. 73.00 (ISBN 0-12-040907-0). Acad Pr.

--Applied Biology, 3 vols. Vol. 1, 1977. 69.00 (ISBN 0-12-040901-1); Vol. 2, 1977. 55.00 (ISBN 0-12-040902-X); Vol. 3, 1978. 75.00 (ISBN 0-12-040903-8). Acad Pr.

--Applied Biology, Vol. 4. (Serial Publication). 1979. 59.50 (ISBN 0-12-040904-6). Acad Pr.

Coaker, Tom H., ed. Advances in Applied Biology, Vol. 10. 1984. 85.00 (ISBN 0-12-040910-0). Acad Pr.

Coakes & Holmes-Sellors. An Outline of Opthalmology. 1985. price not set (ISBN 0-7236-0794-X). PSG Pub Co.

Coakley. Handbook of Automated Analysis: Basic Techniques. 160p. 1981. 25.00 (ISBN 0-8247-1392-3). Dekker.

Coakley, Carolyn, jt. auth. see Wolvin, Andrew.

Coakley, Carroll B. Saleable Skills for Adults with Special Needs: Strategies in Adult Distributive Education. LC 78-94075. (Illus.). 1969. pap. text ed. 3.00x (ISBN 0-8134-1118-1, 1118). Interstate.

Coakley, Carroll B., jt. ed. see Danenburg, William P.

Coakley, Davis. Acute Geriatric Medicine. 300p. 1981. 31.00 (ISBN 0-88416-354-7). PSG Pub Co.

Coakley, Davis, ed. Establishing a Geriatric Service. (Illus.). 236p. 1982. text ed. 33.00x (ISBN 0-7099-0700-1). Sheridan.

Coakley, Deirdre, et al. The Day the MGM Grand Hotel Burned. LC 81-14511. (Illus.). 1982. 11.95 (ISBN 0-8184-0318-7). Lyle Stuart.

Coakley, Harriet. Meals & Memories of Helotes. (Illus., Orig.). 1984. pap. text ed. write for info. (ISBN 0-9612736-0-7). Helotes Area.

Coakley, Jay J. Sport in Society: Issues & Controversies. 2nd ed. LC 81-14119. (Illus.). 335p. 1982. pap. text ed. 16.95 (ISBN 0-8016-1119-9). Mosby.

Coakley, Jerry & Harris, Laurence. The City of Capital. 200p. 1984. 39.95x (ISBN 0-631-12805-0); pap. 14.95x (ISBN 0-631-13363-1). Basil Blackwell.

Coakley, Mary L. How to Live Life to the Fullest: A Handbook for Seasoned Citizens. LC 83-63167. 168p. 1984. pap. 4.95 (ISBN 0-87973-628-3, 628). Our Sunday Visitor.

Coal Age Magazine. Coal Age Operating Handbook of Coal Preparation, Vol. III. (Coal Age Library of Operating Handbooks). 1979. 32.50 (ISBN 0-07-011459-5). McGraw.

--Coal Age Operating Handbook of Underground Mining, Vol. II. 2nd ed. (Coal Age Ser.). (Illus.). 430p. 1980. 31.50 (ISBN 0-07-011461-7). McGraw.

Coal Mines Committee, 11th Session, Geneva 1982. Employment & Training With Reference to Health & Safety at Coal Mines, Report II. International Labour Office, ed. iv, 75p. (Orig.). 1982. pap. 7.15 (ISBN 0-686-87162-6). Intl Labour Office.

Coaldrake, O. P. Relocating Government Employment: Recent Commonwealth & State Experience. LC 79-53371. (Centre for Research on Federal Financial Relations - Research Monograph: No. 28). 116p. (Orig.). 1980. pap. text ed. 8.00 (ISBN 0-7081-1161-0, 0487). Australia N U P.

Coale, Ansley J. The Growth & Structure of Human Populations: A Mathematical Investigation. LC 76-166365. (Publications of the Office of Population Research). 232p. 1972. text ed. 27.00 (ISBN 0-691-09357-1). Princeton U Pr.

Coale, Ansley J. & Anderson, Barbara. Human Fertility in Russia Since the Nineteenth Century. LC 78-70284. (Publications of the Office of Population Research). (Illus.). 1979. 32.00 (ISBN 0-691-03122-3). Princeton U Pr.

Coale, Ansley J. & Demeny, Paul. Regional Model Life Tables & Stable Populations: Monograph. (Studies in Population). 1983. 48.50 (ISBN 0-12-177080-X). Acad Pr.

Coale, Ansley J. & Zelnik, Melvin. New Estimates of Fertility & Population in the United States: A Study of Annual White Births from 1855 to 1960 & of Completeness of Enumeration from 1880 to 1960. (Office of Pupulation Research Ser.). 1963. 22.50 (ISBN 0-691-09322-9). Princeton U Pr.

Coale, Ansley J. & Watkins, Susan C., eds. The Decline of Fertility in Europe. LC 85-42682. (Illus.). 352p. 1985. 55.00 (ISBN 0-691-09416-0); pap. 14.50 (ISBN 0-691-10176-0). Princeton U Pr.

Coale, Ansley J., et al, eds. Aspects of the Analysis of Family Structure. 1965. 29.00x (ISBN 0-691-09306-7). Princeton U Pr.

Coale, Joseph M., III, jt. auth. see Papenfuse, Edward C.

Coale, Robert D., jt. auth. see Brost, Fred B.

Coale, Samuel. Anthony Burgess. LC 81-40459. (Literature and Life Ser.). 234p. 1981. 16.50 (ISBN 0-8044-2124-2). Ungar.

--John Cheever. LC 77-4829. (Literature and Life Ser.). 124p. 1977. 12.95 (ISBN 0-8044-2126-9). Ungar.

--John Cheever. price not set. Ungar.

Coale, Samuel C. In Hawthorne's Shadow: American Romance from Melville to Mailer. LC 84-25792. 264p. 1985. 24.00 (ISBN 0-8131-1545-0). U Pr of Ky.

Coale, Willis B. The Professional Needs of Teachers of English. LC 75-176655. (Columbia University. Teachers College. Contributions to Education: No. 334). Repr. of 1928 ed. 22.50 (ISBN 0-404-55334-6). AMS Pr.

Coalition for Child Advocacy Staff. Touching. (Illus.). 32p. (Orig.). (ps). 1985. pap. 5.95 (ISBN 0-934671-00-1). Whatcom Cty Opp.

Coalition on Women & Religion. The Women's Bible: Study Guide. 1975. 5.95 (ISBN 0-9603042-2-3). Coalition Women-Relig.

Coalson, E. Lucille. Writings from the Heart. 1981. 5.75 (ISBN 0-8062-1851-7). Carlton.

Coalson, George O. The Development of the Migratory Farm Labor System in Texas, 1900-1954. LC 76-24727. 1977. soft bdg. 11.95 (ISBN 0-88247-413-8). R & E Pubs.

Coalson, Glo, tr. see Wasson, Valentina P.

Coan & Coan. Microsoft BASIC for the Macintosh. 1985. 18.95 (ISBN 0-8104-6558-2). Hayden.

Coan, Blair. Red Web. (Americanist Classics Ser). 1965. pap. 1.00 pocketsize (ISBN 0-88279-029-3). Western Islands.

Coan, D. R. Programming Standards, 2 vols. National Computing Centre Ltd. & National Computing Centre Ltd., eds. Incl. Vol. 1. Documentation. write for info. (ISBN 0-685-30481-7); Vol. 2. Techniques. 180p. 1972. 47.50x (ISBN 0-85012-071-3). 240p. 1973. Intl Pubns Serv.

--Standards Management. LC 78-303077. (Illus.). 1977. pap. 27.50x (ISBN 0-85012-172-8). Intl Pubns Serv.

Coan, Eugene. James Graham Cooper: Pioneer Western Naturalist. LC 80-52313. (GEM Books-Historical & Natural History Ser.). (Illus.). 210p. (Orig.). 1982. pap. 12.95 (ISBN 0-89301-071-5). U Pr of Idaho.

Coan, Eugene, jt. auth. see Keen, A. Myra.

Coan, Eugene V., jt. ed. see Trzyna, Thaddeus C.

Coan, Howard, ed. see Galaid, Ruth C.

Coan, James S. Advanced BASIC: Applications & Problems. Haag, J., ed. (Computer Programming Ser.). 1976. text ed. 17.50x (ISBN 0-8104-5856-X); pap. text ed. 13.95x (ISBN 0-8104-5855-1). Hayden.

--Basic Apple BASIC. 1983. pap. 14.95 (ISBN 0-8104-5626-5, 5626). Hayden.

--Basic BASIC: An Introduction to Computer Programming in BASIC Language. 2nd ed. (gr. 10 up). 1978. text ed. 18.95 (ISBN 0-8104-5107-7); pap. text ed. 14.50 (ISBN 0-8104-5106-9); tchr's. guide 1.40 (ISBN 0-8104-5108-5). Hayden.

--Basic Commodore 64 BASIC. 304p. 1984. pap. 14.95 (6456). Hayden.

--Basic Microsoft BASIC. 256p. pap. 16.95 (6263). Hayden.

Coan, James S. & Kushner, Richard. Basic Atari BASIC. 256p. pap. 14.95 (6526). Hayden.

Coan, Peter. Taxi, the Harry Chapin Story. LC 85-9125. 1985. 16.95 (ISBN 0-87949-262-7). Ashley Bks.

Coan, Richard. Psychologists: Personal & Theoretical Pathways. LC 79-13711. 195p. 1979. 18.95x (ISBN 0-470-26785-2). Halsted Pr.

--Psychologists: Personal & Theoretical Pathways. 224p. 1979. text ed. 18.95x (ISBN 0-8290-0858-6). Irvington.

Coan, Richard W. Hero, Artist, Sage, or Saint? A Survey of Views on What Is Variously Called Mental Health, Normality Maturity, Self-Actualization, & Human Fulfillment. LC 76-57751. 1977. 30.00x (ISBN 0-231-03806-2); pap. 13.00x (ISBN 0-231-08355-6). Columbia U Pr.

--The Optimal Personality: An Empirical & Theoretical Analysis. LC 74-11498. 242p. 1974. 30.00x (ISBN 0-231-03807-0). Columbia U Pr.

--Psychology of Adjustment: Personal Experience & Development. LC 82-13413. 558p. 1983. text ed. 29.00x (ISBN 0-471-16133-0); write for info tchr's. ed. (ISBN 0-471-87196-6). Wiley.

Coard, P. Vanishing Bath, Revised & Enlarged, Buildings Threatened & Destroyed. 316p. 1981. 30.00x (ISBN 0-901571-67-9, Pub. by Kingsmead Pr England). State Mutual Bk.

Coard, Peter. Portraits of Glastonbury & Wells. (Illus.). 20.00 (ISBN 0-906230-40-3, Pub. by Kingsmead Pr England). State Mutual Bk.

--Portraits of Oxford. (Illus.). 20.00 (ISBN 0-906230-95-0, Pub. by Kingsmead Pr England). State Mutual Bk.

Coase, R. H., ed. see Kessel, Reuben A.

Coast Community Colleges. Humanities Through the Arts: Study Guide for the Televised Course. 3rd ed. (Illus.). 288p. 1983. 16.95 (ISBN 0-07-011474-9). McGraw.

Coast, John. Recruit to Revolution: Adventure & Politics in Indonesia. LC 76-179179. Repr. of 1952 ed. 16.00 (ISBN 0-404-54809-1). AMS Pr.

Coastal Engineering International Conference, 15th, Honolulu, Hawaii, July 1976 & American Society of Civil Engineers. Coastal Engineering: 1976, 4 vols. 2242p. 1977. Set. pap. 110.00x (ISBN 0-87262-083-2). Am Soc Civil Eng.

Coastal Engineering International Conference, 16th, Hamburg, Germany, Aug. 1978. Coastal Engineering: 1978, 3 vols. American Society of Civil Engineers, compiled By. 3096p. 1979. pap. 110.00x (ISBN 0-87262-190-1). Am Soc Civil Eng.

Coastal Research Center. Georges Bank. Backus, Richard H., ed. (Illus.). 1984. write for info. MIT Pr.

Coate, Evelyn. Wanted: Man to Love. (Candlelight Ecstasy Ser.: No. 342). 1985. pap. 2.25 (ISBN 0-440-19358-3). Dell.

Coate, H. H. & Oates, L. F. A Grammar of Ngarinjin, Western Australia. (Aias Linguistics Ser.: No. 10). 1970. pap. text ed. 7.25x (ISBN 0-85575-098-7). Humanities.

Coate, Mary. Social Life in Stuart England. LC 77-109721. (Illus.). 1971. Repr. of 1924 ed. lib. bdg. 15.00x (ISBN 0-8371-4211-3, COSL). Greenwood.

Coate, Roger A. Global Issue Regimes. LC 82-11269. 238p. 1982. 38.95 (ISBN 0-03-059276-3). Praeger.

Coate, Roger A., jt. auth. see Feld, Werner J.

Coates, Adrian. Prelude to History. LC 73-13022. (Illus.). 289p. 1974. Repr. of 1951 ed. lib. bdg. 15.00x (ISBN 0-8371-7109-1, COPH). Greenwood.

Coates, Albert & Paul, James C. The School Segregation Decision: A Report to the Governor of North Carolina on the Decision of the Supreme Court of the United States on the 17th of May 1954. (Law & Government Ser.). x, 132p. 1981. Repr. of 1954 ed. lib. bdg. 22.50x (ISBN 0-8377-2607-7). Rothman.

Coates, Archie. The Amateur Keeper: A Handbook for the Small Shoot. (Illus.). 160p. 1978. 12.95 (ISBN 0-233-96960-8, Andre Deutsch). David & Charles.

--The Amateur Keeper: A Handbook for the Small Shoot. (Illus.). 160p. 1978. 12.95 (ISBN 0-233-96960-8, Pub. by A Deutsch England). David & Charles.

Coates, Austin. City of Broken Promises. (Writing in Asia Ser.). 1978. pap. text ed. 5.95x (ISBN 0-686-65314-9, 00246). Heinemann Ed.

--A Macao Narrative. LC 79-101322. (Asian Studies). 1978. pap. text ed. 8.00x (ISBN 0-686-65321-1, 00128). Heinemann Ed.

--A Mountain of Light. 1977. pap. text ed. 9.95x (ISBN 0-686-60451-2, 00115). Heinemann Ed.

--Myself a Mandarin. (Writing in Asia Ser.). pap. text ed. 7.00x (ISBN 0-686-65638-5, 00203). Heinemann Ed.

--Numerology. 126p. 1980. pap. 3.95 (ISBN 0-8065-0499-4). Citadel Pr.

--Numerology. 128p. 1984. 4.95 (ISBN 0-8065-0892-2). Citadel Pr.

Coates, Belle. Mak. (gr. 5 up). 1981. 8.95 (ISBN 0-395-31603-0, Pub. by Parnassus). HM.

Coates, C. A. John Cowper Powys in Search of a Landscape. LC 81-19081. 204p. 1982. 28.50x (ISBN 0-389-20191-X). B&N Imports.

Coates, C. R. Developing a Commanding Personality. LC 79-23634. 180p. 1981. 17.95x (ISBN 0-88229-414-8). Nelson-Hall.

Coates, Charles H. & Pellegrin, Roland J. Military Sociology. 1965. pap. text ed. 4.95x (ISBN 0-686-00733-6). Md Bk Exch.

Coates, D. The Labour Party & the Struggle for Socialism. LC 74-19526. 272p. 1975. 39.50 (ISBN 0-521-20740-1); pap. 16.95 (ISBN 0-521-09939-0). Cambridge U Pr.

Coates, D. F. Rock Mechanics Principles. 442p. 1981. pap. text ed. 26.40 (ISBN 0-660-10933-6, Pub. by Inst Engineering Australia). Brookfield Pub Co.

Coates, D. R. Geology & Society: A New York Publication. 275p. 1985. 49.95 (ISBN 0-412-25160-4, NO. 5061, Pub. by Chapman & Hall England); pap. 22.50 (ISBN 0-412-25170-1, NO. 5062, Pub. by Chapman & Hall England). Methuen Inc.

Coates, D. R., ed. Environmental Geomorphology & Landscape Conservation: Non-Urban, Vol. 3. LC 72-77882. (Benchmark Papers in Geology: Vol. 8). 483p. 1973. 57.95 (ISBN 0-87933-040-6). Van Nos Reinhold.

--Environmental Geomorphology & Landscape Conservation: Prior to 1900, Vol. 1. LC 72-77882. (Benchmark Papers in Geology: Vol.1). 485p. 1972. 57.95 (ISBN 0-87933-005-8). Van Nos Reinhold.

Coates, David. The Context of British Politics. LC 84-12931. 288p. (Orig.). 1984. pap. 12.95 (ISBN 0-09-159151-1, Pub by Hutchinson Educ). Longwood Pub Group.

--Labour in Power? A Study of the Labour Government 1974-1979. LC 79-42850. pap. 79.00 (ISBN 0-317-27689-1). Bks Demand UMI.

Coates, David & Johnston, Gordon, eds. Socialist Agruments. (Illus.). 248p. 1983. 39.95x (ISBN 0-85520-650-0); pap. 9.95x (ISBN 0-85520-651-9). Basil Blackwell.

Coates, Donald R. Environmental Geology. LC 80-21272. 731p. 1981. text ed. 37.50x (ISBN 0-471-06379-7). Wiley.

Coates, Donald R., ed. Environmental Geomorphology & Landscape Conservation, 2. V. LC 72-77882. (Benchmark Papers in Geology Ser.). (Illus.). 1974. 66.00 (ISBN 0-12-786242-0). Acad Pr.

--Gas Chromatography. 1960. 79.50 (ISBN 0-12-177350-7). Acad Pr.

--Geomorphology & Engineering. (Binghamton Symposia in Geomorphology: International Ser.: No. 7). (Illus.). 384p. 1980. text ed. 45.00x (ISBN 0-04-551040-7). Allen Unwin.

--Glacial Gemorphology: Binghampton Symposia in Geomorphology. (International Ser.: No. 5). (Illus.). 304p. 1981. text ed. 35.00x (ISBN 0-04-551045-8). Allen Unwin.

--Reviews in Engineering Geology, Vol. 3: Landslides. LC 62-51690. (Illus.). 1977. pap. 27.00 (ISBN 0-8137-4103-3). Geol Soc.

Coates, Donald R. & Vitek, John D., eds. Thresholds in Geomorphology. (Binghamton Symposia in Geomorphology Ser.: Vol. 9). (Illus.). 512p. (Orig.). 1980. text ed. 50.00x (ISBN 0-04-551033-4). Allen Unwin.

Coates, Donald R., ed. see Urban Geomorphology Symposium (1974: Miami Beach, Fl.) Staff.

Coates, Edward & Flynn, Richard B., eds. Planning Facilities for Athletics, Physical Education & Recreation. rev. 1984 ed. 1984. 26.95x (ISBN 0-87670-095-4); pap. 21.95x (ISBN 0-87670-096-2). AAHPERD.

Coates, F. G. Marie Corelli: The Writer & the Woman. 1977. lib. bdg. 59.95 (ISBN 0-8490-2208-8). Gordon Pr.

Coates, G. E., et al. Principles of Organometallic Chemistry. 1968. 17.95 (ISBN 0-412-15350-5, NO. 6062, Pub. by Chapman & Hall). Methuen Inc.

Coates, Gary. Resettling America: Energy, Ecology & Community. (Illus.). 400p. 1981. 27.50 (ISBN 0-931790-52-2); pap. 17.95x (ISBN 0-931790-06-9). Brick Hse Pub.

Coates, Gary & Sanker, Joyce. Ali Baba & the Thieves. 1982. pap. 4.95 (ISBN 0-686-38754-6). Eldridge Pub.

Coates, Gary J., ed. Alternative Learning Environments. LC 74-1268. (Community Development Ser: Vol. 7). (Illus.). 387p. 1974. 35.00 (ISBN 0-87933-037-6). Van Nos Reinhold.

Coates, Gary M., jt. auth. see Sanker, Joyce.

Coates, Henry. Palestrina. LC 78-66885. (Encore Music Editions Ser.). (Illus.). 1979. Repr. of 1938 ed. 22.50 (ISBN 0-88355-732-0). Hyperion Conn.

Coates, Henry T., ed. Children's Book of Poetry. facs. ed. LC 70-149101. (Granger Index Reprint Ser). 1879. 36.50 (ISBN 0-8369-6226-5). Ayer Co Pubs.

--Fireside Encyclopedia of Poetry: Comprising the Best Poems of the Most Famous Writers, English & American. facsimile ed. LC 79-160903. (Granger Index Reprint Ser.). Repr. of 1878 ed. 48.00 (ISBN 0-8369-6266-4). Ayer Co Pubs.

Coates, Hugh & Stanford, J. R. Growing Wheat & Making Bread on a Small Scale. (Self-Sufficient Living Ser.). 96p. 1980. 25.00x (ISBN 0-7225-0594-9, Pub. by Thorsons England). State Mutual Bk.

Coates, J. & Coates, Killian. Heavy Loses. 1985. 22.95 (ISBN 0-670-80484-3). Viking.

Coates, James. Photographing the Invisible. LC 72-9189. (The Literature of Photography Ser.). Repr. of 1911 ed. 31.00 (ISBN 0-405-04899-8). Ayer Co Pubs.

Coates, Jennifer. The Semantics of the Modal Auxiliaries. (Illus.). 272p. 1982. 33.00 (ISBN 0-7099-0735-4, Pub. by Vikas India). Longwood Pub Group.

Coates, John. Chesterton & the Edwardian Cultural Crisis. 279p. 1984. pap. text ed. 19.45x (ISBN 0-85958-444-5, Pub. by U Hull England). Humanities.

--The Watsons: Jane Austen's Fragment Continued and Completed by John Coates. 1978. Repr. of 1958 ed. lib. bdg. 25.00 (ISBN 0-8495-0724-3). Arden Lib.

Coates, Ken. Heresies: Resist Much, Obey Little. 158p. 1982. 30.00 (ISBN 0-85124-355-X); pap. 9.50 (ISBN 0-85124-356-8). Dufour.

Coates, Kevin. Geometry, Proportion, & the Art of Lutherie. (Illus.). 224p. 1985. 42.00x (ISBN 0-19-816139-5). Oxford U Pr.

Coates, Killian, jt. auth. see Coates, J.

Coates, Marie E. Germ-Free Animal in Research. LC 68-24698. (Illus.). 1968. 49.00 (ISBN 0-12-177150-4). Acad Pr.

Coates, Marvin & Pederson, Donald. Thinking in English: Practice with the Complex Sentences for Students of ESL. 1984. pap. text ed. 12.95 (ISBN 0-316-14894-6). Little.

Coates, Noel. Lancashire & Yorkshire Railway Miscellany. 160p. price not set (ISBN 0-86093-188-9, Pub. by ORPC Ltd UK). State Mutual Bk.

Coates, Paul. The Realist Fantasy: Fiction & Reality Since Clarissa. LC 83-8637. 225p. 1983. 22.50 (ISBN 0-312-66524-5). St Martin.

--The Story of the Lost Reflection: The Alienation of the Image in Western & Polish Cinema. 208p. (Orig.). 1985. 25.00 (ISBN 0-8052-7262-3, Pub. by Verso England); pap. 9.95 (ISBN 0-8052-7263-1, Pub. by Verso England). Schocken.

--Words after Speech: A Comparative Study of Romanticism & Symbolism. 194p. 1985. 25.00 (ISBN 0-312-88936-4). St Martin.

Coates, Penelope W., et al. Developing & Regenerating Vertebrate Nervous Systems. LC 83-12055. (Neurology & Neurobiology Ser.: Vol. 6). 284p. 1983. 56.00 (ISBN 0-8451-2705-5). A R Liss.

Coates, R., et al. Sructural Analysis. 2nd ed. 1980. pap. 35.95 (ISBN 0-442-30757-8). Van Nos Reinhold.

Coates, R. F. Modern Communication Systems. 2nd ed. (Electronic & Electrical Engineering Ser.). (Illus.). 405p. 1984. text ed. 39.95x (ISBN 0-333-33344-6). Scholium Intl.

Coates, Robert. Investment Strategy. (Illus.). 1978. text ed. 31.95 (ISBN 0-07-011471-4). McGraw.

Coates, Robert M. The Outlaw Years: The History of the Land Pirates of The Natchez Trace. 1979. Repr. of 1930 ed. lib. bdg. 25.00 (ISBN 0-8495-0929-7). Arden Lib.

--The Outlaw Years: The History of the Land Pirates of the Natchez Trace. LC 74-1087. (Illus.). 307p. 1974. Repr. of 1930 ed. 48.00x (ISBN 0-8103-3961-7). Gale.

--Wisteria Cottage. 1985. 5.95 (ISBN 0-87795-710-X). Arbor Hse.

--Yesterday's Burdens: A Novel. LC 74-23583. (Lost American Fiction Ser.). 275p. 1975. 7.95 (ISBN 0-8093-0717-0). S Ill U Pr.

Coates, Robert M., ed. Organic Syntheses, Vol. 59. LC 21-17747. (Series on Organic Synthesis). 1980. 26.95 (ISBN 0-471-05963-3, Pub. by Wiley-Interscience). Wiley.

Coates, Roger. Introduction to Importing. 160p. (Orig.). 1985. pap. 13.50 (ISBN 0-85941-310-1, Pub. by Woodhead-Faulkner). Longwood Pub Group.

Coates, Ruth A. Great American Naturalists. LC 73-21989. (Pull Ahead Bks). Orig. Title: Famous Great American Naturalists. (Illus.). 104p. (gr. 5-10). 1974. PLB 5.95 (ISBN 0-8225-0467-7). Lerner Pubns.

Coates, S. D., et al, eds. Electronic Maintenance, Vol. 1. (Engineering Craftsmen: No. J4). (Illus.). 1969. spiral bdg. 45.00x (ISBN 0-85083-027-3). Trans-Atlantic.

Coates, Sanford E. Physical Research & Spiritism. (Illus.). 117p. 1983. 79.85 (ISBN 0-89920-056-7). Am Inst Psych.

--Psychical Research & Spiritualism. (Illus.). 1980. deluxe ed. 69.75 (ISBN 0-89920-006-0). Am Classical Coll Pr.

Coates, Thomas. The Sermon on the Mount for Today. LC 77-184. 1979. pap. 2.95x (ISBN 0-915644-13-4). Clayton Pub Hse.

Coates, Thomas J. Promoting Adolescent Health: A Dialog in Research & Practice. 444p. 1982. 48.50 (ISBN 0-12-177380-9). Acad Pr.

Coates, Thomas J., jt. auth. see Goodwin, Dwight L.

Coates, William P. & Coates, Zelda. Soviets in Central Asia. LC 73-88983. Repr. of 1951 ed. lib. bdg. 29.75x (ISBN 0-8371-2091-8, COSA). Greenwood.

Coates, Willson H., jt. auth. see Cope, Esther S.

Coates, Willson H., jt. ed. see Cope, Esther S.

Coates, Willson H., ed. see D'Ewes, Simonds.

Coates, Willson H., et al, eds. The Private Journals of the Long Parliament: January 3 to March 5, 1642. LC 81-3323. 630p. 1982. text ed. 77.00x (ISBN 0-300-02545-9). Yale U Pr.

Coates, Zelda, jt. auth. see Coates, William P.

Coatesville-Jefferson Conference on Addiction, 1st, October 1977. Addiction Research & Treatment Converging Trends: Proceedings. Gottheil, E. L., et al, eds. LC 78-23703. 1979. 21.00 (ISBN 0-08-023025-3). Pergamon.

Coats, A. W., ed. Economists in Parliament: An International Comparative Study. LC 81-9858. (Illus.). 383p. 1982. 21.00 (ISBN 0-8223-0459-7). Duke.

Coats, Alice M. Lord Bute. (Lifelines Ser.: No. 27). (Illus.). 64p. (Orig.). 1983. pap. 3.50 (ISBN 0-85263-272-X, Pub. by Shire Pubns England). Seven Hills Bks.

Coats, George W. From Canaan to Egypt: Structural & Theological Context for the Joseph Story. LC 75-11382. (Catholic Biblical Quarterly Monographs: No. 4). xi, 101p. 1976. pap. 2.50 (ISBN 0-915170-03-5). Catholic Biblical.

--Genesis: With an Introduction to Narrative. (Forms of the Old Testament Literature Ser.: Vol. 1). 368p. (Orig.). 1984. pap. 21.95 (ISBN 0-8028-1954-0). Eerdmans.

Coats, Heather & King, Alan. Patient Assessment: A Handbook for Therapists. (Illus.). 1983. pap. 8.75 (ISBN 0-443-02421-9). Churchill.

Coats J & P. Crochet Stitches & Edgings. LC 78-50728. (Illus.). 1978. pap. 2.25 (ISBN 0-684-15642-3, SL796, ScribT). Scribner.

Coats, J. & P. Ltd. Fifty Counted Thread Embroidery Stitches. LC 78-50729. (Illus.). 1978. pap. 2.25 (ISBN 0-684-15643-1, SL797, ScribT). Scribner.

Coats, Joel. Insecticide Mode of Action. 472p. 1982. 59.50 (ISBN 0-12-177120-2). Acad Pr.

Coats, R. B. & Parkin, A. Computer Models in the Social Sciences. (Orig.). 1977. pap. text ed. 17.95 (ISBN 0-316-14890-3). Little.

Coats, R. H. John Galsworthy As a Dramatic Artist. LC 76-22510. Repr. of 1926 ed. lib. bdg. 25.00 (ISBN 0-8414-3580-4). Folcroft.

Coats, Robert B. John Bunyan. LC 77-9277. 1977. lib. bdg. 15.00 (ISBN 0-8414-1804-7). Folcroft.

Coats, Sandra & Sandel, Mary Anne. Paragraph Writing. 320p. 1986. pap. text ed. 13.95 (ISBN 0-13-648569-3). P-H.

Coats, Warren L. & Khatkhate, Deena R., Jr., eds. Money & Monetary Policy in Less Developed Countries: A Survey of Issues & Evidence. LC 79-42703. (Illus.). 834p. 1980. pap. 22.00 (ISBN 0-08-024042-9). Pergamon.

Coats, William S. Geography of Hudson's Bay: Being the Remarks of Captain W. Coats in Many Voyages to That Locality Between the Years 1727-51. Barrow, John, ed. (Hakluyt Society. First Ser.: No. 11). 1964. 24.50 (ISBN 0-8337-0180-0). B Franklin.

Coatsworth, Elizabeth. Cat Who Went to Heaven. LC 58-10917. (Illus.). 72p. (gr. 4-6). 1967. 9.95 (ISBN 0-02-719710-7); pap. 3.95x (ISBN 0-02-042580-5). Macmillan.

--The Cat Who Went to Heaven. LC 58-10917. (gr. 3-6). 1972. pap. 3.95 (ISBN 0-02-042580-5, Collier). Macmillan.

--Littlest House. (Illus.). (gr. 3-5). 1967. 4.25g (ISBN 0-02-721050-2). Macmillan.

--Marra's World. LC 75-9520. (Illus.). 83p. (gr. 3-5). 1975. 11.75 (ISBN 0-688-80007-6); PLB 11.88 (ISBN 0-688-84007-8). Greenwillow.

--Princess & the Lion. (Illus.). (gr. 3-7). 1963. PLB 5.99 (ISBN 0-394-91520-8). Pantheon.

--Pure Magic. LC 72-92435. (Illus.). 80p. (gr. 3-6). 1973. 8.95 (ISBN 0-02-721500-8, 72150). Macmillan.

--Snow Parlor & Other Bedtime Stories. (Illus.). 64p. (gr. k-3). 1972. pap. 0.95 (ISBN 0-448-05442-6, Pub. by Tempo). Ace Bks.

--Under the Green Willow. LC 84-1471. (Illus.). 24p. (gr. k-3). 1984. 9.25 (ISBN 0-688-03845-X); PLB 8.59 (ISBN 0-688-03846-8). Greenwillow.

--The Werefox. LC 74-20675. Orig. Title: Pure Magic. (Illus.). 80p. (gr. 3-6). 1975. pap. 1.25 (ISBN 0-02-042760-3). Macmillan.

Coatsworth, Elizabeth, ed. see Beston, Henry.

Coatsworth, John H. Growth Against Development: The Economic Impact of Railroads in Porfirian Mexico. LC 80-8662. (Origins of Modern Mexico Ser.). (Illus.). 249p. 1981. 20.00 (ISBN 0-87580-075-0). N Ill U Pr.

Cobarrubias, Juan & Fishman, Joshua A., eds. Progress in Language Planning: International Perspectives, No. xi. LC 82-22310. (Contributions to the Sociology of Language Ser.: No. 31). 383p. 1983. 49.95 (ISBN 90-279-3358-8); pap. 24.95 (ISBN 90-279-3388-X). Mouton.

Cobb. Arrest. (The Law in South Carolina Ser.). 24.95 (ISBN 0-686-90974-7). Harrison Co GA.

--For You. 4.00 (ISBN 0-8065-0314-9). Citadel Pr.

--Process & Pattern: Controlled Composition Practice for ESL Students. 1984. write for info. (ISBN 0-534-03705-4). Wadsworth Pub.

--Recommendations for the Practice of Clinical Neurophysiology. 1983. 9.95 (ISBN 0-444-80505-2, I-402-83). Elsevier.

--Settlements: Strategy, Law & Litigation. (The Law in South Carolina Ser.). 24.95 (ISBN 0-686-90984-4). Harrison Co GA.

Cobb & Eldridge. Damages, Georgia Law. 2nd ed. 870p. 1984. 87.95 (ISBN 0-317-14544-4). Harrison Co GA.

Cobb, A. Beatrix. Medical & Psychological Aspects of Disability. (Illus.). 384p. 1977. 40.75x (ISBN 0-398-02653-X). C C Thomas.

Cobb, A. Beatrix, ed. Special Problems in Rehabilitation. (Illus.). 456p. 1974. 25.00x (ISBN 0-398-02787-0). C C Thomas.

Cobb, Alice, jt. auth. see Fahs, Sophia L.

Cobb, Barbara & Williams, David. Medical Surgical Nursing. (Nursing Study Aid Ser.). 1978. pap. 8.00 (ISBN 0-87488-541-8). Med Exam.

Cobb, Boughton. A Field Guide to Ferns & Their Related Families. (Peterson Field Guide Ser.). 1977. 15.95 (ISBN 0-395-07560-2); pap. 10.95 (ISBN 0-395-19431-8). HM.

Cobb, Buell E., Jr. The Sacred Harp: A Tradition & Its Music. LC 76-12680. 256p. 1978. 15.00x (ISBN 0-8203-0426-3). U of Ga Pr.

Cobb, C. G. The Bad Times Primer: A Complete Guide to Survival on a Budget. LC 81-52089. (Illus.). 336p. (Orig.). 1981. pap. 14.95 (ISBN 0-9606608-0-1). Times Pr.

Cobb, Carl W. Contemporary Spanish Poetry: Eighteen Ninety-Eight to Nineteen Sixty-Three. LC 75-23016. (World Authors Ser.). 1976. lib. bdg. 14.50 (ISBN 0-8057-6202-7, Twayne). G K Hall.

--Federico Garcia Lorca. (World Authors Ser.). 1968. lib. bdg. 13.95 (ISBN 0-8057-2544-X, Twayne). G K Hall.

Cobb, Carl W., tr. from Span. Lorca's Romancero Gitano: A Ballad Translation & Critical Study. LC 82-17454. 136p. 1983. text ed. 15.00x (ISBN 0-87805-177-5). U Pr of Miss.

Cobb, Charles K., Jr., et al. Taxation in Italy as of March 1, 1964. LC 64-25047. 1964. 19.00 (ISBN 0-685-08540-6, 4483). Commerce.

Cobb, Charles M. Practical Communication. LC 77-28696. 1978. pap. text ed. 16.90x (ISBN 0-673-16336-9). Scott F.

--The Shapes of Prose. LC 74-14979. 1975. pap. text ed. 14.95 (ISBN 0-03-011326-1, HoltC); instructor's manual 19.95 (ISBN 0-03-013316-5). HR&W.

Cobb, D. Starting to Sail. 2nd ed. (Illus.). 1973. pap. 5.00 (ISBN 0-540-07132-3). Heinman.

Cobb, David A. Guide to U.S. Map Resources. avail. ALA.

--New Hampshire Maps to 1900: An Annotated Checklist. LC 78-63588. 126p. 1981. pap. 14.00x (ISBN 0-87451-166-6). U Pr of New Eng.

Cobb, Douglas. Mastering Symphony. (Illus.). 763p. Date not set. 24.95 (ISBN 0-89588-244-2). SYBEX.

Cobb, Douglas & DeVoney, Chris. Introducing IBM PCjr. LC 83-63252. (Illus.). 245p. 1983. pap. 12.95 (ISBN 0-88022-065-1, 117). Que Corp.

Cobb, Douglas, jt. auth. see Andersen, Dick.

Cobb, Douglas, et al. One-Two-Three for Business. 338p. 1984. pap. 16.95 (ISBN 0-88022-038-4, 34); IBM-PC format. disk 79.90 (240). Que Corp.

Cobb, Douglas F. & Cobb, Gena B. SuperCalc SuperModels for Business. LC 82-42765. (Illus.). 215p. (Orig.). 1983. pap. 16.95 (ISBN 0-88022-007-4, 9); software disk 79.90 ea. Osborne format (221). IBM-PC format (222). Eight-inch SS/SD format (223). Apple II format (224). Que Corp.

--VisiCalc Models for Business. LC 82-42767. (Que's IBM-PC Library). (Illus.). 210p. (Orig.). 1983. pap. 16.95 (ISBN 0-88022-017-1, 7); software disk 79.90 ea. IBM-PC format (225). Apple II (226). Apple III format (227). Que Corp.

Cobb, Douglas F. & LeBlond, Geoffrey. Using 1-2-3. (Illus.). 420p. 1983. pap. 17.95 (ISBN 0-88022-045-7, 39). Que Corp.

Cobb, Douglas F., et al. Multiplan Models for Business. (Illus.). 272p. 1983. pap. 15.95 (ISBN 0-88022-037-6, 33); software disk 79.90 ea. IBM-PC format (260). Eight-inch SS/SD format (263). Apple II format (262). Que Corp.

Cobb, Edwin L. No Cease Fires: The War on Poverty in Roanoke Valley. 192p. 1984. 13.95 (ISBN 0-932020-28-3); pap. 8.95 (ISBN 0-932020-29-1). Seven Locks Pr.

Cobb, G. C., jt. auth. see Murray, R. L.

Cobb, Gena B., jt. auth. see Cobb, Douglas F.

Cobb, Hazel. Around the Keys & Around the Keys Again. 64p. (gr. 3-6). 1960. pap. text ed. 9.95 (ISBN 0-87487-626-5). Birch Tree Gr.

Cobb, Henry V. The Forecast of Fulfillment: A Review of Research on Predictive Assessment of the Adult Retarded for Social & Vocational Adjustment. LC 72-3084. (Illus.). 176p. 1972. 5.35x (ISBN 0-8077-1168-3). Tchrs Coll.

Cobb, Howell. A Scriptural Examination of the Institution of Slavery in the United States: With Its Objects & Purposes. LC 72-6455. (Black Heritage Library Collection Ser). 1972. Repr. of 1856 ed. 16.00 (ISBN 0-8369-9163-X). Ayer Co Pubs.

Cobb, Hubbard. How to Buy & Remodel the Older House. 1972. pap. 8.95 (ISBN 0-02-079300-6, Collier). Macmillan.

Cobb, Hubbard H. Improvements That Increase the Value of Your House. (McGraw-Hill Paperback Ser.). 1976. pap. 6.95 (ISBN 0-07-011488-9). McGraw.

Cobb, Irvin S. Exit Laughing. LC 73-19798. 576p. 1974. Repr. of 1941 ed. 53.00x (ISBN 0-8103-3687-1). Gale.

--Fishead. (H. P. Lovecraft's Favorite Horror Stories Ser.). 14p. (Orig.). 1985. pap. 1.50 (ISBN 0-318-04712-8). Necronomicon.

--Ladies & Gentlemen. facsimile ed. LC 78-106266. (Short Story Index Reprint Ser.). 1927. 18.00 (ISBN 0-8369-3303-6). Ayer Co Pubs.

--Old Judge Priest. LC 75-120561. (BCL Ser.: No. I). Repr. of 1916 ed. 28.00 (ISBN 0-404-01578-6). AMS Pr.

--Speaking of Operations. LC 71-92422. 65p. 1928. Repr. 19.00x (ISBN 0-403-00556-6). Scholarly.

--Those Times & These. LC 72-5862. (Short Story Index Reprint Ser). Repr. of 1917 ed. 21.00 (ISBN 0-8369-4201-9). Ayer Co Pubs.

Cobb, J. B., jt. auth. see Birch, L. C.

Cobb, J. E. Cobb's Baptist Church Manual. 1979. pap. 2.50 (ISBN 0-89114-056-5). Baptist Pub Hse.

Cobb, J. S., jt. auth. see Philips, B. F.

Cobb, J. Stanley & Phillips, Bruce F., eds. The Biology & Management of Lobsters: Vol. 1, Physiology & Behavior. LC 79-6803. 1980. 60.50 (ISBN 0-12-177401-5). Acad Pr.

--The Biology & Management of Lobsters: Vol. 2, Ecology & Management. LC 79-6803. 1980. 49.50 (ISBN 0-12-177402-3). Acad Pr.

Cobb, James, ed. see Brant, Russell A.

Cobb, James C. Industrialization & Southern Society, 1877-1984. LC 84-5083. (New Perspectives on the South Ser.). 200p. 1984. 19.00x (ISBN 0-8131-0304-5). U Pr of Ky.

--The Selling of the South: The Southern Crusade for Industrial Development, 1936 - 1980. LC 81-18594. 293p. 1982. text ed. 25.00x (ISBN 0-8071-0994-0). La State U Pr.

Cobb, James C. & Namorato, Michael V., eds. The New Deal & the South. LC 84-5109. (Chancellor's Symposium Ser.). 184p. 1984. 15.00x (ISBN 0-87805-218-6); pap. 8.95 (ISBN 0-87805-219-4). U Pr of Miss.

Cobb, Jocelyn. Belmullet. 336p. 1983. 12.95 (ISBN 0-312-07473-5). St Martin.

Cobb, John. Babyshock: A Survival Guide for the New Mother. (Illus.). 219p. 1983. 15.95 (ISBN 0-13-056440-0); pap. 7.95 (ISBN 0-13-056432-X). P-H.

Cobb, John B., jt. auth. see Birch, Charles.

Cobb, John B., Jr. Beyond Dialogue: Toward a Mutual Transformation of Christianity & Buddhism. LC 82-8389. 176p. 1982. pap. 8.95 (ISBN 0-8006-1647-2, 1-1647). Fortress.

--Christ in a Pluralistic Age. LC 74-820. 286p. 1984. pap. 11.95 (ISBN 0-664-24522-6). Westminster.

--God & the World. LC 69-11374. 138p. 1969. pap. 5.95 (ISBN 0-664-24860-8). Westminster.

--Praying for Jennifer. (Orig.). 1985. pap. 4.95 (ISBN 0-8358-0520-4). Upper Room.

--Process Theology As Political Theology. LC 82-1845. 174p. (Orig.). 1982. pap. 8.95 (ISBN 0-664-24417-3). Westminster.

--The Structure of Christian Existence. 1979. pap. 6.95 (ISBN 0-8164-2229-X, Pub. by Seabury). Winston Pr.

--Theology & Pastoral Care. Clinebell, Howard J. & Stone, Howard W., eds. LC 76-7862. (Creative Pastoral Care & Counseling Ser.). 96p. 1977. pap. 4.25 (ISBN 0-8006-0557-8, 1-557). Fortress.

--To Pray or Not to Pray. 1974. pap. 1.25x (ISBN 0-8358-0310-4). Upper Room.

Cobb, John B., Jr. & Griffin, David R. Process Theology: An Introductory Exposition. LC 76-10352. 192p. 1976. pap. 7.95 (ISBN 0-664-24743-1). Westminster.

Cobb, John B., Jr., jt. auth. see Tracy, David.

Cobb, John B., Jr. & Gamwell, Franklin I., eds. Existence & Actuality: Conversations with Charles Hartshorne. LC 84-2476. 188p. 1985. 20.00x (ISBN 0-226-11122-9); pap. 9.95x (ISBN 0-226-11123-7). U of Chicago Pr.

Cobb, John B., Jr. & Schroeder, W. Widick, eds. Process Philosophy & Social Thought. LC 80-70781. (Studies in Religion & Society). 263p. 1981. 24.95x (ISBN 0-913348-18-X); pap. 10.95x (ISBN 0-913348-19-8). Ctr Sci Study.

Cobb, John B., Jr., jt. ed. see Griffin, David R.

Cobb, John B., Jr., jt. ed. see Robinson, James M.

Cobb, John E., Jr. Cobb Chronicles. LC 85-71704. (Illus.). 225p. 1985. 27.00 (ISBN 0-9606128-5-8). Durant Pub.

--Cobbs & Cobbs: Early-Virginians. LC 77-151286. (Illus.). 128p. 1981. pap. 12.50 (ISBN 0-9606128-1-5). Durant Pub.

--The Complete Book for Doing the Family History. LC 80-70108. (Illus.). 139p. (Orig.). 1981. pap. 10.00 (ISBN 0-9606128-3-1). Durant Pub.

Cobb, Jonathan & Sennett, Richard. Hidden Injuries of Class. 1973. pap. 4.95 (ISBN 0-394-71940-9, V940, Vin). Random.

Cobb, Joseph J. An Introduction to Educational Law: For Administrators & Teachers. (Illus.). 204p. 1981. 24.50x (ISBN 0-398-04158-X). C C Thomas.

Cobb, Lawrence. DMSO: The Myths & the Facts. 1980. 3.95 (ISBN 0-686-32616-4). Cancer Control Soc.

Cobb, Linda M. The Error. 1985. 5.95 (ISBN 0-8062-2513-0). Carlton.

Cobb, Loren & Thrall, Robert M., eds. Mathematical Frontiers of the Social & Policy Sciences. (AAAS Selected Symposium Ser.: No. 54). 186p. 1980. 27.00x (ISBN 0-89158-953-8). Westview.

Cobb, Louise S. A Study of the Functions of Physical Education in Higher Education. LC 74-176695. (Columbia University. Teachers College. Contributions to Education: No. 876). Repr. of 1943 ed. 22.50 (ISBN 0-404-55876-3). AMS Pr.

Cobb, Margaret G., ed. see Debussy, Claude.

Cobb, Martha. Harlem, Haiti, & Havana: A Comparative Critical Study of Langston Hughes, Jacques Roumain, & Nicolas Guillen. LC 78-19962. (Illus.). 1979. 20.00 (ISBN 0-914478-90-7); pap. 10.00 (ISBN 0-914478-91-5). Three Continents.

Cobb, Miles A. Federal Regulation of Depository Institutions: Enforcement, Powers & Procedures. LC 83-60089. 400p. 1983. 60.00 (ISBN 0-88262-911-5). Warren.

Cobb, Nancy J., jt. auth. see Stevens-Long, Judith.

Cobb, Nathan & Cole, John. Cityside-Countryside. LC 80-16825. 256p. 1980. 12.95 (ISBN 0-8289-0397-2). Greene.

Cobb, Norman B., ed. see Feldman, Nans A.

Cobb, O., et al. A Performance Data Management Program for Solar Thermal Energy Systems. (Progress in Solar Energy Supplements SERI Ser.). 120p. pap. text ed. cancelled (ISBN 0-89553-101-1). Am Solar Energy.

Cobb, Palmer. Influence of E. T. A. Hoffman on the Tales of Edgar Allen Poe. (North Carolina. University. Philological Club: Vol. 3). Repr. of 1908 ed. 19.50 (ISBN 0-8337-4967-6). B Franklin.

Cobb, Pamela. Inside the Devil's Mouth. LC 75-12074. 42p. 1975. pap. 3.00x (ISBN 0-916418-03-0). Lotus.

Cobb, R. M. Karapetoff, ed. Protein & Synthetic Adhesives for Paper Coating. 1st ed. (TAPPI Press Books). 187p. 1952. 9.95 (ISBN 0-317-36039-6, 01-02BM09). TAPPI.

Cobb, Richard. Armees Revolutionnaires, 2 Vols. (Societe Mouvements Sociaux et Ideologies Etudes 3: No. 3). 1961. Set. pap. text ed. 50.40x (ISBN 90-2796-235-9). Mouton.

--A Classical Education. 160p. 1985. 14.95 (ISBN 0-7011-2936-0, Pub. by Chatto & Windus). Merrimack Pub Cir.

--French & Germans, Germans & French: A Personal Interpretation of France under Two Occupations; 1914-1918, 1940-1944. LC 82-40472. (Tauber Institute Ser.: No. 2). 222p. 1983. 18.50x (ISBN 0-87451-225-5); pap. 8.95 (ISBN 0-87451-318-9). U Pr of New Eng.

--Paris & Its Provinces 1792-1802. 1975. 25.00x (ISBN 0-19-212195-2). Oxford U Pr.

--A Sense of Place. 135p. 1978. text ed. 15.50x (ISBN 0-8419-7100-5). Holmes & Meier.

--Still Life. 9.95 (ISBN 0-318-01620-6). Merrimack Pub Cir.

--Still Life: Sketches from a Tunbridge Wells Childhood. 192p. 1984. 15.95 (ISBN 0-7011-2695-7, Pub. by Chatto & Windus-Hogarth Pr.); pap. 9.95 (ISBN 0-7012-1920-3). Merrimack Pub Cir.

Cobb, Richard C. Death in Paris, 1795-1801: The Records of the Basse-Geole De la Seine. 1978. 21.95x (ISBN 0-19-215843-0). Oxford U Pr.

--Police & the People: French Popular Protest, 1789-1820. 1970. pap. 6.95x (ISBN 0-19-881297-3, OPB). Oxford U Pr.

--Reactions to the French Revolution. 1972. 21.95x (ISBN 0-19-212187-1). Oxford U Pr.

Cobb, Roger W. & Elder, Charles D. Participation in American Politics: The Dynamics of Agenda Building. 2nd ed. LC 83-48052. 224p. 1983. pap. 6.95x (ISBN 0-8018-3086-9). Johns Hopkins.

Cobb, Roger W., jt. auth. see Elder, Charles D.

Cobb, Russell L., jt. auth. see Rice, Marion J.

Cobb, Sanford, ed. see American Booksellers Association.

Cobb, Sanford H. The Rise of Religious Liberty in America. 1978. pap. write for info. (ISBN 0-89102-115-9, Artemis). B Franklin.

--Rise of Religious Liberty in America: A History. LC 68-27517. 541p. 1968. Repr. of 1902 ed. 32.50 (ISBN 0-8154-0051-9). Cooper Sq.

--The Rise of Religious Liberty in America: A History. (American Studies). 1970. Repr. of 1902 ed. 30.00 (ISBN 0-384-09445-7). Johnson Repr.

Cobb, Sidney. Frequency of the Rheumatic Diseases. LC 72-158427. (Vital & Health Statistics Monographs, American Public Health Association). (Illus.). 1971. 12.50x (ISBN 0-674-32325-4). Harvard U Pr.

Cobb, Stanley J. The American Lobster: The Biology of Homarus Americanus. (Marine Technical Report Ser: No. 49). 1976. pap. 2.00 (ISBN 0-938412-01-9). URI MAS.

Cobb, Thomas R. Historical Sketch of Slavery. LC 71-92422. 1858. 15.00x (ISBN 0-403-00157-9). Scholarly.

--Historical Sketch of Slavery, from the Earliest Periods. facs. ed. LC 70-83943. (Black Heritage Library Collection). 1858. 17.00 (ISBN 0-8369-8543-5). Ayer Co Pubs.

--An Inquiry into the Law of Negro Slavery in the United States of America. LC 68-55877. Repr. of 1858 ed. cancelled (ISBN 0-8371-0353-3, COI&, Pub. by Negro U Pr). Greenwood.

Cobb, Thomas S., jt. ed. see Showalter, G. H.

Cobb, Vicki. Brave in the Attempt. (Illus.). 128p. (Orig.). 1983. pap. 8.95 (ISBN 0-914771-00-0). Pinwheel Pubs.

--Chemically Active! Experiments You Can Do at Home. LC 83-49490. (Illus.). 160p. (gr. 6 up). 1985. 11.06i (ISBN 0-397-32079-5); PLB 10.89g (ISBN 0-397-32080-9). Lipp Jr Bks.

--Experimentos Cientificos Que Se Pueden Comer. Ortiz, Victoria, ed. LC 78-20550. (Libros Lippincott En Espanol). (Illus.). 1979. PLB 9.89 (ISBN 0-397-31850-2). Lipp Jr Bks.

--Fuzz Does It! LC 81-47758. (Illus.). (gr. 1-3). 1982. 11.06i (ISBN 0-397-31975-4); PLB 10.89g (ISBN 0-397-31976-2); pap. 4.75i (ISBN 0-397-31977-0). Lipp Jr Bks.

--Gobs of Goo. LC 82-48457. (Illus.). 40p. (gr. 1-3). 1983. 10.53i (ISBN 0-397-32021-3); PLB 10.89g (ISBN 0-397-32022-1). Lipp Jr Bks.

--How to Really Fool Yourself: Illusions for All Your Senses. LC 79-9620. (Illus.). 160p. (gr. 5 up). 1981. 10.53i (ISBN 0-397-31906-1); PLB 10.89 (ISBN 0-397-31907-X); pap. 4.95 (ISBN 0-397-31908-8). Lipp Jr Bks.

--Lots of Rot. LC 80-8726. (Illus.). 40p. (gr. 1-3). 1981. 10.89 (ISBN 0-397-31938-X); PLB 9.89 (ISBN 0-397-31939-8); pap. 4.95 (ISBN 0-397-31960-6). Lipp Jr Bks.

--Magic... Naturally: Science Entertainments & Amusements. LC 76-13179. (gr. 6-9). 1976. 10.53i (ISBN 0-397-31631-3); pap. 2.95 (ISBN 0-397-31632-1). Lipp Jr Bks.

--The Monsters Who Died: A Mystery about Dinosaurs. (Illus.). 64p. (gr. 3-6). 1983. 10.95 (ISBN 0-698-20571-5, Coward). Putnam Pub Group.

--More Science Experiments You Can Eat. LC 78-12732. (Illus.). 1979. 9.57i (ISBN 0-397-31828-6); pap. 4.95 (ISBN 0-397-31853-7). Lipp Jr Bks.

--Science Experiments You Can Eat. LC 71-151474. (Illus.). (gr. 7 up). 1972. lib. bdg. 9.89 (ISBN 0-397-31179-6). Lipp Jr Bks.

--Science Experiments You Can Eat. LC 71-151474. (Illus.). 127p. (gr. 5-8). 8.79 (ISBN 0-397-31487-6). Lipp Jr Bks.

--The Scoop on Ice Cream. (How the World Works Science Ser.). (Illus.). 48p. (gr. 4 up). 1985. 10.95 (ISBN 0-316-14895-4); pap. 3.95 (ISBN 0-316-14897-0). Little.

--The Secret Life of Cosmetics: A Science Experiment Book. LC 85-40097. (Illus.). 128p. (gr. 5-9). 1985. 11.06i (ISBN 0-397-32121-X); PLB 10.89g (ISBN 0-397-32122-8). Lipp Jr Bks.

--The Secret Life of Hardware: A Science Experiment Book. LC 81-48607. (Illus.). 96p. (gr. 5 up). 1982. 10.10i (ISBN 0-397-31999-1); PLB 10.89g (ISBN 0-397-32000-0). Lipp Jr Bks.

--The Secret Life of School Supplies. LC 81-47108. (Illus.). 96p. (gr. 5 up). 1981. 9.57i (ISBN 0-397-31924-X); PLB 10.89g (ISBN 0-397-31925-8). Lipp Jr Bks.

--Sneakers Meet Your Feet. (How the World Works Science Ser.). (Illus.). 48p. (gr. 4-6). 1985. 10.05 (ISBN 0-316-14896-2); pap. 3.95 (ISBN 0-316-14898-9). Little.

Cobb, Vicki & Darling, Kathy. Bet You Can! Science Possibilities to Fool You. (Illus.). 112p. (gr. 3-7). 1983. pap. 2.25 (ISBN 0-380-82180-X, 87437-7, Camelot). Avon.

--Bet You Can't! Science Impossibilities to Fool You. LC 79-9254. (Illus.). (gr. 5 up). 1980. 10.00 (ISBN 0-688-41905-4); PLB 10.88 (ISBN 0-688-51905-9). Lothrop.

--Bet You Can't: Science Impossibilities to Fool You. (Illus.). 128p. (gr. 3-7). 1983. pap. 1.95 (ISBN 0-380-54502-0, 60068-4, Camelot). Avon.

Cobb, W. & Morocutti, eds. Evoked Potentials. (Supplements to Electroencephalography & Clinical Neurophysiology: Vol. 26). 218p. (Proceedings). 1968. 38.75 (ISBN 0-444-40130-X, Biomedical Pr). Elsevier.

Cobb, W. A. & Van Duyn, H. Contemporary Clinical Neurophysiology. (Electroencephalography & Clinical Neurophysiology Ser.: Vol. 34, Suppl.). 578p. 1978. 110.25 (ISBN 0-444-80056-5, Biomedical Pr). Elsevier.

Cobb, W. A., jt. ed. see Buser, P. A.

Cobb, Walter J., tr. see Hugo, Victor.

Cobb, William. Coming of Age at the Y: Delores Lovelady's Hilarious Adventures in Nashville's Opryland. 1984. 12.00 (ISBN 0-916620-72-7). Portals Pr.

Cobb, William & Price, Andrew. History of the Mingo Indians. 1974. Repr. of 1921 ed. 3.50 (ISBN 0-87012-194-4). McClain.

Cobb, William, et al, trs. see Merleau-Ponty, Maurice.

Cobb, Mrs. Wilton P. History of Dodge County. LC 79-11196. (Illus.). 1979. Repr. of 1932 ed. 21.50 (ISBN 0-87152-293-4). Reprint.

Cobban, A. B. King's Hall Within the University of Cambridge in the Later Middle Ages. LC 69-10193. (Studies in Medieval Life & Thought: No. 1). (Illus.). 1969. 57.50 (ISBN 0-521-04678-5). Cambridge U Pr.

Cobban, Alan B. The King's Hall Within the University of Cambridge in the Later Middle Ages. LC 69-10193. (Cambridge Studies in Medieval Life & Thought: 3rd Ser., Vol. 1). pap. 93.80 (ISBN 0-317-26026-X, 2024432). Bks Demand UMI.

Cobban, Alfred. Ambassadors & Secret Agents: The Diplomacy of the First Earl of Malmesbury at the Hague. LC 78-59012. (Illus.). 1979. Repr. of 1954 ed. 21.00 (ISBN 0-88355-687-1). Hyperion Conn.

--Dictatorship: Its History & Theory. LC 76-122979. (World History Ser., No. 48). 1970. Repr. of 1939 ed. lib. bdg. 49.95x (ISBN 0-8383-1111-3). Haskell.

--Edmund Burke & the Revolt Against the Eighteenth Century: A Study of the Political & Social Thinking of Burke, Wordsworth, Coleridge, & Southey. LC 75-28995. (BCL Ser.: No. II). Repr. of 1929 ed. 27.50 (ISBN 0-404-14006-8). AMS Pr.

--History of Modern France: 3 vols. rev. ed. (Orig.). (YA) (gr. 9 up). pap. 4.95, 1957 (ISBN 0-14-020403-2, Pelican); pap. 4.95, 1961 (ISBN 0-14-020525-X, Pelican); pap. 4.95, 1965 (ISBN 0-14-020711-2, Pelican). Penguin.

--The Myth of the French Revolution. 1978. Repr. of 1955 ed. lib. bdg. 12.50 (ISBN 0-8495-0906-8). Arden Lib.

--Myth of the French Revolution. LC 74-7278. 1955. lib. bdg. 10.00 (ISBN 0-8414-3581-2). Folcroft.

--The Social Interpretation of the French Revolution. LC 71-474746. (Wiles Lectures Ser.: 1962). pap. 50.00 (ISBN 0-317-20617-6, 2024571). Bks Demand UMI.

Cobban, Alfred see Burke, Edmund.

Cobban, Alfred B. Social Interpretation of the French Revolution. LC 64-21535. 1968. pap. 11.95 (ISBN 0-521-09548-4). Cambridge U Pr.

Cobban, Helena. The Making of Modern Lebanon. LC 85-51254. (Illus.). 245p. 1985. 27.50 (ISBN 0-8133-0307-9). Westview.

--The Palestinian Liberation Organization: People, Power, & Politics. LC 83-18915. (Illus.). 305p. 1984. 24.95 (ISBN 0-521-25128-1). Cambridge U Pr.

--The Palestinian Liberation Organization: People, Power & Politics. (Cambridge Middle East Library). (Illus.). 305p. 1985. pap. 8.95 (ISBN 0-521-27216-5). Cambridge U Pr.

Cobban, J. M. & Colebourn, R. Civis Romanus: Reader for the First Two Years of Latin. (Illus., Lat.). (gr. 8-10). 1969. text ed. 13.95 (ISBN 0-312-14175-0). St Martin.

Cobbe, F. P. The Devil: His Origin, Greatness & Decline. 59.95 (ISBN 0-8490-0022-X). Gordon Pr.

Cobbe, Hugh. Cook's Voyages & Peoples of the Pacific. 144p. 1981. 40.00x (ISBN 0-7141-1550-9, Pub. by Brit Lib England); pap. 20.00x (ISBN 0-7141-1551-7). State Mutual Bk.

Cobbe, James H., jt. auth. see Bardill, John E.

Cobbe, William R. Doctor Judas: A Portrayal of the Opium Habit. Grob, Gerald N., ed. LC 80-1218. (Addiction in America Ser.). 1981. Repr. of 1895 ed. lib. bdg. 29.00x (ISBN 0-405-13574-2). Ayer Co Pubs.

Cobbett. Rural Rides. 1973. Repr. of 1912 ed. 9.95x (ISBN 0-460-00638-X, Evman). Biblio Dist.

Cobbett, Anne. The English Housekeeper. 1973. Repr. of 1851 ed. 16.95x (ISBN 0-8464-0378-1). Beekman Pubs.

Cobbett, Thomas. Civil Magistrate's Power in Matters of Religion Modestly Debated, London, 1653. LC 74-141104. (Research Library of Colonial Americana). 1972. Repr. of 1653 ed. 24.50 (ISBN 0-405-03318-4). Ayer Co Pubs.

Cobbett, W. Jews & the Jews in England. 1976. lib. bdg. 59.95 (ISBN 0-8490-2103-0). Gordon Pr.

Cobbett, William. Advice to a Lover. (Illus.). 1829. 2.00 (ISBN 0-87523-041-5). Emerson.

--Advice to Young Men. 1980. Repr. of 1830 ed. 17.95x (ISBN 0-19-212212-6). Oxford U Pr.

--Advice to Young Men. 1887. 10.00 (ISBN 0-8274-1826-4). R West.

--Beauties of Cobbett: Being Extracts from the 12 Vols. of the Porcupine. 1978. Repr. of 1836 ed. lib. bdg. 45.00 (ISBN 0-8495-0763-4). Arden Lib.

--Cobbett. LC 83-45421. 24.50 (ISBN 0-404-20064-8). AMS Pr.

--Democratic Judge Or, the Equal Liberty of the Press. LC 70-125686. (American Journalists Ser). 1970. Repr. of 1798 ed. 13.00 (ISBN 0-405-01663-8). Ayer Co Pubs.

--A Grammar of the English Language. (Costerus New Ser.: No. 39). 185p. 1983. pap. text ed. 23.50x (ISBN 90-6203-685-6, Pub. by Rodopi Holland). Humanities.

--History of the Last Hundred Days of English Freedom. LC 73-114501. 1971. Repr. of 1921 ed. lib. bdg. 15.00x (ISBN 0-8371-4780-8, COLH). Greenwood.

--Journal of a Year's Residence in the U. S. A. 1983. 90.00x (ISBN 0-900000-35-X, Pub. by Centaur Pr England). State Mutual Bk.

--Letters of William Cobbett. Duff, Gerald, ed. (Salzburg Studies in English Literature, Romantic Reassessment: No. 35). 101p. 1974. pap. text ed. 25.50x (ISBN 0-391-01346-7). Humanities.

--Life & Adventures of Peter Porcupine. 1927. 30.00 (ISBN 0-8274-2863-4). R West.

--Parliamentary History of England from the Norman Conquest in 1066 to the Year 1803, 36 Vols. 1966. Repr. of 1820 ed. Set. 2250.00 (ISBN 0-384-09496-1); 65.00 ea. Johnson Repr.

--Poor Man's Friend. LC 75-16290. Repr. of 1829 ed. lib. bdg. 25.00x (ISBN 0-678-01039-0). Kelley.

--Rural Rides. Woodcock, George, ed. (English Library Ser.). 554p. 1963. pap. 4.95 (ISBN 0-14-043023-7). Penguin.

--Year's Residence in the United States of America. LC 70-85139. Repr. of 1819 ed. 45.00x (ISBN 0-678-00516-8). Kelley.

--Year's Residence in the United States of America. LC 64-14796. (Centaur Classics Ser.). 338p. 1964. 19.50x (ISBN 0-8093-0149-0). S Ill U Pr.

Cobbett, William & Hazlitt. Selections with Hazlitt's Essay & Other Critical Estimates. 1925. 12.50 (ISBN 0-8274-3363-8). R West.

Cobbett, William, et al, eds. Parliamentary History of England from the Norman Conquest in 1066 to the Year 1803, 36 Vols. LC 54-54297. Repr. of 1820 ed. Set. 2250.00 (ISBN 0-404-01650-2); 62.50 ea. AMS Pr.

Cobbold, Diana. Evenings Faces. LC 81-71688. 1982. 13.95 (ISBN 0-87795-404-6). Arbor Hse.

Cobbold, Richard. The History of Margaret Catchpole. 386p. 1979. 11.50 (ISBN 0-85115-116-7, Pub. by Boydell & Brewer). Longwood Pub Group.

--The History of Margaret Catchpole, a Suffolk Girl, 3 vols. in 2. LC 79-8253. (Illus.). Repr. of 1845 ed. Set. 84.50 (ISBN 0-404-61823-5). Vol. 1 (ISBN 0-404-61824-3). Vol. 2 (ISBN 0-404-61825-1). AMS Pr.

--Mary Ann Wellington, the Soldier's Daughter, Wife & Widow, 3 vols. in 2. LC 79-8254. (Illus.). Repr. of 1846 ed. Set. 84.50 (ISBN 0-404-61827-8). AMS Pr.

Cobbold, Richard S. Transducers for Biomedical Measurements: Principles & Applications. LC 74-2480. (Biomedical Engineering & Health Systems Ser.). 486p. 1974. 50.95x (ISBN 0-471-16145-4, Pub. by Wiley-Interscience). Wiley.

Cobbs, Alfred L. The Image of America in Postwar German Literature: Reflections & Perceptions. (European Uiversity Studies: No. 1, Vol. 546). 139p. 1982. pap. 14.75 (ISBN 3-261-05039-X). P Lang Pubs.

Cobbs, C. Glenn & Griffin, Frank M., Jr. Infectious Diseases Case Studies. 3rd ed. 1981. 19.00 (ISBN 0-87488-011-4). Med Exam.

Cobbs, C. Glenn, et al. Infectious Diseases Case Studies. 4th ed. 1985. pap. text ed. write for info. (ISBN 0-87488-224-9). Med Exam.

Cobbs, Chris. Marcus Allen: Super Raider. (Illus.). 128p. (Orig.). (gr. 7 up). 1984. pap. 2.25 (ISBN 0-590-33375-5). Scholastic Inc.

Cobbs, Chris, jt. auth. see Leitner, Ted.

Cobbs, John J. Owen Wister. (United States Authors Ser.: No. 475). 1984. lib. bdg. 15.95 (ISBN 0-8057-7416-5, Twayne). G K Hall.

Cobbs, Price M., jt. auth. see Grier, William H.

Cobden, J. C. The White Slaves of England: Compiled from Official Documents. (The Development of Industrial Society Ser.). 498p. 1971. Repr. of 1860 ed. 35.00x (ISBN 0-7165-1585-7, Pub. by Irish Academic Pr). Biblio Dist.

Cobden, R. Speeches on Peace, Financial Reform, Colonial Reform, & Other Subjects. rev. ed. Repr. of 1849 ed. 17.50 (ISBN 0-527-18210-9). Kraus Repr.

--Speeches on Questions of Public Policy, 2 Vols. in 1. 3rd ed. Repr. of 1908 ed. 38.00 (ISBN 0-527-18220-6). Kraus Repr.

--Three Panics: An Historical Episode. 3rd. ed. Repr. of 1862 ed. 15.00 (ISBN 0-527-18230-3). Kraus Repr.

Cobden, Richard. England, Ireland, & America. LC 77-28350. 136p. 1980. text ed. 17.50 (ISBN 0-915980-44-4). ISHI PA.

--The Political Writings of Richard Cobden. 59.95 (ISBN 0-8490-0875-1). Gordon Pr.

--Political Writings of Richard Cobden, 2 Vols in 1. 4th ed. LC 4-8568. 1969. Repr. of 1903 ed. 36.00 (ISBN 0-527-18200-1). Kraus Repr.

--Political Writings of the Rich, 2 vols. LC 73-147495. (Library of War & Peace; the Political Economy of War). Set. lib. bdg. 84.00 (ISBN 0-8240-0288-1); lib. bdg. 92.00. Garland Pub.

Cobden, Richard, ed. see Chevalier, Michel.

Cobden-Sanderson, Thomas J. Credo. 1978. wrappers 10.00 (ISBN 0-913537-01-2). Arif.

--The Ideal Book or Book Beautiful. (Illus.). 1982. 75.00 (ISBN 0-913537-07-1). Arif.

--Journals: Eighteen Seventy-Nine to Nineteen Hundred, 2 vols. Incl. The Ideal Book or Book Beautiful. Repr. of 1926 ed. Set. 47.00 (ISBN 0-8337-0612-8). B Franklin.

--Shakesperian Punctuation. LC 73-108427. (Bibliography & Reference Ser.: No. 301). 1970. Repr. of 1912 ed. text ed. 11.50 (ISBN 0-8337-0609-8). B Franklin.

Cobelli, C. & Bergman, R. N., eds. Carbohydrate Metabolism: Quantitative Physiology & Mathematical Modelling. LC 80-41383. 440p. 1981. 82.95 (ISBN 0-471-27912-9, Pub. by Wiley Interscience). Wiley.
Coben, Lawrence A. & Ferster, Dorothy C. Japanese Cloisonne: History, Technique & Appreciation. LC 82-2568. (Illus.). 320p. 1982. 65.00 (ISBN 0-8348-0171-X). Weatherhill.
Coben, Stanley. A. Mitchell Palmer: Politician. LC 79-180787. (Civil Liberties in American History Ser). (Illus.). 352p. 1972. Repr. of 1963 ed. lib. bdg. 42.50 (ISBN 0-306-70208-8). Da Capo.
Coben, Stanley, jt. auth. see Link, Arthur S.
Coben, Stanley, ed. The Development of An American Culture. 2nd ed. Ratner, Lorman. LC 82-60465. 275p. 1983. text ed. 17.95 (ISBN 0-312-19665-2); pap. text ed. 12.95 (ISBN 0-312-19666-0). St Martin.
--Reform, War & Reaction: 1912-1932. LC 72-12667. (Documentary History of the United States). xxii, 466p. 1973. 19.95x (ISBN 0-87249-277-X). U of SC Pr.
Cober, Alan E. Cober's Choice. LC 79-11882. 1979. 10.95 (ISBN 0-525-28065-0, Unicorn Bk.). Dutton.
Cober, Kenneth L. Shaping the Church's Educational Ministry. LC 75-139502. (Illus.). 1971. pap. 3.95 (ISBN 0-8170-0519-6); pap. 1.95 spanish ed (ISBN 0-8170-0603-6). Judson.
Coberly, Lenore M., et al. Writers Have No Age: Creative Writing with Older Adults. LC 84-15715. (Activities Adaptation & Aging Ser.: Vol. 6, No. 2). 144p. 1985. text ed. 22.95 (ISBN 0-86656-320-2); pap. text ed. 14.95 (ISBN 0-86656-351-2). Haworth Pr.
Coberly, Rich. The No-Hit Hall of Fame. LC 85-71539. 224p. (Orig.). 1985. pap. 15.95 (ISBN 0-934289-00-X). Triple Play Pubns.
Cobes, Jon P., jt. auth. see Heck, Shirley.
Cobey, Katharine E. Thrift. LC 78-5146. (Ser. Three). (Illus.). 1978. pap. 2.00 (ISBN 0-931846-06-4). Wash Writers Pub.
Cobham, C. The Patriarchs of Constantinople. 106p. 1974. 15.00 (ISBN 0-89005-028-7). Ares.
Cobham, Catherine, tr. see Idris, Yusuf.
Cobham, David. The Economics of International Trade. 117p. (Orig.). 1979. 10.25 (ISBN 0-85941-094-3). Woodhead-Faulkner.
Cobham, E. M., ed. Mary Everest Boole: Collected Works. 1980. 25.00x (ISBN 0-85207-014-4, Pub. by Daniel Co England). State Mutual Bk.
Cobham, Rosemary. Kaleidoscope Plus. 160p. 1982. 12.95 (ISBN 0-85683-046-1, Pub. by Shepheard-Walwyn). Flatiron Book Dist.
Cobian, Ricardo. Para Todos los Panes no Estan Todos Presentes. Alurista & Xelina, eds. LC 84-60899. (Milpa Poetica). 64p. (Orig.). 1985. pap. 5.00x (ISBN 0-939558-07-6). Maize Pr.
Cobin, Martin. From Convincement to Conversion. LC 64-17424. (Orig.). 1964. pap. 2.30x (ISBN 0-87574-134-7). Pendle Hill.
Coblans, H., et al. Science & Technology Policies Information Exchange System (SPINES) Feasibility Study. (Science Policy Studies & Documents: No. 33). (Illus.). 115p. (Orig.). 1974. pap. 6.00 (ISBN 92-3-101185-5, U571, UNESCO). Unipub.
Coble, A. B. Algebraic Geometry & Theta Functions. LC 30-12679. (Colloquium Pbns. Ser.: Vol. 10). 289p. 1982. Repr. of 1929 ed. 46.00 (ISBN 0-8218-1010-3, COLL-10). Am Math.
Coble, Betty J. The Private Life of the Minister's Wife. LC 81-65385. 1981. pap. 5.95 (ISBN 0-8054-6935-4). Broadman.
--Woman: Aware & Choosing. new ed. LC 75-7943. 156p. 1975. 8.50 (ISBN 0-8054-5613-9). Broadman.
Coble, Charles. Nuclear Energy. LC 82-9790. (A Look Inside). (Illus.). 48p. (gr. 4 up). 1983. PLB 15.52 (ISBN 0-8172-1416-X). Raintree Pubs.
--Nuclear Energy. LC 82-9790. (A Look Inside Ser.). (Illus.). 48p. (gr. 4-7). 1985. pap. 9.27 (ISBN 0-8172-1432-1). Raintree Pubs.
Coble, Charles & Hounshell, Paul. Mainstreaming Language Arts & Social Studies: Special Activities for the Whole Class. LC 76-13164. (Illus.). 1977. 11.95 (ISBN 0-673-16388-1). Scott F.
Coble, Cindy & Stoffel, Maureen. Survival Basics for Kids. (Illus.). 32p. pap. 2.50 (ISBN 0-913724-26-2). Survival Ed Assoc.
Coble, Parks M. The Shanghai Capitalists & the Nationalist Government, Nineteen Twenty-Seven to Nineteen Thirty-Seven. (Harvard East Asian Monographs: No. 94). 350p. 1981. text ed. 22.50x (ISBN 0-674-80535-6). Harvard U Pr.
Cobleigh, Ira U. & Dorfman, Bruce K. The Dowbeaters: How to Buy Stocks That Go Up. 179p. 1984. 13.95 (ISBN 0-02-526490-7). Macmillan.
Cobleigh, Ira W. Double Your Dollars in 600 Days. 224p. 1979. 1.98 (ISBN 0-517-53777-X, Harmony). Crown.
Coblentz. After Twelve Thousand Years. 5.00 (ISBN 0-686-00464-7); pap. 2.00 (ISBN 0-686-00465-5). Fantasy Pub Co.
--Planet of Youth. 1952. 3.50 (ISBN 0-686-21530-3); pap. 1.00 (ISBN 0-686-21531-1). Fantasy Pub Co.
Coblentz, A. M. & Walter, J. R., eds. Systems Science in Health Care. LC 77-21046. 1978. text ed. 35.00 (ISBN 0-89433-067-5). Petrocelli.
--Systems Science in Health Care. 452p. 1977. cancelled (ISBN 0-85066-118-8). Taylor & Francis.
Coblentz, Catherine C. The Blue Cat of Castle Town. (Illus.). 136p. (gr. 3-7). 1983. pap. 5.95 (ISBN 0-914378-05-8). Countryman.
Coblentz, Edmond E., ed. Newsmen Speak: Journalists on Their Craft. facs. ed. LC 68-14900. (Essay Index Reprint Ser). 1954. 17.00 (ISBN 0-8369-0318-8). Ayer Co Pubs.
Coblentz, Patricia, jt. auth. see Bishop, Robert.
Coblentz, Stanton. Avarice: A History. 1965. 7.00 (ISBN 0-8183-0151-1). Pub Aff Pr.
--Paradox of Man's Greatness. 1966. 9.00 (ISBN 0-8183-0188-0). Pub Aff Pr.
Coblentz, Stanton A. After Twelve Thousand Years. Del Rey, Lester, ed. LC 75-398. (Library of Science Fiction). 1975. lib. bdg. 21.00 (ISBN 0-8240-1404-9). Garland Pub.
--In Caverns Below. Del Ray, Lester, ed. LC 75-399. (Library of Science Fiction). 1975. lib. bdg. 21.00 (ISBN 0-8240-1405-7). Garland Pub.
--Light Beyond: The Wonderworld of Parapsychology. LC 80-69585. (Illus.). 256p. 1981. 14.95 (ISBN 0-8453-4712-8). Cornwall Bks.
--Literary Revolution. LC 72-94308. (BCL Ser.: No. I). Repr. of 1927 ed. 10.00 (ISBN 0-404-01579-4). AMS Pr.
--The Literary Revolution. (American Studies Ser). 1969. Repr. of 1927 ed. 18.00 (ISBN 0-384-09455-4). Johnson Repr.
--Modern American Lyrics: An Anthology. 1924. 10.00 (ISBN 0-8274-2745-X). R West.
--When the Birds Fly South. Reginald, R. & Melville, Douglas, eds. LC 77-84212. (Lost Race & Adult Fantasy Ser.). 1978. Repr. of 1945 ed. lib. bdg. 20.00x (ISBN 0-405-10967-9). Ayer Co Pubs.
--When the Birds Fly South. Reginald, R. & Menville, Douglas, eds. LC 80-23935. (Newcastle Forgotten Fantasy Library Ser.: Vol. 23). 223p. 1980. Repr. lib. bdg. 12.95x (ISBN 0-89370-522-5). Borgo Pr.
--When the Birds Fly South. (Newcastle Forgotten Fantasy Library: Vol. 23). 1980. pap. 4.95 (ISBN 0-87877-122-0). Newcastle Pub.
Coblentz, Stanton A., ed. Modern American Lyrics. 1977. Repr. of 1924 ed. lib. bdg. 17.50 (ISBN 0-8495-0714-6). Arden Lib.
--Modern American Lyrics: An Anthology. facsimile ed. LC 76-167476. (Granger Index Reprint Ser.). Repr. of 1924 ed. 17.00 (ISBN 0-8369-6281-8). Ayer Co Pubs.
--Modern British Lyrics. LC 78-73483. (Granger Poetry Library). 1979. Repr. of 1925 ed. 19.75x (ISBN 0-89609-109-0). Granger Bk.
--Modern British Lyrics: An Anthology. facsimile ed. LC 70-38596. (Granger Index Reprint Ser.). Repr. of 1925 ed. 14.00 (ISBN 0-8369-6328-8). Ayer Co Pubs.
--The Music Makers: An Anthology of Recent American Poetry. LC 77-94806. (Granger Poetry Library). 1978. Repr. of 1945 ed. 24.50x (ISBN 0-89609-081-7). Granger Bk.
Cobley, L. S. An Introduction to the Botany of Tropical Crops. 2nd ed. LC 76-7447. (Longman Text Ser.). (Illus.). 1977. pap. text ed. 18.95x (ISBN 0-582-44153-6). Longman.
Cobliner, W. Godfrey, jt. auth. see Spitz, Rene A.
Cobo, Bernabe. History of the Inca Empire. Hamilton, Roland, tr. from Sp. (Texas Pan American Ser.). 301p. 1979. text ed. 20.00x (ISBN 0-292-73008-X). U of Tex Pr.
--History of the Inca Empire: Customs, Legends, History & Sociology. Hamilton, Roland, tr. from Spanish. (Texas Pan American Ser.). (Illus.). 301p. 1983. pap. 8.95 (ISBN 0-292-73025-X). U of Tex Pr.
Cobos, Ruben. A Dictionary of New Mexico & Southern Colorado Spanish. 200p. (Mexican & Span.). 1983. pap. text ed. 7.95 (ISBN 0-89013-142-2). Museum NM Pr.
--Refranes: Southwestern Spanish Proverbs. rev., bilingual ed. (Illus.). 128p. 1985. pap. 7.95 (ISBN 0-89013-177-5). Museum NM Pr.
Coburn, Alexander. The Heian Period in the Evolution of Buddhist Architecture in Japan. (Illus.). 176p. 1985. Repr. of 1930 ed. 187.50 (ISBN 0-86650-167-3). Gloucester Art.
Coburn, Alvin L. Alvin Langdon Coburn, Photographer: An Autobiography. Helmut & Gernsheim, Alison, eds. (Illus.). 1978. pap. 7.95 (ISBN 0-486-23685-4). Dover.
--Alvin Langdon Coburn, Photographer: An Autobiography. Gernsheim, Helmut & Gernsheim, Alison, eds. (Illus.). 14.50 (ISBN 0-8446-5745-X). Peter Smith.
Coburn, Andrew. The Babysitter. 1982. pap. 2.95 (ISBN 0-671-82864-9). PB.
--Off Duty. 1983. pap. 2.95 (ISBN 0-671-83688-9). PB.
--Sweetheart: A Novel of Revenge. 288p. 1985. 15.95 (ISBN 0-02-526530-X). Macmillan.
--The Trespassers. (Orig.). 1980. pap. 2.50 (ISBN 0-671-83048-1). PB.
Coburn, Broughton. Nepali Aama: Portrait of a Napalese Hill Woman. (Illus.). 165p. (Orig.). 1982. pap. 9.95 (ISBN 0-915520-45-1). Ross-Erikson.
Coburn, D. L. The Gin Game. LC 78-16784. 88p. 1978. 7.95 (ISBN 0-89676-002-2). Drama Bk.
Coburn, Daniel R., jt. auth. see Knowlton, Robert E.
Coburn, Edward J. Microcomputers: Hardware, Software, & Programming. 352p. (gr. 11-12). 1984. pap. text ed. 15.35 scp (ISBN 0-672-98445-8); scp instr's. guide 3.67 (ISBN 0-672-98446-6); wkbk 8.75 (ISBN 0-672-98355-9). Bobbs.
Coburn, George M. The Contract Disputes Act of 1978. 233p. 1982. text ed. 25.00 (ISBN 0-686-80911-4, A1-1286). PLI.
Coburn, Gordon C. The Emerging Conflict Between the United States & Europe for the New Leadership of the World. (Illus.). 1979. deluxe ed. 67.45x (ISBN 0-930008-30-8). Inst Econ Pol.
--The Emerging Conflict Between the United States & Europe for the New Leadership of the World. (Illus.). 141p. 1984. 97.85x (ISBN 0-86722-065-1). Inst Econ Pol.
Coburn, J. W. & Massry, S. G., eds. Uses & Actions of 1,25 Dihyroxyvitamin D3 in Uremia. (Contributions to Nephrology: Vol. 18). (Illus.). x, 218p. 1980. 34.50 (ISBN 3-8055-3064-1). S Karger.
Coburn, Jack, jt. ed. see Bronner, Felix.
Coburn, Jack W. & Klein, Gordon L., eds. Metabolic Bone Disease in Total Parenteral Nutrition. (Illus.). 158p. 1984. pap. text ed. 29.00 (ISBN 0-8067-0351-2). Urban & S.
Coburn, Jack W., jt. ed. see Bronner, Felix.
Coburn, Jesse L. Letters of Gold. (Illus.). 400p. 1984. 35.00 (ISBN 0-9603548-1-6). Philatelic Found.
Coburn, Jewell R. Encircled Kingdom: Legends & Folktales of Laos. LC 79-53838. (Illus.). 100p. 1979. 12.50 (ISBN 0-918060-03-6). Burn-Hart.
--Khmers, Tigers, & Talismans: From the History & Legends of Mysterious Cambodia. LC 77-14887. (Illus.). 100p. 1978. 12.50 (ISBN 0-918060-02-8). Burn-Hart.
Coburn, Jewell R., jt. auth. see Van Duong, Quyen.
Coburn, John. A Life to Live - a Way to Pray. 160p. (Orig.). 1973. pap. 5.95 (ISBN 0-8164-2079-3, SP80, Pub. by Seabury). Winston Pr.
Coburn, John B. Anne & the Sand Dobbies: A Story of Death for Children & Their Parents. 120p. 1980. 6.95 (ISBN 0-8164-3003-9, Pub. by Seabury); pap. 3.95 (ISBN 0-8164-2041-6). Winston Pr.
--Christ's Life, Our Life. LC 77-17172. 112p. 1978. 4.00 (ISBN 0-8164-0384-8, Pub. by Seabury); pap. 4.95 (ISBN 0-8164-2616-3). Winston Pr.
--Deliver Us from Evil: The Prayer of Our Lord. 96p. 1976. pap. 4.95 (ISBN 0-8164-2124-2, Pub. by Seabury). Winston Pr.
--Feeding Fire. LC 80-81103. 62p. 1980. 8.95 (ISBN 0-8192-1281-4). Morehouse.
--Prayer & Personal Religion. LC 57-5397. (Layman's Theological Library). 96p. 1957. pap. 4.95 (ISBN 0-664-24005-4). Westminster.
Coburn, K., ed. see Coleridge, Samuel T.
Coburn, Kathleen. The Grandmothers. LC 83-45422. Repr. of 1949 ed. 29.50 (ISBN 0-404-20065-6, PR6005). AMS Pr.
Coburn, Kathleen, ed. Coleridge: Collection of Critical Essays. 1967. 12.95 (ISBN 0-13-139568-8, Spec). P-H.
--Inquiring Spirit. rev. ed. 1979. o. p. 27.50x (ISBN 0-8020-2340-1); pap. 10.95 (ISBN 0-8020-6361-6). U of Toronto Pr.
--The Letters of Sara Hutchinson from 1800-1835. 1979. Repr. of 1954 ed. lib. bdg. 45.00 (ISBN 0-8495-0920-3). Arden Lib.
Coburn, Kathleen, ed. see Coleridge, Samuel T.
Coburn, Kathleen, et al, eds. The Collected Works of Samuel Taylor Coleridge: Marginalia, Part 2, Vol. 12. LC 68-10201. (Bollingen Ser.: Vol. 75). (Illus.). 1280p. 1985. 90.00x (ISBN 0-691-09889-1). Princeton U Pr.
Coburn, L. J. Caleb Thorn No. 1: The First Shot. 144p. 1982. 15.00x (ISBN 0-7278-0545-2, Pub. by Severn Hse). State Mutual Bk.
--Caleb Thorn No. 2: The Raiders. 144p. 1982. 15.00x (ISBN 0-7278-0550-9, Pub. by Severn Hse). State Mutual Bk.
Coburn, Louis. Library Media Center Problems - Case Studies. LC 73-2857. 144p. 1973. lib. bdg. 13.00 (ISBN 0-379-00019-4). Oceana.
Coburn, Louisa V., jt. ed. see Anderson, Scarvia B.
Coburn, O., tr. see Lasserre, Jean.
Coburn, Oliver, tr. see Schaefer, Udo.
Coburn, Peter, et al. A Practical Guide to Computers in Education. LC 82-1718. (Computers in Education Ser.). (Illus.). 192p. 1982. pap. text ed. 12.95 (ISBN 0-201-10563-2). Addison-Wesley.
Coburn, Raymond A. Ancestors & Descendants of James William Coburn, 1850-1929. 1982. 12.00 (ISBN 0-87012-436-6). McClain.
Coburn, Seymour K., ed. Corrosion: Source Book. 1984. 49.00 (ISBN 0-87170-177-4). Am Soc Pub Admin.
Coburn, Stephen P. The Chemistry & Metabolism of the Vitamin B6 Antagonist, 4' Deoxypyridoxine. 224p. 1981. 69.00 (ISBN 0-8493-5783-7). CRC Pr.
Coburn, Thomas. Devi Mahatmya. 1985. 18.50x (ISBN 0-686-42973-7). South Asia Bks.
Coburn, Walt. Drift Fence. 1978. pap. 1.25 (ISBN 0-505-51236-X, Pub. by Tower Bks). Dorchester Pub Co.
--Fast Gun. 1978. pap. 1.25 (ISBN 0-505-51227-0, Pub. by Tower Bks). Dorchester Pub Co.
--Invitation to a Hanging. 1977. pap. 1.25 (ISBN 0-505-51196-7, Pub. by Tower Bks). Dorchester Pub Co.
--The Night Branders. 1979. pap. 1.50 (ISBN 0-505-51348-X, Pub. by Tower Bks). Dorchester Pub Co.
--Spiderweb Ridge. 1978. pap. 1.25 (ISBN 0-8439-0539-5, Leisure Bks). Dorchester Pub Co.
--The Square Shooter. 1978. pap. 1.25 (ISBN 0-505-51228-9, Pub. by Tower Bks). Dorchester Pub Co.
Coburn, William A. The Asuka & Nara Periods of Buddhist Architecture in Japan. (Illus.). 149p. 1984. 117.50 (ISBN 0-86650-120-7). Gloucester Art.
Coca, Arthur F. Familial Non-Reaginic Food Alergy. 304p. 1982. 40.00 (ISBN 0-8184-0334-9). Lyle Stuart.
--Familial Non-Reaginic Food Allergy. 3rd ed. 300p. 1953. 24.50x (ISBN 0-398-04229-2). C C Thomas.
--Pulse Test. 1968. pap. 2.50 (ISBN 0-668-01792-9). Arco.
--The Pulse Test. 192p. 1982. 12.00 (ISBN 0-686-94665-0). Lyle Stuart.
Coca, Arthur F., et al. Asthma & Hay Fever in Theory & Practice. (Illus.). 876p. 1931. photocopy ed. 87.50 (ISBN 0-398-05146-1). C C Thomas.
Cocalis, Susan, ed. The Defiant Muse: German Feminist Poems from the Middle Ages to the Present. 225p. (Orig., Ger.). 1985. text ed. 24.95 (ISBN 0-935312-49-8); pap. text ed. 9.95 (ISBN 0-935312-53-6). Feminist Pr.
Cocannouer, Joseph. Water & the Cycle of Life. 10.95 (ISBN 0-8159-7202-4). Devin.
--Weeds: Guardians of the Soil. (Illus.). pap. 7.95 (ISBN 0-8159-7205-9). Devin.
Cocanower, Naomi. Turquoise. (Illus.). 64p. 24.00 (ISBN 0-88014-010-0). Mosaic Pr OH.
Coccheri, S. & Donati, Maria B., eds. International Congress on Fibrinolysis, 7th Abstracts: Venice, March 1984. (Journal: Haemostasis: Vol. 14, No. 1). 156p. 1984. pap. 22.25 (ISBN 3-8055-3882-0). S Karger.
Cocchi. Italian Opera Librettos. Brown, Howard & Weimer, Eric, eds. (Italian Opera Ser., 1640-1770: No. 2). 83.00 (ISBN 0-317-20351-7). Garland PUb.
Cocchi, John. The Westerns: A Picture Quiz Book. (Film Ser.). (Illus.). 128p. (Orig.). 1976. pap. 3.50 (ISBN 0-486-23288-3). Dover.
Cocchia, Aldo. The Hunters & the Hunted. Gwyer, M., tr. LC 79-6106. (Navies & Men Ser.). (Illus.). 1980. Repr. of 1958 ed. lib. bdg. 18.00x (ISBN 0-405-13035-X). Ayer Co Pubs.
Cocchiara, Giuseppe. The History of Folklore in Europe. McDaniel, John N., tr. from Ital. LC 80-17823. (Translations in Folklore Studies). 730p. 1981. text ed. 26.95 (ISBN 0-915980-99-1). ISHI PA.
Coccia. Caterina di Guisa. (Italian Opera Ser., 1810-1840). 1985. text ed. 85.00 (ISBN 0-8240-6553-0). Garland Pub.
Coccia, Carlo & Gossett, Philip. Edoardo in Iscozia & Excerpts from Maria Stuarda, Vol. 3. (Italian Opera Ser., 1810-1840). 85.00 (ISBN 0-8240-6552-2). Garland Pub.
Coccione, jt. auth. see Winter.
Coce, John William. The Life & Theatrical Times of Charles Kean, 2 vols. (Victorian Muse Ser.). 778p. 1985. lib. bdg. 100.00 (ISBN 0-8240-8602-3). Garland Pub.
Coceani, Flavio, jt. auth. see Brazier, Mary A.
Coceani, Flavio & Olley, Peter M., eds. Prostaglandins & Perinatal Medicine. LC 77-17758. (Advances in Prostaglandin & Thromboxane Research Ser.: Vol. 4). 428p. 1978. 63.00 (ISBN 0-89004-216-0). Raven.
Cochard, G. & Kessler, P., eds. Photon-Photon Collisions: Proceedings. (Lecture Notes in Physics Ser.: Vol. 134). 400p. 1980. pap. 32.00 (ISBN 0-387-10262-0). Springer-Verlag.
Coche, A. G. Report of the Symposium on Finfish Nutrition & Feed Technology: Hamburg, Fed. Rep. of Germany, 20-23 June 1978. (European Inland Fisheries Advisory Commission (EIFAC): Technical Papers: No. 31). 41p. (Eng. & Fr.). 1978. pap. 7.50 (ISBN 92-5-100642-3, F1514, FAO). Unipub.
Coche, A. G. & Wal, H. Van der. Water for Freshwater Fish Culture: Simple Methods for Aquaculture. (Training Ser.: No. 4). 111p. 1981. pap. text ed. 20.25 (ISBN 92-5-101112-5, F2409, FAO). Unipub.
Coche, Andre, ed. Aquaculture in Marine Waters: A List of Reference Books, 1962-1982. (Fisheries Circulars: No. 723, Rev. 1). 18p. 1982. pap. 7.50 (F2358, FAO). Unipub.
Coche, Andre G., ed. Coastal Aquaculture: Development Perspectives in Africa & Case Studies from Other Regions. (Commission for Inland Fisheries of Africa (CIFA): Technical Papers: No. 9). 264p. (Eng. & Fr.). 1983. pap. text ed. 19.00 (ISBN 92-5-001300-0, F2422, FAO). Unipub.
--A List of FAO Publications Related to Aquaculture: 1966-1982. (Fisheries Circulars: No. 744). 21p. 1982. pap. 7.50 (F2359, FAO). Unipub.
Coche, Richard. Veronese. (Oresko-Jupiter Art Bks). (Illus.). 1981. 17.95 (ISBN 0-933516-80-0, Pub. by Oresko-Jupiter England). Hippocrene Bks.
Cochelet, C. Narrative of the Shipwreck of the Sophia. 59.95 (ISBN 0-8490-0709-7). Gordon Pr.

Cochrane, Rexmond C. Measures for Progress: A History of the National Bureau of Standards. LC 75-22808. (America in Two Centuries Ser). (Illus.). 1976. Repr. of 1966 ed. 56.50x (ISBN 0-405-07679-7). Ayer Co Pubs.

Cochrane, Robert. The Treasury of British Eloquence. 1902. Repr. 50.00 (ISBN 0-8274-3644-0). R West.

--The Treasury of Modern Biography: A Gallery of Literary Sketches of Eminent Men & Women of the 19th Century. 1881. Repr. 50.00 (ISBN 0-8274-3645-9). R West.

Cochrane, Robert, ed. The English Essayists: A Comprehensive Selection from the Works of the Great Essayists from Lord Bacon to John Ruskin. 1978. Repr. of 1881 ed. lib. bdg. 40.00 (ISBN 0-8495-0721-9). Arden Lib.

--The Treasury of Modern Biography: A Gallery of Literary Sketches of Eminent Men & Women of the Nineteenth Century. 544p. 1984. Repr. of 1885 ed. lib. bdg. 75.00 (ISBN 0-918377-20-X). Russell Pr.

Cochrane, Rollin. ETC.-Problemes Du Francais Ecrit. LC 72-9378. (Illus.). 304p. 1973. text ed. 16.95 (ISBN 0-13-289983-3). P-H.

Cochrane, Shirley. Burnsite. LC 79-63170. (Series Four). 1979. pap. 2.50 (ISBN 0-931846-11-0). Wash Writers Pub.

Cochrane, Shirley, ed. see Hughes, Riley.

Cochrane, Shirley G., ed. see McKenna, Richard.

Cochrane, Susan H. Fertility & Education: What Do We Really Know? LC 78-26070. (World Bank Staff Occasional Paper Ser.: No. 26). (Orig.). 1979. pap. text ed. 6.95x (ISBN 0-8018-2140-1). Johns Hopkins.

Cochrane, Susan H. & Zachariah, K. C. Infant & Child Mortality as a Determinant of Fertility: The Policy Implications. (Staff Working Paper: No. 556). 44p. 1983. 3.00 (ISBN 0-8213-0147-0, WP 0556). World Bank.

Cochrane, Susan H., jt. auth. see Arnold, Fred.

Cochrane, Susan H., et al. The Effects of Education on Health. (Working Paper: No. 405). 95p. 1980. 5.00 (ISBN 0-686-36037-0, WP-0405). World Bank.

Cochrane, Wilbur W. The Shans. LC 77-87485. (Illus.). 272p. Repr. of 1915 ed. 32.50 (ISBN 0-404-16805-1). AMS Pr.

Cochrane, Willard W. The Development of American Agriculture: A Historical Analysis. (Illus.). 1979. pap. 12.95x (ISBN 0-8166-0929-2). U of Minn Pr.

--Farm Prices Myth & Reality. LC 74-10472. 189p. 1974. Repr. of 1958 ed. lib. bdg. 22.50x (ISBN 0-8371-7688-3, COFP). Greenwood.

Cochrane, Willard W. & Ryan, Mary E. American Farm Policy, Nineteen Forty-Eight to Nineteen Seventy-Three. 1976. 29.50x (ISBN 0-8166-0783-4). U of Minn Pr.

Cochran-Smith, Marilyn. The Making of a Reader. Wallat, Cynthia & Green, Judith, eds. LC 83-25795. (Language & Learning for Human Service Professions Ser.). 288p. 1984. text ed. 29.50 (ISBN 0-89391-187-9); pap. 17.95 (ISBN 0-89391-219-0). Ablex Pub.

Cochrun, John W. Avoid Financial Shocks in Your Family's Future. LC 77-77536. (Illus.). 1976. pap. 9.95 (ISBN 0-9601050-0-X). Cochrun.

Cock, J., jt. auth. see Nestel, B.

Cock, Jacklyn. Maids & Madams: A Study in the Politics of Exploitation. (Illus.). 410p. 1982. pap. 19.95 (ISBN 0-317-17851-2, Pub. by Ravan Pr). Ohio U Pr.

Cock, James H. Cassava. (IADS Development-Oriented Literature Ser.). 175p. 1984. 25.00x (ISBN 0-86531-356-3). Westview.

Cock, Valerie. Dressmaking Simplified. 3rd ed. (Illus.). 239p. 1982. text ed. 12.00 (ISBN 0-246-11501-7, Granada England). Brookfield Pub Co.

--Dressmaking Simplified. 3rd ed. (Illus.). 240p. 1984. pap. text ed. 12.95x (ISBN 0-246-12551-9, Pub. by Granada England). Sheridan.

Cockain, G. D., jt. auth. see Gorman, C. N.

Cockayne, B. & Jones, D. W., eds. Modern Oxide Materials: Preparation, Properties & Device Applications. 1972. 59.50 (ISBN 0-12-177750-2). Acad Pr.

Cockayne, O., ed. Hali Meidenhad, Alliterative Homily of 13th Century. (EETS OS Ser.: No. 18). Repr. of 1922 ed. 11.00 (ISBN 0-527-00020-5). Kraus Repr.

Cockayne, O. & Brock, E., eds. Liflade of St. Juliana: Two Versions with Translations. (EETS OS Ser.: Vol. 51). Repr. of 1872 ed. 15.00 (ISBN 0-317-15655-1). Kraus Repr.

Cockayne, Oswald, ed. Leechdoms, Wortcunning, & Starcraft of Early England: Being a Collection of Documents Illustrating the History of Science in This Country Before the Norman Conquest, 3 vols. (Rolls Ser.: No. 35). Repr. of 1866 ed. Set. 132.00 (ISBN 0-317-16682-4). Kraus Repr.

Cockborn, Andrew. The Threat: Inside the Soviet Military Machine. 333p. 1983. 16.95 (ISBN 0-394-52402-0). Random.

Cockburn, Aidan. The Evolution & Eradication of Infectious Diseases. LC 83-10883. xi, 255p. 1983. Repr. of 1963 ed. lib. bdg. 42.50x (ISBN 0-313-24118-X, COEV). Greenwood.

Cockburn, Aiden & Cockburn, Eve. Mummies, Diseases & Ancient Cultures. Abridged ed. LC 79-25682. (Illus.). 256p. 1983. 18.95 (ISBN 0-521-27237-8). Cambridge U Pr.

Cockburn, Amy. Herbs & Spices. (Picture-Perfect Miniatures Ser.). (Illus.). 48p. 1983. 4.95 (ISBN 0-8253-0176-9). Beaufort Bks NY.

Cockburn, Andrew. The Threat: Inside the Soviet Military Machine. 1984. pap. 4.95 (ISBN 0-394-72379-1, Vin). Random.

Cockburn, Andrew, jt. auth. see Lee, A. K.

Cockburn, C. C. see Diamond, Donald R. & McLoughlin, J. B.

Cockburn, Claude. Cockburn Sums Up. 1981. 17.95 (ISBN 0-7043-2266-8, Pub. by Quartet England). Charles River Bks.

Cockburn, Cynthia. Brothers: Male Dominance & Technological Change. 254p. (Orig.). 1983. pap. 8.95 (ISBN 0-86104-384-7). Pluto Pr.

Cockburn, Eve, jt. auth. see Cockburn, Aiden.

Cockburn, F., jt. ed. see Gray, O. P.

Cockburn, Forrester & Gitzelmann, Richard, eds. Inborn Errors of Metabolism in Humans. LC 82-12709. 308p. 1982. 54.00 (ISBN 0-8451-3008-0). A R Liss.

Cockburn, Henry. Examination of the Trials for Sedition Which Have Hitherto Occured in Scotland, 2 vols in 1. LC 73-100122. Repr. of 1888 ed. lib. bdg. 50.00x (ISBN 0-678-00586-9). Kelley.

Cockburn, Henry T. Life of Lord Jeffrey with a Selection from His Correspondence, 2 vols. in 1. LC 70-148763. Repr. of 1857 ed. 41.50 (ISBN 0-404-07297-6). AMS Pr.

--Memorials of His Time. LC 73-148764. Repr. of 1856 ed. 27.50 (ISBN 0-685-05895-6). AMS Pr.

Cockburn, J. S. Crime in England. LC 77-2867. 1977. 38.00 (ISBN 0-691-05258-1). Princeton U Pr.

--A History of English Assizes, Fifteen Fifty Eight to Seventeen Fourteen. LC 70-179164. (Cambridge Studies in English Legal History). 428p. 1972. 65.00 (ISBN 0-521-08449-0). Cambridge U Pr.

Cockburn, Robert H. The Novels of Hugh MacLennan. LC 76-109579. pap. 41.30 (ISBN 0-317-28408-8, 2022288). Bks Demand UMI.

Cockcroft, A. N. Nicholl's Seamanship & Nautical Knowledge. 1981. 45.00x (ISBN 0-85174-362-5, Pub. by Nautical England). State Mutual Bk.

Cockcroft, A. N. & Lameijer, J. N. Guide to the Collision Avoidance Rules. 3rd ed. (Illus.). 240p. 1982. text ed. 17.50x (ISBN 0-540-07278-8). Sheridan.

--A Guide to the Collision Avoidance Rules: International Regulations for Preventing Collision at Sea, 1972, in Force 1977. 2nd ed. (Illus.). 1978. 17.50 (ISBN 0-540-07272-9). Heinman.

Cockcroft, Ann. Pirate's Promise. (Tapestry Romance Ser.: No. 45). 320p. (Orig.). 1984. pap. 2.95 (ISBN 0-671-53018-6). PB.

Cockcroft, James D. Intellectual Precursors of the Mexican Revolution, 1900-1913. (Latin American Monographs: No. 14). 351p. 1969. pap. 9.95x (ISBN 0-292-73808-0). U of Tex Pr.

--Outlaws in the Promised Land: Mexican Immigrant Workers & America's Future. 288p. (Orig.). 1985. cloth 27.50 (ISBN 0-394-54592-3); pap. 8.95 (ISBN 0-394-62365-7). Grove.

Cockcroft, T. G. Index to the Weird Fiction Magazines, 2 vols. in 1. LC 74-15955. (Science Fiction Ser). (Illus.). 101p. 1975. 12.00x (ISBN 0-405-06322-9). Ayer Co Pubs.

Cocke, Charles F. Parish Lines, Diocese of Southern Virginia. (Virginia State Library Publications: No. 22). 287p. 1979. Repr. of 1964 ed. 5.00 (ISBN 0-88490-049-5). VA State Lib.

--Parish Lines, Diocese of Southwestern Virginia. (Virginia State Library Publications: No. 14). 196p. 1980. Repr. of 1960 ed. 5.00 (ISBN 0-686-74611-2). VA State Lib.

--Parish Lines, Diocese of Virginia. LC 78-19035. (Virginia State Library Publications: No. 28). xv, 321p. 1978. Repr. of 1967 ed. 5.00 (ISBN 0-88490-062-2). VA State Lib.

Cocke, Hugh. A Summary of the Principal Legal Decisions Affecting Auditors. Brief, Richard P., ed. LC 80-1480. (Dimensions of Accounting Theory & Practice Ser.). 1981. Repr. of 1946 ed. lib. bdg. 14.00x (ISBN 0-405-13510-6). Ayer Co Pubs.

Cocke, Marian J. I Called Him Babe: Elvis Presley's Nurse Remembers. LC 79-124443. (Twentieth Century Reminiscences Ser.). (Illus.). 160p. 1979. 10.95 (ISBN 0-87870-053-6); deluxe ed. 25.00 (ISBN 0-87870-056-0). Memphis St Univ.

Cocke, Richard. Raphael. 1981. 60.00x (ISBN 0-906379-19-9, Pub. by Jupiter England). State Mutual Bk.

--Veronese. 1981. 27.00x (ISBN 0-906379-41-5, Pub. by Jupiter England). State Mutual Bk.

--Veronese's Drawings: With a "Catalogue Raisonne". LC 84-70788. (Illus.). 464p. 1984. 95.00x (ISBN 0-8014-1732-5). Cornell U Pr.

Cocke, S. J. Old Mammy Tales from Dixieland. Repr. of 1926 ed. 22.00 (ISBN 0-527-18400-4). Kraus Repr.

Cocke, Sarah J. Bypaths in Dixie: Folk Tales of the South. LC 72-6501. (Black Heritage Library Collection Ser.). 1972. Repr. of 1911 ed. 19.00 (ISBN 0-8369-9164-8). Ayer Co Pubs.

--Bypaths in Dixie: Folktales of the South. 1976. lib. bdg. 59.95 (ISBN 0-8490-1562-6). Gordon Pr.

Cocke, William, et al. Essentials of Plastic Surgery. 1979. 13.95 (ISBN 0-316-14921-7). Little.

Cocke, William M., Jr. Breast Reconstruction Following Mastectomy for Carcinoma. 1977. text ed. 27.50 (ISBN 0-316-14920-9, Little Med Div). Little.

Cocke, William R., III. Hanover County Chancery Wills & Notes. LC 78-60961. 215p. 1978. Repr. of 1940 ed. 15.00 (ISBN 0-8063-0824-9). Genealog Pub.

Cocker, H., jt. auth. see Pizetti, I.

Cocker, M. P. The Observer's Directory of Royal Naval Submarines 1901-1982. 128p. 1983. 21.95 (ISBN 0-87021-946-4). Naval Inst Pr.

Cockeram, Henry. English Dictionary: An Interpreter of Hard English Words. 1970. Repr. of 1626 ed. 39.50x (ISBN 3-4870-2632-5). Adlers Foreign Bks.

Cockerell, Douglas. Bookbinding & the Care of Books. 1978. pap. 9.95 (ISBN 0-8008-0946-7, Pentalic). Taplinger.

Cockerell, H. A. & Dickinson, G. M. Motor Insurance & the Consumer. 184p. 1980. 22.50 (ISBN 0-85941-146-X). Woodhead-Faulkner.

Cockerell, H. A. & Green, Edwin. The British Insurance Business 1547-1970: An Introduction & Guide to Historical Records in the United Kingdom. 142p. 1976. text ed. 16.50x (ISBN 0-8419-5315-5). Holmes & Meier.

Cockerell, Hugh. Lloyd's of London: A Portrait. LC 84-70597. 150p. 1984. 22.50 (ISBN 0-87094-570-X). Dow Jones-Irwin.

--What Goes on In Insurance? (Illus.). 96p. 1982. 10.50 (ISBN 0-85941-160-5). Woodhead-Faulkner.

Cockerell, P. J. Using BBC BASIC. 380p. 1983. pap. 16.95 (ISBN 0-471-90242-X). Wiley.

Cockerham, Allan W. The Apostolic Succession in the Liberal Catholic Church. 2nd ed. (Illus.). 1980. pap. text ed. 2.80 (ISBN 0-918980-09-7). St Alban Pr.

Cockerham, H., ed. see Gautier, Theophile.

Cockerham, William. Medical Sociology. 2nd ed. 250p. 1982. 27.95 (ISBN 0-13-573410-X). P-H.

Cockerham, William C. Medical Sociology. 3rd ed. (Illus.). 380p. 1986. 26.95 (ISBN 0-13-573429-0). P-H.

--Sociology of Mental Disorder. (Series in Sociology). (Illus.). 300p. 1981. text ed. 27.95 (ISBN 0-13-820886-7). P-H.

Cockerill, Art. Sons of the Brave: The History of the Boy Soldiers. (Illus.). 256p. 1984. 24.95 (ISBN 0-436-10294-3, Pub. by Secker & Warburg UK). David & Charles.

Cockerill, P. E. Information & the Practice of Medicine: Report of the Medical Information Review Panel. 1980. 40.00x (ISBN 0-905984-64-1, Pub. by Brit Lib England). State Mutual Bk.

Cockerill, T., jt. auth. see Jones, T.

Cockerill, T. A., jt. ed. see Pickering, J. F.

Cockett, A. T. & Koshiba, K. Manual of Urologic Surgery. (Comprehensive Manuals of Surgical Specialties Ser.). (Illus.). 284p. 1979. 150.00 (ISBN 0-387-90423-9). Springer-Verlag.

Cockett, A. T. & Urry, Ronald L., eds. Male Infertility: Workup, Treatment & Research. LC 76-30630. 352p. 1977. 46.50 (ISBN 0-8089-0987-8, 790870). Grune.

Cockett, Frank B., jt. auth. see Dodd, Harold.

Cockfield, Jamie H., ed. Dollars & Diplomacy: Ambassador David Rowland Francis & the Fall of Tsarism, 1916-17. LC 80-19786. xi, 149p. 1981. 16.75 (ISBN 0-8223-2445-8). Duke.

Cocking, Clive. Following the Leaders: A Media Watcher's Diary of Campaign '79. LC 79-7842. 1980. 14.95 (ISBN 0-385-14395-8). Doubleday.

Cocking, J. M. Proust: Collected Essays on the Writer & His Art. LC 81-6105. (Cambridge Studies in French: No. 1). (Illus.). 344p. 1982. 54.50 (ISBN 0-521-23790-4); pap. 15.95 (ISBN 0-521-28799-5). Cambridge U Pr.

Cocking, Rodney R., jt. auth. see Sigel, Irving E.

Cocking, Walter D. Administrative Procedures in Curriculum Making in Public Schools. LC 79-176656. (Columbia University. Teachers College. Contributions to Education: No. 329). Repr. of 1928 ed. 22.50 (ISBN 0-404-55329-X). AMS Pr.

Cockle, G. R. Giants of the West. LC 81-65098. (Overland Railbook). (Illus.). 208p. 1982. pap. 23.50 (ISBN 0-916160-12-2). G R Cockle.

--Those Bicentennials...from American Rails. LC 78-50294. (Illus.). 1986. 35.00 (ISBN 0-916160-04-1). G R Cockle.

--Union Pacific's Snow Fighters. LC 81-65095. (Overland Railbook Ser.). (Illus.). 208p. 1984. pap. 23.50 (ISBN 0-916160-09-2). G R Cockle.

Cockle, George R. Centennials in Action. LC 78-51541. (Overland Railbook Ser.). (Illus.). 1980. pap. 11.95 (ISBN 0-916160-05-X). G R Cockle.

--Frisco in Transition. (Overland Railbook Ser.). (Illus.). 208p. 1985. pap. 23.50 (ISBN 0-916160-13-0). G R Cockle.

--Union Pacific Forties...on the Move. LC 81-65096. (Overland Railbook Ser.). (Illus.). 208p. 1985. pap. 23.50 (ISBN 0-916160-10-6). G R Cockle.

--Union Pacific...Nineteen Seventy-Seven to Nineteen Eighty. LC 77-81546. (Illus.). 208p. 1980. pap. 18.95 (ISBN 0-916160-03-3). G R Cockle.

Cockle, Maurice J. A Bibliography of Military Books up to Sixteen Forty-Two. (Illus.). xlii, 268p. 1978. Repr. of 1957 ed. 65.00 (ISBN 0-900470-70-4). Oak Knoll.

Cockle, Paul, jt. auth. see Chandler, John.

Cockle, Paul, ed. Public Expenditure Policy, Nineteen Eighty-Four to Nineteen Eighty-Five. LC 84-23733. 256p. 1984. 27.50 (ISBN 0-312-65459-6). St Martin.

Cockley, Dave. Atlanta Is a Cuddly Kind of Place. 32p. Date not set. pap. 1.95 (ISBN 0-86551-007-5). Corinthian.

--Benjamin & the Big Game. LC 82-74515. 32p. pap. 2.95 (ISBN 0-86551-022-9). Corinthian.

--Cleveland Is a Warm Fuzzy Place. 4th ed. 32p. Date not set. pap. 2.50 (ISBN 0-86551-003-2). Corinthian.

--Cleveland Is a Wild Woolly Place. 3rd ed. 32p. Date not set. pap. 2.50 (ISBN 0-86551-005-9). Corinthian.

--Detroit Is a Huggable Place. 32p. Date not set. pap. 2.25 (ISBN 0-86551-009-1). Corinthian.

Cockley, David H. Over the Falls: A Child's Guide to Chagrin Falls. (Illus.). 24p. (Orig.). (gr. 1-6). 1981. pap. 2.25 (ISBN 0-940900-00-9). Ashley Pr.

Cockman, F. G. British Railways' Steam Locomotives. (History in Camera Ser.). (Illus.). 64p. (Orig.). 1980. pap. 6.95 (ISBN 0-85263-531-1, Pub. by Shire Pubns England). Seven Hills Bks.

--Discovering Lost Railways. (Discovering Ser.: No. 178). (Illus., Orig.). 1985. pap. 4.95 (ISBN 0-85263-722-5, Pub. by Shire Pubns England). Seven Hills Bks.

--Discovering Preserved Railways. (Discovering Ser.: No. 253). 1985. pap. 4.95 (ISBN 0-85263-723-3, Pub. by Shire Pubns England). Seven Hills Bks.

Cockman, Thomas, tr. see Cicero.

Cockran, Daniel S. & Arnold, Danny. Effective Communication Skills. 1986. price not set (ISBN 0-256-03166-5). Business Pubns.

Cockrell, Cathy. Undershirts & Other Stories. 1982. pap. 4.00 (ISBN 0-914610-30-9). Hanging Loose.

Cockrell, Wilburn A., ed. In the Realm of Gold: The Proceedings of the Tenth Conference on Underwater Archaeology. (Illus.). 255p. (Orig.). 1981. pap. text ed. 8.00x (ISBN 0-910651-00-0). Fathom Eight.

Cockrill, W. The Buffaloes of China. (Illus.). 96p. 1976. pap. 18.50 (ISBN 92-5-101578-3, F85, FAO). Unipub.

Cockrill, W. R., ed. Husbandry & Health of the Domestic Buffalo. (Illus.). 993p. (2nd Printing 1976). 1974. 50.00 (ISBN 92-5-101580-5, F235, FAO). Unipub.

Cockroft, A. N., ed. Nicholls's Seamanship & Nautical Knowledge. 24th ed. 443p. 1979. 26.50x (ISBN 0-85174-362-5). Sheridan.

Cockroft, James. Mexico: Class Formation, Capital Accumulation, & the State. LC 81-84740. 416p. 1982. 25.00 (ISBN 0-85345-560-0); pap. 12.50 (ISBN 0-85345-561-9). Monthly Rev.

Cockrum, Dave. The Futurians. (Graphic Novel Ser.: No. 9). 6.95 (ISBN 0-939766-81-7). Marvel Comics.

Cockrum, E. Lendell. Mammals of the Southwest. LC 81-21834. 176p. 1982. pap. 5.95 (ISBN 0-8165-0759-7); pap. 14.95 o. p. (ISBN 0-8165-0810-0). U of Ariz Pr.

--The Recent Mammals of Arizona: Their Taxonomy & Distribution. LC 60-15914. (Illus.). 276p. 1960. 12.50x (ISBN 0-8165-0076-2). U of Ariz Pr.

Cockrum, E. Lendell & Fitch, Kenneth L. Geographic Variation in Red-Backed Mice (Genus Clethrionomys) of the Southern Rocky Mountain Region. (Museum Ser.: Vol. 5, No. 22). 12p. 1952. pap. 1.25 (ISBN 0-317-04975-5). U of KS Mus Nat Hist.

Cockrum, E. Lendell, jt. auth. see Hall, E. Raymond.

Cockrum, Lendell E. A New Pocket Mouse (Genus Perognathus) from Kansas. (Museum Ser.: Vol. 5, Vol. 11). 4p. 1951. pap. 1.25 (ISBN 0-317-04967-4). U of KS Mus Nat Hist.

Cockrum, William M. History of the Underground Railroad As It Was Conducted by the Anti Slavery League. LC 73-97361. (Illus.). Repr. of 1915 ed. 15.75x (ISBN 0-8371-2406-9, CUR&, Pub. by Negro U Pr). Greenwood.

Cocks, Anna S. Courtly Jewelry. (The Victoria & Albert Museum Introduction to the Decorative Arts Ser.). (Illus.). 48p. 1982. 9.95 (ISBN 0-88045-001-0). Stemmer Hse.

Cocks, Anna S. & Truman, Charles. Renaissance Jewels, Gold Boxes, & Objects de Vertu from the Thyssen-Bornemisza Collection. De Pury, Simon, ed. LC 84-7342. (Illus.). 384p. 1984. 95.00 (ISBN 0-86565-044-6). Vendome.

Cocks, Charles, tr. see Michelet, Jules.

Cocks, Geoffrey. Psychotherapy in the Third Reich: The Goring Institute. (Illus.). 344p. 1985. 24.95 (ISBN 0-19-503461-9). Oxford U Pr.

Cocks, George, jt. auth. see Preis, Sandra.

Cocks, H. Lovell. The Religious Life of Oliver Cromwell. LC 61-47823. 1961. text ed. 6.00x (ISBN 0-8401-0443-X). A R Allenson.

Cocks, K. D., jt. auth. see Austin, M. P.

Cocks, L. R., ed. The Evolving Earth. LC 80-42171. (Chance, Change & Challenge Ser.). (Illus.). 290p. 1981. 89.50 (ISBN 0-521-23810-2); pap. 27.95 (ISBN 0-521-28229-2). Cambridge U Pr.

Cocks, Leonard R., jt. auth. see Bassett, Michael G.

Cocks, Paul, et al. The Dynamics of Soviet Politics. (Russian Research Center Studies). 1977. 22.50x (ISBN 0-674-21881-7). Harvard U Pr.

Cocks, Richard. Diary of Richard Cocks, Cape Merchant in the English Factory in Japan: 1615-1622, 2 Vols. Thompson, Edward M., ed. (Hakluyt Society. First Ser.: Nos. 66-67). 1965. Set. 59.00 (ISBN 0-8337-3518-7). B Franklin.

Cocks, S. W. Tales & Legends of Ancient Burma. new ed. LC 78-67697. (The Folktale). Repr. of 1916 ed. 17.00 (ISBN 0-404-16068-9). AMS Pr.

Cockshott & Middlemiss. Clinical Radiology in the Tropics. (Illus.). 1979. text ed. 50.00 (ISBN 0-443-01676-3). Churchill.

Cockshott, Gerald. Music & Nature: A Study of Aldous Huxley. (Salzburger Studien: No. 11). 1980. pap. text ed. 39.50x (ISBN 0-391-02158-3). Humanities.

Cockshott, J. S. British Bus Fleets No. 9 Yorkshire Company Operators. pap. 4.00x (ISBN 0-392-08801-0, SpS). Sportshelf.

Cockshut, A. O. The Art of Autobiography in Nineteeth & Twentieth Century England. LC 84-40183. 230p. 1984. 20.00x (ISBN 0-300-03235-8). Yale U Pr.

Cockshut, A. O., intro. by. The Novel to Nineteen Hundred, 1 of 7 vols. (The Great Writers Library). 313p. pap. 9.95 (ISBN 0-312-34707-3). Academy Chi Pubs.

Cockshut, A. O., ed. Religious Controversies of the Nineteenth Century: Selected Documents. LC 66-18225. vi, 265p. 1966. 19.95x (ISBN 0-8032-0019-6). U of Nebr Pr.

Coco, Al. Finding the Law: A Workbook on Legal Research for Laypersons. (Illus.). 283p. 1982. pap. 28.00 (ISBN 0-86587-061-6). Gov Insts.

Coco, Charlene D. Intravenous Therapy: A Handbook for Practice. LC 79-19930. 170p. 1980. pap. text ed. 14.95 (ISBN 0-8016-0995-X). Mosby.

Coco, James & Paone, Marion. The James Coco Diet. 288p. (Orig.). 1985. pap. 3.95 (ISBN 0-553-24514-7). Bantam.

Cocomas Committee & Nakanishi, Motoo. Corporate Design Systems. (Illus.). 125p. 32.50 (ISBN 0-686-61692-8). Art Dir.

--Corporate Design Systems Two. LC 84-22778. (Illus.). 128p. 1985. 34.95 (ISBN 0-86636-004-2). PBC Intl Inc.

Cocoran, Eileen L. Using the Telephone. 1983. pap. 3.00x (ISBN 0-88323-179-4, 259). Richards Pub.

Cocoran, John, ed. see Han, Bong Soo.

Cocoran, John, ed. see Marchini, Ron & Fong, Leo.

Cocoran, John, ed. see Norris, Chuck.

Cocoris, G. Michael. Evangelism: A Biblical Approach. (Orig.). 1984. pap. 6.95 (ISBN 0-8024-2396-5). Moody.

--Lordship Salvation-Is It Biblical? 24p. (Orig.). 1983. pap. 1.25 (ISBN 0-9607576-2-7). Redencion Viva.

Cocozzoli, Gary, jt. ed. see Keresztesi, Michael.

Cocteau, Jean. Agenda: Leoun, Vol. 2, Nos. 2 & 3. Cookson, William, ed. 1977. Repr. of 1961 ed. lib. bdg. 17.50 (ISBN 0-8495-0004-4). Arden Lib.

--L' Aigle a Deux Tetes. (Folio 328). 1973. 3.95 (ISBN 0-686-54511-7). French & Eur.

--Antigone: Avec les Maries de la Tour Eiffel. (Folio 908). 3.95 (ISBN 0-686-54512-5). French & Eur.

--Appogiatures: Bilingual. 1983. 6.00 (ISBN 0-686-38844-5). Man-Root.

--Beauty & the Beast: Diary of a Film. LC 77-130640. (Dover Film Ser.). Orig. Title: Diary of a Film. 1972. pap. 5.95 (ISBN 0-486-22776-6). Dover.

--Beauty & the Beast: Diary of a Film. (Illus.). 14.00 (ISBN 0-8446-4527-3). Peter Smith.

--Le Bel Indifferent. 9.95 (ISBN 0-686-54513-3). French & Eur.

--La Belle et la Bete. (Illus.). 256p. 1975. 23.50 (ISBN 0-686-54514-1). French & Eur.

--Cahiers Jean Cocteau, Vol. 2. 152p. 1971. 8.95 (ISBN 0-686-54515-X). French & Eur.

--Call to Order. LC 74-30365. (Studies in French Literature, No. 45). 1974. lib. bdg. 49.95x (ISBN 0-8383-2056-2). Haskell.

--Le Cap de Bonne Esperance. 247p. (Poesie). 1967. 3.95 (ISBN 0-686-54516-8). French & Eur.

--Cocteau on the Film: Conversations with Jean Cocteau Recorded by Andre Fraigneau. LC 82-49220. (Cinema Classics Ser.). 140p. 1985. lib. bdg. 25.00 (ISBN 0-8240-5755-4). Garland Pub.

--Colette. 113p. 1955. 8.95 (ISBN 0-686-54517-6). French & Eur.

--La Comtesse de Noailles: Oui et Non. (Illus.). 296p. 1963. 13.50 (ISBN 0-686-54518-4). French & Eur.

--Le Cordon Ombilical. 96p. 1962. 3.95 (ISBN 0-686-54519-2). French & Eur.

--La Corrida du 1er Mai. 214p. 1957. 8.95 (ISBN 0-686-54520-6). French & Eur.

--La Difficulte d'Etre. 183p. 1964. 4.95 (ISBN 0-686-54521-4). French & Eur.

--Le Discours d'Oxford. 64p. 1956. 2.95 (ISBN 0-686-54522-2). French & Eur.

--Drawings: One-Hundred & Twenty-Nine Drawings from "Dessins". Appelbaum, Stanley, tr. from Fr. LC 78-182100. (Illus.). 140p. 1972. pap. 5.95 (ISBN 0-486-20781-1). Dover.

--Les Enfants Terribles. (Easy Readers, B). (Illus.). 1975. pap. text ed. 4.25 (ISBN 0-88436-286-8, 40276). EMC.

--Les Enfants Terribles. 218p. 1952. 9.95 (ISBN 0-686-54524-9); pap. 3.95 (ISBN 0-686-54525-7). French & Eur.

--Enfants Terribles. 1958. 7.50 (ISBN 0-685-11161-X). French and Eur.

--Entre Picasso et Radiquet. 194p. 1967. 9.95 (ISBN 0-686-54526-5). French & Eur.

--Faire-Part: 91 Poemes Inedits. 128p. 1969. 14.95 (ISBN 0-686-54529-X). French & Eur.

--Hand of a Stranger. facsimile ed. Brown, Alec, tr. LC 79-99626. (Essay Index Reprint Ser). 1959. 18.00 (ISBN 0-8369-1401-5). Ayer Co Pubs.

--The Holy Terrors. Lehmann, Rosamond, tr. LC 56-13357. Orig. Title: Les Enfants Terribles. (Illus.). 1957. pap. 5.95 (ISBN 0-8112-0021-3, NDP212). New Directions.

--L' Impromptu Du Palais Royal. 80p. 1962. 3.95 (ISBN 0-686-54530-3). French & Eur.

--The Infernal Machine & Other Plays. LC 63-18631. (Translations by W. H. Auden, Albert Bermel, E. E. Cummings, Dudley Fitts, Mary Hoeck & John Savacool). 1967. pap. 10.25 (ISBN 0-8112-0022-1, NDP235). New Directions.

--Jean Cocteau En Verve. 128p. 4.95 (ISBN 0-686-54532-X). French & Eur.

--Jean Marais. (Illus.). 136p. 1975. 12.50 (ISBN 0-686-54533-8). French & Eur.

--Journal d'un Inconnu. 240p. 1952. 8.95 (ISBN 0-686-54534-6). French & Eur.

--Lettre a Maritain, Reponse De Maritain a Cocteau. 146p. 1964. 8.95 (ISBN 0-686-54535-4). French & Eur.

--Lettre Aux Americains. 102p. 1949. 8.95 (ISBN 0-686-54536-2). French & Eur.

--Lettres a Andre Gide: Avec: Responses d'Andre Gide. 224p. 1970. 8.95 (ISBN 0-686-54537-0). French & Eur.

--Lettres a Milorad: 1955-1963. 214p. 1975. 14.50 (ISBN 0-686-54538-9). French & Eur.

--Maalesh: A Theatrical Tour in the Middle-East. Hoeck, Mary C., tr. LC 77-26022. (Illus.). 1978. Repr. of 1956 ed. lib. bdg. 19.75x (ISBN 0-313-20054-8, COMT). Greenwood.

--Maalesh: Journal d'une Tournee de Theatre. 240p. 1950. 4.95 (ISBN 0-686-54539-7). French & Eur.

--La Machine Infernale. new ed. (Documentation thematique). (Illus.). 158p. (Fr.). 1975. pap. 2.95 (ISBN 0-685-57558-6, 53). Larousse.

--Machine Infernale: Theatre. 1962. 8.50 (ISBN 0-685-11299-3, 854); pap. 3.95 (ISBN 0-686-66429-9). French & Eur.

--Opera. 121p. 1959. 8.95 (ISBN 0-686-54543-5). French & Eur.

--Opera: Avec: Plain-Chant. 159p. 1967. pap. 3.95 (ISBN 0-686-54542-7). French & Eur.

--Opium. 1972. 3.95 (ISBN 0-686-54544-3). French & Eur.

--Opium: Journal D'une Desintoxication. 1930. pap. 15.75 (ISBN 0-685-11469-4). French & Eur.

--Opium: The Diary of a Cure. Crosland, Margaret & Road, Sinclair, trs. LC 58-5967. (Illus.). 176p. 1980. pap. 6.95 (ISBN 0-394-17737-1, E771, Ever). Grove.

--Orphee. Freeman, E., ed. (French Texts Ser.). (Illus.). 176p. 1976. pap. 9.95x (ISBN 0-631-00720-2). Basil Blackwell.

--Orphee. (Illus.). 116p. 1961. 4.95 (ISBN 0-686-54545-1). French & Eur.

--Les Parents Terribles. 192p. (Folio 129). 1972. pap. 3.95 (ISBN 0-686-54546-X). French & Eur.

--Les Parents Terribles: Avec: La Machine a Ecrire. 282p. 1971. 16.95 (ISBN 0-686-54547-8). French & Eur.

--Picasso: Avec: Le Potomak, Le Grand Ecart. (Illus.). 329p. 1971. 17.50 (ISBN 0-686-54549-4). French & Eur.

--Poesie Critique, Vol. 1. 352p. 1959. 5.95 (ISBN 0-686-54550-8). French & Eur.

--Poesie du Journalisme. 260p. 1973. 12.50 (ISBN 0-686-54551-6). French & Eur.

--Poesie Graphique. (Illus.). 1974. 25.00 (ISBN 0-686-54552-4). French & Eur.

--Portraits Souvenir: 1900-1914. (Illus.). 216p. 1977. 12.95 (ISBN 0-686-54553-2). French & Eur.

--Le Potomak. 352p. 1951. 4.95 (ISBN 0-686-54554-0). French & Eur.

--La Princess de Cleves. Delannoy, ed. 9.95 (ISBN 0-686-54555-9). French & Eur.

--Le Rappel a l'Ordre. 1949. 6.95 (ISBN 0-686-54556-7). French & Eur.

--Reines de la France. 168p. 1952. 8.95 (ISBN 0-686-54557-5). French & Eur.

--Le Requiem. 180p. 1962. 8.95 (ISBN 0-686-54558-3). French & Eur.

--Saint-Blaise-Des-Simples. (Illus.). 32p. 1973. 8.95 (ISBN 0-686-54560-5). French & Eur.

--Theatre, Tome I. Incl. Antigone; Les Maries de la Tour Eiffel; Les Chevaliers de la Table Ronde; Les Parents Terribles. (Fr.). 1948-49. pap. 11.75 (ISBN 0-685-36056-3). French & Eur.

--Theatre, Tome II. Incl. Les Monstres Sacres; La Machine a Ecrire; Renaud et Armide; L' Aigle a Deux Tetes. 1948-49. pap. 10.95 (ISBN 0-685-36059-8). French & Eur.

--Thomas L'Imposteur: Roman. 1971. 18.95 (ISBN 0-685-11596-8); pap. 3.95 (ISBN 0-686-66430-2). French & Eur.

--Two Screenplays. Martin-Sperry, Carol, tr. from Fr. Incl. Blood of the Poet; Testament of Orpheus. (Illus.). 152p. 1985. pap. 6.95 (ISBN 0-7145-0580-3). M Boyars.

--La Voix Humaine. pap. 6.95 (ISBN 0-685-37277-4). French & Eur.

Cocteau, Jean & Fifield, William. Jean Cocteau: Entretiens avec William Fifield. 176p. 1973. 10.95 (ISBN 0-686-54531-1). French & Eur.

Cocteau, Jean & Jahan, Pierre. La Mort et les Statues. (Illus.). 64p. 1978. 27.50 (ISBN 0-686-54541-9). French & Eur.

Cocteau, Jean & Manuel, Robert. Erik Satie: Son Temps et Ses Amis. (Illus.). 154p. 1952. 12.50 (ISBN 0-686-54528-1). French & Eur.

Cocteau, Jean & Radiquet, Raymond. Paul et Virginie. 128p. 1973. 10.95 (ISBN 0-686-54548-6). French & Eur.

Cocteau, Jean & Trinka, J. Le Rossignol de l'Empereur de Chine. 9.95 (ISBN 0-686-54559-1). French & Eur.

Cocteau, Jean, jt. auth. see Aragon, Louis.

Cocteau, Jean see Dent, Anthony.

Cocteau, Jean see Moliere.

Cocteau, Jean, et al. Du Cinematographe. (Illus.). 205p. 1973. 12.95 (ISBN 0-686-54523-0). French & Eur.

--Entretiens Sur le Cinematographe: Andre Fraigneau, Georges Michel Bovay, Jean Domarchi, Jean-Louis Laugier. (Illus.). 203p. 1973. 12.50 (ISBN 0-686-54527-3). French & Eur.

--Venise. 68p. 1951. 27.50 (ISBN 0-686-54561-3). French & Eur.

--Moretti: L'Homme, l'Ouvre, le Monstre. (Illus.). 228p. 1973. 110.00 (ISBN 0-686-54540-0). French & Eur.

Cocuzza, Gininne, ed. see Lang, Franz.

Cocuzza, Ginnine & Cohen-Stratyner, Barbara N., eds. Performing Arts Resources, Vol. 8: Stage Design: Papers from the 15th International Congress of SIBMAS. (Illus.). xix, 94p. 1983. 25.00 (ISBN 0-932610-04-8); members 10.00. Theatre Lib.

Cocuzza, Ginnine, ed. see Gordon, Mel.

Coda-Messerle, Margaret, jt. auth. see Covino, William A.

CODATA, ed. Data in Modern Biology: Selected Papers from the 9th International CODATA Conference, Jerusalem, Israel, June 1984. (Illus.). 63p. 1985. pap. 10.00 (ISBN 0-08-032483-5). Pergamon.

Codata - Committee on Data for Science & Technology of the International Council of Scientific Unions. Inventory of Data Sources in Science & Technology: A Preliminary Survey. 229p. 1982. pap. 18.75 (ISBN 92-3-102048-X, U1254, UNESCO). Unipub.

Codd, Clara M. Ageless Wisdom of Life. LC 67-8630. 1967. pap. 1.75 (ISBN 0-8356-0145-5, Quest). Theos Pub Hse.

--Meditation, Its Practice & Results. 4th ed. 1968. 2.25 (ISBN 0-8356-7212-3). Theos Pub Hse.

--Technique of the Spiritual Life. 2nd ed. 1963. 2.95 (ISBN 0-8356-7090-2). Theos Pub Hse.

--Trust Yourself to Life. LC 75-4245. 116p. 1975. pap. 1.75 (ISBN 0-8356-0464-0, Quest). Theos Pub Hse.

Codd, E. F. Cellular Automata. (ACM Ser). 1968. 37.00 (ISBN 0-12-178850-4). Acad Pr.

Codd, Geoffrey A., ed. Aspects of Microbial Metabolism & Ecology. (Social Publication Society General Microbiology Ser.: No. 11). 1984. 52.00 (ISBN 0-12-178050-3). Acad Pr.

Codd, L. W., jt. auth. see Terpstra, P.

Codding, George A., Jr. The International Telecommunication Union: An Experiment in International Cooperation. LC 72-4663. (International Propaganda & Communications Ser.). 523p. 1972. Repr. of 1952 ed. 27.50 (ISBN 0-405-04744-4). Ayer Co Pubs.

Codding, George A., Jr. & Rutkowski, Anthony. The ITU in a Changing World. (Artech Telecommunications Library). 350p. 1982. 46.00 (ISBN 0-89006-113-0). Artech Hse.

Codding, George A., Jr. & Safran, William. Ideology & Politics: The Socialist Party of France. (Westview Special Studies in European Politics & Society). 1978. lib. bdg. 31.50x (ISBN 0-89158-182-0). Westview.

Coddington, Alan. Keynesian Economics: The Search for First Principles. 128p. 1984. pap. text ed. 7.95x (ISBN 0-04-330341-2). Allen Unwin.

Coddington, E. A. & De Snoo, H. S. Regular Boundary Value Problems Associated with Pairs of Ordinary Differential Expressions. (Lecture Notes in Mathematics Ser.: Vol. 858). 225p. 1981. pap. 16.00 (ISBN 0-387-10706-1). Springer-Verlag.

Coddington, Earl A. Extension Theory of Formally Normal & Symmetric Subspaces. LC 73-7870. (Memoirs: No. 134). 80p. 1973. pap. 10.00 (ISBN 0-8218-1834-1, MEMO-134). Am Math.

Coddington, Earl A. & Levinson, Norman. Theory of Ordinary Differential Equations. LC 84-4438. 444p. 1984. Repr. of 1955 ed. lib. bdg. 31.50 (ISBN 0-89874-755-4). Krieger.

Coddington, Edwin B. The Gettysburg Campaign. 1979. Repr. 40.00 (ISBN 0-89029-049-0). Pr of Morningside.

--The Gettysburg Campaign: A Study in Command. (Illus.). 880p. 1984. pap. 17.95 (ISBN 0-684-18152-5, ScribT). Scribner.

Coddington, Edwin F. & Marshall, Oscar J. Least Squares in Engineering. pap. 20.00 (ISBN 0-317-08909-9, 2014168). Bks Demand UMI.

Coddington, Joseph. Sting of the Scorpion. (Orig.). 1981. pap. 1.95 (ISBN 0-505-51699-3, Pub. by Tower Bks). Dorchester Pub Co.

Coddington, L. Quick COBOL. 2nd ed. (Computer Monograph Ser.: Vol. 16). 308p. 1978. 31.25 (ISBN 0-444-19460-6). Elsevier.

Coddington, Mary. In Search of the Healing Energy. 208p. (Orig.). 1983. pap. 6.95 (ISBN 0-89281-051-3). Destiny Bks.

Coddington, R. Dean & Wallick, Mollie M. Child Psychiatry Handbook. 320p. 1985. 35.00 (ISBN 0-87527-361-0). Green.

Coddleson, Arthur G., ed. A Vision of Art Treasures from Japan. (Illus.). 121p. 1981. 71.55 (ISBN 0-86650-011-1). Gloucester Art.

Code, Charles F., ed. Handbook of Physiology: Section 6: Alimentary Canal, 5 vols. Incl. Vol. 1: Control of Food & Water Intake. 486p. 22.00 (ISBN 0-683-01951-1); Vol. 2: Secretion. 662p. 32.00 (ISBN 0-683-01952-X); Vol. 3: Intestinal Absorption. 490p. 22.00 (ISBN 0-683-01953-8); Vol. 4: Motility. 804p. 38.50 (ISBN 0-683-01954-6); Vol. 5: Bile, Digestion, Ruminal Physiology. 582p. 30.00 (ISBN 0-683-01955-4). (American Physiological Society Ser.). (Illus.). 1967-68. Williams & Wilkins.

Code, Charles F., et al. An Atlas of Esophageal Motility in Health & Disease. (Illus.). 144p. 1958. photocopy ed. 19.75x (ISBN 0-398-00320-3). C C Thomas.

Code, Chris & Ball, Martin, eds. Instrumentation in Speech-Language Pathology. LC 83-26363. (Illus.). 264p. 1984. 25.00 (ISBN 0-933014-25-2). College-Hill.

Code, Chris & Muller, D. J., eds. Aphasia Therapy. (Studies in Language Disability & Remediation). 240p. 1983. pap. text ed. 18.95 (ISBN 0-7131-6369-0). E Arnold.

Code, Grant. This Undying Quest. 106p. 1971. 5.95 (ISBN 0-88361-070-1). Stanton & Lee.

Code, Grant, ed. see Murray, Joan.

Code, Joseph B. Great American Foundresses. facs. ed. LC 68-20291. (Essay Index Reprint Ser). 1929. 21.50 (ISBN 0-8369-0319-6). Ayer Co Pubs.

Code, Keith. A Twist of the Wrist: The Motorcycle Road Racers Handbook. LC 82-73771. (Illus.). 120p. 1983. 14.95 (ISBN 0-918226-08-2). Acrobat.

Code, Murray. Order & Organism: Steps Toward a Whiteheadian Philosophy of Mathematics & the Natural Sciences. (SUNY Series in Philosophy). 250p. 1985. lib. bdg. 39.50x (ISBN 0-87395-919-1); pap. text ed. 12.95x (ISBN 0-317-17706-0). State U NY Pr.

Codel, Martin, ed. Radio & Its Future. LC 73-161135. (History of Broadcasting: Radio to Television Ser). 1971. Repr. of 1930 ed. 29.00 (ISBN 0-405-03559-4). Ayer Co Pubs.

Coder, Maxwell S. Judas: Los Hechos de los Apostatas (Comentario Biblico Portavoz) Orig. Title: Jude: the Acts of the Apostates (Everyman's Bible Commentary. 134p. (Span.). 1980. pap. 3.95 (ISBN 0-8254-1125-4). Kregel.

Coder, S. Maxwell. The Final Chapter. 318p. 1984. pap. 7.95 (ISBN 0-8423-0866-0). Tyndale.

--Jude: The Acts of the Apostates. (Everyman's Bible Commentary Ser). 1967. pap. 5.95 (ISBN 0-8024-2065-6). Moody.

Coder, S. Maxwell, jt. auth. see Nave, Orville J.

Coder, S. Maxwell, ed. NASB Gospel of John: Horton Edition. (Acorn Ser.). 96p. (Orig.). 1976. pap. 7.50 package of 10 (ISBN 0-8024-3193-3). Moody.

Codera Martin, Jose. Diccionario De Derecho Mercantil. 286p. (Span.). 1979. leatherette 22.50 (ISBN 84-368-0115-6, S-50178). French & Eur.

Codera Martin, Jose M. Diccionario De Contabilidad. 2nd ed. (Span.). leatherette 16.50 (ISBN 84-368-0061-3, S-50180). French & Eur.

Codere, Helen, ed. see Boas, Franz.

Codere, Helen, ed. & intro. by see Boas, Franz.

Codevilla, Angelo. Modern France. LC 74-56. 272p. 1974. 19.95 (ISBN 0-87548-150-7). Open Court.

Codex Alimentarius Commission. Codex Alimentarius Procedural Manual. 5th ed. (Joint FAO-WHO Food Standards Programme). 120p. (Eng., Fr. & Span.). 1982. pap. 9.00 (ISBN 92-5-101141-9, F2299, FAO). Unipub.

--Reports of the Joint FAO-WHO Codex Alimentarius Commission. Incl. Twelfth Session. 1979. pap. 7.50 (ISBN 92-5-100628-8, F1511); Thirteenth Session, Rome, 3-14 December 1979. 103p. 1981. pap. 8.00 (ISBN 92-5-100912-0, F2071); Fourteenth Session, Geneva, June-July 1981. 112p. (Eng., Fr. & Span.). 1982. pap. 8.00 (ISBN 92-5-101119-2, F2235). FAO). Unipub.

Codex Exoniensis. Exeter Book. LC 73-178532. Repr. of 1842 ed. 45.00 (ISBN 0-404-56598-0). AMS Pr.

Codex Theodosianus. The Theodosian Code & Novels, & the Sirmondian Constitutions. Pharr, Clyde, tr. LC 71-91756. xxvi, 643p. Repr. of 1952 ed. lib. bdg. 85.00x (ISBN 0-8371-2494-8, THC). Greenwood.

Codino, Fausto. Einfuehrung in Homer. Enking, Ragna, tr. (Ger). 1970. Repr. of 1965 ed. 15.20x (ISBN 3-11-002819-0). De Gruyter.

Codlin, Ellen M. ASLIB Directory, Vol. 1: Information Sources in Science, Technology & Commerce. 634p. 1977. 90.00x (Pub. by Aslib England). State Mutual Bk.

Codlin, Ellen M., ed. ASLIB Directory: Information Sources in the Social Sciences, Medicine & the Humanities, Vol. 2. 4th ed. 871p. 1981. 135.00x (ISBN 0-85142-130-X, Pub. by Aslib England). Gale.
Codman, E. A. The Shoulder, Rupture of the Supraspinatus Tension & Other Lesions in or about the Subacronial Bursa. LC 83-25154. 495p. 1984. Repr. of 1934 ed. lib. bdg. 55.00 (ISBN 0-89874-731-7). Krieger.
Codman, John T. Brook Farm. 59.95 (ISBN 0-87968-795-9). Gordon Pr.
--Brook Farm: Historic & Personal Memoirs. LC 71-134371. Repr. of 1894 ed. 24.50 (ISBN 0-404-08419-2). AMS Pr.
--Mormon Country. LC 70-134392. Repr. of 1874 ed. 18.25 (ISBN 0-404-08481-8). AMS Pr.
Codman, Ogden, Jr., jt. auth. see Wharton, Edith.
Codol, J. P. & Leyens, J. P. The Cognitive Analysis of Social Behavior. 1982. 39.50 (ISBN 90-247-2701-4, Pub. by Martinus Nijhoff Netherlands). Kluwer Academic.
Codrescu, Andrei. For Max Jacob. LC 74-24555. 32p. (Orig.). 1975. pap. 3.00 (ISBN 0-686-10820-5). Tree Bks.
--In America's Shoes. 256p. 1983. pap. 6.95 (ISBN 0-87286-148-1). City Lights.
--License to Carry a Gun: Poems. LC 73-109893. 1970. 4.95 (ISBN 0-695-80137-6). Small Pr Dist.
--The Life & Times of an Involuntary Genius: Autobiography of a Poet's Youth & Exile to America of the 60's. 192p. 1975. 7.95 (ISBN 0-8076-0773-8). Braziller.
--Necrocorrida. 80p. (gr. 11 up). 1980. pap. 4.50 (ISBN 0-915572-53-2). Panjandrum.
--Selected Poems, Nineteen Seventy to Nineteen Eighty. LC 82-19532. 137p. 1983. pap. 7.00 (ISBN 0-915342-38-3). SUN.
Codrescu, Andrei & Notley, Alice. Three Zero, Turning Thirty. Wright, Keith & Wright, Jeff, eds. (Illus.). 54p. (Orig.). 1982. pap. 5.00 (ISBN 0-938878-14-X). Hard Pr.
Codrington, Humphrey W. Short History of Ceylon. facs. ed. LC 72-140353. (Select Bibliographies Reprint Ser). 1926. 26.00 (ISBN 0-8369-5596-X). Ayer Co Pubs.
Codrington, O. A Manual of Musulman Numismatics. (Illus.). 1980. pap. 20.00 (ISBN 0-89005-200-X). Ares.
Codrington, Robert H. The Melanesian Languages. LC 75-32811. Repr. of 1885 ed. 46.50 (ISBN 0-404-14115-3). AMS Pr.
Codrington, W. S. Know Your Horse. (Illus.). 7.95 (ISBN 0-85131-207-1, BL6839, Dist. by Miller); pap. 9.75 (ISBN 0-85131-208-X). J A Allen.
--Know Your Horse. (Illus.). 220p. pap. 12.95x (ISBN 0-317-11569-3). Diamond Farm Bk.
Cody, Aelred. Ezekiel: With Excursus on Old Testament Priesthood. (Old Testament Message Ser.: Vol. 11). 1984. 12.95 (ISBN 0-89453-411-4); pap. 9.95 (ISBN 0-89453-245-6). M Glazier.
Cody, Al. Broken Wheels. 1976. pap. 1.25 (ISBN 0-532-12453-7). Woodhill.
--The Cry of the Cat. (YA) 1980. 8.95 (ISBN 0-686-73934-5, Avalon). Bouregy.
--Dead Man's Gold. 1980. pap. 1.75 (ISBN 0-8439-0821-1, Pub. by Nordon Pubns). Dorchester Pub Co.
--Flame in the Forest. 1977. pap. 1.50 (ISBN 0-532-15287-5). Woodhill.
--Forbidden River. 192p. 1977. pap. 1.25 (ISBN 0-532-12472-3). Woodhill.
--Gunsong at Twilight. 192p. 1974. pap. 0.95 (ISBN 0-532-12388-3). Woodhill.
--The Heart of Texas. 1981. pap. 1.95 (ISBN 0-8439-0861-0, Leisure Bks). Dorchester Pub Co.
--High Lonesome. 1978. pap. 1.25 (ISBN 0-532-12585-1). Woodhill.
--Iron Horse Country. 192p. 1976. pap. 1.25 (ISBN 0-532-12448-0). Woodhill.
--The Mine at Lost Mountain. 1978. pap. 1.25 (ISBN 0-532-12567-3). Woodhill.
--Once a Sheriff. 1977. pap. 1.25 (ISBN 0-532-12497-9). Woodhill.
--The Outcasts. 1975. pap. 0.95 (ISBN 0-532-95412-2). Woodhill.
--Powdersmoke Payoff. 1980. pap. 1.75 (ISBN 0-8439-0834-3, Pub. by Nordon Pubns). Dorchester Pub Co.
--Ranch at Powder River. 1976. pap. 1.25 (ISBN 0-532-12436-7). Woodhill.
--Return to Texas. 1978. pap. 1.25 (ISBN 0-532-12571-1). Woodhill.
--Rim of the Range. 1980. pap. 1.75 (ISBN 0-8439-0822-X, Pub. by Nordon Pubns). Dorchester Pub Co.
--Rimrock Vengeance. 1981. pap. 1.75 (ISBN 0-8439-0879-3, Leisure Bks). Dorchester Pub Co.
--Shannahan's Feud. 176p. 1975. pap. 0.95 (ISBN 0-532-95395-9). Woodhill.
--The Sheriff of Singing River. 1981. pap. 1.75 (ISBN 0-8439-0862-9, Leisure Bks). Dorchester Pub Co.
--The Three McMahons. 1977. pap. 1.25 (ISBN 0-532-12517-7). Woodhill.
--Thunder to the West. 1980. pap. 1.75 (ISBN 0-8439-0848-3, Pub. by Nordon Pubns). Dorchester Pub Co.
--Triple Cross Trail. 1977. pap. 1.25 (ISBN 0-532-12519-3). Woodhill.
--Trouble at Sudden Creek. 144p. 1975. pap. 0.95 (ISBN 0-532-95427-0). Woodhill.
--West from Abilene. 1978. pap. 1.25 (ISBN 0-532-12565-7). Woodhill.
--West from Deadwood. 1980. pap. 1.95 (ISBN 0-8439-0850-5, Pub. by Nordon Pubns). Dorchester Pub Co.
--West of Sundown. 1978. pap. 1.25 (ISBN 0-532-12544-4). Woodhill.
--Winter Range. 224p. 1975. pap. 0.95 (ISBN 0-532-95432-7). Woodhill.
Cody, Bruce D., ed. Selected Papers in Illinois History, 1981. 1982. pap. 7.50 (ISBN 0-912226-14-5). Ill St Hist Soc.
Cody, Buffalo Bill, jt. auth. see Inman, Henry.
Cody, D. Diseases of the Ears, Nose & Throat. 1980. 47.50 (ISBN 0-8151-1798-1). Year Bk Med.
Cody, E. G., ed. see Leslie, John.
Cody, Eugene O. The Piper Pays. 1984. 5.95 (ISBN 0-8062-2245-X). Carlton.
Cody, Iron Eyes. Indian Talk: Hand Signals of the North American Indians. LC 73-16246. (Illus.). 112p. (gr. 1 up). 1970. 10.95 (ISBN 0-911010-83-1); pap. 4.95 (ISBN 0-911010-82-3). Naturegraph.
Cody, Iron-Eyes. Iron Eyes: My Life As a Hollywood Indian. (Illus.). 384p. 1982. 14.95 (ISBN 0-89696-111-7, An Everest House Book). Dodd.
Cody, James. Eagle: First Sweat. (Illus., Orig.). 1984. pap. 2.00 (ISBN 0-916908-42-9). Place Herons.
--Ritual Songs. (Illus., Orig.). 1982. pap. 2.00 (ISBN 0-916908-41-0). Place Herons.
Cody, James, ed. see Villanueva, Alma.
Cody, James M. Return. (Illus.). 1981. lib. bdg. 20.00 (ISBN 0-916908-31-3); pap. 3.50 (ISBN 0-916908-04-6). Place Herons.
Cody, John. After Great Pain: The Inner Life of Emily Dickinson. LC 79-148937. 1971. 25.00 (ISBN 0-674-00878-2, Belknap Pr). Harvard U Pr.
--Atlas of Foreshortening: The Artist's Model in Deep Perspective. LC 84-3644. (Illus.). 352p. 1984. pap. 19.95 (ISBN 0-442-21595-9). Van Nos Reinhold.
Cody, John, et al, eds. Policies for Industrial Progress in Developing Countries. (World Bank Research Publications Ser.). (Illus.). 1980. text ed. 24.95x (ISBN 0-19-520176-0); pap. text ed. 9.95x (ISBN 0-19-520177-9). Oxford U Pr.
Cody, John F. Loving to Be Loved. 46p. 1980. 5.00 (ISBN 0-682-49620-0). Exposition Pr FL.
Cody, Liza. Bad Company. 260p. 1982. 11.95 (ISBN 0-684-17760-9, ScribT). Scribner.
--Bad Company. 288p. 1984. pap. 2.95 (ISBN 0-446-30738-6). Warner Bks.
--Dupe. 252p. 1981. 10.95 (ISBN 0-684-17153-8, ScribT). Scribner.
--Dupe. 1984. pap. 2.95 (ISBN 0-446-30527-8). Warner Bks.
--Stalker: A Mystery. 168p. 1985. 11.95 (ISBN 0-684-18234-3, ScribT). Scribner.
Cody, Martin L. Competition & the Structure of Bird Communities. (Monographs in Population Biology: No. 7). (Illus.). 352p. 1974. 32.00x (ISBN 0-691-08134-4); pap. 13.50x (ISBN 0-691-08135-2). Princeton U Pr.
Cody, Martin L., ed. Habitat Selection in Birds. (Physiology Ecology Ser.). 1985. 69.50 (ISBN 0-12-178080-5). Acad Pr.
Cody, Martin L. & Diamond, Jared M., eds. Ecology & Evolution of Communities. LC 74-27749. (Illus.). 838p. 1975. (Belknap Pr); pap. 15.00x (ISBN 0-674-22446-9). Harvard U Pr.
Cody, Martin L., jt. ed. see Case, Ted J.
Cody, Morrill & Ford, Hugh. The Women of Montparnasse. LC 81-71638. (Illus.). 192p. 1984. 16.95 (ISBN 0-8453-4747-0). Cornwall Bks.
Cody, Ronald P. & Smith, Jeffrey K. Applied Statistics & the SAS Programming Language. 187p. 1985. pap. 14.95 (ISBN 0-444-00889-6). Elsevier.
Cody, Sherwin. Four American Poets. LC 77-24729. 1977. Repr. of 1899 ed. lib. bdg. 25.00 (ISBN 0-8414-1811-X). Folcroft.
--Selection from the Great English Poets. 1905. 18.50 (ISBN 0-8274-3351-4). R West.
Cody, Sherwin, ed. Selection from the Best English Essays, Illustrative of the History of English Prose Style. facs. ed. LC 68-8448. (Essay Index Reprint Ser.). 1903. 21.50 (ISBN 0-8369-0320-X). Ayer Co Pubs.
--Selection from the Great English Poets. facs. ed. LC 76-128152. (Granger Index Reprint Ser.). 1905. 32.00 (ISBN 0-8369-6179-X). Ayer Co Pubs.
--A Selection from the Great English Poets. LC 76-128152. (Granger Index Reprint Ser.). 576p. Repr. of 1905 ed. lib. bdg. 16.50 (ISBN 0-8290-0516-1). Irvington.
Cody, W. F. Story of the Wild West & Camp-Fire Chats: A Full & Complete History of the Renowned Pioneer Quartette, Boone, Crocket, Carson, & Buffalo Bill. facsimile ed. LC 75-109620. (Select Bibliographies Reprint Ser). 1888. 46.50 (ISBN 0-8369-5229-4). Ayer Co Pubs.
Cody, W. F., jt. auth. see Inman, H.
Cody, William. The Life of Buffalo Bill. 1976. pap. 1.25 (ISBN 0-685-73456-0, L*B399, Leisure Bks). Dorchester Pub Co.
Cody, William F. Life & Adventures of 'Buffalo Bill' facsimile ed. LC 74-169755. (Select Bibliographies Reprint Ser). Repr. of 1917 ed. 26.00 (ISBN 0-8369-5975-2). Ayer Co Pubs.
--The Life of Hon. William F. Cody: Known As Buffalo Bill, the Famous Hunter, Scout & Guide. LC 78-18732. (Illus.). xviii, 365p. 1978. pap. 4.95 (ISBN 0-8032-6303-1, BB 686, Bison). U of Nebr Pr.
Cody, William F. see Buffalo Bill, pseud.
Cody, William F., jt. auth. see Inman, Henry.
Cody, William J. & Porsild, A. Erling. Vascular Plants of Continental Northwest Territories. (Illus.). 676p. 1980. lib. bdg. 85.00x (ISBN 0-660-00119-5, 56546-7, Pub. by Natl Mus Canada). U of Chicago Pr.
Cody, William J., Jr. & White, William. Software Manual for the Elementary Functions. (Illus.). 288p. 1980. text ed. 29.95 (ISBN 0-13-822064-6). P-H.
Cody-Rutter, Elizabeth M., tr. see Sergeichuk, S.
Coe, Ada M. Entertainment in the Little Theatres of Madrid 1959 - 1919. 144p. (Sp.). 2.75 (ISBN 0-318-14261-9). Hispanic Inst.
Coe, Andrew. The Smallholder's Vet Book. (Illus.). 224p. 1985. 16.95 (ISBN 0-7134-4149-6, Pub. by Batsford England). David & Charles.
Coe, Ben. Christian Churches at the Crossroads. LC 80-27624. 160p. (Orig.). 1980. pap. 4.95 (ISBN 0-87808-178-X). William Carey Lib.
Coe, Boyer & Coe, Valerie. Boyer & Valerie Coe's Weight Training Book. (Illus.). 192p. 1982. pap. 8.95 (ISBN 0-8092-5825-0). Contemp Bks.
Coe, Brian. Guide to Early Photographic Processes. (Illus.). 112p. (Orig.). 1984. pap. 18.95 (ISBN 0-905209-40-0, Pub. by Victoria & Albert Mus UK). Faber & Faber.
--The History of Movie Photography. (Illus.). 176p. 1982. 24.95 (ISBN 0-904069-38-9). NY Zoetrope.
--Jacques Henri Lartigue. (Masters of Photography Ser.). (Illus.). 64p. 1985. pap. 10.95 (ISBN 0-356-10509-1, Pub by Salem Hse Ltd). Merrimack Pub Cir.
Coe, Brian, jt. auth. see Millward, Michael.
Coe, Charles. Understanding Risk Management: A Guide for Governments. 70p. (Orig.). 1980. pap. 7.50x (ISBN 0-89854-063-1). U of GA Inst Govt.
Coe, Charles H. Red Patriots: The Story of the Seminoles. Tebeau, Charlton W., intro. by. LC 73-5702. (Floridiana Facsimile & Reprint Ser.). 347p. 1974. Repr. of 1898 ed. 12.00 (ISBN 0-8130-0401-2). U Presses Fla.
Coe, Charles K. Banking. (Getting the Most from Professional Services Ser.). 20p. (Orig.). 1979. pap. 4.00 (ISBN 0-89854-047-X). U of GA Inst Govt.
--Consulting Engineer. (Getting the Most from Professional Services Ser.). 38p. (Orig.). 1979. pap. 4.00 (ISBN 0-89854-046-1). U of GA Inst Govt.
--Cutting Costs with a Safety Program. 2nd ed. 120p. 1983. pap. text ed. 8.95 (ISBN 0-89854-085-2). U of GA Inst Govt.
--Fiscal Advisor. (Getting the Most from Professional Services Ser.). 28p. (Orig.). 1979. pap. 4.00 (ISBN 0-89854-048-8). U of GA Inst Govt.
--Maximizing Revenue: Minimizing Expenditure. 76p. (Orig.). 1981. pap. 7.50 (ISBN 0-89854-070-4). U of GA Inst Govt.
--Outside Auditor. 2nd ed. (Getting the Most from Professional Services Ser.). 20p. 1981. pap. 4.00 (ISBN 0-89854-019-4). U of GA Inst Govt.
Coe, Charles K., ed. Cutting Costs with a Safety Program. 2nd ed. 120p. 1983. pap. 7.95 (ISBN 0-686-45076-0). U of GA Inst Govt.
Coe, Charles K., et al. Changing Local Government Fire Rates. 2nd ed. 115p. 1983. pap. 5.75 (ISBN 0-686-39616-2). U of GA Inst Govt.
Coe, Charles N. Shakespeare's Villains. LC 72-455. Repr. of 1957 ed. 11.50 (ISBN 0-404-01585-9). AMS Pr.
--Wordsworth & the Literature of Travel. 1979. Repr. of 1953 ed. lib. bdg. 16.00x (ISBN 0-374-91791-4). Octagon.
Coe, Christopher L., jt. auth. see Rosenblum, Leonard A.
Coe, David, ed. & intro. by. Mine Eyes Have Seen the Glory: Combat Diaries of Union Sergeant Hamlin Alexander Coe. LC 74-5896. 240p. 1975. 22.50 (ISBN 0-8386-1492-2). Fairleigh Dickinson.
Coe, Edith C. Hertzler Heritage. Vandergriff, James, ed. LC 75-32001. (Illus.). 172p. 1975. 7.50x (ISBN 0-686-13109-6). Emporia State.
Coe, Evan, et al, eds. Images of America: Selected Readings Based on Alistair Cooke's America. 1977. pap. text ed. 17.00 (ISBN 0-394-32118-9, KnopfC). Knopf.
Coe, Fredric L. Hypercalciuric States: Pathogenesis, Consequences & Treatment. 464p. 1984. 69.50 (ISBN 0-8089-1620-3, 790871). Grune.
--Nephrolithiasis: Pathogenesis & Treatment. (Illus.). 1978. 36.50 (ISBN 0-8151-1799-X). Year Bk Med.
Coe, Fredric L., et al, eds. Nephrolithiasis. (Contemporary Issues in Nephrology Ser.: Vol. 5). (Illus.). 280p. 1980. text ed. 40.00 (ISBN 0-443-08048-8). Churchill.
Coe, George A. The Motives of Men. LC 75-3112. Repr. of 1928 ed. 18.50 (ISBN 0-404-59108-6). AMS Pr.
--The Psychology of Religion. LC 75-3113. Repr. of 1916 ed. 31.50 (ISBN 0-404-59109-4). AMS Pr.
--The Psychology of Religion. Repr. of 1916 ed. 25.00 (ISBN 0-89987-046-5). Darby Bks.
--Social Theory of Religious Education. LC 78-89164. (American Education: Its Men, Institutions & Ideas, Ser. 1). 1969. Repr. of 1917 ed. 24.50 (ISBN 0-405-01402-3). Ayer Co Pubs.
Coe, Gigi, jt. ed. see De Moll, Lane.
Coe, Gigi, et al. The Home Energy Decision Book: Remodeling Your Home for Low-Cost Energy Efficiency. LC 83-19574. (Tools for Today Bks.). (Illus.). 180p. (Orig.). 1984. pap. 9.95 (ISBN 0-87156-811-X). Sierra.
Coe, Graham. Colloquial English. (Illus.). 192p. (Orig.). 1981. pap. 6.95 (ISBN 0-7100-0740-X); cassette 12.95 (ISBN 0-7100-0967-4). Routledge & Kegan.
Coe, Greg, jt. auth. see Coe, Jolene.
Coe, Joffre L. The Formative Cultures of the Carolina Piedmont. LC 64-21423. (Transaction Ser.: Vol. 54, Pt. 5). 1981. Repr. of 1964 ed. 10.00 (ISBN 0-87169-545-6). Am Philos.
Coe, Jolene & Coe, Greg. The Mormon Experience: A Young Couple's Fascinating Journey to Truth. 176p. (Orig.). 1985. pap. 5.95 (ISBN 0-89081-486-4). Harvest Hse.
Coe, Joyce. The Donkey Who Served the King. (Arch Bk. Ser.: No. 15). (Illus.). (gr. k-3). 1978. 0.99 (ISBN 0-570-06120-2, 59-1238). Concordia.
Coe, Kenneth. Buridan's Mule. LC 81-82692. 263p. 1982. 15.00 (ISBN 0-8022-2392-3). Philos Lib.
Coe, Linda C., ed. Funding Sources for Cultural Facilities: Private & Federal Support for Capital Projects. 72p. 1980. pap. 3.00 (ISBN 0-89062-184-5, Pub. by Natl Encow Arts). Pub Ctr Cult Res.
Coe, M. E. How to Write for Television. 160p. 1980. 2.98 (ISBN 0-517-53850-4, Michelman Bks). Crown.
Coe, Malcolm. Islands in the Bush: A Natural History of the Kora National Reserve, Kenya. (Illus.). 256p. 1985. 29.95 (ISBN 0-540-01086-3, Pub. by G Philip UK). Sheridan.
Coe, Marguerite. Basic Skills Parts of Speech Workbook. (Basic Skills Workbooks). 32p. (gr. 5-9). 1983. 0.99 (ISBN 0-8209-0547-X, EW-2). ESP.
--Capitalization Skills. (English Ser.). 24p. (gr. 4-7). 1979. wkbk. 5.00 (ISBN 0-8209-0183-0, E-11). ESP.
--The Eight Parts of Speech. (English Ser.). 24p. (gr. 4-7). 1979. wkbk. 5.00 (ISBN 0-8209-0181-4, E-9). ESP.
Coe, Marian. Women-in-Transition. 1984. pap. 8.95 (ISBN 0-911197-03-6). Miracle Pub Co.
--Women in Transition. softcover 8.95 (ISBN 0-911197-03-6). Randall Bk Co.
Coe, Mary J., ed. Certification of Public Librarians in the U.S. 1979. 3rd ed. 57p. 4.50 (ISBN 0-317-34816-7). Library Admin.
Coe, Mary Lee. Growing with Community Gardening. (Illus., Orig.). 1978. 8.95 (ISBN 0-914378-36-8); pap. 6.95 (ISBN 0-914378-22-8). Countryman.
Coe, Michael D. Classic Maya Pottery at Dumbarton Oaks. LC 75-1727. (Illus.). 1975. 25.00x (ISBN 0-88402-063-0). Dumbarton Oaks.
--An Early Stone Pectoral from Southeastern Mexico. LC 66-16019. (Studies in Pre-Columbian Art & Archaeology Ser.: No. 1). (Illus.). 18p. 1966. pap. 2.50x (ISBN 0-88402-013-4). Dumbarton Oaks.
--Lords of the Underworld: Masterpieces of Classical Mayan Ceramics. LC 77-72144. (Illus.). 1978. 60.00x (ISBN 0-691-03917-8). Princeton U Pr.
--The Maya. 3rd, rev. ed. LC 83-72969. (Ancient Peoples & Places Ser.). (Illus.). 207p. 1984. pap. 9.95f (ISBN 0-500-27327-8). Thames Hudson.
--Mexico. 3rd, rev. ed. LC 83-72968. (Ancient Peoples & Places Ser.). (Illus.). 216p. 1984. 19.95f (ISBN 0-500-02105-8); pap. 9.95f (ISBN 0-500-27328-6). Thames Hudson.
--Old Gods & Young Heroes: The Pearlman Collection of Maya Ceramics. LC 82-70987. (Illus.). 130p. 1982. 42.50x (ISBN 0-295-95970-3, Pub. by Israel Museum); pap. 24.95 (ISBN 0-295-95981-9). U of Wash Pr.
Coe, Michael D. & Benson, Elizabeth P. Three Maya Relief Panels at Dumbarton Oaks. LC 66-30016. (Studies in Pre-Columbian Art & Archaeology: No. 2). (Illus.). 1966. pap. 3.00x (ISBN 0-88402-014-2). Dumbarton Oaks.
Coe, Michael D. & Diehl, Richard A. In the Land of the Olmec, 2 vols. (Illus.). 1980. Set. 100.00x (ISBN 0-292-77549-0); Vol. 1, The Archaeology Of San Lorenzo Techochtitan, 436pp. Vol. 2, The People of the River, 204pp. U of Tex Pr.
Coe, Peter, jt. auth. see Coe, Sebastian.
Coe, R. T., ed. see Schuyler, Montgomery.
Coe, Ralph T. Dale Eldred: Sculpture into Environment. LC 77-5896. (Illus.). 1978. 35.00 (ISBN 0-7006-0159-7). U Pr of KS.
--The Magic Theater. LC 78-115920. (Illus.). 261p. (Orig.). 1970. pap. 3.00 (ISBN 0-942614-00-3). Nelson Atkins.
--Sacred Circles: Two Thousand Years of North American Indian Art. LC 77-153583. (Illus.). 260p. 1977. pap. 15.00 (ISBN 0-295-95584-8). U of Wash Pr.
--Sacred Circles: Two Thousand Years of North American Indian Art. Hoare, Irena, ed. (Illus.). 252p. 1977. pap. 12.95 (ISBN 0-942614-05-4). Nelson Atkins.
Coe, Richard. Form & Substance: An Advanced Rhetoric. LC 81-630. 428p. 1981. text ed. 19.50x (ISBN 0-673-15660-5). Scott F.
Coe, Richard, tr. see Stendhal.

Coffey, Michael. Roman Satire. LC 76-28824. 1976. 16.95x (ISBN 0-416-85120-7, NO. 2146); pap. 16.95x (ISBN 0-416-85130-4, NO. 2147). Methuen Inc.

Coffey, Peter. The European Monetary System-Past, Present & Future. 1984. lib. bdg. 25.50 (ISBN 90-247-3080-5, Pub. by Martinus Nijhoff Netherlands). Kluwer Academic.

--Main Economic Policy Areas of the EEC. 1983. lib. bdg. 28.00 (ISBN 90-247-2793-6, Pub. by Martinus Nijhoff Netherlands). Kluwer Academic.

--Ontology. 14.50 (ISBN 0-8446-1119-0). Peter Smith.

--Science of Logic, Vol. 2. 15.00 ea. (ISBN 0-8446-1120-4). Peter Smith.

--The Social Economy of France. LC 73-85269. 160p. 1974. 22.50 (ISBN 0-312-73220-1). St Martin.

--World Monetary Crisis. LC 74-14711. 128p. 1974. 25.00 (ISBN 0-312-89180-6). St Martin.

Coffey, Peter, ed. The Economic Policies of the Common Market. LC 78-11747. 1979. 26.00x (ISBN 0-312-23447-3). St Martin.

Coffey, Richard A. A Midwestern Village. Deegan, Paul, ed. LC 70-156065. (World's People Ser.). (Illus.). (gr. 5-9). 1971. text ed. 7.95 (ISBN 0-87191-077-2). Creative Ed.

Coffey, Robert E., et al. Behavior in Organizations: A Multi-Dimensional View. 2nd ed. LC 74-12372. (Illus.). 608p. 1975. 29.95 (ISBN 0-13-073148-X). P-H.

Coffey, Rosalie L. & Glenn, John S. Completing the Promise. (Religious Awards for Boy Scouts Ser.). 1984. pap. 4.95x (ISBN 0-938758-17-9). MTM Pub Co.

Coffey, S. Rodd's Chemistry of Carbon Compounds, Vol. 4, Pt. A: Three, Four & Five Membered Heterocyclic Compounds. 1973. 159.50 (ISBN 0-444-41093-7). Elsevier.

--Rodd's Chemistry of Carbon Compounds, Vol. 4, Pt. E: Heterocyclic Compounds; Six-Membered Monoeterocyclic Compounds. 522p. 1978. 136.25 (ISBN 0-444-41363-4). Elsevier.

--Rodd's Chemistry of Carbon Compounds, Vol. 4, Pt. J: Proteins. Date not set. price not set (ISBN 0-685-84873-6). Elsevier.

--Rodd's Chemistry of Carbon Compounds, Vol. 4, Pt. K: Six Membered Heterocyclic Compounds with Two or More Hetero-Atoms. 552p. 1979. 144.75 (ISBN 0-444-41647-1). Elsevier.

Coffey, S. see Rodd, E. H.

Coffey, S., ed. Rodd's Chemistry of Carbon Compounds, Vol. 4, Pts. B & F. 2nd ed. Incl. Pt. B. Five-Membered Heterocyclic Compounds, Alkaloids, Dyes & Pigments. Coffey, S., ed. 1977. 127.75 (ISBN 0-444-41504-1); Pt. F. Six Membered Heterocyclic Compounds with a Single Atom in the Rind, Pyridine, Polymethyl-Epyridines, Quinoline, Isoquinoline & Their Derivatives. Coffey, S. 1977. 127.75 (ISBN 0-444-41503-3). LC 64-4605. Elsevier.

--Rodd's Chemistry of Carbon Compounds, Vol. 4, Pt. H: Heterocyclic Compounds. 2nd ed. 1978. 136.25 (ISBN 0-444-41575-0). Elsevier.

--Rodd's Chemistry of Carbon Compounds, Vol. 4, Pt. L: Heterocyclic Compounds, Fused-Ring Heterocycles with Three or More N Atoms. 506p. 1980. 144.75 (ISBN 0-444-40664-6). Elsevier.

Coffey, S., ed. see Rodd, E. H.

Coffey, S. see Rodd, E. H.

Coffey, Susan C. Peter Paul Rubens. (Illus.). 32p. (Orig.). 1984. pap. 8.95 (ISBN 0-295-96210-0). U of Wash Pr.

Coffey, Thomas M. The Donkey's Gift. (Illus.). 133p. 1984. 11.95 (ISBN 0-517-55414-3). Crown.

--Hap: The Story of the U. S. Air Force & the Man Who Built It, Gen. Henry "Hap" Arnold. LC 81-69928. 390p. 1982. 19.95 (ISBN 0-670-36069-4). Viking.

--The Long Thirst: Prohibition in America 1920-1933. 346p. 1975. 9.95 (ISBN 0-393-05557-4). Norton.

Coffey, Thomas P. A Candle in the Wind: My Thirty Years in Book Publishing. 222p. 1985. pap. 5.95 (ISBN 0-87193-212-1). Dimension Bks.

--There Is a Singing Underneath: Meditations in Central Park. 128p. 1985. pap. 5.95 (ISBN 0-87193-217-2). Dimension Bks.

Coffey, Vincent J. Battle of Gettysburg. LC 84-40834. (Turning Points in American History Ser.). (Illus.). 64p. 1985. 13.96 (ISBN 0-382-06830-0). Silver.

Coffey, Wayne. Three Hundred Three of the World's Worst Predictions. LC 83-9128. (Illus.). 96p. (Orig.). 1983. pap. 3.95 (ISBN 0-943392-19-5). Tribeca Comm.

--The World's Worst Predictions. (Tripbrobooks Ser.). (Illus.). 192p. 1985. 4.98 (ISBN 0-943392-59-4). Tribeca Comm.

Coffey, Wayne, jt. auth. see Young, Faye.

Coffey, Wayne R., jt. auth. see Schatzki, Michael.

Coffey, William & Evans, Myron. Molecular Diffusion & Spectra. LC 83-16681. 378p. 1984. 49.95x (ISBN 0-471-87539-2, Pub. by Wiley Interscience). Wiley.

Coffey, William E., et al. West Virginia Government. Buckalew, Marshall & Thoenen, Eugenia G., eds. (Illus.). 112p. (Orig.). (gr. 8). 1984. pap. 10.00 (ISBN 0-914498-05-3). Educ Found.

Coffey, William J. Geography: Towards a General Spatial Systems Approach. 320p. 1981. pap. 13.95x (ISBN 0-416-30980-1, NO. 3605). Methuen Inc.

Coffey-Lewis, Lou. Be Restored to Health. 304p. 1984. pap. 2.95 (ISBN 0-345-31645-2). Ballantine.

Coffield, Frank & Goodings, Richard, eds. Sacred Cows in Education. 214p. 1984. pap. 16.00x (ISBN 0-85224-484-3, Pub. by Edinburgh U Pr Scotland). Columbia U Pr.

Coffield, Frank, et al. A Cycle of Deprivation? 1981. text ed. 24.00x (ISBN 0-435-82145-8). Gower Pub Co.

Coffin. Mainstays of Maine. 1978. pap. 3.75 (ISBN 0-89272-042-5). Down East.

Coffin, Arthur B. Robinson Jeffers: Poet of Inhumanism. LC 74-121767. 324p. 1971. 32.50x (ISBN 0-299-05840-9). U of Wis Pr.

Coffin, Berton. Coffin's Overtones of Bel Canto: Phonetic Basis of Artistic Singing with One Hundred Chromatic Vowel-Chart Exercises. LC 80-21958. 254p. 1980. text ed. 30.00 set (ISBN 0-8108-1370-X). Scarecrow.

--The Singer's Repertoire, 4 vols. 2nd ed. Incl. Vol. 1. Coloratura, Lyric & Dramatic Soprano (ISBN 0-8108-0188-4); Vol. 2. Mezzo Soprano & Contralto (ISBN 0-8108-0189-2); Vol. 3. Lyric & Dramatic Tenor (ISBN 0-8108-0190-6); Vol. 4. Baritone & Bass (ISBN 0-8108-0191-4). LC 60-7265. 1960. Set. 52.50 (ISBN 0-8108-0187-6); 16.00 ea. Scarecrow.

Coffin, Berton & Errolle, Ralph. Phonetic Readings of Songs & Arias: With Revised German Transcriptions. 2nd ed. LC 82-874. 400p. 1982. pap. text ed. 17.00 (ISBN 0-8108-1533-8). Scarecrow.

Coffin, Berton & Singer, Werner. Program Notes for the Singer's Repertoire. LC 60-7265. 230p. 1962. 16.00 (ISBN 0-8108-0169-8). Scarecrow.

Coffin, Berton, et al. Word-by-Word Translations of Songs & Arias, Pt. 1: German & French. LC 66-13746. 620p. 1966. 27.50 (ISBN 0-8108-0149-3). Scarecrow.

Coffin, Carlyn. Noel & His Friends. (Illus.). 130p. (gr. 3-6). 1985. pap. price not set over boards (ISBN 0-931474-30-2). TBW Bks.

Coffin, Charles C. Caleb Krinkle. facs. ed. LC 79-83932. (Black Heritage Library Collection Ser.). 1874. 20.75 (ISBN 0-8369-8545-1). Ayer Co Pubs.

--Four Years of Fighting. LC 74-125687. (American Journalists Ser.). 1970. Repr. of 1866 ed. 32.00 (ISBN 0-405-01664-6). Ayer Co Pubs.

Coffin, Charles M. John Donne & the New Philosophy. 1958. Repr. of 1937 ed. text ed. 13.00x (ISBN 0-391-00444-1). Humanities.

Coffin, Charles M. & Roelofs, Gerrit H., eds. The Major Poets: English & American. 2nd ed. 581p. 1969. pap. text ed. 15.95 (ISBN 0-15-554545-0, HC). HarBraceJ.

Coffin, Charles M., ed. see Donne, John.

Coffin, Chris, jt. auth. see Wadman, Ted.

Coffin, David R. The Villa in the Life of Renaissance Rome. LC 78-9049. (Monographs in Art & Archaeology: XLIII). 1979. 68.00x (ISBN 0-691-03942-9). Princeton U Pr.

Coffin, Edna A. Lessons in Modern Hebrew, 2 vols. LC 76-49149. 1977. Vol. I. 14.95x (ISBN 0-472-08225-6); Vol. II. 14.95x (ISBN 0-472-08226-4). U of Mich Pr.

Coffin, Elizabeth, ed. see Di Curcio, Robert A.

Coffin, Frank. The Ways of a Judge: Reflections from the Federal Apellate Bench. 288p. 1980. 10.95 (ISBN 0-395-29461-4). HM.

Coffin, Frank M. A Lexicon of Oral Advocacy. 112p. 1985. 12.95 (ISBN 0-318-11874-2). Natl Inst Trial Ad.

Coffin, George. Bridge Summary Complete. (Illus., Orig.). pap. 3.00 (ISBN 0-8283-1427-6, 40, IPL). Branden Pub CO.

--Endplays in Bridge: Eliminations, Squeezes, & Coups. 6th ed. 224p. 1982. pap. 4.95 (ISBN 0-486-24230-7). Dover.

Coffin, George, jt. auth. see Andrews, Joseph.

Coffin, George, ed. see Lavinthal, Hy.

Coffin, George S. Acol & the New Point Count. 56p. 1977. 10.95 (ISBN 0-7156-0001-X, BPX-02532, Pub. by Duckworth England). Biblio Dist.

--Bridge Play from A to Z. 4th ed. (Illus.). 1979. pap. 5.00 (ISBN 0-486-23891-1). Dover.

Coffin, Glenyce. Intercession-Intervention. 32p. (Orig.). 1982. pap. 0.95 (ISBN 0-930756-71-1, 541010). Aglow Pubns.

--Run to Win: Training for the Overcoming Life. (Mini-Book Ser.). 40p. 1984. pap. 2.50 (ISBN 0-930756-87-8, 533010). Aglow Pubns.

Coffin, Henry S. In a Day of Social Rebuilding: Lectures on the Ministry of the Church. 1919. 29.50x (ISBN 0-686-51402-5). Elliots Bks.

--The Public Worship of God: A Source Book. 16.00 (ISBN 0-8369-7272-4, 8071). Ayer Co Pubs.

--Religion Yesterday & Today. facs. ed. LC 75-117769. (Essay Index Reprint Ser.). 1940. 18.00 (ISBN 0-8369-1790-1). Ayer Co Pubs.

--Some Christian Convictions: A Practical Restatement in Terms of Present-Day Thinking. LC 79-167328. (Essay Index Reprint Ser.). Repr. of 1915 ed. 17.00 (ISBN 0-8369-2763-X). Ayer Co Pubs.

--What Men Are Asking. facs. ed. LC 70-117770. (Essay Index Reprint Ser). 1933. 12.50 (ISBN 0-8369-1791-X). Ayer Co Pubs.

Coffin, James L., jt. auth. see Driver, Harold E.

Coffin, Joshua & Pinckney, Thomas. Slave Insurrections: Selected Documents. LC 68-55927. Repr. of 1860 ed. lib. bdg. 15.00x (ISBN 0-8371-1798-4, SID&, Pub. by Negro U Pr). Greenwood.

Coffin, Kenneth B., jt. auth. see Leslie, Louis A.

Coffin, Levi. Reminiscences of Levi Coffin. LC 79-113578. Repr. of 1876 ed. 15.00 (ISBN 0-404-00143-2). AMS Pr.

--Reminiscences of Levi Coffin. LC 68-55510. Repr. of 1876 ed. 45.00x (ISBN 0-678-00430-7). Kelley.

--Reminiscences of Levi Coffin, the Reputed President of the Underground Railroad. LC 68-28991. (American Negro: His History & Literature Ser., No. 1). 1968. Repr. of 1898 ed. 21.00 (ISBN 0-405-01810-X). Ayer Co Pubs.

Coffin, Lewis A. Children's Nutrition: A Consumer's Guide. LC 83-26131. (Illus.). 184p. 1984. pap. 8.95 (ISBN 0-88496-213-X). Capra Pr.

Coffin, Lyn. The Poetry of Wickedness & Other Poems. LC 81-20085. 65p. (Orig.). 1981. pap. 4.00 (ISBN 0-87886-116-5). Ithaca Hse.

Coffin, Lyn, tr. see Akhmatova, Anna.

Coffin, R. P. The Dukes of Buckingham: Playboys of the Stuart World. 358p. 1980. Repr. of 1931 ed. lib. bdg. 35.00 (ISBN 0-89760-110-6). Telegraph Bks.

Coffin, Raymond. Poetry for Crazy Cowboys & Zen Monks. (Illus.). 72p. 1980. pap. 4.95 (ISBN 0-915520-26-5). Ross-Erikson.

Coffin, Robert P. The Dukes of Buckingham. Repr. of 1931 ed. 30.00 (ISBN 0-686-19879-4). Ridgeway Bks.

--Kennebec: Cradle of Americans. (Rivers of America Ser.). (Illus.). 292p. 1975. pap. 3.75 (ISBN 0-89272-012-3, 194). Down East.

--Lost Paradise: A Boyhood on a Maine Coast Farm. LC 78-144951. 1971. Repr. of 1947 ed. 49.00x (ISBN 0-403-00904-9). Scholarly.

Coffin, Royce A. The Negotiator: A Manual for Winners. LC 73-75768. pap. 43.50 (ISBN 0-317-10208-7, 2022618). Bks Demand UMI.

Coffin, Sharon. Product Hazards: A Case History Guidebook. 1981. 89.00 (ISBN 0-914176-16-1). Wash Busn Info.

Coffin, Tristram P. Great Game for a Girl. 124p. 1980. 7.00 (ISBN 0-682-49566-2). Exposition Pr FL.

--Uncertain Glory: Folklore & the American Revolution. LC 77-147812. 284p. 1971. 35.00x (ISBN 0-8103-5040-8). Gale.

Coffin, Tristram P. & Renwick, Roger D. The British Traditional Ballad in North America. rev. ed. LC 76-52476. (AFS Bibliographical & Special Ser.: No. 29). 315p. 1977. text ed. 20.00x (ISBN 0-292-70719-3). U of Tex Pr.

Coffin, Tristram P., ed. Indian Tales of North America: An Anthology for the Adult Reader. LC 61-11866. (American Folklore Soc. Bibliographical & Special Ser.: No. 13). 175p. 1961. pap. 6.95 (ISBN 0-292-73506-5). U of Tex Pr.

Coffin, Tristram P., jt. ed. see Cohen, Hennig.

Coffin, Tristram P., jt. ed. see Leach, MacEdward.

Coffin, Victor. Province of Quebec & the Early American Revolution. LC 74-120873. (American Bicentennial Ser.). 1970. Repr. of 1896 ed. 29.00x (ISBN 0-8046-1266-8, Pub. by Kennikat). Assoc Faculty Pr.

Coffin, William S. The Courage to Love. LC 83-48977. 112p. 1984. pap. 5.72 (ISBN 0-06-061509-5, RD 515, HarpR). Har-Row.

--Living the Truth in a World of Illusions. LC 84-48766. 160p. 1985. 12.45 (ISBN 0-06-061512-5, HarpR). Har-Row.

Coffin, William S., Jr. The Courage to Love. LC 81-48386. 128p. 1982. pap. 6.68i (ISBN 0-06-061508-7, RD515, HarpR). Har-Row.

Coffin, William S., Jr & Leibman, Morris I. Civil Disobedience: Aid or Hindrance to Justice. 93p. 1972. 11.25 (ISBN 0-8447-2031-3). Am Enterprise.

Coffinberger, Richard L. & Samuels, Linda B. Business & Its Legal Environment: Study Guide & Workbook. 176p. 1983. 11.95 (ISBN 0-13-101022-0). P-H.

Coffinberry, A. S., ed. see World Metallurgical Congress 1957, Chicago.

Coffler, Gail H. Melville's Classical Allusions: A Comprehensive Index & Glossary. xvi, 153p. 1985. lib. bdg. 37.50 (ISBN 0-313-24626-2, CMV/). Greenwood.

Coffman, Ardis. Terror at Octagon House. (Orig.). 1979. pap. 1.95 (ISBN 0-686-62760-1). Woodhill.

Coffman, Barbara F. His Name Was John: The Life Story of John S. Coffman, an Early Mennonite Leader. LC 64-18732. (Illus.). 352p. 1964. 6.95 (ISBN 0-8361-1486-8). Herald Pr.

Coffman, Burton. Commentary on James, First & Second; Peter, First, Second & Third, John, Jude. (Firm Foundation Commentary Ser.). 1979. cancelled 10.95 (ISBN 0-88027-075-6). Firm Foun Pub.

Coffman, C. DeWitt. Hospitality for Sale: Techniques of Promoting Business for Hospitality Establishments. LC 79-28567. (Illus.). 339p. 1980. 17.56x (ISBN 0-86612-000-9); text ed. 28.95. Educ Inst Am Hotel.

Coffman, C. V. & Fix, G. J. Constructive Approaches to Mathematical Models. LC 79-51673. 1979. 69.50 (ISBN 0-12-178150-X). Acad Pr.

Coffman, Carl. Unto a Perfect Man. 4th ed. 209p. 1982. pap. 8.95 (ISBN 0-943872-83-9). Andrews Univ Pr.

Coffman, Dewitt. Marketing for a Full House. (Illus.). 1984. pap. 10.00 (ISBN 0-937056-03-0). Cornell U Sch Hotel.

Coffman, Edward G., Jr. & Denning, Peter J. Operating Systems Theory. LC 73-491. 400p. 1973. ref. ed. 34.95 (ISBN 0-13-637868-4). P-H.

Coffman, Edward M. Hilt of the Sword: The Career of Peyton C. March. (Illus.). 360p. 1966. 27.50x (ISBN 0-299-03910-2). U of Wis Pr.

Coffman, Edward N. & Jensen, Daniel L. Accounting for Changing Prices. 1984. pap. text ed. 17.95 (ISBN 0-8359-0038-X). Reston.

Coffman, Edward N., jt. auth. see Burns, Thomas J.

Coffman, F. A., ed. Oats & Oat Improvement. (Illus.). 1961. 4.50 (ISBN 0-89118-009-5). Am Soc Agron.

Coffman, James B. Commentary on Acts. (Firm Foundation Commentary Ser). 1976. cancelled 10.95 (ISBN 0-88027-069-1). Firm Foun Pub.

--Commentary on First & Second Corinthians. (Firm Foundation Commentary Ser.). 1977. cancelled 10.95 (ISBN 0-88027-071-3). Firm Foun Pub.

--Commentary on First & Second Thessalonians, I & II Timothy, Titus & Philemon. (Firm Foundation Commentary Ser.). 1978. 10.95 (ISBN 0-88027-073-X). Firm Foun Pub.

--Commentary on Galatians, Ephesians, Phillipians, Colossians. (Firm Foundation Commentary Ser.). 1977. cancelled 10.95 (ISBN 0-88027-072-1). Firm Foun Pub.

--Commentary on Hebrews. (Firm Foundation Commentary Ser.). 1971. cancelled 10.95 (ISBN 0-88027-074-8). Firm Foun Pub.

--Commentary on John. (Firm Foundation Commentary Ser.). 1974. cancelled 10.95 (ISBN 0-88027-068-3). Firm Foun Pub.

--Commentary on Luke. (Firm Foundation Commentary Ser.). 1975. cancelled 10.95 (ISBN 0-88027-067-5). Firm Foun Pub.

--Commentary on Mark. (Firm Foundation Commentary Ser.). 1975. cancelled 10.95 (ISBN 0-88027-066-7). Firm Foun Pub.

--Commentary on Matthew. (Firm Foundation Commentary Ser.). 1968. cancelled 10.95 (ISBN 0-88027-065-9). Firm Foun Pub.

--Commentary on Revelation. (Commentary Ser.). cancelled (ISBN 0-88027-076-4). Firm Foun Pub.

--Commentary on Romans. (Firm Foundation Commentary Ser.). cancelled (ISBN 0-88027-070-5). Firm Foun Pub.

--Commentary on the Minor Prophets, Vol. 1. (Firm Foundation Commentary Ser.). 360p. 1981. cancelled 8.95 (ISBN 0-88027-078-0). Firm Foun Pub.

--Commentary on the Minor Prophets, Vol. 2. (Firm Foundation Commentary Ser.). 383p. 1981. cancelled 8.95 (ISBN 0-88027-079-9). Firm Foun Pub.

--Commentary on the Minor Prophets, Vol. 3. (Commmentary Ser.). 322p. 1983. cancelled 10.95 (ISBN 0-88027-107-8). Firm Foun Pub.

--Commentary on the Minor Prophets, Vol. 4. (Commentary Ser.). 1983. cancelled 10.95 (ISBN 0-88027-108-6). Firm Foun Pub.

--Commentary on the New Testament, 12 vols. (Commentary Ser.). cancelled 125.00 (ISBN 0-88027-077-2). Firm Foun Pub.

--The Mystery of Redemption. 1976. 5.95 (ISBN 0-88027-089-6). Firm Foun Pub.

--The Ten Commandments Yesterday & Today. pap. 4.50 (ISBN 0-88027-094-2). Firm Foun Pub.

Coffman, James P. Introduction to Professional Food Service. rev. ed. 322p. 1972. pap. 16.95 (ISBN 0-8436-2056-0). Van Nos Reinhold.

Coffman, Jay, jt. auth. see Mannick, John.

Coffman, John S. & Funk, J. F., eds. Confession of Faith & Minister's Manual. 134p. 1890. 3.95 (ISBN 0-8361-1354-3). Herald Pr.

Coffman, Lotus D. The Social Composition of the Teaching Population. LC 72-176657. (Columbia University. Teachers College. Contributions to Education: No. 41). Repr. of 1911 ed. 22.50 (ISBN 0-404-55041-X). AMS Pr.

Coffman, M. E. Schaum's Outline of French Vocabulary. (Schaum's Outline Ser.). 256p. 1984. 5.95 (ISBN 0-07-011561-3). McGraw.

Coffman, Mary. Schaum's Outline of French Grammar. (Schaum's Outline Ser.). 288p. 1980. pap. 6.95 (ISBN 0-07-011553-2). McGraw.

Coffman, Mary, jt. auth. see Butturff, Diane.

Coffman, Noah B. Old Lewis County, Oregon Territory. facs. ed. (Shorey Historical Ser.). 32p. pap. 3.95 (ISBN 0-8466-0162-1, S162). Shorey.

Coffman, Rodney, jt. auth. see Barker, Wayne G.

Coffman, S. F., ed. Church Hymnal. 536p. (657 hymns). 1927. 6.95x (ISBN 0-8361-1106-0). Herald Pr.

--Life Songs Number Two. 288p. (With Responsive Readings). 1938. 6.95x (ISBN 0-8361-1116-8). Herald Pr.

Coffman, Sara J. How to Improve Your Test-Taking Skills. 3rd ed. 1982. pap. text ed. 4.50x (ISBN 0-89917-373-X). TIS Inc.

--How to Survive at College. 4th ed. 1984. pap. text ed. 13.95x (ISBN 0-89917-311-X). TIS Inc.

Coffman, Sue E. Music of Finer Tone: Musical Imagery of the Major Romantic Poets. (Salzburg Studies in English Literature, Romantic Reassessment: No. 89). (Orig.). 1979. pap. text ed. 25.50x (ISBN 0-391-01672-5). Humanities.

Coffman, Taylor. Hearst Castle: The Story of William Randolph Hearst & San Simeon. 1985. 19.95 (ISBN 0-86679-022-5); pap. 9.95 (ISBN 0-86679-017-9). Oak Tree Pubns.

Coffman, Tom. Catch a Wave: A Case Study of Hawaii's New Politics. rev. 2nd ed. LC 72-98011. 227p. 1973. pap. text ed. 6.95x (ISBN 0-8248-0270-5). UH Pr.

Coffman, Virginia. Dark Winds. 1985. 16.95 (ISBN 0-87795-631-6). Arbor Hse.

--Dinah Faire. (Reader's Request). 1980. lib. bdg. 15.95 (ISBN 0-8161-3046-9, Large Print Bks). G K Hall.

--Dynasty of Desire. 464p. 1984. pap. 3.95 (ISBN 0-8217-1422-8). Zebra.

--Dynasty of Dreams. 1984. pap. 3.95 (ISBN 0-8217-1370-1). Zebra.

--Fire Dawn. 1978. pap. 1.95 (ISBN 0-449-23640-4, Crest). Fawcett.

--The Gaynor Women. 1979. pap. 1.95 (ISBN 0-449-24075-4, Crest). Fawcett.

--The Gaynor Women. (Reader's Request Ser.). 1980. lib. bdg. 16.95 (ISBN 0-8161-3047-7, Large Print Bks). G K Hall.

--Hyde Place. (General Ser.). 1981. lib. bdg. 14.95 (ISBN 0-8161-3256-9, Large Print Bks). G K Hall.

--The Lombard Cavalcade. LC 81-67523. 464p. 1982. 15.50 (ISBN 0-87795-355-4). Arbor Hse.

--The Lombard Heiress. LC 82-72071. 304p. 1982. 14.95 (ISBN 0-87795-434-8). Arbor Hse.

--Marsanne. (Reader's Request Ser.). 1980. lib. bdg. 14.95 (ISBN 0-8161-3049-3, Large Print Bks). G K Hall.

--The Orchid Tree. 1984. 15.95 (ISBN 0-87795-532-8). Arbor Hse.

--Pacific Cavalcade. 560p. 1982. pap. 3.50 (ISBN 0-449-20002-7, Crest). Fawcett.

--Pacific Cavalcade. LC 80-66502. 1981. 12.95 (ISBN 0-87795-277-9). Arbor Hse.

--Veronique. (Reader's Request Ser.). 1980. lib. bdg. 17.50 (ISBN 0-8161-3048-5, Large Print Bks). G K Hall.

Coffman, William E., jt. ed. see Randhawa, Bikkar S.

Coffrey, Marie B. Four Women. (Orig.). 1980. pap. text ed. 2.25 (ISBN 0-505-51578-4, Pub. by Tower Bks). Dorchester Pub Co.

Coffron, J. Understanding & Troubleshooting the Microprocessors. 1980. 28.95 (ISBN 0-13-936625-3). P-H.

Coffron, James. Using & Troubleshooting the MC68000. 1983. 16.95 (ISBN 0-8359-8159-2). Reston.

--Using & Troubleshooting the Z-8000. 1982. text ed. 29.95 (ISBN 0-8359-8157-6); pap. text ed. 16.95 (ISBN 0-8359-8156-8). Reston.

Coffron, James & Harmon, Bill. Microprocessor Interfacing Techniques, Vol. II. 300p. pap. cancelled (ISBN 0-89588-196-9). SYBEX.

Coffron, James W. The Apple Connection. LC 82-50620. (Illus.). 263p. 1982. pap. 14.95 (ISBN 0-89588-085-7, C405). SYBEX.

--The Commodore 64 Connection. LC 84-51242. 250p. 1984. pap. 14.95 (ISBN 0-89588-192-6). SYBEX.

--Eighty Eighty-Six Applications. 250p. 1984. pap. cancelled (ISBN 0-89588-191-8). SYBEX.

--Getting Started with 8080, 8085, Z80, & 6800 Microprocessor Systems. (Illus.). 352p. 1984. pap. 14.95 (ISBN 0-13-354663-2). P-H.

--The IBM PC Connection. LC 83-51571. (Illus.). 264p. 1984. pap. 16.95 (ISBN 0-89588-127-6). SYBEX.

--Practical Hardware Details for 8080, 8085, Z80, & 6800 Microprocessor Systems. (Illus.). 352p. 1981. text ed. 29.95 (ISBN 0-13-691089-0). P-H.

--Practical Troubleshooting for Microprocessors. (Illus.). 256p. 1981. text ed. 27.95 (ISBN 0-13-694273-3). P-H.

--Programming the 8086-8088. LC 83-50228. (Illus.). 311p. 1983. pap. 15.95 (ISBN 0-89588-120-9). SYBEX.

--Proven Techniques for Troubleshooting the Microprocessor & Home Computer Systems. (Illus.). 256p. 1984. pap. 14.95 (ISBN 0-13-731738-7). P-H.

--The VIC-20 Connection. LC 83-50227. (Illus.). 273p. 1983. pap. 9.95 (ISBN 0-89588-128-4). SYBEX.

--Your First Microprocessor: Organizing, Construction, Debugging. LC 83-62032. (Illus.). 352p. 1984. pap. 14.95 (ISBN 0-13-978446-2). P-H.

--Z80 Applications. LC 83-60950. (Illus.). 295p. 1983. pap. 15.95 (ISBN 0-89588-094-6). SYBEX.

Coffron, James W. & Long, William E. Practical Interfacing Techniques for Microprocessor Systems. (Illus.). 432p. 1983. 31.95 (ISBN 0-13-691394-6). P-H.

Cofield, Roger E., Jr. Design Manual for High Temperature Hot Water & Steam Systems. LC 83-1135. 340p. 1984. 46.50x (ISBN 0-471-89363-3, Pub. by Wiley-Interscience). Wiley.

Cofone, Charles J., ed. Elizabeth Rogers, Hir Virginall Booke. LC 73-94344. 144p. (Orig.). 1975. pap. 7.95 (ISBN 0-486-23138-0). Dover.

--Favorite Christmas Carols. (Illus.). 64p. 1975. pap. 3.00 (ISBN 0-486-20445-6). Dover.

Cogan, Adrian. Microwave Semiconductor Engineering. 1985. text ed. 50.00 (ISBN 0-89006-168-8). Artech Hse.

Cogan, Arlene & Goodman, Charles. Elvis, This One's for You. (Illus.). 304p. 1985. 19.95 (ISBN 0-916693-05-8). Castle Bks.

Cogan, B. H. & Smith, K. G. Insects: Instructions for Collectors, No. 4a. 5th rev. ed. (Illus.). vi, 169p. 1974. pap. 7.00x (ISBN 0-565-05705-7, Pub. by Brit Mus Nat Hist). Sabbot-Natural Hist Bks.

Cogan, David G. Neurology of the Ocular Muscles. 2nd ed. (Illus.). 320p. 1978. photocopy ed. 34.75x (ISBN 0-398-00321-1). C C Thomas.

--Neurology of the Visual System. (Illus.). 424p. 1980. photocopy ed. 45.75x (ISBN 0-398-00322-X). C C Thomas.

--Ophthalmic Manifestations of Systemic Vascular Disease. LC 74-4556. (Major Problem in Internal Medicine Ser.: Vol. 3). (Illus.). 225p. 1974. 15.95 (ISBN 0-7216-2648-3). Saunders.

Cogan, Elaine & Padrow, Ben. You Can Talk to (Almost) Anyone about (Almost) Anything: A Speaking Guide for Business & Professional People. LC 84-15531. (Illus.). 116p. (Orig.). 1984. lib. bdg. 14.95 (ISBN 0-87678-021-4); pap. 7.95 (ISBN 0-87678-022-2). Continuing Ed Pubns.

Cogan, John J. & Schneider, Donald O., eds. Perspectives on Japan: A Guide for Teachers. LC 83-61859. (Illus.). 128p. (Orig.). 1983. pap. 10.95 (ISBN 0-87986-045-6). Nat Coun Soc Studies.

Cogan, Lee. Negroes for Medicine. LC 68-31769. (Josiah Macy Foundation Ser). Repr. of 1968 ed. 21.30 (ISBN 0-8357-9280-3, 2015689). Bks Demand UMI.

Cogan, Lee, ed. Kreuzer & Cogan's Literature for Composition. 2nd ed. LC 75-29337. 1976. text ed. 14.95 (ISBN 0-03-015511-8, HoltC). HR&W.

Cogan, Lee, jt. ed. see Kreuzer, James R.

Cogan, Marc. The Human Thing: The Speeches & Principles of Thucydides' History. LC 80-24226. (Chicago Originals Paperback Ser.). 248p. 1981. lib. bdg. 20.00x (ISBN 0-226-11194-6). U of Chicago Pr.

Cogan, Martin G. & Garovoy, Marvin E., eds. Introduction to Dialysis. (Illus.). 320p. 1985. text ed. 38.50 (ISBN 0-443-08305-3). Churchill.

Cogan, Sr. Mary De Paul. Sisters of Maryknoll: Through Troubled Waters. LC 72-167329. (Essay Index Reprint Ser.). Repr. of 1947 ed. 18.00 (ISBN 0-8369-2764-8). Ayer Co Pubs.

Cogan, Morris L. Clinical Supervision. LC 72-85906. 250p. 1973. text ed. 31.95 (ISBN 0-395-14027-7). HM.

Cogan, Morton. Imperialism & Religion: Assyria, Judah & Israel in the Eighth & Seventh Centuries B.C.E. LC 73-83723. (Society of Biblical Literature. Monograph). 1974. pap. 9.95 (ISBN 0-89130-331-6, 00-06-19). Scholars Pr GA.

Cogan, Philip. Complete Sonatas for Piano Solo. Temperley, Nicholas, ed. (The London Pianoforte School 1770-1860 Ser.). 300p. 1984. lib. bdg. 75.00 (ISBN 0-8240-6157-8). Garland Pub.

Cogan, Robert. New Images of Musical Sound. (Illus.). 224p. 1984. text ed. 25.00x (ISBN 0-674-61585-9). Harvard U Pr.

Cogan, Robert & Escot, Pozzi. Sonic Design: The Nature of Sound & Music. (Illus.). 544p. 1976. 24.95. P-H.

Cogan, Rosemary & Logan, Suzanne. Lamaze for the Joy of it. (Avery's Childbirth Education Ser.). (Illus.). 112p. 1984. pap. text ed. 6.95 plastic comb (ISBN 0-89529-205-X). Avery Pub.

Cogan, Sara, compiled by. The Jews of San Francisco & the Greater Bay Area: 1849 to 1919. (Western Jewish Americana Ser.: No. 2). 1972. 22.00 (ISBN 0-943376-03-3). Magnes Mus.

--The Jews of Los Angeles, No. 3. (Western Jewish Americana Ser. Publications). 237p. 1980. 24.95 (ISBN 0-943376-12-2); pap. 14.95 (ISBN 0-943376-11-4). Magnes Mus.

Cogan, Sara G., compiled by. Pioneer Jews of the California Mother Lode: 1849 to 1880. (Western Jewish Americana Ser.: No. 1). 1968. 7.50 (ISBN 0-943376-01-7). Magnes Mus.

Cogburn, Buddy. All-Round Cowboys with a Texas Limp. LC 85-50955. (Illus.). 112p. (Orig.). 1985. pap. 2.75 (ISBN 0-9614896-1-8). Trails End.

Cogburn, Shirley B., jt. auth. see Hilt, Nancy E.

Cogdell, J. R. An Introduction to Circuits & Electronics. (Illus.). 560p. 1986. text ed. 38.95 (ISBN 0-13-479346-3). P-H.

Cogdell, Roy & Wilson, Sybil. Black Communication in White Society. LC 79-93302. 160p. 1980. 14.00 (ISBN 0-86548-004-4). R & E Pubs.

Cogell, Elizabeth C. Ursula K. Le Guin: A Primary & Secondary Bibliography. 1983. lib. bdg. 45.00 (ISBN 0-8161-8155-1, Hall Reference). G K Hall.

Coger, Dalvan M., jt. auth. see Hess, Robert L.

Coger, Leslie I. & White, Melvin R. Reader's Theatre Handbook. 3rd ed. 1982. pap. text ed. 15.80x (ISBN 0-673-15270-7). Scott F.

Coggan, D. Relevance of the Bible for Today. 1967. pap. 1.75x (ISBN 0-85564-005-7, Pub. by U of W Austral Pr). Intl Spec Bk.

Coggan, W. Readings in Child Psychology. 1969. pap. text ed. 7.95x (ISBN 0-8422-0033-9). Irvington.

Cogger, Harold G. Reptiles & Amphibians of Australia. 3rd ed. (Illus.). 660p. 1983. 59.50 (ISBN 0-88359-012-3). R Curtis Bks.

Cogger, Susan K. Fitting Contact Lenses. 136p. 1985. pap. 13.50 (ISBN 0-88167-042-1). Raven.

Coggeshall, Almy & Coggeshall, Anne. Twenty-Five Ski Tours in the Adirondacks: Cross-Country Skiing Adventures in the Southern Adirondacks, the Capital District & Tug Hill. LC 79-88594. (Twenty-Five Ski Tours Ser.). (Illus.). 144p. 1979. pap. 5.95 (ISBN 0-89725-008-7). Backcountry Pubns.

Coggeshall, Anne, jt. auth. see Coggeshall, Almy.

Coggeshall, Charles P. & Coggeshall, Thellwell R. The Coggeshalls in America: Genealogy of the Descendants of John Coggeshall of Newport with a Brief Notice of Their English Antecedents. LC 83-3163. (Illus.). 424p. 1983. Repr. of 1930 ed. 35.00 (ISBN 0-87152-374-4). Reprint.

Coggeshall, R. E., jt. ed. see Willis, W. D.

Coggeshall, Rosanne. Hymn for Drum. LC 77-28154. 96p. 1978. 13.95x (ISBN 0-8071-0361-6); pap. 4.95 (ISBN 0-8071-0362-4). La State U Pr.

--Traffic, with Ghosts. 13.95 (ISBN 0-395-36508-2); pap. 7.95 (ISBN 0-395-36509-0). HM.

Coggeshall, Thellwell R., jt. auth. see Coggeshall, Charles P.

Coggeshall, William T. The Poets & Poetry of the West: With Biographical & Critical Notices. facsimile ed. LC 75-92. (Mid-American Frontier Ser.). 1975. Repr. of 1860 ed. 52.00x (ISBN 0-405-06859-X). Ayer Co Pubs.

Coggin & Spooner. How to Build a Bus Ministry. 1.95 (ISBN 0-8054-9405-7). Broadman.

Coggin, James K., et al. Manual for Sharpening Hand Woodworking Tools. (Illus.). 1943. pap. 3.35 (ISBN 0-8134-0100-3, 100); 2.50x. Interstate.

Coggin, Patricia A., jt. auth. see Newton, Carolyn S.

Coggins, Clemency C., et al. Cenote of Sacrifice: Maya Treasures from the Sacred Well at Chichen Itza. (Illus.). 176p. 1984. 35.00x (ISBN 0-292-71097-6); pap. 24.50 (ISBN 0-292-71098-4). U of Tex Pr.

Coggins, Dixie L. Complete Six Week Course in Disco Dance Instruction. (Ballroom Dance Ser.). 1985. lib. bdg. 74.00 (ISBN 0-87700-826-4). Revisionist Pr.

Coggins, Frank W. Clocks: Construction, Maintenance & Repair. (Illus.). 256p. 1984. 18.95 (ISBN 0-8306-0269-0, 1569); pap. 13.50 (ISBN 0-8306-0169-4). TAB Bks.

--The Woodturner's Handbook. (Illus.). 224p. 21.95 (ISBN 0-8306-0769-2, 1769); pap. 12.95 (ISBN 0-8306-1769-8). TAB Bks.

Coggins, George C. & Wilkinson, Charles F. Federal Public Land & Resources Law, Statutory Supplement. (University Casebook Ser.). 413p. 1984. pap. text ed. 14.00 (ISBN 0-88277-197-3). Foundation Pr.

--Federal Public Land & Resources Law. LC 80-28034. (University Casebook Ser.). 849p. 1981. text ed. 24.50 (ISBN 0-88277-022-5); Supplement, 215p. write for info. (ISBN 0-88277-144-2). Foundation Pr.

Coggins, Jack. Horseman's Bible. rev. ed. Stoneridge, M. A., rev. by. LC 83-16500. (Outdoor Bible Ser.). (Illus.). 192p. 1984. pap. 5.95 (ISBN 0-385-18343-7). Doubleday.

Coggins, R. J. The Books of Ezra & Nehemiah. LC 75-26278. (Cambridge Bible Commentary on the New English Bible, Old Testament Ser.). (Illus.). 200p. 1976. 22.95 (ISBN 0-521-08648-5); pap. 9.95x (ISBN 0-521-09759-2). Cambridge U Pr.

--The First & Second Book of the Chronicles. LC 75-17117. (Cambridge Bible Commentary on the New English Bible, Old Testament Ser.). (Illus.). 256p. 1976. 39.50 (ISBN 0-521-08647-7); pap. 16.95x (ISBN 0-521-09758-4). Cambridge U Pr.

Coggins, R. J. & Knibb, M. A. The First & Second Books of Esdras: Cambridge Bible Commentary on the New English Bible. LC 78-16420. (Old Testament Ser.). 1979. pap. 15.95 (ISBN 0-521-09757-6). Cambridge U Pr.

Coggins, R. J. & Phillips, Anthony C., eds. Israel's Prophetic Tradition. LC 81-17065. (Illus.). 290p. 1982. 44.50 (ISBN 0-521-24223-1). Cambridge U Pr.

Coggins, Richard. Who's Who in the Bible. (Illus.). 232p. 1981. 26.50x (ISBN 0-389-20183-9). B&N Imports.

Coggins, Richard, et al, eds. Israel's Prophetic Tradition: Essays in Honour of Peter Ackroyd. 294p. 1985. 18.95 (ISBN 0-521-31886-6). Cambridge U Pr.

Coggins, Richard J. & Re'emi, Paul S. Nahum, Obadiah, Esther: Israel among the Nations. Holmgren, Frederick & Knight, George A., eds. (International Theological Commentary Ser.). 128p. (Orig.). 1985. pap. 6.95 (ISBN 0-8028-0048-3). Eerdmans.

Coggins, Wade T. & Frizen, Edwin L., Jr. Reaching Our Generation. LC 82-9751. (Illus., Orig.). 1982. pap. 5.95 (ISBN 0-87808-188-7). William Carey Lib.

Coggins, Wade T. see Frizen, Edwin L.

Coggle, John E. Biological Effects of Radiation. 2nd ed. LC 83-80197. (Illus.). 247p. 1983. 28.00x (ISBN 0-8002-3075-2). Taylor & Francis.

Coghill, George E. Early Embryonic Somatic Movements in Birds & Mammals Other Than Man. (SRCD M Ser.). 1940. pap. 15.00 (ISBN 0-527-01514-8). Kraus Repr.

Coghill, Mrs. Harry. The Autobiography & Letters of Mrs. M. O. W. Oliphant. 1973. Repr. of 1899 ed. 25.00 (ISBN 0-8274-1655-5). R West.

Coghill, Mary A. Games & Simulatons in Industrial & Labor Relations Training. (Key Issues Ser.: No. 7). 32p. 1971. pap. 2.00 (ISBN 0-87546-207-3). ILR Pr.

--Lie Detector in Employment. (Key Issues Ser.: No. 2). 40p. 1973. pap. 2.00 (ISBN 0-87546-208-1). ILR Pr.

Coghill, Mary A., jt. auth. see Miller, Frank B.

Coghill, Mary A., jt. auth. see Shafer, Richard A.

Coghill, Nevil, tr. see Chaucer, Geoffrey.

Coghill, Nevill. The Pardon of Piers Plowman. 1978. Repr. of 1946 ed. lib. bdg. 10.00 (ISBN 0-8495-0907-6). Arden Lib.

--Pardon of Piers Plowman. LC 73-4674. 1945. lib. bdg. 8.50 (ISBN 0-8414-3350-X). Folcroft.

--Shakespeare's Professional Skills. 1964. 47.50 (ISBN 0-521-04681-5). Cambridge U Pr.

Coghill, Nevill & Bradbrook, M. C. British Writers & Their Work: Geoffrey Chaucer & Sir Thomas Malory, No. 1. LC 63-63096. pap. 28.80 (ISBN 0-317-19813-0, 2023207). Bks Demand UMI.

Coghill, Nevill, tr. see Chaucer, Geoffrey.

Coghlan see Sohn, David A.

Coghlan, David A. Automotive Brake System. 1980. pap. text ed. write for info. (ISBN 0-534-00822-4, Breton Pubs). Wadsworth Pub.

--Automotive Chassis Systems: Steering, Suspension, Alignment, & Brakes. 2nd ed. (Illus.). 440p. 1985. pap. text ed. 19.00 (ISBN 0-534-04848-X, 77F6066). Breton Pubs.

Coghlan, John P., jt. ed. see Denton, Derek A.

Coghlan, Margaret. Memoirs of Mrs. Coghlan, Daughter of the Late Major Moncrieffe. LC 75-140859. (Eyewitness Accounts of the American Revolution Ser., No. 3). 1970. Repr. of 1864 ed. 16.00 (ISBN 0-405-01213-6). Ayer Co Pubs.

Coghlan, Richard. Landscape Gardening in the Tropics. (Illus.). 1975. 30.00x (ISBN 0-8464-0545-8). Beekman Pubs.

--Money Credit & the Economy. (Illus.). 192p. 1981. text ed. 29.50x (ISBN 0-04-332079-1). Allen Unwin.

Coghlan, Richard & Sykes, Carolyn. The Use & Abuse of Monetary Policy. 224p. 1985. write for info. (ISBN 0-85941-164-8, Pub. by Woodhead-Faulkner). Longwood Pub Group.

Coghlan, Richard T., jt. ed. see Boeckh, J. Anthony.

Coghlan, Ronan. Pocket Dictionary of Irish Myth & Legend. (Pocket Bk.). (Illus.). 96p. (Orig.). 1985. pap. 3.95 (ISBN 0-86281-152-X, Pub. by Appletree Pr). Irish Bks Media.

--Pocket Guide to Irish First Names. (Pocket Bk.). 72p. (Orig.). 1985. pap. 3.95 (ISBN 0-86281-153-8, Pub. by Appletree Pr). Irish Bks Media.

Coghland, Richard & Sykes, Carolyn. Managing the Money Supply. 224p. 1980. 21.00x (ISBN 0-85941-164-8, Pub. by Woodhead-Faulkner England). State Mutual Bk.

Cogley, John. Catholic America. 240p. 1974. pap. 3.95 (ISBN 0-385-08916-3, Im). Doubleday.

--Report on Blacklisting: Part One, the Movies. LC 79-169349. (Arno Press Cinema Program). 326p. 1972. Repr. of 1956 ed. 24.50 (ISBN 0-405-03915-8). Ayer Co Pubs.

Cogley, John, jt. auth. see Miller, Merle.

Cogley, Thomas S. The Law of Strikes, Lockouts & Labor Organizations. xiv, 377p. 1981. Repr. of 1894 ed. lib. bdg. 32.50x (ISBN 0-8377-0435-9). Rothman.

Cognard, Jacques. Alignment of Nematic Liquid Crystals & Their Mixtures. (Molecular Crystals & Liquid Crystals Supplement Ser.). 78p. 1982. 28.50 (ISBN 0-677-05905-1). Gordon.

Cognazzo, Maria, jt. auth. see Bussi, Luciano.

Cognet, G., jt. ed. see Delhaye, J. M.

Cognia, Raymond & Elgar, Frank. Illustrated Dictionary of Impressionism. (Pocket Art Ser.). (Illus., Eng.). (gr. 10-12). 1979. pap. 3.95 (ISBN 0-8120-0986-X). Barron.

Cogniat, Raymond. Bonnard. (QLP Art Ser.). (Illus.). 1968. 9.95 (ISBN 0-517-09889-X). Crown.

--Braque. (Library of Great Painters). (Illus.). 1980. 40.00 (ISBN 0-8109-0703-8). Abrams.

--Braque. (Quality-Low-Price Art Ser.). 1970. 9.95 (ISBN 0-517-03300-3). Crown.

--The Century of the Impressionists. (Illus.). 1968. 12.98 (ISBN 0-517-01320-7). Outlet Bk Co.

--Chagall. (QLP Art Ser.). (Illus.). 1965. 9.95 (ISBN 0-517-03719-X). Crown.

--Dufy. (QLP Art Ser.). (Illus.). 9.95 (ISBN 0-517-03721-1). Crown.

--Pissarro. (Q L P Art Ser.). 1976. 9.95 (ISBN 0-517-52477-5). Crown.

--Sisley: Q.L.P. (Illus.). 1978. 9.95 (ISBN 0-517-53321-9). Crown.

--Soutine. (Q L P Art Ser.). (Illus.). 96p. 1974. 9.95 (ISBN 0-517-51136-3). Crown.

Cogniaux, Alfredus. Orchidaceae, 4 vols. (Flora Brasiliensis Ser.: Vol. 3, Pts. 4-6). (Illus.). 970p. (Lat.). 1975. Repr. Set. lib. bdg. 157.50x (ISBN 3-87429-080-8). Lubrecht & Cramer.

Cogny, Pierre. L' Education Sentimentale de Flaubert: Le Monde en Creux. new ed. (Collection Themes et Textes). 270p. (Orig., Fr.). 1975. pap. 6.75 (ISBN 2-03-035030-3, 2685). Larousse.
Cogny, Pierre, jt. auth. see Maupassant, Guy de.
Cogoli, John, et al. Graphic Arts Photography: Black & White. (Illus.). 412p. 1981. 32.00 (ISBN 0-318-17928-8); members 16.00 (ISBN 0-318-17929-6). Graphic Arts Tech Found.
Cogoli, John E. Photo-Offset Fundamentals. 4th ed. (Illus.). (gr. 10-12). 1980. text ed. 19.96 (ISBN 0-87345-235-6); study guide 6.00 (ISBN 0-87345-236-4); filmstrips & ans. avail. 398.00 (ISBN 0-685-42198-8). McKnight.
Cogolin, Joseph B. Chabert De see Chabert De Cogolin, Joseph B.
Cogswell, Betty E. & Sussman, Marvin B., eds. Family Medicine: A New Approach to Health Care. LC 81-6980. (Marriage & Family Review Ser.: Vol. 4, Nos. 1 & 2). 187p. 1982. text ed. 29.95 (ISBN 0-917724-25-9, B25); pap. text ed. 12.95 (ISBN 0-917724-80-1). Haworth Pr.
Cogswell, F. N. Polymer Melt Rheology: A Guide for Industrial Practice. LC 80-41762. 225p. 1981. 53.95x (ISBN 0-470-27102-7). Halsted Pr.
Cogswell, Fred, ed. The Poetry of Modern Quebec: An Anthology. LC 77-362075. (French Writers of Canada Ser.). pap. 51.50 (ISBN 0-317-29053-3, 2023750). Bks Demand UMI.
Cogswell, Georgia. Golden Obsession. 1979. pap. 2.25 (ISBN 0-89083-467-9). Zebra.
Cogswell, Howard L. Water Birds of California. (Natural History Guides Ser.). 1977. 12.95 (ISBN 0-520-02994-1); pap. 5.75 (ISBN 0-520-02699-3). U of Cal Pr.
Cogswell, James. No Place Left Called Home. (Orig.). 1983. pap. 5.50 (ISBN 0-377-00128-7). Friend Pr.
Cogswell, Leander W. History of the Town of Henniker. LC 72-94786. (Illus.). 1973. Repr. of 1880 ed. 45.00X (ISBN 0-912274-29-8). NH Pub Co.
Cogswell, Margaret, ed. see Breitenbach, Edgar.
Cogswell, Philip, Jr. Capitol Names: Individuals Woven into Oregon's History. LC 76-56657. (Illus.). 133p. 1977. 4.95 (ISBN 0-87595-076-0); pap. 2.95 (ISBN 0-87595-054-X). Oreg Hist Soc.
Cogswell, William R., jt. auth. see Hutchinngs, Mary H.
Cohalan, Florence D. A Popular History of the Archdiocese of New York. LC 82-84246. (USCHS Monograph: Vol. 37). (Illus.). xviii, 354p. 1983. 15.00 (ISBN 0-930060-17-2). US Cath Hist.
Cohan & Yoshikawa. Retail Nursery Management. 1982. text ed. 18.95 (ISBN 0-8359-6684-4). Reston.
Cohan, A. Theories of Revolution. 1975. pap. 14.95 (ISBN 0-442-30700-4). Van Nos Reinhold.
Cohan, Christopher J. & Olstad, Walter B. Space Transportation Systems: 1980-2000. LC 78-24171. (Illus.). 91p. 1978. 12.50 (ISBN 0-915928-27-2, AAS1); members 12.50 (ISBN 0-317-32196-X). AIAA.
Cohan, George M. Twenty Years on Broadway & the Years It Took to Get There: The True Story of a Trouper's Life from the Cradle to the Closed Shop. LC 76-138106. (Illus.). 264p. 1972. Repr. of 1925 ed. lib. bdg. 24.75x (ISBN 0-8371-5682-3, COTY). Greenwood.
Cohan, John R., ed. Drafting California Irrevocable Inter Vivos Trusts. LC 73-623473. (California Practice Book Ser.: No. 63). xiii, 490p. 1973. 60.00 (ISBN 0-88124-025-7). Cal Cont Ed Bar.
--Drafting California Revocable Living Trusts. 2nd ed. 491p. 1985. 90.00 (ISBN 0-88124-136-9). Cal Cont Ed Bar.
Cohan, Leonard, ed. Readers Advisory Service: Selected Topical Booklists, Vol. 10. 1983. 115.00 (ISBN 0-685-79403-2). Sci Assoc Intl.
Cohan, Steven. Violation & Repair in the English Novel: The Paradigm of Experience from Richardson to Woolf. 236p. 1985. 19.95 (ISBN 0-8143-1794-4). Wayne St U Pr.
Cohan, Steven, ed. see Boaden, James.
Cohan, Tony. The Flame: Notes on the Writer's Art. LC 82-73826. 63p. (Orig.). 1983. 12.00 (ISBN 0-918226-09-0); pap. 6.00 (ISBN 0-918226-10-4). Acrobat.
--Opium. 463p. 1984. 19.95 (ISBN 0-671-47327-1). S&S.
Cohausen, Johann H. Hermippus Redivivus. Kastenbaum, Robert, ed. LC 78-22194. (Aging & Old Age Ser.). 1979. Repr. of 1771 ed. lib. bdg. 19.00x (ISBN 0-405-11811-2). Ayer Co Pubs.
Cohen. Film & Fiction. LC 79-64073. 1979. 19.50x (ISBN 0-300-02366-9). Yale U Pr.
--The Neutron Bomb: Political, Technological & Military Issues. 1978. pap. 6.50 (ISBN 0-89549-009-9, IFPA7, IFPA). Unipub.
--Special People: A Brighter Future for Everyone with Physical, Mental & Emotional Disabilities. (Psychology in Action Series). 1977. text ed. 11.95 (ISBN 0-13-826511-9, Spec); pap. text ed. 5.95 (ISBN 0-13-826503-8). P-H.
Cohen & Cameron. Intermediate Algebra. 1985. 30.31 (ISBN 0-205-07172-4, 567172). Allyn.
Cohen & Glombiewski. Public Personnel Update. (Public Administration & Public Policy Ser.). 352p. 1984. 39.75 (ISBN 0-8247-7237-7). Dekker.
Cohen & Holliday. Statistics For the Social Sciences. 320p. 1982. text ed. 31.50 (ISBN 0-06-318219-X, Pub. by Har-Row Ltd England); pap. text ed. 18.50 (ISBN 0-06-318220-3, Pub. by Har-Row Ltd England). Har-Row.
Cohen & Miller. Consumer Bankruptcy Manual. 1985. 72.00 (ISBN 0-88712-272-8). Warren.
Cohen, jt. auth. see Cox.
Cohen, jt. auth. see Neal.
Cohen, ed. see De Ronsard, Pierre.
Cohen, et al. Teaching Science As a Decision Making Process. 296p. 1984. pap. text ed. 14.50 (ISBN 0-8403-3402-8). Kendall-Hunt.
Cohen, A. Ancient Jewish Proverbs. Cranmer-Byng, L. & Kapadia, S. A., eds. 127p. 1980. Repr. of 1911 ed. lib. bdg. 16.50 (ISBN 0-8414-9991-8). Folcroft.
--Ancient Jewish Proverbs, 1911. 1977. 17.50 (ISBN 0-686-19671-6). Mill Bks.
--Biomedical Scanning Electron Micro Handbook. 1986. cancelled (ISBN 0-442-25160-2). Van Nos Reinhold.
--Deviance & Control. 1966. 14.95 (ISBN 0-13-208389-2). P-H.
--Ezekiel. 350p. 1950. 10.95 (ISBN 0-900689-30-7). Soncino Pr NY.
--Isaiah One & Two. 330p. 1949. 10.95 (ISBN 0-900689-28-5). Soncino Pr NY.
--Jeremiah. 369p. 1949. 10.95 (ISBN 0-900689-29-3). Soncino Pr NY.
--Job. 233p. 1946. 10.95 (ISBN 0-900689-34-X). Soncino Pr NY.
--Kings One & Two. 337p. 1950. 10.95 (ISBN 0-900689-27-7). Soncino Pr NY.
--Proverbs. 223p. 1946. 10.95 (ISBN 0-900689-33-1). Soncino Pr NY.
--The Psalms. 488p. 1945. 10.95 (ISBN 0-900689-32-3). Soncino Pr NY.
--The Soncino Chumash. 1203p. 1947. 22.50 (ISBN 0-900689-24-2). Soncino Pr NY.
--The Twelve Prophets. 368p. 1948. 10.95 (ISBN 0-900689-31-5). Soncino Pr NY.
Cohen, A., ed. Chronicles. 358p. 1952. 10.95 (ISBN 0-900689-37-4). Soncino Pr NY.
--Joshua & Judges. 332p. 1950. 10.95 (ISBN 0-900689-20-X). Soncino Pr NY.
--Samuel. 361p. 1949. 10.95 (ISBN 0-900689-26-9). Soncino Pr NY.
Cohen, A., ed. see Nehemiah, Ezra.
Cohen, A., ed. see Symposium on Dynamic Aspects of Speech Perception Held at I.P.O.,Eindhoven, the Netherlands,Aug.4-6,1975.
Cohen, A. D., jt. ed. see Given, P. H.
Cohen, A. J., jt. auth. see Elias, P. S.
Cohen, A. K. Delinquent Boys. LC 55-7337. 1955. 17.00 (ISBN 0-02-905760-4); pap. text ed. 7.95 (ISBN 0-02-905770-1). Free Pr.
Cohen, Aaron & Cohen, Elaine. Automation, Space Management, & Productivity: A Guide for Librarians. 221p. 1981. 39.95 (ISBN 0-8352-1398-6). Bowker.
--Designing & Space Planning for Libraries: A Behavioral Guide. LC 79-12478. (Illus.). 1979. 32.50 (ISBN 0-8352-1150-9). Bowker.
--Planning the Electronic Office. (Illus.). 256p. 1983. 37.50 (ISBN 0-07-011583-4). McGraw.
Cohen, Aaron I. International Discography of Women Composers. LC 83-26445. (Discographies Ser.: No. 10). xi, 254p. 1984. lib. bdg. 35.00 (ISBN 0-313-24272-0, CID/). Greenwood.
Cohen, Abner. Arab Border-Villages in Israel. 1965. text ed. 30.25x (ISBN 0-7190-0251-6). Humanities.
--Custom & Politics in Urban Africa: A Study of Hausa Migrants in Yoruba Towns. LC 68-55743. 1969. 36.50x (ISBN 0-520-01571-1); pap. 8.50x (ISBN 0-520-01836-2, CAMPUS43). U of Cal Pr.
--The Politics of Elite Culture: Explorations in the Dramaturgy of Power in a Modern African Society. LC 80-5469. 200p. 1981. 28.50x (ISBN 0-520-04120-8); pap. 8.50x (ISBN 0-520-04275-1, CAMPUS 270). U of Cal Pr.
--Two-Dimensional Man: An Essay on the Anthropology of Power & Symbolism in Complex Society. LC 72-93525. 1974. pap. 6.95x (ISBN 0-520-03241-1). U of Cal Pr.
Cohen, Abraham. Confrontation Analysis: Theory & Practice. 528p. 1981. 45.00 (ISBN 0-8089-1417-0, 790876). Grune.
--Everyman's Talmud. LC 75-10750. 446p. 1975. pap. 11.25 (ISBN 0-8052-0497-0). Schocken.
--Hi-Fi Loudspeakers & Enclosures. 2nd, rev. ed. (Illus.). 1968. 11.60 (ISBN 0-8104-0721-3). Hayden.
--Sabbath Sermons. 12.50x (ISBN 0-685-01038-4). Bloch.
Cohen, Adele. Diary of an Exhibition. 36p. 1983. pap. 3.75x (ISBN 0-89822-032-7). Visual Studies.
Cohen, Adir. The Educational Philosophy of Martin Buber. LC 81-68074. 350p. 1983. 32.50 (ISBN 0-8386-3098-7). Fairleigh Dickinson.
Cohen, Alan. The Dragon Doesn't Live Here Anymore: Loving Fully Living Freely. (Illus.). 400p. (Orig.). 1981. pap. 8.95 (ISBN 0-910367-30-2). Eden Co.
--Have You Hugged a Monster Today. (Illus.). 64p. (Orig.). 1984. pap. 3.95 (ISBN 0-910367-32-9). Eden Co.
--Have You Hugged a Monster Today? 2nd ed. (Illus.). 64p. 1983. pap. 5.00 (ISBN 0-942494-73-3). Coleman Pub.
--If We Only Have Love. (Illus.). 15p. (Orig.). 1984. pap. 1.00 (ISBN 0-910367-34-5). Eden Co.
--If We Only Have Love. (Illus., Orig.). 1984. pap. 2.00 (ISBN 0-942494-86-5). Coleman Pub.
--Rising in Love. 150p. (Orig.). 1982. pap. 5.95 (ISBN 0-910367-31-0). Eden Co.
--Setting the Seen: Creative Visualization for Healing. 36p. (Orig.). 1982. pap. 3.95 (ISBN 0-910367-33-7). Eden Co.
--Structure, Logic & Program Design. LC 83-10207. 287p. 1983. 37.95x (ISBN 0-471-16400-3, Pub. by Wiley-Interscience). Wiley.
Cohen, Alan, jt. ed. see Sherwood, William.
Cohen, Alan B., jt. auth. see Steinberg, Carl P.
Cohen, Alan S., ed. Progress in Clinical Rheumatology, Vol. I. 224p. 1984. 33.00 (ISBN 0-8089-1646-7, 790881). Grune.
--Rheumatology & Immunology. (The Science & Practice of Clinical Medicine Ser.). 464p. 1979. 46.50 (ISBN 0-8089-1118-X, 790875). Grune.
Cohen, Alan S. & Combes, John R., eds. Medical Emergencies: Diagnostic Management Procedures from the Boston City Hospital. 2nd ed. 314p. 1983. text ed. 29.50 (ISBN 0-316-14988-8). Little.
Cohen, Albert. Music in the French Royal Academy of Sciences: A Study in the Evolution of Musical Thought. LC 81-47118. (Illus.). 168p. 1981. 20.00 (ISBN 0-691-09127-7). Princeton U Pr.
Cohen, Albert, ed. Elements or Principles of Music. (Musical Theorists in Translation Ser.: Vol. VI). 1966. lib. bdg. 25.00 (ISBN 0-912024-26-7). Inst Mediaeval Mus.
Cohen, Alfred J. A Marriage Below Zero. LC 78-63985. (The Gay Experience). Repr. of 1889 ed. 26.50 (ISBN 0-404-61504-X). AMS Pr.
Cohen, Alfred S. Halacha & Contemporary Society. LC 84-741. 1985. pap. 9.95 (ISBN 0-88125-043-0). Ktav.
Cohen, Allan R. & Gadon, Herman. Alternative Work Schedules: Integrating Individual & Organizational Needs. LC 78-52506. 1978. pap. text ed. 10.50 (ISBN 0-201-01052-6). Addison-Wesley.
Cohen, Allan R., jt. auth. see Bradford, David L.
Cohen, Allan R., et al. Effective Behaviour in Organizations. 3rd ed. 1984. 28.95 (ISBN 0-256-03023-5). Irwin.
--Effective Behavior in Organizations: Learning from the Interplay of Cases, Concepts & Student Experiences. 3rd ed. 1984. 28.95x (ISBN 0-256-03023-5); tchr's. manual avail. Irwin.
Cohen, Allen, ed. see Pizzuto, Joseph.
Cohen, Allen C. Beyond Basic Textiles. (Illus.). 350p. 1982. loose-leaf 16.50 (ISBN 0-87005-407-4). Fairchild.
Cohen, Allen Y., jt. auth. see Marin, Peter.
Cohen, Alvin P. Grammar Notes for Introductory Classical Chinese. (Occasional Ser.: No. 31). 1975. pap. 3.25x (ISBN 0-89644-419-8). Chinese Materials.
Cohen, Alvin P., ed. see Boodberg, Peter A.
Cohen, Amnon. Jewish Life under Islam: Jerusalem in the Sixteenth Century. (Illus.). 288p. 1984. text ed. 30.00x (ISBN 0-674-47436-8). Harvard U Pr.
--Palestine in the Eighteenth Century: Patterns of Government & Administration. 344p. 1973. text ed. 35.50x (Pub. by Magnes Israel). Humanities.
--Political Parties in the West Bank under the Jordanian Regime (1949-1967) 344p. 1983. 25.00x (ISBN 0-8014-1321-4). Cornell U Pr.
Cohen, Amnon & Lewis, Bernard. Population & Revenue in the Towns of Palestine in the Sixteenth Century. LC 78-51160. (Illus.). 1978. 32.00 (ISBN 0-691-09375-X). Princeton U Pr.
Cohen, Amnon & Baer, Gabriel, eds. Egypt & Palestine: A Millennium of Association (868-1948) LC 84-16109. 400p. 1984. 32.50 (ISBN 0-312-23927-0). St Martin.
Cohen, Andrew. British Policy in Changing Africa. LC 59-6733. (Northwestern University, Evanston, Ill. African Studies: No. 2). pap. 31.50 (ISBN 0-317-11335-6, 2006942). Bks Demand UMI.
Cohen, Andrew D. Describing Bilingual Education Classrooms: The Role of the Teacher in Evaluation. LC 80-80307. 52p. (Orig.). 1980. pap. 4.50 (ISBN 0-89763-050-5). Natl Clearinghse Bilingual.
--Testing Language Ability in the Classroom. 1981. pap. text ed. 11.95 (ISBN 0-88377-155-1). Newbury Hse.
Cohen, Andrew D., et al. Evaluating Evaluation. LC 79-56013. (Bilingual Ed. Ser.: No. 6). 70p. 1979. pap. text ed. 7.25x (ISBN 0-15-599048-9). Ctr Appl Ling.
Cohen, Anne B. Poor Pearl, Poor Girl! The Murdered Girl Stereotype in Ballad & Newspaper. LC 73-7919. (American Folklore Society Memoir Ser.: No. 58). (Illus.). 147p. 1973. pap. 5.95 (ISBN 0-292-76468-5). U of Tex Pr.
Cohen, Annette R. & Druley, Ray M. The Buffalo Nickel. (Illus.). 130p. (Orig.). 1979. pap. 7.50 (ISBN 0-939836-00-9). Potomac Ent.
Cohen, Anthea. Angel of Death. LC 84-13599. (Crime Club Ser.). 192p. 1985. pap. 11.95 (ISBN 0-385-19125-1). Doubleday.
--Angel of Vengeance. LC 83-25512. (Crime Club Ser.). 192p. 1984. 11.95 (ISBN 0-385-19126-X). Doubleday.
--Angel Without Mercy. LC 83-14060. (Crime Club Ser.). 1984. 11.95 (ISBN 0-385-19104-9). Doubleday.
--Guardian Angel. LC 84-13771. 192p. 1985. 12.95 (ISBN 0-385-19871-X). Doubleday.
Cohen, Anthony P. The Social Construction of Community. (Key Ideas Ser.). 150p. 1985. 13.95 (ISBN 0-85312-814-6, 9582, Pub. by Tavistock England); pap. 6.50 (ISBN 0-85312-855-3, 9583, Pub. by Tavistock England). Methuen Inc.
--The Symbolic Construction of Community. 150p. 1985. 13.95 (ISBN 0-85312-814-6, 9582, Pub. by Tavistock England); pap. 6.50 (ISBN 0-85312-855-3, 9583). Methuen Inc.
Cohen, Arnold B. Bankruptcy, Secured Transaction & Other Debtor-Creditor Matters. 646p. 1981. Supplement 1985. 55.00 (ISBN 0-87215-398-3); 15.00 (ISBN 0-87215-905-1). Michie Co.
--Debtor-Creditor Relations Under the Bankruptcy Act of 1978. (Contemporary Legal Education Ser.). 1100p. 1979. 27.00 (ISBN 0-672-81784-5); Statutory Appendix. 5.00 (ISBN 0-672-83853-2); Supplement 1981. 7.00 (ISBN 0-672-84376-5). Michie Co.
Cohen, Arnold B. & Zaretsky, Barry L. Debtors' & Creditors' Rights. 390p. 1984. pap. 20.00 (ISBN 0-87215-762-8, 11020). Michie Co.
Cohen, Arnold W. Emergencies in Obstetrics & Gynecology. (Clinics in Emergency Medicine Ser.: Vol. 1). (Illus.). 224p. 1981. text ed. 22.00 (ISBN 0-443-08130-1). Churchill.
Cohen, Arthur, jt. auth. see Halverson, Marvin.
Cohen, Arthur A. An Admirable Woman. LC 82-49342. 240p. 1983. 14.95 (ISBN 0-87923-474-1). Godine.
--Communism of Mao Tse-Tung. LC 64-23420. 1964. pap. 2.95x (ISBN 0-226-11282-9, P207, Phoen). U of Chicago Pr.
--Herbert Bayer: The Complete Work. (Illus.). 448p. 1984. text ed. 65.00x (ISBN 0-262-02206-0). MIT Pr.
--In the Days of Simon Stern. LC 72-11429. 472p. 1985. pap. 12.50 (ISBN 0-87923-559-4). Godine.
--The Natural & the Supernatural Jew: An Historical and Theological Introduction. LC 79-13038. 1979. pap. text ed. 6.95x (ISBN 0-87441-291-9). Behrman.
--The Tremendum: A Theological Interpretation of the Holocaust. 144p. 1981. 9.95 (ISBN 0-8245-0006-7). Crossroad NY.
Cohen, Arthur A., jt. auth. see Kaplan, Mordecai M.
Cohen, Arthur A., ed. see Delauney, Robert & Delauney, Sonia.
Cohen, Arthur A., et al, eds. Humanistic Education & Western Civilization: Essays for Robert M. Hutchins. LC 72-13226. (Essay Index Reprint Ser.). Repr. of 1964 ed. 15.00 (ISBN 0-8369-8150-2). Ayer Co Pubs.
Cohen, Arthur M. & Brawer, Florence B. The American Community College. LC 81-19319. (Higher Education Ser.). 1982. text ed. 18.95x (ISBN 0-87589-511-5). Jossey-Bass.
Cohen, Arthur M., jt. auth. see Epperly, Robert W.
Cohen, Arthur M., et al. College Responses to Community Demands: The Community College in Challenging Times. LC 74-27912. (Higher Education Ser.). 224p. 1975. 18.95x (ISBN 0-87589-252-3). Jossey-Bass.
Cohen, Arthur R. Attitude Change & Social Influence. LC 64-22400. 1964. text ed. 10.95x (ISBN 0-465-00565-9). Basic.
Cohen, Avner & Lee, Steven, eds. Nuclear Weapons & the Future of Humanity: The Fundamental Questions. LC 84-18362. (Philosophy & Society Ser.). 224p. 1985. 38.50x (ISBN 0-8476-7257-3); pap. 16.95x (ISBN 0-8476-7258-1). Rowman & Allanheld.
Cohen, B. Developing Sociological Knowledge: Theory & Method. 1980. pap. 22.95 (ISBN 0-13-205153-2). P-H.
--Scientific Foundations of Dentistry. (Illus.). 1976. 96.95 (ISBN 0-8151-1800-7). Year Bk Med.
Cohen, B. Bernard. Writing about Literature. rev ed. 256p. 1973. pap. 9.75x (ISBN 0-673-07653-9). Scott F.
Cohen, B. Bernard, ed. The Recognition of Nathaniel Hawthorne: Selected Criticism since 1828. LC 70-83454. pap. 80.00 (ISBN 0-317-29153-X, 2055609). Bks Demand UMI.
Cohen, B. G. F., ed. Human Aspects in Office Automation. (Elsevier Series in Office Automation: no. 1). 340p. 1984. 50.00 (ISBN 0-444-42327-3, I-133-84). Elsevier.
Cohen, Barbara. The Binding of Issac. LC 77-90367. (Illus.). (gr. 1 up). 1978. 11.25 (ISBN 0-688-41830-9); PLB 11.88 (ISBN 0-688-51830-3). Lothrop.
--The Carp in the Bathtub. (Illus.). 48p. (gr. 1-5). 1972. 11.25 (ISBN 0-688-41627-6); PLB 11.88 (ISBN 0-688-51627-0). Lothrop.
--Coasting. LC 85-230. 160p. 1985. 10.25 (ISBN 0-688-05849-3). Lothrop.
--The Demon Who Would Not Die. LC 82-1739. (Illus.). 32p. (gr. k-3). 1982. 11.95 (ISBN 0-689-30917-1). Atheneum.
--Fat Jack. LC 80-12510. 192p. (gr. 6 up). 1980. 9.95 (ISBN 0-689-30772-1). Atheneum.
--Gooseberries to Oranges. (gr. 1-3). 1982. 11.75 (ISBN 0-688-00690-6); PLB 11.88 (ISBN 0-688-00691-4). Lothrop.

--Here Come the Purim Players! LC 83-14878. (Illus.). 32p. (gr. 1-4). 1984. 12.00 (ISBN 0-688-02106-9); PLB 11.04 (ISBN 0-688-02108-5). Lothrop.
--I Am Joseph. LC 79-20001. (Illus.). (gr. 2 up). 1980. 13.00 (ISBN 0-688-41933-X); PLB 12.88 (ISBN 0-688-51933-4). Lothrop.
--The Innkeeper's Daughter. LC 79-2421. (gr. 5 up). 1979. 11.25 (ISBN 0-688-41906-2); PLB 11.88 (ISBN 0-688-51906-7). Lothrop.
--King of the Seventh Grade. (gr. 4 up). 1982. 11.75 (ISBN 0-688-01302-3). Lothrop.
--Lovers' Games. LC 83-2641. 252p. (gr. 5-9). 1983. 12.95 (ISBN 0-689-30981-3). Atheneum.
--Lovers' Games. (Two Hearts Romances Ser.). (gr. 7 up). 1984. pap. 2.25 (ISBN 0-399-21081-4). Putnam Pub Group.
--Molly's Pilgrim. LC 83-797. (Illus.). 32p. (gr. 2-5). 1983. 11.75 (ISBN 0-688-02103-4); PLB 11.88 (ISBN 0-688-02104-2). Lothrop.
--Queen for a Day. LC 80-28115. (gr. 5 up). 1981. 11.25 (ISBN 0-688-00437-7); PLB 11.88 (ISBN 0-688-00438-5). Lothrop.
--R My Name Is Rosie. LC 77-28867. (gr. 3-7). 1978. 11.25 (ISBN 0-688-41839-2); PLB 11.88 (ISBN 0-688-51839-7). Lothrop.
--Roses. LC 83-23881. (Illus.). 224p. (gr. 6 up). 1984. 11.50 (ISBN 0-688-02166-2). Lothrop.
--Roses. 256p. (gr. 7 up). 1985. pap. 2.25 (ISBN 0-590-33602-9, Point). Scholastic Inc.
--Thank You, Jackie Robinson. LC 73-17703. (Illus.). 128p. (gr. 3-7). 1974. PLB 11.88 (ISBN 0-688-51580-0). Lothrop.
--Unicorns in the Rain. LC 79-22082. 1980. 10.95 (ISBN 0-689-30735-7, Argo). Atheneum.
--Yussel's Prayer. LC 80-25377. (Illus.). 32p. (gr. k-4). 1981. 11.25 (ISBN 0-688-00460-1); PLB 11.88 (ISBN 0-688-00461-X). Lothrop.
Cohen, Barbara & Lovejoy, Bahija. Seven Daughters & Seven Sons. LC 81-8092. 216p. (gr. 5-9). 1982. 12.95 (ISBN 0-689-30875-2). Atheneum.
Cohen, Barney. Blood on the Moon. 288p. 1984. pap. 2.95 (ISBN 0-8125-3335-6). Tor Bks.
--Sting: Every Breath He Takes. 192p. 1984. pap. 2.95 (ISBN 0-425-07638-5). Berkley Pub.
Cohen, Barney & Baen, Jim. The Taking of Satcon Station. 288p. (Orig.). 1982. pap. 2.95 (ISBN 0-523-48531-X). Pinnacle Bks.
Cohen, Barry, jt. auth. see Quinn, Jim.
Cohen, Barry, jt. ed. see Mohamed A. El-Khawas.
Cohen, Barry D., ed. see Jospe, Michael, et al.
Cohen, Becky, jt. auth. see Oliveros, Pauline.
Cohen, Ben. Your Lead, Partner. 1974. pap. 4.50 (ISBN 0-04-793021-7). Allen Unwin.
Cohen, Ben & Lederer, Rhoda. ABC of Contract Bridge. 4th rev. ed. (Unwin Paperback). 1979. pap. 5.95 (ISBN 0-04-793040-3). Allen Unwin.
--All about Acol. 4th ed. (Unwin Paperbacks). 1979. pap. 5.50 (ISBN 0-04-793032-2). Allen Unwin.
--Basic Acol. 3rd rev. ed. (Unwin Paperback). 1979. pap. 5.50 (ISBN 0-04-793038-1). Allen Unwin.
Cohen, Benjamin, ed. Banks & the Balance of Payments: Private Lending in the International Adjustment Process. LC 81-1805. 256p. 1981. 34.50x (ISBN 0-86598-038-1). Allanheld.
Cohen, Benjamin I. Multinational Firms & Asian Exports. LC 74-17551. (Illus.). 192p. 1975. 21.00x (ISBN 0-300-01812-6). Yale U Pr.
Cohen, Benjamin J. The European Monetary System: An Outsider's View. LC 81-4167. (Essays in International Finance Ser.: No. 142). 1981. pap. text ed. 2.50x (ISBN 0-88165-049-8). Princeton U Int Finan Econ.
--The Question of Imperialism: The Political Economy of Dominance & Dependence. LC 73-81036. (Illus.). 245p. 1973. text ed. 14.95x (ISBN 0-465-06780-8). Basic.
Cohen, Benjamin V. United Nations: Constitutional Developments, Growth & Possibilities. LC 61-16691. (Oliver Wendell Holmes Lectures Ser: 1961). 1961. 10.00x (ISBN 0-674-92265-4). Harvard U Pr.
Cohen, Bernard. Sociocultural Changes in American Jewish Life As Reflected in Selected Jewish Literature. LC 75-146162. 282p. 1972. 24.50 (ISBN 0-8386-7848-3). Fairleigh Dickinson.
Cohen, Bernard, ed. Vestibular & Oculomotor Physiology: International Meeting of the Barany Society, Vol. 374. LC 81-14230. 892p. 1981. 177.00x (ISBN 0-89766-137-0); pap. 177.00x (ISBN 0-89766-138-9). NY Acad Sci.
Cohen, Bernard, ed. see International Symposium on Immunologic Monitoring of the Transplant Patient, 2nd, Netherlands, et al.
Cohen, Bernard C. Political Process & Foreign Policy: The Making of the Japanese Peace Settlement. LC 80-19832. x, 293p. 1980. Repr. of 1957 ed. lib. bdg. 42.50x (ISBN 0-313-22715-2, COPF). Greenwood.
--The Press & Foreign Policy. LC 83-12989. ix, 288p. 1983. Repr. of 1963 ed. lib. bdg. 42.50x (ISBN 0-313-24215-1, CPFP). Greenwood.
--The Public's Impact on Foreign Policy. LC 83-6550. 236p. 1983. pap. text ed. 11.00 (ISBN 0-8191-3244-6). U Pr of Amer.
Cohen, Bernard L. Before It's Too Late: A Scientist's Case for Nuclear Energy. 310p. 1983. (full discount avail.) 16.95 (ISBN 0-306-41425-2, Plenum Press). Plenum Pub.
--Jews Among the Nations. LC 77-79171. 1978. 10.00 (ISBN 0-8022-2209-9). Philos Lib.
Cohen, Bernice H., et al. Selected Genetic Markers of Blood & Secretions for Youth 12-17 Years of Age, United States. (Ser. 11: No. 168). 1979. pap. text ed. 1.75 (ISBN 0-8406-0171-9). Natl Ctr Health Stats.
--Genetic Issues in Public Health & Medicine. (Illus.). 512p. 1978. 54.50x (ISBN 0-398-03659-4). C C Thomas.
Cohen, Beth. Attic Bilingual Vases & Their Painters. LC 77-94689. (Outstanding Dissertations in the Fine Arts Ser.). 1978. lib. bdg. 97.00 (ISBN 0-8240-3220-9). Garland Pub.
Cohen, Boaz. Jewish & Roman Law, 2 Vols. 1966. Set. 15.00x (ISBN 0-8381-4100-5). United Syn Bk.
--Law & Tradition in Judaism. 1959. 12.50x (ISBN 0-87068-023-4). Ktav.
Cohen, Boaz & Katz, Steven, eds. Saadia Anniversary Volume. LC 79-7168. (Jewish Philosophy, Mysticism & History of Ideas Ser.). 1980. Repr. of 1943 ed. lib. bdg. 28.50x (ISBN 0-405-12244-6). Ayer Co Pubs.
Cohen, Brenda. Education & the Individual. (Unwin Education Books). 144p. 1981. text ed. 19.95x (ISBN 0-04-370108-6). Allen Unwin.
--Means & Ends in Education. (Introduction Studies in Philosophy of Education). 128p. 1982. text ed. 19.50x (ISBN 0-04-370122-1); pap. text ed. 7.50x (ISBN 0-04-370123-X). Allen Unwin.
Cohen, Bruce I., jt. ed. see Brackbill, Jeremiah U.
Cohen, Bruce J. Horton-Hunt: Sociology. 6th ed. Date not set. pap. text ed. 9.95c (ISBN 0-07-030446-7). McGraw.
--Introductor to Sociology. (Schaum's Outline Ser.). 1979. pap. 6.95 (ISBN 0-07-011591-5). McGraw.
Cohen, Bruce J., ed. Crime in America: Perspectives on Criminal & Delinquent Behavior. 2nd ed. LC 76-53276. 519p. 1977. pap. text ed. 14.95 (ISBN 0-87581-202-3, 202). Peacock Pubs.
Cohen, Burton I., jt. auth. see Shapiro, Alexander M.
Cohen, Burton J. Cost-Effective Information Systems. LC 78-152375. pap. 20.00 (ISBN 0-317-10661-9, 2050389). Bks Demand UMI.
Cohen, Bydr A., ed. The Five Megilloth. 252p. 1946. 10.95 (ISBN 0-900689-35-8). Soncino Pr NY.
Cohen, C. & Sivan, D. The Ugaritic Hippiatric Texts: A Critical Edition. (American Oriental Essays Ser.: No. 9). 1983. pap. 12.50x (ISBN 0-940490-99-4). Am Orient Soc.
Cohen, C. D. Agenda for Britain One: Micro Policy. 236p. 1982. text ed. 30.00x (ISBN 0-86003-034-2, Pub. by Philip Allan Pubs England); pap. text ed. 15.25x (ISBN 0-86003-132-2). Humanities.
--Agenda For Britain Two: Macro Policy. 161p. 1982. text ed. 21.50x (ISBN 0-86003-041-5, Pub. by Allan Pubs England); pap. text ed. 11.00x (ISBN 0-86003-138-1). Humanities.
Cohen, Carl. Communism, Fascism, & Democracy. 2nd ed. 620p. 1972. pap. text ed. 15.00x (ISBN 0-394-31319-4, RanC). Random.
--Democracy. LC 77-142911. 1973. pap. text ed. 4.95 (ISBN 0-02-906100-8). Free Pr.
--Four Systems. 256p. 1982. pap. text ed. 8.95 (ISBN 0-394-32531-1, RanC). Random.
Cohen, Carl see Dewey, John.
Cohen, Caron L. Sally Ann Thunder Ann Whirlwind Crockett. LC 84-7978. (Illus.). 40p. (gr. 1-3). 1985. 10.25 (ISBN 0-688-04006-3); PLB 10.88 (ISBN 0-688-04007-1). Greenwillow.
Cohen, Chapman. Essays in Freethinking, 4 vols. Vol. I 1980, 112p. pap. 5.00 ea. Vol. II, 1981, 110p. Vol. III 1980, 102p. Vol. IV 1981. Set. pap. 20.00. Am Atheist.
--Primitive Survivals in Modern Thought. LC 74-169207. (Atheist Viewpoint Ser). 142p. 1972. Repr. of 1935 ed. 13.00 (ISBN 0-405-03807-0). Ayer Co Pubs.
--Religion & Sex. LC 72-9631. Repr. of 1919 ed. 22.50 (ISBN 0-404-57430-0). AMS Pr.
Cohen, Charles P., et al. Psychotherapy & Drug Addiction I: Diagnosis & Treatment. LC 73-11097. (Drug Abuse Ser.). 263p. 1974. text ed. 24.00x (ISBN 0-8422-7143-0). Irvington.
Cohen, Charles Z. Your Future As a Lawyer. (Careers in Depth Ser.). (YA) 1977. PLB 7.97 (ISBN 0-8239-0382-6). Rosen Group.
--Your Future As a Lawyer. rev. ed. 1983. 8.97. Rosen Group.
Cohen, Chester G. Shtetl Finder. 1980. pap. 8.25 (ISBN 0-9605586-0-8). Periday.
Cohen, D. Crucial Ten Per Cent That Really Counts for Trial Victories. 1974. 59.50 (ISBN 0-13-194878-4). P-H.
--How to Win Criminal Cases by Establishing a Reasonable Doubt. 1970. 79.50 (ISBN 0-13-439505-0). P-H.
--Sleep & Dreaming: Origins, Nature, & Functions. (International Ser. Experimental Psychology: Vol. 23). (Illus.). 315p. 1981. pap. 18.25 (ISBN 0-08-027400-5). Pergamon.
Cohen, D., jt. ed. see Caquot, Andre.
Cohen, D. Bernard, ed. see Bond, William C.
Cohen, D. I. Basic Techniques of Combinatorial Theory. 297p. 1978. 35.50 (ISBN 0-471-03535-1). Wiley.
Cohen, D. Walter, jt. auth. see Goldman, Henry M.
Cohen, D. Walter, ed. see Abrams, Leonard.
Cohen, D. Walter, ed. see Amsterdam, Morton.
Cohen, D. Walter, ed. see Casullo, Daniel P. & Matarazzo, Francis S.
Cohen, D. Walter, ed. see Corn, Herman.
Cohen, D. Walter, ed. see Coslet, J. George.
Cohen, D. Walter, ed. see Isaacson, George.
Cohen, D. Walter, ed. see Johnson, Ronald.
Cohen, D. Walter, ed. see Rubelman, Peter A.
Cohen, D. Walter, ed. see Seibert, J. S.
Cohen, D. Walter, ed. see Vanarsdall, Robert L., Jr.
Cohen, D. Walter, ed. see Weisgold, Arnold.
Cohen, D. Walter, et al. Educating the Dentist of the Future: The Pennsylvania Experiment. LC 84-19602. (Illus.). 250p. 1985. text ed. 17.95 (ISBN 0-8122-7933-6). U of Pa Pr.
Cohen, Dan. The Case of the Battling Ball Clubs. LC 79-84356. (Carolrhoda Mini-Mystery Ser.). (Illus.). (gr. k-4). 1979. PLB 4.95g (ISBN 0-87614-101-7). Carolrhoda Bks.
--The Case of the Long Lost Twin. LC 79-84357. (Carolrhoda Mini-Mysteries Ser.). (Illus.). (gr. k-4). 1979. PLB 4.95g (ISBN 0-87614-094-0). Carolrhoda Bks.
--The Case of the Missing Poodle. LC 79-84358. (Carolrhoda Mini-Mysteries Ser.). (Illus.). (gr. k-4). 1979. PLB 4.95g (ISBN 0-87614-095-9). Carolrhoda Bks.
--The Case of the Runaway Rabbit. LC 79-84359. (Carolrhoda Mini-Mysteries Ser.). (Illus.). (gr. k-4). 1979. PLB 4.95g (ISBN 0-87614-096-7). Carolrhoda Bks.
--The Case of the Spanish Stamps. LC 79-56197. (The Carolrhoda Mini-Mysteries Ser.). (Illus.). (gr. 1-4). 1980. PLB 4.95g (ISBN 0-87614-117-3). Carolrhoda Bks.
--The Case of the Supermarket Swindle. LC 79-56199. (The Carolrhoda Mini-Mysteries Ser.). (Illus.). (gr. 1-4). 1980. PLB 4.95g (ISBN 0-87614-119-X). Carolrhoda Bks.
--The Mystery of the Faded Footprint. LC 79-84360. (Carolrhoda Mini-Mysteries Ser.). (Illus.). (gr. k-4). 1979. PLB 4.95g (ISBN 0-87614-097-5). Carolrhoda Bks.
--The Mystery of the Hidden Camera. LC 79-84362. (Carolrhoda Mini-Mysteries Ser.). (Illus.). (gr. k-4). 1979. PLB 4.95g (ISBN 0-87614-098-3). Carolrhoda Bks.
--The Mystery of the Locked Door. LC 79-50786. (Carolrhoda Mini-Mysteries Ser.). (Illus.). (gr. k-4). 1979. PLB 4.95g (ISBN 0-87614-099-1). Carolrhoda Bks.
--The Mystery of the Marked Money. LC 79-50788. (Carolrhoda Mini-Mysteries Ser.). (Illus.). (gr. k-4). 1979. PLB 4.95g (ISBN 0-87614-100-9). Carolrhoda Bks.
--The Mystery of the Mellafeller Elephant. LC 79-56198. (The Carolrhoda Mini-Mysteries Ser.). (Illus.). (gr. 1-4). 1980. PLB 4.95g (ISBN 0-87614-118-1). Carolrhoda Bks.
--The Mystery of the Missing Ring. LC 79-56200. (The Carolrhoda Mini-Mysteries Ser.). (Illus.). (gr. 1-4). 1980. PLB 4.95g (ISBN 0-87614-120-3). Carolrhoda Bks.
--Undefeated: The Life of Hubert H. Humphrey. LC 78-53933. (Adult & Young Adult Bks.). (Illus.). 1978. 25.00 (ISBN 0-8225-9953-8). Lerner Pubns.
Cohen, Daniel. America's Very Own Ghosts. (Illus.). 48p. (gr. 2-5). 1985. 9.95 (ISBN 0-396-08505-9). Dodd.
--America's Very Own Monsters. LC 82-4961. (Illus.). 48p. (gr. 2-4). 1982. 7.95 (ISBN 0-396-08069-3). Dodd.
--Animal Territories. (Illus.). 96p. (gr. 4-8). 1975. 7.95g (ISBN 0-8038-0368-0). Hastings.
--Bigfoot: America's Number One Monster. (A Hi-Lo Bk.). (Illus.). (gr. 4 up). 1982. pap. 1.75 (ISBN 0-671-43919-7). Archway.
--Biorhythms in Your Life. 1981. pap. 2.50 (ISBN 0-449-14168-3, GM). Fawcett.
--A Close Look at Close Encounters. LC 80-2784. (Illus.). 160p. (gr. 7 up). 1981. PLB 8.95 (ISBN 0-396-07927-X). Dodd.
--Computers. Barish, Wendy, ed. (A Question & Answer Bk.). (Illus.). 128p. (gr. 5-6). 1983. 6.95 (ISBN 0-671-49340-X). Wanderer Bks.
--Creativity: What Is It? LC 77-23481. (Illus.). 160p. (gr. 7 up). 1977. 5.95 (ISBN 0-87131-245-X). M Evans.
--Creatures from UFO's. (A Hilo Book). (Illus.). (gr. 4 up). 1979. pap. 1.50 (ISBN 0-671-29951-4). Archway.
--Creatures from UFO's. LC 78-7730. (High Interest-Low Vocabulary Book). (Illus.). (gr. 4-9). 1978. 8.95 (ISBN 0-396-07582-7). Dodd.
--Curses, Hexes, & Spells. LC 74-6425. (Weird & Horrible Library). (Illus.). 128p. (gr. 6 up). 1974. 10.89 (ISBN 0-397-31493-0). Lipp Jr Bks.
--Dealing with the Devil. LC 79-14692. (Illus.). (gr. 7 up). 1979. 10.95 (ISBN 0-396-07700-5). Dodd.
--The Encyclopedia of Ghosts. (Illus.). 320p. 1984. 14.95 (ISBN 0-396-08308-0). Dodd.
--The Encyclopedia of Monsters. LC 82-4574. (Illus.). 304p. 1983. 14.95 (ISBN 0-396-08102-9). Dodd.
--The Encyclopedia of the Strange. 256p. 1985. 16.95 (ISBN 0-396-08656-X). Dodd.
--ESP: The Search Beyond the Senses. LC 77-3615. (Illus.). (gr. 7 up). 1977. pap. 1.75 (ISBN 0-15-629045-6, VoyB). HarBraceJ.
--Famous Curses. (Illus.). (gr. 4 up). pap. 1.95 (ISBN 0-671-41867-X). Archway.
--Famous Curses. LC 79-52039. (High Interest-Low Vocabulary Ser.). (Illus.). (gr. 4-9). 1979. 8.95 (ISBN 0-396-07712-9). Dodd.
--Frauds & Hoaxes & Swindles. 96p. (YA) (gr. 5 up). pap. 1.50 (ISBN 0-440-92699-8, LE). Dell.
--Ghostly Terrors. (High Interest, Low Vocabulary Ser.). (Illus.). 112p. (gr. 4-9). 1981. PLB 8.95 (ISBN 0-396-07996-2). Dodd.
--Ghostly Terrors. (gr. 4 up). 1983. pap. 1.95 (ISBN 0-671-45856-6). Archway.
--Gold: The Fascinating Study of the Noble Metal Through the Ages. LC 76-18067. (Illus.). 192p. (gr. 7 up). 1976. 6.95 (ISBN 0-87131-218-2). M Evans.
--The Great Airship Mystery: A UFO of the 1890's. LC 81-5529. (Illus.). 256p. 1981. 9.95 (ISBN 0-396-07990-3). Dodd.
--Great Mistakes. LC 79-18036. (Illus.). 144p. (gr. 4 up). 1979. 6.95 (ISBN 0-87131-306-5). M Evans.
--The Greatest Monsters in the World. (Illus.). (gr. 4 up). 1977. pap. 1.75 (ISBN 0-671-44229-5). Archway.
--The Greatest Monsters in the World. 96p. (gr. 4 up). 1984. pap. 2.25 (ISBN 0-671-54552-3). Archway.
--The Headless Roommate & Other Tales of Terror. LC 80-18821. (Illus.). 128p. (gr. 8 up). 1980. 7.95 (ISBN 0-87131-327-8). M Evans.
--Henry Stanley & the Quest for the Source of the Nile. (gr. 7 up). 11.95 (ISBN 0-87131-445-2). M Evans.
--Hiram Bingham & the Dream of Gold. (gr. 7 up). 1984. 10.95 (ISBN 0-87131-433-9). M Evans.
--Horror in the Movies. (Illus.). 96p. (gr. 3 up). 1982. 10.50 (ISBN 0-89919-074-X, Clarion). HM.
--Horror in the Movies. 128p. (gr. 5 up). 1984. pap. 2.25 (ISBN 0-671-47678-5). Archway.
--How to Buy a Car. LC 82-6899. (Triumph Bks.). (Illus.). 96p. (gr. 9 up). 1982. PLB 8.90 (ISBN 0-531-04494-7). Watts.
--How To Test Your ESP. LC 81-15142. (Illus.). 96p. (gr. 9 up). 1982. 8.95 (ISBN 0-525-45109-9, 0869-260, Skinny Bk). Dutton.
--Intelligence: What Is It? LC 73-80178. (Illus.). 160p. (gr. 5 up). 1974. 7.95 (ISBN 0-87131-127-5). M Evans.
--Introduction to Computer Theory. 1985. text ed. write for info. (ISBN 0-471-80271-9); tchr's ed. avail. (ISBN 0-471-80766-4). Wiley.
--The Julian Messner Question & Answer Books: Computers. LC 83-10355. (Illus.). 128p. (gr. 5 up). 1983. 9.29 (ISBN 0-671-49750-2). Childrens.
--The Last Hundred Years: Household Technology. LC 82-15442. (Illus.). 192p. (gr. 5 up). 1982. 8.95 (ISBN 0-87131-386-3). M Evans.
--The Last Hundred Years: Medicine. LC 81-14357. (Illus.). 192p. (gr. 5 up). 1981. 8.95 (ISBN 0-87131-356-1). M Evans.
--Masters of Horror. LC 83-14402. (Illus.). 128p. (gr. 6up). 1984. PLB 11.95 (ISBN 0-89919-221-1, Clarion). HM.
--Missing: Stories of Strange Disappearances. (Illus.). (gr. 4 up). 1980. pap. 1.95 (ISBN 0-671-56052-2). Archway.
--Missing! Stories of Strange Disappearances. LC 78-25729. (High Interest-Low Vocabulary Ser.). (Illus.). (gr. 4-9). 1979. 8.95 (ISBN 0-396-07648-3). Dodd.
--Monster Dinosaur. LC 82-48460. (Illus.). 192p. (gr. 3-6). 1983. 9.57i (ISBN 0-397-31953-3); PLB 9.89g (ISBN 0-397-31954-1). Lipp Jr Bks.
--Monster Hunting Today. LC 83-7496. (gr. 6-8). 8.95 (ISBN 0-396-08184-3). Dodd.
--The Monsters of Star Trek. (Illus.). 128p. (Orig.). (gr. 4 up). 1984. pap. 1.95 (ISBN 0-671-52360-0). Archway.
--Monsters You Never Heard of. LC 79-23641. (High Interest, Low Vocabulary Ser.). (Illus.). (gr. 4-9). 1980. 8.95 (ISBN 0-396-07789-7). Dodd.
--Re-Thinking: How to Succeed by Learning How to Think. LC 82-1472. 216p. 1982. 11.95 (ISBN 0-87131-369-3). M Evans.
--Real Ghosts. (Illus.). (gr. 4 up). 1979. pap. 1.50 (ISBN 0-671-29908-5). Archway.
--Real Ghosts. LC 77-6502. (Illus.). (gr. 4-9). 1977. 8.95 (ISBN 0-396-07454-5). Dodd.
--Real Ghosts. (Illus.). 128p. (gr. 4 up). 1984. pap. 1.95 (ISBN 0-671-52641-3). Archway.
--Real Magic. LC 82-45388. (High Interest, Low Vocabulary Ser.). (Illus.). 112p. (gr. 4). 1982. 8.95 (ISBN 0-396-08095-2). Dodd.
--The Restless Dead: Ghostly Tales from Around the World. LC 83-27447. (High Interest, Low Vocabulary Ser.). (Illus.). 123p. (gr. 4-9). 1984. PLB 8.95 (ISBN 0-396-08325-0). Dodd.
--Science Fiction's Greatest Monsters. LC 80-1087. (High Interest-Low Vocabulary Ser.). (Illus.). (gr. 4-9). 1980. 8.95 (ISBN 0-396-07859-1). Dodd.
--The Science of Spying. (gr. 7-12). 1977. PLB 9.95 (ISBN 0-07-011578-8). McGraw.
--The Simon & Schuster Question & Answer Book: Computers. (gr. 9-12). 1983. PLB 9.29 (ISBN 0-671-49750-2). S&S.
--Southern Fried Rat & Other Gruesome Tales. LC 82-25120. (Illus.). 128p. (gr. 7 up). 1983. 9.95 (ISBN 0-87131-400-2). M Evans.
--Supermonsters. (Illus.). (gr. 4 up). 1978. pap. 1.75 (ISBN 0-671-44231-7, HI-LO). Archway.
--The Tomb Robbers. LC 79-22760. (Illus.). 96p. (gr. 5-8). 1980. 10.95 (ISBN 0-07-011566-4). McGraw.

--Video Games. (Illus.). (gr. 4 up). 1982. pap. 1.95 (ISBN 0-671-45872-8). Archway.
--Waiting for the Apocalypse: Doomsday Deferred. rev. ed. LC 83-62189. (Illus.). 260p. 1983. pap. 10.95 (ISBN 0-87975-223-8). Prometheus Bks.
--What's Happening to Our Weather. LC 79-732. (Illus.). 160p. (gr. 6 up). 1979. 6.95 (ISBN 0-87131-288-3). M Evans.
--World of UFO's. LC 77-11659. (Illus.). 160p. (gr. 4-6). 1978. 11.49i (ISBN 0-397-31780-8). Lipp Jr Bks.
--The World's Most Famous Ghosts. (Illus.). (gr. 4 up). 1985. pap. 2.25 (ISBN 0-671-54630-9). Archway.
--The World's Most Famous Ghosts. (Illus.). (gr. 4-9). 1978. 8.95 (ISBN 0-396-07543-6). Dodd.
Cohen, Daniel & Cohen, Susan. The Kid's Guide to Home Computers. (Illus., Orig.). (gr. 4 up). 1983. pap. 1.95 (ISBN 0-671-49361-2). Archway.
--The Kid's Guide to Home Video. (Orig.). (gr. 4 up). 1984. pap. 2.25 (ISBN 0-671-52731-2). Archway.
--A Six-Pack & a Fake I.D. Teens Look at the Drinking Question. 176p. (YA) (gr. 7 up). 1986. 11.95 (ISBN 0-87131-459-2). M Evans.
--Teenage Stress: Understanding the Tensions You Feel at Home, at School & among Your Friends. LC 83-16477. 160p. (gr. 5 up). 1984. PLB 10.95 (ISBN 0-87131-423-1). M Evans.
Cohen, David. Admit the Act & Win the Criminal Case. 1980. 74.50 (ISBN 0-13-008656-8). Exec Reports.
--Dictionnaire des Racines Semitiques, Vol. 1. (Fr.). 1974. pap. 27.50 (ISBN 0-686-56862-1, M-6640, Pub. by Mouton). French & Eur.
--Dictionnaire des Racines Semitiques, Vol. 2. 76p. (Fr.). 1976. pap. 29.95 (ISBN 0-686-56863-X, M-6641). French & Eur.
--Dictionnaire Des Racines Semitiques Ou Attestees Dans les Langues Semitiques: Comprenant un Fichier Comparatif De Jean Cantineau. 36p. (Fr.). 1970. pap. text ed. 12.80x (ISBN 0-686-27743-0). Mouton.
--Dictionnaire Des Racines Semitiques: Ou Attestees Dans les Langues Semitiques. (Fr.). 1976. pap. text ed. 16.80x (ISBN 90-2796-441-6). Mouton.
--Etudes De Linguistique Semitique Et Arabe. (Janua Linguarum, Ser. Practica: No. 81). (Orig.). 1970. text ed. 28.80x (ISBN 90-2790-732-3). Mouton.
--Explaining Linguistic Phenomena. LC 74-12463. 1974. 12.95x (ISBN 0-470-16425-5). Halsted Pr.
--Fixed Base Operators: Management Handbook. Jones, David & Hurst, M. Dale, eds. (Aviation Management Ser.). 107p. 1980. pap. text ed. 8.95 (ISBN 0-89100-148-4, EA-148-4). Aviation Maintenance.
--How to Win Criminal Cases by Establishing a Reasonable Doubt. 1970. 29.50 (ISBN 0-13-439505-0). Exec Reports.
--Le Parler Arabe Des Juifs de Tunis: Tome 2, Etude Linguistique. LC 72-94452. (Janua Linguarum, Ser. Practica: No. 161). 318p. (Fr.). 1975. 44.40x (ISBN 90-2793-296-4). Mouton.
--Piaget: Critique & Reassessment. LC 83-17680. 176p. 1983. 25.00 (ISBN 0-312-60921-3). St Martin.
--The Political Process. (Task Force on the Eighties Ser.). 34p. 1981. pap. 2.50 (ISBN 0-87495-040-6). Am Jewish Comm.
--Precalculus. (Illus.). 625p. 1984. text ed. 26.95 (ISBN 0-314-77871-3); instrs.' manual avail. (ISBN 0-314-79135-3). West Pub.
--Psychologists on Psychology. 1976. 12.95 (ISBN 0-8008-6557-X); pap. 6.50 (ISBN 0-8008-6558-8). Taplinger.
--The Ramapo Mountain People. (Illus.). 300p. 1974. 25.00x (ISBN 0-8135-0768-5). Rutgers U Pr.
Cohen, David, jt. auth. see Smolan, Rick.
Cohen, David, ed. Melanges Marcel Cohen: Etudes de Linguistique, Ethnographie et Sciences Connexes Offertes par Ses Amis et Ses Eleves a lL'Occasion dDe Son 80eme Anniversaire. (Janua Linguarum, Series Maior: No. 27). 1970. 90.00x (ISBN 0-686-21253-3). Mouton.
--Multi-Ethnic Media: Selected Bibliographies in Print. 1975. pap. text ed. 3.00x (ISBN 0-8389-3170-7). ALA.
Cohen, David S. The Folklore & Folklife of New Jersey. 223p. 1983. text ed. 25.00 (ISBN 0-8135-0964-5); pap. 11.95 (ISBN 0-8135-0989-0). Rutgers U Pr.
Cohen, David W. Womunafu's Bunafu: A Study of Authority in a Nineteenth-Century African Community. LC 77-71976. (Illus.). 1977. 23.50 (ISBN 0-691-03093-6). Princeton U Pr.
Cohen, David W. & Greene, Jack P., eds. Neither Slave nor Free: The Freedman of African Descent in the Slave Societies of the New World. LC 79-184238. (Symposia in Comparative History Ser.). 357p. 1972. pap. 8.95x (ISBN 0-8018-1647-5). Johns Hopkins.
Cohen, Davis K., jt. auth. see Lindblom, Charles E.
Cohen, Dian & Shannon, Kristin. The Next Canadian Economy. 224p. 1984. pap. 9.95 (ISBN 0-920792-44-8). Eden Pr.
Cohen, Donald & Cameron, Roy. Elementary Algebra. 480p. 1982. pap. text ed. 29.29 (ISBN 0-205-07308-5, 567308); tchr's manual 7.86 (ISBN 0-205-07309-3, 567309). Allyn.
Cohen, Donald N. Knowledge-Based Theorem Proving & Learning. Stone, Harold, ed. LC 81-7494. (Computer Science Ser.: Artificial Intelligence: No. 4). 212p. 1981. 44.95 (ISBN 0-8357-1202-8). UMI Res Pr.
Cohen, Donald S, ed. see Society for Industrial & Applied Mathematical - American Mathematical Society Symposia - New York - April, 1974.
Cohen, Donna, jt. auth. see Eisdorfer, Carl.
Cohen, Doris & Jones, Robert T. High Speed Wing Theory. (Aeronautical Paperbacks Ser.: Vol. 6). (Orig.). 1960. pap. 20.00 (ISBN 0-691-07975-7). Princeton U Pr.
Cohen, Doron J. & Brillinger, Peter C. Introduction to Data Structures & Non-Numeric Computation. (Illus.). 656p. 1972. ref. ed. 32.95 (ISBN 0-13-479899-6). P-H.
Cohen, Dorothy. Consumer Behavior. 504p. 1981. text ed. 27.00 (ISBN 0-394-31160-4, RanC). Random.
Cohen, Dorothy & Stern, Virginia. Observing & Recording the Behavior of Young Children. 3rd, rev. ed. 1983. pap. text ed. 11.95x (ISBN 0-8077-2713-X). Tchrs Coll.
Cohen, Dorothy H. The Learning Child. 1972. pap. 3.95. Pantheon.
--The Learning Child. 384p. (YA) 1973. pap. 3.95 (ISBN 0-394-71877-1, Vin). Random.
Cohen, Dorothy H., jt. auth. see Rudolph, Marguerita.
Cohen, Dovid. The Relevancy of Torah to the Social & Ethical Issues of Our Time. (Annual Fryer Memorial Lecture Ser.). 0.50 (ISBN 0-914131-57-5, I36). Torah Umesorah.
Cohen, E. G., ed. see Symposium on the Boltzmann Equation, Vienna, 1972.
Cohen, E. G. D., ed. Fundamental Problems in Statistical Mechanics: Proceedings of the 5th International Summer School, Eschede, Netherlands-1980, Vol.5. 388p. 1981. 72.50 (ISBN 0-444-86137-8, North-Holland). Elsevier.
Cohen, Eddi. Disasters! An Emergency Care Workbook. Eubanks, David H. & Smith, Beth, eds. LC 85-4154. (Illus.). 209p. 1985. pap. text ed. 23.00 (ISBN 0-933195-01-X). Cal College Pr.
Cohen, Edie L., jt. auth. see Emery, Sherman R.
Cohen, Edie L. & Emery, Sherman R., eds. Dining by Design. (Illus.). 224p. 45.00 (ISBN 0-943370-04-3). Van Nos Reinhold.
Cohen, Edmond. Man Is the Last One to Be Tamed by X. LC 83-61901. 124p. 1983. pap. 5.00 (ISBN 0-910795-07-X, 2). Ondine Pr.
Cohen, Edmund D. C. G. Jung & the Scientific Attitude. (Quality Paperback Ser.: No. 322). 167p. 1976. pap. 4.95x (ISBN 0-8226-0322-5). Littlefield.
--C. G. Jung & the Scientific Attitude. LC 73-88705. 1974. 7.50 (ISBN 0-685-48949-3). Philos Lib.
Cohen, Edward, jt. auth. see Kong, F.
Cohen, Edward H. Works & Criticism of Gerard Manley Hopkins: A Comprehensive Bibliography. LC 68-31683. pap. 29.30 (ISBN 0-317-10563-9, 2022585). Bks Demand UMI.
Cohen, Edward M., ed. New Jewish Voices: Plays Produced by the Jewish Repertory Theatre. (SUNY Series in Modern Jewish Literature & Culture). 260p. 1985. lib. bdg. 34.50x (ISBN 0-87395-996-5); pap. text ed. 10.95x (ISBN 0-87395-997-3). State U NY Pr.
Cohen, Edward P. & Kohler, Heinz, eds. Membranes, Receptors, & the Immune Response: Eighty Years after Ehrlich's Side Chain Theory. LC 80-7811. (Progress in Clinical & Biological Research Ser.: Vol. 42). 404p. 1980. 45.00 (ISBN 0-8451-0042-4). A R Liss.
Cohen, Edward R. Materials for a Basic Course in Property. LC 78-17714. (American Casebook Ser.). 526p. 1978. text ed. 21.95 (ISBN 0-8299-2008-0). West Pub.
Cohen, Edwin. Speaking the Speech. 2nd ed. 1983. pap. text ed. 15.95 (ISBN 0-03-062006-6). HR&W.
Cohen, Edwin, jt. auth. see Eaton, J. Robert.
Cohen, Einya, et al. A New Dictionary of Sign Language: Employing the Eshkol-Wachmann Movement Notation System. (Approaches to Semiotics Ser.: No. 50). 1977. text ed. 59.20x (ISBN 90-279-3334-0). Mouton.
Cohen, Elaine, jt. auth. see Cohen, Aaron.
Cohen, Elaine L. & Poppino, Mary A. Discovering College Reading: Thinking & Study Skills. 1982. pap. text ed. 15.95 (ISBN 0-03-058626-7). HR&W.
--Reading Faster for Ideas. LC 83-18586. 1984. pap. text ed. 14.95 (ISBN 0-03-061959-9). HR&W.
Cohen, Elaine P. & Gainer, Ruth S. Art: Another Language for Learning. LC 84-5409. (Illus.). 272p. 1984. pap. 9.95 (ISBN 0-8052-0769-4). Schocken.
Cohen, Elaine R. Reading Comprehension Space Stories. (Let's Learn Ser.). (Illus.). 32p. (gr. 4-6). 1984. pap. 1.79 (ISBN 0-88724-088-7, CD-7027). Carson-Dellos.
--Spring Activity Book. (Stick-Out-Your Neck Ser.). (Illus.). 32p. (gr. 4 up). 1984. pap. 1.79 (ISBN 0-88724-068-2, CD-8052). Carson-Dellos.
--Winter Activity Book. (Stick-Out-Your-Neck Ser.). (Illus.). 32p. (gr. 4-7). 1984. pap. 1.79 (ISBN 0-88724-064-X, CD-8044). Carson-Dellos.
Cohen, Eleanor, ed. Expanding the Environmental Responsibility of Local Government: Claremont's Environmental Task Force & Its Recommendations. LC 72-83451. (Environmental Studies Ser: No. 3). 1972. pap. 10.00x (ISBN 0-912102-07-1). Cal Inst Public.
Cohen, Eleanor M., ed. How Can Land Be Saved for Agriculture? Proceedings of a Working Conference to Find Solutions for California. LC 83-10107. (Illus.). 64p. (Orig.). 1983. pap. 15.00 (ISBN 0-912102-65-9). Cal Inst Public.
--Local Farmlands Protection in California: Studies of Problems, Programs, & Politics in Seven Counties. (California Farmlands Project Working Paper: No. 2). 56p. (Orig.). 1983. pap. 10.00 (ISBN 0-912102-63-2). Cal Inst Public.
Cohen, Eli E. & Kapp, Louise, eds. Manpower Policies for Youth. LC 66-27479. 152p. 1966. 25.00x (ISBN 0-231-02970-5). Columbia U Pr.
Cohen, Elias. Recognition Proteins, Receptors, & Probes: Invertebrates. LC 84-7878. (Progress in Clinical & Biological Research Ser.: Vol. 157). 228p. 1984. 38.00 (ISBN 0-8451-5007-3). A R Liss.
Cohen, Elias & Singal, Dharam P. Non-HLA Antigens in Health, Aging, & Malignancy. LC 83-13533. (Progress in Clinical & Biological Research Ser.: Vol. 133). 288p. 1983. 44.00 (ISBN 0-8451-0133-1). A R Liss.
Cohen, Elias, ed. see Symposium, Woods Hole, Mass., October, 1978.
Cohen, Elie A. Human Behavior in the Concentration Camp. LC 84-544. 295p. 1984. Repr. of 1953 ed. lib. bdg. 35.00x (ISBN 0-313-24417-0, CHBE/). Greenwood.
Cohen, Eliot A. Citizens & Soldiers: The Dilemmas of Military Service. LC 84-14266. (Studies in Security Affairs). 227p. 1985. 22.50x (ISBN 0-8014-1581-0). Cornell U Pr.
--Commandos & Politicians: Elite Military Units in Modern Democracies. LC 78-57287. (Studies in International Affairs: No. 40). (gr. 10 up). 1978. PLB 8.95x (ISBN 0-87674-042-5); pap. text ed. 3.95x (ISBN 0-87674-041-7). Harvard U Intl Aff.
--Commandos & Politicians: Elite Military Units in Modern Democracies. 136p. 1984. lib. bdg. 14.95 (ISBN 0-8191-4060-0); pap. text ed. 8.25 (ISBN 0-8191-4061-9). U Pr of Amer.
Cohen, Elliot D. Making Value Judgements: Principles of Sound Reasoning. LC 84-28874. 180p. 1985. pap. text ed. 7.50 (ISBN 0-89874-802-X). Krieger.
Cohen, Ellis N. Anesthetic Exposure in the Workplace. LC 79-16694. (Illus.). 212p. 1980. 26.00 (ISBN 0-88416-252-4). PSG Pub Co.
Cohen, Emily C. American Jewish Year Book Index. 1968. 25.00x (ISBN 0-87068-040-4). Ktav.
Cohen, Emmeline. Growth of the British Civil Service, 1780-1939. 221p. 1965. Repr. of 1941 ed. 27.50x (ISBN 0-7146-1293-6, BHA-01293, F Cass Co). Biblio Dist.
Cohen, Erik & Lissak, Moshe, eds. Comparative Social Dynamics: Essays in Honor of S. N. Eisenstadt. 300p. 1985. 25.00x (ISBN 0-86531-633-3). Westview.
Cohen, Esther. No Charge for Looking. LC 84-1435. 192p. 1984. 13.50 (ISBN 0-8052-3919-7). Schocken.
Cohen, Esther R. Human Rights in the Israeli-Occupied Territories: 1967-1982. LC 85-7111. 300p. 1985. 42.00 (ISBN 0-7190-1726-2, Pub. by Manchester Univ Pr). Longwood Pub Group.
Cohen, Eugene J. Guide to Ritual Circumcision & Redemption of the First-Born Son. 210p. 1984. 15.00x (ISBN 0-88125-017-1). Ktav.
Cohen, Eugene N. & Eames, Edwin. Cultural Anthropology. (Orig.). 1982. pap. text ed. 18.95 (ISBN 0-316-14991-8); tchrs'. manual avail. (ISBN 0-316-14989-6). Little.
Cohen, Eva, jt. auth. see Bliss, Ann.
Cohen, F. R. The Homology of Iterated Loop Spaces. (Lecture Notes in Mathematics: Vol. 533). 1976. soft cover 34.00 (ISBN 0-387-07984-X). Springer-Verlag.
Cohen, Fay G., et al. Treaties on Trial: The Continuing Controversy over Northwest Indian Fishing Rights. LC 85-40396. (Illus.). 280p. 1985. 20.00x (ISBN 0-295-96263-1); pap. 9.95 (ISBN 0-295-96268-2). U of Wash Pr.
Cohen, Felissa L. Clinical Genetics in Nursing Practice. (Illus.). 448p. 1984. pap. text ed. 19.50 (ISBN 0-397-54407-3, 64-03489, Lippincott Nursing). Lippincott.
Cohen, Felix. Ethical Systems & Legal Ideals: An Essay on the Foundations of Legal Criticism. LC 75-40440. 303p. 1976. Repr. of 1933 ed. lib. bdg. 19.25x (ISBN 0-8371-8643-9, COETS). Greenwood.
Cohen, Felix S. Legal Conscience, Selected Papers. Cohen, Lucy K., ed. 505p. 1970. Repr. of 1960 ed. 30.00 (ISBN 0-208-00813-6, Archon). Shoe String.
Cohen, Frank J., ed. Youth & Crime: Proceeding of the Law Enforcement Institute Held at NYU. pap. 9.95 (ISBN 0-317-31438-6, 24480). Intl Univs Pr.
Cohen, Fred. The Law of Deprivation of Liberty: A Study in Social Control Cases & Materials. LC 79-26667. (American Casebook Ser.). 755p. 1980. text ed. 23.95 (ISBN 0-8299-2079-X). West Pub.
--Standards Relating to Dispositional Procedures. LC 76-14414. (IJA-ABA Juvenile Justice Standards Project Ser.). 80p. 1980. prof ref 17.50 (ISBN 0-88410-233-5); pap. 10.00 prof ref (ISBN 0-88410-808-2). Ballinger Pub.
Cohen, Fred, jt. auth. see Rutherford, Andrew.
Cohen, Fritz G. The Poetry of Christian Hofmann Von Hofmannswaldau: A New Reading. (Studies in German Literature, Linguistics, & Culture: Vol. 22). (Illus.). 180p. 1985. 28.00x (ISBN 0-938100-38-6). Camden Hse.
Cohen, G. Creating Technical Manuals: A Step-by-Step Approach to Writing User-Friendly Instructions. 1984. 16.95 (ISBN 0-07-011584-2). McGraw.
Cohen, G. & Greenwald, M. D., eds. Oxy Radicals & Their Scavenger Systems, Vol. 1. 339p. 1983. 80.00 (ISBN 0-444-00746-6, Biomedical Pr). Elsevier.
Cohen, G. A. Karl Marx's Theory of History: A Defence. LC 78-51206. 392p. 1980. 27.50x (ISBN 0-691-07175-6); pap. 9.95 (ISBN 0-691-02008-6). Princeton U Pr.
Cohen, Gail A., ed. The Learning Traveler: U. S. College-Sponsored Programs Abroad-Academic Year, Vol. I. 192p. 1984. pap. text ed. 9.95 (ISBN 0-87206-151-5). Inst Intl Educ.
--Learning Traveler: Vacation Study Abroad, Vol. 2. 185p. 1984. pap. text ed. 9.95 (ISBN 0-87206-150-7). Inst Intl Educ.
Cohen, Gary. Horsemen Are Coming. 1979. pap. 2.95 (ISBN 0-8024-1568-7). Moody.
Cohen, Gary & Kirban, Salem. Israel, Land of Promise, Land of Peace. LC 74-77252. (Illus.). 1974. pap. 3.95 (ISBN 0-912582-16-2). Kirban.
Cohen, Gary, jt. auth. see Kirban, Salem.
Cohen, Gary & Vandermey, H. Ronald, eds. Hosea & Amos. (Everyman's Bible Commentary). 128p. 1981. pap. 5.95 (ISBN 0-8024-2028-1). Moody.
Cohen, Gary B. The Politics of Ethnic Survival: Germans in Prague, 1861-1914. LC 81-47119. (Illus.). 316p. 1981. 35.00x (ISBN 0-691-05332-4). Princeton U Pr.
Cohen, Gary G. Biblical Separation Defended. 1966. pap. 3.50 (ISBN 0-87552-147-9). Presby & Reformed.
Cohen, Gary G. & Runyon, Catherine. Weep Not for Me. LC 80-10773. 192p. 1980. pap. 3.95 (ISBN 0-8024-4309-5). Moody.
Cohen, Gene D., jt. ed. see Miller, Nancy.
Cohen, Gerald L. Origin of the Term Shyster. (Forum Anglicum: Vol. 12). 136p. 1982. pap. 16.30 (ISBN 3-8204-7216-9). P Lang Pubs.
Cohen, Gerald L., ed. Names & Etymology. (The International Library of Names). 400p. Date not set. text ed. price not set (ISBN 0-8290-1218-4). Irvington.
Cohen, Gershon. Hebrew Incanabula: Mendel Gottesman Library of Hebraica Judiaica, Yeshiva University. text ed. 29.50x (ISBN 0-88125-080-5, Pub. by Yeshiva Univ Pr). Ktav.
Cohen, Gillian. Psychology of Cognition. 2nd ed. 1983. 35.00 (ISBN 0-12-178760-5); pap. 17.50 (ISBN 0-12-178762-1). Acad Pr.
Cohen, Gourevitch. France in the Troubled World Economy. 1982. text ed. 45.00 (ISBN 0-408-10787-1). Butterworth.
Cohen, Gustav, tr. see Hanslick, Eduard.
Cohen, Gustave, ed. Recueil De Farces Francaises Inedites Du XVe Siecle. 1949. 20.00x (ISBN 0-910956-21-9). Medieval Acad.
Cohen, H., ed. see Gladstone, W. E.
Cohen, H., et al. Gas Turbine Theory. 2nd ed. 337p. 1979. 39.95 (ISBN 0-470-26781-X). Halsted Pr.
Cohen, H. F. Quantifying Music. 1984. lib. bdg. 54.50 (ISBN 90-277-1637-4, Pub. by Reidel Holland). Kluwer Academic.
Cohen, H. J., et al. Coin Inscriptions & Abbreviations of Imperial Rome. 1977. 15.00 (ISBN 0-89005-227-1). Ares.
Cohen, H. L. The Ballad. 59.95 (ISBN 0-87968-696-0). Gordon Pr.
Cohen, Harold, et al. Art & Computers: The First Artificial Intelligence Coloring Book. (Illus.). 1984. 19.95 (ISBN 0-86576-060-8). W Kaufmann.
--The First Artificial Intelligence Coloring Book. (Illus.). 128p. 1985. 19.95 (ISBN 0-86576-060-8). W Kaufmann.
Cohen, Harold L. & Filipczak, James. A New Learning Environment: A Case for Learning. LC 70-151108. (Social & Behavioral Science Ser.). 1971. 23.95x (ISBN 0-87589-101-2). Jossey-Bass.
Cohen, Harold R. Biblical Hapax Legomena in the Light of Akkadian & Ugaritic: Society of Biblical Literature, No.37. LC 77-13422. (Dissertation Ser.). pap. 50.30 (ISBN 0-8357-9565-9, 2017528). Bks Demand UMI.
Cohen, Harry. Connections: Understanding Social Relationships. 256p. 1981. text ed. 15.50x (ISBN 0-8138-1745-5). Iowa St U Pr.
Cohen, Harry, ed. see Kimchi, David B.
Cohen, Haskel & Weil, Geraldine R. Tasks of Emotional Development. LC 75-42572. 359p. 1975. 18.00 (ISBN 0-916598-02-0); pap. 12.00 manual (ISBN 0-317-00903-6); 49 pictures 25.00 (ISBN 0-317-00904-4). T E D Assocs.
Cohen, Hayyim J. Jews of the Middle East (1860-1972) 224p. 1973. casebound 12.95x (ISBN 0-87855-169-7). Transaction Bks.
Cohen, Helen A. The Nurse's Quest for a Professional Identity. 1981. 21.95 (ISBN 0-201-00956-0, Med-Nurse); pap. 19.95 (ISBN 0-201-01157-3). Addison-Wesley.
Cohen, Helen L. The Ballade. 1978. lib. bdg. 50.00 (ISBN 0-8414-9982-9). Folcroft.

--The Ballade. 398p. 1981. Repr. of 1915 ed. lib. bdg. 40.00 (ISBN 0-89760-153-X). Telegraph Bks.
--Educating Superior Students. 1935. 30.00 (ISBN 0-932062-27-X). Sharon Hill.
--One-Act Plays by Modern Authors. 1978. Repr. of 1921 ed. lib. bdg. 22.50 (ISBN 0-8495-0722-7). Arden Lib.
Cohen, Helen L., ed. The Junior Play Book. (Illus.). 388p. 1981. Repr. of 1923 ed. lib. bdg. 30.00 (ISBN 0-89984-110-4). Century Bookbindery.
--More One-Act Plays by Modern Authors. 369p. 1981. Repr. of 1927 ed. lib. bdg. 35.00 (ISBN 0-89760-152-1). Telegraph Bks.
Cohen, Hennig & Coffin, Tristram P., eds. Folklore of American Holidays. 1986. 75.00x (ISBN 0-8103-2126-2). Gale.
Cohen, Hennig & Dillingham, William B., eds. Humor of the Old Southwest. 2nd ed. LC 74-13512. 456p. 1975. pap. 10.00x (ISBN 0-8203-0358-5). U of Ga Pr.
Cohen, Hennig, jt. ed. see Levernier, James.
Cohen, Henry. Brutal Justice: The Ordeal of an American City. LC 79-26797. 248p. 1980. lib. bdg. 10.00x (ISBN 0-89444-027-6). John Jay Pr.
--Business & Politics in America from the Age of Jackson to the Civil War: The Career Biography of W. W. Corcoran. LC 79-98708. (Illus.). 409p. 1971. lib. bdg. 35.00 (ISBN 0-8371-3300-9, CBP/). Greenwood.
--Why Judaism? A Search for Meaning in Jewish Identity. 192p. 1973. pap. 5.00 (ISBN 0-8074-0077-7, 161901). UAHC.
Cohen, Henry, ed. Criminal Justice History: An International Annual,1983, Vol. IV. 350p. 1984. 49.50x (ISBN 0-930466-70-5). Meckler Pub.
--Criminal Justice History: An International Annual, 1981, Vol. II. 1981. 49.50 (ISBN 0-930466-68-3). Meckler Pub.
--Criminal Justice History: An International Annual, 1982, Vol. III. 359p. 1983. 49.50x (ISBN 0-930466-69-1). Meckler Pub.
--Criminal Justice History: An International Annual, 1980, Vol. I. 49.50 (ISBN 0-930466-67-5). Meckler Pub.
--The Public Enemy. LC 80-52292. (Wisconsin-Warner Bros. Screenplay Ser.). (Illus.). 190p. (Orig.). 1981. 17.50x (ISBN 0-299-08460-4); pap. 6.95 (ISBN 0-299-08464-7). U of Wis Pr.
Cohen, Henry B. The Home Video Book: How to Understand & Use Home Video, Home Computers & Electronic Games. (Illus.). 192p. 1983. pap. 9.95 (ISBN 0-8174-3993-5, Amphoto). Watson-Guptill.
Cohen, Henry E., ed. see Proudhon, P. J.
Cohen, Herb. You Can Negotiate Anything. 1982. pap. 3.95 (ISBN 0-553-23455-2). Bantam.
--You Can Negotiate Anything. 1980. 12.00 (ISBN 0-8184-0305-5). Lyle Stuart.
--You Can Negotiate Anything. 264p. 1983. pap. 5.95 (ISBN 0-8065-0847-7). Citadel Pr.
Cohen, Herbert J. Page One: Major Events As Presented in the New York Times, 1920-1981. 16.95 (ISBN 0-405-14350-8, 19818). Ayer Co Pubs.
--Page One: Major Events, Nineten-Twenty to Nineteen Eighty As Presented in the New York Times. 16.95 (ISBN 0-405-13698-6). Ayer Co Pubs.
Cohen, Herbert J. & Kligler, David. Urban Community Care for the Developmentally Disabled. (Illus.). 360p. 1980. 25.50x (ISBN 0-398-03945-3). C C Thomas.
Cohen, Herbert J., jt. auth. see Birenbaum, Arnold.
Cohen, Hermann. Hermann Cohen's Judische Schriften, 3 vols. Katz, Steven, ed. LC 79-7128. (Jewish Philosophy, Mysticism & History of Ideas Ser.). 1980. Repr. of 1924 ed. lib. bdg. 103.50x (ISBN 0-405-12245-4). Ayer Co Pubs.
Cohen, Hermann & Strauss, Bruno. Judische Schriften, Vol. 3. 34.50 (ISBN 0-405-12303-5). Ayer Co Pubs.
--Judische Schriften, Vol. 1. 34.50 (ISBN 0-405-12298-5). Ayer Co Pubs.
--Judische Schriften, Vol. 2. 34.50 (ISBN 0-405-12299-3). Ayer Co Pubs.
Cohen, Howard. Equal Rights for Children. (Quality Paperback Ser.: No. 350). 172p. (Orig.). 1980. pap. 4.95 (ISBN 0-8226-0350-0). Littlefield.
--Equal Rights for Children. LC 80-16005. 182p. 1980. 13.50x (ISBN 0-8476-6772-3). Rowman.
Cohen, Howard M. The Relationship of the Prison Program to Changes in Attitudes & Self Concepts of Inmates. LC 74-28609. 1975. soft bdg. 12.00 (ISBN 0-88247-330-1). R & E Pubs.
Cohen, I. Bernard. Album of Science: From Leonardo to Lavoisier, 1450-1800. LC 80-15542. (Illus.). 1980. 55.00 (ISBN 0-684-15377-7, ScribR). Scribner.
--The Birth of a New Physics. rev. & expanded ed. 1985. 17.95 (ISBN 0-393-01994-2); pap. 5.95 (ISBN 0-393-30045-5). Norton.
--Cotton Mather & American Science & Medicine: With Studies & Documents Concerning the Introduction of Innoculation or Variolation, Vol. 1. 37.50 (ISBN 0-405-12520-8). Ayer Co Pubs.
--Cotton Mather & American Science & Medicine: With Studies & Documents Concerning the Introduction of Inoculation or Variolation, Vol. 2. 37.50 (ISBN 0-405-12521-6). Ayer Co Pubs.
--Introduction to Newton's Principia. LC 76-28770. 1971. pap. text ed. 12.00x (ISBN 0-674-46193-2). Harvard U Pr.
--Isaac Newton's Papers & Letters on Natural Philosophy & Related Documents. 2nd ed. 1978. 32.50x (ISBN 0-674-46853-8). Harvard U Pr.
--The Leibniz-Clarke Correspondence. LC 80-2100. (Development of Science Ser.). (Illus.). 1981. lib. bdg. 50.00x (ISBN 0-405-13865-2). Ayer Co Pubs.
--The Life & Scientific & Medical Career of Benjamin Waterhouse: With Some Account of the Introduction of Vaccination in America, Vol. 1. 34.50 (ISBN 0-405-12522-4). Ayer Co Pubs.
--The Life & Scientific & Medical Career of Benjamin Waterhouse: With Some Account of the Introduction of Vaccination in America, Vol. 2. 34.50 (ISBN 0-405-12523-2). Ayer Co Pubs.
--The Newtonian Revolution. LC 79-18637. 1981. 49.50 (ISBN 0-521-22964-2). Cambridge U Pr.
--The Newtonian Revolution: With Illustrations of the Transformation of Scientific Ideas. LC 79-18637. (Illus.). 404p. 1983. pap. 17.95 (ISBN 0-521-27380-3). Cambridge U Pr.
--Revolution in Science. (Illus.). 704p. 1985. 25.00 (ISBN 0-674-76777-2, Belknap Pr). Harvard U Pr.
Cohen, I. Bernard, jt. auth. see Jones, Howard M.
Cohen, I. Bernard, ed. Andrew N. Meldrum. LC 80-2096. (Development of Science Ser.). (Illus.). lib. bdg. 45.00x (ISBN 0-405-13861-X). Ayer Co Pubs.
--Aspects of Astronomy in America in the Nineteenth Century: An Original Anthology. LC 79-7948. (Three Centuries of Science in America Ser.). (Illus.). 1980. lib. bdg. 44.00x (ISBN 0-405-12529-1). Ayer Co Pubs.
--Benjamin Peirce: Father of Pure Mathematics in America. An Original Anthology. LC 79-7981. (Three Centuries of Science in America Ser.). (Illus.). 1980. lib. bdg. 32.50x (ISBN 0-405-12563-1). Ayer Co Pubs.
--The Conservation of Energy & the Principle of Least Action. LC 80-2097. (Development of Science Ser.). (Illus.). 1981. lib. bdg. 45.00x (ISBN 0-405-13862-8). Ayer Co Pubs.
--Cotton Mather & American Science & Medicine: With Studies & Documents Concerning the Introduction of Inoculation or Variolation, 2 vols. LC 79-7974. (Three Centuries of Science in America Ser.). (Illus.). 1980. lib. bdg. 75.00x (ISBN 0-405-12556-9). Ayer Co Pubs.
--The Development of Science Series, 63 vols. 1981. Set. lib. bdg. 2004.00x (ISBN 0-405-13850-4). Ayer Co Pubs.
--Electro-Magnetism. LC 80-2098. (Development of Science Ser.). (Illus.). 1981. lib. bdg. 32.00x (ISBN 0-405-13863-6). Ayer Co Pubs.
--Gravitation, Heat & X-Rays. LC 80-2104. (Development of Science Ser.). (Illus.). 1981. lib. bdg. 35.00x (ISBN 0-405-13869-5). Ayer Co Pubs.
--Laws of Gases. LC 80-2099. (Development of Science Ser.). (Illus.). 1981. lib. bdg. 35.00x (ISBN 0-405-13864-4). Ayer Co Pubs.
--The Life & Scientific Work of Othniel Charles Marsh: An Original Anthology. LC 79-7973. (Three Centuries of Science in America Ser.). (Illus.). 1980. lib. bdg. 57.50x (ISBN 0-405-12555-0). Ayer Co Pubs.
--The Life & the Scientific & Medical Career of Benjamin Waterhouse: With Some Account of the Introduction of Vaccination in America, An Original Anthology, 2 vols. LC 79-8004. (Three Centuries of Science in America Ser.). (Illus.). 1980. Set. lib. bdg. 69.00x (ISBN 0-405-12591-7). Ayer Co Pubs.
--Research & Technology. LC 79-7982. (Three Centuries of Science in America Ser.). (Illus.). 1980. lib. bdg. 23.00x (ISBN 0-405-12564-X). Ayer Co Pubs.
--Studies on William Harvey. LC 80-2101. (Development of Science Ser.). (Illus.). 1981. lib. bdg. 65.00x (ISBN 0-405-13866-0). Ayer Co Pubs.
--Theory of Solutions & Stereo-Chemistry. LC 80-2103. (Development of Science Ser.). (Illus.). 1981. lib. bdg. 35.00x (ISBN 0-405-13868-7). Ayer Co Pubs.
--Thomas Jefferson & the Sciences: An Original Anthology. LC 79-7970. (Three Centuries of Science in America Ser.). (Illus.). 1980. 57.50x (ISBN 0-405-12552-6). Ayer Co Pubs.
--Three Centuries of Science in America Series, 66 bks. (Illus.). 1980. Set. lib. bdg. 2939.000.00x (ISBN 0-405-12525-9). Ayer Co Pubs.
--The Wave Theory of Light & Spectra. LC 80-2102. (Development of Science Ser.). (Illus.). 1981. lib. bdg. 35.00x (ISBN 0-405-13867-9). Ayer Co Pubs.
Cohen, I. Bernard, ed. see Ackerknecht, Erwin H.
Cohen, I. Bernard, ed. see Adams, John Q.
Cohen, I. Bernard, jt. ed. see Airy, George B.
Cohen, I. Bernard, jt. ed. see Anderson, David L.
Cohen, I. Bernard, ed. see Archibald, Raymond C.
Cohen, I. Bernard, ed. see Beaumont, William.
Cohen, I. Bernard, ed. see Beer, John.
Cohen, I. Bernard, ed. see Bowditch, Henry P.
Cohen, I. Bernard, ed. see Bridgman, Percy W.
Cohen, I. Bernard, jt. ed. see Brown, Theodore.
Cohen, I. Bernard, ed. see Bush, Vannevar.
Cohen, I. Bernard, ed. see Cajori, Florian.
Cohen, I. Bernard, ed. see Cheyne, Charles H.
Cohen, I. Bernard, jt. ed. see Coleman, William.
Cohen, I. Bernard, ed. see Cooper, Thomas.
Cohen, I. Bernard, ed. see Dalton, John C.
Cohen, I. Bernard, ed. see Darton, Nelson H.
Cohen, I. Bernard, ed. see De Candolle, Alphonse.
Cohen, I. Bernard, jt. ed. see Domson, Charles.
Cohen, I. Bernard, jt. ed. see Donahue, William H.
Cohen, I. Bernard, ed. see Dupree, A. Hunter.
Cohen, I. Bernard, ed. see Ellicott, Andrew.
Cohen, I. Bernard, jt. ed. see Farrell, Maureen.
Cohen, I. Bernard, ed. see Fulton, John F.
Cohen, I. Bernard, ed. see Gardner, Walter M.
Cohen, I. Bernard, ed. see Getman, Frederick H.
Cohen, I. Bernard, ed. see Godfray, Hugh.
Cohen, I. Bernard, ed. see Goode, George B.
Cohen, I. Bernard, ed. see Graetzerk, Hans G. & Anderson, David L.
Cohen, I. Bernard, ed. see Grimaux, Edouard.
Cohen, I. Bernard, ed. see Hale, George E.
Cohen, I. Bernard, ed. see Hall, Diana L.
Cohen, I. Bernard, jt. ed. see Hall, Marie B.
Cohen, I. Bernard, ed. see Hannequin, Arthur.
Cohen, I. Bernard, ed. see Harding, T. Swann.
Cohen, I. Bernard, ed. see Harvey-Gibson, Robert J.
Cohen, I. Bernard, jt. ed. see Heibron, John L.
Cohen, I. Bernard, ed. see Heidel, William A.
Cohen, I. Bernard, jt. ed. see Herschel, John F.
Cohen, I. Bernard, ed. see Hiebert, Erwin N.
Cohen, I. Bernard, jt. ed. see Hilts, Victor L.
Cohen, I. Bernard, ed. see Hindle, Brooke.
Cohen, I. Bernard, jt. ed. see Hindle, Brooke.
Cohen, I. Bernard, ed. see Holden, Edward S.
Cohen, I. Bernard, ed. see Home, Roderick W.
Cohen, I. Bernard, ed. see Howard, Leland O.
Cohen, I. Bernard, ed. see Jaffe, Bernard.
Cohen, I. Bernard, ed. see Karpinski, Louis C.
Cohen, I. Bernard, ed. see Loomis, Elias.
Cohen, I. Bernard, ed. see Maeir, Clifford L.
Cohen, I. Bernard, ed. see Merill, Elmer D.
Cohen, I. Bernard, ed. see Meyer, Kirstine B.
Cohen, I. Bernard, ed. see Millikan, Robert A.
Cohen, I. Bernard, ed. see Milne-Edwards, Henri.
Cohen, I. Bernard, ed. see Mitchel, Ormsby M.
Cohen, I. Bernard, ed. see Mouy, Paul.
Cohen, I. Bernard, ed. see Olmsted, J. M. D.
Cohen, I. Bernard, ed. see Organisation for Economic Co-Operation & Development.
Cohen, I. Bernard, ed. see Packard, Alpheus S.
Cohen, I. Bernard, ed. see Partington, J. R. & McKie, D.
Cohen, I. Bernard, ed. see Priestly, Joseph.
Cohen, I. Bernard, ed. see Pupin, Michael.
Cohen, I. Bernard, ed. see Quetelet, Adolphe J.
Cohen, I. Bernard, ed. see Rhees, William J.
Cohen, I. Bernard, jt. ed. see Roe, Shirley A.
Cohen, I. Bernard, ed. see Sayili, Aydin.
Cohen, I. Bernard, ed. see Schofield, Christine J.
Cohen, I. Bernard, ed. see Scott, William B.
Cohen, I. Bernard, ed. see Shirley, John W.
Cohen, I. Bernard, ed. see Shryock, Richard H.
Cohen, I. Bernard, ed. see Shute, Michael.
Cohen, I. Bernard, ed. see Silliman, Benjamin.
Cohen, I. Bernard, ed. see Silliman, Benjamin, Jr.
Cohen, I. Bernard, ed. see Smith, David E. & Ginsberg, Jekuthiel.
Cohen, I. Bernard, ed. see Smith, Edgar F.
Cohen, I. Bernard, ed. see Sopka, Katherine.
Cohen, I. Bernard, ed. see Steelman, John R. & President's Scientific Research Board.
Cohen, I. Bernard, ed. see Stewart, Irvin.
Cohen, I. Bernard, jt. ed. see Stigler, Stephen M.
Cohen, I. Bernard, ed. see Trowbridge, John.
Cohen, I. Bernard, ed. see True, Alfred.
Cohen, I. Bernard, jt. ed. see True, Frederick.
Cohen, I. Bernard, ed. see Turner, Dorothy M.
Cohen, I. Bernard, ed. see Tyndall, John.
Cohen, I. Bernard, ed. see U. S. House of Representatives, 55th Congress, 2nd Session, Doc. No. 575, Pt. 3.
Cohen, I. Bernard, ed. see U. S. National Resources Committee.
Cohen, I. Bernard, ed. see U. S. Senate (49th Congress, 1st Session, Mis. Doc. No. 82).
Cohen, I. Bernard, ed. see Wilhelm, Friedrich G.
Cohen, I. Bernard, ed. see Wool, Harry.
Cohen, I. Bernard, ed. see Wurtz, Adolf.
Cohen, I. Bernard, ed. see Youmans, Edward L.
Cohen, I. Bernard, ed. see Zloczower, A.
Cohen, I. L. Darwin Was Wrong: A Study in Probabilities. Murphy, G., ed. LC 84-22613. (Illus.). 225p. 1985. 16.95 (ISBN 0-910891-02-8). New Research.
--The Secret of Stonehenge. Murphy, G., ed. LC 82-19107. (Illus.). 310p. 1982. 16.95 (ISBN 0-910891-01-X). New Research.
--Urim & Thumim: The Secret of God. Murphy, G., ed. LC 82-24578. (Illus.). 280p. 1983. 16.95 (ISBN 0-910891-00-1). New Research.
Cohen, Ira H. Ideology & Unconsciousness: Reich, Freud & Marx. 256p. 1982. 32.50x (ISBN 0-8147-1383-1). NYU Pr.
Cohen, Ira S. Scientific Handicapping: Tested Way to Win at the Race Track. (Illus., Orig.). 1966. pap. 3.95 (ISBN 0-13-795880-3). P-H.
Cohen, Irun, jt. auth. see Rosenberg, Eugene.
Cohen, Irving S., jt. auth. see Logan, Rayford W.
Cohen, Israel, ed. The Rebirth of Israel. LC 75-6427. (The Rise of Jewish Nationalism & the Middle East Ser.). 338p. 1975. Repr. of 1952 ed. 25.85 (ISBN 0-88355-314-7). Hyperion Conn.
--Zionist Work in Palestine. LC 75-6428. (The Rise of Jewish Nationalism & the Middle East Ser.). (Illus.). 208p. 1975. Repr. of 1911 ed. 22.50 (ISBN 0-88355-315-5). Hyperion Conn.
Cohen, J. Living Embryos. 3rd ed. 1967. 21.00 (ISBN 0-08-025926-X); pap. 7.95 (ISBN 0-08-025925-1). Pergamon.
--Single Server Queue. 2nd ed. (Applied Mathematics & Mechanics Ser.: Vol. 8). 694p. 1982. 89.50 (ISBN 0-444-85452-5, North-Holland). Elsevier.
--Special Bibliography in Monetary Economics & Finance. 214p. 1976. 76.50 (ISBN 0-677-00690-X). Gordon.
Cohen, J. B. & Hilliard, J. E., eds. Local Atomic Arrangements Studied by X-ray Diffraction, Chicago, Illionis, Feruary 15, 1965. LC 66-28062. (Metallurgical Society Conferences: Vol. 36). pap. 98.30 (ISBN 0-317-10549-3, 2001525). Bks Demand UMI.
Cohen, J. Craig, jt. ed. see Rothschild, Henry.
Cohen, J. J., et al, eds. Nephrology Forum. (Illus.). 376p. 1983. pap. 39.50 (ISBN 0-387-90764-5). Springer-Verlag.
Cohen, J. L., et al, eds. Logic, Methodology & Philosophy of Science, Vol. 6. (Studies in Logic & the Foundation of Mathematics: Vol. 104). 104p. 1983. 125.75 (ISBN 0-444-85423-1, North Holland). Elsevier.
Cohen, J. M. Stable Homotopy. LC 77-139950. (Lecture Notes in Mathematics: Vol. 165). 1970. pap. 11.00 (ISBN 0-387-05192-9). Springer-Verlag.
Cohen, J. M. & Cohen, M. J. The Penguin Dictionary of Modern Quotations. rev. ed. (Reference Ser.). 496p. 1971. pap. 6.95 (ISBN 0-14-051038-9). Penguin.
Cohen, J. M. & Phipps, J. F. The Common Experience. LC 81-16651. 266p. (Orig.). 1982. Repr. of 1979 ed. 15.00 (ISBN 0-87477-204-4). J P Tarcher.
Cohen, J. M., tr. see Cervantes de Saavedra, Miguel.
Cohen, J. M., tr. see Eliade, Mircea.
Cohen, J. M., tr. see Montaigne.
Cohen, J. S. Magnetic Resonance in Biology, Vol. 1. 309p. 1980. 63.50 (ISBN 0-471-05176-4). Wiley.
Cohen, J. Simcha. The Six Hundred Thirteenth Commandment: An Analysis of the Mitzvah to Write a Sefer Torah (Derush VeChiddush) LC 83-8436. 162p. 1983. 9.95x (ISBN 0-88125-027-9). Ktav.
Cohen, J. W. & Boxma, O. J. Boundary Value Problems in Queueing Systems Analysis. (Mathematical Studies: Vol. 79). 1983. 42.75 (ISBN 0-444-86567-5, I-010-83). Elsevier.
Cohen, Jack, tr. see Marx, Karl.
Cohen, Jack, et al. Nuclear Magnetic Resonance in Biology & Medicine. (Life Chemistry Reports Ser.: Vol. 1, No. 4). 175p. 1983. 36.50 (ISBN 3-7186-0171-0). Harwood Academic.
Cohen, Jack S. The Jewish Heart: Essays on Jewish Sensitivities. LC 84-27837. 217p. 1985. 15.00 (ISBN 0-88125-065-1). Ktav.
--Magnetic Resonance in Biology, Vol. 2. LC 80-13070. (Magnetic Resonance in Biology Ser.). 308p. 1983. 74.95 (ISBN 0-471-05175-6, Pub. by Wiley-Interscience). Wiley.
Cohen, Jack S., jt. auth. see Portugal, Franklin H.
Cohen, Jack S., ed. Noninvasive Probes of Tissue Metabolism. LC 81-10436. 286p. 1982. 58.50 (ISBN 0-471-08893-5). Krieger.
Cohen, Jacob. Statistical Power Analysis for the Behavioral Sciences. rev. ed. 1977. 50.00 (ISBN 0-12-179060-6). Acad Pr.
Cohen, Jacob & Cohen, Patricia. Applied Multiple Regression: Correlation Analysis for the Behavioral Sciences. 2nd ed. 545p. 1983. text ed. 29.95x (ISBN 0-89859-268-2). L Erlbaum Assocs.
Cohen, Jacob, jt. auth. see Williams, Edward.
Cohen, James S. & Stieglitz, Maria N. Career Education For Physically Disabled Students: Classroom Business Ventures. LC 79-91614. (Illus.). 50p. 1980. 5.00 (ISBN 0-686-38798-8). Human Res Ctr.
Cohen, James S., jt. auth. see Stieglitz, Maria.
Cohen, James S., jt. auth. see Stieglitz, Maria N.
Cohen, Jane R. Charles Dickens & His Original Illustrators. LC 79-21570. (Illus.). 1980. 32.50. Ohio St U Pr.
Cohen, Jean & Dourlen-Rollier, Anne Marie. Dictionnaire de la Vie Affective et Sexuelle. 272p. (Fr.). 1974. 15.95 (ISBN 0-686-56827-3, M-6605). French & Eur.
Cohen, Jean, et al. Encyclopedie De la Vie Sexuelle, 1: De la Physiologie a la Psychologie, 7-9 Ans. 48p. (Fr.). 1973. 9.95 (ISBN 0-686-56950-4, M-6072). French & Eur.
--Encyclopedie De la Vie Sexuelle, 2. 96p. (Fr.). 1973. 11.95 (ISBN 0-686-56951-2, M-6073). French & Eur.
--Encyclopedie De la Vie Sexuelle, 3: De la Physiologie a la Psychologie, 14-16 Ans. 160p. (Fr.). 1973. 15.95 (ISBN 0-686-56952-0, M-6074). French & Eur.
--Encyclopedie De la Vie Sexuelle, 4: De la Physiologie a la Psychologie, 17-18 Ans. 48p. (Fr.). 1973. 16.95 (ISBN 0-686-56953-9, M-6075). French & Eur.
--Encyclopedie De la Vie Sexuelle, 5: De la Physiologie a la Psychologie, Adultes. 48p. (Fr.). 1973. 21.95 (ISBN 0-686-56954-7, M-6076). French & Eur.

Cohen, Jean L. Class & Civil Society: The Limits of Marxian Critical Theory. LC 82-11104. 276p. 1983. lib. bdg. 22.50x (ISBN 0-87023-380-7). U of Mass Pr.

Cohen, Jean P. & Goirand, Roger. Your Baby: Pregnancy, Delivery, & Infant Care. (Illus.). 304p. 1982. 17.95 (ISBN 0-13-978130-7, Spec); pap. 8.95 (ISBN 0-13-978122-6). P-H.

Cohen, Jean-Pierre. Childhood: The First Six Years. (Illus.). 256p. 1983. 17.95 (ISBN 0-13-131300-2); pap. 8.95 (ISBN 0-13-131292-8). P-H.

Cohen, Jeffrey M. Understanding the High Holyday Service. 218p. 1983. 12.50 (ISBN 0-317-26854-6). Hebrew Pub.

Cohen, Jeremy. The Friars & the Jews: The Evolution of Medieval Anti-Judaism. LC 81-15210. 304p. 1982. 27.50x (ISBN 0-8014-1406-7). Cornell U Pr.

--The Friars & the Jews: The Evolution of Medieval Anti-Judaism. LC 81-15210. 304p. 1984. pap. 9.95x (ISBN 0-8014-9266-1). Cornell U Pr.

Cohen, Jerome, et al, eds. Psychosocial Aspects of Cancer. Orig. Title: Research Issues in Psychological Dimensions of Cancer. 336p. 1982. text ed. 48.00 (ISBN 0-89004-494-5). Raven.

Cohen, Jerome A. & Chiu, Hungdah. People's China & International Law, 2 vols. LC 73-2475. (Studies in East Asian Law). 1974. Set. 155.00x (ISBN 0-691-09229-X). Princeton U Pr.

Cohen, Jerome A. & Practising Law Institute. Legal Aspects of Doing Business in China, 1983. LC 82-62773. (Commercial Law & Practice Course Handbook Ser.: No. 293). 600p. 1983. 35.00. PLI.

Cohen, Jerome A., jt. auth. see Cohen, Joan L.

Cohen, Jerome A., ed. China's Practice of International Law: Some Case Studies. LC 72-80656. (Studies in East Asian Law: No. 6). (Illus.). 420p. 1973. 27.50x (ISBN 0-674-11975-4). Harvard U Pr.

--Criminal Process in the People's Republic of China, 1949-1963: An Introduction. LC 68-14252. (Studies in East Asian Law: No. 2). (Illus.). 1968. 40.00x (ISBN 0-674-17650-2). Harvard U Pr.

--The Dynamics of China's Foreign Relations. LC 78-133219. (East Asian Monographs Ser: No. 39). 129p. 1970. soft cover 11.00x (ISBN 0-674-21875-2). Harvard U Pr.

Cohen, Jerome A., et al, eds. Contemporary Chinese Law: Research Problems & Perspectives. LC 74-106957. (Studies in East Asian Law: No. 4). 1970. 25.00x (ISBN 0-674-16675-2). Harvard U Pr.

--Essays on China's Legal Tradition. LC 79-3197. (Studies in East Asian Law, Harvard U). 1980. 42.00 (ISBN 0-691-09238-9). Princeton U Pr.

Cohen, Jerome A., et al, trs. from Chinese. The Criminal Law & the Criminal Procedure Law of China. 298p. (Orig., Eng.). 1984. pap. 6.95 (ISBN 0-8351-1015-X). China Bks.

Cohen, Jerome B. Personal Finance. 6th ed. 1979. 25.95x (ISBN 0-256-02154-6). Irwin.

--Personal Finance. 3rd ed. (Plaid Ser.). 1981. 9.95 (ISBN 0-256-02126-0). Dow Jones-Irwin.

Cohen, Jerome B., et al. Guide to Intelligent Investing. LC 77-83590. 1978. 19.95 (ISBN 0-87094-152-6). Dow Jones-Irwin.

--Investment Analysis & Portfolio Management. 4th ed. 1982. text ed. 29.50x (ISBN 0-256-02501-0). Irwin.

Cohen, Jerome B., et al, eds. Advances in X-Ray Analysis, Vol. 27. 579p. 1984. 69.50x (ISBN 0-306-41712-X, Plenum Pr). Plenum Pub.

Cohen, Jerrold & Greenfield, Roy. UR-U. S. Double Tax Treaties Guide. 224p. 1980. 50.00x (ISBN 0-85120-475-9, Pub. by Oyez England). State Mutual Bk.

Cohen, Jerry S., jt. auth. see Mintz, Morton.

Cohen, Joan L. & Cohen, Jerome A. China Today: And Her Ancient Treasures. 3rd ed. (Illus.). 448p. 1985. 45.00 (ISBN 0-8109-0798-4). Abrams.

Cohen, Joan Mandel. Form & Realism in Six Novels of Anthony Trollope. (De Proprietatibus Litterarum, Ser. Practica: No. 87). 1976. pap. text ed. 12.80x (ISBN 90-2793-464-9). Mouton.

Cohen, Joel & Snitzer, Herb. Reprise: The Extraordinary Revival of Early Music. 224p. 1985. 25.00 (ISBN 0-316-15037-1). Little.

Cohen, Joel, jt. auth. see Mizerak, Steve.

Cohen, Joel, jt. auth. see Seixas, Vic, Jr.

Cohen, Joel A., frwd. by. The Act of Renunciation of Allegiance Adopted by the General Assembly of Rhode Island & Providence Plantations on the Fourth Day of May 1776. 1976. pap. 3.00 ltd. ed. (ISBN 0-917012-47-X). RI Hist Soc.

Cohen, Joel E. Casual Groups of Monkeys & Men: Stochastic Models of Elemental Social Systems. LC 73-133215. (Illus.). 1971. 10.00x (ISBN 0-674-09981-8). Harvard U Pr.

--Food Webs & Niche Space. (Monographs in Population Biology: No. 11). 1978. text ed. 23.00 (ISBN 0-691-08201-4); pap. 9.95 (ISBN 0-691-08202-2). Princeton U Pr.

--A Model of Simple Competition. LC 66-23470. (Annals of the Computation Laboratory). (Illus.). 138p. 1966. 10.00x (ISBN 0-674-57800-7). Harvard U Pr.

Cohen, Joel H., jt. auth. see Dayney, Randy.

Cohen, Joel H., jt. auth. see Mizerak, Steve.

Cohen, John. The Lineaments of Mind. LC 79-21794. (Illus.). 325p. 1980. text ed. 23.95 (ISBN 0-7167-1175-3). W H Freeman.

Cohen, John & Clark, John H. Medicine, Mind, & Man. LC 78-27201. (Illus.). 401p. 1979. text ed. 24.95x (ISBN 0-7167-1089-7); pap. text ed. 13.95x (ISBN 0-7167-1090-0). W H Freeman.

Cohen, John I. & Travers, Robert M., eds. Education for Democracy. facs. ed. LC 72-128222. (Essay Index Reprint Ser). 1939. 27.50 (ISBN 0-8369-1944-0). Ayer Co Pubs.

Cohen, John M. & Cohen, M. J. Penguin Dictionary of Quotations. (Reference Ser.). (Orig.). 1960. pap. 6.95 (ISBN 0-14-051016-8). Penguin.

Cohen, John M. & Uphoff, John M. Rural Development Participation: Concepts & Measures for Project Design, Implementation & Evaluation. (Monograph: No. 2). 317p. (Orig.). 1977. pap. text ed. 14.25 (ISBN 0-86731-001-4). RDC Ctr Intl Stud.

Cohen, John M. & Weintraub, Dov. Land & Peasants in Imperial Ethiopia: The Social Background to a Revolution. 115p. (Orig.). 1975. pap. text ed. 21.25x (ISBN 90-232-1291-6). Humanities.

Cohen, John M., tr. see De Cervantes, Miguel.

Cohen, John M., tr. see Diaz Del Castillo, Bernal.

Cohen, John M., tr. see Rabelais, Francois.

Cohen, John M., tr. see Rousseau, Jean-Jacques.

Cohen, John M., et al. Revolution & Land Reform in Ethiopia: Peasant Associations, Local Government & Rural Development. (Occasional Paper Ser.: No. 6). 127p. (Orig.). 1976. pap. text ed. 8.40 (ISBN 0-86731-019-7). RDC Ctr Intl Stud.

Cohen, Jon, jt. auth. see Scaravelli, Paola.

Cohen, Jon S. Finance & Industrialization in Italy, 1894-1914. Bruchey, Stuart, ed. LC 77-81825. (Dissertations in European Economic History Ser.). (Illus.). 1977. lib. bdg. 24.50x (ISBN 0-405-10777-3). Ayer Co Pubs.

Cohen, Jonathan, jt. ed. see Keylin, Arleen.

Cohen, Jonathan, tr. see Cardenal, Ernesto.

Cohen, Jonathan, et al, trs. see Lihn, Enrique.

Cohen, Jordan J. & Kassirer, Jerome P. Acid-Base. 1982. text ed. 49.95 (ISBN 0-316-15011-8). Little.

Cohen, Joseph. The Jewish Anarchist Movement in the United States. 1977. lib. bdg. 59.95 (ISBN 0-685-74872-3). Gordon Pr.

Cohen, Joseph, ed. The Poetry of Dannie Abse: Critical Essays & Reminiscences. 187p. 1984. 15.00 (ISBN 0-86051-243-6, Pub. by Salem Acad). Merrimack Pub Cir.

Cohen, Joseph E. Anarchism & Libertarian Socialism in Israel: A Study of Anti-Statist Movements. 1979. lib. bdg. 42.95 (ISBN 0-686-24784-1). M Buber Pr.

Cohen, Joseph J. In Quest of Heaven: The Story of the Sunrise Cooperative Farm Community. LC 74-26760. (American Utopian Adventure Ser). (Illus.). 255p. 1975. Repr. of 1957 ed. lib. bdg. 25.00x (ISBN 0-87991-023-2). Porcupine Pr.

Cohen, Josh & Rogers, Joel. On Democracy: Toward a Transformation of American Society. 231p. (Orig.). 1983. pap. 6.95 (ISBN 0-14-006781-7). Penguin.

Cohen, Joyce T., compiled by. Insights: Self-Portraits by Women. LC 78-58501. (Illus.). 144p. 1978. 20.00x (ISBN 0-87923-246-3); pap. 8.95 (ISBN 0-87923-247-1). Godine.

Cohen, Judith & Cohen, Michael. The Spot. 1984. 4.95 (ISBN 0-533-06029-X). Vantage.

Cohen, Judith, jt. auth. see Gordon, Sol.

Cohen, Judith B. Parenthood after Thirty: A Guide to Personal Choice. LC 84-48826. 176p. 1985. 20.00x (ISBN 0-669-09844-2); pap. 8.95 (ISBN 0-669-09845-0). Lexington Bks.

--Seasons. LC 83-63240. 224p. 1984. 16.95 (ISBN 0-932966-38-1). Permanent Pr.

Cohen, Judith H. Handbook of Resource Room Teaching. LC 81-20599. 324p. 1982. text ed. 31.00 (ISBN 0-89443-653-8). Aspen Systems.

Cohen, Jules & McKinney, Catherine S. How to Microcomputerize Your Small Business. (Illus.). 182p. 1983. 18.95 (ISBN 0-13-423897-4); pap. 9.95 (ISBN 0-13-423889-3). P-H.

Cohen, Julius, et al. Parental Authority: The Community & the Law. LC 80-153. (Illus.). xii, 301p. 1980. Repr. of 1958 ed. lib. bdg. 32.50x (ISBN 0-313-22351-3, COPR). Greenwood.

Cohen, Julius H. The Law: Business or Profession? 1980. lib. bdg. 79.95 (ISBN 0-8490-3133-8). Gordon Pr.

--They Builded Better Than They Knew. facsimile ed. LC 70-156633. (Essay Index Reprint Ser). Repr. of 1946 ed. 21.50 (ISBN 0-8369-2350-2). Ayer Co Pubs.

Cohen, Kalman J. & Cyert, Richard M. Theory of the Firm: Resource Allocation in a Market Economy. 2nd ed. (Illus.). 640p. 1975. 31.95 (ISBN 0-13-913798-X). P-H.

Cohen, Kalman J. & Gibson, Stephen E., eds. Management Science in Banking. LC 78-60934. 549p. 1978. text ed. 42.50 (ISBN 0-471-87748-4). Wiley.

Cohen, Karen, et al. Models of Efficient Reading. (Development of the Reading Process Ser.). 1979. pap. text ed. 4.00 (ISBN 0-87207-524-9, 524). Intl Reading.

Cohen, Karen C., ed. see Anderson, M. & Lee, R.

Cohen, Karen C., ed. see Belding, John A.

Cohen, Karen C., ed. see Cho, Chun H.

Cohen, Karen C., ed. see Conta, Lewis D.

Cohen, Karen C., ed. see Dyer, D., et al.

Cohen, Karen C., ed. see Eckerlin, H. & Boyers, A.

Cohen, Karen C., ed. see Furbush, S. A.

Cohen, Karen C., ed. see Furgerson, W. F.

Cohen, Karen C., jt. ed. see Gyftopoulos, Elias P.

Cohen, Karen C., ed. see Harrison, Michael R.

Cohen, Karen C., ed. see Keller, George E., II.

Cohen, Karen C., ed. see Kenney, W. F.

Cohen, Karen C., ed. see Mix, T. W. & Dweck, J. S.

Cohen, Karen C., ed. see Monroe, Elmer S., Jr.

Cohen, Karen C., ed. see Seader, J. D.

Cohen, Karen C., ed. see Shinskey, F. G.

Cohen, Karen C., ed. see Stephanopoulos, G.

Cohen, Kathleen R. Metamorphosis of a Death Symbol: The Transi Tomb in the Late Middle Ages & the Renaissance. LC 78-138511. (California Studies in the History of Art: Vol. 15). 1974. 77.00x (ISBN 0-520-01844-3). U of Cal Pr.

Cohen, Keith. Natural Settings. LC 81-22133. 96p. (Orig.). 1982. 17.95 (ISBN 0-916190-14-5); pap. 6.00 (ISBN 0-916190-15-3). Full Court NY.

Cohen, Kenneth K. Imagine That! A Child's Guide to Yoga. (Illus.). 48p. 1983. pap. 8.95 (ISBN 0-915520-55-9). Santa Barb Pr.

Cohen, Kenneth P. Hospice: Prescription for Terminal Care. LC 79-13341. 302p. 1979. text ed. 37.00 (ISBN 0-89443-151-X). Aspen Systems.

Cohen, Kesarwani. Linear Algebra. 256p. 1984. pap. text ed. 11.95 (ISBN 0-8403-3494-X). Kendall Hunt.

Cohen, Kitty. The Throne & the Chariot: Studies in Milton's Hebraism. (Studies in English Literature: No. 97). 1975. text ed. 23.20x (ISBN 0-686-22628-3). Mouton.

Cohen, L. Readings in Education & Psychology. 1969. pap. text ed. 5.95x (ISBN 0-8422-0028-2). Irvington.

Cohen, L. J. & Hesse, M. B., eds. Applications of Inductive Logic: Proceedings of a Conference at the Queen's College, Oxford, August 1978. (Illus.). 1980. 59.00x (ISBN 0-19-824584-X). Oxford U Pr.

Cohen, L. Jonathan. The Probable & the Provable. (Clarendon Library of Logic & Philosophy). 1977. 39.95x (ISBN 0-19-824412-6). Oxford U Pr.

Cohen, Laura. My Big FunThinker Book of Light. (FunThinkers Ser). (Illus., Basic Set includes: 8" x 10" activity-experiment book, 2 mylar sheets, 4 colored plastic filters, cardboard tube with 2 plastic covers, 3 cardboard printed patterns, magnifying glass, diffracting grading plastic, matte plastic, flexible straw, plastic bag, nail, parent's manual & box. Ensemble includes: Basic Set plus polarizing filter, prism, 1 cardboard piece & carrying case.). (gr. 3-6). 1983. pap. 8.00 Basic Set (ISBN 0-88679-009-3, EI-5626); pap. 12.00 Ensemble (ISBN 0-88679-008-5, EI-5606). Educ Insights.

Cohen, Lawrence. A Synopsis of Medicine in Dentistry. 2nd ed. LC 77-24482. (Illus.). 254p. 1977. text ed. 10.50 (ISBN 0-8121-0608-3). Lea & Febiger.

Cohen, Lawrence & Claiborn, William L., eds. Crisis Intervention. 2nd ed. (Community-Clinical Psychology Ser.: Vol. IV). (Illus.). 208p. 1982. 29.95x (ISBN 0-89885-107-6); pap. 14.95x (ISBN 0-89885-108-4). Human Sci Pr.

Cohen, Lawrence S. & Mock, Michael B. Physical Conditioning & Cardiovascular Rehabilitation. LC 80-23058. 342p. 32.50 (ISBN 0-471-08713-0). Krieger.

Cohen, Leah, jt. auth. see Backhouse, Constance.

Cohen, Leo. The Titanic Revisited. LC 84-60508. (Illus.). 78p. 1984. pap. 4.95 (ISBN 0-9613366-0-9). L Cohen.

Cohen, Leo J. Creating & Planning the Corporate Data Base Project. 2nd ed. (Illus.). 323p. pap. 29.50 (ISBN 0-89435-116-8). QED Info Sci.

--Creating & Planning the Corporate Data Base System Project. LC 80-85044. (Illus.). 400p. 1981. 34.95 (ISBN 0-939274-00-0). Mntn Hse Pub.

--Creating & Planning the Corporate Data Base System Project. (Q.E.D. Information Sciences Inc. Ser.). (Illus.). 336p. 1983. text ed. 37.50 (ISBN 0-13-189093-X). P-H.

--Operating System Analysis & Design. LC 79-118984. 1971. text ed. 13.25 (ISBN 0-8104-5643-5). Hayden.

Cohen, Leon J. Listen & Learn French. 3.50 (ISBN 0-486-20875-3); with records 16.95 (ISBN 0-486-98875-9). Dover.

--Say It in French. (Orig.). pap. 2.50 (ISBN 0-486-20803-6). Dover.

--Say It in French. LC 55-13819. 1962. lib. bdg. 8.50x (ISBN 0-88307-555-5). Gannon.

--Say It in Spanish. LC 56-20451. 1960. lib. bdg. 8.50x (ISBN 0-88307-561-X). Gannon.

Cohen, Leon J. & Rogers, A. C. Digalo En Ingles, (Say It in English for Spanish-Speaking People) (Orig.). pap. 1.50 (ISBN 0-486-20802-8). Dover.

--Say It in Spanish. (Orig.). 1951. pap. 1.95 (ISBN 0-486-20811-7). Dover.

Cohen, Leon W. & Ehrich, Gertrude. The Structure of the Real Number System. rev. ed. LC 76-7512. 122p. 1977. Repr. of 1963 ed. 9.95 (ISBN 0-88275-396-7). Krieger.

Cohen, Leonard. Book of Mercy. LC 84-40174. 88p. 1984. 9.45 (ISBN 0-394-53949-4, Pub. by Villard Bks). Random.

--Death of a Lady's Man. (Penguin Poetry Ser). 1979. pap. 4.95 (ISBN 0-14-042275-7). Penguin.

--Songs of Leonard Cohen. (Illus.). 1969. pap. 3.95 (ISBN 0-02-060290-1, Collier). Macmillan.

Cohen, Leonard & Warwick, Paul V. Political Cohesion in a Fragile Mosaic: The Yugoslav Experience. (Replica Edition Ser.). 175p. 1983. pap. 22.00x (ISBN 0-86531-967-7). Westview.

Cohen, Leslie. Nourishing a Happy Affair: Nutrition Alternatives for Individual & Family Needs. LC 82-16226. (Illus.). 150p. (Orig.). 1983. pap. 6.95 smyth-sewn bdg. (ISBN 0-943914-02-7, Dist by Kampmann & Co.). Larson Pubns Inc.

Cohen, Leslie B. & Salapatek, Philip, eds. Infant Perception: From Sensation to Cognition, 2 vols. Incl. Vol. 1. Basic Visual Processes. 1975. 60.00 (ISBN 0-12-178601-3); Vol. 2. Perception of Space, Speech, & Sound. 1975. 49.50 (ISBN 0-12-178602-1). (Child Psychology Ser.). 1975. Acad Pr.

Cohen, Lester H. The Revolutionary Histories: Contemporary Narratives of the American Revolution. LC 80-11243. 286p. 1980. 24.95x (ISBN 0-8014-1277-3). Cornell U Pr.

Cohen, Lillian. Communication Aids for the Brain Damaged Adult. Rev. ed. 30p. 1977. 5.50 (ISBN 0-88440-024-7). Sis Kenny Inst.

Cohen, Lily & Oppedisano-Reich, Marie. Funding in Aging: Public, Private, & Voluntary. 1979. pap. 18.80 (ISBN 0-88461-006-3). Adelphi Univ.

Cohen, Lily Y. Lost Spirituals. facsimile ed. LC 74-39081. (Black Heritage Library Collection). (Illus.). Repr. of 1928 ed. 17.25 (ISBN 0-8369-9019-6). Ayer Co Pubs.

Cohen, Linda, jt. auth. see Victor, Richard B.

Cohen, Lionel, ed. Biophysical Models in Radiation Oncology. 192p. 1982. 66.00 (ISBN 0-8493-6055-2). CRC Pr.

Cohen, Lois K. & Bryant, Patricia S., eds. Social Sciences & Dentistry, Vol. II. 429p. 1984. pap. text ed. 50.00x (ISBN 0-317-19760-6). Quint Pub Co.

Cohen, Lorraine. Scenes for Young Actors. (gr. 6 up). 1973. pap. 4.95 (ISBN 0-380-00997-8, 69829-3, Bard). Avon.

Cohen, Louis & Holliday, Michael. Statistics for Education. 1979. text ed. 18.95 (ISBN 0-06-318092-8, Pub. by Har-Row Ltd England); pap. text ed. 12.50 (ISBN 0-06-318093-6). Har-Row.

--Statistics for Social Scientists: An Introductory Text with Computer Programmes in Basic. 382p. 1983. pap. text ed. 20.95 (ISBN 0-06-041321-2, HarpC). Har-Row.

Cohen, Louis & Manion, Lawrence. A Guide to Teaching Practice. 2nd ed. LC 83-13190. 300p. 1984. 25.00x (ISBN 0-416-34090-3, NO. 3998); pap. 13.95x (ISBN 0-416-34100-4, NO. 3999). Methuen Inc.

--Multicultural Classrooms: Perspectives for Teachers. 240p. 1982. 27.25 (Pub. by Croom Helm Ltd); pap. 11.50 (ISBN 0-7099-0747-8). Longwood Pub Group.

--Research Methods in Education. (Illus.). 328p. 1980. 25.50 (ISBN 0-85664-917-1, Pub. by Croom Helm Ltd). Longwood Pub Group.

--Research Methods in Education. 2nd ed. LC 85-362. 432p. (Orig.). 1985. pap. 17.00 (ISBN 0-7099-3438-6, Pub. by Croom Helm Ltd). Longwood Pub Group.

Cohen, Louis, et al, eds. Educational Research & Development in Britain 1970-1980. 592p. 1982. 100.00x (ISBN 0-85633-243-7, Pub. by NFER Nelson UK). Taylor & Francis.

Cohen, Louis H. The Cultural-Political Traditions & Development of the Soviet Cinema: 1917-1972. LC 74-2077. (Dissertations on Film Ser.: Vol. 1). 724p. 1974. 46.50x (ISBN 0-405-04876-9). Ayer Co Pubs.

Cohen, Louis S. How to Teach Eureka! A Discovery Approach to the Basics in Math. new ed. 1976. manual & cassettes 179.50 (ISBN 0-917792-00-9). Math Hse.

Cohen, Louise E. Pantheism. LC 79-118531. 1971. Repr. of 1926 ed. 19.50x (ISBN 0-8046-1154-8, Pub. by Kennikat). ASsoc Faculty Pr.

Cohen, Louise G., et al, eds. see Gomez, Antonio E.

Cohen, Lucy K., ed. see Cohen, Felix S.

Cohen, Lucy M. Chinese in the Post-Civil War South: A People Without a History. LC 83-19626. 288p. 1984. text ed. 22.50x (ISBN 0-8071-1122-8). LA State U Pr.

Cohen, Lucy M., jt. auth. see Weber, George H.

Cohen, M. Lost Art of Hand Woodworking. 1986. cancelled (ISBN 0-442-24656-0). Van Nos Reinhold.

Cohen, M. & Mitchell, J. S. Cobalt-60 Teletherapy: A Compendium of International Practice. 695p. 1984. 89.75 (ISBN 92-0-112084-2, ISP413, IAEA). Unipub.

Cohen, M., et al, eds. Central Axis Depth Dose Data for Use in Radiotherapy. 1980. 25.00x (ISBN 0-686-69941-6, Pub. by Brit Inst Radiology England). State Mutual Bk.

--Equality & Preferential Treatment. (Philosophy & Public Affairs Readers). 1976. 22.00 (ISBN 0-691-07213-2); pap. 7.95 (ISBN 0-691-01988-6). Princeton U Pr.

--Rights & Wrongs of Abortion. (Philosophy & Public Affairs Readers). 1974. 17.50x (ISBN 0-691-07197-7); pap. 7.50 (ISBN 0-691-01979-7). Princeton U Pr.

--War & Moral Responsibility. (Philosophy & Public Affairs Readers). 1974. pap. 6.95x (ISBN 0-691-01980-0). Princeton U Pr.

Cohen, M. Bruce, jt. auth. see Jones, Seymour.

Cohen, M. J., jt. auth. see Cohen, J. M.
Cohen, M. J., jt. auth. see Cohen, John M.
Cohen, M. K. Old Houses into New: Successful Real Estate Renovation for Profit. (Illus.). 134p. 1982. 11.95 (ISBN 0-13-633966-2); pap. 5.95 (ISBN 0-13-633958-1). P-H.
Cohen, M. M. A Course in Simple Homotopy Theory. LC 72-93439. (Graduate Texts in Mathematics: Vol. 10). (Illus.). 114p. 1973. text ed. 21.00 (ISBN 0-387-90056-X); pap. text ed. 10.70 (ISBN 0-387-90055-1). Springer-Verlag.
--Notices of Florida & the Campaigns. Tyler, O. Z., Jr., ed. LC 64-19153. (Floridiana Facsimile & Reprint Ser.). 1964. Repr. of 1836 ed. 10.75 (ISBN 0-8130-0048-3). U Presses Fla.
Cohen, M. M., et al, eds. Biochemistry, Ultrastructure & Physiology of Cerebral Anoxia, Hypoxia & Ischaemia. (Monographs in Neural Science: Vol. 1). (Illus.). 1973. 21.00 (ISBN 3-8055-1420-4). S Karger.
Cohen, M. Michael, Jr. The Child with Multiple Birth Defects. 206p. 1982. text ed. 42.00 (ISBN 0-89004-496-1, 453). Raven.
Cohen, M. Michael, Jr., ed. see Jirasek, Jan E.
Cohen, M. R. Preface to Logic. 12.00 (ISBN 0-8446-1878-0). Peter Smith.
Cohen, Malcom S. On the Feasibility of a Labor Market Information System, 3 vols. 1974. pap. 10.95x set (ISBN 0-87736-331-5); pap. 3.95x ea. U of Mich Inst Labor.
Cohen, Marc J., jt. ed. see Biro, Lajos.
Cohen, Marcel. Language: Its Structure & Evolution. Muller, Leonard, tr. from Fr. 157p. 1970. pap. text ed. 5.95 (ISBN 0-8464-1156-3). Beekman Pubs.
--Language: Its Structure & Evolution. Muller, Leonard R., tr. LC 78-102695. (Miami Linguistics Ser: No. 7). 1970. 9.95x (ISBN 0-87024-154-0). U of Miami Pr.
Cohen, Marcelo. El Instrumento Mas Caro de la Tierra. 168p. (Span.). 1981. pap. 7.00 (ISBN 84-85859-24-3, 2003). Ediciones Norte.
Cohen, Marcia, jt. auth. see Simon, Gil.
Cohen, Margo P. & Foa, Piero P. Special Topics in Endocrinology & Metabolism, Vol. 6. 274p. 1984. 58.00 (ISBN 0-8451-0705-4). A R Liss.
Cohen, Margo P. & Foa, Piero P., eds. Special Topics in Endocrinology & Metabolism, Vol. 1. 154p. 1979. 22.00x (ISBN 0-8451-0700-3). A R Liss.
--Special Topics in Endocrinology & Metabolism, Vol. 2. 174p. 1981. 24.00 (ISBN 0-8451-0701-1). A R Liss.
Cohen, Margo P & Foa, Piero P., eds. Special Topics in Endocrinology & Metabolism, Vol. 3. (Special Topics in Endocrinology & Metabolism Ser.). 142p. 1982. 28.00 (ISBN 0-8451-0702-X). A R Liss.
Cohen, Margo P. & Foa, Piero P., eds. Special Topics in Endocrinology & Metabolism, Vol. 4. (Special Topics in Endocrinology & Metabolism). 270p. 1982. 38.00 (ISBN 0-8451-0703-8). A R Liss.
Cohen, Marilyn. Reginald Marsh's New York: Paintings, Drawings, Prints & Photographs. 1984. 18.25 (ISBN 0-317-06297-2). Peter Smith.
Cohen, Marilyn & Gross, Pamela. The Developmental Resource: A Behavioral Resource for Assessment & Programming, 2 vols. 1978. Vol. 1, 224pps. 30.00 (ISBN 0-8089-1122-8, 790877); Vol. 2, 256pps. 31.00 (ISBN 0-8089-1157-0, 790878). Grune.
--The Measurement Manual: How to Measure Child Performance. (Illus.). 304p. (Orig.). 1985. pap. text ed. 32.50 (ISBN 0-87562-077-9). Spec Child.
Cohen, Marion. The Weirdest Is the Sphere. (Poetry Chapbooks: No. 3). 32p. 1979. pap. 2.50 (ISBN 0-913282-15-4). Seven Woods Pr.
Cohen, Marion, compiled by. Limits of Miracles: Poems about the Loss of Babies. 64p. 1984. 14.95 (ISBN 0-89789-066-3); pap. 5.95 (ISBN 0-89789-058-2). Bergin & Garvey.
Cohen, Marion D. An Ambitious Sort of Grief: Woman, Reproduction & Neo-Natal Loss. LC 83-8482. (Woman In History Ser.: Vol. 72). (Illus.). 130p. (Orig.). 1983. lib. bdg. 15.95 (ISBN 0-86663-090-2); pap. text ed. 10.95 (ISBN 0-86663-091-0). Ide Hse.
Cohen, Marjorie A. Shopper's Guide to New York: For International & U. S. Visitors. 288p. 1981. pap. 6.95 (ISBN 0-525-20330-3). Dutton.
Cohen, Marjorie A., jt. auth. see Council on International Educational Exchange.
Cohen, Marjorie A., ed. see Council on International Educational Exchange & Commission on Voluntary Service & Action.
Cohen, Mark E. Sumerian Hymnology: The Ersemma. 1981. 18.75x (ISBN 0-87820-601-9). Ktav.
Cohen, Mark N. The Food Crisis in Prehistory: Over Population & Origins of Agriculture. LC 76-41858. 1979. pap. 10.95x (ISBN 0-300-02351-0). Yale U Pr.
Cohen, Mark N. & Armelagos, George J., eds. Paleopathology at the Origins of Agriculture. LC 83-17235. (MS-Repro Symposium). 1984. 59.00 (ISBN 0-12-179080-0). Acad Pr.
Cohen, Mark N., et al, eds. Biosocial Mechanisms of Population Regulation. LC 79-19023. (Illus.). 1980. 31.00x (ISBN 0-300-02399-5). Yale U Pr.
Cohen, Mark R. Jewish Self-Government in Medieval Egypt: The Origins of the Office of the Head of the Jews, Ca. 1065-1125. LC 80-7514. (Princeton Studies on the Near East). 425p. 1981. 39.00 (ISBN 0-691-05307-3). Princeton U Pr.
Cohen, Marsha. The Pencil Stencil Book: Or Any Other Writing Instrument You Want to Use. (Illus.). 15p. (gr. 2 up). 1981. plastic spiral bdg. 2.95 (ISBN 0-394-84910-8). Random.
Cohen, Marshall. Ronald Dworkin & Contemporary Jurisprudence. 316p. 1984. 29.95 (ISBN 0-8476-7124-0); pap. 11.95 (ISBN 0-8476-7324-3). Biblio Dist.
Cohen, Marshall, jt. auth. see Copeland, Roger.
Cohen, Marshall, ed. Ronald Dworkin & Contemporary Jurisprudence. LC 83-11091. (Philosophy & Society Ser.). 316p. 1984. text ed. 29.95 (ISBN 0-8476-7124-0); pap. text ed. 11.95 (ISBN 0-8476-7324-3). Rowman & Allanheld.
--Ronald Dworkin & Contemporary Jurisprudence. LC 83-11091. (Philosophy & Society Ser.). 316p. 1984. pap. 11.95x (ISBN 0-8476-7324-3). Rowman & Allanheld.
Cohen, Marshall, jt. ed. see Mast, Gerald.
Cohen, Marshall, ed. see Smith, Bruce J.
Cohen, Marshall, ed. see Wolff, Robert P.
Cohen, Marshall, et al, eds. Marx, Justice & History. LC 79-5478. (Philosophy & Public Affairs Reader Ser.). 306p. 1980. 22.50 (ISBN 0-691-07252-3); pap. 9.95 (ISBN 0-691-02009-4). Princeton U Pr.
--Medicine & Moral Philosophy. LC 81-47986. (A Philosophy & Public Affairs Reader). 300p. 1982. 25.00 (ISBN 0-691-07268-X); pap. 8.95x (ISBN 0-691-02020-5). Princeton U Pr.
Cohen, Marshall J. Charles Horton Cooley & the Social Self in American Thought. LC 80-8477. (Modern American History Ser.). 278p. 1982. lib. bdg. 43.00 (ISBN 0-8240-4852-0). Garland Pub.
Cohen, Martin. In Quest of Telescopes. (Illus.). 131p. 1980. 13.95 (ISBN 0-933346-25-5, 6255). Sky Pub.
--In Quest of Telescopes. 131p. 1982. 13.95 (ISBN 0-521-24989-9). Cambridge U Pr.
--Jewish Experience in Latin America, 2 Vols. 1971. Set. 50.00x (ISBN 0-87068-136-2, Pub by Am Jewish Hist Soc). Ktav.
--The Marine Corps 3X Fitness Program. (Illus.). 1986. pap. 5.95 (ISBN 0-316-15017-7). Little.
Cohen, Martin, jt. auth. see Anderson, James L.
Cohen, Martin, ed. The Poems & Letters of Digby Mackworth Dolben: 1848-1867. 174p. 1982. text ed. 38.50x (ISBN 0-86127-219-6, Pub. by Avebury England). Humanities.
Cohen, Martin & O'Reilly, Timothy, eds. Fragments of an Evolving Language. 200p. (Orig.). 1984. pap. 8.95x (ISBN 0-9607066-1-5). Comm Con Ev.
Cohen, Martin, et al. The Executive Woman's Coloring Book: Or You've Come a Long Way, Person. 24p. 1984. pap. 3.95 (ISBN 0-8431-0774-X). Price Stern.
Cohen, Martin A. see Klenicki, Leon.
Cohen, Martin A. & Croner, Helga, eds. Christian Mission-Jewish Mission. LC 82-60856. 1982. pap. 7.95 (ISBN 0-8091-2475-0). Paulist Pr.
Cohen, Martin A., tr. see Usque, Samuel.
Cohen, Martin S. The Shiur Qomah: Liturgy & Theurgy in Pre-Kabbalistic Jewish Mysticism. 300p. (Orig.). 1983. lib. bdg. 24.75 (ISBN 0-8191-3272-1); pap. text ed. 13.25 (ISBN 0-8191-3273-X). U Pr of Amer.
Cohen, Marty. A Traveller's Alphabet. Gale, Vi, ed. LC 79-84509. (Prescott First Bk). (Illus.). 1979. ltd. ed. 20.00 (ISBN 0-915986-15-9); pap. 5.00 (ISBN 0-915986-16-7). Prescott St Pr.
Cohen, Marty, jt. auth. see Aloff, Mindy.
Cohen, Marvin. Baseball the Beautiful. 1974. 12.50 (ISBN 0-8256-3030-4); pap. 5.00 (ISBN 0-8256-3034-7). Ultramarine Pub.
--Fables at Life's Expense. 1975. 5.00 (ISBN 0-685-78967-5). Latitudes Pr.
--The Monday Rhetoric of the Love Club & Other Parables. LC 72-93979. 128p. 1973. pap. 3.75 (ISBN 0-8112-0475-8, NDP352). New Directions.
--The Monday Rhetoric of the Love Club & other Parables. LC 72-93979. 128p. 1973. 10.00 (ISBN 0-8112-0474-X). Ultramarine Pub.
--Others, Including Morstive Sternbump: A Novel. LC 76-11615. 247p. 1976. 15.00 (ISBN 0-672-52145-8). Ultramarine Pub.
Cohen, Marvin M. Introduction to the Quantum Theory of Semiconductors. LC 79-123485. (Illus.). 310p. 1972. 57.75 (ISBN 0-677-02980-2). Gordon.
Cohen, Marylin. Reginald Marsh's New York Paintings, Drawings, Prints & Photographs. LC 83-6465. (Fine Art Ser.). (Illus.). 115p. (Orig.). 1983. pap. 8.95 (ISBN 0-486-24594-2). Dover.
Cohen, Matt. The Expatriate: Collected Short Stories. 304p. 1983. pap. 3.95 (ISBN 0-7736-7018-1). Beaufort Bks NY.
--Life on This Planet & Other Stories. 192p. 1985. 14.95 (ISBN 0-8253-0313-3). Beaufort Bks NY.
--The Spanish Doctor. LC 84-6426. 352p. 1985. 16.95 (ISBN 0-8253-0227-7). Beaufort Bks NY.
Cohen, Max, ed. Biological Protection with Prostaglandins, Vol. I. 320p. 1985. price not set (ISBN 0-8493-5962-7). CRC Pr.
Cohen, Melvin, jt. auth. see Strumwasser, Felix.
Cohen, Melvin J., jt. ed. see Gordon, Solon A.
Cohen, Melvin R. Laparoscopy, Culdoscopy & Gynecography: Technique & Atlas. LC 79-126452. (Major Problems in Obstetrics & Gynecology Ser.: Vol. 1). pap. 44.30 (ISBN 0-317-08678-2, 2016657). Bks Demand UMI.
Cohen, Mervyn D. Soccer for Children & Their Parents. (Illus.). 47p. (Orig.). 1983. pap. 3.50 (ISBN 0-931494-42-7). Brunswick Pub.
Cohen, Michael. Urban Growth & Economic Development in the Sahel. (Working Paper: No. 315). 120p. 1979. 5.00 (ISBN 0-686-36230-6, WP-0315). World Bank.
Cohen, Michael, jt. auth. see Bourdette, Robert E., Jr.
Cohen, Michael, jt. auth. see Cohen, Judith.
Cohen, Michael A. Urban Policy & Political Conflict in Africa: A Study of the Ivory Coast. LC 73-90942. 262p. 1974. 18.00x (ISBN 0-226-11223-3). U of Chicago Pr.
Cohen, Michael E. & Duffner, Patricia K. Brain Tumors in Children: Principles of Diagnosis & Treatment. (International Review of Child Neurology Ser.). (Illus.). 390p. 1984. text ed. 54.50 (ISBN 0-89004-935-1). Raven.
Cohen, Michael H. On the Job Survival. 94p. (Orig.). 1984. pap. 5.95 (ISBN 0-9613768-0-5). Canoe Press.
Cohen, Michael J. Across the Running Tide. (Illus.). 1979. pap. 6.00 (ISBN 0-89166-010-0). Cobblesmith.
--Churchill & the Jews. 408p. 1985. 25.00x (ISBN 0-7146-3254-6, F Cass Co). Biblio Dist.
--Drugs & the Special Child. 1979. 25.00 (ISBN 0-89876-070-4). Gardner Pr.
--Our Classroom Is Wild America. LC 74-76019. (Illus.). 1978. pap. 6.00 (ISBN 0-89166-011-9). Cobblesmith.
--Palestine & the Great Powers, Nineteen Forty-Five to Nineteen Forty-Eight. (Illus.). 411p. 1982. 40.00 (ISBN 0-691-05371-5). Princeton U Pr.
--Palestine, Retreat from the Mandate: The Making of British Policy, 1936-45. LC 78-933. 239p. 1978. text ed. 35.00x (ISBN 0-8419-0373-5). Holmes & Meier.
--Prejudice Against Nature. (Illus.). 1983. pap. 7.50 (ISBN 0-89166-016-X). Cobblesmith.
Cohen, Michael J., ed. Drugs & the Special Child. LC 77-10151. 258p. 1979. 18.95 (ISBN 0-470-99278-6). Halsted Pr.
Cohen, Michael, Jr., ed. Craniosynostosis. 290p. 1985. 70.00 (ISBN 0-89004-469-4, 524). Raven.
Cohen, Michael M. Dr. Cohen's Healthy Sailor Book. LC 83-47889. 272p. 1983. 17.95 (ISBN 0-87742-166-8, D345). Intl Marine.
Cohen, Michael M., Jr. & Rollnick, Beverly R. Craniofacial Dysmorphology: Studies in Honor of Samuel Pruzansky. 325p. 1985. write for info. A R Liss.
Cohen, Michael P. The Pathless Way: John Muir & American Wilderness. LC 83-40260. 500p. 1984. 25.00 (ISBN 0-299-09720-X). U of Wis Pr.
Cohen, Michael R., jt. auth. see Davis, Neil M.
Cohen, Michael V. Coronary Collaterals: Clinical & Experimental Observations. (Illus.). 468p. 1985. 69.50 (ISBN 0-87993-168-X). Futura Pub.
--Correlative Atlas of Adult Cardiac Disorders: Noninvasive Diagnostic Techniques. LC 80-66333. (Illus.). 432p. 1980. 48.50 (ISBN 0-87993-149-3). Futura Pub.
Cohen, Michele, tr. see Broyelle, Claudie.
Cohen, Mindy, et al. Thin Kids: The Proven, Healthy, Sensible Program for Children. (Illus.). 256p. 1985. 17.95 (ISBN 0-8253-0276-5); pap. 9.95 (ISBN 0-8253-0277-3). Beaufort Bks NY.
Cohen, Miriam. Bee My Valentine. LC 77-21950. (Illus.). 32p. (gr. k-3). 1978. PLB 11.88 (ISBN 0-688-84129-5). Greenwillow.
--Bee My Valentine! (Welcome to First Grade Ser.). (Illus.). (gr. k-3). 1983. pap. 1.95 (ISBN 0-440-40507-6, YB). Dell.
--Best Friends. LC 70-146620. (Illus.). 32p. (ps-1). 1971. 9.95 (ISBN 0-02-722800-2); pap. 2.50x (ISBN 0-02-042610-0). Macmillan.
--Best Friends. LC 70-146620. (Illus.). 32p. (gr. k-3). 1973. pap. 2.50 (ISBN 0-02-042610-0, Collier). Macmillan.
--Born to Dance Samba. LC 83-47690. (Illus.). 160p. (gr. 4-7). 1984. 10.53i (ISBN 0-06-021358-2); PLB 10.89g (ISBN 0-06-021359-0). HarpJ.
--First Grade Takes a Test. LC 80-10316. (Illus.). 32p. (ps-3). 1980. 11.75 (ISBN 0-688-80265-6); PLB 11.88 (ISBN 0-688-84265-8). Greenwillow.
--First Grade Takes a Test. (Welcome to First Grade Ser.). (Illus.). (gr. k-3). 1983. pap. 1.95 (ISBN 0-440-42500-X, YB). Dell.
--Jim Meets the Thing. LC 81-1026. (Illus.). 32p. (gr. k-3). 1981. 11.75 (ISBN 0-688-00616-7); PLB 11.88 (ISBN 0-688-00617-5). Greenwillow.
--Jim's Dog Muffins. LC 83-14090. (Illus.). 32p. (gr. k-3). 1984. 11.75 (ISBN 0-688-02564-1); PLB 11.88 (ISBN 0-688-02565-X). Greenwillow.
--Liar, Liar, Pants on Fire! LC 84-25869. (Illus.). 32p. (gr. k-3). 1985. 11.75 (ISBN 0-688-04244-9); lib. bdg. 11.88 (ISBN 0-688-04245-7). Greenwillow.
--Lost in the Museum. LC 78-16765. (Illus.). (gr. k-3). 1979. 11.75 (ISBN 0-688-80187-0); PLB 11.88 (ISBN 0-688-84187-2). Greenwillow.
--Lost in the Museum. (Welcome to First Grade Ser.). (Illus.). (gr. k-3). pap. 1.95 (ISBN 0-440-44780-1, YB). Dell.
--The New Teacher. LC 78-165239. (Illus.). 32p. (ps-1). 1974. pap. 3.95 (ISBN 0-02-042390-X, 04239, Collier). Macmillan.
--No Good in Art. LC 79-16566. (Illus.). 32p. (gr. k-3). 1980. 11.75 (ISBN 0-688-80234-6); PLB 11.88 (ISBN 0-688-84234-8). Greenwillow.
--See You Tomorrow, Charles. LC 82-11834. (Illus.). 32p. (gr. k-3). 1983. 11.75 (ISBN 0-688-01804-1); PLB 11.88 (ISBN 0-688-01805-X). Greenwillow.
--So What? LC 81-20101. (Illus.). 32p. (gr. k-3). 1982. 11.75 (ISBN 0-688-01202-7); PLB 11.88 (ISBN 0-688-01203-5). Greenwillow.
--Starring First Grade. LC 84-5929. (Illus.). 32p. (gr. k-3). 1985. 11.75 (ISBN 0-688-04029-2); PLB 11.88 (ISBN 0-688-04030-6). Greenwillow.
--When Will I Read? LC 76-28320. 32p. (ps-3). 1977. 11.75 (ISBN 0-688-80073-4); PLB 11.88 (ISBN 0-688-84073-6). Greenwillow.
--When Will I Read? (Welcome to First Grade Ser.). (Illus.). (gr. k-3). 1983. pap. 1.95 (ISBN 0-440-49333-1, YB). Dell.
--Will I Have a Friend? LC 67-10127. (Illus.). 32p. (gr. k-1). 1967. 10.95 (ISBN 0-02-722790-1); pap. 3.95x (ISBN 0-02-042620-8). Macmillan.
--Will I Have a Friend? LC 67-5219. (Illus.). (gr. k-1). 1971. pap. 3.95 (ISBN 0-02-042620-8, Collier). Macmillan.
Cohen, Mirian. Marijuana: Its Effects on Mind & Body. (Encyclopedia of Psychoactive Drugs Ser.). (Illus.). 1985. PLB 15.95x (ISBN 0-87754-754-8). Chelsea Hse.
Cohen, Mitch, ed. Berlin: Contemporary Writing from Berlin. LC 77-642342. (Rockbottom Specials Ser.). (Illus., Eng. & Ger.). 1983. 20.00x (ISBN 0-930012-23-2); pap. 8.50x o.s.i (ISBN 0-930012-22-4). Bandanna Bks.
Cohen, Mitchell, ed. see Borochov, Ber.
Cohen, Monroe D. Excellent Paperbacks for Children. 56p. 1979. 4.20 (ISBN 0-87173-001-4). ACEI.
Cohen, Monroe D., ed. Testing & Evaluation: New Views. 2nd, 1980 ed. LC 74-34211. 64p. 1980. Repr. of 1975 ed. 4.20x (ISBN 0-87173-000-6). ACEI.
Cohen, Monroe D. & Rice, Susan, eds. Children Are Centers for Understanding Media. LC 72-92022. (Illus., Orig.). 1978. Repr. of 1973 ed. 4.75x (ISBN 0-87173-017-0). ACEI.
Cohen, Monroe D., ed. see Ballenger, Marcus, et al.
Cohen, Monroe D., ed. see Gillies, Emily.
Cohen, Monroe D., ed. see Langstaff, Nancy & Sproul, Adelaide.
Cohen, Monroe D., ed. see McCune, Shirley D., et al.
Cohen, Morrel H., ed. Superconductivity in Science & Technology. LC 67-25534. pap. 42.80 (ISBN 0-317-08095-4, 2020047). Bks Demand UMI.
Cohen, Morris, jt. auth. see Hynd, George.
Cohen, Morris L. Legal Research in a Nutshell. 4th ed. LC 84-21929. (Nutshell Ser.). 425p. 1985. pap. 10.95 (ISBN 0-314-83243-2). West Pub.
Cohen, Morris L. & Berring, Robert C. Finding the Law: An Abridged Edition of How to Find the Law. 8th ed. LC 83-23463. (American Casebook Ser.). 556p. 1983. pap. text ed. 12.95 (ISBN 0-314-80504-4). West Pub.
Cohen, Morris L., ed. Bibliography of Early American Law. 1986. lib. bdg. price not set (ISBN 0-527-18676-7). Kraus Intl.
Cohen, Morris L. & Ronen, Naomi, eds. Law & Science: A Selected Bibliography. rev. ed. 155p. 1980. 25.00x (ISBN 0-262-03073-X). MIT Pr.
Cohen, Morris L., et al. Law & Science: A Selected Bibliography. Shelanski, Vivien B. & La Follette, Marcel C., eds. (Orig.). 1978. pap. text ed. 7.50 (ISBN 0-932564-00-3). STHV.
Cohen, Morris M. An Introduction to the Study of Constitution: A Study Showing the Play of Physical & Social Factors in the Creation of Institutional Law. LC 78-64255. (Johns Hopkins University. Studies in the Social Sciences. Extra Volumes: 11). Repr. of 1892 ed. 22.00 (ISBN 0-404-61359-4). AMS Pr.
Cohen, Morris R. A Dreamer's Journey: The Autobiography of Morris Raphael Cohen. facsimile ed. LC 74-27972. (Modern Jewish Experience Ser.). (Illus.). 1975. Repr. of 1949 ed. 30.00x (ISBN 0-405-06702-X). Ayer Co Pubs.
--Faith of a Liberal. facsimile ed. LC 76-111820. (Essay Index Reprint Ser). 1946. 26.00 (ISBN 0-8369-1598-4). Ayer Co Pubs.
--Law & the Social Order: Essays in Legal Philosophy. xii, 403p. 1967. Repr. of 1933 ed. 27.50 (ISBN 0-208-00484-X, Archon). Shoe String.
--Law & the Social Order: Essays in Legal Philosophy. Supplemented by Cohen's "Moral Aspects of Criminal Law". LC 81-4394. (Social & Moral Thought Ser.). 520p. (Orig.). 1982. pap. 19.95 (ISBN 0-87855-876-4). Transaction Bks.
--The Meaning of Human History. 2nd ed. LC 61-10174. (The Paul Carus Lectures Ser.). (Illus.). ix, 320p. 1961. 24.95 (ISBN 0-87548-100-0); pap. 7.95 (ISBN 0-87548-101-9). Open Court.
--A Preface to Logic. LC 77-75235. 1977. pap. 5.95 (ISBN 0-486-23517-3). Dover.
--Reason & Nature. 1978. pap. 7.50 (ISBN 0-486-23633-1). Dover.
--Reason & Nature: An Essay on the Meaning of Scientific Method. 469p. 1985. Repr. of 1931 ed. lib. bdg. 65.00 (ISBN 0-8414-1996-5). Folcroft.
Cohen, Morris R. & Drabkin, Israel E. Source Book in Greek Science. LC 58-12979. (Source Books in the History of the Sciences Ser). (Illus.). 1948. text ed. 35.00x (ISBN 0-674-82320-7). Harvard U Pr.
Cohen, Morris R. & Nagel, Ernest. An Introduction to Logic. LC 62-21468. 1962. pap. 3.95 (ISBN 0-15-645125-5, Harv). HarBraceJ.

--An Introduction to Logic & Scientific Method. 467p. 1982. Repr. of 1934 ed. lib. bdg. 50.00 (ISBN 0-89987-130-5). Darby Bks.

Cohen, Morris R., ed. see De Tourtoulon, Pierre.

Cohen, Mortimer J. Pathways Through the Bible. rev. ed. (Illus.). 574p. 1946. 9.95 (ISBN 0-8276-0155-7, 167). Jewish Pubns.

Cohen, Mortimer T. From Prologue to Epilogue in Vietnam. LC 79-54798. 612p. 22.50 (ISBN 0-686-28498-4). Retriever.

--Poems of Morris Rosenfield Transliterated. LC 79-54799. 140p. pap. 12.50 (ISBN 0-686-28499-2). Retriever.

Cohen, Morton. Rudyard Kipling to Rider Haggard. LC 68-22229. 196p. 1968. 18.00 (ISBN 0-8386-6881-X). Fairleigh Dickinson.

Cohen, Morton, jt. auth. see Carroll, Lewis.

Cohen, Morton H., ed. see Carroll, Lewis.

Cohen, Morton N., ed. see Liddon, Henry P.

Cohen, Morton N., tr. see Carroll, Lewis.

Cohen, Murray. Sensible Words: Linguistic Practice in England, 1640-1785. LC 77-1856. (Illus.). 1977. text ed. 20.00x (ISBN 0-8018-1924-5). Johns Hopkins.

Cohen, Myles J., jt. auth. see Johnson, Moulton K.

Cohen, Myron. Myron Cohen's Big Joke Book. 410p. 1983. pap. 5.95 (ISBN 0-8065-0853-1). Citadel Pr.

Cohen, Myron L. House United, House Divided: A Chinese Family in Taiwan. LC 75-28473. (Studies of the East Asian Institute). (Illus.). 272p. 1975. 25.00x (ISBN 0-231-03849-6). Columbia U Pr.

Cohen, Myron S., jt. auth. see Henderson, Gail E.

Cohen, Nancy W. & Estner, Lois J. Silent Knife: Vaginal Birth After Cesarean (VBAC) & Cesarean Prevention. 464p. 1983. 11.95 (ISBN 0-318-17499-5). Cesareans Ed.

Cohen, Nancy Wainer & Estner, Lois J. Silent Knife: Cesarean Prevention & Vaginal Birth after Cesarean (VBAC) (Illus.). 464p. 1983. 29.95 (ISBN 0-89789-026-4); pap. 14.95 (ISBN 0-89789-027-2). Bergin & Garvey.

Cohen, Naomi. American Jews & the Zionist Idea. pap. 9.95x (ISBN 0-87068-272-5). Ktav.

--Encounter with Emancipation: The German Jews in the United States, 1830 to 1914. (Illus.). 407p. 1984. 25.95 (ISBN 0-8276-0236-7). Jewish Pubns.

Cohen, Nathan M. Library Science Dissertations, Nineteen Twenty-Five to Nineteen Sixty: An Annotated Bibliography of Doctoral Studies. (Library Science Ser.). 1980. lib. bdg. 55.00 (ISBN 0-8490-3167-2). Gordon Pr.

Cohen, Neal P., jt. auth. see Kugel, Yerachmiel.

Cohen, Neil & Graff, Lois. Financial Analysis with Lotus 1-2-3. (Illus.). 336p. 1984. pap. 19.95 (ISBN 0-89303-451-7); bk. diskette 44.95 (ISBN 0-89303-452-5); diskette 25.00 (ISBN 0-89303-453-3); kit 44.95 (ISBN 0-89303-452-5). Brady Comm.

Cohen, Neil, jt. auth. see Graff, Lois.

Cohen, Neil P. & Gobert, James J. Problems in Criminal Law. LC 75-46199. (American Casebook Ser.). 1976. pap. 6.95 (ISBN 0-685-71457-8). West Pub.

Cohen, Neil P., jt. auth. see Gobert, James J.

Cohen, Nicholas, jt. auth. see Dumont, Rene.

Cohen, Nicholas & Sigel, Michael, eds. The Reticuloendothelial System - A Comprehensive Treatise: Phylogeny & Ontogeny of the RES, Vol. 3. 789p. 1982. 89.50x (ISBN 0-306-40928-3, Plenum Pr). Plenum Pub.

Cohen, Nicholas, jt. ed. see Marchalonis, John J.

Cohen, Norm. Long Steel Rail: The Railroad in American Folksong. LC 80-14874. (Music in American Life Ser.). (Illus.). 738p. 1984. 49.95x (ISBN 0-252-00343-8); pap. 17.50 (ISBN 0-252-01145-7). U of Ill Pr.

Cohen, Norm, ed. see Randolph, Vance.

Cohen, Norman. Ada as a Second Language. 1984. pap. 26.95 (ISBN 0-07-011589-3). McGraw.

Cohen, Nurit, jt. auth. see Cohen, William A.

Cohen, Octavus R. Bigger & Blacker. facsimile ed. LC 78-106268. (Short Story Index Reprint Ser.). 1925. 19.00 (ISBN 0-8369-3305-2). Ayer Co Pubs.

--Black & Blue. facsimile ed. LC 71-106269. (Short Story Index Reprint Ser.). 1926. 18.00 (ISBN 0-8369-3306-0). Ayer Co Pubs.

--Florian Slappey Goes Abroad. LC 70-130054. (Short Story Index Reprint Ser). 1928. 17.00 (ISBN 0-8369-3570-5). Ayer Co Pubs.

--Polished Ebony. LC 74-128725. (Short Story Index Reprint Ser). (Illus.). 1919. 19.00 (ISBN 0-8369-3616-7). Ayer Co Pubs.

Cohen, Oscar, jt. auth. see Lukoff, Irving F.

Cohen, P. Enzyme Regulation by Reversible Phosphorylation. (Molecular Aspects of Cell Regulation Ser.: Vol. 3). 1984. 75.00 (ISBN 0-444-80525-7, I-173-84). Elsevier.

Cohen, P., ed. Recently Discovered Systems of Enzyme Regulation by Reversible Posphorylation. (Molecular Aspects of Cell Regulation Ser.: Vol. 1). 274p. 1980. 69.00 (ISBN 0-444-80226-6, Biomedical Pr). Elsevier.

Cohen, P. & Van Heyningen, S., eds. Molecular Actions of Toxins & Viruses. (Molecular Aspects of Cellular Regulation Ser.: Vol. 2). 370p. 1982. 79.25 (ISBN 0-444-80400-5, I-143-82, Biomedical Pr). Elsevier.

Cohen, P., jt. ed. see Perry, S. V.

Cohen, P. S., ed. Jewish Radicals & Radical Jews. LC 80-41227. 1981. 38.00 (ISBN 0-12-178780-X). Acad Pr.

Cohen, Patricia. A Calculating People: The Spread of Numeracy in Early America. LC 82-7089. (Illus.). 272p. 1985. lib. bdg. 22.50x (ISBN 0-226-11283-7); pap. 9.95 (ISBN 0-226-11284-5). U of Chicago Pr.

Cohen, Patricia, jt. auth. see Cohen, Jacob.

Cohen, Patricia F., jt. auth. see Neal, Margo C.

Cohen, Paul. Discovering History in China: American Historical Writing on the Recent Chinese Past. 264p. 1984. 26.50 (ISBN 0-231-05810-1). Columbia U Pr.

--Water Coolant Technology of Power Reactors. Wallin, Diane, ed. LC 79-57306. (Monograph Ser.). 250p. 1980. Repr. of 1969 ed. write for info. (ISBN 0-89448-020-0, 300016). Am Nuclear Soc.

Cohen, Paul, jt. auth. see Bernstein, Joanne.

Cohen, Paul, jt. auth. see Bernstein, Joanne E.

Cohen, Paul, jt. auth. see Wind Power Publishing.

Cohen, Paul A. Between Tradition & Modernity: Wang T'ao & Reform in Late Ch'ing China. LC 74-75109. (East Asian Ser.: No. 77). 336p. 1974. text ed. 20.00x (ISBN 0-674-06875-0). Harvard U Pr.

--China & Christianity: The Missionary Movement & the Growth of Chinese Antiforeignism, 1860-1870. LC 63-19135. (East Asian Ser: No. 11). (Illus.). 1963. 27.50x (ISBN 0-674-11701-8). Harvard U Pr.

--Discovering History in China: American Historical Writing on the Recent Chinese Past. 243p. 1985. pap. 14.00 (ISBN 0-231-05811-X). Columbia U Pr.

Cohen, Paul A. & Schrecker, John E., eds. Reform in Nineteenth-Century China. (East Asian Monographs: No. 72). 1976. pap. 11.00x (ISBN 0-674-75281-3). Harvard U Pr.

Cohen, Paul J. Set Theory & the Continuum Hypothesis. (Math Lecture Notes Ser.: No. 3). (Orig.). 1966. pap. 28.95 (ISBN 0-8053-2327-9, Adv Bk Prog). Benjamin-Cummings.

Cohen, Paul R. Heuristic Reasoning about Uncertainty: An Artificial Intelligence Approach. (Research Notes in Artificial Intelligence Ser.). 1985. pap. text ed. 19.50 (ISBN 0-273-08667-7). Pitman Pub MA.

Cohen, Pauline c. & Krause, Merto S. Casework with Wives of Alcoholics. 164p. 1971. pap. 5.95 (ISBN 0-318-15301-7). Natl Coun Alcoholism.

Cohen, Percy S., jt. ed. see Shack, William A.

Cohen, Peter. The Gospel According to the Harvard Business School. 336p. 1974. pap. 5.95 (ISBN 0-14-003912-0). Penguin.

Cohen, Peter Z. Calm Horse, Wild Night. LC 82-1746. 168p. (gr. 4-8). 1982. 10.95 (ISBN 0-689-30918-X). Atheneum.

--The Great Red River Raft. Fay, Ann, ed. (Illus.). 40p. (gr. 3 up). 1984. PLB 9.25 (ISBN 0-8075-3039-5). A Whitman.

--Morena. LC 71-115081. (Illus.). 144p. (gr. 3-7). 1970. PLB 5.95 (ISBN 0-689-20595-3); pap. 0.95 (ISBN 0-689-70353-8). Atheneum.

--Muskie Hook. LC 69-13525. (Illus.). 160p. (gr. 3-7). 1969. pap. 0.95 (ISBN 0-689-70314-7, A-17, Aladdin). Atheneum.

Cohen, Phil. The Three-D Animated Apple. 1984. 21.50 (ISBN 0-13-920224-2). P-H.

Cohen, Phil, ed. It Ain't Half Racist, Mum: Fighting Racism in the Media. 1982. 36.00x (ISBN 0-906890-31-4); pap. 25.00x (ISBN 0-906890-30-6). State Mutual Bk.

Cohen, Philip. Control of Enzyme Activity. 2nd ed. (Outlines Studies in Biology). 1983. pap. 7.50 (ISBN 0-412-25560-X, 6870, Pub. by Chapman & Hall). Methuen Inc.

Cohen, Philip, ed. see American Water Resources Association.

Cohen, Philip K. The Moral Vision of Oscar Wilde. LC 76-50283. (Illus.). 287p. 1978. 25.00 (ISBN 0-8386-2052-3). Fairleigh Dickinson.

Cohen, Phillip M. Bathymetric Navigation & Charting. LC 79-6107. (Navies & Men Ser.). (Illus.). 1980. Repr. of 1970 ed. lib. bdg. 14.00x (ISBN 0-405-13036-8). Ayer Co Pubs.

Cohen, R. Dominance & Defiance: A Study of Martial Instability in an Islamic African Society. 1971. pap. 4.00 (ISBN 0-686-36563-1). Am Anthro Assn.

--The Jewish Nation in Surinam: Historical Essays. (Illus.). 120p. 1982. pap. 35.00 (ISBN 0-8390-0296-3). Abner Schram Ltd.

Cohen, R., jt. ed. see Pilkey, W. D.

Cohen, R. Carl. Beating the Blackjack Slot Machines. 32p. (Orig.). 1985. pap. text ed. 4.95 (ISBN 0-9614943-2-8). Cohen Pub.

Cohen, R. S. Physical Sciences. LC 75-24791. 1976. text ed. 33.95 (ISBN 0-03-012686-X, HoltC). HR&W.

Cohen, R. S. & Seeger, R. J., eds. Boston Studies in the Philosophy of Science: Ernst Mach, Physicist & Philosopher, Vol. 6. (Synthese Library: No. 27). 295p. 1970. 29.00 (ISBN 90-277-0016-8, Pub. by Reidel Holland). Kluwer Academic.

Cohen, R. S. & Stachel, J., eds. Leon Rosenfeld: Selected Papers. (Synthese Library Ser.: No. 100). 1976. lib. bdg. 97.50 (ISBN 90-277-0651-4, Pub. by Reidel Holland); pap. 37.00 (ISBN 90-277-0652-2). Kluwer Academic.

Cohen, R. S., ed. see American Association for the Advancement of Science, Section, L, 1949.

Cohen, R. S., ed. see Colloquium for Philosophy of Science, Boston, 1966-1969.

Cohen, R. S., ed. see Colloquium for the Philosophy of Science, Boston, 1964-1966.

Cohen, R. S., ed. see Colloquium for the Philosophy of Science, Boston, 1966-68.

Cohen, R. S., ed. see Colloquium for the Philosophy of Science, Boston, 1969-1972.

Cohen, R. S., ed. see Colloquium for the Philosophy of Sciences, Boston, 1969-72.

Cohen, R. S., ed. see Helmholtz, H. von.

Cohen, R. S., ed. see Mittelstaedt, Peter.

Cohen, R. S., jt. ed. see Neurath, M.

Cohen, R. S., ed. see Philosophy of Science Association, Biennial Meeting, 1970.

Cohen, R. S., ed. see Philosophy of Science Association, 1972.

Cohen, R. S., ed. see Philosophy of Science Association 1974 Biennial Meeting.

Cohen, R. S., tr. see Helmholtz, H. von.

Cohen, R. S., et al, eds. Essays in Memory of Imre Lakatos. new ed. LC 76-16770. (Synthese Library Ser.: No. 99). 1976. lib. bdg. 87.00 (ISBN 90-277-0654-9, Pub. by Reidel Holland); pap. 47.50 (ISBN 90-277-0655-7, Pub. by Reidel Holland). Kluwer Academic.

--Boston Studies in the Philosophy of Science, Vol. 15: Scientific, Historical & Political Essays in Honor of Dirk J. Struik. LC 73-83556. (Synthese Library: No. 61). 652p. 1974. 76.00 (ISBN 90-277-0393-0, Pub. by Reidel Holland); pap. 47.50- (ISBN 90-277-0379-5). Kluwer Academic.

Cohen, Ralph. The Unfolding of the Seasons. LC 70-82867. pap. 87.50 (ISBN 0-317-19884-X, 2023088). Bks Demand UMI.

Cohen, Ralph, ed. New Directions in Literary History. LC 73-8115. 272p. 1974. 25.00x (ISBN 0-8018-1549-5). Johns Hopkins.

--Studies in Eighteenth Century British Art & Aesthetics. LC 84-2693. 1985. 24.95x (ISBN 0-520-05258-7). U of Cal Pr.

Cohen, Ralph L. Odd Primary Infinite Families in Stable Homotopy Theory. LC 80-28537. (MEMO Ser.: No. 242). 92p. 9.00 (ISBN 0-8218-2242-X, MEMO-242). Am Math.

Cohen, Randy. Easy Answers to Hard Questions. 1979. pap. 4.95 (ISBN 0-449-90011-8, Columbine). Fawcett.

--Modest Proposals: The Official Correspondence of Randy Cohen. 128p. 1981. pap. 3.95 (ISBN 0-312-54365-4); Prepack of 10 39.50 (ISBN 0-312-54366-2). St Martin.

Cohen, Randy & Anderson, Alexandra. Why Didn't I Think of That. (Illus.). 1980. pap. 5.95 (ISBN 0-449-90037-1, Columbine). Fawcett.

Cohen, Raquel & Ahearn, Frederick. Handbook for Mental Health Care of Disaster Victims. 144p. 1980. text ed. 16.50x (ISBN 0-8018-2427-3). Johns Hopkins.

Cohen, Raymond. International Politics: The Rules of the Game. LC 80-41594. 186p. (Orig.). 1981. pap. text ed. 8.50x (ISBN 0-582-29558-0). Longman.

--Threat Perception in International Crisis. LC 79-3964. 214p. 1979. 25.00x (ISBN 0-299-08000-5). U of Wis Pr.

Cohen, Rebecca, et al, eds. Parenthood: A Psychodynamic Perspective. LC 82-18370. (Psychiatry Ser.). 426p. 1984. text ed. 30.00 (ISBN 0-89862-225-5, 2225). Guilford Pr.

Cohen, Richard, tr. see Levinas, Emmanuel.

Cohen, Richard, et al. Nontariff Barrier to High Technology Trade. (International Economics & Business Ser.). 142p. 1985. pap. text ed. 16.50x (ISBN 0-8133-7075-2). Westview.

Cohen, Richard I., ed. Vision & Conflict in the Holy Land. LC 85-1972. 350p. 1985. 29.95 (ISBN 0-312-84967-2). St Martin.

Cohen, Richard L. Applications of Mossbauer Spectroscopy, Vol. 2. 1980. 60.00 (ISBN 0-12-178402-9). Acad Pr.

Cohen, Richard L. see Nospnitz, Joseph D.

Cohen, Richard M., jt. auth. see Neft, David S.

Cohen, Rip. Thirty-Two Cantigas d'Amigo of Dom Diniz: Typology of a Portuguese Renunciation. (Portuguese Ser.: No. 1). 1985. write for info. (ISBN 0-942260-55-4). Hispanic Seminary.

Cohen, Robert. Acting One. 1983. pap. 16.95 (ISBN 0-87484-669-2). Mayfield Pub.

--Acting Power. LC 77-89918. 266p. 1978. text ed. 18.95 (ISBN 0-87484-408-8). Mayfield Pub.

--Acting Professionally: Raw Facts About Careers in Acting. 3rd ed. 1982. pap. 4.76i (ISBN 0-06-463453-1, EH 570, EH). B&N NY.

--Acting Professionally: Raw Facts About Careers in Acting. 3rd ed. LC 81-81275. 122p. 1981. pap. 6.95 (ISBN 0-87484-539-4). Mayfield Pub.

--Color of Man. (Illus.). (gr. 5-9). 1968. (BYR). Random.

--The Development of Spatial Cognition. 416p. 1985. 39.95 (ISBN 0-89859-543-6). L Erlbaum Assocs.

--Giraudoux: Three Faces of Destiny. LC 68-29058. 1970. pap. 2.45 (ISBN 0-226-11248-9, P371, Phoen). U of Chicago Pr.

--New Careers Grows Older: A Perspective on the Paraprofessional Experience, 1965-1975. LC 76-26036. (Policy Studies in Employment & Welfare: No. 26). pap. 36.00 (ISBN 0-317-19881-5, 2023089). Bks Demand UMI.

--The Theatre. LC 80-84012. (Illus.). 433p. 1981. pap. text ed. 18.95 (ISBN 0-87484-459-2). Mayfield Pub.

--There Is a Country. LC 78-108181. (Illus.). 1978. pap. text ed. 1.00 (ISBN 0-931122-08-2). West End.

Cohen, Robert & Harrop, John. Creative Play Direction. 2nd ed. (Illus.). 352p. 1984. 22.95 (ISBN 0-13-190926-6). P-H.

Cohen, Robert & Wartofsky, Marx. Language, Logic & Method. 1983. 69.50 (ISBN 90-277-0725-1, Pub. by Reidel Holland). Kluwer Academic.

Cohen, Robert, ed. Children's Conceptions of Spatial Relationships. LC 81-48564. (Child Development Ser.: No. 15). 1982. 8.95x (ISBN 0-87589-875-0). Jossey-Bass.

Cohen, Robert, jt. ed. see Agassi, Joseph.

Cohen, Robert, et al, eds. Psych City. LC 72-11593. 348p. 1974. pap. text ed. 14.00 (ISBN 0-08-017083-8). Pergamon.

Cohen, Robert M., jt. auth. see Marangos, Paul J.

Cohen, Robert S. Physical Sciences & the History of Physics. 1984. lib. bdg. 39.50 (ISBN 90-277-1615-3, Pub by Reidel Holland). Kluwer Academic.

Cohen, Robert S. & Hempel, Carl G. Physics, Philosophy & Psychoanalysis. 1983. lib. bdg. 59.00 (ISBN 90-277-1533-5, Pub. by Reidel Holland). Kluwer Academic.

Cohen, Robert S. & Wartofsky, Marx. Epistemology, Methodology, & the Social Sciences. 1983. lib. bdg. 48.00 (ISBN 90-277-1454-1, Pub. by Reidel Holland). Kluwer Academic.

--Hegel & the Sciences. 1984. lib. bdg. 61.50 (ISBN 90-277-0726-X, Pub. by Reidel Holland). Kluwer Academic.

Cohen, Robert S., ed. Herbert Feigl: Inquiries & Provocations, Selected Writings. 1929 to 1974. (Vienna Circle Collection: No. 14). 450p. 1980. lib. bdg. 50.00 (ISBN 90-277-1101-1, Pub. by Reidel Holland); pap. 23.50 (ISBN 90-277-1102-X). Kluwer Academic.

Cohen, Robert S. & Schnelle, Thomas, eds. Cognition & Fact: Materials On Ludwik Fleck. 1985. lib. bdg. 59.50 (ISBN 90-277-1902-0, Reidel Holland). Kluwer Academic.

Cohen, Robert S., ed. see Neurath, Otto.

Cohen, Robert S., ed. see Schaff, Adam.

Cohen, Robert S., et al, eds. Studies in the Philosophy of J. N. Findlay. (Philosophy Ser.). 464p. 1985. 49.50x (ISBN 0-87395-795-4); pap. 23.50x (ISBN 0-87395-794-6). State U NY Pr.

Cohen, Roberta G. & Lipkin, Gladys B. Therapeutic Group Work for Health Professionals. LC 79-12388. 1979. pap. text ed. 12.50 (ISBN 0-8261-2311-2). Springer Pub.

Cohen, Roberta G., jt. auth. see Lipkin, Gladys B.

Cohen, Robin. Forced Labour in Colonial Africa. 1982. lib. bdg. 34.50 (ISBN 0-686-45050-7). Porter.

--Labour & Politics in Nigeria. 2nd ed. xv, 304p. (Orig.). 1982. pap. text ed. 12.50x (ISBN 0-435-96150-0). Heinemann Ed.

Cohen, Robin, jt. auth. see Sandbrook, Richard.

Cohen, Robin, ed. African Islands & Enclaves. (Sage Series on African Modernization & Development: Vol. 7). 280p. 1983. 29.95 (ISBN 0-8039-1966-2). Sage.

Cohen, Robin & Gutkind, C. W., eds. Peasants & Proletarians: The Struggles of Third World Workers. LC 79-10020. 1980. pap. 7.50 (ISBN 0-85345-505-8). Monthly Rev.

Cohen, Robin, jt. ed. see Ambursley, Fitzroy.

Cohen, Robin, ed. see Nzula, A., et al.

Cohen, Robin, jt. ed. see Sandbrook, Richard.

Cohen, Robin, et al, eds. Peasants & Proletarians: The Struggles of Third World Workers. LC 79-10020. 505p. 1979. 16.00 (ISBN 0-85345-421-3, CL4213). Monthly Rev.

Cohen, Rona, jt. auth. see Bagley, Vicky.

Cohen, Ronald & Mohl, Raymond. The Paradox of Progressive Education: The Gary Plan & Urban Schooling. (National University Publications,Interdisciplinary Urban Ser). 1979. 20.00x (ISBN 0-8046-9237-8, Pub. by Kennikat). Assoc Faculty Pr.

Cohen, Ronald & Service, Elman R., eds. Origins of the State: The Anthropology of Political Evolution. LC 77-19091. 240p. 1978. text ed. 16.50x (ISBN 0-915980-68-1); pap. text ed. 7.95 (ISBN 0-915980-84-3). ISHI PA.

Cohen, Ronald, jt. ed. see Britan, Gerald M.

Cohen, Ronald, jt. ed. see Greenberg, Jerald.

Cohen, Ronald J. Malpractice: A Guide for Mental Health Professionals. LC 78-72147. 1979. 17.95 (ISBN 0-02-905790-6). Free Pr.

Cohen, Ronald J. & Maiano, William E. Legal Guidebook in Mental Health. (Illus.). 624p. 1982. text ed. 39.95 (ISBN 0-02-905740-X). Free Pr.

Cohen, Rose. Out of the Shadow. LC 77-145475. (The American Immigration Library). 352p. 1971. Repr. of 1918 ed. lib. bdg. 17.95x (ISBN 0-89198-007-5). Ozer.

Cohen, Rose N. The Financial Control of Education in the Consolidated City of New York. LC 79-176700. (Columbia University. Teachers College. Contributions to Education: No. 943). Repr. of 1948 ed. 22.50 (ISBN 0-404-55943-3). AMS Pr.

Cohen, Rosetta M. Domestic Scenes. 1982. pap. 4.00 (ISBN 0-936600-02-0). Riverstone Foothills.

Cohen, Rudolf. Patterns of Personality Judgement. Schaeffer, Dirk L., tr. 1973. 63.00 (ISBN 0-12-178950-0). Acad Pr.

Cohen, Steven M. & Hyman, Paula E., eds. Perspectives on the Jewish Family. 256p. 1984. text ed. 30.00x (ISBN 0-8419-0860-5). Holmes & Meier.

Cohen, Steven M., et al, eds. Perspectives in Jewish Population Research. LC 84-50660. (Replica Edition). 275p. 1984. pap. 22.50x (ISBN 0-86531-853-0). Westview.

Cohen, Stewart & Comiskey, Thomas, eds. Child Development: Contemporary Perspectives. LC 76-53264. 373p. 1977. pap. text ed. 16.95 (ISBN 0-87581-203-1). Peacock Pubs.

Cohen, Stuart A., jt. auth. see Elazar, Daniel J.

Cohen, Suleiman. Agrarian Structures & Agrarian Reform. (Studies in Development & Planning: Vol. 8). 1978. lib. bdg. 15.50 (ISBN 90-207-0764-7, Pub. by Martinus Nijhoff Netherlands). Kluwer Academic.

Cohen, Susan, jt. auth. see Cohen, Daniel.

Cohen, Susan E., jt. ed. see Johnson, William S.

Cohen, Sydney & Warren, Kenneth, eds. Immunology of Parasitic Infections. 2nd ed. (Illus.). 864p. 1982. text ed. 96.00x (ISBN 0-632-00852-0). Blackwell Pubns.

Cohen, Sylvan H., jt. auth. see Gabriel, Richard A.

Cohen, Tamara & Skutch, Judith. Double Vision. (Illus.). 280p. (Orig.). 1985. pap. 8.95 (ISBN 0-89087-411-5). Celestial Arts.

Cohen, Ted & Guyer, Paul. Essays in Kant's Aesthetics. LC 81-13091. 1982. lib. bdg. 25.00x (ISBN 0-226-11226-8). U of Chicago Pr.

Cohen, Ted & Guyer, Paul, eds. Essays in Kant's Aesthetics. LC 81-13091. x, 324p. 1985. pap. 11.95 (ISBN 0-226-11227-6). U of Chicago Pr.

Cohen, Tirza, jt. ed. see Bonne-Tamir, Batsheva.

Cohen, Ulrike & Osterloh, Karl-Heinz. Zimmerfrei. Incl. Student Text. 81p. 6.25 (ISBN 3-468-49420-3); Workbook. 57p. 3.95 (ISBN 3-468-49421-1); Teacher's Suppplement. 32p. 3.50 (ISBN 3-468-49422-X); Text-Cassette. 11.50 (ISBN 3-468-84440-9). Langenscheidt.

Cohen, Uriel & Hunter, John. Teaching Design for Mainstreaming the Handicapped. (Illus.). vi, 120p. 1981. 7.00 (ISBN 0-938744-17-8, R81-1). U of Wis Ctr Arch-Urban.

Cohen, Uriel, et al. Case Studies of Child Play Areas & Child Support Facilities. (Publications in Architecture & Urban Planning Ser.: R78-2). (Illus.). v, 405p. 1978. 18.00 (ISBN 0-938744-03-8). U of Wis Ctr Arch-Urban.

--Mainstreaming the Handicapped: A Design Guide. (Publications in Architecture & Urban Planning Ser.: R79-5). (Illus.). iv, 64p. 1979. 7.00 (ISBN 0-686-27456-3). U of Wis Ctr Arch-Urban.

--Recommendations for Child Play Areas. (Publications in Architecture & Urban Planning Ser.: R79-1). (Illus.). vi, 380p. 1979. 18.00 (ISBN 0-938744-07-0). U of Wis Ctr Arch-Urban.

--Case Studies of Child Play Areas & Child Support Facilities: Appendix-Research Forms. (Illus.). iii, 25p. 4.00 (ISBN 0-938744-10-0, R78-3). U of Wis Ctr Arch-Urban.

Cohen, W. Direct Response Marketing. 496p. 1984. 35.45 (ISBN 0-471-88684-X). Wiley.

Cohen, Walter. Drama of a Nation: Public Theater in Renaissance England & Spain. LC 85-2633. 416p. 1985. text ed. 35.00x (ISBN 0-8014-1793-7). Cornell U Pr.

Cohen, Warren I. The American Revisionists: The Lessons of Intervention in World War I. LC 66-20594. pap. 66.50 (ISBN 0-317-09669-9, 2020046). Bks Demand UMI.

--America's Response to China: An Interpretive History of Simo-American Relations. 2nd ed. 271p. 1980. pap. text ed. 7.95 (ISBN 0-394-34169-4, RanC). Random.

--Dean Rusk. LC 80-10943. (The American Secretaries of State & Their Diplomacy: Vol. XIX). 388p. 1980. 23.50 (ISBN 0-8154-0519-7). Cooper Sq.

Cohen, Warren I., ed. New Frontiers in American-East Asian Relations. (Studies of the East Asian Institute). 344p. 1983. 37.00x (ISBN 0-231-05630-3); pap. 16.00 (ISBN 0-231-05631-1). Columbia U Pr.

Cohen, Warren I., et al. The Chinese Connection. LC 77-18101. (Studies of the East Asian Institute). 322p. 1978. 29.00x (ISBN 0-231-04444-5). Columbia U Pr.

Cohen, Wayne R. & Friedman, Emanuel A., eds. Management of Labor. (Illus.). 384p. 1983. text ed. 37.00 (ISBN 0-8391-1816-3, 17884). Univ Park.

Cohen, Wilbur J. & Heffernan, W. Joseph. Welfare Reform: State & Federal Roles. (Policy Research Project Report Ser.: No. 59). 163p. 1984. 9.95 (ISBN 0-89940-661-0). LBJ Sch Public Affairs.

Cohen, Wilbur J. & Westoff, Charles F. Demographic Dynamics in America. LC 77-80227. 1977. 14.95 (ISBN 0-02-905780-9). Free Pr.

Cohen, Wilbur J., jt. auth. see Friedman, Milton.

Cohen, Wilbur J., ed. The New Deal Fifty Years after: A Historical Assessment. LC 84-82347. (Symposia Ser.). 178p. 1984. 10.50 (ISBN 0-89940-415-4). LBJ Sch Pub Aff.

Cohen, William & Kaplan, John. Constitutional Law, Civil Liberty & Individual Rights. 2nd ed. LC 82-5186. (University Casebook Ser.). 924p. 1982. text ed. 22.50 (ISBN 0-88277-062-4). Foundation Pr.

--Constitutional Law, Civil Liberty & Individual Rights: Second Edition, 1983 Supplement. (University Casebook Ser.). 50p. 1983. pap. text ed. 2.50 (ISBN 0-88277-149-3). Foundation Pr.

Cohen, William, jt. auth. see Barrett, Edward, Jr.

Cohen, William, jt. auth. see Barrett, Edward L., Jr.

Cohen, William, ed. European Empire Building. LC 79-57459. (Problems in Civilization Ser.). (Orig.). 1980. pap. text ed. 5.95x (ISBN 0-88273-410-5). Forum Pr IL.

Cohen, William A. Building a Mail Order Business. 2nd ed. 584p. 1985. 19.95 (ISBN 0-471-81062-2). Wiley.

--Building a Mail Order Business: A Complete Manual for Success. LC 81-16071. 442p. 1982. 17.95 (ISBN 0-471-08803-X, Pub. by Wiley-Interscience). Wiley.

--The Corporate Strategist's Guide to Corporate Planning. (Wiley Series on Business Strategy). 1985. 21.95 (ISBN 0-471-81935-2). Wiley.

--The Entrepreneur & Small Business Problem Solver: A Complete Guide to Owning & Operating Your Own Business. 653p. 1983. 42.95x (ISBN 0-471-86740-3, Pub. by Ronald Pr). Wiley.

--The Entrepreneur & Small Business Problem Solver: An Encyclopedia Reference & Guide. 655p. 1983. pap. text ed. 19.95 (ISBN 0-471-80795-8). Wiley.

--The Executive's Guide to Finding a Superior Job. 224p. 1983. 17.95 (ISBN 0-8144-5766-5). AMACOM.

--The Executive's Guide to Finding a Superior Job. LC 78-7370. pap. 44.00 (ISBN 0-317-27060-5, 2023543). Bks Demand UMI.

--How to Make It Big as a Consultant. LC 85-47678. 304p. 1985. 17.95 (ISBN 0-8144-5821-1). Amacom.

--Principles of Technical Management. LC 79-54829. pap. 58.50 (ISBN 0-317-26710-8, 2023515). Bks Demand UMI.

Cohen, William A. & Cohen, Nurit. Top Executive Performance: Eleven Keys to Success & Power. LC 83-21775. 254p. 1984. 19.95 (ISBN 0-471-89687-X, Pub by Ronald Pr). Wiley.

Cohen, William A. & Reddick, Marshall E. Successful Marketing for Small Business. 288p. 1981. 17.95 (ISBN 0-8144-5611-1). AMACOM.

--Successful Marketing for Small Business. LC 80-69699. pap. 72.00 (ISBN 0-317-19830-0, 2023077). Bks Demand UMI.

Cohen, William B. The French Encounter with Africans: White Response to Blacks, 1530-1880. LC 79-84260. (Illus.). 384p. 1980. 25.00x (ISBN 0-253-34922-2). Ind U Pr.

--Rulers of Empire: The French Colonial Service in Africa. LC 76-137405. (Publications Ser.: No. 95). 1971. 11.95x (ISBN 0-8179-1951-1). Hoover Inst Pr.

Cohen, William D. Blood Cells of Marine Invertebrates. LC 84-26174. (MBL Ser.: Vol. 6). 280p. 1985. 66.00 (ISBN 0-8451-2205-3). A R Liss.

Cohen, William S. & Hart, Gary. The Double Man. LC 85-267. 384p. 1985. 16.95 (ISBN 0-688-04167-1). Morrow.

Cohen, William S. & Lasson, Kenneth. Getting the Most Out of Washington: Using Congress to Move the Federal Bureaucracy. 256p. 1982. 15.95x (ISBN 0-87196-537-2). Facts on File.

Cohen, Yehoshua S. Diffusion of an Innovation in an Urban System: The Spread of Planned Regional Shopping Centers in the United States, 1949-1968. LC 72-76011. (Research Papers Ser.: No. 140). 136p. 1972. pap. 10.00 (ISBN 0-89065-047-0). U Chicago Dept Geog.

Cohen, Yehoshua S. & Berry, Brian J. Spatial Components of Manufacturing Change, 1950-1960. LC 75-33654. (Research Papers Ser: No. 172). (Illus.). 1976. pap. 10.00 (ISBN 0-89065-079-9). U Chicago Dept Geog.

Cohen, Yehudi A., ed. Man in Adaptation. Incl. Biosocial Background. 2nd ed. LC 74-169511. 1974. Vol. 1. lib. bdg. 39.95x (ISBN 0-202-01111-9); pap. 16.95x (ISBN 0-202-01112-7); Cultural Present. 2nd ed. 1974. Vol. 2. lib. bdg. 39.95x (ISBN 0-202-01109-7); pap. 16.95x (ISBN 0-202-01110-0); Institutional Framework. 1971. Vol. 3. 39.95x (ISBN 0-202-01095-3); pap. 16.95x (ISBN 0-202-01096-1). 533p. pap. Aldine Pub.

Cohen, Yona. Jerusalem Under Siege. Shefer, Dorothea, tr. from Hebrew. LC 81-5146. (Illus.). 326p. 1981. text ed. 16.00 (ISBN 0-86628-017-0). Ridgefield Pub.

Cohen, Youseff, et al. Representation & Development in Brazil, Nineteen Seventy-Two to Nineteen Seventy-Three. 2nd ed. LC 80-84095. 1980. write for info., codebk (ISBN 0-89138-950-4). ICPSR.

Cohen-Adad. Alkali-Metal Chlorides (Binary Systems) Solubilities of Solids. (IUPAC Solubility Data Ser.). 1986. 100.00 (ISBN 0-08-023918-8). Pergamon.

Cohen-Stratyner, Barbara. Biographical Dictionary of Dance. 1982. lib. bdg. 75.00x (ISBN 0-02-870260-3). Schirmer Bks.

Cohen-Stratyner, Barbara N., jt. ed. see Cocuzza, Ginnine.

Cohen-Stratyner, Barbara N., ed. see Gordon, Mel.

Cohen-Stratyner, Barbarba N., ed. see Lang, Franz.

Cohen-Tannoudji, Claude, et al. Quantum Mechanics, 2 vols. LC 76-5874. 1977. Vol. 1. 48.95 (ISBN 0-471-16432-1, Pub. by Wiley-Interscience); 43.95 (ISBN 0-471-16434-8); Vol. 1 898pp. pap. 41.50 (ISBN 0-471-16433-X); Vol. 2 626pp. pap. 37.50 (ISBN 0-471-16435-6). Wiley.

Coherent Laser Divison of Coherent, Inc. Lasers: Operation; Equipment; Practical Application; Design. (Illus.). 1980. 36.50 (ISBN 0-07-011593-1). McGraw.

Cohler, Bertram J. & Grunebaum, Henry U. Mothers, Grandmothers & Daughters: Personality & Child-Care in Three Generation Families. LC 80-17979. (Personality Processes Ser.). 456p. 1981. 35.00x (ISBN 0-471-05900-5, Pub. by Wiley-Interscience). Wiley.

Cohler, Bertram J. & Musick, Judith S., eds. Intervention Among Psychiatrically Disabled Parents & Their Young Children. LC 83-82732. (Mental Health Services Ser.: No. 24). 1984. pap. text ed. 9.95x (ISBN 0-87589-781-9). Jossey-Bass.

Cohler, David K. Broadcast Journalism: A Guide for the Presentation of Radio & Television News. (Illus.). 352p. 1985. text ed. 23.95 (ISBN 0-13-083155-7). P-H.

Cohn. Asymptomatic Coronary Artery Disease. (Basic & Clinical Cardiology Ser.). 208p. 1985. price not set. Dekker.

--Mallarme's Masterwork. (Coll. De Proprietatibus Litterarum, Series Practica). 22.50 (ISBN 0-685-34939-X). French & Eur.

--Pancreatic Cancer: New Directions in Therapeutic Management. LC 81-4945. (Masson Cancer Management Ser.). 128p. 1981. 35.00x (ISBN 0-89352-133-7). Masson Pub.

Cohn & Dunifon. Paul Revere Slept Here & Other Great Real Estate Ad Ideas. 1983. pap. 12.95 (ISBN 0-8359-5475-7). Reston.

Cohn, Adrian, jt. auth. see Bell, James K.

Cohn, Adrian A., jt. auth. see Bell, James K.

Cohn, Alan M. & Collins, K. K., eds. Cumulated Dickens Checklist. LC 81-52807. 1982. 30.00x (ISBN 0-87875-230-7). Whitston Pub.

Cohn, Albert. Shakespeare in Germany in the Sixteenth & Seventeenth Centuries. LC 75-166208. (Studies in Shakespeare, No. 24). 1971. Repr. of 1865 ed. lib. bdg. 58.95x (ISBN 0-8383-1330-2). Haskell.

Cohn, Albert & Miller, Leta E. Music in the Paris Academy of Sciences. LC 78-70025. (Detroit Studies in Music Bibliography Ser.: No. 43). 1979. 8.50 (ISBN 0-911772-96-0). Info Coord.

Cohn, Alfred & Udolf, Roy. Criminal Justice System & Its Psychology. 1979. 22.50 (ISBN 0-442-28882-4). Van Nos Reinhold.

Cohn, Alfred E. Medicine, Science & Art. facs. ed. LC 72-86742. (Essay Index Reprint Ser). 1931. 18.50 (ISBN 0-8369-1126-1). Ayer Co Pubs.

--Medicine, Science & Art. (Essay Index Reprint Ser.). 1982. Repr. of 1931 ed. lib. bdg. 15.50 (ISBN 0-8290-0840-3). Irvington.

--Minerva's Progress. LC 68-8197. (Essay & General Literature Index Reprint Ser). 1969. Repr. of 1946 ed. 15.00x (ISBN 0-8046-0082-1, Pub. by Kennikat). Assoc Faculty Pr.

--No Retreat from Reason. LC 68-8198. (Essay & General Literature Index Reprint Ser). 1969. Repr. of 1931 ed. 21.00x (ISBN 0-8046-0083-X, Pub. by Kennikat). Assoc Faculty Pr.

Cohn, Alvin W., jt. auth. see Viano, Emilio.

Cohn, Alvin W., ed. Criminal Justice Planning & Development. LC 77-81154. (Sage Research Progress Series in Criminology: Vol. 4). 134p. 1977. 20.00 (ISBN 0-8039-0918-7); pap. 9.95 (ISBN 0-8039-0913-6). Sage.

--The Future of Policing. LC 77-92833. (Sage Criminal Justice System Annuals: Vol. 9). 308p. 1978. 28.00 (ISBN 0-8039-0702-8); pap. 14.00 (ISBN 0-8039-0703-6). Sage.

Cohn, Alvin W. & Ward, Benjamin, eds. Improving Management in Criminal Justice. LC 80-18331. (Sage Research Progress Ser. in Criminology: Vol. 17). (Illus.). 159p. 1980. 20.00 (ISBN 0-8039-1515-2); pap. 9.95 (ISBN 0-8039-1516-0). Sage.

Cohn, Angelo. Wonderful World of Paper. LC 67-23557. (Illus.). (gr. 5-10). 1967. 10.53i (ISBN 0-200-71665-4, B92190, AbS-J). Har-Row.

Cohn, Arthur. The Collector's Twentieth-Century Music in the Western Hemisphere. LC 74-167848. (Music Ser.). 1972. Repr. of 1961 ed. 29.50 (ISBN 0-306-70404-8). Da Capo.

--Recorded Classical Music: A Critical Guide to Compositions & Performances. (A Schirmer Book). 2164p. 1981. 75.00 (ISBN 0-02-870640-4). Macmillan.

--Twentieth-Century Music in Western Europe: The Compositions & Recordings. LC 70-39297. 510p. 1972. Repr. of 1965 ed. lib. bdg. 45.00 (ISBN 0-306-70460-9). Da Capo.

Cohn, Bernard S., jt. ed. see Singer, Milton.

Cohn, D. V., et al. Endocrine Control of Bone & Calcium Metabolism, Vol. 8A. (International Congress Ser.: Vol. 619). 1984. 107.50 (ISBN 0-444-80589-3). Elsevier.

--Endocrine Control of Bone & Calcium Metabolism, Vol. 8B. (International Congress Ser.: Vol. 635). 1984. 102.00 (ISBN 0-444-80590-7). Elsevier.

Cohn, D. V., et al, eds. Hormonal Control of Calcium Metabolism. (International Congress Ser.: No. 511). 506p. 1981. 98.75 (ISBN 0-444-90193-0, Excerpta Medica). Elsevier.

Cohn, David. Where I Was Born & Raised. 1967. pap. 9.95x (ISBN 0-268-00299-1). U of Notre Dame Pr.

Cohn, David L. The Good Old Days. LC 75-22809. (America in Two Centuries Ser). (Illus.). 1976. Repr. of 1940 ed. 45.50x (ISBN 0-405-07680-0). Ayer Co Pubs.

--Life & Times of King Cotton. LC 73-11996. 286p. 1974. Repr. of 1956 ed. lib. bdg. 15.75x (ISBN 0-8371-7115-6, COKC). Greenwood.

Cohn, Davis L., jt. auth. see Melsa, James L.

Cohn, Don J., tr. see Lao She.

Cohn, Donald. Measure Theory. 276p. 1980. 24.95x (ISBN 0-8176-3003-1). Birkhauser.

Cohn, Dorritt. Transparent Minds: Narrative Modes for Presenting Consciousness in Fiction. LC 78-51161. 1978. 28.50x (ISBN 0-691-06369-9); pap. 11.50 (ISBN 0-691-10156-6). Princeton U Pr.

Cohn, E. J. Manual of German Law, 2 Vols. LC 67-28195. 1968-71. Set. 58.00 (ISBN 0-686-96820-4); Vol. 1. 35.00 (ISBN 0-379-00296-5); Vol. 2. 23.00 (ISBN 0-379-00297-3). Oceana.

Cohn, E. J., et al, eds. Handbook of Institutional Arbitration in International Trade: Rules, Facts & Figures. 302p. 1977. 64.00 (ISBN 0-7204-0567-X, North-Holland). Elsevier.

Cohn, Einar. Danmark under Den Store Krig: En Okonomisk Oversigt. (Verdenskrigens Okonomiske Og Sociale Historie (Skandinavisk Serie)). (Ger.). 1928. 85.00x (ISBN 0-317-27428-7). Elliots Bks.

Cohn, Elchanan. The Economics of Education. rev ed. LC 78-13277. 472p. 1978. text ed. 25.00 (ISBN 0-88410-185-1). Ballinger Pub.

Cohn, Elchanan, et al. Input-Output Analysis in Public Education. LC 75-19249. 160p. 1975. prof ref 25.00 (ISBN 0-88410-155-X). Ballinger Pub.

Cohn, Ellen R. & McWilliams, Betty J. Clinical Orofacial Assessment. 200p. 1984. text ed. 20.00 (ISBN 0-941158-13-6, D1078-8). Mosby.

Cohn, Emil B. This Immortal People: A Short History of the Jewish People. 180p. (Orig.). 1985. pap. 5.95t (ISBN 0-8091-2693-1). Paulist Pr.

Cohn, Georg. Existentialism & Legal Science. LC 67-14397. 148p. 1967. 12.00 (ISBN 0-379-00302-3). Oceana.

Cohn, H. The Trial & Death of Jesus. 14.95x (ISBN 0-87068-432-9). Ktav.

Cohn, H. A., ed. see Heming, William.

Cohn, Haim H. Human Rights in Jewish Law. LC 83-14846. 266p. 1984. 20.00x (ISBN 0-88125-036-8). Ktav.

Cohn, Harvey. Advanced Number Theory. (Illus.). 1980. pap. 5.00 (ISBN 0-486-64023-X). Dover.

--Conformal Mapping on Riemann Surfaces. (Illus.). 352p. 1980. pap. text ed. 7.50 (ISBN 0-486-64025-6). Dover.

--Introduction to the Construction of Class Fields. (Cambridge Studies in Advanced Mathematics: No. 6). (Illus.). 225p. Date not set. price not set (ISBN 0-521-24762-4). Cambridge U Pr.

Cohn, Helen & Tingle, Joyce E. Manual for Nurses in Family & Community Health. 2nd ed. LC 73-17662. 99p. 1974. pap. 8.95 spiral bdg. (ISBN 0-316-15031-2). Little.

Cohn, J. A., jt. auth. see Biegeleisen, J. I.

Cohn, J. N. & Rittinghausen, R., eds. Mononitrates. (International Boehringer Mannheim Symposia). (Illus.). 345p. 1985. pap. 34.50 (ISBN 0-387-15107-9). Springer-Verlag.

Cohn, Jacob. The Royal Table: Outline of the Dietary Laws of Israel. 5.95 (ISBN 0-87306-098-9). Feldheim.

Cohn, Jan. Improbable Fiction: The Life of Mary Roberts Rinehart. LC 79-3997. 1980. 16.95 (ISBN 0-8229-3401-9). U of Pittsburgh Pr.

--The Palace or the Poorhouse: The American House As a Cultural Symbol. 1979. 15.00x (ISBN 0-87013-211-3). Mich St U Pr.

Cohn, Jay N., ed. Hypertension: Neural, Vascular & Hormonal Factors. LC 66-7606. (Hypertension Ser.: Vol. 24). 1976. pap. 3.00 (ISBN 0-87493-048-0, 73-215A). Am Heart.

--Hypertension XXV: Hypertension - Experimental & Clinical Studies. LC 77-76010. (Circulation Research Journal Suppl. Ser.: Vol. 40, No. 5). 1977. pap. 4.00 (ISBN 0-87493-053-7, 73-216A). Am Heart.

--Hypertension XXVI. (AHA Monograph: No. 58). 1978. 5.00 (ISBN 0-87493-024-3, 73-044-A). Am Heart.

Cohn, Jill W. Writing: The Personal Voice. 214p. (Orig.). 1975. pap. text ed. 10.95 (ISBN 0-15-597787-3, HC). HarBraceJ.

Cohn, Jules. The Conscience of the Corporations: Business & Urban Affairs, 1967-1970. LC 77-135533. (Policy Studies in Employment & Welfare: No. 6). pap. 34.00 (ISBN 0-317-19880-7, 2023090). Bks Demand UMI.

Cohn, Jules & Shah, Prauin M., eds. Symposium on Cardiachypertrophy & Cardiomyopathy. (AHA Monograph: No. 43). 210p. 1974. cancelled (ISBN 0-87493-039-1, 73-030A). Am Heart.

Cohn, Keith, et al. Coming Back: A Guide to Recovering from Heart Attack & Living Confidently with Coronary Disease. 1979. pap. 7.95 (ISBN 0-201-04561-3). Addison-Wesley.

Coke, Van Deren, ed. One Hundred Years of Photographic History: Essays in Honor of Beaumont Newhall. 1st ed. LC 74-83381. pap. 47.50 (ISBN 0-317-27141-5, 2024679). Bks Demand UMI.

Cokelet, Giles R., et al, eds. Erythrocyte Mechanics & Blood Flow. LC 79-5473. (Kroc Foundation Ser.: Vol. 13). 286p. 1980. 40.00x (ISBN 0-8451-0303-2). A R Liss.

Cokely, Dennis & Baker, Charlotte. American Sign Language: A Student Text, Units 1-9. 1980. Set. 18.95x (ISBN 0-932666-08-6); Set. pap. 14.95x (ISBN 0-932666-06-X). T J Pubs.

--American Sign Language: A Student Text, Units 19-27. 1981. Set. 18.95x (ISBN 0-932666-14-0); pap. 14.95x (ISBN 0-932666-13-2). T J Pubs.

--American Sign Language: A Teacher's Resource Text on Curriculum, Methods, & Evaluation. 1980. 20.95x (ISBN 0-932666-22-1); pap. 16.95x (ISBN 0-932666-05-1). T J Pubs.

Cokely, Dennis, jt. auth. see Baker, Charlotte.

Coker, Alec. Craft of Straw Decoration. (Illus.). 86p. 1971. 10.95 (ISBN 0-7134-4967-5, Pub. by Batsford England). David & Charles.

Coker, Alice. The Craft of Straw Decoration. (Illus.). 108p. 1984. 10.95 (ISBN 0-85219-078-6, Pub. by Batsford England). David & Charles.

Coker, Carolyn. The Other David. 224p. 1984. 13.95 (ISBN 0-396-08390-0). Dodd.

--The Other David. 1985. pap. 2.95 (ISBN 0-451-13918-6, Sig). NAL.

Coker, Christopher. The Future of the Atlantic Alliance. 224p. 1985. 22.00x (ISBN 0-333-37546-7, Pub. by Salem Acad). Merrimack Pub Cir.

--NATO, the Warsaw Pact & Africa. 320p. 1985. 32.50 (ISBN 0-312-56066-4). St Martin.

--Soviet Union, Eastern Europe & New Economic Order. (Washington Papers: Vol. XII, No. 111). 128p. 1984. pap. 7.95 (ISBN 0-03-002789-6). Praeger.

--U. S. Military Power in the 1980's. 176p. 1984. 24.00x (ISBN 0-333-35834-1, Pub. by Salem Acad). Merrimack Pub Cir.

Coker, Donald W. Complete Guide to Income Property Financing & Loan Packaging. LC 83-22574. 408p. 1984. 125.00 (ISBN 0-87624-099-6). Inst Busn Plan.

Coker, Ed & Stuttard, Geoffrey, eds. Industrial Studies I: The Key Skills. 1975. pap. 1.95 (ISBN 0-09-911210-8, Pub. by Hutchinson). Merrimack Pub Cir.

Coker, Francis W. Organismic Theories of the State. LC 74-120061. (Columbia University Studies in the Social Sciences: No. 101). Repr. of 1910 ed. 16.50 (ISBN 0-404-51101-5). AMS Pr.

Coker, Hazel P., jt. auth. see Coker, William S.

Coker, James L. History of Company G, Ninth S.C. Regiment, Infantry, S.C. Army: And of Company E, Sixth S.C. Regiment, Infantry, S.C. Army. 210p. 1979. Repr. 12.50 (ISBN 0-87921-051-6). Attic Pr.

Coker, Jerry. Listening to Jazz. 148p. 1982. pap. 6.95 (ISBN 0-13-537225-9). P-H.

Coker, Lawrence T. & Gaddis, Robert S., eds. Maintenance Painting Program for Maximum Return on Investment. (TAPPI Press Reports Ser.). 58p. 1982. 39.95 (ISBN 0-89852-395-8, 01-01-R095). TAPPI.

Coker, Michael G., jt. auth. see Oldfield, John S., Jr.

Coker, Paul, jt. auth. see Hart, Stan.

Coker, Paul, jt. auth. see Hart, Stan, Jr.

Coker, Paul, Jr. The Mad Pet Book. 192p. 1983. pap. 2.25 (ISBN 0-446-32632-1). Warner Bks.

Coker, Paul, Jr., jt. auth. see Ficarra, John.

Coker, Robert E. This Great & Wide Sea: An Introduction to Oceanography & Marine Biology. (Illus.). pap. 4.95xi (ISBN 0-06-130551-0, TB551, Torch). Har-Row.

Coker, W. Music & Meaning. LC 72-142358. 1972. 14.95 (ISBN 0-02-906350-7). Free Pr.

Coker, W. C. The Clavarias of the United States & Canada. 1932. Repr. 28.00 (ISBN 3-7682-0913-X). Lubrecht & Cramer.

--The Saprolegniaceae with Notes on Other Water Molds. (Illus.). 1969. Repr. of 1923 ed. 22.40 (ISBN 3-7682-0620-3). Lubrecht & Cramer.

Coker, W. C. & Beers, A. H. The Stipitate Hydnums of the Eastern U.S. (Illus.). 1970. Repr. of 1951 ed. 22.40 (ISBN 3-7682-0695-5). Lubrecht & Cramer.

Coker, W. C. & Couch, J. N. The Gastromycetes of the Eastern U. S. & Canada. 1969. pap. 22.40 (ISBN 3-7682-0602-5). Lubrecht & Cramer.

Coker, William C. The Club & Coral Mushrooms (Clavarias) of the United States & Canada. LC 74-82202. (Illus.). 320p. 1975. pap. 7.95 (ISBN 0-486-23101-1). Dover.

--The Club & Coral Mushrooms (Clavarias) of the United States & Canada. (Illus.). 12.00 (ISBN 0-8446-5171-0). Peter Smith.

Coker, William C. & Beers, Alma. The Boleti of North Carolina. (Illus.). 163p. 1974. pap. 5.50 (ISBN 0-486-20377-8). Dover.

Coker, William C. & Beers, Alma H. The Boleti of North Carolina. (Illus.). 10.00 (ISBN 0-8446-5016-1). Peter Smith.

Coker, William C. & Couch, John N. The Gasteromycetes of Eastern United States & Canada. Bd. with The Gasteromycetes of Ohio. Johnson, Minne M. (Illus.). 11.25 (ISBN 0-8446-5017-X). Peter Smith.

--The Gasteromycetes of the Eastern United States & Canada. LC 73-91490. (Illus.). 447p. 1974. pap. 8.95 (ISBN 0-486-23033-3). Dover.

Coker, William C., ed. Studies in Science. LC 77-39098. (Essay Index Reprint Ser.). (University of North Carolina sesquicentennial publications). Repr. of 1946 ed. 40.00 (ISBN 0-8369-2683-8). Ayer Co Pubs.

Coker, William S. The Financial History of Pensacola's Spanish Presidios, 1698-1763. (Illus.). 20p. pap. 2.50x (ISBN 0-686-32057-3). Pensacola Hist.

--John Forbes & Company & the War of 1812 in the Spanish Borderlands. (The Spanish Borderlands Ser.). (Illus.). 37p. (YA) 1979. pap. 2.50 (ISBN 0-933776-08-X). Perdido Bay.

--The Last Battle of the War of 1812: New Orleans. No, Fort Bowyer! (Illus.). 22p. 1981. pap. 2.50x (ISBN 0-933776-09-8). Perdido Bay.

Coker, William S. & Coker, Hazel P. The Siege of Mobile, Seventeen Eighty in Maps: With Data on Troop Strength, Military Units, Ships, Casualties, & Prisoners of War. LC 82-675288. (Spanish Borderlands Ser.: Vol. 9). (Illus.). 131p. (Orig.). 1982. pap. text ed. 12.95x (ISBN 0-933776-11-X). Perdido Bay.

--The Siege of Pensacola, 1781. LC 81-675060. (The Spanish Borderlands Ser.: Vol. VIII). (Illus.). 132p. 1981. pap. text ed. 12.00 (ISBN 0-933776-07-1). Perdido Bay.

Coker, William S. & Watson, Thomas D. Indian Traders of the Southeastern Spanish Border Lands: Panton, Leslie & Company & John Forbes & Company, 1783 to 1847. LC 84-25806. (Illus.). 450p. 1985. 35.00 (ISBN 0-8130-0801-8). U Presses Fla.

Coker, William S., ed. Hispanic-American Essays in Honor of Max Leon Moorhead. LC 79-11210. (Spanish Borderlands Ser.: Vol. 1). (Illus.). 193p. 1979. 16.95x (ISBN 0-933776-00-4); pap. 9.95 (ISBN 0-933776-01-2). Perdido Bay.

Coker, William S. & Inglis, G. Douglas, eds. The Spanish Censuses of Pensacola, Seventeen Eighty-Four to Eighteen Twenty, Vol. 3. LC 80-26615. (Spanish Borderlands Ser.). (Illus.). 198p. 1980. pap. 20.00 (ISBN 0-933776-04-7). Perdido Bay.

Coker, William S. & Rea, Rober R., eds. Anglo-Spanish Confrontation on the Gulf Coast During the American Revolution: Proceedings of the Gulf Coast History & Humanities Conference, Vol IX. 1983. pap. 6.95 (ISBN 0-940836-17-3); bound 10.95 (ISBN 0-940836-16-5). U of W Fla.

Coker, William S., intro. by see Coxe, Daniel.

Cokes, Curtis & Kayser, Hugh. The Complete Book of Boxing. (Illus.). 1980. 10.95 (ISBN 0-88280-073-6); pap. 5.95 (ISBN 0-88280-074-4). ETC Pubns.

Cokonis, T. J. see International Computers in Engineering Conference & Exhibit, 1983.

Col Educ. Preliminary Plan for the College of Education. 77p. (First draft; prepared by first staff of eight). 1956. 12.00 (ISBN 0-318-17033-7, 59). Am-Nepal Ed.

Col, U Legis. U. S. Constitutions, Vol. 1 & 2. 1967. 130.00 (ISBN 0-379-00186-1). Oceana.

Colaclides, Helen, tr. see Megas, Georgios A.

Colacurcio, Michael J. Province of Piety: Moral History in Hawthorne's Early Tales. LC 83-26586. 688p. 1984. text ed. 30.00x (ISBN 0-674-71957-3). Harvard U Pr.

Colacurcio, Michael J., ed. New Essays on "The Scarlet Letter". (The American Novel Ser.). 192p. Date not set. price not set (ISBN 0-521-26676-9); pap. price not set (ISBN 0-521-31998-6). Cambridge U Pr.

Coladarci, Arthur P., jt. auth. see Koosis, Donald J.

Coladarci, Arthur P., ed. Educational Psychology, a Book of Readings. LC 79-97341. Repr. of 1955 ed. lib. bdg. 25.50x (ISBN 0-8371-2827-7, COEP). Greenwood.

Colaiacovo, Juan Luis, et al see Czinkota, Michael R.

Colaianne, A. J. Piers Plowman: An Annotated Bibliography of Editions & Criticism, 1550-1977. LC 78-7631. (Garland Reference Library of the Humanities: Vol. 121). 217p. 1978. lib. bdg. 28.00 (ISBN 0-8240-9822-6). Garland Pub.

Colaico, James A. James Fitzjames Stephens & the Crisis of Victorian Thought. LC 80-13699. 1983. 20.00 (ISBN 0-312-43961-X). St Martin.

Colakovic, Branko A. Yugoslav Migrations to America. LC 73-76007. (Illus.). 1973. softcover 9.00 (ISBN 0-88247-209-7). Ragusan Pr.

Colander, David C. Solutions to Unemployment. 229p. 1981. pap. text ed. 9.95 (ISBN 0-15-582456-2, HC). HarBraceJ.

Colander, David C., jt. auth. see Lerner, Abba P.

Colander, David C., ed. Incentive-Based Incomes Policies: Theoretical & Adminstrative Advances. 240p. 1985. prof. ref. 29.95 (ISBN 0-88730-082-0). Ballinger Pub.

--Selected Economic Writings of Abba P. Lerner. (Selected Economic Writings Ser.). 752p. 1983. 65.00X (ISBN 0-8147-1385-8). NYU Pr.

--Solutions to Inflation. 220p. 1979. pap. text ed. 9.95 (ISBN 0-15-582450-3, HC). HarBraceJ.

Colander, Pat. Hugh Hefner's First Funeral & Other True Tales of Love & Death in Chicago. 176p. 1985. pap. 8.95 (ISBN 0-8092-5545-6). Contemp Bks.

Colangelo, Cheryl & Gottlieb, Linda L. A Normal Baby: The Sensorimotor Processes of the First Year. 2nd, rev. ed. (Illus.). 1985. pap. text ed. 12.50 (ISBN 0-911681-03-5). Valhalla Rehab.

Colangelo, Cheryl, jt. auth. see Berger, Adrienne F.

Colangelo, Nicholas & Zaffrann, Ronald T. New Voices in Counseling the Gifted. 1979. pap. text ed. 16.95 (ISBN 0-8403-1998-3). Kendall-Hunt.

Colangelo, Nicholas, jt. auth. see Pulvino, Charles J.

Colangelo, Nicholas, et al. Multicultural Nonsexist Education: A Human Relations Approach. 1979. pap. text ed. 15.95 (ISBN 0-8403-2052-3). Kendall-Hunt.

Colangelo, V. & Thornton, P. A. Engineering Aspects of Product Liability. 1981. 85.00 (ISBN 0-87170-103-0). ASM.

Colangelo, V. J. & Heiser, F. A. Analysis of Metallurgical Failures. (Illus.). 368p. 1974. 42.20 (ISBN 0-318-17222-4, 1196). Am Soc Nondestructive.

Colangelo, Vito, jt. auth. see Thornton, Peter A.

Colangelo, Vito J. & Heiser, F. A. Analysis of Metallurgical Failures. LC 73-19773. (Science & Technology of Materials Ser.). 361p. 1974. 49.50x (ISBN 0-471-16450-X, Pub. by Wiley-Interscience). Wiley.

Colantuono, Susan L. Build Your Career: A Workbook for Advancing in an Organization. (Illus.). 94p. (Orig.). 1982. 10.00 (ISBN 0-914234-59-5). Human Res Dev.

Colao, Flora & Hosansky, Tamar. Your Children Should Know. 208p. 1985. pap. 3.50 (ISBN 0-425-07457-9). Berkley Pub.

--Your Children Should Know: Teach Your Children the Strategies That Will Keep Them Safe from Assault & Crime. LC 83-5981. (Illus.). 192p. 1983. 16.95 (ISBN 0-672-52777-4). Bobbs.

Colapinto, V., jt. auth. see McCallum, R. W.

Colarusso, C. A. & Nemiroff, R. A. Adult Development: A New Dimension in Psychodynamic Theory & Practice. (Critical Issues in Psychiatry Ser.). 320p. 1981. 24.50x (ISBN 0-306-40619-5, Plenum Pr). Plenum Pub.

Colarusso, Calvin, jt. ed. see Nemiroff, Robert A.

Colarusso, Calvin A. & Nemiroff, Robert A. Adult Development. 300p. 1981. 22.50. Da Capo.

Colasanti, Ardvino. Italian Painting of the Quattrocento in the Marches. LC 73-81681. lib. bdg. write for info. (ISBN 0-87817-141-X). Hacker.

Colasanti, G., jt. ed. see D'Amico, G.

Colasse. Lexique de Comptabilite et de Gestion. (Fr.). 1975. pap. 14.95 (ISBN 0-686-56768-4, M-6079). French & Eur.

Colasurdo, James F., jt. auth. see Weiner, Richard.

Colavita, Francis B. Sensory Changes in the Elderly. (Illus.). 152p. 1978. 18.50x (ISBN 0-398-03829-5). C C Thomas.

Colbach, Edward M. & Fosterling, Charles D. Police Social Work. 168p. 1976. 13.50x (ISBN 0-398-03505-9). C C Thomas.

Colbath, Arnold. Two Plays. 1980. pap. text ed. 5.95 (ISBN 0-913006-17-3). Puckerbrush.

Colbaugh, Lloyd N. The Gospel Behind Bars. LC 79-53942. (Radiant Life Ser.). 96p. (Orig.). 1979. pap. 1.50 (ISBN 0-88243-503-5, 02-0503). Gospel Pub.

Colbeck, John. Pottery: Techniques of Decoration. 1983. 24.95 (ISBN 0-442-21692-0). Van Nos Reinhold.

--Pottery: The Technique of Throwing. LC 69-12654. (Illus.). 144p. 1969. 19.50 (ISBN 0-8230-4250-2). Watson-Guptill.

Colbeck, Maurice. Yorkshire Moorlands. (Illus.). 160p. 1983. 18.95 (ISBN 0-7134-3803-7, Pub. by Batsford England). David & Charles.

Colbeck, Samuel C. Dynamics of Snow & Ice Masses. LC 79-17949. 1980. 55.00 (ISBN 0-12-179450-4). Acad Pr.

Colberg, Fran. Makeagames. 1974. pap. 8.50x inclds. manual & 10 game sheets (ISBN 0-87879-088-8). Acad Therapy.

Colberg, Marshall R. Social Security Retirement Test: Right or Wrong? 1978. pap. 4.25 (ISBN 0-8447-3307-5). Am Enterprise.

Colberg, Marshall R., et al. Business Economics: Principles & Cases. 6th ed. 1980. 27.95x (ISBN 0-256-02155-4). Irwin.

Colberg, Stephen. Lessons on How to Love a Crocodile. 1985. 6.50 (ISBN 0-8233-0400-0). Golden Quill.

Colbert, Edwin. Dinosaurs of the Colorado Plateau, Vol. 54, No. 2 & 3. 48p. pap. 5.00 (ISBN 0-686-46250-5). Mus Northern Ariz.

Colbert, Edwin H. Age of Reptiles. (World Naturalist Ser.). (Illus.). 1966. pap. 4.95 (ISBN 0-393-00374-4, Norton Lib). Norton.

--The Dinosaur World. LC 76-16586. (Illus.). 1977. 8.95 (ISBN 0-87396-081-5). Stravon.

--Dinosaurs: An Illustrated History. LC 82-23273. (Illus.). 224p. 1983. 30.00 (ISBN 0-8437-3332-2). Hammond Inc.

--Evolution of the Vertebrates: A History of the Backboned Animals Through Time. 3rd ed. LC 79-27621. 510p. 1980. 39.50x (ISBN 0-471-04966-2, Pub. by Wiley Interscience). Wiley.

--The Great Dinosaur Hunters & Their Discoveries. LC 84-4204. 384p. 1984. pap. 6.95 (ISBN 0-486-24701-5). Dover.

--An Outline of Vertebrate Evolution. Head, J. J., ed. LC 81-67987. (Carolina Biology Readers Ser.). (Illus.). 32p. (gr. 10 up). 1983. pap. 2.00 (ISBN 0-89278-331-1, 45-9731). Carolina Biological.

--A Primitive Ornithischian Dinosaur from the Kayenta Formation of Arizona. (MNA Bulletin Ser. No. 53). (Illus.). 1981. pap. 7.95 (ISBN 0-686-76171-5). Mus Northern Ariz.

--Wandering Lands & Animals: The Story of Continental Drift & Animal Populations. 352p. 1985. pap. 7.95 (ISBN 0-486-24918-2). Dover.

Colbert, Edwin H., jt. auth. see Kay, Marshall.

Colbert, Edwin H. & Johnson, R. Roy, eds. The Petrified Forest Through the Ages: Seventy-Fifth Anniversary Symposium. LC 84-62519. (Bulletin Ser.: No. 54). (Illus.). 104p. (Orig.). pap. 12.50 (ISBN 0-89734-056-6). Mus Northern Ariz.

Colbert, Evelyn. Southeast Asia in International Politics, 1941-1956. LC 76-28008. 384p. 1977. 39.95x (ISBN 0-8014-0971-3). Cornell U Pr.

Colbert, Evelyn S. The Left Wing in Japanese Politics. LC 73-5263. 353p. 1973. Repr. of 1952 ed. lib. bdg. 18.50x (ISBN 0-8371-6880-5, COJP). Greenwood.

Colbert, J. C., ed. Foam & Emulsion Control Agents & Processes: Recent Developments. LC 81-2364. (Chemical Technology Review: No. 188). (Illus.). 419p. 1981. 48.00 (ISBN 0-8155-0846-8). Noyes.

--Modern Coating Technology: Radiation Curing, Electrostatic, Plasma, & Laser Methods. LC 81-18900. (Chemical Technology Review: No. 201). (Illus.). 317p. 1982. 48.00 (ISBN 0-8155-0882-4). Noyes.

Colbert, Paul. Life is a Spiritual Experience. LC 82-70932. 91p. 1982. pap. 4.95 (ISBN 0-9608164-0-2). Flower Truth.

Colbert, R. W. & Hyder, William D., eds. Medallic Portraits of Adolf Hitler. (Illus.). 160p. 1981. 13.95 (ISBN 0-918492-04-1). TAMS.

Colbert, Richard P. The Seven Contemporary Tragedies of the Large Corporation. 1978. deluxe ed. 59.75x (ISBN 0-918968-17-8). Inst Econ Finan.

Colbert, W. Who Wrote That Song: Popular Songs in America & Their Composers. 1974. lib. bdg. 69.95 (ISBN 0-87700-216-9). Revisionist Pr.

Colbert-Thornton, Mollie. God's Purpose for Man: The Spirit & the Flesh. 141p. 1984. 8.95 (ISBN 0-533-05913-5). Vantage.

Colbin, Annemarie. The Book of Whole Meals: A Seasonal Guide to Assembling Balanced Vegetarian Breakfasts, Lunches & Dinners. 240p. (Orig.). 1983. pap. 7.95 (ISBN 0-345-30982-0). Ballantine.

Colbo, M. H., jt. auth. see Matthysee, J. G.

Colborn, J. G. The Thermal Structure of the Indian Ocean. (International Indian Ocean Expedition Oceanographic Monographs: No. 2). 181p. 1975. text ed. 22.00x (ISBN 0-8248-0349-3, Eastwest Ctr). UH Pr.

Colborne, Robert. Fundamentals of Merchandise Presentation. LC 82-61469. (Illus.). 208p. 1982. 18.00 (ISBN 0-911380-59-0). Signs of Times.

Colbourn, H. Trevor, ed. & intro. by see Adair, Douglass.

Colbrunn, Ethel B., jt. auth. see Allen, Eliot D.

Colburn, Alan. Squash: The Ambitious Player's Guide. 112p. 1984. pap. 9.95 (ISBN 0-571-13361-4). Faber & Faber.

Colburn, Bettye V. A Tapestry of Childhood. (Illus.). 230p. 1979. 9.00 (ISBN 0-682-49297-3). Exposition Pr FL.

Colburn, David R. Racial Change & Community Crisis: St. Augustine, Florida, 1877-1980. 320p. 1985. 27.50s (ISBN 0-231-06046-7). Columbia U Pr.

Colburn, David R. & Scher, Richard K. Florida's Gubernatorial Politics in the Twentieth Century. LC 80-10277. (Illus.). viii, 342p. 1981. 19.95 (ISBN 0-8130-0644-9). U Presses Fla.

Colburn, David R. & Pozzetta, George E., eds. America & the New Ethnicity. (National University Pubns Urban Ser.). 1979. 24.00x (ISBN 0-8046-9222-X, Pub. by Kennikat); pap. 12.00x (ISBN 0-8046-9246-7). Assoc Faculty Pr.

--Reform & Reformers in the Progressive Era. LC 82-6140. (Contributions in American History: No. 101). (Illus.). xi, 196p. 1983. lib. bdg. 29.95 (ISBN 0-313-22907-4, CRP/). Greenwood.

Colburn, David R., jt. ed. see Jacoway, Elizabeth.

Colburn, Forrest D. Paraprofesionales en Salud Rural en Guatemala. 55p. (Span.). 1981. pap. text ed. 6.45 (ISBN 0-86731-058-8). RDC Ctr Intl Stud.

Colburn, Francis. Letters Home & Further Indiscretions. 96p. 1978. 10.00 (ISBN 0-933050-00-3); pap. 6.95 (ISBN 0-933050-01-1). New Eng Pr VT.

Colburn, Frona E. Yermah the Dorado: The Story of a Lost Race. LC 76-42722. Repr. of 1913 ed. 30.00 (ISBN 0-404-60057-3). AMS Pr.

Colburn, Jeremiah, ed. see Wood, William.

Colburn, Laura. Death in a Small World. (Mystery Puzzlers: No. 23). (Illus., Orig.). 1979. pap. 1.95 (ISBN 0-89083-477-6). Zebra.

Colburn, Robert E. Fire Protection & Suppression. Williams, Carlton, ed. (Illus.). 352p. 1975. text ed. 29.95 (ISBN 0-07-011680-6, 11680-6). McGraw.

Colburn, Steven E., ed. see Sexton, Anne.

Colby, Anita Y., jt. ed. see Palmer, James C.
Colby, Averil. Patchwork. (Illus.). 202p. 1982. pap. 12.95 (ISBN 0-684-17605-X, ScribT). Scribner.
--Patchwork Quilts. 1965. 17.50 (ISBN 0-7134-3025-7, Pub. by Batsford England). David & Charles.
--Quilting. LC 73-140506. (Illus.). 1979. pap. 11.95 (ISBN 0-684-16058-7, SL839, ScribT). Scribner.
--Samplers. (Illus.). 266p. 1985. 19.95 (ISBN 0-7134-4646-3, Pub. by Batsford England). David & Charles.
Colby, Benjamin. A Guide to Health. rev. & enl. ed. 6.95 (ISBN 0-89557-013-0). Bi World Indus.
Colby, Benjamin N. Ethnic Relations in the Chiapas Highlands of Mexico. (Illus.). 1966. pap. 3.95 (ISBN 0-89013-020-5). Museum NM Pr.
Colby, Benjamin N. & Colby, Lore M. The Daykeeper: The Life & Discource of As Ixtil Dviner. (Illus.). 352p. 1981. text ed. 25.00x (ISBN 0-674-19409-8). Harvard U Pr.
Colby, Benjamin N. & Van Den Berghe, Pierre L. Ixil Country: A Plural Society in Highland Guatemala. LC 68-16740. 1969. 32.00x (ISBN 0-520-01515-0). U of Cal Pr.
Colby, C. B. Arms of Our Fighting Men: Personnel Weapons, Bazookas, Big Guns. rev. ed. (Illus.). (gr. 4-7). 1972. PLB 6.99 (ISBN 0-698-30432-2, Coward). Putnam Pub Group.
--Civil War Weapons: Small Arms, & Artillery of the Blue & Gray. (Illus.). (gr. 4-7). 1962. PLB 6.99 (ISBN 0-698-30046-7, Coward). Putnam Pub Group.
--Fighting Gear of World War One: Equipment & Weapons of the American Doughboy. (Illus.). (gr. 4-7). 1961. PLB 6.99 (ISBN 0-698-30077-7, Coward). Putnam Pub Group.
--Fighting Gear of World War Two: Equipment & Weapons of the American G. I. (Illus.). (gr. 4-7). 1961. PLB 6.99 (ISBN 0-698-30078-5, Coward). Putnam Pub Group.
--Two Centuries of Weapons: 1776-1976. LC 75-10459. (Illus.). 48p. (gr. 4-7). 1976. PLB 6.99 (ISBN 0-698-30596-5, Coward). Putnam Pub Group.
Colby, C. B., ed. Camper's & Backpacker's Bible. (Illus.). 480p. pap. 7.95 (ISBN 0-88317-033-7). Stoeger Pub Co.
Colby, Charles C. North Atlantic Arena: Water Transport in the World Order. LC 65-13062. (Illus.). 256p. 1966. 7.50x (ISBN 0-8093-0203-9). S Ill U Pr.
--Pilot Study of Southern Illinois. LC 56-8262. 108p. 1956. 7.50x (ISBN 0-8093-0005-2). S Ill U Pr.
Colby, Charles C., ed. Geographic Aspects of International Relations. facsimile ed. LC 76-99687. (Essay Index Reprint Ser.). 1938. 30.00 (ISBN 0-8369-1402-3). Ayer Co Pubs.
--Geographic Aspects of International Relations. LC 73-113283. 1970. Repr. of 1938 ed. 27.50x (ISBN 0-8046-1320-6, Pub. by Kennikat). Assoc Faculty Pr.
Colby, Constance T., intro. by see Taber, Gladys.
Colby, Curtis. Bill's Great Idea. LC 73-14590. (Adventures in the Glen Ser.). 1973. pap. 3.95 (ISBN 0-88436-023-7, 004055). EMC.
--The Fight for the Glen. LC 73-14586. (His Adventures in the Glen Ser). 1973. pap. 3.95 (ISBN 0-88436-028-8, ELA 004057). EMC.
--Goose Rescue. LC 73-14585. (Adventures in the Glen Ser.). 1973. pap. 3.95 (ISBN 0-88436-019-9, ELA 004053). EMC.
--Night Watch in the Glen. LC 73-14596. (Adventures in the Glen Ser.). 1973. pap. 3.95 (ISBN 0-88436-017-2, ELA 004052). EMC.
--Otter in Danger. LC 73-14591. (His Adventures in the Glen Ser). 1973. pap. 3.95 (ISBN 0-88436-021-0, ELA 004054). EMC.
--Wilderness Adventure. LC 73-14603. (Adventure in the Glen Ser.). 1973. pap. 3.95 (ISBN 0-88436-026-1, ELA 004056). EMC.
Colby, Douglas. As the Curtain Rises: On Contemporary British Drama 1966-1976. LC 77-92566. 103p. 1978. 15.00 (ISBN 0-8386-2194-5). Fairleigh Dickinson.
Colby, Elbridge. Early American Comedy. LC 74-5461. 1919. lib. bdg. 8.50 (ISBN 0-8414-3597-9). Folcroft.
--English Catholic Poets, Chaucer to Dryden. facs. ed. LC 67-28733. (Essay Index Reprint Ser.). 1936. 18.00 (ISBN 0-8369-0321-8). Ayer Co Pubs.
--The National Guard of the United States: A Half Century of Progress. 369p. 1977. pap. text ed. 36.00x (ISBN 0-89126-037-4). MA-AH Pub.
--Theodore Winthrop. (Twayne's United States Authors Ser). 1965. pap. 5.95x (ISBN 0-8084-0296-X, T84, Twayne). New Coll U Pr.
Colby, Elbridge, ed. see Holcroft, Thomas.
Colby, F., jt. auth. see Romain, E.
Colby, Frank M. Constrained Attitudes. facs. ed. LC 68-8449. (Essay Index Reprint Ser.). 1968. Repr. of 1910 ed. 17.00 (ISBN 0-8369-0322-6). Ayer Co Pubs.
--Imaginary Obligations. facs. ed. LC 76-128223. (Essay Index Reprint Ser). 1904. 19.00 (ISBN 0-8369-1870-3). Ayer Co Pubs.
Colby, Gerald. Du Pont Dynasty: Behind the Nylon Curtain. 960p. 1954. 30.00 (ISBN 0-8184-0352-7). Lyle Stuart.
Colby, J. Rose. Literature & Life in School. (Educational Ser.). 1906. Repr. 10.00 (ISBN 0-8482-3580-0). Norwood Edns.
Colby, Jennifer. Birds & Animals in Cross-Stitch: 41 Charted Designs of Lovebirds, Koalas, Angelfish, Butterflies & Other Colorful Creatures. (Embroidery, Needlepoint, Charted Designs Ser.). 48p. (Orig.). 1983. pap. 2.50 (ISBN 0-486-24573-X). Dover.
Colby, Joan. Blue Woman Dancing in the Nerve. LC 79-22754. 1979. pap. 3.50 (ISBN 0-934184-02-X). Alembic Pr.
--How the Sky Begins to Fall. 64p. 1982. pap. 4.50 (ISBN 0-933180-32-2). Spoon Riv Poetry.
Colby, John H., ed. Littleton: Crossroads of Northern New Hampshire. LC 84-4941. 702p. 1984. 34.95 (ISBN 0-914659-03-0). Phoenix Pub.
Colby, John K. A Latin Crossword Puzzle Book. (gr. 9-12). text ed. 2.00x (ISBN 0-88334-045-3). Ind Sch Pr.
--Latin Word Lists. 1978. pap. text ed. 2.25x (ISBN 0-88334-097-6). Ind Sch Pr.
--Lively Latin. (gr. 8-10). 1971. pap. text ed. 3.75x (ISBN 0-88334-035-6). Ind Sch Pr.
--Review Latin Grammar. (gr. 8-10). 1971. pap. text ed. 3.50x (ISBN 0-88334-034-8). Ind Sch Pr.
Colby, John K., jt. auth. see Buehner, William J.
Colby, K. M. Artificial Paranoia: A Computer Simulation of Paranoid Processes. 1975. pap. text ed. 10.75 (ISBN 0-08-018161-9). Pergamon.
Colby, Kenneth M. Primer for Psychotherapists. 167p. 1951. 25.50 (ISBN 0-471-06901-9, Pub. by Wiley-Interscience). Wiley.
Colby, Kenneth M. & Spar, James E. The Fundamental Crisis in Psychiatry: Unreliability of Diagnosis. (Illus.). 246p. 1983. 24.75x (ISBN 0-398-04788-X). C C Thomas.
Colby, Kenneth M., jt. ed. see Schank, Roger C.
Colby, Lore M., jt. auth. see Colby, Benjamin N.
Colby, Marvelle S. Test Your Management I. Q. 128p. 1984. 5.95 (ISBN 0-671-49366-3). Monarch Pr.
Colby, Marvelle S., jt. auth. see Straughn, Charles T.
Colby, P. J. & McNicol, R. E. Synopsis of Biological Data on the Walleye: Stizostedion V. Vitreum (Mitchell 1818) (Fisheries Synopses: No. 119). (Illus.). 147p. 1979. pap. 11.75 (ISBN 92-5-100757-8, F1622, FAO). Unipub.
Colby, Peter W., ed. New York State Today: Politics, Government, Public Policy. 416p. 1984. lib. bdg. 34.50 (ISBN 0-87395-960-4); pap. text ed. 12.95 (ISBN 0-87395-961-2). State U NY Pr.
Colby, Robert A. Thackeray's Canvass of Humanity: An Author & His Public. LC 78-27465. (Illus.). 1979. 25.00 (ISBN 0-8142-0282-9). Ohio St U Pr.
Colby, Robert A., jt. auth. see Colby, Vineta.
Colby, Robert W. Auditing Practice Manual. 1984. 295.00 (ISBN 0-88712-135-7). Warren.
Colby, Roy. The War of Words. LC 83-82792. 256p. 1985. 8.95 (ISBN 0-87319-029-7). C Hallberg.
Colby, Thomas E., 3rd, ed. see Hesse, Hermann.
Colby, Vineta. The Singular Anomaly: Women Novelists of the Nineteenth Century. LC 70-92522. (Gotham Library). 1970. 30.00x (ISBN 0-8147-0096-9). NYU Pr.
Colby, Vineta & Colby, Robert A. Equivocal Virtue: Mrs. Oliphant & the Victorian Literary Marketplace. LC 66-12770. Repr. of 1966 ed. 56.10 (ISBN 0-8357-9582-9, 2015413). Bks Demand UMI.
Colby, Vineta, jt. ed. see Kunitz, Stanley J.
Colby, W. E. A Century of Transportation in Shasta County 1821-1920. (ANCRR Occasional Paper: No. 7). 105p. 1982. 7.50 (ISBN 0-686-38931-X). Assn NC Records.
Colchie, Elizabeth S. Ready When You Are: Company Food That's a Fete Accomplie. (Illus.). 352p. 1982. 15.95 (ISBN 0-517-54367-2). Crown.
Colchie, Elizabeth S., jt. auth. see Witty, Helen.
Colchie, Thomas, tr. see Angelo, Ivan.
Colchie, Thomas, tr. see Puig, Manuel.
Colchie, Thomas, tr. see Rubiao, Murilo.
Colclaser, R. A. & Nagle, S. D. Materials & Devices for Electrical Engineers & Physicists. 304p. 1984. 36.50 (ISBN 0-07-011693-8). McGraw.
Colclaser, Roy A. Microelectronics Process & Device Design. 333p. 1980. 39.45 (ISBN 0-471-04339-7); solutions manual 8.50 (ISBN 0-471-08709-2). Wiley.
Colclaser, Roy A., et al. Electronic Circuit Analysis: Basic Principles. LC 83-21743. 574p. 1984. text ed. 39.50 (ISBN 0-471-86626-1). Wiley.
Colclasure, Chuck. Proverbs, God's Powerhouse of Wisdom. 1981. pap. 2.50 (ISBN 0-8423-4928-6). Tyndale.
Colclough, Christopher. Primary Schooling & Economic Development: A Review of the Evidence. (World Bank Staff Working Paper: No. 399). 31p. 1980. pap. 3.00 (ISBN 0-686-39726-6, WP-0399). World Bank.
Colclough, Christopher & McCarthy, Stephen. The Politocal Economy of Botswana: A Study of Growth & Distribution. (Illus.). 1980. 39.95x (ISBN 0-19-877136-3). Oxford U Pr.
Colcord, Joanna C. Sea Language Comes Ashore. Dorsen, Richard M., ed. (International Folklore Ser.). 1977. Repr. of 1945 ed. lib. bdg. 17.00x (ISBN 0-405-10089-2). Ayer Co Pubs.
--Sea Language Comes Ashore. LC 45-966. 222p. 1945. pap. 5.00 (ISBN 0-87033-095-0). Cornell Maritime.
Colcord, Lincoln. Game of Life & Death. facsimile ed. LC 76-106270. (Short Story Index Reprint Ser). 1914. 18.00 (ISBN 0-8369-3307-9). Ayer Co Pubs.
--An Instrument of the Gods: And Other Stories of the Sea, Vol. 1. LC 72-5863. (Short Story Index Reprint Ser). Repr. of 1922 ed. 23.50 (ISBN 0-8369-4202-7). Ayer Co Pubs.
Cold Spring Harbor, N. Y., Biological Laboratory. Cold Spring Harbor Symposia on Quantitative Biology, 11 vols, Vols. 1-8 & 10-12. Repr. of 1933 ed. Set. 295.00 (ISBN 0-384-09523-2); 27.00 ea. Johnson Repr.
Cold Spring Harbor Symposia On Quantitative Biology. Heredity & Variation in Microorganisms: Proceedings, Vol. 11. Repr. of 1946 ed. 27.00 (ISBN 0-384-22475-X). Johnson Repr.
--Nucleic Acids & Nucleoproteins: Proceedings, Vol. 12. Repr. of 1947 ed. 27.00 (ISBN 0-384-42250-0). Johnson Repr.
--Relation of Hormones to Development: Proceedings, Vol. 10. Repr. of 1942 ed. 27.00 (ISBN 0-384-50250-4). Johnson Repr.
Colden, Cadwallader. The History of the Five Indian Nations. 250p. 1958. pap. 6.95x (ISBN 0-8014-9086-3, CP86). Cornell U Pr.
--The History of the Five Indian Nations of Canada Which Are Dependent on the Province of New York, & Are a Barrier Between the English & the French. LC 72-2827. (American Explorers Ser.). Repr. of 1922 ed. 55.00 (ISBN 0-404-54908-X). AMS Pr.
--The Letters & Papers of Cadwallader Colden: New-York Historical Society Collections 1917-23, 1934, 1935, 9 vols. LC 19-15059. 60.00x set (ISBN 0-685-73909-0). U Pr of Va.
--Letters & Papers of Cadwallader Colden, 1711-1775, 9 vols. LC 72-996. Repr. of 1937 ed. Set. 270.00 (ISBN 0-404-01690-1). AMS Pr.
Colden, J. Botanic Manuscript. Rickett, H. W. & Hall, E. C., eds. (Illus.). 1963. 10.00 (ISBN 0-934454-15-9). Lubrecht & Cramer.
Coldham, Margaret, jt. auth. see Cyriax, James.
Coldham, Peter W. American Loyalist Claims, No. 45. LC 80-8609. 615p. 25.50 (ISBN 0-915156-45-8). Natl Genealogical.
--Bonded Passengers to America, 9 vols. in 3. LC 82-83231. (Illus.). 1426p. 1983. Set. 75.00 (ISBN 0-8063-1003-0). Genealog Pub.
--English Adventurers & Emigrants, 1609-1660: Abstracts of Examinations in the High Court of Admiralty with Reference to Colonial America. LC 84-80790. 219p. 1984. 18.50 (ISBN 0-8063-1082-0). Genealog Pub.
--English Adventures & Emigrants, 1661-733: Abstracts of Examinations in the High Court of Admirality with Reference to Colonial America. LC 85-70011. 238p. 1985. 20.00 (ISBN 0-8063-1119-3). Genealog Pub.
--English Convicts in Colonial America: Vol. 1, Middlesex 1617-1775. 1975. 20.00 (ISBN 0-686-20862-5). Polyanthos.
--English Convicts in Colonial America: Vol. 2, the City of London 1656-1775. 1976. 20.00 (ISBN 0-686-20863-3). Polyanthos.
--English Estates of American Colonists: American Wills & Administrations in the Prerogative Court of Canterbury, 1610-1699. LC 80-68237. 72p. 1983. 10.00 (ISBN 0-8063-0905-9). Genealog Pub.
--English Estates of American Settlers: American Wills & Administrationsin the Prerogative Court of Canterbury, 1800-1858. LC 81-80888. 103p. 1981. 12.50 (ISBN 0-8063-0936-9). Genealog Pub.
--Lord Mayor's Court of London: Depositions Relating to Americans 1641-1736. LC 80-80349. 119p. lib. bdg. 11.00 (ISBN 0-915156-23-7, SP 44); pap. 7.00 (ISBN 0-686-27217-X). Natl Genealogical.
Coldiron, Ronn W. Possible Functions of Ornament in Labryinthodont Amphibians. (Occasional Papers: No. 33). 19p. 1974. pap. 1.25 (ISBN 0-686-79813-9). U of KS Mus Nat Hist.
Coldren, Sharon. The Constant Quest: Raising Billions Through Capital Campaigns. 1982. 12.00 (ISBN 0-02-906450-3). ACE.
Coldrey, C. Courses for Horses. new ed. 1978. 12.95 (ISBN 0-85131-305-1, BL2331, Dist. by Miller). J A Allen.
Coldrey, Jennifer. The Silkworm Story. LC 85-71250. (Illus.). 32p. (ps-3). 1985. 9.95 (ISBN 0-233-97553-5). Andre Deutsch.
Coldrey, Jenny. Penguins. (Nature's Way Ser.). (Illus.). 32p. (gr. 2-5). 1984. 9.95 (ISBN 0-233-97524-1). Andre Deutsch.
Coldrick, A. P. & Jones, Philip, eds. The International Directory of the Trade Union Movement. 1392p. 1979. lib. bdg. 55.00x (ISBN 0-87196-374-4). Facts on File.
Coldsborough, June. Little Puppy. (Shaggies Ser.). (Illus.). 12p. (ps-2). 1982. board 3.95 (ISBN 0-671-43159-5, Little Simon). S&S.
Coldsmith, Don. Daughter of the Eagle. LC 83-45564. (Double D Western Ser.). 192p. 1984. 11.95 (ISBN 0-385-18092-6). Doubleday.
--Horsin' Around Again. LC 81-67743. (Illus.). 188p. 1981. 14.00 (ISBN 0-931722-13-6); pap. 7.95 (ISBN 0-931722-14-4). Corona Pub.
--Man of the Shadows. LC 82-46078. (Double D Western Ser.). 192p. 1983. 11.95 (ISBN 0-385-18091-8). Doubleday.
--Moon of Thunder. LC 84-13516. (Double D Westerns Ser.). 192p. 1985. 11.95 (ISBN 0-385-18923-0). Doubleday.
--The Sacred Hills. LC 84-28710. (Double D Western Ser.). 1985. 12.95 (ISBN 0-385-18924-9). Doubleday.
Coldstream, J. N. Geometric Greece. LC 77-78085. (Illus.). 1977. 35.00x (ISBN 0-312-32365-4). St Martin.
Coldstream, J. N. & Huxley, G. L., eds. Kythera: Excavation & Studies Conducted by the University of Pennsylvania Museum & the British School of Athens. LC 72-87476. (Illus.). 574p. 1973. 48.00 (ISBN 0-8155-5017-0, NP). Noyes.
Coldwell, David F., ed. Virgil's Aeneid, 4 vols. Douglas, Gavin, tr. (Scottish.). 1964. Repr. of 1957 ed. 115.00 (ISBN 0-384-12439-9). Johnson Repr.
Coldwell, Lynn & Robinson, Marilyn, eds. Flood Nineteen Eighty-Three: What Happened & Why. (Illus.). 64p. 1983. pap. 7.95 (ISBN 0-910141-09-6). Kino Pubns.
Cole. Geography of the Soviet Union. 3rd ed. 1984. text ed. 29.95 (ISBN 0-408-49752-1). Butterworth.
--Harriet Lane Handbook. 10th ed. 1984. 16.50 (ISBN 0-8151-4923-9). Year Bk Med.
Cole & Foxcroft. Control of Pig Reproduction. 1982. text ed. 119.95 (ISBN 0-408-10768-5). Butterworth.
Cole, jt. auth. see Haresign.
Cole & Hallowell, eds. The Southern Political Scene 1938-1948. 1948. pap. 6.50 (ISBN 0-317-27701-4). Kallman.
Cole, et al. Where Do I Stand? Challenges in the Social Studies. (gr. 9-12). pap. 9.95 (ISBN 0-8224-9880-4). Pitman Learning.
Cole, A. J. Macro Processors. 2nd ed. LC 81-10068. (Cambridge Computer Science Texts Ser.: No. 4). 240p. 1982. 29.95 (ISBN 0-521-24259-2); pap. 14.95 (ISBN 0-521-28560-7). Cambridge U Pr.
Cole, A. J. & Morrison, R. An Introduction to Programming with S-Algol. LC 82-14568. 192p. 1983. 16.95 (ISBN 0-521-25001-3). Cambridge U Pr.
Cole, A. J., ed. Numerical Taxonomy. 1969. 55.00 (ISBN 0-12-179650-7). Acad Pr.
Cole, A. R., et al, eds. The Role of Laboratory Teaching in University Courses. 1979. text ed. 18.00 (ISBN 0-08-023914-5). Pergamon.
Cole, Adrian. Moorstones. 128p. 1984. 12.95 (ISBN 0-907349-30-7, Pub. by Salem Hse Ltd). Merrimack Pub Cir.
Cole, Alan. The Epistle of Paul to the Galatians. (Tyndale Bible Commentaries). 1964. pap. 4.95 (ISBN 0-8028-1408-5). Eerdmans.
--Gospel According to St. Mark. (Tyndale Bible Commentaries Ser.). 1962. pap. 5.95 (ISBN 0-8028-1401-8). Eerdmans.
--Introduction to the Atmosphere Lab Manual. 1980. loose leaf shrink wrapped 6.95 (ISBN 0-88252-110-1). Paladin Hse.
--Isajah Forty-Jeremiah. 1983. pap. 4.50 (ISBN 0-87508-161-4). Chr Lit.
Cole, Alexander. The Auction. 336p. 1983. pap. 3.50 (ISBN 0-515-06534-X); pap. text ed. 3.95 (ISBN 0-515-07361-X). Jove Pubns.
Cole, Allan & Bunch, Chris. The Court of a Thousand Suns. 288p. (Orig.). 1986. pap. 2.95 (ISBN 0-345-31681-9, Pub. by Del Rey). Ballantine.
--Sten. 288p. 1982. pap. 2.50 (ISBN 0-345-28503-4, Del Rey). Ballantine.
--The Wolf Worlds. 304p. 1984. pap. 2.95 (ISBN 0-345-31229-5, Del Rey). Ballantine.
Cole, Allan B. Conflict in Indo-China & International Repercussions: A Documentary History, 1945-1955. LC 56-14338. (Fletcher School Studies in International Affairs). pap. 73.80 (ISBN 0-317-08458-5, 2000570). Bks Demand UMI.
Cole, Allan Burnett, et al. Socialist Parties in Postwar Japan. LC 66-21511. (Illus.). pap. 127.00 (ISBN 0-317-09609-5, 2021989). Bks Demand UMI.
Cole, Allison. Back Toward Lisbon. 224p. 1985. 14.95 (ISBN 0-396-08708-6). Dodd.
Cole, Ann & Haas, Carolyn. Purple Cow to the Rescue. LC 82-47913. (Illus.). 160p. (gr. 1-5). 1982. 12.95 (ISBN 0-316-15104-1); pap. 8.95 (ISBN 0-316-15106-8). Little.
Cole, Ann, et al. Children Are Children Are Children: An Activity Approach to Exploring Brazil, France, Iran, Japan, Nigeria, & the U. S. S. R. (Illus.). 1978. 11.95 (ISBN 0-316-15114-9); pap. 7.95 (ISBN 0-316-15113-0). Little.
--I Saw a Purple Cow & 100 Other Recipes for Learning. (Illus.). 96p. (gr. 4 up). 1972. 9.95 (ISBN 0-316-15174-2); pap. 5.95 (ISBN 0-316-15175-0). Little.
--A Pumpkin in a Pear Tree: Creative Ideas for Twelve Months of Holiday Fun. (Illus.). 112p. (gr. 1 up). 1976. 10.95g (ISBN 0-316-15110-6); pap. 6.95 (ISBN 0-316-15111-4). Little.
Cole, Arthur C. Era of the Civil War, 1848-1870. facsimile ed. LC 72-148875. (Select Bibliographies Reprint Ser). Repr. of 1919 ed. 26.00 (ISBN 0-8369-5646-X). Ayer Co Pubs.
--Irrepressible Conflict Eighteen Fifty to Eighteen Sixty-Five. LC 71-144952. (Illus.). 1971. Repr. of 1938 ed. 59.00x (ISBN 0-403-00930-8). Scholarly.
--The Whig Party in the South. 1959. 13.25 (ISBN 0-8446-1126-3). Peter Smith.

Cole, Arthur C., ed. The Constitutional Debates of 1847. LC 20-21984. (Illinois Historical Collections Ser.: Vol. 14). 1919. 10.00 (ISBN 0-912154-25-X). Ill St Hist Lib.

Cole, Arthur H. Business Enterprise in Its Social Setting. LC 59-7649. 1959. 17.50x (ISBN 0-674-08751-8). Harvard U Pr.

--The Great Mirror of Folly. (Kress Library Publications: No. 6). 1949. pap. 8.95x (ISBN 0-678-09901-4, Baker Lib). Kelley.

--Measures of Business Change. LC 72-7502. 444p. 1974. Repr. of 1952 ed. lib. bdg. 24.75x (ISBN 0-8371-6513-X, COBC). Greenwood.

--Wholesale Commodity Prices in the United States, 1700-1861, 2 Vols in 1. (History of American Economy Ser.). 1969. Repr. of 1938 ed. 50.00 (ISBN 0-384-09530-5). Johnson Repr.

Cole, Arthur H. & Watts, George B. The Handicrafts of France As Recorded in the Description Des Arts et Metiers, 1761-1788. (Kress Library Publications: No. 8). (Illus.). 1952. pap. 8.95x (ISBN 0-678-09903-0, Baker Lib). Kelley.

Cole, Arthur H., ed. see Hamilton, Alexander.

Cole, B. C. Beyond Word Processing: How to Use Your Personal Computer As a Processor. 1985. 12.95 (ISBN 0-07-011698-9). McGraw.

Cole, B. R., jt. auth. see Hume-Rothery, W.

Cole, Babette. The Hairy Book. LC 84-11496. (Illus.). 40p. (gr. 1-7). 1985. PLB 6.99 (ISBN 0-394-97026-8, BYR); pap. 5.95 (ISBN 0-394-87026-3). Random.

--Nungu & the Hippopotamus. LC 78-12382. (Illus.). (gr. k-2). 1980. 7.95 (ISBN 0-07-011695-4). McGraw.

--The Trouble with Mom. (Illus.). 32p. (gr. k-3). 1984. 9.95 (ISBN 0-698-20597-9, Coward). Putnam Pub Group.

Cole, Barbie C., et al. William Lescaze. (Illus.). 120p. 1982. pap. 18.50 (ISBN 0-8478-0428-3). Rizzoli Intl.

Cole, Barry. Vanessa in the City. 1971. 3.75 (ISBN 0-685-27777-1, Pub. by Trigram Pr); signed 12.50 (ISBN 0-685-27778-X); pap. 1.50 (ISBN 0-685-27779-8). Small Pr Dist.

Cole, Barry, ed. Television Today: A Close-up View, Readings from TV Guide. (Galaxy Book Ser.: No. 618). 1981. pap. 12.95 (ISBN 0-19-502799-X, GB). Oxford U Pr.

Cole, Barry L. A Visual Aid to Electronics. pap. 1.25x (ISBN 0-89741-011-4). Roadrunner Tech.

Cole, Bernard D. Gunboats & Marines: The United States Navy in China, Nineteen Twenty-Five to Nineteen Twenty-Eight. LC 81-72063. (Illus.). 232p. 1982. 24.50 (ISBN 0-87413-203-7). U Delaware Pr.

Cole, Bill. John Coltrane. LC 76-14289. (Illus.). 1978. pap. 10.95 (ISBN 0-02-870500-9). Schirmer Bks.

--John Coltrane. LC 76-14289. (Illus.). 1976. 14.95 (ISBN 0-02-870660-9). Schirmer Bks.

Cole, Bonnie C. see Tennessee. Supreme Court & Michie Company.

Cole, Brenda Maudlin see Mauldin, Brenda C.

Cole, Brock. The King at the Door. LC 78-20064. (Illus.). 32p. (gr. k-3). 1979. 7.95a (ISBN 0-385-14718-X); PLB (ISBN 0-385-14719-8). Doubleday.

--No More Baths. LC 78-22790. (Illus.). 32p. (gr. 1-3). 1980. 10.95a (ISBN 0-385-14714-7); PLB (ISBN 0-385-14715-5). Doubleday.

--The Winter Wren. LC 84-1583. (Illus.). 32p. (gr. 2 up). 1984. 12.95 (ISBN 0-374-38454-1). FS&G.

Cole, Bruce. Giotto & Florentine Painting, 1280-1375. LC 75-7632. (Icon Editions). (Illus.). 1977. pap. 7.95 (ISBN 0-06-430071-4, IN71, HarpT). Har-Row.

--I Was Needled by Uncle Sam. Ashton, Sylvia, ed. LC 78-5413. cancelled (ISBN 0-87949-123-X). Ashley Bks.

--Masaccio & the Art of Early Renaissance Florence. LC 79-2601. (Illus.). 270p. 1980. 25.00x (ISBN 0-253-12298-8). Ind U Pr.

--The Renaissance Artist at Work: From Pisano to Titian. LC 82-48102. (Icon Editions). (Illus.). 208p. 1983. 20.00 (ISBN 0-06-430902-9, HarpT). Har-Row.

--Sienese Painting: From Its Origins to the Fifteenth Century. LC 79-3670. (Icon Editions Ser.). (Illus.). 224p. 1980. 25.00i (ISBN 0-06-430901-0, HarpT). Har-Row.

--Sienese Painting in the Age of the Renaissance. LC 84-48246. (Illus.). 256p. 1985. 37.50x (ISBN 0-253-18130-5). Ind U Pr.

Cole, Bruce, jt. ed. see Thompson, Norma H.

Cole, C. Donald. Basic Christian Faith. LC 84-72008. 256p. (Orig.). 1985. pap. 6.95 (ISBN 0-89107-338-8). Good News.

--Christian Perspectives on Controversial Issues. 128p. (Orig.). 1983. pap. 2.95 (ISBN 0-8024-0165-1). Moody.

--Have I Committed the Unpardonable Sin? And Other Questions You Were Afraid to Ask about the Christian Faith. LC 84-71421. 128p. 1984. pap. 5.95 (ISBN 0-89107-317-5, Crossway Bks). Good News.

--I Believe... 160p. 1983. pap. 3.95 (ISBN 0-8024-0353-0). Moody.

Cole, C. McCall. Left Handed Hunter-Shadow at Jackson Hole. 1980. pap. 2.25 (ISBN 0-8439-0715-0, Leisure Bks). Dorchester Pub Co.

Cole, C. Robert & Moody, Michael E., eds. The Dissenting Tradition: Essays for Leland H. Carlson. LC 74-27706. xxiii, 272p. 1975. 17.00x (ISBN 0-8214-0176-9, 82-81735). Ohio U Pr.

Cole, Carole O., jt. auth. see McIntosh, Carol P.

Cole, Charles A., ed. Memorials of Henry V, King of England. (Rolls Ser.: No. 11). Repr. of 1858 ed. 44.00 (ISBN 0-317-16658-1). Kraus Repr.

Cole, Charles B. Tool Design: Fundamental Principles of Design as Applied to Tooling for Production. LC 41-19998. (Illus.). pap. 148.80 (ISBN 0-317-11004-7, 2004574). Bks Demand UMI.

Cole, Charles C., Jr. Social Ideas of the Northern Evangelists, Eighteen Twenty-Six to Eighteen Sixty. 1966. lib. bdg. 20.50x (ISBN 0-374-91843-0). Octagon.

Cole, Charles E., ed. Something More Than Human: Biographies of Leaders in American Methodist Higher Education. (Illus.). 300p. 1985. 9.95 (ISBN 0-317-18293-5). United Meth Educ.

Cole, Charles J., jt. auth. see Hardy, Laurence M.

Cole, Charles W. French Mercantilism, 1683-1700. 1965. lib. bdg. 23.00x (ISBN 0-374-91824-4). Octagon.

--French Mercantilist Doctrines Before Colbert. LC 79-96178. 1970. Repr. of 1931 ed. lib. bdg. 19.00x (ISBN 0-374-91805-8). Octagon.

Cole, Christopher & Cheesman, E. F. The Air Defence of Britain, 1914-18. (A Putnam Aeronautical Bk.). (Illus.). 416p. 1984. 35.00 (ISBN 0-370-30538-8, Pub. by the Bodley Head). Merrimack Pub Cir.

Cole, Claire G., jt. auth. see Hutchins, David E.

Cole, Clara. Basic Needs. (Social Studies). 24p. (gr. 2-3). 1977. wkbk. 5.00 (ISBN 0-8209-0259-4, SS-26). ESP.

--Personal Health. (Health Ser.). 24p. (gr. 4-9). 1979. wkbk. 5.00 (ISBN 0-8209-0346-9, H-7). ESP.

Cole, Clifford A. The Mighty Act of God. 192p. 1984. pap. text ed. 12.00 (ISBN 0-8309-0393-3). Herald Hse.

Cole, Clifford A., jt. auth. see Judd, Peter A.

Cole, Clifford A., ed. The Priesthood Manual. rev. ed. LC 81-7220. 1985. 12.00 (ISBN 0-8309-0420-4). Herald Hse.

Cole, D. J., ed. Pig Production. LC 70-38754. (Illus.). 434p. 1972. 32.50x (ISBN 0-271-01114-9). Pa St U Pr.

Cole, D. J. & Haresign, W., eds. Recent Developments in Pig Nutrition. 336p. 1985. pap. text ed. 25.95 (ISBN 0-407-00339-8). Butterworth.

Cole, D. J., jt. ed. see Haresign, W.

Cole, David. The Theatrical Event: A "Mythos," a Vocabulary, a Perspective. LC 74-21922. (Illus.). 1975. 16.00x (ISBN 0-8195-4078-1); pap. 9.00x (ISBN 0-8195-6047-2). Wesleyan U Pr.

--The Work of Sir Gilbert Scott. (Illus.). 256p. 1980. 60.00 (ISBN 0-85139-723-9). Eastview.

Cole, David & Kostelanetz, Richard, eds. Eleventh Assembling: Pilot Proposals. LC 81-71598. 96p. 1981. pap. 10.00 (ISBN 0-686-92630-7). Assembling Pr.

Cole, David, et al. Three Places in New Inkland. LC 77-72826. 1977. pap. 5.95 (ISBN 0-9605610-1-3). Zartscorp.

Cole, David C. & Lim, Youngil. The Korean Economy: Issues of Development. LC 79-620015. (Korean Research Monograph Ser.: No. 1). pap. 22.50 (ISBN 0-317-27747-2, 2019466). Bks Demand UMI.

Cole, David C. & Park, Yung C. Financial Development in Korea, 1945-1978. (Harvard East Asian Monographs: No. 106). 340p. 1983. text ed. 17.50x (ISBN 0-674-30147-1). Harvard U Pr.

Cole, David E., et al, eds. Strategic & Product Planning for the Automotive Industry. 1981. 12.00 (ISBN 0-938654-30-6). Indus Dev Inst Sci.

Cole, David L. The Quest for Industrial Peace. LC 77-26873. (Meyer Kestnbaum Lectures). 1978. Repr. of 1962 ed. lib. bdg. 17.00x (ISBN 0-313-20072-6, COQI). Greenwood.

Cole, David R. Helping: Origins & Development of the Major Psychotherapies. 390p. 1983. pap. 19.95x (ISBN 0-409-82407-0, NO. 5071). Methuen Inc.

Cole, Deborah D., jt. auth. see Selig, W. George.

Cole, Desmond T., et al. Lithops. LC 68-22957. (Illus.). 114p. 1968. 60.00 (ISBN 0-8386-6902-6). Fairleigh Dickinson.

Cole, Donald B. Jacksonian Democracy in New Hampshire, 1800-1851. LC 79-127878. 1970. 17.50x (ISBN 0-674-46990-9). Harvard U Pr.

--Martin Van Buren & the American Politcal System. (Illus.). 256p. 1984. 45.00x (ISBN 0-691-04715-4). Princeton U Pr.

Cole, Donald B. & Blum, John M. Handbook of American History. (Illus.). 337p. (Orig.). 1968. pap. text ed. 13.95 (ISBN 0-15-530830-0, HC). HarBraceJ.

Cole, Donald B. & Cornell, Robert H., eds. Respecting the Pupil, Essays on Teaching Able Students by Members of the Faculty of Phillips Exeter Academy. 2nd 1984 ed. LC 81-81104. (Illus.). 132p. 1981. pap. 6.95 (ISBN 0-939618-01-X). Phillips Exeter.

Cole, Donald P. Nomads of the Nomads: The Al Murrah Bedouin of the Empty Quarter. LC 74-18211. (Worlds of Man Ser.). 192p. 1975. pap. 8.95x (ISBN 0-88295-605-1). Harlan Davidson.

Cole, Donald W. Professional Suicide. 256p. 1980. 19.95 (ISBN 0-07-011697-0). McGraw.

Cole, Dora J. & Wichman, Juliet R. Early Kauai Hospitality: A Family Cookbook of Receipts, 1820-1920. 1977. 12.00 (ISBN 0-686-86235-X). Kauai Museum.

Cole, Doris. Eleanor Raymond, Architect. LC 80-67474. (Illus.). 160p. 1981. 35.00 (ISBN 0-87982-036-5). Art Alliance.

--From Tipi to Skyscraper: A History of Women in Architecture. 1978. pap. 6.95x (ISBN 0-262-53033-3). MIT Pr.

Cole, Douglas. Captured Heritage: The Scramble for the Northwest Coast Artifacts. LC 84-40674. (Illus.). 336p. 1985. 17.50 (ISBN 0-295-96215-1). U of Wash Pr.

Cole, Douglas, ed. Renaissance Drama New Series XI. LC 67-29872. 211p. 1981. 24.95 (ISBN 0-8101-0546-2). Northwestern U Pr.

Cole, Duane. Conquest of Lines & Symmetry: Aerobatics. pap. 6.95x (ISBN 0-911721-41-X, Pub. by Cole). Aviation.

--Happy Flying, Safely. LC 77-79892. (Illus.). 1977. pap. 6.95x (ISBN 0-911721-19-3, Pub. by Cole). Aviation.

--Roll Around a Point: Aerobatics. pap. 6.95x (ISBN 0-911721-28-2, Pub. by Cole). Aviation.

Cole, E. R. Ding an Sich: Anapoems. LC 85-80051. 72p. 1985. 12.95 (ISBN 0-934553-02-5). Wainwright PA.

Cole, E. V., jt. auth. see Pruett, Jakie L.

Cole, Eddie C. Now Techniques for Today's Poets. 76p. 1977. pap. 10.95 (ISBN 0-317-17453-3). World Poetry Pr.

Cole, Eddie L. The Family Treasury of Great Poems. 256p. 1982. 39.95 (ISBN 0-317-17452-5). World Poetry Pr.

Cole, Eddie-Lou, ed. Best-Loved Contemporary Poems. 39.95 (ISBN 0-317-29086-X). World Poetry Pr.

--Great Contemporary Poems. 25.00 (ISBN 0-317-29078-9). World Poetry Pr.

--Great Poems of the Western World. 39.95 (ISBN 0-317-29093-2). World Poetry Pr.

--The Great Treasury of World Poems. 39.95 (ISBN 0-317-29097-5). World Poetry Pr.

--Today's Best Poems. 39.95 (ISBN 0-317-29091-6). World Poetry Pr.

--World Treasury of Great Poems. 39.95 (ISBN 0-317-29095-9). World Poetry Pr.

--The World's Great Contemporary Poems. 39.95 (ISBN 0-317-29100-9). World Poetry Pr.

Cole, Edward C., jt. auth. see Burris-Meyer, Harold.

Cole, Edwin L. Maximized Manhood. 176p. (Orig.). 1982. pap. text ed. 3.50 (ISBN 0-88368-107-2). Whitaker Hse.

--The Potential Principle. 144p. (Orig.). 1984. pap. 3.50 (ISBN 0-88368-144-7). Whitaker Hse.

Cole, Ethel. American Farmer. (Social Studies). 24p. (gr. 5-9). 1976. wkbk. 5.00 (ISBN 0-8209-0245-4, SS-12). ESP.

Cole, Evan T. Poems. 1985. 5.95 (ISBN 0-533-06090-7). Vantage.

Cole, Everett B., jt. auth. see Pruett, Jakie L.

Cole, F. C. Chinese Pottery in the Philippines-the Wild Tribes of Davao District, Mindanao. (Chicago Field Museum of Natural History Fieldiana Anthropology Ser). 1912-13. 41.00 (ISBN 0-527-01872-4). Kraus Repr.

--Traditions of the Tinguian, a Study in Philippine Folk-Lore: The Tinguian Social Religious & Economic Life of a Philippine Tribe. (Chicago Field Museum of Natural History Fieldiana Anthropology Ser). Repr. of 1922 ed. 51.00 (ISBN 0-527-01874-0). Kraus Repr.

Cole, F. J. A History of Comparative Anatomy: From Aristotle to the Eighteenth Century. LC 75-12173. (Illus.). 544p. 1975. pap. 8.50 (ISBN 0-486-60224-9). Dover.

--A History of Comparative Anatomy, from Aristotle to the 18th Century. (Illus.). 13.25 (ISBN 0-8446-5172-9). Peter Smith.

Cole, Fay C. Traditions of the Tinguian. LC 78-67698. (The Folktale). Repr. of 1915 ed. 22.50 (ISBN 0-404-16069-7). AMS Pr.

Cole, Fay-Cooper & Deuel, Thorne. Rediscovering Illinois: Archaeological Explorations in & Around Fulton County. (Midway Reprint Ser.). (Illus.). xvi, 296p. 1975. pap. text ed. 12.50x (ISBN 0-226-11336-1). U of Chicago Pr.

Cole, Francis J. A History of Comparative Anatomy, from Aristotle to the 18th Century. LC 75-23696. (Illus.). Repr. of 1944 ed. 42.50 (ISBN 0-404-13245-6). AMS Pr.

Cole, Frank. The Doctor's Shorthand. LC 71-132176. pap. 47.30 (ISBN 0-317-26240-8, 2052143). Bks Demand UMI.

Cole, Frank R. & Schlinger, Evert L. The Flies of Western North America. LC 68-10687. (Illus.). 1969. 95.00x (ISBN 0-520-01516-9). U of Cal Pr.

Cole, Frank W. Reservoir Engineering Manual. 2nd ed. LC 60-16853. (Illus.). 386p. 1969. 28.95x (ISBN 0-87201-779-6). Gulf Pub.

Cole, Frank W., jt. auth. see McCray, Arthur W.

Cole, Franklin P. They Preached Liberty. LC 76-26327. 1976. 5.95 (ISBN 0-913966-16-9, Liberty Pr); pap. 1.25 (ISBN 0-913966-20-7). Liberty Fund.

Cole, Franklyn W. Introduction to Meteorology. 3rd ed. LC 79-1212. 505p. 1980. text ed. 35.50 (ISBN 0-471-04705-8). Wiley.

Cole, G. Management Principles & Practice. 1980. 20.00x (ISBN 0-905435-10-9, Pub. by DP Pubns). State Mutual Bk.

Cole, G., ed. see Jonson, Ben.

Cole, G. A. Management: Theory & Practice. 450p. 1982. 35.00x (ISBN 0-905435-26-5, Pub. by DP Pubns). State Mutual Bk.

Cole, G. D. Guild Socialism Restated. (Social Science Classics Ser.). 224p. 1980. text ed. 29.95 (ISBN 0-87855-386-X); pap. text ed. 6.95 (ISBN 0-87855-817-9). Transaction Bks.

--Labour in the Coal-Mining Industry (1914-1921) (Economic & Social History of the World War, British Ser.). 1923. 75.00x (ISBN 0-317-27503-8). Elliots Bks.

--The Next Ten Years in British Social & Economic Policy. Leventhal, F. M., ed. (English Workers & the Coming of the Welfare State Ser., 1918-1945). 459p. 1985. lib. bdg. 55.00 (ISBN 0-8240-7607-9). Garland Pub.

--Politics & Literature. LC 73-1577. 1973. Repr. of 1929 ed. lib. bdg. 15.00 (ISBN 0-8414-1806-3). Folcroft.

--The Post-War Condition of Britain. LC 75-2625. 483p. 1975. Repr. of 1956 ed. lib. bdg. 22.50x (ISBN 0-8371-8043-0, COPC). Greenwood.

--Samuel Butler. LC 75-43778. 1976. lib. bdg. 10.00 (ISBN 0-8414-3619-3). Folcroft.

--Social Theory. 1920. 15.00 (ISBN 0-8482-3597-5). Norwood Edns.

--William Cobbett. LC 72-13697. 1973. Repr. of 1925 ed. lib. bdg. 6.50 (ISBN 0-8414-1268-5). Folcroft.

--William Morris As a Socialist. LC 73-17131. 1960. lib. bdg. 10.00 (ISBN 0-8414-3508-1). Folcroft.

--Workshop Organization. (Economic & Social History of the World War, British Ser.). 1923. 75.00x (ISBN 0-317-27662-X). Elliots Bks.

Cole, G. D. & Cole, M. I. The Condition of Britain. 471p. 1985. lib. bdg. 55.00 (ISBN 0-8240-7608-7). Garland Pub.

Cole, G. D. & Cole, Margaret. The Murder at Crome House. LC 75-44966. (Crime Fiction Ser). 1976. Repr. of 1927 ed. lib. bdg. 21.00 (ISBN 0-8240-2361-7). Garland Pub.

Cole, G. D. & Postgate, Raymond. The Common People: Seventeen Forty-Six to Nineteen Forty-Six. 4th ed. 1961. pap. 16.95x (ISBN 0-416-67720-7, NO.2149). Methuen Inc.

Cole, G. D. & Philip, Andre, eds. A Report on the UNESCO La Breviere Seminar on Workers. (UNESCO Education Studies & Documents: No. 11). pap. 16.00 (ISBN 0-317-15998-4). Kraus Repr.

Cole, G. D., ed. see Drayton, Michael.

Cole, G. D., ed. see Morris, William.

Cole, G. H. The Physics of Planetary Interiors. 224p. 1984. 39.00 (ISBN 0-9903000-4-8, Pub. by A Hilger Techo Hse UK); pap. 17.00 (ISBN 0-9903000-8-0, Pub. by A Hilger Techo Hse UK). Heyden.

--The Structure of Planets. (Wykeham Science Ser.: No. 45). 232p. 1977. write for info. (ISBN 0-85109-610-7); pap. cancelled (ISBN 0-85109-600-X). Taylor & Francis.

Cole, G. H. & Watton, W. G. The Structure of Planets. LC 77-18646. (Wykeham Science Ser.: No. 45). 232p. 1977. 19.50x (ISBN 0-8448-1309-5). Crane-Russak Co.

Cole, G. T. & Kendrick, B. Biology of Conidial Fungi, 2 vols. 1981. Vol. 1. 49.50 (ISBN 0-12-179501-2); Vol. 2. 69.50 (ISBN 0-12-179502-0); Set. 101.50. Acad Pr.

Cole, G. W., compiled by see Church, E. D.

Cole, Garold. American Travelers in Mexico, 1821-1975: A Descriptive Bibliography. LC 76-21469. 1978. 12.50x (ISBN 0-87875-136-X). Whitston Pub.

Cole, Garold L. Travels in America: From the Voyages of Discovery to the Present: An Annotated Bibliography of Travel Articles in Periodicals, 1955-1980. LC 84-40273. 344p. 1985. 48.50x (ISBN 0-8061-1791-5). U of Okla Pr.

Cole, Garry T. & Samson, Robert A. Patterns of Development in Conidial Fungi. (Pitman International Ser. in Bioscience). 190p. 1979. text ed. 75.95 (ISBN 0-273-08407-0). Pitman Pub MA.

Cole, George. Studies in Class Structure. LC 76-2503. 195p. 1976. Repr. of 1955 ed. lib. bdg. 22.50x (ISBN 0-8371-8779-6, COSS). Greenwood.

--Water Boundaries. (Riparian Boundaries: No. 1). (Illus.). 68p. 1984. pap. 10.00 (ISBN 0-910845-13-1, 645). Landmark Ent.

Cole, George D. Attempts at General Union: A Study in British Trade Union History, 1818-1834. LC 78-20457. 1980. Repr. of 1953 ed. 21.45 (ISBN 0-88355-836-X). Hyperion Conn.

--The British Co-operative Movement in a Socialist Society. LC 76-22523. 168p. 1976. Repr. of 1951 ed. lib. bdg. 22.50x (ISBN 0-8371-9002-9, COBCM). Greenwood.

--Chartist Portraits. LC 74-22738. Repr. of 1941 ed. 23.00 (ISBN 0-404-58490-X). AMS Pr.

--Economic Planning. LC 79-137935. (Economic Thought, History & Challenge Ser). 1971. Repr. of 1935 ed. 27.50 (ISBN 0-8046-1440-7, Pub. by Kennikat). Assoc Faculty Pr.

--Essays in Social Theory. LC 78-14118. 1979. Repr. of 1950 ed. 21.00 (ISBN 0-88355-783-5). Hyperion Conn.

--Fabian Socialism. 164p. 1971. Repr. of 1943 ed. 27.50x (ISBN 0-7146-1553-6, F Cass Co). Biblio Dist.

--Labour in the Commonwealth: Book for the Younger Generation. facsimile ed. LC 75-157330. (Select Bibliographies Reprint Ser). Repr. of 1918 ed. 16.00 (ISBN 0-8369-5790-3). Ayer Co Pubs.

--Life of Robert Owen. 349p. 1965. 30.00x (ISBN 0-7146-1464-5, F Cass Co). Biblio Dist.

--Persons & Periods. LC 73-75412. Repr. of 1938 ed. 27.50x (ISBN 0-678-00495-1). Kelley.

--Persons & Periods: Studies. facs. ed. LC 67-26726. (Essay Index Reprint Ser). 1938. 18.00 (ISBN 0-8369-0323-4). Ayer Co Pubs.

--Self-Government in Industry. facsimile ed. LC 71-152979. (Select Bibliographies Reprint Ser). Repr. of 1918 ed. 21.00 (ISBN 0-8369-5731-8). Ayer Co Pubs.

--Studies in World Economics. facs. ed. LC 67-23195. (Essay Index Reprint Ser). 1934. 18.00 (ISBN 0-8369-0324-2). Ayer Co Pubs.

--What Marx Really Meant. LC 79-90489. Repr. of 1934 ed. lib. bdg. 19.25x (ISBN 0-8371-3082-4, COWM). Greenwood.

Cole, George F. The American System of Criminal Justice. 3rd. ed. LC 82-43092. (Criminal Justice Ser.). 500p. 1982. text ed. 22.00 pub net (ISBN 0-534-01178-0). Brooks-Cole.

--The American System of Criminal Justice. 4th ed. (Criminal Justice Ser.). 576p. 1985. text ed. 30.50 (pub net) (ISBN 0-534-05226-6). Brooks-Cole.

--Criminal Justice: Law & Politics. 4th ed. LC 83-7501. 1983. pap. text ed. 12.25 pub net (ISBN 0-534-02767-9). Brooks-Cole.

Cole, George F., et al, eds. Major Criminal Justice Systems. LC 81-9211. (Sage Focus Editions: Vol. 32). 300p. 1981. 24.00 (ISBN 0-8039-1671-X); pap. 12.00 (ISBN 0-8039-1672-8). Sage.

Cole, Gerald & Farrell, Wes. The Fondas: Portrait of a Dynasty. (Illus.). 192p. 1985. 14.95 (ISBN 0-317-29664-7). St Martin.

Cole, Gerald A. Textbook of Limnology. 3rd ed. LC 82-10607. (Illus.). 401p. 1983. text ed. 24.95 (ISBN 0-8016-1004-4). Mosby.

Cole, Ginny & Durfey, Carolyn, eds. Come to the Banquet. 200p. 1983. pap. text ed. 7.00 (ISBN 0-913991-00-7). Off Christian Fellowship.

Cole, H. A., ed. Petroleum & the Continental Shelf of Northwest Europe, Vol. 2. (Illus.). 126p. 1975. 20.50 (ISBN 0-85334-656-9, Pub. by Elsevier Applied Sci England). Elsevier.

--Petroleum & the Continental Shelf of North-West Europe, Vol. 2: Environmental Protection. LC 75-14329. 126p. 1975. 44.95x (ISBN 0-470-16483-2). Halsted Pr.

Cole, H. A., ed. see Royal Society.

Cole, H. H., ed. Introduction to Livestock Production: Including Dairy & Poultry. 2nd ed. LC 66-16377. (Illus.). 827p. 1966. 35.95 (ISBN 0-7167-0812-4). W H Freeman.

Cole, H. H. & Cupps, P. T., eds. Reproduction in Domestic Animals. 3rd ed. 1977. 53.00 (ISBN 0-12-179252-8). Acad Pr.

Cole, H. H. & Garrett, W. N., eds. Animal Agriculture: The Biology, Husbandry, & Use of Domestic Animals. 2nd ed. LC 79-18984. (Animal Science Ser.). (Illus.). 739p. 1980. text ed. 28.95 (ISBN 0-7167-1099-4). W H Freeman.

Cole, H. S. see Levine, R. & Tuft, R.

Cole, H. S. D., et al, eds. Models of Doom: A Critique of The Limits to Growth. LC 72-97037. (Illus.). 252p. (Orig.). 1973. 10.00x (ISBN 0-87663-184-7); pap. 5.00x (ISBN 0-87663-905-8). Universe.

Cole, Harold S. see Levine, R. & Tuft, R.

Cole, Harry B. The British Labour Party: A Functioning Participatory Democracy. 1977. pap. text ed. 5.75 (ISBN 0-08-021811-3). Pergamon.

Cole, Harry E. Stage Coach & Tavern Tales of the Old Northwest. Kellogg, Louise P., ed. LC 77-137353. 376p. 1972. Repr. of 1930 ed. 46.00x (ISBN 0-8103-3073-3). Gale.

Cole, Henderson, ed. Instrumentation for Tomorrow's Crystallography. (Transactions of the American Crystallographic Association Ser.: Vol. 12). 146p. 1976. pap. 15.00 (ISBN 0-686-60382-6). Polycrystal Bk Serv.

Cole, Henry, tr. see Luther, Martin.

Cole, Henry P. Process Education: The New Direction for Elementary-Secondary Schools. LC 79-178843. 288p. 1972. 26.95 (ISBN 0-87778-030-7). Educ Tech Pubns.

Cole, Henry P., et al. Measuring Learning in Continuing Education for Engineers & Scientists. LC 83-11392. 144p. 1984. lib. bdg. 55.00 (ISBN 0-89774-075-0). Oryx Pr.

Cole, Herbert. Heraldry & Floral Forms As Used in Decoration. LC 74-164180. (Tower Bks). (Illus.). 248p. 1971. Repr. of 1922 ed. 46.00x (ISBN 0-8103-3913-7). Gale.

Cole, Herbert M. Mbari: Art & Life Among the Owerri Igbo. LC 80-8094. (Traditional Arts of Africa Ser.). (Illus.). 288p. 1982. 35.00x (ISBN 0-253-30397-4). Ind U Pr.

Cole, Herbert M. & Aniakor, Chike C. Igbo Arts: Community & Cosmos. LC 84-51463. (Illus.). 256p. (Orig.). 1984. text ed. 30.00 (ISBN 0-930741-00-5); pap. text ed. 17.50 (ISBN 0-930741-01-3). UCLA Mus Hist.

Cole, Herbert M., ed. & intro. by. I Am Not Myself: The Art of African Masquerade. LC 84-62940. (Monograph Ser.: No. 26). (Illus.). 112p. (Orig.). 1985. 18.00 (ISBN 0-930741-02-1). UCLA Mus Hist.

Cole, Herbert M., jt. ed. see Fraser, Douglas.

Cole, Hilary. My Darling Detective. (To Have & to Hold Ser.: No. 34). 192p. 1984. pap. 1.95 (ISBN 0-515-07836-0). Jove Pubns.

--The Sweetheart Trust. (Second Chance At Love Ser.: No. 290). 192p. 1985. pap. 2.25 (ISBN 0-425-08512-0). Berkley Pub.

Cole, Howard. Formation Badges of World War II: Britain, Commonwealth & Empire. (Illus.). 192p. 1985. 14.95 (ISBN 0-85368-078-7, Pub. by Arms & Armour). Sterling.

Cole, Howard, ed. Tables of Wavenumbers for the Calibration of Infrared Spectrometers, Vol. 9. 2nd ed. 1977. text ed. 44.00 (ISBN 0-08-021247-6). Pergamon.

Cole, Howard C. The All's Well Story from Boccaccio to Shakespeare. LC 81-2474. 192p. 1981. 13.50x (ISBN 0-252-00883-9). U of Ill Pr.

--Quest of Inquirie: Some Contexts of Tudor Literature. LC 73-91621. 1973. text ed. 39.50x (ISBN 0-672-53583-1). Irvington.

Cole, Howard N. Coronation & Royal Commemorative Medals 1887-1977. 68p. 1981. 25.00x (ISBN 0-903754-11-8, Pub. by Picton England). State Mutual Bk.

Cole, Hubert. Josephine. 1979. pap. 1.95 (ISBN 0-505-51351-X, Pub. by Tower Bks). Dorchester Pub Co.

--The Wars of the Roses. 1979. 11.95x (ISBN 0-8464-0099-5). Beekman Pubs.

Cole, Hugo. Sounds & Signs: Aspects of Musical Notation. 1974. pap. 7.50x (ISBN 0-19-317105-8). Oxford U Pr.

Cole, Hunter, jt. ed. see Wells, Dean F.

Cole, I., jt. auth. see Pritchard, J. A.

Cole, J. A. Prince of Spies. LC 83-20793. (Illus.). 192p. 1984. 19.95 (ISBN 0-571-13233-2). Faber & Faber.

Cole, J. A., tr. see Yang, et al.

Cole, J. D., jt. auth. see Kevorkian, J.

Cole, J. David, jt. auth. see Watson, Virginia D.

Cole, J. F. see Chapman, R. W.

Cole, J. O., et al, eds. Depression: Biology, Psychodynamics, & Treatment. LC 77-13161. (Illus.). 262p. 1977. 35.00x (ISBN 0-306-31062-7, Plenum Pr). Plenum Pub.

Cole, J. P. The Development Gaps: A Spatial Analysis of World Poverty & Inequality. LC 80-40284. 454p. 1981. 59.95x (ISBN 0-471-27796-7, Pub. by Wiley-Interscience). Wiley.

--Geography of World Affairs. 1959. 10.00 (ISBN 0-686-17720-7). Quest Edns.

--Geography of World Affairs. 6th ed. (Illus.). 288p. 1983. pap. text ed. 29.95 (ISBN 0-408-10842-8). Butterworth.

Cole, J. W. Perry. ANSI FORTRAN IV with FORTRAN 77 Extensions: A Sructured Programming Approach. 2nd ed. 720p. 1983. pap. write for info. (ISBN 0-697-08172-9); instr's. manual avail. (ISBN 0-697-08177-X). Wm C Brown.

Cole, Jack. Walk Softly on the Green. LC 80-52463. 288p. 1981. 8.95 (ISBN 0-938556-00-2). Taugus Hse.

Cole, Jack & Cole, Martha. Language Lessons for the Special Education Classroom. LC 82-24469. 224p. 1983. looseleaf 39.95 (ISBN 0-89443-932-4). Aspen Systems.

Cole, Jack, et al. Executive Selection. 63p. 1983. pap. 7.50x (ISBN 0-88035-031-8). Human Kinetics.

Cole, Jack T., jt. auth. see Cole, Martha L.

Cole, Jacquelyn M. & Cole, Maurice F. Advisory Councils: A Theoretical & Practical Guide for Program Planners. (Illus.). 224p. 1983. text ed. 24.95 (ISBN 0-13-018184-6). P-H.

Cole, James H. The People Versus the Taipings: Bao Lisheng's "Righteous Army of Dongan". (China Research Monographs: No. 21). 72p. 1981. pap. 6.00x (ISBN 0-912966-39-4). IEAS.

Cole, James K., ed. Nebraska Symposium on Motivation, 1971. LC 53-11655. (Nebraska Symposia on Motivation Ser: Vol. 19). xii, 304p. 1972. 23.50x (ISBN 0-8032-0613-5); pap. 5.50x (ISBN 0-8032-5619-1). U of Nebr Pr.

Cole, James K. & Dienstbier, Richard A., eds. Nebraska Symposium on Motivation, 1973: Human Sexuality. LC 53-11655. (Nebraska Symposia on Motivation Ser: Vol. 21). (Illus.). xvi, 323p. 1974. 24.95x (ISBN 0-8032-0615-1); pap. 6.50x (ISBN 0-8032-5621-3). U of Nebr Pr.

Cole, James K & Jensen, Donald D., eds. Nebraska Symposium on Motivation, 1972. LC 53-11655. (Nebraska Symposia on Motivation Ser: Vol. 20). xiv, 343p. 1973. 24.50x (ISBN 0-8032-0614-3); pap. 6.95x (ISBN 0-8032-5620-5). U of Nebr Pr.

Cole, James K. & Sonderegger, Theo B., eds. Nebraska Symposium on Motivation, 1974: Brain Research. LC 53-11655. (Nebraska Symposia on Motivation Ser: Vol. 22). xviii, 310p. 1975. 23.95x (ISBN 0-8032-0617-8); pap. 6.95x (ISBN 0-8032-5622-1). U of Nebr Pr.

Cole, James K., jt. ed. see Spaulding, William D.

Cole, James S. Technological Innovations in the 80's. (American Assembly Ser.). 192p. 1984. 12.95 (ISBN 0-13-902123-X); pap. 6.95 (ISBN 0-13-902115-9). P-H.

Cole, James W., jt. auth. see Baldus, David C.

Cole, Jean M. Exile in the Wilderness: The Life of Chief Factor Archibald McDonald, 1790-1853. LC 79-5361. (Illus.). 288p. 1980. 22.50x (ISBN 0-295-95704-2). U of Wash Pr.

Cole, Jeffrey A. The Potosi Mita, 1573-1700: Compulsory Indian Labor in the Andes. LC 84-40331. (Illus.). 224p. 1985. 35.00x (ISBN 0-8047-1256-5). Stanford U Pr.

Cole, Jerryne, jt. auth. see Potter, Louise.

Cole, Jim. Controllers-A View of Our Responsibility. 1971. pap. 2.75 (ISBN 0-9601200-2-5). J Cole.

--The Controllers: A View of Our Responsibility. (Illus.). 1971. pap. 2.75 (ISBN 0-88310-004-5). Publishers Consult.

--The Facade-a View of Our Behavior. 1970. pap. 2.75 (ISBN 0-9601200-1-7). J Cole.

--The Facade: A View of Our Behavior. (Illus.). 64p. 1970. pap. 2.75 (ISBN 0-88310-003-7). Publishers Consult.

--Fifty More Programs in BASIC for the Home, School & Office. 96p. (Orig.). 1981. pap. 9.95 (ISBN 0-86668-003-9). ARCsoft.

--Fifty Programs in BASIC for the Home, School & Office. 2nd ed. (Illus.). 96p. 1981. pap. 9.95 (ISBN 0-86668-502-2). ARCsoft.

--Forty-four Programs for the TRS-80 Model 100 Portable Computer. 96p. 1983. 8.95 (ISBN 0-86668-034-9). ARCsoft.

--The Helpers-a View of Our Helpfulness. 1973. pap. 3.25 (ISBN 0-9601200-3-3). J Cole.

--The Helpers: A View of Our Helpfulness. (Illus.). 1973. pap. 3.25 (ISBN 0-88310-005-3). Publishers Consult.

--The Holder-A View of Our Relationship. 1975. pap. 3.75 (ISBN 0-9601200-4-1). J Cole.

--Holder: A View of Our Relationships. (Illus.). pap. 3.95 (ISBN 0-88310-006-1). Publishers Consult.

--Holding in: A View of Anger. 1985. pap. 4.75 (ISBN 0-9601200-5-X). J Cole.

--Murder in the Mansion & Other Computer Adventures. 2nd ed. (Illus.). 96p. (Pocket BASIC for the TRS-80). 1981. pap. 6.95 (ISBN 0-86668-501-4). ARCsoft.

--Ninety-Nine Tips & Tricks for the New Pocket Computers. 128p. (Orig.). 1982. pap. 7.95 (ISBN 0-86668-019-5). ARCsoft.

--One Hundred One Pocket Computer Programming Tips & Tricks. (Illus.). 128p. (Orig.). 1982. pap. 7.95 (ISBN 0-86668-004-7). ARCsoft.

--Pocket Computer Program Writing Workbook. 96p. 1983. 4.95 (ISBN 0-86668-817-X). ARCsoft.

--Pocket Computer Programming Made Easy. (Illus.). 128p. (Orig.). 1982. pap. 8.95 (ISBN 0-86668-009-8). ARCsoft.

--Practical PC-2-PC-1500 Pocket Computer Programs. 96p. 1983. 7.95 (ISBN 0-86668-028-4). Arcsoft.

--Thirty-Five Practical Programs for the Casio Pocket Computer. (Illus.). 96p. Date not set. 8.95 (ISBN 0-86668-014-4). ARCsoft.

Cole, Jim E. & Griffin, David E. Notes Worth Noting: Notes Used in AACR2 Serials Cataloging. LC 84-60637. (Current Issues in Serials Management Ser.: No. 4). 128p. 1984. 12.50 (ISBN 0-87650-181-1). Pierian.

Cole, Joan. A Lenten Journey with Jesus. 48p. 1982. pap. 1.50 (ISBN 0-89243-172-5). Liguori Pubns.

--Our Hearts Wait: Daily Prayer for Advent. 48p. 1984. pap. 1.50 (ISBN 0-89243-215-2). Liguori Pubns.

Cole, Joanna. Aren't You Forgetting Something, Fiona? LC 83-13457. (Illus.). 48p. (ps-3). 1984. 5.95 (ISBN 0-8193-1121-9). Parents.

--Best Loved Folktales of the World. LC 81-43288. (Anchor Folktale Library). 816p. 1983. pap. 8.95 (ISBN 0-385-18949-4, Anch). Doubleday.

--A Bird's Body. LC 82-6446. (Illus.). 48p. (gr. k-3). 1982. 10.25 (ISBN 0-688-01470-4); lib. bdg. 10.88 (ISBN 0-688-01471-2). Morrow.

--Cars & How They Go. LC 82-45575. (Illus.). 32p. (gr. 2-6). 1983. 10.53i (ISBN 0-690-04261-2); PLB 9.89g (ISBN 0-690-04262-0). Crowell Jr Bks.

--A Cat's Body. LC 81-22386. (Illus.). 48p. (gr. k-3). 1982. 10.25 (ISBN 0-688-01052-0). lib. bdg. 10.88 (ISBN 0-688-01054-7). Morrow.

--A Chick Hatches. (Illus.). 48p. (gr. k-3). 1976. PLB 11.88 (ISBN 0-688-32087-2). Morrow.

--The Clown-Arounds. LC 81-4662. (Illus.). 48p. (ps-3). 1981. 5.95 (ISBN 0-8193-1059-X); PLB 5.95 (ISBN 0-8193-1060-3). Parents.

--The Clown-Arounds Go on Vacation. LC 83-13480. (Illus.). 48p. (ps-3). 1984. 5.95 (ISBN 0-8193-1120-0). Parents.

--The Clown-Arounds Have a Party. LC 82-2128. (Illus.). 48p. (ps-3). 1982. 5.95 (ISBN 0-8193-1085-9); PLB 5.95 (ISBN 0-8193-1086-7). Parents.

--Cuts, Breaks, Bruises & Burns: How Your Body Heals. LC 84-45335. (Illus.). 48p. (gr. 2-6). 1985. 10.10i (ISBN 0-690-04437-2); PLB 9.89g (ISBN 0-690-04438-0). Crowell Jr Bks.

--Dinosaur Story. LC 74-5931. (Illus.). 32p. (gr. k-3). 1974. PLB 10.88 (ISBN 0-688-31826-6). Morrow.

--A Dog's Body. cancelled (ISBN 0-688-04153-1, Morrow Junior Books); PLB cancelled (ISBN 0-688-04154-X). Morrow.

--Find the Hidden Insect. LC 79-18648. (Illus.). 40p. (gr. k-3). 1979. 10.00 (ISBN 0-688-22203-X); PLB 10.88 (ISBN 0-688-32203-4). Morrow.

--A Fish Hatches. (Illus.). (gr. k-3). 1978. 11.75 (ISBN 0-688-22153-X); PLB 11.88 (ISBN 0-688-32153-4). Morrow.

--A Frog's Body. LC 80-10705. (Illus.). 48p. (gr. k-3). 1980. 10.00 (ISBN 0-688-22228-5); PLB 10.88 (ISBN 0-688-32228-X). Morrow.

--Get Well, Clown-Arounds! LC 82-8148. (Illus.). 48p. (ps-3). 1983. 5.95 (ISBN 0-8193-1095-6); PLB 5.95 (ISBN 0-8193-1096-4). Parents.

--Golly Gump Swallowed a Fly. LC 81-11072. (Illus.). 48p. (ps-3). 1982. 5.95 (ISBN 0-8193-1069-7). Parents.

--A Horse's Body. LC 80-28147. (Illus.). 48p. (gr. k-3). 1981. 10.00 (ISBN 0-688-00362-1); PLB 10.88 (ISBN 0-688-00363-X). Morrow.

--How You Were Born. LC 83-17314. (Illus.). 48p. (ps-3). 1984. 10.25 (ISBN 0-688-01710-X, Morrow Junior Books); lib. bdg. 9.55 (ISBN 0-688-01709-6, Morrow Junior Books). Morrow.

--How You Were Born. LC 83-17314. (Illus.). 48p. (Orig.). (ps-3). 1985. pap. 4.95 (ISBN 0-688-05801-9, Morrow Junior Books). Morrow.

--An Insect's Body. LC 83-22027. (Illus.). 48p. (ps-3). 1984. 10.25 (ISBN 0-688-02771-7); PLB 10.88 (ISBN 0-688-02772-5). Morrow.

--Monster Manners. (Illus.). 48p. (Orig.). (gr. k-3). 1985. pap. 2.25 (ISBN 0-590-33592-8, Lucky Star). Scholastic Inc.

--My Puppy Is Born. LC 72-14201. (Illus.). 40p. (gr. k-3). 1973. PLB 10.88 (ISBN 0-688-30078-2). Morrow.

--The New Baby at Your House. (Illus.). 48p. (ps-3). 1985. 10.25 (ISBN 0-688-05806-X); lib. bdg. 10.88 (ISBN 0-688-05807-8). Morrow.

--New Treasury of Children's Poetry. LC 83-20821. (Illus.). 224p. (ps-8). 1984. 12.95 (ISBN 0-385-18539-1). Doubleday.

--Nighttime Animals. LC 85-7593. (Large As Life Ser.). (Illus.). (gr. 4-8). 1985. PLB 11.99 (ISBN 0-394-97189-2); pap. 9.95 (ISBN 0-394-87189-8). Knopf.

--The Parents Book of Toilet Teaching. LC 82-91150. 144p. 1983. pap. 2.50 (ISBN 0-345-30444-6). Ballantine.

--Plants in Winter. LC 73-1771. (A Let's Read & Find Out Science Bk). (Illus.). (ps-3). 1973. PLB 11.89 (ISBN 0-690-62886-2). Crowell Jr Bks.

--Saber-Toothed Tiger & Other Ice-Age Mammals. (Illus.). (gr. 1-5). 1977. PLB 11.88 (ISBN 0-688-32120-8). Morrow.

--A Snake's Body. LC 81-9443. (Illus.). 48p. (gr. k-3). 1981. 11.25 (ISBN 0-688-00702-3); 11.88 (ISBN 0-688-00703-1). Morrow.

--Sweet Dreams, Clown-Arounds. LC 85-6348. (Illus.). 48p. (ps-3). 1985. 5.95 (ISBN 0-8193-1138-3). Parents.

Cole, Joanna & Lilly, Kenneth. Daytime Animals. LC 85-4301. (Large As Life Ser.). (Illus.). (gr. 4-8). 1985. PLB 11.99 (ISBN 0-394-97188-4); pap. 9.95 (ISBN 0-394-87188-X). Knopf.

Cole, Joanna, ed. Best-Loved Folktales of the World. LC 81-43288. (Illus.). 984p. (YA) (gr. 7 up). 1982. pap. 8.95 (ISBN 0-385-18949-4). Doubleday.

Cole, Johanna. Fleas. (Illus.). 64p. (gr. 3-7). 1973. PLB 10.88 (ISBN 0-688-31844-4). Morrow.

Cole, John & Wing, Cha. Breaking New Ground: Planning, Siting, Designing & Constructing Your Own Compact House. Brady, Upton, ed. (Illus.). 240p. 1985. 24.95 (ISBN 0-87113-019-X, Pub. by Atlantic Monthly Pr); pap. 14.95 (ISBN 0-87113-028-9, Pub. by Atlantic Monthly Pr). Little.

Cole, John & Wing, Charles. From the Ground Up. 1976. pap. 14.45i (ISBN 0-316-15112-2, Pub. by Atlantic Monthly Pr). Little.

Cole, John, jt. auth. see Cobb, Nathan.

Cole, John A., ed. Groundwater Pollution in Europe. LC 74-84820. (Illus.). 547p. 1975. text ed. 28.00 (ISBN 0-912394-12-9). Water Info.

Cole, John N. Striper: A Story of Fish & Man. LC 78-15003. 1978. (Pub. by Atlantic Monthly Pr); pap. 6.95 (ISBN 0-316-15109-2). Little.

Cole, John W. & Wolf, Eric R. The Hidden Frontier: Ecology & Ethnicity in an Alpine Valley. (Studies in Social Discontinuity Ser.). 1974. 39.50 (ISBN 0-12-785132-1). Acad Pr.

Cole, John W., tr. see Guizot, Francois P.

Cole, Johnathan O., jt. auth. see Evans, Wayne O.

Cole, Johnetta B., ed. Anthropology for the Eighties: Introductory Readings. LC 81-69764. pap. text ed. 13.95 (ISBN 0-02-906430-9). Free Pr.

Cole, Jonathan, et al. Peer Review in the National Science Foundation: Phase One of a Study. 1978. pap. text ed. 11.75 (ISBN 0-309-02788-8). Natl Acad Pr.

Cole, Jonathan O. Anxiety, Depression, & Organic Disease. (Illus.). 1976. pap. text ed. 20.50 (ISBN 0-89147-100-6). CAS.

--Mental Illness & Psychotropic Medications, 2 vols. (Illus.). 131p. 1977. Set. 65.00 (ISBN 0-685-62203-7); Bk. 1. 28.50 (ISBN 0-89147-036-0); Bk. 2. 36.50 (ISBN 0-89147-037-9). CAS.

Cole, Jonathan O., jt. auth. see Schatzberg, Alan F.

Cole, Jonathan O., ed. Psychopharmacology Update. LC 79-48064. 195p. 1980. 16.95 (ISBN 0-669-03695-1, Collomore Pr). Heath.

Cole, Jonathan O. & Barrett, James E., eds. Psychopathology in the Aged. (American Psychopathology Association Ser.). 322p. 1980. text ed. 46.00 (ISBN 0-89004-406-6). Raven.
Cole, Jonathan R. & Cole, Stephen. Social Stratification in Science. LC 73-78166. 1973. 20.00x (ISBN 0-226-11338-8); pap. 10.00x (ISBN 0-226-11339-6). U of Chicago Pr.
Cole, Jonathon O., et al, eds. see American Psychopathological Association.
Cole, Jonathon R. Fair Science: Women in the Scientific Community. LC 79-7341. (Illus.). 1979. 24.95 (ISBN 0-02-906360-4). Free Pr.
Cole, Juan R. & Momen, Moojan, eds. Studies in Babi & Baha'i History: Vol. 2: From Iran East & West. (Studies in Babi & Baha'i History). (Illus.). 205p. 1984. 19.95 (ISBN 0-933770-40-5). Kalimat.
Cole, Juan R., tr. see Abu'l-Fadl, Mirza.
Cole, Justine. The Copeland Bride. (Orig.). 1983. pap. 3.50 (ISBN 0-440-11235-4). Dell.
Cole, K. C. Sympathetic Vibrations: Reflections on Physics As a Way of Life. LC 84-60547. (Illus.). 288p. 1984. 16.95 (ISBN 0-688-03968-5). Morrow.
--Sympathetic Vibrations: Reflections on Physics As a Way of Life. LC 85-7555. (Illus.). 352p. 1985. pap. 7.95 (ISBN 0-553-34234-7). Bantam.
--What Only a Mother Can Tell You about Having a Baby. 320p. 1984. pap. 3.95 (ISBN 0-425-07495-1). Berkley Pub.
Cole, Katherine W., ed. Minority Organizations: A National Directory. LC 79-640122. (Illus.). 810p. 1982. pap. 30.00 (ISBN 0-912048-30-1). Garrett Pk.
Cole, Kathleen & Cole, William R. Mosby's Medical Speller. LC 83-8562. 468p. 1983. pap. 7.95 (ISBN 0-8016-3532-2). Mosby.
Cole, Kenneth J. The Headhunter Strategy: How to Make It Work for You. LC 84-27025. 200p. 1985. 15.95 (ISBN 0-471-81943-3). Wiley.
Cole, Kenneth S. Membranes, Ions & Impulses: A Chapter of Classical Biophysics. LC 67-24121. (Biophysics Ser.: No. 1). (Illus.). 1971. 53.00x (ISBN 0-520-00251-2). U of Cal Pr.
Cole, Lawrence T. The Basis of Early Christian Theism. lib. bdg. 59.95 (ISBN 0-8490-1478-6). Gordon Pr.
Cole, Lee S. Claims, Costs & Crimes. 110p. 1984. pap. 11.00 (ISBN 0-939818-08-6). Lee Bks.
--Handling Vehicle Theft Losses. 56p. (Orig.). 1979. pap. 4.00 (ISBN 0-939818-02-7). Lee Bks.
--The Investigation of Motor Vehicle Fires. 65p. 1980. pap. 5.00 (ISBN 0-939818-04-3). Lee Bks.
--The Investigation of Motor Vehicle Fires. 2nd ed. 114p. 1985. pap. 9.00 (ISBN 0-939818-10-8). Lee Bks.
--Vehicle Identification: 1938-1968. 75p. 1980. pap. 5.00 (ISBN 0-939818-03-5). Lee Bks.
--Vehicle Identification: 1969-1982. 136p. (Orig.). 1982. pap. 6.00 (ISBN 0-939818-05-1). Lee Bks.
--Vehicle Identification, 1983. (Illus.). 80p. (Orig.). 1983. pap. 6.50 (ISBN 0-939818-06-X). Lee Bks.
--Vehicle Identification: 1984-1985. 164p. (Orig.). 1984. pap. 15.00 (ISBN 0-939818-09-4). Lee Bks.
Cole, Lee S. & Herold, Robert C. The Investigation of Recreational Boat Fires. (Illus.). 65p. (Orig.). 1983. pap. 6.50 (ISBN 0-939818-07-8). Lee Bks.
Cole, Leonard A. Blacks in Power: A Comparative Study of Black & White Elected Officials. LC 75-2985. 264p. 1975. 32.00x (ISBN 0-691-07573-5). Princeton U Pr.
--Politics & the Restraint of Science. LC 83-2992. (Illus.). 200p. 1983. 17.95 (ISBN 0-86598-125-6). Rowman & Allanheld.
Cole, Leslie. Construction Superintending. 240p. (Orig.). 1982. pap. 22.00 (ISBN 0-910460-88-4). Craftsman.
--Waste Management in the States. LC 82-147343. pap. 20.00 (ISBN 0-317-10672-4, 2020427). Bks Demand UMI.
Cole, Lester. Hollywood Red: The Autobiography of Lester Cole. LC 81-51701. (Illus.). 450p. 1981. 12.95 (ISBN 0-87867-085-8). Ramparts.
Cole, Lisa A., jt. auth. see Harrell, Rhett D.
Cole, Lucy. Cooking for the One You Love. LC 82-71743. 288p. 1982. 16.95 (ISBN 0-8119-0448-2); pap. 9.95 (ISBN 0-8119-0597-7). Fell.
--Gourmet Cooking for Two When Minutes Matter. 1985. 15.95 (ISBN 0-8119-0644-2). Fell.
--Gourmet Cooking When Minutes Matter. 228p. 1984. 15.95 (ISBN 0-8119-0688-4). Fell.
Cole, Luella. Attaining Maturity. 212p. 1981. Repr. of 1944 ed. lib. bdg. 25.00 (ISBN 0-8495-0954-8). Arden Lib.
Cole, M., tr. see Parent, D. P.
Cole, M. I., jt. auth. see Cole, G. D.
Cole, M. I., ed. see Drayton, Michael.
Cole, M. R., tr. Pastores. (AFS M Ser.). (Illus., Span.). Repr. of 1907 ed. 21.00 (ISBN 0-527-01061-8). Kraus Repr.
Cole, Mabel. Philippine Folk Tales. LC 78-67699. (The Folktale). (Illus.). Repr. of 1916 ed. 27.00 (ISBN 0-404-16073-5). AMS Pr.
Cole, Madeleine B. Distant Footsteps. 92p. 1984. 4.33 (ISBN 0-89697-208-9). Intl Univ Pr.
Cole, Maija J., jt. ed. see Keeler, Mary F.
Cole, Malcolm S. & Barclay, Barbara. Armseelchen: The Life & Music of Eric Zeisl. LC 84-520. (Contributions to the Study of Music & Dance Ser.: No. 6). xxvi, 444p. 1984. lib. bdg. 35.00 (ISBN 0-313-23800-6, CAR/). Greenwood.
Cole, Margaret. The Story of Fabian Socialism. LC 61-16949. (Illus.). 1961. 27.50x (ISBN 0-8047-0091-5); pap. 9.95 (ISBN 0-8047-0092-3, SP105). Stanford U Pr.
Cole, Margaret, jt. auth. see Cole, G. D.
Cole, Margaret, jt. auth. see H, G. D.
Cole, Margaret I. Marriage: Past & Present. LC 72-9632. Repr. of 1939 ed. 24.50 (ISBN 0-404-57431-9). AMS Pr.
--Robert Owen of New Lanark. LC 75-77254. Repr. of 1953 ed. 25.00x (ISBN 0-678-00565-6). Kelley.
--Women of To-Day. facs. ed. LC 68-16920. (Essay Index Reprint Ser). 1938. 20.00 (ISBN 0-8369-0325-0). Ayer Co Pubs.
Cole, Margaret I., ed. The Webbs & Their Work. LC 84-22459. (Illus.). xvi, 304p. 1985. Repr. of 1949 ed. lib. bdg. 39.75 (ISBN 0-313-24677-7, COWW). Greenwood.
Cole, Margaret I. & Smith, Charles, eds. Democratic Sweden. facs. ed. LC 70-128224. (Essay Index Reprint Ser). 1939. 19.00 (ISBN 0-8369-1871-1). Ayer Co Pubs.
Cole, Marianne. Shining Promise, No. 171. 192p. 1984. pap. 1.95 (ISBN 0-515-07586-8). Jove Pubns.
Cole, Marion & Cole, Olivia H. Things to Make & Do for Easter. LC 78-12457. (Things to Make & Do Ser.). (Illus.). (gr. k-3). 1979. PLB 8.90 (ISBN 0-531-01463-0). Watts.
Cole, Marion, ed. see National Fire Protection Association.
Cole, Marley. Living Destiny. (Illus.). 260p. pap. 10.95 (ISBN 0-9613657-0-6). Proguides.
Cole, Martha, jt. auth. see Cole, Jack.
Cole, Martha L. & Cole, Jack T. Effective Intervention with the Language Impaired Child. LC 80-28037. 291p. 1981. text ed. 31.50 (ISBN 0-89443-344-X). Aspen Systems.
Cole, Martin, jt. auth. see Birch, Alan.
Cole, Mary I. Cooperation Between the Faculty of the Campus Elementary Training School & the Other Departments of Teachers Colleges & Normal Schools. LC 76-176658. (Columbia University. Teachers College. Contributions to Education: No. 746). Repr. of 1939 ed. 22.50 (ISBN 0-404-55746-5). AMS Pr.
Cole, Mary N. Eggs Before Breakfast: One Woman's Collection of Recipes & Recollections. (Illus.). 192p. (Orig.). 1985. pap. write for info. (ISBN 0-931515-03-3). Triumph Pr.
Cole, Maurice F. Michigan's Courthouses Old & New. (Illus.). 167p. 1963. 10.00 (ISBN 0-317-18875-5, Pub. by M F Cole). Hardscrabble Bks.
Cole, Maurice F., jt. auth. see Cole, Jacquelyn M.
Cole, Michael. Soviet Developmental Psychology: An Anthology. LC 77-85709. 1977. pap. 160.00 (ISBN 0-317-08144-6, 2021854). Bks Demand UMI.
Cole, Michael & Frampton, Susan. Dining in Vail. (Dining In Ser.). (Illus.). Date not set. pap. 8.95 (ISBN 0-89716-059-2). Peanut Butter.
Cole, Michael & Means, Barbara. Comparative Studies of How People Think: An Introduction. LC 80-23825. (Illus.). 208p. 1981. text ed. 16.50x (ISBN 0-674-15260-3). Harvard U Pr.
Cole, Michael & Scribner, Sylvia. Culture & Thought: A Psychological Introduction. LC 73-16360. 227p. 1974. pap. 17.95 (ISBN 0-471-16477-1). Wiley.
Cole, Michael, jt. auth. see Scribner, Sylvia.
Cole, Michael, ed. The Selected Writings of A. R. Luria. LC 78-64342. 320p. 1978. 32.50 (ISBN 0-87332-127-8). M E Sharpe.
Cole, Michael, ed. see Luria, A. R.
Cole, Michael, et al, eds. see Vygotsky, L. S.
Cole, Mitchell & Blinn, James D., eds. Pathways to Risk Management Information Systems. 160p. avail. (ISBN 0-937802-21-2). Risk Management.
Cole, Myron C. Myron Here. LC 82-61064. (Illus.). 260p. (Orig.). 1983. pap. 5.00 (ISBN 0-935356-04-5). Mills Pub Co.
Cole, Natalie. Little Dog. (Little Book Ser). (Illus.). (gr. k-6). 1975. pap. 0.50 (ISBN 0-89409-001-1). Childrens Art.
Cole, Olivia H., jt. auth. see Cole, Marion.
Cole, P. Imbabura Quechua. (Descriptive Grammars Ser.). 250p. 1985. 40.00 (ISBN 0-7099-3444-0, Pub. by Croom Helm Ltd). Longwood Pub Group.
Cole, Patricia. Language Disorders in PreSchool Children. 208p. 1982. 25.95 (ISBN 0-13-522862-X). P-H.
Cole, Paul M., jt. ed. see Taylor, William J., Jr.
Cole, Paul M., Jr. & Taylor, William J., eds. The Nuclear Freeze Debate: Arms Control Issues for the 1980's. LC 83-10628. (Replica Edition Ser.). 245p. 1983. pap. 21.50x (ISBN 0-86531-995-2). Westview.
Cole, Peggy R. Egypt. (Ancient Worlds Curriculum Guides Ser.). (Illus.). 65p. (gr. 6). 1985. tchr.'s ed. 10.00 (ISBN 0-940744-51-1). Chrysler Mus.
Cole, Percival R. Herbart & Froebel: An Attempt at Synthesis. LC 70-176659. (Columbia University. Teachers College. Contributions to Education Ser.: No. 14). Repr. of 1907 ed. 22.50 (ISBN 0-404-55014-2). AMS Pr.
--A History of Educational Thought. LC 74-138214. 316p. 1972. Repr. of 1931 ed. lib. bdg. 22.00x (ISBN 0-8371-5569-X, COET). Greenwood.
--Later Roman Education in Ausonius Capella & the Theodosian Code. LC 74-176660. (Columbia University. Teachers College. Contributions to Education: No. 27). Repr. of 1909 ed. 22.50 (ISBN 0-404-55027-4). AMS Pr.
Cole, Peter, ed. Radical Pragmatics. 1981. 38.50 (ISBN 0-12-179660-4). Acad Pr.
--Studies in Modern Hebrew Syntax & Semantics: Transformational Generative Approach. new ed. (North Holland Linguistics Ser.: Vol. 32). 286p. 1976. pap. 38.50 (ISBN 0-7204-0543-2, North-Holland). Elsevier.
Cole, Phil. Cook Is a Four Letter Word. 160p. (Orig.). 1981. pap. 7.95 (ISBN 0-938400-04-5). Donahoe Pubs.
--Cooking for Dummies. 59p. 1980. pap. 6.95 (ISBN 0-938400-02-9). Donahoe Pubs.
Cole, R. Alan. Exodus: Tyndale Old Testament Commentary. LC 72-97952. 243p. 1973. 10.95 (ISBN 0-87784-865-3); pap. 6.95 (ISBN 0-87784-252-3). Inter-Varsity.
Cole, R. B. Drug Treatment of Respiratory Disease. (Monographs in Clinical Pharmacology). (Illus.). 1981. text ed. 31.00 (ISBN 0-443-08012-7). Churchill.
Cole, R. E. A Glossary of Words Used in South-West Lincolnshire: Wapentake of Graffoe. (English Dialect Society Publications Ser.: No. 52). pap. 20.00 (ISBN 0-317-15943-7). Kraus Repr.
Cole, R. T. The Recollections of R. Taylor Cole: Educator, Emmissary, Development Planner. LC 82-14758. (Illus.). 256p. 1983. 14.95t (ISBN 0-8223-0488-0). Duke.
Cole, R. T., jt. ed. see Canavan, Francis S.
Cole, R. Wellesley. Kossoh Town Boy. (Illus.). 1960. 7.95 (ISBN 0-521-04686-6). Cambridge U Pr.
Cole, Raymond & Bhaerman, Steve. Exercising Your Wellpower for Optimal Physical Health. (Illus.). 233p. (Orig.). 1984. pap. 9.95 (ISBN 0-917073-00-2). Wellpower.
Cole, Rex V. Artistic Anatomy of Trees. 2nd ed. (Illus.). 1951. pap. 5.95 (ISBN 0-486-21475-3). Dover.
--Perspective for Artists. LC 77-15743. (Illus.). 288p. 1976. pap. 4.00 (ISBN 0-486-22487-2). Dover.
Cole, Richard, et al. The Quality of Life in Texas Cities: A Ranking & Assessment of Living Conditions in Texas' Largest Communities. 175p. 1984. pap. 12.50 (ISBN 0-936440-54-6). Inst Urban Studies.
Cole, Richard B. The Application of Security Systems & Hardware. 272p. 1970. photocopy ed. 27.95x (ISBN 0-398-00332-7). C C Thomas.
--Executive Security: A Corporate Guide to Effective Response to Abduction & Terrorism. LC 80-14662. 323p. 1980. 48.50x (ISBN 0-471-07736-4, Pub. by Wiley Interscience). Wiley.
--Principles & Practice of Protection. (Illus.). 432p. 1980. 29.00x (ISBN 0-398-03920-8). C C Thomas.
--Protect Your Property: The Applications of Burglar Alarm Hardware. (Illus.). 192p. 1971. photo copy ed. 19.50x (ISBN 0-398-02262-3). C C Thomas.
Cole, Richard J. & Cox, Richard H., eds. Handbook of Toxic Fungal Metabolites. LC 81-4082. 1981. 87.00 (ISBN 0-12-179760-0). Acad Pr.
Cole, Richard L. Introduction to Political Research. (Illus.). 1980. pap. text ed. write for info. (ISBN 0-02-323350-8). Macmillan.
--Love-Feasts: A History of the Christian Agape. 59.95 (ISBN 0-8490-0563-9). Gordon Pr.
Cole, Robert. The Book of Houses: An Astrological Guide to the Harvest Cycle in Human Life. LC 80-16931. 132p. 1980. pap. 6.95 (ISBN 0-934558-01-9). Entwhistle Bks.
--Computer Communications. 200p. 1982. pap. 17.95 (ISBN 0-387-91204-5). Springer-Verlag.
Cole, Robert E. Japanese Blue Collar: The Changing Tradition. LC 77-107656. 1971. pap. 10.95 (ISBN 0-520-02354-4, CAMPUS86). U of Cal Pr.
--Work, Mobility, & Participation: A Comparative Study of American & Japanese Industry. LC 77-80468. 304p. 1979. 26.50x (ISBN 0-520-03542-9); pap. 8.95x (ISBN 0-520-04204-2, CAMPUS 263). U of Cal Pr.
Cole, Robert H. Consumer & Commercial Credit Management. 7th ed. 1984. 28.50 (ISBN 0-256-03015-4). Irwin.
Cole, Robert H., ed. see Kirkwood, John G.
Cole, Robert S. The Practical Handbook of Public Relations. (Illus.). 224p. 1981. text ed. 19.95 (ISBN 0-13-691162-5, Spec); pap. text ed. 8.95 (ISBN 0-13-691154-4). P-H.
Cole, Roger W., ed. Current Issues in Linguistic Theory. LC 76-26427. (Illus.). 312p. 1977. 25.00x (ISBN 0-253-31608-1); pap. 9.95x (ISBN 0-253-11262-1). Ind U Pr.
Cole, Roland J. & Tegeler, Philip D. Government Requirements of Small Business. LC 79-3046. (Human Affairs Research Center Ser.). 192p. 1980. 24.50x (ISBN 0-669-03307-3). Lexington Bks.
Cole, Ronald A., ed. Perception & Production of Fluent Speech. LC 79-25481. (Illus.). 576p. 1980. text ed. 49.95x (ISBN 0-89859-019-1). L Erlbaum Assocs.
Cole, Sam. Global Models & the International Economic Order. LC 77-30175. 1978. pap. text ed. 4.80 (ISBN 0-08-022025-8). Pergamon.
Cole, Sam & Miles, Ian. Worlds Apart: Technology & North-South Relations in the Global Economy. 256p. 1984. 18.95x (ISBN 0-8476-7374-X). Rowman.
Cole, Sam, jt. auth. see Bessant, John.
Cole, Sam, ed. Models, Planning & Basic Needs: Conference on the Applicability of Global Modelling to Integrated Planning & Developing Countries. (Illus.). 1979. text ed. 33.00 (ISBN 0-08-023732-0). Pergamon.
Cole, Sam, jt. ed. see Bessant, John.
Cole, Sharon A. The Emperor's New Clothes. (Illus.). 30p. 1976. pap. 1.75 (ISBN 0-88680-045-5); royalty 20.00 (ISBN 0-317-03604-1). I E Clark.
Cole, Sheila. When the Tide Is Low. LC 84-10023. (Illus.). 32p. (ps-1). 1985. PLB 11.88 (ISBN 0-688-04067-5); 11.75 (ISBN 0-688-04066-7). Lothrop.
Cole, Sheila, ed. see Luria, A. R.
Cole, Shelia. Working Kids on Working. LC 80-14043. (Illus.). 224p. (gr. 5 up). 1980. 12.50 (ISBN 0-688-41959-3); PLB 12.88 (ISBN 0-688-51959-8). Lothrop.
Cole, Stanely. Amphoto Guide to Basic Photography. (Illus.). 1978. (Amphoto); pap. 7.95 (ISBN 0-8174-2115-7). Watson-Guptill.
Cole, Stephen. The Sociological Method. 3rd ed. 1980. pap. 13.95 (ISBN 0-395-30857-7). HM.
--The Sociological Orientation. 2nd ed. 1979. pap. 20.95 (ISBN 0-395-30579-9); instr's. manual 2.50 (ISBN 0-395-30580-2). HM.
--The Unionization of Teachers: A Case Study of the UFT. Zuckerman, Harriet & Merton, Robert K., eds. LC 79-8986. (Dissertations on Sociology Ser.). 1980. Repr. of 1969 ed. lib. bdg. 20.00x (ISBN 0-405-12959-9). Ayer Co Pubs.
Cole, Stephen, jt. auth. see Cole, Jonathan R.
Cole, Stewart G. History of Fundamentalism. LC 70-138107. 1971. Repr. of 1931 ed. lib. bdg. 19.50x (ISBN 0-8371-5683-1, COHF). Greenwood.
Cole, Storrs. Stratigraphic & Paleontologic Studies of Wells in Florida. (Illus.). 160p. 1945. 1.00 (ISBN 0-318-17291-7, B 28). FL Bureau Geology.
Cole, Susan, jt. auth. see Porter, Douglas R.
Cole, Susan D. Richmond-Windows to the Past. LC 79-57178. (Illus.). 96p. (Orig.). 1980. pap. 6.95 (ISBN 0-936034-00-9). Wildcat Canyon.
--The Woman's Guide to the East Bay Singles' Scene. (Illus.). 120p. (Orig.). 1983. pap. 6.95 (ISBN 0-936034-01-7). Wildcat Canyon.
Cole, Susan D., ed. Mary Ann's Best of Helpful Needlecraft Hints. LC 81-68620. (Illus.). 96p. (Orig.). 1981. pap. 4.95 (ISBN 0-9607224-0-8, N21). Craftways.
Cole, Susan L. The Absent One: Mourning Ritual, Tragedy & the Performance of Ambivalence. LC 84-43063. 179p. 1985. 18.95x (ISBN 0-271-00391-X). Pa ST U Pr.
Cole, Sylvan, Jr. Raphael Soyer: Fifty Years of Printmaking, 1917-1967. LC 67-29917. (Graphic Art Ser.). 1967. 32.50 (ISBN 0-306-70986-4). Da Capo.
Cole, Sylvan, Jr., compiled by. Kleinholz-Graphics 1940-1975. LC 74-31266. (Illus.). 1975. pap. 7.50 (ISBN 0-916224-18-X). Banyan Bks.
Cole, Taylor. Canadian Bureaucracy & Federalism, Nineteen Forty-Seven to Sixty-Five. (Monograph Series in World Affairs: Vol. 3, 1965-66, Bk. 3). (Orig.). pap. 3.95 (ISBN 0-87940-009-9). Monograph Series.
Cole, Terrence. E. T. Barnette: The Strange Story of the Man Who Founded Fairbanks. LC 81-3452. (Illus.). 176p. 1981. pap. 7.95 (ISBN 0-88240-154-8). Alaska Northwest.
Cole, Terry J. Reaching. 1984. 5.95 (ISBN 0-8062-2231-X). Carlton.
Cole, Thacker. Clipart Book of Owls in Action. LC 73-94337. 1974. pap. 7.95 (ISBN 0-87874-011-2). Galloway.
Cole, Thomas. Thomas Cole's Poetry: The Collected Poems of America's Foremost Painter of the Hudson River School, Reflecting His Feelings for Nature & the Romantic Spirit of the 19th Century. Tymn, Marshall B., ed. LC 72-7843. (Illus.). 1972. casebound 15.00 (ISBN 0-87387-057-3). Shumway.
Cole, Toby. Acting: A Handbook of the Stanislavski Method. 1955. pap. 6.95 (ISBN 0-517-05035-8). Crown.
Cole, Toby & Chinoy, Helen Krich. Directors on Directing: A Sourcebook of the Modern Theatre. 479p. 1963. pap. text ed. write for info. (ISBN 0-02-323330-3). Macmillan.
Cole, Toby, ed. Florence: A Traveler's Anthology. 288p. 1981. 12.95 (ISBN 0-88208-126-8). Lawrence Hill.
--Playwrights on Playwriting: The Meaning & Making of Modern Drama. (Drama Book Ser.). 299p. (Orig.). 1961. pap. 5.95 (ISBN 0-8090-0529-8). Hill & Wang.
--Venice: A Portable Reader. LC 78-19857. 1979. 12.00 (ISBN 0-88208-097-0); pap. 6.95 1980 (ISBN 0-88208-107-1). Lawrence Hill.
Cole, Toby & Chinoy, Helen K., eds. Actors on Acting. rev. ed. 736p. 1980. pap. 9.95 (ISBN 0-517-54048-7). Crown.
--Directors on Directing. rev. ed. LC 62-20686. Orig. Title: Directing the Play. 1963. pap. 13.24 scp (ISBN 0-672-60622-4). Bobbs.
Cole, Tom. A Short History of San Francisco. LC 81-2588. (Illus.). 144p. (Orig.). 1981. pap. 9.95 (ISBN 0-938530-00-3, 00-3). Lexikos.

Cole, Tom, jt. auth. see Allen, Dorothy S.
Cole, Tom, ed. see Allen, Dorothy S.
Cole, W. A., jt. auth. see Deane, Phyllis.
Cole, W. Douglas. When Families Hurt. LC 79-51133. 1979. 6.50 (ISBN 0-8054-5638-4). Broadman.
Cole, W. Owen. Five Religions in the Twentieth Century. LC 81-68724. (Illus.). 256p. 1981. pap. 11.95 (ISBN 0-8023-1272-1). Dufour.
--The Guru in Sikhism. 1984. pap. 7.00x (ISBN 0-8364-1238-9, Pub. by D Longman & Todd). South Asia Bks.
--Sikhism & Its Indian Context, 1469-1708. 1984. 38.50x (ISBN 0-8364-1237-0, Pub. by D Longman & Todd); text ed. 27.50x (ISBN 0-8364-1106-4, Pub. by D Longman & Todd). South Asia Bks.
--World Faiths in Education. (Unwin Education Books). (Illus.). 1978. text ed. 22.50x (ISBN 0-04-371054-9); pap. text ed. 8.95x (ISBN 0-04-371055-7). Allen Unwin.
Cole, W. Owen & Sambhi, Piara S. The Sikhs: Their Religious Beliefs & Practices. (Library of Religious Beliefs & Practices). 1978. 23.95x (ISBN 0-7100-8842-6); pap. 9.00 (ISBN 0-7100-8843-4). Routledge & Kegan.
Cole, W. R. A Checklist of Science-Fiction Anthologies. LC 74-15956. (Science Fiction Ser). (Illus.). 390p. 1975. Repr. of 1964 ed. 27.50x (ISBN 0-405-06323-7). Ayer Co Pubs.
Cole, Warren H., ed. Chemotherapy of Cancer. LC 74-85838. (Illus.). pap. 89.80 (ISBN 0-317-07858-5, 2014535). Bks Demand UMI.
Cole, Wayne S. America First: The Battle Against Intervention, 1940-1941. LC 74-159174. 1971. Repr. of 1953 ed. lib. bdg. 20.50x (ISBN 0-374-91800-7). Octagon.
--Roosevelt & the Isolationists, 1932-1945. LC 82-8624. xii, 698p. 1983. 26.50x (ISBN 0-8032-1410-3). U of Nebr Pr.
--Senator Gerald P. Nye & American Foreign Relations. LC 80-17370. (Illus.). 293p. 1980. Repr. of 1962 ed. lib. bdg. 27.50x (ISBN 0-313-22660-1, COSN). Greenwood.
Cole, Wendell. Kyoto in the Momoyama Period. LC 67-15586. (The Centers of Civilization Ser.: Vol. 12). pap. 45.00 (ISBN 0-317-26312-9, 2052146). Bks Demand UMI.
Cole, Wendell, ed. see Grube, Max.
Cole, William. A Boy Named Mary Jane, & Other Silly Verse. (Illus.). 64p. (gr. 3-5). 1979. pap. 1.50 (ISBN 0-380-45955-8, 45955-8, Camelot). Avon.
--Give Up? (Illus.). 48p. 1981. pap. 1.95 (ISBN 0-380-56069-0, 56069-0, Camelot). Avon.
--Oh, Such Foolishness! LC 78-1622. (Illus.). (gr. 3-6). 1978. 11.49i (ISBN 0-397-31807-3). Lipp Jr Bks.
--Oh, That's Ridiculous. LC 70-183934. (Illus.). 80p. (gr. 4-7). 1972. PLB 8.95 (ISBN 0-670-52107-8). Viking.
Cole, William & Thaler, Mike. Monster Knock Knocks. (Illus., Orig.). (gr. 3-5). 1982. pap. 1.75 (ISBN 0-671-44254-6). Archway.
Cole, William, ed. An Arkful of Animals: Poems for the Very Young. (Illus.). 128p. (gr. 3-7). 1978. 6.95 (ISBN 0-395-27205-X). HM.
--Poem Stew. LC 81-47106. (Illus.). 96p. (gr. 3-6). 1981. 10.89 (ISBN 0-397-31963-0); PLB 9.98g (ISBN 0-397-31964-9). Lipp Jr Bks.
--Poem Stew. LC 81-47106. (Trophy Bk.). (Illus.). 96p. (gr. 1-7). 1983. pap. 3.95 (ISBN 0-06-440136-7, Trophy). HarpJ.
--The Poetry of Horses. LC 79-9228. 1979. 8.95 (ISBN 0-684-16330-6, ScribT). Scribner.
Cole, William E., jt. auth. see Harris, Diana K.
Cole, William H., ed. Some Aspects of Amino Acid Supplementation. pap. 24.30 (ISBN 0-317-08913-7, 2050492). Bks Demand UMI.
Cole, William M. Accounts: Their Construction & Interpretation for Business Men & Students of Affairs. LC 75-18462. (History of Accounting Ser.). 1976. 23.50x (ISBN 0-405-07546-4). Ayer Co Pubs.
Cole, William M. & Geddes, Anne E. The Fundamentals of Accounting: With a List of Best Books in Accounting. Brief, Richard P., ed. LC 77-87265. (Development of Contemporary Accounting Thought Ser). 1978. Repr. of 1921 ed. lib. bdg. 34.50x (ISBN 0-405-10894-X). Ayer Co Pubs.
Cole, William R., jt. auth. see Cole, Kathleen.
Colean, M. L. Housing for Defense: A Review of the Role of Housing in Relation to America's Defense & a Program for Actions. LC 77-74932. (American Federalism-the Urban Dimension). (Illus.). 1978. Repr. of 1940 ed. lib. bdg. 20.00x (ISBN 0-405-10480-4). Ayer Co Pubs.
Colean, Miles L. Renewing Our Cities. LC 53-9616. 1975. Repr. of 1953 ed. 13.00 (ISBN 0-527-02802-9). Kraus Repr.
Coleberd, Frances. Hidden Country Villages of California. LC 77-21926. (Illus.). 180p. 1982. pap. 7.95 (ISBN 0-87701-252-0). Chronicle Bks.
Colebourn, R., jt. auth. see Cobban, J. M.
Colebrook, Binda. Winter Gardening in the Maritime Northwest: Cool Season Crops for the Year-Round Gardener. 2nd rev. ed. (Illus.). 170p. (Orig.). 1984. pap. 9.50 (ISBN 0-916239-00-4). Maritime Pubns.
Colebrook, C. Spider, Egg, & Microcosm: Three Men & Three Worlds of Science. LC 55-9287. 1955. 8.00 (ISBN 0-9600476-1-1). E Kinkead.
Colebrook, Val. Shades of Jade. LC 80-52170. (Illus.). 52p. (Orig.). 1980. pap. 3.50 (ISBN 0-932384-11-0). Tashmoo.
Coleburn, ed. Mentor Book CV. 1969. 9.95 (ISBN 0-312-52990-2). St Martin.
Colecchia, Francesca. Garcia Lorca: An Annotated Bibliography of Criticism. LC 78-68301. (Reference Library of Humanities Ser.). 1979. lib. bdg. 41.00 (ISBN 0-8240-9800-5). Garland Pub.
--Repaso Oral. 1967. text ed. 9.95x (ISBN 0-669-31419-6); tapes. 5 reels o.p. 25.00 (ISBN 0-669-34140-1). Heath.
Colecchia, Francesca, ed. Garcia Lorca: An Annotated Primary Bibliography. LC 79-3509. 305p. 1982. lib. bdg. 48.00 (ISBN 0-8240-9496-4). Garland Pub.
Colecchia, Francesca & Matas, Julio, trs. Selected Latin American One-Act Plays. LC 72-92696. (Pitt Latin American Ser.). 1974. pap. 6.95x (ISBN 0-8229-5241-6). U of Pittsburgh Pr.
Colegate, Isabel. Colegate: Three Novels: The Blackmailer, Man of Power, & The Great Occasion. 544p. (Orig.). 1984. pap. 8.95 (ISBN 0-14-006975-5). Penguin.
--A Glimpse of Sion's Glory & Other Stories. (Elisabeth Sifton Bks). 153p. 1985. 14.95 (ISBN 0-670-80897-0). Viking.
--The Orlando Trilogy. 464p. 1984. pap. 7.95 (ISBN 0-14-006546-6). Penguin.
--The Shooting Party. 208p. 1982. pap. 3.50 (ISBN 0-380-59543-5, 60297-0, Bard). Avon.
--Statues in a Garden. 1982. pap. 2.95 (ISBN 0-380-60368-3, 60368-3, Bard). Avon.
--Three Novels: The Blackmailer, A Man of Power, The Great Occasion. 536p. 1984. 25.00 (ISBN 0-670-52409-3); pap. 8.95 (ISBN 0-14-006975-5). Viking.
Colegrove, C. Lee. A Critical Edition of Thomas Middleton's Your Five Gallants. LC 78-66747. (Renaissance Drama Ser.). 382p. 1982. lib. bdg. 51.00 (ISBN 0-8240-9747-5). Garland Pub.
Colegrove, Kenneth, ed. see Cadenhead, I. E.
Colegrove, Kenneth, ed. see Lindsey, David.
Colegrove, Kenneth, ed. see Pancake, John S.
Colegrove, William & Goodman, Frances B. Episodes: Texas Dow Nineteen Forty to Nineteen Seventy-Six. 218p. 1983. 11.95 (ISBN 0-89896-073-8). Larksdale.
Coleiro, E. Introduction to Vergil's Bucolics. 1979. pap. text ed. 46.50x (ISBN 90-6032-117-0). Humanities.
--Tematica E Struttura Dell'Eneide di Virgilio. 148p. (Orig., Italian.). 1983. pap. 18.00x (ISBN 0-317-07596-9, Pub. by B R Gruener Netherlands). Benjamins North Am.
Colella, A. Nuovo Dizionario di Elettrotecnic e di Elettronica: Italiano-Inglese, Inglese-Italiano. 541p. (Ital. & Eng.). 1977. 95.00 (ISBN 0-686-92200-X, M-9296). French & Eur.
Colella, Albert M. & O'Sullivan, Michael J. Systems Simulation: Methods & Applications. LC 73-11645. 320p. 1974. 25.00 (ISBN 0-669-90308-6). Lexington Bks.
Coleman & Brownlee. Financial Accounting for Management. LC 81-65306. (Accounting Ser.). 441p. 29.95 (ISBN 0-936328-03-7); text ed. 25.95 (ISBN 0-686-83172-1). Dame Inc.
Coleman & Newton. Teach Yourself Spanish Phrase Book. (Teach Yourself Ser.). 3.95 (ISBN 0-679-10237-X). McKay.
Coleman, A. Creative Sewing Machine. 1981. pap. 12.50 (ISBN 0-7134-3310-8, Pub. by Batsford England). David & Charles.
--Flaubert's Literary Development in the Light of His Memories D'un Fou Novembre, & Education Sentimentale. (Elliott Monographs: Vol. 1). 1914. 14.00 (ISBN 0-527-02605-0). Kraus Repr.
--Sources & Structure of Flaubert's Salammbo. (Elliott Monographs). 1914. pap. 15.00 (ISBN 0-527-02606-9). Kraus Repr.
Coleman, A., jt. auth. see Price, Steven D.
Coleman, A. D. Light Readings: A Photography Critic's Writings, 1968-1978. (Illus.). 1979. pap. 9.95 (ISBN 0-19-503196-2, GB 700, GB). Oxford U Pr.
--Lucinda Bunnen Collection. LC 83-81149. (Illus.). 56p. 1983. pap. 6.95 (ISBN 0-939802-17-1). High Mus Art.
Coleman, A. D., et al. Photography A-V Program Directory. LC 80-83469. (Illus.). 224p. 1980. 28.00x (ISBN 0-936524-00-6). PMI Inc.
Coleman, A. R., et al. Financial Accounting & Statement Analysis: A Manager's Guide. 1983. pap. 15.95 (ISBN 0-8359-1988-9). Reston.
--Financial Accounting for Management. 1983. text ed. 27.95 (ISBN 0-8359-1987-0). Reston.
Coleman, Alexander. Eca de Queiros & European Realism. LC 79-3011. (The Gotham Library). 1980. 40.00x (ISBN 0-8147-1378-5). NYU Pr.
Coleman, Alexander, ed. Cinco Maestros: Cuentos Modernos de Hispanoamerica. 318p. (Span.). 1969. pap. text ed. 12.95 (ISBN 0-15-507551-9, HC); instr's manual avail. (ISBN 0-15-507552-7, HC). HarBraceJ.
Coleman, Alice. Utopia on Trial: Vision & Reality in Planned Housing. (Illus.). 228p. 1985. 24.00 (ISBN 0-948096-00-4, Pub. by Hilary Shipman Ltd); pap. 11.95 (ISBN 0-948096-01-2). Longwood Pub Group.
Coleman, Allan D. Confirmation. 2nd ed. (Illus.). 48p. 1982. pap. 4.00 (ISBN 0-9608870-0-8). ADCO Enterp.
Coleman, Ann R. Victorian Lady on the Texas Frontier: The Journal of Ann Raney Coleman. King, Richard, ed. LC 69-16721. pap. 56.80 (ISBN 0-317-28704-4, 2055510). Bks Demand UMI.
Coleman, Anne. Fabrics & Threads for Schools. 1977. 9.95 (ISBN 0-7134-0187-7, Pub. by Batsford England). David & Charles.
Coleman, Antony & Hammond, Antony, eds. Poetry & Drama, Fifteen Seventy to Seventeen Hundred: Essays in Honor of Harold F. Brooks. LC 81-18813. 1982. 31.00x (ISBN 0-416-74470-2, NO. 3607). Methuen Inc.
Coleman, Antony, ed. see Vanbrugh, John.
Coleman, Arthur. A Case in Point. LC 78-68669. 1977. 8.95 (ISBN 0-88370-006-9). Watermill Pubs.
--Epic & Romance Criticism, Vol. II. LC 73-75805. 1975. 15.50 (ISBN 0-685-74733-6). Watermill Pubs.
--Epic & Romance Criticism, Vol. I. LC 73-75805. 1973. 15.50 (ISBN 0-88370-001-8). Watermill Pubs.
Coleman, Arthur & Tyler, Gary R. Drama Criticism, 2 vols. Incl. Vol. 1. A Checklist of Interpretation Since 1940 of English & American Plays. LC 66-30426. 457p. 1966. 18.00x (ISBN 0-8040-0069-7, 82-70456); Vol. 2. A Checklist of Continental Interpretation Since 1940 of Classical & Continental Plays. LC 66-30426. 446p. 1970. 18.00x (ISBN 0-8040-0500-1, 82-72437). Pub. by Swallow). Ohio U Pr.
Coleman, Arthur P. Humor in the Russian Comedy from Catherine to Gogòl. LC 25-11187. Repr. of 1925 ed. 12.50 (ISBN 0-404-01589-1). AMS Pr.
--Ice Ages Recent & Ancient. LC 77-105678. (BCL Ser.: Ii). Repr. of 1926 ed. 24.50 (ISBN 0-404-01596-4). AMS Pr.
--The Last Million Years: A History of the Pleistocene in North America. LC 75-41062. (BCL Ser.: Ii). Repr. of 1941 ed. 21.50 (ISBN 0-404-14656-2). AMS Pr.
Coleman, Arthur P., tr. see Slowacki, Juliusz.
Coleman, B. Better Basketball. (Illus.). 96p. 1980. 9.95 (ISBN 0-7182-1462-5, Pub. by Kaye & Ward). David & Charles.
Coleman, B. D., ed. see CISM (International Center for Mechanical Sciences), Dept. of Mechanics of Solids.
Coleman, B. D., et al. Viscometric Flows of Non-Newtonian Fluids: Theory & Experiment. (Springer Tracts in Natural Philosophy Ser.: Vol. 5). (Illus.). 1966. 21.00 (ISBN 0-387-03672-5). Springer-Verlag.
Coleman, Barbara. Primer on Employee Retirement Income Security Act. 166p. 1985. pap. text ed. 18.00 (ISBN 0-87179-476-4). BNA.
Coleman, Bernard & LaBud, Verona. Masinaigans: The Little Book. (Illus.). 368p. 1972. 10.00 (ISBN 0-686-05025-8). North Central.
Coleman, Bill & Coleman, Patty. God's Own Child. rev. ed. 64p. 1983. Parent's Book. pap. text ed. 3.95x (ISBN 0-89622-188-1); Leader's Guide. wkbk. 1.00 (ISBN 0-89622-187-3). Twenty-Third.
--My Confirmation Journal. 95p. (gr. 7-9). 1979. pap. 3.95 (ISBN 0-89622-114-8). Twenty-Third.
--Only Love Can Make It Easy, 2 vols. rev. ed. LC 80-52360. 1981. Couples' Wkbk. pap. 2.95x (ISBN 0-89622-131-8); Leader's Guide. pap. 8.50. Twenty-Third.
Coleman, Bob. The Small Business Survival Guide: A Handbook. LC 83-42678. 1984. 18.95 (ISBN 0-393-01768-0). Norton.
Coleman, Brian. Better Basketball. 17.95x (ISBN 0-7182-1462-5, SpS). Sportshelf.
Coleman, Brian & Ray, Peter. Basketball. (Sports Ser.). (Illus.). 1977. 6.95 (ISBN 0-7158-0587-8). Charles River Bks.
Coleman, Bruce & Hileman, Josephine. Coming to America. (Newbury House Readers Ser.: Stage 3 - Intermediate). 56p. (Orig.). (gr. 7-12). 1981. pap. text ed. 2.95 (ISBN 0-88377-196-9). Newbury Hse.
Coleman, C., jt. auth. see Gisolfi, A. M.
Coleman, Candy. Santa Claus in My Kitchen. Coleman, Candy, ed. (Illus.). 48p. (Orig.). 1979. pap. text ed. 3.00 (ISBN 0-943768-01-2). C Coleman.
--Super Menus for Football Fans. (Illus.). 48p. (Orig.). 1981. pap. text ed. 3.00 (ISBN 0-943768-04-7). C Coleman.
--Tailgate Picnics for the Southwest Conference. (Illus.). 48p. (Orig.). 1981. pap. text ed. 3.00 (ISBN 0-943768-05-5). C Coleman.
--There's a One-Armed Bandit in My Kitchen. (Illus.). 48p. (Orig.). 1980. pap. text ed. 3.00 (ISBN 0-943768-03-9). C Coleman.
--The Way to a Man's Heart. (Illus.). 32p. (Orig.). 1979. pap. text ed. 3.00 (ISBN 0-943768-02-0). C Coleman.
Coleman, Mrs. Chapman. Life of John J. Crittenden, 2 Vols. LC 72-99469. (American Public Figures Ser). 1970. Repr. of 1871 ed. Set. lib. bdg. 89.50 (ISBN 0-306-71843-X). Da Capo.
Coleman, Charles G. Divine Guidance: That Voice Behind You. LC 77-6796. 1977. pap. 2.50 (ISBN 0-87213-087-8). Loizeaux.
--Shining Sword. LC 56-31266. 1956. pap. 1.75 (ISBN 0-87213-086-X). Loizeaux.
Coleman, Charles H. Election of Eighteen Sixty-Eight. LC 70-155636. (Columbia University Studies in the Social Sciences: No. 392). Repr. of 1933 ed. 12.00 (ISBN 0-404-51392-1). AMS Pr.
--Election of Eighteen Sixty-Eight: The Democratic Effort to Regain Control. LC 73-159242. 1971. Repr. of 1933 ed. lib. bdg. 29.00x (ISBN 0-374-91848-1). Octagon.
Coleman, Charles J. Personnel: An Open System Approach. 1979. text ed. 20.95 (ISBN 0-316-15124-6); Tchr's ed. avail. (ISBN 0-316-15125-4). Little.
Coleman, Christopher B. Constantine the Great & Christianity. LC 70-155636. (Columbia University Studies in the Social Sciences: No. 146). Repr. of 1914 ed. 18.50 (ISBN 0-404-51146-5). AMS Pr.
Coleman, Cindy. A Shady Affair. (Illus.). 16p. 1983. pap. 5.95 (ISBN 0-910585-01-6). Willcraft.
Coleman, Clive, jt. auth. see Bottomley, Keith.
Coleman, D. A., ed. Demography of Immigrants & Minority Groups in the United Kingdom. 1983. pap. 36.00 (ISBN 0-12-179780-5). Acad Pr.
Coleman, D. C. Courtaulds: An Economic & Social History Vol. III: Crisis & Change 1940-65. (Illus.). 1980. 47.50x (ISBN 0-19-920111-0). Oxford U Pr.
--The Economy of England 1450-1750. (Opus 81). (Illus.). 1976. pap. 7.95x (ISBN 0-19-289070-0). Oxford U Pr.
--Industry in Tudor & Stuart England. (Studies in Economic & Social History Ser.). 80p. 1975. pap. text ed. 6.00x (ISBN 0-333-14351-5). Humanities.
Coleman, David. For the Long Term. LC 78-59906. 1979. 12.95 (ISBN 0-930726-05-7); pap. 8.95 (ISBN 0-930726-04-9). Concept Pub.
--The Game of Society. LC 79-52348. 12.95 (ISBN 0-930726-07-3); pap. 8.95 (ISBN 0-930726-06-5). Concept Pub.
--Management of the Firm. LC 77-86276. 1979. 13.95 (ISBN 0-930726-03-0); pap. 9.95 (ISBN 0-930726-02-2). Concept Pub.
Coleman, David, jt. auth. see Fox, Phyllis W.
Coleman, David, jt. auth. see Gaines, George.
Coleman, David, jt. ed. see Sors, Andrew I.
Coleman, David S., jt. auth. see Gaines, George.
Coleman, David S., jt. auth. see Gaines, George, Jr.
Coleman, David W., jt. auth. see Zollinger, Robert M.
Coleman, Deborah D., ed. Experiential Education in the Workplace: An Annotated Bibliography. 67p. 1979. 4.50 (ISBN 0-318-15470-6, BB 47). Natl Ctr Res Voc Ed.
Coleman, Denis R., jt. auth. see Edge, Alfred G.
Coleman, Derek. A Structured Programming Approach to Data. 222p. 1979. pap. 16.50 (ISBN 0-387-91138-3). Springer-Verlag.
Coleman, Donald C. The British Paper Industry, Fourteen Ninety-Five to Eighteen Sixty: A Study in Industrial Growth. LC 75-74. (Illus.). 367p. 1975. Repr. of 1958 ed. lib. bdg. 25.00x (ISBN 0-8371-8015-5, COBP). Greenwood.
--Sir John Banks, Baronet & Businessman. LC 74-30845. (Illus.). 215p. 1975. Repr. of 1963 ed. lib. bdg. 17.00x (ISBN 0-8371-7932-7, COJB). Greenwood.
Coleman, Donald C. & Mathias, Peter, eds. Enterprise & History: Essays in Honour of Charles Wilson. (Illus.). 312p. 1984. 49.50 (ISBN 0-521-24951-1). Cambridge U Pr.
Coleman, Donald G. Woodworking Factbook: Basic Information on Wood for Wood Carvers, Home Woodshop Craftsmen, Tradesmen & Instructors. (Illus.). 18.95 (ISBN 0-8315-0024-7). Speller.
Coleman, Dorothy. The Gallo-Roman Muse. LC 79-71. 1979. 39.50 (ISBN 0-521-22254-0). Cambridge U Pr.
--Rabelais: A Critical Study in Prose Fiction. LC 76-173822. 1971. pap. 13.95 (ISBN 0-521-29458-4). Cambridge U Pr.
Coleman, Dorothy G., jt. ed. see Bayley, Peter.
Coleman, Dorothy S., et al. Collector's Encyclopedia of Dolls. (Illus.). 1968. 35.00 (ISBN 0-517-00059-8). Crown.
--The Collector's Book of Dolls' Clothes: Costumes in Miniature, 1700-1929. (Illus.). 640p. 1975. 35.00 (ISBN 0-517-52031-1). Crown.
--Doll Collectors' Manual, 1973, Vol. 8. LC 65-29362. 1978. 8.00x (ISBN 0-9603210-0-4). Doll Collect Am.
Coleman, Dulcie V., jt. ed. see Koss, Leopold G.
Coleman, Earle J. Philosophy of Painting by Shih-T'ao. (Studies in Philosophy: No. 19). 1978. pap. text ed. 15.60x (ISBN 90-279-7756-9). Mouton.
Coleman, Earle J., ed. Varieties of Aesthetic Experience. LC 83-6781. 268p. (Orig.). 1983. lib. bdg. 26.75 (ISBN 0-8191-3276-4); pap. text ed. 12.75 (ISBN 0-8191-3277-2). U Pr of Amer.
Coleman, Edmund T. The First Ascent of Mount Baker: Mountaineering on the Pacific. (Shorey Historical Ser.). (Illus.). 28p. 1975. pap. 2.95 (ISBN 0-8466-0133-8). Shorey.
--Mountaineering on the Pacific in 1868. Jones, William R., ed. (Illus.). 24p. 1977. pap. 1.00 (ISBN 0-89646-014-2). Outbooks.
Coleman, Edward D. Bible in English Drama: An Annotated Bibliography. rev. ed. 1969. 25.00x (ISBN 0-87068-034-X). Ktav.
--Bible in English Drama: An Annotated List of Plays. 1969. 6.95 (ISBN 0-87104-021-2, Co-Pub by Ktav). NY Pub Lib.

--Jew in English Drama: An Annotated Bibliography. rev. ed. LC 67-11901. 1969. 25.00x (ISBN 0-87068-011-0). Ktav.

--Jew in English Drama: An Annotated Bibliography. LC 67-11901. 1968. Repr. of 1943 ed. with The Jew in Western Drama by Edgar Rosenberg 8.95 (ISBN 0-87104-101-4, Co-Pub by Ktav). NY Pub Lib.

--Plays of Jewish Interest on the American Stage. 59.95 (ISBN 0-8490-0842-5). Gordon Pr.

Coleman, Eleanor S. Captain Gustavus Conyingham, U.S.N. Pirate or Privateer, 1747-1819. LC 82-13596. (Illus.). 196p. 1983. lib. bdg. 25.25 (ISBN 0-8191-2692-6); pap. text ed. 11.25 (ISBN 0-8191-2693-4). U Pr of Amer.

Coleman, Elizabeth A. Changing Fashions 1800-1970. LC 72-79563. (Illus.). 72p. (Orig.). 1972. pap. 2.50 (ISBN 0-686-63618-X). Bklyn Mus.

--The Genius of Charles James. (Illus.). 176p. 1982. 25.50 (ISBN 0-03-062588-2). HR&W.

--Of Men Only: Men's & Boys' Fashions, 1750-1975. (Illus.). 32p. 1975. pap. 3.95 (ISBN 0-87273-053-0). Bklyn Mus.

Coleman, Elliot, tr. see Poulet, Georges.

Coleman, Elliott, tr. see Poulet, Georges.

Coleman, Emily & Edwards, Betty. Brief Encounters. LC 77-16908. 1979. pap. 9.95 (ISBN 0-385-15579-4, Anch). Doubleday.

Coleman, Emma L. New England Captives Carried to Canada Between Sixteen Seventy-Seven & Seventeen Sixty During the French & Indian Wars. 44.00 (ISBN 0-8369-6970-7, 7851). Ayer Co Pubs.

Coleman, Ernest A. The Dramatic Use of Bawdy in Shakespeare. LC 73-86132. pap. 60.00 (ISBN 0-317-27691-3, 2025220). Bks Demand UMI.

Coleman, Evelyn. Nineteen Fourteen Marshall Field & Company Doll Catalog. 102p. 1980. pap. 7.95 (ISBN 0-87588-157-2). Hobby Hse.

Coleman, F. Guide to Surgical Terminology. 3rd ed. 1978. pap. 18.95 (ISBN 0-87489-191-4). Med Economics.

Coleman, F. G., tr. see McDonald, Hope.

Coleman, F. L. The Northern Rhodesia Copperbelt, 1889-1962. 226p. 1971. 18.50 (ISBN 0-7190-0419-5, Pub. by Manchester Univ Pr). Longwood Pub Group.

Coleman, Floyd W., jt. auth. see Richardson, John A.

Coleman, Francis. The Deunionizing Handbook. LC 82-84086. (Illus.). ii, 201p. 1983. 65.00 (ISBN 0-318-00258-2). Fed Pubns Inc.

--Great Britain. LC 75-44870. (Countries Ser.). (Illus.). (gr. 6 up). 1976. PLB 13.96 (ISBN 0-382-06102-0). Silver.

Coleman, Francis see Frost, David.

Coleman, Francis L. The Northern Rhodesia Copperbelt, 1899-1962. LC 72-149805. (Illus.). 206p. 1971. lib. bdg. 25.00x (ISBN 0-678-06784-8). Kelley.

Coleman, Francis X. The Harmony of Reason: A Study in Kant's Aesthetics. LC 74-4520. 1974. 17.95x (ISBN 0-8229-3282-2). U of Pittsburgh Pr.

Coleman, Frank M. Hobbes & America: Exploring the Constitutional Foundations. LC 76-46434. 1977. pap. 8.95 (ISBN 0-8020-6374-8). U of Toronto Pr.

--Politics, Policy & the Constitution. LC 80-52138. 363p. 1982. pap. text ed. 11.95 (ISBN 0-312-62942-7). St Martin.

Coleman, Freada A., jt. ed. see McDermott, Beatrice S.

Coleman, Frederic. The Far East Unveiled: An Inner History of Events in Japan & China in the Year 1916. LC 72-82090. (Japan Library). 1973. Repr. of 1916 ed. lib. bdg. 27.00 (ISBN 0-8420-1385-7). Scholarly Res Inc.

Coleman, Gary. Member Missionary: Hey, I Can Do That. LC 83-80527. 79p. 1983. pap. 4.95 (ISBN 0-88290-220-2). Horizon-Utah.

Coleman, Gary J. How Great Will Be Your Joy! 1977. 3.95 (ISBN 0-89036-086-3). Hawkes Pub Inc.

--A Look at Mormonism. pap. 3.95 (ISBN 0-89036-142-8). Hawkes Pub Inc.

Coleman, Gerald. Homosexuality - an Appraisal. 1978. 0.75 (ISBN 0-685-89391-X). Franciscan Herald.

Coleman, Glen. The Man Who Fenced the West. Schoonover, Shirley, ed. (Illus.). 104p. 1984. 20.00 (ISBN 0-9614346-0-0). Osthoff-Thalden.

Coleman, H. S. Teach Yourself Modelcraft. 10.00x (ISBN 0-392-08233-0, SpS). Sportshelf.

Coleman, H. W. & Pfund, P. A., eds. Engineering Applications of Laser Velocimetry. 1982. 40.00 (H00230). ASME.

Coleman, Harry. Camping Out with Your New Van or Minibus: A Survival Manual for International Campers. LC 81-794. 360p. 1983. 19.95 (ISBN 0-87196-308-6). Facts on File.

Coleman, Henry. Church Organist. 2nd ed. 1968. 9.75 (ISBN 0-19-322100-4). Oxford U Pr.

Coleman, Herbert T. Public Education in Upper Canada. LC 78-176661. (Columbia University. Teachers College. Contributions to Education: No. 15). Repr. of 1907 ed. 22.50 (ISBN 0-404-55015-0). AMS Pr.

Coleman, Horace. The Apple IIc BASIC Programming Book. 1986. pap. 19.95 (ISBN 0-673-18278-9). Scott F.

Coleman, Howard W. Case Studies in Broadcast Management. rev.,enl.,2nd ed. 1978. 10.75 (ISBN 0-8038-1220-5); pap. text ed. 6.50x (ISBN 0-8038-1221-3). Hastings.

Coleman, Hywel. Petroleum: Upstream. (Science & Technical Readers Ser.). (Orig.). 1980. pap. text ed. 2.95x (ISBN 0-435-29001-0). Heinemann Ed.

Coleman, Irene S., jt. auth. see Coleman, James C.

Coleman, J. P. Choctaw County Chronicles: A History of Choctaw County Mississippi 1830-1973. LC 81-19886. (Illus.). 484p. 1982. Repr. of 1974 ed. 12.50 (ISBN 0-87152-358-2). Reprint.

Coleman, J. R. Comparative Economic Systems. (gr. 9-12). 1974. text ed. 16.08 (ISBN 0-03-080093-5, HoltE); tchr's guide 16.08 (ISBN 0-03-080094-3). HR&W.

Coleman, J. Walter. The Molly Maguire Riots: Industrial Conflict in the Pennsylvania Coal Region. LC 78-89724. (American Labor, from Conspiracy to Collective Bargaining, Ser. 1). 189p. Repr. of 1936 ed. 20.00 (ISBN 0-405-02112-7). Ayer Co Pubs.

Coleman, J. Winston, Jr. Three Kentucky Artists: Hart, Price, & Troye. LC 74-7873. (Kentucky Bicentennial Bookshelf Ser.). (Illus.). 96p. 1974. 6.95 (ISBN 0-8131-0202-2). U Pr of Ky.

Coleman, James. Microwave Devices. 1982. text ed. 28.95 (ISBN 0-8359-4386-0). Reston.

Coleman, James & Cressey, Donald. Social Problems. 2nd ed. 639p. 1984. text ed. 21.95 scp (ISBN 0-06-041327-1, HarpC); write for info. instr's manual (ISBN 0-06-361331-X). Har-row.

Coleman, James C. Intimate Relationships, Marriage & Family. 624p. 1984. text ed. 24.15 scp (ISBN 0-672-61539-8); scp instr's. guide 7.33 (ISBN 0-672-61619-X); scp wkbk. 8.75 (ISBN 0-672-61620-3). Bobbs.

--Intimate Relationships, Marriage, & Family. 624p. 1984. text ed. write for info (ISBN 0-02-323470-9). Macmillan.

Coleman, James C. & Butcher, James N. Abnormal Psychology & Modern Life. 7th ed. 1984. text ed. 32.60x (ISBN 0-673-15886-1). Scott F.

Coleman, James C. & Coleman, Irene S. Pensacola Fortifications, 1698-1980: Guardians of the Gulf. (Illus.). 120p. 1983. pap. 7.95x (ISBN 0-939566-02-8). Pensacola Hist.

Coleman, James C. & Glaros, Alan G. Contemporary Psychology & Effective Behavior. 5th ed. 1983. text ed. 25.80x (ISBN 0-673-15640-0). Scott F.

Coleman, James J., Jr. Gilbert Antoine de St. Maxent: The Spanish-Frenchman of New Orleans. LC 68-54600. 136p. 1980. 12.50 (ISBN 0-911116-06-0). Pelican.

Coleman, James K. State Administration in South Carolina. LC 70-76647. (Columbia University Studies in the Social Sciences: No. 406). Repr. of 1935 ed. 22.50 (ISBN 0-404-51406-5). AMS Pr.

Coleman, James M. Aesculapius on the Colorado. 1971. 10.00 (ISBN 0-88426-028-3). Encino Pr.

Coleman, James S. Adolescent Society. LC 61-14725. 1971. pap. text ed. 8.95 (ISBN 0-02-906410-4). Free Pr.

--The Asymmetric Society. LC 81-23255. (Frank W. Abrams Lecture Ser.). 192p. 1982. 18.00x (ISBN 0-8156-0172-7); pap. 9.95x (ISBN 0-8156-0174-3). Syracuse U Pr.

--Community Conflict. 1957. pap. text ed. 3.95 (ISBN 0-02-906480-5). Free Pr.

--Introduction to Mathematical Sociology. 1964. 22.95 (ISBN 0-02-906520-8). Free Pr.

--Longitudinal Data Analysis. LC 80-66309. 1981. text ed. 22.50x (ISBN 0-465-04224-4). Basic.

--Nigeria: Background to Nationalism. LC 58-10286. (California Library Reprint Series: No. 28). 1971. 47.50x (ISBN 0-520-02070-7). U of Cal Pr.

--Power & the Structure of Society. new ed. 1974. pap. 4.95x (ISBN 0-393-09327-1). Norton.

--Resources for Social Change: Race in the United States. LC 77-152494. 134p. 1971. 12.75 (ISBN 0-471-16493-3). Krieger.

Coleman, James S. & Karweit, Nancy L. Information Systems & Performance Measures in Schools. LC 72-79547. 152p. 1972. 21.95 (ISBN 0-87778-038-2). Educ Tech Pubns.

Coleman, James S., jt. auth. see United States Office of Education.

Coleman, James S., jt. auth. see United States Office of Equal Opportunity.

Coleman, James S., ed. Education & Political Development. (Studies in Political Development: No. 4). 1965. 46.00 (ISBN 0-691-07506-9). Princeton U Pr.

Coleman, James S., jt. ed. see Almond, Gabriel A.

Coleman, James S., et al. Equality of Educational Opportunity, 2 vols. Coser, Lewis A. & Powell, Walter W., eds. LC 79-6990. (Perennial Works in Sociology Ser.). (Illus.). 1979. Repr. of 1966 ed. Set. lib. bdg. 76.00x (ISBN 0-405-12088-5); lib. bdg. 38.00x ea. Vol. 1 (ISBN 0-405-12089-3). Vol. 2 (ISBN 0-405-12090-7). Ayer Co Pubs.

--Parents, Teachers & Children: Prospects for Choice in American Education. LC 77-89164. 336p. 1977. pap. text ed. 5.95 (ISBN 0-917616-18-9). ICS Pr.

--Parents, Teachers, & Children: Prospects for Choice in American Education. 336p. 1977. pap. 5.95 (ISBN 0-318-04474-9). ICS Pr.

--Youth: Transition to Adulthood-Report on Youth of the President's Advisory Committee. LC 73-92757. 1974. pap. 2.45x (ISBN 0-226-11342-6, P589, Phoen). U of Chicago Pr.

--High School Achievement: Public, Catholic, & Private Schools Compared. LC 81-68411. 1982. 20.75 (ISBN 0-465-02956-6). Basic.

--The Adolescent Society: The Social Life of the Teenager & Its Impact on Education. LC 81-1737. (Illus.). xvi, 368p. 1981. Repr. of 1961 ed. lib. bdg. 35.00x (ISBN 0-313-22934-1, COADS). Greenwood.

Coleman, James W. The Criminal Elite: The Sociology of White Collar Crime. LC 84-51840. 288p. 1985. pap. text ed. 13.95 (ISBN 0-312-17209-5). St Martin.

Coleman, Janet. Medieval Readers & Writers: Literature & Society, 1350-1400. 320p. 1981. 30.00x (ISBN 0-231-05364-9). Columbia U Pr.

Coleman, Jean. Chapter Twenty-Nine. 1979. pap. 2.50 (ISBN 0-88270-436-2). Bridge Pub.

Coleman, Jill P. & Kemp, Robert S., Jr. Issues in Unfunded Pension Liabilities: Accounting Treatment & Investor's Perceptions of Risk. 61p. (Orig.). 1981. pap. text ed. 3.00 (ISBN 0-89154-153-5). Intl Found Employ.

Coleman, John. Charles Reade As I Knew Him. 428p. 1981. lib. bdg. 50.00 (ISBN 0-89987-118-6). Darby Bks.

--Charles Reade As I Knew Him. 1973. Repr. of 1903 ed. 50.00 (ISBN 0-8274-1424-2). R West.

--Your Book of Veteran & Edwardian Cars. (gr. 7 up). 1972. 5.95 (ISBN 0-571-09375-2). Transatlantic.

--Your Book of Vintage Cars. (Illus.). (gr. 7 up). 1969. 4.50 (ISBN 0-571-08276-9). Transatlantic.

Coleman, John & Baum, Gregory, eds. Youth Without A Fututre? (Concilium Ser.: Vol. 181). 120p. pap. 6.95 (ISBN 0-317-31478-5, 30-30061-1902); pap. 9.05 Canada (ISBN 0-317-31479-3). Fortress.

Coleman, John, jt. ed. see Baum, Gregory.

Coleman, John, jt. ed. see Baum, Gregory B.

Coleman, John A. The Evolution of Dutch Catholicism, Nineteen Fifty-Eight to Nineteen Seventy-Four. LC 74-22958. 1979. 40.00x (ISBN 0-520-02885-6). U of Cal Pr.

--Other Voices: A Study of the Late Poetry of Luis Cernuda. (Studies in the Romance Languages & Literatures: No. 81). 186p. 1969. pap. 9.50x (ISBN 0-8078-9081-2). U of NC Pr.

Coleman, John C. Nature of Adolescence. 1980. 10.95x (ISBN 0-416-72620-8, NO. 2894). Methuen Inc.

Coleman, John C., ed. The School Years: Current Issues in the Socialization of Young People. (Psychology in Progress Ser.). 180p. 1979. 25.00x (ISBN 0-416-71190-1, NO. 2898); pap. 12.95x (ISBN 0-416-71200-2, NO. 2899). Methuen Inc.

Coleman, John D. Do Yourself a Favor: Love Your Wife. 1976. wkbk. 1.25 (ISBN 0-88270-162-2, Pub. by Logos). Bridge Pub.

Coleman, John E. Commercial Pilot Questions Answers Explanations. rev. ed. (Illus.). 312p. (Orig.). 1985. pap. text ed. 12.95x. Astro Pubs.

--Flight Instructor: Questions, Answers, Explanations. rev. ed. (Illus.). 220p. 1985. pap. text ed. 12.95 (ISBN 0-941272-23-0). Astro Pubs.

--Instrument Rating Questions-Answers-Explanations (QAE 8080-7) rev. ed. (Illus.). 240p. 1984. pap. text ed. 13.95. Astro Pubs.

--Kephala: A Late Neolithic Settlement & Cemetery. LC 76-13187. (Keos Ser: Vol. 1). 1977. pap. 35.00x (ISBN 0-87661-701-1). Am Sch Athens.

--Military Competency Examination: Questions-Answers-Explanations (QAE-82) Includes FARs. (Illus.). 68p. 1982. pap. text ed. 8.95 (ISBN 0-941272-01-X). Astro Pubs.

--Private Pilot Airplane: Questions-Answers-Explanations. (Illus.). 208p. 1984. pap. text ed. 10.95 (ISBN 0-317-18180-7, QAE 8080-1). Astro Pubs.

--Questions-Answers-Explanations: Private Pilot Airplane Written Test Guide. (Illus.). 168p. 1982. pap. text ed. 10.95 (ISBN 0-941272-10-9, QAE 32C). Astro Pubs.

--Questions-Answers-Explanations: Private Pilot Airplane Written Test Guide. rev. ed. (Illus.). 212p. 1984. pap. text ed. 11.95 (ISBN 0-941272-24-9, QAE-32C). Astro Pubs.

Coleman, John F. The Disruption of the Pennsylvania Democracy, 1848-1860. LC 75-623874. (Illus.). 184p. 1975. 7.95 (ISBN 0-911124-82-9). Pa Hist & Mus.

Coleman, John H. Written Composition Interests of Junior & Senior High School Pupils. LC 71-176662. (Columbia University. Teachers College. Contributions to Education: No. 494). Repr. of 1931 ed. 22.50 (ISBN 0-404-55494-6). AMS Pr.

Coleman, John M. Thomas McKean. LC 74-19952. 1975. 16.95 (ISBN 0-912834-07-2). Am Faculty Pr.

Coleman, John R. Blue-Collar Journal: A College President's Sabbatical. LC 73-21902. 1974. 11.49i (ISBN 0-397-01030-3). Har-Row.

Coleman, John S., Jr. Bataan & Beyond: Memories of an American P.O.W. LC 78-6365. (Centennial Series of the Associatioc of Former Students: No. 6). (Illus.). 224p. 1978. 14.95 (ISBN 0-89096-055-0). Tex A&M Univ Pr.

Coleman, John W. A Bibliography of Kentucky History. LC 49-11965. pap. 133.50 (ISBN 0-317-10456-X, 2001468). Bks Demand UMI.

Coleman, John W., Jr. Slavery Times in Kentucky. LC 40-31785. (Basic Afro-American Reprint Library Ser). (Illus.). 1970. Repr. of 1940 ed. 22.00 (ISBN 0-384-09535-6). Johnson Repr.

Coleman, Jonathan. At Mother's Request: A True Story of Money, Murder, & Betrayal. LC 84-45616. (Illus.). 640p. 1985. 19.95 (ISBN 0-689-11547-4). Atheneum.

Coleman, Joseph. Apple Lisa: A User-Friendly Handbook. (Illus.). 320p. (Orig.). 1984. 24.95 (ISBN 0-8306-0691-2, 1691); pap. text ed. 16.95 (ISBN 0-8306-1691-8). TAB Bks.

--TRS-80 Model 100: A User's Guide. 288p. (Orig.). 1984. 21.95 (ISBN 0-8306-0651-3, 1651); pap. 15.50 (ISBN 0-8306-1651-9). TAB Bks.

--Word Processing Simplified & Self-Taught. LC 82-24501. (Simplified & Self-Taught Ser.). (Illus.). 128p. 1983. lib. bdg. 11.95 (ISBN 0-668-05599-5); pap. 4.95 (ISBN 0-668-05601-0). Arco.

Coleman, Jules L., jt. auth. see Murphy, Jeffrie G.

Coleman, Ken & Valenti, Dan. Diary of a Sportscaster. LC 82-82096. 176p. (Orig.). 1982. pap. 6.95 (ISBN 0-943514-03-7). Literations.

--Rain Delays: Interviews with Baseball Legends. (Illus.). 200p. 1985. pap. 9.95 (ISBN 0-943514-04-5). Literations.

Coleman, Kenneth. American Revolution in Georgia, 1763-1789. LC 58-59848. 360p. 1958. 25.00x (ISBN 0-8203-0015-2). U of Ga Pr.

--America's Endangered Banks: Check the Safety of Your Savings. 36p. 1984. pap. 9.95 (ISBN 0-317-17173-9). Seraphim Pr.

--Colonial Georgia: A History. (A History of the American Colonies Ser.). 1976. lib. bdg. 35.00 (ISBN 0-527-18712-7). Kraus Intl.

--Confederate Athens. write for info. U of Ga Pr.

--Georgia History in Outline. rev. ed. LC 78-14087. 136p. 1978. pap. text ed. 5.00x (ISBN 0-8203-0467-0). U of Ga Pr.

--The Misdirection Conspiracy: or, Who Really Killed the American Dream? (Exposed by Reality Investing) LC 82-50091. (Illus.). 216p. 1983. pap. 10.95 (ISBN 0-942632-00-1). Seraphim Pr.

--U. S. Financial Institutions in Crisis: How Safe are Your Savings? rev. ed. Chambers, Catherine & Lewis, David, eds. 24p. 1984. pap. 9.95 (ISBN 0-942632-01-X). Seraphim Pr.

Coleman, Kenneth, ed. The Colonial Records of the State of Georgia, Vol. 30. LC 84-24141. 376p. 1985. 30.00x (ISBN 0-8203-0774-2). U of Ga Pr.

--A History of Georgia. LC 77-73640. (Illus.). 462p. 1977. 18.00 (ISBN 0-8203-0427-1); text ed. 15.00x (ISBN 0-8203-0433-6). U of Ga Pr.

Coleman, Kenneth & Gurr, Charles S., eds. Dictionary of Georgia Biography, 2 vols. LC 82-17341. 1144p. 1983. Set. 60.00x (ISBN 0-8203-0662-2). U of Ga Pr.

Coleman, Kenneth & Ready, Milton, eds. The Colonial Records of the State of Georgia, Vol. 20. LC 82-2573. (Colonial Records Ser.). 536p. 1982. 30.00x (ISBN 0-8203-0598-7). U of Ga Pr.

--The Colonial Records of the State of Georgia, Vol. 27. LC 77-6466. (Colonial Records Ser.). 320p. 1978. 22.00x (ISBN 0-8203-0423-9). U of Ga Pr.

--The Colonial Records of the State of Georgia, Vol. 28, Pt. II. LC 79-14348. (The Colonial Records Ser.). 446p. 1979. 30.00x (ISBN 0-8203-0481-6). U of Ga Pr.

--The Colonial Records of the State of Georgia, Vol. 28, Pt I. LC 74-30679. (Colonial Records Ser.). 496p. 1975. 30.00x (ISBN 0-8203-0379-8). U of Ga Pr.

--The Colonial Records of the State of Georgia, Vol. 29. LC 84-24142. 372p. 1985. text ed. 30.00x (ISBN 0-8203-0773-4). U of Ga Pr.

Coleman, Kenneth M. Public Opinion in Mexico City about the Electoral System. LC 72-78930. (James Sprunt Studies Ser.). x, 94p. 1972. pap. text ed. 10.00 (ISBN 0-8078-5053-5). U of NC Pr.

Coleman, Kenneth M. & Herring, George C., eds. The Central American Crisis: Sources of Conflict & the Failure of U. S. Policy. LC 84-27624. 224p. 1985. 30.00 (ISBN 0-8420-2238-4); pap. text ed. 9.95 (ISBN 0-8420-2240-6). Scholarly Res Inc.

Coleman, L. F. Aspects of Indian Civilization As Revealed in Representative Mexican Novels. 59.95 (ISBN 0-87968-670-7). Gordon Pr.

Coleman, Laurence V. Historic House Museums. LC 71-175318. (Illus.). xii, 187p. 1973. Repr. of 1933 ed. 43.00x (ISBN 0-8103-3118-7). Gale.

Coleman, Lee. The Reign of Error: Psychiatry, Authority, & the Law. LC 83-71943. 316p. 1985. 18.95 (ISBN 0-8070-0481-2, 702); pap. 9.95 (ISBN 0-8070-0479-0, BP702). Beacon Pr.

Coleman, Les & Pedemonti, Richard D. Squeal. (Illus.). 1982. 15.95 (ISBN 0-939026-03-1). Spoonwood Pr.

Coleman, Libby, jt. auth. see Bing, Elizabeth.

Coleman, Linda, ed. see PACE - Grace Lutheran School.

Coleman, Lonnie. Beulah Land. 1980. pap. 4.95 (ISBN 0-440-11393-8). Dell.

--The Legacy of Beulah Land. 1981. pap. 4.95 (ISBN 0-440-15085-X). Dell.

--The Legacy of Beulah Land. LC 79-7516. 1980. 14.95 (ISBN 0-385-15459-3). Doubleday.

--Look Away Beulah Land. 1979. pap. 4.95 (ISBN 0-440-14654-2). Dell.

Coleman, Loren. Curious Encounters: Phantom Trains, Spooky Spots & Other Mysterious Wonders. LC 85-10132. (Illus.). 170p. (Orig.). 1985. pap. 9.95 (ISBN 0-571-12542-5). Faber & Faber.

--Mysterious America. (Illus.). 176p. (Orig.). 1983. pap. 9.95 (ISBN 0-571-12524-7). Faber & Faber.

Coleman, Louis, tr. see Mariengof, Anatol.

Coleman, Lucien E. The Exciting Christian Life: Bible Study on Christian Growth. 36p. 1982. pap. 3.50 (ISBN 0-939298-11-2). J M Prods.

Coleman, Lucien E., Jr. Como Ensenar la Biblia. Diaz, Jorge E., tr. Orig. Title: How to Teach the Bible. 265p. (Span.). 1982. 7.95 (ISBN 0-311-11039-8). Casa Bautista.

--How to Teach the Bible. LC 79-52001. 1980. 9.95 (ISBN 0-8054-3428-3). Broadman.

--Why the Church Must Teach. LC 84-4966. 1984. pap. 6.95 (ISBN 0-8054-3234-5). Broadman.

Coleman, Lucile. December Twenty-Fifth. Edwards, G. F., ed. 1978. LEB2. pap. 1.00 (ISBN 0-932318-01-0, Little Economy Bks). G F Edwards.

--Hunter of Time: Gnomic Verses. Eng, Steve, ed. (Blue Meadow Poetry Ser.: No. 1). 20p. (Orig.). 1984. pap. 3.50 (ISBN 0-910151-02-4). Depot Pr.

--The Lyric Return. LC 77-82088. 62p. (Orig.). 1977. pap. 2.95x (ISBN 0-9614716-0-3). A to Z Bk Serv.

--Safety Signposts. Edwards, G. F., ed. 1978. Leb3. pap. 1.00 (ISBN 0-932318-02-9, Little Economy Bks). G F Edwards.

--This Laughing Dust. 2nd ed. 80p. 1980. pap. 3.00x (ISBN 0-9614716-1-1). A to Z Bk Serv.

Coleman, Lyman. Body Building. (Free University Ser.). (Orig.). 1981. pap. 4.95 leader's guide (ISBN 0-687-37306-9); pap. 1.25 student's bk. (ISBN 0-687-37307-7). Abingdon.

--Coping: O God, I'm Struggling. (Serendipity Ser.). (Orig.). 1981. pap. 4.95 leader's guide 64 pgs. (ISBN 0-687-37310-7); pap. 1.25 student's bk. 32 pgs. (ISBN 0-687-37311-5). Abingdon.

--Moral Issues: If Christ Is Lord. (Serendipity Ser.). (Orig.). 1981. pap. 4.95 leader's guide 64 pgs. (ISBN 0-687-37330-1); pap. 1.25 student's bk 32 pgs (ISBN 0-687-37331-X). Abingdon.

--My Calling: Here I Am Lord. (Serendipity Ser.). (Orig.). 1981. pap. 4.95 leader's guide 64 pgs (ISBN 0-687-37336-0); pap. 1.25 student's bk 32 pgs (ISBN 0-687-37337-9). Abingdon.

--Self Profile: The Me Nobody Knows. (Free University - Lay Academy in Christian Discipleship Ser.). (Orig.). 1981. pap. 4.95 leader's guide (ISBN 0-687-37346-8); pap. 1.25 (ISBN 0-687-37347-6). Abingdon.

--Spiritual Basics: New Life in Christ. (Free University - Lay Academy in Christian Discipleship Ser.). (Orig.). 1981. pap. 1.25 student's bk. (ISBN 0-687-37355-7); pap. 4.95 tchr's bk. (ISBN 0-687-37354-9). Abingdon.

Coleman, M., ed. Autistic Syndromes. 1976. 35.50 (ISBN 0-7204-0590-4, North Holland). Elsevier.

Coleman, M. Clare. Downham-In-The-Isle: A Study of an Ecclesiastical Manor in the 13th & 14th Centuries. (Illus.). 166p. 1984. 22.50 (ISBN 0-85115-401-8, Pub. by Boydell & Brewer). Longwood Pub Group.

Coleman, M. M. Our Other World: A Polish Scrapbook. (Illus.). 1978. 6.00 (ISBN 0-685-63579-1). Alliance Coll.

Coleman, McAlister. Eugene V. Debs: A Man Unafraid. LC 75-310. (The Radical Tradition in America Ser.). 345p. 1975. Repr. of 1930 ed. 27.50 (ISBN 0-88355-214-0). Hyperion Conn.

--Men & Coal. LC 71-89725. (American Labor, from Conspiracy to Collective Bargaining Ser., No. 1). 350p. 1969. Repr. of 1943 ed. 20.00 (ISBN 0-405-02111-9). Ayer Co Pubs.

--Pioneers of Freedom. facs. ed. LC 68-20292. (Essay Index Reprint Ser). 1968. Repr. of 1929 ed. 17.00 (ISBN 0-8369-0326-9). Ayer Co Pubs.

--Red Neck. LC 74-22772. (Labor Movement in Fiction & Non-Fiction). Repr. of 1936 ed. 24.50 (ISBN 0-404-58412-8). AMS Pr.

Coleman, Margaret C. Behavior Disorders: Theory & Practice. (Illus.). 352p. 1986. text ed. 22.95 (ISBN 0-13-071770-3). P-H.

Coleman, Marie & Eigen, Michael. Evil: Self & Culture. (Self-in-Process Ser.: Vol. 4). 352p. 1984. 29.95 (ISBN 0-89885-143-2). Human Sci Pr.

Coleman, Marion M. Fair Rosalind: The American Career of Helena Modjeska, 1877-1907. LC 69-10370. (Illus.). 1969. 20.00 (ISBN 0-910366-07-1). Alliance Coll.

--Zosia & Thaddeus. 1st ed. LC 73-93707. 115p. 1974. pap. 4.00 (ISBN 0-910366-17-9). Alliance Coll.

Coleman, Marion M., ed. see Sienkiewicz, Henryk.

Coleman, Marion M., tr. see Dyboski, Roman.

Coleman, Marion M., tr. see Slowacki, Juliusz.

Coleman, Mary & Gillberg, Christopher. The Biology of the Autistic Syndromes. LC 84-26402. 272p. 1985. 36.95x (ISBN 0-03-000834-4). Praeger.

Coleman, Mary, ed. Neonatal Neurology. (Illus.). 444p. 1981. text ed. 72.00 (ISBN 0-8391-1584-9). Univ Park.

Coleman, Mary E. How to Astro-Analyze Yourself & Others. (Illus.). 256p. (Orig.). 1985. pap. 6.95 (ISBN 0-85030-400-8, Pub. by Aquarian Pr England). Sterling.

Coleman, Matthew, ed. see Miller Freeman Publications, Inc.

Coleman, Michael. Michael Coleman. (Illus.). 52p. 1979. pap. 12.95 (ISBN 0-8032-6305-8, Buffalo Bill Hist. Ctr.). U of Nebr Pr.

Coleman, Michael C. Presbyterian Missionary Attitudes Toward American Indians, 1837-1893. (Illus.). 1985. 25.00x (ISBN 0-87805-278-X). U Pr of Miss.

Coleman, Mildred H., ed. Frances Virginia Tearoom Cook Book. LC 81-83889. 189p. 1982. 8.95 (ISBN 0-931948-23-1). Peachtree Pubs.

Coleman, N. Eugene V. Debs: A Man Unafraid. 59.95 (ISBN 0-8490-0136-6). Gordon Pr.

Coleman, P. G. & Sharma, S. C., eds. Positron Annihilation: Proceedings of the Sixth International Conference on Positron Annihilation, the University of Texas at Arlington, April 3-7, 1982. 1016p. 1983. 132.00 (ISBN 0-444-86534-9, North Holland). Elsevier.

Coleman, Patricia. Whose Problem? Library Services to the Disadvantaged, 1981. 1981. 16.00x (ISBN 0-900092-37-8, Pub. by Hill & Son England). State Mutual Bk.

Coleman, Patty, jt. auth. see Coleman, Bill.

Coleman, Peter & Shrubb, Lee, eds. Quadrant: Twenty-Five Years. LC 82-19998. 568p. 1983. 22.50 (ISBN 0-7022-1820-0). U of Queensland Pr.

Coleman, Peter J. Debtors & Creditors in America: Insolvency, Imprisonment for Debt, & Bankruptcy 1607-1900. LC 74-502. 375p. 1974. 17.50 (ISBN 0-87020-141-7). State Hist Soc Wis.

--The Transformation of Rhode Island, 1790-1860. LC 84-27932. xiv, 314p. 1985. Repr. of 1969 ed. lib. bdg. 45.00x (ISBN 0-313-24796-X, COTR). Greenwood.

Coleman, R. V., ed. Solid State Physics. (Methods of Experimental Physics Ser.: Vol. 11). 1974. 90.00 (ISBN 0-12-475911-4). Acad Pr.

Coleman, Ray. Lennon. 1985. 24.95 (ISBN 0-07-011786-1); pap. 19.95 (ISBN 0-07-011786-1). McGraw.

Coleman, Raymond. Multiple Choice Questions in Histology. 285p. (Orig.). 1983. pap. text ed. 10.50 (ISBN 0-272-79733-2, Pub. by Pitman Bks Ltd UK). Urban & S.

Coleman, Richard. Gospel-Telling: The Art & Theology of Children's Sermons. 128p. (Orig.). 1982. pap. 5.95 (ISBN 0-8028-1927-3). Eerdmans.

--Is Your Prescription Killing You? Richards, Carolyn, ed. LC 79-28294. 1981. 12.95 (ISBN 0-87949-164-7). Ashley Bks.

Coleman, Richard J. Issues of Theological Conflict: Evangelicals & Liberals. Rev. ed. LC 79-19494. pap. 74.00 (ISBN 0-317-19816-5, 2023209). Bks Demand UMI.

Coleman, Richard P. & Neugarten, Bernice L. Social Status in the City. LC 70-132820. (Jossey-Bass Behavioral Science Ser.). Repr. of 1971 ed. 64.30 (ISBN 0-8357-9348-6, 2013782). Bks Demand UMI.

Coleman, Richard P., et al. Social Standing in America: New Dimensions of Class. LC 77-20426. 353p. 1981. pap. 8.95x (ISBN 0-465-07929-6, TB-5072). Basic.

Coleman, Robert. The Development of Informal Geometry. LC 78-176696. (Columbia University. Teachers College. Contributions to Education: No. 865). Repr. of 1942 ed. 22.50 (ISBN 0-404-55865-8). AMS Pr.

--The New Covenant. 132p. 1985. pap. 4.95 (ISBN 0-89109-524-1). NavPress.

Coleman, Robert, ed. see Virgil.

Coleman, Robert A. Structural Systems Design. (Illus.). 400p. 1983. 44.95 (ISBN 0-13-853978-2). P-H.

Coleman, Robert E. Dry Bones Can Live Again. pap. 4.95 (ISBN 0-8007-5154-X, Power Bks). Revell.

--Evangelism in Perspective. LC 75-31306. 3.95 (ISBN 0-87509-080-X); pap. 2.00 (ISBN 0-87509-081-8). Chr Pubns.

--Growing in the Word. 272p. 1982. pap. 2.95 (ISBN 0-8007-8448-0, Spire Bks). Revell.

--The Heartbeat of Evangelism. 40p. 1985. pap. 1.50 (ISBN 0-89109-400-8). NavPress.

--The Master Plan of Evangelism. 128p. 1978. pap. 5.95 (ISBN 0-8007-5007-1, Power Bks); pap. 2.50 (ISBN 0-8007-8303-4, Spire Bks). Revell.

--The Mind of the Master. 128p. 4.95 (ISBN 0-8007-0880-6); 4.95 (ISBN 0-8007-5155-8, Power Bks). Revell.

--Songs of Heaven. 160p. 1982. pap. 5.95 (ISBN 0-8007-5097-7, Power Bks). Revell.

--They Meet the Master. 1979. pap. 5.95 (ISBN 0-8007-1037-1). Revell.

Coleman, Ron J. Opportunities in Fire Protection Services. (VGM Career Bks). (Illus.). 160p. 1983. 7.95 (ISBN 0-8442-6264-1, 6264-1, Passport Bks.); pap. 5.95 (ISBN 0-8442-6266-8, 6266-8). Natl Textbk.

Coleman, Ronald L. Sculpture: A Basic Handbook for Students. 2nd ed. 336p. 1980. text ed. write for info. (ISBN 0-697-03335-X). Wm C Brown.

Coleman, Ronny J. & Russell, Raymond M. Fire Truck Toys for Men & Boys. (Catalogue of Toy Fire Apparatus Ser.: Vol. II). (Illus.). 168p. 1982. pap. 10.95 (ISBN 0-910105-01-4). Phenix Pub.

--Fire Truck Toys for Men & Boys. (Catalogue of Toy Fire Apparatus Ser.: Vol. I). (Illus.). 168p. 1981. pap. 9.95 (ISBN 0-910105-00-6). Phenix Pub.

Coleman, S. Aspects of Symmetry: The Erice Lectures. (Illus.). 416p. Date not set. price not set (ISBN 0-521-26706-4). Cambridge U Pr.

--Measurement & Analysis of Political Systems: A Science of Social Behavior. LC 75-8704. 219p. 1972. 14.00 (ISBN 0-471-16492-5). Krieger.

Coleman, Samuel. Family Planning in Japanese Society: Traditional Birth Control in a Modern Urban Culture. LC 83-42552. 227p. 1983. 25.00x (ISBN 0-691-03133-9). Princeton U Pr.

Coleman, Sandra, ed. Failures in Family Therapy. LC 84-19325. (Family Therapy Ser.). 444p. 1985. 27.50 (ISBN 0-89862-048-1, 2048). Guilford Pr.

Coleman, Satis N. Bells, Their History, Legends, Making, & Uses. LC 70-109722. (Illus.). ix, 462p. Repr. of 1928 ed. lib. bdg. 24.75x (ISBN 0-8371-4212-1, COBE). Greenwood.

Coleman, Satis N. & Bregman, Adolph, eds. Songs of American Folks. facsimile ed. LC 68-57060. (Granger Index Reprint Ser). 1942. 13.00 (ISBN 0-8369-6011-4). Ayer Co Pubs.

Coleman, Sherman S. Complex Foot Deformities in Children. LC 82-15249. (Illus.). 301p. 1983. text ed. 52.50 (ISBN 0-8121-0857-4). Lea & Febiger.

Coleman, Susan, jt. auth. see Smith, Franci.

Coleman, T. F. Large Sparse Numerical Optimization. (Lecture Notes in Computer Science: Vol. 165). v, 105p. 1984. pap. 11.50 (ISBN 0-387-12914-6). Springer Verlag.

Coleman, Terry. The Scented Brawl: Selected Articles & Interviews. 1979. 19.95 (ISBN 0-241-10042-9, Pub. by Hamish Hamilton England). David & Charles.

--Southern Cross. 480p. 1980. pap. 2.75 (ISBN 0-345-28365-1). Ballantine.

Coleman, Thomas E. Modern Drug Store Merchandising: How to Increase Your Sales & Profits. LC 75-28348. 214p. 1975. 15.95 (ISBN 0-86730-401-4). Lebhar Friedman.

--Retail Drug Store Management & Control. LC 78-70424. 1978. 19.95 (ISBN 0-86730-402-2). Lebhar Friedman.

Coleman, Thomas G. Blood Pressure Control, Vol. 1. 248p. 1981. 32.50 (ISBN 0-88831-088-9). Eden Pr.

Coleman, Thomas G., ed. Computer Simulation of Physiological Systems. 40p. pap. 10.00 (ISBN 0-686-36684-0). Soc Computer Sim.

Coleman, Thomas R. Motivational Workshops for Low Achieving High School Students in Order to Help Them Improve Career Maturity. LC 77-90365. 1978. soft cover 10.00 (ISBN 0-88247-543-6). R & E Pubs.

Coleman, Thomas R., ed. Abnormal Psychology. 185p. 1974. pap. text ed. 9.95x (ISBN 0-8422-0465-2). Irvington.

Coleman, Thomas W. English Mystics of the Fourteenth Century. LC 74-109723. 1971. Repr. of 1938 ed. lib. bdg. 15.00x (ISBN 0-8371-4213-X, COEM). Greenwood.

Coleman, Vernon. A Guide to Child Health: A Practical Guide. 256p. (Orig.). 1985. pap. 9.95 (ISBN 0-7102-0269-5). Routledge & Kegan.

--Stress Control. 214p. 1979. 20.00 (ISBN 0-85117-167-2). Transatlantic.

Coleman, W. Biology in the Nineteenth Century. LC 77-83989. (Cambridge History of Science Ser.). (Illus.). 1978. pap. 11.95 (ISBN 0-521-29293-X). Cambridge U Pr.

Coleman, Wanda. Imagoes. 174p. (Orig.). 1983. 14.00 (ISBN 0-87685-510-9); pap. 7.50 (ISBN 0-87685-509-5); deluxe ed. 25.00 signed ed. (ISBN 0-87685-511-7). Black Sparrow.

Coleman, William. Animals That Show & Tell. 144p. (gr. 2-7). 1985. pap. 4.95 (ISBN 0-87123-807-1). Bethany Hse.

--Bernie Smithwick & the Purple Shoestring. (Early Readers Ser.). 64p. (gr. 1-4). 1984. 4.95 (58248); pap. 2.95 (ISBN 0-89191-824-8). Cook.

--Bernie Smithwick & the Super Red Ball. (Early Readers Ser.). 64p. (gr. 1-4). 1984. 4.95 (58222); pap. 2.95 (ISBN 0-89191-822-1). Cook.

--Bouncing Back: Finding Acceptance in the Face of Rejection. (Orig.). 1985. pap. 4.95 (ISBN 0-89081-455-4). Harvest Hse.

--Chesapeake Charlie & Blackbeard's Treasure. LC 80-70573. (Chesapeake Charlie Ser.). 128p. (Orig.). (gr. 5-9). 1981. pap. 2.95 (ISBN 0-87123-116-6, 200116). Bethany Hse.

--Chesapeake Charlie & the Bay Bank Robbers. LC 80-66638. (Chesapeake Charlie Ser.). 112p. (Orig.). 1980. pap. 2.95 (ISBN 0-87123-113-1, 200113). Bethany Hse.

--Counting Stars. LC 76-28973. 128p. 1976. 4.95 (ISBN 0-87123-055-0, 210055). Bethany Hse.

--Courageous Christians. (Wonderful World of the Bible Ser.). (gr. 4-8). 1983. 9.95 (ISBN 0-89191-558-3). Cook.

--Death Is a Social Disease: Public Health & Political Economy in Early Industrial France. 354p. 1982. text ed. 35.00x (ISBN 0-299-08950-9). U of Wis Pr.

--Earning Your Wings. 144p. (gr. 7 up). 1984. pap. 4.95 (ISBN 0-87123-311-8). Bethany Hse.

--Getting Ready for Our New Baby. LC 84-432. 112p. (ps-2). 1984. pap. 4.95 (ISBN 0-87123-295-2). Bethany Hse.

--The Good Night Book. LC 79-20002. (Illus.). 128p. (ps). 1980. pap. 4.95 (ISBN 0-87123-187-5, 210187). Bethany Hse.

--The Great Date Wait & Other Hazards. LC 82-1233. 138p. (Orig.). (gr. 7 up). 1982. pap. 4.95 (ISBN 0-87123-348-7, 210348). Bethany Hse.

--How, Why, When, Where. Bks. 1 & 2. 23p. (gr. 1-6). 1984. Bk. 1. pap. 2.95 (ISBN 0-89191-717-9, 57174, Chariot Bks.); Bk. 2. pap. 2.95 (ISBN 0-89191-942-2, 59428, Chariot Bks.). Cook.

--How, Why, When, Where Book, Vol. 3. 23p. (gr. 1-6). 1985. pap. 2.95 (ISBN 0-89191-927-9, 59279, Chariot Bks). Cook.

--How, Why, When, Where Book, Vol. 4. 23p. (gr. 1-6). 1985. pap. 2.95 (ISBN 0-89191-929-5, 59295, Chariot Bks). Cook.

--Jesus, My Forever Friend. (Wonderful World of the Bible Ser.). (Illus.). (gr. 4-8). 1981. 9.95 (ISBN 0-89191-370-X, 53702). Cook.

--The Newlywed Book. 150p. (Orig.). 1985. pap. 4.95 (ISBN 0-87123-799-7). Bethany Hse.

--On Your Mark. LC 79-16458. 112p. (gr. 5-9). 1979. pap. 4.95 (ISBN 0-87123-490-4, 210490). Bethany Hse.

--The Palestine Herald, 4 vols. (The Palestine Herald Ser.). (gr. 4 up). No. 1. 2.95 (ISBN 0-89191-981-3); No. 2. 2.95 (ISBN 0-89191-982-1); No. 3. 2.95 (ISBN 0-89191-983-X); No. 4. 2.95 (ISBN 0-89191-984-8). Cook.

--Peter. LC 81-85894. 160p. (Orig.). 1982. pap. 4.95 (ISBN 0-89081-305-1). Harvest Hse.

--The Pharisees' Guide To Total Holiness. LC 82-4551. 147p. 1982. 8.95 (ISBN 0-87123-473-4, 210473); pap. 4.95 (ISBN 0-87123-472-6, 210472). Bethany Hse.

--The Warm Hug Book. 128p. (Orig.). (ps). 1985. pap. 4.95 (ISBN 0-87123-794-6). Bethany Hse.

--The Who, What, When, Where Bible Busy Book. 32p. (gr. 2-8). 1984. pap. 1.50 (ISBN 0-89191-853-1). Cook.

--The Who, What, When, Where Book about the Bible. (gr. 1-5). 1980. 11.95 (ISBN 0-89191-291-6). Cook.

--You Can Be Creative. LC 83-80474. 160p. (Orig.). 1984. pap. 3.95 (ISBN 0-89081-387-6, 3876). Harvest Hse.

Coleman, William & Limoges, Camille. Studies in the History of Biology, Vol. 2. LC 76-47139. (Historical Studies in the Life Sciences). (Illus.). 1978. text ed. 23.00x (ISBN 0-8018-2034-0). Johns Hopkins.

--Studies in the History of Biology, Vol. 4. LC 76-47139. 1979. text ed. 20.00x (ISBN 0-8018-2362-5). Johns Hopkins.

Coleman, William, jt. auth. see Von Baer, Carl E.

Coleman, William & Cohen, I. Bernard, eds. French Views of German Science. LC 80-2106. (Development of Science Ser.). (Illus.). 1981. lib. bdg. 45.00x (ISBN 0-405-13871-7). Ayer Co Pubs.

--Physiological Programmatics of the Nineteenth Century. LC 80-2107. (Development of Science Ser.). (Illus.). 1981. lib. bdg. 50.00x (ISBN 0-405-13872-5). Ayer Co Pubs.

Coleman, William & Limoges, Camille, eds. Studies in History of Biology, Vol. 3. 304p. 1979. 25.00x (ISBN 0-8018-2215-7). Johns Hopkins.

--Studies in History of Biology, Vol. 5. LC 78-647138. 224p. 1981. text ed. 22.00x (ISBN 0-8018-2566-0). Johns Hopkins.

--Studies in History of Biology, Vol. 6. LC 76-47139. 240p. 1983. text ed. 25.00x (ISBN 0-8018-2856-2). Johns Hopkins.

--Studies in History of Biology, Vol. 7. LC 78-647138. 160p. 1984. text ed. 20.00x (ISBN 0-8018-2995-X). Johns Hopkins.

--Studies in History of Biology, Vol. 1. LC 76-47139. (Historical Studies in the Life Sciences). 232p. 1977. 23.00x (ISBN 0-8018-1862-1). Johns Hopkins.

Coleman, William, ed. see Hamilton, Alexander.

Coleman, William, tr. & intro. by. The Interpretation of Animal Form. (The Sources of Science: No. 15). (Illus.). 191p. 1968. Repr. of 1888 ed. 20.00 (ISBN 0-384-28525-2). Johnson Repr.

Coleman, William, et al, eds. A Casebook of Grant Proposals in the Humanities. LC 81-18859. 248p. 1982. 35.00 (ISBN 0-918212-45-6). Neal-Schuman.

Coleman, William D. The Independence Movement in Quebec 1945-1980. (Studies in the Structures of Power: No. 11). 288p. 1984. 30.00x (ISBN 0-8020-2529-3); pap. 12.95x (ISBN 0-8020-6542-2). U of Toronto Pr.

Coleman, William E. Grants in the Humanities: A Scholar's Guide to Funding Sources. 2nd ed. 175p. 1984. lib. bdg. 24.95 (ISBN 0-918212-80-4). Neal-Schuman.

--On the Discrimination of Gothicisms. rev. ed. Varma, Devendra P., ed. LC 79-8447. (Gothic Studies & Dissertations Ser.). 1980. lib. bdg. 28.50x (ISBN 0-405-12651-4). Ayer Co Pubs.

Coleman, William H. Historical Sketch Book & Guide to New Orleans & Environs. (Illus.). text ed. 21.75 (ISBN 0-8369-9238-5, 9092). Ayer Co Pubs.

Coleman, William L. Chesapeake Charlie & the Haunted Ship. (Chesapeake Charlie Ser.). 112p. (Orig.). 1983. pap. 2.95 (ISBN 0-87123-282-0). Bethany Hse.

--Chesapeake Charlie & the Stolen Diamonds. LC 81-68077. (Chesapeake Charlie Ser.). 112p. (Orig.). (gr. 5-8). 1981. pap. 2.95 (ISBN 0-87123-170-0, 200117). Bethany Hse.

--Engaged. 1980. pap. 4.95 (ISBN 0-8423-0693-5). Tyndale.

--Escucha a los Animales. 144p. 1981. 2.75 (ISBN 0-88113-063-X). Edit Betania.

--Getting Ready for My First Day of School. 128p. (Orig.). (gr. k). 1983. pap. 4.95 (ISBN 0-87123-274-X). Bethany Hse.

--Listen to the Animals. LC 79-11312. 128p. (ps-6). 1979. pap. 4.95 (ISBN 0-87123-341-X, 210341). Bethany Hse.
--Making TV Work for Your Family. LC 83-11881. 112p. (Orig.). 1983. pap. 4.95 (ISBN 0-87123-322-3). Bethany Hse.
--Mi Maquina Maravillosa. 144p. 1982. 3.25 (ISBN 0-88113-309-4). Edit Betania.
--My Hospital Book. LC 81-10094. (Illus.). 96p. (Orig.). (gr. 2-7). 1981. pap. 3.95 (ISBN 0-87123-354-1, 210354). Bethany Hse.
--My Magnificient Machine. LC 78-5035. 144p. 1978. pap. 4.95 (ISBN 0-87123-381-9, 210381). Bethany Hse.
--Singing Penguins & Puffed-up Toads. 125p. (ps-4). 1981. pap. 4.95 (ISBN 0-87123-554-4, 210554). Bethany Hse.
--The Sleep Tight Book. LC 82-12953. (Devotionals for Young Children Ser.). 125p. (Orig.). (ps up). 1982. pap. 4.95 (ISBN 0-87123-577-3, 210577). Bethany Hse.
--Today I Feel Like a Warm Fuzzy. LC 80-19708. 126p. (Orig.). 1980. pap. 4.95 (ISBN 0-87123-565-X, 210565). Bethany Hse.
--Today I Feel Loved! LC 82-4184. 128p. (Orig.). (ps-4). 1982. pap. 4.95 (ISBN 0-87123-566-8, 210566). Bethany Hse.
--Today I Feel Shy. LC 83-9216. 128p. (Orig.). (gr. 3-4). 1983. pap. 4.95 (ISBN 0-87123-588-9). Bethany Hse.
--Today's Handbook of Bible Times & Customs. (Illus.). 306p. 1984. 11.95 (ISBN 0-87123-594-3). Bethany Hse.
--What Children Need to Know When Parents Get Divorced. 91p. (gr. k-5). 1983. pap. 3.95 (ISBN 0-87123-612-5). Bethany Hse.
Coleman, William P., jt. auth. see Colman, William P.
Coleman, William P., III & McBurney, Elizabeth. Pediatric Dermatology: New Directions in Therapy. 1981. pap. text ed. 30.50 (ISBN 0-87488-698-8). Med Exam.
Coleman, William V. Finding a Way to Follow. 1977. pap. 4.95 (ISBN 0-8192-1227-X). Morehouse.
--Prayer-Talk: Casual Conversations with God. LC 82-74085. 112p. (Orig.). 1983. pap. 3.95 (ISBN 0-87793-265-4). Ave Maria.
Coleman Brawer, Catherine & Wu, Geri. Trade Winds: The Lure of the China Trade 16th-19th Centuries. (Illus.). 24p. 1985. 6.00 (ISBN 0-915171-01-5). Katonah Gal.
Coleman-Norton, Paul R., ed. Studies in Roman Economic & Social History in Honor of Allan Chester Johnson. facs. ed. LC 70-80384. (Essay Index Reprint Ser). 1951. 23.75 (ISBN 0-8369-1027-3). Ayer Co Pubs.
Colemant, Patrick K. & Lamb, Charles R. The Nonpartisan League; 1915-1922: An Annotated Bibliography. 88p. (Orig.). 1985. pap. 12.95 (ISBN 0-87351-189-1). Minn Hist.
Colen, Alexandra. A Syntactic & Semantic Study of English Predicative Nominals. 224p. (Orig.). 1984. pap. 19.00 (ISBN 90-6569-342-4, Pub. by Brepols Belgium). Benjamins North Am.
Colen, B. D. The COPD Medical Diary-365 Days of Better Breathing: Chronic Obstructive Pulmonary Disease. (Mosby Medical Library). 1983. pap. 8.95 (ISBN 0-452-25458-2, Plume). NAL.
--Diabetic's Three Hundred Sixty-Five Day Medical Diary. (The Mosby Medical Library Ser.). 1983. pap. 7.95 (ISBN 0-452-25403-5, Plume). NAL.
--The Family Medical Diary. (Orig.). 1982. pap. 7.95 (ISBN 0-440-52515-2, Dell Trade Pbks). Dell.
--Take Care: Patients' Guide to Personal Health. LC 83-63295. 224p. 1984. pap. 8.70 (ISBN 0-688-02636-2, Quill). Morrow.
Colen, Bruce D., jt. auth. see Haraszty, Eszter.
Colen, John N., jt. ed. see McNeely, R. L.
Colenbrander, Joanna. A Portrait of a Fryn: A Biography of F. Tennyson Jesse. (Illus.). 320p. 1984. 24.95 (ISBN 0-233-97572-1). Andre Deutsch.
--A Portrait of Fryn: Biography of F. Tennyson Jesse. (Illus.). 320p. 1984. 24.95 (ISBN 0-233-97572-1, Pub. by A Deutsch England). David & Charles.
Colenso, Frances E. History of the Zulu War & Its Origin. LC 70-132643. Repr. of 1880 ed. 28.00x (ISBN 0-8371-3654-7, CZW&, Pub. by Negro U Pr). Greenwood.
Colenso, John W., ed. see Vijn, Cornelius.
Colenso, M., tr. see Vainshtein, Sevyan.
Coleoni, Angelo. U. S. Interventions: A Brief History. 244p. 1984. text ed. 25.00x (ISBN 0-86590-312-3, Sterling Pubs India). Apt Bks.
Coler, Christfried. Diccionario por Fechas de Historia Universal. 2nd ed. 480p. (Span.). 1977. 50.95 (ISBN 84-261-5799-8, S-50366). French & Eur.
Coler, Mark D. The Investor's Guide to Discount Brokerage Houses. 1983. 24.95 (ISBN 0-686-89524-X). Facts on File.
--Seventy Percent Off: The Investor's Guide to Discount Brokerage Houses. LC 83-9025. (Illus.). 320p. 1983. 24.95 (ISBN 0-87196-823-1). Facts on File.
Coler, Mark D. & Ratner, Ellis M., eds. The Discount Brokerage Directory. 400p. 1983. 110.00 (ISBN 0-939300-40-0). Grey Hse Pub.
Coleridge, A. D., tr. see Hauptmann, Moritz.
Coleridge, A. D., tr. see Moscheles, Ignaz.
Coleridge, A. D., tr. see Schone, Alfred & Hiller, Ferdinand.
Coleridge, A. D., tr. see Von Dittersdorf, Karl D.
Coleridge, A. D., tr. see Von Hellborn, Heinrich K.
Coleridge, Arthur. Arthur Coleridge Reminiscences. Fuller-Maitland, J. A., ed. LC 77-75179. 1977. Repr. of 1921 ed. lib. bdg. 25.00 (ISBN 0-89341-055-1). Longwood Pub Group.
Coleridge, Christabel. Charlotte Mary Yonge, Her Life & Letters. LC 77-75961. (Library of Lives & Letters). 412p. 1969. Repr. of 1903 ed. 43.00x (ISBN 0-8103-3891-2). Gale.
--Charlotte Mary Yonge: Her Life & Letters. 1903. 16.00 (ISBN 0-8274-2048-X). R West.
Coleridge, E. H., ed. see Byron, George G.
Coleridge, E. H., ed. see Coleridge, Samuel T.
Coleridge, Ernest H., ed. see Coleridge, Samuel T.
Coleridge, Ernest Hartley, ed. see Coleridge, Samuel Taylor.
Coleridge, Hartley. Essays & Marginalia, 2 vols. LC 72-13289. (Essay Index Reprint Ser.). Repr. of 1851 ed. Set. 41.50 (ISBN 0-8369-8151-0). Ayer Co Pubs.
--Essays: On Parties in Poetry & on the Character of Hamlet. LC 73-450. 1973. lib. bdg. 7.50 (ISBN 0-8414-1407-6). Folcroft.
--Letters of Hartley Coleridge. Griggs, Grace E. & Griggs, Earl L., eds. LC 75-41063. Repr. of 1936 ed. 24.50 (ISBN 0-404-14524-8). AMS Pr.
--New Poems: Including a Selection from His Published Poetry. Griggs, Earl L., ed. LC 73-136059. (Illus.). 135p. Repr. lib. bdg. 24.75x (ISBN 0-8371-5209-7, CONP). Greenwood.
--The Poetical Works of Bowles, Lamb & Hartley Coleridge. Tirebuck, William, ed. 1887. 20.00 (ISBN 0-8274-3170-8). R West.
--The Worthies of Yorkshire & Lancashire: Being Lives of the Most Distinguished Persons That Have Been Born in, or Connected with Those Provinces. 1836. 100.00 (ISBN 0-8274-3771-4). R West.
Coleridge, Henry N. Six Months in the West Indies in Eighteen Twenty-Five. LC 72-100284. Repr. of 1826 ed. 19.75x (ISBN 0-8371-2948-6, CSM&). Greenwood.
Coleridge, Henry N., ed. see Coleridge, Samuel T.
Coleridge, J. T. A Memoir of the Rev. John Keble, 2 vols. 1869. Repr. 50.00 (ISBN 0-8274-2702-6). R West.
Coleridge, John T. A Memoir of the Rev. John Keble, 2 vols. in 1. 2nd rev. ed. LC 75-30019. Repr. of 1869 ed. 38.50 (ISBN 0-404-14024-6). AMS Pr.
Coleridge, K. A. A Descriptive Catalogue of the Milton Collection in the Alexander Turnbull Library, Wellington, New Zealand. (Illus.). 1980. 105.00x (ISBN 0-19-920110-2). Oxford U Pr.
Coleridge, M. E. Non Sequitur. 1900. Repr. 25.00 (ISBN 0-8274-3043-4). R West.
Coleridge, Mary E. Gathered Leaves from the Prose of Mary E. Coleridge: With a Memoir by Edith Sichel. facsimile ed. LC 70-169545. (Short Story Index Reprint Ser.). Repr. of 1910 ed. 20.00 (ISBN 0-8369-4006-7). Ayer Co Pubs.
--The King with Two Faces: An Historical Romance. LC 79-8255. Repr. of 1897 ed. 44.50 (ISBN 0-404-61831-6). AMS Pr.
Coleridge, Nicholas. Around the World in Seventy-Eight Days. 224p. 1985. 14.95 (ISBN 0-07-011699-7). McGraw.
--Shooting Stars. 211p. 1985. 14.95 (ISBN 0-434-14062-7, Pub. by W Heinmann Ltd). David & Charles.
Coleridge, Phillis M. Short Sketch of the Life of Samuel Tayor Coleridge Poet & Philosopher. LC 77-3510. lib. bdg. 8.50 (ISBN 0-8414-3553-7). Folcroft.
Coleridge, Samuel, jt. auth. see Wordsworth, William.
Coleridge, Samuel T. Die Ancient Mariner und Christabel: Mit Literarhistorischer Einleitung und Kommentar. Eichler, A., ed. 1907. pap. 25.00 (ISBN 0-384-09540-2). Johnson Repr.
--Anima Poetae from the Unpublished Note-Books. Coleridge, Ernest H., ed. LC 77-16768. 1895. lib. bdg. 25.00 (ISBN 0-8414-0904-8). Folcroft.
--Animal Poets. 1978. Repr. of 1895 ed. lib. bdg. 40.00 (ISBN 0-8482-3547-9). Norwood Edns.
--Biographia Literaria. Watson, George, ed. 1978. pap. 5.95x (ISBN 0-460-11011-X, Evman). Biblio Dist.
--Biographia Literaria, 2 Vols. Shawcross, John, ed. 1907. Set. 54.00x (ISBN 0-19-811317-X). Oxford U Pr.
--Coleridge on the Seventeenth Century. Brinkley, Roberta F., ed. LC 69-10076. (Illus.). 1968. Repr. of 1955 ed. lib. bdg. 47.50x (ISBN 0-8371-0049-6, COSC). Greenwood.
--Coleridge: Poems & Prose. (Penguin Poetry Library). 304p. 1985. pap. 4.95 (ISBN 0-14-058501-X). Penguin.
--Coleridge: Selected Poems. Bald, R. C., ed. LC 56-6819. (Crofts Classics Ser.). 1956. pap. text ed. 3.75x (ISBN 0-88295-023-1). Harlan Davidson.
--Coleridge's Poems: A Facsimile Reproduction of the Proofs & MSS of Some of the Poems. Campbell, James D., ed. LC 72-5259. 1899. lib. bdg. 20.00 (ISBN 0-8414-0020-2). Folcroft.
--Collected Letters of Samuel Taylor Coleridge, 6 vols. Griggs, Earl L., ed. Vols. 1 & 2. 1956. 98.00x (ISBN 0-19-811318-8); Vols. 5 & 6 1971. 89.00x (ISBN 0-19-811458-3). Oxford U Pr.
--Collected Works of Samuel T. Coleridge, Vols. 1-4 & 6. Coburn, K. & Winer, B., eds. Incl. Vol. 1. Lectures, 1795. 1970. 44.00x (ISBN 0-691-09861-1); Vol. 2. The Watchman. Patton, Lewis, et al, eds. 490p. 1970. 37.50x (ISBN 0-691-09719-4); Vol. 3. Essays on His Time, 3 vols. Erdman, D. V., ed. 1975. 135.00x (ISBN 0-691-09871-9); Vol. 4. The Friend, 2 vols. Rooke, B., et al, eds. 1969. Set. 75.00x (ISBN 0-691-09854-9); Vol. 6. Lay Sermons. White, R. J., et al, eds. 1972. 33.00x (ISBN 0-691-09873-5); Vol. 7. Biographia Literaria. 70.00 (ISBN 0-691-09874-3). LC 68-10210. (Bollingen Series, Vol. 75). Princeton U Pr.
--The Collected Works of Samuel Taylor Coleridge: Logic, Vol. 13. Jackson, J. R., ed. LC 68-10201. (Bollingen Ser.: No. LXXV). 1981. 44.00x (ISBN 0-691-09880-8). Princeton U Pr.
--The Collected Works of Samuel Taylor Coleridge, Vol. 10: On the Constitution of the Church & State. Colmer, J. & Winer, B., eds. (Bollingen Ser.: No. 75). (Illus.). 245p. 1975. 31.00x (ISBN 0-691-09877-8). Princeton U Pr.
--Confessions of an Inquiring Spirit. Hart, H. S., ed. 1957. pap. 3.25 (ISBN 0-8047-0331-0, SP48). Stanford U Pr.
--Critical Annotations. Taylor, William F., ed. LC 72-187518. 1889. lib. bdg. 10.00 (ISBN 0-8414-3046-2). Folcroft.
--Essays on His Own Times, 3 Vols. Coleridge, Sara, ed. LC 72-113579. Repr. of 1850 ed. Set. 110.00 (ISBN 0-404-01700-2). Vol. 1 (ISBN 0-404-01701-0). Vol. 2 (ISBN 0-404-01702-9). Vol. 3 (ISBN 0-404-01703-7). AMS Pr.
--The Friend: A Series of Essays. facsimile ed. LC 75-154146. (Select Bibliographies Reprint Ser). Repr. of 1867 ed. 23.50 (ISBN 0-8369-5762-8). Ayer Co Pubs.
--Inquiring Spirit: A New Presentation of Coleridge from His Published & Unpublished Writings. Coburn, Kathleen, ed. LC 78-65606. 1980. Repr. of 1951 ed. 35.00 (ISBN 0-88355-837-8). Hyperion Conn.
--Lectures & Notes on Shakespeare & Other English Poets: Now First Collected by T. Ashe. LC 70-38347. (Select Bibliographies Reprint Ser). Repr. of 1884 ed. 25.00 (ISBN 0-8369-6764-X). Ayer Co Pubs.
--Literary Remains of Samuel Taylor Coleridge, 4 Vols. Coleridge, Henry N., ed. Repr. of 1839 ed. Set. 165.00 (ISBN 0-404-01710-X). Vol. 1 (ISBN 0-404-01711-8). Vol. 2 (ISBN 0-404-01712-6). Vol. 3 (ISBN 0-404-01713-4). Vol. 4 (ISBN 0-404-01714-2). AMS Pr.
--Notebooks. Coburn, Kathleen, ed. Incl. Vol. 1. 1794-1804, 2 pts. 1957. 110.00x (ISBN 0-691-09802-6); Vol. 2. 1804-1808, 2 pts. 1961. 100.00x (ISBN 0-691-09803-4); Vol. 3. 1808-1819, 2 pts. 1973. 105.00x (ISBN 0-691-09804-2). LC 56-13196. (Bollingen Series, Vol. 50). (Illus.). Princeton U Pr.
--On the Constitution of the Church & State. Barrell, John, ed. & intro. by. (Rowman & Littlefield University Library). 170p. 1972. 6.25x (ISBN 0-87471-419-2); pap. 3.50x (ISBN 0-87471-423-0). Rowman.
--Poems. Beer, John, ed. 1974. 12.95x (ISBN 0-460-00043-8, Evman); pap. 4.50x (ISBN 0-460-01043-3, Evman). Biblio Dist.
--Poems of Samuel Taylor Coleridge. Coleridge, E. H., ed. (Oxford Standard Authors Ser.). 1912. 29.95 (ISBN 0-19-254120-X); pap. 8.95x (ISBN 0-19-281051-0). Oxford U Pr.
--Portable Coleridge. Richards, Ivor A., ed. (Viking Portable Library: No. 48). (gr. 10 up). 1977. pap. 7.95 (ISBN 0-14-015048-X, P48). Penguin.
--The Rime of the Ancient Mariner. (Illus.). 36p. 1979. 8.50 (ISBN 0-7011-2277-3, Pub. by Chatto & Windus). Merrimack Pub Cir.
--Selected Poetry & Prose. Stauffer, Donald, ed. (Modern Library College Editions). 1951. pap. text ed. 6.00 (ISBN 0-394-30952-9, T52, RanC). Random.
--Seven Lectures on Shakespeare & Milton. Collier, John P., ed. LC 72-962. Repr. of 1856 ed. 12.50 (ISBN 0-404-01617-0). AMS Pr.
--Seven Lectures on Shakespeare & Milton. LC 68-56787. (Research & Source Works Ser.: No. 276). 1969. Repr. of 1856 ed. 13.50 (ISBN 0-8337-0618-7). B Franklin.
--Shakespearean Criticism, Vol. 1. 1974. Repr. of 1960 ed. 12.95x (ISBN 0-460-00162-0, Evman). Biblio Dist.
--Shakespearean Criticism, Vol. 2. 1980. Repr. of 1960 ed. 12.95x (ISBN 0-460-00183-3, Evman). Biblio Dist.
--Unpublished Letters from Samuel Tayler Coleridge to the Rev. John Prior Estlin. 1978. Repr. of 1884 ed. lib. bdg. 20.00 (ISBN 0-8495-0909-2). Arden Lib.
--Unpublished Letters from Samuel Taylor Coleridge to the Reverend John Prior Estlin. Bright, Henry A., ed. LC 72-190701. 1893. lib. bdg. 15.00 (ISBN 0-8414-2501-9). Folcroft.
Coleridge, Samuel T. & Whalley, George. The Collected Works of Samuel Taylor Coleridge: Marginalia, Part 1, Vol. 12. LC 68-10201. 1152p. 1980. 90.00x (ISBN 0-691-09879-4). Princeton U Pr.
Coleridge, Samuel T., jt. auth. see Wordsworth, William.
Coleridge, Samuel Taylor. Biographia Literaria, Vol. 7. Engell, James & Bate, W. Jackson, eds. LC 83-63186. (Collected Works of Samuel Taylor Coleridge Ser.). (Illus.). 864p. 1984. pap. 19.95 (ISBN 0-691-01861-8). Princeton U Pr.
--Letters of Samuel Taylor Coleridge, 2 vols. Coleridge, Ernest Hartley, ed. 1895. 85.00 set (ISBN 0-8274-2846-4). R West.
--The Poetical Works of Samuel Taylor Coleridge, 2 vols. Ashe, T., ed. 1890. 50.00 set (ISBN 0-8274-3172-4). R West.
--The Rime of the Ancient Mariner. Dorbe, Gustave, ed. 16.95 (ISBN 0-405-11896-1). Ayer Co Pubs.
--Table Talk of Samuel Taylor Coleridge. 1884. 30.00 (ISBN 0-8274-3563-0). R West.
Coleridge, Sara. Memoir & Letters of Sara Coleridge. LC 76-37677. Repr. of 1874 ed. 42.50 (ISBN 0-404-56736-3). AMS Pr.
--Memoir & Letters of Sara Coleridge. 1874. 24.50 (ISBN 0-8274-2701-8). R West.
--Minnow Among Tritons: Mrs. S. T. Coleridge's Letters to Thomas Poole, 1799-1834. Potter, Stephen, ed. LC 75-38028. Repr. of 1934 ed. 24.50 (ISBN 0-404-56737-1). AMS Pr.
Coleridge, Sara, ed. see Coleridge, Samuel T.
Coleridge, Stephen. An Evening in My Library: The English Poets. 217p. 1980. Repr. of 1916 ed. lib. bdg. 20.00 (ISBN 0-89984-105-8). Century Bookbindery.
--Memories. 1973. lib. bdg. 20.00 (ISBN 0-8414-3039-X). Folcroft.
--Quiet Hours in Poets' Corner. 131p. 1980. Repr. lib. bdg. 20.00 (ISBN 0-89987-109-7). Darby Bks.
Coleridge, Susan, jt. auth. see Nichols, Arline.
Coleridge-Taylor, S. Twenty-Four Negro Melodies. (Music Reprint Ser.: 1980). 1980. Repr. of 1905 ed. lib. bdg. 29.50 (ISBN 0-306-76023-1). Da Capo.
Colerus, Egmont. Mathematics for Everyman: From Simple Numbers to Calculus. (Illus.). 1976. 11.95 (ISBN 0-89490-110-9). Enslow Pubs.
Coles, Adland & Bradley, David. Creeks & Harbours of the Solent. 144p. 1982. 60.00x (ISBN 0-333-31808-0, Pub. by Nautical England). State Mutual Bk.
Coles, Adlard. The Shell Pilot to the English Channel, Part 1: South Coast Habours, Ramsgate to the Scillies. 6th ed. Coote, John, rev. by. (Illus.). 256p. 1985. 27.95 (ISBN 0-571-13540-4). Faber & Faber.
Coles, Adlard & Black. North Biscay Pilot. 3rd ed. (Illus.). 400p. 1982. 55.00 (ISBN 0-229-11661-2). Sheridan.
Coles, Alan. Three Before Breakfast: A True & Dramatic Account of How a German U-Boat Sank Three Cruisers in One Desperate Hour. (Illus.). 192p. 1979. 13.50 (ISBN 0-85937-168-9). Sheridan.
Coles, Blanche. Julius Caesar. (Skakespeare Studies). 281p. 1983. Repr. of 1940 ed. text ed. 40.00 (ISBN 0-89984-149-X). Century Bookbindery.
--Shakespeare Studies: Julius Caesar. LC 72-86174. Repr. of 1940 ed. 21.00 (ISBN 0-404-01597-2). AMS Pr.
--Shakespeare Studies: Julius Caesar. 281p. 1981. Repr. of 1940 ed. lib. bdg. 35.00 (ISBN 0-89987-127-5). Darby Bks.
--Shakespeare Studies: Macbeth. LC 70-86176. Repr. of 1938 ed. 21.00 (ISBN 0-404-01598-0). AMS Pr.
--Shakespeare's Four Giants. 1957. 5.50 (ISBN 0-87233-809-6). Bauhan.
Coles, C. L. Game Conservation in a Changing Countryside. 16.50x (ISBN 0-273-40133-5, SpS). Sportshelf.
Coles, Clarence W. & Glenn, Harold T. Glenn's Complete Bicycle Manual: Selection, Maintenance, Repair. (Illus.). 352p. 1973. pap. 10.95 (ISBN 0-517-50093-0). Crown.
Coles, E. An English Dictionary. Repr. of 1676 ed. 55.00x (ISBN 3-4870-4748-9). Adlers Foreign Bks.
Coles, E. K. Maverick of the Education Family: Two Essays on Non-Formal Education. (Illus.). 120p. 1982. 17.50 (ISBN 0-08-025239-7). Pergamon.
Coles, E. M. Clinical Psychopathology. (Introductions to Modern Psychology Ser.), 480p. 1982. 32.00x (ISBN 0-7100-0864-3). Routledge & Kegan.
Coles, Embert H. Veterinary Clinical Pathology. 3rd ed. LC 78-65966. (Illus.). 562p. 1980. text ed. 34.00 (ISBN 0-7216-2644-0). Saunders.
Coles, Embert H. & Moore, William E. Veterinary Interpretive Clinical Pathology. (Illus.). 350p. Date not set. price not set (ISBN 0-7216-2654-8). Saunders.
Coles, Flournoy A., Jr. Black Economic Development. LC 74-30495. 232p. 1975. 22.95x (ISBN 0-88229-176-9). Nelson-Hall.
Coles, G. H., jt. ed. see Porges, S. W.
Coles, Gladys M. Flower of Light: A Biography of Mary Webb. (Illus.). 386p. 1979. 28.00x (ISBN 0-7156-1120-8, Pub. by Duckworth England). Biblio Dist.
Coles, H. M. Paediatrics. 1976. 30.00x (ISBN 0-272-00102-3). State Mutual Bk.
--Paediatrics. 312p. pap. text ed. cancelled (ISBN 0-272-79536-4, Pub. by Pitman Bks Ltd UK). Pitman Pub MA.
Coles, H. M., ed. Pediatrics: An Interdisciplinary Approach. (Illus.). 1976. text ed. 33.00x (ISBN 0-8464-0708-6). Beekman Pubs.

Coles, Harry L. A History of the Administration of Federal Land Policies & Land Tenure in Louisiana, 1803-1860. Bruchey, Stuart, ed. LC 78-56718. (Management in Public Lands in the U. S. Ser.). (Illus.). 1979. lib. bdg. 28.50x (ISBN 0-405-11327-7). Ayer Co Pubs.
--War of Eighteen Twelve. LC 65-17283. (Chicago History of American Civilization Ser: No. 22). (Illus.). 1965. pap. 10.00x (ISBN 0-226-11350-7, CHAC22). U of Chicago Pr.
Coles, J. M. & Harding, A. F. The Bronze Age in Europe: An Introduction to the Prehistory of Europe, 2000-700 BC. LC 79-14507. (Illus.). 1980. 45.00 (ISBN 0-312-10597-5). St Martin.
Coles, J. M. & Simpson, D. D., eds. Studies in Ancient Europe: Essays Presented to Stuart Piggott. (Illus.). 1968. text ed. 20.00x (ISBN 0-7185-1079-8, Leicester). Humanities.
Coles, Jane H., jt. auth. see Coles, Robert.
Coles, Jessie V. The Consumer-Buyer & the Market. Assael, Henry, ed. LC 78-265. (Century of Marketing Ser.). (Illus.). 1978. lib. bdg. 46.50x (ISBN 0-405-11168-1). Ayer Co Pubs.
Coles, John. Archaeology of the Wetlands. 120p. 1984. pap. 10.00x (ISBN 0-85224-448-7, Pub. by Edinburgh U Pr Scotland). Columbia U Pr.
--Experimental Archaeology. LC 79-41520. 1980. 39.00 (ISBN 0-12-179750-3); pap. 19.00 (ISBN 0-12-179752-X). Acad Pr.
--Field Archaeology in Britain. 267p. 1972. pap. 12.95x (ISBN 0-416-76540-8, NO. 2621). Methuen Inc.
Coles, K. A. Channel Harbours & Anchorages. 5th ed. 198p. 1980. 24.00 (ISBN 0-245-53086-X, Pub. by Nautical England). State Mutual Bk.
--The Shell Pilot to the South Coast Harbours. 6th ed. Coote, J. O., ed. (Illus.). 224p. 1982. Repr. 24.95 (ISBN 0-571-18060-4). Faber & Faber.
Coles, K. Adlard. Heavy Weather Sailing. 3rd rev. ed. LC 80-71018. 1981. 18.50 (ISBN 0-8286-0086-4). J De Graff.
--North Brittainy Pilot. 1979. 34.95x (ISBN 0-8464-0071-5). Beekman Pubs.
--Sailing Years: An Autobiography. LC 80-1216. 1981. 18.50 (ISBN 0-8286-0089-9). J De Graff.
Coles, K. Adlard & Black, A. N. North Biscay Pilot. 1979. 44.95x (ISBN 0-8464-0072-3). Beekman Pubs.
Coles, Manning. Drink to Yesterday. (Seagull Lib. of Mystery & Suspense Ser). 1967. Repr. 4.50 (ISBN 0-393-08550-3). Norton.
--Night Train to Paris. 192p. 1985. pap. 3.50 (ISBN 0-88184-205-2). Carroll & Graf.
--No Entry. 192p. 1985. pap. 3.50 (ISBN 0-88184-204-4). Carroll & Graf.
--Toast to Tomorrow. (Spies & Intrigues Ser.: No. 3). 310p. 1984. pap. 5.95 (ISBN 0-918172-15-2). Leetes Isl.
--Without Lawful Authority. (Spies and Intrigues Ser.: No. 4). 246p. 1984. pap. 5.95 (ISBN 0-918172-16-0). Leetes Isl.
Coles, Michael, et al. Psychophysiological Perspectives: Festchrift for Beatrice & John Lacey. 320p. 1984. 29.50 (ISBN 0-442-21746-3). Van Nos Reinhold.
Coles, Michael G., et al. Handbook of Psychophysiology: Systems, Processes, & Applications. 1985. text ed. write for info. (ISBN 0-89862-640-4). Guilford Pr.
Coles, R. A. A New Oxyrhynchus Papyrus: The Hypothesis of Euripides Alexandros. 70p. 1981. 35.00x (ISBN 0-900587-30-X, Pub. by Inst Class Stud England). State Mutual Bk.
Coles, Richard N. Dynamic Chess: The Modern Style of Aggressive Play. rev. & enl. ed. (Illus.). 1966. pap. 3.95 (ISBN 0-486-21676-4). Dover.
Coles, Robert. Children of Crisis, Vol. 1: A Study of Courage & Fear. (Children of Crisis Ser.). (Illus.). 1967. (Pub. by Atlantic Monthly Pr); pap. 10.95 (ISBN 0-316-15154-8). Little.
--Children of Crisis, Vol. 2: Migrants, Sharecroppers, Mountaineers. (Children of Crisis Ser.). (Illus.). 1972. (Pub. by Atlantic Monthly Pr); pap. 10.95 (ISBN 0-316-15176-9). Little.
--Children of Crisis, Vol. 3: The South Goes North. LC 70-162332. (Children of Crisis Ser.). (Illus.). 704p. 1972. (Pub. by Atlantic Monthly Pr); pap. 10.95 (ISBN 0-316-15177-5). Little.
--Children of Crisis Vol. 5: Privileged Ones: the Well-off & Rich in America. LC 73-10825. (Children of Crisis Ser.). (Illus.). 1978. (Pub. by Atlantic-Little Brown); pap. 12.95 (ISBN 0-316-15177-7). Little.
--The Darkness & the Light. LC 74-76878. (Illus.). 112p. 1974. 20.00 (ISBN 0-912334-60-6). Aperture.
--Dorothea Lange: Photographs of a Lifetime. (Illus.). 192p. 1982. 40.00 (ISBN 0-89381-100-9). Aperture.
--Dorothea Lange: Photographs of a Lifetime. LC 81-66771. (Illus.). 184p. 1984. pap. 25.00 (ISBN 0-89381-139-4). Aperture.
--A Festering Sweetness: Poems of American People. LC 77-15736. (Pitt Poetry Ser.). 1978. limited ed. 20.00x (ISBN 0-8229-3360-8, Dist. by Harper & Row Publishers); 12.95 (ISBN 0-8229-3371-3); pap. 5.95 (ISBN 0-8229-5290-4). U of Pittsburgh Pr.
--Flannery O'Connor's South. LC 79-23057. (Walter Lynwood Fleming Lectures in Southern History). xii, 228p. 1980. 20.00 (ISBN 0-8071-0655-0). La State U Pr.
--Headsparks. (gr. 7 up). 1975. 5.95 (ISBN 0-316-15156-4, Pub. by Atlantic Monthly Pr.). Little.
--Irony in the Mind's Life. LC 78-6651. 1978. pap. 4.95 (ISBN 0-8112-0689-0, NDP459). New Directions.
--Irony in the Mind's Life: Essays on Novels by James Agee, Elizabeth Bowen, & George Eliot. LC 74-5260. (University of Virginia Page-Barbour Lecture Ser.). 210p. 1974. 14.95x (ISBN 0-8139-0550-8). U Pr of Va.
--The Last & First Eskimos. LC 78-7065. (Illus.). 1978. 24.95 (ISBN 0-8212-0737-7, 512494). NYGS.
--The Moral Life of Children. 1986. write for info. Atlantic Monthly.
--The Old Ones of New Mexico. (Illus.). 96p. 1984. pap. 12.95 (ISBN 0-15-668508-6, Harv). HarBraceJ.
--The Political Life of Children. 1986. write for info. Atlantic Monthly.
--Uprooted Children: The Early Life of Migrant Farm Workers. LC 70-98270. (Horace Mann Lecture Ser). 1970. 12.95x (ISBN 0-8229-3192-3). U of Pittsburgh Pr.
--William Carlos Williams: The Knack of Survival in America. 1975. 17.50x (ISBN 0-8135-0998-X); pap. 7.95 (ISBN 0-8135-0996-3). Rutgers U Pr.
Coles, Robert & Coles, Jane H. Women of Crisis. 304p. 1979. pap. 8.95 (ISBN 0-385-29169-8, Delta). Dell.
--Women of Crisis II: Lives of Work & Dreams. 256p. pap. 6.95 (Delta). Dell.
Coles, Robert & Stokes, Geoffrey. Sex & the American Teenager. LC 84-48147. 1985. pap. 5.95 (ISBN 0-06-096002-7, PL). Har-Row.
Coles, Robert, jt. auth. see Catledge, Oraien E.
Coles, Robert, intro. by see Namias, June.
Coles, Robert, ed. see Williams, William C.
Coles, Robert, intro. by. Walker Evans. (Aperture History of Photography Ser.: No. 12). (Illus.). 96p. 1980. pap. 8.95 over boards (ISBN 0-89381-042-8). Aperture.
Coles, Robert M., frwd. by see Sheehan, Susan.
Coles, W. Alfred Stevens. 1977. pap. 12.50 (ISBN 0-912303-12-3). Michigan Mus.
Coles, W. Crosbie & Owen, James G. Kingsley's Country: A Guide to Bideford & District. 1894. Repr. 20.00 (ISBN 0-8274-2652-6). R West.
Coles, William A. & Reed, Henry H., Jr., eds. Architecture in America: A Battle of Styles. LC 61-5653. (Illus., Orig.). 1961. pap. text ed. 11.95x (ISBN 0-89197-029-0). Irvington.
Coles, William A., ed. see Van Brunt, Henry.
Coles, William E., Jr Composing II: Writing As a Self-Creating Process. LC 80-24820. 128p. (Orig.). 1980. pap. text ed. 7.00x (ISBN 0-8104-6118-8). Boynton Cook Pubs.
--Composing: Writing As a Self-Creating Process. 128p. (Orig.). 1974. pap. text ed. 5.95x (ISBN 0-8104-5838-1). Hayden.
--Composing: Writing As a Self-Creating Process. 128p. (Orig.). 1974. pap. text ed. 7.00x (ISBN 0-86709-119-3). Boynton Cook Pubs.
Coles, William H., jt. auth. see Haik, George M.
Coles-Mogford, A. M., jt. auth. see Drummond, A. M.
Colet, John. John Colet's Commentary on First Corinthians. O'Kelly, Bernard & Jarrott, C. A. L., eds. O'Kelly, Bernard, tr. from Lat. LC 82-12403. (Medieval & Renaissance Texts & Studies: Vol. 21). 352p. 1985. 20.00 (ISBN 0-86698-056-3). Medieval & Renaissance NY.
Colet, Roger, tr. see De Maupassant, Guy.
Coleta, Anthony. Working Together: A Guide to Parent Involvement. Fritts, Susan R., tr. LC 76-26758. 1976. pap. text ed. 14.95 (ISBN 0-89334-002-2). Humanics Ltd.
Colett, Simone. Ecstasy. 13.95 (ISBN 0-8488-0075-3, Pub. by Amereon Hse). Amereon Ltd.
Coletta, Mary & Wright, Peggy W. Hello, Central: Give Me Heaven. 200p. 1985. 14.95 (ISBN 0-9613837-0-4). Heather Pubs.
Coletta, P. Multiploy. 1982. lib. bdg. 24.95 (ISBN 0-8359-4742-4). Reston.
Coletta, Paolo. American Secretaries of the Navy, 2 vols. LC 78-70967. (Illus.). 1028p. 1980. Set. slipcased 59.95x (ISBN 0-87021-073-4). Naval Inst Pr.
Coletta, Paolo, ed. American Secretaries of the Navy, 2 Vols. (Illus.). 1028p. 1980. Set. 59.95x (ISBN 0-87021-073-4); bulk rates avail. Naval Inst Pr.
Coletta, Paolo E. Admiral Bradley A. Fiske & The American Navy. LC 78-16525. 1979. 27.50x (ISBN 0-7006-0181-3). U Pr of KS.
--The American Naval Heritage in Brief. 2nd ed. LC 79-66035. 689p. 1980. 28.75 (ISBN 0-8191-0927-4); pap. 14.00 (ISBN 0-8191-0928-2). U Pr of Amer.
--The American Naval Heritage in Brief. 1978. pap. text ed. 14.00 (ISBN 0-8191-0390-X). U Pr of Amer.
--Bowman Hendry McCalla: A Fighting Sailor. LC 79-66975. (Illus.). 1979. pap. text ed. 13.00 (ISBN 0-8191-0863-4). U Pr of Amer.
--Presidency of William Howard Taft. LC 72-92564. (American Presidency Ser.). (Illus.). 296p. 1973. 19.95x (ISBN 0-7006-0096-5). U Pr of KS.
--The United States Navy & Defense Unification, 1947-1953. LC 77-74410. (Illus.). 550p. 1981. 37.50 (ISBN 0-87413-126-X). U Delaware Pr.
--William Jennings Bryan. Incl. Vol. 1. Political Evangelist, 1860-1908. (Illus.). xiv, 486p. 1964. 29.95x (ISBN 0-8032-0022-6); Vol. 3. Political Puritan, 1915-1925. (Illus.). xiv, 334p. 1969. 25.50x (ISBN 0-8032-0024-2). LC 64-11352. (Illus.). U of Nebr Pr.
Coletta, Paolo E., ed. A Bibliography of American Naval History. LC 80-24864. 453p. 1981. 15.95x (ISBN 0-87021-105-6). Naval Inst Pr.
--A Bibliography of American Naval History. (Illus.). 453p. 1981. 15.95x (ISBN 0-87021-105-6); bulk rates avail. Naval Inst Pr.
Coletta, Paolo E. & Bauer, K. Jack, eds. United States Navy & Marine Corps Bases, Domestic. LC 84-4468. xv, 740p. 1985. lib. bdg. 95.00 (ISBN 0-313-23133-8, CUN/). Greenwood.
--United States Navy & Marine Corps Bases, Overseas. LC 84-4470. 480p. 1985. lib. bdg. 75.00 (ISBN 0-313-24504-5, COU/). Greenwood.
Coletta, Paul. Apple Graphics Games. LC 82-23161. 1983. 16.95 (ISBN 0-8359-0325-7); disk 15.00 (ISBN 0-8359-0313-3); bk. & disk o.p. 34.95 (ISBN 0-8359-0326-5). Reston.
Colette. Bella Vista: Avec: Trois, Six, Neuf. 1974. pap. 3.95 (ISBN 0-686-54562-1). French & Eur.
--Betes Libres et Prisonnieres. 219p. 1958. 5.95 (ISBN 0-686-54563-X). French & Eur.
--The Blue Lantern. Senhouse, Roger, tr. from Fr. 168p. 1977. 10.00 (ISBN 0-374-11497-8); pap. 2.95 (ISBN 0-374-51387-2). FS&G.
--Break of Day. McLeod, Enid, tr. from Fr. LC 99-906555. 143p. 1974. pap. 5.25 (ISBN 0-374-51221-3). FS&G.
--Break of Day. 128p. 1983. pap. 2.50 (ISBN 0-345-30858-1). Ballantine.
--Break of Day. 1983. 13.00 (ISBN 0-8446-5981-9). Peter Smith.
--Chats. (Illus.). 1950. pap. 5.95 (ISBN 0-686-54564-8). French & Eur.
--La Chatte. 212p. 1950. 11.95 (ISBN 0-686-54565-6). French & Eur.
--Cheri. Flanner, Janet, tr. from Fr. 112p. 1983. limited ed. 215.00x. G F Ritchie.
--Cheri & the Last of Cheri. Senhouse, Roger, tr. from Fr. 304p. 1976. 7.95 (ISBN 0-374-12102-8). FS&G.
--Cheri & the Last of Cheri. 240p. 1982. pap. 2.50 (ISBN 0-345-30057-2). Ballantine.
--Chiens. (Illus.). 1957. pap. 5.95 (ISBN 0-686-54566-4). French & Eur.
--Les Claudine. 256p. 1969. pap. 3.95 (ISBN 0-686-54567-2). French & Eur.
--Claudine at School. 224p. 1982. pap. 2.50 (ISBN 0-345-30056-4). Ballantine.
--Claudine et Menage. 256p. 1973. pap. 3.95 (ISBN 0-686-54568-0). French & Eur.
--Claudine in Paris. 192p. 1982. pap. 2.50 (ISBN 0-345-30708-9). Ballantine.
--Colette at the Movies: Criticism & Screenplays. Virmaux, Alain & Virmaux, Odette, eds. Smith, Sarah W., tr. from Fr. LC 79-6148. (Ungar Film Library). (Illus.). 300p. 1980. 12.95x (ISBN 0-8044-2125-0); pap. 6.95 (ISBN 0-8044-6086-8). Ungar.
--Colette Par Colette: La Jeunesse de Claudine. 25.00 (ISBN 0-686-54569-9). French & Eur.
--The Collected Stories of Colette. Phelps, Robert G., ed. Ward, Matthew & White, Antonia, trs. from Fr. LC 83-16449. 605p. 1983. 19.95 (ISBN 0-374-12629-1); pap. 9.95 (ISBN 0-374-51865-3). FS&G.
--The Complete Claudine. White, Antonia, tr. from Fr. Incl. Claudine at School; Claudine & Annie; Claudine in Paris; Claudine Married. 632p. 1976. pap. 10.95 (ISBN 0-374-51379-1). FS&G.
--Contes Des Milles et un Matins. 248p. 1970. pap. 9.95 (ISBN 0-686-54570-2). French & Eur.
--Creatures Great & Small. McLeod, Enid, tr. from Fr. 292p. 1978. 10.00 (ISBN 0-374-13102-3); pap. 3.95 (ISBN 0-374-51467-4). FS&G.
--Dialogue Avec les Betes. 160p. 1974. 7.95 (ISBN 0-686-54571-0). French & Eur.
--Dialogues de Betes. 1975. pap. 3.95 (ISBN 0-686-54572-9). French & Eur.
--Earthly Paradise: An Autobiography of Colette Drawn from Her Lifetime Writings. Phelps, Robert, ed. Briffault, Herma, tr. from Fr. 540p. 1966. pap. 10.95 (ISBN 0-374-51308-2). FS&G.
--L' Enfants et les Sortileges. (Illus.). 38p. 1967. 10.95 (ISBN 0-686-54573-7). French & Eur.
--Le Fanal Bleu. 160p. 1975. pap. 3.95 (ISBN 0-686-54574-5). French & Eur.
--Flowers & Fruit. Phelps, Roberts, intro. by. Ward, Matthew, tr. from Fr. 208p. 1985. 14.95 (ISBN 0-374-15683-2). FS&G.
--Gigi & Julie De Carneilhan. 11.95 (ISBN 0-88411-298-5, Pub. by Aeonian Pr). Amereon Ltd.
--Gigi, Julie De Carneilhan, Chance Acquaintances. Senhouse, Roger & Fermor, Patrick, trs. from Fr. 320p. 1976. 11.95 (ISBN 0-374-16223-9); pap. 7.95 (ISBN 0-374-51317-1). FS&G.
--Histoire et Absolu: Essai Sur Kierkegaard. 19.95 (ISBN 0-686-54575-3). French & Eur.
--Histoires Pour Bel Gazou. 7th ed. 192p. 1977. 6.95 (ISBN 0-686-54576-1). French & Eur.
--L' Ingenue Libertine. 256p. 1973. 11.95 (ISBN 0-686-54577-X); pap. 3.95 (ISBN 0-686-54578-8). French & Eur.
--The Innocent Libertine. White, Antonia, tr. from Fr. 216p. 1978. 10.00 (ISBN 0-374-17682-5). FS&G.
--Letters from Colette. Phelps, Robert, tr. from Fr. & ed. 224p. 1980. 12.95 (ISBN 0-374-18509-3). FS&G.
--Lettres a Helene Picard. 240p. 1958. 7.95 (ISBN 0-686-54579-6). French & Eur.
--Lettres a Marguerite Moreno. 360p. 1959. 14.95 (ISBN 0-686-54580-X). French & Eur.
--Lettres a Ses Pairs: Correspondances Inedite De Colette a Marcel Proust, Alfred Jarry, Paul Leautaud. 456p. 1973. 22.50 (ISBN 0-686-54581-8). French & Eur.
--Lettres Au Petit Corsaire. 160p. 1963. 7.95 (ISBN 0-686-54582-6). French & Eur.
--La Maison de Claudine. (Illus.). 256p. 1976. 12.95 (ISBN 0-686-54583-4). French & Eur.
--Mitsou & Music-Hall Sidelights. new ed. Postgate, Raymond & Callimachi, Anne-Marie, trs. from Fr. 242p. 1976. pap. 2.95 (ISBN 0-374-51377-5). FS&G.
--My Apprenticeships. Beauclerk, Helen, tr. from Fr. 144p. 1978. 10.00 (ISBN 0-374-21660-6); pap. 4.95 (ISBN 0-374-51458-5). FS&G.
--My Mother's House & Sido. Troubridge, Una V. & McLeod, Enid, trs. from Fr. Incl. 219p. 1975. 7.95 (ISBN 0-374-21735-1); pap. 6.95 (ISBN 0-374-51218-3). FS&G.
--Oeuvres Completes, 16 vols. (Edition du Centenaire). 1973. Set. 650.00 (ISBN 0-686-54600-8). French & Eur.
--Oeuvres Completes: Belles Saisons, Nudite, Le Fanal Bleu, Vol. 11. 1974. 95.00 (ISBN 0-686-54594-X). French & Eur.
--Oeuvres Completes: Chambre d'Hotel, la Lune de pluie, Julie de Carneilhan, Vol. 9. 1974. 95.00 (ISBN 0-686-54592-3). French & Eur.
--Oeuvres Completes: Claudine a l'Ecole, Claudine a Paris, Claudine en Menage, Vol. 1. (Illus.). 1973. 95.00 (ISBN 0-686-54584-2). French & Eur.
--Oeuvres Completes: Claudine s'en va, La Retraite Sentimentale, L'Ingenue Libertine, Vol. 2. 1973. 95.00 (ISBN 0-686-54585-0). French & Eur.
--Oeuvres Completes: De ma Fenetre, Trois, Six, Neuf, Gigi, Vol. 10. 1974. 95.00 (ISBN 0-686-54593-1). French & Eur.
--Oeuvres Completes: Duo, Le Toutounier, Mes Apprentissages, Vol. 8. 1974. 95.00 (ISBN 0-686-54591-5). French & Eur.
--Oeuvres Completes: La Chambre Eclairee, Cheri, La Fin de Cheri, Vol. 5. 1974. 95.00 (ISBN 0-686-54588-5). French & Eur.
--Oeuvres Completes: La Jumelle Noire, Vol. 12. 1975. 95.00 (ISBN 0-686-54595-8). French & Eur.
--Oeuvres Completes: La Maison de Claudine, Sido Noces, Vol. 6. 1974. 95.00 (ISBN 0-686-54589-3). French & Eur.
--Oeuvres Completes: La Seconde, Prisons et Paradis, Le Pur et l'Impur, Vol. 7. 1974. 95.00 (ISBN 0-686-54590-7). French & Eur.
--Oeuvres Completes: L'Entrave, L'Envers du Musichall, La Paix chez les Betes, Vol. 4. 1974. 95.00 (ISBN 0-686-54587-7). French & Eur.
--Oeuvres Completes: Les Vrilles de la Vigne, Douze Dialogues de Betes, Autres Betes, Vol. 3. 1973. 95.00 (ISBN 0-686-54586-9). French & Eur.
--Oeuvres Completes: Lettres au Petit Corsaire, Lettres a ses Pairs, Vol. 16. 1976. 95.00 (ISBN 0-686-54599-0). French & Eur.
--Oeuvres Completes: Lettres de Vagabonde, Lettres a Helene Picard, Vol. 15. 1976. 95.00 (ISBN 0-686-54598-2). French & Eur.
--Oeuvres Completes: Melanges, Derniers Ecrits, Discours de Reception, Vol. 14. 1975. 95.00 (ISBN 0-686-54597-4). French & Eur.
--Oeuvres Completes: Theatre: Cheri, La Vagabonde, L'Enfant et les Sortileges, Vol. 13. 1975. 95.00 (ISBN 0-686-54596-6). French & Eur.
--The Other One. Tait, Elizabeth & Senhouse, Roger, trs. from Fr. 160p. 1977. 10.00 (ISBN 0-374-22801-9); pap. 2.95 (ISBN 0-374-51388-0). FS&G.
--The Other One. Tait, Elizabeth & Senhouse, Roger, trs. LC 70-178783. 160p. 1960. Repr. lib. bdg. 18.75x (ISBN 0-8371-6295-5, COTO). Greenwood.
--The Other Woman. LC 79-173201. Orig. Title: Mon Ami Valentine. 1972. 5.95 (ISBN 0-672-51651-9). Bobbs.
--The Other Woman: A Short Novel & Stories. Crosland, Margaret, tr. 1984. pap. 4.95 (ISBN 0-452-00685-6, Mer). NAL.
--La Paix Chez les Betes. 192p. 1976. 5.95 (ISBN 0-686-54601-6). French & Eur.
--Paris de ma Fenetre. 160p. 1976. pap. 3.95 (ISBN 0-686-54602-4). French & Eur.
--Prison et Paradis. 1973. pap. 3.95 (ISBN 0-686-54603-2). French & Eur.
--Le Pur et l'Impur. 191p. 1971. pap. 3.95 (ISBN 0-686-54604-0). French & Eur.
--The Pure & the Impure. Briffault, Herma, tr. from Fr. 175p. 1975. 7.95 (ISBN 0-374-23920-7); pap. 6.25 (ISBN 0-374-50692-2). FS&G.
--Retreat from Love. Crosland, Margaret, tr. LC 79-19831. 1980. pap. 4.95 (ISBN 0-15-676588-8, Harv). HarBraceJ.
--The Ripening Seed. Senhouse, Roger, tr. from Fr. 186p. 1975. 7.95 (ISBN 0-374-25069-3); pap. 5.95 (ISBN 0-374-51264-7). FS&G.

--Ripening Seed. Senhouse, Roger, tr. LC 73-178784. 152p. 1955. Repr. lib. bdg. 24.75x (ISBN 0-8371-6292-0, CORS). Greenwood.
--The Shackle. 1982. pap. 2.95 (ISBN 0-345-30058-0). Ballantine.
--The Shackle. White, Antonia, tr. from Fr. 224p. 1976. 7.95 (ISBN 0-374-26184-9); pap. 3.95 (ISBN 0-374-51311-2). FS&G.
--The Tender Shoot & Other Stories. White, Antonia, tr. from Fr. 404p. 1975. 10.00 (ISBN 0-374-27310-3); pap. 7.95 (ISBN 0-374-51258-2). FS&G.
--Trois, Six, Neuf. 1970. 3.95 (ISBN 0-686-54605-9). French & Eur.
--The Vagabond. 1982. pap. 2.50 (ISBN 0-345-30061-0). Ballantine.
--The Vagabond. McLeod, Enid, tr. from Fr. LC 55-5832. 223p. 1975. 8.95 (ISBN 0-374-28233-1); pap. 4.95 (ISBN 0-374-51175-6). FS&G.
Colette, Sidonie-Gabrielle. Le Ble en Herbe. Pichois, ed. (Coll. GF). pap. 3.95 (ISBN 0-685-37279-0). French & Eur.
--Chambre D'Hotel. 1964. pap. 3.95 (ISBN 0-685-11073-7, 1312). French & Eur.
--La Chatte. 1955. pap. 3.95 (ISBN 0-685-23926-8). French & Eur.
--Cheri. 1958. pap. 3.95 (ISBN 0-685-11079-6, 307). French & Eur.
--Claudine a L'Ecole. 1956. pap. 3.95 (ISBN 0-685-11086-9). French & Eur.
--Claudine a Paris. 1957. pap. 3.95 (ISBN 0-685-11087-7). French & Eur.
--Claudine S'en Va. 1957. pap. 3.95 (ISBN 0-685-11088-5). French & Eur.
--Duo. Incl. Le Toutounier. pap. 3.95 (ISBN 0-685-36058-X). French & Eur.
--L' Entrave. pap. 3.95 (ISBN 0-685-37280-4). French & Eur.
--La Femme Cachee. pap. 3.95 (ISBN 0-685-37281-2). French & Eur.
--Gigi. (Illus.). 1959. 12.50 (ISBN 0-685-11214-4, 89); pap. 3.95 (ISBN 0-686-66424-8). French & Eur.
--Maison De Claudine. 1977. pap. 3.95 (ISBN 0-685-11331-0, 763). French & Eur.
--La Naissance du Jour. pap. 3.95 (ISBN 0-685-37283-9). French & Eur.
--La Retraite Sentimentale. 12.95 (ISBN 0-685-37284-7); pap. 3.95 (ISBN 0-686-66858-8). French & Eur.
--Seconde. 1955. pap. 3.95 (ISBN 0-685-11558-5). French & Eur.
--Sido. Bd. with Les Vrilles De la Vigne. 1958. pap. 3.95 (ISBN 0-685-36057-1, 373). French & Eur.
--Vagabonde. 1957. pap. 3.95 (ISBN 0-685-11614-X, 283). French & Eur.
Coletti, Jack J., jt. auth. see Pettit, Tom.
Coletti, Mina S. & Giesea, Roberta. Family Ideal, Bk. 2. LC 82-14612. 279p. 1982. pap. 6.95 (ISBN 0-87747-925-9). Deseret Bk.
Coletti, Mina S. & Giesea, Roberta K. The Family Idea Book. LC 80-10921. 210p. 1980. pap. 6.95 (ISBN 0-87747-813-9). Deseret Bk.
Coletti, Ralph M. Using the Timex-Sinclair 1000 & 1500. 88p. 1984. pap. 9.95 (ISBN 0-88006-065-4, BK7397). Green Pub Inc.
Cole-Whittaker, Terry. How to Have More in a Have-Not World. 1983. 13.95 (ISBN 0-89256-247-1). Rawson Assocs.
--How to Have More in a Have-Not World. 320p. 1985. pap. 3.50 (ISBN 0-449-20673-4, Crest). Fawcett.
--The Inner Path from Where You Are to Where You Want to Be: A Spiritual Odyssey. 256p. 1986. 14.95 (ISBN 0-89256-283-8). Rawson Assocs.
Coley, Betty A., ed. see Browning, Vivienne.
Coley, Betty A., jt. ed. see Kelley, Philip.
Coley, Christopher, jt. auth. see Wolfe, Sidney M.
Coley, Christopher M., jt. auth. see Wolfe, Sidney M.
Coley, Elizabeth A., jt. auth. see Jones, Antonia J.
Coley, George. Reflections of the Colony of New South Wales. 16.50x (ISBN 0-392-04392-0, ABC). Sportshelf.
Coley, N. G., et al. Chemists by Profession. 352p. 1977. pap. 32.00x (ISBN 0-335-00041-X, Pub. by Open Univ Pr). Taylor & Francis.
Coley, W. B., jt. ed. see Ohmann, Richard.
Coley, William, ed. see Fielding, Henry.
Coley, William B., jt. tr. see Wensinger, Arthur S.
Coley-Smith, J. R., et al, eds. The Biology of Botrytis. LC 80-41041. 1981. 69.50 (ISBN 0-12-179850-X). Acad Pr.
Colfax, Henry G. The Most Critical Stations in the Love Experience. (Illus.). 1979. deluxe ed. 47.45 (ISBN 0-930582-22-5). Gloucester Art.
Colfer, George R. Handbook for Coaching Cross-Country & Running Events. 1977. 16.95 (ISBN 0-13-377051-6, Parker). P-H.
Colfer, George R. & Chevrette, John M. Running for Fun & Fitness: A Self-Styled Program for Aerobic Running & Phyhsical Fitness. (Orig.). 1980. pap. text ed. 5.95 (ISBN 0-8403-2135-X). Kendall-Hunt.
Colfer, George R., et al. Contemporary Physical Education. 432p. 1986. pap. text ed. price not set; price not set instr's. manual (ISBN 0-697-00559-3). Wm C Brown.
Colfer, Michael A. Morality, Kindred, & Ethnic Boundary: A Study of the Oregon Old Believers. LC 83-45351. (Immigrant Communities & Ethnic Minorities in the U. S. & Canada Ser.: No. 3). (Illus.). 175p. 1985. 32.50 (ISBN 0-404-19404-4). AMS Pr.
Colflesh, Trudy. Too Precious to Die. LC 84-71121. 248p. 1984. pap. 4.95 (ISBN 0-88270-573-3). Bridge Pub.
Colford, Paul D., jt. auth. see Egan, John P.
Colford, William E. Juan Melendez Valdes. 369p. 3.50 (ISBN 0-318-14278-3). Hispanic Inst.
Colford, William E., tr. see Calderon, Pedro.
Colford, William E., tr. see De Vega, Lope.
Colgan, Arthur R. & Colgan, Mary C. How to Earn Money with Cookbooks. LC 85-71061. (Illus.). Date not set. pap. 4.95 (ISBN 0-934045-00-3). ARCI Assocs.
Colgan, Bill. World War II Fighter Bomber Pilot. (Illus.). 208p. (Orig.). 1985. pap. 13.95 (ISBN 0-8306-2368-X). TAB Bks.
Colgan, Helen H., et al. Eight Writers Seeking Readers. Evans, Robert L., ed. (Illus.). 1985. pap. 6.00 (ISBN 0-9606698-2-5). R L Evans.
Colgan, Mary C., jt. auth. see Colgan, Arthur R.
Colgan, Michael. Your Personal Vitamin Profile: A Medical Scientist Shows You How to Chart Your Individual Vitamin & Mineral Formala. 1982. 14.95 (ISBN 0-688-01505-0); pap. 8.95 (ISBN 0-688-01506-9). Morrow.
Colgan, Patrick. Comparative Social Recognition. 281p. 1983. 37.50 (ISBN 0-471-09350-5, Pub. by Wiley-Interscience). Wiley.
Colgan, Patrick W. Quantitative Ethology. LC 78-999. 364p. 1978. 47.50x (ISBN 0-471-02236-5, Pub. by Wiley-Interscience). Wiley.
Colgan, Susan, jt. ed. see Madigan, Mary Jean.
Colgate, C., Jr., ed. see Columbia Books Staff.
Colgate, Craig & Evans, Laurie A., eds. National Recreational, Sporting & Hobby Organizations of the United States, 1981. LC 80-70429. 130p. 1981. pap. 25.00 (ISBN 0-910416-36-2). Columbia Bks.
Colgate, Craig, Jr. & Russell, John. Washington '85. 2nd ed. 843p. 1985. pap. 40.00 (ISBN 0-910416-55-9). Columbia Bks.
Colgate, Craig, Jr., ed. National Trade & Professional Associations of the United States 1982. 17th annual ed. LC 74-647774. 377p. 1982. pap. 35.00 (ISBN 0-910416-39-7). Columbia Bks.
--National Trade & Professional Associations of the United States, 1983. 18th ed. LC 74-647774. 390p. 1983. pap. 40.00 (ISBN 0-910416-43-5). Columbia Bks.
--National Trade & Professional Associations of the United States, 1984. 19th ed. LC 74-647774. 404p. 1984. pap. 40.00 (ISBN 0-910416-47-8). Columbia Bks.
Colgate, Craig, Jr. & Broida, Patricia, eds. National Trade & Professional Associations of the United State & Canada & Labor Unions, 1979. 14th ed. LC 74-647774. 1979. pap. 30.00x (ISBN 0-910416-30-3). Columbia Bks.
Colgate, Craig, Jr. & Close, Arthur C., eds. Washington Representatives, 1979. 3rd ed. LC 76-21152. 1979. pap. 30.00x (ISBN 0-910416-31-1). Columbia Bks.
Colgate, Craig, Jr. & Evans, Laurie A., eds. National Recreational, Sporting & Hobby Organizations of the United States, 1982. LC 80-70429. 145p. 1982. pap. 25.00 (ISBN 0-910416-41-9). Columbia Bks.
Colgate, Craig, Jr. & Freedman, Stephany J., eds. National Recreational Sporting & Hobby Organizations of the United States, 1983. 150p. 1983. pap. 25.00 (ISBN 0-910416-44-3). Columbia Bks.
--National Recreational, Sporting & Hobby Organizations of the United States, 1984. LC 80-70429. 134p. 1984. pap. 25.00 (ISBN 0-910416-48-6). Columbia Bks.
Colgate, Craig, Jr. & Germain, Regina, eds. National Recreational, Sporting & Hobby Organizations of the U. S., 1985. 5th ed. LC 80-70429. 140p. 1985. pap. 30.00 (ISBN 0-910416-53-2). Columbia Bks.
Colgate, Craig, Jr. & Russell, John, eds. National Trade & Professional Associations of the United States, 1985. 20th ed. LC 74-647774. (Twentieth Annual Edition Ser.). 428p. 1985. pap. 45.00 (ISBN 0-910416-52-4). Columbia Bks.
Colgate, Craig, Jr., jt. ed. see Close, Arthur C.
Colgate, John A. Administration of Intramural & Recreational Activities: Everyone Can Participate. LC 77-9265. 278p. 1978. text ed. 33.45 (ISBN 0-471-01728-0). Wiley.
Colgate, Stephen. Fundamentals of Sailing, Cruising, & Racing. (Illus.). 1978. 21.95 (ISBN 0-393-03215-9). Norton.
Colgin, Mary L. Chants for Children. LC 81-68685. 75p. (Orig.). (ps-8). 1982. pap. 8.95 (ISBN 0-9604582-1-2). Colgin Pub.
--Chords & Strums for Guitar & Autoharp. 37p. (ps-8). 1979. pap. 8.95 (ISBN 0-9604582-0-4). Colgin Pub.
Colglazier, E. W., ed. Politics of Nuclear Waste: Social, Political & Institutional Issues. (Pergamon Policy Studies on Energy). (Illus.). 275p. 1982. 30.00 (ISBN 0-08-026323-2). Pergamon.
Colgrave, Bertram. The Earliest Saint's Lives Written in England. 1978. Repr. of 1958 ed. lib. bdg. 7.50 (ISBN 0-8495-0739-1). Arden Lib.
--Earliest Saints Lives Written in England. LC 72-193175. 1958. lib. bdg. 12.50 (ISBN 0-8414-2353-9). Folcroft.
Colgrave, Bertram, ed. Two Lives of Saint Cuthbert. LC 69-13862. 1969. Repr. of 1940 ed. lib. bdg. 70.00x (ISBN 0-8371-0355-X, COST). Greenwood.
Colgrave, Bertram, ed. see Bede the Venerable.
Colgren, John. The Computer Revolution. (gr. 4-8). 1982. 5.95 (ISBN 0-86653-067-3, GA 421). Good Apple.
Colhoun, Will, et al. Trio Poetry One. 72p. 1980. pap. 6.95 (ISBN 0-85640-164-1, Pub. by Blackstaff Pr). Longwood Pub Group.
Colie, Rosalie. Paradoxia Epidemica: The Renaissance Tradition of Paradox. xx, 553p. 1976. Repr. of 1966 ed. 32.50 (ISBN 0-208-01604-X, Archon). Shoe String.
--The Resources of Kind: Genre-Theory in the Renaissance. LC 72-95307. 1974. 28.50x (ISBN 0-520-02397-8). U of Cal Pr.
Colie, Rosalie L. Atlantic Wall & Other Poems. LC 74-2963. 100p. 1974. 14.00x (ISBN 0-691-06273-0); pap. 5.95 (ISBN 0-691-01314-4). Princeton U Pr.
--Light & Enlightenment: A Syudy of the Cambridge Platonists & the Dutch Arminans. pap. 44.00 (ISBN 0-317-08829-7, 2050767). Bks Demand UMI.
--Shakespeare's Living Art. LC 72-6520. 450p. 1974. 40.00x (ISBN 0-691-06248-X). Princeton U Pr.
Colie, Rosalie L. & Flahiff, F. T., eds. Some Facets of King Lear: Essays in Prismatic Criticism. LC 73-81755. pap. 64.00 (ISBN 0-317-27054-0, 2023616). Bks Demand UMI.
Coligny-Saligny, Jean De see De Coligny-Saligny, Jean.
Colijn, H. Mechanical Conveyors for Bulk Solids. (Studies in Mechanical Engineering: No. 4). 510p. 1985. 99.75 (ISBN 0-444-42403-2); pap. 35.00 (ISBN 0-444-42414-8). Elsevier.
Colijn, Helen. Of Dutch Ways. (Illus.). 240p. 1984. pap. 5.72 (ISBN 0-06-464076-0, BN 4076). Har-Row.
Colijn, Hendrik. Weighing & Proportioning of Bulk Solids. 2nd ed. LC 74-77792. (Bulk Materials Handling Ser.). (Illus.). 362p. 1983. 60.00 (ISBN 0-87849-047-7). Trans Tech.
--Weighing & Proportioning of Bulk Solids. 2nd ed. LC 83-81909. (Illus.). 412p. 1984. 59.95x (ISBN 0-87201-914-4). Gulf Pub.
Colimore, Vincent J., ed. Selected Readings in Modern Language Teaching. 92p. 1969. pap. text ed. 6.95x (ISBN 0-8290-1091-2). Irvington.
--Selected Readings in Scholasticism & Education. 115p. 1971. pap. text ed. 8.95x (ISBN 0-8422-0142-4). Irvington.
Colin, Curtis. The Routemaster Bus. 96p. 1983. 30.00x (ISBN 0-85936-281-7, Pub. by Baton Pr Ltd UK). State Mutual Bk.
Colin, Henri & Excoffier, Jean-Louis. A Guide to the HPLC Literature 1980-1981, Vol. 2. LC 84-11967. 922p. 1984. text ed. 110.00 (ISBN 0-471-87992-4). Wiley.
--A Guide to the HPLC Literature 1982, Vol. 3. 532p. 1984. text ed. 60.00 (ISBN 0-471-80687-0); Three-Volume Set. text ed. write for info. (ISBN 0-471-82056-3). Wiley.
Colin, Henri, et al. A Guide to the HPLC Literature: 1966-1979, Vol. 1. 900p. 1984. text ed. 125.00 (ISBN 0-471-87993-2, Pub. by Wiley-Interscience). Wiley.
Colin, Jean L. The Transformations of War. LC 77-1125. (West Point Military Library). 1977. Repr. of 1912 ed. lib. bdg. 24.75x (ISBN 0-8371-9510-1, COTW). Greenwood.
Colin, Patrick. Neon Gobies. (Illus.). 304p. 1976. 19.95 (ISBN 0-87666-450-8, H-957). TFH Pubns.
Colin, Patrick I. Caribbean Reef Invertebrates & Plants. (Illus.). 1978. 29.95 (ISBN 0-87666-460-5, H-971). TFH Pubns.
Colin, Paul. One Hundred Posters of Paul Colin. (Illus.). 1977. 19.95 (ISBN 0-89545-004-6); pap. 8.95 (ISBN 0-89545-005-4). Images Graphiques.
Colin, Paul, jt. auth. see Lippman, Deborah.
Colin S. The MX ICBM: Multiple Protective Structure (MPS) Basing & Arms Control. 114p. 1979. 15.00 (ISBN 0-318-14349-6, HI2977P). Hudson Inst.
Colin, Sid. And the Bands Played On: An Informal History of British Dance Bands. (Illus.). 160p. 1980. pap. 8.50 (ISBN 0-241-10448-3, Pub. by Hamish Hamilton England). David & Charles.
Colin, Sid & Stavearce, Tony. Al Bowlly. 1979. 24.00 (ISBN 0-241-10057-7, Pub. by Hamish Hamilton England). David & Charles.
Colina, Tessa. Ark Full of Animals. (Illus.). 1985. comb bdg. 4.95 (ISBN 0-317-30647-2, R2707). Standard Pub.
--My Bible Dictionary. (gr. 1-4). 1954. pap. 1.95 (ISBN 0-87239-292-7, 3040). Standard Pub.
--You & Me. Buerger, Jane, ed. (Illus.). 112p. 1980. 5.95 (ISBN 0-89565-179-3, 4936). Standard Pub.
Colina, Tessa, jt. auth. see Moncure, Jane B.
Colina, Tessa, ed. Jesus, My Friend. (Jesus & Me Pupil Activities Books: No. 3). (Illus.). (gr. 1-5). 1978. pap. 1.25 (ISBN 0-87239-270-8, 2442). Standard Pub.
--Jesus, My Lord. (Jesus & Me Pupil Activities Books: No. 4). (Illus.). (gr. 1-5). 1978. pap. 1.25 (ISBN 0-87239-271-6, 2443). Standard Pub.
--Jesus, My Saviour. (Jesus & Me Pupil Activities Books: No. 1). (Illus.). (gr. 1-5). 1978. pap. 1.25 (ISBN 0-87239-268-6, 2440). Standard Pub.
--Jesus, My Teacher: (Pupil Activities Book Two) (Jesus & Me Ser.). (Illus.). 16p. (gr. 1-5). 1978. pap. 1.25 (ISBN 0-87239-269-4, 2441). Standard Pub.
Colina, Tessa & Westers, Jacqueline, eds. Jesus & Me Teacher: Primary Study in the Life of Christ. 1978. pap. 7.95 (ISBN 0-87239-165-5, 3243). Standard Pub.
Colinari, John, jt. auth. see Lipton, Gladys.
Colinvaux, P. Basic Ecology. 704p. 1985. write for info. (ISBN 0-471-16502-6). Wiley.
Colinvaux, P A., ed. The Environment of Crowded Men. 1970. pap. text ed. 6.95x (ISBN 0-8422-0086-X). Irvington.
Colinvaux, Paul. Why Big Fierce Animals Are Rare: An Ecologist's Perspective. LC 77-71977. 1978. lib. bdg. 25.00x (ISBN 0-691-08194-8); pap. 7.95x (ISBN 0-691-02364-6). Princeton U Pr.
Colinvaux, Paul A. Basic Ecology. 2nd ed. LC 72-3788. 621p. 1973. text ed. 39.50x (ISBN 0-471-16498-4). Wiley.
Colish, Marcia L. The Mirror of Language: A Study in the Medieval Theory of Knowledge. rev. ed. LC 83-3599. xviii, 339p. 1983. 25.00x (ISBN 0-8032-1418-9). U of Nebr Pr.
Colker, Marvin L., ed. Analecta Dublinensia: Three Mediaeval Latin Texts in the Library of Trinity College Dublin. LC 75-1954. 1975. 22.00X (ISBN 0-910956-56-1). Medieval Acad.
Colkmire, Lance. Reasoning with Juniors for Christs Sake. 1982. pap. 5.95 (ISBN 0-87148-736-5). Pathway Pr.
Colkrey, Jennifer, et al. The Silk Worm Story. Royds, Pamela, ed. (Illus.). 32p. (ps-2). 1985. 9.95 (ISBN 0-233-97553-5). Andre Deutsch.
Coll, Alberto R. The Western Heritage & American Values: Law, Theology & History. Thompson, Kenneth W., ed. LC 81-43761. (American Values Projected Abroad Ser.: Vol. I). 126p. 1982. lib. bdg. 21.50 (ISBN 0-8191-2526-1); pap. text ed. 8.00 (ISBN 0-8191-2527-X). U Pr of Amer.
--The Wisdom of Statecraft: Sir Herbert Butterfield & the Philosophy of International Politics. 208p. 1985. 25.00 (ISBN 0-8223-0607-7). Duke.
Coll, Alberto R. & Arend, Anthony C., eds. The Falklands War: Lessons for Strategy, Diplomacy & International Law. 220p. 1985. text ed. 27.50x (ISBN 0-04-327075-1); pap. text ed. 12.50X (ISBN 0-04-327076-X). Allen Unwin.
Coll, Edna. Indice Informativo de la Novela Hispano Americana: Centroamerica, Vol. 2. LC 74-235886. 1977. 9.35 (ISBN 0-8477-2003-9). U of PR Pr.
--Indice Informativo de la Novela Hispano-Americana: Vol. 1, las Antillas. LC 74-235886. 9.35 (ISBN 0-8477-2001-2). U of PR Pr.
--Indice Informativo de la Novela Hispanoamericana: Venezuela, Tomo III. LC 74-235886. 1978. 9.35 (ISBN 0-8477-2004-7). U of PR Pr.
--Indice Informativo de la Novela Hispanoamericana: Vol. IV: Colombia. LC 74-235886. (Sp.). 1979. 15.00 (ISBN 0-8477-2008-X). U of PR Pr.
Coll, Regina. Women & Religion: A Reader for the Clergy. 128p. 1982. pap. 4.95 (ISBN 0-8091-2461-0). Paulist Pr.
Coll, S., jt. auth. see Sumpter, A. B.
Collabs, jt. auth. see Huber, P. J.
Collacott, R. A. Mechanical Fault Diagnosis & Condition Monitoring. 1977. 81.00x (ISBN 0-412-12930-2, NO. 3005, Pub. by Chapman & Hall). Methuen Inc.
Collacott, Ralph A. Vibration Monitoring & Diagnosis: Techniques for Cost-Effective Plant Maintenance. LC 78-13602. pap. 91.30 (ISBN 0-317-27642-5, 2025209). Bks Demand UMI.
Collander, Carl E., Sr. Excursion to Europe. Collander, Lloyd, ed. LC 83-91463. (Illus.). 100p. 1983. pap. 5.95 (ISBN 0-9613100-0-6, 100A). Three Crowns Indus.
Collander, David C., jt. auth. see Hunt, Elgin F.
Collander, Lloyd, ed. see Collander, Carl E., Sr.
Collange, J. F. Enigmes De la Deuxienne Epitre De Paul Aux Corinthiens: Etudes Exegetique De 2 Cor. LC 71-154504. (Society for New Testament Studies Monographs: No. 18). 1972. 49.50 (ISBN 0-521-08135-1). Cambridge U Pr.
Collard, Alexandra. Two Young Dancers: Their World of Ballet. (Illus.). 192p. (gr. 7 up). 1984. 10.29 (ISBN 0-671-47074-4). Messner.
Collard, Christopher, compiled by. Composite Index to the 'Clarendon' Commentaries on Euripides 1938-1971. 82p. (Orig.). 1981. pap. 12.00x (ISBN 90-6088-074-9, Pub. by Boumas Boekhuis Netherlands). Benjamins North Am.
Collard, Christopher, ed. Euripides: Supplices, 2 vols. 472p. 1975. Set. 62.00 (ISBN 90-6088-046-3, Pub. by Boumas Boekhuis Netherlands). Vol. 1, Introduction & Text, xxii, 102pgs. Vol. 2, Commentary, 369pgs. Benjamins North AM.
Collard, D. A., et al, eds. Economic Theory & Hicksian Themes. 1984. pap. 11.95x (ISBN 0-19-828493-4). Oxford U Pr.
Collard, David, et al. Income Distribution: The Limits to Redistribution. 267p. 1981. 44.95x (ISBN 0-470-27099-3). Halsted Pr.

Collard, Elizabeth. Nineteenth-Century Pottery & Porcelain in Canada. 2nd ed. (Illus.). 496p. 1984. 39.95x (ISBN 0-7735-0392-7); pap. 22.50 (ISBN 0-7735-0393-5). McGill-Queens U Pr.
--The Potters' View of Canada: Canadian Scenes on Nineteenth Century Earthenware. (Illus.). 196p. 1983. 29.95 (ISBN 0-7735-0421-4). McGill Queens U Pr.
Collard, Elizabeth, jt. auth. see Collard, Howard.
Collard, H. R., et al see Hellwege, K. H.
Collard, Howard & Collard, Elizabeth. Vocabulario Mayo, Vol. 6. rev. ed. 225p. (Span.). 1974. pap. 7.50x (ISBN 0-88312-657-5); microfiche 3.00 (ISBN 0-88312-318-5). Summer Inst Ling.
Collard, Jean, jt. auth. see Brannen, Julia.
Collard, Laurie. Here's to Health. 1982. 8.50 (ISBN 0-394-33279-2, RanC). Random.
Collard, Patrick. The Development of Microbiology. LC 75-40987. pap. 52.50 (ISBN 0-317-07740-6, 2022443). Bks Demand UMI.
Collard, Paul M. Cambodge et Cambodgiens: Metamorphose du Royaume Khmer par une Methode Francaise de Protectorat. LC 77-87068. Repr. of 1925 ed. 25.50 (ISBN 0-404-16806-X). AMS Pr.
Collard, Sharon. Animal Friends to Color. (Illus.). 12p. (Orig.). (gr. k-3). 1981. pap. 0.49 (ISBN 0-88290-179-6, 4522). Horizon Utah.
Collas, Phil, jt. auth. see Hals, Nathan.
Collasse, Pascal. Les Saisons. Soumis, Louis, ed. (Chefs-d'oeuvre classiques de l'opera francais Ser.: Vol. 8). (Illus.). 226p. (Fr.). 1972. pap. 25.00x (ISBN 0-8450-1108-1). Broude.
--Thetis et Pelee. Soumis, Louis, ed. (Chefs-d'oeuvre classiques de l'opera francais Ser.: Vol. 9). (Illus.). 320p. (Fr.). 1972. pap. 27.50x (ISBN 0-8450-1109-X). Broude.
Collatz, L. & Wetterling, W. Optimization Problems. Hadsack, P. R., tr. from Ger. (Applied Mathematical Sciences Ser.: Vol. 17). (Illus.). 370p. (Orig.). 1975. pap. text ed. 22.00 (ISBN 0-387-90143-4). Springer-Verlag.
Collatz, L. & Hadeler, K. P., eds. Numerische Behandlung von Eigenwertaufgaben. (International Series of Numerical Mathematics: No. 24). (Illus.). 142p. (Ger.). 1974. 30.25x (ISBN 0-8176-0739-0). Birkhauser.
Collatz, L. & Mainardus, G., eds. Numerische Methoden der Approximationstheorie, 4 vols. (International Series of Numerical Mathematics: Nos. 16, 26, 30 & 42). (Illus., Ger.). 1972-78. Vol. 1, 256p. 36.95x (ISBN 0-8176-0633-5); Vol. 2, 199p. 32.95x (ISBN 0-8176-0764-1); Vol. 3, 334p. pap. 37.95x (ISBN 0-8176-0824-9); Vol. 4, 344p. pap. 46.95x (ISBN 0-8176-1025-1). Birkhauser.
Collatz, L. & Meinardus, G., eds. Differential Difference Equations: Applications & Numerical Problems. (International Series of Numerical Mathematics: Vol. 62). 196p. (Eng. & Ger.). 1983. text ed. 24.95 (ISBN 0-8176-1499-0). Birkhauser.
--Numerische Methoden bei Graphentheoretischen und Kombinatorischen Problemen, Vol. 1. (International Series of Numerical Mathematics: No. 29). (Illus.). 159p. (Ger.). 1975. 27.95x (ISBN 0-8176-0786-2). Birkhauser.
Collatz, L. & Unger, H., eds. Funktionalanalytische Methoden der Numerischen Mathematik. (International Ser. of Numerical Mathematics: No. 12). 143p. (Ger.). 1969. 28.95x (ISBN 0-8176-0195-3). Birkhauser.
Collatz, L., jt. ed. see Albrecht, J.
Collatz, L., et al, eds. Numerical Methods of Approximation Theory, Vol. 7. (International Series of Numerical Mathematics: Vol. 67). 148p. (Eng. & Ger.). 1984. 24.95 (ISBN 3-7643-1580-6). Birkhauser.
--Numerische Mathematik, Differentialgleichungen, Approximationstheorie. (International Series of Numerical Mathematics: No. 9). (Illus.). 401p. (Ger.). 1968. 54.95x (ISBN 0-8176-0193-7). Birkhauser.
--Iterationsverfahren-Numerische Mathematik-Approximationstheorie. (International Ser. of Numerical Mathematics: No. 15). 257p. (Ger.). 1970. 37.95x (ISBN 0-8176-0547-9). Birkhauser.
--Numerische Methoden bei Graphentheoretischen und Kombinatorishen Problemen: Vol. II. (International Series of Numerical Mathematics: No. 46). (Illus.). 255p. (Ger. & Eng.). 1979. pap. 37.95 (ISBN 0-8176-1078-2). Birkhauser.
--Numerische Methoden bei Optimierungsaufgaben, 3 vols. (International Series of Numerical Mathematics: Nos. 17, 23 & 36). (Illus., Ger.). 1973-77. Vol. 1, 136p. 27.95x (ISBN 0-8176-0668-8); Vol. 2, 166p. 32.95x (ISBN 0-8176-0732-3); Vol. 3, 216p. 36.95x (ISBN 0-8176-0918-0). Birkhauser.
Collatz, L., jt. ed. see Albrecht, J.
Collatz, Lothar. Functional Analysis & Numerical Mathematics. Oser, H., tr. 1966. 82.50 (ISBN 0-12-180450-X). Acad Pr.
Collatz, Lothar, jt. ed. see Albrecht, Julius.
Collatz, Lothar, et al, eds. Constructive Methods for Nonlinear Boundary Value Problems & Nonlinear Oscillations. (International Series of Numerical Mathematics: Vol. 48). 192p. 1979. pap. 22.95x (ISBN 0-8176-1098-7). Birkhauser.
--Numerical Methods of Approximation, Vol. 5. (International Ser. of Numerical Mathematics: No. 52). 337p. 1980. pap. 33.95x (ISBN 0-8176-1103-7). Birkhauser.
Collazo, Javier L. English-Spanish Spanish-English Encyclopedic Dictionary of Technical Terms, 3 vols. LC 79-16074. (Eng. & Span.). 1980. Set, English Edition. 154.00 (ISBN 0-07-079172-4); Set, Spanish Edition. 154.00 (ISBN 0-07-079162-7). McGraw.
Collazo de Camacho, Loida see Camacho, Loida C.
Collcutt, Martin. Five Mountains: The Rinzai Zen Monastic Institution in Medieval Japan. (Harvard East Asian Monograph: Vol. 85). (Illus.). 450p. 1980. 27.50x (ISBN 0-674-30497-7). Harvard U Pr.
Collden, Lisa. Tresors De la Tradition Orale Sakata: Proverbes, Mythes, Legendes, Fabls, Chansons et Devinettes De Sakata. (Uppsala Studies in Cultural Anthropology: No. 2). 446p. (Fr.). 1979. pap. text ed. 40.50x (ISBN 91-554-0898-2). Humanities.
Colle, Vivienne & Katz, Marjorie. Vivienne Colle's Make-It-Yourself Boutique. LC 67-18533. (Illus.). 256p. 1967. 4.95 (ISBN 0-87131-102-X). M Evans.
Colle, Vivienne & Katz, Marjorie P. Make It Yourself Boutique. LC 67-18533. (Illus.). 256p. 1985. 4.95 (ISBN 0-87131-102-X). M Evans.
Collective Bargaining Negotiations & Contracts Editors. Basic Patterns in Union Contracts. 10th ed. 128p. 1979. pap. 15.00 (ISBN 0-87179-302-4). BNA.
Collective Bargaining Negotiations & Contracts Staff, ed. Basic Patterns in Union Contracts. 10th ed. 128p. 1983. pap. text ed. 15.00 (ISBN 0-87179-423-3). BNA.
Collective Investigation Committee. Epidemic Poliomyelitis: Report on the New York Epidemic of 1907. (Nervous & Mental Disease Monographs: No. 6). 1910. 19.00 (ISBN 0-384-14495-0). Johnson Repr.
Collectors Club Library. New York. Philately: The Catalog of the Collectors Club Library. 1974. lib. bdg. 120.00 (ISBN 0-8161-1047-6, Hall Library). G K Hall.
Colledge, Edmund, tr. see Guigo II.
Colledge, Edmund, et al, eds. Julian of Norwich, "Showings". LC 77-90953. (Classics of Western Spirituality). 384p. 1978. 11.95 (ISBN 0-8091-0234-X); pap. 9.95 (ISBN 0-8091-2091-7). Paulist Pr.
Colledge, Eric, tr. see Tauler, John.
Colledge, James J. Ships of the Royal Navy: An Historical Index, 2 vols. Incl. Vol. 1. Major Ships. 50.00x (ISBN 0-678-05300-6); Vol. 2. Navy-Built Trawlers, Drifters, Tugs & Requisitioned Ships. 37.50x (ISBN 0-678-05301-4). LC 69-10859. 1969-70. Set. 75.00x (ISBN 0-678-05514-9). Kelley.
Colledge, Malcolm A. Parthian Art. LC 77-74919. (Illus.). 240p. 1977. 39.95x (ISBN 0-8014-1111-4). Cornell U Pr.
Collee, J. G. Applied Medical Microbiology. (Illus.). 158p. 1981. pap. text ed. 11.95x (ISBN 0-632-00853-9). Blackwell Pubns.
Collee, John. Kingsley's Touch. 1984. 12.95 (ISBN 0-312-45617-4). St Martin.
College & Education Division. Barron's Profiles of American Colleges: Regional Editions. (gr. 10-12). 1981. Northeast. pap. text ed. 6.95 (ISBN 0-8120-2467-2). Barron.
College Board. The College Board Achievement Tests: 14 Tests in 13 Subjects. 350p. (Orig.). (gr. 11-12). 1983. pap. 9.95 (ISBN 0-87447-162-1, 001621). College Bd.
--Index of Majors, 1984-85. 7th ed. 620p. (Orig.). 1984. pap. 11.95 (ISBN 0-87447-186-9, 001869). College Bd.
College Board & Policy Studies in Education. Training by Contract: College-Employer Profiles. 96p. (Orig.). 1983. pap. 8.95 (ISBN 0-87447-175-3, 001753). College Bd.
College Division of Barron's Educational Ser., Inc. Barron's Compact Guide to Colleges. 2nd ed. LC 80-26124. (Illus.). 352p. (gr. 11-12). 1980. pap. 3.95 (ISBN 0-8120-2826-0). Barron.
College Entrance Examination Board. End-of-Year Examinations in English for College-Bound Students: Grades 9-12. 193p. 1963. 7.00 (ISBN 0-317-35266-0, 13451); members 5.00 (ISBN 0-317-35267-9). NCTE.
--Examining the Examination in English: A Report. 1931. 24.00 (ISBN 0-384-09555-0). Johnson Repr.
College of Home Economics, Iowa State University. Families of the Future: A Search for Meaning. facsimile ed. (Illus.). 1972. pap. 7.65x (ISBN 0-8138-2370-6). Iowa St U Pr.
College of the University of Chicago Social Sciences Staff. The People Shall Judge: Readings in the Formation of American Policy, 2 pts, Vol. 1. LC 49-3028. 1949. 11.00x (P703, Phoen); Pt. 1. 5.95x (ISBN 0-226-77049-4, P702); Pt. 2. (ISBN 0-226-77050-8, P703). U of Chicago Pr.
College Placement Council, jt. auth. see Battle, Lynne D.
Collegium Internationale Allergologicum, 8th Symposium, Montreux, 1970. Cellular & Molecular Mechanisms of Cell-Mediated Allergic Reactions, Chemistry of Allergens & Transactions: Proceedings. Kallos, P., et al, eds. (International Archives of Allergy & Applied Immunology: Vol. 41, No. 1). 1971. pap. 23.00 (ISBN 3-8055-1191-4). S Karger.
Collegium Internationale Allergologicum Symposium, 10th, Copenhagen, 1974. Molecular & Cellular Aspects of Allergy: Transactions. Diamant, B., et al, eds. (International Archives of Allergy & Applied Immunology: Vol. 49, No. 1-2). (Illus.). 250p. 1975. pap. 43.50 (ISBN 3-8055-2166-9). S Karger.
Collegium Internationale Allergologicum, 9th, London, Sept. 1972. The Theoretical & Practical Aspects of Allergic Disorders: Proceedings. Parker, D., et al, eds. (International Archives of Allergy & Applied Immunology: Vol. 45, Nos. 1-2). (Illus.). 1973. pap. 32.25 (ISBN 3-8055-1605-3). S Karger.
Collegium Internationale Neuro-Psychopharmacologicum; Congress. Monoamine Oxidase Inhibitors: The State of the Art. Youdim, M. B. & Paykel, E. S., eds. LC 80-41258. (A Wiley-Interscience Publication). pap. 58.00 (ISBN 0-317-27704-9, 2052101). Bks Demand UMI.
Collen, Morris F., jt. ed. see Lindberg, Donald A.
Collen, Robert. A Few Pianos. LC 77-83731. 1978. pap. 3.00 (ISBN 0-89924-016-X). Lynx Hse.
Collender, Stanley E. The Guide to the Federal Budget: Fiscal 1985 Edition. (Orig.). 1984. pap. text ed. 10.00x (ISBN 0-87766-331-9). Urban Inst.
--The Guide to the Federal Budget: Fiscal 1986. 156p. (Orig.). 1984. text ed. 10.00x (ISBN 0-87766-360-2). Urban Inst.
Collens, Gina. Guilt Without Sex. 1981. pap. 1.75 (ISBN 0-8431-0541-0). Price Stern.
Collens, T. Wharton. Eden of Labor, or, the Christian Utopia. LC 79-154435. (Utopian Literature Ser). (Illus.). 1971. Repr. of 1876 ed. 20.00 (ISBN 0-405-03518-7). Ayer Co Pubs.
Colleran, Joseph M., tr. from Latin. see Anselm of Canterbury.
Colleran, Joseph M., tr. see Augustine, St.
Colleran, P. K., ed. Walking with Contemplation: A Walker's Guide. (Illus.). 230p. (Orig.). 1983. pap. 4.95 (ISBN 0-9609102-0-4). CAFH Found Inc.
Colles, H. C. Brahms. LC 77-94550. 1979. Repr. of 1908 ed. lib. bdg. 20.00 (ISBN 0-89341-402-6). Longwood Pub Group.
--The Growth of Music. 4th ed. 1978. 15.95x (ISBN 0-19-316116-8). Oxford U Pr.
Colles, H. C. see Hadow, William H.
Colles, Henry C. Brahms. LC 74-24060. (The Music of the Masters Ser.). Repr. of 1908 ed. 16.50 (ISBN 0-404-12883-1). AMS Pr.
--The Chamber Music of Brahms. LC 74-24061. Repr. of 1933 ed. 11.50 (ISBN 0-404-12884-X). AMS Pr.
--Essays & Lectures. facs. ed. LC 73-128225. (Essay Index Reprint Ser). 1945. 18.80 (ISBN 0-8369-1910-6). Ayer Co Pubs.
--Essays & Lectures. 1945. Repr. 10.00 (ISBN 0-8274-2296-2). R West.
--Voice & Verse: A Study in English Song. LC 78-19562. (Encore Music Editions Ser.). (Illus.). 1979. Repr. of 1928 ed. 16.50 (ISBN 0-88355-733-9). Hyperion Conn.
Colles, W. Morris & Cresswell, Henry. Success in Literature. LC 70-105771. 1970. Repr. of 1911 ed. 25.50x (ISBN 0-8046-0944-6, Pub. by Kennikat). Assoc Faculty Pr.
--Success in Literature. 1911. 20.00 (ISBN 0-8274-3902-4). R West.
Colles, William M. Literature & the Pension List. 1973. Repr. of 1889 ed. 17.50 (ISBN 0-8274-1656-3). R West.
Colles, William M. & Cresswell, Henry. Success in Literature. 360p. 1980. Repr. of 1911 ed. lib. bdg. 20.00 (ISBN 0-89760-116-5). Telegraph Bks.
Collester, J. Bryan, ed. European Communities: A Guide to Information Sources. LC 73-17506. (International Relations Information Guide Ser.: Vol. 3). 304p. 1979. 60.00x (ISBN 0-8103-1322-7). Gale.
Collet, Georges-Paul, ed. see Mauriac, Francois & Blanche, Jacques-Emile.
Collet, Pierre & Eckman, Jean-Pierre. Iterated Maps on the Interval As Dynamical Systems. (Progress in Physics, Ser.: No. 1). 227p. 1980. text ed. 19.95x (ISBN 0-8176-3026-0). Birkhauser.
Collet, Stephen. Relics of Literature. 1973. Repr. of 1823 ed. 45.00 (ISBN 0-8274-1664-4). R West.
Colleton, John. Barefoot on Jill. 1983. pap. 3.50 (ISBN 0-451-13499-0, Sig). NAL.
--Between Cloris & Amy. 1976. pap. 2.75 (ISBN 0-451-11256-3, AE1256, Sig). NAL.
--The Delights of Anna. (Orig.). 1980. pap. 3.50 (ISBN 0-451-12188-0, AE2188, Sig). NAL.
--The Enjoyment of Amy. 1983. pap. 3.95 (ISBN 0-671-47766-8). PB.
--The Enticement of Cindy. 1981. pap. 2.95 (ISBN 0-451-11019-6, AE1019, Sig). NAL.
--The Naked Countess of Liechtenstein. 1983. pap. 3.95 (ISBN 0-671-47645-9). PB.
--On or About the First Day in June. (Orig.). 1978. pap. 2.95 (ISBN 0-451-11584-8, AE3140, Sig). NAL.
--The Pleasures of Cloris. 176p. 1974. pap. 2.95 (ISBN 0-451-12938-5, AE2938, Sig). NAL.
--Replenishing Jennifer. (Orig.). 1975. pap. 2.50 (ISBN 0-451-11585-6, AE1585, Sig). NAL.
--The Seduction of Marianna. (Orig.). 1980. pap. 2.95 (ISBN 0-451-12167-8, AE2167, Sig). NAL.
--Trembling of a Leaf. 1983. pap. 3.95 (ISBN 0-671-47767-6). PB.
--Two Nymphs Named Melissa. 1979. pap. 2.95 (ISBN 0-451-12940-7, AE2940, Sig). NAL.
--Up in Mamie's Diary. (Orig.). 1975. pap. 2.95 (ISBN 0-451-13134-7, Sig). NAL.
Collet-Sandars, W., tr. see Rosengarten, A.
Collett, Dorothy. Troubled Kisses. (YA) 1984. 8.95 (ISBN 0-8034-8417-8, Avalon). Bouregy.
Collett, George. Suzuki GT 380, 550 '72 - '77. new ed. (Owners Workshop Manuals Ser.: No. 216). 1979. 10.50 (ISBN 0-85696-216-3, Pub. by J H Haynes England). Haynes Pubns.
Collett, George & Witcomb, John. Honda 500 & 450 Twins '66 - '78. (Owners Workshop Manuals Ser.: No. 211). 1980. 10.50 (ISBN 0-85696-211-2, Pub. by J H Haynes England). Haynes Pubns.
Collett, H. Flora Simlensis. 1978. Repr. of 1902 ed. 31.25x (ISBN 0-89955-268-4, Pub. by Intl Bk Dist). Intl Spec Bk.
Collett, Peter, ed. Social Rules & Social Behaviour. 185p. 1977. 16.50x (ISBN 0-87471-903-8). Rowman.
Collett, Ritter. Men of the Machine. (Illus.). 254p. 1977. 8.95 (ISBN 0-913428-28-0). Landfall Pr.
--Straight Arrow: The Art Schlichter Story. (Illus.). 160p. 1981. 10.95 (ISBN 0-913428-33-7). Landfall Pr.
--Super Stripes: Paul Brown & the Super Bowl Bengals. LC 82-83268. (Illus.). 224p. 1982. 13.95 (ISBN 0-913428-34-5). Landfall Pr.
Collett, Sidney. All about the Bible: A Popular Handbook. 324p. 1972. Repr. 11.95 (ISBN 0-8007-0004-X). Revell.
Collett, Walter. The Nuclear Bomb Patch: A Children's Play in One Act. (Orig.). (gr. k-12). 1984. spiral bdg. 4.00 (ISBN 0-916843-00-9, 101). Inst Human Soc.
Colletta, Nat J. American Schools for the Natives of Ponape: A Study of Education & Culture Change in Micronesia. 203p. 1980. pap. text ed. 11.00x (ISBN 0-8248-0634-4, Eastwest Ctr). UH Pr.
--Worker-Peasant Education in the People's Republic of China. (World Bank Staff Working Paper: No. 527). 94p. 1982. pap. 3.00 (ISBN 0-8213-0050-4). World Bank.
Colletta, Nat J., jt. auth. see Knight, Peter T.
Colletta, Nat J. & Todd, Trudy A., eds. Human Resource Development: An Annotated Bibliography on Social & Cultural Influences. vi, 165p. (Orig.). 1982. pap. 14.25 (ISBN 0-913178-74-8). Redgrave Pub Co.
Collette, Alfred T. & Chiapetta, Eugene L. Science Instruction in the Middle & Secondary Schools. (Illus.). 592p. 1984. text ed. 24.95 (ISBN 0-8016-1095-8). Mosby.
Collette, Bruce B. & Nauen, Cornelia E. FAO Species Catalogue: Vol. 2: Scombrids of the World: An Annotated & Illustrated Catalogue of Tunas, Mackerels, Bonitos & Related Species Known to Date. (Fisheries Synopsis Ser.: No. 125, Vol. 2). 137p. (Orig.). 1984. pap. text ed. 10.50 (ISBN 92-5-101381-0, F2546, FAO). Unipub.
Collette, J. M. La Recherche-Developpement en Grande-Bretagne. (Economies et Societes Series T: No. 2). 1961. pap. 19.00 (ISBN 0-317-16554-2). Kraus Repr.
--Recherche-Developpement et Progres Economique en U. R. S. S. (Economies et Societes Series G: No. 15). 1962. pap. 19.00 (ISBN 0-317-16016-8). Kraus Repr.
--Le Taux de Croissance du Revenu National Sovietique. (Economies et Societes Series G: No. 12). 1961. pap. 19.00 (ISBN 0-317-16850-9). Kraus Repr.
Collette, Paul & Wright, Robert. Huddles. (Orig.). (gr. 3-12). 1985. pap. text ed. 5.00 (ISBN 0-88734-512-3). Players Pr.
Colletti. The Art of Wood Carving. 160p. 1977. (Spec); pap. 4.95 (ISBN 0-13-049239-6). P-H.
--De Rousseau a Lenine. (Publications Gramma Ser.). 318p. 1972. 38.50 (ISBN 0-677-50645-7). Gordon.
Colletti, Anthony B. Audio-Visual Program, No. 5. (Keystone Publications' Audio-Visual Program Ser.). 1979. 215.00 (ISBN 0-912126-39-6); instrs's. guide 7.07 (ISBN 0-912126-37-X); student wkbk. 1.79 (ISBN 0-912126-38-8). Keystone Pubns.
--A Complete Question & Answer Guide to Hairdressing & Cosmetology. 1978. text ed. 16.00 (ISBN 0-912126-48-5, 1258-01); pap. text ed. 14.21 (ISBN 0-912126-49-3, 1258-00). Keystone Pubns.
--La Cosmetologia, la Guia Keystone para Aprender el Arte de Embellecer. (Illus., Span.). 1979. text ed. 15.43 (ISBN 0-912126-34-5); pap. text ed. 11.00 (ISBN 0-912126-35-3). Keystone Pubns.
--La Cosmetologia, la Guia Keystone para Aprender el Arte de Embellecer. rev. ed. (Span.). 1981. text ed. 16.78 (ISBN 0-912126-61-2, 1260-00); pap. text ed. 12.15 (ISBN 0-912126-62-0, 1261-00). Keystone Pubns.
--Cosmetology. (Illus.). 1981. 16.50x (ISBN 0-912126-59-0). Sheridan.

--Cosmetology Instructor's Guide, No. 1. (Keystone Publications' Audio-Visual Program Ser.). 88p. 1976. 7.10 (ISBN 0-912126-16-7). Keystone Pubns.

--Cosmetology Instructor's Guide, No. 2. (Keystone Publications' Audio-Visual Program Ser.). 80p. 1976. 7.10311 (ISBN 0-912126-17-5). Keystone Pubns.

--Cosmetology Instructor's Guide, No. 3. (Keystone's Publications' Audio-Visual Program Ser.). 136p. 1976. 7.10 (ISBN 0-912126-18-3). Keystone Pubns.

--Cosmetology Instructor's Guide, No. 4. (Keystone Publications' Audio-Visual Program Ser.). 112p. 7.10 (ISBN 0-912126-19-1). Keystone Pubns.

--Cosmetology Review Book. 1981. write for info. (ISBN 0-912126-56-6, 1267-00); pap. write for info. (ISBN 0-912126-64-7). Keystone Pubns.

--Cosmetology: The Keystone Guide to Beauty Culture. rev. ed. 1981. text ed. 10.00 (ISBN 0-912126-59-0, 1248-00); pap. text ed. 7.14 (ISBN 0-912126-60-4, 1249-00). Keystone Pubns.

--Dictionary of Cosmetology & Related Sciences. (Illus.). 1981. 25.00x (ISBN 0-912126-58-2). Sheridan.

--A Dictionary of Cosmetology & Related Services. Chiranky, Gary, ed. 1981. text ed. 23.57 (ISBN 0-912126-58-2, 1275-00). Keystone Pubns.

--Everything You Always Wanted to Know About Beauty. 1978. 14.21 (ISBN 0-912126-40-X). Keystone Pubns.

--Libro de Repaso de la Cosmetologia. 1978. pap. text ed. 5.72 (ISBN 0-912126-44-2, 1267-02). Keystone Pubns.

--Revista a los Examenes De Cosmetologia Que Hace la Junta Estatal (State Board Review Examinations in Cosmetology) 1976. pap. 6.00 (ISBN 0-912126-12-4, 1271-00). Keystone Pubns.

--State Board Review Examinations in Cosmetology. 1976. pap. 4.28 (ISBN 0-912126-11-6). Keystone Pubns.

--Trichology: The Keystone Guide to Hair Analysis As Related to the Practice of Cosmetology & Barbering. (Illus.). 1981. text ed. 11.36 (ISBN 0-912126-57-4). Keystone Pubns.

--Twenty-Four Practice Hairstyles. rev. ed. 1981. pap. text ed. 5.00 (ISBN 0-912126-47-7, 1265-00). Keystone Pubns.

Colletti, Jack J. & Colletti, Paul J. A Freehand Approach to Technical Drawing. 336p. 1974. pap. 22.95 ref. ed. (ISBN 0-13-330548-1). P-H.

Colletti, Jerome, jt. auth. see Metzger, Bert.

Colletti, Lucio. From Rousseau to Lenin: Studies in Ideology & Society. Merringer, John, tr. LC 72-92035. 240p. 1975. pap. 5.95 (ISBN 0-85345-350-0). Monthly Rev.

--Marxism & Hegel. 1979. 20.00x (ISBN 0-8052-7020-5, Pub. by NLB); pap. 7.25 (ISBN 0-8052-7061-2). Schocken.

Colletti, Ned. Golden Glory: A Game-by-Game History of the Purdue-Notre Dame Football Rivalry. LC 83-80696. (Illus.). 320p. (Orig.). 1983. pap. 12.95 (ISBN 0-88011-198-4). Leisure Pr.

--You Gotta Have Heart: Dallas Green's Rebuilding of the Cubs. LC 85-4405. (Illus.). 272p. 1985. 15.95 (ISBN 0-912083-11-5). Diamond Communications.

Colletti, Paul J., jt. auth. see Colletti, Jack J.

Colletti, Paul J., jt. auth. see Weinberg, Norman.

Colletti, V. & Stephens, S. D., eds. Disorders with Defective Hearing. (Advances in Audiology: Vol. 3). (Illus.). viii, 216p. 1985. 70.00 (ISBN 3-8055-3965-7). S Karger.

Collett-Sandars, W., tr. see Rosengarten, A.

Collewijn, H. The Oculomotor System of the Rabbit & Its Plasticity. (Studies of Brain Function: Vol. 5). (Illus.). 200p. 1981. 42.00 (ISBN 0-387-10678-2). Springer-Verlag.

Colley, Ann C. Tennyson & Madness. LC 82-13689. 192p. 1983. 20.00x (ISBN 0-8203-0648-7). U of Ga Pr.

Colley, B. Practical Manual of Site Development. 256p. 1985. 37.50 (ISBN 0-07-011803-5). Mcgraw.

Colley, David. Sound Waves. 240p. 1985. 14.95 (ISBN 0-312-74607-5). St Martin.

Colley, Iain. Dos Passos & the Fiction of Despair. 170p. 1978. 26.00x (ISBN 0-8476-6020-6). Rowman.

Colley, John. Corporate & Divisional Planning. 1984. text ed. 26.95 (ISBN 0-8359-1075-X); sol. manual avail. (ISBN 0-8359-1076-8). Reston.

Colley, John S. John Marston's Theatrical Drama. (Salzburg Studies in English Literature, Jacobean Drama Studies: No. 33). 202p. 1974. pap. text ed. 25.50x (ISBN 0-391-01347-5). Humanities.

Colley, Linda. The Defiance of Oligarchy: The Tory Party, 1714-60. Date not set. pap. price not set (ISBN 0-521-31311-2). Cambridge U Pr.

--In Defiance of Oligarchy: The Tory Party 1714-1760. LC 81-10004. 360p. 1982. 52.50 (ISBN 0-521-23982-6). Cambridge U Pr.

Colli, C. & Montinari, M. Nietzsche-Briefwechsel: Briefe an Nietzsche 1869-1872, Vol. 2, Section 2. 1977. 55.20x (ISBN 3-11-006635-1). De Gruyter.

Colli, Carlo. The Spirit of Mornese. 198p. (Orig.). 1982. pap. 4.95 (ISBN 0-89944-064-9, P-064-9). Don Bosco Multimedia.

Colli, G. & Montinari, M. Nietzsche-Briefwechsel: Briefe April 1869-1872, Vol. 2, Section 1. 1977. 34.40x (ISBN 3-11-006633-5). De Gruyter.

Colli, Giorgio & Montinari, Mazzino, eds. Nietzsche - Werke: Kritische Gesamtausgabe. (Vol. 1, Sect. 7). 1976. 55.20x (ISBN 3-11-004979-1). De Gruyter.

Colli, Giorgio, ed. see Nietzsche, Friedrich.

Colli, Giorgio, et al, eds. Nietzsche - Briefwechsel. (Ger.). 1983. write for info. De Gruyter.

Colli, Jean-Claude, jt. auth. see Bernard, Yves.

Colliander, Roland, et al. Spokane Sketchbook. LC 73-22207. (Illus.). 96p. 1974. 12.95 (ISBN 0-295-95326-8). U of Wash Pr.

Colliander, Tito. The Way of the Ascetics. 130p. Repr. of 1960 ed. cancelled 5.95 (ISBN 0-913026-22-0). St Nectarios.

Collias, Elsie C., jt. auth. see Collias, Nicholas E.

Collias, Elsie C., jt. ed. see Collias, Nicholas E.

Collias, Eugene E. & Andreeva, Svetlana I. Puget Sound Marine Environment: An Annotated Bibliography. LC 77-24231. 402p. 1978. pap. 13.50x (ISBN 0-295-95570-8, Pub. by Washington Sea Grant). U of Wash Pr.

Collias, Eugene E., et al. An Atlas of Physical & Chemical Properties of Puget Sound & Its Approaches. LC 74-10057. (Illus.). 248p. 1974. pap. 25.00x (ISBN 0-295-95345-4, Pub. by Washington Sea Grant). U of Wash Pr.

Collias, Joe G. The Last of Steam. LC 60-14067. (Illus.). 1960. 25.00 (ISBN 0-8310-7018-8). Howell-North.

--Mopac Power. (Illus.). 352p. 1980. 35.00 (ISBN 0-8310-7117-6). Howell-North.

--The Search for Steam. LC 72-86957. (Illus.). 1972. 25.00 (ISBN 0-8310-7092-7). Howell-North.

Collias, Nicholas E. & Collias, Elsie C. Nest Building & Bird Behavior. LC 84-42585. (Illus.). 360p. 1984. 45.00x (ISBN 0-691-08358-4); pap. 16.50x (ISBN 0-691-08359-2). Princeton U Pr.

Collias, Nicholas E. & Collias, Elsie C., eds. External Construction by Animals. LC 75-34185. (Benchmark Papers in Animal Behavior: Vol. 4). 1976. 63.00 (ISBN 0-12-786250-1). Acad Pr.

Collicott, Howard E. & Bauer, Paul E. Spacecraft Thermal Control, Design & Operation. 45.00 (ISBN 0-915928-75-2). AIAA.

Collicott, Howard E., jt. auth. see Bauer, Paul E.

Collidge, Susan. What Katy Did. Date not set. 12.00 (ISBN 0-8446-6184-8). Peter Smith.

Collie, C. H. Kinetic Theory & Entropy. LC 81-8332. (Illus.). 416p. 1983. pap. text ed. 21.95x (ISBN 0-582-44368-7). Longman.

Collie Club of America. The New Collie. LC 82-19049. (Complete Breed Book Ser.). 304p. 1985. 15.95 (ISBN 0-87605-130-1). Howell Bk.

Collie, David, ed. see Ssu Shu.

Collie, M. J. Stirling Engine Design & Feasibility for Automotive Use. LC 79-13444. (Energy Technology Review Ser.: No. 47). (Illus.). 470p. 1979. 36.00 (ISBN 0-8155-0763-1). Noyes.

Collie, M. J., ed. Corrosion Inhibitors: Developments since 1980. LC 83-13055. (Chemical Technology Review No. 223). 379p. 1984. 48.00 (ISBN 0-8155-0957-X). Noyes.

--Etching Compositions & Processes. LC 82-7894. (Chemical Technology Review Ser.: No. 210). (Illus.). 308p. 1983. 42.00 (ISBN 0-8155-0913-8). Noyes.

--Extractive Metallurgy: Developments since 1980. LC 83-21996. (Chemical Technology Review Ser.: No. 227). (Illus.). 323p. 1984. 45.00 (ISBN 0-8155-0978-2). Noyes.

--Geothermal Energy: Recent Developments. LC 78-61893. (Energy Technology Review: No. 32). (Illus.). 1979. 40.00 (ISBN 0-8155-0727-5). Noyes.

--Heat Pump Technology for Saving Energy. LC 79-83902. (Energy Technology Review Ser.: No. 39). (Illus.). 348p. 1979. 39.00 (ISBN 0-8155-0744-5). Noyes.

--Industrial Abrasive Materials & Compositions. LC 81-38326. (Chem. Tech. Rev. Ser. 190). (Illus.). 351p. 1981. 45.00 (ISBN 0-8155-0851-4). Noyes.

--Industrial Water Treatment Chemicals & Processes: Developments Since 1978. LC 83-2411. (Chem. Tech. Rev. 217; Pollution Tech. Rev. 98). (Illus.). 319p. (Orig.). 1983. 42.00 (ISBN 0-8155-0936-7). Noyes.

Collie, Michael. The Alien Art: A Critical Study of George Gissing's Novels. vii, 197p. 1978. 19.50 (ISBN 0-208-01731-3, Archon). Shoe String.

--George Borrow: Eccentric. LC 82-4397. (Illus.). 250p. 1983. 42.50 (ISBN 0-521-24615-6). Cambridge U Pr.

--George Gissing: A Biography. 189p. 1977. 19.50 (ISBN 0-208-01700-3, Archon). Shoe String.

--George Gissino: A Bibliography. LC 75-22129. pap. 35.80 (ISBN 0-317-26933-X, 2023603). Bks Demand UMI.

--George Meredith: A Bibiliography. LC 73-85962. 290p. 1983. 25.00 (ISBN 0-7129-0636-3). U Pr of Va.

--Gissing: A Bibliographical Study. (Illus.). 192p. 1985. 35.00x (ISBN 0-906795-29-X, Pub. by St. Pauls Biblios England). U Pr of Va.

--Jules LaForgue. (French Poets Ser.). 134p. 1977. 32.50 (ISBN 0-485-14606-1, Pub. by Athlone Pr Ltd); pap. 14.95 (ISBN 0-485-12206-5). Longwood Pub Group.

Collie, Michael & Fraser, Angus. George Borrow: A Bibliographical Study. LC 84-119368. (St. Paul's Bibliographies Ser.). 240p. 1984. text ed. 35.00 (ISBN 0-906795-24-9). U Pr of Va.

Collie, Michael, ed. see LaForgue, Jules.

Collier. Collier Bankruptcy Manual: Release 8. 3rd ed. 1983. write for info. Bender.

--Collier Bankruptcy Practice Guide: Release 2. 1983. write for info. Bender.

--Collier Forms Manual: Release 4. 3rd ed. 1983. write for info. Bender.

--Collier on Bankruptcy: Release 10. 15th ed. 1983. write for info. Bender.

Collier & Helfrich. Mount Desert Island & Acadia National Park. (Illus.). 1978. pap. 8.95 (ISBN 0-89272-044-1). Down East.

Collier, et al. Kids' Stuff: Kindergarten - Nursery School. rev. ed. LC 78-70904. (The Kids' Stuff Set). 264p. (ps-k). 1982. pap. 10.95 (ISBN 0-913916-61-7, IP005). Incentive Pubns.

Collier, A. M. A Handbook of Textiles. 3rd ed. 7.80 (ISBN 0-08-024974-4); pap. 5.75 (ISBN 0-08-018057-4). Pergamon.

Collier, Albert, jt. auth. see Warr, Diana.

Collier, Ann. Creative Design in Bobbin Lace. (Illus.). 144p. 1982. 21.95 (ISBN 0-8231-5059-3). Branford.

Collier, Arthur. Clavis Universalis: New Inquiry after Truth, Being a Demonstration of the Non-Existence or Impossibility of an External World. Wellek, Rene, ed. LC 75-11208. (British Philosophers & Theologians of the 17th & 18th Centuries Ser.). 150p. lib. bdg. 51.00 (ISBN 0-8240-1763-3). Garland Pub.

Collier, B. A. Maverick Trail. (YA) 1978. 8.95 (ISBN 0-685-05592-2, Avalon). Bouregy.

--Montana Graves. 1983. 8.95 (ISBN 0-8034-8320-1, Avalon). Bouregy.

--Mustangs for Montana. (YA) 1980. 8.95 (ISBN 0-686-59789-3, Avalon). Bouregy.

--One Foot in the Stirrup. (YA) 1978. 8.95 (ISBN 0-685-53392-1, Avalon). Bouregy.

--Trouble at Crossed Forks. (YA) 1979. 8.95 (ISBN 0-685-93880-8, Avalon). Bouregy.

Collier, Basil. Arms & the Men: The Arms Trade & Governments. (Illus.). 320p. 1980. 26.50 (ISBN 0-241-10308-8, Pub. by Hamish Hamilton England). David & Charles.

--Hidden Weapons. 386p. 1982. 32.00 (ISBN 0-241-10788-1, Pub. by Hamish Hamilton England). David & Charles.

--Japanese Aircraft of World War Two. LC 78-27558. (Illus.). 1979. 12.50 (ISBN 0-8317-5137-1, Mayflower Bks). Smith Pubs.

--The Second World War: A Military History. 19.00 (ISBN 0-8446-4724-1). Peter Smith.

Collier, Bertrand. Advanced Architectural Drawing. (Illus.). 137p. 1986. 175.50 (ISBN 0-86650-174-6). Gloucester Art.

Collier, C. Patrick. Geometry for Teachers. 2nd ed. (Illus.). 308p. 1984. text ed. 20.95x (ISBN 0-88133-046-9). Waveland Pr.

Collier, Calhoun C. & Houston, Robert W. Modern Elementary Education: Teaching & Learning. (Illus.). 352p. 1976. text ed. write for info. (ISBN 0-02-323770-8, 32377). Macmillan.

Collier, Calvin L. War Child's Children: A Story of the Third Arkansas Cavalry. (Illus.). 139p. 1965. 19.95. J W Bell.

Collier, Carole. Five Hundred Five Wine Questions Your Friends Can't Answer. (Five Hundred Five Quiz Ser.). 160p. (Orig.). 1983. 10.95 (ISBN 0-8027-0730-0); pap. 3.95 (ISBN 0-8027-7209-9). Walker & Co.

--The Magical Art of Cake Decorating. (Illus.). 168p. 1984. 18.95 (ISBN 0-442-28207-9). Van Nos Reinhold.

--The Natural, Sugarless Dessert Cookbook. 192p. 1980. 12.95 (ISBN 0-8027-0647-9). Walker & Co.

--The Natural Sugarless Dessert Cookbook. LC 79-91252. (Illus.). 192p. 1983. pap. 5.95 (ISBN 0-8027-7201-3). Walker & Co.

--Woman's Day Serving Food with Style. LC 81-43116. 176p. 1982. 13.95 (ISBN 0-385-18517-0). Doubleday.

Collier, Carolyn R., jt. auth. see Lipsitt, Lewis P.

Collier, Carvel, ed. see Faulkner, William.

Collier, Charles. Essay on the Principles of Education, Physiologically Considered. Bd. with Art of Instructing the Infant Deaf & Dumb. (Contributions to the History of Psychology, Vol. V, Pt. B: Psychometrics & Educational Psychology). 1980. Repr. of 1856 ed. 30.00 (ISBN 0-89093-319-7). U Pubns Amer.

Collier, Christopher. Roger Sherman's Connecticut: Yankee Politics & the American Revolution. LC 78-153104. (Illus.). 1971. 25.00x (ISBN 0-8195-4035-8). Wesleyan U Pr.

Collier, Christopher, jt. auth. see Collier, James L.

Collier, Christopher see Weaver, Glenn.

Collier, Courtland A. & Halperin, Don A. Construction Funding: Where the Money Comes From. LC 83-21753. (Practical Construction Guides Ser.: 1-344). 294p. 1984. 28.50x (ISBN 0-471-89065-0, Pub. by Wiley-Interscience). Wiley.

Collier, Courtland A. & Ledbetter, William B. Engineering Cost Analysis. 528p. 1982. text ed. 28.95 scp (ISBN 0-06-041329-8, HarpC); solutions manual avail. (ISBN 0-06-361330-1). Har-Row.

Collier, David. Chinese-English Dictionary of Colloquial Terms Used in Modern Chinese Literature. 11.95 (ISBN 0-88710-016-3). Far Eastern Pubns.

--Squatters & Oligarchs: Authoritarian Rule & Policy Change in Peru. LC 75-34112. (Illus.). 200p. 1976. 18.50x (ISBN 0-8018-1748-X). Johns Hopkins.

Collier, David, ed. The New Authoritarianism in Latin America. LC 79-83982. 1979. 46.50 (ISBN 0-691-07616-2); pap. 9.95 (ISBN 0-691-02194-5). Princeton U Pr.

Collier, David A. Service Management: The Automation of Services. 1985. pap. 17.95 (ISBN 0-8359-4166-3); instr's manual avail. (ISBN 0-8359-6908-8). Reston.

Collier, David E., jt. auth. see Quigley, Mary A.

Collier, Elsie, jt. auth. see Collier, John.

Collier, Eugenia W., jt. ed. see Long, Richard A.

Collier, Frances. Family Economy of the Working Classes in the Cotton Industry 1784-1833. Fitton, R. S., ed. LC 66-1166. 1965. 17.50x (ISBN 0-678-06756-2). Kelley.

Collier, Francis, et al. Quantitative Laboratory Experiments in General Chemistry. LC 75-26087. (Illus.). 288p. 1976. spiral bdg. 17.50 (ISBN 0-395-18982-9). HM.

Collier, G. Jazz. (Resources of Music Ser.). (Illus.). 200p. 1975. tape o.p. 16.95 (ISBN 0-521-20854-8); record 13.95 (ISBN 0-521-20563-8). Cambridge U Pr.

Collier, Gary. Emotional Expression. 264p. 1985. text ed. 27.50 (ISBN 0-89859-505-3). L Erlbaum Assocs.

Collier, George, ed. The Inca & Aztec States, Fourteen Hundred t0 Eighteen Hundred: Anthropology & History. (Studies in Anthropology Ser.). 438p. 1982. 49.00 (ISBN 0-12-181180-8). Acad Pr.

Collier, George A. Fields of the Tzotzil: The Ecological Bases of Tradition in Highland Chiapas. LC 75-12840. (Texas Pan American Ser.). (Illus.). 270p. 1975. 17.50x (ISBN 0-292-72412-8). U of Tex Pr.

Collier, Gerald, ed. The Management of Peer-Group Learning: Syndicate Methods in Higher Education. 129p. 1983. 20.00 (ISBN 0-900868-96-1). Taylor & Francis.

Collier, Gordon, tr. see Grabes, Herbert.

Collier, Graham. Form, Space, & Vision: An Introduction to Drawing & Design. 4th ed. (Illus.). 320p. 1985. pap. text ed. 25.95 (ISBN 0-13-329442-0). P-H.

Collier, Haiba. English Essentials. Land, Jennifer, ed. 100p. 1985. pap. text ed. 20.00 (ISBN 0-933195-03-6). Cal College Pr.

Collier, Harry, et al, eds. Electronic Publishing Review: The International Journal of the Transfer of Published Information via Videotex & Online Media. 1984. per year 66.00 (ISBN 0-317-00229-5). Learned Info.

Collier, Helen V. Counseling Women: A Guide for Therapists. (Illus.). 352p. 1982. text ed. 24.95 (ISBN 0-02-905840-6). Free Pr.

Collier, Herbert L. How to Help Your Child Get Better Grades. 288p. 1981. pap. 3.50 (ISBN 0-523-40185-X). Pinnacle Bks.

Collier, Howard E. Experiment with a Life. (Orig.). 1953. pap. 2.30x (ISBN 0-87574-069-3). Pendle Hill.

--The Quaker Meeting. 1983. pap. 5.00x (ISBN 0-87574-026-X, 026). Pendle Hill.

Collier, Hugh. Developing Electrical Power: Thirty Years of World Bank Experience. LC 83-22655. 200p. 1984. text ed. 22.50x (ISBN 0-8018-3222-5). Johns Hopkins.

Collier, I., jt. auth. see Lewis, S.

Collier, J., jt. ed. see Phillips, I.

Collier, J. G. Convective Boiling & Condensation. 2nd ed. (Illus.). 460p. 1981. text ed. 85.00 (ISBN 0-07-011798-5). McGraw.

Collier, J. P. Lives of Shakespearian Actors, Memoirs of the Principal Actors in the Plays of Shakespeare. (Shakespeare Society of London Ser.: Vol. 161). pap. 28.00 (ISBN 0-317-16541-0). Kraus Repr.

--The Stationer's Company: Extracts, 2 vols in 1, Vols. 1-2. (Shakespeare Society of London Ser.: Vol. 12). pap. 42.00 (ISBN 0-317-16539-9). Kraus Repr.

Collier, J. P., ed. Henslowe & Alleyn: The Diary of Philip Henslowe, 2 vols. (Shakespeare Society of London: No. 7). pap. 42.00 (ISBN 0-317-16534-8). Kraus Repr.

--Henslowe & Alleyn: Vol. 1, 2 vols. Incl. Memoirs of Edward Alleyn; The Alleyn Papers, a Collection of Original Documents. (Shakespeare Society of London: Vol. 81). pap. 42.00 (ISBN 0-317-16537-2). Kraus Repr.

Collier, J. Payne. Bibliographical & Critical Account of the Rarest Books in the English Language, 4 Vols. Repr. of 1866 ed. Set. 70.00 (ISBN 0-404-01720-7); 17.50 ea. Vol. 1 (ISBN 0-404-01721-5). Vol. 2 (ISBN 0-404-01722-3). Vol. 3 (ISBN 0-404-01723-1). Vol. 4 (ISBN 0-404-01724-X). AMS Pr.

--Farther Particulars Regarding Shakespeare & His Works. LC 70-113581. Repr. of 1839 ed. 12.50 (ISBN 0-404-01607-3). AMS Pr.

--History of English Dramatic Poetry to the Time of Shakespeare, & the Annals of the Stage to the Restoration, 3 vols. LC 74-113582. Repr. of 1831 ed. Set. 145.00 (ISBN 0-404-01730-4). AMS Pr.

--Memoirs of the Principal Actors in the Plays of Shakespeare. LC 77-113580. Repr. of 1846 ed. 24.50 (ISBN 0-404-01599-9). AMS Pr.

--New Facts Regarding the Life of Shakespeare. LC 78-113583. (BCL Ser.: I). Repr. of 1835 ed. 16.50 (ISBN 0-404-01609-X). AMS Pr.

--New Particulars Regarding the Works of Shakespeare. LC 71-113584. Repr. of 1836 ed. 11.50 (ISBN 0-404-01614-6). AMS Pr.

--Notes & Emendations to the Text of Shakespeare's Plays from Early Manuscript Corrections in a Copy of the Folio, 1632. LC 74-106408. (Research & Source Work: No. 401). 1970. Repr. of 1853 ed. lib. bdg. 25.50 (ISBN 0-8337-0627-6). B Franklin.

--Notes & Emendations to the Text of Shakespeare's Plays from Early Manuscript Corrections in a Copy of the Folio. 1973. Repr. of 1853 ed. 19.45 (ISBN 0-8274-1707-1). R West.

--Old Man's Diary Forty Years Ago, 1823-33, 4 Vols. in 1. Repr. of 1872 ed. 29.00 (ISBN 0-404-07289-5). AMS Pr.

--Reasons for a New Edition of Shakespeare's Works. LC 79-113586. Repr. of 1842 ed. 11.50 (ISBN 0-404-01616-2). AMS Pr.

Collier, J. Payne, ed. Broadside Black-Letter Ballads Printed in the Sixteenth & Seventeenth Centuries. LC 68-56803. (Research & Source Works Ser.: No. 288). (Illus.). 1968. Repr. of 1868 ed. 21.00 (ISBN 0-8337-0626-8). B Franklin.

Collier, J. Payne, ed. see Bale, John.

Collier, J. Payne, ed. see Dowdall, John.

Collier, J. Payne, ed. see Egerton, Francis.

Collier, J. Payne, et al, eds. see Trevelyan.

Collier, James L. Give Dad My Best. 192p. (gr. 7 up). 1982. pap. 1.95 (ISBN 0-590-32634-1). Scholastic Inc.

--Louis Armstrong: An American Genius. (Illus.). 1983. 19.95 (ISBN 0-19-503377-9). Oxford U Pr.

--Louis Armstrong: An American Success Story. (Illus.). 176p. (gr. 5-9). 1985. 11.95 (ISBN 0-02-722830-4). Macmillan.

--The Making of Jazz: A Comprehensive History. 560p. (gr. 7 up). 1979. pap. 13.95 (ISBN 0-385-28668-6, Delta). Dell.

--Planet out of the Past. LC 83-9365. 168p. (gr. 5-9). 1983. 10.95 (ISBN 0-02-722860-6). Macmillan.

--The Teddy Bear Habit. 13.50 (ISBN 0-8446-6191-0). Peter Smith.

Collier, James L. & Collier, Christopher. The Bloody Country. 240p. (YA) (gr. 7 up). 1985. pap. 2.25 (ISBN 0-317-17367-7, Point). Scholastic Inc.

--Jump Ship to Freedom. LC 81-65492. 192p. (gr. 4-6). 1981. 12.95 (ISBN 0-385-28484-5). Delacorte.

--Meeting in Philadelphia: The Constitutional Convention of 1787. LC 84-45750. Date not set. price not set (ISBN 0-394-52346-6). Random.

--My Brother Sam Is Dead. 240p. (gr. 7 up). 1985. pap. 2.25 (ISBN 0-590-33694-0, Point). Scholastic Inc.

--War Comes to Willy Freeman. LC 82-70317. 192p. (YA) (gr. 4-6). 1983. 13.95 (ISBN 0-385-29235-X). Delacorte.

--Who Is Carrie? LC 83-23947. 192p. (gr. 4-6). 1984. 14.95 (ISBN 0-385-29295-3). Delacorte.

--The Winter Hero. 208p. (YA) (gr. 7 up). 1985. pap. 2.25 (ISBN 0-590-33696-7, Point). Scholastic Inc.

Collier, James R. Yachting Signal Book. LC 84-45262. (Illus.). 128p. 1985. 17.50 (ISBN 0-87033-324-0). Cornell Maritime.

Collier, Jane F. Law & Social Change in Zinacantan. LC 72-91678. (Illus.). xiv, 282p. 1973. 22.50x (ISBN 0-8047-0821-5). Stanford U Pr.

Collier, Jaunell & Hill, Marie. I Love You. (Children's Coloring Book Ser.). 27p. (Orig.). 1983. write for info. (ISBN 0-918464-58-7). Irresistible.

Collier, Jeremy. A Defence of the Short View off the Profaneness & Immorality of the English Stage. LC 72-170444. (The English Stage Ser.: Vol. 30). lib. bdg. 61.00 (ISBN 0-8240-0613-5). Garland Pub.

--Essays upon Several Moral Subjects, 4 Pts in 3 Vols. 1969. Repr. of 1698 ed. Set. 134.00 (ISBN 3-4870-2389-X). Adlers Foreign Bks.

--A Second Defence of the Short View of the English Stage. LC 76-170445. (The English Stage Ser.: Vol. 34). lib. bdg. 61.00 (ISBN 0-8240-0617-8). Garland Pub.

--Short View of the Immorality, & Profaneness of the English Stage. 3rd ed. LC 74-3401. Repr. of 1698 ed. 21.50 (ISBN 0-404-01619-7). AMS Pr.

--Short View of the Profaneness & Immorality of the English Stage. 1969. Repr. of 1730 ed. 31.25x (ISBN 3-4870-2589-2). Adlers Foreign Bks.

Collier, John. His Monkey Wife. (Twentieth-Century Classics Ser.). 1983. pap. 5.95 (ISBN 0-19-281407-9). Oxford U Pr.

--On the Gleaming Way: Navajos, Eastern Pueblos, Zunis, Hopis, Apaches & Their Land, & Their Meanings to the World. LC 62-12407. 163p. (Photos, Orig). 1962. pap. 5.95 (ISBN 0-8040-0232-0, 82-71595, SB). Ohio U Pr.

Collier, John & Collier, Elsie. China's Socialist Revolution. LC 74-7782. 286p. 1976. pap. 4.95 (ISBN 0-85345-368-3). Monthly Rev.

Collier, John P., ed. Illustrations of Early English Popular Literature, 2 Vols. LC 65-16234. Repr. of 1863 ed. Set. 40.00 (ISBN 0-405-08366-1, Blom Pubns); 20.00; Vol. 1. 22.00 (ISBN 0-405-08367-X). Vol. 2 (ISBN 0-405-08368-8). Ayer Co Pubs.

--Illustrations of Old English Literature, 3 Vols. LC 65-16233. Repr. of 1866 ed. Set. 66.00 (ISBN 0-405-08369-6, Blom Pubns); 22.00 ea. Vol. 1 (ISBN 0-405-08370-X). Vol. 2 (ISBN 0-405-08371-8). Vol. 3 (ISBN 0-405-08372-6). Ayer Co Pubs.

Collier, John P., ed. see Coleridge, Samuel T.

Collier, John P., ed. see Gosson, Stephen.

Collier, John P., ed. see Shakespeare, William.

Collier, Joseph M., ed. Unity & Diversity: Twelve Original Essays on America's Ethnics & Minorities. 1983. pap. text ed. 9.95 (ISBN 0-942738-01-2). Amer Studies.

Collier, Katherine B. Cosmogonies of Our Fathers. 1968. lib. bdg. 29.00x (ISBN 0-374-91862-7). Octagon.

Collier, Kathleen W. & Ross, Mary C. The Photography of Joseph Collier. LC 82-15147. (Illus.). 1983. 24.95 (ISBN 0-87108-633-6). Pruett.

Collier, Keith. Construction Contracts. (Illus.). 1979. ref. ed. 26.95 (ISBN 0-8359-0912-3). Reston.

--Estimating Construction Costs: A Conceptual Approach. text ed. 25.95 (ISBN 0-8359-1792-4). Reston.

--Fundamentals of Construction Estimating & Cost Accounting. (Illus.). 400p. 1974. 30.95 (ISBN 0-13-335604-3). P-H.

--Managing Construction Contracts. 1981. text ed. 28.95 (ISBN 0-8359-4227-9). Reston.

Collier, L. D. Spanish, Everyday. (Teach Yourself Ser.). 1974. pap. 3.95 (ISBN 0-679-10169-1). McKay.

Collier, L. H. & Oxford, J., eds. Developments in Antiviral Therapy. LC 80-41168. 1981. 55.00 (ISBN 0-12-181150-6). Acad Pr.

Collier, Larry. Building & Flying the Mitchell Wing. (Illus.). 176p. 1982. pap. 7.95 (ISBN 0-8306-2302-7, 2302). TAB Bks.

--How to Fly Helicopters. (Modern Aviation Ser.). (Illus.). 1979. pap. 10.95 (ISBN 0-8306-2264-0, 2264). TAB Bks.

Collier, Leona. Change of Heart. (Orig.). 1981. pap. 1.75 (ISBN 0-8439-8028-1, Tiara Bks). Dorchester Pub Co.

--The Ghostly Bridegroom. (Orig.). 1981. pap. 1.75 (ISBN 0-8439-8015-X, Tiara Bks). Dorchester Pub Co.

Collier, Leontine, jt. auth. see Harrigan, Violetta C.

Collier, Louise W. Pilgrimage: A Tale of Old Natchez. 424p. (Orig.). 1983. pap. 9.95 (ISBN 0-918518-26-1). St Luke TN.

--Pilgrimage: A Tale of Old Natchez. 426p. 1984. 14.95 (ISBN 0-918518-32-6). St Luke TN.

Collier, Mel. Local Area Networks: The Implications for Library & Information Science. (LIR Report Ser.: No. 19). 53p. (Orig.). 1984. pap. 14.25 (ISBN 0-7123-3028-3, Pub. by British Lib). Longwood Pub Group.

Collier, Patricia. The Thatched Kitchen: Harvest & Holiday Cookbook. LC 72-87655. 1972. 5.95 (ISBN 0-88351-008-1). Test Recipe.

Collier, Paul & Lal, Deepak. Poverty & Growth in Kenya. (Working Paper: No. 389). 76p. 1980. 5.00 (ISBN 0-686-36149-0, WP-0389). World Bank.

Collier, Peter & Horowitz, David. The Kennedys: An American Drama. LC 84-2502. (Illus.). 608p. 1984. 19.95 (ISBN 0-671-44793-9). Summit Bks.

--The Kennedys: An American Drama. 720p. 1985. pap. 4.95 (ISBN 0-446-32702-6). Warner Bks.

--The Rockefellers: An American Dynasty. (Illus.). 1977. pap. 4.95 (ISBN 0-451-13455-9, Sig). NAL.

Collier, Peter, jt. auth. see Chace, William M.

Collier, Philip E. It Seems to Me. 1982. 4.95 (ISBN 0-86544-019-0). Salvation Army.

Collier, Phyllis. How to Marry a Winner. 203p. 1982. 11.95 (ISBN 0-13-423624-6); pap. 5.95 (ISBN 0-13-423616-5). P-H.

Collier, Price. America & the Americans from a French Point of View. text ed. 15.75 (ISBN 0-8369-9215-6, 9071). Ayer Co Pubs.

Collier, R., et al, eds. Optical Holography. 2nd ed. 1977. student ed. 27.50 (ISBN 0-12-181052-6). Acad Pr.

Collier, R. B. Pleneurethic: A New Approach to Life & Health. Myers, Iris, ed. (Illus.). 1974. text ed. 4.50 (ISBN 0-533-01143-4, Pub. by Vantage). Pleneurethic Intl.

--Pleneurethic & the Brain. LC 65-81608. 2.50 (ISBN 0-686-17437-2). Pleneurethic Intl.

Collier, Raymond O., Jr. & Hummel, Thomas J., eds. Experimental Design & Interpretation. LC 76-18039. (Readings in Educational Research Ser.). 1977. 32.50x (ISBN 0-8211-0225-7); text ed. 29.50x 10 or more copies. McCutchan.

Collier, Richard. The Freedom Road: 1944-1945. LC 83-45066. (Illus.). 336p. (Orig.). 1984. 17.95 (ISBN 0-689-11392-7). Atheneum.

--Poetry & Drama in the York Corpus Christi Play. 303p. 1977. 21.00 (ISBN 0-208-01611-2, Archon). Shoe String.

--The Rainbow People: A Gaudy World of the Very Rich & Those Who Serve Them. (Illus.). 304p. 1984. 17.95 (ISBN 0-396-08389-7). Dodd.

--War in the Desert. LC 77-81945. (World War 11 Ser.). (gr. 7 up). 1977. lib. bdg. 22.60 (ISBN 0-8094-2475-4, Pub. by Time-Life). Silver.

--War in the Desert. (World War II Ser.). 1977. 14.95 (ISBN 0-8094-2474-6). Time-Life.

Collier, Richard B. Pleneurethic: A World Class Philosophy. (Illus.). 368p. 1981. 20.00 (ISBN 0-682-49753-3). Exposition Pr FL.

--Pleneurethic: Its Evolution & Scientific Basis. 318p. 1980. 15.00 (ISBN 0-682-49623-5). Exposition Pr FL.

--Pleneurethic: Way of Life, System of Therapeutics. (Illus.). 1979. 10.00 (ISBN 0-682-49372-4). Exposition Pr FL.

Collier, Robert. The Amazing Secrets of the Masters of the Far East. 10.95 (ISBN 0-912576-02-2). R Collier.

--Be Rich. 1970. pap. 2.95 (ISBN 0-910140-24-3). C & R Anthony.

--Be Rich. pap. 2.95 (ISBN 0-912576-05-7). R Collier.

--Prayer Works. 1950. pap. 3.95 (ISBN 0-910140-04-9). C & R Anthony.

--Prayer Works! 3.50 (ISBN 0-912576-01-4). R Collier.

--Riches Within Your Reach. 1984. deluxe ed. 14.95 (ISBN 0-912576-14-6); pap. 6.95 (ISBN 0-912576-13-8). R Collier.

--Secret of the Ages. rev. ed. 1984. deluxe ed. 14.95 (ISBN 0-912576-12-X); pap. 6.95 (ISBN 0-912576-11-1). R Collier.

Collier, Robert J., et al. Optical Holography. 1971. 76.00 (ISBN 0-12-181050-X). Acad Pr.

Collier, Ruth B. Regimes in Tropical Africa: Changing Forms of Supremacy, 1945-1975. LC 80-28445. 240p. 1982. 32.00x (ISBN 0-520-04313-8). U of Cal Pr.

Collier, S. Ideas & Politics of Chilean Independence, 1808-1833. (Cambridge Latin American Studies). 1968. 54.50 (ISBN 0-521-04690-4). Cambridge U Pr.

Collier, S. I., ed. Petroleum Mechanical Engineering Conference & Workshop 1979. 114p. 1979. 20.00 (ISBN 0-317-33580-4, 100125); members 10.00 (ISBN 0-317-33581-2). ASME.

Collier, S. L. Mud Pump Handbook. LC 82-20743. 242p. 1983. 31.95x (ISBN 0-87201-568-8). Gulf Pub.

Collier, Simon & Blakemore, Harold, eds. The Cambridge Encyclopedia of Latin America & the Caribbean. (Illus.). 446p. 1985. 39.50 (ISBN 0-521-26263-1). Cambridge U Pr.

Collier, William, ed. see Parkinson, John.

Collier, William L. Social & Economic Aspects of Tidal Swamp Land Development in Indonesia. (Development Studies Centre-Occasional Paper: No. 15). 71p. (Orig.). 1980. pap. 2.00 (ISBN 0-909150-90-7, 0567, Pub. by ANUP Australia). Australia N U P.

Collier, William L., et al. Income, Employment & Food Systems in Javanese Coastal Villages. LC 77-620017. (Papers in International Studies: Southeast Asia Ser.: No. 44). (Illus.). 1977. pap. 10.00x (ISBN 0-89680-031-8, 82-90454, Ohio U Ctr Intl). Ohio U Pr.

Collier, Yvonne. Local Area Networks: A European Directory of Suppliers & Systems. 190p. 1985. pap. text ed. 100.00x (ISBN 0-86353-043-5, Pub. by Online). Brookfield Pub Co.

Collier, Zena. Next Time I'll Know. 176p. (Orig.). (gr. 7-12). 1981. pap. 1.75 (ISBN 0-590-31612-5). Scholastic Inc.

Collieu, A. & Powney, Derek J. The Mechanical & Thermal Properties of Materials. LC 72-85498. 294p. 1973. 19.50x (ISBN 0-8448-0074-0). Crane-Russak Co.

Collieu, A., jt. auth. see Hulme, H. R.

Colligan, Doug, jt. auth. see Colligan, Louise.

Colligan, Doug, jt. auth. see Teresi, Dick.

Colligan, Douglas. Creative Insomnia. 1979. pap. 3.95 (ISBN 0-07-011797-7). McGraw.

--Video Avenger. (Twistaplot Ser.). (Illus.). 96p. (Orig.). (gr. 7 up). 1984. pap. 1.95 (ISBN 0-590-32869-7). Scholastic Inc.

Colligan, Douglas, jt. auth. see Locke, Steven.

Colligan, Elsa. The Aerialist. LC 78-71901. 1979. 12.95 (ISBN 0-87929-056-0). Barlenmir.

Colligan, John & Colligan, Kathleen. Evenings for Parish Ministers: Leader's Guide. LC 84-60266. 53p. (Orig.). 1984. pap. text ed. 2.95 (ISBN 0-911905-20-0); wkbk. 1.95 (ISBN 0-911905-16-2). Past & Mat Rene Ctr.

Colligan, John, et al. Calling Disciples. 54p. (Orig.). 1984. 1.95 (ISBN 0-911905-22-7). Past & Mat Rene Ctr.

--Calling Disciples, Mentality. LC 84-60459. (Calling Disciples Ser.: Bk. 2). 67p. (Orig.). 1984. pap. text ed. 2.95 (ISBN 0-911905-21-9). Past & Mat Rene Ctr.

--The Extended Catholic Family: Rediscovering Our Catholic Identity Through Intimate Relationships with Fellow Catholics. LC 83-62198. 110p. (Orig.). 1983. pap. text ed. 4.95 (ISBN 0-911905-06-5). Past & Mat Rene Ctr.

--A Guide for Using Charisms in the Parish. LC 83-62985. 63p. (Orig.). 1983. pap. text ed. 2.95 (ISBN 0-911905-10-3). Past & Mat Rene Ctr.

--Mission & Ministry: A Vision for the Church. LC 83-62365. 84p. (Orig.). 1983. pap. text ed. 3.95 (ISBN 0-911905-07-3). Past & Mat Rene Ctr.

Colligan, Kathleen, jt. auth. see Colligan, John.

Colligan, Louise. A Plus Guide to Book Reports. (Scholastic A Plus Guides Ser.). 96p. (gr. 7 up). 1984. pap. 2.25 (ISBN 0-590-33313-5). Scholastic Inc.

--A Plus Guide to Research & Term Papers. (Scholastic A Plus Guides Ser.). 128p. (gr. 7 up). 1984. pap. 2.25 (ISBN 0-590-33317-8). Scholastic Inc.

--A Plus Guide to Taking Tests. (Scholastic A Plus Guides Ser.). 112p. (gr. 7 up). 1984. pap. 2.25 (ISBN 0-590-33318-6). Scholastic Inc.

--How to Use the Thesaurus. (gr. 7-12). 1978. pap. 1.50 (ISBN 0-590-11860-9). Scholastic Inc.

Colligan, Louise & Colligan, Doug. A Plus Guide to Good Grades. (Scholastic A Plus Guides Ser.). 144p. (gr. 7 up). 1984. pap. 2.25. Scholastic Inc.

Colligan, Michael J., et al, eds. Mass Psychogenic Illness: A Social Psychological Analysis. 272p. 1982. 29.95x (ISBN 0-89859-160-0). L Erlbaum Assocs.

Colligan, Owen A., ed. Saint John Damascene: Dialectica, Version of Robert Grosseteste. (Text Ser.). 1953. 3.50 (ISBN 0-686-11552-X). Franciscan Inst.

Colligan, Owen A., tr. see Faccin, Dominic.

Colligan, Paddy. Soweto Remembered: Conversations with Freedom Fighters. (Illus.). xiv, 115p. (Orig.). 1981. pap. 3.25 (ISBN 0-89567-050-X). WV Pubs.

--Soweto Remembered: Conversations with Freedom Fighters. 115p. 3.25 (ISBN 0-89567-050-X). World View Pubns.

Colligan, Robert & Osborne, David. The MMPI: A Contemporary Normative Study. 448p. 1983. 50.00 (ISBN 0-03-063601-9). Praeger.

Collignon, Jean, ed. see Mauriac, Francois.

Collignon, M. Manual of Mythology in Relation to Greek Art. Harrison, J. E., tr. xvi, 335p. 1982. Repr. of 1899 ed. lib. bdg. 50.00x (ISBN 0-89241-141-4). Caratzas.

Collígón, J. S., ed. Directory of Manufacturers of Vacuum Plant, Components & Associated Equipment in the UK, 1982. 56p. 1982. pap. 13.25 (ISBN 0-08-029323-9, C145, A145). Pergamon.

Collin, Christiane C., jt. auth. see Collins, George R.

Collin, Dorothy, ed. see Gaskell, Elizabeth.

Collin, Francis J., Jr., et al. Drafting the Durable Power of Attorney: A Systems Approach. 250p. 1984. text ed. 59.95 (ISBN 0-9608450-1-1). R P W Pub.

Collin, Francoise, et al, eds. Harrap's French & English Business Dictionary. 508p. (Fr. & Eng.). 1983. 45.00 (ISBN 0-8442-1878-2, 1878-2). Natl Textbk.

Collin, H. B., jt. auth. see Augusteyn, R. C.

Collin, J. E. British Flies: Empididae, Vol. 6. 790p. 1961. 75.00x (ISBN 0-317-07046-0, Pub. by EW Classey UK). State Mutual Bk.

Collin, Laure. Histoire Abregee de la Musique et es Musiciens. (Music Reprint Ser.). (Fr.). 1977. Repr. of 1897 ed. lib. bdg. 37.50 (ISBN 0-306-70875-2). Da Capo.

Collin, P. H., et al, eds. see Mansion, J. E.

Collin, R. E. Antennas & Radiowave Propagation. 528p. 1985. 45.95 (ISBN 0-07-011808-6). McGraw.

Collin, Raeto C. Programming the Commodore 64. COMPUTE Editors, ed. 609p. (Orig.). 1985. pap. 19.95 (ISBN 0-942386-50-7). Compute Pubns.

Collin, Richard, jt. auth. see Collin, Rima.

Collin, Richard H. Theodore Roosevelt, Culture, Diplomacy & Expansion: A New View of American Imperialism. LC 84-25094. 272p. 1985. text ed. 25.00x (ISBN 0-8071-1214-3). La State U Pr.

Collin, Rima & Collin, Richard. The New Orleans Cookbook. LC 74-7729. (Illus.). 320p. 1975. 18.95 (ISBN 0-394-48898-9). Knopf.

Collin, Robert E. Foundations for Microwave Engineering. 1966. 59.00 (ISBN 0-07-011801-9). McGraw.

Collin, Rodney. The Christian Mystery. 1984. pap. 3.95 (ISBN 0-916411-26-5, Pub. by Sure Fire). Holmes Pub.

--The Herald of Harmony. 1984. pap. 3.95 (ISBN 0-916411-27-3, Pub. by Sure Fire). Holmes Pub.

--The Mirror of Light. LC 84-22141. 89p. 1985. pap. 6.95 (ISBN 0-87773-314-7, 72698-7). Shambhala Pubns.

--The Theory of Celestial Influence: Man, The Universe, & Cosmic Mystery. LC 83-20286. (Illus.). 392p. (Orig.). 1984. pap. 10.95 (ISBN 0-87773-267-1, 72391-0). Shambhala Pubns.

--The Theory of Conscious Harmony. 1981. 25.00x (ISBN 0-7224-0152-3, Pub. by Watkins England). State Mutual Bk.

--The Theory of Conscious Harmony. LC 84-5494. 211p. 1984. pap. 8.95 (ISBN 0-87773-285-X, 72698-7). Shambhala Pubns.

--The Theory of Eternal Life. LC 83-20288. (Illus.). 132p. (Orig.). 1984. pap. 5.95 (ISBN 0-87773-273-6, 72399-6). Shambhala Pubns.

Collin, W. G. Computers in Distribution. LC 75-326180. (Illus.). 1975. pap. 26.50x (ISBN 0-85012-127-2). Intl Pubns Serv.

--Introducing Computer Programming. LC 73-89965. 330p. 1979. 15.00x (ISBN 0-85012-210-4). Intl Pubns Serv.

Collin, Wilkie. The Moonstone. (Bantam Classics Ser.). 464p. (YA) (gr. 9-12). 1982. pap. 3.50 (ISBN 0-553-21156-0). Bantam.

Collin, William E. The White Savannahs. LC 73-92516. (Literature of Canada, Poetry & Prose in Reprint: No. 15). pap. 95.80 (ISBN 0-317-26932-1, 2023604). Bks Demand UMI.

Collin De Plancy, J. A. Dictionnaire des Sciences Occultes, 2 vols. Migne, J. P., ed. (Encyclopedie Theologique Ser.: Vols. 48-49). 1116p. (Fr.). Repr. of 1848 ed. lib. bdg. 143.00x (ISBN 0-89241-252-6). Caratzas.
Collinder, Bjorn. Comparative Grammar of the Uralic Languages. 419p. 1960. lib. bdg. 30.00x (ISBN 3-87118-189-7, Pub. by Helmut Buske Verlag Hamburg). Benjamins North Am.
--Fenno-Ugric Vocabulary: An Etymological Dictionary of the Uralic Languages. 2nd rev. ed. 158p. (Finnish & Hungarian.). 1977. text ed. 41.00x (ISBN 3-87118-187-0, Pub. by Helmut Buske Verlag Hamburg). Benjamins North Am.
--Lapps. LC 73-90490. Repr. of 1949 ed. lib. bdg. 15.00x (ISBN 0-8371-2213-9, COL). Greenwood.
--Survey of the Uralic Languages. 2nd rev. ed. 554p. 1969. lib. bdg. 36.00x (ISBN 3-87118-188-9, Pub. by Helmut Buske Verlag Hamburg). Benjamins North Am.
Collinet. Le Monde Litteraire de La Fontaine. 33.95 (ISBN 0-685-34231-X). French & Eur.
Colling, Aubrey, ed. Coronary Care in the Community. 226p. 1977. 31.00x (ISBN 0-85664-481-1, Pub. by Croom Helm Ltd). Longwood Pub Group.
Colling, Gene. The Bicyclist's Guide to Glacier National Park. (Illus.). 48p. pap. cancelled (ISBN 0-934318-17-4). Falcon Pr MT.
--The Bicyclist's Guide to Yellowstone National Park. (Illus.). 64p. (Orig.). 1984. pap. 3.95 (ISBN 0-934318-15-8). Falcon Pr MT.
Colling, Rex. The Biko Inquest. Blair, F. & Fenton, T., trs. 20.00x (ISBN 0-86036-086-5, Pub. by R Collings UK). State Mutual Bk.
Colling, Russell L. Hospital Security. 2nd ed. 1982. text ed. 29.95 (ISBN 0-409-95048-3). Butterworth.
Collinge, N. E. Collectanea Linguistica: Essays in General & Genetic Linguistics. LC 76-129298. (Janua Linguarum, Ser. Minor: No. 21). (Orig.). 1971. pap. text ed. 16.80x (ISBN 0-686-22392-6). Mouton.
Collingridge, David. Critical Decision Making: A New Theory of Social Choice. LC 82-6017. 1982. 26.00x (ISBN 0-312-17418-7). St Martin.
--The Social Control of Technology. 1981. 27.50 (ISBN 0-312-73168-X). St Martin.
--The Social Control of Technology. 200p. 1981. pap. 16.00x (ISBN 0-335-10031-7, Pub. by Open Univ Pr). Taylor & Francis.
--Technology in the Policy Process: The Control of Nuclear Power. LC 83-9801. 200p. 1983. 22.50 (ISBN 0-312-79005-8). St Martin.
Collingridge, L. T., jt. auth. see Wills, William A.
Collingridge, Ruth & Sekowsky, JoAnne. Introduction to Praise. (Workshop Ser.). (Orig.). 1981. pap. 4.95 (ISBN 0-930756-60-6, 581001). Aglow Pubns.
Collings, jt. auth. see McBurney, D.
Collings, A. J. & Luxon, S. G. Safe Use of Solvents. 1982. 49.00 (ISBN 0-12-181250-2). Acad Pr.
Collings, E. W. Applied Superconductivity, Metallurgy, & Physics of Titanium Alloys Vol. 2: Applications. (The International Cryogenics Monograph Ser.). 623p. 1985. 87.50x (ISBN 0-306-41691-3, Plenum Pr). Plenum Pub.
--Applied Superconductivity, Metallurgy, & Physics of Titanuim Alloys, Vol. 2: Fundamentals. (The International Cryogenics Monograph Ser.). 775p. 1985. 97.50x (ISBN 0-306-41690-5, Plenum Pr). Plenum Pub.
--Design & Fabrication of Conventional & Unconventional Superconductors. LC 84-5923. (Illus.). 225p. 1984. 32.00 (ISBN 0-8155-0989-8). Noyes.
--A Sourcebook of Titanium Alloy Superconductivity. 550p. 1983. 79.50x (ISBN 0-306-41344-2, Plenum Pr). Plenum Pub.
Collings, E. W. & Gegel, H. L., eds. Physics of Solid Solution Strengthening. LC 75-33368. 306p. 1975. 45.00x (ISBN 0-306-30890-8, Plenum Pr). Plenum Pub.
Collings, E. W., ed. see Metallurgical Society of AIME.
Collings, Judith, jt. auth. see Collings, Michael.
Collings, Kent J. Second Time Around: Finding a Civilian Career in Mid-Life. LC 77-156600. (Illus., Orig.). 1971. pap. 6.75 (ISBN 0-910328-04-8). Carroll Pr.
Collings, Lawrence & Ruhen, Olaf. On & Around Sydney Harbour. 128p. 1980. 13.95 (ISBN 0-00-216407-8, Pub. by W Collins Australia). Intl Spec Bk.
Collings, Michael. Season of Calm Weather. 68p. 1974. 2.00 (ISBN 0-89036-030-8). Hawkes Pub Inc.
Collings, Michael & Collings, Judith. Whole Wheat Harvest-Recipes for Unground Wheat. pap. 2.95 (ISBN 0-89036-143-6). Hawkes Pub Inc.
Collings, Michael R. Brian Aldiss. (Reader's Guides to Contemporary Science Fiction & Fantasy Authors Ser.: No. 28). (Illus., Orig.). 1985. 14.95x (ISBN 0-317-28343-X); pap. 6.95x. Starmont Hse.
--The Films of Stephen King. (Studies in Literary Criticism: No. 12). (Illus., Orig.). 1985. 19.95x (ISBN 0-930261-11-9); pap. 9.95x (ISBN 0-930261-10-0). Starmont Hse.
--The Many Facets of Stephen King. (Starmont Studies in Literary Criticism: No. 11). 128p. 1985. Repr. lib. bdg. 17.95x (ISBN 0-89370-983-2). Borgo Pr.
--The Many Facets of Stephen King. (Studies in Literary Criticism: No. 11). (Illus., Orig.). 1985. 17.95x (ISBN 0-930261-15-1); pap. 9.95x (ISBN 0-930261-14-3). Starmont Hse.
--Piers Anthony. LC 84-1917. (Starmont Reader's Guide: No. 20). 96p. 1984. Repr. lib. bdg. 13.95x (ISBN 0-89370-058-4). Borgo Pr.
--Reader's Guide to Piers Anthony. Schlobin, Roger C., ed. LC 83-2466. (Starmont Reader's Guides to Contemporary Science Fiction & Fantasy Authors Ser.: Vol. 20). (Illus., Orig.). 1983. 13.95x (ISBN 0-916732-53-3); pap. text ed. 5.95x (ISBN 0-916732-52-5). Starmont Hse.
--Stephen King As Richard Bachman. (Starmont Studies in Literary Criticism: No. 10). 128p. 1985. Repr. lib. bdg. 17.95x (ISBN 0-89370-982-4). Borgo Pr.
--Stephen King as Richard Bachman. LC 85-2832. (Studies in Literary Criticism: No. 10). (Illus.). 176p. (Orig.). 1985. 17.95x (ISBN 0-930261-01-1); pap. 9.95x (ISBN 0-930261-00-3). Starmont Hse.
--The Stephen King Phenomenon. (Studies in Literary Criticism: No. 14). (Illus., Orig.). 1985. 17.95x (ISBN 0-930261-13-5); pap. 9.95x (ISBN 0-930261-12-7). Starmont Hse.
Collings, Michael R. & Engebretson, David. The Shorter Works of Stephen King. (Starmont Studies in Literary Criticism: No. 9). 128p. 1985. Repr. lib. bdg. 17.95x (ISBN 0-89370-981-6). Borgo Pr.
--The Shorter Works of Stephen King. LC 85-2822. (Studies in Literary Criticism: No. 9). (Illus., Orig.). 1985. 17.95x (ISBN 0-930261-03-8); pap. 9.95x (ISBN 0-930261-02-X). Starmont Hse.
Collings, Randy. California. 1982. 9.95 (ISBN 0-933692-16-1). A R Collings.
--Grand Canyon: Shrine of the Ages. 1982. 9.95 (ISBN 0-933692-22-6). A R Collings.
--How to Be a Total Californian. 1982. 4.95 (ISBN 0-933692-25-0). A R Collings.
--Sequoia: Kings Canyon National Parks. 1982. 7.95 (ISBN 0-933692-23-4). A R Collings.
--Southern California. 1982. 12.95 (ISBN 0-933692-17-X). A R Collings.
--Utah. 1982. 7.95 (ISBN 0-933692-24-2). A R Collings.
--Yellowstone: The Grand Old Park. (Illus.). 80p. 1982. pap. 8.95 (ISBN 0-933692-21-8). A R Collings.
Collings, Virginia B., jt. auth. see McBurney, Donald H.
Collingswood, Hermann. A Collection of Fifty-Five Dramatic Illustrations in Full Colours of the Cathedral Cities of Italy. (The Masterpieces of World Architectual Library). (Illus.). 107p. 1983. Repr. of 1911 ed. 287.75 (ISBN 0-89901-081-4). Found Class Reprints.
Collingwood, et al. Craft of the Weaver. 1984. pap. 12.95 (ISBN 0-937274-10-0). Dodd.
Collingwood, Edward F. & Lohwater, A. J. The Theory of Cluster Sets. LC 66-18115. (Cambridge Tracts in Mathematics & Mathematical Physics: No. 56). pap. 55.80 (ISBN 0-317-08574-3, 2013053). Bks Demand UMI.
Collingwood, G. & Brush, W. Knowing Your Trees. 9.50 (ISBN 0-686-26731-1, 23). Am Forestry.
Collingwood, Guillermo. Las Dos Naturalezas del Creyente. 2nd ed. Bennett, Gordon H., ed. Bautista, Sara, tr. from Eng. (La Serie Diamante). 52p. (Span.). 1982. pap. 0.85 (ISBN 0-942504-03-8). Overcomer Pr.
Collingwood, Harris. Stripping the Trees. (Chapbook Ser.: No. 2). 48p. (Orig.). 1980. pap. 4.95 (ISBN 0-937672-01-7). Rowan Tree.
Collingwood, Lucy. Reaching Up Reproducibles. (Perspectives II Ser.). 129p. (gr. 7-12). 1982. pap. 10.00 (ISBN 0-87879-322-4, High Noon Books). Acad Therapy.
Collingwood, Peter. Peter Collingwood: His Weaves & Weaving. Tidball, Harriet, ed. LC 63-2332. (Shuttle Craft Guild Monograph: No. 8). (Illus.). 46p. 1963. pap. 8.45 (ISBN 0-916658-08-2). HTH Pubs.
--Techniques of Rug Weaving. LC 68-24486. (Illus.). 480p. 1969. 35.00 (ISBN 0-8230-5200-1). Watson-Guptill.
--The Techniques of Sprang. LC 73-17319. (Illus.). 300p. 1974. 21.95 (ISBN 0-8230-5220-6). Watson-Guptill.
--The Techniques of Tablet Weaving. (Illus.). 416p. 1982. 35.00 (ISBN 0-8230-5255-9). Watson-Guptill.
Collingwood, R. C., tr. see De Ruggiero, Guido.
Collingwood, R. G. An Essay on Metaphysics. 366p. 1984. pap. 10.25 (ISBN 0-8191-3315-9). U Pr of Amer.
--Human Nature & Human History. (Studies in Philosophy, No. 40). 1972. Repr. of 1936 ed. lib. bdg. 24.95x (ISBN 0-8383-0132-0). Haskell.
Collingwood, R. G. & Richmond, Ian. The Archaeology of Roman Britain. 2nd ed. 1969. 55.00x (ISBN 0-416-27580-X, NO.2152). Methuen Inc.
Collingwood, R. G., tr. see Croce, Benedetto.
Collingwood, Robin G. Autobiography. 1939. 9.95x (ISBN 0-19-824694-3). Oxford U Pr.
--Essay on Philosophical Method. 1933. 39.95x (ISBN 0-19-824123-2). Oxford U Pr.
--Essays in the Philosophy of History. Winks, Robin W., ed. LC 83-49174. (History & Historiography Ser.). 148p. 1985. lib. bdg. 20.00 (ISBN 0-8240-6355-4). Garland Pub.
--Idea of History. Knox, T. M., ed. 1946. pap. 9.95 (ISBN 0-19-500205-9, 1, GB). Oxford U Pr.
--Idea of Nature. 1960. pap. 7.95 (ISBN 0-19-500217-2, GB). Oxford U Pr.
--The New Leviathan: Man, Society, Civilization & Barbarism. LC 84-19284. viii, 387p. 1984. Repr. of 1942 ed. lib. bdg. 47.50x (ISBN 0-313-24621-1, CONL). Greenwood.
--The New Leviathan: Or, Man, Society, Civilization & Barbarism. LC 83-45423. Repr. of 1942 ed. 40.00 (ISBN 0-404-20066-4). AMS Pr.
--Outlines of a Philosophy of Art. LC 25-26891. 104p. 1925. Repr. 39.00x (ISBN 0-403-07231-X). Somerset Pub.
--Principles of Art. 1958. pap. 9.95 (ISBN 0-19-500209-1, GB). Oxford U Pr.
--Speculum Mentis: The Map of Knowledge. LC 82-15552. 327p. 1982. Repr. of 1924 ed. lib. bdg. 39.75x (ISBN 0-313-23701-8, COSM). Greenwood.
Collingwood, Robin G. & Myres, J. N. Roman Britain & the English Settlements. 2nd ed. (Oxford History of England Ser.). (Illus.). 1937. 29.95x (ISBN 0-19-821703-X). Oxford U Pr.
Collingwood, Stuart D. Life & Letters of Lewis Carroll. LC 67-23871. 472p. 1967. Repr. of 1899 ed. 45.00x (ISBN 0-8103-3061-X). Gale.
--The Unknown Lewis Carroll: Eight Major Works & Many Minor. (Illus.). 9.00 (ISBN 0-8446-0065-2). Peter Smith.
Collingwood, Tom & Carkhuff, Robert R. Get Fit for Living. LC 76-4341. (Illus.). 100p. (Orig.). 1976. pap. text ed. 10.00x (ISBN 0-914234-26-9); trainer's guide 12.95x (ISBN 0-914234-27-7). Human Res Dev Pr.
Collingwood, W. G. The Life of Ruskin. 1973. Repr. of 1902 ed. 20.00 (ISBN 0-8274-1709-8). R West.
--Ruskin Relics. 1973. Repr. of 1903 ed. 20.00 (ISBN 0-8274-1710-1). R West.
Collingwood, W. G. & Steffanson, Jon, trs. Life & Death of Cormac the Skald. LC 76-43948. (Viking Society for Northern Research: Translation Ser.: Vol. 1). (Illus.). 416p. Repr. of 1902 ed. 32.50 (ISBN -0404-60011-5). AMS Pr.
Collingwood, W. G., tr. see Chretien de Troyes.
Collingwood, W. Gershom, tr. see Xenophon.
Collingwood, William G. The Art Teaching of John Ruskin. LC 77-17888. 1977. Repr. of 1891 ed. lib. bdg. 35.00 (ISBN 0-8414-9975-6). Folcroft.
Collini, Stefan. Liberalism & Sociology: L. T. Hobhouse & Political Argument in English, 1880-1914. LC 78-23779. 1979. 37.50 (ISBN 0-521-22304-0). Cambridge U Pr.
--Liberalism & Sociology: L. T. Hobhouse & Political Argument in England 1880-1914. LC 78-23779. 288p. 1983. pap. 15.95 (ISBN 0-521-27408-7). Cambridge U Pr.
Collini, Stefan, et al. That Noble Science of Politics: A Study in Nineteenth-Century Intellectual History. LC 83-7697. 352p. 1984. 49.50 (ISBN 0-521-25762-X); pap. 14.95 (ISBN 0-521-27770-1). Cambridge U Pr.
Collins. Synopsis of Chest Diseases. 224p. 1979. pap. 18.50 (ISBN 0-7236-0526-2). PSG Pub Co.
--Takeoffs & Landings. 1983. write for info. Macmillan.
Collins & Lyne. Microbiological Methods. 5th ed. 1984. text ed. 34.95 (ISBN 0-408-70957-X). Butterworth.
Collins, et al. Aleutian Islands: Their People & Natural History. facsimile ed. (Illus.). 157p. Shorey.
--Handbook for Dental Hygienists. 320p. 1978. 20.00 (ISBN 0-7236-0497-5). PSG Pub Co.
--Handbook for Dental Hygientists. 1986. price not set. Psg Pub Co.
--British Bus Fleets No. 4 East Anglia. pap. 4.00x (ISBN 0-392-08703-0, SpS). Sportshelf.
Collins, A., et al, eds. DNA Repair & Its Inhibition. (Nucleic Acids Symposium Ser.: No. 13). (Illus.). 372p. (Orig.). 1984. pap. 55.00 (ISBN 0-904147-73-8). IRL Pr.
Collins, A. Frederick & Hertzberg, Robert. The Radio Amateur's Handbook. 15th, rev. ed. LC 82-48666. (Illus.). 416p. 1983. 14.37i (ISBN 0-06-181366-4, HarpT). Har-Row.
Collins, A. J. Inventory of the Jewels & Plate of Queen Elizabeth I. 608p. 1981. 50.00x (ISBN 0-7141-0445-0, Pub. by Brit Lib England). State Mutual Bk.
Collins, A. J., jt. auth. see Chatfield, C.
Collins, A. S. Profession of Letters: A Study of the Relation of Author to Patron Publisher, & Public 1780-1832. LC 77-134832. Repr. of 1928 ed. lib. bdg. 27.50x (ISBN 0-678-00789-6). Kelley.
Collins, A. S., ed. Treasury of English Verse: New & Old. facsimile ed. LC 79-168778. (Granger Index Reprint Ser.). Repr. of 1931 ed. 22.00 (ISBN 0-8369-6298-2). Ayer Co Pubs.
Collins, Ace, jt. auth. see Mandrell, Louise.
Collins, Adela, ed. Feminist Perspectives on Biblical Scholarship. (Society of Bliblical Literature Centennial Biblical Scholarship in North America Ser.: No. 10). 13.95 (ISBN 0-317-17344-8, 06 11 10); pap. 9.50 (ISBN 0-317-17345-6). Scholars Pr GA.
Collins, Adela Y. Apocalypse. Harrington, Wilfrid & Senior, Donald, eds. (New Testament Message Ser.: Vol. 22). 172p. 1979. 9.95 (ISBN 0-89453-210-3); pap. 6.95 (ISBN 0-89453-145-X). M Glazier.
--Crisis & Catharsis: The Power of the Apocalypse. LC 83-26084. 180p. 1984. pap. 11.95 (ISBN 0-664-24521-8). Westminster.
Collins, Adela Y. & Rice, Charles. Pentecost Two. LC 79-7377. (Proclamation 2: Aids for Interpreting the Lessons of the Church Year, Series B). 64p. 1982. pap. 3.50 (ISBN 0-8006-4090-X, 1-4090). Fortress.
Collins, Adrian. The Use & Abuse of History: Nietzsche. Date not set. pap. text ed. price not set (ISBN 0-02-323730-9). MacMillan.
Collins, Adrian, tr. see Nietzsche, Friedrich W.
Collins, Alice H. The Human Services: An Introduction. LC 72-10176. Orig. Title: People to People - an Introduction to the Human Services. 1973. pap. 7.87 scp (ISBN 0-672-63081-8). Odyssey Pr.
Collins, Alice H. & Pancoast, Diane L. Natural Helping Networks: A Strategy for Prevention. LC 76-10027. 144p. 1976. pap. 6.95x (ISBN 0-87101-070-4). Natl Assn Soc Wkrs.
Collins, Alice H. & Watson, Eunice L. Family Day Care: A Practical Guide for Parents, Caregivers, & Professionals. LC 75-36039. 160p. 1976. 12.50x (ISBN 0-8070-3158-5). Beacon Pr.
Collins, Allen R. The Family Budget Primer. 14p. 1982. pap. text ed. 1.25x (ISBN 0-913453-00-5). Lehigh Info.
Collins, Ann. How to Use a Fake Book. (Fake Bk.). (Illus.). 80p. 1985. saddle-stitch 7.95 (ISBN 0-88188-395-6). H Leonard Pub Corp.
Collins, Ann & Clary, Linda. Sing & Play--Preschool Piano Book One. (Illus.). 40p. (ps). 1981. spiral bdg. 3.75 (ISBN 0-87563-216-5). Stipes.
Collins, Ann M. The Great Sun Must Die. 96p. (Orig.). 1985. pap. 2.95 (ISBN 0-88120-731-4). C C Pubns.
Collins, Anthony. A Disclosure on Free-Thinking. LC 75-11209. (British Philosophers & Theologians of the 17th & 18th Centuries Ser.). 395p. 1976. lib. bdg. 51.00 (ISBN 0-8240-1764-1). Garland Pub.
--A Discourse on the Grounds & Reasons of the Christian Religion. Wellek, Rene, ed. LC 75-11212. (British Philosophers & Theologians of the 17th & 18th Centuries: Vol. 15). 1976. Repr. of 1724 ed. lib. bdg. 51.00 (ISBN 0-8240-1766-8). Garland Pub.
--An Essay Concerning the Use of Reason in Propositions, the Evidence Whereof Depends upon Human Testimony. LC 83-48566. (The Philosophy of John Lock Ser.). 240p. 1984. lib. bdg. 30.00 (ISBN 0-8240-5601-9). Garland Pub.
Collins, Arthur. Collin's Peerage of England, 9 Vols. LC 70-115003. Repr. of 1812 ed. Set. 427.50 (ISBN 0-404-01740-1); 47.50 ea. AMS Pr.
--Letters & Memorials of State, in the Reigns of Queen Mary, Queen Elizabeth, King James, King Charles the First, Part of the Reign of King Charles the Second, & Oliver's Usurpation, 2 Vols. LC 72-997. Repr. of 1746 ed. Set. lib. bdg. 185.00 (ISBN 0-404-01631-6). AMS Pr.
Collins, Arthur S., Jr. Common Sense Training: A Working Philosophy For Leaders. LC 77-19077. 248p. 1978. pap. 8.95 (ISBN 0-89141-067-8). Presidio Pr.
Collins, Arthur W. Thought & Nature: Studies in Rationalist Philosophy. LC 84-4023. 272p. 1985. text ed. 24.95 (ISBN 0-268-01856-1, 85-18565). U of Notre Dame Pr.
Collins, Barry. Judgement. 1984. pap. 6.95 (ISBN 0-87910-213-6). Limelight Edns.
Collins, Barry E., jt. auth. see Gross, Alan E.
Collins, Barry E., ed. Public & Private Conformity: Competing Explanations by Improvisation, Cognitive Dissonance & Attribution Theories. LC 73-7252. (Illus.). 182p. 1974. pap. text ed. 9.95x (ISBN 0-8422-9105-9). Irvington.
Collins, Barry E., jt. ed. see Brewer, Marilynn B.
Collins, Beverley & Mees, Inger. The Sounds of English & Dutch. 293p. 1982. 39.50 (ISBN 90-6021-477-3, Pub. by Martinus Nijhoff Netherlands). Kluwer Academic.
Collins, Billy. Video Poems. LC 79-50762. 1979. pap. 2.50 (ISBN 0-930090-05-5). Applezaba.
Collins, Blackie. Knife Throwing: Sport..Survival..Defense. (Illus.). 31p. (Orig.). 1978. pap. 3.00 (ISBN 0-940362-03-1). Knife World.
Collins, Blackie & Collins, Michael. How to Scrimshaw & Carve Ivory. LC 81-162210. (Illus.). 45p. 1978. pap. 6.95 (ISBN 0-940362-01-5). Knife World.
Collins, Bob. Thought You'd Never Ask. 226p. 1984. pap. 6.95 (ISBN 0-89651-782-9). Icarus.
Collins, Bobby & White, Fred. Elementary Forestry. 1981. text ed. 19.95 (ISBN 0-8359-1647-2). Reston.
Collins, Brad. Hot Cargo. (Perspectives II Ser.). (Illus.). 48p. (gr. 7-12). 1982. pap. 2.50 (ISBN 0-87879-313-5, High Noon Books). Acad Therapy.
Collins, Bruce. Origins of America's Civil War. LC 81-81340. 165p. 1981. text ed. 24.50x (ISBN 0-8419-0714-5); pap. text ed. 13.50x (ISBN 0-8419-0715-3). Holmes & Meier.

Collins, Henry B. Archaeology of the Bering Sea Region. facsimile ed. (Shorey Historical Ser.). 30p. pap. 3.95 (ISBN 0-8466-0092-7, S92). Shorey.

--Prehistoric Art of Alaskan Eskimo. (Shorey Indian Ser.). 78p. pap. 6.95 (ISBN 0-8466-4009-0, I9). Shorey.

Collins, Henry H. & Boyajian, Ned R. Familiar Garden Birds of America: An Illustrated Guide to the Birds in Your Own Backyard. (Nonfiction Ser.). 1985. pap. 9.95 (ISBN 0-8398-2852-7). G K Hall.

Collins, Henry H., Jr. What Bird Is This? Orig. Title: Birdwatcher's Quiz Book. (Illus.). 1961. pap. 2.95 (ISBN 0-486-21490-7). Dover.

Collins, Henry H., Jr. & Boyajian, N. R. Familiar Garden Birds of America. LC 65-21006. (Familiar Nature Series). (Illus.). 1966. PLB 9.87i (ISBN 0-06-070691-0, HarpT). Har-Row.

Collins, Henry H., Jr. & Ransom, Jay E., eds. Harper & Row's Complete Field Guide to North American Wildlife: Eastern Edition. LC 80-8198. (Illus.). 810p. 1981. 17.50i (ISBN 0-690-01977-7, HarpT); flexible vinyl cover 12.95i (ISBN 0-690-01969-6); western edition 17.50i (ISBN 0-690-01979-3). Har-Row.

Collins, Herbert R. Threads of History: Americana Recorded on Cloth - 1775 to the Present. LC 79-16166. (Illus.). 566p. 1979. 60.00x (ISBN 0-87474-326-5). Smithsonian.

Collins, Herbert R. & Weaver, David B. Wills of the U.S. Presidents. LC 75-32100. (Illus.). 1976. 29.95 (ISBN 0-916164-01-2). Stravon.

Collins, Howard S., ed. see Trinity College of Quezon City.

Collins, Hugh. Marxism & Law. LC 84-7199. (Marxist Introductions Ser.). (Illus.). 1982. 19.95x (ISBN 0-19-876093-0); 5.95 (ISBN 0-19-285144-6). Oxford U Pr.

Collins, Irene. Napoleon & His Parliaments, Eighteen Hundred to Eighteen Fifteen. 1979. 26.00x (ISBN 0-312-55892-9). St Martin.

Collins, Irene, ed. Government & Society in France: Eighteen Fourteen to Eighteen Forty-Eight. LC 78-143997. (Documents of Modern History Ser). 1971. 22.50 (ISBN 0-312-34160-1). St Martin.

Collins, Ivan L. Horse Power Days: Popular Vehicles of Nineteenth Century America. LC 52-12857. (Illus.). pap. 25.50 (ISBN 0-317-10799-2, 2051086). Bks Demand UMI.

Collins, J. A. Failure of Materials in Mechanical Design: Analysis, Prediction, Prevention. LC 80-20674. 629p. 1981. 55.95x (ISBN 0-471-05024-5, Pub. by Wiley-Interscience). Wiley.

Collins, J. A., ed. Eighth British Robot Association Annual Conference: Robotic Trends-Applications, Research, Education, & Safety: Proceedings of the Conference, Birmingham, U. K., 14-17 May 1985. 350p. 1985. 79.75 (ISBN 0-444-87768-1, North-Holland). Elsevier.

Collins, J. C. Miltonic Myths & Their Authors in Studies of Poetry & Criticism. 1905. Repr. 30.00 (ISBN 0-8274-2739-5). R West.

Collins, J. Churton. Bolingbroke: A Historical Study & Voltaire in England. 1886. Repr. 20.00 (ISBN 0-8274-3918-0). R West.

--Critical Essays & Literary Fragments. LC 64-16745. (Arber's an English Garner Ser.). 1964. Repr. of 1890 ed. 22.50 (ISBN 0-8154-0052-7). Cooper Sq.

--Greek Influence on English Poetry. LC 72-3186. (English Literature Ser., No. 33). 1972. Repr. of 1910 ed. lib. bdg. 47.95x (ISBN 0-8383-1498-8). Haskell.

--Voltaire, Montesquieu & Rousseau in England. 293p. 1980. Repr. of 1908 ed. lib. bdg. 36.00 (ISBN 0-8414-3032-2). Folcroft.

Collins, J. Churton, ed. see Greene, Robert.

Collins, J. H. The Mineralogy of Cornwall & Devon. 1981. 50.00x (ISBN 0-686-97167-1, Pub. by D B Barton England). State Mutual Bk.

--Ten Miracles. 1975. pap. 0.50 (ISBN 0-8198-0479-7). Dghtrs St Paul.

Collins, J. H. & Masotti, L. Computer-Aided Design of Surface Acoustic Wave Devices, Vol. 2. 308p. 1976. 68.00 (ISBN 0-444-41476-2). Elsevier.

Collins, J. L. & Opitz, Glenn. Women Artists in America: Eighteenth Century to Present. rev. ed. (Illus.). 1981. 60.00 (ISBN 0-938290-00-2). Apollo.

Collins, J. Lawton. Lightning Joe: An Autobiography. LC 78-27375. (Illus.). xx, 462p. 1979. 27.50x (ISBN 0-8071-0499-X). La State U Pr.

Collins, Jackie. The Bitch. 256p. 1985. pap. 3.95 (ISBN 0-671-60219-5). PB.

--Chances. LC 81-638. 816p. (Orig.). 1982. 14.95 (ISBN 0-446-51237-0); pap. 4.50 (ISBN 0-446-32249-0). Warner Bks.

--Hollywood Wives. LC 83-4772. 512p. 1983. 16.95 (ISBN 0-671-47406-5). S&S.

--Hollywood Wives. 560p. 1984. pap. 4.50 (ISBN 0-671-49227-6). PB.

--The Love Killers. Orig. Title: Love Head. 192p. 1975. pap. 2.95 (ISBN 0-446-30816-1). Warner Bks.

--Lovers & Gamblers. 592p. 1980. pap. 3.95 (ISBN 0-446-30782-3). Warner Bks.

--Lucky: A Novel. 1985. 17.95 (ISBN 0-671-52493-3). S&S.

--Sinners. 1984. pap. 3.95 (ISBN 0-671-50793-1). PB.

--The Stud. 1982. pap. 3.95 (ISBN 0-451-13235-1, Sig). NAL.

--The World Is Full of Divorced Women. 416p. (Orig.). 1981. pap. 3.95 (ISBN 0-446-30783-1). Warner Bks.

--The World Is Full of Married Men. 1984. pap. 3.95 (ISBN 0-671-50791-5). PB.

Collins, Jacquelin, jt. auth. see Blakeley, Brian L.

Collins, James. Interpreting Modern Philosophy. LC 70-160259. 1972. 44.00 (ISBN 0-691-07179-9); pap. 13.50 (ISBN 0-691-01985-1). Princeton U Pr.

--Meditations with Dante. 130p. (Orig.). 1984. pap. 6.95 (ISBN 0-939680-18-1). Bear & Co.

--The Mind of Kierkegaard: With a New Preface & Updated Bibliographical Note. LC 83-60464. 320p. 1983. 27.50x (ISBN 0-691-07279-5); pap. 8.95x (ISBN 0-691-02027-2). Princeton U Pr.

--Pilgrim in Love: An Introduction to Dante & His Spirituality. 312p. 1984. 12.95 (ISBN 0-8294-0453-8). Loyola.

Collins, James, jt. auth. see Miller, Jim.

Collins, James, ed. Spinoza on Nature. 360p. 1984. 32.50 (ISBN 0-8093-1160-7). S Ill U Pr.

Collins, James A. Contemporary Theater in Puerto Rico: The Decade of the Seventies. LC 81-12946. (Illus.). xxiii, 261p. (Orig.). 1982. pap. 30.00 (ISBN 0-8477-3174-X). U of PR Pr.

Collins, James C. Accident Reconstruction. (Illus.). 308p. 1979. 23.75x (ISBN 0-398-03907-0). C C Thomas.

Collins, James C. & Morris, Joe L. Highway Collision Analysis. (Illus.). 304p. 1974. photocopy ed. 27.50x (ISBN 0-398-03042-1). C C Thomas.

Collins, James D. The Existentialists: A Critical Study. LC 77-2918. 1977. Repr. of 1952 ed. lib. bdg. 22.50x (ISBN 0-8371-9565-9, COEX). Greenwood.

--God in Modern Philosophy. LC 77-25963. 1978. Repr. of 1959 ed. lib. bdg. 32.75x (ISBN 0-313-20079-3, COGM). Greenwood.

--Lure of Wisdom. (Aquinas Ser.). 1962. 7.95 (ISBN 0-87462-127-5). Marquette.

Collins, James F., ed. Handbook of Clinical Ophthalmology. LC 82-12657. 823p. 1982. 34.75 (ISBN 0-89352-190-6). Masson Pub.

Collins, James J., ed. Drinking & Crime. LC 80-28046. (Alcohol Studies Ser.). 356p. 1981. 25.00 (ISBN 0-89862-163-1, 2163). Guilford Pr.

Collins, James L. Women Artists in America II. (Women Artists in America: Vol. 2). (Illus.). 1975. 15.00x (ISBN 0-8150-0899-6). Wittenborn.

Collins, James L., jt. auth. see Craig, William N.

Collins, James L., ed. Teaching All the Children to Write. 100p. 1983. pap. text ed. 5.00 (ISBN 0-930348-10-9). NY St Eng Coun.

Collins, James L. & Sommers, Elizabeth A., eds. Writing-on-Line: Using Computers in the Teaching of Writing. 176p. 1985. pap. text ed. 9.75x (ISBN 0-317-19861-0). Boynton Cook Pubs.

Collins, James P. Autobiography of a Revolutionary Soldier. Kohn, Richard H., ed. LC 78-22378. (American Military Experience Ser.). 1979. Repr. of 1859 ed. lib. bdg. 12.00x (ISBN 0-405-11855-4). Ayer Co Pubs.

Collins, James R., et al, eds. Hines Insurance Counsel: 1984-85. 76th ed. 1984. 15.00 (ISBN 0-910911-04-5). Hines Legal Dir.

Collins, Jane S. Free at Last. facsimile ed. LC 71-37586. (Black Heritage Library Collection). Repr. of 1896 ed. 16.75 (ISBN 0-8369-8962-7). Ayer Co Pubs.

Collins, Jean E., jt. auth. see Ozer, Mark N.

Collins, Jennifer, designed by see Thompson, Joyce.

Collins, Jim. The Bermuda Triangle. LC 77-21808. (Great Unsolved Mysteries). (Illus.). (gr. 4-5). 1977. PLB 14.25 (ISBN 0-8172-1050-4). Raintree Pubs.

--The Bermuda Triangle. LC 77-21808. (Great Unsolved Mysteries Ser.). (Illus.). 48p. (gr. 4up). 1983. pap. 9.27 (ISBN 0-8172-2153-0). Raintree Pubs.

--The Strange Story of Uri Geller. LC 77-24501. (Myth, Magic & Superstition). (Illus.). (gr. 4-5). 1977. PLB 14.25 (ISBN 0-8172-1037-7). Raintree Pubs.

--Unidentified Flying Objects. LC 77-13040. (Great Unsolved Mysteries). (Illus.). (gr. 4-5). 1977. PLB 14.25 (ISBN 0-8172-1065-2). Raintree Pubs.

--Unidentified Flying Objects. LC 77-13040. (Great Unsolved Mysteries Ser.). (Illus.). 48p. (gr. 4up). 1983. pap. 9.27 (ISBN 0-8172-2169-7). Raintree Pubs.

Collins, Joan. Future Terrific! (Illus.). 1985. pap. 3.95 (ISBN 0-317-13932-0). Berkley Pub.

--Past Imperfect. 336p. 1985. pap. 3.95 (ISBN 0-425-07786-1). Berkley Pub.

--Past Imperfect: An Autobiography. LC 84-1263. 336p. 1984. 16.95 (ISBN 0-671-47360-3). S&S.

Collins, Jodie. Codeword: Catherine. 240p. (Orig.). 1984. pap. 6.95 (ISBN 0-8423-0301-4). Tyndale.

--Codeword Catherine. 384p. cancelled (ISBN 0-8423-0302-2). Tyndale.

Collins, Joe. Chevelle vs. the Pack. (Pack Ser.). (Illus.). 128p. 1985. pap. 10.95 (ISBN 0-934780-70-6). Bookman Dan.

--New Series Olds 4-4-2 vs. the Pack. (Pack Ser.). (Illus.). 128p. 1985. pap. 10.95 (ISBN 0-934780-69-2). Bookman Dan.

--Z-28. (Source Bks.). (Illus.). 144p. 1984. pap. 12.95 (ISBN 0-934780-36-6). Bookman Dan.

Collins, John. Achieving Change in Social Work. (Community Care Practice Handbook Ser.). (Orig.). 1981. pap. text ed. 8.50x (ISBN 0-435-82186-5). Gower Pub Co.

--Apocalyptic Imagination. 288p. 1984. 24.50 (ISBN 0-8245-0623-5). Crossroad NY.

--Daniel, One-Two Maccabees, with Excursus on Apocalyptic Genre. (Old Testament Message Ser.: Vol. 15). 1982. 12.95 (ISBN 0-89453-415-7); pap. 9.95 (ISBN 0-89453-250-2). M Glazier.

--A Dictionary of Spanish Proverbs. LC 77-25483. (Span.). 1977. Repr. of 1823 ed. lib. bdg. 45.00 (ISBN 0-8414-1101-8). Folcroft.

--MusicMakers of West Africa. LC 81-51651. (Illus.). 150p. 1985. 20.00 (ISBN 0-89410-075-0); pap. 10.00 (ISBN 0-89410-076-9). Three Continents.

Collins, John, jt. auth. see Barker, Nicolas.

Collins, John, ed. see Carter, John & Pollard, Graham.

Collins, John A., jt. auth. see Collins, Sheila D.

Collins, John A. & Murawski, Kris, eds. Massive Transfusion in Surgery & Trauma. LC 82-18657. (Progress in Clinical & Biological Research Ser.: Vol. 108). 334p. 1982. 32.00 (ISBN 0-8451-0108-0). A R Liss.

Collins, John C. Critical Essays & Literary Fragments. 1912. lib. bdg. 11.00 (ISBN 0-8414-2357-1). Folcroft.

--Essays & Studies. 1978. Repr. of 1895 ed. lib. bdg. 30.00 (ISBN 0-8495-0753-7). Arden Lib.

--Essays & Studies. 1895. lib. bdg. 25.00 (ISBN 0-8414-2360-1). Folcroft.

--Essays & Studies. 369p. 1983. Repr. of 1895 ed. lib. bdg. 45.00 (ISBN 0-89987-142-9). Darby Bks.

--Greek Influence on English Poetry. LC 72-3186. 1910. lib. bdg. 15.00 (ISBN 0-8414-2362-8). Folcroft.

--Illustrations of Tennyson. LC 77-148765. Repr. of 1891 ed. 9.00 (ISBN 0-404-08738-8). AMS Pr.

--Illustrations of Tennyson. 1973. lib. bdg. 10.00 (ISBN 0-8414-2363-6). Folcroft.

--Jonathan Swift: A Biographical & Critical Study. LC 72-195913. 1893. lib. bdg. 30.00 (ISBN 0-8414-3605-3). Folcroft.

--Jonathan Swift: A Biographical & Critical Study. 59.95 (ISBN 0-8490-0461-6). Gordon Pr.

--Posthumous Essays of John Churton Collins. Collins, L. C., ed. 1912. lib. bdg. 30.00 (ISBN 0-8414-0946-3). Folcroft.

--Renormalization: An Introduction to Renormalization, the Renormalization Group, & the Operator-Product Expansion. (Monographs on Mathematical Physics). (Illus.). 400p. 1984. 69.50 (ISBN 0-521-24261-4). Cambridge U Pr.

--Studies in Poetry & Criticism. LC 72-12568. 1973. lib. bdg. 25.00 (ISBN 0-8414-0928-5). Folcroft.

--Studies in Shakespeare. LC 72-944. Repr. of 1904 ed. 12.50 (ISBN 0-404-01637-5). AMS Pr.

--The Study of English Literature. 1891. lib. bdg. 17.50 (ISBN 0-8414-2365-2). Folcroft.

Collins, John C., ed. see Greene, Robert.

Collins, John C., ed. see Herbert, Edward H.

Collins, John F. A Primer of Ecclesiastical Latin. LC 84-22957. 250p. 1985. 24.95x (ISBN 0-8132-0610-3). Cath U Pr.

Collins, John G. Physician Visits: Volume & Internal Since Last Visit, United States, 1980. Shipp, Audrey, ed. 55p. 1983. pap. text ed. 1.95 (ISBN 0-8406-0276-6). Natl Ctr Health Stats.

Collins, John H. Mystical Body of Christ. 1977. 2.00 (ISBN 0-8198-0435-5); pap. 0.95 (ISBN 0-8198-0436-3). Dghtrs St Paul.

Collins, John J. The Apocalyptic Vision of the Book of Daniel. LC 77-23124. (Harvard Semitic Monograph). 1977. text ed. 11.95 (ISBN 0-89130-133-X, 040016). Scholars Pr GA.

--Bargaining at the Local Level. LC 73-81503. xii, 191p. 1974. 20.00 (ISBN 0-8232-0972-5). Fordham.

--Between Athens & Jerusalem: Jewish Indentity in the Hellenistic Diaspora. 272p. 1983. 22.50 (ISBN 0-8245-0491-7). Crossroad NY.

--Daniel: With an Introduction to Apocalyptic Literature. Knierim, Rolf, et al, eds. (The Forms of the Old Testament Literature Ser.: Vol. XX). 160p. (Orig.). 1984. pap. 12.95 (ISBN 0-8028-0020-3). Eerdmans.

--Primitive Religion. (Quality Paperback Ser.: No. 342). 256p. 1978. pap. 4.95 (ISBN 0-8226-0342-X). Littlefield.

--Proverbs & Ecclesiastes. LC 79-92067. (Knox Preaching Guides Ser.). 117p. (Orig., John Hayes series editor). 1980. pap. 4.95 (ISBN 0-8042-3218-0). John Knox.

Collins, John J. & Nickelsburg, George W., eds. Ideal Figures in Ancient Judaism: Profiles & Paradigms. LC 80-19878. 1980. 17.95 (ISBN 0-89130-434-7, 060412); pap. 11.95 (ISBN 0-89130-435-5). Scholars Pr GA.

Collins, John J., jt. ed. see Mason, Dean T.

Collins, John M. American & Soviet Military Trends: Since the Cuban Missile Crisis. LC 78-58310. (Illus.). 1978. text ed. 14.95 (ISBN 0-89206-003-4); pap. 10.95 (ISBN 0-89206-002-6). CSI Studies.

--U. S. Defense Planning: A Critique. LC 82-51148. 338p. 1982. lib. bdg. 31.50x (ISBN 0-86531-549-3); pap. text ed. 12.50x (ISBN 0-86531-554-X). Westview.

--U. S. Soviet Military Balance Nineteen Eighty to Nineteen Eighty-Five. (Illus.). 400p. 1985. 50.00 (ISBN 0-08-033131-9, Pub. by P-B); pap. 29.95 (ISBN 0-08-033130-0). Pergamon.

Collins, John M. & Cordesman, Anthony H. Imbalance of Power: Shifting U.S.-Soviet Military Strengths. LC 77-91933. (Illus.). 316p. 1978. pap. 6.95 (ISBN 0-89141-059-7). Presidio Pr.

Collins, John W., et al. Business Law: Cases & Materials. 1150p. Date not set. price not set (ISBN 0-471-04075-4). Wiley.

Collins, Joseph. Agrarian Reform & Counter-Reform in Chile. (Illus.). 24p. pap. text ed. 1.45 (ISBN 0-935028-02-1). Inst Food & Develop.

--Idling in Italy. facs. ed. LC 77-128226. (Essay Index Reprint Ser). 1920. 19.00 (ISBN 0-8369-1824-X). Ayer Co Pubs.

Collins, Joseph, jt. auth. see Lappe, Frances M.

Collins, Joseph, et al. Nicaragua: What Difference Could a Revolution Make? LC 85-80393. 328p. 1985. pap. 8.95 (ISBN 0-935028-20-X). Inst Food & Develop.

--What Difference Could a Revolution Make? Food & Farming in the New Nicaragua. LC 82-21032. 200p. 1982. pap. 5.95 (ISBN 0-935028-10-2). Inst Food & Develop.

Collins, Joseph J. The Soviet Invasion of Afghanistan: A Study in the Use of Force in Soviet Foreign Policy. LC 85-45167. (Illus.). 1985. price not set (ISBN 0-669-11259-3). Lexington Bks.

Collins, Joseph T., jt. auth. see Cross, Frank B.

Collins, Joseph T., ed. Amphibians & Reptiles in Kansas. (University of Kansas, Museum of Natural History Public Education Ser. No. 8). (Illus.). 356p. (Orig.). 1982. 17.00 (ISBN 0-89338-013-X); pap. 12.00 (ISBN 0-89338-012-1). U of KS Mus Nat Hist.

--Natural Kansas. LC 85-7542. (Illus.). 224p. 1985. 25.00 (ISBN 0-7006-0258-5). U Pr of KS.

Collins, Joseph T., ed. see Armstrong, Barry L. & Murphy, James B.

Collins, Joseph T., ed. see Bee, James W., et al.

Collins, Joseph T., ed. see O'Brien, Patricia.

Collins, Joseph T., ed. see Reisz, Robert R.

Collins, Joseph T., ed. see Wilson, Larry D. & Porras, Louis.

Collins, Joseph W. Atari Color Graphics: A Beginner's Workbook. pap. 12.95 (ISBN 0-912003-19-7). Bk Co.

Collins, Judith. The Omega Workshops. LC 83-18285. (Illus.). x, 310p. 1985. lib. bdg. 25.00x (ISBN 0-226-11374-4); pap. 17.50 (ISBN 0-226-11375-2). U of Chicago Pr.

Collins, Judith & Finer, Ruth. National Acquistion Policies & Systems: A Comparative Study of Existing Systems & Possible Models. 221p. 1982. 56.00x (ISBN 0-85350-185-8, Pub. by Pubns Sec Brit Lib England). State Mutual Bk.

Collins, Judith G. Josh's Scary Dad. 32p. (Orig.). (gr. 3-5). 1983. pap. 4.95 (ISBN 0-687-20546-8). Abingdon.

Collins, Judy. Judy Collins Song Book. (Illus.). 1969. pap. 8.95 (ISBN 0-448-01918-3, G&D). Putnam Pub Group.

Collins, June M. Valley of the Spirits: The Upper Skagit Indians of Western Washington. LC 74-8719. (Illus.). 282p. 1974. text ed. 20.00x (ISBN 0-295-95327-6); pap. text ed. 9.95x (ISBN 0-295-95734-4). U of Wash Pr.

Collins, June M., jt. auth. see Collins, Orvis.

Collins, K. J. Hypothermia. (The Facts Ser.). (Illus.). 1983. 13.95 (ISBN 0-19-261360-X). Oxford U Pr.

Collins, K. J. & Roberts, D. F., eds. The Capacity for Work in the Tropics. (Society for the Study of Human Biology Symposium Ser.: No. 26). (Illus.). 300p. Date not set. price not set (ISBN 0-521-30935-2). Cambridge U Pr.

Collins, K. J., jt. ed. see Bittles, A. H.

Collins, K. K., jt. ed. see Cohn, Alan M.

Collins, Kathleen, tr. see Mars, Louis B.

Collins, Kathryn. The Wings of Night. (Superromances Ser.). 384p. 1984. pap. 2.95 (ISBN 0-373-70097-0, Pub. by Worldwide). Harlequin Bks.

Collins, Kathryn, jt. auth. see Maughan, Jackie J.

Collins, Kathy. Complete Carob Cookbook. 1981. pap. 7.95x (ISBN 0-317-07298-6, Regent House). B of A.

Collins, Keith E. Black Los Angeles: The Maturing of the Ghetto. LC 79-65254. 145p. 1980. 12.95 (ISBN 0-86548-005-2). R & E Pubs.

Collins, L. A. Collecting Books in New England. LC 83-81117. (Illus.). 184p. (Orig.). 1983. pap. 6.50 (ISBN 0-913125-00-8). R J Diefendorf.

Collins, L. C., ed. see Collins, John C.

Collins, L. W., jt. ed. see Wendlandt, W. W.

Collins, Larry. Fall from Grace. 1985. 17.95 (ISBN 0-671-43609-0). S&S.

Collins, Larry & La Pierre, Dominique. The Fifth Horseman. 496p. 1981. pap. 3.95 (ISBN 0-380-54734-1, 67306-1). Avon.

Collins, Larry & Lapierre, Dominique. Freedom at Midnight. 608p. 1976. pap. 4.95 (ISBN 0-380-00693-6, 61747-1). Avon.

--O Jerusalem. 1980. pap. 3.95 (ISBN 0-671-83684-6). PB.

Collins, Laura & Collins, Virginia. Levels of Mind. 1984. 6.50 (ISBN 0-8062-2357-X). Carlton.

Collins, Lauren F., jt. auth. see Mitchell, Charlie R.

Collins, Lee. Oh, Didn't He Ramble: The Life Story of Lee Collins As Told to Mary Collins. Gillis, Frank J. & Miner, John W., eds. LC 73-85485. (Music in American Life Ser.). (Illus.). 174p. 1974. 12.50 (ISBN 0-252-00234-2). U of Ill Pr.

Collins, Leighton. Take-offs & Landings. 1982. 17.95 (ISBN 0-02-527240-3). Macmillan.

Collins, Leo C. Hercules Seghers. LC 77-73729. (Illus.). 1978. Repr. of 1953 ed. lib. bdg. 50.00 (ISBN 0-87817-209-2). Hacker.

Collins, Lewis. Historical Sketches of Kentucky Embracing Its History, Antiquities, & Natural Curiosities, Geographical, Statistical, & Geological Description. LC 77-146385. (First American Frontier Ser). (Illus.). 1971. Repr. of 1848 ed. 33.00 (ISBN 0-405-02836-9). Ayer Co Pubs.

Collins, Lewis & Collins, Richard H. A History of Kentucky. Set. 90.00 (ISBN 0-89308-168-X); Vol. 1, 683 pp. (ISBN 0-89308-166-3); Vol. 2, 804 pp. (ISBN 0-89308-167-1). Southern Hist Pr.

Collins, M. B., jt. auth. see Banner, F. T.

Collins, M. B., et al, eds. Industrialised Embayments & Their Environmental Problems - a Case Study of Swansea Bay: Proceedings of an Interdisciplinary Symposium Held at University College, Swansea, 26-28 Sept. 1979. LC 80-40507. (Illus.). 608p. 1980. 88.00 (ISBN 0-08-023992-7). Pergamon.

Collins, M. E. Conquest & Colonisation. (History of Ireland Ser.: Vol. 2). (Illus.). 240p. 1969. pap. text ed. 8.50 (ISBN 0-7171-0256-4). Irish Bk Ctr.

--Ireland, Forteen Seventy-Seven to Sixteen Ten. (Illus.). 283p. (Orig.). 1980. pap. 13.50 (ISBN 0-318-03208-2, Pub. by Educ Co Ireland). Irish Bk Ctr.

--Ireland Three: Eighteen Hundred to the Present Day. (Illus.). 264p. (Orig.). 1972. pap. 11.95 (ISBN 0-318-03226-0, Pub. by Educ Co Ireland). Irish Bk Ctr.

Collins, M. E. & Gough, H. Modern Times: Ireland & Europe Since 1870. (Illus.). 340p. (Orig.). 1978. pap. 13.50 (ISBN 0-914916-75-0, Pub. by Educ Co Ireland). Irish Bk Ctr.

Collins, M. Fred. Space Shots. LC 78-68713. (Illus.). 1979. pap. 7.95 (ISBN 0-8129-0823-6). Times Bks.

Collins, Mabel. Idyll of the White Lotus. LC 74-7341. 128p. 1974. pap. 1.25 (ISBN 0-8356-0301-6, Quest). Theos Pub Hse.

--Light on the Path. 1970. pap. 1.75 (ISBN 0-8356-0299-0, Quest). Theos Pub Hse.

--Light on the Path. Incl. Through the Gates of Gold. verbatim ed. LC 68-21157. 1976. 7.50 (ISBN 0-911500-37-5); pap. 4.00 (ISBN 0-911500-38-3). Theos U Pr.

Collins, Mabel C. Light on the Path. leatherette 2.50 (ISBN 0-911662-13-8). Yoga.

Collins, Mal & Harker, Dave, eds. Big Red Songbook. (Illus.). 128p. 1977. pap. 5.95 (ISBN 0-86104-356-1). Pluto Pr.

Collins, Mallary M. & Fontenelle, Don, 2nd. Changing Student Behaviors: A Positive Approach. 192p. 1981. text ed. 11.25x (ISBN 0-87073-657-4). Schenkman Bks Inc.

Collins, Marcia & Land, Norman E. Early Books on Art, 1500 to 1800. (Illus.). 74p. (Orig.). 1977. pap. 4.00x (ISBN 0-910501-04-1). U of Missouri Mus Art Arch.

Collins, Marcia R. & Anderson, Linda. Libraries for Small Museums. 3rd ed. Feldman, Lawrence, ed. LC 78-620740. (Miscellaneous Publications in Anthropology Ser.: No. 4). 1977. pap. text ed. 2.50x (ISBN 0-913134-90-2). Mus Anthro Mo.

Collins, Marie, tr. see Michaud, Guy.

Collins, Marilyn C. Child Abuser: A Study of Child Abusers in Self-Help Group Therapy. LC 76-47866. 124p. 1978. pap. 12.00 (ISBN 0-88416-186-2). PSG Pub Co.

Collins, Marjorie. Bible Quizzes on Bible Themes. 48p. (gr. 5 up). 1983. pap. 1.95 (ISBN 0-87239-658-4, 3138). Standard Pub.

Collins, Marjorie A. Manual for Missionaries on Furlough. LC 72-92747. 1978. pap. 4.45 (ISBN 0-87808-119-4). William Carey Lib.

Collins, Marnie. Green Things in Small Spaces. 9.95 (ISBN 0-686-66147-8, NO. 0002). Methuen Inc.

Collins, Martha. The Catastrophe of Rainbows. (CSU Poetry Ser.: No. XVII). 67p. (Orig.). 1985. pap. 6.00 (ISBN 0-914946-48-X). Cleveland St Univ Poetry Ctr.

--Critical Essays on Louise Bogan. (Critical Essays on American Literature Ser.). 184p. 1984. 35.00 (ISBN 0-8161-8680-4). G K Hall.

Collins, Martha D., jt. auth. see Cheek, Earl H., Jr.

Collins, Martin. The French Coast: A Visitor's Guide. (Illus.). 160p. (Orig.). 1985. pap. 9.95 (ISBN 0-86190-136-3, Pub. by Moorland Pr UK). Bradt Ent.

--Urban Ecology: A Teacher's Resource Book. (Illus.). 160p. 1984. 19.95 (ISBN 0-521-30085-1); pap. 11.95 (ISBN 0-521-27803-1). Cambridge U Pr.

Collins, Martin, ed. Ireland after Britain. 192p. (Orig.). 1985. pap. 5.95 (ISBN 0-7453-0046-4, Pub. by Pluto Pr). Longwood Pub Group.

Collins, Martin, ed. see Brush, Stephen G., et al.

Collins, Mary & Power, David, eds. A Creative Tradition. (Concilium 1983: Vol. 162). 128p. (Orig.). 1983. pap. 6.95 (ISBN 0-8164-2442-X, Pub. by Seabury). Winston Pr.

Collins, Mary, jt. ed. see Fiorenza, Elisabeth S.

Collins, Mary, jt. ed. see Power, David.

Collins, Mary S., jt. auth. see Baker, John A.

Collins, Mattie. Communication in Health Care: The Human Connection in the Life Cycle. 2nd ed. LC 82-3482. (Illus.). 276p. 1983. pap. text ed. 12.95 (ISBN 0-8016-1081-8). Mosby.

Collins, Max. The Baby Blue Rip-Off. 1983. 11.95 (ISBN 0-8027-5475-9). Walker & Co.

--Hard Cash. (Nolan Ser.: No. 5). 192p. (Orig.). 1982. pap. 1.95 (ISBN 0-523-41163-4). Pinnacle Bks.

--Hush Money. (Nolan Ser.: No.4). 192p. (Orig.). 1981. pap. 1.95 (ISBN 0-523-41162-6). Pinnacle Bks.

--No Cure for Death. 192p. 1983. 12.95 (ISBN 0-8027-5488-0). Walker & Co.

--Nolan, Number Six: Scratch Fever. 192p. (Orig.). 1982. pap. 1.95 (ISBN 0-523-41164-2). Pinnacle Bks.

Collins, Max A. Kill Your Darlings. 192p. 1984. 13.95 (ISBN 0-8027-5594-1). Walker & Co.

--Quarry. 217p. 1985. pap. 4.50 (ISBN 0-88150-057-7, Foul Play). Countryman.

--Quarry's List. 186p. 1985. pap. 4.95 (ISBN 0-88150-058-5). Countryman.

--A Shroud for Aquarius. (A Mallory Mystery Ser.). 175p. 1985. 14.95 (ISBN 0-8027-5629-8). Walker & Co.

--True Crime. 1984. 15.95 (ISBN 0-312-82045-3). St Martin.

--True Detective. (Illus.). 368p. 1983. 14.95 (ISBN 0-312-82051-8). St Martin.

Collins, Max A. & Traylor, James L. One Lonely Knight: Mickey Spillane's Mike Hammer. LC 84-71256. 186p. 1984. 19.95 (ISBN 0-87972-301-7); pap. 8.95 (ISBN 0-87972-302-5). Bowling Green Univ.

Collins, Max A., ed. see Spillane, Mickey.

Collins, Meghan. The Willow Maiden. LC 85-1533. (Illus.). 40p. (gr. k up). 1985. 11.95 (ISBN 0-8037-0217-5); PLB 11.89 (ISBN 0-8037-0218-3). Dial Bks Young.

Collins, Meghan R. Maiden Crown. (gr. 7 up). 1979. 8.95 (ISBN 0-395-28639-5). HM.

Collins, Michael. Flying to the Moon & Other Strange Places. LC 76-25496. (Illus.). 159p. (gr. 4 up). 1976. 10.95 (ISBN 0-374-32412-3); pap. 3.45 (ISBN 0-374-42355-5). FS&G.

--Freak. 216p. 1983. 10.95 (ISBN 0-396-08104-5). Dodd.

--From a Fiberglass Hull. (Illus.). 132p. 1979. 15.00 (ISBN 0-229-11616-7). Sheridan.

Collins, Michael, jt. auth. see Bullard, Scott R.

Collins, Michael, jt. auth. see Capie, Forrest.

Collins, Michael, jt. auth. see Collins, Blackie.

Collins, Michael & Kirk, Elise K., eds. Opera & Vivaldi. LC 83-23557. (Illus.). 406p. 1984. text ed. 35.00x (ISBN 0-292-70746-0). U of Tex Pr.

Collins, Michael, ed. see Scarlatti.

Collins, Michael A. Aldehyde Adducts in Alcoholism. (PCBR Ser.). 248p. 1985. 46.00 (ISBN 0-8451-5033-2). A R Liss.

Collins, Michael D. Cultured Mexico. 297p. 1974. lib. bdg. 69.95 (ISBN 0-87968-973-0). Gordon Pr.

Collins, Michael F. & Pharoah, Timothy M. Transport Organisation in a Great City: The Case of London. LC 74-77339. pap. 160.00 (ISBN 0-317-29604-3, 2021877). Bks Demand UMI.

Collins, Michael J., ed. Finite Simple Groups, II. LC 77-149703. 1981. 60.00 (ISBN 0-12-181480-7). Acad Pr.

Collins, Michael M. Genetics & Ecology of a Hybrid Zone in Hyalophora. LC 83-18019. (Entomology Ser.: Vol. 104). 112p. 1984. lib. bdg. 11.50x (ISBN 0-520-09953-2). U of Cal Pr.

Collins, Myrtle T. & Collins, Dwane R. Survival Kit for Teachers (& Parents) LC 74-10230. 1975. pap. 11.95 (ISBN 0-673-16443-8). Scott F.

Collins, Nancy J. Building a Life. (Character Foundation Curriculum Ser.). (gr. 3). 1981. tchr's. ed 7.00 (ISBN 0-8007-7032-3, Christian School Curriculum); wkbk. 2.95 (ISBN 0-8007-7031-5). Revell.

Collins, Nancy W. Professional Women & Their Mentors: A Practical Guide to Mentoring for the Woman Who Wants to Get Ahead. 163p. 1982. 12.95 (ISBN 0-13-725994-8); pap. 6.95 (ISBN 0-13-725986-7). P-H.

Collins, Nell & Moster, Mary Beth. The Valley Is Bright. LC 82-24562. 102p. 1983. pap. 4.95 (ISBN 0-8407-5835-9). Nelson.

Collins, Norman. Facts of Fiction. facsimile ed. LC 70-111821. (Essay Index Reprint Ser). 1933. 18.00 (ISBN 0-8369-1599-2). Ayer Co Pubs.

Collins, Orvis & Collins, June M. Interaction & Social Structure. (Approaches to Semiotics Ser: No. 32). 1973. text ed. 23.20x (ISBN 0-686-22559-7). Mouton.

Collins, Orvis F., et al. Enterprising Man. LC 64-63821. 1964. 7.50 (ISBN 0-87744-027-1). Mich St U Pr.

Collins, P. D. An Introduction to Regge Theory & High-Energy Physics. LC 76-2233. (Cambridge Monographs on Mathematical Physics). (Illus.). 1977. 125.00 (ISBN 0-521-21245-6). Cambridge U Pr.

Collins, P. D. & Squires, E. J. Regge Poles in Particle Physics. (Springer Tracts in Modern Physics: Vol. 45). 1968. 58.50 (ISBN 0-387-04339-X). Springer-Verlag.

Collins, Pat. How to Be a Really Nice Person: Doing the Right Thing-Your Way. LC 83-1759. 192p. 1983. 12.95 (ISBN 0-87131-406-1). M Evans.

Collins, Pat L. My Friend Andrew. (Illus.). (ps-2). 1980. 9.95x (ISBN 0-13-608844-9). P-H.

--Tumble, Tumble, Tumbleweed. Fay, Ann, ed. LC 81-23968. (Illus.). 32p. (gr. 1-3). 1982. PLB 10.75 (ISBN 0-8075-8122-4). A Whitman.

Collins, Patricia W. Cambria County, PA Willbook Index. 59p. 1983. pap. text ed. 9.50 (ISBN 0-933227-08-6). Closson Pr.

--Marriages & Deaths from the Cambria Tribune, Vol. 4. 242p. (Orig.). 1985. perfect bdg. 18.00 (ISBN 0-318-03863-3). Closson Pr.

Collins, Patrick. Currency Convertibility: The Return to Sound Money. LC 84-18197. 208p. 1985. 29.95 (ISBN 0-312-17915-4). St Martin.

--Living in Troubled Lands: The Complete Guide to Personal Security Abroad. 200p. 1980. 14.95 (ISBN 0-87364-205-8). Paladin Pr.

Collins, Patrick J. The N-Town Plays & Medieval Picture Cycles. (Early Drama, Art, & Music Ser.). (Illus.). 1979. pap. 4.95x (ISBN 0-918720-03-6). Medieval Inst.

Collins, Patrick W. More Than Meets the Eye: Ritual & Parish Liturgy. LC 82-62920. 160p. (Orig.). 1983. pap. 6.95 (ISBN 0-8091-2539-0). Paulist Pr.

Collins, Paul, ed. Administration for Development in Nigeria: Introduction & Readings. 337p. (Orig.). 1980. pap. text ed. 11.95x (ISBN 978-2308-00-5). Transaction Bks.

Collins, Peggie V. & Collins, Shirley W. Beyond Interior Design, Quality-the Third Dimension. Rev. ed. LC 83-73400. 212p. 1984. text ed. 21.00 (ISBN 0-915587-01-7); pap. text ed. 16.00 (ISBN 0-915587-00-9). Bid Pub Co.

Collins, Peter. Architectural Judgement. (Illus.). 1971. 12.50x (ISBN 0-7735-0114-2). McGill-Queens U Pr.

--Changing Ideals in Modern Architecture. (Illus.). 1965. pap. 12.95 (ISBN 0-7735-0048-0). McGill-Queens U Pr.

Collins, Peter & Graham, Colin. Coarse Fishing. (Know the Game Ser.). (Illus.). 1975. pap. 2.50 (ISBN 0-7158-0209-7). Charles River Bks.

Collins, Philip. Thackeray: Interviews & Recollections, 2 vols. LC 81-21327. 20.00 ea. (ISBN 0-312-79488-6). St Martin.

Collins, Philip, ed. Dickens: Interviews & Recollections, 2 vols. (Illus.). 1981. 28.50x ea. Vol. 1, 210 1 Pgs (ISBN 0-389-20042-5). Vol. 2, 200 Pgs (ISBN 0-389-20043-3). B&N Imports.

Collins, Philip, ed. see Dickens, Charles.

Collins, Phillip, ed. Thackeray: Interviews & Recollections, 2 Vols. LC 81-21327. 394p. 1983. Vol. 1. 20.00 (ISBN 0-312-79488-6); Vol. 2. 20.00 (ISBN 0-312-79489-4). St Martin.

Collins, R. & Van Der Werff, T. J. Mathematical Models of the Dynamics of the Human Eye. (Lecture Notes in Biomathematics Ser.: Vol. 34). 99p. 1980. pap. 13.00 (ISBN 0-387-09751-1). Springer-Verlag.

Collins, R. Douglas. Dynamic Differential Diagnosis. (Illus.). 195p. 1981. text ed. 44.50 (ISBN 0-397-50467-5, 65-06083, Lippincott Medical). Lippincott.

--Illustrated Manual of Fluid & Electrolyte Disorders. 2nd ed. (Illus.). 224p. 1983. text ed. 39.50 (ISBN 0-397-50516-7, 65-06604, Lippincott Medical). Lippincott.

--Illustrated Manual of Laboratory Diagnosis: Indications & Interpretations. 2nd ed. LC 74-23530. (Illus.). 344p. 1975. 49.50 (ISBN 0-397-50340-7, 65-00854, Lippincott Medical). Lippincott.

--Illustrated Manual of Neurologic Diagnosis. 2nd ed. (Illus.). 272p. 1982. text ed. 38.50 (ISBN 0-397-50515-9, 65-06612, Lippincott Medical). Lippincott.

Collins, R. S. The Artist in Modern German Drama, 1885-1939. 59.95 (ISBN 0-87968-663-4). Gordon Pr.

Collins Radio Company. Amateur Single Sideband. LC 77-71665. (Illus.). 1977. pap. text ed. 4.95 (ISBN 0-918232-05-8, HR-SSB). Comm Tech.

Collins, Randall. Conflict Sociology: Toward an Explanatory Science. 1975. 55.00 (ISBN 0-12-181350-9). Acad Pr.

--The Credential Society: A Historical Sociology of Education & Stratification. LC 78-20042. 1979. 16.00 (ISBN 0-12-181360-6). Acad Pr.

--Sociological Insight: An Introduction to Non-Obvious Sociology. 1982. pap. text ed. 4.95x (ISBN 0-19-503037-0). Oxford U Pr.

--Sociology since Midcentury: Essays in Theory Cumulation. LC 81-13034. 1981. 28.50 (ISBN 0-12-181340-1). Acad Pr.

--Three Sociological Traditions. 270p. 1985. pap. 8.95x (ISBN 0-19-503519-4). Oxford U Pr.

--Three Sociological Traditions: Selected Readings. 284p. 1985. pap. 9.95 (ISBN 0-19-503521-6). Oxford U Pr.

Collins, Randall & Makowsky, Michael. Discovery of Society. 3rd ed. 275p. 1983. pap. text ed. 11.00 (ISBN 0-394-33153-2, RanC). Random.

Collins, Randall, ed. Sociological Theory 1983. (Social & Behavioral Science Ser.). 1983. text ed. 25.95x (ISBN 0-87589-557-3). Jossey-Bass.

--Sociological Theory 1984. (Social & Behavioral Science Ser.). 1984. 29.95x (ISBN 0-87589-587-5). Jossey-Bass.

Collins, Raymond A., ed. The Giant Handbook of Electronic Circuits. (Illus.). 882p. 1980. pap. 19.95 (ISBN -08306-9662-8, 1300). TAB Bks.

Collins, Raymond F. Introduction to the New Testament. LC 82-45070. (Illus.). 480p. 1983. 24.95 (ISBN 0-385-18126-4). Doubleday.

--Models of Theological Reflections. LC 83-21733. (Illus.). 240p. (Orig.). 1984. lib. bdg. 23.25 (ISBN 0-8191-3661-1); pap. text ed. 12.00 (ISBN 0-8191-3662-X). U Pr of Amer.

Collins, Richard. Flight Level Flying. 160p. 1985. 18.95 (ISBN 0-02-527310-8). MacMillan.

--Foolscape. Peters, Robert, intro. by. LC 83-60865. 73p. 1983. pap. 6.95 (ISBN 0-912288-23-X). Perivale Pr.

Collins, Richard H., jt. auth. see Collins, Lewis.

Collins, Richard L. Dick Collins Tips to Fly By. 1982. 11.95 (ISBN 0-02-527220-9). Macmillan.

--Flying Safely. rev. ed. 1982. 12.95 (ISBN 0-02-527230-6). Macmillan.

--Flying the Weathermap. 1982. 12.50 (ISBN 0-02-527200-4). Macmillan.

--Thunderstorms & Planes. 1982. 14.95 (ISBN 0-02-527250-0). Macmillan.

Collins, Richard L. & Bradley, Patrick E. Instrument Flying Refresher. rev. ed. (An Eleanor Friede Bk.). 304p. 1984. 17.95 (ISBN 0-02-527160-1). Macmillan.

Collins, Rip & Whitehead, Steve. Double Your Sales Commission Using a Personal Computer. (Micropower Ser.). 240p. 1985. pap. 14.95 (ISBN 0-697-00802-9). Wm C Brown.

Collins, Rob. Software by Design. (Illus.). 352p. 1984. pap. 19.95 (ISBN 0-88056-310-9). Dilithium Pr.

Collins, Robert & Deng, Francis, eds. The British in the Sudan, 1898-1956: The Sweetness & the Sorrow. (Publications Ser.). (Illus.). 258p. 1985. 29.95x (ISBN 0-317-18672-8). Hoover Inst Pr.

Collins, Robert A. & Pearce, Howard D., eds. The Scope of the Fantastic-Culture, Biography, Themes, Children's Literature: Selected Essays from the First International Conference on the Fantastic in Literature & Film. LC 84-530. (Contributions to the Study of Science Fiction & Fantasy Ser.: No. 11). (Illus.). 288p. 1985. lib. bdg. 35.00 (ISBN 0-313-23448-5, COF/02). Greenwood.

--The Scope of the Fantastic-Theory, Technique, Major Authors: Selected Essays from the First International Conference on the Fantastic in Literature & Film. LC 84-538. (Contributions to the Study of Science Fiction & Fantasy Ser.: No. 10). (Illus.). xii, 295p. 1985. lib. bdg. 35.00 (ISBN 0-313-23447-7, COF/01). Greenwood.

Collins, Robert C., jt. ed. see Pearlman, Alan L.

Collins, Robert E. Theodore Parker: American Transcendentalist: A Critical Essay & a Collection of His Writings. LC 73-9593. 277p. 1973. 16.00 (ISBN 0-8108-0641-X). Scarecrow.

Collins, Robert G. Critical Essays on John Cheever. (Critical Essays on American Literature Ser.). 1982. lib. bdg. 33.50 (ISBN 0-8161-8623-5). G K Hall.

Collins, Robert M. The Business Response to Keynes, Nineteen Twenty-Nine to Nineteen Sixty-Four. LC 81-3898. (Contemporary American History Ser.). 320p. 1981. 30.00x (ISBN 0-231-04486-0). Columbia U Pr.

Collins, Robert O. King Leopold, England & the Upper Nile, 1899-1909. LC 68-27750. (Illus.). Repr. of 1968 ed. 69.20 (ISBN 0-8357-9376-1, 2011095). Bks Demand UMI.

--Shadows in the Grass: Britain in the Southern Sudan, 1918-1956. 1983. 41.00 (ISBN 0-300-02922-5). Yale U Pr.

--The Southern Sudan in Historical Perspective. 101p. 1976. pap. text ed. 9.95x (ISBN 0-87855-616-8). Transaction Bks.

Collins, Robert O. & Nash, Roderick. The Big Drops: Ten Legendary Rapids. LC 78-5821. (Illus.). 240p. 1978. 18.50 (ISBN 0-87156-217-0). Sierra.

Collins, Roger. Early Medieval Spain: Unity in Diversity, 400-1000. LC 83-15931. 320p. 1983. 27.50 (ISBN 0-312-22464-8). St Martin.

Collins, Ronald K., ed. Constitutional Government in America. LC 79-51944. 504p. 1980. 35.00 (ISBN 0-89089-131-1). Carolina Acad Pr.

Collins, Rosemary, jt. ed. see Close, Paul.

Collins, Ross W. Catholicism & the Second French Republic, 1848-1852. 1980. lib. bdg. 27.50x (ISBN 0-374-91868-6). Octagon.

Collins, Rowland L., ed. see Beowulf.

Collins, S. H. Emigrant's Guide to the United States of America, Containing All Things Necessary to Be Known by Every Class of Persons Emigrating to That Continent. LC 70-145476. (The American Immigration Library). vi, 144p. 1971. Repr. of 1830 ed. lib. bdg. 9.95x (ISBN 0-89198-008-3). Ozer.

Collins, S. M. & Skorton, D. Cardiac Imaging & Image Processing. 608p. 1985. write for info. (ISBN 0-07-057912-1). McGraw.

Collins, Sarah H. & Tuttle, Frederick B., Jr. Technical & Scientific Writing. 127p. 1979. pap. 6.95 (ISBN 0-8106-1718-8). NEA.

Collins, Selwyn D. & Tibbitts, Clark. Research Memorandum on Social Aspects of Health in the Depression. LC 72-162846. (Studies in the Social Aspects of the Depression). 1971. Repr. of 1937 ed. 17.00 (ISBN 0-405-00849-X). Ayer Co Pubs.

Collins, Sheila. From Melting Pot to Rainbow Coalition: The Emergence of Race in American Politics. 256p. (Orig.). 1986. 26.00 (ISBN 0-85345-690-9); pap. 10.00 (ISBN 0-85345-691-7). Monthly Rev.

--Half a Winter to Go. LC 76-12003. (Sunburst Originals Ser.: No. 4). 52p. (Orig.). 1976. pap. 2.25 (ISBN 0-934648-04-2). Sunburst Pr.

Collins, Sheila D. A Different Heaven & Earth. LC 74-2890. 256p. 1974. 8.95 (ISBN 0-8170-0620-6). Judson.

Collins, Sheila D. & Collins, John A. In Your Midst: Perspectives on Christian Mission. (Orig.). 1980. pap. 3.25 (ISBN 0-377-00101-5). Friend Pr.

Collins, Shelia, jt. auth. see Golden, Renny.

Collins, Shirley W., jt. auth. see Collins, Peggie V.

Collins, Stephanie. A Page a Day for Advent & the Christmas Season, 1985. (Orig.). 1985. pap. 1.95 (ISBN 0-8091-2700-8). Paulist Pr.

Collins, Stephen N. Down to the Sea with Books: NAUI International Bibliography of Diving & Related Science. 1973. 2.95 (ISBN 0-916974-04-9, NO. 106). NAUI.

Collins, Steven. Selfless Persons: Imagery & Thought in Theravada Buddhism. LC 81-16998. 1982. 44.50 (ISBN 0-521-24081-6). Cambridge U Pr.

Collins, Steven, jt. ed. see Carrithers, Micheal.

Collins, Susan. The Me Book: An Illustrated Manual for Remodeling Yourself. pap. 7.95 (ISBN 0-915677-24-5). Roundtable Pub.

--The Me Book: Developing Your Inner Model. LC 84-60763. (Illus.). 240p. 1985. cancelled (ISBN 0-915677-06-7). Roundtable Pub.

--Once Removed. LC 81-83735. (Illus.). 100p. (Orig.). 1981. pap. 5.95 (ISBN 0-941356-00-0). Little Lady's Pr.

Collins, Susan B. Baldwin's Ohio Bank Law & Regulation Manual. 3rd ed. (Ohio Practice Ser.). 764p. 1982. annual 60.00 (ISBN 0-8322-0022-0); pap. text ed. 10.00. Banks-Baldwin.

Collins, Susan B., ed. Ohio Bank Manual Text. 1981. 10.00 (ISBN 0-8322-0001-8). Banks-Baldwin.

Collins, Susan M., jt. auth. see Henderson, Jane O.

Collins, Susanna. Breathless Dawn. (Second Chance at Love Ser.: No. 94). 192p. 1983. pap. 1.75 (ISBN 0-515-06858-6). Jove Pubns.

--Brief Enchantment. (Second Chance at Love: No. 201). 192p. 1984. pap. 1.95 (ISBN 0-515-07817-4). Jove Pubns.

--On Wings of Magic. (Second Chance at Love Ser.: No. 62). 192p. 1982. pap. 1.75 (ISBN 0-515-06650-8). Jove Pubns.

--Parisain Nights. (Second Chance at Love Ser.: No. 134). 192p. 1983. pap. 1.95 (ISBN 0-515-07222-2). Jove Pubns.

--Wrapped in Rainbows. 192p. 1984. pap. 1.95 (ISBN 0-515-07587-6). Jove Pubns.

Collins, T. & Bruce, T. Staff Support & Staff Training. (Residential Social Work Ser.). 168p. 1984. pap. 10.95 (ISBN 0-422-76920-7, 4003, Pub. by Tavistock England). Methuen Inc.

Collins, Thomas. Nightside. (Orig.). 1979. pap. 2.25 (ISBN 0-532-23143-0). Woodhill.

Collins, Thomas C., jt. auth. see Reynolds, Donald C.

Collins, Thomas W., ed. Cities in a Larger Context. LC 79-54361. (Southern Anthropological Society Proceedings Ser.: No. 14). 160p. 1980. 14.00x (ISBN 0-8203-0504-9); pap. 7.00x (ISBN 0-8203-0505-7). U of Ga Pr.

Collins, Tom. The Centre Cannot Hold: Britain's Failure in Northern Ireland. (Illus.). 190p. 1985. pap. 9.95 (ISBN 0-946968-00-4). Devin.

--Steven Spielberg: Creator of E. T. (Taking Part Ser.). (Illus.). 48p. (gr. 3 up). 1983. PLB 8.95 (ISBN 0-87518-249-6). Dillon.

Collins, Tom, ed. see Lovecraft, Howard P.

Collins, Tom, et al. Collins Backroom Cooking Secrets: Wild Game, Fish & Other Savories. (Orig.). 1983. pap. 8.95 (ISBN 0-931674-02-6). Waldman Hse Pr.

Collins, Trish. Grinkles: A Keen Halloween Story. (Easy-Read Story Bks.). (Illus.). 32p. (gr. k-3). 1981. 8.60 (ISBN 0-531-02471-7). Watts.

Collins, V. H., pseud. A Book of English Idioms with Explanations. LC 85-12617. xiii, 258p. 1984. Repr. of 1958 ed. lib. bdg. 39.75x (ISBN 0-8371-8152-6, COEI). Greenwood.

Collins, V. H. A Book of Narrative Verse. 1930. 16.00 (ISBN 0-686-17677-4). Quaker City.

--A Book of Victorian Verse. 1928. 12.50 (ISBN 0-686-17678-2). Quaker City.

Collins, V. H., ed. A Book of Victorian Verse: Chiefly Lyrical. 1979. Repr. of 1928 ed. lib. bdg. 20.00 (ISBN 0-8495-0779-0). Arden Lib.

--Selected Letters of Byron. 1928. 17.50 (ISBN 0-8274-3350-6). R West.

Collins, V. H., ed. see Byron, George G.

Collins, Val. The Beginner's Guide to Microwave Cookery. (Illus.). 120p. 1982. 9.95 (ISBN 0-7153-8316-7). David & Charles.

--Microwave Baking. (Illus.). 128p. 1980. 14.95 (ISBN 0-7153-8018-4). David & Charles.

--Microwave Fish Cookbook. (Illus.). 120p. 1983. 14.95 (ISBN 0-7153-8393-0). David & Charles.

--The Microwave Fruit & Vegetable Cookbook. LC 81-65958. (Illus.). 120p. 1981. 14.95 (ISBN 0-7153-8199-7). David & Charles.

Collins, Varnum L. President Witherspoon. LC 78-83416. (Religion in America, Ser. 1). 1969. Repr. of 1925 ed. 30.00 (ISBN 0-405-00242-4). Ayer Co Pubs.

Collins, Varnum L., ed. Brief Narrative of the Ravages of the British & Hessians at Princeton in 1776-1777. LC 67-29024. (Eyewitness Accounts of the American Revolution, Ser. No. 1). 1968. Repr. of 1906 ed. 13.50 (ISBN 0-405-01110-5). Ayer Co Pubs.

Collins, Varnum L., ed. see Witherspoon, John.

Collins, Vere H. A Book of English Proverbs, with Origins & Explanations. LC 73-16945. 144p. 1974. Repr. of 1959 ed. lib. bdg. 29.75x (ISBN 0-8371-7242-X, COEN). Greenwood.

--Talks with Thomas Hardy at Max Gate. 2nd ed. 85p. 1978. 13.50x (ISBN 0-7156-1280-8, Pub. by Duckworth England). Biblio Dist.

--Talks with Thomas Hardy at Max Gate, 1920-1922. LC 74-28383. 1928. 16.50 (ISBN 0-8414-3615-0). Folcroft.

Collins, Vere H., ed. Three Centuries of English Essays: From Francis Bacon to Max Beerbohm. facs. ed. LC 67-26727. (Essay Index Reprint Ser). 1931. 11.00 (ISBN 0-8369-0327-7). Ayer Co Pubs.

Collins, Victor, tr. see Gougaud, Dom L.

Collins, Vincent J. Principles of Anesthesiology. 2nd ed. LC 76-2054. (Illus.). 1671p. 1976. text ed. 60.00 (ISBN 0-8121-0463-3). Lea & Febiger.

Collins, Vincent P. Me, Myself & You. rev. ed. LC 74-17734. 1974. pap. 2.95 (ISBN 0-87029-001-0, 20033-7). Abbey.

Collins, Violet F. The Magical Maze. 2nd ed. LC 80-67536. (Illus.). 100p. (gr. 1-6). 1981. PLB cancelled (ISBN 0-9604578-2-8); pap. cancelled (ISBN 0-9604578-0-1); cancelled tchr's ed (ISBN 0-9604578-1-X). Baraka Bk.

Collins, Virgil D. World Marketing. Assael, Henry, ed. LC 78-271. (Century of Marketing Ser.). 1978. Repr. of 1935 ed. lib. bdg. 26.50x (ISBN 0-405-11186-X). Ayer Co Pubs.

Collins, Virginia, jt. auth. see Collins, Laura.

Collins, W. Cathedral Cities of Spain. 1976. lib. bdg. 59.95 (ISBN 0-8490-1585-5). Gordon Pr.

--The Poems. facsimile ed. Bronson, Walter C., ed. 135p. Repr. of 1898 ed. 23.75x (ISBN 3-4870-4665-2). Adlers Foreign Bks.

Collins, W., jt. auth. see Leyden, D.

Collins, W. A., ed. Minnesota Symposia on Child Psychology, Vol. 11. 286p. 1978. 29.95x (ISBN 0-89859-113-9). L Erlbaum Assocs.

Collins, W. Andrew, ed. Aspects of the Development of Competence. LC 80-20568. (Minnesota Symposia on Child Psychology: Vol. 14). 288p. 1981. 24.95x (ISBN 0-89859-070-1). L Erlbaum Assocs.

--Children's Language & Communication. LC 79-364. (The Minnesota Symposia on Child Psychology Ser.: Vol. 12). (Illus.). 256p. 1979. text ed. 29.95x (ISBN 0-89859-000-0). L Erlbaum Assocs.

--The Concept of Development. (The Minnesota Symposia on Child Psychology: Vol. 15). 182p. 1982. 29.95x (ISBN 0-89859-159-7). L Erlbaum Assocs.

--Development of Cognition, Affect, & Social Relations. LC 79-27560. (The Minnesota Symposia on Child Psychology Ser.: Vol. 13). (Illus.). 320p. 1980. text ed. 29.95x (ISBN 0-89859-023-X). L Erlbaum Assocs.

Collins, W. Andrews, jt. auth. see Sprinthall, Norman A.

Collins, W. B. They Went to Bush. 231p. 6.00 (ISBN 0-685-26801-2). Univ Place.

Collins, W. J. Intermediate Pascal Programming: A Case Study Approach. (Computer Science Ser.). 416p. 1985. price not set (ISBN 0-07-044652-0). McGraw.

Collins, W. J., ed. see Scott, Alexander.

Collins, W. L. The Iliad. 1877. Repr. 25.00 (ISBN 0-8274-2552-X). R West.

--The Odyssey. 1877. Repr. 25.00 (ISBN 0-8274-3056-6). R West.

Collins, W. Lucas. Aristophanes. 1877. 25.00 (ISBN 0-8274-1877-9). R West.

--Butler. 1881. 25.00 (ISBN 0-8274-1987-2). R West.

--Cicero. 1876. 25.00 (ISBN 0-8274-2061-7). R West.

--La Fontaine & Other French Fabulists. 1973. Repr. of 1882 ed. 25.00 (ISBN 0-8274-1792-6). R West.

--Lucian. 180p. 1981. Repr. lib. bdg. 30.00 (ISBN 0-89987-113-5). Darby Bks.

--Lucian. 1877. Repr. 25.00 (ISBN 0-8274-3005-1). R West.

--Montagne. 192p. 1982. Repr. of 1879 ed. lib. bdg. 25.00 (ISBN 0-89760-166-1). Telegraph Bks.

--Montaigne. 1979. Repr. of 1879 ed. lib. bdg. 20.00 (ISBN 0-8495-0930-0). Arden Lib.

--Montaigne. 1973. Repr. of 1879 ed. 25.00 (ISBN 0-8274-1781-0). R West.

--Virgil. 1877. Repr. 25.00 (ISBN 0-8274-3674-2). R West.

Collins, W. P., ed. Alternative Immunoassays. 1985. 44.95 (ISBN 0-471-90669-7). Wiley.

Collins, Wilkie. Armadale. LC 76-23984. (Illus.). 597p. 1977. pap. 7.95 (ISBN 0-486-23429-0). Dover.

--Armadale, 2 vols. LC 70-107168. (Illus.). 1972. Repr. of 1866 ed. Set. 69.00x (ISBN 0-403-00433-0). Scholarly.

--Basil. 352p. 1980. pap. 5.95 (ISBN 0-486-24015-0). Dover.

--The Dead Secret. LC 78-74113. (Illus.). 384p. 1979. pap. 5.00 (ISBN 0-486-23775-3). Dover.

--The Haunted Hotel. (Mystery Ser.). 127p. 1982. pap. 3.00 (ISBN 0-486-24333-8). Dover.

--Hide & Seek: Or, the Mystery of Mary Grice. 1983. 12.75 (ISBN 0-8446-5952-5). Peter Smith.

--Hide & Seek: The Mystery of Mary Grice. (Illus.). 384p. 1982. pap. 5.95 (ISBN 0-486-24211-0). Dover.

--Little Novels. LC 77-74566. 1978. pap. 5.95 (ISBN 0-486-23506-8). Dover.

--Mad Monkton & Other Stories. Repr. lib. bdg. 12.95x (ISBN 0-89190-247-3, Pub. by River City Pr). Amereon Ltd.

--Man & Wife. (Illus.). 239p. 1983. pap. 5.95 (ISBN 0-486-24451-2). Dover.

--Miss Bertha & the Yankee & Other Stories. Repr. lib. bdg. 11.95 (ISBN 0-89190-248-1, Pub. by River City Pr). Amereon Ltd.

--The Moonstone. 1976. Repr. of 1868 ed. lib. bdg. 24.95 (ISBN 0-89190-241-4, Pub. by River City Pr). Amereon Ltd.

--The Moonstone. 1977. 8.95x (ISBN 0-460-00979-6, Evman); pap. 4.50x (ISBN 0-460-01979-1, Evman). Biblio Dist.

--Moonstone. (English Library Ser.). 1966. pap. 3.95 (ISBN 0-14-043014-8). Penguin.

--The Moonstone. Trodd, Anthea, ed. (World's Classics Ser.). 1982. pap. 3.95 (ISBN 0-19-281579-2). Oxford U Pr.

--The Moonstone. 1984. pap. 2.95 (ISBN 0-451-51837-3, Sig Classics). NAL.

--Moonstone: Abridged & Adapted to Grade 2 Reading Level. Laklan, Carli, ed. LC 67-25786. (Pacemaker Classics Ser.). (Illus.). 1967. pap. 4.92 (ISBN 0-8224-9220-2); tchrs' manual free. Pitman Learning.

--No Name. LC 77-92478. (Illus.). 1978. pap. 6.95 (ISBN 0-486-23605-6). Dover.

--Poor Miss Finch: A Novel. LC 77-131672. (Literature Ser.). (Illus.). 454p. 1972. Repr. of 1872 ed. 49.00x (ISBN 0-403-00559-0). Scholarly.

--The Queen of Hearts. LC 75-32740. (Literature of Mystery & Detection Ser.). 1976. Repr. of 1859 ed. 35.50x (ISBN 0-405-07868-4). Ayer Co Pubs.

--Rambles Beyond Railways. 196p. 1982. pap. 7.50 (ISBN 0-907746-05-5, Pub. by A Mott Ltd). Longwood Pub Group.

--A Rogue's Life: From His Birth to His Marriage. 192p. 1985. pap. 4.50 (ISBN 0-486-24947-6). Dover.

--Tales of Terror & the Supernatural. Van Thal, Herbert, ed. & intro. by. LC 75-189974. 305p. (Orig.). 1972. pap. 4.00 (ISBN 0-486-20307-7). Dover.

--Tales of Terror & the Supernatural. Van Thal, Herbert, ed. 11.00 (ISBN 0-8446-4725-X). Peter Smith.

--Woman in White. 1976. Repr. of 1860 ed. lib. bdg. 27.95x (ISBN 0-89190-242-2, Pub. by River City Pr). Amereon Ltd.

--Woman in White. 1982. pap. 4.95x (ISBN 0-460-01464-1, Evman). Biblio Dist.

--The Woman in White. Sucksmith, Harvey, ed. (World's Classics Paperback Ser.). 1981. pap. 3.95 (ISBN 0-19-281534-2). Oxford U Pr.

--The Woman in White. Symons, Julian, ed. (English Library Ser.). 656p. (Orig.). 1975. pap. 3.95 (ISBN 0-14-043096-2). Penguin.

--Works of Wilkie Collins, 30 Vols. Repr. of 1900 ed. Set. 1200.00 (ISBN 0-404-01750-9); 40.00 ea. AMS Pr.

Collins, Wilkie see Bleiler, E. F.

Collins, William. Introduction to Computer Programming with Pascal. 350p. Date not set. pap. text ed. price not set (ISBN 0-02-323780-5). Macmillan.

--The Works of William Collins. Wendorf, Richard & Ryskamp, Charles, eds. (English Texts Ser.). (Illus.). 1979. text ed. 52.00x (ISBN 0-19-812749-9). Oxford U Pr.

Collins, William, jt. auth. see Holstrum, Gary L.

Collins, William A., jt. auth. see Gleim, Irvin N.

Collins, William E., ed. Archbishop Laud Commemoration, 1895. (Bibliography & Reference Ser: No. 257). 1969. Repr. of 1895 ed. 23.50 (ISBN 0-8337-0628-4). B Franklin.

Collins, William W. Memoirs of the Life of William Collins. 720p. 60.00x (ISBN 0-686-45466-9, Pub. by EP Pub England). State Mutual Bk.

--Moonstone. (Classics Ser). (gr. 10 up). pap. 1.95 (ISBN 0-8049-0076-0, CL-76). Airmont.

--The Moonstone. (Regents Illustrated Classics Ser.). 62p. (gr. 7-12). 1982. pap. text ed. 2.75 (ISBN 0-88345-474-2, 20420). Regents Pub.

--The Woman in White. 624p. 1985. pap. 3.50 (ISBN 0-553-21186-2). Bantam.

Collins, Zipporah W. & Wood, Linda J. Basic PersonaL Injury Anatomy. LC 66-63016. 1966. 37.50 (ISBN 0-88124-002-8, TO-30540). Cal Cont Ed Bar.

Collins-Cheek, Martha & Cheek, Earl H., Jr. Diagnostic-Prescriptive Reading Instruction: A Guide for Classroom Teachers. 2nd ed. 496p. 1984. pap. text ed. write for info. (ISBN 0-697-00086-9); instr's. manual avail. (ISBN 0-697-06072-1). Wm C Brown.

Collins-Fantozzi, Lynn, jt. auth. see Bluestein, Jane E.

Collinson, A. S. Introduction to World Vegetation. 1977. pap. text ed. 10.95 (ISBN 0-04-581013-3). Allen Unwin.

Collinson, D. W., ed. Methods in Rock Magnetism & Palaeomagnetism: Techniques & Instrumentation. (Illus.). 528p. 1983. 79.95 (ISBN 0-412-22980-3, NO. 6752, Chapman & Hall). Methuen Inc.

Collinson, Francis. The Traditional & National Music of Scotland. (Illus.). 1972. Repr. of 1966 ed. 25.00 (ISBN 0-7100-1213-6). Routledge & Kegan.

Collinson, Francis, jt. ed. see Campbell, John L.

Collinson, J D. & Thompson, D B. Sedimentary Structuress. (Illus.). 240p. 1982. text ed. 40.00x (ISBN 0-04-552017-8); pap. text ed. 17.95x (ISBN 0-04-552018-6). Allen Unwin.

Collinson, J. D. & Lewin, J., eds. Modern & Ancient Fluvial Systems. (Illus.). 584p. 1983. pap. text ed. 56.00x (ISBN 0-632-00997-7). Blackwell Pubns.

Collinson, John. The History & Antiquities of the County of Somerset. 2001p. 1983. text ed. 168.50x (ISBN 0-86299-003-3, Pub. by Alan Sutton England). Humanities.

Collinson, M. P. Farm Management in Peasant Agriculture. (Encore Edition Ser.). 470p. 1983. softcover 31.50X (ISBN 0-86531-558-2). Westview.

Collinson, Patrick. Archbishop Grindal, 1519-1589: The Struggle for a Reformed Church in England. LC 78-65474. 1979. 46.00x (ISBN 0-520-03831-2). U of Cal Pr.

--The Elizabethan Puritan Movement. (Library Reprints Ser.). 528p. 1982. 55.00x (ISBN 0-416-34000-8, NO. 3701). Methuen Inc.

--Godly People: Essays on English Protestantism & Puritanism. (No. 23). 634p. 1983. 40.00 (ISBN 0-907628-15-X). Hambledon Press.

--The Religion of Protestants: The Church in English Society 1559-1625. 1982. pap. 14.95x (ISBN 0-19-820053-6). Oxford U Pr.

Collinson, Richard. Journal of H.M.S. Enterprise on the Expedition in Search of Sir John Franklin's Ships by Behring Strait: 1850-55. LC 74-5830. 1976. Repr. of 1889 ed. 37.50 (ISBN 0-404-11636-1). AMS Pr.

Collinson, Richard, ed. see Best, George.

Collinson, William E. & Morris, A. V. Indication: A Study of Demonstratives, Articles & Other Indicators. (LM Ser.). 1937. pap. 16.00 (ISBN 0-527-00821-4). Kraus Repr.

Collip, Bruce G. Buoyancy, Stability & Trim. (Rotary Drilling Ser.: Unit V, Lesson 3). (Illus.). 30p. (Orig.). 1976. pap. text ed. 4.50 (ISBN 0-88698-071-2, 2.50310). PETEX.

Collipp, Platon J. & Castro-Magana, Mariano. Pediatric & Adolescent Endocrinology Case Studies. (Case Studies). 1983. pap. text ed. 35.00 (ISBN 0-87488-054-8). Med Exam.

Collipp, Platon J., ed. Childhood Obesity. 2nd ed. LC 79-16052. (Illus.). 448p. 1980. 33.50 (ISBN 0-88416-221-4). PSG Pub Co.

Collis, Edgar L. & Greenwood, Major. The Health of the Industrial Worker. Stein, Leon, ed. LC 77-70489. (Work Ser.). (Illus.). 1977. Repr. of 1921 ed. lib. bdg. 38.50x (ISBN 0-405-10161-9). Ayer Co Pubs.

Collis, Eirene, tr. see Sand, George.

Collis, Harry. Colloquial English. (Illus.). 96p. (gr. 9-12). 1981. pap. text ed. 4.25 (ISBN 0-88345-428-9, 18197). Regents Pub.

Collis, J., tr. from Ger. Cinderella. (Illus.). 23p. (gr. 2-3). 1978. 10.95 (ISBN 0-85440-332-9, Pub. by Steinerbooks). Anthroposophic.

Collis, J. S. Shaw. 1925. Repr. 20.00 (ISBN 0-8274-3387-5). R West.

Collis, Johanna, tr. see Grosse, Rudolf.

Collis, John. The European Iron Age. (Illus.). 256p. 1984. 26.50 (ISBN 0-8052-3941-3). Schocken.

Collis, John S. Living with a Stranger: A Discourse on the Human Body. LC 78-21307. 1979. 8.95 (ISBN 0-8076-0912-9); pap. 4.95 (ISBN 0-8076-0968-4). Braziller.

--The Vision of Glory: The Extraordinary Nature of the Ordinary. new ed. LC 73-79347. 272p. 1973. 8.95 (ISBN 0-8076-0697-9). Braziller.

--Worm Forgives the Plough. LC 73-92678. (Illus.). 160p. 1975. 7.95 (ISBN 0-8076-0745-2). Braziller.

Collis, John S., jt. ed. see Watkins, Robert G.

Collis, John S., Jr. Lumbar Discography. (Illus.). 192p. 1963. photocopy ed. 22.75x (ISBN 0-398-00336-X). C C Thomas.

Collis, Joyce. All about the Bearded Collie. (Illus.). 144p. 1981. 12.95 (ISBN 0-7207-1128-2, Pub. by Michael Joseph). Merrimack Pub Cir.

--All about the Bearded Collie. (Illus.). 144p. 1985. 15.95 (ISBN 0-7207-1615-2, Pub. by Michael Joseph). Merrimack Pub Cir.

Collis, Kevin, jt. auth. see Biggs, John B.

Collis, Kevin F. Language Development & Intellectual Functioning. (APEID Occasional Papers: No. 10). 20p. 1983. pap. 5.00 (ISBN 0-686-44024-2, UB125, UB). Unipub.

Collis, L., jt. auth. see Fookes, P. J.

Collis, Louise. Memoirs of a Medieval Woman. LC 82-48226. (Illus.). 288p. 1983. pap. 6.68i (ISBN 0-06-090992-7, CN 992, CN). Har-Row.

Collis, Maurice. Cortez & Montezuma. 1978. pap. 3.95 (ISBN 0-380-40402-8, 60178-8, Discus). Avon.

--First Holy One. LC 70-110819. Repr. of 1948 ed. lib. bdg. 15.75x (ISBN 0-8371-3222-3, COFH). Greenwood.

--Foreign Mud Anglo-Chinese Opium War. (Illus.). 312p. 1980. pap. 10.00 (ISBN 9-971-99010-5, Pub. by Graham Brash Singapore). Three Continents.

--Great Within. facs. ed. LC 72-128876. (Select Bibliographies Reprint Ser). 1941. 23.50 (ISBN 0-8369-5496-3). Ayer Co Pubs.

--The Land of the Great Image. 256p. (Orig.). 1985. pap. 9.95 (ISBN 0-8112-0972-5, NDP612). New Directions.

--Lords of the Sunset: A Tour in the Shan States. LC 77-87074. Repr. of 1938 ed. 26.50 (ISBN 0-404-16807-8). AMS Pr.

--Raffles. 216p. 1982. pap. 10.00 (ISBN 0-317-07091-6, Pub. by Graham Brash Singapore). Three Continents.

--Trials in Burma. LC 74-179181. Repr. 16.00 (ISBN 0-404-54812-1). AMS Pr.

Collision, Robert L., ed. see Grant, Eric G.

Collison, Beth, jt. ed. see Harris, Diana.

Collison, David. Stage Sound. 2nd, rev. ed. (Illus.). 192p. 1982. 20.00x (ISBN 0-304-30987-7). Drama Bk.

Collison, Kathleen & Webb, Warren. Forty-Eight Hours More or Less: A Retreat Resource. 111p. (Orig.). pap. 11.00 (ISBN 0-941988-03-1). K Q Assocs.

Collison, Kathleen, jt. auth. see Brockmeyer, Lloyd.

Collison, Mary, jt. auth. see Collison, Robert.

Collison, Mary, jt. auth. see Collison, Robert L.

Collison, Mike, jt. ed. see Carlen, Pat.

Collison, R. L. Dictionaries of English & Foreign Languages. 2nd ed. 1971. 20.50x (ISBN 0-02-843110-3). Hafner.

--A History of Foreign-Language Dictionaries. (Language Library). 214p. 1982. pap. 24.95x (ISBN 0-233-97310-9). Basil Blackwell.

Collison, Robert. A History of Foreign-Language Dictionaries. 216p. 1982. 75.00x (ISBN 0-233-97310-9, Pub. by A Deutsch England). State Mutual Bk.

Collison, Robert & Collison, Mary. Dictionary of Foreign Quotations. LC 81-22090. 416p. 1982. pap. 11.95 (ISBN 0-89696-158-3, An Everest House Book). Dodd.

--Dictionary of Foreign Quotations. 416p. 1980. 29.95 (ISBN 0-87196-428-7). Facts on File.

Collison, Robert, ed. A Bibliography of English Dictionaries. LC 82-48974. 1986. lib. bdg. price not set (ISBN 0-527-18676-7). Kraus Intl.

Collison, Robert L. Kenya. (World Bibliographical Ser.: No. 25). 157p. 1982. lib. bdg. 25.25 (ISBN 0-903450-34-8). ABC-Clio.

--Library Assistance to Readers. rev. 4th ed. LC 75-141261. (Illus.). 139p. 1972. Repr. of 1963 ed. lib. bdg. 15.00x (ISBN 0-8371-5858-3, COLA). Greenwood.

--Library Assistance to Readers. 1963. 4.75 (ISBN 0-8022-0284-5). Philos Lib.

--Uganda. (World Bibliographical Ser.: No. 11). 159p. 1981. lib. bdg. 25.20 (ISBN 0-903450-17-8). ABC-Clio.

Collison, Robert L. & Collison, Mary. Dictionary of Foreign Quotations. LC 81-124080. pap. 103.80 (ISBN 0-317-20687-7, 2025151). Bks Demand UMI.

Collison, Robert L., ed. Dictionary of Dates. LC 77-95116. Repr. of 1961 ed. lib. bdg. 23.00x (ISBN 0-8371-2495-6, CODD). Greenwood.

Collison, Robert L., ed. see Clogg, Mary Jo & Clogg, Richard.

Collison, Robert L., ed. see Findlay, Allan M., et al.

Collison, Robert L., ed. see Pollak, Oliver & Pollak, Karen.

Collison, Robert L., ed. see Tee, Lim H.

Collison-Macy, Lacy. Giuseppe Baretti: With an Account of His Literary Friendships & Feuds in Italy & in England in the Days of Dr. Johnson. 1909. Repr. 30.00 (ISBN 0-8274-2412-4). R West.

Collison-Morley, Lacy. Shakespeare in Italy. LC 67-23862. Repr. of 1916 ed. 16.00 (ISBN 0-405-08373-4, Blom Pubns). Ayer Co Pubs.

--Shakespeare in Italy. 1973. Repr. of 1916 ed. 9.50 (ISBN 0-8274-1759-4). R West.

Collister, Edward A., jt. auth. see Harrison, Alice W.

Collister, H. The Sulivans & the Slave Trade. Rex Collings Ltd., ed. 49.00x (ISBN 0-86036-121-7, Pub. by R Collings UK). State Mutual Bk.

Collister, Peter. The Sulivans & the Slave Trade. (Illus.). 199p. 1980. 14.95x (ISBN 0-8476-3611-9). Rowman.

Collitz, K. H. Verbs of Motion in Their Semantic Divergence. (LM Ser.). 1931. pap. 16.00 (ISBN 0-527-00812-5). Kraus Repr.

Colliver, David J. Compound Semiconductor Technology. LC 75-31377. 1976. pap. 20.00 (ISBN 0-89006-052-5). Artech Hse.

Collman, Charles A. Our Mysterious Panics, 1830-1930: A Story of Events & the Men Involved. LC 68-28621. 1968. Repr. of 1931 ed. lib. bdg. 22.50x (ISBN 0-8371-0050-X, COMP). Greenwood.

Collman, Ed, jt. auth. see Brown, Robert L.

Collman, Herbert L., ed. see Roxburghe Club.

Collman, James P. & Hegedus, Louis S. Principles & Applications of Organotransition Metal Chemistry. LC 79-57228. 715p. 1980. 30.00 (ISBN 0-935702-03-2). Univ Sci Bks.

Collman, Russ, ed. see Crouter, George.

Collman, Russ, ed. see Jones, Robert C.

Collman, Russ, ed. see Shoemaker, Len.

Collman, Russell, jt. auth. see McCoy, Dell.

Collmann, Robin D. The Psychogalvanic Reactions of Exceptional & Normal School Children. LC 79-176664. (Columbia University. Teachers College. Contributions to Education: No. 469). Repr. of 1931 ed. 22.50 (ISBN 0-404-55469-5). AMS Pr.

Collmer, Candace W. see Hetherington, E. Mavis.

Collmer, H., ed. see Huygens, L., et al.

Collmer, Robert G. & Herring, Jack W., eds. American Bypaths: Essays in Honor of E. Hudson Long. LC 80-82061. 250p. 1980. 19.50 (ISBN 0-918954-22-3). Baylor Univ Pr.

Collmore, Ben & Collmore, Sarah. Nutrition & Your Body. 1981. pap. 18.95x (ISBN 0-317-07274-9, Regent House). B of A.

Collmore, Sarah, jt. auth. see Collmore, Ben.

Collocott, E. E. V. Tales & Poems of Tonga. (BMB Ser.: No. 46). Repr. of 1928 ed. 22.00 (ISBN 0-527-02152-0). Kraus Repr.

Collocott, T. C., ed. Chambers Biographical Dictionary, 2 vols. rev. ed. 1974. pap. 7.95 set (ISBN 0-8226-0498-1). Littlefield.

--Chambers' English Dictionary. (Quality Paperback Ser.: No. 166). 380p. 1965. pap. 2.95 (ISBN 0-8226-0166-4). Littlefield.

Collocott, T. C., et al, eds. Chambers Diccionario Cientifico y Tecnologico-Technical Dictionary with Reverse Indices: Spanish-English-French-German, 2 vols. 3rd ed. 1979. Set. 165.00x (ISBN 84-282-0531-0). Adlers Foreign Bks.

Collodi. Pinocchio. (Easy Reader, B). pap. 4.25 (ISBN 0-88436-050-4, 55254). EMC.

Collodi, C., pseud. The Adventures of Pinocchio: Tale of a Puppet. Rosenthal, M. L., tr. LC 83-801. (Illus.). 256p. (gr. 3 up). 1983. 17.50 (ISBN 0-688-02267-7). Lothrop.

Collodi, Carla. Pinocchio. 15.95 (ISBN 0-88411-249-7, Pub. by Aeonian Pr). Amereon Ltd.

Collodi, Carlo. Adventures of Pinocchio. (Classics Ser). (Illus.). (gr. 4 up). pap. 1.25 (ISBN 0-8049-0101-5, CL-101). Airmont.

--Adventures of Pinocchio. (Illus.). (gr. 4-6). 1982. pap. 5.95 (ISBN 0-448-11001-6, G&D); deluxe ed. 10.95 (ISBN 0-448-06001-9). Putnam Pub Group.

--The Adventures of Pinocchio. (Bambi Classics Ser.). (Illus.). 256p. (Orig.). 1981. pap. 3.95 (ISBN 0-89531-069-4, 0221-48). Sharon Pubns.

--Adventures of Pinocchio. (Illus.). 96p. (gr. 3-6). 1982. 9.95 (ISBN 0-528-82071-0). Rand.

--The Adventures of Pinocchio. (Looking Glass Library). (Illus.). 64p. (gr. k-3). 1983. 6.95 (ISBN 0-394-85910-3); PLB 7.99 (ISBN 0-394-95910-8). Random.

--The Adventures of Pinocchio. 256p. 1984. lib. bdg. 16.95x (ISBN 0-89968-257-X). Lightyear.

--Pinocchio. (Illus., Fr.). (gr. 3-8). 5.95 (ISBN 0-685-11495-3). French & Eur.

--Pinocchio. Harden, E., tr. 1974. pap. 2.95 (ISBN 0-14-030230-1, Puffin). Penguin.

--Pinocchio. Date not set. pap. 2.25 (ISBN 0-14-035037-3). Penguin.

--Pinocchio & the Great Whale. LC 81-16026. (Adventures of Pinocchio Ser.). (Illus.). 32p. (gr. 2-5). 1982. PLB 9.79 (ISBN 0-89375-720-9); pap. text ed. 2.50 (ISBN 0-89375-721-7). Troll Assocs.

--Pinocchio & the Puppet Show. LC 81-16001. (Adventures of Pinocchio Ser.). (Illus.). 32p. (gr. 2-5). 1982. PLB 9.79 (ISBN 0-89375-714-4); pap. text ed. 2.50 (ISBN 0-89375-715-2); avail.cassettes. Troll Assocs.

--Pinocchio Goes to School. LC 81-15312. (Adventures of Pinocchio Ser.). (Illus.). 32p. (gr. 2-5). 1982. PLB 9.79 (ISBN 0-89375-718-7); pap. text ed. 2.50 (ISBN 0-89375-719-5). Troll Assocs.

--Pinocchio Meets the Cat & Fox. LC 81-16427. (Adventures of Pinocchio Ser.). (Illus.). 32p. (gr. 2-5). 1982. PLB 9.79 (ISBN 0-89375-716-0); pap. text ed. 2.50 (ISBN 0-89375-717-9). Troll Assocs.

Collom, Jack. Blue Heron & IBC. 1970. signed 6.00 (ISBN 0-685-78954-3, Pub. by Grosseteste); sewn in wrappers 2.00 (ISBN 0-685-78955-1). Small Pr Dist.

--Moving Windows: Evaluating the Poetry Children Write. 200p. (Orig.). 1985. pap. 9.95 (ISBN 0-915924-55-2). Tchrs & Writers Coll.

Colloms, Brenda. Victorian Country Parsons. LC 77-82027. (Illus.). 284p. 1978. 19.95x (ISBN 0-8032-0981-9). U of Nebr Pr.

--Victorian Visionaries. 272p. 1981. 39.00x (ISBN 0-09-463370-3, Pub. by Constable Pubs). State Mutual Bk.

Colloms, M. High Performance Loudspeakers. 3rd ed. 1985. 29.95 (ISBN 0-470-20107-X). Halsted Pr.

Colloms, Martin. Computer Controlled Testing & Instrumentation: An Introduction to the IEC-625: IEEE-488 Bus. 151p. 1983. 27.95x (ISBN 0-470-27406-9). Halsted Pr.

--High Performance Loudspeakers. 2nd ed. LC 79-21318. 245p. 1979. 29.95x (ISBN 0-470-26875-1). Halsted Pr.

Collon, Dominique. Catalogue of the Western Asiatic Seals in the British Museum: Cylinder Seals II. (Akkadian-Post Akkadian-Ur III Periods). 240p. 1982. 110.00x (ISBN 0-7141-1104-X, Pub. by Brit Mus Pubns England). State Mutual Bk.

Collons, Roger D., ed. see Del Mar, Donald.

Collop, John. Poems of John Collop. Hilberry, Conrad, ed. 240p. 1962. 40.00x (ISBN 0-299-02490-3). U of Wis Pr.

Colloque du Club Jules Gonin, 7th & Assemblee de la Societe Suisse d'ophtalmologie, 63rd, Lausanne, 1970. Secondary Detachment of the Retina: Proceedings. Dufour, R., ed. (Modern Problems in Ophthalmology: Vol. 10). (Illus.). 1972. 68.25 (ISBN 3-8055-1300-3). S Karger.

Colloquim for the History of Romance Studies, Trier 2-4 Okt 1975. In Memoriam Friedrich Diez: Atken De Colloquiums Zur Wissenschaftsgeschichte der Romanistik Actes Du Colloque Sur L'histoire Des Etudes Romanes. Niederehe, Hans-Josef & Haarmann, H., eds. (Studies in the History of Linguistics: No. 9). 1976. text ed. 47.25x (ISBN 0-391-01650-4). Humanities.

Colloquium for Philosophy of Science, Boston, 1966-1969. Boston Studies in the Philosophy of Science: Proceedings, Vol. 5. Cohen, R. S. & Wartofsky, M. W., eds. (Synthese Library: No. 19). 482p. 1969. 42.00 (ISBN 90-277-0015-X, Pub. by Reidel Holland). Kluwer Academic.

Colloquium for the Philosophy of Science, Boston, 1961-1962. Boston Studies in the Philosophy of Science: Proceedings, Vol. 1. Wartofsky, M. W., ed. (Synthese Library: No. 6). 212p. 1963. 24.00 (ISBN 90-277-0021-4, Pub. by Reidel Holland). Kluwer Academic.

Colloquium for the Philosophy of Science, Boston, 1966-68. Boston Studies in the Philosophy of Science: Proceedings, Vol. 4. Cohen, R. S. & Wartofsky, M. W, eds. (Synthese Library: No. 18). 537p. 1969. 45.00 (ISBN 90-277-0014-1, Pub. by Reidel Holland). Kluwer Academic.

Colloquium for the Philosophy of Science, Boston, 1969-1972. Boston Studies in the Philosophy of Science, Vol. 13: Logical & Epistemological Studies in Contemporary Physics, Proceedings. Cohen, R. S. & Wartofsky, M. W., eds. LC 73-83557. (Synthese Library: No.59). 462p. 1974. 53.00 (ISBN 90-277-0391-4); pap. 28.95 (ISBN 90-277-0377-9). Kluwer Academic.

Colloquium for the Philosophy of Sciences, Boston, 1969-72. Boston Studies in the Philosophy of Science, Vol. 14: Methodological & Historical Essays in the Natural & Social Sciences, Proceedings. Cohen, R. S. & Wartofsky, M. W., eds. LC 73-83558. (Synthese Library: No.60). 405p. 1974. 48.50 (ISBN 90-277-0392-2, Pub. by Reidel Holland); pap. 26.00 (ISBN 90-277-0378-7). Kluwer Academic.

Colloquium for the Philosophy of Science, Boston, 1964-1966. Boston Studies in the Philosophy of Science, Vol 3: In Memory of Norwood Russell Hanson. Cohen, R. S. & Wartofsky, M. W., eds. (Synthese Library: No. 14). 489p. 1967. 45.00 (ISBN 90-277-0013-3, Pub. by Reidel Holland). Kluwer Academic.

Colloquium Held at Dijon, June 17-22, 1974, et al. Differential Topology & Geometry: Proceedings. Joubert, G. P. & Moussu, R. P., eds. LC 75-25927. (Lecture Notes in Mathematics: Vol. 484). ix, 287p. 1975. pap. 14.70 (ISBN 0-387-07405-8). Springer-Verlag.

Colloquium in the Philosophy of Science, Salzburg, 1969. Induction, Physics, & Ethics: Proceedings. Weingartner, P. & Zecha, G., eds. LC 78-118137. (Synthese Library: No. 31). 382p. 1970. lib. bdg. 39.50 (ISBN 90-277-0158-X, Pub. by Reidel Holland). Kluwer Academic.

Colloquium, International Union of History & Philosophy of Sciences, Utrecht, 1960. The Concept & the Role of the Model in Mathematics & Natural & Social Sciences: Proceedings. Freudenthal, H., ed. (Synthese Library: No. 3). 194p. 1961. 24.00 (ISBN 90-277-0017-6, Pub. by Reidel Holland). Kluwer Academic.

Colloquium of Linguistics Association of Great Britain, Historical Section, Univ. of London, March 18-20, 1970. Hamito-Semitica: Proceedings. Bynon, James & Bynon, Theodora, eds. LC 74-81134. (Janua Linguarum, Series Practice: No. 200). (Illus.). 518p. (Orig.). 1975. 88.00x (ISBN 0-686-22584-8); pap. 67.50x (ISBN 90-2793-092-9). Mouton.

Colloquium of the Gesellschaft Fuer Biologische Chemie, 26th, Mosbach, Baden, Germany, April 10-12, 1975. Molecular Basis of Motility. Heilmeyer, L., ed. (Illus.). 260p. 1976. 40.00 (ISBN 0-387-07576-3). Springer-Verlag.

Colloquium of the Workshop for Biological Chemistry, April 29 - May 1, 1976, Mosbach-Baden. The Immune System: Proceedings. Melchers, F., ed. (Illus.). 1976. 49.00 (ISBN 0-387-07976-9). Springer-Verlag.

Colloquium on Complex Analysis, Joensuu, Finland, August 24-27, 1978. Complex Analysis: Proceedings. Laine, I., et al, eds. (Lecture Notes in Mathematics: Vol. 747). 1979. pap. 26.00 (ISBN 0-387-09553-5). Springer-Verlag.

Colloquium on Computer Assisted Mass Appraisal Potential for Commercial & Industrial Real Property. Proceedings. (Lincoln Institute Monograph: 77-10). (Orig.). 1978. pap. text ed. 9.00 (ISBN 0-686-25525-9). Lincoln Inst Land.

Colloquium on Electronic Transition Lasers, 4th, Munich, June 20-22, 1977. High-Power Lasers & Applications: Proceedings. Kompa, K. L. & Walter, H., eds. (Springer Series in Optical Sciences: Vol. 9). (Illus.). 1979. 37.00 (ISBN 0-387-08641-2). Springer-Verlag.

Colloquium on Mathematical Analysis, Jyvaskyla, 1970, et al. Topics in Analysis: Proceedings. Louhivaara, I. S., et al, eds. LC 74-20555. (Lecture Notes in Mathematics Ser.: Vol. 419). xiii, 392p. 1974. pap. 23.00 (ISBN 0-387-06965-8). Springer-Verlag.

Colloquium on Mathematics & Cybernetics in the Economy, Berlin, 1964. Pseudo-Boolean Programming & Applications. Ivanescu, P. L., ed. (Lecture Notes in Mathematics: Vol. 9). 1965. pap. 10.70 (ISBN 0-387-03352-1). Springer-Verlag.

Colloquium on Methods of Optimization, Novosibirsk USSR, 1968. Proceedings. Moiseev, N. N., ed. LC 77-106194. (Lecture Notes in Mathematics: Vol. 112). (Eng. & Fr.). 1970. pap. 14.70 (ISBN 0-387-04901-0). Springer-Verlag.

Colloquium on Myth in Literature, Bucknell & Susquehanna Universities, Mar. 21-2, 1974. The Binding of Proteus, Perspectives on Myth & the Literary Process: Proceedings. McCune, Marjorie W. & Orbison, T. Tucker, eds. LC 76-49774. 352p. 1978. 28.50 (ISBN 0-8387-1708-X). Bucknell U Pr.

Colloquium on Protides of the Biological Fluids, 27th, Brussels, Apr. 30-May 3, 1979. Protides of the Biological Fluids: Proceedings. Peeters, H., ed. LC 58-5908. (Illus.). 895p. 1980. 165.00 (ISBN 0-08-024933-7). Pergamon.

Colloquium on the Law of Outer Space -International Institute of Space Law of the International Astronautical Federation, 12th, 1969. Proceedings. Schwartz, Mortimer D., ed. iii, 336p. (Orig.). 1970. pap. text ed. 27.50x (ISBN 0-8377-0407-3). Rothman.

Colloquium on the Law of Outer Space - International Institute of Space Law of the International Astronautical Federation, 9th, 1966. Proceedings. Schwartz, Mortimer D., ed. 221p. 1967. pap. text ed. 27.50x (ISBN 0-8377-0403-0). Rothman.

Colloquium on the Law of Outer Space - International Institute of Space Law of the International Astronautical Federation, 10th, 1967. Proceedings. Schwartz, Mortimer D., ed. 279p. 1968. pap. text ed. 27.50x (ISBN 0-8377-0405-7). Rothman.

Colloquium on the Law of Outer Space--International Institute of Space Law of the International Astronautical Federation, 11th, 1968. Proceedings. Schwartz, Mortimer D., ed. iii, 394p. (Orig.). 1969. pap. text ed. 27.50x (ISBN 0-8377-0406-5). Rothman.

Colloquium on the Law of Outer Space-International Institute of Space Law of the International Astronautical Federation, 13th, 1970. Proceedings. Schwartz, Mortimer D., ed. iii, 381p. 1971. pap. text ed. 27.50x (ISBN 0-8377-0408-1). Rothman.

Colloquium on the Law of Outer Space-International Institute of Space Law of the International Astronautical Federation, 14th, 1971. Proceedings. Schwartz, Mortimer D., ed. iv, 298p. 1972. pap. text ed. 27.50x (ISBN 0-8377-0409-X). Rothman.

Colloquium on the Law of Outer Space - International Institute of Space Law of the International Astronautical Federation 15th, 1972. Proceedings. Schwartz, Mortimer, ed. iv, 284p. 1973. pap. text ed. 27.50x (ISBN 0-8377-0410-3). Rothman.

Colloquium on the Law of Outer Space - International Institute of Space Law of the International Astronautical Federation, 16th, 1973. Proceedings. Schwartz, Mortimer, ed. vi, 408p. 1974. pap. text ed. 27.50x (ISBN 0-8377-0411-1). Rothman.

Colloquium on the Law of Outer Space - International Institute of Space Law of the International Astronautical Federation, 20th, 1977. Proceedings. Schwartz, Mortimer D., ed. v, 524p. 1978. pap. text ed. 32.50x (ISBN 0-8377-0439-1). Rothman.

Colloquium on the Law of Outer Space - International Institute of Space Law of the International Astronautical Federation, 21st, 1978. Proceedings. Schwartz, Mortimer D., ed. v, 291p. 1979. pap. text ed. 32.50x (ISBN 0-8377-0440-5). Rothman.

Colloquium on the Law of Outer Space - International Institute of the Space Law of the International Astronautical Federation, 18th, 1975. Proceedings. Schwartz, Mortimer D., ed. v, 201p. 1976. pap. text ed. 27.50x (ISBN 0-8377-0413-8). Rothman.

Colloquium on the Law of Outer Space - International Institute of Space Law of the International Astronautical Federation, 19th, 1976. Proceedings. Schwartz, Mortimer D., ed. 419p. 1977. pap. text ed. 27.50x (ISBN 0-8377-0414-6). Rothman.

Colloquium on the Law of Outer Space-International Institute of Space Law of the International Astronautical Federation, 17th, 1974. Proceedings. Schwartz, Mortimer D., ed. vi, 401p. 1975. pap. text ed. 27.50x (ISBN 0-8377-0412-X). Rothman.

Colloquium Spectroscopicum Internationale. Atomic Spectroscopy: XXI Colloquium Spectroscopicum Internationale, 8th International Conferenceon Atomic Spectroscopy, Cambridge, July 1-6, 1979: Keynote Lectures. LC 81-197242. pap. 71.30 (ISBN 0-317-29347-8, 2024000). Bks Demand UMI.

Collord, Marjorie, jt. auth. see Miller, Ann.

Collot, Georges H. Journey in North America, 3 Vols. LC 72-1001. Repr. of 1924 ed. Set. 295.00 (ISBN 0-404-01790-8). AMS Pr.

Collotti-Pischel, Enrica & Robertazzi, Chiara. L' Internationale Communiste et les Problemes Coloniaux, 1919-1935. (Materiaux Pour L'histoire Du Socialisme International, Essais Bibliographiques: No. 2). 1968. pap. 40.00x (ISBN 90-2796-149-2). Mouton.

Colls, Robert. The Collier's Rant: Folk-Song & Culture in the Industrial Village. 216p. 1977. 15.00x (ISBN 0-87471-941-0). Rowman.

Colls, Robert, jt. ed. see Dodd, Philip.

Collu, R., et al, eds. Brain Neurotransmitters & Hormones. 428p. 1982. text ed. 66.00 (ISBN 0-89004-763-4). Raven.

Collu, Robert, et al, eds. Central Nervous System Effects of Hypothalamic Hormones & Other Peptides. LC 77-94310. 453p. 1979. text ed. 59.00 (ISBN 0-89004-347-7). Raven.

--Pediatric Endocrinology. (Comprehensive Endocrinology Ser.). 660p. 1981. text ed. 86.00 (ISBN 0-89004-543-7). Raven.

Collum, V. C., tr. see Morgan, Jacques J.

Colluthus see Oppian.

Collver, Donald L. Scientific Blackjack & Complete Casino Guide. LC 66-23116. (Illus.). 1967. pap. 1.95 (ISBN 0-668-02420-8). Arco.

Collver, O. Andrew. Birth Rates in Latin America: New Estimates of Historical Trends & Fluctuations. (Research Ser.: No. 7). 1965. pap. 2.50x (ISBN 0-87725-107-X). U of Cal Intl St.

Coll Y Cuchi, Cayetano. Historias Que Parecen Cuentos. (UPREX, Ensayo Ser.: No. 11). pap. 1.85 (ISBN 0-8477-0011-9). U of PR Pr.

Collyear, John. Management Precepts. 1975. 90.95x (ISBN 0-903763-14-1, Pub. by MCB Pubns). State Mutual Bk.

--The Practice of First Level Management. 1976. 90.00x (ISBN 0-903763-55-9, Pub. by MCB Pubns). State Mutual Bk.

Collyer, David. Fly Dressing Two. LC 81-50000. (Illus.). 224p. 1981. 29.95 (ISBN 0-7153-8145-8). David & Charles.

Collyer, David J. Fly-Dressing. LC 74-20454. (Illus.). 240p. 1975. 25.00 (ISBN 0-7153-6719-6). David & Charles.

Collyer, Mary. Virtuous Orphan; or, the Life of Marianne, Countess of ---, 4 vols. Paulson, Ronald, ed. LC 78-60843. (Novel 1720-1805 Ser.). 1979. lib. bdg. 150.00 (ISBN 0-8240-3652-2). Garland Pub.

Collyer, Moses W., jt. auth. see Verplanck, William.

Collyns, Charles. Alternatives to the Central Bank in the Developing World. (Occasional Papers: No. 20). 23p. 1983. pap. 5.00 (ISBN 0-317-04017-0). Intl Monetary.

Colm, G. & Lehmann, F. Economic Consequences of Recent American Tax Policy. (Social Research Supplement: No. 1). 1938. pap. 10.00 (ISBN 0-527-00861-3). Kraus Repr.

Colm, Hanna. The Existentialist Approach to Psychotherapy with Adults & Children. (Illus.). 240p. 1966. 37.00 (ISBN 0-8089-0102-8, 790882). Grune.

Colm, Luibheid, tr. from Egyptian. John Cassian: Conferences. 04/1985 ed. 12.95 (ISBN 0-317-18083-5); pap. 9.95 (ISBN 0-317-18084-3). Paulist Pr.

Colman. Triangle of Love. Date not set. pap. 2.25 (ISBN 0-671-49631-X). Archway.

Colman, A. Game Theory & Experimental Games: The Study of Strategic Interaction. (International Series in Experimental Social Psychology: Vol. 4). 300p. 1982. 42.00 (ISBN 0-08-026070-5); pap. 17.95 (ISBN 0-08-026069-1). Pergamon.

Colman, Andrew. Cooperation & Competition in Humans & Animals. 1982. 35.75 (ISBN 0-442-30521-4). Van Nos Reinhold.

Colman, Arthur & Colman, Libby. Earth Father-Sky Father: The Changing Concept of Fathering. (Illus.). 206p. 1981. 12.95 (ISBN 0-13-223032-1, Spec); pap. 5.95 (ISBN 0-13-223024-0). P-H.

Colman, B. H. & Pfaltz, C. R., eds. Modern Perspectives in Otology. (Advances in Oto-Rhino-Laryngology: Vol. 31). (Illus.). xii, 252p. 1983. 84.25 (ISBN 3-8055-3641-0). S Karger.

Colman, Barry S. Sex & the Single Christian. 1982. pap. write for info. (ISBN 0-937762-02-4). Dark Horse.

Colman, Bernard H., jt. auth. see Hall, Ian S.

Colman, Carol. Love & Money. 400p. 1984. pap. 3.95 (ISBN 0-8217-1412-0). Zebra.

Colman, Carol & Perelman, Michael. Late Bloomers: How to Achieve Your Potential at Any Age. 224p. 1985. 15.95 (ISBN 0-02-527320-5). Macmillan.

Colman, Cathy. Robert Glenn Ketchum. 32p. (Orig.). 1983. art catalogue 10.00 (ISBN 0-9610972-0-5). PWBBA Prod.

Colman, David & Nixson, Frederick. Economics of Change in Less Developed Countries. 2nd ed. LC 84-24361. 320p. 1985. 31.50x (ISBN 0-389-20548-6, 08109); pap. 19.75x (ISBN 0-389-20550-8, 08110). B&N Imports.

Colman, E. A., ed. King Lear. (The Challis Shakespeare Ser). 1981. pap. 9.00x (ISBN 0-424-00082-2, Pub. by Sydney U Pr Australia). Intl Spec Bk.

Colman, George. Broad Grins: Comprising, with New Additional Tales in Verse, Those Formerly Published Under the Title of "My Nightgown & Slippers", Repr. Of 1802 Ed. Bd. with Eccentricities for Edinburgh. Repr. of 1816 ed. LC 75-31180. (Romantic Context: Poetry 1789-1830 Ser.: Vol. 33). 1977. lib. bdg. 57.00 (ISBN 0-8240-2132-0). Garland Pub.

--New Brooms! & the Manager in Distress. LC 80-14205. 35.00x (ISBN 0-8201-1353-0). Schol Facsimiles.

--Poetical Vagaries, Repr. Of 1812 Ed. Bd. with Vagaries Vindicated: Or, Hypocritick Hypocriticks: a Poem Addressed to the Reviewers. Repr. of 1813 ed. LC 75-31182. (Romantic Context: Poetry 1789-1830 Ser.: Vol. 34). 1976. lib. bdg. 52.00 (ISBN 0-8240-2133-9). Garland Pub.

Colman, George & Morton, Thomas. Plays by George Colman the Younger & Thomas Morton: Inkle & Yarico; The Surrender of Calis; The Children in the Wood, Blue Beard & Speed the Plough. Sutcliffe, Barry, ed. LC 83-5156. (British & American Playwrights Ser.: 1750-1920). (Illus.). 246p. 1983. 47.50 (ISBN 0-521-24019-0); pap. 14.95 (ISBN 0-521-28400-7). Cambridge U Pr.

Colman, George, jt. auth. see Garrick, David.

Colman, George the Younger. The Plays of George Colman, the Younger. Tasch, Peter A., ed. (Eighteenth Century English Drama Ser.). 1981. lib. bdg. 145.00 (ISBN 0-8240-3585-2). Garland Pub.

Colman, Henry, ed. Divine Meditations (Sixteen Forty) 1979. 27.50x (ISBN 0-300-02305-7). Yale U Pr.

Colman, Hila. Accident. (gr. 7-9). 1981. pap. 1.95 (ISBN 0-671-46123-0). Archway.

--Accident. LC 80-20509. 160p. (gr. 7-9). 1980. 11.25 (ISBN 0-688-22238-2); PLB 11.88 (ISBN 0-688-32238-7). Morrow.

--Claudia, Where Are You? (gr. 7-9). 1976. pap. 1.95 (ISBN 0-671-42450-5). Archway.

--Confession of a Storyteller. (Orig.). (gr. 6-8). 1984. pap. 1.95 (ISBN 0-671-45659-8). Archway.

--Confession of a Storyteller. 1984. pap. write for info. Archway.

--Diary of a Frantic Kid Sister. (gr. 4-6). 1975. pap. 1.95 (ISBN 0-671-46376-4). Archway.

--Don't Tell Me That You Love Me. (Orig.). (gr. 7 up). 1983. pap. 1.95 (ISBN 0-317-02464-7). Archway.

--Ellie's Inheritance. LC 79-19009. (gr. 7-9). 1979. PLB 10.88 (ISBN 0-688-32204-2). Morrow.

--The Family Trap. 192p. 1982. 10.25 (ISBN 0-688-01472-0). Morrow.

--Family Trap. 1982. write for info. Macmillan.

--A Fragile Love. (gr. 7-10). 1985. pap. 2.25 (ISBN 0-671-55655-X). PB.

--Girl Meets Boy. 144p. (gr. 7 up). 1982. pap. 1.95 (ISBN 0-590-31988-4). Scholastic Inc.

--Just the Two of Us. 176p. (Orig.). (gr. 7 up). 1984. pap. 2.25 (ISBN 0-590-32512-4, Point). Scholastic Inc.

--My Friend, My Love. (gr. 12 up). 1983. write for info. Archway.

--Nobody Has to Be a Kid Forever. (gr. 5-7). 1977. pap. 1.95 (ISBN 0-671-46122-2). Archway.

--Nobody Told Me What I Need to Know. 176p. (gr. 7 up). 1984. 10.25 (ISBN 0-688-03869-7, Morrow Junior Books). Morrow.

--Not for Love. LC 83-6120. 192p. (gr. 5 up). 1984. PLB 10.25 (ISBN 0-688-02419-X). Morrow.

--Not for Love. 160p. 1984. pap. 2.25 (ISBN 0-449-70100-X, Juniper). Fawcett.

--Rachel's Legacy. (gr. 7 up). 1978. PLB 11.88 (ISBN 0-688-32154-2). Morrow.

--The Secret Life of Harold the Bird Watcher. LC 77-11559. (Illus.). (gr. 3-6). 1978. 9.57i (ISBN 0-690-01306-X). Crowell Jr Bks.

--Sometimes I Don't Love My Mother. (gr. 7 up). 1977. 11.25 (ISBN 0-688-22121-1); PLB 11.88 (ISBN 0-688-32121-6). Morrow.

--Sometimes I Don't Love My Mother. (gr. 7 up). 1979. pap. 1.95 (ISBN 0-590-32424-1). Scholastic Inc.

--Tell Me No Lies. (gr. 7-9). 1980. pap. 1.75 (ISBN 0-671-29920-4). Archway.

--That's the Way It Is, Amigo. LC 74-30398. (Illus.). 96p. (gr. 6 up). 1975. 10.10i (ISBN 0-690-00750-7). Crowell Jr Bks.

--Weekend Sisters. LC 85-5665. 192p. (gr. 7 up). 1985. 10.25 (ISBN 0-688-05785-3, Morrow Junior Books). Morrow.

--What's the Matter with the Dobsons. (gr. 5-7). 1982. pap. 1.95 (ISBN 0-671-43143-9). Archway.

Colman, Hila, jt. auth. see Morris, Richard.

Colman, J. Barry, ed. Readings in Church History: From Pentecost to the Protestant Revolt, Vol. 1. pap. 14.95 (ISBN 0-8091-1962-5). Paulist Pr.

Colman, John. John Locke's Moral Philosophy. 282p. 1983. 28.50x (ISBN 0-686-82135-1, Pub. by Edinburgh U Pr Scotland). Columbia U Pr.

Colman, Libby, jt. auth. see Colman, Arthur.

Colman, Louis. Lumber. LC 74-22773. (Labor Movement in Fiction & Non-Fiction Ser.). Repr. of 1931 ed. 22.00 (ISBN 0-404-58413-6). AMS Pr.

Colman, Raphael. The Dynamic Growth of the Thinking Processes in the Child & the Teenager. (Illus.). 1977. 51.50 (ISBN 0-89266-327-8). Am Classical Coll Pr.

--How to Develop the Learning Powers of the Child & of the Teenager. (Illus.). 1977. 49.50 (ISBN 0-89266-086-4). Am Classical Coll Pr.

--Maximal Exercises to Promote Mental Agility & the Power of Dynamic Thinking. (Illus.). 121p. 1983. 69.85x (ISBN 0-89266-428-2). Am Classical Coll Pr.

--Mental Exercises to Develop Thinking Abilities. (Illus.). 220p. 1976. 57.85 (ISBN 0-89266-008-2). Am Classical Coll Pr.

Colman, Robert W., ed. Disorders of Thrombin Formation. (Methods in Hematology: Vol. 7). (Illus.). 161p. 1983. text ed. 40.00 (ISBN 0-443-08184-0). Churchill.

Colman, Robert W. & Hirsh, Jack, eds. Hemostasis & Thrombosis. LC 65-5671. (Illus.). 1248p. 1982. text ed. 125.00x (ISBN 0-397-50435-7, Lippincott Medical). Lippincott.

Colman, Rosalie M. English As a Second Language & the Saladbowl Concept. (TWEC World Education Monograph Ser.). 11p. 1981. 1.50. Thut World Ed Ctr.

Colman, Samuel. Nature's Harmonic Unity: A Treatise on Its Relation to Proportional Form. LC 78-177520. (Illus.). Repr. of 1912 ed. 25.00 (ISBN 0-405-08374-2). Ayer Co Pubs.

Colman, T. S. History of the Parish of Barwick-In-Elmet in the County of York. 1908. 34.00 (ISBN 0-384-09565-8). Johnson Repr.

Colman, William G. Cities, Suburbs & States: Governing & Financing Urban America. LC 75-2810. (Illus.). 1975. 20.95 (ISBN 0-02-906490-2). Free Pr.

Colman, William P. & Coleman, William P. Outpatient Surgery of the Skin. (Advanced Textbk.). 1983. text ed. 49.50 (ISBN 0-87488-185-4). Med Exam.

Colmbaro, Pasqualino, tr. see Ferrarotti, Franco.

Colmer, Francis. Shakespeare in Time of War. LC 76-30691. (Studies in Shakespeare, No. 24). 1977. lib. bdg. 42.95x (ISBN 0-8383-2165-8). Haskell.

Colmer, J., ed. see Coleridge, Samuel T.

Colmer, John. E. M. Forster: The Personal Voice. 256p. 1975. 21.00x (ISBN 0-7100-8209-6). Routledge & Kegan.

--E. M. Forster: The Personal Voice. 1983. pap. 8.95 (ISBN 0-7100-9496-5). Routledge & Kegan.

--Patrick White. 96p. 1984. pap. 4.75 (ISBN 0-416-36790-9, NO. 4066). Methuen Inc.

Colmey, Mary J. Red, Yellow, & Blue. (Second Grade Bk.). (Illus.). (gr. 2-3). PLB 1.88 (ISBN 0-513-00398-3). Denison.

Colmore, Gertrude. Suffragettes: Sally. 320p. (Orig.). 1984. pap. 8.95 (ISBN 0-86358-041-6, Pandora Pr). Routledge & Kegan.

Colnaghi, Maria I., et al, eds. Markers for Diagnosis & Monitoring of Human Cancer. (Serono Symposia Ser.: No. 46). 1982. 45.00 (ISBN 0-12-181520-X). Acad Pr.

Colodner, Solomon. Concepts & Values. LC 68-58503. 140p. 1968. 10.00 (ISBN 0-88400-020-6). Shengold.

Colodny, Robert G., ed. Beyond the Edge of Certainty: Essays in Contemporary Science & Philosophy. LC 83-1162. (CPS Publications in Philosophy of Science Ser.). (Illus.). 298p. 1983. text ed. 26.75 (ISBN 0-8191-3057-5); pap. text ed. 14.00 (ISBN 0-8191-3058-3). U Pr of Amer.

--Frontiers of Science & Philosophy. LC 61-9401. (Philosophy of Science Ser.). 1962. 26.95x (ISBN 0-8229-3100-1). U of Pittsburgh Pr.

--Frontiers of Science & Philosophy. LC 83-1212. (SPS Publications in Philosophy of Science Ser.). (Illus.). 296p. 1983. text ed. 26.75 (ISBN 0-8191-3060-5); pap. text ed. 14.00 (ISBN 0-8191-3061-3). U Pr of Amer.

--Logic, Laws, & Life: Some Philosophical Complications. LC 76-50886. (Philosophy of Science Ser.). 1977. 24.95x (ISBN 0-8229-3346-2). U of Pittsburgh Pr.

--Mind & Cosmos: Essays in Contemporary Science & Philosophy. LC 83-21662. (CPS Publications in Philosophy of Science). (Illus.). 380p. 1984. lib. bdg. 27.25 (ISBN 0-8191-3649-2); pap. text ed. 15.50 (ISBN 0-8191-3650-6). U Pr of Amer.

--Paradigms & Paradoxes: The Philosophical Challenge of the Quantum Domain. LC 79-158189. (Philosophy of Science Ser). 1972. 39.95x (ISBN 0-8229-3235-0). U of Pittsburgh Pr.

Colodny, Robert G., ed. see Nalimov, V. V.

Cologne Symposium, Third, June 16-19, 1976. Brain & Heart Infarct: Proceedings. Zulch, K. J., et al, eds. (Illus.). 1977. 45.00 (ISBN 0-387-08270-0). Springer-Verlag.

Cology, Lorry. Psychology, Study Guide with Practice Tests (by Landy) (Illus.). 288p. 1984. text ed. 9.95 (ISBN 0-13-733544-X). P-H.

Colojoara, I. & Foias, C. Theory of Generalized Spectral Operators. LC 68-24488. (Mathematics & Its Applications Ser.). 248p. 1968. 69.50 (ISBN 0-677-01480-5). Gordon.

Colokathis, Jane. Comprehensive Index to CPL Exchange Bibliographies, No. 1-1565: A Numerical Index. (CPL Bibliographies: No. 3). 89p. 1979. pap. 9.00 (ISBN 0-86602-003-9). CPL Biblios.

--Comprehensive Index to CPL Exchange Bibliographies, No. 1-1565: A Subject Index. (CPL Bibliographies: No. 1). 119p. 1979. pap. 12.00 (ISBN 0-86602-001-2, Z5942). CPL Biblios.

--Comprehensive Index to CPL Exchange Bibliographies, Nos. 1-1565: An Author Index. (CPL Bibliographies: No. 2). 100p. 1979. pap. 10.00 (ISBN 0-86602-002-0). CPL Biblios.

Coloma, Jose M. Leico De Politica. 6th ed. 200p. (Span.). 1976. pap. 8.75 (ISBN 84-7222-752-9, S-50039). French & Eur.

Colomb, A. La Tribu de Wagap (Nouvelle-Caledonie) LC 75-32812. Repr. of 1890 ed. 19.50 (ISBN 0-404-14116-1). AMS Pr.

Colomb, F. R., jt. auth. see Bajada, E.

Colomb, John C. Slave-Catching in the Indian Ocean. LC 72-78367. (Illus.). Repr. of 1873 ed. cancelled (ISBN 0-8371-1339-3). Greenwood.

Colomb, P., et al. The Great War of 189- A Forecast. LC 74-16390. (Science Fiction Ser). (Illus.). 320p. 1975. Repr. of 1893 ed. 20.00x (ISBN 0-685-51336-X). Ayer Co Pubs.

Colombani, Alfredo. L'Opera Italiana Nel Secolo XIX: Dono Agli Abbonati Del Corriere Della Sera. LC 80-2266. Repr. of 1900 ed. 61.00 (ISBN 0-404-18819-2). AMS Pr.

Colombe, Paul D. see De Sainte Colombe, Paul.

Colombe, Sainte. Grapho-Therapeutics. pap. 8.95 (ISBN 0-87516-297-5). Borden.

Colombeau, J. F. Differential Calculus & Holomorphy. (Mathematical Studies: Vol. 64). 456p. 1982. 59.75 (ISBN 0-444-86397-4, North-Holland). Elsevier.

--Elementary Introduction to New Generalized Functions. (Mathematics Studies: Vol. 113). 290p. 1985. 44.50 (ISBN 0-444-87756-8, North Holland). Elsevier.

--New Generalized Functions & Multiplication of Distributions. (Mathematics Studies: No. 84). 376p. 1984. 38.50 (ISBN 0-444-86830-5, North-Holland). Elsevier.

Colombetti, Giuliano & Lenci, Francesco, eds. Membranes & Sensory Transduction. 375p. 1984. 52.50x (ISBN 0-306-41439-2, Plenum Pr). Plenum Pub.

Colombetti, Giuliano, jt. ed. see Lenci, Francesco.

Colombetti, Giuliano, et al, eds. Sensory Perception & Transduction in Aneural Organisms. (NATO ASI Series A, UFE Sciences: Vol. 89). 338p. 1985. 52.50x (ISBN 0-306-42000-7, Plenum Pr). Plenum Pub.

Colombetti, L. Radiotracers in Biology & Medicine, Vol. I. 447p. 1982. write for info. (ISBN 0-8493-6027-7). CRC Pr.

Colombetti, Lelio G. Principles of Radiopharmacology, Vol. III. 352p. 1979. 86.00 (ISBN 0-8493-5467-6). CRC Pr.

Colombetti, Lelio G., ed. Biological Transport of Radiotracers. 344p. 1982. 96.00 (ISBN 0-8493-6017-X). CRC Pr.

Colombia Ministerio De Obras Publicas Y Transporte & Inter-American Development Bank. The Impact of Energy Costs on the Transport Sector in Latin America: Proceedings of a Seminar Held in Bogota, Colombia Between December 1-3, 1983. LC 83-189959. (Illus.). v, 405p. Date not set. price not set. IADB.

Colombiere, Claude De La see Saint-Jure, Jean B. & De La Colombiere, Claude.

Colombo, Attilio. Fantastic Photographs. LC 79-1877. 1979. 17.95 (ISBN 0-394-50733-9); pap. 8.95 (ISBN 0-394-73785-7). Pantheon.

Colombo, Furio. God in America: Religion & Politics in the United States. Jarrat, Kristin, tr. from Ital. LC 84-4278. 208p. 1984. 17.95x (ISBN 0-231-05972-8). Columbia U Pr.

Colombo, Henry J., et al. The New Complete Beagle. 3rd ed. Madden, et al, eds. LC 70-161397. (Complete Breed Book Ser.). (Illus.). 1971. 12.95 (ISBN 0-87605-024-0). Howell Bk.

Colombo, J. P., ed. see Eastham, R. C.

Colombo, J. P., ed. see Richterich, R.

Colombo, Jean-Pierre, jt. ed. see Richterich, R.

Colombo, John R. Colombo's Canadian References. 1976. 35.00x (ISBN 0-19-540253-7). Oxford U Pr.

--Windigo: An Anthology of Fact & Fantastic Fiction. (Illus.). vii, 208p. 1982. 17.95 (ISBN 0-88833-097-9, Pub. by West Prod CN). U of Nebr Pr.

Colombo, Umberto see Hannay, N. Bruce.

Colombo, Umberto, jt. ed. see Parker, Earl R.

Colome, Jaime S., jt. auth. see Cano, Raul J.

Colomer del Castillo, Jordi. Diccionari Ingles-Catala, Catala-Ingles. 3rd ed. 253p. (Eng. & Catalan.). 1978. pap. 8.75 (ISBN 84-7306-091-1, S-50414). French & Eur.

Colon, A. R. Pediatric Hepatology. (Medical Outline Ser.). 1983. pap. text ed. 26.00 (ISBN 0-87488-407-1). Med Exam.

Colon, E., et al, eds. Evoked Potential Manual. 1984. lib. bdg. 52.50 (ISBN 0-89838-614-4, Pub. by Martinus Nijhoff Netherlands). Kluwer Academic.

Colon, Eliseo. Ritmos y Melodias. (Lecturas Faciles). 67p. (Spanish.). 1983. pap. 3.75 (ISBN 0-88345-529-3, 21294). Regents Pub.
Colon, Elizabeth. Community Efforts to Improve Local Schools: Pt. I, A Case Study of District Planning. 21p. (Orig.). 1983. pap. 2.00 (ISBN 0-88156-013-8). Comm Serv Soc NY.
Colon, Fernando. The Life of Admiral Christopher Columbus by His Son Ferdinand. Keen, Benjamin, tr. from Ital. LC 77-27400. (Illus.). 1978. Repr. of 1959 ed. lib. bdg. 28.50x (ISBN 0-313-20175-7, COAC). Greenwood.
Colon, Jesus. A Puerto Rican in New York & Other Sketches. LC 74-14229. (The Puerto Rican Experience Ser). 206p. 1975. Repr. 18.00x (ISBN 0-405-06218-4). Ayer Co Pubs.
--A Puerto Rican in New York & Other Sketches. LC 82-6100. (Illus.). 220p. (Orig.). 1982. pap. 3.75 (ISBN 0-7178-0589-1). Intl Pubs Co.
Colon, Laurent E. Selling by Mail Order, Tips & Techniques: How to Make a Fortune. LC 81-68458. (With All the Secrets of Mail Order Trading). (Illus.). 189p. (Orig.). 1982. 12.95 (ISBN 0-941286-01-0, DIP-7-82-000); pap. 7.95 (ISBN 0-941286-00-2). Dynamic Info.
Colon, Matilde, et al. Antologia de Literatura Hispanica Contemporanea: Espanol 3101-3102, Vol. 2. LC 84-20849. 240p. (Span.). 1984. pap. 5.00 (ISBN 0-8477-3514-1). U of PR Pr.
Colon, Robert, jt. auth. see Tedeschi, Frank P.
Colon Cora, Rafael. The Professor's Attitude & Performance. LC 78-12813. 1979. pap. 6.25 (ISBN 0-8477-2450-6). U of PR Pr.
Colon De Zalduondo, Baltazara. The Growing Puerto Rican Economy: Saving & Consumption Variables. 1976. lib. bdg. 69.95 (ISBN 0-8490-1357-7). Gordon Pr.
Colonell, J. M. & Stockholm, H. K., eds. Port Valdez, Alaska: Environmental Studies, Nineteen Seventy-Six to Nineteen Seventy-Nine. (Occasional Publications Ser.: No. 5). (Illus.). 373p. 1980. 45.00 (ISBN 0-914500-09-0). U of AK Inst Marine.
Colonial Dames Of America - Chapter 1 Baltimore. Ancestral Records & Portraits: A Compilation from the Archives, 2 Vols. LC 68-57950. (Illus.). 835p. 1969. Repr. of 1910 ed. Set. 45.00 (ISBN 0-8063-0078-7). Genealog Pub.
Colonial Society of Massachusetts. Architecture in Colonial Massachusetts. Cummings, Abbot L., ed. 1983. 30.00x (ISBN 0-686-89627-0). U Pr of Va.
--Sibley's Heir: A Volume in Memory of Clifford Kenyon Shipton. Allis, Frederick S., Jr., ed. 1983. 30.00x (ISBN 0-686-89628-9). U Pr of Va.
Colonial Williamsburg Foundation. The Apprentice. (Annual Ser.). (Illus.). 40p. (Orig.). (gr. 5-7). 1984. pap. 2.50 (ISBN 0-87935-103-9). Williamsburg.
Colonial Williamsburg Foundation Staff. Apothecary in Eighteenth-Century Williamsburg. (Williamsburg Craft Ser). (Illus.). 37p. (Orig.). 1965. pap. 1.25 (ISBN 0-910412-16-2). Williamsburg.
--Blacksmith in Eighteenth-Century Williamsburg. (Williamsburg Craft Ser). (Illus.). 30p. (Orig.). 1970. pap. 1.25 (ISBN 0-910412-83-9). Williamsburg.
--Bookbinder in Eighteenth Century Williamsburg. (Williamsburg Craft Ser). (Illus.). 32p. (Orig.). pap. 1.25 (ISBN 0-910412-15-4). Williamsburg.
--Colonial Williamsburg: A Guide for Deaf & Hearing Impaired Visitors. (Illus.). (gr. 7 up). 1983. pap. 1.00 (ISBN 0-87935-070-9). Williamsburg.
--Favorite Meals from Williamsburg: A Menu Cookbook. Sheppard, Donna, ed. (Illus.). 1982. 10.00 (ISBN 0-03-062433-9). HR&W.
--Gardens of Williamsburg. LC 70-140635. (Illus.). 48p. (Orig.). 1970. pap. 4.95 (ISBN 0-910412-89-8). Williamsburg.
--Leatherworker in Eighteenth-Century Williamsburg. (Williamsburg Craft Ser). (Illus.). 36p. (Orig.). 1967. pap. 1.25 (ISBN 0-910412-18-9). Williamsburg.
--Legacy from the Past. LC 73-173788. (Illus.). 78p. (Orig.). 1971. pap. 6.95 (ISBN 0-910412-98-7). Williamsburg.
--Miller in Eighteenth Century Virginia. (Williamsburg Craft Ser). (Illus.). 32p. (Orig.). 1958. pap. 1.25 (ISBN 0-910412-19-7). Williamsburg.
--Printer in Eighteenth Century Williamsburg. (Williamsburg Craft Ser.). (Illus.). 34p. (Orig.). 1955. pap. 1.25 (ISBN 0-910412-20-0). Williamsburg.
--Silversmith in Eighteenth Century Williamsburg. (Williamsburg Craft Ser). (Illus.). 37p. (Orig.). 1956. pap. 1.25 (ISBN 0-910412-21-9). Williamsburg.
--Wigmaker in Eighteenth Century Williamsburg. (Williamsburg Craft Ser). (Illus.). 36p. (Orig.). 1959. pap. 1.25 (ISBN 0-910412-22-7). Williamsburg.
--The Williamsburg Collection of Antique Furnishing. LC 73-86811. 1974. 11.95 (ISBN 0-03-089492-1). HR&W.
--The Williamsburg Collection of Antique Furnishings. LC 73-86811. (Decorative Art Ser). (Illus.). 120p. (Orig.). 1973. pap. 6.95 (ISBN 0-87935-017-2). Williamsburg.
Colonias, John S. Particle Accelerator Design Computer Programs. 1974. 70.50 (ISBN 0-12-181550-1). Acad Pr.
Colonna, Egidio. Li Livres Du gouvernement des rois: A 13th Century French Version of Egidio Colonna's Treatise "De Regimine Principium". Molenaer, Samuel P., ed. LC 99-434. (Columbia University. Studies in Romance Philology & Literature: No. 1). Repr. of 1899 ed. 33.50 (ISBN 0-404-50601-1). AMS Pr.
Colonna, Francesco. Hypnerotomachia: The Strife of Love in a Dreame (1592). Dallington, Robert, tr. from Latin. LC 73-16223. 208p. 1973. Repr. lib. bdg. 40.00x (ISBN 0-8201-1124-4). Schol Facsimiles.
--Hypnerotomachia, the Strife of Love in a Dreame. LC 75-27858. (Renaissance & the Gods Ser.: Vol. 15). (Illus.). 1976. Repr. of 1592 ed. lib. bdg. 88.00 (ISBN 0-8240-2064-2). Garland Pub.
--Hypnerotomachia: The Strife of Love in a Dreame. Dallington, R., tr. LC 73-6347. (English Experience Ser.: No. 87). 200p. 1969. Repr. of 1592 ed. 28.50 (ISBN 90-221-0087-1). Walter J Johnson.
Colonna, Phyllia & Phillips, Ana M. The Power of Caring. LC 81-50388. (Power Tales Ser.). pap. write for info. (ISBN 0-911712-87-9). Promised Land.
Colonna, Phyllis & Ramussen, Della M. The Power of Courage. LC 80-85338. (Power Tales Ser.). write for info. Promised Land.
Colonna, Phyllis & Rasmussen, Della M. The Power of Cheerfulness. LC 80-85337. (Power Tales Ser.). pap. write for info. Promised Land.
--The Power of Determination. LC 80-85339. (Power Tales Ser.). pap. write for info. Promised Land.
--The Power of Enthusiasm. LC 81-50864. (Power Tales Ser.). pap. write for info. Promised Land.
--The Power of Integrity. LC 81-50390. (Power Tales Ser.). pap. write for info. (ISBN 0-911712-85-2). Promised Land.
--The Power of Sportsmanship. LC 81-50868. (Power Tales Ser.). pap. write for info. (ISBN 0-911712-94-1). Promised Land.
--The Power of Trying Again. LC 81-50389. (Power Tales Ser.). pap. write for info. (ISBN 0-911712-86-0). Promised Land.
Colonne, G. Delle see Delle Colonne, G.
Colonnese, Louis. Human Rights & the Liberation of Man. 304p. 1970. 17.95 (ISBN 0-268-00424-2). U of Notre Dame Pr.
Colonnese, Tom & Owens, Louis. Native American Indian Novelists: An Annotated Critical Bibliography. LC 84-49135. (Reference Library of the Humanities). 178p. 1983. lib. bdg. 31.00 (ISBN 0-8240-9199-X). Garland Pub.
Colon-Osorio, Fernando C., jt. auth. see Glorioso, Robert M.
Colony, Horatio. The Amazon's Hero. 6.00 (ISBN 0-8283-1340-7). Branden Pub Co.
--The Antique Thorn. LC 73-93388. 100p. 1974. 6.00 (ISBN 0-8283-1534-5). Branden Pub Co.
--Collected Works: Drama, Verse, Novels, 2 vols. 1500p. 1982. 60.00 set. Vol. 1 (ISBN 0-8283-1741-0). Branden Pub Co.
--Collected Works of Horatio Colony, 2 vols. 1982. 60.00 set. Branden Pub Co.
--Demon in Love. 6.00 (ISBN 0-8283-1214-1). Branden Pub Co.
--Early Land. 1967. 6.00 (ISBN 0-8283-1216-8). Branden Pub Co.
--The Emperor & the Bee Boy. 1000p. 1976. 6.00 (ISBN 0-8283-1638-4). Branden Pub Co.
--Flying Ones. 1967. 6.00 (ISBN 0-8283-1218-4). Branden Pub Co.
--Magic Child. 6.00 (ISBN 0-8283-1215-X). Branden Pub Co.
--Some Phoenix Blood. LC 69-11622. 1969. 6.00 (ISBN 0-8283-1008-4). Branden Pub Co.
--Three Loves the Same. 1967. 6.00 (ISBN 0-8283-1217-6). Branden Pub Co.
Colony, Horatio, ed. Flower Myth. 6.00 (ISBN 0-8283-1278-8). Branden Pub Co.
Colony, Robert G., ed. see Maxwell, Grover, et al.
Colorado, Antonio J., tr. see Mathews, Thomas.
Colorado School of Mines. Subject Catalog of the Arthur Lakes Library of the Colorado School of Mines. 1977. lib. bdg. 595.00 (ISBN 0-8161-0072-1, Hall Library). G K Hall.
Colorado Springs Fine Arts Center. Woodworking in the Rockies. LC 82-71534. (Illus.). 1982. 6.00 (ISBN 0-686-37084-8). Taylor Museum.
--Woodworking in the Rockies. LC 82-71534. (Illus.). 52p. (Orig.). 1982. pap. 6.00 (ISBN 0-686-35850-3). CO Springs Fine Arts.
Colorado Supreme Court, et al. Civil Rules Annotated. LC 84-51233. Date not set. price not set. West Pub.
Colorni, Evelina. Singers' Italian: A Manual of Diction & Phonetics. LC 71-113927. 1970. pap. text ed. 9.50 (ISBN 0-02-870620-X). Schirmer Bks.
Colose, Thomas R. & Rynecki, Steven, eds. Federal Legislation for Public Sector Collective Bargaining. new ed. 250p. 1975. pap. 6.00 (ISBN 0-87373-148-4). Intl Personnel Mgmt.
Colouris, G. F. see Halpern, M., et al.
Colourpictur Publishers. Scenic Utah. (Travel Ser.: No. L-23). (Illus.). 32p. 1981. pap. text ed. 2.50 (ISBN 0-938440-48-9). Colourpicture.
Colourpicture Publishing Co. New Orleans. (Travel Ser.: No. L-38). (Illus.). 72p. (Orig.). 1981. pap. text ed. 6.95 (ISBN 0-938440-04-7). Colourpicture.
Colourpicture Staff. Grand Teton National Park. (Travel Ser.: No. L-23). (Illus.). 32p. (Orig.). 1981. pap. text ed. 2.50 (ISBN 0-938440-45-4). Colourpicture.
Colowick & Kaplan, eds. Methods in Enzymology: Glutamate, Glutamine, Glutathione, & Related Compounds, Vol. 113. Date not set. 75.00 (ISBN 0-12-182013-0). Acad Pr.
Colowick, Kaplan, ed. Methods in Enzymology: Diffraction Methods for Biological Macromolecules, Part B, Vol. 115. Date not set. price not set (ISBN 0-12-182015-7). Acad Pr.
Colowick, S. & Ginsburg, Victor, eds. Methods in Enzymology: Complex Carbohydrates, Vol. 83, Pt. D. 1982. 69.50 (ISBN 0-12-181983-3). Acad Pr.
Colowick, S. & Langone, John, eds. Methods in Enzymology: Immunological Techniques, Vol. 84, Pt. D. LC 82-1678. 736p. 1982. 70.00 (ISBN 0-12-181984-1). Acad Pr.
Colowick, S. & Lorand, L., eds. Methods in Enzymology: Proteolytic Enzymes, Vol. 80, Pt. C. 1982. 77.00 (ISBN 0-12-181980-9). Acad Pr.
Colowick, S. P. & Lands, William, eds. Methods in Enzymology: Prostaglandins & Arachidonate Metabolites, Vol. 86. LC 82-6791. 1982. 73.50 (ISBN 0-12-181986-8). Acad Pr.
Colowick, S. P., et al, eds. Methods in Enzymology: Lipids, Vol. 71, Pt. C. 1981. 76.50 (ISBN 0-12-181971-X). Acad Pr.
--Methods in Enzymology: Lipids, Vol. 72. (Serial Publications: Pt. D). 1981. 76.50 (ISBN 0-12-181972-8). Acad Pr.
--Methods in Enzymology: Immunochemical Techniques, Vol. 70, Pt. A. (Serial Publications Ser.). 1980. 65.00 (ISBN 0-12-181970-1). Acad Pr.
Colowick, Sidney & Antonini, Eraldo, eds. Methods in Enzymology: Hemoglobins, Vol. 76. 1981. 76.00 (ISBN 0-12-181976-0). Acad Pr.
Colowick, Sidney & Cunningham, Leon, eds. Methods in Enzymology: Structural & Contractile Proteins: Extracellular Matrix, Vol. 82, Pt. A. 1982. 75.00 (ISBN 0-12-181982-5). Acad Pr.
Colowick, Sidney & Dennis, Martha, eds. Methods in Enzymology: Cumulative Subject Index, Vols. 31, 32 & 34. (Serial Publication: Vol. 75). 1982. 85.00 (ISBN 0-12-181975-2). Acad Pr.
Colowick, Sidney & Jakoby, William, eds. Methods in Enzymology: Detoxication & Drug Metabolism: Conjugation & Related Systems, Vol. 77. (Methods in Enzymology Ser.). 1981. 55.00 (ISBN 0-12-181977-9). Acad Pr.
Colowick, Sidney & Kaplan, Nathan, eds. Methods in Enzymology: Photosynthesis & Nitrogen Fixation, Vol. 69, Pt. C. LC 54-9110. 1980. 75.00 (ISBN 0-12-181969-8). Acad Pr.
Colowick, Sidney & Packer, Leslie, eds. Methods in Enzymology: Biomembranes: Visual Pigments & Purple Membranes, I, Vol. 81, Pt. H. LC 82-1736. 1982. 85.00 (ISBN 0-12-181981-7). Acad Pr.
Colowick, Sidney & Packer, Lester, eds. Methods in Enzymology: Biomembranes - Visual Pigments & Purple Membranes, Vol. 88. 750p. 1982. 78.00 (ISBN 0-12-181988-4). Acad Pr.
Colowick, Sidney & Pestka, Sidney, eds. Methods in Enzymology: Interferons, Vol. 78, Pt. A. 1981. 67.50 (ISBN 0-12-181978-7). Acad Pr.
--Methods in Enzymology: Interferons, Vol. 79, Pt. B. 1981. 69.50 (ISBN 0-12-181979-5). Acad Pr.
Colowick, Sidney & Wood, Willis, eds. Methods in Enzymology: Carbohydrate Metabolism. (Vol. 89. Pt. D). 656p. 1982. 66.00 (ISBN 0-12-181989-2). Acad Pr.
--Methods in Enzymology: Carbohydrate Metabolism, Vol. 90, Pt. E. 559p. 1982. 65.00 (ISBN 0-12-181990-6). Acad Pr.
Colowick, Sidney, et al, eds. Methods in Enzymology: Immunochemical Techniques, Vol. 73, Pt. B. 1981. 70.00 (ISBN 0-12-181973-6). Acad Pr.
--Methods in Enzymology: Vitamins & Coenzymes, Vol. 67, Pt F. 1980. 70.00 (ISBN 0-12-181967-1). Acad Pr.
Colowick, Sidney P. & Kaplan, Nathan O. Methods in Enzymology: Enzyme Purification & Related Techniques, Vol. 104, Pt. C. 1984. 60.00 (ISBN 0-12-182004-1). Acad Pr.
--Methods in Enzymology: Oxygen Radicals in Biological Systems, Vol. 105. 1984. 70.00 (ISBN 0-12-182005-X). Acad Pr.
--Methods in Enzymology: Posttranslational Modification, Vol. 107, Pt. B. 1984. 69.50 (ISBN 0-12-182007-6). Acad Pr.
Colowick, Sidney P. & Frederiksen, D. W., eds. Methods in Enzymology: Structural & Contractile Proteins-The Contractile Apparatus & the Cytoskeleton, Vol. 85. 774p. 1982. 75.00 (ISBN 0-12-181985-X). Acad Pr.
Colowick, Sidney P. & Kaplan, Nathan, eds. Methods in Enzymology: Postranslational Modifications, Vol. 106, Pt. A. 1984. 65.00 (ISBN 0-12-182006-8). Acad Pr.
Colowick, Sidney P. & Kaplan, Nathan O., eds. Methods in Enzymology, Vols. 1-15. Incl. Vol. 1. Preparation & Assay of Enzymes. 1955. 89.50 (ISBN 0-12-181801-2); Vol. 2. Preparation & Assay of Enzymes, Continued. 1955. 89.50 (ISBN 0-12-181802-0); Vol. 3. Preparation & Assay of Substrates. 1957. 94.00 (ISBN 0-12-181803-9); Vol. 4. Special Techniques for the Enzymologist. 1957. 94.00 (ISBN 0-12-181804-7); Vol. 5. Preparation & Assay of Enzymes, Supplement to Vols. 1 & 2. 1961. 94.00 (ISBN 0-12-181805-5); Vol. 6. Preparation & Assay of Enzymes, Continued & Preparation & Assay of Substrates, Special Techniques. 1963. 94.00 (ISBN 0-12-181806-3); Vol. 7. General Subject Index. 1964; Vol. 8. Complex Carbohydrates. Neufeld, Elizabeth F. & Ginsberg, Victor, eds. 1966. 90.00 (ISBN 0-12-181808-X); Vol. 9. Carbohydrate Metabolism. Wood, W. A., ed. 1967. 90.00 (ISBN 0-12-181809-8); Vol. 10. Oxidation & Phosphorylation. Estabrook, Ronald W. & Pullman, Maynard E., eds. 1967. 90.00 (ISBN 0-12-181850-0); Vol. 11. Enzyme Structure. Hirs, C. Werner, ed. 1967. 93.00 (ISBN 0-12-181860-8); Vol. 12. Nucleic Acids, Pts. A-B. Grossman, Lawrence & Moldave, Kivic, eds. Pt. A, 1967. 90.00 (ISBN 0-12-181854-3); Pt. B, 1968. 93.00 (ISBN 0-12-181856-X); Vol. 13. Citric Acid Cycle. Lowenstein, J. M., ed. 1969. 83.50 (ISBN 0-12-181870-5); Vol. 14. Lipids. Lowenstein, J. M. 1969. 83.50 (ISBN 0-12-181871-3); Vol. 15. Steroids & Terpenoids. Clayton, R. B., ed. 1969. 93.00 (ISBN 0-12-181872-1). Acad Pr.
--Methods in Enzymology, Vol. 87. 752p. 1982. 74.50 (ISBN 0-12-181987-6). Acad Pr.
--Methods in Enzymology: Diffraction Methods for Biological Macromolecules, Vol. 114, Pt. A. Edited Treatise ed. Date not set. price not set (ISBN 0-12-182014-9). Acad Pr.
--Methods in Enzymology: Drug & Enzyme Targeting, Vol. 112. 1985. 69.00 (ISBN 0-12-182012-2). Acad Pr.
--Methods in Enzymology: Enzyme Kinetics & Mechanism, Initial Rate & Inhibiter Methods, Vol. 63. LC 54-9110. (Serial Publication: Pt. A). 1979. 65.00 (ISBN 0-12-181963-9). Acad Pr.
--Methods in Enzymology: Enzyme Structure, Vol. 117, Pt. J. Date not set. price not set (ISBN 0-12-182017-3). Acad Pr.
--Methods in Enzymology: Enzyme Structure, Vol. 91, Pt. 1. 1983. 71.50 (ISBN 0-12-181991-4). Acad Pr.
--Methods in Enzymology: Hormone Action; Peptide Hormones, Vol. 109, Pt. I. 1985. 85.00 (ISBN 0-12-182009-2). Acad Pr.
--Methods in Enzymology: Immunochemical Techniques, Conventional Antibodies, FC Receptors & Cytotoxicity, Vol. 93, Pt. F. 393p. 1983. 55.00 (ISBN 0-12-181993-0). Acad Pr.
--Methods in Enzymology: Immunochemical Techniques: Effectors & Mediators of Lymphoid Cell, Vol. 116. (Methods in Enzymology Ser.: Pt. H). Date not set. price not set (ISBN 0-12-182016-5). Acad Pr.
--Methods in Enzymology: Monoclonal Antibodies & General Immonoassay Methods, Vol. 92, Pt. E. 1983. 69.50 (ISBN 0-12-181992-2). Acad Pr.
--Methods in Enzymology: Recombinant DNA. LC 79-26584. 1983. Vol. 100: Pt. B. 65.00 (ISBN 0-12-182000-9); Vol. 101: Pt. C. 70.00 (ISBN 0-12-182001-7). Acad Pr.
--Methods in Enzymology: Steroids & Isoprenoids, Vol. 110, Pt. A. 1985. 55.00 (ISBN 0-12-182010-6). Acad Pr.
--Methods in Enzymology: Steroids & Isoprenoids, Vol. 111, Pt. B. 1985. 66.50 (ISBN 0-12-182011-4). Acad Pr.
--Methods in Enzymology: Vitamins & Coenzymes, Vol. 66, Pt.E. LC 54-9110. 1980. 71.50 (ISBN 0-12-181966-3). Acad Pr.
Colowick, Sidney P., et al, eds. Glutathione: A Symposium. 1954. 65.00 (ISBN 0-12-181876-4). Acad Pr.
--Methods in Enzymology: Enzyme Kinetics & Mechanism, Vol. 64. LC 54-9110. (150 tape probes & complex enzyme systems pt B). 1980. 55.00 (ISBN 0-12-181964-7). Acad Pr.
--Methods in Enzymology: Nucleic Acids, Vol. 65. LC 54-9110. (Methods in Enzymology Ser.: Pt. 1). 1980. 69.50 (ISBN 0-12-181965-5). Acad Pr.
--Methods in Enzymology: Recombinant Dna, Vol. 68. LC 54-9110. (Methods in Enzymology Ser.). 1980. 59.50 (ISBN 0-12-181968-X). Acad Pr.
Colp, Ralph, Jr. To Be an Invalid: The Illnes of Charles Darwin. LC 76-17698. 1977. 25.00x (ISBN 0-226-11401-5). U of Chicago Pr.
Colpitt, Frances & Brougher, Kerry. Mark Lere: New & Selected Work. LC 84-43091. (Illus.). 80p. 1985. pap. 12.95 (ISBN 0-295-96279-8). U of Wash Pr.
Colpitt, Frances, et al. Changing Trends: Content & Style. (Illus.). 86p. (Orig.). 1982. pap. write for info. (ISBN 0-911291-00-8). Fellows Cont Art.
Colpron, Gilles. Les Anglicismes au Quebec. 247p. (Fr. & Eng.). 1979. 17.50 (ISBN 0-686-56957-1, M-6080). French & Eur.
Colquhoun, A., tr. see Lampedusa, Giuseppe Di.

Colquhoun, Alan. Essays in Architectural Criticism: Modern Architecture & Historical Change. (Oppositions Bks.). (Illus.). 224p. 1985. 37.50x (ISBN 0-262-03076-4); pap. 12.50 (ISBN 0-262-53063-5). MIT Pr.

Colquhoun, Archibald. Manzoni & His Times: A Biography of the Author of The Betrothed (I Promessi Sposi) LC 78-59013. (Illus.). 1979. Repr. of 1954 ed. 25.00 (ISBN 0-88355-688-X). Hyperion Conn.

Colquhoun, Archibald, tr. see Calvino, Italo.

Colquhoun, Archibald, tr. see Manzoni, Alessandro.

Colquhoun, Archibald R. Mastery of the Pacific. LC 70-111750. (American Imperialism: Viewpoints of United States Foreign Policy, Ser.1898-1941). 1970. Repr. of 1904 ed. 26.50 (ISBN 0-405-02009-0). Ayer Co Pubs.

Colquhoun, Frank. Christ's Ambassadors. (Canterbury Bks.). pap. 2.50 (ISBN 0-8010-2428-5). Baker Bk.

--Family Prayers. 80p. 1984. pap. 1.35 (ISBN 0-88028-040-9). Forward Movement.

--Four Portraits of Jesus. LC 85-4248. Orig. Title: Fourfold Portrait of Jesus. 84p. 1985. pap. 2.95 (ISBN 0-87784-450-X). Inter-Varsity.

--A Hymn Companion. 288p. 1985. pap. 8.95 (ISBN 0-8192-1368-3). Morehouse.

--Hymns That Live. LC 81-1458. 320p. 1981. pap. 6.95 (ISBN 0-87784-473-9). Inter Varsity.

Colquhoun, Frank, ed. Prayers for Every Occasion. Orig. Title: Parish Prayers. 445p. 1974. Repr. of 1967 ed. kivar 14.95 (ISBN 0-8192-1280-6). Morehouse.

Colquhoun, H. M., et al. New Pathways for Organic Synthesis: Practical Applications of Transition Metals. 430p. 1983. 59.50x (ISBN 0-306-41318-3, Plenum Pr). Plenum Pub.

Colquhoun, J. C., jt. auth. see Committee of the Medical Section of the French Royal Academy of Sciences, Jun 21-28th, 1831.

Colquhoun, Keith. Filthy Rich. 174p. 1983. 11.95 (ISBN 0-89733-081-1). Academy Chi Pubs.

--Goebbels & Gladys: A Novel of Fleet Street. 188p. 1985. 13.95 (ISBN 0-89733-130-3). Academy Chi Pubs.

Colquhoun, Norman. Painting: A Creative Approach. LC 68-21280. 1969. pap. 3.50 (ISBN 0-486-22000-1). Dover.

--Painting: A Creative Approach, Guide to Modern Methods & Materials. 2nd rev. ed. Orig. Title: Paint Your Own Pictures. 10.00 (ISBN 0-8446-1882-9). Peter Smith.

Colquhoun, P. A New & Appropriate New System of Education for the Labouring People. 98p. 1971. Repr. of 1806 ed. 15.00x (ISBN 0-7165-1773-6, Pub. by Irish Academic Pr Ireland). Biblio Dist.

Colquhoun, Patrick. Treatise on the Commerce & Police of the River Thames. LC 69-14917. (Criminology, Law Enforcement & Social Problems Ser.: No. 41). (Map). 1969. Repr. of 1800 ed. 30.00x (ISBN 0-87585-041-3). Patterson Smith.

--Treatise on the Police of the Metropolis. 7th ed. LC 69-14918. (Criminology, Law Enforcement & Social Problems Ser.: No. 42). 1969. Repr. of 1806 ed. 30.00x (ISBN 0-87585-042-1). Patterson Smith.

--A Treatise on the Wealth, Power & Resources of the British Empire. 2nd ed. 1815. 60.00 (ISBN 0-384-09710-3). Johnson Repr.

Colquhoun, Robert. Life Begins at Midnight. 15.00 (ISBN 0-392-08555-0, SpS). Sportshelf.

Colquhoun, W. P., ed. Biological Rhythms & Human Performance. 1971. 49.50 (ISBN 0-12-182050-5). Acad Pr.

Colquhoun, W. P. & Rutenfanz, J., eds. Studies of Shiftwork. (Illus.). 468p. 1980. 44.00x (ISBN 0-85066-210-9). Taylor & Francis.

Colson, B., et al. Southeast Litigation Guide, 16 Vols. 1981. 60.00 ea.; Supplement 1982. 35.00 (ISBN 0-686-46752-3). Bender.

Colson, Bill. Southeast Litigation Guide, 12 vols. 1981. Updates avail. looseleaf 720.00 (633); looseleaf 1983 97.50; looseleaf 1984 167.00. Bender.

Colson, Bill, et al. Southeast Litigation Guide, 12 vols. 1981. Updates avail. looseleaf 720.00 (ISBN 0-317-09801-2, 633); looseleaf 1983 97.50; looseleaf 1984 167.00. Bender.

Colson, Charles. Born Again. 352p. 1976. lib. bdg. 7.95 (ISBN 0-310-60640-3). Zondervan.

--Naci de Nuevo. Ward, Rhode, tr. from Eng. LC 77-81645. 419p. (Span.). 1977. pap. 6.25 (ISBN 0-89922-087-8). Edit Caribe.

--Who Speaks for God? LC 85-71892. 192p. (Orig.). 1985. pap. 6.95 (ISBN 0-89107-372-8, Crossway Bks). Good News.

Colson, Charles W. Cadena Perpetua. 304p. (Orig., Span.). 1983. pap. 6.95 (ISBN 0-89922-221-8). Edit Caribe.

--Life Sentence. (Illus.). 320p. 1981. pap. 7.95 (ISBN 0-8007-5059-4, Power Bks). Revell.

--Loving God. 288p. 1983. 11.95 (ISBN 0-310-47030-7). Zondervan.

Colson, Earl M. Capital Gains & Losses. 251p. 1975. Incl. suppl. 22.00 (ISBN 0-317-30768-1, B266); Suppl. only. pap. 2.00 (ISBN 0-317-30769-X, B267). Am Law Inst.

--Nontax & Tax Aspects of Life Insurance. 53p. 1980. pap. 10.00 (ISBN 0-686-29225-1, B401). Am Law Inst.

Colson, Edna M. The Analysis of the Specific References to Negroes in Selected Curricula for the Education of Teachers. LC 75-17663. (Columbia University. Teachers College. Contributions to Education: No. 822). Repr. of 1940 ed. 22.50 (ISBN 0-404-55822-4). AMS Pr.

Colson, Elise, ed. see Stanley, Charles A.

Colson, Elizabeth. The Makah Indians. LC 73-15051. (Illus.). 308p. 1974. Repr. of 1953 ed. lib. bdg. 21.00x (ISBN 0-8371-7153-9, COMI). Greenwood.

--Tradition & Contract: The Problem of Order. LC 74-82603. 152p. 1974. 14.95x (ISBN 0-202-01131-3). Aldine Pub.

Colson, Elizabeth, jt. auth. see Scudder, Thayer.

Colson, Ethel M. How to Read Poetry. LC 74-11276. 1974. Repr. of 1918 ed. lib. bdg. 22.50 (ISBN 0-8414-3519-7). Folcroft.

Colson, Ethelm M. How to Write Poetry. 1973. Repr. of 1919 ed. 15.00 (ISBN 0-8274-1661-X). R West.

Colson, F. H., ed. Cicero: Pro Milone. 148p. 25.00x (ISBN 0-906515-50-5, Pub. by Bristol Classical Pr). State Mutual Bk.

Colson, Francis H. The Week. LC 73-7697. 126p. 1974. Repr. of 1926 ed. lib. bdg. 22.50x (ISBN 0-8371-6940-2, CTHW). Greenwood.

Colson, Howard P. & Rigdon, Raymond M. Understanding Your Church's Curriculum. rev. ed. LC 80-67351. 1981. pap. 5.95 (ISBN 0-8054-3201-9). Broadman.

Colson, John H. Progressive Exercise Therapy in Rehabilitation & Physical Education. 4th ed. (Illus.). 249p. 1983. pap. text ed. 18.50 (ISBN 0-7236-0665-X). PSG Pub Co.

Colson, John H. & Armour, William J. Sports Injuries & Their Treatment. rev. ed. (Illus.). 234p. 1983. text ed. 32.95x (ISBN 0-09-124180-4, SpS). Sportshelf.

Colson, Lucy W., jt. auth. see Colson, Robert E.

Colson, Percy. Georgian Portraits. 1973. Repr. of 1939 ed. 17.50 (ISBN 0-8274-1662-8). R West.

--Their Ruling Passions. facs. ed. LC 70-136645. (Biography Index Reprint Ser.). 1949. 21.00 (ISBN 0-8369-8040-9). Ayer Co Pubs.

--Victorian Portraits. facs. ed. LC 68-16921. (Essay Index Reprint Ser). 1932. 15.00 (ISBN 0-8369-0328-5). Ayer Co Pubs.

Colson, Rene, et al, eds. Memories Originaus Des Createurs de la Photographic. LC 76-23043. (Sources of Modern Photography Ser.). (Fr.). 1979. Repr. of 1898 ed. lib. bdg. 17.00x (ISBN 0-405-09605-4). Ayer Co Pubs.

Colson, Robert E. & Colson, Lucy W. Monroe & Conecuh Counties, Alabama, Marriages, 1833-1880. 172p. 1983. 20.00 (ISBN 0-89308-335-6). Southern Hist Pr.

Colston, Lowell G. Pastoral Care with Handicapped Persons. Clinebell, Howard J. & Stone, Howard W., eds. LC 77-15229. (Creative Pastoral Care & Counseling Ser). 96p. (Orig.). 1978. pap. 4.50 (ISBN 0-8006-0560-8, 1-560). Fortress.

Colston, Stephanie, jt. auth. see Carr, T. R.

Colt, C. F. & Miall, Antony. The Early Piano. (Illus.). 160p. 1981. 85.00x (ISBN 0-389-20187-1). B&N Imports.

Colt, Clem. Coyote Song. 1978. pap. 1.50 (ISBN 0-505-51317-X, Pub. by Tower Bks). Dorchester Pub Co.

Colt, H. Dunscombe, ed. Excavations at Nessana, Vol. I. (Colt Archaeological Institute). (Illus.). 311p. 1962. text ed. 72.50x (ISBN 0-85668-071-0, Pub. by Aris & Phillips England). Humanities.

Colt, John. Computation of Dissolved Gas Concentrations as Functions of Temperature, Salinity, & Pressure. (Special Publication Ser.: No. 14). 154p. 1984. 18.00 (ISBN 0-913235-02-4). Am Fisheries Soc.

Colt, Zandra. Cactus Rose. (Second Chance at Love Ser.: No. 40). (Orig.). 1982. pap. 1.75 (ISBN 0-515-06540-9). Jove Pubns.

--Splendid Savage. (Second Chance at Love Ser.: No. 92). 1982. pap. 1.75 (ISBN 0-515-06854-3). Jove Pubns.

Coltas, J. A. Railway Stations of Britain: Just a Glimpse. (Illus.). 1979. 9.00 (ISBN 0-916170-09-8). J-B Pub.

Colter, Cyrus. Beach Umbrella. LC 72-122919. 225p. 1971. pap. 4.95 (ISBN 0-8040-0555-9, 82-72916, Pub. by Swallow). Ohio U Pr.

--The Beach Umbrella. LC 72-122919. (The Iowa School of Letters Award for Short Fiction Ser.: No. 1). 225p. 1970. 15.00 (ISBN 0-87745-005-6). U of Iowa Pr.

--The Hippodrome: A Novel. LC 72-96164. 213p. 1973. 10.95 (ISBN 0-8040-0625-3, 82-73385, Pub. by Swallow). Ohio U Pr.

--Night Studies: A Novel. LC 79-642952. 775p. 1979. 19.95 (ISBN 0-8040-0827-2, 82-75992, Pub. by Swallow). Ohio U Pr.

--Rivers of Eros: A Novel. LC 73-189191. 219p. 1972. 10.95 (ISBN 0-8040-0563-X, 82-72965, Pub. by Swallow) Ohio U Pr.

Colter, Janet, jt. auth. see Colter, Rudyard.

Colter, John S. & Paranchych, William. Molecular Biology of Viruses. 1967. 90.00 (ISBN 0-12-182250-8). Acad Pr.

Colter, Mel A., jt. auth. see Couger, J. Daniel.

Colter, Rob. Grammar to Go: An Informal Guide to Correct Usage. rev. ed. 176p. 1981. text ed. 4.95 (ISBN 0-88784-077-9, Pub. by Hse Anansi Pr Canada). U of Toronto Pr.

Colter, Rudyard & Colter, Janet. Favorite Vermont Ski Inns & Lodging Guide. (McGraw-Hill Paperbacks). 1977. pap. 5.95 (ISBN 0-07-012085-4). McGraw.

Coltharp, Barbara. Colonel Neverfail's Christmas. Sandifer, Shannon & Woolfolk, Doug, eds. (Illus., Orig.). 1981. 7.95 (ISBN 0-86518-019-9). Moran Pub Corp.

Coltharp, Joe & Benjiuja, Nisim. Production of Two by Two Inch Slides. rev. ed. Hazelton, Jane, ed. (Bridges for Ideas Handbook Ser.). 1983. pap. text ed. 6.00x (ISBN 0-913648-05-1). U Tex Austin Film Lib.

Coltheart, Max, et al, eds. Deep Dyslexia. (International Library of Psychology). 1980. 50.00x (ISBN 0-7100-0456-7). Routledge & Kegan.

Coltman, Charles A., Jr. & Golomb, Harvey, eds. Hodgkin's & Non-Hodgkin's Lymphomas. (Seminars in Oncology Reprint Ser.). 288p. 1980. 40.00 (ISBN 0-8089-1354-9, 790884). Grune.

Coltman, Derek, tr. see Belmont, Nicole.

Coltman, Derek, tr. see Blais, Marie-Claire.

Coltman, Derek, tr. see Doubrovsky, Serge.

Coltman, Derek, tr. see Dumezil, Georges.

Coltman, Derek, tr. see Duroselle, Jean B.

Coltman, Derek, tr. see Eliade, Mircea.

Coltman, Derek, tr. see Leduc, Violette.

Coltman, Derek, tr. see Leites, Nathan C.

Coltman, Derek, tr. see Marceau, Felicien.

Coltman, Derek, tr. see Piaget, Jean, et al.

Coltman, Derek, tr. see Pierrot, Jean.

Coltman, Derek, tr. see Touraine, Alain.

Coltman, Derek, tr. see Varenne, Jean.

Coltman, Irene. Private Men & Public Causes: Philosophy & Politics in the English Civil War. LC 66-4931. 1962. text ed. 12.50x (ISBN 0-8401-0450-2). Allenson-Breckinridge.

Coltman, Michael M. Buying & Selling a Business. 137p. (Orig.). 1983. pap. 6.95 (ISBN 0-88908-569-2). Self Counsel Pr.

--Buying & Selling a Small Business. 168p. Date not set. pap. 6.95 (ISBN 0-317-30523-9, 9518, Pub. by Intl Self-Counsel Pr). TAB Bks.

--Cost Control for the Hospitality Industry. 1980. 18.95 (ISBN 0-8436-2193-1). Van Nos Reinhold.

--Financial Control for the Small Business: A Practical Primer for Keeping a Tighter Rein on Your Profits & Cash Flow. 12/1982 ed. (Illus.). 119p. (Orig.). pap. 5.50 (ISBN 0-88908-911-6, 9503, Pub. by Intl Self-Counsel Pr). TAB Bks.

--Financial Control for the Small Business. 1st ed. (Canadian Edition). 1982. 5.50 (ISBN 0-88908-550-1). Self Counsel Pr.

--Financial Management for the Hospitality Industry. LC 79-378. 1980. 18.95 (ISBN 0-8436-2141-9). Van Nos Reinhold.

--Franchising in Canada: Pros & Cons. 1st ed. 137p. 1982. 5.95 (ISBN 0-88908-092-5). Self Counsel Pr.

--Franchising in the U. S. Pros & Cons. 148p. 1982. pap. text ed. 5.95 (ISBN 0-88908-909-4, 9504, Pub. by Intl Self-Counsel Pr). TAB Bks.

--Hospitality Management Accounting. 2nd ed. 400p. 1982. 18.95 (ISBN 0-8436-0866-8); 8.95 (ISBN 0-8436-0874-9). Van Nos Reinhold.

--A Practical Guide to Financial Management: Tips & Techniques for the Non-Financial Manager. 160p. 1984. pap. 5.50 (ISBN 0-88908-600-1, 9531, Pub. by Intl Self-Counsel Pr). TAB Bks.

--Resort Condos & Timesharing: Buyer Beware! 119p. (Orig.). 1981. pap. 4.50 (ISBN 0-88908-079-8, 9510, Pub. by Intl Self-Counsel Pr). TAB Bks.

--Start & Run a Profitable Restaurant. (Illus.). 168p. (Orig.). 1983. pap. 10.95 (ISBN 0-88908-567-6, 9523, Pub. by Intl Self-Counsel Pr). TAB Bks.

--Start & Run a Profitable Retail Business: A Complete Step-by-Step Business Plan. 160p. (Orig.). 1983. pap. 11.95 (ISBN 0-88908-570-6, 9520, Pub. by Intl Self-Counsel Pr). TAB Bks.

Coltman, Paul. Tog the Ribber: Or Granny's Tales. LC 84-82555. (Illus.). 32p. (ps-5). 1985. 11.95 (ISBN 0-374-37630-1). FS&G.

Coltman, Robert. Chinese. LC 72-4164. (Select Bibliographies Reprint Ser.). 1972. Repr. of 1891 ed. 23.50 (ISBN 0-8369-6874-3). Ayer Co Pubs.

Colton, Ann R. Draughts of Remembrance. 177p. 1959. 8.95 (ISBN 0-917187-09-1). A R C Pub.

--Ethical ESP. LC 78-149600. 367p. 1971. 11.50 (ISBN 0-917187-03-2). A R C Pub.

--The Human Spirit. 289p. 1966. 8.95 (ISBN 0-917187-05-9). A R C Pub.

--Islands of Light. 203p. 1953. 6.95 (ISBN 0-917187-14-8). A R C Pub.

--The Jesus Story. 396p. 1969. 10.00 (ISBN 0-917187-04-0). A R C Pub.

--The King. 72p. 1968. 5.00 (ISBN 0-917187-08-3). A R C Pub.

--Kundalini West. (Illus.). 403p. 1978. 12.95 (ISBN 0-917187-01-6). A R C Pub.

--The Lively Oracles. 151p. 1962. 5.95 (ISBN 0-917187-13-X). A R C Pub.

--Men in White Apparel. (Illus.). 202p. 1961. 6.95 (ISBN 0-917187-10-5). A R C Pub.

--Precepts for the Young. 66p. (gr. 1-8). 1959. pap. 2.50 (ISBN 0-917187-15-6). A R C Pub.

--The Soul & the Ethic. 262p. 1965. 7.95 (ISBN 0-917187-07-5). A R C Pub.

--The Third Music. LC 82-71249. (Illus.). 432p. 1982. 15.95 (ISBN 0-917187-00-8). A R C Pub.

--The Venerable One. 166p. 1963. 5.95 (ISBN 0-917187-11-3). A R C Pub.

--Vision for the Future. 139p. 1960. 5.95 (ISBN 0-917187-12-1). A R C Pub.

--Watch Your Dreams. LC 72-90911. (Illus.). 414p. 1973. 10.00 (ISBN 0-917187-02-4). A R C Pub.

Colton, Ann R. & Murro, Jonathan. Galaxy Gate, 2 vols. Incl. Vol. 1. The Holy Universe. LC 84-70851 (ISBN 0-917189-02-7); Vol. II. The Angel Kingdom. LC 84-70850 (ISBN 0-917189-03-5). LC 84-70851. (Illus.). 1984. Set. 33.90 (ISBN 0-917189-01-9); 16.95 ea. Colton Found.

--The Pelican & the Chela. LC 85-70766. (Illus.). 420p. 1985. price not set (ISBN 0-917189-04-3). Colton Found.

--Prophet for the Archangels. (Illus.). 289p. 1964. 8.95 (ISBN 0-917187-06-7). A R C Pub.

Colton, Arthur W. Delectable Mountains. facs. ed. LC 71-86139. (Short Story Index Reprint Ser). 1901. 17.00 (ISBN 0-8369-3043-6). Ayer Co Pubs.

Colton, C. C. Remarks on Don Juan. 1978. Repr. of 1826 ed. lib. bdg. 10.00 (ISBN 0-8495-0908-4). Arden Lib.

Colton, C. E. The Faithfulness of Faith. 1985. pap. 4.95 (ISBN 0-8054-1534-3). Broadman.

--Revelation: Book of Mystery & Hope. LC 79-52981. 1979. pap. 3.50 (ISBN 0-8054-1384-7). Broadman.

Colton, Calvin. Abolition a Sedition. LC 72-1054. Repr. of 1839 ed. 16.00 (ISBN 0-404-00017-7). AMS Pr.

--Abolition a Sedition, by a Northern Man. facs. ed. LC 73-133152. (Black Heritage Library Collection Ser). 1839. 14.50 (ISBN 0-8369-8707-1). Ayer Co Pubs.

--History & Character of American Revivals of Religion. LC 72-1008. Repr. of 1832 ed. 22.50 (ISBN 0-404-00018-5). AMS Pr.

--The Junius Tracts. (The Neglected American Economists Ser.). 1975. lib. bdg. 61.00 (ISBN 0-8240-1009-4). Garland Pub.

--The Life & Times of Henry Clay, 2 vols. (The Neglected American Economists Ser.). 1975. lib. bdg. 110.00. Garland Pub.

--Manual for Emigrants to America. LC 69-18767. (American Immigration Collection Ser., No. 1). 1969. Repr. of 1832 ed. 10.00 (ISBN 0-405-00515-6). Ayer Co Pubs.

--Public Economy for the United States. 2nd ed. LC 68-30517. Repr. of 1848 ed. 39.50x (ISBN 0-678-00513-3). Kelley.

Colton, Calvin, ed. see Clay, Henry.

Colton, Charles C. Remarks on Don Juan. LC 75-33020. 1975. Repr. of 1826 ed. lib. bdg. 10.00 (ISBN 0-8414-3641-X). Folcroft.

Colton, D. L. Analytic Theory of Partial Differential Equations. LC 80-14112. (Monographs & Studies in Mathematics Ser.: No. 8). 240p. 1980. text ed. 72.50 (ISBN 0-273-08462-3). Pitman Pub MA.

--Solution of Boundary Value Problems by the Method of Integral Operators. (Research Notes in Mathematics Ser.: No. 6). 148p. (Orig.). 1976. pap. text ed. 21.95 (ISBN 0-273-00307-0). Pitman Pub MA.

Colton, D. L. & Gilbert, R. P., eds. Constructive & Computational Methods for Differential & Integral Equations. (Lecture Notes in Mathematics Ser.: Vol. 430). vii, 476p. 1974. pap. 23.00 (ISBN 0-387-07021-4). Springer-Verlag.

Colton, David & Kress, Rainer. Integral Equation Methods in Scattering Theory. LC 82-21870. (Pure & Applied Mathematics Ser.). 271p. 1983. 43.50x (ISBN 0-471-86420-X, Pub. by Wiley-Interscience). Wiley.

Colton, David L. & Graber, Edith E. Teacher Strikes & the Courts. LC 81-47887. 144p. 1982. 21.00 (ISBN 0-669-05121-7). Lexington Bks.

Colton, Ethan T. Four Patterns of Revolution. facs. ed. LC 79-121456. (Essay Index Reprint Ser.). 1935. 19.00 (ISBN 0-8369-1747-2). Ayer Co Pubs.

Colton, G. Q. Shakespeare & the Bible. LC 74-8569. 1888. lib. bdg. 20.00 (ISBN 0-685-45608-0). Folcroft.

Colton, Gary P. Praise & Prayer. 1978. 7.95 (ISBN 0-8198-0593-9). Dghtrs St Paul.

Colton, H. S., jt. auth. see Colton, M. R.

Colton, Harold S. Black Sand: Prehistory in Northern Arizona. LC 73-13454. (Illus.). 132p. 1974. Repr. of 1960 ed. lib. bdg. 22.50x (ISBN 0-8371-7137-7, COBS). Greenwood.

--Hopi Kachina Dolls with a Key to Their Identification. rev ed. LC 59-5480. (Illus.). 150p. 1971. pap. 8.95 (ISBN 0-8263-0180-0). U of NM Pr.

--A Survey of Prehistoric Sites in the Region of Flagstaff, Arizona. Repr. of 1932 ed. 29.00x (ISBN 0-403-03702-6). Scholarly.

Colton, Harold S. & Hargrave, Lyndon L. Handbook of Northern Arizona Pottery Wares. LC 76-43677. (Museum of Northern Arizona Bulletin: No. 11). Repr. of 1937 ed. 32.50 (ISBN 0-404-15511-1). AMS Pr.

Colton, Helen. The Gift of Touch: How Physical Contact Improves Communication, Pleasure & Health. 224p. 1983. 14.95 (ISBN 0-399-31014-2, Seaview). Putnam Pub Group.

--Touch Therapy. 1985. pap. 3.50 (ISBN 0-8217-1595-X). Zebra.

Colton, Joel, jt. auth. see Palmer, R. R.

Colton, Joel, jt. auth. see Palmer, Robert R.

Colton, Kent W. & Kramer, Kenneth L., eds. Computers & Banking. LC 79-9307. (Applications of Modern Technology in Business Ser.). (Illus.). 325p. 1979. 39.50x (ISBN 0-306-40255-6, Plenum Pr). Plenum Pub.

Colton, M. R. & Colton, H. S. Little-Known Small House Ruins in the Coconino Forest. LC 19-15014. (Amer Anthro Assn Memoirs). 1918. pap. 15.00 (ISBN 0-527-00523-1). Kraus Repr.

Colton, Mary-Russell F. Hopi Dyes. 2nd ed. LC 78-60236. (Illus.). pap. 4.95 (ISBN 0-89734-000-0). Mus Northern Ariz.

Colton, Ray C. The Civil War in the Western Territories: Arizona, Colorado, New Mexico, & Utah. 1959. 5.00 (ISBN 0-686-88887-1). U of Okla Pr.

--The Civil War in the Western Territories: Arizona, Colorado, New Mexico, & Utah. LC 59-7964. (Illus.). 240p. (Orig.). 1984. pap. 8.95 (ISBN 0-8061-1902-0). U of Okla Pr.

Colton, Raymond R. & Rohrs, Walter F. Industrial Purchasing & Effective Materials Management. 1984. text ed. 23.95 (ISBN 0-8359-3096-3); instr's manual avail. (ISBN 0-8359-3097-1). Reston.

Colton, Raymond R., jt. auth. see Arkin, Herbert.

Colton, Theodore. Statistics in Medicine. LC 73-1413. 400p. 1975. pap. 22.50 (ISBN 0-316-15250-1). Little.

Colton, Timothy J. Big Daddy: Frederick G. Gardiner & the Building of Metropolitan Toronto. 224p. 1980. 15.00 (ISBN 0-8020-2393-2). U of Toronto Pr.

--Commissars, Commanders, & Civilian Authority: The Structure of Soviet Military Politics. LC 78-23342. (Russian Research Center Studies: No. 79). (Illus.). 1979. 25.00x (ISBN 0-674-14535-6). Harvard U Pr.

--The Dilemma of Reform in the Soviet Union. 128p. 1984. pap. 6.95 (ISBN 0-87609-002-1). Coun Foreign.

Colton, Walter. Three Years in California. Cortes, Carlos E., ed. LC 76-1221. (Chicano Heritage Ser.). (Illus.). 1976. Repr. of 1854 ed. 35.50x (ISBN 0-405-09496-5). Ayer Co Pubs.

Coltrera, Joseph T., ed. Lives, Events & Other Plays: Studies in Psychobiography. LC 79-51911. (Downstate Psychoanalytic Institute Twenty-Fifth Anniversary Ser.: Vol. IV). 1979. 25.00x (ISBN 0-87668-369-3). Aronson.

Coltrin, Peter & Marchet, Jean-Francois. Lamborghini Miura. (Illus.). 160p. 1982. 24.95 (ISBN 0-85045-469-7, Pub. by Osprey England). Motorbooks Intl.

Coltrin, Peter, jt. auth. see Marchet, Jean-Francois.

Colucci, Joseph M. & Gallopoulos, Nicholas E., eds. Future Automotive Fuels: Prospects, Performance, Perspective. LC 76-30757. (General Motors Research Symposia Ser.). 380p. 1977. 59.50x (ISBN 0-306-31017-1, Plenum Pr). Plenum Pub.

Colum, Mary. From These Roots: The Ideas That Have Made Modern Literature. LC 67-25260. Repr. of 1937 ed. 28.50x (ISBN 0-8046-0084-8, Pub. by Kennikat). Assoc Faculty Pr.

Colum, Mary & Colum, Padraic. Our Friend James Joyce. 11.25 (ISBN 0-8446-1122-0). Peter Smith.

Colum, Padraic. The Children of Odin. Repr. of 1920 ed. 35.00 (ISBN 0-89987-140-2). Darby Bks.

--The Children of Odin. 1920. 40.00 (ISBN 0-686-18157-3). Havertown Bks.

--The Children of Odin: The Book of Northern Myths. LC 83-20367. (Illus.). 280p. (gr. 5up). 1984. 10.95 (ISBN 0-02-722890-8); pap. 5.95 (ISBN 0-02-042100-1). Macmillan.

--The Children's Homer: The Adventure of Odysseus & the Tale of Troy. LC 82-12643. (Illus.). 256p. (gr. 5 up). 1982. pap. 5.95x (ISBN 0-02-042520-1). Macmillan.

--Collected Poems. 12.00 (ISBN 0-8159-5203-1). Devin.

--The Golden Fleece: And the Heroes Who Lived Before Achilles. LC 82-21667. 320p. (gr. 5 up). 1983. 12.95 (ISBN 0-02-723620-X); pap. 5.95x (ISBN 0-02-042260-1). Macmillan.

--Half-Day's Ride. facsimile ed. LC 77-90625. (Essay Index Reprint Ser). 1932. 18.00 (ISBN 0-8369-1282-9). Ayer Co Pubs.

Colum, Padraic, jt. auth. see Colum, Mary.

Colum, Padraic, ed. Treasury of Irish Folklore. rev. ed. (YA) (gr. 9 up). 1969. 14.95 (ISBN 0-517-50294-1). Crown.

Colum, Padraic, ed. see MacDonagh, Thomas P., et al.

Colum, Padraic, et al. Homage to James Joyce. LC 73-14976. 1974. lib. bdg. 10.00 (ISBN 0-8414-3482-4). Folcroft.

--On James Stephens. LC 73-181227. lib. bdg. 9.50 (ISBN 0-8414-3524-3). Folcroft.

Colum, Padriac. Legends of Hawaii. (Illus.). 1937. 26.00x (ISBN 0-300-00376-5). Yale U Pr.

Columbanus, Saint Columbanus in His Own Words. O'Fiaich, Thomas, tr. pap. 4.95 (ISBN 0-686-19381-4). Eastern Orthodox.

Columbaro, Barbara, tr. see Ferrarotti, Franco.

Columbaro, Pasqualino, tr. see Ferrarotti, Franco.

Columbe, Bob, jt. auth. see Crescenti, Peter.

Columbetti, Lelio G., ed. Principles of Radiopharmacology, 2 vols. 1979. Vol. 1, 304p. 81.00 (ISBN 0-8493-5465-X); Vol. 2, 288p. 76.00 (ISBN 0-8493-5466-8). CRC Pr.

Columbia Books Staff. Washington '84. 6th ed. Colgate, C., Jr., ed. (Yes Ser.). 445p. (Orig.). 1982. pap. 40.00 (ISBN 0-910416-50-8). Columbia Bks.

Columbia College - Contemporary Civilization Staff. Introduction to Contemporary Civilization in the West, 2 Vols. 3rd ed. LC 60-16650. 1960-61. Vol. 1. text ed. 25.00x (ISBN 0-231-02423-1); Vol. 2. text ed. 25.00x (ISBN 0-231-02477-0). Columbia U Pr.

Columbia Journalism Review Editors. Squad Helps Dog Bite Victim & Other Flubs from the Nation's Press. LC 79-8553. (Illus.). 128p. 1980. pap. 4.95 (ISBN 0-385-15828-9, Dolp). Doubleday.

Columbia Law Review. Essays on International Law. 462p. 1967. 20.00 (ISBN 0-379-00330-9); pap. 8.50. Oceana.

--Essays on Jurisprudence from the Columbia Law Review. LC 77-10131. xii, 413p. 1977. Repr. of 1963 ed. lib. bdg. 29.00x (ISBN 0-8371-9776-7, CLEJ). Greenwood.

Columbia Law School Alumni Association & Columbia Law School Association of the United Kingdom. The U. S. Transnational Business & the Law. 1985. lib. bdg. 25.00 (ISBN 0-379-20029-5). Oceana.

Columbia Law School Association of the United Kingdom, jt. auth. see Columbia Law School Alumni Association.

Columbia Sailing Club Cookbook Committee Members. Southern Cooking. LC 75-32400. (Illus.). 215p. 1975. pap. 5.95 (ISBN 0-87844-030-5). Sandlapper Pub Co.

Columbia University. Avery Index to Architectural Periodicals, 15 vols. 2nd ed. 1973. Set. lib. bdg. 1485.00 (ISBN 0-8161-1067-0, Hall Library). G K Hall.

--Avery Index to Architectural Periodicals, First Supplement. 2nd ed. 1975. lib. bdg. 145.00 (ISBN 0-8161-0018-7, Hall Library). G K Hall.

--Avery Index to Architectural Periodicals: Third Supplement. 1979. lib. bdg. 140.00 (ISBN 0-8161-0282-1, Hall Library). G K Hall.

--Catalog of the Avery Memorial Architectural Library, 19 Vols. 2nd, enl. ed. 1968. Set. 1590.00 (ISBN 0-8161-0779-3, Hall Library). G K Hall.

--Catalog of the Avery Memorial Architectural Library, Columbia University, Second Supplement, 4 vols. 1975. Set. lib. bdg. 440.00 (ISBN 0-8161-1070-0, Hall Library). G K Hall.

--Catalog of the Avery Memorial Architectural Library, First Supplement, 4 vols. 3166p. 1973. Set. lib. bdg. 440.00 (ISBN 0-8161-0780-7, Hall Library). G K Hall.

--Catalog of the Avery Memorial Architectural Library, Second Edition, Fourth Supplement. 1980. lib. bdg. 340.00 (ISBN 0-8161-0283-X, Hall Library). G K Hall.

--Columbia University Contributions to Anthropology, 37 nos. in 42 vols. Repr. of 1956 ed. Set. 1433.50 (ISBN 0-404-50500-7). AMS Pr.

--Columbia University Contributions to Oriental History & Philology, 13 Vols. Repr. of 1927 ed. Set. 175.00 (ISBN 0-404-50530-9). AMS Pr.

--Columbia University Germanic Studies, Old Ser, Vols. 1-35, 1900-1931, New Ser., Vols. 1-14, 1936-1941. Repr. of 1941 ed. Set. 864.50 (ISBN 0-404-50400-0). AMS Pr.

--Columbia University Indo-Iranian Ser, 14 Vols. Repr. of 1932 ed. Set. 295.50 (ISBN 0-404-50470-1). AMS Pr.

--Columbia University Oriental Studies, 28 Vols. Repr. of 1928 ed. Set. 508.50 (ISBN 0-404-50490-6). AMS Pr.

--Columbia University Studies in Romance Philology & Literature, 40 Vols. Repr. of 1925 ed. Set. 780.00 (ISBN 0-404-50600-3). AMS Pr.

--Columbia University Studies in the Social Sciences, Nos. 1-608. Orig. Title: Studies in History, Economics & Public Law. Repr. of 1966 ed. Set. 9354.00 (ISBN 0-404-51000-0). AMS Pr.

--Dictionary Catalog of the Library of the School of Library Service, 7 Vols. 1962. Set. lib. bdg. 695.00 (ISBN 0-8161-0634-7, Hall Library). G K Hall.

--Dictionary Catalog of the Library of the School of Library Service, 1st Suppl, 4 vols. 1976. Set. lib. bdg. 480.00 (ISBN 0-8161-1166-9, Hall Library). G K Hall.

--Dictionary Catalog of the Teachers College Library, 36 vols. 1970. Set. lib. bdg. 3900.00 (ISBN 0-8161-0855-2, Hall Library). G K Hall.

--Dictionary Catalog of the Teachers College Library, First Supplement, 5 vols. 1971. Set. lib. bdg. 550.00 (ISBN 0-8161-0958-3, Hall Library). G K Hall.

--Dictionary Catalog of the Teachers College Library, Second Supplement, 2 vols. 1973. Set. lib. bdg. 275.00 (ISBN 0-8161-1039-5, Hall Library). G K Hall.

--Lectures on Literature. facs. ed. LC 67-22059. (Essay Index Reprint Ser). 1911. 20.00 (ISBN 0-8369-0329-3). Ayer Co Pubs.

--Quarter Century of Learning, 1904-1929. facs. ed. LC 68-58780. (Essay Index Reprint Ser). 1931. 21.50 (ISBN 0-8369-1028-1). Ayer Co Pubs.

--Spinoza Bibliography. Oko, Adolph S., compiled by. 1964. lib. bdg. 79.00 (ISBN 0-8161-0699-1, Hall Library). G K Hall.

Columbia University. Ancient Near East Society. Journal, Vols. 1-13. Repr. of 1981 ed. Set. buckram 487.50 (ISBN 0-686-57766-3); buckram 37.50 ea. AMS Pr.

Columbia University Center for Advanced Research in Urban & Environmental Affairs. Fifteen Families in Akcalan. (Working Papers Ser.: 2). (Illus.). 1977. pap. 15.00 (ISBN 0-686-19303-2). Pr of Nova Scotia.

Columbia University: Center for Advanced Research in Urban & Environmental Affairs. The New York Federal Archive Building: A Proposal for Mixed Re-Use. (Working Papers Ser.: 1). (Illus.). 1976. pap. 7.95 (ISBN 0-686-20829-3). Pr of Nova Scotia.

Columbia University Center for Advanced Research in Urban & Enviornmental Affairs. Working Paper 2. (Working Papers Ser.: 2). (Illus.). 1977. pap. 15.00 (ISBN 0-686-19302-4). Pr of Nova Scotia.

Columbia University-Department Of Classical Philology. Greek Literature. facs. ed. LC 69-18922. (Essay Index Reprint Ser.). 1912. 17.00 (ISBN 0-8369-0038-3). Ayer Co Pubs.

Columbia University, Dept. of Philosophy, ed. Studies in the History of Ideas, 3 Vols. LC 79-130993. Repr. of 1935 ed. Set. 90.00 (ISBN 0-404-19510-5). AMS Pr.

Columbia University, East Asian Library, New York, 1962. Index to Learned Chinese Periodicals. 1962. lib. bdg. 78.00 (ISBN 0-8161-0644-4, Hall Library). G K Hall.

Columbia University. English Institute. Annual Publications. Approaches to Poetics. Chatman, Seymour, ed. & frwd. by. Repr. of 1973 ed. write for info. (ISBN 0-685-42527-4). AMS Pr.

--Aspects of Narrative. Miller, J. H., ed. & frwd. by. Repr. of 1971 ed. write for info. (ISBN 0-685-42525-8); 12.50 ea. AMS Pr.

Columbia University. English Institute. English Institute Annual. Kirk, Rudolf, ed. Set. write for info. Vol. 1 (ISBN 0-404-52201-7). Vol. 2 (ISBN 0-404-52202-5). Vol. 3 (ISBN 0-404-52203-3). Vol. 4 (ISBN 0-404-52204-1). AMS Pr.

--English Institute Essays. Repr. of 1947 ed. write for info. (ISBN 0-404-52206-8). AMS Pr.

--English Institute Essays. Robertson, D. A., Jr., ed. Repr. of 1948 ed. write for info. (ISBN 0-404-52207-6). AMS Pr.

--English Institute Essays, 4 vols. Downer, Alan S., ed. Set. write for info. (ISBN 0-404-52200-9). Vol. 1 (ISBN 0-404-52208-4). Vol. 2 (ISBN 0-404-52209-2). Vol. 3 (ISBN 0-404-52210-6). Vol. 4 (ISBN 0-404-52211-4). AMS Pr.

--English Institute Essays. Incl. Sound & Poetry. Frye, Northrop, ed. Repr. of 1956 ed; Literature & Belief. Abrams, M. H., ed. Repr. of 1957 ed; Style in Prose Fiction. Martin, Harold C., ed. Repr. of 1958 ed; Edwardians & Late Victorians. Ellmann, Richard, ed. Repr. of 1959 ed; Form & Convention in the Poetry of Edmund Spenser. Nelson, William, ed. Repr. of 1961 ed; Explication As Criticism. Wimsatt, W. K., Jr., ed. & frwd. by. Repr. of 1963 ed; Romanticism Reconsidered. Frye, Northrop, ed. Repr. of 1963 ed. Set. write for info. (ISBN 0-404-52200-9). AMS Pr.

--English Institute Essays. Incl. The Critical Significance of Biographical Evidence; the Methods of Literary Studies. Repr. of 1946 ed (ISBN 0-404-52205-X); English Stage Comedy. Wimsatt, W. K., Jr., ed. Repr. of 1954 ed (ISBN 0-404-52212-2); Motive & Method in The Cantos of Ezra Pound. Leary, Lewis, ed. Repr. of 1954 ed (ISBN 0-404-52213-0); Society & Self in the Novel. Schorer, Mark, ed. Repr. of 1955 ed (ISBN 0-404-52214-9). Set. write for info. (ISBN 0-404-52200-9). AMS Pr.

Columbia University. English Institute. Annual Publications. Forms of Lyric. Brower, Reuben, ed. & frwd. by. Repr. of 1970 ed. write for info. (ISBN 0-685-42524-X). AMS Pr.

--New Perspectives on Coleridge & Wordsworth. Hartman, Geoffrey H., ed. & frwd. by. Repr. of 1972 ed. write for info. (ISBN 0-685-42526-6). AMS Pr.

--Reinterpretations of Elizabethan Drama. Rabkin, Norman, ed. & frwd. by. Repr. of 1969 ed. write for info. (ISBN 0-685-42523-1). AMS Pr.

Columbia University. English Institute. Selected Papers from the English Institute. Incl. Critical Approaches to Medieval Literature. Bethurum, Dorothy, ed. Repr. of 1959 ed (ISBN 0-404-52219-X); The Presence of Walt Whitman. Lewis, R. W., ed. Repr. of 1962 ed (ISBN 0-404-52221-1); Ideas in the Drama. Gassner, John, ed. Repr. of 1964 ed (ISBN 0-404-52224-6); The Lyric & Dramatic Milton. Summers, Joseph H., ed. & frwd. by. Repr. of 1965 ed (ISBN 0-404-52225-4); Northrop Frye in Modern Criticism. Krieger, Murray, ed. & intro. by. Repr. of 1966 ed (ISBN 0-404-52226-2); Literary Criticism & Historical Understanding. Damon, Phillip, ed. & intro. by. Repr. of 1967 ed (ISBN 0-404-52227-0); Experience in the Novel. Pearce, Roy H., ed. & intro. by. Repr. of 1968 ed. write for info. (ISBN 0-404-52228-9). AMS Pr.

Columbia University Law Library, New York. Dictionary Catalog of the Columbia University Law Library, 28 Vols. 1969. Set. lib. bdg. 2860.00 (ISBN 0-8161-0800-5, Hall Library). G K Hall.

--Dictionary Catalog of the Columbia University Law Library, First Supplement, 7 vols. 1973. Set. lib. bdg. 940.00 (ISBN 0-8161-0802-1, Hall Library). G K Hall.

Columbia University Legislative Drafting Research Fund. Constitutions of the United States, 1974-80: National & State, 7 bdgs. 2nd ed. LC 61-18391. looseleaf 75.00 ea. (ISBN 0-379-00186-1); index digest 35.00; 520.00 set. Oceana.

Columbia University, New York. Cumulative Author Index to Psychological Index, 1894 to 1935, & Psychological Abstracts, 1927 to 1958, 5 vols. 1960. Set. 460.00 (ISBN 0-8161-0470-0, Hall Library); first supplement (1959-1963) 110.00 (ISBN 0-8161-0598-7); second supplement (1964-1968) 2 vols. 290.00 (ISBN 0-8161-0749-1). G K Hall.

Columbia University Press. The Concise Columbia Encyclopedia. (Illus.). 960p. 1983. pap. 14.95 (ISBN 0-380-63396-5, 63396-5). Avon.

Columbia University School of Social Work. Counseling in Abortion Services: Physician-Nurse-Social Worker. 1974. 3.00 (ISBN 0-686-09562-6). Univ Bk Serv.

Columbia University. Teachers College. Contributions to Education: Numbers 1-974. Repr. of 1951 ed. Set. 2188.00 (ISBN 0-404-55000-2); 22.50 ea. AMS Pr.

Columbia University, Teachers College Library. Dictionary Catalog of the Teachers College Library, Columbia University, Third Supplement. 1977. lib. bdg. 1095.00 (ISBN 0-8161-0017-9, Hall Library). G K Hall.

Columbia's Graduate School of Architecture Student & Faculty. Precis V: Beyond Style. (Illus.). 160p. 1984. pap. 15.00 (ISBN 0-8478-5391-8). Rizzoli Intl.

Columbo, Anita & Columbu, Franco. Firm up Your Thighs in Fifteen Minutes a Day. (Anita & Franco Columbu's Shape up in Minutes-a-Day Program). (Illus., Orig.). 1980. pap. 1.95 (ISBN 0-8092-7078-1); prepack 93.60 (ISBN 0-8092-7022-6). Contemp Bks.

--Flatten Your Stomach in Fifteen Minutes a Day. (Anita & Franco Columbu's Shape up in Minutes-a-Day Program Ser.). (Illus., Orig.). 1980. pap. 2.45 (ISBN 0-8092-7076-5). Contemp Bks.

Columbo, Serge. Holomorphic Functions of One Variable. 286p. (Fr.). 1983. 39.50 (ISBN 0-677-05950-7). Gordon.

Columbu, Anita & Columbu, Franco. Anita & Franco Columbu's Firm-Up Your Thighs in 15 Minutes a Day. 1.95 (ISBN 0-8092-7078-1). Contemp Bks.

--Anita & Franco Columbu's Flatten Your Stomach in 15 Minutes a Day. 2.45 (ISBN 0-8092-7076-5). Contemp Bks.

--Redesign Your Body: The 90 Day Real Body Makeover. 160p. 1985. 14.95 (ISBN 0-525-24290-2, 01451-440). Dutton.

Columbu, Anita, jt. auth. see Columbu, Franco.

Columbu, Franco. The Businessman's Minutes-A-Day Guide to Shaping Up. (Illus.). 192p. 1983. 16.95 (ISBN 0-8092-5580-4). Contemp Bks.

--The Businessman's Minutes-a-Day Guide to Shaping up. (Illus.). 200p. 1985. pap. 8.95 (ISBN 0-8092-5579-0). Contemp Bks.

--Franco Columbu's Complete Book of Bodybuilding. (Illus.). 160p. 1983. pap. 9.95 (ISBN 0-8092-5983-4). Contemp Bks.

Columbu, Franco & Columbu, Anita. Starbodies: The Women's Weight Training Book. 1978. pap. 10.95 (ISBN 0-525-47527-3, 01063-320). Dutton.

Columbu, Franco & Fels, George. Winning Bodybuilding. LC 76-42436. (Winning Ser.). (Illus.). 1977. 9.95 (ISBN 0-8092-8110-4); pap. 7.95 (ISBN 0-8092-8109-0). Contemp Bks.

Columbu, Franco & Fragomeni, Lydia. The Bodybuilder's Nutrition Book. (Illus.). 192p. (Orig.). 1985. pap. 8.95 (ISBN 0-8092-5457-3). Contemp Bks.

Columbu, Franco & Tyler, Dick. Weight Training & Body Building for Young Athletes. (Illus.). (gr. 4-8). 1979. pap. 6.95 (ISBN 0-671-33006-3). Wanderer Bks.

Columbu, Franco & Tyler, Richard. Winning Weight Lifting & Powerlifting. 1979. pap. 6.95 (ISBN 0-8092-7428-0). Contemp Bks.

Columbu, Franco, jt. auth. see Columbo, Anita.

Columbu, Franco, jt. auth. see Columbu, Anita.

Columbu, Franco, et al. Weight Training for Young Athletes. 1979. o. p. 9.95 (ISBN 0-8092-7479-5); pap. 6.95 (ISBN 0-8092-7478-7). Contemp Bks.

Columbus, Christopher. Four Voyages to the New World. Major, R. H., tr. & ed. 16.75 (ISBN 0-8446-1883-7). Peter Smith.

--Journal of Christopher Columbus (During His First Voyage, 1492-93) & Documents Relating to the Voyages of John Cabot & Gaspar Corte Real. Markham, Clements R., ed. LC 77-178001. (Hakluyt Society Ser: No. 86). 320p. 1972. Repr. lib. bdg. 29.50 (ISBN 0-8337-2230-1). B Franklin.

--Journal of First Voyage to America. LC 77-150177. (Select Bibliographies Reprint Ser.). 1972. Repr. of 1924 ed. 16.00 (ISBN 0-8369-5690-7). Ayer Co Pubs.

--Letter of Christopher Columbus to Rafael Sanchez. (Illus.). 1970. Repr. of 1493 ed. 5.00 (ISBN 0-930230-14-0). Johnson NC.

Columbus, Frederick. Introductory Workbook in Historical Phonology. (Orig.). 1974. pap. 3.50 (ISBN 0-89357-018-4). Slavica.

Columbus Museum of Art. Catalog of the Collection. LC 78-74705. (Illus.). 249p. (Orig.). 1978. pap. 7.50x (ISBN 0-918881-02-1). Columbus Mus Art.

--The Frederick W. Schumacher Collection. LC 76-28630. (Illus.). 280p. (Orig.). 1976. 15.00x (ISBN 0-918881-00-5); pap. 8.00x (ISBN 0-918881-01-3). Columbus Mus Art.

--Images of Ancient Mexico: Pre-Columbian Art from Columbus Collections. LC 80-65728. (Illus.). 60p. (Orig.). 1980. pap. 6.00x (ISBN 0-918881-06-4). Columbus Mus Art.

--Looms of Splendor: Oriental Rugs from Columbus Collections. (Illus.). 91p. (Orig.). 1980. pap. 18.00x (ISBN 0-918881-08-0). Columbus Mus Art.

--One Hundred & Thirty Years of Ohio Photography. LC 78-74247. (Illus.). 72p. (Orig.). 1978. pap. 4.00x (ISBN 0-918881-04-8). Columbus Mus Art.

--Shadow of the Dragon: Chinese Domestic & Trade Ceramics. (Illus.). 100p. (Orig.). 1982. pap. 21.00x (ISBN 0-918881-10-2). Columbus Mus Art.

--Three Hundred Years of Venetian Glass: Selection from the Museo Vetrario-Murano. (Illus.). 32p. (Orig.). 1983. pap. 3.50x (ISBN 0-918881-11-0). Columbus Mus Art.

--Two Hundred Selections from the Permanent Collection. LC 78-74706. (Illus.). 130p. (Orig.). 1978. pap. 2.50x (ISBN 0-918881-03-X). Columbus Mus Art.

Columbus Museum of Art Ser. George Bellows: Painting, Drawing & Prints. LC 78-74708. (Illus.). 90p. (Orig.). 1979. pap. 7.00x (ISBN 0-918881-05-6). Columbus Mus Art.

Columbus Museum of Art Staff. Art in Columbus: Fifty Years. (Illus.). 86p. (Orig.). 1980. pap. 3.00x (ISBN 0-918881-07-2). Columbus Mus Art.

--Art of Glass: Selections from Columbus Collections. (Illus.). 96p. (Orig.). 1981. pap. 6.50x (ISBN 0-918881-09-9). Columbus Mus Art.

--Oriental Images. (Illus.). 20p. (Orig.). 1985. pap. 4.00x (ISBN 0-918881-13-7). Columbus Mus Art.

Columella. De Re Rustica, 3 Vols. (Loeb Classical Library: No. 361, 407, 408). 12.50x ea. Vol. 1 (ISBN 0-674-99398-5). Vol. 2 (ISBN 0-674-99448-5). Vol. 3 (ISBN 0-674-99449-3). Harvard U Pr.

Colussi, G. Finnish-Italian Dictionary. 302p. (Finnish & Italian.). 1978. 29.95 (ISBN 951-0-08233-3, M-9650). French & Eur.

--Finnish-Italian-Finnish Dictionary. 532p. (Ital. & Finnish.). 1981. pap. 14.95 (ISBN 951-0-07998-7, M-9640). French & Eur.

Colussi, G., ed. Dizionario Italiano-Finlandes, Finlandes-Italiano. (Ital. & Finnish.). leatherette 5.95 (ISBN 0-686-92443-6, M-9170). French & Eur.

Coluzzi, Giansanti. The Trains on Avenue De Rumine. (Illus.). 1983. 75.00 (ISBN 0-517-55170-5). Crown.

Colvard, Dean W. Mixed Emotions. 208p. 1985. pap. text ed. 7.95x (ISBN 0-8134-2496-8, 2496). Interstate.

Colver, A. Wayne, ed. see Hume, David.

Colver, A. Wayne, jt. ed. see Vavoulis, Alexander.

Colver, Anne. Abraham Lincoln. (Illus.). 76p. (gr. 1-7). 1966. pap. 2.25 (ISBN 0-440-40001-5, YB). Dell.

--Abraham Lincoln: For the People. LC 60-7079. (Discovery Bks.). (gr. 2-5). 1960. PLB 7.47 (ISBN 0-8116-6253-5). Garrard.

--Bread-&-Butter Indian. (Illus.). (gr. 3-6). 1972. pap. 1.75 (ISBN 0-380-00699-5, 52092-3, Camelot). Avon.

--Bread & Butter Journey. (Illus.). 132p. (gr. 3-7). 1971. pap. 1.75 (ISBN 0-380-00708-8, 55715-0, Camelot). Avon.

--Pluto: Brave Lipizzaner Stallion. LC 78-3463. (Famous Animal Stories Ser.). (Illus.). (gr. 2-5). 1978. PLB 7.68 (ISBN 0-8116-4863-X). Garrard.

Colver, Jay. The Colver Trading Method for Winning the Commodity Game. 1983. 50.00 (ISBN 0-318-00211-6). Windsor.

Colver, Margaret, jt. auth. see Dickson, Elizabeth.

Colverd, Edward C. & Less, Menahem. Teaching Driver Education To The Physically Disabled: A Sample Course. 40p. 1978. 4.25 (ISBN 0-686-38805-4). Human Res Ctr.

Colverd, Edward C., jt. auth. see Less, Menaham.

Colverd, Edward C., jt. auth. see Less, Menahem.

Colvert, DeLynn C. Play Winning Cribbage. LC 80-67576. (Illus.). 142p. 1980. lib. bdg. 13.95 (ISBN 0-9612548-1-5); pap. 9.95 (ISBN 0-9612548-0-7). Starr Studios.

Colvert, J., ed. see Crane, Stephen.

Colvert, James B. Stephen Crane. LC 84-3805. (Album Biographies Ser.). (Illus.). 352p. 1984. 24.95 (ISBN 0-15-184958-7). HarBraceJ.

--Stephen Crane. (Album Biographies Ser.). (Illus.). 352p. 1984. pap. 12.95 (ISBN 0-15-684946-1, Harv). HarBraceJ.

Colvig, Richard, jt. auth. see Coover, James.

Colvile, Kenneth N. Fame's Twilight. facs. ed. LC 73-117771. (Essay Index Reprint Ser). 1923. 19.00 (ISBN 0-8369-1703-0). Ayer Co Pubs.

Colville, Derek. The Teaching of Wordsworth. (American University Studies IV: English Language & Literature: Vol. 7). 128p. (Orig.). 1984. pap. text ed. 12.55 (ISBN 0-8204-0077-7). P Lang Pubs.

--Victorian Poetry & the Romantic Religion. LC 76-97213. 1970. pap. 19.95x (ISBN 0-87395-074-7). State U NY Pr.

Colville, John. The Fringes of Power: Ten Downing Street Diaries, 1939-1955. (Illus.). 1985. 25.00 (ISBN 0-393-02223-4). Norton.

--Historie & Life of King James the Sext. LC 72-1010. (Bannatyne Club, Edinburgh. Publications Ser.: No. 13). Repr. of 1825 ed. 37.50 (ISBN 0-404-52713-2). AMS Pr.

--Original Letters. Laing, David, ed. LC 72-976. (Bannatyne Club, Edinburgh. Publications: No. 104). Repr. of 1858 ed. 45.00 (ISBN 0-404-52859-7). AMS Pr.

Colville, Joseph H. Is It To Die? 224p. 10.95 (ISBN 0-89962-291-7). Todd & Honeywell.

Colville, Josephine. Growing Up. 1979. 6.25 (ISBN 0-8198-0575-0); pap. 5.00 (ISBN 0-8198-0576-9). Dghtrs St Paul.

Colville, W. J. Ancient Mystery & Modern Revelation. 366p. 1985. pap. 18.50 (ISBN 0-89540-122-3, SB 122). Sun Pub.

Colvin & Viall. The Manufacture of Model 1903 Springfield Service Rifle. Wolfe, Dave, ed. 392p. 1984. Repr. of 1917 ed. 19.50 (ISBN 0-935632-20-4). Wolfe Pub Co.

Colvin, jt. auth. see Gleeson.

Colvin, Angela S. Melted Tears: A Poetic True Story. LC 81-71494. (A Poetry Book: Vol. 1). (Illus.). 54p. 1982. pap. 4.95 (ISBN 0-938512-03-X). Brigadoon.

Colvin, Brenda. Land & Landscape: Evolution, Design & Control. 2nd ed. (Illus.). 1971. 28.00 (ISBN 0-7195-1800-8). Transatlantic.

Colvin, Christina, ed. see Edgeworth, Maria.

Colvin, Clare, jt. auth. see Causey, Andrew.

Colvin, Ernest W. Silicon in Organic Synthesis. LC 85-19. 360p. 1985. Repr. of 1981 ed. lib. bdg. write for info. (ISBN 0-89874-843-7). Krieger.

Colvin, Geoffrey, jt. auth. see Prendergast, Curt.

Colvin, Gerald. Now I Will Sing. 136p. 1983. pap. 6.95 (ISBN 0-89390-043-5). Resource Pubns.

Colvin, Goeffrey, jt. auth. see Engelmann, Siegfried.

Colvin, Howard. A Biographical Dictionary of British Architects, 1600-1840. 1088p. 75.00x (ISBN 0-87196-442-2). Facts on File.

--Calke Abbey, Derbyshire: A Hidden House Revealed. (Illus.). 128p. 1985. 24.95 (ISBN 0-540-01084-7, Pub. by G Philip Uk). Sheridan.

--English Architectural History: A Guide to Sources. 23p. 1976. 25.00x (ISBN 0-901262-16-1, Pub. by Pinhorns UK). State Mutual BK.

--Unbuilt Oxford. LC 83-42870. (Illus.). 208p. 1983. text ed. 42.00 (ISBN 0-300-03016-9); pap. 14.95x (ISBN 0-300-03126-2, Y-481). Yale U Pr.

Colvin, Howard & Newman, John. Of Building: Roger North's Writings on Architects. (Illus.). 1981. 49.00x (ISBN 0-19-817325-3). Oxford U Pr.

Colvin, Howard M. Guide to the Sources of English Architectural History. 40.00x (ISBN 0-901262-01-3, Pub. by Pinhorns UK). State Mutual Bk.

Colvin, Ian. Chamberlain Cabinet: How the Meetings in 10 Downing Street, 1937-9, Led to the Second World War. LC 73-155803. 1971. 8.95 (ISBN 0-8008-1433-9). Taplinger.

Colvin, Ian D. Germans in England, 1066-1598. LC 73-118464. 1971. Repr. of 1915 ed. 13.50x (ISBN 0-8046-1213-7, Pub. by Kennikat). Assoc Faculty Pr.

Colvin, Ian D., ed. Cape of Adventure. LC 76-94309. (Illus.). 1969. Repr. of 1912 ed. 32.50 (ISBN 0-404-01638-3). Ams Pr.

Colvin, Lucie G. Historical Dictionary of Senegal. LC 80-25466. (African Historical Dictionaries Ser.: No. 23). 355p. 1981. 22.50 (ISBN 0-8108-1369-6). Scarecrow.

Colvin, Lucie G., et al. The Uprooted of the Western Sahel: Migrants' Quest for Cash in the Senegambia. LC 81-5005. 400p. 1981. 46.95 (ISBN 0-03-057599-0). Praeger.

Colvin, Maggie. Pure Fabrication. LC 84-71909. 192p. (Orig.). 1985. pap. 19.95 (ISBN 0-8019-7603-0). Chilton.

Colvin, Margaret, jt. auth. see Dickson, Elizabeth.

Colvin, Mary N., ed. see Guilelmus.

Colvin, Nola R. & Finholt, Joan M. Guidelines for Physical Educators of Mentally Handicapped Youth: Curriculum, Assessment, IEP's. 90p. 1981. spiral 16.75x (ISBN 0-398-04640-9). C C Thomas.

Colvin, Phyllis. The Economic Ideal in British Government. LC 85-2978. 1985. 30.00 (ISBN 0-7190-1744-0, Pub. by Manchester Univ Pr). Longwood Pub Group.

Colvin, Robert, et al. Keeping it Off: Winning at Weight Loss. 1985. 15.95 (ISBN 0-671-53294-4). S&S.

Colvin, Ruth, jt. auth. see Root, Jane.

Colvin, Ruth J. I Speak English. 103p. 1980. pap. 7.75 (ISBN 0-930713-28-1). Lit Vol Am.

Colvin, S. John Keats: His Life & Poetry. 59.95 (ISBN 0-8490-0453-5). Gordon Pr.

Colvin, Sidney. Keats. Morley, John, ed. LC 68-58373. (English Men of Letters). Repr. of 1889 ed. lib. bdg. 12.50 (ISBN 0-404-51706-4). AMS Pr.

--Keats. 1978. Repr. of 1887 ed. lib. bdg. 15.00 (ISBN 0-8495-0734-0). Arden Lib.

--Keats. 1979. Repr. of 1906 ed. lib. bdg. 15.00 (ISBN 0-8482-7575-6). Norwood Edns.

--Landor. Morley, John, ed. LC 68-58374. (English Men of Letters). Repr. of 1888 ed. lib. bdg. 12.50 (ISBN 0-404-51705-6). AMS Pr.

--Landor. 1979. Repr. of 1881 ed. lib. bdg. 15.00 (ISBN 0-89987-100-3). Darby Bks.

--Landor. 224p. Repr. of 1888 ed. lib. bdg. 20.00 (ISBN 0-918377-61-7). Russell Pr.

--Robert Louis Stevenson. 1978. Repr. of 1902 ed. lib. bdg. 30.00 (ISBN 0-8482-7559-4). Norwood Edns.

--Selections from the Writings of Walter Savage Landor. 1979. Repr. of 1895 ed. lib. bdg. 15.00 (ISBN 0-8492-4039-5). R West.

Colvin, Sidney, ed. Letters & Miscellanies of Robert Louis Stevenson, 2 vols. 465p. 1983. Repr. of 1901 ed. Set. lib. bdg. 50.00 (ISBN 0-89987-847-4). Darby Bks.

--Letters of John Keats to His Family & Friends. 398p. 1984. Repr. of 1925 ed. lib. bdg. 35.00 (ISBN 0-89987-198-4). Darby Bks.

--The Letters of Robert Louis Stevenson to His Family & Friends, 2 Vols. 389p. 1982. Repr. of 1910 ed. Set. lib. bdg. 65.00 (ISBN 0-8495-5054-8). Arden Lib.

Colvin, Sidney, ed. see Finiguerra, Maso.

Colvin, Sidney, ed. see Stevenson, Robert Louis.

Colvin, Sidney, et al. Keats. 1902. lib. bdg. 12.00 (ISBN 0-8414-2371-7). Folcroft.

Colvin, Stephen S. An Introduction to High School Teaching. 451p. Repr. of 1924 ed. lib. bdg. 35.00 (ISBN 0-89984-141-4). Century Bookbindery.

Colvin, Stephen S., ed. see Burrow, N. Trigant.

Colvin, Thomas. Cruising Designs. (Illus.). 112p. 1977. pap. 5.95 (ISBN 0-915160-17-X). Seven Seas.

--Cruising Wrinkles. 112p. 1975. pap. 5.95 (ISBN 0-915160-14-5). Seven Seas.

--Practical Steel Boatbuilding, Vol. 2. (Illus.). 224p. 1985. 25.00 (ISBN 0-87742-203-6). Intl Marine.

--Practical Steel Boatbuilding, Vol. 1. LC 84-48520. (Illus.). 288p. 1985. 30.00 (ISBN 0-87742-189-7). Intl Marine.

Colvin, Thomas, jt. auth. see Klingel, Gilbert.

Colvin, Thomas E. Coastwise & Offshore Cruising Wrinkles. pap. 5.95 (ISBN 0-915160-14-5). Seven Seas.

--Cruising As a Way of Life. LC 79-66980. (Illus.). 232p. 1979. 13.95 (ISBN 0-915160-22-6). Seven Seas.

--Cruising Designs from the Board of Thomas E. Colvin. (Illus.). 112p. 1977. 5.95 (ISBN 0-915160-17-X). Seven Seas.

Colwell. Pathogens & Toxins in the Marine Environment. 1985. write for info. (ISBN 0-471-82593-X). Wiley.

Colwell, A. R., Jr. Understanding Your Diabetes. (Illus.). 184p. 1978. spiral 23.75x (ISBN 0-398-03682-9). C C Thomas.

Colwell, Eileen. Storytelling. 96p. 1983. 8.95 (ISBN 0-370-30228-1, Pub. by the Bodley Head). Merrimack Pub Cir.

Colwell, Eileen, ed. The Magic Umbrella & Other Stories for Telling. (Illus.). 160p. (gr. 2-5). 1981. 9.95 (ISBN 0-370-11020-X, Pub. by the Bodley Head). Merrimack Pub Cir.

Colwell, Ernest C. Study of the Bible. rev. ed. LC 64-23411. (Midway Reprint Ser.). (Orig.). 1964. pap. 8.00x (ISBN 0-226-11420-1). U of Chicago Pr.

Colwell, Ernest C. & Tune, E. W. A Beginner's Reader-Grammar for New Testament Greek. 1965. 12.00xi (ISBN 0-06-061530-3, HarpR). Har-Row.

Colwell, J. D. Computations for Studies of Soil Fertility & Fertilizer Requirements. 297p. 1978. pap. 60.00x (ISBN 0-85198-437-1, Pub. by CAB Bks England). State Mutual Bk.

Colwell, John A. & Lizarralde, German. Diabetes Enocrinology & Metabolic Disorders Continuing Education Review. 1981. 12.00 (ISBN 0-87488-362-8); pap. 27.50. Med Exam.

Colwell, L. V., et al. Research in Support of Numerical & Adaptive Control in Manufacturing. (Illus.). 94p. 1969. 12.00 (ISBN 0-938654-06-3, RESNA). Indus Dev Inst Sci.

Colwell, M. Electronic Components. (Newnes Constructor's Guide Ser.). (Illus.). 1976. pap. 7.50 (ISBN 0-408-00202-6, 5444-0, Pub. by Newnes-Butterworth). Hayden.

Colwell, M., jt. auth. see Hughes, M.

Colwell, M. A., jt. auth. see Ainslie, Alan C.

Colwell, Maggie. West of England Market Towns. (Illus.). 192p. 1983. 14.95 (ISBN 0-7134-2780-9, Pub. by Batsford England). David & Charles.

Colwell, Marian. Think Like an MBA. (Clear & Simple Ser.). (Orig.). 1984. pap. 3.95 (ISBN 0-440-58646-1, Dell Trade Pbks). Dell.

Colwell, Morris A. Project Planning & Building. (Newnes Constructor's Guides Ser.). (Illus.). (gr. 10 up). 1976. pap. 6.95 (ISBN 0-408-00229-8, 5449-1). Hayden.

Colwell, Peter. Blaschke Products: Bounded Analytic Functions. 152p. 1985. text ed. 15.00x (ISBN 0-472-10065-3). U of Mich Pr.

Colwell, Richard & Colwell, Ruth. Concepts for a Musical Foundation. LC 73-4749. (Illus.). 320p. 1974. pap. text ed. 23.95 (ISBN 0-13-166298-8). P-H.

Colwell, Richard, ed. Bulletin Council for Research in Music Education. 96p. 10.00 (ISBN 0-686-37032-5). U IL Sch Music.

--Symposium in Music Education: A Festschrift for Charles Leonhard. LC 81-71592. 329p. 15.00 (ISBN 0-686-38473-3). U IL Sch Music.

Colwell, Richard J. Teaching of Instrumental Music. (Illus.). 1969. 26.95 (ISBN 0-13-893131-3). P-H.

Colwell, Rita, et al, eds. Biotechnology of Marine Polysaccharides. LC 84-25221. (Illus.). 550p. 1985. 79.95 (ISBN 0-89116-433-2). Hemisphere Pub.

Colwell, Rita R., ed. Vibrios in the Environment. LC 83-21720. (Enviromental Science & Technology Ser.: 1-121). 634p. 1983. 45.00x (ISBN 0-471-87343-8, Pub. by Wiley-Interscience). Wiley.

Colwell, Rita R. & Foster, J., eds. Aquatic Microbial Ecology: Proceedings of the ASM Conference. pap. 8.00 (ISBN 0-943676-07-X). MD Sea Grant Col.

Colwell, Rita R. & Hatem, Mary, eds. Microbial Hazards of Diving in Polluted Waters. 3.00 (ISBN 0-943676-08-8). MD Sea Grant Col.

Colwell, Rita R. & Pariser, E. Ray, eds. Biotechnology in the Marine Sciences: Proceedings of the First Annual MIT Sea Grant Lecture & Seminar. 1984. text ed. 37.50 (ISBN 0-471-88276-3, Pub. by Wiley-Interscience). Wiley.

Colwell, Robert N., ed. Manual of Remote Sensing, 2 vols. 2nd ed. LC 83-6055. 2724p. 1983. Set. (106.00 member) 132.00 (ISBN 0-937294-52-7). Vol. I (ISBN 0-937294-41-1). Vol. II (ISBN 0-937294-42-X). ASP & RS.

Colwell, Ruth, jt. auth. see Colwell, Richard.

Colwell, Stella. The Family History Book. (Illus.). 176p. 1985. pap. 9.95 (ISBN 0-7148-2372-4, Pub. by Salem Hse Ltd). Merrimack Pub Cir.

--Tracing Your Family Tree. LC 84-8084. (Illus.). 108p. 1984. 14.95 (ISBN 0-571-13246-4). Faber & Faber.

--Tracing Your Family Tree. LC 84-8084. (Illus.). 112p. (gr. 7 up). 1985. pap. 7.95 (ISBN 0-571-13590-0). Faber & Faber.

Colwell, Stephen. New Themes for the Protestant Clergy. LC 71-83417. (Religion in America, Ser. 1). 1969. Repr. of 1851 ed. 32.00 (ISBN 0-405-00243-2). Ayer Co Pubs.

--The Position of Christianity in the United States, in Its Relations with Our Political Institutions, & Specially with Reference to Religious Instruction in the Public Schools. LC 78-38444. (Religion in America, Ser. 2). 180p. 1972. Repr. of 1854 ed. 17.00 (ISBN 0-405-04063-6). Ayer Co Pubs.

--Ways & Means of Payment. LC 65-23212. Repr. of 1859 ed. 45.00x (ISBN 0-678-00110-3). Kelley.

Colwill, Nina. The New Partnership: Women & Men in Organizations. 216p. 1982. pap. 9.95 (ISBN 0-87484-509-2). Mayfield Pub.

Colwill, Nina L., jt. auth. see Lips, Hilary M.

Colwill, Stephen, jt. auth. see Barrett, Terry.

Colwill, Stiles T. Francis Guy: Seventeen Sixty to Eighteen Twenty. LC 81-81085. (Illus.). 140p. (Orig.). 1981. pap. 15.00 (ISBN 0-938420-20-8). Md Hist.

Colwill, Stiles T., jt. auth. see Klots, Alfred P.

Colwin, Laurie. Family Happiness. LC 82-23. 1982. 12.95 (ISBN 0-394-52511-6). Knopf.

--Family Happiness. 1983. pap. 2.95 (ISBN 0-449-20275-5, Crest). Fawcett.

--Happy All the Time. (General Ser.). 1979. lib. bdg. 13.95 (ISBN 0-8161-6683-8, Large Print Bks). G K Hall.

--Happy All the Time. LC 78-2425. 1978. 12.95 (ISBN 0-394-50190-X). Knopf.

--Happy All the Time. 224p. 1985. pap. 5.95 (ISBN 0-14-007687-5). Penguin.

--The Lone Pilgrim. LC 80-24572. 224p. 1981. 9.95 (ISBN 0-394-51453-X). Knopf.

--The Lone Pilgrim. 1982. pap. 3.95 (ISBN 0-671-43489-6). WSP.

--Passion & Affect. 192p. 1984. pap. 5.95 (ISBN 0-14-007415-5). Penguin.

--Shine On, Bright & Dangerous Object. 192p. 1984. pap. 5.95 (ISBN 0-14-007414-7). Penguin.

Coly, Lisette, ed. see International Conference, Montreal Canada, Aug. 24-25, 1978.

Coly, Lisette, ed. see International Conference, New York, Dec. 6, 1980.

Coly, Lisette, ed. see Proceedings of the International Conference, Paris, France, Aug. 24-26, 1977.

Coly, Lisette, jt. ed. see Shapin, Betty.

Colyer, Frank. Old Instruments Used for Extracting Teeth. LC 77-13129. 1977. Repr. of 1952 ed. lib. bdg. 25.00 (ISBN 0-89341-500-6). Longwood Pub Group.

Colyer, Penrose. I Can Read Italian: My First English Italian Word Book. LC 83-124942. (I Can Read Bks.). (Illus.). 116p. (gr. 2 up). 1983. PLB 9.40 (ISBN 0-531-04601-X). Watts.

--I Can Read Spanish. (I Can Read Ser.). (gr. 2 up). 1981. PLB 9.40 (ISBN 0-531-04285-5). Watts.

--PB: Passeport pour la France. (Illus.). 80p. (Fr.). 1983. pap. text ed. 6.95 (ISBN 0-8219-0046-3, 40294). EMC.

Colyer, Richard J. The Welsh Cattle Drovers. 55p. 1976. text ed. 17.25x (ISBN 0-7083-0592-X, Pub. by Univ of Wales Pr England). Humanities.

Colyer, Vincent. Peace with the Apaches of New Mexico & Arizona. facsimile ed. LC 70-165622. (Select Bibliographies Reprint Ser). Repr. of 1872 ed. 12.00 (ISBN 0-8369-5929-9). Ayer Co Pubs.

Colyer-Fergusson, T. C. see Le Fanu, Thomas P.

Coma, Anthony S. Dry Ice. 1982. 6.50 (ISBN 0-8062-1970-X). Carlton.

Coman, Katharine. Economic Beginnings of the Far West: How We Won the Land Beyond the Mississippi, 2 Vols. Incl. Vol. 1. Explorers & Colonizers; Vol. 2. American Settlers. LC 67-29510. Repr. of 1912 ed. Set. 67.50x (ISBN 0-678-00422-6). Kelley.
--The Industrial History of the United States. LC 73-1999. (Big Business; Economic Power in a Free Society Ser.). Repr. of 1910 ed. 33.00 (ISBN 0-405-05080-1). Ayer Co Pubs.

Coman, Katharine, jt. ed. see Bates, Katharine L.

Coman, Katherine & Lind, Andrew W. The History of Contract Labor in the Hawaiian Islands & Hawaii's Japanese, 2 vols. in 1. Daniels, Roger, ed. LC 78-54813. (Asian Experience in North America Ser.). (Illus.). 1979. Repr. of 1946 ed. lib. bdg. 25.50x (ISBN 0-405-11269-6). Ayer Co Pubs.

Coman, Katherine, jt. ed. see Bates, Katherine L.

Coman, Peter. Catholics & the Welfare State. LC 76-49523. pap. 32.00 (ISBN 0-317-08456-9, 2011288). Bks Demand UMI.

Comanor, William S. National Health Insurance in Ontario: Effects of a Policy of Cost Control. 1980. pap. 4.25 (ISBN 0-8447-3379-2). Am Enterprise.

Comanor, William S. & Wilson, Thomas A. Advertising & Market Power. Caves, Richard E., frwd. by. LC 73-90849. (Economic Studies: No. 144). 1974. text ed. 17.50x (ISBN 0-674-00580-5). Harvard U Pr.

Comant, Kenneth J. Carolingian & Romanesque Architecture: 800-1200. 4th, rev ed. (History of Art Ser: No. 13). (Illus.). 1978. pap. 18.95 (ISBN 0-14-056113-7, Pelican). Penguin.
--Carolingian & Romanesque Architecture. (Pelican History of Art Ser.: No. 13). 1959. 50.00 (ISBN 0-670-20527-3). Viking.

Comar, C. L. & Bronner, Felix, eds. Mineral Metabolism: An Advanced Treatise, 3 vols. Incl. Vol. 1, Pt. A. Principles, Processes & Systems. 1960. 72.00 (ISBN 0-12-183201-5); Vol. 1, Pt. B. Principles, Processes & Systems. 1961. 84.00 (ISBN 0-12-183241-4); Vol. 2, Pt. A. The Elements. 1964. 94.00 (ISBN 0-12-183202-3); Vol. 2, Pt. B. The Elements. 1962. 88.00 (ISBN 0-12-183242-2); Vol. 3. Supplementary Volume. 1969. 84.00 (ISBN 0-12-183250-3). Set. 342.00. Acad Pr.

Comaroff, J., ed. The Meaning of Marriage Payments. (Studies in Anthropology: No. 7). 1980. 39.00 (ISBN 0-12-183450-6). Acad Pr.

Comaroff, Jean. Body of Power, Spirit of Resistance: The Culture & History of a South African People. LC 84-24012. (Illus.). 304p. 1985. lib. bdg. 32.00x (ISBN 0-226-11422-8); pap. 14.95x (ISBN 0-226-11423-6). U of Chicago Pr.

Comaroff, John L. & Roberts, Simon. Rules & Processes: The Cultural Logic of Dispute in An African Context. LC 80-26640. (Illus.). 1981. lib. bdg. 27.50x (ISBN 0-226-11424-4). U of Chicago Pr.

Comaromi, John P. Book Numbers: A Historical Study & Practical Guide to Their Use. LC 81-13691. 145p. 1981. lib. bdg. 25.00 (ISBN 0-87287-251-3). Libs Unl.
--The Dewey Decimal Classification: Eighteen Editions. LC 76-10604. 678p. 1976. 11.00x (ISBN 0-910608-17-2). Forest Pr.

Comaromi, John P. & Warren, Margaret J. Dewey Decimal Classification: Manual on the Use of the DDC: Edition 19. LC 82-1516. 551p. 1982. pap. text ed. 21.00 (ISBN 0-910608-32-6). Forest Pr.

Comas, Juan. Racial Myths. LC 76-5909. (Race Question in Modern Science Ser.). 51p. 1976. Repr. of 1965 ed. lib. bdg. 17.50 (ISBN 0-8371-8801-6, CORM). Greenwood.

Comba, Emilio. History of the Waldenses of Italy: From Their Origin to the Reformation. LC 77-84713. Repr. of 1889 ed. 28.50 (ISBN 0-404-16119-7). AMS Pr.

Combas-Guerra, Eliseo. Presidentes de los Estados Unidos: Anecdotario. LC 83-21647. (Coleccion Uprex, 65 Serie Biografias). viii, 168p. (Orig., Span.). 1984. pap. 3.00 (ISBN 0-8477-0065-8). U of PR Pr.

Combe, Andrew. Observations on Mental Derangement: Being an Application of the Principles of Phrenology to the Elucidation of the Causes, Symptoms, Nature, Treatment of Insanity. LC 72-161928. (History of Psychology Ser.). Repr. of 1834 ed. 50.00x (ISBN 0-8201-1089-2). Schol Facsimiles.

Combe, David A., tr. see Seruzier, Charles.

Combe, G. S., ed. see Harmer, Lewis.

Combe, George. The Constitution of Man Considered in Relation to External Objects. 2nd ed. LC 74-16109. (Hist. of Psych. Ser.). 313p. 1974. Repr. of 1833 ed. 35.00x (ISBN 0-8201-1136-8). Schol Facsimiles.
--Notes on the United States of North America During a Phrenological Visit in 1838-1940, 2 vols. in 1. LC 73-13125. (Foreign Travelers in America, 1810-1935 Ser.). 780p. 1974. Repr. 53.00x (ISBN 0-405-05448-3). Ayer Co Pubs.

Combe, Iris. Border Collies. (Illus.). 198p. 1978. 15.95 (ISBN 0-571-11173-4). Faber & Faber.

Combe, T. G. & Rickard, P. French Language: History, Practice, & Stylistics. 1970. 22.95x (ISBN 0-245-59995-9). Intl Ideas.

Combe, Thomas. Theatre of Fine Devices. Fasc. ed. (Illus.). 120p. 1982. pap. 5.00 (ISBN 0-87328-075-X). Huntington Lib.

Combee, Jerry H. & Hall, Cline E. Designed for Destiny. 112p. 1985. 4.95 (ISBN 0-317-27096-6). Tyndale.

Comber, Chris, jt. auth. see Paris, Mike.

Comber, L. & Hogg, M. Animals in Schools: Vol. 2, Terrestrial Invertebrates. LC 79-670193. (Orig.). 1980. pap. text ed. 9.50x (ISBN 0-435-59401-X). Heinemann Ed.

Comber, Leon. Chinese Magic & Superstitions in Malaya. LC 77-87023. (Illus.). 104p. Repr. of 1960 ed. 16.50 (ISBN 0-404-16808-6). AMS Pr.
--Favourite Chinese Stories. bilingual ed. (The Favourite Stories Series). (Orig.). 1981. pap. text ed. 2.50x (ISBN 9971-64-005-8, 00330). Heinemann Ed.
--Favourite Stories from Asia. bilingual ed. (The Favourite Stories Ser.). (Orig.). 1981. pap. text ed. 2.50x (ISBN 9-97164-007-4, 00332). Heinemann Ed.
--Favourite Stories from Malaysia. bilingual ed. (The Favourite Stories Ser.). (Orig.). 1981. pap. text ed. 2.50x (ISBN 0-686-73752-0, 00336). Heinemann Ed.
--Favourite Stories from the Philippines. bilingual ed. (The Favourite Stories Ser.). 1981. pap. text ed. 2.50x (ISBN 0-686-73754-7, 00337). Heinemann Ed.
--Further Favourite Stories from Asia. bilingual ed. (The Favourite Stories Ser.). (gr. 5). 1981. pap. text ed. 2.50x (ISBN 0-686-73756-3, 00334). Heinemann Ed.
--More Favourite Chinese Stories. bilingual ed. (The Favourite Stories Ser.). (Orig.). 1981. pap. 2.50x (ISBN 0-686-73757-1, 00331). Heinemann Ed.
--More Favourite Stories from Asia. bilingual ed. (The Favourite Stories Ser.). (Orig.). 1981. pap. text ed. 2.50x (ISBN 0-686-73758-X, 00333). Heinemann Ed.
--More Favourite Stories from Asia. (Favourite Stories Ser.). pap. text ed. 2.50x (ISBN 0-686-65637-7, 00301). Heinemann Ed.
--The Strange Cases of Magistrate Pao. (Writing in Asia Ser.). 1972. pap. text ed. 5.50x (ISBN 0-686-65343-2, 00200). Heinemann Ed.
--Thirteen May 1969: A Historical Survey of Sinomalay Relations. (Illus.). xviii, 134p. 1983. pap. text ed. 10.00x (ISBN 967-925-001-6). Heinemann Ed.

Comber, Leon & Shuttleworth, Charles. Favourite Stories from Taiwan. (Orig.). 1975. pap. text ed. 2.50x (ISBN 0-686-97707-6, 00317). Heinemann Ed.

Comber, Leon, retold by. Favourite Chinese Stories. 1967. pap. text ed. 2.50x (ISBN 0-686-60353-2, 00303). Heinemann Ed.
--Favourite Stories from Borneo. (Favourite Stories Ser.). 1975. pap. text ed. 2.50x (ISBN 0-686-60355-9, 00306). Heinemann Ed.
--Favourite Stories from Hong Kong. (Favourite Stories Ser.). 1978. pap. text ed. 2.50x (ISBN 0-686-60358-3, 00310). Heinemann Ed.

Comber, Leon, jt. ed. see Ly, Singko.

Comber, Leon, tr. Favourite Stories from Asia. (Favourite Stories Ser.). 1971. pap. text ed. 2.50x (ISBN 0-686-65609-1, 00300). Heinemann Ed.

Comber, Leon, retold by. Favourite Stories from Malaysia. (Favourite Stories Ser.). 1972. pap. text ed. 2.50x (ISBN 0-686-60425-3, 00314). Heinemann Ed.
--Favourite Stories from the Philippines. (Favourite Stories Ser.). 1978. pap. text ed. 2.50x (ISBN 0-686-60426-1, 00315). Heinemann Ed.

Combes, John R., jt. ed. see Cohen, Alan S.

Combes, Laura. Winning Women's Bodybuilding. Reynolds, Bill, ed. (Illus.). 176p. (Orig.). 1983. pap. 7.95 (ISBN 0-8092-5616-9). Contemp Bks.

Combes, Maria, ed. see Bean, Betty.

Combes, Peter, jt. auth. see Tiffin, John.

Combes, Sharon. Caly. 288p. (Orig.). 1980. pap. 2.50 (ISBN 0-89083-624-8). Zebra.
--Cherron. 336p. (Orig.). 1981. pap. 2.75 (ISBN 0-89083-700-7). Zebra.

Combes, Sharon M. So Little Time. 1982. pap. 2.50 (ISBN 0-89083-974-3). Zebra.
--So Little Time. (Orig.). 1980. pap. 2.50 (ISBN 0-89083-585-3). Zebra.

Combinational Theory Seminar, Eindhoven University of Technology. Proceedings. Van Lint, J. H., ed. (Lecture Notes in Mathematics: Vol. 382). vi, 131p. 1974. pap. text ed. 13.00 (ISBN 0-387-06735-3). Springer-Verlag.

Comblin, Jose. The Church & the National Security State. LC 79-10881. 256p. (Orig.). 1979. pap. 8.95 (ISBN 0-88344-082-2). Orbis Bks.
--Jesus of Nazareth: Meditations on His Humanity. Kabat, Carl, tr. from Port. LC 75-29580. Orig. Title: Jesus De Nazare. 176p. (Orig.). 1976. pap. 6.95 (ISBN 0-88344-239-6). Orbis Bks.
--The Meaning of Mission: Jesus, Christians & the Wayfaring Church. Drury, John, tr. from Spanish. LC 76-41723. Orig. Title: Teologia de la Mision. 142p. 1977. pap. 4.95 (ISBN 0-88344-305-8). Orbis Bks.
--Sent from the Father: Meditations on the Fourth Gospel. Kabat, Carl, tr. from Port. LC 78-16750. Orig. Title: O Enviado do Pai. 115p. (Orig.). 1979. pap. 4.95 (ISBN 0-88344-453-4). Orbis Bks.

Combray, Richard de see De Combray, Richard.

Combs. Percussion Manual. 1977. write for info. (ISBN 0-534-00504-7). Wadsworth Pub.

Combs, Ann. Helter Shelter. 1979. 11.49i (ISBN 0-397-01334-5). Har-Row.
--Smith College Never Taught Me How to Salute. LC 80-8227. 216p. 1981. 12.45i (ISBN 0-690-02012-0, HarpT). Har-Row.
--We'll Laugh about This... Someday. LC 83-45067. 320p. 1983. 14.95 (ISBN 0-689-11393-5). Atheneum.

Combs, Arthur W. Florida Studies in the Helping Professions. LC 71-625778. (University of Florida Social Sciences Monographs: No. 37). 1969. pap. 4.50 (ISBN 0-8130-0271-0). U Presses Fla.
--Myths in Education: Beliefs That Hinder Progress & Their Alternatives. 1978. pap. text ed. 19.29 (ISBN 0-205-05984-8, 2359847). Allyn.
--A Personal Approach to Teaching: Beliefs That Make a Difference. 200p. 1982. 24.95 (ISBN 0-205-07604-1, 247604); pap. text ed. 17.14 (ISBN 0-205-07643-2, 2476436). Allyn.

Combs, Arthur W. & Avila. Helping Relationships. 3rd ed. 250p. (Orig.). 1985. pap. text ed. 20.65 net (ISBN 0-205-08325-0, 248325). Allyn.

Combs, Arthur W., et al. Perceiving, Behaving, Becoming: A New Focus for Education. new ed. LC 44-6213. (ASCD Yearbook: 1962). 264p. 1962. 5.00 (ISBN 0-87120-050-3, 610-17278). Assn Supervision.
--Humanistic Education: Objectives & Assessment. 1978. pap. 4.75 (ISBN 0-87120-089-9, 611-78136). Assn Supervision.
--Perceptual Psychology: A Humanistic Approach to the Study of Persons. 492p. 1976. pap. text ed. 20.95 scp (ISBN 0-06-041346-8, HarpC). Har-Row.

Combs, B., et al. An Invitation to Health: Your Personal Responsibility. 1980. pap. 16.95 (ISBN 0-8053-2301-5). Addison-Wesley.

Combs, Barbara, et al. An Invitation to Health: Your Personal Responsibility. 2nd ed. 1983. 25.95 (ISBN 0-8053-2290-6); instr's guide 6.95 (ISBN 0-8053-2291-4). Benjamin-Cummings.

Combs, Barry, jt. auth. see Creger, Ralph.

Combs, Barry B. Westward to Promontory: Building the Union Pacific Across the Plains & Mountains. (Illus.). 79p. 1969. 10.00 (ISBN 0-318-12737-7). Am Geographical.

Combs, Bert T. The Public Papers of Governor Bert T. Combs, 1959-1963. Robinson, George W. & Sexton, Robert F., eds. LC 78-58103. (The Public Papers of the Governors of Kentucky). 568p. 1980. 28.00x (ISBN 0-8131-0604-4). U Pr of Ky.

Combs, Bob, jt. auth. see Coffelt, Kenneth.

Combs, C. Murphy, ed. Illustrated Family Medical Encyclopedia: Based on Parr's Medical Encyclopedia. LC 76-16457. (Illus.). 1976. 10.95 (ISBN 0-8326-2213-3, 7499); pap. 5.95 (ISBN 0-8326-2259-1). Delair.
--Illustrated Medical Dictionary. (Medical Adviser Ser.). (Illus.). 224p. 1979. pap. 3.95 (ISBN 0-8326-2237-0, 7455). Delair.

Combs, David. Sleepwalker. 320p. 1983. pap. 2.95 (ISBN 0-380-85183-0, 85183-0). Avon.

Combs, Diana W. Early Gravestone Art in Georgia & South Carolina. LC 85-1129. (Illus.). 304p. 1985. text ed. 35.00 (ISBN 0-8203-0788-2). U of Ga Pr.

Combs, Eugene, ed. Modernity & Responsibility: Essays for George Grant. 160p. 1984. 20.00x (ISBN 0-8020-2445-9). U of Toronto Pr.

Combs, Eunice A., jt. auth. see Lyons, Beth.

Combs, Eunice A., ed. see Crump, Claudia.

Combs, Eunice A., ed. see Davis, James.

Combs, Eunice A., ed. see Davis, James E.

Combs, Eunice A., ed. see Fink, Barbara.

Combs, Eunice A., ed. see Haist, Linda.

Combs, Eunice A., ed. see Laudenschlager, David D.

Combs, Eunice A., ed. see Lyons, Beth.

Combs, Eunice A., ed. see Moore, Dean.

Combs, Eunice A., ed. see Shockley, Carol & Wilkins, Phelps.

Combs, Eunice A., ed. see Swank, Pamela.

Combs, Eunice B., ed. see Superka, D. P. & Singleton, L. R.

Combs, Gerald. Brief U. S. Foreign Policy. 1986. text ed. 24.95 (ISBN 0-394-34146-5, KnopfC). Knopf.

Combs, H. C. & Sullens, Z. R. Concordance to the English Poems of John Donne. LC 74-92960. (Studies in Poetry, No. 38). 1970. Repr. of 1940 ed. lib. bdg. write for info. (ISBN 0-8383-0969-0). Haskell.

Combs, Homer C., ed. see Donne, John.

Combs, J. Who's Who in the World Zionist Conspiracy. 1982. lib. bdg. 75.00 (ISBN 0-87700-327-0). Revisionist Pr.

Combs, J., jt. auth. see Nimmo, D.

Combs, James. Polpop: Politics & Popular Culture in America. LC 83-73574. 1984. 24.95 (ISBN 0-87972-276-2); pap. 9.95 (ISBN 0-87972-277-0). Bowling Green Univ.

Combs, James E. & Mansfield, Michael. Drama in Life: The Uses of Communication in Society. (Humanistic Studies in the Communication Arts). 1976. 19.95 (ISBN 0-8038-1555-7); pap. 10.50x (ISBN 0-8038-1556-5). Hastings.

Combs, James E. & Nimmo, Dan. The Student's Prince: Primer of Politics. 496p. 1984. pap. text ed. write for info. (ISBN 0-02-324100-4). Macmillan.

Combs, James E., jt. auth. see Nimmo, Dan.

Combs, Jerald A. American Diplomatic History: Two Centuries of Changing Interpretations. LC 81-24067. 400p. 1982. 39.50x (ISBN 0-520-04590-4). U of Cal Pr.
--The Jay Treaty: Political Battleground of the Founding Fathers. LC 70-84044. 1970. 32.00x (ISBN 0-520-01573-8). U of Cal Pr.

Combs, Jim. Dimensions of Political Drama. 1979. pap. text ed. 14.70x (ISBN 0-673-16259-1). Scott F.

Combs, Jim & Robinson, Jeff. Vega Service, Repair Handbook 1971-1977 Models. 3rd ed. (Illus.). pap. 13.95 (ISBN 0-89287-130-X, A135). Clymer Pubns.

Combs, Josiah H. Folk-Songs of the Southern United States. Wilgus, D. K., ed. (AFS Bibliographic & Special Ser.: No. 19). 282p. 1967. 15.95x (ISBN 0-292-73692-4). U of Tex Pr.

Combs, Richard & Gillen, Stephen E. A Canoeing & Kayaking Guide to the Streams of Ohio, Vol. II. LC 83-13502. (Illus.). 160p. (Orig.). 1983. pap. 9.95 (ISBN 0-89732-013-1). Menasha Ridge.
--A Canoeing & Kayaking Guide to the Streams of Ohio, Vol. I. LC 83-13502. (Illus.). 160p. (Orig.). 1983. pap. 9.95 (ISBN 0-89732-012-3). Menasha Ridge.

Combs, Roger. Holsters & Other Gun Leather: Gun Digest Bk. LC 83-70139. 256p. 1983. pap. 11.95 (ISBN 0-910676-55-0). DBI.

Combs, Roger, ed. Digest Book of Backpacking. LC 79-50065. 96p. pap. 3.95 (ISBN 0-695-81282-3). DBI.

Combs, Roger & Lewis, Jack, eds. Gun Digest Book of Knives. 2nd ed. LC 73-83465. 288p. 1982. 10.95 (ISBN 0-910676-37-2). DBI.

Combs, Steve & Frank, Chuck. Winning Wrestling. (Winning Ser.). (Illus.). 127p. 1980. pap. 7.95 (ISBN 0-8092-7086-2). Contemp Bks.

Combs, Tram. Saint Thomas: Poems. LC 65-14050. (Wesleyan Poetry Program: Vol. 25). (Orig.). 1965. 15.00x (ISBN 0-8195-2025-X); pap. 6.95 (ISBN 0-8195-1025-4). Wesleyan U Pr.

Combs, Trey. Steelhead Fly Fishing & Flies. (Illus.). 118p. (Orig.). 1976. pap. 12.00 (ISBN 0-936608-03-X). F Amato Pubns.

Combs, W. V. First Federal Issue 1798-1801: U. S. Embossed Revenue Stamped Paper. (APS Handbook Ser.). (Illus.). 1979. 17.00 (ISBN 0-933580-01-0). Am Philatelic Society.

Combs, William L. Voice of the S. S. A History of the S. S. Journal "Das Schwarze Korps". (Amercan University Studies IX: Vol. 1). 350p. 1985. text ed. 42.50 (ISBN 0-8204-0083-1). P Lang Pubs.

Combustion Dynamics & Toong, T. Y. Dynamics of Chemically Reacting Fluids. (Energy, Combustion, & Enviroment Ser.). (Illus.). 336p. 1983. text ed. 56.00 (ISBN 0-07-064976-6). McGraw.

Comden, Betty, et al. On the Twentieth Century. LC 79-28365. (Illus.). 152p. 1981. 8.95 (ISBN 0-89676-033-2). Drama Bk.

Come, Patricia C. Diagnostic Cardiology: Non-Invasive Imaging Techniques. LC 65-7313. (Illus.). 608p. 1984. text ed. 67.50 (ISBN 0-397-50572-8, Lippincott Medical). Lippincott.

Comeau, Alexander De see De Comeau, Alexander.

Comeau, Bill. Doubters & Dreamers. 1973. pap. 1.25x (ISBN 0-8358-0278-7). Upper Room.

Comeau, Paul T. Workbook for Wheelock's Latin: An Introductory Course. 112p. (Orig.). 1979. pap. 4.95i (ISBN 0-06-460192-7, CO-192). Har-Row.

Comeau, Raymond F. & Lamoureux, Normand J. Echanges. (Fr.). 1982. text ed. 27.95 (ISBN 0-03-043596-X); instr's manual 19.95 (ISBN 0-03-058078-1); wkbk.-lab manual 11.95 (ISBN 0-03-043601-X); tapes 350.00 (ISBN 0-03-043606-0). HR&W.

Comeau, Raymond F., et al. Ensemble: Culture et Societe. 2nd ed. LC 76-49630. 1982. pap. text ed. 15.95 (ISBN 0-03-060087-1, HoltC). HR&W.
--Ensemble: Grammaire. 2nd ed. LC 76-49636. 1982. text ed. 17.95 (ISBN 0-03-060082-0, HoltC); lab manual 11.95 (ISBN 0-03-060083-9). tapes avail. (ISBN 0-03-060084-7). HR&W.
--Ensemble: Literature. 2nd ed. LC 76-48930. 1982. pap. text ed. 15.95 (ISBN 0-03-060086-3, HoltC). HR&W.

Comeaux, Malcolm L. Arizona: A Geography. LC 80-13119. (Geographies of the United States Ser.). (Illus.). 336p. 1981. 37.50x (ISBN 0-89158-563-X); text ed. 20.00. Westview.

Comeaux, Maureen N., jt. auth. see Ristow, Kate S.

Comel, M., ed. see Symposia Angiologica Santoriana, 3rd Intl. Symposium, Fribourg, 1970.

Comel, M., ed. see Symposia Angiologica Santoriana, 4th International Symposium, Fribourg-Nyon, 1972.

Comeliau, Christian, jt. auth. see OECD Staff.

Comenius, John A. Orbis Pictus of John Amos Comenius. Bardeen, Charles W., ed. LC 67-23933. (Illus.). 232p. (Eng. & Lat.). 1968. Repr. of 1887 ed. 40.00x (ISBN 0-8103-3476-3). Gale.

Comer, Cornelia A. Book of Martyrs. facsimile ed. LC 77-94711. (Short Story Index Reprint Ser.). 1896. 14.50 (ISBN 0-8369-3090-8). Ayer Co Pubs.
--Preliminaries, & Other Stories. LC 78-128726. (Short Story Index Reprint Ser). 1912. 14.00 (ISBN 0-8369-3617-5). Ayer Co Pubs.

Comer, David J. Digital Logic & State Machine Design. 1984. text ed. 39.95 (ISBN 0-03-063731-7). HR&W.

--Electronic Design with Integrated Circuits. LC 80-23365. (Electrical Engineering Ser.). (Illus.). 416p. 1981. text ed. 27.95 (ISBN 0-201-03931-1); solutions manual 1.50 (ISBN 0-201-03932-X). Addison-Wesley.

--Modern Electronic Circuit Design. LC 75-9008. 704p. 1976. text ed. 36.95 (ISBN 0-201-01008-9). Addison-Wesley.

Comer, Douglas. Operating System Design: The Xinu Approach. (P-H Software Ser.). (Illus.). 496p. 1984. text ed. 34.95 (ISBN 0-13-637539-1). P-H.

Comer, J. W. The Continuous Struggle, Bk. 1. LC 73-81488. 160p. 1973. text ed. 2.95 (ISBN 0-88429-900-7). Collegiate Pub.

Comer, James M. & Dubinsky, Alan J. Managing Effective Sales Personnel. LC 84-48359. 160p. 1984. 18.00x (ISBN 0-669-09200-2). Lexington Bks.

Comer, James P. School Power: Implications of an Intervention Project. LC 80-757. 1980. 14.95 (ISBN 0-02-906550-X). Free Pr.

Comer, John C., jt. auth. see Welch, Susan.

Comer, John P. Forging of the Federal Indigent Code. LC 66-16505. 248p. 1966. 6.00 (ISBN 0-911536-07-8). Trinity U Pr.

--Legislative Functions of National Administrative Authorities. LC 68-57566. (Columbia University Studies in the Social Sciences: No. 289). Repr. of 1927 ed. 21.00 (ISBN 0-404-51289-5). AMS Pr.

Comer, Joyce B. Pharmacology in Critical Care. LC 81-65332. (Series in Critical Care Nursing). (Illus.). 169p. (Orig.). 1981. pap. text ed. 15.95 (ISBN 0-471-88805-2). Wiley.

Comer, M. Corporate Fraud. 2nd ed. 416p. 1985. 24.95 (ISBN 0-07-084791-6). McGraw.

Comer, Michael J. Corporate Fraud. LC 85-11686. Date not set. 16.50 (ISBN 0-07-084791-6). McGraw.

Comer, William L. Freedom, Taxes & You. LC 81-71702. 274p. (Orig.). 1982. pap. 14.95 (ISBN 0-942360-00-1). Finan Freedom.

Comerchero, Victor. Nathanael West: The Ironic Prophet. LC 64-23342. 202p. 1967. pap. 5.95x (ISBN 0-295-97876-7, WP30). U of Wash Pr.

Comerchero, Victor, ed. Values in Conflict: Christianity, Marxism, Psychoanalysis & Existentialism. LC 74-111099. 986p. (Orig., Free booklet, "Suggestions for Instructors," available). 1970. pap. text ed. 19.95x (ISBN 0-89197-463-6). Irvington.

Comerci, George D., et al. Adolescent Medicine Case Studies. LC 78-61736. 1979. pap. 24.00 (ISBN 0-87488-053-X). Med Exam.

Comerford, Brian E. Journal of Taxation Digest: Annual. 1984. 35.75 (ISBN 0-88262-983-2). Warren.

Comerford, Brian E. & Sacks, Mason J. Federal Tax Deductions: Annual Cumulative Supplement. 1st ed. 1982. 65.00 (ISBN 0-88262-755-4). Warren.

Comerford, R. V. Charles J. Kickham (1828-1882) A Study in Irish Nationalism & Literature. 256p. 1979. 14.95 (ISBN 0-905473-14-0, Pub. by Wolfhound Pr Ireland). Irish Bks Media.

--The Fenians in Context: Irish Politics & Society, 1848-82. 272p. 1985. text ed. 33.25x (ISBN 0-391-03312-3, Pub. by Wolfhound Pr). Humanities.

Comerford, R. V., ed. see O'Shea, James.

Comerford, Robert A. & Callaghan, Dennis W., eds. Strategic Management: Text, Tools, & Cases for Business Policy. LC 84-27827. 880p. 1985. text ed. write for info. (ISBN 0-534-04518-9). Kent Pub Co.

Comes, F. J. & Muller, A., eds. Spectroscopy in Chemistry & Physics: Modern Trends. (Studies in Physical & Theoretical Chemistry: Vol. 8). 342p. 1980. 81.00 (ISBN 0-444-41856-3). Elsevier.

Comes, Natalis. Mythologiae. LC 75-27853. (Renaissance & the Gods Ser.: Vol. 11). (Illus.). 1976. Repr. of 1567 ed. lib. bdg. 88.00 (ISBN 0-8240-2060-X). Garland Pub.

Cometti, Elizabeth, ed. The American Journals of Lt. John Enys. (Illus.). 377p. 1976. 17.95 (ISBN 0-686-74830-1). Adirondack Mus.

--The American Journals of Lt. John Enys. (Illus.). 377p. 1976. 17.95 (ISBN 0-317-32101-3). Adirondack Mus.

Cometti, Elizabeth, ed. see Dal Verme, Francesco.

Comey, Arthur C. Transition Zoning. LC 73-2903. (Metropolitan America Ser.). (Illus.). 184p. 1974. Repr. 10.00 (ISBN 0-405-05392-4). Ayer Co Pubs.

Comey, David, ed. see Zinoviev, A. A., et al.

Comey, David, tr. see Zinoviev, A. A., et al.

Comey, Dennis J. The Waterfront Peacemaker. LC 82-60025. 202p. 1983. pap. 5.95 (ISBN 0-916101-03-7). St Joseph.

Comfort, jt. auth. see Terrass.

Comfort, A. The Biology of Senescence. 3rd ed. 414p. 1979. 31.50 (ISBN 0-444-00266-9, Biomedical Pr). Elsevier.

--Practice of Geriatric Psychiatry. 1980. 26.95 (ISBN 0-444-00360-6, Biomedical Pr). Elsevier.

Comfort, A., et al. Aging in Cold Blooded Animals, Vol. 2. 236p. 1974. text ed. 21.50x (ISBN 0-8422-7209-7). Irvington.

Comfort, Alex. Barbarism & Sexual Freedom. LC 76-30586. (Anarchy & Anarchism: No. 99). 1977. lib. bdg. 32.95x (ISBN 0-8383-2147-X). Haskell.

--Boxed Set of Joy of Sex & More Joy of Sex. (Illus.). 1975. pap. 22.95 (ISBN 0-671-22178-7, Fireside). S&S.

--The Joy of Sex. 1972. 17.95 (ISBN 0-517-50148-1); non-illus 7.95 (ISBN 0-517-50149-X). Crown.

--The Joy of Sex. (Illus.). 1974. pap. 11.95 (ISBN 0-671-21649-X, Fireside). S&S.

--Joy of Sex. 1985. pap. 12.95 (ISBN 0-317-26736-1, Wallaby). PB.

--Koka Shastra. LC 65-13605. 1977. pap. 3.95 (ISBN 0-8128-2259-5). Stein & Day.

--More Joy of Sex. (Illus.). 234p. 1975. pap. 12.95 (ISBN 0-671-22124-8, Fireside). S&S.

--Novel & Our Time. LC 76-57724. 1948. lib. bdg. 15.00 (ISBN 0-8414-3415-8). Folcroft.

--Reality & Empathy: Physics, Mind & Science in the 21st Century. LC 83-9318. 1984. 39.50x (ISBN 0-87395-762-8); pap. 14.95 (ISBN 0-87395-763-6). State U NY Pr.

--Reality & Empathy: Physics, Mind, & Science in the 21st Century. LC 83-9318. 1985. 14.95 (ISBN 0-913729-09-4). Paragon Hse.

--Sexual Consequences of Disability. (Illus.). 1978. text ed. 24.50x (ISBN 0-89313-008-7); pap. 17.00 (ISBN 0-89313-013-3). G F Stickley Co.

--What Is a Doctor? LC 80-51834. 240p. 1980. 10.95 (ISBN 0-89313-022-2). G F Stickley Co.

Comfort, Alex, ed. The Joy of Sex & More Joy of Sex, 2 vols. 1976. boxed set 23.95 (ISBN 0-517-52732-4). Crown.

Comfort, B. Green Mountain Murder. 1984. pap. 3.95 (ISBN 0-317-14857-5). Landgrove Pr.

--Vermont Village Murder. 192p. (Orig.). 1982. 4.00 (ISBN 0-9608726-0-4). Landgrove Pr.

Comfort, Daniel B. To the Top of the Mountain. LC 82-99918. 226p. 1983. 12.95 (ISBN 0-938316-02-8). Bridges Sound.

Comfort, Daniel B., Jr. Through the Winds Rain. rev. ed. LC 80-53436. 64p. 1981. 7.95 (ISBN 0-938316-00-1). Bridges Sound.

Comfort, J. M., et al. Business Reports in English. (Illus.). 128p. 1985. pap. 6.95 (ISBN 0-521-27294-7). Cambridge U Pr.

Comfort, Jeremy, et al. Basic Technical English. (Illus.). 1982. pap. 6.25x student's ed. (ISBN 0-19-457382-6); pap. 6.95x tchr.'s ed (ISBN 0-19-457383-4). Oxford U Pr.

Comfort, Louise K. Education Policy & Evaluation: A Chance for Change. (Pergamon Policy Studies on Public Administration Ser.). 200p. 1982. 25.00 (ISBN 0-08-023856-4). Pergamon.

Comfort, Randy L. & Williams, Constance D. The Child Care Catalog: A Handbook of Resources & Information on Child Care. 200p. 1985. lib. bdg. 23.50 (ISBN 0-87287-458-3). Libs Unl.

Comfort, Richard A. Revolutionary Hamburg: Labor Politics in the Early Weimar Republic. 1966. 18.50x (ISBN 0-8047-0284-5). Stanford U Pr.

Comfort, W. W. French Romantic Prose. 1977. Repr. of 1928 ed. 20.00 (ISBN 0-89984-167-8). Century Bookbindery.

Comfort, W. W. & Negrepontis, S. Continuous Pseudometrics. (Lecture Notes in Pure & Applied Mathematics Ser.: Vol. 14). 136p. 1975. 35.00 (ISBN 0-8247-6294-0). Dekker.

--The Theory of Ultra Filters. (Die Grundlehren der Mathematischen Wissenschaften Ser.: Vol. 211). 480p. 1974. 55.00 (ISBN 0-387-06604-7). Springer-Verlag.

Comfort, W. W., tr. see Chretien De Troyes.

Comfort, Will L. Apache. 1976. Repr. of 1931 ed. lib. bdg. 16.95x (ISBN 0-89190-851-X, Pub. by River City Pr). Amereon Ltd.

--Routledge Rides Alone. 1976. Repr. of 1910 ed. lib. bdg. 17.95 (ISBN 0-89190-852-8, Pub. by River City Pr). Amereon Ltd.

--Trooper Tales. 1976. Repr. of 1899 ed. lib. bdg. 15.95x (ISBN 0-89190-853-6, Pub. by River City Pr). Amereon Ltd.

--Trooper Tales. facsimile ed. LC 70-106271. (Short Story Index Reprint Ser.). 1899. 18.00 (ISBN 0-8369-3308-7). Ayer Co Pubs.

Comfort, William W. William Penn & Our Liberties. 146p. 1976. pap. 3.00 (ISBN 0-941308-02-2). Religious Soc Friends.

Comhaire, Jean & Rahnman, Werner J. How the Cities Grew. 4th ed. 196p. 1971. pap. 5.95 (ISBN 0-912598-23-9). Florham.

Comhaire-Sylvain, Suzanne. Les Contes Haitiens, 2 vols. in 1. LC 78-67701. (The Folktale). Repr. of 1937 ed. 33.50 (ISBN 0-404-16074-3). AMS Pr.

Comics, Harvey. Casper in Sky-Jinks, No. 16. 128p. 1984. pap. 1.95 (ISBN 0-441-09243-8). Ace Bks.

Comines, Philippe de. History of Comines, 2 Vols. Danett, Thomas, tr. (Tudor Translations, First Ser.: Nos. 17-18). Repr. of 1897 ed. Set. 90.00 (ISBN 0-404-51890-7); 45.00 ea. Vol. 1 (ISBN 0-404-51891-5). Vol. 2 (ISBN 0-404-51892-3). AMS Pr.

Comings, John. Participatory Communication in Nonformal Education, No. 17. (Technical Notes Ser.). 15p. (Orig.). 1981. pap. 1.50 (ISBN 0-932288-62-6). Ctr Intl Ed U of MA.

Comings, John, jt. auth. see Cain, Bonnie.

Comings, Lois L., ed. see Kent, Henry W.

Comini, Alessandra. Egon Schiele. (Illus.). pap. 14.95 (ISBN 0-8076-0820-3). Braziller.

--Egon Schiele's Portraits. (California Studies in the History of Art: Vol. 17). (Illus.). 1974. 70.00 (ISBN 0-520-01726-9). U of Cal Pr.

--Gustav Klimt. LC 75-10965. (Illus.). 112p. 1975. pap. 12.95 (ISBN 0-8076-0806-8). Braziller.

Comins, Ethel M. Caroline: Oxbow's American Bonaparte. 208p. 1985. 13.95 (ISBN 0-912526-38-6). Lib Res.

--Love's Impossible Dream. 1982. 8.95 (ISBN 0-686-84736-9, Avalon). Bouregy.

--Love's Tangled Web. (YA) 1978. 8.95 (ISBN 0-685-19061-7, Avalon). Bouregy.

Comins, N. R. & Clark, J. B., eds. Specialty Steels & Hard Materials: Proceedings of the International Conference (Materials Development '82), Pretoria, South Africa, 9-12 November 1982. 450p. 1983. 100.00 (ISBN 0-08-029358-1). Pergamon.

Comish, Newel W. Effective Leadership of Voluntary Organizations. LC 76-23694. (Management Ser.). (Illus.). 1976. 12.95 (ISBN 0-89305-001-6). Anna Pub.

Comision International De Redaccion, jt. auth. see Ibarruri, Dolores.

Comiskey, James C. Negotiating the Purchase or Sale of a Business. (Successful Business Library). 200p. 1985. 3-ring binder 32.95 (ISBN 0-916378-69-1, Oasis). PSI Res.

Comiskey, Kate, ed. see Baird, Chuck, et al.

Comiskey, Kate, ed. see Blattner, John W., et al.

Comiskey, Kate, ed. see Blechman, Fred, et al.

Comiskey, Kate, ed. see Domuret, Allan J., et al.

Comiskey, Kate, jt. ed. see Putnam, Katherine.

Comiskey, Thomas, jt. ed. see Cohen, Stewart.

Comissiong, Barbara, jt. auth. see Jordan, Alma.

Comisso. Worker's Control under Plan & Market. 1979. text ed. 33.00x (ISBN 0-300-02334-0). Yale U Pr.

Comitas, Lambros. Caribbeana, 1900-1965: A Topical Bibliography. LC 68-14239. (Illus.). 930p. 1968. 27.50x (ISBN 0-295-73970-3). U of Wash Pr.

--The Complete Caribbeana 1900-1975: A Bibliographic Guide to the Scholarly Literature, 4 Vols. LC 76-56709. 1977. Set. lib. bdg. 265.00 (ISBN 0-527-18820-4). Kraus Intl.

Comitas, Lambros, jt. auth. see Rubin, Vera.

Comite Central del Partido Comunista del la URSS. Historia Del Partido Comunista "Bolchevique" De la URSS. 429p. 1975. pap. text ed. 6.95 (ISBN 0-89380-024-4). Proletarian Pubs.

Comite des Archives de la Louisiane, compiled by. History of Pointe Coupee Parish, Louisiana, Vol. I. (Illus.). 363p. 1983. 43.50 (ISBN 0-88107-005-X). Natl ShareGraphics.

Comite Interagencial De la Estrategia De Puerto Rico. El Desarrollo Economico De Puerto Rico: Una Estrategia Para la Proxima Decada. (Illus., Span.). 1976. pap. 3.75x (ISBN 0-8477-2215-5). U of PR Pr.

Comite International D'Historie de l'Art, ed. Glossarium Artis. 1985. lib. bdg. 36.00 (ISBN 0-317-11845-5). Tome 9: Stadtbaukunst-Urbanisme-Town Planning (ISBN 3-598-10461-8). Tome 10: Holzbaukunst-Architecture en Bois-Architecture of Wood (ISBN 3-598-10460-X). K G Saur.

Comite Para el Estudio De las Finanzas De Puerto Rico. Informe Al Gobernador Del Comite Para el Estudio De las Finanzas De Puerto Rico (Informe Tobin) Velilla Robertin, Angie, tr. from Eng. Orig. Title: Report to the Governor the Committee to Study P.R's Finances. (Illus., Span.). 1976. pap. text ed. 5.00 (ISBN 0-8477-2216-3). U of PR Pr.

Comitini, Salvatore & Hardjolukito, Sutanto. Indonesian Marine Fisheries Development & Strategy under Extended Maritime Jurisdiction. LC 83-14208. (Research Report Series of the East-West Environment & Policy Institute:: No. 13). (Illus.). vi, 69p. 1983. pap. text ed. 3.00 (ISBN 0-86638-048-5). E W Center HI.

Comito, Terry. The Idea of the Garden in the Renaissance. 1978. 27.50x (ISBN 0-8135-0841-X). Rutgers U Pr.

Comito, Terry, ed. Touch of Evil, Orson Wells, Director. (Rutgers Films in Print Ser.). (Illus.). 250p. 1985. 25.00 (ISBN 0-8135-1096-1); pap. 10.00 (ISBN 0-8135-1097-X). Rutgers U Pr.

Comjean, Marlies I., tr. see Bruckner, Christine.

Comley, Nancy R., jt. auth. see Scholes, Robert.

Comley, Nancy R., et al, eds. Fields of Writing: Readings Across the Disciplines. LC 83-61621. (Illus.). 700p. 1984. pap. text ed. 12.95 (ISBN 0-312-28837-9); instr's manual avail. St Martin.

Commager, A., ed. Documents of American History, 2 vols. 9th ed. 1974. Vol. 1. pap. 21.95 (ISBN 0-13-216994-0); Vol. 2. pap. 21.95 (ISBN 0-13-217000-0). P-H.

Commager, H. S. Theodore Parker: Yankee Crusader. 11.25 (ISBN 0-8446-1884-5). Peter Smith.

Commager, H. Steele, ed. see Knight, William F.

Commager, Henry. The Defeat of the Confederacy. LC 78-25755. (Anvil Ser.). 189p. 1964. pap. 6.95 (ISBN 0-442-00071-5). Krieger.

Commager, Henry S. The American Mind: An Interpretation of American Thought & Character Since the 1800's. 1950. pap. 10.95x (ISBN 0-300-00046-4, Y7). Yale U Pr.

--The Blue & the Gray, Vols. 1 & 2. 1973. pap. 3.95 ea. (Ment); Vol. 1. pap. (ISBN 0-451-62166-2, ME2166); Vol. 2. pap. (ISBN 0-451-62278-2, ME2278). NAL.

--The Empire of Reason: How Europe Imagined & America Realized the Enlightenment. 1982. pap. 9.95 (ISBN 0-19-503062-1, GB 664, GB). Oxford U Pr.

--The Empire of Reason: How Europe Imagined & America Realized the Enlightenment. 1984. 17.25 (ISBN 0-8446-6088-4). Peter Smith.

--The Era of Reform Eighteen Thirty to Eighteen Sixty. LC 82-15190. 192p. (Orig.). 1982. pap. 6.95 (ISBN 0-89874-498-9). Krieger.

--Fifty Basic Civil War Documents. LC 82-15187. 192p. 1982. pap. 6.95 (ISBN 0-89874-497-0). Krieger.

--Freedom, Loyalty, Dissent. 1954. 14.95x (ISBN 0-19-500510-4). Oxford U Pr.

--Great Constitution. LC 61-7914. (gr. 6-10). 1961. 7.50 (ISBN 0-672-50299-2). Bobbs.

--Jefferson, Nationalism, & the Enlightenment: Spread of Enlightenment from Old World to New. LC 74-80659. 224p. 1975. 7.50 (ISBN 0-8076-0765-7). Braziller.

--Majority Rule & Minority Rights. 11.25 (ISBN 0-8446-1123-9). Peter Smith.

--The Nature & Study of History. Winks, Robin W., ed. LC 83-49173. (History & Historiography Ser.). 155p. 1985. lib. bdg. 20.00 (ISBN 0-8240-6356-2). Garland Pub.

--Noah Webster's American Spelling Book. LC 62-21960. (Classics in Education Ser.). 1963. pap. text ed. 5.00x (ISBN 0-8077-1176-4). Tchrs Coll.

--The People & Their Schools. LC 76-23913. (Fastback Ser.: No.79). (Orig.). 1976. pap. 0.75 (ISBN 0-87367-079-5). Phi Delta Kappa.

--Theodore Parker. 1982. pap. 6.45 (ISBN 0-933840-15-2). Unitarian Univ.

Commager, Henry S. & Muessig, Raymond H. The Study & Teaching of History. 2nd ed. (Social Science Seminar, Secondary Education Ser.: No. C28). 136p. 1980. pap. text ed. 8.95 (ISBN 0-675-08317-6). Merrill.

Commager, Henry S., jt. auth. see Nevins, Allan.

Commager, Henry S., ed. The Blue & the Gray, 2 vols. (Illus.). 1296p. 1982. Set. 9.98 (ISBN 0-517-38379-9). Outlet Bk Co.

--The Blue & the Gray: The Story of the Civil War As Told by Participants, 2 vols. in 1. (Illus.). (gr. 11-12). Repr. of 1950 ed. text ed. 50.00x (ISBN 0-8290-0033-X). Irvington.

--Lester Ward & the Welfare State. LC 66-22579. 1967. 37.50x (ISBN 0-672-50998-9). Irvington.

Commager, Henry S. & Doherty, Stephen M., eds. The American Spirit. (Illus.). 352p. 1985. 49.50 (ISBN 0-8109-1838-2). Abrams.

Commager, Henry S., ed. see Garraty, John A.

Commager, Henry S., ed. see Hamilton, et al.

Commager, Henry S., ed. see Savage, Henry, Jr.

Commager, Henry S., ed. see Smelser, Marshal L.

Commager, Henry S., ed. see Smelser, Marshall.

Commager, Henry S., ed. see Thomas, Emory M.

Commager, Henry S., et al. Civil Liberties Under Attack: Publications of the William J. Cooper Foundation, Swarthmore College. facs. ed. LC 68-14899. (Essay Index Reprint Ser). 1951. 17.00 (ISBN 0-8369-0308-0). Ayer Co Pubs.

Commager, Henry Steele. Freedom & Order. LC 66-15755. 1966. 6.50 (ISBN 0-8076-0384-8). Braziller.

Commager, Steele, ed. see Bae Hrens, Aemilius.

Commager, Steele, ed. see Bridges, Robert, et al.

Commager, Steele, ed. see Brinton, Anna C.

Commager, Steele, ed. see Cousin, Jean.

Commager, Steele, ed. see Crump, Mary M.

Commager, Steele, ed. see Daryusl, A. A., et al.

Commager, Steele, ed. see Deutsch, Rosamund E.

Commager, Steele, ed. see Enk, P. J.

Commager, Steele, ed. see Ewbank, William W.

Commager, Steele, ed. see Fowler, H. W., et al.

Commager, Steele, ed. see Kroll, Wilhelm.

Commager, Steele, ed. see Lier, Bruno, et al.

Commager, Steele, ed. see Lilja, Saara.

Commager, Steele, ed. see Onions, C. T., et al.

Commager, Steele, ed. see Piwonka, Mario P.

Commager, Steele, ed. see Richardson, Lawrence.

Commager, Steele, ed. see Robinson, Ellis.

Commager, Steele, ed. see Rothstein, Maximilian.

Commager, Steele, ed. see Smith, Logan P., et al.

Commager, Steele, ed. see Sparrow, John.

Commager, Steele, ed. see Wagenvoort, Hendrik.

Commager, Steele, ed. see Winbolt, Samuel E.

Commance, Ashtar, ed. New World Order. (Illus.). 72p. (Orig.). 1982. 8.95 (ISBN 0-938294-12-1). Global Comm.

Command of the Army Council. Pistol: Browning, F. N. 9mm. No. 2, Mark 1. 1982. pap. text ed. 0.95 (ISBN 0-86663-991-8). Ide Hse.

Commander, Lydia K. The American Idea. LC 77-169378. (Family in America Ser.). 352p. 1972. Repr. of 1907 ed. 18.00 (ISBN 0-405-03855-0). Ayer Co Pubs.

Commanger, Steele H. see Commager, Henry S.

Commerce & Community Affairs Dept. Fire Protection Administration for Small Communities & Fire Protection Districts. LC 79-93086. (Illus.). 330p. 1980. pap. text ed. 15.00 (ISBN 0-87939-037-9). Intl Fire Serv.

Commerce Clearing House. Corporation-Partnership-Fiduciary Filled-in Tax Return Forms-1986. 152p. 1985. 6.50 (ISBN 0-317-30573-5, 5926). Commerce.

--Federal Income Taxes of Decedents & Estates. LC 82-244462. (CCH Tax Analysis Ser.). 1982. pap. 8.00 (ISBN 0-686-46282-3). Commerce.

--Interest & Dividends: Witholding, Information Returns. Date not set. price not set. Commerce.

--New Zealand Master Tax Guide: 1981. 550p. 1981. 24.50 (ISBN 0-686-75923-0). Commerce.

--Tax-Saving Plans for Self-Employed. LC 82-233494. 48p. Date not set. price not set. Commerce.

Commerce Clearing House & United States Federal Energy Regulatory Commission. Federal Energy Regulatory Commission Reporter. LC 84-153382. Date not set. price not set. Commerce.

Commerce Clearing House, jt. auth. see United States Equal Opportunity Commission.

Commerce Clearing House, Inc. AICPA Audit & Accounting Manual, As of June 1, 1984. 752p. 1984. 17.00 (ISBN 0-317-30612-X, 4813). Commerce.

--AICPA Codification of Statements on Auditing Standards: Numbers 1-49. 880p. 1985. 19.50 (ISBN 0-317-30613-8, 4755). Commerce.

--Business Expense Log-1985: Mid-Year Edition. 64p. 1985. 2.50 (ISBN 0-317-30581-6, 4704). Commerce.

--Business Recordkeeping: New Substantiation Rules ITC-Depreciation for Luxury Automobiles. 40p. 1985. 4.00 (ISBN 0-317-30582-4, 4710). Commerce.

--CCH Federal Tax Manual-1986. 2100p. 1985. looseleaf 85.00 (ISBN 0-317-30575-1, 5816). Commerce.

--Estate Planning for California Residents. 272p. 1985. 14.00 (ISBN 0-317-30609-X, 5834). Commerce.

--Federal Estate & Gift Taxes: Code & Regulations-As of March 1985-Including Federal Income Taxes of Estates & Trusts (Subchapter J) 1024p. 1985. 13.00 (ISBN 0-317-30566-2, 4745). Commerce.

--Federal Estate & Gift Taxes Explained: 1985 Edition. 400p. 1985. 13.00 (ISBN 0-317-30568-9, 4746). Commerce.

--Federal Tax Computation-1986. 40p. 1985. 2.00 (ISBN 0-317-30586-7, 4376). Commerce.

--Federal Tax Course-1986: General Edition. 400p. 1985. 52.50 (ISBN 0-317-30584-0, 4719). Commerce.

--Foreign Sales Corporations under Tax Reform Act of 1984. 80p. 1985. 15.00 (ISBN 0-317-30579-4, 4753). Commerce.

--Guidebook to Florida Taxes. 128p. 1986. 14.00 (ISBN 0-317-30593-X, 4737). Commerce.

--Guidebook to Illinois Taxes. 288p. 1986. 14.00 (ISBN 0-317-30595-6, 4736). Commerce.

--Guidebook to Labor Relations-1985. 416p. 1984. 10.50 (ISBN 0-317-30616-2, 4766). Commerce.

--Guidebook to Massachusetts Taxes 1986. 184p. 1986. 14.00 (ISBN 0-317-30596-4, 4735). Commerce.

--Guidebook to Michigan Taxes 1986. 328p. 1986. 14.00 (ISBN 0-317-30598-0, 4734). Commerce.

--Guidebook to New Jersey Taxes 1986. 232p. 1986. 14.00 (ISBN 0-317-30601-4, 4732). Commerce.

--Guidebook to New York Taxes-1986. 384p. 1986. 14.00 (ISBN 0-317-30602-2, 4732). Commerce.

--Guidebook to North Carolina Taxes-1986. 264p. 1986. 14.00 (ISBN 0-317-30603-0, 4731). Commerce.

--Guidebook to Ohio Taxes-1986. 272p. 1986. 14.00 (ISBN 0-317-30605-7, 4730). Commerce.

--Guidebook to Pennsylvania Taxes. 232p. 1986. 14.00 (ISBN 0-317-30606-5, 4729). Commerce.

--Guidebook to Wisconsin Taxes-1986. 328p. 1986. 14.00 (ISBN 0-317-30607-3, 4728). Commerce.

--Income Tax Regulations, As of June 1985, 4 vols. 7216p. 1985. 37.00 (ISBN 0-317-30563-8, 4702). Commerce.

--Individuals' Filled-in Tax Return Forms-1986. 152p. 1985. 6.00 (ISBN 0-317-30574-3, 5936). Commerce.

--Internal Revenue Code: Income, Employment, Estate & Gift Tax Provisions, As of June 1985. 3408p. 1985. 20.50 (ISBN 0-317-30560-3, 4703). Commerce.

--IRS Classification Handbook. 64p. 1985. 8.00 (ISBN 0-317-30578-6, 4754). Commerce.

--Minimum Wages & Overtime Pay: The Answer Book on Federal Law. 48p. 1985. 3.50 (ISBN 0-317-30619-7, 4727). Commerce.

--Occupational Safety & Health Standards for General Industry. 544p. 1984. 8.50 (ISBN 0-317-30620-0, 4789). Commerce.

--Pension & Employee Benefits, Code-ERISA-Regulations, As of April 5, 1985. 2568p. 1985. 27.00 (ISBN 0-317-30621-9, 4721). Commerce.

--Planning for Your Retirement-IRAs & Keogh Plans. 112p. 1984. 2.50 (ISBN 0-317-30622-7, 4761). Commerce.

--Pocketax-1986. 32p. 1985. 1.50 (ISBN 0-317-30588-3, 4396). Commerce.

--Responsibilities of Corporate Officers & Directors under Federal Securities Law. 128p. 1985. 10.00 (ISBN 0-317-30611-1, 4752). Commerce.

--Security Transactions-1985. 32p. 1985. 2.00 (ISBN 0-317-30590-5, 4366). Commerce.

--Small Business Investment Companies. Bruchey, Stuart & Carosso, Vincent P., eds. LC 78-18958. (Small Business Enterprise in America Ser.). 1979. Repr. of 1959 ed. lib. bdg. 12.00x (ISBN 0-405-11462-1). Ayer Co Pubs.

--Social Security Benefits, Including Medicare, January 1, Nineteen Eighty-Five. 48p. 1985. 2.00 (ISBN 0-317-30615-4, 4771). Commerce.

--Social Security Explained Nineteen Eighty-Five. 256p. 1985. 9.00 (ISBN 0-317-30614-6, 4765). Commerce.

--Tax Law of the State of New York, As of November, 1984. 720p. 1985. 27.50 (ISBN 0-317-30608-1, 5834). Commerce.

--U. S. Excise Tax Guide-1985. 256p. 1985. 9.00 (ISBN 0-317-30585-9, 5905). Commerce.

--U. S. Master Tax Guide-1986. 576p. 1985. pap. 14.50 (ISBN 0-317-30558-1, 5956); 21.00 (ISBN 0-317-30559-X, 5886). Commerce.

--VEBAs Explained. 32p. 1985. 2.00 (ISBN 0-317-30623-5, 4750). Commerce.

Commerce Clearing House Staff. Divorce: How It Affects Your Taxes. 64p. 1985. 3.00 (ISBN 0-317-30583-2, 4741). Commerce.

--Government Contracts Reporter: Laws, Regulations, Rulings, Topically Arranged, Full Explanations, Currently Supplemented, Completely Indexed. LC 83-460243. Date not set. price not set. Commerce.

--Labor Law Guide. LC 83-460244. Date not set. price not set. Commerce.

Commerce Clearing House Staff, et al. Contract Appeals Decisions: Reporting Full Text Decisions, Armed Services Board of Appeals. LC 83-460264. Date not set. price not set. Commerce.

Commercial & Financial Trust Company Limited. British Virgin Islands Business Law. 257p. 1980. 50.00x (ISBN 0-89499-011-X). Bks Business.

Commins, Dorothy. What Is an Editor? Saxe Commins at Work. LC 77-81716. 256p. pap. 5.95 (ISBN 0-226-11428-7, Phoen). U of Chicago Pr.

Commins, Elaine. Bloomin' Bulletin Boards. LC 83-81432. 175p. (Orig.). 1984. pap. 12.95 (ISBN 0-89334-047-2). Humanics Ltd.

--Early Childhood Activities: A Treasury of Ideas from Worldwide Sources. LC 81-83051. 260p. 1981. pap. 16.95 (ISBN 0-89334-066-9). Humanics Ltd.

Commins, Eugene D. & Bucksbaum, Philip H. Weak Interactions of Leptons & Quarks. LC 82-4452. (Illus.). 674p. 1983. 72.50 (ISBN 0-521-23092-6); pap. 29.95 (ISBN 0-521-27370-6). Cambridge U Pr.

Commins, Lloyd T. Winning at Craps. 1965. pap. 4.00 (ISBN 0-87980-345-2). Wilshire.

Commins, Saxe, ed. see Stevenson, Robert Louis.

Commins, Saxe D. & Linscott, Robert N., eds. Man & Man: The Social Philosophers. (Orig.). (gr. 9-12). pap. 0.75 (ISBN 0-671-47075-2). WSP.

--Man & Spirit: The Speculative Philosophers. (gr. 9-12). pap. 0.75 (ISBN 0-671-47076-0). WSP.

--Man & the Universe: The Philosophers of Science. pap. 0.75 (ISBN 0-671-47078-7). WSP.

Commins, Stephen, jt. ed. see Cesaretti, C. A.

Commins, Stephen K., et al, eds. Africa's Agrarian Crisis: The Roots of Famine. (Food in Africa Ser.). 225p. 1985. lib. bdg. 23.00x (ISBN 0-931477-60-3). Lynne Rienner.

Commire, Anne, ed. Something about the Author, Vol. 40. (Something about the Author Ser.). (Illus.). 300p. 1985. 64.00x (ISBN 0-8103-2250-1). Gale.

--Something About the Author, Vo. 41. LC 72-27107. (Something About the Author Ser.). 300p. 1985. 64.00x (ISBN 0-8103-2251-X). Gale.

--Something about the Author: Facts & Pictures about Contemporary Authors & Illustrators of Books for Young People. Incl. Vol. 1. 1971 (ISBN 0-8103-0050-8); Vol. 2. 1972 (ISBN 0-8103-0052-4); Vol. 3. 1972 (ISBN 0-8103-0054-0); Vol. 4. 1973 (ISBN 0-8103-0056-7); Vol. 5. 1973 (ISBN 0-8103-0058-3); Vol. 6. 1974 (ISBN 0-8103-0060-5); Vol. 7. 1975 (ISBN 0-8103-0062-1); Vol. 8. 1975. (ISBN 0-8103-0064-8); Vol. 9. 1976. (ISBN 0-8103-0066-4); Vol. 10. 1976. (ISBN 0-8103-0068-0); Vol. 11. 1977. (ISBN 0-8103-0070-2); Vol. 12. 1977. (ISBN 0-8103-0072-9); Vol. 13. 1978. (ISBN 0-685-43929-1); Vol. 14. 1978 (ISBN 0-8103-0095-8); Vol. 15. 1979 (ISBN 0-8103-0096-6); Vol. 16. 1979 (ISBN 0-8103-0097-4); Vol. 17. 1979 (ISBN 0-8103-0098-2); Vol. 18. 1980 (ISBN 0-8103-0099-0); Vol. 19. 1979 (ISBN 0-8103-0051-6); Vol. 20. 1980 (ISBN 0-8103-0053-2); Vol. 21. 1980 (ISBN 0-8103-0093-1); Vol. 22. 1980 (ISBN 0-8103-0085-0); Vol. 23. 1981 (ISBN 0-8103-0086-9); Vol. 24. 1981 (ISBN 0-8103-0087-7); Vol. 25. 1981 (ISBN 0-8103-0084-2); Vol. 26. 1982 (ISBN 0-8103-0089-3); Vol. 27. 1982 (ISBN 0-8103-0083-4); Vol. 28. 296p (ISBN 0-8103-0082-6); Vol. 29. 328p (ISBN 0-8103-0081-8). LC 72-27107. (Illus.). (gr. 7-12). 62.00x ea. Gale.

--Something about the Author: Facts & Pictures about Contemporary Authors & Illustrators of Books for Young People. Incl. Vol. 31. 272p. 1984 (ISBN 0-8103-0057-5); Vol.32. 288p. 1983 (ISBN 0-8103-0059-1); Vol. 33. 1984 (ISBN 0-8103-0061-3); Vol. 35. 250p. 1984 (ISBN 0-8103-0065-6); Vol. 36. 250p. 1984 (ISBN 0-8103-0067-2); Vol. 37. 250p. 1984 (ISBN 0-8103-0069-9); Vol. 38. 250p. 1985 (ISBN 0-8103-0071-0); Vol. 39. 300p. 1985 (ISBN 0-8103-0074-5). LC 72-27107. (Illus.). 62.00x ea. Gale.

--Yesterday's Authors of Books for Children: Facts & Pictures about Authors & Illustrators of Books for Young People, 2 vols. LC 76-17501. (Yesterday's Authors of Books for Children Ser.). (Illus.). (YA) (gr. 7-12). 62.00x ea.; Vol. 1, 1977. (ISBN 0-8103-0073-7); Vol. 2 1978. (ISBN 0-8103-0090-7). Gale.

Commissariat a l'Energie Atomique. Dictionnaire des Sciences et Techniques Nucleaires. 3rd ed. 492p. (Fr.). 1975. 67.50 (ISBN 0-686-56958-X, M-6081). French & Eur.

Commission Christian Lit. Bible Translations. 1981. pap. 0.79 (ISBN 0-8100-0132-2, 04N1212). Northwest Pub.

Commission for Aeronautical Meteorology, 5th Session, 1971. Report. pap. 20.00 (ISBN 0-686-93916-6, W119, WMO). Unipub.

Commission for Basic Systems, 6th Session, 1974. Report. pap. 25.00 (ISBN 0-686-93919-0, W151, WMO). Unipub.

Commission For Christian Literature, ed. Is Evolutionism the Answer. (Truth Unchanging Series). (Illus.). 1968. pap. 2.50 (ISBN 0-8100-0023-7, 12-0331). Northwest Pub.

Commission for Instruments & Methods of Observation, 6th Session. Abridged Final Report of the Sixth Session. 98p. (Orig.). 1974. pap. 20.00 (ISBN 0-685-40958-9, W459, WMO). Unipub.

Commission for Investigation of Health Hazards of Chemical Compounds in the Work Area Staff. Maximum Concentrations at the Workplace & Biological Tolerance Values for Working Materials 1983. 75p. 1984. pap. text ed. 10.00x (ISBN 0-89573-202-5). VCH Pubs.

Commission for Special Applications of Meteorology & Climatology, 6th Session, 1973. Report. pap. 25.00 (ISBN 0-686-93925-5, W142, WMO). Unipub.

Commission for the Advancement of Public Interest Organizations. Periodicals of Public Interest Organizations: A Citizen's Guide. LC 79-88697. (Illus.). 1982. pap. 5.00 (ISBN 0-9602744-1-3). Comm Adv Public Interest.

Commission For The Compilation Of The History Of The Kuomintang, ed. see Sun Yat-Sen.

Commission of Architecture of AEA. Architecture for Adult Education. 74p. 1953. 2.30 (ISBN 0-88379-008-4). A A A C E.

Commission of European Communities, ed. Plutonium Recycling Scenario in Light Water Reactors: Assessment of Environmental Impact in the European Community. 240p. 1982. 29.50 (ISBN 3-7186-0118-4). Harwood Academic.

--Research & Development on Radioactive Waste Management & Storage: First Annual Progress Report of the European Community Programme 1980-84. (Radioactive Waste Management Ser.: Vol. 4). 129p. 1982. 19.75 (ISBN 3-7186-0115-X). Harwood Academic.

Commission of International Trade & Investment Policy. U. S. International Economic Policy in an Interdependent World, 4 vols. (Final Reports & Compendium of Papers: Nos. 1 & 2). 1985. Repr. of 1971 ed. Set. lib. bdg. 160.00 (ISBN 0-89941-420-6). W S Hein.

Commission of the Central Committee of the C.P.S.U. (B.), ed. History of the Communist Party of the Soviet Union (Bolsheviks) LC 75-2470. 364p. 1975. Repr. of 1939 ed. lib. bdg. 19.75x (ISBN 0-8371-8018-X, HICP). Greenwood.

Commission of the European Communities, jt. auth. see International Agency for Research on Cancer Workshop. Brussels, Belgium, June 9-12, 1975.

Commission of the European Communities Directorate-General for Research, Science & Education, ed. see International Conference, Varese, Italy, March 26-29, 1979.

Commission of the European Communities Staff, ed. Agricultural Economics & Rural Sociology-Multilingual Thesaurus, 5 Vols. (Thesauri Ser.). 456p. 1979. lib. bdg. 110.00 (ISBN 3-598-10097-3). K G Saur.

Commission of the European Communities, Luxembourg. Better Translation for Better Communication: A Survey of the Translation Market, Present & Future, Prepared for the Commission of the European Communities, Directorate-General Information Market & Innovation. (Commission of the European Communities Ser.). 200p. 1983. 24.00 (ISBN 0-08-030534-2). Pergamon.

Commission of the European Communities. Coke Oven Techniques. 350p. 1983. pap. 40.00x (ISBN 0-8448-1422-9). Crane-Russak Co.

--Conference on the Quality of the Environment & the Iron & Steel Industry: 24-26 Sept. 1974. 1977. Eng. Ed. 105.00 (ISBN 0-08-020915-7); Ger. Ed. 97.00 (ISBN 0-08-020917-3); Fr. Ed. 97.00 (ISBN 0-08-020916-5). Pergamon.

--Criteria (Dose-Effect Relationships) for Cadmium. LC 77-30193. 1977. text ed. 33.00 (ISBN 0-08-022024-X). Pergamon.

--Electronic Document Delivery II. 1980. 45.00 (ISBN 0-317-00235-X). Learned Info.

Commission of the European Communities, Brussels, Belgium. Energy Research & Development Programme, 2 vols. in one. 1979. lib. bdg. 121.00 (ISBN 90-247-2220-9, Pub. by Martinus Nijhoff Netherlands). Kluwer Academic.

Commission of the European Communities, ed. Energy Research & Development Programme, Status Report 1977. 1977. pap. 24.00 (ISBN 90-247-2059-1, Pub. by Martinus Nijhoff Netherlands). Kluwer Academic.

Commission of the European Communities. European Community Oil & Gas Research & Development Projects. 250p. 1982. 99.00x (ISBN 0-86010-393-5, Pub. by Graham & Trotman England). State Mutual Bk.

Commission of the European Communities Staff, ed. Food-Multilingual Thesaurus, 5 Vols. (Thesauri Ser.). 724p. 1979. lib. bdg. 162.00 (ISBN 3-598-10105-8). K G Saur.

Commission of the European Communities, Luxembourg. Fusion Technology: Proceedings of the 11th Symposium, Oxford, England, Sept. 15-19, 1980, 2 vols. (Illus.). 1000p. 1981. Set. 165.00 (ISBN 0-08-025697-X). Pergamon.

Commission of the European Communities, Luxembourg, ed. Fusion Technology: Proceedings of the 12th Symposium (SOFT), Julich Laboratory, Federal Republic of Germany, 13-17 September 1982, 2 Vols. (International School of Fusion Reactor Technology (CEC) Ser.). 1564p. 1983. Set. pap. 250.00 (ISBN 0-08-029977-6). Pergamon.

Commission of the European Communities. Fusion Technology 1984: Proceedings of the 13th Symposium (SOFT), Varese, Italy, 24-28 Sept. 1984, 2 vols. (International School of Fusion Reactor Tecnology (CEC) Ser.). (Illus.). 1749p. 1985. Set. pap. 250.00 (ISBN 0-08-032559-9, Pub. by PPI). Pergamon.

--The Law & Practice Relating to Pollution Control in the Member States of the European Communities. Environmental Resources Ltd, ed. Incl. Vol. 1 (ISBN 0-86010-040-5); Vol. 2a (ISBN 0-86010-041-3); Vol. 3 (ISBN 0-86010-029-4); Vol. 4 (ISBN 0-86010-033-2); Vol. 4a (ISBN 0-86010-035-9); Vol. 5 (ISBN 0-86010-032-4); Vol. 5a (ISBN 0-86010-034-0); Vol. 6 (ISBN 0-86010-031-6); Vol. 7 (ISBN 0-86010-039-1); Vol. 7a (ISBN 0-86010-042-1); Vol. 8 (ISBN 0-86010-030-8); Vol. 9 (ISBN 0-86010-037-5); Vol. 11 (ISBN 0-86010-038-3). 1983. 29.00 ea. (Pub. by Graham & Trotman England); complete set 288.00. State Mutual Bk.

--Law & Practice Relating to Pollution Control in the Member States of the European Communities: France. 1983. 40.00x (ISBN 0-8448-1442-3). Crane-Russak.

--Law & Practice Relating to Pollution Control in the Member States of the European Communities: Greece. 1983. 40.00x (ISBN 0-8448-1445-8). Crane-Russak.

--Law & Practice Relating to Pollution Control in the Member States of the European Communities: Federal Republic of Germany. 1983. 40.00x (ISBN 0-8448-1443-1). Crane-Russak.

--Law & Practice Relating to Pollution Control in the Member States of the European Communities: Denmark. 1983. 40.00x (ISBN 0-8448-1441-5). Crane-Russak.

--Law & Practice Relating to Pollution Control in the Member States of the European Communities: Italy. 1983. 40.00x (ISBN 0-8448-1447-4). Crane-Russak.

--Law & Practice Relating to Pollution Control in the Member States of the European Communities: Belgium & Luxembourg. 1983. 40.00x (ISBN 0-8448-1435-0). Crane-Russak.

--Law & Practice Relating to Pollution Control in the Member States of the European Communities: Netherlands. 1983. 40.00x (ISBN 0-8448-1448-2). Crane-Russak.

--Law & Practice Relating to Pollution Control in the Member States of the European Communities: Ireland. 1983. 40.00x (ISBN 0-8448-1446-6). Crane-Russak.

--Law & Practice Relating to Pollution Control in the Member States of the European Communities: Comparative Volume. 1983. 40.00x (ISBN 0-8448-1450-4). Crane-Russak.

--Law & Practice Relating to Pollution Control in the Member States of the European Communities: United Kingdom. 1983. 40.00x (ISBN 0-8448-1449-0). Crane-Russak.

--New Technologies for Exploration & Exploitation of Oil & Gas Resources, Vol. 1. 800p. 1979. 90.00x (ISBN 0-86010-158-4, Pub. by Graham & Trotman England). State Mutual Bk.

--New Technologies for Exploration & Exploitation of Oil & Gas Resources, Vol. 11. 600p. 1979. 75.00x (ISBN 0-86010-159-2, Pub. by Graham & Trotman England). State Mutual Bk.

--Organophosphorus Pesticides Criteria (Dose-Effect Relationships) for Organophosphorus Compounds. Derache, R., ed. 1977. pap. text ed. 44.00 (ISBN 0-08-021993-4). Pergamon.

--Public Health Risks of Exposure to Asbestos. Zielhuis, R. L., ed. LC 76-51964. 1977. pap. text ed. 25.00 (ISBN 0-08-021580-7). Pergamon.

Commission of the European Communities, Staff, ed. Veterinary Multilingual Thesaurus, 5 Vols. (Thesauri Ser.). 122p. 1979. lib. bdg. 270.00 (ISBN 3-598-10109-0). K G Saur.

Commission on Accreditation. Handbook of Accreditation Standards & Procedures. rev. ed. LC 84-4268. 200p. 1984. pap. 20.00 (ISBN 0-87293-009-3). Coun Soc Wk Ed.

Commission on Advertising Staff. Bar Association Advertising: A How-To Manual. 17p. 1979. 7.00 (ISBN 0-317-30628-6). Amer Bar Assn.

Commission on Cancer Control, Cancer Detection Committee. Cancer Detection. 2nd rev. ed. (UICC Monograph: Vol. 4). (Illus.). vii, 51p. 1974. pap. 22.00 (ISBN 0-387-06976-3). Springer-Verlag.

Commission on Chicago Historical & Architectural Landmarks. Landmark Neighborhoods in Chicago. (Illus.). 64p. (Orig.). 1981. pap. 3.50 (ISBN 0-934076-02-2). Chicago Review.

Commission on Country Life. Report of the Commission on Country Life. facsimile ed. McCurry, Dan C. & Rubenstein, Richard E., eds. LC 74-30625. (American Farmers & the Rise of Agribusiness Ser.). 1975. Repr. of 1911 ed. 17.00x (ISBN 0-405-06787-9). Ayer Co Pubs.

Commission on Critical Choices. The Soviet Empire: Expansion & Detente. Griffith, William E., ed. LC 75-44727. (Critical Choices for Americans Ser.: Vol. IX). 1976. 26.50 (ISBN 0-669-00421-9). Lexington Bks.

Commission on Education for Health Administration. Report of the Commission on Education for Health Administration, Vol. 1. LC 74-17538. 190p. 1975. 7.50x (ISBN 0-914904-04-3). Health Admin Pr.

--Report of the Commission on Education for Health Administration, Vol. 3. DeVries, Robert A., frwd. by. (Illus.). 1977. text ed. 7.50x (ISBN 0-914904-23-X). Health Admin Pr.

--Selected Papers of the Commission on Education for Health Administration, Vol. 2. LC 74-17537. 330p. 1975. 12.50x (ISBN 0-914904-05-1). Health Admin Pr.

Commission On Education In Agriculture & Natural Resources. Undergraduate Education in the Plant & Soil Sciences. LC 71-600161. (Orig.). 1969. pap. 4.25 (ISBN 0-309-01704-1). Natl Acad Pr.

--Undergraduate Teaching in the Animal Sciences. 1967. pap. 5.25 (ISBN 0-309-01486-7). Natl Acad Pr.

Commission on Engineering & Technical Systems, National Research Council. Toward Safer Underground Coal Mines. 1982. pap. text ed. 10.50 (ISBN 0-309-03298-9). Natl Acad Pr.

Commission On English, ed. End-of-Year Examinations in English for College-Bound Students, Grades 9-12: Sample Questions in Language, Literature & Composition; Sample Responses by Students; Evaluation of the Responses. 101p. 1963. pap. 4.00 spiral bound (ISBN 0-87447-040-4, 224315). College Bd.

--Twelve Thousand Students & Their English Teachers: Tested Units in Teaching Literature, Language, Composition. LC 67-30437. 389p. 1968. pap. 8.50 spiral bdg. (ISBN 0-87447-097-8, 295725). College Bd.

Commission on Foundations & Private Philanthropy. Foundations: Private Giving & Public Policy. LC 78-139831. 1970. 15.00x (ISBN 0-226-66286-1). U of Chicago Pr.

Commission on Freedom of the Press, ed. see Leigh, Robert D.

Commission on Human Resources. A Century of Doctorates. LC 78-5644. 173p. 1978. pap. text ed. 11.95 (ISBN 0-309-02738-1). Natl Acad Pr.

Commission on Hydrometeorology, 1972. Report. pap. 20.00 (ISBN 0-685-57278-1, W124, WMO). Unipub.

Commission on International Relations. Astronomy in China. 109p. 1979. pap. 7.75 (ISBN 0-309-02867-1). Natl Acad Pr.

--Oral Contraceptives & Steroid Chemistry in People's Republic of China. 1977. pap. 9.00 (ISBN 0-309-02638-5). Natl Acad Pr.

--Wheat Studies in the People's Republic of China. 1977. pap. 11.50 (ISBN 0-309-02637-7). Natl Acad Pr.

Commission on International Relations, National Research Council. World Food & Nutrition Study: Interim Report. LC 75-37120. xix, 82p. 1975. pap. 6.95 (ISBN 0-309-02436-6). Natl Acad Pr.

Commission on International Relations. World Food & Nutrition Study: Supporting Papers, 5 vols. 1977. Vol. I. pap. 8.25 (ISBN 0-309-02647-4); Vol. II. pap. 8.25 (ISBN 0-309-02726-8); Vol. III. pap. 8.50 (ISBN 0-309-02730-6); Vol. IV. pap. 7.50 (ISBN 0-309-02727-6); Vol. V. pap. 7.50 (ISBN 0-309-02646-6). Natl Acad Pr.

Commission on Museums for a New Century. Museums for a New Century. LC 84-72051. (Illus.). 144p. (Orig.). 1984. pap. 17.95 (ISBN 0-931201-08-X). Am Assn Mus.

Commission on National Parks & Protected Areas (CNPPA), jt. auth. see International Union for Conservation of Nature & Natural Resources (IUCN).

Commission on Natural Resources. Environmental Monitoring. 1977. pap. 9.25 (ISBN 0-309-02639-3). Natl Acad Pr.

--Perspectives on Technical Information for Environmental Protection. 1977. pap. 7.75 (ISBN 0-309-02623-7). Natl Acad Pr.

Commission on Natural Resources, National Research Council. The Shallow Land Burial of Low-Level Radioactively Contaminated Solid Waste. LC 76-56928. 1976. pap. 8.50 (ISBN 0-309-02535-4). Natl Acad Pr.

Commission on Non-traditional Study. Diversity by Design. 1st ed. LC 73-3772. (Jossey-Bass Series in Higher Education). pap. 52.00 (ISBN 0-317-27219-5, 2023875). Bks Demand UMI.

Commission on Secondary Schools. Policies & Procedures. 88p. 15.00 (ISBN 0-318-14823-4, CSS 9); members free. Mid St Coll & Schl.

Commission on Sociotechnical Systems, National Research Council. The Integrity of Frozen Spermatozoa. LC 77-940301. (Illus.). 1978. pap. text ed. 11.25 (ISBN 0-309-02645-8). Natl Acad Pr.

Commission on Sociotechnical Systems. N R C Trans-Bus Study. 1979. pap. 1.50 (ISBN 0-309-02929-5). Natl Acad Pr.

Commission on Sociotechnical Systems, National Research Council. A Program of Studies on Socioeconomic Effects of Earthquake Predictions. 1978. pap. text ed. 9.95 (ISBN 0-309-02789-6). Natl Acad Pr.

Commission on the Humanities. The Humanities in American Life: Report of the Commission on the Humanities. LC 80-14084. 1980. 14.50 (ISBN 0-520-04183-6); pap. 5.95 (ISBN 0-520-04208-5). U of Cal Pr.

Commission on Theological Concerns of the Christian Conference of Asia, ed. Minjung Theology: People As the Subjects of History. LC 83-7279. 224p. (Orig.). 1983. pap. 9.95 (ISBN 0-88344-336-8). Orbis Bks.

Commission on U.S.-Latin American Relations. The Americas in a Changing World. 1975. 10.00 (ISBN 0-685-59068-2). Ayer Co Pubs.

Commission on Voluntary Service & Action, jt. auth. see Council on International Educational Exchange.

Commission Studies. Wiretapping & Electronic Surveillance. (Illus.). 1983. pap. 10.95 (ISBN 0-317-03315-8). Loompanics.

Commission to Study the Organization of Peace. Building Peace: Reports of the Commission to Study the Organization of Peace, 1939-1972, 2 vols. LC 73-4845. 1973. Repr. Set. 40.00 (ISBN 0-8108-0621-5). Scarecrow.

--New Dimensions for the United Nations. Eichelberger, Clark M., ed. LC 42-18205. 246p. 1966. 15.00 (ISBN 0-379-13351-2). Oceana.

--Organizing Peace in the Nuclear Age. Holcombe, Arthur N., ed. LC 75-31831. 245p. 1975. Repr. of 1959 ed. lib. bdg. 17.00x (ISBN 0-8371-8441-X, HOOP). Greenwood.

Commission to Study the Organization of Peace & Holcombe, Arthur N. Strengthening the United Nations. LC 74-7536. 276p. 1976. Repr. of 1957 ed. lib. bdg. 18.50x (ISBN 0-8371-7579-8, HOUN). Greenwood.

Commission to Study the Organization of Peace. Thirtieth Report. LC 82-219541. Date not set. 4.00. Comm Peace.

--United Nations & Human Rights. Eichelberger, Clark M., et al, eds. LC 42-18205. 224p. 1968. 15.00 (ISBN 0-379-13352-0). Oceana.

--The United Nations: The Next Twenty Five Years. Sohn, Louis B., ed. LC 42-18205. 1971. 15.00 (ISBN 0-379-13353-9). Oceana.

Commissioner Of Education In The District Of Columbia. History of Schools for the Colored Population. LC 74-101516. (American Negro: His History & Literature, Ser. No. 3). 1970. Repr. of 1871 ed. 13.00 (ISBN 0-405-01918-1). Ayer Co Pubs.

Commisssion of the European Communities. Oil & Gas Multilingual Glossary. 500p. 1979. 44.00x (ISBN 0-86010-170-3, Pub. by Graham & Trotman England). State Mutual Bk.

Committe on Corporate Laws of the Section of Corporation, Banking & Business Law of the American Bar Association. Official Forms for Use Under the Model Business Corporation Act. 130p. 1969. pap. 3.00 (ISBN 0-317-32245-1, B143). Am Law Inst.

Committe on International Collaborative Activities, ed. International Directory of Specialized Cancer Research & Treatment Establishment. 3rd ed. (UICC Technical Report Ser.: Vol. 66). 727p. 1983. text ed. 97.50 (ISBN 92-9018-066-8, Pub. by Intl Union Against Cancer Switzerland). J K Burgess.

Committe, Thomas C., et al. Managerial Finance for the Seventies. (Finance Ser.). 1972. text ed. 35.95 (ISBN 0-07-012371-3). McGraw.

Committee D-2 on Petroleum Products & Lubricants. Multi-Cylinder Test Sequences for Evaluating Automotive Engine Oils, Pt. 3, Sequence V-D-STP 315H. LC 83-68369. 146p. pap. 24.00 (ISBN 0-8031-0238-0, 04-315100-12); 20.00 (ISBN 0-8031-0525-8). ASTM.

Committee E-10 on Radioisotopes & Radiation Effects. Space Radiation Effects on Materials. LC 62-20905. (American Society for Testing & Materials. Special Technical Publication Ser.: No. 330). pap. 20.00 (ISBN 0-317-09203-0, 2000123). Bks Demand UMI.

Committee f the American Association of Vet. Lab Diagnosticians, ed. Culture Methods for the Detection of Animal Salmonellosis & Arizonosis. 88p. 1975. pap. text ed. 5.50x (ISBN 0-8138-1455-3). Iowa St U Pr.

Committee for Economic Development. An Approach to Federal Urban Policy. LC 77-27893. 1977. lib. bdg. 4.00 (ISBN 0-87186-765-6); pap. 2.50 (ISBN 0-87186-065-1). Comm Econ Dev.

--Broadcasting & Cable Television: Policies for Diversity & Change. LC 75-6536. 120p. 1975. pap. 2.50 (ISBN 0-87186-058-9). Comm Econ Dev.

--Budgeting for National Objectives. LC 66-17307. 72p. 1966. lib. bdg. 2.50 (ISBN 0-87186-721-4); pap. 1.50 (ISBN 0-87186-021-X). Comm Econ Dev.

--Building a National Health-Care System. LC 73-75244. 105p. 1973. pap. 2.00 (ISBN 0-87186-049-X). Comm Econ Dev.

--Congressional Decision Making for National Security. LC 74-12944. 1974. lib. bdg. 3.50 (ISBN 0-87186-755-9); pap. 2.00 (ISBN 0-87186-055-4). Comm Econ Dev.

--Development Assistance to Southeast Asia. LC 73-133144. 96p. 1970. lib. bdg. 2.50 (ISBN 0-87186-738-9); pap. 1.50 (ISBN 0-87186-038-4). Comm Econ Dev.

--Economic Aspects of North Atlantic Security: A Statement on National Policy by the Research & Policy Committee of the Committee Foe Economic Development. LC 51-5321. pap. 20.00 (ISBN 0-317-08292-2, 2007008). Bks Demand UMI.

--Economic Development Issues: Latin America. LC 67-29353. 356p. 1967. pap. 4.25 (ISBN 0-87186-221-2). Comm Econ Dev.

--Educating Tomorrow's Managers. LC 68-8483. 52p. 1964. pap. 1.00 (ISBN 0-87186-015-5). Comm Econ Dev.

--Education for the Urban Disadvantaged from Preschool to Employment. LC 75-153374. 1971. pap. 1.50 (ISBN 0-87186-041-4). Comm Econ Dev.

--Financing a Better Election System. LC 68-59440. 84p. 1968. lib. bdg. 2.00 (ISBN 0-87186-731-1); pap. 1.00 (ISBN 0-87186-031-7). Comm Econ Dev.

--Financing the Nation's Housing Needs. LC 73-77093. 69p. 1973. pap. 1.50 (ISBN 0-87186-050-3). Comm Econ Dev.

--Fiscal & Monetary Policies for Steady Economic Growth. LC 76-76619. 85p. 1969. pap. 1.00 (ISBN 0-87186-032-5). Comm Econ Dev.

--Further Weapons Against Inflation. LC 70-141683. 96p. 1970. lib. bdg. 2.50 (ISBN 0-87186-740-0); pap. 1.50 (ISBN 0-87186-040-6). Comm Econ Dev.

--Helping Insure Our Energy Future: A Program for Developing Synthetic Fuel Plants Now. 1979. lib. bdg. 6.00 (ISBN 0-87186-769-9); pap. 4.50 (ISBN 0-87186-069-4). Comm Econ Dev.

--High Employment Without Inflation: A Positive Program for Economic Stabilization. LC 72-86317. 76p. 1972. pap. 1.50 (ISBN 0-87186-747-8); lib. bdg. 2.50. Comm Econ Dev.

--Improving Executive Management in the Federal Government. LC 64-25240. 80p. 1964. pap. 1.50 (ISBN 0-87186-014-7). Comm Econ Dev.

--Improving Federal Program Performance. LC 70-173676. 86p. 1971. pap. 1.50 (ISBN 0-87186-043-0). Comm Econ Dev.

--Improving Productivity in State & Local Government. LC 76-2408. 1976. pap. 8.50 (ISBN 0-87186-060-0). Comm Econ Dev.

--International Economic Consequences of High-Priced Energy. LC 75-22468. 116p. 1975. pap. 2.50 (ISBN 0-87186-059-7). Comm Econ Dev.

--Making Congress More Effective. LC 70-136764. 84p. 1970. lib. bdg. 2.00 (ISBN 0-87186-739-7); pap. 1.00 (ISBN 0-87186-039-2). Comm Econ Dev.

--The Management & Financing of Colleges. LC 73-86038. 95p. 1973. pap. 1.50 (ISBN 0-87186-052-X). Comm Econ Dev.

--Military Manpower & National Security. LC 78-189538. 48p. 1972. lib. bdg. 2.00 (ISBN 0-87186-745-1); pap. 1.00 (ISBN 0-87186-045-7). Comm Econ Dev.

--Modernizing Local Government. LC 66-26939. 84p. 1966. lib. bdg. 2.50 (ISBN 0-87186-723-0); pap. 1.50 (ISBN 0-87186-023-6). Comm Econ Dev.

--Modernizing State Government. LC 67-27541. 85p. 1967. lib. bdg. 2.50 (ISBN 0-87186-728-1); pap. 1.50 (ISBN 0-87186-028-7). Comm Econ Dev.

--National Security & Our Individual Freedom: A Statement on National Policy by the Research & Policy Committee of the Committee for Economic Department. LC 50-2569. pap. 20.00 (ISBN 0-317-08296-5, 2007001). Bks Demand UMI.

--A New Trade Policy Toward Communist Countries. LC 72-87311. (Illus.). 60p. 1972. pap. 1.50 (ISBN 0-87186-048-1). Comm Econ Dev.

--New U. S. Farm Policy for Changing World Food Needs. LC 74-84123. 1974. pap. 2.00 (ISBN 0-87186-056-2). Comm Econ Dev.

--Nuclear Energy & National Security. LC 76-28795. 1976. pap. 2.50 (ISBN 0-87186-062-7). Comm Econ Dev.

--The Problem of National Security, Some Economic & Administrative Aspects: A Statement on National Policy by the Research & Policy Committee of the Committee for Economic Development. LC 58-13649. pap. 21.50 (ISBN 0-317-08288-4, 2007033). Bks Demand UMI.

--Public-Private Partnership in American Cities: Seven Case Studies. Fosler, R. Scott & Berger, Renee A., eds. LC 82-48016. 320p. (Orig.). 1982. pap. 19.95 (ISBN 0-87186-334-0). Comm Econ Dev.

--Redefining Government's Role in the Market System. 1979. lib. bdg. 6.50 (ISBN 0-87186-768-0); pap. 5.00 (ISBN 0-87186-068-6). Comm Econ Dev.

--Reducing Crime & Assuring Justice. LC 72-81298. 86p. 1972. lib. bdg. 2.50 (ISBN 0-87186-746-X); pap. 1.50 (ISBN 0-87186-046-5). Comm Econ Dev.

--Toward a New International Economic System: A Joint Japanese-American View. LC 74-79477. 64p. 1974. pap. 2.00 (ISBN 0-87186-054-6). Comm Econ Dev.

--Training & Jobs for the Urban Poor. LC 78-130757. 78p. 1970. pap. 1.50 (ISBN 0-87186-037-6). Comm Econ Dev.

--Transnactional Corporations & Developing Countries: New Policies for a Changing World Economy. 96p. 1981. lib. bdg. 6.50 (ISBN 0-87186-772-9); pap. 5.00 (ISBN 0-87186-072-4). Comm Econ Dev.

Committee for Economic Development & the Conservation Foundation. Energy Prices & Public Policy. LC 82-7428. (CED Statement on National Policy Ser.). 88p. 1982. lib. bdg. 9.50 (ISBN 0-87186-775-3); pap. 7.50 (ISBN 0-87186-075-9). Comm Econ Dev.

Committee for Economic Development in Cooperation with Work in America Institute, Inc. Training & Jobs Programs in Action: Case Studies in Private-Sector Initiatives for the Hard-To-Employ. 1978. pap. 5.00 (ISBN 0-87186-332-4). Comm Econ Dev.

Committee for Economic Development Staff. Productivity Policy: Key to the Nation's Economic Future. (CED Statement on National Policy Ser.). 122p. (Orig.). 1983. 10.50x (ISBN 0-87186-776-1); pap. 8.50x (ISBN 0-87186-076-7). Comm Econ Dev.

Committee For Freedom of Choice. Sloan-Kettering (Laetrile) Studies. 3.50x (ISBN 0-686-29895-0). Cancer Control Soc.

Committee for Fundamental Metallurgy, ed. Slag Atlas. 1981. 135.00 (ISBN 0-9960086-2-4, Pub. by Verlag Stahleisen W Germany). Heyden.

Committee for Nonviolent Revolution. Alternative, Vols. 1-3, No. 5. 1948-1951. Repr. lib. bdg. 11.00x (ISBN 0-8371-9124-6, A100). Greenwood.

Committee for Rational Development. Sri Lanka: The Ethnic Conflict: Myths, Realities & Perspectives. 1985. 35.00x (ISBN 0-8364-1292-3, Pub. by Navrang). South Asia Bks.

Committee for Reporting Tribunal Jurisprudence. Matrimonial Jurisprudence United States, 1975-1976: Summaries of Selected Cases. 158p. (Orig.). 1977. pap. 3.50 (ISBN 0-943616-11-5). Canon Law Soc.

Committee for Study of Environmental Manpower. Manpower for Environmental Pollution Control. 1977. 12.75 (ISBN 0-309-02634-2). Natl Acad Pr.

Committee for the Bicentennial National Conference of Catholic Bishops. Liberty & Justice for All: A Discussion Guide. 1.50, 10 copies 1.25 (ISBN 0-686-11440-X). US Catholic.

Committee for the Compilation of Materials on the Damage of the Atomic Bombs in Hiroshima & Nagasaki. Hiroshima & Nagasaki: The Physical, Medical, & Social Effects of the Atomic Bombings. LC 80-68179. (Illus.). 1981. 39.00 (ISBN 0-465-02985-X); pap. 15.95 (ISBN 0-465-02987-6, CN-5088). Basic.

Committee for the Development of Subject Access to Chicano Literature. A Cumulative Index to Selected Chicano Periodicals Published Between 1967 and 1978. 1981. lib. bdg. 100.00 (ISBN 0-8161-0363-1, Hall Library). G K Hall.

Committee for the Inauguration of Wendell R. Anderson. Governors of Minnesota: 1849-1971. (Illus.). 22p. 1971. pap. 2.00 (ISBN 0-685-47097-0). Minn Hist.

Committee for the Publication of the Biography of Master Hsuan Hua. Records of the Life of Tripitaka Master Hua, Vol. 1. (Illus.). 90p. (Orig.). 1981. pap. 5.00 (ISBN 0-917512-78-2). Buddhist Text.

--Records of the Life of Tripitaka Master Hua, Vol. 2. (Illus.). 229p. (Orig.). 1976. pap. 8.00 (ISBN 0-917512-10-3). Buddhist Text.

Committee for the Study of Nursing Education. Nursing & Nursing Education in the United States. Reverby, Susan, ed. LC 83-49182. (History of American Nursing Ser.). 585p. 1984. Repr. of 1923 ed. lib. bdg. 70.00 (ISBN 0-8240-6506-9). Garland Pub.

Committee for the Survey of Chemistry. Theoretical Chemistry. 1966. pap. 3.00 (ISBN 0-309-01292-9). Natl Acad Pr.

Committee for Truth in History. The Six Million Reconsidered. Grimstad, William N., ed. (Illus.). 1979. pap. 8.00 (ISBN 0-911038-50-7). Noontide.

Committee for Truth in History & Grimstad, William. Six Million Reconsidered: An Examination of Jewish Genocide. 1982. lib. bdg. 69.95 (ISBN 0-87700-445-5). Revisionist Pr.

Committee from the Editorial Board of Psychosomatic Medicine, ed. Psychosomatic Classics: Selected Papers from Psychosomatic Medicine, 1939-1958. 1972. pap. 15.25 (ISBN 3-8055-1232-5). S Karger.

Committee of Community Social Researchers, 1976. Social Indicators in Community Research: Proceedings. 1976. 2.00 (ISBN 0-86671-034-5). Comm Coun Great NY.

Committee Of Fifty. Liquor Problem: A Summary of Investigations Conducted by the Committee of Fifty, 1893-1903. LC 70-112533. (Rise of Urban America). 1970. Repr. of 1905 ed. 17.00 (ISBN 0-405-02444-4). Ayer Co Pubs.

Committee of Injury. A Voice for All Children: Report of an Independent Committee of Injury. 54p. (Orig.). 1982. pap. text ed. 6.95x (ISBN 0-7199-1090-0, Pub. by Bedford England). Brookfield Pub Co.

Committee of Scholarly Communication with the People's Republic of China, National Research Council. Herbal Pharmacology in the People's Republic of China: A Trip Report of the American Herbal Pharmacology Delegation. LC 75-39772. v, 169p. 1975. pap. 9.50 (ISBN 0-309-02438-2). Natl Acad Pr.

Committee of the American Neurological Association for the Investigation of Eugenical Sterilization. Eugenical Sterilization. Grob, Gerald N., ed. LC 78-22556. (Historical Issues in Mental Health Ser.). (Illus.). 1979. Repr. of 1936 ed. lib. bdg. 16.00x (ISBN 0-405-11910-0). Ayer Co Pubs.

Committee of the Children's Services Division. I Read; You Read; We Read. I See; You See; We See. I Hear; You Hear; We Hear. I Learn; You Learn; We Learn. LC 76-152684. (gr. k-6). 1971. pap. 4.00x (ISBN 0-8389-3124-3). ALA.

Committee of the Junior League, ed. see Junior League of the Palm Beaches Inc.

Committee of the Junior League, ed. see Junior League of the Palm Beaches, Inc.

Committee of the Medical Section of the French Royal Academy of Sciences, Jun 21-28th, 1831 & Colquhoun, J. C. Report of the Experiments on Animal Magnetism: Proceedings. LC 75-7371. (Perspectives in Psychical Research Ser.). 1975. Repr. of 1833 ed. 23.50x (ISBN 0-405-07022-5). Ayer Co Pubs.

Committee of the President's Conference on Unemployment. Business Cycles & Unemployment: Proceedings. LC 75-19697. (National Bureau of Economic Research Ser.). (Illus.). 1975. Repr. 33.00x (ISBN 0-405-07577-4). Ayer Co Pubs.

Committee on a Multimedium Approach to Municipal Sludge Management, National Research Council. Multimedium Management of Municipal Sludge. LC 77-93086. (Analytical Studies for the U. S. Environmental Protection Agency Ser.). (Illus.). 1978. pap. text ed. 9.50 (ISBN 0-309-02733-0). Natl Acad Pr.

Committee on Accident & Poison Prevention, American Academy of Pediatrics. Handbook of Common Poisonings in Children. 2nd ed. LC 82-72740. (Illus.). 175p. 1983. pap. text ed. 15.00 (ISBN 0-910761-03-5). Am Acad Pediat.

Committee on Advanced Nuclear Systems National Research Council. Advanced Nuclear Systems for Portable Power in Space. 60p. 1983. pap. 13.50 (ISBN 0-309-03427-2). Natl Acad Pr.

Committee on Agriculture, U.S. House of Representatives. Oleomargarine. LC 75-26318. (World Food Supply Ser). (Illus.). 1976. Repr. of 1949 ed. 31.00x (ISBN 0-405-07794-7). Ayer Co Pubs.

Committee on an Assessment of Quality-Related Characteristics of Research-Doctorate Programs in the U. S., National Research Council. An Assessment of Research-Doctorate Programs in the U. S. Biological Sciences. 264p. 1982. pap. text ed. 11.50 (ISBN 0-309-03340-3). Natl Acad Pr.

--An Assessment of Research-Doctorate Programs in the U. S. Engineering. 193p. 1982. pap. text ed. 11.50 (ISBN 0-309-03336-5). Natl Acad Pr.

--An Assessment of Research-Doctorate Programs in the United States: Humanities. 244p. 1982. pap. text ed. 11.50 (ISBN 0-309-03333-0). Natl Acad Pr.

--An Assessment of Research-Doctorate Programs in the U. S. Mathematical & Physical Sciences. 243p. 1982. pap. text ed. 11.50 (ISBN 0-309-03299-7). Natl Acad Pr.

--An Assessment of Research-Doctorate Programs in the U. S. Social & Behavioral Sciences. 256p. 1982. pap. text ed. 11.50 (ISBN 0-309-03342-X). Natl Acad Pr.

Committee on an Assessment of Quality-Related Characteristics of Research Doctorate Programs in the United States, National Research Council. An Assessment of Research-Doctorate Programs in the United States, 5 vols. 1982. Set. pap. text ed. 47.25 set (ISBN 0-309-03344-6). Natl Acad Pr.

Committee on Animal Health. A Nationwide System for Animal Health Surveillance. LC 74-19048. 1974. pap. 5.25 (ISBN 0-309-02243-6). Natl Acad Pr.

Committee on Animal Nutrition. Effects of Fluorides in Animals. LC 74-4061. (Illus.). 76p. 1974. pap. 5.75 (ISBN 0-309-02219-3). Natl Acad Pr.

--Nutrient Requirements of Dairy Cattle, 1978. 5th ed. (Nutrient Requirements of Domestic Animals Ser). 76p. 1978. pap. text ed. 6.50 (ISBN 0-309-02749-7). Natl Acad Pr.

--Nutrient Requirements of Dogs. 71p. 1975. pap. 8.50 (ISBN 0-309-02315-7). Natl Acad Pr.

--Nutrient Requirements of Rabbits. rev. 7th ed. LC 77-6318. 1977. pap. 5.95 (ISBN 0-309-02607-5). Natl Acad Pr.

Committee on Animal Nutrition Board on Agriculture & Renewable Resources, National Research Council. Nutrient Requirements of Beef Cattle. 5th, rev. ed. LC 75-43977. (Nutrient Requirements of Domestic Animals Ser.). 56p. 1976. pap. 8.95 (ISBN 0-309-02419-6). Natl Acad Pr.

Committee on Animal Nutrition, Board of Agriculture, National Research Council. Selenium in Nutrition. rev. ed. 1983. pap. text ed. 14.50 (ISBN 0-309-03375-6). Natl Acad Pr.

Committee on Animal Nutrition, National Research Council. Nutrient Requirements of Cats. LC 78-5976. (Nutrient Requirements of Domestic Animals Ser.). 49p. 1978. pap. text ed. 6.95 (ISBN 0-309-02743-8). Natl Acad Pr.

--Nutritional Energetics of Domestic Animals & Glossary of Energy Terms. 54p. (Orig.). 1981. pap. text ed. 5.25 (ISBN 0-309-03127-3). Natl Acad Pr.

Committee on Animal Production. Plant & Animal Products in the U. S. Food System. 254p. 1978. pap. 12.25 (ISBN 0-309-02769-1). Natl Acad Pr.

Committee On Atmospheric Sciences. Atmospheric Sciences & Man's Needs: Priorities for the Future. LC 70-611003. 88p. (Orig.). 1971. pap. text ed. 5.50 (ISBN 0-309-01912-5). Natl Acad Pr.

--Atmospheric Sciences: Problems & Applications. 124p. 1977. pap. 9.25 (ISBN 0-309-02626-1). Natl Acad Pr.

--Weather & Climate Modification. (Illus.). 256p. 1973. pap. 10.25 (ISBN 0-309-02121-9). Natl Acad Pr.

Committee on Atmospheric Sciences, ed. Severe Storms: Predicion, Detection & Warning. LC 77-77588. (Illus.). 1977. pap. text ed. 7.95 (ISBN 0-309-02613-X). Natl Acad Pr.

Committee on Banking & Currency. Commercial Banks & Their Trust Activities, 2 vols. LC 75-81987. Repr. of 1968 ed. Set. 36.00 (ISBN 0-405-00011-1); 18.25 ea. Vol. 1 (ISBN 0-405-00012-X). Vol. 2 (ISBN 0-405-00013-8). Ayer Co Pubs.

Committee On Banking And Currency - Staff Report. Growth of Unregistered Bank Holding Companies: Problems & Prospects. LC 75-81988. 1969. Repr. of 1969 ed. 20.00 (ISBN 0-405-00019-7). Ayer Co Pubs.

Committee on Banking & Currency, U. S. Congressional House. Report of the Committee Appointed Pursuant to House Resolutions 429 & 504 to Investigate the Concentration of Control of Money & Credit. facsimile ed. LC 75-2677. (Wall Street & the Security Market Ser.). 1975. Repr. of 1913 ed. 20.00x (ISBN 0-405-07239-2). Ayer Co Pubs.

Committee on Banking & Currency, U. S. Senate, 1934. Stock Exchange Practices. facsimile ed. LC 75-2678. (Wall Street & the Security Market Ser.). 1975. Repr. of 1934 ed. 31.00x (ISBN 0-405-07240-6). Ayer Co Pubs.

Committee on Basic Auditing Concepts. A Statement of Basic Auditing Concepts, Vol. 6. (Studies in Accounting Research). 58p. 1973. 6.00 (ISBN 0-86539-018-5); members 4.00. Am Accounting.

Committee on Basic Library Lists, ed. A Basic Library List for Two-Year College. 66p. 1980. pap. 9.50 (ISBN 0-88385-436-8). Math Assn.

Committee on Basic Research in the Behavioral & Social Sciences, National Research Council. Behavioral & Social Science Research: A National Resource, Part II. 604p. 1982. pap. text ed. 27.50 (ISBN 0-309-03297-0). Natl Acad Pr.

Committee on Biologic Effects of Atmosphere Pollutants. Particulate Polycyclic Organic Matter. (Biologic Effects of Atmospheric Pollutants Ser.). (Illus.). 336p. 1972. pap. 12.95 (ISBN 0-309-02027-1). Natl Acad Pr.

Committee on Biological Effects of Atmospheric Pollutants. Lead: Airborne Lead in Perspective. LC 71-186214. (Biological Effects of Atmospheric Pollutants Ser.). (Illus.). 1972. pap. 10.95 (ISBN 0-309-01941-9). Natl Acad Pr.

Committee on Boarding Schools. International Students in the Independent School: A Handbook. 1981. pap. 7.00 (ISBN 0-686-83733-9). NAIS.

Committee on Business Archives of the International Council on Archives, ed. Business Archives: Studies on International Practices. 167p. 1983. pap. text ed. 25.00 (ISBN 3-598-10516-9). K G Saur.

Committee on Byssinosis, National Research Council. Byssinosis: Clinical & Research Issues. 143p. 1982. pap. text ed. 10.95 (ISBN 0-309-03276-8). Natl Acad Pr.

Committee on Child Development Research & Public Policy, National Research Council. Learning from Experience: Evaluating Early Childhood Demonstration Programs. 271p. 1982. pap. text ed. 13.50 (ISBN 0-309-03232-6). Natl Acad Pr.

Committee on Classroom Practices, jt. ed. see Carter, Candy.

Committee on Colorimetry of the Optical Society of America. The Science of Color. LC 52-7039. (Illus.). 340p. 1963. 20.00x (ISBN 0-9600380-1-9). Optical Soc.

Committee on Concepts & Standards for External Financial Reports. Statement on Accounting Theory & Theory Acceptance. 61p. 6.00 (ISBN 0-86539-010-X); members 3.00. Am Accounting.

Committee on Contingency Plans for Chromium Utilization, National Research Council. Contingency Plans for Chromium Utilization. LC 77-95193. (Illus.). 1978. 11.95 (ISBN 0-309-02737-3). Natl Acad Pr.

Committee on Continuing Legal Education for Wisconsin, et al. Labor & Employment Law: ALI-ABA Course of Study Materials. LC 84-225565. Date not set. price not set. Am Law Inst.

Committee on Continuity in Academic Research Performance. Research Excellence Through the Year 2000. LC 79-67784. xiv, 241p. 1979. pap. 10.50 (ISBN 0-309-02938-4). Natl Acad Pr.

Committee on Corporate Laws of the American Bar Association of Corporation, Banking, & Business Law. Model Business Corporation Act. 3rd ed. 177p. 1979. pap. 10.00 (ISBN 0-317-32241-9, B142). Am Law Inst.

Committee on Corporate Laws of the ABA Section of Corporation, Banking & Business Law. Model Business Corporation Act: No. B142. 3rd ed. 177p. 1979. pap. 10.00 (ISBN 0-317-30811-4). Am Law Inst.

Committee on Corporate Laws of the Section of Corporation, Banking & Business Law of the American Bar Association. Model Nonprofit Corporation Act. 119p. 1964. pap. 2.50 (ISBN 0-317-32243-5, B144). Am Law Inst.

--Model Nonprofit Corporation Act: No. B144. 119p. 1964. pap. 2.50 (ISBN 0-317-30814-9). Am Law Inst.

Committee on Criminal Justice & the Military, American Bar Association. Comparative Analysis: Federal Rules of Criminal Procedure & Military Practice & Procedure. LC 83-104791. 135p. 1982. 11.25 (ISBN 0-89707-099-2, 509-0014). Amer Bar Assn.

Committee On Data For Science And Technology Of The International Council Of Scientific Unions. International Compendium of Numerical Data Projects. 1969. 38.00 (ISBN 0-387-04570-8). Springer-Verlag.

Committee on Development in Business Financing of the Section of Corporation, Banking & Business Law, American Bar Association. Term Loan Handbook. McCann, John J., ed. 300p. 1983. 55.00 (ISBN -15-100056-5, H4285X). HarBraceJ.

Committee on Diet, Nutrition, & Cancer, National Research Council. Diet, Nutrition, & Cancer: Directions for Research, Vol. 8. 74p. 1983. pap. text ed. 7.95 (ISBN 0-309-03385-3). Natl Acad Pr.

Committee on Drinking Water, National Research Council. Drinking Water & Health. Incl. Vol. I. 1977. 26.50 (ISBN 0-309-02619-9); Vol. II. 1980. 15.50 (ISBN 0-309-02931-7); Vol. III. 1980. 17.00 (ISBN 0-309-02932-5). Natl Acad Pr.

Committee on Education & Labor, U.S. Senate, 76th Congress, 3rd Session. Violations of Free Speech & Rights of Labor: Hearings Before a Subcommittee on Education & Labor, 3 vols. in 1. facsimile ed. McCurry, Dan C. & Rubenstein, Richard E., eds. LC 74-30659. (American Farmers & the Rise of Agribusiness Ser.). 1975. Repr. of 1941 ed. 87.00x (ISBN 0-405-06836-0). Ayer Co Pubs.

Committee on Env. Geochem., National Research Council. Geochemistry & the Environment: Distribution of Trace Elements Related to the Occurrence of Certain Cancers, Cardiovascular Diseases, & Urolithiasis, Vol. III. (Geochemistry & the Environment Ser.). 1978. pap. text ed. 15.50 (ISBN 0-309-02795-0). Natl Acad Pr.

Committee on Environmental Pollutants, National Research Council. Nitrates: An Environmental Assessment. (Scientific & Technical Assessments of Environmental Pollutants Ser.). 1978. pap. text ed. 16.75 (ISBN 0-309-02785-3). Natl Acad Pr.

Committee on Evaluation of Media Programs, AECT. Evaluating Media Programs: District & School. (Illus.). 77p. 1980. wkbk. 8.95 (ISBN 0-89240-039-0). Assn Ed Comm Tech.

Committee on Evaluation of Poverty Research. Evaluating Federal Support for Poverty Research. 1979. pap. 7.95 (ISBN 0-309-02894-9). Natl Acad Pr.

Committee on Evaluation of Sound Spectrograms, National Research Council. On the Theory & Practice of Voice Identification. 1979. pap. text ed. 7.50 (ISBN 0-309-02873-6). Natl Acad Pr.

Committee on Federal Agency Evaluation Research, National Research Council. Protecting Individual Privacy in Evaluation Research. LC 75-18591. 133p. 1975. pap. 8.50 (ISBN 0-309-02406-4). Natl Acad Pr.

Committee on Fire Research & Committee on Toxicology Staff. An Appraisal of Halogenated Fire Extinguishing Agents. (Illus.). 360p. 1972. pap. 9.25 (ISBN 0-309-02111-1). Natl Acad Pr.

Committee on Fire Research, National Research Council. Air Quality & Smoke from Urban & Forest Fires. LC 76-8356. (Illus.). 381p. 1976. pap. 11.75 (ISBN 0-309-02500-1). Natl Acad Pr.

--Directory of Fire Research. 8th ed. 1978. pap. text ed. 9.95 (ISBN 0-309-02799-3). Natl Acad Pr.

--Fire Detection for Life Safety. LC 76-53105. 1977. pap. 9.25 (ISBN 0-309-02600-8). Natl Acad Pr.

--Physiological & Toxicological Aspects of Combustion Products. LC 76-24955. 1976. pap. 9.50 (ISBN 0-309-02521-4). Natl Acad Pr.

Committee on Food Stability, National Research Council. Objective Methods for Food Evaluation. LC 76-26723. 1976. pap. 10.25 (ISBN 0-309-02520-6). Natl Acad Pr.

Committee on Foreign Affairs, House of Representatives. Test of Proposed China Aid Bill & Background Information on Economic Assistance Program for China. Myers, Ramon H., ed. (The Modern Chinese Economy Ser.). 67.00 (ISBN 0-8240-4289-1). Garland Pub.

Committee On Foreign Relations. Decade of American Foreign Policy, Basic Documents 1941-1949. 1968. 65.00x (ISBN 0-403-00008-4). Scholarly.

Committee on Gas Production Opportunities. Potential for Increasing Production of Natural Gas from Existing Fields in the Near Term. 1978. pap. 7.75 (ISBN 0-309-02784-5). Natl Acad Pr.

Committee on Geodesy, National Research Council. Procedures & Standards for a Multipurpose Cadastre. 1983. pap. text ed. 8.50 (ISBN 0-309-03343-8). Natl Acad Pr.

Committee on Germplasm Resources. Conservation of Germplasm Resource: An Imperative. 1978. pap. 7.95 (ISBN 0-309-02744-6). Natl Acad Pr.

Committee on Hazardous Materials. Pressure Relieving Systems for Marine Bulk Liquid Cargo Containers. (Illus.). 168p. 1973. pap. 11.75 (ISBN 0-309-02122-7). Natl Acad Pr.

Committee on Hazardous Substances in the Laboratory, National Research Council. Prudent Practices for Handling Hazardous Chemicals in Laboratories. 291p. 1981. 16.95 (ISBN 0-309-03128-1); pap. text ed. 9.95 (ISBN 0-309-03234-2). Natl Acad Pr.

Committee on Hearing, Bioacoustics, & Biomechanics, National Research Council. Tinnitus: Facts, Theories, & Treatments. 1983. pap. text ed. 11.25 (ISBN 0-309-03328-4). Natl Acad Pr.

Committee on Homosexual Offences & Prostitution, Home Office, Scottish Home Department. Report. LC 76-24924. (Great Britain Parliament Papers by Command: No. 247). 1976. Repr. of 1968 ed. lib. bdg. 15.00x (ISBN 0-8371-8839-3, RECH). Greenwood.

Committee on Impacts of Stratospheric Change, National Research Council. Halocarbons: Environmental Effects of Chlorofluoromethane Release. 125p. 1976. pap. 7.75 (ISBN 0-309-02529-X). Natl Acad Pr.

Committee on Impacts of Stratospheric Change, et al. Protection Against Depletion of Stratospheric Ozone by Chlorofluorocarbons. LC 79-57247. xvii, 392p. (Orig.). 1979. pap. text ed. 10.25 (ISBN 0-309-02947-3). Natl Acad Pr.

Committee on Interior Lighting for Public Conveyances of the IES. Public Conveyances: Road-Rail Interior Lighting. new ed. (Illus.). 20p. 1974. tech. manual 6.50 (ISBN 0-87995-004-8, IES CP-12); member 3.25. Illum Eng.

Committee on International Disaster Assistance. Assessing International Disaster Needs. 146p. 1979. pap. 6.50 (ISBN 0-309-02893-0). Natl Acad Pr.

Committee on Interplay of Engineering with Biology & Medicine. Study of Engineering in Medicine & Health Care. LC 74-7253. 80p. 1974. pap. 4.95 (ISBN 0-309-02148-0). Natl Acad Pr.

Committee on Jury Standards & American Bar Association. Standards Relating to Juror Use & Management. 196p. 1982. pap. 10.00 (ISBN 0-89656-063-5). Natl Ctr St Courts.

Committee on Literature in the Elementary Language Arts & Lamme, Linda. Learning to Love Literature: Preschool Through Grade Three. LC 81-14076. (Illus.). 98p. 1981. 6.50 (ISBN 0-8141-2787-8). NCTE.

Committee on Materials Specifications, Testing Methods & Standards, National Research Council. Materials & Process Specifications & Standards. LC 77-92433. (Illus.). 1977. pap. text ed. 9.95 (ISBN 0-309-02731-4). Natl Acad Pr.

Committee on Medical & Biologic Effects of Environmental Pollutants, National Research Council. Selenium. LC 76-40687. (Medical & Biologic Effects of Environmental Pollutants Ser). 203p. 1976. pap. 11.75 (ISBN 0-309-02503-6). Natl Acad Pr.

Committee on Medical & Biological Effects of Environmental Pollutants. Nickel. 277p. 1975. pap. 16.50 (ISBN 0-309-02314-9). Natl Acad Pr.

Committee on Mineral Resources & Environment, National Research Council. Reserves & Resources of Uranium in the United States: Mineral Resources & the Environment Supplementary Report. ix, 236p. 1975. pap. 8.50 (ISBN 0-309-02423-4). Natl Acad Pr.

Committee on Mineral Resources & the Environment, National Research Council. Coal Workers' Pneumoconiosis-Medical Considerations, Some Social Implications: Mineral Resources & the Environment Supplementary Report. LC 75-39531. 149p. 1976. pap. 7.50 (ISBN 0-309-02424-2). Natl Acad Pr.

--Resource Recovery from Municipal Solid Wastes: Mineral Resources & the Environment Supplementary Report. 432p. 1975. pap. 10.75 (ISBN 0-309-02422-6). Natl Acad Pr.

Committee on National Statistics. Privacy & Confidentiality As Factors in Survey Response. 1979. pap. 14.25 (ISBN 0-309-02878-7). Natl Acad Pr.

Committee on National Statistics, National Research Council. Counting the People in 1980: An Appraisal of Census Plans. 1978. pap. text ed. 10.95 (ISBN 0-309-02797-7). Natl Acad Pr.

--Estimating Population & Income of Small Areas. 1981. pap. text ed. 14.25 (ISBN 0-309-03096-X). Natl Acad Pr.

--Surveying Crime. Penick, Bettye, ed. LC 76-50120. 1977. pap. 12.50 (ISBN 0-309-02524-9). Natl Acad Pr.

Committee on National Urban Policy, National Research Council. Critical Issues for National Urban Policy: A Reconnaissance & Agenda for Further Study. 112p. 1982. pap. text ed. 8.50 (ISBN 0-309-03242-3). Natl Acad Pr.

Committee on Natural Resources. Working Group Meeting on Energy Planning: Proceedings, 5th Session. (Energy Resources Development Ser.: No. 20). 151p. 1980. pap. 12.00 (ISBN 0-686-70131-3, UN792F11, UN). Unipub.

Committee on Nitrate Accumulation. Accumulation of Nitrate. vii, 106p. 1972. pap. text ed. 7.50 (ISBN 0-309-02038-7). Natl Acad Pr.

Committee on Nuclear & Alternative Energy Sources. Alternative Energy Demand Futures to 2010. 281p. 1979. pap. 10.50 (ISBN 0-309-02939-2). Natl Acad Pr.

Committee on Nuclear & Alternative Energy Systems, National Research Council. Controlled Nuclear Fusion: Current Research & Potential Progress. 1978. pap. text ed. 5.25 (ISBN 0-309-02863-9). Natl Acad Pr.

Committee on Nuclear & Alternative Energy Systems. Domestic Potential of Solar & Other Renewable Energy Sources. 1979. pap. 8.50 (ISBN 0-309-02927-9). Natl Acad Pr.

Committee on Nuclear & Alternative Energy Systems, National Research Council. Geothermal Resources & Technology in the U. S. 1979. pap. text ed. 5.95 (ISBN 0-309-02874-4). Natl Acad Pr.

Committee on Nuclear & Alternative Energy Systems. Problems of U. S. Uranium Resources & Supply to the Year 2010. 1978. pap. 7.50 (ISBN 0-309-02782-9). Natl Acad Pr.

--U. S. Energy Supply Prospects to 2010. 1979. pap. 9.25 (ISBN 0-309-02936-8). Natl Acad Pr.

Committee On Nuclear Sciences. Geochronology of North America. 1965. pap. 7.00 (ISBN 0-309-01276-7). Natl Acad Pr.

Committee on Nutrition of the Mother & Preschool Child, Food & Nutrition Board, National Research Council. Alternative Dietary Practices & Nutritional Abuses in Pregnancy: Proceedings of a Workshop. 211p. 1982. pap. text ed. 14.50 (ISBN 0-309-03327-6). Natl Acad Pr.

Committee on Occupational Classification & Analysis. Job Evaluation: An Analytical Review. 170p. 1979. pap. 9.95 (ISBN 0-309-02882-5). Natl Acad Pr.

Committee On Ocean Engineering, jt. auth. see Committee On Oceanography.

Committee On Oceanography & Committee On Ocean Engineering. Oceanic Quest: The International Decade of Ocean Exploration. (Orig.). 1969. pap. 6.00 (ISBN 0-309-01709-2). Natl Acad Pr.

Committee on Particulate Control Technology, National Research Council. Controlling Airborne Particles. xi, 114p. (Orig.). 1980. pap. text ed. 9.50 (ISBN 0-309-03035-8). Natl Acad Pr.

Committee On Patent Policy. Nonprofit Research & Patent Management in the United States. 1956. pap. 2.75 (ISBN 0-309-00371-7). Natl Acad Pr.

Committee on Pattern Jury Charges of the State Bar of Texas. Texas Pattern Jury Charges, Vol. 3. LC 78-13954. 380p. 1982. 65.00 (ISBN 0-938160-28-1, 6315). State Bar TX.

--Texas Pattern Jury Charges: 1984 Cumulative Supplement, Vol. 3. LC 78-13954. 45p. 1985. 20.00 (ISBN 0-938160-39-7, 6286). State Bar TX.

Committee on Pesticide Decision Making, National Research Council. Pesticide Decision Making. LC 77-94524. (Analytical Studies for the U. S. Environmental Protection Agency Ser.). (Illus.). 1978. pap. text ed. 7.50 (ISBN 0-309-02734-9). Natl Acad Pr.

Committee On Police Conditions Of Service. Report of the Committee on Police Conditions of Service. LC 76-156281. (Police in Great Britain Ser). 1971. Repr. of 1949 ed. 19.00 (ISBN 0-405-03392-3). Ayer Co Pubs.

Committee on Population & Demography, National Research Council. The Estimation of Recent Trends in Fertility & Mortality in Egypt: Report No. Nine. 1982. pap. text ed. 7.25 (ISBN 0-309-03238-5). Natl Acad Pr.

--Trends in Fertility & Mortality in Turkey, 1935-1975: Report No. 8. 1982. pap. text ed. 6.95 (ISBN 0-309-03239-3). Natl Acad Pr.

Committee on Postdoctorals in Science & Engineering, National Research Council. Postdoctoral Appointments & Disappointments. 1981. pap. text ed. 15.75 (ISBN 0-309-03132-X). Natl Acad Pr.

Committee on Power Plant Siting. Engineering for Resolution of the Energy-Environment Dilemma. LC 79-186370. (Illus.). 1972. pap. 12.25 (ISBN 0-309-01943-5). Natl Acad Pr.

Committee on Pre-Postoperative Care. Manual of Preoperative & Postoperative Care. 3rd ed. (Illus.). 848p. 1983. 38.95 (ISBN 0-7216-1164-8). Saunders.

Committee on Price Determination, jt. auth. see Conference on Price Research.

Committee on Private Sector Participation in Government Energy RD&D Planning. Private Sector Participation in Federal Energy RD&D Planning. 1978. pap. 7.95 (ISBN 0-309-02783-7). Natl Acad Pr.

Committee on Prosthetics Research & Development. The Child with an Acquired Amputation. (Illus.). 162p. 1972. pap. 9.25 (ISBN 0-309-02047-6). Natl Acad Pr.

--Comprehensive Management of Musculoskeletal Disorders in Hemophilia. (Illus.). 200p. 1973. pap. 10.25 (ISBN 0-309-02139-1). Natl Acad Pr.

Committee on Prototype Explicit Analysis for Pesticides. Regulating Pesticides. xiii, 288p. 1980. pap. text ed. 12.50 (ISBN 0-309-02946-5). Natl Acad Pr.

Committee on Radioactive Waste Management. An Evaluation of the Concept of Storing Radioactive Wastes in Bedrock Below the Savannah River Plant Site. (Illus.). 88p. 1972. pap. 4.95 (ISBN 0-309-02035-2). Natl Acad Pr.

--A Review of the Swedish KBS-II Plan for Disposal of Spent Nuclear Fuel. Subcommittee for Review of the KBS-II Plan, ed. LC 80-80362. xiii, 91p. 1980. pap. text ed. 9.25 (ISBN 0-309-03036-6). Natl Acad Pr.

Committee on Research on Law Enforcement & Criminal Justice. Rehabilitation of Criminal Offenders: Problems & Prospects. 1979. pap. 15.25 (ISBN 0-309-02895-7). Natl Acad Pr.

--Understanding Crime. 1977. 13.50 (ISBN 0-309-02635-0). Natl Acad Pr.

Committee on Research Priorities in Tropical Biology. Research Priorities in Tropical Biology. xii, 116p. 1980. pap. text ed. 9.75 (ISBN 0-309-03043-9). Natl Acad Pr.

Committee on Scholarly Communication with the People's Republic of China. Acupuncture Anesthesia in the People's Republic of China: A Trip Report of the American Acupuncture Anesthesia Study Group. LC 76-22856. 73p. 1976. pap. 7.25 (ISBN 0-309-02517-6). Natl Acad Pr.

Committee on Scholarly Communication with the People's Republic of China, National Research Council. Animal Agriculture in China. 197p. 1980. pap. text ed. 13.25 (ISBN 0-309-03092-7). Natl Acad Pr.

Committee on Scholarly Communication with the People's Republic of China (CSCPRC) Insect Control in the People's Republic of China: A Trip Report of the American Insect Control Delegation. LC 76-52849. (CSCPRC Report: No. 2). 1977. pap. 12.75 (ISBN 0-309-02525-7). Natl Acad Pr.

Committee on Scholarly Communications with the People's Republic of China National Research Council. Pure & Applied Mathematics in the People's Republic of China. 1977. pap. 14.50 (ISBN 0-686-25566-6, PB279 509); microfiche 4.50 (ISBN 0-686-25567-4). Natl Tech Info.

Committee on Science & Public Policy, jt. auth. see National Research Council National Academy of Sciences.

Committee on Science, Engineering, & Public Policy, Offices of Public Sector AAAS, ed. Guide to Education in Science, Engineering, & Public Policy. 91p. 1985. pap. text ed. 3.00 ea (ISBN 0-87168-271-0). AAAS.

Committee on Science, Engineering & Public Policy. Research Briefing 1983. 92p. 1983. pap. text ed. 8.50 (ISBN 0-309-03437-X). Natl Acad Pr.

--Strengthening the Government-University Partnership in Science. 188p. 1983. 14.50 (ISBN 0-309-03380-2). Natl Acad Pr.

Committee On Secondary School Studies. Report of the Committee on Secondary School Studies, Appointed at the Meeting of the National Education Association. LC 70-89222. (American Education: Its Men, Institutions & Ideas, Ser. 1). 1969. Repr. of 1893 ed. 19.00 (ISBN 0-405-01403-1). Ayer Co Pubs.

Committee on Seismology, ed. Global Earthquake Monitoring: Its Uses, Potentials, & Support Requirements. LC 77-5219. 1977. pap. text ed. 7.75 (ISBN 0-309-02608-3). Natl Acad Pr.

Committee on Seismology, National Research Council. Predicting Earthquakes: A Scientific & Technical Evaluation--with Implications for Society. LC 76-40493. 1976. pap. 6.75 (ISBN 0-309-02527-3). Natl Acad Pr.

--U. S. Earthquake Observatories: Recommendations for a New National Network. 122p. (Orig.). 1980. pap. 7.00x (ISBN 0-309-03131-1). Natl Acad Pr.

Committee on Social Development & World Peace. The Farm Family. United States Catholic Conference, ed. (Illus., Orig.). 1979. pap. 0.75 (ISBN 0-686-24814-7). US Catholic.

Committee on Sports Medicine. Sports Medicine: Health Care for the Young Athlete. LC 82-73444. 326p. 1983. pap. 15.00 (ISBN 0-910761-02-7). Am Acad Pediat.

Committee on Substance Abuse & Habitual Behavior. Issues in Controlled Substance Use. Maloff, Deborah R. & Levison, Peter K., eds. LC 80-81027. ix, 183p. 1980. pap. text ed. 8.75 (ISBN 0-309-03041-2). Natl Acad Pr.

Committee on Substance Abuse & Habitual Behavior, National Research Council. Reduced Tar & Nicotine Cigarettes: Smoking Behavior & Health. 1982. pap. text ed. 3.95 (ISBN 0-686-43976-7). Natl Acad Pr.

Committee on Taxation, Resources & Economic Development, jt. auth. see Break, George F.

Committee on Taxation Resources & Economic Development Symposium, 4th. Land & Building Taxes: Their Effect on Economic Development: Proceedings. Becker, Arthur P., ed. (Illus.). 324p. 1969. 25.00x (ISBN 0-299-05460-8). U of Wis Pr.

Committee On Taxation - Resources - & Economic Development Symposium - 1967. Property Tax & Its Administration: Proceedings. Lynn, Arthur D., Jr., ed. (Committee on Taxation, Resources & Economic Development Ser., No. 3). 260p. 1969. 25.00x (ISBN 0-299-05210-9); pap. 7.50x (ISBN 0-299-05214-1). U of Wis Pr.

Committee on Taxation, Resources, & Economic Development. Property Taxation, Land Use & Public Policy. Lynn, Arthur D., Jr., ed. 268p. 1976. 27.50x (ISBN 0-299-06920-6). U of Wis Pr.

Committee On Telecommunications. Reports on Selected Topics in Telecommunications. (Orig.). 1969. pap. 6.75 (ISBN 0-309-01751-3). Natl Acad Pr.

Committee on the Alaska Earthquake. The Great Alaska Earthquake of 1964: Biology. (Illus.). 320p. 1972. text ed. 23.50 (ISBN 0-309-01604-5). Natl Acad Pr.

--The Great Alaska Earthquake of 1964: Geology. (Illus.). 848p. 1972. text ed. 36.50 (ISBN 0-309-01601-0). Natl Acad Pr.

--Great Alaska Earthquake of 1964: Human Ecology. 1970. 31.00 (ISBN 0-309-01607-X). Natl Acad Pr.

--Great Alaska Earthquake of 1964: Hydrology. (Great Alaskan Earthquake Ser.). (Illus.). 1968. 26.50 (ISBN 0-309-01603-7). Natl Acad Pr.

--The Great Alaska Earthquake of 1964: Oceanography & Coastal Engineering. LC 68-60037. (Illus.). 624p. 1972. 34.00 (ISBN 0-309-01605-3). Natl Acad Pr.

--The Great Alaska Earthquake of 1964: Seismology & Geodesy. LC 68-60037. (Illus.). 592p. 1972. 25.50 (ISBN 0-309-01602-9). Natl Acad Pr.

--The Great Alaska Earthquake of 1964: Summary & Recommendations Including Index to Series. (Illus.). 288p. 1973. 17.50 (ISBN 0-309-01608-8). Natl Acad Pr.

Committee on the Costs of Medical Care, October 1932. Medical Care for the American People: The Final Report of the Committee on the Costs of Medical Care. LC 75-180569. (Medicine & Society in America Ser). 242p. 1972. Repr. of 1932 ed. 17.00 (ISBN 0-405-03944-1). Ayer Co Pubs.

Committee on the Education & Employment of Women in Science & Engineering. Climbing the Ladder II: An Update on the Status of Doctoral Women Scientists & Engineers. Office of Scientific & Engineering Personnel, National Research Council, ed. 112p. 1983. pap. text ed. 8.95 (ISBN 0-309-03341-1). Natl Acad Pr.

--Women Scientists in Industry & Government: How Much Progress in the 1970's. LC 80-80079. vii, 56p. 1980. pap. text ed. 5.50 (ISBN 0-309-03023-4). Natl Acad Pr.

Committee on the Family of the Group for the Advancement of Psychiatry. New Trends in Child Custody Determinations. 183p. 1981. 25.00 (ISBN -15-100039-5, H40016). HarBraceJ.

Committee on the Grading of Nursing Schools. Nurses, Patients & Pocketbooks. Reverby, Susan, ed. LC 83-49181. (History of American Nursing Ser.). 618p. 1984. Repr. of 1928 ed. lib. bdg. 75.00 (ISBN 0-8240-6507-7). Garland Pub.

Committee on the Great Alaska Earthquake of 1964. The Great Alaska Earthquake of 1964: Engineering. (The Great Alaska Earthquake of 1964 Ser.). (Illus.). 1210p. 1973. 39.00 (ISBN 0-309-01606-1). Natl Acad Pr.

Committee on the Infant & Preschool Child & Anderson, John E. Nursery Education: A Survey of the Day Nurseries, Nursery Schools, Private Kindergartens in the United States. Rothman, Sheila, ed. (Women & Children First Ser.). 25.00 (ISBN 0-8240-7655-9). Garland Pub.

Committee on the Institutional Means for Assessment of Risks to Public Health, National Research Council. Risk Assessment in the Federal Government: Managing the Process. 191p. 1983. pap. text ed. 11.75 (ISBN 0-309-03349-7). Natl Acad Pr.

Committee on the Junior High & Middle School Booklist & Christensen, Jane. Your Reading: A Booklist for Junior High & Middle School Students. 764p. 1983. pap. 12.00 (ISBN 0-8141-5938-9); pap. 10.00 members. NCTE.

Committee on the Medical Aspects of Sports, jt. ed. see Subcommittee on Classification of Sports in Injuries.

Committee On The Police Service. Minutes of Evidence of the Committee Appointed to Consider & Report Whether Any & What Changes Should Be Made in the Method of Recruiting for, the Conditions of Service of, & the Rates of Pay, Pensions, & Allowances of the Police Forces of England, Wales & Scotland. LC 70-156282. (Police in Great Britain Ser). 1971. Repr. of 1920 ed. 66.00 (ISBN 0-405-03393-1). Ayer Co Pubs.

Committee on the Safety of Nuclear Installations Specialist Meeting. Transient Two-Phase Flow: Proceedings. Plesset, Milton, et al, eds. LC 82-23422. (Illus.). 736p. 1983. text ed. 75.00 (ISBN 0-89116-258-5). Hemisphere Pub.

Committee on the Senior High School Booklist see Small, Robert C., Jr.

Committee on the Undergraduate Program in Mathematics. A Basic Library List for Four Year Colleges. 106p. 1977. pap. 10.50 (ISBN 0-88385-423-6). Math Assn.

Committee on Toxicology Staff, jt. auth. see Committee on Fire Research.

Committee on Transport & Chemical Transformation in Acid Precipitation, Nation Research Council. Acid Deposition: Atmospheric Process in Eastern North America. 1983. pap. text ed. 16.50 (ISBN 0-309-03389-6). Natl Acad Pr.

Committee on Transportation, Assembly of Engineering, Natl. Research Council. A Review of Short Haul Passenger Transportation. 1976. pap. 7.75 (ISBN 0-309-02445-5). Natl Acad Pr.

Committee On Urban Technology - Division Of Engineering. Long-Range Planning for Urban Research & Development: Technological Considerations. (Illus., Orig.). 1969. pap. 5.75 (ISBN 0-309-01729-7). Natl Acad Pr.

Committee on Urban Waterfront Lands. Urban Waterfront Lands. xii, 243p. 1980. pap. text ed. 12.95 (ISBN 0-309-02940-6). Natl Acad Pr.

Committee on Veterinary Medical Research & Education. New Horizons for Veterinary Medicine. LC 74-181827. 176p. (Orig.). 1972. pap. 6.95 (ISBN 0-309-01935-4). Natl Acad Pr.

Committee on Vision. Color Vision. (Illus.). 1973. pap. 8.00 (ISBN 0-309-02105-7). Natl Acad Pr.

--Visual Search. (Illus.). 152p. 1973. pap. 9.25 (ISBN 0-309-02103-0). Natl Acad Pr.

Committee on Vocational Education Research & Development, National Research Council. Assessing Vocational Education Research & Development. LC 76-46196. 131p. 1976. pap. 9.50 (ISBN 0-309-02526-5). Natl Acad Pr.

Committee on Water Treatment Chemicals, National Research Council. Water Chemicals Codex. 1982. pap. text ed. 7.25 (ISBN 0-309-03338-1). Natl Acad Pr.

Committee on Water Well Standards, National Water Well Association. Water Well Specifications: A Manual of Technical Standards & General Contractual Conditions for Construction of Water Wells. LC 80-80552. (Illus.). 156p. 1981. 13.00 (ISBN 0-912722-04-5). Prem Press.

Committee to Prepare a Statement of Basic Accounting Theory. A Statement of Basic Accounting Theory. 100p. 6.00 (ISBN 0-86539-008-8); members 3.00. Am Accounting.

--A Statement of Basic Accounting Theory. 100p. 6.00 (ISBN 0-318-12348-7); members 3.00 (ISBN 0-318-12349-5). Am Accounting.

Committee to Revise High Interest-Easy Reading & Agee, Hugh, eds. High Interest-Easy Reading: For Junior & Senior High School Students. 4th, rev. ed. 96p. (gr. 7-12). 1984. pap. 5.00 (ISBN 0-8141-2095-4). NCTE.

Committee to Study Foreign Investment in the U. S. A Guide to Foreign Investment under United States Law. Roth, Allan R., ed. 608p. 1979. 55.00 (ISBN 0-317-06002-3, H3976X, Law & Business). HarBraceJ.

Committee to Study Foreign Investment in the United States of the Section of Corporation, Banking & Business Law of the American Bar Association. A Guide to Foreign Investment Under United States Law. 626p. 1979. 55.00 (ISBN 0-317-29404-0, #H39808). HarBraceJ.

Committee To Support Middle-East Liberation, jt. auth. see Jewish Liberation Project.

Committee to the Human Health Effects of Subtherapeutic Antibiotic Use in Animal Feeds. The Effects on Human Health of Subtherapeutic Use of Antimicrobials in Animal Feeds. LC 80-81486. 376p. 1980. pap. text ed. 10.75 (ISBN 0-309-03044-7). Natl Acad Pr.

Commodore Computer. VIC-20 Programming Reference Guide. 304p. 1982. 16.95 (ISBN 0-672-21948-4, 21948). Sams.

Commodore Computer Staff. Commodore Software Encyclopedia. 3rd ed. 896p. 1983. pap. text ed. 19.95 (ISBN 0-672-22091-1, 22091). Sams.

--Commodore 64 User's Guide. 166p. 1983. pap. 12.95 (ISBN 0-672-22010-5, 22010). Sams.

Commomwealth Fund, jt. auth. see Littlefield, John W.

Common, Alfred. How to Repair Violins & Other Musical Instruments. 1977. lib. bdg. 59.95 (ISBN 0-8490-2023-9). Gordon Pr.

Common, Alfred F. How to Repair Violins. Repr. lib. bdg. 29.00x (ISBN 0-403-03871-5). Scholarly.

Common Council for American Unity. The Alien & the Immigration Law. LC 72-6923. 388p. Repr. of 1958 ed. lib. bdg. 20.75x (ISBN 0-8371-6503-2, ALIL). Greenwood.

Common Ground Community Restaurant, Inc. The Common Ground Dessert Cookbook. Kolzrman, Katherine & Graham, Carol, eds. LC 83-440. 224p. (Orig.). 1983. pap. 6.95 (ISBN 0-89815-113-9). Ten Speed Pr.

Common, I. F. & Waterhouse, D. F. Butterflies of Australia. 682p. 1972. 75.00x (ISBN 0-207-14236-X, Pub. by Angus & Robertson). State Mutual Bk.

Common, Michael S. Basic Econometrics. LC 76-7466. (Modern Economics Ser.). pap. 131.80 (ISBN 0-317-27820-7, 2025244). Bks Demand UMI.

Common, Thomas, tr. see Nietzsche, Friedrich.

Common Women Collective Staff. Women in U. S. History: An Annotated Bibliography. LC 77-350179. (Illus.). 2.60 (ISBN 0-9601122-1-9). Common Women.

Commoner, Barry. The Politics of Energy. 1979. pap. 4.95 (ISBN 0-394-73808-X). Knopf.

--The Poverty of Power. (YA) 1976. 10.00 (ISBN 0-394-40371-1). Knopf.

Commoner, Barry & Boksenbaum, Howard, eds. Energy & Human Welfare: Alternative Technologies for Power Production, Vol. 2. LC 75-8987. 1975. 14.95 (ISBN 0-02-468430-9). Macmillan Info.

--Energy & Human Welfare: Human Welfare: the End Use for Power, Vol. 3. LC 75-8992. 1975. 14.95 (ISBN 0-02-468440-6). Macmillan Info.

--Energy & Human Welfare: The Social Costs of Power Production, Vol. 1. LC 75-8986. 1975. 14.95 (ISBN 0-02-468420-1). Macmillan Info.

Commoner, Barry, et al, eds. Energy & Human Welfare: A Critical Analysis, 3 vols. 1975. 40.00 set (ISBN 0-02-468410-4). Macmillan Info.

Commons, Dorman L. Tender Offer: The Sneak Attack in Corporate Takeovers. LC 85-1182. 1985. 14.95 (ISBN 0-520-05583-7). U of Cal Pr.

Commons, John R. Distribution of Wealth. LC 64-54864. Repr. of 1893 ed. 27.50x (ISBN 0-678-00002-6). Kelley.

--Industrial Goodwill. LC 75-89726. (American Labor, from Conspiracy to Collective Bargaining Ser. 1). 213p. 1969. Repr. of 1919 ed. 16.00 (ISBN 0-405-02113-5). Ayer Co Pubs.

--Institutional Economics: It's Place in Political Economy. xii, 921p. Repr. of 1934 ed. lib. bdg. 37.50x (ISBN 0-87991-094-1). Porcupine Pr.

--Labor & Administration. LC 64-17404. Repr. of 1913 ed. 35.00x (ISBN 0-678-00035-2). Kelley.

--Legal Foundations of Capitalism. LC 75-184663. Repr. of 1924 ed. lib. bdg. 35.00x (ISBN 0-678-00897-3). Kelley.

--Proportional Representation. 2nd ed. LC 66-21662. Repr. of 1907 ed. 35.00x (ISBN 0-678-00222-3). Kelley.

--Races & Immigrants in America. 2nd ed. LC 67-27834. Repr. of 1920 ed. 25.00x (ISBN 0-678-00321-1). Kelley.

--Social Reform & the Church. LC 66-21663. Repr. of 1894 ed. 22.50x (ISBN 0-678-00286-X). Kelley.

--Sociological View of Sovereignty. LC 64-17405. Repr. of 1899 ed. 19.50x (ISBN 0-678-00090-5). Kelley.

Commons, John R. & Andrews, John B. Principles of Labor Legislation. 4th ed. LC 66-22620. Repr. of 1936 ed. 45.00x (ISBN 0-678-00207-X). Kelley.

--Principles of Labor Legislation. 1916. 15.00 (ISBN 0-686-17721-5). Quest Edns.

Commons, John R., ed. Trade Unionism & Labor Problems. LC 66-21664. Repr. of 1905 ed. 45.00x (ISBN 0-678-00221-5). Kelley.

--Trade Unionism & Labor Problems, 2nd Series. LC 66-21665. Repr. of 1921 ed. 50.00x (ISBN 0-678-00287-8). Kelley.

Commons, John R., et al. History of Labor in the United States, 4 Vols. LC 66-18557. Repr. of 1918 ed. 175.00x (ISBN 0-678-00142-1); 50.00 ea. Vol. 1 (ISBN 0-678-04036-2). Vol. 2 (ISBN 0-678-04037-0). Vol. 3 (ISBN 0-678-04038-9). Vol. 4 (ISBN 0-678-04039-7). Kelley.

--Industrial Government. LC 79-89727. (American Labor, from Conspiracy to Collective Bargaining Ser. 1). 425p. 1969. Repr. of 1921 ed. 23.50 (ISBN 0-405-02114-3). Ayer Co Pubs.

Commons, Michael & Nevin, John A., eds. Discriminative Properties of Reinforcement Schedules. LC 81-2654. (The Quantitative Analysis of Behavior Ser.: Vol. I). 480p. 1981. prof ref 45.00x (ISBN 0-88410-377-3). Ballinger Pub.

Commons, Michael L., ed. Beyond Formal Operations: Late Adolescent & Adult Cognitive Development. Richards, Francis A. & Armon, Cheryl. LC 83-21142. 494p. 1984. 31.95x (ISBN 0-03-062559-9). Praeger.

Commons, Michael L. & Mazur, James E., eds. Reinforcer Values: The Effects of Delay & Intervening Events. LC 81-2654. (The Quantitative Analyses of Behavior Ser.: Vol. V). 350p. 1985. prof. ref. 50.00x (ISBN 0-88410-893-7). Ballinger Pub.

Commons, Michael L. & Shettleworth, A. Kacelnick, eds. Qualitative Analysis of Behavior: Foraging, Vol. 6. (Roitblat-Bever Olton: Comparative Cognition & Neuroscience Ser.). 350p. Date not set. text ed. price not set (ISBN 0-89859-550-9). L Erlbaum Assocs.

Commons, Michael L., et al, eds. Acquisition. (The Quantitative Analyses of Behavior Ser.: Vol. III). 496p. 1984. prof ref 55.00x (ISBN 0-88410-740-X). Ballinger Pub.

--Matching & Maximizing Accounts, Vol II. LC 81-2654. (The Quantitative Analyses of Behavior Ser.). 624p. 1982. prof ref 55.00x (ISBN 0-88410-739-6). Ballinger Pub.

--Discrimination Processes, Vol. IV. LC 81-2654. (The Quantitative Analyses of Behavior Ser.). 376p. 1984. 55.00x (ISBN 0-88410-741-8). Ballinger Pub.

--Quantitative Analyses of Behavior: The Effects of Delay & of Intervening Events on Reinforcement Value, Vol. 5. (Roitblat-Bever-Olton: Comparative Cognition & Neuroscience Ser.). Date not set. text ed. write for info. (ISBN 0-89859-800-1). L Erlbaum Assocs.

Commonwealth Associates, Inc Nuclear Power Plant Siting-A Generalized Process (AIF-NESP-002) (National Environmental Studies Project: NESP Reports). 95p. 1974. 7.00 (ISBN 0-318-13586-8). Atomic Indus Forum.

Commonwealth Institute & Heathcote, David. The Arts of the Hausa. LC 77-4274. 1977. 2 color fiches incl. 30.00 (ISBN 0-226-68899-2, Chicago Visual Lib). U of Chicago Pr.

Commonwealth Institute Seminar, Nov. 26, 1980, London. The Commonwealth & World Peace: A Report by the English-Speaking Union of the Commonwealth & the International Peace Academy. (IPA Report Ser.: No. 11). 62p. 1981. 6.00x (ISBN 0-937722-16-2). Intl Peace.

Commonwealth Relations Office, Great Britain. Catalogue of European Printed Books, India Office Library, 10 Vols. 1964. Set. 835.00 (ISBN 0-8161-0671-1, Hall Library). G K Hall.

--Index of Post-Nineteen Thirty Seven European Manuscript Accessions. India Office Library. 1964. 100.00 (ISBN 0-8161-0687-8, Hall Library). G K Hall.

Commonwealth Scientific & Industrial Research Institute. A Curious & Diverse Flora. Commonwealth Scientific & Industrial Research Institute & Australian Academy of Science, eds. 1982. slides 35.00x (ISBN 0-89955-361-3, Pub. by CSIRO). Intl Spec Bk.

--Scientific & Common Names of Insects & Allied Forms Occuring in Australia. 100p. (Orig.). 1980. pap. 6.00x (ISBN 0-643-00386-X, Pub. by CSIRO Australia). Intl Spec Bk.

Commonwealth Universities Association London, ed. Scholarships Guide for Commonwealth Postgraduate Students, 1983-85. 5th ed. LC 77-643818. 328p. (Orig.). 1982. pap. 25.00x (ISBN 0-85143-078-3). Intl Pubns Serv.

Communications Research Machines, Inc. & Sherrod, Drury. Social Psychology: Explorations in Understanding. (CRM Bks.). 1980. text ed. 23.00x (ISBN 0-394-32099-9, RanC). Random.

Communications Research Machines, Inc. Understanding Psychology. 4th ed. LC 79-19647. 498p. 1983. text ed. 26.00 (ISBN 0-394-34280-1, RanC); wkbk. 7.95 (ISBN 0-394-33823-5). Random.

Communications Trends, Inc. Editors. Computer Industry Advertising & Marketing Forecast 1984. 98p. 1984. looseleaf binders 250.00 (ISBN 0-88709-004-4). Comm Trends Inc.

--Computer Industry Advertising & Marketing Forecast: 1985. 2nd. ed. 122p. 1985. looseleaf binders 375.00 (ISBN 0-88709-007-9). Comm Trends Inc.

Communist Labor Party. Revolutionary Age, Vols. 1-2, No. 7. Repr. of 1918 ed. lib. bdg. 99.00x (ISBN 0-8371-9236-6, RA10). Greenwood.

--Revolutionary Age (Weekly Organ of the Communist Party U.S.A., Majority Group, Vols. 1-3, No. 5. Repr. of 1929 ed. lib. bdg. 180.00x (ISBN 0-8371-9237-4, RA20). Greenwood.

Communist League of America. Militant, Vols. 1-7, No. 48. Repr. of 1928 ed. lib. bdg. 310.00x (ISBN 0-8371-9201-3, MI00). Greenwood.

Communist League of Struggle. Class Struggle, Vols. 1-7, No. 9. 1931-37. Repr. lib. bdg. 110.00x (ISBN 0-8371-9144-0, C200). Greenwood.

Communist Party. Party Organizer, Vols. 1-11, No. 8. 1927-38. Repr. of 1927 ed. lib. bdg. 215.00x (ISBN 0-8371-9149-1, PO00). Greenwood.

Communist Party Central Committee, ed. Our Nation's Crisis & How to Solve It: Main Political Resolution, Communist Party Twentieth National Convention. 96p. 1972. pap. 0.65 (ISBN 0-87898-087-3). New Outlook.

Communist Party National Committee. National Issues: A Survey of Politics & Legislation, Nos. 1-9. 1939. Repr. of 1939 ed. lib. bdg. 28.00x (ISBN 0-8371-9210-2, NS00). Greenwood.

Communist Party of America. Communist. 1919-21. Repr. lib. bdg. 83.00x (ISBN 0-8371-9147-5, CC00). Greenwood.

Communist Party of America, International Labor Defense Staff. Equal Justice, Vols. 1-6, No. 3. 1926-42. Repr. lib. bdg. 270.00x (ISBN 0-8371-9152-1, EJ00). Greenwood.

Communist Party of the United States of America, Convention & Hall, Gus. For Peace, Jobs, Equality: Prevent "The Day After," Defeat Reaganism - Report to the 23rd Convention of the Communist Party, U. S. A., Cleveland, Ohio, November 10-13, 1983. LC 84-1976. Date not set. price not set (ISBN 0-87898-156-X). New Outlook.

Communist Party Steel & Metal Workers Commission. Steel Mill or Treadmill? How to Stop the Big Steel Steal. 1971. pap. 0.15 (ISBN 0-87898-069-5). New Outlook.

Communist Party Twentieth National Convention. La Lucha De los Chicanos Por la Liberacion: La Posicion Del Partido Comunista. 24p. (Span.). 1972. pap. 0.40 (ISBN 0-87898-092-X). New Outlook.

Community & Family Study Center. Family Planning Resume, Vol. II. Bogue, Donald J. & Rumsey, George W., eds. LC 79-54259. (Orig.). pap. 12.00 (ISBN 0-89836-027-7). Comm & Family.

Community Association Institute. Financial Management of Condominium & Homeowner's Associations. LC 76-21960. (Special Report Ser.). 102p. 1975. 19.00 (ISBN 0-87420-569-7, F03); members 14.25. Urban Land.

Community Associations Institute & Wolfe, David B. Condominium & Homeowner Associations that Work: On Paper & In Action. 136p. 1978. 27.00 (ISBN 0-87420-583-2, C15); pap. 22.00 members. Urban Land.

Community Foundation of Greater Washington. Directory of Foundations of the Greater Washington Area, 1984. 125p. 1984. 10.00 (ISBN 0-318-03830-7). Comm Foun DC.

Community Service Editors. Bottom-up Democracy. 1954. pap. 1.50 (ISBN 0-910420-07-6). Comm Serv.

--Community in Economic Pioneering. 1973. pap. 1.00 (ISBN 0-910420-21-1). Comm Serv.

--Pioneering in Education Requires Pioneering in Community. 1973. pap. 1.50 (ISBN 0-910420-15-7). Comm Serv.

--Wholeness in Interaction. 1976. pap. 1.00 (ISBN 0-910420-10-6). Comm Serv.

--World's Economic Plight & Community Responsibility. 1977. pap. 1.00 (ISBN 0-910420-24-6). Comm Serv.

Community Service Society, jt. auth. see Citizen's Committee for New York City.

Community Service Society of New York. Family in a Democratic Society. facsimile ed. LC 77-167330. (Essay Index Reprint Ser). Repr. of 1949 ed. 20.00 (ISBN 0-8369-2491-6). Ayer Co Pubs.

--Social Agency Research - What's Involved? 14p. 1967. pap. 1.50 (ISBN 0-87304-066-X). Family Serv.

Community Service Staff, ed. Guidebook for Intentional Communities. 1977. pap. 2.00 (ISBN 0-910420-01-7). Comm Serv.

Comnena, Anna. The Alexiad of the Princess Anna Comnena. Dawes, Elizabeth A., tr. LC 76-29821. Repr. of 1928 ed. 36.00 (ISBN 0-404-15414-X). AMS Pr.

Comnock, Robert M., compiled by. Comnock's School Speaker: Rhetorical Recitations for Boys & Girls. LC 73-2838. (Granger Index Reprint Ser.). 1973. Repr. of 1883 ed. 21.00 (ISBN 0-8369-6412-8). Ayer Co Pubs.

Como, James T., ed. C. S. Lewis at the Breakfast Table & Other Reminiscences. 336p. 1985. pap. 8.95 (ISBN 0-02-049700-8). MacMillan.

Como, Jay. Surviving on the Job. 1982. 6.36 (ISBN 0-686-36298-5); instr's. guide 5.28 (ISBN 0-686-37287-5). McKnight.

Como, Perry & Hagner, David. Community Work Development. 90p. (Orig.). 1985. pap. price not set (ISBN 0-916671-65-8). Material Dev.

Comoedia Sine Nominee. Etudes sur le Theatre Francais du Quatorzieme et du Quinzieme Siecle. LC 78-53041. (Research & Source Works Ser.: No. 669). 1971. Repr. of 1901 ed. lib. bdg. 34.50 (ISBN 0-8337-3085-1). B Franklin.

Comoglio, P. M., et al, eds. see Immunochemistry of the Cell Membrane, Ravello, 1975.

Comoss, Patricia M., et al. Cardiac Rehabilitation: A Comprehensive Nursing Approach. LC 79-13050. 1979. text ed. 24.75i (ISBN 0-397-54322-0, Lippincott Nursing). Lippincott.

Compagno, Leonard. FAO Species Catalogue: Sharks of the World, Vol. 4, Pt. 2. (Fisheries Synopsis Ser.: No. 125). 655p. 1985. pap. 30.00 (ISBN 92-5-101383-7, F2726, FAO). Unipub.

Compaine, Benjamin. Understanding New Media: Trends & Issues in Electronic Distribution of Information. 400p. 1984. professional reference 29.95x (ISBN 0-88410-977-1). Ballinger Pub.

Compaine, Benjamin M. The Book Industry in Transition: An Economic Study of Book Distribution & Marketing. LC 78-7527. (Communications Library Ser.). (Illus.). 235p. 1978. professional 29.95 (ISBN 0-914236-16-4, 402-BW). Knowledge Indus.

--The Business of Consumer Magazines. LC 82-180. (Communications Library). 197p. 1982. professional 32.95 (ISBN 0-86729-020-X, 404-BW). Knowledge Indus.

--The Newspaper Industry in the 1980s: An Assessment of Economics & Technology. LC 80-10121. (Communications Library). 290p. 1980. professional 29.95 (ISBN 0-914236-37-7, 415-BW). Knowledge Indus.

Compaine, Benjamin M. & Litro, Robert F. Business: An Introduction. 540p. 1984. text ed. 29.95x (ISBN 0-03-059902-4); study guide 13.95x (ISBN 0-03-063618-3). Dryden Pr.

Compaine, Benjamin M., ed. Who Owns the Media? Concentration of Ownership in the Communications Industry. 2nd ed. LC 82-13039. (Communications Library Ser.). 529p. 1982. professional 45.00 (ISBN 0-86729-007-2, 423-BW). Knowledge Indus.

--Who Owns the Media? Concentration of Ownership in the Mass Communication Industry. (Illus.). 300p. 1980. 15.95 (ISBN 0-517-54058-4, Harmony); pap. 2.98 (ISBN 0-517-54059-2). Crown.

Compaine, Benjamin M., et al. Anatomy of the Communications Industry: Who Owns the Media? 2nd ed. LC 83-12012. (Communications Library). 529p. 1982. pap. text ed. 24.95 professional (ISBN 0-86729-007-2). Knowledge Indus.

Companion, Audrey L. Chemical Bonding. 2nd ed. (Illus.). 1979. pap. text ed. 14.95 (ISBN 0-07-012379-9). McGraw.

Compans, R. W., jt. ed. see Bishop, D. H.

Compans, Richard W. & Bishop, David H., eds. Segmented Negative Strand Viruses: Arenaviruses, Bunyaviruses & Orthomyxoviruses, Vol. 1. 1984. 49.00 (ISBN 0-12-183501-4). Acad Pr.

Compans, Richard W., jt. ed. see Bishop, David H.

Company for the Propagation of the Gospel in New England & the Parts Adjacent in America, London. Some Correspondence Between the Governors & Treasurers of the New England Company in London & the Commissioners of the United Colonies in America, the Missionaries of the Company & Others Between the Years 1657 & 1712. Ford, John W., ed. LC 73-126413. (Research & Source Works: No. 524). 1970. Repr. of 1896 ed. lib. bdg. 29.50 (ISBN 0-8337-1185-7). B Franklin.

Comparaetti, Domenico see Consigleri, Pederoso.

Comparato, Frank E. Books for the Millions: A History of the Men Whose Methods & Machines Packaged the Printed Word. (Illus.). 374p. 1971. 12.50 (ISBN 0-8117-0263-4). Labyrinthos.

--Chronicles of Genius & Folly: R. Hoe & Company & the Printing Press As a Service to Democracy. (Illus.). 846p. 1979. 39.95 (ISBN 0-911437-00-2); 24.95 (ISBN 0-911437-10-X). Labyrinthos.

Comparato, Frank E., ed. see Garcia de Palacios, Diego.

Comparato, Frank E., ed. see Villagutierre, Juan.

Compareil, Gabriel. The Courses of Study & Methods of Teaching of the Early Universities, 2 vols. (Illus.). 325p. Date not set. Repr. of 1893 ed. Set. 227.45 (ISBN 0-89901-155-1). Found Class Reprints.

Comparette, Louis. Aes Signatum. (Illus.). 1978. 20.00 (ISBN 0-89005-270-0). Ares.

Comparette, T. Louis. Aes Signatum. (Illus.). 1978. 20.00 (ISBN 0-916710-39-4). Obol Intl.

Comparetti, Marco M., tr. see Gedda, Luigi.

Compass, jt. auth. see Assecuranz.

Compayre, Gabriel. Abelard & the Origin & Early History of the Universities. LC 75-90094. (BCL Ser.: II). 1969. Repr. of 1893 ed. 11.50 (ISBN 0-404-01639-1). AMS Pr.

--Abelard & the Origin & Early History of the Universities. 1893. 10.00x (ISBN 0-403-00009-2). Scholarly.

--History of Pedagogy. Payne, W. H., ed. LC 70-136417. (BCL Ser.: I). Repr. of 1886 ed. 28.00 (ISBN 0-404-01648-0). AMS Pr.

--The History of Pedagogy. Payne, W. H., tr. 1977. Repr. of 1891 ed. lib. bdg. 45.00 (ISBN 0-8492-0534-4). R West.

--History of Pedagogy. Payne, W. H., tr. LC 72-108467. 1970. Repr. of 1900 ed. 79.00x (ISBN 0-403-00205-2). Scholarly.

--Jean Jacques Rousseau & Education from Nature. Jago, R. P., tr. LC 76-168273. (Philosophy Monograph Ser: No. 86). 128p. 1972. Repr. of 1907 ed. lib. bdg. 18.50 (ISBN 0-8337-4053-9). B Franklin.

--Jean Jacques Rousseau & Education from Nature. 1907. Repr. 17.00 (ISBN 0-8274-2607-0). R West.

--Michel de Montaigne. (Educational Ser.). 1908. Repr. 20.00 (ISBN 0-8482-3586-X). Norwood Edns.

--Montaigne & Education of the Judgment. 1973. Repr. of 1908 ed. 10.95 (ISBN 0-8274-1780-2). R West.

--Montaigne & the Education of the Judgement. Mansion, J. E., tr. LC 77-166439. (Research & Source Works Ser: No. 782). 1971. Repr. of 1908 ed. lib. bdg. 17.00 (ISBN 0-8337-4054-7). B Franklin.

Compayre, Gabriel & Payne, W. H. A History of Pedagogy. 1979. Repr. of 1905 ed. lib. bdg. 30.00 (ISBN 0-8492-2162-5). R West.

Comper, Frances M. M. & Kastenbaum, Robert, eds. The Book of the Craft of Dying & Other Early English Tracts Concerning Death. LC 76-19564. (Death & Dying Ser.). 1977. Repr. of 1917 ed. lib. bdg. 19.00x (ISBN 0-405-09560-0). Ayer Co Pubs.

Comper, Francis M., ed. see Rolle, Richard.

Comper, W. D. Heparin (& Related Polysaccharides) Structural & Functional Properties. 280p. 1981. 64.95 (ISBN 0-677-05040-2). Gordon.

Comper, W. D., et al. Solar Energy Phase Transfer Catalysis Transport Processes. (Advances in Polymer Sciences: Vol. 55). (Illus.). 170p. 1984. 41.00 (ISBN 0-387-12592-2). Springer-Verlag.

Compere, Edward L. Orthopedic Surgery. (Illus.). 323p. 1974. 36.50 (ISBN 0-8151-1814-7). Year Bk Med.

Compernolle, Theo, jt. auth. see Bisschop, Marijke.

Compesi & Sherriffs. Small Format Television Production. 1985. write for info. (ISBN 0-205-08455-9, 488456). Allyn.

Compressed Gas Association. Handbook of Compressed Gases. 2nd ed. 1981. 46.50 (ISBN 0-442-25419-9). Van Nos Reinhold.

Comprone, Joseph. A Concise Guide to Writing About Literature. (Illus.). 104p. 1974. text ed. 3.75 (ISBN 0-685-53503-7). Collegiate Pub.

Comprone, Joseph & Holte, James, eds. The Modern Essays, Writing from Experience. rev. ed. 1973-74. text ed. 4.95 perfect bdg. (ISBN 0-685-48767-9). Collegiate Pub.

Comprone, Joseph J. From Experience to Expression: A College Rhetoric. 2nd ed. LC 80-82348. (Illus.). 528p. 1981. text ed. 18.95 (ISBN 0-395-29310-3); instr's manual 0.75 (ISBN 0-395-29311-1). HM.

Comptex Associates Incorporated. Getting the Job you Want with the Audiovisual Portfolio: A Practical Guide for Job Hunters & Career Changers. 1981. 9.50 (ISBN 0-686-37449-5). Competent Assocs.

Compton, Al. Armonia Familiar. 32p. 1981. pap. 1.30 (ISBN 0-311-46078-X). Casa Bautista.

Compton, Alan. Comunicacion Cristiana. 168p. 1982. Repr. of 1979 ed. 4.15 (ISBN 0-311-13833-0). Casa Bautista.

Compton, Anne E. Sorcerer. LC 82-61042. 176p. 1983. pap. 9.95 (ISBN 0-933256-37-X). Second Chance.

Compton, Arthur H. Freedom of Man. LC 70-95117. Repr. of 1935 ed. lib. bdg. 15.00x (ISBN 0-8371-2543-X, COFM). Greenwood.

--Man's Destiny in Eternity. LC 75-117821. (Essay Index Reprint Ser). 1949. 19.00 (ISBN 0-8369-1762-6). Ayer Co Pubs.

--Scientific Papers of Arthur Holly Compton. Shankland, Robert S., ed. 1974. 50.00x (ISBN 0-226-11430-9). U of Chicago Pr.

Compton, Beulah & Galaway, Burt. Social Work Processes. 3rd ed. 1984. pap. 23.00x (ISBN 0-256-02866-4). Dorsey.

Compton, Beulah R. Introduction to Social Welfare & Social Work: Structure, Function, & Process. 1980. 28.00x (ISBN 0-256-02093-0). Dorsey.

Compton, Boyd, ed. & tr. Mao's China: Party Reform Documents, 1942-44. LC 51-12273. (Publications on Asia of the International Studies: No. 1). (Illus.). 332p. 1966. pap. 6.95x (ISBN 0-295-74011-6). U of Wash Pr.

Compton, Boyd, tr. see Mao Tse-Tung.

Compton, Carol J. Courting Poetry in Laos: A Textual & Linguistic Analysis. (Special Report Ser.: No. 18). (Illus.). 1979. pap. 9.00x (ISBN 0-686-25222-5, Ctr South & Southeast Asian Studies). Cellar.

Compton, Charles. Inside Chemistry. (Illus.). 1979. text ed. 29.95 (ISBN 0-07-012350-0). McGraw.

Compton, Charles H. Memories of a Librarian. 1954. 5.00 (ISBN 0-937322-06-7). St Louis Pub Lib.

--Who Reads What? facs. ed. LC 69-18923. (Essay Index Reprint Ser). 1934. 14.00 (ISBN 0-8369-0012-X). Ayer Co Pubs.

Compton, Charles H., et al. Twenty-Five Crucial Years of the St. Louis Public Library, 1927 to 1952. 1953. 5.00 (ISBN 0-937322-00-8). St Louis Pub Lib.

Compton, D. G. Ascendancies. 224p. 1985. pap. 2.95 (ISBN 0-441-03088-2). Ace Bks.

--Chronocules. 1980. pap. 1.95 (ISBN 0-671-83079-1, Timescape). PB.

--Farewell, Earth's Bliss. LC 79-12824. 1979. lib. bdg. 12.95x (ISBN 0-89370-135-1); pap. 4.95x (ISBN 0-89370-235-8). Borgo Pr.

--Farewell, Earth's Bliss. 160p. 1979. pap. 4.95 (ISBN 0-87877-235-9). Newcastle Pub.

--The Steel Crocodile. (Orig.). 1980. pap. 2.25 (ISBN 0-671-83078-3, Timescape). PB.

--Synthajoy. 1977. Repr. of 1968 ed. lib. bdg. 13.00 (ISBN 0-8398-2373-8, Gregg). G K Hall.

--The Unsleeping Eye. 1980. pap. 2.25 (ISBN 0-671-83077-5, Timescape). PB.

--A Usual Lunacy. LC 78-14953. (Illus.). 1978. lib. bdg. 12.95x (ISBN 0-89370-125-4); pap. 4.95x (ISBN 0-89370-225-0). Borgo Pr.

--A Usual Lunacy. 1983. pap. 2.75 (ISBN 0-441-84760-9, Ace Science Fiction). Ace Bks.

--A Usual Lunacy. 160p. 1978. pap. 4.95 (ISBN 0-87877-225-1). Newcastle Pub.

--Windows. LC 79-921. 1983. pap. 2.95 (ISBN 0-441-89230-2). Ace Bks.

Compton, David, jt. auth. see Edginton, Christopher.

Compton, David W. & Benson, Charles D. Living & Working in Space: A History of Skylab. (NASA SP 4208, NASA History Ser.). 462p. 20.00 (ISBN 0-318-11796-7). Gov Printing Office.

Compton, Eric N. Inside Commercial Banking. 2nd ed. LC 83-10278. 288p. 1983. 32.50x (ISBN 0-471-89561-X, Pub. by Wiley-Interscience). Wiley.

Compton, Grant. What Does a Meteorologist Do? (What Do They Do Ser.). (Illus.). 80p. (gr. 5 up). 1981. PLB 9.95 (ISBN 0-396-07931-8). Dodd.

Compton, H. K. Storehouse & Stockyard Management. 2nd ed. (Illus.). 544p. 1981. text ed. 42.50x (ISBN 0-7121-1965-5, Pub. by Macdonald & Evans). Trans-Atlantic.

--Supplies & Materials Management. 2nd ed. (Illus.). 512p. 1979. text ed. 37.50x (ISBN 0-7121-1964-7, Pub. by Macdonald & Evans England). Trans-Atlantic.

Compton, J. Lin, ed. The Transformation of International Agricultural Research & Development. (Westview Special Studies in Agriculture Science & Policy). 275p. 1985. pap. 19.85x (ISBN 0-8133-0057-6). Westview.

Compton, Jay. The Power of Construction Management Using Lotus 1-2-3. (Illus.). 300p. 1984. pap. 29.95 (ISBN 0-943518-17-2); pap. 44.95, incl. disk (ISBN 0-317-11824-2). Mgmt Info Inc.

--The Power of Construction Management Using Multiplan. (Illus.). 300p. 1984. 29.95 (ISBN 0-943518-18-0); 44.95, incl. disk (ISBN 0-317-11827-7). Mgmt Info Inc.

Compton, Jay C. Power of Construction Management Using Multiplan. 220p. 1984. pap. 29.95 (ISBN 0-13-688086-X); pap. text ed. 44.95 with disk (ISBN 0-13-688094-0). P-H.

--Power of Construction Management Using 1-2-3. 220p. 1984. pap. 29.95 (ISBN 0-13-688235-8); pap. text ed. 44.95 with disk (ISBN 0-13-688243-9). P-H.

Compton, Joan. Enjoy Your Flowers. 14.50 (ISBN 0-392-02805-0, LTB). Sportshelf.

Compton, Joy B. A Decade of Glory. (Illus.). 64p. 1983. 10.50 (ISBN 0-89962-322-0). Todd & Honeywell.

Compton, LaNell. Looking Forward to a New Day. 1984. 7.95 (ISBN 0-8158-0418-0). Chris Mass.

Compton, Martha, ed. An Accent Guide: Easy Cooking. 128p. 1982. pap. 3.25 (ISBN 0-915708-12-4). Cheever Pub.

Compton, Mary F. A Source Book for the Middle School. LC 78-52470. 1978. 4.00x (ISBN 0-918772-06-0). Ed Assocs.

Compton, Merlin D. Ricardo Palma. (World Authors Ser.). 1982. lib. bdg. 16.95 (ISBN 0-8057-6435-6, Twayne). G K Hall.

Compton, Michael. Looking at Pictures in the Tate Gallery. (Illus.). 72p. 1985. pap. 6.95 (ISBN 0-905005-61-9, Pub. by Salem Hse Ltd). Merrimack Pub Cir.

--New Art: At the Tate Gallery 1983. (Illus.). 72p. pap. 9.95 (ISBN 0-905005-79-1, Pub. by Salem Hse Ltd). Merrimack Pub Cir.

Compton, Michael, intro. by. Towards a New Art: Essays on the Background to Abstract Art 1910-20. (Illus.). 239p. 16.95 (ISBN 0-905005-22-8, Pub. by Salem Hse Ltd). Merrimack Pub Cir.

Compton, Michael M. Understanding Robots: How They Work, What They Can Do, What They Will Become. Ledin, George, Jr., ed. LC 83-15149. (Handy Guide Series to Computers). (Illus.). 47p. 1983. pap. 3.50 (ISBN 0-88284-248-X). Alfred Pub.

Compton, Neil. The High Ozarks: A Vision of Eden. LC 82-60891. (Illus.). iv, 97p. 1982. 27.95 (ISBN 0-912456-06-X). Ozark Soc Bks.

Compton, Paul & Pesci, Marton. Environmental Management. (Studies in Geography in Hungary: 16). 264p. 1984. 32.00 (ISBN 963-05-3696-X, Pub. by Akademiai Kaido Hungary). Heyden.

Compton, Paul A. Northern Ireland: A Census Atlas. 1978. text ed. 39.50x (ISBN 0-7171-0891-0). Humanities.

Compton, R., jt. auth. see Harvey, M.

Compton, R. R. Manual of Field Geology. LC 61-17357. 378p. 1962. 28.95 (ISBN 0-471-16698-7). Wiley.

Compton, Rae. Complete Book of Traditional Knitting. LC 82-62119. (Illus.). 240p. 1983. 22.50 (ISBN 0-684-17866-4, ScribT). Scribner.

Compton, Robert. La Teologia de la Liberacion: Una Introduccion. 112p. (Orig., Span.). 1985. pap. 3.75 (ISBN 0-311-09106-7). Casa Bautista.

Compton, Robert W. Design Notes Log, G.O.D. 2nd ed. (Illus.). 330p. 1984. pap. 10.00 (ISBN 0-9607376-1-8). Pi Rho.

Compton, Susan, ed. Chagall. (Illus.). 240p. 1985. 25.00 (ISBN 0-8109-0797-6). Abrams.

Compton, W. Dale, ed. The Interaction of Science & Technology. LC 75-83548. 137p. 1969. 12.50x (ISBN 0-252-00024-2). U of Ill Pr.

Compton, W. H. Special Day Sermons. 1972. 3.25 (ISBN 0-87148-752-7); pap. 2.50 (ISBN 0-87148-753-5). Pathway Pr.

Compton-Burnet, Ivy. Bullivant & the Lambs. LC 83-45737. 1948. Repr. of 1948 ed. 29.50 (ISBN 0-404-20067-2, PR6005). AMS Pr.

Compton-Burnett, I. Elders & Betters. 1944. 14.95 (ISBN 0-575-02371-6, Pub. by Gollancz England). David & Charles.

--A Family & a Fortune. 1939. 14.95 (ISBN 0-575-02579-4, Pub. by Gollancz England). David & Charles.

--A Heritage & its History. 1959. 12.95 (ISBN 0-575-02723-1, Pub by Gollancz England). David & Charles.

--Manservant & Maidservant. 1947. 14.95 (ISBN 0-575-02706-1, Pub. by Gollancz England). David & Charles.

--The Mighty & Their Fall. 1961. 12.95 (ISBN 0-575-02704-5, Pub. by Gollancz England). David & Charles.

--More Women Than Men. 1933. 14.95 (ISBN 0-575-01959-X, Pub. by Gollancz England). David & Charles.

--Pastors & Masters. 1952. 12.95 (ISBN 0-575-02705-3, Pub. by Gollancz England). David & Charles.

--The Present & the Past. 1953. 12.95 (ISBN 0-575-01416-4, Pub by Gollancz England). David & Charles.

--Two Worlds & Their Ways. 1949. 14.95 (ISBN 0-575-02610-3, Pub by Gollancz England). David & Charles.

Compton-Burnett, Ivy. Brothers & Sisters. 1950. 14.95 (ISBN 0-575-01894-1, Pub. by Gollancz England). David & Charles.

--Brothers & Sisters. 230p. 1984. pap. write for info. (ISBN 0-8052-8213-0, Pub. by Allison & Busby England). Schocken.

--Collector's Edition (All 19 Titles, 19 vols. 1950. Set. 250.00 (ISBN 0-575-03683-4, Pub. by Gollancz England). David & Charles.

--Darkness & Day. 248p. 1951. 14.95 (ISBN 0-575-03477-7, Pub. by Gollancz England). David & Charles.

--Daughters & Sons. 1937. 14.95 (ISBN 0-575-01796-1, Pub. by Gollancz England). David & Charles.

--Daughters & Sons. 208p. 1984. pap. 5.95 (ISBN 0-8052-8214-9, Pub. by Allison & Busby, England). Schocken.

--Dolores. 330p. 1981. 15.00x (ISBN 0-85158-104-8, Pub. by Blackwood & Sons England). State Mutual Bk.

--Elders & Betters. 304p. 1984. pap. 5.95 (ISBN 0-8052-8211-4, Pub. by Allison & Busby, England). Schocken.

--A Family & a Fortune. (Penguin Modern Classics Ser.). 304p. 1983. pap. 4.95 (ISBN 0-14-001713-5). Penguin.

--A Father & His Fate. 216p. 1957. 14.95 (ISBN 0-575-03476-9, Pub. by Gollancz England). David & Charles.

--A Father & His Fate. (Twentieth-Century Classics). 224p. 1985. pap. 5.95 (ISBN 0-19-281853-8). Oxford U Pr.

--A God & His Gifts. 1963. 12.95 (ISBN 0-575-02578-6, Pub by Gollancz England). David & Charles.

--A God & His Gifts. (Penguin Modern Classics Ser.). 176p. 1983. pap. 3.95 (ISBN 0-14-006125-8). Penguin.

--A House & Its Head. (Modern Classics Ser.). 280p. 1983. pap. 4.95 (ISBN 0-14-001317-2). Penguin.

--A House & Its Head. 1966. 14.95 (ISBN 0-575-01579-9, Pub. by Gollancz England). David & Charles.

--The Last & the First. 216p. 1971. 12.95 (ISBN 0-575-00614-5, Pub. by Gollancz England). David & Charles.

--Manservant & Maidservant. (Twentieth-Century Classics Ser.). 312p. 1984. pap. 5.95 (ISBN 0-19-281380-3). Oxford U Pr.

--Men & Wives. 288p. 1984. pap. 5.95 (ISBN 0-8052-8215-7, Pub. by Allison & Busby, England). Schocken.

--Men & Wives. 1966. 14.95 (ISBN 0-575-01581-0, Pub. by Gollancz England). David & Charles.

--More Women Than Men. 231p. 1984. pap. 5.95 (ISBN 0-8052-8210-6, Pub. by Allison & Busby England). Schocken.

--Parents & Children. 1941. 14.95 (ISBN 0-575-01578-0, Pub. by Gollancz England). David & Charles.

--Pastors & Masters. 96p. 1984. pap. 5.95 (ISBN 0-8052-8212-2, Pub. by Allison & Busby England). Schocken.

Compton-Burnett, J. Brothers & Sisters. 1981. 20.00x (Pub. by Gollancz England). State Mutual Bk.

--Mother & Son. 1981. 20.00x (ISBN 0-575-02353-8, Pub. by Gollancz England). State Mutual Bk.

Compton-Burnett, J., tr. see Steiner, Rudolf.

Compton-Burnett, Judith, tr. see Steiner, Rudolf.

Compton-Burnett, Juliet, tr. see Savitch, Marie.

Compton-Burnett, V., tr. see Steiner, Rudolf.

Compton Burnett, V. see Steiner, Rudolf.

Compton-Burnett, V., et al, trs. see Steiner, Rudolf.

Compton-Hall, P. R., ed. The Submariner's World One: An Annual Underwater Digest. (Illus.). 144p. 1983. 19.95 (ISBN 0-85937-303-7, Pub. by K Mason). Sheridan.

Compton-Hall, Richard. Submarine Boats: The Beginning of Underwater Warfare. LC 83-7128. (Illus.). 192p. 1984. 19.95 (ISBN 0-668-05924-9). Arco.

--The Underwater War 1939-1945. (Illus.). 165p. 1982. 19.95 (ISBN 0-7137-1131-0, Pub. by Blandford Pr England). Sterling.

Compton-Rickett, Arthur. A History of English Literature. Repr. 20.00 (ISBN 0-8274-2507-4). R West.

--The London Life of Yesterday. 1979. Repr. of 1909 ed. lib. bdg. 40.00 (ISBN 0-8482-7573-X). Norwood Edns.

--Our Poets at School & Other Fancies in Prose & Verse. 1979. Repr. of 1921 ed. lib. bdg. 20.00 (ISBN 0-8495-0924-6). Arden Lib.

--Personal Forces in Modern Literature. LC 72-973. Repr. of 1906 ed. 19.25 (ISBN 0-404-01649-9). AMS Pr.

--Personal Forces in Modern Literature. facs. ed. LC 68-54367. (Essay Index Reprint Ser). 1906. 17.00 (ISBN 0-8369-0824-4). Ayer Co Pubs.

--Personal Forces in Modern Literature. 1973. lib. bdg. 15.00 (ISBN 0-8414-2373-3). Folcroft.

--Portraits & Personalities. 1973. Repr. of 1937 ed. 20.00 (ISBN 0-8274-1761-6). R West.

--Robert Browning: Humanist. 1979. Repr. of 1925 ed. lib. bdg. 25.00 (ISBN 0-8495-0926-2). Arden Lib.

--Robert Browning, Humanist. LC 73-20319. 1925. lib. bdg. 25.00 (ISBN 0-8414-3540-5). Folcroft.

--William Morris: A Study in Personality. 1978. Repr. of 1913 ed. lib. bdg. 30.00 (ISBN 0-8495-0801-0). Arden Lib.

--William Morris: A Study in Personality. LC 73-160749. 1971. Repr. of 1913 ed. 25.00x (ISBN 0-8046-1563-2, Pub. by Kennikat). Assoc Faculty Pr.

Compton-Rickett, Arthur, jt. auth. see Hake, Thomas.

Compton-Rickett, Arthur, jt. auth. see Short, Ernest H.

Compton-Rickett, R. William Morris: A Study in Personality. LC 72-195148. 1973. lib. bdg. 20.00 (ISBN 0-8414-2374-1). Folcroft.

Compute!, ed. see Guzelimian, Vahe.

Compute, ed. see Heilborn, John.

Compute!, ed. see Larsen, Elmer.

Compute!, ed. see Leemon, Sheldon & Levitan, Arlan.

Compute!, ed. see Metcalf, Chris & Sugiyama, Marc.

Compute!, ed. see Standage, Blaine D., et al.

Compute Editors. Compute's Commodore Collection, Vol. I. 224p. (Orig.). 1984. pap. 12.95 (ISBN 0-942386-55-8). Compute Pubns.

--Compute's Commodore Collection, Vol. 2. (Orig.). 1984. pap. 12.95 (ISBN 0-942386-70-1). Compute Pubns.

--Compute's First Book of Apple. (Orig.). 1984. pap. 12.95 (ISBN 0-942386-69-8). Compute Pubns.

--Compute's First Book of Commodore 64. 264p. 1983. 12.95 (ISBN 0-942386-20-5). Compute Pubns.

--Compute's First Book of Commodore 64 Sound & Graphics. 275p. (Orig.). 1983. pap. 12.95 (ISBN 0-942386-21-3). Compute Pubns.

--Compute's Second Book of Apple. (Orig.). 1985. pap. 12.95 (ISBN 0-87455-008-4). Compute Pubns.

--Compute's Telecomputing on the Commodore 64. (Orig.). 1985. pap. 12.95 (ISBN 0-87455-009-2). Compute Pubns.

Compute Editors, ed. Compute's Commodore 64-128 Collection. (Orig.). 1985. pap. 12.95 (ISBN 0-942386-97-3). Compute Pubns.

--MacOffice: Using the Macintosh for Everything. (Orig.). 1985. pap. 18.95 (ISBN 0-87455-006-8). Compute Pubns.

Compute Editors, ed. see Brannon, Charles.

Compute Editors, ed. see Brannon, Charles & Martin, Kevin.

Compute Editors, ed. see Carlson, Edward H.

Compute Editors, ed. see Chadwick, Ian.

COMPUTE Editors, ed. see Collin, Raeto C.

Compute Editors, ed. see Davies, Russ.

Compute Editors, ed. see Dorf, Richard C.

Compute Editors, ed. see Enright, Thomas E., et al.

Compute Editors, ed. see Flynn, Brian.

Compute Editors, ed. see Flynn, Christopher.

Compute Editors, ed. see Freiberger, Paul & McNeill, Dan.

Compute Editors, ed. see Gutman, Dan & Adams, Shay.

Compute Editors, ed. see Heeb, Dan.

Compute Editors, ed. see Kidd, Clark & Kidd, Kathy.

Compute Editors, ed. see Kidd, Clark & Kidd, Kathy H.

Compute Editors, ed. see Levitan, Arlan R. & Leemon, Sheldon.

Compute Editors, ed. see Mansfield, Richard.

Compute Editors, ed. see Trivette, Donald.

Compute Magazine, ed. Compute's First Book of PET-CBM. (Illus.). 244p. (Orig.). 1981. pap. 12.95 (ISBN 0-942386-01-9). Compute Pubns.

Compute! Magazine, ed. see Mansfield, Richard, et al.

Compute! Magazine, ed. see Wilkinson, Bill.

Compute Magazine Staff. Compute's First Book of Atari. (Illus.). 184p. (Orig.). 1981. pap. 12.95 (ISBN 0-942386-00-0). Compute Pubns.

Compute! Magazine Staff. Compute's First Book of Atari Games. 232p. (Orig.). 1983. pap. 12.95 (ISBN 0-942386-14-0). Compute Pubns.

--Compute's First Book of Commodore 64 Games. 217p. (Orig.). 1983. pap. 12.95 (ISBN 0-942386-34-5). Compute Pubns.

--Compute's First Book of TI Games. Regena, C., ed. 211p. (Orig.). 1983. pap. 12.95 (ISBN 0-942386-17-5). Compute Pubns.

--Compute's First Book of VIC. (Illus.). 212p. (Orig.). 1982. pap. 12.95 (ISBN 0-942386-07-8). Compute Pubns.

--Compute's First Book of VIC Games. 201p. 1983. 12.95 (ISBN 0-942386-13-2). Compute Pubns.

--Positive Philosophy. Martineau, Harriet, tr. LC 70-174979. Repr. of 1855 ed. 38.50 (ISBN 0-404-08209-2). AMS Pr.

--Positivist Library of Auguste Comte, 1798-1854. Harrison, Frederic, ed. LC 73-162317. (Bibliography & Reference Ser.: No. 419). 1971. Repr. of 1886 ed. lib. bdg. 14.50 (ISBN 0-8337-0631-4). B Franklin.

Comte, Edward Le see Le Comte, Edward.

Comte, Edward Le see LeComte, Edward.

Comte, Edward Le see Le Comte, Edward.

Comte, Edward S. Le see Le Comte, Edward S.

Comte, R. & Pernin, A. Lexique des Industries Graphiques. 128p. (Fr.). 1975. pap. 17.50 (ISBN 0-686-56959-8, M-6082). French & Eur.

Comtet, L. Advanced Combinatorics: The Art of Finite & Infinite Expansions. enl. & rev. ed. Nienhuys, J., tr. LC 73-86091. 1974. lib. bdg. 60.50 (ISBN 90-277-0380-9, Pub. by Reidel Holland); pap. text ed. 34.00 (ISBN 90-277-0441-4, Pub. by Reidel Holland). Kluwer Academic.

Comtex Staff. Artificial Intelligence Reports from Bolt, Beranek & Newman. 1984. write for info. (ISBN 0-471-82286-8). Wiley.

--Artificial Intelligence Reports from Carnegie Mellon University. 1984. write for info. (ISBN 0-471-82289-2). Wiley.

--Artificial Intelligence Reports from Carnegie Mellon University, Pt. 1. 1984. write for info. (ISBN 0-471-82288-4). Wiley.

--Artificial Intelligence Reports from Carnegie Mellon University, Pt. 2. 1984. write for info. (ISBN 0-471-82287-6). Wiley.

--Artificial Intelligence Reports from the University of Illinois. 1985. write for info. (ISBN 0-471-82284-1). Wiley.

--Artificial Intelligence Reports from the University of Pennsylvania. 1984. write for info. (ISBN 0-471-82283-3). Wiley.

--Artificial Intelligence Reports from Yale University. 1985. write for info. (ISBN 0-471-82285-X). Wiley.

Comtois, M. F. & Miller, Lynn F. Contemporary American Theatre Critics: A Dictionary & Anthology of Their Works. LC 77-23063. 1977. 50.00 (ISBN 0-8108-1057-3). Scarecrow.

Comyn, J. Polymer Permeability. 1985. 67.50 (ISBN 0-85334-322-5, Pub. by Elsevier Applied Sci England). Elsevier.

Comyn, James. Lost Causes. 208p. (Orig.). 1982. 18.00 (ISBN 0-436-10581-0, Pub. by Secker & Warburg UK). David & Charles.

Comyns, Barbara. Our Spoons Came from Woolworths. LC 83-45186. 224p. 1983. pap. 6.95 (ISBN 0-385-27960-4, Virago). Doubleday.

--The Vets Daughter. LC 81-9702. (Virago Modern Classic Ser.). 1981. pap. 5.95 (ISBN 0-385-27190-5, Virago). Doubleday.

Conable, Barber B., Jr., et al. Future of the Social Security System. 1977. pap. 3.75 (ISBN 0-8447-2114-X). Am Enterprise.

Conable, Charlotte W. Women at Cornell: The Myth of Equal Education. LC 77-3117. (Illus.). 176p. 1977. 17.50x (ISBN 0-8014-1098-3); pap. 6.50x (ISBN 0-8014-9167-3). Cornell U Pr.

Conacher, D. J. Aeschylus' "Prometheus Bound". A Literary Commentary. 128p. 1980. 25.00x (ISBN 0-8020-2391-6); pap. 8.50 (ISBN 0-8020-6416-7). U of Toronto Pr.

Conacher, J. B. The Peelites & the Party System, 1846-52. (Library of Politics & Society Ser.). 246p. 1972. 17.50 (ISBN 0-208-01268-0, Archon). Shoe String.

Conacher, James B., ed. see Du Creux, Francois.

Conaghan, John, ed. Dryden: A Selection. 1978. 19.50 (ISBN 0-416-80160-9, NO.2622); pap. 19.50x (ISBN 0-416-80170-6, NO.2623). Methuen Inc.

Conahan, Judith M. Helping Your Elderly Patients: A Guide for Nursing Assistants. LC 75-40507. (Illus.). 128p. 1976. pap. 4.95 (ISBN 0-913292-29-X). Tiresias Pr.

Conahan, Thomas J., III. Cardiac Anesthesia. 1981. 39.50 (ISBN 0-201-04097-2, 04097, Med-Nurse). Addison-Wesley.

Conaire, P. O. Padraic O'Conaire Stories. 192p. 1982. pap. 4.95 (ISBN 0-905169-54-9, Pub. by Poolbeg Pr Ireland). Irish Bks Media.

Conan, Laure. Angeline de Montbrun. LC 73-82585. (Literature of Canada, Poetry & Prose in Reprint: No. 14). pap. 50.50 (ISBN 0-317-26930-5, 2023605). Bks Demand UMI.

Conan Doyle, Arthur see Doyle, Arthur Conan.

Conant, Charles A. History of Modern Banks of Issue. 6th ed. Nadler, M., ed. LC 68-30519. Repr. of 1927 ed. 57.50x (ISBN 0-678-00505-2). Kelley.

--A History of Modern Banks of Issue. 1897. 50.00 (ISBN 0-686-17722-3). Quest Edns.

--United States in the Orient. LC 72-137936. (Economic Thought, History & Challenge Ser.). 1971. Repr. of 1900 ed. 24.50x (ISBN 0-8046-1441-5, Pub by Kennikat). Assoc Faculty Pr.

--Wall Street & the Country: A Study of Recent Financial Tendencies. LC 68-28622. 1968. Repr. of 1904 ed. lib. bdg. 22.50x (ISBN 0-8371-0358-4, COWS). Greenwood.

Conant, D. C. The Earnest Man; or the Character & Labors of Adoniram Judson. 1978. Repr. of 1856 ed. lib. bdg. 20.00 (ISBN 0-8492-3943-5). R West.

Conant, Francis, et al, eds. Resource Inventory & Baseline Study Methods for Developing Countries. LC 83-15493. 539p. 1983. 22.95 (ISBN 0-87168-258-3). AAAS.

Conant, Helen S., tr. see Charnay, Desire.

Conant, James B. The Citadel of Learning. LC 77-22592. 1977. Repr. of 1956 ed. lib. bdg. 15.00x (ISBN 0-8371-9733-3, COCL). Greenwood.

--Education in a Divided World: The Function of the Public Schools in Our Unique Society. LC 78-94580. Repr. of 1948 ed. lib. bdg. 15.00x (ISBN 0-8371-2548-0, COEW). Greenwood.

--Modern Science & Modern Man. LC 83-12753. 111p. 1983. Repr. of 1952 ed. lib. bdg. 27.50x (ISBN 0-313-24119-8, CMOS). Greenwood.

--The Overthrow of the Phlogiston Theory: The Chemical Revolution of 1775-1789. LC 50-8087. (Harvard Case Histories in Experimental Science: No. 2). pap. 20.00 (ISBN 0-317-09099-2, 2017681). BKs Demand UMI.

Conant, James B., ed. Robert Boyle's Experiments in Pneumatics. (Havard Case Histories in Experimental Science: Case 1). (Illus.). pap. 20.00 (ISBN 0-317-08773-8, 2022240). Bks Demand UMI.

Conant, James B., et al. Harvard Case Histories in Experimental Science, 2 Vols. Roller, Duane & Roller, Duane H., eds. LC 57-12843. (Illus.). 1957. Set. 40.00x (ISBN 0-674-37400-2). Harvard U Pr.

Conant, Jonathan B. Cochran's German Review Grammar. 3rd ed. LC 73-21535. 384p. 1974. text ed. 22.95 (ISBN 0-13-139501-7). P-H.

Conant, Julia, jt. auth. see Pyeritz, Reed E.

Conant, Lynn, jt. auth. see North, Douglass A.

Conant, Margaret E. The Construction of a Diagnostic Reading Test for Senior High School Students & College Freshmen. LC 71-176697. (Columbia University. Teachers College. Contributions to Education: No. 861). Repr. of 1942 ed. 22.50 (ISBN 0-404-55861-5). AMS Pr.

Conant, Martha P. Oriental Tale in England in the Eighteenth Century. 1967. lib. bdg. 21.50x (ISBN 0-374-91900-3). Octagon.

Conant, Melvin. Heralds of Their Age. (Illus.). 24p. pap. 1.00 (ISBN 0-913344-04-4). South St Sea Mus.

--The Long Polar Watch: Canada & the Defense of North America. LC 74-9874. (Published for the Council on Foreign Relations Ser). (Illus.). 204p. 1974. Repr. of 1962 ed. lib. bdg. 18.75x (ISBN 0-8371-7613-1, COPW). Greenwood.

--The Long Polar Watch: Canada & the Defence of North America. 1st ed. LC 62-14889. pap. 54.00 (ISBN 0-317-08303-1, 2002151). Bks Demand UMI.

Conant, Melvin, ed. see Levy, Walter J.

Conant, Melvin A. Access to Energy: Two Thousand & After. Davis, Vincent, ed. LC 79-15015. (Essays for the Third Century Ser.). 144p. 1979. 13.00x (ISBN 0-8131-0401-7). U Pr of Ky.

--The Oil Factor in U. S. Foreign Policy: 1980-1990. LC 81-47714. (A Council on Foreign Relations Book Ser.). (Illus.). 144p. 1981. 17.00 (ISBN 0-669-04728-7); pap. 9.50 (ISBN 0-669-05206-X). Lexington Bks.

Conant, Michael. Antitrust in the Motion Picture Industry. Jowett, Garth S., ed. LC 77-11372. (Aspects of Film Ser.). (Illus.). 1978. Repr. of 1960 ed. lib. bdg. 26.50x (ISBN 0-405-11128-2). Ayer Co Pubs.

--Railroad Mergers & Abandonments. LC 82-15834. (Publications of the Institute of Business & Economic Research, University of California). xiii, 212p. 1982. Repr. of 1964 ed. lib. bdg. 29.75x (ISBN 0-313-23694-1, CORAM). Greenwood.

Conant, Miriam B., ed. see Aron, Raymond.

Conant, Newton. Changed by Beholding Him. 1972. pap. 2.95 (ISBN 0-87508-147-9). Chr Lit.

Conant, Ralph W. The Conant Report: A Study of the Education of Librarians. 1980. 25.00x (ISBN 0-262-03072-1). MIT Pr.

Conant, Ralph W., jt. auth. see Easton, Thomas A.

Conant, Robert, jt. auth. see Bedford, Frances.

Conant, Roger. A Field Guide to Reptiles & Amphibians of Eastern & Central North America. 2nd ed. LC 74-13425. (Peterson Field Guide Ser.). 448p. 1975. 16.95 (ISBN 0-395-19979-4); pap. 11.95 (ISBN 0-395-19977-8). HM.

--The Political Poetry & Ideology of F. I. Tiutchev. (Ardis Essay Ser.: No. 6). 1983. 10.00 (ISBN 0-88233-624-X). Ardis Pubs.

Conant, Roger, ed. see Ashby, W. Ross.

Conant, Susan J., et al. Teaching Language-Disabled Children: A Communication Games Intervention. LC 83-27303. 185p. 1983. 19.95 (ISBN 0-914797-04-2). Brookline Book.

Conard, Alfred F., et al. Enterprise Organization: Cases, Statutes & Analysis on Licensing, Employment, Agency, Partnerships, Associations, & Corporations. 3rd ed. LC 82-10902. (University Casebook Ser.). 1243p. 1982. text ed. 27.50 (ISBN 0-88277-058-6); Editor's Notes. write for info. (ISBN 0-88277-108-6). Foundation Pr.

--Agency, Associations, Employment, Licensing & Partnerships: Cases, Statutes & Analysis. 3rd ed. LC 82-82863. (University Casebook Ser.). 656p. 1982. pap. 20.00 (ISBN 0-88277-080-2). Foundation Pr.

Conard, Henry S. The Background of Plant Ecology: Translation from the German the Plant Life of the Danube Basin. Egerton, Frank N., 3rd, ed. LC 77-74234. (History of Ecology Ser.). 1978. Repr. of 1951 ed. lib. bdg. 19.00 (ISBN 0-405-10403-0). Ayer Co Pubs.

Conard, Henry S. & Redfearn, Paul L., Jr. How to Know the Mosses & Liverworts. 2nd ed. (Pict. Key Nature Ser.). 320p. 1979. wire coil write for info. (ISBN 0-697-04768-7). Wm C Brown.

Conard, Henry S., tr. see Braun-Blanquet, J.

Conard, Howard L. Uncle Dick Wootton: The Pioneer Frontiersman of the Rocky Mountain Region. Quaife, Milo M., ed. LC 79-19038. (Illus.). xxiv, 462p. 1980. 29.95x (ISBN 0-8032-1408-1); pap. 7.50 (ISBN 0-8032-6306-6, BB 730, Bison). U of Nebr Pr.

Conard, Joseph W. Behavior of Interest Rates: A Progress Report. (General Ser.: No. 81). 159p. 1966. 9.50 (ISBN 0-87014-081-7, Dist. by Columbia U Pr). Natl Bur Econ Res.

Conard, Rebecca & Nelson, Christopher H. Santa Barbara: A Guide to El Pueblo Viejo. Days, Mary L., ed. LC 84-72199. (Illus.). 160p. (Orig.). 1986. pap. 9.95 (ISBN 0-88496-226-1). Capra Pr.

Conard, Robert, ed. see Hesse, Herman.

Conard, Robert C. Heinrich Boll. (World Authors Ser.). 15.95 (ISBN 0-8057-6464-X, Twayne). G K Hall.

Conarroe, Joel. John Berryman: An Introduction to the Poetry. LC 77-8461. (Columbia Introductions to Twentieth-Century American Poetry). 215p. 1977. 20.00x (ISBN 0-231-03811-9). Columbia U Pr.

--William Carlos Williams' Paterson: Language & Landscape. LC 73-92854. 1974. pap. 9.95 (ISBN 0-8122-1046-8). U of Pa Pr.

Conarroe, Richard R. Bravely, Bravely...in Business. (AMACOM Executive Bks). 1978. pap. 3.95 (ISBN 0-8144-7509-4). AMACOM.

Conason, Emil & Metz, Ella. The Salt-Free Diet Cook Book. pap. 4.95 (ISBN 0-399-51052-4, G&D). Putnam Pub Group.

Conason, Robert, jt. auth. see Baum, David B.

Conati, Marcello. Encounters with Verdi. Stokes, Richard, tr. LC 83-73736. (Illus.). 417p. 1984. 25.00 (ISBN 0-8014-1717-1). Cornell U Pr.

Conaway, J. C. Death Style. 1977. pap. 1.50 (ISBN 0-505-51160-6, Pub. by Tower Bks). Dorchester Pub Co.

--Quarrel with the Moon. 320p. (Orig.). 1982. pap. 2.95 (ISBN 0-523-48033-4). Pinnacle Bks.

Conaway, Jim. The Deadly Spring. 1976. pap. 1.50 (ISBN 0-685-72567-7, LB395, Pub. by Nordon Pubns). Dorchester Pub Co.

--They Do It with Mirrors. 1977. pap. 1.50 (ISBN 0-505-51190-8, Pub. by Tower Bks). Dorchester Pub Co.

Conaway, Judith. Detective Tricks You Can Do. (Illus.). 48p. (gr. 1-5). 1986. PLB 9.49 (ISBN 0-8167-0672-7); pap. text ed. 1.95 (ISBN 0-8167-0673-5). Troll Assocs.

--The Discovery Book of Size. LC 76-46471. (Discovery). (Illus.). (gr. k-3). 1977. PLB 13.31 (ISBN 0-8172-0252-8). Raintree Pubs.

--The Discovery Book of Up & Down. LC 76-46470. (Discovery). (Illus.). (gr. k-3). 1977. PLB 13.31 (ISBN 0-8172-0251-X). Raintree Pubs.

--Easy-to-Make Christmas Crafts. (Illus.). 48p. (gr. 1-5). 1986. PLB 9.49 (ISBN 0-8167-0674-3); pap. text ed. 1.95 (ISBN 0-8167-0675-1). Troll Assocs.

--Great Gifts to Make. (Illus.). 48p. (gr. 1-5). 1986. PLB 9.49 (ISBN 0-8167-0676-X); pap. text ed. 1.95 (ISBN 0-8167-0677-8). Troll Assocs.

--Great Indoor Games from Trash & Other Things. LC 77-7383. (Games & Activities). (Illus.). (gr. k-4). 1977. PLB 13.31 (ISBN 0-8172-0952-2). Raintree Pubs.

--Great Outdoor Games from Trash & Other Things. LC 77-7785. (Games & Activities). (Illus.). (gr. k-4). 1977. PLB 13.31 (ISBN 0-8172-0950-6). Raintree Pubs.

--Happy Haunting: Halloween Costumes You Can Make. (Illus.). 48p. (gr. 1-5). 1985. PLB 9.49 (ISBN 0-8167-0666-2); pap. text ed. 1.95 (ISBN 0-8167-0667-0). Troll Assocs.

--Happy Thanksgiving: Things to Make & Do. (Illus.). 48p. (gr. 1-5). 1986. PLB 9.49 (ISBN 0-8167-0668-9); pap. text ed. 1.95 (ISBN 0-8167-0669-7). Troll Assocs.

--Springtime Surprises: Things to Make & Do. (Illus.). 48p. (gr. 1-5). 1986. PLB 9.49 (ISBN 0-8167-0670-0); pap. text ed. 1.95 (ISBN 0-8167-0671-9). Troll Assocs.

--Unsolved Mysteries...with Sherlock Holmes & Dr. Watson. (gr. 7-9). 1976. 225.00 (ISBN 0-89290-113-6, CM-37). Soc for Visual.

Conaway, Judith, adapted by. King Kong. LC 82-15078. (Step-Up Adventures Ser.). (Illus.). 96p. (gr. 2-5). 1983. 2.50 (ISBN 0-394-85617-1); PLB 4.99 (ISBN 0-394-95617-6). Random.

--Twenty-Thousand Leagues under the Sea. (Step-Up Adventures Ser.: No. 6). (Illus.). 96p. (gr. 2-5). 1983. 2.95 (ISBN 0-394-85333-4); PLB 4.99 (ISBN 0-394-95333-9). Random.

Conaway, Mary E. Circular Migration: A Summary & Bibliography. 1977. 1.50 (ISBN 0-686-19108-0, 1250). CPL Biblios.

Conboy, William A., ed. The Challenge of the Future: Visions & Versions. LC 80-621213. 162p. (Orig.). 1979. pap. text ed. 6.95 (ISBN 0-936352-03-5, B277). U of KS Cont Ed.

Concannon, G. J. George Orwell. 1976. lib. bdg. 59.95 (ISBN 0-87700-253-3). Revisionist Pr.

Concannon, Joe, jt. auth. see Rodgers, Bill.

Con-Cannon, Tom. Using Media for Creative Teaching. 76p. 1979. pap. text ed. 5.95 (ISBN 0-932720-85-4). New Plays Bks.

Conceicao Fernandes, Julio Da. Diccionario Manual Espanol-Portugues, Portugues-Espanol. 3rd ed. 1974p. (Span. & Port.). 1978. 12.25 (ISBN 84-7183-001-9, S-50428). French & Eur.

--Diccionario Portugues-Espanol. 2nd ed. 916p. (Port. & Span.). 1978. 6.95 (ISBN 0-686-57351-X, S-31570). French & Eur.

Concepcion, Sara I., jt. auth. see Cordova, Gonzalo F.

Concept-Research & Reference Division, ed. Who's Who of Indian Geographers. 139p. 1982. text ed. 15.75x (ISBN 0-391-02808-1, Pub. by Concept India). Humanities.

Concepta, Sr. Maria. Making of a Sister-Teacher. 250p. 1965. 14.95x (ISBN 0-268-00381-5). U of Notre Dame Pr.

Concetta. In the Light of the Bible, Vols. 1 & 2. 1976. Vol. 1. 2.00 (ISBN 0-8198-0426-6); Vol. 2. pap. 2.00 (ISBN 0-8198-0427-4). Dghtrs St Paul.

Concha, Joseph. Chokecherry Hunters & Other Poems. 31p. 1976. pap. 2.25 (ISBN 0-913270-57-1). Sunstone Pr.

Concheff, Beatrice J. Bibliography of Old Catalan Texts. (Bibliographical Ser.: No. 5). 1985. write for info. (ISBN 0-942260-61-9). Hispanic Seminary.

Concone, J. Twenty Etudes Chantantes (The Singing Touch) for Piano, Op. 30: The Singing Touch for Piano, Op. 30. Gahm, Joseph, ed. (Carl Fischer Music Library: No. 514). 1918. pap. 4.75 (ISBN 0-8258-0131-1, L514). Fischer Inc NY.

Concord Reference Books Inc. The New American Desk Encyclopedia. 1984. pap. 6.95 (ISBN 0-451-12803-6, Sig). NAL.

Concordia, Charles. Synchronous Machines Theory & Performance. (General Electric Ser.). (Illus.). pap. 58.50 (ISBN 0-317-08837-8, 2011865). Bks Demand UMI.

Concordia Historical Institute. Heritage of Cooking. Kramer, Gerhardt, ed. 1981. pap. 5.00 (ISBN 0-318-02225-7). Concordia Hist.

Concordia Historical Institute Staff & Lutheran Historical Conference Staff. Lutheran Historical Conference: Essays & Reports. Suelflow, August R., ed. 7.50 (ISBN 0-318-04799-3). Concordia Hist.

Concrete Society, ed. see International Conference, Newcastle upon Tyne 1st, 1981.

Condax, Kate D. Riding: An Illustrated Guide. LC 82-16460. (Illus.). 208p. 1983. 14.95 (ISBN 0-668-05424-7, 5424). Arco.

Condax, Philip L. Selections from the Spira Collection: An Exhibition at George Eastman House Sept. 26, 1980 - Jan. 11, 1981. (Illus.). 24p. (Orig.). 1981. pap. 4.00 (ISBN 0-935398-04-X). Intl Mus Photo.

Conde, Alexander De see De Conde, Alexander.

Conde, D. F., jt. auth. see Harris, Norman C.

Conde, John A. The Cars That Hudson Built. LC 80-53376. (Illus.). 224p. 1980. 19.95 (ISBN 0-9605048-0-X). Arnold-Porter Pub.

--Cars with Personalities. LC 82-73487. (Illus.). 256p. 1982. 21.95 (ISBN 0-9605048-1-8). Arnold Porter Pub.

Conde, Jose A. History of the Dominion of the Arabs in Spain, 3 Vols. Foster, Mrs. Jonathan, tr. Repr. of 1855 ed. Set. 55.00 (ISBN 0-404-09270-5); 18.50 ea. Vol. 1 (ISBN 0-404-09271-3). Vol. 2 (ISBN 0-404-09272-1). Vol. 3 (ISBN 0-404-09273-X). AMS Pr.

Conde, Julian, jt. auth. see Zachariah, K. C.

Conde, Julien, et al. Mortality in Developing Countries. OECD Deveopment Centre, ed. (Development Centre Studies). (Orig.). 1980. Tome 1 & 2, 1266p. pap. 85.00 (ISBN 9-2640-2097-7, 41-80-05-3); Tome 3, 550p. pap. 30.00 (ISBN 9-2640-2120-5, 41-80-06-1). OECD.

Conde, Maryse. Heremakhonon. Philcox, Richard, tr. LC 81-51667. 188p. 1982. 17.00 (ISBN 0-89410-232-X); pap. 8.00 (ISBN 0-89410-233-8). Three Continents.

Conde Nast, ed. see Bride's Magazine Editors.

Conde, Nicholas. The Legend. 1984. pap. 3.95 (ISBN 0-451-13266-1, Sig). NAL.

Conde, Teresa del see Mexican Ministry Art Staff & Del Conde, Teresa.

Condee, Nancy. Explosion in the Puzzle Factory. (Poetry Ser.). 32p. (Orig.). 1983. pap. 3.00 (ISBN 0-930901-18-5). Burning Deck.

Condee, Ralph W. Milton's Theories Concerning Epic Poetry. LC 77-861. 1977. lib. bdg. 8.50 (ISBN 0-8414-3421-2). Folcroft.

--Structure in Milton's Poetry: From the Foundation to the Pinnacles. LC 73-12934. 240p. 1974. 23.50x (ISBN 0-271-01133-5). Pa St U Pr.

Conder, C. R. Judas Maccabaeus. 1982. 45.00x (ISBN 0-686-45726-9, Pub. by Palestine Explo England). State Mutual Bk.

Conder, Claude R. The Latin Kingdom of Jerusalem. LC 78-180331. Repr. of 1897 ed. 40.00 (ISBN 0-404-56238-8). AMS Pr.

--Mishmash & the Big Fat Problem. (Mishmash Ser.). (Illus.). 96p. (gr. 3-5). 1984. pap. 2.25 (ISBN 0-671-46290-3). Archway.

--Mishmash & The Robot. (Illus.). (gr. 3-5). 1982. pap. 1.75 (ISBN 0-671-44064-0). Archway.

--Mishmash & The Robot. (Illus.). (gr. 2-5). 1981. 7.95 (ISBN 0-395-30345-1). HM.

--Mishmash & The Sauerkraut Mystery. (Illus.). (gr. 3-5). 1979. pap. 1.75 (ISBN 0-671-43135-8). Archway.

--Mishmash & The Sauerkraut Mystery. (Illus.). (gr. 4-6). 1965. 8.95 (ISBN 0-395-06702-2); pap. 0.95 (ISBN 0-395-18556-4). HM.

--Mishmash & the Substitute Teacher. (Illus.). (gr. 3-5). 1979. pap. 1.95 (ISBN 0-671-45920-1). Archway.

--Mishmash & The Substitute Teacher. (Illus.). (gr. 2-5). 1963. 10.95 (ISBN 0-395-06709-X). HM.

--Mishmash & The Venus Flytrap. (Illus.). (gr. 3-5). 1979. pap. 1.75 (ISBN 0-671-45069-7). Archway.

--Mishmash & The Venus Flytrap. LC 75-44380. (Illus.). 128p. (gr. 2-5). 1976. 6.95 (ISBN 0-395-24376-9). HM.

--Mishmash & Uncle Looey. (Illus.). (gr. 3-5). 1979. pap. 1.75 (ISBN 0-671-43682-1). Archway.

--Number Four. LC 72-2758. (Illus.). 160p. (gr. 5-9). 1972. 6.95 (ISBN 0-395-13889-2). HM.

--Paul David Silverman Is a Father. LC 82-18205. (Illus.). 64p. (gr. 2 up). 1983. 8.95 (ISBN 0-525-44050-X, 0869-260). Dutton.

--Promise Is a Promise. (Illus.). (gr. 7-9). 1964. 8.95 (ISBN 0-395-06703-0). HM.

--Purim. LC 67-10071. (Holiday Ser.). (Illus.). (gr. k-3). 1967. PLB 10.89 (ISBN 0-690-65922-9). Crowell Jr Bks.

--Ringling Brothers. LC 70-132295. (Biography Ser). (Illus.). (gr. 2-5). 1971. 11.49 (ISBN 0-690-70287-6); PLB 11.89 (ISBN 0-690-70288-4). Crowell Jr Bks.

Cone, Nancy, ed. see Zepke, Brent E.

Cone, Paul. What You Need to Know about Computers. (Clear & Simple Ser.). (Orig.). 1984. pap. 3.95 (ISBN 0-440-59577-0, Dell Trade Pbks). Dell.

Cone, Polly & Harper, Prudence O., eds. Essays on Near Eastern Art & Archaeology in Honor of Charles K. Wilkinson. (Illus.). 96p. pap. 15.00 (ISBN 0-87099-324-0). Metro Mus Art.

Cone, Polly, ed. see Harper, Prudence O. & Meyers, Pieter.

Cone, Polly, ed. see Metropolitan Museum of Art Curators from European Paintings, European Sculpture & Decorative Arts & Medieval Art.

Cone, Polly, ed. see Schimmel, Annemarie, et al.

Cone, Poly, et al, eds. see Ettesvold, Paul M.

Cone, Richard A. & Dowling, John E., eds. Membrane Transduction Mechanisms. LC 78-65280. (Society of General Physiologists Ser.: Vol. 33). 248p. 1979. text ed. 42.00 (ISBN 0-89004-236-5). Raven.

Cone, Sydney M. & American Bar Association. Committee on Comparative Procedure & Practice. The Regulation of Foreign Lawyers. LC 84-72263. 110p. Date not set. price not set (ISBN 0-89707-155-7). Amer Bar Assn.

Cone, Thomas E., Jr. History of American Pediatrics. 1980. 24.50 (ISBN 0-316-15289-7). Little.

Cone, Thomas E., Jr., ed. see Children's Hospital, Boston, Department of Medicine Staff.

Cone, Thomas E., Jr., ed. see Children's Hospital Medical Center, Boston.

Cone, William F. Supervising Employees Effectively. (Illus.). 180p. 1974. 9.95 (ISBN 0-201-01154-9). Addison-Wesley.

Conell, E. B., jt. ed. see Beynon, L. R.

Conerly, Luke W., jt. auth. see Williams, E. Russ.

Cones, Vanessa C. & Malinowski, Gregory P. Small-Scale Hydroelectric Power Development: Potential Sources of Federal Financial Support for Low-Income Communities. (Illus.). 267p. 1980. pressboard binder cover 25.00 (ISBN 0-936130-00-8). Intl Sci Tech.

Conesa, Salvador H. & Argote, M. L. A Visual Aid to the Examination of Nerve Roots. (Illus.). 1976. text ed. 12.95 (ISBN 0-7216-0737-3, Pub. by Bailliere-Tindall). Saunders.

Coney, John C. Exploring the Known & Unknown Factors in the Rates of Alcoholism Among Black & White Females. LC 77-90385. 1978. pap. 12.00 perfect bdg. (ISBN 0-88247-509-6). R & E Pubs.

--The Precipitating Factors in the Use of Alcoholic Treatment Services: A Comparative Study of Black & White Alcoholics. LC 76-24721. 1977. soft bdg 11.95 (ISBN 0-88247-414-6). R & E Pubs.

Coney, Michael. Cat Karina. 304p. 1982. pap. 2.75 (ISBN 0-441-09254-3). Ace Bks.

--The Celestial Steam Locomotive. LC 83-8567. 1983. 13.95 (ISBN 0-395-34395-X). HM.

--Gods of the Greataway. (The Song of the Earth Ser.: Vol. II). 1984. 15.95 (ISBN 0-395-35337-8). HM.

Coney, Michael G. Neptune's Cauldron. 240p. (Orig.). 1981. pap. 2.25 (ISBN 0-505-51755-8, Pub. by Tower Bks). Dorchester Pub Co.

Confalonieri, Cardinal Carlo. Pius Eleventh: A Close up. Barwig, Regis N., tr. & pref. by. 1975. pap. 8.50 (ISBN 0-686-18877-2). Benziger Sis.

Confalonieri, Giulio. Prigionia Di un Artista: Il Romanzo Di Luigi Cherubini, 2 vols. LC 80-2267. Repr. of 1948 ed. 78.00 (ISBN 0-404-18820-6). AMS Pr.

Confederate Memorial Literary Society - Richmond - 1908. Calendar of Confederate Papers, Preliminary Report. Freeman, Douglas S., ed. LC 68-28850. 1968. 40.00 (ISBN 0-527-18900-6). Kraus Repr.

Confederate States of America. Laws & Joint Resolutions of the Last Session of the Confederate Congress. Repr. of 1941 ed. 16.50 (ISBN 0-404-05222-3). AMS Pr.

Confederate States Of America - Congress. Journal of the Congress of the Confederate States of America, 1861-1865, 7 Vols. Repr. of 1905 ed. Set. 512.00 (ISBN 0-527-18930-8). Kraus Repr.

Confederate States of America - Constitutional Convention. Constitution of the Confederate States of America with the Inaugural Address of President Jefferson Davis. Davis, Jefferson, ed. pap. 2.95 (ISBN 0-686-25517-8). British Am Bks.

Confederate States Of America - War Department. Southern History of the War. Repr. of 1863 ed. 47.00 (ISBN 0-527-18950-2). Kraus Repr.

Confederation Fiscale Europeenne, ed. see European Tax Consultants Congress, Strasbourg, October 1978.

Confederation of British Industry Marketed. West European Living Costs: Nineteen Seventy-Nine. 72p. 1979. 26.00x (ISBN 0-86010-169-X, Pub. by Graham & Trotman England). State Mutual Bk.

Confer, Grayce. Faith & Fried Potatoes. 184p. 1982. pap. 4.95 (ISBN 0-8341-0732-5). Beacon Hill.

Confer, Vincent. France & Algeria: The Problem of Civil & Political Reform, 1870-1920. LC 66-24455. 1966. 12.00x (ISBN 0-8156-2099-3). Syracuse U Pr.

Confer, William N. & Ables, Billie S. Multiple Personality: Etiology, Diagnosis & Treatment. LC 82-2969. 1983. 29.95 (ISBN 0-89885-081-9). Human Sci Pr.

Conference, Bethesda, Md, June, 1981 & Chan-Palay, Victoria. Cytochemical Methods in Neuroanatomy: Proceedings. LC 82-7826. (Neurology & Neurobiology Ser.: Vol. 1). 584p. 1982. 96.00 (ISBN 0-8451-2700-4). A R Liss.

Conference Board. Challenge to Leadership: Managing in a Changing World. LC 73-1861. (Orig.). 1973. pap. 5.95 (ISBN 0-02-906570-4). Free Pr.

--The Impact of the Anti-Inflation Program: A Framework for Analysis. (Canadian Technical Papers). 88p. 1979. 15.00 (ISBN 0-317-34004-2, CTP-4); members 5.00 (ISBN 0-317-34005-0). Conference Bd.

Conference Center, Madison, Wisconsin, May 14, 1971. Assistance to Libraries in Developing Nations: Papers on Comparative Studies - Proceedings. Williamson, William L., ed. 68p. 1971. pap. 3.00 (ISBN 0-936442-03-4). U Wis Lib Sch.

Conference: February 14-15, 1977, Brussels, Belgium. Laboratory Testing for Cancer. Schoenfeld, H., et al, eds. (Antibiotics & Chemotherapy: Vol. 22). (Illus.). 1977. 32.50 (ISBN 3-8055-2765-9). S Karger.

Conference for the Study of Problems Concerning Negro City Life. Social & Physical Condition of Negroes in Cities. (Atlanta Univ. Publ. Ser.: No. 2). (Orig.). Repr. of 1897 ed. 14.00 (ISBN 0-527-03109-7). Kraus Repr.

Conference Group on Correctional Organization. Theoretical Studies in Social Organization of the Prison. LC 60-7249. 1960. pap. 6.00 (ISBN 0-527-03303-0). Kraus Repr.

Conference Held at Jackson Laboratory, Bar Harbor, Maine, Sept. 1976. Genetic Effects on Aging: Proceedings. Harrison, David E. & Bergsma, Daniel, eds. LC 77-20249. (Birth Defects Original Article Ser.: Vol. 14, No. 1). 550p. 1978. 70.00x (ISBN 0-8451-1016-0). A R Liss.

Conference Held at Manheim, 21-25 July, 1975. Categorical Topology: Proceedings. Binz, E., ed. (Lecture Notes in Mathematics: Vol. 540). 1976. soft cover 33.00 (ISBN 0-387-07859-2). Springer-Verlag.

Conference Held at Oberwolfach, Nov. 17-23, 1974, et al. Optimization & Optimal Control: Proceedings. Bulirsch, R. & Oettli, W., eds. LC 75-23372. (Lecture Notes in Mathematics: Vol. 477). vii, 294p. 1975. pap. 18.00 (ISBN 0-387-07393-0). Springer-Verlag.

Conference Held at Silver Spring, Maryland, Mar. 1978. Membrane Mechanisms of Drugs of Abuse: Proceedings. Abood, Leo G. & Sharp, Charles W., eds. LC 78-19682. (Progress in Clinical & Biological Research: Vol. 27). 280p. 1979. 29.00 (ISBN 0-8451-0027-0). A R Liss.

Conference Hoechst, 5th, Kitzbuhel, 5-9 Oct. 1976. Pancreatic Beta Cell Culture: Proceedings. Von Wasielewski, E. & Chick, W. L., eds. (International Congress Ser.: No. 408). 1977. 48.50 (ISBN 0-444-15262-8, Excerpta Medica). Elsevier.

Conference in Honor of Anna Goldfeder, Feb 17-19, 1982. Cell Proliferation, Cancer, & Cancer Therapy, Vol. 397. Baserga, Renato, ed. 328p. 1982. 65.00x (ISBN 0-89766-184-2); pap. 65.00x (ISBN 0-89766-185-0). NY Acad Sci.

Conference in Mathematical Logic, London, 1970. Proceedings. Hodges, W., ed. (Lecture Notes in Mathematics: Vol. 255). 351p. 1972. pap. 13.00 (ISBN 0-387-05744-7). Springer-Verlag.

Conference in Orders, Group Rings & Related Topics. Proceedings. Hsia, J. S., et al, eds. (Lecture Notes in Mathematics: Vol. 353). 224p. 1973. pap. 16.00 (ISBN 0-387-06518-0). Springer-Verlag.

Conference in Topological Dynamics, Yale University, June 19-23, 1972. Recent Advances in Topological Dynamics: Proceedings. Beck, A., ed. LC 73-76674. viii, 285p. 1973. pap. 16.00 (ISBN 0-387-06187-8). Springer-Verlag.

Conference Internationale d'Histoire Economique, 3rd, Munich, 1965. Proceedings, 5 vols. (Congres et Colioques Ser.: No. 10). (Illus.). 504p. (Fr.). 1974. text ed. 123.00x set (ISBN 0-686-22580-5). Mouton.

Conference, Murat-le-Quaire, March 1976. Convex Analysis & Its Applications: Proceedings. Auslender, A., ed. (Lecture Notes in Economics & Mathematical Systems: Vol. 144). 1977. soft cover 18.00 (ISBN 0-387-08149-6). Springer-Verlag.

Conference, Oberwolfach, Germany, July 4-10, 1976. Numerical Treatment of Differential Equations: Proceedings. Bulirsch, R., et al, eds. (Lecture Notes in Mathematics Ser.: Vol. 631). (Eng. & Ger.). 1978. pap. 18.00 (ISBN 0-387-08539-4). Springer-Verlag.

Conference, Oct. 18-21, 1970 & Gallardo, Jose M. Education of Puerto Rican Children on the Mainland: Proceedings. LC 74-14235. (The Puerto Rican Experience Ser). (Illus.). 200p. 1975. Repr. 13.00x (ISBN 0-405-06224-9). Ayer Co Pubs.

Conference of ASME, 1976. Present Status & Research Needs in Energy Recovery from Wastes: Proceedings. Matula, Richard A., ed. 1977. pap. text ed. 35.00 (ISBN 0-685-81974-4, H00091). ASME.

Conference of Economic Staff, jt. auth. see Keyserling, Leon H.

Conference of European Statisticians. Correspondence Table Between the Standard International Trade Classification of the United Nations (SITC) & the Standard Foreign Trade Classification of the Council for Mutual Economic Assistance (SFTC). 22.00 (ISBN 0-686-43224-X, E/R.82.II.E.10). UN.

--Standardized Input-Output Tables of ECE Countries for Years around 1970. 198p. 1983. pap. text ed. 16.50 (ISBN 0-317-00302-X, UN82/2E23, UN). Unipub.

Conference of Gifted Children 1958, University of Minnesota. Talent & Education: Present Status & Future Directions. Torrance, Ellis P., ed. LC 60-15896. (The Modern School Practice Ser.: No. 4). pap. 55.00 (ISBN 0-317-28174-7, 2055966). Bks Demand UMI.

Conference of Scientology Ministers. The American Inquisition: U. S. Government Agency Harassment, Religious Persecution & Abuse of Power. 1977. pap. 7.00 (ISBN 0-915598-16-7). Church of Scient Info.

Conference of State Bank Supervisors. A Profile of State-Chartered Banking. 10th, rev. ed. (Illus.). 283p. 1984. 50.00 (ISBN 0-916361-01-2). Conf St Bank.

Conference of the Academy of Marketing Science. Developments in Marketing Science: Proceedings of the Sixth Annual Conference of the Academy of Marketing Science, 1982, Vol. 5. Kothari, Vinay, ed. pap. 160.00 (ISBN 0-317-26533-4, 2023984). Bks Demand UMI.

--Developments in Marketing Science: Proceedings of the Seventh Annual Conference of the Academy of Marketing Science, 1983, Vol. 6. Rogers, John C., III, ed. pap. 160.00 (ISBN 0-317-26534-2, 2023985). Bks Demand UMI.

Conference of the American Council of Learned Societies & Corning Glass Works,May 17-19,1951, Corning, New York. Creating an Industrial Civilization: Proceedings. Stein, Leon & Staley, Eugene, eds. LC 77-70536. (Work Ser.). 1977. Repr. of 1952 ed. lib. bdg. 32.00x (ISBN 0-405-10204-6). Ayer Co Pubs.

Conference of the British Educational Research Association 1980. Microcomputers in Secondary Education: Proceedings. Howe, Jim & Ross, Peter, eds. 162p. 1981. pap. 23.50 (ISBN 0-89397-108-1). Nichols Pub.

Conference of the Cryogenic Society of America, 5th, 1972. Application of Cryogenic Technology: Proceedings, Vol. 5. Carr, Robert H., ed. LC 68-57815. 352p. 1973. text ed. 30.00x (ISBN 0-87936-001-1). Scholium Intl.

Conference of the Cryogenic Society of America, 1973. Applications of Cryogenic Technology: Proceedings, Vol. 6. Vance, Robert H. & Booth, Sterling H., eds. LC 68-57815. (Illus.). 290p. 1974. text ed. 30.00x (ISBN 0-87936-003-8). Scholium Intl.

Conference of the European Cooperation in Informatics, 1976. Proceedings. Samelson, K., et al, eds. (Lecture Notes in Computer Science: Vol. 44). 1976. soft cover 20.00 (ISBN 0-387-07804-5). Springer-Verlag.

Conference of the European Society for Microcirculation, 9th, Antwerp, July 5-9, 1976. Recent Advances in Basic Microcirculatory Research: Proceedings, Pt. 1. Wolf-Heidegger, G. & Lewis, D. H., eds. (Bibliotheca Anatomica: No. 15). (Illus.). 1977. 84.25 (ISBN 3-8055-2757-8). S Karger.

--Recent Advances in Basic Microcirculatory Research: Proceedings, Pt. 2. Wolf-Heidegger, G. & Lewis, D. H., eds. (Bibliotheca Anatomica: No. 16). (Illus.). 1977. 84.25 (ISBN 3-8055-2758-6). S Karger.

Conference of the Institute of Industrial Relations. The Development of Prepaid Legal Services: Proceedings. 1972. 4.50 (ISBN 0-89215-039-4). U Cal LA Indus Rel.

--Dispute Settlement Procedures in Five Western European Countries: Proceedings. Aaron, Benjamin, ed. 1969. 3.00 (ISBN 0-89215-036-X). U Cal LA Indus Rel.

--Welfare: a National Policy: Proceedings. 64p. 1973. 3.00 (ISBN 0-89215-041-6). U Cal LA Indus Rel.

Conference of the International Society of Geographical Pathology, 12th, Zurich, Sept. 1975, et al. Inflammatory Vascular Diseases-Endo-Myocardial Fibrosis-Pulmonary Hypertension: Proceedings. Ruettner, J. R., ed. (Pathologia et Microbiologia: Vol. 43, No. 1-2). (Illus.). 180p. 1976. 33.25 (ISBN 3-8055-2311-4). S Karger.

Conference of the International Society for Psychoneuroendocrinology, Mieken, Sept., 1973. Psychoneuroendocrinology: Proceedings. Hatotani, N., ed. (Illus.). 450p. 1974. 57.25 (ISBN 3-8055-1711-4). S Karger.

Conference of the Summer School, Banff Centre, Banff, Alberta, Canada, August 14-26, 1972. Relativity, Astrophysics & Cosmology: Proceedings. Israel, Werner, ed. LC 72-97957. (Astrophysics & Space Science Library: Vol. 38). 340p. 1973. lib. bdg. 52.65 (ISBN 90-277-0369-8, Pub. by Reidel Holland). Kluwer Academic.

Conference of the Universities. Aspects of Labor Economics: Proceedings. LC 75-19698. (National Bureau of Economic Research Ser.). (Illus.). 1975. Repr. 27.50x (ISBN 0-405-07578-2). Ayer Co Pubs.

--Business Concentration & Price Policy: Proceedings. LC 75-19699. (National Bureau of Economic Research Ser.). 1975. Repr. 38.50x (ISBN 0-405-07579-0). Ayer Co Pubs.

--Capital Formation & Economic Growth: Proceedings. LC 75-19700. (National Bureau of Economic Research Ser.). (Illus.). 1975. Repr. 49.50x (ISBN 0-405-07580-4). Ayer Co Pubs.

--Policies to Combat Depression: Proceedings. LC 75-19701. (National Bureau of Economic Research Ser.). (Illus.). 1975. Repr. 32.00x (ISBN 0-405-07581-2). Ayer Co Pubs.

--The Rate & Direction of Inventive Activity: Economic & Social Factors: Proceedings. LC 75-19703. (National Bureau of Economic Research Ser.). (Illus.). 1975. Repr. 46.50x (ISBN 0-405-07583-9). Ayer Co Pubs.

--The State of Monetary Economics: Proceedings. LC 75-19702. (National Bureau of Economic Research Ser.). (Illus.). 1975. Repr. of 1963 ed. 17.00x (ISBN 0-405-07582-0). Ayer Co Pubs.

Conference of U.S. Schools of Pharmacy, Oct. 1975. Guidelines for Pharm.D Programs. 5.00 (ISBN 0-937526-05-3). Am Assn Coll Pharm.

Conference on a Century of Russian Foreign Policy, Yale University, 1961. Russian Foreign Policy: Essays in Historical Perspective. Lederer, Ivo J., ed. LC 62-8251. pap. 160.00 (ISBN 0-317-09483-1, 2003061). Bks Demand UMI.

Conference on African Linguistics, Seventh. Language & Linguistic Problems in Africa: Proceedings. Kotey, Paul F. & Der-Houssikian, Haig, eds. 1977p. pap. text ed. 8.75 (ISBN 0-917496-08-6). Hornbeam Pr.

Conference on Aging, 2nd, University of Michigan. Planning the Older Years. Donohue, Wilma & Tibbitts, Clark, eds. Repr. of 1950 ed. lib. bdg. 20.50x (ISBN 0-8371-0386-X, MIUA). Greenwood.

Conference on Aging, 5th, University of Michigan, 1952. Housing the Aging. LC 76-26114. (Conference on Aging). 1976. Repr. of 1954 ed. lib. bdg. 20.50x (ISBN 0-8371-9043-6, DORO). Greenwood.

Conference on Ambulatory Monitoring, 3rd, 1977. The Scope of Ambulatory Monitoring in Ischemic Heart Disease: Proceedings. Jacobsen, Nancy K., et al, eds. 1978. 18.50 (ISBN 0-917054-15-6). Med Communications.

Conference on Analytical Theory of Differential Equations, Kalamazoo, Mich, 1970. Analytic Theory of Differential Equations: Proceedings. Hsieh, P. F. & Stoddart, A. W., eds. LC 77-153467. (Lecture Notes in Mathematics: Vol. 183). (Illus.). 1971. 13.00 (ISBN 0-387-05369-7). Springer-Verlag.

Conference on Antenatal Diagnosis. Antenatal Diagnosis. LC 78-177973. (NICHO-Mental Retardation Research Centers Ser.). pap. 74.50 (ISBN 0-317-28223-9, 2019961). Bks Demand UMI.

Conference on Antenatal Diagnosis (1970: University of Chicago) Antenatal Diagnosis. Dorfman, Albert, ed. LC 78-177973. pap. 74.50 (ISBN 0-317-26152-5, 2024112). Bks Demand UMI.

Conference on Applications of Numerical Analysis, Dundee, Scotland, 1971. Proceedings. Morris, J. L., ed. (Lecture Notes in Mathematics: Vol. 228). 358p. 1971. pap. 18.00 (ISBN 0-387-05656-4). Springer-Verlag.

Conference on Applications of X-Ray Analysis. Advances in X-Ray Analysis, Vol. 3: Proceedings of the Eighth Annual Conference on Applications of X-Ray Analysis Held August 12-14, 1959. Mueller, William M., ed. LC 58-35928. (Illus.). pap. 96.00 (ISBN 0-317-08356-2, 2019407). Bks Demand UMI.

Conference on Bioavailability of Drugs, Washington, D.C., Nov. 1971. Bioavailability of Drugs: Proceedings. Brodie, B. B. & Heller, W. M., eds. (Pharmacology: Vol. 8, Nos. 1-3). (Illus.). 1972. 27.75 (ISBN 3-8055-1456-5). S Karger.

Conference on Blood Viscosity in Heart Disease, Thromboembo-Lism & Cancer, Sydney Australia, May, 1978. Health Needs & Health Services in Rural Ghana. De Kadt, E., et al, eds. 140p. 1981. pap. 16.25 (ISBN 0-08-028136-2). Pergamon.

Conference on Book Publishing in Wisconsin, May 6, 1977, et al. Book Publishing in Wisconsin: Proceedings. Clarke, Jack A. & Aslakson, Sarah Z., eds. 101p. 1977. pap. 4.00 (ISBN 0-936442-06-9). U Wis Lib Sch.

Conference on Canberra, 1973. The Myocardium: Proceedings. Reader, Ralph, ed. (Advances in Cardiology: Vol. 12). 300p. 1974. 57.50 (ISBN 3-8055-1690-8). S Karger.

Conference on Cardiovascular Disease, 2nd, Snowmass-at-Aspen, Colorado, 1971. Long-Term Prognosis Following Valve Replacement: Proceedings. Vogel, J. H., ed. (Advances in Cardiology: Vol. 7). 1972. 42.25 (ISBN 3-8055-1299-6). S Karger.

Conference on Carpatho-Ruthenian Immigration, 8 June 1974. Proceedings. Renoff, Richard & Reynolds, Stephen, eds. LC 75-24033. (Sources & Documents Ser.). (Orig.). 1975. pap. 5.00x (ISBN 0-916458-00-8). Harvard Ukrainian.

Conference on Changing Career Opportunities, Pennsylvania State Univ., Aug. 1977. Physics Careers, Employment & Education. Perl, Martin L., ed. LC 77-9403. (AIP Conference Proceedings: No. 39). (Illus.). 1978. lib. bdg. 18.50 (ISBN 0-88318-138-X). Am Inst Physics.

Conference on Communication, Language & Sex, 1st Annual. Communication, Language, & Sex: Proceedings. Berryman-Fink, Cynthia & Eman-Wheeless, Virginia, eds. 1980. pap. text ed. 15.95 (ISBN 0-88377-136-5). Newbury Hse.

Conference on Commutative Algebra. Proceedings. Brewer, J. W. & Rutter, E. A., eds. LC 72-96859. (Lecture Notes in Mathematics: Vol. 311). 251p. 1973. pap. 14.00 (ISBN 0-387-06140-1). Springer-Verlag.

Conference on Compact Transformation Groups, 2nd. Proceedings, Pt. 1. LC 72-95314. (Lecture Notes in Mathematics: Vol. 298). xii, 453p. 1972. pap. 19.00 (ISBN 0-387-06077-4). Springer-Verlag.

--Proceedings, Pt. 2. LC 72-95314. (Lecture Notes in Mathematics: Vol. 299). xi, 327p. 1972. pap. 16.00 (ISBN 0-387-06078-2). Springer-Verlag.

Conference on Computer Simulation Staff. UKSC '84: Proceedings. Murray-Smith, D. J., ed. (Illus.). 560p. 1984. text ed. 89.00 (ISBN 0-408-01504-7). Butterworth.

Conference on Consumerism. Consumerism: New Challenges for Marketing. LC 77-7370. (American Marketing Association, Proceedings Ser.). pap. 55.00 (ISBN 0-317-20077-1, 2023359). Bks Demand UMI.

Conference on Contemporary Issues in Thematic Apperceptive Methods. Contemporary Issues in Thematic Apperceptive Methods. Kagan, Jerome & Lesser, Gerald S., eds. LC 76-7536. 1976. Repr. of 1961 ed. lib. bdg. 24.75x (ISBN 0-8371-8842-3, KACI). Greenwood.

Conference on Creativity & the Gifted-Talented & Bruch, Catherine B. The Faces & Forms of Creativity. 212p. 14.95 (ISBN 0-318-16002-1, 28). NSLTIGT.

Conference on Design Criteria & Equipment for Transmission at 400 KV & High Voltages(1965: London) Conference on Design Criteria & Equipment for Transmission at 400 KV & High Voltages: Contributions, Pt. 1. LC 66-1977. (Institution of Electrical Engineers Conference Publications: No. 15). pap. 58.50 (ISBN 0-317-10161-7, 2007389). Bks Demand UMI.

Conference on Disposal of Solid Waste Materials (1977, University of Michigan) Geotechnical Practice for Disposal of Solid Waste Material: Proceedings of the Conference on June 13-15, 1977, University of Michigan, Ann Arbor, Michigan. LC 77-152066. (Illus.). pap. 160.00 (ISBN 0-317-10625-2, 2019547). Bks Demand UMI.

Conference on Economic Development, jt. auth. see Nelson, Eastin.

Conference on Economic Progress Staff, jt. auth. see Keyserling, Leon H.

Conference on Economic Progress Staff & Conference on Economic Progress Staff. The Coming Crisis in Housing. (Illus.). 1972. 1.00 (ISBN 0-685-41557-0). Conf Econ Prog.

Conference On Educational Problems Of Special Cultural Groups - Teachers College - Columbia University - 1949. Cultural Groups & Human Relations. facs. ed. Allport, G. W., et al, eds. LC 77-117772. (Essay Index Reprint Ser). 1951. 18.00 (ISBN 0-8369-1792-8). Ayer Co Pubs.

Conference on Electrical Insulation & Dielectric Phenomena. Annual Report. Incl. 1952. 61p; 1957. 69p; 1958. 57p; 1963. 144p. 5.00 (ISBN 0-309-01141-8); 1964. 146p. 5.00 (ISBN 0-309-01238-4); 1965. 139p. 5.00 (ISBN 0-686-64609-6); 1966. 129p. 10.00 (ISBN 0-309-01484-0); 1967. 201p. 10.00 (ISBN 0-309-01578-2); 1968. 204p. 10.00 (ISBN 0-309-01705-X); 1969. 193p. 15.00 (ISBN 0-309-01764-5); 1970. 258p. 15.00 (ISBN 0-309-01870-6); 1971. 289p. 15.00 (ISBN 0-309-02032-8); 1972. 496p. 20.00 (ISBN 0-309-02112-X); 1973. 638p. 25.00 (ISBN 0-309-02229-0); 1974. 706p. 25.00 (ISBN 0-309-02416-1); 1975. 544p. 22.00 (ISBN 0-686-64610-X); 1976. 576p. 25.00 (ISBN 0-686-64611-8); 1977. 596p. 25.00 (ISBN 0-309-02866-3); 1978. 405p. 25.00 (ISBN 0-309-02861-2); 1979. 25.00 (ISBN 0-309-02933-3). Natl Acad Pr.

--Digest of Literature on Dielectrics, Vols. 11-13, 18-42. Incl. Vol. 11. 1947; Vol. 12. 1948; Vol. 13. 1949; Vol. 18. 1954; Vol. 19. 1955; Vol. 20. 1956; Vol. 21. 1957; Vol. 22. 1958; Vol. 24. 1960; Vol. 25. 1961. 15.00 (ISBN 0-309-01034-9); Vol. 26. 1962; Vol. 27. 1963. 15.00 (ISBN 0-309-01230-9); Vol. 28. 1964. 27.00 (ISBN 0-309-01342-9); Vol. 29. 1965. 27.00 (ISBN 0-309-01461-1); Vol. 30. 1966. 27.00 (ISBN 0-309-01496-4); Vol. 31. 1967. 27.00 (ISBN 0-309-01595-2); Vol. 32. 1968. 35.00 (ISBN 0-309-01732-7); Vol. 33. 1969. 35.00 (ISBN 0-309-01856-0); Vol. 34. 1970. 35.00 (ISBN 0-309-01920-6); Vol. 35. 1971. 40.00 (ISBN 0-309-02049-2); Vol. 36. 1972. 40.00 (ISBN 0-309-02316-5); Vol. 37. 1973. 40.00 (ISBN 0-309-02437-4); Vol. 38, 1977. 40.00 (ISBN 0-309-02643-1); Vol. 39, 1975. 45.00 (ISBN 0-309-02748-9); Vol. 40, 1976. 45.00 (ISBN 0-309-02787-X); Vol. 41, 1979. 45.00 (ISBN 0-309-02886-8); Vol. 42, 1979. 45.00 (ISBN 0-309-02934-1). Natl Acad Pr.

Conference on Electronic Structures in Solids (2nd, 1968: Chania, Crete) Electronic Structures in Solids. Haidemenakis, E. D., ed. LC 71-82759. pap. 118.80 (ISBN 0-317-08215-9, 2019394). Bks Demand UMI.

Conference on Experimental Medicine & Surgery in Primates, 2nd, New York, 1969. Medical Primatology, 1970: Proceedings. Goldsmith, E. I. & Moor-Jankowski, J., eds. 1971. 119.25 (ISBN 3-8055-1227-9). S Karger.

Conference on Experimental Medicine & Surgery in Primates, 3rd, Lyon, June 1972. Medical Primatology 1972: Selected Papers, Proceedings, 3 pts. Goldsmith, E. I. & Moor-Jankowski, J., eds. Incl. Pt. 1. General Primatology, Reproduction, & Perinatal Studies, Genetics, Phylogenetics, & Evolution. 450p. 59.75 (ISBN 3-8055-1486-7); Pt. 2. Surgery, Transplantation, Oral Medicine, Neurophysiology & Psychology. 350p. 51.25 (ISBN 3-8055-1487-5); Pt. 3. Infectious Diseases, Oncology, Pharmacology & Toxicology, Cardiovascular Studies. 400p. 59.75 (ISBN 3-8055-1488-3). 1972. Set. 149.00 (ISBN 3-8055-1489-1). S Karger.

Conference on Federal Taxation & Land Use. Proceedings. (Lincoln Institute Monograph: 78-7). (Orig.). 1978. pap. text ed. 5.00 (ISBN 0-686-25526-7). Lincoln Inst Land.

Conference on Fetal Homeostasis, 1964. Fetal Homeostasis: Proceedings, Vol. 2. Wynn, Ralph M., ed. pap. 93.00 (ISBN 0-317-26278-5, 2055700). Bks Demand UMI.

Conference on Finite Elements Applied to Thin Shells & Curved Members (1974: University College, Cardiff, Wales) Finite Elements for Thin Shells & Curved Members. Ashwell, D. G. & Gallagher, R. H., eds. LC 75-37654. (Illus.). pap. 70.00 (ISBN 0-317-08377-5, 2016448). Bks Demand UMI.

Conference on Frequency Generation & Control for Radio Systems(1967: London) Conference on Frequency Generation & Control for Radio Systems. LC 67-112020. (Institution of Electrical Engineers Conference Publications: No. 31). pap. 49.80 (ISBN 0-317-10119-6, 2007383). Bks Demand UMI.

Conference on Functional Analysis & Related Fields, University of Chicago, 1968. Proceedings. Browder, Felix E., ed. LC 74-79552. (Illus.). 1970. 43.00 (ISBN 0-387-05104-X). Springer-Verlag.

Conference on Graph Theory - Western Michigan University - Kalamazoo - 1972. Graph Theory & Applications: Proceedings. Alavi, Y., et al, eds. LC 72-95978. (Lecture Notes in Mathematics: Vol. 303). 329p. 1973. pap. 16.00 (ISBN 0-387-06096-0). Springer-Verlag.

Conference On Graph Theory - Western Michigan University - Kalamazoo - 1968. Many Facets of Graph Theory: Proceedings. Chartrand, G. & Kapoor, S. F., eds. LC 70-101693. (Lecture Notes in Mathematics: Vol. 110). (Illus.). 1970. pap. 14.70 (ISBN 0-387-04629-1). Springer-Verlag.

Conference on Group Theory, University of Wisconsin-Parkside, 1972. Proceedings. Gatterdam, R. W. & Weston, K. W., eds. LC 73-76679. (Lecture Notes in Mathematics: Vol. 319). v, 188p. 1973. pap. 13.00 (ISBN 0-387-06205-X). Springer-Verlag.

Conference on Harmonic Analysis, College Park, Md., 1971. Proceedings. Gulick, D. & Lipsman, R. L., eds. LC 72-80302. (Lecture Notes in Mathematics: Vol. 266). 329p. 1972. pap. 13.00 (ISBN 0-387-05856-7). Springer-Verlag.

Conference on Hokan Languages, San Diego, California, April, 1970. Hokan Studies: Proceedings. Langdon, Margaret & Silver, Shirley, eds. (Janua Linguarum Ser. Practica: No. 181). 1976. pap. text ed. 51.20x (ISBN 90-2793-124-0). Mouton.

Conference on Hyperfunctions & Pseudo-Differential Equations, Katata 1971. Proceedings. Komatsu, H., ed. LC 72-88782. (Lecture Notes in Mathematics: Vol. 287). vii, 529p. 1973. pap. 23.00 (ISBN 0-387-06218-1). Springer-Verlag.

Conference on Income Support Policies for the Aging-University of Chicago. Income Support Policies for the Aged. Tolley, George S. & Burkhauser, Richard V., eds. LC 77-4155. 1977. prof ref 19.50 (ISBN 0-88410-359-5). Ballinger Pub.

Conference on Intellectual Freedom. Freedom of Inquiry: Supporting the Library Bill of Rights. LC 65-24954. pap. 20.00 (ISBN 0-317-26826-0, 2024198). Bks Demand UMI.

Conference on Interference Problems Associated with the Operation of Microwave Communication Systems(1968: London) Conference on Interference Problems Associated with the Operation of Microwave Communication Systems, 23rd-24th April, 1968. LC 71-586382. (Institution of Electrical Engineers Conference Publications: No. 39). pap. 52.00 (ISBN 0-317-10149-8, 2007388). Bks Demand UMI.

Conference on International Negotiation, et al. International Negotiation, Art & Science: Report of a Conference on International Negotiation, June 9-10, 1983. LC 84-601062. Date not set. price not set. Gov Printing Office.

Conference on Invertebrate Nervous Systems-California Institute of Technology, ed. see Wiersma, Cornelius G.

Conference on Issues in Educational Measurement, 2nd, Carmel, Cal., 1974. Aptitude - Achievement Distinction: Proceedings. Green, Donald R., ed. LC 73-20415. 1973. 9.95 (ISBN 0-07-024272-0, 99815). CTB McGraw-Hill.

Conference On Jewish Social Studies. Negro-Jewish Relations in the United States. 1966. pap. 1.50 (ISBN 0-8065-0092-1, 218). Citadel Pr.

Conference on Junior College Libraries. Junior College Libraries: Development, Needs, & Perspectives. LC 68-56370. (ACRL Monograph: No. 30). pap. 29.00 (ISBN 0-317-29357-5, 2024206). Bks Demand UMI.

Conference on K-Theory & Operator Algebras, University of Georgia, Athens, Ga., Apr. 21-25, 1975. K-Theory & Operator Algebras: Proceedings. Morrel, B. B. & Singer, I. M., eds. (Lecture Notes in Mathematics: Vol. 575). 1977. soft cover 13.00 (ISBN 0-387-08133-X). Springer-Verlag.

Conference on Latin-American Fine Arts, Texas University, College of Fine Arts. Proceedings. Repr. of 1952 ed. lib. bdg. 15.00x (ISBN 0-8371-7442-2, TLFA). Greenwood.

Conference on Library Manpower. Library Manpower: Needs & Utilization. Asheim, Lester, ed. LC 72-3089. pap. 20.00 (ISBN 0-317-29368-0, 2024209). Bks Demand UMI.

Conference on Life Insurance Company Products & American Law Institute-American Bar Association Committee on Continuing Professional Education. Conference on Life Insurance Company Products: Current Securities & Tax Issues: ALI-ABA Course of Study Materials. LC 84-103561. (Illus.). write for info. Am Law Inst.

Conference on Magnetism & Magnetic Materials 20th, Dec 3-6, 1974 San Francisco. Magnetism & Magnetic Materials: Proceedings, 1974. Graham, C. D., Jr., et al, eds. LC 75-2647. (AIP Conference Proceedings: No. 24). 792p. 1975. 30.00 (ISBN 0-88318-123-1). Am Inst Physics.

Conference on Magnetism & Magnetic Materials. Magnetism & Magnetic Materials: Proceedings of the Seventh Conference. Osborn, J. A., ed. LC 72-623469. pap. 95.80 (ISBN 0-317-08214-0, 2019389). Bks Demand UMI.

Conference on Marketing Management (6th: 1962: University of Michigan) Changing Perspectives in Marketing Management: Sixth Annual Conference on Marketing Management, March 30, 1962. Warshaw, Martin R., ed. (Michigan Business Papers Ser.: No. 37). pap. 28.00 (ISBN 0-317-28859-8, 2022082). Bks Demand UMI.

Conference on Marmosets in Experimental Medicine, Oak Ridge Tenn., March 16-18, 1977. Marmosets in Experimental Medicine: Proceedings. Moor-Jankowski, J., et al, eds. (Primates in Medicine: Vol. 10). (Illus.). 1977. 65.25 (ISBN 3-8055-2750-0). S Karger.

Conference on Martingales, Oberwolfach Germany, 1970. Proceedings. Dinges, H., ed. (Lecture Notes in Mathematics: Vol. 190). 1971. pap. 11.00 (ISBN 0-387-05396-4). Springer-Verlag.

Conference on Microcirculation, 6th, Aalborg, 1970. Proceedings. Ditzel, J. & Lewis, D. H., eds. (Illus.). 1971. 100.00 (ISBN 3-8055-1234-1). S Karger.

Conference on Microcirculation, 6th European, Aalborg, 1970. Microcirculatory Approaches to Current Therapeutic Problems: Lung in Shock, Organ Transplantation, Diabetic Microangiopathy. Proceedings. Ditzel, J. & Lewis, D. H., eds. (Illus.). 1971. 22.25 (ISBN 3-8055-1186-8). S Karger.

Conference on Molecular Spectroscopy. Molecular Spectroscopy: Proceedings of the 6th Conference on Molecular Spectroscopy, Organized by the Institute of Petroleum, Hydrocarbon Research Group, & Held at the University of Durham, 30 March-2 April, 1976. West, A. R., ed. LC 78-320788. pap. 149.50 (ISBN 0-317-29410-5, 2024013). Bks Demand UMI.

Conference on Mononuclear Phagocytes, Third, Noorwijk aan Zee, The Netherlands, Sept. 17-24, 1978. Functional Aspects of Mononuclear Phagocytes: Proceedings, 2 vols. Ralph, ed. 1980. Set. lib. bdg. 189.50 (ISBN 90-247-2211-X, Pub. by Martinus Nijhoff Netherlands). Kluwer Academic.

Conference on Natural Gas Research & Technology (2nd: 1972: Atlanta) Staff. Proceedings of the Second Conference on Natural Gas Research & Technology Sponsored by American Gas Association & Institute of Gas Technology, Atlanta, Georgia, June 5-7, 1972. White, Jack W. & Kragulski, Maryann, eds. pap. 160.00 (ISBN 0-317-26319-6, 2024236). Bks Demand UMI.

Conference on Numerical Solution of Ordinary Differential Equations. Proceedings. Bettis, D. G., ed. LC 73-20914. (Lecture Notes in Mathematics Ser.: Vol. 362). viii, 490p. 1974. pap. 22.00 (ISBN 0-387-06602-0). Springer-Verlag.

Conference on Operator Theory, Dalhousie Univ., Halifax, 1973. Proceedings. Fillmore, P. A., ed. LC 73-14482. (Lecture Notes in Mathematics: Vol. 345). pap. 16.00 (ISBN 0-387-06496-6). Springer-Verlag.

Conference on Optimisation Techniques in Circuit & Control Applications(1970: London) Conference on Optimisation Techniques in Circuit & Control Applications, 29-30 June 1970. LC 71-595801. (Institution of Electrical Engineers Conference Publications: No. 66). pap. 20.50 (ISBN 0-317-10170-6, 2050329). Bks Demand UMI.

Conference on Optimization Techniques, 5th. Proceedings, Pt. 2. Ruberti, A., ed. (Lecture Notes in Computer Science: Vol. 4). (Illus.). 389p. 1973. pap. 21.00 (ISBN 0-387-06600-4). Springer-Verlag.

Conference on Oriental Classics in General Education (1958: Columbia University) Staff. Approaches to the Oriental Classics: Asian Literature & Thought in General Education. De Bary, W. Theodore, ed. LC 59-9905. pap. 68.80 (ISBN 0-317-29070-3, 2023746). Bks Demand UMI.

Conference on Origins of Life, 3rd, California, 1970. Planetary Astronomy: Proceedings. Margulis, L., ed. LC 72-91514. (Illus.). 268p. 1973. 30.00 (ISBN 0-387-06065-0). Springer-Verlag.

Conference on Particle Induced X-Ray Emissions & Its Applications, Lund, August 23-26, 1976 & Johansson, S. E. Particle Induced X-Ray Emission & Its Analytical Applications: Proceedings. (Nuclear Instruments & Methods Ser.: Vol. 142 Pts. 1-2). Date not set. price not set (ISBN 0-7204-0715-X, North-Holland). Elsevier.

Conference on Periodical Publishing in Wisconsin, May 11-12, 1978, et al. Periodical Publishing in Wisconsin: Proceedings. Arnold, Barbara J. & Clarke, Jack A., eds. 233p. 1980. pap. 6.50 (ISBN 0-936442-08-5). U Wis Lib Sch.

Conference on Physics of the Magnetosphere, Boston College, 1967. Physics of the Magnetosphere: Proceedings. Carovillano, R. L. & McClay, J. F., eds. (Astrophysics & Space Science Library: No.10). 686p. 1968. lib. bdg. 68.50 (ISBN 90-277-0111-3, Pub. by Reidel Holland). Kluwer Academic.

Conference on Poverty in America. Poverty in America. Gordon, M. S., ed. (New Reprints in Essays & General Literature Index Ser.). 1975. Repr. of 1965 ed. 31.00 (ISBN 0-518-10197-5, 10197). Ayer Co Pubs.

Conference on Power Applications of Controllable Semi-Conductor Devices(1965: London) Conference on Power Applications of Controllable Semi-Conductor Devices: Contributions. LC 66-9749. (Institution of Electrical Engineers Conference Publications: No. 17). pap. 20.00 (ISBN 0-317-10168-4, 2050327). Bks Demand UMI.

Conference on Price Research & Committee on Price Determination. Cost Behavior & Price Policy. 24.50 (ISBN 0-405-19043-3, 7). Ayer Co Pubs.

Conference on Propogation of Radio Waves at Frequencies above 10 GHz(1973: London) Conference on Propogation of Radio Waves at Frequencies above 10 GHz, 10-13 April, 1973. (Institution of Electrical Engineers Conference Publications: NO. 98). pap. 67.50 (ISBN 0-317-10088-2, 2012132). Bks Demand UMI.

Conference on Proposed Legislation in The United States & on the British National Health Care Experience. National Health Insurance Schemes: Proceedings. 75p. 1972. 3.00 (ISBN 0-89215-038-6). U Cal LA Indus Rel.

Conference on Propranolol & Schizophrenia, Santa Ynez, Calif., Dec. 5-8, 1976, et al. Propranolol & Schizophrenia: Proceedings. Roberts, Eugene & Amacher, Peter, eds. LC 78-1781. (Kroc Foundation Ser.: Vol. 10). 162p. 1978. 24.00 (ISBN 0-8451-0300-8). A R Liss.

Conference on Quantitative Flourescence Techniques As Applied to Cell Biology, Seattle, Wash. Fluorescence Techniques in Cell Biology: Proceedings. Thaer, A. & Sernetz, M., eds. LC 73-11950. (Illus.). 450p. 1973. 35.00 (ISBN 0-387-06421-4). Springer-Verlag.

Conference on Race Relations in World Perspective, Honolulu, 1954. Race Relations in World Perspective: Papers. Lind, Andrew W., ed. LC 73-7074. 488p. 1973. Repr. of 1955 ed. lib. bdg. 22.50x (ISBN 0-8371-6907-0, RRWP). Greenwood.

Conference on Reading - University Of Chicago. Reading: Seventy-Five Years of Progress. Robinson, H. Alan, ed. LC 66-23696. 1966. 7.50x (ISBN 0-226-72178-7, SEM96). U of Chicago Pr.

Conference On Reading - University Of Chicago - 1965. Recent Developments in Reading. Robinson, H. Alan, ed. LC 66-23696. (Supplementary Educational Monographs Ser: No. 95). 1965. 6.50x (ISBN 0-226-72177-9). U of Chicago Pr.

Conference on Recombinant DNA, Committee on Genetic Experimentation (COGENE) & the Royal Society of London, Wye College, Kent, UK, April, 1979. Recombinant DNA & Genetic Experimentation: Proceedings. Morgan, Joan & Whelan, W. J., eds. LC 79-40962. (Illus.). 334p. 1979. 73.00 (ISBN 0-08-024427-0). Pergamon.

Conference on Regional Accounts Staff. Elements of Regional Accounts: Papers Presented at the Conference on Regional Accounts, 1962. Werner, Hirsch Z., ed. LC 64-16309. pap. 59.80 (ISBN 0-317-28472-X, 2020740). Bks Demand UMI.

Conference on Remotely Manned Systems, 2nd, June 1975. Robots & Manipulator Systems: Papers, 2 pts. Heer, E., ed. LC 77-73105. 336p. 1977. pap. text ed. 32.00 ea. Pt. 1 (ISBN 0-08-021727-3). Pt. 2 (ISBN 0-08-022681-7). Pergamon.

Conference on Research in Family Planning. Research in Family Planning. Kiser, Clyde V., ed. LC 62-7409. pap. 160.00 (ISBN 0-317-29432-6, 2024297). Bks Demand UMI.

Conference on Research in Income & Wealth. Input-Output Analysis: An Appraisal. LC 75-19705. (National Bureau of Economic Research Ser.). (Illus.). 1975. Repr. of 1955 ed. 29.00x (ISBN 0-405-07585-5). Ayer Co Pubs.

--Long-Range Economic Projection. (Studies in Income & Wealth: No. 16). 468p. 1954. 44.00 (ISBN 0-691-04141-5, Dist. by Princeton U Pr). Natl Bur Econ Res.

Conference on Research in Income & Wealth, 88th Congress, 2nd Session. Measuring the Nation's Wealth: Proceedings. LC 75-19737. (National Bureau of Economic Research Ser.). (Illus.). 1975. Repr. 64.00x (ISBN 0-405-07614-2). Ayer Co Pubs.

Conference On Research In Income And Wealth. Output, Input & Productivity Measurement. (Studies in Income & Wealth: No. 25). 1961. 16.00x (ISBN 0-87014-181-3, Dist. by Princeton U Pr). Natl Bur Econ Res.

Conference on Research in Income & Wealth. Output, Input, & Productivity Measurement. LC 60-12234. (National Bureau of Economic Research. Studies in Income & Wealth: Vol. 25). pap. 129.00 (ISBN 0-317-29949-2, 2051702). Bks Demand UMI.

--Problems of Capital Formation: Concepts, Measurement, & Controlling Factors. LC 75-19707. (National Bureau of Economic Research Ser.). (Illus.). 1975. Repr. of 1957 ed. 45.50x (ISBN 0-405-07587-1). Ayer Co Pubs.

--Trends in the American Economy in the Nineteenth Century. LC 75-19709. (National Bureau of Economic Research Ser.). (Illus.). 1975. Repr. of 1960 ed. 58.50x (ISBN 0-405-07588-X). Ayer Co Pubs.

Conference on Research in National Income & Wealth. Studies in Income & Wealth. LC 75-19704. (National Bureau of Economic Research Ser.). (Illus.). 1975. Repr. 26.50x (ISBN 0-405-07589-8). Ayer Co Pubs.

Conference on Rock Engineering for Foundations & Slopes, University of Colorado. Rock Engineering for Foundations & Slopes: Proceedings of a Specialty Conference, University of Colorado, Boulder, Colorado, August 15-18, 1976, 2 vols. LC 77-368041. Vol. 1. pap. 112.30 (ISBN 0-317-10584-1, 2019552); Vol. 2. pap. 67.50 (ISBN 0-317-10585-X). Bks Demand UMI.

Conference on Rural Environmental Engineering. Water Pollution Control in Low Density Areas: Proceedings. Jewell, William J. & Swan, Rita, eds. LC 74-82975. (Illus.). 518p. 1975. 45.00x (ISBN 0-87451-105-4). U Pr of New Eng.

Conference on Science & Values. Science & Values: Patterns of Tradition & Change. Thackray, Arnold & Mendelsohn, Everett, eds. 1974. text ed. 11.50x (ISBN 0-391-00234-1). Humanities.

Conference on Science - Philosophy & Religion - 6th Symposium. Approaches to Group Understanding. Bryson, L., et al, eds. 858p. 1964. Repr. of 1947 ed. 35.00 (ISBN 0-8154-0036-5). Cooper Sq.

Conference on Science, Philosophy & Religion in Their Relation to the Democratic Way of Life, 6th. Approaches to Group Understanding: Proceedings. Repr. of 1947 ed. 24.00 (ISBN 0-527-00653-X). Kraus Repr.

Conference on Science-Philosophy & Religion in Their Relation to the Democratic Way of Life - 4th. Approaches to World Peace: Proceedings. 1944. 70.00 (ISBN 0-527-00651-3). Kraus Repr.

Conference On Science - Philosophy And Religion - 7th Symposium. Conflicts of Power in Modern Culture. Bryson, L., et al, eds. 703p. 1964. Repr. of 1947 ed. 35.00 (ISBN 0-8154-0037-3). Cooper Sq.

Conference on Science-Philosophy & Religion in Their Religion to the Democratic Way of Life, New York. Ethics & Bigness: Proceedings. 1962. 41.00 (ISBN 0-527-00664-5). Kraus Repr.

Conference on Science-Philosophy & Religion in Their Relation to the Democratic Way of Life, 11th. Foundations of World Organization: A Political & Cultural Appraisal: Proceeding. 37.00 (ISBN 0-527-00658-0). Kraus Repr.

Conference on Science-Philosophy & Religion in Their Relation to the Democratic Way of Live, 12th, New York. Freedom & Authority in Our Time: Proceeding. 1953. 51.00 (ISBN 0-527-00659-9). Kraus Repr.

Conference on Science-Philosophy & Religion in Their Relation to the Democratic Way of Life - 9th. Goals for American Education: Proceedings. 1950. 28.00 (ISBN 0-527-00656-4). Kraus Repr.

Conference on Science, Philosophy & Religion in Their Relation to the Democratic Way of Life, 3rd. Science, Philosophy, & Religion: Proceedings. 1943. 37.00 (ISBN 0-527-00650-5). Kraus Repr.

Conference on Science, Philosophy & Religion in Their Relation to the Democratic Way of Life, 2nd. Science, Philosophy, & Religion: Proceedings. 1942. 37.00 (ISBN 0-527-00649-1). Kraus Repr.

Conference on Science, Philosophy & Religion & Their Relation to the Democratic Way of Life, 1st. Science, Philosophy, & Religion: Proceedings. 1941. 37.00 (ISBN 0-527-00648-3). Kraus Repr.

Conference on Science-Philosophy & Religion-13th Symposium. Symbols & Values. Bryson, L., et al, eds. 827p. 1964. Repr. of 1954 ed. 35.00 (ISBN 0-8154-0038-1). Cooper Sq.

Conference on Science-Philosphy & Religion in Their Relation to the Democratic Way of Life - 5th. Approaches to National Unity: Proceedings. 1945. 70.00 (ISBN 0-527-00652-1). Kraus Repr.

Conference on Scientific Management, 1st. Addresses & Discussions at the Conference on Scientific Management: Proceedings. LC 72-90030. (Management History Ser.: No. 9). 399p. Repr. of 1912 ed. 22.50 (ISBN 0-87960-014-4). Hive Pub.

Conference on Set-Valued Mappings, SUNY, Buffalo, 1969. Set-Valued Mappings, Selections & Topological Properties of 2x: Proceedings. Fleischman, W. M., ed. (Lecture Notes in Mathematics: Vol. 171). 1970. pap. 11.00 (ISBN 0-387-05293-3). Springer-Verlag.

Conference on Shock, 4th, Marco Island, Florida, June, 1981 & Reichard, Sherwood M. Advances in Shock Research: Proceedings. LC 79-63007. 1982. Vol. 7, Pt. 1 254pgs. 44.00 (ISBN 0-8451-0606-6); Vol. 8, Pt. 2, 288pgs. 48.00 (ISBN 0-8451-0607-4). A R Liss.

Conference on Silicon Carbide, 3rd, 1973. Silicon Carbide: Proceedings. Marshall, R. C. & Faust, John W., Jr., eds. LC 74-2394. (Illus.). 692p. 1974. 29.95x (ISBN 0-87249-315-6). U of SC Pr.

Conference On Social Psychology - University Of Oklahoma - 1950. Social Psychology at the Crossroads. facsimile ed. Rohrer, John N. & Sherif, Muzafer, eds. LC 73-111822. (Essay Index Reprint Ser). 1951. 26.00 (ISBN 0-8369-1600-X). Ayer Co Pubs.

Conference on Software Engineering for Telecommunication Switching Systems(1973: University of Essex) Conference on Software Engineering for Telecommunication Switching Systems. (Institution of Electrical Engineers Conference Publications: No. 97). pap. 86.50 (ISBN 0-317-10093-9, 2012131). Bks Demand UMI.

Conference on Soviet Agricultural & Peasant Affairs. Soviet Agricultural & Peasant Affairs. Laird, Roy D., frwd. by. LC 81-20287. (Slavic Studies: No. 1). xi, 335p. 1982. Repr. of 1963 ed. lib. bdg. 35.00x (ISBN 0-313-23450-7, COSO). Greenwood.

Conference on Systems & Computer Science, 1965: University of Western Ontario. Systems & Computer Science. Hart, John F. & Takasu, Satoru, eds. LC 68-114245. pap. 65.30 (ISBN 0-317-10999-5, 2014240). Bks Demand UMI.

Conference on Telecommunication Transmission (1975: London) Conference on Telecommunication Transmission, September 9-11, 1975. LC 76-371266. (Institution of Electrical Engineers Conference Publication Ser.: No. 131). pap. 51.50 (ISBN 0-317-10159-5, 2012128). Bks Demand UMI.

Conference on Tensions in Development, Oxford Univ. Restless Nations: A Study of World Tensions & Development. LC 73-3751. 217p. 1974. Repr. of 1962 ed. lib. bdg. 15.00x (ISBN 0-8371-6846-5, RENA). Greenwood.

Conference on the Aging, 4th, University of Michican, 1951. Rehabilitation of the Older Worker: Proceedings. Donahue, Wilma, et al, eds. LC 76-44290. 1976. Repr. of 1953 ed. lib. bdg. 22.50x (ISBN 0-8371-9042-8, DORO). Greenwood.

Conference on the Application of Large Industrial Drives(1965: London) Conference on the Application of Large Industrial Drives. LC 67-2581. (Institution of Electrical Engineers Conference Publication Ser.: No. 10). pap. 68.80 (ISBN 0-317-11158-2, 2050326); pap. 20.00 Supplement (ISBN 0-317-11159-0). Bks Demand UMI.

Conference on The Care Of Dependent Children. Proceedings of the Conference on the Care of Dependent Children. LC 79-137182. (Poverty U. S. A. Historical Record Ser). 1971. Repr. of 1909 ed. 20.00 (ISBN 0-405-03120-3). Ayer Co Pubs.

Conference on the Electrical Tansport & Optical Properties of Inhomogeneous Media, 1st, Ohio State Univ., Sept. 1977. Electrical Transport & Optical Properties of Inhomogeneous Media. Garland, J. C. & Tanner, D. B., eds. LC 78-54319. (AIP Conference Proceedings: No. 40). 1978. lib. bdg. 21.00 (ISBN 0-88318-139-8). Am Inst Physics.

Conference on the Environment & Airlie House. Recovery for Exposure to Hazardous Substance: The Superfund Section 301(E) Report & Beyond: Presentations Delivered at the Twelfth Annual Conference on the Environment, May6-7, 1983. LC 84-70640. Date not set. price not set (ISBN 0-89707-139-5). Amer Bar Assn.

Conference on the Federal Election Commission, jt. auth. see American Bar Association Special Committee on Election Law & Voter Participation.

Conference on the History of Medicinal Drug Control (1968: National Library of Medicine. Safeguarding the Public: Historical Aspects of Medicinal Drug Control. Blake, John B., ed. LC 76-84651. pap. 53.30 (ISBN 0-317-19888-2, 2023084). Bks Demand UMI.

Conference on the HP-1000 International Users Group, 1st. Minicomputer Research & Applications: Proceedings. Brown, H. K., ed. LC 81-5134. (Illus.). 392p. 1981. 44.00 (ISBN 0-08-027567-2). Pergamon.

Conference on the Human Environment, Founex, Switzerland, June 4-12, 1971. Development & Environment: Proceedings. Strong, Maurice F., ed. LC 72-75446. (Illus.). 225p. (Orig.). 1973. pap. text ed. 12.80x (ISBN 90-2796-990-6). Mouton.

Conference on the Nature of the Surface of the Moon. The Nature of the Lunar Surface: Proceedings of the 1965 IAU-NASA Symposium, Greenbelt, MD. Hess, Wilmot N., et al, eds. LC 65-27671. (Illus.). pap. 82.00 (ISBN 0-317-07805-4, 2003844). Bks Demand UMI.

Conference on the Numerical Solution of Differential Equations. Proceedings. Morris, J. L., ed. LC 77-101372. (Lecture Notes in Mathematics: Vol. 109). 1969. pap. 14.70 (ISBN 0-387-04628-3). Springer-Verlag.

--Proceedings. Watson, G. A., ed. (Lecture Notes in Mathematics Ser.: Vol. 363). ix, 221p. 1974. pap. 14.00 (ISBN 0-387-06617-9). Springer-Verlag.

Conference on the Optimal Preparation for the Study of Medicine, 1967. Preparation for the Study of Medicine: Proceedings. Page, Robert G. & Littlemeyer, Mary H., eds. LC 69-19280. pap. 73.80 (ISBN 0-317-20632-X, 2024123). Bks Demand UMI.

Conference on the Present Status of Weak Interaction Physics, Indiana Univ., Bloomington, May 16-17, 1977. Weak Interaction Physics: Nineteen Seventy-Seven Proceedings. Lichtenberg, D. B., ed. LC 77-83344. (AIP Conference Proceedings: Vol. 37). (Illus.). 1977. lib. bdg. 13.00 (ISBN 0-88318-136-3). Am Inst Physics.

Conference on the Public Land Law Review Commission Report, Dec. 1970. America's Public Lands: Politics, Economics, & Administration. Nathan, Harriet, ed. LC 72-4850. (Illus.). 395p. (Orig.). 1972. pap. 7.00x (ISBN 0-87772-084-3). Inst Gov Stud Berk.

Conference On The Scientific Spirit & Democratic Faith - 2nd. Authoritarian Attempt to Capture Education. facs. ed. (Essay Index Reprint Ser.). 1945. 15.00 (ISBN 0-8369-1819-3). Ayer Co Pubs.

Conference On The Scientific Spirit And Democratic Faith - 3rd. Science for Democracy. facs. ed. LC 70-121459. (Essay Index Reprint Ser.). 1946. 18.00 (ISBN 0-8369-1793-6). Ayer Co Pubs.

Conference On The Scientific Spirit And Democratic Faith-1st-New York-1943. Scientific Spirit & Democratic Faith. facs. ed. LC 72-121457. (Essay Index Reprint Ser). 1944. 14.00 (ISBN 0-8369-1872-X). Ayer Co Pubs.

Conference on the Theory of Ordinary & Partial Differential Equations, Dundee, Scotland, 1972. Proceedings. Everitt, W. N. & Sleeman, B. D., eds. LC 72-87925. (Lecture Notes in Mathematics: Vol. 280). (Illus.). xv, 367p. 1972. pap. 13.00 (ISBN 0-387-05962-8). Springer-Verlag.

Conference on the Theory of Ordinary & Partial Differential Equations, Dundee, Scotland, 1974. Proceedings. Sleeman, B. D. & McRae, I. M., eds. LC 74-18467. (Lecture Notes in Mathematics Ser.: Vol. 415). xvii, 447p. 1974. pap. 24.00 (ISBN 0-387-06959-3). Springer-Verlag.

Conference on the Undergraduate & Lifetime Reading Interest. Reading for Life: Developing the College Student's Lifetime Reading Interest. Price, Jacob M., ed. LC 68-54775. Repr. of 1959 ed. lib. bdg. 19.75x (ISBN 0-8371-0359-2, REFL). Greenwood.

Conference on the Use of Orbiting Spacecraft in Geographic Research - Houston - Tex 1965. Spacecraft in Geographic Research. 1966. pap. 4.00 (ISBN 0-309-01353-4). Natl Acad Pr.

Conference on Topological Methods in Algebraic Topology, SUNY, Binghamton, Oct. 1973. Algebraic & Geometrical Methods in Topology: Proceedings. McAuley, L. F., ed. (Lecture Notes in Mathematics Ser.: Vol. 428). xi, 280p. 1974. pap. 18.00 (ISBN 0-387-07019-2). Springer-Verlag.

Conference on Transformation Groups - New Orleans - 1967. Proceedings. Mostert, P. S., ed. LC 68-27313. (Illus.). 1968. 47.50 (ISBN 0-387-04299-7). Springer-Verlag.

Conference on Trend in On-Line Computer Control Systems, 2nd., University of Sheffield, 1975. Trend in On-Line Computer Control Systems: 21-24 April, 1975. LC 76-355944. (Institution of Electrical Engineers Conference Publication Ser.: 127). (Illus.). pap. 72.50 (ISBN 0-317-10838-7, 2012129). Bks Demand UMI.

Conference on Understanding Profits. Profits in the Modern Economy: Selected Papers. Stevenson, Harold W. & Nelson, J. Russell, eds. LC 67-13120. pap. 53.50 (ISBN 0-317-29470-9, 2055919). Bks Demand UMI.

Conference On Unemployment - Washington D. C. - 1921. Recent Economic Changes in the United States, 2 Vols. in 1. 1929. 70.00 (ISBN 0-384-09745-6). Johnson Repr.

Conference on Vacuum Microbalance Techniques (9th: 1970: Berlin, Germany) Progress in Vacuum Microbalance Techniques: Proceedings of the Ninth Conference on Vacuum Microbalance Techniques, Technical University, Berlin, Germany, June, 1970, Vol. 1. Gast, Th. & Robens, E., eds. LC 72-82129. pap. 104.80 (ISBN 0-317-29331-1, 2024022). Bks Demand UMI.

Conference on Vacuum Microbalance Techniques (10th: 1972: Uxbridge, England. Progress in Vacuum Microbalance Techniques: Proceedings of the 10th Conference on Vacuum Microbalance Techniques, Brunal University, Uxbridge, England, June 1972, Vol. 2. Bevan, S. C. & Gregg, S. J., eds. LC 72-82129. pap. 66.50 (ISBN 0-317-29333-8, 2024023). Bks Demand UMI.

Conference on Vacuum Microbalance Techniques (12th: 1974: Lyon, France) Progress in Vacuum Microbalance Techniques: Proceedings of the 12th Conference on Vacuum Microbalance Techniques, Lyon University, Lyon, France, September 1974, Vol. 3. Eyraud, C. & Escoubes, M., eds. LC 72-82189. pap. 115.30 (ISBN 0-317-29334-6, 2024024). Bks Demand UMI.

Conference on Waste Heat Management & Utilization, Miami Beach, May 9-11, 1977. Waste Heat Management & Utilization: Proceedings, 3 vols. new ed. Lee, S. S. & Sengupta, S., eds. LC 78-13267. (Illus.). 2541p. 1979. Set. text ed. 340.00 (ISBN 0-89116-158-9). Hemisphere Pub.

Conference Sponsored by ASCE Construction Division, May 1980, San Francisco, CA. Social & Economic Impact of Earthquakes on Utility Lifelines: Seismic Considerations in Lifelines Planning, Siting and Design. Isenberg, J., ed. LC 80-69153. 250p. 1981. pap. 21.00x (ISBN 0-87262-254-1). Am Soc Civil Eng.

Conference Sponsored by National Foundation-March of Dimes, Key Biscayne, Florida, Nov. 1975. Iron Metabolism & Thalassemia: Proceedings. Bergsma, Daniel, et al, eds. LC 76-25835. (Birth Defects Original Article Ser.: Vol. 12, No. 8). 212p. 1976. 34.00x (ISBN 0-8451-1006-3). A R Liss.

Conference, 5th, Oberwolfach, Germany, Jan. 29 - Feb. 4, 1978. Probability Measures on Groups: Proceedings. Heyer, H., ed. (Lecture Notes in Mathematics: Vol. 706). 1979. pap. 22.00 (ISBN 0-387-09124-6). Springer-Verlag.

Conferences on Brain & Behavior, Los Angeles. Brain & Behavior: Proceedings, 2 vols. Brazier, M. A., ed. Incl. Vol. 1. Brain & Behavior. First Conference, 1961 (ISBN 0-934454-17-5); Vol. 2. The Internal Environment & Alimentary Behavior. Second Conference, 1962 (ISBN 0-934454-18-3). 7.75 ea. Lubrecht & Cramer.

Confino, M. & Shamir, Shimon, eds. U. S. S. R. & the Middle East. 441p. 1973. casebound 21.95x (ISBN 0-87855-160-3). Transaction Bks.

Confino, Michael. Daughter of a Revolutionary: Natalie Herzen & the Bakunin-Nechayev Circle. LC 73-86555. 416p. 1974. 19.95 (ISBN 0-912050-15-2, Library Pr). Open Court.

--Systemes Agraires & Progres Agricole - L'assolement Triennal En Russie Au XVIIIe-XIXe Siecles. (Etudes Sur L'histoire, L'economie & la Sociologie Des Pays Slaves: No. 14). 1970. pap. 34.40 (ISBN 90-2796-294-4). Mouton.

Confino, Vico. The Wrath of Condo. 171p. (Orig.). 1985. pap. 7.95 (ISBN 0-9615100-0-5). River Bend Club.

Conford, Ellen. The Alfred G. Graebner Memorial High School Handbook of Rules & Regulations: A Novel. (gr. 7-9). 1977. pap. 1.95 (ISBN 0-671-41673-1). Archway.

--The Alfred G. Graebner Memorial High School Handbook of Rules & Regulations. (gr. 7-12). 1976. 14.45 (ISBN 0-316-15293-5). Little.

--Alfred G. Graebner Memorial High School Handbook of Rules & Regulations: A Novel. (YA) (gr. 7-9). 1983. pap. 2.25 (ISBN 0-671-47039-6). PB.

--And This Is Laura. (gr. 5-7). 1978. pap. 2.25 (ISBN 0-671-44379-8). Archway.

--And This Is Laura. (gr. 4-6). 1977. 12.45 (ISBN 0-316-15300-1). Little.

--Anything for a Friend. (gr. 5-7). 1981. pap. 1.95 (ISBN 0-671-44379-8). Archway.

--Anything for a Friend. LC 78-27843. (gr. 3-7). 1979. 12.45i (ISBN 0-316-15308-7). Little.

--Dear Lovey Hart: I Am Desperate. 224p. (gr. 4-6). 1975. 12.45i (ISBN 0-316-15306-0). Little.

--Dear Lovey Hart, I Am Desperate. (gr. 7 up). 1977. pap. 2.25 (ISBN 0-590-33738-6, Point). Scholastic Inc.

--Dreams of Victory. (Illus.). 144p. (gr. 4-6). 1973. 12.45i (ISBN 0-316-15294-3). Little.

--Dreams of Victory. 112p. (gr. 4-6). 1982. pap. 1.95 (ISBN 0-590-31954-X, Apple Paperbacks). Scholastic Inc.

--Felicia, the Critic. (gr. 4-6). 1978. pap. 1.95 (ISBN 0-671-43924-3). Archway.

--Felicia the Critic. (Illus.). (gr. 4-6). 1973. 12.45i (ISBN 0-316-15295-1). Little.

--Hail, Hail, Camp Timberwood. (Illus.). (gr. 4-6). 1980. pap. 1.95 (ISBN 0-671-42685-0). Archway.

--Hail, Hail Camp Timberwood. LC 78-18715. (Illus.). (gr. 3-7). 1978. 14.45i (ISBN 0-316-15291-9). Little.

--Hello, You're on the Air. 160p. (gr. 7 up). 1985. 11.95. Putnam Pub Group.

--If This Is Love, I'll Take Spaghetti. 176p. (gr. 7 up). 1984. pap. 2.25 (ISBN 0-590-32338-5, Point). Scholastic Inc.

--Impossible Possum. (Illus.). (gr. 1-3). 1971. 10.45i (ISBN 0-316-15297-8). Little.

--Just the Thing for Geraldine. (Illus.). 32p. (gr. 1-3). 1974. 7.95 (ISBN 0-316-15304-4). Little.

--Lenny Kandell, Smart Aleck. 128p. (gr. 4-6). 1983. 11.45i (ISBN 0-316-15313-3). Little.

--Lenny Kandell, Smart Aleck. 160p. (gr. 4-7). 1984. pap. 1.95 (ISBN 0-671-50078-3). Archway.

--The Luck of Pokey Bloom. (Illus.). (gr. 4-6). 1983. 1.95 (ISBN 0-671-44233-3). Archway.

--The Luck of Pokey Bloom. (Illus.). 144p. (gr. 4-6). 1975. 10.45i (ISBN 0-316-15305-2). Little.

--Me & the Terrible Two. (Illus.). (gr. 4-6). 1977. pap. 2.25 (ISBN 0-671-41769-X). Archway.

--Me & the Terrible Two. (Illus.). 128p. (gr. 4-6). 1974. 12.45i (ISBN 0-316-15303-6). Little.

--Me & the Terrible Two. 1985. pap. 2.25 (ISBN 0-671-55388-7). PB.

--The Revenge of the Incredible Dr. Rancid & His Youthful Assistant, Jeffrey. 132p. (gr. 1-8). 1980. 6.70i (ISBN 0-316-15288-9). Little.

--Revenge of the Incredible Dr. Rancid & His Youthful Assistant, Jeffrey. (gr. 4-6). 1983. pap. 2.25 (ISBN 0-590-33746-7, Apple Paperbacks). Scholastic Inc.

--The Revenge of the Incredible Dr. Rancid & His Youthful Assistant, Jeffrey. 128p. (gr. 4-6). 1982. pap. 1.95 (ISBN 0-590-31794-6, Apple Paperbacks). Scholastic Inc.

--Seven Days to a Brand-New Me. 96p. (gr. 5 up). 1981. 10.45i (ISBN 0-316-15311-7). Little.

--Seven Days to a Brand-New Me. 128p. (gr. 7 up). 1982. pap. 2.25 (ISBN 0-590-33926-5, Point). Scholastic Inc.

--Strictly for Laughs. 160p. (gr. 7 up). 1985. 12.95 (ISBN 0-448-47754-8, Putnam). Putnam Pub Group.

--To All My Fans, with Love from Sylvie. 192p. (gr. 7 up). 1982. 12.45i (ISBN 0-316-15312-5). Little.

--To All My Fans, with Love from Sylvie. (gr. 7 up). 1983. pap. 2.25 (ISBN 0-686-44321-7). Archway.

--We Interrupt This Semester for an Important Bulletin. LC 79-9133. (Illus.). (gr. 5 up). 1979. 10.45i (ISBN 0-316-15309-5). Little.

--We Interrupt This Semester for an Important Bulletin. 192p. (Orig.). (YA) (gr. 7 up). 1979. pap. 1.95 (ISBN 0-590-32830-1). Scholastic Inc.

Conforti, Joseph A. Samuel Hopkins & the New Divinity Movement: Calvinism, the Congregational Ministry, & Reform in New England Between the Great Awakenings. LC 80-28268. pap. 62.30 (ISBN 0-317-08398-8, 2020840). Bks Demand UMI.

Conforti, Michael, et al. English Ceramics from Northern California Collections. LC 80-65652. (Illus.). 56p. 1980. pap. 3.95 (ISBN 0-88401-035-X). Fine Arts Mus.

Conforto, Giovanni. Breve e Facile Maniera. (Monuments of Music Literature in Facsimile: Ser. II, Vol. 115). 1978. Repr. of 1593 ed. 22.50x (ISBN 0-8450-2315-2). Broude.

Confucius. The Analects. Lau, D. C., tr. 1979. pap. 3.95 (ISBN 0-14-044348-7). Penguin.

--Analects. Waley, Arthur, tr. 1966. pap. 4.95 (ISBN 0-394-70173-9, V173, Vin). Random.

--The Analects of Confucius. (Illus.). 149p. 1986. 88.85 (ISBN 0-89266-538-6). Am Classical Coll Pr.

--Confucian Analects, the Great Learning & the Doctrine of the Mean. Legge, James, ed. 1893. pap. 7.95 (ISBN 0-486-22746-4). Dover.

--Confucian Analects, the Great Learning & the Doctrine of the Mean. Legge, James, tr. 15.50 (ISBN 0-8446-0067-9). Peter Smith.

--Confucius: The Great Digest, the Unwobbling Pivot, the Analects. Pound, Ezra, tr. LC 74-87911. 1969. pap. 7.95 (ISBN 0-8112-0154-6, NDP285). New Directions.

--The Great Learning & the Doctrine of the Mean. (Illus.). 151p. 1986. 88.85 (ISBN 0-89266-539-4). Am Classical Coll Pr.

--The Most Compelling Sayings by Confucius. Lynall, Leonard D., tr. (Most Meaningful Classics in World Culture Ser.). (Illus.). 166p. 1983. 83.45 (ISBN 0-89266-387-1). Am Classical Coll Pr.

--Sayings of Confucius. Ware, James R., tr. (Orig.). pap. 3.95 (ISBN 0-451-62391-6, Ment). NAL.

--The Wisdom of Confucius. (Illus.). 131p. 1982. 63.45 (ISBN 0-89266-359-6). Am Classical Coll Pr.

--Wisdom of Confucius. 1965. 4.95 (ISBN 0-88088-100-3). Peter Pauper.

--The Wisdom of Confucius. Yutang, Lin, ed. LC 38-27366. 1938. 5.95 (ISBN 0-394-60426-1). Modern Lib.

Congar, Samuel H., ed. Records of the Town of Newark, New Jersey, from its Settlement in 1666 to its Incorporation as a City in 1836, Vol. 6. 308p. 1966. pap. 8.50 (ISBN 0-686-81799-0). NJ Hist Soc.

Congar, Yves. Diversity & Communion. 240p. 1985. pap. text ed. 9.95 (ISBN 0-89622-275-6). Twenty-Third.

--Droit ancient et structures ecclesiales: Eleven Studies in French 1958-78. 312p. 1982. 75.00x (ISBN 0-86078-107-0, Pub. by Variorum England). State Mutual Bk.

--I Believe in the Holy Spirit, 3 Vols. Smith, David, tr. from Fr. Incl. Vol. I. The Experience of the Spirit. 173p. 24.95 (ISBN 0-8164-0518-2); Vol. 2. Lord & Giver of Life. 230p. 24.95 (ISBN 0-8164-0535-2); Vol. 3. The River of Life Flows in the East & in the West. 274p. 24.95 (ISBN 0-8164-0537-9). 300p. 1983. Set. 70.00 (ISBN 0-8164-0540-9, Pub. by Seabury). Winston Pr.

--Lay People in the Church. 518p. 1985. pap. 14.95 (ISBN 0-87061-114-3). Chr Classics.

Congar, Yves & Siegwalt, Gerard. Vocabulaire Oecumenique. 428p. (Fr.). pap. 22.50 (ISBN 0-686-56960-1, M-6083). French & Eur.

Congdon, Allan R. Training in High-School Mathematics Essential for Success in Certain College Subjects. (Columbia University. Teachers College. Contributions to Education: No. 403). Repr. of 1930 ed. 22.50 (ISBN 0-404-55403-2). AMS Pr.

Congdon, Brenda, ed. Annotated Media Bibliography. 138p. 1985. 14.00 (ISBN 0-318-18156-8); members 9.00 (ISBN 0-318-18157-6). Assn Care Child.

Congdon, Charles T. Tribune Essays. facsimile ed. LC 79-154147. (Select Bibliographies Reprint Ser). Repr. of 1869 ed. 24.50 (ISBN 0-8369-5763-6). Ayer Co Pubs.

Congdon, Don, ed. Combat World War II, 2 vols. Incl. European Theater of Operations. 608p. 24.95 (ISBN 0-87795-457-7); Pacific Theater of Operations. 24.95 (ISBN 0-87795-458-5). (Illus.). 1983. Arbor Hse.

Congdon, Herbert W. Covered Bridge. (Illus.). 1970. pap. 4.95 (ISBN 0-911570-05-5). Vermont Bks.

--Dake of Castleton, House-Joiner Extra Ordinary. (Illus.). 36p. 1949. pap. 1.25x (ISBN 0-934720-13-4). VT Hist Soc.

--Early American Homes for Today: A Treasury of Decorative Details & Restoration Procedures. 1985. pap. 12.95 (ISBN 0-87233-065-6). Bauhan.

--Old Vermont Houses, 1763-1850. 1968. pap. 7.95 (ISBN 0-87233-001-X). Bauhan.

Congdon, Howard K. The Pursuit of Death. LC 76-44308. Repr. of 1977 ed. 36.30 (ISBN 0-8357-9022-3, 2016395). Bks Demand UMI.

Congdon, Kirby. Contemporary Poets in American Anthologies 1960-1977. LC 78-13772. 236p. 1978. 17.50 (ISBN 0-8108-1168-5). Scarecrow.

Congdon, Lee. The Young Lukacs. LC 82-11162. xiii, 256p. 1983. 22.50 (ISBN 0-8078-1538-1). U of NC Pr.

Congdon, S. Perry, 2nd. The Drama Reader: Full-Length Plays for the Secondary School. LC 62-13409. 1962. pap. text ed. 7.20 scp (ISBN 0-672-73220-3). Odyssey Pr.

Conger, Amy. Edward Weston in Mexico, Nineteen Twenty-Three to Nineteen Twenty-Six. (Illus.). 128p. 1983. pap. 15.95 (ISBN 0-8263-0666-7). U of NM Pr.

Conger, Amy, jt. ed. see Newhall, Beaumont.

Conger, Arthur L. Rise of U. S. Grant. facs. ed. LC 74-137371. (Select Bibliographies Reprint Ser). (Illus.). 1931. 23.50 (ISBN 0-8369-5572-2). Ayer Co Pubs.

Conger, Arthur L., ed. see De Purucker, G.

Conger, B. V., ed. Cloning Agricultural Plants via In Vitro Techniques. LC 80-23852. 280p. 1981. 85.00 (ISBN 0-8493-5797-7). CRC Pr.

Conger, Ben, jt. auth. see Jacob, Bart.

Conger, Donald. Closeout. 1980. pap. 1.75 (ISBN 0-8439-0722-3, Leisure Bks). Dorchester Pub Co.

Conger, Eric. The Fairy & the Princess: Tales from Heather's Diary. LC 85-71342. 66p. (gr. 6-8). 1985. pap. 2.25 (ISBN 0-932365-03-5, FP-035). DeWitt & Sheppard.

Conger, Flora S. & Rose, Irene B. Child Care Aide Skills. (Careers in Home Economics Ser.). (Illus.). 1979. pap. text ed. 18.80 (ISBN 0-07-012420-5). McGraw.

Conger, George P. Ideologies of Religion. facsimile ed. LC 70-93329. (Essay Index Reprint Ser). 1940. 19.00 (ISBN 0-8369-1283-7). Ayer Co Pubs.

Conger, Horace. In Search of Gold. (Illus.). 1983. pap. 9.95 (ISBN 0-88240-239-0). Alaska Northwest.

Conger, Jean. Velvet Paw. (Illus.). 1963. 7.95 (ISBN 0-8392-1125-2). Astor-Honor.

Conger, John. Adolescence: Generation under Pressure. (Life Cycle Ser.). 1980. pap. text ed. 4.76I (ISBN 0-06-384744-2, HarpC). Har-Row.

Conger, John J. Current Issues in Adolescent Development. (Master Lectures on Developmental Psychology: Manuscript No. 1334). 7.50x (ISBN 0-912704-20-9). Am Psychol.

Conger, John J. & Peterson, Anne C. Adolescence & Youth: Psychological Development in a Changing World. 3rd ed. 732p. 1983. text ed. 26.50 (ISBN 0-06-041357-3, HarpC); instr's manual avail. (ISBN 0-06-361342-5). Har-Row.

Conger, Margaret. Combined Chronology for Use with the Mahatma Letters to A. P. Sinnett & the Letters of H. P. Blavatsky to A. P. Sinnett. LC 73-92461. 1973. pap. 3.00 (ISBN 0-911500-17-0). Theos U Pr.

Conger, Roger. Pictorial History of Waco. (Illus.). 292p. 1969. 15.95 (ISBN 0-87244-026-5). Texian.

Conger, Shirley & Moore, Kay. Social Work in Long-Term Care Facilities. 160p. 1981. pap. 18.95 (ISBN 0-8436-0850-1). Van Nos Reinhold.

Conger, Syndy M. Matthew G. Lewis, Charles Robert Maturin & the Germans: An Interpretative Study of the Influence of German Literature on Two Gothic Novels. Varma, Devendra P., ed. LC 79-8448. (Gothic Studies & Dissertations Ser.). 1980. Repr. of 1977 ed. lib. bdg. 32.50x (ISBN 0-405-12652-2). Ayer Co Pubs.

Conger, Syndy M. & Welsch, Janice R., eds. Narrative Strategies: Original Essays in Film & Prose Fiction. LC 80-53296. (Essays in Literature Ser.: Bk. 4). 140p. (Orig.). 1981. pap. 8.00x (ISBN 0-934312-03-6). Western Ill Univ.

Conger, Wilda L. & Cushman, Elizabeth. Forever Is Now. 1964. pap. 6.95 (ISBN 0-8158-0077-0). Chris Mass.

Conger, Yves M. After Nine Hundred Years: The Background of the Schism Between the Eastern & Western Churches. LC 78-6154. 1978. Repr. of 1959 ed. lib. bdg. 22.50x (ISBN 0-313-20493-4, COAN). Greenwood.

Congessional Quarterly Inc., ed. see Schroeder, Richard.

Cong-Huyen-Ton-Nu, Wha-Trang. Vietnamese Folklore: An Introductory & Annotated Bibliography. (Occasional Papers: No. 7). 60p. 1983. pap. text ed. 10.00 (ISBN 0-8191-3135-0, Co-pub. by Ctr S SE Asia). U Pr of Amer.

Congleton, Henry B. On Financial Reform. 3rd ed. LC 68-56560. Repr. of 1831 ed. 37.50x (ISBN 0-678-00452-8). Kelley.

Congleton, J. E. Theories of Pastoral Poetry in England, 1684-1798. LC 68-29735. (Studies in Poetry, No. 38). 1969. Repr. of 1952 ed. lib. bdg. 75.00x (ISBN 0-8383-0329-3). Haskell.

Congo, David & Congo, Janet. Less Stress: The Ten-Minute Stress Reduction Program. 1985. pap. price not set (ISBN 0-8307-0968-1, 5418240). Regal.

Congo, Janet. Finding Inner Security: A Woman's Quest for Interdependence. 1985. pap. price not set (ISBN 0-8307-1045-0, 5418511). Regal.

Congo, Janet, jt. auth. see Congo, David.

Congrat-Butlar, Stefan, ed. Russian Vest Pocket Dictionary. (Rus.). 1974. 3.95 (ISBN 0-394-40068-2). Random.

Congrat-Butlar, Stefan, compiled by. Translation & Translators. LC 79-6965. 241p. 1979. 35.00 (ISBN 0-8352-1158-4). Bowker.

Congres International de la Preparation des Minerais, ed. Lexique Quadrilinque de la Preparation des Minerais. 260p. (Ger., Eng., Fr. & Rus., Four-Language Lexicon of Ore Preparation). 1963. pap. 25.00 (ISBN 0-686-56795-1). French & Eur.

Congresional Information Service, Inc. Staff. Statistical Reference Index Annual, 1982, 2 Vols. 1954p. 1983. Set 435.00 (ISBN 0-912380-06-3). Index Vol (ISBN 0-912380-07-1). Abstract Vol. Cong Info.

Congress For Cultural Freedom - Berlin - 1960. History & Hope. facs. ed. Jelenski, K. A., ed. LC 70-117773. (Essay Index Reprint Ser.). 1962. 18.00 (ISBN 0-8369-1794-4). Ayer Co Pubs.

Congress of Accountants, World Fair, St Louis, September 26-28th, 1904. Official Record of the Congress of Accountants: Proceedings. Brief, Richard P., ed. LC 77-87266. (Development of Contemporary Accounting Thought Ser). 1978. Repr. of 1904 ed. lib. bdg. 20.00x (ISBN 0-405-10895-8). Ayer Co Pubs.

Congress of International College of Psychosomatic Medicine, 2nd, Amsterdam, June 18-21, 1973. Mechanisms in Symptom Formation: Proceedings. Musaph, H., ed. (Psychotherapy & Psychosomatics: Vol. 23, No. 1-6). 300p. 1974. 41.00 (ISBN 3-8055-1689-4). S Karger.

Congress of International Society of Development Biologists, Basel, Switzerland, Aug. 28-Sept. 1, 1981 & Burger, Max M. Embryonic Development. LC 82-15351. (Progress in Clinical & Biological Research Ser.: Vols. 85 A & B). 1982. Pt. A: Genetic Aspects 520 pgs. 50.00 (ISBN 0-8451-0163-3); Pt. B: Cellular Aspects, 698 pgs. 68.00 (ISBN 0-8451-0164-1). Set (ISBN 0-8451-0085-8). A R Liss.

Congress of Pediatric Dermatology, 2nd, Mexico City, October 20-23, 1976. Pediatric Dermatology & Internal Medicine: Internal Medicine & External Medicine, Proceedings. Ruiz-Maldonado, R., ed. (Modern Problems in Pediatrics: Vol. 20). (Illus.). 1978. 41.75 (ISBN 3-8055-2703-9). S Karger.

Congress of Psychosomatic Obstetrics & Gynecology 4th, Israel, 1974. The Family: Proceeding. Hirsh, H., et al, eds. 600p. 1975. 75.00 (ISBN 3-8055-2206-1). S Karger.

Congress of the International Astronautical Federation, 22nd, Brussels, Sept. 1971. Astronautical Research 1971: Proceedings. Napolitano, L. G., ed. LC 72-92536. (Illus.). 586p. 1973. lib. bdg. 76.00 (ISBN 90-277-0306-X, Pub. by Reidel Holland). Kluwer Academic.

Congress On Africa. Africa & the American Negro. facs. ed. Bowen, J. W., ed. LC 74-79020. (Black Heritage Library Collection Ser). 1896. 15.50 (ISBN 0-8369-8547-8). Ayer Co Pubs.

Congress on Electrocardiology, 1st, Wiesbaden, Oct. 1974. Proceedings. Abel, H., ed. (Advances in Cardiology: Vol. 16). 1976. 54.50 (ISBN 3-8055-2197-9). S Karger.

Congress on Haematology Society, 13th International, Munich, 1970. Nucleic Acid Metabolism in Normal & Leukemic Cells: Proceedings. Polli, E., ed. 1971. pap. 8.75 (ISBN 3-8055-1230-9). S Karger.

Congress on Metallic Corrosion. Metallic Corrosion: Proceedings of the 8th International Congress on Metallic Corrosion, Mainz, Germany, Sept. 1981 (111th Event, 8th ICMC, 7th CEFC, 3 Vols. (Dechema Proceedings Ser.). 2300p. 1982. Set. pap. text ed. 150.00x (ISBN 3-921567-36-X, Pub. by Dechema Germany). Scholium Intl.

Congress on Occupational Therapy, 5th International, Zurich, 1970. Occupational Therapy Today, Tomorrow, Proceedings: Its Present Position & the Possibilities of Development. Binswanger, Rotraut & De Spindler, Irene, eds. 1971. pap. 21.50 (ISBN 3-8055-1223-6). S Karger.

Congress on Perinatal Medicine, 2nd European, London, 1970. Perinatal Medicine: Proceedings. Huntingford, P. J., et al, eds. 1971. 34.25 (ISBN 3-8055-1224-4). S Karger.

Congress on Toxic Nephropathies, 6th, Parma, June 1977. Toxic Nephropathies: Proceedings. Berlyne, G. M., et al, eds. (Contributions to Nephrology: Vol. 10). (Illus.). 1978. 21.00 (ISBN 3-8055-2832-9). S Karger.

Congress Organizing Committee. Electron Microscopy, 1982: Material Sciences, Vol. 2. 1982. 150.00 (ISBN 0-9960099-7-3, Pub. by Wissenschaftliche W Germany). Heyden.

Congress, 75th, 1st Session, House Document No. 360. Technological Trends & National Policy, Including the Social Implications of New Inventions: National Resources Committee, Report of the Subcommittee on Technology. LC 72-5084. (Technology & Society Ser.). (Illus.). 398p. 1972. Repr. of 1937 ed. 30.00 (ISBN 0-405-04732-0). Ayer Co Pubs.

Congressional Information Serivce Staff. CIS U. S. Serial Set Index, Pt. IX, 3 vols. LC 75-27448. 1108p. 1975. Set. 520.00 (ISBN 0-912380-27-6). Cong Info.

Congressional Information Service, Inc. American Statistics Index: A Comprehensive Guide to the Statistical Publications of the U. S. Government, 3 vols. write for info. Cong Info.

Congressional Information Service, Inc. Staff. ASI Annual & Retrospective Edition, 3 vols. LC 73-82599. 2072p. 1974. Set. 490.00 (ISBN 0-912380-16-0). Index Vol (ISBN 0-912380-17-9). Abstract Vol. I (ISBN 0-912380-18-7). Abstract Vol. II (ISBN 0-912380-19-5). Cong Info.

--ASI Annual, 1974, 2 Vols. LC 73-82599. 1393p. 1975. 400.00 set (ISBN 0-912380-23-3). Index Vol (ISBN 0-912380-24-1). Abstract Vol (ISBN 0-912380-25-X). Cong Info.

--ASI Annual, 1975, 2 vols. LC 73-82599. 1776p. 1976. Set. 400.00 (ISBN 0-912380-35-7). Index Vol (ISBN 0-912380-36-5). Abstract Vol (ISBN 0-912380-37-3). Cong Info.

--ASI Annual, 1976, 2 vols. LC 73-82599. 2036p. 1977. Set. 400.00 (ISBN 0-912380-44-6). Index Vol (ISBN 0-912380-45-4). Abstract Vol (ISBN 0-912380-46-2). Cong Info.
--ASI Annual, 1977, 2 vols. LC 73-82599. 2146p. 1978. 490.00 set (ISBN 0-912380-53-5). Index Vol (ISBN 0-912380-54-3). Abstract Vol (ISBN 0-912380-55-1). Cong Info.
--ASI Annual, 1978, 2 vols. LC 73-82599. 2055p. 1979. Set. 490.00 (ISBN 0-912380-64-0). Index Vol (ISBN 0-912380-65-9). Abstract Vol (ISBN 0-912380-66-7). Cong Info.
--ASI Annual, 1979, 2 vols. LC 73-82599. 2085p. 1980. lib. bdg. 525.00 set (ISBN 0-912380-76-4). Index Vol (ISBN 0-912380-77-2). Abstract Vol (ISBN 0-912380-78-0). Cong Info.
--ASI Annual, 1980, 2 vols. LC 73-82599. 2262p. 1981. lib. bdg. 590.00 set (ISBN 0-912380-83-7). Index Vol (ISBN 0-912380-84-5). Abstract Vol (ISBN 0-912380-85-3). Cong Info.
--ASI Annual, 1981, 2 Vols. LC 73-82599. 2241p. 1982. 715.00 set (ISBN 0-912380-95-0). Index Vol (ISBN 0-912380-96-9). Abstract Vol (ISBN 0-912380-97-7). Cong Info.
Congressional Information Service Inc. Staff. ASI Annual, 1982, 2 vols. LC 73-82599. 2188p. 1983. 825.00 (ISBN 0-686-46980-1). Cong Info.
Congressional Information Service, Inc. CIS Federal Register Index. 1984. write for info. Cong Info.
Congressional Information Service, Inc. Staff. CIS Five-Year Cumulative Index: 1970-1974, 2 vols. LC 75-27390. 2465p. 1975. Set. lib. bdg. 385.00 (ISBN 0-912380-28-4). Index Vol. I (ISBN 0-912380-29-2). Index Vol. II (ISBN 0-912380-30-6). Cong Info.
--CIS Four-Year Cumulative Index: 1975-1978, 3 vols. 3363p. 1979. Set. lib. bdg. 655.00 (ISBN 0-912380-69-1). Index Vol. I (ISBN 0-912380-70-5). Index Vol. II (ISBN 0-912380-71-3). Index Vol. III (ISBN 0-912380-72-1). Cong Info.
--CIS Index 1975 Annual, 2 Vols. LC 79-158879. 1819p. 1976. 220.00 set (ISBN 0-912380-32-2). Index Vol (ISBN 0-912380-33-0). Abstract Vol (ISBN 0-912380-34-9). Cong Info.
--CIS Index 1976 Annual, 2 Vols. LC 79-158879. 2089p. 1977. 220.00 set (ISBN 0-912380-41-1). Index Vol (ISBN 0-912380-42-X). Abstract Vol (ISBN 0-912380-43-8). Cong Info.
--CIS Index 1977 Annual, 2 vols. LC 79-158879. 2044p. 1978. Set. 260.00 (ISBN 0-912380-50-0); Index Vol. (ISBN 0-912380-51-9); Abstract Vol. (ISBN 0-912380-52-7). Cong Info.
--CIS Index 1978 Annual, 2 Vols. LC 79-158879. 2246p. 1979. 260.00 set (ISBN 0-912380-60-8). Index Vol (ISBN 0-912380-61-6). Abstract Vol (ISBN 0-912380-62-4). Cong Info.
--CIS Index 1979 Annual, 2 vols. LC 79-158879. 2040p. 1980. lib. bdg. 300.00 set (ISBN 0-912380-73-X). Index Vol (ISBN 0-912380-74-8). Abstract Vol (ISBN 0-912380-75-6). Cong Info.
--CIS Index 1980 Annual, 2 vols. LC 79-158879. 2214p. 1981. lib. bdg. 320.00 set (ISBN 0-912380-80-2). Index Vol (ISBN 0-912380-81-0). Abstract Vol (ISBN 0-912380-82-9). Cong Info.
--CIS Index 1981 Annual, 2 Vols. LC 79-158879. 1927p. 1982. 370.00 set (ISBN 0-912380-92-6). Index Vol (ISBN 0-912380-93-4). Abstract Vol. Cong Info.
--CIS Index 1982 Annual. LC 79-158879. 2042p. 1983. Set. 550.00 (ISBN 0-686-47669-7). Cong Info.
--CIS Online User Guide & Thesaurus. 400p. 1982. loose-leaf guide 75.00 (ISBN 0-912380-98-5). Thesaurus (ISBN 0-912380-99-3). Cong Info.
Congressional Information Service, Inc. CIS U. S. Congressional Committee Hearings Index: Part IV, 74th-78th Congresses (1935-1944) 1985. write for info. Cong Info.
--CIS U. S. Congressional Committee Hearings Index: Part II, 65th-68th Congresses, (Apr. 1917-Mar. 1925) 1984. write for info. Cong Info.
--CIS U. S. Congressional Committee Hearings Index: Part I, 23rd-64th Congresses (ca. 1833-Mar. 1917) 1985. write for info. Cong Info.
Congressional Information Service, Inc. Staff. CIS U. S. Congressional Committee Hearings Index: Pt. VIII, 1965-1969, 5 Vols. 3283p. 1981. Set 1625.00 (ISBN 0-686-84196-4). Cong Info.
--CIS U. S. Congressional Committee Hearings Index: Pt. VII, 1959-1964, 5 Vols. 3357p. 1982. Set 1625.00 (ISBN 0-686-84197-2). Cong Info.
--CIS U. S. Congressional Committee Hearings Index: Part VI, 1953-1958. 3600p. 1982. 1625.00 (ISBN 0-686-43134-0). Cong Info.
Congressional Information Service, Inc. CIS U. S. Congressional Committee Hearings Index: Part V, 1945-1952. 1985. write for info. Cong Info.
Congressional Information Service Inc. Staff. CIS U. S. Congressional Committee Prints Index, 5 vols. LC 80-24837. 3136p. 1980. lib. bdg. 1475.00 Set (ISBN 0-912380-57-8). Cong Info.
Congressional Information Service, Inc. Staff. CIS U. S. Serial Set Index, 36 vols. lib. bdg. 4920.00 set (ISBN 0-912380-26-8). Cong Info.
Congressional Information Service, Inc. CIS U. S. Serial Set Index, Pt. II: 35th-45th Congress (1857-1879) write for info. Cong Info.
Congressional Information Service, Inc. Staff. CIS U. S. Serial Set Index, Pt. I, 3 vols. LC 75-27448. 2668p. 1977. 400.00 (ISBN 0-912380-47-0). Cong Info.
Congressional Information Service, Inc. Directory of Government Document Collections & Librarians. 4th ed. 1984. write for info. Cong Info.
--Index to International Statistics: A Detailed Guide to the Statistical Publications of International Intergovernmental Organizations. 1983. write for info. Cong Info.
--National Statistical Compendiums. write for info. Cong Info.
Congressional Information Service, Inc. Staff, ed. State Constitutional Conventions, Commissions, & Amendments, 1959-78: An Annotated Bibliography. LC 81-3206. 1391p. 1981. lib. bdg. 350.00 (ISBN 0-912380-79-9). Cong Info.
Congressional Information Service, Inc. Staff. Statistical Reference Index Annual, 1980, 2 Vols. 1659p. 1981. lib. bdg. 365.00 (ISBN 0-912380-86-1). Index Vol (ISBN 0-912380-87-X). Abstract Vol (ISBN 0-912380-88-8). Cong Info.
--Statistical Reference Index Annual, 1981, 2 Vols. 1886p. Set 380.00 (ISBN 0-912380-89-6). Index Vol (ISBN 0-912380-90-X). Abstract Vol (ISBN 0-912380-89-6). Cong Info.
Congressional Information Service, Inc. U. S. Reports: The Official Compilation of Supreme Court Decisions & Orders. write for info. Cong Info.
Congressional Information Service Staff. ASI Annual 1983, 2 vols. LC 75-82599. 1984. Set. 890.00 (ISBN 0-88692-020-5). Index Vol (ISBN 0-88692-022-1). Abstracts Vol. Cong Info.
--CIS Four-Year Cumulative Index: 1979-1982, 3 vols. 3958p. 1983. Set. 940.00 (ISBN 0-88692-000-0). Cong Info.
--CIS Index 1970 Annual, 2 vols. LC 79-158879. 1971. Set. write for info. (ISBN 0-912380-00-4); Vol. 1, Index. write for info. (ISBN 0-912380-01-2); Vol. 2, Abstracts. write for info. (ISBN 0-912380-02-0). Cong Info.
--CIS Index 1971 Annual, 2 vols. 1122p. 1972. Set. write for info. (ISBN 0-912380-03-9); Vol. 1, Index. write for info. (ISBN 0-912380-04-7); Vol. 2, Abstracts. write for info. (ISBN 0-912380-05-5). Cong Info.
--CIS Index 1973 Annual, 2 vols. LC 79-158879. 1296p. 1974. Set. write for info (ISBN 0-912380-12-8); Index Vol. write for info. (ISBN 0-912380-13-6); Abstracts Vol. write for info. (ISBN 0-912380-14-4). Cong Info.
--CIS Index 1974 Annual, 2 vols. LC 79-158879. 1507p. 1975. Set. write for info. (ISBN 0-912380-20-9). Index Vol (ISBN 0-912380-21-7). Abstracts Vol (ISBN 0-912380-22-5). Cong Info.
--CIS U. S. Congressional Committee Hearings Index, Pt. III, 6 vols. 1984. Set. 1700.00 (ISBN 0-88692-025-6). Cong Info.
--CIS U. S. Congressional Committee Hearings Index, Pt. VI, 6 vols. 3580p. 1983. Set. 1700.00 (ISBN 0-88692-004-3). Cong Info.
--CIS U. S. Serial Set Index, Pt. III, 3 vols. LC 75-27448. 1641p. 1978. Set. 520.00 (ISBN 0-912380-56-X). Cong Info.
--CIS U. S. Serial Set Index, Pt. IV, 3 vols. LC 75-27448. 1355p. 1978. Set. 520.00 (ISBN 0-912380-58-6). Cong Info.
--CIS U. S. Serial Set Index, Pt. V, 3 vols. LC 75-27448. 983p. 1978. Set. 520.00 (ISBN 0-912380-59-4). Cong Info.
--CIS U. S. Serial Set Index, Pt. VIII, 3 vols. LC 75-27448. 1432p. 1979. Set. 520.00 (ISBN 0-912380-67-5). Cong Info.
--CIS U. S. Serial Set Index, Pt. VII, 3 vols. LC 75-27448. 1103p. 1979. Set. 520.00 (ISBN 0-912380-68-3). Cong Info.
--CIS U. S. Serial Set Index, Pt. X, 3 vols. LC 75-27448. 2018p. 1976. Set. 520.00 (ISBN 0-912380-31-4). Cong Info.
--CIS U. S. Serial Set Index, Pt. XI, 3 vols. LC 75-27448. 2159p. 1976. Set. 520.00. Cong Info.
--CIS U. S. Serial Set Index, Pt. XII, 3 vols. LC 75-27448. 1519p. 1976. Set. 520.00 (ISBN 0-912380-40-3). Cong Info.
--Complete Guide to Citing Government Documents. LC 84-11357. 154p. 1984. 12.95 (ISBN 0-88692-023-X). Cong Info.
--Directory of Government Documents, 1984: Collections & Librarians. 4th ed. write for info. (ISBN 0-88692-024-8). Cong Info.
--IIS 1983 Annual, 2 vols. 1095p. 1984. Set. 350.00 (ISBN 0-88692-011-6). Index Vol (ISBN 0-88692-013-2). Abstracts Vol (ISBN 0-88692-012-4). Cong Info.
--Statistical Reference Index Annual 1983, 2 vols. 1883p. 1984. Set. 480.00 (ISBN 0-88692-014-0). Index Vol (ISBN 0-88692-016-7). Abstracts Vol (ISBN 0-88692-015-9). Cong Info.
Congressional Information Services, Inc. Index to the Code of Federal Regulations, 1977. LC 78-379. (Orig.). 1981. pap. text ed. write for info. (ISBN 0-89847-007-2). Cong Info.
Congressional Informational Service Staff. CIS Index 1983 Annual, 2 vols. LC 79-158879. 1986p. 1984. Set. 600.00 (ISBN 0-88692-017-5). Index Vol. Abstracts Vol. Cong Info.
--CIS U. S. Serial Set Index, Pt. VI, 3 vols. LC 75-27448. 1354p. 1979. Set. 520.00 (ISBN 0-912380-63-2). Cong Info.
Congressional Office of Technology Assessment. The Direct Use of Coal: Prospects & Problems of Production & Combustion. 432p. 1981. prof ref. 35.00x (ISBN 0-88410-648-9). Ballinger Pub.
--Energy from Biological Processes: Technical & Environmental Analyses. 248p. 1981. prof ref 35.00x (ISBN 0-88410-647-0). Ballinger Pub.
Congressional Quarterly Inc. Advances in Science. LC 78-25601. (Editorial Research Reports). 188p. 1979. pap. 7.95 (ISBN 0-87187-142-4). Congr Quarterly.
Congressional Quarterly, Inc. America in the 1980's. LC 79-25320. (Editorial Research Reports Ser.). 186p. 1980. pap. 7.95 (ISBN 0-87187-194-7). Congr Quarterly.
Congressional Quarterly Inc. America Votes, Vol. 15. LC 56-10132. 404p. 1983. 75.00 (ISBN 0-87187-265-X). Congr Quarterly.
--American Regionalism: Our Economic, Cultural & Political Makeup. LC 80-18934. (Editorial Research Reports). 199p. 1980. pap. 7.95 (ISBN 0-87187-156-4). Congr Quarterly.
--America's Needy: Care & Cutbacks - LC 84-4359. 1984. 9.25 (ISBN 0-87187-322-2). Congr Quarterly.
--Changing American Family. LC 79-12753. (Editorial Research Reports). 207p. 1979. pap. 7.95 (ISBN 0-87187-149-1). Congr Quarterly.
--Congressional Districts in the 1980's. LC 83-18988. 650p. 1983. 95.00 (ISBN 0-87187-264-1). Congr Quarterly.
--Congressional Quarterly Almanac: 1978. (Almanac Ser.). 1979. 82.00 (ISBN 0-87187-141-6). Congr Quarterly.
--Congressional Quarterly Almanac, 1979. (Almanac Ser.). 1980. 82.00 (ISBN 0-87187-192-0). Congr Quarterly.
--Congressional Quarterly Almanac: 1981. LC 47-41081. 1043p. 1982. 105.00 (ISBN 0-87187-231-5). Congr Quarterly.
--Congressional Quarterly Almanac: 1982. LC 47-41081. 1040p. 1983. 115.00 (ISBN 0-87187-251-X). Congr Quarterly.
--Congressional Quarterly Almanac, 1984. 1000p. 1985. pap. 135.00 (ISBN 0-87187-346-X). Congr Quarterly.
--Congressional Quarterly Service. 1983. Annual subscription. 756.00 (ISBN 0-686-89358-1); Editorial Rights. annually 240.00 (ISBN 0-686-89359-X). Congr Quarterly.
--Congressional Roll Call, 1976. LC 72-77849. 1977. pap. text ed. 12.00 (ISBN 0-87187-106-8). Congr Quarterly.
--Congressional Roll Call, 1977. LC 72-77849. 1977. pap. text ed. 12.00 (ISBN 0-87187-121-1). Congr Quarterly.
--Congressional Roll Call, 1978. 1979. pap. text ed. 12.00 (ISBN 0-87187-146-7). Congr Quarterly.
--Congressional Roll Call 1979. (Roll Call Ser.). 1980. pap. text ed. 12.00 (ISBN 0-87187-191-2). Congr Quarterly.
--Congressional Roll Call, 1980: A Chronology & Analysis of Notes in the House & Senate. 320p. (Orig.). 1981. pap. 12.95 (ISBN 0-87187-168-8). Congr Quarterly.
--Congressional Roll Call, 1982. LC 82-77849. 272p. 1983. pap. 13.95 (ISBN 0-87187-252-8). Congr Quarterly.
--Dollar Politics. 3rd ed. LC 81-19572. 163p. 1982. pap. 9.75 (ISBN 0-87187-220-X). Congr Quarterly.
--Editorial Research Reports, 2 Vols. 1983. Vol. I: 1983, 800p. write for info. (ISBN 0-87187-273-0); Vol. II: 1982, 972p. 75.00 (ISBN 0-87187-271-4). Congr Quarterly.
--Editorial Research Reports, Vol. II: 1984. 1985. 75.00 (ISBN 0-87187-354-0). Congr Quarterly.
--Education in America: Quality vs. Cost. LC 81-12621. (Editorial Research Reports Ser.). 202p. 1981. pap. 8.95 (ISBN 0-87187-212-9). Congr Quarterly.
Congressional Quarterly, Inc. Elections, 1982. LC 82-2347. 104p. (Orig.). 1982. pap. 9.25 (ISBN 0-87187-228-5). Congr Quarterly.
Congressional Quarterly Inc. Employment in America. LC 83-10131. 208p. 1983. pap. 9.95 (ISBN 0-87187-272-2). Congr Quarterly.
--Energy Issues: New Directions & Goals. LC 82-2523. (Editorial Research Reports Ser.). 204p. 1982. pap. 9.25 (ISBN 0-87187-234-X). Congr Quarterly.
--Energy Policy. 2nd ed. LC 81-1225. 274p. 1981. pap. 10.25 (ISBN 0-87187-167-X). Congr Quarterly.
--Environment & Health. LC 81-15155. 227p. 1981. pap. 10.25 (ISBN 0-87187-224-2). Congr Quarterly.
--Environmental Issues: Prospects & Problems. LC 82-4975. (Editorial Research Reports Ser.). 161p. 1982. pap. 9.25 (ISBN 0-87187-238-2). Congr Quarterly.
--Farm Policy: The Politics of Soil, Surpluses, & Subsidies. 179p. 1984. pap. 9.95 (ISBN 0-87187-286-2). Congr Quarterly.
--Federal Regulatory Directory: 1983-1984. LC 79-644368. 893p. 1983. 35.95 (ISBN 0-87187-250-1). Congr Quarterly.
--Going Public: New Strategies of Presidential Leadership. 220p. 1985. 14.95 (ISBN 0-87187-382-6); pap. 10.95 (ISBN 0-87187-381-8). Congr Quarterly.
--Guide to Congress. 3rd ed. LC 82-14148. 1185p. 1982. 100.00 (ISBN 0-87187-239-0). Congr Quarterly.
--Guide to Current American Government, Fall 1980. 190p. 1980. pap. text ed. 6.95 (ISBN 0-87187-151-3). Congr Quarterly.
--Guide to Current American Government, Fall 1981. 167p. 1981. pap. text ed. 6.75 (ISBN 0-87187-209-9). Congr Quarterly.
--Guide to Current American Government: Fall 1983. LC 61-16893. 156p. 1983. pap. 8.95 (ISBN 0-87187-261-7). Congr Quarterly.
--Guide to Current American Government, Spring 1982. 167p. 1981. pap. text ed. 6.75 (ISBN 0-87187-219-6). Congr Quarterly.
--Guide to Current American Government: Spring 1983. LC 61-16893. 156p. 1982. pap. 7.95 (ISBN 0-87187-245-5). Congr Quarterly.
--Guide to Current American Government: Spring 1984. LC 61-16893. 164p. 1983. pap. 8.95 (ISBN 0-87187-267-6). Congr Quarterly.
--Guide to Current American Government: Spring 1985. 164p. 1984. pap. 8.95 (ISBN 0-87187-326-5). Congr Quarterly.
--Guide to Current American Government: Spring 1981 Edition. 160p. 1980. pap. text ed. 6.95 (ISBN 0-87187-159-9). Congr Quarterly.
--Guide to the U. S. Supreme Court. LC 79-20210. 1022p. 1979. 95.00 (ISBN 0-87187-184-X). Congr Quarterly.
--Guide to U. S. Elections. 2nd ed. LC 75-659. 1200p. 1985. 100.00 (ISBN 0-87187-339-7). Congr Quarterly.
Congressional Quarterly, Inc. Historic Documents, Vols. 1-5. 1973-77. 65.00 ea. Vol. 1: 1972, 987p (ISBN 0-87187-043-6). Vol. 2: 1973, 1020p (ISBN 0-87187-054-1). Vol. 3: 1974, 982p (ISBN 0-87187-069-X). Vol. 4: 1975, 982p (ISBN 0-87187-090-8). Vol. 5: 1976, 1003p (ISBN 0-87187-103-3). Congr Quarterly.
Congressional Quarterly Inc. Historic Documents: 1982, Vol. XI. LC 72-97888. 1000p. 1983. 65.00 (ISBN 0-87187-257-9). Congr Quarterly.
--Historic Documents 1984. LC 85-6912. 1000p. 1985. 69.00 (ISBN 0-87187-324-9). Congr Quarterly.
--How Congress Works. LC 83-5244. (Illus.). 219p. 1983. pap. 10.50 (ISBN 0-87187-254-4). Congr Quarterly.
--Jobs for Americans. LC 77-18994. (Editorial Research Reports). 189p. 1978. pap. 7.95 (ISBN 0-87187-120-3). Congr Quarterly.
--Members of Congress since 1789. 3rd ed. LC 84-27504. 192p. 1985. pap. 9.95 (ISBN 0-87187-335-4). Congr Quarterly.
--Middle East. 5th ed. LC 81-15206. 275p. (Orig.). 1981. pap. 10.50 (ISBN 0-87187-211-0). Congr Quarterly.
--National Health Issues. LC 77-12770. (Editorial Research Reports Ser.). 207p. 1977. pap. 7.95 (ISBN 0-87187-118-1). Congr Quarterly.
--Ninety-Ninth Congress Committees 1985-86. LC 85-12786. 114p. 1985. pap. 9.25 (ISBN 0-87187-351-6). Congr Quarterly.
Congressional Quarterly, Inc. Origins & Development of Congress. 2nd ed. LC 82-7372. 346p. 1982. pap. 9.50 (ISBN 0-87187-235-8). Congr Quarterly.
Congressional Quarterly Inc. Powers of Congress. 2nd ed. LC 82-14331. 380p. 1982. pap. 9.50 (ISBN 0-87187-242-0). Congr Quarterly.
--President Carter, 1980. LC 81-3255. 187p. (Orig.). 1981. pap. 7.95 (ISBN 0-87187-206-4). Congr Quarterly.
--President Reagan. LC 81-2283. (Presidency Ser.). 123p. (Orig.). 1981. pap. 8.95 (ISBN 0-87187-172-6). Congr Quarterly.
--Presidential Elections since 1789. 3rd ed. LC 83-1864. 211p. 1983. pap. 10.25 (ISBN 0-87187-268-4). Congr Quarterly.
--The Public's Right to Know. LC 80-20610. (Editorial Research Reports). 187p. 1980. pap. 7.95 (ISBN 0-87187-157-2). Congr Quarterly.
--Reagan: The Next Four Years. 168p. 1985. pap. 9.95 (ISBN 0-87187-352-4). Congr Quarterly.
--Regulation: Process & Politics. LC 82-14292. 184p. 1982. pap. 9.95 (ISBN 0-87187-243-9). Congr Quarterly.
--The Rights Revolution. LC 78-31931. (Editorial Research Reports). 217p. 1979. pap. 7.95 (ISBN 0-87187-144-0). Congr Quarterly.
--Roll Call 1983. 296p. 1984. pap. 13.95 (ISBN 0-87187-313-3). Congr Quarterly.
--Social Security & Retirement: Private Goals & Public Policy. LC 83-14349. 246p. 1983. 9.95 (ISBN 0-87187-274-9). Congr Quarterly.
Congressional Quarterly, Inc. Soviet Union. LC 82-2408. 280p. (Orig.). 1982. pap. 10.50 (ISBN 0-87187-232-3). Congr Quarterly.
--State Politics & Redistricting, 2 Pts. LC 82-7261. (Orig.). 1982. Pt. I, 199 pp., Pt. II, 231pp. pap. 16.00 set (ISBN 0-87187-233-1). Congr Quarterly.
Congressional Quarterly Inc. Supreme Court & Individual Rights. LC 79-26967. 303p. (Orig.). 1980. pap. 10.50 (ISBN 0-87187-195-5). Congr Quarterly.

--Supreme Court, Justice & the Law. 3rd ed. LC 83-2120. 194p. 1983. pap. 10.50 (ISBN 0-87187-253-6). Congr Quarterly.

--U. S. Defense Policy. 3rd ed. LC 83-7555. 248p. 1983. pap. 10.50 (ISBN 0-87187-258-7). Congr Quarterly.

--Washington Information Directory, 1984-85. LC 75-646321. 902p. 1984. 35.95 (ISBN 0-87187-295-1). Congr Quarterly.

--Washington Information Directory, 1985-86. LC 75-646321. 900p. 1985. 39.95 (ISBN 0-87187-340-0). Congr Quarterly.

--The Washington Lobby. 4th ed. LC 82-12525. 179p. 1982. pap. 10.25 (ISBN 0-87187-240-4). Congr Quarterly.

--Youth Problems. LC 82-18222. (Editorial Research Reports Ser.). 176p. 1982. pap. 9.25 (ISBN 0-87187-244-7). Congr Quarterly.

Congressional Quarterly Inc. & Beyle, Thad L. State Government: CQ's Guide to Current Issues & Activities 1985-1986. 218p. 1985. pap. 8.95 (ISBN 0-87187-353-2). Congr Quarterly.

Congressional Quarterly Inc., ed. America Votes, Vol. 14. LC 56-10132. 427p. 1981. 75.00 (ISBN 0-87187-218-8). Congr Quarterly.

--Budgeting for America. LC 81-17376. 227p. (Orig.). 1982. pap. 9.75 (ISBN 0-87187-214-5). Congr Quarterly.

--China: U. S. Policy since 1945. LC 79-27840. 387p. (Orig.). 1980. pap. 12.95 (ISBN 0-87187-188-2). Congr Quarterly.

--Congress & the Nation: 1977-1980, Vol. 5. 1240p. 1981. 95.00 (ISBN 0-87187-216-1). Congr Quarterly.

--Congressional Quarterly Almanac, 1980. (Almanac Ser.). 1000p. 1981. 96.00 (ISBN 0-87187-170-X). Congr Quarterly.

--Consumer Protection: Gains & Setbacks. LC 78-2927. 209p. 1978. pap. 7.95 (ISBN 0-87187-130-0). Congr Quarterly.

Congressional Quarterly Inc., ed. see Arrandale, Thomas.

Congressional Quarterly Inc. Staff. America Votes Sixteen. 400p. 1985. 85.00 (ISBN 0-87187-380-X). Congr Quarterly.

--A Different Justice: Reagan & the Supreme Court. 220p. 1985. 10.50 (ISBN 0-87187-367-2). Congr Quarterly.

--Energy & Environment: The Unfinished Business. 180p. 1985. 9.95 (ISBN 0-87187-360-5). Congr Quarterly.

--U. S. Foreign Policy: The Reagan Imprint. 180p. 1985. pap. 10.95 (ISBN 0-87187-366-4). Congr Quarterly.

Congressional Quarterly Press Staff. Roll Call 1984. 225p. 1985. pap. 13.95 (ISBN 0-87187-347-8). Congr Quarterly.

Congressional Quarterly Service. Congress & the Nation, 4 vols. Incl. Vol. 1: 1945-1964. 2015p. 1965. 95.00 (ISBN 0-685-28880-3); Vol. 2: 1965-1968. 1120p. 1969. 95.00 (ISBN 0-87187-004-5); Vol. 3, 1969-1972. 1178p. 1973. 95.00 (ISBN 0-87187-055-X); Vol. 4, 1972-1976. 1217p. 1977. 95.00 (ISBN 0-87187-112-2). LC 65-22351. Congr Quarterly.

Congressional Quarterly Staff. Congress & the Nation VI. LC 65-22351. 1000p. 1985. 110.00 (ISBN 0-87187-334-6). Congr Quarterly.

--Congressional Quarterly Almanac, 1977. (Almanac Ser.). 1977. 82.00 (ISBN 0-87187-123-8). Congr Quarterly.

--Current American Government, Fall 1985. LC 61-16893. 164p. 1985. pap. 8.95 (ISBN 0-87187-379-6). Congr Quarterly.

--Guide to U. S. Elections. LC 75-659. 1103p. 1975. 60.00 (ISBN 0-87187-072-X). Congr Quarterly.

Congressional Research Service, ed. Major Studies & Issue Briefs of the Congressional Research Service: 1916-1981. 1974. 490.00 (ISBN 0-89093-405-3). U Pubns Amer.

Congresso Internazionale di Linguistica e Filologia Romanza, 14th Napoli, 15-20 Aprile 1974. Atti, Vol. 3. Varvaro, Alberto, ed. 561p. 1980. pap. text ed. 70.00x (ISBN 90-272-0944-8). Humanities.

Congresso Internazionale di Linguistica e Filologia Romanza, 14th, Napole, 15-20 April 1974. Atti: Proceedings, Vols. 1, 2 & 4. Vavaro, Alberto, ed. (Orig.). 1979. pap. text ed. 70.00x ea. Vol. 1 (ISBN 90-272-0942-1). Vol. 2 (ISBN 90-272-0943-X). Vol. 4 (ISBN 90-272-0945-6). Humanities.

Congreve, Carola, tr. see Van Lysebeth, Andre.

Congreve, Lillian. The Way of the World. Gibbons, Brian, ed. (New Mermaid Ser.). 1976. pap. 5.95x (ISBN 0-393-90004-5). Norton.

Congreve, Richard, tr. see Comte, Auguste.

Congreve, William. Amendments of Mr. Collier's False & Imperfect Citations: From the Old Batchelour, Double Dealer, Love for Love, Mourning Bride, Vol. 23. LC 73-170439. (The English Stage Ser.). lib. bdg. 61.00 (ISBN 0-8240-0606-2). Garland Pub.

--The Comedies of William Congreve: The Old Bachelor, the Double Dealer, Love for Love, the Way of the World. Henderson, Anthony, ed. LC 82-1182. (Plays by Renaissance & Restoration Dramatists Ser.). 407p. 1982. 42.50 (ISBN 0-521-24747-0); pap. 14.95 (ISBN 0-521-28932-7). Cambridge U Pr.

--Complete Plays of William Congreve. Davis, Herbert, ed. LC 66-20598. 1967. 35.00x (ISBN 0-226-11485-6). U of Chicago Pr.

--Love for Love. Kelsall, Malcolm, ed. (New Mermaid Ser.). 1976. pap. 2.95x (ISBN 0-393-90003-7). Norton.

--Love for Love. Avery, Emmett L., ed. LC 66-20827. (Regents Restoration Drama Ser). xviii, 147p. 1966. 14.50x (ISBN 0-8032-0353-5); pap. 3.95x (ISBN 0-8032-5353-2, BB 259, Bison). U of Nebr Pr.

--The Way of the World. Perry, Henry T., ed. LC 51-6756. (Crofts Classics Ser.). 1951. pap. text ed. 3.75x (ISBN 0-88295-024-X). Harlan Davidson.

--The Way of the World. Lynch, Kathleen M., ed. LC 65-10543. (Regents Restoration Drama Ser.). xxii, 136p. 1965. 13.50x (ISBN 0-8032-0354-3); pap. 3.50x (ISBN 0-8032-5354-0, BB 251, Bison). U of Nebr Pr.

Congreve, William see Harris, Brice.

Congreve, William see Wilson, John H.

Congwen, Shen. Border Town & Other Stories. 1981. pap. 2.50 (ISBN 0-8351-0852-X). China Bks.

Conheim, Cathy, jt. auth. see Carmody, Leie.

Coni, N., et al. Aids to Prescribing. 144p. 1983. pap. text ed. 12.95 (ISBN 0-632-00599-8, B1041-9). Mosby.

Coni, Nicholas, et al. Ageing: The Facts. 205p. 1984. 13.95x (ISBN 0-19-261429-0). Oxford U Pr.

Coniaris, A. Gems from the Sunday Gospel Lessons in the Orthodox Church, Vol. II. pap. 5.95 (ISBN 0-937032-13-1). Light&Life Pub Co MN.

--Gems from the Sunday Gospel Lessons in the Orthodox Church, Vol. I. 1975. pap. 5.95 (ISBN 0-937032-12-3). Light&Life Pub Co MN.

--Getting Ready for Marriage in the Orthodox Church. 1972. pap. 1.25 (ISBN 0-937032-11-5). Light&Life Pub Co MN.

--Sermons on the Major Holy Days of the Orthodox Church. 1978. pap. 5.95 (ISBN 0-937032-10-7). Light&Life Pub Co MN.

--Sixty-One Talks for Orthodox Funerals. 1969. pap. 4.95 (ISBN 0-937032-02-6). Light&Life Pub Co MN.

Coniaris, A. M. Christ's Comfort for Those Who Sorrow. 1978. pap. 3.95 (ISBN 0-937032-00-X). Light&Life Pub Co MN.

--Eastern Orthodoxy: A Way of Life. 1966. pap. 5.95 (ISBN 0-937032-14-X). Light&Life Pub Co MN.

--Eighty Talks for Orthodox Young People. 1975. pap. 4.50 (ISBN 0-937032-16-6). Light&Life Pub Co MN.

--God Speaks from the Cross. 1984. pap. 4.95 (ISBN 0-937032-33-6). Light&Life Pub Co MN.

--The Great I Came's of Jesus. 1980. pap. 7.95 (ISBN 0-686-27069-X). Light&Life Pub Co MN.

--Introducing the Orthodox Church. 1982. pap. 7.95. Light&Life Pub Co MN.

--Making God Real in the Orthodox Christian Home. 1977. pap. 5.95 (ISBN 0-937032-07-7). Light&Life Pub Co MN.

--The Message of the Sunday Gospel Readings, Vol. 1. 1982. pap. 6.95 (ISBN 0-937032-26-3). Light&Life Pub Co MN.

--The Message of the Sunday Gospels, Vol. 2. 1983. pap. 6.95 (ISBN 0-937032-29-8). Light&Life Pub Co MN.

--No Man Ever Spoke As This Man. 1969. pap. 4.50 (ISBN 0-937032-18-2). Light&Life Pub Co MN.

--Orthodoxy: A Creed for Today. 1972. pap. 6.95 (ISBN 0-937032-19-0). Light&Life Pub Co MN.

--Perspectives on Living the Orthodox Faith. 1985. pap. 7.95 (ISBN 0-937032-36-0). Light&Life Pub Co MN.

--These Are the Sacraments. 1981. pap. 6.95 (ISBN 0-937032-22-0). Light&Life Pub Co MN.

--Treasures from Paul's Letters, Vol. I. 1978. pap. 6.95 (ISBN 0-937032-05-0). Light&Life Pub Co MN.

--Treasures from Paul's Letters, Vol. II. 1979. pap. 6.95 (ISBN 0-937032-06-9). Light&Life Pub Co MN.

--Where Moth & Rust Do Not Consume. 1983. pap. 5.95 (ISBN 0-937032-30-1). Light&Life Pub Co MN.

Coniff, Milton. Meet Burma. Chadbourne, Bill, ed. LC 77-75669. (Milton Coniff's Terry & the Pirates Ser.: Vol. 3). (Illus.). 1977. pap. 6.95 (ISBN 0-87897-015-0). Nostalgia Pr.

Coniker, Jerome F. Devotions & Prayers in Honor of St. Joseph. (Living Meditation & Prayer Bklt. Library). (Illus.). 34p. (Orig.). 1978. pap. text ed. 2.50 (ISBN 0-932406-04-1). AFC.

--Peaceful Seed Living, Vols. 1 & 2. 2nd ed. LC 78-66369. (Living Meditation & Prayerbook Ser.). (Illus.). 156p. 1981. pap. text ed. 3.00 ea. (ISBN 0-932406-00-9). AFC.

--Prayers & Recommended Practices. 2nd ed. LC 78-66374. (Living Meditation & Prayerbook Ser.). (Illus.). 91p. pap. text ed. 3.00 (ISBN 0-932406-01-7). AFC.

Coniker, Jerome F., ed. see Seeley, Burns K.

Conil, Jean & Franklin, Fay. Cuisine Vegetarienne Francaise. (Illus.). 192p. 1985. pap. 12.95 (ISBN 0-7225-1070-5). Thorsons Pubs.

Coningsby, W., jt. auth. see Day-Lewis, J.

Coninx, Raymond G. Foreign Exchange Dealer's Manual. 168p. 1983. 50.00x (ISBN 0-85941-152-4, Pub. by Woodhead-Faulkner England). State Mutual Bk.

--Foreign Exchange Today. rev. ed. 171p. 1980. 24.95x (ISBN 0-470-27025-X). Halsted Pr.

Conisbee, L. R. A List of Names Proposed for Genera & Subgenera of Recent Mammals from the Publication of T. S. Palmer's Index Generum Mammalium 1904 to the End of 1951. 110p. 1953. 11.00x (ISBN 0-565-00210-4). Sabbot-Natural Hist Bks.

Conisbee, Philip. Chardin. LC 84-23259. (Illus.). 240p. 1985. 55.00 (ISBN 0-8387-5091-5). Bucknell U Pr.

--Paintings in Eighteenth-Century France. LC 81-66151. 224p. 1981. 60.00x (ISBN 0-8014-1424-5). Cornell U Pr.

Conk, Margo A. The United States Census & Labor Force Change: A History of Occupation Statistics, 1870-1940. Berkhofer, Robert, ed. LC 79-28085. (Studies in American History & Culture: No. 11). 240p. 1980. 39.95 (ISBN 0-8357-1078-5). UMI Res Pr.

Conkey, Kathleen. The Postal Precipice: Can the U. S. Postal Service Be Saved. 515p. 1983. pap. text ed. 30.00 (ISBN 0-936758-09-0). Ctr Responsive Law.

Conkin, Barbara M. & Conkin, James E. Stratigraphy: Foundation & Concepts. 1984. 45.00 (ISBN 0-442-21747-1). Van Nos Reinhold.

Conkin, James E., jt. auth. see Conkin, Barbara M.

Conkin, Paul K. American Christianity in Crisis. LC 81-80738. (Charles Edmondson Historical Lectures Ser.). 48p. (Orig.). 1981. pap. 4.50 (ISBN 0-918954-24-X). Baylor Univ Pr.

--Gone with the Ivy: A Biography of Vanderbilt University. LC 84-19714. 824p. 1985. 49.50x (ISBN 0-87049-452-X). U Of Tenn Pr.

--New Deal. 2nd ed. LC 75-1148. (American History Ser.). (Illus.). 1975. pap. 5.95x (ISBN 0-88295-722-8). Harlan Davidson.

--Prophets of Prosperity: America's First Political Economists. LC 79-3251. 352p. 1980. 25.00x (ISBN 0-253-30843-7). Ind U Pr.

--Puritans & Pragmatists: Eight Eminent American Thinkers. LC 75-34730. (Midland Bks.: No. 197). 512p. 1976. 20.00x (ISBN 0-253-34720-3); pap. 6.95x (ISBN 0-253-20197-7). Ind U Pr.

--Self-Evident Truths: Being a Discourse on the Origins & Development of the First Principles of American Government. LC 73-16525. (Midland Bks.: No. 198). 228p. 1974. pap. 6.95x (ISBN 0-253-20198-5). Ind U Pr.

--Two Paths to Utopia: The Hutterites & the Llano Colony. LC 83-16639. viii, 212p. 1983. Repr. of 1964 ed. lib. bdg. 27.50x (ISBN 0-313-24248-8, C0TP). Greenwood.

Conkin, Paul K., jt. ed. see Hargrove, Erwin C.

Conkin, Paul K., jt. ed. see Highan, John.

Conkis, William T. The Complete Collection of the Original Herbal Manuscript. 169p. 1982. pap. 7.95 (ISBN 0-943638-00-3). Herbal Perception.

--The Electrical Technical Man. Date not set. price not set. Herbal Perception.

Conkle, E. P. No Time for Heaven. 76p. 1955. pap. 2.75 (ISBN 0-88680-140-0); royalty 35.00 (ISBN 0-317-03590-8). I E Clark.

--No Time for Heaven. (Illus.). 107p. (Director's Production Script). 1955. pap. 10.00 (ISBN 0-88680-141-9). I E Clark.

Conklin, Agnes M. Failure of Highly Intelligent Pupils: A Study of Their Behavior by Means of the Control Group. LC 76-176666. (Columbia University. Teachers College. Contributions to Education Ser.: No. 792). Repr. of 1940 ed. 22.50 (ISBN 0-404-55792-9). AMS Pr.

Conklin, Barbara. Goodbye, Forever. (Sweet Dreams Ser.: No. 72). 144p. (Orig.). (YA) 1984. pap. 2.25 (ISBN 0-553-24356-X). Bantam.

--I Believe in You. (Sweet Dreams Ser.: No. 67). 160p. (Orig.). 1984. pap. 2.25 (ISBN 0-553-24180-X). Bantam.

--P. S. I Love You. (Teenage Romance Ser.). (Orig.). 1981. pap. 2.25 (ISBN 0-553-24460-4). Bantam.

--The Summer Jenny Fell in Love. (Sweet Dreams Ser.). 1982. pap. 2.25 (ISBN 0-553-24333-0). Bantam.

Conklin, Cathleen. St. Nicholas. (Illus.). Date not set. pap. 11.95 (ISBN 0-915520-82-6). Ross-Erikson.

Conklin, Dick. PC Graphics: Charts, Graphs, Games, & Art on the IBM-PC. LC 83-5797. (IBM Personal Computer Ser.). 182p. 1983. pap. text ed. 15.95 (ISBN 0-471-89207-6, 1-646, Pub. by Wiley Pr); book & program disk 40.90 (ISBN 0-471-88541-X). Wiley.

Conklin, Dick & Schwaderer, David. The IBM PCjr Book. 382p. 1985. pap. 14.95 (ISBN 0-471-81192-0, Pub. by Wiley Pr). Wiley.

Conklin, Edmund S. Three Diagnostic Scorings for the Thurstone Personality Schedule. LC 37-28256. (Science Ser.: No. 6). 1937. pap. 20.00 (ISBN 0-317-08001-6, 2055229). Bks Demand UMI.

Conklin, Edwin G. Heredity & Environment in the Development of Men. 6th rev. ed. (Illus.). 1930. 28.00 (ISBN 0-384-09755-3). Johnson Repr.

--Heredity & Environment in the Development of Men. 533p. 1984. Repr. of 1915 ed. lib. bdg. 45.00 (ISBN 0-89984-025-6). Century Bookbindery.

Conklin, G. D. The Laws Regulating Human Development & The Role of Inheritance in the Growth of Man. (Illus.). 166p. 1984. 88.75 (ISBN 0-89266-484-3). Am Classical Coll Pr.

Conklin, George. Conklin's Vest-Pocket Argument Settler: 1914 Edition. 1981. 4.95 (ISBN 0-8065-0788-8). Citadel Pr.

Conklin, Gladys. I Watch Flies. LC 76-26532. (Illus.). 32p. (gr. 1-4). 1977. reinforced bdg 6.95 (ISBN 0-8234-0290-8). Holiday.

--Praying Mantis: The Garden Dinosaur. LC 77-27007. (Illus.). 32p. (gr. k-3). 1978. reinforced bdg. 6.95 (ISBN 0-8234-0323-8). Holiday.

--Tarantula, the Giant Spider. LC 72-75596. (Illus.). 32p. (gr. k-3). 1972. reinforced bdg. 6.95 (ISBN 0-8234-0208-8). Holiday.

--When Insects Are Babies. (Illus.). 40p. (gr. k-3). 1969. reinforced bdg. 7.95 (ISBN 0-8234-0134-0). Holiday.

Conklin, Groff, ed. Great Science Fiction by Scientists. (Orig.). 1962. pap. 2.95 (ISBN 0-02-019030-1, Collier). Macmillan.

--Science Fiction Thinking Machines. LC 54-6995. 1954. 8.95 (ISBN 0-8149-0040-2). Vanguard.

--Treasury of Science Fiction. 6.98 (ISBN 0-517-30618-2). Outlet Bk Co.

Conklin, Groff, jt. ed. see Asimov, Isaac.

Conklin, Harold C. Ethnographic Atlas of Ifugao. LC 79-689774. (Illus.). 124p. 1980. text ed. 100.00x (ISBN 0-300-02529-7). Yale U Pr.

--Folk Classification: A Topically Arranged Bibliography of Contemporary & Background References Through 1971. rev. ed. LC 80-80582. 521p. 1980. pap. text ed. 8.50 (ISBN 0-913516-02-3). Yale U Anthro.

--Hanunoo Agriculture: A Report on an Integral System of Shifting Cultivation in the Phillipines FAO Forestry Development Paper No. 12. LC 75-28745. (Illus.). 209p. 1975. text ed. 19.50x scholars (ISBN 0-911830-22-7); pap. 29.50x institutions (ISBN 0-685-69785-1). Elliots Bks.

--Ifugao Bibliography. LC 68-29881. (Bibliography Ser.: No. 11). vi, 75p. 1968. 5.50x (ISBN 0-938692-18-6). Yale U SE Asia.

Conklin, Henry. Through Poverty's Vale: A Hardscrabble Boyhood in Upstate New York, 1832-1862. Tripp, Wendell, ed. LC 73-19980. (Illus.). 280p. 1974. 8.50 (ISBN 0-8156-0098-4); pap. 5.95 (ISBN 0-8156-0117-4). Syracuse U Pr.

Conklin, John. Introduction to Criminology. 1981. text ed. write for info. (ISBN 0-02-324180-2). Macmillan.

Conklin, John E. Criminology. 2nd ed. 923p. 1986. text ed. price not set (ISBN 0-02-323790-2). Macmillan.

--Sociology: An Introduction. 656p. 1984. text ed. write for info. (ISBN 0-02-324190-X). Macmillan.

Conklin, Les. Betting Horses to Win. pap. 3.00 (ISBN 0-87980-265-0). Wilshire.

--Payday at the Races. pap. 3.00 (ISBN 0-87980-269-3). Wilshire.

Conklin, Lynn, jt. auth. see Moore, Elaine.

Conklin, Marie E. Genetic & Biochemical Aspects of the Development of Datura. Wolsky, A., ed. (Monographs in Developmental Biology: Vol. 12). (Illus.). 170p. 1976. 32.00 (ISBN 3-8055-2307-6). S Karger.

Conklin, Mike. Inside Football. 114p. 1978. pap. 7.95 (ISBN 0-8092-7585-6). Contemp Bks.

Conklin, Mike, jt. auth. see Sands, Bill.

Conklin, Mike, jt. auth. see Zolna, Ed.

Conklin, Nancy, jt. auth. see Lourie, Margaret.

Conklin, Paul. Tomorrow a New World. (FDR & the Era of the New Deal Ser.). 1976. Repr. of 1959 ed. lib. bdg. 39.50 (ISBN 0-306-70805-1). Da Capo.

Conklin, Robert. How to Get People to Do Things. 1982. pap. 2.50 (ISBN 0-345-28752-5). Ballantine.

--How to Get People to Do Things. 192p. 1979. 11.95 (ISBN 0-8092-7358-6). Contemp Bks.

Conklin, W. E. In Defense of Fundamental Rights. 326p. 1979. 57.50x (ISBN 90-286-0389-1). Sijthoff & Noordhoff.

Conklin, William A. Nature's Art: The Inner & Outer Dimensions of the Shell. (Illus.). 160p. 1985. 35.00 (ISBN 0-87249-467-5). U of SC Pr.

Conkling. Chemistry & Pyrotechnics: Basic Principles & Theory. 216p. 1985. 49.75 (ISBN 0-8247-7443-4). Dekker.

Conkling, Alfred. Treatise on the Organization, Jurisdiction & Practice of the Courts of the U. S., to Which Is Added an Appendix. LC 85-80031. 1985. Repr. of 1831 ed. lib. bdg. 75.00x (ISBN 0-912004-26-6). W W Gaunt.

Conkling, Alfred R. Appleton's Guide to Mexico. 1976. lib. bdg. 59.95 (ISBN 0-8490-1443-3). Gordon Pr.

Conkling, Edgar C., jt. auth. see Berry, Brian J. L.

Conkling, Philip. Islands in Time. LC 80-70610. (Illus.). 242p. 1981. pap. 8.95 (ISBN 0-89272-111-1). Down East.

Conkwright, Nelson B. Introduction to the Theory of Equations. LC 58-2094. pap. 56.30 (ISBN 0-317-08691-X, 2000509). Bks Demand UMI.

Conlan, Irene, jt. auth. see Conlan, John.

Conlan, Jim. IBM PC Pascal. (IBM Personal Computer Ser.). 318p. 1984. pap. 17.95 (ISBN 0-471-87936-3). Wiley.

Conlan, Jim, jt. auth. see Inman, Don.

Conlan, John & Conlan, Irene. Beyond Nineteen Eighty-Four. LC 84-8035. 170p. (Orig.). 1984. pap. 5.95 (ISBN 0-942770-01-3). FaithAmerica.

Conlen, William J. Vignettes of Mexico. 1937. 25.00 (ISBN 0-686-17227-2). Scholars Ref Lib.

Conlen, Wolliam J. Vignettes of Mexico. 1978. Repr. of 1937 ed. lib. bdg. 15.00 (ISBN 0-8495-0806-1). Arden Lib.

Conley, Bernard E. Social & Economic Aspects of Drug Utilization Research. LC 76-9598. 1976. 47.50 (ISBN 0-914768-02-6). Drug Intl Pubns.

Conley, Bruce H. Butterflies, Grandpa & Me. (Illus.). 23p. 1976. pap. 2.00 (ISBN 0-685-65885-6). Thum Print.

Conley, C. Isolated Invariant Sets & the Morse Index. LC 78-1577. (Conference Board of the Mathematical Sciences Ser.: No. 38). 89p. 1982. pap. 15.00 (ISBN 0-8218-1688-8, CBMS 38). Am Math.

Conley, C. H. First English Translators of the Classics. LC 67-27587. Repr. of 1927 ed. 19.00x (ISBN 0-8046-0085-6, Pub. by Kennikat). Assoc Faculty Pr.

--The Reader's Johnson: A Representative Selection of His Writings. 1977. Repr. of 1940 ed. lib. bdg. 30.00 (ISBN 0-8495-0708-1). Arden Lib.

Conley, Cort. Idaho for the Curious: A Guide. (Illus.). 700p. (Orig.). 1982. pap. 14.95 (ISBN 0-9603566-3-0). Backeddy Bks.

Conley, Cort & Carrey, John. The Middle Fork & the Sheepeater War. LC 80-17367. 1977. pap. 9.95 (ISBN 0-9603566-1-4). Backeddy Bks.

--River of No Return. LC 78-52373. 1978. pap. 10.95 (ISBN 0-9603566-2-2). Backeddy Bks.

--Snake River, of Hells Canyon. LC 79-55450. (Orig.). 1979. pap. 11.95 (ISBN 0-9603566-0-6). Backeddy Bks.

Conley, Cort, selected by. Gathered Waters: An Anthology of River Poems. 1985. pap. 9.95 (ISBN 0-317-17262-X). Backeddy Bks.

Conley, Darrell. First Corinthians (Adult Workbook) pap. 2.50 (ISBN 0-89315-052-5). Lambert Bk.

--The Gospel Vs. Occultism. pap. 1.50 (ISBN 0-89315-078-9). Lambert Bk.

Conley, Diane, ed. Graduate & Professional Programs: An Overview 1985. 19th ed. (Annual Guides-Graduate Study Ser.). 885p. (Orig.). 1984. pap. 15.95 (ISBN 0-87866-234-0). Petersons Guides.

--Summer Opportunities for Kids & Teenagers 1985. 2nd ed. (Annual Guides Ser.). (Illus.). 499p. (Orig.). 1984. pap. 9.95 (ISBN 0-87866-275-8). Petersons Guides.

Conley, Diane & Goldstein, Amy J., eds. Graduate Programs in the Humanities & Social Sciences 1985. 19th ed. (Annual Guides to Graduate Study Ser.). 1576p. (Orig.). 1984. pap. 22.95 (ISBN 0-87866-235-9). Petersons Guides.

Conley, Diane & Granade, Charles, eds. Graduate Programs in Engineering & Applied Sciences 1985. 19th ed. (Annual Guides to Graduate Study Ser.). 885p. (Orig.). 1984. pap. 21.95 (ISBN 0-87866-238-3). Petersons Guides.

--Graduate Programs in the Physical Sciences & Mathematics 1985. 19th ed. (Annual Guides to Graduate Study Ser.). 640p. (Orig.). 1984. pap. 19.95 (ISBN 0-87866-237-5). Petersons Guides.

Conley, Diane & Ready, Barbara C., eds. Graduate Programs in the Biological, Agricultural, & Health Sciences 1985. 19th ed. (Annual Guides-Graduate Study Ser.). 2038p. (Orig.). 1984. pap. 25.95 (ISBN 0-87866-236-7). Petersons Guides.

Conley, Ellen A. Soho Madonna. 1980. pap. 2.25 (ISBN 0-380-75614-5, 75614). Avon.

--Soon to Be Immortal. LC 81-23188. 224p. 1982. 13.95 (ISBN 0-312-74504-4). St Martin.

Conley, J. & Huffman, W. Readings in Marriage-Sex Education in Human Sexuality. 1972. pap. 6.50x (ISBN 0-87563-047-2). Stipes.

Conley, J., jt. auth. see Moldaver, J.

Conley, J., et al. The Mirror of Everyman's Salvation: A Prose Translation of the Original Everyman. (Costerus New Ser.: Vol. 49). 101p. 1985. pap. text ed. 12.00x (ISBN 90-6203-865-4, Pub. by Rodopi Holland). Humanities.

Conley, John. Complications of Head & Neck Surgery. LC 79-416. (Illus.). 1979. text ed. 49.50 (ISBN 0-7216-2649-1). Saunders.

--Concepts in Head & Neck Surgery. (Illus.). 300p. 1970. 141.00 (ISBN 0-8089-0631-3, 790888). Grune.

--Face-Lift Operation. (Illus.). 132p. 1968. photocopy ed. 24.75x (ISBN 0-398-00340-8). C C Thomas.

Conley, John & Dickinson, John T., eds. Plastic & Reconstructive Surgery of the Face & Neck, 2 vols. Incl. Vol. 1. Aesthetic Surgery. 264p; Vol. 2. Rehabilitative Surgery. 392p. 119.00 (ISBN 0-8089-0751-4, 790892). (Illus.). 1972. Grune.

Conley, John A., ed. Theory & Research in Criminal Justice: Current Perspectives. 150p. 1979. softcover 5.00 (ISBN 0-87084-014-2). Anderson Pub Co.

Conley, John J. Salivary Glands & the Facial Nerve. 330p. 1975. 199.00 (ISBN 0-8089-0872-3, 790895). Grune.

Conley, Joyce, jt. auth. see Clough, John.

Conley, Lucy. Gone to the Zoo. 1979. 5.90 (ISBN 0-686-25258-6). Rod & Staff.

--The Priceless Privilege. 1981. 6.65 (ISBN 0-686-30773-9). Rod & Staff.

Conley, Lucy, jt. auth. see Birky, Lela.

Conley, Lucy A. Tattletale Sparkie. 1983. 6.75 (ISBN 0-318-01337-1). Rod & Staff.

Conley, Luke G., III. The Conley Helpful Format Wordmaster Bald Dictionary. (Gamemaster Edition Ser.). 1950p. 1985. 37.50 (ISBN 0-930725-00-X); lib. bdg. 40.00 (ISBN 0-930725-01-8); pap. 32.50 (ISBN 0-930725-02-6). Pathfound Pubs.

Conley, Patrick & Campbell, Paul. Providence: A Pictorial History. LC 80-27671. 208p. 1983. 19.95 (ISBN 0-89865-128-X). Donning Co.

Conley, Patrick T. The Blackstone Valley: A Sketch of Its River, Its Canal & Its People. 19p. 1983. pap. 2.75 (ISBN 0-917012-41-0). RI Pubns Soc.

--The Constitutional Significance of Trevett vs. Weeden (1786) (Illus.). 10p. 1976. pap. 1.25 (ISBN 0-917012-43-7). RI Pubns Soc.

--Democracy in Decline: Rhode Island Constitutional Development, 1776-1841. LC 77-76314. (Illus.). 1977. 13.95 (ISBN 0-917012-09-7). RI Pubns Soc.

--Democracy in Decline: Rhode Island's Constitutional Development, 1776-1841. 1977. 13.95 (ISBN 0-685-67662-5). RI Hist Soc.

--The Dorr Rebellion: Rhode Island's Crisis in Constitutional Government. 13p. (Orig.). 1976. pap. 2.00 (ISBN 0-917012-49-6). RI Pubns Soc.

--North Kingstown: An Historical Sketch. (Illus., Orig.). 1976. pap. 1.50 (ISBN 0-917012-53-4). RI Pubns Soc.

--Rhode Island Catholicism: A Historical Guide. 24p. (Orig.). 1984. pap. 2.95 (ISBN 0-917012-56-9). RI Pubns Soc.

--Rhode Island Constitutional Development, 1636-1775: A Survey. 35p. 1968. pap. 2.75 (ISBN 0-917012-42-9). RI Pubns Soc.

--Rhode Island Profile. LC 82-62009. (Illus.). 60p. (Orig.). 1983. pap. 1.25 (ISBN 0-917012-40-2). RI Pubns Soc.

Conley, Patrick T. & Campbell, Paul R. Rhode Island Historical Development: An Interpretative Essay. 64p. 1985. pap. cancelled (ISBN 0-917012-69-0). RI Pubns Soc.

Conley, Patrick T. & Smith, Matthew J. Catholicism in Rhode Island: The Formative Era. LC 76-62863. 1976. 12.50 (ISBN 0-917012-13-5). RI Pubns Soc.

Conley, Patrick T., ed. see Cunha, M. Rachel, et al.

Conley, Patrick T., ed. see Gelenian, Ara A.

Conley, Patrick T., ed. see Sickinger, Raymond L. & Primeau, John K.

Conley, Pauline C. The Code Breaker. (Orig.). 1983. pap. 3.00 (ISBN 0-87602-241-7). Anchorage.

Conley, Robert J. The Rattlesnake Band & Other Poems. Bilingual ed. Feelings, Durbin, tr. (Illus.). 124p. (Orig.). 1984. pap. 5.00 (ISBN 0-940392-13-5). Indian U Pr OK.

Conley, Robert J., ed. see Tahlequah Indian Writer's Group.

Conley, Ronald. The Economics of Mental Retardation. LC 72-12345. 390p. 1973. 33.50x (ISBN 0-8018-1410-3). Johns Hopkins.

Conley, Verena A. Helene Cixous: Writing the Feminine. LC 83-23600. x, 181p. 1984. 16.95x (ISBN 0-8032-1424-3). U of Nebr Pr.

Conley, Virginia & Freisner, Arlyne. Evaluation of Students in Baccalaureate Nursing Programs. 98p. 1977. 8.95 (0-88737-245-1). Natl League Nurse.

Conley, Virginia, jt. auth. see Epstein, Rhoda.

Conley, Virginia C. Curriculum & Instruction in Nursing. 1973. 22.50 (ISBN 0-316-15307-9). Little.

Conley, William. Computer Optimization Techniques. 1980. 25.00 (ISBN 0-89433-111-6). Petrocelli.

--The Kalimantan Kenyah: A Study of Tribal Conversion in Terms of Dynamic Cultural Themes. 1973. pap. 4.95 (ISBN 0-87552-148-7). Presby & Reformed.

--Optimization: A Simplified Approach. (Illus.). 272p. 1981. 20.00 (ISBN 0-89433-121-3). Petrocelli.

Conley, William C. Advanced BASIC. (Illus.). 160p. 1983. pap. 10.95 (ISBN 0-89433-202-3). Petrocelli.

--BASIC II Advanced. 160p. 1983. pap. 10.95 (ISBN 0-89433-202-3). Van Nos Reinhold.

--Computer Optimization Techniques. rev. ed. (Illus.). 350p. 1984. text ed. 29.95 (ISBN 0-89433-213-9). Petrocelli.

Conley, William E. BASIC for Beginners. (Illus.). 144p. 1982. pap. text ed. 10.95 (ISBN 0-89433-141-8). Petrocelli.

Conlin, Bill. The Rutledge Book of Baseball. 128p. 1981. 10.95 (ISBN 0-8317-7596-3, Rutledge Pr). Smith Pubs.

Conlin, David, et al. Intellectual Property Rights in Biotechnology Worldwide. 320p. 1986. pap. 80.00x (ISBN 0-943818-15-X). Stockton Pr.

Conlin, Jean M. & Conlin, Robert G. Word Processing Training on the Wang. 400p. 1985. pap. 26.95 (ISBN 0-13-963406-1). P-H.

Conlin, Joseph. The Troubles: A Jaundiced Glance Back at the Movement of the Sixties. 368p. 1982. 16.95 (ISBN 0-531-09856-7). Watts.

Conlin, Joseph R. The American Past: A Survey of American History, 1 Vol, Pts. One & Two. Incl. Pt. One. A Survey of American History to 1877. 462p. pap. text ed. 17.95 (ISBN 0-15-502310-1); Pt. Two. A Survey of American History Since 1865. 514p. pap. text ed. 17.95 (ISBN 0-15-502311-X). 910p. 1984. text ed. 26.95 (ISBN 0-15-502309-8, HC); Pt. I. study guide 6.95 (ISBN 0-15-502313-6); Pt. II. study guide 6.95 (ISBN 0-15-502314-4); test manual avail. (ISBN 0-15-502312-8). HarBraceJ.

--The American Radical Press: Eighteen Eighty to Nineteen Sixty, 2 vols. LC 72-9825. 1974. Set. lib. bdg. 60.00 (ISBN 0-8371-6625-X, AMR/). Greenwood.

--Big Bill Haywood & the Radical Union Movement. LC 79-80015. (Men & Movements Ser). (Illus.). 1969. 15.95x (ISBN 0-8156-2140-X). Syracuse U Pr.

--Bread & Roses Too. LC 79-95505. (Contributions in American History Ser.: No. 1). 1970. lib. bdg. 27.50 (ISBN 0-8371-2344-5, COB/). Greenwood.

--The Morrow Book of Quotations in American History. LC 84-60613. 320p. 1984. 17.95 (ISBN 0-688-02068-2). Morrow.

Conlin, Joseph R., ed. At the Point of Production: The Local History of the I.W.W. LC 80-1708. (Contributions in Labor History Ser.: No. 10). viii, 329p. 1981. lib. bdg. 29.95 (ISBN 0-313-22046-8, CPP/). Greenwood.

Conlin, Marion. Marion Conlin's Home Cooking School. rev. ed. 224p. 1981. Repr. of 1972 ed. 12.95 (ISBN 0-87518-216-X). Dillon.

Conlin, Mary L. Patterns Plus: A Short Prose Reader with Argumentation. LC 84-81972. 448p. 1984. pap. text ed. write for info. (ISBN 0-395-35761-6); instr's manual avail. (ISBN 0-395-36397-7). HM.

Conlin, Mary Lou. Concepts of Communication: Reading, Ideas Module, Inferences Module. LC 77-78895. (Illus.). 1978. pap. text ed. 17.50 (ISBN 0-395-25492-2); instr's. guide 1.00 (ISBN 0-395-25493-0). HM.

--Concepts of Communication: Writing Skills Module. 2nd ed. LC 79-49830. 1980. pap. text ed. 17.50 (ISBN 0-395-28484-8). HM.

--Concepts of Communication: Writing: Summary, Paragraph, Essay-Test, Theme Module. 2nd ed. LC 79-49830. 1980. pap. text ed. 16.50 (ISBN 0-395-28735-9); instr's. manual 1.10. HM.

--Patterns: A Short Prose Reader. 400p. 1983. pap. text ed. 11.95 (ISBN 0-395-32599-4); instr's. manual 2.00 (ISBN 0-395-32600-1). HM.

Conlin, Robert G., jt. auth. see Conlin, Jean M.

Conlon, Ann, ed. see Gayley, Rano.

Conlon, Dalys. Presenting Australia. (Illus.). 336p. 1985. 29.95 (ISBN 0-88162-118-8, Pub. by Salem Hse Ltd). Merrimack Pub Cir.

Conlon, Denis J. Li Romans de Witasse le Moine. (Studies in the Romance Languages & Literatures: No. 126). 142p. 1973. pap. 8.50x (ISBN 0-8078-9126-6). U of NC Pr.

Conlon, Denis J., ed. Richard Sans Peur. (Studies in the Romance Languages & Literatures: No.192). 120p. (Orig.). 1978. pap. 9.00x (ISBN 0-8078-9192-4). U of NC Pr.

Conlon, Elizabeth, jt. auth. see Alarie, Julia.

Conlon, Faith, et al, eds. The Things That Divide Us. 192p. (Orig.). 1985. pap. 7.95 (ISBN 0-931188-32-6). Seal Pr Feminist.

Conlon, Frank F. A Caste in a Changing World: The Chitrapur Saraswat Brahmans, 1700-1935. LC 75-7192. 1977. 38.50x (ISBN 0-520-02998-4). U of Cal Pr.

Conlon, Frank S., ed. see Blee, Ben W.

Conlon, Grace W. The View from the Top: How Chief Executives Look at Planning. 100p. 1982. pap. 8.00 (ISBN 0-912841-16-8, 04). Planning Forum.

Conlon, Hazel M. Ballroom Variations: One Hundred Steps & Combinations with Lesson Plans for 10 Hour Course Class Instruction. (Ballroom Dance Ser.). 1985. lib. bdg. 79.00 (ISBN 0-87700-663-6). Revisionist Pr.

Conlon, James, tr. see De Carcaradec, Maria.

Conlon, John J. Walter Pater & the French Tradition. LC 81-65458. 180p. 1982. 21.50 (ISBN 0-8387-5016-8). Bucknell U Pr.

Conlon, Kathleen. The Best of Friends. 368p. 1984. 14.95 (ISBN 0-312-07714-9). St Martin.

--A Move in the Game. LC 78-66255. 336p. 1979. pap. 3.50 (ISBN 0-8128-8118-4). Stein & Day.

Conlon, Tom. PILOT: The Language & How to Use It. (Illus.). 1984. pap. 17.95 (ISBN 0-13-676247-6). P-H.

Conn, Bruce C. Horror of Cabrini-Green. 224p. (Orig.). 1975. pap. 2.25 (ISBN 0-87067-023-9, BH023). Holloway.

Conn, Charles P. A Faith to Keep. LC 77-70783. pap. 1.99 (ISBN 0-87148-016-6). Pathway Pr.

--Father Care. 90p. 1985. pap. 3.95 (ISBN 0-8499-4169-5, 4169-5). Word Bks.

--FatherCare: What It Means to Be God's Child. 1983. 7.95 (ISBN 0-8499-0339-4). Word Bks.

--Fathercare: What It Means to Be Gods Child. 128p. 1984. pap. 2.95 (ISBN 0-425-07305-X). Berkley Pub.

--Making It Happen. 128p. 1983. pap. 2.95 (ISBN 0-425-07185-5). Berkley Pub.

--The Man from Galilee. LC 74-83547. 1974. pap. 1.99 (ISBN 0-87148-565-6). Pathway Pr.

--The Meaning of Marriage. LC 76-26408. (Illus.). (gr. 10-12). pap. 1.99 (ISBN 0-87148-569-9). Pathway Pr.

--Promises to Keep: The Amway Phenomenon & How It Works. 320p. 1985. 16.95 (ISBN 0-399-13059-4). Putnam Pub Group.

--Promises to Keep: The Amway Phenomenon & How it Works. 128p. 1986. 11.95 (ISBN 0-399-13059-4). Putnam Pub Group.

--An Uncommon Freedom: The Amway Experience & Why It Grows. 208p. 1983. pap. 2.95 (ISBN 0-425-05870-0). Berkley Pub.

--The Winner's Circle. 160p. 1983. pap. 2.95 (ISBN 0-425-06306-2). Berkley Pub.

Conn, Charles P. & Aultman, Donald S. Studies in Discipleship. LC 75-14887. 1975. pap. 1.99 (ISBN 0-87148-772-1). Pathway Pr.

Conn, Charles P. & Conn, Charles W. The Relevant Record. LC 76-2969. (Illus.). 1976. pap. 1.99 (ISBN 0-87148-732-2). Pathway Pr.

--What Is the Church? 1977. pap. 1.99 (ISBN 0-87148-907-4). Pathway Pr.

Conn, Charles P. & Miller, Barbara. Kathy. 1983. pap. 2.95 (ISBN 0-425-06570-7). Berkley Pub.

Conn, Charles P., jt. auth. see Devos, Richard.

Conn, Charles P., jt. auth. see DeVos, Richard M.

Conn, Charles P., jt. auth. see Devos, Richard M.

Conn, Charles P., jt. auth. see Miller, Barbara.

Conn, Charles P., jt. auth. see Mitchell, William.

Conn, Charles P., jt. auth. see Walker, Paul L.

Conn, Charles W. The Acts of the Apostles. 1966. pap. 4.25 (ISBN 0-87148-010-7). Pathway Pr.

--Anatomy of Evil. 1984. pap. text ed. 6.95 (ISBN 0-87148-018-2). Pathway Pr.

--A Balanced Church. 1983. pap. 6.95 (ISBN 0-87148-017-4). Pathway Pr.

--The Bible: Books of Books. 1977. pap. 4.25 (ISBN 0-87148-102-2). Pathway Pr.

--A Certain Journey. 152p. 1965. 4.25 (ISBN 0-87148-000-X); pap. 3.25 (ISBN 0-87148-001-8). Pathway Pr.

--Christ & the Gospels. 109p. 1964. pap. 4.25 (ISBN 0-87148-150-2). Pathway Pr.

--The Evangel Reader. 1958. 3.25 (ISBN 0-87148-275-4). Pathway Pr.

--A Guide to the Pentateuch. 109p. 1963. 5.25 (ISBN 0-87148-004-2); pap. 4.25 (ISBN 0-87148-005-0). Pathway Pr.

--Highlights of Hebrew History. 1975. pap. 4.25 (ISBN 0-87148-401-3); instrs. guide 5.25 (ISBN 0-87148-404-8). Pathway Pr.

--Like a Mighty Army. rev. ed. LC 77-82067. 1977. 12.95 (ISBN 0-87148-510-9). Pathway Pr.

--Like a Mighty Army. 1955. 7.95 (ISBN 0-87148-505-2). Pathway Pr.

--Pillars of Pentecost. 148p. 1979. 6.95 (ISBN 0-87148-681-4). Pathway Pr.

--Poets & Prophets of Israel. 1981. 5.25 (ISBN 0-87148-707-1); pap. 4.25 (ISBN 0-87148-708-X). Pathway Pr.

--Rudder & the Rock. 1976. pap. 4.25 (ISBN 0-87148-733-0). Pathway Pr.

--A Survey of the Epistles. 112p. 1969. 5.25 (ISBN 0-87148-007-7); pap. 4.25 (ISBN 0-87148-008-5). Pathway Pr.

--Why Men Go Back. 1983. 6.95 (ISBN 0-87148-902-3); pap. 5.95 (ISBN 0-87148-917-1). Pathway Pr.

Conn, Charles W., jt. auth. see Conn, Charles P.

Conn, Charles W., ed. La Biblia, el Libro de los Libros. 116p. (Span.). 1979. pap. 3.95 (ISBN 0-87148-523-0). Pathway Pr.

--Una Iglesia Blanceada. 165p. (Span.). 1979. pap. 4.95 (ISBN 0-87148-882-5). Pathway Pr.

Conn, David. A Theory of Economic Systems. LC 80-8619. (Outstanding Dissertations in Economics Ser.). 1984. lib. bdg. 24.00 (ISBN 0-8240-4176-3). Garland Pub.

Conn, E. E., jt. ed. see Stumpf, P. K.

Conn, Eric E. & Stumpf, Paul K. Outlines of Biochemistry. 4th ed. LC 75-34288. 629p. 1976. text ed. 40.95x (ISBN 0-471-16843-2). Wiley.

Conn, Floyd & Conn, Sadie. They Followed The Rivers. (Illus.). 241p. 1981. 14.50x (ISBN 0-9607602-0-2). Kiowa Pr.

Conn, Frances G. & Fromer, Margot J. How to Quit Smoking in Thirty Days Without Cracking Up. (Illus.). 84p. (Orig.). 1982. pap. 5.95 (ISBN 0-910107-00-9). Phillips Neuman.

Conn, G. K. & Fowler, G. N., eds. Essays in Physics. Vol. 4. 1972. pap. 24.00 (ISBN 0-12-184804-3); Vol. 5, 1974. pap. 25.00 (ISBN 0-12-184805-1); Vol. 6, 1976. pap. 24.00 (ISBN 0-12-184806-X). Acad Pr.

Conn, George H. Horse Selection & Care for Beginners. pap. 5.00 (ISBN 0-87980-193-X). Wilshire.

--Treating Common Diseases of Your Horse. pap. 5.00 (ISBN 0-87980-255-3). Wilshire.

Conn, H. L., et al. Prostaglandins, Lipids: New Developments in Arteriosclerosis. 152p. 1981. 44.00 (ISBN 0-444-00566-8, Biomedical Pr). Elsevier.

Conn, H. W. The Story of Germ Life. 1904. 10.00 (ISBN 0-8274-4192-4). R West.

Conn, Hadley L. & Horwitz, Orville, eds. Cardiac & Vascular Diseases, 2 Vol. LC 71-98493. pap. 160.00 ea. (2055998). Bks Demand UMI.

Conn, Harold O. & Wood, Clive, eds. International Workshop on Plus Cyanidanol-Three in Diseases of the Liver. (Royal Society of Medicine International Congress & Symposium Ser.: No. 47). 1981. 40.50 (ISBN 0-8089-1433-2, 790898). Grune.

Conn, Harry. Four Trojan Horses of Humanism. 141p. 1982. pap. 5.95 (ISBN 0-88062-009-9). Mott Media.

Conn, Harvie. Evangelism: Doing Justice & Preaching Grace. 112p. (Orig.). 1982. pap. 3.95 (ISBN 0-310-45311-9). Zondervan.

Conn, Harvie M. Bible Studies on World Evangelization & the Simple Lifestyle. 1981. pap. 1.50 (ISBN 0-87552-208-4). Presby & Reformed.
--Contemporary World Theology. 1974. pap. 4.95 (ISBN 0-87552-149-5). Presby & Reformed.
--Eternal Word & Changing Worlds: Theology, Anthropology & Mission in Trialogue. 336p. 1984. pap. 10.95 (ISBN 0-310-45321-6, 11647P, Pub. by Academie Bks). Zondervan.
--Theological Perspectives on Church Growth. 1976. kivar 4.95 (ISBN 0-87552-150-9). Presby & Reformed.
Conn, Harvie M. & Rowen, Samuel F., eds. Missions & Theological Education in World Perspective. LC 84-72527. 484p. (Orig.). 1984. pap. text ed. 11.95 (ISBN 0-930957-00-8). Assocs Urbanus.
Conn, Herb & Conn, Jan. The Jewel Cave Adventure. (Illus.). 240p. 1981. pap. 6.95 (ISBN 0-939748-01-0). Cave Bks Mo.
Conn, Howard F. & Conn, Rex B., Jr. Current Diagnosis Six. (Illus.). 1424p. 1980. text ed. 58.00 (ISBN 0-7216-2707-2). Saunders.
Conn, Howard F., ed. Current Therapy 1983: The Latest Methods of Treatment for the Practicing Physician. (Illus.). 1100p. 1983. 42.00 (ISBN 0-7216-2711-0). Saunders.
Conn, Jack F. Non-Abelian Minimal Closed Ideals of Transitive Lie Algebras. LC 79-5479. (Mathematical Notes Ser.: 25). 216p. 1980. pap. 11.50x (ISBN 0-691-08251-0). Princeton U Pr.
Conn, Jan, jt. auth. see Conn, Herb.
Conn, Jerry D. Preston Smith: The Making of a Texas Governor. (Illus.). 173p. 8.50 (ISBN 0-8363-0078-5). Jenkins.
Conn, Michael, ed. Methods in Enzymology: Hormone Action: Neuroendocrine Peptides, Vol. 103, Pt. H. 1983. 69.50 (ISBN 0-12-182003-3). Acad Pr.
Conn, Michael P., ed. Cellular Regulation of Secretion & Release. (Cell Biology Ser.). 514p. 1982. 65.00 (ISBN 0-12-185058-7). Acad Pr.
Conn, P. Michael, ed. The Receptors, Vol. 1. 1984. 78.00 (ISBN 0-12-185201-6). Acad Pr.
Conn, Paul. The Possible Dream. 1982. pap. 2.75 (ISBN 0-425-05491-8). Berkley Pub.
Conn, Paul, jt. auth. see Moore, Pat.
Conn, Peter. The Divided Mind: Ideology & Imagination in America 1898-1917. LC 82-23661. (Studies in American Literature & Culture). 384p. 1983. 29.95 (ISBN 0-521-25392-6). Cambridge U Pr.
Conn, Phoebe. Captive Heart. 1985. pap. 3.95 (ISBN 0-8217-1569-0). Zebra.
--Love's Elusive Flame. 1983. pap. 3.75 (ISBN 0-8217-1267-5). Zebra.
--Savage Fire. 512p. 1984. pap. 3.75 (ISBN 0-8217-1397-3). Zebra.
Conn, Rex B., ed. Current Diagnosis Seven. 1250p. 1984. write for info. (ISBN 0-7216-2713-7). Saunders.
Conn, Rex B., Jr., jt. auth. see Conn, Howard F.
Conn, Richard. Circles of the World: Traditional Art of the Plains Indians. LC 82-70497. (Illus.). 152p. 1982. pap. 14.95 (ISBN 0-914738-27-5, Dist. by U of Wash Pr). Denver Art Mus.
--Circles of the World: Traditional Art of the Plains Indians. LC 82-70497. (Illus.). 152p. (Orig.). 1982. pap. 14.95 (ISBN 0-295-96229-1). U of Wash Pr.
--Native American Art in the Denver Art Museum. LC 78-62396. (Illus.). 1979. 40.00 (ISBN 0-295-95637-2, Dist. by U of Wash Pr); pap. 19.95 (ISBN 0-295-95638-0). Denver Art Mus.
--Native American Art in the Denver Art Museum. LC 78-62396. (Illus.). 352p. 40.00x (ISBN 0-295-95637-2). U of Wash Pr.
--Robes of White Shell & Sunrise. LC 74-16739. (Illus.). 1974. pap. 7.50 (ISBN 0-914738-04-6). Denver Art Mus.
--ZCPR3: The Manual. LC 84-61790. 352p. (Orig.). 1985. pap. 19.95 (ISBN 0-918432-59-6). NY Zoetrope.
Conn, Robert & Clapp, Steve. Methods of Bible Study. (C-Four Youth Bible Materials Ser.). (Illus.). 91p. (Orig.). 1982. pap. 8.00 (ISBN 0-914527-14-2). C-Four Res.
Conn, Robert L., jt. auth. see Bolten, Steven E.
Conn, Sadie, jt. auth. see Conn, Floyd.
Conn, Stephen, tr. see Krumeich, Gerd.
Conn, Stewart. The Aquarium. 1980. pap. 4.95 (ISBN 0-7145-3560-5). Riverrun NY.
--Burning. pap. 4.95 (ISBN 0-7145-0832-2). Riverrun NY.
Conn, Walter E. Conscience: Development & Self-Transcendence. LC 80-24043. 230p. (Orig.). 1981. pap. 12.95 (ISBN 0-89135-025-X). Religious Educ.
--Conversion: Perspectives on Personal & Social Transformation. LC 78-19079. 1978. pap. 9.95 (ISBN 0-8189-0368-6). Alba.
Conn, Walter E., jt. ed. see Swidler, Arlene.
Connah, Graham. Australian Field Archaeology: A Guide to Techniques. 182p. 1983. pap. text ed. 19.75x (ISBN 0-85575-136-3, Pub. by Australian Inst. Australia). Humanities.
--Three Thousand Years in Africa: Man & His Environment in the Lake Chad Region of Nigeria. LC 79-41508. (New Studies in Archaeology). (Illus.). 268p. 1981. 72.50 (ISBN 0-521-22848-4). Cambridge U Pr.

Connaissance des Arts Editorial Staff, ed. French Cabinetmakers of the 18th Century. (Connaissance des Arts Collection Ser.). 280p. (Fr.). 1966. 150.00 (ISBN 0-686-46617-9). French & Eur.
--French Master Goldsmiths & Silversmiths from the Seventeenth to the Nineteenth Century. (Connaissance des Arts Collection Ser.). 280p. (Fr.). 1966. 50.00 (ISBN 0-686-46618-7). French & Eur.
Connaissance des Arts Editorial Staff. Gardens & Flowers: Their Design & Arrangement. (Connaissance des Arts Collection). (Illus.). 280p. 1966. 50.00 (ISBN 0-686-46620-9). French & Eur.
Connaissance des Arts Editors. Les Ebenistes du Huitieme Siecle Francais. (Illus., Fr. & Eng., Avail. in Fr. & Eng. eds.). 75.00 (ISBN 0-685-11206-3). French & Eur.
--Les Orfevres de Louis XIII a Charles X. (Illus.). 75.00 (ISBN 0-685-11470-8). French & Eur.
--Les Porcelainiers du Huitieme Siecle Francais. (Illus., Fr.). 75.00 (ISBN 0-685-11208-X). French & Eur.
Connally, Andrew M. Dangers of Liberalism. 1985. pap. 4.00 (ISBN 0-934916-07-1). Natl Christian Pr.
Connally, Andrew M. & Hicks, Olan. Connally-Hicks Debate on Divorce & Remarriage. 1979. pap. 13.00 (ISBN 0-934916-31-4). Natl Christian Pr.
Connally, Eugenia H., ed. National Parks in Crisis. 220p. 1982. 13.95 (ISBN 0-318-17829-X). Natl Parks & Cons.
Connally, Eugenia M. Bienvenido a Washington. (Illus.). 36p. (Orig., Span.). 1980. pap. 3.95 (ISBN 0-936478-00-4). Interpretive Pubns.
--Bienvenue a Washington. (Illus.). 36p. (Orig., Fr.). 1980. pap. 3.95 (ISBN 0-936478-01-2). Interpretive Pubns.
--Welcome to Washington. (Illus.). 36p. (Orig., Japanese.). 1981. pap. 3.95 (ISBN 0-936478-04-7). Interpretive Pubns.
--Welcome to Washington. (Illus.). 36p. 1981. pap. 3.95 (ISBN 0-936478-03-9). Interpretive Pubns.
--Willkommen in Washington. (Illus.). 36p. (Orig., Ger.). 1980. 3.95 (ISBN 0-936478-02-0). Interpretive Pubns.
Connally, Walter J. The Failure of the World Leaders & the Explosive Pauperization of the World. (Illus.). 121p. 1983. 99.55x (ISBN 0-86722-056-2). Inst Econ Pol.
Connatser, Larry A. The Effect of an Academic Program on the Moral Development of Incarcerated Young Adults. LC 77-91446. 1978. pap. 9.95 perfect bdg. (ISBN 0-88247-510-X). R & E Pubs.
Connaway, John M. The Wilsford Site 22-Co-516, Coahoma County Mississippi. LC 84-620008. (Mississippi Department of Archives & History Archaeological Reports Ser.: No. 14). 222p. (Orig.). pap. 15.00. Mississippi De.
Conne, John. Ignatius His Conclave, or His Inthronisation in a Late Election in Hell. LC 77-6876. (English Experience Ser.: No. 868). 1977. Repr. of 1611 ed. lib. bdg. 11.50 (ISBN 90-221-0868-6). Walter J Johnson.
Conneau, Theophilus. A Slaver's Log Book: Or, 20 Years' Residence in Africa. 1972. pap. 2.75 (ISBN 0-380-01773-3, 35063, Discus). Avon.
Connechen, James, et al. Pharmacology for Nurses. 5th ed. 384p. 1983. pap. 9.95 (ISBN 0-7216-0803-5, Pub. by Bailliere-Tindall). Saunders.
Connecticut General Assembly. Minutes of the Testimony Taken Before John Q. Wilson, Joseph Eaton, & Morris Woodruff, Committee from the General Assembly, to Inquire into the Condition of the Connecticut State Prison. facsimile ed. LC 74-3819. (Criminal Justice in America Ser.). 1974. Repr. of 1834 ed. 12.00x (ISBN 0-405-06140-4). Ayer Co Pubs.
Connecticut Historical Society. Collections of the Connecticut Historical Society, 20 vols. LC 74-19612. Repr. of 1920 ed. Set. 500.00 (ISBN 0-404-12383-X); 25.00 ea. AMS Pr.
Connecticut Law Tribune Company. The Connecticut Law Tribune Cumulative Index 1981-1983. 360p. 1984. pap. 50.00 (ISBN 0-910051-02-X). CT Law Trib.
Connell, jt. auth. see Brown.
Connell, et al. Touche Ross Guide to Personal Financial Management: 1985 Edition. LC 85-3492. 300p. 1995. 79.95 (Busn); pap. 19.95 (ISBN 0-317-29367-2). P-H.
Connell, Abby. Spring Fever. 176p. 1985. pap. 2.25 (ISBN 0-345-32399-8). Ballantine.
--Two by Two Romance, No. 2: Jed & Jessie. 192p. (Orig.). 1983. pap. 1.95 (ISBN 0-446-30802-1). Warner Bks.
Connell, Brian, tr. see Von Papen, Franz.
Connell, Charles. Hidden Catch. (Illus.). 176p. pap. 12.95x (ISBN 0-86695-005-2). Interserv Pub.
--They Gave Us Shakespeare: John Heminge & Henry Condell. (Illus.). 110p. 1982. 15.95x (ISBN 0-85362-193-4, Oriel). Routledge & Kegan.
Connell, Charles J. Land Revenue Policy in Northern India. 203p. 1983. text ed. 27.95x (ISBN 0-86590-144-9). Apt Bks.
Connell, D. W. Water Pollution: Causes & Effects in Australia & New Zealand. 2nd ed. (Australian Environment Ser.: Vol. 2). (Illus.). 203p. 1981. pap. text ed. 10.50x (ISBN 0-7022-1781-6). U of Queensland Pr.

Connell, D. W., jt. auth. see Vowles, P. D.
Connell, Des W. & Miller, Gregory. Chemistry & Exotoxicology of Pollution: Environmental Science & Technology. LC 83-16794. (A Wiley-Interscience Series of Text & Monographs: No. 1121). 444p. 1984. 44.50x (ISBN 0-471-86249-5, Pub. by Wiley-Interscience). Wiley.
Connell, Donna. Itl Early Writing Program. (gr. k-1). 1985. 89.50 (ISBN 0-88671-194-0). Am Guidance.
--My ITL Book. (ITL Early Writing Program Ser.). (ps-1). 1985. Set of twenty-five. 49.50 (ISBN 0-88671-196-7); lesson guide 20.00 (ISBN 0-88671-197-5); contains 59 lessons 20.00. Am Guidance.
--Writing Is Childs Play. (ITL Early Writing Program Ser.). 1985. pap. 7.95 (ISBN 0-88671-195-9). Am Guidance.
Connell, Ed. Reinsman of the West: Bridles & Bits. 1977. pap. 5.00 (ISBN 0-87980-333-9). Wilshire.
Connell, Ed C. Hackamore Reinsman. (Illus.). 1952. 5.00 (ISBN 0-914208-03-9). Longhorn Pr.
Connell, Elizabeth, et al. Family Planning & Reproductive Health. 60p. 1985. Boxed Set. 270.00 (ISBN 0-918473-08-X). Sci-Thru-Media.
Connell, Elizabeth B. & Tatum, Howard J. Barrier Methods of Contraception. LC 84-71598. 1985. 7.95 (ISBN 0-917634-17-9). Creative Infomatics.
--Sexually Transmitted Diseases: Diagnosis & Treatment. LC 85-70298. 1985. pap. 7.95 (ISBN 0-317-18815-1). Creative Infomatics.
Connell, Evan S. Anatomy Lesson, & Other Stories. facsimile ed. LC 79-38719. (Short Story Index Reprint Ser.). Repr. of 1957 ed. 15.00 (ISBN 0-8369-4132-2). Ayer Co Pubs.
--A Long Desire. LC 78-14175. 288p. 1980. 10.95 (ISBN 0-03-046161-8); pap. 4.95 (ISBN 0-03-057793-4). HR&W.
--Mr. Bridge. LC 81-81513. 384p. 1981. pap. 10.50 (ISBN 0-86547-054-5); boxed, set hardcover trade with Evan Connell's Mrs. Bridge 35.00 (ISBN 0-86547-057-X). N Point Pr.
--Mrs. Bridge. LC 81-81514. 256p. 1981. pap. 9.50 (ISBN 0-86547-056-1); boxed set hardcover trade with Evan Connell's Mr. Bridge 35.00 (ISBN 0-86547-057-X). N Point Pr.
--Notes from a Bottle Found on the Beach at Carmel. 256p. 1984. pap. 10.00 (ISBN 0-86547-144-4). N Point Pr.
--Points for a Compass Rose. 256p. 1985. pap. 12.50 (ISBN 0-86547-205-X). N Point Pr.
--Saint Augustine's Pigeon: The Selected Stories. Blaisdell, Gus, ed. LC 80-18186. 304p. 1980. 15.00 (ISBN 0-86547-013-8); pap. 10.00 (ISBN 0-86547-014-6). N Point Pr.
--Son of the Morning Star: Custer & the Little Bighorn. 464p. 1984. 20.00 (ISBN 0-86547-160-6). N Point Pr.
--Son of the Morning Star: Custer & the Little Bighorn. LC 85-42560. (Illus.). 448p. 1985. pap. 8.95 (ISBN 0-06-097003-0, PL 7003, PL). Har-Row.
--White Lantern. 1981. pap. 5.95 (ISBN 0-03-059154-6). HR&W.
Connell, G. Spanish Poetry of the Grupo Poetico De 1927. text ed. 16.25 (ISBN 0-08-016950-3). Pergamon.
Connell, George. To Be One Thing: Personal Unity in Kierkegaard's Thought. xx, 198p. 1985. 17.95x (ISBN 0-86554-156-6, MUP/H146). Mercer Univ Pr.
Connell, I. Modern Algebra: A Constructive Introduction. 452p. 1981. 30.00 (ISBN 0-444-00609-5, North-Holland). Elsevier.
Connell, J. J. Control of Fish Quality. 1978. 40.00 (ISBN 0-685-63397-7). State Mutual Bk.
--Control of Fish Quality. 2nd ed. (Illus.). 240p. 1980. 33.25 (ISBN 0-85238-105-0, FN83, FNB). Unipub.
Connell, J. J. & Hardy, R. Trends in Fish Utilization. 116p. 1982. 25.00x (ISBN 0-85238-120-4, Pub. by Fishing News England). State Mutual Bk.
--Trends in Fish Utilization. (Illus.). 116p. 1982. pap. 19.00 (ISBN 0-85238-120-4, FN96, FNB). Unipub.
Connell, J. J., ed. Advances in Fish Science & Technology. 528p. 1980. cloth 118.50x (ISBN 0-85238-108-5, Pub. by Fishing News England). State Mutual Bk.
--Advances in Fish Science & Technology. (Illus.). 528p. 1980. pap. 150.00 (ISBN 0-85238-108-5, FN87, FNB). Unipub.
Connell, Joan. The Roman Catholic Church in England: 1553-1850, Vol. 158. LC 83-71299. (Memoirs Ser.). 1984. 12.00 (ISBN 0-87169-158-2). Am Philos.
--The Roman Catholic Church in England 1780-1850: A Study in Internal Politics. 215p. 1984. 14.00 (ISBN 0-87169-158-2). Am Philos.
Connell, John. Tiam Bilong Mani: The Evolution of Agriculture in a Solomon Is. Society. (Development Studies Monograph: No. 12). (Orig.). 1978. pap. text ed. 9.00x (ISBN 0-909150-66-4, 506, Pub. by ANUP Australia). Australia N U P.
--W. E. Henley. LC 78-160750. 1971. Repr. of 1949 ed. 32.50x (ISBN 0-8046-1566-7, Pub. by Kennikat). Assoc Faculty Pr.
--W. E. Henley. 1977. Repr. of 1949 ed. lib. bdg. 20.00 (ISBN 0-8492-0441-0). R West.
Connell, John, jt. ed. see Moore, Mick.

Connell, Jon & Sutherland, Douglas. Fraud. LC 78-66247. (Illus.). 1979. 12.95 (ISBN 0-8128-2602-7). Stein & Day.
Connell, Kenneth F. & Smith, Robert B. Analysis of Causes & Determination of Possible Means of Prevention of External Damage to Pipelines. 100p. 1968. 2.50 (ISBN 0-318-12584-6, U78173). Am Gas Assn.
Connell, Kenneth H. The Population of Ireland, 1750-1845. LC 74-9165. 293p. 1975. Repr. of 1950 ed. lib. bdg. 27.50x (ISBN 0-8371-7620-4, COPI). Greenwood.
Connell, Mary U. Biology Laboratory Manual, Pt. I. 146p. (Orig.). 1983. lab manual 8.95x (ISBN 0-89459-216-5). Hunter Textbks.
--Biology Laboratory Manual, Pt. II. 166p. 1983. lab manual 8.95x (ISBN 0-89459-217-3). Hunter Textbks.
Connell, Maureen. Mary Lacey. LC 80-7893. 288p. 1981. 13.41i (ISBN 0-690-01950-5, HarpT). Har-Row.
Connell, R. W. The Childs Construction of Politics. 251p. 1975. pap. 15.50x (ISBN 0-522-84006-X, Pub. by Melbourne U Pr). Intl Spec Bk.
--Ruling Class, Ruling Culture. LC 76-22981. (Illus.). 1977. 39.50 (ISBN 0-521-21392-4); pap. 12.95 (ISBN 0-521-29133-X). Cambridge U Pr.
--Teacher's Work. 212p. 1985. text ed. 20.00x (ISBN 0-86861-752-0); pap. text ed. 9.00x (ISBN 0-86861-760-1). Allen Unwin.
--Which Way Is Up? 224p. 1983. text ed. 28.50x (ISBN 0-86861-366-5). Allen Unwin.
--Which Way Is up? 224p. 1984. pap. 9.95 (ISBN 0-86861-374-6). Allen Unwin.
Connell, R. W., et al. Making the Difference: Schools, Families & Social Division. 224p. 1982. pap. 7.95 (ISBN 0-86861-132-8). Allen Unwin.
Connell, Richard E. Apes & Angels. facsimile ed. LC 73-106272. (Short Story Index Reprint Ser.). 1924. 18.00 (ISBN 0-8369-3309-5). Ayer Co Pubs.
--Sin of Monsieur Pettipon & Other Humorous Stories. facsimile ed. LC 77-106273. (Short Story Index Reprint Ser.). 1922. 18.00 (ISBN 0-8369-3310-9). Ayer Co Pubs.
Connell, Robert H. Serial Tagging Exercises for the OCLC System, 2 Vols. (AMIGOS Training Ser.: No. 3). 1981. Set. pap. 15.00 (ISBN 0-938288-02-4). Vol. A, 66 p. Vol. B, 32 p. AMIGOS Biblio.
Connell, Royal W., jt. auth. see Mack, William P.
Connell, Stephen & Galbraith, Ian A. Electronic Mail: A Revolution in Business Communications. LC 82-44. (Information & Communications Management Guides Ser.). 141p. 1982. text ed. 32.95 (ISBN 0-86729-015-3, 702-BW); pap. text ed. 22.95 (ISBN 0-86729-016-1). Knowledge Indus.
--Electronic Mail: A Revolution in Business Communications. (Illus.). 152p. 1983. pap. 14.95 (ISBN 0-442-21691-2). Van Nos Reinhold.
Connell, Tim, jt. auth. see Kattan-Ibarra, Juan.
Connell, W., jt. auth. see Mack, William P.
Connell, W. F. A History of Education in the Twentieth Century World. 1981. text ed. 29.95x (ISBN 0-8077-8024-3). Tchrs Coll.
Connell, William F. Educational Thought & Influence of Matthew Arnold. LC 74-109305. 1971. Repr. of 1950 ed. lib. bdg. 18.25x (ISBN 0-8371-3580-X, COMA). Greenwood.
Connellan, Leo. Another Poet in New York. new ed. LC 75-24029. 54p. 1975. pap. 4.95 (ISBN 0-915726-01-7). Living Poets.
--The Clear Blue Lobster-Water Country: A Trilogy. 150p. 1985. 15.95 (ISBN 0-15-118135-7, Harv); pap. 8.95 (ISBN 0-15-618054-5). HarBraceJ.
--Crossing America. 48p. 1976. 20.00, signed ed. (ISBN 0-915778-11-4); pap. 4.00 (ISBN 0-915778-12-2). Penmaen Pr.
--First Selected Poems. LC 75-29152. (Pitt Poetry Ser.). 1976. pap. 5.95 (ISBN 0-8229-5268-8). U of Pittsburgh Pr.
--Massachusetts Poems. (Hollow Spring Poetry Ser.). 60p. (Orig.). 1981. pap. 6.95 (ISBN 0-936198-02-8). Hollow Spring Pr.
--Shatterhouse. (Hollow Spring Poetry Ser.). 50p. (Orig.). 1983. pap. 6.95 (ISBN 0-936198-04-4). Hollow Spring Pr.
Connellan, Owen, ed. Imtheacht Ne Tromdhaimhe; or, the Proceedings of the Great Bardic Institution. 340p. Repr. of 1860 ed. 21.00 (ISBN 0-384-09757-X). Johnson Repr.
Connellan, Thomas K. Getting Yours: Success Strategies for the 1980's. 244p. 1982. 12.95 (ISBN 0-8184-0330-6). Lyle Stuart.
--How to Grow People into Self Starters. LC 80-65657. 238p. 1980. 19.95 (ISBN 0-936452-00-5). Achievement Inst.
--How to Improve Human Performance: Behaviorism in Business & Industry. (Continuing Management Education Ser.). 1978. text ed. 14.37l (ISBN 0-06-041349-2, HarpC). Har-Row.
Connelley, William E. John Brown. facs. ed. LC 71-164383. (Black Heritage Library Collection). Repr. of 1900 ed. 23.50 (ISBN 0-8369-8842-6). Ayer Co Pubs.
--Wild Bill & His Era: The Life & Adventures of James Butler Hickok. LC 76-187842. (Illus.). xii, 244p. 1972. Repr. of 1933 ed. 22.50 (ISBN 0-8154-0413-1). Cooper Sq.

Connell-Smith, Gordon. Forerunners of Drake. LC 75-7237. (Royal Empire Society Imperial Studies Ser). (Illus.). 264p. 1975. Repr. of 1954 ed. lib. bdg. 22.50x (ISBN 0-8371-8100-3, COFOD). Greenwood.

Connell-Tatum, Elizabeth & Tatum, Howard J. Managing Patients with IntrauterineDevices: A Clinic Manual. LC 84-71601. 1985. 8.95 (ISBN 0-917634-11-X). Creative Infomatics.

Connell-Tatum, Elizabeth & Tatum, Howard. Reproductive Health Care Manual. LC 84-70995. 1985. 8.65 (ISBN 0-917634-12-8). Creative Infomatics.

Connelly, Donald P., et al, eds. Clinical Decisions & Laboratory Use. LC 81-19825. (Continuing Medical Education Ser.: Vol. 1). 416p. 1982. 29.50x (ISBN 0-8166-1001-0). U of Minn Pr.

Connelly, Finbarr & Burns, Peter. The Ten Commandments & Today's Christian. 48p. 1985. pap. 1.50 (ISBN 0-89243-233-0). Liguori Pubns.

Connelly, Gwen, illus. Adventures. LC 83-25212. (The Shape of Poetry Ser.). (Illus.). 32p. (gr. k-3). 1984. PLB 7.45 (ISBN 0-89565-265-X). Childs World.

Connelly, H. W. Forty-Seven Object Lessons for Youth Programs. (Object Lesson Ser). (YA) 1964. pap. 3.45 (ISBN 0-8010-2314-9). Baker Bk.

Connelly, J. A. Analog Integrated Circuits: Devices, Circuits, Systems & Applications. LC 74-20947. 401p. 1975. 48.50x (ISBN 0-471-16854-8, Pub. by Wiley-Interscience). Wiley.

Connelly, James F. & Fratangelo, Robert A. Elementary Technical Mathematics. (Illus.). 1978. text ed. write for info. (ISBN 0-02-324430-5). Macmillan.

--Elementary Technical Mathematics with Calculus. 1979. write for info. (ISBN 0-02-324440-2). Macmillan.

--Precalculus Mathematics: A Functional Approach. 2nd ed. (Illus.). 1980. text ed. write for info. (ISBN 0-02-324400-3); write for info. study guide (ISBN 0-02-324420-8). Macmillan.

Connelly, Jerry, jt. auth. see Ristoedt, Larry.

Connelly, John P. You're Too Sweet. (gr. 4-9). 1968. 5.95 (ISBN 0-8392-1173-2). Astor-Honor.

Connelly, Kevin J., jt. auth. see Garofalo, James.

Connelly, Lisa. Lean & Firm. (Illus.). 128p. (Orig.). 1985. pap. 7.95 (ISBN 0-399-51074-5, Perigee). Putnam Pub Group.

Connelly, Marc. Green Pastures, a Play. LC 30-16400. 1959. pap. 6.95 (ISBN 0-03-028805-3). HR&W.

Connelly, Mark T. The Response to Prostitution in the Progressive Era. LC 79-24038. x, 261p. 1980. 22.50 (ISBN 0-8078-1424-5). U of NC Pr.

Connelly, Michael, jt. auth. see Sims, Jean.

Connelly, Naomi, jt. auth. see Goldberg, E. Maltilda.

Connelly, Naomi, jt. ed. see Goldberg, Mitilda E.

Connelly, Owen. The Epoch of Napoleon. LC 77-13473. 208p. 1978. pap. text ed. 6.95 (ISBN 0-88275-622-2). Krieger.

--French Revolution: Napoleonic Era. LC 77-85509. 1979. text ed. 23.95 (ISBN 0-03-091558-9, HoltC). HR&W.

--Napoleon's Satellite Kingdoms. LC 66-10336. 1970. pap. 5.95 (ISBN 0-02-906600-X). Free Pr.

Connelly, Owen, et al, eds. Historical Dictionary of Napoleonic France, 1799-1815. LC 83-22754. (Illus.). xv, 586p. 1985. lib. bdg. 65.00 (ISBN 0-313-21321-6, CNF/). Greenwood.

Connelly, Patricia A., jt. auth. see Barry, Kenneth H.

Connelly, Peter. Hannibal & the Enemies of Rome. LC 79-65844. (Armies of the Past Ser.). PLB 13.96 (ISBN 0-382-06307-4). Silver.

Connelly, Robert J. Last Rights: Death & Dying in Texas Law & Experience. LC 82-73384. 182p. 1983. pap. text ed. 9.95 (ISBN 0-931722-21-7). Corona Pub.

Connelly, Stephen E. Allan Seager. (United States Authors Ser.). 1983. lib. bdg. 17.95 (ISBN 0-8057-7386-X, Twayne). G K Hall.

Connelly, Thomas, jt. auth. see McDonough, James L.

Connelly, Thomas G., et al, eds. Morphogenesis & Pattern Formation. 312p. 1981. 50.50 (ISBN 0-89004-635-2). Raven.

Connelly, Thomas L. Army of the Heartland: The Army of Tennessee, 1861-1862. LC 67-21373. (Illus.). xvi, 306p. 1967. 22.50x (ISBN 0-8071-0404-3). La State U Pr.

--Autumn of Glory: The Army of Tennessee, 1862-1865. LC 70-122353. (Illus.). 1971. 27.50x (ISBN 0-8071-0445-0). La State U Pr.

--Civil War Tennessee: Battles & Leaders. LC 79-14885. (Tennessee Three Star Bks.). (Illus.). 1979. lib. bdg. 8.50x (ISBN 0-87049-284-5); pap. 3.50 (ISBN 0-87049-261-6). U of Tenn Pr.

--The Marble Man: Robert E. Lee & His Image in American Society. LC 76-41778. 1977. pap. 7.95 (ISBN 0-8071-0474-4). La State U Pr.

--Will Campbell & the Soul of the South. 176p. 1982. 10.95 (ISBN 0-8264-0182-1). Continuum.

Connelly, Thomas L. & Bellows, Barbara. God & General Longstreet: The Lost Cause & the Southern Mind. 1982. 14.95 (ISBN 0-8071-1020-5). La State U Pr.

Connelly, Thomas L. & Jones, Archer. The Politics of Command: Factions & Ideas in Confederate Strategy. LC 72-89113. xvi, 235p. 1973. 22.50x (ISBN 0-8071-0228-8). La State U Pr.

Connelly, Tony & Holley, Cindy. Holiday Stories. Champlin, John, ed. (Hi-Lo Write & Read Ser.). (Illus.). 38p. (gr. 3-6). 1982. pap. 8.95 (ISBN 0-938594-02-8). Spec Lit Pr.

Connelly, Vivian. Five Ports to Danger. (Crime Court Mystery Ser.). 208p. pap. 2.50 (ISBN 0-8439-2282-6, Leisure Bks). Dorchester Pub Co.

Connelly, Will. The Musician's Guide to Independent Record Production. (Illus.). 1981. 12.95 (ISBN 0-8092-5969-9); pap. 9.95 (ISBN 0-8092-5968-0). Contemp Bks.

Connely, Willard. Adventures in Biography: A Chronicle of Encounters & Findings,W.B. Yeats, Augustus John, Robert Browning, Margaret Fuller, Robert Lewis Stevenson. 1977. lib. bdg. 22.50 (ISBN 0-8495-0709-X). Arden Lib.

--Brawny Wycherley. LC 71-93060. 1969. Repr. of 1930 ed. 28.25 (ISBN 0-8046-0673-0, Pub. by Kennikat). Assoc Faculty Pr.

--Brawny Wycherley. 1930. 30.00 (ISBN 0-8274-1974-0). R West.

--Laurence Sterne As Yorick. LC 79-17312. (Illus.). 1979. Repr. of 1958 ed. lib. bdg. 27.50x (ISBN 0-313-22000-X, COLS). Greenwood.

--Louis Sullivan: A Biography. 1971. 5.95 (ISBN 0-8180-0230-1). Horizon.

--Sir Richard Steele. LC 67-27588. 1934. Repr. 32.75x (ISBN 0-8046-0086-4, Pub. by Kennikat). Assoc Faculty Pr.

--Sir Richard Steele. 1973. 30.00 (ISBN 0-8274-0053-5). R West.

--Young George Farquhar. 333p. 1980. Repr. of 1949 ed. lib. bdg. 25.00 (ISBN 0-8495-0787-1). Arden Lib.

Conner, Albert Z., jt. auth. see Poirier, Robert G.

Conner, Bart & Ziert, Paul. Bart Conner: Winning the Gold. 192p. 1985. text ed. 15.50 (ISBN 0-446-51333-4). Warner Bks.

Conner, Berenice G. Dyes from Your Garden. LC 75-33970. (Illus.). 128p. 1976. spiral bdg. 7.95 (ISBN 0-912458-61-5). E A Seemann.

Conner, Bettina, jt. auth. see Ridgeway, James.

Conner, Christopher S., jt. auth. see Watanabe, Arthur S.

Conner, Daniel & Miller, Lorraine. Master Mariner: Captain James Cook & the Peoples of the Pacific. LC 78-2989. (Illus.). 176p. 1978. 25.00x (ISBN 0-295-95621-6). U of Wash Pr.

Conner, David A., jt. auth. see Winter, John V.

Conner, Dennis J. & Bueso, Alberto T. Managerial Finance: Theory & Techniques. (Illus.). 320p. 1981. 31.95 (ISBN 0-13-550269-1); Self Correcting Approach. pap. 12.95 (ISBN 0-13-550293-4). P-H.

Conner, Douglas L. & Marszalek, John F. A Black Physician's Story: Bringing Hope in Mississippi. (Illus.). 1985. 14.95x (ISBN 0-87805-279-8). U Pr of Miss.

Conner, Floyd & Snyder, John. Baseball's Footnote Players. (Illus.). 300p. 1985. 15.95 (ISBN 0-89651-059-X); pap. 9.95 (ISBN 0-89651-060-3). Icarus.

--Day-by-Day in Cincinnati Bengals History. LC 83-80858. (Illus.). 320p. (Orig.). 1984. pap. 12.95 (ISBN 0-88011-218-2). Leisure Pr.

--Day-by-Day in Cincinnati Reds History. LC 82-83938. (Illus.). 300p. (Orig.). 1983. pap. 12.95 (ISBN 0-88011-106-2). Leisure Pr.

Conner, J. Richard & Loehman, Edna, eds. Economics & Decision-Making for Environmental Quality. LC 74-6056. 1974. pap. 6.00 (ISBN 0-8130-0508-6). U Presses Fla.

Conner, Janette V. Children's Stories Youngsters Will Like. 1984. 6.50 (ISBN 0-8062-2364-2). Carlton.

Conner, John T., jt. ed. see Hessel, Dietert T.

Conner, Judith & Yoshida, Mayumi. Tokyo City Guide. LC 85-40064. (Illus.). 364p. 1985. pap. 12.95 (ISBN 0-87011-725-4). Kodansha.

Conner, Kevin. Acts. 3rd ed. 136p. 1975. 7.50 (ISBN 0-914936-16-6). Bible Temple.

--The Name of God. (Illus.). 90p. 1975. 10.50 (ISBN 0-914936-15-8). Bible Temple.

--The Shepherds & Sheep. 15p. 1973. 0.75 (ISBN 0-914936-07-7). Bible Temple.

--Tabernacle of Moses. 119p. 1974. 5.95 (ISBN 0-914936-08-5). Bible Temple.

Conner, Kevin J. Feasts of Israel. (Illus.). 122p. 1980. pap. 6.95 (ISBN 0-914936-42-5). Bible Temple.

--Foundations of Christian Doctrine. 313p. (gr. 10-12). 1979. pap. 14.95 (ISBN 0-914936-38-7). Bible Temple.

--Interpreting Symbols & Types. 73p. 1980. pap. 5.50 (ISBN 0-914936-40-9). Bible Temple.

--The Tabernacle of David. 230p. 1976. pap. 9.75 (ISBN 0-914936-19-0). Bible Temple.

Conner, Kevin J. & Iverson, K. R. Principles of Church Life. (Illus.). 92p. 1977. ring-binder 4.95 (ISBN 0-914936-23-9). Bible Temple.

Conner, Kevin J. & Malmin, Ken. The Covenants. 112p. 1976. pap. 8.75 (ISBN 0-949829-02-1). Bible Temple.

Conner, Kevin J. & Malmin, Ken P. Interpreting the Scriptures. 1976. pap. 9.95 (ISBN 0-914936-20-4). Bible Temple.

Conner, Michael D., ed. The Hill Creek Homestead & the Late Mississippian Settlement in the Lower Illinois Valley. LC 85-2642. (Kampsville Archeological Center Research Ser.: No. 1). (Illus.). 239p. (Orig.). 1985. pap. 9.95 (ISBN 0-942118-18-9). Ctr Amer Arche.

Conner, Michael D., jt. ed. see McGimsey, Charles R.

Conner, Mike. Groupmind. 224p. 1984. pap. 2.95 (ISBN 0-425-07191-X). Berkley Pub.

Conner, P. E. Differentiable Periodic Maps. 2nd ed. (Lecture Notes in Mathematics: Vol. 738). 1979. pap. 14.00 (ISBN 0-387-09535-7). Springer-Verlag.

--Neumann's Problem for Differential Forms on Riemannian Manifolds. LC 52-42839. (Memoirs Ser.: No. 20). 58p. 1979. pap. 10.00 (ISBN 0-8218-1220-3, MEMO-20). Am Math.

--Notes on the Witt Classification of Hermitian Innerproduct Spaces over a Ring of Algebraic Integers. 157p. 1979. text ed. 20.00x (ISBN 0-292-75516-3). U of Tex Pr.

Conner, Patrick. Michael Angelo Rooker. (British Water-Colour Ser.). (Illus.). 192p. 1985. 28.00 (ISBN 0-7134-3756-1, Pub. by Batsford England); pap. 16.95 (ISBN 0-7134-3757-X). David & Charles.

--People at Home. LC 82-1832. (Looking at Art Ser.). (Illus.). 48p. (gr. 5up). 1982. 11.95 (ISBN 0-689-50252-4, McElderry Bk). Atheneum.

--People at Work. LC 82-1812. (Looking at Art Ser.). (Illus.). 48p. (gr. 5up). 1982. 11.95 (ISBN 0-689-50253-2, McElderry Bk). Atheneum.

--Savage Ruskin. LC 78-17051. 234p. 1979. 14.95x (ISBN 0-8143-1619-0). Wayne St U Pr.

Conner, Paul W. Poor Richard's Politicks: Benjamin Franklin & His New American Order. LC 80-21490. xiv, 285p. 1980. Repr. of 1965 ed. lib. bdg. 29.75x (ISBN 0-313-22695-4, COPRP). Greenwood.

Conner, Pierre E. Lectures on the Action of a Finite Group. LC 68-57940. (Lecture Notes in Mathematics: Vol. 73). 1968. pap. 10.70 (ISBN 0-387-04243-1). Springer-Verlag.

Conner, Pierre E. & Floyd, E. E. Relation of Corbordism to K-Theories. (Lecture Notes in Mathematics: Vol. 28). 1966. pap. 10.70 (ISBN 0-387-03610-5). Springer-Verlag.

Conner, Ralph. Chronicle of a Cop. 1983. 7.95 (ISBN 0-8062-2018-X). Carlton.

Conner, Robert, jt. auth. see Ulrich, Heinz.

Conner, Roger. Breaking down the Barriers: The Changing Relationship Between Illegal Immigration & Welfare. 1982. pap. text ed. 2.50 (ISBN 0-935776-03-6). F A I R.

Conner, Ross F. Methodological Advances in Evaluation Research. (Sage Research Progress Series in Evaluation: Vol. 10). 152p. 1981. 20.00 (ISBN 0-8039-1727-9); pap. 9.95 (ISBN 0-8039-1728-7). Sage.

Conner, Ross F. & Huff, C. Ronald. Attorneys as Activists: Evaluating the American Bar Association's BASICS Program. LC 79-19830. (Contemporary Evaluation Research Ser.: Vol. 1). pap. 66.00 (ISBN 0-317-29601-9, 2021878). Bks Demand UMI.

Conner, T. Doctrina Cristiana. Robleto, Adolfo, tr. Orig. Title: Christian Doctrine. 408p. (Span.). 1981. pap. 7.50 (ISBN 0-311-09012-5). Casa Bautista.

Conner, Terri & Sanderson, Joyce. Live Love Laugh. Dowdney, Donna, ed. (Illus.). 52p. (Orig.). 1981. pap. 4.57 (ISBN 0-9606904-0-9). Conner & Sanderson.

Conner, Thomas L. see Berger, Joseph, et al.

Conner, Valerie J. The National War Labor Board: Stability, Social Justice, & the Voluntary State in World War I. LC 82-13362. (Supplementary Volumes to The Papers of Woodrow Wilson). vii, 232p. 1983. 23.50x (ISBN 0-8078-1539-X). U of NC Pr.

Conner, W. T. The Work of the Holy Spirit. LC 78-54244. 1978. pap. 3.95 (ISBN 0-8054-1618-8). Broadman.

Conner, Walter T. Christian Doctrine. 1940. 14.95 (ISBN 0-8054-1701-X). Broadman.

Conner, William, ed. see Milling, Bryan E. & Olson, David O.

Conner, William B. Math's & Music's Metasonics, 2 vols. Incl. Vol. 1-Creativity through Calculator Harmonic Braiding. LC 82-5100. 140p (ISBN 0-9603536-5-8); Vol. 2-Creativity through Keyboard Harmonic Braiding. LC 82-74235. 213p (ISBN 0-9603536-6-6). (Orig.). 1983. Set. pap. text ed. 36.50 GBC punched (ISBN 0-9603536-7-4). Tesla Bk Co.

Conner-Ogorzaly, M., jt. auth. see Simpson, B. B.

Conners, Bernard F. Dancehall. LC 82-17793. 360p. 1983. 14.95 (ISBN 0-672-52757-X). Bobbs.

--Dancehall. 352p. 1985. pap. 3.95 (ISBN 0-425-08173-7). Berkley Pub.

Conners, C. Keith. Food Additives for Hyperactive Children. LC 80-66. 180p. 1980. 22.50x (ISBN 0-306-40400-1, Plenum Pr). Plenum Pub.

Conners, John R. Advice to a Freshman. 104p. 1984. pap. text ed. 12.25x (ISBN 0-89917-416-7). Tichenor Pub.

Conners, Kenneth W. Lord, Have You Got a Minute? LC 78-15297. 1979. pap. 4.95 (ISBN 0-8170-0816-0). Judson.

Conners, Michael F. Rising Germanophobia: The Chief Obstacle to Current World War II Revisionism. (Studies in Revisionist Historiography). 1980. lib. bdg. 59.95 (ISBN 0-686-59416-9). Revisionist Pr.

Conners, William J. California Surety & Fidelty Bond Practice. LC 74-625114. 475p. 1966. 50.00 (ISBN 0-88124-010-9, BV-30130). Cal Cont Ed Bar.

Connerton, P. The Tragedy of Enlightenment. LC 79-16102. (Cambridge Studies in the History & Theory of Politics). 1980. 37.50 (ISBN 0-521-22842-5). Cambridge U Pr.

Connery, Donald S. The Inner Source: Exploring Hypnosis with Dr. Herbert Spiegel. 1982. 15.50 (ISBN 0-03-046496-X). HR&W.

--The Inner Source: Exploring Hypnosis with Dr. Herbert Spiegel. 1984. pap. 7.95 (ISBN 0-03-000439-X, Owl Bks). HR&W.

Connery, John. Abortion: The Development of the Roman Catholic Perspective. LC 76-51217. 1977. 12.95 (ISBN 0-8294-0257-8). Loyola.

Connery, John, jt. ed. see Malone, Richard.

Connery, Liz N. Loving Letters. (Illus.). 60p. (Orig.). 1985. pap. text ed. 4.95 (ISBN 0-9614333-0-2). L Newkirk Connery.

Connery, R. H. & Leach, R. H. The Federal Government & Metropolitan Areas. LC 77-74936. (American Federalism-the Urban Dimension). 1978. Repr. of 1960 ed. lib. bdg. 24.50x (ISBN 0-405-10483-9). Ayer Co Pubs.

Connery, R. H., ed. see Academy of Political Science.

Connery, Robert H. Governmental Problems in Wild Life Conservation. LC 68-58560. (Columbia University Studies in the Social Sciences: No. 411). Repr. of 1935 ed. 20.00 (ISBN 0-404-51411-1). AMS Pr.

Connery, Robert H. & Benjamin, Gerald. Rockefeller of New York: Executive Power in the Statehouse. LC 78-23947. (Illus.). 480p. 1979. 32.50x (ISBN 0-8014-1188-2). Cornell U Pr.

Connery, Robert H., et al. The Politics of Mental Health: Organizing Community Mental Health in Metropolitan Areas. LC 68-28396. (Illus.). 595p. 1968. 37.00x (ISBN 0-231-03029-0). Columbia U Pr.

Connery, Robert Howe. The Navy & the Industrial Mobilization in World War II. LC 73-166951. (FDR & the Era of the New Deal Ser). 526p. 1972. Repr. of 1951 ed. lib. bdg. 59.50 (ISBN 0-306-70322-X). Da Capo.

Connes, G. Dictionary of the Characters & Scenes in the Novels, Romances & Short Stories of H. G. Wells. LC 73-174698. (Reference Ser., No. 44). 1971. Repr. of 1926 ed. lib. bdg. 46.95x (ISBN 0-8383-1353-1). Haskell.

Connes, G. A. Dictionary of the Characters & Scenes in the Novels, Romances & Short Stories of H. G. Wells. 1926. lib. bdg. 36.00 (ISBN 0-8414-2376-8). Folcroft.

Connes, Georges. Etat Present Des Etudes: Shakespeariennes. 116p. 1980. Repr. of 1932 ed. lib. bdg. 25.00 (ISBN 0-8495-0951-3). Arden Lib.

Connes, Georges, jt. auth. see Merimee, Prosper.

Connes, Keith. Know Your Airplane! 176p. 1985. 19.95 (ISBN 0-8138-1056-6). Iowa St U Pr.

--The Loran, RNAV & Nav-Comm Book. (Illus.). 1985. pap. 14.95 (ISBN 0-932579-01-9). Butterfield Pr.

Connett, Eugene. Duck Decoys. 1980. 12.50 (ISBN 0-911764-00-3). Durrell.

Connett, P. H. Inorganic Elements in Biochemistry. (Structure & Bonding: Vol. 54). (Illus.). 190p. 1983. 39.00 (ISBN 0-387-12542-6). Springer-Verlag.

Connett, W. C. & Schwartz, Alan Lee. The Theory of Ultraspherical Multipliers. LC 76-58958. (Memoirs: No. 183). 92p. 1977. pap. 13.00 (ISBN 0-8218-2183-0, MEMO-183). Am Math.

Connick, C. Milo. Jesus: The Man, the Mission, & the Message. 2nd ed. (Illus.). 512p. 1974. 27.95 (ISBN 0-13-509521-2). P-H.

Conniff, Gregory. Common Ground. LC 84-40669. 128p. 1985. 35.00x (ISBN 0-300-03407-5). Yale U Pr.

Conniff, Michael, ed. Latin American Populism in Comparative Perspective. LC 80-54572. (Illus.). 272p. 1981. pap. 12.95x (ISBN 0-8263-0581-4). U of NM Pr.

Conniff, Michael L. Black Labor on a White Canal: Panama, 1904-1981. LC 84-21970. (Pitt Latin American Ser.). (Illus.). 239p. 1985. 29.95x (ISBN 0-8229-3509-0). U of Pittsburgh Pr.

--Urban Politics in Brazil: The Rise of Populism, 1925-1945. LC 80-54060. (Pitt Latin American Ser.). (Illus.). 280p. 1981. 23.95x (ISBN 0-8229-3438-8). U of Pittsburgh Pr.

Conniff, Richard, ed. The Devil's Book of Verse. (Illus.). 256p. 1983. 15.95 (ISBN 0-89696-186-9, An Everest House Book). Dodd.

Conniffe, Patricia. Computer Dictionary. pap. 4.95 (ISBN 0-317-33054-3); tchr's guide 1.50 (ISBN 0-317-06582-3). Scholastic Inc.

Conningham, Frederic A. Currier & Ives Prints: An Illustrated Checklist. 14.95 (ISBN 0-517-55115-2); pap. 9.95 (ISBN 0-517-55116-0). Crown.

Connis, Richard T. Training the Mentally Handicapped for Employment: A Comprehensive Manual. LC 81-1979. 192p. 1981. 19.95 (ISBN 0-89885-001-0). Human Sci Pr.

Connor, W. R., ed. see Taylor, Michael.

Connock, Marion. Nadia of Romania. (Illus.). 132p. 1977. 13.50 (ISBN 0-7156-1241-7, Pub. by Duckworth England); (Pub. by Duckworth England). Biblio Dist.

Connolly, Ann M., jt. auth. see Munnell, Alicia H.

Connolly, Arlene F. & Kelley, Jean. Curriculum in Graduate Education in Nursing: Part III - Development & Improvement of Graduate Education in Nursing. 46p. 1977. 5.95 (ISBN 0-88737-190-6, 15-1679). Natl League Nurse.
Connolly, Austin J. Keymath Attribute Blocks Manual. (Illus.). 58p. 1980. pap. text ed. 8.25 (ISBN 0-913476-93-5). Am Guidance.
--KeyMath Balance Manual. (Illus.). 46p. 1980. pap. text ed. 7.25 (ISBN 0-913476-95-1). Am Guidance.
--KeyMath Boards Manual. (Illus.). 110p. 1980. pap. text ed. 9.50 (ISBN 0-913476-96-X). Am Guidance.
--KeyMath Card Decks Manual. (Illus.). 76p. 1980. pap. text ed. 8.25 (ISBN 0-913476-97-8). Am Guidance.
--KeyMath Chips Manual. (Illus.). 71p. 1980. pap. text ed. 8.25 (ISBN 0-913476-98-6). Am Guidance.
--KeyMath Cubes Manual. (Illus.). 134p. 1980. pap. text ed. 13.00 (ISBN 0-913476-94-3). Am Guidance.
--KeyMath Early Steps. (Illus.). 64p. 1982. pap. 7.25 tchr's.guide (ISBN 0-913476-90-0). Am Guidance.
--KeyMath Early Steps. (Illus.). 294p. 1982. text ed. 24.00 instr. manual (ISBN 0-913476-91-9). Am Guidance.
--KeyMath Early Steps. (Illus.). 1982. of printed materials 63.50 set (ISBN 0-913476-92-7). Am Guidance.
--KeyMath Teach & Practice. (gr. k-6). 1985. 97.50 (ISBN 0-88671-240-8). Am Guidance.
--KeyMath Teach & Practice Teacher's Guide. (KeyMath Teach & Practice Ser.). 1985. 7.95 (ISBN 0-88671-241-6). Am Guidance.
--KeyMath Tumblers Manual. (Illus.). 74p. 1980. pap. text ed. 8.25 (ISBN 0-913476-99-4). Am Guidance.
Connolly, B. W., jt. ed. see Oliveira-Pinto, F.
Connolly, Bob. Paper Collectibles. 2nd ed. 400p. 1981. pap. 9.95 (ISBN 0-517-54403-2, Americana). Crown.
Connolly, Charles. On Being Catholics. 96p. Date not set. pap. 5.00 (ISBN 0-912414-37-5). Lumen Christi.
Connolly, Christopher, jt. auth. see Campbell, Roy.
Connolly, Christopher, jt. auth. see Syer, John.
Connolly, Cornelius J. External Morphology of the Primate Brain. (Illus.). 386p. 1950. photocopy ed. 36.50x (ISBN 0-398-04230-6). C C Thomas.
Connolly, Cyril. Enemies of Promise. 268p. pap. 6.95 (ISBN 0-89255-078-3). Persea Bks.
--The Evening Colonnade. 492p. 1985. pap. 8.95 (ISBN 0-15-629060-X, Harv). HarBraceJ.
--The Rock Pool. 190p. 1982. cancelled 12.95 (ISBN 0-89255-073-2); pap. 5.95 (ISBN 0-89255-059-7). Persea Bks.
--The Selected Essays of Cyril Connolly. Quennell, Peter, ed. 312p. 1984. 17.95 (ISBN 0-89255-072-4). Persea Bks.
--The Unquiet Grave. 156p. 1982. cancelled 12.95 (ISBN 0-89255-074-0); pap. 5.95 (ISBN 0-89255-058-9). Persea Bks.
Connolly, Cyril, tr. see Jarry, Alfred.
Connolly, Edward F. & Harding, Christopher, eds. A Cop's Cop. (Illus.). 300p. 23.95 (ISBN 0-317-17306-5). Quinlan Pr.
Connolly, Edward S. & Lieberman, Philip. Introducing the Apple Macintosh. LC 84-50035. 192p. 1984. 12.95 (ISBN 0-672-22361-9). Sams.
Connolly, Eileen. Earthdance. LC 84-24172. 304p. 1984. Repr. of 1984 ed. lib. bdg. 16.95x (ISBN 0-89370-676-0). Borgo Pr.
--Earthdance. 256p. (Orig.). 1984. pap. 6.95 (ISBN 0-87877-076-3). Newcastle Pub.
--Tarot: A New Handbook for the Apprentice. LC 80-22271. 244p. 1980. Repr. of 1979 ed. lib. bdg. 21.95x (ISBN 0-89370-645-0). Borgo Pr.
--The Tarot: A New Handbook for the Apprentice. LC 79-15303. (Illus.). 1979. pap. 9.95 (ISBN 0-87877-045-3). Newcastle Pub.
Connolly, Finbarr. God & Man in Modern Spirituality. 276p. 1984. pap. 9.95 (ISBN 0-87061-108-9). Chr Classics.
Connolly, Frank, ed. see Moore, Christy.
Connolly, Harold X. A Ghetto Grows in Brooklyn. LC 77-2471. (Illus.). 1977. 25.00x (ISBN 0-8147-1371-8). NYU Pr.
Connolly, J. L. John Gerson: Reformer & Mystic. (Medieval Studies Ser.). (Illus.). Repr. of 1928 ed. lib. bdg. 44.00x (ISBN 0-697-00031-1). Irvington.
Connolly, James. James Connolly: Selected Writings. Ellis, P. Berresford, ed. 317p. 1973. pap. 6.25 (ISBN 0-14-021613-8, Pub. by Penguin England). Irish Bk Ctr.
--Sax's Songs. (Illus.). 1975. pap. 4.00 (ISBN 0-916906-05-1). Konglomerati.
Connolly, James B. Deep Sea's Toll. facsimile ed. LC 78-37262. (Short Story Index Reprint Ser.). (Illus.). Repr. of 1905 ed. 21.00 (ISBN 0-8369-4073-3). Ayer Co Pubs.
--Out of Gloucester. facsimile ed. LC 70-94712. (Short Story Index Reprint Ser.). 1902. 18.00 (ISBN 0-8369-3091-6). Ayer Co Pubs.
Connolly, James E. Public Speaking As Communication. LC 73-90806. 1974. pap. text ed. 8.95x (ISBN 0-8087-0344-7). Burgess.
Connolly, James E., ed. Why the Possum's Tail Is Bare: And Other North American Indian Nature Tales. (Illus.). 56p. (gr. 3 up). 1985. PLB 12.95 (ISBN 0-88045-069-X). Stemmer Hse.
Connolly, John. A Study of Hamlet. LC 73-517. 1973. Repr. of 1863 ed. lib. bdg. 17.00 (ISBN 0-8414-1490-4). Folcroft.
Connolly, John F., ed. DePalma's the Management of Fractures & Dislocations: An Atlas, 2 vols. 3rd ed. (Illus.). 2000p. 1981. Set. text ed. 120.00 (ISBN 0-7216-2666-1); Vol. 1. 60.00 (ISBN 0-7216-2702-1); Vol. 2. 60.00 (ISBN 0-7216-2703-X). Saunders.
Connolly, John G., ed. Carcinoma of the Bladder. (Progress in Cancer Research & Therapy Ser.: Vol. 18). 310p. 1981. 46.00 (ISBN 0-89004-536-4). Raven.
Connolly, John R. Dimensions of Belief & Unbelief. LC 80-67241. 373p. 1981. lib. bdg. 27.50 (ISBN 0-8191-1389-1); pap. text ed. 15.50 (ISBN 0-8191-1390-5). U Pr of Amer.
Connolly, John S. Photochemical Conversion & Storage of Solar Energy. LC 81-12853. 1981. 55.00 (ISBN 0-12-185880-4). Acad Pr.
Connolly, Joseph. Modern First Editions: Their Value to Collectors. (Illus.). 1985. 20.00 (ISBN 0-85613-657-3, Pub. by Salem Hse Ltd). Merrimack Pub Cir.
--P. G. Wodehouse. (Illus.). 160p. 1980. text ed. 18.75x (ISBN 0-85613-235-7). Humanities.
--P. G. Wodehouse: An Illustrated Biography. (Illus.). 160p. 1983. 17.95 (ISBN 0-8253-0147-5). Beaufort Bks NY.
Connolly, Julian W. Ivan Bunin. (World Authors Ser.). 1982. lib. bdg. 19.95 (ISBN 0-8057-6513-1, Twayne). G K Hall.
Connolly, K. G. Mechanisms of Motor Skill Development. 1971. 70.00 (ISBN 0-12-185950-9). Acad Pr.
Connolly, K. J., jt. auth. see Smith, P. K.
Connolly, K. J. & Prechtl, H. F., eds. Maturation & Development-Biological & Psychological Perspectives. (Clinics in Developmental Medicine Ser.: Vols. 77 & 78). 326p. 1981. text ed. 39.50 (ISBN 0-433-06415-3, Pub. by Spastics Intl England). Lippincott.
Connolly, Mary G. Mental Illness & Use of Community Res. LC 74-28600. 1975. soft bdg. 12.95 (ISBN 0-88247-326-3). R & E Pubs.
Connolly, Michael & Adeniran, Iunde, eds. The International Monetary System: Choices for the Future. LC 82-7483. 352p. 1982. 39.95 (ISBN 0-03-061794-4). Praeger.
Connolly, Michael B. International Trade & Lending. LC 84-26254. 144p. 1985. 28.95 (ISBN 0-03-071166-5). Praeger.
Connolly, Michael B. & McDermott, John, eds. The Economics of the Caribbean Basin. LC 85-3419. 306p. 1985. 41.95 (ISBN 0-03-001674-6). Praeger.
Connolly, Michael J., ed. see Black, Henry C.
Connolly, Myles. Mister Blue. pap. 3.50 (ISBN 0-385-02866-0, Im). Doubleday.
--Mister Blue. 1928. 12.95 (ISBN 0-02-527460-0). Macmillan.
Connolly, Pat. Guide to Living Foods. rev. ed. LC 78-70856. (Illus.). 10.00 (ISBN 0-916764-05-2). Price-Pottenger.
Connolly, Pat & Associates of Price Pottinger Nutrition Foundation. Candida Albicans Yeast-Free Cookbook. 168p. (Orig.). 1985. pap. 9.95 (ISBN 0-87983-409-9). Keats.
Connolly, Patrick. Love, Dad. (Illus.). 200p. (Orig.). 1985. pap. 5.95 (ISBN 0-8362-7927-1). Andrews McMeel Parker.
Connolly, Paul H. Building Family: An Act of Faith. LC 82-74073. 96p. 1982. pap. 4.95 (ISBN 0-87029-186-6, 20277-0). Abbey.
--On Essays: A Reader for Writers. 318p. 1981. pap. text ed. 9.50 scp (ISBN 0-06-041345-X, HarpC). Har-Row.
Connolly, Paul M. Promotional Practices & Policies. (Studies in Productivity: Highlights of the Literature Ser.: Vol. 41). 1985. 35.00 (ISBN 0-08-029515-0). Work in Amer.
Connolly, Peter. The Greek Armies. LC 79-65846. (Armies of the Past Ser.). PLB 13.96 (ISBN 0-382-06308-2). Silver.
--The Greek Armies. (Armies of the Past Ser.). 80p. (gr. 4 up). 1985. pap. 8.75 (ISBN 0-382-06909-9). Silver.
--Hannibal & the Enemies of Rome. (Armies of the Past Ser.). 80p. (gr. 4 up). 1985. pap. 8.75 (ISBN 0-382-06911-0). Silver.
--The Roman Army. LC 79-65845. (Armies of the Past Ser.). PLB 13.96 (ISBN 0-382-06306-6); pap. 8.75 (ISBN 0-382-06910-2). Silver.
Connolly, Peter, ed. Literature & the Changing Ireland. LC 81-14930. (Irish Literary Studies: No. 9). 240p. 1982. 28.50x (ISBN 0-389-20234-7). B&N Imports.
Connolly, Ray. The Sun Place. 368p. 1981. pap. 2.95 (ISBN 0-380-78816-0, 78816-0). Avon.
Connolly, Robert D. The New Collector's Directory. 1976. pap. 3.50 (ISBN 0-914598-36-8). Padre Prods.
--The New Collector's Directory for the 1980's. rev. 2nd ed. (Illus.). 168p. 1980. pap. 5.95 (ISBN 0-914598-38-4). Padre Prods.
--Paper Collectibles, Identification & Value Guide. 2nd ed. (Illus.). 364p. pap. 9.95 (ISBN 0-89689-022-8). Wallace-Homestead.
Connolly, Sean. Priests & People in Pre-Famine Ireland, 1780-1845. LC 81-16526. 340p. 1982. 30.00x (ISBN 0-312-64411-6). St Martin.
Connolly, T. F., et al. Solid State Physics Literature Guides, 10 vols. Incl. Vol. 2. Semiconductors: Preparation, Crystal Growth & Selected Properties. LC 74-133269. 230p. 1972. 75.00x (ISBN 0-306-68322-9); Vol. 3. Groups IV, V & VI Transition Metals & Compounds: Preparation & Properties. LC 74-133269. 225p. 1972. 75.00x (ISBN 0-306-68323-7); Vol. 4. Electrical Properties of Solids: Surface Preparation & Methods of Measurement. LC 74-133269. 120p. 1972. 75.00x (ISBN 0-306-68324-5); Vol. 5. Bibliography of Magnetic Materials & Tabulation of Magnetic Transition Temperatures. LC 74-133269. 187p. 1972. 75.00x (ISBN 0-306-68325-3); Vol. 6. Ferroelectrics Literature Index. LC 74-4363. 718p. 1974. 110.00x (ISBN 0-306-68326-1); Vol. 9. Laser Window & Mirror Materials. LC 77-20174. 302p. 1977. 95.00x (ISBN 0-306-68329-6). IFI Plenum). Plenum Pub.
Connolly, Terence L. An Introduction to Chaucer & Langland. LC 76-40470. 1925. lib. bdg. 12.50 (ISBN 0-8414-3586-3). Folcroft.
Connolly, Terence L., ed. see Thompson, Francis.
Connolly, Thomas E. Swinburne's Theory of Poetry. LC 64-17576. 1965. 22.50x (ISBN 0-87395-013-5). State U NY Pr.
Connolly, Thomas E., ed. Joyce's "Portrait". Criticisms & Critiques. LC 62-14861. (Goldentree Books in English Literature). (Orig.). 1962. pap. text ed. 10.95x (ISBN 0-89197-253-6). Irvington.
Connolly, Thomas E., notes by see Hawthorne, Nathaniel.
Connolly, Thomas J. Foundations of Nuclear Engineering. LC 77-26916. 344p. 1978. text ed. 48.75x (ISBN 0-471-16858-0). Wiley.
Connolly, Vivian. Five Ports to Danger. (Orig.). 1980. pap. 1.75 (ISBN 0-505-51518-0, Pub. by Tower Bks). Dorchester Pub Co.
--I Know My Love. (To Have & to Hold Ser.: No. 10). 1983. pap. 1.95 (ISBN 0-317-04568-7). Jove Pubns.
--I Know My Love, No. 10. 192p. 1983. pap. 1.95 (ISBN 0-515-06937-X). Jove Pubns.
--Love in Exile. (Superromance Ser.). 295p. 1983. pap. 2.95 (ISBN 0-373-70063-6, Pub. by Worldwide). Harlequin Bks.
--Moonlight & Magnolias. (To Have & to Hold: No. 21). 1984. pap. 1.95 (ISBN 0-515-06948-5). Jove Pubns.
--Promises to Keep. (To Have & to Hold Ser.: No. 30). 192p. 1984. pap. 1.95 (ISBN 0-515-07832-8). Jove Pubns.
--Sweet Country Music. (To Have & To Hold Ser.: No. 49). 192p. 1985. pap. 1.95 (ISBN 0-425-07780-2). Berkley Pub.
Connolly, W. E. Appearance & Reality in Politics. 224p. 1981. 34.50 (ISBN 0-521-23026-8). Cambridge U Pr.
Connolly, William & Lukes, Steven, eds. Legitimacy & the State. (Readings in Social & Political Theory). 256p. 1984. 30.00x (ISBN 0-8147-1394-7); pap. 12.50x (ISBN 0-8147-1395-5). NYU Pr.
Connolly, William E. The Terms of Political Discourse. exp. ed. LC 83-42928. 240p. 1983. 30.00x (ISBN 0-691-07664-2); pap. 9.95x (ISBN 0-691-02223-2). Princeton U Pr.
Connolly, William E., jt. auth. see Best, Michael H.
Connolly, William G. The New York Times Guide to Buying or Building a Home. LC 84-40111. 1984. 16.95 (ISBN 0-8129-1119-9). Times Bks.
Connolly, William H. & Gordon, Glen. Social Structure & Political Theory. 1974. pap. text ed. 5.95x (ISBN 0-669-83923-X). Heath.
Connolly, William J., jt. auth. see Barry, William A.
Connoly, Vivian. Cecilia. 224p. 1981. pap. 1.95 (ISBN 0-449-50211-2, Crest). Fawcett.
Connon, J. J. An Introductory Textbook of Medicine. 374p. 1977. 49.00x (ISBN 0-686-79476-1, Pub. by Lloyd-Luke England). State Mutual Bk.
Connor & Bristow. Coronary Heart Disease: Prevention, Complications, & Treatment. LC 65-7289. 1984. 45.00 (ISBN 0-397-50569-8, Lippincott Medical). Lippincott.
Connor, Anthony J. Baseball for the Love of It: Hall of Famers Tell It Like It Was. (Illus.). 288p. 1982. 16.95 (ISBN 0-02-527500-3). Macmillan.
--Voices from Cooperstown: Baseball's Hall of Famers Tell it Like it Was. 352p. 1984. pap. 7.95 (ISBN 0-02-028210-9, Collier). Macmillan.
Connor, Brooke, jt. auth. see Kittelson, Pat.
Connor, Dennis A. Information System Specification & Design Road Map. (Illus.). 240p. 1985. text ed. 32.95 (ISBN 0-13-464868-4). P-H.
Connor, Dixie. Shining Mountain Shadows. (Illus.). 1977. pap. 5.00x (ISBN 0-918292-02-6). Griggs Print.
Connor, E. S., jt. ed. see Bruce, A. M.
Connor, Edward. Prophecy for Today. LC 83-70408. 135p. 1984. pap. 3.00 (ISBN 0-89555-212-4). TAN Bks Pubs.
Connor, Elizabeth. Methodist Trail Blazer: Philip Gatch. rev. ed. LC 76-101704. (Illus.). 260p. pap. 12.00 smythsewn (ISBN 0-914960-51-2). Academy Bks.
Connor, Elizabeth, tr. see Aelred of Rievaulx.
Connor, F. R. Electronic Devices. 244p. 1982. scp 18.16 (ISBN 0-205-07780-3, 327780). Allyn.
--Modulation. (Introductory Topics in Electronics & Telecommunication Ser.). (Illus.). 1973. pap. text ed. 17.95x (ISBN 0-7131-3303-1). Intl Ideas.
--Modulation. 2nd ed. (Introductory Topics in Electronics & Telecommunication). 144p. 1982. pap. text ed. 9.95 (ISBN 0-7131-3457-7). E Arnold.
--Networks. (Introductory Topics in Electronics & Telecommunication Ser.). (Illus.). 1972. pap. text ed. 17.95x (ISBN 0-7131-3258-2). Intl Ideas.
--Noise. (Introductory Topics in Electronics & Telecommunication Ser.). (Illus.). 1973. pap. text ed. 17.95x (ISBN 0-7131-3306-6). Intl Ideas.
--Noise. 2nd ed. (Introductory Topics in Electronics & Telecommunications). 144p. 1982. pap. text ed. 9.95 (ISBN 0-7131-3459-3). E Arnold.
--Signals. (Introductory Topics in Electronics & Telecommunications Ser.). (Illus.). 1972. pap. text ed. 17.95x (ISBN 0-7131-3262-0). Intl Ideas.
--Signals. 2nd ed. (Introductory Topics in Electronics & Telecommunication). 144p. 1982. pap. text ed. 9.95 (ISBN 0-7131-3458-5). E Arnold.
--Wave Transmission. (Introductory Topics in Electronics & Telecommunications Ser.). (Illus.). 1972. pap. text ed. 17.95x (ISBN 0-7131-3278-7). Intl Ideas.
Connor, Floyd, et al. Day-by-Day in Montreal Expos History. LC 84-47514. (Illus.). 304p. 1984. pap. 10.95 (ISBN 0-88011-207-7). Leisure Pr.
Connor, Frances P. Education of Homebound or Hospitalized Children. LC 64-16622. (Orig.). 1964. pap. text ed. 4.25x (ISBN 0-8077-1185-3). Tchrs Coll.
Connor, Frances P., et al. Program Guide for Infants & Toddlers with Neuromotor & Other Developmental Disabilities. LC 77-28188. 1978. pap. 15.95x (ISBN 0-8077-2546-3). Tchrs Coll.
Connor, Frank. Sky Pilot. 1973. pap. 0.95 (ISBN 0-380-01552-8, 17905). Avon.
Connor, J. J., jt. auth. see Brebbia, C. A.
Connor, J. M. Soft Tissue Ossification. (Illus.). 176p. 1983. 50.00 (ISBN 0-387-12530-2). Springer-Verlag.
Connor, James P. Classroom Activities for Helping Hyperactive Children. 1974. pap. 6.40x (ISBN 0-87628-200-1). Ctr Appl Res.
Connor, Jeannette M., ed. Colonial Records of Spanish Florida: Letters & Reports of Governors & Secular Persons, 2 vols. LC 74-19720. Repr. of 1930 ed. Set. 55.00 (ISBN 0-404-12475-5). AMS Pr.
Connor, Jeannette T., tr. see Solis De Meras, Gonzalo.
Connor, Jerome J., jt. ed. see Chryssostomidis, Chryssostomos.
Connor, John J. On-the-Job-Training. (Illus.). 89p. 1983. pap. text ed. 21.00 (ISBN 0-934634-56-4). Intl Human Res.
Connor, John J. & Carson, William M. Manpower Planning & Development: The Developing World. LC 82-81030. (Illus.). 150p. 1982. text ed. 30.00 (ISBN 0-934634-32-7). Intl Human Res.
Connor, John M., et al. The Food Manufacturing Industries. LC 83-49504. 496p. 1984. 38.00x (ISBN 0-669-08203-1). Lexington Bks.
Connor, John W. A Study of the Marital Stability of Japanese War Brides. LC 75-36569. 1976. perfect bdg. softcover 10.00 (ISBN 0-88247-376-X). R & E Pubs.
--Tradition & Change in Three Generations of Japanese Americans. LC 76-28999. 382p. 1977. 25.95x (ISBN 0-88229-288-9). Nelson-Hall.
Connor, Joseph. Marine Fire Prevention, Fire Fighting & Fire Safety. (Illus.). 404p. 1979. pap. text ed. 16.95 (ISBN 0-87618-994-X). Brady Comm.
Connor, Joseph E. & Devos, Burnell H., Jr., eds. Guide to Accounting Controls: Establishing, Evaluating, & Monitoring Control Systems, Annual Supplement. LC 79-64169. 1979. 96.00 (ISBN 0-88262-333-8). Warren.
Connor, Larry J., et al. Managing the Farm Business. (Illus.). 384p. 1981. text ed. 27.95 (ISBN 0-13-550376-0). P-H.
Connor, Leo E. Administration of Special Education Programs. LC 61-11500. 1961. pap. text ed. 4.75x (ISBN 0-8077-1182-9). Tchrs Coll.
--Speech for the Deaf Child: Knowledge & Use. LC 71-175247. 1971. pap. text ed. 8.75 (ISBN 0-88200-085-3, A1118). Alexander Graham.
Connor, Marlene K., jt. auth. see Woman's Day Editors.
Connor, Michael. Duty Free: Smuggling Made Easy. (Illus.). 80p. 1983. pap. 10.00 (ISBN 0-87364-264-3). Paladin Pr.
--How to Hide Anything. (Illus.). 120p. (Orig.). 1984. pap. 10.00 (ISBN 0-87364-289-9). Paladin Pr.
--Sneak It Through. (Illus.). 112p. (Orig.). 1984. pap. 10.00 (ISBN 0-87364-282-1). Paladin Pr.
Connor, N. E., jt. auth. see Pritchard, R. Guy.
Connor, P. E. & Perils, R. A Survey of Trace Forms of Algebraic Number Fields. (Lecture Notes on Pure Mathematics: Vol. 2). 325p. 1984. 35.00x (ISBN 9971-966-04-2, Pub. by World Sci Singapore); pap. 19.00x (ISBN 9971-966-05-0, Pub. by World Sci Singapore). Taylor & Francis.
Connor, P. J., tr. see Home, R. W.
Connor, Patrick E. Dimensions in Modern Management. 3rd ed. LC 81-84072. 1982. pap. 19.50 (ISBN 0-395-31723-1). HM.

--Organizations: Theory & Design. 1980. text ed. 29.95 (ISBN 0-574-19380-4, 13-2380); instr's guide avail. (ISBN 0-574-19381-2, 13-2381). SRA.
Connor, Paula. Walking in the Garden: Inner Peace from the Flowers of God. (Illus.). 170p. 1984. 14.95 (ISBN 0-13-944280-4); pap. 5.95 (ISBN 0-13-944264-2). P-H.
Connor, Pierre E. & Floyd, E. E. Torsion in SU-bordism. LC 52-42839. (Memoirs: No. 60). 74p. 1969. pap. 10.00 (ISBN 0-8218-1260-2, MEMO-60). Am Math.
Connor, R. D. Ante-Bellum Builders of North Carolina. LC 70-149342. 123p. 1971. Repr. of 1930 ed. 10.00 (ISBN 0-87152-064-8). Reprint.
--Race Elements in the White Population of North Carolina. Jackson, W. C., ed. LC 73-149343. 115p. 1971. Repr. of 1920 ed. 10.00 (ISBN 0-87152-062-1). Reprint.
Connor, R. W., ed. see Isocrates.
Connor, Ralph. Black Rock. 1973. pap. 0.95 (ISBN 0-380-01065-8, 17301). Avon.
--Black Rock: A Tale of the Selkirks. 1976. lib. bdg. 12.95x (ISBN 0-89968-014-3). Lightyear.
--The Doctor: A Tale of the Rockies. 1976. lib. bdg. 17.25x (ISBN 0-89968-015-1). Lightyear.
--The Major. 1976. lib. bdg. 16.75x (ISBN 0-89968-014-3). Lightyear.
--The Man from Glengarry. 1976. lib. bdg. 19.50x (ISBN 0-89968-017-8). Lightyear.
--The Sky Pilot, a Tale of the Foothills. 1976. lib. bdg. 14.25x (ISBN 0-89968-019-4). Lightyear.
--The Sky Pilot: A Tale of the Foothills. LC 73-104767. (Novel As American Social History Ser.). 304p. 1970. 20.00x (ISBN 0-8131-1210-9); pap. 8.00x (ISBN 0-8131-0130-1). U Pr of Ky.
--The Sky Pilot in No Man's Land. 1976. lib. bdg. 15.75x (ISBN 0-89968-018-6). Lightyear.
Connor, Reardon. Shake Hands with the Devil. 312p. Repr. of 1934 ed. lib. bdg. 17.95x (ISBN 0-89190-449-2, Pub. by River City Pr). Amereon Ltd.
Connor, Richard A., Jr. & Davidson, Jeffrey P. Marketing Your Consulting & Professional Services. 219p. 1985. 19.95 (ISBN 0-471-81827-5). Wiley.
Connor, Robert D. Cornelius Harnett: An Essay in North Carolina History. facsimile ed. LC 76-148876. (Select Bibliographies Reprint Ser). Repr. of 1909 ed. 18.00 (ISBN 0-8369-5647-8). Ayer Co Pubs.
Connor, Robert W., ed. Greek Orations: Lysias, Isocrates, Demosthenes, Aeschines, Hyperides. LC 66-17355. 1966. 6.95 (ISBN 0-472-24250-4); pap. 6.95 (ISBN 0-472-06116-X). U of Mich Pr.
Connor, Ross F., ed. Evaluation Studies Review Annual, Vol. 9. LC 76-15865. 752p. 1984. 40.00 (ISBN 0-8039-2386-4). Sage.
Connor, Ruth. The Scholastic Behavior of a Selected Group of Undergraduate Home Economics Students. LC 70-176667. (Columbia University. Teachers College. Contributions to Education: No. 497). Repr. of 1931 ed. 22.50 (ISBN 0-404-55497-0). AMS Pr.
Connor, Samuel R. The Handbook for Effective Job Development. 101p. 1981. pap. 14.95 (ISBN 0-89361-027-5). Work in Amer.
Connor, Samuel R. & Pelletier, Mary B. The Handbook for Effective Job Development. Work in America Institute, ed. (Work in America Institute in Productivity). 101p. (Orig.). pap. 14.95 (ISBN 0-89361-027-5). Pergamon.
Connor, Seymour, ed. Dear America. LC 70-172388. 1971. 8.50 (ISBN 0-685-02299-4). Jenkins.
Connor, Seymour V. Kentucky Colonization in Texas: A History of the Peters Colony. LC 83-80997. 153p. 1983. Repr. of 1954 ed. 15.00 (ISBN 0-8063-1032-4). Genealog Pub.
--Texas: A History. LC 71-136037. (Illus., Orig.). 1971. text ed. 24.95x (ISBN 0-88295-724-4). Harlan Davidson.
--Texas in Seventeen Seventy-Six. LC 75-37049. 1975. 14.95 (ISBN 0-8363-0136-6). Jenkins.
Connor, Seymour V. & Skaggs, Jimmy M. Broadcloth & Britches: The Santa Fe Trade. LC 76-17978. 252p. 1977. 16.50 (ISBN 0-89096-022-4); pap. 7.95 (ISBN 0-89096-191-3). Tex A&M Univ Pr.
Connor, Stephen. Charles Dickens. (Rereading Literature Ser.). 192p. 1985. cloth 24.95x (ISBN 0-631-13441-7); pap. 6.95x (ISBN 0-631-13512-X). Basil Blackwell.
Connor, Susan, jt. auth. see Kendig, Lane H.
Connor, Susan F. A Comprehensive Review Manual for the Nurse Practitioner. 1984. spiral text 18.95 (ISBN 0-316-15317-6). Little.
Connor, Tony. New & Selected Poems. LC 81-16148. 160p. 1982. 14.00x (ISBN 0-8203-0605-3); pap. 6.95 (ISBN 0-8203-0606-1). U of Ga Pr.
Connor, Ursula. How to Select & Buy a Personal Computer: For Small Business, for Department Heads, for the Home, for Self-Employed Professionals. (Illus.). 177p. 1983. pap. 9.95 (ISBN 0-8159-5717-3). Devin.
Connor, W. R. Roman Augury & Etruscan Divination. LC 75-10649. (Ancient Religion & Mythology Ser.). 1976. 14.00x (ISBN 0-405-07273-2). Ayer Co Pubs.
Connor, W. R., ed. The Acts of the Pagan Martyrs. LC 78-18588. (Greek Texts & Commentaries Ser.). 1979. Repr. of 1954 ed. lib. bdg. 25.50x (ISBN 0-405-11430-3). Ayer Co Pubs.
--Ancient Religion & Mythology, 32 vols. (Illus.). 1976. Set. 1039.00x (ISBN 0-405-07001-2). Ayer Co Pubs.
--Chion of Heraclea. LC 78-18571. (Greek Texts & Commentaries Ser.). 1979. Repr. of 1951 ed. lib. bdg. 14.00x (ISBN 0-405-11415-X). Ayer Co Pubs.
--Greek History, 27 bks. 1973. Set. 881.00 (ISBN 0-405-04775-4). Ayer Co Pubs.
--Greek Texts & Commentaries Series, 40 bks. (Illus.). 1979. lib. bdg. 1007.50xset (ISBN 0-405-11412-5). Ayer Co Pubs.
--Latin Texts & Commentaries Series, 30 bks. (Illus.). 1979. Set. lib. bdg. 643.50 (ISBN 0-405-11594-6). Ayer Co Pubs.
Connor, W. R. & Dilke, O. A., eds. Statius Achilled. LC 78-67127. (Latin Texts & Commentaries Ser.). (Latin & Eng.). 1979. Repr. of 1954 ed. lib. bdg. 14.00x (ISBN 0-405-11598-9). Ayer Co Pubs.
Connor, W. R. & Magnus, Hugo, eds. Metamorphoseon, Libri XV. LC 78-67140. (Latin Texts & Commentaries Ser.). (Latin & Eng.). 1979. Repr. of 1914 ed. lib. bdg. 55.50x (ISBN 0-405-11609-8). Ayer Co Pubs.
Connor, W. R., ed. see Adler, Eve.
Connor, W. R., ed. see Aeschines.
Connor, W. R., ed. see Aeschylus.
Connor, W. R., ed. see Alcman.
Connor, W. R., ed. see Apollonius, Rhodius.
Connor, W. R., ed. see Aristophanes.
Connor, W. R., ed. see Arnould, Dominique.
Connor, W. R., ed. see Augustine.
Connor, W. R., ed. see Block, Elizabeth.
Connor, W. R., ed. see Bowie, Angus M.
Connor, W. R., ed. see Brooks, Robert A.
Connor, W. R., ed. see Brumfield, Allaire C.
Connor, W. R., ed. see Caesar.
Connor, W. R., ed. see Callimachus.
Connor, W. R., ed. see Carey, Christopher.
Connor, W. R., ed. see Cicero.
Connor, W. R., ed. see David, Ephraim.
Connor, W. R., ed. see Davies, John K.
Connor, W. R., ed. see Demetrius.
Connor, W. R., ed. see Demosthenes.
Connor, W. R., ed. see Doenges, Norman A.
Connor, W. R., ed. see Euripides.
Connor, W. R., ed. see Figueira, Thomas J.
Connor, W. R., ed. see Furley, William D.
Connor, W. R., ed. see Geffcken, John.
Connor, W. R., ed. see Ginsberg, Judith.
Connor, W. R., ed. see Hall, Jennifer.
Connor, W. R., ed. see Hammond, N. G.
Connor, W. R., ed. see Herodas.
Connor, W. R., ed. see Hesiod.
Connor, W. R., ed. see Hillyard, Brian P.
Connor, W. R., ed. see Hine, Harry M.
Connor, W. R., ed. see Hippocrates.
Connor, W. R., ed. see Homer.
Connor, W. R., ed. see Horace.
Connor, W. R., ed. see Horrocks, Geoffrey C.
Connor, W. R., ed. see Isaeus.
Connor, W. R., ed. see Isocrates.
Connor, W. R., ed. see Juvenal.
Connor, W. R., ed. see Lipovsky, James.
Connor, W. R., ed. see Longus.
Connor, W. R., ed. see Lucan.
Connor, W. R., ed. see Lycophron.
Connor, W. R., ed. see Lysias.
Connor, W. R., ed. see McCabe, Donald F.
Connor, W. R., ed. see Nicander.
Connor, W. R., ed. see Parry, Adam M.
Connor, W. R., ed. see Pernot, Laurent.
Connor, W. R., ed. see Persius.
Connor, W. R., ed. see Philippides, Dia M.
Connor, W. R., ed. see Philo.
Connor, W. R., ed. see Pindar.
Connor, W. R., ed. see Plautus.
Connor, W. R., ed. see Plutarch.
Connor, W. R., ed. see Propertius.
Connor, W. R., ed. see Rash, James N.
Connor, W. R., ed. see Robinson, Thomas M.
Connor, W. R., ed. see Skinner, Marilyn B.
Connor, W. R., ed. see Sophocles.
Connor, W. R., ed. see Spofford, Edward W.
Connor, W. R., ed. see Stone, Laura M.
Connor, W. R., ed. see Suetonius.
Connor, W. R., ed. see Szegedy-Maszak, Andrew.
Connor, W. R., ed. see Terence.
Connor, W. R., ed. see Theognis.
Connor, W. R., ed. see Theophrastus.
Connor, W. R., ed. see Tibullus.
Connor, W. R., ed. see Varro.
Connor, W. R., ed. see Walker, B.
Connor, W. R., ed. see White, F. C.
Connor, W. R., ed. see Xenophon.
Connor, W. R., ed. see Zetzel, James E.
Connor, W. R., ed. see Ziolkowiski, John E.
Connor, W. R., et al, eds. Monographs in Classical Studies, 32 vols. 1981. Set. lib. bdg. 1055.00 (ISBN 0-405-14025-8). Ayer Co Pubs.
Connor, W. Robert. Thucydides. LC 83-43066. 256p. 1984. 30.00x (ISBN 0-691-03569-5). Princeton U Pr.
Connor, Walker. The National Question in Marxist-Leninist Theory & Strategy. LC 83-43067. 600p. 1984. 47.50x (ISBN 0-691-07655-3); pap. 14.50 (ISBN 0-691-10163-9). Princeton U Pr.
Connor, Walker, ed. Mexican Americans in Comparative Perspective: Conference Volume. 400p. 1985. text ed. price not set (ISBN 0-87766-389-0); pap. text ed. price not set (ISBN 0-87766-390-4). Urban Inst.
Connor, Walter D. Deviance in Soviet Society: Crime, Delinquency, Alcoholism. LC 71-180044. 327p. 1972. 32.50x (ISBN 0-231-03439-3). Columbia U Pr.
--Socialism, Politics & Equality: Hierarchy & Change in Eastern Europe & the USSR. (Illus.). 1979. 36.00x (ISBN 0-231-04318-X); pap. 15.00x (ISBN 0-231-04319-8). Columbia U Pr.
Connor, Walter R. Theopompus & Fifth-Century Athens. LC 68-14253. (Center for Hellenic Studies Ser.). Repr. of 1968 ed. 62.20 (ISBN 0-8357-9180-7, 2016543). Bks Demand UMI.
Connors, Andree. Amateur People. LC 76-47836. 1977. 8.95 (ISBN 0-914590-30-8); pap. 3.95 (ISBN 0-914590-31-6). Fiction Coll.
Connors, Bill, ed. How to Steal a Job. 120p. 1977. 10.00 (ISBN 0-930566-03-3). Morrison Peterson Pub.
Connors, Debra J., et al, eds. With the Power of Each Breath: A Disabled Women's Anthology. (Illus.). 360p. 1985. pap. 9.95 (ISBN 0-939416-06-9). Cleis Pr.
Connors, Dennis, ed. Onondaga: Portrait of a Native People. (Iroquois Bks.). (Illus.). 120p. (Orig.). 1985. pap. 12.50 (ISBN 0-8156-0198-0). Syracuse U Pr.
Connors, Eugene T. Educational Tort Liability & Malpractice. LC 81-82884. 180p. (Orig.). 1981. pap. 6.00 (ISBN 0-87367-774-9). Phi Delta Kappa.
--Student Discipline & the Law. LC 79-83625. (Fastback Ser.: No. 121). 60p. 1979. pap. 0.75 (ISBN 0-87367-121-X). Phi Delta Kappa.
Connors, John M., jt. auth. see Perlin, Marc G.
Connors, Joseph. The Robie House of Frank LLoyd Wright. LC 83-4891. (Illus.). 1984. lib. bdg. 25.00x (ISBN 0-226-11541-0). U of Chicago Pr.
--Robie House of Frank Lloyd Wright. LC 83-4891. (Illus.). 1984. pap. 8.95 (ISBN 0-226-11542-9). U of Chicago Pr.
Connors, Joseph J. Borromini & the Roman Oratory: Style & Society. (Illus.). 528p. 1980. 55.00x (ISBN 0-262-03071-3). MIT Pr.
Connors, Kenneth A. A Textbook of Pharmaceutical Analysis. 3rd ed. LC 81-19742. 664p. 1982. 55.00x (ISBN 0-471-09034-4, Pub. by Wiley-Interscience). Wiley.
Connors, Kenneth A., et al. Chemical Stability of Pharmaceuticals: A Handbook for Pharmacists. LC 78-1759. 367p. 1979. 42.50x (ISBN 0-471-02653-0, Pub. by Wiley-Interscience). Wiley.
Connors, Marie. Chickasaw Gardens. LC 84-26212. (Raccoon Bks.). 24p. 1985. 5.00 (ISBN 0-918518-37-7). St Luke TN.
Connors, Marie, jt. ed. see Yellin, David G.
Connors, Martin, jt. ed. see Schmittroth, John, Jr.
Connors, Michael. Dealing in Hate. 40p. 1979. pap. 2.50 (ISBN 0-911038-55-8). Inst Hist Rev.
--Dealing in Hate: The Development of Anti-German Propaganda. 1981. lib. bdg. 59.95 (ISBN 0-686-73180-8). Revisionist Pr.
Connors, Richard J. The Process of Constitutional Revision in New Jersey: 1940-1947. 219p. 1970. 1.00 (ISBN 0-318-15813-2). Citizens Forum Gov.
Connors, Richard J. & Dunham, William J. The Government of New Jersey: An Introduction. LC 84-12005. 252p. (Orig.). 1984. lib. bdg. 23.50 (ISBN 0-8191-4123-2); pap. text ed. 12.00 (ISBN 0-8191-4124-0). U Pr of Amer.
Connors, Robert J., et al, eds. Essays on Classical Rhetoric & Modern Discourse. LC 83-14718. 308p. 1984. pap. 11.95x (ISBN 0-8093-1134-8). S Ill U Pr.
Connors, T. A. & Roberts, J. J., eds. Platinum Coordination Complexes in Cancer Chemotherapy. (Recent Results in Cancer Research Ser.: Vol. 48). (Illus.). 220p. 1974. 45.00 (ISBN 0-387-06793-0). Springer-Verlag.
Connors, T. A., jt. ed. see Hellmann, K.
Connors, Thomas E. Abstract Relations. LC 79-50423. (Illus.). 128p. 1980. pap. 5.95x (ISBN 0-913204-12-9). December Pr.
Connors, Tracy D. Longman Dictionary of the Mass Media & Communication. LC 82-92. (Public Communication Ser.). (Illus.). 256p. 1982. text ed. 24.95x (ISBN 0-582-28337-X); pap. text ed. 13.95x (ISBN 0-582-28336-1). Longman.
--The Nonprofit Organization Handbook. LC 78-26691. (Illus.). 1979. 54.95 (ISBN 0-07-012422-1). McGraw.
Connors, Tracy D., ed. The Nonprofit Organization Handbook. 740p. 1980. cloth 36.75 (ISBN 0-318-17168-6, C43). Natl Ctr Cit Involv.
Connors, Tracy D. & Callaghan, Christopher T., eds. Financial Management for Nonprofit Organizations. LC 81-69355. pap. 86.50 (ISBN 0-317-26714-0, 2023517). Bks Demand UMI.
Connotillo, Barbara C., ed. Practical Guide for Foreign Visitors. 49p. 1979. 3.50 (ISBN 0-87206-096-9). Inst Intl Educ.
--Specialized Study Options U S A. 180p. 1984. pap. text ed. 11.95 (ISBN 0-87206-127-2). Inst Intl Educ.
--Study of Agriculture in the U. S. A Guide for Foreign Students. LC 79-90889. 1980. pap. text ed. 4.50 (ISBN 0-87206-097-7). Inst Intl Educ.
--Summer Learning Options U. S. A. A Guide for Foreign Nationals. 137p. (Orig.). 1983. pap. text ed. 8.95 (ISBN 0-87206-122-1). Inst Intl Educ.
--Teaching Abroad. 160p. 1984. pap. text ed. 11.95 (ISBN 0-87206-124-8). Inst Intl Educ.
Conoley, Collie W., jt. auth. see Conoley, Jane C.
Conoley, Jane C. & Conoley, Collie W. School Consultation: A Guide to Practice & Training. (Pergamon General Psychology Ser.: No. 111). (Illus.). 260p. 1982. 28.00 (ISBN 0-08-027566-4); pap. 12.95 (ISBN 0-08-027565-6). Pergamon.
Conoley, Jane C., jt. auth. see Apter, Steven J.
Conoley, Jane C., ed. Consultation in Schools: Theory, Research Procedures. LC 80-2329. (Educational Technology Ser.). 1981. 38.50 (ISBN 0-12-186020-5). Acad Pr.
Conoley, William N., Jr. Waterfowl Heritage: North Carolina Decoys & Gunning Lore. (Illus.). 336p. 1983. 39.95 (ISBN 0-9610358-1-1); limited ed. 200.00 (ISBN 0-317-13566-X). Webfoot Inc.
Conolly, B. Techniques in Operational Research: Models, Search & Randomization, Vol. 2. LC 80-41741. (Mathematics & Its Applications Ser.). 340p. 1981. 89.95x (ISBN 0-470-27130-2). Halsted Pr.
Conolly, Brian. Lecture Notes in Queueing Systems. LC 75-7788. 176p. 1975. pap. 19.95x (ISBN 0-470-16857-9). Halsted Pr.
Conolly, J. Construction & Government of Lunatic Asylums & Hospitals for the Insane. (Illus.). 215p. 1968. Repr. of 1847 ed. 19.95x (ISBN 0-8464-0275-0). Beekman Pubs.
--Inquiry Concerning the Indications of Insanity with Suggestions for the Better Protection & Care of the Insane. (Illus.). 469p. 1964. Repr. of 1830 ed. 25.00x (ISBN 0-8464-0515-6). Beekman Pubs.
Conolly, John. Indications of Insanity. 1964. Repr. 21.00x (ISBN 0-8464-0507-5). Beekman Pubs.
--On Some of the Forms of Insanity. Bd. with Inquiry Concerning the Indications of Insanity. (Contributions to the History of Psychology Ser.: Vol. XIII, Pt. A). 1983. Repr. of 1850 ed. 30.00 (ISBN 0-89093-315-4). U Pubns Amer.
--Study of Hamlet. LC 72-942. Repr. of 1863 ed. 17.00 (ISBN 0-404-01695-2). AMS Pr.
--The Treatment of the Insane Without Mechanical Restraints. LC 73-2392. (Mental Illness & Social Policy; the American Experience Ser.). Repr. of 1856 ed. 25.50 (ISBN 0-405-05200-6). Ayer Co Pubs.
Conolly, L. W., ed. Theatrical Touring & Founding in North America. LC 81-23766. (Contributions in Drama & Theatre Studies: No. 5). (Illus.). xiv, 245p. 1982. lib. bdg. 29.95 (ISBN 0-313-22595-8, CTH/). Greenwood.
Conolly, Leonard W. The Censorship of English Drama Seventeen Thirty-Seven to Eighteen Twenty-Four. LC 75-32840. (Illus.). 223p. 1976. 15.00 (ISBN 0-87328-068-7). Huntington Lib.
Conolly, Leonard W. & Wearing, J. P., eds. English Drama & Theatre, 1800-1900: A Guide to Information Sources. LC 73-16975. (American Literature, English Literature, & World Literatures in English Information Guide Ser.: Vol. 12). 528p. 1978. 60.00x (ISBN 0-8103-1225-5). Gale.
Conolly, Violet. Siberia Today & Tomorrow. LC 75-26327. (Illus.). 260p. 1976. 20.00 (ISBN 0-8008-7182-0). Taplinger.
--Soviet Economic Policy in the East: Turkey, Persia, Afghanistan, Mongolia & Tana Tuva, Sin Kiang. LC 79-5205. (Illus.). 168p. 1980. Repr. of 1933 ed. 17.00 (ISBN 0-8305-0065-0). Hyperion Conn.
--Soviet Trade from the Pacific to the Levant: With an Economic Study of the Soviet Far Eastern Region. LC 79-5206. (Illus.). 238p. 1980. Repr. of 1935 ed. 21.50 (ISBN 0-8305-0066-9). Hyperion Conn.
Conolly, Vivian. The Counterfeit Bride. (Coventry Romance Ser.: No. 68). 224p. 1980. pap. 1.75 (ISBN 0-449-50099-3, Coventry). Fawcett.
Conolly, W. Bruce. Color Atlas of Hand Conditions. (Illus.). 366p. 1980. 99.95 (ISBN 0-8151-1836-8). Year Bk Med.
--Surgical Procedures: Treatment of Carpal Tunnel Syndrome, Vol. 9. (Single Surgical Procedures Ser.). 1984. 25.95 (ISBN 0-87489-510-3). Med Economics.
Conolly, W. Bruce & Kilgore, Eugene S. Hand Injuries & Infections: An Illustrated Guide. (Illus.). 1979. 49.95 (ISBN 0-8151-1833-3). Year Bk Med.
Conomos, Dimitri. Byzantine Hymnography & Byzantine Chant. Vaporis, N. M., intro. by. (Nicholas E. Kulukundis Lectures in Hellenism Ser.). 56p. (Orig.). 1984. pap. text ed. 4.00 (ISBN 0-917653-04-1). Hellenic Coll Pr.
Conomos, Dimitri E. The Late Byzantine & Slavonic Communion Cycle: Liturgy & Music, Vol. 21. LC 84-12176. (Dumbarton Oaks Studies). (Illus.). 222p. 1985. 25.00x (ISBN 0-88402-134-3). Dumbarton Oaks.
Conomos, T. J., ed. San Francisco Bay: The Urbanized Estuary. 469p. (Orig.). 1979. 16.95 (ISBN 0-934394-00-8). AAASPD.
Conot, Robert E. Justice at Nuremberg. 594p. 1984. pap. 10.95 (ISBN 0-88184-032-7). Carroll & Graf.
--Justice at Nuremberg: The First Comprehensive, Dramatic Account of the Trial of the Leaders. LC 82-48395. (Illus.). 640p. 1983. 21.63i (ISBN 0-06-015117-X, HarpT). Har-Row.

Conover, Chris. Six Little Ducks. LC 75-22155. (Illus.). 32p. (gr. k-2). 1976. 10.10i (ISBN 0-690-01036-2); PLB 10.89 (ISBN 0-690-01037-0). Crowell Jr Bks.
--The Wizard's Daughter: A Viking Legend. LC 84-12613. (Magical Northland Ser.). (Illus.). 32p. (gr. 3-5). 1984. 12.95 (ISBN 0-316-15314-1). Little.
Conover, Donald W., jt. auth. see Woodson, Wesley E.
Conover, Grandin. Ten Years. LC 72-77578. 76p. 1971. 7.50x (ISBN 0-87023-116-2); pap. 3.50 (ISBN 0-87023-117-0). U of Mass Pr.
Conover, Helen F. A Guide to Bibliographic Tools for Research in Foreign Affairs, 2 vols. lib. bdg. 250.00 (ISBN 0-8490-1917-6). Gordon Pr.
Conover, Helen F., jt. auth. see Mugridge, Donald H.
Conover, Herbert S. Grounds Maintenance Handbook. 3rd ed. (Illus.). 512p. 1976. 47.50 (ISBN 0-07-012412-4). McGraw.
Conover, Hobart & Berlye, Milton. Business Dynamics. 481p. 1982. text ed. 18.76 scp (ISBN 0-672-97973-X); scp tchr's ed. 7.33 (ISBN 0-672-97978-0); scp wkbk 7.20 (ISBN 0-672-97977-2). Bobbs.
Conover, Jewel H. Nineteenth-Century Houses in Western New York. LC 66-63788. (Illus.). 1966. 19.50x (ISBN 0-87395-017-8). State U NY Pr.
Conover, Joseph A. How to Make Big Profits from Land in Transition. 1975. 59.50 (ISBN 0-13-418012-7). Exec Reports.
Conover, Mary. Understanding Electrocardiography: Physiological & Interpretive Concepts. 4th ed. (Illus.). 272p. 1984. pap. text ed. 19.95 (ISBN 0-8016-1123-7). Mosby.
Conover, Mary B. Electrocardiography: A Home Study Course. (Illus.). 1984. pap. text ed. 12.95 (ISBN 0-8016-1179-2). Mosby.
--Understanding Electrocardiography: Physiological & Interpretive Concepts. 3rd ed. LC 80-14104. (Illus.). 288p. 1980. pap. text ed. 16.95 (ISBN 0-8016-5676-1). Mosby.
Conover, Mary B., jt. auth. see Tilkian, Ara G.
Conover, Mary H. Cardiac Arrhythmias: Exercises in Pattern Interpretation. 2nd ed. LC 77-24509. (Illus.). 1978. pap. text ed. 15.95 (ISBN 0-8016-1024-9). Mosby.
Conover, Mary H., jt. auth. see Marriott, Henry J.
Conover, Milton. The Federal Power Commission: Its History, Activities & Organization. LC 72-3035. (Brookings Institution. Institute for Government Research. Service Monographs of the U.S. Government: No. 17). Repr. of 1923 ed. 24.00 (ISBN 0-404-57117-4). AMS Pr.
--The General Land Office: Its History, Activities & Organization. LC 72-3026. (Brookings Institution. Institute for Government Research. Service Monographs of the U.S. Government: No. 13). Repr. of 1923 ed. 30.00 (ISBN 0-404-57113-1). AMS Pr.
--The Office of Experiment Stations: Its History, Activities & Organization. LC 72-3047. (Brookings Institution. Institute for Government Research. Service Monographs of the U.S. Government: No. 32). Repr. of 1924 ed. 25.00 (ISBN 0-404-57132-8). AMS Pr.
Conover, Pamela J. & Gray, Virginia. Feminism & the New Right: Conflict Over the American Family. 272p. 1983. 34.95 (ISBN 0-03-060237-8). Praeger.
Conover, Robert, jt. auth. see Futcher, Jane.
Conover, Ted. Rolling Nowhere. (Illus.). 247p. 1984. 15.95 (ISBN 0-670-60319-8). Viking.
--Rolling Nowhere. (Travel Library). 272p. 1985. pap. 5.95 (ISBN 0-14-009550-0). Penguin.
Conover, Theodore E. Graphic Communications Today. (Illus.). 450p. 1985. text ed. 24.95 (ISBN 0-314-85225-5). West Pub.
Conover, W. J. Practical Nonparametric Statistics. 2nd ed. LC 80-301. (Probability & Mathematical Statistics Ser.). 493p. 1980. 43.50 (ISBN 0-471-02867-3). Wiley.
Conover, W. J. & Iman, Ronald L. Introduction to Modern Business Statistics. 525p. 1983. 32.50 (ISBN 0-471-09669-5). Wiley.
--Study Guide to Accompany Introduction to Modern Business Statistics. 204p. 1983. pap. 13.95 (ISBN 0-471-09664-4). Wiley.
Conover, W. J., jt. auth. see Iman, R. L.
Conoway, Judith, jt. auth. see Tilkin, Sheldon.
Conoway, Judith, jt. auth. see Tilkin, Sheldon L.
Conoway, Judith, jt. auth. see Tlkin, Sheldon L.
Conpayre, G. Montaigne & Education of the Judgement. Mansion, J. E., tr. 139p. 1980. Repr. lib. bdg. 30.00 (ISBN 0-8492-4046-8). R West.
Conquest, Ned. The Gun & the Glory of Granite Hendley. 1979. pap. 1.25 (ISBN 0-8439-0685-5, Leisure Bks). Dorchester Pub Co.
Conquest, Plesanton, Jr. At Large: Poetry. 1933. 1.00 (ISBN 0-685-09006-X). Dietz.
Conquest, Robert. Inside Stalin's Secret Police: NKVD Politics, 1936-1939. LC 84-29765. (Publication Ser.). 1985. 22.95 (ISBN 0-8179-8241-8). Hoover Inst Pr.
--Kolyma: The Arctic Death Camps. (Illus.). 1979. pap. 5.95 (ISBN 0-19-285091-1, GB 591, GB). Oxford U Pr.
--Kolyma: The Artic Death Camps. 1978. 14.95 (ISBN 0-670-41499-9). Viking.
--The Pasternak Affair: Courage of Genius. LC 79-4117. 1979. Repr. of 1962 ed. lib. bdg. 18.00x (ISBN 0-374-91913-5). Octagon.
--The Politics of Ideas in the U. S. S. R. LC 76-27307. 1976. Repr. of 1967 ed. lib. bdg. 19.00x (ISBN 0-8371-9049-5, COPO). Greenwood.
Conquest, Robert, ed. The Last Empire: Nationality & the Soviet Future. (Publication Ser.: No. 325). 500p. 1986. lib. bdg. price not set (ISBN 0-8179-8251-5). Hoover Inst Pr.
Conquest, Robert, jt. ed. see Amis, Kingsley.
Conquest, Robert, intro. by see Sahaydak, Maksym.
Conquest, Robert, tr. see Solzhenitsyn, Alexander.
Conrac Corporation Staff. Raster Graphics Handbook. 2nd ed. (Illus.). 360p. 1985. 37.50 (ISBN 0-442-21608-4). Van Nos Reinhold.
Conrad & Magar, eds. Physical Principles of Neuronal & Organismic Behavior. 256p. 1973. 59.25 (ISBN 0-677-12290-X). Gordon.
Conrad, Agnes C., jt. auth. see Gast, Ross H.
Conrad, Aiken. Modern American Poets. 1979. Repr. of 1927 ed. lib. bdg. 20.00 (ISBN 0-8492-3246-5). R West.
Conrad, Alfred F., et al. Automobile Accident Costs & Payments: Studies in the Economics of Injury Protection. LC 64-17437. (Michigan Legal Publications). xxviii, 506p. 1983. Repr. of 1964 ed. lib. bdg. 38.50 (ISBN 0-89941-315-3). W S Hein.
--Enterprise Organization: Corporation & Partnership Statutes, Rules & Forms to Accompany 3rd ed. (University Casebook Ser.). 339p. 1982. pap. text ed. 5.50 (ISBN 0-88277-088-8). Foundation Pr.
Conrad, Andree, tr. see Donoso, Jose.
Conrad, Barnaby. A Revolting Transaction. (Illus.). 200p. 1983. 16.95 (ISBN 0-87795-534-4). Arbor Hse.
Conrad, Barnaby & Mastorakis, Nico. Keepers of the Secret. 256p. 1983. pap. 2.95 (ISBN 0-515-05544-1). Jove Pubns.
Conrad, Borys. My Father Joseph Conrad. 12.95 (ISBN 0-7145-0018-6). Riverrun NY.
Conrad, Charles. Strategic Organizational Communication. 1985. text ed. 24.95 (ISBN 0-03-061669-7). HR&W.
Conrad, Clifton F. At the Crossroads: General Education in Comunity Colleges. (Horizons Issues Monograph Ser.). 72p. 1983. pap. 5.00 (ISBN 0-87117-130-9). Am Assn Comm Jr Coll.
Conrad, Clifton F., jt. auth. see Bullock, G. William, Jr.
Conrad, Daniel & Hedin, Diane, eds. Youth Participation & Experiential Education: Theory, Research, & Programs. LC 81-20114. (Child & Youth Services Ser.: Vol. 4, Nos. 3 & 4). 156p. 1982. text ed. 24.95 (ISBN 0-917724-99-2, B99). Haworth Pr.
Conrad, Daniel E. Learning from the Field Experience: A Guide for Student Reflection in Youth Participation Programs. 59p. 1982. pap. 5.00. Natl Comm Res Youth.
Conrad, Daniel L. How to Get Federal Grants. 2nd ed. LC 79-53107. 1979. 3 ring binder 49.00x (ISBN 0-916664-10-4). Public Management.
--How to Solicit Big Gifts. LC 78-53209. 1978. 3 ring binder 49.00x (ISBN 0-916664-04-X). Public Management.
--The Quick Proposal Workbook. LC 80-84209. 119p. 1980. 19.00x (ISBN 0-916664-38-4). Public Management.
--Techniques of Fund-Raising. 1974. 25.00 (ISBN 0-8184-0169-9). Lyle Stuart.
Conrad, Daniel L. & Public Management Institute Staff. Successful Fund Raising Techniques. 2nd ed. LC 76-49799. 1976. 3 ring binder 39.00x (ISBN 0-916664-03-1). Public Management.
Conrad, Daniel L. & Research & Development Staff of Public Management Institute. The New Grants Planner. rev. ed. LC 80-84395. 1980. 3 ring binder 49.00x (ISBN 0-916664-31-7). Public Management.
Conrad, David E. The Forgotten Farmers: The Story of Sharecroppers in the New Deal. LC 82-955. 223p. 1982. Repr. of 1965 ed. lib. bdg. 27.50x (ISBN 0-313-23358-6, COFF). Greenwood.
Conrad, David R. Education for Transformation: Implications in Lewis Mumford's Ecohumanism. LC 75-25867. 1976. 14.95 (ISBN 0-88280-030-2). ETC Pubns.
Conrad, Dick. Tony Dorsett: From Heisman to Super Bowl in One Year. LC 78-11378. (Sports Stars Ser.). (Illus.). 48p. (gr. 2-8). 1979. PLB 9.25 (ISBN 0-516-04305-6); pap. 2.95 (ISBN 0-516-44305-4). Childrens.
--Walter Payton: The Running Machine. LC 78-11378. (Sports Stars Ser.). (Illus.). 48p. (gr. 2-8). 1979. PLB 9.25 (ISBN 0-516-04306-4); pap. 2.95 (ISBN 0-516-44306-2). Childrens.
Conrad, Earl. Gulf Stream North. LC 80-50244. 248p. 1980. 15.95 (ISBN 0-933256-13-2); pap. 7.95 (ISBN 0-933256-17-5). Second Chance.
--Invention of the Negro. LC 66-26645. 1969. Repr. of 1967 ed. 5.95 (ISBN 0-8397-3700-9). Eriksson.
Conrad, Eva & Maul, Terry. Introduction to Experimental Psychology. LC 81-1647. 542p. 1981. text ed. 30.50 (ISBN 0-471-06005-4). Wiley.
Conrad, Geoffrey W. & Demarest, Arthur A. Religion & Empire: The Dynamics of Aztec & Inca Expansionism. LC 83-14414. (New Studies in Archaeology). 256p. 1984. 49.50 (ISBN 0-521-24357-2); pap. 17.95 (ISBN 0-521-31896-3). Cambridge U Pr.
Conrad, Geoffrey W., jt. auth. see Bawden, Garth.
Conrad, Glenn. First Families of L. A, 2 vols. 1969. Set. 25.00 (ISBN 0-87511-356-7). Claitors.
Conrad, Glenn R. & Brasseaux, Carl A. A Selected Bibliography of Scholarly Literature on Colonial Louisiana & New France. 150p. 6.95 (ISBN 0-940984-06-7). U of SW LA Ctr LA Studies.
Conrad, Glenn R., ed. The Cajuns: Essays on Their History & Culture. LC 83-70891. (U. S. L. History Ser.). 280p. 1983. 15.00 (ISBN 0-940984-10-5). U of SW LA Ctr LA Studies.
Conrad, Glenn R. & Baker, Vaughan B., eds. Louisiana Gothic. LC 83-7000732. (Illus.). 150p. 1984. 25.00 (ISBN 0-940984-19-9). U of SW LA Ctr LA Studies.
Conrad, Glenn R., ed. see De la Harpe, Jean-Baptiste.
Conrad, Glenn R., ed. see De Villiers du Terrage, Marc.
Conrad, H., jt. ed. see Westbrook, J. H.
Conrad, Harold. Dear Muffo: Thirty Five Years in the Fast Lane. LC 81-40811. (Illus.). 226p. 1982. 14.95 (ISBN 0-8128-2842-9). Stein & Day.
Conrad, Helen. A Stroke of Genius. (Candlelight Ecstasy Ser.: No. 386). (Orig.). 1985. pap. 2.25 (ISBN 0-440-18345-6). Dell.
--Undercover Affair. 208p. (Orig.). 1984. pap. 2.25 (ISBN 0-553-21676-7). Bantam.
Conrad, Herbert S., ed. Studies in Human Development: Selections from the Publications & Addresses of Harold Ellis Jones. (Century Psychology Ser.). (Illus.). 1966. 46.50x (ISBN 0-89197-581-0). Irvington.
Conrad, J., ed. Society, Technology & Risk Assessment. LC 80-40533. 1980. 47.00 (ISBN 0-12-186450-2). Acad Pr.
Conrad, Jack R. The Horn & the Sword. LC 72-9822. (Illus.). 222p. 1973. Repr. of 1957 ed. lib. bdg. 15.50x (ISBN 0-8371-6604-7, COHO). Greenwood.
Conrad, James. Higher Level Protocols. 300p. pap. text ed. 59.95 (ISBN 0-935506-31-4). Carnegie Pr.
Conrad, James H. Reference Sources in Social Work: An Annotated Bibliography. LC 81-21219. 207p. 1982. 16.00 (ISBN 0-8108-1503-6). Scarecrow.
Conrad, James H., jt. ed. see Sitton, Thad.
Conrad, James W. Standard & Protocols For Communications Network. 397p. 1982. 59.95 (ISBN 0-935506-03-9). Carnegie Pr.
Conrad, Jeff, ed. see Terres, John K.
Conrad, Jessie. Joseph Conrad As I Knew Him. facs. ed. LC 76-128877. (Select Bibliographies Reprint Ser). 1925. 15.00 (ISBN 0-8369-5497-1). Ayer Co Pubs.
--Joseph Conrad As I Knew Him. LC 70-131673. (Illus.). xxi, 162p. 1972. Repr. of 1926 ed. 29.00x (ISBN 0-403-00560-4). Scholarly.
Conrad, John. Joseph Conrad-Times Remembered. LC 79-41596. (Illus.). 212p. 1981. 22.95 (ISBN 0-521-22805-0). Cambridge U Pr.
Conrad, John J., jt. auth. see Cox, Steven M.
Conrad, John P. The Dangerous & the Endangered. LC 78-405. (The Dangerous Offender Project Ser.). 176p. 1985. 19.00x (ISBN 0-669-02184-9). Lexington Bks.
--Future of Corrections. Sellin, Thorsten, ed. LC 69-16927. (Annals: No. 381). 1969. pap. 7.95 (ISBN 0-87761-112-2). Am Acad Pol Soc Sci.
--Justice & Consequences. LC 78-348. 192p. 1981. 20.00 (ISBN 0-669-02190-3). Lexington Bks.
Conrad, John P. & Dinitz, Simon. In Fear of Each Other: Studies of Dangerousness in America. LC 77-286. (The Dangerous Offender Project). 1977. 19.50x (ISBN 0-669-01478-8). Lexington Bks.
Conrad, John P., jt. auth. see Van den Haag, Ernest.
Conrad, John P., ed. The Evolution of Criminal Justice: A Guide for Practical Criminologists. LC 78-19610. (Sage Research Progress Series in Criminology: Vol. 7). 160p. 1978. 20.00 (ISBN 0-8039-1146-7); pap. 9.95 (ISBN 0-8039-1147-5). Sage.
Conrad, John P., jt. ed. see Flynn, Edith E.
Conrad, John W. Contemporary Ceramic Formulas. (Illus.). 261p. 1981. 19.95 (ISBN 0-02-527640-9). Macmillan.
--Contemporary Ceramic Techniques. 1979. 24.95 (ISBN 0-13-169540-1). P-H.
Conrad, Joseph. Almayer's Folly. LC 79-184735. 224p. 1971. Repr. lib. bdg. 12.50x (ISBN 0-8376-0408-7). Bentley.
--Almayer's Folly. 321p. 1983. lib. bdg. 15.95x (ISBN 0-89966-056-8). Buccaneer Bks.
--Almayer's Folly. 1976. pap. 3.95 (ISBN 0-14-000036-4). Penguin.
--Chance. 432p. (Orig.). 1984. pap. 7.95 (ISBN 0-7012-1911-4). Merrimack Pub Cir.
--Chance. 352p. 1985. pap. 3.95 (ISBN 0-553-21177-3). Bantam.
--The Collected Letters of Joseph Conrad: 1861 to 1897, Vol. 1. Karl, Frederick & Davies, Laurence, eds. LC 82-14643. (Illus.). 480p. 1983. 39.50 (ISBN 0-521-24216-9). Cambridge U Pr.
--The Conrad Reader. Hoppe, A. J., ed. 1978. Repr. of 1945 ed. lib. bdg. 30.00 (ISBN 0-8274-0002-0). R West.
--Conrad's Prefaces to His Works. facsimile ed. LC 72-160963. (Select Bibliographies Reprint Ser). Repr. of 1937 ed. 16.00 (ISBN 0-8369-5831-4). Ayer Co Pubs.
--Conrad's Prefaces to His Works. LC 70-163112. (English Literature Ser., No. 33). 1971. lib. bdg. 39.95x (ISBN 0-8383-1304-3). Haskell.
--Great Short Works of Joseph Conrad. Allen, Jerry, ed. pap. 3.80i (ISBN 0-06-083039-5, P3039, PL). Har-Row.
--Great Short Works: The Lagoon, the Nigger of Narcissus, Youth, Heart of Darkness, Typhoon, the Secret Sharer. 13.75 (ISBN 0-8446-0068-7). Peter Smith.
--Heart of Darkness. Bd. with End of the Tether. (Classics Ser). (gr. 11up). pap. 1.50 (ISBN 0-8049-0112-0, CL-112). Airmont.
--Heart of Darkness. Walker, Franklin, ed. Bd. with The Secret Sharer. (Bantam Classics Ser.). 204p. (Critical suppl. includes biography, reviews, essays). (gr. 10-12,RL 10). 1981. pap. 1.75 (ISBN 0-553-21088-2). Bantam.
--Heart of Darkness. LC 81-38511. 128p. 1982. Repr. of 1926 ed. 12.50x (ISBN 0-8376-0458-3). Bentley.
--Heart of Darkness. rev. ed. Kimbrough, Robert, ed. LC 78-152308. (Norton Critical Edition Series). 1972. pap. 4.95x (ISBN 0-393-09773-0, NortonC). Norton.
--Heart of Darkness. (Enriched Classics Ser.). (gr. 10 up). 1972. pap. 1.95 (ISBN 0-671-48936-4, RE). PB.
--Heart of Darkness. Shefter, Harry, ed. (Enriched Classics Edition Ser.). 178p. pap. 2.95 (ISBN 0-671-00817-X). WSP.
--Heart of Darkness. O'Prey, Paul, ed. (Penguin English Library). 128p. 1984. pap. 1.95 (ISBN 0-14-043168-3). Penguin.
--Heart of Darkness & the Secret Sharer. 1978. Repr. of 1910 ed. lib. bdg. 14.95x (ISBN 0-89966-054-1). Buccaneer Bks.
--Heart of Darkness & the Secret Sharer. 1971. pap. 1.75 (ISBN 0-451-51893-4, Sig Classics). NAL.
--Joseph Conrad. LC 73-19979. 1956. lib. bdg. 7.50 (ISBN 0-8414-2949-9). Folcroft.
--Joseph Conrad: A Sketch. 1924. lib. bdg. 7.50 (ISBN 0-8414-2377-6). Folcroft.
--Joseph Conrad on Fiction. Wright, Walter F., ed. LC 64-11355. (Regents Critics Ser). xvi, 236p. 1964. 19.95x (ISBN 0-8032-0452-3); pap. 4.95x (ISBN 0-8032-5452-0, BB 400, Bison). U of Nebr Pr.
--Last Essays. facs. ed. LC 75-117777. (Essay Index Reprint Ser). 1926. 17.00 (ISBN 0-8369-1795-2). Ayer Co Pubs.
--Lord Jim. (Classics Ser). (gr. 10 up). pap. 1.50 (ISBN 0-8049-0054-X, CL-54). Airmont.
--Lord Jim. (Literature Ser). (gr. 7-12). 1969. pap. text ed. 5.17 (ISBN 0-87720-708-9). AMSCO Sch.
--Lord Jim. (Bantam Classics Ser.). 271p. (gr. 9-12). 1981. pap. 1.95 (ISBN 0-553-21027-0). Bantam.
--Lord Jim. LC 75-184734. 320p. 1971. Repr. lib. bdg. 12.50x (ISBN 0-8376-0409-5). Bentley.
--Lord Jim. 1974. pap. 1.95x (ISBN 0-460-01925-2, Evman). Biblio Dist.
--Lord Jim. lib. bdg. 16.95 (ISBN 0-89966-057-6). Buccaneer Bks.
--Lord Jim. Zabel, M. D., ed. LC 58-3202. 1958. pap. 5.50 (ISBN 0-395-05121-5, RivEd). HM.
--Lord Jim. 1961. pap. 1.95 (ISBN 0-451-51195-6, CJ1195, Sig Classics). NAL.
--Lord Jim. Moser, Thomas, ed. (Critical Editions Ser.). (Annotated). 1968. pap. text ed. 8.95x (ISBN 0-393-09656-4). Norton.
--Lord Jim. (Now Age Illustrated V Ser.). (Illus.). 64p. (gr. 4-12). 1979. text ed. 5.00 (ISBN 0-88301-403-3); pap. text ed. 1.95 (ISBN 0-88301-391-6); student activity bk. 1.25 (ISBN 0-88301-415-7). Pendulum Pr.
--Lord Jim. (Modern Classics Ser). 1971. pap. 1.95 (ISBN 0-14-000529-3). Penguin.
--Lord Jim. Batchelor, John, ed. (The World's Classics-Paperback Ser.). 1983. pap. 1.95 (ISBN 0-19-281625-X). Oxford U Pr.
--Lord Jim, with Reader's Guide. (Literature Program Ser.). (Orig.). (gr. 9-12). 1973. pap. text ed. 6.00 (ISBN 0-87720-820-4); tchr's ed. 3.80 (ISBN 0-87720-920-0). AMSCO Sch.
--Nigger of "Narcissus", Typhoon, Falk, & Other Stories. Sherry, Norman, ed. 1978. 12.95x (ISBN 0-460-00980-X, Evman); pap. 3.50x (ISBN 0-460-01980-5, Evman). Biblio Dist.
--Nigger of the Narcissus. lib. bdg. 15.95x (ISBN 0-89966-055-X). Buccaneer Bks.
--Nigger of the Narcissus. LC 59-1937. 5.95 (ISBN 0-385-04328-7). Doubleday.
--The Nigger of the "Narcissus". Kimbrough, Robert, ed. (Norton Critical Editions). (Illus.). 1979. pap. 4.95x (ISBN 0-393-09019-1). Norton.
--The Nigger of the "Narcissus". Berthoud, Jacques, ed. (World's Classics Ser.). 1984. pap. 3.50 (ISBN 0-19-281623-3). Oxford U Pr.
--Nigger of the Narcissus, Typhoon & Other Stories. 1963. pap. 2.95 (ISBN 0-14-002061-6). Penguin.
--Nostromo. 1979. 14.95x (ISBN 0-460-00038-1, Evman); pap. 2.95x (ISBN 0-460-01038-7, Evman). Biblio Dist.
--Nostromo. pap. 2.95 (ISBN 0-451-51455-6, CE1455, Sig Classics). NAL.
--Nostromo. 464p. 1984. pap. 3.95 (ISBN 0-14-043171-3). Penguin.
--Nostromo. 449p. 30.00 (ISBN 0-913720-27-5, Sandstone); leather bound 65.00 (ISBN 0-913720-26-7). Beil.

--Nostromo. LC 82-42865. 1950. 8.95 (ISBN 0-394-60431-8). Modern Lib.
--Nostromo. 566p. 1983. Repr. lib. bdg. 18.95x (ISBN 0-89966-311-7). Buccaneer Bks.
--Nostromo. Carabine, Keith, ed. (World's Classics Ser.). 1984. pap. 3.95 (ISBN 0-19-281624-1). Oxford U Pr.
--Notes on Life & Letters. LC 72-1327. (Essay Index Reprint Ser.). Repr. of 1921 ed. 16.00 (ISBN 0-8369-2842-3). Ayer Co Pubs.
--Outcast of the Islands. (Classics Ser). (gr. 9 up). pap. 1.50 (ISBN 0-8049-0113-9, CL-113). Airmont.
--An Outcast of the Islands. 345p. 1983. lib. bdg. 16.95x (ISBN 0-89966-263-3). Buccaneer Bks.
--An Outcast of the Islands. 296p. 1976. pap. 3.95 (ISBN 0-14-004054-4). Penguin.
--A Personal Record. LC 82-73728. xvii, 220p. 1982. pap. 6.95 (ISBN 0-910395-05-5). Marlboro Pr.
--Portable Conrad. rev. ed. Zabel, Morton D. & Karl, Frederick R., eds. (Viking Portable Library: No. 33). 1976. pap. 7.95 (ISBN 0-14-015033-1, P33). Penguin.
--Sea Stories. 272p. (Orig.). 1984. pap. 11.50 (ISBN 0-246-12426-1, Pub. by Granada England). Sheridan.
--Sea Stories. 272p. 1985. pap. 8.95 (ISBN 0-88184-177-3). Carroll & Graf.
--The Secret Agent. lib. bdg. 16.95x (ISBN 0-89966-058-4). Buccaneer Bks.
--Secret Agent. 1953. pap. 4.95 (ISBN 0-385-09352-7, Anch). Doubleday.
--The Secret Agent. 240p. (Orig.). 1984. pap. text ed. 2.50 (ISBN 0-553-21134-X). Bantam.
--The Secret Agent. 240p. 1983. pap. 2.50 (ISBN 0-451-51804-7, Sig Classics). NAL.
--The Secret Agent. 239p. 1975. pap. 3.95 (ISBN 0-330-24129-X, 00239756, Pub. by Pan Classics). Academy Chi Pubs.
--The Secret Agent. Seymour-Smith, Martin, ed. (English Library). 272p. 1985. pap. 2.50 (ISBN 0-14-043228-0). Penguin.
--A Set of Six. 395p. 1983. lib. bdg. 18.95x (ISBN 0-89966-264-1). Buccaneer Bks.
--The Shadow Line. Hawthorn, Jeremy, ed. (WC-P Ser.). 176p. 1985. pap. 3.95 (ISBN 0-19-281686-1). Oxford U Pr.
--Shorter Tales. LC 71-128727. (Short Story Index Reprint Ser). 1924. 22.00 (ISBN 0-8369-3618-3). Ayer Co Pubs.
--Tales of Unrest. 75.00 (ISBN 0-87968-086-5). Gordon Pr.
--Tales of Unrest. 1977. pap. 2.95 (ISBN 0-14-003885-X). Penguin.
--Three Great Tales. Incl. Nigger of the Narcissus; Heart of Darkness; Typhoon. 1958. pap. 3.95 (ISBN 0-394-70155-0, V-155, Vin). Random.
--Typhoon & Other Tales. pap. 3.95 (ISBN 0-451-51779-2, CE1779, Sig Classics). NAL.
--Typhoon & Youth. Clay, N. L., ed. (Guide Novel Ser.). pap. text ed. 2.95x (ISBN 0-435-16181-4). Heinemann Ed.
--Under Western Eyes. LC 63-8112. 1963. pap. 1.95 (ISBN 0-385-03001-0, Anch). Doubleday.
--Under Western Eyes. Ford, Boris, ed. (Classics Ser.). 352p. 1986. pap. 3.95 (ISBN 0-14-043243-4). Penguin.
--Victory. LC 32-26954. 1957. pap. 5.50 (ISBN 0-385-09314-4, Anch). Doubleday.
--Wisdom & Beauty from Conrad. Capes, Harriett, ed. LC 76-51355. (Studies in Conrad, No. 8). 1977. lib. bdg. 47.95x (ISBN 0-8383-2125-9). Haskell.
--The Works of Joseph Conrad. 3900.00 (ISBN 0-384-55125-4). Johnson Repr.
--Youth & the End of the Tether. 176p. 1976. pap. 2.95 (ISBN 0-14-004055-2). Penguin.
--Youth, Heart of Darkness. Kimbrough, Robert, ed. (World's Classics Ser.). 1984. pap. 2.95 (ISBN 0-19-281626-8). Oxford U Pr.
--Youth, Heart of Darkness, & the End of the Tether. 1978. 12.95x (ISBN 0-460-00694-0, Evman); pap. 3.95x (ISBN 0-460-01694-6, Evman). Biblio Dist.
--Youth, Heart of Darkness, Typhoon, The Secret Sharer. (Literature Ser.). (gr. 10-12). 1970. pap. text ed. 5.25 (ISBN 0-87720-748-8). AMSCO Sch.
--Youth, Heart of Darkness, Typhoon, The Secret Sharer. with Reader's Guide. (AMSCO Literature Program). (gr. 9-12). 1974. pap. text ed. 6.67 (ISBN 0-87720-819-0); tchr's ed. 4.20 (ISBN 0-87720-919-7). AMSCO Sch.
Conrad, Joseph & Ford, Ford M. The Inheritors. 228p. 1985. pap. 7.95 (ISBN 0-88184-136-6). Carroll & Graf.
--Romance. 558p. 1985. pap. 8.95 (ISBN 0-88184-166-8). Carroll & Graf.
Conrad, Joseph see Swan, D. K.
Conrad, Joseph, ed. see Ford, Ford Madox.
Conrad, Joseph, et al. Conrad under Familial Eyes. Zdzislaw, Najder, ed. Carroll-Najder, Halina, tr. LC 83-5187. 282p. 1984. 37.50 (ISBN 0-521-25082-X). Cambridge U Pr.
--Hugh Walpole. LC 73-1133. lib. bdg. 7.50 (ISBN 0-8414-1800-4). Folcroft.
--Fifty Great Sea Stories. 768p. 1980. Repr. lib. bdg. 35.00 (ISBN 0-8495-1712-5). Arden Lib.
Conrad, Joseph H., et al. Mineraux pour les Ruminants de Paturage des Regions Tropicales. LC 84-72137. (Illus., Orig., Fr.). 1984. write for info. extension billetin (ISBN 0-916287-02-5, Pub. by Ctr Tropical Agri). Univ Fla Food.
--Minerais Para Ruminantes em Pastejo em Regioes Tropicais. Euclides, Valeria P., tr. from Eng. LC 84-72136. (Illus., Orig., Portuguese.). 1984. write for info. extension bulletin (ISBN 0-916287-03-3, Pub. by Ctr Tropical Agri). Univ Fla Food.
Conrad, Joyner. The American Politician. LC 70-160811. pap. 61.80 (ISBN 0-317-26804-X, 2024318). Bks Demand UMI.
Conrad, Kenneth & Bressler, Rubin. Drug Therapy for the Elderly. LC 81-38398. (Illus.). 371p. 1982. pap. text ed. 23.95 (ISBN 0-8016-0782-5). Mosby.
Conrad, L. K., tr. see Guaresch, Giovanni.
Conrad, Lawrence H. Temper. LC 74-22774. (Labor Movement in Fiction & Non-Fiction). Repr. of 1924 ed. 22.50 (ISBN 0-404-58414-4). AMS Pr.
Conrad, Lawrence I., ed. & tr. see Duri, A. A.
Conrad, Leo, jt. auth. see Zimmerman, Steven.
Conrad, Michael. Adaptability: The Significance of Variability from Molecule to Ecosystem. LC 82-24558. 408p. 1983. 45.00x (ISBN 0-306-41223-3, Plenum Pr). Plenum Pub.
Conrad, Pam. I Don't Live Here! LC 84-7125. (Illus.). 80p. (gr. 2-6). 1984. 9.95 (ISBN 0-525-44080-1, 0966-290). Dutton.
Conrad, Pamela. Amanda. (Orig.). 1980. pap. 2.25 (ISBN 0-505-51554-7, Pub. by Tower Bks). Dorchester Pub Co.
--Prairie Songs. LC 85-42633. (Illus.). 176p. (gr. 5 up). 1985. 11.06i (ISBN 0-06-021336-1); PLB 10.89g (ISBN 0-06-021337-X). HarpJ.
Conrad, Peter. The Art of the City: Views & Versions of New York. (Illus.). 1984. 18.95 (ISBN 0-19-503408-2). Oxford U Pr.
--Imagining America. (Illus.). 1980. 16.95x (ISBN 0-19-502651-9). Oxford U Pr.
--Imagining America. 336p. 1982. pap. 3.95 (ISBN 0-380-59899-X, 59899-X, Discus). Avon.
--Romantic Opera & Literary Form. (Quantum Bk.). (Illus.). 185p. 1981. 19.50x (ISBN 0-520-03258-6, CAL 527); pap. 6.95 (ISBN 0-520-04508-4, CAL527). U of Cal Pr.
--Shandyism: The Character of the Romantic Irony. (Illus.). 190p. 1978. text ed. 26.50x (ISBN 0-06-491267-1). B&N Imports.
Conrad, Peter & Schneider, Joseph W. Deviance & Medicalization: From Badness to Sickness. LC 79-20333. 1980. pap. text ed. 15.95 (ISBN 0-8016-1025-7). Mosby.
Conrad, Peter, jt. auth. see Schneider, Joseph W.
Conrad, Peter, ed. Television: The Medium & Its Manners. 180p. 1982. 14.95x (ISBN 0-7100-9040-4); pap. 7.95x (ISBN 0-7100-9041-2). Routledge & Kegan.
Conrad, Peter & Kern, Rochelle, eds. Sociology of Health & Illness: Critical Perspectives. 500p. 1981. pap. text ed. 18.95x (ISBN 0-312-74066-2). St Martin.
Conrad, Peter & Reinharz, Shulamit, eds. Computers & Qualitative Data: A Special Issue of Qualitative Sociology. 212p. 1984. pap. 16.95 (ISBN 0-89885-218-8). Human Sci Pr.
Conrad, Randall, tr. see Benayon, Robert.
Conrad, Randy. Your Community & Recreation Planning: A Guide for Local Involvement in Comprehensive Recreation Planning. 160p. 1977. pap. 5.00 (ISBN 0-943272-14-9). Inst Recreation Res.
Conrad, Robert, ed. Brazilian Slavery: An Annotated Research Bibliography. 1977. lib. bdg. 20.00 (ISBN 0-8161-7855-0, Hall Reference). G K Hall.
Conrad, Robert & Hool, Bryce, eds. Taxation of Mineral Resources. LC 80-8392. (Lincoln Institute of Land Policy Book). 1980. 20.50x (ISBN 0-669-04104-1). Lexington Bks.
Conrad, Robert, ed. see Nabuco, Joaquim.
Conrad, Robert E., ed. & tr. from Portugese. Children of God's Fire: A Documentary History of Black Slavery in Brazil. LC 83-42553. (Illus.). 520p. 1983. 50.00x (ISBN 0-691-07658-8); pap. 16.50x L.P.E. (ISBN 0-691-10153-1). Princeton U Pr.
Conrad, Robert T., ed. General Scott & His Staff: Comprising Memoirs of General Scott, Twiggs, Smith, Quitman, Shields, Pillow, Lane, Cadwalader, Patterson, & Pierce, Colonels Childs, Riley, Harney, & Butler, & Other Distinguished Officers Attached to General Scott's Army. facsimile ed. LC 77-109626. (Select Bibliographies Reprint Ser). 1848. 26.50 (ISBN 0-8369-5235-9). Ayer Co Pubs.
Conrad, Stephen A., et al, eds. Pulmonary Function Testing: Principles & Practice. (Illus.). 378p. 1984. text ed. 33.50 (ISBN 0-443-08182-4). Churchill.
Conrad, Susan P. Perish the Thought: Intellectual Women in Romantic America 1830-1860. 1978. pap. 5.95 (ISBN 0-8065-0650-4). Citadel Pr.
--Perish the Thought: Intellectual Women in Romantic America, 1830-1860. LC 75-25463. (Illus.). 1976. 22.50x (ISBN 0-19-501995-4). Oxford U Pr.
Conrad, Tony & Broughel, Barbara. The Animal. (Illus.). 24p. 1984. pap. 6.00 (ISBN 0-939784-09-2). CEPA Gall.
Conrad, William R., Jr. & Glenn, William E. The Effective Voluntary Board of Directors: What It Is & How It Works. LC 76-13425. (Illus.). 186p. 1976. pap. 8.95x (ISBN 0-8040-0735-7, 82-74060, Pub. by Swallow). Ohio U Pr.
--The Effective Voluntary Board of Directors: What It Is & How It Works. rev. ed. LC 82-8240. (Illus.). xx, 244p. 1983. pap. text ed. 9.95 (ISBN 0-8040-0836-1, 82-76081, Swallow). Ohio U Pr.
Conrader, Constance, jt. auth. see Conrader, Jay.
Conrader, Jay & Conrader, Constance. The Northwoods Wildlife Region. LC 83-6257. (American Wildlife Region Ser.: No. 9). (Illus.). 192p. (Orig.). 1983. lib. bdg. 13.95 (ISBN 0-87961-126-X); pap. 7.95 (ISBN 0-87961-127-8). Naturegraph.
Conradi, Peter J. Iris Murdoch: The Saint & the Artist. 194p. 1985. 25.00 (ISBN 0-312-43614-9). St Martin.
--John Fowles. (Contemporary Writers Ser.). 1982. pap. 4.75x (ISBN 0-416-32250-6, NO. 3664). Methuen Inc.
Conrads, Ulrich, ed. Programs & Manifestoes on 20th-Century Architecture. 1971. pap. 5.95 (ISBN 0-262-53030-9). MIT Pr.
Conradt, David P. German Polity. 2nd ed. (Illus.). 256p. 1984. pap. text ed. 15.95 (ISBN 0-582-28191-1). Longman.
Conran, Shirley. Lace. 1984. pap. text ed. 4.50 (ISBN 0-671-54755-0). PB.
--Lace II. (Orig.). 1985. pap. 3.95 (ISBN 0-671-54603-1). PB.
--The Legend. 1985. write for info. (ISBN 0-671-50149-6). S&S.
Conran, Terence. The House Book. (Illus.). 448p. 1982. pap. 14.95 (ISBN 0-517-54654-X). Crown.
--The Kitchen Book. (Illus.). 1977. 35.95 (ISBN 0-517-53131-3). Crown.
--The Kitchen Book. (Illus.). 1984. pap. 14.95 (ISBN 0-517-55453-4). Crown.
Conrath, David, et al. Evaluating Telecommunications Technology in Medicine. LC 83-71833. (Illus.). 250p. 1983. 50.00 (ISBN 0-89006-126-2). Artech Hse.
Conrod, J. Computer Bible Games, Bk. 1. 192p. (Orig.). 1983. pap. 6.95 (ISBN 0-89636-126-8). Accent Bks.
Conrod, John. Computer Bible Games, Bk. 2. 160p. (Orig.). (YA) 1984. pap. 6.95 (ISBN 0-89636-141-1). Accent Bks.
Conron, John, ed. The American Landscape: A Critical Anthology of Prose & Poetry. (Illus.). 1974. pap. text ed. 16.95x (ISBN 0-19-501767-6). Oxford U Pr.
Conron, John P. Socorro: A Historic Survey. LC 79-56821. (Illus.). 144p. 1980. 14.95 (ISBN 0-8263-0528-8). U of NM Pr.
Conrow, Robert. The Great Diamond Hoax & Other True Tales. (Wyoming Frontier Ser.). (Illus.). 64p. (Orig.). 1983. pap. 3.95 (ISBN 0-933472-75-7). Johnson Bks.
Conrow, Robert & Hecksel, Arlene. Herbal Pathfinders: A Sourcebook for the Herbal Renaissance. LC 83-12350. (Illus.). 288p. 1983. pap. 9.95 (ISBN 0-88007-128-1); 15.95 (ISBN 0-88007-142-7). Woodbridge Pr.
Conroy, Ann P. & Conroy, Michael C. Fun Birds. LC 85-70679. (Illus.). 110p. 1985. 12.95 (ISBN 0-931494-65-6); pap. 7.95 (ISBN 0-931494-64-8). Brunswick Pub.
Conroy, Barbara. Learning Packaged to Go: A Directory & Guide to Staff Development & Training Packages. LC 82-42921. 244p. 1984. pap. 75.00x (ISBN 0-89774-065-3). Oryx Pr.
--Library Staff Development & Continuing Education: Principles & Practices. LC 78-18887. 296p. 1978. 30.00 (ISBN 0-87287-177-0). Libs Unl.
--Library Staff Development Profile Pages. 52p. (Orig.). 1979. 10.00 (ISBN 0-686-27541-1). B Conroy.
Conroy, Charles. First & Second Samuel, First & Second Kings, with Excursus on Davidic Dynasty & Holy City Zion. (Old Testament Message Ser.: Vol. 6). 12.95 (ISBN 0-89453-406-8); pap. 8.95 (ISBN 0-89453-241-3). M Glazier.
Conroy, D. A. Evaluation of the Present State of World Trade in Ornamental Fish. (Fisheries Technical Papers: No. 146). 133p. (2nd Printing 1976). 1975. pap. 9.00 (ISBN 92-5-101911-8, F877, FAO). Unipub.
Conroy, Frank. Midair. 160p. 1985. 15.95 (ISBN 0-525-24319-4, 01549-460, Seymour Lawrence). Dutton.
--Stop-Time. 1977. pap. 4.95 (ISBN 0-14-004446-9). Penguin.
Conroy, G. Teen Involvement: A Teen Counselor Training Manual. (gr. 7-12). 1972. text ed. 6.44 (ISBN 0-03-091272-5, HoltE); teachers edition 6.12 (ISBN 0-03-091273-3). HR&W.
Conroy, G. C. Primate Postcranial Remains from the Oligocene of Egypt. (Contributions to Primatology: Vol.8). 140p. 1976. 27.00 (ISBN 3-8055-2333-5). S Karger.
Conroy, Hilary. The Japanese Frontier in Hawaii, 1868-1898. Daniels, Roger, ed. LC 78-54840. (Asian Experience in North America). 1979. Repr. of 1953 ed. lib. bdg. 13.00x (ISBN 0-405-11306-4). Ayer Co Pubs.
--The Japanese Seizure of Korea, 1868-1910: A Study of Realism & Idealism in International Relations. LC 60-6936. 544p. 1974. pap. 11.95x (ISBN 0-8122-1074-3). U of Pa Pr.
Conroy, Hilary, jt. ed. see Wray, Harry.
Conroy, Hilary, et al, eds. Japan in Transition: Thought & Action in the Meiji Era 1868-1912. LC 83-48577. (Illus.). 320p. 1984. 35.00 (ISBN 0-8386-3169-X). Fairleigh Dickinson.
Conroy, Jack. The Disinherited. LC 78-26296. 1979. Repr. of 1933 ed. lib. bdg. 12.50x (ISBN 0-8376-0426-5). Bentley.
--The Disinherited. xii, 310p. 1982. pap. 6.95 (ISBN 0-88208-150-0). Lawrence Hill.
--The Weed King & Other Stories. 1985. 17.95; pap. 9.95 (ISBN 0-317-14861-3). Lawrence Hill.
Conroy, Jack, jt. auth. see Bontemps, Arna.
Conroy, Jack & Johnson, Curt, eds. Writers in Revolt: The Anvil Anthology, 1933-1940. LC 73-81748. 256p. 1973. 8.95 (ISBN 0-88208-025-3); pap. 4.95 (ISBN 0-88208-026-1). Lawrence Hill.
Conroy, John. Northern Ireland. 1985. write for info. (ISBN 0-670-51557-4). Viking.
Conroy, John, jt. auth. see Kraft, Eve.
Conroy, Joseph F. Aventure En Normandie: Reader 2. LC 81-7784. (A L'Aventure! Ser.). (Illus.). 40p. (Orig., Fr.). (YA) (gr. 7-12). 1982. pap. 1.95 (ISBN 0-88436-855-6, 40260). EMC.
--Danger sur la Cote d'azur: Reader 4. LC 81-7820. (A l'Aventure! Ser.). (Illus.). 40p. (Orig., Fr.). (YA) (gr. 7-12). 1982. pap. 1.95 (ISBN 0-88436-857-2, 40262). EMC.
--Destination: France! Reader 1. LC 81-7816. (A L'aventure! Ser.). (Illus.). 40p. (Orig., Fr.). (YA) (gr. 7-12). 1982. pap. 1.95 (ISBN 0-88436-854-8, 40259). EMC.
--Guide Terrestre, ou La Terre et Ses Singes. (Orig.). (gr. 7-12). 1975. pap. text ed. 6.17 (ISBN 0-87720-461-6). AMSCO Sch.
--Le Monstre dans le Metro et d'Autres Merveilles. (gr. 7-12). 1974. wkbk. 6.17 (ISBN 0-87720-469-1). AMSCO Sch.
--Sur la Route de la Contrebande. LC 81-7817. (A L'aventure! Ser.: Reader 3). (Illus.). 40p. (Orig., French.). (YA) (gr. 7-12). pap. 1.95 (ISBN 0-88436-856-4, 40261). EMC.
Conroy, Kathleen. Valuing the Timeshare Property. 97p. 1981. 15.00 (ISBN 0-911780-50-5). Am Inst Real Estate Appraisers.
Conroy, Kathleen & DiChiara, James. Timeshare Property Assesment & Taxation. Smith, Jeanette E., ed. (Illus., Orig.). 1983. 31.00 (ISBN 0-318-04658-X). Am Land Dev.
Conroy, Larry & O'Connell, Paul. The Consumer Cost Guide to Car Repair. (Illus.). 144p. 1983. text ed. 13.95 (ISBN 0-13-168872-3); pap. 6.95 (ISBN 0-13-168864-2). P-H.
Conroy, Lawrence E., et al. General Chemistry Laboratory Operation. 3rd ed. 1977. pap. write for info. (ISBN 0-02-324330-9, 32433). Macmillan.
Conroy, Lois. The Gardner Museum Cafe Cookbook. (Illus.). 176p. (Orig.). 1985. pap. 10.95 (ISBN 0-916782-71-9). Harvard Common Pr.
Conroy, Mark. Modernism & Authority: Strategies of Legitimation in Flaubert & Conrad. LC 84-21848. 256p. 1985. text ed. 20.00x (ISBN 0-8018-2480-X). Johns Hopkins.
Conroy, Mary. Complete Book of Crazy Patchwork: A Step-By-Step Guide to Crazy Patch-Work Projects. LC 85-50179. (Illus.). 110p. 1985. 19.95 (ISBN 0-8069-5548-1); pap. 9.95 (ISBN 0-8069-7966-6). Sterling.
Conroy, Mary & Ritvo, Edward. Every Woman Can: A Common-Sense Guide to Safety, Security & Self-Defense. LC 82-82355. 224p. (Orig.). 1982. pap. 6.95 (ISBN 0-399-51044-3, G&D). Putnam Pub Group.
Conroy, Michael. Cincinnati Jones. 1976. 7.95 (ISBN 0-915626-07-1). Yellow Jacket.
Conroy, Michael, jt. ed. see Walbek, Norman V.
Conroy, Michael C., jt. auth. see Conroy, Ann P.
Conroy, Michael R. Bong Sai. 1976. 1.50 (ISBN 0-915626-06-3). Yellow Jacket.
--Crusaders. 1975. 19.95 (ISBN 0-915626-02-0). Yellow Jacket.
--Fourth Down & Bedroom to Go. 1976. 9.95 (ISBN 0-915626-03-9). Yellow Jacket.
--Knight Flight! Travers, Mary A., ed. 1977. pap. 1.50 (ISBN 0-915626-09-8). Yellow Jacket.
--Mission at San y Sydro. LC 74-18207. 1975. 12.95 (ISBN 0-915626-01-2). Yellow Jacket.
--Summon the Brave. 1980. 2.50 (ISBN 0-686-27985-9). Yellow Jackett.
--Susurrations. 1976. 1.00 (ISBN 0-915626-05-5). Yellow Jacket.
Conroy, Pat. The Boo. 1983. Repr. of 1970 ed. 13.95 (ISBN 0-937036-02-1). Old NY Bk Shop.
--The Great Santini. 1977. pap. 3.95 (ISBN 0-380-00991-9, 65961-1). Avon.
--The Great Santini. 536p. Repr. of 1976 ed. 11.95 (ISBN 0-937036-00-5). Old NY Bk Shop.
--The Lords of Discipline. 512p. 1982. pap. 3.95 (ISBN 0-553-23396-3). Bantam.
--The Lords of Discipline. 544p. 1980. 12.95 (ISBN 0-395-29462-2). HM.
--The Water Is Wide. 1979. pap. 3.95 (ISBN 0-380-46037-8, 67124-7). Avon.
--The Water Is Wide. LC 70-177537. 1972. 9.95 (ISBN 0-395-13644-X). HM.
Conroy, Patricia, tr. see Andersen, Hans Christian.

Conry, Edward J., et al. The Legal Environment of Business. 624p. 1986. text ed. price not set (ISBN 0-697-00361-2); price not set instr's. manual (ISBN 0-697-00865-7); price not set student study guide (ISBN 0-697-00864-9). Wm C Brown.

Cons, Louis L. Auteur De la Farce De Pathelin. (Elliott Monographs: Vol. 17). 1926. 18.00 (ISBN 0-527-02620-4). Kraus Repr.

Conseil International De la Langue Francaise, ed. Vocabulaire De la Publicite. (Fr.). 1976. pap. 14.50 (ISBN 0-686-57251-3, M-6559). French & Eur.

--Vocabulaire de L'Environnement. (Fr.). 1976. pap. 14.95 (ISBN 0-686-57283-1, M-4648). French & Eur.

--Vocabulaire d'Ecologie. (Fr.). 1974. pap. 9.95 (ISBN 0-686-57284-X, M-4641). French & Eur.

Conseil International De la Langue Francais. Vocabulaire Du Beton. 192p. (Fr.). 1976. pap. 39.95 (ISBN 0-686-56961-X, M-6084). French & Eur.

Conseil International Des Machines a Combustion. Lexique: Machines a Combustion. 96p. (Fr., Eng., Span., It., Ger. & Dutch.). pap. 23.95 (ISBN 84-600-0836-3, S-30858). French & Eur.

Conseiller, C., ed. Liver-Anaesthesia & Critical Care. 256p. 1980. 58.25 (ISBN 90-219-0445-4, Excerpta Medica). Elsevier.

Conseiller, C. & Cousin, M. T., eds. Complications of Anaesthesia Operative Risk: Post Graduate Course. 370p. 1983. 76.75 (ISBN 0-444-90326-7, I-130-83, Excerpta Medica). Elsevier.

--Morphinomimetic & Antagonist Drugs: Post Graduate Course. 289p. 1983. 64.00 (ISBN 0-444-90327-5, I-142-83, Excerpta Medica). Elsevier.

Conseiller, C., et al, eds. Curare & Curarisation. 368p. 1980. 73.50 (ISBN 90-219-0443-8, Excerpta Medica). Elsevier.

--Anaesthesia & Postoperative Care in Uncommon Diseases: Post Graduate Course, Proceedings of International Meeting of Anaesthesiology & Resuscitation, XIIth, C. H. U. PetieSalpetriere, Paris 1980. 442p. 1982. 73.75 (ISBN 90-2-190473-X, Excerpta Medica). Elsevier.

--Volatile Halogenated Anaesthetics: Post Graduate Course. Proceedings of International Meeting of Anaesthesiology & Resuscitation, C. H. U. PetieSalpetriere, Paris, 1980. 242p. 1981. 55.25 (ISBN 90-219-0474-8, Excerpta Medica). Elsevier.

Conselman, Frank B., ed. Frontiers of the Semi-Arid World: An International Symposium. 96p. 1977. 3.00 (ISBN 0-318-14553-7, 77-2). Intl Ctr Arid & Semi-Arid.

Conser, James A., jt. auth. see Swank, Calvin J.

Conser, Walter H., Jr. Church & Confession: Conservative Theologians in Germany, England, & America, 1815-1866. LC 84-18990. viii, 360p. 1984. 28.95x (ISBN 0-86554-119-1, MUP/H109). Mercer Univ Pr.

Conservation Commission of the World Energy Conference. Energy, Two Thousand to Two Thousand & Twenty: World Prospects & Regional Stresses. 327p. 1984. 48.00x (ISBN 0-8448-1481-4). Crane-Russak Co.

Conservation Education Association. Critical Index of Films on Man & His Environment. LC 65-23951. 32p. 1972. pap. text ed. 1.25x (ISBN 0-8134-1374-5, 1374). Interstate.

--Education: Key to Conservation. Incl. 8p. 1965; Bk. 2. Planning a State Program in Conservation Education. (Illus.). 16p. 1965. pap. text ed. 0.30 (ISBN 0-8134-0870-9, 870); Bk. 3. Twenty-Five Key Guides for Preparing Conservation Education Publications & Visual Aids. (Illus.). 16p. 1965. pap. text ed. 0.30 (ISBN 0-8134-0871-7, 871); Bk. 5. A Selected List of Filmstrips on the Conservation of Natural Resources. (Illus.). 48p. 1968. pap. text ed. 0.50 (ISBN 0-8134-1040-1, 1040). LC 65-23951. pap. text ed. Interstate.

--Education, Key to Conservation: Critical Index of Films on Man & His Environment, Bk. 8. 32p. 1972. pap. text ed. 1.25 (ISBN 0-8134-1374-5). Interstate.

--Education, Key to Conservation: Environmental Conservation Education, a Selected Annotated Bibliography. LC 73-92152. 70p. 1974. pap. text ed. 2.50x (ISBN 0-8134-1633-7, 1633). Interstate.

--Environmental Conservation Education: A Selected Annotated Bibliography-1977 Supplement. 32p. 1978. pap. text ed. 1.50x (ISBN 0-8134-2027-X, 2027). Interstate.

--Environmental Conservation Education: A Selected Annotated Bibliography-1976 Supplement. LC 73-92152. 44p. 1977. pap. text ed. 1.50x (ISBN 0-8134-1899-2, 1899). Interstate.

--Environmental Conservation Education: A Selected Annotated Bibliography, 1975 Supplement. LC 73-92152. 32p. 1975. pap. text ed. 1.00 (ISBN 0-8134-1763-5, 1763). Interstate.

Conservation Foundation. Conservation & New Economic Realities. LC 78-68250. 1978. pap. 4.00 (ISBN 0-89164-049-5). Conservation Foun.

--National Parks for A New Generation: Visions, Realities, Prospects. LC 85-10948. (Illus.). 407p. (Orig.). 1985. pap. 19.95 (ISBN 0-89164-090-8). Conservation Foun.

--National Parks for the Future. LC 89-567. 254p. 1974. pap. 7.00 (ISBN 0-89164-009-6). Conservation Foun.

--Paying for Pollution: Water Quality & Effluent Charges. LC 78-52289. (Conservation Foundation: Issue Reports). pap. 20.00 (ISBN 0-317-11226-0, 2015784). Bks Demand UMI.

--Toward Clean Water: A Guide to Citizen Action. 1976. pap. 8.00 (ISBN 0-89164-034-7). Conservation Foun.

Conservation Foundation Staff. Risk Assessment & Risk Control. LC 85-5743. 69p. 1985. pap. 7.50 (ISBN 0-89164-091-6). Conservation Foun.

--State of the Environment: An Assessment at Mid-Decade. LC 84-12651. (Illus.). 620p. (Orig.). 1984. pap. 16.00 (ISBN 0-89164-084-3). Conservation Foun.

--State of the Environment 1982. LC 82-8257. (Illus.). 439p. (Orig.). 1982. pap. 15.00 (ISBN 0-89164-070-3). Conservation Foun.

Conservation of Human Resources Project Staff & Ginzberg, Eli, eds. From Health Dollars to Health Services. (Conservation of Human Resources Ser.: No. 25). 168p. 1985. text ed. 29.50x (ISBN 0-8476-7440-1). Rowman & Allanheld.

Conservation of Human Resources Staff, jt. auth. see Ginzberg, Eli.

Considerant, Victor P. Au Texas: With the Great West & European Colonization in Texas. LC 74-32216. (American Utopian Adventure Ser.). 432p. (Fr.). Repr. of 1855 ed. lib. bdg. 37.50x (ISBN 0-87991-021-6). Porcupine Pr.

Considine, Bob. They Rose Above It. 1978. pap. 1.75 (ISBN 0-449-23417-7, Crest). Fawcett.

Considine, Bob, ed. see Stripling, Robert E.

Considine, Brian. World Almanac's Puzzlink. 48p. (Orig.). 1985. pap. 2.95 (ISBN 0-911818-82-0). World Almanac.

--World Almanac's Puzzlink, No. 2. 48p. (Orig.). 1985. pap. 2.95 (ISBN 0-911818-89-8). World Almanac.

Considine, David M. The Cinema of Adolescence. LC 84-24604. (Illus.). 304p. 1985. lib. bdg. 19.95x (ISBN 0-89950-123-0). McFarland & Co.

Considine, Douglas M. Chemical & Process Technology Encyclopedia. 1184p. 1974. 82.50 (ISBN 0-07-012423-X). McGraw.

--Encyclopedia of Instrumentation & Control. LC 80-24422. 814p. 1981. Repr. of 1971 ed. text ed. 49.50 (ISBN 0-89874-281-1). Krieger.

--Energy Technology Handbook. 1977. 82.50 (ISBN 0-07-012430-2). McGraw.

--Handbook of Food Growth Technology. 1986. cancelled (ISBN 0-442-21614-9). Van Nos Reinhold.

--Handbook on World Food Production. 1986. cancelled (ISBN 0-442-21613-0). Van Nos Reinhold.

--Van Nostrand's Scientific Encyclopedia. 6th ed. (Illus.). 3100p. 1984. 2 vol. ed. 139.50 (ISBN 0-442-25164-5); 1 vol. ed. 107.50 (ISBN 0-442-25161-0). Van Nos Reinhold.

Considine, Douglas M. & Considine, Glenn D. Foods & Food Production Encyclopedia. LC 81-19728. (Illus.). 2560p. 1982. 195.00 (ISBN 0-442-21612-2). Van Nos Reinhold.

Considine, Douglas M., ed. Encyclopedia of Chemistry. 4th ed. (Illus.). 1168p. 1984. 89.50 (ISBN 0-442-22572-5). Van Nos Reinhold.

--Process Instruments & Controls Handbook. 3rd ed. (Illus.). 1593p. 1985. 89.50 (ISBN 0-07-012436-1). McGraw.

--Van Nostrand's Scientific Encyclopedia. 6th ed. (Illus.). 3100p. Date not set. One volume. 107.50 (ISBN 0-317-31219-7); Two volume set. 139.50 (ISBN 0-317-31220-0). Van Nos Reinhold.

--VNR Encyclopedia of Chemistry. 4th ed. (Illus.). 1168p. Date not set. 89.50 (ISBN 0-317-31236-7). Van Nos Reinhold.

Considine, Douglas M. & Ross, S. D., eds. Handbook of Applied Instrumentation. LC 81-19336. 1179p. 1982. Repr. of 1964 ed. 64.50 (ISBN 0-89874-397-4). Krieger.

Considine, Glenn D., jt. auth. see Considine, Douglas M.

Considine, Harvey & Trimberger, George W. Dairy Goat Judging Techniques. 15.95 (ISBN 0-686-26692-7). Dairy Goat.

Considine, J. D. Van Halen! LC 84-62455. (Illus.). 352p. (Orig.). 1985. pap. 9.95 (ISBN 0-688-04299-6, Quill). Morrow.

Considine, John J. New Horizons in Latin America. facs. ed. LC 74-93330. (Essay Index Reprint Ser.). 1958. 27.50 (ISBN 0-8369-1561-5). Ayer Co Pubs.

Considine, Robert, ed. see Wainwright, Jonathan M.

Considine, Shaun. Barbra Streisand: The Woman, the Myth, the Music. (Illus.). 288p. 1985. 17.95 (ISBN 0-385-29390-9). Delacorte.

Considine, Tim. The Language of Sport. Doering, Henry & Fisher, Patricia, eds. 336p. 1982. pap. 7.95 (ISBN 0-911818-24-3). World Almanac.

--The Language of Sport. LC 82-1544. 355p. 1983. 15.95x (ISBN 0-87196-653-0). Facts on File.

--The Language of Sport. LC 82-61797. 336p. 1983. pap. 7.95 (ISBN 0-911818-25-1). World Almanac.

--The Language of Sport. 1983. pap. 7.95 (ISBN 0-911818-25-1, World Almanac). Newspaper Ent.

Consigleri, Pederoso. Portuguese Folk-Tales. Montfiro, H., tr. Bd. with Researches Respecting the Books of Sindibad. Comparaetti, Domenico. (Folk-Lore Society, London: vol. 9). pap. 14.00 (ISBN 0-317-16024-9). Kraus Repr.

Consigliere-Pedroso, Z. Portuguese Folk-Tales. LC 68-57186. 1969. Repr. of 1882 ed. 10.00 (ISBN 0-405-08375-0, Blom Pubns). Ayer Co Pubs.

Consilvio, Thomas. Snapshooters. LC 73-81972. (Illus.). 40p. 1974. pap. 4.95 (ISBN 0-913968-00-5). Mouse Pr.

Conso, P. La Gestion Financiee De L'entreprise, 2 vols. 5th ed. 768p. (Fr.). 1979. Set. 39.95 (ISBN 0-686-56962-8, M-6085). French & Eur.

Consolazio, C. F. Nutrition & Performance, Vol 7/1-2. (Illus.). 200p. 1983. pap. 84.00 (ISBN 0-08-031013-3, 38). Pergamon.

Consolloy, Patricia, ed. After Scholarships, What? Creative Ways to Lower Your College Costs & the Colleges That Offer Them. LC 81-8478. 386p. 1981. pap. 8.00 (ISBN 0-87866-129-8). Petersons Guides.

Constabel, F., jt. ed. see Fowke, L. C.

Constable & Reynolds, Graham. Constable with His Friends in 1806, 5 vols. ltd. ed. (Illus.). 1981. Set. hand bound leather 316.00 (ISBN 0-904351-20-3). Vol. 1-28 pg. Vol. 2-44 pg. Vol. 3-90 pg. Vol. 4-36 pg. Vol. 5-56 pg. Genesis Pubns.

Constable, Anthony. Early Wireless. 1981. 40.00x (ISBN 0-85936-125-X, Pub. by Midas Bks England). State Mutual Bk.

Constable, Benjamin. Art, the Metaphysics of Love & Its Universal Mystical Symbols. (Illus.). 1977. 47.25 (ISBN 0-89266-046-5). Am Classical Coll Pr.

--God & the "New" Psychology of Sex. (Illus.). 265p. 1976. 53.75 (ISBN 0-89266-043-0). Am Classical Coll Pr.

--The Mystical Symbolism of Universal Love. (Illus.). 1978. 47.50 (ISBN 0-89266-113-5). Am Classical Coll Pr.

Constable, David, tr. see Calvin, Jean.

Constable, Frank C. The Curse of the Intellect. LC 79-8297. Repr. of 1895 ed. 44.50 (ISBN 0-404-61835-9). AMS Pr.

Constable, Freda. John Constable. (Illus.). 1979. 20.00 (ISBN 0-900963-54-9, Pub. by Terence Dalton England). State Mutual Bk.

Constable, Freda & Simon, Sue. The England of Eric Raviliousv. 1982. 37.50 (ISBN 0-85967-580-7). Scolar.

Constable, G. & Smith, B., eds. Libellus De Diversis Ordinibus et Professionibus Qui Sunt in Aecclesia: Orders & Callings of the Church. (Oxford Medieval Texts Ser). 1972. 42.00x (ISBN 0-19-822218-1). Oxford u Pr.

Constable, Giles. Attitudes Toward Self-Inflicted Suffering in the Middle Ages. (Stephen J. Brademas Lectures Ser.). 28p. (Orig.). pap. text ed. 2.50 (ISBN 0-916586-87-1). Hellenic Coll Pr.

--Cluniac Studies. 326p. 1980. 60.00x (ISBN 0-86078-054-6, Pub. by Variorum). State Mutual Bk.

--Medieval Monasticism: A Select Bibliography. LC 75-42284. 1976. 20.00x (ISBN 0-8020-2200-6); pap. 7.50 (ISBN 0-8020-6280-6). U of Toronto Pr.

Constable, Giles, jt. auth. see Kazhdan, Alexander.

Constable, Giles, jt. ed. see Benson, Robert L.

Constable, Giles, ed. see Peter The Venerable.

Constable, Giles, jt. ed. see Benson, Robert L.

Constable, John. Correspondence & Discourses of John Constable, R.A, 8 vols. Beckett, R. B., ed. Incl. No. 1. The Family at East Bergholt, 1807-1837. (Illus.). 337p. 1976. Repr. 22.75x (ISBN 0-8476-1252-X); No. 2. Early Friends & Marie Bicknell (Mrs. Constable) (Illus.). 474p. 18.75x (ISBN 0-8476-1253-8); No. 3. The Correspondence with C.R. Leslie R.A. 12.50x (ISBN 0-8476-1254-6); No. 4. Patrons, Dealers & Fellow Artists. (Illus.). 481p. 18.75x (ISBN 0-8476-1255-4); No. 5. Various Friends with Charles Boner & the Artist's Children. (Illus.). 229p. 12.50x (ISBN 0-8476-1256-2); No. 6. The Fishers. Grigson, Geoffrey, pref. by. (Illus.). 294p. 18.50x (ISBN 0-8476-1257-0); No. 7. Discourses. (Illus.). 109p. 12.50x (ISBN 0-8476-1258-9); No. 8. Further Correspondence & Documents. Paris, Leslie, et al, eds. (Illus.). 371p. 1976. 30.00x (ISBN 0-8476-1259-7). Set. 145.00x (ISBN 0-8476-1260-0). Rowman.

Constable, R. L., et al. An Introduction to the Pl-CV2 Programming Logic. (Lecture Notes in Computer Science: Vol. 135). 292p. 1982. pap. 20.00 (ISBN 0-387-11492-0). Springer-Verlag.

Constable, Robert. Prerogativa Regis: Tertia Lectura Roberti Constable De Lyncolnis Inne. Thorne, Samuel E., ed. 1949. 59.50x (ISBN 0-685-69876-9). Elliots Bks.

Constable, Robert L. & O'Donnell, Michael J. A Programming Logic: With an Introduction to the PL-CV Verifier. 1978. text ed. 24.95 (ISBN 0-316-15316-8). Little.

Constable, Robert T. & Flynn, John P. School Social Work: Practice & Research Perspectives. 1982. pap. 17.00x (ISBN 0-256-02775-7). Dorsey.

Constable, Robin, jt. auth. see Clapham, Adam.

Constable, Thomas. Archibald Constable & His Literary Correspondents, 3 vols. LC 70-148766. Repr. of 1873 ed. 145.00 set (ISBN 0-404-07640-8). AMS Pr.

Constable, Trevor, jt. auth. see Toliver, Raymond.

Constable, Trevor J. The Cosmic Pulse of Life: The Revolutionary Biological Power Behind UFO's. 432p. 25.00x (ISBN 0-85435-194-9, Pub. by Spearman England). State Mutual Bk.

Constable, Trevor J. & Toliver, Raymond F. Fighter Aces of the Luftwaffe. LC 77-79516. 1977. 19.95 (ISBN 0-8168-5790-3). Aero.

Constable, Trevor J., jt. auth. see Toliver, Raymond F.

Constable, W. G. The Painter's Workshop. (Illus.). 1980. pap. 4.50 (ISBN 0-486-23836-9). Dover.

Constabulary Force Commissioners, Great Britain. First Report of the Constabulary Force Commissioners Appointed to Inquire As to the Best Means of Establishing an Efficient Constabulary Force in the Countries of England & Wales. LC 76-172561. (Criminology, Law Enforcement, & Social Problems Ser.: No. 165). (Intro. added). Date not set. cancelled 15.00 (ISBN 0-87585-165-7). Patterson Smith.

Constance. Controlling In-Plant Airborne Contaminants. (Mechanical Engineering Ser.). 352p. 1983. 45.00 (ISBN 0-8247-1900-X). Dekker.

Constance, Diana, jt. auth. see Crossland, John.

Constance, Garnett, tr. see Tolstoy, Leo.

Constance, J. Mechanical Engineering for Professional Engineers' Examinations. 4th ed. 624p. 1985. 34.95 (ISBN 0-07-012452-3). McGraw.

Constance, J. D. Mechanical Engineering for Professional Engineers' Examinations. 3rd ed. 1981. 19.95 (ISBN 0-07-012457-4). McGraw.

Constanda, C., tr. see Tsypkin, Yakov Z.

Constandinidou, Loula D. Hellenic Hours: Or It All Happened in Greece. Hogan, Maria P., tr. 1982. 6.95 (ISBN 0-533-05279-3). Vantage.

Constandse, A. K. & Hofstee, E. W. Rural Sociology in Action. (Economic & Social Development Papers: No. 10). 64p. 1964. pap. 5.25 (ISBN 92-5-100470-6, F1459, FAO). Unipub.

Constandse, William. Dewi. 168p. (Orig.). 1983. pap. 6.95 (ISBN 0-317-01757-8). Utama Pubns Inc.

--How to Select Your Own Computer. 132p. 1983. 12.95 (ISBN 0-8119-0596-9). Fell.

--Inside Indonesia. 128p. (Orig.). 1983. pap. 6.95 (ISBN 0-911527-00-1). Utama Pubns Inc.

--A Tribute to the Women of Santa Fe. 149p. (Orig.). 1983. pap. 6.95 (ISBN 0-911527-01-X). Utama Pubns Inc.

--Why I Became a Buddhist. 130p. (Orig.). 1985. pap. 6.95 (ISBN 0-911527-02-8). Utama Pubns Inc.

Constandse, William J. Dewi. 168p. 1982. pap. 9.00 (ISBN 0-686-88954-1, Pub. by Graham Brash Singapore). Three Continents.

Constanduros, Bob. Brabham. (Kiberley's Grand Prix Team Guide Ser.: No. 2). (Illus.). 24p. 1982. pap. 4.95 (ISBN 0-946132-00-3, Pub by Kiberleys England). Motorbooks Intl.

--Derek Bell: Kimberley's Driver's Guide. (Kimberley's Driver Guides: No. 3). (Illus.). 24p. 1985. pap. 4.95 (ISBN 0-946132-19-4, Pub by Kimberley's England). Motorbooks Intl.

--Ferrari. (Kimberley's Grand Prix Team Guide Ser.: No. 3). (Illus.). 24p. 1982. pap. 4.95 (ISBN 0-946132-02-X, Pub by Kimberleys England). Motorbooks Intl.

--Lotus. (Kimberley's Grand Prix Team Guide Ser.: No. 6). (Illus.). 24p. 1983. pap. 4.95 (ISBN 0-946132-05-4, Pub by Kimberleys England). Motorbooks Intl.

--McLearen. (Kimberley's Grand Prix Team Guide Ser.: No. 5). (Illus.). 24p. 1908. pap. 4.95 (ISBN 0-946132-04-6, Pub by Kimberleys England). Motorbooks Intl.

--Renault. (Kimberley's Grand Prix Team Guide Ser.: No. 4). (Illus.). 1982. pap. 4.95 (ISBN 0-946132-03-8, Pub by Kimberleys England). Motorbooks Intl.

--Williams. (Kimberley's Grand Prix Team Guide: No. 1). (Illus.). 24p. 1982. pap. 4.95 (ISBN 0-946132-01-1, Pub by Kimberleys England). Motorbooks Intl.

Constans, H. Philip, Jr. Fit for Freedom. LC 79-6405. 141p. 1980. pap. text ed. 9.25 (ISBN 0-8191-0945-2). U Pr of Amer.

Constans, J., et al, eds. Neurology. (International Congress ser.: No. 94). (Abstracts - 8th Intl. Congress, Vienna, 1965). 1965. pap. 16.50 (ISBN 90-219-1128-0, Excerpta Medica). Elsevier.

Constans, Jacques A. Marine Sources of Energy. (Pergamon Policy Studies). (Illus.). 1980. 33.00 (ISBN 0-08-023897-1). Pergamon.

--Marine Sources of Energy. 125p. 15.00 (ISBN 0-318-15624-5). Natl Environment Pros.

Constant, A. L. Dictionnaire de la Litterature Chretienne, Vol. 7. Migne, J. P., ed. (Nouvelle Encyclopedie Theologique Ser.). 626p. (Fr.). Repr. of 1851 ed. lib. bdg. 80.00x (ISBN 0-89241-257-7). Caratzas.

Constant, Alberta W. Does Anyone Care About Lou Emma Miller? LC 78-4774. (gr. 3-7). 1979. 11.49i (ISBN 0-690-01335-3); PLB 11.89 (ISBN 0-690-03890-9). Crowell Jr Bks.

Constant, Benjamin. Adolphe. 1973. 27.50 (ISBN 0-685-10981-X); pap. 4.50 (ISBN 0-686-66412-4). French & Eur.

--Adolphe. Tancock, L. W., tr. (Penguin Classics). 1980. pap. 4.95 (ISBN 0-14-044134-4). Penguin.

--Adolphe. 2nd ed. Rudler, G., ed. (Modern French Texts Ser.). 148p. (Fr.). 1941. pap. text ed. 4.95 (ISBN 0-7190-0142-0, Pub. by Manchester Univ Pr). Longwood Pub Group.

--De la Perfectibilite de l'Espece Humaine. 1967. 7.95 (ISBN 0-686-54608-3). French & Eur.

--De l'Esprit de Conquete. 72p. 1947. 4.95 (ISBN 0-686-54609-1). French & Eur.
--Ecrits et Discours Politiques, 2 vols. (Illus.). 256p. Set. 29.95 (ISBN 0-686-54610-5). French & Eur.
--Journal Intimes. 6.95 (ISBN 0-686-54611-3). French & Eur.
--Journaux Intimes. 1965. 9.95 (ISBN 0-686-54612-1). French & Eur.
--Memoires sur les Cent Jours. 348p. 14.95 (ISBN 0-686-54614-8). French & Eur.
--Oeuvres. Roulin, ed. (Bibliotheque De la Pleiade). 1957. 29.95 (ISBN 0-685-11435-X). French & Eur.
Constant, Benjamin & Constant, R. de. Correspondance 1786-1830. 6.95 (ISBN 0-686-54606-7). French & Eur.
Constant, Benjamin & Derre, Jean Rene. Wallstein: Edition Critique. 264p. 1965. 19.95 (ISBN 0-686-54616-4). French & Eur.
Constant, Benjamin & Goyet de la Sarthe, Charles L. Correspondance 1818-1822. 1973. 75.00 (ISBN 0-686-54607-5). French & Eur.
Constant, Benjamin & Harpaz, Ephraim. Recueil d'Articles, 2 vols. 1566p. 1972. Set. 99.50 (ISBN 0-686-54615-6). French & Eur.
Constant, Benjamin, tr. see Godwin, William.
Constant, Benjamin, et al. Lettres a un Ami: Cent Onze Lettres Inedites a Claude Hochet. 256p. 1949. 11.95 (ISBN 0-686-54613-X). French & Eur.
Constant, Caroline. The Palladio Guide. (Illus.). 160p. 1985. pap. 17.00 (ISBN 0-910413-10-X). Princeton Arch.
Constant, Constantine. Earth Science: Intermediate Level. (gr. 7-10). 1972. wkbk. ed. 9.00 (ISBN 0-87720-154-4). AMSCO Sch.
--Review Text in Earth Science, Intermediate Level. (Orig.). (gr. 7-9). 1971. pap. text ed. 7.83 (ISBN 0-87720-152-8). AMSCO Sch.
--Student Earth Scientist Explores Changing Earth. LC 75-8906. (Student Scientist Ser.). (YA) (gr. 7-12). 1975. PLB 8.97 (ISBN 0-8239-0330-3). Rosen Group.
--The Student Earth Scientist Explores Earth & Its Materials. LC 74-23283. (Student Scientist Ser.). (Illus.). (YA) (gr. 7-12). 1975. PLB 8.97 (ISBN 0-8239-0306-0). Rosen Group.
--The Student Earth Scientist Explores Weather. LC 74-13746. (Student Scientist Ser.). (Illus.). 190p. (gr. 7-12). 1975. PLB 8.97 (ISBN 0-8239-0303-6). Rosen Group.
Constant, D'Estournelles De see De Constant, D'Estaurnelles.
Constant, Edward W., II. The Origins of the Turbojet Revolution. LC 80-11802. (JH Studies in the History of Technology). 328p. 1981. 29.50x (ISBN 0-8018-2222-X). Johns Hopkins.
Constant, F. Woodbridge. Theoretical Physics: Mechanics of Particles, Rigid & Elastic Bodies & Heat Flow. LC 78-14353. 296p. 1979. Repr. of 1954 ed. lib. bdg. 20.50 (ISBN 0-88275-738-5). Krieger.
Constant, Gustave L. The Reformation in England. Scantlebury, R. E., tr. LC 83-45576. Date not set. Repr. of 1934 ed. 85.00 (ISBN 0-404-19895-3). AMS Pr.
Constant, Jacques see Otten, Anna.
Constant, James. Gravitational Action. 114p. 1978. pap. 15.00 (ISBN 0-914330-16-0). RCS Assocs.
Constant, James N. Fundamentals of Strategic Weapons. 940p. 1981. 140.00 (ISBN 90-286-0129-5). Sijthoff & Noordhoff.
--Fundamentals of Strategic Weapons, 2 Vols. 1982. lib. bdg. 195.00 (ISBN 90-247-2545-3, Pub. by Martinus Nijhoff Netherlands). Kluwer Academic.
--Invention Secrecy Score: Government 30,000-Inventors 0. 97p. (Orig.). 1984. pap. 15.00 ltd. ed. (ISBN 0-930293-00-2). RCS Assocs.
Constant, Jules. Bedside Cardiology. 2nd ed. 1976. 39.95 (ISBN 0-316-15319-2). Little.
--Learning Electrocardiography: A Complete Course. 2nd ed. (Illus.). 1981. text ed. 39.50 (ISBN 0-316-15322-2). Little.
Constant, Nicholas J. Improved Recovery. LC 83-62119. (Oil & Gas Production Ser.: Lesson 8). (Illus., Orig.). 1983. pap. text ed. 7.50 (ISBN 0-88698-044-5, 3.30810). PETEX.
Constant, R. de, jt. auth. see Constant, Benjamin.
Constant de Rebecque, Henri B. Cours de Politique Constitutionnelle, 2 vols. Mayer, J. P., ed. LC 78-67347. (European Political Thought Ser.). (Fr.). 1979. Repr. of 1872 ed. Set. lib. bdg. 80.00x (ISBN 0-405-11686-1). Ayer Co Pubs.
Constantelos, D. J. Marriage, Sexuality & Celibacy: A Greek Orthodox Perspective. 1975. pap. 4.50 (ISBN 0-937032-15-8). Light&Life Pub Co MN.
Constantelos, Demetrios J. Byzantine Philanthropy & Social Welfare, Vol. I. rev. ed. (Studies in Byzantine Religious & Social History). 384p. 1985. lib. bdg. 50.00 (ISBN 0-89241-402-2). Caratzas.
--Byzantine Society & Church Philanthropy: From the Fourth Crusade Through the Fall, Vol. 2. (Studies in Byzantine Religious & Social History). 352p. 1985. lib. bdg. 50.00 (ISBN 0-89241-401-4). Caratzas.
--Understanding the Greek Orthodox Church: Its Faith, History & Practice. 214p. 1982. (Pub. by Seabury); pap. 9.95 (ISBN 0-8164-2367-9). WInston Pr.
Constantelos, Demetrios J., intro. by. Orthodox Theology & Diakonia: Trends & Prospects. 398p. 1981. 24.95 (ISBN 0-916586-79-0); pap. 17.95 (ISBN 0-916586-80-4). Hellenic Coll Pr.
Constantian, Mark B., ed. Pressure Ulcers: Principles & Techniques of Management. 320p. 1980. text ed. 45.00 (ISBN 0-316-15330-3). Little.
Constantindes, P. Ultrastructural Pathobiology. 1984. 120.00 (ISBN 0-444-80440-4, I-194-84). Elsevier.
Constantine & Hobbs. Know Your Woods. 1975. text ed. 17.95 (ISBN 0-02-664790-7). Bennett IL.
Constantine, et al. Traveler's Dictionary. 1985. 5.95 (ISBN 0-8120-3557-7). Barron.
--Traveler's Phrasebook. 1985. 6.95 (ISBN 0-8120-3558-5). Barron.
Constantine, Albert. Know Your Woods. rev. ed. 1975. 19.95 (ISBN 0-684-14115-9, ScribT). Scribner.
Constantine, Archimandrite. Antichrist, Orthodoxy or Heterodoxy. pap. 0.25 (ISBN 0-686-11505-8). Eastern Orthodox.
Constantine, David. Early Greek Travellers & the Hellenic Ideal. LC 83-18860. (Illus.). 256p. 1984. 49.50 (ISBN 0-521-25342-X). Cambridge U Pr.
Constantine, Greg. Leonardo Visits Los Angeles. Scudellari, R. D., ed. LC 85-40222. (Illus.). 80p. 1985. pap. 7.95 (ISBN 0-394-73555-2). Knopf.
--Vincent van Gogh Visits New York. LC 83-48011. 1983. pap. 7.95 (ISBN 0-394-72180-2). Knopf.
Constantine, H. F. William Strang R. A. Eighteen Fifty-Nine to Nineteen Twenty-One: Painter-Etcher. (Illus.). 86p. 1981. 18.50 (ISBN 0-8390-0280-7). Abner Schram Ltd.
Constantine, J., jt. auth. see Clifford, H. T.
Constantine, John & Wallis, Julia. The Thames & Hudson Manual of Professional Photography. LC 82-50814. (Thames & Hudson Manual Ser.). (Illus.). 1983. pap. 10.95 (ISBN 0-500-68025-6). Thames Hudson.
Constantine, K. C. Always a Body to Trade. (Crime Monthly Ser.). 256p. 1984. pap. 3.50 (ISBN 0-14-007059-1). Penguin.
--Always a Body to Trade: A Mario Balzic Mystery. LC 82-48700. 256p. 1983. 13.95 (ISBN 0-87923-458-X). Godine.
--The Man Who Liked Slow Tomatoes. LC 81-47321. (Balzic Mystery Ser.: No. 5). 256p. 1982. 13.95 (ISBN 0-87923-407-5). Godine.
--The Man Who Liked Slow Tomatoes. 224p. 1983. pap. 2.95 (ISBN 0-14-006621-7). Penguin.
--The Man Who Liked to Look at Himself. Barzun, J. & Taylor, W. H., eds. LC 81-47346. (Crime Fiction 1950-1975 Ser.). 151p. 1983. lib. bdg. 18.00 (ISBN 0-8240-4955-1). Garland Pub.
--The Man Who Liked to Look at Himself & a Fix Like This. LC 83-47507. (Double Detective Ser.: No. 3). 352p. (Orig.). 1983. pap. 8.95 (ISBN 0-87923-468-7). Godine.
--Rocksburg Railroad Murders: The Blank Page. LC 81-47322. (Double Detective Ser.: No. 1). 356p. 1982. pap. 7.95 (ISBN 0-317-27085-0). Godine.
Constantine, K C. Upon Some Midnights Clear. LC 84-48748. (A Mario Balzic Mystery Ser.). 256p. 1985. 15.95 (ISBN 0-87923-570-5). Godine.
Constantine, Larry L. & Martinson, Floyd. Children & Sex: New Findings, New Perspectives. 1981. text ed. 24.50 (ISBN 0-316-15331-1). Little.
Constantine, Larry L., jt. auth. see Yourdon, Edward.
Constantine, M. Whole Cloth. 1986. cancelled. Van Nos Reinhold.
Constantine, Mildred. Tina Modotti: A Fragile Life. (Illus.). 224p. 1983. 30.00 (ISBN 0-8478-0480-1). Rizzoli Intl.
Constantine, Mildred & Fern, Alan. Revolutionary Soviet Film Posters. LC 74-6817. (Illus.). 112p. 1974. 18.50x (ISBN 0-8018-1641-6); pap. 8.95 (ISBN 0-8018-1760-9). Johns Hopkins.
Constantine, Mildred, jt. auth. see Selz, Peter.
Constantine, Mildred, jt. ed. see Selz, Peter.
Constantine, Murray. The Devil, Poor Devil: A Novel. Reginald, R. & Melville, Douglas, eds. LC 77-84214. (Lost Race & Adult Fantasy Ser.). 1978. Repr. of 1934 ed. lib. bdg. 22.00x (ISBN 0-405-10969-5). Ayer Co Pubs.
Constantine, Stephen. The Making of British Colonial Development Policy, 1914-1940. (Illus.). 340p. 1984. text ed. 32.50x (ISBN 0-7146-3204-X, BHA-03204, F Cass Co). Biblio Dist.
Constantine, Steven. Social Conditions in Britain Nineteen Eighteen to Nineteen Thirty-Nine. (Lancaster Pamphlets). 55p. 1983. pap. 3.95 (ISBN 0-416-36010-6, NO. 3983). Methuen Inc.
Constantine I. A Treatise of the Donation of Gyfts & Endowment of Possessyons Gyven & Graunted Unto Sylvester Pope of Rome by Constantyne Emperour of Rome. Marshall, William, tr. LC 79-84096. (English Experience Ser.: No. 916). 152p. (Eng.). 1979. Repr. of 1534 ed. lib. bdg. 24.00 (ISBN 90-221-0916-X). Walter J Johnson.
Constantinesco, I. Soil Conservation for Developing Countries. (Soils Bulletins: No. 30). (Illus.). 104p. (Eng., Fr. & Span., 3rd Printing 1981). 1976. pap. 7.75 (ISBN 92-5-100101-4, F1172, FAO). Unipub.
Constantinescu, C. Duality in Measure Theory. (Lecture Notes in Mathematics: Vol. 796). 197p. 1980. pap. 17.00 (ISBN 0-387-09989-1). Springer-Verlag.
Constantinescu, C. & Cornea, A. Potential Theory on Harmonic Spaces. LC 72-86117. (Die Grundlehren der Mathematischen Wissenschaften: Vol. 158). 1972. 65.00 (ISBN 0-387-05916-4). Springer-Verlag.
Constantinescu, Corneliu. Spaces of Measures. LC 84-5815. (Studies in Mathematics: No. 4). 444p. 1984. 59.95x (ISBN 3-11-008784-7). De Gruyter.
Constantinescu, Corneliu, et al. Integration Theory: Measure & Integral, Vol. I. (Pure & Applied Mathematics Ser.). 576p. 1985. text ed. 48.50x (ISBN 0-471-04479-2, Pub. by Wiley-Interscience). Wiley.
Constantinescu, F. & Magyari, E. Problems in Quantum Mechanics. 1971. text ed. 28.00 (ISBN 0-08-019008-1). Pergamon.
Constantinescu, Ilinca, tr. see Vasiliu, Emanuel & Golopentia-Eretescu, Sanda.
Constantinescu, V. N. Gas Lubrication: Translated from the Rumanian. Wehe, Robert L., ed. Technica, Scripta, tr. LC 78-93540. 630p. 1969. pap. 19.50 (ISBN 0-685-06526-X, G00015). ASME.
Constantinescu, V. N., et al. Sliding Bearings. xx, 543p. 1984. 80.00x (ISBN 0-89864-011-3). Allerton Pr.
Constantinescu, Virgiliu N. Gas Lubrication. Wehe, Robert L., ed. Scripta Technica, tr. LC 78-93540. pap. 160.00 (ISBN 0-317-26212-2, 2052120). Bks Demand UMI.
Constantini, Humberto. The Gods, the Little Guys & the Police. Talbot, Toby, tr. from Span. LC 83-48339. 230p. 1984. 14.37x (ISBN 0-06-015252-4, HarpT). Har-Row.
Constantinides, A., et al, eds. see Biochemical Engineering Conference, 2nd, Henniker, New Hampshire, July 13-18, 1980.
Constantinides, A. G., jt. ed. see Bogner, R. E.
Constantinides, A. G., jt. ed. see Cappelini, V.
Constantinides, A. G., jt. ed. see Cappellini, V.
Constantinides, George C. Intelligence & Espionage: An Analytical Bibliography. LC 83-3519. 559p. 1983. 60.00x (ISBN 0-86531-545-0). Westview.
Constantinides, P., et al. Immunity & Atherosclerosis. (Serono Symposia Ser.: No.24). 1980. 39.50 (ISBN 0-12-186250-X). Acad Pr.
Constantinides, Paris. Functional Electronic Histology. 244p. 1974. 110.25 (ISBN 0-444-40998-X, Biomedical Pr). Elsevier.
Constantino, Anthony. Fight City Hall. (Illus.). 44p. 1981. 5.00 (ISBN 0-682-49785-1). Exposition Pr FL.
Constantino, Ernesto. Ilokano Dictionary. McKaughan, Howard P., ed. (PALI Language Texts: Philippines). 510p. (Orig.). 1971. pap. text ed. 12.00x (ISBN 0-87022-152-3). UH Pr.
Constantinon, P. How to Say It in Modern Greek. 12.50 (ISBN 0-87559-171-X). Shalom.
Constantopoulos, E. Aesop's Fables. (Illus.). 160p. (gr. 2-3). 3.20 (ISBN 0-686-79630-6); wkbk. 2.50 (ISBN 0-686-79631-4). Divry.
Constantopoulos, G. First Greek Reader. (Illus.). 96p. 3.70 (ISBN 0-686-79626-8). Divry.
--Second Greek Reader. (Illus.). 96p. 3.70 (ISBN 0-686-79627-6). Divry.
Constanz, Bernold Von see Von Constanz, Bernold.
Constas, Michael & Harroch, Richard D. Private Real Estate Syndications. LC 83-9417. 1984. looseleaf 70.00. NY Law Pub.
Constas, Robert. Death Does Not Exist: Psychology of Becoming Oneself. 1979. pap. 2.00 (ISBN 0-911794-48-4). Aqua Educ.
Consterdine, Guy. Readership Research. 200p. 1986. text ed. price not set (ISBN 0-566-05071-4). Gower Pub Co.
Constiner, Merle. The Fourth Gunman. 176p. 1985. pap. 2.50 (ISBN 0-441-24927-2). Ace Bks.
--Killers Corral. 1978. pap. 1.25 (ISBN 0-505-51237-8, Pub. by Tower Bks). Dorchester Pub Co.
Constinett, jt. auth. see Warshawsky.
Constitutional Convention of South Carolina. Proceedings. LC 68-29018. (American Negro: His History & Literature Ser., No. 1). 1968. Repr. of 1868 ed. 35.50 (ISBN 0-405-01837-1). Ayer Co Pubs.
Consultants Bureau. Physics & Heat Technology of Reactors. LC 59-958. (Soviet Journal of Atomic Energy. Supplement 1958: No. 1). pap. 45.00 (ISBN 0-317-08314-7, 2020654). Bks Demand UMI.
--Primary Acts in Radiation Chemical Processes: A Portion of proceedings of the First All-Union Conference on Radiation Chemistry, Moscow, 1957 in English Translation. pap. 20.00 (ISBN 0-317-09397-5, 2020688). Bks Demand UMI.
--Production of Isotopes: A Portion of the Proceedings of the All-Union Scientific & Technical Conference on Applications of Radioactive Isotopes. LC 59-14487. pap. 34.80 (ISBN 0-317-09120-4, 2020655). Bks Demand UMI.
Consultants Bureau Staff. Contemporary Equipment for Work with Radioactive Isotopes: Collected Reports. LC 59-14767. (Soviet Journal of Atomic Energy, Supplement, 1958: No. 5). pap. 20.00 (ISBN 0-317-28013-9, 2055800). Bks Demand UMI.
--The Geology of Uranium. LC 59-24987. (Soviet Journal of Atomic Energy, Supplement: 1957; No. 6). Repr. of 1958 ed. 33.50 (ISBN 0-317-27110-5, 2024705). Bks Demand UMI.
Consultants, jt. auth. see Hoard, Samuel L.
Consulting Staff. The CIA & the NSA. 1985. 95.00 (ISBN 0-938124-08-0). P R Lees-Haley.
Consumer Automotive Press. The Used Car Book. (Orig.). 1985. pap. 6.95 (ISBN 0-449-90144-0, Columbine). Fawcett.
Consumer Credit Project. New Credit Rights for Women. LC 78-55596. (Illus.). 1978. pap. text ed. 2.00x (ISBN 0-931786-00-2). Consumer Credit Project.
Consumer Digest Editors, ed. How to Win at Apple Computer Games. 64p. 1984. spiral bound 8.95 (ISBN 0-671-49559-3). S&S.
Consumer Electronics Group. New World of Audio: A Music Lover's Guide. LC 82-50019. 164p. 1983. pap. 8.95 (ISBN 0-672-21946-8). Sams.
Consumer Group, ed. Prescription Drugs. 287p. 1985. 24.00 (ISBN 0-317-19972-2). Porter.
Consumer Group, Inc., jt. auth. see Darack, Arthur.
Consumer Group, Inc. Staff, jt. auth. see Darack, Arthur.
Consumer Guide. The Food Processor Bread Cookbook. (Illus.). 1980. (Fireside); pap. 7.95 (ISBN 0-671-25138-4). S&S.
--The Vitamin Book. 1979. (Fireside); pap. 5.95 (ISBN 0-671-24819-7). S&S.
Consumer Guide, ed. Family Medical Guide: The Illustrated Medical & Health Advisor. LC 83-13105. (Illus.). 576p. 1983. FPT 12.95 (ISBN 0-688-02210-3). Morrow.
Consumer Guide Editions. Do It Yourself & Save Money. LC 80-7585. (Illus.). 636p. 1980. 14.95i (ISBN 0-06-010861-4, HarpT). Har-Row.
Consumer Guide Editors. Atari Software: Rating the Best. LC 83-737274. 154p. 1984. spiral bd. 1.98 (ISBN 0-517-42474-6). Outlet Bk Co.
--Baby Equipment Buying Guide. 1985. pap. 3.95 (ISBN 0-451-13825-2, Sig). NAL.
--Book of Personal Computers & Games. 54p. 1984. spiral bdg. 3.98 (ISBN 0-517-41595-X, Pub. by Beekman Hse). Outlet Bk Co.
--The Complete Book of Prefabs, Kits & Manufactured Houses. 160p. 1981. pap. 7.95 (ISBN 0-449-90051-7, Columbine). Fawcett.
--Computer Careers: Where the Jobs Are & How to Get Them. 256p. 1981. 6.95 (ISBN 0-449-90064-9, Columbine). Fawcett.
--Computer Careers: Where the Jobs Are & How to Get Them. 256p. 1984. pap. 6.95 (ISBN 0-449-90127-0, Columbine). Fawcett.
--Consumer Guide - 1985 Buying Guide. 1985. pap. 3.95 (ISBN 0-451-13422-2, Sig). NAL.
--Decorating Your Office for Success. LC 78-20157. (Illus.). 1979. 13.41i (ISBN 0-06-010854-1, HarpT). Har-Row.
--The Dieter's Complete Guide to Calories, Carbohydrates, Sodium, Fats & Cholesterol. 192p. (Orig.). 1981. pap. 5.95 (ISBN 0-449-90050-9, Columbine). Fawcett.
--An Easy-to-Understand Guide to Home Computers. 1982. pap. 3.95 (ISBN 0-451-12031-0, Sig). NAL.
--Easy-to-Understand Guide to Home Computers. 95p. 1984. pap. 3.95 (ISBN 0-517-42584-X, Pub. by Beekman Hse). Outlet Bk Co.
--Favorite Brand Name Recipes: Casseroles. 144p. 1985. pap. 2.50 (ISBN 0-449-20209-7, Crest). Fawcett.
--Favorite Brand Name Recipes: Salads. 144p. 1985. pap. 2.50 (ISBN 0-449-20210-0, Crest). Fawcett.
--Flatten Your Stomach for Men & Women. 1983. pap. 2.95 (ISBN 0-671-47312-3). PB.
--Gas Savers Guide. (Orig.). 1979. pap. 1.95 (ISBN 0-449-80000-8, Columbine). Fawcett.
--Health Careers: Where the Jobs Are & How to Get Them. 1982. pap. 6.95 (ISBN 0-449-90075-4, Columbine). Fawcett.
--The Home Energy Saver. (Orig.). 1979. pap. 1.95 (ISBN 0-449-80002-4, Columbine). Fawcett.
--Home Repair Money Saver. 1981. pap. 2.50 (ISBN 0-449-90027-4, Columbine). Fawcett.
--How to Win at Atari Computer Games. (Illus.). 64p. 1983. pap. 8.95 spiral bound cancelled (ISBN 0-671-49558-5, Fireside). S&S.
--How to Win at Donkey Kong. 32p. (Orig.). 1982. pap. 1.95 (ISBN 0-671-45840-X). PB.
--How to Win at E.T. the Video Game. 32p. 1983. pap. 2.50 (ISBN 0-440-13767-5). Dell.
--How to Win at Pac-Man. (Orig.). 1982. pap. 2.25 (ISBN 0-671-46072-2). PB.
--How to Win at Video Games. 1984. spiral bdg. 1.98 (ISBN 0-517-42470-3). Outlet Bk Co.
--How to Win Video Games. 96p. (Orig.). 1982. pap. 2.95 (ISBN 0-671-45841-8). PB.
--The Insiders Guide to Computer Networking. 192p. 1984. pap. cancelled (ISBN 0-671-47806-0, Touchstone). S&S.
--The Perfect Dessert. 1985. pap. 9.95 (ISBN 0-452-25688-7, Plume). NAL.
--Slimming Your Hips & Thighs. 1983. pap. 2.95 (ISBN 0-671-47311-5). PB.
--Social Security Benefits. 1980. pap. 2.50 (ISBN 0-449-90029-0, Columbine). Fawcett.
--The User's Guide to Apple II, II Plus & IIe Computers, Software & Peripherals. 1983. spiral bdg. 2.98 (ISBN 0-517-41678-6). Outlet Bk Co.

--The User's Guide to APPLE 1000, 2000. (Orig.). 1983. pap. 3.95 (ISBN 0-671-49502-X). PB.

--The User's Guide to Atari, 400, 800, 1200XL. (Orig.). 1983. pap. 3.95 (ISBN 0-671-49503-8). PB.

--The User's Guide to Commodore 64 & VIC-20 Computers, Software & Peripherals. 80p. pap. 4.98 (ISBN 0-318-02641-4). Pubns Intl Ltd.

--The User's Guide to Texas Instruments. (Orig.). 1983. pap. 3.95 (ISBN 0-671-49504-6). PB.

--Whole Car Catalog. (Illus.). 1978. pap. 7.95 (ISBN 0-671-23022-0, Fireside). S&S.

--Whole Sewing Catalog. Rev ed. 256p. 1982. pap. 11.95 (ISBN 0-671-45189-8, Fireside). S&S.

--The Woman's "No Sweat" Exercise Book. 1981. pap. 2.50 (ISBN 0-449-90028-2, Columbine). Fawcett.

--Your Home Is Money: Managing Your Home for Profit. 1978. pap. 6.95 (ISBN 0-07-018997-8). McGraw.

Consumer Guide Editors & Adams, Roe R., III. Apple Software: Rating the Best. LC 83-73275. 154p. 1984. pap. 4.98 spiral bdg. (ISBN 0-517-42475-4). Outlet Bk Co.

Consumer Guide Editors & Goodman, Danny. A Parent's Guide to Personal Computers & Software. 80p. 1983. pap. 6.95 (ISBN 0-671-49173-3, 22083, Touchstone). S&S.

Consumer Guide Editors & Mosher, Charles. Emergency First Aid. 96p. 1980. pap. 2.50 (ISBN 0-449-90023-1, Columbine). Fawcett.

Consumer Guide Editors & Ojakangas, Beatrice A. The Convection Oven Cookbook. (Illus.). 1980. pap. 6.95 (ISBN 0-449-90042-8, Columbine). Fawcett.

Consumer Guide Editors, jt. auth. see Gibbons, Barbara.

Consumer Guide Editors, jt. auth. see Kay, Sophie.

Consumer Guide Editors, jt. auth. see Kuntzleman, Beth A.

Consumer Guide Editors, jt. auth. see Kuntzleman, Charles T.

Consumer Guide Editors, ed. Consumer Guide Family Health & Medical Guide. 1985. pap. 4.95 (ISBN 0-451-13839-2, Sig). NAL.

--Consumer Guide to a Flatter Stomach. (Illus.). 1983. pap. 2.95 (ISBN 0-671-49702-2). PB.

--The Fastest, Cheapest, Best Way to Clean Everything. 288p. 1982. pap. 8.95 (ISBN 0-671-25468-5, Fireside). S&S.

--How It Works & How to Fix It. 1985. pap. 4.50 (ISBN 0-451-13871-6, Sig). NAL.

--Two Hundred Favorite Brand Name Recipes Cookbook. 1984. pap. 2.95 (ISBN 0-517-55395-3). Crown.

--The Video Equipment Buying Guide. 1985. pap. 3.95 (ISBN 0-451-13752-3, Sig). NAL.

--The Whole House Catalog. Rev ed. 384p. 1981. pap. 9.50 (ISBN 0-671-43640-6, Fireside). S&S.

Consumer Guide Editors, ed. see Berland, Theodore.

Consumer Guide Editors, jt. ed. see Video Times Editors.

Consumer Guide Editors, et al. The Illustrated Computer Dictionary. Horowitz, Shirley, ed. (Computer Bks.). (Illus.). 180p. (gr. 4 up). 1983. PLB 13.25 (ISBN 0-516-00815-3). Childrens.

Consumer Guide Publications International Ltd. Computer Careers: Where the Jobs Are & How to Get Them. 256p. 1984. pap. 6.95. Ballantine.

Consumer Guide Publications International Editors. Favorite Brand Name Recipes, Appetizers, Dips & Snacks. 144p. (Orig.). 1982. pap. 2.50 (ISBN 0-449-24568-3, Crest). Fawcett.

--Favorite Brands Name Recipes, Soups & Sandwiches. 144p. (Orig.). 1982. pap. 2.50 (ISBN 0-449-24571-3, Crest). Fawcett.

Consumer Guide Staff. Computer Buying Guide 1985. 380p. pap. cancelled (ISBN 0-451-13244-0, Sig). NAL.

--Consumer Guide Prescription Drugs. 1985. pap. 5.95 (ISBN 0-451-13838-4, Sig). NAL.

--Favorite Brand Name Recipe Cookbook. (Illus.). 416p. 1982. 7.98 (ISBN 0-517-54619-1, Pub. by Beekman Hse). Outlet Bk Co.

Consumer Guide Staff, ed. Consumer Guide to Used Cars, 1985. 1985. pap. 3.95 (ISBN 0-451-13583-0, Sig). NAL.

Consumer Liaison Committee of the American National Metric Council. Metric Reference for Consumers. 1976. pap. text ed. 2.50 (ISBN 0-916148-10-6). Am Natl.

Consumer Liaison Committee of the Council. Metrication & the Consumer: The Issue of Deception in the Marketplace & Planning for Practical Metric Packaging. Boselovic, Len, ed. (Illus.). 1978. pap. text ed. 5.00 (ISBN 0-916148-14-9). Am Natl.

Consumer Reports Books Editors & Brecher, Edward M. Love, Sex, & Aging: A Consumers Union Report. 384p. 1984. 19.45i (ISBN 0-316-10718-2). Little.

Consumer Reports Books Editors, jt. auth. see Florman, Monte.

Consumer Reports Editors. The Consumers Union Report on Life Insurance: A Guide to Planning & Buying the Protection You Need. 384p. 1981. pap. 8.95 (ISBN 0-03-059108-2). HR&W.

Consumer Reports Editors & Brecher, Edward M. Licit & Illicit Drugs: The Consumers Union Report on Narcotics, Stimulants, Depressants, Inhalants, Hallucinogens, & Marijuana - Including Caffeine, Nicotine, & Alcohol. 1972. pap. 10.45 (ISBN 0-316-10717-4). Little.

Consumers' Checkbook Staff & Krughoff, Robert. The Complete Guide to Lower Phone Costs. 68p. (Orig.). 1984. pap. 6.95 (ISBN 0-9611432-0-7). Consumers Checkbk.

Consumers Guide Editors. Food Processor Cookbook. 1980. pap. 2.95 (ISBN 0-671-42284-7). PB.

Consumers Guide Editors, ed. The User's Guide to Commodore. (Orig.). 1983. pap. 3.95 (ISBN 0-671-49505-4). PB.

Consumers Power Company. Fundamentals of Electricity, 2 vols. Incl. Vol. 1. Basic Principles. pap. 15.95 (ISBN 0-201-01185-9); Vol. 2. Alternating Current. pap. 15.95 (ISBN 0-201-01186-7). (gr. 9 up). 1966. pap. Addison-Wesley.

--Fundamentals of Natural Gas. LC 74-100858. (Supervision Ser.). 1970. pap. text ed. 14.95 (ISBN 0-201-01180-8). Addison-Wesley.

Consumers Union. Consumer Reports Buying Guide, 1986. 1985. pap. 5.95 (ISBN 0-385-23293-4). Doubleday.

Consumption, Location, & Occupational Patterns Resource Group Systhesis Panel of the Committee on Nuclear & Alternative Energy Systems. Energy Choices in a Democratic Society. LC 80-81335. (Study of Nuclear & Alternative Energy Systems Ser.). xvii, 136p. 1980. pap. text ed. 7.95 (ISBN 0-309-03045-5). Natl Acad Pr.

Conta, Lewis D. Energy Conservation in Space Conditioning. Gyftopoulos, Elias P. & Cohen, Karen C., eds. (Industrial Energy-Conservation Manuals Ser.: No. 7). (Illus.). 120p. 1982. loose-leaf 20.00x (ISBN 0-262-03084-5). MIT Pr.

Conta, Marcia & Reardon, Maureen. Feelings Between Kids & Grownups. LC 75-19383. (Moods & Emotions). (Illus.). 32p. (gr. k-3). 1975. Repr. of 1974 ed. PLB 13.31 (ISBN 0-8172-0043-6). Raintree Pubs.

Conta, Marcia M. Women for Human Rights. LC 79-13331. (Movers & Shapers Ser.). (Illus.). (gr. 4-8). 1979. PLB 13.31 (ISBN 0-8172-1378-3). Raintree Pubs.

Contact, pseud. Cavalry of the Clouds. LC 76-169411. (Literature & History of Aviation Ser). 1972. Repr. of 1918 ed. 22.00 (ISBN 0-405-03756-2). Ayer Co Pubs.

Contag, Victoria. Chinese Masters of the Seventeenth Century. 148p. 1980. 70.00x (ISBN 0-85331-240-0, Pub. by Humphries England). State Mutual Bk.

Containe, Phillipe. La France Au XIVe et XVe Siecles: Hommes, Mentalites, Guerre et Paix. 360p. 1981. 69.00x (ISBN 0-86078-091-0, Pub. by Variorum). State Mutual Bk.

Contamine, Philippe. War in the Middle Ages. 387p. 1984. 24.95 (ISBN 0-631-13142-6). Basil Blackwell.

Contant, Clement & De Filippi, Joseph. Parallele des Principaux Theatres Moderns de l'Europe, 2 vols in 1. LC 68-21209. (Illus.). 1968. Repr. 60.50 (ISBN 0-405-08376-9). Ayer Co Pubs.

Contant, H. & Duthie, H. C. The Phytoplankton of Lac St-Jean, Quebec. (Bibliotheca Phycologica Ser.: No. 40). (Illus.). 1978. pap. text ed. 14.00x (ISBN 3-7682-1198-3). Lubrecht & Cramer.

Contanto, William. Index to Science Fiction: Anthologies & Collections, Supplement. 1984. lib. bdg. 45.00 (ISBN 0-8161-8554-9, Hall Reference). G K Hall.

Contarini, Amrogio, jt. auth. see Barbaro, Josafa.

Contarini, Arthur. Just Thinking. 48p. 1986. 5.95 (ISBN 0-89962-502-9). Todd & Honeywell.

Contarini, Gasparo. The Commonwealth & Government of Venice. Lewkenor, Lewis, tr. LC 71-6159. (English Experience Ser.: No. 101). 230p. 1969. Repr. of 1599 ed. 25.00 (ISBN 90-221-0101-0). Walter J Johnson.

Contat, Michel, ed. see Sartre, Jean-Paul.

Conte & Polk. Antibiotic Prophylaxis in Surgery: A Comprehensive Review. LC 65-8378. 1984. 22.50 (ISBN 0-397-50671-6, Lippincott Medical). Lippincott.

Conte, A., ed. Algebraic Threefolds, Varenna, Italy 1981, Second Session: Proceedings. (Lecture Notes in Mathematics: Vol. 947). 315p. 1982. pap. 19.50 (ISBN 0-387-11587-0). Springer-Verlag.

Conte, Christine. Maya Culture & Costume: A Catalogue of the Taylor Museum's E. B. Ricketson Collection of Guatemalan Textiles. LC 84-40115. (Illus.). 120p. (Orig.). 1984. pap. 15.00 (ISBN 0-916537-00-5). Taylor Museum.

Conte, Gianni & Del Corso, Dante, eds. Multi-Microprocesser Systems for Real-Time Applications. 1985. lib. bdg. 44.00 (ISBN 90-277-2054-1, Pub. by Reidel Netherlands). Kluwer Academic.

Conte, Giuseppe. Woerterbuch der Deutschen und Italienischen Wirtschafts und Rechtssprache, Vol. 1. 2nd ed. (Ital. & Ger.). 1971. 30.00 (ISBN 3-406-01195-0, M-7028). French & Eur.

--Woerterbuch der Deutschen und Italienischen Wirtschafts und Rechtssprache, Vol. 2. 2nd ed. (Ger. & Ital.). 1969. 30.00 (ISBN 3-406-00887-9, M-7027). French & Eur.

Conte, John E., Jr. & Barriere, Steven L. Manual of Antibiotics & Infectious Diseases. 5th ed. LC 83-18725. (Illus.). 351p. 1984. pap. 18.50 (ISBN 0-8121-0908-2). Lea & Febiger.

Conte, Jon R. & Shore, David A., eds. Social Work & Child Sexual Abuse. LC 82-11952. (Journal of Social Work & Human Sexuality Ser.: Vol. 1, Nos. 1 & 2). 184p. 1982. text ed. 24.95 (ISBN 0-917724-50-X, B50); pap. text ed. 9.95 (ISBN 0-86656-212-5). Haworth Pr.

Conte, Joseph Le see Le Conte, Joseph.

Conte, Michael, et al. Employee Ownership. 70p. (Orig.). 1981. pap. 10.00x (ISBN 0-87944-255-7). Inst Soc Res.

Conte, S. D. & De Boor, C. Elementary Numerical Analysis: An Algorithmic Approach. 3rd ed. 1980. 37.95 (ISBN 0-07-012447-7). McGraw.

Conte, Sylvester B. & Kemme, Douglas G. Positioning Technique Handbook for Radiologic Technologists. LC 78-5245. 289p. 1978. pap. text ed. 16.95 (ISBN 0-8016-1031-1). Mosby.

Conte, William, jt. auth. see Murray, Diane.

Conte, William R. Old Cripple Creek Stage Road. (Illus.). 60p. (Orig.). 1984. pap. 3.50 (ISBN 0-936564-30-X). Little London.

Contemporary Arts Center, Cincinnati & Byrd Hoffman Foundation, New York. Robert Wilson: The Theater of Images. LC 83-48839. (Illus.). 160p. 1984. 23.99 (ISBN 0-06-015289-3, HarpT). Har-Row.

--Robert Wilson: The Theater of Images. LC 83-48839. (Illus.). 160p. 1984. pap. 14.37 (ISBN 0-06-091138-7, CN 1138, CN). Har-Row.

Contemporary China Institute, ed. A Bibliography of Chinese Newspapers & Periodicals in European Libraries. LC 75-12135. (Contemporary China Institute Publications). 1100p. 1975. 115.00 (ISBN 0-521-20950-1). Cambridge U Pr.

Contemporary Folk Poetry Staff. Quechua Peoples Poetry. 70p. 1982. pap. 6.00 (ISBN 0-686-97207-4). Curbstone.

Contemporary Perspectives, Inc. High Action Treasure Chest Books. (Incl. 44 bks., skill cards & tchr's guide). (gr. 4-6). 1981. write for info (ISBN 0-87895-295-0). Modern Curr.

--Problem Solving in Mathematics: Level A. (Problem Solving in Mathematics Ser.). 96p. (gr. 1). 1982. text ed. write for info. (ISBN 0-87895-198-9); tchrs. guide avail. (ISBN 0-87895-199-7). Modern Curr.

--Problem Solving in Mathematics: Level C. (Problem Solving in Mathematics Ser.). 96p. (gr. 3). 1982. text ed. write for info.; tchrs. guide avail. (ISBN 0-87895-349-3). Modern Curr.

--Problem Solving in Mathematics: Level D. (Problem Solving in Mathematics Ser.). 96p. (gr. 4). 1982. text ed. write for info. (ISBN 0-87895-448-1); tchrs. guide avail. (ISBN 0-87895-449-X). Modern Curr.

--Problem Solving in Mathematics: Level E. (Problem Solving in Mathematics Ser.). 96p. (gr. 5). 1982. text ed. write for info. (ISBN 0-87895-548-8); tchrs. guide avail. (ISBN 0-87895-549-6). Modern Curr.

--Problem Solving in Mathematics: Level F. (Problem Solving in Mathematics Ser.). 96p. (gr. 6). 1982. text ed. write for info. (ISBN 0-87895-648-4); tchrs. guide avail. (ISBN 0-87895-649-2). Modern Curr.

Contemporary Prespectives, Inc. Problem Solving in Mathematics: Level B. (Problem Solving in Mathematics Ser.). 96p. (gr. 2). 1982. text ed. write for info. (ISBN 0-87895-248-9); tchrs. guide avail. (ISBN 0-87895-249-7). Modern Curr.

Contemporary Programs Inc. Woman's Contemporary Image: A Personal & Professional Guide. 1975. 23.95 (ISBN 0-13-962274-8). P-H.

Contemporary Research Associates, Inc. Staff. Directory of Regional Economic & Business Information Sources, Vol. 1. 220p. 69.00 (ISBN 0-935061-01-0); Spiral bdg. 46.00 (ISBN 0-935061-00-2). Contemp Res.

Contemporary Research, Inc. An Investigation of the Application of Programmed Inert Gas Multiple Electrode Arc Welding to the Fabrication of Automotive Heat Exchangers. 63p. 9.45 (ISBN 0-317-34534-6, 134). Intl Copper.

Contemporary Testimony Committee of the Christian Reformed Church. Our World Belongs to God: A Contemporary Testimony (Study Version) 1984. pap. 0.85 (ISBN 0-933140-91-6). Bd of Pubns CRC.

Content, C. S. A Geologist's Sketch Book. 56p. 1977. pap. 8.75x (ISBN 0-87262-089-1). Am Soc Civil Eng.

Content, Robin, jt. auth. see Smelser, Neil J.

Conteurs Francais du XVI Siecle. Les Cent Nouvelles Nouvelles. 1520p. 41.50 (ISBN 0-686-56489-8). French & Eur.

Conti, jt. auth. see Pansini.

Conti, C. Richard, ed. Cardiac Drug Therapy. LC 83-15440. (Cardiovascular Clinics Ser.: Vol. 14, No. 3). (Illus.). 309p. 1983. text ed. 45.00 (ISBN 0-8036-1975-8). Davis Co.

Conti, David J., ed. see Elinsky, Peter I.

Conti, F., et al, eds. Physical Methods on Biological Membranes & Their Model Systems. (NATO ASI Series A, Life Sciences: Vol. 71). 470p. 1985. 65.00x (ISBN 0-306-41480-5, Plenum Press). Plenum Pub.

Conti, Francesco. Don Chisciotte in Sierra Morena. Brown, Howard M. & Weimer, Eric, eds. (Italian Opera Ser., 1640-1770: No. 2). 83.00 (ISBN 0-8240-4808-3). Garland Pub.

Conti, Francesco B., et al. Italians in Vienna. Brook, Barry S., ed. LC 83-11708. (The Symphony Ser.). 1983. lib. bdg. 90.00 (ISBN 0-8240-3830-4). Garland Pub.

Conti, Peter S. & De Loore, C. W., eds. Mass Loss & Evolution of O-Type Stars. (International Astronomical Union Symposium Ser.: No. 83). 1979. lib. bdg. 63.00 (ISBN 90-277-0988-2, Pub. by Reidel Holland); pap. 31.50 (ISBN 90-277-0989-0, Pub. by Reidel Holland). Kluwer Academic.

Conti, R. Institutiones Mathematicae: Linear Differential Equations & Control, Vol. 1. 1977. 34.50 (ISBN 0-12-363601-9). Acad Pr.

Conti, Roberto, ed. Recent Advances in Differential Equations. LC 81-15042. 1981. 47.50 (ISBN 0-12-186280-1). Acad Pr.

Conti, Samuel D., et al, eds. see National Center for State Courts.

Conti, Vittorio. The Gem in the Wire. Lewis, Barbara E., tr. from Ital. 101p. 1984. 8.95 (ISBN 0-533-05810-4). Vantage.

Continental Assocation of Funeral & Memorial Societies, Inc & Memorial Society Association of Canadacompiled by. Handbook for Funeral & Memorial Societies. Fleming, Peggy, ed. LC 72-7963. 1976. pap. 3.50 (ISBN 0-686-18088-7). Continent Assn Funeral.

Continental Historical Society. Queen Victoria's "Alice in Wonderland". 2nd ed. Orig. Title: Queen Victoria Secret Diaries, Vol. I. (Illus.). 290p. 1984. pap. 9.95 (ISBN 0-9609900-1-1). Cont Hist Soc.

--Queen Victoria's Secret Diaries, Vol. I. 289p. (Orig.). 1983. pap. 14.95 (ISBN 0-9609900-0-3). Cont Hist Soc.

--Queen Victoria's Through the Looking Glass. (Illus.). 319p. 1984. pap. 10.95 (ISBN 0-9609900-2-X). Cont Hist Soc.

Continental Language System, tr. see Rouillard, Dominique.

Continental Software. The Home Accountant - Apple. (Orig.). 1985. pap. 9.95 manual (ISBN 0-538-01010-X, AO11). SW Pub.

--The Home Accountant - IBM PC. 1985. manual 9.95 (ISBN 0-538-01012-6, A013). SW Pub.

--The Home Accountant - TRS 80. 1985. manual 9.95 (ISBN 0-538-01011-8, A012). SW Pub.

Contini, Paolo. Somali Republic: An Experiment in Legal Integration. 92p. 1969. 28.50x (ISBN 0-7146-2395-4, F Cass Co). Biblio Dist.

Contis & Phillips, Donald. Investigating Chemistry: Up'N Atom. 176p. 1982. pap. text ed. 13.95 (ISBN 0-8403-2640-8). Kendall-Hunt.

Conton, William. The African. (African Writers Ser.). 1964. pap. text ed. 4.00x (ISBN 0-435-90012-9). Heinemann Ed.

Contopoulos, G., ed. Reports on Astronomy, 3 pts. (Transactions of the International Astronomical Union: Vol. XVIA). 1976. Pt. 1. lib. bdg. 47.50 (ISBN 90-277-0739-1, Pub. by Reidel Holland); Pt. 2. lib. bdg. 47.50 (ISBN 90-277-0740-5); Pt. 3. lib. bdg. 47.50 (ISBN 90-277-0741-3); Set. lib. bdg. 126.00 (ISBN 90-277-0703-0). Kluwer Academic.

Contopoulos, G., ed. see General Assembly 15th,Sydney,1973 & Extraordinary General Assembly,Poland,1973.

Contopoulos, G., ed. see I.A.U. General Assembly, 14th.

Contopoulos, G., ed. see I.A.U. Symposium, 38th, Basel, Switzerland, 1969.

Contos, Leonidas, tr. see Kalokyris, Konstantin.

Contos, Leonidas C. Two Thousand & One the Church in Crisis. 60p. 1981. pap. 2.95 (ISBN 0-916586-46-4). Holy Cross Orthodox.

Contoski, Edmund. Makers & Takers. lib. bdg. cancelled (ISBN 0-933028-25-3); pap. price not set (ISBN 0-933028-26-1). Fisher Inst.

Contoski, J. Bocheck in Poland. 54p. 1983. 10.00 (ISBN 0-317-36707-2). Kosciuszko.

Contoski, Victor. Astronomers, Madonnas & Prophesies. (Juniper Bk.: No. 8). 1970. 4.00 (ISBN 0-686-61864-5). Juniper Pr WI.

--Broken Treaties. 1973. 5.00 (ISBN 0-685-29868-X); signed ltd. ed. 10.00 (ISBN 0-685-29869-8); pap. 2.50 (ISBN 0-685-29870-1). New Rivers Pr.

Contoski, Victor, tr. see Harasymowicz, Jerzy.

Contosta, David R. Henry Adams & the American Experiment. (Library of American Biography). 176p. (Orig.). 1980. pap. 6.95 (ISBN 0-316-15400-8). Little.

Contra Viento y Marea, jt. auth. see Iturralde, Iraida.

Contractor, Farok J. International Technology Licensing: Compensation, Costs, & Negotiation. LC 80-8768. 208p. 1981. 29.50 (ISBN 0-669-04359-1). Lexington Bks.

--Licensing in International Strategy: A Guide for Planning & Negotiations. LC 84-22756. (Illus.). 288p. 1985. lib. bdg. 45.00 (ISBN 0-89930-024-3, CLI/, Quorum). Greenwood.

Contractor, Farok J., jt. auth. see Sagafi-Nejad, Tagi.

Contreni, J. J., tr. see Riche, Pierre.

Contreras, Arnoldo, jt. auth. see Gregersen, Hans M.

Contreras, Arnoldo H., jt. auth. see Gregerson, Hans.

Contreras, Belisario R. Tradition & Innovation in New Deal Art. LC 81-65861. (Illus.). 256p. 1983. 35.00 (ISBN 0-8387-5032-X). Bucknell U Pr.
Contreras, Eduardo, et al. Cross-Cultural Broadcasting. (Reports & Papers on Mass Communication: No. 77). 49p. 1976. pap. 5.00 (ISBN 92-3-101353-X, U107, UNESCO). Unipub.
Contreras, Gloria, jt. ed. see Simms, Richard L.
Contreras, Moyra, tr. see Rodieck, Jorma.
Contributors Friends of Philadelphia Orchestra. The Philadelphia Orchestra Cookbook. Krout, Anne M. & Roberts, Doris L., eds. 400p. 1980. pap. 10.75 (ISBN 0-9607586-0-7). W Phila Womens Comm.
Control Theory Centre Symposium, University of Warwick, 1972. Stability of Stochastic Dynamical Systems: Proceedings. Curtain, R. F., ed. LC 72-91895. (Lecture Notes in Mathematics: Vol. 294). (Illus.). 332p. 1972. pap. 13.00 (ISBN 0-387-06050-2). Springer-Verlag.
Controller of Exams. Courses of Study for SLC Exam. Amended ed. 64p. (Outlines of Content). 1951. 6.00 (ISBN 0-318-17031-0, 55). Am-Nepal Ed.
Controversies in Nephrology Conference Sponsored by the American Kidney Fund. Controversies in Nephrology, Vol. 2: Proceedings. Schreiner, George E., ed. (Controversies in Nephrology, 2nd). 390p. 1981. text ed. 59.50x (ISBN 0-89352-144-2). Masson Pub.
Controvich, James T, compiled by. United States Army Unit Histories: A Reference & Bibliography. 591p. 1983. 60.00x (ISBN 0-89126-121-4). MA-AH Pub.
Contrucci, Peg. The Home Office: How to Set It Up, Operate It, & Make It Pay Off. 300p. 1985. 24.95 (ISBN 0-13-393034-3); pap. 12.95 (ISBN 0-13-393026-2). P-H.
Conture, Edward G. Stuttering. (Illus.). 208p. 1982. ref. ed. 26.95 (ISBN 0-13-858977-1). P-H.
Contz, Otto. Isle of the Shapeshifters. 224p. (gr. 5 up). 1985. pap. 2.50 (ISBN 0-553-24801-4). Bantam.
Conus, Leon & Conus, Olga. Fundamentals of Piano Technique, Bks. 1 & 2. rev. ed. McKeever, James, ed. 64p. 1984. pap. text ed. 9.95 (ISBN 0-87487-660-5). Birch Tree Gr.
Conus, Olga, jt. auth. see Conus, Leon.
Conveney, James & Moore, Shiela J. Lexique De Termes Anglais-Francais De Gestion: Les Cycle Au Superieur, Ecoles Superieures De Gestion. 160p. (Eng. & Fr.). 1972. pap. 9.95 (ISBN 0-686-56963-6, M-6087). French & Eur.
Convention of Friends of Agricultural Education, Chicago. Early View of the Land-Grant Colleges. LC 67-20999. 162p. 1967. 15.95x (ISBN 0-252-72463-1). U of Ill Pr.
Convention on International Trade in Endangered Species of Wild Fauna & Flora. Guidelines for the Transport & Preparation of Shipment of Live Wild Animals & Plants. 109p. 1981. pap. 13.00 (ISBN 0-686-93565-9, UPB100, UNEP); pap. 13.00 Fr. ed. (ISBN 0-686-99140-0, UPB102); pap. 13.00 Span. ed. (ISBN 0-686-99141-9, UPB101). Unipub.
Convention on International Trade in Endangered Species of Wild Fauna & Flora, Geneva, 1977. Special Working Session of the Conference Parties (CITES) Proceedings. 271p. 1978. pap. 22.50 (ISBN 0-686-74017-3, CIT001, IUCN). Unipub.
Converse, Hugh, jt. ed. see Magoon, Orville T.
Converse, J. M., jt. auth. see Ballantyne, D. L.
Converse, James, ed. see Moore, Ruth N.
Converse, Jane. Alias Miss Saunders, R.N. Large print ed. LC 81-14529. 266p. 1981. Repr. of 1962 ed. 10.95 (ISBN 0-89621-315-3). Thorndike Pr.
Converse, Jean M. & Schuman, Howard. Conversations at Random: Survey Research as Interviewers See It. LC 73-15840. (Illus.). 121p. 1974. pap. 8.00x (ISBN 0-87944-248-4). Inst Soc Res.
Converse, John M., ed. Reconstructive Plastic Surgery: Principles & Procedures in Correction Reconstruction & Transplantation, 7 vols. 2nd ed. LC 74-21010. (Illus.). 1977. Set. text ed. 395.00 (ISBN 0-7216-2691-2); Vol. 1. text ed. 58.00 (ISBN 0-7216-2680-7); Vol. 2. text ed. 58.00 (ISBN 0-7216-2681-5); Vol. 3. text ed. 58.00 (ISBN 0-7216-2682-3); Vol. 4. text ed. 58.00 (ISBN 0-7216-2683-1); Vol. 5. text ed. 58.00 (ISBN 0-7216-2684-X); Vol. 6. text ed. 58.00 (ISBN 0-7216-2685-8); Vol. 7. text ed. 58.00 (ISBN 0-7216-2686-6). Saunders.
Converse, John M., jt. ed. see Rapaport, Felix T.
Converse, Mary, ed. see Skurka, Margaret F.
Converse, Paul D. The Beginning of Marketing Thought in the United States, 2 vols. in one. Assael, Henry, ed. LC 78-282. (Century of Marketing Ser.). 1978. Repr. of 1959 ed. lib. bdg. 19.00x (ISBN 0-405-11161-4). Ayer Co Pubs.
Converse, Philip, et al. Canadian National Election Study, 1965. 1972. codebook write for info. (ISBN 0-89138-058-2). ICPSR.
Converse, Philip E., jt. ed. see Campbell, Angus.
Converse, Philip E., et al. American Social Attitudes Data Sourcebook: 1947-1978. 392p. 1980. spiral bdg. 27.50x (ISBN 0-674-02880-5). Harvard U Pr.
Converse, Phillip E., jt. auth. see Campbell, Angus.
Converse, T., et al. Reflex in Business. 352p. 1985. 16.95 (ISBN 0-07-020230-3). McGraw.
Conversi, M., ed. Evolution of Particle Physics. 1970. 82.50 (ISBN 0-12-186150-3). Acad Pr.
--Selected Topics on Elementary Particle Physics. (Italian Physical Society: Course 26). 1964. 75.00 (ISBN 0-12-368826-4). Acad Pr.
Conversi, M., et al, eds. Some Perspectives on Fundamental Nuclear & High Energy Research. 350p. 1983. pap. text ed. 50.00x (ISBN 0-911767-10-X). Hadronic Pr Inc.
Conversino da Ravenna, Giovanni di see Di Conversino da Ravenna, Giovanni.
Convert, Claudine, jt. auth. see Rochester, Myrna B.
Convert, Pierre & Forsyth, J. Bruce, eds. Position-Sensitive Detection of Thermal Neutrons. 1984. 39.00 (ISBN 0-12-186180-5). Acad Pr.
Convey, John, jt. auth. see Houghton, Bernard.
Conveyor Equipment Manufacturers Association. Belt Conveyors for Bulk Materials. 2nd ed. LC 78-31987. 384p. 1979. 34.95 (ISBN 0-8436-1008-5). Van Nos Reinhold.
Conway. The Female Experience in the Eighteenth & Nineteenth Centuries, Vol. I. 1985. pap. 17.00 (ISBN 0-8240-8951-0). Garland Pub.
--The Female Experience in the Twentieth Century, Vol. 2. 1985. lib. bdg. 40.00 (ISBN 0-8240-9259-7). Garland Pub.
Conway & Malloy, eds. Hazardous Solid Waste Testing: First Conference - STP 760. 352p. 1982. 39.00 (ISBN 0-8031-0795-1, 04-760000-16). ASTM.
Conway, Agnes. Henry Seventh's Relations with Scotland & Ireland, 1485-1498. 1972. lib. bdg. 20.00x (ISBN 0-374-91915-1). Octagon.
Conway, Alan. Reconstruction of Georgia. 1966. 10.00x (ISBN 0-8166-0392-8). U of Minn Pr.
Conway, Alan, jt. ed. see Baylen, Joseph O.
Conway, Alice. The Green Branch. 257p. 10.67 (ISBN 0-89697-254-2). Intl Univ Pr.
Conway, Anne. The Conway Letters: Being the Correspondence of Anne, Viscountess Conway, Henry More & Their Friends. Nicolson, M. H., ed. 1930. 75.00x (ISBN 0-685-89745-1). Elliots Bks.
--The Principles of the Most Ancient & Modern Philosophy. 1982. 35.00 (ISBN 90-247-2671-9, Pub. by Martinus Nijhoff Netherlands). Kluwer Academic.
Conway, Arthur L. Strange Ways of Dragons. LC 85-50093. (Illus.). 64p. (Orig.). 1985. pap. 4.95 (ISBN 0-938232-70-3). Winston-Derek.
--Walking Through the Mist of Life. LC 82-61883. 56p. 1983. pap. 4.95 (ISBN 0-938232-18-5). Winston-Derek.
Conway, B. E. Electrochemical Data. LC 69-10078. (Illus.). 1969. Repr. of 1952 ed. lib. bdg. 22.50x (ISBN 0-8371-1630-9, COED). Greenwood.
--Electrochemical Data. Date not set. price not set. Elsevier.
--Ionic Hydration in Chemistry & Biophysics. (Studies in Physical & Theoretical Chemistry: Vol. 12). 774p. 1981. 132.00 (ISBN 0-444-41947-0). Elsevier.
--Theory & Principals of Electrode Processes. LC 65-17090. 302p. 1965. 20.50 (ISBN 0-686-74216-8). Krieger.
Conway, B. E. & Bockris, J. O'M., eds. Modern Aspects of Electrochemistry, No. 13. LC 54-12732. (Illus.). 441p. 1979. 57.50x (ISBN 0-306-40256-4, Plenum Pr). Plenum Pub.
Conway, Bertrand L., tr. see Vacandard, Elphege.
Conway, Brian E., et al, eds. Comprehensive Treatise of Electrochemistry, Vol. 5: Thermodynamics & Transport Properties of Aqueous & Molten Electrolytes. 405p. 1983. text ed. 59.50 (ISBN 0-306-40866-X, Plenum Pr). Plenum Pub.
Conway, Brian E., jt. ed. see Bockris, J. O'M.
Conway, Bryant W. Successful Hints on Hunting White Tail Deer. 2nd ed. 1967. pap. 3.98 (ISBN 0-87511-589-6). Claitors.
Conway, Carle. The Joy of Soaring: A Training Manual. LC 73-98038. (Illus.). 134p. 1969. 17.00 (ISBN 0-911720-54-5, Pub. by Soaring). Aviation.
Conway, Daniel. Autobiography Memories & Experiences of Moncure Daniel Conway: Emerson, Hawthorne, Whitman, 2 Vols. 404p. 1984. Repr. of 1904 ed. Set. lib. bdg. 150.00 (ISBN 0-8495-0970-X). Arden Lib.
Conway, Donald, jt. auth. see Hydge, Debra M.
Conway, Donald J., ed. Human Response to Tall Buildings. LC 76-58917. (Community Development Ser.: Vol. 34). (Illus.). 1977. 46.50 (ISBN 0-87933-268-9). Van Nos Reinhold.
Conway, Edward S. Comprehending Comprehensives: The J.F.S. Experience. (Illus.). 176p. 1983. 27.50x (ISBN 0-7130-4008-4, Pub. by Woburn Pr England). Biblio Dist.
--Comprehending Comprehensives: The J.F.S. Experience. (Illus.). 176p. 1985. pap. 18.50x (ISBN 0-7130-0172-0, Pub. by Woburn Pr England). Biblio Dist.
Conway, Flo & Siegelman, Jim. Holy Terror: The Fundamentalist War on America's Freedoms in Religion, Politics, & Our Private Lives. 504p. 1984. pap. 10.95 (ISBN 0-385-29286-4, Delta). Dell.
--Snapping. 272p. pap. 8.95 (ISBN 0-385-28928-6, Delta). Dell.
Conway, Geoffrey S., tr. from Gr. The Odes of Pindar. (Rowman & Littlefield University Library). 268p. 1972. pap. 5.00x (ISBN 0-87471-420-6). Rowman.
Conway, Gordon R. Pest & Pathogen Control: Strategy, Tactics & Policy Models. (ILASA International Series on Applied Systems Analysis). 508p. 1984. 60.00x (ISBN 0-471-90349-3, 1-696, Pub. by Wiley-Interscience). Wiley.
Conway, H. G. Bugatti "le pur - sang des automobiles". 3rd ed. LC 74-80931. (Illus.). 463p. 1974. 24.95 (ISBN 0-85429-158-X, G. T. Foulis England). Motorbooks Intl.
--Grand Prix! Bugatti. (Illus.). 272p. 39.95 (ISBN 0-85429-293-4, F293). Haynes Pubns.
Conway, H. M. & Liston, Linda L. The Good Life Index: How to Compare Quality of Life Throughout the U.S. & Around the World. LC 81-68204. (Illus.). 1981. 11.95 (ISBN 0-910436-22-3). Conway Data.
Conway, H. McKinley. Disaster Survival: How to Choose Secure Sites & Make Practical Escape Plans. LC 80-68816. (Illus.). 1980. 12.95 (ISBN 0-910436-17-7). Conway Data.
--Industrial Park Growth. LC 78-74931. 508p. 1978. pap. 12.9500150741xxx (ISBN 0-910436-09-6). Conway Data.
--Legislative Climates for Economic Development. LC 78-73392. 540p. 1978. 48.00x (ISBN 0-910436-10-X). Conway Data.
--Marketing Industrial Buildings & Sites. LC 78-74933. 358p. 1980. 9.95 (ISBN 0-910436-15-0). Conway Data.
--New Industries of the Seventies. LC 78-62201. 1978. pap. 65.00x (ISBN 0-910436-07-X). Conway Data.
--Pitfalls in Development. LC 78-62198. 1980. pap. 9.95 (ISBN 0-910436-19-3). Conway Data.
Conway, H. McKinley & Liston, Linda L. Industrial Facilities Planning. LC 76-49711. 330p. 1976. pap. 35.00x (ISBN 0-910436-05-3). Conway Data.
Conway, H. McKinley, Jr. & Liston, Linda L., eds. The Weather Handbook. rev. ed. LC 79-54253. (Illus.). 1974. 12.95 (ISBN 0-910436-00-2). Conway Data.
Conway, Hazel. Ernest Race. (Design Council Ser.). (Illus.). 96p. 1982. pap. text ed. 12.50x (ISBN 0-87663-573-7). Universe.
Conway, J. A Course in Functional Analysis. (Graduate Texts in Mathematics Ser.: Vol. 96). 350p. 1985. 38.00 (ISBN 0-387-96042-2). Springer-Verlag.
Conway, J. B. Functions of One Complex Variable. 2nd ed. (Graduate Texts in Mathematics Ser.: Vol. 11). (Illus.). 1978. 29.80 (ISBN 0-387-90328-3). Springer-Verlag.
--Functions of One Complex Variable. Halmos, P. R., ed. LC 72-96938. (Lecture Notes in Mathematics: Vol. 11). (Illus.). xiv, 314p. 1975. text ed. 10.70 (ISBN 0-387-07028-1). Springer-Verlag.
--Numerical Methods for Creep & Rupture Analysis. 212p. 1967. 57.75 (ISBN 0-677-01090-7). Gordon.
--Stress-Rupture Parameters: Origin, Calculation, & Use. 318p. 1969. 80.95 (ISBN 0-677-01860-6). Gordon.
Conway, J. B. & Flagella, P. N. Creep-Rupture Data for the Refractory Metals to High Temperatures. 798p. 1971. 205.75 (ISBN 0-677-02660-9). Gordon.
Conway, J. B. & Olin, R. F. A Functional Calculus for Subnormal Operators, II. LC 77-3937. (Memoirs Ser.: No. 184). 61p. 1977. pap. 12.00 (ISBN 0-8218-2184-9, MEMO-184). Am Math.
Conway, Jack. Compass Course, One Hundred Eighty Degrees. 1978. 7.50 (ISBN 0-8158-0367-2); pap. 4.95 (ISBN 0-8158-0410-5). Chris Mass.
Conway, James. Night of the Wolf. 1979. pap. 1.75 (ISBN 0-8439-0700-2, Leisure Bks). Dorchester Pub Co.
Conway, James V. Evidential Documents. (Illus.). 288p. 1978. 29.75x (ISBN 0-398-00342-4). C C Thomas.
Conway, Jill K. The Female Experience in Eighteenth & Nineteenth Century America: A Guide to the History of American Women. LC 82-48081. 314p. 1982. lib. bdg. 34.00 (ISBN 0-8240-9936-2). Garland Pub.
--Society & the Sexes in Early Industrial America: Part One of a Bibliographical Guide to the Study of the History of American Women. LC 82-48041. 350p. 1984. lib. bdg. 31.00 (ISBN 0-8240-9936-2). Garland Pub.
Conway, Jill K., et al. The Female Experience in Eighteenth & Nineteenth Century America: A Guide to the History of American Women. 314p. 1985. pap. 14.50 (ISBN 0-691-00599-0). Princeton U Pr.
Conway, Jim. Los Hombres En Su Crisis de Media Vida. Orig. Title: Men in Mid-Life Crisis. 256p. (Span.). 1982. pap. 5.95 (ISBN 0-311-46088-7, Edit Mundo). Casa Bautista.
--Men in Mid-Life Crisis. LC 78-67098. 1978. text ed. 6.95 (ISBN 0-89191-145-6). Cook.
Conway, Jim & Conway, Sally. La Mujer en su Crisis de Media Vida. De Zorzoli, Alicia, tr. from Span. 352p. 1985. pap. write for info. (ISBN 0-311-46105-0). Casa Bautista.
--Women in Mid-Life Crisis. 391p. 1983. 10.95 (ISBN 0-8423-8382-4); pap. 7.95 (ISBN 0-8423-8379-4). Tyndale.
Conway, Jim, et al. Your Family: A Love & Maintenance Manual for People with Parents & Other Relatives. LC 81-20809. 120p. (Orig.). 1982. pap. 3.95 (ISBN 0-87784-370-8). Inter-Varsity.
Conway, John. On Numbers & Games. (London Mathematical Society Monographs). 1976. 34.50 (ISBN 0-12-186350-6). Acad Pr.
Conway, John B. Subnormal Operators. LC 81-231. (Research Notes in Mathematics: No. 51). 400p. 1981. pap. text ed. 29.95 (ISBN 0-273-08520-4). Pitman Pub MA.
Conway, John H., et al, eds. Atlas of Finite Groups: Maximal Subgroups & Ordinary Characters for Simple Groups. 250p. 1984. text ed. 45.00x (ISBN 0-19-853199-0). Oxford U Pr.
Conway, John T., jt. ed. see Grogan, John C.
Conway, Joyce E., jt. auth. see Giles, Marsha J.
Conway, Judith, jt. auth. see Tilkin, Sheldon L.
Conway, L. M. Goal Getters. (Values & Feelings Ser.). 48p. (gr. 4-6). 1984. 4.95 (ISBN 0-88160-105-5, LW 245). Learning Wks.
Conway, Lorraine. Animals. (gr. 5-8). 1980. 5.95 (ISBN 0-916456-68-4, GA 177). Good Apple.
--Chemistry Concepts. (Illus.). 64p. (gr. 5-8). 1983. wkbk. 5.95 (ISBN 0-86653-100-9, GA 460). Good Apple.
--Heredity & Embryology. (gr. 5-8). 1980. 4.95 (ISBN 0-916456-90-0, GA 179). Good Apple.
--The Human Body. (gr. 5-8). 1980. 5.95 (ISBN 0-916456-67-6, GA 178). Good Apple.
--Marine Biology. (gr. 5-8). 1982. 5.95 (ISBN 0-86653-056-8, GA 400). Good Apple.
--Oceanography. (gr. 5-8). 1982. 5.95 (ISBN 0-86653-066-5, GA401). Good Apple.
--Plants. (gr. 5-8). 1980. 5.95 (ISBN 0-916456-69-2, GA 176). Good Apple.
--Science Graphs & Word Games. (Superific Science Ser.: Bk. V). 48p. (gr. 5-8). 1981. 4.95 (ISBN 0-86653-029-0, GA 257). Good Apple.
Conway, Lynn, jt. auth. see Mead, Carver.
Conway, M. D. Life of Nathaniel Hawthorne. LC 68-24935. (Studies in Hawthorne, No. 15). 1969. Repr. of 1890 ed. lib. bdg. 49.95x (ISBN 0-8383-0931-3). Haskell.
--Omitted Chapters of History Disclosed in the Life & Papers of Edmund Randolph. LC 73-124041. (American Public Figures Ser). 1971. Repr. of 1888 ed. lib. bdg. 52.50 (ISBN 0-306-70995-3). Da Capo.
Conway, M. Margaret. Political Participation in the U. S. LC 85-15186. 170p. 1985. pap. 10.95 (ISBN 0-87187-331-1). Congr Quarterly.
Conway, McKinley. The Airport City: Development Concepts for the Twenty-First Century. rev. ed. LC 80-65254. (Illus.). 227p. 1980. 9.95 (ISBN 0-910436-14-2). Conway Data.
Conway, McKinley, ed. see Myhra, David.
Conway, Madeleine, jt. auth. see Moss, Lydia.
Conway Maritime Editors. Conway's All the World's Fighting Ships Eighteen Sixty to Nineteen Hundred & Five. LC 79-11466. (Illus.). 1979. 35.00 (ISBN 0-8317-0302-4, Mayflower Bks). Smith Pubs.
Conway Maritime Press, ed. All the World's Fighting Ships, 1922-1946. (Illus.). 448p. 1980. 65.00 (ISBN 0-8317-0303-2, Mayflower Bks). Smith Pubs.
Conway Maritime Press Ltd., ed. Conway's All the World's Fighting Ships 1947-1982. 480p. 125.00x (ISBN 0-85177-225-0, Pub. by Conway Maritime England). State Mutual Bk.
Conway, Martin. Harpers Ferry-Time Remembered. Mehrkam, Deborah, ed. LC 80-65777. (Illus.). 160p. 1981. 14.95 (ISBN 0-938634-00-3). Carabelle.
--The Outer Banks: An Historical Adventure from Kitty Hawk to Ocracoke. Knott, Susan, ed. LC 84-71012. (Illus.). 96p. 1984. text ed. 12.95 (ISBN 0-938634-05-4). Carabelle.
--Outer Banks: An Historical Adventure from Kitty Hawk to Ocracoke. Knott, Susan, ed. (Illus.). 100p. 1985. pap. text ed. 9.95 (ISBN 0-938634-06-2). Carabelle.
Conway, Mary, jt. ed. see Hardy, Margaret E.
Conway, Mary E. & Andruskiw, Olga, eds. Administrative Theory & Practice: Issues in Higher Education in Nursing. 430p. 1983. 22.50 (ISBN 0-8385-0074-9). ACC.
Conway, Melvin E. American National Standard MUMPS Programmers Reference Manual. 1985. 17.00 (ISBN 0-918118-29-8). MUMPS.
Conway, Michael & Ricci, Mark. Films of Jean Harlow. 1969. pap. 7.95 (ISBN 0-8065-0147-2). Citadel Pr.
--Films of Marilyn Monroe. (Illus.). 1968. 12.00 (ISBN 0-8065-0395-5, C265); pap. 7.95 (ISBN 0-8065-0145-6, C265). Citadel Pr.
Conway, Moncure. Autobiography: Memoirs, & Experiences of Moncure Daniel Conway, 2 Vols. LC 76-87495. (American Public Figures Ser.). (Illus.). 1970. Repr. of 1904 ed. lib. bdg. 115.00 (ISBN 0-306-71402-7). Da Capo.
Conway, Moncure D. Autobiography; Memories & Experiences, 2 vols. LC 71-88405. (Illus.). Repr. of 1904 ed. Set. 40.00x (ISBN 0-8371-2478-6, CMC&, Pub. by Negro U Pr). Greenwood.
--Autobiography, Memories & Experiences, 2 vols. 1973. Set. 35.00 (ISBN 0-8274-1730-6). R West.
--Demonology & Devil-Lore, 2 vols. Set. 250.00 (ISBN 0-8490-0017-3). Gordon Pr.
--Emerson at Home & Abroad. LC 68-24934. (Studies in Emerson, No. 12). 1969. Repr. of 1883 ed. lib. bdg. 49.95x (ISBN 0-8383-0930-5). Haskell.

--Golden Hour. LC 79-97447. Repr. of 1862 ed. 15.00x (ISBN 0-8371-2683-5, COG&, Pub. by Negro U Pr). Greenwood.

--Life of Thomas Paine. LC 74-9716. 1973. lib. bdg. 37.50 (ISBN 0-8414-3511-1). Folcroft.

--The Life of Thomas Paine. 1909. 37.50 (ISBN 0-8482-3579-7). Norwood Edns.

--Solomon & Solomonic Literature. LC 72-2032. (Studies in Comparative Literature, No. 35). 1972. Repr. of 1899 ed. lib. bdg. 49.95x (ISBN 0-8383-1478-3). Haskell.

--Testimonies Concerning Slavery. LC 77-82187. (Anti-Slavery Crusade in America Ser). 1969. Repr. of 1865 ed. 13.00 (ISBN 0-405-00625-X). Ayer Co Pubs.

--Thomas Carlyle. LC 77-648. 1973. Repr. of 1881 ed. lib. bdg. 15.00 (ISBN 0-8414-3411-5). Folcroft.

--Thomas Carlyle. 1978. lib. bdg. 25.00 (ISBN 0-8482-3541-X). Norwood Edns.

Conway, Moncure D., ed. Dial: A Monthly Magazine for Literature, Philosophy & Religion, Vol. 1, Nos. 1-12. Repr. of 1860 ed. lib. bdg. 47.50 (ISBN 0-404-19515-6). AMS Pr.

Conway, Moncure D., ed. see Paine, Thomas.

Conway, Neville. An Atlas of Cardiology: ECG's & Chest X-Rays. (Illus.). 1978. 49.95 (ISBN 0-8151-1846-5). Year Bk Med.

--A Pocket Atlas of Arrhythmias. (Illus.). 1975. pap. 15.50 (ISBN 0-8151-5950-1). Year Bk Med.

Conway, P. Development of Volitional Competence: Selected Readings. 1975. text ed. 19.50x (ISBN 0-8290-1077-7); pap. text ed. 6.00x (ISBN 0-8422-0424-5). Irvington.

Conway, Patricia, jt. auth. see Jensen, Robert.

Conway, R. A. & Gulledge, W. P., eds. Hazardous & Industrial Solid Waste Testing: 2nd Symposium. LC 84-70420. (Special Technical Publications: No. 805). 332p. 1983. text ed. 44.00 (ISBN 0-8031-0246-1, 04-805000-16). ASTM.

Conway, R. S. The Making of Latin: An Introduction to Latin, Greek & English Etymology. 1983. 25.00 (ISBN 0-89241-335-2); pap. 12.50 (ISBN 0-89241-341-7). Caratzas.

Conway, R. S. see Livy.

Conway, R. S., et al see Livy.

Conway, Richard. A Primer on Disciplined Programming: Using PL-1, PL-CS, & PL-CT. (Orig.). 1978. pap. text ed. 16.95 (ISBN 0-316-15426-1). Little.

Conway, Richard & Archer, James. Programming for Poets: A Gentle Introduction Using BASIC. (Orig.). 1979. pap. text ed. 16.95 (ISBN 0-316-15412-1). Little.

--Programming for Poets: A Gentle Introduction Using FORTRAN with WATFIV. (Orig.). 1978. pap. text ed. 16.95 (ISBN 0-316-15421-0). Little.

Conway, Richard & Gries, David. An Introduction to Programming: A Structured Approach Using PL-1 & PL-C. 3rd ed. 728p. 1978. pap. text ed. 24.95 (ISBN 0-316-15414-8). Little.

--Primer on Structured Programming: Using PL-1, PL-C & PL-CT. (Orig.). 1976. pap. text ed. 16.95 (ISBN 0-316-15425-3). Little.

Conway, Richard, et al. Programming for Poets: A Gentle Introduction Using Pascal. (Orig.). 1979. pap. text ed. 16.95 (ISBN 0-316-15411-3). Little.

--A Primer on Pascal. 2nd ed. 430p. 1981. pap. text ed. 16.95 (ISBN 0-316-15416-4). Little.

Conway, Richard A. Environmental Risk Analysis of Chemicals. (Environmental Engineering Ser.). 640p. 1981. 42.50 (ISBN 0-442-21650-5). Van Nos Reinhold.

Conway, Richard A. & Ross, Richard D. Handbook of Industrial Waste Disposal. 576p. 1980. text ed. 39.50 (ISBN 0-442-27053-4). Van Nos Reinhold.

Conway, Robert S. Ancient Italy & Modern Religion. LC 77-27141. (Hibbert Lectures: 1932). Repr. of 1933 ed. 17.00 (ISBN 0-404-60428-5). AMS Pr.

--Harvard Lectures on the Vergilian Age. LC 67-13861. 1928. 10.00x (ISBN 0-8196-0182-9). Biblo.

--Harvard Lectures on the Vergilian Age. 1975. Repr. of 1928 ed. 7.25 (ISBN 0-8274-4045-6). R West.

--Makers of Europe: Dickinson College, James Henry Morgan Lectures, 1930. facsimile ed. LC 67-28748. (Essay Index Reprint Ser). 1931. 13.00 (ISBN 0-8369-0330-7). Ayer Co Pubs.

Conway, Robert S., et al. Prae-Italic Dialects, 3 Vols. 1967. Repr. of 1933 ed. Set. 175.00x (ISBN 3-4870-1889-6). Adlers Foreign Bks.

Conway, Rosanne, jt. auth. see Scott, Kenneth.

Conway, Sally. You & Your Husband's Mid-Life Crisis. (Orig.). 1980. pap. 5.95 (ISBN 0-89191-318-1). Cook.

Conway, Sally, jt. auth. see Conway, Jim.

Conway, Shirley & Wilson, Jean. Steiff Teddy Bears, Dolls & Toys with Prices. 152p. pap. 14.95 (ISBN 0-87069-415-4). Wallace-Homestead.

Conway, Stephen M., jt. ed. see Flint, Christine E.

Conway, Steve. Timber Cutting Practices. 3rd ed. LC 78-53017. (A Forest Industries Book). (Illus.). 192p. 1978. 20.00 (ISBN 0-87930-021-3). Miller Freeman.

Conway, Theresa. Crimson Glory. 1979. pap. 2.25 (ISBN 0-449-14112-8, GM). Fawcett.

--Honor Bound. 352p. (Orig.). 1980. pap. 2.50 (ISBN 0-449-14340-6, GM). Fawcett.

--Love Chase. (Tapestry Romance Ser.). 1983. pap. 2.50 (ISBN 0-671-46054-4). PB.

--Paloma. 672p. (Orig.). 1984. pap. 3.95 (ISBN 0-345-31566-9). Ballantine.

--Silver Clouds, Golden Dreams. 608p. 1985. pap. 3.95 (ISBN 0-425-08075-7). Berkley Pub.

--Wine of Paradise. 384p. (Orig.). 1982. pap. 2.95 (ISBN 0-449-24553-5, Crest). Fawcett.

Conway, Thomas, Jr. & Patterson, Ernest M. The Operations of the New Bank Act. Bruchey, Stuart, ed. LC 80-1141. (The Rise of Commercial Banking Ser.). 1981. Repr. of 1914 ed. lib. bdg. 39.00x (ISBN 0-405-13643-9). Ayer Co Pubs.

Conway, Tom & Egli, Audrey. The Real Estate Planning Guide. 300p. 1984. 24.95 (ISBN 0-88192-011-8). Timber.

Conway, W. D., jt. auth. see Hueper, W. C.

Conway, W. Martin, ed. Early Dutch & English Voyages to Spitzbergen in the Seventeenth Century. (Hakluyt Society Works Ser.: No. 2, Vol. 11). (Illus.). Repr. of 1902 ed. 25.00 (ISBN 0-317-16770-7). Kraus Repr.

Conway, William M. The Van Eycks & Their Followers. LC 75-41065. (BCL Ser.: Ii). Repr. of 1921 ed. 37.50 (ISBN 0-404-14657-0). AMS Pr.

Conway-Rutkowski, Barbara & Rutkowski, Arthur D. Labor Relations in Hospitals. 320p. 1984. 35.95 (ISBN 0-89443-582-5). Aspen Systems.

Conway-Rutkowski, Barbara L. Carini & Owens' Neurological & Neurosurgical Nursing. 8th ed. LC 81-14161. (Illus.). 803p. 1982. pap. text ed. 25.95 (ISBN 0-8016-1035-4). Mosby.

Conwell, Esther M. High Field Transport in Semiconductors. (Solid State Physics Ser.: Suppl. 9). 1967. 64.50 (ISBN 0-12-607769-X). Acad Pr.

Conwell, Marilyn & Juilland, Alphonse. Louisiana French Grammar, Vol. 1, Phonology, Morphology, & Syntax. (Janua Linguarum, Ser. Practica: No. 1). 1963. text ed. 28.80x (ISBN 90-2790-621-1). Mouton.

Conwell, Russell H. Acres of Diamonds. 1915. Repr. of 1931 ed. 8.95i (ISBN 0-06-010845-2, HarpT). Har-Row.

--Acres of Diamonds. 1982. pap. 2.25 (ISBN 0-515-06168-9, V2762). Jove Pubns.

--Acres of Diamonds. (Inspirational Classics Ser.). 64p. 1975. 6.95 (ISBN 0-8007-1141-6); pap. 2.25 (ISBN 0-8007-8091-4, Spire Bks). Revell.

Conwill, R. H. Life of Bayard Taylor. 1879. Repr. 25.00 (ISBN 0-8274-2920-7). R West.

Conybeare, C. E. Lithostratigraphic Analysis of Sedimentary Basins. LC 79-6951. 1979. 59.50 (ISBN 0-12-186050-7). Acad Pr.

Conybeare, C. E. B. Oil Search in Australia. LC 80-65047. (Illus.). 151p. 1980. pap. text ed. 10.50 (ISBN 0-7081-1164-5, 0593). Australia N U P.

Conybeare, Charles A. Place of Iceland in the History of European Institutions, Being the Lothian Prize Essay, 1877. Repr. of 1877 ed. 15.00 (ISBN 0-404-01696-0). AMS Pr.

Conybeare, F. C. & Stock, George, eds. Selections from the Septuagint. (College Classical Ser.). vi, 313p. 1981. lib. bdg. 25.00x (ISBN 0-89241-366-2); pap. 12.50 (ISBN 0-89241-114-7). Caratzas.

Conybeare, Mrs. F. C., tr. see Scherer, W., et al.

Conybeare, Fred C. The Key of Truth. cancelled 93.00 (ISBN 0-686-12403-0). Church History.

Conybeare, Frederick C. Russian Dissenters. LC 79-2897. 370p. 1980. Repr. of 1921 ed. 29.25 (ISBN 0-8305-0068-5). Hyperion Conn.

Conybeare, Frederick C. & Stock, G. A Grammar of Septuagint Greek. 80p. 1980. pap. 6.95 (ISBN 0-310-43001-1). Zondervan.

Conybeare, John J. Illustrations of Anglo-Saxon Poetry. LC 65-15875. (Studies in Poetry, No. 38). 1969. Repr. of 1826 ed. lib. bdg. 52.95x (ISBN 0-8383-0530-X). Haskell.

Conybeare, W. D. & Phillips, William. Outlines of the Geology of England & Wales: General Principles of That Science, & Comparative Views of the Structure of Foreign Countries. Albritton, Claude C., Jr., ed. LC 77-6516. (History of Geology Ser.). 1978. Repr. of 1822 ed. lib. bdg. 37.50x (ISBN 0-405-10438-3). Ayer Co Pubs.

Conybeare, W. J. & Howson, J. S. Life & Epistles of St. Paul. 1949. 16.95 (ISBN 0-8028-8086-X). Eerdmans.

--The Life & Epistles of St. Paul. 1977. lib. bdg. 59.95 (ISBN 0-8490-2160-X). Gordon Pr.

Conyers, D. Rural Regional Planning: Towards An Operational Theory. 66p. 1984. pap. 20.00 (ISBN 0-08-032351-0). Pergamon.

Conyers, D. & Hills, P. An Introduction to Development Planning in the Third World: Public Administration in Developing Countries. 271p. 1984. 32.95 (ISBN 0-471-90231-4). Wiley.

Conyers, DeWitt. Animal Poems for Children. (Golden Storytime Bks.). (Illus.). 24p. (ps-1). 1982. 1.95 (ISBN 0-307-11954-8, Golden Bks). Western Pub.

--Santa Claus the Movie: Santa's Sleigh. (Fast Rolling Bks.). (Illus.). 12p. (ps). 1985. 5.95 (ISBN 0-448-10282-X, G&D). Putnam Pub Group.

Conyers, Diana. An Introduction to Social Planning in the Third World. LC 80-14714. 224p. 1981. 44.95x (ISBN 0-471-10043-9, Pub. by Wiley-Interscience). Wiley.

Conyers, James E. & Wallace, Walter L. Black Elected Officials: A Study of Black Americans Holding Governmental Office. LC 74-30881. 208p. 1976. 9.95x (ISBN 0-87154-206-4). Russell Sage.

Conyers, Marshall. How Many Feathers Does it Take to Make An Eagle Fly. 80p. (gr. 1 up). 1985. 9.95 (ISBN 0-914007-00-9). Bonner Pub Co.

Conyers, Peggy. Because You Asked Me: Inspirational Poems. 1984. 6.95 (ISBN 0-916620-74-3). Portals Pr.

Conyers, Samuel. Jail Letters from Samuel. large print ed. 27p. 1984. pap. 8.00 (ISBN 0-914009-09-5). Chr Overeaters Bks.

Conyne, Robert K. & Clack, R. James. Environmental Assessment & Design: A New Tool for the Applied Behavioral Scientist. LC 80-24816. 204p. 1981. 32.95 (ISBN 0-03-057948-1). Praeger.

Conyne, Robert K., ed. The Group Workers' Handbook: Varieties of Group Experience. 340p. 1985. 34.50x (ISBN 0-398-05049-X). C C Thomas.

Conyngham, William J. Industrial Management in the Soviet Union: The Role of the CPSU in Industrial Decision-Making, 1917-1970. LC 74-170206. (Publications Ser.: No. 116). 389p. 1973. 12.95x (ISBN 0-8179-6161-5). Hoover Inst Pr.

--The Modernization of Soviet Industrial Management: Socio-Economic Development & the Search for Viability. LC 81-21630. (Soviet & East European Studies). (Illus.). 256p. 1982. 39.50 (ISBN 0-521-24381-5). Cambridge U Pr.

Conyngton, Mary. How to Help: A Manual of Practical Charity. LC 77-137160. (Poverty U.S.A. Historical Record Ser). 1971. Repr. of 1909 ed. 22.00 (ISBN 0-405-03099-1). Ayer Co Pubs.

Conyngton, Thomas. A Manual of Partnership Relations. LC 6-693. (Business Enterprises Reprint Ser.). 221p. 1982. Repr. of 1905 ed. lib. bdg. 30.00 (ISBN 0-89941-178-9). W S Hein.

Conynham, David P. The Irish Brigade & Its Campaigns: With Some Accounts of the Corcoran Legion, 63rd, 69th, 88th N. Y., 28th Mass., 116th Pa. 599p. 1985. Repr. of 1869 ed. 35.00x (ISBN 0-913419-15-X). Butternut Pr.

Conze, E., tr. Buddha's Law Among Birds. 1975. Repr. 4.50 (ISBN 0-85181-033-0). Orient Bk Dist.

Conze, Edward. Buddhism: Its Essence & Development. 17.50 (ISBN 0-8446-1889-6). Peter Smith.

--Buddhism: It's Essence & Development. 1982. pap. 4.95 (ISBN 0-06-130058-6, TB 58, Torch). Har-Row.

--Buddhist Meditation. 190p. 1972. pap. 6.95 (ISBN 0-04-294073-7). Allen Unwin.

--Buddhist Studies Nineteen Thirty-Four to Nineteen Seventy-Two. 512p. 1977. Repr. 20.00 (ISBN 0-686-48400-2). Wheelwright Pr.

--Buddhist Thought in India. 1967. pap. 8.95 (ISBN 0-472-06129-1, 129, AA). U of Mich Pr.

--The Large Sutra on Perfect Wisdom: With the Divisions of the Abhisamayalankara. LC 71-189224. 697p. 1985. pap. 12.95 (ISBN 0-520-05321-4, CAL 668). U of Cal Pr.

--A Short History of Buddhism. 1982. text ed. 12.50x (ISBN 0-04-294109-1); pap. 5.95 (ISBN 0-04-294123-7). Allen Unwin.

Conze, Edward, jt. auth. see Wilkinson, Ellen C.

Conze, Edward, ed. & tr. The Large Sutra on Perfect Wisdom, with the Divisions of the Abhisamayalankara. LC 71-189224. 1975. 60.00x (ISBN 0-520-02240-8). U of Cal Pr.

Conze, Edward & Lancaster, Lewis, eds. Buddhist Scriptures: A Bibliography. LC 77-83380. (Reference Library of the Humanities: Vol. 113). 161p. 1982. lib. bdg. 31.00 (ISBN 0-8240-9848-X). Garland Pub.

Conze, Edward, tr. Buddhist Scriptures. (Classics Ser.). (Orig.). 1959. pap. 3.95 (ISBN 0-14-044088-7). Penguin.

Conze, Edward, tr. from Sanskrit. & pref. by. The Perfection of Wisdom in Eight Thousand Lines & Its Verse Summary. LC 72-76540. (Wheel Ser.: No. 1). 348p. 1973. 15.00 (ISBN 0-87704-048-6); pap. 8.95 (ISBN 0-87704-049-4). Four Seasons Foun.

Conze, Werner & Hertz-Eichenrode, Dieter. Karl Marx: Manuskripte Uber Die Polnische Frage (1863-64) (Quellen & Untersuchungen Zur Geschichte der Deutschen & Desterreichischen Arbeiterbewegung: No. 4). 1961. 23.20x (ISBN 90-2790-153-8). Mouton.

Conzelmann, Hans. First Corinthians. MacRae, George W., ed. Leitch, James W., tr. from Ger. LC 73-88360. (Hermeneia: a Critical & Historical Commentary on the Bible). 352p. 1975. 25.95x (ISBN 0-8006-6005-6, 20-6005). Fortress.

--History of Primitive Christianity. Steely, John E., tr. from Ger. LC 72-8818. Orig. Title: Geschichte Des Unchristentums. 192p. 1973. pap. 8.95 (ISBN 0-687-17252-7). Abingdon.

--Jesus. Reumann, John, ed. Lord, J. Raymond, tr. from Gr. LC 73-79011. 128p. 1973. pap. 3.95 (ISBN 0-8006-1000-8, 1-1000). Fortress.

--The Theology of St. Luke. LC 82-2372. 256p. 1982. pap. 9.95 (ISBN 0-8006-1650-2, 1-1650). Fortress.

Conzelmann, Hans, jt. auth. see Dibelius, Martin.

Conzen, Kathleen N. Immigrant Milwaukee, Eigtheen Thirty-six to Eighteen Sixty. (Studies in Urban History). 1976. text ed. 18.00x (ISBN 0-674-44436-1). Harvard U Pr.

Conzen, Michael P. & Lewis, Geroge K. Boston: A Geographical Portrait. LC 76-4791. (Contemporary Metropolitan Analysis Ser.). 104p. 1976. pap. 14.95 (ISBN 0-88410-432-X). Ballinger Pub.

Conzen, Michael P., ed. Chicago Mapmakers: Essays on the Rise of the City's Map Trade. LC 84-5853. (Illus.). 76p. 1984. 12.00 (ISBN 0-916789-01-2). Chicago Map.

Coo, Bill. Scenic Rail Guide to Central & Atlantic Canada. (Illus.). 160p. 1983. pap. 9.95 (ISBN 0-919872-76-X). NY Zoetrope.

--Scenic Rail Guide to Western Canada. (Illus.). 192p. 1983. pap. 9.95 (ISBN 0-919872-77-8). NY Zoetrope.

Cooch, Daphne & Judetz, Nancy. Curdling the Cream. 43p. (Orig.). pap. 4.95 (ISBN 0-913244-80-5). Hapi Pr.

Coode, Thomas H. & Bauman, John F. People, Poverty, & Politics: Pennsylvanians During the Great Depression. LC 78-75198. 276p. 1981. 24.50 (ISBN 0-8387-2320-9). Bucknell U Pr.

Coodley. Geriatric Heart Disease. 1985. 49.50 (ISBN 0-88416-468-3). PSG Pub Co.

Coodley, Eugene, et al, eds. Internal Medicine Update, Nineteen Seventy-Nine to Nineteen Eighty. (Hahnemann Symposia). 416p. 1979. 62.00 (ISBN 0-8089-1172-4, 790897). Grune.

Coodleyt, Eugene L., ed. Diagnostic Enzymology. LC 78-85839. pap. 84.00 (ISBN 0-317-07924-7, 2055417). Bks Demand UMI.

Coodsworth, Elizabeth. The Snow Parlor. 64p. 1983. pap. 0.95 (ISBN 0-448-05442-6). Ace Bks.

Coody, Betty. Using Literature with Young Children. 3rd ed. 256p. 1982. pap. text ed. write for info. (ISBN 0-697-06068-3). Wm C Brown.

Coody, Betty & Nelson, David. Teaching Elementary Language Arts. 416p. 1981. text ed. write for info. (ISBN 0-534-01022-9). Wadsworth Pub.

--Teaching Elementary Language Arts: A Literature Approach. (Illus.). 390p. 1985. Repr. of 1982 ed. text ed. 23.95x (ISBN 0-88133-187-2). Waveland Pr.

Coogan, C. K., et al. Magnetic Resonance. LC 70-119613. 386p. 1970. 37.50x (ISBN 0-306-30487-2, Plenum Pr). Plenum Pub.

Coogan, Daniel, tr. see Goethe, Johann W.

Coogan, Gertrude. Lawful Money Explained. 1979. lib. bdg. 59.95 (ISBN 0-8490-2956-2). Gordon Pr.

Coogan, Gertrude M. Money Creators. 69.95 (ISBN 0-87968-317-1). Gordon Pr.

Coogan, John W. The End of Neutrality: The United States, Britain & Maritime Rights, 1899-1915. LC 81-66645. 256p. 1981. 24.95x (ISBN 0-8014-1407-5). Cornell U Pr.

Coogan, Michael D., ed. Stories from Ancient Canaan. LC 77-20022. 120p. 1978. pap. 6.95 (ISBN 0-664-24184-0). Westminster.

Coogan, Peter, et al. Secured Transactions Under the Uniform Commercial Code, 4 vols. (Bender's Uniform Commercial Code Service: Volumes 1, 1A, 1B & 1C). 1963. Updates avail. 280.00 (615); looseleaf 1983 165.00; looseleaf 1984 185.00. Bender.

Coogan, Tim P. The I. R. A. 620p. 1971. pap. 7.25 (ISBN 0-00-635932-9, Pub. by Fontana England). Irish Bk Ctr.

--On the Blanket: The H-Block Story. 6.95 (ISBN 0-907085-01-6). Turtle Isl Foun.

Coogan, Timothy P. Ireland Since the Rising. LC 75-35333. (Illus.). 355p. 1976. Repr. of 1966 ed. lib. bdg. 27.50x (ISBN 0-8371-8560-2, COIR). Greenwood.

Coogan, William H. & Woshinsky, Oliver H. The Science of Politics: An Introduction to Hypothesis Formation & Testing. 242p. (Orig.). 1982. lib. bdg. 25.25 (ISBN 0-8191-2652-7); pap. text ed. 12.00 (ISBN 0-8191-2653-5). U Pr of Amer.

Coogler, J. Gordon. Purely Original Verse. (Illus.). 1974. Repr. limited ed. 6.00 (ISBN 0-686-09908-7). C H Neuffer.

Coogler, O. J. Structured Mediation in Divorce Settlements: A Handbook for Marital Mediators. LC 77-15814. 1978. o. p. 20.00 (ISBN 0-669-02343-4); pap. 10.00 (ISBN 0-669-09747-0). Lexington Bks.

Cook. Drawing Cats. (The Grosset Art Instruction Ser.: No. 8). (Illus.). 48p. pap. 3.95 (ISBN 0-399-51039-7, G&D). Putnam Pub Group.

--Drawing Dogs. (The Grosset Art Instruction Ser.: No. 10). (Illus.). 48p. 1966. pap. 2.95 (ISBN 0-399-51034-6, G&D). Putnam Pub Group.

--Faith Planning. 1983. 3.95 (ISBN 0-88207-299-4). Victor Bks.

--New Testament Holiness. 4.95 (ISBN 0-686-12895-8). Schmul Pub Co.

--Osiris. 1985. Repr. of 1931 ed. 12.50 (ISBN 0-89005-287-5). Ares.

Cook & Forti. Professional Secretary's Handbook. 354p. 1984. 28.50 (ISBN 0-85013-151-0). Dartnell Corp.

Cook & Marchant. Advanced Greek Unseens. Bowen, Anthony, ed. 1981. 20.00x (ISBN 0-906515-47-5, Pub. by Bristol Classical Pr). State Mutual Bk.

Cook, jt. auth. see Blance.

Cook, jt. auth. see Perard.

Cook, et al. Family Mediation Workbook. Polk, Donice, ed. 90p. (Orig.). 1980. pap. 10.00 (ISBN 0-686-29084-4). D Polk.

Cook, A. A. Diseases of Tropical Fruits & Nuts. LC 75-18737. 1975. 35.00x (ISBN 0-02-843070-0). Hafner.

Cook, A. H. Gravity & the Earth. (The Wykeham Science Ser.: No. 6). 108p. 1969. pap. cancelled (ISBN 0-85109-070-2). Taylor & Francis.

--Interiors of the Planets. (Cambridge Planetary Science Ser.: No. 1). (Illus.). 360p. 1981. 72.50 (ISBN 0-521-23214-7). Cambridge U Pr.

Cook, A. H. & Saunders, V. T. Gravity & the Earth. (Wykeham Science Ser.: No. 6). 108p. 1969. 9.95x (ISBN 0-8448-1108-4). Crane Russak Co.

Cook, A. M. A Latin Anthology. 187p. 1981. Repr. of 1912 ed. lib. bdg. 30.00 (ISBN 0-89987-126-7). Darby Bks.

--A Latin Anthology. 1912. 25.00 (ISBN 0-8274-3942-3). R West.

Cook, A. S. Biblical Quotations in Old English Prose Writers. 59.95 (ISBN 0-87968-731-2). Gordon Pr.

--Concordance to Beowulf. LC 68-26349. (Beowulf & Literature of the Anglo Saxons Ser., No. 2). 1969. Repr. of 1911 ed. lib. bdg. 49.95x (ISBN 0-8383-0273-4). Haskell.

Cook, A. S., ed. The Dream of the Rood: An Old English Poem Attributed to Cynewulf. 1977. lib. bdg. 59.95 (ISBN 0-8490-1733-5). Gordon Pr.

Cook, Ablert, tr. see Homer.

Cook, Adrian. The Armies of the Streets: The New York City Draft Riots of 1863. LC 73-80463. (Illus.). 336p. 1974. 28.00x (ISBN 0-8131-1298-2). U Pr of Ky.

Cook, Alan H. The Astronomer As Natural Philosopher: An Inaugural Lecture. LC 73-89007. (Illus.). pap. 20.00 (ISBN 0-317-07952-2, 2051372). Bks Demand UMI.

Cook, Albert. Adapt the Living. LC 80-17828. viii, 83p. 1980. 12.95x (ISBN 0-8040-0350-5, 82-75018, Pub by Swallow); pap. 6.95 (ISBN 0-8040-0359-9, 82-75026). Ohio U Pr.

--Changing the Signs: The Fifteenth-Century Breakthrough. LC 84-17280. (Illus.). xiv, 168p. 1985. 26.50x (ISBN 0-8032-1425-1). U of Nebr Pr.

--Charges. LC 70-112872. 154p. 1970. 10.95 (ISBN 0-8040-0036-0, 82-70241, Pub. by Swallow); pap. 5.95 (ISBN 0-8040-0037-9, 82-70258, Pub. by Swallow). Ohio U Pr.

--Dark Voyage & the Golden Mean. 1966. pap. 1.75x (ISBN 0-393-00357-4, Norton Lib). Norton.

--Enactment: Greek Tragedy. LC 78-153076. 175p. 1971. 15.00x (ISBN 0-8040-0539-7, 82-72742, Pub by Swallow). Ohio U Pr.

--Figural Choice in Poetry & Art. LC 84-40582. (Illus.). 272p. 1985. 20.00x (ISBN 0-87451-333-2). U Pr of New Eng.

--French Tragedy: The Power of Enchantment. LC 80-39611. xvi, 124p. 1981. 15.00x (ISBN 0-8040-0548-6, 82-75737, Pub. by Swallow). Ohio U Pr.

--Myth & Language. LC 79-84259. 352p. 1980. 25.00x (ISBN 0-253-14027-7). Ind U Pr.

--Oedipus Rex: A Mirror for Greek Drama. LC 81-71992. 178p. 1982. pap. text ed. 5.95x (ISBN 0-917974-84-0). Waveland Pr.

--Shakespeare's Enactment: The Dynamics of Renaissance Theatre. LC 76-3128. 257p. 1975. 15.00x (ISBN 0-8040-0695-4, 82-73849, Pub. by Swallow). Ohio U Pr.

Cook, Albert, ed. see Aeschylus & Sophocles.

Cook, Albert, ed. see Homer.

Cook, Albert, ed. & tr. see Homer.

Cook, Albert M. & Webster, John G., eds. Clinical Engineering: Principles & Practices. (Illus.). 1979. text ed. 43.95 (ISBN 0-13-137737-X). P-H.

--Therapeutic Medical Devices: Application & Design. (Illus.). 656p. 1981. 47.95 (ISBN 0-13-914796-9). P-H.

Cook, Albert S. The Authorized Version & Its Influence. LC 76-41905. Repr. of 1910 ed. lib. bdg. 8.50 (ISBN 0-8414-3559-6). Folcroft.

--The Bible & English Prose Style. LC 72-192049. Repr. of 1892 ed. lib. bdg. 8.50 (ISBN 0-8414-1134-4). Folcroft.

--Biblical Quotations in Old English Prose Writers. LC 74-2465. 1898. lib. bdg. 40.00 (ISBN 0-8414-3552-9). Folcroft.

--Biblical Quotations in Old English Prose Writers: Second Series. LC 74-7275. 1903. lib. bdg. 40.00 (ISBN 0-686-96720-8). Folcroft.

--Chaucerian Papers. LC 72-1040. Repr. of 1919 ed. 11.50 (ISBN 0-404-01697-9). AMS Pr.

--Christ of Cynewulf: A Poem in Three Parts, the Advent, the Ascension, & the Last Judgement. (Select Bibliographies Reprint Ser.). 1982. Repr. of 1900 ed. lib. bdg. 13.95 (ISBN 0-8290-0846-2). Irvington.

--Concordance to Beowulf. LC 74-46. 1911. lib. bdg. 40.00 (ISBN 0-8414-3456-5). Folcroft.

--Concordance to Beowulf. LC 68-23146. 440p. 1968. Repr. of 1911 ed. 40.00x (ISBN 0-8103-3169-1). Gale.

--A Concordance to English Poems of Thomas Gray. LC 74-8062. Repr. of 1908 ed. lib. bdg. 30.00 (ISBN 0-8414-3355-0). Folcroft.

--A Concordance to the English Poems of Thomas Gray. 16.50 (ISBN 0-8446-1124-7). Peter Smith.

--Historical Background of Chaucer's Knight. LC 68-1564. (Studies in Chaucer, No. 6). 1969. Repr. of 1916 ed. lib. bdg. 39.95x (ISBN 0-8383-0531-8). Haskell.

--Last Months of Chaucer's Earliest Patron. LC 72-1000. Repr. of 1916 ed. 14.50 (ISBN 0-404-01698-7). AMS Pr.

--A Literary Middle English Reader. LC 73-9745. Repr. of 1915 ed. lib. bdg. 50.00 (ISBN 0-8414-1823-3). Folcroft.

--Old English Physiologus. LC 73-4487. 1921. lib. bdg. 10.00 (ISBN 0-8414-1843-8). Folcroft.

--Possible Begetter of the Old English Beowulf & Widsith. (Beowulf & Literature of the Anlgo-Saxons Ser., No. 2). 1970. pap. 19.95x (ISBN 0-8383-0018-9). Haskell.

--Progressions & Other Poems. LC 63-11976. pap. 32.00 (ISBN 0-317-28649-8, 2055348). Bks Demand UMI.

--Select Translations from Old English Poetry. 1902. lib. bdg. 17.50 (ISBN 0-8414-2381-4). Folcroft.

--Sidney's The Defense of Poesy. 1890. lib. bdg. 22.50 (ISBN 0-8414-2382-2). Folcroft.

--Thresholds: Studies in the Romantic Experience. LC 85-40365. 432p. 1985. text ed. 37.50x (ISBN 0-299-10300-5). U of Wis Pr.

Cook, Albert S., ed. The Christ of Cynewulf: A Poem in Three Parts, the Advent, the Ascension & the Last Judgment. 1900. 14.95 (ISBN 0-8274-2052-8). R West.

--Judith, an Old English Epic Fragment. LC 70-144441. (Belles Lettres Ser. Section I: No. 7). Repr. of 1904 ed. 12.50 (ISBN 0-404-53608-5). AMS Pr.

Cook, Albert S. & Tinker, Chauncey B., eds. Select Translations from Old English Poetry. rev. ed. LC 68-59036. 1968. Repr. of 1902 ed. 9.00x (ISBN 0-87752-024-0). Gordian.

--Select Translations from Old English Poetry. LC 73-89014. Repr. of 1902 ed. lib. bdg. 18.75x (ISBN 0-8371-3083-2, COOE). Greenwood.

--Select Translations from Old English Prose. LC 68-57700. 1968. Repr. of 1908 ed. 10.00x (ISBN 0-87752-025-9). Gordian.

Cook, Albert S., ed. see Cynewulf.

Cook, Albert S., ed. see Eglamour.

Cook, Albert S., ed. see Hunt, Leigh.

Cook, Albert S., ed. see Pierce, Frederick E.

Cook, Albert S., tr. see Sievers, Eduard.

Cook, Albert S., et al. Translations from the Old English. Incl. Andreas: The Legend of St. Andrew: No. 7. Root, Robert K. Repr. of 1899 ed; Elene of Cynewulf: No. 21. Holt, Lucius H. Repr. of 1904 ed; Genesis: No. 48. Mason, Lawrence A. Repr. of 1915 ed; King Alfred's Version of St. Augustine's Soliloquies: No. 22. Hargrove, Henry L. Repr. of 1904 ed; Old English Physiologus: No. 63. Cook, Albert S. & Pitman, James H. Repr. of 1921 ed. (Yale Studies in English Ser.). 274p. 1970. Set. 25.00 (ISBN 0-208-00909-4, Archon). Shoe String.

Cook, Alice & Kirk, Gwyn. Greenham Women Everywhere: Dreams, Ideas & Actions from the Womens' Peace Movement. 128p. 1983. pap. 6.50 (ISBN 0-89608-199-0). South End Pr.

Cook, Alice H. Comparable Worth: The Problem & States' Approaches to Wage Equity. (Occasional Publication Ser.). 84p. 1983. 4.00 (ISBN -0318-04752-7). U Hawaii.

--Introduction to Japanese Trade Unionism. LC 66-63380. 228p. 1966. pap. 5.00 (ISBN 0-87546-014-3). ILR Pr.

--The Working Mother: A Survey of Problems & Programs in Nine Countries. 2nd rev. ed. LC 78-620004. 84p. 1978. pap. 4.75 (ISBN 0-87546-067-4). ILR Pr.

Cook, Alice H. & Douty, Agnes M. Labor Education Outside the Unions: A Review of Postwar Programs in Western Europe & the United States. 148p. 1958. pap. 2.00 (ISBN 0-87546-015-1); pap. 6.00 special hard bdg. (ISBN 0-87546-267-7). ILR Pr.

Cook, Alice H. & Hayashi, Hiroko. Working Women in Japan: Discrimination, Resistance, & Reform. LC 80-17706. (Cornell International Industrial & Labor Relations Reports: No. 10). 128p. 1980. pap. 7.95 (ISBN 0-87546-079-8). ILR Pr.

Cook, Alice H. & Lorwin, Val R., eds. Women & Trade Unions in Eleven Industrialized Countries. LC 83-17946. (Women in the Political Economy Ser.). 327p. 1984. text ed. 34.95 (ISBN 0-87722-319-X). Temple U Pr.

Cook, Alice H., et al. Public Employee Labor Relations in Japan: Three Aspects. LC 71-634401. (Comparative Studies in Public Employment Labor Relations Ser.). 1971. 5.00x (ISBN 0-87736-019-7); pap. 3.00x (ISBN 0-87736-020-0). U of Mich Inst Labor.

Cook, Alicia S. Contemporary Perspectives on Adulthood & Aging. 384p. 1983. text ed. write for info. (ISBN 0-02-324600-6). Macmillan.

Cook, Allan. Akin to Slavery. 81p. 1982. pap. 1.25 (ISBN 0-904759-48-2). Intl Defense & Aid.

Cook, Allen. Akin to Slavery: Prison Labor in South Africa. 81p. 1982. 2.00 (ISBN 0-317-36648-3). Africa Fund.

Cook, Allyn A. Diseases of Tropical & Subtropical Field, Fiber & Oil Plants. (Illus.). 545p. 1981. text ed. 45.00x (ISBN 0-02-949300-5). Macmillan.

--Diseases of Tropical & Subtropical Vegetables & Other Food Plants. LC 78-57055. 1978. 35.00x (ISBN 0-02-843080-8). Hafner.

Cook, Alta L., tr. see Tougas, Gerard.

Cook, Andrea, jt. auth. see Cook, Frank.

Cook, Ann & Mack, Herb. Robot & the Flea Market. (Illus.). 32p. (Orig.). (ps-3). 1982. pap. 1.95 (ISBN 0-440-47506-6, YB). Dell.

--Robot Comes to Stay. (Illus.). 32p. (Orig.). (ps-3). 1982. pap. 1.95 (ISBN 0-440-47507-4, YB). Dell.

--Robot Goes Collecting. (Illus.). 32p. (Orig.). (ps-3). 1982. pap. 1.95 (ISBN 0-440-47518-X, YB). Dell.

--Robot in Danger. (Illus.). 32p. (Orig.) (ps-3). 1982. pap. 1.95 (ISBN 0-440-47535-X, YB). Dell.

--Robot Saves the Day. (Illus.). 32p. (Orig.). (ps-3). 1982. pap. 1.95 (ISBN 0-440-47520-1, YB). Dell.

--Robot Visits School. (Illus.). 32p. (Orig.). (ps-3). 1982. pap. 1.95 (ISBN 0-440-47548-1, YB). Dell.

Cook, Ann J. The Privileged Playgoers of Shakespeare's London, 1576-1642. LC 80-8542. (Illus.). 280p. 1981. 26.00 (ISBN 0-691-06454-7). Princeton U Pr.

Cook, Anna M. History of Baldwin County Georgia. LC 78-13226. 1978. Repr. of 1925 ed. 25.00 (ISBN 0-87152-279-9). Reprint.

Cook, Arlene. Forever Yours. (Rhapsody Romance Ser.). 1984. pap. 2.95 (ISBN 0-89081-438-4). Harvest Hse.

--Love's Destiny. (Orig.). 1985. pap. 4.95 (ISBN 0-89081-470-8). Harvest Hse.

--One True Love. (Rhapsody Romance Ser.). 192p. 1984. 2.95 (ISBN 0-89081-416-3). Harvest Hse.

Cook, Arthur B. Zeus: A Study of Ancient Religion, 2 vols. Incl. Vol. 1. Zeus, God of the Bright Sky. LC 64-25839. (Illus.). 885p. Repr. of 1914 ed. 50.00x (ISBN 0-8196-0148-9); Vol. 2. Zeus, God of the Dark Sky: Thunder & Lightning, 2 pts. LC 64-25839. Repr. of 1925 ed. 100.00xset (ISBN 0-8196-0156-X); Vol. 2, Pt. 1. Text & Notes. xliii, 858p; Vol. 2, Pt. 2. Appendixes & Index. (Illus.). 539p. Biblo.

Cook, Arthur N. Africa: Past & Present. (Quality Paperback Ser.: No. 73). 374p. (Orig.). 1969. pap. 3.95 (ISBN 0-8226-0073-0). Littlefield.

--British Enterprise in Nigeria. 330p. 1964. Repr. of 1943 ed. 30.00x (ISBN 0-7146-1644-3, F Cass Co). Biblio Dist.

Cook, B. F. The Elgin Marbles. 72p. 1984. pap. 6.95 (ISBN 0-674-24626-8). Harvard U Pr.

Cook, B. F., ed. Greek & Roman Art in the British Museum. (British Museum Publications Ser.). (Illus.). 1977. pap. 7.95 (ISBN 0-8120-0903-7). Barron.

Cook, B. G., jt. ed. see Moore, A. W.

Cook, B. W. & Jones, K. A Programmed Introduction to Infrared Spectroscopy. 207p. 1972. 43.95 (ISBN 0-471-25644-7, Wiley Heyden); pap. 35.95 (ISBN 0-471-25643-9). Wiley.

Cook, Barbara. How to Raise Good Kids. LC 78-7844. 192p. 1978. pap. 4.95 (ISBN 0-87123-233-2, 210233). Bethany Hse.

Cook, Barbara, jt. auth. see Cook, Jerry.

Cook, Barbara, jt. auth. see Rothberg, Diane.

Cook, Barbara, et al. Any Time's a Party. rev. ed. (The Quail Ridge Press Cookbook Ser.: No. 5). Orig. Title: The Party Calendar Cookbook. (Illus.). 80p. 1983. pap. 4.95 (ISBN 0-937552-12-7). Quail Ridge.

Cook, Barbara E. & Rothberg, Diane S. Employee Benefits for Part-Timers. LC 85-70631. 60p. 1985. pap. 7.95 (ISBN 0-917449-01-0). Assn Part-Time.

Cook, Ben. Legend in Crimson: A Photo History of Alabama Football. Wells, Lawrence, ed. (Illus.). 192p. 1982. 29.95 (ISBN 0-916242-20-X, Pub. by Sports Yearbook Company). Yoknapatawpha.

Cook, Bernard A. & Watson, James R. Louisiana Labor: From Slavery to "Right-To-Work". LC 85-10457. 314p. (Orig.). 1985. lib. bdg. 26.75 (ISBN 0-8191-4746-X); pap. text ed. 14.50 (ISBN 0-8191-4747-8). U Pr of Amer.

Cook, Beryl. Beryl Cook's New York. Janeway, Carol B., ed. LC 85-48535. (Illus.). 64p. 1985. 13.95 (ISBN 0-394-53517-0). Knopf.

Cook, Bill J. Saints & Sinners. 64p. 1981. pap. 3.95 (ISBN 0-938400-05-3). Donahoe Pubs.

Cook, Blanche. Max & Crystal Eastman on Peace, Revolution & War. Chatfield, Charles & Cooper, Sandi, eds. (Library of War & Peace). 46.00 (ISBN 0-317-20455-6). Garland Pub.

Cook, Blanche, et al. Sermons on War by Theodore Parker. LC 70-149546. (Library of War & Peace; Relig. & Ethical Positions on War). 1973. lib. bdg. 46.00 (ISBN 0-8240-0499-X). Garland Pub.

Cook, Blanche, et al, eds. see Gandhi, Mahatma.

Cook, Blanche W. The Declassified Eisenhower: A Divided Legacy. LC 80-699. 432p. 1981. 17.95 (ISBN 0-385-05456-4). Doubleday.

--The Declassified Eisenhower: A Divided Legacy of Peace & Political Warfare. LC 84-4293. 1984. 8.95 (ISBN 0-14-007061-3). Penguin.

Cook, Blanche W., ed. Crystal Eastman on Women & Revolution. (Illus.). 1978. 25.00x (ISBN 0-19-502445-1); pap. 9.95 (ISBN 0-19-502446-X, GB 556). Oxford U Pr.

Cook, Blanche W., ed. see Dix, Otto.

Cook, Blanche W., ed. see Eastman, Crystal.

Cook, Blanche W., et al, eds. Garland Library of War & Peace, 327 vols. Incl. International Organization, Arbitration & Law, 22 vols; International Law, 19 vols; Kellogg Pact & the Outlawry of War, 4 vols; Non-Resistance & Non-Violence, 37 vols; Conscription & Conscientious Objection, 14 vols; Religious & Ethical Positions on War, 14 vols; Artist on War, 9 vols; Documentary Anthologies, 14 vols. Set. lib. bdg. 9470.00. Garland Pub.

Cook, Blanche W., et al, eds. see Mayr, Kaspar.

Cook, Bob. Speaking in Tongues: Is That All There Is? LC 88243000935000009. (Discovery Bks.). 48p. (YA) (gr. 9-12). 1982. pap. text ed. 1.50 (ISBN 0-88243-932-4, 02-0932); tchr's ed. 3.95 (02-0935). Gospel Pub.

--Today with the King. 408p. 1985. 14.95 (ISBN 0-89693-364-4). Victor Bks.

Cook, Bob, et al. The Baby Book for Grandparents. (Illus.). 40p. 1985. pap. 4.95 (ISBN 0-916043-02-9). Light Hearted Pub Co.

Cook, Bridget. Introduction to Bobbin Lace Patterns. LC 84-47815. (Illus.). 96p. 1984. 15.95 (ISBN 0-88332-364-8). Larousse.

Cook, Bridget & Stott, Geraldine. An Introduction to Bobbin Lace Stitches. (Illus.). 96p. 1983. 16.95 (ISBN 0-7134-4261-1, Pub. by Batsford England); pap. text ed. 9.95 (ISBN 0-7134-4262-X). David & Charles.

Cook, Bridget, jt. auth. see Stott, Geraldine.

Cook, Bridget M. & Stott, Geraldine. The Book of Bobbin Lace Stitches. (Illus.). 144p. 1980. 18.50 (ISBN 0-8231-5057-7). Branford.

Cook, Bruce. The Beat Generation. LC 82-20918. 248p. 1983. Repr. of 1971 ed. lib. bdg. 35.00x (ISBN 0-313-23073-0, COBG). Greenwood.

--Brecht in Exile. LC 82-2926. 240p. 1983. 17.95 (ISBN 0-03-060278-5). HR&W.

--Sex Life. LC 78-13487. 294p. 1979. 9.95 (ISBN 0-87131-263-8). M Evans.

Cook, C. D. Water Plants of the World. (Illus.). 1974. 125.00 (ISBN 9-0619-3024-3). Heinman.

Cook, C. D., jt. auth. see Whittle, Tyler.

Cook, C Donald, ed. The Future of the Union Catalogue: Proceedings of the International Symposium on the Future of the Union Catalogue, University of Toronto, May 21-22, 1981. LC 82-6238. (Cataloging & Classification Quarterly Ser.: Vol. 2, Nos. 1 & 2). 130p. 1982. text ed. 24.95 (ISBN 0-86656-175-7, B175). Haworth Pr.

Cook, C. E., et al, eds. Spread-Spectrum Communications. Ellersick, F. W. 286p. 1983. 39.95x (ISBN 0-471-87886-3, Pub. by Wiley Interscience). Wiley.

--Spread-Spectrum Communications. LC 83-12665. 296p. 1983. 39.95 (ISBN 0-87942-170-3, PC01636). Inst Electrical.

Cook, Carole & Carlisle, Jody. Challenges for Children: Creative Activities for Gifted & Talented Primary Children. 240p. 1984. tchng. aid 16.50x (ISBN 0-87628-196-X). Ctr Appl Res.

Cook, Catherine E., ed. see Carus, Paul.

Cook, Cathleen, tr. see Alexeyev, Sergei.

Cook, Cecil. Marquette: The Biography of an Iowa Railroad Town. LC 75-7184. (Illus.). 240p. 1975. 9.95 (ISBN 0-942240-03-0). W & M Pr.

Cook, Charles, ed. Daily Meditations for Prayer. Gift Ed. 9.95 (ISBN 0-89107-160-1). Good News.

Cook, Charles C. A Study of the Interrelationship of Massachusetts Assessment Level & Assessment Quality. (Lincoln Institute Monograph: No. 76-41). 1976. pap. text ed. 1.00 (ISBN 0-686-23015-9). Lincoln Inst Land.

Cook, Charles C., pref. by. Land Valuation Methods, Rural & Transitionary Land. (Lincoln Institute Monograph: No. 80-2). 1980. pap. text ed. 10.00 (ISBN 0-686-27944-1). Lincoln Inst Land.

Cook, Charles C., intro. by. Land Valuation Methods: Urban Land. (Lincoln Institute Monograph: No. 80-1). (Illus.). 200p. 1980. pap. text ed. 10.00 (ISBN 0-686-29505-6). Lincoln Inst Land.

Cook, Charles C., illus. Spatial Algorithms for Processing Land Data with a Microcomputer: Lincoln Institute Monograph. (84-2). 278p. 1984. pap. text ed. 9.00 (ISBN 0-318-03877-3). Lincoln Inst Land.

Cook, Charles E. & Bernfeld, Marvin. Radar Signals: An Introduction to Theory & Application. (Electrical Science Ser.). 1967. 85.00 (ISBN 0-12-186750-1). Acad Pr.

Cook, Charles M. The American Codification Movement: A Study of Antebellum Legal Reform. LC 80-662. (Contributions in Legal Studies Ser.: No. 14). xi, 234p. 1981. lib. bdg. 35.00 (ISBN 0-313-21314-3, CAC/). Greenwood.

Cook, Charles T, ed. see Spurgeon, Charles H.

Cook, Charles T., ed. see Spurgeon, Charles H.

Cook, Charles T, ed. see Spurgeon, Charles H.

Cook, Charles T., ed. see Spurgeon, Charles H. C. H.

Cook, Chester L. Inventor's Guide in a Series of Four Parts: How to Protect, Search, Compile Facts & Sell Your Invention. rev. ed. (Illus.). 52p. 1981. Repr. of 1979 ed. saddle stitch 11.95 (ISBN 0-9604670-1-7). C L Cook.

Cook, Chris. Dictionary of Historical Terms: A Guide to Names & Events of Over 1,000 Years of World History. LC 83-13377. 304p. 1984. 15.95x (ISBN 0-911745-16-5). P Bedrick Bks.

--The First European Elections: A Handbook & Guide. 1979. text ed. 21.25x (ISBN 0-391-00989-3); pap. text ed. 8.25x (ISBN 0-391-00990-7). Humanities.

--Pears Cyclopaedia. 94th ed. (Illus.). 1056p. 1985. 14.95 (ISBN 0-7207-1523-7, Pub. by Michael Joseph). Merrimack Pub Cir.

--Pears Cylopaedia. 92nd ed. (Illus.). 1056p. 1983. 14.95 (ISBN 0-7207-1459-1, Pub. by Michael Joseph). Merrimack Pub Cir.

--A Short History of the Liberal Party, 1900-1984. 2nd ed. 256p. 1984. 24.00x (ISBN 0-333-37026-0, Pub. by Salem Acad); pap. 9.95x (ISBN 0-333-37324-3). Merrimack Pub Cir.

--A Short History of the Liberal Party, 1900-1984. 2nd ed. LC 85-111247. Date not set. price not set. Macmillan.

--Sources in British Political History, 1900-1951, Vols. 3 & 4. Incl. Vol. 3. A Guide to the Private Papers of Members of Parliament, A-K. LC 77-71207 (ISBN 0-312-74656-3); Vol. 4. A Guide to the Private Papers of Members of Parliament, L-Z. LC 77-71188 (ISBN 0-312-74657-1). 1977. 27.50x ea. St Martin.

--Sources in British Political History, 1900-1951: A Guide to the Papers of Selected Public Servants. LC 75-15220. 320p. 1975. Vol. 1. 27.50 (ISBN 0-312-74620-2); Vol. 2. 27.50 (ISBN 0-312-74655-5). St Martin.

--Sources in British Political History, 1900-1950, Consolidated Vol. 6. LC 75-4012. 256p. 1985. 32.50 (ISBN 0-312-74659-8). St Martin.

Cook, Chris & Keith, Brendan. British Historical Facts: Eighteen Thirty to Nineteen Hundred. LC 74-76689. 279p. 1984. Repr. of 1975 ed. 29.95 (ISBN 0-312-10290-9). St Martin.

Cook, Chris & Killingray, David. African Political Facts since Nineteen Forty-Five. LC 81-17514. 256p. 1983. 19.95x (ISBN 0-87196-381-7). Facts on File.

Cook, Chris & Paxton, John. Commonwealth Political Facts. (Chronology Ser.). 308p. 1979. lib. bdg. 20.00 (ISBN 0-87196-378-7). Facts on File.

Cook, Chris & Ramsden, John. By-Elections in British Politics. LC 73-87075. 224p. 1974. 27.50 (ISBN 0-312-11095-2). St Martin.

Cook, Chris & Stevenson, John. British Historical Facts 1760 to 1830. ix, 197p. 1980. 32.50 (ISBN 0-208-01868-9, Archon). Shoe String.

Cook, Chris & Taylor, Ian. The Labour Party. (Illus.). 208p. 1980. text ed. 27.00x (ISBN 0-582-49038-3); pap. text ed. 10.95x (ISBN 0-582-49039-1). Longman.

Cook, Chris & Weeks, Jeffery. Sources in British Political History 1900-1951: A Guide to the Private Papers of Selected Writers, Intellectuals & Publicists, Vol. 5. LC 75-4012. 1978. 27.50 (ISBN 0-312-74658-X). St Martin.

Cook, Chris & Wroughton, John. English Historical Facts: 1603-1688. 231p. 1980. 32.50x (ISBN 0-8476-6295-0). Rowman.

Cook, Chris, jt. auth. see Sked, Alan.

Cook, Chris & Paxton, John, eds. European Political Facts 1789-1973, 3 vols. new ed. 1978. Vol. 1, 1789-1848. lib. bdg. 19.95x, 212 pg. (ISBN 0-87196-379-5); Vol. II, 1848-1918. lib. bdg. 19.95x 356 pg. (ISBN 0-87196-376-0); Vol. III, 1918-1973. lib. bdg. 19.95x, 376 pg. (ISBN 0-87196-377-9). Facts on File.

Cook, Chris & Ramsden, John, eds. Trends in British Politics Since 1945. LC 77-17789. 1978. 25.00x (ISBN 0-312-81754-1). St Martin.

Cook, Chris, jt. ed. see Awdry, W. V.

Cook, Chris, jt. ed. see Peele, Gillian.

Cook, Chris, jt. ed. see Pimlott, Ben.

Cook, Chris, jt. ed. see Sked, Alan.

Cook, Christopher. The Lion & the Dragon. (Illus.). 192p. 1985. 22.50 (ISBN 0-241-11411-X, Pub. by Hamish Hamilton England). David & Charles.

Cook, Christopher, jt. auth. see McKie, David.

Cook, Claire K. Line by Line: How to Edit Your Own Writing. 256p. 14.95 (ISBN 0-395-38944-5). HM.

Cook, Clarence. Art & Artists of Our Time, 3 vols. Weinberg, H. Barbara, ed. LC 75-28881. (Art Experience in Late 19th Century America Ser.: Vol. 15). (Illus.). 1976. Repr. of 1888 ed. Set. lib. bdg. 303.00 (ISBN 0-8240-2239-4). Garland Pub.

--The House Beautiful: Essays on Beds & Tables, Stools & Candlesticks. LC 78-14326. (Illus.). 336p. 1980. Repr. of 1878 ed. 35.00 (ISBN 0-88427-029-7). North River.

Cook, Clarence, ed. see Lubke, Wilhelm.

Cook, Clarence C. A Description of the New York Central Park. LC 70-174831. (Illus.). Repr. of 1869 ed. 20.00 (ISBN 0-405-08377-7, Blom Pubns). Ayer Co Pubs.

Cook, Claude W. A Practical Guide to the Basics of Physical Evidence: A Reference Text for the Criminalist, Investigator, Student & Attorney. (Illus.). 288p. 1984. 29.75x (ISBN 0-398-04933-5). C C Thomas.

Cook, Clayton B., et al, eds. Cellular Interactions in Symbiosis & Parasitism. LC 79-23304. (Ohio State University Biosciences Colloquia: No. 5). (Illus.). 321p. 1980. 25.00x (ISBN 0-8142-0315-9). Ohio St U Pr.

Cook, Clifford. String Teaching & Some Related Topics. 5.00 (ISBN 0-318-18115-0). Am String Tchrs.

Cook, Clifford A. Suzuki Education in Action: A Story of Talent Training from Japan. LC 74-136977. 1970. 7.50 (ISBN 0-682-47192-5, University). Exposition Pr FL.

Cook, Constance E. Nuclear Power & Legal Advocacy: The Environmentalists & the Courts. LC 79-3277. 176p. 1980. 21.50 (ISBN 0-669-03441-X). Lexington Bks.

Cook, Cornelia. Joyce Cary: Liberal Principles. (Critical Studies). 242p. 1981. 28.50x (ISBN 0-389-20201-0). B&N Imports.

Cook, Curtis W., jt. auth. see Basil, Douglas.

Cook, D., et al, eds. Social Work Treatment of Alcohol Problems. LC 82-620033. (NIAAA-RUCAS Alcoholism Treatment Ser.: No. 5). 1983. pap. 15.00 (ISBN 0-911290-15-X). Rutgers Ctr Alcohol.

Cook, D. J., ed. Cook & Deal. 1982. pap. 10.95 (ISBN 0-939114-53-4). Wimmer Bks.

Cook, Dan, jt. auth. see Toman, Jim.

Cook, Daniel. Language in the Philosophy of Hegel. (Janua Linguarum, Ser. Minor: No. 135). 198p. (Orig.). 1973. pap. text ed. 18.00x (ISBN 90-2792-402-3). Mouton.

Cook, Daniel, ed. see Chaucer, Geoffrey.

Cook, Daniel J., tr. see Leibniz, Gottfried W.

Cook, Daniel W., jt. auth. see Bolton, Brian.

Cook, Darius B. Six Months among Indians. (Illus.). 101p. 1974. Repr. of 1889 ed. 4.50 (ISBN 0-915056-03-8). Hardscrabble Bks.

Cook, David. Birds. LC 84-11398. (Our Endangered Earth Ser.). 32p. (gr. 3-7). 1985. bds. 5.95 (ISBN 0-517-55431-3). Crown.

--Birds. LC 84-11398. (Our Endangered Earth Ser.). (Illus.). 32p. (gr. 3-7). 1985. pap. 5.95 (ISBN 0-517-55431-3). Crown.

--Environment. LC 84-11417. (Our Endangered Earth Ser.). (Illus.). 32p. (gr. 3-7). 1985. pap. 5.95 (ISBN 0-517-55428-3). Crown.

--Land Animals. LC 84-12072. (Our Endangered Earth Ser.). 32p. (gr. 3-7). bds. 5.95 (ISBN 0-517-55430-5). Crown.

--Northrop Frye: A Vision of the New World. (New World Perspectives Ser.). 130p. (Orig.). 1985. 19.95 (ISBN 0-312-57916-0); pap. 7.95 (ISBN 0-312-57917-9). St Martin.

--Ocean Life. LC 84-12065. (Our Endangered Earth Ser.). 32p. (gr. 3-7). 1985. bds. 5.95 (ISBN 0-517-55429-1). Crown.

--Small World of Ants. LC 80-85049. (Gloucester Press Ser.). (gr. k-3). 1981. PLB 7.90 (ISBN 0-531-03452-6). Watts.

--Small World of Bees & Wasps. LC 80-85050. (Gloucester Press Ser.). (gr. k-3). 1981. PLB 7.90 (ISBN 0-531-03453-4). Watts.

--Small World of Butterflies & Moths. LC 80-85051. (Gloucester Press Ser.). (gr. k-3). 1981. PLB 7.40 (ISBN 0-531-03454-2). Watts.

--Small World of Reptiles. LC 80-85052. (Gloucester Press Ser.). (gr. k-3). 1981. PLB 7.90 (ISBN 0-531-03455-0). Watts.

--Studies on Neotropical Water Mites. (Memoirs Ser.: No. 31). (Illus.). 644p. 1980. 50.00x (ISBN 0-686-27979-4). Am Entom Inst.

--Walter. LC 84-5116. 206p. 1985. 15.95 (ISBN 0-87951-972-X). Overlook Pr.

--Water Mite Genera & Subgenera. (Memoris Ser: No. 21). (Illus.). 860p. 1974. 60.00x (ISBN 0-686-08749-6). Am Entom Inst.

--Winter Doves. 224p. 1979. 14.95 (ISBN 0-436-10673-6, Pub. by Secker & Warburg UK). David & Charles.

--Winter Doves: A Love Story. LC 84-22678. 213p. 1985. 15.95 (ISBN 0-87951-994-0). Overlook Pr.

Cook, David & Okenimkpe, Micheal. Ngugi Wa Thiong'o: An Exploration of His Writings. (Studies in African Literature). 250p. (Orig.). 1983. pap. text ed. 11.50x (ISBN 0-435-91174-0). Heinemann Ed.

Cook, David, jt. auth. see Prasad, Vikram.

Cook, David, jt. auth. see Scalisi, Philip.

Cook, David, jt. auth. see Spence, Robin.

Cook, David, ed. Origin East Africa. (African Writers Ser.). 1965. pap. text ed. 3.50x (ISBN 0-435-90015-3). Heinemann Ed.

Cook, David & Lee, Miles, eds. Short East African Plays in English. (African Writers Ser.). 1970. pap. text ed. 5.00x (ISBN 0-435-90028-5). Heinemann Ed.

Cook, David & Rubadiri, David, eds. Poems from East Africa. (African Writers Ser.). 1971. pap. text ed. 5.50x (ISBN 0-435-90096-X). Heinemann Ed.

Cook, David, ed. see Jonson, Ben.

Cook, David, ed. see Wycherley, William.

Cook, David, et al, eds. Psychosocial Issues in the Treatment of Alcoholism. LC 84-28966. (Alcoholism Treatment Quarterly: Vol. 2, No. 1). 152p. 1985. text ed. 22.95 (ISBN 0-86656-363-6); pap. text ed. 16.95 (ISBN 0-86656-401-2). Haworth Pr.

Cook, David A. A History of Narrative Film, 1889-1979. (Illus.). 1981. 24.95 (ISBN 0-393-01370-7); pap. text ed. 19.95x (ISBN 0-393-09022-1). Norton.

Cook, David A., tr. see Henrichsen, Walter A.

Cook, David A., tr. see Stott, John R.

Cook, David A., tr. see Wagner, Maurice.

Cook, David G., jt. ed. see Brinkhurst, Ralph O.

Cook, David M. The Theory of the Electromagnetic Field. (Illus.). 560p. 1975. ref. ed. 39.95 (ISBN 0-13-913293-7). P-H.

Cook, David M. & Swauger, Craig G., eds. The Small Town in American Literature. 2nd ed. 1977. pap. text ed. 12.85 scp (ISBN 0-06-041354-9, HarpC). Har-Row.

Cook, David R. Water Mites from India. (Memoirs Ser: No. 9). (Illus.). 411p. 1967. 30.00x (ISBN 0-686-17145-4). Am Entom Inst.

--The Water Mites of Liberia. (Memoirs Ser: No. 6). (Illus.). 418p. 1966. 30.00x (ISBN 0-686-17144-6). Am Entom Inst.

Cook, Davis R. Lancastrians & Yorkists: The Wars of the Roses. (Seminar Studies in History). (Illus.). 1984. pap. 6.25 (ISBN 0-317-14000-0). Longman.

Cook, Denys. Presidents of the U. S. A. LC 80-85497. 256p. 1981. 22.50 (ISBN 0-7153-8067-2). David & Charles.

Cook, Desmond L. Program Evaluation & Review Technique: Applications in Education. LC 78-57981. 1978. pap. text ed. 7.25 (ISBN 0-8191-0657-7). U Pr of Amer.

Cook, Don. Charles de Gaulle: A Biography. 432p. 1985. pap. 10.95 (ISBN 0-399-51143-1, Perigee). Putnam Pub Group.

--Charles DeGaulle: A Biography. LC 83-4637. 544p. 1984. 22.95 (ISBN 0-399-12858-1, Putnam). Putnam Pub Group.

Cook, Don L., ed. see Howells, William D.

Cook, Donald, jt. ed. see Schimmelpfeng, Richard H.

Cook, Donald C., et al. Future of American Enterprise. (Michigan Business Papers: No. 46). 1967. pap. 1.50 (ISBN 0-87712-095-1). U Mich Busn Div Res.

Cook, Donald L., ed. see Tyler, Royall.

Cook, Doris E. Sherlock Holmes & Much More. (Illus.). 112p. 1970. pap. 3.50x (ISBN 0-940748-42-8). Conn Hist Soc.

Cook, Dorothy E. & Monro, Isabel S., eds. Short Story Index: Basic Volume, 1900-1949. Incl. Supplement 1950-1954. Cook, Dorothy E. & Fidell, Estelle A., eds. 394p. 1956. 18.00 (ISBN 0-686-66648-8); Supplement 1955-1958. Fidell, Estelle A. & Flory, Esther V., eds. 341p. 1960. 18.00 (ISBN 0-686-66649-6); Supplement 1959-1963. Fidell, Estelle A., ed. 487p. 1965. 22.00 (ISBN 0-686-66650-X); Supplement 1964-1968. Fidell, Estelle A., ed. 599p. 1969. 28.00 (ISBN 0-686-66651-8); Supplement 1969-1973. Fidell, Estelle A., ed. 1974. 40.00 (ISBN 0-686-66652-6); Supplement 1974. Bogart, Gary L. & Fidell, Estelle A., eds. 1975; 1976; 1977; Supplement, 1974-1978. Bogart, Gary L., ed. 70.00 (ISBN 0-686-66656-9). 1553p. 1953. 27.00 (ISBN 0-8242-0384-4). Wilson.

Cook, Dorothy L. Love: Lost & Found. 1984. 5.95 (ISBN 0-533-05901-1). Vantage.

Cook, Douglas. The Military History of Canada. 1985. lib. bdg. 45.00 (ISBN 0-8240-8964-2). Garland Pub.

Cook, Dutton. A Book of the Play: Studies & Illustrations of Histrionic Story, Life, & Character, 2 vols. LC 72-13278. (Essay Index Reprint Ser.). Repr. of 1876 ed. 38.00 (ISBN 0-8369-8152-9). Ayer Co Pubs.

--A Book of the Play: Studies & Illustrations of Historic Story, Life & Character. 1975. Repr. of 1882 ed. 25.00 (ISBN 0-8274-4113-4). R West.

Cook, E. A. Scottish Rite Masonry, 2 vols. Set. 18.00x (ISBN 0-685-22097-4). Wehman.

Cook, E. H. Knight Templarism. 9.50 (ISBN 0-685-19481-7). Powner.

Cook, E. T. The Century Book of Gardening. 610p. 1980. Repr. lib. bdg. 100.00 (ISBN 0-8495-0793-6). Arden Lib.

--Homes & Haunts of John Ruskin. 1973. Repr. of 1912 ed. 35.00 (ISBN 0-8274-1758-6). R West.

--The Life of John Ruskin, 2 vols. (Illus.). 1979. Repr. of 1912 ed. lib. bdg. 100.00 set (ISBN 0-8495-0918-1). Arden Lib.

Cook, Earl. Energy: The Ultimate Resource? Natoli, Salvatore J., ed. LC 77-87402. (Resource Papers for College Geography). (Illus.). 1978. pap. 4.00 (ISBN 0-89291-127-1). Assn Am Geographers.

--Man, Energy, Society. LC 75-33774. (Illus.). 478p. 1976. text ed. 25.95 (ISBN 0-7167-0725-X); pap. text ed. 13.95 (ISBN 0-7167-0724-1). W H Freeman.

Cook, Earl F., ed. Tufflavas & Ignimbrites. 1966. 23.95 (ISBN 0-444-00008-9, North Holland). Elsevier.

Cook, Earleen H. Desertification & Deforestation: A Selected Bibliography of English Language Sources. (Public Administration Ser.: Bibliography P 1641). 1985. pap. 3.75 (ISBN 0-89028-331-1). Vance Biblios.

--The Insance or Mentally ImpairedDefendant: A Selected Bibliography from the Professional Literature. (Public Administration Ser.: Bibliography P1125). 57p. 1983. pap. 8.25 (ISBN 0-88066-355-3). Vance Biblios.

--The Peace & Nuclear Freeze Movements. (Public Administration Ser.: P-1470). 50p. 1984. pap. 7.50 (ISBN 0-89028-010-X). Vance Biblios.

Cook, Earleen H., jt. auth. see Cook, Joseph L.

Cook, Edward. Literary Recreations: Arnold, Browning, Byron, Coleridge, Dickens, FitzGerald, Hardy, Johnson, Ruskin, Tennyson, Swinburne, Thackeray, Wordsworth. 1918. Repr. 15.50 (ISBN 0-8274-2959-2). R West.

--More Literary Recreations. 1973. Repr. of 1919 ed. 23.50 (ISBN 0-8274-1660-1). R West.

Cook, Edward M., Jr. The Fathers of the Towns: Leadership & Community Structure in Eighteenth Century New England. LC 75-36937. (Studies in Historical & Political Sciences: Ninety-Fourth Series NO.2 (1976)). (Illus.). 296p. 1976. o. p. 25.00x (ISBN 0-8018-1741-2); pap. 9.95 (ISBN 0-8018-2149-5). Johns Hopkins.

Cook, Edward T. Life of John Ruskin, 2 vols. LC 68-24903. (English Biography Ser., No. 31). 1969. Repr. lib. bdg. 79.95x (ISBN 0-8383-0155-X). Haskell.

--Literary Recreations. facs. ed. LC 68-54340. (Essay Index Reprint Ser). 1918. 18.00 (ISBN 0-8369-0331-5). Ayer Co Pubs.

--More Literary Recreations. facsimile ed. LC 76-105005. (Essay Index Reprint Ser.). 1919. 26.50 (ISBN 0-8369-1457-0). Ayer Co Pubs.

--Studies in Ruskin: Some Aspects of the Work & Teaching of John Ruskin. 1978. Repr. of 1890 ed. lib. bdg. 25.00 (ISBN 0-8495-0728-6). Arden Lib.

Cook, Eleanor, et al, eds. Centre & Labyrinth: Essays in Honour of Northrop Frye. 360p. 1982. 30.00x (ISBN 0-8020-2496-3). U of Toronto Pr.

Cook, Elisabeth E., jt. auth. see Cook, John S.

Cook, Elizabeth. The Ordinary & the Fabulous. 2nd ed. LC 75-7213. 204p. 1976. pap. 11.95 (ISBN 0-521-09961-7). Cambridge U Pr.

--Visual Play: A Green Dance in Three Acts. (Illus.). 30p. 1983. metalring bd. 10.00 (ISBN 0-915066-55-6). Assembling Pr.

Cook, Elizabeth, jt. ed. see Dow, Michael.

Cook, Ellen P. see Piel Cook, Ellen.

Cook, Emilie C. Winnie the Witch & the Frightened Ghost. Gilleo, Alma, ed. LC 74-734865. (Holiday Tales). (Illus., Books & cassettes sold as 10 book set only). (ps). 1977. 22.00 (ISBN 0-89290-012-1). Soc for Visual.

Cook, Emilie C., jt. auth. see Quinn, Daniel.

Cook, Eugene A., ed. see Texas Attorneys or Professors of Law.

Cook, Eung-Do & Gerdts, Donna B. Syntax & Semantics: Vol. 16: The Syntax of Native American Languages. LC 83-17265. (Serial Publication). 1984. 59.00 (ISBN 0-12-613516-9). Acad Pr.

Cook, F. C., ed. The Bible Commentary, 10 vols. 6803p. 1981. Repr. 195.00 (ISBN 0-8010-2431-5). Baker Bk.

Cook, Francis D. How to Raise an Ox. LC 78-12025. (Orig.). 1978. pap. 7.95x (ISBN 0-916820-07-6). Center Pubns.

Cook, Francis H. Hua-Yen Buddhism: The Jewel Net of Indra. LC 76-43288. (Institute for Advanced Study of World Religions Ser.). 1977. 19.95x (ISBN 0-271-01245-5). Pa St U Pr.

--The Territory of Washington in 1879. Oliphant, J. Orin, ed. 39p. 1972. Repr. of 1925 ed. pap. 3.00 (ISBN 0-87770-085-0). Ye Galleon.

Cook, Francis R. Introduction to Canadian Amphibians & Reptiles. (National Museum of Science Ser.). 200p. 1984. pap. text ed. 12.95x (ISBN 0-317-03314-X, 56396-0, Pub. by Natl Mus Canada). U of Chicago Pr.

Cook, Frank & Cook, Andrea. The Casualty Roll For the Crimes 1854-1855. 269p. 1981. 90.00 (ISBN 0-686-98448-X, Pub. by Picton England). State Mutual Bk.

Cook, Frank X., jt. auth. see Maxim, L. Daniel.

Cook, Fred B., Jr. Cyprus & Beyond. LC 84-90790. (Orig.). 1984. pap. write for info. (ISBN 0-9614001-0-2, 24A). Cook MO.

Cook, Fred J. The Crimes of Watergate. LC 81-10497. (Illus.). 192p. (gr. 9 up). 1981. lib. bdg. 9.90 (ISBN 0-531-04353-3). Watts.

--Maverick: Fifty Years of Investigative Reporting. LC 84-4813. 320p. 1984. 18.95 (ISBN 0-399-12993-6, Putnam). Putnam Pub Group.

--A Two-Dollar Bet Means Murder. LC 72-854. 248p. 1972. Repr. of 1961 ed. lib. bdg. 15.00x (ISBN 0-8371-5927-X, COTD). Greenwood.

Cook, Frederick, jt. auth. see Sullivan, John.

Cook, Frederick A. Through the First Antarctic Night, Eighteen Ninety-Eight to Eighteen Ninety-Nine. (Illus.). 478p. 1980. 49.00x (ISBN 0-7735-0514-8). McGill-Queens U Pr.

Cook, G. C. & Phipps, Lloyd J. Six Hundred More Things to Make for the Farm & Home. (Illus.). (gr. 9-12). 1952. 19.35 (ISBN 0-8134-0198-4); text ed. 14.50x. Interstate.

Cook, G. D., & Co. Illustrated Catalogue of Carriages & Special Business Advertiser. 1970. pap. 7.50 (ISBN 0-486-22364-7). Dover.

Cook, Gail C., ed. Opportunity for Choice: A Goal for Women in Canada. (Illus.). 217p. 1977. pap. 6.95 (ISBN 0-685-76673-X, SSC67, SSC). Unipub.

Cook, Gail C. A., ed. Opportunity for Choice: A Goal for Women in Canada. (Illus.). 217p. (Eng. & Fr.). 1976. 4.50 (ISBN 0-88806-016-5). Inst C D Howe.

Cook, Gary D., ed. see Hardenbrook, Harry.

Cook, Geoffrey, tr. Basket of Chestnuts: From the Miscellanea of Venantius Fortunatus. LC 79-17109. 80p. 1981. 15.00x (ISBN 0-916156-38-9); pap. 5.00x (ISBN 0-916156-40-0). Cherry Valley.

Cook, George A. John Wise, Early American Democrat. 1967. lib. bdg. 18.50x (ISBN 0-374-91919-4). Octagon.

Cook, Gillian. Spatial Dynamics of Business Growth in the Witwatersrand. LC 73-92654. (Research Papers Ser.: No. 157). (Illus.). 143p. 1975. pap. 10.00 (ISBN 0-89065-064-0). U Chicago Dept Geog.

Cook, Glen. All Darkness Met: Dread Empire No. 3. 336p. 1984. pap. 2.50 (ISBN 0-425-06541-3). Berkley Pub.

--The Black Company. 320p. (Orig.). 1984. pap. 2.95 (ISBN 0-8125-3370-4). Tor Bks.

--Darkwar Trilogy: Warlock, No. 2. (Orig.). 1985. pap. 2.95 (ISBN 0-445-20049-9, Pub. by Popular Lib). Warner Bks.

--Doomstalker. 1985. pap. 2.95 (Pub. by Popular Lib). Warner Bks.

--The Fire in His Hands. (Orig.). 1984. pap. 2.95 (ISBN 0-671-45907-4, Timescape). PB.

--A Matter of Time. 272p. 1985. pap. 2.95 (ISBN 0-441-52213-0, Pub. by Ace Science Fiction). Ace Bks.

--October's Baby. (Orig.). 1984. pap. 2.50 (ISBN 0-425-06538-3). Berkley Pub.
--October's Baby. (Dread Empire Ser.: No. 2). 256p. 1984. pap. 2.50 (ISBN 0-425-06538-3). Berkley Pub.
--Passage at Arms. 272p. (Orig.). 1985. pap. 2.95 (ISBN 0-445-20006-5, Pub. by Popular Lib). Warner Bks.
--A Shadow of All Night Falling. 256p. 1983. pap. 2.50 (ISBN 0-425-06320-8). Berkley Pub.
--Shadows Linger. 320p. (Orig.). 1984. pap. 2.95 (ISBN 0-8125-3372-0). Tor Bks.
--Stars' End. 352p. (Orig.). 1982. pap. 2.95 (ISBN 0-446-30156-6). Warner Bks.
--The Swordbearer. (Orig.). 1982. pap. 2.75 (ISBN 0-671-83687-0, Timescape). PB.
--The White Rose. (The Black Company Trilogy Ser.: Vol. 3). 320p. 1985. pap. 2.95 (ISBN 0-8125-3374-7). Tor Bks.
Cook, Glenn C. Five Hundred More Things to Make for Farm & Home. (Illus.). 471p. (gr. 9-12). 1944. 19.35 (ISBN 0-8134-0038-4); text ed. 14.50x. Interstate.
Cook, Graeme. Commandos in Action. LC 73-13016. (Illus.). 176p. 1974. 6.95 (ISBN 0-8008-1749-4). Taplinger.
Cook, Guillermo. The Expectation of the Poor: Latin American Base Ecclesial Communities in Protestant Perspective. LC 85-5131. 256p. (Orig.). 1985. pap. 13.95 (ISBN 0-88344-209-4). Orbis Bks.
Cook, Hal. Arranging: The Basics of Contemporary Floral Design. LC 84-61862. 174p. 1985. 19.95 (ISBN 0-688-02572-2, Pub. by Quarto Bks). Morrow.
Cook, Harold E. Shaker Music: A Manifestation of American Folk Culture. LC 71-161507. 312p. 1973. 25.00 (ISBN 0-8387-7953-0). Bucknell U Pr.
Cook, Harold J. Tales of the 04 Ranch: Recollections of Harold J. Cook, 1887-1909. LC 68-25320. (Illus.). xviii, 221p. 1968. 17.95x (ISBN 0-8032-0027-7). U of Nebr Pr.
Cook, Harriet N. Bible Alphabet of Animals. rev. ed. (Illus.). pap. 3.50 (ISBN 0-686-15488-6). Rod & Staff.
Cook, Howard. Swifter Than Eagles: The Battle of Athens-1946. LC 80-69421. (Illus.). 354p. 1981. 15.00x (ISBN 0-938212-00-1). Friendly City.
Cook, Hugh, ed. Cracked Wheat & Other Stories. LC 84-18878. 127p. (Orig.). 1984. 12.95 (ISBN 0-931940-09-5); pap. 6.95 (ISBN 0-931940-08-7). Middleburg Pr.
Cook, Hulet H. Paul Hervieu & French Classicism. LC 45-37189. (Indiana University Humanities Ser.: No. 14). pap. 20.00 (ISBN 0-317-09054-2, 2055223). Bks Demand UMI.
Cook, Iva D. Occupational Notebook Program. 48p. (Orig.). (gr. 7-12). 1977. pap. text ed. 2.25 (ISBN 0-86703-000-3); 5.50 (ISBN 0-86703-001-1). Opportunities Learn.
Cook, J. Award-Winning Passive Solar Designs: Professional Edition. 288p. 1983. 39.95 (ISBN 0-07-012478-7). McGraw.
Cook, J. & Carruthers, W. Progress in Organic Chemistry, Vol. 7. 176p. 1968. 32.50x (ISBN 0-306-30637-9, Plenum Pr). Plenum Pub.
Cook, J. E. & Earlley, Elsie C. Remediating Reading Disabilities: Simple Things That Work. LC 79-20412. 266p. 1979. text ed. 32.00 (ISBN 0-89443-154-4). Aspen Systems.
Cook, J. Gordon. ABC of Plant Terms. 293p. 1968. 39.00x (ISBN 0-900541-56-3, Pub. by Meadowfield Pr England). State Mutual Bk.
--Handbook of Polyolefin Fibers. 608p. 1967. 90.00x (ISBN 0-900541-50-4, Pub. by Meadowfield Pr England). State Mutual Bk.
--Handbook of Textile Fibers. 1160p. 1968. 125.00x (ISBN 0-900541-00-8, Pub. by Meadowfield Pr England). State Mutual Bk.
--Science for Everyman Encylopedia. 643p. 1964. 40.00x (ISBN 0-900541-51-2, Pub. by Meadowfield Pr England). State Mutual Bk.
--Your Guide to Plant Growth. 184p. 1967. 39.00x (ISBN 0-900541-54-7, Pub. by Meadowfield Pr England). State Mutual Bk.
--Your Guide to Plastics. 320p. 1968. 40.00x (ISBN 0-900541-52-0, Pub. by Meadowfield Pr England). State Mutual Bk.
--Your Guide to the Plant Kingdom. 304p. 40.00x (ISBN 0-900541-55-5, Pub. by Meadowfield Pr England). State Mutual Bk.
--Your Guide to the Soil. 480p. 1965. 40.00x (ISBN 0-900541-53-9, Pub. by Meadowfield Pr England). State Mutual Bk.
Cook, J. Keith. The First Parish: A Pastor's Survival Manual. LC 83-6940. 154p. (Orig.). 1983. pap. 8.95 (ISBN 0-664-24442-4). Westminster.
Cook, J. Lennox. Six Great Travellers. (gr. 4-8). 1960. 7.00 (ISBN 0-8023-9031-5). Dufour.
Cook, Jacqueline. The River Between. Severance, Anne, ed. 1985. pap. 2.50 (ISBN 0-317-18753-8, Serenade-Saga). Zondervan.
Cook, James. Bibliography of the Writings of Charles Dickens. 59.95 (ISBN 0-87968-744-4). Gordon Pr.
--Explorations of Captain James Cook in the Pacific, as Told by Selections of His Own Journals, 1768-1779. Price, A. Grenfell, ed. (Illus.). 292p. pap. 6.00 (ISBN 0-486-22766-9). Dover.
--The Explorations of Captain James Cook in the Pacific as Told by Selections of His Own Journals 1768-1779. Price, A. Grenfell, ed. (Illus.). 14.00 (ISBN 0-8446-4531-1). Peter Smith.
--Remedies & Rackets: The Truth About Patent Medicines Today. LC 75-39284. (Getting & Spending: the Consumer's Dilemma). 1976. Repr. of 1958 ed. 20.00x (ISBN 0-405-08059-X). Ayer Co Pubs.
--The Start-Up Entrepreneur: How You Can Succeed at Building Your Own Company or Enterprise Starting from Scratch. 320p. 1986. 18.50 (ISBN 0-525-24372-0, 01796-540). Dutton.
--Voyages of Discovery. Barrow, John, ed. 1976. 10.95x (ISBN 0-460-00099-3, Evman). Biblio Dist.
Cook, James, et al. James Cook's Journal of HMS Endeavor, 1768-71. ltd. ed. (Illus.). 600p. 1977. hand bound leather 460.00 (ISBN 0-904351-02-5). Genesis Pubns.
--James Cook's Journal of HMS Resolution, 1772-75. (Illus.). 900p. 1981. 460.00 (ISBN 0-904351-06-8). Genesis Pubns.
Cook, James D. Iron. (Methods in Hematology Ser.: Vol. 1). (Illus.). 224p. 1980. 34.00 (ISBN 0-443-08118-2). Churchill.
Cook, James E. Arizona One Hundred One: An Irreverent Short Course for New Arrivals. rev. ed. (Illus.). 80p. 1981. pap. 3.25 (ISBN 0-9606366-0-9). Cocinero Pr.
Cook, James E., jt. ed. see Ketner, Kenneth L.
Cook, James E. see Ketner, Kenneth L.
Cook, James F. Governors of Georgia. LC 77-71397. (Illus.). 320p. 1979. 12.95 (ISBN 0-686-83449-6). Strode.
Cook, James H. Fifty Years on the Old Frontier As Cowboy, Hunter, Guide, Scout, & Ranchman. LC 57-5951. 310p. 1957. 18.95 (ISBN 0-8061-0364-7). U of Okla Pr.
--Fifty Years on the Old Frontier As Cowboy, Hunter, Guide, Scout, & Ranchman. LC 57-5951. (Illus.). 310p. 1981. pap. 9.95 (ISBN 0-8061-1761-3). U of Okla Pr.
--Longhorn Cowboy. Driggs, Howard R., ed. LC 84-7283. (The Western Frontier Library: Vol. 55). (Illus.). 256p. 1984. Repr. of 1942 ed. 14.95 (ISBN 0-8061-1877-6). U of Okla Pr.
Cook, James I. Edgar Johnson Goodspeed: Articulate Scholar. Richards, Kent, ed. LC 80-21070. (Biblical Scholarship in North America). 1981. pap. 15.00 (ISBN 0-686-86729-7, 061104); pap. write for info. (ISBN 0-89130-439-8). Scholars Pr GA.
Cook, James I., ed. Saved by Hope: Essays in Honor of Richard C. Oudersluys. LC 78-5416. Repr. of 1978 ed. 49.50 (ISBN 0-8357-9132-7, 2016060). Bks Demand UMI.
Cook, James R. & Baker, Kenneth F. Nature & Practice of Biological Control of Plant Pathogens. LC 83-71224. (Illus.). 539p. 1983. text ed. 43.00 (ISBN 0-89054-053-5). Am Phytopathol Soc.
Cook, Jan L. The Mysterious Undersea World. LC 79-1791. (Series One). (Illus.). 104p. (gr. 3-8). 1980. 6.95 (ISBN 0-87044-317-8); PLB 8.50 (ISBN 0-87044-322-4). Natl Geog.
Cook, Jane, ed. Innovations in Activities for the Elderly. LC 84-28996. (Activities, Adaptations & Aging Ser.: Vol. 6, No. 3). 136p. 1985. text ed. 19.95 (ISBN 0-86656-389-X). Haworth Pr.
Cook, Janice E., ed. see Lynch, Laura B.
Cook, Jeffrey. Award-Winning Passive Solar House Designs. Stetson, Fred, ed. (Illus.). 176p. 1983. pap. 14.95 (ISBN 0-88266-313-5). Garden Way Pub.
Cook, Jeffrey & Prowler, Donald, eds. Passive Systems Seventy-Eight: A Selection of the Leading Passive Solar Papers of the Year Presented at National Solar Conferences in Philadelphia & Denver. 1978. pap. text ed. 27.00x (ISBN 0-89553-016-3). Am Solar Energy.
Cook, Jennifer & Wolf, Michael D. Body Type Beautiful. (Illus.). 160p. (Orig.). 1984. pap. 9.95 (ISBN 0-8092-5411-5). Contemp Bks.
Cook, Jerry & Baldwin, Stanley C. Love, Acceptance & Forgiveness. LC 79-63763. 128p. 1979. pap. 4.95 (ISBN 0-8307-0654-2, 5411106). Regal.
Cook, Jerry & Cook, Barbara. Choosing to Love. LC 81-84566. 144p. (Orig.). 1983. pap. 4.95 (ISBN 0-8307-0897-9). Regal.
Cook, Jerry O., jt. auth. see Clapp, Steve.
Cook, Jerry O., ed. see Taylor, Blaine, et al.
Cook, Jim. Arizona Landmarks. Holden, John W., ed. (Illus.). 160p. (Orig.). 1985. 35.00 (ISBN 0-916179-04-4). Ariz Hwy.
Cook, Jim & Lewington, Mike, eds. Images of Alcoholism. (British Film Institute Bks.). (Illus.). 82p. 1979. pap. 5.95 (ISBN 0-85170-091-8). U of Ill Pr.
Cook, Joel. Switzerland: Picturesque & Descriptive. 1977. lib. bdg. 59.95 (ISBN 0-8490-2721-7). Gordon Pr.
Cook, John, ed. School Librarianship. (Illus.). 272p. 1981. 28.00 (ISBN 0-08-024814-4); pap. 17.50 (ISBN 0-08-024813-6). Pergamon.
Cook, John, et al, eds. The Experience of Work: A Compendium & Review of Measures & their Use. (Organizational & Occupational Psychology Ser.). 1981. 44.00 (ISBN 0-12-187050-2). Acad Pr.
Cook, John A. Neo-Classic Drama in Spain. Archival ed. LC 74-5771. 576p. 1974. Repr. of 1959 ed. lib. bdg. 75.00x (ISBN 0-8371-7518-6, CONC). Greenwood.
--Pursuing the Whale: A Quarter Century of Whaling in the Arctic. 1977. lib. bdg. 59.95 (ISBN 0-8490-2493-5). Gordon Pr.
Cook, John A., jt. auth. see Wool, Robert.
Cook, John B. Gems of Mental Magic. Date not set. 5.00 (ISBN 0-87505-222-3). Borden.
Cook, John B., jt. auth. see Buckley, Arthur H.
Cook, John E. What You Should Know about Data Processing. LC 69-19799. (Business Almanac Ser.: No. 15). 90p. 1969. text ed. 5.95 (ISBN 0-379-11215-9). Oceana.
Cook, John E., jt. auth. see Burns, John H.
Cook, John H. A Study of the Mill Schools of North Carolina. LC 73-176668. (Columbia University. Teachers College. Contributions to Education: No. 178). Repr. of 1925 ed. 22.50 (ISBN 0-404-55178-5). AMS Pr.
Cook, John L., et al. A New Way to Proficiency in English. 2nd ed. 320p. 1980. pap. 9.95x (ISBN 0-631-12652-X). Basil Blackwell.
Cook, John M. The Persian Empire. LC 82-10382. (Illus.). 275p. 1983. 30.00 (ISBN 0-8052-3846-8). Schocken.
--The Sanctuary of Hemithea at Kastabos. Plommer, W. H., ed. LC 66-10449. pap. 55.50 (ISBN 0-317-11302-X, 2051471). Bks Demand UMI.
Cook, John P. Composite Construction Methods. LC 76-26020. (Practical Construction Guides Ser.). 330p. 1977. 51.50 (ISBN 0-471-16905-6, Pub by Wiley-Interscience). Wiley.
--Composite Construction Methods. LC 84-5770. 346p. 1985. Repr. of 1977 ed. lib. bdg. 47.95 (ISBN 0-89874-760-0). Krieger.
Cook, John Philip, jt. auth. see Panek, Julian R.
Cook, John S. & Cook, Elisabeth E. The Financing of Hospital Capital. 23p. 1984. pap. text ed. 4.00 (ISBN 0-930228-25-1). Healthcare Fin Mgmt Assn.
Cook, John S., ed. Biogenesis & Turnover of Membrane Macromolecules. LC 75-25111. (Society of General Physiologists Ser.: Vol. 31). 304p. 1976. 40.00 (ISBN 0-89004-092-3). Raven.
Cook, John W. & Winkle, Gary M. Auditing. 3rd ed. LC 83-81026. 656p. 1983. text ed. 31.95 (ISBN 0-395-34318-6); instr's manual 3.50 (ISBN 0-395-34319-4). HM.
Cook, Joseph G. Constitutional Rights of the Accused: Post-Trial. new ed. LC 75-160369. (Criminal Law Library). 1976. 66.50 (ISBN 0-686-20646-0); Suppl. 1984. 20.50; Suppl. 1983. 18.50. Lawyers Co-Op.
--Constitutional Rights of the Accused: Trial Rights. LC 75-160369. (Criminal Law Library). 1974. 66.50 (ISBN 0-686-14499-6); Suppl. 1984. 21.50; Suppl. 1983. 19.50. Lawyers Co-Op.
--Constitutional Rights of the Accused: Pretrial Rights. LC 75-160369. 1972. 66.50 (ISBN 0-686-14498-8); Suppl. 1984. 21.50; Suppl. 1983. 19.50. Lawyers Co-Op.
Cook, Joseph G. & Marcus, Paul. Criminal Law. LC 82-73299. (Analysis & Skills Ser.). Date not set. price not set. Bender.
Cook, Joseph G. & Sobieski, John L. Civil Rights Actions. LC 83-70748. Date not set. price not set, loose leaf. Bender.
--Civil Rights Actions, 4 vols. 1983. Updates avail. looseleaf 320.00 (ISBN 0-317-09752-0, 199); looseleaf 1984 125.00. Bender.
Cook, Joseph L. & Cook, Earleen H. Employment-at-Will. (Public Administration Ser.: Bibliography P 1630). 1985. pap. 3.75 (ISBN 0-89028-300-1). Vance Biblios.
--Industrial Spying & Espionage. (Public Administration Ser.: P-1707). 49p. 1985. pap. 7.50 (ISBN 0-89028-457-1). Vance Biblios.
Cook, Joyce L., jt. auth. see Bull, T. R.
Cook, Judith. Apprentices of Freedom. 7.95 (ISBN 0-7043-3368-6, Pub. by Quartet England). Charles River Bks.
--Close to the Earth: Living the Social History of the British Isles. (Illus.). 160p. 1984. 19.95 (ISBN 0-7100-9634-8). Routledge & Kegan.
Cook, K. M., tr. see Anikin, Andrei V.
Cook, Karen S., jt. ed. see Messick, David M.
Cook, Kathleen, tr. see Pogorelsky, A.
Cook, Keningale. The Fathers of Jesus: A Study of the Lineage of the Christian Doctrine & Tradition, 2 vols. 1977. lib. bdg. 250.00 (ISBN 0-8490-1807-2). Gordon Pr.
Cook, Kenneth. Play Little Victims. LC 79-303356. 1978. text ed. 8.25 (ISBN 0-08-023123-3). Pergamon.
Cook, L., jt. ed. see Gordy, W.
Cook, L. H., ed. The Minerals Sector & the Australian Economy. Porter, M. G. 352p. 1984. pap. text ed. 20.00x (ISBN 0-86861-410-6). Allen Unwin.
Cook, L. M. Coefficients of Natural Selection. 1971. text ed. 8.25x (ISBN 0-09-104190-2, Hutchinson U Lib). Humanities.
--Population Genetics: Outline Studies in Biology. 1976. pap. 6.95 (ISBN 0-412-13930-8, NO. 6064, Pub. by Chapman & Hall). Methuen Inc.
Cook, L. M., ed. Case Studies in Population Biology. LC 84-19451. 1985. text ed. 35.00 (ISBN 0-7190-1740-8, Pub. by Manchester Univ Pr). Longwood Pub Group.
Cook, L. M., jt. ed. see Bishop, J. A.
Cook, Laurel, jt. auth. see Cooper, Patricia.
Cook, Lawrence S., ed. Lighting in America: From Colonial Rushlights to Victorian Chandeliers. rev. ed. LC 84-897. (Illus.). 176p. 1984. pap. 10.95 (ISBN 0-915590-40-9). Main Street.
Cook, LeRoy. One Hundred & One Things to Do with Your Private License. (Illus.). 224p. (Orig.). 1985. pap. 12.95 (ISBN 0-8306-2359-0, 2359). TAB Bks.
Cook, Lewis C., ed. see Pollard, Stewart M.
Cook, Lloyd A., ed. Toward Better Human Relations. facsimile ed. LC 70-90626. (Essay Index Reprint Ser). 1952. 17.00 (ISBN 0-8369-1284-5). Ayer Co Pubs.
Cook, Louis. Beautiful Michigan. 2nd ed. LC 78-105527. (Illus.). 80p. 1985. 16.95 (ISBN 0-89802-438-2); pap. 9.95 (ISBN 0-89802-437-4). Beautiful Am.
Cook, Lurana H., et al. Provincetown Massachusetts Cemetery Inscriptions. 255p. 1980. 25.00 (ISBN 0-917890-18-3). Heritage Bk.
Cook, Lyndon W. & Cannon, Donald Q. A New Light Breaks Forth. pap. 7.95 (ISBN 0-89036-148-7). Hawkes Pub Inc.
Cook, Lyndon W. & Cannon, Donald W. Exodus & Beyond. (Essays in Mormon History Ser.). 264p. 1980. pap. 7.95 (ISBN 0-89036-151-7). Hawkes Pub Inc.
Cook, Lyndon W., jt. ed. see Cannon, Donald Q.
Cook, M. Early Muslim Dogma. 256p. 1981. 54.50 (ISBN 0-521-23379-8). Cambridge U Pr.
Cook, M., jt. auth. see Argyle, M.
Cook, M., jt. auth. see Crone, Patricia.
Cook, M. A., ed. The History of the Ottoman Empire to Seventeen Thirty. LC 75-38188. (Illus.). 232p. 1976. 44.50 (ISBN 0-521-20891-2); pap. 14.95 (ISBN 0-521-09991-9). Cambridge U Pr.
--Studies in the Economic History of the Middle East: From the Rise of Islam to the Present Day. 1970. 29.95x (ISBN 0-19-713561-7). Oxford U Pr.
Cook, Malcolm. Soccer Coaching & Team Management. (Illus.). 160p. (Orig.). 1983. pap. 7.95 (ISBN 0-7158-0795-1, Pub. by EP Publishing England). Sterling.
--Soccer Coaching & Team Management. 160p. 1982. cased 40.00x (ISBN 0-7158-0833-8, Pub. by EP Pub England); pap. 30.00x (ISBN 0-7158-0795-1, Pub. by EP Pub England). State Mutual Bk.
Cook, Malcolm, jt. auth. see Whitehead, Nick.
Cook, Margaret. Bibliography of Fund-Raising Cook Books: America's Charitable Cooks (1861-1915) 25.00x (ISBN 0-686-52884-0). Corner.
Cook, Margaret, tr. see Piaget, Jean.
Cook, Margaret G. New Library Key. 3rd ed. LC 75-11754. (Illus.). 264p. 1975. pap. 8.00 (ISBN 0-8242-0541-3). Wilson.
Cook, Margaret J. The Anatomy of the Laboratory Mouse. 1976. 34.00 (ISBN 0-12-186956-3). Acad Pr.
Cook, Marjorie. To Walk on Two Feet. LC 77-17369. 96p. 1978. 8.95 (ISBN 0-664-32628-5). Westminster.
Cook, Mark. Levels of Personality. LC 88-47779. 208p. 1984. pap. 16.95 (ISBN 0-03-071999-2). Praeger.
--Perceiving Others: The Psychology of Interpersonal Perception. 180p. 1979. pap. 9.95x (ISBN 0-416-71560-5, 2838). Methuen Inc.
Cook, Mark & McHenry, R. Sexual Attraction. 1978. pap. text ed. 8.25 (ISBN 0-08-022230-7). Pergamon.
Cook, Mark, ed. The Bases of Human Sexual Attraction. LC 81-66378. 1981. 36.00 (ISBN 0-12-187220-3). Acad Pr.
--Issues in Personal Perception. (Psychology in Progress Ser.). 280p. 1984. 33.00 (ISBN 0-416-32450-9, NO. 4173); pap. 12.95 (ISBN 0-416-32460-6, NO. 4170). Methuen Inc.
Cook, Mark & Howells, Kevin, eds. Adult Sexual Interest in Children. LC 80-41318. (Personality & Psychopathology Ser.). 1981. 44.00 (ISBN 0-12-187250-5). Acad Pr.
Cook, Mark & Wilson, Glenn, eds. Love & Attraction: An International Conference. LC 78-40286. 1979. text ed. 85.00 (ISBN 0-08-022234-X). Pergamon.
Cook, Mary F. Human Resource Director's Handbook. LC 83-17810. 320p. 1984. 59.95x (ISBN 0-13-445859-1, Busn). P-H.
--Personnel Manager's Portfolio of Model Letters. LC 84-15065. 198p. 1984. 60.00 (ISBN 0-13-659251-1, Busn). P-H.
Cook, Mary J. Trouble Spots of English Grammar: A Text-Workbook for ESL, 2 Vols. 290p. 1983. Vol. 1. pap. text ed. 11.95 (ISBN 0-15-592370-6, HC); Vol. 2. pap. text ed. 11.95 (ISBN 0-15-592371-4); answer key avail. (ISBN 0-15-592372-2). HarbraceJ.
Cook, Melva. Cassie's Busy Day. LC 82-72989. (ps). 1984. 5.95 (ISBN 0-8054-4162-X, 4241-62). Broadman.
Cook, Melva, jt. auth. see Brown, Richard.
Cook, Melva, jt. auth. see Hinkle, Joseph.
Cook, Melvin A. The Science of High Explosives. LC 58-10260. (A C S Ser: No. 139). 456p. 1970. Repr. of 1958 ed. 37.50 (ISBN 0-88275-010-0). Krieger.
Cook, Mercer. The Haitian Novel. 59.95 (ISBN 0-8490-0275-3). Gordon Pr.

Cook, Mercer & Henderson, Stephen E. Militant Black Writer in Africa & the United States. LC 69-17324. 150p. 1969. pap. 8.95x (ISBN 0-299-05394-6). U of Wis Pr.

Cook, Mercer, ed. & tr. see Diop, Cheikh A.

Cook, Michael. Archives & the Computer. LC 80-41286. 152p. 1981. text ed. 49.95 (ISBN 0-408-10734-0). Butterworth.

--Muhammad. (Past Masters Ser.). (Illus.). 1983. 12.95 (ISBN 0-19-287606-6); pap. 3.95 (ISBN 0-19-287606-6). Oxford U Pr.

--The Triumph Spitfire. (Illus.). 144p. 1982. pap. 6.95 (ISBN 0-8306-2079-6, 2079). TAB Bks.

Cook, Michael L. Dime Novel Roundup: Annotated Index 1931-1981. LC 82-73847. 1983. 12.95 (ISBN 0-87972-227-4); pap. 6.95 (ISBN 0-87972-228-2). Bowling Green Univ.

--The Jesus of Faith: A Study in Christology. LC 80-84510. 192p. (Orig.). pap. 6.95 (ISBN 0-8091-2349-5). Paulist Pr.

--Murder by Mail: Inside the Mystery Book Clubs. LC 83-82013. 1983. 15.95 (ISBN 0-87972-264-9). Bowling Green Univ.

--Mystery, Detective, & Espionage Magazines. LC 82-20977. (Historical Guides to the World's Periodicals & Newspapers). xxiv, 793p. 1983. lib. bdg. 65.00 (ISBN 0-313-23310-1, CMD/). Greenwood.

--Mystery Fanfare: A Composite Annotated Index to Mystery & Related Fanzines 1963-1981. LC 82-73848. 1983. 21.95 (ISBN 0-87972-229-0); pap. 12.95 (ISBN 0-87972-230-4). Bowling Green Univ.

Cook, Michael L., jt. auth. see Miller, Harvey R.

Cook, Michael L., ed. Monthly Murders: A Checklist & Chronological Listing of Fiction in the Digest-size Mystery Magazines in the United States & England. LC 81-6986. xv, 1147p. 1982. lib. bdg. 49.95 (ISBN 0-313-23126-5, CMM/). Greenwood.

Cook, N. G. Problems in Rock Mechanics. (Illus.). 1985. 19.95x (ISBN 0-412-24110-2, NO. 6750, Pub. by Chapman & Hall). Methuen Inc.

Cook, N. G., jt. auth. see Jaeger, J. C.

Cook, Nancy G., jt. auth. see Stengel, Erwin.

Cook, Nathan H. Mechanics & Materials for Design. LC 83-11337. (Illus.). 496p. 1984. text ed. 34.00x (ISBN 0-07-012486-8). McGraw.

Cook, Nigel P. Microwave Principles & Systems. (Illus.). 224p. 1986. text ed. 29.95 (ISBN 0-13-581596-7). P-H.

Cook, Noble D. Demographic Collapse: Indian Peru 1520-1620. LC 81-9950. (Latin American Studies: No. 41). (Illus.). 320p. 1982. 42.50 (ISBN 0-521-23995-8). Cambridge U Pr.

Cook, Olive. English Cottages & Farmhouses. LC 82-80247. (Illus.). 1984. pap. 10.95 (ISBN 0-500-27341-3). Thames Hudson.

--The English Country House: An Art & Way of Life. (Illus.). 240p. 1984. pap. 10.95f (ISBN 0-500-27309-X). Thames-Hudson.

--The English House Through Seven Centuries. LC 83-4013. (Illus.). 320p. 45.00 (ISBN 0-87951-183-4). Overlook Pr.

Cook, P. J. & Shergold, J. H., eds. Proterozoic-Cambrian Phosphorites. 1979. pap. text ed. 6.00 (ISBN 0-7081-1159-9, 0522, Pub. by ANUP Australia). Australia N U P.

Cook, Patsy A., ed. Directory of Oral History Programs in the United States. 138p. 59.95 (ISBN 0-667-00680-X). Microfilming Corp.

--New York Times Oral History Guide, No. 2. 134p. 1979. pap. 17.50 (ISBN 0-667-00620-6). Microfilming Corp.

Cook, Paul. The Alejandra Variations. 256p. 1984. pap. 2.75 (ISBN 0-441-01240-X). Ace Bks.

--Tintagel. 224p. 1985. pap. 2.75 (ISBN 0-441-81298-8). Ace Bks.

Cook, Paul B. Academicians in Government from Roosevelt to Roosevelt. LC 80-8470. (Modern American History Ser.: Vol. 2). 210p. 1982. lib. bdg. 31.00 (ISBN 0-8240-4853-9). Garland Pub.

Cook, Paul D., jt. auth. see Cook, Wade B.

Cook, Paul E. Communion Handbook. 96p. 1980. 6.95 (ISBN 0-8170-0877-2). Judson.

Cook, Paul J. Bidding for the General Contractor. Gardner, Michael, ed. 232p. 1985. text ed. 37.95 (ISBN 0-911950-77-X). R S Means.

--Estimating for the General Contractor. LC 82-208250. 225p. 1982. text ed. 35.95 (ISBN 0-911950-48-6); pap. 30.95 (ISBN 0-911950-49-4). R S Means.

Cook, Paul M., jt. auth. see Bitter, Gary G.

Cook, Peter. Strolling Through London. (Illus.). 96p. 1982. pap. 6.95 (ISBN 0-9506503-1-5, Pub. by British Tourist Authority). Merrimack Pub Cir.

Cook, Peter, contrib. by. Richard Rogers & Partners: An Architectural Monograph. (Academy Architecture Ser.). (Illus.). 160p. 1985. 35.00 (ISBN 0-312-68208-5); pap. 24.95 (ISBN 0-312-68207-7). St Martin.

Cook, Peter & Webb, Barbara, eds. The Complete Book of Sailing. LC 76-19620. (Illus.). 1977. 19.00 (ISBN 0-385-11531-8). Doubleday.

Cook, Peter D. Start & Run Your Own Succussful Business: An Entrepreneur's Guide. LC 82-4336. 256p. 1982. 14.95 (ISBN 0-8253-0107-6). Beaufort Bks NY.

Cook, Philip J. & Lambert, Richard D., eds. Gun Control. (The Annals of the American Academy of Political & Social Science Ser.: No. 455). 250p. 1981. pap. 7.95x (ISBN 0-87761-263-3). Am Acad Pol Soc Sci.

Cook, Phillip. How to Enjoy Theatre. Bragg, Melvyn, ed. (How to Enjoy Ser.). (Illus.). 192p. 1984. 15.00 (ISBN 0-86188-142-7, Pub. by Salem Hse Ltd). Merrimack Pub Cir.

Cook, R. B., jt. ed. see Bolin, B.

Cook, R. D. & Weisberg, S. Residuals & Influence in Regression. (Monographs on Statistics & Applied Probability). 200p. 1982. 28.95 (ISBN 0-412-24280-X, NO. 6718, Pub. by Chapman & Hall). Methuen Inc.

--Residuals & Influence in Regression. 200p. 1982. 60.00x (ISBN 0-412-24280-X, Pub. by Chapman & Hall England). State Mutual Bk.

Cook, R. F., jt. auth. see Bart, B. F.

Cook, R. J., jt. auth. see Baker, K. F.

Cook, R. James, jt. auth. see Baker, Kenneth F.

Cook, R. James, et al, eds. Annual Review of Phytopathology, Vol. 23. LC 63-8847. (Illus.). 535p. 1985. text ed. 27.00 (ISBN 0-8243-1323-2). Annual Reviews.

Cook, R. M. Greek Painted Pottery. 2nd ed. (Illus.). 400p. 1972. 80.00x (ISBN 0-416-76170-4, NO. 2153). Methuen Inc.

Cook, R. M. & Charleston, R. J. Greek & Roman Pottery. Charleston, Robert J., ed. LC 78-55079. (Masterpieces & Western & Near Eastern Ceramics Ser.: Vol. 2). (Illus.). 1979. 250.00 (ISBN 0-87011-343-7). Kodansha.

Cook, Ralph T. The City Lights Pocket Poets Series: A Descriptive Bibliography. 1982. 22.50 (ISBN 0-910938-90-3); pap. 12.50 (ISBN 0-910938-89-X). McGilvery.

Cook, Ramsay, ed. Confederation. LC 23-16213. (Canadian Historical Readings Ser.: No. 3). 1967. pap. 4.95x (ISBN 0-8020-1456-9). U of Toronto Pr.

--Politics of Discontent. LC 23-16213. (Canadian Historical Readings Ser.: No. 4). 1967. pap. 4.00x (ISBN 0-8020-1453-4). U of Toronto Pr.

Cook, Ray. The Dance Director. 2nd rev. ed. (Illus.). 178p. (Orig.). 1981. pap. text ed. 12.00 (ISBN 0-9602002-1-5). R G Cook.

--One Hundred & Sixteen Modern Classroom Combinations. (Illus.). 40p. (Orig.). 1979. pap. text ed. 7.00 (ISBN 0-9602002-2-3). R G Cook.

--Theme & Variation. 59p. (Orig.). 1981. pap. text ed. 10.00 (ISBN 0-9602002-3-1). R G Cook.

Cook, Ray, jt. auth. see Swanson, Margo.

Cook, Ray, ed. see Becker, Svea & Winn, Laurie.

Cook, Ray, jt. ed. see Dance Notation Bureau Staff.

Cook, Ray G. The Three Ivans. (Illus.). 30p. (Orig.). 1985. pap. text ed. 7.00 (ISBN 0-9602002-8-2). R G Cook.

Cook, Ray G., ed. The Wombat Duet. (Illus.). 22p. 1984. pap. 7.00 (ISBN 0-9602002-6-6). R G Cook.

Cook, Ray L. Soil Management for Conservation & Production. LC 62-8770. (Illus.). 527p. 1962. 40.50 (ISBN 0-471-16995-1). Wiley.

Cook, Raymond A. Mountain Singer: The Life & the Legacy of Byron Herbert Reece. LC 80-8067. (Illus.). 368p. 1980. bds. 14.95 (ISBN 0-87797-051-3). Cherokee.

Cook, Reginald L. The Concord Saunterer. LC 80-2504. Repr. of 1940 ed. 22.50 (ISBN 0-404-19052-9). AMS Pr.

--Robert Frost: A Living Voice. LC 74-78982. (New England Writers Ser.). 360p. 1974. 20.00x (ISBN 0-87023-165-0). U of Mass Pr.

Cook, Reginald L., ed. see Emerson, Ralph Waldo.

Cook, Richard B. Mountaineer Pride, Prospects for Renewal in Southern West Virginia. 100p. (Orig.). 1985. pap. 7.95 (ISBN 0-9615033-0-0). Mercer Pr.

--The Story of the Baptists: In All Ages & Countries. LC 76-54582. (Illus.). 416p. 1976. Repr. of 1884 ed. 11.95 (ISBN 0-87921-023-0). Attic Pr.

Cook, Richard I. Jonathan Swift As a Tory Pamphleteer. LC 67-21199. (Illus.). 184p. 1967. 15.00x (ISBN 0-295-97870-8). U of Wash Pr.

Cook, Richard J. Super Power Steam Locomotives. LC 66-29787. (Illus.). 144p. 1966. 20.95 (ISBN 0-87095-010-X). Golden West.

Cook, Richard J. & Gardi, Gavin L. How to Design & Build Thermosiphoning Air Panels. iv, 36p. (Orig.). 1982. pap. 2.00 (ISBN 0-939294-13-3, TH-7413-C-66). Beech Leaf.

Cook, Richard M. Carson McCullers. LC 75-2789. (Literature & Life Ser.). 160p. 1975. 12.95 (ISBN 0-8044-2128-5). Ungar.

--Carson McCullers. (Literature & Life Ser.). 160p. 1984. pap. 7.95 (ISBN 0-8044-6087-6). Ungar.

Cook, Rick. Using Cassette Recorders with Computers. 175p. pap. 11.95 (ISBN 0-89588-169-1). SYBEX.

Cook, Rick & Vaughan, Frank. All about Home Satellite Television. (Illus.). 336p. (Orig.). 1983. o.p 19.95 (ISBN 0-8306-0519-3); pap. 13.50 (ISBN 0-8306-1519-9, 1519). TAB Bks.

Cook, Robert. Ahora que Creo. Orig. Title: Now That I Believe. 128p. (Span.). 1984. pap. 2.95 (ISBN 0-8254-1137-8). Kregel.

Cook, Robert, tr. see Thordarson, Agnar.

Cook, Robert A. In Step with God. 1978p. write for info. (ISBN 0-86693-010-8). Christian Herald.

--Now That I Believe. 1956. pap. 2.95 (ISBN 0-8024-5982-X). Moody.

--Walk with the King Today. LC 78-56977. 1978. pap. 4.95 (ISBN 0-915684-42-X). Christian Herald.

Cook, Robert C. Human Fertility: The Modern Dilemma. LC 72-156185. 1971. Repr. of 1951 ed. lib. bdg. 18.75x (ISBN 0-8371-6128-2, COHU). Greenwood.

Cook, Robert D. Concepts & Applications of Finite Element Analysis. 2nd ed. LC 80-26255. 537p. 1981. text ed. 49.45 (ISBN 0-471-03050-3); 30.00 (ISBN 0-471-08200-7). Wiley.

Cook, Robert D. & Young, Warren C. Advanced Mechanics of Materials. 1985. text ed. write for info. (ISBN 0-02-324620-0). Macmillan.

Cook, Robert F. Chanson D'antioche, Chanson de Geste: Le Cycle De la Croisade Est-Il Epique? (Purdue University Monographs in Romance Languages Ser.: No. 2). vi, 107p. 1979. 16.00x (ISBN 90-272-1712-2). Benjamins North Am.

Cook, Robert F., tr. see Murat, Ines.

Cook, Robin. Brain. 1982. pap. 3.50 (ISBN 0-451-11260-1, AE1260, Sig). NAL.

--Coma. 1977. pap. 3.50 (ISBN 0-451-12740-4, AE2740, Sig). NAL.

--Fever. (General Ser.). 1982. lib. bdg. 15.95 (ISBN 0-8161-3420-0, Large Print Bks). G K Hall.

--Fever. 320p. 1983. pap. 3.95 (ISBN 0-451-11993-2, AE1993, Sig). NAL.

--Godplayer. 368p. 1983. 14.95 (ISBN 0-399-12764-X, Putnam). Putnam Pub Group.

--Godplayer. 1983. pap. 4.50 (ISBN 0-451-12950-4, Sig). NAL.

--Godplayer. (General Ser.). 1984. lib. bdg. 16.95 (ISBN 0-8161-3620-3, Large Print). G K Hall.

--Mindbend. LC 84-24954. 368p. 1985. 15.95 (ISBN 0-399-12966-9, Putnam). Putnam Pub Group.

--Mindbend. (Large Print Books General Ser.). 1985. lib. bdg. 17.95 (ISBN 0-8161-3804-4). G K Hall.

--Sphinx. 1980. pap. 3.95 (ISBN 0-451-13147-9, AE3147, Sig). NAL.

--Year of the Intern. pap. 2.50 (ISBN 0-451-13133-9, AE3133, Sig). NAL.

Cook, Robin, jt. ed. see Brown, Gordon.

Cook, Roger & Zimmermann, Karl. Western Maryland Railway. LC 81-1176. (Illus.). 320p. 1981. 25.00 (ISBN 0-8310-7139-7). Howell-North.

Cook, Roy J., compiled by. One Hundred & One Famous Poems. gift ed. (Illus.). 186p. 1986. 12.95 (ISBN 0-8092-5833-1). Contemp Bks.

--One Hundred One Famous Poems. 186p. 1985. leatherette 7.95 (ISBN 0-8092-8831-1); 12.95 (ISBN 0-8092-5833-1); pap. 5.95 (ISBN 0-8092-8834-6). Contemp Bks.

Cook, Ruth E. & Armbruster, Virginia B. Adapting Early Childhood Curricula: Suggestions for Meeting Special Needs. (Illus.). 386p. 1982. pap. text ed. 17.95 (ISBN 0-8016-1149-0). Mosby.

Cook, S. A. The Religion of Ancient Palestine in the Light of Archaeology. (British Academy, London, Schweich Lectures on Biblical Archaeology Series, 1925). pap. 28.00 (ISBN 0-317-15791-4). Kraus Repr.

Cook, Sandra. Books in Wandswoth. (BNB RF Report 18). (Orig.). 1985. pap. 16.50 (ISBN 0-7123-3048-8, Pub. by British Lib). Longwood Pub Group.

Cook, Sarah S. Children & Dying, an Exploration & Selective Bibliographies. 106p. 1974. pap. 5.95 (ISBN 0-930194-87-X). Ctr Thanatology.

Cook, Scott. Peasant Capitalist Industry: Piecework & Enterprise in Southern Mexican Brickyards. (Illus.). 256p. 1985. lib. bdg. 24.75 (ISBN 0-8191-4321-9); pap. text ed. 13.50 (ISBN 0-8191-4322-7). U Pr of Amer.

--Zapotec Stoneworkers: The Dynamics of Rural Simple Commodity Production in Modern Mexican Capitalism. LC 81-40584. (Illus.). 454p. (Orig.). 1982. lib. bdg. 32.25 (ISBN 0-8191-2419-2); pap. text ed. 18.25 (ISBN 0-8191-2420-6). U Pr of Amer.

Cook, Scott & Diskin, Martin, eds. Markets in Oaxaca. (Institute of Latin American Studies-Special Publication). 349p. 1975. 17.50x (ISBN 0-292-75014-5). U of Tex Pr.

Cook, Sherburne F. The Conflict Between the California Indian & White Civilization, 4 vols. in 1. LC 76-43678. (Ibero-Americana: 21-24). Repr. of 1943 ed. 27.50 (ISBN 0-404-15512-X). AMS Pr.

--The Conflict Between the California Indian & White Civilization. LC 75-23860. 1976. 48.50x (ISBN 0-520-03142-3); pap. 6.95 (ISBN 0-520-03143-1, CAL332). U of Cal Pr.

--The Population of the California Indians 1769-1970. LC 74-27287. 1976. 32.00s (ISBN 0-520-02923-2). U of Cal Pr.

Cook, Sherburne F. & Borah, Woodrow. Essays in Population History, 3 vols. Incl. Vols. 1 & 2. Mexico & the Caribbean. 1971. 43.00x ea. Vol. 1 (ISBN 0-520-01764-1). Vol. 2 (ISBN 0-520-02272-6); Vol. 3. Mexico & California. 1979. 39.50x (ISBN 0-520-03560-7). U of Cal Pr.

Cook, Sherburne F. & Simpson, Lesley B. The Population of Central Mexico in the Sixteenth Century. LC 76-29408. (Ibero-Americana: 31). Repr. of 1948 ed. 23.00 (ISBN 0-404-15333-X). AMS Pr.

Cook, Sherwin L. Torchlight Parade. facs. ed. LC 70-128227. (Essay Index Reprint Ser). 1929. 21.00 (ISBN 0-8369-1911-4). Ayer Co Pubs.

Cook, Shirley. Diary of a Fat Housewife. LC 77-71003. (Illus.). 128p. 1982. pap. 2.25 (ISBN 0-89081-295-0). Harvest Hse.

--I'm No Spring Chicken, but It's Fun Being Over Forty. 2nd ed. LC 81-85512. 128p. 1982. pap. 2.25 (ISBN 0-89081-083-4, 0834). Harvest Hse.

--The Marriage Puzzle. 128p. (Orig.). 1985. pap. 5.95 (ISBN 0-310-33611-2, Pub. by Pyranee). Zondervan.

Cook, Stanley A. An Introduction to the Bible. LC 78-12762. 1979. Repr. of 1945 ed. lib. bdg. 22.50x (ISBN 0-313-21028-4, COIB). Greenwood.

--The Old Testament. 1936. 35.00 (ISBN 0-8274-3060-4). R West.

Cook, Stanley A., ed. see Smith, William R.

Cook, Stanley J. & Suter, Richard W. The Scope of Grammar: A Study of Modern English. Talkington, William A., ed. (Illus.). 1980. text ed. 26.95x (ISBN 0-07-012460-4). McGraw.

Cook, Stephani & Lumiere, Richard. Healthy Sex...& Keeping it That Way. (Orig.). 1983. pap. 5.95 (ISBN 0-671-45899-X). S&S.

Cook, Stephanie. Second Life. 384p. 1982. pap. 3.95 (ISBN 0-345-30675-9). Ballantine.

Cook, Sterling & Southard, Edna C. Annette Covington: Paintings & Drawings. LC 82-82113. (Illus.). 50p. (Orig.). 1982. pap. 5.00 (ISBN 0-940784-02-5). Miami Univ Art.

Cook, Sue C. The Numbers Book: Student Syllabus, 2 vols. (gr. k-2). 1974. Vol. 1. pap. text ed. 11.85 ea. packs of 10 (ISBN 0-89420-081-X, 193050); Vol. 2. pap. text ed. 11.85 ea. packs of 10 (ISBN 0-89420-082-8, 193051); cassette recordings 17.36 (ISBN 0-89420-208-1, 193000). Natl Book.

Cook, Susan & LaMay, Thomasin. The Virtuoso Female Performer in the Italian Renaissance, 1600-1630: An Annotated Bibliography & Guide. LC 82-49141. 150p. 1983. lib. bdg. 20.00 (ISBN 0-8240-9138-8). Garland Pub.

Cook, Susanne. The Open Goal of My Life. LC 84-90269. 74p. 1985. 7.95 (ISBN 0-533-06303-5). Vantage.

Cook, Sy & Moffett, Martha. The Sharing. 224p. (Orig.). 1984. pap. 2.95 (ISBN 0-380-86538-6, 86538). Avon.

Cook, Sylvia J. From Tobacco Road to Route 66: The Southern Poor White in Fiction. LC 75-35822. xiv, 208p. 1976. 18.00x (ISBN 0-8078-1264-1). U of NC Pr.

Cook, T., ed. Vagrancy: Some New Perspectives. 1979. 33.00 (ISBN 0-12-187550-4); pap. 14.50 1981 (ISBN 0-12-187560-1). Acad Pr.

Cook, T. A. The Story of Rouen. (Medieval Towns Ser.: Vol. 24). pap. 44.00 (ISBN 0-317-16435-X). Kraus Repr.

Cook, T. D. Stratigraphic Atlas: North & Central America. 1977. 70.00x (ISBN 0-691-08189-1); spiral bdg 22.00x (ISBN 0-691-08193-X). Princeton U Pr.

Cook, T. M. & Cullen, D. J. Chemical Plant & Its Operation (Including Safety & Health Aspects) 2nd ed. (Illus.). 1980. text ed. 22.00 (ISBN 0-08-023812-2); pap. text ed. 10.00 (ISBN 0-08-023813-0). Pergamon.

Cook, T. S., jt. auth. see Lee, Joanna.

Cook, T. W. see Ruckwick, Christian A.

Cook, Tennessee C. Constitutional Equality: A Right of Woman. LC 75-21812. (Pioneers of the Woman's Movement: an International Perspective Ser.). 148p. 1976. Repr. of 1871 ed. 16.50 (ISBN 0-88355-263-9). Hyperion-Conn.

Cook, Terri. Family Guide to Honolulu & the Island of Oahu. LC 77-85698. 1977. soft bdg. 2.95 (ISBN 0-930492-00-5). Hawaiian Serv.

Cook, Theodore A. The Curves of Life. 1979. pap. 6.95 (ISBN 0-486-23701-X). Dover.

--The Curves of Life. (Illus.). 16.50 (ISBN 0-8446-5746-8). Peter Smith.

Cook, Theodore A., ed. An Anthology of Humorous Verse. Repr. of 1902 ed. 15.00 (ISBN 0-8274-4152-5). R West.

Cook, Theodore S. City Planning Theory. 5.00 (ISBN 0-685-28344-5). Philos Lib.

Cook, Thomas. Tabernacle. 352p. 1985. pap. 3.50 (ISBN 0-523-42338-1). Pinnacle Bks.

Cook, Thomas & Campbell, Donald T. Quasi-Experimentation. 1979. pap. 22.95 (ISBN 0-395-30790-2). HM.

Cook, Thomas, jt. ed. see Scioli, Frank.

Cook, Thomas C., Jr., jt. auth. see Thorson, James A.

Cook, Thomas D. & Reichardt, Charles S., eds. Qualitative & Quantitative Methods in Evaluation Research. LC 79-20962. (Sage Research Progress Ser. in Evaluation: Vol. 1). (Illus.). 160p. 1979. pap. 9.95 (ISBN 0-8039-1301-X). Sage.

Cook, Thomas D., et al. Sesame Street Revisited. LC 74-25853. 420p. 1975. 15.00x (ISBN 0-87154-207-2). Russell Sage.

Cook, Thomas D., et al, eds. Evaluation Studies Review Annual, Vol. 3. LC 76-15865. 783p. 1978. 40.00x (ISBN 0-8039-1075-4). Sage.

Cook, Thomas G. Koster: An Artifact Analysis. LC 82-101459. (Prehistoric Records Ser.: No. 1). (Illus.). 218p. 1976. 18.00 (ISBN 0-942118-04-9); pap. 12.00 (ISBN 0-942118-05-7). Ctr Amer Arche.

Cook, Thomas H. The Orchids. 252p. 1982. 12.95 (ISBN 0-395-32503-X). HM.

--Tabernacle. 1983. 13.95 (ISBN 0-395-34396-8). HM.

Cook, Thomas I., ed. & intro. by see Locke, John.

Cook, Thomas J., jt. auth. see King, Francis P.

Cook, Thomas M. & Russell, Robert A. Contemporary Operations Management: Text & Cases. 2nd ed. (Illus.). 528p. 1984. 30.95 (ISBN 0-13-170449-4). P-H.
--Introduction to Management Science. 3rd ed. (Illus.). 784p. 1985. text ed. 31.95 (ISBN 0-13-487026-3); study guide 12.95 (ISBN 0-13-487042-5). P-H.
Cook, Thomas M., jt. auth. see Shurr, Donald.
Cook, Thomas R., ed. Essays in Modern Thought. facs. ed. LC 68-16922. (Essay Index Reprint Ser). 1935. 15.00 (ISBN 0-8369-0332-3). Ayer Co Pubs.
Cook, Thomas W. Ants of California. (Illus.). 1953. 29.95x (ISBN 0-87015-036-7). Pacific Bks.
Cook, Tim, jt. auth. see Miller, Joshua.
Cook, V. Analysis of Distance Protection. Date not set. 39.95 (ISBN 0-471-90749-9). Wiley.
Cook, W. Sabrina Kane. 288p. 1982. pap. 2.95 (ISBN 0-441-74554-7). Ace Bks.
Cook, W, jt. auth. see Hartnell, Tim.
Cook, W. A. Electrostatics in Reprography. (Reprographic Lib.). 1970. 8.95 (ISBN 0-8038-1899-8). Hastings.
Cook, W. D. & Kuhn, W. D. Planning Processes in Developing Countries: Techniques & Achievements. (TIMS Studies in the Management Sciences: Vol. 17). 416p. 1982. 64.00 (ISBN 0-444-86344-3, North Holland). Elsevier.
Cook, W. Paul. Lovecraft: In Memoriam. 1977. pap. 4.95 (ISBN 0-686-19171-4). Necronomicon.
Cook, W. W. The Corporation Problem: The Public Phases of Corporations, Their Uses, Abuses. Repr. of 1891 ed. 20.00 (ISBN 0-527-19200-7). Kraus Repr.
Cook, Wade. One Hundred One Ways to Buy Real Estate Without Cash. 1985. pap. 10.95 (ISBN 0-910019-13-4). Invest Tax Pubn.
--Real Wealth. 1985. 16.95 (ISBN 0-910019-12-6). Invest Tax Pubn.
Cook, Wade B. Cook's Book on Creative Real Estate. 172p. (Orig.). 1982. pap. 24.95 (ISBN 0-910019-02-9). Invest Tax Pubn.
--The First National Bank of Real Estate Clauses. 204p. (Orig.). pap. 34.95 (ISBN 0-910019-08-8). Invest Tax Pubn.
--How to Build a Real Estate Money Machine. 2nd ed. 221p. 1983. 14.95 (ISBN 0-910019-00-2). Invest Tax Pubn.
--How to Pick up Foreclosures. (Orig.). 1982. 14.95 (ISBN 0-910019-04-5). Invest Tax Pubn.
--Pay No Taxes. rev. ed. (Illus.). 170p. 1981. pap. 24.95 (ISBN 0-910019-01-0). Invest Tax Pubn.
--Real Estate: The Best Game in Town. 143p. (Orig.). pap. 11.95 (ISBN 0-910019-10-X). Invest Tax Pubn.
Cook, Wade B. & Cook, Paul D. Big Bucks by Selling Your Property. (Orig.). pap. 24.95 (ISBN 0-910019-09-6). Invest Tax Pubn.
Cook, Walter. Investing in Oil. LC 83-63203. (Illus.). 192p. 1985. 13.95 (ISBN 0-915677-05-9). Roundtable Pub.
Cook, Walter A. Case Grammar: Development of the Matrix Model (1970-1978) LC 79-11067. 223p. 1979. pap. text ed. 8.95 (ISBN 0-87840-174-1). Georgetown U Pr.
--Introduction to Tagmemic Analysis. LC 78-1268. 210p. 1978. pap. text ed. 7.95 (ISBN 0-87840-171-7). Georgetown U Pr.
Cook, Walter L. Table Prayers for Children. (Illus.). (gr. k-4). 1977. pap. 2.95 (ISBN 0-8272-3621-2). CBP.
--Table Prayers for the Family Circle. 96p. (Orig.). 1982. pap. 3.45 (ISBN 0-8010-2471-4). Baker Bk.
--Worship Stories. (Object Lesson Ser.). 64p. 1980. pap. 3.50 (ISBN 0-8010-2445-5). Baker Bk.
Cook, Walter W. The Logical & Legal Bases of the Conflict of Laws. LC 43-268. (Harvard Studies in the Conflict of Laws: Vol.5). xx, 473p. 1978. Repr. of 1942 ed. lib. bdg. 35.00 (ISBN 0-89941-130-4). W S Hein.
Cook, Wanda D. Adult Literacy Education in the United States. LC 76-58957. 1977. pap. 4.50 (ISBN 0-87207-934-1). Intl Reading.
Cook, Warren L. Flood Tide of Empire: Spain & the Pacific Northwest, 1543-1819. LC 72-75187. (Western Americana Ser.: No. 24). (Illus.). 672p. 1973. 45.00x (ISBN 0-300-01577-1). Yale U Pr.
Cook, Will C. Elizabeth, by Name. (Illus.). 320p. 1983. pap. 1.95 (ISBN 0-441-20391-4, Pub. by Charter Bks). Ace Bks.
Cook, William A. Natural Childbirth: Fact & Fallacy. LC 81-19021. 216p. 1982. text ed. 18.95x (ISBN 0-88229-655-8). Nelson-Hall.
Cook, William H. Success, Motivation, & the Scriptures. new ed. LC 74-82582. 192p. 1975. kivar 6.95 (ISBN 0-8054-5226-5). Broadman.
Cook, William J. Confidence in Fact. 1969. pap. 3.95 (ISBN 0-89137-700-X). Quality Pubns.
--The Joy of Computer Communications. 192p. (Orig.). 1984. pap. 5.95 (ISBN 0-440-54412-2, Dell Trade Pbks). Dell.
Cook, William J. & Ma, Christopher. The Telephone Survival Guide. 1985. pap. 5.95 (ISBN 0-671-55400-X, Wallaby). PB.
Cook, William J., jt. auth. see Fellinger, Robert C.
Cook, William J., Jr. Masks, Modes, & Morals: The Art of Evelyn Waugh. LC 73-118125. 352p. 1971. 27.50 (ISBN 0-8386-7707-X). Fairleigh Dickinson.
--Security Systems: Considerations, Layout, Performance. LC 82-50653. 144p. 1983. pap. 10.95 (ISBN 0-672-21949-2, 21953). Sams.
Cook, William R. & Herzman, Ronald B. The Medieval World View: An Introduction. (Illus.). 1983. 15.95x (ISBN 0-19-503089-3); pap. 8.95x (ISBN 0-19-503090-7). Oxford U Pr.
Cook, William W. Adrift in the Unknown: Queer Adventures in a Queer Realm. LC 74-15957. (Science Fiction Ser). 305p. 1975. Repr. 23.50x (ISBN 0-405-06283-4). Ayer Co Pubs.
--Cast Away at the Pole. Reginald, R. & Melville, Douglas, eds. LC 77-84215. (Lost Race & Adult Fantasy Ser.). 1978. Repr. of 1904 ed. lib. bdg. 26.50x (ISBN 0-405-10970-9). Ayer Co Pubs.
--Round Trip to the Year Two Thousand. LC 75-13250. (Classics of Science Fiction Ser.). 318p. 1974. pap. 10.95 (ISBN 0-88355-135-7). Hyperion Conn.
Cook, Zena. Impact of Advertising: Implications for Consumer Education. 75p. 6.00 (ISBN 0-318-16279-2, A-17). Public Int Econ.
--Implementation of the Jobs Project & Transition Problems. 84p. 5.90 (ISBN 0-318-16283-0, G-17). Public Int Econ.
Cook, Zena & Booth, James. Employment Stimulus Tools: Subsidy Approaches & Design Options. 62p. 4.30 (ISBN 0-318-16264-4, G-11). Public Int Econ.
Cook, Zena & Rittner, Debra. A Taxonomy of Policy Tools for Increasing Labor Force Participation. 80p. 6.50 (ISBN 0-318-16307-1, H-3). Public Int Econ.
Cook, Zena, jt. auth. see Ferguson, Allen.
Cook-Bey, William. The Way It Came. (Orig.). 1983. pap. 2.25 (ISBN 0-87067-208-8, BH208). Holloway.
Cookbook Committee, compiled by. Country Roads. (Illus., Orig.). 1983. pap. 8.95 (ISBN 0-9611640-2-6). Chapin PTO.
Cookbook Committee of Holy Trinity Episcopal Church, ed. Not by Bread Alone. (Illus.). 304p. 1985. pap. 11.95 (ISBN 0-9615284-0-0). Holy Episcopal.
Cookbook Committee, 1979, ed. Indianapolis Collects & Cooks. (Illus.). 208p. 1980. pap. text ed. 11.75 (ISBN 0-936260-00-9). Ind Mus Art.
Cookbook Consortium. Apples: Uses for the Whole Apple Recipes & Suggestions. 14p. 1984. pap. text ed. 1.95 (Pub. by Cookbk Consort). Prosperity & Profits.
--Coconut: Uses for the Entire Coconut Recipes & Suggestions. 1984. pap. text ed. 1.95 (Pub. by Cookbk Consort). Prosperity & Profits.
--Coffee Substitutes with Medicinal Additives: A Recipe Book. 1984. pap. text ed. 1.95 (ISBN 0-318-04305-X, Pub. by Cookbk Consorts). Prosperity & Profits.
--Corn Starch Drink Recipe Substitution Book. 1984. pap. text ed. 2.50 (ISBN 0-318-04308-4, Pub. by Cookbk Consorts). Prosperity & Profits.
--Corn: Uses for the Whole Corn Recipe & Suggestion Book. 1984. pap. text ed. 5.95 (Pub. by Cookbk Consort). Prosperity & Profits.
--The Dandelion: Uses for the Whole Dandelion Recipe & Suggestion Book. 1984. pap. text ed. 1.95 (Pub. by Cookbk Consort). Prosperity & Profits.
--Dumb Cake Recipe Ingredient Substitution Cookbook. 1984. pap. text ed. 1.95 (ISBN 0-318-04310-6, Pub. by Cookbk Consorts). Prosperity & Profits.
--Egg: Uses for the Entire Egg Recipes & Suggestions. 1984. pap. text ed. 1.95 (Pub. by Cookbk Consort). Prosperity & Profits.
--Family Meals Recipe & Cookbook Research Correspondence Course. 1985. pap. text ed. 5.95 (ISBN 0-318-04311-4, Pub. by Cookbk Consorts). Prosperity & Profits.
--Food Businesses: Snack Shops, Specialty Food, Restaurants, & Other Ideas with Business & Cookbook Bibliography. 35p. 1984. pap. text ed. 5.95 (ISBN 0-318-01299-5, Pub. by Cookbk Consort). Prosperity & Profits.
--Fruits, Nuts, Etc: Snack Mix Ingredient Substitution Recipe Book. 1984. pap. text ed. 2.50 (ISBN 0-318-04312-2, Pub. by Cookbk Consorts). Prosperity & Profits.
--Honey Basic Information Rhyme. 1984. pap. text ed. 0.75 (ISBN 0-318-01298-7, Pub. by Cookbk Consort). Prosperity & Profits.
--Lemon: Uses for the Entire Lemon Recipes & Suggestions. 1984. pap. text ed. 1.95 (Pub. by Cookbk Consort). Prosperity & Profits.
--Mock Champagne Ingredient Substitution Recipe Book. 1984. pap. text ed. 2.50 (ISBN 0-318-04313-0, Pub. by Cookbk Consorts). Prosperity & Profits.
--No Cook Recipe Substitution Book for Pastries & Deserts, Bk. 1. 1984. pap. text ed. 4.95 (ISBN 0-318-04314-9, Pub. by Cookbk Consorts). Prosperity & Profits.
--Orange: Uses for the Whole Orange Recipes & Suggestions. 1984. pap. text ed. 1.95 (Pub. by Cookbk Consort). Prosperity & Profits.
--Peach Preserve Ingredient Substitution Cookbook. 1984. pap. text ed. 6.95 (ISBN 0-318-04315-7, Pub. by Cookbk Consorts). Prosperity & Profits.
--Peanut Powder Suggestion Rhyme. 1984. pap. text ed. 1.50 (ISBN 0-318-01295-2, Pub. by Cookbk Consort). Prosperity & Profits.
--Pie Crust Ingredient Substitution Cookbook. 1984. pap. text ed. 2.50 (ISBN 0-318-04316-5, Pub. by Cookbk Consorts). Prosperity & Profits.
--Puffed Corn Natural Snack or Breakfast Pack Recipe Book. 1984. pap. text ed. 2.75 (ISBN 0-318-04317-3, Pub. by Cookbk Consorts). Prosperity & Profits.
--Puffed Millet Rhyming Natural Snack or Breakfast Pack Recipe Book. 1984. pap. text ed. 2.75 (ISBN 0-318-04318-1, Pub. by Cookbk Consortium). Prosperity & Profits.
--Rice Powder, Peanut Powder & Soybean Powder Suggestion Rhymes. 1984. pap. text ed. 1.50 (ISBN 0-318-01294-4, Pub. by Cookbk Consort). Prosperity & Profits.
--Rice Powder Suggestion Rhyme. 1984. pap. text ed. 1.50 (ISBN 0-318-01296-0, Pub. by Cookbk Consort). Prosperity & Profits.
--Rinds & Peels: A Cookbook. 1986. pap. text ed. 1.95 (ISBN 0-318-01303-7, Pub. by Cookbk Consort). Prosperity & Profits.
--Same Task: Different Mask Fundraising Cookbook. 1985. pap. 1.95 (ISBN 0-318-04323-8, Pub. by Cookbk Consorts). Prosperity & Profits.
--Shells, Skins & Hulls: A Recyling Bibliography. Date not set. pap. text ed. 1.95 (ISBN 0-318-01292-8, Pub. by Cookbk Consort). Prosperity & Profits.
--Soybean Powder Suggestion Rhyme. 1984. pap. text ed. 1.50 (ISBN 0-318-01297-9, Pub. by Cookbk Consort). Prosperity & Profits.
--Tea Ingredient Centerpiece Recipe Book. 1984. pap. text ed. 2.35 (ISBN 0-318-04324-6, Pub. by Cookbk Consorts). Prosperity & Profits.
--Tortillo, Taco, Pita, & More Ingredient Substitution Recipe Book. 1984. pap. text ed. 2.75 (ISBN 0-318-04325-4, Pub. by Cookbk Consorts). Prosperity & Profits.
--Using the Total Fruit or Vegetable, Bk. I. (Waste Not Ser.). 1984. pap. text ed. 6.95 (Pub. by Cookbk Consort). Prosperity & Profits.
--Watermelon: Uses for the Entire Watermelon Recipes & Suggestions. 1984. pap. text ed. 1.95 (Pub. by Cookbk Consort). Prosperity & Profits.
Cookbook Consortium, ed. Decorative Food Gifts Ingredient Substitution Book. 40p. 1984. pap. 3.00 (ISBN 0-318-00209-4, Pub. by Cookbk Consort). Prosperity & Profits.
Cookbook Consortium Editors, ed. Bread Pudding Ingredient Substitution Recipe Book. 1984. pap. 1.00 (ISBN 0-318-00205-1, Pub. by Cookbk Consort). Prosperity & Profits.
Cookbook Consortium Educ. Division. Recipe Research Correspondence Course for Pastries & Deserts. 1984. pap. text ed. 9.95 (ISBN 0-318-04320-3, Pub. by Cookbk Consorts). Prosperity & Profits.
Cookbook Consortium Educational Division. Cookbook Research Correspondence Course. 25p. 1984. pap. text ed. 12.95 (ISBN 0-318-04307-6, Pub. by Cookbk Consorts). Prosperity & Profits.
--Diabetic Recipe & Cookbook Research Correspondence Course. 25p. 1984. pap. text ed. 9.95 (ISBN 0-318-04309-2, Pub. by Cookbk Consorts). Prosperity & Profits.
--Recipe Research Correspondence Course. 1984. pap. text ed. 9.95 (ISBN 0-318-04319-X, Pub. by Cookbk Consorts). Prosperity & Profits.
--Regional Cookbook, Recipe & Cookbook Research Correspondence Course. 1985. pap. text ed. 9.95 (ISBN 0-318-04321-1, Pub. by Cookbk Consorts). Prosperity & Profits.
Cookbook Consortium Information Division, ed. Baby Food Cookbooks & Recipe References: An Index. 60p. 1984. pap. text ed. 4.95 (ISBN 0-318-00119-5, Pub. by Cookbk Consort). Prosperity & Profits.
Cookbook Consortium Information Division Staff, ed. Food Gifts: Simple Gifts to Make with Food, a Bibliography. 26p. 1984. pap. text ed. 1.95 (ISBN 0-318-00121-7, Pub. by Cookbk Consort). Prosperity & Profits.
Cookbook Consortium Information Division, ed. Singles Cookbooks: An Index. 70p. 1984. pap. text ed. 3.95 (ISBN 0-318-00120-9, Pub. by Cookbk Consort). Prosperity & Profits.
Cookbook Consortium Staff. Food Variations Suggestion Rhymes, Bk. 1. 1984. pap. text ed. 2.75 (ISBN 0-318-01300-2, Pub. by Cookbk Consort). Prosperity & Profits.
--Fruit Basket Ingredient Substitution Book. 13p. 1984. pap. 2.00 (ISBN 0-318-00208-6, Pub. by Cookbk Consort). Prosperity & Profits.
--Potato: Uses for the Whole Potato Plus Recipes & Suggestions. 1984. pap. text ed. 1.95 (Pub. by Cookbk Consort). Prosperity & Profits.
--Roses: Uses for the Whole Rose Recipe & Suggestions Book. 1984. pap. text ed. 1.95 (Pub. by Cookbk Consort). Prosperity & Profits.
Cooke. Applied Finite Element Analysis: An Apple II Implementation. 1984. pap. write for info. (ISBN 0-471-82337-6); supplementary material avail. Wiley.
--Dependent Development in United Kingdom Regions with Particular Reference to Wales. (Progress in Planning Ser.: Vol. 15, Part 1). 90p. 1980. pap. 14.75 (ISBN 0-08-026809-9). Pergamon.
Cooke, A. M., ed. A History of the Royal College of Physicians of London, Vol. 3. (Illus.). 1972. 19.00x (ISBN 0-19-920031-9). Oxford U Pr.
Cooke, Aileen H. Out of the Mouth of Babes: Extrasensory Perception in Children. 192p. 1968. 8.50 (ISBN 0-227-67736-6). Attic Pr.
Cooke, Alan, ed. see Universite Laval,Centre d'Etudes Nordiques, Quebec.
Cooke, Alistair. Alistair Cooke's America. 1973. 30.00 (ISBN 0-394-48726-5). Knopf.
--Alistair Cooke's America. 1977. pap. 15.95 (ISBN 0-394-73449-1). Knopf.
--The Americans. 1980. pap. 2.95 (ISBN 0-425-04681-8). Berkley Pub.
--The Americans: Fifty Talks on Our Life & Times. LC 79-2218. 1979. 10.95 (ISBN 0-394-50364-3). Knopf.
--A Generation on Trial: U. S. A. vs Alger Hiss. LC 82-11870. 371p. 1982. Repr. of 1968 ed. lib. bdg. 35.00x (ISBN 0-313-23373-X, COGE). Greenwood.
--Masterpieces: A Decade of Masterpiece Theatre. LC 80-2707. (Illus.). 240p. 1981. 25.00 (ISBN 0-394-51907-8). Knopf.
Cooke, Alistair, jt. auth. see Cameron, Robert.
Cooke, Alistair, ed. see Mencken, Henry L.
Cooke, Ann. Giraffes at Home. LC 79-158686. (A Let's-Read-&-Find-Out Science Bk.). (Illus.). (gr. k-3). 1972. 11.49i (ISBN 0-690-33082-0); PLB 11.89 (ISBN 0-690-33083-9). Crowell Jr Bks.
--The Grandfather Clock. 1984. 5.95 (ISBN 0-533-05997-6). Vantage.
Cooke, Ann & Cooke, Frank. Cooking with Music. LC 83-82333. (Illus.). 310p. 1983. cassette included 18.95 (ISBN 0-940076-01-2). Fiesta City.
Cooke, Barclay. Paradoxes & Probabilities: One Hundred Eighty Backgammon Problems. (Illus.). 1978. 8.95 (ISBN 0-394-50126-8). Random.
Cooke, Barclay & Bradshaw, Jon. Backgammon, the Cruelest Game: The Art of Winning. LC 74-8725. (Illus.). 1974. pap. 6.95 (ISBN 0-394-73243-X). Random.
Cooke, Barclay & Orlean, Rene. Championship Backgammon: Learning Through Master Play. LC 79-13353. (Illus.). 1979. 19.95. P-H.
Cooke, Bernard. Formation of Faith. LC 65-27619. (Pastoral Ser). 1965. pap. 2.00 (ISBN 0-8294-0014-1). Loyola.
--Ministry to Word & Sacraments: History & Theology. LC 75-36459. 688p. 1980. pap. 16.95 (ISBN 0-8006-1440-2, 1-1440). Fortress.
--Sacraments & Sacramentality. 240p. 1983. pap. 7.95 (ISBN 0-89622-161-X). Twenty-Third.
Cooke, Bernard J. Beyond Trinity. (Acquinas Lecutre). 1969. 7.95 (ISBN 0-87462-134-8). Marquette.
Cooke, C. M., Jr. Land Snail Genus Carelia. (BMB Ser.: No. 85). Repr. of 1931 ed. 12.00 (ISBN 0-527-02191-1). Kraus Repr.
Cooke, C. M., Jr. & Kondo, Y. Revision of Tornatellinidae & Achatinellidae. (BMB Ser.: No. 221). Repr. of 1960 ed. 32.00 (ISBN 0-527-02329-9). Kraus Repr.
Cooke, C. W., jt. auth. see Cushman, J. A.
Cooke, Catherine. Iakov Chernikhov: Fantasy & Construction. (Academy Architecture Ser.). (Illus.). 88p. 1985. pap. 14.95 (ISBN 0-312-40313-5). St Martin.
--Mask of the Wizard. 320p. 1985. pap. 2.95 (ISBN 0-8125-3384-4). Tor Bks.
Cooke, Catherine, ed. The Russian Avant-Garde: Art & Architecture. (Academy Editions Ser.). (Illus.). 96p. 1984. pap. 14.95 (ISBN 0-312-69612-4). St Martin.
Cooke, Charles. Playing the Piano for Pleasure. LC 70-110824. (Illus.). Repr. of 1941 ed. lib. bdg. 19.75x (ISBN 0-8371-3224-X, COPP). Greenwood.
--Playing the Piano for Pleasure. 1960. pap. 5.95 (ISBN 0-671-57801-4, Fireside). S&S.
Cooke, Charles E. & Van Vogt, A. E. Hypnotism Handbook. 14.95 (ISBN 0-87505-086-7). Borden.
Cooke, Cynthia W. & Dworkin, Susan. The Ms. Guide to a Woman's Health. 528p. 1984. pap. 4.95 (ISBN 0-425-07313-0). Berkley Pub.
Cooke, D., jt. auth. see Clarke, G. M.
Cooke, D., jt. ed. see Hiorns, R. W.
Cooke, D., et al. BASIC Statistical Computing. 176p. 1982. pap. text ed. 14.95 (ISBN 0-7131-3441-0). E Arnold.
Cooke, D. J. & Bez, H. E. Computer Mathematics. LC 83-7588. (Cambridge Computer Science Texts Ser.: No. 18). (Illus.). 425p. 1984. 49.50 (ISBN 0-521-25341-1); pap. 19.95 (ISBN 0-521-27324-2). Cambridge U Pr.
Cooke, D. J., jt. auth. see Solymar, L.
Cooke, Delmar G. William Dean Howells: A Critical Study. 1978. Repr. of 1922 ed. lib. bdg. 45.00 (ISBN 0-8495-0833-9). Arden Lib.
--William Dean Howells: A Critical Study. LC 73-10412. 1922. lib. bdg. 25.00 (ISBN 0-8414-3380-1). Folcroft.
Cooke, Deryck. Gustav Mahler: An Introduction to His Music. 1980. 27.95 (ISBN 0-521-23175-2); pap. 8.95 (ISBN 0-521-29847-4). Cambridge U Pr.
--I Saw the World End: A Study of Wagner's Ring. 1979. 25.00 (ISBN 0-19-315316-5). Oxford U Pr.
--Language of Music. 1959. pap. 11.50x (ISBN 0-19-284004-5, OPB). Oxford U Pr.
--Vindications: Essays on Romantic Music. LC 82-4295. 160p. 1982. 29.95 (ISBN 0-521-24765-9); pap. 9.95 (ISBN 0-521-28947-5). Cambridge U Pr.

Cooke, Donald A. Life & Death of Stars. LC 84-4266. 228p. 1985. 29.95 (ISBN 0-517-55268-X). Crown.

Cooke, Donald E. Atlas of the Presidents. rev. ed. LC 81-6525. (Profile Ser.). (Illus.). 96p. (gr. 6 up). 1984. 8.95 (ISBN 0-8437-1045-4). Hammond Inc.

Cooke, Dorian, tr. see Djilas, Milovan.

Cooke, Dwight. There Is No Asia. LC 79-118487. (Essay & General Literature Index Reprint Ser). 1971. Repr. of 1954 ed. 27.50x (ISBN 0-8046-1404-0, Pub by Kennikat). Assoc Faculty Pr.

Cooke, E. I. & Cooke, R. W. Gardner's Chemical Synonyms & Trade Names: A Dictionary & Commercial Handbook Containing Over 35,500 Definitions & Identifications. 8th ed. 776p. 1980. 150.00x (ISBN 0-291-39678-X, Pub. by Tech Pr). State Mutual Bk.

Cooke, E. M. & Gibson, G. L. Essential Clinical Microbiology: An Introductory Text. 276p. 1983. pap. 16.95 (ISBN 0-471-90017-6, Pub. by Wiley Med). Wiley.

Cooke, E. Thornton. Speaking Dust: Thomas & Jane Carlyle. 1938. 20.00 (ISBN 0-8274-3478-2). R West.

Cooke, Edward & Rogers, Woodes. English Privateers at Cabo San Lucas. The Descriptive Accounts of Puerto Seguro. Andrews, Thomas F., ed. (Los Angeles Miscellany Ser.). 36.00 (ISBN 0-317-11599-5). Dawsons.

Cooke, Edward F. Detailed Analysis of the Constitution. 4th ed. (Quality Paperback Ser.: No. 36). (Orig.). 1977. pap. 3.95 (ISBN 0-8226-0036-6). Littlefield.

--A Detailed Analysis of the Constitution. 5th rev. ed. LC 83-24628. (Helix Bks.: No. 383). 190p. 1984. 7.95 (ISBN 0-8226-0383-7). Rowman & Allanheld.

--A Detailed Analysis of the Constitution. 5th ed. LC 83-24628. (Helix Ser.: No. 383). 190p. 1984. pap. 7.95 (ISBN 0-8226-0383-7). Littlefield.

Cooke, Edward F. & Janosik, G. Edward. Guide to Pennsylvania Politics. LC 79-14132. (Illus.). 1980. Repr. of 1957 ed. lib. bdg. 19.75x (ISBN 0-313-21994-X, COGP). Greenwood.

Cooke, Edward I., jt. auth. see Gardner, William.

Cooke, Edward I., ed. Handbook of Chemical Synonyms & Trade Names. 8th ed. 776p. 1978. 66.00 (ISBN 0-685-56918-7). CRC Pr.

Cooke, Edwin D., Jr. Interpersonal Orientation of Elementary Teachers with Mexican-American Pupils. LC 74-76566. 1975. Repr. of 1967 ed. soft bdg. 11.95 (ISBN 0-88247-352-2). R & E Pubs.

Cooke, Francis B. Seamanship for Yachtsmen. 1977. lib. bdg. 69.95 (ISBN 0-8490-2582-6). Gordon Pr.

Cooke, Frank, jt. auth. see Cooke, Ann.

Cooke, Frank E. Kids Can Write Songs, Too! (Illus.). 120p. (Orig.). (gr. 6-12). 1985. pap. 6.95 (ISBN 0-940076-02-0). Fiesta City.

--Write That Song! How to Get Started & Where to Go from There. Rev. ed. LC 81-90107. (Illus.). 132p. (Orig.). 1982. pap. 3.95 (ISBN 0-940076-00-4, RB101). Fiesta City.

Cooke, Fred J. Ku Klux Klan: America's Recurring Nightmare. LC 80-19325. (Illus.). 160p. (YA) (gr. 7 up). 1981. PLB 9.79 (ISBN 0-671-34055-7). Messner.

Cooke, Frederick H. The Law of Trade & Labor Combinations As Applicable to Boycotts, Strikes, Trade Conspiracies, Monopolies, Pools, Trusts, & Kindred Topics. xxv, 214p. 1981. Repr. of 1898 ed. lib. bdg. 24.00x (ISBN 0-8377-0430-8). Rothman.

Cooke, G. Elton. A Funeral to Prepare. Date not set. pap. cancelled (ISBN 0-8054-2302-8). Broadman.

Cooke, G. W. Agricultural Research Nineteen Thirty-One to Nineteen Eighty-One. 367p. 1981. 90.00x (ISBN 0-7084-0180-5, Pub. by CAB Bks England). State Mutual Bk.

--Fertilizing for Maximum Yield. 3rd ed. 320p. 1982. write for info. Macmillan.

--Fertilizing for Maximum Yield. 3rd ed. 473p. 1982. 32.50 (ISBN 0-02-949310-2). Free Pr.

Cooke, Gail, ed. see Hosck, Martha A.

Cooke, Gary. Butterfish & Other Poems. (Flowering Quince Poetry Ser.: No. 2). (Illus.). 24p. (Orig.). 1978. pap. 4.50 (ISBN 0-940592-03-7). Heyeck Pr.

Cooke, Geoffrey, et al. Youth & Justice: Young Offenders in Ireland. (Turoe Press Ser.). 230p. pap. 15.00 (ISBN 0-905223-24-1, Dist. by Scribner). M Boyars.

Cooke, George W. A Bibliography of James Russell Lowell. LC 77-13536. 1977. Repr. of 1906 ed. lib. bdg. 20.00 (ISBN 0-89341-453-0). Longwood Pub Group.

--Bibliography of Ralph Waldo Emerson. 1908. 32.00 (ISBN 0-527-19250-3). Kraus Repr.

--China: Being "The Times" Special Correspondence from China in the Years 1857-1858. LC 72-79814. (China Library Ser.). (Illus.). 1972. Repr. of 1858 ed. lib. bdg. 37.00 (ISBN 0-8420-1371-7). Scholarly Res Inc.

--George Eliot: A Critical Study of the Life, Writings & Philosophy. LC 73-11158. 1883. lib. bdg. 49.50 (ISBN 0-8414-3376-3). Folcroft.

--John Sullivan Dwight: A Biography. LC 79-90210. (Music Reprint Ser). 1969. Repr. of 1898 ed. 35.00 (ISBN 0-306-71818-9). Da Capo.

--Letters of George Wm. Curtis to John S. Dwight: Brook Farm & Concord. 1898. Repr. 20.00 (ISBN 0-8274-2840-5). R West.

--Poets & Problems: Tennyson, Ruskin, Browning. LC 72-196438. 1886. lib. bdg. 25.00 (ISBN 0-8414-2385-7). Folcroft.

--The Poets of Transcendentalism: An Anthology. 59.95 (ISBN 0-8490-0868-9). Gordon Pr.

--Ralph Waldo Emerson. LC 74-8996. 1882. lib. bdg. 30.00 (ISBN 0-8414-3367-4). Folcroft.

--Unitarianism in America. LC 72-155153. Repr. of 1902 ed. 12.50 (ISBN 0-404-01699-5). AMS Pr.

Cooke, George W., ed. Poets of Transcendentalism: An Anthology. LC 72-126410. (Literature & Criticism Ser). 1971. Repr. of 1903 ed. lib. bdg. 21.00 (ISBN 0-8337-0652-7). B Franklin.

Cooke, George W., ed. see Curtis, George W.

Cooke, George Willis, ed. Early Letters of George Williamm Curtis to John S. Dwight: Brook Farm & Cincord. 1978. Repr. of 1898 ed. lib. bdg. 30.00 (ISBN 0-8414-9976-4). Folcroft.

Cooke, Gerald. The Role of the Forensic Psychologist. 432p. 1980. 44.75x (ISBN 0-398-03905-4). C C Thomas.

Cooke, Grace. The Illumined Ones. (Illus.). 1966. pap. 5.95 (ISBN 0-85487-058-X). De Vorss.

--The Jewel in the Lotus. 1973. pap. 5.95 (ISBN 0-85487-032-6). De Vorss.

--Meditation. 1955. pap. 4.95 (ISBN 0-85487-059-8). De Vorss.

--The New Mediumship. 1965. pap. 4.95 (ISBN 0-85487-013-X). De Vorss.

--Sun Men of the Americas. pap. 5.95 (ISBN 0-85487-057-1). De Vorss.

Cooke, Grace & Cooke, Ivan. The Light in Britain. (Illus.). 1971. pap. 5.95 (ISBN 0-85487-056-3). De Vorss.

--The Return of Arthur Conan Doyle. (Illus.). 1963. 9.95 (ISBN 0-85487-037-7). De Vorss.

Cooke, Grace M. The Grapple. LC 74-22775. (Labor Movement in Fiction & Non-Fiction). Repr. of 1905 ed. 27.50 (ISBN 0-404-58415-2). AMS Pr.

Cooke, H. B., jt. ed. see Maglio, Vincent J.

Cooke, Hereward Lester. Painting Techniques of the Masters. rev. & enl. ed. LC 75-188323. (Illus.). 272p. 1972. 24.50 (ISBN 0-8230-3863-7). Watson-Guptill.

Cooke, Hope. Time Change: An American Women's Extraordinary Story. 336p. 1982. pap. 3.50 (ISBN 0-425-05497-7). Berkley Pub.

Cooke, Ivan. Healing by the Spirit. 1955. pap. 7.95 (ISBN 0-85487-039-3). De Vorss.

Cooke, Ivan, jt. auth. see Cooke, Grace.

Cooke, J. F. Great Men & Famous Musicians. 59.95 (ISBN 0-8490-0259-1). Gordon Pr.

--Music Masters Old & New. 59.95 (ISBN 0-8490-0682-1). Gordon Pr.

--Standard History of Music. 59.95 (ISBN 0-8490-1120-5). Gordon Pr.

Cooke, Jacob E. Alexander Hamilton: A Biography. (Illus.). 288p. 1982. 17.95 (ISBN 0-684-17344-1, ScribT). Scribner.

--Tench Coxe & the Early Republic. (Institute of Early American History & Culture Ser.). (Illus.). xiv, 573p. 1978. 32.50 (ISBN 0-8078-1308-7). U of NC Pr.

Cooke, Jacob E., ed. The Federalist. LC 61-6971. 1961. 35.00x (ISBN 0-8195-3016-6). Wesleyan U Pr.

--The Federalist. LC 82-2815. 704p. 1982. pap. 12.95 (ISBN 0-8195-6077-4). Wesleyan U Pr.

Cooke, Jacqueline, jt. auth. see Travers, Robert M.

Cooke, James F. Great Pianists on Piano Playing. LC 74-27332. Repr. of 1913 ed. 27.50 (ISBN 0-404-12885-8). AMS Pr.

--Great Singers on the Art of Singing. LC 74-27333. Repr. of 1921 ed. 24.50 (ISBN 0-404-12886-6). AMS Pr.

Cooke, James J. France: 1789-1962. (Modern History Reference Ser.). 287p. 1975. 22.00 (ISBN 0-208-01510-8, Archon). Shoe String.

--The New French Imperialism, 1880-1910: The Third Republic & Colonial Expansion. (Library of Politics & Society Ser.). 224p. 1973. 18.50 (ISBN 0-208-01320-2, Archon). Shoe String.

Cooke, James J., ed. see French Colonial Historical Society.

Cooke, James J., ed. see French Colonial Historical Society, 5th Meeting.

Cooke, James J., jt. ed. see Heggoy, Alf A.

Cooke, James J., jt. ed. see Owens, Harry P.

Cooke, Jean, et al. Archaeology. rev. ed. (Modern Knowledge Library). (Illus.). 48p. (gr. 5 up). 1982. PLB 9.90 (ISBN 0-531-09051-5, Warwick). Watts.

Cooke, Jo. Greene's Tu Quoque. LC 72-133649. (Tudor Facsimile Texts. Old English Plays: No. 131). Repr. of 1913 ed. 49.50 (ISBN 0-404-53431-7). AMS Pr.

Cooke, John. John Milton: 1608-1674. LC 74-5138. 1973. Repr. of 1908 ed. lib. bdg. 10.00 (ISBN 0-8414-3549-9). Folcroft.

--John Milton: 1608-1674. 56p. 1980. Repr. of 1908 ed. lib. bdg. 12.50 (ISBN 0-8482-3553-3). Norwood Edns.

--The Novels of Nadine Gordimer: Private Lives-Public Landscapes. 248p. 1985. text ed. 27.50 (ISBN 0-8071-1247-X). La State U Pr.

Cooke, John, ed. The Dublin Book of Irish Verse, Seventeen Twenty-Eight - Nineteen Hundred Nine. facsimile ed. LC 70-152148. (Granger Index Reprint Ser.). Repr. of 1909 ed. 38.50 (ISBN 0-8369-6251-6). Ayer Co Pubs.

Cooke, John B. The Snowblind Moon: A Novel of the West. 687p. 1985. 19.95 (ISBN 0-671-45089-1). S&S.

Cooke, John D. Minor Victorian Poets. 1977. Repr. of 1928 ed. 20.00 (ISBN 0-89984-169-4). Century Bookbindery.

Cooke, John D. & Stevenson, Lionel. English Literature of the Victorian Period. LC 70-102481. (Illus.). 1971. Repr. of 1949 ed. 19.00x (ISBN 0-8462-1509-8). Russell.

Cooke, John E. Georges Bernanos: A Study of Christian Commitment. 197p. 1981. text ed. 38.50x (ISBN 0-86127-202-1, Pub. by Avebury England). Humanities.

--The Life of Stonewall Jackson. facsimile ed. LC 76-179511. (Select Bibliographies Reprint Ser). Repr. of 1863 ed. 18.00 (ISBN 0-8369-6640-6). Ayer Co Pubs.

--Mohun. LC 68-20008. (Americans in Fiction Ser.). (Illus.). lib. bdg. 16.00 (ISBN 0-8398-0271-4); pap. text ed. 4.95x (ISBN 0-89197-856-9). Irvington.

--My Lady Pokahontas. LC 68-20009. (Americans in Fiction Ser.). lib. bdg. 15.00 (ISBN 0-8398-0272-2); pap. text ed. 4.95x (ISBN 0-89197-862-3). Irvington.

--Pretty Mrs. Gaston & Other Stories. facsimile ed. LC 74-94713. (Short Story Index Reprint Ser.). 1874. 18.00 (ISBN 0-8369-3092-4). Ayer Co Pubs.

--Surry of Eagle's Nest. LC 68-23718. (Americans in Fiction Ser.). Repr. of 1866 ed. lib. bdg. 14.00 (ISBN 0-8398-0273-0). Irvington.

--Virginia: A History of the People. LC 72-3765. (American Commonwealths: No. 1). Repr. of 1903 ed. 42.00 (ISBN 0-404-57201-4). AMS Pr.

--The Virginia Comedians. LC 68-23717. (Americans in Fiction Ser.). Repr. of 1854 ed. lib. bdg. 17.00 (ISBN 0-8398-0274-9). Irvington.

--Wearing the Grey: Being Personal Portraits, Scenes & Adventures of the War. LC 59-13533. (Indiana University Civil War Centennial Ser.). (Illus.). 1968. Repr. of 1959 ed. 36.00 (ISBN 0-527-19270-8). Kraus Repr.

Cooke, K. L., jt. ed. see Ludwig, D.

Cooke, Kenneth, jt. auth. see Busenberg, Stavros.

Cooke, Kenneth, jt. ed. see Renfrew, Colin.

Cooke, Kenneth L., jt. auth. see Bellman, Richard.

Cooke, Kenneth L., jt. auth. see Bellman, Richard E.

Cooke, M. Brazil on the March. 1976. lib. bdg. 59.95 (ISBN 0-8490-1546-4). Gordon Pr.

Cooke, M. & Dennis, A. J., eds. Polynuclear Aromatic Hydrocarbons V: Chemical & Biological Fate Symposium. 770p. 1982. 49.95 (ISBN 0-387-47009-3). Springer-Verlag.

Cooke, M., ed. see Grosseteste, Robert.

Cooke, Marcus & Dennis, Anthony J. Polynuclear Aromatic Hydrocarbons: Formation, Metabolism & Measurement. (International Poynuclear Aromatic Symposium on Hydrocarbons). 1301p. 1983. 65.00 (ISBN 0-935470-16-6). Battelle.

--Polynuclear Aromatic Hydrocarbons: Mechanisms, Methods & Metabolism. (International Symposium on Polynuclear Aromatic Hydrocarbons Ser.). 1504p. 1984. 75.00 (ISBN 0-935470-22-0). Battelle.

Cooke, Marcus & Dennis, Anthony J., eds. Chemical Analysis & Biological Fate: Polynuclear Aromatic Hydrocarbons. (International Symposium on Polynuclear Aromatic Hydrocarbons Ser.). 770p. 1981. 59.95 (ISBN 0-935470-09-3). Battelle.

--Polynuclear Aromatic Hydrocarbons: Physical & Biological Chemistry. (International Symposium on Polynuclear Aromatic Hydrocarbons, Sixth). 947p. 1982. 65.00 (ISBN 0-935470-13-1). Battelle.

Cooke, Marjorie. Never Too Late. 157p. 1980. pap. 2.75 (ISBN 0-89877-019-X). Jeremy Bks.

Cooke, Marjorie B. Dramatic Episodes. LC 79-50023. (One-Act Plays in Reprint Ser.). 1980. Repr. of 1904 ed. 19.50x (ISBN 0-8486-2047-X). Core Collection.

Cooke, Michael. Acts of Inclusion: Studies Bearing on an Elementary Theory of Romanticism. LC 78-21909. (Illus.). 1979. 27.00x (ISBN 0-300-02303-0). Yale U Pr.

--The Ancient Curse of the Baskervilles. LC 82-83499. 63p. 1984. 11.95 (ISBN 0-934468-14-1). Gaslight.

Cooke, Michael G. Afro-American Literature in the Twentieth Century: The Achievement of Intimacy. LC 84-5066. 234p. 1984. 18.50x (ISBN 0-300-03218-8). Yale U Pr.

--Blind Man Traces the Circle: On the Patterns & Philosophy of Byron's Poetry. LC 68-27406. pap. 60.80 (ISBN 0-8357-9495-4, 2009053). Bks Demand UMI.

Cooke, Miriam. The Anatomy of an Egyptian Intellectual: Yahya Haqqi. LC 83-70809. 188p. 1984. 24.00 (ISBN 0-89410-395-4); pap. 14.00 (ISBN 0-89410-396-2). Three Continents.

Cooke, Morris L. & Murray, Philip. Organized Labor & Production: Next Steps in Industrial Democracy. LC 73-156409. (American Labor Ser., No. 2). 1971. Repr. of 1946 ed. 20.00 (ISBN 0-405-02918-7). Ayer Co Pubs.

Cooke, Nelson M. & Adams, Herbert F. Arithmetic Review for Electronics. 1968. 23.85 (ISBN 0-07-012516-3). McGraw.

Cooke, Nelson M., et al. Basic Mathematics for Electronics. 5th ed. LC 82-226. (Illus.). 688p. 1982. 32.00x (ISBN 0-07-012514-7). McGraw.

Cooke, Nicholas F. Satan in Society. LC 73-20617. (Sex, Marriage & Society Ser.). 412p. 1974. Repr. of 1876 ed. 31.00x (ISBN 0-405-05796-2). Ayer Co Pubs.

Cooke, P. Region, Class & Gender: A European Comparison. (Illus.). 62p. 1984. pap. 20.00 (ISBN 0-08-032303-0). Pergamon.

Cooke, P. & Woodward, F. Controlling Company Car Costs. 200p. 1985. text ed. price not set (ISBN 0-566-02474-8). Gower Pub Co.

Cooke, P., jt. ed. see Loveday, P.

Cooke, Peter. Financing the Transport Function. 1975. 90.00x (ISBN 0-903763-56-7, Pub. by MCB Pubns). State Mutual Bk.

Cooke, Peter N. The Company Car: Its Allocation, Acquisition & Administration. 128p. 1975. text ed. 34.00x (ISBN 0-7161-0272-2). Gower Pub Co.

--Energy Saving in Distribution. 288p. 1981. text ed. 54.00x (ISBN 0-566-02155-2). Gower Pub Co.

--Inflation Management in Motor Transport Operations. 192p. 1978. text ed. 41.95x (ISBN 0-566-02056-4). Gower Pub Co.

Cooke, Philip. Theories of Planning & Spatial Development. (The Built Environment Ser.). 311p. 1984. pap. 11.95 (ISBN 0-09-153001-6, Pub. by Hutchinson Educ). Longwood Pub Group.

Cooke, Philip & Van der Beek, Jan M. Tax Aspects of Acquisition & Mergers. 2nd ed. (Orig.). 1983. pap. text ed. 31.00 (ISBN 90-654-4151-4, Pub. by Kluwer Law & Taxation). Kluwer Academic.

Cooke, Philip & Van der Beek, Jan M., eds. Tax Aspects of Acquisitions & Mergers. 148p. 1982. pap. 35.00 cancelled (ISBN 90-200-0629-0, Pub. by Kluwer Law Netherlands). Kluwer Academic.

Cooke, Philip P. Froissart Ballads, & Other Poems. LC 72-4959. (The Romantic Tradition in American Literature Ser.). 220p. 1972. Repr. of 1847 ed. 20.00 (ISBN 0-405-04631-6). Ayer Co Pubs.

Cooke, Philip St. G. The Conquest of New Mexico & California: An Historical & Personal Narrative. 1977. Repr. lib. bdg. 59.00x (ISBN 0-403-07682-X). Scholarly.

Cooke, Philip St. George see St. George Cooke, Philip.

Cooke, Philip St George. The Conquest of New Mexico & California: An Historical & Personal Narrative. Cortes, Carlos E., ed. LC 76-1244. (Chicano Heritage Ser.). 1976. Repr. of 1878 ed. 24.50x (ISBN 0-405-09497-3). Ayer Co Pubs.

Cooke, Phillip S., ed. The Second Symposium on American Cuisine. 256p. 1984. 39.95 (ISBN 0-442-21743-9). Van Nos Reinhold.

Cooke, R. The Mathematics of Sonya Kovalevskaya. (Illus.). 275p. 1984. 29.80 (ISBN 0-387-96030-9). Springer-Verlag.

Cooke, R. C. & Rayner, A. D. Ecology of Saprotrophic Fungi. (Illus.). 384p. 1984. text ed. 50.00 (ISBN 0-582-44260-5). Longman.

Cooke, R. J., jt. auth. see Trevena, D. H.

Cooke, R. U. Geomorphological Hazards in Los Angeles: A Study of Slope & Sediment Problems in a Metropolitan County. LC 84-9234. (London Research Series in Geography: No. 7). (Illus.). 192p. 1984. text ed. 35.00x (ISBN 0-04-551090-3). Allen Unwin.

Cooke, R. U. & Brunsden, D. Urban Geomorphology in Drylands. 1982. 32.00x (ISBN 0-19-823239-X). Oxford U Pr.

Cooke, R. V. & Johnson, J. H. Trends in Geography: An Introductory Survey. 1969. pap. 7.00 (ISBN 0-08-006674-7). Pergamon.

Cooke, R. W., jt. auth. see Cooke, E. I.

Cooke, Rebecca. Witch's D. 1984. 5.75 (ISBN 0-8062-2329-4). Carlton.

Cooke, Robert, jt. auth. see Rosenfeld, Charles.

Cooke, Robert A., jt. auth. see Georgopoulos, Basil S.

Cooke, Robert A., jt. auth. see Kornbluh, Hyman.

Cooke, Robert E., jt. ed. see Osler, Sonia F.

Cooke, Ronald J. Money-Making Ideas for Retirees: Your Guide to Starting a Second Career or Earning More Income. 1984. 8.95 (ISBN 0-7736-1126-6). Beaufort Bks NY.

Cooke, Ronald U. & Doornkamp, John C. Geomorphology in Environmental Management: An Introduction. (Illus.). 1974. pap. text ed. 15.95x (ISBN 0-19-874021-2). Oxford U Pr.

Cooke, Ronald U. & Reeves, Richard W. Arroyos & Environmental Change in the American South-West. (Oxford Research Studies in Geography Ser.). (Illus.). 1976. 37.50x (ISBN 0-19-823213-6). Oxford U Pr.

Cooke, Ronald U. & Warren, Andrew. Geomorphology in Deserts. 1974. 40.00x (ISBN 0-520-02280-7). U of Cal Pr.

Cooke, Rose. Huckleberries Gathered from New England Hills. 1972. Repr. of 1891 ed. 24.00 (ISBN 0-8422-8029-4). Irvington.

--Root-Bound. LC 68-23719. (Americans in Fiction Ser.). (Illus.). lib. bdg. 14.00x (ISBN 0-8398-0275-7); pap. text ed. 4.95x (ISBN 0-89197-924-7). Irvington.

--Somebody's Neighbors. 1972. Repr. of 1881 ed. lib. bdg. 26.00 (ISBN 0-8422-8028-6). Irvington.

Cooke, Sidney R. & Davenport, E. H. The Oil Trusts & Anglo-American Relations. LC 75-6467. (The History & Politics of Oil Ser). (Illus.). xii, 272p. 1976. Repr. of 1923 ed. 19.75 (ISBN 0-88355-286-8). Hyperion Conn.

Cooke, Thomas, tr. see Hesiodus.

Cooke, Thomas D. The Old French & Chaucerian Fabliaux: A Study of Their Comic Climax. LC 77-77861. 224p. 1978. 18.00x (ISBN 0-8262-0225-X). U of Mo Pr.
Cooke, Thomas D., ed. The Present State of Scholarship in Fourteenth Century Literature. (Illus.). 352p. 1983. 24.80 (ISBN 0-8262-0379-5). U of MO Pr.
Cooke, Thomas D. & Honeycutt, Benjamin L., eds. The Humor of the Fabliaux: A Collection of Critical Essays. LC 74-82563. 224p. 1974. 18.00x (ISBN 0-8262-0168-7). U of Mo Pr.
Cooke, Thomas P., jt. ed. see Apolloni, Tony.
Cooke, Tom, illus. Bert & Ernie on the Go. LC 80-54574. (Sesame Street Pop-Up Ser.: No. 15). (Illus.). 16p. (ps-2). 1981. 5.95 (ISBN 0-394-84869-1). Random.
--Sesame Street Playtime Book. (Illus.). (ps-1). 1982. pap. 6.95 (ISBN 0-394-85279-6). Random.
Cooke, Virginia & Trussler, Simon, eds. Beckett on File. (Writers on File Ser.). 96p. (Orig.). 1985. pap. 6.50 (ISBN 0-413-54560-1). Methuen Inc.
Cooke, W. Bridge. Ecology of Fungi. 288p. 1979. 84.50 (ISBN 0-8493-5343-2). CRC Pr.
Cooke, W. P. Quantitative Methods for Management Decisions. 704p. 1985. 33.95 (ISBN 0-07-012518-X); study guide 13.95 (ISBN 0-07-012519-8). McGraw.
Cooke, W. T. & Holmes, G. K. Coeliac Disease. (Illus.). 281p. 1984. text ed. 55.00 (ISBN 0-317-19629-4). Churchill.
Cooke, William. Elements of Dramatic Criticism. Repr. of 1775 ed. 27.00x (ISBN 3-4870-4277-0). Adlers Foreign Bks.
--Memoirs of Charles Macklin. LC 72-82822. 1804. 27.50 (ISBN 0-405-08378-5, Blom Pubns). Ayer Co Pubs.
--The Nemesis Conjecture. 1980. pap. 2.25 (ISBN 0-8439-0802-5, Pub by Nordon Pubns). Dorchester Pub Co.
--Orion's Shroud. 1981. pap. 2.75 (ISBN 0-8439-0886-6, Pub. by Nordon Pubns). Dorchester Pub Co.
Cooke, William, ed. The Table-Talk & Bon-Mots of Samuel Foote. Repr. of 1902 ed. 20.00 (ISBN 0-8274-4153-3). R West.
Cooke-Macgregor, Frances. After Plastic Surgery: Adaptation & Adjustment. 160p. 1979. 25.95x (ISBN 0-686-84385-1). Bergin & Garvey.
Cookenboo, Leslie, Jr. Crude Oil Pipe Lines & Competition in the Oil Industry & Costs of Operating Crude Oil Pipe Lines. Bruchey, Stuart, ed. LC 78-22669. (Rice Institute Pamphlet: Energy in the American Economy Ser.: Vol. 41, No. 1). (Illus.). 1979. Repr. of 1955 ed. lib. bdg. 25.50x (ISBN 0-405-11973-9). Ayer Co Pubs.
Cookey, S. J. S. King Jaja of the Niger Delta: His Life & Times 1821-1891. LC 73-88683. 192p. 1974. text ed. 18.95x (ISBN 0-88357-026-2). Nok Pubs.
Cooking Committee of Concord Alternative Residence, Inc., ed. Family Occasions: A Cookbook. LC 83-51249. (Illus.). 216p. 1984. pap. 5.95 (ISBN 0-89909-029-X). Yankee Bks.
Cooklin, Lawrence. Profitable Mail Order Marketing. 1976. 19.95x (ISBN 0-434-90259-4). Intl Ideas.
Cookman, jt. auth. see Teacher.
Cookridge, E. H. George Blake: Double Agent. (Espionage-Intelligence Library). 256p. 1982. pap. 2.75 (ISBN 0-345-30264-8). Ballantine.
--The Orient Express: The Life & Time of the World's Most Famous Train. 1978. 12.95 (ISBN 0-394-41176-5). Random.
--The Orient Express: The Life & Times of the World's Most Famous Train. LC 78-57119. (Illus.). 1980. pap. 6.95i (ISBN 0-06-090770-3, CN 770, CN). Har-Row.
Cooks, R. G, ed. Collision Spectroscopy. LC 77-10761. (Illus.). 459p. 1977. 65.00x (ISBN 0-306-31044-9, Plenum Pr). Plenum Pub.
Cooks, R. G., et al. Metastable Ions. LC 72-97419. 296p. 1973. 68.00 (ISBN 0-444-41119-4). Elsevier.
Cooks, Robert, jt. auth. see Rosenfeld, Charles.
Cooksey, Brian, jt. auth. see Blakemore, Kenneth.
Cooksey, John. Clinical Vectorcardiography & Electrocardiography. 2nd ed. (Illus.). 1977. 68.50 (ISBN 0-8151-1851-1). Year Bk Med.
Cooksey, Tom, et al. The Complete Guide to American Pocket Watches. 5th ed. (Illus.). 376p. 1985. pap. 10.95 (ISBN 0-89145-293-1). Overstreet.
Cookson, Catherine. The Bannaman Legacy. 528p. 1985. 18.95 (ISBN 0-671-53024-0). Summit Bks.
--The Black Velvet Gown. 368p. 1984. 15.95 (ISBN 0-671-46788-3). Summit Bks.
--The Black Velvet Gown. 1985. pap. 3.95 (ISBN 0-317-19318-X). PB.
--Glass Virgin. LC 70-81283. 1969. 6.95 (ISBN 0-672-50685-8). Bobbs.
--Lanky Jones. LC 80-22676. 192p. (gr. 6 up). 1981. 11.25 (ISBN 0-688-00430-X); PLB 11.88 (ISBN 0-688-00431-8). Lothrop.
--The Man Who Cried. LC 79-87976. 1979. 10.95 (ISBN 0-688-03520-5). Morrow.
--Mary Ann & Bill. LC 78-64881. 1979. 8.95 (ISBN 0-688-03393-8). Morrow.
--Mary Ann's Angels. LC 78-53413. 1978. 7.95 (ISBN 0-688-03317-2). Morrow.
--Our John Willie. LC 73-22687. 224p. 1974. 6.95 (ISBN 0-672-51897-X). Bobbs.
--Tilly. 1982. pap. 3.50 (ISBN 0-671-45219-3). PB.
--Tilly Alone. LC 81-11203. 272p. 1982. 13.50 (ISBN 0-688-00455-5). Morrow.
--Tilly Alone. 1983. pap. 3.50 (ISBN 0-671-42606-0). PB.
--Tilly Wed. Orig. Title: Tilly Trotter Wed. 384p. 1980. 11.95 (ISBN 0-688-00188-2). Morrow.
--Tilly Wed. 1982. pap. 3.50 (ISBN 0-671-42605-2). PB.
--The Whip. 384p. 1983. 14.95 (ISBN 0-686-37591-2). Summit Bks.
--The Whip. 1984. pap. 3.95 (ISBN 0-671-46545-7). PB.
Cookson, G. M., tr. see Aeschylus.
Cookson, J. E. The Friends of Peace: Anti-War Liberalism in England 1793-1815. LC 81-3909. 320p. 1982. 44.50 (ISBN 0-521-23928-1). Cambridge U Pr.
--Lord Liverpool's Administration: The Crucial Years, 1815-1822. xii, 422p. 1975. 30.00 (ISBN 0-208-01495-0, Archon). Shoe String.
Cookson, John & Nottingham, Judith. Survey of Chemical & Biological Warfare. LC 79-128595. 432p. pap. 3.95 (ISBN 0-85345-223-7). Monthly Rev.
Cookson, John W. The Retired Investor's Guide to Financial Security. LC 83-11161. 237p. 1983. 17.95 (ISBN 0-13-778977-7); pap. 7.95 (ISBN 0-13-778969-6). P-H.
Cookson, Peter W., Jr. & Persell, Carolina H. Preparing for Power: America's Elite Boarding Schools. LC 85-47559. 288p. 1986. 20.95 (ISBN 0-465-06268-7). Basic.
Cookson, R. F., jt. auth. see Chesseman, G. W.
Cookson, William. Advanced Methods for Sheet Metal Work. 6th ed. (Illus.). 1975. 39.95x (ISBN 0-291-39427-2). Intl Ideas.
--A Guide to the Cantos of Ezra Pound. (Persea Lamplighter Titles Ser.). 300p. 1985. 24.95 (ISBN 0-89255-081-3); pap. 14.95 (ISBN 0-89255-082-1). Persea Bks.
Cookson, William, ed. Agenda Double Issue: Hugh Macdiarmid & Scottish Poetry, Vol. 5, No. 4 & Vol. 6, No. 1. 1977. lib. bdg. 17.50 (ISBN 0-8495-0005-2). Arden Lib.
--Agenda: English Poetry Today, Vol. 6, No. 2. 1977. Repr. of 1968 ed. lib. bdg. 17.00 (ISBN 0-8495-0006-0). Arden Lib.
--Agenda: Francois Villon, Ezra Pound, Charles Tomlinson, Paul Celan, Peter Dale, Anne Beresford, Peter Porter, Kathleen Rainde, Hugh Gordon Porteus. 1977. lib. bdg. 17.50 (ISBN 0-8495-0014-1). Arden Lib.
--Agenda: Peter Dale, Michael Hamburger, Wallace Kaufman, Peter Dent, William Stafford, Herbert Reed, Basil Bunting, Tom Scott, Vol. 7 No. 2. 1977. lib. bdg. 17.50 (ISBN 0-8495-0009-5). Arden Lib.
--Agenda: Special Issue in Honour or Ezra Pound's Eighty-Fifth Birthday, Vol. 8 Nos. 3-4. 1977. lib. bdg. 27.50 (ISBN 0-8495-0012-5). Arden Lib.
--Agenda: Wyndham Lewis Special Issue. 1977. Repr. of 1970 ed. lib. bdg. 28.50 (ISBN 0-8495-0010-9). Arden Lib.
Cookson, William, ed. see Cocteau, Jean.
Cookson, William, ed. see Pound, Ezra.
Cookson, William, et al, eds. Agenda: M. Hamburger, K. Bosley, C. Clothier, K. Crossley-Holland, P. Dent, D. Harsent, Vol. 9 No. 1. 1977. lib. bdg. 17.50 (ISBN 0-8495-0013-3). Arden Lib.
Cool, J. & Smith, E. L., eds. Frontiers in Visual Science: Proceedings of the University of Houston College of Optometry Dedication Symposium, Houston Texas, March, 1977. LC 78-24191. (Springer Series in Optical Sciences: Vol. 8). (Illus.). 1978. 54.00 (ISBN 0-387-09185-8). Springer-Verlag.
Cool, Jeannie. Word Picture Puzzles. 1985. pap. 0.69 pocket size (ISBN 0-87239-822-6, 2812). Standard Pub.
Cool, Joyce. The Kidnapping of Courtney Van Allen & What's-Her-Name. LC 80-28455. 192p. (gr. 4-7). 1981. 8.95 (ISBN 0-394-84822-5); PLB 8.99 (ISBN 0-394-94822-X). Knopf.
--The Kidnapping of Courtney Van Allen & What's-Her-Name. (Bantam Starfire Bks.). 176p. (YA) 1984. pap. 2.25 (ISBN 0-553-23917-1). Bantam.
Cool, Phyllis, et al. The Psychology of Human Behavior: A Study Guide for Psychology, 100, 1984-1985. 165p. 1984. write for info. (ISBN 0-314-80337-8). West Pub.
Cool, Wouter. With the Dutch in the East: An Outline of the Military Operations in Lombock, 1894. Taylor, E. J., tr. from Dutch. LC 77-86968. (Illus.). Repr. of 1897 ed. 32.00 (ISBN 0-404-16702-0). AMS Pr.
Coolbrith, Ina, ed. see Stoddard, Charles W.
Coole, Arthur B. Ch'i Heavy Sword Coins of the Chou Dynasty, Vol. 5. LC 72-86801. (Encyclopedia of Chinese Coins Ser.: Vol. 5). (Illus.). 1976. 35.00x (ISBN 0-88000-014-7). Quarterman.
--Coins in China's History. 4th ed. (Illus.). 1965. 25.00 (ISBN 0-912706-01-5). M Akers.
--The Earliest Round Coins of China. LC 80-54408. (Encyclopedia of Chinese Coins Ser.: Vol. 7). 325p. 1981. lib. bdg. 40.00x (ISBN 0-88000-122-4). Quarterman.
--The Early Coins of the Chou Dynasty. LC 72-86804. (Encyclopedia of Chinese Coins: Vol. 2). (Illus.). 550p. 1973. 35.00x (ISBN 0-88000-010-4). Quarterman.
--Pointed Spade Coins of the Chou Dynasty. LC 72-86806. (Encyclopedia of Chinese Coins Ser: Vol. 4). (Illus.). 464p. 1975. 35.00x (ISBN 0-88000-012-0). Quarterman.
--Spade Coin Types of the Chou Dynasty. LC 76-86803. (Encyclopedia of Chinese Coins Ser.: Vol. 3). (Illus.). 1973. 35.00x (ISBN 0-88000-011-2). Quarterman.
--State of Ming Coin Knives & Minor Knife Coins. LC 72-86802. (Encyclopedia of Chinese Coins Ser.: Vol. 6). (Illus.). 1977. 35.00x (ISBN 0-88000-013-9). Quarterman.
--A Trouble Shooter for God in China. (Illus.). 1976. 20.00 (ISBN 0-912706-05-8). M Akers.
Coole, Arthur B., et al. Encyclopedia of Chinese Coins, Vol. 1, Bibliography Of Far Eastern Numismatology & A Coin Index. (Illus.). 1967. 35.00 (ISBN 0-912706-04-X). M Akers.
Coolen, Edward J. Nicholls's Concise Guide to the Navigation Examinations, Vol. 2. 11th ed. (Illus.). 512p. 1984. text ed. 60.00x (ISBN 0-85174-480-X, Pub. by Brown Son & Ferguson). Sheridan.
Coolen, John, jt. auth. see Roddy, Dennis.
Cooley, Adelaide N. The Monument Maker: A Biography of Frederick Ernst Triebel. 1978. 5.00 (ISBN 0-682-49051-2). Exposition Pr FL.
Cooley, Arnold J. The Toilet & Cosmetic Arts in Ancient & Modern Times: With a Review of All the Different Theories of Beauty, & Copious Allied Information Social, Hygienic, & Medical. LC 78-80248. (Research & Source Ser.: No. 511). 1970. Repr. of 1866 ed. 43.00 (ISBN 0-8337-0653-5). B Franklin.
Cooley, Charles H. Human Nature & the Social Order. LC 82-11002. (Social Science Classics Ser.). (Illus.). 482p. 1983. 19.95 (ISBN 0-87855-918-3). Transaction Bks.
--Social Organization: A Study of the Larger Mind. LC 80-15746. (Social Science Classics Ser.). 457p. 1983. pap. 19.95 (ISBN 0-87855-824-1). Transaction Bks.
--Social Process. LC 65-12395. (Arcturus Books Paperbacks). 494p. 1966. pap. 3.45 (ISBN 0-8093-0201-2). S Ill U Pr.
--Social Process. LC 65-12395. (Perspectives in Sociology Ser.). 494p. 1966. 10.00x (ISBN 0-8093-0200-4). S Ill U Pr.
--Sociological Theory & Social Research. LC 69-18159. Repr. of 1930 ed. 29.50x (ISBN 0-678-00477-3). Kelley.
Cooley, Denton A. Reflections & Observations. (Illus.). 240p. 1984. 14.95 (ISBN 0-89015-455-4). Eakin Pubns.
--Techniques in Cardiac Surgery. 2nd ed. (Illus.). 416p. 1984. 75.00 (ISBN 0-7216-2701-3). Saunders.
Cooley, Donald G. Science Book of Wonder Drugs. facsimile ed. LC 72-99627. (Essay Index Reprint Ser.). 1954. 20.00 (ISBN 0-8369-1562-3). Ayer Co Pubs.
Cooley, Doris H., ed. Ritual of Music. 12p. 1968. pap. text ed. 1.25 (ISBN 0-88053-318-8, S-79). Macoy Pub.
Cooley, Earl. Trimotor & Trail. (Illus.). 288p. 1984. 14.95 (ISBN 0-87842-173-4). Mountain Pr.
Cooley, Edwin J. Problem of Delinquency: The Study & Treatment of the Individual Delinquent. 1927. 17.50 (ISBN 0-8482-3591-6). Norwood Edns.
Cooley, Eli F. Genealogy of Early Settlers in Trenton & Ewing, "Old Hunterdon County", New Jersey. 1976. Repr. of 1883 ed. 15.00 (ISBN 0-912606-03-7). Hunterdon Hse.
Cooley, Eli F. & Cooley, William S. Genealogy of Early Settlers in Trenton & Ewing, "Old Hunterdon County", New Jersey. LC 76-45636. 336p. 1977. Repr. of 1883 ed. 17.50 (ISBN 0-8063-0744-7). Genealog Pub.
Cooley, Frank L. Indonesia: Church & Society. (Orig.). 1968. pap. 1.95 (ISBN 0-377-18021-1). Friend Pr.
Cooley, Henry B. Chartering & Charter Parties. LC 47-27564. pap. 41.50 (2022552). Bks Demand UMI.
Cooley, Henry S. A Study of Slavery in New Jersey. LC 78-63853. (Johns Hopkins University. Studies in the Social Sciences. Fourteenth Ser. 1896: 9-10). Repr. of 1896 ed. 11.50 (ISBN 0-404-61109-5). AMS Pr.
--A Study of Slavery in New Jersey. 1973. pap. 9.00 (ISBN 0-384-09779-0). Johnson Repr.
Cooley, John. Savages & Naturals: Black Portraits by White Writers in Modern American Literature. 208p. 1982. 21.50 (ISBN 0-87413-167-7). U Delaware Pr.
Cooley, John K. Libyan Sandstorm: The Complete Account of Qaddafi's Revolution. 1982. 16.50 (ISBN 0-03-060414-1). HR&W.
Cooley, June H. & Gooley, Frank B., eds. Trends in Ecological Research for the Nineteen Eighties. (NATO Conference Series I, Ecology: Vol. 7). 328p. 1985. 52.50x (ISBN 0-306-41889-4, Plenum Pr). Plenum Pub.
Cooley, Leland. The Dancer. 440p. 1984. pap. 3.95 (ISBN 0-8128-8073-0). Stein & Day.
Cooley, Leland F. California. LC 84-40237. 612p. 1984. 17.95 (ISBN 0-8128-2987-5). Stein & Day.
--Imaginology. 180p. 1984. 14.95 (ISBN 0-13-451386-X); pap. 5.95 (ISBN 0-13-451378-9). P-H.
Cooley, Marcia & Shaffer, Carol. Fundamentals of Nursing for Human Needs. 1982. text ed. 19.95 (ISBN 0-8359-2175-1); instrs'. manual avail. (ISBN 0-8359-2176-X). Reston.
--Nursing Skills for Human Needs. 1982. pap. text ed. 14.95 (ISBN 0-8359-5038-7). Reston.
Cooley, Marilyn, jt. auth. see Schlayer, Mary E.
Cooley, Maurice E., jt. auth. see Eddy, Frank W.
Cooley, Mike. Architect or Bee? The Human Technology Relationship. 150p. 1982. pap. 7.00 (ISBN 0-89608-131-1). South End Pr.
Cooley, Mortimer E. Scientific Blacksmith. LC 72-5041. (Technology & Society Ser.). (Illus.). 290p. 1972. Repr. of 1947 ed. 18.00 (ISBN 0-405-04693-6). Ayer Co Pubs.
--Scientific Blacksmith: An Autobiography of Mortimer E. Cooley. 290p. 1947. 4.50 (ISBN 0-317-33611-8, A00010); members 2.25 (ISBN 0-317-33612-6). ASME.
Cooley, Peter. The Company of Strangers. LC 75-23387. (Breakthrough Bks.). 80p. 1975. 6.95 (ISBN 0-8262-0191-1). U of Mo Pr.
--Miracle, Miracles. (Juniper Bk.: 18). 1975. 4.00 (ISBN 0-686-61874-2). Juniper Pr WI.
--Nightseasons. LC 82-74302. 1983. 14.95 (ISBN 0-915604-82-5); pap. 6.95 (ISBN 0-915604-83-3). Carnegie-Mellon.
--The Room Where Summer Ends. LC 79-51605. (Poetry Ser.). 1979. 8.95 (ISBN 0-915604-27-2); pap. 4.50 (ISBN 0-915604-28-0). Carnegie-Mellon.
Cooley, Peter, jt. auth. see Bennett, John.
Cooley, Phil. How to Value an Oil Jobbership for Purchase or Sale. 238p. 1982. 65.00 (ISBN 0-318-16167-2, F-3); members 50.00 (ISBN 0-318-16168-0). Petro Mktg Ed Found.
Cooley, Philip L. Financial Characteristics of Petroleum Marketers. 65p. 65.00 (ISBN 0-318-16164-8, F-1); members 45.00 (ISBN 0-318-16165-6). Petro Mktg Ed Found.
Cooley, Rossa B. Homes of the Freed. LC 76-100285. Repr. cancelled (ISBN 0-8371-2929-X, COF&, Pub. by Negro U Pr). Greenwood.
--School Acres: An Adventure in Rural Education. LC 71-106853. (Illus.). Repr. of 1930 ed. 17.50x (ISBN 0-8371-3475-7, CSC&). Greenwood.
Cooley, Stella G., jt. auth. see Jensen, Joyce D.
Cooley, Susan D. Country Walks in Connecticut: A Guide to The Nature Conservancy Preserves. (Country Walks Ser.). (Illus.). 218p. (Orig.). 1982. pap. 6.95 (ISBN 0-910146-41-1). Appalach Mtn.
Cooley, Thomas. Educated Lives: The Rise of Modern Autobiography in America. LC 76-28952. 1977. 12.00 (ISBN 0-8142-0263-2). Ohio St U Pr.
--The Norton Sampler. 3rd ed. 1985. pap. text ed. 7.95 (ISBN 0-393-95412-9); instructor's manual avail. (ISBN 0-393-95415-3). Norton.
Cooley, Thomas, ed. The Norton Sampler: Short Essays for Composition. 2nd ed. (gr. 12). 1981. pap. text ed. 8.95x (ISBN 0-393-95179-0); write for info. instrs'. hdbk. (ISBN 0-393-95183-9). Norton.
--The Norton Sampler: Short Essays for Composition. 1978. instructor's handbook free (ISBN 0-393-95047-6). Norton.
Cooley, Thomas M. Michigan, a History of Governments. rev. ed. LC 72-3764. (American Commonwealths: No. 5). Repr. of 1905 ed. 35.00 (ISBN 0-404-57205-7). AMS Pr.
--A Treatise on the Constitutional Limitations. LC 78-87510. (American Constitutional & Legal History Ser). 720p. 1972. Repr. of 1868 ed. lib. bdg. 75.00 (ISBN 0-306-71403-5). Da Capo.
--A Treatise on the Law of Taxation: Including the Law of Local Assessments. 2nd ed. Repr. of 1886 ed. 63.00 (ISBN 0-384-09775-8). Johnson Repr.
Cooley, W. C., ed. see Ayruni, A. T.
Cooley, W. C., ed. see Smoldyrev, A. Ye.
Cooley, W. D. Negroland of the Arabs. rev ed. 143p. 1966. 28.50x (ISBN 0-7146-1799-7, F Cass Co). Biblio Dist.
Cooley, W. D., ed. see Maynarde, Thomas.
Cooley, William D. Inner Africa Laid Open. LC 70-76486. (Illus.). Repr. of 1852 ed. cancelled (ISBN 0-8371-1095-5, COA&, Pub. by Negro U Pr). Greenwood.
Cooley, William S., jt. auth. see Cooley, Eli F.
Cooley, William W. & Lohnes, Paul R. Evaluation Research in Education: Theory, Principles & Practice. 368p. 1976. text ed. 19.95x (ISBN 0-8290-0410-6). Irvington.
--Multivariate Data Analysis. LC 84-15438. 376p. 1985. Repr. of 1971 ed. 30.50 (ISBN 0-89874-781-3). Krieger.
Coolican, Alice, jt. auth. see Frenkel, Stephen J.
Coolidge, Archibald C. The U. S. As a World Power. 1981. Repr. lib. bdg. 59.00 (ISBN 0-403-00907-3). Scholarly.
Coolidge, Archibald C., jt. auth. see Channing, Edward.
Coolidge, Archibald C., ed. see Harris, Joel C.
Coolidge, Calvin. Autobiography of Calvin Coolidge. 246p. 1972. Repr. of 1929 ed. 8.50 (ISBN 0-914960-02-4, Pub. by Academy Bks). C E Tuttle.
--Foundations of the Republic. facs. ed. LC 68-8450. (Essay Index Reprint Ser). 1926. 21.00 (ISBN 0-8369-0333-1). Ayer Co Pubs.
Coolidge, Charles E. Zig-Zag. 1983. 6.95 (ISBN 0-686-84429-7). Vantage.

Coolidge, Clark. American Ones. 48p. (Orig.). 1981. pap. 5.00 (ISBN 0-939180-17-0). Tombouctou.
Coolidge, Clark & Katz, Alex. Smithsonian Depositions & Subject to a Film. 88p. 1980. pap. 6.00 (ISBN 0-931428-30-0). Vehicle Edns.
Coolidge, Clark, ed. Joglars (Three Issues) (Avant-Garde Magazines Ser.). 230p. 1972. Repr. of 1964 ed. Set. 15.00 (ISBN 0-405-01755-3). Ayer Co Pubs.
Coolidge, Dane. Arizona Cowboys. LC 83-27439. (Illus.). 160p. 1984. pap. 7.95 (ISBN 0-8165-0858-5). U of Ariz Pr.
--California Cowboys. LC 84-28001. 1985. pap. 7.95 (ISBN 0-8165-0862-3). U of Ariz Pr.
--The Desert Trail. 1975. lib. bdg. 13.85x (ISBN 0-89966-059-2). Buccaneer Bks.
--Fighting Men of the West. facs. ed. LC 68-24846. (Essay Index Reprint Ser.). (Illus.). 1968. Repr. of 1932 ed. 19.50 (ISBN 0-8369-0334-X). Ayer Co Pubs.
--Hidden Water. 1975. lib. bdg. 20.10x (ISBN 0-89966-062-2). Buccaneer Bks.
--Texas Cowboys. 1985. pap. 7.95 (ISBN 0-8165-0947-6). U of Ariz Pr.
--The Texican. 1975. lib. bdg. 16.30x (ISBN 0-89966-065-7). Buccaneer Bks.
Coolidge, Dane & Coolidge, Mary R. Last of the Seris: The Aboriginal Indians of Kino Bay, Sonora, Mexico. LC 71-153199. (Beautiful Rio Grande Classics Ser.). (Illus.). 340p. 1983. Repr. of 1939 ed. lib. bdg. 15.00 (ISBN 0-87380-078-8). Rio Grande.
--The Navajo Indians. LC 76-43679. Repr. of 1930 ed. 28.50 (ISBN 0-404-15513-8). AMS Pr.
Coolidge, Edna M. Celestial Gems Books, Vol. 1. rev. ed. LC 73-88209. 150p. 10.00 (ISBN 0-914154-00-1). Celestial Gems.
--Celestial Gems Books, Vols. 2-3. LC 73-88209. (Illus.). 48p. 1972. spiral bdg. 10.00 ea. Vol. 2 (ISBN 0-914154-01-X). Celestial Gems.
--Celestial Gems Books, Vol. 4. LC 73-88209. 65p. 1974. spiral bdg. 10.00 (ISBN 0-914154-03-6). Celestial Gems.
--Celestial Gems Books, Vols. 5-6. LC 73-88209. (Illus.). 150p. 1975. 10.00 ea.; Vol. 5. (ISBN 0-914154-05-2). Celestial Gems.
Coolidge, Grace. Teepee Neighbors. LC 83-40487. 200p. 1984. pap. 7.95 (ISBN 0-8061-1889-X). U of Okla Pr.
Coolidge, Guy O. The French Occupation of the Champlain Valley: From 1609-1759. LC 79-13458. 1979. Repr. of 1938 ed. 9.75 (ISBN 0-916346-34-X). Harbor Hill Bks.
Coolidge, Harold J. & Lord, Robert H. Archibald Cary Coolidge: Life & Letters. facsimile ed. LC 70-179512. (Select Bibliographies Reprint Ser). Repr. of 1932 ed. 24.50 (ISBN 0-8369-6641-4). Ayer Co Pubs.
Coolidge, Julian L. Treatise on the Circle & the Sphere. LC 78-128872. 1971. text ed. 27.50 (ISBN 0-8284-0236-1). Chelsea Pub.
Coolidge, Louis A. Old-Fashioned Senator: Orville H. Platt of Connecticut, 2 Vols. LC 74-137907. (American History & Culture in the Nineteenth Century Ser). 1971. Repr. of 1910 ed. Set. 62.50x (ISBN 0-8046-1475-X, Pub. by Kennikat). Assoc Faculty PR.
--Ulysses S. Grant. Morse, John T., Jr., ed. LC 75-128953. (American Statesmen: No. 32). Repr. of 1917 ed. 43.00 (ISBN 0-404-50894-4). AMS Pr.
Coolidge, Mary E. The Rain-Makers: Indians of Arizona & New Mexico. LC 76-43681. (Illus.). 376p. Repr. of 1929 ed. 35.00 (ISBN 0-404-15514-6). AMS Pr.
Coolidge, Mary R. Chinese Immigration. LC 69-18768. (American Immigration Collection Ser.: No. 1). (Illus.). 1969. Repr. of 1909 ed. 24.00 (ISBN 0-405-00516-4). Ayer Co Pubs.
--Why Women Are So. LC 72-2595. (American Women Ser: Images & Realities). 376p. 1972. Repr. of 1912 ed. 23.50 (ISBN 0-405-04452-6). Ayer Co Pubs.
Coolidge, Mary R., jt. auth. see Coolidge, Dane.
Coolidge, Oliver. Golden Days of Greece. LC 68-21599. (Illus.). (gr. 5 up). 1968. 13.50i (ISBN 0-690-33473-7). Crowell Jr Bks.
Coolidge, Olivia. Greek Myths. (Illus.). 256p. (gr. 7 up). 1949. 13.95 (ISBN 0-395-06721-9). HM.
--Legends of the North. (Illus.). (gr. 7 up). 1951. 13.95 (ISBN 0-395-06726-X). HM.
--Trojan War. (Illus.). (gr. 7-12). 1952. 14.95 (ISBN 0-395-06731-6). HM.
--Hercules & Other Tales from Greek Myths. abr. ed. Orig. Title: Greek Myths. (gr. 6-9). pap. 1.95 (ISBN 0-590-08542-5). Scholastic Inc.
Coolidge, Philip, et al, eds. The OECD Guidelines for Multinational Enterprises: A Business Appraisal. LC 77-90874. (Orig.). 1977. pap. text ed. 10.00 (ISBN 0-935328-02-5). Intl Law Inst.
Coolidge, Susan. What Katy Did. (Puffin Classics Ser.). 176p. (gr. 3-7). 1983. pap. 2.25 (ISBN 0-14-035011-X, Puffin). Penguin.
--What Katy Did at School. 1985. pap. 2.25 (ISBN 0-14-035043-8). Penguin.
Cooling, B. F., jt. auth. see Millett, Allan R.
Cooling, B. Franklin. Benjamin Franklin Tracy: Father of the Modern American Fighting Navy. (Illus.). xvi, 211p. 1973. 17.50 (ISBN 0-208-01336-9, Archon). Shoe String.
--Gray Steel & Blue Water Navy: The Formative Years of America's Military-Industrial Complex 1881-1917. 286p. 1979. 19.50 (ISBN 0-208-01771-2, Archon). Shoe String.
--War, Business, & American Society: Historical Perspectives on the Military-Industrial Complex. LC 76-18163. (National University Pubns. Ser. in American Studies). 1977. 19.50x (ISBN 0-8046-9156-8, Pub. by Kennikat). Assoc Faculty Pr.
Cooling, B. Franklin, 3rd, ed. New American State Papers, Seventeen Eighty-Nine to Eighteen Sixty: Military Affairs, 19 vols. LC 79-110. 1979. Set. lib. bdg. 1100.00 (ISBN 0-8420-2137-X). Scholarly Res Inc.
Cooling, Benjamin F., ed. War, Business, & World Military-Industrial Complexes. (National University Publications, Political Science Ser.). 1981. 19.50x (ISBN 0-8046-9276-9, Pub. by Kennikat). Assoc Faculty Pr.
Cooling, W. Colebrook. Low-Cost Maintenance Control. LC 73-75670. (Illus.). pap. 20.00 (ISBN 0-317-11041-1, 2051529). Bks Demand UMI.
--Simplified Low-Cost Maintenance Control. rev. ed. 128p. 1983. 24.95 (ISBN 0-8144-5657-X). Am Mgmt Assns.
Cooling, Wilmer. Simplified Low-cost Maintenance Control. LC 82-18380. pap. 30.50 (ISBN 0-317-20412-2, 2023501). Bks Demand UMI.
Cooljar, Mahendranath. Sweet Remembrance of Silberkugel & Christmas Holiday in Summer. LC 82-90563. 92p. 1983. 7.95 (ISBN 0-533-05490-7). Vantage.
Coolman, Anne, ed. see Beckstrom, Bob.
Coolman, Anne, ed. see Craig, Tracy & Ballard, Gay.
Coolman, Anne, ed. see Scheer, Cynthia.
Coolman, Anne, ed. see Snow, Diane, et al.
Coolman, Anne, ed. see Snow, Diane.
Coolman, Anne, ed. see Walker, Charlotte.
Coolman, J., jt. auth. see Birchfield, E.
Coolsaet, B., ed. see Annual Meeting of the International Continence Society, 6th, Antwerp, Sept. 1976.
Coomann, Heiner. Die Kohaerenztheorie der Wahrheit: Eine Kritische Darstellung der Theorie Reschers vor ihrem Historischen Hintergrund, Vol. 3. (Studia Philosphica et Historica). 258p. (Ger.). 1983. 32.10 (ISBN 3-8204-7540-0). P Lang Pubs.
Coomara, Swamy M., intro. by. Sutta Nipata: Or Dialogues & Discourses of Gotama Buddha. LC 78-70125. 1980. Repr. of 1874 ed. 23.00 (ISBN 0-404-17384-5). AMS Pr.
Coomaraswamy. Coomaraswamy. Lipsey, Roger, ed. Incl. Vol. 1. Selected Papers: Traditional Art & Symbolism. 1977. 50.00 (ISBN 0-691-09885-9); Vol. 2. Selected Papers: Metaphysics. 1977. 47.00 (ISBN 0-691-09932-4); Set Vols. 1 & 2. 82.50 (ISBN 0-686-68004-9); Vol. 3. His Life & Work. 1977. 33.00 (ISBN 0-691-09931-6). LC 76-41158. (Bollingen Ser: No. 89). (Illus.). 1977. Princeton U Pr.
Coomaraswamy, A. K. The Arts & Crafts of India & Ceylon. (Illus.). 256p: Repr. 12.00 (ISBN 0-686-33376-4, Pub. by Messers Today & Tomorrows Printers & Publishers India). Scholarly Pubns.
--Symbolism of Indian Architecture. 80p. 1983. text ed. 16.50x (ISBN 0-391-03118-X, Pub. by Hist Res India). Humanities.
Coomaraswamy, A. K. & Noble, M. E. Myths of the Hindus & Buddhists. (Illus.). 15.25 (ISBN 0-8446-1896-9). Peter Smith.
Coomaraswamy, Ananda. The Dance of Siva: Essays on Indian Art & Culture. (Fine Art Ser.). 192p. 1985. pap. 5.95 (ISBN 0-486-24817-8). Dover.
Coomaraswamy, Ananda K. Am I My Brother's Keeper? facs. ed. LC 67-23196. (Essay Index Reprint Ser.). 1947. 12.00 (ISBN 0-8369-0335-8). Ayer Co Pubs.
--Christian & Oriental Philosophy of Art. 1957. pap. 3.00 (ISBN 0-486-20378-6). Dover.
--Christian & Oriental Philosophy of Art. Orig. Title: Why Exhibit Works of Art. 13.75 (ISBN 0-8446-0553-0). Peter Smith.
--Hinduism & Buddhism. LC 78-138215. 1971. Repr. of 1943 ed. lib. bdg. 22.50x (ISBN 0-8371-5570-3, COHB). Greenwood.
--History of Indian & Indonesian Art. 295p. 1985. pap. 8.95 (ISBN 0-486-25005-9). Dover.
--Rajput Painting, 2 vols. in 1. LC 72-87768. 1975. Repr. of 1916 ed. lib. bdg. 75.00 (ISBN 0-87817-118-5). Hacker.
--Rajput Painting, 2 vols. 2nd ed. (Illus.). 221p. 1976. Set. 100.00 (ISBN 0-89581-113-8). Asian Human Pr.
--Rajput Painting, 2 vols. 2nd ed. (Illus.). 1976. Set. 150.00 (ISBN 0-89684-301-7). Orient Bk Dist.
--Spiritual Authority & Temporal Power in the Indian Theory of Government. (Amer Oriental Soc Ser.). 1942. pap. 16.00 (ISBN 0-527-02696-4). Kraus Repr.
--Traditional Art & Symbolism. Lipsey, Roger, ed. (Bollingen Ser.: No. LXXXIX). (Illus.). 620p. 1985. text ed. 50.00 (ISBN 0-691-09885-9); pap. text ed. 12.95 (ISBN 0-691-01869-3). Princeton U Pr.
--Transformation of Nature in Art. 1937. pap. 4.95 (ISBN 0-486-20368-9). Dover.
--The Transformation of Nature in Art. 11.25 (ISBN 0-8446-0554-9). Peter Smith.
Coomaraswamy, Ananda K. & Horner, I. B. The Living Thoughts of Gotama, the Buddha. LC 78-72397. Repr. of 1948 ed. 34.50 (ISBN 0-404-17256-3). AMS Pr.
Coomaraswamy, Ananda K. & Nivedita, Sr. Myths of the Hindus & Buddhists. (Illus.). 400p. (gr. 4-8). pap. 5.95 (ISBN 0-486-21759-0). Dover.
Coomaraswamy, Ananda K., ed. see Devi, Ratan.
Coomaraswamy, Radhika. Sri Lanka: The Crisis of the Anglo-American Constitutional Tradition in a Developing Society. 194p. 1983. text ed. 25.00x (ISBN 0-7069-2472-X, Pub. by Vikas India). Advent NY.
Coomarawaswamy, A. Dance of Siva. 69.95 (ISBN 0-87968-245-0). Gordon Pr.
Coombe, Jack & Goodman, James. The Temptation. 1984. pap. 6.95 (ISBN 0-89896-127-0). Larksdale.
Coomber, D. I., ed. Radiochemical Methods in Analysis. LC 72-95069. 498p. 1975. 65.00 (ISBN 0-306-30738-3, Plenum Pr). Plenum Pub.
Coomber, I. M. Datsun 310 '78-'81. (No. 679). 12.95 (ISBN 0-85696-977-X). Haynes Pubns.
--MGA '56-'62. (No. 475). 12.95 (ISBN 0-85696-475-1). Haynes Pubns.
--Toyota Corolla '80 thru '82. (No. 961). 12.95 (ISBN 0-85696-961-3). Haynes Pubns.
--Triumph GT6 Vitesse '62 - '74. (Owners Workshop Manuals Ser.: No. 112). 1983. 12.95 (ISBN 0-85696-612-6, Pub. by J H Haynes England). Haynes Pubns.
Coomber, I. M., jt. auth. see Haynes, J. H.
Coomber, James E., jt. auth. see Peet, Howard D.
Coombes, Allen J. Timber Press Dictionary of Plant Names. 210p. 1985. 9.95 (ISBN 0-88192-023-1, Dist. by Intl Spec Bk). Timber.
Coombes, Archie J. Some Australian Poets. facsimile ed. LC 76-107688. (Essay Index Reprint Ser). 1938. 12.00 (ISBN 0-8369-1492-9). Ayer Co Pubs.
Coombes, B., ed. Vehicle Body Building, Pt. 2, 2 vols. (Engineering Craftsmen: No. E22). (Illus.). 1969. Set. spiral bdg. 82.50x (ISBN 0-85083-063-X). Intl Ideas.
Coombes, B., et al, eds. Vehicle Body Building: Pt. 1. (Engineering Craftsmen: Pt. 2). (Illus.). 1968. 49.95x (ISBN 0-89563-035-4). Intl Ideas.
Coombes, C. G., ed. Printed Circuits Handbook. 536p. 50.00 (ISBN 0-318-12558-7); members 42.00 (ISBN 0-318-12559-5). Am Electroplate.
Coombes, D. & Walkland, S. A., eds. Parliaments & Economic Affairs. 1981. text ed. 42.00x (ISBN 0-435-83804-0). Gower Pub Co.
Coombes, David. The Future of the European Parliament. 136p. 1981. 29.00x (ISBN 0-686-87338-6, Pub. by Policy Studies). State Mutual Bk.
--Representative Government & Economic Power. (Policy Studies Institute Ser.). vi, 208p. 1982. text ed. 45.00x (ISBN 0-435-83180-1). Gower Pub Co.
Coombes, H. T. F. Powys. Repr. of 1960 ed. 20.00 (ISBN 0-8274-4333-1). R West.
Coombes, John. Capital Transfer Tax. 90.00 (ISBN 0-903486-25-3, Pub. by Prof Bks England). State Mutual Bk.
Coombes, Karenna, ed. see Ergonomics Society, UK.
Coombes, R. C., et al, eds. Breast Cancer Management: The Experience of the Combined Breast Clinic, St. George's Hospital-Royal Marsden Hospital. 1981. 50.00 (ISBN 0-8089-1348-4, 790899). Grune.
Coombs. Developments in Expert Systems. 1984. 15.00 (ISBN 0-12-187580-6). Acad Pr.
Coombs, Ann. The Fire Within. 1978. pap. 2.25 (ISBN 0-532-22137-0). Woodhill.
Coombs, Bryan. Pitman Shorthand Speedbuilder. (Illus.). 128p. (Orig.). 1975. pap. 7.95x (ISBN 0-8464-0721-3). Beekman Pubs.
Coombs, Charles. Auto Racing. LC 73-153770. (Illus.). (gr. 5-9). 1971. 11.25 (ISBN 0-688-21053-8); PLB 8.59 (ISBN 0-688-31053-2). Morrow.
--Be a Winner in Windsurfing. LC 82-2165. (Illus.). 128p. (gr. 4-6). 1982. 11.75 (ISBN 0-688-01060-1). Morrow.
--BMX: A Guide to Bicycle Motocross. LC 82-20904. (Illus.). 144p. (gr. 4-6). 1983. 10.25 (ISBN 0-688-01867-X). Morrow.
--Coal in the Energy Crisis. LC 80-13701. (Illus.). 128p. (gr. 4-6). 1980. 10.00 (ISBN 0-688-22239-0); PLB 10.88 (ISBN 0-688-32239-5). Morrow.
--Detective Stories. (Young Readers Bookshelf). (Illus.). (gr. 4-7). PLB 6.19 (ISBN 0-8313-0025-6). Lantern.
--Drag Racing. (Illus.). (gr. 5-9). 1970. PLB 11.88 (ISBN 0-688-31243-8). Morrow.
--Gold & Other Precious Metals. LC 81-38414. (Illus.). 128p. (gr. 4-6). 1981. 11.25 (ISBN 0-688-00542-X); PLB 11.88 (ISBN 0-688-00543-8). Morrow.
--Hot-Air Ballooning. LC 80-26704. (Illus.). 128p. (gr. 4-6). 1981. 11.25 (ISBN 0-688-00364-8); PLB 11.88 (ISBN 0-688-00365-6). Morrow.
--Mopeding. (Illus.). (gr. 4-6). 1978. 10.00 (ISBN 0-688-22155-6); PLB 10.88 (ISBN 0-688-32155-0). Morrow.
--Passage to Space: The Shuttle Transportation System. LC 79-1176. (Illus.). (gr. 4-6). 1979. 11.25 (ISBN 0-688-22188-2); PLB 11.88 (ISBN 0-688-32188-7). Morrow.
--Pipeline Across Alaska. LC 77-28986. (Illus.). (gr. 5-9). 1978. 10.00 (ISBN 0-688-22139-4); PLB 10.88 (ISBN 0-688-32139-9). Morrow.
--Tankers, Giants of the Sea. LC 79-9376. (Illus.). 128p. (gr. 4-6). 1979. 10.00 (ISBN 0-688-22205-6); PLB 10.88 (ISBN 0-688-32205-0). Morrow.
--Ultralights: The Flying Featherweights. LC 83-17411. (Illus.). 160p. (gr. 5 up). 1984. 11.00 (ISBN 0-688-02775-X). Morrow.
--Water Sports. (Young Readers Bookshelf Ser.). (Illus.). (gr. 4-7). PLB 6.19 (ISBN 0-8313-3444-4). Lantern.
--Young Atom Detective. (Illus.). (gr. 4-7). PLB 6.19 (ISBN 0-8313-0021-3). Lantern.
Coombs, Charles A. The Arena of International Finance. LC 76-19093. (Illus.). pap. 65.80 (ISBN 0-317-09371-1, 2016463). Bks Demand UMI.
Coombs, Charles A., jt. auth. see Guindey, Guillaume.
Coombs, Clyde F. Printed Circuits Handbook. 1979. 48.50 (ISBN 0-07-012608-9). McGraw.
Coombs, Clyde F., Jr. Basic Electronic Instrument Handbook. LC 72-1394. (Handbook Ser.). (Illus.). 832p. 1972. 56.50 (ISBN 0-07-012615-1). McGraw.
Coombs, Clyde H. Psychology & Mathematics: An Essay on Theory. 104p. 1983. text ed. 12.50x (ISBN 0-472-10034-3). U of Mich Pr.
--A Theory of Psychological Scaling. LC 75-41413. (Illus.). 94p. 1976. Repr. of 1951 ed. lib. bdg. 18.75x (ISBN 0-8371-8646-3, COPS). Greenwood.
Coombs, David. The Antique Collector's Picture Guide to Prices. 192p. 1981. 35.00x (ISBN 0-85223-161-X, Pub. by Ebury Pr England). State Mutual Bk.
Coombs, David, ed. Antique Collecting for Pleasure. 192p. 1981. 30.00x (ISBN 0-85223-136-9, Pub. by Ebury Pr England). State Mutual Bk.
Coombs, Fred, jt. auth. see Branson, Margaret.
Coombs, G. H., jt. auth. see Gutteridge, W. E.
Coombs, Gary B. Goleta Depot: The History of a Rural Railroad Station. LC 82-83472. (Illus.). 96p. 1982. pap. 5.00x (ISBN 0-911773-01-0). Inst Am Res.
Coombs, Gary B., jt. auth. see Everett, William B.
Coombs, H. C. Kulinma: Listening to Aboriginal Australians. (Illus.). 1979. text ed. 19.50 (ISBN 0-7081-1149-1, Pub. by ANUP Australia); pap. text ed. 14.95 (ISBN 0-7081-1156-4). Australia N U P.
--Some Ingredients for Growth: Edward Shann Memorial Lectures in Economics. 1963. pap. 3.00x (ISBN 0-85564-033-2, Pub. by U of W Austral Pr). Intl Spec Bk.
Coombs, H. Samm. Teenage Survival Manual: How to Enjoy the Trip to Twenty. (Illus.). 1978. pap. 4.95 (ISBN 0-87516-277-0). De Vorss.
Coombs, J. Biomass Directory. 1986. pap. 80.00x (ISBN 0-943818-19-2). Stockton Pr.
Coombs, J., jt. auth. see Hall, David O.
Coombs, J. & Hall, D., eds. Techniques in Bioproductivity & Photosynthesis. (Illus.). 160p. 1981. 40.00 (ISBN 0-08-027382-3); pap. 17.50 (ISBN 0-08-027383-1). Pergamon.
Coombs, J., et al. Plants As Solar Collectors: Optimizing Productivity for Energy. 1983. lib. bdg. 32.50 (ISBN 90-277-1625-0, Pub. by Reidel Holland). Kluwer Academic.
Coombs, Jan. Living with the Disabled: You Can Help; A Family Guide. LC 83-24298. 1984. pap. 7.95 (ISBN 0-8069-7840-6). Sterling.
Coombs, Jim. The Biotechnology Directory 1985. 464p. 1985. pap. 130.00x (ISBN 0-943818-06-0). Stockton Pr.
--The International Biotechnology Directory 1984: Products, Companies, Research & Organizations. LC 83-12138. 426p. 1983. 100.00 (ISBN 0-943818-03-6, Nature Pr). Groves Dict Music.
Coombs, John, tr. see Schwendowius, Barbara & Domling, Wolfgang.
Coombs, L. F. Harrow Railway Disaster 1952. 1977. 14.95 (ISBN 0-7153-7409-5). David & Charles.
Coombs, Lolagene C., jt. auth. see Freedman, Ronald.
Coombs, M. J. & Alty, J. L. Computing Skills & the User Interface. LC 80-2768. (Computers & People Ser.). 1981. 49.50 (ISBN 0-12-186520-7). Acad Pr.
Coombs, Margery C. Large Mammalian Clawed Herbivores: A Comparative Study. LC 83-71301. (Transactions Ser.: Vol. 73, Pt. 7). 1983. 20.00 (ISBN 0-87169-737-8). Am Philos.
Coombs, Marian, ed. see Yuen, Aubrey.
Coombs, Marie T., jt. auth. see Nemeck, Francis K.
Coombs, Michael J. see Sime, Max S.
Coombs, Nina. Forbidden Joy. (Rapture Romance Ser.: No. 32). 1983. pap. 1.95 (ISBN 0-451-12513-4, Sig). NAL.
--Love So Fearful. (Rapture Romance Ser.: No. 1). 1983. pap. 1.95 (ISBN 0-451-12003-5, AJ2003, Sig). NAL.
Coombs, Patricia. Dorrie & the Amazing Magic Elixir. (Illus.). (gr. k-6). 1982. pap. 1.75 (ISBN 0-440-41684-1, YB). Dell.
--Dorrie & the Blue Witch. (Illus.). 48p. (gr. k-6). 1980. pap. 2.50 (ISBN 0-440-42210-8, YB). Dell.
--Dorrie & the Dreamyard Monsters. LC 77-1373. (gr. 1-5). 1977. 10.00 (ISBN 0-688-41807-4); PLB 10.88 o. p. (ISBN 0-688-51807-9). Lothrop.
--Dorrie & the Dreamyard Monsters. (Illus.). 48p. (gr. k-6). 1982. pap. 1.75 (ISBN 0-440-40896-2, YB). Dell.
--Dorrie & the Goblin. 48p. (gr. 1-5). 1983. pap. 1.75 (ISBN 0-440-41700-7, YB). Dell.
--Dorrie & the Halloween Plot. LC 76-3643. (Illus.). (gr. 1-5). 1976. PLB 10.88 (ISBN 0-688-51764-1). Lothrop.

--Dorrie & the Halloween Plot. 48p. (gr. k-6). 1982. pap. 1.75 (ISBN 0-440-42076-8, YB). Dell.

--Dorrie & the Haunted House. 48p. (gr. k-6). 1980. pap. 1.50 (ISBN 0-440-42212-4, YB). Dell.

--Dorrie & the Witch Doctor. LC 67-25293. (Illus.). (gr. 1-5). 1967. PLB 10.88 (ISBN 0-688-51311-5). Lothrop.

--Dorrie & the Witches' Camp. LC 82-9986. (Illus.). 48p. (gr. 1-5). 1983. 10.25 (ISBN 0-688-01507-7); PLB 10.88 (ISBN 0-688-01508-5). Lothrop.

--Dorrie & the Witch's Imp. 48p. (gr. k-6). 1982. pap. 1.75 (ISBN 0-440-40889-X, YB). Dell.

--Dorrie & the Wizard's Spell. LC 68-27601. (Illus.). (gr. 1-5). 1968. PLB 11.88 (ISBN 0-688-51083-3). Lothrop.

--The Magician & McTree. LC 83-11984. (Illus.). (gr. 1-4). 1984. 10.00 (ISBN 0-688-02109-3); PLB 9.12 (ISBN 0-688-02111-5). Lothrop.

Coombs, Philip H. New Strategies for Improving Rural Family Life. 72p. 1981. 3.00 (ISBN 0-318-16926-6). ICED Pubns.

--The World Crisis in Education: A View from the Eighties. LC 84-5713. 310p. 1985. 19.95 (ISBN 0-19-503502-X); pap. 10.95 (ISBN 0-19-503503-8). Oxford U Pr.

Coombs, Philip H. & Ahmed, Manzoor. Attacking Rural Poverty: How Non-Formal Education Can Help. LC 73-19350. (The World Bank Ser). (Illus.). 308p. 1974. pap. 10.95x (ISBN 0-8018-1601-7). Johns Hopkins.

Coombs, Philip H., ed. Meeting the Basic Needs of the Rural Poor: The Integrated, Community-Based Approach. LC 80-19838. (Pergamon Policy Studies on International Development). 828p. 1980. 54.00 (ISBN 0-08-026306-2). Pergamon.

Coombs, Robert, et al, eds. Socialization in Drug Abuse. LC 75-37067. 496p. 1976. pap. text ed. 11.95x (ISBN 0-87073-489-X). Schenkman Bks Inc.

Coombs, Robert H. Mastering Medicine: Professional Socialization in Medical School. LC 77-85351. 1978. 17.95 (ISBN 0-02-906640-9). Free Pr.

Coombs, Robert H. & Vincent, Clark E., eds. Psychosocial Aspects of Medical Training. (Illus.). 584p. 1971. 59.50x (ISBN 0-398-00343-2). C C Thomas.

Coombs, Robert H., et al. Making It in Medical School. 184p. 1981. pap. 7.95 (ISBN 0-87866-297-9). Petersons Guides.

Coombs, Rod, jt. auth. see Green, K.

Coombs, Roy E. Violets: The History & Cultivation of Scented Violets. (Illus.). 144p. 1981. 17.00 (ISBN 0-7099-0704-4, Pub. by Croom Helm Ltd). Longwood Pub Group.

Coombs, Steven L., jt. auth. see MacKuen, Michael B.

Coombs, W. E. & Palmer, W. J. A Handbook of Construction Accounting & Financial Management. 3rd ed. 576p. 1983. 41.95 (ISBN 0-07-012611-9). McGraw.

Coombs, Whitney. Wages of Unskilled Labor in Manufacturing Industries in the United States, 1890-1924. LC 76-76686. (Columbia University Studies in the Social Sciences: No. 283). Repr. of 1926 ed. 16.50 (ISBN 0-404-51283-6). AMS Pr.

Coomer, James C., ed. Quest for a Sustainable Society. LC 80-24158. (Pergamon Policy Studies on International Development). 230p. 1981. 29.00 (ISBN 0-08-027168-5). Pergamon.

Coomer, Joe. The Decatur Road: A Novel of the Appalachian Hill Country. 208p. 1983. 12.95 (ISBN 0-312-18998-2, Pub. by Marek). St Martin.

--Kentucky Love. 192p. 1985. 12.95 (ISBN 0-312-45161-X, Pub. by Marek). St Martin.

Coon, Alma S. The Mouse & the Mill & the Bottle Babies. (Illus.). 44p. (ps-1). 1982. 3.95 (ISBN 0-87935-061-X). Williamsburg.

Coon, Betty. Seaward. 36p. (Orig.). 1978. pap. 3.00 (ISBN 0-917658-08-6). BPW & P.

Coon, C. S. Caravan: The Story of the Middle East. rev. ed. LC 75-45344. 390p. 1976. Repr. of 1958 ed. 19.50 (ISBN 0-88275-393-2). Krieger.

Coon, C. S., et al. Races: A Study of the Problems of Race Formation in Man. (Illus.). 164p. 1950. photocopy ed. 14.75x (ISBN 0-398-04231-4). C C Thomas.

Coon, Carleton S. The Hunting People. (Illus.). 412p. 1979. 10.95 (ISBN 0-224-00685-1, Pub. by Jonathan Cape). Merrimack Pub Cir.

--Mountains of Giants: A Racial & Cultural Study of the North Albanian Mountain Ghegs. (HU. PMP: Vol. 23, No. 3). Repr. of 1950 ed. 18.00 (ISBN 0-527-01258-0). Kraus Repr.

--The Races of Europe. LC 76-184840. (Illus.). 739p. 1972. Repr. of 1939 ed. lib. bdg. 47.50x (ISBN 0-8371-6328-5, CORE). Greenwood.

--Racial Adaptations. LC 82-8010. (Illus.). 1982. text ed. 24.95 (ISBN 0-8304-1012-0); pap. text ed. 12.95 (ISBN 0-88229-806-2). Nelson-Hall.

--A Reader in Cultural Anthropology. LC 76-78. 634p. 1977. Repr. of 1948 ed. lib. bdg. 26.50 (ISBN 0-88275-394-0). Krieger.

--The Seven Caves: Archaeological Explorations in the Middle East. LC 80-24503. (Illus.). xx, 354p. 1981. Repr. of 1957 ed. lib. bdg. 31.50x (ISBN 0-313-22824-8, COSCA). Greenwood.

--Tribes of the Rif. (Harvard African Studies: Vol. 9). 1931. 72.00 (ISBN 0-527-01032-4). Kraus Repr.

Coon, Carleton S., et al. Yengema Cave Report. (University Museum Monographs: No. 31). (Illus.). 77p. 1968. 8.75x (ISBN 0-934718-23-7). Univ Mus of U PA.

--Races: A Study of the Problems of Race Formation in Man. LC 80-24479. (American Lecture Ser.: No. 77). (Illus.). xiv, 153p. 1981. Repr. of 1950 ed. lib. bdg. 19.75x (ISBN 0-313-22878-7, CORA). Greenwood.

Coon, Carlton S. Adventures & Discoveries: The Autobiography of Carlton S. Coon. (Illus.). 404p. 1981. 16.95 (ISBN 0-13-014027-9). P-H.

Coon, Carlton S., jt. auth. see Chapple, Eliot D.

Coon, Dennis. Essentials of Psychology. 3rd ed. (Illus.). 650p. 1985. pap. text ed. 23.95 (ISBN 0-314-85226-3). West Pub.

--Essentials of Psychology: Exploration & Application. 2nd ed. (Illus.). 550p. 1982. pap. text ed. 20.95 (ISBN 0-314-63162-3). West Pub.

--Introduction to Psychology. 3rd ed. (Exploration & Application Ser.). (Illus.). 686p. 1983. text ed. 27.95 (ISBN 0-314-69642-3); tchrs.' manual avail. (ISBN 0-314-71085-X); mastery study guide 8.95 (ISBN 0-314-72291-2); test bank avail. (ISBN 0-314-72619-5). West Pub.

--The Psychology of Human Behavior: A Study Guide for Psychology 100. 162p. 1981. 4.50 (ISBN 0-314-62828-2). West Pub.

Coon, Dennis, ed. see Bingham, Mindy & Edmondson, Judy.

Coon, Dennis J. Instructor's Handbook for Use With Introduction to Psychology: Exploration & Application. 3rd ed. 1983. write for info. (ISBN 0-314-72290-4); write for info. instr's handbook. West Pub.

Coon, Helen C. The House at the Back of the Lot. LC 82-83883. (Illus.). 147p. (Orig.). (gr. 4-9). 1982. pap. 6.95 (ISBN 0-87303-077-X). Faith & Life.

Coon, Julius, jt. ed. see Hathcock, John N.

Coon, Minor J., ed. Microsomes, Drug Oxidations & Chemical Carcinogenesis, Vol. 1. LC 80-11363. 1980. 55.00 (ISBN 0-12-187701-9). Acad Pr.

--Microsomes, Drug Oxidations & Chemical Carcinogenesis, Vol. 2. LC 80-11363. 1980. 60.00 (ISBN 0-12-187702-7). Acad Pr.

Coon, Nelson. Using Wild & Wayside Plants. (Illus.). 288p. 1980. pap. 5.95 (ISBN 0-486-23936-5). Dover.

Coon, Pam. The Vowel Van. (Reading Ser.). 72p. (gr. 1-3). 1980. 6.95 (ISBN 0-88160-010-5, LW 115). Learning Wks.

Coon, Roger. A Gift of Light. Coffen, Richard W., ed. LC 83-17811. (Better Living Ser.). (Illus.). 63p. (Orig.). 1983. pap. 0.99 (ISBN 0-8280-0229-0). Review & Herald.

Coon, Sevren, ed. see Bingham, Mindy & Edmondson, Judy.

Coon, Susan. Cassilee. 1983. pap. 2.25 (ISBN 0-380-75887-3, 75887). Avon.

Cooney. Activated Charcoal: Antidotal & Other Medical Uses. (Drugs & the Pharmaceutical Sciences Ser.: Vol. 9). 1980. 37.50 (ISBN 0-8247-6913-9). Dekker.

Cooney, Barbara. Christmas. LC 67-18510. (Holiday Ser.). (Illus.). (gr. k-3). 1967. PLB 10.89 (ISBN 0-690-19201-0). Crowell Jr Bks.

--Little Brother & Little Sister. LC 81-43058. (Illus.). 48p. (gr. 2-3). 1982. 10.95 (ISBN 0-385-14583-7); PLB (ISBN 0-385-14584-5). Doubleday.

--The Little Juggler. LC 61-10576. (Illus.). 48p. (gr. 5 up). Repr. of 1961 ed. 9.95 (ISBN 0-8038-4239-2). Hastings.

--Little Prayer. (Illus.). (gr. k-3). 1967. 3.50 (ISBN 0-8038-4243-0). Hastings.

--Miss Rumphius. LC 82-2837. (Illus.). 32p. (gr. k-3). 1982. 13.95 (ISBN 0-670-47958-6). Viking.

--Miss Rumphius. LC 85-40447. (Illus.). 32p. (ps-3). 1985. pap. 4.95 (ISBN 0-14-050539-3, Puffin). Penguin.

Cooney, Barbara, jt. auth. see Godden, Rumer.

Cooney, Barbara, jt. auth. see Preston, Edna M.

Cooney, Barbara, tr. see Hall, Donald.

Cooney, Caroline. I'm Not Your Other Half. 160p. 1985. pap. 2.25 (ISBN 0-425-08421-3, Pub. by Berkley-Pacer). Berkley Pub.

--Invasion of the Mutants. (Which Way Bk.: No. 17). (gr. 6 up). 1.95 (ISBN 0-671-53161-1). Archway.

--Racing to Love. (Follow Your Heart Romance Ser.: No. 7). (Orig.). (gr. 5 up). 1985. pap. 2.25 (ISBN 0-671-53161-1). Archway.

--A Stage Set for Love. (Follow Your Heart Romances Ser.). (Orig.). (gr. 5 up). 1983. pap. 1.95 (ISBN 0-671-47396-4). Archway.

Cooney, Caroline B. All the Way. (Cheerleader Ser.: No. 5). 176p. (Orig.). (gr. 7 up). 1985. pap. 2.25 (ISBN 0-590-33406-9). Scholastic Inc.

--An April Love Story. 176p. (Orig.). (YA) 1981. pap. 1.95 (ISBN 0-590-31858-6, Wildfire). Scholastic Inc.

--The Bad & the Beautiful. (Chrystal Falls Ser.: No. 3). 192p. (Orig.). (gr. 7 up). 1985. pap. 2.50 (ISBN 0-590-33690-8). Scholastic Inc.

--He Loves Me Not. 160p. (Orig.). (gr. 7 up). 1982. pap. 1.95 (ISBN 0-590-32190-0, Wildfire). Scholastic Inc.

--Holly in Love. (Orig.). (gr. 7 up). 1983. pap. 1.95 (ISBN 0-590-32558-2, Wildfire). Scholastic Inc.

--I'm Not Your Other Half. LC 84-7768. (Pacer Bks.). 160p. (gr. 7 up). 1984. 10.95 (ISBN 0-399-21134-9). Putnam Pub Group.

--The Morning After. (Chrystal Falls Ser.: No. 4). (gr. 7 up). 1985. pap. 2.50 (ISBN 0-590-33691-6). Scholastic Inc.

--Nancy & Nick. 176p. (Orig.). (gr. 7 up). 1982. pap. 1.95 (ISBN 0-590-31981-7, Wildfire). Scholastic Inc.

--Nice Girls Don't. 192p. (Orig.). (gr. 7 up). 1984. pap. 2.25 (ISBN 0-590-32846-8, Wildfire). Scholastic Inc.

--Rumors. (Cheerleaders Ser.: No. 3). 208p. (Orig.). (gr. 7 up). 1985. pap. 2.25 (ISBN 0-590-33404-2). Scholastic Inc.

--Sand Trap. 192p. pap. 2.50 (ISBN 0-380-83295-X, 83295). Avon.

--Sun, Sea, & Boys. (Follow Your Heart Ser.: No. 4). (Orig.). (gr. 5 up). 1984. pap. 1.95 (ISBN 0-671-47580-0). Archway.

--Trying Out. (Cheerleaders Ser.: No. 1). 192p. (Orig.). (gr. 7 up). 1985. pap. 2.25 (ISBN 0-590-33402-6). Scholastic Inc.

Cooney, Charles L., jt. ed. see Olson, Alfred.

Cooney, David, ed. Biomedical Engineering Principles: An Introduction to Fluid, Heat and Mass Transport Processes. (Biomedical Engineering & Instrumentation Ser.: Vol. 2). 464p. 1976. 49.50 (ISBN 0-8247-6347-5); text ed. 26.50. Dekker.

Cooney, Ellen. House Holding. LC 83-72996. (Illus.). 111p. (Orig.). 1984. pap. 7.95 (ISBN 0-9602912-6-1). Duir Press.

--The Quest for the Holy Grail. LC 80-67333. 85p. (Orig.). 1981. pap. 5.95 (ISBN 0-9602912-3-7). Duir Press.

--The Silver Rose. LC 79-52862. 99p. (Orig.). 1979. pap. 5.95 (ISBN 0-9602912-8-8). Duir Press.

--Small Town Girl. LC 82-23379. 208p. (gr. 5 up). 1983. 9.95 (ISBN 0-395-33881-6). HM.

Cooney, James A., jt. ed. see Rice, Michael.

Cooney, John. The American Pope. 1986. pap. 4.50 (ISBN 0-440-10194-8). Dell.

--The American Pope: The Life & Times of Francis Cardinal Spellman 1889-1967. LC 84-40096. (Illus.). 416p. 1984. 19.95 (ISBN 0-8129-1120-2). Times Bks.

Cooney, John, jt. auth. see Barrington, Ruth.

Cooney, John D. Amarna Reliefs from Hermopolis in American Collections. LC 65-17172. (Illus.). 1965. 8.00 (ISBN 0-913696-01-3). Bklyn Mus.

--Late Egyptian & Coptic Art: An Introduction to the Collections in the Brooklyn Museum. (Illus.). 1974. Repr. of 1943 ed. 9.00 (ISBN 0-913696-23-4). Bklyn Mus.

Cooney, Linda A. Alone Together. (Couples Ser.: No. 3). 185p. (Orig.). (gr. 7 up). 1985. pap. 2.50 (ISBN 0-590-33392-5). Scholastic Inc.

--A Chance to Make it. (Orig.). 1986. pap. 2.50 (ISBN 0-449-70156-5, Juniper). Fawcett.

--Change of Hearts. (Couples Ser.: No. 1). 288p. (Orig.). (gr. 7 up). 1985. pap. 2.50 (ISBN 0-590-33390-9). Scholastic Inc.

--Deadly Design. (Moonstone Novels Ser.: No. 1). 160p. (Orig.). (gr. 5 up). 1985. pap. 2.25 (ISBN 0-671-50782-6). Archway.

--Don't Look Now. (Moonstone Ser.: No. 4). (Orig.). (gr. 5 up). 1984. pap. write for info. (ISBN 0-671-50784-2). Archway.

--Fire & Ice. (Couples Ser.: No. 2). 208p. (Orig.). (gr. 7 up). 1985. pap. 2.50 (ISBN 0-590-33391-7). Scholastic Inc.

--Getting Experienced. (Orig.). 1986. pap. 2.50 (ISBN 0-449-70144-1, Juniper). Fawcett.

Cooney, Margaret, jt. auth. see Talbott, G. Douglas.

Cooney, Nancy. The Wobbly Tooth. LC 77-14943. (Illus.). 1981. pap. 4.95 (ISBN 0-399-20776-7). Putnam Pub Group.

Cooney, Nancy E. The Blanket That Had to Go. (Illus.). 32p. (gr. 4-8). 1981. 8.95 (ISBN 0-399-20716-3, Putnam); pap. 4.95 (ISBN 0-399-21054-7, Putnam). Putnam Pub Group.

Cooney, Nancy H. Sex, Sexuality, & You: A Handbook for Growing Christians. 100p. (Orig.). 1980. pap. text ed. 3.50 (ISBN 0-697-01741-9); tchrs.' resource guide 1.00 (ISBN 0-697-01742-7). Wm C Brown.

Cooney, Rian. Icarus. LC 82-2865. (Kestrel Chap Bks.). 48p. (Orig.). 1982. pap. 4.00 (ISBN 0-914974-35-1). Holmgangers.

Cooney, Rosemary S., jt. auth. see Rogler, Lloyd H.

Cooney, Seamus, jt. auth. see Morrow, Bradford.

Cooney, Seamus & Morrow, Bradford, eds. Blast Three. (Illus.). 300p. (Orig.). 1984. deluxe ed. 30.00 (ISBN 0-87685-592-3); pap. 20.00 (ISBN 0-87685-591-5). Black Sparrow.

Cooney, Seamus, ed. see Miller, Henry.

Cooney, Seamus, ed. see Reznikoff, Charles.

Cooney, Sean, jt. auth. see Wakin, Edward.

Cooney, Stephanie H. & Bagby, Sara A. The Individual as Teacher: Caring, Creating & Coping. 1978. 3.00 (ISBN 0-686-26997-7, 261-08434). Home Econ Educ.

Cooney, Thomas J. & Davis, Edward J. Dynamics of Teaching Secondary School Mathematics. 448p. 1983. text ed. 24.95x (ISBN 0-88133-061-2). Waveland Pr.

Cooney, Timothy J. Telling Right from Wrong: What Is Moral, What Is Immoral & What Is Neither One nor the Other. 158p. 1985. 17.95 (ISBN 0-87975-297-1). Prometheus Bks.

Cooney, William P., jt. auth. see Brooker, Andrew F.

Coonfield, Ed. Enduro Secrets Revealed. LC 84-62945. (Illus.). 176p. (Orig.). 1985. pap. 11.95 (ISBN 0-932479-24-3). Hourglass Pub.

Cooley, Douglas R. Wind: Making It Work for You. LC 78-31772. (Illus., Orig.). (gr. 7 up). 1979. pap. 3.50 (ISBN 0-89168-008-X). L Erlbaum Assocs.

Coonrod, J. Donald, et al, eds. The Direct Detection of Micro-Organisms in Clinical Samples. 1983. 56.00 (ISBN 0-12-187780-9). Acad Pr.

Coonrod, Renita J. Learning to Think. (Character Foundation Curriculum Ser.). (gr. 2). 1981. pap. 2.95 (ISBN 0-8007-7029-3); tchr's ed. 7.00 (ISBN 0-8007-7030-7). Revell.

Coons, Alvin E. & Glaze, Bert T. Housing Market Analysis & the Growth of Home Ownership. 1963. 5.00x (ISBN 0-87776-115-9, R115). Ohio St U Admin Sci.

Coons, Alvin E., jt. ed. see Stogdill, Ralph M.

Coons, John E. & Sugarman, Stephen D. Education by Choice: The Case for Family Control. LC 77-20318. 1978. 20.00x (ISBN 0-520-03613-1); pap. 4.95 (ISBN 0-520-03837-1). U of Cal Pr.

--Family Choice in Education: A Model State System for Vouchers. LC 70-169912. 118p. (Orig.). 1971. pap. 2.50x (ISBN 0-87772-082-7). Inst Gov Stud Berk.

Coons, Kenelm. Seasons for the Seafood Buyer-How to Plan Profitable Purchasing of Fish & Shellfish: A Guide to Natural Cycles & Regulatory Controls. Dore, Ian, ed. LC 84-2385. (Osprey Seafood Handbooks). 1985. 54.00x (ISBN 0-943738-02-4). Osprey Bks.

Coons, Quentin & Krusell, Cynthia H. The Winslows of "Careswell". Before & after the Mayflower. 1975. 3.00 (ISBN 0-940628-02-3). Pilgrim Hall.

Coontz, Otto. Hornswoggle Magic. (gr. 3-7). 1981. 8.95 (ISBN 0-316-15536-5). Little.

--Isle of the Shapeshifters. 224p. (gr. 5up). 1983. 6.95 (ISBN 0-395-34552-9). HM.

--Mystery Madness. (gr. 4-9). 1982. 8.95 (ISBN 0-395-32079-8). HM.

--The Night Walkers. LC 82-6161. (gr. 5 up). 1982. 9.95 (ISBN 0-395-32557-9). HM.

--The Night Walkers. 176p. (gr. 7-10). 1983. pap. 2.25 (ISBN 0-671-47523-1). Archway.

Coontz, Stephanie, ed. & intro. by. Life in Capitalist America. LC 74-14164. 288p. 1975. 20.00 (ISBN 0-87348-406-1). Path Pr NY.

Coontz, Stephanie & Henderson, Peta, eds. Women's Work, Men's Property: The Origins of Gender & Class. 220p. (Orig.). 1985. 28.00 (ISBN 0-8052-7254-2, Pub. by Verso England); pap. 8.95 (ISBN 0-8052-7255-0, Pub. by Verso England). Schocken.

Coontz, Sydney H. Productive Labour & Effective Demand, Including a Critique of Keynesian Economics. LC 66-15567. (Illus.). 1966. 25.00x (ISBN 0-678-06511-X). Kelley.

Coop, J. E. Sheep & Goat Production. (World Animal Science Ser.: Vol. 1C). 492p. 1982. 121.50 (ISBN 0-444-41989-6). Elsevier.

Coop, Richard H., jt. auth. see McCandless, Boyd R.

Coop, William L. Pacific People Sing Out Strong. (Orig.). 1982. pap. 4.95 (ISBN 0-377-00118-X). Friend Pr.

Coope, Christopher, et al. Wittgenstein Workbook. LC 79-135161. 1970. pap. 3.95x (ISBN 0-520-01840-0, CAMPUS48). U of Cal Pr.

Coope, Geoffrey G., jt. ed. see Beckwith, John A.

Coope, Jean. The Menopause. LC 83-19648. (Illus.). 112p. (Orig.). 1984. 12.95 (ISBN 0-668-05819-6); pap. 7.95 (ISBN 0-668-05821-8). Arco.

Coope, Rosalys. Salomon de Brosse & the Development of the Classical Style in French Architecture from 1565 to 1630. LC 70-127381. (Illus.). 295p. 1972. 60.00x (ISBN 0-271-00140-2). Pa St U Pr.

Cooper. Introduction to Japanese History & Culture. 1971. pap. 3.94 (ISBN 0-08-017484-1). Pergamon.

--Introduction to Queuing Theory. 2nd ed. 348p. 1980. 30.50 (ISBN 0-444-00379-7, North-Holland). Elsevier.

--The Pathfinder. (American Classics Ser.). (gr. 9-12). 1977. pap. text ed. 3.99 (ISBN 0-88343-406-7); cassettes 52.00 (ISBN 0-88343-422-9). McDougal-Littell.

--Software Quality Management. 1979. 25.00 (ISBN 0-89433-093-4). Petrocelli.

--Stress, Immunity & Aging. (Immunology Ser.). 352p. 1984. 59.75 (ISBN 0-8247-7114-1). Dekker.

--Tennessee Forms for Trial Practice. 2nd ed. incl. latest pocket part supplement 59.95 (ISBN 0-686-90996-8); separate pocket part supplement, 1984 16.95 (ISBN 0-686-90997-6). Harrison Co GA.

--The Tools of Biochemistry. 2nd ed. 1985. price not set (ISBN 0-471-82358-9). Wiley.

Cooper & Neal. Diagnosing Stress in Your Nursing World. 1985. 7.50 (ISBN 0-683-09540-4). Williams & Wilkins.

Cooper, jt. auth. see Walker.

Cooper, et al. Eli Whitney & the Whitney Armory. (Illus.). 95p. 8.95 (ISBN 0-9603662-0-2); pap. 4.95 (ISBN 0-686-63873-5). Arma Pr.

--Nursing Care Planning Guides for Maternity & Pediatric Care. 382p. 1982. 19.95 (ISBN 0-683-09533-1). Williams & Wilkins.

--Money: The Financial System & Economic Policy. (Finance Ser.). 576p. 1984. text ed. 34.95 (ISBN 0-201-03994-X); pap. 20.00 (ISBN 0-201-03995-8). Addison-Wesley.

--Nurse Care Planning Guides, 5 bks. 2nd ed. Date not set. Set. 47.80 (ISBN 0-683-09541-2); 12.95 ea. Vol. (ISBN 0-683-09519-6). Vol. 2 (ISBN 0-683-09520-X). Vol. 3 (ISBN 0-683-09521-8). Vol. 4 (ISBN 0-683-09522-6). Vol. 5 (ISBN 0-683-09523-4). Williams & Wilkins.

Cooper, A. A. An Inquiry Concerning Virtue, or Merit. Walford, D. E., ed. 152p. 1977. 15.50 (ISBN 0-7190-0657-0, Pub. by Manchester Univ Pr). Longwood Pub Group.

--Speeches of the Earl of Shaftesbury. 456p. 1971. Repr. of 1868 ed. 35.00x (ISBN 0-7165-1765-5, BBA 03100, Pub. by Irish Academic Pr). Biblio Dist.

Cooper, A. J. Root Temperature & Plant Growth. 73p. 1973. 30.00x (ISBN 0-85198-271-9, Pub. by CAB Bks England). State Mutual Bk.

Cooper, A. M. How to Supervise People. 4th ed. 1958. pap. 5.95 (ISBN 0-07-012779-4). McGraw.

Cooper, A. R. & Heuer, A. H., eds. Mass Transport Phenomena in Ceramics. LC 75-20154. (Materials Science Research Ser.: Vol. 9). 515p. 1975. 75.00x (ISBN 0-306-38509-0, Plenum Pr). Plenum Pub.

Cooper, Al. World of Logotypes, Vol. 1. LC 75-29774. 1976. 27.50 (ISBN 0-910158-20-7). Art Dir.

--World of Logotypes, Vol. 2. LC 75-29774. (Illus.). 1978. 27.50 (ISBN 0-910158-34-7). Art Dir.

--World of Logotypes, Vol. 3. LC 75-29774. (Illus.). 356p. 1982. 28.50 (ISBN 0-910158-82-7). Art Dir.

Cooper, Alan. Electricity. LC 83-50223. (Visual Science Ser.). 48p. (gr. 6 up). 1983. 13.72 (ISBN 0-382-06715-0); pap. 6.75 (ISBN 0-382-09999-0). Silver.

Cooper, Alan, jt. auth. see Single, Alan.

Cooper, Alice P. Authors & Others. facsimile ed. LC 70-107689. (Essay Index Reprint Ser.). 1927. 19.00 (ISBN 0-8369-1493-7). Ayer Co Pubs.

Cooper, Allan D. U. S. Economic Power & Political Influence in Namibia, 1700-1982. (Replica Edition). 222p. 1982. softcover 23.50x (ISBN 0-86531-920-0). Westview.

Cooper & Lybrand. Non-Pension Benefits for Retired Employees: Survey of Benefits & Accounting Practices. Hewitt Associates, ed. 1985. 12.00 (ISBN 0-317-20195-6). Finan Exec.

Cooper & Lybrand International Tax Network. International Tax Summaries, 1985: A Guide for Planning & Decisions. (Professional Accounting & Business Ser.). 904p. 65.00 (ISBN 0-471-82836-X). Wiley.

Cooper, Anna J. Voice from the South. LC 77-78762. Repr. of 1892 ed. 19.75x (ISBN 0-8371-1384-9, COV&). Greenwood.

Cooper, Anne M., jt. auth. see Wamsley, James S.

Cooper, Anthony R., ed. Polymeric Separation Media. LC 82-3668. (Polymer Science & Technology Ser.: Vol. 16). 285p. 1982. 49.50 (ISBN 0-306-40902-X, Plenum Pr). Plenum Pub.

--Ultrafiltration Membranes & Applications. LC 80-18685. (Polymer Science & Technology Ser.: Vol. 13). 724p. 1981. 95.00x (ISBN 0-306-40548-2, Plenum Pr). Plenum Pub.

Cooper, Arlene, jt. auth. see School, Beverly.

Cooper, Artemis, ed. A Durable Fire: The Letters of Duff & Diana Cooper 1913-1950. 332p. 1984. 17.95 (ISBN 0-531-09827-3). Watts.

Cooper, Arthur, tr. see Po, Li & Fu, Tu.

Cooper, Arthur R. North American Pseudophyllidean Cestodes from Fishes. (Illus.). 1919. 19.00 (ISBN 0-384-09785-5). Johnson Repr.

Cooper, Arthur R., jt. auth. see Kampmeier, Otto F.

Cooper, B. L. A Popular Music Handbook: A Resource for Teacher's, Librarians, & Media Specialists. 1983. lib. bdg. 27.50 (ISBN 0-87287-393-5). Libs Unl.

Cooper, B. Lee. Images of American Society in Popular Music: A Guide to Reflective Teaching. LC 81-18790. 1982. 23.95x (ISBN 0-88229-514-4); pap. 11.95x (ISBN 0-88229-798-8). Nelson-Hall.

Cooper, B. R. & Petrakis, L., eds. Chemistry & Physics of Coal Utilization - 1980 (APS, Morgantown) LC 81-65106. (AIP Conference Proceedings: No. 70). 472p. 1981. lib. bdg. 34.50 (ISBN 0-88318-169-X). Am Inst Physics.

Cooper, B. S., jt. auth. see Westwood, W.

Cooper, Barbara A. Winds of Passion. 1981. pap. 2.75 (ISBN 0-89083-778-3). Zebra.

Cooper, Barbara E., jt. auth. see Somer, John L.

Cooper, Barry. The End of History: An Essay on Modern Hegelianism. 400p. 1984. 45.00x (ISBN 0-8020-5625-3). U of Toronto Pr.

--Merleau-Ponty & Marxism: From Terror to Reform. LC 78-16829. 1979. 30.00x (ISBN 0-8020-5435-8). U of Toronto Pr.

--Michel Foucault: An Introduction to the Study of his Thought. LC 82-8260. (Studies in Religion & Society: Vol. 2). 176p. 1982. 39.95x (ISBN 0-88946-867-2). E Mellen.

--Renegotiating Secondary School Mathematics: A Study of Curriculum Change & Stability. (Studies in Curriculum History Ser.). 300p. 1985. 29.00x (ISBN 1-85000-014-X, Pub. by Falmer Pr); pap. 17.00x (ISBN 1-85000-013-1, Pub. by Falmer Pr). Taylor & Francis.

Cooper, Barry, tr. see Baechler, Jean.

Cooper, Bernard R., ed. Scientific Problems of Coal Utilization: Proceedings. LC 78-9553. (DOE Symposium Ser.). 424p. 1978. pap. 18.50 (ISBN 0-87079-400-0, CONF-770509); microfiche 4.50 (ISBN 0-87079-378-0, CONF-770509). DOE.

Cooper, Bernard R. & Ellingson, William A., eds. The Science & Technology of Coal & Coal Utilization. 682p. 1984. 85.00x (ISBN 0-306-41436-8, Plenum Pr). Plenum Pub.

Cooper, Bette, jt. auth. see Martin, Jim.

Cooper, Bev, jt. auth. see McCullough, Bonnie.

Cooper, Bobbi G., jt. auth. see Erskine, Jim.

Cooper, Brian & Morgan, H. G. Epidemiological Psychiatry. (Illus.). 232p. 1973. 25.75x (ISBN 0-398-02581-9). C C Thomas.

Cooper, Brian, ed. Assessing the Handicaps & Needs of Mentally Retarded Children. LC 81-66374. 1981. 38.50 (ISBN 0-12-188020-6). Acad Pr.

Cooper, Brian G. Meeting Famous Christians. (Illus.). 111p. 1977. pap. text ed. 5.95 (ISBN 0-85597-205-X). Attic Pr.

Cooper, Bruce C. & Hart, Gene. The Hockey Trivia Book. LC 84-757. (Illus.). 128p. (Orig.). 1984. pap. 8.95 (ISBN 0-88011-233-6). Leisure Pr.

Cooper, Bruce C., jt. auth. see Croce, Pat.

Cooper, Bruce S. Collective Bargaining, Strikes, & Financial Costs in Public Education: A Comparative Review. LC 81-71248. xix, 120p. (Orig.). 1982. pap. 7.85 (ISBN 0-86552-079-8). U of Oreg ERIC.

Cooper, Bryan. The Battle of the Torpedo Boats. (Zebra World at War Ser.: No. 16). 1979. pap. 2.50 (ISBN 0-89083-532-2). Zebra.

Cooper, C. A. & Clark, J. A., eds. Employment, Economics & Technology: The Impact of Technological Change on the Labor Market. LC 82-42543. 180p. 1982. 25.00x (ISBN 0-312-24459-2). St Martin.

Cooper, C. Everett. Up Your Asteroid! A Science Fiction Farce. LC 77-866. 1977. lib. bdg. 12.95x (ISBN 0-89370-106-8); pap. 4.95x (ISBN 0-89370-206-4). Borgo Pr.

--Up Your Asteroid! A Science Fiction Farce. 50p. 1977. pap. 4.95 (ISBN 0-87877-206-5). Newcastle Pub.

Cooper, C. L. Psychosocial Stress & Cancer. 263p. 1984. 29.95 (ISBN 0-471-90477-5). Wiley.

Cooper, C. L., jt. auth. see Davidson, M. J.

Cooper, C. L., ed. Group Training for Individual & Organizational Development. (Interpersonal Development: Vol. 3, Nos. 1-4). (Illus.). 1973. 25.75 (ISBN 3-8055-1481-6). S Karger.

Cooper, C. L. & Marshall, J., eds. White Collar & Professional Stress. LC 79-41779. (Studies in Occupational Stress). 257p. 1980. 53.95x (ISBN 0-471-27760-6, Pub. by Wiley-Interscience). Wiley.

Cooper, Carl, jt. auth. see Humble, Lance.

Cooper, Carlton R. The Word in Stanzas. 1983. 6.95 (ISBN 0-533-05458-3). Vantage.

Cooper, Carole L., jt. auth. see Stanley, David T.

Cooper, Carolyn. Creative Computer Video. (Computer Awareness Ser.). (Illus.). 72p. (gr. 4-6). 1985. PLB 9.40 (ISBN 0-531-10037-5). Watts.

--Electronic Bulletin Boards. (Computer Activity, First Bk. Ser.). (Illus.). 72p. (gr. 4 up). 1985. lib. bdg. 9.40 (ISBN 0-531-04907-8). Watts.

Cooper, Carolyn C., jt. auth. see Russett, Bruce M.

Cooper, Cary. Developing Managers for the 1980's. LC 80-15212. 160p. 1981. text ed. 44.50x (ISBN 0-8419-0649-1). Holmes & Meier.

--Psychology & Management. (Psychology for Professional Groups Ser.). 275p. 1981. text ed. 28.25x (ISBN 0-333-31856-0, Pub. by Macmillan England); pap. text ed. 11.50x (ISBN 0-333-31875-7). Humanities.

Cooper, Cary & Torrington, Derek P. After Forty: The Time for Achievement. 211p. 1981. 31.95x (ISBN 0-471-28043-7, Pub. by Wiley Interscience). Wiley.

Cooper, Cary, jt. auth. see Davidson, Marilyn.

Cooper, Cary L. Executive Families Under Stress: How Male & Female Executives Can Keep Their Pressures Out of Their Homes. 170p. 1981. 11.95 (ISBN 0-13-294074-4); pap. 5.95 (ISBN 0-13-294066-3). P-H.

--Improving Interpersonal Relationships. (Illus.). 145p. 1982. 11.95 (ISBN 0-13-452714-3); pap. 5.95 (ISBN 0-13-452706-2). P-H.

--Learning from Others in Groups: Experimental Learning Approaches. LC 78-26987. (Illus.). 1979. lib. bdg. 29.95 (ISBN 0-313-20922-7, COL/). Greenwood.

--The Stress Check: Coping with the Stresses of Life & Work. (Illus.). 176p. 1980. 11.95 (ISBN 0-13-852640-0, Spec); pap. 5.95 (ISBN 0-13-852632-X). P-H.

--Stress Research: Issues for the Eighties. LC 82-11049. 149p. 1982. 32.95 (ISBN 0-471-10246-6, Pub. by Wiley-Interscience). Wiley.

--Theories of Group Processes. LC 74-28089. (Individuals, Groups & Organizations Ser.). 275p. 1975. (Pub. by Wiley-Interscience); pap. text ed. 22.00 (ISBN 0-471-99452-9). Wiley.

Cooper, Cary L. & Marshall, Judi. Understanding Executive Stress. LC 77-16077. 1978. text ed. 14.00 (ISBN 0-89433-059-4). Petrocelli.

Cooper, Cary L., jt. auth. see Jones, Andrew N.

Cooper, Cary L., jt. auth. see Marshall, Judi.

Cooper, Cary L., jt. auth. see Robinson, Ivan T.

Cooper, Cary L., ed. Organizational Development in the U. K., U. S. A. A Joint Evaluation. LC 77-15084. 1978. text ed. 10.00 (ISBN 0-89433-069-1). Petrocelli.

--Theories of Group Processes. LC 74-28089. pap. 55.00 (ISBN 0-317-09544-7, 2051855). Bks Demand UMI.

Cooper, Cary L. & Alderfer, Clayton, eds. Advances in Experiential Social Processes. LC 77-22060. (Advances in Experiential Social Processes Ser.: Vol. 1). 1978. 49.95 (ISBN 0-471-99546-0, Pub. by Wiley-Interscience). Wiley.

Cooper, Cary L. & Mumford, Enid, eds. The Quality of Working Life in Western & Eastern Europe. LC 78-27692. (Contributions in Economics & Economic History: No. 25). 1979. lib. bdg. 35.00 (ISBN 0-313-20957-X, CWL/). Greenwood.

Cooper, Cary L., jt. ed. see Alderfer, Clayton P.

Cooper, Cary L., ed. see Freedman, Richard D.

Cooper, Cary L., jt. ed. see Marshall, Judi.

Cooper, Cary L., jt. ed. see Payne, Roy.

Cooper, Cary L., et al, eds. Current Concerns in Occupational Stress. LC 79-40641. (Wiley Series on Studies in Occupational Stress). (Illus.). pap. 88.30 (ISBN 0-317-09649-4, 2020971). Bks Demand UMI.

Cooper, Catherine R., jt. ed. see Grotevant, Harold D.

Cooper, Catherine R., jt. ed. see Moore, Shirley G.

Cooper, Catherine R., jt. ed. see Mueller, Edward C.

Cooper, Charles. English Table in History & Literature. LC 68-21760. 244p. 1968. Repr. of 1929 ed. 35.00x (ISBN 0-8103-3520-4). Gale.

--Policy Interventions for Technological Innovation in Developing Countries. (Working Paper: No. 441). 59p. 1980. 5.00 (ISBN 0-686-36148-2, WP-0441). World Bank.

--Researching Response to Literature & the Teaching of Literature. LC 83-11826. 400p. 1985. text ed. 39.50 (ISBN 0-89391-184-4); pap. 22.50 (ISBN 0-89391-323-5). Ablex Pub.

Cooper, Charles & Clark, John. Employment, Economics & Technology: The Impact of Technical Change on the Labour Market. 1982. 60.00x (ISBN 0-7108-0157-2, Pub. by Harvester Pr England). State Mutual Bk.

Cooper, Charles, ed. Science, Technology & Development: Political Economy of Technical Advance in Underdeveloped Countries. 204p. 1973. 29.50x (ISBN 0-7146-2999-5, F Cass Co). Biblio Dist.

Cooper, Charles R. Measuring Growth in Appreciation of Literature. (Reading Information Ser: Where Do We Go?). 1972. 2.00 (ISBN 0-87207-865-5). Intl Reading.

Cooper, Charles R., jt. auth. see Axelrod, Rise B.

Cooper, Charles R., ed. The Nature & Measurement of Competency in English. LC 80-26964. 176p. 1981. pap. 13.00 (ISBN 0-8141-3262-6). NCTE.

Cooper, Charles R. & Odell, Lee, eds. Evaluating Writing: Describing, Measuring, Judging. LC 77-11991. 156p. (Orig.). 1977. pap. 7.00 (ISBN 0-8141-1622-1). NCTE.

--Research on Composing: Points of Departure. LC 78-18251. 203p. 1978. pap. 9.25 (ISBN 0-8141-4069-6). NCTE.

Cooper, Charles W. & Robins, Edmund J. The Term Paper: A Manual & Model. 4th ed. 1967. pap. 1.25x (ISBN 0-8047-0348-5). Stanford U Pr.

Cooper, Charles W., jt. auth. see Zingaro, Ralph.

Cooper, Chester L., ed. Growth in America. LC 75-35359. (Contributions in American Studies: No. 21). (Illus.). 320p. 1976. lib. bdg. 35.00 (ISBN 0-8371-8596-3, CGA/). Greenwood.

Cooper, Chris & Osman, Tony. How Everyday Things Work. LC 84-1654. (The Junior World of Science Ser.). (gr. 7 up). 9.95 (ISBN 0-87196-988-2). Facts on File.

Cooper, Christine J., jt. auth. see Schaffer, Matthew.

Cooper, Clara. The Relation Between Morality & Intellect: A Compendium of Evidence Contributed by Psychology, Criminology, & Sociology. LC 71-176638. (Columbia University. Teachers College. Contributions to Education: No. 607). Repr. of 1935 ed. 22.50 (ISBN 0-404-55607-8). AMS Pr.

Cooper, Clare C. Easter Hill Village: Some Social Implications of Design. LC 74-10311. (Illus.). 1975. 17.95 (ISBN 0-02-906670-0). Free Pr.

Cooper, Clyde B. Some Elizabethan Opinions of the Poetry & Character of Ovid. LC 76-43057. 1914. lib. bdg. 10.00 (ISBN 0-8414-3573-1). Folcroft.

Cooper, Constance, et al. Public Education: Toward Equality, Equity & Excellence. 280p. 1981. pap. text ed. 12.95 (ISBN 0-8403-2384-0). Kendall-Hunt.

Cooper, D. B. Ha-Ha-Ha by D. B. Cooper. (Illus.). 330p. 1983. pap. 3.95 (ISBN 0-9612034-0-4). Signum Bks.

--The Pursuit of D. B. Cooper. 1981. pap. 2.50 (ISBN 0-440-17167-9). Dell.

Cooper, D. E., jt. auth. see Cooper, M. G.

Cooper, D. K. & Lanza, R. P., eds. Heart Transplantation. 1984. lib. bdg. 71.00 (ISBN 0-85200-862-7, Pub. by MTP Pr England). Kluwer Academic.

Cooper, D. L., jt. auth. see Richards, W. G.

Cooper, Dale, tr. see Verkuyl, Johannes.

Cooper, Dale J. Psalms: A Study Guide. (Revelation Series for Adults). 1979. pap. text ed. 2.25 (ISBN 0-933140-08-8). Bd of Pubns CRC.

Cooper, Daniel & Cooper, Suzanne. Being Yourself: Twenty-Four Ways to See the Light. (Illus.). 72p. (Orig.). 1981. pap. 3.95 (ISBN 0-941648-00-1). Perfect Prods.

Cooper, Darien. How to Be Happy Though Young. (Illus.). 224p. 1979. 5.95 (ISBN 0-8007-5048-9, Power Bks). Revell.

Cooper, Darien B. The Beauty of Beholding God. 168p. 1982. pap. 4.95 (ISBN 0-88207-350-8). Victor Bks.

--You Can Be the Wife of a Happy Husband. LC 74-77450. 156p. 1974. pap. 4.95 (ISBN 0-88207-711-2). Victor Bks.

Cooper, Darien B. & Carroll, Anne K. We Became Wives of Happy Husbands. LC 76-4314. 165p. 1976. pap. 4.95 (ISBN 0-88207-731-7). Victor Bks.

Cooper, David D. The Lesson of the Scaffold: The Public Execution Controversy in Victorian England. LC 73-92901. (Illus.). xi, 212p. 1974. 13.95x (ISBN 0-8214-0148-3, 82-81511). Ohio U Pr.

Cooper, David E. Authenticity & Learning: Nietzsche's Educational Philosophy. (International Library of the Philosophy of Education). 200p. 1983. 24.95X (ISBN 0-7100-9552-X). Routledge & Kegan.

--Presupposition. (Janua Linguarum, Ser. Minor: No. 203). 130p. 1974. pap. text ed. 13.60x (ISBN 90-2793-152-6). Mouton.

Cooper, David G. & Laing, R. D. Reason & Violence. pap. 5.95 (ISBN 0-394-71582-9, V-43, Vin). Random.

Cooper, David J. Brooks Range Passage. (Illus.). 208p. 1982. 14.95 (ISBN 0-89886-061-X). Mountaineers.

Cooper, David L., jt. auth. see Richards, W. Graham.

Cooper, David Y., et al, eds. Cytochromes P-450 & B5: Structure, Function, & Interaction. LC 75-15625. (Advances in Experimental Medicine & Biology Ser.: Vol. 58). 565p. 1975. 69.50x (ISBN 0-306-39058-2, Plenum Pr). Plenum Pub.

Cooper, Davis. Daily Devotions for Newlyweds. LC 81-67204. 1983. 7.50 (ISBN 0-8054-5646-5). Broadman.

Cooper, Denis. Coins & Minting. (Albums Ser.: No. 106). (Illus.). 32p. (Orig.). 1983. pap. 2.95 (ISBN 0-85263-639-3, Pub. by Shire Pubns England). Seven Hills Bks.

Cooper, Denis A., ed. Public Utilities Law Anthology, Vol. 4. LC 74-77644. (National Law Anthology Ser.). 1977. text ed. 59.95 (ISBN 0-914250-16-7). Intl Lib.

--Public Utilities Law Anthology, Vol. 5. LC 74-77644. (National Law Anthology Ser.). 1979. 59.95 (ISBN 0-914250-19-1). Intl Lib.

Cooper, Dennis. He Cried: Poems & Stories. 32p. 1984. pap. 5.00 (ISBN 0-9607630-1-5). Black Star.

--Idols. LC 79-66660. 1979. pap. 5.95 (ISBN 0-686-28355-4). Sea Horse.

--Safe. LC 83-51376. 110p. (Orig.). 1984. pap. 5.95 (ISBN 0-933322-16-X). Sea Horse.

--Tenderness of the Wolves. LC 81-15104. 76p. 1981. 15.95 (ISBN 0-89594-066-3); pap. 5.95 (ISBN 0-89594-065-5). Crossing Pr.

Cooper, Derek. Guide to the Whiskies of Scotland. 1979. 2.95 (ISBN 0-346-12425-5). Cornerstone.

--The Road to Mingulay. (Illus.). 224p. 1985. 25.00 (ISBN 0-317-30921-8). Routledge & Kegan.

--Skye. (Illus.). 242p. 1983. pap. 11.95 (ISBN 0-7100-9565-1). Routledge & Kegan.

Cooper, Dermot M. F. & Seamon, Kenneth B., eds. Dual Regulation of Adenylate Cyclase. (Advances in Cyclic Nucleotide & Protein Phosphorylation Research Ser.: Vol. 19). (Illus.). 352p. 1985. text ed. 59.00 (ISBN 0-88167-079-0). Raven.

Cooper, Diana. Animal Hotel. 224p. 1983. 12.95 (ISBN 0-312-03782-1). St Martin.

--Autobiography: The Rainbow Comes & Goes, the Light of Common Day, Trumpets from the Steep. 752p. 1985. pap. 12.95 (ISBN 0-88184-131-5). Carroll & Graf.

--Up to Scratch. 224p. 1983. 12.95 (ISBN 0-312-83391-1). St Martin.

Cooper, Dominic. The Dead of Winter. 2nd ed. LC 85-10226. 216p. 1985. pap. 7.95 (ISBN 0-571-13601-X). Faber & Faber.

Cooper, Donald, jt. auth. see Murdick, R. G.

Cooper, Donald, photos by. Theatre Year. 4th ed. (Illus.). 129p. 1984. pap. 11.95 (ISBN 0-9507578-3-7, NO. 3996). Methuen Inc.

Cooper, Doug. Standard Pascal User Reference Manual. 1983. pap. 12.95 (ISBN 0-393-30121-4). Norton.

Cooper, Doug & Clancy, Michael. Oh! Pascal! 1982. pap. 20.95x (ISBN 0-393-95205-3). Norton.

--Oh! Pascal! 2nd ed. 1985. pap. text ed. 23.95x (ISBN 0-393-95445-5); instructor's manual avail. (ISBN 0-393-95447-1). Norton.

Cooper, Douglas. Living God's Joy. LC 78-71158. (Redwood Ser.). 1979. pap. 4.95 (ISBN 0-8163-0241-3). Pacific Pr Pub Assn.

--Living God's Love. LC 74-27171. (Redwood Ser.). 1975. pap. 4.95 (ISBN 0-8163-0176-X, 12523-7). Pacific Pr Pub Assn.

--Living in Our Finest Hour. Phillips, Max, ed. (RWD Ser.). 112p. 1982. pap. 4.95 (ISBN 0-8163-0465-3). Pacific Pr Pub Assn.

--Living Spirit-Filled Life. (Red Ser.). 1985. pap. 4.95 (ISBN 0-8163-0595-1). Pacific Pr Pub Assn.

--Living We've Just Begun. (Redwood Ser.). 96p. 1983. pap. 4.95 (ISBN 0-8163-0505-6). Pacific Pr Pub Assn.

--Toulouse-Lautrec. (Library of Great Painters Ser). (Illus.). 1956. 40.00 (ISBN 0-8109-0512-4). Abrams.

--Toulouse-Lautrec. (Masters of Art Ser.). 1984. 19.95 (ISBN 0-8109-1678-9). Abrams.
--Toulouse-Lautrec: Twenty-Five Masterworks. 1983. 14.95 (ISBN 0-8109-2270-3). Abrams.
Cooper, Douglas & Tinterow, Gary. Essential Cubism. LC 83-22348. (Illus.). 448p. 1984. 45.00 (ISBN 0-8076-1092-5). Braziller.
Cooper, Duff. Sergeant Shakespeare. LC 76-30696. (Studies in Shakespeare, No. 24). 1977. lib. bdg. 46.95x (ISBN 0-8383-2152-6). Haskell.
--Talleyrand. 1932. 25.00x (ISBN 0-8047-0616-6). Stanford U Pr.
Cooper, E., ed. see Martin, Lance & Dicke, Robert, Jr.
Cooper, E. H. Introduction to Economic Geography. 1981. 25.00x (ISBN 0-7231-0709-2, Pub. by Univ Tutorial England). State Mutual Bk.
Cooper, E. L. General Immunology. LC 80-42218. (Illus.). 300p. 1982. 53.00 (ISBN 0-08-026368-2); pap. 22.00 (ISBN 0-08-026369-0). Pergamon.
Cooper, E. S. The Language of Medicine: A Guide for Stenotypists. 1977. pap. 13.95 (ISBN 0-87489-045-4). Med Economics.
Cooper, Earle, jt. auth. see Cahn, Nguyen Van.
Cooper, Ed, photos by. Portrait of Seattle. LC 79-55980. (Portrait of America Ser.). (Illus.). 80p. (Orig., Text by Archie Satterfield). 1980. pap. 7.50 (ISBN 0-912856-56-4). Graphic Arts Ctr.
--San Juan Islands. LC 83-80329. (Illus.). 128p. (Text by Ruth Kirk). 1983. 32.50 (ISBN 0-912856-84-X). Graphic Arts Ctr.
Cooper, Edmund. The Tenth Planet. 1973. 15.00 (ISBN 0-399-11187-5). Ultramarine Pub.
Cooper, Edward & Poda, Christopher L., eds. Broadband Network Technology: An Overview for the Data & Telecommunications Industries. LC 83-51319. (Illus.). 163p. (Orig.). 1984. pap. 19.95 (ISBN 0-9613248-0-5). Sytek Pr.
Cooper, Edwin & Brazier, Mary. Developmental Immunology: Clinical Problems & Aging. LC 82-4035. (UCLA Forum in Medical Sciences Ser.: No. 25). 1982. 35.00 (ISBN 0-12-188040-0). Acad Pr.
Cooper, Edwin L. Fishes of Pennsylvania & the Northeastern United States. LC 82-18052. (Illus.). 256p. 1983. 32.50x (ISBN 0-271-00337-5). Pa St U Pr.
Cooper, Edwin L., ed. Contemporary Topics in Immunobiology, Vol. 4: Invertebrate Immunology. LC 78-165398. (Illus.). 316p. 1974. 32.50x (ISBN 0-306-37804-3, Plenum Pr). Plenum Pub.
Cooper, Edwin L., ed. see International Symposium of the American Society of Zoologists, Toronto, December 27-30, 1977.
Cooper, Edythe, ed. see Martin, Lance.
Cooper, Eli L. Am Seguliah: A Treasured People. LC 82-91010. 148p. 1984. 10.00 (ISBN 0-533-05673-X). Vantage.
Cooper, Elizabeth. Harim & the Purdah: Studies of Oriental Women. LC 68-23147. 312p. 1975. Repr. of 1915 ed. 43.00x (ISBN 0-8103-3167-5). Gale.
--The Harim & the Purdah: Studies of Oriental Women. (Illus.). 309p. 1983. text ed. 35.00x (ISBN 0-86590-137-6). Apt Bks.
--A Primer of Cooking & Housekeeping. (Illus.). 192p. 1979. 8.95 (ISBN 0-89496-023-7); pap. 5.95 (ISBN 0-89496-015-6). Ross Bks.
--The Women of Egypt. LC 79-2934. (Illus.). 380p. 1981. Repr. of 1914 ed. 28.25 (ISBN 0-8305-0102-9). Hyperion Conn.
Cooper, Elizabeth I., jt. ed. see Bailey, N. Louise.
Cooper, Ella G., jt. auth. see Goodall, Helen S.
Cooper, Emmanuel. Electric Kiln Pottery: The Complete Guide. (Illus.). 144p. 1982. 24.95 (ISBN 0-7134-4037-6, Pub. by Batsford England). David & Charles.
Cooper, Eugene. The Woodcarvers of Hong Kong. LC 78-75255. (Cambridge Studies in Social Anthropology: No. 29). (Illus.). 1980. 34.50 (ISBN 0-521-22699-6). Cambridge U Pr.
Cooper, F. T. Some American Story Tellers. 1977. lib. bdg. 59.95 (ISBN 0-8490-2623-7). Gordon Pr.
Cooper, F. T. & Maurice, A. B. History of the Nineteenth Century in Caricature. 59.95 (ISBN 0-8490-0359-8). Gordon Pr.
Cooper, F. T., tr. see Donauer, Friedrich.
Cooper, Frank & Knight, Jesse F. The Romantic Revival-Setting the Record Straight. Villegas, Robert, ed. LC 79-50797. (gr. 7 up). 1980. pap. 2.95 (ISBN 0-930962-02-8). Lion Ent.
Cooper, Frank E. Administrative Agencies & the Courts. LC 51-62547. (Michigan Legal Publications Ser.). xxv, 470p. 1982. Repr. of 1951 ed. lib. bdg. 32.50 (ISBN 0-89941-171-1). W S Hein.
--Writing in Law Practice. 556p. 1963. text ed. 19.00 (ISBN 0-672-81021-2, Bobbs-Merrill Law). Michie Co.
Cooper, Franklin S., jt. ed. see Sawashima, Masayuki.
Cooper, Fred C. Advertising Law Anthology, 1982-1983, Vol. VIII. LC 73-87656. (National Law Anthology Ser.). 1984. text ed. 59.95 (ISBN 0-914250-25-6). Intl Lib.
--Banking Law Anthology, Nineteen Eighty-Three, Vol.1. (National Law Anthology Ser.). 1983. 59.97 (ISBN 0-914250-23-X). Intl Lib.
Cooper, Fred C., ed. Insurance Law Anthology, Vol. 1. (National Law Anthology Ser.). Date not set. text ed. 59.95 (ISBN 0-914250-21-3). Intl Lib.
--Public Utilities Law Anthology, 1980-1981, Vol. 6. LC 74-77644. (National Law Anthology Ser.). text ed. 59.95 (ISBN 0-914250-24-8). Intl Lib.
--Public Utilities Law Anthology, 1982-1983, Vol. 7. LC 74-77644. (National Law Anthology Ser.). 1984. 59.95 (ISBN 0-914250-26-4). Intl Lib.
Cooper, Frederic T. The Craftsmanship of Writing. 275p. 1980. Repr. of 1911 ed. lib. bdg. 25.00 (ISBN 0-89984-106-6). Century Bookbindery.
--The Craftsmanship of Writing. 1973. Repr. of 1911 ed. 12.50 (ISBN 0-8274-1665-2). R West.
--Some American Story Tellers. facs. ed. LC 68-8451. (Essay Index Reprint Ser). 1968. Repr. of 1911 ed. 21.50 (ISBN 0-8369-0336-6). Ayer Co Pubs.
--Some English Story Tellers. facs. ed. LC 68-54341. (Essay Index Reprint Ser). 1912. 21.50 (ISBN 0-8369-0337-4). Ayer Co Pubs.
--Some English Story Tellers: A Book of the Younger Novelists. 1977. lib. bdg. 59.95 (ISBN 0-8490-2627-X). Gordon Pr.
--Some English Story Tellers: A Book of the Younger Novelists. 1912. 13.50 (ISBN 0-8274-3455-3). R West.
Cooper, Frederic T., jt. auth. see Maurice, Arthur B.
Cooper, Frederick. From Slaves to Squatters: Plantation Labor & Agriculture in Zanibar & Coastal Kenya, 1890-1925. LC 80-5391. 352p. 1981. text ed. 33.00x (ISBN 0-300-02454-1). Yale U Pr.
--Plantation Slavery on the East Coast of Africa. LC 76-41308. (Yale Historical Publications, Miscellany: No. 113). (Illus.). 1977. 31.00x (ISBN 0-300-02041-4). Yale U Pr.
Cooper, Frederick, ed. Struggle for the City: Migrant Labor, Capital & the State in Urban Africa. (Sage Series on African Modernization & Development: Vol. 8). 304p. 1983. 29.95 (ISBN 0-8039-2067-9). Sage.
Cooper, Frederick T., jt. auth. see Maurice, Arthur B.
Cooper, G. Arthur. Brachiopods from the Caribbean Sea & Adjacent Waters. LC 75-4757. (Studies in Tropical Oceanography: No. 14). 1977. 29.95x (ISBN 0-87024-277-6). U Miami Marine.
Cooper, G. R. & McGillem, C. D. Modern Communications & Spread Spectrum. 544p. 1985. 51.95 (ISBN 0-07-012951-7). McGraw.
Cooper, G. S., jt. auth. see Rahman, H.
Cooper, Gale. Animal People. (Illus.). 224p. 1983. 15.95 (ISBN 0-395-32198-0); pap. 8.95 (ISBN 0-395-34838-2). HM.
--One Unicorn. (Illus.). 32p. (ps up). 1981. 10.50 (ISBN 0-525-36438-2, 01019-310, Unicorn Bk). Dutton.
Cooper, Gale & Schiller, Alan L. Anatomy of the Guinea Pig. LC 74-81866. (Commonwealth Fund Ser.). (Illus.). 432p. 1975. text ed. 40.00x (ISBN 0-674-03159-8). Harvard U Pr.
Cooper, Gayle. Checklist of American Imprints for 1830: Items 1-5609. (Checklist of American Imprints Ser.: Vol. 1830). 1972. 27.50 (ISBN 0-8108-0520-0). Scarecrow.
Cooper, Gayle, ed. see Shoemaker, Richard H.
Cooper, Geoffrey & Wortham, Christopher, eds. Everyman. 64p. 1980. pap. 5.50x (ISBN 0-85564-167-3, Pub. by U of W Austral Pr). Intl Spec Bk.
Cooper, George. A Voluntary Tax? New Perspectives on Sophisticated Estate Tax Avoidance. LC 78-20853. (Studies of Government Finance). 1979. 16.95 (ISBN 0-8157-1552-8); pap. 6.95 (ISBN 0-8157-1551-X). Brookings.
Cooper, George R. & McGillem, Clare D. Probabilistic Methods of Signal & System Analysis. LC 73-136170. 1971. text ed. 41.95 (ISBN 0-03-084291-3). HR&W.
Cooper, George R., jt. auth. see McGillem, C. D.
Cooper, Gerald. Selected Methods of Clinical Chemistry, Vol. 8. LC 53-7099. 209p. 1977. 30.00 (ISBN 0-915274-05-1); members 20.00. Am Assn Clinical Chem.
Cooper, Gerald R., ed. Selected Methods of Clinical Chemistry, Vol. 10. 234p. 1983. AACC member 40.00 (ISBN 0-915274-21-3); non-member 30.00. Am Assn Clinical Chem.
Cooper, Grace C. Guide to Teaching Early Child Development: A Comprehensive Curriculum. LC 75-15336. 344p. 1975. pap. 15.00 (ISBN 0-87868-154-X, 010-0006). Child Welfare.
Cooper, Grace R. The Sewing Machine: Its Invention & Development. LC 75-619415. (Illus.). 238p. 1977. 27.50x (ISBN 0-87474-330-3). Smithsonian.
Cooper, Grosvenor. Learning to Listen: A Handbook for Music. LC 57-8579. 1962. pap. 7.00x (ISBN 0-226-11519-4, P79, Phoen). U of Chicago Pr.
Cooper, Grosvenor & Meyer, Leonard B. Rhythmic Structure of Music. LC 60-14068. 1960. pap. 6.95x (ISBN 0-226-11522-4, P118, Phoen). U of Chicago Pr.
Cooper, Gwen & Haas, Evelyn. Wade a Little Deeper, Dear. (Illus.). 108p. 1979. pap. 4.50 (ISBN 0-89395-013-0). Synergistic Pr.
--Wade a Little Deeper Dear. 1978. pap. 4.50 (ISBN 0-87735-044-2). Wade Bks.
Cooper, Gwen, jt. auth. see Haas, Evelyn.
Cooper, H. H. On Assassination. 224p. 1984. 14.95 (ISBN 0-87364-290-2). Paladin Pr.
Cooper, H. H., jt. auth. see Kobetz, Richard W.
Cooper, H. R. Practical Dredging. 1981. 60.00x (ISBN 0-85174-079-0, Pub. by Nautical England). State Mutual Bk.
Cooper, Harold. Believing Truth about the Church. (Illus.). 122p. (gr. 8-9). 1975. pap. 1.50 (ISBN 0-89114-070-0); tchr's ed. 1.00 (ISBN 0-89114-071-9). Baptist Pub Hse.
--Discovering Christ in the Home. 1974. pap. 1.00 (ISBN 0-89114-019-0); tchr's guide 1.00 (ISBN 0-89114-018-2). Baptist Pub Hse.
--Doctrines from Beloved Disciple: Outlined Gospel of John. 1972. pap. 1.00 (ISBN 0-89114-054-9). Baptist Pub Hse.
--Living Jesus. (Illus.). 106p. 1977. pap. text ed. 1.50 (ISBN 0-89114-077-8); tchrs. ed. 1.00 (ISBN 0-89114-078-6). Baptist Pub Hse.
--True Science. 1973. pap. 1.50 (ISBN 0-89114-029-8); tchr's guide 1.50 (ISBN 0-89114-028-X). Baptist Pub Hse.
--True Service. (Illus.). 110p. 1973. pap. text ed. 1.50 (ISBN 0-89114-081-6); tchrs. ed. 1.25 (ISBN 0-89114-082-4). Baptist Pub Hse.
Cooper, Harris M. & Good, Thomas L. Pygmalion Grows Up. LC 82-14876. (Research in Writing Ser.). (Illus.). 224p. 1982. 25.00x (ISBN 0-582-28401-5). Longman.
Cooper, Helen. The Basic Guide to How to Read Music. (Illus.). 80p. (Orig.). 1985. pap. 7.95 (ISBN 0-399-51122-9, Perigee). Putnam Pub Group.
--John Trumbull: The Hand & Spirit of a Painter. LC 82-50609. (University Art Gallery Publication Ser.). (Illus.). 256p. 1982. text ed. 47.00x (ISBN 0-300-02928-4); pap. 19.95x (ISBN 0-300-02932-2). Yale U Pr.
--Pastoral: Mediaeval into Renaissance. 257p. 1977. 32.50x (ISBN 0-87471-906-2). Rowman.
--The Structure of the "Canterbury Tales". LC 83-13997. 256p. 1984. pap. 12.00x (ISBN 0-8203-0781-5). U of Ga Pr.
Cooper, Helen, ed. see Burnham, Patricia M. & Price, Martin.
Cooper, Henry R. The Igor Tale: An Annotated Bibliography of Twentieth-Century Non-Soviet Scholarship on the Slovo O polku Igoreve. LC 77-85703. 140p. 1978. 27.50 (ISBN 0-87332-111-1). M E Sharpe.
Cooper, Henry R., Jr. France Preseren. (World Authors Ser.). 1981. lib. bdg. 16.95 (ISBN 0-8057-6462-3, Twayne). G K Hall.
Cooper, Henry R., Jr., jt. ed. see Lencek, Rado L.
Cooper, Henry S., Jr. Imaging Saturn. LC 83-10. (Illus.). 224p. 1985. pap. 8.95 (ISBN 0-03-005614-4, Owl Bks.). HR&W.
--The Search for Life on Mars. LC 79-20061. 276p. 1980. 10.95 (ISBN 0-03-046166-9). HR&W.
--The Search for Life on Mars. LC 81-2440. 264p. 1981. pap. 6.95 (ISBN 0-03-059818-4, Owl Bk). HR&W.
Cooper, Herbert, jt. auth. see Mullish, Henry.
Cooper, Herbert K., et al, eds. Cleft Palate & Cleft Lip: A Team Approach to Clinical Management & Rehabilitation of the Patient. LC 76-41536. pap. 146.00 (ISBN 0-317-26127-4, 2025168). Bks Demand UMI.
Cooper, Herbert K., Sr., et al, eds. Cleft Palate & Cleft Lip: A Team Approach to Clinical Management & Rehabilitation of the Patient. LC 76-41536. (Illus.). 1978. text ed. 54.00 (ISBN 0-7216-2687-4). Saunders.
Cooper, Hermann. An Accounting of Progress & Attendance of Rural School Children in Delaware. LC 77-176669. (Columbia University. Teachers College. Contributions to Education: No. 422). Repr. of 1930 ed. 22.50 (ISBN 0-404-55422-9). AMS Pr.
Cooper-Hewitt Museum-Rizzoli. The Phenomenon of Change. Taylor, Lisa, ed. (Illus.). 192p. 1984. pap. 15.95 (ISBN 0-8478-0537-9). Rizzoli Intl.
Cooper, Homer C., jt. auth. see Campbell, Angus.
Cooper, Horton. North Carolina Folklore & Miscellany. (Illus.). 168p. 1972. 9.50 (ISBN 0-930230-18-3). Johnson NC.
Cooper, I. S. The Victim Is Always the Same. (Illus.). 160p. 1976. pap. 2.95 (ISBN 0-393-00817-7, Norton Lib). Norton.
--The Vital Probe: My Life As a Brain Surgeon. (Illus.). 1981. 15.95 (ISBN 0-393-01469-X). Norton.
Cooper, I. S., ed. Cerebellar Stimulation in Man. LC 77-76925. 232p. 1978. 41.00 (ISBN 0-89004-206-3). Raven.
Cooper, Ian, jt. ed. see Powell, James A.
Cooper, Ilene. Susan B. Anthony. (Impact Biography Ser.). 128p. (gr. 7 up). 1984. lib. bdg. 9.90 (ISBN 0-531-04750-4). Watts.
Cooper, Ilene, jt. ed. see Wilms, Denise.
Cooper, Irving, et al, eds. The Cerebellum, Epilepsy & Behavior. LC 73-21971. 413p. 1974. 39.50x (ISBN 0-306-30775-8, Plenum Pr). Plenum Pub.
Cooper, Irving S. Reincarnation: A Hope of the World. LC 79-11475. 1979. pap. 3.95 (ISBN 0-8356-0528-0, Quest). Theos Pub Hse.
--Secret of Happiness. LC 75-26815. 75p. 1976. pap. 1.75 (ISBN 0-8356-0469-1, Quest). Theos Pub Hse.
--Theosophy Simplified. 59.95 (ISBN 0-8490-1191-4). Gordon Pr.
--Theosophy Simplified. new ed. LC 78-64905. 1979. pap. 3.25 (ISBN 0-8356-0519-1, Quest). Theos Pub Hse.
Cooper, Irving S., et al. The Pulvinar-LP Complex. (Illus.). 312p. 1974. photocopy ed. 39.50x (ISBN 0-398-02849-4). C C Thomas.
Cooper, Isabella M. Bibliography on Educational Broadcasting. LC 76-161184. (History of Broadcasting: Radio to Television Ser). 1971. Repr. of 1942 ed. 46.50 (ISBN 0-405-03587-X). Ayer Co Pubs.
Cooper, Iver P. Biotechnology & the Law. LC 82-12957. 1982. 86.50 (ISBN 0-87632-311-5). Boardman.
Cooper, J. Microprocessor Background for Management Personnel. 208p. 1981. 23.95 (ISBN 0-13-580829-4). P-H.
--The Minolta Systems Handbook. 1976. 29.95 (ISBN 0-13-584599-8, Spec). P-H.
--Minolta Systems Handbook. 2nd ed. 1979. 34.95 (ISBN 0-13-584581-5, Spec). P-H.
--Plastic Containers for Pharmaceuticals: Testing & Control. (Offset Pub.: No. 4). (Also avail. in French). 1974. pap. 12.80 (ISBN 92-4-170004-1). World Health.
Cooper, J., jt. ed. see Rose, J. W.
Cooper, J. C. Fairy Tales: Allegories of the Inner Life. 128p. 1983. pap. 7.95 (ISBN 0-85030-313-3). Newcastle Pub.
--An Illustrated Encyclopaedia of Traditional Symbols. (Illus.). 1979. 19.95 (ISBN 0-500-01201-6). Thames Hudson.
--Symbolism: The Universal Language. 128p. 1983. pap. 7.95 (ISBN 0-85030-279-X). Newcastle Pub.
--Taoism: The Way of the Mystic. 1973. pap. 7.95 (ISBN 0-85030-096-7). Weiser.
Cooper, J. California. A Piece of Mine: A New Short Story Collection. 124p. (Orig.). 1984. pap. 7.95 (ISBN 0-931125-00-6). Wild Trees Press.
Cooper, J. David & Worden, Thomas W. The Classroom Reading Program in the Elementary School: Assessment, Organization, & Management. 416p. 1983. text ed. write for info. (ISBN 0-02-324660-X). Macmillan.
Cooper, J. David, et al. Decision Making for the Diagnostic Teacher: A Laboratory Manual. LC 70-175165. 155p. 1972. pap. text ed. 10.95 (ISBN 0-03-080274-1). HR&W.
--The What & How of Reading Instruction. 1979. pap. text ed. 19.95 (ISBN 0-675-08287-0). Additional supplements may be obtained from publisher. Merrill.
Cooper, J. E. & Eley, J. T. First Aid & Care of Wild Birds. 1979. 24.95 (ISBN 0-7153-7664-0). David & Charles.
Cooper, J. E. & Jackson, O. F., eds. Diseases of the Reptilia, 2 vols. LC 81-66390. 1982. Vol. 1. 66.00 (ISBN 0-12-187901-1); Vol. 2. 47.50 (ISBN 0-12-187902-X). Acad Pr.
Cooper, J. I. & MacCallum, F. O. Viruses & the Environment. (Illus.). 190p. 1984. 32.00x (ISBN 0-412-22870-X, NO. 6437); pap. 15.95x (ISBN 0-412-22880-7, NO. 6869). Methuen Inc.
Cooper, J. L., jt. auth. see Moran, T. K.
Cooper, J. P. Land, Men & Beliefs: Studies in Early-Modern History. Aylmer, G. E. & Morrill, J. S., eds. (No. 24). 300p. 1983. 27.00 (ISBN 0-907628-26-5). Hambledon Press.
Cooper, J. P., ed. Photosynthesis & Productivity in Different Environments. (International Biological Programme Ser.: No. 3). (Illus.). 550p. 1975. 110.00 (ISBN 0-521-20573-5). Cambridge U Pr.
Cooper, J. T. & Hagan, Paul. Dr. Cooper's Fabulous Fructose Diet. LC 78-27346. 216p. 1979. 8.95 (ISBN 0-87131-280-8). M Evans.
Cooper, J. T. & Hagen, P. Dr. Cooper's Fabulous Fructose Diet. 224p. 1981. pap. 2.50 (ISBN 0-449-24299-4, Crest). Fawcett.
Cooper, J. W. Introduction to Pascal for Scientists. LC 80-28452. 260p. 1981. 28.95x (ISBN 0-471-08785-8, Pub. by Wiley-Interscience). Wiley.
Cooper, Jack R. & Bloom, Floyd E. The Biochemical Basis of Neuropharmacology. 4th ed. (Illus.). 1982. text ed. 24.95x (ISBN 0-19-503093-1); 12.95 (ISBN 0-19-503094-X). Oxford U Pr.
Cooper, Jackie & Kleiner, Dick. Please Don't Shoot My Dog. 1984. pap. 3.95 (ISBN 0-425-07483-8). Berkley Pub.
Cooper, Jackie, et al. Mackintosh Architecture. (Illus.). 128p. 1984. pap. 19.95 (ISBN 0-312-50243-5). St Martin.
Cooper, Jacqueline. Angus & the Mona Lisa. LC 80-13506. (Illus.). 32p. (gr. 1-3). 1981. 12.50 (ISBN 0-688-41972-0); PLB 12.88 (ISBN 0-688-51972-5). Lothrop.
Cooper, James A. Computer-Security Technology. LC 82-49206. (Illus.). 192p. 1984. 26.50x (ISBN 0-669-06436-X). Lexington Bks.
Cooper, James F. Afloat & Ashore: A Sea Tale. 549p. 1980. Repr. of 1844 ed. lib. bdg. 18.25x (ISBN 0-89968-212-X). Lightyear.
--The American Democrat. LC 80-83794. 280p. 1981. 10.00 (ISBN 0-913966-91-6, Liberty Clas); pap. 5.00 (ISBN 0-913966-92-4). Liberty Fund.
--Borderers: Or, the Wept of Wish-Ton-Wish. LC 74-162892. (Bentley's Standard Novels Ser.: No. 33). (Illus.). Repr. of 1833 ed. 15.50 (ISBN 0-404-54433-9). AMS Pr.
--The Bravo. Ringe, Donald A., ed. (Masterworks of Literature Ser.). 1963. 10.95x (ISBN 0-8084-0065-7); pap. 7.95x (ISBN 0-8084-0066-5). New Coll U Pr.
--Chainbearer: Or, the Littlepage Manuscripts, 2 vols. in 1. LC 70-37651. Repr. of 1845 ed. 21.50 (ISBN 0-404-01704-5). AMS Pr.

--Chainbearer or the Littlepage Manuscripts, 2 vols. in 1. LC 6-32149. 1981. Repr. of 1845 ed. 19.00x (ISBN 0-403-00135-8). Scholarly.
--Correspondence of James Fenimore Cooper, 2 vols. facsimile ed. LC 70-164597. (Select Bibliographies Reprint Ser). Repr. of 1922 ed. Set. 53.00 (ISBN 0-8369-5881-0). Ayer Co Pubs.
--Correspondence of James Fenimore Cooper, 2 Vols. LC 71-160159. (American Biography Ser., No. 32). 1971. Repr. of 1922 ed. Set. lib. bdg. 79.95x (ISBN 0-8383-1295-0). Haskell.
--The Crater: Or, Vulcan's Peak. (John Harvard Library, Belknap Press). 501p. 1962. text ed. 18.50x (ISBN 0-674-17550-6). Harvard U Pr.
--The Crater: Or, Vulcan's Peak; a Tale of the Pacific. LC 76-42723. Repr. of 1896 ed. 37.50 (ISBN 0-404-60058-1). AMS Pr.
--Deerslayer. (YA) (gr. 6 up). 1964. pap. 1.25 (ISBN 0-8049-0031-0, CL31). Airmont.
--Deerslayer. (RL 7). pap. 2.95 (ISBN 0-451-51645-1, CE1645, Sig Classics). NAL.
--The Deerslayer. 5th ed. (Bantam Classics Ser.). 528p. (YA) (gr. 9-12). 1982. pap. 2.95 (ISBN 0-553-21085-8). Bantam.
--Early Critical Essays, 1820-1822. LC 55-11038. 1977. Repr. 40.00x (ISBN 0-8201-1228-3). Schol Facsimiles.
--Gleanings in Europe, 2 Vols. Spiller, Robert E., ed. Repr. of 1928 ed. Set. 41.00 (ISBN 0-527-19400-X). Kraus Repr.
--Gleanings in Europe: France. Philbrick, Thomas & Denne, Constance A., eds. (The Writings of James Fenimore Cooper Ser.). 380p. 1983. 44.50x (ISBN 0-87395-368-1); pap. 14.95x (ISBN 0-87395-596-X). State U NY Pr.
--Gleanings in Europe: Italy. Denne, Constance A., ed. (The Writings of James Fenimore Cooper Ser.). 1981. 44.50x (ISBN 0-87395-365-7); pap. 14.95x (ISBN 0-87395-460-2). State U NY Pr.
--Gleanings in Europe: Switzerland. Staggs, Kenneth & Elliot, James P., eds. LC 79-13133. (Writings of James Fenimore Cooper Ser.). 1980. 44.50x (ISBN 0-87395-364-9); pap. 14.95x (ISBN 0-87395-422-X). State U NY Pr.
--James Fenimore Cooper: New Critical Essays. Clark, Robert, ed. (Critical Studies Ser.). 224p. 1985. 28.50x (ISBN 0-389-20592-3). B&N Imports.
--Last of the Mohicans. (Classics Ser). (gr. 6 up). 1964. pap. 1.95 (ISBN 0-8049-0005-1, CL-5). Airmont.
--Last of the Mohicans. (Orig.). (RL 7). pap. 2.50 (ISBN 0-451-51495-5, CE1495, Sig Classics). NAL.
--The Last of the Mohicans. new & abr. ed. Farr, Naunerle, ed. (Now Illustrated III Ser.). (Illus.). (gr. 4-12). 1977. text ed. 5.00 (ISBN 0-88301-279-0); pap. text ed. 1.95 (ISBN 0-88301-267-7). Pendulum Pr.
--The Last of the Mohicans. 450p. 1983. Repr. lib. bdg. 18.95x (ISBN 0-89966-312-5). Buccaneer Bks.
--The Last of the Mohicans. 21.95 (ISBN 0-89190-895-1, Pub. by Am Repr). Amereon Ltd.
--Last of the Mohicans: Abridged & Adapted to Grade 2 Reading Level. Hurdy, John M., ed. LC 67-25787. (Pacemaker Classics Ser.). (Illus.). 1967. pap. 4.92 (ISBN 0-8224-9215-6); tchr's manual free. Pitman Learning.
--The Leatherstocking Saga. 30.95 (ISBN 0-8488-0059-1, Pub. by Amereon Hse). Amereon Ltd.
--Letters & Journals of James Fenimore Cooper, 6 vols. Beard, James F., ed. Incl. 1960; Vols. 3-4. 1964. Set. 50.00x (ISBN 0-674-52551-5); Vols. 5-6. 1968. Set. 50.00x (ISBN 0-674-52552-3). (Illus., Belknap Pr). Harvard U Pr.
--Lionel Lincoln or the Leaguer of Boston. Ringe, Donald A. & Ringe, Lucy B., eds. LC 84-8675. (The Writings of James Fenimore Cooper Ser.). 400p. 1984. 44.50x (ISBN 0-87395-416-5); pap. 14.95x (ISBN 0-87395-671-0). State U NY Pr.
--New York: Being an Introduction to an Unpublished Manuscript by the Author, Entitled The Towns of Manhattan. LC 73-16206. 1930. lib. bdg. 15.00 (ISBN 0-8414-3500-6). Folcroft.
--Pathfinder. (Classics Ser). (gr. 6 up). 1964. pap. 2.95 (ISBN 0-8049-0035-3, CL-35). Airmont.
--Pathfinder. 1976. lib. bdg. 18.95 (ISBN 0-89968-159-X). Lightyear.
--Pathfinder. (YA) (RL 10). 1964. pap. 3.50 (ISBN 0-451-51708-3, CE1708, Sig Classics). NAL.
--The Pathfinder. Dixson, Robert J., ed. (American Classics Ser.: Bk. 4). (gr. 9 up). 1973. pap. text ed. 3.80 (ISBN 0-88345-200-6, 18123); cassettes 45.00 (ISBN 0-685-38992-8, 58223). Regents Pub.
--The Pathfinder. 419p. 1984. Repr. lib. bdg. 18.95 (ISBN 0-89966-491-1). Buccaneer Bks.
--The Pathfinder: Or the Inland Sea. (Writings of James Fenimore Cooper Ser.). 1980. 44.50x (ISBN 0-87395-360-6); pap. 14.95x (ISBN 0-87395-477-7). State U NY Pr.
--Pioneers. (Classics Ser). (gr. 8 up). 1964. pap. 1.95 (ISBN 0-8049-0049-3, CL-49). Airmont.
--The Pioneers. 1976. lib. bdg. 18.95 (ISBN 0-89968-157-3). Lightyear.
--Pioneers. (YA) (RL 10). pap. 3.50 (ISBN 0-451-51621-4, CE1621, Sig Classics). NAL.
--The Pioneers. Beard, James F., ed. LC 77-21795. (Writings of James Fenimore Cooper Ser.). 1980. 44.50x (ISBN 0-87395-359-2); pap. 14.95x (ISBN 0-87395-423-8). State U NY Pr.
--The Pioneers. 493p. 1984. Repr. lib. bdg. 18.95 (ISBN 0-89966-492-X). Buccaneer Bks.
--The Pioneers. Date not set. pap. 3.95 (ISBN 0-14-039007-3). Penguin.
--Prairie. (Classics Ser). (gr. 8 up). 1964. pap. 1.95 (ISBN 0-8049-0041-8, CL-41). Airmont.
--The Prairie. 1976. lib. bdg. 19.95 (ISBN 0-89968-160-3). Lightyear.
--Prairie. (Orig.). (YA) (RL 10). 1964. pap. 3.95 (ISBN 0-451-51780-6, CE1780, Sig Classics). NAL.
--The Prairie. Elliot, James P., ed. (The Writings of James Fenimore Cooper Ser.). 450p. 1984. 44.50x (ISBN 0-87395-363-0); pap. 14.95x (ISBN 0-87395-672-9). State U NY Pr.
--Precaution, 2 vols. LC 73-1898. (BCL Ser.: No. I). Repr. of 1820 ed. Set. 12.50 (ISBN 0-404-01707-X). AMS Pr.
--Precaution. LC 6-29686. Repr. of 1820 ed. 11.00x (ISBN 0-403-00101-3). Scholarly.
--The Red Rover. 1976. lib. bdg. 16.95x (ISBN 0-89968-158-1). Lightyear.
--Representative Selections, with Introduction, Bibliography & Notes. Spiller, R. E., ed. LC 76-48040. (Illus.). 1977. Repr. of 1936 ed. lib. bdg. 32.50x (ISBN 0-8371-9317-6, CORES). Greenwood.
--Satanstoe. LC 62-9515. (A Bison Book: BB138). pap. 110.50 (ISBN 0-317-29729-5, 2022205). Bks Demand UMI.
--Sea Lions. Walker, Warren S., ed. LC 65-18416. (Illus.). Repr. of 1965 ed. 133.30 (ISBN 0-8357-9714-7, 2016027). Bks Demand UMI.
--The Spy. Pickering, James H., ed. (Masterworks of Literature Ser.). 1971. pap. 8.95x (ISBN 0-8084-0027-4). New Coll U Pr.
--The Spy. 1976. lib. bdg. 19.95 (ISBN 0-89968-161-1). Lightyear.
--Tales for Fifteen. LC 59-6525. 1977. Repr. of 1823 ed. 45.00x (ISBN 0-8201-1247-X). Schol Facsimiles.
--Water-Witch. (BCL Ser.). Repr. of 1896 ed. 14.50 (ISBN 0-404-00629-9). AMS Pr.
--Water-Witch: Or, the Skimmer of the Seas. LC 4-15437. 1896. 13.00x (ISBN 0-403-00244-3). Scholarly.
--The Ways of the Hour. LC 68-57518. (The Muckrakers Ser.). Repr. of 1850 ed. lib. bdg. 27.00 (ISBN 0-8398-0277-3). Irvington.
--Wept of Wish-Ton-Wish, 2 vols. in one. (BCL I). Repr. of 1829 ed. 18.00 (ISBN 0-404-01715-0). AMS Pr.
--The Wept of Wish-Ton-Wish. LC 75-127081. (Merrill Standard Ser). 1975. pap. 4.00 (ISBN 0-685-56437-1). Brown Bk.
--Wept of Wish Ton-Wish, 2 Vols in 1. LC 74-107169. 1971. Repr. of 1829 ed. 13.00x (ISBN 0-403-00432-2). Scholarly.
--Works. LC 69-13864. 1891-1893. Repr. lib. bdg. 330.00x (ISBN 0-8371-2672-X, COWO). Greenwood.
--Works of Fenimore Cooper, 16 vols. 250.00 (ISBN 0-8274-3762-5). R West.
--Wyandotte. Philbrick, Thomas & Philbrick, Marianne, eds. (The Writings of James Fenimore Cooper Ser.). 518p. 1981. 44.50x (ISBN 0-87395-414-9); pap. 14.95x (ISBN 0-87395-469-6). State U NY Pr.

Cooper, James F; see Swan, D. K.

Cooper, James F., ed. Correspondence of James Fenimore Cooper, 2 Vols. 776p. 1983. Repr. of 1922 ed. lib. bdg. 200.00 set (ISBN 0-89760-167-X). Telegraph Bks.

Cooper, James F., et al. Gleanings in Europe: England. Ringe, Donald A. & Staggs, Kenneth W., eds. (The Writings of James Fenimore Cooper Ser.). 383p. 1981. 44.50x (ISBN 0-87395-367-3); pap. 14.95x (ISBN 0-87395-459-9). State U NY Pr.

Cooper, James Fenimore. Deerslayer. (Great Il. Classics). (gr. 9 up). 1979. 8.95 (ISBN 0-396-07746-3). Dodd.
--Deerslayer. 1976. lib. bdg. 19.95 (ISBN 0-89968-162-X). Lightyear.
--The Deerslayer. 517p. 1984. lib. bdg. 19.95x (ISBN 0-89966-490-3). Buccaneer Bks.
--Gleanings in Europe: France. Spiller, Robert E., ed. 1979. Repr. of 1928 ed. lib. bdg. 40.00 (ISBN 0-8492-4022-0). R West.
--Last of the Mohicans. (Literature Ser). (gr. 7-12). 1970. pap. text ed. 5.00 (ISBN 0-87720-731-3). AMSCO Sch.
--The Last of the Mohicans. (Bantam Classics Ser.). 384p. (Orig.). (gr. 7-12). 1981. pap. 2.50 (ISBN 0-553-21103-X). Bantam.
--The Last of the Mohicans. (Regents Illustrated Classics Ser.). (gr. 7-12). 1982. pap. text ed. 2.75 (ISBN 0-88345-480-7, 20569). Regents Pub.
--The Last of the Mohicans. Sappenfield, James A. & Feltskog, E. N., eds. (Definitive Edition of the Writings of James Fenimore Cooper Ser.). 500p. 1982. 44.50x (ISBN 0-87395-362-2); pap. 14.95x (ISBN 0-87395-470-X). State U NY Pr.
--The Last of the Mohicans. (Illus.). 414p. 1984. 12.95 (ISBN 0-396-08260-2). Dodd.
--The Last of the Mohicans. LC 84-61431. (Illus.). 432p. 1984. 12.95 (ISBN 0-89577-199-3). RD Assn.
--Leatherstocking Saga. Nevins, Allan, ed. 840p. 1980. pap. 8.95 (ISBN 0-380-58453-0, 58453-0). Avon.
--The Leatherstocking Tales, 2 vols. Nevius, Blake, ed. LC 84-25060. 1250p. 1985. Vol. I. 27.50 (ISBN 0-940450-20-8). Vol. II (ISBN 0-940450-21-6). Library of America.
--The Oak Openings. 520p. 1984. Repr. of 1848 ed. 40.00 (ISBN 0-938190-33-4). North Atlantic.

Cooper, James Fenimore see Fenimore Cooper, James.

Cooper, James M. Developing Skills for Instructional Supervision. 480p. 1984. 17.95 (ISBN 0-582-29019-8). Longman.

Cooper, James M. & DeVault, M. Vere. Competency Based Teacher Education. LC 72-83478. 123p. 1973. 22.75x (ISBN 0-8211-0010-6); text ed. 20.50x. McCutchan.

Cooper, James M., jt. auth. see Ryan, Kevin.

Cooper, James M., et al. Classroom Teaching Skills: A Handbook. 2nd ed. 544p. 1982. pap. text ed. 16.95 (ISBN 0-669-04369-9); instr's guide 1.95 (ISBN 0-669-04370-2). Heath.

Cooper, James R. & Phyrr, Stephen A. Real Estate Investment: Strategy, Analysis, Decision - Problems & Casebook. 45p. (Orig.). 1983. pap. 16.95 (ISBN 0-88406-169-8). Ga St U Busn Pub.

Cooper, James R., jt. auth. see Pyhrr, Stephen A.

Cooper, James W. The Laboratory Microcomputer: Programming in Pascal & MC68000 Assembly Language on the IBM System 9000. LC 84-10437. 328p. 1984. text ed. 29.00 (ISBN 0-471-81036-3, Pub. by Wiley-Interscience). Wiley.
--The Minicomputer in the Laboratory. 2nd ed. LC 82-8490. 381p. 1982. cloth 31.50 (ISBN 0-471-09012-3, Pub. by Wiley-Interscience). Wiley.
--Spectroscopic Techniques for Organic Chemists. LC 79-23952. 1980. 29.50x (ISBN 0-471-05166-7, Pub. by Wiley-Interscience). Wiley.

Cooper, Jan, et al. Teaching College Students to Read Analytically: An Individualized Approach. LC 85-5081. 58p. (Orig.). 1985. pap. 5.00 (ISBN 0-8141-5059-4). NCTE.

Cooper, Jane. Woodstove Cookery: At Home on the Range. LC 77-10640. (Illus.). 208p. 1977. pap. 6.95 (ISBN 0-88266-108-6). Garden Way Pub.

Cooper, Jane, et al, eds. Extended Outlooks: The Iowa Review Collection of Contemporary Women Writers. 400p. 1982. pap. 9.95 (ISBN 0-02-049690-7). Macmillan.

Cooper, Jane T. Entering Pisces. 1984. pap. 5.00 (ISBN 0-930502-02-7). Pine Pr.

Cooper, Jay L., jt. ed. see Spiegel, Irwin O.

Cooper, Jay S. & Pizzarello, Donald J. Concepts in Cancer Care: A Practical Explanation of Radiotherapy & Chemotherapy for Primary Care Physicians. LC 80-10334. (Illus.). 273p. 1980. text ed. 16.50 (ISBN 0-8121-0716-0). Lea & Febiger.

Cooper, Jean, et al. Helping Language Development. LC 77-27524. 1978. 17.95 (ISBN 0-312-36757-0). St Martin.

Cooper, Jeff. Building a Recording Studio: The Complete Guide to Studio Design & Construction. rev. ed. LC 84-90061. (Illus.). 209p. 1984. pap. text ed. 30.00 comb bdg. (ISBN 0-916899-00-4). Synergy Group.
--Fireworks: A Gunsite Anthology. LC 80-83992. 1981. 19.95 (ISBN 0-916172-07-4). Janus Pr.
--Principles of Personal Defense. 30p. 1972. pap. 5.00 (ISBN 0-87364-001-2). Paladin Pr.

Cooper, Jeffrey. Bonnie's Blues. 144p. (Orig.). 1985. pap. 2.25 (ISBN 0-449-70140-9, Juniper). Fawcett.
--How to Make Love to an Extraterrestrial. LC 82-62491. 96p. (Orig.). 1983. pap. 3.50 (ISBN 0-688-01888-2, Quill). Morrow.

Cooper, Jeffrey H. The Rise of Instrumental Music & Concert Series in Paris, 1828-1871. Buelow, George, ed. LC 83-1062. (Studies in Musicology: No. 65). 402p. 1983. 49.95 (ISBN 0-8357-1403-9). UMI Res Pr.

Cooper, Jeremy. Dealing with Dealers. (Illus.). 1985. 12.95 (ISBN 0-500-01354-3). Thames Hudson.

Cooper, Jerrold S. The Curse of Agade. LC 82-14885. (Near Eastern Studies). 304p. 1983. text ed. 30.00x (ISBN 0-8018-2846-5). Johns Hopkins.
--Reconstructing History from Ancient Inscriptions: The Lagash-Umma Border Conflict. (Sources from the Ancient Near East Ser.: Vol. 2, Issue 1). (Illus.). 61p. 1983. 8.65 (ISBN 0-89003-003-0). Undena Pubns.

Cooper, Jerry M. The Army & Civil Disorder: Federal Military Intervention in Labor Disputes, 1877-1900. LC 79-7064. (Contributions in Military History: No. 19). 1980. lib. bdg. 29.95 (ISBN 0-313-20958-8, CAD/). Greenwood.

Cooper, Jilly. Animals in War. (Illus.). 168p. 1984. 14.95 (ISBN 0-434-14370-7, Pub. by W Heinemann Ltd). David & Charles.
--Bella. 192p. 1981. pap. 2.25. Fawcett.
--Emily. 192p. 1981. pap. 1.95 (ISBN 0-449-24410-5, Crest). Fawcett.
--Harriet. 224p. 1981. pap. 1.95 (ISBN 0-449-24442-3, Crest). Fawcett.
--Imogen. 224p. 1982. pap. 2.25 (ISBN 0-449-24491-1, Crest). Fawcett.
--Octavia. 224p. 1982. pap. 2.25 (ISBN 0-449-24545-4, Crest). Fawcett.
--Prudence. 192p. 1981. pap. 1.95 (ISBN 0-449-24361-3, Crest). Fawcett.

Cooper, Jilly & Hartman, Tom, eds. Beyond Bartlett: Quotations by & about Women. LC 83-42961. (Illus.). 240p. 1983. pap. 8.95 (ISBN 0-8128-6192-2). Stein & Day.
--Violets & Vinegar: An Anthology of Women's Writings & Sayings. 231p. 1982. 15.95 (ISBN 0-8128-2813-5). Stein & Day.

Cooper, Jo. Handfeeding Baby Birds. (Illus.). 1979. 4.95 (ISBN 0-87666-992-5, KW-017). TFH Pubns.

Cooper, Joan. The Creation of the British Personal Social Services 1962-74. (Studies in Social Policy & Welfare: Vol. XVIII). 224p. 1983. text ed. 30.00x (ISBN 0-435-82188-1). Gower Pub Co.

Cooper, Joel, jt. auth. see Worchel, Stephen.

Cooper, John. The Management & Regulation of Banks. LC 83-40162. 256p. 1983. 27.95 (ISBN 0-312-51224-4). St Martin.

Cooper, John A. & Malek, Dorothy, eds. Residential Solid Fuels: Environmental Impacts & Solutions. (Proceedings of the 1981 International Conference on Residential Solid Fuels, Portland, Oregon, June 1-4, 1981). (Illus.). 1300p. 1981. lib. bdg. 80.00x (ISBN 0-686-46045-6, Pub. by OGC). Scholium Intl.

Cooper, John C. Religious Pied Pipers. 128p. 1981. pap. 5.95 (ISBN 0-8170-0907-8). Judson.
--Throwing the Sticks: Occult Self-Therapy-The Arts of Self-Transcendence in Post-Freudian Modes of Thought. 175p. (Orig.). 1985. pap. 8.95 (ISBN 0-932269-49-4). Wyndham Hall.

Cooper, John C., jt. auth. see McManus, Una.

Cooper, John L. The Anti-Gravity Force. LC 80-83402. 160p. 1981. pap. text ed. 11.95 (ISBN 0-8403-2300-X). Kendall-Hunt.
--The Police & the Ghetto. (National University Publications, Multi-Disciplinary Studies in the Law). 1980. 16.50x (ISBN 0-8046-9250-5, Pub. by Kennikat). Assoc Faculty Pr.
--You Can Hear Them Knocking: A Study in the Policing of America. 128p. 1981. 14.50x (ISBN 0-317-08102-0, 9285). Assoc Faculty Pr.

Cooper, John M. The Northern Algonquian Supreme Being. LC 76-43682. (Catholic University of America Anthropological Ser.: No. 2). Repr. of 1934 ed. 14.00 (ISBN 0-404-15515-4). AMS Pr.
--Reason & Human Good in Aristotle. LC 74-30852. 224p. 1975. text ed. 16.50x (ISBN 0-674-74952-9). Harvard U Pr.
--Snares, Deadfalls & Other Traps of the Northern Algonquian & Northern Athapaskans. LC 76-43683. (Catholic University of America Anthropological Ser.: No. 5). Repr. of 1938 ed. 17.50 (ISBN 0-404-15516-2). AMS Pr.
--The Warrior & the Priest: Woodrow Wilson & Theodore Roosevelt. (Illus.). 448p. 1983. 20.00 (ISBN 0-674-94750-9, Belknap). Harvard U Pr.

Cooper, John M. & Siedentop, Daryl. The Theory & Science of Basketball. 2nd ed. LC 74-4376. (Illus.). 253p. 1975. pap. 7.00 (ISBN 0-8121-0502-8). Lea & Febiger.

Cooper, John M., ed. Biomechanics. LC 78-159585. 1971. pap. 5.00 (ISBN 0-87670-852-1). Athletic Inst.

Cooper, John M., et al. Kinesiology. 5th ed. LC 81-11116. (Illus.). 452p. 1982. text ed. 23.95 (ISBN 0-8016-1040-0). Mosby.

Cooper, John M., Jr. The Vanity of Power: American Isolationism & the First World War. LC 70-95508. (Contributions in American History: No. 3). 1969. lib. bdg. 29.95 (ISBN 0-8371-2342-9, COP/). Greenwood.
--Walter Hines Page: The Southerner As American, 1855-1918. xxx, 457p. 1977. 32.50 (ISBN 0-8078-1298-6). U of NC Pr.
--The Warrior & the Priest: Woodrow Wilson & Theodore Roosevelt. (Illus.). 480p. 1985. pap. 9.95 (ISBN 0-674-94751-7, Belknap Pr). Harvard U Pr.

Cooper, John N., jt. auth. see Smith, Alpheus.

Cooper, John R. Mel Martin: First Base Jinx. (Mel Martin Baseball Stories Ser.: No. 4). 208p. (gr. 3-7). 1982. 8.95 (ISBN 0-671-44539-1); pap. 2.95 (ISBN 0-671-44548-0). Wanderer Bks.
--Mel Martin: The Mystery at the Ball Park. (Mel Martin Baseball Stories Ser.: No. 1). 208p. (gr. 3-7). 1982. 8.95 (ISBN 0-671-44536-7); pap. 2.95 (ISBN 0-671-44545-6). Wanderer Bks.
--Mel Martin: The Phantom Homer. (Mel Martin Baseball Stories Ser.: No. 3). 208p. (gr. 3-7). 1982. 8.95 (ISBN 0-671-44538-3); pap. 2.95 (ISBN 0-671-44547-2). Wanderer Bks.
--Mel Martin: The Southpaw's Secret. (Mel Martin Baseball Stories Ser.: No. 2). 208p. (gr. 3-7). 1982. 8.95 (ISBN 0-671-44537-5); pap. 2.95 (ISBN 0-671-44546-4). Wanderer Bks.

Cooper, John W. The Theology of Freedom: The Legacy of Jacque Maritain & Reinhold Niebuhr. ix, 186p. 1985. text ed. 16.95x (ISBN 0-86554-172-8, MUP-H162). Mercer Univ Pr.

Cooper, John W., jt. ed. see Novak, Michael.

Cooper, Joseph. Lost Continent, or Slavery & the Slave Trade in Africa. 130p. 1968. Repr. of 1875 ed. 26.00x (ISBN 0-7146-1890-X, BHA-01890, F Cass Co). Biblio Dist.
--Origins of the Standing Committees & Development of the Modern House. (Rice University Studies: Vol. 56, No. 3). 167p. 1970. pap. 10.00x (ISBN 0-89263-205-4). Rice Univ.

Cooper, Joseph & Mackenzie, G. Calvin, eds. The House at Work. 376p. 1981. text ed. 32.50x (ISBN 0-292-73017-9). U of Tex Pr.

Cooper, Joseph, jt. ed. see Maisel, Louis.

Cooper, Joseph, jt. ed. see Maisel, Louis S.

Cooper, Joseph, jt. ed. see Meisel, Louis.

Cooper, Joseph B. Comparative Psychology. LC 70-190204. (Illus.). pap. 118.00 (ISBN 0-317-10465-9, 2012477). Bks Demand UMI.

Cooper, Joshua, tr. from Rus. Four Russian Plays. (Penguin Classics Ser.). 400p. 1972. pap. 5.95 (ISBN 0-14-044258-8). Penguin.

Cooper, Judith. Ubu Roi: An Analytical Study, Vol. 6. 120p. 1974. pap. 7.00 (ISBN 0-912788-05-4). Tulane Romance Lang.

Cooper, Judith A., jt. ed. see Ludlow, Christy L.

Cooper, Julian, jt. ed. see Amann, Ronald.

Cooper, K. E., ed. see Pharmacology of Thermoregulation, 3rd Symposium, Banff, Alberta, Sept. 1976, et al.

Cooper, K. E., ed. see Symposium, Calgary, Alberta, May, 1973.

Cooper, Kay. Who Put the Cannon in the Courthouse Square: A Guide to Uncovering the Past. (Illus.). (gr. 4 up). 1984. cancelled (ISBN 0-8027-6547-5); PLB 11.85 set (ISBN 0-8027-6561-0). Walker & Co.

Cooper, Keith H. & Mills, Colin C. Canada at the Pension Crossroads. LC 79-51782. 1979. 8.00 (ISBN 0-910586-27-6). Finan Exec.

Cooper, Ken. Bodybusiness: The Sender's & Receiver's Guide to Nonverbal Communications. LC 78-25971. 224p. 1981. 5.95 (ISBN 0-8144-7545-0). Am Mgmt Assns.

Cooper, Kenneth. Aerobics. 1968. 3.95x (ISBN 0-553-20992-2). Cancer Control Soc.

--The Aerobics Program for Total Well-Being: Exercise, Diet & Emotional Balance. LC 82-16361. (Illus.). 320p. 1982. 16.95 (ISBN 0-87131-380-4). M Evans.

--New Aerobics. 1970. pap. 3.95 (ISBN 0-553-23415-3). Bantam.

Cooper, Kenneth, jt. auth. see Cooper, Mildred.

Cooper, Kenneth, ed. see Monteverdi, Claudio.

Cooper, Kenneth C. Stop It Now: How Targets & Managers Can End Sexual Harassment. LC 85-1280. (Illus.). 212p. (Orig.). 1985. pap. 9.95 (ISBN 0-932801-00-5). Total Comm Pr.

Cooper, Kenneth H. Aerobics. (Illus.). 192p. 1972. pap. 3.95 (ISBN 0-553-23546-X). Bantam.

--Aerobics. LC 67-27297. 256p. 1968. 8.95 (ISBN 0-87131-029-5). M Evans.

--The Aerobics Program for Total Well-Being. 1983. pap. 10.95 (ISBN 0-553-34151-0). Bantam.

--The Aerobics Program for Total Well-Being. 16.95 (ISBN 0-87131-380-4, 01646-490). M Evans.

--The Aerobics Way. 1978. pap. 3.95 (ISBN 0-553-23348-3). Bantam.

--The Aerobics Way: New Data on the Worlds Most Popular Exercise Program. LC 77-22129. (Illus.). 336p. 1977. 10.00 (ISBN 0-87131-210-7). M Evans.

--The New Aerobics. LC 78-88699. 192p. 1970. 8.95 (ISBN 0-87131-028-7). M Evans.

--The New Aerobics. LC 78-88699. (Illus.). 192p. 1985. 8.95 (ISBN 0-87131-028-7). M Evans.

--Running Without Fear: How to Reduce the Risk of Heart Attack & Sudden Death During Aerobic Exercise. Katz, Herb, ed. LC 85-4501. (Illus.). 240p. 1985. 12.95 (ISBN 0-87131-456-8). M Evans.

--Total Well-Being: The Complete Aerobics Program for Radiant Health through Exercise & Diet. (Illus.). 288p. 1982. 15.95 (ISBN 0-87131-380-4). M Evans.

Cooper, Kenneth H., jt. auth. see Cooper, Mildred.

Cooper, Kent. Barriers Down. LC 73-94560. 1969. Repr. of 1942 ed. 25.25x (ISBN 0-8046-0689-7, Pub.by Kennikat). Assoc Faculty Pr.

--Below Houston Street. 1979. pap. 1.50 (ISBN 0-532-15365-0). Woodhill.

--The Minnesota Strip. 1978. pap. 1.95 (ISBN 0-532-19211-7). Woodhill.

Cooper, Kent & Palmer, Fred. Sonny Terry's Country Blues Harmonica. LC 74-23037. (Illus.). 96p. (Orig.). 1975. pap. 7.95 with recording (ISBN 0-8256-0166-5, Oak). Music Sales.

Cooper, Kirk. William Lauderdale: General Andrew Jackson's Warrior. 292p. 1982. 15.00x (ISBN 0-8103-0341-8, Pub. by Manatee Bks). Gale.

Cooper, L. Aristotelian Theory of Comedy. Repr. of 1922 ed. 17.00 (ISBN 0-527-19420-4). Kraus Repr.

Cooper, L. & Cooper, Mary W. Introduction to Dynamic Programming. LC 79-42640. (International Ser. in Modern Applied Mathematics & Computer Science: Vol. 1). (Illus.). 256p. 1981. 36.00 (ISBN 0-08-025065-3); pap. 21.00 (ISBN 0-08-025064-5). Pergamon.

Cooper, L., ed. Concordance of the Latin, Greek, & Italian Poems of John Milton. Repr. of 1923 ed. 14.00 (ISBN 0-527-19440-9). Kraus Repr.

Cooper, L. C. Horse Show Organization. new ed. 1978. 9.95 (ISBN 0-85131-310-8, BL2441, Dist. by Miller). J A Allen.

--Horse Show Organization. (Illus.). 15.00 (ISBN 0-87556-621-9). Saifer.

Cooper, Lane. Aristotle on the Art of Poetry. 1913. Repr. 20.00 (ISBN 0-8274-3797-8). R West.

--Aristotle on the Art of Poetry: An Amplified Version with Supplementary Illustrations. rev. ed. (Illus.). 129p. 1962. pap. 3.95x (ISBN 0-8014-9044-8, CP44). Cornell U Pr.

--Evolution & Repentance: Mixed Essays & Addresses. facsimile ed. LC 78-152166. (Essay Index Reprint Ser). Repr. of 1935 ed. 18.00 (ISBN 0-8369-2222-0). Ayer Co Pubs.

--Louis Agassiz As a Teacher. (Educational Ser.). 1917. Repr. 10.00 (ISBN 0-8482-3582-7). Norwood Edns.

--A Manual of American Literature. 59.95 (ISBN 0-8490-0580-9). Gordon Pr.

--Methods & Aims in the Study of Literature. (Illus.). 1978. Repr. of 1915 ed. 30.00 (ISBN 0-8492-4002-6). R West.

--Methods & Aims in the Study of Literature. 239p. 1981. Repr. of 1915 ed. lib. bdg. 35.00 (ISBN 0-89760-120-3). Telegraph Bks.

--Poetics of Aristotle. LC 63-10307. (Our Debt to Greece & Rome Ser). 157p. 1963. Repr. of 1930 ed. 18.50 (ISBN 0-8154-0053-5). Cooper Sq.

--The Poetics of Aristotle: Its Meaning & Influence. LC 78-152592. 157p. 1972. Repr. of 1956 ed. lib. bdg. 18.75x (ISBN 0-8371-6025-1, COPA). Greenwood.

--Prose Poetry of Thomas De Quincey. LC 74-6177. 1902. lib. bdg. 10.00 (ISBN 0-8414-3595-2). Folcroft.

Cooper, Lane, ed. Art of the Writer: Essays, Excerpts, & Translations. rev. & enl. facsimile ed. LC 73-37837. (Essay Index Reprint Ser). Repr. of 1952 ed. 23.00 (ISBN 0-8369-2586-6). Ayer Co Pubs.

--Theories of Style. (Research & Source Works Ser: No. 173). 1968. Repr. of 1907 ed. 26.00 (ISBN 0-8337-0654-3). B Franklin.

Cooper, Lane, ed. see Meredith, George.

Cooper, Lane, tr. Plato on the Trial & Death of Socrates: Euthyphro, Apology, Crito, Phaedo. 214p. 1967. 4.95x (ISBN 0-8014-9049-9). Cornell U Pr.

--Rhetoric of Aristotle. (Orig.). 1960. pap. text ed. 18.95 (ISBN 0-13-780692-2). P-H.

Cooper, Laura G. & Smith, Marilyn Z. Standard FORTRAN: A Problem-Solving Approach. LC 72-4395. 288p. (Orig.). 1973. pap. text ed. 22.50 (ISBN 0-395-14028-5). HM.

Cooper, Lauren E. Designing the Site & Service Plot Allocation Process: Lessons from Project Experience. (Urban Development Technical Paper: No. 3). 30p. 1982. pap. 3.00 (ISBN 0-686-39778-9, UD-0003). World Bank.

Cooper, Lee. Chinese Language for Beginners. LC 70-151121. 1971. pap. 3.25 (ISBN 0-8048-0918-6). C E Tuttle.

--Fun with German. (Illus.). (gr. 3 up). 1965. 13.45i (ISBN 0-316-15588-8). Little.

--More Fun with Spanish. (Illus.). (gr. 4-6). 1967. 14.45i (ISBN 0-316-15616-7). Little.

Cooper, Lee W. How to Get to the Wilderness Without a Car. (Illus.). 192p. (Orig.). 1982. pap. 7.95 (ISBN 0-9607116-0-0). Cooper.

Cooper, Lettice. Blackberry's Kitten. LC 63-13798. (Illus.). (gr. 1-4). 1963. 3.00 (ISBN 0-8149-0291-X). Vanguard.

--Robert Louis Stevenson. LC 73-12552. 1947. lib. bdg. 12.50 (ISBN 0-8414-3443-3). Folcroft.

Cooper, Linn F. & Erickson, Milton H. Time Distortion in Hypnosis: An Experimental & Clinical Investigation. 2nd ed. LC 82-663. (Illus.). 206p. 1982. Repr. of 1959 ed. text ed. 26.50x (ISBN 0-8290-0702-4). Irvington.

Cooper, Liz, et al. The Other Secret Service: Press Distributors & Press Censorship. 20.00x (ISBN 0-906890-15-2, Pub. by Comedia England). State Mutual Bk.

Cooper, Lloyd G. & Maltby, Gregory P., eds. New Directions for Education. 249p. 1975. pap. text ed. 9.75x (ISBN 0-8422-0504-7). Irvington.

Cooper, Louise. The Initiate. 288p. (Orig.). 1985. pap. 2.95 (ISBN 0-8125-3392-5, Dist. by Warner Pub Services & St. Martin). Tor Bks.

Cooper, Lucy & Hosman, Bob. Miami Herald Dining Guide. 122p. 1984. write for info. (ISBN 0-918878-02-0). WICC Bks.

Cooper, Lucy & Hosmon, Bob. Them Miami Herald Dining Guide. (Illus.). 144p. (Orig.). 1984. pap. text ed. 3.95 (ISBN 0-918878-02-0). Wanderer Bks.

Cooper, Lynn & Platt, Anthony. Policing America. 224p. 1974. pap. 2.95x (ISBN 0-13-684902-4, Spec). P-H.

Cooper, Lynn A., jt. auth. see Shepard, Roger N.

Cooper, Lynna. The Hired Wife. Bd. with The Moon in Eclipse. Slack, Claudia. 1981. pap. 2.75 (ISBN 0-451-11089-7, AE1089, Sig). NAL.

Cooper, M. & Culyer, A. J. Price of Blood. (Institute of Economic Affairs Hobart Papers Ser.: No. 41). 1977. pap. 2.50 technical (ISBN 0-255-69626-4). Transatlantic.

Cooper, M. & Wallace, E. King Kong. 1982. Repr. lib. bdg. 17.95x (ISBN 0-89966-440-7). Buccaneer Bks.

Cooper, M., et al, eds. Current Topics in Microbiology & Immunology, Vol. 102. (Illus.). 152p. 1983. pap. 38.00 (ISBN 0-387-12133-1). Springer-Verlag.

--B Lymphocytes in the Immune Response. (Developments in Immunology Ser.: Vol. 3). 396p. 1979. 76.50 (ISBN 0-444-00319-3, Biomedical Pr). Elsevier.

Cooper, M. A. Fundamentals of Survey Measurement & Analysis: Introduction to the Analysis of Survey Data. 115p. 1982. pap. 18.00x (ISBN 0-246-11917-9, Pub. by Granada England). Sheridan.

--Fundamentals of Survey Measurement & Analysis. (Aspects of Modern Land Surveying Ser.). 107p. 1974. text ed. 17.00x (ISBN 0-258-96871-0, Pub. by Granada England). Brookfield Pub Co.

--Modern Theodolites & Levels. 2nd ed. 288p. 1982. 45.00x (ISBN 0-246-11502-5, NO. 6721). Methuen Inc.

Cooper, M. D., et al, eds. Immune Deficiency. (Illus.). 1979. pap. 23.30 (ISBN 0-387-09490-3). Springer-Verlag.

Cooper, M. E. Broken Hearts. (Couples Ser.: No. 9). 192p. (Orig.). (gr. 7 up). 1986. pap. 2.50 (ISBN 0-590-40159-9). Scholastic Inc.

--Crazy Love. (Couples Ser.: No. 6). 192p. (Orig.). (gr. 7 up). 1985. pap. 2.50 (ISBN 0-590-33395-X). Scholastic Inc.

--Made for Each Other. (Couples Ser.: No. 4). 192p. (Orig.). (gr. 7up). 1985. pap. 2.50 (ISBN 0-590-33393-3). Scholastic Inc.

--Making Promises. (Couples Ser.: No. 8). 192p. (Orig.). (gr. 7 up). 1986. pap. 2.50 (ISBN 0-590-33971-0). Scholastic Inc.

--Moving Too Fast. (Couples Ser.: No. 5). 192p. (Orig.). (gr. 7 up). 1985. pap. 2.50 (ISBN 0-590-33394-1). Scholastic Inc.

Cooper, M. Frances. A Checklist of American Imprints, Eighteen Twenty to Eighteen Twenty-Nine: Title Index. (Checklist of American Imprints Ser.). 1972. 30.00 (ISBN 0-8108-0513-8). Scarecrow.

--A Checklist of American Imprints Eighteen Twenty to Eighteen Twenty-Nine: Author Index, Corrections & Sources. 1973. 15.00 (ISBN 0-8108-0567-7). Scarecrow.

Cooper, M. G. & Cooper, D. E. The Medical Assistant. 5th ed. 704p. 1985. price not set (ISBN 0-07-012755-7). McGraw.

Cooper, M. G., ed. Risk: Man-Made Hazards to Man. (Illus.). 160p. 1985. 21.95 (ISBN 0-19-854154-6); pap. 12.95 (ISBN 0-19-854155-4). Oxford U Pr.

Cooper, M. H. Prices & Profits in the Pharmaceutical Industry. 1967. pap. 12.75 (ISBN 0-08-012177-2). Pergamon.

Cooper, M. J., jt. auth. see Hanley, W. S.

Cooper, M. K. Managerial Tools. 1986. cancelled (ISBN 0-442-21609-2). Van Nos Reinhold.

Cooper, M. McG. & Morris, D. W. Grass Farming. 5th ed. (Illus.). 256p. 1983. 19.95 (ISBN 0-85236-140-8, Pub. by Farming Pr UK). Diamond Farm Bk.

Cooper, M. McG. & Thomas, R. J. Profitable Sheep Farming. 5th ed. (Illus.). 192p. 1982. 18.95 (ISBN 0-85236-117-3, Pub. by Farming Pr UK). Diamond Farm Bk.

Cooper, M. McG. & Willis, M. B., eds. Profitable Beef Production. 3rd ed. (Illus.). 160p. 1979. 16.95 (ISBN 0-85236-093-2, Pub. by Farming Pr UK). Diamond Farm Bk.

Cooper, Marcia. Pica: A Survey of the Historical Literature As Well As Reports from the Fields of Veterinary Medicine & Anthropology, the Present Study of Pica in Young Children, & a Discussion of Its Pediatric & Psychological Implications. (Illus.). 120p. 1957. 14.50x (ISBN 0-398-04232-2). C C Thomas.

Cooper, Marcia H., jt. auth. see Cooper, Morton.

Cooper, Marcia M. Evaluation of the Mother's Advisory Service. (SRCD M Ser.). 1947. pap. 16.00 (ISBN 0-527-01540-7). Kraus Repr.

Cooper, Margaret. Inventions of Leonardo Da Vinci. LC 65-13592. (Illus.). 192p. (gr. 7 up). 1968. 9.95 (ISBN 0-02-724490-3). Macmillan.

Cooper, Margaret C. Code Name: Clone. (Illus.). 192p. (gr. 4-6). 1982. 8.95 (ISBN 0-8027-6474-6); PLB 9.85 (ISBN 0-8027-6475-4). Walker & Co.

--Solution: Escape. LC 80-50496. (Illus.). 94p. (gr. 3-7). 1981. 8.85 (ISBN 0-8027-6404-5); PLB 8.85 (ISBN 0-8027-6405-3). Walker & Co.

Cooper, Marian & Bredow, Miriam. The Medical Assistant. 4th ed. (Illus.). 1978. text ed. 29.00 (ISBN 0-07-012751-4). McGraw.

Cooper, Mario. Flower Painting in Watercolor. rev. ed. LC 72-186773. pap. 35.80 (ISBN 0-317-10020-3, 2005809). Bks Demand UMI.

Cooper, Mark N. The Transformation of Egypt. LC 82-15317. 288p. 1982. text ed. 27.00x (ISBN 0-8018-2836-8). Johns Hopkins.

Cooper, Mark N. & Sullivan, Theodore L. Equity & Energy: Rising Energy Prices & the Living Standards of Lower Income Americans. LC 83-14642. 302p. 1983. softcover 30.00 (ISBN 0-86531-999-5). Westview.

Cooper, Martha & Chalfant, Henry. Subway Art. LC 84-620. (Illus.). 104p. 1984. pap. 14.95 (ISBN 0-03-071963-1, Owl Bks). HR&W.

Cooper, Martha, jt. auth. see Levitan, Sar A.

Cooper, Martin. Beethoven: The Last Decade, 1817-1827. (Illus.). 496p. 1985. pap. 14.95 (ISBN 0-19-315321-1). Oxford U Pr.

--French Music: From the Death of Berlioz to the Death of Faure. 1951. pap. 8.95x (ISBN 0-19-316202-4). Oxford U Pr.

--Georges Bizet. LC 71-138216. (Illus.). 1971. Repr. of 1938 ed. lib. bdg. 25.00 (ISBN 0-8371-5571-1, COGB). Greenwood.

--Gluck. LC 74-181129. 293p. 1935. Repr. 39.00x (ISBN 0-403-01526-X). Scholarly.

--Opera Comique. LC 70-181128. 1949. Repr. 39.00x (ISBN 0-403-01527-8). Scholarly.

--Russian Opera. LC 77-181127. 65p. 1951. Repr. 29.00x (ISBN 0-403-01528-6). Scholarly.

Cooper, Martin see Abraham, Gerald, et al.

Cooper, Martin, tr. see Druskin, Mikhail S.

Cooper, Martin, tr. see Warrack, John.

Cooper, Martin M. Academy Awards, 1979: Oscar Annual. (Illus.). 1979. lib. bdg. 14.95x (ISBN 0-912076-33-X); pap. 9.95x (ISBN 0-912076-34-8). ESE Calif.

Cooper, Mary P. The Early English Kitchen Garden. (The Lost Art of Kitchen Gardening Ser.). (Illus.). 126p. (Orig.). 1984. pap. 6.00 (ISBN 0-9613313-0-5). M P Cooper.

Cooper, Mary W., jt. auth. see Cooper, L.

Cooper, Matthew. The German Army: Vol. 2 Conquest 1933-1945. (World at War Ser.: No. 14). 1979. pap. 2.50 (ISBN 0-89083-485-7). Zebra.

--The German Army: Vol. 3 Decline & Fall. (World at War Ser.: No. 15). 1979. pap. 2.50 (ISBN 0-89083-493-8). Zebra.

--The Nazi War Against Soviet Partisans. LC 78-24689. (Illus.). 1979. 16.95 (ISBN 0-8128-2600-0). Stein & Day.

Cooper, Matthew, jt. ed. see Rodman, Margaret.

Cooper, Matthew H. To Ride a Tiger. 247p. 1985. 13.95 (ISBN 0-8149-0903-5). Vanguard.

--When Fish Begin to Smell. 224p. 1984. 13.95 (ISBN 0-8149-0893-4). Vanguard.

Cooper, Max D. & Dayton, Delbert H., eds. Development of Host Defenses. LC 76-51866. 320p. 1977. 45.50 (ISBN 0-89004-117-2). Raven.

Cooper, Max D. & Warner, Noel L., eds. Contemporary Topics in Immunobiology, Vol. 3. LC 68-26769. (Illus.). 281p. 1974. 32.50x (ISBN 0-306-37803-5, Plenum Pr). Plenum Pub.

Cooper, Max D., jt. ed. see Warner, Noel L.

Cooper, Michael. Exploring Kamakura. LC 79-11997. (Illus.). 1979. pap. 7.50 (ISBN 0-8348-0144-2). Weatherhill.

--This Island of Japon: Joao Rodrigues' Account of 16th Century Japan. LC 72-93533. (Illus.). 354p. 1973. 16.95x (ISBN 0-87011-194-9). Kodansha.

Cooper, Michael, compiled by. They Came to Japan: An Anthology of European Reports on Japan, 1543-1640. (Center for Japanese & Korean Studies, UC Berkley). 447p. pap. 8.95 (ISBN 0-520-04509-2, CAL 532). U of Cal Pr.

Cooper, Michael D. California's Demand for Librarians: Projecting Future Requirements. LC 78-8919. 1978. pap. 6.50x (ISBN 0-87772-256-0). Inst Gov Stud Berk.

Cooper, Michele & Mannella, Donna. The One Minute Los Angeles Ticket Guide. LC 84-71262. (Illus.). 130p. (Orig.). 1984. pap. 4.95 (ISBN 0-918853-00-1). Big Apple Co.

Cooper, Mildred & Cooper, Kenneth. Aerobics for Women. 160p. 1973. pap. 3.95 (ISBN 0-553-24788-3). Bantam.

Cooper, Mildred & Cooper, Kenneth H. Aerobics for Women. LC 77-164548. 160p. 1972. 8.95 (ISBN 0-87131-030-9). M Evans.

Cooper, Mildred & Fanning, Martha. What Every Woman Still Knows: A Celebration of the Christian Liberated Woman. LC 78-17182. 182p. 1978. 7.95 (ISBN 0-87131-271-9). M Evans.

Cooper, Miriam. Snap! Photography. LC 81-88. (Illus.). 64p. (gr. 3 up). 1981. 8.59 (ISBN 0-671-34021-2, 770). Messner.

Cooper, Montgomery & Allyn, Jane. Dance for Life: Ballet in South Africa. (Illus.). 160p. 1980. 22.00x (ISBN 0-8476-3286-5). Rowman.

Cooper, Morley. The Cruising Yacht: What to Buy, How to Equip It & How to Handle It on Long & Short Cruises. 1977. lib. bdg. 69.95 (ISBN 0-8490-1688-6). Gordon Pr.

Cooper, Morton. Change Your Voice, Change Your Life. 192p. 1985. pap. text ed. 5.72i (ISBN 0-06-463712-3, EH 712). B&N NY.

--Change Your Voice-Change Your Life: A Quick, Simple Plan for Finding Your Natural, Dynamic Voice. (Illus.). 192p. 1984. 13.95 (ISBN 0-02-528040-6). Macmillan.

--Modern Techniques of Vocal Rehabilitation. (Illus.). 384p. 1977. 39.75x (ISBN 0-398-02451-0). C C Thomas.

Cooper, Morton & Cooper, Marcia H. Approaches to Vocal Rehabilitation. (Illus.). 420p. 1977. 45.50x (ISBN 0-398-03517-2). C C Thomas.

Cooper, Murray S., ed. Quality Control in the Pharmaceutical Industry, 3 vols. Vol. 1, 1972. 59.50 (ISBN 0-12-187601-2); Vol. 2, 1973. 71.50 (ISBN 0-12-187602-0); Vol. 3, 1979. 49.50 (ISBN 0-12-187603-9). Acad Pr.

Cooper, Myrtle E. From Tent Town to City: A Chronological History of Billings, Montana 1882-1935. Von Vogt, Janice, ed. (Illus.). 79p. (Orig.). (gr. 6-8). 1982. pap. 5.95 (ISBN 0-9613224-0-3). Parmly Lib.

Cooper, N. The Opulent Eye. (Illus.). 264p. 1980. pap. text ed. 18.80x (ISBN 0-85139-506-6, Pub. by Architectural Pr England). Humanities.

Cooper, Nancy, jt. auth. see Bin-Nun, Judy.

Cooper, Neil. The Diversity of Moral Thinking. (CLLP Ser.). (Illus.). 1981. text ed. 39.00x (ISBN 0-19-824423-1). Oxford U Pr.

Cooper, Norman W. Finding Your Self. new ed. 96p. 1974. pap. 4.50 (ISBN 0-87516-183-9). De Vorss.

--Love That Heals. 1977. pap. 4.50 (ISBN 0-87516-228-2). De Vorss.

Cooper, P., jt. ed. see Gopalakrishnan, S.

Cooper, P. F. & Atkinson, B., eds. Biological Fluidised Bed Treatment of Water & Wastewater. LC 80-41740. 411p. 1981. 106.95 (ISBN 0-470-27112-4). Halsted Pr.

Cooper, P. I., jt. auth. see Morse, R. N.

Cooper, Page, jt. auth. see Wagner, Friedelind.

Cooper, Pamela & Stewart, Lea. Language Skills in the Classroom. 32p. 1982. 2.50 (ISBN 0-8106-1056-6). NEA.

Cooper, Pamela J. Speech Communication for the Classroom Teacher. 2nd ed. 296p. 1984. pap. text ed. 18.95x (ISBN 0-89787-319-X). Gorsuch Scarisbrick.

Cooper, Parley J. Las Feministas. new ed. Lopez, Javier, tr. from Eng. (Compadre Collection Ser.). Orig. Title: The Feminists. 160p. (Span.). 1974. pap. 0.75 (ISBN 0-88473-607-5). Fiesta Pub.

--Golden Fever. (Orig.). 1981. pap. 2.75 (ISBN 0-671-81476-1). PB.

Cooper, Patricia & Buferd, Norma B. The Quilters: Women & Domestic Art. LC 76-2765. (Illus.). 1977. 15.95 (ISBN 0-385-12039-7, Anch). Doubleday.

Cooper, Patricia & Cook, Laurel. Hots Springs & Spas of California. LC 78-10665. (Illus.). 1978. pap. 3.95 (ISBN 0-89286-145-2). One Hund One Prods.

Cooper, Patricia J., ed. Better Homes & Gardens Woman's Health & Medical Guide. LC 79-55161. (Illus.). 696p. 1981. 29.95 (ISBN 0-696-00275-2). BH&G.

Cooper, Paul. Dimensions of Sight Singing: An Anthology. LC 79-22146. (Longman Music Ser.). 320p. (Orig.). 1981. pap. text ed. 14.95x (ISBN 0-582-28159-8). Longman.

--Perspectives in Music Theory: An Historical-Analytical Approach. 2nd ed. LC 78-26448. 1980. text ed. 20.50 scp (ISBN 0-06-041373-5, HarpC); Vol. 1. wkbk. scp 13.95 (ISBN 0-06-041374-3); Vol. 2. wkbk. scp 13.95 (ISBN 0-06-041375-1). Har-Row.

Cooper, Paul, jt. auth. see Rowland, A. J.

Cooper, Paul, ed. Polyphase Flow in Turbomachinery. 1978. 40.00 (ISBN 0-685-66809-6, H00123). ASME.

Cooper, Paul G., jt. ed. see Bolton, Brian.

Cooper, Paulette, ed. Growing up Puerto Rican. LC 79-184881. 256p. 1972. 6.95 (ISBN 0-87795-033-4, A4319). Arbor Hse.

Cooper, Peter. An Index of Adverse Reactions to Drugs. 213p. 1971. 30.00x (ISBN 0-686-79487-7, Pub. by Lloyd-Luke England). State Mutual Bk.

--The Secret Papers of Julia Templeton. 160p. (gr. 6-9). 1985. pap. 6.95 (ISBN 0-89272-197-9). Down East.

--Style in Piano Playing. 1980. 11.95 (ISBN 0-7145-3512-5); pap. 6.95 (ISBN 0-7145-3505-2). Riverrun NY.

Cooper, Peter L. Signs & Symptoms: Thomas Pynchon & the Contemporary World. LC 82-6929. 288p. 1983. 22.50 (ISBN 0-520-04537-8). U of Cal Pr.

Cooper, Philip, jt. auth. see Wansbrough, Nancy.

Cooper, Philip D. & Robinson, Larry M. Health Care Marketing Mamagement: A Case Approach. LC 82-3904. 361p. 1982. text ed. 38.50 (ISBN 0-89443-394-6). Aspen Systems.

Cooper, Philip D., et al, eds. An Annotated & Extended Bibliography of Health Care Marketing. LC 84-16795. (Bibliography Ser.). 186p. 1984. pap. text ed. 8.00 (ISBN 0-87757-171-6). AMACOM.

--Marketing & Preventive Health Care: Interdisciplinary & Interorganizational Perspectives. LC 77-25849. (American Marketing Association Proceedings Ser.). pap. 35.50 (ISBN 0-317-28849-0, 2017779). Bks Demand UMI.

Cooper, Phillip J. Public Law & Public Administration. LC 82-73742. 474p. 1983. text ed. 24.95 (ISBN 0-87484-526-2). Mayfield Pub.

Cooper, Phyllis. Feminine Gymnastics. 3rd ed. LC 80-65135. 1980. spiral bdg. 14.95x (ISBN 0-8087-2962-4). Burgess.

Cooper, Phyllis & Trnka, Milan. Teaching Gymnastic Skills to Men & Women. (Illus.). 224p. 1982. spiral bdg. 14.95x (ISBN 0-8087-2990-X). Burgess.

Cooper, Priscilla H. Call Me Black Woman. 50p. (Orig.). Date not set. price not set (ISBN 0-933865-04-X, 004); pap. price not set (ISBN 0-933865-02-3). Doris Pubns.

Cooper, R. & Osselton, J. W. EEG Technology. 3rd ed. Shaw, J. C., ed. (Illus.). 304p. 1981. text ed. 39.95 (ISBN 0-407-16002-7). Butterworth.

Cooper, R. A. & Weekes, A. J. Data, Models & Statistical Analysis. LC 82-25110. (Illus.). 416p. 1983. text ed. 30.00x (ISBN 0-389-20382-3); pap. text ed. 19.50x (ISBN 0-389-20383-1). B&N Imports.

Cooper, R. G. Resource Scarcity & the Hmong Response. 314p. 1984. text ed. 22.95 (ISBN 9971-69-070-5, Pub. by Singapore U Pr). Ohio U Pr.

Cooper, R. H., jt. auth. see Johnson, L. F.

Cooper, R. John & Sanford, Bruce W. First Amendment & Libel: The Experts Look at Print, Broadcast & Cable. Law & Business Inc., ed. LC 83-234206. Date not set. price not set (Law & Business). HarBraceJ.

Cooper, Raymond D. & Wood, Robert W., eds. Physical Mechanisms in Radiation Biology: Proceedings. AEC Technical Information Center. LC 74-600124. 332p. 1974. pap. 16.25 (CONF-721001); microfiche 4.50 (ISBN 0-87079-303-9, CONF-721001). DOE.

Cooper, Rebecca. The Logical Influence of Hegel on Marx. 1974. lib. bdg. 75.00 (ISBN 0-8490-0550-7). Gordon Pr.

Cooper, Richard N. The Economics of Interdependence. (Council on Foreign Relations Ser.). 316p. 1980. 30.00x (ISBN 0-231-05070-4); pap. 13.00x (ISBN 0-231-05071-2). Columbia U Pr.

Cooper, Richard N., et al. Towards a Renovated International System. 1977. 15.00 (ISBN 0-318-02792-5); pap. 4.95 (ISBN 0-318-02793-3). Trilateral Comm.

Cooper, Robert. An Essay on the Art of Richard Crashaw. (Salzburg-Elizabethan & Renaissance Studies: No. 102). 96p. 1982. pap. text ed. 25.50x (ISBN 0-391-02702-6, Pub. by Salzburg Austria). Humanities.

Cooper, Robert B., Jr., jt. auth. see Harrington, Thomas P.

Cooper, Robert D. Health & Welfare Fund Operations & Expenses: Summary Report & Fact Book for Multiemployer Plans. 47p. (Orig.). 1982. pap. 12.50 (ISBN 0-89154-200-0). Intl Found Employ.

--Health Care Cost Management: Issues, Strategies & Current Practices; Final Report & Fact Book. Brennan, Mary E., ed. 91p. (Orig.). 1984. pap. 17.50 (ISBN 0-89154-243-4). Intl Found Employ.

--Health Care Cost Survey Results. 10p. 1981. 5.00 (ISBN 0-89154-166-7). Intl Found Employ.

--Multiemployer Health & Welfare Plan Operations & Expenses: The Technical Report. 127p. 1983. pap. text ed. 27.50 (ISBN 0-89154-208-6). Intl Found Employ.

--Pension Fund Operating Expenses: The Summary Report & Fact Book. (Illus.). 53p. (Orig.). 1984. pap. 12.00 (ISBN 0-89154-247-7). Intl Found Employ.

Cooper, Robert D. & Carlsen, Melody A. Pension Fund Operations & Expenses: The Technical Report. (Illus.). 149p. (Orig.). 1980. pap. 15.00 (ISBN 0-89154-139-X). Intl Found Employ.

Cooper, Robert D. & Crabb, Connie A. Health Care Costs: Labor & Management at the Crossroads. 67p. (Orig.). 1984. pap. 17.50 (ISBN 0-89154-240-X). Intl Found Employ.

Cooper, Robert D., et al. Pension Fund Operations & Expenses: The Technical Report 1984. 102p. (Orig.). 1984. pap. text ed. 30.00 (ISBN 0-89154-248-5). Intl Found Employ.

Cooper, Robert L., ed. Language Spread: Studies in Diffusion & Social Change. LC 81-47567. 368p. 1982. 20.00 (ISBN 0-253-32000-3). Ind U Pr.

Cooper, Robert M. A Concordance to the English Poetry of Richard Crashan. LC 80-51219. 536p. 1980. 35.00x (ISBN 0-87875-188-2). Whitston Pub.

--Essays on Richard Crashaw. (Salzburg Studies in Elizabethan Literature: No. 83). 1980. pap. text ed. 25.50x (ISBN 0-391-01910-4). Humanities.

--The Literary Guide & Companion to Southern England. LC 84-25409. xviii, 387p. 1985. text ed. 28.95x (ISBN 0-8214-0790-2). Ohio U Pr.

--Lost on Both Sides, Dante Gabriel Rossetti: Critic & Poet. LC 71-91957. 268p. 1970. 15.50x (ISBN 0-8214-0069-X, 82-80752). Ohio U Pr.

Cooper, Robert W. An Historical Analysis of the Tontine Principle. LC 72-92061. (S. S. Huebner Foundation Monographs: No. 1). 69p. 1972. pap. 9.00 (ISBN 0-918930-01-4). Huebner Foun Insur.

--Investment Return & Property-Liability Insurance Ratemaking. 1974. 11.75x (ISBN 0-256-01605-4). Irwin.

Cooper, Robert W., jt. auth. see Rosenblum, Leonard A.

Cooper, Robin. Quantifications & Syntactic Theory. 1983. lib. bdg. 47.50 (ISBN 90-277-1484-3, Pub. by Reidel Holland). Kluwer Academic.

Cooper, Rodney H., jt. auth. see Johnson, Leroy F.

Cooper, Rosaleen & Palmer, Ann. Games from an Edwardian Childhood. (Illus.). 96p. 1983. 9.95 (ISBN 0-7153-8317-5). David & Charles.

Cooper, Rosalind. The Home Bartender. LC 99-943979. (Illus.). 160p. 1984. 6.95 (ISBN 0-307-49273-7, Golden Pr). Western Pub.

--The Wine Book. (Illus.). 1981. pap. 7.95 (ISBN 0-89586-131-3). H P Bks.

Cooper, Ross, jt. auth. see Pike, Andrew.

Cooper, Roy. Calf Roping. Witte, Randy, ed. (Illus.). 144p. (Orig.). 1984. pap. 9.95 (ISBN 0-911647-04-X). Western Horseman.

Cooper, Russell M. & Fisher, Margaret B. The Vision of a Contemporary University: A Case Study of Expansion & Development in American Higher Education, 1950-75. LC 80-29022. (Illus.). xiv, 318p. 1982. 12.95 (ISBN 0-8130-0702-X). U Presses Fla.

Cooper, Ruth P. Enameling on Glass, Porcelain Bisque, China. Thompson, Bill, ed. 50p. 1985. 9.95 (ISBN 0-318-04481-1). Scott Pubns MI.

Cooper, S. & Wanerman, L. Children in Treatment: A Primer for Beginning Therapists. LC 77-7637. 1977. pap. 15.95 (ISBN 0-87630-333-5). Brunner-Mazel.

Cooper, S. G. The Textile Industry: Environmental Control & Energy Conservation. LC 78-53999. 385p. (Pollution technology review no. 42; energy technology review no. 28). 1978. 42.00 (ISBN 0-8155-0702-X). Noyes.

Cooper, S. J., jt. auth. see Levens, A. S.

Cooper, S. J., ed. Theory of Psychopharmacology, Vol. I. 1982. 49.50 (ISBN 0-12-188001-X). Acad Pr.

Cooper, S. J., jt. ed. see Brown, K.

Cooper, S. K. & Fraser, D. R. The Financial Marketplace. 1982. 35.95 (ISBN 0-201-00196-9); instrs' guide 9.95 (ISBN 0-201-10196-3). Addison-Wesley.

Cooper, S. Kerry & Fraser, Donald R. Banking Deregulation & the New Competition in Financial Services. 296p. 1984. professional reference 32.00 (ISBN 0-88410-712-4). Ballinger Pub.

Cooper, S. Kerry, jt. auth. see Gaertner, James F.

Cooper, St. G. The Natural Resources of Trinidad & Tobago. Bacon, P. R., ed. 225p. 1981. 44.50x (ISBN 0-8448-1416-4). Crane-Russak Co.

Cooper, Samuel W. Think & Thank: A Tale. facsimile ed. LC 74-27975. (Modern Jewish Experience Ser.). 1975. Repr. of 1890 ed. 14.00x (ISBN 0-405-06704-6). Ayer Co Pubs.

Cooper, Sandi. Soups & Salads. Lawrence, Betsy, ed. LC 81-70441. (Great American Cooking Schools Ser.). (Illus.). 84p. 1982. pap. 5.95 (ISBN 0-941034-13-5). I Chalmers.

--Soups & Salads. LC 82-48659. (Great American Cooking Schools Ser.). (Illus.). 80p. 1983. 8.61 (ISBN 0-06-015151-X, HarpT). Har-Row.

Cooper, Sandi, ed. Internationalism in Nineteenth Century Europe. LC 74-147743. (Library of War & Peace; Documentary Anthologies). 1976. lib. bdg. 46.00 (ISBN 0-8240-0505-8). Garland Pub.

--Peace & Civilization: The Writings of Jacques Novicow, 1849-1912. LC 78-147744. (Library of War & Peace; Documentary Anthologies). lib. bdg. 46.00 (ISBN 0-8240-0506-6). Garland Pub.

Cooper, Sandi, ed. see Cook, Blanche.

Cooper, Sandra F., jt. auth. see Mertens, Thomas R.

Cooper, Saul & Hodges, William F., eds. The Mental Health Consultation Field, Vol. XI. 224p. 1983. text ed. 26.95x (ISBN 0-89885-130-0). Human Sci Pr.

Cooper, Shawn. The Clinical Use & Interpretation of the Wechsler Intelligence Scale for Children-Revised. (Illus.). 310p. 1982. 26.50x (ISBN 0-398-04750-2). C C Thomas.

Cooper, Shirley & Wanerman, Leon. A Casebook of Child Psychotherapy: Strategies & Techniques. LC 84-12678. 286p. 1984. 27.50 (ISBN 0-87630-369-6). Brunner-Mazel.

Cooper, Signe S. The Practice of Continuing Education in Nursing. LC 82-13872. 340p. 1982. 31.50 (ISBN 0-89443-664-3). Aspen Systems.

Cooper, Signe S. & Neal, Margo C. Perspectives on Continuing Education in Nursing. (Illus.). 312p. 1980. 15.95 (ISBN 0-683-09536-6). Williams & Wilkins.

Cooper, Signe S., ed. Self-Directed Learning in Nursing. LC 80-80088. 160p. 1980. pap. 20.95 (ISBN 0-913654-64-7). Aspen Systems.

Cooper, Signe S., jt. ed. see Neal, Margo C.

Cooper, Sol E. & Chen, Andrew C. Designing Steel Structures: Methods & Cases. (Illus.). 832p. 1985. text ed. 37.95 (ISBN 0-13-201385-1). P-H.

Cooper, Sonni. Black Fire. (Orig.). 1983. pap. 2.95 (ISBN 0-671-83632-3, Timescape). PB.

Cooper, Stephanie. Public Housing & Private Property. 200p. Date not set. text ed. write for info. (ISBN 0-566-05004-8). Gower Pub Co.

Cooper, Stephanie, jt. auth. see Jaffe, Marjorie.

Cooper, Stephen. ESL Theses & Dissertations: 1979-80. LC 81-15436. (Language in Education Ser.: No. 35). 20p. 1981. pap. 3.95x (ISBN 0-15-599049-7). Ctr Appl Ling.

--Graduate Theses & Dissertations in ESL: 1977-78. (Language in Education Ser.: No. 15). 20p. 1979. pap. 3.95x (ISBN 0-15-599051-9). Ctr Appl Ling.

--Graduate Theses & Dissertations in ESL: 1978-79. (Language in Education Ser.: No. 27). 38p. 1980. pap. 3.95x (ISBN 0-15-599052-7). Ctr Appl Ling.

--Graduate Theses Dissertations in ESL: 1976-77. (Language in Education Ser.: No. 3). 27p. 1978. pap. 3.95x (ISBN 0-15-599051-9). Ctr Appl Ling.

Cooper, Steven J., ed. Theory in Psychopharmacology, Vol. 2. 1983. 49.00 (ISBN 0-12-188002-8). Acad Pr.

Cooper, Stuart L. & Estes, Gerald M., eds. Multiphase Polymers. LC 79-10972. (Advances in Chemistry Ser.: No. 176). 1979. 64.95 (ISBN 0-8412-0457-8). Am Chemical.

Cooper, Stuart L. & Peppas, Nicholas A., eds. Biomaterials: Interfacial Phenomena & Applications. LC 82-6763. (ACS Advances in Chemistry Ser.: No. 199). 539p. 1982. lib. bdg. 69.95x (ISBN 0-8412-0631-7). Am Chemical.

Cooper, Susan. The Dark Is Rising. (YA) 1976. pap. 3.95 (ISBN 0-689-70420-8, A-51, Aladdin). Atheneum.

--The Dark Is Rising. LC 72-85916. 232p. (gr. 6 up). 1973. 11.95 (ISBN 0-689-30317-3, McElderry Bk); pap. 3.95 (ISBN 0-689-70420-8). Atheneum.

--Dawn of Fear. LC 71-115755. (Illus.). (gr. 3-7). 1970. 5.95 (ISBN 0-15-266201-4, HJ). HarBraceJ.

--Greenwitch. LC 73-85319. 148p. (gr. 4-7). 1973. 13.95 (ISBN 0-689-30426-9, McElderry Bk); pap. 3.95 (ISBN 0-689-70431-3). Atheneum.

--The Grey King. (Illus.). 1978. pap. 3.50 (ISBN 0-689-70448-8, A-78, Aladdin). Atheneum.

--The Grey King. LC 75-8526. 224p. (gr. 4-9). 1975. 12.95 (ISBN 0-689-50029-7, McElderry Bk); pap. 3.50 (ISBN 0-689-70448-8). Atheneum.

--Jethro & the Jumbie. LC 79-14667. (Illus.). 32p. (ps-4). 1979. 7.95 (ISBN 0-689-50140-4, McElderry Bk). Atheneum.

--Over Sea, Under Stone. LC 66-11199. (gr. 4-6). 1966. 10.95 (ISBN 0-15-259034-X, HJ). HarBraceJ.

--Over Sea, under Stone. LC 79-10489. (Illus.). (gr. 4-7). 1979. pap. 4.95 (ISBN 0-15-670542-7, VoyB). HarBraceJ.

--Seaward. LC 83-7055. 180p. (gr. 7up). 1983. 10.95 (ISBN 0-689-50275-3, Argo). Atheneum.

--The Silver Cow: A Welsh Tale. LC 82-13928. (Illus.). 32p. (ps-4). 1983. 12.95 (ISBN 0-689-50236-2, McElderry Bk). Atheneum.

--Silver on the Tree. LC 77-5361. 256p. (gr. 5-9). 1977. pap. 13.95 (ISBN 0-689-50088-2, McElderry Bk); 4.95 (ISBN 0-689-70467-4). Atheneum.

Cooper, Susan & Heenan, Cathy. Preparing, Designing, Leading Workshops. 1980. pap. 12.95 (ISBN 0-442-21722-6). Van Nos Reinhold.

Cooper, Susan, jt. auth. see Heenan, Cathy.

Cooper, Suzanne, jt. auth. see Cooper, Daniel.

Cooper, T. G. & Singleton, Carol. America Onstage. LC 83-73436. (DJH Theatre Library). 144p. (Orig.). 1984. pap. 8.95 (ISBN 0-915833-22-0). Drama Jazz Hse Inc.

Cooper, T. P. With Dickens in Yorkshire. 1973. 15.00 (ISBN 0-8274-0054-3). R West.

Cooper, Terrance C. The Tools of Biochemistry. LC 76-30910. 423p. 1977. 34.95x (ISBN 0-471-17116-6, Pub. by Wiley-Interscience). Wiley.

Cooper, Terry & Gent, John. Around London by Tram. 1982. 25.00x (ISBN 0-9505458-4-8, Pub. by Sheaf Pub England). State Mutual Bk.

Cooper, Terry L. The Responsible Administrator: An Approach to Ethics for the Administrative Role. (Political Science Ser.). 180p. 1982. 17.50x (ISBN 0-8046-9292-0, Pub. by Kennikat). Assoc Faculty Pr.

Cooper, Terry T. & Ratner, Marilyn. Many Friends Cooking. LC 79-24832. (gr. 3 up). spiral bdg. 7.00 (ISBN 0-935738-00-2, 5065). US Comm Unicef.

Cooper, Theodore W. By Popular Choice: Why Not Vocalize the Silent Majority? 2nd ed. LC 75-1656. 152p. 1975. 8.50 (ISBN 0-915428-01-6); pap. 3.95 (ISBN 0-915428-02-4). Technicon Pubs.

--Functionality: A Revelation for Science. LC 83-51463. (Illus.). 562p. 1984. tchr's ed 55.00 (ISBN 0-915428-05-9). Technicon Pubs.

Cooper, Thomas. An Answer in Defence of the Truth Against the Apology of Private Mass. 1850. 21.00 (ISBN 0-384-09790-1). Johnson Repr.

--Introductory Lecture & Discourse on the Connexion Between Chemistry & Medicine, 2 vols. in 1. Cohen, I. Bernard, ed. LC 79-7956. (Three Centuries of Science in America Ser.). 1980. Repr. of 1818 ed. lib. bdg. 23.00x (ISBN 0-405-12537-2). Ayer Co Pubs.

--Lectures on the Elements of Political Economy. 2nd ed. LC 66-21666. Repr. of 1829 ed. lib. bdg. 37.50x (ISBN 0-678-00776-4). Kelley.

--Some Information Respecting America. LC 67-29498. (Illus.). Repr. of 1794 ed. 29.50x (ISBN 0-678-00570-2). Kelley.

--Treatise on the Law of Libel & the Liberty of the Press, Showing the Origin, Use & Abuse of the Law of Libel. LC 78-125688. (American Journalists Ser). 1970. Repr. of 1830 ed. 20.00 (ISBN 0-405-01665-4). Ayer Co Pubs.

--Treatise on the Law of Libel & the Liberty of the Press. LC 71-107408. (Civil Liberties in American History Ser). 1970. Repr. of 1833 ed. lib. bdg. 25.00 (ISBN 0-306-71892-8). Da Capo.

--Two Essays: On the Foundation of Civil Government & On the Constitution of the United States. LC 72-99477. (American Constitutional & Legal History Ser). 1970. Repr. of 1826 ed. lib. bdg. 19.50 (ISBN 0-306-71852-9). Da Capo.

Cooper, Thomas & Hill, Paul. Dialogue with Photography. (Illus.). 448p. 1979. 12.95 (ISBN 0-374-13893-1); pap. 6.95 (ISBN 0-374-51544-1). FS&G.

Cooper, Thomas, tr. see Broussais, Francois J.

Cooper, Thomas, et al. Sentence Combining in Second Language Instruction. (Language in Education Ser.: No. 31). 75p. 1980. pap. 6.95x (ISBN 0-15-599053-5). Ctr Appl Ling.

Cooper, Thomas J. Guidebook to Biblical Truth. Cooper, Willia S., ed. (Make the Path Clear Ser.: Vol. 1). 99p. (Orig.). 1984. pap. 4.95 (ISBN 0-931429-01-3). Cooper & Cooper Pub.

--Guidebook to Biblical Truth. Cooper, Willia S., ed. (The Ministry of Women in God's Plan Ser.: Vol. 6). 50p. (Orig.). 1985. pap. 4.00 (ISBN 0-931429-06-4). Cooper & Cooper Pub.

--Guidebook to Biblical Truth. Cooper, Willia S., ed. (The Master of Light & Darkness Ser.: Vol. 5). 70p. (Orig.). 1985. pap. 4.75 (ISBN 0-931429-05-6). Cooper & Cooper Pub.

--Investigate the Demons (Did Jesus Have a Christology?) Cooper, Willia S., ed. (Guidebook to Biblical Truth Ser.: Vol. 2). 45p. (Orig.). 1984. pap. 3.75 (ISBN 0-931429-02-1, TXU 104-636). Cooper & Cooper Pub.

Cooper, Thomas J. & Cooper, Willia S. Christian Message for Today. (Guidebook to Biblical Truth Ser.: Vol. 3). 60p. (Orig.). 1984. pap. 4.50 (ISBN 0-931429-03-X, TXU 109-949). Cooper & Cooper Pub.

--Guidebook to Biblical Truth. (Stewardship Ser.: Vol. 4). 60p. (Orig.). 1985. Set. write for info. (ISBN 0-931429-00-5); Vol. 4. pap. 4.50 (ISBN 0-931429-04-8). Cooper & Cooper Pub.

Cooper, Thomas M. & DiBiaggio, John A. Applied Practice Management: A Strategy for Stress Control. LC 79-15266. (Illus.). 208p. 1979. text ed. 34.95 (ISBN 0-8016-1082-6). Mosby.

Cooper, Tom C., ed. Iowa's Natural Heritage. (Illus.). 352p. 1984. 39.95 (ISBN 0-317-13131-1). Iowa Nat Heritage.

Cooper, V. Student's Manual of Auditing. 2nd ed. 1979. pap. 32.50 (ISBN 0-85258-175-0). Van Nos Reinhold.

Cooper, W. Warm Air Heating for Climate Control. 1980. 29.95 (ISBN 0-13-944231-6). P-H.

Cooper, W. A., tr. see Fontane, Theodor.

Cooper, W. D. & Helfrick, A. D. Electronic Instrumentation & Measurement Techniques. 3rd ed. (Illus.). 496p. 1985. text ed. 32.95 (ISBN 0-13-250721-8). P-H.

Cooper, W. E. ABC of Garden Pests & Diseases. (Illus.). 12.50 (LTB). Sportshelf.

Cooper, W. E. & Sorensen, J. M. Fundamental Frequency in Sentence Production. (Illus.). 213p. 1981. 30.50 (ISBN 0-387-90510-3). Springer-Verlag.

Cooper, W. Norman. Dance with God. LC 81-69932. 128p. (Orig.). 1982. 7.50 (ISBN 0-87516-491-9); pap. 4.50 (ISBN 0-87516-468-4). De Vorss.

--The Non-Thinking Self. 112p. 1980. 7.50 (ISBN 0-87516-414-5); pap. 4.50 (ISBN 0-87516-403-X). De Vorss.

--The Ultimate Destination. 95p. 1980. 7.50 (ISBN 0-87516-413-7); pap. 4.50 (ISBN 0-87516-381-5). De Vorss.

Cooper, W. R. An Archaic Dictionary. 59.95 (ISBN 0-87968-653-7). Gordon Pr.

Cooper, W. W. & Ljiri, Yuji. Kohler's Dictionary for Accountants. 6th ed. (Illus.). 592p. 1983. 49.95 (ISBN 0-13-516658-6). P-H.

Cooper, W. W., jt. auth. see Charnes, Abraham.

Cooper, Walter G. Official History of Fulton County. LC 78-12918. 1978. Repr. of 1934 ed. 25.00 (ISBN 0-87152-280-2). Reprint.

Cooper, Weldon & Morris, Thomas R. Virginia Government & Politics: Readings & Comments. LC 75-44333. 450p. 1976. 12.95x (ISBN 0-8139-0677-6). U Pr of Va.

Cooper, Wendy. In Praise of America: American Decolative Arts, Sixteen Fifty to Eighteen Thirty. LC 79-3477. (Illus.). 1980. 25.00 (ISBN 0-394-50994-3). Knopf.

Cooper, Wendy & Smith, Tim. Beyond Our Limits: What Ordinary Humans Can Do in Extremis. LC 81-48443. 224p. 1982. 14.95 (ISBN 0-8128-2867-4). Stein & Day.

Cooper, Willia S., jt. auth. see Cooper, Thomas J.

Cooper, Willia S., ed. see Cooper, Thomas J.

Cooper, William. Guide in the Wilderness. facs. ed. LC 79-140352. (Select Bibliographies Reprint Ser). 1810. 12.00 (ISBN 0-8369-5595-1). Ayer Co Pubs.

--Liberty & Slavery: Southern Politics to 1860. LC 83-4311. 336p. 1983. pap. text ed. 6.95 (ISBN 0-394-32382-3, KnopfC). Knopf.

--Scenes from Married Life & Scenes from Later Life. LC 84-70466. 508p. 1984. 18.95 (ISBN 0-525-24258-9, 01840-550). Dutton.

--Scenes from Provincial Life & Scenes from Metropolitan Life. 432p. 1984. pap. 4.95 (ISBN 0-380-69302-X, Bard). Avon.

--Scenes from the Provincial Life & Scenes from Metropolitan Life. 422p. 1983. 17.95 (ISBN 0-525-24198-1, 01743-520). Dutton.

Cooper, William & Wiesbecker, Henry. Solid State Devices & Integrated Circuits. 1982. text ed. 29.95 (ISBN 0-8359-7045-0); solutions manual avail. (ISBN 0-8359-7046-9). Reston.

Cooper, William, ed. see Pennsylvania University Bicentennial Conference.

Cooper, William A., tr. see Bielschowsky, Albert.

Cooper, William B. Licensed Operator's Key to Refrigeration. LC 74-14660. (Illus.). 1975. 14.95 (ISBN 0-912524-11-1). Busn News.

Cooper, William C. In Search of the Golden Apple: An Adventure in Citrus Science & Travel. 1981. 14.95 (ISBN 0-533-04803-6). Vantage.

Cooper, William D., ed. List of Foreign Protestants, & Aliens, Resident in England, 1618-1688. 1862. 19.00 (ISBN 0-384-09795-2). Johnson Repr.

--Lists of Foreign Protestants & Aliens Resident in England 1618-1688. Repr. of 1862 ed. 19.00 (ISBN 0-404-50182-6). AMS Pr.

Cooper, William E. Speech Perception & Production. LC 79-17281. (Language & Being Ser.). 1979. 29.50 (ISBN 0-89391-027-9). Ablex Pub.

Cooper, William E. & Paccia-Cooper, Jeanne. Syntax & Speech. LC 80-16614. (Cognitive Science Ser.: No. 3). 284p. 1980. text ed. 22.50x (ISBN 0-674-86075-6). Harvard U Pr.

Cooper, William E., ed. Cognitive Aspects of Skilled Typewriting. (Illus.). 417p. 1983. 37.00 (ISBN 0-387-90774-2). Springer-Verlag.

Cooper, William H., ed. see Buch, Jane.

Cooper, William H., ed. see Butrick, Lyn M.

Cooper, William H., ed. see Leonard, Mary K.

Cooper, William H., ed. see McCarthy, Donald.

Cooper, William H., ed. see McCarthy, Donald W.

Cooper, William H., ed. see Oana, Katherine.

Cooper, William H., ed. see Shuster, Albert H., et al.

Cooper, William H., ed. see Shuster, Albert H. & Miller, Russell R.

Cooper, William J., Jr. Liberty & Slavery: Southern Politics to Eighteen Sixty. LC 83-4311. 1983. 17.95 (ISBN 0-394-53289-9). Knopf.

--South & the Politics of Slavery, 1828-1856. LC 78-751. 456p. 1978. 35.00x (ISBN 0-8071-0385-3); pap. 7.95x (ISBN 0-8071-0775-1). La State U Pr.

Cooper, William J., Jr., ed. see Bauer, K. Jack.

Cooper, William J., Jr., ed. see Dillon, Merton L.

Cooper, William J., Jr., ed. see Hundley, Daniel R.

Cooper, William R. Archaic Dictionary. LC 73-76018. 688p. 1969. Repr. of 1876 ed. 75.00x (ISBN 0-8103-3885-8). Gale.

Cooper, William R., ed. see Butrick, Lyn M.

Cooper, William S. Foundations of Logico-Linguistics. (Synthese Language Library: No. 2). 1978. lib. bdg. 34.00 (ISBN 90-277-0864-9, Pub. by Reidel Holland); pap. text ed. 16.00 (ISBN 90-277-0876-2, Pub. by Reidel Holland). Kluwer Academic.

--Set Theory & Syntactic Description. (Janua Linguarum, Ser. Minor: No. 34). 52p. 1974. pap. text ed. 6.80x (ISBN 90-2792-704-9). Mouton.

Cooper, William W., jt. ed. see Charnes, Abraham.

Cooper, Wyatt. Families: A Memoir & a Celebration. LC 75-9347. (Illus.). 224p. 1975. 12.45i (ISBN 0-06-010857-6, HarpT). Har-Row.

Cooperation in Documentation & Communication. Bibliographical Notes for Understanding the Transnational Corporations & the Third World. Strharsky, Harry & Riesch, Mary, eds. LC 75-8120. 1975. pap. 6.95 (ISBN 0-914958-03-8). CoDoC.

Cooperative Housing Foundation. Operations Handbook for Rural Cooperative Housing. 300p. 1980. 35.95 (ISBN 0-318-01746-6). Rural America.

Cooperative Whole Grain Educational Association. Uprisings: The Whole Grain Bakers Book. LC 83-50137. 304p. (Orig.). 1983. pap. write for info. (ISBN 0-9611600-0-4). Uprisings Pub Co.

--Uprisings: The Whole Grain Bakers' Book. (Illus.). 296p. (Orig.). 1984. pap. 12.95 (ISBN 0-938432-12-5). Mother Earth.

Cooperberg, Judy A. Beyond Twilight. rev. ed. Scoggins, Sharon S., ed. 126p. 1983. 6.00 (ISBN 0-912077-01-8). Creat Image Assocs.

Cooperberg, Peter L., jt. ed. see Winsberg, Fred.

Cooper-Clark, Diana. Designs of Darkness: Interviews with Detective Novelists. LC 82-74452. 1983. 19.95 (ISBN 0-87972-223-1); pap. 9.95 (ISBN 0-87972-224-X). Bowling Green Univ.

--Interviews with Contemporary Novelists. 256p. 1985. 25.00 (ISBN 0-312-42534-1). St Martin.

Cooper-Hill, James & Greenberg, Martin J. Cases & Materials on Mortgages & Real Estate Finance. (Contemporary Legal Education Ser.). 632p. 1982. 27.50 (ISBN 0-87215-499-8). Michie Co.

Cooper Madlener, Judith. The Sea Vegetable Gelatin Cookbook. LC 80-29228. (Illus., Orig.). 1981. pap. 7.95 (ISBN 0-912800-76-3). Woodbridge Pr.

Cooperman. Collection of Accounts. (The Law in Connecticut Ser.). 24.95 (ISBN 0-686-90157-6). Harrison Co GA.

--Collection of Accounts. (The Law in Florida Ser.). incl. latest pocket part supplement 24.95 (ISBN 0-686-90229-7); separate pocket part supplement, 1982 9.45 (ISBN 0-686-90230-0). Harrison Co GA.

--Collection of Accounts. (The Law in Georgia Ser.). incl. latest pocket part supplement 24.95 (ISBN 0-686-90384-6); separate pocket part supplement, 1984 11.95. Harrison Co GA.

--Collection of Accounts. (The Law in New York Ser.). 24.95 (ISBN 0-686-90795-7). Harrison Co GA.

--Collection of Accounts. (The Law in Oklahoma Ser.). 24.95 (ISBN 0-686-90964-X). Harrison Co GA.

--Collection of Accounts. (The Law in South Carolina Ser.). 24.95 (ISBN 0-686-90980-1). Harrison Co GA.

--Collection of Accounts. (The Law in Tennessee Ser.). 24.95 (ISBN 0-686-90998-4); separate pocket part supplement, 1983 9.95 (ISBN 0-686-90999-2). Harrison Co GA.

--Collection of Accounts. (The Law in Texas Ser.). 24.95 (ISBN 0-686-91019-2). Harrison Co GA.

Cooperman, Avram M. & Hoerr, Stanley O. Surgery of the Pancreas: A Text & Atlas. LC 77-23621. (Illus.). 1978. 54.50 (ISBN 0-8016-1032-X). Mosby.

Cooperman, Bernard D., ed. Jewish Thought in the Sixteenth Century. (Center for Jewish Studies Ser.). 500p. 1982. text ed. 30.00x (ISBN 0-674-47461-9); pap. text ed. 14.95x (ISBN 0-674-47462-7). Harvard U Pr.

Cooperman, Carolyn & Rhoades, Chuck. New Methods for Puberty Education. (Illus.). 1983. 20.00 (ISBN 0-9609366-0-2). NW Plan Parent.

Cooperman, David N. Fascinations. 96p. 1984. pap. 4.50 (ISBN 0-682-40150-1). Exposition Pr FL.

Cooperman, Hasye. The Making of a Woman. 112p. 1984. pap. 6.95 (ISBN 0-89962-402-2). Todd & Honeywell.

Cooperman, Jehiel B., ed. America in Yiddish Poetry: An Anthology. Cooperman, Sarah C., tr. 1967. 10.00 (ISBN 0-682-46879-7, Banner). Exposition Pr FL.

Cooperman, Lee H., jt. ed. see Orkin, Frederick K.

Cooperman, Marc. Intestinal Ischemia. LC 83-80584. (Illus.). 432p. 1983. monograph 49.50 (ISBN 0-87993-197-3). Futura Pub.

Cooperman, Sarah C., tr. see Cooperman, Jehiel B.

Cooperman, Stanley. Monarch Notes on Hemingway's Major Novels. (Orig.). pap. 2.75 (ISBN 0-671-00621-5). Monarch Pr.

--World War One & the American Novel. 264p. 1967. pap. 6.95x (ISBN 0-8018-1151-1). Johns Hopkins.

Cooper-Prichard, A. H. Conversations with Oscar Wilde. LC 72-12952. 1973. lib. bdg. 30.00 (ISBN 0-8414-0996-X). Folcroft.

Cooperrider, Edward A., tr. see Rommel, Kurt.

Cooperrider, Edward A., tr. see Steinwede, Dietrich.

Cooperrider, Tom S., ed. Endangered & Threatened Plants of Ohio. LC 81-82268. 1982. 10.00 (ISBN 0-86727-091-8). Ohio Bio Survey.

Coopers & Lybrand. The Early History of Coopers & Lybrand. LC 83-49108. (Accounting History & the Development of a Profession Ser.). 187p. 1984. lib. bdg. 25.00 (ISBN 0-8240-6319-8). Garland Pub.

--Employer Accounting for Pension Costs & Other Post-Retirement Benefits. LC 81-68568. 1981. 8.00 (ISBN 0-686-83748-7). Finan Exec.

--International Tax Summaries 1982: A Guide for Planning & Decisions. (Wiley Ronald Series in Professional Accounting & Business). 912p. 1982. 55.00x (ISBN 0-471-87576-7, Pub. by Ronald Pr). Wiley.

Coopers, jt. auth. see Pomeranz, Felix.

Coopers & Lybrand. Accounting for Pensions: Results of Applying the FASB's Preliminary Views. LC 83-82954. 1983. 10.00 (ISBN 0-910586-53-5). Finan Exec.

Coopers & Lybrand International Tax Network, jt. ed. see Berger, Alexander.

Coopers & Lybrand Staff. International Insurance Industry Guide. 288p. 1985. 60.00 (ISBN 1-85044-046-8). Lloyds London Pr.

Cooper-Schluter, H. K., tr. see Hansen, H. G. & Graucob, E.

Coopersmith, Georgia. Directions in Metal: Work Produced at the Johnson Atelier Technical Institute of Sculpture. (Illus.). 24p. (Orig.). 1982. pap. 8.00 (ISBN 0-942746-02-3). Brainerd.

--Twentieth Anniversary Exhibition of the Vogels Collection. (Illus.). 94p. 1982. pap. 12.50 (ISBN 0-942746-03-1). Brainerd.

--Variations on a Theme: Four Figurative Painters. (Illus.). 32p. 1985. pap. 8.00 (ISBN 0-942746-08-2). Brainerd.

Coopersmith, Georgia, jt. ed. see Hildreth, Joseph.

Coopersmith, Harry. Companion Volume to the Songs We Sing. 1950. 3.50x (ISBN 0-8381-0210-7). United Syn Bk.

--New Jewish Songbook. LC 65-14593. pap. 9.95x (ISBN 0-87441-060-6). Behrman.

--Songs We Sing. (Illus.). 1950. 22.50x (ISBN 0-8381-0723-0). United Syn Bk.

Coopersmith, Harry, ed. More of the Songs We Sing. (Illus.). 288p. (Eng. & Heb.). (gr. 4-10). 1970. 9.50x (ISBN 0-8381-0217-4). United Syn Bk.

Cooper-Smith, John H., jt. auth. see Eatwell, David.

Coopersmith, Stanley. Antecedents of Self-Esteem. 2nd ed. (Illus.). xii, 296p. 1981. pap. 13.25 (ISBN 0-89106-017-0, 7283). Consulting Psychol.

Cooperstein, Bruce, jt. ed. see Mason, Geoffrey.

Cooperstein, S. J. & Watkins, Dudley, eds. The Islets of Langerhans: Biochemistry, Physiology, & Pathology. LC 81-10895. 1981. 65.00 (ISBN 0-12-187820-1). Acad Pr.

Coopey, Judith R., jt. auth. see Mentzer, Michael.

Coopland. Letter to King Richard II. 186p. 1982. 53.00x (ISBN 0-85323-283-0, Pub. by Liverpool Univ England). State Mutual Bk.

Coopola, Gary M., jt. auth. see Schuster, Herbert F.

Coops, W. E., jt. ed. see Koops, Willem R.

Cooray, L. J. Conventions, the Australian Constitution & the Future. xix, 235p. 1979. 24.00x (ISBN 0-9596568-1-2, Pub. by Legal Bks.NY Ltd. Sydney). Rothman.

Coordinating Committee for Continuing Education in Thoracic Surgery. Self-Education-Self Assessment in Thoracic Surgery. LC 80-84130. 208p. 1983. 100.00 (ISBN 0-8403-3156-8, 40315601). Kendall-Hunt.

Coors, Holly. Joy Is the Promise. 1978. pap. 1.50 (ISBN 0-88419-182-6). Creation Hse.

Coortice, F. C., jt. auth. see Yoffey, J. M.

Coote, J. O., ed. see Coles, K. A.

Coote, Jack. North Sea Harbours & Pilotage: Calais to Den Helder. 5th ed. (Adlard Coles Pilotage Ser.). (Illus.). 128p. 1983. 32.50 (ISBN 0-229-11686-8, Pub. by Adlard Coles). Sheridan.

Coote, Jack, ed. Total Loss. (Illus.). 256p. 1985. 24.95 (ISBN 0-229-11684-1, Pub. by Adlard Coles). Sheridan.

Coote, Jack H. Monochrome Darkroom Practice. (Illus.). 320p. 1982. 31.50 (ISBN 0-240-51061-5); pap. 13.95 (ISBN 0-240-51700-8). Focal Pr.

Coote, John. The Shell Pilot to the English Channel, Pt. 2: Harbours in Northern France & the Channel Islands, Dunkerque to Brest. (Illus.). 1985. 27.95 (ISBN 0-571-13486-6). Faber & Faber.

Coote, John, rev. by see Coles, Adlard.

Coote, Robert, jt. auth. see Stott, John R.

Coote, Robert B. Amos among the Prophets: Composition & Theology. LC 80-8054. 144p. 1981. pap. 5.95 (ISBN 0-8006-1400-3, 1-1400). Fortress.

Coote, Stephen, ed. The Penguin Book of Homosexual Verse. 416p. 1983. pap. 6.95 (ISBN 0-14-042293-5). Penguin.

Cooter, Roger. The Cultural Meaning of Popular Science: Phrenology & the Organization of Consent in Nineteenth Century Britain. (History of Medicine Ser.). (Illus.). 448p. 1985. 37.50 (ISBN 0-521-22743-7). Cambridge U Pr.

Cootes, R. J. The Middle Ages. (Longman Secondary Histories Ser.). (Illus.). 208p. (Orig.). (gr. 6-12). 1980. pap. text ed. 9.95 (ISBN 0-582-20510-7); 3.50 (ISBN 0-582-36691-7). Longman.

Cootes, R. J. & Snellgrove, L. E. The Ancient World. (Longman Secondary Histories Ser.). (Illus.). 208p. (YA) (gr. 6-12). 1978. pap. text ed. 9.95x (ISBN 0-582-20503-4); paper 3.95. Longman.

Cotner, Cathryn. Tent & Town: Rugs & Embroideries from Central Asia. LC 82-49068. (The H. McCoy Jones Collection). (Illus.). 16p. 1982. pap. 2.95x (ISBN 0-88401-043-0). Fine Arts Mus.

Cootner, Cathryn M., jt. ed. see Sharpe, William F.

Cootner, Cathryn M., et al. Flat-Woven Textiles: The Arthur D. Jenkins Collection. LC 81-84336. (Illus.). 224p. 1981. 110.00 (ISBN 0-87405-018-9). Textile Mus.

Cootner, Paul H. & Lof, George O. Water Demand for Steam Electric Generation: An Economic Projection Model. LC 65-27669. pap. 39.00 (ISBN 0-317-09080-1, 2020959). Bks Demand UMI.

Coots, Max. Seasons of the Self. LC 71-158676. (Illus.). 1971. 3.50 (ISBN 0-687-37140-6). Unitarian.

Coover, J. F. see Hayes, Joseph W.

Coover, James. Musical Instrument Collections: Catalogs & Cognate Literature. LC 81-19901. (Detroit Studies in Music Bibliography Ser.: No. 47). 1981. 25.00 (ISBN 0-89990-013-5). Info Coord.

Coover, James & Colvig, Richard. Medieval & Renaissance Music on Long-Playing Records. (Detroit Studies in Music Bibliography Ser.: No. 6). 1964. pap. 2.00 (ISBN 0-911772-26-X). Info Coord.

--Medieval & Renaissance Music on Long-Playing Records: Supplement 1962-1971. (Detroit Studies in Music Bibliography: No. 26). 1973. 5.00 (ISBN 0-911772-44-8); pap. 2.00 (ISBN 0-89990-008-9). Info Coord.

Coover, John E. Experiments in Psychical Research at Leland Stanford Junior University. LC 75-7372. (Perspectives in Psychical Research Ser.). (Illus.). 1975. Repr. of 1917 ed. 49.50x (ISBN 0-405-07023-3). Ayer Co Pubs.

Coover, Robert. After Lazarus: A Filmscript. 1980. 35.00 (ISBN 0-89723-020-5). Bruccoli.

--The Convention. 30p. 1981. limited signed ed. 35.00 (ISBN 0-935716-13-0). Lord John.

--Gerald's Party. 1986. 16.95 (ISBN 0-317-19276-0, Linden Pr). S&S.

--Hair O'The Chine. 1979. ltd. ed 40.00 (ISBN 0-89723-019-1). Bruccoli.

--In Bed One Night & Other Brief Encounters. (Fiction Ser.). 60p. 1983. pap. 4.00 (ISBN 0-930901-17-7). Burning Deck.

--The Origin of the Brunists. (Richard Seaver Bk). 1978. 12.50 (ISBN 0-670-52863-3). Viking.

--Pricksongs & Descants. 1970. pap. 5.95 (ISBN 0-452-25480-9, Z5480, Plume). NAL.

--Spanking the Maid. 1981. 50.00 (ISBN 0-89723-023-X); specially bound manuscript ed. 100.00 (ISBN 0-89723-024-8). Bruccoli.

--Spanking the Maid. LC 81-48546. 256p. 1982. 10.95 (ISBN 0-394-52561-2, GP-850). Grove.

--Spanking the Maid. 256p. 1981. pap. 4.95 (ISBN 0-394-17971-4, E804, Ever). Grove.

--The Universal Baseball Association Inc., J.Henry Waugh, Prop. pap. 6.95 (ISBN 0-452-25553-8, Z5553, Plume). NAL.

Coover, Virginia, et al. Resource Manual for a Living Revolution. 330p. 1985. lib. bdg. 19.95 (ISBN 0-86571-015-5); pap. 9.95 (ISBN 0-86571-056-2). New Soc Pubs.

Coox, Alvin D. The Anatomy of a Small War: The Soviet-Japanese Struggle for Changkufeng-Khasan, 1938. LC 76-51924. (Contributions in Military History: No. 13). 1977. lib. bdg. 35.00 (ISBN 0-8371-9479-2, CSJ/). Greenwood.

--Nomonhan: Japan Against Russia, 1939, 2 vols. LC 81-85447. (Illus.). 1200p. 1985. Set. 95.00x (ISBN 0-8047-1160-7). Stanford U Pr.

Copa, G. & Moss, J. Planning & Vocational Education. 208p. 1983. 17.00 (ISBN 0-07-013049-3). McGraw.

Copans, Stuart & Singer, Thomas. Who's the Patient Here? Portraits of the Young Psychotherapist. (Illus.). 1978. pap. 8.95 (ISBN 0-19-502386-2, GB545, GB). Oxford U Pr.

Copass, Michael K. & Eisenberg, Mickey. The Paramedic Manual. (Blue Book Ser.). (Illus.). 304p. 1980. spiral bdg. 12.95 (ISBN 0-7216-2716-1). Saunders.

Copass, Michael K., jt. auth. see Eisenberg, Mickey S.

Cope, C. B. & Fuller, W. H. The Scientific Management of Hazardous Wastes. LC 82-14650. (Illus.). 375p. 1983. 75.00 (ISBN 0-521-25100-1). Cambridge U Pr.

Cope, D. R., et al, eds. Energy Policy & Land-Use Planning: An International Perspective. (Urban & Regional Planning Ser.). 328p. 1984. 40.00 (ISBN 0-08-031323-X); pap. 22.50. Pergamon.

Cope, David. New Music Composition. LC 76-21376. 1977. pap. text ed. 13.95 (ISBN 0-02-870630-7). Schirmer Bks.

--New Music Notation. LC 75-32585. 1976. perfect bdg. 9.95 (ISBN 0-8403-1315-2). Kendall-Hunt.

--Quiet Lives. LC 83-172. (Vox Humana Ser.). 1983. 12.95 (ISBN 0-89603-048-2); pap. 4.95 (ISBN 0-89603-049-0). Humana.

Cope, David, jt. auth. see Goldman, Myer.

Cope, David E. Organisation Development & Action Research in Hospitals. 176p. 1982. text ed. 44.50x (ISBN 0-566-00387-2). Gower Pub Co.

Cope, David H. New Directions in Music. 4th ed. 416p. 1983. pap. text ed. write for info. (ISBN 0-697-03607-3). Wm C Brown.

Cope, Dawn & Cope, Peter. Humpty Dumpty's Favourite Nursery Rhymes. (Illus.). 64p. 1981. 9.95 (ISBN 0-03-059907-5). Webb & Bower.

--Red Riding Hood's Favourite Fairy Tales. (Illus.). 64p. 1981. 9.95 (ISBN 0-03-059906-7). Webb & Bower.

Cope, Dawn & Cope, Peter, eds. Christmas Carols for Young Children. (Illus.). 32p. (gr. 5-12). 1981. pap. 4.75 (ISBN 0-914510-12-6). Evergreen.

Cope, Dawn, et al. Illustrators of Postcards From the Nursery. (Illus.). 64p. 1983. pap. 5.95 (ISBN 0-904499-05-7, Pub. by Salem Hse Ltd). Merrimack Pub Cir.

Cope, Dwight W. & Schoude, Lee E. Plastics. LC 77-21618. (Illus.). 112p. 1982. text ed. 6.40 (ISBN 0-87006-426-6). Goodheart.

Cope, E. D. Batrachia of North America. (Illus.). 1963. 10.00 (ISBN 0-910914-01-X). J Johnson.

Cope, E. M. Introduction to Aristotle's Rhetoric with Analysis, Notes, & Appendices. (Classical Studies Ser.). Repr. of 1867 ed. lib. bdg. 45.00x (ISBN 0-697-00032-X). Irvington.

--The Rhetoric of Aristotle with a Commentary, 3 vols. Sandys, J. E., ed. (Classical Studies Ser.). (Gr. & Eng.). Repr. of 1877 ed. Vol. 1. lib. bdg. 59.00x (ISBN 0-697-00033-8); Vol. 2. lib. bdg. 59.00x (ISBN 0-697-00034-6); Vol. 3. lib. bdg. 59.00x (ISBN 0-697-00035-4). Irvington.

Cope, Eddie. Agatha Christie Made Me Do It. (Illus.). 62p. 1975. pap. 2.75 (ISBN 0-88680-001-3); royalty 35.00 (ISBN 0-317-03592-4). I E Clark.

--Airport Nineteen Hundred Four. 96p. (Piano-Vocal Score, Music & Lyrics by Buster Cearley). 1981. pap. 10.00 (ISBN 0-88680-003-X). I E Clark.

--Don't Print That! A Three-Act Melodrama. (Illus.). 40p. 1983. pap. 2.50x (ISBN 0-88680-042-0). I E Clark.

--Frankenstein's Centerfold. 40p. (Orig.). 1984. pap. 2.75 (ISBN 0-88680-222-9). I E Clark.

--The Invisible Man. (Illus.). 48p. 1980. pap. 2.50 (ISBN 0-88680-094-3); royalty 35.00. I E Clark.

--No Cheers for the Cheerleaders (Smart Assets) 48p. 1979. pap. 2.50 (ISBN 0-88680-139-7); royalty 35.00 (ISBN 0-317-03562-2). I E Clark.

--Soon to Be a Major Motion Picture. 52p. 1976. pap. 2.50 (ISBN 0-88680-179-6); royalty 35.00 (ISBN 0-317-03589-4). I E Clark.

Cope, Eddie & Cearley, Buster. Airport Nineteen Hundred Four. (Illus.). 40p. 1981. pap. 2.75 (ISBN 0-317-03627-0); royalty 35.00 (ISBN 0-317-03628-9). I E Clark.

Cope, Edward D. The Origin of the Fittest: Essays on Evolution & the Primary Factors of Organic Evolution, 2 vols. in one. LC 73-17813. (Natural Sciencesin America Ser.). 1066p. 1974. Repr. 69.50x (ISBN 0-405-05729-6). Ayer Co Pubs.

--The Vertebrata of the Tertiary Formations of the West, 1 vol. in two, Vol. 3. Sterling, Keir B., ed. LC 77-81093. (Biologists & Their World Ser.). (Illus.). 1978. Repr. of 1883 ed. Set. lib. bdg. 108.00x (ISBN 0-405-10672-6); Vol. 1. lib. bdg. 41.00x (ISBN 0-405-10673-4); Vol. 2. 45.50x (ISBN 0-405-10674-2). Ayer Co Pubs.

Cope, Emma E. How to Decipher & Study Old Documents: Being a Guide to the Reading of Ancient Manuscripts, the Key to the Family Deed Chest. 2nd ed. LC 73-18446. 170p. 1974. Repr. of 1903 ed. 43.00x (ISBN 0-8103-3701-0). Gale.

Cope, Esther. The Life of a Public Man: Edward, First Baron Montague of Boughton. LC 79-54279. (Memoirs Ser.: Vol. 142). 1981. 12.00 (ISBN 0-87169-142-6). Am Philos.

Cope, Esther S. & Coates, Willson H. Short Parliament of Sixteen-Forty: Proceedings. 340p. 1977. 18.50x (ISBN 0-8476-1473-5). Rowman.

Cope, Esther S. & Coates, Willson H., eds. Proceedings of the Short Parliament of 1640, Vol. 19. (RHS Camden Fourth Ser.). 340p. 1977. 15.00 (ISBN 0-901050-37-7, Pub. by Boydell & Brewer). Longwood Pub Group.

Cope, Gabriele E. Coping with the OCLC Subsystems. LC 84-81906. (Illus.). 330p. (Orig.). 1984. 27.75x (ISBN 0-933540-03-5). Ego Bks.

Cope, Gaylor E, Jr. Secret of Success. Russ, Herman, ed. 67p. (Orig.). 1982. pap. 10.00 (ISBN 0-9613391-0-1, SOS-1). G E C.

Cope, Gilbert. Symbolism in the Bible & the Church. 1959. 10.00 (ISBN 0-8022-0300-0). Philos Lib.

Cope, Glen H. & Wilson, Robert. The Effects of State Government on Economic Development in Texas Cities. LC 84-81929. (Policy Research Project Ser.: No. 63). 230p. 1985. 9.00 (ISBN 0-89940-665-3). LBJ Sch Pub Aff.

Cope, Jack. The Adversary Within. 208p. 1982. text ed. 23.75x (ISBN 0-391-02697-6, 40255, Pub. by David Philip Pub Africa). Humanities.

Cope, Jackson. The Metaphoric Structure of Paradise Lost. 1979. Repr. of 1962 ed. lib. bdg. 19.00x (ISBN 0-374-91920-8). Octagon.

Cope, Jackson I. Dramaturgy of the Daemonic: Studies in Anti-Generic Theater from Ruzante to Grimaldi. LC 83-23886. 184p. 1984. text ed. 20.00x (ISBN 0-8018-3120-2). Johns Hopkins.

--Joyce's Cities: Archaeologies of the Soul. LC 80-8056. 176p. 1981. text ed. 15.00x (ISBN 0-8018-2543-1). Johns Hopkins.

Cope, Jackson I. & Green, Geoffrey, eds. Novel vs. Fiction. 168p. 1982. 16.95 (ISBN 0-937664-53-7). Pilgrim Bks OK.

Cope, James B., jt. auth. see Humphrey, Stephen R.

Cope, Jeff & Goddard, Kenneth. Weaponless Control: For Law Enforcement & Security Personnel. (Illus.). 302p. 1979. photocopy ed. 32.75x (ISBN 0-398-03902-X). C C Thomas.

Cope, Ken. Angling Times Book of the Severn. LC 79-51088. (Illus.). 1979. 19.95 (ISBN 0-7153-7791-4). David & Charles.

--Fishing Canals. LC 79-55994. (Illus.). 1980. 17.95 (ISBN 0-7153-7887-2). David & Charles.

Cope, Lloyd. Astrologer's Forecasting Workbook. 182p. 1982. 16.95 (ISBN 0-86690-041-1, 2642-01). Am Fed Astrologers.

Cope, Maurice E. The Venetiam Chapel of the Sacrament in the Sixteenth Century. LC 78-74363. (Outstanding Dissertations in the Fine Arts Ser.). 653p. 1980. lib. bdg. 74.00 (ISBN 0-8240-3952-1). Garland Pub.

Cope, O. Lamar. Matthew: A Scribe Trained for the Kingdom of Heaven. LC 75-36778. (Catholic Biblical Quarterly Monographs: No. 5). 142p. 1976. pap. 3.00 (ISBN 0-915170-04-3). Catholic Biblical.

Cope, Peter, jt. auth. see Cope, Dawn.

Cope, Peter, jt. ed. see Cope, Dawn.

Cope, R. & Sawko, F. Computer Methods for Civil Engineering. 336p. 1982. 19.00 (ISBN 0-07-084129-2). McGraw.

Cope, R. J. & Clark, L. A., eds. Concrete Slabs: Analysis & Design. (Illus.). 512p. 1984. 64.50 (ISBN 0-85334-254-7, I-216-84, Pub. by Elsevier Applied Sci England). Elsevier.

Cope, Robert E. Successful Participative Management in Smaller Companies. 125p. (Orig.). 1982. pap. text ed. 18.00 (ISBN 0-9610044-0-1). QDP Inc.

Cope, Stuart, jt. auth. see Baker, Glenn A.

Cope, Thom K. Executive Guide to Employment Practices. LC 84-62043. 176p. (Orig.). 1984. pap. 19.95 (ISBN 0-939644-14-2). Media Prods & Mktg.

Cope, Thomas P. Philadelphia Merchant: The Diary of Thomas P. Cope, 1800-1851. Harrison, Eliza Cope, intro. by. LC 78-60231. (Illus.). 1978. 19.95 (ISBN 0-89526-689-X). Regnery-Gateway.

Cope, Tonia. Computing Using BASIC: An Interactive Approach. (Computers & Their Applications). 290p. 1981. pap. 19.95x (ISBN 0-470-27280-5). Halsted Pr.

Cope, William, ed. A Glossary of Hampshire Words & Phrases. (English Dialect Society Publications Ser.: No.40). pap. 12.00 (ISBN 0-317-15900-3). Kraus Repr.

Cope, Zachary. History of the Acute Abdomen. 1965. 19.50x (ISBN 0-19-265104-8). Oxford U Pr.

Copeau, Jacques, jt. auth. see Martin du Gard, Roger.

Copel, Sidney L. Psychodiagnostic Study of Children & Adolescents. 216p. 1967. 14.75x (ISBN 0-398-00346-7). C C Thomas.

Copelan, Rachel. How to Hypnotize Yourself & Others. 240p. 1982. pap. text ed. 5.72i (ISBN 0-06-463554-6, EH 554, EH). B&N NY.

--How to Hypnotize Yourself & Others. LC 80-70951. 240p. 1981. 10.95 (ISBN 0-8119-0418-0). Fell.

Copeland, Adrian D. Textbook of Adolescent Psychopathology & Treatment. (Illus.). 152p. 1974. spiral 16.50x (ISBN 0-398-03114-2). C C Thomas.

Copeland, Benny R. & Sullivan, Nelson G. Cost Accounting: Accumulation, Analysis, & Control. 1977. text ed. 26.95 (ISBN 0-8299-0122-1); check figures bklt. avail. (ISBN 0-8299-0470-0); solutions manual avail. (ISBN 0-8299-0469-7). West Pub.

Copeland, Betsy, ed. see Junior League of Jackson, Mississippi.

Copeland, C. T., ed. see Carlyle, Thomas.

Copeland, Carolyn F. Language & Time & Gertrude Stein. LC 75-16491. 192p. 1975. text ed. 15.00x (ISBN 0-87745-059-5); pap. text ed. 7.50 (ISBN 0-87745-062-5). U of Iowa Pr.

Copeland, Charles T. Representative Biographies of English Men of Letters. 1973. Repr. of 1910 ed. 30.00 (ISBN 0-8274-1658-X). R West.

Copeland, Charles Townsend, ed. Letters of Thomas Carlyle to His Youngest Sister. Carlyle, Thomas. 1899. 25.00 (ISBN 0-8274-2848-0). R West.

--Letters of Thomas Carlyle to His Youngest Sister. 276p. 1983. Repr. of 1899 ed. lib. bdg. 48.50 (ISBN 0-8495-0979-3). Arden Lib.

Copeland, Colene. Priscilla. LC 81-80663. (Illus.). 212p. (Orig.). (gr. 3 up). 1981. 6.95 (ISBN 0-939810-01-8); pap. 2.95 (ISBN 0-939810-02-6). Jordan Valley.

Copeland, Colene M. Family Trees & Pedigrees. LC 84-81951. (Illus.). 104p. 1984. pap. 5.95 (ISBN 0-939810-03-4). Jordan Valley.

Copeland, Donna R., et al. The Mind of the Child Who is Said to be Sick. (Illus.). 322p. 1983. 32.75x (ISBN 0-398-04793-6). C C Thomas.

Copeland, E. B. Ferns of Fiji. (BMB Ser.). Repr. of 1929 ed. 14.00 (ISBN 0-527-02165-2). Kraus Repr.

--Hymenophyllum. Bd. with Trichomanes; Genera Hymenophyllacearum. (Illus.). 460p. (Repr. of 1933-38 eds.). 1975. lib. bdg. 56.00x (ISBN 3-87429-079-4). Lubrecht & Cramer.

--Pteridophytes of the Society Islands. (BMB Ser.). Repr. of 1932 ed. 12.00 (ISBN 0-527-02199-7). Kraus Repr.

Copeland, E. L. El Cristianismo y Otras Religiones. Mora, Abdias A., tr. Orig. Title: Christianity & World Religious. (Illus.). 192p. (Span.). 1981. pap. 3.50 (ISBN 0-311-05760-8, Edit Mundo). Casa Bautista.

Copeland, E. Luther. World Mission & World Survival. LC 84-14963. 1985. pap. 5.95 (ISBN 0-8054-6335-6). Broadman.

Copeland, Edward M. Surgical Oncology. LC 82-8608. 723p. 1982. cloth 66.00x (ISBN 0-471-07997-9, Pub. by Wiley Med). Wiley.

Copeland, Gene, jt. auth. see Trever, John.

Copeland, Herbert F. Classification of Lower Organisms. LC 56-7944. (Illus.). 1956. 17.95x (ISBN 0-87015-059-6). Pacific Bks.

Copeland, Irene, jt. auth. see Seidel, Linda.

Copeland, J. E., ed. see Linguistic Association of Canada & the U.S.

Copeland, J. Isaac, jt. ed. see Green, Fletcher M.

Copeland, J. Isaac, ed. see Green, Fletcher M.

Copeland, J. L. Transport Properties of Ionic Liquids. 84p. 1974. 28.95 (ISBN 0-677-02830-X). Gordon.

Copeland, James C. & Marzluf, George A., eds. Regulatory Biology. LC 77-2256. (Ohio State University Biosciences Colloquia: No. 2). (Illus.). 1977. 20.00x (ISBN 0-8142-0262-4). Ohio St U Pr.

Copeland, James E. Stepmatricial Generative Phonology of German. 1970. pap. text ed. 11.20x (ISBN 0-686-22396-9). Mouton.

Copeland, James E., ed. New Directions in Linguistics & Semiotics. LC 83-62329. (New Ser.: No. 2). (Illus.). 269p. 1984. text ed. 25.00x (ISBN 0-89263-253-4). Rice Univ.

Copeland, James E., ed. see Bennett, Michael, et al.

Copeland, John A. A Study of Daniel. 1973. pap. 4.25 (ISBN 0-89137-703-4). Quality Pubns.

--A Study of the Revelation. 1971. pap. 4.25 (ISBN 0-89137-702-6). Quality Pubns.

Copeland, John G. & Kite, Ralph. Puertas a la Lengua Espanola. 2nd ed. 357p. (appendix). 1986. text ed. 18.00 (ISBN 0-394-34247-X, RanC); Puertas al mundo reader. pap. text ed. 12.00 (ISBN 0-394-34246-1); Puertas a la communication activity manual. pap. text ed. 12.00 (ISBN 0-394-34245-3); 9.00 (ISBN 0-394-34244-5); 9.00 (ISBN 0-394-34243-7). Random.

Copeland, John G., et al. Intermediate Spanish: Civilizacion y Cultura. 2nd ed. (Span.). 1981. pap. text ed. 14.96 (ISBN 0-03-057606-7). HR&W.

--Intermediate Spanish: Conversacion y Repaso. 2nd ed. (Span.). 1981. pap. text ed. 18.95 (ISBN 0-03-057601-6); lab manual 11.95 (ISBN 0-03-057603-2); tapes 150.00 (ISBN 0-03-057602-4). HR&W.

--Intermediate Spanish: Literatura y Arte. 2nd ed. (Span.). 1981. pap. text ed. 14.95 (ISBN 0-03-057604-0). HR&W.

--Literatura y Arte. 3rd ed. 272p. 1985. pap. text ed. 12.95 (ISBN 0-03-071629-2). HR&W.

--Telemundo: A Basic Reader. 264p. 1980. pap. text ed. 8.95 (ISBN 0-394-32374-2, RanC). Random.

Copeland, Judith. Modular Crochet: A Revolutionary New Method for Creating Custom-Design Pull-Overs. LC 78-3704. (Illus.). 192p. 1978. 17.50 (ISBN 0-87131-256-5). M Evans.

Copeland, Keith, ed. Aids for the Severely Handicapped. (Illus.). 150p. 1975. 37.00 (ISBN 0-8089-0866-9, 790900). Grune.

Copeland, L. L., jt. auth. see Liddicoat, Richard T., Jr.

Copeland, Lawrence O. Principles of Seed Science & Technology. 2nd ed. (Illus.). 384p. 1984. text ed. write for info. (ISBN 0-8087-4849-1). Burgess.

Copeland, Lennie & Griggs, Lewis. Going International. LC 85-1985. 288p. 1985. 19.95 (ISBN 0-394-54450-1). Random.

Copeland, Lewis. Popular Quotations for All Uses. 29.95 (ISBN 0-89190-474-3, Pub. by Am Repr). Amereon Ltd.

Copeland, Lewis, ed. High School Subjects Self Taught. 3rd rev. ed. LC 64-13835. 1967. 24.95 (ISBN 0-385-04949-8). Doubleday.

--Ten Thousand Jokes, Toasts & Stories. LC 66-737. 1965. 17.95 (ISBN 0-385-00163-0). Doubleday.

Copeland, Lewis & Lamm, Lawrence, eds. World's Great Speeches. 3rd rev. ed. 1958. pap. 9.95 (ISBN 0-486-20468-5). Dover.

Copeland, Lori. All or Nothing. (Candlelight Ecstasy Ser.: No. 217). 192p. (Orig.). 1984. pap. 1.95 (ISBN 0-440-10120-4). Dell.

--Forever After. (Candlelight Ecstasy Ser.: No. 320). (Orig.). 1985. pap. 1.95 (ISBN 0-440-12681-9). Dell.

--High Voltage. (Candlelight Supreme Ser.: No. 76). 288p. (Orig.). 1985. pap. 2.75 (ISBN 0-440-13604-0). Dell.

--A Love of Our Own. (Candlelight Ecstasy Ser.: No. 406). (Orig.). 1986. pap. 2.25 (ISBN 0-440-15009-4). Dell.

--More Than She Bargained For. (Candlelight Supreme Ser.: No. 89). (Orig.). 1985. pap. 2.75 (ISBN 0-440-15820-6). Dell.

--Only the Best. (Candlelight Ecstacy Supreme Ser.: No. 52). (Orig.). 1984. pap. 2.50 (ISBN 0-440-16615-2). Dell.

--Out of Control. (Candlelight Ecstasy Ser.: No. 239). (Orig.). 1984. pap. 1.95 (ISBN 0-440-16751-5). Dell.

--Playing for Keeps. (Candlelight Ecstasy Ser.: No. 134). (Orig.). 1983. pap. 1.95 (ISBN 0-440-17171-7). Dell.

--Rainbow's End. (Candlelight Ecstasy Ser.: No. 294). (Orig.). 1984. pap. 1.95 (ISBN 0-440-17239-X). Dell.

--Spitfire. (Candlelight Ecstasy Romance Ser.: No. 350). (Orig.). 1985. pap. 2.25 (ISBN 0-440-18155-0). Dell.

--A Tempting Stranger. (Candlelight Ecstasy Ser.: No. 181). 192p. (Orig.). 1983. pap. 1.95 (ISBN 0-440-19085-1). Dell.

--Two of a Kind. (Candlelight Ecstasy Supreme Ser.: No. 39). 288p. (Orig.). 1984. pap. 2.50 (ISBN 0-440-19082-7). Dell.

--A Winning Combination. (Candlelight Ecstasy Ser.: No. 267). 192p. (Orig.). 1984. pap. 1.95 (ISBN 0-440-19715-5). Dell.

Copeland, Marion W. Charles Alexander Eastman (Ohiyesa) LC 78-52562. (Western Writers Ser.: No. 33). 1978. pap. 2.00x (ISBN 0-88430-057-9). Boise St Univ.

Copeland, Melvin T. Cotton Manufacturing Industry of the United States. LC 66-23981. Repr. of 1917 ed. lib. bdg. 37.50x (ISBN 0-678-00196-0). Kelley.

--Principles of Merchandising. Assael, Henry, ed. LC 78-277. (Century of Marketing Ser.). 1978. Repr. of 1924 ed. lib. bdg. 30.00x (ISBN 0-405-11182-7). Ayer Co Pubs.

Copeland, Melvin T. & Rogers, Elliot C. The Saga of Cape Ann. 1984. 14.75 (ISBN 0-8446-6067-1). Peter Smith.

Copeland, Mildred, et al. Occupational Therapy for Mentally Retarded Children: Guidelines for Occupational Therapy Aides & Certified Occupational Therapy Assistants. (Illus.). 238p. 1976. pap. text ed. 21.00 (ISBN 0-8391-0930-X). Univ Park.

Copeland, Morris A. Fact & Theory in Economics. Morse, Chandler, ed. LC 73-8564. 347p. 1973. Repr. of 1958 ed. lib. bdg. 65.00x (ISBN 0-8371-6965-8, COFA). Greenwood.

--Trends in Government Financing. LC 75-19710. (National Bureau of Economic Research Ser.). (Illus.). 1975. Repr. 18.00x (ISBN 0-405-07590-1). Ayer Co Pubs.

Copeland, Pamela C. & MacMaster, Richard K. The Five George Masons: Patriots & Planters of Virginia & Maryland. LC 75-8565. (Illus.). 332p. 1975. 19.95x (ISBN 0-8139-0550-8). U Pr of Va.

Copeland, Paul W. The Land & People of Jordan. rev. ed. LC 72-5362. (Portraits of the Nation Ser.). (Illus.). (gr. 6 up). 1972. 11.49i (ISBN 0-397-31403-5). Lipp Jr Bks.

--The Land & People of Syria. rev. ed. LC 77-37732. (Portraits of the Nations Ser.). (Illus.). (gr. 6 up). 1972. lib. bdg. 10.89 (ISBN 0-397-31537-6). Lipp Jr Bks.

Copeland, Peter. Civil War Uniforms Coloring Book. (Illus.). 1977. pap. 2.50 (ISBN 0-486-23535-1). Dover.

--From Antietam to Gettysburg: A Civil War Coloring Book. (Illus.). 48p. (Orig.). (gr. 3 up). 1983. pap. 2.50 (ISBN 0-486-24476-8). Dover.

--Uniforms of the American Revolution Coloring Book. (Illus.). pap. 2.75 (ISBN 0-486-21850-3). Dover.

--Uniforms of the Napoleonic Wars Coloring Book. (Coloring Bks.). (Illus.). 48p. (Orig.). (gr. 3 up). 1982. pap. 2.50 (ISBN 0-486-24390-7). Dover.

Copeland, Peter & Martin, John. Story of Glass Coloring Book. (Illus.). pap. 2.00 (ISBN 0-486-24199-8). Dover.

Copeland, Peter & Peterson, Harold L. America's Fighting Men, Sixteen Hundred Seven to Eighteen Sixty-Four. LC 70-162560. (Illus.). 1976. boxed, ltd. signed ed. (1000 copies) 100.00 (ISBN 0-8212-0403-3). Arma Pr.

Copeland, Peter F. American Military Uniforms, 1639-1968: A Coloring Book. (Coloring Book Ser.). 48p. (Orig.). 1976. pap. 2.50 (ISBN 0-486-23239-5). Dover.

--Antique Airplanes Coloring Book. (Coloring Book Ser.). (Illus.). 48p. (Orig.). 1975. pap. 2.50 (ISBN 0-486-21524-5). Dover.

--Early American Trades Coloring Book. (Illus.). 48p. (Orig.). 1980. pap. 2.50 (ISBN 0-486-23846-6). Dover.

--Everyday Dress of the American Revolution Coloring Book. (Coloring Book Ser.). (Illus.). 48p. (Orig.). 1975. pap. 2.25 (ISBN 0-486-23109-7). Dover.

--Pirates & Buccaneers Coloring Book. (Illus.). 1977. pap. 2.50 (ISBN 0-486-23393-6). Dover.
--Working Dress in Colonial & Revolutionary America. LC 76-15309. (Contributions in American History: No. 58). (Illus.). 1977. lib. bdg. 45.00 (ISBN 0-8371-9033-9, COD/). Greenwood.
--World War One Uniforms Coloring Book. (Illus.). pap. 2.00 (ISBN 0-486-23579-3). Dover.
Copeland, Peter F., illus. The Lewis & Clark Expedition Coloring Book. (Coloring Bks). (Illus.). 48p. (Orig.). (gr. 3up). pap. 2.50 (ISBN 0-486-24557-8). Dover.
Copeland, R. M., et al. Financial Accounting. LC 79-18276. 517p. 1980. 36.45x (ISBN 0-471-17173-5); wkp 340 p. 18.45x (ISBN 0-471-05994-3); S.G. 205 p. 17.45x (ISBN 0-471-02289-6). Wiley.
Copeland, Rachel. Sexually Fulfilled Man. pap. 5.00 (ISBN 0-87980-403-3). Wilshire.
--Sexually Fulfilled Woman. 1983. pap. 5.00 (ISBN 0-87980-402-5). Wilshire.
Copeland, Richard W. How Children Learn Mathematics: Teaching Implications of Piaget's Research. 4th ed. 448p. 1984. text ed. write for info. (ISBN 0-02-324770-3). Macmillan.
--Math Activities for Children: A Diagnostic Approach. (Elementary Curriculum Ser.). 1979. pap. text ed. 13.95 (ISBN 0-675-08316-8). Merrill.
Copeland, Robert. Blue & White Transfer-Printed Pottery. (Album Ser.: No. 97). (Illus.). 32p. (Orig.). 1983. pap. 2.95 (ISBN 0-85263-620-2, Pub. by Shire Pubns England). Seven Hills Bks.
Copeland, Roger & Cohen, Marshall. What Is Dance? Readings in Theory & Criticism. (Illus.). 1983. 25.00 (ISBN 0-19-503217-9); pap. 12.95 GB (ISBN 0-19-503197-0). Oxford U Pr.
Copeland, Ronald M. & Dascher, Paul E. Managerial Accounting: An Introduction to Planning, Information Processing & Control. 2nd ed. LC 74-5147. 658p. 1978. text ed. 38.45x (ISBN 0-471-17171-9); S.G. 15.45x (ISBN 0-471-02346-9). Wiley.
Copeland, Ronald M. & Ingram, Robert W. Municipal Financial Reporting & Disclosure Quality. LC 82-11580. (Illus.). 156p. 1983. pap. text ed. 10.50 (ISBN 0-201-10197-1). Addison-Wesley.
Copeland, Thomas E. & Weston, J. Fred. Financial Theory & Corporate Policy. 2nd ed. LC 82-11662. (Illus.). 704p. 1983. text ed. 36.95 (ISBN 0-201-10292-7); student solution manual 11.50 (ISBN 0-201-10292-7). Addison-Wesley.
Copeland, Thomas E., jt. auth. see Weston, J. Fred.
Copeland, Thomas W. Our Eminent Friend Edmund Burke, Six Essays. LC 76-104217. Repr. of 1949 ed. lib. bdg. 15.00x (ISBN 0-8371-3334-3, COEB). Greenwood.
Copeland, Thomas W. see Burke, Edmund.
Copeland, Tom, ed. Parents in the Workplace: A Management Resource for Employers. (Illus.). 30p. folder 10.00 (ISBN 0-934140-17-0). Toys N Things.
Copeland, Vince. The Built-in U. S. War Drive. 106p. 1980. pap. 2.25 (ISBN 0-89567-038-0). WV Pubs.
--The Built-in U. S. War Drive. 106p. 2.25 (ISBN 0-89567-038-0). World View Pubns.
--Expanding Empire. 68p. 1.50 (ISBN 0-317-36177-5). World View Pubns.
--Southern Populism & Black Labor. 62p. 1.50 (ISBN 0-317-36178-3). World View Pubns.
Copeland, Vince, ed. see Anderson, Osborne P.
Copeland, Vincent. Southern Populism & Black Labor. 62p. pap. 2.00 (ISBN 0-317-03152-X). WV Pubs.
Copeland, Vincent, jt. auth. see Marcy, Sam.
Copeland, W. J., et al, eds. Library of Anglo-Catholic Theology, 18 titles in 81 vols. Repr. of 1841 ed. Set. 2627.50 (ISBN 0-404-52010-3); individual vols. avail. AMS Pr.
Copeland, Wilfred. The World Monetary Chaos & the Cowardice of the United States & of the World Bankers. (Illus.). 1979. deluxe ed. 79.85x (ISBN 0-930008-20-0). Inst Econ Pol.
Copely, Ursula E., jt. ed. see Slater, Don.
Copeman, George. The Managing Director. 2nd ed. 283p. 1982. text ed. 36.75x (ISBN 0-09-147280-6, Pub. by Busn Bks England). Brookfield Pub Co.
Copeman, George, et al. Shared Ownership: How to Use Capital Incentives to Sustain Business Growth. LC 84-12929. 251p. 1984. text ed. 38.50x (ISBN 0-566-02533-7). Gower Pub Co.
Copen, Melvyn R., jt. auth. see Richman, Barry M.
Copenhaver, Brian. Symphorien Champier & the Reception of the Occultist Tradition in Renaissance France. 1978. text ed. 38.80x (ISBN 90-279-7647-3). Mouton.
Copenhaver, Edward H. Surgery of the Vulva & Vagina: A Practical Guide. (Illus.). 100p. 1981. text ed. 31.95 (ISBN 0-7216-2718-8). Saunders.
Copernicus, Nicholas. De Revolutionibus Orbium Coelestium. 1965. Repr. of 1543 ed. Facsimile Ed. 50.00 (ISBN 0-384-09806-1). Johnson Repr.
--On the Revolutions: Manuscript. facsimile ed. (Illus.). 1972. Repr. 85.00 (ISBN 0-384-09805-3). Johnson Repr.
Copes, W. S., jt. auth. see Sacco, W. J.
Copetas, A. Craig. Metal Men: Marc Rich & the Ten Billion Dollar Scam. LC 85-6540. 224p. 1985. 17.95 (ISBN 0-399-13078-0). Putnam Pub Group.
Copi. Plays: Includes Eva Peron, Vol. 1. Taylor, Lee, tr. 1980. pap. 4.95 (ISBN 0-7145-3563-X). Riverrun NY.
Copi, Irving M. Informal Logic. 520p. 1986. pap. text ed. price not set (ISBN 0-02-324940-4). Macmillan.
--Introduction to Logic. 6th ed. 1982. text ed. write for info. (ISBN 0-02-324920-X). Macmillan.
--An Introduction to Logic. 7th ed. 1986. text ed. price not set (ISBN 0-02-325020-8). Macmillan.
--Symbolic Logic. 5th ed. 1979. text ed. write for info. (ISBN 0-02-324980-3). Macmillan.
Copi, Irving M. & Beard, Robert W. Essays on Wittgenstein's Tractatus. LC 72-91932. 1973. 20.50h (ISBN 0-02-843180-4). Hafner.
Copinger, H. B., ed. see Merryweather, F. Somner.
Copinschi, G. & Jaquet, P., eds. Lipo-Corticotropic Hormones & Cushing's Disease. (Journal: Hormone Research: Vol. 13, No. 4-5). (Illus.). 152p. 1981. pap. 28.25 (ISBN 3-8055-3410-8). S Karger.
Copinschi, G., jt. ed. see Van Cauter, E.
Coplan, Kate. Effective Library Exhibits: How to Prepare & Promote Good Displays. rev., 2nd ed. LC 74-4428. (Illus.). 176p. 1974. lib. bdg. 12.50 (ISBN 0-379-00265-5). Oceana.
--Poster Ideas & Bulletin Board Techniques. 2nd ed. LC 80-24871. 248p. 1981. lib. bdg. 25.00 (ISBN 0-379-20333-2). Oceana.
Coplan, Kate & Rosenthal, Constance. Guide to Better Bulletin Boards. LC 76-102937. 232p. 1970. 20.00 (ISBN 0-379-00369-4). Oceana.
Copland, Aaron. Copland on Music. LC 76-13512. 1976. Repr. of 1960 ed. lib. bdg. 29.50 (ISBN 0-306-70775-6). Da Capo.
--Copland on Music. 1963. pap. 7.95 (ISBN 0-393-00198-9, Norton Lib). Norton.
--Music & Imagination. LC 52-9385. (Charles Eliot Norton Lectures Ser: 1951-1952). 1952. pap. 3.95 (ISBN 0-674-58915-7). Harvard U Pr.
--New Music: 1900-1960. rev. ed. LC 68-10878. 1968 o.p. 7.50; pap. 5.95, 1969 (ISBN 0-393-00239-X). Norton.
--What to Listen for in Music. rev. ed. (Illus.). 1957. 16.95 (ISBN 0-07-013089-2). McGraw.
--What to Listen for in Music. rev. ed. (YA) (RL 9). 1964. pap. 2.75 (ISBN 0-451-62373-8, ME2265, Ment). NAL.
Copland, Aaron & Perlis, Vivian. Copland: Nineteen Hundred to Nineteen Forty-Two, Vol. 1. 412p. 1984. 24.95 (ISBN 0-312-16962-0). St Martin.
Copland, Douglas B. Australia in the World Crisis, 1929-1933. LC 74-111474. (BCL Ser. I). Repr. of 1934 ed. 19.00 (ISBN 0-404-01718-5). AMS Pr.
--The Changing Structure of the Western Economy. LC 65-9230. (Beatty Memorial Lectures Ser.). pap. 24.00 (ISBN 0-317-20720-2, 2023827). Bks Demand UMI.
Copland, Ian. The British Raj & the Indian Prices: Paramountcy in Western India, 1857-1930. 358p. 1982. cloth 45.00x (Pub. by Sangam Bks England). State Mutual Bk.
--The British Raj & the Indian Princes. 1982. 18.50x (ISBN 0-8364-0893-4, Pub. by Macmillan India). South Asia Bks.
--Jawaharlal Nehru of India Eighteen Eighty-Nine to Nineteen Sixty-Four. (Leaders of Asia Ser.). 53p. (Orig.). 1980. pap. 3.00x (ISBN 0-7022-1506-6). U of Queensland Pr.
Copland, Robert, tr. see Aristotle.
Copland, Samuel. History of the Island of Madagascar. LC 72-106856. Repr. of 1822 ed. 20.75x (ISBN 0-8371-3478-1, CMA&, Pub. by Negro U Pr). Greenwood.
Coplans, John. Don Judd. LC 78-162345. (Pasadena Art Museum Publications). (Illus.). 1971. 7.95x (ISBN 0-912158-72-7). Hennessey.
Coplans, M. P. & Green, R. A. Anaesthesia & Sedation in Dentistry. (Monographs in Anaesthesiology: Vol. 12). 1983. 64.00 (ISBN 0-444-80503-6, I-449-83). Elsevier.
Coplen, Ron, compiled by. Special Libraries: A Cumulative Index, 1971-1980. 94p. 1982. lib. bdg. 18.75 (ISBN 0-87111-314-7). SLA.
Copleston, Edward. Advice to a Young Reviewer. 1927. Repr. 10.00 (ISBN 0-8274-1825-6). R West.
Copleston, F. C. Aquinas. 272p. 1956. pap. 4.95 (ISBN 0-14-020349-4, Pelican). Penguin.
Copleston, F. W., et al, eds. Advanced Pipe & Tube Welding. (Engineering Craftsmen Ser.: No. F21). (Illus.). 1970. spiral bdg. 45.00x (ISBN 0-85083-131-8). Trans-Atlantic.
Copleston, Frederick. Arthur Schopenhauer: Philosopher of Pessimism. 216p. 1975. Repr. of 1946 ed. text ed. 18.50x (ISBN 0-06-491281-7). B&N Imports.
--Friedrich Nietzsche: Philosopher of Culture. 2nd ed. LC 74-15182. 273p. 1975. text ed. 16.50x (ISBN 0-06-491283-3). B&N Imports.
--History of Philosophy, 10 vols. Incl. Vol. 1. Greece & Rome. 17.95 (ISBN 0-8091-0065-7); Vol. 2. Medieval Philosophy - Augustine to Scotus. 18.95 (ISBN 0-8091-0066-5); Vol. 3. Ockham to Suarez. 17.95 (ISBN 0-8091-0067-3); Vol. 4. Descartes to Leibniz. 16.95 (ISBN 0-8091-0068-1); Vol. 5. Hobbes to Hume. 17.95 (ISBN 0-8091-0069-X); Vol. 6. Wolff to Kant. 17.95 (ISBN 0-8091-0070-3); Vol. 7. Fichte to Nietzsche. 17.95 (ISBN 0-8091-0071-1); Vol. 8. Bentham to Russell. 18.95 (ISBN 0-8091-0072-X); Vol. 9. Maine de Bira to Sartre. 1976. 17.95 (ISBN 0-8091-0196-3). Vols. 1-9. Paulist Pr.
--History of Philosophy, Vols. I-III. LC 84-25889. 1640p. 1985. Bk. I. pap. 16.95 (ISBN 0-385-23031-1, Im). Doubleday.
--History of Philosophy, Vols. IV-VI. LC 84-25889. 1343p. 1985. Bk. 2. pap. 16.95 (ISBN 0-385-23032-X, Im). Doubleday.
--History of Philosophy, Vols. VII-IX. LC 84-25889. 1608p. 1985. Bk. 3. pap. 16.95 (ISBN 0-385-23033-8, Im). Doubleday.
--History of Philosophy: Greece & Rome, 2 pts, Vol. 1. Pt. 1. pap. 5.50 (ISBN 0-385-00210-6, Im); Pt. 2. pap. 4.50 (ISBN 0-385-00211-4). Doubleday.
--History of Philosophy: Late Mediaeval & Renaissance Philosophy, Vol. 3. 1953. (Im); pap. 4.95 pt. 2 (ISBN 0-385-06532-9, Im, D136B). Doubleday.
--History of Philosophy: Mediaeval Philosophy, 2 pts, Vol. 2. Pt. 1. pap. 4.95 (ISBN 0-385-01631-X, Im); Pt. 2. pap. 5.50 (ISBN 0-385-03235-8, Im). Doubleday.
--History of Philosophy: Modern Philosophy: The French Enlightenment to Kant, Vol. 6. (Im); Pt. 2. pap. 4.50 (ISBN 0-385-06541-8, Im). Doubleday.
--History of Philosophy: Seventeenth & Eighteenth Century British Philosophers, 2 pts, Vol. 5. Pt. 1. pap. 3.95 (ISBN 0-385-06540-X, Im); Pt. 2. pap. 3.95 (ISBN 0-385-01634-4). Doubleday.
--On the History of Philosophy. LC 79-56223. 160p. 1980. text ed. 24.50x (ISBN 0-06-491285-X). B&N Imports.
--Philosophers & Philosophies. 272p. 1976. Repr. of 1955 ed. 24.50x (ISBN 0-06-491278-7). B&N Imports.
--Philosophies & Cultures. 1980. 19.95x (ISBN 0-19-213960-6). Oxford U Pr.
--Religion & the One: Philosophies East & West. LC 81-5372. (Gifford Lectures, 1980 Ser.). 320p. 1981. 17.50 (ISBN 0-8245-0092-X). Crossroad NY.
--Religion & the One: Philosophies East & West. 288p. 1982. 60.00x (ISBN 0-85532-510-0, Pub. by Search Pr England). State Mutual Bk.
--Thomas Aquinas. LC 76-46842. 272p. 1976. Repr. of 1955 ed. text ed. 24.50x (ISBN 0-06-491277-9). B&N Imports.
Copleston, Frederick C. Medieval Philosophy. LC 53-2190. (Methuen's Home Study Bks.). pap. 50.00 (ISBN 0-317-09453-X, 2013153). Bks Demand UMi.
Copleston, Frederick J. A History of Philosophy-Maine De Biran to Sartre: Part II Bengson to Sartre, Vol. 9. 1977. pap. 4.50 (ISBN 0-385-12926-2, Im). Doubleday.
Copleston, Fredrick C. Philosophy in Russia: Herzen to Lenin. LC 85-40601. 320p. 1985. text ed. 29.95x (ISBN 0-268-01558-9, 85-15587, Dist. by Har-Row). U of Notre Dame Pr.
Copleston, Reginald S. Aeschylus. 1901. 25.00 (ISBN 0-8274-1828-0). R West.
--Buddhism, Primitive & Present in Magdha & in Ceylon. 2nd ed. LC 78-72398. Repr. of 1908 ed. 28.00 (ISBN 0-404-17257-1). AMS Pr.
Copley. Political Career of C. Rajagopalachari, 1937-1954. 1980. 18.00x (ISBN 0-8364-0586-2, Pub. by Macmillan India). South Asia Bks.
Copley, Alfred L. & Seaman, Geoffrey V., eds. Surface Phenomena in Hemorheology: Their Theoretical, Experimental & Clinical Aspects, Vol. 416. 155.00x (ISBN 0-89766-226-1); pap. 155.00x (ISBN 0-89766-227-X). NY Acad Sci.
Copley, Anthony. Fig for Fortune. (Spencer Society Publications Ser.: No. 35). 1966. Repr. of 1596 ed. 24.50 (ISBN 0-8337-0656-X). B Franklin.
Copley, Eleanor. The User Friendly Cookbook: Easy to Use Recipes for Busy People. 200p. 1985. 14.95 (ISBN 0-943066-05-0). CTPI NVP.
Copley, F. O., tr. see Lucretius.
Copley, Frank B. Frederick W. Taylor, Father of Scientific Management, 2 Vols. LC 68-55515. (Illus.). Repr. of 1923 ed. 67.50x (ISBN 0-678-00461-7). Kelley.
Copley, Frank O. The Aeneid Second Vergil. 1975. pap. text ed. write for info. Macmillan.
--Exclusus Amator: A Study in Latin Love Poetry. (APA Philological Monographs). pap. 18.00 (ISBN 0-89130-708-7, 40-00-17). Scholars Pr GA.
--Menaechmi: Plautus. 1956. pap. text ed. write for info. (ISBN 0-02-325060-7). Macmillan.
Copley, Frank O. & Hadas, Moses. Nine Plays of Terence, Platetus, & Seneca: Roman Drama. 1965. pap. text ed. write for info. (ISBN 0-02-325040-2). Macmillan.
Copley, Frank O., ed. see Terence.
Copley, Frank O., ed. & tr. see Virgil.
Copley, Frank O., tr. Roman Drama: Nine Plays of Terence, Plautus & Seneca. LC 64-66074. (YA) (gr. 11 up). 1965. pap. 11.49 scp (ISBN 0-672-60455-8, LLA209). Bobbs.
Copley, Frank O., tr. see Cicero, M. T.
Copley, Frank O., tr. see Plautus.
Copley, Frank O., tr. see Terence.
Copley, Frank S. A Set of Alphabets in Modern Use with Examples of Each Style; Letters, Cyphers, Figures, Monograms, Borders, Compasses & Flourishes. 200p. pap. 15.00 (ISBN 0-87556-490-9). Saifer.
Copley, Frederick S. Art Deco Alphabets: A Treasury of Original Alphabets from the 1920s and 1930s. (Graphic Arts Archives Ser.). (Illus.). 128p. (Orig.). 1985. pap. 8.95 (ISBN 0-915590-77-8). Main Street.
Copley, J. Shift of Meaning. 1978. Repr. of 1961 ed. lib. bdg. 25.00 (ISBN 0-8495-0719-7). Arden Lib.
Copley, J. A. The Music of Peter Warlock: A Critical Survey of One of the Great Song-Writers of the English Tradition. 334p. 1981. 45.00x (ISBN 0-234-77249-2, Pub. by Dobson Bks England). State Mutual Bk.
Copley, John S. Letters & Papers of John Singleton Copley & Henry Pelham, 1739-1776. LC 78-100615. (Library of American Art Ser.). (Illus.). 1970. Repr. of 1914 ed. lib. bdg. 45.00 (ISBN 0-306-71406-X). Da Capo.
Copley, John S. & Pelham, Henry. Letters & Papers of J. S. Copley & Henry Pelham, 1739-1776. LC 72-456. Repr. of 1914 ed. 27.50 (ISBN 0-404-01719-3). AMS Pr.
Copley, R. Evan. Harmony: Baroque to Contemporary, Pt. I. 198p. 1978. pap. text ed. 10.60x (ISBN 0-87563-158-4). Stipes.
--Harmony: Baroque to Contemporary, Pt. II. 198p. 1979. pap. text ed. 11.60x (ISBN 0-87563-175-4). Stipes.
Copley, Stephen. Literature & the Social Order in Eighteenth Century England. LC 84-14940. 204p. 1984. 31.00 (ISBN 0-7099-0755-9, Pub. by Croom Helm Ltd); pap. 15.50 (ISBN 0-7099-3400-9). Longwood Pub Group.
Copley, Thomas. Letters of Sir Thomas Copley to Queen Elizabeth & Her Ministers. Christie, Richard C., ed. LC 74-80263. (Research & Source Works Ser.: No. 631). 1971. Repr. lib. bdg. 32.00 (ISBN 0-8337-0655-1). B Franklin.
Copley, William N. CPLY: Reflection on a Past Life. 1979. pap. 3.00 (ISBN 0-686-51194-8). Inst for the Arts.
Coplin, Maxine. A National Guide to Guest Homes. (Illus., Orig.). 1981. pap. 4.95 (ISBN 0-686-29699-0, 0-96057804). Home on Arrange.
Coplin, William. Teaching Policy Studies. 1978. pap. 8.00 (ISBN 0-918592-26-7). Policy Studies.
Coplin, William D. & O'Leary, Michael K. Introduction to Political Risk Analysis. (Learning Packages in the Policy Sciences Ser.: No. 24). (Illus.). 104p. (Orig.). 1983. pap. text ed. 5.75x (ISBN 0-936826-19-3). Pol Stud Assocs.
--Political Analysis Through the Prince System. (Learning Packages in the Policy Sciences Ser.: No. 23). (Illus.). 100p. (Orig.). 1983. pap. text ed. 5.50x (ISBN 0-936826-18-5). Pol Stud Assocs.
Coplin, William D. & Rochester, J. Martin. Dyadic Disputes, 1920-1968. 2nd ed. 1976. codebk write for info. (ISBN 0-89138-021-3). ICPSR.
Coplin, William D. & O'Leary, Michael K., eds. Basic Policy Studies Skills. (Illus.). 170p. 1981. pap. text ed. 7.50x (ISBN 0-936826-14-2). Pol Stud Assocs.
Coplon, Jennifer, jt. auth. see Barnes, Beverly C.
Copp, David & Wendell, Susan, eds. Pornography & Censorship. LC 83-61031. 414p. 1982. 23.95 (ISBN 0-87975-181-9); pap. 14.95 (ISBN 0-87975-182-7). Prometheus Bks.
Copp, David & Zimmerman, David, eds. Morality, Reason & Truth: New Essays on the Foundations of Ethics. LC 84-13424. 342p. 1985. 36.50x (ISBN 0-8476-7368-5); pap. 17.95x (ISBN 0-8476-7369-3). Rowman & Allanheld.
Copp, David H., jt. auth. see Crawford, Rudd A., Jr.
Copp, Dewitt S. A Few Great Captains. LC 78-22310. (Illus.). 1980. 19.95 (ISBN 0-385-13310-3). Doubleday.
--Forged in Fire. LC 81-43265. (Illus.). 528p. 1982. 19.95 (ISBN 0-385-15911-0). Doubleday.
Copp, E. Anthony. Regulating Competition in Oil: Government Intervention in the U.S. Refining Industry, 1948-1975. LC 76-19795. (Texas A&M University Economics Ser.: No. 1). 304p. 1976. 24.50x (ISBN 0-89096-014-3). Tex A&M Univ Pr.
Copp, Henry N. Manual for the Use of Prospectors on the Mineral Lands of the U. S. 5th ed. Bruchey, Stuart, ed. LC 78-53538. (Development of Public Lands Law in the U. S. Ser.). 1979. Repr. of 1897 ed. lib. bdg. 13.00x (ISBN 0-405-11371-4). Ayer Co Pubs.
--Public Land Laws. Bruchey, Stuart, ed. LC 78-53559. (Development of Public Land Law in the U. S. Ser.). 1979. Repr. of 1875 ed. lib. bdg. 63.00x (ISBN 0-405-11372-2). Ayer Co Pubs.
--United States Mineral Lands. Bruchey, Stuart, ed. LC 78-53539. (Development of Public Land Law in the U. S. Ser.). 1979. Repr. of 1882 ed. lib. bdg. 45.00x (ISBN 0-405-11373-0). Ayer Co Pubs.
Copp, James H., ed. see Iowa State University-Center For Agricultural And Economic Development.
Copp, John D. & Pula, Faafouina I. The Samoan Dance of Life: An Anthropological Narrative. LC 83-26370. xvi, 176p. 1984. Repr. of 1950 ed. lib. bdg. 27.50x (ISBN 0-313-24244-5, COSD). Greenwood.
Copp, Laurel A., ed. Care of the Aging. (Recent Advances in Nursing Ser.: Vol. 2). (Illus.). 238p. 1981. pap. text ed. 16.25 (ISBN 0-443-02187-2). Churchill.

Coradini, A. & Fulchignoni, M., eds. The Comparative Study of the Planets. 1982. 59.50 (ISBN 90-277-1406-1, Pub. by Reidel Holland). Kluwer Academic.

Coram, T. C. & Hill, R. W., eds. New Ideas in Industrial Marketing. (Illus.). 319p. 1970. text ed. 25.00x (ISBN 0-8464-1266-7). Beekman Pubs.

Coran, James L., jt. auth. see Neslon-Rees, W. A.

Coran, Terence. Enciclopedia De la Decoracion. 3rd ed. 343p. (Espn.). 1978. 65.00 (ISBN 84-278-0451-2, S-50463). French & Eur.

Corapcioglu, M. Yavuz, jt. ed. see Bear, Jacob.

Corasco, Francesco, ed. see Matulich, Loretta K.

Coray, G., jt. ed. see Nievergelt, J.

Corballis, Michael C. Human Laterality. (Perspectives in Neurolinguistics & Psycholinguistics Ser.). 1983. 29.50 (ISBN 0-12-188180-6). Acad Pr.

Corballis, Michael C. & Beale, Ivan L. The Ambivalent Mind: The Neuropsychology of Left & Right. LC 83-4026. (Illus.). 328p. 1983. lib. bdg. 25.95x (ISBN 0-88229-475-X). Nelson-Hall.

--The Psychology of Left & Right. 240p. 1976. text ed. 24.95x (ISBN 0-89859-114-7). L Erlbaum Assocs.

Corballis, R. & Harding, J. M. John Webster Concordance, Vol. 2, Pt. 3. (Jacobean Drama Studies: No. 70). 1979. pap. text ed. 25.50x (ISBN 0-391-01761-6). Humanities.

Corballis, Richard. A Concordance to the Works of John Webster, Vol. 2, Pt. 3. Harding, J. M., ed. (Salzburg Institute for English Literature Ser.: Vol. 70). 1979. pap. text ed. 25.50x (ISBN 0-391-01760-8). Humanities.

--George Chapman's Minor Translations. (Salzburg-Jacobean Drama Studies: No. 98). 115p. 1984. pap. text ed. 25.50x (ISBN 0-391-03211-9, Pub. by Salzburg Austria). Humanities.

--Stoppard: The Mystery & the Clockwork. 208p. 1984. pap. 9.95 (ISBN 0-416-00981-6, NO. 9148); 20.00 (ISBN 0-416-01011-3, NO. 9172). Methuen Inc.

Corballis, Richard & Harding, J. M. A Concordance to the Works of John Webster, Vol. 1 Pt. 2. (Salzburg Studies in English Literature, Jacobean Drama: No. 70-1). (Orig.). 1980. pap. text ed. 25.50x (ISBN 0-391-01316-5). Humanities.

--A Concordance to the Works of John Webster, Vol. 1 Pt. 3. (Salzburg Studies in English Literature, Jacobean Drama Ser.: 70). (Orig.). 1979. pap. text ed. 25.50x (ISBN 0-391-01723-3). Humanities.

--A Concordance to the Works of John Webster, Vol. 1 Pt. 4. (Salzburg Studies in English Literature, Jacobean Drama Ser.). (Orig.). 1979. pap. text ed. 25.50x (ISBN 0-391-01717-9). Humanities.

--A Concordance to the Works of John Webster, Vol. 2, Pt. 4. (Salzburg Studies in English Literature, Jacobean Drama: No. 70-2). 1979. pap. text ed. 25.50x (ISBN 0-391-01317-3). Humanities.

--A Concordance to the Works of John Webster, Vol. 2, Pt. 1. (Salzburg Studies in English Literature, Jacobean Drame Ser.: 70). (Orig.). 1979. pap. text ed. 25.50x (ISBN 0-391-01724-1). Humanities.

--A Concordance to the Works of John Webster, Vol. 3 Pt. 1. (Salzburg Studies in English Literature, Jacobean Drama: No. 70-3). (Orig.). 1980. pap. text ed. 25.50x (ISBN 0-391-01318-1). Humanities.

--A Concordance to the Works of John Webster: Vol. 4, Appendix, Sir Thomas Wyatt. (Salzburg Studies in English Literature, Jacobean Drama Ser.: No. 70-4). (Orig.). 1979. pap. text ed. 25.50x (ISBN 0-391-01213-4). Humanities.

Corballis, Richard & Harding, John. A Concordance to the Works of John Webster, Vol. 2 Pt. 2. (Salzburg Studies in English Literature, Jacobean Drama Ser.: 70). (Orig.). 1979. pap. text ed. 25.50x (ISBN 0-391-01737-3). Humanities.

Corbally, John E., jt. ed. see Sergiovanni, Thomas J.

Corbally, Marguerite. The Partners. LC 77-74121. 1977. pap. text ed. 4.95x (ISBN 0-8134-1953-0). Interstate.

Corban, Herbert C. Classical & Quantum Theories of Spinning Partiles. LC 68-5706. pap. 73.30 (ISBN 0-317-08304-X, 2016288). Bks Demand UMI.

Corbeil, J., ed. see Viller, M. & Drollet, A.

Corbeil, Richard L., Sr. Tele-Robotics: The New Medium for Marketing, Sales, & Politics: An Innovative Breakthrough in Communications & Target Marketing. (Illus.). 112p. 1984. 10.00 (ISBN 0-682-40137-4). Exposition Pr FL.

Corbeiller, Clare Le see Parker, James & Le Corbeiller, Clare.

Corbeiller, Philippe E. Le see Le Corbeiller, Philippe E.

Corben, H. C. & Stehle, Philip. Classical Mechanics. 2nd ed. LC 74-141. 402p. 1974. Repr. of 1960 ed. 25.00 (ISBN 0-88275-162-X). Krieger.

Corben, Richard. Den: Muvovum. (Den Ser.). (Illus.). 120p. 1984. pap. 10.95 (ISBN 0-87416-004-9). Catalan Communs.

--Den: Neverwhere. 2nd ed. (Den Ser.). (Illus.). 120p. (Orig.). 1984. pap. 10.95 (ISBN 0-87416-003-0). Catalan Communs.

--Werewolf. (Illus.). 76p. 1985. 12.95 (ISBN 0-87416-007-3). Catalan Communs.

Corben, Richard, et al. Underground. (Richard Corben Complete Works: No. 1). (Illus.). 80p. (Orig.). 1985. pap. 10.95 (ISBN 0-87416-018-9). Catalan Communs.

Corbet & Pendlebury. Butterflies of the Malay Peninsular. 3rd, rev. ed. Eliot, J. N., rev. by. 90.00x (ISBN 0-317-07045-2, Pub. by EW Classey UK). State Mutual Bk.

Corbet, jt. auth. see Ovenden.

Corbet, G. B. The Mammals of the Palaearctic Region: A Taxonomic Review. LC 77-90899. (Illus.). 350p. 1978. 55.00x (ISBN 0-8014-1171-8). Cornell U Pr.

--Mammals of the Palaearctic Region: A Taxonomic Review - Supplement. 46p. 1984. pap. text ed. 12.00 (ISBN 0-565-00944-3, Pub by Brit Mus Nat Hist England). Sabbot-Natural Hist Bks.

--Terrestrial Mammals of Western Europe. LC 66-23640. (Illus.). 1966. 14.95 (ISBN 0-8023-1030-3). Dufour.

Corbet, G. B. & Hill, J. E. A World List of Mammalian Species. LC 79-53396. 226p. 1980. 49.50x (ISBN 0-8014-1260-9). Cornell U Pr.

Corbet, John H. Physical Geography Manual. 1976. pap. text ed. 13.95 (ISBN 0-8403-0963-5). Kendall-Hunt.

Corbet, Philip S. A Biology of Dragonflies. 247p. 1983. 69.00x (ISBN 0-317-07032-0, Pub. by EW Classey UK). State Mutual Bk.

Corbet, Philip S., jt. auth. see Walker, Edmund M.

Corbett. Roman Art. 2.98 (ISBN 0-517-30375-2). Outlet Bk Co.

Corbett & Ovenden. The Mammals of Britain & Europe. pap. 15.95 (ISBN 0-00-219774-X, Collins Pub England). Greene.

Corbett, Arthur. History of the Institution of Engineers: Australia 1919-1969. 288p. 1973. text ed. 19.50x (ISBN 0-207-12516-3, Pub. by Inst Engineering Australia). Brookfield Pub Co.

Corbett, Bayliss, compiled by. Spectrum: A Guide to the Independent Press & Informative Organizations. 15th ed. LC 81-642893. 62p. 1985. pap. 10.00 (ISBN 0-933152-06-X). Bayliss Corbett.

Corbett, Bernard. Boston Sports Trivia. LC 89-70069. (Illus.). 180p. (Orig.). 1985. pap. 7.95 (ISBN 0-933341-02-4). Quinlan Pr.

Corbett, Bernard, jt. auth. see White, Morgan, Jr.

Corbett, Bill. Runaway Pond. 1981. pap. 3.95 (ISBN 0-918222-26-5). Apple Wood.

Corbett, Charles D. The Latin American Military As a Socio-Political Force: Case Studies of Bolivia & Argentina. new ed. LC 72-86566. (Monographs in International Affairs). 143p. 1972. text ed. 6.95 (ISBN 0-933074-18-2); pap. text ed. 4.95 (ISBN 0-933074-19-0). AISI.

Corbett, Doris S., jt. auth. see Wright, J. E.

Corbett, E. V. Introduction to Librarianship. 1968. 12.50 (ISBN 0-8022-0303-5). Philos Lib.

Corbett, Edmund V. Illustrations Collection: Its Formation, Classification & Exploitation. LC 72-164185. (Illus.). 164p. 1971. Repr. of 1941 ed. 40.00x (ISBN 0-8103-3786-X). Gale.

Corbett, Edward E. & Jensema, Carl J. Teachers of the Deaf: Descriptive Profiles. LC 80-84605. xviii, 158p. 1981. 3.25 (ISBN 0-913580-64-3). Gallaudet Coll.

Corbett, Edward P. Classical Rhetoric for the Modern Student. 2nd ed. 1971. text ed. 19.95x (ISBN 0-19-501382-4). Oxford U Pr.

--Little English Handbook: Choices & Conventions. 4th ed. 1984. pap. text ed. 9.25x (ISBN 0-673-15879-9). Scott F.

--The Little Rhetoric. LC 76-45081. 1977. pap. text ed. 13.65x (ISBN 0-673-15663-X). Scott F.

--The Little Rhetoric & Handbook. 2nd ed. 550p. 1982. pap. text ed. 16.55x (ISBN 0-673-15733-4). Scott F.

Corbett, Edward P. & Burke, Virginia M., eds. The New Century Composition-Rhetoric. LC 73-150594. 1971. 34.50x (ISBN 0-89197-315-X); pap. text ed. 19.95x (ISBN 0-89197-865-8). Irvington.

Corbett, Edward P., jt. ed. see Tate, Gary.

Corbett, Edward P. J. The Little Rhetoric & Handbook with Readings. 1983. pap. text ed. 18.65x (ISBN 0-673-15830-6). Scott F.

Corbett, Grahame. What Number Now? LC 82-70034. (Very First Bk.). (Illus.). 14p. (ps-k). 1982. bds. 3.50 (ISBN 0-8037-9735-4). Dial Bks Young.

--Who Is Next? LC 82-70036. (Very First Bk.). (Illus.). 14p. (ps-k). 1982. 3.50 (ISBN 0-8037-9759-1). Dial Bks Young.

--Who's Inside? LC 82-70033. (Very First Bk.). (Illus.). 14p. (ps-k). 1982. 3.50 (ISBN 0-8037-9726-5). Dial Bks Young.

Corbett, Greville. Hierarchies, Targets & Controllers: Agreement Patterns in Slavic. LC 83-61325. 272p. 1983. text ed. 24.95x (ISBN 0-271-00354-5). Pa St U Pr.

Corbett, H. Dickson, et al. School Context & School Change: Implications for Effective Planning. 1984. text ed. 18.95x (ISBN 0-8077-2704-0). Tchrs Coll.

Corbett, H. Roger, Jr. Virginia White Water. 1977. pap. 8.95 (ISBN 0-686-22838-3). Corbett.

Corbett, J. R., et al, eds. The Biochemical Mode of Action of Pesticides. 2nd ed. 1984. 65.00 (ISBN 0-12-187860-0). Acad Pr.

Corbett, J. S. Sir Francis Drake. LC 68-25228. (English Biography Ser., No. 31). 1969. Repr. of 1890 ed. lib. bdg. 49.95x (ISBN 0-8383-0932-1). Haskell.

Corbett, J. W. & Watkins, G. D. Radiation Effects in Semiconductors. 456p. 1971. 119.25 (ISBN 0-677-15080-6). Gordon.

Corbett, Jack. Hark! Who's That Yoohooing in My Jungle? LC 79-88235. (Illus.). 1979. pap. 3.95 (ISBN 0-934574-00-6). JC-DC Cartoons.

Corbett, James A. Praepostini Tractatus De Officiis. (Mediaeval Studies Ser.: Vol. 21). (Lat). 1969. 21.95x (ISBN 0-268-00326-2). U of Notre Dame Pr.

Corbett, James A., ed. Catalog of Medieval & Renaissance Manuscripts of the University of Notre Dame. 1978. text ed. 25.00x (ISBN 0-268-00723-3). U of Notre Dame Pr.

--De Instructione Puerorum of William of Tournai. (Text & Studies Ser). pap. 6.00x (ISBN 0-268-00075-1). U of Notre Dame Pr.

Corbett, James A. & Garvin, Joseph N., eds. Summa Contra Haereticos. (Mediaeval Studies Ser.: No. 15). (Lat). 1968. 23.95 (ISBN 0-268-00268-1). U of Notre Dame Pr.

Corbett, James A. & Moore, Philip S., eds. Petri Pictaviensis Allegoriae Super Tabernaculum Moysi. (Mediaeval Studies Ser.: No. 3). 1938. 17.95 (ISBN 0-268-00207-X). U of Notre Dame Pr.

Corbett, James J. The Roar of the Crowd. LC 76-6330. (Irish American Ser). 1976. Repr. of 1925 ed. 26.50 (ISBN 0-405-09326-8). Ayer Co Pubs.

Corbett, James W. & Ianniello, Louis C., eds. Radiation-Induced Voids in Metals: Proceedings. LC 72-600048. (AEC Symposium Ser.). 884p. 1972. pap. 30.00 (ISBN 0-87079-320-9, CONF-710601); microfiche 4.50 (ISBN 0-87079-321-7, CONF-710601). DOE.

Corbett, Jan. Creative Youth Leadership. LC 77-778950. 1977. pap. 4.95 (ISBN 0-8170-0761-X). Judson.

Corbett, Jan, ed. Respond, Vol. 2. 144p. (Orig.). 1972. pap. 5.95 (ISBN 0-8170-0561-7). Judson.

Corbett, Jane V. Diagnostic Procedures in Nursing Practice. 186p. (Orig.). 1983. pap. 12.95 (ISBN 0-8385-1597-5). ACC.

--Laboratory Tests in Nursing Practice. 464p. 1982. pap. 19.95 (ISBN 0-8385-5585-3). ACC.

Corbett, Janice M., ed. Explore, Vol.1. LC 74-8574. 144p. (Orig.). 1974. pap. 6.95 (ISBN 0-8170-0646-X). Judson.

Corbett, Jim. Jim Corbett's India: Stories Selected by R. E. Hawkins. Hawkins, R. E., ed. (Illus.). 1978. 22.50x (ISBN 0-19-212968-6). Oxford U Pr.

Corbett, John, ed. Basic Metric Style Manual for Secretaries. new ed. 1976. pap. 3.50x (ISBN 0-912702-04-4). Global Eng.

Corbett, John P. Europe & the Social Order. LC 78-20459. 1980. Repr. of 1959 ed. text ed. 19.25 (ISBN 0-88355-843-2). Hyperion Conn.

Corbett, Julia, ed. see Kemper, Donald W., et al.

Corbett, Julian. Monk. facsimile ed. LC 72-154148. (Select Bibliographies Reprint Ser). Repr. of 1889 ed. 18.00 (ISBN 0-8369-5764-4). Ayer Co Pubs.

--Sir Thomas Drake. 1916. lib. bdg. 17.50 (ISBN 0-8414-2388-1). Folcroft.

Corbett, Julian S. The Campaign of Trafalgar, 2 vols. in 1. LC 70-154131. (Illus.). Repr. of 1919 ed. 44.50 (ISBN 0-404-09234-9). AMS Pr.

--England in the Seven Years War, 2 Vols. 2nd ed. LC 76-154130. Repr. of 1918 ed. Set. 72.50 (ISBN 0-404-09224-1). AMS Pr.

--Naval Operations, 1914-1918, 5 vols. Incl. Vol. 1, Pt. 1 (ISBN 0-404-09281-0); Vol. 1, Pt. 2 (ISBN 0-404-09282-9); Vol. 2 (ISBN 0-404-09283-7); Vol. 3, Pt. 1 (ISBN 0-404-09284-5); Vol. 3, Pt. 2 (ISBN 0-404-09285-3); Vol. 4, Pt. 1 (ISBN 0-404-09286-1); Vol. 4, Pt. 2 (ISBN 0-404-09287-X); Vol. 5, Pt. 1 (ISBN 0-404-09288-8); Vol. 5, Pt. 2 (ISBN 0-404-09289-6). (Illus.). Repr. of 1931 ed. Set. 420.00 (ISBN 0-404-09280-2). AMS Pr.

--Sir Francis Drake. LC 77-105513. (BCL Ser. II). Repr. of 1890 ed. 10.00 (ISBN 0-404-01725-8). AMS Pr.

--Sir Francis Drake. LC 69-13865. Repr. of 1890 ed. lib. bdg. 15.00x (ISBN 0-8371-4086-2, COFD). Greenwood.

--Some Principles of Maritime Strategy. LC 76-154122. (BCL Ser. II). Repr. of 1911 ed. 24.50 (ISBN 0-404-09227-6). AMS Pr.

--Successors of Drake. (Research & Source Works Ser.: No. 176). 1968. Repr. of 1900 ed. 25.50 (ISBN 0-8337-0662-4). B Franklin.

Corbett, Julian S., ed. Fighting Instructions, 1530-1816. LC 68-3777. 366p. 1905. Repr. 20.50 (ISBN 0-8337-0660-8). B Franklin.

--Papers Relating to the Navy During the Spanish War 1585-1587. LC 72-132676. (Research & Source Works: No. 562). 1970. Repr. of 1898 ed. lib. bdg. 22.50 (ISBN 0-8337-0661-6). B Franklin.

Corbett, Kathleen, jt. auth. see Borgin, Karl.

Corbett, Lily, jt. auth. see Sternberg, Martin.

Corbett, Margaret D. Help Yourself to Better Sight. pap. 3.00 (ISBN 0-87980-048-8). Wilshire.

Corbett, Margery, tr. see De Chantelou, Paul F.

Corbett, Marjorie R., ed. Greenline Parks: Land Conservation Trends for the Eighties & Beyond. 142p. 1984. 9.95 (ISBN 0-318-17826-5). Natl Parks & Cons.

Corbett, Maurice N. Harp of Ethiopia. facs. ed. LC 74-152918. (Black Heritage Library Collection Ser). 1914. 18.75 (ISBN 0-8369-8762-4). Ayer Co Pubs.

Corbett, Michael. Political Tolerance in America: Freedom & Equality in Political Attitudes. LC 81-11799. (Illus.). 240p. 1982. pap. text ed. 12.95 (ISBN 0-582-28262-4). Longman.

Corbett, Nancy A. & Beveridge, Phyllis. Computer Simulations for Clinical Nursing, Vol. 2. 1984. Apple II version. 495.00 (ISBN 0-7216-1343-8); IBM-PC version. 495.00 (ISBN 0-7216-1368-3). Saunders.

--Computer Simulations in Clinical Nursing, Vol. 1. 1984. Apple II Complete Package. 495.00 (ISBN 0-7216-1023-4); Apple II. additional wkbk. 9.95 (ISBN 0-7216-1154-0); IBM-PC Version. 495.00 (ISBN 0-7216-1365-9). Saunders.

Corbett, Nancy Ann & Beveridge, Phyllis. Clinical Simulations in Nursing Practice. LC 78-52724. 332p. 1980. pap. text ed. 10.95 (ISBN 0-7216-2722-6). Saunders.

Corbett, P. E., tr. see De Visscher, Charles.

Corbett, Patricia, jt. auth. see Eisler, Colin.

Corbett, Paula. Fantasy Fling. (Creative Writing Ser.). 56p. (gr. 5-8). 1984. 6.95 (ISBN 0-88160-112-8, LW 247). Learning Wks.

--Learning BASIC Programming on the Apple. (Learning BASIC Programming Ser.). (Illus.). 64p. (Orig.). (gr. 2-8). Date not set. pap. 3.95 (ISBN 0-88190-489-9, 489). Datamost.

--Learning BASIC Programming on the Atari Home Computer. (Learning BASIC Programming Ser.). (Illus.). 64p. (Orig.). (gr. 2-8). Date not set. pap. 3.95 (ISBN 0-88190-490-2, 490). Datamost.

--Learning BASIC Programming on the Commodore. (Learning BASIC Programming Ser.). (Illus.). 64p. (Orig.). (gr. 2-8). Date not set. pap. 3.95 (ISBN 0-88190-491-0, 491). Datamost.

Corbett, Paula & Huntsman, Leslee. Quick Change Displays. (Teacher Aid Ser.). 43p. 1985. saddle-stitch 6.95 (ISBN 0-513-01772-0). Denison.

Corbett, Percy E. Growth of World Law. LC 70-132236. 1971. 23.00 (ISBN 0-691-09223-0). Princeton U Pr.

--Law in Diplomacy. 14.50 (ISBN 0-8446-1125-5). Peter Smith.

Corbett, Percy E., jt. auth. see Joynt, Carey B.

Corbett, Roger & Matacia, Louis J. An Illustrated Guide to Ten Beginner & Intermediate Canoe Trips. 4th rev. ed. (Blue Ridge Voyages: Vol. 1). (Illus., Orig.). 1973. pap. 3.50x (ISBN 0-686-08918-9). Matacia.

Corbett, Roger, jt. auth. see Matacia, Louis J.

Corbett, Roger, Jr., et al. Blue Ridge Voyages, 3 Vols. 1974. write for info. Appalachian Bks.

Corbett, Ruth. Art As a Living. LC 82-74158. 176p. 1984. 9.95 (ISBN 0-88108-000-4); pap. 6.95 (ISBN 0-88108-008-X). Art Dir.

Corbett, S. E. The Diver's Reference Dictionary. Date not set. text ed. price not set (ISBN 0-941332-03-9). Best Pub Co.

Corbett, Scott. The Black Mask Trick. (Illus.). (gr. 4-7). 1976. 8.95 (ISBN 0-316-15656-6, Pub. by Atlantic Monthly Pr). Little.

--The Boy Who Walked on Air. (Illus.). 48p. (gr. 1-5). 1975. 5.95 (ISBN 0-316-15723-6, Pub. by Atlantic Monthly Pr). Little.

--Captain Butcher's Body. (Illus.). 144p. (gr. 4-6). 1976. 8.95 (ISBN 0-316-15727-9, Pub. by Atlantic Monthly Pr). Little.

--The Case of the Burgled Blessing Box. (Illus.). 128p. (gr. 4-6). 1975. 6.95g (ISBN 0-316-15724-4, Pub. by Atlantic Monthly Pr.). Little.

--The Case of the Silver Skull. (Illus.). 128p. (gr. 4-6). 1974. 9.70i (ISBN 0-316-15711-2, Pub. by Atlantic Monthly Pr). Little.

--The Case of the Ticklish Tooth. (gr. 4-6). 1971. 5.95 (ISBN 0-316-15720-1, Pub. by Atlantic Monthly Pr.). Little.

--Cop's Kid. (Illus.). (gr. 4-6). 1968. 6.95 (ISBN 0-316-15660-4, Pub. by Atlantic Monthly Pr). Little.

--The Deadly Hoax. LC 80-26552. (gr. 5 up). 1981. 9.25 (ISBN 0-525-28585-7, 0898-270). Dutton.

--The Discontented Ghost. (gr. 7 up). 1978. 10.95 (ISBN 0-525-28775-2, 01064-310, Unicorn Bk). Dutton.

--The Donkey Planet. LC 78-11455. (Illus.). (gr. 4-7). 1979. 7.95 (ISBN 0-525-28825-2, Unicorn Bk). Dutton.

--Down with Wimps! LC 84-1579. (Illus.). 96p. (gr. 3-6). 1984. 10.95 (ISBN 0-525-44108-5, 01063-320). Dutton.

--The Foolish Dinosaur Fiasco. (Illus.). (gr. 1-3). 1978. 8.70i (ISBN 0-316-15657-4, Pub. by Atlantic Monthly Pr). Little.

--Grave Doubts. LC 82-47916. 144p. (gr. 3-7). 1982. 12.45i (ISBN 0-316-15659-0, Pub. by Atlantic Monthly Pr). Little.

--The Great Custard Pie Panic. (Illus.). 48p. (gr. 1-3). 1974. 8.95 (ISBN 0-316-15714-7, Pub. by Atlantic Monthly Pr.). Little.

--Great McGoniggle Rides Shotgun. 52p. (gr. k-6). 1980. pap. 1.25 (ISBN 0-440-43313-4, YB). Dell.

--The Great McGoniggle Rides Shotgun. (Illus.). (gr. 1-3). 1977. 10.45i (ISBN 0-316-15729-5, Atlantic-Little, Brown). Little.

--The Great McGoniggle Switches Pitches. (Illus.). 64p. (gr. 2 up). 1980. 10.45i (ISBN 0-316-15710-4, Pub. by Atlantic Monthly Pr). Little.

--The Great McGoniggle's Gray Ghost. (Illus.). (gr. 1-3). 1975. 10.45i (ISBN 0-316-15725-2, Pub. by Atlantic Monthly Pr). Little.

--The Great McGoniggle's Key Play. (Illus.). (gr. 1-3). 1976. 6.95 (ISBN 0-316-15726-0, Pub. by Atlantic Monthly Pr). Little.

--The Hairy Horror Trick. LC 70-77443. (The Trick Ser.). (Illus.). (gr. 4-6). 1969. 10.45i (ISBN 0-316-15702-3, Pub. by Atlantic Monthly Pr). Little.
--The Hairy Horror Trick. (Illus.). 112p. (gr. 4-6). 1985. pap. 2.25 (ISBN 0-590-32195-1, Apple Paperbacks). Scholastic Inc.
--The Hangman's Ghost Trick. (The Truck Ser.). (Illus.). (gr. 4-6). 1977. 13.45i (ISBN 0-316-15728-7, Atlantic-Little, Brown). Little.
--The Hangman's Ghost Trick. (Illus.). 96p. (gr. 4-6). 1983. pap. 2.25 (ISBN 0-590-40126-2, Apple Paperbacks). Scholastic Inc.
--Here Lies the Body. (Illus.). 128p. (gr. 4-6). 1974. 10.45i (ISBN 0-316-15717-1, Pub. by Atlantic Monthly Pr.). Little.
--The Hockey Girls. 112p. (gr. 5-6). 1976. 8.95 (ISBN 0-525-32065-2). Dutton.
--The Hockey Trick. (The Trick Ser.). (Illus.). 112p. (gr. 4-6). 1974. 7.95 (ISBN 0-316-15716-3, Pub. by Atlantic Monthly Pr). Little.
--Home Computers: A Simple & Informative Guide. (Illus.). 128p. (gr. 5 up). 1980. 6.70i (ISBN 0-316-15658-2, Pub. by Atlantic Monthly Pr); pap. 6.70i (ISBN 0-316-15712-0). Little.
--Jokes to Read in the Dark. LC 79-23129. (Illus.). 80p. (gr. 5-9). 1980. 10.95 (ISBN 0-525-32796-7, 01063-320, Unicorn Bk.). Dutton.
--Jokes to Tell to Your Worst Enemy. LC 83-16564. (Illus.). 80p. (gr. 2-6). 1984. 9.95 (ISBN 0-525-44082-8, 0966-290). Dutton.
--The Lemonade Trick. (The Trick Ser). (Illus.). (gr. 4-6). 1960. 10.45i (ISBN 0-316-15694-9, Pub. by Atlantic Monthly Pr). Little.
--The Mailbox Trick. (The Trick Ser). (Illus.). (gr. 4-6). 1961. 7.95 (ISBN 0-316-15701-5, Pub. by Atlantic Monthly Pr). Little.
--The Mysterious Zetabet. LC 78-23243. (Illus.). (gr. 1-3). 1979. 7.95 (ISBN 0-316-15730-9, Pub. by Atlantic Monthly Pr). Little.
--The Red Room Riddle. (A Corbett Riddle Bk.). (Illus.). 128p. (gr. 4-6). 1972. 9.40i (ISBN 0-316-15719-8, Pub. by Atlantic Monthly Pr.). Little.
--Run for the Money. (Illus.). (gr. 4-6). 1973. 5.95 (ISBN 0-316-15707-4, Pub. by Atlantic Monthly Pr). Little.
--The Trouble with Diamonds. LC 84-18762. (Illus.). (gr. 3-7). 1985. 9.95 (ISBN 0-525-44190-5, 0966-290). Dutton.
--We Chose Cape Cod. LC 52-13127. 1970. pap. 6.95 (ISBN 0-85699-007-8). Chatham Pr.
--We Chose Cape Cod. 320p. 1984. pap. 8.95 (ISBN 0-940160-27-7). Parnassus Imprints.
--What Makes a Boat Float? LC 76-94498. (gr. 4-6). 1970. 6.95 (ISBN 0-316-15713-9, Pub. by Atlantic Monthly Pr). Little.
--Witch Hunt. Kroupa, Melanie, ed. LC 85-47783. 176p. (gr. 5 up). 1985. 13.95 (ISBN 0-87113-040-8, 157503). Atlantic Monthly.
Corbett, Thomas H. Cancer & Chemicals. LC 76-54270. 220p. 1977. 20.95x (ISBN 0-88229-305-2); pap. 10.95 (ISBN 0-88229-465-2). Nelson-Hall.
Corbett, Tiffany K., ed. see Summit Junior Fortnightly Club.
Corbett, W. J. The Song of Pentecost. (Illus.). 224p. (gr. 5 up). 1983. 10.95 (ISBN 0-525-44051-8, 01063-320). Dutton.
--The Song Pentecost. (gr. k-6). 1985. pap. 3.25 (ISBN 0-440-48092-2, YB). Dell.
Corbett, William. Collected Poems, Nineteen Sixty-Eight to Nineteen Eighty-Four. LC 84-71923. (Poets Ser.). 140p. (Orig.). 1984. 15.95 (ISBN 0-915032-45-7); pap. 9.95 (ISBN 0-915032-46-5). Natl Poet Foun.
Corbiere. Amours Jaunes. (Documentation thematique). (Fr). pap. 2.95 (ISBN 0-685-13797-X, 61). Larousse.
--The Centenary Corbiere. Warner, Val, tr. from Fr. LC 74-18607. 171p. 1975. 14.00 (ISBN 0-8023-1256-X). Dufour.
Corbiere, Tristan. Poems. McElroy, Walter, tr. from Fr. LC 77-10257. 80p. Repr. of 1947 ed. 16.50 (ISBN 0-404-16312-2). AMS Pr.
Corbiere, Tristan, jt. auth. see Cros, Charles.
Corbierre, Anne. Paris. LC 80-50996. (Rand McNally Pocket Guide Ser.). (Illus.). 1983. pap. 4.95 (ISBN 0-528-84294-3). Rand.
Corbin. How to Relax in a Busy World. pap. 4.95 (ISBN 0-87505-263-0). Borden.
Corbin, Alan, jt. ed. see Briggs, Michael.
Corbin, Arthur L. Contracts. (Text Ser.). 1224p. 1952. Student edition 20.95 (ISBN 0-317-00014-4). West Pub.
Corbin, Carol L. John Lennon. (Impact Bks.). (Illus.). 128p. (gr. 7 up). 1982. PLB 9.90 (ISBN 0-531-04478-5). Watts.
Corbin, Carole L. The Right to Vote. (Issues in American History Ser.). (Illus.). 112p. (YA) (gr. 7 up). 1985. lib. bdg. 10.90 (ISBN 0-531-04932-9). Watts.
Corbin, Charles & Lindsey, Ruth. The Ultimate Fitness Book: Physical Fitness Forever. (Illus.). 224p. 1984. pap. 12.95 (ISBN 0-88011-232-8). Leisure Pr.
Corbin, Charles B. The Athletic Snowball. (Illus.). 64p. 1977. pap. text ed. 3.00x (ISBN 0-931250-07-2, BCOR0007). Human Kinetics.
--Becoming Physically Educated in the Elementary School. 2nd ed. LC 75-25894. (Illus.). 305p. 1976. pap. 10.00 (ISBN 0-8121-0536-2). Lea & Febiger.
--A Textbook of Motor Development. 2nd ed. 336p. 1980. pap. text ed. write for info. (ISBN 0-697-07266-5). Wm C Brown.
Corbin, Charles B. & Corbin, David E. Homemade Play Equipment. (Illus.). 115p. 1981. pap. text ed. 3.95x (ISBN 0-89641-058-7). American Pr.
Corbin, Charles B. & Laurie, David R. Teaching Lifetime Fitness, 5 vols. LC 81-81868. (Advanced Ser.). 1981. Set. 3-ring notebook contains slides & tapes 695.00 (ISBN 0-914607-07-3). Vol. 1 (ISBN 0-914607-08-1). Vol. 2 (ISBN 0-914607-09-X). Vol. 3 (ISBN 0-914607-10-3). Vol. 4 (ISBN 0-914607-11-1). Vol. 5 (ISBN 0-914607-12-X). Master Tchr.
--Teaching Lifetime Fitness, 3 vols. Incl. Vol. 1-Primary Level. 235.00x (ISBN 0-914607-14-6); Vol. II-Intermediate Level. 205.00x (ISBN 0-914607-15-4); Vol. III-Middle J.H.S Level. 245.00x (ISBN 0-914607-16-2). LC 83-61293. (gr. 1-9). 1982. text ed. 685.00x (ISBN 0-914607-13-8). Master Tchr.
Corbin, Charles B. & Lindsey, Ruth. Concepts in Physical Fitness with Laboratories. 5th ed. 272p. 1985. pap. write for info. (ISBN 0-697-07232-0); instr's. manual avail. (ISBN 0-697-00560-7). Wm C Brown.
Corbin, Cheryl. Nutrition. LC 80-11138. (Illus.). 208p. 1981. pap. 8.95 (ISBN 0-03-048276-3, Owl Bks.). HR&W.
Corbin, David A. Life, Work, & Rebellion in the Coal Fields: Southern West Virginia Miners, 1880-1920. LC 80-25493. (The Working Class in American History). (Illus.). 282p. 1981. 24.95x (ISBN 0-252-00850-2). U of Ill Pr.
Corbin, David E., jt. auth. see Corbin, Charles B.
Corbin, Eve, jt. auth. see Corbin, Floyd.
Corbin, Floyd & Corbin, Eve. How to Relax in a Busy World. 7th ed. LC 62-13196. 222p. 1980. pap. text ed. 4.95 (ISBN 0-87516-461-7). De Vorss.
Corbin, Henry. Avicenna & the Visionary Recital. Trask, Willard R., tr. from French. (Dunquin Ser.: No. 13). 314p. 1980. pap. 14.50 (ISBN 0-88214-213-5). Spring Pubns.
--Avicenna & the Visionary Recital. 420p. 1980. pap. 12.50 (ISBN 0-88214-213-5). Weiser.
--Creative Imagination in the Sufism of Ibn'Arabi. Manheim, R., tr. (Bollingen Ser.: Vol. 91). 1969. 38.00 (ISBN 0-691-09852-2); pap. 11.95 (ISBN 0-691-01828-6). Princeton U Pr.
--Cyclical Time & Ismaili Gnosis. (Islamic Texts & Contexts Ser.). 193p. 1983. 24.95x (ISBN 0-7103-0047-6, Kegan Paul); pap. 13.95 (ISBN 0-7103-0048-4). Routledge & Kegan.
--Spiritual Body & Celestial Earth: From Mazdean Iran to Shi Ite Iran. Pearson, Nancy, tr. (Bollingen Ser: No. 91). 1977. text ed. 38.00x (ISBN 0-691-09937-5). Princeton U Pr.
Corbin, Jackie D. & Hardman, Joel D., eds. Methods in Enzymology: Hormone Action: Protein Kinases, Vol. 99, Pt F. 1983. 55.00 (ISBN 0-12-181999-X). Acad Pr.
Corbin, John. The Anarchist Passion: An Anthropological Perspective on Class Conflict in Southern Spain (1810-1965) 1985. text ed. write for info. (ISBN 0-566-00667-7). Gower Pub Co.
--Elizabethan Hamlet. LC 70-134608. Repr. of 1895 ed. 12.50 (ISBN 0-404-01726-6). AMS Pr.
--Managing the Library Automation Project. LC 85-45154. (Illus.). 176p. 1985. lib. bdg. 32.50 (ISBN 0-89774-151-X). Oryx Pr.
--Unkown Washington. LC 72-1273. (Select Bibliographies Reprint Ser). 1972. Repr. of 1930 ed. 21.00 (ISBN 0-8369-6823-9). Ayer Co Pubs.
Corbin, John B. Technical Services Manual for Small Libraries. LC 70-156885. 206p. 1971. 15.00 (ISBN 0-8108-0388-7). Scarecrow.
Corbin, John B., compiled by. An Index of State Geological Survey Publications Issued in Series: Supplement, Nineteen Sixty-Three to Nineteen Eighty. LC 81-18501. 461p. 1982. 37.50 (ISBN 0-8108-1501-X). Scarecrow.
Corbin, John R. & Corbin, Marie P. Compromising Relations: Kith, Kin & Class in Southern Spain. 05/1984 ed. LC 83-20729. (Studies in Spanish Anthropology, 1). 153p. text ed. 32.95x (ISBN 0-566-00669-3). Gower Pub Co.
Corbin, Jonathan, jt. auth. see Corbin, Richard.
Corbin, Linda. Following Jesus. Dys, Pat, ed. (Studies for Kids Ser.: Pt. 2). (Illus.). 48p. (gr. 3-7). 1985. 2.95 (ISBN 0-87239-904-4, 3303). Standard Pub.
Corbin, Linda & Dys, Pat. Following Jesus. (Studies for Kids Ser.: Pt. 1). (Illus.). 48p. (gr. 3-7). 1985. 2.95 (ISBN 0-87239-903-6, 3304). Standard Pub.
Corbin, Marie, ed. The Couple. 1978. pap. 3.95 (ISBN 0-14-021969-2, Pelican). Penguin.
Corbin, Marie P., jt. auth. see Corbin, John R.
Corbin, Patricia. Gardens of Earthly Delight. (Illus.). 1985. 35.00 (ISBN 0-525-24335-6, 03398-1020). Dutton.
--Summer Cottages & Castles: Scenes from the Good Life. (Illus.). 144p. 1983. 29.95 (ISBN 0-525-66696-6, 02908-870). Dutton.
Corbin, Richard & Corbin, Jonathan. Research Papers: A Guided Writing Experience for Senior High Students. 2nd rev. ed. 1978. pap. text ed. 2.00 (ISBN 0-930348-00-1). NY St Eng Coun.
Corbin, Richard & Belf, Miriam, eds. Twelve American Plays. LC 69-11437. 480p. 1969. pap. text ed. 9.95 (ISBN 0-02-325180-8, Pub. by Scribner). Macmillan.
Corbit, Julia. Julia's Book. Sonnack, Iver & Hatchimonji, Mike, eds. LC 79-66049. (Illus.). 1979. 14.95 (ISBN 0-934724-00-8). Xenos Bks.
Corbitt, David L. Formation of the North Carolina Counties, 1663-1943. xxix, 323p. 1975. pap. 9.00 (ISBN 0-86526-032-X). NC Archives.
Corbitt, Helen. The Helen Corbitt Collection. Johnson, Elizabeth A., ed. LC 81-4259. (Illus.). 490p. 1981. 27.95 (ISBN 0-395-31295-7). HM.
--Helen Corbitt Cooks for Company. LC 74-599. 1974. 14.95 (ISBN 0-395-18491-6). HM.
--Helen Corbitt Cooks for Looks: An Adventure in Low-Calorie Eating. 1967. 6.95 (ISBN 0-395-07575-0). HM.
--Helen Corbitt's Greenhouse Cookbook. 1979. 9.95 (ISBN 0-395-25729-8). HM.
Corbitt, Helen, ed. Mexico Through My Kitchen Window. 1961. 10.95 (ISBN 0-395-07579-3). HM.
Corbitt, Helen L. Helen Corbitt's Cookbook. (Illus.). 1976. 11.95 (ISBN 0-395-07577-7). HM.
--Helen Corbitt's Potluck Cookbook. 1962. 11.95 (ISBN 0-395-07576-9). HM.
Corbitt, Joan, illus. Benji's Riddle Book. (Illus.). 12p. (gr. 1-5). 1982. pap. 2.95 (ISBN 0-89954-203-4). Antioch Pub Co.
--The Gary Coleman Show: What If Elephants Had Pink Stripes? (Saturday Morning Bks.). (Illus.). 22p. (ps-2). 1983. 2.50 (ISBN 0-89954-223-9). Antioch Pub Co.
--Is It Saturday Yet? Joke & Riddle Book. (Illus.). 24p. (gr. 1-5). 1983. pap. 1.95 (ISBN 0-89954-208-5). Antioch Pub Co.
Corbitt, Mary K., ed. Results from the Second Mathematics Assessment of the NAEP. LC 81-4322. 167p. 1981. 9.00 (ISBN 0-87353-172-8). NCTM.
Corbitt, Theodore, jt. auth. see Finnerty, Gertrude B.
Corbman, B. Textiles: Fiber to Fabric. 6th ed. 608p. 1982. text ed. 29.00 (ISBN 0-07-013137-6). McGraw.
Corbman, Bernard P. Textiles: Fiber to Fabric. 5th ed. (Illus.). 512p. (gr. 12). 1975. text ed. 29.00 (ISBN 0-07-013125-2). McGraw.
Corbman, Bernard P. & Krieger, Murray. Mathematics of Retail Merchandising. 2nd ed. 450p. 1972. cloth 37.95x (ISBN 0-471-06587-0, Pub. by Ronald Pr). Wiley.
--Mathematics of Retail Merchandising. 2nd ed. LC 85-5161. 420p. 1985. Repr. of 1972 ed. lib. bdg. 32.50 (ISBN 0-89874-846-1). Krieger.
Corbo, Margaret S. & Barras, Diane M. Arnie, the Darling Starling. (General Ser.). 1984. lib. bdg. 12.95 (ISBN 0-8161-3638-6, Large Print Bks). G K Hall.
Corbo, Margarete S. & Barras, Diane M. Arnie & a House Full of Company. (Illus.). 240p. 1985. 11.95 (ISBN 0-395-38167-3). HM.
--Arnie, the Darling Starling. (Illus.). 288p. 1983. 9.95 (ISBN 0-395-34390-9). HM.
Corbo, Vittorio & Krueger, Anne. Export-Oriented Development Strategies: The Success of Five Newly Industrializing Countries. (Replica Edition). 340p. 1985. softcover 28.00x (ISBN 0-8133-7016-7). Westview.
Corboy, J. M. The Retinoscopy Book: A Manual for Beginners. rev. ed. LC 79-65451. 143p. 1979. text ed. 19.50 (ISBN 0-913590-67-3). Slack Inc.
Corbridge, D. E. Phosphorus: An Outline of Its Chemistry, Biochemistry & Technology. 2nd ed. 1980. 93.75 (ISBN 0-444-41887-3). Elsevier.
--Phosphorus: An Outline of Its Chemistry, Biochemistry & Technology, No. 6. 3rd ed. (Studies in Inorganic Chemistry). 762p. 1985. 157.50 (ISBN 0-444-42468-7). Elsevier.
Corbridge, S. The Structural Chemistry of Phosphorus. LC 64-4605. 560p. 1974. 106.50 (ISBN 0-444-41073-2). Elsevier.
Corbridge-Patkaniowska, M. Polish. (Teach Yourself Ser.). 1974. pap. 4.95 (ISBN 0-679-10232-9). McKay.
Corbus, Howard F. & Swanson, Laura L. Adopting the Problem-Oriented Medical Record in Nursing Homes: A Do-It-Yourself Manual. LC 78-53068. 98p. 1978. pap. 12.95 (ISBN 0-913654-44-2). Aspen Systems.
Corbusier, Le see Le Corbusier.
Corbusier, le see Le Corbusier.
Corby, Jane. Girl in the Tower. 1978. pap. 1.50 (ISBN 0-8439-0538-7, Leisure Bks). Dorchester Pub Co.
--Riverwood. 1975. pap. 1.25 (ISBN 0-685-61049-7, LB317, Leisure Bks). Dorchester Pub Co.
--The Shadow & the Fear. 1977. pap. 1.50 (ISBN 0-505-51174-6, Pub. by Tower Bks). Dorchester Pub Co.
Corby, Michael, jt. auth. see Geare, Michael.
Corcao, Gustavo. Who If I Cry Out. Wilson, Clotilde, tr. from Portuguese. (Texas Pan American Ser). 229p. 1967. 9.95x (ISBN 0-292-73669-X). U of Tex Pr.
Corchado, Veronica & McHugh, Kathleen. Selecting the Right Word Processing Software for the IBM PC. LC 84-50991. 96p. 1984. pap. 11.95 (ISBN 0-89588-177-2). SYBEX.
Corchado, Veronica, jt. auth. see McHugh, Kathleen.
Corchado y Juarbe, Manuel. Complete Works of Manuel Corchado y Juarbe, 2 vols. (Puerto Rico Ser.). 1979. Set. lib. bdg. 250.00 (ISBN 0-8490-2897-3). Gordon Pr.
Corcoran, A. Wayne. Costs: Accounting, Analysis & Control. LC 77-18798. (Wiley Series Accounting & Information Systems). 786p. 1978. text ed. 48.50x (ISBN 0-471-17251-0). Wiley.
Corcoran, Barbara. Abigail. 160p. (Orig.). 1981. pap. 1.95 (ISBN 0-345-28669-3). Ballantine.
--August, Die She Must. LC 83-15657. 180p. (gr. 5-9). 1984. 11.95 (ISBN 0-689-31012-9). Atheneum.
--Beloved Enemy. 160p. (Orig.). 1981. pap. 1.95 (ISBN 0-345-28667-7). Ballantine.
--By the Silvery Moon. 1982. pap. 1.95 (ISBN 0-345-30259-1). Ballantine.
--Cabin in the Sky. LC 76-17. 204p. (gr. 5-9). 1976. 7.95 (ISBN 0-689-30521-4). Atheneum.
--The Call of the Heart. (Orig.). 1981. pap. 1.95 (ISBN 0-345-28668-5). Ballantine.
--Child of the Morning. LC 81-8057. 132p. (gr. 5-9). 1982. PLB 11.95 (ISBN 0-689-30876-0). Atheneum.
--The Clown. LC 75-8759. 192p. (gr. 5-9). 1975. 8.95 (ISBN 0-689-30465-X). Atheneum.
--A Dance to Still Music. LC 74-75558. 192p. (gr. 4-8). 1974. 9.95 (ISBN 0-689-30406-4); pap. 1.95 (ISBN 0-689-70440-2). Atheneum.
--Face the Music. LC 85-7453. 204p. (gr. 7 up). 1985. 12.95 (ISBN 0-689-31139-7). Atheneum.
--Hey, That's My Soul You're Stomping on. LC 77-13499. 144p. (gr. 5-9). 1978. 7.95 (ISBN 0-689-30617-2); pap. 2.95 (ISBN 0-689-70486-0). Atheneum.
--Long Journey. LC 79-115067. (Illus.). 192p. (gr. 3-7). 1970. pap. 1.25 (ISBN 0-689-70404-6, A-41, Aladdin). Atheneum.
--Love Is Not Enough. 1981. pap. 1.95 (ISBN 0-345-29011-9). Ballantine.
--Making It. (gr. 7-10). 1985. pap. 2.25 (ISBN 0-671-44219-8). Archway.
--Mystery on Ice. LC 84-21559. 156p. (gr. 4-7). 1985. 10.95 (ISBN 0-689-31089-7). Atheneum.
--The Person in the Potting Shed. LC 80-12299. 132p. (gr. 6 up). 1980. 9.95 (ISBN 0-689-30774-8). Atheneum.
--Sam. LC 67-18994. 224p. (gr. 5-9). 1967. pap. 0.95 (ISBN 0-689-70312-0, A-15, Aladdin). Atheneum.
--Sasha, My Friend. (Illus.). (gr. 5-9). 1973. pap. 0.95 (ISBN 0-689-70358-9, A-29, Aladdin). Atheneum.
--The Shadowed Path. (Moonstone Novels Ser.: No. 2). 160p. (Orig.). (gr. 5 up). 1985. pap. 2.25 (ISBN 0-671-50781-8). Archway.
--Song for Two Voices. 128p. 1981. pap. 1.95 (ISBN 0-345-29012-7). Ballantine.
--Strike! LC 82-13759. 168p. (gr. 6-9). 1983. 12.95 (ISBN 0-689-30952-X). Atheneum.
--A Watery Grave. LC 82-1726. 180p. (gr. 3-7). 1982. 14.95 (ISBN 0-689-30919-8). Atheneum.
--Which Witch Is Which. LC 83-3900. (Escapade Ser.). 128p. (gr. 3-7). 1983. 3.95 (ISBN 0-689-31373-X). Atheneum.
--Winds of Time. LC 73-84823. (Illus.). 176p. (gr. 4-7). 1974. 7.95 (ISBN 0-689-30133-2). Atheneum.
--The Woman in Your Life. LC 84-2942. 192p. (gr. 8 up). 1984. 10.95 (ISBN 0-689-31044-7). Atheneum.
--You're Allegro Dead. LC 81-1906. 144p. (gr. 3-7). 1981. PLB 11.95 (ISBN 0-689-30840-X). Atheneum.
Corcoran, Barbara, jt. auth. see Angier, Bradford.
Corcoran, Eileen. Gaining Skills in Using the Library. (Illus.). 1980. pap. 3.00x (ISBN 0-88323-158-1, 247); 1.00x (ISBN 0-88323-163-8). Richards Pub.
--Meeting Basic Competencies in Communications. 1979. pap. 3.00x (ISBN 0-88323-152-2, 242); tchr's. answer key 1.00x (ISBN 0-88323-156-5, 246). Richards Pub.
--Meeting Basic Competencies in Math. 1984. pap. text ed. 3.00x (ISBN 0-88323-203-0, 227); tchr's. answer key avail. (ISBN 0-88323-141-7, 230). Richards Pub.
--Reading for Survival. 1984. pap. 3.00x (ISBN 0-88323-205-7, 234); tchr's. answer key (ISBN 0-88323-151-4, 240). Richards Pub.
Corcoran, Eileen L. Finding Ourselves. 1983. pap. text ed. 3.00x (ISBN 0-88323-190-5, 114). Richards Pub.
--Know Your Signs - Be a Better Driver, Bk. 1. (Know Your Signs Ser.). 1982. pap. 4.25x (ISBN 0-88323-175-1, 258). Richards Pub.
--Know Your Signs - Be a Better Driver: Driving Interstate & Superhighways. (Know Your Signs Ser.). 1973. pap. 4.25x (ISBN 0-88323-112-3, 200). Richards Pub.
--Meeting Basic Competencies in Practical Science & Health: A Workstudy Book to Improve Daily Living Skills. (Illus.). 1985. 3.00x (ISBN 0-88323-210-3, 237); tchr's. answer key avail. (ISBN 0-88323-154-9, 245). Richards Pub.
--Meeting Basic Competencies in Reading. 1977. pap. text ed. 3.00x (ISBN 0-88323-134-4, 221); tchr's. answer key 1.00 (ISBN 0-88323-144-1, 232). Richards Pub.
--Weather & Us, Bk. 1. (Science Ser.). 1967. pap. 1.50x (ISBN 0-88323-078-X, 175). Richards Pub.
Corcoran, Eileen L. & Pavka, John. What Is Electricity? (Science Ser.). 1966. pap. 1.50x (ISBN 0-88323-080-1, 177). Richards Pub.
Corcoran, Frances, jt. auth. see Blickle, Calvin.
Corcoran, J., ed. see Buffalo Symposium on Modernist Interpretation of Ancient Logic, 21 & 22 April, 1972.

Corcoran, J. W., ed. Biosynthesis. (Antibiotics Ser.: Vol. 4). (Illus.). 380p. 1981. 105.00 (ISBN 0-387-10186-1). Springer-Verlag.

Corcoran, J. W. & Hahn, F. E., eds. Mechanism of Action of Antimicrobial & Antitumor Agents. LC 74-34. (Antibiotics Ser.: Vol. 3). (Illus.). xii, 743p. 1975. 115.00 (ISBN 0-387-06653-5). Springer-Verlag.

Corcoran, John, jt. auth. see Farkas, Emil.

Corcoran, John, ed. see Soo, Kim Pyung.

Corcoran, John, ed. see Tarski, Alfred.

Corcoran, John, ed. see Tulleners, Tonny.

Corcoran, Kevin, et al. Saudi Arabia: Keys to Business Success. 204p. 1982. 44.00x (ISBN 0-07-084567-0). McGraw.

Corcoran, Lawrence. Outboard Service Guide. Corcoran, Lynn, ed. 1977. pap. text ed. 3.25 (ISBN 0-686-24789-2). L Corcoran.

Corcoran, Lynn, ed. see Corcoran, Lawrence.

Corcoran, M. I. Milton's Paradise with Reference to the Hexameral Background. LC 45-3381. 149p. 1967. pap. 5.95x (ISBN 0-8132-0335-X). Cath U Pr.

Corcoran, Mark, illus. Star Wars: The Mystery of the Rebellious Robot. LC 78-19701. (Illus.). 1979. (BYR); pap. 1.95 (ISBN 0-394-84086-0). Random.

Corcoran, Mary B., tr. see Thalmann, Marianne.

Corcoran, Mary E. & Peterson, Marvin W., eds. Institutional Research in Transition. LC 84-82373. (Institutional Research Ser.: No. 46). (Orig.). 1985. pap. text ed. 9.95x (ISBN 0-87589-752-5). Jossey-Bass.

Corcoran, Sr. Mary H., ed. see Hojeda, Diego de.

Corcoran, N., tr. see Manenc, J.

Corcoran, N., tr. see Tremillon, B.

Corcoran, Neil. The Song of Deeds: A Study of the Anathemata of David Jones. 120p. 1982. text ed. 22.00x (ISBN 0-7083-0806-6, Pub. by Univ of Wales Pr England). Humanities.

Corcoran, Paul A. With All Due Respect. 1983. 3.75 (ISBN 0-89536-609-6). CSS of Ohio.

Corcoran, Paul E. Political Language & Rhetoric. LC 79-63529. 234p. 1979. text ed. 20.00x (ISBN 0-292-76458-8). U of Tex Pr.

Corcoran, Paul E., ed. Before Marx: Socialism & Communism in France 1830-48. LC 82-21557. 240p. 1983. 28.50 (ISBN 0-312-07158-2). St Martin.

Corcoran, S., jt. auth. see Gustafson, M.

Corcoran, Theresa S. Vida Dutton Scudder. (United States Authors Ser.). 1982. lib. bdg. 16.95 (ISBN 0-8057-7354-1, Twayne). G K Hall.

Corcoran, Thom. Mount St. Helens: The Story Behind the Scenery. LC 85-50108. (Illus.). 48p. (Orig.). 1985. pap. 3.75 (ISBN 0-88714-000-9). KC Pubns.

Corcoran, Thomas H., tr. see Seneca.

Corcoran, Thomas J. Outline of Classical Origins: Rome. (Illus.). 77p. 4.85 (ISBN 0-318-12455-6, B34). Amer Classical.

Corcoran, Wayne A. & Istvan, Donald F. Audit & the Punched Card: An Introduction. 1961. pap. text ed. 2.00x (ISBN 0-87776-101-9, R101). Ohio St U Admin Sci.

Corcoran, William H., et al. Momentum Transfer in Fluids. 1956. 65.00 (ISBN 0-12-188050-8). Acad Pr.

Corcoran, William S. & Reyes-Guerra, David, Sr., eds. Engineering Education: Aims & Goals for the Eighties. LC 82-71877. 186p. (Orig.). 1982. pap. 25.00 (ISBN 0-939204-13-4, 81-29). Eng Found.

Cord, Barry. Deadly Amigos: Two Graves for a Gunman. 1979. pap. 2.25 (ISBN 0-505-51419-2, Pub. by Tower Bks). Dorchester Pub Co.

--Gun Junction. 1979. pap. 1.25 (ISBN 0-8439-0612-X, Leisure Bks). Dorchester Pub Co.

--The Gun Shy Kid. 1979. pap. 1.25 (ISBN 0-505-51379-X, Pub. by Tower Bks). Dorchester Pub Co.

--The Guns of Hammer. 1979. pap. 1.25 (ISBN 0-505-51338-2, Pub. by Tower Bks). Dorchester Pub Co.

--Hell in Paradise Valley. 1978. pap. 1.25 (ISBN 0-505-51316-1, Pub. by Tower Bks). Dorchester Pub Co.

--Last Chance at Devil's Canyon. 1979. pap. 1.25 (ISBN 0-8439-0613-8, Leisure Bks). Dorchester Pub Co.

--Last Stage to Gomorrah. 1979. pap. 1.25 (ISBN 0-505-51339-0, Pub. by Tower Bks). Dorchester Pub Co.

--The Long Wire. 1978. pap. 1.25 (ISBN 0-505-51238-6, Pub. by Tower Bks). Dorchester Pub Co.

--Shadow Valley. 1978. pap. 1.25 (ISBN 0-505-51329-3, Pub. by Tower Bks). Dorchester Pub Co.

--The Third Rider. 1978. pap. 1.25 (ISBN 0-505-51318-8, Pub. by Tower Bks). Dorchester Pub Co.

--Trail Boss from Texas. 1979. pap. 1.25 (ISBN 0-505-51337-4, Pub. by Tower Bks). Dorchester Pub Co.

Cord, Robert L. Separation of Church & State: Historical Fact & Current Fiction. 307p. 1982. 19.95x (ISBN 0-931186-03-X). Lambeth Pr.

Cord, Steven. Catalyst! 115p. 1979. pap. 5.00 (ISBN 0-911312-29-3). Schalkenbach.

Cord, Steven B., ed. Henry George: Dreamer or Realist? 272p. 1984. pap. 5.00 (ISBN 0-911312-26-9). Schalkenbach.

Cord, William O. An Introduction to Richard Wagner's Der Ring Des Nibelungen: A Handbook. LC 82-14417. (Illus.). xii, 163p. 1983. text ed. 19.95x (ISBN 0-8214-0648-5, 82-84176); pap. 11.95 (ISBN 0-8214-0708-2, 82-84770). Ohio U Pr.

Corda, A. C. Icones Fungorum Hucusque Cognitorum. 1963. 133.00 (ISBN 3-7682-7050-5). Lubrecht & Cramer.

Cordano, Vira. Levi Scott: Oregon Trailblazer. LC 81-70857. (Illus.). 1982. pap. 7.50 (ISBN 0-8323-0400-X). Binford.

Cordaro, Philip. Lecturas Italianas, 3 bks. Incl. Bk. 1. Apprendere Leggendo. pap. 1.55 (ISBN 0-8477-3302-5); pap. 1.50 (ISBN 0-8477-3303-3); Bk. 2. Raccontini Divertenti. pap. 0.90 (ISBN 0-8477-3304-1); Bk. 3. Obra De Pirandello. pap. 3.75 (ISBN 0-8477-3305-X). Set. pap. (ISBN 0-8477-3301-7). U of PR Pr.

Cordaro, Philip, ed. see Dante Alighieri.

Cordasco, F., intro. by. Bibliography of Publications of the U. S. Office of Education, Eighteen Sixty-Seven to Nineteen Fifty-Nine, 3 vols. in 1. 372p. 1971. Repr. 27.50x (ISBN 0-87471-011-1). Rowman.

Cordasco, Farncesco, ed. see Mondello, Salvatore A.

Cordasco, Francesco. American Medical Imprints, 1820-1910: A Checklist of Publications Illustrating the History & Progress of Medical Science & Education & the Healing Arts in the United States, 2 vols. 1654p. 1985. 245.00 (ISBN 0-940198-01-0). Junius-Vaughn.

--American Medical Imprints, 1820-1910: A Checklist of Publications Illustrating the History & Progress of Medical Science, Medical Education, & the Healing Arts in the United States: A Preliminary Contribution, 2 vols. LC 84-11829. 1680p. 1985. Set. 245.00x (ISBN 0-8476-7338-3). Rowman.

--Bohn Libraries: A History & a Checklist. 1951. 16.50 (ISBN 0-8337-0663-2). B Franklin.

--A Brief History of Education. 2nd rev. ed. (Quality Paperback Ser.: No. 67). 1976. pap. 5.95 (ISBN 0-8226-0067-6). Littlefield.

--Immigrant Children in American Schools: A Classified & Annotated Bibliography with Selected Source Documents. LC 76-45096. 1976. lib. bdg. 47.50x (ISBN 0-678-00743-8). Kelley.

--The Italian-American Experience. new ed. LC 74-10922. (Ethnic Bibliographical Guides Ser). (Illus.). xxiii, 183p. 1974. lib. bdg. 14.95 (ISBN 0-89102-028-4). B Franklin.

--Italian Mass Emigration: The Exodus of a Latin People--A Bibliographical Guide to the "Bollettino Dell'Emigrazione, 1902-1927. (Illus.). 307p. 1980. 47.50x (ISBN 0-8476-6283-7). Rowman.

--Junius & His Works: A History of the Letters of Junius & the Authorship Controversy. 450p. Date not set. 27.50 (ISBN 0-940198-03-7). Junius-Vaughn.

--Junius Bibliography. rev ed. 1973. 19.50 (ISBN 0-8337-0664-0). B Franklin.

--Puerto Ricans & Educational Opportunity: An Orginal Anthology. LC 74-14246. (A Puerto Rican Experience Ser). (Illus.). 1975. Repr. 20.00x (ISBN 0-405-06231-1). Ayer Co Pubs.

--The Puerto Ricans, Fourteen Ninety-Three to Nineteen Seventy-Three: A Chronology & Fact Book. LC 73-5840. (Ethnic Chronology Ser.: No. 11). 137p. 1973. lib. bdg. 8.50 (ISBN 0-379-00509-3). Oceana.

--The Puerto Ricans: Migration & General Bibliography. LC 74-14245. (An Puerto Rican Experience Ser). (Illus.). 1975. Repr. 35.50x (ISBN 0-405-06232-X). Ayer Co Pubs.

--Register of Eighteenth Century Bibliographies & References: A Chronological Quarter-Century Survey Relating to English Literature, Booksellers, Newspapers, Periodicals, Printing & Publishing, Aesthetics, Art & Music, Economics, History & Science, a Preliminary Contribution. LC 76-4182. 80p. 1968. Repr. of 1950 ed. 35.00x (ISBN 0-8103-3521-2). Gale.

--Tobias George Smollett: A Bibliographical Guide. LC 77-83136. (AMS Studies in the Eighteenth Century: No. 2). lib. bdg. 32.50 (ISBN 0-404-16018-2). AMS Pr.

Cordasco, Francesco & Alloway, David N. American Ethnic Groups: The European Heritage. LC 80-28775. 376p. 1981. 19.00 (ISBN 0-8108-1405-6). Scarecrow.

--Crime in America: Historical Patterns & Contemporary Realities: An Annotated Bibliography. LC 84-48123. (Reference Library of Social Science). 275p. 1985. lib. bdg. 42.00 (ISBN 0-8240-8901-4). Garland Pub.

Cordasco, Francesco & Bucchioni, Eugene. The Puerto Rican Community & Its Children on the Mainland: A Source Book for Teachers, Social Workers & Other Professionals. rev., 3rd ed. LC 81-21250. 469p. 1982. 22.50 (ISBN 0-8108-1506-0). Scarecrow.

Cordasco, Francesco & Cordasco, Michael. Italians in the United States. 225p. 1981. 20.00 (ISBN 0-940198-00-2). Junius Vaughn.

Cordasco, Francesco & Gatner, Elliott S. Research & Report Writing. rev. ed. (Quality Paperback Ser.: No. 277). 146p. 1974. pap. 4.95 (ISBN 0-8226-0277-6). Littlefield.

Cordasco, Francesco & Pitkin, Thomas M. The White Slave Trade & the Immigrants: A Chapter in American Social History. LC 80-25556. 1981. 16.50 (ISBN 0-87917-077-8); pap. 6.95 (ISBN 0-87917-076-X). Ethridge.

Cordasco, Francesco & Rivera Alvarez, Pablo. Useful Spanish for Medical & Hospital Personnel with a Bibliography on Hispanic Peoples in the United States. LC 77-16566. 1977. pap. 7.95 (ISBN 0-87917-062-X). Ethridge.

Cordasco, Francesco see Dickinson, Joan Y.

Cordasco, Francesco, jt. auth. see Pitkin, Thomas M.

Cordasco, Francesco, ed. American Ethnic Groups, 47 bks. (The European Heritage Ser.). 1981. Set. lib. bdg. 1580.00x (ISBN 0-405-13400-2). Ayer Co Pubs.

--A Bibliography of Vocational Education: An Annotated Guide. LC 76-5961. (American Studies in Education: No. 4). 42.50 (ISBN 0-404-10125-9). AMS Pr.

--The Bilingual-Bicultural Child & the Question of Intelligence: An Original Anthology. LC 77-90568. (Bilingual-Bicultural Education in the U. S. Ser.). 1978. lib. bdg. 43.00x (ISBN 0-405-11107-X). Ayer Co Pubs.

--Bilingual-Bicultural Education in the U. S. Series, 37 bks. (Illus.). 1978. Set. lib. bdg. 1090.00x (ISBN 0-405-11071-5). Ayer Co Pubs.

--Bilingual Education in American Schools: A Guide to Information Sources. Bernstein, George. LC 79-15787. (Education Information Guide Ser.: Vol. 3). 328p. 1979. 60.00x (ISBN 0-8103-1447-9). Gale.

--Bilingual Education in New York City. LC 77-92284. (Bilingual-Bicultural Education in the U. S. Ser.). 1978. lib. bdg. 33.00x (ISBN 0-405-11081-2). Ayer Co Pubs.

--Bilingualism & the Bilingual Child: Challenges & Problems (an Original Anthology) LC 77-90569. (Bilingual-Bicultural Education in the U. S. Ser.). 1979. lib. bdg. 46.50x (ISBN 0-405-11108-8). Ayer Co Pubs.

--Italian Americans: A Guide to Information Sources. LC 78-4833. (Ethnic Studies Information Guide Ser.: Vol. 2). 248p. 1978. 60.00x (ISBN 0-8103-1397-9). Gale.

--The Italian Community & Its Language in the United States: The Annual Reports of the Italian Teachers Association. 472p. 1975. 27.50x (ISBN 0-87471-585-7). Rowman.

--Italians in the City: An Original Anthology. LC 74-17933. (Italian American Experience Ser). (Illus.). 1975. Repr. 13.00x (ISBN 0-405-06405-5). Ayer Co Pubs.

--Italians in the United States: An Original Anthology. LC 74-17934. (Italian American Experience Ser). (Illus.). 1975. Repr. 43.00x (ISBN 0-405-06406-3). Ayer Co Pubs.

--Jacob Riis Revisited. LC 72-93134. Repr. of 1970 ed. lib. bdg. 35.00x (ISBN 0-678-00706-3). Kelley.

--Materials & Human Resources for Teaching Ethnic Studies. LC 77-17706. (Bilingual-Bicultural Education in the U. S. Ser.). 1978. Repr. of 1975 ed. lib. bdg. 26.50x (ISBN 0-405-11088-X). Ayer Co Pubs.

--Protestant Evangelism among Italians in America. LC 74-17943. (Italian American Experience Ser.). (Illus.). 276p. 1975. Repr. 21.00x (ISBN 0-405-06414-4). Ayer Co Pubs.

--The Puerto Rican Experience. (Illus.). 10610p. 1975. 827.50 set (ISBN 0-405-06210-9). Ayer Co Pubs.

--La Societa Italiana Di Fronte Alle Prime Migrazioni Di Massa: Italian Society at the Beginnings of the Mass Migrations. LC 74-17954. (Italian American Experience Ser). (Illus.). 524p. 1975. Repr. 32.00x (ISBN 0-405-06423-3). Ayer Co Pubs.

--Studies in Italian-American Social History: Essays in Honor of Leonard Covello. (Illus.). 264p. 1975. 27.50x (ISBN 0-87471-705-1). Rowman.

Cordasco, Francesco & Alloway, David N., eds. Medical Education in the United States: A Guide to Information Sources. LC 79-24030. (Education Information Guide Ser.: Vol. 8). 426p. 1980. 58.00x (ISBN 0-8103-1458-4). Gale.

--Sociology of Education: A Guide to Information Sources. LC 78-10310. (Education Information Guide Ser.: Vol. 2). 280p. 1979. 60.00x (ISBN 0-8103-1436-3). Gale.

Cordasco, Francesco & Brickman, William W., eds. A Bibliography of American Educational History: An Annotated & Classified Guide. LC 74-29140. (American Studies in Educaion: No. 3). 1975. 42.50 (ISBN 0-404-12661-8). AMS Pr.

Cordasco, Francesco, ed. see Allen, Harold B.

Cordasco, Francesco, ed. see Allen, Virginia F. & Forman, Sidney.

Cordasco, Francesco, ed. see Appel, John J.

Cordasco, Francesco, ed. see Aucamp, A. J.

Cordasco, Francesco, ed. see Axelrod, Herman C.

Cordasco, Francesco, ed. see Bayer, Alan E.

Cordasco, Francesco, ed. see Bengelsdorf, Winnie.

Cordasco, Francesco, ed. see Berger, Morris I.

Cordasco, Francesco, ed. see Berman, Myron.

Cordasco, Francesco, ed. see Berrol, Selma C.

Cordasco, Francesco, ed. see Buxbaum, Edwin C.

Cordasco, Francesco, ed. see Castelli, Joseph R.

Cordasco, Francesco, ed. see Costantakos, Chrysie M.

Cordasco, Francesco, ed. see Covello, Leonard.

Cordasco, Francesco, ed. see Dissemination Center for Bilingual-Bicultural Education.

Cordasco, Francesco, ed. see Dissemination Center For Bilingual Bicultural Education.

Cordasco, Francesco, ed. see Dobbert, Guido A.

Cordasco, Francesco, ed. see Farrell, John J.

Cordasco, Francesco, ed. see Ferroni, Charles D.

Cordasco, Francesco, ed. see Fishman, Joshua A., et al.

Cordasco, Francesco, ed. see Flores, Solomon H.

Cordasco, Francesco, ed. see Gabriel, Richard A.

Cordasco, Francesco, ed. see Galvan, Robert R.

Cordasco, Francesco, ed. see Glasco, Laurence A.

Cordasco, Francesco, ed. see Gobetz, Giles E.

Cordasco, Francesco, ed. see Hansen, Judith E.

Cordasco, Francesco, ed. see Harper, Richard C.

Cordasco, Francesco, ed. see Hill, Robert F.

Cordasco, Francesco, ed. see Hosay, Philip M.

Cordasco, Francesco, ed. see Illinois State Advisory Committee, the United States Commission on Civil Rights.

Cordasco, Francesco, ed. see Iorizzo, John L.

Cordasco, Francesco, ed. see Juliani, Richard N.

Cordasco, Francesco, ed. see Knoche, Carl H.

Cordasco, Francesco, ed. see Kolm, Richard.

Cordasco, Francesco, ed. see Kraus, Harry P.

Cordasco, Francesco, ed. see Leder, Hans H.

Cordasco, Francesco, ed. see Leonard, Henry B.

Cordasco, Francesco, ed. see Levy-Salomone, Rosemary.

Cordasco, Francesco, ed. see Lindberg, Duane R.

Cordasco, Francesco, ed. see Malherbe, Ernst G.

Cordasco, Francesco, ed. see Mandera, Franklin R.

Cordasco, Francesco, ed. see Medina, Amelia C.

Cordasco, Francesco, ed. see Mostwin, Danuta.

Cordasco, Francesco, ed. see Munguia, Juan C.

Cordasco, Francesco, ed. see Nam, Charles B.

Cordasco, Francesco, ed. see National Advisory Council on Bilingual Education.

Cordasco, Francesco, ed. see Neuringer, Sheldon M.

Cordasco, Francesco, ed. see Newton, Lewis W.

Cordasco, Francesco, ed. see Obidinski, Eugene E.

Cordasco, Francesco, ed. see Peebles, Robert W.

Cordasco, Francesco, ed. see Reyes, Vinicio H.

Cordasco, Francesco, ed. see Royal Commission on Bilingualism & Biculturalism.

Cordasco, Francesco, ed. see Schelbert, Leo.

Cordasco, Francesco, ed. see Scherini, Rose D.

Cordasco, Francesco, ed. see Scourby, Alice.

Cordasco, Francesco, ed. see Spengler, Paul A.

Cordasco, Francesco, ed. see Stein, Howard F.

Cordasco, Francesco, ed. see Streiff, Virginia.

Cordasco, Francesco, ed. see Strelff, Paul R.

Cordasco, Francesco, ed. see Theriault, George F.

Cordasco, Francesco, ed. see Thompson, Bryan.

Cordasco, Francesco, ed. see Ulrich, Robert J.

Cordasco, Francesco, ed. see United Kingdom, Dept. of Education & Science, National Commission for U. N. E. S. C. O.

Cordasco, Francesco, ed. see United Nations Educational Scientific & Cultural Organization.

Cordasco, Francesco, ed. see U. S. Bureau of Indian Affairs.

Cordasco, Francesco, ed. see U. S. Commission on Civil Rights.

Cordasco, Francesco, ed. see U. S. House of Representatives, Committee on Education & Labor, General Subcommittee on Education.

Cordasco, Francesco, ed. see U. S. House of Representatives, General Subcommittee on Education & Labor.

Cordasco, Francesco, ed. see U. S. Office of Education, Bureau of Research.

Cordasco, Francesco, ed. see U. S. Senate, Committee on Labor & Public Welfare.

Cordasco, Francesco, ed. see Viereck, Louis.

Cordasco, Francesco, ed. see Wilhelm, Hubert G.

Cordasco, Francesco, et al. The Puerto Rican Experience: A Sociological Sourcebook. (Quality Paperback: No. 259). 370p. (Orig.). 1975. pap. 5.95 (ISBN 0-8226-0259-8). Littlefield.

--Puerto Ricans on the United States Mainland: A Bibliography of Reports, Texts, Critical Studies & Related Materials. 146p. 1972. 15.00x (ISBN 0-87471-017-0). Rowman.

--The Equality of Educational Opportunity: A Bibliography of Selected References. (Quality Paperback Ser.: No. 264). 139p. (Orig.). 1973. pap. 1.00 (ISBN 0-8226-0264-4). Littlefield.

Cordasco, Francesco, et al, eds. History of American Education: A Guide to Information Sources. LC 79-23010. (Education Information Guide Ser.: Vol. 7). 328p. 1979. 60.00x (ISBN 0-8103-1382-0). Gale.

--The School in the Social Order: A Sociological Introduction to Educational Understanding. LC 81-40495. 438p. 1981. pap. text ed. 18.50 (ISBN 0-8191-1731-5). U Pr of Amer.

Cordasco, Fransecso, ed. see Olson, Audrey L.

Cordasco, Fransecso, ed. see Romano, Louis A.

Cordasco, Fransecso, ed. see Scarpaci, Jean A.

Cordasco, Michael, jt. auth. see Cordasco, Francesco.

Cordavero, Moses. Or Nerev: Hebrew Text. 1980. 10.00 (ISBN 0-943688-17-5). Res Ctr Kabbalah.

Corday, Eliot, ed. Controversies in Cardiology. LC 76-54825. (Cardiovascular Clinics Ser: Vol, 8, No. 1). 1977. text ed. 35.00x (ISBN 0-8036-1980-4). Davis Co.

Corday, Eliot & Swan, H. J. C., eds. Clinical Strategies in Ischemic Heart Disease: New Concepts & Current Controversies. LC 78-22068. 632p. 56.00 (ISBN 0-683-02080-3). Krieger.

Corddry, Thomas. Kibby & the Red Elephant. LC 72-13771. (Illus.). (gr. 3-6). 1973. 6.95 (ISBN 0-87955-106-2). O'Hara.

Cordeiro, Aquiles, tr. see Jackins, Harvey.

Cordeiro, Daniel R., ed. A Bibliography of Latin American Bibliographies: Social Sciences & Humanities, Supplement No. 2 to Arthur E. Gropp's A Bibliography of Latin American Bibliographies, Vol. 1. LC 78-11935. 1979. lib. bdg. 20.00 (ISBN 0-8108-1170-7). Scarecrow.

Cordelier, Jeanne. The Life: Memoirs of a French Hooker. 1980. pap. 2.75 (ISBN 0-380-45609-5, 45609-5). Avon.

Cordelier, M., jt. auth. see Harrison, P. W.

Cordell, A. Robert & Ellison, Robert. Complications of Intrathoracic Surgery. 1979. 47.50 (ISBN 0-316-15732-5). Little.

Cordell, Arthur J. & Gilmour, James, eds. The Role & Function of Government Laboratories & the Transfer of Technology to the Manufacturing Sector. (Science Council of Canada Background Studies: No. 35). 1976. pap. 12.00 (ISBN 0-685-77314-0, SSC72, SSC). Unipub.

Cordell, Benjamin. The World Truth Bible. 219p. 1981. 12.50 (ISBN 0-682-49758-4). Exposition Pr FL.

Cordell, Brad. My Name on a Bullet. 1979. pap. 1.25 (ISBN 0-505-51411-7, Pub. by Tower Bks). Dorchester Pub Co.

Cordell, Dennis D. Dar Al-Kuti & the Last Years of the Trans-Saharan Slave Trade. LC 84-40147. (Illus.). 352p. 1985. 35.00x (ISBN 0-299-09520-7). U of Wis Pr.

Cordell, Frank & Gieber, Gale. Take Ten to Grow. LC 78-60169. 1978. 3.95 (ISBN 0-89505-017-X). Argus Comm.

Cordell, Geoffrey A. Introduction to Alkaloids: A Biogenetic Approach. LC 80-39651. 1056p. 1981. cloth 171.50 (ISBN 0-471-03478-9, Pub. by Wiley-Interscience). Wiley.

Cordell, H. Ken & Stanley-Saunders, Barbara. The Private Sector Role in Rural Outdoor Recreation in the United States: An Annotated Bibliography. (Bibliographic Ser.: No. 8). 118p. 1984. 20.00 (ISBN 0-88329-135-5). Intl Assess.

Cordell, Ken & Stanley-Saunders, Barbara. The Private Sector Role in Rural Outdoor Recreation in the U.S. An Annotated Bibliography. (CPL Bibliographies Ser.: No. 106). 118p. 1983. 15.00 (ISBN 0-86602-106-X). Coun Plan Librarians.

Cordell, Linda S. Prehistory of the South West. (New World Archaeological Record Ser.). 1984. 49.00 (ISBN 0-12-188220-9); pap. 25.00 (ISBN 0-12-188222-5). Acad Pr.

Cordell, Linda S., ed. Tijeras Canyon: Analyses of the Past. (Maxwell Mus. Anthropology Publ. Ser.). (Illus.). 232p. 1980. 19.95 (ISBN 0-8263-0553-9). U of NM Pr.

Cordell, Linda S. & Beckerman, Stephen, eds. The Versatility of Kinship. LC 80-525. (Studies in Anthropology). 1980. 47.50 (ISBN 0-12-188250-0). Acad Pr.

Cordell, Melissa. Bond of Evil. 1977. pap. 1.75 (ISBN 0-532-17163-2). Woodhill.

--Shades of Peril. 1977. pap. 1.50 (ISBN 0-532-15280-8). Woodhill.

Cordell, Richard A. Henry Arthur Jones & the Modern Drama. LC 68-26274. 1968. Repr. of 1932 ed. 21.00x (ISBN 0-8046-0089-9, Pub. by Kennikat). Assoc Faculty Pr.

Cordellos, Harry C. Breaking Through. LC 78-23270. (Illus.). 240p. (Orig.). 1981. pap. 7.95 (ISBN 0-89037-168-7). Anderson World.

Cordemoy, Geraud De. A Philosophical Discourse Concerning Speech. Bd. with A Discourse Written by a Learned Frier. Repr. of 1670 ed. LC 78-147961. Repr. of 1668 ed. 15.00 (ISBN 0-404-08211-4). AMS Pr.

--Philosophical Discourse Concerning Speech (1668) & a Discourse Written to a Learned Frier (1670) LC 72-6400. (History of Psychology Ser.). 232p. 1972. Repr. 35.00x (ISBN 0-8201-1106-6). Schol Facsimiles.

Corden, W. M. Inflation, Exchange Rates, & the World Economy: Lectures on Int'l Monetary Economics. rev. ed. (Studies in Business & Society Ser.). 160p. 1981. 15.00x (ISBN 0-226-11585-2). U of Chicago Pr.

--Inflation, Exchange Rates, & the World Economy: Lectures on International Monetary Economics. 2nd ed. (Business & Society Studies). 1980. pap. 6.00x (ISBN 0-226-11584-4). U of Chicago Pr.

--Theory of Protection. (Illus.). 1971. 18.95x (ISBN 0-19-828171-4). Oxford U Pr.

--Trade Policy & Economic Welfare. (Illus.). 1974. text ed. 44.50x o. p. (ISBN 0-19-828199-4); pap. text ed. 17.95x (ISBN 0-19-828401-2). Oxford U Pr.

Cordenoy, E. Jacob De. Flore De l'Ile De la Reunion (Mascarene Islands) 1972. Repr. of 1895 ed. 52.50 (ISBN 3-7682-0758-7). Lubrecht & Cramer.

Corder, Brice W. Preparing for Medical School: A Guide to Requirements, Admission, Financial Aid, & More. LC 83-71087. (Illus.). 200p. (Orig.). 1983. pap. 8.95 (ISBN 0-913011-00-2). Ambleside.

Corder, Brice W., et al. Health: Current Perspectives. 3rd ed. 384p. 1981. pap. text ed. write for info. (ISBN 0-697-07388-2); instructor's manual avail. (ISBN 0-697-07389-0). Wm C Brown.

Corder, E. M. The Deer Hunter. 1979. pap. 1.95 (ISBN 0-515-05321-X). Jove Pubns.

Corder, Frederick. Ferencz (Francois) Liszt. LC 74-24062. Repr. of 1925 ed. 18.50 (ISBN 0-404-12888-2). AMS Pr.

Corder, Gene L. The Five Deadly Mistakes That Lead to Bankruptcy! A Successful Business Handbook for Today's Men & Women. LC 81-50762. 208p. (gr. 12). 1981. pap. 9.95x (ISBN 0-939588-01-3). Redcor Bk.

Corder, George E. Your Brain-Image Power: How to Selfsex & Imagize Your Way to Super-Successful Living. LC 82-90505. 200p. 1983. lib. bdg. 25.00 (ISBN 0-9609246-0-4). Brain-Image.

Corder, Henry. Liberia Under Military Rule. 1980. 8.50 (ISBN 0-686-33169-9). Liberian Studies.

Corder, Henry, ed. New Voices from West Africa. 1979. 6.00 (ISBN 0-686-33149-4). Liberian Studies.

Corder, Jim W. Contemporary Writing: Process & Practice. 2nd ed. 1983. pap. text ed. 17.35x (ISBN 0-673-15430-0). Scott F.

--Contemporary Writing with Handbook. 2nd ed. 1983. text ed. 19.50x (ISBN 0-673-15443-2). Scott F.

Corder, Jim W. & Ruszkiewicz, John J. Handbook of Current English. 7th ed. 1985. text ed. 12.95x (ISBN 0-673-15968-X). Scott F.

Corder, S. Pit. Error Analysis & Interlanguage. 1981. pap. text ed. 11.95x (ISBN 0-19-437073-9). Oxford U Pr.

Corder, Suzanne & Thompson, Gay. Of Magnolia & Mesquite. (Illus.). 352p. (Orig.). pap. 12.95 (ISBN 0-9614184-0-0). Hart Graphics.

Corderman, Esther B. Echo from Rose Hill. 1983. write for info. (ISBN 0-9611892-0-7). McClain.

Cordero, Raymond & Serjeantson, Richard, eds. Iron & Steel Works of the World 1978. 7th ed. LC 75-314459. 1978. 100.00x (ISBN 0-900542-21-7). Intl Pubns Serv.

Cordes, Carole V., jt. auth. see Babin, Edith H.

Cordes, E. H., ed. Reaction Kinetics in Micelles. LC 72-94823. 157p. 1973. 39.50x (ISBN 0-306-30722-7, Plenum Pr). Plenum Pub.

Cordes, H. O. Elliptic Pseudo-Differential Operators: An Abstract Theory. (Lecture Notes in Mathematics: Vol. 756). 1979. pap. 23.00 (ISBN 0-387-09704-X). Springer-Verlag.

Cordes, Lianne. The Reflecting Pond. 148p. 1980. pap. 5.95 (ISBN 0-89486-121-2). Hazelden.

Cordes, Rainer & Scholz, Fred. Bedouins, Wealth, & Change: A Study of Rural Development in the United Arab Emirates & the Sultanate of Oman. 64p. 1980. pap. 11.75 (ISBN 92-808-0143-0, TUNU086, UNU). Unipub.

Cordes, Ron, ed. see Kaufmann, Randall.

Cordesman, Anthony H. The Gulf & the Search for Strategic Stability: Saudi Arabia, the Military Balance in the Gulf, & Trends in the Arab-Israeli Military Balance. (Special Studies on the Middle East). 1000p. 1984. lib. bdg. 45.00x (ISBN 0-86531-619-8). Westview.

--Jordanian Arms & the Middle East Balance. (Illus.). 186p. (Orig.). 1983. pap. 15.00 (ISBN 0-916808-20-3). Mid East Inst.

--U. S. - Arab Relations: The Iran-Iraq War & U. S.-Iraq Relations: An Iraqi Perspective, No. 11. 40p. (Orig.). pap. 5.00 (ISBN 0-916729-09-5). Natl Coun Arab.

--U. S. - Arab Relations: The Strategic Dimension, No. 8. 80p. (Orig.). 1984. pap. 8.00 (ISBN 0-916729-08-7). Natl Coun Arab.

Cordesman, Anthony H, jt. auth. see Collins, John M.

Cordier, Andrew, ed. Public Papers of the Secretaries-General of the United Nations, Vol. 8: U Thant 1968-1971. LC 68-8873. 1977. 50.00x (ISBN 0-231-04232-9). Columbia U Pr.

Cordier, Andrew W., ed. Columbia Essays in International Affairs: The Dean's Papers, Vol. 2, 1966. LC 66-14078. 324p. 1967. 34.00x (ISBN 0-231-03047-9). Columbia U Pr.

--Columbia Essays in International Affairs: The Dean's Papers, Vol. 3, 1967. LC 66-14078. 441p. 1968. 34.00x (ISBN 0-231-03156-4). Columbia U Pr.

--Columbia Essays in International Affairs: The Dean's Papers, Vol. 4, 1968. LC 66-14078. 295p. 1969. 34.00x (ISBN 0-231-03270-6). Columbia U Pr.

--Columbia Essays in International Affairs: The Dean's Papers, Vol. 5, 1969. LC 66-14078. 328p. 1970. 34.00x (ISBN 0-231-03487-3). Columbia U Pr.

--Columbia Essays in International Affairs: The Dean's Papers, Vol. 6, 1970. LC 66-14078. 232p. 1971. 34.00x (ISBN 0-231-03550-0). Columbia U Pr.

--Columbia Essays in International Affairs: The Dean's Papers, Vol. 7, 1971. LC 66-14078. 261p. 1972. 34.00x (ISBN 0-231-03667-1). Columbia U Pr.

--Paths to World Order. LC 67-19877. 161p. (Orig.). 1967. pap. 12.00x (ISBN 0-231-08578-8). Columbia U Pr.

Cordier, Andrew W. & Foote, Wilder, eds. Public Papers of the Secretaries-General of the United Nations, Vol 1: Trygve Lie, 1946-1953. LC 68-8873. 535p. 1969. 36.00x (ISBN 0-231-03137-8). Columbia U Pr.

--Public Papers of the Secretaries-General of the United Nations, Vol. 2: Dag Hammarskjold, 1953-1956. LC 68-8873. 115p. 1972. 36.00x (ISBN 0-231-03633-7). Columbia U Pr.

--Public Papers of the Secretaries-General of the United Nations, Vol. 5: Dag Hammarskjold, 1960-1961. LC 68-8873. 592p. 1975. 36.00x (ISBN 0-231-03897-6). Columbia U Pr.

--Public Papers of the Secretaries-General of the United Nations, Vol. 3: Dag Hammarskjold, 1956-1957, Vol. 3. 729p. 1973. 36.00x (ISBN 0-231-03735-X). Columbia U Pr.

--Public Papers of the Secretaries General of the United Nations, Vol 4: Dag Hammarskjold, 1958-1960, Vol. 4. LC 68-8873. 659p. 1974. 36.00x (ISBN 0-231-03810-0). Columbia U Pr.

Cordier, Andrew W. & Harrelson, Max, eds. Public Papers of the Secretaries-General of the United Nations, Vol. 6: U Thant, 1961-1964. LC 68-8873. 708p. 1976. 36.00x (ISBN 0-231-03966-2). Columbia U Pr.

--Public Papers of the Secretaries General of the United Nations, Vol. 7: U Thant, 1965-1967. LC 68-8873. 633p. 1976. 36.00 (ISBN 0-231-04098-9). Columbia U Pr.

Cordier, Henri. Bibliographie Stendhalienne. LC 68-58476. (Bibliography & Reference Ser.: No. 259). (Fr). 1969. Repr. of 1914 ed. 29.00 (ISBN 0-8337-0672-1). B Franklin.

--Bibliotheca Indosinica. Dictionnaire bibliographique des ouvrages relatifs a la peninsule indo-chinoise, 5 vols. in 3. (Span. & Indonesian.). 1912-32. Set. 197.00 (ISBN 0-8337-0676-4). B Franklin.

--Bibliotheca Sinica, dictionnaire bibliographique des ouvrages relatifs a l'Empire chinois, 6 vols. in 5. 2nd ed. LC 68-58196. (Bibliography & Research Ser.: No. 250). (Span., Chinese & Fr.). 1969. Repr. of 1922 ed. 200.00 (ISBN 0-8337-0671-3). B Franklin.

--L' Expedition de Chine de 1857-1858: Histoire diplomatique. LC 72-38062. Repr. of 1905 ed. 24.00 (ISBN 0-404-56922-6). AMS Pr.

--L' Expedition de Chine De 1860: Histoire diplomatique. LC 76-38063. Repr. of 1906 ed. 24.00 (ISBN 0-404-56923-4). AMS Pr.

Cordier, Henri, ed. Cathay & the Way Thither, 4 vols. new rev. ed. (Hakluyt Society Works Ser.: No. 2, Vols. 33, 37 & 41). (Illus.). Repr. of 1913 ed. Set. 145.00 (ISBN 0-317-16772-3). Kraus Repr.

Cordier, J., jt. ed. see Lowenthal, F.

Cordier, Sherwood S. The Air & Sea Lanes of the North Atlantic: Their Security in the Nineteen Eighties. LC 81-40180. 90p. (Orig.). 1981. pap. text ed. 7.50 (ISBN 0-8191-1587-8). U Pr of Amer.

--Calculus of Power: The Current Soviet-American Conventional Military Balance in Central Europe. 3rd ed. LC 79-5435. 1980. pap. text ed. 9.00 (ISBN 0-8191-0883-9). U Pr of Amer.

--U. S. Military Power & Rapid Deployment Requirements in the 1980s. 156p. 1983. pap. 18.50x (ISBN 0-86531-968-5). Westview.

Cordilla, Ann. The Making of an Inmate. 133p. 1983. 15.25 (ISBN 0-87073-722-8); pap. 8.95 (ISBN 0-87073-723-6). Schenkman Bks Inc.

Cording, Edward J., ed. see Rock Mechanics Symposium Participants.

Cording, Ruth. Joy of Remembering Our Children. 1984. gift padded cover 9.95 (ISBN 0-87162-281-5, J1022). Warner Pr.

--The Joy of Remembering Our Guests. 1982. gift padded cover 7.95 (ISBN 0-87162-258-0, J1016). Warner Pr.

--The Joy of Remembering-Special Friends, Moments, Days. 1981. gift padded cover 7.95 (ISBN 0-87162-247-5, J1015). Warner Pr.

--Larry the Lamb. (God's Animals Story Bks.). 1983. pap. 1.50 (ISBN 0-87162-286-6, D5600). Warner Pr.

Cordingley, E. W. Principles & Practice of Naturopathy. 25p. 1971. pap. 2.95 (ISBN 0-88697-034-2). Life Science.

Cordingley, Patrick, jt. auth. see Limb, Sue.

Cordingly, David. Painters of the Sea. (Illus.). 1980. pap. 14.95 (ISBN 0-85331-425-X). Eastview.

Cordner, Gary W., jt. auth. see Hudzik, John.

Cordner, Gary W., jt. auth. see Sheehan, Robert.

Cordner, J. W. Manual of Operating Room Management. 1982. pap. 14.95 (ISBN 0-87489-260-0). Med Economics.

Cordner, Jacqueline W. Logic of Operating Room Nursing. 3rd ed. LC 83-20385. 1984. pap. 13.95 prof. (ISBN 0-87489-359-3). Med Economics.

Cordner, Michael, ed. see Etherege, George.

Cordner, Michael, ed. see Farquhar, George.

Cordoba, Pedro De see De Cordoba, Pedro.

Cordon, Faustino. An Introduction to the Biological Basis of Feeding: Essential Biological Ideas Necessary to a Study of Living Beings from the Evolutionary Standpoint. LC 79-40933. (Illus.). 250p. 1980. pap. 37.00 (ISBN 0-08-025484-5). Pergamon.

--The Origin, Nature & Evolution of Protoplasmic Individuals & their Associations: Protoplasmic Action & Experience. (Illus.). 650p. 1982. 110.00 (ISBN 0-08-027990-2). Pergamon.

Cordon, Mary J. Clinical Calculations for Nurses: With Basic Mathematics Review. (Illus.). 240p. 1984. pap. text ed. 16.95 (ISBN 0-13-137679-9). P-H.

Cordon, Mary J. & Yamato, Yoshiko. Mastering Mathematical Concepts. 480p. 1985. pap. text ed. 25.95x (ISBN 0-89863-084-3). Star Pub CA.

Cordon, William A. Freezing & Thawing of Concrete: Mechanisms & Control. LC 66-14390. (American Concrete Institute Monograph: No. 3). pap. 27.80 (ISBN 0-317-08526-3, 2012299). Bks Demand UMI.

--Properties, Evaluation & Control of Engineering Materials. 1979. text ed. 45.00 (ISBN 0-07-013123-6). McGraw.

Cordor, Henry. Africa, from People to People. 1979. 5.00 (ISBN 0-686-33168-0). Liberian Studies.

--Facing the Realities of the Liberian Nation. 1980. 6.50 (ISBN 0-686-34401-4). Liberian Studies.

Cordova, Efren. Conciliation Services: Structures, Functions & Techniques. (Labour-Management Relations Ser.: No. 62). 141p. (Orig.). 1984. pap. 10.00 (ISBN 92-2-103236-1, ILO299 5071, ILO). Unipub.

Cordova, Efren, jt. auth. see Morris, James O.

Cordova, Efren, ed. Industrial Relations in Latin America. LC 83-24480. 304p. 1984. 28.95 (ISBN 0-03-070284-4). Praeger.

--Selected Basic Agreements & Joint Declarations on Labour-Management Relations. (Labour-Management Relations Ser.: No. 63). 299p. (Orig.). 1984. pap. 14.25 (ISBN 92-2-103460-7, ILO300, ILO). Unipub.

Cordova, Efren, intro. by see International Labour Office, et al.

Cordova, Gonzalo F. & Concepcion, Sara I. Santiago Iglesias: Creador del Movimiento Obrero de Puerto Rico. LC 78-14404. (Illus., Span.). 1979. pap. 6.50 (ISBN 0-8477-0857-8). U of PR Pr.

Cordova, Lieban. Luis Munoz Marin y Sus Campanas Politicas. LC 83-26083. (Illus.). 175p. (Orig., Span.). 1984. pap. 7.00 (ISBN 0-317-17287-5). U of PR Pr.

Cordova, Lorenzo de see De Cordova, Lorenzo.

Cordovano, Steven & Sechi, Stephan M. The Compleat Alchemist. (The Compleat Fantasy Ser.). (Illus.). 45p. 1983. pap. text ed. 7.50 (ISBN 0-9610770-0-X, 4801). Bard Games.

Cordovano, Steven, ed. see Sechi, Stephan M., et al.

Cordovano, Steven, ed. see Sechi, Stephan M. & Taylor, Vernie J.

Cordovero, Moses. The Palm Tree of Deborah. Jacobs, Louis, tr. from Heb. LC 80-54594. (The Judaic Studies Library: No. SPH8). 133p. 1981. pap. 7.95 (ISBN 0-87203-097-0). Hermon.

Cordry, Donald. Mexican Masks. LC 73-92100. (Illus.). 36p. 1973. pap. 3.00 (ISBN 0-88360-004-8). Amon Carter.

--Mexican Masks. (Illus.). 304p. 1980. 49.95 (ISBN 0-292-75050-1). U of Tex Pr.

--Mexican Masks. pap. 3.00 (ISBN 0-88360-004-8, Dist. by Univ. of Texas Pr.). Amon Carter.

Cordry, Donald & Cordry, Dorothy. Mexican Indian Costumes. (Texas Pan American Ser.). (Illus.). 393p. 1968. 39.95 (ISBN 0-292-73426-3). U of Tex Pr.

Cordry, Donald B. Costumes & Weaving of the Zoque Indians of Chiapas, Mexico. 130p. 1941. 5.00 (ISBN 0-916561-17-8). Southwest Mus.

Cordry, Dorothy, jt. auth. see Cordry, Donald.

Cords, Nicholas & Gerster, Patrick. Myth & the American Experience, Vol. 1. 2nd ed. 1978. pap. text ed. write for info. (ISBN 0-02-471880-7). Macmillan.

Cords, Nicholas, jt. auth. see Gerster, Patrick.

Corduan, Winfried. Handmaid to Theology. 176p. (Orig.). 1981. pap. 7.95 (ISBN 0-8010-2468-4). Baker Bk.

Corduneanu, Constantin. Integral Equations & Stability of Feedback Systems. (Mathematics in Science & Engineering Ser.). 1973. 60.00 (ISBN 0-12-188350-7). Acad Pr.

--Principles of Differential & Integral Equations. 2nd ed. LC 77-2962. 1977. text ed. 14.95 (ISBN 0-8284-0295-7). Chelsea Pub.

Cordwell, Justine, ed. The Visual Arts: Plastic & Graphic. (World Anthropology Ser.). 1979. text ed. 56.00x (ISBN 90-279-7820-4). Mouton.

Cordwell, Justine & Schwartz, Ronald A., eds. The Fabrics of Culture: The Anthology of Clothing & Adornment. (World Anthropology Ser.). 1979. text ed. 4.20x (ISBN 90-279-7910-3). Mouton.

Cordy, Don. The Protein Book. LC 75-44132. (Illus.). 86p. (Orig.). 1976. 10.95 (ISBN 0-87961-045-X); pap. 4.95 (ISBN 0-87961-044-1). Naturegraph.

Cordy, Donald. Mexican Masks. (Illus.). 304p. 1982. pap. 19.95 (ISBN 0-292-75074-9). U of Tex Pr.

Cordy, Peter. Creative Source. 6th ed. (Illus.). 392p. 1985. 49.50 (ISBN 0-920986-06-4). R Silver.

Cordy, Peter, ed. Creative Source: Fifth Annual. (Illus.). 442p. 1984. 47.50 (ISBN 0-920986-04-8). Wilcord Pubns.

--Creative Source: Seventh Annual. (Illus.). 480p. 1985. 51.50 (ISBN 0-317-19811-4, Pub. by Rotovision). R Silver.

Cordy, Ross. A Study of Prehistoric Social Change: The Development of Complex Societies in the Hawaiian Islands. LC 81-10825. (Studies in Archaeology). 1981. 36.00 (ISBN 0-12-188450-3). Acad Pr.
Cordy-Collins, Alana. Pre-Columbian Art History. rev. ed. (Illus.). 400p. 1982. pap. text ed. 14.95 (ISBN 0-917962-71-0). Peek Pubns.
Cordy-Collins, Alana & Nicholson, H. B. Pre-Columbian Art from the Land Collection. Land, L. K., ed. (Illus.). 272p. (Orig.). 1979. pap. 25.00 (ISBN 0-940228-03-3). Calif Acad Sci.
Cordy-Collins, Alana, jt. auth. see Nicholson, H. B.
Core, Arthur C. Otterbein (Philip William) 1968. 4.00 (ISBN 0-687-30917-4); pap. 2.25 (ISBN 0-687-30918-2). Abingdon.
Core, Earl. Monongalia Story: Five, Sophistication. 1984. 35.00 (ISBN 0-87012-465-X). McClain.
Core, Earl L. Chronicles of Core. 3rd ed. 1975. 10.00 (ISBN 0-87012-227-4). McClain.
--Monongalia Story: Four, Industrialization. 1982. 30.00 (ISBN 0-87012-411-0). McClain.
--The Monongalia Story: One Prelude. 1974. 25.00 (ISBN 0-87012-169-3). McClain.
--Monongalia Story: Three, Discord. 1979. 30.00 (ISBN 0-87012-309-2). McClain.
--The Monongalia Story, Two: The Pioneers. 1977. 25.00 (ISBN 0-87012-245-2). McClain.
--Morgantown Disciples. (Illus.). 1960. 8.00 (ISBN 0-87012-024-7). McClain.
--Spring Wild Flowers of West Virginia. LC 81-50933. 1981. 4.00 (ISBN 0-937058-02-5). West Va U Pr.
Core, Earl L. & Ammons, Nelle P. Woody Plants in Winter. (Illus., Orig.). (YA) (gr. 9 up). 1958. text ed. 9.95x (ISBN 0-910286-21-3); pap. text ed. 7.95x (ISBN 0-910286-02-7). Boxwood.
Core, Earl L., jt. auth. see Strausbaugh, P. D.
Core, George & Sullivan, Walter. Writing from the Inside. 1983. 8.95x (ISBN 0-393-95246-0); instr. manual avail. (ISBN 0-393-95337-8). Norton.
Core, George, jt. ed. see Young, Thomas Daniel.
Core, Harold, et al. Wood Structure & Identification. 2nd ed. 1979. pap. 12.95x (ISBN 0-8156-5043-4). Syracuse U Pr.
Core, Lucy & Calhoun, David, eds. The Louisiana Almanac, 1984-85 Edition. (Illus.). 496p. (Orig.). 1984. pap. 11.95 (ISBN 0-88289-297-5). Pelican.
Core, Lucy, ed. see Women of Christ Church Cathedral.
Core, Marianne S., jt. auth. see Corey, Gerald.
Core, Philip. Camp: The Lie That Tells the Truth. (Illus.). 192p. (Orig.). 1984. pap. 12.95 (ISBN 0-933328-83-4). Delilah Bks.
--The Original Eye: Creators of Twentieth Century Style. LC 83-22924. (Illus.). 192p. 1984. 24.95 (ISBN 0-13-642455-4). P-H.
--Paintings Nineteen Seventy-Five to Nineteen Eighty-Five. (Illus.). 96p. 1985. 24.95 (ISBN 0-907040-67-5, Pub. by GMP England). Alyson Pubns.
Corea, G. Need for Change: Towards the New International Economic Order. flexi-cover 17.25 (ISBN 0-08-027411-0). Pergamon.
Corea, Gamani. Development & Recovery: The Realities of the New Interdependence: Report by the Secretary-General of the United Nations Conference on Trade & Development to the Sixth Session of the Conference. 60p. 1985. pap. 6.00 (UN84/2D4, UN). Unipub.
--Need for Change: Towards the New International Economic Order. LC 80-40800. 350p. 1980. 33.00 (ISBN 0-08-026095-0). Pergamon.
Corea, Gena. The Hidden Malpractice: How American Medicine Mistreats Women. Upd. ed. LC 84-48149. 384p. 1984. pap. 7.64i (ISBN 0-06-091215-4, CN 1215, CN). Har-Row.
--The Mother Machine: Reproductive Technologies from Artificial Insemination to Artificial Wombs. LC 84-48150. 352p. 1985. 17.26i (ISBN 0-06-015390-3, HarpT). Har-Row.
Corea, Nicholas J. Cleaner Breed. 1974. pap. 1.25 (ISBN 0-380-00167-5, 21311). Avon.
Coreil, Judith, jt. auth. see Reck, Carleen.
Corell, Richard A. Representative Modern Plays British & American from Robertson to O'Neill. 654p. Repr. of 1929 ed. lib. bdg. 75.00 (ISBN 0-8492-7309-9). R West.
Corelli, A. La Folio for Violin & Piano. David, Ferd & Auer, Leopold, eds. (Carl Fischer Music Library: No. 877). 1922. pap. 5.00 (ISBN 0-8258-0093-5). Fischer Inc NY.
Corelli, Marie. Ardath. pap. 4.95 (ISBN 0-910122-04-0). Amherst Pr.
--Barabbas. pap. 4.95 (ISBN 0-910122-00-8). Amherst Pr.
--Barabras: A Dream of the World's Tragedy. 317p. 1983. Repr. of 1893 ed. lib. bdg. 12.50 (ISBN 0-89987-149-6). Darby Bks.
--Cameos. facsimile ed. LC 75-106278. (Short Story Index Reprint Ser.). 1895. 16.00 (ISBN 0-8369-3316-8). Ayer Co Pubs.
--Free Opinions Freely Expressed on Certain Phases of Modern Social Life & Conduct. LC 76-37685. Repr. of 1905 ed. 34.00 (ISBN 0-404-56739-8). AMS Pr.
--Innocent. pap. 4.95 (ISBN 0-910122-37-7). Amherst Pr.
--Life Everlasting. pap. 8.95 deluxe (ISBN 0-87505-092-1). Borden.
--Master Christian. pap. 4.95 (ISBN 0-910122-02-4). Amherst Pr.
--The Master Christian. 604p. 1983. Repr. of 1900 ed. lib. bdg. 45.00 (ISBN 0-8495-0961-0). Arden Lib.
--The Mighty Atom. 1896. lib. bdg. 25.00 (ISBN 0-8414-2390-3). Folcroft.
--Romance of Two Worlds. (Illus.). pap. 4.95 (ISBN 0-910122-03-2). Amherst Pr.
--A Romance of Two Worlds. Wolff, Robert L., ed. LC 75-484. (Victorian Fiction Ser.). 1975. Repr. of 1886 ed. lib. bdg. 73.00 (ISBN 0-8240-1561-4). Garland Pub.
--A Romance of Two Worlds. LC 83-83171. (Spiritual Fiction Publications Ser.: Vol. 3). 328p. 1985. cloth 15.00 (ISBN 0-8334-0002-9, Spiritual Fiction). Garber Comm.
--Secret Power. pap. 4.95 (ISBN 0-910122-07-5). Amherst Pr.
--Song of Miriam: And Other Stories, Vol. 1. LC 71-37263. (Short Story Index Reprint Ser). Repr. of 1898 ed. 15.00 (ISBN 0-8369-4074-1). Ayer Co Pubs.
--Sorrows of Satan. (Illus.). pap. 4.95 (ISBN 0-910122-06-7). Amherst Pr.
--Soul of Lilith. (Illus.). pap. 4.95 (ISBN 0-910122-05-9). Amherst Pr.
--Temporal Power. pap. 4.95 (ISBN 0-910122-26-1). Amherst Pr.
--Thelma. lib. bdg. 30.00 (ISBN 0-8414-2391-1). Folcroft.
--Vendetta. pap. 4.95 (ISBN 0-910122-27-X). Amherst Pr.
--Wormwood. pap. 4.95 (ISBN 0-910122-38-5). Amherst Pr.
--The Writings of Marie Corelli, 28 vols. 1976. lib. bdg. 34.95 ea. Gordon Pr.
--Ziska. pap. 4.95 (ISBN 0-910122-28-8). Amherst Pr.
Corelli, Stephen, ed. The Charlottesville Tapes. (Illus.). 224p. 1985. 25.00 (ISBN 0-8478-0538-7); pap. 25.00. Rizzoli Intl.
Coren, Alan. Arthur & the Great Detective. (The Arthur Ser.). (Illus.). 80p. (gr. 3-7). 1980. 7.95 (ISBN 0-316-15736-8). Little.
--Arthur & the Purple Panic. LC 83-61281. (Illus.). 64p. (gr. 4-6). 1984. 6.50 (ISBN 0-88186-001-8). Parkwest Pubns.
--Arthur the Kid. (The Arthur Ser.). (Illus.). (gr. 4-6). 1978. 7.95 (ISBN 0-316-15734-1). Little.
--Arthur the Kid. (Skylark Bks.). 80p. (gr. 4-6). 1984. pap. text ed. 2.25 (ISBN 0-553-15169-X, Skylark). Bantam.
--Arthur Versus the Rest. (Illus.). 64p. (gr. 3). 1985. 6.50 (ISBN 0-88186-000-X). Parkwest Pubns.
--Arthur's Last Stand. LC 79-14052. (The Arthur Ser.). (Illus.). (gr. 4-6). 1979. 7.95 (ISBN 0-316-15742-2). Little.
--Bumf. 160p. 1985. 12.95 (ISBN 0-88186-026-3). Parkwest Pubns.
--The Cricklewood Diet. LC 83-61287. 176p. 1984. 9.95 (ISBN 0-88186-050-6). Parkwest Pubns.
--Pick of Punch. (Illus.). 192p. 1985. 14.95 (ISBN 0-09-158790-5). Beaufort Bks NY.
Coren, Alan, ed. The Punch Book of Kids. (Illus.). 192p. (Orig.). 1985. pap. 6.95 (ISBN 0-88186-826-4). Parkwest Pubns.
--The Punch Book of Short Stories II. 192p. 1981. 9.95 (ISBN 0-312-65577-0). St Martin.
Coren, Arthur. The Lone Arthur. LC 78-6459. (The Arthur Ser). (Illus.). (gr. 4-6). 1978. 7.95 (ISBN 0-316-15739-2). Little.
Coren, Michael. Theatre Royal: One Hundred Years of Stratford East. (Illus.). 192p. 1985. 17.95 (ISBN 0-7043-2474-1, Pub. by Quartet Bks). Merrimack Pub Cir.
Coren, Michael, jt. auth. see Pilger, John.
Coren, S. & Girgus, J. S. Seeing Is Deceiving: The Psychology of Visual Illusions. 272p. 1978. 29.95x (ISBN 0-89859-463-4). L Erlbaum Assocs.
Coren, S., jt. auth. see Porac, C.
Coren, Stanley & Girgus, Joan S. Seeing Is Deceiving: The Psychology of Visual Illusions. LC 78-13509. (Complex Human Behavior Ser.). 255p. 1978. cloth 18.00x (ISBN 0-470-26522-1). Halsted Pr.
Coren, Stanley, et al. Sensation & Perception. 2nd ed. 1984. 22.00i (ISBN 0-12-188555-0); pap. 5.00i instr's. manual (ISBN 0-12-188556-9). Acad Pr.
Cores, Lucy. Destiny's Passion. 1982. pap. 3.50 (ISBN 0-8217-1061-3). Zebra.
--Katya. 384p. 1982. pap. 2.95 (ISBN 0-441-43233-6). Ace Bks.
Coret, Harriette. In & Out the Windows. (Sundown Fiction Ser.). 64p. 1982. 2.25 (ISBN 0-88336-751-3). New Readers.
Coretto, Carlo, frwd. by. The Jerusalem Community: Rule of Life. 144p. (Orig.). 1985. pap. 5.95 (ISBN 0-8091-2712-1). Paulist Pr.
Corey, A. Raymond. The Development of Markets for New Materials: A Study of Building New End-Product Markets for Aluminum, Fibrous Glass, & the Plastics. LC 56-9764. pap. 69.80 (ISBN 0-317-29992-1, 2051840). Bks Demand UMI.
Corey, Arthur. Behind the Scenes with the Metaphysicians. 7.50 (ISBN 0-87516-014-X). De Vorss.
--More Class Notes. pap. 2.50 (ISBN 0-87516-016-6). De Vorss.
Corey, Arthur, jt. auth. see Merritt, Robert E.
Corey, Arthur T. Mechanics of Heterogeneous Fluids in Porous Media. LC 77-71937. 1977. 25.00 (ISBN 0-918334-17-9). WRP.
Corey, Charles Henry, ed. The Oregon & Proceedings & Debates of the Constitutional Convention of 1857. 543p. 1926. 14.95 (ISBN 0-87595-092-2, Western Imprints). Oreg Hist Soc.
Corey, Cindy. Exploring the Lighthouses of North Carolina. (Illus.). softbound 6.95 (ISBN 0-318-00388-0). Provincial Pr.
Corey, D. Q. & Maas, J. P. The Energy Couple: The New Sexuality. (Illus.). 160p. 1980. 9.95 (ISBN 0-398-03964-X). C C Thomas.
Corey, Dallas. The Christmas Legend of Monkey Joe. 1979. 2.98 (ISBN 0-933208-00-6). Monkey Joe Ent.
Corey, Dorothy. Everybody Takes Turns. Ann, Fay, ed. LC 79-18652. (Self-Starter Ser.). (Illus.). (ps-1). 1980. PLB 9.25 (ISBN 0-8075-2166-3). A Whitman.
--New Shoes! Fay, Ann, ed. LC 84-17381. (Illus.). 32p. (ps-2). 1985. 10.75 (ISBN 0-8075-5583-5). A Whitman.
--No Company was Coming to Samuel's House: No Llegaban Invitados a la Casa De Samuel. LC 76-21301. (Illus., Eng. & Span.). (gr. k-3). 1976. 5.95 (ISBN 0-87917-055-7). Ethridge.
--Tomorrow You Can. Rubin, Caroline, ed. LC 77-12789. (Self-Starter Ser.). (Illus.). (ps-1). 1977. PLB 9.25 (ISBN 0-8075-8015-5). A Whitman.
--We All Share. Fay, Ann, ed. LC 80-18988. (Self-Starter Bks.). (Illus.). 32p. (ps-1). 1980. PLB 9.25 (ISBN 0-8075-8696-X). A Whitman.
--You Go Away. LC 75-33015. (Self Starter Bks.). (Illus.). 32p. (ps). 1975. PLB 9.25 (ISBN 0-8075-9441-5). A Whitman.
Corey, Douglas Q. & Maas, Jeannette P. The Existential Bible, a Genesis of Creativity, Vol. I. new ed. LC 76-281. (Illus.). 288p. 1976. 10.50 (ISBN 0-917132-01-7). Na Pali Pub.
Corey, E. Raymond. Procurement Management: Strategy, Organization & Decision-Making. LC 78-5826. 320p. 1978. 22.50 (ISBN 0-8436-0759-9). Van Nos Reinhold.
Corey, E. Raymond & Star, Steven H. Organization Strategy: A Marketing Approach. LC 79-132151. 1971. 27.95x (ISBN 0-87584-088-4). Harvard Busn.
Corey, Faris J. Exploring the Country Inns of North Carolina. softbound 5.95 (ISBN 0-686-34610-6). Provincial Pr.
--Exploring the Mountains of North Carolina. (Illus.). 6.95 (ISBN 0-686-34612-2); pap. 6.95 (ISBN 0-686-35707-8). Provincial Pr.
--Exploring the Villages of North Carolina. (Illus.). softbound 6.95 (ISBN 0-686-34616-5). Provincial Pr.
--North Carolina Superlatives. (Illus.). softbound 6.95 (ISBN 0-686-34619-X). Provincial Pr.
Corey, Gerald. A Case Approach to Counseling & Psychotherapy. 2nd ed. LC 85-9683. (Psychology-Counseling Ser.). 320p. 1985. pap. 14.25 (pub net) (ISBN 0-534-05262-2). Brooks-Cole.
--I Never Knew I Had a Choice. 2nd. ed. LC 82-4300. (Psychology Ser.). 400p. 1982. pap. text ed. 14.00 pub net (ISBN 0-534-01201-9). Brooks-Cole.
--I Never Knew I Had a Choice. 3rd. ed. LC 85-11306. (Psychology-Counseling Ser.). 520p. 1985. pap. 19.75 (pub net) (ISBN 0-534-05418-8). Brooks-Cole.
--Manual for Theory & Practice of Counseling & Psychotherapy. 2nd ed. 150p. (Orig.). 1981. pap. text ed. 7.25 pub net (ISBN 0-8185-0457-9). Brooks-Cole.
--Manual for Theory & Practice of Group Counseling. 2nd ed. (Psychology-Counseling Ser.). 160p. 1984. pap. text ed. 7.50 pub net (ISBN 0-534-03428-4). Brooks-Cole.
--Theory & Practice of Counseling & Psychotherapy. 2nd ed. LC 81-6139. 270p. 1981. text ed. 18.00 pub net (ISBN 0-8185-0455-2). Brooks-Cole.
--Theory & Practice of Counseling & Psychotherapy. 3rd. ed. Incl. Manual for Theory & Practice of Counseling & Psychotherapy. 192p. pap. 7.50 (pub net) (ISBN 0-534-05077-8). LC 85-6676. (Counseling Ser.). 400p. 1985. text ed. 24.50 (pub net) (ISBN 0-534-05076-X). Brooks-Cole.
--Theory & Practice of Group Counseling. 2nd ed. LC 84-5026. (Psychology-Counseling Ser.). 600p. 1984. text ed. 21.75 pub net (ISBN 0-534-03223-0). Brooks-Cole.
Corey, Gerald & Core, Marianne S. Issues & Ethics in the Helping Professions. 2nd ed. LC 83-10119. (Psychology-Counseling Ser.). 480p. 1983. pap. text ed. 13.00 pub net (ISBN 0-534-02819-5). Brooks-Cole.
Corey, Gerald & Corey, Marianne S. Groups: Process & Practice. 2nd ed. LC 82-4117. (Psychology Ser.). 352p. 1982. pap. text ed. 12.50 pub net (ISBN 0-534-01174-8). Brooks-Cole.
Corey, Helen. Art of Syrian Cookery. LC 61-18785. (Illus.). 1962. 12.95 (ISBN 0-385-00295-5). Doubleday.
Corey, Irene. The Mask of Reality: An Approach to Design for Theatre. (Illus.). 1968. 22.50 (ISBN 0-87602-007-4); pap. 17.50 o. p. (ISBN 0-87602-006-6). Anchorage.
Corey, Jane. Exploring the Seacoast of North Carolina. (Illus.). softbound 5.95 (ISBN 0-686-34602-5). Provincial Pr.
Corey, Jane, ed. North Carolina: A Camera Profile. (Illus.). softbound 5.95 (ISBN 0-686-34605-X). Provincial Pr.
Corey, Joseph, jt. auth. see Bodle, Yvonne.
Corey, Kenneth E. Deconcentrated Urbanization in Sri Lanka: A Case of Policy Serendipity. (Working Paper Ser.: No. 2). 47p. 1984. 4.00 (ISBN 0-317-20440-8). U MD Geography.
--Qualitative Planning Methodology: An Application in Development Planning Research to South Korea & Sri Lanka. (Working Paper Ser.). 23p. 1985. 3.00 (ISBN 0-317-20445-9). U MD Geography.
Corey, Lawrence, et al. Medicine in a Changing Society. 2nd ed. LC 76-46313. (Illus.). 1977. pap. 12.50 (ISBN 0-8016-1044-3). Mosby.
Corey, Lee. The Abode of Life. 1982. pap. 2.95 (ISBN 0-671-47719-6, Timescape). PB.
--Shuttle Down. 224p. (Orig.). 1981. pap. 2.25 (ISBN 0-345-29262-6, Del Rey). Ballantine.
--Space Doctor. 256p. 1985. pap. 2.95 (ISBN 0-345-32486-2, Del Rey). Ballantine.
Corey, Lewis. The Decline of American Capitalism. LC 70-38265. (The Evolution of Capitalism Ser.). 628p. 1972. Repr. of 1934 ed. 35.00 (ISBN 0-405-04116-0). Ayer Co Pubs.
--House of Morgan. LC 78-94469. Repr. of 1930 ed. 32.50 (ISBN 0-404-01728-2). AMS Pr.
--The Unfinished Task: Economic Reconstruction for Democracy. 1942. 15.00 (ISBN 0-686-17723-1). Quest Edns.
Corey, M., ed. see Verdon, Rene & Norman, Rachel H.
Corey, Marianne S., jt. auth. see Corey, Gerald.
Corey, Orlin. The Book of Job. 1961. 5.00 (ISBN 0-87602-000-7). Anchorage.
Corey, Paul. Do Cats Think? 1980. pap. 2.50 (ISBN 0-515-05841-6). Jove Pubns.
Corey, Stephen. Gentle Iron Lace. 28p. 1984. pap. 12.50 (ISBN 0-912960-16-7). Nightowl.
--The Last Magician. LC 81-50605. (Illus.). 64p. (Orig.). 1981. pap. 6.50 (ISBN 0-931956-05-6); hand made paper jacket O.P. 10.00 (ISBN 0-931956-12-9); handbound 60.00 (ISBN 0-931956-10-2). Water Mark.
--Synchronized Swimming. 88p. (Orig.). 1985. 13.95 (ISBN 0-930501-03-9); pap. 6.95 (ISBN 0-930501-01-2). Swallows Tale Pr.
Corey, Stephen, et al. Award Highlights. (Illus., Orig.). 1981. 45.00 (ISBN 0-931956-07-2); pap. 12.00 (ISBN 0-931956-08-0). Water Mark.
Corfe, T. St. Patrick & Irish Christianity. LC 73-75862. (Cambridge Introduction to the Hoistory of Mankind Ser.). 48p. 1973. 4.50 (ISBN 0-521-20228-0). Cambridge U Pr.
Corfe, Tom. The Murder of Archbishop Thomas. LC 76-22419. (Cambridge Topic Bks). (Illus.). (gr. 5-10). 1977. PLB 7.95 (ISBN 0-8225-1202-5). Lerner Pubns.
--St. Patrick & Irish Christianity. LC 78-56811. (Cambridge Topic Bks). (Illus.). (gr. 5-10). 1978. PLB 7.95 (ISBN 0-8225-1217-3). Lerner Pubns.
Corfiato, H. O., jt. auth. see Richardson, Albert E.
Corfield, P. J. The Impact of English Towns, Seventeen Hundred to Eighteen Hundred. (Oxford Paperbacks University Ser.). 1982. 25.95x (ISBN 0-19-215830-9); pap. 9.95x (ISBN 0-19-289093-X). Oxford U Pr.
Corgan, James X., ed. The Geological Sciences in the Antebellum South. LC 81-2993. (Illus.). 208p. 1982. 17.50 (ISBN 0-8173-0076-7). U of Ala Pr.
Corgel, John B. & Smith, Albert C. Concept & Estimation of Economic Life in the Residential Appraisal Process. 115p. 1981. 9.50 (ISBN 0-317-36922-9). Soc Real Estate Appraisers.
Coriat, Isador H. What Is Psychoanalysis? LC 73-2393. (Mental Illness & Social Policy; the American Experience Ser.). Repr. of 1917 ed. 11.50 (ISBN 0-405-05201-4). Ayer Co Pubs.
Corica, jt. auth. see Presley.
Coriden, James A., et al. The Art of Interpretation: Selected Studies on the Interpretation of Canon Law. v, 79p. (Orig.). 1983. pap. 3.75 (ISBN 0-943616-18-2). Canon Law Soc.
Coriden, James A., et al, eds. The Code of Canon Law: A Text & Commentary. 39.95 (ISBN 0-317-14083-3). Paulist Pr.
Coriell, Rebekah, jt. auth. see Coriell, Ron.
Coriell, Ron & Coriell, Rebekah. Caring & Sharing. (Character Builders Ser.). (ps-2). 1980. pap. 1.35 (ISBN 0-8007-7013-7, Christian School Curricium). Revell.
--A Child's Book of Character Building. (Illus.). 128p. (ps-2). 1980. 10.95 (ISBN 0-8007-1197-1). Revell.
--A Child's Book of Character Building, Bk. Two. 128p. (ps-2). 1981. 10.95 (ISBN 0-8007-1265-X). Revell.
--Doing Unto Others. (Character Builders Ser.). (ps-2). 1980. pap. 1.35 (ISBN 0-8007-7012-9, Christian School Curriculum). Revell.
--Faithful Followers. (Character Builders Ser.). (gr. 3-6). 1980. pap. 1.35 (ISBN 0-8007-7014-5, Christian School Curriculum). Revell.
--Fashioning the Faith. (Character Builders Ser.). (gr. 7-10). 1980. pap. 1.35 (ISBN 0-8007-7010-2, Christian School Curriculum). Revell.
--Happy Hearts. (Character Builders Ser.). (ps-2). 1980. pap. 1.35 (ISBN 0-8007-7006-4, Christian School Curriculum). Revell.

--His Mind, His Heart. (Character Builders Ser.). (gr. 7-10). 1980. pap. 1.35 (ISBN 0-8007-7002-1, Christian School Curriculum). Revell.
--Learning Lessons. (Character Builders Ser.). (ps-2). 1980. pap. 1.35 (ISBN 0-8007-7004-8, Christian School Curriculum). Revell.
--Learning to Listen. (Character Builders Ser.). (gr. 3-6). 1980. pap. 1.35 (ISBN 0-8007-7008-0, Christian School Curriculum). Revell.
--Listen, Look & Live. (Character Builders Ser.). (ps-2). 1980. pap. 1.35 (ISBN 0-8007-7001-3, Christian School Curriculum). Revell.
--Living Like Him. (Character Builders Ser.). (ps-2). 1980. pap. 1.35 (ISBN 0-8007-7005-6, Christian School Curriculum). Revell.
--Planning to Please. (Character Builders Ser.). (gr. 6-8). 1981. pap. 1.35 (ISBN 0-8007-7020-X). Revell.
--Putting up with Others. (Character Builders Ser.). (gr. 3-6). 1981. pap. 1.35 (ISBN 0-8007-7017-X). Revell.
--Rejoicing in Truth. (Character Builder Ser.). (gr. 7-10). 1980. 1.35 (ISBN 0-8007-7011-0, Christian School Curriculum). Revell.
--Seeing & Being Like Him. (Character Builders Ser.). (ps-2). 1980. 1.35 (ISBN 0-8007-7000-5, Christian School Curriculum). Revell.
--Starting His Way. (Character Builders Ser.). (gr. 7-10). 1981. pap. 1.35 (ISBN 0-8007-7023-4). Revell.
--True & Happy. (Character Builders Ser.). (gr. 3-6). 1980. pap. 1.35 (ISBN 0-8007-7009-9, Christian School Curriculum). Revell.
--Walking His Way. (Character Builders Ser.). (gr. 3-6). 1980. pap. 1.35 (ISBN 0-8007-7003-X, Christian School Curriculum). Revell.
--Willing to Work. (Character Builders Ser.). (gr. 7-10). 1981. pap. 1.35 (ISBN 0-8007-7021-8). Revell.
--Wise Eyes & Wise Ways. (Character Builders Ser.). (gr. 3-6). 1980. pap. 1.35 (ISBN 0-8007-7015-3, Christian School Curriculum). Revell.

Corillion, Robert. Les Charophycees de France et de l'Europe Occidentale. 1972. 61.60 (ISBN 3-87429-014-X). Lubrecht & Cramer.

Corin, James. Mating, Marriage & the Status of Women. LC 72-9633. Repr. of 1910 ed. 17.25 (ISBN 0-404-57432-7). AMS Pr.

Corinne, Tee. Labiaflowers. 48p. (Orig.). 1981. pap. 3.95 (ISBN 0-930044-20-7). Naiad Pr.
--Yantras of Womanlove. 100p. (Orig.). 1982. pap. 6.95 (ISBN 0-930044-30-4). Naiad Pr.

Corinth, Kay. Fashion Showmanship: Everything You Need to Know to Give a Fashion Show. LC 83-19446. 288p. 1984. Repr. of 1970 ed. 24.95x (ISBN 0-89874-697-3). Krieger.

Corio, P. L. Structure of High Resolution Nuclear Magnetic Resonance Spectra. 1966. 81.00 (ISBN 0-12-188750-2). Acad Pr.

Coriolan, John. Christy Dancing. rev. ed. LC 83-22665. 224p. 1984. pap. 7.95 (ISBN 0-912516-87-9). Grey Fox.
--Dream Stud & Other Stories. 192p. (Orig.). 1985. pap. 7.95 (ISBN 0-917342-04-6). Gay Sunshine.
--A Sand Fortress. rev. ed. 224p. 1984. pap. 8.95 (ISBN 0-917342-46-1). Gay Sunshine.
--The Smile of Eros. 192p. (Orig.). 1984. pap. 7.95 (ISBN 0-917342-39-9). Gay Sunshine.
--Unzipped: A Novella & Six Short Stories. (Illus.). 160p. 1983. pap. 7.95 (ISBN 0-917342-31-3). Gay Sunshine.

Coriolano, Marcello. The Absolutely Guaranteed Guide on How to Live Beyond 100. (Illus.). 87p. 1984. 27.95 (ISBN 0-89266-478-9). Am Classical Coll Pr.

Coripio Perez, Fernando. Diccionario Etimologico Abreviado. 2nd ed. 320p. (Span.). 1976. pap. 3.50 (ISBN 84-02-03901-4, S-50161). French & Eur.

Corippus, Flavius C. In Laudem Iustini Augusti Minoris. Cameron, Averil, ed. (Illus.). 224p. 1976. 90.00 (ISBN 0-485-11157-8, Pub. by Athlone Pr Ltd). Longwood Pub Group.

Corish, Patrick J. The Catholic Community in the 17th & 18th Centuries. (Helicon History of Ireland Ser.: Vol. 5). 156p. 1981. 22.95 (ISBN 0-318-03185-X, Pub. by Educ Co Ireland); pap. 9.95 (ISBN 0-318-03186-8, Pub. by Educ Co Ireland). Irish Bk Ctr.

Corish, Patrick J., ed. Radicals, Rebels & Establishments. 256p. 1985. 24.00 (ISBN 0-86281-131-7, Pub. by Salem Acad). Merrimack Pub Cir.

Corita Communications Editors. The Mail Order Guide: For the Beginner Interested in a Part or Full Time Business (in Mail Order) 1979. 10.95 (ISBN 0-933016-02-6). Corita Comm.

Cork. Wild Animals. (First Nature Bk.). (gr. 2-5). 1982. 6.95 (ISBN 0-86020-629-7, Usborne-Hayes); PLB 11.95 (ISBN 0-88110-077-3); pap. 2.95 (ISBN 0-86020-628-9). EDC.

Cork, jt. auth. see Cox.

Cork, B. & Bramwell, M. Rocks & Fossils. (Young Scientist Ser.). (Illus.). 32p. (gr. 5-8). 1983. 7.95 (ISBN 0-86020-766-8); PLB 12.95 (ISBN 0-88110-159-1); pap. 4.95 (ISBN 0-86020-765-X). EDC.

Cork, Barbara. Mysteries & Marvels of Plant Life. (Mysteries & Marvels Ser.). 32p. (gr. 6up). 1984. 7.95 (ISBN 0-86020-756-0); PLB 12.95 (ISBN 0-88110-169-9); pap. 4.95 (ISBN 0-86020-755-2). EDC.

Cork, Barbara & Morris, R. Mysteries & Marvels of Nature. (Mysteries & Marvels Ser.). (Illus.). 96p. (gr. 3-6). 1983. 12.95 (ISBN 0-86020-757-9). EDC.

Cork, Barbara, ed. see Hill.

Cork, Dorothy. A La Poursuite D'Orion. (Harlequin Romantique Ser.). 192p. 1984. pap. 1.95 (ISBN 0-373-41239-8). Harlequin Bks.
--Retour a Coolabah Creek. (Harlequin Romantique Ser.). 192p. 1983. pap. 1.95 (ISBN 0-373-41205-3). Harlequin Bks.
--Where Black Swans Fly, Summer Mountain, Butterfly Montane. (Harlequin Romances Ser.). 576p. pap. 3.50 (ISBN 0-373-20068-4). Harlequin Bks.

Cork, Kenneth & Weiss, G. A., eds. European Insolvency Practitioners' Handbook. LC 83-24567. 324p. 1984. 40.00 (ISBN 0-312-27069-0). St Martin.

Cork, R. Margaret. The Forgotten Children. 112p. 1969. pap. 1.50 (ISBN 0-318-15326-2, Pub. by Addiction Res. Foun.). Natl Coun Alcoholism.

Cork, Richard. Art Beyond the Gallery in Early Twentieth Century England. LC 84-52240. (Illus.). 352p. 1985. 65.00 (ISBN 0-300-03236-6). Yale U Pr.
--The Social Role of Art. 128p. 1981. 30.00x (ISBN 0-86092-048-8, Pub. by Fraser Bks). State Mutual Bk.
--Vorticism & Abstract Art in the First Machine Age, 2 vols. Incl. Vol. 1. Origins & Development. 1976 (ISBN 0-520-03154-7); Vol. 2. Synthesis & Decline. 1977 (ISBN 0-520-03269-1). LC 75-37227. 75.00 ea. U of Cal Pr.

Cork, Seamus. Irish Erotic Art. 96p. 1981. 5.95 (ISBN 0-312-43601-7); prepack 29.75 (ISBN 0-312-43602-5). St Martin.

Corke, Bettina, ed. Who Is Who in Latin America: Government & Politics. 532p. (Span. & Eng.). 1984. 65.00 (ISBN 0-910365-02-4). Decade Media.

Corke, C. F. Self-Assessment for MRCP, Pt. 1. 224p. 1981. pap. text ed. 16.75 (ISBN 0-632-00819-9, B 1059-1). Mosby.

Corke, D. K. Production Control in Engineering. 2nd ed. (Illus.). 1977. 42.50x (ISBN 0-7131-3380-5). Intl Ideas.

Corke, Helen. D. H. Lawrence's Princess. LC 73-18344. 1899. lib. bdg. 10.00 (ISBN 0-8414-3528-6). Folcroft.

Corkery, Christopher J. Blessing. LC 84-42879. (Series of Contemporary Poets). 64p. 1985. text ed. 13.95x (ISBN 0-691-06631-0); pap. 7.50x (ISBN 0-691-01418-3). Princeton U Pr.

Corkery, Daniel. Fohnam the Sculptor. (The Lost Play Ser.). Date not set. pap. 1.25x (ISBN 0-912262-32-X). Proscenium.
--The Hidden Ireland. 1967. pap. 7.95 (ISBN 0-7171-0079-0). Irish Bk Ctr.
--Hounds of Banba. LC 75-128728. (Short Story Index Reprint Ser). 1920. 14.00 (ISBN 0-8369-3619-1). Ayer Co Pubs.
--The Wager & Other Stories. (Illus.). 1950. 8.50 (ISBN 0-8159-7200-8). Devin.

Corkery, J. F. & Stone, R. C. Weimar Germany & the Third Reich. (Illus.). 68p. (Orig.). 1982. pap. text ed. 5.50x (ISBN 0-86863-510-3, 00566). Heinemann Ed.

Corkery, Tom. Tom Corkery's Dublin. (Illus.). 128p. 1980. 13.95 (ISBN 0-900068-53-1, Pub. by Anvil Bks Ireland). Irish Bks Media.

Corkhill, J. W., jt. auth. see Park, W. W.

Corkhill, Thomas. The Complete Dictionary of Wood. LC 79-10183. (Illus.). 672p. 1982. pap. 14.95 (ISBN 0-8128-6142-6). Stein & Day.
--The Complete Dictionary of Wood. LC 79-10183. (Illus.). 664p. 1980. 19.95 (ISBN 0-8128-2708-2). Stein & Day.

Corkill, W. A. Railway Modelling: An Introduction. 1979. 12.95 (ISBN 0-7153-7571-7). David & Charles.

Corkindale, David & Newall, John. Advertising Thresholds & Wearout. 1978. 90.00x (ISBN 0-905440-66-8, Pub. by MCB Pubns). State Mutual Bk.

Corkindale, David, jt. auth. see Kennedy, Sherril.

Corkindale, David R., jt. auth. see Kennedy, Sherrie H.

Corkran, Alice. The Poet's Corner or Haunts & Homes of the Poets. Repr. 35.00 (ISBN 0-8274-3163-5). R West.
--The Romance of Woman's Influence: (Dorothy Wordsworth) 377p. 1981. Repr. of 1906 ed. lib. bdg. 50.00 (ISBN 0-89987-149-6). Darby Bks.

Corkran, Herbert. Mini-Nations & Macro-Cooperation: The Caribbean & the South Pacific. 1977. 15.00 (ISBN 0-88265-011-4). North Am Intl.

Corkran, Herbert, Jr. Patterns of International Cooperation in the Caribbean, 1942-1969. LC 74-128122. 1970. 11.95 (ISBN 0-87074-033-4). SMU Press.

Corl, Heth. Lectionary Worship Aids B: (Common) 1984. 7.75 (ISBN 0-89536-690-8, 4868). CSS of Ohio.

Corl, Heth H. Continuity in Contemporary Worship. 124p. (Orig.). 1975. pap. 5.00 (ISBN 0-89536-042-X). CSS of Ohio.
--Lectionary Worship Aids. rev. ed. (Ser. B.). pap. cancelled (ISBN 0-89536-523-5). CSS of Ohio.
--Lectionary Worship Aids "B". 1978. pap. 7.75 (ISBN 0-89536-319-4). CSS of Ohio.
--Lectionary Worship Aids: Series A. 1977. pap. 7.75 (ISBN 0-89536-147-7). CSS of Ohio.
--Lectionary Worship Aids: Series C. rev. ed. 1976. pap. 3.10 (ISBN 0-89536-142-6). CSS of Ohio.

Corle, Clyde G. Teaching Mathematics in the Elementary School. LC 64-13943. pap. 98.80 (ISBN 0-317-08697-9, 2012479). Bks Demand UMI.

Corle, Clyde G., jt. auth. see Bouwsma, Ward D.

Corle, Edwin. Billy the Kid. LC 79-4930. (Zia Books). 1979. pap. 6.95 (ISBN 0-8263-0509-1). U of NM Pr.
--Fig Tree John. 1971. 7.95 (ISBN 0-87140-518-0); pap. 2.95 (ISBN 0-87140-242-4). Liveright.
--The Gila: River of the Southwest. LC 51-6152. (Illus.). xii, 402p. 1964. pap. 8.95 (ISBN 0-8032-5040-1, BB 305, Bison). U of Nebr Pr.

Corle, Edwin, ed. see Armitage, Merle.

Corless, Brian. Formal English. LC 78-73637. 1979. pap. 4.95 (ISBN 0-7081-1157-2, Pub. by ANUP Australia). Australia N U P.

Corless, Roger. I Am Food: The Mass in Planetary Perspective. LC 81-7836. 112p. 1981. 8.95 (ISBN 0-8245-0077-6). Crossroad NY.

Corlett, D. Shelby. God in the Present Tense. 176p. 1974. 1.95 (ISBN 0-8341-0248-X). Beacon Hill.

Corlett, E. N. & Richardson, J. Stress, Work Design & Productivity. LC 81-13075. (Studies in Occupational Stress). 271p. 1981. 42.95x (ISBN 0-471-28044-5, Pub. by Wiley-Interscience). Wiley.

Corlett, E. N., jt. auth. see Clarke, T. S.

Corlett, E. N., jt. ed. see Gudnason, C. H.

Corlett, Ewan. The Revolution in Merchant Shipping. (The Ship Ser.). (Illus.). 60p. 1981. 10.95 (ISBN 0-11-290320-7). Sheridan.

Corlett, John. Aviation in Ulster. (Illus.). 148p. 1981. pap. 8.95 (ISBN 0-85640-252-4, Pub. by Blackstaff Pr). Longwood Pub Group.

Corlett, P. N. Practical Programming. 2nd ed. LC 75-161295. (School Mathematics Project Handbooks). (Illus.). 1971. pap. 12.95x (ISBN 0-521-09740-1). Cambridge U Pr.

Corlett, Stan & Cain, John. Getting Started with the Epson HX-20 Portable Computer. 118p. 1984. pap. 12.95 (ISBN 0-946576-02-5, Pub. by Phoenix Pub). David & Charles.

Corlett, William. The Bloxworth Blue. LC 85-42916. 192p. (YA) (gr. 7 up). 1985. 11.06i (ISBN 0-06-021343-4); PLB 10.89g (ISBN 0-06-021344-2). HarpJ.

Corlett, William T. The Medicine-Man of the American Indian & His Cultural Background. LC 75-23699. Repr. of 1935 ed. 33.50 (ISBN 0-404-13249-9). AMS Pr.
--Medicine Man of the Early American Indian & His Cultural Background. (Illus.). 369p. 1935. 34.50x00121904x (ISBN 0-398-04233-0). C C Thomas.

Corlew, Robert E. Tennessee: A Short History. 2nd ed. LC 80-13553. (Illus.). 652p. 1981. 22.50 (ISBN 0-87049-258-6); pap. text ed. 14.50x (ISBN 0-87049-302-7). U of Tenn Pr.

Corlew, Robert E., jt. auth. see Nicholson, James L.

Corlew, Robert E., ed. see Burns, G. Frank.

Corlew, Robert E., III, ed. see Pittard, Mabel.

Corley, jt. auth. see Gamble.

Corley, Bruce, jt. auth. see Vaughan, Curtis.

Corley, Bruce C., ed. Colloquy on New Testament Studies: A Time for Reappraisal & Fresh Approaches. LC 83-8192. 1983. 21.50x (ISBN 0-86554-082-9, H54). Mercer Univ Pr.

Corley, C. F. Riding & Schooling the Western Performance Horse. LC 81-3550. (Illus.). 256p. 1982. 19.95 (ISBN 0-668-05083-7, 5083). Arco.

Corley, Donald. Haunted Jester. facsimile ed. LC 79-106279. (Short Story Index Reprint Ser.). 1931. 18.00 (ISBN 0-8369-3317-6). Ayer Co Pubs.
--House of Lost Identity: Tales & Drawings. facsimile ed. LC 73-106280. (Short Story Index Reprint Ser.). Repr. of 1927 ed. 21.00 (ISBN 0-8369-4007-5). Ayer Co Pubs.

Corley, Edwin. The Jesus Factor. 320p. 1984. pap. 3.95 (ISBN 0-8128-8104-4). Stein & Day.
--Seige. 1984. pap. 3.95 (ISBN 0-8128-8052-8). Stein & Day.
--Shadows. LC 75-11832. 300p. 1975. pap. 1.95 (ISBN 0-8128-7002-6). Stein & Day.

Corley, Elizabeth A. Tell Me about Death Tell Me about Funerals. (Illus.). 36p. (Orig.). (gr. 3-6). 1973. pap. text ed. 2.00 (ISBN 0-686-02638-1). Grammatical Sci.

Corley, Hugh. Organic Small Farming. Bargyla & Rateaver, Gylver, eds. LC 74-33122. (Conservation Gardening & Farming Ser: Ser. C). 1975. pap. 10.00 (ISBN 0-9600698-4-4). Rateavers.

Corley, Jane. The House Next Door. (Sharon Romance Ser.). 128p. (Orig.). 1981. pap. 2.25 (ISBN 0-89531-136-4, 0198-96). Sharon Pubns.

Corley, John B. Evaluating Residency Training. LC 80-833. (N. A. Ser.). 320p. 1982. 23.95 (ISBN 0-669-03859-8, Collamore). Heath.

Corley, Mary A., jt. auth. see Coyle, Joseph M.

Corley, Mary A., ed. American History Reader. 96p. (Orig.). (gr. 7-12). 1983. pap. text ed. 5.95 (ISBN 0-88499-700-6). Inst Mod Lang.

Corley, Mary Ann & Hancock, Charles. Speak English, Text 3. (Speak English Ser.). (Illus.). 80p. (Orig.). 1981. pap. text ed. 4.95 (ISBN 0-88499-655-7). Inst Mod Lang.

Corley, Mary Ann & Smallwood, Betty. Speak English, Text 2. (Speak English Ser.). (Illus.). 96p. (Orig.). 1981. pap. 4.95 (ISBN 0-88499-653-0). Inst Mod Lang.
--Speak English, Workbook 2. (Speak English Ser.). (Illus.). 72p. (Orig.). 1981. pap. 4.95 (ISBN 0-88499-654-9). Inst Mod Lang.

Corley, Mary Ann & Steurer, Stephen. Basic Beginner Book. (Speak English! Ser.). (Illus.). 80p. (Orig.). 1980. pap. text ed. 4.95 (ISBN 0-88499-652-2). Inst Mod Lang.

Corley, Nora T., ed. Travel in Canada: A Guide to Information Sources. (Geography & Travel Information Guide Ser.: Vol. 4). 350p. 1982. 60.00x (ISBN 0-8103-1493-2). Gale.

Corley, R. H., et al, eds. Oil Palm Research. (Developments in Crop Science Ser.: Vol. 1). 532p. 1976. 117.00 (ISBN 0-444-41471-1). Elsevier.

Corley, Robert, jt. auth. see Windal, Floyd.

Corley, Robert N. & Holmes, Eric M. Principles of Business Law. 12th ed. (Illus.). 960p. 1983. 31.95 (ISBN 0-13-701250-0); student gd. & wkbk. 11.95 (ISBN 0-13-701276-4). P-H.

Corley, Robert N., et al. Fundamentals of Business Law. 3rd ed. (Illus.). 800p. 1982. text ed. 28.95 (ISBN 0-13-332189-4); study guide 9.95 (ISBN 0-13-332247-5). P-H.
--Principles of Business Law. 13th ed. (Illus.). 1120p. 1986. text ed. 33.95 (ISBN 0-13-701186-5). P-H.
--Director's & Officer's Deskbook of Business Law. LC 84-24946. 1985. 39.95 (ISBN 0-13-214891-9). P-H.
--Fundamentals of Business Law. 4th ed. (Illus.). 896p. 1986. text ed. 28.95 (ISBN 0-13-331844-3). P-H.
--Real Estate & the Law. 453p. 1982. text ed. 32.00 (ISBN 0-394-32546-X, RanC). Random.

Corley, Thomas A. Democratic Despot: A Life a Napoleon III. LC 74-8651. (Illus.). 402p. 1974. Repr. of 1961 ed. lib. bdg. 22.50x (ISBN 0-8371-7587-9, CODC). Greenwood.

Corley, Winnie. Echoes from the Hills. 1981. lib. bdg. 14.95x (ISBN 0-934188-06-8). Evans Pubns.

Corlin, Judith R. & Miller, Mary S. The Scarsdale Nutritionist's Weight-Loss Program for Teenagers. 208p. 1983. 8.95 (ISBN 0-671-46262-8, Fireside). S&S.

Corlin, Richard, et al. Converting Enzyme Inhibition in Heart Failure: Management Strategies for the Eighties. 54p. 1983. write for info. (ISBN 0-911741-03-8). Advanced Thera Comm.

Corliss, Augustus, compiled by. Old Times of North Yarmouth, Maine. LC 76-52883. (Illus.). 1977. 55.00x (ISBN 0-912274-72-7). NH Pub Co.

Corliss, Carlton J. Rural Railroads-Prelude: Trails to Rails. 76p. 1976. Repr. 6.00 (ISBN 0-686-27589-6). E S Cunningham.

Corliss, Clark E. Patten's Elements of Embryology. (Illus.). 1976. text ed. 30.00 (ISBN 0-07-013150-3). McGraw.

Corliss, Dennis, jt. auth. see Beekman, George.

Corliss, Hazel B. Hilltop Housewife Cookbook. (Illus.). 258p. 1973. pap. 4.95x (ISBN 0-9600712-4-5). Sourcebook.

Corliss, John O. The Ciliated Protozoa: Characterization, Classification & Guide to the Literature. 2nd ed. LC 78-41075. (Illus.). 1979. text ed. 58.00 (ISBN 0-08-018752-8). Pergamon.

Corliss, Richard. Talking Pictures: Screenwriters in the American Cinema. pap. 10.95 (ISBN 0-87951-159-1). Overlook Pr.

Corliss, William R. Ancient Man: A Handbook of Puzzling Artifacts. LC 77-99243. (Illus.). 1978. 16.95 (ISBN 0-915554-05-4). Sourcebook.
--Earthquakes, Tides, Unidentified Sounds & Related Phenomena. LC 83-50781. (Catalog of Geophysical Anomalies Ser.). (Illus.). 214p. 1983. 12.95 (ISBN 0-915554-11-9). Sourcebook.
--Incredible Life: A Handbook of Biological Mysteries. LC 80-53971. (Illus.). 1050p. 1981. 22.50 (ISBN 0-915554-07-0). Sourcebook.
--Lightning, Auroras, Nocturnal Lights & Related Luminous Phenomena. LC 82-99902. (A Catalog of Geophysical Anomalies Ser.). (Illus.). 248p. 1982. 11.95 (ISBN 0-915554-09-7). Sourcebook.
--Mysterious Universe: A Handbook of Astronomical Anomalies. LC 78-65616. (Illus.). 1979. 16.95 (ISBN 0-915554-05-4). Sourcebook.
--Rare Halos, Mirages, Anomalous Rainbows, & Related Electromagnetic Phenomena. (Catalog of Geophysical Anomalies Ser.). (Illus.). 244p. 1984. 12.95 (ISBN 0-915554-12-7). Sourcebook.
--Strange Artifacts: A Sourcebook on Ancient Man, Vol. M1. LC 74-75256. (Illus.). 268p. 1974. 8.95x (ISBN 0-9600712-2-9). Sourcebook.
--Strange Artifacts: A Sourcebook on Ancient Man, Vol. M2. LC 74-75256. (Illus.). 275p. 1976. 8.95x (ISBN 0-9600712-6-1). Sourcebook.
--Strange Life: A Sourcebook on the Mysteries of Organic Nature. LC 75-6128. (Strange Life Ser.: Vol. B1). (Illus.). 275p. 1975. 8.95x (ISBN 0-9600712-8-8). Sourcebook.
--Strange Minds: A Sourcebook of Unusual Mental Phenomena, Vol. P1. LC 76-12666. 280p. 1976. 8.95x (ISBN 0-915554-00-3). Sourcebook.
--Strange Phenomena: A Sourcebook of Unusual Natural Phenomena, Vol. G2. LC 73-9148. 1974. 8.95x (ISBN 0-9600712-5-3). Sourcebook.

--Strange Planet: A Sourcebook of Unusual Geological Facts. LC 74-26226. (Strange Planet Ser.: Vol. E2). 1978. 8.95x (ISBN 0-915554-04-6). Sourcebook.
--Strange Planet: A Sourcebook of Unusual Geological Facts, Vol. E1. LC 74-26226. (Illus.). 283p. 1975. 8.95x (ISBN 0-9600712-3-7). Sourcebook.
--Tornadoes, Dark Days, Anomalous Precipitation & Related Weather Phenomena. LC 82-63156. (Catalog of Geophysical Anomalies Ser.). (Illus.). 196p. 1983. 11.95 (ISBN 0-915554-10-0). Sourcebook.
--The Unfathomed Mind: A Handbook of Unusual Mental Phenomena. LC 81-85081. (Illus.). 760p. 1982. 19.95 (ISBN 0-915554-08-9). Sourcebook.
--Unknown Earth: A Handbook of Geological Enigmas. LC 80-50159. (Illus.). 839p. 1980. 19.95 (ISBN 0-915554-06-2). Sourcebook.
Corliss, William R., ed. The Moon & the Planets. LC 85-61380. (Catalog of Astronomical Anomalies Ser.). (Illus.). 380p. 1985. 18.95 (ISBN 0-915554-19-4). Sourcebook.
Cormack, A. J. Famous Pistols & Hand Guns. (Illus.). 160p. (Orig.). 1983. pap. 9.95 (ISBN 0-668-05867-6, 5867). Arco.
Cormack, D. Criteria for the Selection of Oil Spill Containment & Recovery Equipment for Use at Sea, 1979. 1981. 40.00x (ISBN 0-686-97051-9, Pub. by W Spring England). State Mutual Bk.
--Response to Oil & Chemical Marine Pollution. (Illus.). 531p. 1983. 87.00 (ISBN 0-85334-182-6, Pub. by Elsevier Applied Sci England). Elsevier.
Cormack, D. & Nichols, J. A. Feasability Study of Aerial Application of Oil Dispersant Concentrates for Oil Spill Clearance, 1977. 1981. 40.00x (ISBN 0-686-97078-0, Pub. by W Spring England). State Mutual Bk.
Cormack, D., jt. auth. see Martinelli, F. N.
Cormack, D., jt. auth. see Parker, H. D.
Cormack, D., et al. Oil Mop Device for Oil Recovery on the Open Sea, 1979. 1982. 39.00x (ISBN 0-686-97137-X, Pub. by W Spring England). State Mutual Bk.
Cormack, David H. Introduction to Histology. (Illus.). 512p. 1984. text ed. 19.75 (ISBN 0-397-52114-6, 65-07338, Lippincott Medical). Lippincott.
Cormack, David H., jt. auth. see Ham, Arthur W.
Cormack, Desmond F. Psychiatric Nursing Described. LC 82-9447. (Studies in Nursing Ser.). (Illus.). 224p. 1983. pap. text ed. 16.00 (ISBN 0-443-02722-6). Churchill.
Cormack, Malcolm. Selection II: British Watercolors & Drawings from the Museum's Collection. (Illus.). 1972. 6.50 (ISBN 0-686-05414-8). Mus of Art RI.
Cormack, Margaret L. The Hindu Woman. LC 74-6750. 207p. 1974. Repr. of 1953 ed. lib. bdg. 15.50x (ISBN 0-8371-7557-7, COHW). Greenwood.
Cormack, Margaret L. & Skagen, Kiki. Guidelines for Academic Opportunities in India: Travel, Work, Training, Teaching, Study & Research Information for Faculty & Students. (Occasional Papers: No. 10). 40p. 1983. pap. text ed. 5.75 (ISBN 0-8191-3120-2, Co-pub. by Ctr S SE Asia). U Pr of Amer.
Cormack, Mary P., jt. auth. see Barrett, M. Edgar.
Cormack, Patrick. English Cathedrals. (Illus.). 1984. 14.95 (ISBN 0-517-55409-7, Harmony). Crown.
--Westminster: Palace & Parliament. (Illus.). 192p. 1981. 25.00 (ISBN 0-7232-2681-4). Warne.
Cormack, R. J. & Osborne, R. D., eds. Religion, Education & Employment: Aspects of Equal Opportunity in Northern Ireland. LC 83-135557. (Illus.). 266p. 1984. 28.00x (ISBN 0-904651-87-8, Pub. by Salem Acad). Merrimack Pub Cir.
Cormack, R. M. & Ord, J. K., eds. Spatial & Temporal Analysis in Ecology. (Statistical Ecology Ser.: Vol. 8). 1979. 45.00 (ISBN 0-89974-005-7). Intl Co-Op.
Cormack, R. M., et al, eds. Sampling Biological Populations. (Statistical Ecology Ser.: Vol. 5). 1979. 45.00 (ISBN 0-89974-002-2). Intl Co-Op.
Cormack, Robin. Writing in Gold: Byzantine Society & Its Icons. (Illus.). 256p. 1985. 24.95 (ISBN 0-19-520486-7). Oxford U Pr.
Cormack, Sandy. Small Arms: A Concise History of Their Development. (Illus.). 154p. 1983. 16.95 (ISBN 0-85383-085-1, Profile Pr England). Hippocrene Bks.
Corman, Avery. Kramer Versus Kramer. (Illus.). 1977. 7.95 (ISBN 0-394-41053-X). Random.
--The Old Neighborhood. (General Ser.). 1980. lib. bdg. 13.95 (ISBN 0-8161-3146-5, Large Print Bks). G K Hall.
Corman, Calvin. Commercial Law: Cases & Materials. 2nd ed. 856p. 1983. 32.00 (ISBN 0-316-15746-5). Little.
Corman, Cid. Aegis: Selected Poems Nineteen Seventy-Nineteen to Eighty. 112p. (Orig.). 1983. 14.95 (ISBN 0-930794-57-5); limited, signed ed. 30.00 (ISBN 0-88268-035-8); pap. 5.95 (ISBN 0-930794-58-3). Station Hill Pr.
--And Without End. 1968. 4.00 (ISBN 0-685-00992-0). Elizabeth Pr.
--At Least. 4.00 (ISBN 0-318-11910-2). Great Raven Pr.
--At Their Word: Essays on the Arts of Language, Vol. 2. 220p. (Orig.). 1978. 14.00 (ISBN 0-87685-308-4); pap. 5.00 (ISBN 0-87685-307-6); ltd. signed 17.50 (ISBN 0-87685-309-2). Black Sparrow.
--Auspices. (Orig.). 1978. o. p. limited signed ed. 35.00 (ISBN 0-915316-59-5). Pentagram.
--For Granted. 1967. pap. 4.00 (ISBN 0-685-00991-2). Elizabeth Pr.
--Livingdying. LC 77-103369. 1970. 5.00 (ISBN 0-8112-0261-5); limited ed. 25.00 (ISBN 0-8112-0508-8); pap. 1.75 (ISBN 0-8112-0023-X, NDP289). New Directions.
--Nigh. 1970. pap. 4.00 (ISBN 0-685-00996-3). Elizabeth Pr.
--No Less. 1968. pap. 4.00 (ISBN 0-685-00993-9). Elizabeth Pr.
--No More. 1969. pap. 4.00 (ISBN 0-685-00994-7). Elizabeth Pr.
--O-I. 1974. pap. 8.00 (ISBN 0-685-41063-3). Elizabeth Pr.
--Plight. 1970. 5.00 (ISBN 0-685-00995-5). Elizabeth Pr.
--S. 1976. boards 16.00 (ISBN 0-686-63994-4); pap. 8.00 (ISBN 0-686-63995-2). Elizabeth Pr.
--So Far. 1973. signed 6.00 (ISBN 0-685-36864-5); wrappers 8.00, signed ed (ISBN 0-685-36865-3). Elizabeth Pr.
--Stead. 1966. pap. 6.00 (ISBN 0-685-00990-4). Elizabeth Pr.
--Sun Rock Man. LC 73-140033. (Orig.). 1970. pap. 1.75 (ISBN 0-8112-0024-8, NDP318). New Directions.
--Tu. 48p. 1983. pap. 12.50 (ISBN 0-915124-79-3, Pub. by Toothpaste). Coffee Hse.
--William Bronk: An Essay. 112p. 1976. 4.00 (ISBN 0-916562-06-9). Truck Pr.
--Word for Word: Essays on the Arts of Language, Vol.I. 180p. (Orig.). 1977. 14.00 (ISBN 0-87685-276-2); pap. 5.00 (ISBN 0-87685-275-4); ltd. signed 17.50 (ISBN 0-87685-277-0). Black Sparrow.
--Yet. 1974. pap. 6.00 (ISBN 0-685-40886-8); pap. 8.00 signed ed. (ISBN 0-685-40887-6). Elizabeth Pr.
Corman, Cid, jt. ed. see Niedecker, Lorine.
Corman, Cid, tr. Back Roads to Far Towns: Basno's Travel Journal. 1985. 7.50 (ISBN 0-934834-65-2). White Pine.
Corman, Cid, tr. see Basho, et al.
Corman, Cid, tr. see Jaccottet, Philippe.
Corman, Cid, tr. see Kusano, Shimpei.
Corman, Cid, et al, trs. see Sanesi, Roberto.
Corman, James W. Materialism & Sensations. LC 75-151570. pap. 91.50 (ISBN 0-317-08064-4, 2021990). Bks Demand UMI.
Corman, Marvin L. Colon & Rectal Surgery. LC 65-8113. (Illus.). 784p. 1984. text ed. 89.00 (ISBN 0-397-50647-3, Lippincott Medical). Lippincott.
Corman, Nicole S., tr. see Ingold, Gerard.
Cormane, Rudi H. & Asghar, Syed S. Immunology & Skin Disease. 224p. 1981. 75.00x (ISBN 0-7131-4346-0, Pub. by E Arnold England). State Mutual Bk.
Cormann, Enzo. Cabale. Schein, Gideon Y., tr. from Fr. (Ubu Repertory Theater Publications Ser.: No. 12). (Orig.). 1985. pap. text ed. 6.25 (ISBN 0-913745-09-X, Dist. by Publishing Center for Cultural Resources). Ubu Repertory.
Cormany, Robert B. Competency & Remediation: Testing Procedures & Instructional Strategies. 1985. write for info. (ISBN 0-931802-02-4). Prof Assocs.
Cormick, G. W., jt. ed. see Chalmers, W. E.
Cormier, E. D., ed. see Laviana, Ken.
Cormier, E. D., ed. see Laviana, Kenneth J.
Cormier, Frank. Presidents Are People Too. 1966. 11.00 (ISBN 0-8183-0198-8). Pub Aff Pr.
Cormier, Frank & Deakin, James. The White House Press on the Presidency: News Management & Co-option. Thompson, Kenneth W., ed. LC 83-6708. (The Presidency & the Press Ser.: Vol. IV). 92p. (Orig.). 1983. lib. bdg. 18.75 (ISBN 0-8191-3254-3, Pub. by White Miller Center); pap. text ed. 7.50 (ISBN 0-8191-3255-1). U Pr of Amer.
Cormier, J. M., jt. auth. see Ward, A. S.
Cormier, Jay. Giving Good Homilies. LC 84-70383. 96p. 1984. pap. 3.95 (ISBN 0-87793-317-0). Ave Maria.
Cormier, L. Sherilyn & Cormier, William H. Interviewing & Helping Skills for Health Professionals. LC 83-14596. 350p. 1983. pap. text ed. 13.50 pub net (ISBN 0-534-02849-7). Brooks-Cole.
Cormier, L. Sherilyn, jt. auth. see Cormier, William H.
Cormier, M. J., et al, eds. Chemiluminescence & Bioluminescence. LC 73-76169. 515p. 1973. 55.00x (ISBN 0-306-30733-2, Plenum Pr). Plenum Pub.
Cormier, Patricia P. & Levy, Joyce I. Community Oral Health: A Systems Approach for the Dental Health Profession. (Illus.). 237p. 1981. pap. 16.95 (ISBN 0-8385-1184-8). ACC.
Cormier, Ramona & Pallister, Janis L. Waiting for Death: The Philosophical Significance of Beckett's En Attendant Godot. LC 76-10218. (Studies in Humanities: No. 19). 176p. 1979. 14.25 (ISBN 0-8173-7605-4). U of Ala Pr.
Cormier, Raymond J. One Heart, One Mind: The Rebirth of Virgil's Hero in Medieval French Romance. LC 73-81571. (Romance Monographs: No. 3). 1973. pap. 16.00x (ISBN 8-4399-1292-7). Romance.
Cormier, Raymond J., ed. Three Ovidian Tales. LC 84-48061. 130p. 1985. lib. bdg. 20.00 (ISBN 0-8240-8956-1). Garland Pub.
--Voices of Conscience: Essays on Medieval & Modern French Literature in Memory of James D. Powell & Rosemary Hodgins. LC 76-15343. 282p. 1977. 34.95 (ISBN 0-87722-090-5). Temple U Pr.
Cormier, Raymond J. & Holmes, Urban T., eds. Essays in Honor of Louis Francis Solano. (Studies in the Romance Languages & Literatures: No. 92). 204p. 1970. pap. 11.00x (ISBN 0-8078-9092-8). U of NC Pr.
Cormier, Raymond J., tr. see Frappier, Jean.
Cormier, Rita M. Soul on Fire. LC 84-51433. 46p. 1984. 5.95 (ISBN 0-317-11630-4). Winston-Derek.
Cormier, Robert. After the First Death. 224p. 1983. pap. 2.50 (ISBN 0-380-48652-0, 62885-6, Flare). Avon.
--After the First Death. LC 78-11770. (Illus.). (YA) 1979. 7.95 (ISBN 0-394-84122-0); PLB 9.99 (ISBN 0-394-94122-5). Pantheon.
--Beyond the Chocolate War. LC 84-22865. (Books for Young Readers). 288p. (gr. 9 up). 11.95 (ISBN 0-394-87343-2); PLB 11.99 (ISBN 0-394-97343-7). Knopf.
--The Bumblebee Flies Anyway. LC 83-2458. 256p. (gr. 8 up). 1983. 10.95 (ISBN 0-394-86120-5); PLB 10.99 (ISBN 0-394-96120-X). Knopf.
--The Bumblebee Flies Anyway. 256p. (gr. 5 up). 1984. pap. 2.75 (ISBN 0-440-90871-X, LFL). Dell.
--The Chocolate War. 192p. (gr. 7 up). 1975. pap. 2.50 (ISBN 0-440-94459-7, LFL); tchr's. guide by Lou Stanek 0.50. Dell.
--The Chocolate War. LC 73-15109. 272p. (gr. 7-9). 1974. 13.95 (ISBN 0-394-82805-4). Pantheon.
--Eight Plus One. 1980. 7.95 (ISBN 0-394-84595-1); PLB 7.99 (ISBN 0-394-94595-6). Pantheon.
--Eight Plus One. 192p. 1982. pap. 2.50 (ISBN 0-553-25153-8). Bantam.
--I Am the Cheese. 224p. (gr. 7 up). 1978. pap. 2.50 (ISBN 0-440-94060-5, LFL); tchr's. guide by Lou Stanek 0.50. Dell.
--I Am the Cheese. LC 76-55948. (YA) 1977. 11.95 (ISBN 0-394-83462-3). Pantheon.
--I Am the Cheese. LC 76-55948. 224p. (gr. 7-12). 1977. 11.95 (ISBN 0-394-83462-3). Pantheon.
Cormier, Robert & Paquette, Laurence. RPG II Programming: A Building Block Approach. 206p. 1982. pap. write for info. Wadsworth Pub.
--RPG Two Programming: A Building Block Approach. 224p. 1981. pap. text ed. write for info. (ISBN 0-534-01018-0). Wadsworth Pub.
Cormier, Sherilyn, jt. auth. see Cormier, William H.
Cormier, Sherilyn N., jt. auth. see Hackney, Harold L.
Cormier, William H. & Cormier, L. Sherilyn. Interviewing Strategies for Helpers: A Guide to Assessment, Treatment & Evaluation. LC 78-12849. (Psychology Ser.). (Illus.). 1979. text ed. 23.00 pub net (ISBN 0-8185-0282-7). Brooks-Cole.
Cormier, William H. & Cormier, Sherilyn. Interviewing Strategies for Helpers-Fundamental Skills & Cognitive Behavioral Interventions. 2nd ed. LC 84-19837. (Counseling Ser.). 640p. 1985. text ed. 22.50 pub net (ISBN 0-534-04416-6). Brooks-Cole.
Cormier, William H., jt. auth. see Cormier, L. Sherilyn.
Cormley, Beatrice. The Ghastly Glasses. Amper, Julie, ed. LC 85-10112. (Illus.). 144p. (gr. 2-6). 1985. 11.95 (ISBN 0-525-44215-4). Dutton.
Corn, Alfred. A Call in the Midst of the Crowd. (Poetry Ser.). 1978. pap. 6.95 (ISBN 0-14-042257-9). Penguin.
--A Call in the Midst of the Crowd. 1978. 9.95 (ISBN 0-670-19979-6). Viking.
--Notes from a Child of Paradise. (Poetry Ser.). 112p. 1984. pap. 8.95 (ISBN 0-14-042327-3). Penguin.
--Notes from a Child of Paradise. 112p. 1984. pap. 14.95 (ISBN 0-670-51707-0). Viking.
--The Various Light. 1980. pap. 7.95 (ISBN 0-14-042284-6). Penguin.
--The Various Light. 96p. 1980. 12.95 (ISBN 0-670-74322-4). Viking.
Corn, Anne, et al. Are You Really Blind? 56p. 1985. 3.00 (ISBN 0-89128-134-7). Am Foun Blind.
Corn, David, jt. auth. see O'Brien, Kevin.
Corn, David & Vladimer, Randi, eds. Yours for the Asking: A Cornucopia of Free Information. 102p. 1981. 5.00 (ISBN 0-936758-02-3). Ctr Responsive Law.
Corn, Esther, ed. see Argaman, Shmuel.
Corn, Frederick L. Basketball's Magnificent Bird: The Larry Bird Story. LC 82-580. (Random House Sports Library). (Illus.). 144p. (gr. 5-9). 1982. pap. 1.95 (ISBN 0-394-85019-X). Random.
Corn, Herman. The Intergration of a Preventive Dentistry Program into a Dental Practice. Cohen, D. Walter, ed. (Continuing Dental Education Series). 182p. 1981. pap. 18.00 (ISBN 0-931386-25-X). Quint Pub Co.
Corn, Ira, Jr. Scalpel. 1984. pap. 3.50 (ISBN 0-8217-1371-X). Zebra.
Corn, Joseph J. & Horrigan, Brian, eds. Yesterday's Tomorrows: Past Visions of the American Future. (Illus.). 208p. (Orig.). 1984. 29.95 (ISBN 0-671-54276-1); pap. 17.95 (ISBN 0-671-54133-1). Summit Bks.
Corn, Wanda M. Grant Wood: The Regionalist Vision. LC 83-3514. 220p. 1983. 35.00x (ISBN 0-300-03103-3). Yale U Pr.
--Grant Wood: The Regionalist Vision. LC 83-3514. 220p. 1985. pap. 15.95x (ISBN 0-300-03401-6, Y-520). Yale U Pr.
Corn, Wanda M., ed. The Art of Andrew Wyeth. LC 73-93900. (Illus.). 176p. 1973. 29.95 (ISBN 0-8212-0516-1, 052515); pap. 19.95 (ISBN 0-8212-0685-0, 052280). NYGS.
Cornaby, W. Arthur. A String of Chinese Peach-Stones. LC 70-175730. (Illus.). 502p. 1974. Repr. of 1895 ed. 43.00x (ISBN 0-8103-3125-X). Gale.
Cornacchia, Harold J. & Barrett, Stephen. Consumer Health: A Guide to Intelligent Decisions. 2nd ed. LC 80-11515. (Illus.). 338p. 1980. pap. text ed. 16.95 (ISBN 0-8016-1037-0). Mosby.
--Shopping for Health Care: The Essential Guide to Products & Services. 1982. pap. 9.95 (ISBN 0-452-25366-7, Plume). NAL.
--Shopping for Health Care: The Essential Guide to Products & Services. LC 82-6405. (Mosby Medical Library). 381p. 1982. pap. 9.95 (ISBN 0-452-25366-7, 1140-7). Mosby.
Cornacchia, Harold J., et al. Health in Elementary Schools. 6th ed. LC 82-24000. (Illus.). 479p. 1983. text ed. 22.95 (ISBN 0-8016-1076-1). Mosby.
Cornacchia, Pete, ed. see Fabian, John.
Cornaro, Alvise. How to Beat Death: The Art to Live a Healthy Life Till 117. (Illus.). 127p. 1984. 96.85x (ISBN 0-89266-470-3). Am Classical Coll Pr.
Cornaro, Luigi. The Art of Living Long. Kastenbaum, Robert, ed. LC 78-22195. (Aging & Old Age Ser.). (Illus.). 1979. Repr. of 1917 ed. lib. bdg. 16.00x (ISBN 0-405-11812-0). Ayer Co Pubs.
Cornaro, Luigi, jt. auth. see Lessius, Leonard.
Cornatzer, W. E., jt. ed. see Mertz, Walter.
Cornazano, Antonio. The Book on the Art of Dancing. Inglehearn, Madeleine, et al, trs. from Ital. 52p. 1981. text ed. 11.95 (ISBN 0-903102-63-3, Pub. by Dance Bks England). Princeton Bk Co.
Cornberg, Sol & Gebauer, Emanuel L. Stage Crew Handbook. rev. ed. LC 56-11916. (Illus.). 1957. 13.41xi (ISBN 0-06-031560-1, HarpT). Har-Row.
Cornblath, Marvin & Schwartz, Robert. Disorders of Carbohydrate Metabolism in Infancy. 2nd ed. LC 75-31298. (Major Problems in Clinical Pediatrics Ser.: No. 3). (Illus.). 1976. 25.00 (ISBN 0-7216-2721-8). Saunders.
--Disorders of Carbohydrate Metabolism in Infancy. LC 66-12410. (Major Problems in Clinical Pediatrics Ser.: Vol. 3). pap. 77.80 (ISBN 0-317-26428-1, 2024984). Bks Demand UMI.
Cornbleet, S. Microwave & Optical Ray Geometry. LC 83-16737. 152p. 1984. cloth 36.95x (ISBN 0-471-90315-9, Pub. by Wiley-Interscience). Wiley.
Cornbleet, Sidney. Microwave Optics: The Optics of Microwave Antenna Design. (Pure & Applied Physics Ser.). 1977. 69.50 (ISBN 0-12-189650-1). Acad Pr.
Corncob, Jonathan. The Adventures of Jonathan Corncob. Perrin, Noel, ed. LC 75-43348. (Illus.). 128p. 1976. 12.95 (ISBN 0-87923-184-X); pap. 7.95 (ISBN 0-87923-283-8). Godine.
Corne, Chris. Seychelles Creole Grammar. Elements for Indian Ocean Proto-Creole Reconstruction. (Tuebinger Beitraege Zur Linguistik Ser.: No. 91). (Illus.). 240p. (Orig.). 1977. pap. 18.00x (ISBN 3-87808-091-3). Benjamins North Am.
Corne, Chris, jt. auth. see Baker, Philip.
Corne, Michele F. American Neptune Pictorial Supplements, Vol. 14. pap. 3.50 (ISBN 0-87577-101-7). Peabody Mus Salem.
Cornea, A. & Licea, G. Order & Potential Resolvent Familiers of Kernels. (Lecture Notes in Mathematics: Vol. 494). iv, 154p. 1975. pap. 13.00 (ISBN 0-387-07531-3). Springer-Verlag.
Cornea, A., jt. auth. see Constantinescu, C.
Cornebise, Alfred. The Amaroc News: The Daily Newspaper of the American Forces in Germany, 1919-1923. LC 80-27275. (New Horizons in Journalism Ser.). 272p. 1981. 24.95x (ISBN 0-8093-1001-5). S Ill U Pr.
Cornebise, Alfred C., ed. Doughboy Doggeral: Verse of the American Expeditionary Force, 1918-1919. LC 82-85561. 100p. 1985. text ed. 19.50 (ISBN 0-8214-0798-8). Ohio U Pr.
Cornebise, Alfred E. The Stars & Stripes: Doughboy Journalism in World War I. LC 83-12863. (Contributions in Military History Ser.: No. 37). (Illus.). xiii, 221p. 1984. lib. bdg. 29.95 (ISBN 0-313-24230-5, COS/). Greenwood.
--Typhus & Doughboys: The American Polish Typhus Relief Expedition, Nineteen Nineteen to Nineteen Twenty-One. LC 81-70530. (Illus.). 240p. 1982. 23.50 (ISBN 0-87413-216-9). U Delaware Pr.
--War as Advertised: The Four Minute Men & America's Crusade, 1917-1918. LC 83-73279. (Memoirs Ser.: Vol. 156). 1984. 15.00 (ISBN 0-87169-156-6). Am Philos.
Cornehls, James V., jt. auth. see Taebel, Delbert A.
Corneille. L' Illusion Comique. Marks, T., ed. (Modern French Texts). 162p. (Fr.). 1969. pap. text ed. 5.95 (ISBN 0-7190-0323-7, Pub. by Manchester Univ Pr). Longwood Pub Group.

Corneille, Pierre. Attila. 1965. pap. 4.50 (ISBN 0-685-11019-2). French & Eur.

--Attila. (Nouveaux Classiques Larousse Ser.). (Illus., Fr). pap. 2.95 (ISBN 0-685-13803-8, 62). Larousse.

--Chief Plays of Corneille. Lockert, L., tr. 1957. 38.00x (ISBN 0-691-06016-9). Princeton U Pr.

--Cid. Feltenstein, Rosalie, tr. from Fr. (YA) 1953. pap. text ed. 2.50 (ISBN 0-8120-0041-2). Barron.

--Le Cid. 1965. pap. 2.95 (ISBN 0-685-11082-6). French & Eur.

--Le Cid. Lapp, John C., ed. & tr. LC 55-9014. (Crofts Classics Ser.). 1955. pap. text ed. 3.25x (ISBN 0-88295-026-6). Harlan Davidson.

--Le Cid. Nurse, Peter, ed. 144p. 1978. 16.95x (ISBN 0-8071-0470-1). La State U Pr.

--Le Cid. (Documentation thematique). (Illus., Fr.). pap. 2.95 (ISBN 0-685-13829-1, 63). Larousse.

--The Cid, Cinna, the Theatrical Illusion. Cairncross, John, tr. from Fr. (Penguin Classics). 1976. pap. 3.95 (ISBN 0-14-044312-6). Penguin.

--Cinna. 1965. pap. 2.95 (ISBN 0-685-11084-2). French & Eur.

--Cinna. (Documentation thematique). (Illus., Fr). pap. 2.95 (ISBN 0-685-13831-3, 65); tchrs. manual avail. (ISBN 0-685-13832-1). Larousse.

--Clitandre ou l'Innocence Delivree. 151p. 1949. 4.95 (ISBN 0-686-54617-2). French & Eur.

--Horace. 1966. pap. 2.95 (ISBN 0-685-11236-5). French & Eur.

--Horace. (Documentation thematique). pap. 2.95 (ISBN 0-685-13941-7, 66). Larousse.

--L' Illusion Comique. (Univers des Lettres Bordas). pap. 3.95 (ISBN 0-685-34208-5). French & Eur.

--Illusion comique. (Documentation thematique). pap. 2.95 (ISBN 0-685-13943-3, 69). Larousse.

--L' Imitation de Jesus-Christ. 68p. 1941. 2.95 (ISBN 0-686-54618-0). French & Eur.

--Melite ou les Fausses Lettres. 147p. 1950. 4.95 (ISBN 0-686-54619-9). French & Eur.

--Mort de Pompee. (Nouveaux Classiques Larousse). (Illus., Fr). pap. 2.95 (ISBN 0-685-13995-6, 71). Larousse.

--La Mort de Solon: Piece Attribuee a Corneille Par Elisabeth M. Fraser. 136p. 1949. 4.95 (ISBN 0-686-54620-2). French & Eur.

--Nicomede. 1964. pap. 3.95 (ISBN 0-685-11421-X). French & Eur.

--Nicomede. (Documentation thematique). pap. 2.95 (ISBN 0-685-14000-8, 73). Larousse.

--Oeuvres Completes. 1970. 25.00 (ISBN 0-686-54621-0). French & Eur.

--Otho. 172p. (Fren. Ger.). 1974. 11.00 (ISBN 0-917396-01-4); pap. 6.50 (ISBN 0-917396-02-2). H Linder.

--Polyeucte. Sayce, R. A., ed. (French Text Ser.). 112p. 1962. pap. 9.95x (ISBN 0-631-00480-7). Basil Blackwell.

--Polyeucte. 1965. pap. 3.95 (ISBN 0-685-11500-3). French & Eur.

--Polyeucte. (Documentation thematique). (Illus., Fr). pap. 2.95 (ISBN 0-685-14054-7, 74). Larousse.

--Polyeuctus, the Liar, Nicomedes. Cairncross, John, tr. from Fr. (Penguin Classics). 1980. pap. 4.95 (ISBN 0-14-044349-5). Penguin.

--Rodogune. 1963. pap. 3.95 (ISBN 0-685-11532-1). French & Eur.

--Rodogune. new ed. (Documentation thematique). (Illus.). 173p. (Fr.). 1975. pap. 2.95 (ISBN 0-685-62581-8, 75). Larousse.

--Rodogune: The French Text with a Facing English Translation. Clubb, William G., ed. & tr. LC 73-86397. xxxviii, 132p. 1974. 14.50x (ISBN 0-8032-0501-5). U of Nebr Pr.

--Sertorius. 160p. 1959. 4.95 (ISBN 0-686-54622-9). French & Eur.

--Surena, General Des Parthes. 248p. 1970. 12.95 (ISBN 0-686-54623-7). French & Eur.

--Theatre, 12 vols. facsimile ed. (Illus.). 1975. Set. 1500.00 (ISBN 0-686-54624-5). French & Eur.

--Theatre Complet, 2 tomes. Lievre & Callois, eds. (Bibl. de la Pleiade). 1934. Set. 59.95 (ISBN 0-685-11592-5). French & Eur.

--La Veuve Ou le Traitre Puni. 154p. 1954. 4.95 (ISBN 0-686-54625-3). French & Eur.

Corneille, Pierre see Guicharnaud, Jacques.

Corneille, Thomas. Ariadne: A Tragedy in Five Acts. Mandel, Oscar, tr. LC 80-24597. xii, 84p. 1982. 10.00 (ISBN 0-8130-0698-8). U Presses Fla.

Cornelia, Elizabeth. Australia. LC 78-56592. (Countries Ser.). (Illus.). 1978. PLB 13.96 (ISBN 0-382-06182-9). Silver.

Cornelia, Marie. The Function of the Masque in Jacobean Tragedy & Tragicomedy. (Salzburg Studies in English Literature, Jacobean Drama Studies: No. 77). 1978. pap. text ed. 25.50x (ISBN 0-391-01350-8). Humanities.

Cornelia, Mary P. & Tarr, G. Alan, eds. State Supreme Courts: Policymakers in the Federal System. LC 81-13431. (Contributions in Legal Studies Ser.: No. 24). (Illus.). xxvii, 221p. 1982. lib. bdg. 35.00 (ISBN 0-313-22942-2, PSC/). Greenwood.

Cornelia, Nicholas, jt. auth. see Pasewark, William R.

Cornelia, Nicholas J., et al. Curso de Maquinas de Oficina. (Span.). 1977. text ed. 5.15 (ISBN 0-538-22790-7, V79). SW Pub.

Cornelisen, Ann. Any Four Women... Could Rob the Bank of Italy. LC 83-4342. 288p. 1983. 15.95 (ISBN 0-03-063254-4). HR&W.

--Any Four Women Could Rob the Bank of Italy. 3rd ed. (Penguin Crime Fiction Ser.). 304p. 1985. pap. 5.95 (ISBN 0-14-007599-2). Penguin.

--Strangers & Pilgrims. (McGraw-Hill Paperbacks Ser.). 324p. 1981. pap. 5.95 (ISBN 0-07-013192-9). McGraw.

--Strangers & Pilgrims: The Last Italian Migration. LC 79-3429. 320p. 1980. 12.95 (ISBN 0-03-044285-0). HR&W.

--Women of the Shadows. 1977. pap. 4.95 (ISBN 0-394-72345-7, Vin). Random.

Cornelison, Gayle, compiled by. A Directory of Children's Theatres in the United States. 164p. 1983. pap. text ed. 14.00 (ISBN 0-8191-3526-7, Co-pub. by Am Theat Assn). U Pr of Amer.

Cornelison, Isaac J. The Relation of Religion to Civil Government in the United States. LC 75-107409. (Civil Liberties in American History Ser). 1970. Repr. of 1895 ed. lib. bdg. 45.00 (ISBN 0-306-71890-1). Da Capo.

Cornelison, Kathy D., jt. auth. see Risser, Paul G.

Cornelison, Lynn E. Asleep in a Wildflower Sanctuary. 82p. 1983. 5.00 (ISBN 0-9614329-0-X). L Cornelison.

Cornelisse, J. W., et al. Rocket Propulsion & Spaceflight Dynamics. LC 78-40059. (Aerospace Engineering Ser.). 505p. 1979. text ed. 89.95 (ISBN 0-273-01141-3). Pitman Pub MA.

Cornelissen, Christian. Theorie de la valeur. 2nd ed. LC 77-147839. (Research & Source Works Ser.: No. 649). 1971. Repr. of 1913 ed. 29.50 (ISBN 0-8337-0681-0). B Franklin.

Cornelius. Food Service Careers. 1979. text ed. 20.20 (ISBN 0-02-664010-4); tchr's guide 2.00 (ISBN 0-02-664020-1); student's guide 5.32 (ISBN 0-02-663990-4). Bennett IL.

Cornelius, Betty, jt. auth. see Silver, Edith.

Cornelius, C. A. see Brandly, C. A. & Jungherr, E. L.

Cornelius, C. E. & Simpson, C. F., eds. Advances in Veterinary Science & Comparative Medicine, Vol. 25. (Serial Publication Ser.). 1981. 70.00 (ISBN 0-12-039225-9); lib. ed. 80.00 (ISBN 0-12-039286-0); microfiche 40.00 (ISBN 0-12-039287-9). Acad Pr.

Cornelius, C. E., jt. ed. see Brandly, C. A.

Cornelius, C. E., jt. ed. see Kaneko, J. J.

Cornelius, Carol. Bobbin's Land. LC 78-2399. (Illus.). (ps-4). 1978. PLB 6.95 (ISBN 0-913778-99-0). Childs World.

--Isabella Wooly Bear Tiger Moth. LC 77-28423. (Illus.). (ps-4). 1978. PLB 6.95 (ISBN 0-913778-97-4). Childs World.

--Polka Dots, Checks, & Stripes. LC 78-983. (Illus.). (ps-4). 1978. PLB 6.95 (ISBN 0-89565-017-7). Childs World.

Cornelius, Charles E. & Simpson, Charles F., eds. Advances in Veterinary Science & Comparative Medicine, Vol. 27. (Serial Publication Ser.). 1983. 58.00 (ISBN 0-12-039227-5). Acad Pr.

--Advances in Veterinary Science & Comparative Medicine, Vol. 29. (Serial Publication). Date not set. price not set (ISBN 0-12-039229-1). Acad Pr.

Cornelius, Charles E. & Simpson, Charles, eds. Advances in Veterinary Science & Comparative Medicine, Vol. 30. (Serial Publication). Date not set. price not set (ISBN 0-12-039230-5). Acad Pr.

Cornelius, Chase, jt. auth. see Cornelius, Sue.

Cornelius, Debra. Who Cares? Handbook on Sex Education & Counseling Services for Disabled People. (Illus.). 276p. 1982. pap. 17.00 (ISBN 0-8391-1727-2). Pro Ed.

Cornelius, E. T., Jr., jt. auth. see Alexander, L. G.

Cornelius, Edwin T., jt. auth. see Byrne, Donn.

Cornelius, Edwin T., Jr. ACT: Accomplishing Advanced Communicative Tasks: Perfecting Communicative Abilities. (New Technology English Ser.: Vol. 11). (Illus.). 247p. 1984. text ed. 8.95 (ISBN 0-89209-117-7); pap. text ed. 6.95 (ISBN 0-89209-410-9); Set of 12. audiocassettes 50.00 (ISBN 0-89209-118-5). Pace Intl Res.

--ACT Interaction. (New Technology English Ser.: Vol. 12). (Illus.). 173p. 1984. text ed. 8.95 (ISBN 0-89209-169-X); pap. text ed. 6.25 (ISBN 0-89209-411-7); Set of 8. audiocassettes 36.00 (ISBN 0-89209-162-2). Pace Intl Res.

--Comprehension. (New Technology English Ser.: Vol. 9). (Illus.). 155p. 1984. text ed. 8.95 (ISBN 0-89209-157-6); pap. text ed. 6.25 (ISBN 0-89209-408-7); Set of 8. audiocassettes 36.00 (ISBN 0-89209-183-5). Pace Intl Res.

--Interaction. (New Technology English Ser.: Vol. 8). (Illus.). 153p. 1984. text ed. 8.95 (ISBN 0-89209-159-2); pap. text ed. 6.25 (ISBN 0-89209-407-9); Set of 4. audiocassettes 17.00 (ISBN 0-89209-160-6). Pace Intl Res.

--Interview: Listening Comprehension for High Intermediate & Advanced Students. (English As a Second Language Bk.). (Illus.). 128p. 1981. pap. text ed. 6.50x (ISBN 0-582-79700-4); cassette 14.75x (ISBN 0-582-79702-0); bk. & cassette in tote 18.95x (ISBN 0-582-79782-9). Longman.

--New English Course, 6 bks. Incl. Book 1. student text 4.75 (ISBN 0-89285-125-2); tchr's. annotated ed. 6.95 (ISBN 0-89285-137-6); wkbk. 2.00 (ISBN 0-89285-131-7); cassette 120.00 (ISBN 0-89285-119-8); cassette tape 18.00 (ISBN 0-89285-113-9); Book 2. student text 4.75 (ISBN 0-89285-126-0); tchr's annotated ed. 6.95 (ISBN 0-89285-138-4); wkbk. 2.00 (ISBN 0-89285-132-5); cassette 120.00 (ISBN 0-89285-120-1); cassette tape 18.00 (ISBN 0-89285-114-7); Book 3. student text 4.75 (ISBN 0-89285-127-9); tchr's annotated ed. 6.95 (ISBN 0-89285-139-2); wkbk. 2.00 (ISBN 0-89285-133-3); cassette 120.00 (ISBN 0-89285-121-X); cassette tape 18.00 (ISBN 0-89285-115-5); Book 4. student text 4.75 (ISBN 0-89285-128-7); tchr's annotated ed. 6.95 (ISBN 0-89285-140-6); wkbk. 2.00 (ISBN 0-89285-134-1); cassette 120.00 (ISBN 0-89285-122-8); cassette tape 18.00 (ISBN 0-89285-116-3); Book 5. student text 4.75 (ISBN 0-89285-129-5); tchr's annotated ed. 6.95 (ISBN 0-89285-141-4); wkbk. 2.00 (ISBN 0-89285-135-X); cassette 120.00 (ISBN 0-89285-123-6); cassette tape 18.00 (ISBN 0-89285-117-1); Book 6. student text 4.75 (ISBN 0-89285-130-9); tchr's annotated ed. 6.95 (ISBN 0-89285-142-2); wkbk. 2.00 (ISBN 0-89285-136-8); cassette 120.00 (ISBN 0-89285-124-4); cassette tape 18.00 (ISBN 0-89285-118-X); Bks. 1-6. progress quizzes & placement tests avail.. (Illus.). 1979. pap. text ed. 4.75 ea. English Lang.

--NTE (New Technology English) Book 1: Handling Social Conventions. (New Technology English Ser.: Vol. 4). (Illus.). 147p. 1984. text ed. 8.95 (ISBN 0-89209-109-6); pap. text ed. 6.25 (ISBN 0-89209-403-6); Set of 6. audiocassettes 25.00 (ISBN 0-89209-113-4). Pace Intl Res.

--NTE (New Technology English) Book 2: Interacting in Social & Business Settings. (New Technology English Ser.: Vol. 5). (Illus.). 150p. 1984. text ed. 8.95 (ISBN 0-89209-110-X); pap. text ed. 6.25 (ISBN 0-89209-404-4); audiocassettes (Set of 6) 25.00 (ISBN 0-89209-114-2). Pace Intl Res.

--NTE (New Technology English) Book 3: Expressing & Finding Out Attitudes. (New Technology English Ser.: Vol. 6). (Illus.). 151p. 1984. text ed. 8.95 (ISBN 0-89209-111-8); pap. text ed. 6.25 (ISBN 0-89209-405-2); audiocassettes (Set of 6) 25.00 (ISBN 0-89209-115-0). Pace Intl Res.

--NTE (New Technology English) Book 4: Extending Personal Abilities. (New Technology English Ser.: Vol. 7). (Illus.). 152p. 1984. text ed. 8.95 (ISBN 0-89209-112-6); pap. text ed. 6.25 (ISBN 0-89209-406-0); audiocassettes (Set of 6) 25.00 (ISBN 0-89209-116-9). Pace Intl Res.

--NTE Progress & Performance. (New Technology English Ser.: Vol. 10). (Illus.). 1984. text ed. 8.95; pap. text ed. 6.95 (ISBN 0-89209-409-5); audiocassettes (Set of 8) 36.00 (ISBN 0-89209-158-4). Pace Intl Res.

--PAL (Preliminary Achievement Level) Book 1: Giving Information & Socializing. (New Technology English Ser.: Vol. 1). (Illus.). 148p. 1984. text ed. 8.95 (ISBN 0-89209-105-3); pap. text ed. 6.25 (ISBN 0-89209-400-1); audiocassettes (Set of 6) 25.00 (ISBN 0-89209-107-X). Pace Intl Res.

--PAL (Preliminary Achievement Level) Book 2: Taking an Active Role in Conversations. (New Technology English Ser.: Vol. 2). 151p. 1984. text ed. 8.95 (ISBN 0-89209-106-1); pap. text ed. 6.25 (ISBN 0-89209-401-X); audiocassettes (Set of 6) 25.00 (ISBN 0-89209-108-8). Pace Intl Res.

--Progress & Performance. (New Technology English Ser.: Vol. 3). 125p. 1984. text ed. 8.95 (ISBN 0-89209-164-9); pap. text ed. 6.25 (ISBN 0-89209-402-8); audiocassettes (Set of 4) 17.00 (ISBN 0-89209-165-7). Pace Intl Res.

Cornelius, Edwin T., Jr., jt. auth. see O'Neill, Robert.

Cornelius, Edwin T., Jr., et al. Magazine U. S. A. (Illus.). 160p. 1984. pap. text ed. 6.95 (ISBN 0-89209-269-6); audiocassettes (10 C-60) 75.00 (ISBN 0-89209-270-X). Pace Intl Res.

Cornelius, Hal & Lewis, William. Career Blazer Guide to Sales & Marketing. (Career Blazers Guides). 1983. pap. 8.95 (ISBN 0-671-47169-4). Monarch Pr.

--A Career Blazer Guide to Word Processing. (Career Blazers Guides Ser.). 192p. 1983. pap. 7.95 (ISBN 0-671-45869-8). Monarch Pr.

Cornelius, Janet. Constitution Making in Illinois, 1818-1970. LC 72-76864. (Studies in Illinois Constitution Making Ser.). 190p. 1972. pap. 10.00 (ISBN 0-252-00251-2). U of Ill Pr.

Cornelius, L. A. Grammar & Composition for Schools. 390p. 1981. pap. text ed. 5.95x (ISBN 0-86131-291-0, Pub. by Orient Longman Ltd India). Apt Bks.

Cornelius, Martin P., III. Til Death Do Us Part: A Basic Education in Total Health: How to Keep Body & Soul Happily Together. 256p. (Orig.). 1981. pap. 15.00 (ISBN 0-9607142-0-0). Health Ed & Life Exp Res.

Cornelius, Michael, ed. Teaching Mathematics. 268p. 1982. pap. 15.95. Nichols Pub.

--Teaching Mathematics. LC 82-6404. (Illus.). 248p. 1982. pap. 16.50. Nichols Pub.

Cornelius, Patsy S. E. K.'s Commentary on The Shepheardes Calendar. (Salzburg Studies in English Literature, Elizabethan & Renaissance Studies: No. 31). 111p. 1974. pap. text ed. 25.50x (ISBN 0-391-01350-5). Humanities.

Cornelius, Peter. Literarische Werke, 1904-1905, 4 vols. Repr. 190.00 (ISBN 0-384-09845-2). Johnson Repr.

Cornelius, R. M. Christopher Marlowe's Use of the Bible. LC 84-21280. (American University Studies IV (English Language & Literature): Vol. 23). (Illus.). 335p. 1985. text ed. 32.00 (ISBN 0-8204-0193-5). P Lang Pubs.

Cornelius, Ruth. All Together: A Manual of Cooperative Games. 1950. 3.00 (ISBN 0-318-01694-X). Peace Res Lab.

Cornelius, Stephen. Contribution to the Life History of Black Drum & Analysis of the Commercial Fishery in Baffin Bay, Vol. 11. LC 83-71622. 75p. 1984. pap. 5.50 (ISBN 0-912229-07-1). CK Wildlife Res.

--An Ecological Survey of Alazan Bay, Texas, Vol. 1. LC 83-71623. 160p. 1984. pap. 8.50 (ISBN 0-912229-06-3). CK Wildlife Res.

Cornelius, Sue & Cornelius, Chase. City in Art. LC 65-29036. (Fine Art Bks.). (Illus.). (gr. 5-11). 1966. PLB 5.95 (ISBN 0-8225-0159-7). Lerner Pubns.

Cornelius, Temple H. & Marshall, John B. Golden Treasures of the San Juan. LC 61-9435. 235p. 1961. pap. 6.95 (ISBN 0-8040-0636-9, 82-73450, SB). Ohio U Pr.

Cornelius, W. & Agnew, W. G., eds. Emissions from Continuous Combustion Systems. LC 72-80343. (General Motors Symposia Ser.). 479p. 1972. 69.50x (ISBN 0-306-30702-2, Plenum Pr). Plenum Pub.

Cornelius, Wanda & Short, Thayne. Ding Hao: America's Air War in China, 1937-1945. LC 80-19337. (Illus.). 502p. 1980. 19.95 (ISBN 0-88289-253-3). Pelican.

Cornelius, Wayne A. Politics & the Migrant Poor in Mexico City. LC 75-179. (Illus.). xiv, 319p. 1975. 25.00x (ISBN 0-8047-0880-0). Stanford U Pr.

Cornelius, Wayne A. & Kemper, Robert V., eds. Metropolitan Latin America: The Challenge & the Response. LC 77-79867. (Latin American Urban Research Ser.: Vol. 6). pap. 86.50 (ISBN 0-317-29599-3, 2021881). Bks Demand UMI.

Cornelius, Wayne A. & Trueblood, Felicity M., eds. Anthropological Perspectives on Latin American Urbanization. LC 73-86706. (Latin American Urban Research Ser.: Vol. 4). (Illus.). pap. 74.00 (ISBN 0-317-08986-2, 2021880). Bks Demand UMI.

--Urbanization & Inequality: The Political Economy of Urban & Rural Development in Latin America. LC 74-83000. (Latin American Urban Research Ser.: Vol. 5). (Illus.). pap. 79.50 (ISBN 0-317-08989-7, 2021879). Bks Demand UMI.

Cornelius, William L. Beginning & Intermediate Gymnastics. (Illus.). 112p. 1983. pap. text ed. 8.95x (ISBN 0-88136-017-1). Jostens.

--Beginning & Intermediate Gymnastics. (Illus.). 112p. 1983. pap. text ed. 8.95x (ISBN 0-89582-134-6). Morton Pub.

Cornelius Nepus see Florus.

Cornell. Sanyo Programming & Software Applications. 1985. pap. 16.95 (ISBN 0-471-82496-8). Wiley.

--Statistical Methods for Cancer Studies. (Statistics: Textbooks & Monographs). 344p. 1984. Repr. of 1972 ed. 59.50 (ISBN 0-8247-7169-9). Dekker.

Cornell, jt. auth. see Fry.

Cornell, A. D., jt. auth. see Gauld, Alan.

Cornell, Alexander H. The Decision-Maker's Handbook. (Illus.). 1980. 13.95 (ISBN 0-13-198218-4, Spec); pap. 7.95 (ISBN 0-13-198200-1, Spec). P-H.

--International Collaboration in Weapons & Equipment Development & Production by the NATO Allies. (Atlantic Ser.: No. 2). 248p. lib. bdg. 54.50 (ISBN 90-247-2564-X, Pub. by Martinus Nijhoff Netherlands). Kluwer Academic.

Cornell, Claire P., jt. auth. see Gelles, Richard J.

Cornell, Dale D. & Erickson, Frances G. Marriage: The Phoenix Contract. 1985. 22.50 (ISBN 0-87527-264-9). Green.

Cornell, David, ed. The Spider Anthology: Contemporary American Poets on Spiders. LC 83-72508. (Illus.). 67p. 1983. pap. 5.95 (ISBN 0-9611940-0-6). Arachnes Muse.

Cornell, Dewey G. Families of Gifted Children. Nathan, Peter E., ed. LC 84-3578. (Research in Clinical Psychology Ser.: No. 11). 170p. 1984. 34.95 (ISBN 0-8357-1550-7). UMI Res Pr.

Cornell, Elizabeth see Rose, Louisa, et al.

Cornell, F. M. & Hoffman, A. C. American Merchant Seamans Manual. 6th ed. Hayler, William B., ed. LC 56-12402. (Illus.). 635p. 1981. 22.50x (ISBN 0-87033-267-8). Cornell Maritime.

Cornell, Francis G. A Measure of Tax-Paying Ability of Local School Administrative Units. LC 71-176670. (Columbia University. Teachers College. Contributions to Education Ser.: No. 698). Repr. of 1936 ed. 22.50 (ISBN 0-404-55698-1). AMS Pr.

Cornell, G., tr. see Scharlau, W. & Opolka, H.

Cornell, Gary & Abikoff, William. The BASIC Apple IIc: A Self-Teaching Guide. 512p. 1985. pap. 15.95 (ISBN 0-471-82021-0); Book with program disk. 44.95 (ISBN 0-471-82617-0). Wiley.

Cornell, Gary, jt. auth. see Abikoff, William.

Cornell, Gwenda. Pacific Odyssey. (Illus.). 224p. (Orig.). 1985. pap. 12.95 (ISBN 0-229-11758-9, Pub. by Adlar Coles). Sheridan.

Cornell, H. L. Encyclopedia of Medical Astrology. rev. 3rd ed. 958p. 1972. 27.50 (ISBN 0-87728-212-9). Weiser.

Cornell, James. The First Stargazers: An Introduction to the Origins of Astronomy. 1981. 15.95 (ISBN 0-684-16799-9, ScribT). Scribner.

--The Great International Disaster Book. 1979. pap. 2.75 (ISBN 0-671-81951-8). PB.

--The Great International Disaster Book. 3rd ed. (Illus.). 464p. 1982. encore ed. 5.95 (ISBN 0-684-17345-X, ScribT). Scribner.

--The Monster of Loch Ness. (gr. 7 up). 1978. pap. 1.95 (ISBN 0-590-11872-2). Scholastic Inc.

Cornell, James & Carr, John, eds. Infinite Vistas: How the Space Telescope & Other Advances Are Revolutionizing Our Knowledge of the Universe. 256p. 1985. 18.95 (ISBN 0-684-18287-4, ScribT). Scribner.

Cornell, James & Gorenstein, Paul, eds. Astronomy from Space: Sputnik to Space Telescope. (Illus.). 264p. 1983. 20.00x (ISBN 0-262-03097-7). MIT Pr.

--Astronomy from Space: Sputnik to Space Telescope. 264p. 1985. pap. 8.95 (ISBN 0-262-53061-9). MIT Pr.

Cornell, James & Lightman, Alan P., eds. Revealing the Universe: Prediction & Proof in Astronomy. (Illus.). 264p. 1981. pap. text ed. 8.95 (ISBN 0-262-53043-0). MIT Pr.

Cornell, Jane. The Art of Gift Wrapping. LC 80-14156. (Illus.). 96p. (Orig.). 1980. 13.95 (ISBN 0-446-51212-5); pap. 7.95 (ISBN 0-446-97474-9). Warner Bks.

--The Art of Table Decoration. LC 80-1447. (Illus.). 96p. (Orig.). 1980. 13.95 (ISBN 0-446-51213-3); pap. 7.95 (ISBN 0-446-97475-7). Warner Bks.

Cornell, Jean G. Mahalia Jackson: Queen of Gospel Song. LC 73-14713. (Americans All Ser.). (Illus.). 96p. (gr. 3-6). 1974. PLB 7.98 (ISBN 0-8116-4581-9). Garrard.

--Ralph Bunche: Champion of Peace. LC 75-20368. (Americans All Ser.). 96p. (gr. 3-6). 1976. PLB 7.98 (ISBN 0-8116-4583-5). Garrard.

Cornell, Jimmy. Modern Ocean Cruising: Boats, Gear & Crews Surveyed. (Illus.). 250p. 1985. write for info. (ISBN 0-229-11687-6, Pub. by Adlard Coles). Sheridan.

Cornell, John A. Experiments with Mixtures: Designs, Models & the Analysis of Mixtures Data. LC 80-22153. (Probability & Mathematical Statistics Ser.). 305p. 1981. 41.50x (ISBN 0-471-07916-2, Pub. by Wiley-Interscience). Wiley.

Cornell, Joseph A. Computers in Hospital Pharmacy Management: Fundamentals & Applications. LC 82-24381. 228p. 1983. 32.00 (ISBN 0-89443-673-2). Aspen Systems.

Cornell, Joseph B. Sharing Nature with Children. LC 78-74650. (Illus.). 143p. 1979. pap. 6.95 (ISBN 0-916124-14-2). Ananda.

Cornell, Julien. Conscience & the State. Bd. with Conscientious Objector & the Law. Cornell, Julien. LC 70-147636. (Library of War & Peace; Conscrip. & Cons. Object.). lib. bdg. 46.00 (ISBN 0-8240-0412-4). Garland Pub.

Cornell, Julien D. The Conscientious Objector & the Law. Bd. with Conscience & the State: Legal & Administrative Problems of Conscientious Objectors, 1943-1944. LC 75-137532. (Peace Movement in America Ser). 264p. 1972. Repr. of 1943 ed. lib. bdg. 16.95x (ISBN 0-89198-060-1). Ozer.

Cornell, Kenneth. Post-Symbolist Period: French Poetic Currents, 1900-1920. vi, 182p. 1970. Repr. of 1958 ed. 17.50 (ISBN 0-208-00822-5, Archon). Shoe String.

--Symbolist Movement. LC 70-121755. ix, 217p. 1970. Repr. of 1951 ed. 18.50 (ISBN 0-208-00947-7, Archon). Shoe String.

Cornell, Luis L. Kipling in India. 224p. 1982. Repr. of 1966 ed. lib. bdg. 35.00 (ISBN 0-89760-165-3). Telegraph Bks.

Cornell, M., jt. auth. see Fry, Lionel.

Cornell, Margaret, jt. auth. see Belgrave, Robert.

Cornell, Meriss & Yocum, James C. Census Tract Street Directory, 1966: Columbus & Franklin County. 1966. pap. 4.00x (ISBN 0-87776-130-2, R130). Ohio St U Admin Sci.

Cornell, N. W., jt. ed. see Harris, R. A.

Cornell, Pat. Search N Shade. Jacobs, Alan, ed. (Illus.). (gr. 4-9). 1979. pap. 7.50 (ISBN 0-918272-07-6). Jacobs.

Cornell, Richard. Revolutionary Vanguard: The Early Years of the Communist Youth International, 1914-1924. 368p. 1982. 35.00x (ISBN 0-8020-5559-1). U of Toronto Pr.

Cornell, Robert H., jt. ed. see Cole, Donald B.

Cornell, Ross, jt. auth. see Dudick, Thomas S.

Cornell, S. A. Flying Carrots. (Illus.). 48p. (gr. 1-3). 1986. PLB 8.59 (ISBN 0-8167-0640-9); pap. text ed. 1.95 (ISBN 0-8167-0641-7). Troll Assocs.

--Little Eagle Learns to Fly. (Illus.). 48p. (Orig.). (gr. 1-3). 1986. lib. bdg. 8.59 (ISBN 0-8167-0618-2); pap. text ed. 1.95 (ISBN 0-8167-0619-0). Troll Assocs.

Cornell, Sara. Art: A History of Changing Style. 456p. 1983. 27.95 (ISBN 0-13-047126-7); pap. text ed. 36.95 (ISBN 0-13-047118-6). P-H.

Cornell, Stephen, jt. auth. see Galbraith, Ian A.

Cornell, Steven H. The Roentgenographic Diagnosis of Diseases of the Thoracic Aorta. (Illus.). 292p. 1973. photocopy ed. 33.75 (ISBN 0-398-02687-4). C C Thomas.

Cornell, Tim & Matthews, John. Atlas of the Roman World. (Cultural Atlas Ser.). (Illus.). 240p. 1982. 35.00 (ISBN 0-87196-652-2). Facts on File.

Cornell University. Catalog of the Southeast Asia Collection, Cornell University: First Supplement. 1887p. 1983. lib. bdg. 505.00 (ISBN 0-8161-0383-6, Hall Library). G K Hall.

--Third Supplement to the Cumulation of the Library Catalog Supplements of the New York State School of Industrial & Labor Relations. 1979. lib. bdg. 190.00 (ISBN 0-8161-0260-0, Hall Library). G K Hall.

Cornell University. Libraries. Catalogue of the Witchcraft Collection in Cornell University Library. LC 76-41552. 1977. lib. bdg. 120.00 (ISBN 0-527-19705-X). Kraus Intl.

Cornell University, Martin P. Catherwood Library. Cumulation of the Library Catalog Supplements of the New York State School of Industrial & Labor Relations, First Supplement. 1977. lib. bdg. 125.00 (ISBN 0-8161-0055-1, Hall Library). G K Hall.

Cornell University New York State School of Industrial & Labor Relations. Cumulation of the Library Catalog Supplements of Martin P. Catherwood Library of the New York State School of Industrial & Labor Relations, 9 vols. 1976. Set. lib. bdg. 1285.00 (ISBN 0-8161-0022-5, Hall Library). G K Hall.

Cornell University, New York State School of Industrial & Labor Ralations Staff. Library Catalog of the Martin P. Catherwood Library of the New York State School of Industrial & Labor Relations, 12 vols. 1967. Set. lib. bdg. 1190.00 (ISBN 0-8161-0757-2, Hall Library). G K Hall.

Cornell University, New York State School of Industrial & Labor Relations. Library Catalog of the Martin P. Catherwood Library of the New York State School of Industrial & Labor Relations, First Supplement. 873p. 1967. lib. bdg. 115.00 (ISBN 0-8161-0772-6, Hall Library). G K Hall.

Cornell University, New York State School of Industrial & Labor Relations Staff. Library Catalog of the Martin P. Catherwood Library of the New York State School of Industrial & Labor Relations, Second Supplement. 1968. lib. bdg. 125.00 (ISBN 0-8161-0844-7, Hall Library). G K Hall.

--Library Catalog of the Martin P. Catherwood Library of the New York State School of Industrial & Labor Relations, Third Supplement. 1969. lib. bdg. 125.00 (ISBN 0-8161-0878-1, Hall Library). G K Hall.

--Library Catalog of the Martin P. Catherwood Library of the New York State School of Industrial & Labor Relations, Fourth Supplement. 1970. lib. bdg. 125.00 (ISBN 0-8161-0911-7, Hall Library). G K Hall.

--Library Catalog of the Martin P. Catherwood Library of the New York State School of Industrial & Labor Relations, Fifth Supplement. 1972. 125.00 (ISBN 0-8161-0986-9, Hall Library). G K Hall.

--Library Catalog of the Martin P. Catherwood Library of the New York State School of Industrial & Labor Relations, Sixth Supplement. 1973. lib. bdg. 125.00 (ISBN 0-8161-1072-7, Hall Library). G K Hall.

--Library Catalog of the Martin P. Catherwood Library of the New York State School of Industrial & Labor Relations, Seventh Supplement. 1974. lib. bdg. 125.00 (ISBN 0-8161-1079-4, Hall Library). G K Hall.

Cornell University Staff. Libraries, Cornell University: Southeast Asia Catalog, 7 vols. 1976. Set. lib. bdg. 695.00 (Hall Library). G K Hall.

Cornell University, Summer Seminar, 1965. Relativity Theory & Astrophysics: Galactic Structure, Vol. 9. Ehlers, J., ed. LC 62-21481. (Lectures in Applied Mathematics). 220p. 1974. Repr. of 1967 ed. 24.00 (ISBN 0-8218-1109-6, LAM-9). Am Math.

Cornell, Vincent J., tr. see Abu 'Uthman 'Amr Ibn Bahr Al-Jahiz.

Cornell, Wallace L., tr. see Isoardi, Gian C.

Cornell, William. Understanding Pennsylvania Civics. (gr. 7-12). 1985. pap. 6.95 (ISBN 0-931992-45-1). Penns Valley.

Cornell, William A. & Altland, Millard. Our Pennsylvania Heritage. LC 78-50430. (gr. 7-12). 1983. 15.45 (ISBN 0-931992-21-4). Penns Valley.

Cornell, William K. Adolphe Rette, 1863-1930. (Yale Romanic Studies: No. 20). Repr. of 1942 ed. 32.00 (ISBN 0-404-53220-9). AMS Pr.

Corner, Betsy C., ed. see Fothergill, John.

Corner, C. M., jt. auth. see Gunston, C. A.

Corner, Desmond C. & Mayes, David G., eds. Modern Portfolio Theory & Financial Institutions. 1983. text ed. 35.00 (ISBN 0-8419-5093-8). Holmes & Meier.

Corner, E. A Monograph of Thelephora. (Illus.). 1968. 14.00 (ISBN 3-7682-5427-5). Lubrecht & Cramer.

--Supplement to "A Monograph of Clavaria & Allied Genera". (Illus.). 1970. pap. 42.00 (ISBN 3-7682-5433-X). Lubrecht & Cramer.

Corner, E. J. Ad Polyporaceae I. Amauroderma & Canoderma. (Nova Hedwigia Beift Ser.: No. 75). (Illus.). 182p. 1983. text ed. 28.00x (ISBN 3-7682-5475-5). Lubrecht & Cramer.

--As Poyporaceas II & III. (Illus.). 222p. 1984. lib. bdg. 42.00x (ISBN 3-7682-5478-X). Lubrecht & Cramer.

--The Life of Plants. LC 81-11436. 1981. 10.95 (ISBN 0-226-11586-0, Phoen). U of Chicago Pr.

--Phylloporus Quel & Paxillus Fr. in Malaya & Borneo. (Illus.). 1971. pap. 10.50 (ISBN 3-7682-0741-2). Lubrecht & Cramer.

Corner, E. J. H. The Seeds of Dicotyledons, 2 vols. LC 74-14434. (Illus.). 860p. 1976. Vol. 1. 99.50 (ISBN 0-521-20688-X); Vol. 2. 145.00 (ISBN 0-521-20687-1). Cambridge U Pr.

Corner, George W. Anatomical Texts of the Earlier Middle Ages. LC 75-23700. (Carnegie Institution of Washington. Publication: No. 364). Repr. of 1927 ed. 22.50 (ISBN 0-404-13250-2). AMS Pr.

--Anatomist at Large. facs. ed. LC 76-86743. (Essay Index Reprint Ser). 1958. 18.00 (ISBN 0-8369-1176-8). Ayer Co Pubs.

--Anatomy. LC 75-23652. (Clio Medica: 3). (Illus.). Repr. of 1930 ed. 9.50 (ISBN 0-404-58903-0). AMS Pr.

--Dr. Kane of the Arctic Seas. LC 72-88531. 319p. 1972. 24.95 (ISBN 0-87722-022-0). Temple U Pr.

--A History of the Rockefeller Institute 1901-1953. LC 64-24275. (Illus.). 652p. 1965. 25.00x (ISBN 0-87470-003-5). Rockefeller.

--Ourselves Unborn: An Embryologist's Essay on Man. Repr. of 1944 ed. 25.00 (ISBN 0-8492-9970-5). R West.

--Ourselves Unborn: An Embryologist's Essay on Man. LC 71-143884. 188p. 1972. Repr. of 1944 ed. 16.50 (ISBN 0-685-02973-5, Archon). Shoe String.

Corner, George W., ed. see Rush, Benjamin.

Corner, George W., Sr. The Seven Ages of a Medical Scientist: An Autobiography. LC 81-51143. (Illus.). 406p. 1981. 30.00x (ISBN 0-8122-7811-9). U of Pa Pr.

Corner, J. & Hawthorn, J. Communication Studies: An Introductory Reader. 256p. 1980. pap. text ed. 14.95 (ISBN 0-7131-6278-3). E Arnold.

Corner, Paul. Fascism in Ferrara Nineteen Fifteen to Nineteen Twenty-Five. (Oxford Historical Monographs). 1975. 45.00x (ISBN 0-19-821857-5). Oxford U Pr.

Corner, Philip. Ear Journeys: Water. (Illus.). 1979. box 7.00 (ISBN 0-914162-30-6). Printed Edns.

--I Can Walk Through the World As Music, Pt. 1. 1980. pap. 6.00 (ISBN 0-914162-19-5). Printed Edns.

--Popular Entertainments. 16p. 1981. pap. 3.00 (ISBN 0-914162-56-X). Printed Edns.

Corner, Trevor, ed. Education in Multicultural Societies. LC 84-40038. 288p. 1984. 25.00 (ISBN 0-312-23726-X). St Martin.

Cornes, D. L. Design Liability in the Construction Industry. 2nd ed. 240p. 1985. 35.00x (ISBN 0-00-383020-9, Pub. by Collins England). Sheridan.

Cornes, Paul. The Future of Work & People with Disabilities: A View from Great Britain. (International Exchange of Experts & Information in Rehabilitation Ser.: No. 28). 96p. 1984. pap. write for info. (ISBN 0-939986-42-6). World Rehab Fund.

Cornes, Phil. Commodore 64: Step by Step Programming Guides. 64p. 1984. book 1 9.95 (ISBN 0-13-152141-1); 19.95 (ISBN 0-13-152117-9); 9.95 (ISBN 0-13-152158-6). P-H.

Cornet, Joseph. Art from Zaire-L'art Du Zaire: One Hundred Masterworks from the National Collection. LC 75-21768. (Illus.). 98p. (Orig.). 1975. pap. 5.00 (ISBN 0-686-66073-0). AAI.

Cornett, Charles F., jt. auth. see Cornett, Claudia E.

Cornett, Claudia E. What You Should Know about Teaching & Learning Styles. LC 82-63062. (Fastback Ser.: No. 191). 50p. 1983. pap. 0.75 (ISBN 0-87367-191-0). Phi Delta Kappa.

Cornett, Claudia E. & Cornett, Charles F. Bibliotherapy: The Right Book at the Right Time. LC 80-82684. (Fastback Ser.: No. 151). 1980. pap. 0.75 (ISBN 0-87367-151-1). Phi Delta Kappa.

Cornett, Emily F., jt. auth. see Blume, Dorothy M.

Cornett, Jim. Coachella Valley Nature Guide. (Illus.). 36p. (Orig.). 1980. pap. 3.95 (ISBN 0-937794-02-3). Nature Trails.

--Wildlife of the Southwest Deserts. 2nd ed. (Illus.). 240p. 1985. pap. 5.95 (ISBN 0-937794-06-6). Nature Trails.

--Wildlife of the Western Mountains. (Illus.). 244p. (Orig.). 1982. pap. 7.95 (ISBN 0-937794-03-1). Nature Trails.

Cornett, Sandra J. & Watson, Joan E. Cardiac Rehabilitation: An Interdisciplinary Team Approach. LC 83-19679. 308p. 1984. pap. text ed. 18.50 (ISBN 0-471-07731-3, Pub. by Wiley Med). Wiley.

Cornetto, Anna Maria, jt. auth. see Bettoja, Jo.

Cornevin, Marianne. Apartheid: Power & Historical Falsification. (Insights Ser.: No. 3). (Illus.). 144p. 1980. pap. 14.50 (ISBN 92-3-101769-1, U970, UNESCO). Unipub.

Corney, Alan. Atomic & Laser Spectroscopy. (Illus.). 1977. text ed. 32.50x (ISBN 0-19-851138-8). Oxford U Pr.

Corney, B. Glanville. The Quest & Occupation of Tahiti, by Emissaries of Spain During the Years 1772-1776, 3 vols. (Hakluyt Society Works Ser.: No. 2, Vols. 32, 36 & 43). (Illus.). Repr. of 1913 ed. Set. 41.00 (ISBN 0-317-16773-1). Kraus Repr.

Corney, Bolton G., ed. The Voyage of Captain Don Felipe Gonzalez to Easter Island in 1770-1771. (Hakluyt Society Works Ser.: No. 2, Vol. 13). (Illus.). Repr. of 1903 ed. 38.00 (ISBN 0-317-16771-5). Kraus Repr.

Corney, G., jt. auth. see Strong, S. J.

Corney, Peter. Early Voyages in the North Pacific, 1813-1818. (Illus.). 1966. Repr. of 1896 ed. 9.95 (ISBN 0-87770-007-9). Ye Galleon.

Corney, R. Problems in Social Care. LC 81-68112. (Problems in Practice Ser.: Vol. 9). (Illus.). 168p. 1983. 20.00x (ISBN 0-8036-1985-5). Davis Co.

Corney, R. H., jt. ed. see Clare, A. W.

Cornfeld, Gaalyah. The Historical Jesus: A Scholarly View of the Man & His World. LC 82-14860. (Illus.). 224p. 1983. 16.95 (ISBN 0-02-528200-X). Macmillan.

Cornfeld, Gaalyah & Freedman, David N., eds. Archaeology of the Bible - Book by Book: An Up-to-Date Archaeological Commentary on the Bible. LC 76-9979. 352p. 1982. pap. 14.37 (ISBN 0-06-061587-7, RD 389, HarpR). Har-Row.

Cornfeld, Gaalyah & Maier, Paul L., eds. Josephus: The Jewish War. 560p. 1982. 44.95 (ISBN 0-310-39210-1). Zondervan.

Cornfeld, I. P., et al. Ergodic Theory. (Grundlehren der Mathematischen Wissenschafter Ser.: Vol. 245). (Illus.). 480p. 1982. 55.00 (ISBN 0-387-90580-4). Springer-Verlag.

Cornfield, Jim. Electronic Flash. (Petersen's Photographic Library Ser.: Vol. 3). (Illus.). 160p. (Orig.). 1980. pap. text ed. 8.95 (ISBN 0-8227-4041-9). Petersen Pub.

Cornfield, Robert, jt. auth. see Martins, Peter.

Cornfield, Ruth R. Foreign Language Instruction: Dimensions & Horizons. LC 66-24055. 1966. text ed. 12.95x (ISBN 0-89197-167-X); pap. text ed. 6.95x (ISBN 0-89197-168-8). Irvington.

Cornford, A., tr. see Thimme, Jurgen.

Cornford, A. J. The Market for Owned Houses in England & Wales since 1945. 342p. 1979. text ed. 49.95x (ISBN 0-566-00195-0). Gower Pub Co.

Cornford, Adam. Shooting Scripts. (Illus.). 1979. pap. 10.00 (ISBN 0-686-28251-5). Black Stone.

Cornford, F. M. From Religion to Philosophy. A Study of the Origins of Western Speculation. 1957-1979. text ed. o. p. (ISBN 0-391-01238-X); pap. text ed. 10.45x (ISBN 0-391-01239-8). Humanities.

--Microcosmographia Academia. 24p. 1980. pap. 2.95 (ISBN 0-370-00145-1, Pub. by the Bodley Head). Merrimack Pub Cir.

--Principium Sapientiae: The Origins of Greek Philosophical Thought. Guthrie, ed. 13.25 (ISBN 0-8446-0069-5). Peter Smith.

Cornford, Francis. Plato's Cosmology: The Timaeus of Plato. 4th ed. (International Library of Psychology, Philosophy & Scientific Method). 1971. text ed. 24.25x (ISBN 0-7100-3126-2); pap. text ed. 25.25x o.p. Humanities.

--Plato's Theory of Knowledge. (International Library of Psychology, Philosophy & Scientific Method). 1967. text ed. 25.25x (ISBN 0-7100-3119-X). Humanities.

Cornford, Francis, ed. Plato & Parmenides. (International Library of Psychology, Philosophy & Scientific Method). 1964. text ed. 29.00x (ISBN 0-7100-3130-0). Humanities.

Cornford, Francis M. Before & After Socrates. 27.95 (ISBN 0-521-04726-9); pap. 8.95 (ISBN 0-521-09113-6). Cambridge U Pr.

--Microcosmographia Academica. 3.50 (ISBN 0-87948-014-9); pap. 1.50 (ISBN 0-685-06828-5). Beatty.

--Plato's Theatetus. 1957. pap. text ed. write for info. (ISBN 0-02-325170-0). Macmillan.

--Plato's Timaeus. Piest, Oskar, ed. 1959. pap. text ed. write for info. (ISBN 0-02-325190-5). Macmillan.

--Unwritten Philosophy & Other Essays. Guthrie, William K., ed. 1967. 27.95 (ISBN 0-521-04727-7). Cambridge U Pr.

Cornford, Francis M., ed. Greek Religious Thought from Homer to the Age of Alexander. LC 79-98637. (Library of Greek Thought: No. 2). Repr. of 1923 ed. 21.50 (ISBN 0-404-01734-7). AMS Pr.

Cornford, Francis M., tr. see Plato.

Cornford, Frank M. Plato's Theory of Knowledge: The Theateus & Sophist. 1957. pap. text ed. write for info. (ISBN 0-02-325160-3). Macmillan.

Cornford, James, ed. The Failure of the State: On the Distribution of Political & Economic Power in Europe. 198p. 1975. 19.50x (ISBN 0-87471-607-1). Rowman.

Cornford, James, jt. ed. see Stubbs, William.

Cornford, Jean, jt. ed. see Callow, Paul.

Cornford, L. William Ernest Henley. 59.95 (ISBN 0-8490-1302-X). Gordon Pr.

Cornford, L. C. William Ernest Henley. LC 72-3679. (English Biography Ser., No. 31). 1972. Repr. of 1913 ed. lib. bdg. 35.95x (ISBN 0-8383-1580-1). Haskell.

--William Ernest Henley. 1973. Repr. of 1913 ed. 19.45 (ISBN 0-8274-1358-0). R West.

Cornford, L. Cope. Interpretations. LC 77-105773. 1970. Repr. of 1926 ed. 19.50x (ISBN 0-8046-0945-4, Pub. by Kennikat). Assoc Faculty Pr.

--Interpretations: W. E. Henley, Dante, Victor Hugo Moliere, Scott, Shakespeare. 1926. Repr. 20.00 (ISBN 0-8274-3857-5). R West.

--Robert Louis Stevenson. 1979. Repr. of 1899 ed. lib. bdg. 20.00 (ISBN 0-8495-0783-9). Arden Lib.

Cornforth, John & Fowler, John. English Decoration on the Eighteenth Century. 2nd rev. ed. 288p. 1981. 50.00x (ISBN 0-214-20552-5, Pub. by Barrie & Jenkins England). State Mutual Bk.

Cornforth, Maurice. Communism & Philosophy. 1980. 30.00x (ISBN 0-686-78817-6, Pub. by Lawrence & Wishart England). State Mutual Bk.

--Communism & Philosophy: Contemporary Dogmas & Revisions of Marxism. 1980. pap. 10.00x (ISBN 0-85315-547-X). Humanities.

--Dialectical Materialism, 3 vols. new ed. Incl. Vol. 1. Materialism & the Dialectical Method. 128p. pap. 1.45 (ISBN 0-7178-0326-0); Vol. 2. Historical Materialism. 148p. pap. 2.50 (ISBN 0-7178-0327-9); Vol. 3. The Theory of Knowledge. 208p. pap. 2.75 (ISBN 0-7178-0328-7). 1971. pap. Intl Pubs Co.

--The Open Philosophy & the Society. 373p. 1977. pap. text ed. 9.25x (ISBN 0-85315-384-1, Pub by Lawrence & Wishart Ltd). Humanities.

--Rebels & Their Causes: Essays in Honour of A. L. Morton. 1957. pap. 20.00x (ISBN 0-85315-426-0). Humanities.

--Science Versus Idealism. LC 72-6924. 463p. 1975. Repr. of 1962 ed. lib. bdg. 25.50x (ISBN 0-8371-6501-6, COSV). Greenwood.

Corngold, Stanley. The Fate of the Self: German Writers & French Theory. 272p. 1985. 28.50x (ISBN 0-231-06174-9). Columbia U Pr.

Corngold, Stanley, tr. see Kafka, Franz.

Corngold, Stanley, et al. Thomas Mann, 1875-1955. (Illus.). 62p. 1975. pap. 3.00 (ISBN 0-87811-021-6). Princeton Lib.

Cornhill, Carl H. The Prophets of Israel: Popular Sketches from Old Testament History. 1977. Repr. of 1913 ed. lib. bdg. 20.00 (ISBN 0-8482-3453-7). Norwood Edns.

Cornia, G. A., jt. ed. see Jolly, R.

Cornia, Ivan E., et al. Art Is Elementary: Teaching Visual Thinking Art Concepts. (Illus.). 464p. (gr. k-7). 1984. tchr's. guide 35.00 (ISBN 0-87905-138-8, Peregrine Smith). Gibbs M Smith.

Cornick, Delroy L. Auditing in the Electronic Environment: Theory, Practice & Literature. LC 80-81813. 316p. 1981. 19.75 (ISBN 0-912338-23-7); microfiche 14.75 (ISBN 0-912338-24-5). Lomond.

Cornick, Delroy L. & Elkin, Robert. Analyzing Costs in a Residential Group Care Facility: A Step-by-Step Manual. LC 78-89708. 116p. 1969. pap. 7.95 (ISBN 0-87868-062-4, I-33). Child Welfare.

Cornick, H. F. Dock & Harbour Engineering: The Design of Docks, Vol. 1. 338p. 200.00x (ISBN 0-85264-037-4, Pub. by Griffin England). State Mutual Bk.

Cornier, Henri. The Humor of Jesus. Heiman, David, tr. from Fr. LC 77-9887. Orig. Title: L Humour De Jesus. 1977. pap. 5.95 (ISBN 0-8189-0356-2). Alba.

Cornillie, O., jt. auth. see Lammineur, P.

Cornillie, O. A. Microprocessors. (EPO Applied Technology Ser.: Vol. 8). 400p. 1985. 80.00 (ISBN 0-08-030575-X). Pergamon.

Cornillier, Pierre. The Survival of the Soul & Its Evolution after Death. lib. bdg. 79.95 (ISBN 0-87968-498-4). Krishna Pr.

Cornillon, Peter. A Guide to Environmental Satellite Data. (Technical Report Ser.: No. 79). 469p. 1982. 20.00 (ISBN 0-938412-21-3, P894). URI MAS.

Cornillon, Susan K., ed. Images of Women in Fiction. 1972. casebound 15.95 (ISBN 0-87972-048-4); pap. 10.95 (ISBN 0-87972-049-2). Bowling Green Univ.

Cornils, Stanley. Thirty-Four Two-Minute Talks for Youth & Adults. 64p. 1985. pap. 2.50 (ISBN 0-87239-868-4, 2883). Standard Pub.

--Twenty-Five Two-Minute Talks for Children. 48p. 1985. pap. 2.50 (ISBN 0-87239-867-6, 2882). Standard Pub.

Corning Glass Museum Staff, ed. The History & Art of Glass: Index of Periodical Articles, 1980-1982. 1984. lib. bdg. 90.00 (ISBN 0-8161-0427-1). G K Hall.

Corning, Howard M. Willamette Landings: Ghost Towns of the River. 2nd ed. LC 73-81023. 272p. 1973. pap. 6.95 (ISBN 0-87595-042-6). Oreg Hist Soc.

Corning, Leavitt, Jr. Baronial Forts of the Big Bend. 2nd. ed. LC 67-23005. (Illus.). 146p. 1969. 4.00 (ISBN 0-911536-08-6). Trinity U Pr.

Corning Museum of Glass. American & European Pressed Glass in the Corning Museum of Glass. (Illus.). 500p. (Orig.). pap. 25.00 (ISBN 0-486-24330-3). Dover.

--The Cut & Engraved Glass of Corning, 1868-1940. (Antiques Series: Pottery, China, Glass). 102p. 1985. pap. 5.00 (ISBN 0-486-24872-0). Dover.

--Masterpieces of Glass from the Corning Museum: 24 Ready-to-Mail Full-Color. (Stationery Ser.). 12p. (Orig.). (gr. 7 up). 1984. pap. 3.50 (ISBN 0-486-24526-8). Dover.

--New Glass: A Worldwide Survey. (Illus.). 286p. 1981. pap. 27.50 (ISBN 0-486-24156-4). Dover.

--New Glass Review 6. LC 81-641214. (Illus.). 52p. (Orig.). 1985. pap. 5.00 (ISBN 0-87290-112-2). Corning.

--Pressed Glass: Eighteen Twenty-Five to Nineteen Twenty-Five. (Antiques Ser.). 48p. (Orig.). 1983. pap. 6.00 (ISBN 0-486-24510-1). Dover.

--A Survey of Glassmaking from Ancient Egypt to the Present. LC 77-15599. 1977. 2 color fiches incl. 30.00 (ISBN 0-226-68902-6, Chicago Visual Lib). U of Chicago Pr.

Corning Museum of Glass & Godstein, Sidney M. Pre-Roman & Early Roman Glass. (Illus.). 312p. (Orig.). 1983. lib. bdg. 40.00 (ISBN 0-486-24329-X). Dover.

Corning Museum of Glass Staff. New Glass Review 5. LC 81-641214. (Illus.). 48p. (Orig., Annual Compendium of Contemporary Glass Made in Previous Calendar Year). 1984. pap. 2.50 (ISBN 0-87290-110-6). Corning.

Corning Musuem of Glass, ed. Czechoslovakian Glass Thirteen Fifty to Nineteen Eighty. (Illus.). 176p. (Orig.). 1981. pap. 17.50 (ISBN 0-486-24237-4). Dover.

Corning, P. A. The Synergism Hypothesis: A Theory of Progressive Evolution. 512p. 1983. 19.95 (ISBN 0-07-013166-X); pap. 12.95 (ISBN 0-07-013172-4). McGraw.

Corning, W. C. & Ratner, S. C., eds. Chemistry of Learning: Invertebrate Research. LC 67-25103. 468p. 1967. 42.50x (ISBN 0-306-30305-1, Plenum Pr). Plenum Pub.

Corning, W. C., et al. Invertebrate Learning. Incl. Vol. 1, Protozoans Through Annelids. 313p. 1973. 37.50x (ISBN 0-306-37671-7); Vol. 2, Arthropods & Gastropod Mollusks. 296p. 1973. 37.50x (ISBN 0-306-37672-5); Vol. 3, Cephalopods & Echinoderms. 231p. 1975. 35.00x (ISBN 0-306-37673-3). LC 72-90335. (Illus., Plenum Pr). Plenum Pub.

Cornish, et al. Sampling Systems for Process Analyzers. 1981. 99.95 (ISBN 0-408-00261-1). Butterworth.

Cornish, Blanche W., ed. Some Family Letters of W. M. Thackeray. LC 74-6225. 1911. lib. bdg. 10.00 (ISBN 0-8414-3649-5). Folcroft.

Cornish, Clive G. Basic Accounting for the Small Business: Simple, Foolproof Techniques for Keeping Your Books Straight & Staying Out of Trouble. 3rd ed. (Illus.). 186p. 1984. pap. 5.95 (ISBN 0-88908-915-9, 9501, Pub. by Intl Self-Counsel Pr). TAB Bks.

Cornish, Derek B., jt. ed. see Clarke, Ronald V.

Cornish, Dudley T. Sable Arm: Negro Troops in the Union Army, 1861-1865. 15.25 (ISBN 0-8446-0557-3). Peter Smith.

Cornish, E. H. Winemaking Simplified. (Illus.). 69p. Date not set. pap. 3.95 (ISBN 0-900841-76-1, Pub. by Aztex Corp). Argus Bks.

Cornish, Edward. The Study of the Future. 310p. 1977. pap. 9.50 (ISBN 0-930242-03-3). Transaction Bks.

Cornish, Edward, ed. Careers Tomorrow: The Outlook for Work in a Changing World. 160p. 1983. pap. 6.95 (ISBN 0-930242-19-X). Transaction Bks.

--Careers Tomorrow: The Outlook for Work in a Changing World. 1983. pap. 6.95 (ISBN 0-930242-19-X). World Future.

--Communications Tomorrow: The Coming of the Information Society. (Illus.). 160p. 1982. pap. text ed. 6.95 (ISBN 0-930242-14-9). Transaction Bks.

--The Computerized Society: Living & Working in an Electronic Age. 160p. 1985. pap. 6.95 (ISBN 0-930242-27-0). Transaction Bks.

--Global Solutions: Innovative Approaches to World Problems. LC 84-50375. 160p. 1984. 6.95 (ISBN 0-930242-22-X). World Future.

--The Great Transformation. 1983. pap. 6.95 (ISBN 0-930242-20-3). World Future.

--Habitats Tomorrow: Homes & Communities in an Exciting Era. 160p. 1984. pap. 6.95 (ISBN 0-930242-24-6). Transaction Bks.

--Habitats Tomorrow: Homes & Communities in an Exciting New Era. LC 84-50376. 160p. 1984. 6.95 (ISBN 0-930242-24-6). World Future.

Cornish, Francis W. Jane Austen. facsimile ed. LC 78-37333. (Select Bibliographies Reprint Ser). Repr. of 1913 ed. 16.00 (ISBN 0-8369-6680-5). Ayer Co Pubs.

Cornish, Geoffrey S. & Whitten, Ronald F. The Golf Course. (Illus.). 320p. 1981. 35.00 (ISBN 0-8317-3947-9, Rutledge Pr). Smith Pubs.

Cornish, Graham. Religious Periodicals Directory. (Clio Periodicals Directories Ser.). 250p. 1985. lib. bdg. 89.00 (ISBN 0-87436-365-9). ABC-Clio.

Cornish, John. Gospel of John & the Mind of Today. 1981. pap. 7.95 (ISBN 0-916786-55-2). St George Bk Serv.

--The Raising of Lazarus. 1979. pap. 2.95 (ISBN 0-916786-36-6). St George Bk Serv.

Cornish, Patty Jo. The Prayer Primer: A Philosophy Book. Quintero, Roberto, ed. LC 84-81741. 68p. (Orig.). pap. 5.95 (ISBN 0-9613717-0-6). Hilltop Hse.

Cornish, Robert L & Mabry, Aleta M. Arkansas: Learning Activities for Elementary Students. 1983. 15.00x (ISBN 0-931510-13-9). Hi Willow.

Cornish, Roger & Orlock, John. Short Plays for the Long Living. 1976. 3.25 (ISBN 0-87440-004-X). Bakers Plays.

Cornish, Roger & Kase, C. Robert, eds. Senior Adult Theatre: The American Theatre Association Handbook. LC 80-23485. (Illus.). 96p. 1981. 8.95x (ISBN 0-271-00276-X); pap. text ed. 5.95x (ISBN 0-271-00275-1). Pa St U Pr.

Cornish, Roger & Ketels, Violet, eds. Landmarks of Modern British Drama, Vol. 1. 688p. (Orig.). 1985. 25.00 (ISBN 0-413-59080-1, 9656); pap. 8.95 (ISBN 0-413-57260-9, 9657). Methuen Inc.

--Landmarks of Modern British Drama, Vol. 2. 640p. 1985. 25.00 (ISBN 0-317-19347-3, 9658); pap. 8.95 (ISBN 0-413-57270-6, 9659). Methuen Inc.

Cornish, Sally, jt. ed. see Jennings, Lane.

Cornish, Sam. Grandmother's Pictures. (Illus.). 1974. pap. 4.00 (ISBN 0-912846-04-6). Bookstore Pr.

Cornish, Vaughan. Great Capitals. LC 70-114503. (Illus.). 1971. Repr. of 1923 ed. lib. bdg. 22.50x (ISBN 0-8371-4782-4, COGC). Greenwood.

Cornish, W. R., et al. Crime & Law in Nineteeth Century Britain. (Government & Society in 19th Century Britain Ser.: Vol. 4). 232p. 1978. 20.00x (ISBN 0-7165-2213-6, BBA 02036, Pub. by Irish Academic Pr Ireland). Biblio Dist.

Cornish-Bowden, A. Basic Mathematics for Biochemists. 1981. 19.95x (ISBN 0-412-23000-3, NO. 6560, Pub. by Chapman & Hall); pap. 10.95 (ISBN 0-412-23010-0, NO. 6559). Methuen Inc.

Cornish-Bowden, A., jt. ed. see Ricard, J.

Cornish-Bowden, Athel. Fundamentals of Enzyme Kinetics. LC 79-40116. (Illus.). 1979. text ed. 24.95 (ISBN 0-408-10617-4). Butterworth.

Cornlorin, J., jt. auth. see Hill, O.

Cornman, James W. Perception, Common Sense & Science. LC 74-29715. 432p. 1975. Yale U Pr.

--Skepticism, Justification, & Explanation. (Philosophical Studies Series in Philosophy: No. 18). 368p. 1980. lib. bdg. 39.50 (ISBN 90-277-1041-4, Pub. by Reidel Holland). Kluwer Academic.

Cornman, James W., et al. Philosophical Problems & Arguments. 3rd ed. 1982. text ed. write for info. (ISBN 0-02-325120-4). Macmillan.

Cornman, John N. & Kincaid, Barbara. Lessons from Rural America: A Case History. 202p. 1984. 13.95 (ISBN 0-932020-24-0). Seven Locks Pr.

Cornog, Martha, jt. auth. see Neufeld, M. Lynne.

Cornold, W. The Yoga of Yama. 64p. 1970. pap. 2.95 (ISBN 0-88697-041-5). Life Science.

Corns, Albert R. Bibliography of Unfinished Books in the English Language. Sparke, Archibald, ed. LC 67-28093. 278p. 1968. Repr. of 1915 ed. 40.00x (ISBN 0-8103-3208-6). Gale.

Corns, Albert R. & Sparke, Archibald. Bibliography of Unfinished Books in the English Language with Annotations. LC 69-17931. 1969. Repr. of 1915 ed. 15.00 (ISBN 0-8337-0682-9). B Franklin.

Corns, Marshall C. Practical Operations & Management of a Bank. 2nd ed. LC 68-17247. 976p. 1968. 39.00 (ISBN 0-87267-005-8). Bankers.

Corns, T. N., jt. auth. see Rudall, B. H.

Corns, Thomas N. The Development of Milton's Prose Style. (Oxford English Monographs). 1982. 27.95x (ISBN 0-19-811717-5). Oxford U Pr.

Cornsweet, Tom N. Visual Perception. 1970. text ed. 23.25i (ISBN 0-12-189750-8). Acad Pr.

Cornu, A. & Massot, R. List of Conversion Factors for Atomic Impurities to PPM by Weight. 1968. 69.95 (ISBN 0-471-25645-5, Pub. by Wiley Heyden). Wiley.

Cornu, A., jt. auth. see Leclerc, J. C.

Cornu, Auguste. The Origins of Marxian Thought. 144p. 1957. 14.50x (ISBN 0-398-04234-9). C C Thomas.

Cornu, Aymbe & Massot, R. List of Conversion Factors for Atomic Impurities to PPM Weight. LC 68-20754. pap. 37.00 (ISBN 0-317-29352-4, 2024003). Bks Demand UMI.

Cornubert, Raymond. Dictionnaire de Chimie Allemand-Francais. 3rd ed. 240p. (Fr. & Ger.). 1977. pap. 29.65 (ISBN 0-686-56964-4, M-6088). French & Eur.

Cornuelle, Richard. The Healing of America. LC 82-24015. 208p. 1983. 14.95 (ISBN 0-399-12785-2, Seaview). Putnam Pub Group.

Cornut, Jacques P. Canadensium Plantarum. 1966. Repr. of 1635 ed. Facsimile Ed. 25.00 (ISBN 0-384-09835-5). Johnson Repr.

Cornwall, Barry. Dramatic Scenes: With Other Poems. 368p. 1981. Repr. lib. bdg. 40.00 (ISBN 0-89987-124-0). Darby Bks.

--The Literary Recollections of Barry Cornwall. Armour, Richard W., intro. by. 1936. Repr. 25.00 (ISBN 0-8274-2958-4). R West.

Cornwall, Claudia. Print-Outs: The Adventures of a Rebel Computer. (Illus.). 78p. (Orig.). 1982. pap. 5.95 (ISBN 0-919325-00-9, Pub. by Nerve Pr Canada). Gay Sunshine.

Cornwall Collective. Your Daughters Shall Prophesy: Feminist Alternatives in Theological Education. LC 80-14891. 155p. 1980. pap. 6.95 (ISBN 0-8298-0404-8). Pilgrim NY.

Cornwall, J. Spencer. Stories of Our Mormon Hymns. 7.95 (ISBN 0-87747-247-5). Deseret Bk.

Cornwall, John. The Conditions for Economic Recovery: A Post-Keynesian Analysis. LC 83-12802. 370p. 1983. pap. 18.95 (ISBN 0-87332-264-9). M E Sharpe.

--Modern Capitalism: Its Growth & Transformation. LC 77-81846. (Illus.). 1978. 25.00 (ISBN 0-312-53784-0). St Martin.

--Modern Capitalism: Its Growth & Transformation. LC 82-5490. 226p. 1982. Repr. of 1977 ed. deluxe ed. 13.95 (ISBN 0-87332-222-3). M E Sharpe.

Cornwall, John, ed. After Stagflation: Alternatives to Economics Decline. LC 83-27140. 194p. 1984. 25.00 (ISBN 0-87332-271-1). M E Sharpe.

Cornwall, Judson. La Alabanza Que Libera. 160p. 1976. 2.50 (ISBN 0-88113-002-8). Edit Betania.

--Elements of Worship. LC 85-61459. 1985. pap. 5.95 (ISBN 0-88270-594-6). Bridge Pub.

--Freeway under Construction. 1978. bklt. .95 (ISBN 0-88270-304-8, Pub. by Logos). Bridge Pub.

--Give Me-Make Me. LC 79-64976. 1979. 1.25 (ISBN 0-88270-387-0). Bridge Pub.

--Let God Arise. 160p. 1982. pap. 5.95 (ISBN 0-8007-5080-2, Power Bks). Revell.

--Let Us Abide. LC 77-23143. 155p. 1984. pap. 4.95 (ISBN 0-8007-5065-9). Bridge Pub.

--Let Us Be Holy. LC 87-70993. 1978. pap. 4.95 (ISBN 0-88270-278-5, Pub. by Logos). Bridge Pub.

--Let Us Draw Near. LC 77-24832. 1977. pap. 4.95 (ISBN 0-88270-226-2, Pub. by Logos). Bridge Pub.

--Let Us Enjoy Forgiveness. LC 78-8306. 159p. 1978. pap. 4.95 (ISBN 0-8007-5090-X). Bridge Pub.

--Let Us Get Together. 192p. 1983. pap. 5.95 (ISBN 0-8007-5103-5, Power Bks). Revell.

--Let Us Praise: A Prominent Charismatic Leader Tells How & Why to Praise God. LC 73-75957. 1973. pap. 4.95 (ISBN 0-88270-039-1, Pub. by Logos). Bridge Pub.

--Let Us See Jesus. LC 80-20645. 160p. 1981. pap. 4.95 (ISBN 0-8007-5052-7). Bridge Pub.

--Let Us Worship. LC 82-74089. 1983. pap. 4.95 (ISBN 0-88270-542-3, Pub. by Logos). Bridge Pub.

--Profiles of a Leader. LC 80-85161. (Orig.). 1980. pap. 4.95 (ISBN 0-88270-503-2, Pub. by Logos). Bridge Pub.

--Unfeigned Faith. 192p. 1981. pap. 4.95 (ISBN 0-8007-5057-8, Power Bks). Revell.

Cornwall, Judson, jt. auth. see Cornwall, Thomas.

Cornwall, Julian. How to Read Old Title Deeds. 25.00x (ISBN 0-317-20328-2, Pub. by Pinhorns UK). State Mutual Bk.

Cornwall, Keith. The Flow of Heat. 1977. pap. 14.95 (ISBN 0-442-30168-5). Van Nos Reinhold.

Cornwall, Peter G. & McBeath, Gerald, eds. Alaska's Rural Development. (Replica Edition Ser.). 165p. 1982. softcover 30.00x (ISBN 0-86531-294-X). Westview.

Cornwall, R. R., ed. Introduction to the Use of General Equilibrium Analysis. (Advanced Textbooks in Economics: Vol. 20). 774p. 1984. 72.50 (ISBN 0-444-86443-1, I-417-83, North Holland). Elsevier.

Cornwall, Rebecca & Arrington, Leonard J. Rescue of the Eighteen Fifty-Six Handcart Companies. Alexander, Thomas G., ed. (Charles Redd Monographs in Western History: No. 11). (Illus.). 59p. pap. 4.95 (ISBN 0-941214-04-4). Signature Bks.

Cornwall, Richard, jt. auth. see Claudon, Michael P.

Cornwall, Susan. Mathematical Manka. (Math Is Everywhere Ser.). (Illus.). (gr. 1-9). 1974. pap. 6.95 (ISBN 0-918932-29-7). Activity Resources.

Cornwall, Thomas & Cornwall, Judson. Please Accept Me. LC 79-90401. pap. 2.50 (ISBN 0-88270-391-9, Pub. by Logos). Bridge Pub.

Cornwallis, Kinahan. The New El Dorado; or, British Columbia. LC 72-9437. (The Far Western Frontier Ser.). (Illus.). 442p. 1973. Repr. of 1858 ed. 26.50 (ISBN 0-405-04967-6). Ayer Co Pubs.

Cornwallis, William. Discourses Upon Seneca the Tragedian. LC 52-10576. 1978. Repr. of 1601 ed. 35.00x (ISBN 0-8201-1220-8). Schol Facsimiles.

Cornwallis-West, George. Edwardian Hey-Days or a Little About a Lot of Things. (Illus.). 1977. Repr. of 1930 ed. 19.95x (ISBN 0-7158-1055-3). Charles River Bks.

--Edwardian Heydays: A Little About a Lot of Things. (Illus.). 338p. 1975. Repr. of 1930 ed. 17.95x (ISBN 0-8464-0356-0). Beekman Pubs.

Cornwallis-West, J. J. see Churchill, J. J.

Cornwall-Jones, A. T. Education for Leadership: The International Administrative Staff Colleges, 1948-1984. (Illus.). 272p. 1985. 29.95x (ISBN 0-7102-0464-7). Routledge & Kegan.

Cornwell, jt. auth. see Davis.

Cornwell, jt. auth. see Levine, Erwin L.

Cornwell, Anita. Black Lesbian in White America. LC 82-18945. 144p. (Orig.). 1983. pap. 7.50 (ISBN 0-930044-41-X). Naiad Pr.

Cornwell, Bernard. Sharpe's Company. LC 81-69930. (Sharpe Ser.: No. 3). 288p. 1982. 14.95 (ISBN 0-670-63942-7). Viking.

--Sharpe's Company: The Seige of Badajoz. 288p. 1984. pap. 4.95 (ISBN 0-14-007023-0). Penguin.

--Sharpe's Eagle. (Illus.). 352p. 1982. pap. 3.25 (ISBN 0-441-76091-0, Pub. by Charter Bks). Ace Bks.

--Sharpe's Eagle. LC 80-54081. 264p. 1981. 12.95 (ISBN 0-670-63944-3). Viking.

--Sharpe's Enemy. LC 83-47925. (Sharpe Saga Ser.). 336p. 1984. 16.95 (ISBN 0-670-63940-0). Viking.

--Sharpe's Enemy: The Defense of Portugal, Chirstmas 1812. (Penguin Fiction Ser.). 368p. 1985. pap. 5.95 (ISBN 0-14-007655-7). Penguin.

--Sharpe's Gold: Richard Sharpe & the Destruction of Almeda August, 1810. LC 81-51908. 252p. 1982. 13.95 (ISBN 0-670-63943-5). Viking.

--Sharpe's Honour: The Vitoria Campaign, Feb-June 1813. (Fiction Ser.). 324p. 1985. 16.95 (ISBN 0-670-80389-8). Viking.
--Sharpe's Sword: Richard Sharpe & the Salamanca Campaign, June & July, 1812. (Sharpe Saga Ser.). 324p. 1983. 15.75 (ISBN 0-670-63941-9). Viking.
--Sharpe's Sword: The Salamanca Campaign. 336p. 1984. pap. 4.95 (ISBN 0-14-007024-9). Penguin.
Cornwell, Clifton, jt. auth. see Gibson, James W.
Cornwell, Debbra & Cornwell, Stephen. Cooking in the Nude: Quickies. (Illus.). 64p. (Orig.). 1984. pap. 3.95 (ISBN 0-943678-01-3). Wellton Bks.
Cornwell, Debbra, jt. auth. see Cornwell, Stephen.
Cornwell, Debra, jt. auth. see Cornwell, Stephen.
Cornwell, Elmer E., Jr. Presidential Leadership of Public Opinion. LC 78-11946. (Illus.). 1979. Repr. of 1965 ed. lib. bdg. 27.50x (ISBN 0-313-21076-4, COPL). Greenwood.
Cornwell, Elmer E., Jr. & Goodman, Jay S. The Politics of the Rhode Island Constitutional Convention. 96p. 1969. 1.00 (ISBN 0-318-15811-6). Citizens Forum Gov.
Cornwell, Elmer E., Jr., jt. ed. see Seligman, Lester G.
Cornwell, Elmer E, Jr., et al. Constitutional Conventions. 96p. 1974. 1.00 (ISBN 0-318-15794-2). Citizens Forum Gov.
Cornwell, H. Campbell. William Stroudley, Craftsman of Steam. LC 68-23836. (Illus.). 1968. 24.95x (ISBN 0-678-05591-2). Kelley.
Cornwell, Ilene J. Travel Guide to the Natchez Trace Parkway Between Natchez, MS, & Nashville, TN. LC 83-51206. (Illus.). 104p. (Orig.). 1984. pap. 7.95x (ISBN 0-915575-00-0). Southern Resources.
Cornwell, Jocelyn. Hard Earned Lives: Accounts of Health & Illness from East London. 250p. (Orig.). 1985. pap. 12.95 (ISBN 0-422-78580-6, 9246, Pub by Tavistock England). Methuen Inc.
Cornwell, John. Earth to Earth. LC 84-6075. (Illus.). 185p. 1984. 12.50 (ISBN 0-88001-069-X). Ecco Pr.
--The Free & the Brave. 1978. pap. 2.25 (ISBN 0-8439-0591-3, Leisure Bks). Dorchester Pub Co.
--The Super. 1972. pap. 2.25 (ISBN 0-8439-0682-0, Leisure Bks). Dorchester Pub Co.
Cornwell, John F. Group Therapy in Physics, Vol. 1. (Techniques of Physics Ser.). 1984. 75.00 (ISBN 0-12-189801-6). Acad Pr.
Cornwell, Malcolm. Formed by His Word: Patterns of Scriptural Prayer. (Orig.). 1978. pap. 2.95 (ISBN 0-914544-20-9). Living Flame Pr.
Cornwell, Malcom. Arise & Renew. 1985. pap. 4.95 (ISBN 0-8146-1441-8). Liturgical Pr.
Cornwell, Mary, ed. see Haywood County Hospital Auxiliary.
Cornwell, N. The Life, Times & Milieu of V. F. Odoyevsky, 1804-1869. 1981. 80.00x (ISBN 0-86127-207-2, Pub. by Avebury Pub England). State Mutual Bk.
Cornwell, Neil. The Life, Times & Milieu of V. F. Odoyevsky: 1804-1869. 240p. 1983. text ed. 57.50x (ISBN 0-86127-207-2, Pub. by Avebury England). Humanities.
Cornwell, Patricia D. A Time for Remembering: The Ruth Bell Graham Story. LC 82-48922. (Illus.). 320p. 1983. 13.41 (ISBN 0-06-061685-7, HarpR). Har-Row.
Cornwell, Peter. Church & the Nation: The Case for Disestablishment. (Faith & the Future Ser.). 160p. 1984. 24.95x (ISBN 0-631-13223-6); pap. 8.95x (ISBN 0-631-13224-4). Basil Blackwell.
Cornwell, R. D. World History in the Twentieth Century. 2nd ed. (Illus.). 1981. pap. text ed. 12.95x (ISBN 0-582-33075-0). Longman.
Cornwell, Regina. The Other Side: European Avant-Garde Cinema, 1960-1980. (Illus.). 100p. 1983. pap. write for info. (ISBN 0-917418-74-3). Am Fed Arts.
--Snow Seen: The Films & Photographs of Michael Snow. (PMA Bks.). (Illus.). 1980. 24.95 (ISBN 0-88778-197-7). NY Zoetrope.
Cornwell, Richard E. & Victor, Buzz. Self-Service Storage: The Handbook for Investors & Managers. rev. ed. Moore, Betty T., ed. LC 81-86050. (Institute of Real Estate Management Monographs: Series on Specific Property Types). (Illus.). 208p. 1983. pap. text ed. 24.35 (ISBN 0-912104-54-6, 853). Inst Real Estate.
Cornwell, Robert C. & Manship, Darwin W. Applied Business Communication. 300p. 1978. text ed. write for info. (ISBN 0-697-08025-0); instr's manual (ISBN 0-697-08072-2). Wm C Brown.
Cornwell, Robert C., jt. auth. see Manship, Darwin.
Cornwell, Rupert. God's Banker: Account of the Life & Death of Roberto Calvi. (Illus.). 260p. 1984. 15.95 (ISBN 0-396-08295-5). Dodd.
Cornwell, Stephen & Cornwell, Debbra. Cooking in the Nude: For Playful Gourmets. (Illus.). 64p. 1982. pap. 3.95 (ISBN 0-943678-00-5). Wellton Bks.
Cornwell, Stephen & Cornwell, Debra. Cooking in the Nude: For Men Only. (Illus.). 64p. 1985. pap. 3.95 (ISBN 0-943678-02-1). Wellton Bks.
--Cooking in the Nude: For Women Only. (Illus.). 64p. 1985. pap. 3.95 (ISBN 0-943678-03-X). Wellton Bks.
Cornwell, Stephen, jt. auth. see Cornwell, Debbra.
Cornweyle, Robert. The Maner of Fortification of Cities, Townes, Castelles, & Other Place,....to Bee Called the Keye of the Treasorie... 79p. 1559. text ed. 33.12x (ISBN 0-576-15141-6, Pub. by Gregg Intl Pubs England). Gregg Intl.
Cornyn, J. H. Mexican Fairy Tales. 59.95 (ISBN 0-8490-0614-7). Gordon Pr.
Cornyn, W. S. Outline of Burmese Grammar. (LD Ser.). 1944. pap. 16.00 (ISBN 0-527-00784-6). Kraus Repr.
Cornyn, William S. Spoken Burmese. (Spoken Language Ser.). 165p. 1979. pap. 10.00x Bk. 1, Units 1-12 (ISBN 0-87950-020-4); 6 dual track cassettes for bk. 1 60.00x (ISBN 0-87950-025-5); cassettes & bk. 1 65.00x (ISBN 0-87950-026-3); pap. 10.00x Bk. 2, Units 13-30 (ISBN 0-87950-021-2). Spoken Lang Serv.
Cornyn, William S. & Roop, D. Haigh. Beginning Burmese. LC 66-21513. (Yale Linguistic Ser.). pap. 131.30 (ISBN 0-317-10142-0, 2011091). Bks Demand UMI.
Corob, Alison. Social Work with Depressed Women. 200p. 1986. text ed. write for info. (ISBN 0-566-05100-1). Gower Pub Co.
Coroles, Yvonne, jt. auth. see Curtis, Lindsay R.
Corominas, Joan. Breve Diccionario Etimologico de la Lengua Espanola. 3rd ed. 628p. (Span.). 1976. 35.95 (ISBN 84-249-1332-9, S-11936). French & Eur.
--Diccionario Critico Etimologico De la Lengua Espanola, 6 vols. 4418p. (Span.). 1976. Set. 200.00 (ISBN 84-249-1322-1, S-11937). French & Eur.
Corona. Site Planning Organization for Transport Infrastructures. Date not set. write for info. (ISBN 0-444-87600-6). Elsevier.
Corona, Simon, tr. see Yates, K. M.
Coronado, Linda, et al. Reading "Three Thousand One Hundred & Four" Study Skill Units. 1978. pap. text ed. 4.95 (ISBN 0-8403-2529-0, 40252901). Kendall-Hunt.
Coronado, Rosa. Cooking the Mexican Way. LC 82-254. (Easy Menu Ethnic Cookbooks Ser.). (Illus.). 48p. (gr. 5 up). 1982. PLB 8.95g (ISBN 0-8225-0907-5). Lerner Pubns.
Coronary Drug Project Research Group. The Coronary Drug Project. 1973. pap. 4.00 (ISBN 0-87493-032-4, EM262J). Am Heart.
Coronel, Gustavo. The Nationalization of the Venezuelan Oil Industry: From Technocratic Success to Political Failure. LC 82-48609. 320p. 1983. 28.50x (ISBN 0-669-06763-6). Lexington Bks.
Coroniti, Samuel C. & Hughes, J., eds. Planetary Electrodynamics, 2 Vols. (Illus.). 1132p. 1969. Set. 216.25 (ISBN 0-677-13600-5). Gordon.
Corosso, Vincent see Kane, Thomas P.
Corporacion Fiduciaria De Panama. Panamanian Business Law. 298p. 1980. 50.00x (ISBN 0-89499-012-8). Bks Business.
Corporate & Securities Law Conference & Mass. Second Annual Corporate & Securities Law Conference. LC 84-60191. (Illus.). Date not set. price not set. Mass CLE.
Corporate Aviation Safety Seminar. Managing Corporate Aviation Safety: Proceedings, 27th Annual Meeting, April 4-6, 1982, Houston Texas. pap. 41.00 (ISBN 0-317-29060-6, 2017828). Bks Demand UMI.
--New Technologies & Corporation Aviation: 25th Annual Meeting of Corporate Aviation Safety Seminar, March 23-25, 1980 St. Louis, Missouri. pap. 43.50 (ISBN 0-317-27621-2, 2014635). Bks Demand UMI.
--Safety in the Terminal Environment: Proceedings, 23rd Annual Meeting, April 9-12, 1978, Arlington Va. pap. 33.50 (ISBN 0-317-10145-5, 2010339). Bks Demand UMI.
Corporate Aviation Safety Seminar (29th: 1984: Montreal, Canada) Staff. Advancing Safety Through Effective Communication (Proceedings) of the 29th Annual Meeting April 1-3, 1984, Le Bonaventure Westin Hotel, Montreal, Canada. pap. 56.00 (ISBN 0-317-26834-1, 2023492). Bks Demand UMI.
Corporate Communnication Studies. The Defense Communication Study: 1984-1985. 338p. 1984. pap. 23.50 (ISBN 0-915683-10-5). Corporate Comm Studies.
Corporate Debt Financing Committee of ABF. Commentaries on Model Debenture Indenture Provisions, 1965; Model Debenture Indenture Provisions, All Registered Issues, 1967, & Certain Negotiable Provisions Which May Be Included in a Particular Incorporating Indenture. xvii, 609p. 1971. 100.00 (ISBN 0-910058-00-8); 2 to 9 copies ea. 87.50 (ISBN 0-317-33320-8); 10-49 copies ea. 75.00 (ISBN 0-317-33321-6). Amer Bar Assn.
Corporation for Com. Col. TV. Contemporary Health Issues. 2nd ed. 1982. pap. text ed. 7.50 (ISBN 0-394-33059-5, RanC). Random.
Corporation for Pacific Northwest Laboratory. Wind Energy Resource Atlas: The East Central Region (Delaware, Kentucky, Maryland, North Carolina, Tennessee, Virginia & West Virginia, Vol. 5. 219p. 1981. pap. 34.50x (ISBN 0-89934-133-0, W-047). Solar Energy Info.
Corpron, Carlotta & Sandweiss, Martha A. Carlotta Corpron: Designer with Light. (Illus.). 64p. 1980. 14.95 (ISBN 0-292-71064-X); pap. 9.95 (ISBN 0-292-71065-8). U of Tex Pr.
Corpus Juris Civilis. The Institutes of Justinian. Sandars, Thomas C., tr. LC 71-98749. ixxx, 608p. Repr. of 1922 ed. lib. bdg. 24.50x (ISBN 0-8371-2920-6, INOJ). Greenwood.
Corpus, Severino F. An Analysis of the Racial Adjustment Activities & Problems of the Filipino-American Christian Fellowship in Los Angeles. LC 75-5330. 1975. soft bdg. 11.00 (ISBN 0-88247-339-5). R & E Pubs.
Corput, Jeannette C. van der see Heusken, Henry C.
Corr, A. M. J., jt. auth. see Plaster, H. J.
Corr, C. A., jt. auth. see Wass, H.
Corr, Charles & Corr, Donna. Hospice Approaches to Pediatric Care. 304p. 1985. 26.95 (ISBN 0-8261-4600-7). Springer Pub.
Corr, Charles, jt. ed. see Wass, Hannelore.
Corr, Charles A. & Corr, Donna M., eds. The Hospice Care: Principles & Practice. (Death & Suicide Ser.: Vol. 5). 1983. text ed. 26.95 (ISBN 0-8261-3540-4); text ed. 22.95 Quantities of 10 or more. Springer Pub.
Corr, Charles A., jt. ed. see Wass, Hannelore.
Corr, Donna, jt. auth. see Corr, Charles.
Corr, Donna M., jt. ed. see Corr, Charles A.
Corr, Edwin G. The Political Process in Colombia. (Monograph Series in World Affairs: Vol. 9, 1971-72 Ser., Bks. 1 & 2). 149p. (Orig.). 1972. 4.95 (ISBN 0-87940-030-7). Monograph Series.
Corr, Michael. Brooming to Paradise. 1976. pap. 2.00 (ISBN 0-935388-03-6). Workingmans Pr.
--Cape Alava. 1981. 3.00 (ISBN 0-934834-20-2). White Pine.
--To Leave the Standing Grain. (Illus.). 1977. 25.00 (ISBN 0-914742-27-2); pap. 5.00 (ISBN 0-914742-27-2). Copper Canyon.
Corr, Michael, ed. Power Consumption & Human Welfare. 1975. write for info. MacMillan Info.
Corradi, Giulio C; see Brown, Howard M.
Corradi, Juan E. The Fitful Republic: Economy, Society, & Politics in Argentina. (Latin American Perspectives Ser.). 200p. 1985. 30.00x (ISBN 0-8133-0110-6); pap. text ed. 15.00x (ISBN 0-317-14728-5). Westview.
Corradini, Claudia. Lab & Exercise Book for Elementary Italian. 2nd ed. 1977. pap. text ed. 10.25 (ISBN 0-8191-0245-8). U Pr of Amer.
Corradini, Enrico. Discorsi Politici: 1902-1923. LC 76-180395. (It.). Repr. of 1923 ed. 41.00 (ISBN 0-404-56116-0). AMS Pr.
Corradini, M. L. & Bishop, A. A., eds. Fuel-Coolant Interactions. (HTD Ser.: Vol. 19). 113p. 1981. 24.00 (ISBN 0-686-34493-6, H00204). ASME.
Corradini, V., tr. see Carducci, Joshua.
Corradini, Virgilio. Italian Power, Italian Democracy & Italian Degeneration. (Illus.). 138p. 1982. 81.75x (ISBN 0-930008-97-9). Inst Econ Pol.
Corradino, R. A., ed. Functional Regulation at the Cellular & Molecular Levels: Proceedings of Conference, Ithaca, N. Y., July 21-24, 1981. 1982. 80.00 (ISBN 0-444-00676-1, Biomedical Pr). Elsevier.
Corrado, Anne Y. No Season. 1984. 6.50 (ISBN 0-8233-0377-2). Golden Quill.
Corrado, Frank M. Media for Managers. (Illus.). 224p. 1984. pap. 15.95 (ISBN 0-13-572446-5). P-H.
Corrado, Joseph. The Family Hour. 1975. 1.25 (ISBN 0-936426-05-5). Play Schs.
Corrado, Joseph & Reed, James. Play - with a Difference. 1970. 1.50 (ISBN 0-936426-06-3). Play Schs.
Corrado, Michael. The Analytic Tradition in Philosophy: Background & Issues. LC 75-9801. pap. 41.30 (ISBN 0-317-26293-9, 2024250). Bks Demand UMI.
Corrado, Raymond R., jt. auth. see Roesch, Ronald.
Corral, Jesus. Caro Amigo: The Autobiography of Jesus Corral. (Illus.). 1984. 11.95 (ISBN 0-87026-059-6). Westernlore.
Corral, Wilfrido, tr. see Lopez-Portillo, J.
Corrales, Fausto L. Calentador De Fiestas. new ed. (Pimienta Collection Ser). 160p. 1974. pap. 1.00 (ISBN 0-88473-219-3). Fiesta Pub.
Corrales, Ramon G., jt. auth. see Barnard, Charles P.
Corrance, Douglas, photos by. Scotland. 18.95 (ISBN 0-318-03147-7, Pub. by Salem Hse Ltd). Merrimack Pub Cir.
Corras, James & Zerowin, Jeffrey. Improving College Admission Test Scores: Verbal Workbook. 184p. (Orig.). (gr. 11-12). 1982. pap. write for info. (ISBN 0-88210-135-8); write for info. tchr's. manual. Natl Assn Principals.
Corre, W. J. & Breimer, T. Nitrate & Nitrite in Vegetables. (Literature Survey Ser.: No. 39). 91p. 1979. pap. 9.75 (ISBN 90-220-0723-5, PDC242, PUDOC). Unipub.
Correa, F. G., tr. see Canright, D. M.
Correa, Gaspar. Three Voyages of Vasco Da Gama. 1964. 23.50 (ISBN 0-8337-3364-8). B Franklin.
Correa, Hector. The Economics of Human Resources. LC 82-6260. (Contributions to Economic Analysis Ser.). ii, 262p. 1982. Repr. lib. bdg. 29.75 (ISBN 0-313-23438-8, COEH). Greenwood.
Correa, Hector & El Torky, Mohamed A. The Biological & Social Determinants of the Demographic Transition. LC 82-16042. (Illus.). 298p. (Orig.). 1983. lib. bdg. 27.50 (ISBN 0-8191-2754-X); pap. text ed. 13.50 (ISBN 0-8191-2755-8). U Pr of Amer.
Correa, Lourdes. Solucionario del Libro "Elementos de Matematica Comercial" de Ruperto Vazquez Cruz. pap. 2.50 (ISBN 0-8477-2604-5). U of PR Pr.
Correa, P. & Haenszel, W. Epidemiology of Cancer of the Digestive Tract. 1982. 48.00 (ISBN 90-247-2601-8, Pub. by Martinus Nijhoff Netherlands). Kluwer Academic.
Correa, Pelayo, jt. ed. see Mizell, Merle.
Correa-Arana, Lourdes. Solucionario del Libro "Estadistica Elemental" de Ruperto Vazques Cruz. LC 77-14570. 1977. pap. 2.50 (ISBN 0-8477-2633-9). U of PR Pr.
Correale, Ernest V. Claws of the Eagle. (Orig.). 1982. pap. 2.95 (ISBN 0-89083-957-3). Zebra.
Correale, William H. A Building Code Primer. (Illus.). 1978. pap. text ed. 23.95x (ISBN 0-07-013171-6). McGraw.
Corredor-Matheos, J., jt. auth. see Artigas, J. Llorens.
Correia, Manning J. & Perachio, Adrian A. Contemporary Sensory Neurobiology. LC 85-142. (Progress in Clinical & Biological Research Ser.: Vol. 176). 372p. 1985. 58.00 (ISBN 0-8451-5026-X). A R Liss.
Correia-Afonso, John, ed. Indo-Portuguese History: Sources & Problems. 1981. 25.00x (ISBN 0-19-561261-2). Oxford U Pr.
Correia-Afonso, John, ed. & tr. Letters from the Mughal Court: The First Jesuit Mission to Akbar (1580-1583) LC 81-81766. (Jesuit Primary Sources in English Translation Ser.: No. 4). (Illus.). 150p. 1982. 9.00 (ISBN 0-912422-57-2). Inst Jesuit.
Correl, Donovan S., jt. auth. see Ames, Oakes.
Correll, Donovan S. Flora of the Bahamian Archipelago. (Illus.). 1692p. 1982. lib. bdg. 105.00x (ISBN 3-7682-1289-0). Lubrecht & Cramer.
--Native Orchids of North America North of Mexico. LC 78-62270. (Illus.). 1950. 35.00x (ISBN 0-8047-0999-8). Stanford U Pr.
--The Potato & Its Wild Relatives: Section Tuberarium of the Genus Solanum. (Illus.). 606p. 1962. lib. bdg. 20.00x (ISBN 0-934454-93-0). Lubrecht & Cramer.
Correll, Donovan S. & Correll, Helen B. Aquatic & Wetland Plants of Southwestern United States, 2 vols. LC 74-82776. (Illus.). 1808p. 1972. Set. 95.00x (ISBN 0-8047-0866-5). Stanford U Pr.
Correll, Helen B., jt. auth. see Correll, Donovan S.
Correll, Marsha M. Teaching the Gifted & Talented. LC 78-61323. (Fastback Ser.: No. 119). 54p. 1978. pap. 0.75 (ISBN 0-87367-119-8). Phi Delta Kappa.
Correll, Philip G. Botanical Gardens & Arboreta of North America: An Organizational Survey. 550p. 1980. 23.00 (ISBN 0-317-36321-2). Am Assn Botanical Gdns.
Correns, Ursula. Die Bildwerke vom Djebelet el Beda in ihrer raeumlichen und zeitlichen Umwelt. (Illus.). viii, 68p. 1972. 59.20x (ISBN 3-11-003877-3). De Gruyter.
Correns, Ursula Moortgat see Correns, Ursula.
Corrente. The House of the Seven Gables (Hawthorne) (Book Note Ser.). 1985. pap. 2.50 (ISBN 0-8120-3519-4). Barron.
Correri, William P., jt. ed. see Yarborough, Michael F.
Corrette, Michel. Le Maitre De Clavecin. (Monuments of Music and Music Literature in Facsimile, Ser II, Vol. 13). 1976. Repr. of 1753 ed. 35.00x (ISBN 0-8450-2213-X). Broude.
--Masters of the Violin, Vol 6. Banat, Gabriel, ed. 75.00 (ISBN 0-384-03186-2). Johnson Repr.
Correu, Larry M. Beyond the Broken Marriage. LC 82-13661. 126p. 1982. pap. 7.95 (ISBN 0-664-24446-7). Westminster.
Correu, Larry M., ed. The Best of These Days. LC 82-13415. 132p. 1983. 8.95 (ISBN 0-664-21391-X). Westminster.
Correy, Lee. Manna. 240p. 1984. pap. 2.95 (ISBN 0-87997-896-1). DAW Bks.
--Star Driver. 1980. pap. 1.95 (ISBN 0-345-28994-3). Ballantine.
Corri, Adrienne. The Search for Gainsborough. (Illus.). 286p. 1985. 15.95 (ISBN 0-8149-0906-X). Vanguard.
Corrick, Frank. Preparing for Your Retirement Years. Rev. ed. LC 70-160362. 59p. (Orig.). 1979. pap. 2.50 (ISBN 0-87576-036-8). Pilot Bks.
Corrick, James A. The Human Brain: Mind & Matter. LC 82-18461. (Arco How-It-Works Ser.). (Illus.). 208p. 1983. 12.95 (ISBN 0-668-05519-7). Arco.
Corrick, Marshall, ed. Handicapped Students Science: Teaching. 88p. 1981. 8.95 (ISBN 0-8106-3179-2). NEA.
Corrie, Bruce A. The Atlantic Coast Conference 1953-1978: Silver Anniversary. LC 78-67832. 246p. 1978. 17.75 (ISBN 0-89089-025-0). Carolina Acad Pr.
Corrie, J. E. T., jt. auth. see Hunter, W. M.
Corrie, Jane. A Cause D'Un Heritage. (Collection Harlequin Ser.). 192p. 1983. pap. 1.95 (ISBN 0-373-49348-7). Harlequin Bks.
--Man with Two Faces. (Harlequin Romances Ser.). 192p. 1983. pap. 1.75 (ISBN 0-373-02551-3). Harlequin Bks.
--Miss Catastrophe. (Collection Harlequin Ser.). 192p. 1983. pap. 1.95 (ISBN 0-373-49336-3). Harlequin Bks.

Corrie, M., et al. Classroom Management Strategies. (SCRE Ser.: No. 78). 103p. 1982. text ed. 20.50x (ISBN 0-901116-82-3, Pub. by Scottish Coun Res UK); pap. text ed. 12.25x (ISBN 0-901116-83-1, Pub. by Scottish Coun Res UK). Humanities.

Corriente Cordoba, Federico. Diccionario Espanol-Arabe. 480p. (Span. & Arabic.). 1970. 18.95 (ISBN 0-686-57345-5, S-50343). French & Eur.

Corrie ten Boom. Jesus Is Victor. 288p. 1984. pap. 6.95 (ISBN 0-8007-5176-0, Power Bks). Revell.

Corriez, Paul, jt. auth. see Lanjalley, Paul.

Corrigan, Adeline. Holiday Ring. LC 75-15975. (Anthologies Ser). (Illus.). 256p. (gr. 3 up). 1975. PLB 11.95 (ISBN 0-8075-3356-4). A Whitman.

Corrigan, B., ed. Two Renaissance Plays: Ariosto, 'Il Negromante', & Trissino, 'Sofonisba' (Italian Texts). 184p. (Ital.). 1975. pap. text ed. 6.50 (Pub. by Manchester Univ Pr). Longwood Pub Group.

Corrigan, B. C. A Profile of General Meade & the Four Military Installations Named for the Victor at Gettysburg. (Historic Marker Ahead Ser.). (Illus., Orig.). 1985. pap. 1.95 (ISBN 0-318-04240-1). ADS Pr.

--Tailgating-The Lincoln-Douglas Debates: A Tour of the Seven Original Debate Sites on the Eve of Their 125th Anniversary. LC 82-73684. (Illus.). 60p. 1984. pap. 2.95 (ISBN 0-9612956-0-0). ADS Pr.

Corrigan, Beatrice, ed. Italian Poets & English Critics, 1755-1859: A Collection of Critical Essays. LC 68-54483. (Patterns of Literary Criticism Ser). 1969. pap. 3.45x (ISBN 0-226-11588-7, PLC7). U of Chicago Pr.

Corrigan, Beatrice, ed. see Erasmus, Desiderius.

Corrigan, Beatrice, tr. see Alfieri, Vittorio.

Corrigan, D. A., jt. ed. see Kudryk, V.

Corrigan, D. Felicitas, tr. see St. Augustine.

Corrigan, Dean C. & Howey, Kenneth R., eds. Special Education in Transition: Concepts to Guide the Education of Experienced Teachers with Implications for PL 94-142. LC 80-68281. 222p. 1980. pap. 6.00 (ISBN 0-86586-109-9). Coun Exc Child.

Corrigan, Dorothy D. The Brain Game: Exploring & Activating Your Body's Most Creative Organ. LC 81-6131. 144p. 1980. 8.95 (ISBN 0-8253-0054-1). Beaufort Bks NY.

--Workbook for a Successful Workshop. (Illus.). 36p. 1967. pap. 3.75x (ISBN 0-8389-5047-7). ALA.

Corrigan, Eileen. Problem Drinkers Seeking Treatment. LC 73-620006. (Rutgers Center of Alcohol Studies: Monograph No. 8). 1974. 5.00 (ISBN 0-911290-39-7). Rutgers Ctr Alcohol.

Corrigan, Eileen M. Alcoholic Women in Treatment. 1980. text ed. 22.95x (ISBN 0-19-502653-5). Oxford U Pr.

--Alcoholic Women in Treatment. 191p. 1980. 14.95 (ISBN 0-318-15283-5). Natl Coun Alcoholism.

Corrigan, Eileen M., jt. auth. see Sauber, Mignon.

Corrigan, Felicitas. The Nun, the Infidel, & the Superman: The Remarkable Frienships of Dame Laurentia MacLachlan. LC 84-52822. (Illus.). 148p. 1985. 14.95 (ISBN 0-226-11589-5). U of Chicago Pr.

Corrigan, Felicitas, ed. More Latin Lyrics. Waddell, Helen, tr. 1977. 12.95x (ISBN 0-393-04469-6). Norton.

Corrigan, Felicitas, tr. see Augustine, St.

Corrigan, Harriett, jt. auth. see Benjamin, Alice.

Corrigan, Jacqueline. Getting a Room on Campus: The Facts about Getting a Space to Live & Surviving It. LC 82-83981. 70p. (Orig.). 1984. pap. text ed. 6.95 (ISBN 0-88247-701-3). R & E Pubs.

Corrigan, James J., Jr. Hemorrhagic & Thrombotic Diseases in Childhood & Adolescence. (Illus.). 216p. 1985. text ed. 29.50 (ISBN 0-443-08425-4). Churchill.

Corrigan, John D., jt. auth. see Bennett, Millard.

Corrigan, John T. Archives: The Light of Faith. (Catholic Library Association Studies in Librarianship: No. 4). 1980. 4.00 (ISBN 0-87507-008-6). Cath Lib Assn.

--Guide for the Organization & Operation of a Religious Resource Center. (Illus.). 1977. pap. 2.50 (ISBN 0-87507-004-3). Cath Lib Assn.

--Librarian-Educator Interdependence. 1976. 3.00 (ISBN 0-87507-002-7). Cath Lib Assn.

Corrigan, John T., jt. auth. see Cargas, Harry J.

Corrigan, John T., ed. Anglo-American Cataloging Rules: One Year Later. (CLA Studies in Librarianship: No. 6). (Illus.). 61p. pap. 8.00 (ISBN 0-87507-023-X). Cath Lib Assn.

--Today's Youth-Today's Librarian. (Catholic Library Assn. Studies in Librarianship: No. 3). 64p. 1980. pap. 5.00 (ISBN 0-87507-007-8). Cath Lib Assn.

--What Today's Youth is Reading & Why. (CLA Studies in Librarianship). 46p. 1981. 5.00 (ISBN 0-686-85772-0). Cath Lib Assn.

Corrigan, John T., ed. see Brown, James, et al.

Corrigan, L. Luan, ed. APHA Drug Names. Shoff, Janet. LC 78-78275. 1979. softcover 18.00 (ISBN 0-917330-24-2). Am Pharm Assn.

Corrigan, Paul. Waiting for the Spring Freshet. 1984. pap. 3.00 (ISBN 0-942396-33-2). Blackberry ME.

Corrigan, Paul & Leonard, Peter. Social Work Practice under Capitalism: A Marxist Approach. (Critical Texts in Social Work & the Welfare State Ser.). 1978. (MacMillian); pap. text ed. 11.00x (ISBN 0-333-21602-4); pap. text ed. 11.00x (ISBN 0-333-21601-6). Humanities.

Corrigan, Philip, et al. For Mao: Essays in Historical Materialism. 1979. text ed. 30.50x (ISBN 0-391-01014-X). Humanities.

--Socialist Construction & Marxist Theory: Bolshevism & Its Critique. LC 78-7591. 232p. 1978. 15.00 (ISBN 0-85345-469-8); pap. 7.50 (ISBN 0-85345-580-5). Monthly Rev.

Corrigan, Phillip, ed. Capitalism, State Formation & Marxist Theory. 9.95 (ISBN 0-7043-3311-2, Pub. by Quartet England). Charles River Bks.

Corrigan, R., ed. Arthur Miller: A Collection of Critical Essays. 1969. 12.95 (ISBN 0-13-582973-9, Spec). P-H.

Corrigan, Robert W. Comedy: Meaning & Form. 2nd ed. 335p. 1981. pap. text ed. 12.85 scp (ISBN 0-06-041370-0, HarpC). Har-Row.

--The Making of Theatre: From Drama to Performance. 1981. pap. text ed. 11.90x (ISBN 0-673-15403-3). Scott F.

--Tragedy: Vision & Form. 2nd ed. 370p. 1981. pap. text ed. 12.85 scp (ISBN 0-06-041371-9, HarpC). Har-Row.

--The World of the Theatre. 1979. text ed. 20.60x (ISBN 0-673-15107-7). Scott F.

Corrigan, Robert W., ed. New American Plays, Vol. 1. Incl. Mister Biggs. Barlow, Anna M; The Hundred & First. Cameron, Kenneth; A Summer Ghost. Fredericks, Claude; Blood Money. Jasudowicz, Dennis; Socrates Wounded. Levinson, Alfred; Constantinople Smith. Mee, Charles L., Jr; Pigeons. Osgood, Lawrence; The Death & Life of Sneaky Fitch. Rosenberg, James L; Ginger Anne. Washburn, Deric; The Golden Bull of Boredom. Yerby, Lorees. (Mermaid Dramabook Ser.). 284p. (Orig.). 1965. pap. 7.95 (ISBN 0-8090-0734-7). Hill & Wang.

Corrigan, Robert W. & Loney, Glenn M., eds. Comedy: A Critical Anthology. LC 78-150137. (Orig.). 1971. pap. text ed. 17.50 (ISBN 0-395-04325-5). HM.

--Forms of Drama. LC 74-150136. 906p. (Orig.). 1972. pap. text ed. 17.50 (ISBN 0-395-04327-1). HM.

Corrigan, Robert W., ed. see Tulane Drama Review.

Corrigan, Timothy. Coleridge, Language & Criticism. LC 81-10433. 232p. 1982. 17.00x (ISBN 0-8203-0593-6). U of Ga Pr.

--New German Film: The Displaced Image. LC 83-10210. (Illus.). 227p. 1983. text ed. 19.95x (ISBN 0-292-71086-0); pap. 8.95 (ISBN 0-292-71087-9). U of Tex Pr.

Corrill, John. Brief History of the Church of Christ of Latter Day Saints. 48p. (Orig.). 1983. pap. 1.95 (ISBN 0-942284-05-4). Restoration Re.

Corrin, Brownlee S; see Mead, Robert G., Jr.

Corrin, Jay P. G. K. Chesterton & Hilaire Belloc: The Battle Against Modernity. LC 81-4756. xvi, 262p. 1981. text ed. 24.95x (ISBN 0-8214-0604-3, 82-83897). Ohio U Pr.

Corrin, Sara & Corrin, Stephen. Pet Stories for Children. (Illus.). 160p. (gr. 2-7). 1985. 11.95 (ISBN 0-571-13642-7). Faber & Faber.

Corrin, Sara & Corrin, Stephen, eds. The Faber Book of Christmas Stories. LC 84-13552. (Illus.). 150p. (gr. 3-7). 1984. 9.95 (ISBN 0-571-13348-7). Faber & Faber.

--The Faber Book of Christmas Stories. 9.95 (ISBN 0-317-31393-2). Faber & Faber.

--The Faber Book of Modern Fairy Tales. (Illus.). 320p. (gr. 3 up). 1981. 13.95 (ISBN 0-571-11768-6). Faber & Faber.

--More Stories for Seven-Year-Olds. LC 79-670248. 184p. (gr. 1-3). 1979. 10.95 (ISBN 0-571-11196-3). Faber & Faber.

--Once upon a Rhyme: One Hundred One Poems for Young Children. (Illus.). 160p. (gr. 1-4). 1982. 11.95 (ISBN 0-571-11913-1). Faber & Faber.

--Round the Christmas Tree. (Illus.). 144p. (ps-5). 1983. 8.95 (ISBN 0-571-13151-4). Faber & Faber.

--Stories for Eight-Year-Olds & Other Young Readers. (Illus.). 192p. (gr. 2-4). 1984. 11.95 (ISBN 0-571-09332-9). Faber & Faber.

--Stories for Nine-Year-Olds. LC 79-670371. (Illus.). 160p. (gr. 2-5). 1979. 11.95 (ISBN 0-571-11409-1). Faber & Faber.

--Stories for Seven-Year-Olds & Other Young Readers. (Illus.). 188p. (gr. 1-3). 1982. 12.95 (ISBN 0-571-05823-X). Faber & Faber.

--Stories for Six-Year Olds & Other Young Readers. (Illus.). 198p. (gr. k-2). 1984. 12.95 (ISBN 0-571-08114-2). Faber & Faber.

--A Time to Laugh: Funny Stories for Children. (Illus.). 208p. (gr. 2-4). 1985. pap. 4.95 (ISBN 0-571-13416-5). Faber & Faber.

Corrin, Sara, et al. Stories for Five Year-Olds & Other Young Readers. Corrin, Stephen, ed. (Illus.). 168p. (ps-5). 1973. 11.95 (ISBN 0-571-10162-3). Faber & Faber.

--Stories for Tens & Over. Corrin, Stephen, ed. (Illus.). 240p. 1976. 9.95 (ISBN 0-571-10873-3). Faber & Faber.

Corrin, Sara, et al, eds. Stories for Under-Fives. (Illus.). 158p. (ps-5). 1974. 9.95 (ISBN 0-571-10371-5). Faber & Faber.

Corrin, Sarah & Corrin, Stephen. Mrs. Fox's Wedding. (Illus.). 32p. (ps-3). 1983. pap. 2.95 (ISBN 0-14-050375-7, Puffin). Penguin.

Corrin, Stephen, jt. auth. see Corrin, Sara.

Corrin, Stephen, jt. auth. see Corrin, Sarah.

Corrin, Stephen, jt. ed. see Corrin, Sara.

Corrin, Stephen, ed. see Corrin, Sara, et al.

Corrin, Stephen, jt. ed. see Corrin, Sara.

Corrin, Stephen, ed. see Corrin, Sara, et al.

Corrin, Stephen, jt. ed. see Corrin, Sara.

Corrin, Stephen, tr. see Ardizzone, Edward.

Corrin, Stephen, tr. see Eliade, Mircea.

Corrington, John W. The Actes & Monuments Stories. LC 78-15325. (Short Fiction Ser.). 144p. 1978. 11.95x (ISBN 0-252-00716-6); pap. 5.95 (ISBN 0-252-00715-8). U of Ill Pr.

--Bombardier. 1970. 15.00 (ISBN 0-399-10096-2). Ultramarine Pub.

--Shad Sentell. 320p. 1984. 15.95 (ISBN 0-312-92765-7). Congdon & Weed.

--Shad Sentell. 1984. 15.95 (ISBN 0-312-92765-7). St Martin.

--The Southern Reporter, Stories. LC 80-26204. 192p. 1981. 14.95 (ISBN 0-8071-0869-3). La State U Pr.

Corrington, Leafy J., jt. auth. see Fink, Bruce.

Corripio Perez, Fernando. Diccionario Abreviado de Sinonimos. 480p. (Span.). 1976. pap. 5.75 (ISBN 84-02-04681-9, S-50157). French & Eur.

--Diccionario Etimologico General de la Lengua Espanola. 2nd ed. (Span.). 18.95 (ISBN 84-02-03344-X, S-50158, French & Eur). French & Eur.

Corris, Peter. The Empty Beach. 160p. 1985. pap. cancelled (ISBN 0-940242-11-7). Fjord Pr.

--Passage, Port & Plantation: A History of Solomon Islands Labour Migration 1870-1914. (Illus.). 201p. 1973. 22.00x (ISBN 0-522-84050-7, Pub. by Melbourne U Pr). Intl Spec Bk.

Corris, Peter, jt. auth. see Keesing, Roger M.

Corris, Peter, ed. & intro. by see Wawn, William T.

Corrothers, James D. Black Cat Club: Negro Humor & Folk-Lore. LC 72-1047. (Illus.). Repr. of 1902 ed. 18.00 (ISBN 0-404-00023-1). AMS Pr.

--In Spite of the Handicap. facsimile ed. LC 75-170694. (Black Heritage Library Collection). Repr. of 1916 ed. 19.25 (ISBN 0-8369-8884-1). Ayer Co Pubs.

--In Spite of the Handicap: An Autobiography. LC 71-111571. (Illus.). 238p. Repr. of 1916 ed. 19.75x (ISBN 0-8371-4596-1, CSH&, Pub. by Negro U Pr). Greenwood.

Corruccini, Robert S., jt. ed. see Ciochon, Russell L.

Corruscini, R. S., jt. ed. see Chiarelli, A. B.

Corruscini, Robert S., et al, eds. Anthropological Studies Related to Health Problems of North American Indians. LC 74-5180. (American Indian Health Ser.: Vol. 4). 148p. 1974. text ed. 19.00x (ISBN 0-8422-7157-0). Irvington.

Corry & Cimbolic. Drugs: Facts, Alternatives & Decisions. 1985. write for info. (ISBN 0-534-04065-9). Wadsworth Pub.

Corry, Davidson. Making the Connection. (Illus.). 1975. pap. 3.50 (ISBN 0-686-14616-6). Pacific Pipeline.

Corry, Emmett. Grants for Libraries: A Guide to Public & Private Funding Programs and Proposal Writing Techniques. LC 81-20886. 240p. 1982. lib. bdg. 22.50 (ISBN 0-87287-262-9). Libs Unl.

Corry, J. E., et al, eds. Isolation & Identification Methods for Food Poisoning Organisms. LC 81-71577. (Society for Applied Bacteriology Technical Ser.: No. 17). 1982. 59.50 (ISBN 0-12-189950-0). Acad Pr.

Corry, James M. Consumer Health: Facts, Skills, & Decisions. 496p. 1983. pap. text ed. write for info. (ISBN 0-534-01355-4). Wadsworth Pub.

Corry, Janet E., jt. auth. see Gould, G. W.

Corry, John P. Indian Affairs in Georgia, 1732-1756. LC 76-43685. Repr. of 1936 ed. 21.50 (ISBN 0-404-15518-9). AMS Pr.

Corry, Joseph. Observations upon the Windward Coast of Africa: Religion, Character, Customs, Etc., of the Natives. (Illus.). 163p. 1968. Repr. of 1807 ed. 28.50x (ISBN 0-7146-1800-4, F Cass Co). Biblio Dist.

Corry, Robert J. & Thompson, John S. Renal Transplantation Case Studies. 1977. spiral bdg. 19.50 (ISBN 0-87488-015-7). Med Exam.

Corsa, Leslie & Oakley, Deborah. Population Planning. (Illus.). 1979. text ed. 22.50x (ISBN 0-472-08243-4). U of Mich Pr.

Corsaro, Frank. Maverick: A Director's Personal Experience in Opera & Theatre. LC 77-77036. (Illus.). 320p. 1978. 17.95 (ISBN 0-8149-0790-3). Vanguard.

Corsaro, Frank & Sendak, Maurice. The Love for Three Oranges. LC 84-47773. (Illus.). 128p. 1984. 30.00 (ISBN 0-374-19286-3). FS&G.

Corsaro, Maria & Korzeniowsky, Carole. STD: A Common Sense Guide to Sexually Transmitted Diseases. (Illus.). 144p. 1982. pap. 5.25 (ISBN 0-03-059914-8, Owl Bks). HR&W.

--A Woman's Guide to a Safe Abortion. LC 82-15652. (Illus.). 200p. 1983. 12.95 (ISBN 0-03-060603-9); pap. 6.95 (ISBN 0-03-060602-0). HR&W.

Corsaro, William. Friendship & Peer Culture in the Early Years. Wallat, Cynthia & Green, Judith, eds. (Language & Learning for Human Service Professions Ser.). 352p. 1985. text ed. 39.95 (ISBN 0-89391-174-7); pap. text ed. 24.95 (ISBN 0-89391-256-5). Ablex Pub.

Corsaut, Maurine J. Hematology Laboratory Manual. (Illus.). 162p. 1982. pap. 21.75x spiral (ISBN 0-398-04524-0). C C Thomas.

Corse, Larry B. & Corse, Sandra B. Articles on American & British Literature: An Index to Selected Periodicals, 1950-1977. LC 81-4010. xii, 413p. 1981. 30.00x (ISBN 0-8040-0408-0, 82-75521, Pub. by Swallow). Ohio U Pr.

Corse, Sandra B., jt. auth. see Corse, Larry B.

Corsel, Ralph, jt. auth. see Graziano, Rocky.

Corsellis, J. A., jt. auth. see Adams.

Corsellis, Jane. Painting Figures in Light. (Illus.). 144p. 1982. 22.50 (ISBN 0-8230-3631-6). Watson-Guptill.

Corser, Frank & Corser, Rose. Tahiti Traveler's Guide. 3rd, rev. ed. (Illus.). 52p. 1981. pap. 3.50 (ISBN 0-686-38091-6). F & R Corser.

Corser, Joan D. The Tales of Mannikin & Bubbikin. (Illus.). 1984. 4.95 (ISBN 0-533-05970-4). Vantage.

Corser, Rose, jt. auth. see Corser, Frank.

Corser, Thomas, ed. Zepheria. LC 72-185712. (Spenser Society Publications Ser: No. 5). 44p. Repr. of 1594 ed. 24.50 (ISBN 0-8337-3920-4). B Franklin.

Corsi, Edward. In the Shadow of Liberty: The Chronicle of Ellis Island. LC 69-18769. (American Immigration Collection Ser., No. 1). (Illus.). 1969. Repr. of 1935 ed. 16.00 (ISBN 0-405-00517-2). Ayer Co Pubs.

Corsi, Jerome R. Judicial Politics: An Introduction. (Illus.). 352p. 1984. pap. text ed. 18.95 (ISBN 0-13-511683-X). P-H.

Corsi, Jerome R. & Hills, William F. Debugging Techniques for IBM PC BASIC. (Illus.). 288p. 1985. pap. 18.95 (ISBN 0-89303-587-4). Brady Comm.

Corsi, Jerome R. & Lippman, Matthew R. Constitutional Law: A Political Science Casebook. 800p. 1985. text ed. 31.95 (ISBN 0-13-167883-3). P-H.

Corsi, M. & Modesto, A. Double Contrast Examination of the Esophagus: An Atlas. (Illus.). 113p. 1981. text ed. 33.00 (ISBN 88-212-0924-5, Pub. by Piccin Italy). J K Burgess.

Corsi, Mario. Tamagno, Il Piu Grande Fenomeno Canoro Dell'ottocento: Tamagno, the Greatest Singing Phenomenon of the Nineteenth Century. Farkas, Andrew, ed. LC 76-29931. (Opera Biographies). (Illus., It.). 1977. Repr. of 1937 ed. lib. bdg. 24.50x (ISBN 0-405-09673-9). Ayer Co Pubs.

Corsi, P., jt. auth. see Chow, G. C.

Corsi, Pietro. Sweet Banana. LC 82-80142. 154p. 1984. 10.95 (ISBN 0-86666-204-9). Natl Lit Guild.

Corsi, Pietro & Weindling, Paul. Information Sources in the History of Science & Medicine. (Illus.). 531p. 1983. 75.00 (ISBN 0-408-10764-2). Butterworth.

Corsiglia, Christina S., et al. The Rita & Frits Markus Collection of European Ceramics & Enamels. Jupe, D. Margaret, ed. LC 83-63520. (Illus.). 287p. 1984. pap. 17.50 (ISBN 0-87846-238-4). Mus Fine Arts Boston.

Corsini, Eugenio. The Apocalypse: The Perennial Revelation of Jesus Christ. Moloney, ed. (Good News Studies: Vol. 5). 1983. pap. 12.95 (ISBN 0-89453-310-X). M Glazier.

Corsini, G. U., jt. ed. see Gessa, G. L.

Corsini, Giovanni U. & Gessa, Gian L., eds. Apomorphine & Other Dopaminomimetics: Clinical Pharmacology. 296p. 1981. text ed. 45.50 (ISBN 0-89004-674-3). Raven.

Corsini, Ray P., ed. see Loos, Anita.

Corsini, Raymond J. & Cardone, Samuel. Roleplaying in Psychotherapy: A Manual. LC 65-22488. 1966. lib. bdg. 21.95x (ISBN 0-202-26007-0). Aldine Pub.

Corsini, Raymond J. & Marsella, Anthony J. Personality Theories, Research & Assessment. LC 82-61261. 703p. 1983. text ed. 26.95 (ISBN 0-87581-288-0). Peacock Pubs.

Corsini, Raymond J. & Painter, Genevieve. The Practical Parent: The ABC's of Child Discipline. LC 74-1801. 262p. 1975. 15.34i (ISBN 0-06-010873-8, HarpT). Har-Row.

Corsini, Raymond J., jt. auth. see Gazda, George M.

Corsini, Raymond J., jt. auth. see Manaster, Guy J.

Corsini, Raymond J., jt. auth. see Painter, Genevieve.

Corsini, Raymond J., jt. auth. see Phillips, Clinton E.

Corsini, Raymond J., ed. Current Psychotherapies. 3rd ed. LC 83-61991. 570p. 1984. pap. text ed. 19.95 (ISBN 0-87581-298-8). Peacock Pubs.

--Handbook of Innovative Psychotherapies. LC 80-29062. (Personality Processes Ser.). 1016p. 1981. 57.95x (ISBN 0-471-06229-4, Pub. by Wiley-Interscience). Wiley.

Corsini, Raymond J. & Ozaki, Bonnie D., eds. Encyclopedia of Psychology, 4 Vol. set. LC 83-16814. 2016p. 1984. Set. 249.95x (ISBN 0-471-86594-X, Pub. by wiley-Interscience). Wiley.

Corsini, Raymond J., jt. ed. see Ignas, Edward.

Corsini, Raymond J., jt. ed. see Wedding, Dan.

Corso, Dante del see Conte, Gianni & Del Corso, Dante.

Corso, Gregory. Earth Egg. (Illus.). 1974. pap. 10.00 (ISBN 0-934450-01-3); pap. 20.00 signed ed. (ISBN 0-934450-00-5). Unmuzzled Ox.

--Elegiac Feelings American. LC 71-122104. (Illus., Orig.). 1970. pap. 3.95 (ISBN 0-8112-0026-4, NDP299). New Directions.

--Gasoline, the Vestal Lady on Brattle. new ed. LC 76-10440. (Pocket Poets Ser., No. 8). (Orig.). pap. 2.95 (ISBN 0-87286-088-4). City Lights.

--The Happy Birthday of Death. LC 59-15018. (Orig.). 1960. pap. 4.95 (ISBN 0-8112-0027-2, NDP86). New Directions.
--Herald of the Autochthonic Spirit. LC 81-9486. 64p. 1981. 12.95 (ISBN 0-8112-0819-2); pap. 4.95 (ISBN 0-8112-0808-7, NDP522). New Directions.
--The Japanese Notebook Ox. 1974. pap. 4.95x (ISBN 0-934450-05-6). Unmuzzled Ox.
--Long Live Man. LC 62-16927. (Orig.). 1962. pap. 3.75 (ISBN 0-8112-0025-6, NDP127). New Directions.
--Writings from Ox. Andre, Michael, ed. (Illus.). 160p. (Orig.). 1981. pap. 6.95 (ISBN 0-934450-10-2). Unmuzzled Ox.
Corso, John F. Aging Sensory Systems & Perception. LC 80-39579. 302p. 1981. 42.95x (ISBN 0-03-058957-6). Praeger.
Corso, S. M. De see Clark, J. S. & De Corso, S. M.
Corson, Blake. My Dear Jennie. 1982. 10.57 (ISBN 0-317-02280-6). Dietz.
Corson, Christopher. Maya Anthropomorphic Figurines from Jaina Island, Campeche. (Studies in Mesoamerican Art, Archaeology & Ethnohistory: No. 1). (Illus.). 218p. 1976. pap. 8.95 (ISBN 0-87919-053-1). Ballena Pr.
Corson, D. The Lexical Bar. (Illus.). 135p. 1985. 24.00 (ISBN 0-08-030858-9, Pub. by PPL); pap. 11.50 (ISBN 0-08-030857-0). Pergamon.
Corson, Dale R., jt. auth. see Lorrain, Paul.
Corson, E. O'Leary, jt. auth. see Corson, S. A.
Corson, Edward M. Introduction to Tensors, Spinors, & Relativistic Wave Equations. 2nd ed. LC 80-85523. 222p. 1981. text ed. 15.95 (ISBN 0-8284-0315-5). Chelsea Pub.
Corson, Elizabeth O., jt. ed. see Corson, Samuel A.
Corson, Elizabeth O., ed. see Korneva, Elena A., et al.
Corson, Helen B. Does Your Diet Work? LC 80-8427. (Illus.). 105p. (Orig.). 1980. pap. 7.95 (ISBN 0-9605358-0-2). MIND.
Corson, Hiram. Index of Proper Names & Subjects to Chaucer's Canterbury Tales. LC 73-3304. 1973. lib. bdg. 17.50 (ISBN 0-8414-1828-4). Folcroft.
--Introduction to the Prose & Poetical Works of John Milton. (Illus.). 335p. Repr. of 1899 ed. 13.50x (ISBN 0-87752-224-3). Gordian.
--Introduction to the Study of Robert Browning's Poetry. facs. ed. LC 74-119929. (Select Bibliographies Reprint Ser). 1901. 21.00 (ISBN 0-8369-5372-X). Ayer Co Pubs.
--Introduction to the Study of Shakespeare. LC 72-1033. Repr. of 1889 ed. 15.00 (ISBN 0-404-01735-5). AMS Pr.
--A Primer of English Verse. 1973. lib. bdg. 10.00 (ISBN 0-8414-2392-X). Folcroft.
Corson, James C. Bibliography of Sir Walter Scott. LC 68-58238. (Bibliography & Reference Ser.: No. 264). 1969. Repr. of 1943 ed. 30.50 (ISBN 0-8337-0683-7). B Franklin.
Corson, James C., ed. Notes & Index to Sir Herbert Grierson's Edition of the Letters of Sir Walter Scott. 1979. 105.00x (ISBN 0-19-812718-9). Oxford U Pr.
Corson, John J. The Governance of Colleges & Universities: Modernizing Structure & Processes. 2nd. ed. 1975. 19.95 (ISBN 0-07-013205-4). McGraw.
Corson, John J. & Harris, Joseph P. Public Administration in Modern Society. LC 81-7262. (Foundations of American Government & Political Science Ser.). 155p. 1985. Repr. of 1963 ed. lib. bdg. 20.75 (ISBN 0-313-22668-7, COPU/). Greenwood.
Corson, John J. & McConnell, John W. Economic Needs of Older People. LC 55-7161. 1975. Repr. of 1956 ed. 25.00 (ISBN 0-527-02803-7). Kraus Repr.
Corson, John J. & Paul, R. S. Men Near the Top: Filling Key Posts in the Federal Service. LC 66-17010. (Committee for Economic Development, Supplementary Paper: No. 20). pap. 52.00 (ISBN 0-317-09396-7, 2020510). Bks Demand UMI.
Corson, John J. & Paul, R. Shale. Men Near the Top: Filling Key Posts in the Federal Service. 192p. 1966. 3.00 (ISBN 0-317-33991-5, 220). Comm Econ Dev.
Corson, John J. & Steiner, George A. Measuring Business's Social Performance: Corporate Social Audit. LC 74-19382. 1975. pap. 4.00 (ISBN 0-87186-239-5). Comm Econ Dev.
Corson, Livingston. Finding List of Political Poems Referring to English Affairs of the 13th & 14th Centuries. LC 72-121222. (Bibliography & Reference Ser.: No. 331). 1970. Repr. of 1910 ed. lib. bdg. 18.50 (ISBN 0-8337-0684-5). B Franklin.
--A Finding List of Political Poems Referring to English Affairs of the Thirteenth & Fourteenth Centuries. LC 72-11719. 1973. Repr. lib. bdg. 18.00 (ISBN 0-8414-0925-0). Folcroft.
Corson, Lynn A. Statistical Report of Compensable Injuries in Michigan's Hazardous Waste Processing & Transporting Industry: 1982. LC 83-720023. 1983. 2.00 (ISBN 0-941872-46-7). MSU Inst Comm Devel.
--A Statistical Report of Hazardous Materials Transportation Incidents in Michigan Communities: January 1979 to September 1981. LC 82-620021. 1982. 1.50 (ISBN 0-941872-39-4). MSU Inst Comm Devel.
Corson, Lynn A. & Johnson, Melinda O. Report of Rail Incidents Involving Cars Carrying Hazardous Materials: State of Michigan, 1977-1982. LC 83-620021. 1983. 1.50 (ISBN 0-941872-47-5). MSU Inst Comm Devel.
Corson, Lynn A., jt. auth. see Sobetzer, John G.
Corson, Richard. Fashions in Eyeglasses. (Illus.). 1980. Repr. of 1967 ed. 50.00 (ISBN 0-7206-3282-X). Dufour.
--Fashions in Eyeglasses: From the 14th Century to the Present Day. rev. ed. (Illus.). 1980. Repr. of 1967 ed. text ed. 70.50x (ISBN 0-7206-3282-X). Humanities.
--Fashions in Hair: The First Five Thousand Years. 3rd rev. ed. (Illus.). 1971. text ed. 75.50x (ISBN 0-391-00167-1). Humanities.
--Fashions in Makeup. 1981. text ed. 78.50x (ISBN 0-7206-0431-1). Humanities.
--Stage Make Up. 7th ed. (Illus.). 448p. 1986. text ed. 33.95 (ISBN 0-13-840521-2). P H.
--Stage Makeup. 6th ed. (Illus.). 464p. 1981. text ed. 33.95 (ISBN 0-13-840512-3). P-H.
Corson, S. A. & Corson, E. O'Leary. Ethology & Nonverbal Communication in Mental Health: An Interdisciplinary Biopsychosocial Exploration. LC 79-41689. (International Ser. in Biopsychosocial Sciences). (Illus.). 290p. 1980. 57.00 (ISBN 0-08-023728-2). Pergamon.
Corson, Samuel A. & Corson, Elizabeth O., eds. Psychiatry & Psychology in the USSR. LC 76-47482. 310p. 1976. 39.50x (ISBN 0-306-30992-0, Plenum Pr). Plenum Pub.
Corson, Samuel A., ed. see Korneva, Elena A., et al.
Corson, Stephen, et al. Fertility Control. 400p. 1984. pap. text ed. 24.50 (ISBN 0-316-15748-1). Little.
Corson, Stephen L. Conquering Infertility. (Illus.). 192p. 1982. 14.95 (ISBN 0-8385-1207-0). ACC.
Corson, Walter & Nicholson, Walter. The Federal Supplemental Benefits Program: An Appraisal of Emergency Extended Unemployment Insurance Benefits. 117p. 1982. pap. 9.95 (ISBN 0-911558-91-8). W E Upjohn.
Corson, Walter E. & Lowe, James L. Publishers' Trademarks Identified. (Illus.). 64p. 1979. 6.95 (ISBN 0-686-39852-1). Deltiologists Am.
Corson, William R. The Consequences of Failure. 1974. 7.95 (ISBN 0-393-05492-6). Norton.
Corson, William R. & Crowley, Robert T. The New KGB: Engine of Soviet Power. LC 85-2911. 560p. 1985. 19.95 (ISBN 0-688-04183-3). Morrow.
Corson-Finnerty, Adam. No More Plastic Jesus: Global Justice & Christian Lifestyle. LC 76-13174. 223p. (Orig.). 1977. pap. 6.95x (ISBN 0-88344-341-4). Orbis Bks.
--World Citizen: Action for Global Justice. LC 81-16918. 192p. (Orig.). 1982. pap. 6.95 (ISBN 0-88344-715-0). Orbis Bks.
Corstanje, Auspicius Van see Van Corstanje, Auspicius.
Corsten, I. C. & Hermans, J., eds. COMPSTAT 1978: Proceedings. 540p. 1978. pap. text ed. 31.00x (ISBN 3-7908-0196-8). Birkhauser.
Corstius, H. Brandt see Brandt Corstius, H.
Cort, David. The Sin of Henry R. Luce: An Anatomy of Journalism. 480p. 1974. 12.50 (ISBN 0-8184-0201-6). Lyle Stuart.
Cort, J. H., ed. see Symposium on Natriuretic Hormone, Czechoslovakia, June, 1969.
Cort, John, ed. see Bhartrhari.
Cort, Joseph. Electrolytes, Fluid Dynamics, & the Nervous System. 1966. 46.00 (ISBN 0-12-190150-5). Acad Pr.
Cort, Louise A. Shigaraki, Potters' Valley. LC 79-89265. (Illus.). 428p. 1980. 65.00 (ISBN 0-87011-382-8). Kodansha.
Cort, Margaret. Little Oleg. LC 77-103606. (Illus.). (gr. k-4). 1971. PLB 3.95g (ISBN 0-87614-007-X). Carolrhoda Bks.
Cort, Rebecca H., jt. auth. see Sapir, Selma.
Cort, William W. Some North American Larval Trematodes. (Illus.). 1915. pap. 8.00 (ISBN 0-384-09870-3). Johnson Repr.
Cortada, James N. & Cortada, James W. United States Foreign Policy in the Caribbean, Cuba, & Central America. LC 84-26629. 270p. 1985. 35.95 (ISBN 0-03-002119-7). Praeger.
Cortada, James W. EDP Cost & Charges: Finance, Budgets & Cost Control in Data Processing. (Data Processing Management Ser.). (Illus.). 1980. text ed. 36.95 (ISBN 0-13-235655-4). P-H.
--Managing DP Hardware: Capacity Planning, Cost Justification, Availability & Energy Management. (Data Processing Management Ser.). (Illus.). 416p. 1983. text ed. 36.95 (ISBN 0-13-550392-2). P-H.
--Spain & the American Civil War: Relations at Mid-Century, 1855 to 1868, Vol. 70, Pt. 4. 1980. 10.00 (ISBN 0-87169-704-1). Am Philos.
--Strategic Data Processing: Considerations for Management. (Illus.). 224p. 1984. text ed. 32.95 (ISBN 0-13-851246-9). P-H.
--Two Nations Over Time: Spain & the United States, 1776-1977. LC 77-94752. (Contributions in American History: No. 74). 1978. lib. bdg. 29.95 (ISBN 0-313-20319-9, CTN/). Greenwood.
Cortada, James W., jt. auth. see Cortada, James N.
Cortada, James W., compiled by. An Annotated Bibliography on the History of Data Processing. LC 83-8539. xlii, 216p. 1983. lib. bdg. 35.00 (ISBN 0-313-24001-9, CDP/). Greenwood.
--Bibliographic Guide to Spanish Diplomatic History: Fourteen Sixty to Nineteen Seventy-Seven. LC 77-4565. 1977. lib. bdg. 39.95 (ISBN 0-8371-9685-X, CBG/). Greenwood.
Cortada, James W., ed. A City in War: American Views on Barcelona & the Spanish Civil War, 1936-39. LC 84-20302. (Illus.). 220p. 1985. 30.00 (ISBN 0-8420-2229-5). Scholarly Res Inc.
--Historical Dictionary of the Spanish Civil War, 1936-1939. LC 81-13424. (Illus.). xxviii, 571p. 1982. lib. bdg. 75.00 (ISBN 0-313-22054-9, CSP/). Greenwood.
--Spain in the Twentieth-Century World: Essays on Spanish Diplomacy, 1898-1978. LC 78-75257. (Contributions in Political Science: No. 30). 1980. lib. bdg. 29.95 (ISBN 0-313-21326-7, CST/). Greenwood.
Cortani, R. M. Diesels of the Espee: Alco PA's. LC 75-38238. (Illus.). 1975. 22.50 (ISBN 0-89685-034-X). Chatham Pub CA.
Cortassi, Hugh, ed. Mitford's Japan: The Memoirs & Recollections, 1866-1906, of Algernon Bertram Mitford, the First Lord of Redesdale. LC 85-15805. 1985. 36.50 (ISBN 0-485-11275-2, Pub. by Athlone Pr Ltd). Longwood Pub Group.
Cortazar, Julio. Around the Day in Eighty Worlds. Christensen, Thomas, tr. from Span. 304p. 1986. 18.75 (ISBN 0-86547-203-3). N Point Pr.
--Blow up & Other Stories. 1985. pap. 6.95 (ISBN 0-394-72881-5). Pantheon.
--A Certain Lucas. Rabassa, Gregory, tr. from Span. LC 83-48850. 139p. 1984. 12.95 (ISBN 0-394-50723-1). Knopf.
--A Change of Light & Other Stories. Rabassa, Gregory, tr. from Span. LC 80-7656. 288p. 1980. 11.95 (ISBN 0-394-50721-5). Knopf.
--Hopscotch. 1974. pap. 5.95 (ISBN 0-380-00372-4, 69825-0, Bard). Avon.
--A Manual for Manuel. Rabassa, Gregory, tr. 394p. 1986. pap. 9.95 (ISBN 0-88184-213-3). Carroll & Graf.
--Paris: The Essence of an Image. (The Master Collection Ser.). (Illus.). 1981. 35.00 (ISBN 2-880460-20-4, Pub. by Roto-Vision). Norton.
--We Love Glenda So Much & Other Tales. Rabassa, Gregory, tr. from Span. LC 82-48732. 1983. 11.95 (ISBN 0-394-52493-4). Knopf.
--We Love Glenda So Much & Other Tales. 1984. pap. 8.95 (ISBN 0-394-72297-3, Vin). Random.
--The Winners. Kerrigan, Elaine, tr. (Modern Writers Ser.). 1984. pap. 8.95 (ISBN 0-394-72301-5). Pantheon.
Cortazzi, Hugh. Dr. Willis in Japan, 1862-1877: A British Medical Pioneer. LC 85-1334. (Illus.). 1985. 29.50 (ISBN 0-485-11264-7, Pub. by Athlone Pr Ltd). Longwood Pub Group.
--Isles of Gold: Antique Maps of Japan. (Illus.). 184p. 1983. 75.00 (ISBN 0-8348-0184-1). Weatherhill.
Cortazzi, Hugh, jt. auth. see Fraser, Mary C.
Cortazzo, Arnold D., jt. auth. see Allen, Robert M.
Cortazzo, Arnold D., jt. ed. see Allen, Robert M.
Cortazzo, Carmen. Nowhere to Go but Home. 176p. (Orig.). 1982. pap. 2.25 (ISBN 0-523-41626-1). Pinnacle Bks.
Corte, Andrea D., ed. Canto E Bel Canto P.F. Tosi: Opinioni De Cantori Antchi E Moderni 1723. LC 80-2268. Repr. of 1933 ed. 31.50 (ISBN 0-404-18823-0). AMS Pr.
Corte, Andrea Della. L' Opera Comica Italiana nel Settecento, Studi ed Appunti, 2 vols. LC 80-2269. Repr. of 1923 ed. Set. 62.50 (ISBN 0-404-18830-3). Vol. 1 (ISBN 0-404-18831-1). Vol. 2 (ISBN 0-404-18832-X). AMS Pr.
Cortelazzo, Manlio. I Dialetti E la Dialettologia in Italia (Fini Al 1800) (ARS Linguistica Ser.: No. 4). 146p. (Orig., Ital.). 1980. pap. 24.00x (ISBN 3-87808-354-8). Benjamins North Am.
Cortellaro, M., jt. ed. see Polli, E. E.
Cortelyou, Irwin F., jt. auth. see Bolton, Theodore.
Cortes, Carlos, ed. & intro. by see Griffin & Foster.
Cortes, Carlos, ed. see Jarratt, et al.
Cortes, Carlos, ed. see Tireman, L. S. & Watson, Mary.
Cortes, Carlos E., ed. Church Views of the Mexican American. LC 73-14198. (The Mexican American Ser.). (Illus.). 58p. 1974. Repr. 45.00x (ISBN 0-405-05672-9). Ayer Co Pubs.
--Cuban Exiles in the United States: An Original Anthology. LC 79-6236. (Hispanics in the United States Ser.). (Illus.). 1981. lib. bdg. 17.00x (ISBN 0-405-13183-6). Ayer Co Pubs.
--The Cuban Experience in the United States: An Original Anthology. LC 79-6230. (Hispanics in the United States Ser.). 1981. lib. bdg. 51.50x (ISBN 0-405-13177-1). Ayer Co Pubs.
--The Cuban Minority in the United States, 2 vols. LC 79-17461. (Hispanics in the United States Ser.). (Illus.). 1981. Set. lib. bdg. 37.50x (ISBN 0-405-13174-7). Ayer Co Pubs.
--Cuban Refugee Programs: An Original Anthology. LC 79-6237. (Hispanics in the United States Ser.). (Orig.). 1981. lib. bdg. 83.00x (ISBN 0-405-13184-4). Ayer Co Pubs.
--Education & the Mexican American. LC 73-14201. (The Mexican American Ser.). 1974. Repr. 36.00x (ISBN 0-405-05675-3). Ayer Co Pubs.
--Hispanics in the United States Series, 30 bks. 1981. Set. lib. bdg. 1080.00 (ISBN 0-405-13150-X). Ayer Co Pubs.
--Juan N. Cortina: Two Interpretations. LC 73-14204. (The Mexican American Ser.). (Illus.). 1974. Repr. 15.00x (ISBN 0-405-05678-8). Ayer Co Pubs.
--The Latin American Brain Drain to the United States: An Original Anthology. LC 79-6229. (Hispanics in the United States Ser.). (Illus.). 1981. lib. bdg. 17.00x (ISBN 0-405-13176-3). Ayer Co Pubs.
--Latinos in the United States: An Original Anthology. LC 79-6232. (Hispanics in the United States Ser.). (Illus.). 1981. lib. bdg. 66.50x (ISBN 0-405-13179-8). Ayer Co Pubs.
--The Mexican American, 21 vols. 1974. 623.00 set (ISBN 0-405-05670-2). Ayer Co Pubs.
--The Mexican American & the Law. LC 73-14207. 1974. Repr. 24.00x (ISBN 0-405-05681-8). Ayer Co Pubs.
--Mexican American Bibliographies. LC 73-14421. (The Mexican American Ser.). 1974. Repr. 27.00x (ISBN 0-405-05682-6). Ayer Co Pubs.
--Mexican Labor in the United States. LC 73-14208. (The Mexican American Ser.). (Illus.). 480p. 1974. Repr. 32.00x (ISBN 0-405-05683-4). Ayer Co Pubs.
--The Mexican Side of the Texas Revolution (1836), by the Chief Mexican Participants. Castenada, Carlos E., tr. LC 76-1215. (Chicano Heritage Ser.). 1976. Repr. of 1928 ed. 30.00x (ISBN 0-405-09487-6). Ayer Co Pubs.
--The New Mexican Hispano. LC 73-14210. (The Mexican American Ser.). (Illus.). 510p. 1974. Repr. 36.00x (ISBN 0-405-05684-2). Ayer Co Pubs.
--Nineteenth Century Latin Americans in the United States: An Original Anthology. LC 79-6234. (Hispanics in the United States Ser.). 1981. lib. bdg. 28.50x (ISBN 0-405-13182-8). Ayer Co Pubs.
--The Penitentes of New Mexico. LC 73-14212. (The Mexican American Ser.). (Illus.). 1974. Repr. 36.00x (ISBN 0-405-05686-9). Ayer Co Pubs.
--Portugese Americans & Spanish Americans: An Original Anthology. LC 79-6233. (Hispanics in the United States Ser.). 1981. lib. bdg. 28.50x (ISBN 0-405-13180-1). Ayer Co Pubs.
--Protestantism & Latinos in the United States: An Original Anthology. LC 79-6266. (Hispanics in the United States Ser.). (Illus.). 1981. lib. bdg. 51.50x (ISBN 0-405-13173-9). Ayer Co Pubs.
--Regional Perspectives on the Puerto Rican Experience. LC 79-6231. (Hispanics in the United States Ser.). lib. bdg. 74.50x (ISBN 0-405-13178-X). Ayer Co Pubs.
--Report of the Select Commission on Western Hemisphere Immigration. LC 80-7574. (Hispanics in the United States Ser.). (Illus.). 1981. Repr. of 1968 ed. lib. bdg. 21.00x (ISBN 0-405-13185-2). Ayer Co Pubs.
--Spanish & Mexican Land Grants. LC 73-14216. (The Mexican American Ser.). (Illus.). 1974. Repr. 30.00x (ISBN 0-405-05690-7). Ayer Co Pubs.
--Spanish & Portugese Languages in the United States: An Original Anthology. LC 79-6234. (Hispanics in the United States Ser.). 1981. lib. bdg. 33.50x (ISBN 0-405-13181-X). Ayer Co Pubs.
Cortes, Carlos E., ed. see Adams, Emma H.
Cortes, Carlos E., ed. see Anderson, Henry P.
Cortes, Carlos E., ed. see Avina, Rose H.
Cortes, Carlos E., ed. see Barker, Ruth L.
Cortes, Carlos E., ed. see Biberman, Herbert.
Cortes, Carlos E., ed. & intro. by see Campa, Arthur.
Cortes, Carlos E., ed. see Colton, Walter.
Cortes, Carlos E., ed. see Cooke, Philip St George.
Cortes, Carlos E., ed. see Cue Canovas, Agustin.
Cortes, Carlos E., ed. see Digges, Jeremiah.
Cortes, Carlos E., ed. see Duran, Daniel F.
Cortes, Carlos E., ed. see Fergusson, Harvey.
Cortes, Carlos E., ed. see Fernandez, Jose.
Cortes, Carlos E., ed. see Fernandez-Florez, Dario.
Cortes, Carlos E., ed. see Francis, Jessie D.
Cortes, Carlos E., ed. see Gallagher, Patrick L.
Cortes, Carlos E., ed. see Getty, Harry T.
Cortes, Carlos E., ed. & intro. by see Griggs, et al.
Cortes, Carlos E., ed. see Guzman, Ralph C.
Cortes, Carlos E., ed. see Harding, George L.
Cortes, Carlos E., ed. see Hayes, Benjamin.
Cortes, Carlos E., ed. see Herrick, Robert.
Cortes, Carlos E., ed. & intro. by see Hill, et al.
Cortes, Carlos E., ed. see Jamieson, Stuart.
Cortes, Carlos E., ed. see Kernstock, Elwyn N.
Cortes, Carlos E., ed. see Landolt, Robert G.
Cortes, Carlos E., ed. see Lane, John H., Jr.
Cortes, Carlos E., ed. see Lewin, Ellen.
Cortes, Carlos E., ed. see Lewis & Emory.
Cortes, Carlos E., ed. see Livermore, Abiel A.
Cortes, Carlos E., ed. see Loyola, Mary.
Cortes, Carlos E., ed. & intro. by see Lucero-White, et al.
Cortes, Carlos E., ed. see Macklin, Barbara J.
Cortes, Carlos E., ed. see McWilliams, Carey.
Cortes, Carlos E., ed. see Miyares, Marcelino.
Cortes, Carlos E., ed. see Morrison, J. Cayce.
Cortes, Carlos E., ed. see Murray, Winifred.
Cortes, Carlos E., ed. see Parigi, Sam F.
Cortes, Carlos E., ed. see Poldervaart, Arie W.
Cortes, Carlos E., ed. see Read, Benjamin M.
Cortes, Carlos E., ed. see Redden, Charlotte A.
Cortes, Carlos E., ed. see Richmond, Marie L.
Cortes, Carlos E., ed. see Rodriguez, Eugene, Jr.
Cortes, Carlos E., ed. see Ropka, Gerald W.

Cortes, Carlos E., ed. see Ross, Elmer L.
Cortes, Carlos E., ed. see Sanchez, Nellie.
Cortes, Carlos E., ed. see Shulman, Irving.
Cortes, Carlos E., ed. & intro. by see Smith, et al.
Cortes, Carlos E., ed. & intro. by see Taylor, et al.
Cortes, Carlos E., ed. see Tireman, L. S.
Cortes, Carlos E., ed. see Tovar, Federico R.
Cortes, Carlos E., ed. see Twitchell, Ralph E.
Cortes, Carlos E., ed. see U. S. House of Representatives.
Cortes, Carlos E., ed. see West, Stanley A.
Cortes, Carlos E., ed. see Woods, Frances J.
Cortes, Carlos E., et al. Understanding You & Them: Tips for Teaching About Ethnicity. 66p. 1976. pap. 7.95 (ISBN 0-89994-187-7). Soc Sci Ed.
Cortes, Carlos E., et al, eds. The Chicano Heritage, 55 vols. 1976. 1746.00x (ISBN 0-405-09480-9). Ayer Co Pubs.
Cortes, F., et al. Systems Analysis for Social Scientists. LC 73-23061. Repr. of 1974 ed. 66.90 (ISBN 0-8357-9990-5, 2016464). Bks Demand UMI.
Cortes, Felix M. The Pericardium & Its Disorders. (Illus.). 320p. 1971. photocopy ed. 27.50x (ISBN 0-398-00348-3). C C Thomas.
Cortes, Hernan. Five Letters. Morris, J. Bayard, tr. 1977. lib. bdg. 59.95 (ISBN 0-8490-1841-2). Gordon Pr.
Cortes, Hernando. The Fifth Letter of Hernando Cortes to the Emperor Charles 5th Containing an Account of His Expedition to Honduras. De Gayangos, Pascual, tr. (Hakluyt Soc. Ser.: No. 401). 1964. 25.50 (ISBN 0-8337-0686-1). B Franklin.
--Five Letters of Cortes. Morris, J. Bayard, tr. Orig. Title: Hernando Cortes Five Letters, 1519-1526. 1969. pap. 6.95x (ISBN 0-393-09877-X, NortonC). Norton.
Cortes, Hernando, et al. Mexican Mosaic. 1978. pap. 4.95 (ISBN 0-914558-01-3). Georgetown Pr.
Cortes, Juan B. & Gatti, Florence M. Delinquency & Crime, a Biopsychosocial Approach: Empirical, Theoretical, & Practical Aspects of Criminal Behavior. LC 76-154390. 480p. 1972. 50.00 (ISBN 0-12-785138-0). Acad Pr.
Cortes, Juan D. & Schramm, Edmund. Ensayo Sobre el Catolicismo, el Liberalismo y el Socialismo & Donoso Cortes, 2 vols. in one. Mayer, J. P., ed. LC 78-67342. (European Political Thought Ser.). (Sp. & Ger.). 1979. Repr. of 1935 ed. lib. bdg. 39.00x (ISBN 0-405-11687-X). Ayer Co Pubs.
Cortes, Mariluz & Bocock, Peter. North-South Technology Transfer: A Case Study of Petrochemicals in Latin America. LC 83-49365. 184p. 1984. text ed. 25.00x (ISBN 0-8018-3259-4). Johns Hopkins.
--The Transfer of Petrochemical Technology to Latin America: An Empirical Study of Participants, Policies, & Processes. LC 83-49365. 200p. 1984. 25.00 (ISBN 0-8018-3259-4, JH 3259). Johns Hopkins.
Cortes, Rosario M. Pangasinan, 1572-1800. 1975. Repr. of 1974 ed. wrps. 4.00x (ISBN 0-686-18692-3). Cellar.
Cortesad, Armando, ed. The Suma Oriental of Tome Pires, an Account of the East Fifteen Twelve to Fifteeen Fifteen & the Book of Francisco Rodriguez, Rutter of a Voyage in the Red Sea: Vol. 89 & Vol. 90, 2 vols. in one. (Hakluyt Society Works Series: No. 2). (Illus.). Repr. of 1944 ed. 72.00 (ISBN 0-317-15630-6). Kraus Repr.
Cortes-Caben, David. Al Final de las Palabras. SLUSA, ed. 110p. (Orig., Sp.). 1984. pap. 4.50 (ISBN 0-9606758-9-2). SLUSA.
Cortes-Conde, Roberto & Hunt, Shane J., eds. Latin American Economies: Growth & the Export Sector, 1880-1930. 300p. 1985. 45.00x (ISBN 0-8419-0771-4). Holmes & Meier.
Cortes Conde, Roberto & Stein, Stanley J., eds. Latin America: A Guide to Economic History 1830-1930. LC 74-30534. 1977. 66.00x (ISBN 0-520-02956-9). U of Cal Pr.
Cortese, Charles F., ed. The Social Impact of Energy Development in the West. 1985. pap. text ed. 12.95x (ISBN 0-8290-1083-1). Irvington.
--The Social Impacts of Energy Development in the West. 1985. text ed. 24.95x (ISBN 0-8290-0235-9). Irvington.
Cortes Funes, H. & Rozencweig, M., eds. New Approaches in Cancer Therapy. (European Organization for Research on Treatment of Cancer (EORTC) Monograph: Vol. 11). 204p. 1982. text ed. 59.00 (ISBN 0-89004-781-2). Raven.
Cortesi, David. A Programmer's Notebook: Utilities for the CP-M-80. 1983. pap. 17.95 (ISBN 0-8359-5641-5); incl. disk 35.95. Reston.
Cortesi, David & Cherry, George. Personal Pascal: Compiled Pascal for the IBM Personal Computer. (Illus.). 1983. text ed. 24.95 (ISBN 0-8359-5523-0); pap. text ed. 17.95 (ISBN 0-8359-5522-2). Reston.
Cortesi, David, jt. auth. see Arnold, David.
Cortesi, David, jt. auth. see Zussman, John.
Cortesi, David E. Inside Concurrent CP-M-86. 1984. 17.95 (ISBN 0-03-070669-6). HR&W.
--Inside CP-M: A Guide for Users & Programmers, with CP-M-86 & MP-M2. 576p. pap. 26.45 (ISBN 0-03-059558-4). HR&W.
--Inside CP-M Plus. 1984. 17.95 (ISBN 0-03-070671-8). HR&W.
--Inside CP-M-86. 1984. 16.95 (ISBN 0-03-062656-0). HR&W.
--Your IBM Personal Computer: Use, Applications, & BASIC. LC 82-15671. 304p. 1983. pap. 19.95 (ISBN 0-03-061979-3). HR&W.
Cortesi, Laurence. Target: Tokyo. 1983. pap. 3.25 (ISBN 0-8217-1256-X). Zebra.
Cortesi, Lawerence. Hitler's Final Siege. (World-at-War Ser.). 1982. pap. 2.50 (ISBN 0-8217-1010-9). Zebra.
--Pacific Strike. (World-at-War Ser.). (Orig.). 1982. pap. 2.95 (ISBN 0-8217-1041-9). Zebra.
Cortesi, Lawrence. The Battle for Manilla. 1984. pap. 3.25 (ISBN 0-8217-1332-9). Zebra.
--Battle of the Bismarck Sea. 1977. pap. 1.50 (ISBN 0-8439-0510-7, Leisure Bks). Dorchester Pub Co.
--Bloody Friday off Guadalcanal. (Orig.). 1981. pap. 2.95 (ISBN 0-89083-870-4). Zebra.
--D-Day Minus One. 1984. pap. 3.25 (ISBN 0-8217-1318-3). Zebra.
--The Deadly Skies. 1983. pap. 3.25 (ISBN 0-8217-1132-6). Zebra.
--Escape from Mindanao. 1978. pap. 1.75 (ISBN 0-8439-0584-0, Leisure Bks). Dorchester Pub Co.
--Forty Fathoms Down. 1979. pap. 1.75 (ISBN 0-505-51445-1, Pub. by Tower Bks). Dorchester Pub Co.
--Gunfight at Powder River. (Orig.). 1980. pap. text ed. 1.95 (ISBN 0-505-51585-7, Pub. by Tower Bks). Dorchester Pub Co.
--Gunfight at Powder River. 224p. 1984. pap. 2.25 (ISBN 0-8439-2140-4). Dorchester Pub Co.
--Justice at Iritara. 224p. (Orig.). 1982. pap. 2.25 (ISBN 0-505-51776-0, Pub. by Tower Bks). Dorchester Pub Co.
--Last Bridge to Victory. 320p. 1984. pap. 2.50 (ISBN 0-8217-1392-2). Zebra.
--The Last Outlaw. (Orig.). 1980. pap. write for info. (ISBN 0-505-51560-1, Pub. by Tower Bks). Dorchester Pub Co.
--The Last Outlaw. 208p. 1985. pap. 2.25 (ISBN 0-8439-2274-5, Leisure Bks). Dorchester Pub Co.
--Mission Incredible. 1979. pap. 1.25 (ISBN 0-505-51346-3, Pub. by Tower Bks). Dorchester Pub Co.
--Operation Bodenplatte. 288p. (Orig.). 1981. pap. 2.50 (ISBN 0-89083-710-4). Zebra.
--Operation Cannibal. 224p. (Orig.). 1982. pap. 2.50 (ISBN 0-8439-1088-7, Leisure Bks). Dorchester Pub Co.
--Operation Cartwheel: The Final Countdown to V-J Day. (World-at-War Ser.). 1982. pap. 2.95 (ISBN 0-89083-989-1). Zebra.
--Pacific Breakthrough. (Orig.). 1981. pap. 2.95 (ISBN 0-89083-814-3). Zebra.
--Pacific Hellfire. (World-at-War Ser.). 1983. pap. 3.25 (ISBN 0-8217-1179-2). Zebra.
--Pacific Seige. pap. 3.25 (ISBN 0-8217-1363-9). Zebra.
--Rogue Sergeant. 224p. 1982. pap. 2.50 (ISBN 0-505-51854-6, Pub. by Tower Bks). Dorchester Pub Co.
--Rogue Sergeant. 224p. 1983. pap. 2.50 (ISBN 0-8439-2016-5, Leisure Bks). Dorchester Pub Co.
--Rommel's Last Stand. 320p. 1984. pap. 3.25 (ISBN 0-8217-1415-5). Zebra.
--Target: Daimler-Benz. 1980. pap. 1.75 (ISBN 0-8439-0713-4, Leisure Bks). Dorchester Pub Co.
--Valor at Leyte. (Orig.). 1983. pap. 3.25 (ISBN 0-8217-1213-6). Zebra.
--Valor at Okinawa. (Orig.). 1981. pap. 2.95 (ISBN 0-89083-904-2). Zebra.
--Valor at Samar. (World at War Ser.: No. 26). (YA) 1981. pap. 2.75 (ISBN 0-89083-742-2). Zebra.
--Valor at Samar. (Orig.). 1983. pap. 2.75 (ISBN 0-8217-1226-8). Zebra.
--Valor in the Sky. 1985. pap. 3.50 (ISBN 0-8217-1578-X). Zebra.
Cortesi, Wendy W. see National Geographic Society.
Cortesini, Rafaello & Rapaport, Felix T., eds. Transplantation Today, Vol. V. (Transplantation Proceedings Reprint Ser.). 1256p. 1979. 91.50 (ISBN 0-8089-1210-0, 790908). Grune.
Cortes-Prieto, J. & De Paz, A. Campos. Research on Fertility & Sterility. (Illus.). 352p. 1981. text ed. 42.00 (ISBN 0-8391-1684-5). Univ Park.
Cortez, Carlos E., ed. United States Congress, Immigration Hearings. LC 80-7793. (Hispanics in the United States Ser.). 1981. Repr. of 1970 ed. lib. bdg. 23.00x (ISBN 0-405-13186-0). Ayer Co Pubs.
--United States Congress, Immigration 1976. LC 80-7794. (Hispanics in the United States Ser.). lib. bdg. 25.00x (ISBN 0-405-13187-9). Ayer Co Pubs.
--Unites States Congress, Western Hemisphere Immigration. LC 80-7795. (Hispanics in the United States Ser.). 1981. Repr. of 1976 ed. lib. bdg. 37.00x (ISBN 0-405-13188-7). Ayer Co Pubs.
Cortez, Edwin M. Contracts, RFP's & Other Procurement Documents for Library Automation. LC 82-48493. 1984. write for info. (ISBN 0-669-06158-1). Lexington Bks.
Cortez, Edwin M. & Kazlauskas, Edward J. Managing Information Systems & Technologies: A Basic Guide for Design, Selection, Evaluation & Use. 250p. 1986. pap. text ed. 35.00 (ISBN 0-918212-92-8). Neal-Schuman.
Cortez, Hernando see Cortes, Hernan.
Cortez, Jayne. Coagulations: New & Selected Poems. LC 83-24180. 96p. (Orig.). 1984. 14.95 (ISBN 0-938410-21-0); pap. 6.95 (ISBN 0-938410-20-2). Thunder's Mouth.
--Firespitter. (Illus.). 48p. (Orig.). 1982. pap. text ed. 4.00 (ISBN 0-9608062-5-3). Bola Pr.
--Mouth on Paper. 1977. 4.00 (ISBN 0-9608062-3-7). Bola Pr.
--Scarifications. 1973. 4.00 (ISBN 0-9608062-2-9). Bola Pr.
Cortez, Joseph J. Goodbye Cruel World: How Soon Can You Leave? LC 83-90330. (Illus.). 160p. (Orig.). 1983. pap. 7.95. HK Pub Co.
Cortez, Julio Garcia. El Santo (La Ocha) 3rd ed. LC 82-84401. (Illus.). 582p. (Orig., Span.). 1983. pap. 19.95 (ISBN 0-89729-322-3). Ediciones.
Corti, E. Reign of the House of Rothschild. 75.00 (ISBN 0-87968-171-3). Gordon Pr.
--Rise of the House of Rothschild. 75.00 (ISBN 0-87968-170-5). Gordon Pr.
Corti, Egon. Downfall of Three Dynasties. facs. ed. LC 79-124230. (Select Bibliographies Reprint Ser). (Illus.). 1934. 21.00 (ISBN 0-8369-5419-X). Ayer Co Pubs.
Corti, Egon C. Maximilian & Charlotte of Mexico, 2 vols. 1976. lib. bdg. 250.00 (ISBN 0-8490-0595-7). Gordon Pr.
--The Rise of the House of Rothschild. 430p. 1972. pap. 4.95 (ISBN 0-88279-112-5). Western Islands.
--The Rise of the House of Rothschild. Lunn, Brian & Lunn, Beatrix, trs. from Ger. 432p. Date not set. Repr. of 1928 ed. lib. bdg. 40.00 (ISBN 0-8482-7590-X). Norwood Edns.
Corti, G. & Frazer, F. The Nation's Oil: A Story of Control. 225p. 1983. 33.00x (ISBN 0-8448-1466-0). Crane-Russak Co.
Corti, M., jt. ed. see Degiorgio, V.
Corti, W. The Philosophy of William James. 1977. pap. 25.90x (ISBN 3-7873-0352-9). Adlers Foreign Bks.
Corti, Walter R. The Philosophy of George Herbert Mead. 1977. pap. 17.75x (ISBN 3-7873-0353-7). Adlers Foreign Bks.
Cortina. Cortina-Ace Basic French Dictionary. (Foreign Language Dictionary Ser.). 384p. (Fr.). 1983. pap. 3.50 (ISBN 0-441-04999-0). Ace Bks.
--Cortina-Ace Basic German Dictionary. (Foreign Language Dictionary Ser.). 384p. 1982. pap. 2.95 (ISBN 0-441-05002-6). Ace Bks.
--Cortina-Ace Basic Italian Dictionary. (Foreign Language Dictionary Ser.). 384p. 1982. pap. 2.95 (ISBN 0-441-05003-4). Ace Bks.
--Cortina-Ace Basic Spanish Dictionary. (Foreign Language Dictionary Ser.). 384p. (Span. & Eng.). 1982. pap. 2.95 (ISBN 0-441-05004-2). Ace Bks.
Cortina Company. Conversational Brazilian-Portuguese in 20 Lessons. 192p. 1980. pap. 3.95 (ISBN 0-06-463607-0, EH 607, EH). B&N NY.
--Conversational Japanese in Twenty Lessons. 256p. 1980. pap. 4.95 (ISBN 0-06-463606-2, EH 606, EH). B&N NY.
--Conversational Modern Greek in Twenty Lessons. 288p. 1980. pap. 4.95 (ISBN 0-06-463604-6, EH 604, EH). B&N NY.
--Conversational Russian in Twenty Lessons. 448p. 1980. pap. 5.95 (ISBN 0-06-463605-4, EH 605, EH). B&N NY.
--Ingles en Viente Lecciones. 384p. 1980. pap. 4.95 (ISBN 0-06-463608-9, EH 608, EH). B&N NY.
Cortina, F. A., ed. see Famous Artists School.
Cortina, F. A., jt. ed. see Reed, Walt.
Cortina, Frank M. Face to Face. LC 76-184745. 301p. 1972. 29.00x (ISBN 0-231-03635-3). Columbia U Pr.
--Stroke a Slain Warrior. LC 70-133197. 231p. 1970. 26.00x (ISBN 0-231-03481-4); pap. 13.00x (ISBN 0-231-08658-X). Columbia U Pr.
Cortina, Lynn E. Spanish-American Women Writers: A Bibliographical Research Checklist. LC 82-48281. 304p. 1983. lib. bdg. 39.00 (ISBN 0-8240-9247-3). Garland Pub.
Cortina, R. D., Co. Conversational French in Twenty Lessons. (EH 600 Ser.). pap. 4.95 (ISBN 0-06-463601-1, EH 601, EH). B&N NY.
--Conversational German in Twenty Lessons. (EH 600 Ser.). pap. 4.95 (ISBN 0-06-463602-X, EH 602, EH). B&N NY.
--Conversational Italian in Twenty Lessons. (EH 600 Ser.). pap. 4.95 (ISBN 0-06-463603-8, EH 603, EH). B&N NY.
--Conversational Spanish in Twenty Lessons. (EH 600 Ser.). pap. 4.95 (ISBN 0-06-463600-3, EH 600, EH). B&N NY.
Cortina, Rodolfo J. & Herrera, Felipe, eds. El Mutualista, Nineteen Forty-Seven to Nineteen Fifty: A Facsimile Edition of a Milwaukee Hispanic Newspaper. 104p. 10.00 (ISBN 0-317-11606-1). Arte Publico.
Cortinez, Carlos, ed. Simply a Man of Letters: Panel Discussion & Papers from the Proceedings of a Symposium on Jorge Luis Borges Held at the University of Maine at Orono. 353p. 1982. pap. 12.50 (ISBN 0-89101-051-3); 25.00x (ISBN 0-89101-052-1). U Maine Orono.
Cortinovis, Dan. Controlling Wastewater Treatment Processes. LC 84-61877. (Illus.). 150p. (Orig.). 1984. pap. 14.95 (ISBN 0-918967-00-7). Ridgeline Pr.
--Pass Your Wastewater Operator Exams. LC 85-60331. 60p. (Orig.). 1985. study manual 9.95 (ISBN 0-918967-01-5). Ridgeline Pr.
Cortissoz, Royal. American Artists. LC 70-121282. (BCL Ser. I). Repr. of 1923 ed. 12.50 (ISBN 0-404-01736-3). AMS Pr.
--American Artists. facs. ed. LC 74-128228. (Essay Index Reprint Ser). 1923. 19.00 (ISBN 0-8369-1825-8). Ayer Co Pubs.
--John Lafarge: A Memoir & A Study. LC 70-87508. (Library of American Art Ser). (Illus.). 1971. Repr. of 1911 ed. lib. bdg. 29.50 (ISBN 0-306-71405-1). Da Capo.
--Personalities in Art. facs. ed. LC 68-55844. (Essay Index Reprint Ser). 1925. 24.50 (ISBN 0-8369-0339-0). Ayer Co Pubs.
Cortland, Barbara. The Magnificent Marriage. 13.95 (ISBN 0-88411-247-0, Pub. by Aeonian Pr). Amereon Ltd.
Cortland, Philip Van see Van Cortlandt, Philip.
Cortland Publishing, Inc. Where the Good Men Are: A Look at the Most Interesting Single Men of the Twin Cities. (Illus.). 216p. (Orig.). 1983. pap. 10.95 (ISBN 0-914825-00-3). Cortland Pub.
Cortner, R. & Lytle, C. Modern Constitutional Law. LC 73-122280. 1971. text ed. 16.95 (ISBN 0-02-906740-5). Free Pr.
Cortner, Richard C. Apportionment Cases. 1972. pap. 2.95x (ISBN 0-393-00637-9, Norton Lib). Norton.
--The Apportionment Cases. LC 75-100408. pap. 74.00 (ISBN 0-317-20139-5, 2023168). Bks Demand UMI.
--The Bureaucracy in Court: Commentaries & Case Studies in Administrative Law. (Multidisciplinary Studies in Law & Jurisprudence). 234p. 1982. 25.00 (ISBN 0-8046-9299-8, 9299, Pub. by Kennikat). Assoc Faculty Pr.
--The Supreme Court & Civil Liberties Policy. LC 75-21071. 225p. 1976. pap. 9.95 (ISBN 0-87484-336-7). Mayfield Pub.
--The Supreme Court & the Second Bill of Rights: The Fourteenth Amendment & the Nationalization of Civil Liberties. 480p. 1981. 32.00x (ISBN 0-299-08390-X). U of Wis Pr.
Cortot, Alfred. French Piano Music. Andrews, Hilda, tr. from Fr. LC 77-4108. (Music Reprint, 1977 Ser.). 1977. Repr. of 1932 ed. 25.00 (ISBN 0-306-70896-5). Da Capo.
--In Search of Chopin. Clarke, Cyril & Clarke, Rena, trs. from Fr. LC 74-33504. (Illus.). 268p. 1975. Repr. of 1952 ed. lib. bdg. 21.75x (ISBN 0-8371-7971-8, COSCH). Greenwood.
Cortrada, John W. United States-Spanish Relations: Wolfram & World War II. 134p. 1971. 10.00 (ISBN 0-939738-11-2). Zubal Inc.
Cortright, Barbara. The Reach of Solitude: The Paintings of Ann Taylor. (Illus.). 1983. 25.00 (ISBN 0-8397-7073-1). Eriksson.
Cortright, David. International Soldiers' Movement. 23p. 1975. 0.50 (ISBN 0-686-43098-0). Recon Pubns.
Corts, Paul, jt. auth. see Kell, Carl.
Corty, Floyd L., jt. ed. see Bertrand, Alvin L.
Corum, Ann K. Easy Cooking: The Island Way. LC 81-19881. (Illus.). 120p. (Orig.). 1982. pap. 4.95 (ISBN 0-916630-24-2). Pr Pacifica.
--Ethnic Foods of Hawaii. LC 83-70358. (Illus.). 160p. 1983. pap. 7.95 (ISBN 0-935848-21-5). Bess Pr.
--Folk Wisdom from Hawaii: Or Don't Take Bananas on a Boat. (Illus.). 120p. 1985. pap. 5.95 (ISBN 0-935848-32-0). Bess Pr.
Corum, Claudia & Smith-Stark, Cedrik, eds. You Take the High Node & I'll Take the Low Node: Proceedings - Papers from the Comparative Syntax Festival. 422p. 1973. pap. 6.00 (ISBN 0-914203-03-7). Chicago Ling.
Corum, Claudia W. An Introduction to the Swazi (Siswati) Language. (African Language Texts Ser.). (Orig.). pap. text ed. 5.00 (ISBN 0-941934-01-2). Indiana Africa.
Corum, J. M., ed. see National Congress on Pressure Vessels & Piping (2nd: 1975: San Francisco.
Corum, Robert T., Jr. Other Worlds & Other Seas: Art & Vision in Saint-Amant's Nature Poetry. LC 78-73094. (French Forum Monographs: 13). (Illus.). 174p. (Orig.). 1979. pap. 12.50x (ISBN 0-917058-12-7). French Forum.
Corvalan-Vasquez, Oscar. Youth Employment & Training in Developing Countries: An Annotated Bibliography. International Labour Office Staff, ed. vii, 172p. (Orig.). 1984. pap. 10.00 (ISBN 92-2-103420-8). Intl Labour Office.
--Youth Employment & Training in Developing Countries: An Annotated Bibliography. 172p. (Orig.). 1984. pap. text ed. 10.00 (ISBN 92-2-103420-8, ILO287, ILO). Unipub.
Corvasse, Frances. Satire & Irony: A Jr. High-Intermediate Language Arts Unit. 1984. text ed. 4.00 (ISBN 0-89824-103-0); tchr's. manual 5.00 (ISBN 0-89824-102-2). Trillium Pr.
Corvilain, H. & Fuss, M., eds. Hormones & Calcium Metabolism. (Journal: HormoneResearch: Vol. 20, No. 1). 92p. 1984. pap. 16.75 (ISBN 3-8055-3888-X). S Karger.
Corvin, R. O. David & His Mighty Men. facs. ed. LC 74-136646. (Biography Index Reprint Ser.). 1950. 17.00 (ISBN 0-8369-8041-7). Ayer Co Pubs.

Corvinus, G. S. Das Carneval der Liebe. 450p. Repr. of 1712 ed. 45.00 (ISBN 0-384-09875-4). Johnson Repr.

Corvisier, Andre. Armies & Societies in Europe: 1494-1789. Siddall, Abigail T., tr. LC 78-62419. 224p. 1979. 15.00x (ISBN 0-253-12985-0). Ind U Pr.

Corvo, Baron. The Armed Hands & Other Stories & Pieces. 137p. 1974. text ed. 16.25x (ISBN 0-900821-13-2, Pub. by C Woolf U K). Humanities.

--Hadrian, the Seventh. 1977. pap. 5.95 (ISBN 0-486-22323-X). Dover.

Corvo, Frederich B. The Songs of Meleager: Made into English with Designs by Frederich Baron Corvo. LC 82-49103. (Degeneration & Regeneration Ser.). 150p. 1984. lib. bdg. 25.00 (ISBN 0-8240-5566-7). Garland Pub.

Corwen, Leonard. Job Hunter's Handbook: How to Sell Yourself & Get the Job You Really Want. LC 75-23578. 104p. 1966. pap. 1.75 (ISBN 0-668-03877-2). Arco.

--There's a Job for You In: Advertising, Commercial Art, Fashion, Films, Public Relations & Publicity, Publishing, Television & Radio, Travel & Tourism. LC 83-8349. (Illus.). 192p. (Orig.). 1983. pap. 8.95 (ISBN 0-8329-0273-X). New Century.

--Your Future in Publishing. LC 72-91800. (Careers in Depth Ser.). (Illus.). 128p. (gr. 7-12). 1973. PLB 8.97 (ISBN 0-8239-0274-9). Rosen Group.

--Your Job: Where to Find It---How to Get It. LC 80-22251. 256p. 1981. lib. bdg. 11.95 (ISBN 0-668-05129-9); pap. 6.95 (ISBN 0-668-05131-0). Arco.

--Your Resume: Key to a Better Job. LC 83-21402. 144p. (Orig.). 1984. pap. 4.95 (ISBN 0-668-05937-0). Arco.

Corwin & Szczarba. Calculus in Vector Spaces. (Pure & Applied Mathematics Ser.: Vol. 52). 1979. 95.00 (ISBN 0-8247-6832-9). Dekker.

--Multivariable Calculus. (Pure and Applied Mathematics Ser.: Vol. 64). 544p. 1982. 59.75 (ISBN 0-8247-6962-7). Dekker.

Corwin, Arthur F., ed. Immigrants & Immigrants: Perspectives on Mexican Labor Migration to the United States. LC 77-84756. (Contributions in Economics & Economic History: No. 17). (Illus.). 1978. lib. bdg. 29.95 (ISBN 0-8371-9848-8, CII/). Greenwood.

Corwin, B. R. A Trip to the Rockies. LC 78-39693. (Select Bibliographies Reprint Ser). 1972. Repr. of 1890 ed. 9.50 (ISBN 0-8369-9934-7). Ayer Co Pubs.

Corwin, Charles, et al. A Dictionary of Japanese & English Idiomatic Equivalents. LC 68-11818. 302p. (Japanese & Eng.). 1980. 18.75 (ISBN 0-87011-111-6). Kodansha.

Corwin, Charles H. Basic Chemistry: Laboratory Experiments. 4th ed. (Illus.). 272p. 1985. lab manual 19.95 (ISBN 0-13-057845-2). P-H.

Corwin, Consuelo, tr. see Fuentes, Norberto.

Corwin, E. S. French Policy & the American Alliance of 1778. 11.75 (ISBN 0-8446-0559-X). Peter Smith.

--Supplement to Edward S. Corwin's Constitution & What It Means Todays. Chase, H. & Ducat, C., eds. 1981. pap. 3.50x (ISBN 0-691-02761-7). Princeton U Pr.

Corwin, E. T., ed. Ecclesiastical Records of the State of New York, 7 Vols. LC 74-19602. Repr. of 1916 ed. Set. 440.00 (ISBN 0-404-12305-8); 63.00 ea.; Vol. 1. (ISBN 0-404-12306-6); Vol. 2. (ISBN 0-404-12307-4); Vol. 3. (ISBN 0-404-12308-2); Vol. 4. (ISBN 0-404-12309-0); Vol. 5. (ISBN 0-404-12310-4); Vol. 6. (ISBN 0-404-12311-2); Vol. 7. (ISBN 0-404-12312-0). AMS Pr.

Corwin, Edward. American Constitutional History: Essays. Mason & Garvey, eds. 11.25 (ISBN 0-8446-0558-1). Peter Smith.

Corwin, Edward S. Commerce Power Versus States Rights. 1959. 11.75 (ISBN 0-8446-1130-1). Peter Smith.

--Constitution & World Organization. facs. ed. LC 73-117869. (Select Bibliographies Reprint Ser). 1944. 13.00 (ISBN 0-8369-5322-3). Ayer Co Pubs.

--Constitutional Revolution, Ltd. LC 77-805. ix, 121p. 1977. Repr. of 1941 ed. lib. bdg. 15.00x (ISBN 0-8371-9498-9, COCO). Greenwood.

--Court Over Constitution: A Study of Judicial As an Instrument of Popular Government. 11.75 (ISBN 0-8446-1129-8). Peter Smith.

--Doctrine of Judicial Review. 11.75 (ISBN 0-8446-1128-X). Peter Smith.

--Edward S. Corwin's, Constitution & What It Means Today. rev. 14th ed. Chase, Harold W. & Ducat, Craig R., eds. LC 78-53809. 374p. 1979. 45.00 (ISBN 0-691-09240-0); pap. 15.50 (ISBN 0-691-02758-7). Princeton U Pr.

--French Policy & the American Alliance of 1778. LC 77-121599. (Research & Source Works Ser: No. 476). 1970. Repr. of 1916 ed. lib. bdg. 21.00 (ISBN 0-8337-0687-X). B Franklin.

--The Higher Law Background of American Constitutional Law. 101p. 1955. pap. 4.95x (ISBN 0-8014-9012-X, CP12). Cornell U Pr.

--John Marshall & the Constitution. 1919. 8.50x (ISBN 0-686-83597-2). Elliots Bks.

--Liberty Against Government: The Rise, Flowering, & Decline of a Famous Judicial Concept. LC 77-4090. xiii, 210p. 1978. Repr. of 1948 ed. lib. bdg. 32.50x (ISBN 0-8371-9589-6, COLAG). Greenwood.

--National Supremacy: Treaty Power Vs. State Power. 1965. 11.75 (ISBN 0-8446-1127-1). Peter Smith.

--The President: Office & Powers. 5th, rev. ed. Bland, Randall W., et al, eds. 600p. 1984. 45.00x (ISBN 0-8147-1390-4); pap. 22.50x (ISBN 0-8147-1391-2). NYU Pr.

--Presidential Power & the Constitution: Essays. Loss, Richard, ed. LC 75-38000. 185p. 1976. 29.95x (ISBN 0-8014-0982-9). Cornell U Pr.

--The President's Control of Foreign Relations. (Political Science Ser.). 1970. Repr. of 1917 ed. 19.00 (ISBN 0-384-09880-0, P540). Johnson Repr.

--Total War & the Constitution. facs. ed. LC 70-127590. (Essay Index Reprint Ser). 1947. 18.00 (ISBN 0-8369-1796-0). Ayer Co Pubs.

--Twilight of the Supreme Court: A History of Our Constitutional Theory. xxvii, 237p. 1970. Repr. of 1934 ed. 17.50 (ISBN 0-208-00839-X, Archon). Shoe String.

Corwin, Edward S see Johnson, Allen & Nevins, Allan.

Corwin, Harold E., ed. see Horacek, Robert G.

Corwin, Harold E., ed. see Ortner, Herbert E.

Corwin, Harold G., et al. Southern Galaxy Catalogue: A Catalogue of 5481 Galaxies South of Declination-17 Degress Found on 1.2m U. K. Schmidt IIIa-J Plates. LC 85-50556. (The University of Texas Monographs in Astronomy: No. 4). 342p. (Orig.). 1985. pap. write for info. (ISBN 0-9603796-3-0). U of Tex Dept Astron.

Corwin, Judith. Easy-to-Make Applique Quilts for Children: Instructions & Full-Size Templates. (Illus.). 48p. pap. 3.50 (ISBN 0-486-24293-5). Dover.

Corwin, Judith H. Christmas Fun. LC 82-60648. (The Holiday Library). (Illus.). 64p. (gr. 3 up). 1982. lib. bdg. 9.29 (ISBN 0-671-45944-9); pap. 5.95 (ISBN 0-671-49583-6). Messner.

--Easter Fun. LC 84-9122. (Messner Holiday Library). (Illus.). 64p. (gr. 7 up). 1984. PLB 9.29 (ISBN 0-671-50798-2); pap. 5.95 (ISBN 0-671-53108-5). Messner.

--Halloween Fun. LC 83-8289. (Holiday Library). 64p. (gr. 3-6). 1983. lib. bdg. 9.29 (ISBN 0-671-49421-X); pap. 5.95 (ISBN 0-671-49756-1). Messner.

--Thanksgiving Fun. LC 83-25062. (Holiday Library). 64p. (gr. 3-6). 1984. PLB 9.29g (ISBN 0-671-49422-8); pap. 5.95 (ISBN 0-671-50849-0). Messner.

--Valentine Fun. LC 82-6047. (Holiday Library). (Illus.). 64p. (gr. 4 up). 1982. PLB 9.29 (ISBN 0-671-45945-7); pap. 5.95 (ISBN 0-671-49755-3). Messner.

Corwin, Judith H., illus. Cookie Fun. (Messner Holiday Library). (Illus.). 64p. (gr. 4 up). 1985. 4.95 (ISBN 0-671-55019-5). Messner.

--Patriotic Fun. (Illus.). 64p. (gr. 3 up). 1985. pap. 4.95 (ISBN 0-671-55378-X). Messner.

Corwin, Margaret & Hoy, Helen. Waterloo: An Actorial History. (Illus.). 200p. 1983. 22.95 (ISBN 0-940286-02-5). Quest Pub IL.

Corwin, Norman. Greater Than the Bomb. (Santa Susana Press Ser.). 1981. 38.00 (ISBN 0-937048-31-3). CSUN.

--Holes in a Stained Glass Window. 1978. 10.00 (ISBN 0-8184-0255-5). Lyle Stuart.

--Trivializing America. 256p. 1983. 14.95 (ISBN 0-8184-0341-1). Lyle Stuart.

Corwin, Phillip. The Way Things Are. 96p. (Orig.). 1985. pap. 5.95 (ISBN 0-933515-06-5). Exile Pr.

Corwin, R. D. Racial Minorities in Banking: New Workers in the Banking Industry. 1971. pap. 5.95x (ISBN 0-8084-0042-8). New Coll U Pr.

Corwin, Ronald G. Education in Crisis: A Sociological Analysis of Schools & Universities in Transition. LC 73-12844. pap. 98.00 (ISBN 0-317-09797-0, 2055111). Bks Demand UMI.

--The Entrepreneurial Bureaucracy: Biographies of Two Federal Programs in Education. LC 82-81210. (Contemporary Studies in Sociology: Vol. 1). 1983. 42.50 (ISBN 0-89232-314-0). JAI Pr.

--Militant Professionalism: A Study of Organizational Conflict in High Schools. LC 75-98400. 1970. text ed. 22.50x (ISBN 0-89197-303-6); pap. text ed. 7.95x (ISBN 0-89197-304-4). Irvington.

--Reform & Organizational Survival. LC 72-10367. 496p. 1973. 27.50 (ISBN 0-471-17519-6, Pub. by Wiley). Krieger.

Corwin, Ronald G., ed. Research in the Sociology of Education & Socialization, Vol. 2. 316p. 1980. 42.50 (ISBN 0-89232-158-X). Jai Pr.

--Research in the Sociology of Education & Socialization, Vol. 3. 325p. 1981. 42.50 (ISBN 0-89232-187-3). Jai Pr.

Corwin, Sheila. Marriage & the Family & Child-Rearing Practices. Zak, Therese A., ed. (Lifeworks Ser.). (Illus.). 160p. 1981. text ed. 7.88 (ISBN 0-07-013198-8). McGraw.

Corwin, Stanley. Acme's Plaintiff's Proof of a Prima Facie Case: 1969-1981. LC 81-10261. write for info. Callaghan.

--Acme's Proof of a Prima Facie Defense: 1969-1981. LC 81-10260. 50.00; Suppl., 1982. 18.00; Suppl., 1983. 26.50. Callaghan.

--Corporation Practice under the BCL: 1965, 1 vol. 85.00. Callaghan.

Corwin, Stanley J. How to Become a Bestselling Author. LC 84-5285. (Illus.). 252p. 1984. 14.95 (ISBN 0-89879-129-4). Writers Digest.

Corwin, Steven D. Crystals & Cobwebs & Jail Bird Blues. Cohen, Steven, ed. LC 85-50213. (Illus.). 70p. (Orig.). 1985. pap. 5.95 (ISBN 0-9614516-0-2). Skokie Valley Pr.

Corwin, T. K., et al. International Technology for the Nonferrous Smelting Industry. LC 82-3434. (Chemical Tech. Rev. 205, Pollution Tech Rev. 90). (Illus.). 413p. 1982. 36.00 (ISBN 0-8155-0894-8). Noyes.

Cory, Beverly. Birdseye Mastery Masters, 4 bks. Incl. Birdseye View Phonics & Spelling (ISBN 0-8224-0703-5); Birdseye View Word Structure (ISBN 0-8224-0704-3); Birdseye View Word Meaning (ISBN 0-8224-0705-1); Birdseye View Grammar & Usage (ISBN 0-8224-0706-X). 1980. 5.95 ea.; 22 spirit duplicating masters per book incl.; comp. set 19.80 (ISBN 0-8224-0707-8). Pitman Learning.

--Birdseye View of Language Arts: Worksheets in Spelling & Phonics, Word Structure, Word Meaning, Grammar & Usage. (Makemaster Bk.). (gr. 4-6). 1977. pap. 15.95 (ISBN 0-8224-0701-9). Pitman Learning.

--Grammar & Usage. (Learning Workbooks Language Arts). (gr. 4-6). pap. 1.95 (ISBN 0-8224-4179-9). Pitman Learning.

--Phonics & Spelling. (Learning Workbooks Language Arts). (gr. 4-6). pap. 1.95 (ISBN 0-8224-4176-4). Pitman Learning.

--Word Meaning. (Learning Workbooks Language Arts). (gr. 4-6). pap. 1.95 (ISBN 0-8224-4178-0). Pitman Learning.

--Word Structure. (Learning Workbooks Language Arts). (gr. 4-6). pap. 1.95 (ISBN 0-8224-4177-2). Pitman Learning.

Cory, Carol & Lintner, Jay. Peace Futuring. (Orig.). 1983. pap. 1.95 leader's bk. (ISBN 0-8298-0677-6); pap. 1.95 student's bk. (ISBN 0-8298-0678-4). Pilgrim NY.

Cory, Charles B. Hunting & Fishing in Florida, Including a Key to the Water Birds. LC 75-125734. (American Environmental Studies). 1970. Repr. of 1896 ed. 19.00 (ISBN 0-405-02657-9). Ayer Co Pubs.

Cory, Daniel, ed. see Santayana, George.

Cory, David M. Faustus Socinus. LC 83-45606. Date not set. Repr. of 1932 ed. 28.50 (ISBN 0-404-19874-0). AMS Pr.

Cory, Desmond. Dead Fall. LC 65-22137. (British Mystery Ser.). 175p. 1984. pap. 2.95 (ISBN 0-8027-3062-0). Walker & Co.

--The Night Hawk. 188p. 1983. pap. 2.95 (ISBN 0-8027-3024-8). Walker & Co.

--Timelock. LC 67-23099. (British Mystery Ser.). 175p. 1984. pap. 2.95 (ISBN 0-8027-3052-3). Walker & Co.

--Undertow. (British Mysteries Ser.). 1983. pap. 2.95 (ISBN 0-8027-3044-2). Walker & Co.

Cory, Donald W. The Homosexual in America: A Subjective Approach. LC 75-12310. (Homosexuality). 1975. Repr. of 1951 ed. 20.00x (ISBN 0-405-07365-8). Ayer Co Pubs.

Cory, George. Head-on with Hurricane Camille. LC 79-21323. (Quest, Adventure, Survival Ser.). (Illus.). (gr. 4-8). 1980. PLB 14.25 (ISBN 0-8172-1565-4). Raintree Pubs.

--Head-On with Hurricane Camille. LC 79-21323. (Quest, Adventure, Survival Ser.). (Illus.). 46p. (gr. 4-9). 1982. pap. 9.27 (ISBN 0-8172-2060-7). Raintree Pubs.

Cory, H. & Hartnoll, M. Customary Law of the Haya Tribe, Tanganyika Territory. 362p. 1971. Repr. of 1945 ed. 30.00x (ISBN 0-7146-2476-4, F Cass Co). Biblio Dist.

Cory, H. M. Compulsory Arbitration of International Disputes. Repr. of 1932 ed. 22.00 (ISBN 0-527-19800-5). Kraus Repr.

Cory, Hans. Customary Law of the Haya Tribe, Tanganyika Territory. LC 75-111572. (Illus.). 299p. Repr. of 1945 ed. cancelled (ISBN 0-8371-4597-X, CLH&, Pub. by Negro U Pr). Greenwood.

--Sukuma Law & Customs. LC 70-106831. (Illus.). 194p. Repr. of 1953 ed. 19.75x (ISBN 0-8371-3453-6, CSL&, Pub. by Negro U Pr). Greenwood.

Cory, Herbert E. Critics of Edmund Spenser. LC 65-15901. (Studies in Spenser, No. 26). 1969. Repr. of 1911 ed. lib. bdg. 49.95x (ISBN 0-8383-0532-6). Haskell.

--The Intellectuals & the Wage Works: A Study in Educational Psychoanalysis. 273p. 1982. Repr. of 1919 ed. lib. bdg. 50.00 (ISBN 0-89987-135-6). Darby Bks.

Cory, Isaac P. Ancient Fragments. enl. ed. LC 74-78000. (Secret Doctrine Reference Ser.). 361p. 1974. Repr. of 1832 ed. 20.00 (ISBN 0-913510-11-4). Wizards.

Cory, Jean-Jacques. Lists. 64p. (Orig.). 1974. pap. 1.50 (ISBN 0-915066-06-8); signed & lettered 10.00 (ISBN 0-685-49923-5). Assembling Pr.

Cory, Lloyd, compiled by. Quotable Quotations. 400p. 1985. pap. 14.95 (ISBN 0-88207-823-2). Victor Bks.

Cory, Tory. The Living Ghost. 1985. 5.95 (ISBN 0-8062-2470-3). Carlton.

Cory, William J. Lucretilis: Pleasant Hill of Horace (William Johnson Cory's Latin Verses) Wilson, Don D., tr. from Lat. 64p. (Orig.). 1982. pap. 6.00 (ISBN 0-9607756-6-8). Singular Speech Pr.

Coryate, Thomas. T. Coryate Traveller for the English Wits: Greetings from the Court of the Great Mogul. LC 68-54628. (English Experience Ser.: No. 30). 56p. 1968. Repr. of 1616 ed. 9.50 (ISBN 90-221-0030-8). Walter J Johnson.

Coryell, Helen M., ed. Progressive Sychronized Swimming Program. 80p. 5.95x (ISBN 0-88035-057-1, 461). YMCA USA.

--Progressive Synchronized Swimming Program. 80p. 1972. pap. text ed. 5.95x (ISBN 0-88035-057-1). Human Kinetics.

Coryell, Jacie. Who Get's Amy's Room? 1985. price not set; pap. price not set. Loiry Pubs Hse.

Coryell, Nancy G. An Evaluation of Extensive & Intensive Teaching of Literature. LC 75-176671. (Columbia University. Teachers College. Contributions to Education Ser.: No. 275). Repr. of 1927 ed. 22.50 (ISBN 0-404-55275-7). AMS Pr.

Cosand, Joseph P. Perspective: Community Colleges in the Nineteen Eighties. (Horizons Issues Monograph Ser.). 60p. (Orig.). pap. 5.00 (ISBN 0-87117-049-3). Am Assn Comm Jr Coll.

Cosby, Michael. Sex in the Bible: An Introduction to What the Scriptures Teach Us about Sexuality. LC 83-16090. 182p. 1984. 12.95 (ISBN 0-13-807280-9); pap. 5.95 (ISBN 0-13-807272-8). P-H.

Coscarelli, Diego, ed. Barron's Regents Exams & Answers: Italian. rev. ed. LC 75-39381. 250p. (gr. 10-12). 1982. pap. text ed. 4.50 (ISBN 0-8120-3149-0). Barron.

Coscarelli, Kate. Fame & Fortune. 336p. 1984. 14.95 (ISBN 0-312-28020-3). St Martin.

--Perfect Order. 352p. 1985. 15.95 (ISBN 0-453-00495-4). NAL.

Coscas, Gabriel J., jt. ed. see Regenbogen, Lucian S.

Coscia, Donald. Computer Applications for Applied Math. 1985. pap. text ed. price not set. (ISBN 0-673-18154-5). Scott F.

Coscia, Joseph F. Reincarnation of Bridgett. 139p. 1981. 6.00 (ISBN 0-682-49699-5). Exposition Pr FL.

Coscia, Louis W., pseud. The Promised One. 192p. 1983. 10.95. Todd & Honeywell.

Cosden, Rose. Help Your Child up the Ladder. Reed, R., ed. LC 81-83630. 100p. 1982. pap. 9.95 (ISBN 0-88247-608-4). R & E Pubs.

Cose, Ellis. Decentralizing Energy Decision: The Rebirth of Community Power. LC 83-14686. 135p. 1983. softcover 17.50x (ISBN 0-86531-801-8). Westview.

--Energy & the Urban Crisis. LC 78-19560. 67p. (Orig.). 1978. pap. 4.95 (ISBN 0-941410-08-0). Jt Ctr Pol Studies.

Cose, Ellis, ed. Energy & Equity: Some Social Concerns. LC 79-84291. 94p. (Orig.). 1979. pap. 8.50 (ISBN 0-941410-09-9). Jt Ctr Pol Studies.

Cose, Elsa T. Introduction to Silk & Metal Thread Embroidery. rev. ed. (Illus.). 40p. 1984. pap. 7.95 (ISBN 0-9614004-0-4). Embroidery.

Cosell, Hilary. Woman on a Seesaw: The Ups & Downs of Making It. 208p. 1985. 14.95 (ISBN 0-399-13034-9, Putnam). Putnam Pub Group.

Cosell, Howard & Bonventure, Peter. I Never Played the Game. 1985. 18.95 (ISBN 0-688-04481-6). Morrow.

Cosens, D. J. & Vince-Prue, D., eds. The Biology of Photoreception. LC 82-22032. (Society for Experimental Biology Symposia Ser.: No. 36). 500p. 1984. 84.50 (ISBN 0-521-25152-4). Cambridge U Pr.

Cosens, D. J., jt. ed. see Laverack, M. S.

Cosentino, Andrew J. The Paintings of Charles Bird King. LC 77-608258. (Illus.). 214p. 1978. 35.00 (ISBN 0-87474-336-2). Smithsonian.

Cosentino, Andrew J. & Glassie, Henry H. The Capital Image: Painters in Washington, 1800-1915. LC 83-600241. (Illus.). 280p. 1983. 39.95 (ISBN 0-87474-338-9); pap. 22.50 (ISBN 0-87474-337-0). Smithsonian.

Cosentino, Christine, jt. ed. see Gerber, Margy.

Cosentino, Donald J. Defiant Maids & Stubborn Farmers: Tradition & Invention in Mende Story Performance. LC 81-15517. (Studies in Oral & Literate Culture: No. 4). (Illus.). 260p. 1982. 37.50 (ISBN 0-521-24197-9). Cambridge U Pr.

Cosentino, Frank J. The Boehm Journey to Egypt, Land of Tutankhamun. (The Boehm Journeys). (Illus.). 1978. 9.50 (ISBN 0-918096-02-2). E M Boehm.

Cosentino, John, ed. Computer Graphics Marketplace 1983-84. 2nd ed. 112p. 1983. pap. 35.00x (ISBN 0-89774-086-6). Oryx Pr.

Cosentino, Rodolfo. Atlas of Anatomy & Surgical Approaches in Orthopaedic Surgery, Vol. 2: Lower Extremity. (Illus.). 276p. 1973. pap. 24.50x spiral (ISBN 0-398-00350-5). C C Thomas.

Cosenza, Mario E., compiled by. Biographical & Bibliographical Dictionary of the Italian Humanists & of the World of Classical Scholarship in Italy, 1300-1800, 5 Vols. 1962. Set. 495.00 (ISBN 0-8161-0626-6, Hall Library); Vol. 6. suppl. (1967) 110.00 (ISBN 0-8161-0765-3). G K Hall.

Cosenza, Mario E., ed. Biographical & Bibliographical Dictionary of the Italian Printers & of Foreign Printers in Italy from the Introduction of the Art of Printing into Italy to 1800. 1968. lib. bdg. 100.00 (ISBN 0-8161-0766-1, Hall Library). G K Hall.

Cosenza, Mario E., compiled by. Checklist of the Non-Italian Humanists, 1300-1800. 1969. lib. bdg. 78.00 (ISBN 0-8161-0839-0, Hall Library). G K Hall.

Cosenza, Mario E., tr. see Pais, Ettore.

Cosenza, Robert, jt. auth. see Davis, Duane.

Coser, Lewis, jt. auth. see Howe, Irving.

Coser, Lewis, tr. see Danns, George.

Coser, Lewis A. Functions of Social Conflict. LC 56-6874. 1964. pap. text ed. 11.95 (ISBN 0-02-906810-X). Free Pr.

--Greedy Institutions. LC 73-10571. 1974. 12.95 (ISBN 0-02-906750-2). Free Pr.

--Masters of Sociological Thought: Ideas in Historical & Social Context. 2nd ed. (Illus.). 611p. 1977. text ed. 24.95 (ISBN 0-15-555130-2, HC). HarBraceJ.

--Men of Ideas. LC 65-10957. 1970. pap. 3.45 (ISBN 0-02-906770-7). Free Pr.

--The Pleasures of Sociology. (Orig.). 1980. pap. 4.50 (ISBN 0-451-62264-2, ME2264, Ment). NAL.

--Refugee Scholars in America: Their Impact & Their Experiences. LC 84-40193. 384p. 1984. 25.00x (ISBN 0-300-03193-9). Yale U Pr.

--Sociology Through Literature. 2nd ed. 544p. 1972. pap. text ed. 24.95 (ISBN 0-13-821538-3). P-H.

Coser, Lewis A. & Rosenberg, Bernard. Sociological Theory. 5th ed. 1982. text ed. write for info. (ISBN 0-02-325220-0). Macmillan.

Coser, Lewis A. & Larsen, Otto N., eds. The Uses of Controversy in Sociology. LC 76-7177. 1976. 17.95 (ISBN 0-02-906830-4). Free Pr.

Coser, Lewis A. & Powell, Walter W., eds. Perennial Works in Sociology, 34 books. (Illus.). 1979. lib. bdg. 1064.00xset (ISBN 0-405-12081-8). Ayer Co Pubs.

Coser, Lewis A., ed. see Abegglen, James C.

Coser, Lewis A., ed. see Aron, Raymond.

Coser, Lewis A., ed. see Bernard, Luther L.

Coser, Lewis A., ed. see Chapin, F. Stuart.

Coser, Lewis A., ed. see Coleman, James S., et al.

Coser, Lewis A., ed. see DeGre, Gerard.

Coser, Lewis A., ed. see Granick, David.

Coser, Lewis A., ed. see Hughes, Everett C.

Coser, Lewis A., ed. see Keller, Suzanne.

Coser, Lewis A., ed. see Lazarsfeld, Paul F. & Kendall, Patricia L.

Coser, Lewis A., ed. see Levy-Bruhl, Lucien.

Coser, Lewis A., ed. see Pareto, Vilfredo.

Coser, Lewis A., ed. see Powdermaker, Hortense.

Coser, Lewis A., ed. see President's Research Committee on Social Trends.

Coser, Lewis A., ed. see Rainwater, Lee, et al.

Coser, Lewis A., ed. see Riesman, David & Glazer, Nathan.

Coser, Lewis A., ed. see Rogoff, Natalie.

Coser, Lewis A., ed. see Rosenberg, Bernard & Fliegel, Norris.

Coser, Lewis A., ed. see Roth, Guenther.

Coser, Lewis A., ed. see Selznick, Philip.

Coser, Lewis A., ed. see Simmel, Georg.

Coser, Lewis A., ed. see Sorokin, Pitirim A.

Coser, Lewis A., ed. see Sumner, William G.

Coser, Lewis A., ed. see Svalastoga, Kaare.

Coser, Lewis A., ed. see Tiryakian, Edward A.

Coser, Lewis A., ed. see Walker, Charles R. & Guest, Robert H.

Coser, Lewis A., ed. see Warner, W. Lloyd & Abegglen, James C.

Coser, Lewis A., ed. see Wood, Robert C.

Coser, Lewis A., et al. Books: The Culture & Commerce of Publishing. LC 81-66100. 350p. 1982. 19.00 (ISBN 0-465-00745-7). Basic.

--Books: The Culture & Commerce of Publishing. xiv, 411p. 1985. pap. 12.50 (ISBN 0-226-11593-3). U of Chicago Pr.

--Introduction to Sociology. 540p. 1983. 25.95 (ISBN 0-15-545910-4, HC); study guide 9.95 (ISBN 0-15-545912-0); instr's manual avail. (ISBN 0-15-545911-2); test file avail. (ISBN 0-15-545913-9). HarBraceJ.

Coser, Rose L. The Family: Its Structure & Functions. 2nd ed. 600p. 1974. pap. text ed. 15.95 (ISBN 0-312-28140-4). St Martin.

--Training in Ambiguity: Learning Through Doing in a Mental Hospital. LC 78-54109. (Illus.). 1979. 18.00 (ISBN 0-02-906580-1). Free Pr.

Coser, Rose L., jt. ed. see Epstein, Cynthia F.

Coseriu, Eugenio & Geckeler, Horst. Trends in Structural Semantics. (Tuebinger Beitraege Zur Linguistik: No. 58). 86p. (Orig.). 1981. pap. 14.00x (ISBN 3-87808-158-8). Benjamins North Am.

Cos-Gayon, C. S. & McDermott, A., eds. Aspects of Human Genetics with Special Reference to X-Linked Disorders. (Illus.). x, 158p. 1984. 41.75 (ISBN 3-8055-3756-5). S Karger.

Cosgrave, Art. Late Medieval Ireland, 1370-1541. (Helicon History of Ireland Ser.: Vol. 3). 134p. 1981. 22.95 (ISBN 0-904916-12-X, Pub. by Educ Co Ireland); pap. 9.95 (ISBN 0-318-03234-1, Pub. by Educ Co Ireland). Irish Bk Ctr.

Cosgrave, D. North Dublin: City & County. 138p. 1977. Repr. of 1909 ed. 6.00x (ISBN 0-906127-02-5, Pub. by Irish Academic Pr Ireland). Biblio Dist.

Cosgrave, Gerald P. Let's Think About You. 1978. pap. text ed. 4.25x (ISBN 0-8077-8064-2, Pub. by Guid Ctr U of Toronto). Tchrs Coll.

--Set Your Course. 1978. pap. text ed. 4.00x (ISBN 0-8077-8063-4, Pub. by Guid Ctr U of Toronto). Tchrs Coll.

Cosgrave, Jessica G. The Psychology of Youth. 234p. 1981. Repr. of 1929 ed. lib. bdg. 20.00 (ISBN 0-89760-121-1). Telegraph Bks.

Cosgriff, Carolyn, jt. auth. see Cosgriff, John.

Cosgriff, James H. Atlas of Diagnostic & Therapeutic Procedures for Emergency Personnel. LC 78-2943. 1978. text ed. 32.50i (ISBN 0-397-54213-5). Har-Row.

Cosgriff, James H., Jr. & Anderson, Diann L. The Practice of Emergency Care. 2nd ed. (Illus.). 652p. 1984. text ed. 34.50 (ISBN 0-397-54357-3, 64-02994, Lippincott Nursing). Lippincott.

Cosgriff, John & Cosgriff, Carolyn. Climb It Right: A High-Tech Genealogy Primer. LC 84-62512. 1985. 14.95 (ISBN 0-917255-01-1); pap. 8.95 preliminary, ltd. ed. (ISBN 0-917255-00-3). Progenesys Pr.

Cosgrove. In Search of the Saveopotomas. (Serendipity Bks.). (Illus.). 32p. (gr. k-4). PLB 8.95 (ISBN 0-317-31022-4). Creative Ed.

--Leo the Lop (Tail Three) (Serendipity Bks.). (Illus.). 32p. (gr. k-4). PLB 8.95 (ISBN 0-317-31019-4). Creative Ed.

--Snaffles. (Serendipity Bks.). (Illus.). 32p. (gr. k-4). PLB 8.95 (ISBN 0-317-31024-0). Creative Ed.

Cosgrove, Art & McGuire, J. I., eds. Parliament & Community. 248p. 1984. 27.00x (ISBN 0-904651-93-2, Pub. by Salem Acad). Merrimack Pub Cir.

Cosgrove, Brian. Wordsworth & the Poetry of Self-Sufficiency: A Study of the Poetic Development, 1796-1814. (Salburg Romantic Reassessment Ser.: No. 93). 327p. 1982. pap. text ed. 25.50x (ISBN 0-391-02848-0, Pub. by Salzburg Austria). Humanities.

Cosgrove, C. B., jt. auth. see Cosgrove, Harriet S.

Cosgrove, Carol A. & Twitchett, Kenneth J. New International Actors: The United Nations & the European Economic Community. LC 73-111412. 1970. 20.00 (ISBN 0-312-56805-3). St Martin.

Cosgrove, Cornelius B. Caves of the Upper Gila & Hueco Areas in New Mexico & Texas. (HU PMP Ser.). 1947. 37.00 (ISBN 0-527-01261-0). Kraus Repr.

Cosgrove, D. J. Inositol Phosphates: Their Chemistry, Biochemistry & Physiology. (Studies in Organic Chemistry: Vol. 4). 192p. 1980. 49.00 (ISBN 0-444-41874-1). Elsevier.

Cosgrove, David O. & McCready, V. Ralph. Ultrasound Imaging: Liver, Spleen, Pancreas. LC 82-1908. 368p. 1982. 75.00x (ISBN 0-471-10068-4, Pub. by Wiley Med). Wiley.

Cosgrove, Denis E. Social Formation & Symbolic Landscape. LC 84-21629. (Illus.). 304p. 1985. 28.50x (ISBN 0-389-20540-0, 08102). B&N Imports.

Cosgrove, Ed, jt. auth. see Cosgrove, Irene.

Cosgrove, Frances. Scenes for Student Actors, 6 Vols. 5.00 ea.; Vol. 1. (ISBN 0-573-69025-1); Vol. 2. (ISBN 0-573-69026-X); Vol. 3. (ISBN 0-573-69027-8); Vol. 4. (ISBN 0-573-69028-6); Vol. 5. (ISBN 0-573-69029-4); Vol. 6. (ISBN 0-573-69030-8). French.

Cosgrove, Francis M. Essentials of Discipleship. LC 79-93015. 192p. 1980. pap. 5.95 (ISBN 0-89109-442-3). NavPress.

--Essentials of New Life. LC 78-54949. (Illus.). 180p. (Orig.). 1978. pap. 4.95 (ISBN 0-89109-427-X, 14274). NavPress.

Cosgrove, Harriet S. & Cosgrove, C. B. Swarts Ruin: A Typical Mimbres Site in Southwestern New Mexico. (HU PMP Ser.). 1932. 54.00 (ISBN 0-527-01234-3). Kraus Repr.

Cosgrove, Irene & Cosgrove, Ed. My Recipes Are for the Birds. LC 76-23757. 62p. 1976. pap. 4.95 (ISBN 0-385-12634-4). Doubleday.

Cosgrove, J. J. History of Sanitation. 1977. lib. bdg. 59.95 (ISBN 0-8490-1985-0). Gordon Pr.

Cosgrove, John, ed. see Wilson, Gilbert.

Cosgrove, Margaret. Its Snowing! LC 80-14254. (A Skylight Bk.). (Illus.). 48p. (gr. 2-5). 1980. PLB 7.95 (ISBN 0-396-07851-6). Dodd.

Cosgrove, Mark & Mallory, James, Jr. Salud Mental: Un Enfoque Cristiano. Vargas, Wesley, tr. from Eng. (Curriculo de la Universidad Cristiana Libre Ser.). 88p. 1982. pap. text ed. 2.75 (ISBN 0-89922-195-5). Edit Caribe.

Cosgrove, Mark P. La Esencia de la Naturaleza Humana. Vargas, Carlos A., tr. from Eng. (Curriculo de la Universidad Cristiana Libre Ser.). 80p. 1982. pap. text ed. 2.75 (ISBN 0-89922-191-2). Edit Caribe.

--The Essence of Human Nature. 1977. pap. 2.95 (ISBN 0-310-35711-X). Zondervan.

Cosgrove, Mark P. & Mallory, James D., Jr. Mental Health: A Christian Approach. 1977. pap. 4.95 (ISBN 0-310-35721-7). Zondervan.

Cosgrove, Patrick & Hussar, Lawrence. Abuse This Word. (Illus.). 1980. pap. 3.95 (ISBN 0-380-76117-3, 76117-3). Avon.

Cosgrove, R., jt. auth. see Stedman, Robert E.

Cosgrove, Ron, jt. auth. see Stedman, Robert.

Cosgrove, Stephen. Bangalle. 1136p. 1977. 1.50 (ISBN 0-8431-0550-X). French & Eur.

--The Bugglar Brothers. (Bugg Ser.). (Illus.). 32p. 1983. 1.00 (ISBN 0-8431-1209-3). Price Stern.

--Bugglar Brothers. (Bugg Bks.). (Orig.). 1984. incl. cassette 3.95 (ISBN 0-8431-1232-8). Price Stern.

--Bumble B. Bear: A Gift for the Giving. (Bear Board Bks.). (Illus.). 1984. 2.50 (ISBN 0-8431-1386-3). Price Stern.

--Bumble B. Bear Cleans Up. (Bear Board Bks.). (Illus.). 1984. 2.50 (ISBN 0-8431-1169-0). Price Stern.

--Bumble B. Bear in the Garden. (Bear Board Bks.). (Illus.). 1984. 2.50 (ISBN 0-8431-1168-2). Price Stern.

--Bumble B. Bear Rides in the Car. (Bear Board Bks.). (Illus.). 1984. 2.50 (ISBN 0-8431-1167-4). Price Stern.

--Bumble B. Bear Takes a Walk. (Bear Board Bks.). (Illus.). 1984. 2.50 (ISBN 0-8431-1170-4). Price Stern.

--Bumble B. Bear: The Christmas Tree. (Bear Board Bks.). (Illus.). 1984. 2.50 (ISBN 0-8431-1387-1). Price Stern.

--Cap'n Smudge. 42p. 1967. 1.50 (ISBN 0-8431-0551-8). French & Eur.

--Catundra. (Serendipity Bks). (Illus.). 32p. (gr. 1-4). 1978. pap. 1.95 (ISBN 0-8431-0571-2). Price Stern.

--Catundra. Manoni, Mary H., ed. (Serendipity Book Cassettes). (Illus.). (gr. 1-3). 1979. pap. text ed. 22.00 (ISBN 0-89290-069-5). Soc for Visual.

--Cooty-Doo. (Bugg Bks.). 32p. (Orig.). 1984. pap. 1.00 (ISBN 0-317-11680-0). Price Stern.

--Crabby Gabby. (Serendipity Bks.). (Illus.). 32p. (Orig.). (gr. 1-4). 1985. pap. 1.95 (ISBN 0-8431-1441-X). Price Stern.

--Crickeette. (Bugg Bks.). (Orig.). 1984. incl. cassette 3.95 (ISBN 0-8431-1226-3). Price Stern.

--Doodle Bugg. (Bugg Bks.). 32p. (Orig.). 1984. pap. 1.00 (ISBN 0-8431-1213-1). Price Stern.

--Dragolin. (Serendipity Storybks.). (Orig.). 1984. pap. 1.95 (ISBN 0-8431-1165-8). Price Stern.

--The Dream Tree. (Serendipity Bks.). (Illus.). (gr. 1-6). 1975. pap. 1.95 (ISBN 0-8431-0553-4). Price Stern.

--Dune Bugg. (Crick-Ette Ser.). (Illus.). 32p. 1983. 1.00 (ISBN 0-8431-1200-X). Price-Stern.

--Dune Bugg. (Bugg Ser.). (Illus.). 32p. 1983. 1.00 (ISBN 0-8431-1206-9). Price Stern.

--Dune Bugg. (Bugg Bks.). (Orig.). 1984. incl. cassette 3.95 (ISBN 0-8431-1235-2). Price Stern.

--Eevil Weevil. (Bugg Ser.). (Illus.). 32p. 1983. 1.00 (ISBN 0-8431-1201-8). Price Stern.

--Eevil Weevil. (Bugg Bks.). (Orig.). 1984. incl. cassette 3.95 (ISBN 0-8431-1227-1). Price Stern.

--Feather Fin. (Serendipity Ser.). (Illus.). 32p. (Orig.). 1983. pap. 1.95 (ISBN 0-8431-0593-3). Price Stern.

--Flutterby. 672p. (Fr.-Esp n13.). pns (ISBN 0-8431-0554-2, S-12416, French & Eur). French & Eur.

--Flutterby. (Serendipity Bks.). 32p. (Orig.). 1984. incl. cassette 4.95 (ISBN 0-8431-1174-7). Price Stern.

--Flutterby Fly. (Serendipity Storybks.). (Illus., Orig.). 1984. pap. 1.95 (ISBN 0-8431-1162-3). Price Stern.

--Gabby. (Serendipity Bks.). (Orig.). 1984. incl. cassette 4.95 (ISBN 0-8431-0607-7). Price Stern.

--Glance. (Bugg Ser.). (Illus.). 32p. 1983. pap. 1.00 (ISBN 0-8431-1211-5). Price Stern.

--Glance. (Bugg Bks.). (Orig.). 1984. incl. cassette 3.95 (ISBN 0-8431-1236-0). Price Stern.

--Glitterby Baby. (Serendipity Bks.). (Illus.). 32p. (Orig.). (gr. 1-4). 1985. pap. 1.95 (ISBN 0-8431-1166-6). Price Stern.

--Grampa-Lop. (Serendipity Bks.). (Illus.). 32p. (Orig.). 1982. pap. 1.95 (ISBN 0-8431-0586-0). Price Stern.

--Grampa Lop. (Serendipity Bks.). 32p. (Orig.). 1984. incl. cassette 4.95 (ISBN 0-8431-1161-5). Price Stern.

--Humbugg. (Bugg Ser.). (Illus.). 32p. 1983. 1.00 (ISBN 0-8431-1202-6). Price Stern.

--Humbugg. (Bugg Bks.). (Orig.). 1984. incl. cassette 3.95 (ISBN 0-8431-1230-1). Price Stern.

--Jake O'Shawnasey. (Serendipity Bks.). (Illus.). 32p. (gr. 1-6). 1975. pap. 1.95 (ISBN 0-8431-0558-5). Price Stern.

--Jingle Bear. (Serendipity Bks.). (Illus.). 32p. (Orig.). (gr. 1-4). 1985. pap. 1.95 (ISBN 0-8431-1440-1). Price Stern.

--Jitterbugg. (Bugg Bks.). (Illus., Orig.). 1984. pap. 1.00 (ISBN 0-8431-1216-6). Price Stern.

--June Bugg. (Bugg Ser.). (Illus.). 32p. 1984. 1.00 (ISBN 0-8431-1203-4). Price Stern.

--June Bugg. (Bugg Bks.). (Orig.). 1984. incl. cassette 3.95 (ISBN 0-8431-1228-X). Price Stern.

--Kartusch. (Serendipity Bks). (Illus.). 1978. pap. 1.95 (ISBN 0-8431-0568-2). Price Stern.

--Kartusch Book Cassette. new ed. Manoni, Mary H., ed. (Serendipity Cassette Books Ser.). (Illus.). 16p. (gr. k-3). pap. 22.00 (ISBN 0-89290-053-9). Soc for Visual.

--Katy-Didd. (Bugg Bks.). (Illus., Orig.). 1984. pap. 1.00 (ISBN 0-8431-1214-X). Price Stern.

--Kiyomi. (Serendipity Storybks.). (Illus., Orig.). 1984. pap. 1.95 (ISBN 0-8431-1164-X). Price Stern.

--Leo the Lop. (Serendipity Bks.). 32p. (Orig.). 1984. incl. cassette 4.95 (ISBN 0-8431-1158-5). Price Stern.

--Leo the Lop - Tail Three. (Serendipity Bks). (Illus.). 32p. 1980. pap. 1.95 (ISBN 0-8431-0577-1). Price Stern.

--Leo the Lop: Tail Three. (Serendipity Bks.). 32p. (Orig.). 1984. 4.95 (ISBN 0-8431-1160-7). Price Stern.

--Leo the Lop (Tail Two) (Serendipity Bks.). (Illus.). 32p. (Orig.). (gr. k-6). 1979. pap. 1.95 (ISBN 0-8431-0572-0). Price Stern.

--Leo the Lop: Tail Two. (Serendipity Bks.). 32p. (Orig.). 1984. incl. cassette 4.95 (ISBN 0-8431-1159-3). Price Stern.

--Little Mouse on the Prairie. (Serendipity Bks.). (Illus.). 32p. (gr. 1-4). 1978. pap. 1.95 (ISBN 0-8431-0569-0). Price Stern.

--Little Mouse on the Prairie. Manoni, Mary H., ed. (Serendipity Book Cassettes). (Illus.). (gr. 1-3). 1979. pap. text ed. 22.00 (ISBN 0-89290-068-7). Soc for Visual.

--Little Mouse on the Prairie. (Serendipity Bks.). (Orig.). 1984. incl. cassette 4.95 (ISBN 0-8431-1069-4). Price Stern.

--Lord & Lady Bugg. (Bugg Ser.). (Illus.). 32p. 1983. 1.00 (ISBN 0-8431-1207-7). Price Stern.

--Lord & Lady Bugg. (Bugg Bks.). (Orig.). 1984. incl. cassette 3.95 (ISBN 0-8431-1233-6). Price Stern.

--Love Bugg. (Bugg Ser.). (Illus.). 32p. 1983. 1.00 (ISBN 0-8431-1208-5). Price Stern.

--Love Bugg. (Bugg Bks.). (Orig.). 1984. incl. cassette 3.95 (ISBN 0-8431-1231-X). Price Stern.

--Maui-Maui. (Serendipity Bks.). (Illus.). 32p. (gr. k-6). 1979. pap. 1.95 (ISBN 0-8431-0573-9). Price Stern.

--Ming Ling. (Serendipity Bks.). (Illus.). 32p. (Orig.). 1983. pap. 1.95 (ISBN 0-8431-0592-5). Price Stern.

--Ming Ling. (Serendipity Bks.). (Orig.). 1984. incl. cassette 4.95 (ISBN 0-8431-1070-8). Price Stern.

--Minikin. (Serendipity Storybooks). (Illus., Orig.). 1984. pap. 1.95 (ISBN 0-8431-1163-1). Price Stern.

--Morgan & Me. (Serendipity Bks.). (Orig.). 1984. incl. cassette 4.95 (ISBN 0-8431-1172-0). Price Stern.

--Morgan & Yew. (Serendipity Bks.). (Orig.). 1984. incl. cassette 4.95 (ISBN 0-8431-1173-9). Price Stern.

--Morgan Mine. (Serendipity Bks.). (Illus.). 32p. (gr. 1-6). 1982. pap. 1.95 (ISBN 0-8431-0590-9). Price Stern.

--Morgan Mine. (Serendipity Bks.). (Orig.). 1984. incl. cassette 4.95 (ISBN 0-8431-1198-4). Price Stern.

--Morgan Morning. (Serendipity Bks.). (Illus.). 32p. (gr. 1-6). 1982. pap. 1.95 (ISBN 0-8431-0591-7). Price Stern.

--Morgan Morning. (Serendipity Books). (Orig.). 1984. incl. cassette 4.95 (ISBN 0-8431-1199-2). Price Stern.

--Muffin Muncher. (Serendipity Bks.). (Illus.). 32p. (gr. 1-6). 1975. pap. 1.95 (ISBN 0-8431-0561-5). Price Stern.

--Nitter Pitter. (Serendipity Bks). (Illus.). 32p. (gr. 1-4). 1978. pap. 1.95 (ISBN 0-8431-0570-4). Price Stern.

--Nitter Pitter. Manoni, Mary H., ed. (Serendipity Book Cassettes). (Illus.). (gr. 1-3). 1979. pap. text ed. 22.00 (ISBN 0-89290-070-9). Soc for Visual.

--Raz-Ma-Taz. (Serendipity Bks.). (Illus.). 32p. (gr. 1-6). 1982. pap. 1.95 (ISBN 0-8431-0588-7). Price Stern.

--Shimmeree. (Serendipity Bks.). (Illus.). 32p. 1980. pap. 1.95 (ISBN 0-8431-0574-7). Price Stern.

--Shutterbugg. (Bugg Bks.). (Illus., Orig.). 1984. pap. 1.00 (ISBN 0-8431-1217-4). Price Stern.

--Snaffles. (Serendipity Bks.). (Illus.). 32p. 1980. pap. 1.95 (ISBN 0-8431-0576-3). Price Stern.

--Snugg. (Bugg Ser.). (Illus.). 32p. 1983. 1.00 (ISBN 0-8431-1204-2). Price Stern.

--Snugg. (Bugg Bks.). (Orig.). 1984. incl. cassette 3.95 (ISBN 0-8431-1225-5). Price Stern.

--Snugg & Shoe-Fly Flu. (Bugg Bks.). (Illus., Orig.). 1984. pap. 1.00 (ISBN 0-8431-1212-3). Price Stern.

--Squeakers. (Serendipity Bks.). (Illus.). 32p. (Orig.). (gr. 1-4). 1985. pap. 1.95 (ISBN 0-8431-1442-8). Price Stern.

--Tee-Tee. (Serendipity Ser.). (Illus.). 32p. (Orig.). 1983. pap. 1.95 (ISBN 0-8431-1400-2). Price Stern.

--Tik Tok. (Bugg Bks.). (Illus.). 32p. 1983. 1.00 (ISBN 0-8431-1210-7). Price Stern.

--Tik Tok. (Bugg Bks.). (Orig.). 1984. incl. cassette 3.95 (ISBN 0-8431-1234-4). Price Stern.

--Trafalgar True. (Serendipity Bks.). (Illus.). 32p. 1980. pap. 1.95 (ISBN 0-8431-0575-5). Price Stern.

--Trafalgar True, Bk. 4. (Serendipity Bks.). (Illus.). 32p. (gr. k-4). 1981. lib. bdg. 8.95 (ISBN 0-87191-794-7). Creative Ed.

--Trapper. (Serendipity Bks.). (Illus.). 32p. 1982. pap. 1.95 (ISBN 0-8431-0587-9). Price Stern.

--Vee-Dubb. (Bugg Ser.). (Illus.). 32p. 1983. 1.00 (ISBN 0-8431-1205-0). Price Stern.

--Vee-Dubb. (Bugg Bks.). (Orig.). 1984. incl. cassette 3.95 (ISBN 0-8431-1229-8). Price Stern.

--Whimsie Storybooks. Incl. Gimme. LC 85-1958 (ISBN 0-394-87451-X); Tattletale. LC 85-42713 (ISBN 0-394-87455-2); Gobble & Gulp. LC 85-42715 (ISBN 0-394-87457-9); Cranky. LC 85-42712 (ISBN 0-394-87454-4); Fibber. LC 85-42714 (ISBN 0-394-87456-0); Giggle. LC 85-42716 (ISBN 0-394-87458-7). (Illus.). 40p. (ps-3). 1985. pap. 3.95 ea. (BYR). Random.

Cosgrove, Steve. Leo the Lop. Tail Two. (Serendipity Bks). (Illus.). (gr. k-4). 1980. PLB 8.95 (ISBN 0-87191-779-3). Creative Ed.

Cosgrove, Steven. Gnome from Nome. (Serenity Bks.). (Illus.). 32p. (gr. 1-6). 1975. pap. 1.95 (ISBN 0-8431-0555-0). Price Stern.

Cosgrove, William. Double Dealer. (New Mermaids Ser.). 1984. pap. text ed. 5.95x (ISBN 0-393-90053-3). Norton.

Cosgrove-Twitchett, Carol. Europe & Africa. 212p. 1978. text ed. 41.95x (ISBN 0-566-00182-9). Gower Pub Co.

Cosi, Liliana. The Young Ballet Dancer. LC 78-62942. (Illus.). 1979. 10.95 (ISBN 0-8128-2570-5). Stein & Day.

Cosic, Dobrica. Reach to Eternity. Heppell, Muriel, tr. LC 79-2234. 1980. 14.95 (ISBN 0-15-175961-8). HarBraceJ.

--South to Destiny. LC 80-8764. 480p. 1981. 19.95 (ISBN 0-15-184486-0). HarBraceJ.

--This Land, This Time, 4 vols. Heppell, Muriel, tr. Incl. Into the Battle. 8.95 (ISBN 0-15-644991-9); Reach to Eternity. 7.95 (ISBN 0-15-676012-6); South to Destiny. 7.95 (ISBN 0-15-683913-X); Time of Death. 7.95 (ISBN 0-15-690445-4). 1983. Repr. of 1978 ed. Set. 29.95 (ISBN 0-15-690026-2, Harv). HarBraceJ.

Cosin, B., et al. School & Society: A Sociological Reader. 1972. pap. 5.95x (ISBN 0-262-53022-8). MIT Pr.

Cosin, John. Complete Works of John Cosin, 5 Vols. LC 72-1028. (Library of Anglo-Catholic Theology: No. 5). Repr. of 1855 ed. Set. 150.00 (ISBN 0-404-52080-4). AMS Pr.

Cosindas, Marie. Marie Cosindas: Color Photographs. LC 78-7064. (Illus.). 1978. 49.95 (ISBN 0-8212-0743-1, 546119). NYGS.

Cosio Villegas, Daniel. American Extremes. Paredes, Americo, tr. from Span. LC 64-11188. (Texas Pan American Ser.). Orig. Title: Extremos de America. 243p. 1964. pap. 6.95x (ISBN 0-292-70069-5). U of Tex Pr.

Coskey, Evelyn. Christmas Crafts for Everyone. LC 76-4916. (Illus.). (YA) 1976. 9.95 (ISBN 0-687-07815-6). Abingdon.

--Easter Eggs for Everyone. LC 72-6680. (Illus.). (gr. 5 up). 1973. 9.95 (ISBN 0-687-11492-6). Abingdon.

Coslet, Dorothy. Madame Jeanne Guyon: Child of Another World. 219p. (Orig.). 1984. pap. 3.95 (ISBN 0-87508-144-4). Chr Lit.

Coslet, J. George. The Incisal Edge Splint & Other Methods of Temporary Stabilization of Periodontally Involved Teeth. Cohen, D. Walter, ed. (Continuing Dental Education Series). 102p. 1980. pap. 18.00 (ISBN 0-931386-22-5). Quint Pub Co.

Cosman, Anna. How to Read & Write Poetry. (First Bks.). (Illus.). (gr. 5-8). 1979. PLB 8.90 s&l (ISBN 0-531-02261-7). Watts.

Cosman, Carol, tr. see Robert, Marthe.

Cosman, Carol, tr. see Sarte, Jean-Paul.

Cosman, Carol, et al, eds. The Penguin Book of Women Poets. (Poetry Ser.). 1979. pap. 6.95 (ISBN 0-14-042225-0). Penguin.

--The Penguin Book of Women Poets. 1979. 14.95 (ISBN 0-670-77856-7). Viking.

Cosman, Madeleine P. Fabulous Feasts: Medieval Cookery & Ceremony. LC 76-15909. (Illus.). 1977. 30.00 (ISBN 0-8076-0832-7); pap. 14.95 (ISBN 0-8076-0898-X). Braziller.

--Kissing the Dragon: The Intelligent Work-Hunter's Companion. LC 84-71095. (Illus.). 128p. 1984. pap. 9.99 (ISBN 0-916491-07-2). Bard Hall Pr.

--The Medieval Baker's Daughter: A Bilingual Adventure in Medieval Life with Costumes, Banners, Music, Food, & a Mystery Play. LC 84-71590. (Illus.). 112p. (gr. 3-12). 1984. pap. 7.95 (ISBN 0-916491-18-8). Bard Hall Pr.

--Medieval Holidays & Festivals. (Illus.). 128p. (gr. 7 up). 1981. 13.95 (ISBN 0-684-17172-4, ScribJ). Scribner.

Cosman, Milein, jt. auth. see Keller, Hans.

Cosmao, Vincent. Changing the World: An Agenda for the Churches. Drury, John, tr. LC 84-5153. 128p. (Orig.). 1984. pap. 8.95 (ISBN 0-88344-107-1). Orbis Bks.

Cosmas, Graham A. An Army for Empire: The United States Army in the Spanish American War. LC 76-149010. (Illus.). 341p. 1971. 20.00x (ISBN 0-8262-0107-5). U of Mo Pr.

Cosmen, Madeleine P., ed. see De Pizan, Christine.

Cosmi, E. V. & Scarpelli, E. M., eds. Pulmonary Surfactant System. (Symposia of the Giovanni Lorenzini Foundation: Vol. 16). 404p. 1984. 88.50 (ISBN 0-444-80514-1, Biomedical Pr). Elsevier.

Cosmi, Ermelando, jt. ed. see Scarpelli, Emilie.

Cosmi, Ermelando V., jt. auth. see Scarpelli, Emile M.

Cosmi, Ermelando V., ed. Obstetric Anesthesia & Perinatology. (Illus.). 769p. 1981. 49.50 (ISBN 0-8385-7196-4). ACC.

Cosmi, Ermelando V., jt. ed. see Scarpelli, Emile M.

Cosminsky, Sheila & Harrison, Ira. Traditional Medicine. LC 82-49196. (Reference Library of Social Science). 275p. 1983. lib. bdg. 43.00 (ISBN 0-8240-9181-7). Garland Pub.

Cosminsky, Sheila, jt. auth. see Harrison, Ira E.

Cosmovici, ed. see International Conference on Supernovae; May 7-11, 1973, Lecce, Italy.

Cosnac, Daniel De see De Cosnac, Daniel.

Cosnard, M., et al, eds. Rhythms in Biology & Other Fields of Application: Deterministic & Stochastic Approaches. (Lecture Notes in Biomathematics: Vol. 49). 400p. 1983. pap. 24.00 (ISBN 0-387-12302-4). Springer-Verlag.

Cosner, Shaaron. Be Your Own Weather Forecaster. LC 81-14006. (Illus.). 96p. (gr. 4 up). 1982. PLB 9.79 (ISBN 0-671-42726-1). Messner.

--Special Effects in Movies & TV. (Illus.). 96p. (gr. 3-7). 1985. 8.79 (ISBN 0-671-46136-2). Messner.

Cosner, Sharon. The Light Bulb: Inventions That Changed Our Lives. LC 83-40398. 64p. 1984. PLB 10.85 (ISBN 0-8027-6527-0). Walker & Co.

--Paper Through the Ages. LC 84-7760. (On My Own Bks.). (Illus.). 48p. (gr. 1-4). 1984. PLB 8.95 (ISBN 0-87614-270-6). Carolrhoda Bks.

Cosofret, V. V. Membrane Electrodes in Drug-Substances Analysis. Thomas, J. D., ed. (Illus.). 376p. 1981. 66.00 (ISBN 0-08-026264-3). Pergamon.

Cospar Committee on the International Reference Atmosphere. CIRA Nineteen Seventy-Two. 58.00 (ISBN 0-08-021997-7). Pergamon.

COSPAR-IAU-IAG-IUGG-IUTAM - May 20-24, 1969. Dynamics of Satellites: Proceedings. Morando, B., ed. (Illus.). vii, 312p. (Eng. & Fr.). 1970. 82.10 (ISBN 0-387-04792-1). Springer-Verlag.

COSPAR-IAU-IUTAM Symposium, Paris, 1965. Trajectories of Artificial Celestial Bodies As Determined from Observations: Proceedings. Kovalevsky, J., ed. (Illus.). 1966. 52.00 (ISBN 0-387-03681-4). Springer-Verlag.

COSPAR-IAU-IUTAM Symposium, Sao Paulo, Brazil, June 19-21, 1974. Satellite Dynamics. Giacaglia, G. E. & Stickland, A. C., eds. (Illus.). 390p. 1975. 37.80 (ISBN 0-387-07087-7). Springer-Verlag.

COSPAR, Twenty-Second Plenary Meeting, Bangalore, India, 1979. Low Latitude Aeronomical Processes: Proceedings. Mitra, A. P., ed. LC 79-41341. 1980. 76.00 (ISBN 0-08-024439-4). Pergamon.

--Non-Solar Gamma-Rays: Proceedings. Cowsik, R. & Wills, R. D., eds. 254p. 1980. 55.00 (ISBN 0-08-024440-8). Pergamon.

COSRIMS, ed. Mathematical Sciences: A Collection of Essays. 1969. pap. 8.95x (ISBN 0-262-53008-2). MIT Pr.

Cossa, Luigi. Introduction to the Study of Political Economy. Dyer, Louise, tr. from It. LC 79-1576. 1981. Repr. of 1893 ed. 42.25 (ISBN 0-88355-882-3). Hyperion Conn.

Cossa, Roberto M. Neustro Fin De Semana. Yates, Donald, ed. (Orig., Span.). 1966. pap. text ed. 2.50x (ISBN 0-685-15661-3). Macmillan.

Cossaboom, Sterling P. Fundamentals of Music Theory. LC 72-87760. 1973. pap. 2.50 (ISBN 0-8008-3102-0, Crescendo). Taplinger.

Cossaboon, John. Let Them Play! A Guide to Youth Soccer. LC 83-18216. (Illus.). 108p. 1983. 9.95 (ISBN 0-87833-376-2). Taylor Pub.

Cossard, Monique & Salazar, Robert. FSI French Basic Course, Units 1-12. 1976. 13.75x (ISBN 0-686-10712-8); Units 1-6. 19 cassettes 114.00x (ISBN 0-686-10713-6); Units 7-12. 29 cassettes 174.00x (ISBN 0-686-10714-4). Intl Learn Syst.

--FSI French Basic Course, Units 13-24. 1976. pap. text ed. 15.00x (ISBN 0-686-10715-2); Units 13-18. 29 cassettes 174.00x (ISBN 0-686-10716-0); Units 19-24. 24 cassettes 144.00x (ISBN 0-686-10717-9). Intl Learn Syst.

Cossart, V., et al. Resolution of Surface Singularities. (Lecture Notes in Mathematics Ser.: Vol. 1101). vii, 132p. 1984. pap. 7.50 (ISBN 0-387-13904-4). Springer-Verlag.

Cossart, Yvonne E. Virus Hepatitis & Its Control. (Illus.). 1978. text ed. 23.95 (ISBN 0-7216-0714-4, Pub. by Bailliere-Tindall). Saunders.

Cosse, Jerome J. De see DeCosse, Jerome J.

Cosse, Thomas J., jt. auth. see Matejka, J. Kenneth.

Cosseboom, Kathy. Grosse Pointe, Michigan: Race Against Race. xiii, 167p. 1972. 7.50. Mich St U Pr.

Cossery, Albert. Proud Beggars. Cushing, Thomas, tr. from Fr. 200p. 1981. 14.00 (ISBN 0-87685-451-X); signed ed. 20.00 (ISBN 0-87685-452-8); pap. 6.50 (ISBN 0-87685-450-1). Black Sparrow.

Cossins, Andrew R. & Sheterline, Peter, eds. Cellular Acclimatisation to Environment Change. LC 82-17804. (Society for Experimental Biology Seminar Ser.: No. 17). (Illus.). 255p. 1983. 65.00 (ISBN 0-521-24384-X). Cambridge U Pr.

Cossio, Aluigi. The Canzoniere of Dante: A Contribution to Its Critical Edition. 1977. lib. bdg. 59.95 (ISBN 0-8490-1569-3). Gordon Pr.

Cosslett, Tess. Science & Religion in the Nineteenth Century. LC 83-7505. (Cambridge English Prose Texts Ser.). 225p. 1984. 39.50 (ISBN 0-521-24402-1); pap. 14.95 (ISBN 0-521-28668-9). Cambridge U Pr.

--The Scientific Movement & Victorian Literature. LC 82-10284. 1983. 22.50x (ISBN 0-312-70298-1). St Martin.

Cosslett, V. E. & Barer, R. Advances in Optical & Electron Microscopy, Vol. 9. LC 62-25134. (Serial Publication Ser.). 1984. 70.00 (ISBN 0-12-029909-7). Acad Pr.

Cosslett, V. E. & Barer, R., eds. Advances in Optical & Electron Microscopy. Vol. 1. 1966. 55.00 (ISBN 0-12-029901-1); Vol. 2. 1968. 75.00 (ISBN 0-12-029902-X); Vol. 3. 1969. 55.00 (ISBN 0-12-029903-8); Vol. 4. 1971. 75.00 (ISBN 0-12-029904-6); Vol. 5. 1973. 70.00 (ISBN 0-12-029905-4); Vol. 6, 1976. 65.00 (ISBN 0-12-029906-2); Vol. 7, 1979. 70.00 (ISBN 0-12-029907-0). Acad Pr.

--Advances in Optical & Electron Microscopy, Vol. 8. (Serial Publication Ser.). 281p. 1982. 65.00 (ISBN 0-12-029908-9). Acad Pr.

Cosslett, V. E., jt. ed. see Brederoo, P.

Cossman, E. Joseph. How I Made One Million Dollars in Mail Order. (Illus.). 1963. 14.95 (ISBN 0-13-397406-5). P-H.

Cosson, Annie, ed. see McDowell, Josh.

Cossons, Neil. The BP Book of Industrial Archaeology. LC 74-20468. (Illus.). 1975. 21.50 (ISBN 0-7153-6250-X). David & Charles.

Cossons, Neil, jt. auth. see Buchanan, R. A.

Cost, Bruce. Ginger East to West: A Cook's Tour with Recipes, Techniques & Lore. LC 84-2842. (Illus.). 192p. (Orig.). 1984. 17.95 (ISBN 0-943186-13-7, 0-671-55803-X); pap. 10.95 (ISBN 0-943186-06-4, 0-671-55840-4). Aris Bks Harris.

Cost, Jacquelyn S. Dietary Management of Renal Disease: A Controlled Protein, Sodium & Potassium Cookbook. LC 75-18657. 135p. 1975. 9.00 (ISBN 0-913590-27-4). Slack Inc.

Cost, Patrica, ed. Selected Bibliography: Color Scanners, Vol. 1. LC 84-40400. 50p. 1984. pap. 15.00 (ISBN 0-89938-018-2). Tech & Ed Ctr Graph Arts RIT.

Cost, Patricia, ed. Selected Bibliography: Computer Graphics. 1984. pap. 30.00 (ISBN 0-89938-021-2). Tech & Ed Ctr Graph Arts RIT.

--Selected Bibliography: Materials Handling. 1984. pap. 22.00 (ISBN 0-89938-020-4). Tech & Ed Ctr Graph Arts RIT.

--Selected Bibliography: Printing Inks, Vol.2. 1984. pap. 22.00 (ISBN 0-89938-019-0). Tech & Ed Ctr Graph Arts RIT.

Costa, Anthony, et al. The Variables: A Descriptive Text for Educational Psychology. 1980. pap. text ed. 7.00 (ISBN 0-89669-047-4). Collegium Bk Pubs.

Costa, Betty & Costa, Marie. A Micro Handbook for Small Libraries & Media Centers. 220p. 1983. lib. bdg. 19.50 (ISBN 0-87287-354-4). Libs Unl.

Costa, C. D., ed. Lucretius: De Rerum Natura V. 160p. 1984. pap. 12.95 (ISBN 0-19-814457-1). Oxford U Pr.

Costa, C. D., ed. see Seneca.

Costa, Corrado. The Complete Films of Corrado Costa. Vangelisti, Paul, tr. from Italian. LC 83-60077. 64p. (Orig.). 1983. pap. 4.00 (ISBN 0-88031-063-4). Invisible-Red Hill.

--Our Positions. bi-lingual ed. Vangelisti, Paul, tr. from Ital. 1975. 2.50 (ISBN 0-88031-021-9). Invisible-Red Hill.

Costa, Dennis. Irenic Apocalypse: Some Uses of Apocalyptic in Dante, Petrarch & Rabelais. (Stanford French & Italian Studies: Vol. 21). vi, 143p. 1981. pap. 25.00 (ISBN 0-915838-18-4). Anma Libri.

Costa, E., ed. The Benzodiazepines: From Molecular Biology to Clinical Practice. 446p. 1983. text ed. 48.00 (ISBN 0-89004-885-1). Raven.

Costa, E & Gessa, G. L., eds. Nonstriatal Dopaminergic Neurons. LC 76-5661. (Advances in Biochemical Psychopharmacology Ser.: Vol. 16). 728p. 1977. 86.00 (ISBN 0-89004-127-X). Raven.

Costa, E. & Racagni, G., eds. Typical & Atypical Antidepressants: Clinical Practice. (Advances in Biochemical Psychopharmacology Ser.: Vol. 32). 422p. 1982. text ed. 57.50 (ISBN 0-89004-830-4). Raven.

--Typical & Atypical Antidepressants: Molecular Mechanisms. (Advances in Biochemical Psychopharmacology Ser.: Vol. 31). 416p. 1982. text ed. 64.50 (ISBN 0-89004-686-7). Raven.

Costa, E. & Trabucci, M., eds. Regulatory Peptides: From Molecular Biology to Function. (Advances in Biochemical Psychopharmacology Ser.: Vol. 33). 588p. 1982. text ed. 85.00 (ISBN 0-89004-797-9). Raven.

Costa, E., jt. ed. see Greengard, P.

Costa, E., et al, eds. Serotonin, New Vistas: Biochemistry & Behavioral & Clinical Studies. LC 73-91166. (Advances in Biochemical Psychopharmacology Ser.: Vol. 11). 446p. 1974. 45.50 (ISBN 0-911216-69-3). Raven.

--Serotonin, New Vistas: Histochemistry & Pharmacology. LC 73-91165. (Advances in Biochemical Psychopharmacology Ser.: Vol. 10). 345p. 1974. 45.50 (ISBN 0-911216-68-5). Raven.

--First & Second Messengers: New Vistas. LC 75-14583. (Advances in Biochemical Psychopharmacology Ser: Vol. 15). 514p. 1976. 59.50 (ISBN 0-89004-084-2). Raven.

Costa, E., jt. ed. see Biggio, G.

Costa, Erminio & Trabucchi, Marco, eds. Neural Peptides & Neuronal Communication. (Advances in Biochemical Psychopharmacology Ser.: Vol. 22). 670p. 1980. text ed. 88.00 (ISBN 0-89004-375-2). Raven.

Costa, Francis D., ed. see Hopko, T., et al.

Costa, Francisco Da see Mickle, M. M. & Da Costa, Francisco.

Costa, Frank J., jt. ed. see Dutt, Ashok K.

Costa, G. & Gatto, R. R., eds. Theory of Fundamental Interactions: Proceedings of the International School of Physics, Enrico Fermi Course LXXXI, Varenna, Italy, July 21 - August 2, 1980. (Enrico Fermi International Summer School of Physics Ser.: Vol. 81). 300p. 1982. 66.00 (ISBN 0-444-86156-4, I-324-82, North Holland). Elsevier.

Costa, Gomes B. De see De Costa, Gomes B.

Costa, Greg. American Short Stories: Exercises in Reading & Writing. 142p. 1983. pap. text ed. 9.95 (ISBN 0-15-502391-8, HC). HarbraceJ.

Costa, J. E. & Fleisher, p. J., eds. Developments & Applications of Geomorphology. (Illus.). 300p. 1984. 44.00 (ISBN 0-387-13457-3). Springer Verlag.

Costa, John. Le Conflict Moral dans les Oeuvres Romanesques de Jean-Pierre Camus: 1584-1652. LC 74-2068. (Illus.). 70p. (Fr.). 1976. lib. bdg. 18.50 (ISBN 0-89102-031-4). B Franklin.

Costa, John E. & Baker, Victor R. Surficial Geology: Building with the Earth. LC 80-22644. 498p. 1981. text ed. 37.50x (ISBN 0-471-03229-8). Wiley.

Costa, Joseph. The Jade Buffalo & Other Solitary Verses. 1982. 5.95 (ISBN 0-533-05016-2). Vantage.

--Oilfield Stories. 1983. 8.95 (ISBN 0-533-05513-X). Vantage.

Costa, Joseph J. Abuse of the Elderly. LC 84-48472. 320p. 1984. 28.50x (ISBN 0-669-06142-5). Lexington Bks.

--Abuse of Women: Legislation, Reporting, & Prevention. LC 81-48512. 688p. 1983. 40.00 (ISBN 0-669-05374-0). Lexington Bks.

Costa, Leon Da. Freedom & Discipline in the Education of Young People. (Science of Man Library Bk). (Illus.). 176p. 1976. lib. bdg. 47.50 (ISBN 0-913314-68-4). Am Classical Coll Pr.

Costa, Louis & Spreen, Otfried, eds. Studies in Neuropsychology: Selected Papers of Arthur Benton. (Illus.). 320p. 1985. 39.50 (ISBN 0-19-503636-0). Oxford U Pr.

Costa, Luiz E. Rio in the Time of the Viceroys. 1976. lib. bdg. 59.95 (ISBN 0-8490-2526-5). Gordon Pr.

Costa, Marie, jt. auth. see Costa, Betty.

Costa, Max. Metal Carcinogenesis Testing: Principles & in Vitro Methods. LC 80-80444. (Biological Methods Ser.). (Illus.). 176p. 1980. 44.50 (ISBN 0-89603-017-2). Humana.

Costa, Michael L. Master Trust: Simplifying Employee Benefits Trust Fund Administration. 288p. 1980. 19.95 (ISBN 0-8144-5622-7). AMACOM.

Costa, Myldred M., tr. The Letters of Marie Madeleine Hachard. 66p. 1974. 6.00 (ISBN 0-686-32517-6). Transitour.

Costa, Nicoletta. The Birthday Party. (Molly & Tom Bks.). (Illus.). 16p. (gr. k-1). 1984. 3.50 (ISBN 0-448-23404-1, G&D). Putnam Pub Group.

--The Clever Dog. LC 85-7140. (Little Bks.). (Illus.). 16p. (ps-k). 1985. bds. 3.95 (ISBN 0-02-724670-1). Macmillan.

--Dressing Up. (Molly & Tom Bks.). (Illus.). 16p. (gr. k). 1984. 3.50 (ISBN 0-448-23401-7, G&D). Putnam Pub Group.

--A Friend Comes to Play. (Molly & Tom Bks.). (Illus.). 16p. (gr. k-1). 1984. 3.50 (ISBN 0-448-23403-3, G&D). Putnam Pub Group.

--The Grown-Up Dog. LC 85-7138. (Little Books). (Illus.). 16p. (ps-k). 1985. bds. 3.95 (ISBN 0-02-724680-9). Macmillan.

--The Missing Cat. (Molly & Tom Bks.). (Illus.). 15p. (gr. k-1). 1984. 3.50 (ISBN 0-448-23402-5, G&D). Putnam Pub Group.

--The Naughty Puppy. LC 85-7151. (Little Books). (Illus.). 16p. (ps-k). 1985. bds. 3.95 (ISBN 0-02-724660-4). Macmillan.

--The New Puppy. LC 85-7139. (Little Books). (Illus.). 16p. (ps-k). bds. 3.51 (ISBN 0-02-724650-7). Macmillan.

Costa, Paul T., Jr., jt. auth. see McCrae, Robert R.

Costa, Philip J. & Cotty, Richard G. Laboratory Textbook in Anatomy & Physiology. 4th ed. 1981. wire coil bdg. 9.95 (ISBN 0-8403-2014-0). Kendall-Hunt.

Costa, Ray. How to Be a Male Exotic Dancer. (Illus.). 114p. (Orig.). pap. text ed. 9.95 (ISBN 0-686-38733-3). Costa.

Costa, Rebecca, et al. A Parent's Guide to Children: The Challenge. LC 77-90090. (Illus., Orig.). 1978. pap. 4.25 (ISBN 0-8015-5734-8, 0413-120, Hawthorn). Dutton.

Costa, Rene de see De Costa, Rene.

Costa, Rene De see De Costa, Rene.

Costa, Richard H. Edmund Wilson: Our Neighbor from Talcottville. LC 80-23453. (York State Bks.). (Illus.). 192p. 1980. 15.95x (ISBN 0-8156-0163-8). Syracuse U Pr.

--H. G. Wells. rev. ed. (English Author Ser.). 1985. lib. bdg. 13.95 (ISBN 0-8057-6887-4, Twayne). G K Hall.

Costa, Roberto. The Adventure of a Roman Lover. 1984. 10.95 (ISBN 0-533-05935-6). Vantage.

Costa, Vasco & Frances, Osvald. Diccionario de Unidadaes y Tablas de Conversion. 3rd ed. 168p. (Span.). 1977. pap. 8.75 (ISBN 84-252-0214-0, S-50579). French & Eur.

Costabel, Eva D. A New England Village. LC 82-13738. (Illus.). 64p. (gr. 3 up). 1983. 12.95 (ISBN 0-689-30972-4). Atheneum.

Costabel-Deutsch, Eva. Design & Make Your Own Floral Applique. LC 76-24568. (Needlework Ser). 1976. 2.95 (ISBN 0-486-23427-4). Dover.
--Full-Color Floral Needlepoint Designs. (Dover Needlework Ser). (Illus., Orig.). 1976. pap. 3.25 (ISBN 0-486-23387-1). Dover.
Costa De Beauregard, Oliver. Precis of Special Relativity. Hoffman, B., tr. 1966. 33.00 (ISBN 0-12-191450-X). Acad Pr.
Costa De Machado, Bernadete, tr. see Seixas, Cid.
Costadoni, A., jt. auth. see Mittarelli, J. H.
Costain, David W., jt. auth. see Green, A. Richard.
Costain, Thomas B. High Towers. (Illus.). 1949. 9.95 (ISBN 0-385-04194-2). Doubleday.
--White & the Gold. LC 53-7236. 5.95 (ISBN 0-385-04526-3); limited ed. o.p. 35.00. Doubleday.
Costales, Bryan. C: From A to Z. 244p. 1985. 21.95 (ISBN 0-13-110057-2); pap. 14.95 (ISBN 0-13-110040-8). P H.
Costales, Claire & Barack, Priscilla. A Secret Hell: Surviving Life with an Alcoholic. LC 83-21275. (Orig.). 1984. pap. 4.95 (ISBN 0-8307-0915-0, 5418062). Regal.
Costales, Claire & Berry, Jo. Staying Dry: A Workable Solution to the Problem of Alcohol Abuse. rev. ed. LC 83-3417. 1983. pap. 5.95 (ISBN 0-8307-0885-5, 5417946). Regal.
Costanso, Miguel. The Costanso Narrative of the Portola Expedition. Brandes, Ray, tr. LC 79-112869. 112p. 1983. Repr. of 1970 ed. lib. bdg. 29.95x (ISBN 0-89370-753-8). Borgo Pr.
Costantakos, Chrysie M. The American-Greek Subculture: Process of Continuity. Cordasco, Francesco, ed. LC 80-848. (Amercian Ethnic Groups Ser.). 1981. lib. bdg. 71.50x (ISBN 0-405-13411-8). Ayer Co Pubs.
Costantini, Costanzo. Are All Italians Lousy Lovers. Walter, Eugene, tr. from It. LC 74-28697. 212p. 1975. 6.95 (ISBN 0-8184-0207-5). Lyle Stuart.
Costantini, Humberto. Gods, the Little Guys & the Police. Talbott, Toby, tr. 240p. 1985. pap. 3.95 (ISBN 0-380-69839-0, Bard). Avon.
--The Long Night of Francisco Sanctis. Di Giovanni, Norman T., tr. LC 84-48151. 224p. 1985. 14.37 (ISBN 0-06-015391-1, HarpT). Har-Row.
Costantini, Humberto, tr. see Slote, Alfred.
Costantino. Italian at a Glance. (Phrase Book-Dictionaries for Travelers). 192p. 1984. pap. 4.95 (ISBN 0-8120-2713-2). Barron.
Costanza, Mary S. The Living Witness: Art in the Concentration Camps & Ghettos. 1982. 19.95 (ISBN 0-02-906660-3). Free Pr.
Costanzi, John J., ed. Clinical Management of Malignant Melanoma. (Cancer Treatment & Research Ser.). 1984. lib. bdg. 38.95 (ISBN 0-89838-656-X, Pub. by Martinus Nijhoff Netherlands). Kluwer Academic.
Costanzo, Christie. Mommy & Me Exercises the Kidnastics Program. (Illus.). 120p. (Orig.). 1983. pap. 7.95 (ISBN 0-917982-28-2). Cougar Bks.
Costanzo, Gerald. In the Aviary. LC 74-84572. (Breakthrough Bks). 72p. 1974. 6.95 (ISBN 0-8262-0169-5). U of Mo Pr.
Costanzo, Gerald & Langton, Daniel J. In the Aviary & Querencia: Poetry Readings by Gerald Costanzo & Daniel J. Langton. LC 76-740443. 1976. 7.95 (ISBN 0-8262-0214-4). U of Mo Pr.
Costanzo, Gerald, ed. Three Rivers Ten Years. 1983. 14.95 (ISBN 0-915604-84-1); pap. 7.95 (ISBN 0-915604-85-X). Carnegie-Mellon.
Costanzo, Gerald, et al. Poems. 62p. 1973. pap. 3.00 (ISBN 0-915596-03-2). West Coast.
Costanzo, P. R., jt. auth. see Shaw, M. E.
Costanzo, William V. Double Exposure: Composing Through Writing & Film. LC 84-16847. 272p. (Orig.). pap. text ed. 10.50x (ISBN 0-86709-051-0). Boynton Cook Pubs.
Costar, Brian & Woodward, Dennis. Country to National: Australian Rural Parties. 150p. 1985. text ed. 27.50x (ISBN 0-86861-708-3). Allen Unwin.
Costas, O., et al, eds. Hacia Una Teologia Evangelica Latinoamericana. 154p. 1984. pap. 3.95 (ISBN 0-89922-238-2). Edit Caribe.
Costas, Orlando. Christ Outside the Gate: Mission Beyond Christendom. LC 82-7892. 272p. (Orig.). 1982. pap. 12.95 (ISBN 0-88344-147-0). Orbis Bks.
--Compromiso y Mision. 159p. (Orig., Span.). 1979. pap. 3.95 (ISBN 0-89922-165-3). Edit Caribe.
Costas, Orlando E. Comunicacion Por Medio de la Predicacion. 255p. (Span.). pap. 6.25 (ISBN 0-89922-021-5). Edit Caribe.
--The Integrity of Mission: The Inner Life & Outreach of the Church. LC 79-1759. 1979. pap. 5.72i (ISBN 0-06-061586-9, RD 235, HarpR). Har-Row.
Costas, Procope S. An Outline History of the Greek Language. 1978. 20.00 (ISBN 0-89005-259-X). Ares.
Coste, Brigitte, jt. auth. see Braude, Beatrice.
Coste, D., jt. ed. see Galisson, R.
Coste, D., tr. see Prokopius Of Caesarea.
Coste, Didier. Sink Your Teeth in the Moon. 11.95 (ISBN 0-7145-1045-9). Riverrun NY.
Coste, Rene. Marxist Analysis & Christian Faith. Couture, Roger A., et al, trs. from Fr. LC 85-3119. 256p. (Orig.). 1985. pap. 11.95 (ISBN 0-88344-342-2). Orbis Bks.
Costeley, Guillaume see Expert, Henry.
Costeley, Guillaume see Janequin, Clement, et al.
Costello. Nicolas Poussin. pap. write for info. (Pub. by Natl Mus Canada). U of Chicago Pr.
--The Siwash: Their Life, Legends & Tales. (Shorey Indian Ser.). (Illus.). 177p. pap. 11.95 (ISBN 0-8466-0164-8, S164). Shorey.
Costello, Andrew. How to Deal with Diffficult People. LC 80-81751. 112p. (Orig.). 1980. pap. 2.95 (ISBN 0-89243-128-8). Liguori Pubns.
Costello, Anita C. Picasso's "Vollard Suite". LC 78-74365. (Outstanding Dissertations in the Fine Arts, Fourth Ser.). 1979. lib. bdg. 57.00 (ISBN 0-8240-3953-X). Garland Pub.
Costello, Anne. Bittergreen. 304p. (Orig.). 1980. pap. 2.25 (ISBN 0-345-28459-3). Ballantine.
Costello, Augustine. Our Police Protectors: History of the New York Police. 3rd ed. LC 79-129324. (Criminology, Law Enforcement, & Social Problems Ser.: No. 127). (Illus.). 653p. (With intro. added). 1972. Repr. of 1885 ed. lib. bdg. 25.00x (ISBN 0-87585-127-4). Patterson Smith.
Costello, Bella, tr. see Kuschevsky, Ivan.
Costello, Bella, tr. see Purishkevich, V. M.
Costello, Bonnie. Marianne Moore: Imaginary Possessions. LC 81-1133. 320p. 1981. text ed. 18.50x (ISBN 0-674-54848-5). Harvard U Pr.
Costello, C. G. Symptoms of Psychopathology: A Handbook. LC 78-88309. Repr. of 1970 ed. 120.00 (ISBN 0-8357-9988-3, 2055186). Bks Demand UMI.
Costello, Charles G. Anxiety & Depression: The Adaptive Emotions. 1976. text ed. 12.50x (ISBN 0-7735-0255-6). McGill-Queens U Pr.
Costello, Chris & Strait, Raymond. Lou's on First: The Biography of Lou Costello. (Illus.). 384p. 1983. pap. 6.95 (ISBN 0-312-49914-0). St Martin.
Costello, D. P., tr. see Hedayat, Sadegh.
Costello, Daniel J., Jr., jt. auth. see Shu Lin.
Costello, David F. The Prairie World. (Illus.). 1980. pap. 8.95 (ISBN 0-8166-0938-1). U of Minn Pr.
--The Seashore World. LC 79-7641. (Illus.). 256p. 1980. 14.37i (ISBN 0-690-01235-7). Har-Row.
--World of the Prairie Dog. LC 70-110650. (Living World Bks Ser.). (Illus.). 1970. 10.53i (ISBN 0-397-00679-9). Har-Row.
Costello, Dennis. New Venture Analysis: Research, Planning & Finance. LC 84-73197. 1985. 35.00 (ISBN 0-87094-505-X). Dow Jones-Irwin.
Costello, Don. For Inner Peace & Strength. 1978. 4.00 (ISBN 0-8198-0380-4); pap. 3.00 (ISBN 0-8198-0381-2). Dghtrs St Paul.
Costello, Donald P. Fellini's Road. LC 82-50286. 224p. 1983. text ed. 16.95 (ISBN 0-268-00958-9); pap. text ed. 9.95 (ISBN 0-268-00961-9). U of Notre Dame Pr.
Costello, E. J., jt. tr. see Gabrieli, Francesco.
Costello, Elaine. Signing: How to Speak with Your Hands. (Illus.). 256p. 1983. pap. 10.95 (ISBN 0-553-34250-9). Bantam.
--Signing: How to Speak with Your Hands. 1983. pap. 9.95 (ISBN 0-317-05935-1). Bantam.
Costello, Frank B. The Political Philosophy of Luis De Molina, S. J. 1974. pap. 18.00 (ISBN 88-7041-338-1). Jesuit Hist.
Costello, Gerald M. Mission to Latin America: The Successes & Failures of a Twentieth-Century Crusade. LC 78-12974. 319p. (Orig.). 1979. pap. 9.95 (ISBN 0-88344-312-0). Orbis Bks.
--Without Fear or Favor. (Illus.). 306p. (Orig.). 1984. pap. 9.95 (ISBN 0-89622-209-8). Twenty-Third.
Costello, Harry T. Josiah Royce's Seminar Nineteen Thirteen to Nineteen Fourteen: As Recorded in the Notebooks of Harry T. Costello. Smith, Grover, ed. LC 81-4213. (Illus.). xxiii, 209p. 1981. Repr. of 1963 ed. lib. bdg. 25.00x (ISBN 0-313-23080-3, C0JR). Greenwood.
--Philosophy of the Real & the Possible. LC 72-972. Repr. of 1954 ed. 15.00 (ISBN 0-404-01737-1). AMS Pr.
Costello, J. P., jt. auth. see Patrick, E. A.
Costello, Jacinta L., jt. auth. see Masterson, James F.
Costello, Jacqueline & Tucker, Amy. A Writing Course by & for ESL Students. 320p. 1984. pap. text ed. 14.95 (ISBN 0-394-33807-3, RanC). Random.
Costello, James A. The Underbelly Poems. 1981. pap. 2.95 (ISBN 0-9605098-0-1). En Passant Poet.
Costello, Jane. Nicolas Poussin: The Martyrdom of Saint Erasmus. (Masterpieces in the National Gallery Ser.). 1975. pap. 3.95 (ISBN 0-88884-258-9, Pub. by Natl Mus Canada). Nat Gal Can.
--An Outline of the History of Art. LC 60-6044. (Orig.). 1959. pap. 3.50x (ISBN 0-8147-0103-5). NYU Pr.
Costello, Janis M., ed. Speech Disorders in Adults: Recent Advances. (Illus.). 250p. 1984. 29.50t (ISBN 0-933014-98-8). College-Hill.
--Speech Disorders in Children: Recent Advances. LC 83-23141. (Illus.). 374p. 1984. 29.50 (ISBN 0-933014-90-2). College-Hill.
Costello, Jeanne & Witty, Doreen. Lighten-Up. Neumayer, Lisa, ed. (Illus.). 288p. (Orig.). 1983. pap. write for info. (ISBN 0-9609894-1-2). Costello & Witty.
Costello, Joan, et al. Growing up American: Contemporary Children & Their Society. 256p. 1985. 18.95 (ISBN 0-87073-303-6); pap. 11.25 (ISBN 0-87073-304-4). Schenkman Bks Inc.
Costello, John. The Pacific War. (Illus.). 1981. 24.00 (ISBN 0-89256-206-4). Rawson Assocs.
--The Pacific War. 1984. pap. 13.95 (ISBN 0-688-01620-0, Quill). Morrow.
--Virtue under Fire. 336p. 1985. 17.45i (ISBN 0-316-73968-5). Little.
Costello, John J., et al. Finite Mathematics with Applications. 524p. 1981. text ed. 24.95 (ISBN 0-15-527400-7, HC); solutions manual avail. (ISBN 0-15-527401-5). HarBraceJ.
--Mathematics for the Management, Life & Social Sciences. 792p. 1982. text ed. 24.95 (ISBN 0-15-555240-6, HC); answers avail. (ISBN 0-15-555241-4). HarBraceJ.
Costello, John R. A Generative Grammar of Old Frisian: German Language & Literature, Vol. 222. (European University Studies: Series 1). xv, 123p. 1977. pap. 16.30 (ISBN 3-261-03047-X). P Lang Pubs.
--Syntactic Change & Syntactic Reconstruction: A Tagmemic Approach. LC 83-60279. (Publications in Linguistics Ser.). 78p. (Orig.). 1983. pap. 9.00 (ISBN 0-88312-092-5). Summer Inst Ling.
Costello, Joseph. Can Modern Man Survive Modern Government? 109p. 1983. 12.95 (ISBN 0-89803-109-5, Dist. by Kampmann). Green Hill.
Costello, Louisa S. Catherine De Medicis. LC 70-162911. (Bentley's Standard Novels: No. 112). Repr. of 1848 ed. 17.00 (ISBN 0-404-54512-2). AMS Pr.
--The Rose Garden of Persia. 1977. Repr. of 1845 ed. 15.00 (ISBN 0-89984-170-8). Century Bookbindery.
Costello, Marjorie & Heiss, Michael. How to Select & Use Home Video Equipment. 144p. 1984. pap. 9.95 (ISBN 0-89586-209-3). H P Bks.
Costello, Marjorie & Katz, Cynthia. Breaking into Video. 1985. 7.95 (ISBN 0-671-50994-2, Pub. by Fireside). S&S.
Costello, Mark. The Murphy Stories. LC 72-86409. 120p. 1973. pap. 5.95 (ISBN 0-252-00309-8). U of Ill Pr.
Costello, Mary C. Between Fixity & Flux. LC 47-5815. 122p. 1966. pap. 5.95x (ISBN 0-8132-0255-8). Cath U Pr.
Costello, Maurice J. & Gibbs, Richard C. Palms & Soles in Medicine. (Illus.). 720p. 1967. photocopy ed. 61.25x (ISBN 0-398-00351-3). C C Thomas.
Costello, Neil & Richardson, Michael, eds. Continuing Education for the Post-Industrial Society. 160p. 1982. pap. 18.00x (ISBN 0-335-10186-0, Pub. by Open Univ Pr). Taylor & Francis.
Costello, Patty & Glossbrenner, Alfred. Bowling. (Illus.). 1977. 8.95 (ISBN 0-442-80375-3). Van Nos Reinhold.
Costello, Peter. James Joyce. (Gill's Irish Lives Ser.). 135p. 1980. 15.95 (ISBN 0-7171-1077-X, Pub. by Gill & Macmillan Ireland); pap. 6.95 (ISBN 0-7171-0986-0). Irish Bk Ctr.
--Leopold Bloom: A Biography. 1983. 17.95 (ISBN 0-7171-1100-8, Pub by Salem Hse Ltd). Merrimack Pub Cir.
Costello, R. B. American Expressions. 192p. 1981. 10.95 (ISBN 0-07-047137-1). McGraw.
Costello, Ralph. The Road to Manhood: The Male Adolescent's Guide to Survival in a Disorderly & Dangerous Age. LC 83-91230. 60p. 1983. pap. 4.95 (ISBN 0-9612900-0-5). R H Costello.
Costello, Tim, jt. auth. see Brecher, Jeremy.
Costello, Tom, jt. auth. see Brecher, Jeremy.
Costelloe, Joseph, tr. see Bouyer, Louis.
Costelloe, M. Joseph, tr. see Schurhammer, Georg.
Costello-Jones, Barry, et al, trs. see Kross, Jaan.
Costeloe, M. P. Church & State in Independent Mexico: A Study of the Patronage Debate, 1821-1857. (Royal Historical Society-Studies in History Ser.: Vol. 8). 207p. 1978. text ed. 32.25x (ISBN 0-901050-46-6, Pub. by Swiftbks England). Humanities.
--Church & State in Independent Mexico: A Study of the Patronage Debate, 1821 to 1857. 1982. 70.00x (ISBN 0-901050-46-6, 07549982, Pub. by Royal Hist Soc England). State Mutual Bk.
Costeloe, Michael P. Mexico State Papers 1744-1843: A Descriptive Catalogue of the G. R. G. Conway Collection in the Institute of Historical Research, University of London. (Institute of Latin American Studies Monographs: No. 6). 153p. 1976. 28.50 (ISBN 0-485-17706-4, Pub. by Athlone Pr Ltd). Longwood Pub Group.
Coster, C. H. Iudicium Quinquevirale. (MED ACAD AMER Pubns). 1935. 16.00 (ISBN 0-527-01694-2). Kraus Repr.
Coster, Charles H. Late Roman Studies. LC 67-22863. 1968. 20.00x (ISBN 0-674-51200-6). Harvard U Pr.
Coster, Charles T. De see De Coster, Charles T.
Coster, Howard. Howard Coster's Celebrity Portraits: One Hundred One Photographs of Personalities in Literature & the Arts. (Illus.). 128p. 1985. pap. 7.95 (ISBN 0-486-24892-5). Dover.
Coster, J., jt. ed. see Lewis, S. M.
Coster, Jean De see De Coster, Jean.
Costero, Isaac. Arterial Hypertension. bilingual ed. 4.35 (ISBN 0-8477-2306-2); pap. 3.75 (ISBN 0-8477-2307-0). U of PR Pr.
Costich, Emmett R. & White, Raymond P., Jr. Fundamentals of Oral Surgery. LC 75-139423. (Illus.). Repr. of 1971 ed. 47.70 (ISBN 0-8357-9546-2, 2013065). Bks Demand UMI.
Costich, Julia F. Antonin Artaud. (World Authors Ser.). 1978. lib. bdg. 16.95 (ISBN 0-8057-6333-3, Twayne). G K Hall.
--The Poetic Structure of Change: A Study of the Surrealist Work of Benjamin Peret. (Studies in the Romance Languages & Literatures: No.206). 1979. pap. 10.50x (ISBN 0-8078-9206-8). U of NC Pr.
Costigan, Daniel M. Electronic Delivery of Documents & Graphics. 1978. text ed. 29.95 (ISBN 0-442-80036-3). Van Nos Reinhold.
--Electronic Delivery of Documents & Graphics. 344p. 1978. 24.25 (ISBN 0-686-98117-0). Telecom Lib.
--Micrographic Systems. 2nd ed. Meyer, Ellen T., ed. LC 75-29532. (Reference Ser.). 268p. 1980. 21.75 (ISBN 0-89258-021-6, R016); member 16.25. Assn Inform & Image Mgmt.
Costigan, Edward P. Public Ownership of Government. LC 68-15821. 1968. Repr. of 1940 ed. 26.75x (ISBN 0-8046-0090-2, Pub. by Kennikat). Assoc Faculty Pr.
Costigan, Giovanni. A History of Modern Ireland: With a Sketch of Earlier Times. LC 69-15699. (Illus.). 1970. pap. 9.63scp (ISBN 0-672-63547-X). Pegasus.
--History of Modern Ireland: With a Sketch of Earlier Times. 1970. pap. text ed. write for info. (ISBN 0-02-325350-9). Macmillan.
Costigan, Madeleine. The Last of the Long Hot Summers & Other Short Stories. 1982. 8.95 (ISBN 0-933184-41-7). Flame Intl.
Costigan, Shirleyann. The Three Bears Get in Shape. (The Three Bears Ser.). (Illus.). 1984. pap. 2.95 (ISBN 0-8224-6929-4). Pitman Learning.
--The Three Bears Go to Camp. (The Three Bears Ser.). (Illus.). 1984. pap. 2.95 (ISBN 0-8224-6933-2). Pitman Learning.
--The Three Bears Go to the Circus. (The Three Bears Ser.). (Illus.). 1984. pap. 2.95 (ISBN 0-8224-6934-0). Pitman Learning.
--The Three Bears Go to Town. (The Three Bears Ser.). (Illus.). 1984. pap. 2.95 (ISBN 0-8224-6931-6). Pitman Learning.
--The Three Bears Go West. (The Three Bears Ser.). (Illus.). 1984. pap. 2.95 (ISBN 0-8224-6932-4). Pitman Learning.
--The Three Bears Series, 6 bks. (Illus.). 1984. Set. pap. 17.70 (ISBN 0-8224-6928-6). Pitman Learning.
--The Three Bears Spot the Clues. (The Three Bears Ser.). (Illus.). 1984. pap. 2.95 (ISBN 0-8224-6935-9). Pitman Learning.
Costigliola, Frank. Awkward Dominion: American Political, Economic, & Cultural Relations with Europe 1919-1933. LC 84-45150. 376p. 1985. 27.50x (ISBN 0-8014-1679-5). Cornell U Pr.
Costikyan, Barbara H. Be Kind to Your Dog At Christmas, & Other Ways to Have Happy Holidays & a Lucky New Year. LC 81-22343. (Illus.). 56p. (gr. 8-11). 1982. 9.95 (ISBN 0-394-84963-9); PLB 9.99 (ISBN 0-394-94963-3). Pantheon.
Costikyan, Edward N. Behind Closed Doors: Politics in the Public Interest. LC 66-123599. 1968. pap. 5.75 (ISBN 0-15-611681-2, Harv). HarBraceJ.
Costikyan, Edward N. & Lehman, Maxwell. New Strategies for Regional Cooperation: A Model for the Tri-State New York-New Jersey-Connecticut Area. LC 73-9388. (Special Studies in U. S. Economic, Social & Political Issues). 1973. 27.50x (ISBN 0-275-28777-7). Irvington.
Costikyan, Edward N & Lehman, Maxwell. Re-Structuring the Government of New York City: Report of the Scott Commission Task Force on Jurisdiction & Structure. LC 72-86838. (Special Studies in U. S. Economic, Social & Political Issues). 1972. 24.50x (ISBN 0-275-06320-8). Irvington.
Costill, David L. A Scientific Approach to Distance Running. LC 78-68880. (Illus., Orig.). 1979. pap. 6.00 (ISBN 0-911520-88-0). Tafnews.
Costin, A. B. & Gray, M. Kosciusko Alpine Flora. 408p. 1979. 45.00 (ISBN 0-643-02473-5, C006, CSIRO). Unipub.
Costin, A. B. & Groves, R. H. Nature Conservation in the Pacific. (Illus.). 337p. 1973. pap. 20.00 (ISBN 2-88032-051-8, IUCN37, IUCN). Unipub.
Costin, A. B., et al. Kosciusko Alpine Flora. 408p. 1982. 85.00x (ISBN 0-643-02473-5, Pub. by CSIRO Australia). State Mutual Bk.
Costin, Alec, et al. Kosciusko Alpine Flora. 408p. 1980. 35.00x (ISBN 0-643-02473-5, Pub. by CSIRO Australia). Intl Spec Bk.
Costin, Alec B., et al. Kosciusko Alpine Flora. (Illus.). 408p. 1979. 35.00x (ISBN 0-643-02473-5, Pub. by Brit Mus Nat Hist England). Sabbot-Natural Hist Bks.
Costin, L. B., jt. auth. see Brieland, D.
Costin, Lela B. Two Sisters for Social Justice: A Biography of Grace & Edith Abbott. LC 82-21790. 336p. 1983. 18.50x (ISBN 0-252-01013-2). U of Ill Pr.
Costin, Lela B. & Gruener, Jennette R. The Licensing of Family Homes in Child Welfare: A Guide for Instructors & Trainees. LC 65-12939. 160p. 1965. 8.95x (ISBN 0-8143-1266-7). Wayne St U Pr.
Costin, Lela B. & Rapp, Charles A. Child Welfare: Policies & Practice. 3rd ed. (Illus.). 608p. 1984. text ed. 28.95 (ISBN 0-07-013244-5). McGraw.

Costin, Michael & Phipps, David. Racing & Sports Car Chassis Design. LC 68-4344. (Illus.). (YA) (gr. 9 up). 1965. pap. 16.95 (ISBN 0-8376-0296-3). Bentley.

Costineti, Sandra. Language of Accounting in English. (English for Careers Ser). (gr. 10-12). 1977. pap. text ed. 4.25 (ISBN 0-88345-281-2, 18512). Regents Pub.

Costinett, Sandra. Advanced Readings & Conversations. 1973. pap. text ed. 4.95 (ISBN 0-88499-050-8). Inst Mod Lang.

--American English for International Businessmen. 1973. text ed. 6.95 (ISBN 0-88499-055-9); Set Of 12 Tapes. 225.00 (ISBN 0-88499-160-1); Set Of 6 Cassettes. 115.00 (ISBN 0-88499-161-X). Inst Mod Lang.

--Spectrum Two: Textbook. (Spectrum Ser.). (gr. 7-12). 1982. pap. text ed. 5.95 (ISBN 0-88345-502-1, 20115). Regents Pub.

Costley, Bill. Rag(a) S. 1978. write for info. (ISBN 0-686-08921-9). Ghost Dance.

Costley, Dan L. & Todd, Ralph. Human Relations in Organizations. 2d ed. (Illus.). 586p. 1983. text ed. 24.95 (ISBN 0-314-69643-1); write for info. instr's. manual (ISBN 0-314-71087-6); transparency masters avail. (ISBN 0-314-74294-8). West Pub.

Costley, Thomas. My Favorite Authors: (Raleigh, Swift, Goldsmith, Cowper, Burns, Longfellow, Ruskin) 1979. Repr. of 1894 ed. lib. bdg. 40.00 (ISBN 0-8482-7576-4). Norwood Edns.

Costlow, J. D. & Tipper, R. C., eds. Marine Biodeterioration. LC 81-85468. (Illus.). 512p. 1983. 29.95x (ISBN 0-87021-530-2). Naval Inst Pr.

--Marine Biodeterioration. (Illus.). 512p. 1982. 29.95 (ISBN 0-87021-530-2); bulk rates avail. Naval Inst Pr.

Costlow, John D., ed. Fertility of the Sea, 2 vols. LC 74-132383. (Illus.). 646p. 1971. Set. 121.50 (ISBN 0-677-14730-9). Gordon.

Costner, Herbert L. The Changing Folkways of Parenthood: A Content Analysis. Zuckerman, Harriet & Merton, Robert K., eds. LC 79-8987. (Dissertations on Sociology Ser.). 1980. lib. bdg. 36.00x (ISBN 0-405-12960-2). Ayer Co Pubs.

Costner, Herbert L., ed. Sociological Methodology 1973-74. LC 73-9071. (Social & Behavioral Science Ser.). 1974. 32.95x (ISBN 0-87589-197-7). Jossey-Bass.

Costner, Susan. Gifts of Food. (Illus.). 1984. 18.95 (ISBN 0-517-55415-1). Crown.

Costo, Rupert, ed. Textbooks & the American Indian. LC 75-119022. 269p. 1969. pap. 5.00 (ISBN 0-913436-00-3). Indian Hist Pr.

Costoff, Allen. Ultrastructure of Rat Adenohypophysis: Correlation with Function. 1973. 49.00 (ISBN 0-12-191550-6). Acad Pr.

Coston, Henry, ed. Dictionnaire des Dynasties Bourgecises et du Monde des Affaires. 599p. (Fr.). 1975. 55.00 (ISBN 0-686-56839-7, M-6617). French & Eur.

Coston, William H. The Spanish-American War Volunteer. 2nd rev. enl. facsimile ed. LC 75-164384. (Black Heritage Library Collection). Repr. of 1899 ed. 26.50 (ISBN 0-8369-8843-4). Ayer Co Pubs.

Costonis, John J. Space Adrift: Landmark Preservation & the Marketplace. LC 73-5405. (Illus.). 229p. 1974. 17.50 (ISBN 0-252-00402-7). U of Ill Pr.

Costonis, John J. & DeVoy, Robert S. The Puerto Rico Plan: Environmental Protection Through Development Rights Transfer. LC 75-15460. pap. 20.00 (ISBN 0-317-26003-0, 2023883). Bks Demand UMI.

Costonis, John J., et al. Regulation V. Compensation in Land Use Control: A Recommended Accommodation, a Critique, & an Interpretation. LC 77-5939. 1977. pap. 4.50x (ISBN 0-87772-226-9). Inst Gov Stud Berk.

Costonis, Maureen, ed. Therapy in Motion. LC 77-9077. 232p. 1977. 15.50 (ISBN 0-252-00586-4). U of Ill Pr.

Costopoulos, Tom. Irlich, the Stalin Assassination. LC 78-70359. 1979. 11.95x (ISBN 0-932634-00-1). NPC Pub Co.

Costopoulos, William C. The Price of Acquittal. 1982. 12.50 (ISBN 0-8062-1944-0). Carlton.

Cosway, R., et al. Trade & Investment in Taiwan: The Legal & Environment in the Republic of China. 783p. 1980. 20.00x (ISBN 0-89955-144-0, Pub. by Mei Ya China). Intl Spec Bk.

Cot, J. International Conciliation. (Europa's International Relations Ser). 368p. 1972. 13.95x (ISBN 0-900362-40-5). Intl Pubns Serv.

Cot, J. P. & Guilhaudi, J. F. Repertory of Disarmament Research. (Illus.). 449p. 1982. 35.00x (ISBN 0-8002-3318-2). Intl Pubns Serv.

Cota, Sancho. Memorias de Sancho Cota. Keniston, Hayward, ed. LC 64-16064. (Studies in Romance Languages: No. 28). 1964. 15.00x (ISBN 0-674-56600-9). Harvard U Pr.

Cotant, Christopher J., jt. auth. see Jenkins, Michael D.

Cotchett, Joseph W. & Elkind, Arnold B. Federal Courtroom Evidence. LC 75-26155. 249p. 1976. incl. 1984 suppl. 47.50 (ISBN 0-911110-20-8). Parker & Son.

Cotchett, Joseph W. & Haight, Fulton. California Courtroom Evidence: 1984 Supplement. 2nd ed. LC 80-85487. 1981. 05/1981 49.50 (ISBN 0-911110-36-4). Parker & Son.

Cotchin, E. & Marchant, J. Animal Tumors of the Female Reproductive Tract. 1977. 21.00 (ISBN 0-387-90209-0). Springer Verlag.

Cote, Joe E. Adventure of a Tumbleweed. 1982. 13.95 (ISBN 0-533-05281-5). Vantage.

Cote, M., ed. see Larouche, L. & Pilon, J.

Cote, N. & Gaumond, J. Nomenclature des Appelations d'emploi dans L' Industrie Papetiere Quebecoise: Anglais-Francais. 114p. (Eng. & Fr.). 1977. pap. 6.95 (ISBN 0-7754-2765-9, M-9234). French & Eur.

Cote, Oliver. Going Down. LC 78-70409. 1979. pap. 3.95 (ISBN 0-917300-08-4). SingleJack Bks.

Cote, R. A., et al, eds. Role of Informatics in Health Data Coding & Classification Systems: Proceedings of the IFIP-IMIA International Working Conference on the Role of Informatics in Health Data Decoding & Classification Systems, Ottawa, Canada, 26-28 September, 1984. 394p. 1985. 59.25 (ISBN 0-444-87682-0, North-Holland). Elsevier.

Cote, Raymond. Business Math Concepts. 336p. 1984. 19.75x (ISBN 0-89702-047-2); solution manual 18.10 (ISBN 0-89702-047-2). PAR Inc.

Cote, Richard G. Could It Be? A Theological Reflections on America. LC 76-11035. 1976. 3.95 (ISBN 0-8189-0330-9). Alba.

Cote, Richard N. The Genealogists Guide to Charleston County, South Carolina. (Illus.). 52p. 1981. pap. 10.00 (ISBN 0-89308-245-7). Southern Hist Pr.

--Local Family History in South Carolina: A Bibliography. 520p. 1981. 27.50 (ISBN 0-89308-200-7); pap. 22.50 (ISBN 0-89308-200-7). Southern Hist Pr.

Cote, Richard N. & Williams, Patricia H., eds. The Dictionary of South Carolina Biography, Vol. 1. (Illus.). 404p. 1985. 30.00 (ISBN 0-89308-275-9). Southern Hist Pr.

Cote, Richard N., ed. see Heitzler, Michael J.

Cote, W. A., jt. auth. see Kollmann, F. F.

Cote, Wilfred A., jt. auth. see Nanko, Heroki.

Cote, Wilfred A., ed. Papermaking Fibers: A Photomicrographic Atlas. (Renewable Materials Institute Ser.). (Illus.). 200p. 1980. pap. text ed. 12.00x (ISBN 0-8156-2228-7). Syracuse U Pr.

Cote, Wilfred A., Jr. Wood Ultrastructure: An Atlas of Electron Micrographs. LC 67-21204. (Illus.). 64p. 1967. pap. 20.00x (ISBN 0-295-97868-6). U of Wash Pr.

Cotellessa, Robert F., ed. Identifying Research Areas in the Computer Industry to 1995. LC 84-16551. (Illus.). 154p. 1985. 32.00 (ISBN 0-8155-1008-X). Noyes.

Cotera, Martha & Hufford, Larry, eds. Bridging Two Cultures: Multidisciplinary Readings in Bilingual Bicultural Education. LC 77-89044. 1980. pap. text ed. 14.95x (ISBN 0-916542-10-6). AAR-Tantalus.

Cotera, Martha P. Austin Hispanic Directory. 144p. 1984. 14.95 (ISBN 0-931738-11-3). Info Systems.

--The Chicana Feminist. 68p. 1977. pap. 5.00x (ISBN 0-931738-01-6). Info Systems.

--Diosa y Hembra: History & Heritage of Chicanas in the U.S. 202p. 1976. pap. 6.95x (ISBN 0-931738-00-8). Info Systems.

--Mexican American Directory of Austin, Texas, 1980. Cunningham, Nella, ed. (Orig.). 1979. pap. 9.00x (ISBN 0-931738-05-9). Info Systems.

--Multicultural Women's Sourcebook: Materials Guide for Use in Women's Studies & Bilingual Multicultural Programs. 160p. 1982. pap. 17.00 (ISBN 0-931738-08-3). Info Systems.

Cotera, Martha P., tr. see Hazen, Nancy.

Cotes, Peter, jt. auth. see Atkins, Harold.

Cotgrave, Randle. A Dictionarie of the French & English Tongues. LC 77-171741. (English Experience Ser.: No. 367). 992p. (Fr. & Eng.). 1971. Repr. of 1611 ed. 105.00 (ISBN 90-221-0367-6). Walter J Johnson.

--Dictionary of the French & English Tongues. (Fr. & Eng.). 1971. Repr. of 1611 ed. 128.00x (ISBN 0-685-05204-4). Adlers Foreign Bks.

Cotgrove, Stephen. Catastrophe or Cornucopia: The Environment, Politics & the Future. LC 81-148827. 1982. 154p. 44.95x, (ISBN 0-471-10079-X, Pub. by Wiley-Interscience); pap. 24.95x, 232p. (ISBN 0-471-10166-4). Wiley.

Cotham, Perry C., ed. Christian Social Ethics Perspective & Problems. 1978. pap. 6.95 (ISBN 0-8010-2424-2). Baker Bk.

Cothen, Grady C. Faith & Higher Education. 1976. pap. 1.50 (ISBN 0-8054-6916-8). Broadman.

--Unto All the World: Bold Mission. LC 79-50341. 1979. pap. 2.25 (ISBN 0-8054-5508-6). Broadman.

Cothen, Joe. Come to Bethlehem: The Christmas Story. LC 75-25503. (Illus.). 64p. (gr. 4 up). 1975. 4.95 (ISBN 0-88289-098-0). Pelican.

Cothen, Joe H. Equipped for Good Work: A Guide for Pastors. LC 80-37964. 336p. 1981. 14.95 (ISBN 0-88289-271-1). Pelican.

Cothen, Joe H. & Strange, John O. The Preacher's Notebook on Isaiah. LC 82-24596. 96p. 1983. pap. 6.95 (ISBN 0-88289-365-3). Pelican.

Cothenet, Edouard, et al. Imitating Christ. Inkel, Sr. Simone, tr. LC 73-94173. (Religious Experience Ser: Vol. 5). 1974. pap. 3.95 (ISBN 0-87029-029-0, 20095-6). Abbey.

Cothran, Jean, ed. The Whang Doodle & Other Stories. LC 72-86904. (Illus.). (gr. 3-7). 1972. 4.95 (ISBN 0-87844-052-6). Sandlapper Pub Co.

Cothren, Paige. Let None Deal Treacherously. 256p. (Orig.). 1981. pap. 5.00 (ISBN 0-937778-03-6). Fulness Hse.

Cothren, William. History of Ancient Woodbury, Connecticut. LC 77-82298. (Illus.). 833p. 1977. Repr. of 1854 ed. 38.50 (ISBN 0-8063-0781-1). Genealog Pub.

Cotich, Felicia, et al. Primavera, V. Heller, Janet R., et al, eds. LC 76-647540. (Illus.). 1979. pap. 4.00 (ISBN 0-916980-05-7). Primavera.

Cotiviela, A., tr. see Schrolder, A. & Bonnet, L.

Cotler, Joanna, jt. auth. see Cristofaro, Cris.

Cotler, Julio & Fagen, Richard R., eds. Latin America & the United States: The Changing Political Realities. LC 73-94487. 429p. 1974. 30.00x (ISBN 0-8047-0860-6); pap. 8.95x (ISBN 0-8047-0861-4). Stanford U Pr.

Cotler, Stephen R. Modifying the Existing Campus Building for Accessibility: Construction Guidelines & Specifications. 89p. 10.50 (ISBN 0-317-33662-2); members 7.50 (ISBN 0-317-33663-0). Assn Phys Plant Admin.

Cotliar, William, jt. auth. see Riordan, John J.

Cotlier, Edward & Maumenee, Irene H., eds. Genetic Eye Diseases: Retinitis Pigmentosa & Other Inherited Eye Disorders. LC 82-13049. (Birth Defects; Original Article Ser.: Vol. 18, No. 6). 772p. 1982. 76.00 (ISBN 0-8451-1050-0). A R Liss.

Cotlier, H., et al. Transplantation. Masshoff, W., ed. (Handbuch der Allgemeinen Pathologie: Bund 6, Teil 8). (Illus.). 1977. 275.00 (ISBN 0-387-07751-0). Springer-Verlag.

Cotman, C. W., jt. ed. see Tapia, R.

Cotman, C. W., et al, eds. Cell Surface & Neuron & Neuronal Function. Nicolson. (Cell Surface Reviews Ser.: Vol. 6). 546p. 1981. 121.75 (ISBN 0-444-80202-9, Biomedical Pr). Elsevier.

Cotman, Carl W. & Jenson, Robert. Behavioral Neuroscience: An Introduction. 1979. instr's. manual 10.00 (ISBN 0-12-191655-3). Acad Pr.

Cotman, Carl W. & McGaugh, James L. Behavioral Neuroscience: An Introduction. LC 79-50214. 1980. 24.00i (ISBN 0-12-191650-2). Acad Pr.

Cotman, Carl W., jt. auth. see Angevine, Jay B., Jr.

Cotman, Carl W., ed. Neuronal Plasticity. LC 77-72807. 349p. 1978. 45.50 (ISBN 0-89004-210-1). Raven.

--Synaptic Plasticity. 460p. text ed. write for info (ISBN 0-89862-654-4). Guilford Pr.

Cotner, Robert, tr. Theodore Foster's Minutes of the Convention Held at South Kingstown, R.I. in March, 1790. (Illus.). 1929. 8.50 (ISBN 0-685-67676-5). RI Hist Soc.

Cotner, Robert C., ed. see Foster, Theodore.

Cotner, Robert C., ed. see Urbantke, Carl.

Cotner, Sam. The Vegetable Book: A Texan's Guide to Gardening. (Illus.). 384p. 1985. 24.95 (ISBN 0-914641-01-8). Texas Gard.

Cotner, Thomas E. Military & Political Career of Jose Joaquin De Herrera, 1792-1854. LC 69-19007. Repr. of 1949 ed. lib. bdg. 22.75x (ISBN 0-8371-1018-1, TICH). Greenwood.

Cotner, Thomas E, ed. see Texas University Institute of Latin American Studies.

Cotran, E., jt. ed. see Rubin, N. N.

Cotran, Eugene, jt. ed. see Rubin, Neville.

Cotran, Eugene, jt. ed. see Rubin, Neville N.

Cotran, Ramzi, jt. auth. see Leaf, Alexander.

Cotran, Ramzi, ed. Tubulo-Interstitial Nephropathies. (Contemporary Issues in Nephrology Ser.: Vol. 10). (Illus.). 381p. 1982. text ed. 49.50 (ISBN 0-443-08258-8). Churchill.

Cotran, Ramzi S., jt. auth. see Robbins, Stanley L.

Cotrell, Allin. Social Classes in Marxist Theory & in Post-War Britain. 330p. (Orig.). 1984. 39.50x (ISBN 0-7100-9906-1). Routledge & Kegan.

Cotroneo, Ross R. History of the Northern Pacific Land Grant, 1900-1952. Bruchey, Stuart, ed. LC 78-56728. (Management in Public Lands in the U. S. Ser.). (Illus.). 1979. lib. bdg. 36.00x (ISBN 0-405-11329-3). Ayer Co Pubs.

Cotruvo, Joseph A., jt. ed. see Rice, Rip G.

Cotsforde, Thomas, tr. see Zwingli, Ulrich.

Cott, Allan, et al. Dr. Cott's Help for Your Learning Disabled Child: The Orthomolecular Treatment. LC 84-40417. 288p. 1985. 16.95 (ISBN 0-8129-1147-4). Times Bks.

Cott, Christine D. Midnight Magic. pap. write for info. Harlequin Bks.

Cott, Christine H. Dangerous Delight. (Superromances Ser.). 384p. 1983. pap. 2.50 (ISBN 0-373-70050-4, Pub. by Worldwide). Harlequin Bks.

--Perfume & Lace. (Superromances). 384p. 1984. pap. 2.95 (ISBN 0-373-70098-9, Pub. by Worldwide). Harlequin Bks.

--Un Sejour a Clifftop. (Harlequin Seduction Ser.). 332p. 1984. pap. 3.25 (ISBN 0-373-45034-6). Harlequin Bks.

--A Tender Wilderness. (SuperRomances Ser.). 384p. 1982. pap. 2.50 (ISBN 0-373-70030-X, Pub. by Worldwide). Harlequin Bks.

--Toute la Tendresse du Monde. (Harlequin Seduction Ser.). 332p. 1983. pap. 3.25 (ISBN 0-373-45015-X). Harlequin Bks.

Cott, J. Pipers at the Gates of Dawn: The Wisdom of Children's Literature. (Paperbacks Ser.). 352p. 1984. pap. 8.95 (ISBN 0-07-013220-8). McGraw.

Cott, Jonathan. Charms. LC 80-28181. 24p. 1980. pap. 4.00 (ISBN 0-915124-48-3, Pub. by Toothpaste). Coffee Hse.

--Conversations with Glenn Gould. 160p. 1984. 15.45i (ISBN 0-316-15777-5); pap. 7.70i (ISBN 0-316-15776-7). Little.

--Pipers at the Gates of Dawn: The Wisdom of Children's Literature. 1983. 19.95 (ISBN 0-394-50464-X). Random.

Cott, Jonathan & Rolling Stone Press. Dylan. LC 84-4049. (Illus.). 256p. 1984. 35.00 (ISBN 0-385-19161-8). Doubleday.

--Dylan. LC 84-4049. (Illus.). 256p. 1985. pap. 15.95 (ISBN 0-385-19162-6, Dolp). Doubleday.

Cott, Jonathan, ed. Beyond the Looking Glass: Extraordinary Works of Fairy Tale & Fantasy. LC 84-22675. (Illus.). 576p. 1985. 19.95 (ISBN 0-87951-995-9). Overlook Pr.

--Masterworks of Children's Literature, Vol. VII: Victorian Color Picture Books. 1984. 50.00 (ISBN 0-87754-381-X). Chelsea Hse.

--Masterworks of Children's Literature: 1550-1900, 8 vols. LC 79-89986. (Illus.). Set. 310.00 (ISBN 0-87754-089-6). Chelsea Hse.

--Victorian Color Picture Books. (Illus.). 184p. 1983. 50.00x (ISBN 0-87754-398-4). Chelsea Hse.

Cott, Nancy, ed. The Roots of Bitterness: Documents of the Social History of American Women. 1972. pap. 9.75 (ISBN 0-525-47328-9, 0947-280). Dutton.

Cott, Nancy F. The Bonds of Womanhood: "Woman's Sphere" in New England, 1780-1835. LC 76-49728. 1978. pap. 6.95x (ISBN 0-300-02289-1). Yale U Pr.

Cott, Nancy F. & Pleck, Elizabeth H. A Heritage of Her Own: Families, Work & Feminism in America. 1980. pap. 11.95 (ISBN 0-317-05160-1, Touchstone Bks.). S&S.

Cotta, Alain. Dictionnaire de la Science Economique. 3rd ed. 448p. (Fr.). pap. 22.50 (ISBN 0-686-56965-2, M-6092). French & Eur.

Cotta, Horst. Orthopedics. (Illus.). 480p. 1980. pap. 20.95 (ISBN 0-8151-1864-3). Year Bk Med.

Cotta, John. A Short Discoverie of the Dangers of Ignorant Practisers of Physicke. LC 72-38168. (English Experience Ser.: No. 445). 144p. 1972. Repr. of 1612 ed. 21.00 (ISBN 90-221-0445-1). Walter J Johnson.

--The Triall of Witch-Craft Shewing the True Methode of the Discovery. LC 68-54629. (English Experience Ser.: No. 39). 128p. 1968. Repr. of 1616 ed. 21.00 (ISBN 90-221-0039-1). Walter J Johnson.

Cotta, Sergio. Montesquieu e la Scienza Della Societa. Mayer, J. P., ed. LC 78-67343. (European Political Thought Ser.). (It.). 1979. Repr. of 1953 ed. lib. bdg. 48.50x (ISBN 0-405-11688-8). Ayer Co Pubs.

--Why Violence? A Philosophical Interpretation. Gullace, Giovanni, tr. from Ital. LC 84-25779. Orig. Title: Perch la violenza? Una Interpretazione Filosofica. 168p. 25.00 (ISBN 0-8130-0804-2); pap. 12.00 (ISBN 0-8130-0824-7). U Presses Fla.

Cottage Crew. Calico Cottage Cook Book. 50p. (Orig.). 1982. pap. 2.00 (ISBN 0-9606508-2-2). Holly Hill.

Cottam, Clarence A., jt. auth. see Zim, Herbert S.

Cottam, K. J., ed. & tr. The Girl from Kashin: Soviet Women in Resistance in World War II. (Illus.). 230p. 1984. pap. 27.00x (ISBN 0-89126-128-1). MA-AH Pub.

--The Golden-Tressed Soldier. 287p. 1983. pap. 33.00x (ISBN 0-89126-119-2). MA-AH Pub.

--In the Sky Above the Front. (Illus.). 270p. 1984. pap. text ed. 31.00x (ISBN 0-89126-126-5). MA-AH Pub.

Cottam, K. J., tr. Soviet Airwomen in Combat in WWII. 141p. 1983. pap. 14.00x (ISBN 0-89126-118-4). MA-AH Pub.

Cottam, Kazimiera J. Boleslaw Limanowski, (1835-1935) (Eastern European Monographs: No. 41). 365p. 1978. 30.00x (ISBN 0-914710-34-6). East Eur Quarterly.

Cottam, Richard W. Competitive Interference & Twentieth Century Diplomacy. LC 67-12925. pap. 62.80 (ISBN 0-317-26637-3, 2025435). Bks Demand UMI.

--Foreign Policy Motivation: A General Theory & a Case Study. LC 76-6659. 1977. 29.95 (ISBN 0-8229-3323-3). U of Pittsburgh Pr.

--Nationalism in Iran: Updated Through 1978. LC 78-12302. 1979. 24.95x (ISBN 0-8229-3396-9); pap. 9.95x (ISBN 0-8229-5299-8). U of Pittsburgh Pr.

Cottam, Walter P., et al. Oak Hybridization at the University of Utah. (State Arboretum of Utah Ser.: Publication No. 1, 1982). (Illus.). 96p. 1982. 15.00 (ISBN 0-942830-00-8); pap. 10.00x (ISBN 0-942830-01-6). State Arbor.

Cottan, G. B. & Glencorss, A. Cumulated Fiction Index Nineteen Forty-Five to Nineteen Sixty. 1981. 60.00x (ISBN 0-900092-09-2, Pub. by Hill & Son England). State Mutual Bk.

Cotte, Sabine. Claude Lorrain. LC 76-137220. (Great Draughtsmen Ser). (Illus.). 1971. 7.95 (ISBN 0-8076-0594-8). Braziller.

Cottrel, P. L. & Aldcroft, D. H., eds. Shipping, Trade & Commerce: Essays in Memory of Ralph Davis. 200p. 1981. text ed. 32.00x. Humanities.

Cottrell, A. H. The Mechanical Properties of Matter. LC 80-12439. 340p. 1981. Repr. of 1964 ed. lib. bdg. 23.50 (ISBN 0-89874-168-8). Krieger.

--Theory of Crystal Dislocations. (Documents on Modern Physics Ser.). 104p. 1964. pap. 27.95 (ISBN 0-677-00175-4). Gordon.

Cottrell, Alan. How Safe Is Nuclear Energy? 1981. pap. text ed. 6.50x (ISBN 0-435-54175-7). Heinemann Ed.

--An Introduction to Metallurgy. LC 75-21731. 598p. 1975. pap. 29.50x (ISBN 0-8448-0767-2). Crane-Russak Co.

Cottrell, Alan P., tr. see Steiner, Rudolf.

Cottrell, Alvin, et al. Arms Transfers & U. S. Foreign & Military Policy, No. 7. LC 80-50062. (Significant Issues Ser.: Vol. 1). 63p. 1980. 5.95 (ISBN 0-89206-013-1). CSI Studies.

Cottrell, Alvin J. Military Response to the Persian Gulf Crisis. 45p. 1982. pap. write for info. (ISBN 0-87855-909-4). Transaction Bks.

--Seapower & Strategy in the Indian Ocean. LC 80-28415. (Illus.). 148p. 1981. 20.00 (ISBN 0-8039-1577-2). Sage.

Cottrell, Alvin J. & Dougherty, James E. Iran's Quest for Security: U. S. Arms Transfers & the Nuclear Option. LC 77-80298. (Foreign Policy Reports Ser.). 59p. 1977. 5.00 (ISBN 0-89549-004-8). Inst Foreign Policy Anal.

Cottrell, Alvin J. & Hahn, Walter F. Naval Race or Arms Control in the Indian Ocean? Some Problems for Negotiating Naval Limitations. 78p. 1978. pap. text ed. 3.95 (ISBN 0-87855-799-7). Transaction Bks.

Cottrell, Alvin J. & Hanks, Robert J. The Military Utility of the U. S. Facilities in the Philippines, No. 11. LC 80-83128. (Significant Issues Ser.: Vol. II). 40p. 1980. 5.95 (ISBN 0-89206-027-1). CSI Studies.

Cottrell, Alvin J., jt. auth. see Adams, Thomas W.

Cottrell, Alvin J., jt. auth. see Hahn, Walter F.

Cottrell, Alvin J., ed. The Persian Gulf States: A General Survey. LC 79-19452. 736p. 1980. text ed. 40.00x (ISBN 0-8018-2204-1). Johns Hopkins.

Cottrell, Barbara J., jt. auth. see Larsen, Lawrence H.

Cottrell, Beekman W., jt. auth. see Slack, Robert C.

Cottrell, Calvert B., jt. auth. see Schneider, David M.

Cottrell, Clayton. The Thirty-Fourth World's Fair Exposition Scrapbook. Nord, Barry, ed. (Illus.). 55p. (Orig.). 1982. pap. 10.95x (ISBN 0-935656-06-5, 101F). Chrome Yellow.

Cottrell, Donald P. Instruction & Instructional Facilities in the Colleges of the United Lutheran Church in America. LC 79-176672. (Columbia University. Teachers College. Contributions to Education: No. 376). Repr. of 1929 ed. 22.50 (ISBN 0-404-55376-1). AMS Pr.

Cottrell, Edyth Y. Mrs. Cottrell's Stretching-the-Food-Dollar Cookbook. LC 80-36894. (Illus.). 128p. (Orig.). 1982. pap. 4.95 (ISBN 0-912800-80-1). Woodbridge Pr.

--The Oats, Peas, Beans & Barley Cookbook: A Complete Vegetarian Cookbook Using Nature's Most Economical Foods. rev. ed. LC 80-80794. (Illus.). 283p. 1980. pap. 7.95 (ISBN 0-912800-85-2). Woodbridge Pr.

--Sugar-Coated Teddy. LC 75-37441. (Illus.). 80p. (Orig.). 1976. pap. 4.95 (ISBN 0-912800-25-9). Woodbridge Pr.

Cottrell, Fred W. The Railroader. (Russell Sage Foundation Reprint Ser). 1971. lib. bdg. 16.00x (ISBN 0-697-00210-1); pap. 6.95x (ISBN 0-89197-916-6). Irvington.

Cottrell, G. W., Jr., ed. see Child, Francis J. & Lowell, James R.

Cottrell, Georgia M. Portrait of Christ in Poetry. (Contemporary Poets of Dorrance Ser.). 100p. 1983. 5.95 (ISBN 0-8059-2888-X). Dorrance.

Cottrell, Glen A., et al, eds. Synapses. 1977. 58.00 (ISBN 0-12-192550-1). Acad Pr.

Cottrell, J. D., et al. Teaching of Public Health in Europe. (Monograph Ser: No. 58). 246p. 1969. 14.40 (ISBN 92-4-140058-7, 550). World Health.

Cottrell, J. E., tr. see Popescu, D. R.

Cottrell, Jack. The Bible Says. 128p. (YA) 1983. pap. 2.25 (ISBN 0-87239-480-8, 41014). Standard Pub.

--His Truth. LC 79-67437. 96p. (Orig.). 1980. pap. 2.25 (ISBN 0-87239-379-8, 40082). Standard Pub.

--What the Bible Says about God the Creator. (What the Bible Says Ser.). 1983. 13.50 (ISBN 0-89900-094-0). College Pr Pub.

Cottrell, James E. & Turndorf, Herman. Anesthesia & Neurosurgery. LC 79-24676. (Illus.). 434p. 1980. text ed. 71.95 (ISBN 0-8016-1036-2). Mosby.

Cottrell, James E., jt. auth. see Newfield, Phillippa.

Cottrell, Jane E. Alberto Moravia. LC 73-84598. (Literature and Life Ser.). 174p. 1974. 12.95 (ISBN 0-8044-2131-5). Ungar.

Cottrell, Jane E., tr. see Alain.

Cottrell, Jim. Skiing--Everyone. 81p. (Orig.). 1981. pap. text ed. 4.95x (ISBN 0-89459-125-8). Hunter Textbks.

Cottrell, Leonard. The Bull of Minos. 15.95 (ISBN 0-88411-469-4, Pub. by Aeonian Pr). Amereon Ltd.

--Lost Pharaohs: The Romance of Egyptian Archaeology. LC 72-90140. Repr. of 1951 ed. lib. bdg. 21.75x (ISBN 0-8371-2260-0, COLP). Greenwood.

--Up in a Balloon. LC 69-17423. (Illus.). (gr. 8 up). 1970. 12.95 (ISBN 0-87599-142-4). S G Phillips.

Cottrell, Leonard S. & Eberhart, Sylvia. American Opinion on World Affairs in the Atomic Age. LC 69-13867. Repr. of 1948 ed. lib. bdg. 15.00x (ISBN 0-8371-0361-4, COAO). Greenwood.

Cottrell, Leonard S., Jr., jt. auth. see Foote, Nelson N.

Cottrell, Leonard S., Jr., et al, eds. see Burgess, Ernest W.

Cottrell, P. J., jt. ed. see Teichova, Alice.

Cottrell, P. L. British Overseas Investment in the 19th Century. (Studies in Economic & Social History). (Illus.). 79p. 1975. pap. text ed. 5.00x (ISBN 0-333-13590-3). Humanities.

--Investment Banking in England, Eighteen Fifty-Six to Eighteen Eighty-Two: A Case Study of the International Financial Society, 2 vols. Mathias, Peter & Bruchey, Stuart, eds. LC 84-45997. (British Economic History Ser.). 1000p. 1985. lib. bdg. 100.00 (ISBN 0-8240-6677-4). Garland Pub.

Cottrell, Ralph. The New You. 1973. pap. 1.00 (ISBN 0-89114-044-1). Baptist Pub Hse.

Cottrell, Robert D. Colette. LC 73-84598. (Literature & Life Ser.). 150p. 1974. 12.95 (ISBN 0-8044-2130-7). Ungar.

--The Grammar of Silence: A Reading of Marguerite de Navarre's Poetry. 300p. 1986. 29.95 (ISBN 0-8132-0615-4). Cath U Pr.

--Sexuality-Textuality: A Study of the Fabric of Montaigne's "Essais". LC 81-2085. 197p. 1981. 15.00 (ISBN 0-8142-0326-4). Ohio St U Pr.

--Simone De Beauvoir. LC 74-34131. (Literature and Life Ser.). 176p. 1975. 12.95 (ISBN 0-8044-2132-3). Ungar.

Cottrell, Robert D., tr. see Alain.

Cottrell, Ron. The Remarkable Spaceship Earth. LC 82-70775. (Accent Imperials Ser.). (Illus.). 64p. (Orig.). 1982. gift book 9.95 (ISBN 0-89636-088-1). Accent Bks.

Cottrell, Stan. No Mountain Too High. (Illus.). 192p. 1984. 12.50 (ISBN 0-8007-1206-4). Revell.

--To Run & Not Be Weary. (Illus.). 192p. 1985. 12.95 (ISBN 0-8007-1444-X). Revell.

Cottrell, William F. Energy & Society: The Relation Between Energy, Social Change & Economic Development. LC 75-100152. Repr. of 1955 ed. lib. bdg. 21.75x (ISBN 0-8371-3679-2, COES). Greenwood.

Cottress, Allin. Social Classes in Marxist Theory. 330p. 1985. 39.50x (ISBN 0-7100-9906-1). Routledge & Kegan.

Cottrill, Phillip K. Automobile Ads List Life Magazine Nineteen Sixty to Nineteen Sixty-Nine. LC 80-52108. 91p. (Orig.). 1980. pap. 9.95 (ISBN 0-937234-60-5). Rigel.

--The Ford Falcon 1960-1963. LC 83-60755. 150p. 1983. pap. 18.50 (ISBN 0-937234-00-1). Rigel.

Cottrol, Robert J. The Afro-Yankees: Providence's Black Community in the Antebellum Era. LC 81-23717. (Contributions in Afro-American & African Studies: No. 68). (Illus.). xviii, 200p. 1982. lib. bdg. 29.95 (ISBN 0-313-22936-8, CBL/). Greenwood.

Cottu, Charles. De L'administration de la Justice Criminelle en Angleterre, et de l'esprit du Gouvernement Anglais. Mayer, J. P., ed. LC 78-67348. (European Political Thought Ser.). (Fr.). 1979. Repr. of 1822 ed. lib. bdg. 20.00x (ISBN 0-405-11689-6). Ayer Co Pubs.

Cottvell, Jack. What the Bible Says about God the Ruler. (What the Bible Says about Ser.). 465p. 13.95 (ISBN 0-89900-094-0). College Pr Pub.

Cotty, Richard G., jt. auth. see Costa, Philip J.

Coty, Francois. Tearing Away the Veils of International Finance. 1979. lib. bdg. 69.95 (ISBN 0-8490-3011-0). Gordon Pr.

Cotzias, George & McDowell, Fletcher, eds. Developments in Treatment for Parkinson's Disease. LC 73-2629. 91p. 1971. pap. 9.95 (ISBN 0-685-90281-1, Pub. by W & W). Krieger.

Couch, A. S., jt. auth. see Armor, D. J.

Couch, Anthony Q. & Du Maurier, Daphne. The Scapegoat. 16.95 (ISBN 0-89190-154-X, Pub. by Am Repr). Amereon Ltd.

Couch, Arthur Q. & Du Maurier, Daphne. Castle D'Or. Repr. lib. bdg. 16.95 (ISBN 0-88411-148-2, Pub. by Aeonian Pr). Amereon Ltd.

Couch, Carl & Hintz, Robert. Constructing Social Life. 1978. pap. text ed. 6.80x (ISBN 0-87563-096-0). Stipes.

Couch, Carl J. Constructing Civilizations. (Contemporary Studies in Sociology: Vol. 5). 1984. 47.50 (ISBN 0-89232-438-4). Jai Pr.

Couch, Herbert N. Classical Civilization: Greece. LC 73-156186. (Illus.). 622p. 1973. Repr. of 1951 ed. lib. bdg. 33.00x (ISBN 0-8371-6129-0, COCC). Greenwood.

Couch, Houston B. Diseases of Turfgrasses. 3rd ed. 1986. price not set (ISBN 0-89874-211-0). Krieger.

--Diseases of Turfgrasses. 2nd ed. LC 73-80742. 376p. 1976. Repr. of 1974 ed. 29.50 (ISBN 0-88275-062-3). Krieger.

Couch, J. Hudson. The Braves First Fifteen Years in Atlanta. LC 84-81647. 436p. (Orig.). 1984. pap. 9.95 (ISBN 0-931083-00-1). Other Alligator.

Couch, J. N., jt. auth. see Coker, W. C.

Couch, James. Fundamentals of Statistics for the Behavioral Sciences. LC 81-51854. 423p. 1982. text ed. 24.95 (ISBN 0-312-31195-8); study guide 6.95 (ISBN 0-312-31197-4); intr's. manual avail. St Martin.

Couch, James H., et al. Una Vez Mas. (gr. 10-12). 1982. pap. 8.50x (ISBN 0-88334-164-6); tests 3.00 (ISBN 0-317-02593-7). Ind Sch Pr.

Couch, Jean & Weaver, Nell. Runner's World Yoga Book. LC 78-68619. (Runners World Instructional Ser.). (Illus.). 228p. 1982. Repr. of 1980 ed. spiral bdg. 11.95 (ISBN 0-89037-206-3). Anderson World.

Couch, John D., jt. auth. see Barrett, William A.

Couch, John N., jt. auth. see Coker, William C.

Couch, John N. & Bland, Charles E., eds. The Genus Coelomomyces. Date not set. 84.50 (ISBN 0-12-192650-8). Acad Pr.

Couch, Larry. Dada Dog. Strahan, Bradley R., ed. (Black Buzzard Illustrated Poetry Chapbook Ser.). (Illus.). 24p. 1983. pap. text ed. 2.50 (ISBN 0-938872-04-4). Black Buzzard.

Couch, Leon W. Digital & Analog Communication Systems. 672p. 1983. text ed. write for info. (ISBN 0-02-325240-5). Macmillan.

Couch, M. E., compiled by. Education in Africa: A Select Bibliography, Pt. 1. 1962. 25.00x (ISBN 0-900008-00-8, Pub. by U of London England). State Mutual Bk.

--Education in Africa: A Select Bibliography, Pt. 2. 1964. 30.00x (ISBN 0-900008-01-6, Pub. by U of London England). State Mutual Bk.

Couch, Margaret. Books, Libraries & Teachers: Towards a History of the London Institute of Education Area Library Service; Essays Presented to Olive Stokes. 1978. 20.00x (ISBN 0-900008-23-7, Pub. by U of London England). State Mutual Bk.

Couch, Robert H. Everyday Is Easter in Alabama. LC 76-21358. (Illus.). 1976. 10.00x (ISBN 0-916624-02-1). Troy State Univ.

Couch, William, Jr., ed. New Black Playwrights: An Anthology. LC 68-31137. pap. 70.50 (ISBN 0-317-29855-0, 2019574). Bks Demand UMI.

Couch, William T. The Human Potential: An Essay on Its Cultivation. LC 72-97940. xii, 410p. 1974. 21.00 (ISBN 0-8223-0300-0). Duke.

Couch, William T., ed. Culture in the South. (Illus.). Repr. of 1934 ed. cancelled (ISBN 0-8371-3759-4, COC&, Pub. by Negro U Pr). Greenwood.

Couchman, Bob & Couchman, Win. James: Hear It! Live It! (Carpenter Studyguide Ser.). 1982. saddle-stitched leader's handbook, 61p 2.95 (ISBN 0-87788-423-4); member's handbook, 64p 1.95 (ISBN 0-87788-422-6). Shaw Pubs.

--Small Groups: Timber to Build up God's House. LC 82-798. (Carpenter Studyguide). 83p. 1982. pap. 2.95 (ISBN 0-87788-097-2). Shaw Pubs.

Couchman, Charles B. The Balance Sheet. LC 82-48355. (Accountancy in Transition Ser.). 300p. 1982. lib. bdg. 33.00 (ISBN 0-8240-5308-7). Garland Pub.

Couchman, Gordon W. This Our Caesar: A Study of Bernard Shaw's "Ceasar & Cleopatra". 1973. pap. text ed. 19.20 (ISBN 90-2792-601-8). Mouton.

Couchman, Jeffrey. Dark August. 160p. 1985. 12.95 (ISBN 0-930689-02-X). Cherryable.

Couchman, Win, jt. auth. see Bob.

Couchman, Win, jt. auth. see Couchman, Bob.

Coudari, C. One-hundred Parties Quebecoises. 222p. 1979. pap. 7.20 (ISBN 0-318-17458-8, FC6); pap. 6.50 members (ISBN 0-318-17459-6). Chess Fed.

Coudenhove-Kalergi, H. Anti-Semitism Through the Ages. 59.95 (ISBN 0-87968-649-9). Gordon Pr.

Coudenhove-Kalergi, Heinrich J. Anti-Semitism Throughout the Ages. Coudenhove-Kalergi, Richard, ed. Rappoport, Angelo S., tr. LC 73-97274. (Illus.). 288p. 1973. Repr. of 1935 ed. lib. bdg. 17.50x (ISBN 0-8371-2595-2, COAS). Greenwood.

Coudenhove-Kalergi, Richard, ed. see Coudenhove-Kalergi, Heinrich J.

Coudert, Allison, jt. auth. see Adams, Laurie.

Coudert, Jo. Advice from a Failure. LC 65-26996. pap. 7.95 (ISBN 0-8128-6182-5). Stein & Day.

--The Alcoholic in Your Life. LC 70-185955. 264p. 1981. pap. 8.95 (ISBN 0-8128-6121-3). Stein & Day.

--The I Never Cooked Before Cookbook. 224p. 1972. pap. 2.95 (ISBN 0-451-12173-2, Sig). NAL.

Coudroglou, Aliki. Work, Women & the Stuggle for Self-Sufficiency: The Win Experience. LC 82-13679. 214p. 1982. lib. bdg. 25.25 (ISBN 0-8191-2654-3); pap. text ed. 12.25 (ISBN 0-8191-2655-1). U Pr of Amer.

Coudroglou, Aliki & Poole, Dennis L. Disability, Work & Social Policy: Models for Social Welfare. LC 83-16843. (Springer Series in Social Work: Vol. 2). 140p. 1984. text ed. 20.95 (ISBN 0-8261-4520-5). Springer Pub.

Coudron, Jill M. Alphabet Activities. 1982. pap. 8.95 (ISBN 0-8224-0297-1). Pitman Learning.

--Alphabet Fun & Games. LC 83-62563. 1984. pap. 8.95 (ISBN 0-8224-0295-5). Pitman Learning.

--Alphabet Puppets. LC 78-72077. 1979. pap. 6.95 (ISBN 0-8224-0298-X). Pitman Learning.

--Alphabet Stories. 1982. pap. 8.95 (ISBN 0-8224-0299-8). Pitman Learning.

Coue, Emile. My Method. 97p. 1985. 6.00 (ISBN 0-89540-147-9, SB-147). Sun Pub.

--My Method. 97p. 1983. pap. 6.00 (ISBN 0-89540-147-9, SB-147). Sun Pub.

--Self Mastery Through Conscious Autosuggestion. 93p. 1981. pap. 4.50 (ISBN 0-89540-095-2, SB-095). Sun Pub.

Coue, Emile & Brooks, C. H. Self Mastery Through Conscious Auto-Suggestion: The Practice of Autosuggestion by the Method of Emile Coue. 160p. 1984. pap. 7.95x (ISBN 0-04-130019-X). Allen Unwin.

Couer de Jesus d' Elbee, Jean du. I Believe In Love. Teichert, Marilyn & Stebbins, Madeline, trs. LC 82-24134. (Fr.). 1983. pap. 3.95 (ISBN 0-932506-21-6). St Bedes Pubns.

Coues, E., ed. see Lewis, Meriwether & Clark, William.

Coues, Elliot, ed. see Fowler, Jacob.

Coues, Elliot, ed. see Lewis, Meriwether & Clark, William.

Coues, Elliott. Audubon & His Journals, 2 vols. 250.00 (ISBN 0-87968-677-4). Gordon Pr.

--Birds of the Colorado Valley: A Repository of Scientific & Popular Information Concerning North American Ornithology, Vol. 11. LC 73-17814. (Natural Sciences in America Ser.). 820p. 1974. Repr. 54.00x (ISBN 0-405-05730-X). Ayer Co Pubs.

--Birds of the Northwest: A Handbook of the Ornithology of the Region Drained by the Missouri River & Its Tributaries. LC 73-17815. (Natural Sciences in America Ser.). 808p. 1974. Repr. 53.00x (ISBN 0-405-05731-8). Ayer Co Pubs.

--Fur-Bearing Animals of North America. LC 79-125735. (American Environmental Studies). (Illus.). 1970. Repr. of 1877 ed. 24.50 (ISBN 0-405-02660-9). Ayer Co Pubs.

--Key to North American Birds: Containing a Concise Account of Every Species of Living & Fossil Bird at Present Known from the Continent North of the Mexican and the United States Boundary, Inclusive of Greenland and Lower California, 2 vols. 5th ed. LC 73-17816. (Natural Sciences in America Ser.). (Illus.). 1189p. 1974. Repr. Set. 77.00x (ISBN 0-405-05732-6); 38.50x ea. Vol. 1 (ISBN 0-405-05774-1). Vol. 2 (ISBN 0-405-05775-X). Ayer Co Pubs.

--War & Christianity. 250.00 (ISBN 0-8490-1276-7). Gordon Pr.

Coues, Elliott, ed. see Fowler, Jacob.

Couey, Dick. Happiness Is Being a Physically Fit Christian. LC 84-12746. 1985. 9.95 (ISBN 0-8054-7525-7). Broadman.

Couey, Richard. Lifelong Fitness & Fulfillment. LC 80-65844. 1980. 7.95 (ISBN 0-8054-5426-8). Broadman.

Coufal, H., jt. ed. see Luscher, E.

Coufal, James E., jt. auth. see Allen, Douglas G.

Couffignal, L. Quelques Notions de Base pour l'Economie. (Economies et Societes Ser. N.: No. 4). 1962. pap. 11.00 (ISBN 0-317-16352-3). Kraus Repr.

--Quelques Notions de Base pour l'Economie. Bd. with La Connaissance Cybernetique de L'Economie et l'Information Statistique. Rouquet-la-Garrigue, V; Methodes Nouvelles d'Expoitation des Courbes-Reponses. Coulmy, G. (Economies et Societes Ser N: No. 4). 1962. pap. 11.00 (ISBN 0-317-16360-4). Kraus Repr.

Couger, Daniel. Computer & the School of Business. 98p. 1967. 4.00 (ISBN 0-89478-006-9). U CO Busn Res Div.

Couger, Daniel & Shannon, Loren E. FORTRAN: A Beginner's Approach. 3rd ed. (Plaid Ser.). 1983. pap. 11.95 (ISBN 0-87094-327-8). Dow Jones-Irwin.

Couger, Daniel J. & Shannon, Loren E. FORTRAN: A Simplified Approach. 3rd, rev. ed. 200p. 11.95 (ISBN 0-87094-327-8). Dow Jones-Irwin.

Couger, Daniel J. & Zawacki, Robert A. Motivating & Managing Computer Personnel. 232p. 1980. members 25.95 (ISBN 0-318-17053-1); (W4) 27.95 (ISBN 0-318-17054-X). Data Process Mgmt.

Couger, J. Daniel & Colter, Mel A. Advanced Systems Development-Feasibility Techniques. 2nd ed. 506p. 1982. 38.50 (ISBN 0-471-03141-0). Wiley.

--Maintenance Programming: Improved Productivity Through Motivation. (Illus.). 192p. 1985. text ed. 39.95 (ISBN 0-13-545450-6). P-H.

Couger, J. Daniel & McFadden, Fred R. First Course in Data Processing with BASIC. 2nd ed. (Computers & Information Processing Systems for Business Ser.). 595p. 1984. pap. 27.95 (ISBN 0-471-86945-7). Wiley.

--First Course in Data Processing with BASIC, COBOL, FORTRAN & RPG. 3rd ed. LC 83-17032. (Wiley Series in Computers & Information Processing Systems for Business: 1-661). 682p. 1984. text ed. 28.95 (ISBN 0-471-86946-5); write for info. tchr's ed. (ISBN 0-471-86952-X); pap. 15.95 student wkbk (ISBN 0-471-86951-1); write for info. tests (ISBN 0-471-88531-2); write for info. slides (ISBN 0-471-88493-6). Wiley.

Couger, J. Daniel & Zawacki, Robert A. Motivating & Managing Computer Personnel. 213p. 1980. 32.95 (ISBN 0-471-08485-9, Pub. by Wiley-Interscience). Wiley.

Coughanowr, Donald R. & Koppel, L. B. Process Systems Analysis & Control. (Chemical Engineering Ser.). (Illus.). 1965. 45.00 (ISBN 0-07-013210-0). McGraw.

Coughenour, Robert A., ed. For Me To Live: Essays Honoring James Leon Kelso. LC 72-89962. 1973. 7.95 (ISBN 0-913228-05-2). Dillon-Liederbach.

Coughlan & Frank Bacon Press. Going Co-op. 248p. 1983. 9.00 (ISBN 0-318-17890-7, H09B). NASCO.

Coughlan, Barry. The Irish Lions Eighteen Ninety-Six to Nineteen Eighty-Three. (Illus.). 247p. 1983. pap. 8.95 (ISBN 0-907085-67-9, Pub. by Ward River Pr Ireland). Irish Bks Media.

Coughlan, Joseph D. & Strand, William K. Depreciation: Accounting, Taxes, & Business Decisions. LC 69-12971. (Illus.). pap. 89.00 (ISBN 0-317-09505-6, 2012410). Bks Demand UMI.

Coughlan, Margaret N., ed. Children's Books 1981. LC 65-60014. 16p. 1982. pap. 2.50 (ISBN 0-686-97938-9). Lib Congress.

Coughlan, Margaret N., jt. ed. see Haviland, Virginia.

Coughlan, Michael P. Molybdenum & Molybdenum-Containing Enzymes. (Illus.). 1980. 110.00 (ISBN 0-08-024398-3). Pergamon.

Coughlan, Neil. Young John Dewey: An Essay in American Intellectual History. LC 74-33519. 200p. 1975. 13.00x (ISBN 0-226-11604-2). U of Chicago Pr.

Coughlan, Peter, tr. see Vagaggini, Cipriano.

Coughlan, Peter, et al. A Christian's Prayer Book: Psalms, Poems & Prayers for the Church's Year. 325p. 1972. pap. 3.50 (ISBN 0-8199-0447-3). Franciscan Herald.

Coughlan, Rupert. Napper Tandy. (Illus.). 1976. 16.25 (ISBN 0-900068-34-5). Irish Bk Ctr.

Coughlan, William & Franke, Monte. Going CO-OP: The Complete Guide to Buying & Owning Your Own Apartment. LC 82-72501. 224p. 1983. 15.00x (ISBN 0-8070-0868-0); pap. 9.95 (ISBN 0-8070-0869-9, BP 650). Beacon Pr.

Coughlin. Father Coughlin on Money & Gold. Carpenter, Kenneth E., ed. LC 74-368. (Gold Ser.: Vol. 4). 1974. Repr. of 1972 ed. 24.50x (ISBN 0-405-05929-9). Ayer Co Pubs.

Coughlin, Ann, et al. You Know You're a Peace Officer's Wife When... 1978. pap. 3.00x (ISBN 0-89368-603-4). Davis Pub Co.

Coughlin, C. E. A Series of Lectures on Social Justice. LC 71-173652. (FDR & the Era of the New Deal). 242p. 1971. Repr. of 1935 ed. lib. bdg. 32.50 (ISBN 0-306-70373-4). Da Capo.

Coughlin, Caroline M., ed. Recurring Library Issues: A Reader. LC 79-14966. 543p. 1979. 22.50 (ISBN 0-8108-1227-4). Scarecrow.

Coughlin, Charles E. Money, Questions & Answers. 1978. pap. 4.00x (ISBN 0-911038-28-0). Noontide.

--Sermons, 2 vols. Set. 250.00 (ISBN 0-8490-1025-X). Gordon Pr.

Coughlin, E., jt. auth. see Wilhite, J.

Coughlin, Edward V., ed. & tr. from Span. Poems by Roberto Sosa. LC 83-72296. 119p. (Orig.). 1984. 14.00x (ISBN 0-938972-06-5). Spanish Lit Pubns.

Coughlin, George C. Law for the Layman. LC 75-547. 320p. 1976. pap. 4.33i (ISBN 0-06-465020-0, PBN 5020, BN). B&N NY.

Coughlin, George G. Dictionary of Law. 224p. 1982. pap. 6.68i (ISBN 0-06-463539-2, EH-539). Har-Row.

--Will Requirements of Various States. LC 84-231653. 40p. 1984. write for info. Am Coll Probate.

--Your Introduction to Law. 4th ed. LC 74-29435. 320p. 1982. pap. 5.72i (ISBN 0-06-463563-5, EH 563, EH). B&N NY.

Coughlin, Joseph W. Jack Dawn & the Vanishing Horses. 140p. (Orig.). (gr. 5-8). 1980. pap. 2.25 (ISBN 0-89323-009-X). Bible Memory.

Coughlin, Kevin. Finding God in Everyday Life. LC 80-84506. 64p. (Orig.). 1981. pap. 2.95 (ISBN 0-8091-2351-7). Paulist Pr.

Coughlin, Mary T., jt. auth. see Brinckloe, William D.

Coughlin, Obert E., et al. An Investigation of Location Factors Influencing the Economy of the Philadelphia Region. (Discussion Paper Ser.: No. 12). 1967. pap. 5.75 (ISBN 0-686-32181-2). Regional Sci Res Inst.

Coughlin, R. E., et al. Urban Analysis for Branch Library System Planning. LC 71-133496. (Contributions in Librarianship & Information Science Ser.: No. 1). 1972. lib. bdg. 29.95 (ISBN 0-8371-5161-9, CLP/). Greenwood.

Coughlin, R. F. & Driscoll, F. F. Semiconductor Fundamentals. (Illus.). 336p. 1976. 31.95x (ISBN 0-13-806406-7). P-H.

Coughlin, Richard J. Double Identity: The Chinese in Modern Thailand. LC 76-42298. (Illus.). 1976. Repr. of 1960 ed. lib. bdg. 22.50x (ISBN 0-8371-9292-7, CODI). Greenwood.

Coughlin, Richard M. Ideology, Public Opinion, & Welfare Policy: Attitudes Toward Taxes & Spending in Industrialized Societies. LC 79-22894. (Research Ser.: No. 42). 1980. pap. 6.50x (ISBN 0-87725-142-8). U of Cal Intl St.

Coughlin, Robert. Principles & Applications of Semiconductors & Circuits. LC 78-149974. (Electronic Technology Ser.). (Illus.). 1971. 32.95 (ISBN 0-13-700971-2). P-H.

Coughlin, Robert E. Criteria for Open Space System Planning: An Exploratory Survey & Synthesis. (Discussion Paper Ser.: No. 83). 1975. pap. 3.25 (ISBN 0-686-32249-5). Regional Sci Res Inst.

--Goal Attainment Levels in One Hundred & One Metropolitan Areas. (Discussion Paper Ser.: No. 41). 1970. pap. 4.50 (ISBN 0-686-32210-X). Regional Sci Res Inst.

--The Perception & Valuation of Water Quality: A Review of Research Method & Findings. (Discussion Paper Ser.: No. 80). 1975. pap. 4.50 (ISBN 0-686-32246-0). Regional Sci Res Inst.

Coughlin, Robert E. & Fritz, James. Land Values & Environmental Characteristics in the Rural-Urban Fringe. (Discussion Paper Ser.: No. 45). 1971. pap. 4.50 (ISBN 0-686-32214-2). Regional Sci Res Inst.

Coughlin, Robert E. & Goldstein, Karen A. The Extent of Agreement Among Observers on Environmental Attractiveness. (Discussion Paper Ser.: No. 37). 1970. pap. 5.75 (ISBN 0-686-32206-1). Regional Sci Res Inst.

--The Public's View of the Outdoor Environment As Interpreted by Magazine Ad-Makers. (Discussion Paper Ser.: No. 25). 1968. pap. 5.75 (ISBN 0-686-32194-4). Regional Sci Res Inst.

Coughlin, Robert E. & Isard, Walter. Planning Efficient Hospital Systems. (Discussion Paper Ser.: No. 1). 1963. pap. 5.75 (ISBN 0-686-32169-3). Regional Sci Res Inst.

Coughlin, Robert E. & Kawashima, Tatsuhiko. Property Values & Open Space in Northwest Philadelphia: An Empirical Analysis. (Discussion Paper Ser.: No. 64). 1973. pap. 4.50 (ISBN 0-686-32230-4). Regional Sci Res Inst.

Coughlin, Robert E. & Plaut, Thomas. The Use of Less-Than-Fee Acquisition for the Preservation of Open Space. (Discussion Paper Ser.: No. 101). 1977. pap. 3.25 (ISBN 0-686-32267-3). Regional Sci Res Inst.

Coughlin, Robert E. & Scherer, Ursala. A Pilot Household Survey of Perception & Use of a Large Urban Park. (Discussion Paper Ser.: No. 59). 1972. pap. 4.50 (ISBN 0-686-32226-6). Regional Sci Res Inst.

Coughlin, Robert E., jt. auth. see Berry, David.

Coughlin, Robert E., jt. auth. see Rabinowitz, Carla B.

Coughlin, Robert E., jt. auth. see Rosenberger, Lisa.

Coughlin, Robert E., jt. auth. see Stevens, Benjamin H.

Coughlin, Robert E., et al. Differential Assessment of Real Property As an Incentive to Open Space Preservation & Farmland Retention. (No. 102). 1978. pap. 3.25 (ISBN 0-686-32268-1). Regional Sci Res Inst.

--The Distribution of Social Service Facilities Within the City of Philadelphia. (Discussion Paper Ser.: No. 93). 1976. pap. 3.25 (ISBN 0-686-32259-2). Regional Sci Res Inst.

--Perception & Use of Streams in Suburban Areas: Effects of Water Quality & of Distance from Residence to Stream. (Discussion Paper Ser.: No. 53). 1972. pap. 4.50 (ISBN 0-686-32220-7). Regional Sci Res Inst.

--The Activity Structure & Transportation Requirements of a Major University Hospital. (Discussion Paper Ser.: No. 4). 1964. pap. 5.75 (ISBN 0-686-32172-3). Regional Sci Res Inst.

--Perceptions of Landfill Operations Held by Nearby Residents. (Discussion Paper Ser.: No. 65). 1973. pap. 4.50 (ISBN 0-686-32231-2). Regional Sci Res Inst.

--The Intensity of Development Along Small & Medium Sized Streams in Surburban Philadelphia. (Discussion Paper Ser.: No. 50). 1971. pap. 4.50 (ISBN 0-686-32218-5). Regional Sci Res Inst.

Coughlin, Robert F. & Driscoll, Frederick F., Jr. Operational Amplifiers & Linear Integrated Circuits. 2nd ed. (Illus.). 400p. 1982. 34.95 (ISBN 0-13-637785-8). P-H.

Coughlin, Robert F., jt. auth. see Driscoll, Fred.

Coughlin, Vincent J. Telecommunication Equipment: Equipment Fundamentals & Network Structures. (Illus.). 144p. 1984. 24.50 (ISBN 0-442-21737-4). Van Nos Reinhold.

Coughlin, William J. The Twelve Apostles. 1985. pap. 3.95 (ISBN 0-451-13604-7, Sig). NAL.

Coughran, JoAnne. Victory at the Supermarket. LC 83-51175. 320p. (Orig.). 1984. pap. 3.95 (ISBN 0-8423-7824-3). Tyndale.

Coughran, Mabel H. Horas Encantadas. (Illus.). 128p. (Span.). 1983. pap. 5.95 (ISBN 0-8442-7656-1, 7656-1, Passport Bks). Natl Textbk.

Coughtrey, P. J. Ecological Aspects of Radionuclide Release. (Illus.). 294p. 1984. pap. 60.00 (ISBN 0-632-01185-8). Blackwell Pubns.

Coughtrey, P. J., jt. auth. see Martin, M. H.

Coughtry, Jay. The Notorious Triangle: Rhode Island & the African Slave Trade, 1700-1807. LC 81-4324. 361p. 1981. 37.95 (ISBN 0-87722-218-5). Temple U Pr.

Couhat, Jean L., ed. Combat Fleets of the World, 1984-85. Baker, A. D., III, tr. (Illus.). 1022p. (Fr.). 1984. 84.95 (ISBN 0-87021-136-6). Naval Inst Pr.

Couhig, Marcelle R. Asphodel Plantation Cookbook & Cook Box. LC 78-24263. 144p. 1980. spiral bdg. 6.95 (ISBN 0-88289-194-4); file box, 256 cards 25.00 (ISBN 0-911116-66-4). Pelican.

Couilland, Xavier, et al. The Other Languages of England. (Language, Education & Society Ser.). 416p. 1985. 37.50x (ISBN 0-7100-9929-0). Routledge & Kegan.

Couisins, Mark & Hussain, Athar. Michel Foucault. LC 84-4843. (Theoretical Traditions in the Social Sciences Ser.). 368p. 1984. 27.95 (ISBN 0-312-53166-4); pap. 11.95 (ISBN 0-312-53167-2). St Martin.

Coukis, Basil & World Bank Transportation Staff & Consultants. Labor-Based Construction Programs: A Practical Guide for Planning & Management. (Illus.). 1983. 24.95x (ISBN 0-19-561511-5); pap. 12.95x (ISBN 0-19-561512-3). Oxford U Pr.

Coukis, Basil P., tr. see Papanoutsos, Evangelos P.

Coukoulis, Peter P. Guru, Psychotherapist & Self: A Comparative Study of the Guru-Disciple Relationship & the Jungian Analytic Process. 1977. 8.00 (ISBN 0-87516-222-3); pap. 4.50 (ISBN 0-87516-221-5). De Vorss.

Coulacos, Spero & Carey, Robert J. How to Recover from Heart Disease. LC 82-82306. 352p. cancelled (ISBN 0-448-07367-6, G&D). Putnam Pub Group.

Coulam, Craig M., ed. Physical Basis of Medical Imaging. (Illus.). 416p. 1981. 62.00 (ISBN 0-8385-7844-6). ACC.

Coulam, Robert F. Illusions of Choice: Robert McNamara, the F-111 & the Problem of Weapons Acquisition Reform. LC 76-24292. 1977. 46.00 (ISBN 0-691-07583-2). Princeton U Pr.

Coulanges, Fustel De see De Coulanges, Fustel.

Coulanges, Numa D. De see De Coulanges, Numa D.

Coulbeck, Neil. The Multinational Banking Industry. 416p. 1985. 55.00x (ISBN 0-8147-1396-3). NYU Pr.

Coulbois, Paul. Le Systeme monetaire international face aux desequilibres: Re port & Proceedings of a Seminar held in Paris, November 23-25, 1981. 165p. (Fr.). 1982. text ed. 5.00 (ISBN 2-7178-0578-8). Intl Monetary.

Coulborn, Rushton, ed. Feudalism in History. xiv, 438p. 1965. Repr. of 1956 ed. 29.50 (ISBN 0-208-00274-X, Archon). Shoe String.

Coulbourn, John. Selection of Teachers in Large City School Systems. LC 72-176673. (Columbia University. Teachers College. Contributions to Education: No. 740). Repr. of 1938 ed. 22.50 (ISBN 0-404-55740-6). AMS Pr.

Coulby, David & Harper, Tim. Preventing Classroom Disruption: Policy, Practice & Evaluation in Urban Schools. 208p. 1985. 23.00 (ISBN 0-7099-3424-6, Pub. by Croom Helm Ltd); pap. 11.50 (ISBN 0-7099-3425-4). Longwood Pub Group.

Couldrey, Vivienne. The Swans of Brhyadr. 224p. 1981. pap. 1.75 (ISBN 0-449-50166-3, Coventry). Fawcett.

Couldridge, Alan. The Hat Book. (Illus.). 128p. 1980. 22.50 (ISBN 0-7134-2385-4, Pub. by Batsford England). David & Charles.

--The Hat Book. 128p. 1981. (Spec); pap. 8.95 (ISBN 0-13-384214-2). P-H.

Coulehan, Robert E. Introduction to Microprocessor Control in Hostile Environments. 160p. 1983. 59.95 (ISBN 0-935506-12-8). Carnegie Pr.

Coulet, Jules. Troubadour Guilhem Montanhagol. Repr. of 1898 ed. 20.00 (ISBN 0-384-39860-X). Johnson Repr.

Coulet-du-Gard, Rene. La Course et la Piraterie en Mediterranee. 315p. (Fr.). Repr. of 1980 ed. 18.00 (ISBN 0-939586-09-6). Edns Des Deux Mondes.

Coulet du Gard, Rene. Dictionary of Spanish Place Names of the Northwest Coast of America: California, Vol. I. 190p. (Span. & Eng.). 1982. 24.00 (ISBN 0-939586-01-0). Edns Des Deux Mondes.

--Dictionary of Spanish Place Names of the Northwest Coast of America: Oregon, Washington State, British Columbia, Alaska, Vol. II. 190p. (Span. & Eng.). 1983. 24.00 (ISBN 0-939586-02-9). Edns Des Deux Mondes.

--Dictionary of Spanish Place Names, Vol. III: New Mexico. 380p. 1983. 39.00 (ISBN 0-939586-03-7). Edns Des Deux Mondes.

Coulet-du-Gard, Rene. Pleure pas P'tit Bonhomme. 320p. (Fr.). Repr. of 1977 ed. 18.00 (ISBN 0-939586-08-8). Edns Des Deux Mondes.

Coulet du Gard, Rene & Western, Dominique. Handbook of American Counties, Parishes & Independent Cities. (Illus.). 500p. 1981. 34.00x (ISBN 0-939586-00-2). Edns Des Deux Mondes.

Coulibaly, S. & Gregory, J. Les Migrations Voltaiques: Tome 1: Importance et Ambivalence de la Migration Voltaique. 180p. 1980. pap. 7.50 (ISBN 0-88936-237-8, IDRC). Unipub.

Couling, David. Solent Yachting Scene: In Bygone Years 1890-1938. (Illus.). 128p. (Orig.). 1984. pap. 12.95 (ISBN 0-540-07280-X, Stanford Maritime). Sheridan.

--Steam Yachts. LC 80-81524. (Illus.). 120p. 1980. 16.95 (ISBN 0-87021-963-4). Naval Inst Pr.

--Steam Yachts. (Illus.). 120p. 1980. 16.95 (ISBN 0-87021-963-4); bulk rates avail. Naval Inst Pr.

Coull, Bruce C., jt. ed. see Tenore, Kenneth R.

Coulling, Sidney. Matthew Arnold & His Critics: A Study of Arnold's Controversies. LC 74-82498. xiv, 351p. 1974. 20.00x (ISBN 0-8214-0161-0, 82-81610). Ohio U Pr.

Coulmas, Florian. A Festschrift for Native Speaker. (Janua Linguarum Series Maior: No. 97). 406p. 1981. 46.00 (ISBN 90-279-3498-3). Mouton.

Coulmas, Florian, ed. Conversational Routine. (Janua Linguarum, Ser. Maior-Rasmus Rask Studies in Pragmatic Linguistics: Vol. 2). 1980. text ed. 36.80x (ISBN 90-279-3098-8). Mouton.

--Linguistic Minorities & Literacy: Language Policy Issues in Developing Countries. LC 84-14746. (Trends in Linguistics, Studies & Monographs: No. 26). (Illus.). x, 133p. 1984. 19.95x (ISBN 3-11-009867-9). Mouton.

Coulmas, Florian & Ehlich, Konrad, eds. Writing in Focus. LC 83-13095. (Trends in Linguistics Studies & Monographs: No. 24). viii, 405p. 1983. 59.95x (ISBN 90-279-3359-6). Mouton.

Coulmy, G; see Couffignal, L.

Coulomb, J. Sea Floor Spreading & Continental Drift. Tanner, R. W., tr. from Fr. LC 79-179891. (Geophysics & Astrophysics Monographs: No. 2). 184p. 1972. lib. bdg. 31.50 (ISBN 90-277-0232-2, Pub. by Reidel Holland); pap. 18.50 (ISBN 90-277-0238-1). Kluwer Academic.

Coulomb, J. & Caputo, M., eds. Mantle & Core in Planetary Physics. (Italian Physical Society: Course 50). 1972. 75.00 (ISBN 0-12-368850-7). Acad Pr.

Coulombe, Deborah. The Seaside Naturalist: A Guide to Nature at the Seashore. 256p. 1984. 19.95 (ISBN 0-13-797259-8); pap. 12.95 (ISBN 0-13-797242-3). P-H.

Coulon, F. de see Kunt, M. & De Coulon, F.

Coulon, Marcel. Poet Under Saturn: The Tragedy of Verlaine. Rickwood, Edgell, tr. LC 77-103176. 1970. Repr. of 1932 ed. 19.50x (ISBN 0-8046-0813-X, Pub. by Kennikat). Assoc Faculty Pr.

Couloumbis, Ted & Wolfe, James. Introduction to International Relations: Power & Justice. 2nd ed. 448p. 1982. 27.95 (ISBN 0-13-485292-3). P-H.

Couloumbis, Theodore A. Greek Political Reaction to American & NATO Influences. LC 66-12491. pap. 65.00 (ISBN 0-317-29585-3, 2021991). Bks Demand UMI.

--The United States, Greece & Turkey: The Troubled Triangle. Rubinstein, Alvin Z., ed. (Studies of Influence in International Relations). 256p. 1983. 29.95 (ISBN 0-03-052551-9); pap. 14.95 (ISBN 0-03-052546-2). Praeger.

Couloumbis, Theodore A. & Wolfe, James H. Introduction to International Relations: Power & Justice. 3rd ed. LC 85-6535. (Illus.). 432p. 1986. text ed. 26.95 (ISBN 0-13-485327-X). P-H.

Coulsen, Kinsell L. Solar & Terrestrial Radiation. 1975. 35.75 (ISBN 0-12-192950-7). Acad Pr.

Coulson & Freiert. Greek & Roman Art & Architecture. 1985. lib. bdg. 47.00 (ISBN 0-8240-8756-9). Garland Pub.

Coulson, Andrew. Tanzania: A Political Economy. (Illus.). 1982. 37.50x (ISBN 0-19-828292-3); pap. 16.95x (ISBN 0-19-828293-1). Oxford U Pr.

Coulson, C. A. The Shape & Structure of Molecules. 2nd ed. McWeeny, Roy, rev. by. 1982. 19.95x (ISBN 0-19-855517-2); pap. 10.95x (ISBN 0-19-855518-0). Oxford U Pr.

Coulson, C. A., et al. Huckell Theory for Organic Chemists. 1978. 44.00 (ISBN 0-12-193250-8). Acad Pr.

Coulson, Charles A. Coulson's Valence. 3rd ed. McWeeny, Roy, ed. (Illus.). 1979. 59.00x (ISBN 0-19-855144-4); pap. 25.95x (ISBN 0-19-855145-2). Oxford U Pr.

--Science, Technology, & the Christian. LC 78-16421. 1978. Repr. of 1960 ed. lib. bdg. 15.75x (ISBN 0-8371-9041-X, COSCI). Greenwood.

Coulson, David & Clarke, James. The Roof of Africa. LC 84-719. (Illus.). 240p. 1984. 25.00 (ISBN 0-03-071766-3). HR&W.

Coulson, Herbert H., jt. auth. see Cave, Roy C.

Coulson, J., ed. The Pocket Oxford Russian-English Dictionary. (Rus. & Eng.). 1975. 12.95x (ISBN 0-19-864113-3). Oxford U Pr.

Coulson, J., et al, eds. The Oxford Illustrated Dictionary. 2nd rev. ed. 1975. 29.50x (ISBN 0-19-861118-8). Oxford U Pr.

Coulson, J. M. Chemical Engineering: An Introduction to Design, Vol. 6. (Illus.). 720p. 1983. 75.00 (ISBN 0-08-022969-7); pap. 29.50 (ISBN 0-08-022970-0). Pergamon.

Coulson, J. M. & Richardson, J. F. Chemical Engineering, 6 vols. Incl. Vol. 1. text ed. 27.50, 3rd ed. 1978 (ISBN 0-08-020614-X); pap. text ed. 15.00 (ISBN 0-08-021015-5); pap. text ed. 13.00, 2nd ed. 1964 (ISBN 0-08-009017-6); Vol. 2. text ed. 25.00 (ISBN 0-08-022919-0); pap. text ed. 18.50, 1968 ed. (ISBN 0-08-013185-9); Vol. 3. 3rd ed. text ed. 17.50 (ISBN 0-08-016438-2); Vol. 4. Problems & Solutions (SI Units) 3rd ed. Backhurst, J. R. & Harker, J. H. text ed. 20.00 (ISBN 0-08-020926-2); pap. 10.50 (ISBN 0-08-020918-1). pap. write for info. Pergamon.

Coulson, J. M., et al. Chemical Engineering, Vol. 5: Solutions to the Problems in Volume Two. 3rd ed. LC 78-40923. (Chemical Engineering Technical Ser.). (Illus.). 1979. 40.00 (ISBN 0-08-022951-4); pap. 16.75 (ISBN 0-08-022952-2). Pergamon.

Coulson, J. R. & Peacock, D. G., eds. Chemical Engineering, Vol. 3. 2nd ed. (Chemical Engineering Ser.: Vol. 3). (Illus.). 1979. text ed. 83.75 (ISBN 0-08-023818-1); pap. text ed. 24.00 (ISBN 0-08-023819-X). Pergamon.

Coulson, Jesse, tr. see Dostoyevsky, Fyodor.

Coulson, Jessie. Dostoevsky: A Self Portrait. LC 75-26212. (Illus.). 279p. 1975. Repr. of 1962 ed. lib. bdg. 29.75x (ISBN 0-8371-8405-3, CODO). Greenwood.
Coulson, Jessie, tr. see Dostoyevsky, Fyodor.
Coulson, Jessie, et al, eds. The Pocket Oxford Russian Dictionary: Russian-English - English-Russian. (Rus. & Eng.). 1981. pap. 10.95x (ISBN 0-19-864122-2). Oxford U Pr.
Coulson, John. Religion & Imagination. 1981. 39.95x (ISBN 0-19-826656-1). Oxford U Pr.
Coulson, John & Allchin, Arthur M., eds. The Rediscovery of Newman: An Oxford Symposium. LC 68-84451. 1967. text ed. 15.00x (ISBN 0-8401-0458-8). A R Allenson.
Coulson, Juanita. Children of the Stars: Bk. 1, Tomorrow's Heritage. 384p. 1981. pap. 2.75 (ISBN 0-345-28178-0, Del Rey). Ballantine.
--Children of the Stars: Bk. 2 Outward Bound. (Orig.). 1982. pap. 2.95 (ISBN 0-345-28179-9, Del Rey). Ballantine.
--The Death God's Citadel. 400p. (Orig.). 1984. pap. 2.95 (ISBN 0-345-31789-0, DEL REY BKS.). Ballantine.
--Tomorrow's Heritage. (Children of the Stars Ser.: Bk. 2). 1982. pap. 2.75 (ISBN 0-345-26235-2, Del Rey). Ballantine.
--The Web of Wizardry. 1984. pap. 2.95 (ISBN 0-345-31788-2, Del Rey Bks). Ballantine.
Coulson, Margaret & Riddell, Carol. Approaching Sociology. rev. ed. 144p. 1980. pap. 6.95x (ISBN 0-7100-0575-X). Routledge & Kegan.
Coulson, Michael, tr. Three Sanskrit Plays. (Penguin Classic Ser.). 1981. pap. 8.95 (ISBN 0-14-044374-6). Penguin.
Coulson, N. J. Contract Law in Saudi Arabia & the Gulf States. 200p. 1980. 55.00x (ISBN 0-86010-217-3, Pub. by Graham & Trotman England). State Mutual Bk.
--Succession in the Muslim Family. 1971. 54.50 (ISBN 0-521-07852-0). Cambridge U Pr.
Coulson, Noel. A History of Islamic Law. 264p. 1964. pap. 10.00 (ISBN 0-85224-354-5, Pub. by Edinburgh U Pr Scotland). Columbia U Pr.
Coulson, Noel J. Conflicts & Tensions in Islamic Jurisprudence. Polk, William R., ed. LC 79-80433. (Publications of the Center for Middle Eastern Studies Ser: No. 5). 1969. 12.00x (ISBN 0-226-11610-7). U of Chicago Pr.
Coulson, Robert. Business Arbitration: What You Need to Know. 2nd ed. 156p. 1982. 10.00. Am Arbitration.
--Business Arbitration: What You Need To Know. 152p. 5.00 (ISBN 0-318-12373-8); members 4.25 (ISBN 0-318-12374-6). Am Arbitration.
--Fighting Fair: Fighting Fair. 191p. 1983. 14.95 (ISBN 0-02-906420-1). Free Pr.
--Labor Arbitration: What You Need to Know. 3rd ed. 172p. 5.00 (ISBN 0-318-12385-1); members 4.25 (ISBN 0-318-12386-X). Am Arbitration.
--Professional Mediation of Civil Disputes. LC 84-72418. 62p. Date not set. price not set. Am Arbitration.
--Professional Mediation of Civil Disputes. 62p. avail. (56). NRCCLS.
--The Termination Handbook. LC 81-66988. 235p. 1981. 17.95 (ISBN 0-02-906700-6). Free Pr.
--The Termination Handbook. 224p. 1981. 15.95 (ISBN 0-02-906700-6). Am Arbitration.
Coulson, Robert N. & Witter, John A. Forest Entomology: Ecology & Management. LC 83-23492. 736p. 1984. text ed. 37.50x (ISBN 0-471-02573-9, Pub. by Wiley-Interscience). Wiley.
Coulson, Suzanne, jt. auth. see Emami, Mary Lou.
Coulson, Suzzanne, jt. auth. see Emami, Mary L.
Coulson, Walter F., ed. Surgical Pathology, 2 vols. LC 78-17028. (Illus.). 1978. 165.00x (ISBN 0-397-50386-5, Lippincott Medical). Lippincott.
Coulson, William D. An Annotated Bibliography of Greek & Roman Art, Architecture, & Archaeology. LC 75-24081. (Reference Library of the Humanities: Vol. 28). 135p. 1975. lib. bdg. 25.00 (ISBN 0-8240-9984-2). Garland Pub.
Coulson, William D. & Leonard, Albert, Jr. Cities of the Delta, Part I: Naukratis. Preliminary Report on the 1977-1978 & 1980 Seasons. LC 81-52798. (American Research Center in Egypt, Reports: Vol. 4). (Illus.). xiv, 118p. (Orig.). 1982. 26.00x (ISBN 0-89003-081-2); pap. 16.00x (ISBN 0-89003-080-4). Undena Pubns.
Coulson, William D., jt. ed. see McDonald, William A.
Coulson, William R. Banding. (Illus.). 63p. (Orig.). 1978. pap. 5.95 (ISBN 0-686-32705-5). Helicon House.
Coulson, William R. & Rogers, Carl R., eds. Man & the Science of Man. 1968. text ed. 9.95 (ISBN 0-675-09599-9). Merrill.
Coulson, Zoe, intro. by. Good Housekeeping Illustrated Cookbook. LC 79-92727. 528p. 1980. 23.50 (ISBN 0-87851-037-0). Hearst Bks.
Coulson-Thomas, Colin. Public Relations Is Your Business. 273p. 1981. text ed. 42.00x (ISBN 0-09-142960-9, Pub. by Busn Bks England). Brookfield Pub Co.
Coulson-Thomas, Colin J. Marketing Communications. (Illus.). 352p. 1984. pap. 18.95 (ISBN 0-434-91930-6, Pub. by W Heinemann Ltd). David & Charles.
Coulston, F. & Korte, F., eds. Environmental Quality: Global Aspects of Chemistry, Toxicology & Technology As Applied to the Environment, 5 vols. Vol. 1, 1972. 29.50 (ISBN 0-12-227001-0); Vol. 2, 1973. 36.00 (ISBN 0-12-227002-9); Vol. 3, 1974. 32.00 (ISBN 0-12-227003-7); Vol.4, 1975. 29.00 (ISBN 0-12-227004-5); Vol. 5, 1976. 27.50 (ISBN 0-12-227005-3). Acad Pr.
Coulston, Frederick & Poochiari, Francesco. Accidental Exposure to Dioxins: Human Health Aspects (Symposium) (Ecotoxicology & Environmental Quality Ser.). 1983. 29.50 (ISBN 0-12-193160-9). Acad Pr.
Coulston, Frederick, ed. Regulatory Aspects of Carcinogenesis & Food Additives: The Delaney Clause. (Ecotoxicology & Environmental Quality Ser.). 1979. 48.50 (ISBN 0-12-192750-4). Acad Pr.
Coulston, Frederick & Dunne, John F., eds. The Potential Carcinogenicity of Nitrosatable Drugs. LC 79-16498. (Illus.). 1980. 35.00x (ISBN 0-89391-022-8). Ablex Pub.
Coulston, Frederick & Mrak, E., eds. Water Quality: Proceedings of an International Symposium. (Ecotoxicology & Environmental Quality Ser.). 1977. 45.00 (ISBN 0-12-193150-1). Acad Pr.
Coulston, Frederick & Shubik, Philippe, eds. Human Epidemiology & Animal Laboratory Correlations in Chemical Carcinogens. LC 79-25466. (Current Topics Biomedical Research Ser.). 1980. text ed. 65.00 (ISBN 0-89391-026-0). Ablex Pub.
Coult, Tony & Kershaw, Baz, eds. Engineers of the Imagination: The Welfare State Handbook. (Illus.). 200p. 1983. pap. 9.95 (ISBN 0-413-52890-1, NO.3896). Methuen Inc.
Coultate, T. P. Food: The Chemistry of Its Components. 202p. (Orig.). 1984. pap. 11.00 (ISBN 0-85186-483-X, Pub by Royal Soc Chem UK). Heyden.
Coulter, C. A. & Shatas, R. A., eds. Topics in Fields & Solids. 228p. 1968. 59.25 (ISBN 0-677-12740-5). Gordon.
Coulter, Carleton, III & Weinroth, Donald M., eds. Building Economics: Solving the Owner's Problems of the 80's. (Illus.). 197p. (Orig.). 1981. pap. 21.00 (ISBN 0-930284-10-0). Am Assn Cost Engineers.
Coulter, Catherine. The Autumn Countess. 1979. pap. 2.25 (ISBN 0-451-11445-0, AE1445, Sig). NAL.
--Chandra. (Scarlet Ribbons Ser.). 352p. 1984. pap. 2.95 (ISBN 0-451-12672-6, Sig). NAL.
--Devil's Daughter. 1985. pap. 3.95 (ISBN 0-317-18405-9, Sig). NAL.
--Devil's Embrace. 1982. pap. 2.95 (ISBN 0-451-11853-7, AE1853, Sig). NAL.
--Fire Song. 1985. pap. 3.95 (ISBN 0-451-14000-1, Sig). NAL.
--The Generous Earl. (Orig.). 1985. pap. 2.50 (ISBN 0-451-13618-7, Sig). NAL.
--An Honorable Offer. (Orig.). 1981. pap. 2.25 (ISBN 0-451-11209-1, Sig). NAL.
--An Intimate Deception. (Regency Romance Ser.). 1983. pap. 2.25 (ISBN 0-451-12236-4, Sig). NAL.
--Lord Deverill's Heir. 1980. pap. 2.50 (ISBN 0-451-11534-1, AE1398, Sig). NAL.
--Lord Harry's Folly. 1980. pap. 2.50 (ISBN 0-451-13765-5, AE1534, Sig). NAL.
--The Rebel Bride. (Orig.). 1979. pap. 2.50 (ISBN 0-451-13837-6, AE1719, Sig). NAL.
--Sweet Surrender. LC 99-943913. 1984. pap. 3.50 (ISBN 0-451-13191-6, Sig). NAL.
Coulter, Catherine R. Portraits of Homoeopathic Medicines: Psychophysical Analyses of Select Constitutional Types. 500p. 1985. 25.00 (ISBN 0-938190-61-X). North Atlantic.
Coulter, Charles W., jt. auth. see Creamer, Daniel.
Coulter, E. Merton. The Civil War & Readjustment in Kentucky. 1926. 12.75 (ISBN 0-8446-1131-X). Peter Smith.
--College Life in the Old South. LC 51-7109. 334p. 1951. 12.50 (ISBN 0-8203-0034-9). U of Ga Pr.
--College Life in the Old South. 2nd ed. LC 83-9210. (Brown Thrasher Bks.). 336p. 1983. pap. 8.95 (ISBN 0-8203-0684-3). U of Ga Pr.
--Confederate States of America, 1861-1865. LC 50-6319. (History of the South, Vol. 7). (Illus.). x, 644p. 1950. 27.50x (ISBN 0-8071-0007-2). La State U Pr.
--Georgia: A Short History. 2nd rev. ed. xii, 537p. 1960. 14.95 (ISBN 0-8078-0786-9). U of NC Pr.
--James Monroe Smith: Georgia Planter. LC 61-9793. 304p. 1961. 23.00 (ISBN 0-8203-0095-0). U of Ga Pr.
--South During Reconstruction Eighteen Sixty-Five to Eighteen Seventy-Seven. LC 48-5161. (History of the South Ser.: Vol. 8). (Illus.). 1947. 27.50x (ISBN 0-8071-0008-0). La State U Pr.
--Travels in the Confederate States: A Bibliography. xiv, 289p. 1981. Repr. of 1948 ed. 25.00 (ISBN 0-916107-02-7). Broadfoot.
--William G. Brownlow: Fighting Parson of the Southern Highlands. LC 71-136309. (Tennesseana Editions Ser.). (Illus.). pap. 114.50 (ISBN 0-8357-9767-8, 2016173). Bks Demand UMI.
Coulter, E. Merton & Saye, Albert B. A List of the Early Settlers of Georgia. LC 83-80998. 111p. 1983. Repr. of 1967 ed. 15.00 (ISBN 0-8063-1031-6). Genealog Pub.
Coulter, E. Merton, ed. Confederate Receipt Book: A Compilation of Over One Hundred Receipts, Adapted to the Times. LC 60-9896. 38p. 1960. pap. 2.50 (ISBN 0-8203-0561-8). U of Ga Pr.
Coulter, Edwin M. Principles of Politics & Government. 2nd ed. 1983. pap. 20.00 scp (ISBN 0-205-08004-9, 768004). Allyn.
Coulter, Francis C. A Manual of Home Vegetable Gardening. (Illus.). 288p. 1973. pap. 1.00 (ISBN 0-486-22945-9). Dover.
--A Manual of Home Vegetable Gardening. (Illus.). 11.25 (ISBN 0-8446-4726-8). Peter Smith.
Coulter, Fredrick L., jt. auth. see Ornelas-Struve, Carole M.
Coulter, Harris. Homoeopathic Science & Modern Medicine: The Physics of Healing with Microdoses. 164p. 1981. 20.00 (ISBN 0-913028-86-X); pap. 5.95 (ISBN 0-913028-84-3). North Atlantic.
Coulter, Harris L. Divided Legacy: The Conflict Between Homoeopathy & the American Medical Association in the Nineteenth & Early Twentieth Centuries. 546p. (Orig.). 1982. pap. 14.95 (ISBN 0-913028-96-7); 25.00 (ISBN 0-938190-57-1). North Atlantic.
--Homoeopathic Influences in Nineteenth-Century Allopathic Therapeutics. LC 73-75139. 1973. pap. 2.50 (ISBN 0-685-64858-3). Formur Intl.
--Homoeopathic Medicine. LC 74-190020. 1972. pap. 1.65 (ISBN 0-89378-072-3). Formur Intl.
Coulter, Harris L. & Fisher, Barbara L. DPT: A Shot in the Dark. LC 84-12933. 416p. 1985. 19.95 (ISBN 0-15-126481-3). HarBraceJ.
Coulter, J. W. Land Utilization in American Samoa. (BMB Ser.). pap. 10.00 (ISBN 0-527-02278-0). Kraus Repr.
--Population & Utilization of Land & Sea in Hawaii. (BMB Ser.). pap. 8.00 (ISBN 0-527-02194-6). Kraus Repr.
Coulter, James. The Literary Microcosm: Theories of Interpretation of the Later Neoplatonists. (Columbia Studies in the Classical Tradition: No. II). 1976. text ed. 28.00x (ISBN 90-04-04489-2). Humanities.
Coulter, Jeff. Approaches to Insanity: A Philosophical & Sociological Study. 180p. 1973. 24.95x (ISBN 0-85520-049-9); pap. 9.95 (ISBN 0-85520-048-0). Basil Blackwell.
--Rethinking Cognitive Theory. LC 83-9639. 190p. 1983. 22.50 (ISBN 0-312-67800-2). St Martin.
--The Social Construction of Mind: Studies in Ethnomethodology & Linguistic Philosophy. 190p. 1979. 18.50x (ISBN 0-8476-6131-8). Rowman.
Coulter, Jeremy. Lamborghini Countach LP400, LP500S. LC 83-15836. (World Supercars Ser.: No. 2). (Illus.). 60p. 1984. 16.95 (ISBN 0-668-05978-8). Arco.
Coulter, John. Adventures on the Western Coast of South America, 2 vols. in 1. LC 77-88570. 1977. Repr. of 1847 ed. lib. bdg. 50.00 (ISBN 0-89341-277-5). Longwood Pub Group.
Coulter, John M. Evolution of Sex in Plants. (Illus.). 1973. Repr. of 1914 ed. lib. bdg. 10.75x (ISBN 0-02-843230-4). Hafner.
Coulter, John S. Physical Therapy. LC 75-23658. (Clio Medica: 8). (Illus.). Repr. of 1932 ed. 13.00 (ISBN 0-404-58908-1). AMS Pr.
Coulter, John W. Drama of Fiji: A Contemporary History. LC 67-14279. 1967. 3.50 (ISBN 0-8048-0146-0). C E Tuttle.
Coulter, M. O. Modern Chlor-Alkali Technology. LC 80-41236. 289p. 1980. 122.95 (ISBN 0-470-27005-5). Halsted Pr.
Coulter, Merle C. Story of the Plant Kingdom. 3rd ed. rev ed. LC 64-10093. (Illus.). 1964. text ed. 17.50x (ISBN 0-226-11621-2). U of Chicago Pr.
--The Story of the Plant Kingdom. rev. ed. Dittmer, Howard J., ed. LC 64-10093. 480p. 1973. pap. text ed. 4.95x (ISBN 0-226-11611-5, P494, Phoen). U of Chicago Pr.
Coulter, N. Arthur, Jr. Leaping into Being. LC 83-50642. (Illus.). 100p. (Orig.). Date not set. pap. 1.95 (ISBN 0-910217-03-3). Synergetics WV.
Coulter, Philip, jt. ed. see Busson, Terry.
Coulter, Philip B., jt. auth. see Bousson, Terry.
Coulter, Rita K. Discover the French Connection Between St. Louis & New Orleans. 1977. 16.95x (ISBN 0-932380-01-8); lib. bdg. 9.95x (ISBN 0-686-96751-8). Interhouse Pub.
Coulthard, Malcolm. Introduction to Discourse Analysis. (Applied Linguistics & Language Study Ser.). 1978. 11.95x (ISBN 0-582-55087-4). Longman.
Coulthard, Malcolm, jt. ed. see Montgomery, Martin.
Coulthard-Clark, C. A Heritage of Spirit: A Biography of General W. T. Bridges. 1979. 22.00x (ISBN 0-522-84170-8, Pub. by Melbourne U Pr Australia). Intl Spec Bk.
Coulton, Claudia J. Social Work Quality Assurance Programs: A Comparative Analysis. LC 79-64941. 102p. 1979. pap. 6.95x (ISBN 0-87101-080-1). Natl Assn Soc Wkrs.
Coulton, G. G. The Autobiography of Guibert Abbot of Nogent Souscoucy. Bland, C. Swinton, tr. Repr. 30.00 (ISBN 0-8274-1902-3). R West.
--Chaucer & His England. (Illus.). 321p. 1976. Repr. of 1909 ed. 18.50 (ISBN 0-87928-068-9). Corner Hse.
--Chaucer & His England. 321p. 1985. Repr. of 1908 ed. lib. bdg. 50.00 (ISBN 0-918377-81-1). Russell Pr.
--Fourscore Years: An Autobiography. 1944. Repr. 20.00 (ISBN 0-8274-2358-6). R West.
--Infant Perdition in the Middle Ages. 1977. lib. bdg. 59.95 (ISBN 0-8490-2058-1). Gordon Pr.
--Inquisition & Liberty. 11.75 (ISBN 0-8446-0560-3). Peter Smith.
--Medieval Panorama: The English Scene from Conquest to Reformation. 816p. 1974. pap. 4.95 (ISBN 0-393-00708-1, Norton Lib). Norton.
--Romanism & Truth. 1977. lib. bdg. 59.95 (ISBN 0-8490-2541-9). Gordon Pr.
--Scottish Abbeys & Social Life. 1977. lib. bdg. 59.95 (ISBN 0-8490-2573-7). Gordon Pr.
--Some Problems in Medieval Historiography. 1974. lib. bdg. 59.95 (ISBN 0-8490-1079-9). Gordon Pr.
--Two Saints: St. Bernard & St. Francis. 1923. lib. bdg. 11.50 (ISBN 0-8414-3513-8). Folcroft.
Coulton, G. G., ed. & tr. see Salimbene Di Adam.
Coulton, George C., compiled by. Social Life in Britain: From the Conquest to the Reformation. (Illus.). 566p. 1968. Repr. of 1918 ed. 15.00x (ISBN 0-87471-309-9). Rowman.
Coulton, George G. Art & the Reformation. (Illus.). xxii, 662p. 1969. Repr. of 1928 ed. 32.50 (ISBN 0-208-00738-5, Archon). Shoe String.
--The Chronicler of European Chivalry. 1978. Repr. of 1930 ed. lib. bdg. 35.00 (ISBN 0-8492-4010-7). R West.
--Inquisition. LC 74-18020. 1974. Repr. of 1929 ed. lib. bdg. 16.50 (ISBN 0-8414-3647-9). Folcroft.
--Life in the Middle Ages. pap. 22.95 (ISBN 0-521-09400-3). Cambridge U Pr.
--Pearl, a Fourteenth-Century Poem. LC 76-44809. 1976. Repr. of 1907 ed. lib. bdg. 15.00 (ISBN 0-8414-3385-2). Folcroft.
Coulton, J. J. Ancient Greek Architects at Work: Problems of Structure & Design. LC 76-44117. 1977. 24.50x (ISBN 0-8014-1077-0). Cornell U Pr.
--Ancient Greek Architects at Work: Problems of Structure & Design. 208p. 1982. pap. 9.95 (ISBN 0-8014-9234-3). Cornell U Pr.
Coulton, Jill. Women's Gymnastics. (Sports Ser.). (Illus.). 1977. 7.95 (ISBN 0-7158-0592-4). Charles River Bks.
Counce, S. J. & Waddington, C. H., eds. Developmental Systems: Insects. 1973. Vol. 1. 53.00 (ISBN 0-12-193301-6); Vol. 2. 97.50 (ISBN 0-12-193302-4). Acad Pr.
Council Envir. Quality. The Global Two Thousand Report to the President: Entering the Twenty-First Century, Vol. I. (Illus.). 766p. 1982. pap. 10.00 (ISBN 0-14-022441-6). Penguin.
Council for Applied Social Research. Proposition Thirteen & Its Consequences for Public Management. Mushkin, Selma J., ed. LC 79-65017. 1979. 18.00 (ISBN 0-89011-536-2). Abt Bks.
Council for Economic Planning & Development (Republic of China) Taiwan Statistical Data Book, 1981. LC 72-219425. (Illus.). 318p. (Orig.). 1981. pap. 12.50x (ISBN 0-8002-2995-9). Intl Pubns Serv.
--Taiwan Statistical Data Book, 1982. LC 72-219425. (Illus.). 318p. (Orig.). 1982. pap. 12.50x (ISBN 0-8002-3027-2). Intl Pubns Serv.
Council for High Blood Pressure. Hypertension in Man & Animals. Hunt, James C., ed. (Hypertension Ser.: Vol. 21). 1973. pap. 5.00 (ISBN 0-87493-034-0, 73-212A). Am Heart.
Council for High Blood Research, 1972. Blood Pressure - Regulation & Control: Proceedings. Hunt, James C., ed. (Hypertension Ser.: Vol. 20). 1972. pap. 5.00 (ISBN 0-87493-026-X, 73-211A). Am Heart.
Council for National Cooperation in Aquatics. The New Science of Skin & Scuba Diving. 6th, rev. ed. (Illus.). 320p. 1985. pap. 10.95. New Century.
Council for Political Excellence Editors. How the American Government Operates: A Practical Guide for All Democracies. 117p. 1985. pap. 37.50 (ISBN 0-86722-117-8). Inst Econ Finan.
Council for Science & Society. Human Procreation: Ethical Aspects of the New Techniques. (Illus.). 1984. pap. 5.95x (ISBN 0-19-857608-0). Oxford U Pr.
Council, Jon D. Profitable People Planning: A Guide to Effective Human Resource Management. (Illus.). 159p. 1978. 12.50 (ISBN 0-682-49104-7). Exposition Pr FL.
Council of American Building Officials. You Can Build It! pap. 1.50 (ISBN 0-318-00062-8). Intl Conf Bldg Off.
Council of Better Business Bureau. Better Business Bureau Guide to Wise Buying. 388p. 17.50x (ISBN 0-87196-419-8). Facts on File.
Council of Better Business Bureaus, Inc. Getting More for Your Money. (Orig.). pap. 7.95 (ISBN 0-87502-097-6). Benjamin Co.
Council of Better Business Bureaus Staff. How to Protect Your Business. 200p. 1985. 8.95 (ISBN 0-13-430539-6). P-H.
Council of Educators in Landscape Architecture. The Landscape: Critical Issues & Resources: Proceedings of the 1983 Conference of Educators in Landscape Architecture, August 6-10, 1983, Utah State University, Logan, Utah. pap. 77.50 (ISBN 0-317-30073-3, 2021081). Bks Demand UMI.
--The Rural Landscape: Abstracts of Papers Presented at the Annual Meeting of CELA, October 23-27, 1982. pap. 31.80 (ISBN 0-317-29834-8, 2019634). Bks Demand UMI.

Council of Educators in Landscape Architecture Staff. Teaching on the Crest of the Third Wave: Proceedings CELA 84. pap. 117.80 (ISBN 0-317-26816-3, 2023482). Bks Demand UMI.

Council of Europe. Harmonisation Measures in the Field of Legal Data Processing in the Member States of the Council of Europe. 25p. 1982. 5.00 (ISBN 92-871-0036-5, Council of Europe). Unipub.

--Harmonisation of Laws Relating to the Requirement of Written Proof & the Admissibility of Reproductions of Documents & Recordings on Computers. 21p. 1982. 6.00 (ISBN 92-871-0044-6, Council of Europe). Unipub.

--Statutory Regulation & Self-Regulation of the Press. (Mass Media Files Ser.: No. 2). 70p. 1982. 12.00 (Council of Europe). Unipub.

--Yearbook of the European Convention on Human Rights, Vol. 21. (Annuaire de la convention europeenne des droits de l'homme, 1978). 1980. lib. bdg. 155.00 (ISBN 90-247-2215-2, Pub. by Martinus Nijhoff Netherlands). Kluwer Academic.

Council of Europe, ed. Collected Edition of the "Travaux Preparatoires of the European Convention on Human Rights". Vol. V Legal Committee-Ad Hoc Joint Committee-Committee of Ministers-Consultative Assembly 23 June - 28 August 1950. 356p. 1979. lib. bdg. 131.60 (ISBN 90-247-1970-4). Kluwer Academic.

--Collected Edition of the "Travaux Preparatories" of the European Convention on Human Rights, Vol. 6. 1978. lib. bdg. 79.00 (ISBN 90-247-1969-0, Pub. by Martinus Nijhoff Netherlands). Kluwer Academic.

--Monument Protection in Europe. 1980. lib. bdg. 31.50 (ISBN 90-268-1107-1, Pub. by Kluwer Law Netherlands). Kluwer Academic.

--Population Decline in Europe: Implications of a Declining or Stationary Population. LC 78-3106. (Illus.). 1978. 37.50x (ISBN 0-312-63125-1). St Martin.

--Yearbook of the European Convention on Human Rights. (European Convention on Human Rights: No. 22). 688p. 1980. lib. bdg. 132.00 (ISBN 90-247-2383-3, Pub. by Martinus Nijhoff Netherlands). Kluwer Academic.

Council of Europe, Directorate of Legal affairs see Criminological Colloquium.

Council of Europe for Cultural Cooperation. Paedogogica Europaea, Vol. 5. 1971. 14.25 (ISBN 0-444-99978-7). Elsevier.

Council of New York Law Associates, ed. By-Laws: A Guide for Not-for-Profit Organizations & Their Lawyers. 20p. 1984. pap. 6.00 (ISBN 0-318-03105-1). Coun NY Law.

--Legal Handbook for Community Development Organizations. 67p. 1983. pap. 25.00 (ISBN 0-318-03110-8). Coun NY Law.

--New York Not-for-Profit Organization Manual. rev. ed. 190p. 1985. pap. 25.00 (ISBN 0-686-37424-X). Coun NY Law.

Council of New York Law Associates, et al, eds. Practicing Law in New York City. 195p. 1975. pap. 3.75 (ISBN 0-318-03111-6). Coun NY Law.

Council of New York Law Associates. Should You Incorporate? 24p. (Eng. & Span.). 1977. 3.00. Coun NY Law.

Council of State Governments. Federal Grants-in-Aid. LC 77-74937. (American Federalism-the Urban Dimension). (Illus.). 1978. Repr. of 1949 ed. lib. bdg. 26.50x (ISBN 0-405-10484-7). Ayer Co Pubs.

--Federal-State Relations. LC 77-74938. (American Federalism-the Urban Dimension). (Illus.). 1978. Repr. of 1949 ed. lib. bdg. 26.50x (ISBN 0-405-10485-5). Ayer Co Pubs.

--The Handbook of Interstate Crime Control. LC 77-2991. vii, 179p. 1977. Repr. of 1966 ed. lib. bdg. 17.25x (ISBN 0-8371-9567-5, CSHI). Greenwood.

--Reorganizing State Government. LC 76-7570. 1976. Repr. of 1950 ed. lib. bdg. 22.50x (ISBN 0-8371-8874-1, RESG). Greenwood.

Council of State Governments see Gardner, Jack & Purcell, L. Edward.

Council of State Governments, ed. Suggested State Legislation, 1941-1980, 39 vols. in 19. LC 72-86156. 1972. Repr. Set. lib. bdg. 895.00x (ISBN 0-912004-05-3). W W Gaunt.

Council of State Governments Staff, ed. State & Local Government Purchasing. 2nd ed. 295p. (Orig.). 1983. pap. 21.00 (ISBN 0-87292-033-X). Coun State Govts.

Council of State Governments Staff. State Elective Officials & the Legislatures: 1983-84. 1983. 15.00 (ISBN 0-87292-034-8). Coun State Govts.

--State Legislative Leadership, Committees & Staff: 1983-84 (Supplement Two to "The Book of the States") 230p. 1983. 15.00 (ISBN 0-87292-036-4). Coun State Govts.

Council of Superior Court Judges of Georgia Committee. Suggested Pattern Jury Instructions: Vol. I: Civil Cases. 2nd ed. 379p. 1984. looseleaf 50.00 (ISBN 0-318-03835-8). U of GA Inst Govt.

Council of Superior Court Judges of Georgia. Suggested Pattern Jury Instructions, Vol. II: Criminal Cases. Institute of Government Staff, ed. 201p. 1985. looseleaf 50.00 (ISBN 0-89854-132-8). U of GA Inst Govt.

Council of the Family Law Section of the State Bar of Texas. Texas Family Law Practice Manual, 3 vols. Tindall, Harry L., ed. LC 84-71042. 2166p. 1984. Set. loose-leaf, tab-divided 325.00 (ISBN 0-938160-36-2, 6260). State Bar TX.

Council of Trent. The Catechism of the Council of Trent. LC 82-50588. 603p. 1983. pap. 15.00 (ISBN 0-89555-185-3). TAN Bks Pubs.

Council on Development Choices for the '80s. The Affordable Community: Adapting Today's Communities to Tomorrow's Needs. (Illus.). 113p. 1982. pap. 16.00 (ISBN 0-87420-627-8, A12); pap. 12.00 members. Urban Land.

Council on Economic Priorities & Buchsbaum, Steven. Jobs & Energy: The Employment & Economic Impacts of Nuclear Power, Conservation, & Other Energy Options. Schwartz, Wendy C., ed. LC 79-91065. 1979. 35.00 (ISBN 0-87871-011-6). CEP.

Council on Economic Priorities & Simcich, Tina L. Women & Minorities in Banking: Shortchanged-Update. LC 76-50522. 188p. 1977. 36.95 (ISBN 0-03-040336-7). Praeger.

Council on Economic Priorities, jt. auth. see DeGrasse, Robert W., Jr.

Council on Economic Priorities (CEP) The Price of Power: Electric Utilities & the Environment. 376p. 1973. pap. 22.50x (ISBN 0-262-53024-4). MIT Pr.

Council on Energy Resources. National Energy Policy: A Continuing Assessment. (Illus.). 395p. 1978. 4.00 (ISBN 0-318-03326-7). Bur Econ Geology.

Council on Environmental Quality. Solar Energy: Progress & Promise. pap. 9.95x (ISBN 0-930978-41-2, V-021). Solar Energy Info.

Council on Foreign Relations, Inc. (New York) Catalog of the Foreign Relations Library, First Supplement. 1979. lib. bdg. 340.00 (ISBN 0-8161-0306-2, Hall Library). G K Hall.

Council on Foreign Relations Inc., New York. Catalog of the Foreign Relations Library, 9 Vols. 1969. Set. lib. bdg. 870.00 (ISBN 0-8161-0840-4, Hall Library). G K Hall.

Council on Hemispheric Affairs (U. S.) & Newspaper Guild. A Survey of Press Freedom in Latin America. LC 83-176225. 1983. 3.95. Coun Hemispheric Aff.

Council on High Blood Pressure Research American Heart Association Cleveland, Oct. 19, 20, 1973. Hypertension: Peptides, Lipids, Electrolytes & Hypertension. Hunt, James C., ed. 225p. 1974. 5.00 (ISBN 0-87493-038-3, 73-213A). Am Heart.

Council on International Educational Exchange & Commission on Voluntary Service & Action. Volunteer! The Comprehensive Guide to Voluntary Service. Cohen, Marjorie A., ed. LC 84-81561. 179p. 1984. pap. 5.50 (ISBN 0-933662-56-4). Intercult Pr.

Council on International Educational Exchange & Cohen, Marjorie A. Where to Stay U. S. A., 1984-85. 448p. 1984. 8.95 (ISBN 0-671-47604-1). Frommer-Pasmantier.

Council on International Educational Exchange Staff. The Whole World Handbook: A Guide to Study, Travel, & Work Abroad. 352p. 1981. pap. 5.75 (ISBN 0-525-93171-6, 0558-017). Dutton.

Council on International Educational Exchange. Work, Study, Travel Abroad 1984-1985: The Whole World Handbook. 7th ed. 352p. 1983. pap. 6.95 (ISBN 0-312-88953-4). St Martin.

Council on Interracial Books for Children, Inc. Chronicles of American Indian Protest. 2nd, rev. ed. 400p. (gr. 11-12). pap. 6.95 (ISBN 0-930040-30-9). CIBC.

--Guidelines for Selecting Bias-Free Textbooks & Storybooks. LC 80-165903. 105p. 1980. pap. 7.95 (ISBN 0-930040-33-3). CIBC.

Council on Interracial Books for Children. Guidelines for Selecting Bias-Free Textbooks & Story Books. (Orig.). 1980. pap. 6.95 (ISBN 0-686-74209-5). Friend Pr.

Council on Interracial Books for Children, Inc. Racism & Sexism in Children's Books. (Interracial Digest Ser.: No. 1). (Illus.). 48p. (Orig.). (gr. 11-12). 1976. pap. 3.50x (ISBN 0-930040-28-7). CIBC.

--Racism & Sexism in Children's Books. (Interracial Digest Ser.: No. 2). (Illus.). 48p. (Orig.). (gr. 11-12). 1978. pap. 4.50 (ISBN 0-930040-29-5). CIBC.

--Stereotypes, Distortions & Omissions in U. S. History Textbooks: A Content Analysis Instrument for Detecting Racism & Sexism. 143p. (gr. 11-12). 1977. pap. 8.95x (ISBN 0-930040-03-1). CIBC.

--Unlearning "Indian" Stereotypes. LC 77-88826. 56p. 1977. pap. 3.95 (ISBN 0-930040-36-8). CIBC.

Council on Learning, jt. auth. see Educational Testing Service.

Council on Legal Education Opportunity. Allan Bakke versus Regents of the University of California, 6 vols. Slocum, Alfred A., ed. LC 78-3573. 1978. lib. bdg. 44.00 ea. (ISBN 0-379-20297-2); Set. lib. bdg. 264.00. Oceana.

Council on Postsecondary Accreditation, jt. auth. see Association of College & Research Libraries.

Council on Resident Education in Obstetrics & Gynecology, ed. see Sloviter, Robert S.

Council on Tall Buildings & Urban Habitat. Developments in Tall Buildings, 1983. 912p. 1984. 75.00 (ISBN 0-87933-048-1). Van Nos Reinhold.

Council on Tall Buildings & Urban Habitats of Fritz Engineering Lab., Lehigh Univ. Structural Design of Tall Concrete & Masonry Buildings. LC 78-60643. 960p. 1978. 62.50x (ISBN 0-87262-152-9). Am Soc Civil Eng.

--Structural Design of Tall Steel Buildings. LC 79-63736. 1077p. 1979. 75.00x (ISBN 0-87262-228-2). Am Soc Civil Eng.

Council on Tall Buildings & Urban Habitat. Tall Building Criteria & Loading. LC 79-56002. (Monographs on the Planning & Design of Tall Buildings: No. 5). 900p. 1980. 50.00x (ISBN 0-87262-237-1). Am Soc Civil Eng.

--Tall Buildings Systems & Concepts. LC 80-65692. (Monographs on Planning & Design of Tall Buildings: No. 4). 669p. 1980. 50.00x (ISBN 0-87262-239-8). Am Soc Civil Eng.

Cound, John J., et al. Cases & Materials on Civil Procedure. 4th ed. (American Casebook Ser.). 1202p. 1985. text ed. write for info. (ISBN 0-314-90276-7). West Pub.

--Civil Procedure, Cases & Materials. 4th ed. (American Casebook Ser.). 258p. 1985. pap. text ed. write for info. (ISBN 0-314-94998-4). West Pub.

--Civil Procedure Supplement for Use with All Pleading & Procedure Casebooks. (American Casebooks Ser.). 435p. 1984. pap. text ed. 8.95 (ISBN 0-314-81152-4). West Pub.

--Civil Procedure Supplement for Use with All Pleading & Procedure Casebooks. (American Casebook Ser.). 435p. 1985. pap. text ed. write for info. (ISBN 0-314-93545-2). West Pub.

Coundakis, Anthony L. Mannerism on Space Communication. 194p. 1981. 12.50 (ISBN 0-682-49734-7). Exposition Pr FL.

Counihan, Martin. A Dictionary of Energy. (Illus.). 200p. 1981. 16.95x (ISBN 0-7100-0847-3). Routledge & Kegan.

Counihan, Rick, jt. auth. see Nemtzow, David.

Counsel, June. But Martin! An Engaging & Whimsical Tale for E. T. Lovers Everywhere. LC 83-25299. (Illus.). 32p. (ps-2). 1984. 7.95 (ISBN 0-571-13349-5). Faber & Faber.

--A Dragon in Class Four. (Illus.). 96p. (gr. 1-4). 1984. 11.95 (ISBN 0-571-13249-9). Faber & Faber.

Counsell, J. N. Natural Colours for Food & Other Uses. (Illus.). 173p. 1981. 29.75 (ISBN 0-85334-933-9, Pub. by Elsevier Applied Sci England). Elsevier.

Counsell, J. N. & Horning, D. H. Vitamin C (Ascorbic Acid) (Illus.). 383p. 1981. 63.00 (ISBN 0-85334-109-5, Pub. by Elsevier Applied Sci England). Elsevier.

Counselman, Mary E. The Face of Fear & Other Poems. Eng, Steve, ed. (Eidolon Poets Ser.). (Illus.). 43p. 1982. pap. 3.95 (ISBN 0-686-35877-5). Eidolon Pr.

--Half in Shadow. 1978. 8.95 (ISBN 0-87054-081-5). Arkham.

Counselor, Fred. Double-O Phudd Saves the World & Other Mysteries for You to Solve, No. 4. (The Phudd Files Ser.). (Illus.). 64p. (gr. 2-4). 1985. pap. 1.50 (ISBN 0-307-13103-3, Pub. by Golden Bks). Western Pub.

--Hopalong Phudd & the Curse of the Crooked Cow & Other Mysteries for You to Solve, No. 3. (The Phudd Files Ser.). (Illus.). 64p. (gr. 2-4). 1985. pap. 1.50 (ISBN 0-307-13102-5, Pub. by Golden Bks). Western Pub.

--Inspector Phudd in the Goldfish Who Knew Too Much & Other Mysteries for You to Solve, No. 1. (The Phudd Files Ser.). (Illus.). 64p. (gr. 2-4). 1985. pap. 1.50 (ISBN 0-307-13100-9, Pub. by Golden Bks). Western Pub.

--Miss Agatha Phudd in the Murder at Motley Manor & Other Mysteries for You to Solve, No. 2. (The Phudd Files Ser.). (Illus.). 64p. (gr. 2-4). 1985. pap. 1.50 (ISBN 0-307-13101-7, Pub. by Golden Bks). Western Pub.

Counsilman, James. Science of Swimming. 1968. ref. ed. 28.95 (ISBN 0-13-795385-2). P-H.

Counsilman, James E. The Complete Book of Swimming. LC 72-82682. (Illus.). 256p. 1977. pap. 5.95 (ISBN 0-689-70583-2, 246). Atheneum.

Counsins, Evert H. Process Thought on the Eve of the Twenty-First Century. 50p. (Orig.). 1985. pap. 3.95 (ISBN 0-932269-25-7). Wyndham Hall.

Count, Brian. Power from Sea Waves. (Institute of Mathematics & Its Applications Conference Ser.). 1981. 65.00 (ISBN 0-12-193550-7). Acad Pr.

Count, Earl W. & Bowles, Gordon T., eds. Fact & Theory in Social Science. LC 64-16921. 1964. 11.95x (ISBN 0-8156-2063-2). Syracuse U Pr.

Count de St. Germain. The Theory of the Mounts of the Hand & the Message They Convey to the Future of Man. (Illus.). 131p. 1983. Repr. of 1898 ed. 115.45 (ISBN 0-89901-110-1). Found Class Reprints.

Counte, Michael A. & Christman, Luther. Interpersonal Behavior & Health Care. (Behavioral Sciences for the Health Care Professional Ser.). 128p. (Orig.). 1981. lib. bdg. 17.00x (ISBN 0-86531-008-4); pap. text ed. 8.00x (ISBN 0-86531-009-2). Westview.

Counte, Michael A., jt. auth. see Christman, Luther.

Counter, Constance & Tani, Karl. Palette in the Kitchen. LC 74-75303. (Illus.). 1973. pap. 5.95 (ISBN 0-913270-28-8). Sunstone Pr.

Counter, Richard. The Yachtsman's Doctor. 148p. 1982. 40.00x (ISBN 0-333-32106-5, Pub. by Nautical England). State Mutual Bk.

Counter, Richard T. Color Atlas of Temporal Bone Surgical Anatomy. (Illus.). 80p. 1980. 47.50 (ISBN 0-8151-1869-4). Year Bk Med.

Counter, S. Allen & Evans, David L. I Sought My Brother: An Afro-American Reunion. (Illus.). 296p. 1981. 19.95 (ISBN 0-262-03079-9). MIT Pr.

Countess, Robert H. The Jehovah's Witnesses' New Testament: A Critical Analysis. 1982. pap. 5.95 (ISBN 0-87552-210-6). Presby & Reformed.

Countess Of Warwick. William Morris: His Homes & Haunts. LC 73-13851. 1912. lib. bdg. 17.50 (ISBN 0-8414-3462-X). Folcroft.

Country Music Foundation Staff. The Country Music Hall of Fame & Museum Book. 48p. 1983. 4.95 (ISBN 0-86558-019-7). Country Music Found.

Countryman, David W. & Sofranko, Denise M., eds. Guiding Land Use Decisions: Planning & Management of Forest & Recreation. LC 81-14281. 304p. 1982. 25.00x (ISBN 0-8018-2650-0). Johns Hopkins.

Countryman, Edward. The American Revolution. Foner, Eric, ed. 256p. 1985. 16.95 (ISBN 0-8090-2563-9); pap. 7.95 (ISBN 0-8090-0162-4). Hill & Wang.

--A People in Revolution: The American Revolution & Political Society in New York, 1760-1790. LC 81-5993. (Studies in Historical & Political Science 99th Series: No. 2). 418p. 1981. text ed. 30.00x (ISBN 0-8018-2625-X). Johns Hopkins.

Countryman, Kathleen M., jt. auth. see Gekas, Alexandra B.

Countryman, L. Wm. The Rich Christian in the Church of the Early Empire: Contradictions & Accomodations. LC 80-81884. (Texts & Studies in Religion: Vol. 7). viii, 248p. 1980. 49.95x (ISBN 0-88946-970-9). E Mellen.

Countryman, Vern. Cases & Materials on Debtor & Creditor. 2nd ed. 1974. 29.00 (ISBN 0-316-15803-8). Little.

--Commercial Law: Selected Statutes. 2nd ed. 1980. 15.00i (ISBN 0-316-15813-5). Little.

--Problems of Professional Responsibility Under the Uniform Commercial Code. 228p. 1969. pap. 10.00 (ISBN 0-317-30891-2, B383). Am Law Inst.

--Un-American Activities in the State of Washington. 1951. 27.00 (ISBN 0-384-09920-3). Johnson Repr.

Countryman, Vern, ed. Discrimination & the Law: Papers. LC 65-24422. pap. 46.00 (ISBN 0-317-26499-0, 2024039). Bks Demand UMI.

Countryman, Vern, ed. see Douglas, William O.

Countryman, Vern, et al. Law in Contemporary Society: The Orgain Lectures. 115p. 1973. 8.95x (ISBN 0-292-74606-7). U of Tex Pr.

--Cases & Materials on Commercial Law. 2nd ed. LC 81-81533. 1326p. 1982. 34.00 (ISBN 0-316-15796-1). Little.

Countryman, William. Biblical Authority or Biblical Tyranny? Scripture & the Christian Pilgrimage. LC 81-70591. 96p. 1982. pap. 6.95 (ISBN 0-8006-1630-8, 1-1630). Fortress.

Countryside Magazine Editors. Country Kitchen: A Project & Idea Book. (Illus.). 144p. (Orig.). 1984. 15.95 (ISBN 0-8306-0354-9); pap. 9.95 (ISBN 0-8306-1354-4, 1354). TAB Bks.

--Country Wisdom: The Art of Successful Homesteading. (Illus.). 544p. 1982. 21.95 (ISBN 0-8306-0076-0); pap. 12.95 (ISBN 0-8306-1356-0, 1356). TAB Bks.

--The Countryside Book of Farming Lore. (Illus.). 288p. (Orig.). 1985. 22.95 (ISBN 0-8306-0952-0, 1952); pap. 13.95 (ISBN 0-8306-1952-6). TAB Bks.

--Raising Animals for Fun & Profit. (Illus.). 304p. (Orig.). 1984. o.p 18.95 (ISBN 0-8306-0666-1, 1666); pap. 13.95 (ISBN 0-8306-1666-7). TAB Bks.

Countryside Press Editors, ed. The Psalms Around Us. (Illus.). 96p. 1974. deluxe ed. 10.95 (ISBN 0-385-01087-7). Doubleday.

Countryside Staff, ed. The Countryside A-Z Guide to Vegetables. (A-Z Ser.). (Orig.). Date not set. pap. 7.95 (ISBN 0-88453-038-8). Countryside Bks.

Counts, Bill, jt. auth. see Narramore, Bruce.

Counts, Charles. Common Clay: Indiana Revisions. (Illus.). 1977. pap. 4.00 (ISBN 0-686-86009-8). Halldin Pub.

--Pottery Workshop. (Illus.). 198p. 1976. pap. 8.95 (ISBN 0-02-011230-0, Collier). Macmillan.

Counts, David R. Grammar of Kaliai-Kove. LC 72-627917. (Oceanic Linguistics Special Publication: No. 6). (Orig.). 1970. pap. text ed. 8.00x (ISBN 0-87022-156-6). UH Pr.

Counts, David R., jt. auth. see Counts, Dorothy A.

Counts, Dorothy A. & Counts, David R. Aging & Its Transformations: Moving Toward Death in Pacific Societies. (Illus.). 348p. (Orig.). 1985. lib. bdg. 26.50 (ISBN 0-8191-4840-7, Co-Pub by Assoc Soc Anthro Oceania); pap. text ed. 14.75 (ISBN 0-8191-4841-5). U Pr of Amer.

Counts, Dorothy A., jt. ed. see Rodman, William L.

Counts, George S. American Road to Culture: A Social Interpretation of Education in the United States. LC 70-165736. (American Education Ser.: No.2).). 1971. Repr. of 1930 ed. 14.00 (ISBN 0-405-03605-1). Ayer Co Pubs.

--Bolshevism, Fascism & Capitalism. 1932. 13.50x (ISBN 0-686-83492-5). Elliots Bks.

--The Challenge of Soviet Education. LC 74-25992. 330p. 1975. Repr. of 1957 ed. lib. bdg. 35.00x (ISBN 0-8371-7877-0, COSE). Greenwood.
--Country of the Blind: The Soviet System of Mind Control. LC 79-100153. Repr. of 1949 ed. lib. bdg. 35.00x (ISBN 0-8371-3680-6, CCOB). Greenwood.
--Dare the School Build a New Social Order? LC 78-18895. (Arcturus Books Paperbacks). 68p. 1978. pap. 4.95x (ISBN 0-8093-0878-9). S Ill U Pr.
--Dare the Schools Build a New Social Order. LC 71-89165. (American Education: Its Men, Institutions & Ideas, Ser. 1). 1969. Repr. of 1932 ed. 10.00 (ISBN 0-405-01496-1). Ayer Co Pubs.
--Education & American Civilization. LC 73-19569. 491p. 1974. Repr. of 1952 ed. lib. bdg. 26.00x (ISBN 0-8371-7293-4, COEA). Greenwood.
--School & Society in Chicago. LC 71-165715. (American Education Ser, No. 2). 1971. Repr. of 1928 ed. 27.50 (ISBN 0-405-03704-X). Ayer Co Pubs.
--Selective Character of American Secondary Education. LC 75-89166. (American Education: Its Men, Institutions & Ideas, Ser. 1). 1969. Repr. of 1922 ed. 14.00 (ISBN 0-405-01404-X). Ayer Co Pubs.
--Social Composition of Boards of Education. LC 79-89167. (American Education: Its Men, Institutions & Ideas, Ser. 1). 1969. Repr. of 1927 ed. 10.00 (ISBN 0-405-01405-8). Ayer Co Pubs.
Counts, Robert, ed. Independent Living Rehabilitation for Severely Handicapped People: A Preliminary Appraisal. 67p. 1978. pap. 6.00x (ISBN 0-87766-228-2, 22600). Urban Inst.
Coupe, B. E. Regional Economic Structure & Environmental Pollution. (Studies in Applied Science: No. 5). 1977. pap. 15.50 (ISBN 90-207-0646-2, Pub. by Martinus Nijhoff Netherlands). Kluwer Academic.
Coupe, Stuart & Baker, Glenn A. The New Rock 'n Roll: The A-Z of Rock in the 80's. LC 83-51778. (Illus.). 192p. 1984. pap. 14.95 (ISBN 0-312-57210-7). St Martin.
Coupe, William A. German Political Satires from the Reformation to the Second World War, 6 vols. (Illus.). 1985. Set. lib. bdg. write for info. (ISBN 0-527-19839-0); Pt. 1-Circa 1500-1848 Commentary. lib. bdg. write for info. (ISBN 0-527-19840-4); Pt. 1: Circa 1500-1848 Plates. lib. bdg. write for info. (ISBN 0-527-19841-2); Pt. 2: 1849-1918 Commentary. lib. bdg. write for info. (ISBN 0-527-19842-0); Pt. 2: 1849-1918 Plates. lib. bdg. write for info. (ISBN 0-527-19843-9); Pt. 3: 1918-1945 Commentary. lib. bdg. write for info. (ISBN 0-527-19844-7); Pt. 3: 1918-1945 Plates. lib. bdg. write for info. (ISBN 0-527-19845-5). Kraus Intl.
Couper, Alastair, ed. The Times Atlas of the Oceans. (Illus.). 256p. 1983. 79.95 (ISBN 0-442-21661-0). Van Nos Reinhold.
Couper, Charles T. Report on the Trial...Against the Directors & the Manager of the City of Glasgow Bank. LC 83-49106. (Accounting History & the Development of a Profession Ser.). 467p. 1984. lib. bdg. 60.00 (ISBN 0-8240-6320-1). Garland Pub.
Couper, Heater & Murtagh, Terence. Heavens Above! (Illus.). 64p. (gr. 5 up). 1981. lib. bdg. 9.90 (ISBN 0-531-04287-1). Watts.
Couper, Heather. Comets & Meteors. (Space Scientist Ser.). (Illus.). 32p. (gr. 7-12). 1985. PLB 9.90 (ISBN 0-531-10000-6). Watts.
--The Planets. (Space Scientist Ser.). (Illus.). 32p. (gr. 7 up). 1985. PLB 9.90 (ISBN 0-531-10001-4). Watts.
--The Universe. (Illus.). 1985. 19.45 (ISBN 0-394-54691-1). Random.
Couper, Heather & Henbest, Nigel. All about Space. (Full Color Fact Bks.). (Illus.). 32p. (gr. 4-12). 1982. PLB 7.95 (ISBN 0-8219-0014-5, 35545). EMC.
--Astronomy. (Science World Ser.). 40p. (gr. 4-6). 1983. PLB 9.90 (ISBN 0-531-04651-6). Watts.
Couper, Heather, jt. auth. see Henbest, Nigel.
Couper, John M. Canterbury Folk. ix, 58p. 1984. 14.25x (ISBN 0-522-84272-0, Pub. by Melbourne Pr). Intl Spec Bk.
Couperie, Pierre, et al. Encyclopedie De la Bande Dessinee, Vol. 1: A-Cap. 173p. (Fr.). pap. 27.50 (ISBN 0-686-56966-0, M-6093). French & Eur.
--Encyclopedie De la Bande Dessinee Vol. 3. 176p. (Fr.). pap. 29.95 (ISBN 0-686-56968-7, M-6095). French & Eur.
Coupers & Lybran. Closing Plants: Planning & Implementing Strategies. 1985. price not set. Finan Exec.
Couperus, L. The Hidden Force. Beekman, E. M., ed. De Mattos, Alexander T., tr. from Dutch. LC 84-16208. (Library of the Indies). 274p. (De Stille Kracht.). 1985. lib. bdg. 24.00x (ISBN 0-87023-465-X). U of Mass Pr.
Coupland, R. E. & Forssmann, W. G., eds. Peripheral Neuroendocrine Interaction. (Illus.). 1978. pap. 51.00 (ISBN 0-387-08779-6). Springer-Verlag.
Coupland, R. T., ed. Grassland Ecosystems of the World. LC 77-83990. (International Biological Programme Ser.: No. 18). 1979. 89.50 (ISBN 0-521-21867-5). Cambridge U Pr.
Coupland, Reginald. The Exploitation of East Africa. 507p. 1967. 17.00x (ISBN 0-89771-008-8). State Mutual Bk.
--Kirk on the Zambesi: A Chapter of African History. Repr. of 1928 ed. 22.50x (ISBN 0-8371-2916-8, COK&, Pub. by Negro U Pr). Greenwood.
--The Quebec Act: A Study in Statesmanship. LC 83-45424. Repr. of 1925 ed. 28.00 (ISBN 0-404-20068-0). AMS Pr.
--Wilberforce, a Narrative. LC 68-55879. Repr. of 1923 ed. 23.00x (ISBN 0-8371-0362-2, COW&). Greenwood.
Coupland, Susan. Beginning to Pray in Old Age, Vol. II. (Parish Life Sourcebks.). 96p. 1985. pap. 6.95 (ISBN 0-936384-29-8). Cowley Pubns.
Courakis, Anthony S., ed. Inflation, Depression & Economic Policy in the West. LC 79-55497. 376p. 1981. text ed. 32.50x (ISBN 0-389-20144-8). B&N Imports.
Courant, ed. see De Beaumarchais, Pierre A.
Courant, Maurice A. Bibliographie Coreenne, Tableau Litteraire De la Coree, 4 vols in 3. (Incl. suppl). Repr. of 1894 ed. Set. 177.00 (ISBN 0-8337-0692-6). B Franklin.
Courant, Paul N. & Gramlich, Edward M. Federal Budget Deficits: America's Great Consumption Binge. (Illus.). 96p. 1986. pap. text ed. 12.95 (ISBN 0-13-308438-8). P-H.
Courant, R. Differential & Integral Calculus, 2 vols. Incl. Vol. 1. 630p. 1937. 43.95 (ISBN 0-471-17820-9); Vol. 2. 692p. 1936. 43.95x (ISBN 0-471-17853-5). Pub. by Wiley-Interscience). Wiley.
Courant, R. & Friedrichs, K. O. Supersonic Flow & Shock Waves. (Applied Mathematical Sciences: Vol. 21.). 1948. 42.00 (ISBN 0-387-90232-5). Springer-Verlag.
Courant, R. & Hilbert, D. Methods of Mathematical Physics, 2 vols. Set. 110.00x (ISBN 0-471-17990-6, Pub. by Wiley-Interscience); Vol. 1, 1953. 51.95x (ISBN 0-470-17952-X); Vol. 2, 1962. 70.95x (ISBN 0-470-17985-6). Wiley.
Courant, R., jt. ed. see Behnke, H.
Courant, Richard & John, J. Fritz. Introduction to Calculus & Analysis, 2 vols. LC 65-16403. Vol. 2, 954p. 1974. 57.50x (ISBN 0-471-17862-4, Pub. by Wiley-Interscience). Wiley.
Courant, Richard & Robbins, Herbert. What Is Mathematics? An Elementary Approach to Ideas & Methods. (Illus.). 1978. pap. 13.95 (ISBN 0-19-502517-2, GB576, GB). Oxford U Pr.
Courbier, R. Basis for a Classification of Cererral Arterial Diseases. (Current Clinical Practice Ser.: Vol. 22). 1985. 83.50 (ISBN 0-444-90411-5). Elsevier.
Courcelle, B., et al, eds. Trees in Algebra & Programming: Proceedings of the Ninth Colloquium, Bordeaux, France, March 1984. 350p. 1984. 39.50 (ISBN 0-521-26750-1). Cambridge U Pr.
Courcelles, M. Extract from the Despatches of Courcelles. Bell, Robert, ed. LC 72-1015. (Bannatyne Club, Edinburgh. Publications: No. 22). Repr. of 1828 ed. 18.50 (ISBN 0-404-52728-0). AMS Pr.
Courcelle-Seneuil, J. G. Traite Elementaire de Comptabilite: Elementary Treatise on Accounting. Brief, Richard P., ed. (Dimensions of Accounting Theory & Practice Ser.). (Fr.). 1981. Repr. of 1869 ed. lib. bdg. 22.00x (ISBN 0-405-13513-0). Ayer Co Pubs.
Courchene, Thomas J. Migration, Income, & Employment: Canada, 1965-68, Vol. 1. (HRI Special Study). (Illus.). 155p. 1974. 3.00 (ISBN 0-88806-009-2). Inst C D Howe.
--Money, Inflation, & the Bank of Canada: An Analysis of Canadian Monetary Policy from 1970 to Early 1975, Vol. 2. (HRI Special Study). (Illus.). 290p. 1976. 5.00 (ISBN 0-88806-015-7). Inst C D Howe.
--Money, Inflation, & the Bank of Canada: An Analysis of Monetary Gradualism, 1975-80. 321p. 1981. 13.00 (ISBN 0-88806-111-0). Inst C D Howe.
--No Place to Stand? Abandoning Monetary Targets: An Evaluation. 101p. 1983. 6.00 (ISBN 0-88806-116-1). Inst C D Howe.
--The Strategy of Gradualism: An Analysis of Bank of Canada Policy from Mid-1975 to Mid-1977. 131p. 1977. 5.00 (ISBN 0-88806-029-7, H*RZ). Inst C D Howe.
Courcier, Helen M. November Burning. 80p. 1974. 6.95 (ISBN 0-87881-012-9). Mojave Bks.
Courcy, G. de, tr. see Revesz, Geza.
Courcy, G. I. C. De Paganini: The Genoese, 2 vols. LC 76-5892. (Music Reprint Series). 1977. Repr. of 1957 ed. Set. lib. bdg. 75.00 (ISBN 0-306-70872-8). Da Capo.
Courcy, G. I. C. De see Ringbom, Nils-Eric.
Courcy, G. I. de see Misch, Ludwig.
Courcy, Pol Potier De see Potier De Courcy, Pol.
Courdy, Jean-Claude. The Japanese: Everyday Life in the Empire of the Rising Sun. Rosenthal, Raymond, tr. from Fr. LC 80-5775. 1984. 22.07 (ISBN 0-06-038010-1). Har-Row.
Couric, Emily. Women Lawyers: Perspectives on Success. LC 83-22811. 259p. 1984. 40.00 (ISBN -- 15-100059-X, H42906). HarBraceJ.
Couric, Emily, ed. The Business of Law: A Handbook on How to Manage Law Firms. 470p. 1984. 55.00 (ISBN 0-15-004290-6, Law & Business). HarBraceJ.
Courier, P. L. Oeuvres Completes. 1088p. 35.95 (ISBN 0-686-56490-1). French & Eur.
Courjon, Jean, et al, eds. Clinical Applications of Evoked Potentials in Neurology. (Advances in Neurology Ser.: Vol. 32). 592p. 1982. text ed. 85.00 (ISBN 0-89004-619-0). Raven.
Courlander, Harold. The African. 1977. 7.95 (ISBN 0-517-50680-7). Crown.
--The Crest & the Hide & Other African Stories. (Illus.). 144p. 1982. 11.95 (ISBN 0-698-20536-7, Coward). Putnam Pub Group.
--The Drum & the Hoe: Life & Lore of the Haitian People. (California Library Reprint Ser.: No. 31). (Illus.). 436p. 1981. Repr. of 1973 ed. 34.00x (ISBN 0-520-02364-1). U of Cal Pr.
--Haiti Singing. LC 72-95270. (Illus.). 274p. 1973. Repr. of 1939 ed. lib. bdg. 23.50 (ISBN 0-8154-0461-1). Cooper Sq.
--King's Drum: And Other African Stories. LC 62-14242. (Illus.). (gr. 3-7). 1970. pap. 3.95 (ISBN 0-15-647190-6, VoyB). HarBraceJ.
--The Master of the Forge: A West African Odyssey. LC 84-28528. 214p. 1985. 16.95 (ISBN 0-517-55807-6). Crown.
--Negro Folk Music, U.S.A. LC 63-18019. 324p. 1963. pap. 13.00x (ISBN 0-231-08634-2). Columbia U Pr.
--Shaping Our Times: What the U. N. Is & Does. rev. ed. LC 60-14790. 242p. (Orig.). 1960. 7.50 (ISBN 0-379-00037-7). Oceana.
--Treasury of African Folklore. 640p. 1975. 14.95 (ISBN 0-517-51670-5). Crown.
--A Treasury of Afro-American Folklore. 1976. 14.95 (ISBN 0-517-52348-5). Crown.
Courlander, Harold & Bastien, Remy. Religion & Politics in Haiti. LC 66-26633. (Illus.). 1970. 3.95 (ISBN 0-911976-00-0). ICR.
Courlander, Harold, ed. Hopi Voices: Recollections, Traditions, & Narratives of the Hopi Indians. 224p. 1982. 17.50 (H-23). U of NM Pr.
Courlander, Harold, ed. see Yava, Albert.
Cournand, Andre & Levy, Maurice. Shaping the Future: Gaston Berger & the Concept of Prospective. LC 72-78388. (Current Topics of Contemporary Thought Ser.). 314p. 1973. 56.75 (ISBN 0-677-12550-X). Gordon.
Cournos, John. Autobiography. LC 78-64010. (Des Imagistes: Literature of the Imagist Movement Ser.). (Illus.). 368p. Repr. of 1935 ed. 35.00 (ISBN 0-404-17084-6). AMS Pr.
--In Exile. LC 78-64011. (Des Imagistes: Literature of the Imagist Movement). Repr. of 1923 ed. 11.50 (ISBN 0-404-17085-4). AMS Pr.
--The Mask. LC 74-26098. (Labor Movement in Fiction & Non-Fiction). Repr. of 1919 ed. 23.00 (ISBN 0-404-58416-0). AMS Pr.
--A Modern Plutarch: Mark Twain. 1928. 25.00 (ISBN 0-8274-2754-9). R West.
Cournos, John, ed. A Treasury of Russian Life & Humor. 676p. 1984. Repr. of 1943 ed. lib. bdg. 45.00 (ISBN 0-89984-146-5). Century Bookbindery.
--A Treasury of Russian Life & Humor. 676p. 1984. Repr. of 1943 ed. lib. bdg. 45.00 (ISBN 0-89987-199-2). Darby Bks.
Cournos, John, tr. from Rus. see Biely, Andrey.
Cournos, John, tr. see Bunin, Ivan A.
Cournos, John, tr. see Esenwein, Joseph B.
Cournos, John, tr. see Remizov, Aleksei M.
Cournos, John, tr. see Sologub, Fiodor K.
Cournot, Antoine A. Considerations Sur la Marche Des Idees et Des Evenements Dans les Temps Modernes. 1971. Repr. of 1872 ed. lib. bdg. 40.50 (ISBN 0-8337-0700-0). B Franklin.
Cournot, Augustin. Researches into the Mathematical Principles of the Theory of Wealth. LC 73-28986. Repr. of 1927 ed. 25.00x (ISBN 0-678-00066-2). Kelley.
--Revue Sommaire Des Doctrines Economiques. LC 68-22372. (Fr). Repr. of 1877 ed. 37.50x (ISBN 0-678-00377-7). Kelley.
Cournoyer, Norman G. & Marshall, Anthony. Hotel, Restaurant & Travel Law. 2nd ed. 1983. text ed. 24.00 (ISBN 0-534-01273-6). Breton Pubs.
Cournulier, Benoit De see De Cornulier, Benoit.
Couro, Ted. San Diego County Indians As Farmers & Wage Earners. pap. 1.00 (ISBN 0-686-69102-4). Acoma Bks.
Couro, Ted & Hutcheson, Christina. Dictionary of Mesa Grande Diegueno. 1973. pap. 5.50 (ISBN 0-939046-14-8). Malki Mus Pr.
Couro, Ted & Langdon, Margaret. Let's Talk 'Iipay Aa: An Introduction to the Mesa Grande Diegueno Language. 1975. pap. 7.50 (ISBN 0-939046-19-9). Malki Mus Pr.
Courot, M., ed. The Male in Farm Animal Reproduction. (Current Topics in Veterinary Medicine Ser.). 1985. lib. bdg. 69.50 (ISBN 0-89838-682-9, Pub. by Martinus Nijhoff Netherlands). Kluwer Academic.
Courrege, Keith. Pecans: From Soup to Nuts. LC 84-70931. (Illus.). 54p. 1984. pap. 5.95 (ISBN 0-9613404-0-1). Cane River.
Courrier, Kathleen. Life after Eighty: Environmental Choices We Can Live With. 280p. 1980. 6.95 (ISBN 0-931790-13-1, 209). Ctr Renew Resources.
Courrier, Kathleen & Munson, Richard, eds. Life after Eighty: Environmental Choices We Can Live With. LC 80-11783. 304p. 1980. pap. 8.95x (ISBN 0-931790-13-1). Brick Hse Pub.
Courrier, Kathleen, ed. see Dover, Michael J.
Courrier, Kathleen, jt. ed. see Gunn, Anita.
Courrier, Kathleen, ed. see Wasserstrom, Robert F. & Wiles, Richard.
Coursault, Jesse H. The Learning Process: Educational Theory Implied in Theory of Knowledge. LC 76-176674. (Columbia University. Teachers College. Contributions to Education: No. 16). Repr. of 1907 ed. 22.50 (ISBN 0-404-55016-9). AMS Pr.
--The Principles of Education. (Educational Ser.). 1920. Repr. 17.50 (ISBN 0-8482-3590-8). Norwood Edns.
Course, A. G. Wheel's Kick & the Wind's Song. 3rd ed. LC 68-23816. 1968. 24.95x (ISBN 0-678-05592-0). Kelley.
Course, A. G. & Oram, R. B. Glossary of Cargo Handling Terms. 1981. 25.00x (ISBN 0-85174-080-4, Pub. by Nautical England). State Mutual Bk.
--Glossary of Cargo Handling Terms. 2nd ed. 96p. 1974. pap. 7.50x (ISBN 0-85174-080-4). Sheridan.
Course, Edwin. Railways Then & Now. 1979. 21.00 (ISBN 0-7134-0533-3, Pub. by Batsford England). David & Charles.
Coursen, H. R. After the War. LC 81-4241. (Illus.). 1981. 13.95 (ISBN 0-918606-06-3); pap. 8.95 (ISBN 0-918606-05-5). Heidelberg Graph.
--The Leasing out of England: Shakespeare's Second Henriad. LC 81-40354. (Illus.). 234p. (Orig.). 1982. PLB 25.25 (ISBN 0-8191-2455-9); pap. text ed. 12.25 (ISBN 0-8191-2456-7). U Pr of Amer.
--Walking Away. 1977. pap. 1.50 (ISBN 0-686-23157-0). Samisdat.
--War Stories: Poems. Turco, Lewis, ed. LC 84-72827. (Illus.). 48p. 1984. 4.00 (ISBN 0-910380-05-8). Cider Mill.
--Winter Dreams. St. Cyr, Napoleon, ed. LC 82-4152. (Orig.). 1982. pap. 4.00 (ISBN 0-910380-04-X). Cider Mill.
Coursen, Herbert R., Jr. Christian Ritual & the World of Shakespeare's Tragedies. 441p. 1976. 32.50 (ISBN 0-8387-1518-4). Bucknell U Pr.
Coursen, Virgene. Bulletin Board Ideas for Sunday School & Church. 32p. 1977. pap. 3.50 (ISBN 0-687-04374-3). Abingdon.
Coursey, Robert D., ed. Program Evaluation for Mental Health: Methods, Strategies & Participants. LC 77-5634. 432p. 1977. 56.00 (ISBN 0-8089-1019-1, 790920). Grune.
Coursey, Rudell. Vortices & Hell. 1968. pap. 1.50 (ISBN 0-686-14909-2). Goliards Pr.
Coursodon, J. P., jt. auth. see Besnard, M.
Courson, R. L., jt. auth. see Curtis, P. E.
Court, Arnold, ed. Eclectic Climatology: Association of Pacific Coast Geographers, Vol. 30. LC 37-13376. (Illus.). 1968. 8.00x (ISBN 0-87071-312-4). Oreg St U Pr.
Court, Artelia. Puck of the Droms: The Lives & Literatures of the Irish Tinkers. 1985. 24.95 (ISBN 0-520-03711-1). U of Cal Pr.
Court, David & Ghai, Dharam, eds. Education, Society & Development: New Perspectives from Kenya. (Illus.). 1974. pap. 8.95x (ISBN 0-19-572345-7). Oxford U Pr.
Court, Franklin E., ed. Walter Pater: An Annotated Bibliography of Writings about Him. LC 78-56125. (Annotated Secondary Bibliography Series on English Literature in Transition: 1880-1920). 411p. 1980. 25.00 (ISBN 0-87580-072-6). N Ill U Pr.
Court, J., jt. auth. see Dierauf, E., Jr.
Court, John M. Helping Your Diabetic Child: A Guide to Parents & to Their Children Who Have Diabetes. LC 78-18312. 1974. 8.95 (ISBN 0-8008-3823-8); pap. 4.95 (ISBN 0-8008-3824-6). Taplinger.
Court, Judith. Ponds & Streams. (Action Science Ser.). 32p. (gr. 1-8). 1985. PLB 9.90 (ISBN 0-531-04952-3). Watts.
Court, Nathan A. Modern Pure Solid Geometry. 2nd ed. LC 64-18134. 1979. text ed. 17.95 (ISBN 0-8284-0147-0). Chelsea Pub.
Court, Pieter De La see De La Court, Pieter.
Court, Rosemary. Sam's System: A Guide to Computers. (Computer Bk.). (Illus.). 48p. (gr. 4 up). 1983. PLB 11.95 (ISBN 0-516-00591-X). Childrens.
Court, Simon. Meditator's Manual: A Practical Introduction to the Art of Meditation. (Illus.). 112p. (Orig.). 1985. pap. 12.95 spiral (ISBN 0-85030-410-5, Pub. by Aquarian Pr England). Sterling.
Court, T. H., jt. auth. see Clay, Reginald S.
Court, Thomas H., jt. auth. see Clay, Reginald S.
Court, W. H. Coal. 1976. 53.00 (ISBN 0-527-35768-5). Kraus Intl.
Court, Wesli. Courses in Lambents. (Illus.). (YA) (gr. 7-12). 1977. 15.00 (ISBN 0-930000-00-5); PLB 8.95 (ISBN 0-930000-01-3); pap. 3.95 (ISBN 0-930000-02-1). Mathom.
--Murgatroyd & Mabel. (Illus.). 42p. (gr. k-2). 1978. PLB 3.95 (ISBN 0-930000-06-4). Mathom.
Court, William H. British Economic History, Eighteen Seventy to Nineteen Fourteen. 1966. 64.50 (ISBN 0-521-04731-5); pap. 19.95x (ISBN 0-521-09362-7). Cambridge U Pr.
--Scarcity & Choice in History. LC 74-113460. 1970. lib. bdg. 27.50x (ISBN 0-678-08017-8). Kelley.
Courtade, Anthony. The Structure of John Webster's Plays. (Salzberg - Jacobean Drama Studies: No. 97). 172p. 1980. pap. text ed. 25.50x (ISBN 0-391-02324-1, Pub. by Inst Lit Austria). Humanities.

Courtauld, Caroline. In Search of Burma. (Illus.). 112p. 1985. 19.95 (ISBN 0-318-11697-9, Pub. by Salem Hse Ltd). Merrimack Pub Cir.

Courtauld, George. An Axe, a Spade & Ten Acres: The Story of a Garden & Nature Reserve. LC 84-10324. (Illus.). 213p. 1985. 19.95 (ISBN 0-374-10749-1); pap. 8.95 (ISBN 0-374-51871-8). FS&G.

Courtauld Institute of Art, London & Troutman, Philip. The Painting Collections of the Courtauld Institute of Art. LC 78-13168. 1979. 5 color fiches incl. 80.00 (ISBN 0-226-68904-2, CVL 24, Chicago Visual Lib). U of Chicago Pr.

Courteau, E. Coins & Tokens of Nova Scotia. (Illus.). 1982. pap. 8.00 (ISBN 0-942666-09-7). S J Durst.

Courteline, Georges. Ah! Jeunesse. 190p. 1965. 3.95 (ISBN 0-686-54626-1). French & Eur.

--Les Balances. 34p. 1946. 2.50 (ISBN 0-686-54627-X). French & Eur.

--Boubouroche, Lidoire et Potiron. 189p. 1964. 3.95 (ISBN 0-686-54628-8). French & Eur.

--Les Femmes d'Amis. 1972. 3.95 (ISBN 0-686-54629-6). French & Eur.

--Le Gendarme Est Sans Pitie: Avec: La Peur des Coupes, Theodore Cherche des Allumettes, La Couche. 1974. 3.95 (ISBN 0-686-54631-8). French & Eur.

--Hortense, Couche-toi: Avec: La Conversion d'Alceste, Monsieur Badinet, Les Boulingrin. 160p. 1975. 3.95 (ISBN 0-686-54632-6). French & Eur.

--Les Linottes. 192p. 1966. 3.95 (ISBN 0-686-54633-4). French & Eur.

--Oeuvres, 2 vols. (Illus.). 1975. Set. 65.00 (ISBN 0-686-54635-0). French & Eur.

--La Paix Chez Soi. 40p. 1966. 2.95 (ISBN 0-686-54636-9). French & Eur.

--Theatre: Avec: Boubouroche, La Peur des Coups. 253p. 1965. 4.50 (ISBN 0-686-54637-7). French & Eur.

--Theatre Complet. 1961. 19.95 (ISBN 0-686-54638-5). French & Eur.

--Le Train de 8h 47. 256p. 1959. 8.95 (ISBN 0-686-54639-3). French & Eur.

Courteline, Georges & Pruner, Francis. Les Gaietes de l'Escadron. 192p. 1962. 3.95 (ISBN 0-686-54630-X). French & Eur.

--Messieurs les Ronds-de-cuirt. 192p. 1966. 3.95 (ISBN 0-686-54634-2). French & Eur.

Courtemanche, Gil W. The New Internal Auditing. (Institute of International Auditng Ser.). 42.00 (ISBN 0-471-82885-8). Wiley.

Courtemanche, Regis, jt. auth. see Curtis, Carl T.

Courtenay, Ashley. Let's Halt Awhile in Great Britain Hotel Guide, 1982. (Orig.). 1982. pap. 14.95 (ISBN 0-8038-4339-9). Hastings.

--Let's Halt Awhile in Ireland 1982 to 1983. (Illus.). 128p. (Orig.). 1982. pap. 5.95 (ISBN 0-8038-4341-0). Hastings.

Courtenay, Thomas P. Commentaries on the Historical Plays of Shakspeare, 2 Vols. LC 72-1030. Repr. of 1840 ed. Set. 57.50 (ISBN 0-404-01781-9). Vol. 1 (ISBN 0-404-01782-7). Vol. 2 (ISBN 0-404-01783-5). AMS Pr.

Courtenay, Walter R., Jr. & Stauffer, Jay R., Jr., eds. Distribution, Biology & Management of Exotic Fishes. LC 83-18723. 448p. 1984. 40.00x (ISBN 0-8018-3037-0). Johns Hopkins.

Courtenay, William J., ed. see Weinberg, Julius R.

Courteney, Sally, jt. auth. see Goeldner, C. R.

Courter, jt. auth. see Hamp-Lyons.

Courter, Gay. The Beansprout Book. (Illus.). 1977. pap. 2.95 (ISBN 0-671-22947-8, Fireside). S&S.

--The Midwife. 512p. 1981. 12.95 (ISBN 0-395-29463-0). HM.

--River of Dreams. LC 83-22747. (Illus.). 544p. 1984. 16.95 (ISBN 0-395-35301-7). HM.

--River of Dreams. (General Ser.). 1984. lib. bdg. 18.95 (ISBN 0-8161-3768-4, Large Print Bks). G K Hall.

--River of Dreams. 1985. pap. 4.50 (ISBN 0-451-13510-5, Sig). NAL.

Courter, J. W. Aladdin, the Magic Name in Lamps. 68p. 17.50 (ISBN 0-87069-001-9, 99001); 3.95 (99002). Wallace-Homestead.

Courtes, G., jt. ed. see Marechal, A.

Courtes, J., jt. auth. see Greimas, A. J.

Courtes, Jean Marie, jt. auth. see Devisse, Jean.

Courthion, Pierre. Impressionism. concise ed. Shepley, John, tr. (Illus.). 1977. pap. 10.95 (ISBN 0-8109-2067-0). Abrams.

--Impressionism. (Illus.). 40.00 (ISBN 0-8109-0202-8). Abrams.

--Impressionism. (Illus.). 160p. 14.98 (ISBN 0-8109-8056-8). Abrams.

--Manet. (Library of Great Painters Ser). (Illus.). 1963. 40.00 (ISBN 0-8109-0260-5). Abrams.

--Manet. (Master of Art Ser.). (Illus.). 19.95 (ISBN 0-8109-1318-6). Abrams.

--Rouault. (Library of Great Painters). (Illus.). 1977. 40.00 (ISBN 0-8109-0459-4). Abrams.

--Seurat. LC 68-13066. (Library of Great Painters Ser.). (Illus.). 1968. 40.00 (ISBN 0-8109-0474-8). Abrams.

Courthope, W. J. Essays on Milton. 1908. lib. bdg. 10.00 (ISBN 0-8414-3599-5). Folcroft.

--Genius of Spenser. 1868. lib. bdg. 8.50 (ISBN 0-8414-3419-0). Folcroft.

--Liberal Movement in English Literature. LC 72-194105. 1885. lib. bdg. 12.50 (ISBN 0-8414-2395-4). Folcroft.

Courthope, William J. Addison. Morley, John, ed. LC 68-58375. (English Men of Letters). Repr. of 1889 ed. lib. bdg. 12.50 (ISBN 0-404-51707-2). AMS Pr.

--Addison. 1973. lib. bdg. 15.00 (ISBN 0-8414-2396-2). Folcroft.

--Liberal Movement in English Literature. LC 72-458. Repr. of 1885 ed. 19.50 (ISBN 0-404-01784-3). AMS Pr.

--Life in Poetry. LC 72-992. Repr. of 1901 ed. 24.50 (ISBN 0-404-01785-1). AMS Pr.

--Life in Poetry. 1973. Repr. of 1901 ed. 13.95 (ISBN 0-8274-1321-1). R West.

Courtial, Donald C., jt. auth. see Rantz, Marilyn.

Courtice, Katie, jt. auth. see Powell, Lenore.

Courtier, Gary. Midwife. 1982. pap. 3.95 (ISBN 0-451-11503-1, AE1503, Sig). NAL.

Courtin, Nicholas, tr. see De Hoyos, Ladislas.

Courtin, Robina, ed. see McDonald, Kathleen.

Courtine, Robert H. Dictionnaire des Fromages. 250p. (Fr.). 1972. pap. 6.95 (ISBN 0-686-56807-9, F-A16). French & Eur.

Courtine, Robert J. Dictionnaire des Fromages. 255p. (Fr.). 1972. pap. 8.50 (ISBN 2-03-075473-0, 3792). Larousse.

--Guide Courtine - Bon Appetit a Paris. 256p. 1976. 7.95 (ISBN 0-8184-0210-5). Lyle Stuart.

--Larousse des fromages. new ed. (Illus.). 253p. (Fr.). 1973. 38.95x (ISBN 2-03-019012-8). Larousse.

Courtine, Robert J., ed. Larousse Gastronomique. (Illus.). 1142p. 1984. 89.95 (ISBN 2-03-506301-9). Larousse.

--The Master Chefs of France Recipe Book. (Illus.). 192p. 1982. 24.95 (ISBN 0-89696-140-0, An Everest House Book). Dodd.

--Nouveau Larousse Gastronomique. 1104p. (Fr.). 1968. 79.50 (ISBN 0-686-57062-6, M-6433). French & Eur.

Courtis, Stuart A., jt. auth. see Caldwell, Otis W.

Courtiss, Eugene H. Male Aesthetic Surgery. 1st ed. LC 81-14147. (Illus.). 426p. 1982. text ed. 89.95 (ISBN 0-8016-1115-6). Mosby.

Courtiss, Eugene H., jt. ed. see Goulian, Dicran.

Courtivron, Isabelle de & Resnick, Margery. Women Writers in Translation: An Annotated Bibliography, 1945-1981. LC 80-9039. (Reference Library of the Humanities). 200p. 1984. lib. bdg. 50.00 (ISBN 0-8240-9332-1). Garland Pub.

Courtivron, Isabelle De see Resnick, Margery & De Cortivron, Isabelle.

Courtivron, Isabelle De see Marks, Elaine & De Courtivron, Isabelle.

Courtman-Davies, Mary. Your Deaf Child's Speech & Language. 296p. 1980. 14.95 (ISBN 0-370-30149-8, Pub. by the Bodley Head). Merrimack Pub Cir.

Courtman-Stock, J, jt. auth. see Clark, A. M.

Courtney, ed. Nationalism & War in the Near East. LC 79-135800. (Eastern Europe Collection Ser). 1970. Repr. of 1915 ed. 25.50 (ISBN 0-405-02742-7). Ayer Co Pubs.

Courtney, Alice E. & Whipple, Thomas W. Sex Stereotyping in Advertising. 256p. 1983. 26.00 (ISBN 0-669-03955-1). Lexington Bks.

Courtney, C. P. A Bibliography of Editions of the Writings of Benjamin Constant to 1833, Vol. 10. 267p. 1981. avail. Modern Humanities Res.

--Montesquieu & Burke. LC 74-2586. 204p. 1975. Repr. of 1963 ed. lib. bdg. 22.50x (ISBN 0-8371-7406-6, COMB). Greenwood.

--A Preliminary Bibliography of Isabelle de Charriere: Belle De Zuylen. 157p. 1981. 90.00x (ISBN 0-7294-0240-1, Pub. by Voltaire Found). State Mutual Bk.

Courtney, Caroline. Dangerous Engagement. (General Ser.). 1980. lib. bdg. 12.95 (ISBN 0-8161-3094-9, Large Print Bks). G K Hall.

--The Daring Heart. (Nightingale Ser.). 313p. 1983. pap. 9.95 (ISBN 0-8161-3493-6, Large Print Bks). G K Hall.

--Destiny's Duchess. (Nightingale Ser.). 1985. pap. 10.95 (ISBN 0-8161-3809-5, Large Print Bks). G K Hall.

--Forbidden Love. (Nightingale Paperbacks Ser.). 1984. pap. 9.95 (ISBN 0-8161-3629-7, Large Print Bks). G K Hall.

--Heart of Honor. (General Ser.). 1981. lib. bdg. 12.95 (ISBN 0-8161-3242-9, Large Print Bks). G K Hall.

--Libertine in Love. 224p. 1980. pap. 2.25 (ISBN 0-446-32591-0). Warner Bks.

--Love in Waiting. (Nightingale Ser.). 1982. pap. 9.95 (ISBN 0-8161-3463-4, Large Print Bks). G K Hall.

--Love Triumphant. (General Ser.). 1981. lib. bdg. 11.95 (ISBN 0-8161-3243-7, Large Print Bks). G K Hall.

--Love Unmasked. (General Ser.). 1980. lib. bdg. 11.95 (ISBN 0-8161-3096-5, Large Print Bks). G K Hall.

--A Lover's Victory. (Nightingale Ser.). 1982. pap. 9.95 (ISBN 0-8161-3268-2, Large Print Bks). G K Hall.

--The Romantic Rivals. (General Ser.). 1982. lib. bdg. 13.95 (ISBN 0-8161-3198-8, Large Print Bks). G K Hall.

--The Tempestuous Affair. (Nightingale Large Print Bk.). 1985. pap. text ed. 10.95 (ISBN 0-8161-3796-X, Large Print Bks). G K Hall.

--A Wager for Love. 1980. pap. 8.95 (ISBN 0-8161-3100-7, Large Print Bks). G K Hall.

Courtney, Damien A., tr. see Pressat, Roland.

Courtney, Dayle. Escape from Eden. LC 81-5710. (Thorne Twins Adventure Bks.). (Illus.). 192p. (Orig.). (gr. 5 up). 1981. pap. 2.98 (ISBN 0-87239-467-0, 2712). Standard Pub.

--Flight to Terror. LC 81-5632. (Thorne Twins Adventure Bks.). (Illus.). 192p. (Orig.). (gr. 5 up). 1981. pap. 2.98 (ISBN 0-87239-468-9, 2713). Standard Pub.

--The Foxworth Hunt. LC 82-5512. (Thorne Twins Adventure Bks.). (Illus.). 224p. (Orig.). (gr. 5 up). 1982. pap. 2.98 (ISBN 0-87239-553-7, 2894). Standard Pub.

--The Great UFO Chase. (Thorne Twins Adventure Bks.). (Illus.). 192p. (Orig.). (gr. 6-10). 1984. pap. 2.98 (ISBN 0-87239-755-6, 2905). Standard Pub.

--The Hidden Cave. LC 82-5510. (Thorne Twins Adventure Bks.). (Illus.). 192p. (Orig.). (gr. 5 up). 1982. pap. 2.98 (ISBN 0-87239-555-3, 2896). Standard Pub.

--The House That Ate People. (Thorne Twins Adventure Ser.). (Illus.). 192p. (Orig.). (gr. 7-12). 1983. pap. 2.98 (ISBN 0-87239-683-5, 2903). Standard Pub.

--The Ivy Plot. LC 81-5631. (Thorne Twins Adventure Bks.). (Illus.). 192p. (Orig.). (gr. 5 up). 1981. pap. 2.98 (ISBN 0-87239-469-7, 2714). Standard Pub.

--Jaws of Terror. LC 82-5511. (Thorne Twins Adventure Bks.). (Illus.). 192p. (Orig.). (gr. 5 up). 1982. pap. 2.98 (ISBN 0-87239-554-5, 2895). Standard Pub.

--The Knife with Eyes. LC 81-5624. (Thorne Twins Adventure Bks.). (Illus.). 192p. (Orig.). (gr. 5 up). 1981. pap. 2.98 (ISBN 0-87239-471-9, 2716). Standard Pub.

--Mysterious Strangers. LC 82-3320. (Thorne Twins Adventure Bks.). (Illus.). 224p. (Orig.). (gr. 5 up). 1982. pap. 2.98 (ISBN 0-87239-552-9, 2893). Standard Pub.

--The Olympic Plot. (Thorne Twins Adventure Bks.). (Illus.). 192p. (Orig.). (gr. 6-10). 1984. pap. 2.98 (ISBN 0-87239-756-4, 2906). Standard Pub.

--Omen of the Flying Light. LC 81-5353. (Thorne Twins Adventure Bks.). (Illus.). 192p. (Orig.). (gr. 5 up). 1981. pap. 2.98 (ISBN 0-87239-470-0, 2715). Standard Pub.

--Operation Doomsday. LC 81-5655. (Thorne Twins Adventure Bks.). (Illus.). 192p. (Orig.). (gr. 5 up). 1981. pap. 2.98 (ISBN 0-87239-466-2, 2711). Standard Pub.

--Secret of Pirates' Cave. (Thorne Twins Adventure Bks.). (Illus.). 192p. (Orig.). (gr. 6-10). 1984. pap. 2.98 (ISBN 0-87239-758-0, 2908). Standard Pub.

--Shadow of Fear. LC 83-4696. (Thorne Twins Adventure Ser.). (Illus.). 192p. (Orig.). (gr. 7-12). 1983. pap. 2.98 (ISBN 0-87239-682-7, 2902). Standard Pub.

--The Sinister Circle. LC 83-4699. (Thorne Twins Adventure Ser.). (Illus.). 192p. (Orig.). (gr. 7-12). 1983. pap. 2.98 (ISBN 0-87239-684-3, 2904). Standard Pub.

--Three-Ring Inferno. LC 82-5561. (Thorne Twins Adventure Bks.). (Illus.). 192p. (Orig.). (gr. 5 up). 1982. pap. 2.98 (ISBN 0-87239-551-0, 2892). Standard Pub.

--Tower of Flames. LC 82-3270. (Thorne Twins Adventure Bks.). (Illus.). 192p. (Orig.). (gr. 5 up). 1982. pap. 2.98 (ISBN 0-87239-556-1, 2897). Standard Pub.

--The Trail of Bigfoot. (Thorne Twins Adventure Ser.). (Illus.). 192p. (Orig.). (gr. 7-12). 1983. pap. 2.98 (ISBN 0-87239-681-9, 2901). Standard Pub.

Courtney, Donald. Simba Gold. (Orig.). 1985. pap. 3.50 (ISBN 0-440-18052-X). Dell.

Courtney, E. A Commentary on the Satires of Juvenal. (Illus.). 650p. 1980. text ed. 110.00 (ISBN 0-485-11190-X, Pub. by Athlone Pr Ltd). Longwood Pub Group.

Courtney, E. C., jt. auth. see Rudd, N.

Courtney, E. Wayne, ed. Applied Research in Education. (Quality Paperback Ser.: No. 92). (Orig.). 1965. pap. 3.50 (ISBN 0-8226-0092-7). Littlefield.

Courtney, Elise & Celeste, Emily. How to Find Music Easily for Good Times in Harmony. LC 80-51888. (Illus.). 317p. (Orig.). 1980. pap. 6.00 (ISBN 0-686-28899-8). Merk.

Courtney, F. M. & Trudgill, S. T. The Soil: An Introduction to Soil Study. 2nd ed. 128p. 1984. pap. text ed. 13.95 (ISBN 0-7131-0995-5). E Arnold.

Courtney, Gerald. High Pressure Center. LC 78-54138. 1980. 14.95 (ISBN 0-87949-127-2). Ashley Bks.

Courtney, James F., Jr. & Jensen, Ronald. The Systems Laboratory for Information Management. 1981. pap. 7.95x (ISBN 0-256-02574-6). Business Pubns.

Courtney, Janet E. Adventurous Thirties: A Chapter in the Women's Movement. facs. ed. LC 67-26728. (Essay Index Reprint Ser). 1933. 18.00 (ISBN 0-8369-0341-2). Ayer Co Pubs.

--Freethinkers of the Nineteenth Century. facs. ed. LC 67-30182. (Essay Index Reprint Ser). 1920. 20.00 (ISBN 0-8369-0342-0). Ayer Co Pubs.

--Freethinkers of the Nineteenth Century. LC 74-8075. 1920. lib. bdg. 30.00 (ISBN 0-8414-3354-2). Folcroft.

--Recollected in Tranquillity. 1973. Repr. of 1926 ed. 20.00 (ISBN 0-8274-1525-7). R West.

--The Women of My Time. (Women Ser.). 1934. 25.00 (ISBN 0-8482-7586-1). Norwood Edns.

Courtney, John C. The Selection of National Party Leaders in Canada. xiv, 278p. 1973. 22.00 (ISBN 0-208-01393-8, Archon). Shoe String.

Courtney, Bro. Leonard, ed. Reading Interaction: The Teacher, the Pupil, the Materials. LC 75-45017. 112p. 1976. pap. text ed. 5.00 (ISBN 0-87207-483-8). Intl Reading.

Courtney, Lisa. A Coming of Age. new ed. LC 78-54786. (Illus.). 1978. 10.95x (ISBN 0-932464-01-7). TREK-CIR.

Courtney, Margaret A. Cornish Feasts & Folk-Lore. LC 77-8082. 1977. lib. bdg. 25.00 (ISBN 0-8414-1829-2). Folcroft.

Courtney, Marguerite. Laurette: The Intimate Biography of Laurette Taylor. LC 84-5649. (Illus.). 448p. 1984. pap. 9.95 (ISBN 0-87910-015-X). Limelight Edns.

Courtney, Max & Seidel, Andrew D. Citizen Attitudes in Texas on Proposed Changes in the State Intoxicated Driver Laws. 68p. (Orig.). 1983. pap. 6.00 (ISBN 0-936440-53-8). Inst Urban Studies.

Courtney, Max, jt. auth. see Seidel, Andrew D.

Courtney, Nicholas. Diana, Princess of Wales. LC 82-83165. 96p. 1983. pap. 7.95 (ISBN 0-03-063229-3, Owl Bks). HR&W.

--Prince Andrew. (Illus.). 64p. (Orig.). 1983. pap. 7.70 (ISBN 0-316-15820-8). Little.

--Queen Elizabeth, the Queen Mother. (Illus.). 128p. 1985. pap. 7.95 (ISBN 0-88162-026-2, Pub. by Salem Hse Ltd). Merrimack Pub Cir.

--The Tiger: Symbol of Freedom. (Illus.). 128p. 1981. 25.00 (ISBN 0-7043-2245-5, Pub. by Quartet England). Charles River Bks.

--The Tiger: Symbol of Freedom. (Illus.). 110p. 1984. pap. 14.95 (ISBN 0-7043-3448-8, Pub. by Quartet Bks). Merrimack Pub Cir.

Courtney, P. P. Plantation Agriculture. (Advanced Economic Geographies Ser.). 296p. 1982. 35.00x (ISBN 0-7135-1256-3, Pub. by Bell & Hyman England). State Mutual Bk.

Courtney, Ragan. Meditations for the Suddenly Single. pap. 5.95 (ISBN 0-310-70301-8). Zondervan.

Courtney, Richard. The Dramatic Curriculum. 144p. 1980. text ed. 10.00x (ISBN 0-89676-061-8); pap. text ed. 7.95x (ISBN 0-89676-062-6). Drama Bk.

--Outline History of British Drama. LC 82-6595. (Quality Paperback Ser.: No. 346). 346p. (Orig.). 1982. pap. text ed. 8.95 (ISBN 0-8226-0373-X). Littlefield.

Courtney, Richard, jt. ed. see Schattner, Gertrud.

Courtney, W. L. The Feminine Note in Fiction. LC 73-4563. 1973. lib. bdg. 20.00 (ISBN 0-8414-1840-3). Folcroft.

--Rosemary's Letter Book: The Record of a Year Edgar A. Poe, Milton, Barrie, Swinburne, Kipling, Fitzgerald, Galsworthy, George Meredith. 1973. Repr. of 1909 ed. 25.00 (ISBN 0-8274-1524-9). R West.

--Studies at Leisure. 1973. Repr. of 1892 ed. 20.00 (ISBN 0-8274-1523-0). R West.

Courtney, William L. Development of Maurice Maeterlinck. LC 74-118408. 1971. Repr. of 1904 ed. 21.00x (ISBN 0-8046-1185-8, Pub. by Kennikat). Assoc Faculty Pr.

--Old Saws & Modern Instances. facs. ed. LC 69-18924. (Essay Index Reprint Ser). 1918. 19.00 (ISBN 0-8369-0039-1). Ayer Co Pubs.

Courtney, William P. Dodsley's Collection of Poetry, Its Contents & Contributors. (Bibliography & Reference Ser.: No. 141). 1969. Repr. of 1910 ed. 23.50 (ISBN 0-8337-0701-9). B Franklin.

--Eight Friends of the Great. LC 74-1376. 1973. Repr. of 1910 ed. lib. bdg. 20.00 (ISBN 0-8414-3546-4). Folcroft.

--Register of National Bibliography, 3 vols in 2. (Bibliography & Reference Ser.: No. 135). 1968. Repr. of 1912 ed. Set. 50.00 (ISBN 0-8337-0704-3). B Franklin.

--The Secrets of Our National Literature. 1908. Repr. 25.00 (ISBN 0-8274-3346-8). R West.

--Secrets of Our National Literature: Chapters in the History of the Anonymous & Pseudonymous Writings of Our Countrymen. LC 68-21761. 264p. 1968. Repr. of 1908 ed. 43.00x (ISBN 0-8103-3140-3). Gale.

Courtney, Winifred F. Young Charles Lamb, 1775-1802. (The Gotham Library). (Illus.). 412p. 1983. pap. 15.00x (ISBN 0-8147-1388-2). NYU Pr.

Courtois, Louis J. Chronologie Critique de la Vie et des Ouvrages de Jean-Jacques Rousseau. LC 72-87246. (Annales J. J. Rousseau, XV). 404p. (Fr.). 1973. Repr. of 1924 ed. lib. bdg. 26.50 (ISBN 0-8337-4058-X). B Franklin.

Courtois, P. J. Decomposability: Queueing & Computer System Applications. (ACM Monagraph Ser.). 1977. 50.00 (ISBN 0-12-193750-X). Acad Pr.

Courton, ed. see Moliere.

Courtot, Marilyn E. & Meyer, Ellen T. An Introduction to Microform Indexing & Retrieval Systems. rev. ed. (Consumer Ser.). 1980. pap. text ed. 5.50 (ISBN 0-89258-071-2, C104); member 5.00. Assn Inform & Image Mgmt.

Courtright, Gordon. Landscape Planting Guide: Garden Success from Proper Planting. 77p. (Orig.). 1962. pap. 2.95 (ISBN 0-89955-415-6, Pub. by Gordon). Intl Spec Bk.

--Trees & Shrubs for Temperate Climates. LC 79-65785. (Illus.). 239p. 1979. 43.00 (ISBN 0-917304-13-6). Timber.

Courtright, John A., jt. auth. see Bowers, John W.

Courts, A., jt. ed. see Ward, A. G.

Courtwright, David T. Dark Paradise: Opiate Addiction in America before 1940. LC 81-6958. (Illus.). 288p. 1982. text ed. 20.00x (ISBN 0-674-19261-3). Harvard U Pr.

Courville, Donovan A. The Exodus Problem & Its Ramifications, 2 vols. 1972. Set. plastic cover 11.95 (ISBN 0-913776-03-3). Crest Challenge.

Courville, Elgerna. How to Grow Roses on the Gulf Coast. 32p. 1985. 5.95 (ISBN 0-89962-469-3). Todd & Honeywell.

Courville, Jacques, et al, eds. The Inferior Olivary Nucleus: Anatomy & Physiology. (Illus.). 407p. 1980. text ed. 70.50 (ISBN 0-89004-414-7). Raven.

Courville, L., et al, eds. Economic Analysis of Telecommunications: Theory & Applications. 414p. 1983. 64.00 (ISBN 0-444-86674-4, I-180-83, North Holland). Elsevier.

Courvoisier, B., et al. Fluoride & Bone. 304p. 1978. 60.00 (ISBN 3-456-80648-5, Pub. by Holdan Bk Ltd UK). State Mutual Bk.

Courvoisier, Donath A. Bone & Tumors. 248p. 1980. 69.00 (ISBN 3-456-80944-1, Pub. by Holdan Bk Ltd UK). State Mutual Bk.

Courvoisier, Karl. Technics of Violin Playing. LC 77-94555. 1978. Repr. of 1899 ed. lib. bdg. 10.00 (ISBN 0-89341-403-4). Longwood Pub Group.

--Technics of Violin Playing. Repr. lib. bdg. 19.00 (ISBN 0-403-03861-8). Scholarly.

Coury, Elaine. Terence's Bembine Phormio: A Palaeographic Examination. (Illus.). 150p. 59.00 (ISBN 0-86516-011-2). Bolchazy-Carducci.

Coury, Elaine, ed. see Terence.

Cousar, Charles. Galatians: The Bible Commentary for Teaching & Preaching. LC 81-82354. (Interpretation Ser.). 168p. (James Mays General Editor of the series, Paul Achtemeier New Testament editor). 1982. 13.95 (ISBN 0-8042-3138-9). John Knox.

Couse. Ohio Form Book (Business & Legal, 3 vols. 2nd ed. 1960. 285.00. Anderson Pub Co.

Cousens, Henry. The Antiquities of Sind: With Historical Outline, Archaeological Survey of India. (Imperial Ser.: Vol. 46). (Illus.). 1975. 24.95x (ISBN 0-19-577197-4). Oxford U Pr.

Cousin, Glynis, tr. see Melossi, Dario & Pavarini, Massimo.

Cousin, Jean. Etudes sur la Poesie Latine: Nature et Mission du Poete. Commager, Steele, ed. LC 77-70760. (Latin Poetry Ser.). 1979. Repr. of 1945 ed. lib. bdg. 34.00 (ISBN 0-8240-2965-8). Garland Pub.

Cousin, M. T., jt. ed. see Conseiller, C.

Cousin, Victor. Elements of Psychology. 3rd. ed. LC 75-3005. Repr. of 1871 ed. 34.00 (ISBN 0-404-59121-3). AMS Pr.

--Lectures on the True, the Beautiful, & the Good. 3rd. ed. Wright, O. W., tr. LC 75-3006. Repr. of 1854 ed. 32.00 (ISBN 0-404-59122-1). AMS Pr.

Cousin Alice, ed. see Bradley, Mary E.

Cousineau, Lise. Le Compagnon de l'agent de sante. 282p. 1981. 10.50 (ISBN 0-933853-07-6). Pathfinder Fund.

Cousins, Albert N. & Nagpaul, Hans. Urban Life: The Sociology of Cities & Urban Society. LC 78-14427. 608p. 1979. text ed. 33.50x (ISBN 0-471-03026-0). Wiley.

Cousins, Basil. Data Independence & Data Flow Systems. 20p. 1983. pap. 7.75x (ISBN 0-471-87934-7). Wiley.

Cousins, D. Book-Keeping. (Teach Yourself Ser.). 1975. pap. 4.95 (ISBN 0-679-10455-0). McKay.

Cousins, Ewert, ed. Bonaventure: The Soul's Journey into God: the Tree of Life, the Life of Francis. LC 78-60723. (Classics of Western Spirituality). 380p. 1978. 11.95 (ISBN 0-8091-0240-4); pap. 9.95 (ISBN 0-8091-2121-2). Paulist Pr.

Cousins, Ewert H. The Coincidence of Opposites in the Theology of Saint Bonaventure. 164p. 1977. 12.95 (ISBN 0-8199-0580-1). Franciscan Herald.

--Process Theology. LC 78-171961. 384p. 1971. pap. 8.95 (ISBN 0-8091-1667-7). Paulist Pr.

Cousins, Frank & Riley, Phil M. Wood Carver of Salem: Samuel McIntire, His Life & Work. LC 74-119649. (BCL Ser. II). Repr. of 1916 ed. 20.00 (ISBN 0-404-01786-X). AMS Pr.

Cousins, H. James. Irish Mythology. 59.95 (ISBN 0-8490-0425-X). Gordon Pr.

Cousins, James H. Modern English Poetry: Its Characteristics & Tendancies. LC 72-197456. lib. bdg. 10.00 (ISBN 0-8414-2397-0). Folcroft.

--Work Promethean. LC 70-105774. 1970. Repr. of 1933 ed. 19.00x (ISBN 0-8046-1011-8, Pub. by Kennikat). Assoc Faculty Pr.

Cousins, L., et al, eds. Buddhist Studies in Honour of I. B. Horner. LC 74-77963. 275p. 1974. lib. bdg. 45.00 (ISBN 90-277-0473-2, Pub. by Reidel Holland). Kluwer Academic.

Cousins, Linda, ed. Ancient Black Youth & Elders Reborn. LC 84-50898. (Illus.). 252p. (Orig.). 1985. pap. 10.00 (ISBN 0-930569-00-8). Univ Black Pr.

Cousins, M. F. Engineering Drawing form the Beginning, Vol. 2. pap. 13.25 (ISBN 0-08-006853-7). Pergamon.

Cousins, Margaret. Ben Franklin of Old Philadelphia. LC 81-806. (Landmark Paperback Ser.: No. 10). 160p. (gr. 5-9). 1981. pap. 2.95 (ISBN 0-394-84928-0). Random.

--The Boy in the Alamo. LC 83-72585. (Illus.). 180p. 1983. pap. 4.95 (ISBN 0-931722-26-8). Corona Pub.

--The Story of Thomas Alva Edison. LC 81-805. (Landmark Paperback Ser.: No. 8). (Illus.). 160p. (gr. 5-9). 1981. pap. 2.95 (ISBN 0-394-84883-7). Random.

Cousins, Margaret & Metcalfe, Jill. Vegetarian on a Diet: The High-Fibre, Low-Sugar, Low-Fat, Whole Food Vegetarian Cookbook. (Illus.). 192p. (Orig.). 1986. pap. 6.95 (ISBN 0-7225-0887-5). Thorsons Pubs.

Cousins, Michael J. & Bridenbaugh, Phillip O. Neural Blockade in Clinical Anesthesia & Management of Pain. (Illus.). 1188p. 1980. text ed. 125.00x (ISBN 0-397-50439-X, 65-05812, Lippincott Medical). Lippincott.

Cousins, Michael J., jt. ed. see Tiengo, Mario.

Cousins, Norman. Albert Schweitzer's Mission: Healing & Peace. 1985. 16.95 (ISBN 0-393-02238-2). Norton.

--Anatomy of an Illness As Perceived by the Patient: Reflections on Healing & Regeneration. 1979. 11.95 (ISBN 0-393-01252-2). Norton.

--Anatomy of an Illness As Perceived by the Patient. 176p. 1981. pap. 5.95 (ISBN 0-553-01491-9). Bantam.

--Healing & Belief. LC 82-81098. 64p. 1982. 65.00 (ISBN 0-88014-041-0). Mosaic Pr OH.

--The Healing Heart. (General Ser.). 1984. lib. bdg. 14.95 (ISBN 0-8161-3669-6, Large Print Bks). G K Hall.

--The Healing Heart. 240p. 1984. pap. 3.95 (ISBN 0-380-69245-7). Avon.

--The Healing Heart: Antidotes to Panic & Helplessness. LC 83-42657. 1983. 13.95 (ISBN 0-393-01816-4). Norton.

--Human Options. 224p. 1983. pap. 5.95 (ISBN 0-425-05875-1). Berkley Pub.

--Human Options: An Autobiographical Notebook. (Illus.). 1981. 9.95 (ISBN 0-393-01430-4). Norton.

--The Improbable Triumvirate: John F. Kennedy, Pope John, Nikita Khrushchev. (Illus.). 176p. 1984. pap. 4.95 (ISBN 0-393-30162-1). Norton.

--The Physician in Literature. 500p. 1982. text ed. 16.95 (ISBN 0-7216-2739-0). Saunders.

--The Trial of Dr. Mesmer: A Play. Date not set. 15.00 (ISBN 0-393-01845-8). Norton.

Cousins, Norman, ed. The Physician in Literature. LC 81-50841. 500p. 1981. 16.95 (ISBN 0-03-059653-X, HoltC). HR&W.

Cousins, Norman, ed. see Saturday Review.

Cousins, Norman, intro. by see Schweitzer, Albert.

Cousins, Ronald B. The Effects of Task & Sex of Co-Actor on Female Expectancy Level & Performance. LC 84-22857. (Landmark Dissertations in Women's Studies). 128p. 1984. 29.95x (ISBN 0-03-064188-8). Praeger.

Cousins, William J. & Goyder, Catherine. Changing Slum Communities. 1979. 10.00 (ISBN 0-8364-0533-1). South Asia Bks.

Cousoneau, Eric & Richardson, Peter R. Gold: The World Industry & Canadian Corporate Strategy. 192p. (Orig.). 1979. pap. text ed. 13.00x (ISBN 0-88757-013-5, Pub. by Ctr Resource Stud Canada). Brookfield Pub Co.

Cousse, Raymond. Death Sty: A Pig's Tale. 1980. 9.50 (ISBN 0-394-50867-X, GP829). Grove.

--Death Sty: A Pig's Tale. LC 79-2349. Orig. Title: Strategie Pour Deux Jambons. 1980. 5.95 (ISBN 0-394-17573-5, E747, Ever). Grove.

Coussemaker, Edmond de see De Coussemaker, Edmond.

Coussemaker, Edmond de see De la Halle, Adam.

Coussemaker, Edmond de see De Coussemaker, Edmond.

Coussemant, F., et al. Les Fonctions D'acidite et Leurs Utilisations en Catalyse Acido-Basique. (Cours & Documents de Chimie Ser.). 238p. (Fr). 1969. 69.50 (ISBN 0-677-50120-X). Gordon.

Coussement, R., jt. ed. see Perez, A.

Coussens, Penrhyn. Poems Children Love. facsimile ed. LC 72-98078. (Granger Index Reprint Ser). 1908. 18.00 (ISBN 0-8369-6073-4). Ayer Co Pubs.

Coussens, Penrhyn W. One Thousand Books for Children. 1977. lib. bdg. 59.95 (ISBN 0-8490-2377-7). Gordon Pr.

Coussy, Jean, jt. ed. see Weiller, Jean.

Cousteau, Jacques. Jacques Cousteau: The Ocean World. (Illus.). 1979. 60.00 (ISBN 0-8109-0777-1). Abrams.

Cousteau, Jacques & Sivirine, Alexis. Jacques Cousteau's Calypso. LC 83-3751. (Illus.). 192p. 1983. 37.50 (ISBN 0-8109-0788-7). Abrams.

Cousteau, Jacques, jt. auth. see Cribb, James.

Cousteau, Jacques-Yves. A Bill of Rights for Future Generations. 33p. (Orig.). 1980. pap. 1.50 (ISBN 0-913098-29-9). Myrin Institute.

--Jacques Cousteau: The Ocean World. (Illus.). 446p. 1985. 24.95 (ISBN 0-8109-8068-1). Abrams.

Cousteau, Jacques-Yves & Cousteau, Philippe. Shark: Splendid Savage of the Sea. 1970. 12.95 (ISBN 0-385-06892-1). Doubleday.

Cousteau, Jacques-Yves & Cousteau Society Staff. The Cousteau Almanac of the Environment: An Inventory of Life on a Water Planet. LC 79-7862. (Illus.). 864p. 1981. 29.95 (ISBN 0-385-14875-5, Dolp); pap. 19.95 (ISBN 0-385-14876-3, Dolp). Doubleday.

Cousteau, Jacques-Yves & Diole, Philippe. Dolphins. LC 74-9481. 340p. 1975. 15.95 (ISBN 0-385-00015-4). Doubleday.

--Octopus & Squid: The Soft Intelligence. LC 72-76141. 304p. 1973. 12.95 (ISBN 0-385-06896-4). Doubleday.

Cousteau, Jacques-Yves & Dumas, Frederic. The Silent World. LC 52-5431. 1953. 15.00i (ISBN 0-06-010890-8, HarpT). Har-Row.

Cousteau, Jacques-Yves & Richards, Mose. Jacques Cousteau's Amazon Journey. (Illus.). 236p. 1984. 35.00 (ISBN 0-8109-1813-7). Abrams.

Cousteau, Philippe, jt. auth. see Cousteau, Jacques-Yves.

Cousteau Society Staff, jt. auth. see Cousteau, Jacques-Yves.

Coustillas, Pierre, ed. Collected Articles on George Gissing. 186p. 1968. 28.50x (ISBN 0-7146-2054-8, F Cass Co). Biblio Dist.

--London & the Life of Literature in Late Victorian England: The Diary of George Gissing, Novelist. LC 77-72970. 617p. 1978. 60.00 (ISBN 0-8387-2145-1). Bucknell U Pr.

Coustillas, Pierre & Partridge, Colin, eds. Gissing: The Critical Heritage. (Critical Heritage Ser.). 1972. 40.00x (ISBN 0-7100-7367-4). Routledge & Kegan.

Coustillas, Pierre, ed. see Gissing, George.

Cousy, Bob, et al. Basketball: Concepts & Techniques. 2nd ed. 502p. 1985. 28.95 (ISBN 0-205-07819-2). Allyn.

Cousy, Robert J. & Power, Frank, Jr. Basketball: Concepts & Techniques. 502p. 1983. 24.95x (ISBN 0-205-07679-3, 237679, Pub. by Longwood Div). Allyn.

Coutanceau, Maurice. Encyclopedie Des Jardins. new ed. 556p. (Fr.). 1973. 45.00 (ISBN 0-686-57141-X, M-6198). French & Eur.

Coutant, Helen. First Snow. LC 74-1187. (Illus.). 48p. (gr. 1-3). 1974. PLB 5.99 (ISBN 0-394-92831-8). Knopf.

--The Gift. LC 82-7810. (Illus.). 48p. (gr. 2-5). 1983. 9.95 (ISBN 0-394-85499-3); lib. bdg. 9.99 (ISBN 0-394-95499-8). Knopf.

Coutant, Helen, tr. see Hanh, Nhat.

Coutant, Victor, tr. see Theophrastus.

Coutchie, Mariann. Jewelry on Display. (Illus.). 1982. pap. 16.95 (ISBN 0-911380-56-6). Signs of Times.

Coute, A. & Tell, G. Ultrastructure de la Paroi Cellulaire des Desmidiacees au Microscope Electronique a Balayage. (Nova Hedwigia Beiheft: No. 68). (Illus.). 228p. (Fr.). 1982. lib. bdg. 52.50x (ISBN 3-7682-5468-2). Lubrecht & Cramer.

Couteau, Paul. Observing Visual Double Stars. Batten, Alan, tr. from Fr. (Illus.). 272p. 1981. 25.00x (ISBN 0-262-03077-2); pap. 8.95x (ISBN 0-262-53046-5). MIT Pr.

--Observing Visual Double Stars. Batten, Alan, tr. 257p. 1981. pap. 8.95x (ISBN 0-262-53046-5). MIT Pr.

Coutinho, A. Pereira. Flora de Portugal. 2A ed. dirigido pel Ruy Telles Plahinha. (Historia Naturalis Classica 98). 1973. Repr. lib. bdg. 70.00x (ISBN 3-7682-0931-8). Lubrecht & Cramer.

Coutinho, Alfranio. An Introduction to Literature in Brazil. Rabassa, Gregory, tr. from Portugese. LC 69-15569. 1969. 31.50x (ISBN 0-231-02993-4). Columbia U Pr.

Coutinho, Elisman M., et al. Prostaglandins II: Clinical Aspects. LC 73-510. 1973. 29.00x (ISBN 0-8422-7109-0). Irvington.

Coutinho, Elsimar M. & Fuchs, Fritz, eds. Physiology & Genetics of Reproduction. LC 74-17494. (Basic Life Sciences: Vol. 4A & 4B). (Illus.). 464p. 1974. Set. Part A 52.50x (ISBN 0-306-36591-X, Plenum Pr); Part B 59.50x (ISBN 0-306-36592-8). Plenum Pub.

Coutinho, John de S. Advanced Systems Development Management: Development Management. LC 83-24815. 464p. 1984. Repr. of 1977 ed. lib. bdg. 42.50 (ISBN 0-89874-727-9). Krieger.

Coutinho, John S. de see Coutinho, John de S.

Coutinho, O., jt. auth. see Sharma, T. C.

Couto, Armando. La Triste Historia De Mi Vida Oscura: A Peticion Popular. LC 78-70332. 1978. pap. 5.95 (ISBN 0-89729-196-4). Ediciones.

Couto, Richard A. Streams of Idealism & Health Care Innovation: An Assessment of Service Learning & Community Mobilization. (Illus.). 1982. text ed. 18.95x (ISBN 0-8077-2724-5). Tchrs Coll.

Coutourat, Louis. De l'Infini Mathematique. LC 68-56776. (Research & Source Works Ser.: No. 262). (Fr). 1969. Repr. of 1896 ed. 35.50 (ISBN 0-8337-0706-X). B Franklin.

Coutsouradis, D., et al, eds. High Temperature Alloys for Gas Turbines. (Illus.). 901p. 1978. 96.25 (ISBN 0-85334-815-4, Pub. by Elsevier Applied Sci England). Elsevier.

Coutts, Alfred. Hans Denck, Fourteen Ninety-Five to Fifteen Twenty-Seven: Humanistic & Heretic. LC 83-45607. Date not set. Repr. of 1927 ed. 32.00 (ISBN 0-404-19825-2). AMS Pr.

Coutts, G. S. Poultry Diseases under Modern Management. (Illus.). 1980. 21.75 (ISBN 0-904558-80-0). Saiga.

Coutts, K., et al. Industrial Pricing in the United Kingdom. LC 77-8976. (Applied Economics Monograph: No. 26). (Illus.). 1978. 34.50 (ISBN 0-521-21725-3). Cambridge U Pr.

Coutts, Lorne. Naked Drawings of Lorne Coutts. (Illus.). 80p. 1982. 50.00 (ISBN 0-88962-206-X, Pub by Mosaic Pr Canada); pap. 14.95 (ISBN 0-88962-146-2). Flatiron Book Dist.

Coutts, Martin. Racing Certainty. 160p. 1984. 12.95 (ISBN 0-89962-339-5). Todd & Honeywell.

Coutts, P. J. The Archaeology of Wilson's Promontory. (Aias Prehistory & Material Culture Ser.: No. 7). 1970. pap. text ed. 11.00x (ISBN 0-391-01944-9). Humanities.

Coutts, Peter J. An Archaeological Perspective of Panay Island, Philippines. (San Carlos Humanities Ser.: No. 13). (Illus.). 342p. (Orig.). 1983. pap. 13.50x (ISBN 971-100-043-1, Pub. by San Carlos Phillipines). Cellar.

Coutts, R. Yukon Places & Names. 256p. 1980. 16.95 (ISBN 0-88826-085-7); pap. 7.95 (ISBN 0-88826-082-2). Superior Pub.

Coutts, R. T., jt. ed. see Baker, G. B.

Coutts, S. R., ed. Functional Morphology of the Human Ovary. (Illus.). 280p. 1981. text ed. 42.00 (ISBN 0-8391-1647-0). Univ Park.

Coutts, T. J. Electrical Conduction in Thin Metal Films. 244p. 1974. 61.75 (ISBN 0-444-41184-4). Elsevier.

Coutts, T. J., ed. Active & Passive Thin Film Devices. 1978. 140.00 (ISBN 0-12-193850-6). Acad Pr.

Coutts, T. J. & Meakin, J. O., eds. Current Topics in Photovoltaics. Date not set. 62.00 (ISBN 0-12-193860-3). Acad Pr.

Coutu, Sr. Albert C. Hispanism in France from Morel-Fatio to the Present. LC 70-94187. (Catholic University of America Studies in Romance Languages & Literatures Ser: No. 49). Repr. of 1954 ed. 23.00 (ISBN 0-404-50349-7). AMS Pr.

Couture, Barbara & Goldstein, Jone R. Cases for Technical & Professional Writing. 1984. pap. text ed. 13.95 (ISBN 0-316-15830-5); tchr's. manual avail. (ISBN 0-316-15831-3). Little.

Couture, Eugene T., jt. ed. see Edelstein, Barry A.

Couture, Roger A., et al, trs. see Coste, Rene.

Couturier, Jean J., jt. auth. see Schick, Richard P.

Couturier, Maurice & Durand, Regis. Donald Barthelme. (Contemporary Writers Ser.). 96p. 1982. pap. 4.75x (ISBN 0-416-31870-3, NO. 3557). Methuen Inc.

Couvares, Francis G. The Remaking of Pittsburgh: Class & Culture in an Industrializing City, 1877-1919. (American Social History Ser.). 208p. 1984. 33.50x (ISBN 0-87395-778-4); pap. 10.95x (ISBN 0-87395-779-2). State U NY Pr.

Couvering, John Van see Berggren, W. A. & Van Couvering, John.

Couvert, Roger. The Evaluation of Literacy Programmes: A Practical Guide. (Illus.). 168p. 1979. pap. 9.25 (ISBN 92-3-101580-X, U911, UNESCO). Unipub.

Couvveur, F. S. Dictionnaire Classique de la Langue Chinoise. 1080p. (Fr. & Chinese.). 1966. 35.00 (ISBN 0-686-56810-9, M-6588). French & Eur.

Couzens, Gerald S. A Baseball Album. LC 79-25044. (Illus.). 256p. 1980. 14.00i (ISBN 0-690-01864-9). Har-Row.

Couzens, Reginald C. Stories of the Months & Days. LC 70-124662. (Illus.). 164p. 1971. Repr. of 1923 ed. 58.00x (ISBN 0-8103-3013-X). Gale.

Couzens, T., jt. auth. see White, L.

Couzens, Tim. The New African: A Study of the Life & Work of H. I. E. Dhlomo. 368p. 1985. pap. text ed. 21.95x (ISBN 0-86975-231-6, Pub. by Ravan Pr). Ohio U Pr.

Couzens, Tim & Patel, Essop, eds. The Return of the Amasi Bird: Black South African Poetry, 1891-1981. 411p. 1982. pap. 12.95 (ISBN 0-86975-195-6, Pub. by Ravan Pr). Ohio U Pr.

Couzens, Tim & Visser, Nick, eds. H. I. E. Dhlomo: Collected Works. 500p. 1985. pap. text ed. 25.95x (ISBN 0-86975-271-5, Pub. by Ravan Pr). Ohio U Pr.

Couzens, Tim, ed. see Plaatje, Solomon T.

Coval, S. C., jt. ed. see Macintosh, J. J.

Covalt, Donald A., ed. Rehabilitation in Industry: A Modern Monograph in Industrial Medicine. LC 58-10361. (Illus.). 166p. 1958. 39.00 (ISBN 0-8089-0104-4, 790925). Grune.

Covalt, Nila K. Bed Exercises for Convalescent Patients. 244p. 1968. 19.75.x (ISBN 0-398-00352-1). C C Thomas.

Covan, Jenny, tr. see Sobol, Andrei M.

Covannier, Henry. St. Francis De Sales. 1973. Repr. 5.00 (ISBN 0-8198-0512-2). Dghtrs St Paul.

Covarrubias, A. J., jt. ed. see Woite, G.

Covarrubias Horozco, Sebastian De see De Covarrubias Horozco, Sebastian.

Covatta, Anthony. Thomas Middleton's City Comedies. LC 72-3261. 187p. 1974. 18.00 (ISBN 0-8387-1196-0). Bucknell U Pr.

Cove, D. J. Genetics. LC 75-160089. (Illus.). 1972. 39.50 (ISBN 0-521-08255-2); pap. text ed. 10.95x (ISBN 0-521-09663-4). Cambridge U Pr.

--Genetics. LC 75-160089. pap. 55.30 (ISBN 0-317-26020-0, 2024430). Bks Demand UMI.

Cove, Joseph W. see Gibbs, Lewis, pseud.

Cove, Mary & Regan, Jane. Teaching Religion Effectively Program. 96p. 1982. pap. 3.50 (ISBN 0-697-01825-3); program manual 24.95 (ISBN 0-697-01826-1). Wm C Brown.

Cove, Mary K. & Mueller, Mary L. Regarding Religious Education. LC 77-10873. 181p. (Orig.). 1977. pap. 8.95 (ISBN 0-89135-011-X). Religious Educ.

Cove, P. B. see Pennar, Davis W.

Covell, Alan C. Ecstasy: Shamanism in Korea. LC 83-81487. (Illus.). 107p. 1983. 19.50x (ISBN 0-930878-33-7). Hollym Intl.

--Shamanist Folk Paintings: Korea's Eternal Spirits. LC 83-82586. (Illus.). 112p. 1984. 19.50x (ISBN 0-930878-39-6). Hollym Intl.

Covell, Alan C., jt. auth. see Covell, Jon C.

Covell, Charles. The Redefinition of Conservatism: Politics & Doctrine. 272p. 1985. 27.50 (ISBN 0-312-66725-6). St Martin.

Covell, Charles V., Jr. A Field Guide to the Moths of Eastern North America. LC 83-26523. (Peterson Field Guide Ser.). (Illus.). 496p. 1984. 18.95 (ISBN 0-395-26056-6); pap. 13.95 (ISBN 0-395-36100-1). HM.

Covell, G., et al. Chemotherapy of Malaria. (Monograph Ser: No. 27). 123p. (Eng. & Fr.). 1955. pap. 5.60 (ISBN 92-4-140027-7). World Health.

Covell, Jamie L., jt. auth. see Feldman, Philip S.

Covell, Jon C. Korea's Cultural Roots. 5th ed. LC 83-81319. (Illus.). 132p. 1983. 19.50x (ISBN 0-930878-32-9). Hollym Intl.

--Korea's Cultural Roots. (Illus.). 122p. 1984. 19.95 (ISBN 0-89346-222-5). Heian Intl.

Covell, Jon C. & Covell, Alan C. Japan's Hidden History: Korean Impact on Japanese Culture. LC 83-81484. (Illus.). 112p. 1984. 19.50x (ISBN 0-930878-34-5). Hollym Intl.

Covell, Jon Carter & Yamada, Abbot S. Unraveling Zen's Red Thread: Ikkyu's Controversial Way. LC 80-81040. (Illus.). 341p. 1980. 21.50x (ISBN 0-930878-19-1). Hollym Intl.

Covell, Mara, et al. The Home Alternative to Hospitals & Nursing Homes. 1985. pap. 9.95 (ISBN 0-03-003922-3, Owl Bks). HR&W.

Covell, Mara B. & Beer, Maurice. The Home Alternative to Hospitals & Nursing Homes: Creating Your Own Home Health Care Center. LC 82-42684. (Illus.). 256p. 1983. 15.95 (ISBN 0-89256-236-6). Rawson Assocs.

Covell, Ralph. W. A. P Martin: Pioneer of Progress in China. LC 77-13321. Repr. of 1978 ed. 59.10 (ISBN 0-8357-9133-5, 2012723). Bks Demand UMI.

Covelli, Pasquale. Borrowing Time: Growing up with Juvenile Diabetes. LC 79-7083. 1979. 11.49 (ISBN 0-690-01841-X). T Y Crowell.

Covello, Charles J. Real Estate Buying - Selling Guide for Washington. 2nd ed. (Illus.). 83p. 1983. pap. 5.95 (ISBN 0-88908-723-7). Self Counsel Pr.

--Real Estate Buying-Selling Guide for Washington. 82p. 1978. 2.95 (ISBN 0-88908-710-5). Self Counsel Pr.

Covello, Leonard. The Social Background of the Italo-American School Child: A Study of the Southern Italian Family Mores and Their Effect on the School Situation in Italy and America. Cordasco, Francesco, ed. xxx, 488p. 1972. Repr. of 1967 ed. 27.50x (ISBN 0-87471-018-9). Rowman.

Covello, Leonard & D'Agnostino, Guido. Teacher in the Urban Community. (Quality Paperback Ser.: No. 242). 275p. 1970. pap. 4.95 (ISBN 0-8226-0242-3). Littlefield.

Covello, Vincent & Abernathy, Mark. Technological Risk: A Bibliography. (Public Administration Ser.: P 1220). 83p. 1983. pap. 12.75 (ISBN 0-88066-550-5). Vance Biblios.

Covello, Vincent, ed. Poverty & Public Policy: An Evaluation of Social Science Research. 288p. 1980. pap. text ed. 13.95x (ISBN 0-87073-889-5). Schenkman Bks Inc.

Covello, Vincent, jt. ed. see Whipple, Chris.

Covello, Vincent T. & Yoshimura, Yuji. Japanese Art of Stone Appreciation: Suiseki & Its Use with Bonsai. LC 84-50508. (Illus.). 166p. 1984. 21.50 (ISBN 0-8048-1485-6). C E Tuttle.

Covello, Vincent T., jt. ed. see Waller, Ray A.

Covello, Vincent T., et al, eds. The Analysis of Actual Versus Perceived Risks. (Advances in Risk Analysis Series: Vol. 1). 400p. 1983. 55.00x (ISBN 0-306-41397-3, Plenum Pr). Plenum Pub.

Coven, Brenda. American Women Dramatists of the Twentieth Century: A Bibliography. LC 82-5942. 244p. 1982. 16.00 (ISBN 0-8108-1562-1). Scarecrow.

Coveney, D., jt. auth. see Medlicott, W. N.

Coveney, J., ed. International Organization Documents for Translation from French. 93p. 1972. 19.00 (ISBN 0-08-016287-8). Pergamon.

Coveney, James. Glossary of German & English Management Terms. (English for Special Purposes Bk.). (Eng. & Ger.). 1977. pap. text ed. 7.50x (ISBN 0-582-55525-6). Longman.

Coveney, James & Amey, J. Glossary of Spanish & English Management Terms. (English for Special Purposes Bk.). (Span. & Eng.). 1978. pap. text ed. 7.50x (ISBN 0-582-55541-8). Longman.

Coveney, James & Moore, Shelia J., eds. Glossary of French & English Management Terms. (English for Special Purposes Bk.). 158p. (Fr. & Eng.). 1972. pap. text ed. 7.50x (ISBN 0-582-55502-7). Longman.

Coveney, Lal, et al. The Sexuality Papers: Male Sexuality & the Social Control of Women. LC 84-12867. (Explorations in Feminism Ser.). 109p. (Orig.). 1984. pap. 4.95 (ISBN 0-09-156971-0, Pub. by Hutchinson Educ). Longwood Pub Group.

Coveney, P. J., ed. France in Crisis, 1620-1675. 273p. 1977. 22.50x (ISBN 0-87471-916-X). Rowman.

Coveney, Peter. Image of Childhood: The Individual & Society, a Study of the Theme in English Literature. 1957. lib. bdg. 17.50x (ISBN 0-88307-064-2). Gannon.

Coveney, Peter, ed. see Eliot, George.

Coveney, Peter, ed. see Twain, Mark.

Covensky, Milton. The Ancient Near Eastern Tradition. (Orig.). 1966. pap. text ed. 10.95 scp (ISBN 0-06-041365-4, HarpC). Har-Row.

Coventry, Camilla, tr. see Shestov, Lev.

Coventry, Camilla, tr. see Veresaev, Vikenti V.

Coventry, Eng. The Coventry Leet Book: Parts I & II. (EETS, OS Ser.: Nos. 134-35). Repr. of 1907 ed. Set. 43.00 (ISBN 0-527-00132-5). Kraus Repr.

--The Coventry Leet Book: Parts III & IV. (EETS, OS Ser.: No. 138). Repr. of 1909 ed. Set. 35.00 (ISBN 0-527-00133-3). Kraus Repr.

Coventry, F., tr. see Grotius, Hugo.

Coventry, F. Leslie. Financial Control for the Small Business. 1st ed. 1982. 40.00x (ISBN 0-907313-03-5, Pub. by Jordan & Sons UK). State Mutual Bk.

Coventry, Francis. The History of Pompey the Little; or, the Life & Adventures of a Lap-Dog, 1751. Shugrue, Michael F., ed. (The Flowering of the Novel, 1740-1775 Ser: Vol. 32). 1974. lib. bdg. 61.00 (ISBN 0-8240-1131-7). Garland Pub.

Coventry, John. Faith in Jesus Christ. 54p. 1982. pap. 3.95 (ISBN 0-86683-620-9). Winston Pr.

Coventry, Mark B., ed. Year Book of Orthopedics, 1981. 1981. 44.95 (ISBN 0-8151-1881-3). Year Bk Med.

--Year Book of Orthopedics, 1982. (Illus.). 1982. 44.95 (ISBN 0-8151-1883-X). Year Bk Med.

--Year Book of Orthopedics, 1983. 1983. 44.95 (ISBN 0-8151-1884-8). Year Bk Med.

--Year Book of Orthopedics, 1984. 1984. 44.95 (ISBN 0-8151-1885-6). Year Bk Med.

Coventry, Martha, tr. see Gallaz, Chrsitophe.

Coventry, W. & Burstiner, I. Management: A Basic Handbook. 1977. (Spec); pap. 9.95 (ISBN 0-13-549170-3, Spec). P-H.

Cover, Arthur B. The Rigns of Saturn. (Time Machine Ser.: No. 6). 144p. (gr. 5 up). 1985. pap. 1.95 (ISBN 0-553-24424-8). Bantam.

Cover, John H. Neighborhood Distribution & Consumption of Meat in Pittsburgh: As Related to Other Social & Economic Factors. LC 75-39353. (Getting & Spending Ser.: the Consumer's Dilemma). 1976. Repr. of 1932 ed. 20.00x (ISBN 0-405-08017-4). Ayer Co Pubs.

Cover, Nelson, compiled by. A Guide to Successful Phonathons. 100p. 1980. pap. 14.50 (ISBN 0-89964-049-4). Coun Adv & Supp Ed.

--A Guide to Successful Phonathons. rev. 1984 ed. 95p. 1984. 14.50 (ISBN 0-89964-227-6). Coun Adv & Supp Ed.

Cover, Robert. Justice Accused: Antislavery & the Judicial Process. LC 74-19573. 334p. 1984. pap. 12.95x (ISBN 0-300-03252-8, Y-509). Yale U Pr.

Coverdale, G. M. Planning Education in Relation to Rural Development. (Fundamentals of Educational Planning: No. 21). 37p. (Orig.). 1974. pap. 5.00 (ISBN 92-803-1062-3, U450, UNESCO). Unipub.

Coverdale, John F. The Basque Phase of Spain's First Carlist War: 1833-1835. LC 83-43068. 312p. 1984. 31.00 (ISBN 0-691-05411-8). Princeton U Pr.

--Italian Intervention in the Spanish Civil War. LC 74-25604. 450p. 1975. 46.00 (ISBN 0-691-05225-5). Princeton U Pr.

--The Political Transformation of Spain after Franco. LC 78-19777. (Praeger Special Studies). 176p. 1979. 36.95 (ISBN 0-03-044326-1). Praeger.

Coverdale, Linda, tr. see Barthes, Roland.

Coverdale, M., tr. from Dutch. The Original & Sprynge of All Sectes & Orders by Whome, Wha or Where (Sic) They Beganne. LC 79-84127. (English Experience Ser.: No. 946). 140p. (Eng.). 1979. Repr. of 1537 ed. lib. bdg. 11.50 (ISBN 90-221-0946-1). Walter J Johnson.

Coverdale, Myles. A Confutacion of That Treatise Which One John Standish Made Agaynst the Protestacion of D. Barnes. LC 79-84096. (English Experience Ser.: No. 917). 212p. 1979. Repr. of 1541 ed. lib. bdg. 16.00 (ISBN 90-221-0917-8). Walter J Johnson.

--Remains of Myles Coverdale, Bishop of Exeter. 1846. 51.00 (ISBN 0-384-09950-5). Johnson Repr.

--Writings & Translations of Myles Coverdale, Bishop of Exeter. 1844. 41.00 (ISBN 0-384-09950-5). Johnson Repr.

Coverdale, Myles, tr. see Bullinger, Heinrich.

Covernton, Mary & Wheeler, Tony. Bali & Lombok - A Travel Survival Kit. (Lonely Planet Travel Guides). 232p. 1984. pap. 6.95 (ISBN 0-908086-51-2, Pub. by Lonely Planet Australia). Hippocrene Bks.

Covert, Alice L. Reflections. 1981. pap. 2.75 (ISBN 0-89083-779-1). Zebra.

--What Price Love. (Orig.). 1979. pap. 2.25 (ISBN 0-89083-491-1). Zebra.

Covert, Catherine L., jt. auth. see Christians, Clifford G.

Covert, Catherine L. & Stevens, John D., eds. Mass Media Between the Wars: Perceptions of Cultural Tensions, 1918-1940. LC 83-20329. 240p. 1984. text ed. 25.00 (ISBN 0-8156-2307-0). Syracuse U Pr.

Covert, Mildred L. & Gerson, Sylvia P. Kosher Creole Cookbook. LC 81-15841. (Illus.). 220p. 1982. spiral bdg. 8.95 (ISBN 0-88289-295-9). Pelican.

Covert, Nadine, jt. ed. see Trojan, Judith.

Covert, Paul. Cages. (New Writers Ser.). 1971. 3.95 (ISBN 0-87140-531-8). Liveright.

Coverte, Robert. A True & Almost Incredible Report of an Englishman That Travelled by Land Through Many Kingdoms. LC 72-186. (English Experience Ser.: No. 302). 1971. Repr. of 1612 ed. 11.50 (ISBN 90-221-0302-1). Walter J Johnson.

Covey, Cyclone, tr. see Cabeza de Vaca, Alvar N.

Covey, Elizabeth, jt. auth. see Ingham, Rosemary.

Covey, Frances A. The Earl Covey Story. (Illus.). 164p. 1979. 10.00 (ISBN 0-682-49443-7). Exposition Pr FL.

Covey, Gerald W. A Plot of Chess. 1984. 7.95 (ISBN 0-8062-2313-8). Carlton.

--Vibrations: Chinese Chippendale. 1983. 5.95 (ISBN 0-8062-1724-3). Carlton.

Covey, Joan. Pony Express '76' 14.00 (ISBN 0-686-37636-6). Snohomish Pub.

Covey, Liz, jt. auth. see Ingham, Rosemary.

Covey, Robert D. Christmas Tree Growers Choose & Cut Handbook. LC 81-85079. 100p. 1982. pap. 20.00 (ISBN 0-910744-04-1). Media Awards.

Covey, Simon, jt. auth. see Grierson, Donald.

Covey, Stephen R. How to Succeed with People. 6.95 (ISBN 0-87747-439-7). Deseret Bk.

--Spiritual Roots of Human Relations. LC 72-119477. 8.95 (ISBN 0-87747-315-3). Deseret Bk.

--Spiritual Roots of Human Relations. 1979. pap. 2.50 (ISBN 0-87747-742-6). Deseret Bk.

Covi, Dario A. The Inscription in Fifteenth-Century Florentine Painting. Freedberg, S. J., ed. (Outstanding Dissertations in Fine Arts Ser.). (Illus.). 800p. 1985. Repr. of 1958 ed. 95.00 (ISBN 0-8240-6853-X). Garland Pub.

Covici, Pascal, ed. Portable Steinbeck. 2nd ed. (Portable Library: No. 2). 1971. 14.95 (ISBN 0-670-66960-1). Viking.

Covici, Pascal, Jr. Mark Twain's Humor: The Image of a World. LC 62-13274. 1962. pap. 9.95 (ISBN 0-87074-166-7). SMU Press.

Covici, Pascal, Jr., ed. see Steinbeck, John.

Covick, Owen, jt. ed. see Blandy, Richard.

Coviello, Carole, ed. see Huber, Helen & Spatz, Audree.

Covill, William E., Jr. Ink Bottles & Inkwells. LC 72-165308. (Illus.). 71. lib. bdg. 22.50x (ISBN 0-88492-004-6). W S Sullwold.

Coville, Alfred, et al, eds. Studies in Anglo-French History During the Eighteenth, Nineteenth & Twentieth Centuries. facs. ed. LC 67-23197. (Essay Index Reprint Ser). 1935. 17.00 (ISBN 0-8369-0343-9). Ayer Co Pubs.

Coville, Bruce. Amulet of Doom. (Twilight Ser.: No. 24). (Orig.). (gr. k-12). 1985. pap. 2.25 (ISBN 0-440-90953-8, LFL). Dell.

--The Monster's Ring. LC 82-3436. (Illus.). 96p. (gr. 8-11). 1982. 8.95 (ISBN 0-394-85320-2); PLB 8.99 (ISBN 0-394-95320-7). Pantheon.

--Sarah & the Dragon. LC 83-48447. (Illus.). 48p. (gr. k-3). 1984. 9.89i (ISBN 0-397-32069-8); PLB 8.89g (ISBN 0-397-32070-1). Lipp Jr Bks.

--Sarah & the Dragon. (Illus.). 8.95 (ISBN 0-397-32069-8). Lippincott.

--Spirits & Spells. (Twilight Ser.: No. 15). 160p. (Orig.). (YA) (gr. 5-9). 1983. pap. 1.95 (ISBN 0-440-98151-4, LFL). Dell.

--Waiting Spirits. (Dark Forces Ser.: No. 11). 160p. (Orig.). (gr. 8-10). 1984. pap. text ed. 1.95 (ISBN 0-553-23731-4). Bantam.

Coville, Bruce & Coville, Katherine. The Foolish Giant. LC 77-18522. (I-Like-to-Read Bks). (Illus.). (gr. k-2). 1978. 8.89 (ISBN 0-397-31800-6). Lipp Jr Bks.

--Sarah's Unicorn. LC 79-2408. (I-Like-to-Read-Bks.). (Illus.). (ps-2). 1979. PLB 8.89 (ISBN 0-397-31873-1). Lipp Jr Bks.

--Sarah's Unicorn. LC 85-42749. (A Trophy Picture Bk.). (Illus.). 48p. (gr. k-3). 1985. pap. 2.84i (ISBN 0-06-443084-7, Trophy). HarpJ.

Coville, Bruce, et al. Seniority Travel Directory. 300p. (Orig.). 1985. pap. 6.95 (ISBN 0-9614965-3-3). Seniority Mag.

Coville, David H., jt. auth. see Nelson, Dee J.

Coville, Katherine, jt. auth. see Coville, Bruce.

Coville, Rollin E. Wasps of the Genus Trypoxylon Subgenus Trypargilum in North America: Hymenoptera: Sphecidae. (Publications in Entomology Ser.: Vol. 97). 1982. pap. 17.00x (ISBN 0-520-09651-7). U of Cal Pr.

Coville, Walter J., et al. Abnormal Psychology. (Orig.). 1960. pap. 5.25 (ISBN 0-06-460094-7, CO 94, COS). B&N NY.

Covin, Theron M., ed. Readings in Human Development: A Humanist Approach. 197p. 1974. pap. text ed. 6.95x (ISBN 0-8422-0439-3). Irvington.

--Readings in the Psychology of Early Childhood. LC 72-85868. 488p. 1976. text ed. 18.50x (ISBN 0-8422-5238-X); pap. text ed. 14.50x (ISBN 0-8422-0491-1). Irvington.

Covina, Gina. The City of Hermits. LC 82-74335. 232p. (Orig.). 1983. 14.95 (ISBN 0-9609626-2-X); pap. 7.95 (ISBN 0-9609626-1-1). Barn Owl Bks.

Covina, Gina & Galana, Laurel, eds. Lesbian Reader. 1975. pap. 5.95 (ISBN 0-9609626-0-3, Pub. by Amazon Pr). Barn Owl Bks.

Covington, A. Ion-Selective Electrodes. 1981. 29.50x (ISBN 0-85186-398-1). State Mutual Bk.

Covington, A. K., ed. Ion Selective Electrode Methodology, 2 vols. 1979. Vol. 1, 272 Pgs. 64.95 (ISBN 0-8493-5247-9); Vol. 2, 144 Pgs. 47.50 (ISBN 0-8493-5248-7). CRC Pr.

Covington, A. K. & Dickinson, T., eds. Physical Chemistry of Organic Solvents Systems. LC 72-77042. 823p. 1973. 110.00 (ISBN 0-306-30569-0, Plenum Pr). Plenum Pub.

Covington, A. K. & Jones, P., eds. Hydrogen-Bonded Solvent Systems. 366p. 1968. cancelled (ISBN 0-85066-025-4). Taylor & Francis.

Covington, Faison, jt. auth. see Owensby, Lou R.

Covington, G. Edwin. What They Believe. 1956. 5.00 (ISBN 0-8022-0310-8). Philos Lib.

Covington, James. The Operative. (Orig.). 1981. pap. 1.95 (ISBN 0-505-51636-5, Pub. by Tower Bks). Dorchester Pub Co.

Covington, James W. The Billy Bowlegs War. LC 82-80100. (Illus.). 100p. 1982. 9.95 (ISBN 0-913122-06-8). Mickler Hse.

--The Terrified. 1979. pap. 1.75 (ISBN 0-532-17206-X). Woodhill.

Covington, Jim. Confessions of a Single Father. LC 82-13232. 192p. 1982. 13.95 (ISBN 0-8298-0412-9). Pilgrim NY.

Covington, Kentucky City & Zoning Commission. Comprehensive Plan for Covington, Kentucky & Environs. LC 73-2904. (Metropolitan America Ser.). 144p. 1974. Repr. 18.00x (ISBN 0-405-05393-2). Ayer Co Pubs.

Covington, M. V. & Berry, R. G. Self-Worth & School Learning. LC 76-2052. 1976. pap. text ed. 11.95 (ISBN 0-03-015286-0, HoltC). HR&W.

Covington, Margaret. Jury Selection Psychology. 1986. price not set looseleaf (ISBN 0-409-25105-4). Butterworth TX.

Covington, Michael. Basic Astrophotography. (Illus.). 224p. Date not set. price not set (ISBN 0-521-25391-8). Cambridge U Pr.

Covington, Michael A. Syntactic Theory in the High Middle Ages: Modistic Models of Sentence Structure. (Studies in Linguistics: No. 39). (Illus.). 200p. 1985. 39.50 (ISBN 0-521-25679-8). Cambridge U Pr.

Covington, Robert N. see Labor Law Group.

Covington, Robert N., jt. ed. see Roady, Thomas G., Jr.

Covington, Sally, ed. The Israeli Invasion of Lebanon: Part II-Press Profile: August 1982-March 1983. (Invasion of Lebanon Ser.). 364p. (Orig.). 1983. pap. 10.00 (ISBN 0-912439-02-5). Claremont.

--The Israeli Occupation of the West Bank Since Camp David: Press Profile: 1979-1983. (Invasion of Lebanon Ser.). 300p. 1984. pap. 10.00 (ISBN 0-912439-04-1). Claremont.

Covington, Timothy R. & Walker, J. Ingram. Current Geriatric Therapy. (Illus.). 463p. 1984. 42.50 (ISBN 0-7216-2743-9). Saunders.

Covington, W. A. History of Colquitt County. LC 80-13117. (Illus.). 424p. 1980. Repr. of 1937 ed. 20.00 (ISBN 0-87152-318-3). Reprint.

Covino, Benjamin & Scott, D. B., eds. Handbook of Epidural Anesthesia & Analgesia. (Illus.). 180p. 1985. 49.50 (ISBN 0-8089-1742-0). Grune.

Covino, Benjamin G. & Vassallo, Helen G. Local Anesthetics: Mechanisms of Action & Clinical Use. LC 75-35749. 192p. 1976. 41.50 (ISBN 0-8089-0918-5, 790930). Grune.

Covino, Benjamin G., jt. ed. see Smith, Graham.

Covino, Frank. Controlled Painting. LC 81-22583. 176p. 1981. 22.50 (ISBN 0-89134-042-4); pap. 14.95 (ISBN 0-89134-044-0). North Light Pub.

--Digest Book of Downhill Skiing. LC 79-51751. 96p. pap. 3.95 (ISBN 0-695-81320-X). DBI.

--Snowballing. (Orig.). 1975. pap. 1.50 (ISBN 0-685-54128-2, LB290DK, Leisure Bks). Dorchester Pub Co.

Covino, Joseph, Jr. And War for All: The Pledge of Subjection. LC 83-61725. (The New Humanities Ser.: Bk. I). 144p. 1983. pap. 11.00 (ISBN 0-935834-19-2). Rainbow Books.

Covino, Marge & Jordan, Pat. Woman's Guide to Shaping Your Body with Weights. (Illus.). 1978. 12.45i (ISBN 0-397-01301-9). Har-Row.

Covino, Michael. Off-Season. 224p. 1985. 13.95 (ISBN 0-89255-099-6). Persea Bks.

--Unfree Associations. 64p. (Orig.). 1982. pap. 3.95. BPW & P.

Covino, Willam A., jt. auth. see Weber, Loraine J.

Covino, William A. & Coda-Messerle, Margaret. GED Reading Skills Test Preparation Guide: High School Equivalency Examination. (Cliffs Test Preparation Ser.). 105p. (Orig.). (gr. 10 up). 1981. pap. 2.95 (ISBN 0-8220-2014-9). Cliffs.

Covino, William A., jt. auth. see Bobrow, Jerry.

Covino, William A., et al. GRE (Graduate Record Examination Aptitude Test) Preparation Guide. (Cliffs Test Preparation Ser.). (Illus.). 267p. (Orig.). 1982. wkbk. 5.95 (ISBN 0-8220-2008-4). Cliffs.

Covitz, Joel D. Emotional Child Abuse: The Family Curse. 200p. (Orig.). 1985. 17.95 (ISBN 0-938434-22-5); pap. 10.95 (ISBN 0-938434-23-3). Sigo Pr.

Covo, Jacqueline. The Blinking Eye: Ralph Waldo Ellison & His American, French, German & Italian Critics, 1952-1971; Bibliographic Essays & a Checklist. LC 74-13042. (Author Bibliographies Ser.: No. 18). 230p. 1974. 20.00 (ISBN 0-8108-0736-X). Scarecrow.

Covvey, H. Dominic & McAlister, Neil H. Computer Choices: Beware of Conspicuous Computing. (Illus.). 192p. pap. 8.95 (ISBN 0-201-10113-0). Addison-Wesley.

--Computer Consciousness: Surviving the Automated Eighties. LC 79-27144. 1980. pap. text ed. 7.95 (ISBN 0-201-01939-6). Addison-Wesley.

--Conspicuous Computing - or Informed Choices for the Computer Age. LC 81-3646. 192p. 1981. pap. 8.95 (ISBN 0-201-10113-0). Addison-Wesley.

Cowals, Dennis A., ed. see Sisson, Daniel J.

Cowan, Anita P., jt. auth. see Stettner, Allison G.

Cowan, Bainard. Exiled Waters: Moby-Dick & the Crisis of Allegory. LC 81-19354. xii, 212p. 1982. text ed. 22.50x (ISBN 0-8071-1002-7). La State U Pr.

Cowan, Brian. Classical Mechanics. (Student Physics Ser.). (Illus.). 128p. (Orig.). 1984. pap. 9.95x (ISBN 0-7102-0280-6). Routledge & Kegan.

Cowan, C. D. & Wolters, O. W., eds. Southeast Asian History & Historiography: Essays Presented to D. G. E. Hall. LC 75-18726. (Illus.). 448p. 1976. 35.00x (ISBN 0-8014-0841-5). Cornell U Pr.

Cowan, C. F. Annotationes Rhopalocerologicae. 90p. 1968-1970. 35.00x (ISBN 0-317-07027-4, Pub. by EW Classey UK). State Mutual Bk.

Cowan, C. F. & Grant, P. M. Adaptive Filters. (Illus.). 368p. 1985. text ed. 41.95 (ISBN 0-13-004037-1). P-H.

Cowan, Connell & Kinder, Melvyn. Smart Women, Foolish Choices: Finding the Right Men & Avoiding the Wrong Ones. 1985. 14.95 (ISBN 0-517-55145-4, C N Potter Bks). Crown.

Cowan, D. O. & Drisko, R. L., eds. Elements of Organic Photochemistry. LC 75-28173. (Illus.). 586p. 1976. 35.00x (ISBN 0-306-30821-5, Plenum Pr). Plenum Pub.

Cowan, D. R. Sales Analysis from the Management Standpoint. LC 67-24325. 210p. 1967. 15.00 (ISBN 0-379-00072-5). Oceana.

Cowan, Dale. Campfire Nights. (Sweet Dreams Ser.: No. 56). (Orig.). 1984. pap. text ed. 2.25 (ISBN 0-553-23965-1). Bantam.

--Deadly Sleep. (Twilight Ser.: No. 1). (gr. 5 up). 1982. pap. 1.95 (ISBN 0-440-91961-4, LFL). Dell.

Cowan, Dale H. Preferred Provider Organizations: Planning, Structure & Operation. 320p. 1984. 35.00 (ISBN 0-89443-593-0). Aspen Systems.

Cowan, Daniel A. Language & Negation: The Two-Level Structure That Prevents Paradox. LC 76-21954. 112p. 1980. pap. 6.00 (ISBN 0-915878-03-8). Joseph Pub Co.

Cowan, David. Introduction to Modern Literary Arabic. 1958. pap. 15.95 (ISBN 0-521-09240-X). Cambridge U Pr.

Cowan, Elizabeth. Readings for Writing. 1983. pap. text ed. 11.40x (ISBN 0-673-15845-4). Scott F.

--Writing: Brief Edition. 1983. pap. text ed. 17.55x (ISBN 0-673-15735-0). Scott F.

Cowan, Elizabeth, jt. auth. see Cowan, Gregory.

Cowan, Elizabeth W. Options for the Teaching of English: The Undergraduate Curriculum. (Options for Teaching Ser.: No. 1). iv, 123p. (Orig.). 1975. pap. 11.00x (ISBN 0-87352-300-8, J200). Modern Lang.

Cowan, Evelyn. Portrait of Alice. LC 78-24598. 1979. 8.95 (ISBN 0-8008-6419-0). Taplinger.

--Spring Remembered: A Scottish Jewish Childhood. LC 78-66450. 1979. 8.50 (ISBN 0-8008-7367-X). Taplinger.

Cowan, Frank. Revi-Lona: A Romance of Love in a Marvelous Land. Reginald, R. & Melville, Douglas, eds. LC 77-84216. (Lost Race & Adult Fantasy Ser.). 1978. Repr. of 1890 ed. lib. bdg. 22.00x (ISBN 0-405-10971-7). Ayer Co Pubs.

Cowan, Frank, Jr., jt. auth. see Moak, Lennox L.

Cowan, Fred F. Pharmacology for the Dental Hygienist: For Students & Practitioners. LC 77-17477. (Illus.). 410p. 1978. pap. 13.50 (ISBN 0-8121-0626-1). Lea & Febiger.

Cowan, Geoffrey. See No Evil. 1980. 4.95 (ISBN 0-671-25411-1, Touchstone). S&S.

Cowan, George S. M., et al, eds. Intravenous Hyperalimentation. LC 70-170734. (Illus.). pap. 62.30 (ISBN 0-317-07911-5, 2014536). Bks Demand UMI.

Cowan, Gregory & Cowan, Elizabeth. Writing. 1980. text ed. 23.75x (ISBN 0-673-15665-6). Scott F.

Cowan, Gregory & McPherson, Elisabeth. Plain English Reader. 3rd ed. 448p. 1982. pap. text ed. 13.00 (ISBN 0-394-32655-5, RanC). Random.

Cowan, Gregory & McPherson, Elisabeth. Plain English Please: A Rhetoric. 4th ed. 477p. 1980. pap. text ed. 13.00 (ISBN 0-394-32367-X, RanC). Random.

Cowan, H. J. An Historical Outline of Architectural Science. 2nd, enl. ed. 200p. 1978. 20.50 (ISBN 0-85334-725-5, Pub. by Applied Sci England). Elsevier.

--Models in Architecture. 1968. 29.75 (ISBN 0-85334-624-0, Pub. by Elsevier Applied Sci England). Elsevier.

--Predictive Methods for the Energy Conserving Design of Buildings. (Illus.). 128p. 1983. pap. 33.50 (ISBN 0-08-029838-9). Pergamon.

Cowan, H. J., jt. auth. see Gero, J. S.

Cowan, H. J., ed. Solar Energy Applications in the Design of Buildings. (Illus.). 164p. 1980. 48.00 (ISBN 0-85334-883-9, Pub. by Elsevier Applied Sci England). Elsevier.

Cowan, Helen I. Charles Williamson. LC 68-55516. Repr. of 1941 ed. 37.50x (ISBN 0-678-00862-0). Kelley.

Cowan, Henry. John Knox: The Hero of the Scottish Reformation. LC 70-133817. (Illus.). Repr. of 1905 ed. 27.50 (ISBN 0-404-01788-6). AMS Pr.

--Landmarks of Church History to the Reformation. new rev. & enl. ed. LC 70-144590. Repr. of 1896 ed. 17.00 (ISBN 0-404-01787-8). AMS Pr.

Cowan, Henry J. Architectual Structures: An Introduction to Structural Mechanics. LC 79-13735. (Civil Engineering Ser.). 320p. 1980. text ed. 34.95 (ISBN 0-273-01054-9). Pitman Pub MA.

--Architectural Structures. 2nd ed. LC 75-26330. 416p. 1976. 31.50 (ISBN 0-444-00177-8). Elsevier.

--The Design of Reinforced Concrete in Accordance with the Metric SAA Concrete Structures Code. (Illus.). 240p. 1975. 26.00x (ISBN 0-424-00000-8, Pub by Sydney U Pr). Intl Spec Bk.

--Design of Reinforced Concrete Structures. (Illus.). 304p. 1982. 31.00 (ISBN 0-13-201376-2). P-H.

--A Dictionary of Architectural Science. LC 73-15839. (Illus.). 354p. 1973. pap. 19.95x (ISBN 0-470-18070-6). Halsted Pr.

--The Master Builders. LC 84-19400. 314p. 1985. Repr. of 1977 ed. lib. bdg. write for info. (ISBN 0-89874-804-6). Krieger.

--Structural System. (Illus.). 356p. 1981. pap. 16.95 (ISBN 0-442-21713-7). Van Nos Reinhold.

Cowan, Henry J. & Dixon, John. Building Science Laboratory Manual. (Illus.). 156p. 1978. 24.00 (ISBN 0-85334-747-6, Pub. by Elsevier Applied Sci England). Elsevier.

Cowan, Henry J. & Smith, Peter R. Environmental Systems. 1983. 26.95 (ISBN 0-442-21490-1); pap. 18.95 (ISBN 0-442-21489-8). Van Nos Reinhold.

Cowan, Ian B. The Scottish Reformation. LC 82-5834. 256p. 1982. 25.00x (ISBN 0-312-70519-0). St Martin.

Cowan, Ian B. & Shaw, Duncan, eds. The Renaissance & Reformation in Scotland. 220p. 1983. 20.00x (ISBN 0-7073-0261-7, Scottish Academic Pr). Columbia U Pr.

Cowan, J. C., jt. auth. see Wolf, W. J.

Cowan, J. I. Manual of Grenades & New Grenade Chart. (War Documents Ser.: No. 23). (Illus.). 49p. pap. 4.95 (ISBN 0-86663-992-6). Ide Hse.

Cowan, J. L. Pleasure & Pain. LC 68-13019. 1968. 22.50 (ISBN 0-312-61705-4). St Martin.

Cowan, J. M., ed. see Wehr, Hans.

Cowan, J Milton, ed. see Wehr, Hans.

Cowan, J. Ronayne & Schuh, Russell G. Spoken Hausa. LC 75-15184. (Spoken Language Ser). 350p. (Programmed book). 1976. pap. text ed. 10.00x (ISBN 0-87950-401-3); cassetes for units 1-12, six dual track 65.00x (ISBN 0-87950-402-1); book & cassettes for units 1-12 70.00x (ISBN 0-87950-403-X); cassettes for units 13-25 (14 hours) 100.00x (ISBN 0-87950-404-8). Spoken Lang Serv.

Cowan, Jack C. & Weintritt, Donald J. Water-Formed Scale Deposits. LC 75-5089. 606p. 1976. 79.95x (ISBN 0-87201-896-2). Gulf Pub.

Cowan, James. Daybreak: A Romance of an Old World. 2nd ed. LC 72-154436. (Utopian Literature Ser). (Illus.). 1971. Repr. of 1896 ed. 25.50 (ISBN 0-405-03519-5). Ayer Co Pubs.

--Fairy Folk Tales of the Maori. 2nd ed. LC 75-35246. Repr. of 1930 ed. 18.00 (ISBN 0-404-14420-9). AMS Pr.

--The Maori Yesterday & to-Day. LC 75-35247. Repr. of 1930 ed. 22.50 (ISBN 0-404-14421-7). AMS Pr.

--New Zealand Wars, 2 Vols. LC 76-100514. (BCL Ser. II). Repr. of 1922 ed. 37.50 (ISBN 0-404-00600-0). AMS Pr.

--Tales of the Maori Bush. LC 75-35248. Repr. of 1934 ed. 24.50 (ISBN 0-404-14422-5). AMS Pr.

Cowan, James C., ed. D. H. Lawrence: An Annotated Bibliography of Writings about Him, Vol. I. LC 80-8664. (The Annotated Secondary Bibliography Series on English Literature in Transition, 1880-1920). 612p. 1982. 35.00 (ISBN 0-87580-077-7). N Ill U Pr.

--D. H. Lawrence: An Annotated Bibliography of Writings About Him, Vol. II. LC 80-8664. (An Annotated Secondary Bibliography Series on English Literature in Transition, 1880-1920). 799p. 1985. 45.00 (ISBN 0-87580-105-6). N Ill U Pr.

Cowan, Joseph L., ed. Studies in Thought & Language. LC 75-89620. 1970. pap. 58.00 (ISBN 0-317-08180-2, 2022755). Bks Demand UMI.

Cowan, L. The Clearing Banks & the Trade Unions. 1984. 25.00x (ISBN 0-317-20362-2, Pub. by Inst Bankers UK). State Mutual Bk.

Cowan, L. Gray. Black Africa: The Growing Pains of Independence. LC 72-75587. (Headline Ser.: No. 210). (Illus., Orig.). 1972. pap. 3.00 (ISBN 0-87124-016-5). Foreign Policy.

Cowan, L. Gray, tr. see Mendes, Candido.

Cowan, Laing G. France & the Saar, 1680-1948. LC 50-3112. (Columbia University Studies in the Social Sciences: No. 561). Repr. of 1950 ed. 20.00 (ISBN 0-404-51561-4). AMS Pr.

--Local Government in West Africa. LC 75-110429. (BCL Ser. I). Repr. of 1958 ed. 23.00 (ISBN 0-404-00144-0). AMS Pr.

Cowan, Les. The Illustrated Computer Dictionary & Handbook. (Illus.). 224p. 1983. pap. 9.95 (ISBN 0-86582-116-X, EN79101). Enrich.

--TI 99-4A for the Beginning Beginner. (Illus.). 176p. (gr. 5 up). 1984. TI 99-4 & -4A Model. pap. 8.95 (ISBN 0-86582-132-1, EN79225). Enrich.

Cowan, Louise S. The Southern Critics. 1971. 3.95x (ISBN 0-918306-01-9). U of Dallas Pr.

Cowan, Lyn. Masochism: A Jungian View. LC 82-16957. 137p. (Orig.). 1982. pap. 12.00 (ISBN 0-88214-320-4). Spring Pubns.

Cowan, Marianne, tr. see Nietzsche, Friedrich.

Cowan, Marvin W. Los Mormones: Sus Doctrinas Refutadas a la Luz De la Biblia. De La Fuente, Tomas, tr. from Eng. 160p. 1981. pap. 3.50 (ISBN 0-311-05763-2). Casa Bautista.

Cowan, Maxwell W. & Shooter, Eric M., eds. Annual Review of Neuroscience, Vol. 8. 500p. 1985. 24.00 (ISBN 0-318-18123-1); members 21.50 (ISBN 0-318-18124-X). Soc Neuroscience.

Cowan, Michael A., jt. auth. see Egan, Gerard.

Cowan, Paul. An Orphan in History. 272p. 1983. pap. 3.50 (ISBN 0-553-23571-0). Bantam.

Cowan, Peter. A Unique Position: A Biography of Edith Dircksey Cowan, 1861-1932. 1979. 24.00x (ISBN 0-85564-135-5, Pub. by U of W Austral Pr). Intl Spec Bk.

Cowan, Peter, ed. The Future of Planning. LC 73-80439. (Centre for Environmental Studies Ser.: Vol. 1). pap. 47.50 (ISBN 0-317-29598-5, 2021882). Bks Demand UMI.

Cowan, Philip. Behind the Beatles Songs. 20.00X (ISBN 0-905150-09-0, Pub. by J Landesman England). State Mutual Bk.

Cowan, R. S., jt. auth. see Stafleu.

Cowan, R. S., jt. ed. see Stafleu, F. A.

Cowan, Rachel. Growing Up Yanqui. 160p. (gr. 7 up). 1975. 6.95 (ISBN 0-670-35597-6). Viking.

Cowan, Richard O. Doctrine & Covenants: Our Modern Scripture. rev. ed. LC 78-19190. (Illus.). 1978. pap. 7.95 (ISBN 0-8425-1316-7). Brigham.

Cowan, Robert. Teleconferencing. 1984. text ed. 25.95 (ISBN 0-8359-7549-5). Reston.

Cowan, Robert D. The Theory of Atomic Structure & Spectra. LC 81-4578. (Los Alamos Ser. in Basic & Applied Sciences). 650p. 1981. 45.00x (ISBN 0-520-03821-5). U of Cal Pr.

Cowan, Robert G. The Admission of the Thirty-First State by the Thirty-First Congress: An Annotated Bibliography of Congressional Speeches upon the Admission of California. 139p. 1984. Repr. of 1962 ed. lib. bdg. 19.95x (ISBN 0-89370-865-8). Borgo Pr.

--A Backward Glance: Los Angeles, 1901-1915. 48p. 1984. Repr. of 1969 ed. lib. bdg. 19.95x (ISBN 0-89370-866-6). Borgo Pr.

--On the Rails of Los Angeles: A Pictorial History of Its Street-Cars. 48p. 1984. Repr. of 1971 ed. lib. bdg. 19.95x (ISBN 0-89370-867-4). Borgo Pr.

--Ranchos of California. 151p. 1984. Repr. of 1977 ed. lib. bdg. 19.95x (ISBN 0-89370-863-1). Borgo Pr.

Cowan, Robert J., jt. ed. see Weintraub, Sam.

Cowan, Ruth S. More Work for Mother: The Ironies of Household Technology from the Open Hearth to the Microwave. LC 83-70759. (Illus.). 350p. 1983. text ed. 17.95 (ISBN 0-465-04731-9). Basic.

--More Work for Mother: The Ironies of Household Technology from the Open Hearth to the Microwave. 350p. 1985. pap. 7.95 (ISBN 0-465-04732-7, CN 5131). Basic.

--Sir Francis Galton & the Study of Heredity in the Nineteenth Century. Rosenberg, Charles, ed. LC 83-48624. (The History of Hereditarian Thought Ser.). 289p. 1985. lib. bdg. 35.00 (ISBN 0-8240-5802-X). Garland Pub.

Cowan, S. D., jt. auth. see Orr, William I.

Cowan, S. T. Cowan & Steel's Manual for the Identification of Medical Bacteria. (Illus.). 240p. 1974. 44.50 (ISBN 0-521-20399-6). Cambridge U Pr.

--A Dictionary of Microbial Taxonomic Usage. 1968. 7.50 (ISBN 0-934454-28-0). Lubrecht & Cramer.

--A Dictionary of Microbial Taxonomy. Hill, L. R., ed. LC 77-85705. (Illus.). 1978. 52.50 (ISBN 0-521-21890-X). Cambridge U Pr.

Cowan, Sada. Pomp & Other Plays. LC 79-50024. (One-Act Plays in Reprint Ser.). 1980. Repr. of 1926 ed. 19.75x (ISBN 0-8486-2048-8). Core Collection.

Cowan, Sam. Handbook of Digital Logic with Practical Applications. LC 84-16049. 309p. 1985. 29.95 (ISBN 0-13-377193-8). P-H.

--Handbook of Modern Electronics Math. LC 82-11260. 254p. 1983. 21.95 (ISBN 0-13-380485-2). P-H.

Cowan, Stuart D., jt. auth. see Orr, William I.

Cowan, Thomas. Beyond the Bath: A Dreamer's Guide. LC 83-61775. (Illus.). 128p. (Orig.). 1983. lib. bdg. 19.80 (ISBN 0-89471-224-1); pap. 8.95 (ISBN 0-89471-223-3). Running Pr.

--Beyond the Bath: A Dreamer's Guide. (Illus.). 128p. 1985. 12.98 (ISBN 0-317-14619-X). Running Pr.

--Beyond the Kitchen: A Dreamer's Guide. LC 84-42923. (Illus.). 128p. (Orig.). 1985. 24.95 (ISBN 0-89471-303-5); pap. 9.95 (ISBN 0-89471-306-X). Running Pr.

--The Gourmet's Guide to Mixed Drinks. (Illus.). 128p. (Orig.). 1984. pap. 6.95 (ISBN 0-688-02502-1, Quill). Morrow.

Cowan, Thomas A., ed. American Jurisprudence Reader. LC 56-12585. (Docket Ser.: Vol. 8). 256p. (Orig.). 1956. 15.00 (ISBN 0-379-11308-2); pap. 2.50. Oceana.

Cowan, Thomas D. How to Tap into Your Own Genius. 192p. 1984. pap. 6.95 (ISBN 0-671-53071-2, Fireside). S&S.

Cowan, Tom. Resumes That Work. LC 83-8332. 192p. 1983. pap. 9.95 (ISBN 0-452-25455-8, Plume). NAL.

Cowan, W. M., et al, eds. Annual Review of Neuroscience, Vol. 5. (Illus.). 1981. text ed. 22.00 (ISBN 0-8243-2405-6). Annual Reviews.

--Annual Review of Neuroscience, Vol. 6. (Illus.). 1983. text ed. 27.00 (ISBN 0-8243-2406-4). Annual Reviews.

--Annual Review of Neuroscience, Vol. 7. (Illus.). 1984. text ed. 27.00 (ISBN 0-8243-2407-2). Annual Reviews.

--Annual Review of Neuroscience, Vol. 4. (Illus.). 1981. text ed. 20.00 (ISBN 0-8243-2404-8). Annual Reviews.

Cowan, W. Maxwell, ed. Studies in Developmental Neurobiology: Essays in Honor of Viktor Hamburger. (Illus.). 1981. text ed. 49.50x (ISBN 0-19-502927-5). Oxford U Pr.

Cowan, W. Maxwell, et al, eds. Annual Review of Neuroscience, Vol. 1. (Illus.). 1978. text ed. 20.00 (ISBN 0-8243-2401-3). Annual Reviews.

--Annual Review of Neuroscience, Vol. 2. (Illus.). 1979. text ed. 20.00 (ISBN 0-8243-2402-1). Annual Reviews.

--Annual Review of Neuroscience, Vol. 3. (Illus.). 1980. text ed. 20.00 (ISBN 0-8243-2403-X). Annual Reviews.

--Annual Review of Neuroscience, Vol. 8. (Illus.). 603p. 1985. text ed. 27.00 (ISBN 0-8243-2408-0). Annual Reviews.

Cowan, Walter G., et al. New Orleans, Yesterday & Today: A Guide to the City. LC 83-772. (Illus.). 288p. 1983. 14.95 (ISBN 0-8071-1108-2); pap. 6.95 (ISBN 0-8071-1109-0). La State U Pr.

Cowan, William & Gadd, Laurence. College Pursuit. 1985. 24.95 (ISBN 0-671-60523-2). S&S.

Coward. Case Presentations: In Renal Medicine. 1983. text ed. 24.95 (ISBN 0-407-00234-0). Butterworth.

Coward, Barry. The Stanleys, Lords Stanley & Earls of Derby 1385-1672: The Origins, Wealth & Power of a Land Owning Family. LC 83-823. 272p. 1983. 35.00 (ISBN 0-7190-1338-0, Pub. by Manchester Univ Pr). Longwood Pub Group.

--The Stuart Age. LC 79-42887. (A History of England Ser.). (Illus.). 512p. 1980. text ed. 32.00x (ISBN 0-582-48279-8); pap. text ed. 19.95x (ISBN 0-582-48833-8). Longman.

Coward, David, tr. see Daumal, Rene.

Coward, E. Walter, ed. Irrigation & Agricultural Development in Asia: Perspectives from the Social Sciences. LC 79-24319. (Illus.). 368p. (Orig.). 1980. 39.95x (ISBN 0-8014-1132-7); pap. 11.95x (ISBN 0-8014-9871-6). Cornell U Pr.

Coward, Harold. Pluralism: Challenge to World Religions. LC 84-14737. 144p. (Orig.). 1985. pap. 8.95 (ISBN 0-88344-710-X). Orbis Bks.

Coward, Harold & Kawamura, Leslie, eds. Religion & Ethnicity. 181p. 1978. pap. text ed. 8.50 (ISBN 0-88920-064-5, Pub. by Wilfred Laurier U Pr Canada). Humanities.

Coward, Harold, ed. see Murty, T. R.

Coward, Harold C. Jung & Eastern Thought. (Series in Transpersonal & Humanistic Philosophy). 229p. 1985. lib. bdg. 34.50x (ISBN 0-88706-052-8); pap. text ed. 12.95 (ISBN 0-88706-051-X). State U NY Pr.

Coward, Harold G. Sphota Theory of Language. 1981. 12.00x (ISBN 0-8364-0692-3). South Asia Bks.

Coward, Harold G., ed. Language in Indian Philosophy & Religion. 98p. 1978. pap. text ed. 8.00x (ISBN 0-919812-07-4, Pub. by Wilfred Laurier U Pr Canada). Humanities.

Coward, Harold G., jt. ed. see Woods, John.

Coward, Henry. Choral Technique & Interpretation. LC 72-1254. (Select Bibliographies Reprint Ser.). 1972. Repr. of 1914 ed. 20.00 (ISBN 0-8369-6824-7). Ayer Co Pubs.

Coward, Jane, ed. see Grisanti, John.

Coward, Joan W. Kentucky in the New Republic: The Process of Constitution Making. LC 77-92920. (Illus.). 232p. 1979. 21.00x (ISBN 0-8131-1380-6). U Pr of Ky.

Coward, Margaret, ed. The Gaines County Story. (Illus.). 544p. 1974. 12.50 (ISBN 0-933512-18-X). Pioneer Bk Tx.

Coward, Noel. The Collected Stories of Noel Coward. LC 83-5704. 600p. 1983. 20.00 (ISBN 0-525-24207-4, 01942-580). Dutton.

--Collected Verse of Noel Coward. Payn, Graham & Tickner, Martin, eds. 222p. 1985. 17.95 (ISBN 0-413-55140-7, NO. 9241). Methuen Inc.
--Future Indefinite: An Autobiography. (Illus.). 352p. 1980. pap. 7.95 (ISBN 0-306-80126-4). Da Capo.
--The Lyrics of Noel Coward. LC 73-77884. (Tusk Bks.). 432p. 1973. 25.00 (ISBN 0-87951-197-4); pap. 9.95 (ISBN 0-87951-187-7). Overlook Pr.
--Plays: Five. 432p. 1983. pap. 9.95 (ISBN 0-394-62456-4, B486, BC). Grove.
--Plays: Four. 512p. (Orig.). 1981. pap. 9.95 (ISBN 0-394-17943-9, B-462, BC). Grove.
--Plays: One. 384p. (Orig.). 1981. pap. 9.95 (ISBN 0-394-17940-4, B-459, BC). Grove.
--Plays: Three. 432p. (Orig.). 1981. pap. 9.95 (ISBN 0-394-17942-0, B-461, BC). Grove.
--Plays: Two. 384p. (Orig.). 1981. pap. 9.95 (ISBN 0-394-17941-2, B-460, BC). Grove.
--Pomp & Circumstance. 17.95 (ISBN 0-89190-219-8, Pub. by Am Repr). Amereon Ltd.
--Pomp & Circumstance: A Novel. 312p. 1982. pap. 5.95 (ISBN 0-525-48019-6, 0578-170, Obelisk). Dutton.
--Present Indicative: An Autobiography. (Illus.). 1980. pap. 7.95 (ISBN 0-306-80112-4). Da Capo.
--Private Lives. 1983. pap. 2.95 (ISBN 0-451-12534-7, Sig). NAL.
--Spangled Unicorn. LC 82-83582. (Illus.). 101p. 1982. Repr. of 1932 ed. 8.95 (ISBN 0-910638-00-4). Frisch H.
--Three Plays. Incl. Blithe Spirit; Hay Fever; Private Lives. 1979. pap. 4.50 (ISBN 0-394-17535-2, E742, Ever). Grove.
Coward, Noel P. Star Quality: Six Stories. LC 75-109288. Repr. of 1951 ed. lib. bdg. 24.75x (ISBN 0-8371-3831-0, COSQ). Greenwood.
Coward, Parnell C. Revelation, Systematically Studied. 1983. pap. 6.95 (ISBN 0-87148-739-X). Pathway Pr.
Coward, Raymond & Lee, Gary. The Elderly in Rural Society: Every Fourth Elder. (Springer Series on Adulthood & Aging: Vol. 13). 288p. 1985. 24.95 (ISBN 0-8261-4120-X). Springer Pub.
Coward, Raymond T., jt. auth. see Sauer, William J.
Coward, Raymond T. & Smith, William M., eds. The Family in Rural Society. (Special Studies in Contemporary Social Issues). 280p. 1981. lib. bdg. 30.00x (ISBN 0-86531-121-8). Westview.
Coward, Raymond T. & Smith, William M., Jr., eds. Family Services: Issues & Opportunities in Contemporary Rural America. LC 83-1267. xviii, 208p. 1983. 18.95x (ISBN 0-8032-1420-0). U of Nebr Pr.
Coward, Rosalind. Female Desires: How They Are Sought, Bought, & Packaged. LC 84-73207. 256p. 1985. 17.50 (ISBN 0-394-54591-5, GP-961); pap. 5.95 (ISBN 0-394-62367-3, E-977, Ever). Grove.
--Patriarchal Precedents: Sexuality & Social Relations. 280p. (Orig.). 1983. pap. 9.95 (ISBN 0-7100-9324-1). Routledge & Kegan.
Coward, Rosalind & Ellis, John. Language & Materialism: Developments in Semiology & the Theory of the Subject. 1977. pap. 8.95x (ISBN 0-7100-8627-X). Routledge & Kegan.
Coward, Stuart, ed. Developmental Regulation: Aspects of Cell Differentiation. (Cell Biology Series). 1973. 59.50 (ISBN 0-12-194050-0). Acad Pr.
Cowardin, David. Handling Elevator Emergencies. Saunders, Laura & Tower, Keith, eds. LC 79-84710. 1979. pap. 18.25 (ISBN 0-87765-146-9, SPP-54). Natl Fire Prot.
Cowardin, David H. The On Scene Emergency Management System. (Illus.). 14.95 (ISBN 0-686-32880-9). Emerg Service Product & Prod.
Cowart, Andrew T. & Brofoss, Karl E. Decisions, Politics & Change: A Study of Norwegian Urban Budgeting. 1979. pap. 15.00x (ISBN 82-00-01882-2, Dist. by Columbia U. Pr.). Universitet.
Cowart, Andrew T. & Brofoss, Karl Erik. Decision, Politics, & Change: A Study of Norweigan Urban Budgeting. 151p. 1979. write for info. Universitet.
Cowart, David. Arches & Light: The Fiction of John Gardner. LC 83-335. 240p. 1983. 19.95 (ISBN 0-8093-1127-5). S Ill U Pr.
--Thomas Pynchon: The Art of Allusion. LC 79-20157. (Crosscurrents-Modern Critiques-New Ser.). 168p. 1980. 15.95 (ISBN 0-8093-0944-0). S Ill U Pr.
Cowart, David, ed. Twentieth-Century American Science Fiction Writers, 2 vols. (Dictionary of Literary Biography Ser.: Vol. 8). 688p. 1981. 170.00x set (ISBN 0-8103-0918-1, Bruccoli Clark). Gale.
Cowart, Georgia. The Origins of Modern Musical Criticism: French & Italian Music, 1600-1750. Buelow, George, ed. LC 81-641. (Studies in Musicology: No. 38). 228p. 1981. 39.95 (ISBN 0-8357-1166-8). UMI Res Pr.
Cowart, J. B., jt. auth. see Osmond, J. K.
Cowart, Jack. New-Photo Realism: Paintings & Sculpture from the 1970's. LC 74-77609. (Illus.). 56p. 1974. pap. 4.50 (ISBN 0-317-13606-2). Wadsworth Atheneum.
--Roy Lichtenstein, 1970-1980. LC 80-28348. (Illus.). 176p. 1981. 35.00 (ISBN 0-933920-14-8); pap. 15.00 museum distribution only (ISBN 0-933920-15-6). Hudson Hills.
Cowart, Jack & Chambers, Karen. Dale Chihuly: A Decade of Glass. (Illus.). 56p. (Orig.). 1984. pap. 14.95 (ISBN 0-942342-03-8). Bellevue Art.
Cowart, Marie & Allen, Rodney, eds. Changing Conceptions of Health Care: Public Policy & Ethical Issues for Nurses. LC 81-51721. 125p. 1981. 14.50 (ISBN 0-913590-81-9). Slack Inc.
Cowasjee, Saros. Stories & Sketches. (Writers Workshop Greenbird Ser.). 85p. 1975. 11.00 (ISBN 0-88253-646-X); pap. text ed. 6.00 (ISBN 0-88253-645-1). Ind-US Inc.
Cowasjee, Saros & Shahane, Vasant A. Modern Indian Fiction. 244p. 1982. 39.00x (ISBN 0-7069-1051-6, Pub. by Garlandfold England). State Mutual Bk.
Cowasjee, Saros & Kumar, Shiv K., eds. Modern Indian Short Stories. 1983. pap. 4.95x (ISBN 0-19-561563-8). Oxford U Pr.
Cowboy Artists of America, illus. Cowboy Artists of America Nineteenth Annual Exhibition Catalog. LC 73-162045. (Yearly CAA Exhibition Catalogs Ser.). (Illus.). 64p. (Orig.). 1984. pap. 16.00 (ISBN 0-87358-355-8). Northland.
Cowden, Dudley J. Measures of Exports of the United States. LC 68-58561. (Columbia University Studies in the Social Sciences: No. 356). 14.50 (ISBN 0-404-51356-5). AMS Pr.
Cowden, Joanna D., jt. ed. see Curry, Richard O.
Cowden, Mary, jt. auth. see Clarke, Chas.
Cowden, Morton. Russian Bolshevism & British Labor: 1917-1921. 238p. 1984. 27.00x (ISBN 0-88033-045-7). East Eur Quarterly.
Cowden, Robert. A Brief Sketch of the Organization & Services of the Fifty-Ninth Regiment of United States Colored Infantry. facsimile ed. LC 74-168514. (Black Heritage Library Collection). Repr. of 1883 ed. 19.50 (ISBN 0-8369-8866-3). Ayer Co Pubs.
Cowden, Robert H. The Chautauqua Opera Association, 1929-1958. Fox, Leland, ed. LC 74-77605. (National Opera Association Monograph Ser.: No. 1). 85p. (Orig.). 1974. pap. 3.50 (ISBN 0-938178-03-2). Natl Opera Assn.
Cowden, Ronald R., jt. ed. see Harrison, Frederick.
Cowden, Ronald R., jt. ed. see Harrison, Frederick W.
Cowden-Clark, Mary. Complete Concordance to Shakespeare. 1973. lib. bdg. 65.00 (ISBN 0-8414-2398-9). Folcroft.
Cowden-Clarke, Mary. Letters to an Enthusiast. Nettleton, Anne U., ed. 1973. Repr. of 1902 ed. 25.00 (ISBN 0-8274-1526-5). R West.
--Shakespeare Proverbs or the Wise Saws of Our Wisest Poet Collected into a Modern Instance. LC 73-3433. 1973. Repr. of 1908 ed. lib. bdg. 27.50 (ISBN 0-8414-1837-3). Folcroft.
Cowdery, M. F. Elementary Moral Lessons for Schools & Families. 1975. Repr. 4.95 (ISBN 0-686-15523-8). St Thomas.
Cowdery, Ray. All American Wonder. (Illus.). 160p. 1986. 24.95 (ISBN 0-910667-09-8); pap. 19.95 (ISBN 0-910667-10-1). Northstar-Maschek.
--Nazi Buckles, Psychology & the Fighting Spirit. (Illus.). 64p. 1982. 9.95 (ISBN 0-910667-01-2); pap. 7.95 (ISBN 0-910667-00-4). Northstar-Maschek.
Cowdery, Ray & Robinson, George C. Nazi Para-Military Organizations & Their Badges. (Illus.). 142p. 1985. 24.95 (ISBN 0-910667-06-3); pap. 19.95 (ISBN 0-910667-05-5). Northstar-Maschek.
Cowdrey, Albert E. This Land, This South: An Environmental History. LC 82-20154. (New Perspectives on the South Ser.). 256p. 1983. 23.00 (ISBN 0-8131-0302-9). U Pr of Ky.
Cowdrey, H. E. The Age of Abbot Desiderius: Montecassino, the Papacy & the Normans in the Eleventh & Early Twelfth Centuries. 1983. 45.00x (ISBN 0-19-821939-3). Oxford U Pr.
--Popes, Monks & Crusaders. (No. 27). 400p. 1983. 40.00 (ISBN 0-907628-34-6). Hambledon Press.
Cowdrey, H. E., ed. see Gregory VII, Pope.
Cowdrey, Michael L. Basic Law for the Allied Health Professions. LC 83-23390. 300p. 1984. pap. text ed. 13.25x pub net (ISBN 0-534-03208-7). Wadsworth Health.
Cowdry, E. V. Aging Better. (Illus.). 500p. 1972. photocopy ed. 49.50x (ISBN 0-398-02263-1). C C Thomas.
Cowdry, E. V., jt. auth. see Emmel, Victor E.
Cowdry, E. V. & Kastenbaum, Robert, eds. Problems of Aging: Biological & Medical Aspects. LC 78-22196. (Aging & Old Age Ser.). (Illus.). 1979. Repr. of 1939 ed. lib. bdg. 53.50x (ISBN 0-405-11813-9). Ayer Co Pubs.
Cowe, Eileen G. Free Play: Organization & Management in the Pre-School & Kindergarten. (Illus.). 100p. 1982. 15.75x (ISBN 0-398-04647-6). C C Thomas.
--A Study of Kindergarten Activities for Language Development. LC 74-83368. 10.00 (ISBN 0-88247-301-8). R & E Pubs.
Cowe, Peter L., jt. auth. see Feld, Raoul.
Cowe, Roger. Handbook of Management Accounting. 2nd ed. 500p. 1986. text ed. price not set (ISBN 0-566-02615-5). Gower Pub Co.
Cowel, Lucinda, jt. auth. see Gilliam, Terry.
Cowell, tr. Buddhist Mahayana Texts. (Sacred Books of the East Ser., Vol. 49). 12.00 (ISBN 0-8446-0518-2). Peter Smith.
Cowell, Barbara, jt. auth. see Wilson, John.
Cowell, Benjamin. Spirit of '76 in Rhode Island. LC 72-10847. 560p. 1973. Repr. of 1850 ed. 25.00 (ISBN 0-8063-0542-8). Genealog Pub.
Cowell, D. W., jt. auth. see Blois, K. J.
Cowell, Don. Marketing of Services. 1977. 125.00x (ISBN 0-686-79198-3, Pub. by MCB Pubns). State Mutual Bk.
Cowell, Donald. The Marketing of Services. (Illus.). 352p. 1985. pap. 22.50 (ISBN 0-434-90263-2, Pub. by W Heinemann Ltd). David & Charles.
Cowell, E. B. The Grammar of Prakrit Language. Orig. Title: Prakrita-Prakasa of Vararuchi. 200p. 1977. Repr. of 1853 ed. lib. bdg. 14.50 (ISBN 0-89684-149-9). Orient Bk Dist.
Cowell, E. B. & Muller, F. Max. Buddhist Mahayana Texts. (Sacred Bks. of the East: Vol. 49). 18.00 (ISBN 0-89581-534-6). Asian Human Pr.
Cowell, E. B., et al. Buddhist Mahayana Texts. Mueller, F. Max, ed. LC 68-9450. (Sacred Books of the East Ser). 1969. Dover.
Cowell, E. R. & Thomas, F. W., trs. Harsa-Carita of Bana. 2nd ed. 1968. pap. 3.95 (ISBN 0-89684-210-X). Orient Bk Dist.
Cowell, F. R. The Garden As Fine Art. 1978. 20.00 (ISBN 0-395-27065-0). HM.
Cowell, Frank R. History, Civilization & Culture: An Introduction to the Historical & Social Philosophy of Pitirum A. Sorokin. LC 78-14112. (Illus.). 1979. Repr. of 1950 ed. 24.75 (ISBN 0-88355-784-3). Hyperion Conn.
Cowell, Henry & Cowell, Sidney. Charles Ives & His Music. (Music Reprint Ser.). x, 253p. 1981. Repr. of 1969 ed. 29.50 (ISBN 0-306-76125-4). Da Capo.
Cowell, Henry, ed. American Composers on American Music: A Symposium. LC 62-9681. 1962. pap. 4.95 (ISBN 0-8044-6088-4). Ungar.
Cowell, Joe. Thirty Years Passed among the Players in England & America. Saxon, Arthur, ed. (Archon Books on Popular Entertainments). (Illus.). viii, 103p. 1979. Repr. of 1844 ed. 15.00 (ISBN 0-208-01778-X, Archon). Shoe String.
Cowell, John. The Begrudgers. 159p. 1978. pap. 4.95 (ISBN 0-905140-38-9, Pub. by O'Brien Pr Ireland). Irish Bks Media.
--The Interpreter: Or, Book Containing the Signification of Words. LC 76-25757. (English Experience Ser.: No. 231). 584p. 1970. Repr. of 1607 ed. 69.00 (ISBN 90-221-0231-9). Walter J Johnson.
--Where They Lived in Dublin. (Illus.). 160p. 1980. 14.95 (ISBN 0-905140-43-5, Pub. by O'Brien Pr Ireland). Irish Bks Media.
Cowell, Mark W. A Reference Grammar of Syrian Arabic. (Richard Slade Harrell Arabic Ser). 579p. 1964. pap. 11.95 (ISBN 0-87840-009-5); of three cassettes 15.50 set (ISBN 0-87840-019-2); write for info set of five-inch reels (ISBN 0-87840-020-6). Georgetown U Pr.
Cowell, Phyllis. A Hugga Bunch Hello. (Hugga Bunch Ser.). (Illus.). 40p. (ps). 1985. 4.00 (ISBN 0-910313-87-3). Parker Bro.
Cowell, Phyllis F. The Baby Hugs Bear & Baby Tugs Bear Alphabet Book. (Young World of Care Bears Ser.). (Illus.). 40p. (ps). 1984. 5.95 (ISBN 0-910313-72-5). Parker Bro.
--Your Best Wishes Can Come True. (Care Bear Ser.). (Illus.). 40p. (ps-3). 1984. 5.95 (ISBN 0-910313-18-0). Parker Bro.
Cowell, Raymond. The Critical Enterprise: English Studies in Higher Education. 156p. 1975. 11.50x (ISBN 0-87471-635-7). Rowman.
Cowell, Raymond, ed. Critics on Wordsworth. (Readings in Literary Criticism). 1973. pap. text ed. 7.95x (ISBN 0-04-801015-4). Allen Unwin.
--Critics on Yeats. LC 78-148725. (Readings in Literary Criticism Ser: No. 10). 1979. pap. 5.95 (ISBN 0-87024-200-8). U of Miami Pr.
Cowell, Sally. Happy Times with Happy Seeds. (Happy Days Bks.). (Illus.). 24p. (ps-2). 1984. 1.39 (ISBN 0-87239-738-6, 3708). Standard Pub.
Cowell, Sidney, jt. auth. see Cowell, Henry.
Cowell, Wayne R., ed. Sources & Development of Mathematical Software. (Illus.). 416p. 1984. text ed. 35.00 (ISBN 0-13-823501-5). P-H.
Cowen & Middaugh. Strategics Planning & Control Systems. 1987. price not set (ISBN 0-471-88747-1). Wiley.
Cowen, Claudine, tr. see Duval, Marguerite.
Cowen, David L. & Segelman, Alvin B. Antibiotics in Historical Perspective. 238p. 1981. write for info. (ISBN 0-911910-71-9). Merck-Sharp-Dohme.
Cowen, Deborah, ed. The Year of Grace of the Lord. 254p. (Orig.). 1980. pap. 8.95 (ISBN 0-913836-68-0). St Vladimirs.
Cowen, Emory L., jt. auth. see Zax, Melvin.
Cowen, Emory L., et al. New Ways in School Mental Health: Early Detection & Prevention of School Maladaptation. LC 74-11815. 396p. 1975. 29.95 (ISBN 0-87705-214-X). Human Sci Pr.
Cowen, Frances. The Gentle Obsession. DeRoin, Gene, ed. (Aston Hall Presents Ser.). (Orig.). 1980. pap. 1.50 (ISBN 0-89936-020-3). Aston Hall.
Cowen, Gerald. Sermon Starters from the Greek New Testament. 1985. pap. 5.95 (ISBN 0-8054-1397-9). Broadman.
Cowen, Ida & Gunther, Irene. A Spy for Freedom: The Story of Sarah Aaronsohn. LC 84-10193. (Jewish Biography Ser.). (Illus.). 176p. (gr. 5 up). 1984. 14.95 (ISBN 0-525-67150-1, 01451-440). Lodestar Bks.
Cowen, Janet, ed. see Malory, Thomas.
Cowen, John E., ed. Teaching Reading through the Arts. 118p. 1983. pap. 7.00 (ISBN 0-87207-733-0). Intl Reading.
Cowen, N. J. Hand Surgery. 1981. 79.50 (ISBN 0-8151-1871-6). Year Bk Med.
Cowen, P. J., jt. auth. see Grahame-Smith, D. G.
Cowen, P. N., jt. auth. see Smiddy, F. G.
Cowen, Philip. Memories of an American Jew. facsimile ed. LC 74-27974. (Modern Jewish Experience Ser.). (Illus.). 1975. Repr. of 1932 ed. 37.50x (ISBN 0-405-06703-8). Ayer Co Pubs.
Cowen, Richard & Lipps, Jere H. Controversies in the Earth Sciences: A Reader. LC 75-1395. (Illus.). 439p. 1975. pap. text ed. 16.95 (ISBN 0-8299-0044-6). West Pub.
Cowen, Robert, ed. International Yearbook of Education, Vol. 33. (Illus.). 253p. 1981. pap. 13.50 (ISBN 92-3-101868-X, U1167, UNESCO). Unipub.
Cowen, Robert & McLean, Martin, eds. International Handbook of Education Systems: Asia, Australasia & Latin America, Vol. 3. (International Handbook of Educational Systems Ser.: 1-670). 844p. 1984. 60.00x (ISBN 0-471-90214-4, Pub. by Wiley-Interscience). Wiley.
Cowen, Zelman. British Commonwealth of Nations in a Changing World: Law, Politics & Prospects. LC 65-12096. (Julius Rosenthal Memorial Lecture Ser: 1964). Repr. of 1965 ed. 24.20 (ISBN 0-8357-9448-2, 2015292). Bks Demand UMI.
Cowen, Zelman & Carter, P. B. Essays on the Law of Evidence. LC 72-11327. 278p. 1973. Repr. of 1956 ed. lib. bdg. 18.25x (ISBN 0-8371-6665-9, COEL). Greenwood.
Cowen, Zelman & Zines, Leslie. Federal Jurisdiction in Australia. 2nd ed. 1979. text ed. 39.95x (ISBN 0-19-550556-5). Oxford U Pr.
Cowger, J. F. Friction Ridge Skin: Comparison & Identification of Fingerprints. (Practical Aspects of Criminal & Forensic Investigation Ser.: Vol. 2). 220p. 1983. 41.75 (ISBN 0-444-00770-9). Elsevier.
Cowgill, et al. History of Laguna De Petenixil: A Small Lake in Northern Guatemala. (Connecticut Academy of Arts Sciences Memoirs Ser.: Vol. 17). (Illus.). 126p. 1966. pap. 15.00 (ISBN 0-208-00784-9). Shoe String.
Cowgill, Carol. Adult Confession: Conversion in Process. 80p. 1984. pap. 3.50 (ISBN 0-697-02030-4). Wm C Brown.
Cowgill, Donald O. Aging Around the World: An Examination of Modernization & Aging. LC 85-7174. 200p. 1985. pap. text ed. write for info (ISBN 0-534-05166-9). Wadsworth Pub.
Cowgill, George R. The Vitamin B: Requirements of Man. 1934. 49.50x (ISBN 0-686-50034-2). Elliots Bks.
Cowgill, George R., jt. auth. see Marxer, Webster L.
Cowgill, Joy. Wagon Train Nineteen Fifty-Eight. (Illus.). 78p. 1980. pap. 5.00 (ISBN 0-916552-21-7). Acoma Bks.
Cowgill, Robert W. & Pardee, Arthur B. Experiments in Biochemical Research Technique. 189p. 1957. 9.50 (ISBN 0-471-18084-X, Pub. by Wiley). Krieger.
Cowgill, Ursula M. Soil Fertility & the Ancient Maya. (Connecticut Academy of Arts & Sciences Transactions Ser.: Vol. 42). 56p. 1961. 12.00 (ISBN 0-317-03798-6). Shoe String.
Cowherd, Raymond G. The Humanitarians & the Ten Hour Movement in England. (Kress Library Publications: No. 10). (Illus.). 1956. pap. 8.95x (ISBN 0-678-09905-7, Baker Lib). Kelley.
--Political Economists & the English Poor Laws: A Historical Study of the Influence of Classical Economics on the Formation of Social Welfare Policy. LC 76-8301. xvii, 300p. 1977. 22.00x (ISBN 0-8214-0233-1, 82-82352). Ohio U Pr.
Cowhey, Peter F. The Problems of Plenty: Energy Policy & International Politics. LC 83-9275. (Science, Technology & the Changing World Order Ser.). 375p. 1985. 36.00x (ISBN 0-520-04693-5). U of Cal Pr.
Cowhey, Peter F. see Aronson, Jonathan D.
Cowie, A. P. & Mackin, Ronald. Oxford Dictionary of Current Idiomatic English: Verbs with Prepositions & Particles, Vol. 1. 1975. 15.00x (ISBN 0-19-431145-7). Oxford U Pr.
Cowie, A. P., et al. Oxford Dictionary of Current Idiomatic English: Phrase, Clause & Sentence Idioms. 448p. 1983. 18.00x (ISBN 0-19-431150-3). Oxford U Pr.
Cowie, A. T., et al. Hormonal Control of Lactation. (Monographs on Endocrinology: Vol. 15). (Illus.). 320p. 1980. 58.00 (ISBN 0-387-09680-9). Springer-Verlag.
Cowie, Alexander. John Trumbull, Connecticut Wit. LC 72-4233. 230p. 1972. Repr. of 1936 ed. lib. bdg. 18.75x (ISBN 0-8371-6094-4, COJT). Greenwood.
Cowie, Frederick J. Pioneers of Catholic Europe. LC 84-62160. 190p. 1985. pap. 6.95 (ISBN 0-87973-713-1, 713). Our Sunday Visitor.

Cowie, Helen, ed. The Development of Children's Imaginative Writing. LC 83-13970. 256p. 1984. 25.00x (ISBN 0-312-19743-8). St Martin.

Cowie, J. M. Polymers: Chemistry & Physics of Modern Materials. (Illus.). 1973. pap. text ed. 27.50x (ISBN 0-7002-0222-6). Intl Ideas.

Cowie, J. M., ed. Alternating Copolymers. (Specialty Polymers Ser.). 294p. 1985. 47.50x (ISBN 0-306-41779-0, Plenumn Pr). Plenum Pub.

Cowie, L. W. Sixteenth Century Europe: The Renaissance & Its Effects. (Illus.). 340p. (Orig.). (gr. 9-12). 1977. pap. text ed. 13.50 (ISBN 0-05-002828-6). Longman.

Cowie, Leonard W. Hanoverian England, 1714-1837. (Bell Modern History Ser.). 1967. text ed. 18.50x o.p (ISBN 0-7135-0234-7); pap. text ed. 15.00x (ISBN 0-7135-0235-5). Humanities.

Cowie, Marian L., ed. see Schott, Peter.

Cowie, Murray A., ed. see Schott, Peter.

Cowie, Peter. The Cinema of Orson Welles. (Quality Paperbacks Ser.). (Illus.). 262p. 1983. pap. 9.95 (ISBN 0-306-80201-5). Da Capo.

--Ingmar Bergman: A Critical Biography. (Illus.). 352p. 1982. 19.95 (ISBN 0-684-17771-4, ScribT). Scribner.

--Ingmar Bergman: A Critical Biography. (Illus.). 416p. 1983. pap. 9.95 (ISBN 0-684-18032-4, ScribT). Scribner.

--International Film Guide: 1984. (Tantivy). (Illus.). 496p. 1983. pap. 11.95 (ISBN 0-900730-15-3). NY Zoetrope.

--World Filmography, Vol.1. 35.00 (ISBN 0-8453-1565-X). Cornwall Bks.

--World Filmography, Vol.2. 35.00 (ISBN 0-8453-1569-2). Cornwall Bks.

Cowie, Peter, ed. International Film Guide 1983. (International Film Guide Ser.). (Illus.). 496p. 1983. pap. 10.95 (ISBN 0-900730-00-5). NY Zoetrope.

--International Film Guide, 1985. (Illus.). 500p. 1985. pap. 12.95 (ISBN 0-900730-22-6, Pub. by Tantivy). NY Zoetrope.

Cowie, Valerie, jt. auth. see Slater, Eliot.

Cowie, Vera. Rich & the Mighty. LC 84-21165. 408p. 1985. 16.95 (ISBN 0-385-19931-7). Doubleday.

Cowin, S. C., ed. Mechanical Properties of Bone. (AMD Ser.: Vol. 45). 238p. 1981. 20.00 (ISBN 0-686-34477-4, G00203). ASME.

--Mechanics Applied to the Transport of Bulk Materials AMD, Vol. 31, Bk. No. G00146. 140p. 1979. 20.00 (ISBN 0-686-58131-8). ASME.

Cowin, Stephen C. & Carroll, Michael M., eds. The Effects of Voids on Material Deformation: AMD, Vol. 16. 192p. 1976. pap. 20.00 (ISBN 0-685-68907-7, I00101). ASME.

Cowing, Cedric B. Populists, Plungers, & Progressives: A Social History of Stock & Commodity Speculation, 1890-1936. LC 65-12988. (Orig.). 1965. 32.00 (ISBN 0-691-04555-0); pap. 9.95 (ISBN 0-691-00563-X). Princeton U Pr.

Cowing, Susan B., tr. see Coedes, G.

Cowing, T. G. & Stevenson, R. E., eds. Productivity Measurement in Regulated Industries. LC 80-1685. (Economic Theory, Econometrics & Mathematical Economic Ser.). 1981. 53.50 (ISBN 0-12-194080-2). Acad Pr.

Cowing, Thomas G. & McFadden, Daniel L. Microeconomics Modeling & Policy Analysis: Studies in Residential Energy Demand. LC 84-6296. (Economic Theory, Econometrics & Mathematical Economics Ser.). 1984. 49.50 (ISBN 0-12-194060-8). Acad Pr.

Cowitt, Philip, ed. see International Currency Analysis.

Cowl, R. P. An Anthology of Imaginative Prose. 1977. 15.00 (ISBN 0-89984-171-6). Century Bookbindery.

Cowl, R. R. Theory of Poetry in England: Its Development in Doctrines & Ideas from the 16th to the 19th Century. LC 75-90366. 1970. Repr. of 1914 ed. 12.00x (ISBN 0-87753-009-2). Phaeton.

Cowl, Richard P. Theory of Poetry in England from the 16th to the 19th Century. 59.95 (ISBN 0-8490-1190-6). Gordon Pr.

Cowle, Jerry. How to Survive Getting Fired - & Win! 224p. 1980. pap. 2.50 (ISBN 0-446-91717-6). Warner Bks.

Cowles, C. S. Family Journey Into Joy. 168p. 1982. pap. 3.95 (ISBN 0-8341-0803-8). Beacon Hill.

Cowles, Fleur. All Too True: Twenty-Nine True Stories that Might Have Been Invented. (Illus.). 156p. 1983. 13.95 (ISBN 0-7043-2327-3, Pub. by Quartet Bks). Merrimack Pub Cir.

--The Flower Game. (Illus.). 140p. 1983. 15.95 (ISBN 0-688-02055-0). Morrow.

--The Love of Tiger Flower. LC 80-20301. (Illus.). 1980. 9.95 (ISBN 0-688-03737-2). Morrow.

Cowles, Fleur, jt. auth. see Vavra, Robert.

Cowles, G. S., jt. auth. see Harrison, C. J.

Cowles, George. The Accessible Wilderness. 96p. (Orig.). 1985. pap. write for info. (ISBN 0-934318-50-6). Falcon Pr MT.

Cowles, H. Robert. Opening the Old Testament. LC 80-65149. (Illus.). 158p. (Orig.). 1980. pap. 4.50 (ISBN 0-87509-279-9); Leader's Guide. 2.95 (ISBN 0-87509-283-7). Chr Pubns.

--Operation Heartbeat. 1976. pap. 3.95 (ISBN 0-87509-115-6). Chr Pubns.

Cowles, Julia. The Diaries of Julia Cowles. Mosely, ed. 1931. 42.50x (ISBN 0-685-89746-X). Elliots Bks.

Cowles, Lawrence G. Transistor Circuit Design. (Illus.). 432p. 1972. 34.95 (ISBN 0-13-930032-5). P-H.

Cowles, Linn Ann. An Index & Guide to an Autobiography: The 1943 Edition, by Frank Lloyd Wright. 1977. spiral bdg. 12.00 (ISBN 0-686-20613-4). Greenwich Des.

Cowles, Milly, jt. auth. see Walsh, Kevin.

Cowles, N. Robert. Opening the New Testament. LC 84-72468. 158p. (Orig.). 1985. pap. write for info (ISBN 0-87509-357-4); leader's guide 2.95 (ISBN 0-87509-358-2). Chr Pubns.

Cowles, Raymond B. Zulu Journal: Field Notes of a Naturalist in South Africa. LC 59-8760. 1959. pap. 1.95 (ISBN 0-520-00276-8, CAL73). U of Cal Pr.

Cowles, Raymond B. & Bakker, Elna S. Desert Journal: Reflections of a Naturalist. 1977. 14.95 (ISBN 0-520-02879-1); pap. 4.95 (ISBN 0-520-03636-0). U of Cal Pr.

Cowles, V. Phantom Major. LC 79-21890. Repr. of 1958 ed. 15.95 (ISBN 0-89201-088-6). Zenger Pub.

Cowles, Virginia. The Great Marlborough & His Duchess. (Illus.). 476p. 1983. 19.95 (ISBN 0-02-528580-7). Macmillan.

--Romanovs. LC 78-156516. (Illus.). 1971. 20.00 (ISBN 0-06-010908-4, HarpT). Har-Row.

--Rugged Ragged Warriors. 320p. 1985. pap. 3.50 (ISBN 0-553-24882-0). Bantam.

Cowles, Willard B. Treaties & Constitutional Law: Property Interferences & Due Process of Law. LC 75-18356. xv, 315p. 1975. Repr. of 1941 ed. lib. bdg. 22.50x (ISBN 0-8371-8316-2, COTC). Greenwood.

Cowley. The Silent One. LC 80-21853. (Illus.). (gr. 4-6). 1981. PLB 8.99 (ISBN 0-394-94761-4). Knopf.

Cowley, jt. auth. see Bode, Ed C.

Cowley, see Yuen, Ko, pseud.

Cowley, A. E. The Hittites. (British Academy, London; Schweich Lectures on Biblical Archaeology Series, 1918). pap. 19.00 (ISBN 0-317-15760-4). Kraus Repr.

Cowley, A. E., ed. see Gesunius, William.

Cowley, Abraham. Complete Works in Verse & Prose. Grosart, Alexander B., ed. LC 73-31054. (Chertsey Worthies' Library: No. 7). 1881. Set. 57.50 (ISBN 0-404-50297-0). Vol. 1 (ISBN 0-404-50390-X). Vol. 2 (ISBN 0-404-50391-8). AMS Pr.

--Cowley: Selected Poetry. Taaffe, James G., ed. LC 79-102036. (Crofts Classics Ser.). 1970. pap. text ed. 1.25x (ISBN 0-88295-027-4). Harlan Davidson.

--Essays, Plays & Sundry Verses. 499p. Repr. of 1906 ed. 69.00x (ISBN 0-403-04057-4). Somerset Pub.

--The Mistress with Other Select Poems. Sparrow, John, ed. LC 72-192025. lib. bdg. 25.00 (ISBN 0-8414-2387-3). Folcroft.

--Poetry & Prose. 1979. Repr. of 1949 ed. lib. bdg. 25.00 (ISBN 0-8495-0927-0). Arden Lib.

Cowley, Alan H., ed. Compounds Containing Phosphorus-Phosphorus Bonds. LC 72-90631. (Benchmark Papers in Inorganic Chemistry Ser: Vol. 3). 322p. 1973. 52.50 (ISBN 0-87933-017-1). Van Nos Reinhold.

--Rings, Clusters, & Polymers of the Main Group Elements. LC 83-15462. (ACS Symposium Ser.: No. 232). 182p. 1983. lib. bdg. 32.95x (ISBN 0-8412-0801-8). Am Chemical.

Cowley, Arthur E., ed. The Samaritan Liturgy, 2 vols. LC 77-87608. Repr. of 1909 ed. Set. 65.00 (ISBN 0-404-16430-7). AMS Pr.

Cowley, Au-Deane S. Family Integration & Mental Health. LC 78-62234. 1978. soft cover 10.00 (ISBN 0-88247-539-8). R & E Pubs.

Cowley, Charles R. Theory of Stellar Spectra. (Topics in Astrophysics & Space Physics Ser.). 272p. 1970. 67.25 (ISBN 0-677-02400-2). Gordon.

Cowley, David. Moulded & Slip Cast Pottery. (Illus.). 120p. 1984. pap. 9.95 (ISBN 0-7134-0972-X, Pub. by Batsford England). David & Charles.

Cowley, Deborah & Serour, Aleya, eds. Cairo: A Practical Guide with Directory & Maps. 5th ed. 1985. 12.95x (ISBN 977-424-024-3, Pub. by Am Univ Cairo Pr). Columbia U Pr.

Cowley, F. G. The Monastic Order in South Wales: 1066-1349. (Studies in Welsh History: No. 1). 325p. 1977. text ed. 32.00x (ISBN 0-7083-0648-9, Pub. by Univ of Wales Pr England). Humanities.

Cowley, G., jt. auth. see MacPhee, I.

Cowley, Hannah. The Plays of Hannah Cowley, 2 vols. Link, Frederick M., ed. LC 78-66646. (Eighteenth-Century English Drama Ser.: Vol. 12). 1980. Set. lib. bdg. 145.00 (ISBN 0-8240-3586-0); lib. bdg. 50.00 ea. Garland Pub.

Cowley, J. Health Education in Schools. 1981. text ed. 26.50 (ISBN 0-06-318178-9, Pub. by Har-Row England Ltd); pap. text ed. 15.50 (ISBN 0-06-318179-7). Har-Row.

Cowley, J. M. Diffraction Physics. 2nd, rev. ed. 1981. 68.00 (ISBN 0-444-86121-1). Elsevier.

Cowley, J. M., et al, eds. Modulated Structures - 1979. LC 79-53846. (AIP Conference Preceedings: No. 53). (Illus.). 1979. lib. bdg. 22.00 (ISBN 0-88318-152-5). Am Inst Physics.

Cowley, James C., jt. auth. see David, Kenneth G.

Cowley, John. The Management of Polytechnic Libraries. 230p. 1985. text ed. write for info. (ISBN 0-566-03525-1). Gower Pub Co.

--Personnel Management in Libraries. 112p. 1982. 13.00 (ISBN 0-85157-324-X, Pub. by Bingley England). Shoe String.

Cowley, John D. Bibliographical Description & Cataloguing. LC 71-122837. (Bibliography & Reference Ser.: No. 341). 1970. Repr. of 1949 ed. lib. bdg. 19.00 (ISBN 0-8337-0708-6). B Franklin.

--Bibliography of Abridgments, Digests, Dictionaries & Indexes of English Law to the Year Eighteen Hundred. LC 79-54199. (Illus.). 1979. Repr. of 1932 ed. lib. bdg. 85.00x (ISBN 0-912004-15-0). W W Gaunt.

Cowley, John M. Diffraction Physics. 2nd, rev. ed. (Personal Library: Vol. 1). 430p. 1985. pap. 27.95 (ISBN 0-444-86925-5, North-Holland). Elsevier.

Cowley, Joy. The Growing Season. LC 77-81785. 7.95 (ISBN 0-385-04449-6). Doubleday.

Cowley, Malcolm. And I Worked at the Writer's Trade. 1978. 12.50 (ISBN 0-670-12291-2). Viking.

--And I Worked at the Writer's Trade: Chapters of Literary History, 1918-1978. 1979. pap. 5.95 (ISBN 0-14-005075-2). Penguin.

--The Dream of the Golden Mountains. (Illus.). 1980. 14.95 (ISBN 0-670-28474-2). Viking.

--The Dream of the Golden Mountains: Remembering the 1930's. 344p. 1981. pap. 5.95 (ISBN 0-14-005919-9). Penguin.

--Exile's Return: A Literary Odyssey of the 1920's. 1976. pap. 6.95 (ISBN 0-14-004392-6). Penguin.

--Exile's Return: A Literary Odyssey of the 1920's. 1983. 11.75 (ISBN 0-8446-6053-1). Peter Smith.

--The Faulkner-Cowley File: Letters & Memories, 1944-1962. 1978. pap. 3.95 (ISBN 0-14-004684-4). Penguin.

--The Flower & the Leaf: A Contemporary Record of American Writing since 1941. Faulkner, Donald W., ed. LC 83-40645. 416p. 1985. 25.00 (ISBN 0-670-32009-9). Viking.

--Many-Windowed House: Collected Essays on American Writers & American Writing. Piper, Henry D., ed. LC 74-112384. 297p. 1970. 14.95x (ISBN 0-8093-0444-9). S Ill U Pr.

--Many-Windowed House: Collected Essays on American Writers & American Writing. Piper, Henry D., ed. LC 72-11923. (Arcturus Books Paperbacks). 297p. 1973. pap. 6.95 (ISBN 0-8093-0626-3). S Ill U Pr.

--A Second Flowering: Works & Days of the Lost Generation. 1980. pap. 5.95 (ISBN 0-14-005498-7). Penguin.

--A Second Flowering: Works & Days of the Lost Generation. (Illus.). 320p. 1973. 10.95 (ISBN 0-670-62826-3). Viking.

--Think Back on Us. A Contemporary Chronicle of the 1930s. Piper, Henry D., ed. LC 67-10024. 416p. 1967. 19.95x (ISBN 0-8093-0232-2). S Ill U Pr.

--Think Back on Us. A Contemporary Chronicle of the 1930s: The Literary Record. Piper, Henry D., ed. LC 72-5606. (Arcturus Books Paperbacks). 210p. (Pt. 2 of the hardbound ed. of Think Back On Us). 1972. pap. 7.95 (ISBN 0-8093-0599-2). S Ill U Pr.

--Think Back on Us. A Contemporary Chronicle of the 1930s: The Social Record. Piper, Henry D., ed. LC 72-5606. (Arcturus Books Paperbacks). 213p. (Pt. 1 of the hardbound ed. of Think Back On Us). 1972. pap. 7.95 (ISBN 0-8093-0598-4). S Ill U Pr.

--Unshaken Friend: A Profile of Maxwell Perkins. 1985. 8.95 (ISBN 0-911797-15-7). R Rinehart Inc.

--The View from Eighty. 1982. pap. 4.95 (ISBN 0-14-006050-2). Penguin.

--The View from Eighty. 96p. 1980. 6.95 (ISBN 0-670-74614-2). Viking.

Cowley, Malcolm, ed. The Portable Faulkner: Anthology. rev. ed. 1967. 14.95 (ISBN 0-670-31002-6). Viking.

--Writers at Work: The Paris Review Interviews, First Series, Vol. 1. 1977. pap. 7.95 (ISBN 0-14-004540-6). Penguin.

Cowley, Malcolm & Smith, Bernard, eds. Books That Changed Our Minds. facs. ed. LC 72-128230. (Essay Index Reprint Ser). 1939. 20.00 (ISBN 0-8369-1912-2). Ayer Co Pubs.

Cowley, Malcolm, jt. ed. see Bode, Carl.

Cowley, Malcolm, ed. see Emerson, Ralph Waldo.

Cowley, Malcolm, ed. see Faulkner, William.

Cowley, Malcolm, ed. see Hawthorne, Nathaniel.

Cowley, Malcolm, jt. ed. see Josephson, Hannah.

Cowley, Malcolm, ed. see Whitman, Walt.

Cowley, R. A., jt. auth. see Bruce, A. D.

Cowley, R. Adams & Trump, Benjamin F. Pathophysiology of Shock, Anoxia & Ischemia. 722p. 1981. 79.00 (ISBN 0-683-02149-4). Williams & Wilkins.

Cowley, R. Adams, ed. Shock Trauma-Critical Care Manual. (Illus.). 616p. 1982. text ed. 50.00 (ISBN 0-8391-1712-4). Univ Park.

Cowley, Robert L. Hogarth's "Marriage A-La-Mode". LC 82-70749. (Illus.). 192p. 1983. 48.50x (ISBN 0-8014-1525-X). Cornell U Pr.

Cowley, Roger W. The Traditional Interpretation of the Apocalypse of St. John in the Ethiopian Orthodox Church. LC 82-19834. (University of Cambridge Oriental Publications Ser.: No. 33). 480p. 1983. 72.50 (ISBN 0-521-24561-3). Cambridge U Pr.

Cowley, Stewart. Space Flight. (Gateway Fact Bks.). (Illus.). 96p. (gr. 4-6). 1982. PLB 8.90 (ISBN 0-531-09204-6, Warwick). Watts.

--Spacebase 2000. (Illus.). 192p. 1985. pap. 14.95 (ISBN 0-312-74940-6). St Martin.

Cowley, W. H. Presidents, Professors, & Trustees: The Evolution of American Academic Government. Williams, Donald T., Jr., ed. LC 79-92461. (Higher Education Ser.). 1980. text ed. 19.95x (ISBN 0-87589-448-8). Jossey-Bass.

Cowling, A. G. & Mailer, C. J. Managing Human Resources. (Illus.). 256p. 1981. pap. text ed. 24.95x (ISBN 0-7131-0569-0). Intl Ideas.

Cowling, E. B., jt. ed. see Horsfall, J. G.

Cowling, E. R., jt. ed. see Horsfall, J. G.

Cowling, Elizabeth. The Cello. LC 74-16824. (Illus.). 218p. 1975. 15.00 (ISBN 0-684-14127-2, ScribT). Scribner.

--The Cello: New Edition. (Illus.). 240p. 1983. 17.95 (ISBN 0-684-17870-2, ScribT). Scribner.

Cowling, Ellis B., jt. ed. see Horsfall, James G.

Cowling, George. Essays in the Use of English. 1973. Repr. of 1934 ed. 25.00 (ISBN 0-8274-1517-6). R West.

Cowling, George H. Chaucer. facsimile ed. LC 74-150179. (Select Bibliographies Reprint Ser). Repr. of 1927 ed. 16.00 (ISBN 0-8369-5692-3). Ayer Co Pubs.

--Music on the Shakespearian Stage. LC 74-24063. Repr. of 1913 ed. 10.00 (ISBN 0-404-12889-0). AMS Pr.

--Shelley, & Other Essays. facs. ed. LC 67-23198. (Essay Index Reprint Ser). 1936. 17.00 (ISBN 0-8369-0344-7). Ayer Co Pubs.

Cowling, K., et al. Resource Structure of Agriculture: An Economic Analysis. LC 70-114570. 1970. 28.00 (ISBN 0-08-015585-5). Pergamon.

Cowling, Keith. Monopoly Capitalism. LC 81-7215. 192p. 1982. 27.95x (ISBN 0-470-27288-0). Halsted Pr.

Cowling, Maurice. Eighteen Sixty-Seven: Disraeli, Gladstone & Revolution. (Cambridge Studies in the History & Theory of Politics). 1967. 57.50 (ISBN 0-521-04740-4). Cambridge U Pr.

--The Impact of Hitler: British Politics & British Policy 1933-1940. LC 74-12968. (Cambridge Studies in the History & Theory of Politics). 448p. 1975. 67.50 (ISBN 0-521-20582-4). Cambridge U Pr.

--The Impact of Hitler: British Politics & British Policy, 1933-1940. 1977. pap. 7.95x (ISBN 0-226-11660-3, P747, Phoen). U of Chicago Pr.

--Mill & Liberalism. LC 63-25851. pap. 44.80 (ISBN 0-317-08783-5, 2051498). Bks Demand UMI.

--The Nature & Limits of Political Science. LC 85-12591. viii, 214p. 1985. Repr. of 1963 ed. lib. bdg. 37.50x (ISBN 0-313-24949-0, CNLI). Greenwood.

--Religion & Public Doctrine in Modern England. (Cambridge Studies in the History & Theory of Politics). 498p. 1981. 59.50 (ISBN 0-521-23289-9). Cambridge U Pr.

Cowling, T. G. Magnetohydrodynamics. Meadows, A. J., ed. (Mas 2). 1976. 32.00 (ISBN 0-9960026-5-0, Pub. by A Hilger England). Heyden.

Cowling, T. G., jt. auth. see Chapman, S.

Cowling, T. M. & Steeley, G. C. Sub-Regional Planning Studies: An Evaluation. LC 73-4476. 1973. text ed. 19.00 (ISBN 0-08-017019-6). Pergamon.

Cowlishaw, Michael F. REXX Language. 176p. 1985. pap. text ed. 21.95 (ISBN 0-13-780735-X). P-H.

Cowman, Charles E. Streams in the Desert Sampler. 128p. 1983. pap. 3.95 (ISBN 0-310-37651-3). Zondervan.

Cowman, Charles E. & Serrano, Antonio. Manantiales en el Desierto. Orig. Title: Stream in the Desert. 1985. pap. 4.95 (ISBN 0-311-40028-0, Edit Mundo). Casa Bautista.

Cowman, Mrs. Charles E. Cumbres De Inspiracion. Robleto, Adolfo, tr. 1982. pap. 4.25 (ISBN 0-311-40026-4). Casa Bautista.

--Mountain Trailways for Youth: Devotions for Young People. 1979. pap. 4.95 (ISBN 0-310-37641-6). Zondervan.

--Springs in the Valley. 1977. large-print ed. kivar 8.95 (ISBN 0-310-22517-5). Zondervan.

--Streams in the Desert. 1974. large print kiver 8.95 (ISBN 0-310-22527-2). Zondervan.

--Streams in the Desert, Vol. 1. 9.95 (ISBN 0-310-22520-5, Pub. by Cowman). Zondervan.

--Streams in the Desert, Vol. 2. 9.95 (ISBN 0-310-22530-2, Pub. by Cowman). Zondervan.

--Streams in the Desert, Vol. 2. large print ed. 384p. 1976. 8.95 (ISBN 0-310-22537-X). Zondervan.

--Traveling Toward Sunrise. large print ed. 272p. 1975. 8.95 (ISBN 0-310-22547-7). Zondervan.

--Words of Comfort & Cheer. pap. 5.95 (ISBN 0-310-22551-5). Zondervan.

Cowman, Mrs. Charles E., ed. Springs in the Valley. 2nd ed. 384p. 1980. pap. 4.95 (ISBN 0-310-22511-6). Zondervan.

Cowper, A. D., tr. see Einstein, Albert.

Cowper, Ann & Young, Cyril. Family Planning: Fundamentals for Health Professionals. (Illus.). 160p. 1981. (Pub. by Croom Helm Ltd); pap. 11.50 (ISBN 0-85664-908-2). Longwood Pub Group.

Cowper, C. J. & Derose, A. J. The Analysis of Gases by Chromatography. LC 83-6207. (Pergamon Series in Analytical Chemistry: Vol. 7). (Illus.). 159p. 1983. 25.00 (ISBN 0-08-024027-5). Pergamon.

Cowper, H. S. The Art of Attack. (Illus.). 1977. Repr. of 1906 ed. 24.00x (ISBN 0-7158-1212-2). Charles River Bks.

--The Art of Attack: Being a Study in the Development of Weapons & Appliances of Offence, from the Earliest Times to the Age of Gunpowder. (Illus.). 312p. 1977. Repr. of 1906 ed. 21.50x (ISBN 0-8476-6061-3). Rowman.

Cowper, J. M. & Manning, Robert, eds. Mediations on the Supper of Our Lord. (EETS, OS Ser.: No. 60). Repr. of 1875 ed. 15.00 (ISBN 0-527-00054-X). Kraus Repr.

Cowper, J. M., ed. see Crowley, Robert.

Cowper, J. M., ed. see Starkey, Thomas.

Cowper, John & Powys, LLewelyn. Confessions of Two Brothers. 272p. 1982. 45.00x (ISBN 0-86300-004-5, Pub. by Sinclair Browne Arch England). State Mutual Bk.

Cowper, Richard. Clone. 1979. pap. 1.75 (ISBN 0-671-82543-7, Timescape). PB.

--The Custodians & Other Stories. 191p. 1985. 11.95 (ISBN 0-575-02096-2, Pub. by Gollancz England). David & Charles.

--The Tithonian Factor. 150p. 1984. 14.95 (ISBN 0-575-03440-8, Pub. by Gollancz). David & Charles.

Cowper, W. Correspondence of William Cowper, 4 Vols. LC 68-24904. (English Biography Ser., No. 31). 1969. Repr. of 1904 ed. lib. bdg. 119.95 (ISBN 0-8383-0156-8). Haskell.

Cowper, William. Correspondence, Arranged in Chronological Order, 4 Vols. Wright, Thomas, ed. LC 68-58329. (BCL Ser. I). Repr. of 1904 ed. Set. 59.50 (ISBN 0-404-01830-0). AMS Pr.

--Correspondence of William Cowper, 4 Vols. Wright, Thomas, ed. (Illus.). 1970. Repr. of 1904 ed. Set. 59.00 (ISBN 0-403-00203-6). Scholarly.

--The Letters & Prose Writings of William Cowper, Vol. III: Letters, 1787-1791. King, James & Ryskamp, Charles, eds. (Illus.). 1982. 84.00x (ISBN 0-19-812608-5). Oxford U Pr.

--The Letters & Prose Writings of William Cowper, Vol. I, 1750-1781 & Vol. II, 1782-1786. King, James & Ryskamp, Charles, eds. (Illus.). 1979. 69.00x (ISBN 0-19-811863-5); Vol. II, 1981 98.00x (ISBN 0-19-812607-7). Oxford U Pr.

--Letters of William Cowper, 2 Vols. facsimile ed. Frazer, J. G., ed. LC 70-103647. (Select Bibliographies Reprint Ser). 1912. Set. 55.00 (ISBN 0-8369-5147-6). Ayer Co Pubs.

--The Poems of William Cowper, Vol. I: 1748 - 1782. Baird, John D. & Ryskamp, Charles, eds. (English Texts Ser.). (Illus.). 1980. text ed. 79.00x (ISBN 0-19-811875-9). Oxford U Pr.

--The Poetical Works of William Cowper. 4th ed. Milford, H. S., ed. LC 75-41066. (BCL Ser. II). Repr. of 1934 ed. 42.50 (ISBN 0-404-14525-6). AMS Pr.

--Works of William Cowper, 15 Vols. Southey, Robert, ed. LC 71-18097. Repr. of 1837 ed. Set. 525.00 (ISBN 0-404-01840-8); 35.00 ea. AMS Pr.

Cowperthwaite, Gordon, et al. College Without Walls. 1984. pap. text ed. 8.50 (ISBN 0-89917-423-X). Tichenor Pub.

Cowser, K. E. & Richmond, C. R., eds. Synthetic Fossil Fuel Technologies. (Illus.). 632p. 1984. text ed. 85.00 (ISBN 0-250-40624-1). Butterworth.

Cowsik, R., ed. see COSPAR, Twenty-Second Plenary Meeting, Bangalore, India, 1979.

Cox. Natural Gas Hydrates. 1983. text ed. 29.95 (ISBN 0-250-40631-4). Butterworth.

--Understanding Zoo Animals. (Animal World Ser.). (gr. 3-6). 1980. 7.95 (ISBN 0-86020-250-X, Usborne-Hayes); PLB 12.95 (ISBN 0-88110-092-7); pap. 4.95 (ISBN 0-86020-251-8). EDC.

Cox & Cohen. Methodological Issues for Health Care Surveys. (Statistics: Textbooks & Monographs). 456p. 1985. 65.00 (ISBN 0-8247-7323-3). Dekker.

Cox & Cork. Birds. (First Nature Book). (gr. 2-5). 1980. 6.95 (ISBN 0-86020-476-6, Usborne-Hayes); PLB 11.95 (ISBN 0-88110-072-2); pap. 2.95 (ISBN 0-86020-475-8). EDC.

--Butterflies & Moths. (First Nature Bks.). (gr. 2-5). 1980. 6.95 (ISBN 0-86020-478-2, Usborne-Hayes); PLB 11.95 (ISBN 0-88110-073-0); pap. 2.95 (ISBN 0-86020-477-4). EDC.

--First Book of Nature. (First Nature Book). (gr. 2-5). 1980. 10.95 (ISBN 0-86020-483-9, Usborne-Hayes). EDC.

--Flowers. (First Nature Books). (gr. 2-5). 1980. 6.95 (ISBN 0-86020-480-4, Usborne-Hayes); PLB 11.95 (ISBN 0-88110-074-9); pap. 2.95 (ISBN 0-86020-479-0). EDC.

Cox, jt. auth. see Enis.

Cox, jt. auth. see Thompson.

Cox, ed. Phytoflagellates. (Developments in Marine Biology Ser.: Vol. 2). 474p. 1980. 76.50 (ISBN 0-444-00363-0, Biomedical Pr). Elsevier.

Cox, Albert W. Sonar & Underwater Sound. LC 74-15547. (Illus.). 1975. 24.00x (ISBN 0-669-95935-9). Lexington Bks.

Cox, Allan. The Cox Report on the American Corporation. 448p. 1982. 21.95 (ISBN 0-385-28177-3). Delacorte.

--The Making of the Achiever: How to Win Distinction in your Company. 288p. 1985. 16.95 (ISBN 0-396-08471-0). Dodd.

Cox, Allan & Hart, Robert B. Plate Tectonics: The Plate Tectonics Game. (Illus.). 350p. 1985. pap. text ed. 14.95 (ISBN 0-86542-313-X). Blackwell Pubns.

Cox, Allan, ed. Plate Tectonics & Geomagnetic Reversals. LC 73-4323. (Geology Ser.). (Illus.). 702p. 1973. text ed. 44.95 (ISBN 0-7167-0259-2); pap. text ed. 30.95 (ISBN 0-7167-0258-4). W H Freeman.

Cox, Alva I., Jr., jt. auth. see O'Connell, William S.

Cox, Alvin J., ed. see International Symposium on Psoriasis-Stanford University, 1971.

Cox, Alwyn & Cox, Angela. Rockingham Pottery & Procelain, 1745-1842. LC 82-25158. (Faber Monographs on Pottery & Porcelain). (Illus.). 240p. 1983. 65.00 (ISBN 0-571-13049-6). Faber & Faber.

Cox, Alwyn see Allen, W. S.

Cox, Alwyn see Milne, John.

Cox, Andrew. Adversary Politics & Land: The Conflict Over Land & Property Policy in Post-War Britain. LC 83-14483. 296p. 1984. 44.50 (ISBN 0-521-25517-1). Cambridge U Pr.

--Politics, Policy & the European Recession. LC 81-14493. 267p. 1982. 25.00 (ISBN 0-312-62949-4). St Martin.

Cox, Andrew, et al. Power in Capitalist Societies: Theory, Explanation & Cases. 224p. 1985. 27.50 (ISBN 0-312-63409-9). St Martin.

Cox, Andrew W., jt. auth. see McKay, David.

Cox, Angela, jt. auth. see Cox, Alwyn.

Cox, Ann R., et al. Child Health Management: Guidelines for Nurse Practitioners. 1985. pap. text ed. 16.95. Reston.

--Steps to Better Health for Children. 1985. pap. 9.95 (ISBN 0-8359-7110-4). Reston.

Cox, Annette. Art-As-Politics: The Abstract Expressionist Avant-Garde & Society. Foster, Stephen, ed. LC 82-4760. (Studies in the Fine Arts: The Avant Garde: No. 26). 216p. 1982. 39.95 (ISBN 0-8357-1318-0). UMI Res Pr.

Cox, Archibald. Freedom of Expression. LC 81-4374. 96p. 1981. 8.95x (ISBN 0-674-31912-5); pap. 2.95 (ISBN 0-674-31913-3). Harvard U Pr.

--Law & the National Labor Policy. (Monograph & Research Ser.: No. 5). 111p. 1960. 5.00 (ISBN 0-89215-007-6). U Cal LA Indus Rel.

--Law & the National Labor Policy. LC 82-20930. 111p. 1983. Repr. of 1960 ed. lib. bdg. 27.50x (ISBN 0-313-23794-8, COLN). Greenwood.

--The Role of the Supreme Court in American Government. x1976 ed. LC 75-29958. 1977. pap. 5.95 (ISBN 0-19-519909-X, 482, GB). Oxford U Pr.

--Warren Court: Constitutional Decision As an Instrument of Reform. LC 68-21971. 1968. pap. 3.95x (ISBN 0-674-94742-8). Harvard U Pr.

Cox, Archibald & Bok, Derek C. Labor Law, Cases & Materials on: 1983 Case Supplement. 9th ed. (University Casebook Ser.). 219p. 1983. pap. text ed. write for info. (ISBN 0-88277-148-5). Foundation Pr.

Cox, Archibald, et al. Civil Rights, the Constitution & the Courts. LC 67-20874. 1967. 7.95x (ISBN 0-674-13300-5). Harvard U Pr.

--Labor Law, Cases & Materials on. 9th ed. LC 81-9731. (University Casebook Ser.). 1215p. 1981. text ed. 25.50 (ISBN 0-88277-027-6). Foundation Pr.

Cox, Arthur. Photographic Optics. 15th ed. (Illus.). 1974. 38.95 (ISBN 0-240-50844-0). Focal Pr.

Cox, B., jt. auth. see Vale, J.

Cox, B., et al, eds. Thermoregulatory Mechanisms & Their Therapeutic Implications: Symposium, 4th, Oxford, July-August, 1979. (Illus.). 1979. 27.75 (ISBN 3-8055-0277-X). S Karger.

Cox, B. G., jt. ed. see Hinshaw, L. B.

Cox, Barbara G. & Macaulay, Janet. Nuevas Fronteras-New Frontiers: Un Programa de Aprendizaje Bilingue para Ninos-A Bilingual Early Learning Program. LC 81-81331. 1982. 636.00 (ISBN 0-08-028280-6). Pergamon.

Cox, Barbara G., ed. Hispanic American Periodicals Index, 1975. LC 75-642408. 1978. lib. bdg. 160.00x (ISBN 0-87903-400-9). UCLA Lat Am Ctr.

--Hispanic American Periodicals Index, 1976. LC 75-642408. 1979. lib. bdg. 160.00x (ISBN 0-87903-401-7). UCLA Lat Am Ctr.

Cox, Barbara G., ed. see International Conference on Hyperbaric Medicine - 3rd - Durham - N. C. - 1965.

Cox, Barry, jt. auth. see Vale, Janet.

Cox, Bernard. Pleasure Steamers. (Illus.). 64p. (Orig.). 1983. 12.50 (ISBN 0-7153-8333-7). David & Charles.

Cox, Bertram, ed. see Smart, George.

Cox, Beverly. Gourmet Minceur: A Week of Gourmet Diet Meals. LC 76-52758. (Illus., Orig.). 1977. pap. 9.95 (ISBN 0-8149-0783-0). Vanguard.

--Minceur Italienne: Slimming Gourmet Menus & Recipes. LC 79-63111. (Gourmet Minceur Ser.). (Illus.). 1979. 9.95 (ISBN 0-8149-0820-9). Vanguard.

Cox, Beverly & Benois, George. Cellulite: Defeat It Through Diet & Exercise. LC 81-1735. (Illus.). 1981. 12.50 (ISBN 0-8149-0845-4); pap. 9.95 (ISBN 0-8149-0846-2). Vanguard.

Cox, Beverly & Whitman, Joan. Cooking Techniques: How to Do Anything a Recipe Tells You to Do. (Illus.). 1981. 29.95 (ISBN 0-316-93752-5). Little.

--Cooking Techniques: How to Do Anything a Recipe Tells You to Do. (Illus.). 544p. pap. 17.45 (ISBN 0-316-93753-3). Little.

Cox, Beverly J. & Anderson, Denna J. Miguel Covarrubias Caricatures. LC 84-22142. (Illus.). 164p. 1985. 24.95 (ISBN 0-87474-340-0, COMC). Smithsonian.

Cox, Bill. The Cameron Aurameter in Action: Step-by-Step Method for Use of the Aurameter in Dowsing. (Illus.). 48p. 1982. perfect stitch 5.75 (ISBN 0-88234-008-5). Life Understanding.

--Techniques of Pendulum Dowsing: Step by Step Method for Use of the Pendulum in Dowsing. (Illus.). 38p. 1971. Saddle-Stitch 3.00 (ISBN 0-88234-006-9). Life Understanding.

--Techniques of Swing-Rod Dowsing: Step-by-Step Method for Use of the Pendulum in Dowsing. (Illus.). 38p. 1971. saddle-stitch 3.00 (ISBN 0-88234-007-7). Life Understanding.

--Unseen Kingdoms: UFOs & Invisible Elemental Forces. (Illus.). 72p. 1983. pap. 9.95 saddle-stitch (ISBN 0-938294-14-8). Global Comm.

Cox, Bill, jt. auth. see Boring, Holland, Sr.

Cox, Bill, ed. see Cameron, Verne L.

Cox, Billy J., jt. auth. see Horsley, F. William.

Cox, Bryan. The Law of Special Educational Needs: A Guide to the Education Act 1981. LC 84-15600. 134p. 1984. 22.50 (ISBN 0-7099-3429-7, Pub. by Croom Helm Ltd). Longwood Pub Group.

Cox, C. B. The Free Spirit: A Study of Liberal Humanism in the Novels of George Eliot, Henry James, E. M. Forster, Virginia Woolf, Angus Wilson. LC 80-13281. 195p. 1980. Repr. of 1963 ed. lib. bdg. 27.50x (ISBN 0-313-22449-8, COFS). Greenwood.

--Joseph Conrad: The Modern Imagination. 191p. 1974. 12.00x (ISBN 0-87471-548-2). Rowman.

Cox, C. B. & Dyson, A. E. Modern Poetry: Studies in Practical Criticism. LC 78-159804. 1971. Repr. of 1963 ed. 39.00x (ISBN 0-403-01306-2). Scholarly.

Cox, C. B. & Moore, P. D. Biogeography: An Ecological & Evolutionary Approach. 4th ed. (Illus.). 272p. 1985. pap. text ed. 19.00x (ISBN 0-632-01332-X). Blackwell Pubns.

Cox, C. B. & Palmer, D. J., eds. Shakespeare's Wide & Universal Stage. LC 84-6061. 240p. 1984. 27.50 (ISBN 0-7190-1075-6, Pub. by Manchester Univ Pr). Longwood Pub Group.

Cox, C. B., jt. ed. see Bellairs, D. A.

Cox, C. Benjamin. The Censorship Game & How to Play It. LC 77-82256. (Bulletin Ser.: No. 50). 1977. pap. 4.20 (ISBN 0-87986-011-1, 498-15258). Nat Coun Soc Studies.

Cox, C. L., ed. see Smart, George.

Cox, C. R. Operation & Control of Water Treatment Processes. (Monograph Ser: No. 49). (Illus.). 390p. (Eng, Fr, Rus, & Span.). 1964. 20.80 (ISBN 92-4-140049-8). World Health.

Cox, C. Robinson. Criminal Justice: Improving Police Report Writing. 280p. 1977. pap. text ed. 8.95x student manual (ISBN 0-8134-1902-6, 1902); instr's. manual 1.75x (ISBN 0-8134-1906-9, 1906). Interstate.

Cox, Carol. The Water in the Pearl. 1982. pap. 4.50 (ISBN 0-914610-28-7). Hanging Loose.

--Woodworking & Places Nearby. 1979. pap. 3.00 (ISBN 0-914610-13-9). Hanging Loose.

Cox, Carol M. Jubilee Time: Celebrating Gods Grace & Justice. 112p. (Orig.). 1984. pap. 8.25 (ISBN 0-687-20609-X). Abingdon.

Cox, Caroline. Sociology: An Introduction for Nurses, Midwives & Health Visitors. 224p. 1983. pap. 16.50 (ISBN 0-407-00231-6). Butterworth.

Cox, Catharine M. The Early Mental Traits of Three Hundred Geniuses. (Genetic Studies of Genius Ser). 1926. 52.50x (ISBN 0-8047-0010-9). Stanford U Pr.

Cox, Charles, jt. auth. see Beck, John.

Cox, Charles & Beck, John, eds. Management Development: Advances in Practice & Theory. 350p. 1984. 39.95x (ISBN 0-471-90388-4). Wiley.

Cox, Charles B., ed. Dylan Thomas: A Collection of Critical Essays. (Illus.). 1966. 12.95 (ISBN 0-13-919381-2, Spec). P-H.

Cox, Charles H. & Cox, Jean W. Wittgenstein's Vision. LC 84-337. 1984. 10.95 (ISBN 0-87212-178-X). Libra.

Cox, Christopher. A Key West Companion. (Illus.). 208p. 1983. 17.95 (ISBN 0-312-45182-2). St Martin.

--A Key West Companion. (Illus.). 224p. 1983. pap. 10.95 (ISBN 0-312-45183-0). St Martin.

Cox, Claude E. The Armenian Translation of Deuteronomy. Stone, Michael E., ed. LC 81-5273. 1981. text ed. 16.50 (ISBN 0-89130-491-6, 21-02-02); pap. text ed. 12.00 (ISBN 0-89130-492-4). Scholars Pr GA.

Cox, Clyde C. Apocalyptic Commentary. 1970. 6.95 (ISBN 0-87148-011-5). Pathway Pr.

--Evangelical Precepts of the Revelation. 1972. 5.95 (ISBN 0-87148-278-9). Pathway Pr.

Cox, D. H. A Third Century Hoard of Tetradrachms from Gordion. (University Museum Monographs: No. 9). (Illus.). v, 20p. 1953. 3.75x (ISBN 0-934718-01-6). Univ Mus of U PA.

Cox, D. R. Analysis of Binary Data. 1970. 15.95 (ISBN 0-412-15340-8, NO.6065, Pub. by Chapman & Hall). Methuen Inc.

--Applied Statistics: Principles & Examples. 1981. 34.00x (ISBN 0-412-16560-0, NO.6549, Pub. by Chapman & Hall); pap. 12.50x (ISBN 0-412-16570-8, NO.6548). Methuen Inc.

--Problems & Solutions in Theoretical Statistics. 1978. pap. 17.50 (ISBN 0-412-15370-X, NO. 6066, Pub. by Chapman & Hall). Methuen Inc.

--Renewal Theory. (Monographs on Statistic & Applied Probability). 1967. pap. 8.95 (ISBN 0-412-20570-X, NO. 6068, Pub. by Chapman & Hall). Methuen Inc.

Cox, D. R. & Hinkley, D. V. Theoretical Statistics. 1979. 21.00x (ISBN 0-412-16160-5, 6069, Pub. by Chapman & Hall). Methuen Inc.

Cox, D. R. & Isham, V. Point Processes. 1980. 18.95 (ISBN 0-412-21910-7, NO. 2962, Pub. by Chapman & Hall England). Methuen Inc.

Cox, D. R. & Lewis, P. A. The Statistical Analysis of Series of Events. (Monographs on Statistics & Applied Probability). 1966. 18.95 (ISBN 0-412-21800-3, 6343, Pub. by Chapman & Hall). Methuen Inc.

Cox, D. R. & Oakes, D. O. Analysis of Survival Data. (Monographs on Statistics & Applied Probabilty). 220p. 1984. 25.00 (ISBN 0-412-24490-X, NO. 6810, Pub. by Chapman & Hall). Methuen Inc.

Cox, D. R. & Smith, W. L. Queues: Receptors & Recognition Series B. Incl. Vol. 13. Receptor Regulation. 59.95 (2245); Vol. 12. Purinergic Receptors. 63.00 (2142); Vol. 11. Membrane Receptors. 49.95 (2156); Vol. 10. Neurotransmitter Receptors, Part 2: Biogenic Amines. 49.95 (49.95); Vol. 9. Neurotransmitter Receptors, Part 1: Amino Acids, Peptides & Benzodiazepines. 49.95 (NO.6456); Vol. 8. Virus Receptors, Part 2: Animal Viruses. 43.00 (NO.6413); Vol. 7. Virus Receptors, Part 1: Bacterial Viruses. 43.00 (NO.6416); Vol. 6. Bacterial Adherence. 69.95 (6453); Vol. 5. Taxis & Behavior. 63.00 (NO.6452); Vol. 4. Specificity of Embryological Interactions. 49.95 (NO.6118); Vol. 3. Microbial Interactions. 49.95 (NO.6236); Vol. 2. Intercellular Junctions & Synapses. 53.00 (NO.6107); Vol. 1. The Specificity & Action of Animal, Bacterial & Plant Toxins. 63.00 (NO. 6078). Pub. by Chapman & Hall England). Methuen Inc.

Cox, David. Ayu & the Perfect Moon. (Illus.). 32p. (ps-k). 1984. pap. 9.95 laminated boards (ISBN 0-370-30533-7, Pub. by the Bodley Head). Merrimack Pub Cir.

--Debussy Orchestral Music. LC 74-19974. (BBC Music Guides). (Illus.). 64p. 1975. pap. 4.95 (ISBN 0-295-95374-8). U of Wash Pr.

--Modern Psychology: The Teachings of Carl Gustav Jung. 1968. pap. 3.95 (ISBN 0-06-463231-8, EH 231, EH). B&N NY.

--Tin Lizzie & Little Nell. (Illus.). 32p. (ps-1). 1984. laminated boards 9.95 (ISBN 0-370-30922-7, Pub. by the Bodley Head). Merrimack Pub Cir.

Cox, David B. & Ernst & Whinney. Energy Resources Tax Reports, 2 vols. LC 83-213523. Date not set. price not set looseleaf. Commerce.

Cox, David R. Planning of Experiments. LC 58-13457. (Probability & Statistics Ser.). (Illus.). 308p. 1958. 48.75x (ISBN 0-471-18183-8). Wiley.

Cox, Deborah & Davis, Juliet. Thirty Days to a Beautiful Bottom. 1982. pap. 2.95 (ISBN 0-553-01472-2). Bantam.

Cox, Dermot. Proverbs, with Introduction to Sapiential Books. (Old Testament Ser.: Vol. 17). 1982. 12.95 (ISBN 0-89453-417-3); pap. 8.95 (ISBN 0-89453-251-0). M Glazier.

Cox, Diane & Peck, Cynthia V. Reading Games in the Classroom. (Illus.). 82p. 1977. pap. text ed. 6.00x (ISBN 0-89061-280-3, 427). Jamestown Pubs.

Cox, Diane L. William Faulkner's "As I Lay Dying": A Critical Casebook. Polk, Noel, ed. LC 82-48496. (Garland Faulkner Casebooks). 246p. 1984. lib. bdg. 45.00 (ISBN 0-8240-9228-7). Garland Pub.

Cox, Don R. Arthur Conan Doyle. LC 84-28050. (Literature & Life Ser.). 250p. 1985. 13.95 (ISBN 0-8044-2146-3). Ungar.

Cox, Don R., jt. auth. see Anderson, W. Steve.

Cox, Don R., ed. Sexuality & Victorian Literature. LC 83-21655. (TSL: No. 27). 280p. 1984. text ed. 21.95x (ISBN 0-87049-424-4); pap. text ed. 10.95x (ISBN 0-87049-438-4). U of Tenn Pr.

Cox, Donald D. Common Flowering Plants of the Northeast. 430p. 1985. lib. bdg. 29.50x (ISBN 0-87395-889-6); pap. text ed. 9.95x (ISBN 0-87395-890-X). State U NY Pr.

Cox, Dorothy. Modern Upholstery. (Illus.). 152p. 1980. pap. 13.50x (ISBN 0-7135-1599-6, LTB). Sportshelf.

Cox, E. Green Count of Savoy, Amadeus Sixth & Transalpine Savoy, in the Fourteenth Century. 1967. 42.00 (ISBN 0-691-05125-9). Princeton U Pr.

Cox, E. G. The Medieval Popular Ballad. 59.95 (ISBN 0-8490-0600-7). Gordon Pr.

Cox, E. M. H. Farrer's Last Journey. LC 76-48121. (Illus.). 1977. Repr. of 1926 ed. write for info (ISBN 0-913728-16-0). Theophrastus.

Cox, E. R. & Bold, H. C. Taxonomic Investigations of Stigeoclonium. (Phycological Studies: No. 7). (Illus.). 1979. pap. text ed. 19.60 (ISBN 3-87429-130-8). Lubrecht & Cramer.

Cox, E. S. Lincoln's Negro Policy. 1982. lib. bdg. 56.95 (ISBN 0-87700-414-5). Revisionist Pr.

--The South's Part in Mongrelizing the Nation. 1982. lib. bdg. 59.95 (ISBN 0-87700-379-3). Revisionist Pr.

Cox, Earnest S. Lincoln's Negro Policy. 1968. 3.00 (ISBN 0-911038-13-2). Noontide.

--Teutonic Unity. 1976. pap. 5.00 (ISBN 0-911038-18-3). Noontide.

Cox, Ed. Waking. 48p. (Orig.). 1977. pap. 2.50 (ISBN 0-917342-56-9). Gay Sunshine.

Cox, Edward F. State & National Voting in Federal Elections, 1910-1970. xv, 280p. 1972. 25.00 (ISBN 0-208-01261-3, Archon). Shoe String.

--Twelve for Twelve. 64p. 1982. pap. 3.50 (ISBN 0-8341-0787-2). Beacon Hill.

Cox, Edward G. Reference Guide to the Literature of Travel, Including Voyages, Geographical Descriptions, Adventures, Shipwrecks & Expeditions, 3 Vols. LC 70-90492. 1935-1949. Repr. Set. lib. bdg. 82.00x (ISBN 0-8371-2506-5, COLT). Greenwood.

Cox, Edward G., tr. see Steenstrup, Johannes C.

Cox, Edward L. Free Coloreds in the Slave Societies of St. Kitts & Grenada, 1763-1833. LC 83-14646. (Illus.). 212p. 1984. text ed. 16.95x (ISBN 0-87049-414-7). U of Tenn Pr.

Cox, Edward W. The Principles of Punishment As Applied in the Administration of the Criminal Law by Judges & Magistrates. LC 83-49234. (Crime & Punishment in England, 1850-1922 Ser.). 226p. 1984. lib. bdg. 30.00 (ISBN 0-8240-6209-4). Garland Pub.

Cox, Edwin B., ed. see Brauns, Robert & Slater, Sarah W.

Cox, Edwin B., et al. The Bank Director's Handbook. (Illus.). 224p. 1981. 27.00 (ISBN 0-86569-056-1). Auburn Hse.

Cox, Eleanor A. Intermezzo, No.14. 224p. 1981. pap. 1.50 (ISBN 0-449-50219-8, Coventry). Fawcett.

--Pegasus. 224p. 1981. pap. 1.95 (ISBN 0-449-50195-7, Coventry). Fawcett.

Cox, Eli P. & Erickson, Leo G. Retail Decentralization. LC 67-63754. 1967. 3.50 (ISBN 0-87744-056-5). Mich St U Pr.

Cox, Eli P., III. Evaluating Complex Business Reports: A Guide for Executives. LC 83-73363. 130p. 1984. 14.95 (ISBN 0-87094-431-2). Dow Jones-Irwin.

Cox, Eli P., 3rd. Marketing Research: Information for Decision Making. 1979. text ed. 24.00 scp (ISBN 0-912212-14-4, HarpC); instr. manual avail. (ISBN 0-06-361361-1). Har-Row.

Cox, Elizabeth. Familiar Ground. LC 84-45055. 205p. 1984. 14.95 (ISBN 0-689-11474-5). Atheneum.

Cox, Erle. Out of the Silence. LC 75-28852. (Classics of Science Fiction Ser.). 1976. 16.00 (ISBN 0-88355-366-X); pap. 5.95 (ISBN 0-88355-451-8). Hyperion Conn.

Cox, Eugene L. The Eagles of Savoy: The House of Savoy in Thirteenth Century Europe. LC 73-16966. 484p. 1974. 49.00 (ISBN 0-691-05216-6). Princeton U Pr.

Cox, Eunice, jt. ed. see Winters, Stanley A.

Cox, Evelyn. Holiday Farm. (Illus.). 192p. 1984. 15.95 (ISBN 0-340-27835-8, Pub. by Hodder & Stoughton UK). David & Charles.

Cox, F. E., ed. Modern Parasitology: A Textbook of Parasitology. (Illus.). 358p. 1982. pap. text ed. 25.00x (ISBN 0-632-00612-9). Blackwell Pubns.

Cox, Frances M. Aging in a Changing Village Society: A Kenyan Experience. (Orig.). 1977. pap. text ed. 3.00 (ISBN 0-910473-03-X). Intl Fed Ageing.

Cox, Francis A. The Life of Philip Melanchthon. LC 83-45641. Date not set. Repr. of 1815 ed. 72.50 (ISBN 0-404-19824-4). AMS Pr.

Cox, Frank D. Human Intimacy: Marriage, the Family & Its Meaning. 2nd ed. (Illus.). 560p. 1981. 22.95 (ISBN 0-8299-0367-4). West Pub.

--Human Intimacy: Marriage, the Family & Its Meaning. 3rd ed. (Illus.). 525p. 1984. text ed. 25.95 (ISBN 0-314-77872-1); instrs.' manual avail. (ISBN 0-314-77873-X); avail. study guide 7.95 (ISBN 0-314-77874-8). West Pub.

--Psychology. 2nd ed. 696p. 1973. pap. text ed. write for info. (ISBN 0-697-06615-0). Wm C Brown.

Cox, Frank L. According to Luke. 1941. pap. 2.75 (ISBN 0-88027-030-6). Firm Foun Pub.

--Bedside Meditations. 1967. pap. 2.00 (ISBN 0-88027-000-4). Firm Foun Pub.

--One Hundred One Sermon Outlines. 1971. 3.00 (ISBN 0-88027-028-4). Firm Foun Pub.

--Sermon Notes on the Miracles. pap. 2.50 (ISBN 0-89225-155-7). Gospel Advocate.

--Seventy-Seven Sermon Outlines. 1958. pap. 1.75 (ISBN 0-88027-052-7). Firm Foun Pub.

Cox, Frank L., jt. auth. see Showalter, G. H.

Cox, Fred M., et al. Strategies of Community Organizations: A Book of Readings. 3rd ed. LC 77-83396. 526p. 1979. pap. text ed. 17.50 (ISBN 0-87581-230-9). Peacock Pubs.

Cox, Fred M., et al, eds. Tactics & Techniques of Community Practice. 2nd ed. Tropman, John E. LC 83-62004. 501p. 1984. pap. text ed. 17.50 (ISBN 0-87581-299-6). Peacock Pubs.

Cox, Frederick A. English Madrigals in the Time of Shakespeare. LC 77-27932. 1899. 25.00 (ISBN 0-8414-1842-X). Folcroft.

Cox, G. E. & Jones, E. H. Popular Romances of the Middle Ages. 1976. lib. bdg. 69.95 (ISBN 0-8490-2456-0). Gordon Pr.

Cox, G. Valentine, tr. see Dahlmann, Friedrich C.

Cox, G. W. An Introduction to the Science of Comparative Mythology & Folklore. 69.95 (ISBN 0-8490-0420-9). Gordon Pr.

Cox, Gary. Tyrant & Victim in Dostoevsky. 119p. 1984. pap. 9.95 (ISBN 0-89357-125-3). Slavica.

Cox, Gary, jt. auth. see Austin, Michael J.

Cox, Geoffrey. See It Happen: The Making of ITN. 256p. 1984. 19.95 (ISBN 0-370-30950-2, Pub. by the Bodley Head). Merrimack Pub Cir.

Cox, Geoffrey J., jt. auth. see Ayling, Tony.

Cox, George, tr. see Otto, Friedrich.

Cox, George W. The Athenian Empire. LC 77-94562. 1979. Repr. of 1890 ed. lib. bdg. 25.00 (ISBN 0-89341-257-0). Longwood Pub Group.

--Athenian Empire. 1889. 10.00 (ISBN 0-8482-3555-X). Norwood Edns.

--The Crusades. Repr. 10.00 (ISBN 0-8482-3560-6). Norwood Edns.

--The Early Empire. Repr. 20.00 (ISBN 0-8482-3557-6). Norwood Edns.

--A General History of Greece. LC 77-94563. 1979. Repr. of 1892 ed. lib. bdg. 75.00 (ISBN 0-89341-258-9). Longwood Pub Group.

--An Introduction to the Science of Comparative Mythology & Folklore. 1976. lib. bdg. 59.95 (ISBN 0-8490-2071-9). Gordon Pr.

--Latin & Teutonic Christendom: An Historical Sketch. LC 77-94557. 1979. Repr. of 1870 ed. lib. bdg. 30.00 (ISBN 0-89341-259-7). Longwood Pub Group.

--Lives of Greek Statesmen. 1975. Repr. of 1885 ed. 15.00 (ISBN 0-8274-4046-4). R West.

--Lives of Greek Statesmen: Ephialtes to Hermokrates. LC 77-94560. 1979. Repr. of 1886 ed. lib. bdg. 30.00 (ISBN 0-89341-260-0). Longwood Pub Group.

--A Manual of Mythology. LC 77-94556. 1979. Repr. of 1867 ed. lib. bdg. 30.00 (ISBN 0-89341-307-0). Longwood Pub Group.

--Mythology of the Aryan Nations, 2 Vols. LC 68-8202. 1969. Repr. of 1870 ed. Set. 65.00x (ISBN 0-8046-0091-0, Pub. by Kennikat). Assoc Faculty Pr.

--Tales of Ancient Greece. LC 77-94559. 1979. Repr. of 1880 ed. lib. bdg. 40.00 (ISBN 0-89341-308-9). Longwood Pub Group.

--Tales of the Gods & Heroes. LC 77-94564. 1979. Repr. of 1895 ed. lib. bdg. 25.00 (ISBN 0-89341-309-7). Longwood Pub Group.

Cox, George W. & Jones, Eustace H. Tales of the Teutonic Lands. LC 77-94558. 1979. Repr. of 1872 ed. lib. bdg. 40.00 (ISBN 0-89341-179-5). Longwood Pub Group.

Cox, Gerald. Wintersigns in the Snow. (Illus.). 80p. 1985. pap. 4.95 (ISBN 0-935576-11-8). Kesend Pub Ltd.

Cox, Gertrude M., jt. auth. see Cochran, William G.

Cox, H. & Morgan, D. City Politics & the Press. LC 72-96678. (Illus.). 200p. 1973. 32.50 (ISBN 0-521-20162-4). Cambridge U Pr.

Cox, Halley J. & Stasack, Edward. Hawaiian Petroglyphs. LC 78-111491. (Special Publication Ser.: No. 60). (Illus.). 108p. 1977. pap. 9.00 (ISBN 0-910240-09-4). Bishop Mus.

Cox, Harold. Economic Liberty. 1920. 15.00 (ISBN 0-686-17724-X). Quest Edns.

--Later Life: The Realities of Aging. (Illus.). 480p. 1984. text ed. 26.95 (ISBN 0-13-524157-X). P-H.

--Technical Manual for the IBM PCjr. 1984. cancelled (ISBN 0-89303-884-9). Brady Comm.

Cox, Harold, jt. auth. see Schieck, Paul.

Cox, Harold E. Early Electric Cars of Baltimore. (Illus.). 92p. (Orig.). 1979. pap. 9.00 (ISBN 0-911940-31-6). Cox.

--Early Electric Cars of Philadelphia 1885-1911. (Illus.). 136p. (Orig.). 1969. pap. 8.00 (ISBN 0-911940-09-X). Cox.

--Philadelphia Car Routes. (Illus.). 168p. (Orig.). 1982. pap. 9.00 (ISBN 0-911940-36-7). Cox.

Cox, Harold E., jt. auth. see Schieck, Paul J.

Cox, Harold E., ed. see Gordon, William R. & Platukis, Joseph G.

Cox, Harvey. Feast of Fools: A Theological Essay on Festivity & Fantasy. LC 75-75914. (William Belden Noble Lectures Ser). 1969. 15.00x (ISBN 0-674-29525-0). Harvard U Pr.

--Just As I Am. LC 82-11631. 160p. 1983. 10.95 (ISBN 0-687-20687-1). Abingdon.

--Religion in the Secular City: Toward a Post-Modern Theology. 320p. 1984. 16.95 (ISBN 0-671-45344-0). S&S.

--Religion in the Secular City: Toward a Postmodern Theology. 304p. 1985. pap. 7.95 (ISBN 0-671-52805-X, Touchstone Bks). S&S.

--Seduction of the Spirit. 1985. pap. 8.95 (ISBN 0-671-21728-3, Touchstone Bks). S&S.

--Turning East: The Promise & Peril of the New Orientalism. 1979. pap. 7.95 (ISBN 0-671-24405-1, Touchstone Bks). S&S.

Cox, Heather & Rickard, Garth. Carols to Sing, Clap & Play: A Companion to the Soprano Recorder Tuition Books. 1984. pap. 4.50 (ISBN 0-918812-36-4). MMB Music.

--Concerts to Sing, Clap, & Play: A Companion to the Soprano Recorder Tuition Books. 1985. pap. 4.00 (ISBN 0-918812-43-7). MMB Music.

--Sing, Clap, & Play the Recorder. (Illus.). 1983. pap. 3.50 ea. Book 1, A Soprano Recorder Book for Beginners (ISBN 0-918812-29-1). Book 2, A Soprano Recorder Book for Intermediate Players (ISBN 0-918812-30-5). MMB Music.

Cox, Helen. Cooking under Pressure. pap. 6.50 (ISBN 0-571-11103-3). Faber & Faber.

Cox, Henry B. & American Bar Association. War, Foreign Affairs, & Constitutional Power, 1829-1901. LC 76-15392. 440p. 1984. prof. ref. 35.00x (ISBN 0-88410-956-9). Ballinger Pub.

Cox, Herman G. Your Dachshund. LC 66-22305. (Your Dog Book Ser). (Illus.). 1966. 7.95 (ISBN 0-87714-021-9); pap. 4.95 (ISBN 0-87714-022-7). Denlingers.

Cox, Homer T. Henry Seton Merriman. LC 66-21746. (English Authors Ser.). 1967. lib. bdg. 12.95 (ISBN 0-89197-785-6); pap. text ed. 6.95x (ISBN 0-89197-992-1). Irvington.

Cox, Isaac J. Nicaragua & the United States. 1976. lib. bdg. 59.95 (ISBN 0-8490-2344-0). Gordon Pr.

Cox, Isaac J, ed. The Journeys of Rene Robert Cavelier, 2 vols. LC 72-2828. (American Explorers Ser.). (Illus.). Repr. of 1922 ed. Set. 75.00 (ISBN 0-404-54917-9). AMS Pr.

Cox, J. Charles. The English Parish Church. (Illus.). 1977. Repr. of 1914 ed. 25.00x (ISBN 0-7158-1174-6). Charles River Bks.

--Parish Registers of England. (Illus.). 290p. 1974. Repr. of 1910 ed. 16.50x (ISBN 0-87471-541-5). Rowman.

Cox, J. D. Thermochemistry of Organic & Organometallic Compounds. 1970. 97.50 (ISBN 0-12-194350-X). Acad Pr.

Cox, J. Gray. The Will at the Crossroads: A Reconstruction of Kant's Moral Philosophy. 220p. (Orig.). 1984. lib. bdg. 22.00 (ISBN 0-8191-3710-3); pap. text ed. 11.50 (ISBN 0-8191-3711-1). U Pr of Amer.

Cox, J. Halley & Davenport, William. Hawaiian Sculpture. LC 73-151453. (Illus.). 208p. 1974. text ed. 20.00x (ISBN 0-8248-0281-0). UH Pr.

Cox, J. P. Theory of Stellar Pulsation. LC 79-3198. (Ser. in Astrophysics: No. 2). (Illus.). 1980. 57.50x (ISBN 0-691-08252-9); pap. 16.50x (ISBN 0-691-08253-7). Princeton U Pr.

Cox, J. P., ed. Principle of Stellar Structure, 2 Vols. LC 68-26755. (Illus.). 1327p. 1968. Set. 350.25 (ISBN 0-677-01950-5). Gordon.

Cox, J. Stevens. Ice Creams of Queen Victoria's Reign. 1.95 (ISBN 0-913714-61-5). Legacy Bks.

Cox, Jack, ed. see Davey, Gilbert.

Cox, Jack R. Gemcutter's Handbook: Cabochon Cutting. pap. 2.50 (ISBN 0-910652-12-0). Gembooks.

Cox, Jack R. & Gems & Minerals Staff. Gem Cutters Handbook: Specialized Gem Cutting. (Illus.). 1970. pap. 2.50 (ISBN 0-910652-13-9). Gembooks.

Cox, Jack R., jt. auth. see Gems & Mineral Magazine Staff.

Cox, Jack R., ed. see Giacomini, Afton.

Cox, Jack R., ed. see Soukup, Edward J.

Cox, Jacob. Atlanta: Campaigns of the Civil War IX. LC 84-14197. 288p. 1984. 14.95 (ISBN 0-87797-080-7). Cherokee.

--The March to the Sea: Campaigns of the Civil War X. LC 84-17069. 278p. 1984. 14.95 (ISBN 0-87797-085-8). Cherokee.

Cox, Jacob D. Battle of Franklin. (Civil War Heritage Ser.: No. 9). 356p. 1983. 30.00 (ISBN 0-89029-072-5). Pr of Morningside.

Cox, James. Corporation. rev. ed. (Sum & Substance Ser.). 1980. 12.95 (ISBN 0-686-28348-1). Josephson-Kluwer Legal Educ Ctrs.

--Financial Information, Accounting & the Law: Cases & Materials. 1980. text ed. 28.00 (ISBN 0-316-15861-5). Little.

Cox, James A. A Century of Light. LC 78-19204. (Illus.). 1979. Set. 17.50 (ISBN 0-87502-062-3). Benjamin Co.

--Put Your Foot in Your Mouth & Other Silly Sayings. LC 80-12877. (Step-up Book: No. 31). (Illus.). 72p. (gr. 2-5). 1980. bds. 3.95 (ISBN 0-394-84503-X); PLB 5.99 (ISBN 0-394-94503-4). Random.

Cox, James D. Corporations. (Sum & Substance Ser.). 1975. 12.95 (ISBN 0-686-18193-X). Josephson-Kluwer Legal Educ Ctrs.

Cox, James E. The Rise of Sentimental Comedy. 1979. Repr. of 1926 ed. lib. bdg. 22.50 (ISBN 0-8495-0945-9). Arden Lib.

--Rise of Sentimental Comedy. LC 74-9974. 1926. lib. bdg. 10.00 (ISBN 0-8414-3360-7). Folcroft.

Cox, James H. Confessions of a Moonlight Writer: A Freelancer's Guide to the Church Market. LC 80-70315. 97p. (Orig.). 1982. pap. 5.95 (ISBN 0-939298-00-7). J M Prods.

Cox, James M. Low Back Pain: Mechanism, Diagnosis & Treatment. 4th ed. (Illus.). 384p. 1985. 80.00 (ISBN 0-683-02151-6). Williams & Wilkins.

--Mark Twain: The Fate of Humor. 1966. 32.00 (ISBN 0-691-06072-X); pap. 11.95 (ISBN 0-691-01327-6). Princeton U Pr.

Cox, James M., ed. Robert Frost: A Collection of Critical Essays. 1962. 12.95 (ISBN 0-13-331512-6, Spec). P-H.

Cox, James S. An Illustrated Dictionary of Hairdressing & Wigmaking. (Illus.). 312p. 1984. text ed. 35.00x (ISBN 0-7134-4208-5, Pub. by Batsford England). Drama Bk.

Cox, James W. Preaching: A Comprehensive Approach to the Design & Delivery of Sermons. LC 84-48214. 320p. 1985. 18.22 (ISBN 0-06-061600-8, HarpR). Har-Row.

Cox, James W., ed. Biblical Preaching: An Expositor's Treasury. LC 83-10518. 368p. (Orig.). 1983. 19.95 (ISBN 0-664-21397-9). Westminster.

--The Minister's Manual for Nineteen Eighty-Five. LC 25-21658. (Doran's Ser.). 288p. 1984. 11.49i (ISBN 0-06-061599-0, HarpR). Har-Row.

--The Ministers Manual for Nineteen Eighty-Six. LC 25-21658. 352p. 1985. 14.37 (ISBN 0-06-061595-8, HarpR). Har-Row.

--The Twentieth-Century Pulpit. LC 77-21997. 1978. pap. 8.95 (ISBN 0-687-42715-0). Abingdon.

Cox, James W. & Cox, Patricia P., eds. Twentieth Century Pulpit, Vol. II. LC 77-21997. 1981. pap. 9.95 (ISBN 0-687-42716-9). Abingdon.

Cox, Jan. Death of Gurdjieff in the Foothills of Georgia: Secret Papers of an American Work Group. 316p. 1980. 9.00 (ISBN 0-936380-03-9). Chan Shal Imi.

--Dialogues of Gurdjieff: An Allegorical Work Adventure. rev., enl. ed. 318p. 1980. 9.00 (ISBN 0-936380-02-0). Chan Shal Imi.

--Magnus Machina: The Great Machine. 1970. 7.95 (ISBN 0-87707-092-X); pap. 5.95 (ISBN 0-686-65960-0). Chan Shal Imi.

Cox, Janet. Valley of Fire. LC 83-20966. 216p. 1983. 8.95 (ISBN 0-87747-985-2). Deseret Bk.

Cox, Jean W., jt. auth. see Cox, Charles H.

Cox, Jeff. From Vines to Wines: The Complete Step-by-Step Guide to Growing Grapes in Your Backyard & Making Your Own Wine. LC 84-48590. (Illus.). 288p. 1985. 16.30 (ISBN 0-06-015427-6, HarpT). Har-Row.

--Gardener's Almanac 1986: Seasonal Celebrations. (Illus.). 160p. 1985. pap. 6.95 (ISBN 0-87857-535-9). Rodale Pr Inc.

Cox, Jeff & Cox, Marilyn. The Perennial Garden: Color Harmonies Through the Season. Halpin, Anne, ed. (Illus.). 288p. 1985. 21.95 (ISBN 0-87857-573-1). Rodale Pr Inc.

Cox, Jeff, jt. auth. see Goldratt, Eliyahu M.

Cox, Jeffrey. The English Churches in a Secular Society: Lambeth, 1870-1930. (Illus.). 1982. 39.95x (ISBN 0-19-503019-2). Oxford U Pr.

Cox, Jim, jt. auth. see Robison, James.

Cox, Jimmie, jt. auth. see Robinson, James.

Cox, Joan. Mindsong. 1979. pap. 2.25 (ISBN 0-380-43638-8, 43638-8). Avon.

Cox, Joan G. & Kriegbaum, Herbert. Growth, Innovation & Employment: An Anglo-German Comparison. 77p. 1982. 30.00x (ISBN 0-905492-31-5, Pub. by Anglo-German Found England). State Mutual Bk.

Cox, John. Overkill: Weapons of the Nuclear Age. LC 77-27663. (Illus.). (gr. 7 up). 1978. PLB 11.89 (ISBN 0-690-03857-7). Crowell Jr Bks.

Cox, John E. Surgery of the Reproductive Tract in Large Animals. 210p. 1982. pap. 40.00x (ISBN 0-686-92031-7, Pub. by Liverpool Univ England). State Mutual Bk.

Cox, John H. The Junior High School & Its Curriculum. (Educational Ser.). 1929. Repr. 10.00 (ISBN 0-8482-3578-9). Norwood Edns.

--Literature in the Common Schools. (Educational Ser.). 1911. Repr. 10.00 (ISBN 0-8482-3581-9). Norwood Edns.

--Literature in the Common Schools. 1911. 20.00 (ISBN 0-932062-41-5). Sharon Hill.

Cox, John H., jt. ed. see Cox, Lawanda.

Cox, John Harrington. Folk-Songs Mainly from West Virginia. Herzog, George & Halpert, Herbert, eds. LC 76-58548. (Music Reprint Series). 1977. Repr. of 1939 ed. lib. bdg. 27.50 (ISBN 0-306-70786-1). Da Capo.

Cox, John J., jt. auth. see Rubinstein, Mark.

Cox, John L., jt. auth. see Vogt, Judith F.

Cox, John S., jt. auth. see Davidson, Frank P.

Cox, Jonathan. Kiss of the Raven. 224p. (Orig.). 1981. pap. 2.25 (ISBN 0-449-14415-1, GM). Fawcett.

Cox, Joseph M. Great Black Men of Masonry: Qualitative Black Achievers Who Were Freemasons. 211p. 1982. 15.00 (ISBN 0-686-82377-X); pap. 8.00 (ISBN 0-686-82378-8). Blue Diamond.

--New & Selected Poems. 196p. 10.00 (ISBN 0-930856-00-7); pap. 5.00 (ISBN 0-930856-01-5). Blue Diamond.

Cox, Joseph W. Champion of Southern Federalism: Robert Goodloe Harper of South Carolina. LC 78-189554. 1972. 21.50x (ISBN 0-8046-9025-1, Pub. by Kennikat). Assoc Faculty Pr.

Cox, June, et al. Educating Able Learners: Programs & Promising Practices. 240p. 1985. 20.00 (ISBN 0-292-70386-4); pap. 12.50 (ISBN 0-292-70387-2). U of Tex Pr.

--Educating Able Learners: Programs & Promising Practices. 240p. 1985. text ed. 20.00x (ISBN 0-292-70386-4); pap. 12.50 (ISBN 0-292-70387-2). U of Tex Pr.

Cox, K. E., ed. see Kermode, R. I., et al.

Cox, K. G., et al. Interpretation of Igneous Rocks. 1979. text ed. 50.00x (ISBN 0-04-552015-1); pap. text ed. 24.95x (ISBN 0-04-552016-X). Allen Unwin.

--An Introduction to the Practical Study of Crystals, Minerals, & Rocks. rev. ed. LC 74-13833. 235p. 1975. pap. 21.95x (ISBN 0-470-18139-7). Halsted Pr.

Cox, Kaludia, ed. see Annest, Joseph L. & Mahaffey, Kathryn.

Cox, Kaludia, ed. see Fingerhut, Loia A.

Cox, Kaludia, ed. see Strahan, Geneive.

Cox, Kay. Being a Health Unit Coordinator. LC 83-15824. (Illus.). 368p. 1984. pap. text ed. 14.95 (ISBN 0-89303-236-0); instr's guide 4.95 (ISBN 0-89303-329-4). Brady Comm.
Cox, Keith, jt. auth. see Kotler, Philip.
Cox, Keith K. & McGinnis, Vern J. Strategic Market Decisions: A Reader. (Illus.). 416p. 1982. pap. text ed. 18.95 (ISBN 0-13-851022-9). P-H.
Cox, Keith K., jt. auth. see Kotler, Phillip.
Cox, Keith K., ed. Readings in Market Research. LC 67-15866. (Illus., Orig.). 1967. pap. text ed. 11.95x (ISBN 0-89197-372-9). Irvington.
Cox, Keith K., jt. ed. see Higginbotham, James B.
Cox, Keller & Frazier, Raymond L. Buck; a Tennessee Boy in Korea. 1982. 9.95 (ISBN 0-9610818-0-5); pap. 4.95 (ISBN 0-9610818-1-3). M K Cox.
Cox, Kenneth E. & Williamson, Kenneth D., Jr., eds. Hydrogen: Its Technology & Implications, Vols. 2-5. Incl. Vol. 2. Transmission & Storage of Hydrogen. 144p. 1977. 51.00 (ISBN 0-8493-5122-7); Vol. 3. Hydrogen Properties. 336p. 1975. 86.50 (ISBN 0-8493-5123-5); Vol. 4. Utilization of Hydrogen. 256p. 1979. 76.50 (ISBN 0-8493-5124-3); Vol. 5. Implications of Hydrogen Energy. 144p. 1979. 51.00 (ISBN 0-8493-5125-1). LC 74-29484. (Uniscience Ser.). CRC Pr.
Cox, Kenneth R. Planning Clinical Experiments. (Illus.). 344p. 1968. 28.50x (ISBN 0-398-00353-X). C C Thomas.
Cox, Kenneth R. & Ewan, Christine E., eds. The Medical Teacher. LC 81-67459. (Illus.). 248p. 1982. pap. text ed. 25.00 (ISBN 0-443-02446-4). Churchill.
Cox, Kenyon. The Classic Point of View. rev. ed. (Illus.). 1980. 14.95 (ISBN 0-393-01320-0); pap. 6.95 (ISBN 0-393-00994-7). Norton.
--Classic Point of View: Six Lectures on Painting. facs. ed. LC 68-22907. (Essay Index Reprint Ser). 1911. 20.00 (ISBN 0-8369-0345-5). Ayer Co Pubs.
--Old Masters & New. facsimile ed. LC 74-90627. (Essay Index Reprint Ser.). 1905. 24.50 (ISBN 0-8369-1403-1). Ayer Co Pubs.
--Painters & Sculptors. facsimile ed. LC 70-105006. (Essay Index Reprint Ser.). 1907. 27.50 (ISBN 0-8369-1458-9). Ayer Co Pubs.
Cox, Kevin. Man, Location & Behavior: An Introduction to Human Geography. LC 72-4790. 414p. 1972. text ed. 21.50 (ISBN 0-471-18150-1). Krieger.
Cox, Kevin R. Location & Public Problems. 352p. 1979. 16.95x (ISBN 0-416-60091-3, NO. 2861). Methuen Inc.
Cox, Kevin R., ed. Conflict, Politics & the Urban Scene. Johnston, R. J. LC 81-16620. 265p. 1983. 28.50 (ISBN 0-312-16233-2). St Martin.
Cox, Kevin R. & Golledge, Reginald G., eds. Behavioural Problems in Geography Revisited. 1982. 27.95x (ISBN 0-416-72430-2, NO. 3533); pap. 13.50x (ISBN 0-416-72440-X, NO. 3534). Methuen Inc.
Cox, Klaudia, ed. Guide for Reporting Occupation & Industry on Death Certificates. 50p. 1983. text ed. 1.50 (ISBN 0-8406-0278-2). Natl Ctr Health Stats.
--Utilization of Family Planning Services by Currently Married Women 15-44 Years of Age: United States, 1973. (Ser. 23, No. 1). 1977. pap. text ed. 1.50 (ISBN 0-8406-0113-1). Natl Ctr Health Stats.
Cox, Klaudia, ed. see Abraham, Sidney, et al.
Cox, Klaudia, ed. see Bloom, Barbara & Jack, Susan S.
Cox, Klaudia, ed. see Borham, Gordon S. & Leaverton, Paul E.
Cox, Klaudia, ed. see Burt, Brian A., et al.
Cox, Klaudia, ed. see Causey, G. Donald, et al.
Cox, Klaudia, ed. see Cypress, Beulah J.
Cox, Klaudia, ed. see Cypress, Beulah K.
Cox, Klaudia, ed. see Dundon, Mary L.
Cox, Klaudia, ed. see Eckard, Eugenia.
Cox, Klaudia, ed. see Foster, Jean & Eckard, Eugenia.
Cox, Klaudia, ed. see Ganley, James P. & Roberts, Jean.
Cox, Klaudia, ed. see Gardocki, Gloria J.
Cox, Klaudia, ed. see Gardocki, Gloria J., et al.
Cox, Klaudia, ed. see Hadden, Wilbur C.
Cox, Klaudia, ed. see Harris, Kenneth W. & French, Dwight K.
Cox, Klaudia, ed. see Haupt, Barbara J.
Cox, Klaudia, ed. see Hing, Ester.
Cox, Klaudia, ed. see Hodgson, Thomas A.
Cox, Klaudia, ed. see Hudson, Bettie L.
Cox, Klaudia, ed. see Jack, Susan S. & Ries, Peter W.
Cox, Klaudia, ed. see Kapantais, G. Gloria.
Cox, Klaudia, ed. see Kozak, Lola J.
Cox, Klaudia, ed. see Landis, J. Richard & Eklund, Stephen A.
Cox, Klaudia, ed. see Maurer, Kurt.
Cox, Klaudia, ed. see O'Brien, Richard J. & Drizd, Terence A.
Cox, Klaudia, ed. see Ries, Peter W.
Cox, Klaudia, ed. see Rowland, Michael.
Cox, Klaudia, ed. see Sanchez, Marcus & Moien, Mary.
Cox, Klaudia, ed. see Sauer, Herbert I.
Cox, Klaudia, ed. see Sirrocco, Al.
Cox, Klaudia, ed. see Taffel, Selma.
Cox, Klaudia, ed. see Vaughn, Barbara, et al.
Cox, Klaudia, ed. see Weed, James A.
Cox, Klaudia, ed. see Wilder, Charles S.
Cox, Klaudia, ed. see Woolsey, Theodore D.
Cox, Klaudia, ed. see Zappolo, Aurora.
Cox, Klaudia, tr. see Fulwood, Robinson & Johnson, Clifford L.
Cox, Kris, jt. auth. see Cox, Mike.
Cox, LaWanda. Lincoln & Black Freedom: A Study in Presidential Leadership. LC 81-3350. 275p. 1981. 17.95x (ISBN 0-87249-400-4). U of SC Pr.
--Lincoln & Black Freedom: A Study in Presidential Leadership. LC 84-16445. (Blacks in the New World Ser.). 272p. 1985. pap. 8.95x (ISBN 0-252-01173-2). U of Ill Pr.
Cox, Lawanda & Cox, John H., eds. Reconstruction, the Negro & the New South. LC 73-5793. (Documentary History of the United States Ser.). xxx, 426p. 1973. 19.95x (ISBN 0-87249-278-8). U of SC Pr.
Cox, Lee S. Figurative Design in "Hamlet". The Significance of the Dumb Show. LC 72-12916. 1973. 8.00 (ISBN 0-8142-0175-X). Ohio St U Pr.
Cox, Leland H. William Faulkner, Biographical & Reference Guide: A Guide to His Life & Career. 304p. 1982. 65.00x (ISBN 0-8103-1117-8). Gale.
--William Faulkner: Critical Collection...A Guide to Critical Studies with Statements by Faulkner & Evaluative Essays on His Works. (Gale Author Handbook Ser.: Vol. 2). 536p. 1982. 70.00x (ISBN 0-8103-1118-6). Gale.
Cox, Leonard. Arte or Crafte of Rhethoryke. Carpenter, Frederic I., ed. LC 73-136371. (Chicago. University. English Studies: No. 5). Repr. of 1899 ed. 18.00 (ISBN 0-404-50265-2). AMS Pr.
--Arte or Crafte of Rhethoryke. Carpenter, Franklin I., ed. LC 72-194750. 1973. Repr. of 1899 ed. lib. bdg. 17.50 (ISBN 0-8414-2402-0). Folcroft.
Cox, Louis A., Jr., jt. auth. see Murray, Charles A.
Cox, M. History of Sir John Deane's Grammar School, Northwich. 1976. 25.00 (ISBN 0-7190-1282-1, Pub. by Manchester Univ Pr). Longwood Pub Group.
Cox, M. E. Practical Laundrywork. 147p. 1961. 11.50x (ISBN 0-85264-080-3, Pub. by Griffin England). State Mutual Bk.
Cox, M. V., ed. Are Young Children Egocentric? 1985. 25.00 (ISBN 0-312-04839-4). St Martin.
Cox, Marcelion. Second Class Suburbanites: White Blue-Collar Suburbs & Black White-Collar Suburbs, No. 739. 1975. 6.00 (ISBN 0-686-20337-2). CPL Biblios.
Cox, Marcia L. Make-up Monsters. 128p. 1983. pap. 1.95 (ISBN 0-441-53581-X). Ace Bks.
Cox, Margaret, ed. The Challenge of Reading Failure. 4.00x (ISBN 0-901225-16-9, Pub. by NFER Nelson UK). Taylor & Francis.
Cox, Marilyn, jt. auth. see Cox, Jeff.
Cox, Martha. Bibliography of Maxwell Anderson. 1977. 20.00 (ISBN 0-685-86326-3). Porter.
--Maxwell Anderson: A Bibliography. LC 74-2451. 1958. lib. bdg. 15.00 (ISBN 0-8414-3606-1). Folcroft.
Cox, Martha & Cox, Roger. Foster Care: Current Issues & Practices. Haskins, Ron & Gallagher, James J., eds. LC 84-20482. (Child & Family Policy Ser.: Vol. 4). 268p. 1985. text ed. 32.50 (ISBN 0-89391-228-X). Ablex Pub.
Cox, Martha H. Maxwell Anderson Bibliography. 117p. 1980. Repr. of 1958 ed. lib. bdg. 20.00 (ISBN 0-8495-0792-8). Arden Lib.
--New Reading Approach to College Writing. rev. ed. 416p. 1974. pap. text ed. 11.50 scp (ISBN 0-8102-0476-2, HarpC). Har-Row.
Cox, Mary K. Sparks from Synergy's Fire. 2nd ed. LC 83-50644. (Illus.). 80p. 1983. pap. 1.95 (ISBN 0-910217-02-5). Synergetics WV.
Cox, Mary S. Leroy, Headed for Stardom: With Danny Boy & Prince David. LC 81-50943. (Illus.). 56p. (Orig.). 1981. pap. 2.99 (ISBN 0-939726-00-9). Sunflowers KS.
--There Will Be an Answer... LC 81-90113. (Illus.). 92p. (Orig.). 1981. pap. 4.50 (ISBN 0-939726-01-7). Sunflowers KS.
Cox, Maureen. The Child's Point of View: The Development of Cognition & Language. 256p. 1985. 27.50 (ISBN 0-312-13250-6). St Martin.
Cox, Meridith B. Standards of Care for the Health Care Professional. Dienstein, Dianne H., ed. (Legal Aspects of Medical & Health Records Ser.). (Illus.). xiii, 130p. 1984. pap. 6.00 (ISBN 0-912665-05-X). Cox Pubns.
Cox, Michael. Handbook of Christian Spirituality: The Major Figures & Teachings from the New Testament to the 20th Century. LC 84-48236. 288p. 1985. 14.37 (ISBN 0-06-061601-6, HarpR). Har-Row.
--Mysticism: The Direct Experience of God. 256p. 1984. pap. 9.95 (ISBN 0-85030-280-3). Newcastle Pub.
Cox, Michael & Crocket, Dresda. The Subversive Vegetarian. LC 80-635. (Illus.). 129p. (Orig.). 1980. pap. 3.95 (ISBN 0-912800-83-6). Woodbridge Pr.
Cox, Michael A. M. R. James: An Informal Portrait. (Illus.). 1983. 32.50x (ISBN 0-19-211765-3). Oxford U Pr.
--Oxycal vs. Arthritis. 171p. (Orig.). 1982. pap. 5.95 (ISBN 0-686-43305-X). R Tanner Assocs Inc.
Cox, Mike. Fred Gipson: Texas Storyteller. (Illus.). 256p. 1980. 15.00 (ISBN 0-88319-054-0). Shoal Creek Pub.
--Red Rooster Country: Stories & Legends of Southwest Texas. (Illus.). 114p. 1970. 6.00 (ISBN 0-933512-09-0). Pioneer Bk Tx.
Cox, Mike & Cox, Kris. Flowers. Wasserman, Dan, ed. (Ten Word Bks.). (Illus.). (gr. k-1). 1979. PLB 5.95 (ISBN 0-89868-076-X); pap. 1.95 (ISBN 0-89868-087-5). ARO Pub.
Cox, Mike, et al. Fire Drill. Wasserman, Dan, ed. (Ten Word Bks.). (Illus.). (gr. k-1). 1979. PLB 5.95 (ISBN 0-89868-071-9); pap. 1.95 (ISBN 0-89868-082-4). ARO Pub.
Cox, Millard. Derby: The Life & Times of the 12th Earl of. (Illus.). 31.50 (ISBN 0-85131-199-7, Dist. by Sporting Book Center). J A Allen.
Cox, Montagu H. & Forrest, G. Topham. Parish of St. Margaret, Westminster: Neighbourhood of Whitehall, Vol. 1. LC 70-138272. (London County Council. Survey of London: No. 13). Repr. of 1930 ed. 74.50 (ISBN 0-404-51663-7). AMS Pr.
Cox, Montagu H., ed. The Parish of St. Margaret, Westminster. LC 70-138272. (London County Council. Survey of London: No. 10). (Illus.). Repr. of 1926 ed. 74.50 (ISBN 0-404-51660-2). AMS Pr.
Cox, Murray. Coding the Therapeutic Process: Emblems of Encounter. LC 77-30463. 1978. text ed. 21.00 (ISBN 0-08-021454-1); pap. text ed. 7.50 (ISBN 0-08-021453-3). Pergamon.
--Structuring the Therapeutic Process: Compromise with Chaos - a Therapist's Response to the Individual & the Group. LC 77-4181. 1978. text ed. 44.00 (ISBN 0-08-020403-1); pap. text ed. 13.75 (ISBN 0-08-020402-3). Pergamon.
Cox, N. S., jt. ed. see Balmforth, C. K.
Cox, Nicola. Country Cooking from Farthinghoe. (Illus.). 156p. 1984. 19.95 (ISBN 0-575-03504-8, Pub. by Gollancz). David & Charles.
--Good Food from Farthinghoe: Recipes for All Occasions. (Illus.). 256p. 1981. 19.95 (ISBN 0-575-02979-X, Pub. by Gollancz England). David & Charles.
Cox, Nicole & Federici, Silvia. Counter-Planning from the Kitchen: Wages for Housework - a Perspective on Capital & the Left. 2nd ed. 24p. 1976. pap. 1.75 (ISBN 0-905046-03-X). Falling Wall.
Cox, Norman W., ed. Encyclopedia of Southern Baptists, Vols. I & II. LC 58-5417. (Illus.). 1958. 39.95 (ISBN 0-8054-6501-4). Broadman.
Cox, Oliver C. Caste, Class, & Race. LC 59-8866. 1970. pap. 7.95 (ISBN 0-85345-116-8). Monthly Rev.
--Race Relations: Elements & Social Dynamics. LC 75-38572. pap. 88.50 (ISBN 0-317-30024-5, 2025022). Bks Demand UMI.
Cox, P. Larger Species of Rhododendrons. 1981. 49.00 (ISBN 0-7134-1747-1, Pub. by Batsford England). David & Charles.
Cox, P. H. Progress in Radiopharmacology 3. 1983. 44.00 (ISBN 90-247-2768-5, Pub. by Martinus Nijhoff Netherlands). Kluwer Academic.
Cox, P. H., jt. ed. see Biersack, H. J.
Cox, Palmer. The Brownies: Their Book. (Illus.). 144p. (gr. 2-6). 1887. pap. 3.95 (ISBN 0-486-21265-3). Dover.
Cox, Patricia. Biography in Late Antiquity: A Quest for the Holy Man. LC 82-4946. 208p. 1983. text ed. 27.50x (ISBN 0-520-04612-9). U of Cal Pr.
Cox, Patricia P., jt. ed. see Cox, James W.
Cox, Paul, jt. auth. see Ball, Richard.
Cox, Penny, jt. auth. see Darlington, Mansur.
Cox, Peter. Cholescintigraphy: Developments in Nuclear Medicine, No. 1. 250p. 1981. 39.00 (ISBN 90-247-2524-0, Pub. by Martinus Nijhoff Netherlands). Kluwer Academic.
--Dwarf Rhododendrons. (Illus.). 296p. 1973. 17.95 (ISBN 0-02-528560-2). Macmillan.
Cox, Peter A. The Smaller Rhododendrons. (Illus.). 216p. 1985. 29.95 (ISBN 0-88192-014-2). Timber.
Cox, Peter H. & King, Christine M. Radiopharmacy & Radiopharmacology Yearbook. 392p. 1985. text ed. 47.00 (ISBN 2-88124-114-X); pap. text ed. 18.00 (ISBN 2-88124-113-1). Gordon.
Cox, Peter R., ed. Demography. 5th ed. LC 70-92245. (Illus.). 1976. 54.50 (ISBN 0-521-21003-8); pap. 22.95 (ISBN 0-521-29020-1). Cambridge U Pr.
Cox, Peter R., et al, eds. see Eugenics Society Annual Symposium, 11th, London, 1973.
Cox, R., jt. auth. see Johnson, R.
Cox, R. A., ed. Offshore Medicine: Medical Care of Employees in the Offshore Oil Industry. (Illus.). 208p. 1982. 35.60 (ISBN 0-387-11111-5). Springer-Verlag.
Cox, R. H., jt. auth. see Leyden, D. E.
Cox, R. J., ed. Photographic Gelatin II. 1976. 66.00 (ISBN 0-12-194452-2). Acad Pr.
Cox, R. J., ed. see Symposium on Photographic Gelatin - 2nd, Trinity College, Cambridge, 1970.
Cox, R. Merritt. Eighteenth Century Spanish Literature. (World Authors Ser.). 1979. lib. bdg. 14.50 (ISBN 0-8057-6367-8, Twayne). G K Hall.
--An English Ilustrado: The Reverend John Bowle, Ibero-Romance Languages & Literatures, Vol. 9. (European University Studies: Ser. 24). 120p. 1977. pap. 18.25 (ISBN 3-261-02981-1). P Lang Pubs.
Cox, Raymond P., jt. ed. see Degen, H.
Cox, Reavis. Competition in the American Tobacco Industry, 1911-1932. LC 68-58562. (Columbia University Studies in the Social Sciences: No. 381). Repr. of 1933 ed. 26.50 (ISBN 0-404-51381-6). AMS Pr.
Cox, Reginald. The Complete Illustrated Manual of Pottery Making. (Illus.). 197p. 1984. 69.75x (ISBN 0-86650-106-1). Gloucester Art.
Cox, Richard. The Botticelli Madonna. 1985. pap. 2.95 (ISBN 0-345-32477-3). Ballantine.
--Figures of Transformation: Rilke & the Example of Valery. (Bithell Series of Dissertations: Vol. 2). 199p. 1979. pap. text ed. 17.50x (ISBN 0-85457-092-6, Pub. by Inst Germanic UK). Humanities.
--Ground Zero. LC 85-40258. 224p. 1985. 14.95 (ISBN 0-8128-3043-1). Stein & Day.
--Teaching Volleyball. LC 80-65110. 1980. pap. text ed. 8.95x (ISBN 0-8087-2929-2). Burgess.
--The Undaunted River. 1966. pap. 1.00x (ISBN 0-88020-080-4). Coach Hse.
Cox, Richard A. Technicians Guide To Programmable Controllers. LC 84-7715. 160p. 1984. pap. text ed. 15.00 (ISBN 0-8273-2420-0); instr's. guide 2.25 (ISBN 0-8273-2421-9). Delmar.
Cox, Richard C. & West, Wilma L. Fundamentals Of Research for Health Professionals. (Illus.). 96p. (Orig.). 1982. pap. text ed. 9.95 (ISBN 0-943596-00-9, RAMSCO 00300). Ramsco Pub.
Cox, Richard G. Singer's Manual of German & French Diction. 1970. pap. text ed. 7.95 (ISBN 0-02-870650-1). Schirmer Bks.
Cox, Richard H. Locke on War & Peace. LC 82-42514. 240p. 1983. pap. text ed. 12.25 (ISBN 0-8191-2662-4). U Pr of Amer.
--Sports Psychology: Concepts & Applications. 400p. 1985. pap. text ed. write for info. (ISBN 0-697-00141-5). Wm C Brown.
Cox, Richard H., jt. ed. see Cole, Richard J.
Cox, Richard H., ed. see Locke, John.
Cox, Richard J., ed. A Name Index to the Baltimore City Tax Records: 1798-1808 of the Baltimore City Archives. 229p. (Orig.). 1981. pap. 12.50 (ISBN 0-916623-01-7). City Baltimore.
Cox, Richard L. & Sullivan, Larry E. Guide to the Research Collection of the Maryland Historical Society. 354p. 1981. 22.00 (ISBN 0-938420-01-1). Md Hist.
Cox, Richard T. Time, Space, & Atoms. LC 33-6773. pap. 42.50 (ISBN 0-317-29503-9, 2055962). Bks Demand UMI.
Cox, Robert & Willard, Charles A. Advances in Argumentation Theory & Research. LC 82-5496. 469p. 1982. 25.00x (ISBN 0-8093-1050-3). S Ill U Pr.
Cox, Robert G., jt. auth. see Wixon, Rufus.
Cox, Robert W., et al. The Anatomy of Influence: Decision Making in International Organization. LC 72-75188. 520p. 1973. 54.00x (ISBN 0-300-01553-4). Yale U Pr.
Cox, Roger, jt. auth. see Cox, Martha.
Cox, Roger A. The Thompson Submachine Gun. (Illus.). 1982. 29.95 (ISBN 0-943850-00-2). Law Enf Ord Co.
Cox, Ross. Adventures on the Columbia River. (Illus.). 124p. 1957. pap. 4.95 (ISBN 0-8323-0083-7). Binford.
Cox, S. & Drysdale, A. H. The Epistle to Philemon. 246p. 1982. lib. bdg. 9.25 Smythe Sewn (ISBN 0-86524-134-1, 7108). Klock & Klock.
Cox, S. & Fuller, T. The Book of Ruth. 393p. 1983. Repr. lib. bdg. 14.75 Smythe Sewn (ISBN 0-86524-140-6, 0701). Klock & Klock.
Cox, S., jt. auth. see Morgan, J.
Cox, S., et al. Wellness R. S. V. P. 1981. 9.95 (ISBN 0-8053-2304-X). Benjamin-Cummings.
Cox, S. W. Microelectronics in Agriculture & Horticulture: Electronics & Computers In Farming. 240p. 1982. pap. text ed. 26.50x (ISBN 0-86598-087-X). Allanheld.
Cox, Samuel. The Pilgrim Psalms: An Exposition of the Songs of Degrees. 255p. 1983. lib. bdg. 9.50 (ISBN 0-86524-159-7, 1903). Klock & Klock.
Cox, Samuel S. Orient Sunbeams: From the Porte to the Pyramids, by Way of Palestine. Davis, Moshe, ed. LC 77-70665. (America & the Holy Land Ser.). (Illus.). 1977. Repr. of 1882 ed. lib. bdg. 33.00x (ISBN 0-405-10238-0). Ayer Co Pubs.
--Three Decades of Federal Legislation 1855 to 1885. facsimile ed. LC 75-114870. (Select Bibliographies Reprint Ser). 1885. 33.00 (ISBN 0-8369-5275-8). Ayer Co Pubs.
--Why We Laugh. 2nd & enl. ed. LC 67-13325. 1969. Repr. of 1880 ed. 26.50 (ISBN 0-405-08379-3, Blom Pubns). Ayer Co Pubs.
--Why We Laugh. 1876. 25.00 (ISBN 0-8274-3702-1). R West.
Cox, Sandford C. Recollections of the Early Settlement of the Wabash Valley. facs. ed. LC 78-117870. (Select Bibliographies Reprint Ser). 1860. 17.00 (ISBN 0-8369-5323-1). Ayer Co Pubs.
Cox, Sarah, jt. auth. see Golden, Robert.
Cox, Shelley. A Personal Name Index to New Directions. LC 37-1751. 167p. 1979. 12.50x (ISBN 0-87875-180-7). Whitston Pub.
Cox, Sidney. Indirections: For Those Who Want to Write. LC 80-39820. 160p. 1981. pap. 5.95 (ISBN 0-87923-389-3, Nonpareil Bks). Godine.
Cox, Soren F., jt. auth. see Clark, Marden J.
Cox, Stephen, tr. see Aron, Raymond.
Cox, Stephen D. The Stranger Within Thee: Concepts of the Self in Late-Eighteenth-Century Literature. LC 80-5252. (Illus.). 195p. 1980. 16.95x (ISBN 0-8229-3424-8). U of Pittsburgh Pr.
Cox, Steve, tr. see Curval, Philippe.
Cox, Steve, tr. see Goubert, Pierre.

Cox, Steve, tr. see Waldberg, Michael.

Cox, Steven G., jt. ed. see Jacks, Irving.

Cox, Steven M. & Conrad, John J. Juvenile Justice: A Guide to Practice & Theory. 320p. 1978. text ed. write for info. (ISBN 0-697-08206-7); instructor's resource manual avail. (ISBN 0-697-08225-3). Wm C Brown.

Cox, Steven M. & Fitzgerald, Jack D. Police & Community Relations: Critical Issues. 208p. 1983. text ed. write for info. (ISBN 0-697-08219-9). Wm C Brown.

Cox, Steven M. & Wade, John E. The Criminal Justice Network: An Introduction. 368p. 1985. pap. text ed. write for info. (ISBN 0-697-00258-6); test item file avail. (ISBN 0-697-00572-0). Wm C Brown.

Cox, Sue, ed. Female Psychology: The Emerging Self. 2nd ed. 480p. 1981. text ed. 21.95x (ISBN 0-312-28742-9); pap. text ed. 16.95x (ISBN 0-312-28743-7). St Martin.

Cox, Susan M. & Budeit, Janice L., eds. Early English Newspapers, Bibliography & Guide to the Microfilm Collection. 1983. 80.00 (ISBN 0-89235-076-8). Res Pubns Conn.

Cox, Susan N. The Collectors Guide to Frankoma Pottery, Bk. 2. (Illus.). 176p. 1982. pap. 15.95 (ISBN 0-9607274-0-X). Page One.

Cox, T. Disadvantaged Eleven Year Olds. 140p. 1983. 18.95 (ISBN 0-08-028911-8). Pergamon.

--Motor Boat & Yachting Manual. 18th ed. (Illus.). 1973. 17.50 (ISBN 0-540-00966-0). Heinman.

--Stress. (Illus.). 208p. 1978. pap. text ed. 20.00 (ISBN 0-8391-1219-X). Univ Park.

Cox, Terence. Rural Sociology in the Soviet Union. LC 78-14956. 106p. 1979. text ed. 25.50x (ISBN 0-8419-0442-1). Holmes & Meier.

Cox, Terri, ed. see D'Addio, Janie.

Cox, Terry & Littlejohn, Gary, eds. Kritsman & the Agrarian Marxists. LC 83-25225. (The Library of Peasant Studies: No. 7). (Illus.). 150p. 1984. 27.50x (ISBN 0-7146-3237-6, BHA-03237, F Cass Co). Biblio Dist.

Cox, Thomas C. Blacks in Topeka, Kansas, 1865-1915: A Social History. LC 81-14310. xiv, 236p. 1982. text ed. 27.50x (ISBN 0-8071-0975-4). La State U Pr.

Cox, Thomas R., et al. This Well-Wooded Land: Americans & Their Forest from Colonial Times to the Present. LC 85-1141. (Illus.). 338p. 1985. 27.95xt (ISBN 0-8032-1426-X). U of Nebr Pr.

Cox, Thomas S. Civil-Military Relations in Sierra Leone: A Case Study of African Soldiers in Politics. 220p. 1976. 18.50x (ISBN 0-674-13290-4). Harvard U Pr.

Cox, Thornton. Thornton Cox Traveller's Guide to Majorca. rev. ed. 1973. 5.95 (ISBN 0-8038-7205-4). Hastings.

--Thornton Cox Traveller's Guide to the Caribbean. (Thornton Cox's Travellers' Guide Ser.). (Illus.). 1974. pap. 4.95 (ISBN 0-8038-7153-8). Hastings.

Cox, Tom. Damned Englishman: A Study of Erskine Childers (1870-1922) LC 73-86542. 1975. 10.00 (ISBN 0-682-47821-0, University). Exposition Pr FL.

--Motor Boat & Yachting Manual. 18th ed. (Illus.). 356p. 1973. 17.95x (ISBN 0-8464-0644-6). Beekman Pubs.

Cox, Trenchard. Jehan Foucquet, Native of Tours. LC 72-7072. (Select Bibliographies Reprint Ser.). 1972. Repr. of 1931 ed. 34.50 (ISBN 0-8369-6926-X). Ayer Co Pubs.

Cox, Victoria, jt. auth. see Applebaum, Stan.

Cox, Vivian, tr. see De Montherlant, Henry.

Cox, Vladimir. The Illustrated Guidebook of Chinese Art. (Illus.). 159p. 1985. 117.50 (ISBN 0-86650-162-2). Gloucester Art.

Cox, W. Miles. The Addictive Personality. (Encyclopedia of Psychoactive Drugs Ser.). (Illus.). 1985. PLB 15.95 (ISBN 0-87754-773-4). Chelsea Hse.

Cox, Warren, jt. auth. see Sullivan, George E.

Cox, Warren E. Book of Pottery & Porcelain. rev. ed. (Illus.). 1970. 25.00 (ISBN 0-517-53931-4). Crown.

Cox, Wesley. Crime Stoppers: Low-Cost, No-Cost Ways to Protect Yourself, Your Family, Your Home, & Your Car. LC 83-6639. (Illus.). 156p. 1983. pap. 1.98 (ISBN 0-517-55102-0). Crown.

--Energy Smarts: Low-Cost, No-Cost Ways to Shrink Your Energy Bills. (Illus.). 1984. pap. 4.95 (ISBN 0-517-55325-2). Crown.

--Kiss Ma Bell Goodbye: How to Install Your Own Telephones, Extensions & Accessories. (Illus.). 1983. pap. 4.95 (ISBN 0-517-54936-0). Crown.

Cox, William E. Amillenialism Today. 1972. pap. 3.95 (ISBN 0-87552-151-7). Presby & Reformed.

--Biblical Studies in Final Things. 1967. pap. 5.95 (ISBN 0-87552-152-5). Presby & Reformed.

--An Examination of Dispensationalism. 1963. pap. 2.25 (ISBN 0-87552-153-3). Presby & Reformed.

--Industrial Marketing Research. LC 78-11480. (Marketing Management Ser.). 468p. 1979. 45.95x (ISBN 0-471-03467-3, Pub. by Wiley-Interscience). Wiley.

--Sir, I Represent Christian Salesmanship. pap. 1.50 (ISBN 0-686-64392-5). Reiner.

--Why I Left Scofieldism. 1975. pap. 0.50 (ISBN 0-87552-154-1). Presby & Reformed.

Cox, William R. Cemetery Jones. 176p. (Orig.). 1985. pap. 2.50 (ISBN 0-449-12810-5, GM). Fawcett.

--The Fourth-of-July Kid. (Orig.). 1981. pap. 2.25 (ISBN 0-505-51621-7, Pub. by Tower Bks). Dorchester Pub Co.

--Home Court Is Where You Find It. LC 79-6641. (gr. 6 up). 1980. 7.95 (ISBN 0-396-07798-6). Dodd.

Cox, Willis F. Conversations about God from the Journal of Willis F. Cox. (Orig.). 1985. 11.95 (ISBN 0-9610758-2-1); pap. 6.95 (ISBN 0-9610758-3-X); pap. text ed. 6.95 (ISBN 0-9610758-1-3). W F Cox.

--Tidbits for Thought: From the Journal of Willis F. Cox. LC 83-90752. (Illus., Orig.). 1983. pap. 6.95 (ISBN 0-9610758-0-5). W F Cox.

Coxall, W. N. Parties & Pressure Groups. (Political Realities Ser.). 168p. 1986. pap. text ed. cancelled (ISBN 0-582-36621-6). Longman.

Coxe see Sohn, David A.

Coxe, Anthony D. A Seat at the Circus. rev. ed. Saxon, Arthur, ed. (Archon Bks. on Popular Entertainments). (Illus.). 258p. 1980. 19.50 (ISBN 0-208-01766-6, Archon). Shoe String.

Coxe, Brinton. An Essay on Judicial Power & Unconstitutional Legislation. LC 79-99476. 1970. Repr. of 1893 ed. 47.50 (ISBN 0-306-71853-7). Da Capo.

Coxe, Brinton, tr. see Guterbock, Carl.

Coxe, Daniel. A Description of the English Province of Carolana, by the Spaniards Call'd Florida, & by the French la Louisiane. Coker, William S., intro. by. LC 76-18184. (Floridiana Facsimile Reprint Ser.). (Illus.). 122p. 1976. Repr. of 1722 ed. 8.50 (ISBN 0-8130-0402-0). U Presses Fla.

Coxe, Francis. A Short Treatise Declaringe the Detestable Wickednesse of Magicall Sciences. LC 72-5971. (English Experience Ser.: No. 501). 32p. 1972. Repr. of 1561 ed. 5.00 (ISBN 90-221-0501-6). Walter J Johnson.

Coxe, George H. Double Identity. 224p. 1974. pap. 1.25 (ISBN 0-532-12204-6). Woodhill.

--Fenner. 224p. 1974. pap. 1.25 (ISBN 0-532-12251-8). Woodhill.

--Murder with Pictures. LC 80-8410. 288p. 1981. pap. 2.25i (ISBN 0-06-080527-7, P 527, PL). Har-Row.

--The Silent Witness. 224p. 1974. pap. 1.25 (ISBN 0-532-12245-3). Woodhill.

Coxe, H. O., ed. Roger of Wendover: Chronica Sive Flores Historiarum, 4 vols. (English History Society Publication Ser.: Vol. 12). Repr. of 1841 ed. Set. 218.00 (ISBN 0-317-15739-6). Kraus Repr.

Coxe, Louis. Enabling Acts: Selected Essays in Criticism. LC 76-4485. 1976. 13.00x (ISBN 0-8262-0200-4). U of Mo Pr.

--Last Hero & Other Poems. LC 65-18544. 1965. 7.95 (ISBN 0-8265-1074-4). Vanderbilt U Pr.

--Nikal Seyn & Decoration Day: A Poem & a Play. LC 66-20049. 1966. 7.95 (ISBN 0-8265-1089-2). Vanderbilt U Pr.

--North Well. LC 84-48752. 80p. 1985. 12.95 (ISBN 0-87923-566-7). Godine.

--Passage: Selected Poems, 1943-1978. LC 78-20382. 128p. 1979. text ed. 9.95 (ISBN 0-8262-0260-8). U of Mo Pr.

Coxe, Louis O. Edwin Arlington Robinson. (Pamphlets on American Writers Ser: No. 17). (Orig.). 1962. pap. 1.25x (ISBN 0-8166-0269-7, MPAW17). U of Minn Pr.

--Edwin Arlington Robinson: The Life of Poetry. LC 69-15698. 1969. 18.50x (ISBN 0-672-53528-9). Irvington.

--The Second Man, & Other Poems. LC 55-9369. pap. 20.00 (ISBN 0-317-27945-9, 2055851). Bks Demand UMI.

--The Wilderness, & Other Poems. LC 58-59912. pap. 20.00 (ISBN 0-317-27943-2, 2055852). Bks Demand UMI.

Coxe, Louis O., jt. auth. see Chapman, Robert.

Coxe, Lyle. The Cocaine Blues Mission. (Orig.). 1979. pap. 1.95 (ISBN 0-532-23316-6). Woodhill.

Coxe, Marian R. Cinderella: Three Hundred Forty-Five Variants. (Folk-Lore Society, London: Vol. 31). pap. 47.00 (ISBN 0-317-16260-8). Kraus Repr.

Coxe, Tench. View of the United States of America Between the Years 1787 & 1794. LC 64-24342. Repr. of 1794 ed. 47.50x (ISBN 0-678-00070-0). Kelley.

Coxe, Weld. Managing Architectural & Engineering Practice. LC 80-17196. 190p. 1980. 22.95 (ISBN 0-471-08203-1). Krieger.

--Managing Architectural & Engineering Practice. 192p. 1980. 21.95 (ISBN 0-442-21736-6). Van Nos Reinhold.

--Marketing Architectural & Engineering Services. 2nd ed. 1982. 26.95 (ISBN 0-442-22011-1). Van Nos Reinhold.

Coxe, William. Account of the Russian Discoveries Between Asia & America. 3rd ed. LC 78-107912. (Illus.). Repr. of 1787 ed. 45.00x (ISBN 0-678-00626-1). Kelley.

--Anecdotes of George Frederick Handel & John Christopher Smith. (Music Reprint Ser.). 1979. Repr. of 1799 ed. 27.50 (ISBN 0-306-79512-4). Da Capo.

--History of the House of Austria: From the Foundation of the Monarchy by Rhodolph of Hapsburgh to the Death of Leopold the Second, 1218-1792, 3 Vols. LC 72-135801. (Eastern Europe Collection Ser). 1970. Repr. of 1847 ed. Set. 106.00x (ISBN 0-405-02743-5); Vol.1. 35.50 (ISBN 0-405-02790-7); Vol.2. 35.50 (ISBN 0-405-02791-5); Vol.3. 35.50 (ISBN 0-405-02792-3). Ayer Co Pubs.

--Memoirs of the Administration of the Right Honourable Henry Pelham, 2 Vols. LC 74-130626. Repr. of 1829 ed. Set. 85.00 (ISBN 0-404-01794-0). Vol. 1 (ISBN 0-404-01795-9). Vol. 2 (ISBN 0-404-01796-7). AMS Pr.

--Travels in Poland & Russia. LC 73-115524. (Russia Observed, Ser.). 1970. Repr. of 1802 ed. 53.00 (ISBN 0-405-03017-7). Ayer Co Pubs.

--Travels into Poland. LC 76-135802. (Eastern Europe Collection Ser). (Illus.). 226p. 1970. Repr. of 1785 ed. 16.00 (ISBN 0-405-02744-3). Ayer Co Pubs.

Coxeter, H. S. Introduction to Geometry. 2nd ed. LC 72-93909. 469p. 1969. 42.00 (ISBN 0-471-18283-4). Wiley.

--Non-Euclidean Geometry. 5th ed. 1965. 30.00 (ISBN 0-8020-1068-7). U of Toronto Pr.

--Projective Geometry. 2nd ed. LC 73-86992. 1974. 17.50 (ISBN 0-8020-2104-2). U of Toronto Pr.

--Regular Polytopes. (Illus.). 321p. 1973. pap. 7.95 (ISBN 0-486-61480-8). Dover.

--Unverganglich Geometrie. 2nd, Rev. ed. (Wissenschaft und Kultur Ser.: 17). 552p. 1982. text ed. 46.95x (ISBN 0-8176-1195-9). Birkhauser.

--Unvergangliche Geometrie. (Science & Civilization Ser.: No. 17). (Illus.). 552p. (Ger.). 1963. 53.35x (ISBN 0-8176-0071-X). Birkhauser.

Coxeter, H. S. & Greitzer, S. L. Geometry Revisited. LC 67-20607. (New Mathematical Library: No. 19). 193p. 1975. pap. 10.00 (ISBN 0-88385-619-0). Math Assn.

Coxeter, H. S. & Moser, W. O. Generators & Relations for Discrete Groups. 3rd rev. ed. LC 72-79063. (Ergebnisse der Mathematik und Ihrer Grenzgebiete: Vol. 14). (Illus.). ix, 169p. 1980. 39.00 (ISBN 0-387-09212-9). Springer-Verlag.

Coxeter, H. S., et al. The Fifty-Nine Icosahedra. (Illus.). 30p. 1982. pap. 15.00 (ISBN 0-387-90770-X). Springer-Verlag.

--Zero-Symmetric Graphs: Trivalent Graphical Regular Representations of Groups. LC 81-4604. 1981. 21.50 (ISBN 0-12-194580-4). Acad Pr.

Coxeter, Harold & Macdonald, Scott. The Real Projective Plane. 2nd ed. LC 60-3540. pap. 59.50 (ISBN 0-317-09189-1, 2050796). Bks Demand UMI.

Coxeter, Harold S. Regular Complex Polytopes. LC 73-75855. (Illus.). 208p. 1975. 62.50 (ISBN 0-521-20125-X). Cambridge U Pr.

Coxford, Lola M. Resume Writing Made Easy. 2nd ed. 128p. 1985. pap. text ed. 6.95 (ISBN 0-89787-805-1). Gorsuch Scarisbrick.

Cox-Gedmark, Jan. Coping with Physical Disability, Vol. 3. LC 79-28275. (Christian Care Books). 118p. 1980. pap. 6.95 (ISBN 0-664-24297-9). Westminster.

Coxhead, David & Hiller, Susan. Dreams: Visions of the Night. 1976. pap. 5.95 (ISBN 0-380-01151-4, 27862). Avon.

--Dreams: Visions of the Night. Purce, Jill, ed. LC 81-67704. (The Illustrated Library of Sacred Imagination). (Illus.). 96p. 1982. 19.95 (ISBN 0-8245-0064-4); pap. 9.95 (ISBN 0-8245-0069-5). Crossroad NY.

Coxhead, Elizabeth. Daughters of Erin. (Orig.). pap. text ed. 7.75x (ISBN 0-901072-60-5). Humanities.

--Lady Gregory: A Literary Portrait. rev. ed. 1976. Repr. of 1961 ed. text ed. 10.00x (ISBN 0-900675-74-8). Humanities.

Cox-ife, William. W. S. Gilbert: Stage Director. 112p. 1981. 35.00x (ISBN 0-234-77206-9, Pub. by Dobson Bks England). State Mutual Bk.

Coxon, A. P. & Jones, C. L. Measurement & Meanings: Techniques & Methods of Studying Occupational Cognition. LC 78-26705. 1980. 32.50x (ISBN 0-312-52418-8). St Martin.

Coxon, A. P., jt. ed. see Davies, P. M.

Coxon, A. P. M. The User's Guide to Multidimensional Scaling. LC 82-9317. 320p. 1982. text ed. 28.00x (ISBN 0-435-82251-9). Heinemann Ed.

Coxon, Anthony P. & Jones, Charles L. Class & Hierarchy: The Social Meaning of Occupations. (Illus.). 1979. 30.00 (ISBN 0-312-14256-0). St Martin.

--The Images of Occupational Prestige: A Study in Social Cognition. LC 77-90093. 1978. 30.00x (ISBN 0-312-40928-1). St Martin.

Coxon, J. M. & Halton, B. Organic Photochemistry. LC 73-82447. (Chemistry Texts Ser). (Illus.). 270p. 1974. pap. 18.95 (ISBN 0-521-09824-6). Cambridge U Pr.

Coxon, Margaret E. Gardening as Therapy: A Resource Manual of Horticultural Therapy Programs for the Summer Season. (Illus.). 32p. 1979. pap. 4.25 (ISBN 0-89955-378-8, Pub. by U BC Pr Canada). Intl Spec Bk.

Coxon, Margaret E., et al. Gardening as Therapy: A Resource Manual for Development of Horticultural Therapy Programs for the Spring Season. (Illus.). 32p. (Orig.). 1978. pap. 4.25 (ISBN 0-89955-377-X, Pub. by U BC Pr Canada). Intl Spec Bk.

Coxon, Roger. Chesterfield & His Critics. LC 76-48055. 1977. Repr. of 1925 ed. lib. bdg. 40.00 (ISBN 0-8414-3461-1). Folcroft.

Cox-Rearick, Janet. The Drawings of Pontormo: A Catalogue Raisonne with Notes on the Paintings, 2 vols. rev. ed. LC 79-93167. (Illus.). 880p. 1981. Set. lib. bdg. 120.00 (ISBN 0-87817-272-6). Hacker.

--Dynasty & Destiny in Medici Art. LC 83-13738. (Illus.). 452p. 1984. 85.00 (ISBN 0-691-04023-0). Princeton U Pr.

Coxwell, C. Fillingham, tr. see Krylov, Ivan H.

Coxwell, Charles F. Siberian & Other Folk-Tales: Primitive Literature from the Empire of the Tsars. LC 78-67702. (The Folktale). 1056p. Repr. of 1925 ed. 74.50 (ISBN 0-404-16076-X). AMS Pr.

Coy, Genevieve. Counsels of Perfection: A Baha'i Guide to Mature Living. 192p. 1979. 6.95 (ISBN 0-85398-079-9). G Ronald Pub.

Coy, Genevieve L. The Interests, Abilities & Achievements of a Special Class for Gifted Childred. LC 70-176675. (Columbia University. Teachers College. Contributions to Education: No. 131). Repr. of 1923 ed. 22.50 (ISBN 0-404-55131-9). AMS Pr.

Coy, Harold. Congress. LC 80-24914. (First Books about Washington Ser.). (gr. 4 up). 1981. PLB 8.90 (ISBN 0-531-04250-2). Watts.

--Presidents. (First Bks.). (Illus.). (gr. 4-6). 1977. PLB 8.90 s&l (ISBN 0-531-02906-9). Watts.

--Supreme Court. LC 80-25701. (First Books About Washington Ser.). (gr. 4 up). 1981. PLB 8.90 (ISBN 0-531-04252-9). Watts.

Coy, Kendrick. Multi-Sensory Educational Aids from Scrap. (Illus.). 232p. 1980. photocopy ed. spiral 28.50x (ISBN 0-398-03934-8). C C Thomas.

Coy, Owen C. California County Boundaries. rev. ed. (Illus.). 1973. Repr. 9.95 (ISBN 0-913548-14-6, Valley Calif). Western Tanager.

Coy, Peter M. Love Song. (Contemporary Poets Ser.). 62p. (Orig.). 1982. pap. 3.95 (ISBN 0-911027-00-9). Fevertree Pr.

Coyaud, Maurice. Classification Nominale En Chinois: Les Particules Numerales. (Materiaux Pour L'etude De L'extreme-Orient Moderne & Contemporain, Etudes Linguistiques: No. 3). 1973. pap. 10.00x (ISBN 90-2797-178-1). Mouton.

Coye, Molly J. & Livingston, Jon, eds. China: Yesterday & Today. rev. ed. (gr. 10 up). 1979. pap. 5.95 (ISBN 0-553-23876-0). Bantam.

Coyecque, Ernest, compiled by see Bibliotheque Nationale, Paris.

Coykendall, Ralf, Jr. Duck Decoys & How to Rig Them. (Illus.). 128p. 1983. 21.95 (ISBN 0-8329-0344-2, Pub. by Winchester Pr). New Century.

Coyle, Alcuin & Bonner, Dismas. The Church Under Tension. 1976. pap. 2.95 (ISBN 0-685-77495-3). Franciscan Herald.

Coyle, Angela. Redundant Women. 160p. 1984. pap. 7.95 (ISBN 0-7043-3923-4, Pub. by Quartet Bks.). Merrimack Pub Cir.

Coyle, Beverly. A Thought to be Rehearsed: Aphorism in Wallace Stevens's Poetry. Litz, Walton, ed. LC 83-5778. (Studies in Modern Literature: No. 9). 130p. 1983. 34.95 (ISBN 0-8357-1414-4). UMI Res Pr.

Coyle, David C. Breakthrough to the Great Society. LC 65-11941. 225p. 1965. 7.50 (ISBN 0-379-00240-X). Oceana.

--Irrepressible Conflict: Business Vs. Finance. facsimile ed. LC 73-103648. (Select Bibliographies Reprint Ser). 1933. 14.00 (ISBN 0-8369-5148-4). Ayer Co Pubs.

--Ordeal of the Presidency. LC 72-10691. (Illus.). 408p. 1973. Repr. of 1960 ed. lib. bdg. 21.00x (ISBN 0-8371-6612-8, COOP). Greenwood.

--Ordeal of the Presidency. 1960. 12.00. Pub Aff Pr.

--Roads to a New America. facsimile ed. LC 77-103649. (Select Bibliographies Reprint Ser). 1938. 29.00 (ISBN 0-8369-5149-2). Ayer Co Pubs.

--U. S. Political System & How It Works. rev. ed. 1954. pap. 1.95 (ISBN 0-451-61980-3, MJ1980, Ment). NAL.

Coyle, David C., et al. American Way. facs. ed. LC 68-58781. (Essay Index Reprint Ser.). 1938. 17.00 (ISBN 0-8369-0107-X). Ayer Co Pubs.

Coyle, Dominick J. Minorities in Revolt. LC 81-65866. (Illus.). 256p. 1982. 28.50 (ISBN 0-8386-3120-7). Fairleigh Dickinson.

Coyle, E. Wallace. The American Revolution: Changing Perspectives. 2nd ed. Fowler, William, ed. LC 79-88424. (Illus.). 231p. 1981. pap. text ed. 9.95x (ISBN 0-930350-21-9). NE U Pr.

Coyle, Elinor. Old Saint Louis Homes, Seventeen Sixty-Four to Eighteen Sixty-Five: The Stories They Tell. 7th ed. LC 79-53544. (Illus.). 1979. 14.95 (ISBN 0-910600-05-8). Folkestone.

--Saint Louis Treasures: 1904 World's Fair Relics. (Illus.). 180p. 1985. 24.95 (ISBN 0-317-28614-5). Folkestone.

Coyle, Elinor, ed. see Miller, W. Robert.

Coyle, J. D., jt. auth. see Barltrop, J. A.

Coyle, J. D. & Hill, R. R., eds. Light, Chemical Change & Life. 420p. 1982. pap. 19.00x (ISBN 0-335-16100-6, Pub. by Open Univ Pr). Taylor & Francis.

Coyle, J. D., et al, eds. Interpretation of NMR Spectra: An Introductory Audio Visual Programme. 62p. 1983. pap. 18.95 (ISBN 0-471-26228-5, Pub. by Wiley-Interscience); wkbk. avail. (ISBN 0-471-90369-8). Wiley.

Coyle, Jeanette & Roberts, Norman C. A Field Guide to the Common & Interesting Plants of Baja California. LC 74-24866. (Illus.). 224p. 1975. pap. 8.50 (ISBN 0-686-12112-0). Nat Hist Pub Co.

Coyle, John, et al. Interpretation of NMR Spectra: An Introductory Audio-Visual Programme. 1984. pap. write for info. (ISBN 0-471-26227-7). Wiley.

Coyle, John J. & Bardi, Edward. The Management of Business Logistics. 2nd ed. 500p. 1980. text ed. 24.95 (ISBN 0-8299-0325-9); instrs.' manual avail. (ISBN 0-8299-0472-7). West Pub.

Coyle, John J. & Bardi, Edward J. The Management of Business Logistics. 3rd ed. (Illus.). 550p. 1984. text ed. 28.95 (ISBN 0-314-77875-6). West Pub.

--The Management of Business Logistics. 3rd ed. 249p. 1984. write for info. instr's manual (ISBN 0-314-80338-6). West Pub.

--Transportation. (Illus.). 542p. 1982. text ed. 28.95 (ISBN 0-314-63158-5). West Pub.

Coyle, Joseph. Read English, Bk. 2. (Speak English Ser.). (Illus.). 64p. (Orig.). 1981. pap. 4.95 (ISBN 0-88499-676-X). Inst Mod Lang.

Coyle, Joseph M. & Corley, Mary A. Speak English, Text 1. (Speak Eng. Ser.). (Illus.). 80p. (Orig.). 1980. pap. text ed. 4.95 (ISBN 0-88499-650-6). Inst Mod Lang.

Coyle, Joseph T. & Enna, S. J., eds. Neuroleptics: Neurochemical, Behavioral, & Clinical Perspectives. (Central Nervous System Pharmacology Set). 342p. 1983. text ed. 71.50 (ISBN 0-89004-735-9). Raven.

Coyle, Karen. RLIN II Processing for UC Online Catalog Input: Bibliographic Specifications. 1984. 5.00 (ISBN 0-317-18069-X). UCDLA.

Coyle, L. Patrick. The World Encyclopedia of Food. (Illus.). 800p. 1982. 40.00x (ISBN 0-87196-417-1). Facts on File.

Coyle, Lee. George Ade. LC 64-20713. (United States Authors Ser.). 1964. lib. bdg. 15.95 (ISBN 0-8057-0004-8). Irvington.

Coyle, Lee P. George Ade. (Twayne's United States Authors Ser.). 1964. pap. 5.95x (ISBN 0-8084-0142-4, T63, Twayne). New Coll U Pr.

Coyle, M., jt. auth. see Peck, J.

Coyle, Neva. Daily Thoughts on Living Free. LC 82-4495. 174p. (Orig.). 1982. pap. 4.95 (ISBN 0-87123-286-3, 210286). Bethany Hse.

--Free to Be Thin Aerobics. 64p. 1983. pap. 9.98 bk., booklet & LP record (ISBN 0-87123-308-8); bk. & cassette 9.98 (ISBN 0-87123-293-6). Bethany Hse.

--The Free to Be Thin Cookbook. 150p. (Orig.). 1982. Spiral Bdg. 6.95 (ISBN 0-87123-255-3, 210255). Bethany Hse.

--Free to Be Thin Daily Planner. 128p. (Orig.). 1983. pap. 4.95 (ISBN 0-87123-284-7). Bethany Hse.

--Free to Be Thin Study Guide Discipline, No. 2. 58p. 1982. pap. 2.25 (ISBN 0-87123-169-7, 210169). Bethany Hse.

--Living Free. 123p. 1981. pap. 3.95 (ISBN 0-87123-346-0, 210346). Bethany Hse.

--Restoration. 50p. (Orig.). 1985. saddlestitched 2.50 (ISBN 0-87123-851-9). Bethany Hse.

Coyle, Neva & Chapian, Marie. Slimming Down & Growing Up. 160p. (Orig.). (gr. 4-7). 1985. pap. 5.95 (ISBN 0-87123-833-0). Bethany Hse.

--There's More to Being Thin Than Being Thin. 176p. (Orig.). 1984. pap. 5.95 (ISBN 0-87123-443-2). Bethany Hse.

Coyle, Neva, compiled by. Scriptures for Living Free. 58p. (Orig.). 1982. pap. 4.95 (ISBN 0-87123-576-5, 210576). Bethany Hse.

Coyle, Patrick L. Jr. Cooks' Books: An Affectionate Guide to the Literature of Food & Good Cooking. (Illus.). 256p. 1984. 17.95 (ISBN 0-87196-683-2); pap. 9.95 (ISBN 0-87196-695-6). Facts On File.

Coyle, R. G. Management System Dynamics. LC 76-40144. 463p. 1977. 89.95x (ISBN 0-471-99444-8, Pub. by Wiley-Interscience); pap. 37.95 (ISBN 0-471-99451-0). Wiley.

Coyle, Rena. My First Cookbook. (A Bialosky & Friends Book). (Illus.). 128p. (Orig.). (gr. 4-8). 1985. pap. 8.95 (ISBN 0-89480-846-X, 846). Workman Pub.

Coyle, Terence, jt. auth. see Hale, Robert B.

Coyle, Terrence, ed. Master Class in Figure Drawing: The Lectures of Robert Beverly Hale. (Illus.). 144p. 1985. 24.95 (ISBN 0-8230-0224-1). Watson-Guptill.

Coyle, Thomas. This Is Our Mass. 144p. 1985. pap. 3.50 (ISBN 0-89622-233-0). Twenty-Third.

Coyle, Wallace. Stanley Kubrick: A Guide to Reference & Resources. 1980. lib. bdg. 27.50 (ISBN 0-8161-8058-X, Hall Reference). G K Hall.

Coyle, Wallace, jt. ed. see Fowler, William M.

Coyle, William. Research Papers. 5th ed. LC 79-14110. 1980. pap. 8.40 scp (ISBN 0-672-61500-2). Bobbs.

--Research Papers. 5th ed. LC 79-14110. 1980. pap. 8.48scp (ISBN 0-672-61500-2). Odyssey Pr.

--Research Papers. 6th ed. 240p. (Orig.). 1985. pap. text ed. 8.48scp (ISBN 0-672-61637-8). Bobbs.

--Research Papers. 5th ed. 224p. 1980. pap. text ed. write for info. (ISBN 0-02-325290-1). Macmillan.

--Research Papers. 6th ed. 1985. pap. text ed. write for info. (ISBN 0-02-325360-6). Macmillan.

Coyle, William, ed. see Frankenstein, John.

Coym, Johannes. Gellerts Lustspiele. 1899. 18.00 (ISBN 0-384-09980-7); pap. 13.00 (ISBN 0-384-09981-5). Johnson Repr.

Coyne. Readings in Managerial Economics. 4th ed. 1985. 16.95x (ISBN 0-256-03056-1). Business Pubns.

Coyne, Anthony M. Introduction to Inductive Reasoning. LC 84-3560. 294p. (Orig.). 1984. pap. text ed. 13.50 (ISBN 0-8191-3883-5). U Pr of Amer.

Coyne, James C., ed. Essential Papers on Depression. 384p. 1985. text ed. 40.00x (ISBN 0-8147-1398-X); pap. text ed. 20.00x (ISBN 0-8147-1399-8). NYU Pr.

Coyne, John. Brothers & Sisters. 1985. 15.50 (ISBN 0-453-00496-2). NAL.

--The Legacy. pap. 3.50 (ISBN 0-425-06745-9). Berkley Pub.

Coyne, John, jt. auth. see Binks, Martin.

Coyne, John, jt. auth. see Hebert, Tom.

Coyne, John, jt. auth. see Wright, Mike.

Coyne, John & Wright, Mike, eds. Divestment & Strategic Change. LC 84-24456. 224p. 1985. 29.50x (ISBN 0-389-20547-8, 08111). B&N Imports.

Coyne, John J., tr. see Schutte, Josef F.

Coyne, Robert, jt. ed. see Levin, Bruce A.

Coyne, Thomas A, compiled by. Federal Rules of Civil Procedure. LC 81-18095. (Federal Practice Ser.). 1982. 50.00 (ISBN 0-87632-114-7). Boardman.

Coyne, Thomas J. Managerial Economics: Analysis & Cases. 5th ed. 1984. 29.50 (ISBN 0-256-02698-X). Business Pubns.

Coyne, William. Our Lady of the Eucharist. 48p. 1.25 (ISBN 0-911988-14-9). AMI Pr.

Coyner, Athleen B., jt. auth. see Zelle, Raeone.

Coynik, David. Film: Real to Reel. (Mass Media Ser.). (Illus.). 273p. (Orig.). (gr. 10-12). 1972. pap. text ed. 7.20 (ISBN 0-88343-304-4); tchrs'. manual 1.50 (ISBN 0-88343-305-2). McDougal-Littell.

--Moviemaking. (Com-Ed Ser.). (Orig.). (gr. 9-11). 1974. pap. text ed. 3.50 (ISBN 0-8294-0229-2); tchr's guide 1.50 (ISBN 0-8294-0230-6). Loyola.

Coysh, A. Dictionary & Picture Postcards 1894-1939. (Illus.). 1984. 49.50 (ISBN 0-907462-55-3). Antique Collect.

Coysh, A. W. Blue & White Transfer Ware 1780-1840. LC 76-146524. (Illus.). 1971. 13.50 (ISBN 0-8048-0975-5). C E Tuttle.

--Blue-Printed Earthenware 1800-1850. (Illus.). 112p. 1972. 12.50 (ISBN 0-8048-1088-5). C E Tuttle.

--British Art Pottery, 1870-1940. LC 76-6748. 1977. 10.00 (ISBN 0-8048-1202-0). C E Tuttle.

--Dictionary of Picture Postcards in Britain 1984-1939. (Illus.). 1984. 49.50 (ISBN 0-907462-55-3). Antique Collect.

Coysh, A. W. & Henrywood, R. K. The Dictionary of Blue & White Pottery. (Illus.). 420p. 1982. 49.50 (ISBN 0-907462-06-5). Antique Collect.

Coysh, A. W. & Stefano, Frank, Jr. Collecting Ceramic Landscapes-British & American Landscapes on Printed Pottery. (Illus.). 80p. 1981. 15.00 (ISBN 0-8048-1407-4, Pub by Lund Humphries England). C E Tuttle.

Cozad, Dale. Water Supply for Fire Protection. (Illus.). 304p. 1981. text ed. 26.95 (ISBN 0-13-945964-2). P-H.

Cozad, R. L., ed. The Speech Clinician & the Hearing-Impaired Child. (Illus.). 232p. 1974. 17.50x (ISBN 0-398-02983-0). C C Thomas.

Cozart, Cheryl L., jt. auth. see Heyman, Louis.

Cozart, Leon. Life: The Pursuit of Happiness & Death. LC 81-90517. 1982. 6.95 (ISBN 0-533-05227-0). Vantage.

Cozby, P. Christopher, jt. auth. see Perlman, Daniel.

Cozby, Paul C. Methods in Behavioral Research. 3rd. ed. 398p. 1985. pap. text ed. 14.95 (ISBN 0-87484-683-8). Mayfield Pub.

--Using Computers in the Behavioral Sciences. 1984. 9.95 (ISBN 0-87484-714-1). Mayfield Pub.

Coze, Minerva de la see De la Coze, Minerva.

Cozen, Lewis. Difficult Orthopedic Diagnosis. (Illus.). 104p. 1971. photocopy ed. 14.75x (ISBN 0-398-02212-7). C C Thomas.

--Office Orthopedics. 4th ed. (Illus.). 588p. 1975. photocopy ed. spiral 64.75x (ISBN 0-398-03068-5). C C Thomas.

Cozens, Frederick W. & Stumpf, Florence S. Sports in American Life. LC 75-22810. (America in Two Centuries Ser). 1976. Repr. of 1953 ed. 29.00x (ISBN 0-405-07681-9). Ayer Co Pubs.

Cozetto. Topics in Family Practice. 1979. 43.95 (ISBN 0-8151-1874-0). Year Bk Med.

Cozyris, George A. Christian Metz & the Reality of Film. Jowett, Garth S., ed. LC 79-6670. (Dissertation on Film, 1980 Ser.). 1980. lib. bdg. 21.00x (ISBN 0-405-12904-1). Ayer Co Pubs.

Cozzarelli, Nicholas R. Mechanisms of DNA Replication & Recombination. LC 83-18710. (UCLA Symposia on Molecular & Cellular Biology, New Ser.: Vol. 10). 902p. 1983. 136.00 (ISBN 0-8451-2609-1). A R Liss.

Cozzens, Frederic S. Sparrowgrass Papers. facs. ed. LC 72-76922. (American Fiction Reprint Ser). 1856. 16.00 (ISBN 0-8369-7001-2). Ayer Co Pubs.

Cozzens, J. H., et al, eds. see International Conference, Kent State U., April 4-5, 1975.

Cozzens, James G. Guard of Honor. LC 48-8544. 1964. pap. 8.95 (ISBN 0-15-637609-1, Harv). HarBraceJ.

--The Just & the Unjust. LC 42-17992. (Modern Classic Ser.). 1950. 11.95 (ISBN 0-15-146577-0). HarBraceJ.

--The Just & the Unjust. LC 42-17992. 1965. pap. 6.95 (ISBN 0-15-646578-7, Harv). HarBraceJ.

--Just Representations: A James Gould Cozzens Reader. Bruccoli, Matthew, ed. & intro. by. LC 78-9357. 1978. pap. 6.95 (ISBN 0-15-646611-2, Harv). HarBraceJ.

--The Last Adam. 301p. 1985. pap. 8.95 (ISBN 0-88184-210-9). Carroll & Graf.

--S. S. San Pedro. LC 67-19206. 1968. pap. 1.15 (ISBN 0-15-684830-9, Harv). HarBraceJ.

--Selected Notebooks: Nineteen Sixty to Nineteen Sixty-Seven. Bruccoli, Matthew J., ed. 1984. 12.00 (ISBN 0-89723-042-6). Bruccoli.

--The Son of Perdition. LC 83-45738. Repr. of 1929 ed. 29.00 (ISBN 0-404-20069-9). AMS Pr.

--A Time of War: Air Force Diaries & Pentagon Memos, 1943-45. Bruccoli, Matthew J., ed. 1984. 29.95 (ISBN 0-89723-043-4). Bruccoli.

Cozzens, James G. see Meriwether, James B.

Cozzens, James Gould. A Flower in Her Hair. 1974. ltd. ed. 40.00 (ISBN 0-89723-011-6). Bruccoli.

--A Rope for Dr. Webster. 1976. ltd. ed. boxed 35.00 (ISBN 0-89723-010-8). Bruccoli.

Cozzens, Samuel W. Marvelous Country. 1967. Repr. 15.00 (ISBN 0-87018-011-8). Ross.

Cozzolino, John M., jt. auth. see Gupta, Shiv K.

CO2-Climate Review Panel Climate Research Committee National Research Council. Carbon Dioxide & Climate: A Second Assessment. 72p. 1982. pap. text ed. 7.25 (ISBN 0-309-03285-7). Natl Acad Pr.

CPRI Researchers, jt. auth. see Alock, Norman Z.

CPUSA. The People vs. Monopoly: Nineteen Eighty Draft Program of the Communist Party, U. S. A. 62p. (Orig.). 1980. pap. 0.50 (ISBN 0-87898-142-X). New Outlook.

Crabb, Arthur. Samuel Lyle Criminologist. LC 74-121531. (Short Story Index Reprint Ser). 1920. 21.00 (ISBN 0-8369-3487-3). Ayer Co Pubs.

Crabb, Cecil V. & Holt, Pat. Invitation to Struggle. 2nd ed. LC 84-5904. 267p. 1984. pap. 11.95 (ISBN 0-87187-308-7). Congr Quarterly.

Crabb, Cecil V., jt. ed. see Sandoz, Ellis.

Crabb, Cecil V., Jr. The American Approach to Foreign Policy: A Pragmatic Perspective. LC 84-29087. (The Credibility of Institutions, Policies & Leadership Ser.: Vol. 2). 102p. (Orig.). 1985. lib. bdg. 16.50 (ISBN 0-8191-4422-3, Co-Pub. by White Miller Center); pap. text ed. 6.75 (ISBN 0-8191-4423-1). U Pr of Amer.

--American Foreign Policy in the Nuclear Age. 4th ed. 614p. 1983. pap. text ed. 18.50 scp (ISBN 0-06-041391-3, HarpC). Har-Row.

--The Doctrines of American Foreign Policy: Their Meaning, Role, & Future. LC 81-20846. 446p. 1982. text ed. 35.00x (ISBN 0-8071-1016-7); pap. text ed. 14.95x (ISBN 0-8071-1060-4). La State U Pr.

Crabb, Connie A., jt. auth. see Cooper, Robert D.

Crabb, Daniel M. Comparative Study of Word Order in Old Spanish & Old French Prose Works. LC 78-94189. (Catholic University of America Studies in Romance Languages & Literatures Ser: No. 51). Repr. of 1955 ed. 19.50 (ISBN 0-404-50351-9). AMS Pr.

Crabb, David W., ed. see Silverman, Martin G.

Crabb, George. English Synonyms. 1966. Repr. of 1916 ed. 27.50 (ISBN 0-7100-1234-9). Routledge & Kegan.

Crabb, John H. French Civil Code. 484p. 1977. 72.00 (ISBN 90-27-1130-68). Kluwer Academic.

Crabb, John H., ed. French Business Enterprise: Basic Legislative Texts (As amended to January 1, 1979) 363p. 1980. 57.00 (ISBN 90-271-1640-7, Pub. by Kluwer Law Netherlands). Kluwer Academic.

Crabb, John H., tr. from Fr. Constitution of Belgium & the Belgian Civil Code As Amended to September 1, 1982 in the Moniteur Belge. LC 82-18059. ix, 428p. 1982. text ed. 65.00x (ISBN 0-8377-0438-3). Rothman.

--French Business Enterprises: Basic Legislative Texts. viii, 355p. 1979. 45.00x (ISBN 0-8377-0425-1). Rothman.

Crabb, John H., tr. The French Civil Code (As Amended to July 1,1976) xx, 443p. 1977. text ed. 60.00x (ISBN 0-8377-0531-2). Rothman.

Crabb, Lawrence J. Effective Biblical Counseling: A Model for Helping Caring Christians Become Capable Counselors. 1977. 9.95 (ISBN 0-310-22570-1). Zondervan.

Crabb, Lawrence J., Jr. Basic Principles of Biblical Counseling. 160p. 1975. 8.95 (ISBN 0-310-22560-4). Zondervan.

--The Marriage Builder: A Blueprint for Couples & Counselors. 176p. 1982. 8.95 (ISBN 0-310-22580-9). Zondervan.

Crabb, Lawrence J., Jr. & Allender, Dan B. Encouragement: The Key to Caring. 144p. 1984. 8.95 (ISBN 0-310-22590-6, 10182, Pub. by Pyranee). Zondervan.

Crabb, Lawrence J., Jr. & Crabb, Lawrence J., Sr. Adventures of Captain Al Scabbard, No. 1. LC 80-27223. 128p. (Orig.). (gr. 6-8). 1981. pap. 3.95 (ISBN 0-8024-0280-1). Moody.

--The Adventures of Captain Al Scabbard, No. 2. LC 80-27358. 128p. (Orig.). (gr. 6-8). 1981. pap. 3.95 (ISBN 0-8024-0281-X). Moody.

Crabb, M. C. ZZ-Two-Homotopy Theory. (London Mathematical Lecture Note Ser.: No. 44). 100p. (Orig.). 1980. pap. 17.95 (ISBN 0-521-28051-6). Cambridge U Pr.

Crabb, Richard. Radio's Beautiful Day. (Illus.). 349p. 1983. pap. 8.95 (ISBN 0-87970-163-3). North Plains.

Crabb, Tom. Making Wood Boxes with a Band Saw. LC 85-8068. (Illus.). 128p. (Orig.). 1985. pap. 8.95 (ISBN 0-8069-6246-1). Sterling.

Crabbe. The Life of George Crabbe. 285p. 1980. Repr. lib. bdg. 25.00 (ISBN 0-8495-0452-X). Arden Lib.

Crabbe, David & McBride, Richard, eds. The World Energy Book: An A-Z, Atlas, & Statistical Sourcebook. (Illus.). 1979. pap. 12.50x (ISBN 0-262-53036-8). MIT Pr.

Crabbe, George. Poems, 3 vols. Ward, Adolphus W., ed. LC 75-41067. (BCL Ser. II). Repr. of 1907 ed. 135.00 set (ISBN 0-404-14860-3). AMS Pr.

--Poetical Works of George Crabbe. Caryle, A. J. & Caryle, R. M., eds. LC 33-27214. 1971. Repr. of 1932 ed. 79.00x (ISBN 0-403-00908-1). Scholarly.

--Tales & Other Selected Poems. Mills, Howard W., ed. 1967. pap. 16.95 (ISBN 0-521-09420-8, 420). Cambridge U Pr.

--Tales, Eighteen Twelve, & Other Selected Poems. Mills, Howard, ed. LC 67-10348. pap. 120.80 (ISBN 0-317-20623-0, 2024577). Bks Demand UMI.

Crabbe, J. A., jt. ed. see Jermy, A. C.

Crabbe, J. C., jt. auth. see Rigter, H.

Crabbe, John. Hector Berlioz: Rational Romantic. LC 78-68765. 192p. 1980. 9.95 (ISBN 0-8008-0718-9, Crescendo). Taplinger.

Crabbe, Katharyn F. J. R. R. Tolkien. LC 81-4793. (Literature and Life Ser.). 200p. 1981. 13.95x (ISBN 0-8044-2134-X); pap. 6.95 (ISBN 0-8044-6091-4). Ungar.

Crabbe, Pierre. ORD & CD in Chemistry & Biochemistry: An Introduction. 1972. 41.50 (ISBN 0-12-194650-9). Acad Pr.

Crabbe, Pierre, ed. Prostaglandin Research. (Organic Chemistry Ser.). 1977. 65.00 (ISBN 0-12-194660-6). Acad Pr.

Crabbs, Jack A., Jr. The Writing of History in Nineteenth Century Egypt: A Study in National Transformation. LC 84-2176. 230p. 1984. pap. 22.50 (ISBN 0-8143-1761-8, Co-Pub Amer. U. of Cairo Pr.). Wayne St U Pr.

Crabbs, Lelah M. Measuring Efficiency in Supervision & Teaching. LC 73-176676. (Columbia University. Teachers College. Contributions to Education: No. 175). Repr. of 1925 ed. 22.50 (ISBN 0-404-55175-0). AMS Pr.

Crabill, Calvin D., jt. auth. see Stein, Sherman K.

Crabill, Delmar. Probability Theory: An Introduction. LC 83-10345. 304p. (Orig.). 1983. pap. text ed. 14.25 (ISBN 0-8191-3332-9). U Pr of Amer.

--Statistical Theory: An Introduction. 296p. (Orig.). 1984. pap. text ed. 12.00 (ISBN 0-8191-3796-0). U Pr of Amer.

Crabill, Delmar C. & Neitzke, John J. Elementary Integral Calculus. (Illus.). 210p. 1983. pap. text ed. 12.25 (ISBN 0-8191-3516-X). U Pr of Amer.

Crabites, Pierre. Gordon, the Sudan & Slavery. LC 72-88999. Repr. of 1933 ed. 22.50x (ISBN 0-8371-1764-X, CRS&, Pub. by Negro U Pr). Greenwood.

Crable, Richard E. Argumentation As Communication: Reasoning with Receivers. 312p. 1976. text ed. 17.50 (ISBN 0-675-08609-4). Merrill.

--One to Another: A Guidebook for Interpersonal Communication. (Illus.). 300p. 1981. pap. text ed. 14.50 scp (ISBN 0-06-041395-6, HarpC); instructor's manual avail. (ISBN 0-06-361405-7). Har-Row.

--Using Communication: A New Introduction for the Nineteen Eightys. 336p. 1982. scp 27.14 (ISBN 0-205-07689-0, 487689). Allyn.

Crabtree, Adam. Animal Magnetism, Early Hypnosis & Psychical Research From 1766-1925: An Annotated Bibliography. Wozniak, R. H., ed. (Bibliographies in the History of Psychology & Psychiatry Ser.). 300p. lib. bdg. write for info (ISBN 0-527-20006-9). Kraus Intl.

--Multiple Man: Explanations in Possession & Multiple Personality. LC 84-3512. 1985. write for info. (ISBN 0-03-005179-7). Praeger.

Crabtree, Beth G. North Carolina Governors,1585-1974: Brief Sketches. rev. ed. (Illus.). viii, 184p. 1974. pap. 4.00 (ISBN 0-86526-033-8). NC Archives.

Crabtree, Beth G. & Patton, James W., eds. Journal of a Secesh Lady: The Diary of Catherine Ann Devereux Edmondston. (Illus.). xxxviii, 850p. 1979. 28.00x (ISBN 0-86526-047-8). NC Archives.

Crabtree, Catherine. A la Texas: Down Home Restaurant Recipes. 1985. pap. 9.95 (ISBN 0-937070-07-6). Crabtree.

Crabtree, Catherine G. A la Aspen. (Illus.). 190p. (Orig.). 1978. softcover 8.95 (ISBN 0-937070-00-9). Crabtree.

--A la Aspen: Restaurant Recipes. rev. ed. 1984. pap. 9.95 (ISBN 0-937070-05-X). Crabtree.
--A la San Francisco: Restaurant Recipes. (Illus.). 240p. (Orig.). 1980. pap. 9.95 (ISBN 0-937070-01-7). Crabtree.
--A la Texas: Restaurant Recipes. 1985. pap. 9.95 (ISBN 0-937070-04-1). Crabtree.
--A'la Vail: Restaurant Recipes. LC 80-67564. pap. 9.95 cancelled (ISBN 0-937070-03-3). Crabtree.
Crabtree, Charles T. This I Believe. LC 81-84913. 160p. (Orig.). 1982. pap. 2.95 (ISBN 0-88243-758-5, 02-0758). Gospel Pub.
Crabtree, Derek & Thirlwall, A. P., eds. Keynes & the Bloomsbury Group. 100p. 1980. text ed. 30.00x (ISBN 0-8419-5066-0). Holmes & Meier.
Crabtree, Elizabeth. From Brioche to Brandy: A Guide to the Best of the Bay Area's Cafes & Bars. Blackaby, Suzy, ed. LC 83-80642. (Illus.). 125p. (Orig.). 1983. pap. 5.95 (ISBN 0-942902-01-7). Knighttime Pubns.
Crabtree, G. W. & Vashishta, P., eds. Novel Materials & Techniques in Condensed Matter. 346p. 1982. 75.00 (ISBN 0-444-00694-X, North-Holland). Elsevier.
Crabtree, Harold. Spinning Tops & Gyroscopic Motion. LC 66-23755. (Illus.). 1977. text ed. 12.95 (ISBN 0-8284-0204-3). Chelsea Pub.
Crabtree, Helen K. Saddle Seat Equitation. rev. ed. LC 81-43770. (Illus.). 384p. 1982. 21.95 (ISBN 0-385-17217-6). Doubleday.
Crabtree, J. Michael & Moyer, Kenneth E., eds. Bibliography of Aggressive Behavior: A Reader's Guide to the Research Literature. LC 77-12900. 442p. 1977. 49.00x (ISBN 0-8451-0200-1). A R Liss.
Crabtree, Judith. The Sparrow's Story At the King's Command. LC 83-670222. (Illus.). 32p. (ps-1). 1983. bds. 10.95 laminated (ISBN 0-19-554359-9, Pub. by Oxford U Pr Childrens). Merrimack Pub Cir.
Crabtree, June. Basic Principles of Effective Teaching. rev. ed. LC 81-16585. (Illus.). 96p. 1982. pap. 7.95 (ISBN 0-87239-454-9, 3653). Standard Pub.
Crabtree, Lou A. Sweet Hollow: Stories. LC 83-16229. (Illus.). 144p. 1984. text ed. 14.95x (ISBN 0-8071-1132-5); pap. 8.95 (ISBN 0-8071-1133-3). La State U Pr.
Crabtree, Mary B. The Secret. 96p. (Orig.). 1985. pap. 2.95 (ISBN 0-88120-734-9). C C Pubns.
--This Summer. 96p. (Orig.). 1985. pap. 2.95 (ISBN 0-88120-730-6). C C Pubns.
Crabtree, Michael, jt. ed. see Moyer, Kenneth E.
Crabtree, Philip, et al, eds. see New Troubadours.
Crabtree, T. T. The Zondervan Pastor's Annual, 1985. 384p. 1984. Kivar 11.95 (ISBN 0-310-22681-3, 11382P, Pub. by Minister Res Lib). Zondervan.
--The Zondervan Pastor's Annual, 1986. 384p. 1985. kivar 11.95 (ISBN 0-310-22691-0, Pub. by Minister Res Lib). Zondervan.
Crabtree, Tom. An A-Z of Children's Emotional Problems. 320p. 1981. 16.95 (ISBN 0-241-10581-1, Pub. by Hamish Hamilton England). David & Charles.
Crace, Max D. & McJunkin, James N. Visions of Vietnam: Drawings & Photographs of the Vietnam War. (Illus.). 248p. 1983. 25.00 (ISBN 0-89141-175-5). Presidio Pr.
Craciunas, Silviu. The Lost Footsteps. 318p. (Orig.). 1982. pap. 4.95 (ISBN 0-88264-176-X). Diane Bks.
Crackanthorpe, David. Hubert Crackanthorpe & English Realism in the 1890s. LC 77-269. (Illus.). 224p. 1977. 17.00x (ISBN 0-8262-0224-1). U of Mo Pr.
Crackanthorpe, Hubert. Collected Stories, 1893-1897, 4 Vols. in 1. LC 74-75379. 1969. 90.00x (ISBN 0-8201-1056-6). Schol Facsimiles.
Crackenthorpe, Hubert. Last Studies: An Appreciation by Henry James. 1897. Repr. 25.00 (ISBN 0-8274-2803-0). R West.
Cracknell, A. P. Magnetism in Crystalline Materials (Applications of the Groups of Cambiant Symmetry) 1975. text ed. 44.00 (ISBN 0-08-017935-5). Pergamon.
--Remote Sensing in Meteorology Oceanography & Hydrology. LC 81-4151. (Environmental Sciences Ser.). 542p. 1981. 112.95x (ISBN 0-470-27183-3). Halsted Pr.
--Ultrasonics. (The Wykeman Science Ser.: No. 55). 200p. 1980. pap. cancelled (ISBN 0-85109-770-7). Taylor & Francis.
Cracknell, A. P. & Clark, J. L. Ultrasonics. LC 79-26250. (Wykeham Science Ser.: No. 55). 200p. 1980. pap. 15.95x (ISBN 0-8448-1330-3). Crane-Russak Co.
Cracknell, A. P. & Wong, K. C. Fermi Surface: Its Concept, Determination & Use in the Physics of Metals. (Monographs on the Physics & Chemistry of Materials). (Illus.). 1973. 69.00x (ISBN 0-19-851330-5). Oxford U Pr.
Cracknell, A. P., et al, eds. Kronecker Product Tables, Vols. 1-4. LC 79-14566. 2600p. 1979. Set. 395.00 (ISBN 0-306-65175-0, IFI Plenum). Plenum Pub.
Cracknell, Arthur P., ed. Remote Sensing Applications in Marine Science & Technology. 1983. lib. bdg. 78.00 (ISBN 90-2771-608-0, Pub. by Reidel Holland). Kluwer Academic.
Cracknell, Brian. The Failure of Admiral Kolchak. 1984. 22.00 (ISBN 0-317-14514-2, Pub. by Selecteditions). State Mutual Bk.
Cracknell, H. L. & Kaufman, R. J., trs. from Fr. Escoffier: Le Guide Culinaire. 646p. 1980. 24.95 (ISBN 0-8317-5478-8, Mayflower Bks). Smith Pubs.
Cracraft, James. The Church Reform of Peter the Great. 1971. 27.50x (ISBN 0-8047-0747-2). Stanford U Pr.
--The Soviet Union Today: An Interpretive Guide. LC 83-1916. (Illus.). x, 348p. 1983. pap. 9.95 (ISBN 0-226-03875-0, 03875-0). U of Chicago Pr.
Cracraft, James, ed. For God & Peter the Great. (East European Monographs: No. 96). 461p. 1982. 32.00x (ISBN 0-914710-90-7). East Eur Quarterly.
--The Soviet Union Today: An Interpretive Guide. (Illus.). 357p. (Orig.). 1983. pap. 9.95 (ISBN 0-941682-06-4). Educ Found for Nucl Sci.
Cracraft, Joel, jt. auth. see Eldredge, Niles.
Cracraft, Joel & Eldredge, Niles, eds. Phylogenetic Analysis & Paleonology. LC 78-31404. (Illus.). 256p. 1979. 39.00x (ISBN 0-231-04692-8); pap. 14.00x (ISBN 0-231-04693-6). Columbia U Pr.
Cracroft, Richard. Washington Irving: The Western Works. LC 74-1973. (Western Writers Ser: No. 14). 1974. pap. 2.00x (ISBN 0-88430-013-7). Boise St Univ.
Craddock, C. H., ed. see Virgil.
Craddock, Campbell, ed. Antarctic Geoscience: Proceedings of 1977 Symposium. (International Union of Geological Sciences Ser. B: No. 4). (Illus.). 1204p. 1982. 50.00x (ISBN 0-299-08410-8). U of Wis Pr.
Craddock, Sr. Clare E. Style Theories As Found in Stylistic Studies of Romance Scholars - 1900-1950. LC 70-94184. (Catholic University of America Studies in Romance Languages & Literatures Ser: No. 43). Repr. of 1952 ed. 26.00 (ISBN 0-404-50343-8). AMS Pr.
Craddock, Fred. Philippians: Interpretation: A Bible Commentary for Teaching & Preaching. Mays, James L. & Miller, Patrick D., eds. LC 84-47797. 96p. 1984. 12.95 (ISBN 0-8042-3140-0). John Knox.
Craddock, Fred B. As One Without Authority. 3rd ed. LC 79-4363. 1979. pap. 7.75 (ISBN 0-687-01930-3). Abingdon.
--The Gospels. LC 80-26270. 160p. (Orig.). 1981. pap. 8.75 (ISBN 0-687-15655-6). Abingdon.
--John. Hayes, John H., ed. LC 82-48095. (Knox Preaching Guides Ser.). 149p. 1982. pap. 6.95 (ISBN 0-8042-3241-5). John Knox.
--Overhearing the Gospel. LC 77-19106. (The Beecher Lectures for 1978). pap. 36.00 (ISBN 0-317-29724-4, 2022209). Bks Demand UMI.
--Preaching. 224p. 1985. 16.95 (ISBN 0-687-33636-8). Abingdon.
Craddock, Fred B., jt. auth. see Saunders, Ernest W.
Craddock, Fred B., et al. Preaching the New Common Lectionary. 176p. (Orig.). 1984. pap. 8.50 (ISBN 0-687-33845-X). Abingdon.
--Preaching the New Common Lectionary: Year B: Lent, Holy Week, Easter. 256p. (Orig.). 1984. pap. 9.95 (ISBN 0-687-33846-8). Abingdon.
--Preaching the New Common Lectionary: Year C-Advent, Christmas, Epiphany. 176p. (Orig.). 1985. pap. 9.50 (ISBN 0-687-33848-4). Abingdon.
--Preaching the New Common Lectionary: Year B, 2 vols. (Orig.). Vol. 2, 256 pgs. pap. 9.95 (ISBN 0-687-33846-8); Vol. 3, 304 pgs. pap. 11.95 (ISBN 0-687-33847-6). Abingdon.
Craddock, J. M. Storage Cataloguing & Retrieval of Meteorological Information. (World Weather Watch Planning Reports: No. 34). xv, 234p. 1974. pap. 32.00 (ISBN 92-63-10366-6, W246, WMO). Unipub.
Craddock, Patricia B. Young Edward Gibbon: Gentleman of Letters. LC 81-13726. 400p. 1982. text ed. 32.50x (ISBN 0-8018-2714-0). Johns Hopkins.
Craddock, Sally. Retired Except on Demand: The Life of Dr. Cicely Williams. 1983. 25.00 (ISBN 0-19-520446-8). Oxford U Pr.
Craddock, Thomas. Charles Lamb. 1979. Repr. of 1867 ed. lib. bdg. 25.00 (ISBN 0-8495-0937-8). Arden Lib.
--Charles Lamb. 1867. lib. bdg. 25.00 (ISBN 0-8414-9984-5). Folcroft.
--Charles Lamb. 216p. 1979. Repr. of 1867 ed. lib. bdg. 25.00 (ISBN 0-8482-7599-3). Norwood Edns.
Craddock, William J. Be Not Content. 2nd ed. 336p. 1985. pap. 7.95 (ISBN 0-917583-04-3). Don't Call Frisco.
Cradock, Chris. A Manual of Clayshooting. (Illus.). 192p. 1983. 24.95 (ISBN 0-88254-880-8). Hippocrene Bks.
Cradock, Eveline. Musical Appreciation in an Infant School. (Illus., Orig.). 1977. pap. text ed. 6.75 (ISBN 0-19-321055-X). Oxford U Pr.
Craemer, Willy De see De Craemer, Willy.
Craemer, Willy De see De Craemer, Willy & Fox, Renee C.
Craeybeckx, A. S. Elsevier's Dictionary of Photography. 660p. (Eng., Fr., & Ger.). 1965. 125.75 (ISBN 0-444-40146-6). Elsevier.
Crafford, F. S. Jan Smuts: A Biography. LC 69-10081. (Illus.). 1968. Repr. of 1943 ed. lib. bdg. 19.25x (ISBN 0-8371-0054-2, CRJS). Greenwood.
Craft, Alma & Bardell, Geoff. Curriculum Opportunities in Multicultural Society. 1984. pap. text ed. 13.50 (ISBN 0-06-318285-8). Har-Row.
Craft, Ann & Craft, Michael. Handicapped Married Couples: A Welsh Study of Couples Handicapped from Birth by Mental, Physical of Personality Disorder. 1979. 25.00x (ISBN 0-7100-0411-7). Routledge & Kegan.
--Sex & The Mentally Handicapped. Rev. ed. 1982. pap. 8.95 (ISBN 0-7100-9293-8). Routledge & Kegan.
Craft, Ann & Craft, Michael, eds. Sex Education & Counselling for Mentally Handicapped People. LC 82-50831. 322p. 1983. pap. 18.00 (ISBN 0-8391-1773-6, 19496). Pro Ed.
Craft, Beniece R. Speedwriting Legal Dictionary. 170p. 1972. pap. 5.99 scp (ISBN 0-672-96142-3). Bobbs.
Craft, Benjamin C. & Hawkins, M. F. Applied Petroleum Reservoir Engineering. 1959. 44.95 (ISBN 0-13-041285-6). P-H.
Craft, Benjamin C., et al. Well Design: Drilling & Production. 1962. ref. ed. 44.95x (ISBN 0-13-950022-7). P-H.
Craft, Berniece, et al. Speedwriting for the Legal Secretary. LC 78-10833. 1979. pap. 17.55 scp (ISBN 0-672-97013-9); tchr's. manual o.p. 3.33 (ISBN 0-672-97014-7). Bobbs.
Craft, Hazel S. Beyond the Stars. 251p. (Orig.). 1985. pap. 15.00 (ISBN 0-9614538-2-6). Scott Craft Pubs.
--Jesus God's Gift of Peace to You. 100p. (Orig.). 1983. pap. 8.95 (ISBN 0-88144-013-2, CPS-013). Christian Pub.
Craft, J. L., ed. see Bouwsma, O. K.
Craft, J. L., jt. ed. see Craig, R. G.
Craft, J. L., jt. ed. see Whelan, A.
Craft, James E. Wheels on the Mountains. (Illus.). 1969. 8.00 (ISBN 0-87012-072-7). McClain.
Craft, John L. & Askling, Lawrence. Statistics & Data Analysis for Social Workers. LC 84-61422. 166p. (Orig.). 1984. pap. text ed. 19.95 (ISBN 0-87581-305-4). Peacock Pubs.
Craft, M., ed. Teaching in a Multicultural Society: The Task for Teacher Education. LC 82-135236. 196p. (Orig.). 1981. pap. 13.00x (ISBN 0-905273-28-1). Taylor & Francis.
Craft, Maurice, ed. Education & Cultural Pluralism. (Contemporary Analyses in Education Ser.). 150p. 1984. pap. 16.00x (ISBN 1-85000-000-X, Pub. by Falmer Pr). Taylor & Francis.
Craft, Maurice, et al. Linking Home & School. 3rd ed. 1980. text ed. 23.65i (ISBN 0-06-318136-3, IntlDept); pap. text ed. 13.10i (ISBN 0-06-318149-5). Har-Row.
Craft, Michael. Mentally Abnormal Offenders: Concepts, Disposal & Treatment. (Illus.). 510p. Date not set. price not set (Pub. by Bailliere-Tindall). Saunders.
Craft, Michael, jt. auth. see Craft, Ann.
Craft, Michael, ed. Tredgold's Mental Retardation. 12th ed. (Illus.). 1980. text ed. 50.00 (ISBN 0-7216-0715-2, Pub. by Bailliere-Tindall). Saunders.
Craft, Michael, jt. ed. see Craft, Ann.
Craft, Quentin. Old Car Value Guide. 1985 ed. (Illus.). 168p. 1985. pap. 10.95 (ISBN 0-911473-03-3). Wallace-Homestead.
--Old Car Value Guide: 1983 Edition. 168p. pap. cancelled (ISBN 0-911473-00-9). Wallace-Homestead.
Craft, Robert. Dearest Bubushkin: Selected Letters & Diaries of Vera & Igor Stravinsky. (Illus.). 1985. 29.95 (ISBN 0-500-01368-3). Thames Hudson.
--Present Perspectives: Critical Writings. LC 83-48886. 416p. Date not set. 18.95 (ISBN 0-394-53073-X). Knopf.
--A Stravinsky Scrapbook. LC 83-50016. (Illus.). 180p. 1984. 24.95f (ISBN 0-500-01310-1). Thames-Hudson.
Craft, Robert, jt. auth. see Stravinsky, Igor.
Craft, Robert, ed. Stravinsky: Selected Correspondence, Vol. I. LC 81-47495. (Illus.). 416p. 1981. 27.50 (ISBN 0-394-51870-5). Knopf.
--Stravinsky: Selected Correspondence, Vol. II. LC 81-47495. (Illus.). 559p. 1984. 30.00 (ISBN 0-394-52813-1). Knopf.
Craft, Robert & Gottlieb, Robert, eds. Stravinsky: Selected Correspondence III. LC 81-47495. (Illus.). 1985. 35.00 (ISBN 0-394-54220-7). Knopf.
Craft, Ruth. Carrie Hepple's Garden. LC 78-397. (Illus.). 32p. (ps-3). 1979. 9.95 (ISBN 0-689-50099-8, McElderry Bk). Atheneum.
--The King's Collection. LC 78-8808. (gr. k-3). 1979. 6.95a (ISBN 0-385-14664-7); PLB (ISBN 0-385-14665-5). Doubleday.
--Pieter Brueghel's The Fair. LC 76-10256. (gr. 2-4). 1976. 11.49i (ISBN 0-397-31698-4). Lipp Jr Bks.
--The Winter Bear. LC 74-18178. (Illus.). 32p. (ps-2). 1975. 12.95 (ISBN 0-689-50017-3, McElderry Bk); pap. 2.50 (ISBN 0-689-70456-9). Atheneum.
Craft, William. Running a Thousand Miles for Freedom: Or, the Escape of William & Ellen Craft from Slavery. facs. ed. LC 77-89417. (Black Heritage Library Collection Ser). 1860. 10.75 (ISBN 0-8369-8549-4). Ayer Co Pubs.
Crafton, Allen & Gard, Robert E. Woman of No Importance. LC 74-82344. 203p. 1974. 8.95 (ISBN 0-88361-032-9). Stanton & Lee.
Crafton, Dennis. Comanche Duel. (Lobo Ser.: No. 2). 208p. (Orig.). 1983. pap. 1.95 (ISBN 0-523-42011-0). Pinnacle Bks.
--The First Hunt. 208p. (Orig.). 1982. pap. 1.95 (ISBN 0-523-41639-3). Pinnacle Bks.
--Lobo, No. 1. 208p. (Orig.). 1982. pap. 1.95 (ISBN 0-523-41734-9). Pinnacle Bks.
Crafton, Donald. Before Mickey: The Animated Film 1898-1928. (Illus.). 352p. 1982. 27.50x (ISBN 0-262-03083-7); VHS video 55.00x (ISBN 0-262-03091-8); Beta-2 video 55.00x (ISBN 0-262-03092-6); U-Matic video 150.00x (ISBN 0-262-03093-4); pap. 9.95 (ISBN 0-262-53058-9). MIT Pr.
Crafton, Helen & Lindgren, Dorothy. The Elsah Landing Restaurant Cookbook. WB Design & Development, Inc., ed. LC 81-43379. (Illus.). 224p. 1981. 12.95 (ISBN 0-9606150-0-8). Elsah Landing.
Crafton, Roy L., jt. auth. see Kramer, Jack.
Crafts, Alden S. Modern Weed Control. LC 74-76383. (Illus.). 1975. 33.00x (ISBN 0-520-02733-7). U of Cal Pr.
Crafts, Alden S. & Crisp, Carl E. Phloem Transport in Plants. LC 71-125130. (Biology Ser.). (Illus.). 481p. 1971. text ed. 39.95 (ISBN 0-7167-0683-0). W H Freeman.
Crafts, Alden S., jt. auth. see Ashton, Floyd M.
Crafts, Glenna C. How to Raise & Train a Norwegian Elkhound. (Orig.). pap. 2.95 (ISBN 0-87666-342-0, DS-1101). TFH Pubns.
Crafts, Kathy & Hauther, Brenda. How to Beat the System: The Student's Guide to Good Grades. rev. ed. LC 81-47643. 192p. 1981. 3.95 (ISBN 0-394-17740-1, B-442, BC). Grove.
Crafts, R. C. & Binhammer, Robert T. A Guide to Regional Dissection & Study of the Human Body. 4th ed. LC 79-14417. 324p. 1979. pap. 17.50 (ISBN 0-471-05154-3). Wiley.
Crafts, Roger C. A Textbook of Human Anatomy. 2nd ed. LC 78-11424. 1979. 42.50x (ISBN 0-471-04454-7, Pub. by Wiley Med). Wiley.
--Textbook of Human Anatomy. 3rd ed. 906p. 1985. 39.95 (ISBN 0-471-88624-6). Wiley.
Crafts, Virginia, ed. National Association for Physical Education in Higher Education Annual Conference: Proceedings, Vol. II. LC 80-85214. 352p. 1981. pap. text ed. 15.00x (ISBN 0-931250-62-5, NPR00002). Human Kinetics.
Crafts, Wilbur F. Successful Men of To-Day: And What They Say of Success. LC 73-2500. (Big Business; Economic Power in a Free Society Ser.). Repr. of 1883 ed. 18.00 (ISBN 0-405-05081-X). Ayer Co Pubs.
Crafts-Lighty, A. Information Sources in Biotechnology. LC 83-17479. 306p. 1983. 80.00 (ISBN 0-943818-04-4, Nature Pr). Groves Dict Music.
Cragan, John F. & Shields, Donald C. Applied Communication Research: A Dramatistic Approach. 432p. 1981. text ed. 18.95x (ISBN 0-917974-53-0). Waveland Pr.
Cragan, John F. & Wright, David W. Communications Small Group Discussions: A Case Study Approach. (Illus.). 400p. 1980. text ed. 19.95 (ISBN 0-8299-0338-0); instrs.' manual avail. (ISBN 0-8299-0474-3). West Pub.
Cragen, Dorothy C. The Boys in the Sky Blue Pants. (Illus.). 1975. 15.00 (ISBN 0-914330-07-1, Pub by Pioneer Pub Co). Panorama West.
Crager, Richard L. & Spriggs, Ann J. The Development of Concepts: A Manual for the Test of Concept Utilization. 104p. 1972. pap. text ed. 18.50x (ISBN 0-87424-119-7). Western Psych.
Cragg, Dan. The Guide to Military Installations. 416p. 1983. pap. 14.95 (ISBN 0-8117-2169-8). Stackpole.
--The NCO Guide. LC 81-23312. (Illus.). 288p. 1982. pap. 12.95 (ISBN 0-8117-2144-2). Stackpole.
Cragg, Dan, jt. auth. see Grose, Francis.
Cragg, Ernest E. The Cragg Commentaries. LC 79-50349. 1979. 9.95 (ISBN 0-87863-176-3). Farnswth Pub.
Cragg, Gerald. Freedom & Authority: A Study of English Thought in the Early Seventeenth Century. 334p. text ed. 15.00 (ISBN 0-664-20738-3). Brown Bk.
Cragg, Gerald R. Church & the Age of Reason. (History of the Church). (Orig.). 1961. pap. 4.95 (ISBN 0-14-020505-5, Pelican). Penguin.
--Puritanism in the Period of the Great Persecution, 1660-1688. LC 76-143557. 1971. Repr. of 1957 ed. 16.00x (ISBN 0-8462-1578-0). Russell.
Cragg, Gerald R., ed. The Cambridge Platonists. 466p. 1985. pap. text ed. 17.50 (ISBN 0-8191-4347-2). U Pr of Amer.
Cragg, Gordon. Organoboranes in Organic Synthesis. (Studies in Organic Chemistry: Vol. 1). 440p. 1973. 75.00 (ISBN 0-8247-6018-2). Dekker.
Cragg, Gordon M., jt. ed. see Pettit, George R.
Cragg, J. B., ed. Advances in Ecological Research. Vol. 1 1963. 45.00 (ISBN 0-12-013901-4); Vol. 2 1965. 50.00 (ISBN 0-12-013902-2); Vol. 3 1966. 60.00 (ISBN 0-12-013903-0); Vol. 4 1967. 60.00 (ISBN 0-12-013904-9); Vol. 6 1969. 60.00 (ISBN 0-12-013906-5); Vol. 7 1971. 60.00 (ISBN 0-12-013907-3); Vol. 8 1974. 75.00 (ISBN 0-12-013908-1); Vol. 9 1975. 70.00 (ISBN 0-12-013909-X); Vol. 10, 1978. 40.00 (ISBN 0-12-013910-3). Acad Pr.
--Advances in Ecological Research, Vol. 11. LC 62-21479. 1980. 70.00 (ISBN 0-12-013911-1). Acad Pr.
--Advances in Ecological Research, Vol. 12. (Serial Publication Ser.). 1982. 46.00 (ISBN 0-12-013912-X). Acad Pr.
--Advances in Ecological Research, Vol. 14. 1984. 46.00 (ISBN 0-12-013914-6). Acad Pr.

Craig, Gerald S. Certain Techniques Used in Developing a Course of Study in Science for the Horace Mann Elementary School. LC 77-176677. (Columbia University. Teachers College. Contributions to Education: No. 276). Repr. of 1927 ed. 22.50 (ISBN 0-404-55276-5). AMS Pr.

Craig, Gordon. The End of Prussia. LC 83-40261. (Merle Curti Lecture Ser.). 96p. 1984. text ed. 15.00x (ISBN 0-299-09730-7). U of Wis Pr.

--On the Art of the Theatre. (Illus.). 1925. pap. 8.95 (ISBN 0-87830-570-X). Theatre Arts.

Craig, Gordon A. The Battle of Koniggratz: Prussia's Victory Over Austria, 1866. LC 75-35334. (Illus.). 211p. 1976. Repr. of 1964 ed. lib. bdg. 25.00x (ISBN 0-8371-8563-7, CRBK). Greenwood.

--Europe: Eighteen Fifteen to Nineteen Fourteen, Vol. 1. 3rd ed. LC 77-140148. (Orig.). 1972. text ed. 19.95 (ISBN 0-03-089194-9, HoltC). HR&W.

--Europe Since Eighteen Fifteen: Alternate Edition. LC 73-4178. 1974. text ed. 26.95 (ISBN 0-03-089211-2, HoltC). HR&W.

--Europe since Nineteen Fourteen. 3rd ed. LC 77-140148. (Orig.). 1972. pap. text ed. 19.95 (ISBN 0-03-089193-0, HoltC). HR&W.

--From Bismarck to Adenau: Aspects of German Statecraft. LC 78-1080. (The Albert Shaw Lectures on Diplomatic History, 1958 Ser.). 1979. Repr. of 1958 ed. lib. bdg. 22.50x (ISBN 0-313-21233-3, CRFB). Greenwood.

--The Germans. 348p. 1982. 15.95 (ISBN 0-399-12436-5, Putnam). Putnam Pub Group.

--The Germans. LC 82-22541. 352p. 1983. pap. 8.95 (ISBN 0-452-00622-8, F622, Mer). NAL.

--Germany, Eighteen Sixty-Six to Nineteen Forty-Five. (History of Modern Europe Ser.). 1978. 27.50x (ISBN 0-19-822113-4); pap. 15.95x (ISBN 0-19-502724-8). Oxford U Pr.

--Politics of the Prussian Army Sixteen Forty - Nineteen Forty-Five. 1964. pap. 9.95x (ISBN 0-19-500257-1). Oxford U Pr.

Craig, Gordon A. & Alexander, George L. Force & Statecraft: Diplomatic Problems of Our Time. LC 81-22304. (Illus.). 1983. 22.50x (ISBN 0-19-503115-6); pap. 9.95x (ISBN 0-19-503116-4). Oxford U Pr.

Craig, Gordon A. & Gilbert, Felix, eds. Diplomats, Nineteen Nineteen to Nineteen Thirty-Nine, 2 Vols. LC 53-6378. 1963. Vol. 1. pap. text ed. 3.45x (ISBN 0-689-70054-7, 41A); Vol. 2. pap. text ed. 4.95x (ISBN 0-689-70055-5, 41B). Atheneum.

Craig, Gordon A., ed. see Kehr, Eckart.

Craig, Grace, jt. auth. see Specht, Riva.

Craig, Grace J. Human Development. 4th ed. (Illus.). 608p. 1986. text ed. 29.95 (ISBN 0-13-445065-5). P-H.

Craig, Grace M. But This Is Our War. 192p. 1981. 15.95 (ISBN 0-8020-2442-4). U of Toronto Pr.

Craig, H. Two Coventry Corpus Christi Plays. 2nd ed. (EETS ES Ser.: Vol. 87). Repr. of 1952 ed. 15.00 (ISBN 0-317-15675-6). Kraus Repr.

Craig, H., ed. see Metham, John.

Craig, H., ed. see Stanford University, School of Letters.

Craig, H. A. Bilal. 14.95 (ISBN 0-7043-2136-X, Pub. by Quartet England); pap. 5.95 (ISBN 0-7043-3160-8, Pub. by Quartet England). Charles River Bks.

Craig, Hardin. The Enchanted Glass: The Elizabethan Mind in Literature. LC 75-11492. 293p. 1975. Repr. of 1952 ed. lib. bdg. 35.00x (ISBN 0-8371-8200-X, CREG). Greenwood.

--English Religious Drama of the Middle Ages. LC 78-6893. 1978. Repr. of 1968 ed. lib. bdg. 37.50x (ISBN 0-313-20496-9, CRER). Greenwood.

--Freedom & Renaissance. LC 74-86007. 1969. Repr. of 1949 ed. 15.00x (ISBN 0-8046-0552-1, Pub. by Kennikat). Assoc Faculty Pr.

--Literary Study & the Scholarly Profession. facs. ed. LC 72-84303. (Essay Index Reprint Ser.). 1944. 16.75 (ISBN 0-8369-1079-6). Ayer Co Pubs.

--A New Look at Shakespeare's Quartos. LC 71-181932. (Stanford University. Stanford Studies in Language & Literature: No. 22). Repr. of 1961 ed. 21.00 (ISBN 0-404-01797-5). AMS Pr.

--Written Word & Other Essays. LC 78-86008. (Essay & General Literature Index Reprint Ser.). 1969. Repr. of 1953 ed. 19.00x (ISBN 0-8046-0551-3, Pub. by Kennikat). Assoc Faculty Pr.

Craig, Hardin & Bevington, David. An Introduction to Shakespeare. 2nd ed. 1975. pap. 13.65x (ISBN 0-673-07972-4). Scott F.

Craig, Hardin, ed. Stanford Studies in Language & Literature. LC 76-25581. 1942. lib. bdg. 37.50 (ISBN 0-8414-3389-5). Folcroft.

Craig, Hardin & Thomas, J. M., eds. English Prose of the Nineteenth Century. 1929. 44.50x (ISBN 0-89197-147-5); pap. text ed. 24.95x (ISBN 0-89197-148-3). Irvington.

Craig, Hardin, jt. ed. see Parrott, Thomas M.

Craig, Hardin, Jr., ed. Rededication of Fondren Library of Rice University. (Rice University Studies: Vol. 55, No. 4). 112p. 1969. pap. 10.00x (ISBN 0-89263-202-X). Rice Univ.

Craig, Helen. The Knight, the Princess & the Dragon. LC 84-19419. (Illus.). 32p. (ps-2). 1985. 8.99 (ISBN 0-394-97212-0); pap. 7.95 (ISBN 0-394-87212-6). Knopf.

--Mouse House Months. LC 79-93307. (Illus.). 30p. (ps-3). 1981. accordian fold, slipcased 2.50 (ISBN 0-394-84580-3). Random.

--The Nights of the Paper Bag Monsters. LC 84-25045. (A Susie & Alfred Bk.). (Illus.). (ps-3). 1985. pap. 7.95 (ISBN 0-394-87307-6); PLB 8.99 (ISBN 0-394-97307-0). Knopf.

Craig, Howard A. Sunward I've Climbed. LC 74-80106. 1975. 10.00 (ISBN 0-87404-049-3). Tex Western.

Craig, Isabel, jt. auth. see Blaustein, Saul J.

Craig, J. Nine Poems & a Play. 1970. text ed. 6.75x (ISBN 0-317-13474-4, Pub. by C Woolf UK). Humanities.

Craig, J. C., et al. Labour Market Structure, Industrial Organization & Low Pay. LC 82-4265. (University of Cambridge Dept. of Applied Economics Occasional Papers: No. 54). 200p. 1982. 29.95 (ISBN 0-521-24579-6). Cambridge U Pr.

Craig, J. DuHadway. The Antiquated American. 1976. pap. 4.50 (ISBN 0-9602042-0-2). J D Craig.

--Luis & les Deux Coins. 1976. 7.00 (ISBN 0-533-02406-4). J D Craig.

Craig, J. W. Design of Lossy Filters. 1970. 25.00x (ISBN 0-262-03038-1). MIT Pr.

Craig, James. Designing with Type. rev. ed. Meyer, Susan, ed. (Illus.). 1980. 22.50 (ISBN 0-8230-1321-9). Watson-Guptill.

--Graphic Design Career Guide: How to Get a Job & Establish a Career in Design. (Illus.). 160p. (Orig.). 1983. pap. 14.95 (ISBN 0-8230-2151-3). Watson-Guptill.

--Phototypesetting: A Design Manual. Malmstrom, Margit, ed. (Illus.). 1978. 22.50 (ISBN 0-8230-4011-9). Watson-Guptill.

--Production for the Graphic Designer. (Illus.). 208p. 1974. 22.50 (ISBN 0-8230-4415-7). Watson-Guptill.

Craig, James D. Fishers of Men: Group Leader Guide. 3rd rev. ed. 116p. 1981. 4.00 (ISBN 0-88151-016-5). Lay Leadership.

--New Life Studies. 2nd rev. abr. ed. 174p. 1983. pap. text ed. 15.00 (ISBN 0-88151-023-8). Lay Leadership.

--New Life Studies: Group Leader's Guide. 2nd rev. abr. ed. 48p. 1983. 4.00 (ISBN 0-88151-025-4). Lay Leadership.

--New Life Studies: Home Study Guide. 2nd rev. abr. ed. 64p. 1983. 8.00 (ISBN 0-88151-024-6). Lay Leadership.

--Rejoice in the Lord. 32p. 1981. pap. 2.49 (ISBN 0-88151-018-1). Lay Leadership.

Craig, James D. & Hill, Donald E. One Hundred Series Implementation Outline. 38p. 1980. pap. 9.95 inc. cassettes (ISBN 0-88151-020-3). Lay Leadership.

Craig, James D., ed. All about Cells. 2nd rev. ed. 32p. 1981. pap. 2.49 (ISBN 0-88151-017-3). Lay Leadership.

--The Care & Feeding of New Converts. 1st ed. 12p. 1981. pap. text ed. 0.49 (ISBN 0-88151-021-1). Lay Leadership.

Craig, James D. & Hill, Donald E., eds. How to Start a Home Cell Ministry. 1st ed. 32p. 1981. pap. 7.95 includes cassettes (ISBN 0-88151-019-X). Lay Leadership.

Craig, James H. & Craig, Marguerite. Synergic Power: Beyond Domination, Beyond Permissiveness. 2nd ed. LC 79-67184. (Illus.). 164p. 1979. pap. 5.95x (ISBN 0-914158-28-7). ProActive Pr.

Craig, James R. Intimacy Training. 249p. (Orig.). 1983. pap. 12.95 (ISBN 0-686-38457-1). J R Craig.

Craig, James R. & Metze, Leroy P. Methods of Psychological Research. LC 77-11333. (Illus.). 1979. text ed. 21.95 (ISBN 0-7216-2738-2). HR&W.

--Methods of Psychological Research. 2nd. ed. LC 85-9656. (Psychology Ser.). 350p. 1985. text ed. 25.00 (pub net) (ISBN 0-534-05358-0). Brooks-Cole.

Craig, James R. & Vaughan, David J. Ore Microscopy. LC 80-39786. 406p. 1981. 37.50 (ISBN 0-471-08596-0, Pub. by Wiley-Interscience). Wiley.

Craig, James R., jt. auth. see Vaughan, David J.

Craig, James T. Gibson see Gibson Craig, James T.

Craig, James V. Domestic Animal Behavior: Causes & Implications for Animal Care & Management. (Illus.). 400p. 1981. text ed. 28.95 (ISBN 0-13-218339-0). P-H.

Craig, Janet. Turtles. LC 81-11448. (Now I Know Ser.). (Illus.). 32p. (gr. k-2). 1982. PLB 9.89 (ISBN 0-89375-664-4); pap. 1.25 (ISBN 0-89375-665-2). Troll Assocs.

--What's under the Ocean. LC 81-11425. (Now I Know Ser.). (Illus.). 32p. (gr. k-2). 1982. PLB 9.89 (ISBN 0-89375-652-0); pap. 1.25 (ISBN 0-89375-653-9). Troll Assocs.

Craig, Jasmine. Dear Adam. (Second Chance at Love Ser.: No. 243). 192p. 1985. pap. 1.95 (ISBN 0-425-07770-5). Berkley Pub.

--Imprisoned Heart. (Second Chance at Love Ser.: No. 118). 192p. 1983. pap. 1.95 (ISBN 0-515-07206-0). Jove Pubns.

--Master Touch. (Second Chance at Love: No. 274). 192p. 1985. pap. 2.25 (ISBN 0-425-08284-9). Berkley Pub.

--Refuge in His Arms, No. 170. 192p. 1984. pap. 1.95 (ISBN 0-515-07585-X). Jove Pubns.

--Surprised by Love. (Second Chance at Love Ser.: No. 187). 192p. 1984. pap. 1.95 (ISBN 0-515-07803-4). Jove Pubns.

Craig, Joan, ed. see Hollands, Jean.

Craig, Joe M. & Craig, Mary. John Toole & Ruth Ann Rankin & Their Descendants. (Illus.). 358p. (Orig.). 1984. pap. text ed. 25.00 (ISBN 0-910513-03-1). Mayfield Printing.

Craig, John. Chappie & Me. 1979. 8.95 (ISBN 0-396-07660-2). Dodd.

--Remarks on Some Fundamental Doctrines of Political Economy. LC 70-121321. Repr. of 1821 ed. lib. bdg. 29.50x (ISBN 0-678-00684-9). Kelley.

--Watersteps: The Locks of the Oxford Canal. (Illus.). 64p. 1982. 70.00x (ISBN 0-904845-50-8, Pub. by Whittington England). State Mutual Bk.

Craig, John C. One Hundred Nineteen Practical Programs for the TRS-80 Pocket Computer. (Illus.). 308p. 1982. 15.95 (ISBN 0-8306-0061-2); pap. 10.25 (ISBN 0-8306-1350-1, 1350). TAB Bks.

Craig, John C. & Bretz, Jeff. IBM PC Graphics. LC 84-8893. (Illus.). 250p. (Orig.). 1984. 19.95 (ISBN 0-8306-0860-5); pap. 13.95 (ISBN 0-8306-1860-0, 1860). TAB Bks.

Craig, John C., jt. auth. see Bretz, Jeff.

Craig, John E. Scholarship & Nation Building: The Universities of Strasbourg & Alsatian Society, 1871-1939. LC 83-24341. 432p. 1984. lib. bdg. 30.00x (ISBN 0-226-11670-0). U of Chicago Pr.

Craig, John R. Don't Marry a Friend: Escape This Divorce Trap... Friends Can Ruin Your Life. LC 85-60318. 144p. (Orig.). 1985. pap. text ed. 2.95 (ISBN 0-9614423-5-2). Rite Bks Pub.

--Ranching with Lords & Commons: Or, Twenty Years on the Range. LC 79-132387. Repr. of 1903 ed. 19.50 (ISBN 0-404-01798-3). AMS Pr.

Craig, Jonathan. Concepts in Jewish Art. LC 84-263. (Judaic Studies). (Illus.). 165p. 1986. 18.50x (ISBN 0-8046-9355-2, 9355, Pub. by Natl U). Assoc Faculty Pr.

Craig, Josmine. Under Cover of Night. (To Have & to Hold Ser.: No. 32). 192p. 1984. pap. 1.95 (ISBN 0-515-07834-4). Jove Pubns.

Craig, Julia F., jt. auth. see McVicar, Marjorie.

Craig, Katherine T. The Fabric of Dreams, Dream Lore & Dream Interpretation, Ancient & Modern. Repr. of 1918 ed. 20.00 (ISBN 0-89987-048-1). Darby Bks.

--Stars of Destiny: The Ancient Science of Astrology & How to Make Use of it Today. 312p. 1981. pap. 15.50 (ISBN 0-89540-115-0, SB-115). Sun Pub.

Craig, Kenneth D. & McMahon, Robert J., eds. Advances in Clinical Behavior Therapy. LC 83-10161. 280p. 1983. 30.00 (ISBN 0-87630-338-6). Brunner-Mazel.

Craig, Linda & Praytor, Phyllis. Criterion Referenced Test Kit: Math. (Criterion Reference Tests Ser.). (Illus.). 54p. (gr. 4). 1978. write for info. (ISBN 0-936394-01-3). Education Ser.

Craig, Lois A. & Federal Architecture Project Staff. The Federal Presence: Architecture, Politics, & National Design. 600p. pap. 20.00 (ISBN 0-262-53059-7). MIT Pr.

Craig, Lois A., jt. auth. see Federal Architecture Project Staff.

Craig, M., jt. auth. see Bhatia, B. D.

Craig, M. Jean. Dinosaurs & More Dinosaurs. (Illus.). (gr. k-3). 1973. pap. 1.95 (ISBN 0-590-32423-3). Scholastic Inc.

--Little Monsters. LC 76-42936. (Illus.). 40p. (ps-3). 1977. PLB 6.29 (ISBN 0-8037-4728-4); 6.50 (ISBN 0-8037-4727-6). Dial Bks Young.

Craig, M. Jean, retold by. The Three Wishes. (gr. k-3). 1971. pap. 1.50 (ISBN 0-590-01621-0). Scholastic Inc.

Craig, M. S. Gillian's Chain. 208p. 1983. 11.95 (ISBN 0-396-08249-1). Dodd.

--The Third Blonde: A Novel of Suspense. 196p. 1985. 14.95 (ISBN 0-396-08418-4). Dodd.

Craig, Malcolm. Successful Investment Strategy. LC 84-3681. 143p. 1984. 22.50 (ISBN 0-85941-247-4, Pub. by Woodhead-Faulkner). Longwood Pub Group.

Craig, Marguerite, jt. auth. see Craig, James H.

Craig, Marguerite, et al. Power from Within: A Guide for Women to Discover Their Power & Express It in Creative, Caring Ways. (Illus., Orig.). 1977. pap. 3.00x (ISBN 0-914158-27-9). ProActive Pr.

Craig, Marjorie. Miss Craig's Face-Saving Exercises. 1970. 12.95 (ISBN 0-394-42412-3). Random.

--Miss Craig's Twenty-One Day Shape up Program for Men & Women. (Illus.). 1968. 13.95 (ISBN 0-394-40993-0). Random.

Craig, Marveen. Ultrasound Exam Review: Sonographer's Self Assessment Guide. 256p. 1985. pap. text ed. 24.50 (ISBN 0-397-50742-9, Lippincott Medical). Lippincott.

Craig, Mary. Mistress of Lost River. 192p. 1976. pap. 1.25 (ISBN 0-532-12396-4, 532-12396-125). Woodhill.

--Mother Teresa. (Profiles Ser.). (Illus.). 64p. (gr. 4-6). 1983. 7.95 (ISBN 0-241-10933-7, Pub. by Hamish Hamilton England). David & Charles.

--Pope John Paul II. (Profiles Ser.). (Illus.). 64p. (gr. 3-6). 1982. 7.95 (ISBN 0-241-10711-3, Pub. by Hamish Hamilton England). David & Charles.

--Pope Paul II. (Illus.). 80p. (gr. 5 up). 1982. pap. 2.50 (ISBN 0-686-40828-4, Pub by Penguin England). Irish Bk Ctr.

--Shadows of the Past. 224p. 1976. pap. 1.25 (ISBN 0-532-12408-1). Woodhill.

--Six Modern Martyrs. 272p. (Orig.). 1985. pap. 9.95 (ISBN 0-8245-0684-7). Crossroad NY.

Craig, Mary, jt. auth. see Craig, Joe M.

Craig, Mary S. Lyon's Pride. 352p. 1983. pap. 3.50 (ISBN 0-515-05295-7). Jove Pubns.

--Pirate's Landing. 352p. 1983. pap. 3.50 (ISBN 0-515-05296-5). Jove Pubns.

Craig, Maurice. Architecture in Ireland. (Aspects of Ireland Ser.). (Illus.). 57p. (Orig.). 1978. pap. 5.95 (ISBN 0-906404-01-0, Pub. by Dept Foreign Ireland). Irish Bks Media.

--The Architecture of Ireland. (Illus.). 240p. 1982. 50.00 (ISBN 0-7134-2586-5, Pub. by Batsford England). David & Charles.

--Classic Irish Houses of the Middle Size. 1977. 18.95 (ISBN 0-8038-0044-4). Architectural.

--Dublin Sixteen Sixty - Eighteen Sixty. (Illus.). 1980. pap. 13.50 (ISBN 0-900372-91-5). Irish Bk Ctr.

Craig, Millie. Mr. Peanut & Mr. Jellybean. 1983. 4.95 (ISBN 0-533-05480-X). Vantage.

Craig, Nathalie. Knit Toys. (Illus.). 144p. 1985. 16.95 (ISBN 0-668-06268-1). Arco.

Craig, Neville B., ed. Olden Time: A Monthly Publication. LC 9-10983. Repr. of 1846 ed. 66.00 (ISBN 0-527-68300-0). Kraus Repr.

Craig Norback & Co. The Gerber Baby Encyclopedia. (Orig.). 1983. pap. write for info. (ISBN 0-440-53292-2). Dell.

Craig, Oman. Childhood Diabetes: The Facts. (The Facts Ser.). (Illus.). 1982. 13.95x (ISBN 0-19-261330-8). Oxford U Pr.

Craig, P. P. & Jungerman, J. A. The Nuclear Arms Race: Technology & Society. 464p. 1985. 23.95 (ISBN 0-07-013345-X). McGraw.

Craig, Paul G. & Yocum, James C. Trends in the Ohio Economy. 1955. pap. text ed. 1.00x (ISBN 0-87776-079-9, R79). Ohio St U Admin Sci.

Craig, Paul P., ed. Energy Decentralization. Levine, Mark D. (AAAS Selected Symposium 72). 175p. 1982. lib. bdg. 21.00x (ISBN 0-86531-407-1). Westview.

Craig, R. Scottish Libraries, Nineteen Seventy-Eight to Nineteen Eighty: A Triennial Review. 1982. 30.00x (ISBN 0-900649-26-7, Pub. by Scot Lib Scotland). State Mutual Bk.

Craig, R., jt. auth. see Jarvis, R. C.

Craig, R. F. Soil Mechanics. 3rd ed. 1983. 32.50 (ISBN 0-442-30568-0); pap. 17.95 (ISBN 0-442-30568-0). Van Nos Reinhold.

Craig, R. G. & Craft, J. L., eds. Applied Geomorphology. (Binghamton Symposia in Geomorphology, International Ser.: No. 11). (Illus.). 272p. 1982. text ed. 35.00x (ISBN 0-04-551050-4). Allen Unwin.

Craig, R. G. & Labovitz, M. L., eds. Future Trends in Geomathematics. 1982. 28.00x (ISBN 0-85086-080-6, NO. 8002, Pub by Pion England). Methuen Inc.

Craig, R. S. The Making of Carlyle: An Experiment in Biographical Information. 1908. 35.00 (ISBN 0-8274-2663-1). R West.

Craig, Richard A. Upper Atmosphere: Meteorology & Physics. (International Geophysics Ser.: Vol. 8). 1965. 49.50 (ISBN 0-12-194850-1). Acad Pr.

Craig, Robert. Trauma. 224p. 1984. pap. 2.95 (ISBN 0-451-12758-7, Sig). Nal.

Craig, Robert C., jt. auth. see Clarizio, Harvey F.

Craig, Robert D. Captain Cook in the Pacific. (Pamphlets Polynesia Ser.: No. 1). (Illus.). pap. 3.50 (ISBN 0-939154-00-5). Inst Polynesian.

Craig, Robert D. & Pera, Vernice W. Tapa Samples from Polynesia. softcover 3.50 (ISBN 0-939154-06-4). Inst Polynesian.

Craig, Robert D. & Clement, Russell T., eds. Who's Who In Oceania: 1980-1981. 1981. 12.95 (ISBN 0-939154-13-7); pap. 7.95 (ISBN 0-939154-14-5). Inst Polynesian.

Craig, Robert D. & King, Frank P., eds. Historical Dictionary of Oceania. LC 80-24779. (Illus.). 416p. 1981. lib. bdg. 55.00 (ISBN 0-313-21060-8, KHD/). Greenwood.

Craig, Robert G. Restorative Dental Materials. 6th ed. LC 80-12105. (Illus.). 478p. 1980. pap. text ed. 29.95 (ISBN 0-8016-3866-6). Mosby.

Craig, Robert G. & O'Brien, William J. Dental Materials: Properties & Manipulation. 3rd ed. Powers, John M., ed. LC 82-12401. (Illus.). 327p. 1983. pap. text ed. 17.95 (ISBN 0-8016-1084-2). Mosby.

Craig, Robert J. & Baker, Stewart L. Drug Dependent Patients: Treatment & Research. (Illus.). 412p. 1982. 45.50x (ISBN 0-398-04562-3). C C Thomas.

Craig, Robert P., jt. auth. see Middleton, Carl L., Jr.

Craig, Robert P., ed. Issues in Philosophy & Education. 128p. 1973. pap. text ed. 8.95x (ISBN 0-8422-0372-9). Irvington.

Craig, Robert S. The Virginia Updikes-Updykes. 1050p. 1985. 37.50 (ISBN 0-9615135-0-0). Craig Pub Hse.

Craig, Robert T. The Mammillaria Handbook. (Illus.). 1945. 30.00 (ISBN 0-384-10090-2). Johnson Repr.

Craig, Robert T. & Tracy, Karen, eds. Conversational Coherence: Form, Structure, & Strategy, Vol. 2. (Sage Series in Interpersonal Communication). 344p. 1983. 28.00 (ISBN 0-8039-2121-7); pap. 14.00 (ISBN 0-8039-2122-5). Sage.

Craig, Robin. Steam Tramps & Cargo Liners. (The Ship Series, National Maritime Museum). (Illus.). 60p. 1980. 10.95 (ISBN 0-11-290315-0). Sheridan.
Craig, Robin, et al. The British Seafarer. 256p. 1982. 45.00x (ISBN 0-563-17852-3, Pub. by BBC Pubns). State Mutual Bk.
Craig, Roger & Plagenhoef, Vern. Inside Pitch: Roger Craig's 1984 Tiger Journal. 256p. (Orig.). 1984. pap. 8.95 (ISBN 0-8028-7048-1). Eerdmans.
Craig, Roy R. Structural Dynamics: An Introduction to Computer Methods. LC 80-39798. 527p. 1981. text ed. 46.50 (ISBN 0-471-04499-7). Wiley.
Craig, Ruth H. Learning the Nemeth Braille Code: A Manual for Teachers. LC 79-15984. (Illus.). 1980. pap. text ed. 1.00x (ISBN 0-8425-1701-4). Brigham.
Craig, S., ed. see Rogers, Jason.
Craig, Samuel, ed. see Calkins, Earnest E. & Holden, Ralph.
Craig, Samuel, jt. ed. see Ghosh, Avijit.
Craig, Samuel, ed. see Lockwood, R. Bigelow.
Craig, Samuel, ed. see Lucas, Darrell B. & Britt, Steuart H.
Craig, Samuel, ed. see Scott, Walter D.
Craig, Samuel, ed. see Woodward, Helen.
Craig, Sandy, ed. Dreams & Deconstructions: Alternative Theatre in Britain. 192p. 1981. text ed. 21.50x (ISBN 0-906399-19-X, Pub. by Amber Lane England); pap. text ed. 13.50x (ISBN 0-906399-20-3, Pub. by Amber Lane England). Humanities.
Craig, Sidney D. Raising Your Child, Not by Force But by Love. LC 72-10436. 192p. 1982. pap. 6.95 (ISBN 0-664-24413-0). Westminster.
Craig, Stephanie, tr. see Reboul, Antoine.
Craig, Stephen R. A Guide to Timeshare Housekeeping. 165p. 1984. pap. 40.00 (ISBN 0-318-03348-8). Am Land Dev.
Craig, T. & Springer, Hugh W., eds. Commonwealth Universities Yearbook 1980, 4 vols. 56th ed. LC 59-24175. (Illus.). 2700p. (Orig.). 1980. Boxed Set. 112.50x (ISBN 0-85143-063-5). Intl Pubns Serv.
Craig, Thomas, ed. Commonwealth Universities Yearbook 1981, 4 vols. 57th ed. LC 59-24175. (Illus.). 2700p. (Orig.). 1981. Set. pap. 155.00x (ISBN 0-85143-066-X). Intl Pubns Serv.
Craig, Timothy. Knots & Fans. 18p. (Orig.). 1984. pap. 10.00 (ISBN 0-914991-01-9). Tamara Pr.
--A Place in the Rain. 48p. (Orig.). 1982. pap. 10.00 (ISBN 0-914991-00-0). Tamara Pr.
Craig, Tom, jt. auth. see Shogan, Robert.
Craig, Tracey L., ed. Directory of Historical Societies & Agencies in the United States & Canada. 12th ed. LC 56-4164. (Illus.). 512p. 1982. pap. 36.00x (ISBN 0-910050-58-9). AASLH Pr.
Craig, Tracy & Ballard, Gay. Home Care & Upkeep. Coolman, Anne, ed. LC 82-63129. (Illus.). 96p. (Orig.). 1983. pap. 5.95 (ISBN 0-89721-014-X). Ortho.
Craig, Victor. Smart Choices. LC 81-70755. (Illus.). 112p. 1982. pap. 9.95 (ISBN 0-941156-00-1). Clear View Pubns.
Craig, W. Doctor Johnson & the Fair Sex: A Study of Contrasts. 59.95 (ISBN 0-8490-0053-X). Gordon Pr.
Craig, W. J., ed. see Shakespeare, William.
Craig, W. L., et al. International Chamber of Commerce Arbitration. 1984. loose-leaf 200.00 (ISBN 0-317-30371-6). Oceana.
Craig, W. Lawrence & Park, William W. International Chamber of Commerce Arbitration. LC 84-7466. 704p. 1984. lib. bdg. 75.00 (ISBN 0-379-10161-0). Oceana.
--International Commercial Arbitration: International Chamber of Commerce Arbitration. 1984. Set. 200.00 (ISBN 0-379-10160-2); binder (looseleaf) 100.00 (ISBN 0-317-07702-3). Oceana.
Craig, Warren. Sweet & Lowdown: America's Popular Song Writers. LC 77-20223. 1978. 37.50 (ISBN 0-8108-1089-1). Scarecrow.
Craig, William. Enemy at the Gates. 1974. pap. 1.95 (ISBN 0-345-23875-3). Ballantine.
--The Fall of Japan. 1979. pap. 6.95 (ISBN 0-14-005261-5). Penguin.
Craig, William H. Doctor Johnson & the Fair Sex: A Study of Contrasts. LC 77-10656. 1977. Repr. of 1895 ed. lib. bdg. 30.00 (ISBN 0-8414-1836-5). Folcroft.
Craig, William L. Apologetics: An Introduction. 1984. 13.95 (ISBN 0-8024-0405-7). Moody.
--The Cosmological Argument from Plato to Leibniz. LC 79-10394. (Library of Philosophy & Religion Ser.). 305p. 1980. text ed. 26.50x (ISBN 0-06-491311-2). B&N Imports.
--The Kalam Cosmological Argument. LC 77-17232. (Library of Philosophy & Religion Ser.). 216p. 1979. text ed. 28.50x (ISBN 0-06-491308-2). B&N Imports.
--The Son Rises. LC 11-267. 260p. 1981. 7.95 (ISBN 0-8024-7948-0). Moody.
Craig, William N. & Collins, James L. New Vistas for Competitive Employment of Deaf. (Monograph: No. 2). 110p. 1970. pap. text ed. 3.00 (ISBN 0-914494-04-X). Am Deaf & Rehab.
Craige, Betty J. Literary Relativity: An Essay on Twentieth Century Narrative. LC 81-69634. (Illus.). 136p. 18.50 (ISBN 0-8387-5034-6). Bucknell U Pr.
Craige, Betty J., ed. Relativism in the Arts. LC 82-4726. 216p. 1983. 19.00x (ISBN 0-8203-0625-8). U of Ga Pr.
Craige, Betty J., tr. The Poetry of Gabriel Celaya. LC 83-45367. 160p. 1984. 24.50 (ISBN 0-8387-5062-1). Bucknell U Pr.
Craige, Betty J., tr. see Machado, Antonio.
Craige, Betty Jean. Lorca's "Poet in New York". The Fall into Consciousness. LC 76-24339. (Studies in Romance Languages: No. 15). 112p. 1977. 11.00x (ISBN 0-8131-1349-0). U Pr of Ky.
Craiger-Smith, Alan. Tin-Glaze Pottery. 1973. 45.00 (ISBN 0-571-09349-3). Faber & Faber.
Craig-Green, Laurence. For... (Illus.). 96p. 1971. pap. 3.50 (ISBN 0-916922-01-4). IDTTC.
--From the Love of... (Illus.). 60p. 1970. pap. 3.50 (ISBN 0-916922-00-6). IDTTC.
--My Child. (Illus.). 120p. 1971. pap. 4.95 (ISBN 0-916922-02-2). IDTTC.
--Perhaps... (Illus.). 64p. 1973. pap. 3.50 (ISBN 0-916922-03-0). IDTTC.
Craighead, Erwin. Craighead's Mobile. Delaney, Caldwell, ed. (Illus.). 221p. 1968. 10.00 (ISBN 0-940882-10-8). Haunted Bk Shop.
Craighead, F. C., jt. auth. see Boving, A. G.
Craighead, Frank C., Jr. Track of the Grizzly. LC 78-8563. (Sierra Club Paperback Library). (Illus.). 272p. 1982. 10.95 (ISBN 0-87156-322-3); pap. 9.95 (ISBN 0-87156-223-5). Sierra.
--Track of the Grizzly. Date not set. 15.75 (ISBN 0-8446-6131-7). Peter Smith.
Craighead, Frank C., Jr. & Craighead, John J. How to Survive on Land & Sea. 4th ed. Smith, Ray E. & Jarvis, Shiras, eds. (Illus.). 488p. 1984. 14.95 (ISBN 0-87021-278-8). Naval Inst Pr.
Craighead, Frank C., Jr., jt. auth. see Craighead, John J.
Craighead, J. J. & Sumner, J. S. A Definitive System for Analysis of Grizzly Bear Habitat & Other Wilderness Resources Utilizing LANDSAT Multispectral Imagery & Computer Technology. Mitchell, J. A. & Lyons, L. J., eds. (Illus.). 279p. (Orig.). 1982. pap. text ed. 27.50 (ISBN 0-910439-01-X). Wildlife-Wildlands.
Craighead, John J. & Craighead, Frank C., Jr. Hawks, Owls & Wildlife. LC 74-81670. 1969. pap. 7.95 (ISBN 0-486-22123-7). Dover.
--Hawks, Owls, & Wildlife. (Illus.). 16.00 (ISBN 0-8446-0562-X). Peter Smith.
Craighead, John J., jt. auth. see Craighead, Frank C., Jr.
Craighead, John J., et al. A Field Guide to Rocky Mountain Wildflowers. LC 63-7093. (Peterson Field Guide Ser.). 1974. 15.95 (ISBN 0-395-07578-5); pap. 10.95 (ISBN 0-395-18324-3). HM.
Craighead, Meinrad. The Mother's Songs: Images of God the Mother. 88p. (Orig.). 1985. pap. 9.95 (ISBN 0-8091-2716-4). Paulist Pr.
Craighead, T. W. Sneaking Through Sociology: An Instructional System for the Introductory Course. 1970. pap. text ed. 9.50x (ISBN 0-8290-1190-0). Irvington.
Craighead, W. Edward, jt. ed. see Meyers, Andrew W.
Craighead, W. Edward, et al. Behavior Modification. 2nd ed. LC 80-83115. 576p. 1981. text ed. 29.50 (ISBN 0-395-29721-4); instr's. manual 1.00 (ISBN 0-395-30090-8). HM.
Craighill, Lloyd R., tr. see Hosono, Masanobu.
Craighton, Jack. Insight into Government. 13.50x (ISBN 0-392-03405-0, SpS). Sportshelf.
Craigie, E. Horne. Laboratory Guide to the Anatomy of the Rabbit. 2nd ed. LC 70-358625. (Illus.). 1966. pap. 8.50x (ISBN 0-8020-2038-0). U of Toronto Pr.
Craigie, E. Horne & Gibson, William C. The World of Ramon y Cajal: With Selections from His Nonscientific Writings. (Illus.). 308p. 1968. 27.50x (ISBN 0-398-00354-8). C C Thomas.
Craigie, Edward H. Craigie's Neuroanatomy of the Rat. rev. ed. Zeman, Wolfgang & Innes, James R., eds. 1963. 52.00 (ISBN 0-12-195450-1). Acad Pr.
Craigie, J. S., jt. auth. see Hellebust, J. A.
Craigie, N. S., et al, eds. Monopoles in Quantum Field Theory: Proceedings of the Monopole Meeting, Trieste, Italy, Dec. 11-15, 1981. xxi, 440p. 1982. 49.00x (ISBN 9971-950-28-6, Pub. by World Sci Singapore); pap. 21.00x (ISBN 9971-950-29-4, Pub. by World Sci Singapore). Taylor & Francis.
Craigie, P. C. Commentary on the Book of Deuteronomy. (New International Commentary of the Old Testament). 520p. 1976. 16.95 (ISBN 0-8028-2355-6). Eerdmans.
Craigie, Peter. Ugarit & the Old Testament. 110p. (Orig.). 1983. pap. 5.95 (ISBN 0-8028-1928-1). Eerdmans.
Craigie, Peter C. Ezekiel. LC 83-7044. (Daily Study Bible-Old Testsment). 332p. 1983. 14.95 (ISBN 0-664-21807-5); pap. 7.95 (ISBN 0-664-24574-9). Westminster.
--Twelve Prophets, Vol. 1. LC 84-2372. (Daily Study Bible-Old Testament Ser.). 1984. 14.95 (ISBN 0-664-21810-5); pap. 7.95 (ISBN 0-664-24577-3). Westminster.
--Twelve Prophets, Vol. 2. LC 84-2372. (The Daily Study Bible-Old Testament). 260p. 1985. 15.95 (ISBN 0-664-21813-X); pap. 8.95 (ISBN 0-664-24582-X). Westminster.
--War in the Old Testament. LC 78-17698. 1979. pap. 3.95 (ISBN 0-8028-1742-4). Eerdmans.
Craigie, W. A. The Religion of Ancient Scandinavia. 59.95 (ISBN 0-8490-0939-1). Gordon Pr.
--Scandinavian Folklore. 59.95 (ISBN 0-8490-0996-0). Gordon Pr.
Craigie, W. A., ed. The Maitland Folio Manuscript, 2 vols. 1927. Repr. of 1919 ed. Set. 59.00 (ISBN 0-384-35077-1). Johnson Repr.
Craigie, W. A., ed. see Asloan, John.
Craigie, William A. The Critique of Pure English. LC 77-970. 1946. lib. bdg. 12.50 (ISBN 0-8414-3403-4). Folcroft.
--The Critiques of Pure English from Caxton to Smollett. 1978. Repr. of 1945 ed. lib. bdg. 12.00 (ISBN 0-8482-7554-3). Norwood Edns.
--English Spelling: Its Rules & Reasons. LC 72-11547. 1928. lib. bdg. 15.00 (ISBN 0-8414-0900-5). Folcroft.
--The Growth of American English. LC 77-769. 1940. lib. bdg. 10.00 (ISBN 0-8414-3563-4). Folcroft.
--Growth of American English. LC 74-109967. 1971. Repr. of 1940 ed. lib. bdg. 18.75x (ISBN 0-8371-4469-8, CRGA). Greenwood.
--The Icelandic Sagas. LC 73-6948. 1913. lib. bdg. 17.50 (ISBN 0-8414-3368-2). Folcroft.
--Icelandic Sagas. LC 13-6314. 1968. Repr. of 1913 ed. 16.00 (ISBN 0-527-20100-6). Kraus Repr.
--The Northern Element in English Literature. LC 77-824. 1931. lib. bdg. 15.00 (ISBN 0-8414-3401-8). Folcroft.
--Northern Words in English Literature. LC 77-1353. 1937. lib. bdg. 12.50 (ISBN 0-8414-3407-7). Folcroft.
--Northern Words in Modern English. 1978. Repr. of 1937 ed. lib. bdg. 12.00 (ISBN 0-8482-3540-1). Norwood Edns.
--Primer of Burns. LC 70-103177. 1970. Repr. of 1896 ed. 19.50x (ISBN 0-8046-0814-8, Pub. by Kennikat). Assoc Faculty Pr.
--Problems of Spelling Reform. LC 77-1365. 1946. lib. bdg. 10.00 (ISBN 0-8414-3584-7). Folcroft.
--Religion of Ancient Scandinavia. facsimile ed. LC 74-99657. (Select Bibliographies Reprint Ser). 1906. 14.50 (ISBN 0-8369-5086-0). Ayer Co Pubs.
--Scandinavian Folklore. LC 74-78129. 466p. 1970. Repr. of 1896 ed. 51.00 (ISBN 0-8103-3587-5). Gale.
--Some Abnormalties of Spelling. 1978. Repr. of 1942 ed. lib. bdg. 12.00 (ISBN 0-8482-3544-4). Norwood Edns.
--Some Anomalies of Spelling. LC 77-766. 1946. lib. bdg. 10.00 (ISBN 0-8414-3409-3). Folcroft.
--The Study of American English. LC 77-965. 1926. lib. bdg. 10.00 (ISBN 0-8414-3405-0). Folcroft.
Craigie, William A. & Hulbert, James R., eds. Dictionary of American English on Historical Principles, 4 Vols. LC 36-21500. 1938-1944. Set. 300.00x (ISBN 0-226-11741-3). U of Chicago Pr.
Craigin, Elisabeth. Either Is Love. LC 75-12311. (Homosexuality). 1975. Repr. of 1937 ed. 11.00x (ISBN 0-405-07379-8). Ayer Co Pubs.
Craigmyle. The Mixed Cranial Nerves. Date not set. price not set (ISBN 0-471-90699-9). Wiley.
Craigmyle, Elizabeth. German Ballads. 20.00 (ISBN 0-89984-225-9). Century Bookbindery.
Craigmyle, M. Color Atlas of Histology. (Year Book Color Atlas Ser.). (Illus.). 320p. 1975. 42.95 (ISBN 0-8151-1888-0). Year Bk Med.
Craigmyle, M. B. & Presley, R. Embryology: (Concise Medical Textbook) 2nd ed. (Illus.). 1975. pap. text ed. 13.50 (ISBN 0-7216-0716-0, Pub. by Bailliere-Tindall). Saunders.
Craigmyle, Marshall B. The Apocrine Glands & the Breast. LC 84-7567. 1984. write for info. (ISBN 0-471-90506-2, Pub. by Wiley Med). Wiley.
--The Aprocrine Glands & the Breast. LC 84-7567. 1984. text ed. write for info (ISBN 0-471-90506-2, Pub. by Wiley Med). Wiley.
Craik, D. J. Structure & Properties of Magnetic Materials. 1971. (Pub. by Pion England); pap. 11.50x (ISBN 0-85086-018-0, 2903). Methuen Inc.
Craik, D. J., jt. auth. see Tebble, R. S.
Craik, Dinah M. Little Lame Prince. (Illus.). (gr. 4-6). companion lib. ed. o.s.i. 7.95 (ISBN 0-448-06017-5, G&D); Illus. Jr. Ed. o.p. 5.95 (ISBN 0-686-66436-1); PLB 3.79 (ISBN 0-448-03255-4). Putnam Pub Group.
--Unkind Word & Other Stories. facsimile ed. LC 70-101278. (Short Story Index Reprint Ser.). 1870. 21.50 (ISBN 0-8369-3215-3). Ayer Co Pubs.
Craik, E. M., ed. Marriage & Property. 208p. 1984. 22.40 (ISBN 0-08-028448-5). Pergamon.
Craik, F. I., jt. ed. see Cermak, L. S.
Craik, Fergus & Trehub, Sandra, eds. Aging & Cognitive Processes. (Advances in the Study of Communications & Affect: Vol. 8). 395p. 1982. 39.50 (ISBN 0-306-40946-1, Plenum Pr). Plenum Pub.
Craik, George L. Bacon: His Writings & His Philosophy. 715p. 1983. Repr. of 1860 ed. lib. bdg. 85.00 (ISBN 0-8495-0871-1). Arden Lib.
--English of Shakespeare. 3rd rev. & corr. ed. LC 79-132387. Repr. of 1864 ed. 24.00 (ISBN 0-404-01799-1). AMS Pr.
--Spenser & His Poetry, 3 vols. in 1. rev. ed. LC 74-99247. Repr. of 1871 ed. 46.00 (ISBN 0-404-01826-2). AMS Pr.
Craik, Harry. Life of Jonathan Swift, 2 Vols. LC 74-82016. (Research & Source Works Ser: No. 379). 1969. Repr. of 1894 ed. lib. bdg. 36.00 (ISBN 0-8337-0714-0). B Franklin.
Craik, Henry. English Prose: Selections with Critical Introductions by Various Writers & General Introductions to Each Period, 6 Vols. 1984. Repr. of 1893 ed. lib. bdg. 350.00 (ISBN 0-89760-184-X). Telegraph Bks.
Craik, Henry, ed. English Prose Selections, 5 Vols. Repr. of 1896 ed. Set. 187.50 (ISBN 0-404-01860-2); 37.50 ea. Vol. 1 (ISBN 0-404-01861-0). Vol. 2 (ISBN 0-404-01862-9). Vol. 3 (ISBN 0-404-01863-7). Vol. 4 (ISBN 0-404-01864-5). Vol. 5 (ISBN 0-404-01865-3). AMS Pr.
Craik, Kenneth & Zube, Ervin H., eds. Perceiving Environmental Quality: Research & Applications. LC 76-13513. (Environmental Science Research Ser.: Vol. 9). (Illus.). 323p. 1976. 45.00x (ISBN 0-306-36309-7, Plenum Pr). Plenum Pub.
Craik, Kenneth H. & McKechnie, George E., eds. Personality & The Environment. LC 77-94068. (Sage Contemporary Social Science Issues Ser.: 42). pap. 32.00 (ISBN 0-317-08224-8, 2021883). Bks Demand UMI.
Craik, Kenneth J. The Nature of Psychology: A Selection of Papers Essays, & Other Writings. LC 65-14851. pap. 51.00 (ISBN 0-317-10478-0, 2051423). Bks Demand UMI.
Craik, Rebecca L., jt. auth. see Bishop, Beverly.
Craik, T. W. I Know When One Is Dead, & When One Lives. 1981. 15.50x (ISBN 0-85672-198-0, Pub. by Brit Acad England). State Mutual Bk.
Craik, T. W., ed. see Marlowe, Christopher.
Craik, T. W., ed. see Shakespeare, William.
Craik, Thomas, et al. Revels History of Drama in English, Vol. 2: 1500-1576. 1980. 55.00x (ISBN 0-416-13030-5, NO. 6365). Methuen Inc.
Craik, W. A. Jane Austen: The Six Novels. (Orig.). 1968. pap. 11.95 (ISBN 0-416-29540-1, NO. 2154). Methuen Inc.
Crail, Lou. The Strange Legacy of Aunt Betina. 1978. pap. 1.50 (ISBN 0-532-15374-X). Woodhill.
Crail, Ted. Apetalk & Whalespeak: The Quest for Interspecies Communication. 320p. 1983. pap. 7.95 (ISBN 0-8092-5527-8). Contemp Bks.
Crain, Cynthia D. Movement & Rhythmic Activities for the Mentally Retarded. (Illus.). 136p. 1981. 14.75x (ISBN 0-398-04174-1). C C Thomas.
Crain, Darrell C. The Arthritis Handbook. LC 72-3319. (Illus.). 220p. 1973. pap. 1.95 (ISBN 0-668-02685-5). Arco.
Crain, Ellen & Gershel, Jeffrey. Pediatric Emergencies. 608p. 1985. pap. text ed. price not set (ISBN 0-8385-1126-0). ACC.
Crain, Ernest, jt. auth. see Maxwell, William E.
Crain, Ernest, et al. The Challenge of Texas Politics: Text with Readings. (Illus.). 1980. pap. 16.95 (ISBN 0-8299-0339-9). West Pub.
Crain, Jim. Historic Country Inns of California. rev. ed. LC 84-3233. (Orig.). 1984. pap. 8.95 (ISBN 0-87701-299-7). Chronicle Bks.
Crain, Jim & Milne, Terry. Camping Around California. 1975. pap. 5.95 (ISBN 0-394-73051-8). Random.
Crain, Mary B., ed. see L. A. Weekly Staff.
Crain, Robert L. Politics of School Desegregation: Comparative Case Studies of Community Structure & Policy-Making. LC 67-27390. (NORC Monographs in Social Research Ser.: No. 14). (Illus.). 1968. 9.95x (ISBN 0-202-30033-1). NORC.
--Southern Schools: An Evaluation of the Emergency School Assistance Program (EASP) & of School Desegregation. (Report Ser: Nos. 124A-124B). 1973. Set. 10.00x (ISBN 0-932132-21-9). NORC.
Crain, Robert L. & Weisman, Carlos S. Discrimination, Personality & Achievement: A Survey of Northern Negroes. LC 72-10104. (Quantitative Studies in Social Relations Er). 1972. 42.00 (ISBN 0-12-785142-9). Acad Pr.
Crain, Robert L., et al. The Politics of Community Conflict: The Fluoridation Decision. LC 68-31777. 1969. pap. text ed. 3.95x (ISBN 0-672-60840-5). Irvington.
--Making Desegregation Work: How Schools Create Social Climates. LC 81-10971. (Rand Educational Policy Study Ser.). 304p. 1982. prof ref 29.95 (ISBN 0-88410-199-1). Ballinger Pub.
Crain, Stanley M. Neurophysiologic Studies in Tissue Culture. LC 75-14567. 292p. 1976. 42.50 (ISBN 0-89004-048-6). Raven.
Crain, Steve. Bible Fun Book, No. 7. (Activity Book Ser.). 32p. (Orig.). (gr. k-4). 1981. oversized saddle stitched .99 (ISBN 0-87123-766-0, 220766). Bethany Hse.
--Bible Fun Book, No. 8. (Activity Book Ser.). 32p. (Orig.). (gr. k-4). 1981. pap. 0.99 saddle-stitched (ISBN 0-87123-772-5, 220772). Bethany Hse.
Crain, W. Mark. Vehicle Safety Inspection Systems: How Effective? 1980. pap. 4.25 (ISBN 0-8447-3361-X). Am Enterprise.
Crain, William C. Theories of Development. 2nd ed. (Illus.). 320p. 1985. pap. text ed. 30.95 (ISBN 0-13-913617-7). P-H.
Crain, William L. Balzac's le Secret des Ruggieri: A Critical Edition. LC 77-105268. 530p. 1970. 30.00x (ISBN 0-8262-0087-7). U of Mo Pr.

Crain, William L., tr. from Fr. Phaedra & Iphigenia. LC 82-81873. (Illus.). 150p. (Orig.). 1982. pap. 14.50 (ISBN 0-88127-002-4). Oracle Pr LA.

Craine, E. R., jt. auth. see Rossano, G. S.

Craine, Eric R. A Handbook of Quasistellar & BL Lacertae Objects. (Astronomy & Astrophysics Ser.: Vol. 4). 292p. 1977. 19.00x (ISBN 0-912918-23-3, 0923). Pachart Pub Hse.

Craine, Eugene R. & Reindorp, Reginald C., eds. Chronicles of Michoacan. LC 69-16726. (Civilization of the American Indian Ser.: No. 98). (Illus.). 1970. 19.50x (ISBN 0-8061-0887-8). U of Okla Pr.

--The Codex Perez & the Book of Chilam Balam of Mani. LC 78-21393. (CAI Ser.: Vol. 150). (Illus.). 1979. 24.95 (ISBN 0-8061-1512-2). U of Okla Pr.

Craine, James F. & Gudeman, Howard E. The Rehabilitation of Brain Functions: Principles, Procedures, & Techniques of Neurotraining. 358p. 1981. pap. 32.50x spiral (ISBN 0-398-04605-0). C C Thomas.

Crakanthorp, Richard. Defensio Ecclesiae Anglicanae. LC 72-1027. (Library of Anglo-Catholic Theology: No. 6). Repr. of 1847 ed. 27.50 (ISBN 0-404-52087-1). AMS Pr.

Craker, Lyle E. & Simon, James E., eds. Herbs, Spices & Medicinal Plants: Recent Advances in Botany, Horticulture & Pharmacology, Vol. 1. (Illus.). 336p. 1985. lib. bdg. 85.00 (ISBN 0-89774-143-9). Oryx Pr.

Cralley. Patty's Industrial Hygiene & Toxicology, Vol. 3B. 2nd ed. 1985. 70.00 (ISBN 0-471-82333-3). Wiley.

Cralley & Cralley. Industrial Hygiene of Plant Operations, Vol. III. 1986. 60.00 (ISBN 0-317-03918-0). Macmillan.

Cralley, Lester & Cralley, Lewis. Industrial Hygiene Aspects of Plant Operations: Process Flows, Vol. I. LC 82-80255. 1982. text ed. 65.00 (ISBN 0-02-949350-1). Macmillan.

Cralley, Lester, jt. auth. see Cralley, Lewis.

Cralley, Lester & Cralley, Lewis, eds. Patty's Industrial Hygiene & Toxicology: Theory & Rationale of Industrial Hygiene Practice, Vol. 3, Pt. A. LC 78-27102. 1979. 87.00 (ISBN 0-471-02698-0, Pub by Wiley-Interscience). Wiley.

Cralley, Lester V., jt. auth. see Cralley, Lewis J.

Cralley, Lester V., ed. Industrial Hygiene Aspects of Plant Operations: Engineering Considerations in Equipment Selection, Layout, & Building Design. Cralley, Lewis J. 752p. 1985. 65.00x (ISBN 0-02-949370-6). Macmillan.

Cralley, Lewis & Cralley, Lester. Industrial Hygiene of Plant Operations: Unit Operations & Product Fabrication, Vol. 2. LC 82-80255. (Industrial Hygiene of Plant Operations Ser.). 1984. 65.00 (ISBN 0-02-949360-9). Macmillan.

Cralley, Lewis, jt. auth. see Cralley, Lester.

Cralley, Lewis, jt. ed. see Cralley, Lester.

Cralley, Lewis J. & Cralley, Lester V. Patty's Industrial Hygiene Toxicology: The Work Environment, Vol. 3A. 2nd ed. 832p. 1985. 95.00 (ISBN 0-471-86137-5). Wiley.

Cralley, Lewis J. see Cralley, Lester V.

Cram, Donald J. Fundamentals of Carbanion Chemistry. (Organic Chemistry Ser.: Vol. 4). 1965. 57.50 (ISBN 0-12-196150-8). Acad Pr.

Cram, Donald J., jt. auth. see Cram, Jane M.

Cram, Ire H., ed. Future Petroleum Provinces of the United States: Their Geology & Potential, 2 vols. LC 73-165867. (American Association of Petroleum Geologists Memoirs: No. 15). Vol. 1. pap. 160.00 (ISBN 0-317-10271-0, 2050024); Vol. 2. pap. 160.00 (ISBN 0-317-10272-9). Bks Demand UMI.

Cram, J. S. Water: Canadian Needs & Resources. 3rd ed. LC 74-171154. (Environment Ser.). pap. 55.00 (ISBN 0-317-28411-8, 2022290). Bks Demand UMI.

Cram, Jane M. & Cram, Donald J. Essence of Organic Chemistry. LC 77-73957. (Chemistry Ser.). 1978. text ed. 29.95 (ISBN 0-201-01031-3); study guide 6.95 (ISBN 0-201-01032-1). Addison-Wesley.

Cram, Jean. Alcohol Stills: Moonshining Made Legal. LC 81-51361. (Illus.). 110p. (Orig.). 1981. pap. 5.95 (ISBN 0-939862-00-X). Washburn Pr MN.

Cram, M. D., jt. auth. see Schauder, D. E.

Cram, Mildred. Born in Time: The Christmas Story. (Illus.). 26p. (Orig.). 1972. pap. 2.50 (ISBN 0-913270-10-5). Sunstone Pr.

--Forever. 1935. 10.95 (ISBN 0-394-42540-5). Knopf.

--Old Seaport Towns of the South. 1973. Repr. of 1917 ed. 30.00 (ISBN 0-8274-1527-3). R West.

--Sir. 1973. 4.95 (ISBN 0-913270-11-3). Sunstone Pr.

--Stranger Things. LC 78-121532. (Short Story Index Reprint Ser). 1923. 17.00 (ISBN 0-8369-3488-1). Ayer Co Pubs.

Cram, Penny Hauser see Hauser-Cram, Penny & Carrozza-Martin, Fay.

Cram, R. A. Impressions of Japanese Architecture & the Allied Arts. (Illus.). 11.25 (ISBN 0-8446-1916-7). Peter Smith.

Cram, Ralph A. Black Spirits & White: A Book of Ghost Stories. facsimile ed. LC 70-167445. (Short Story Index Reprint Ser.). Repr. of 1895 ed. 14.00 (ISBN 0-8369-3971-9). Ayer Co Pubs.

--The Catholic Church & Art. 59.95 (ISBN 0-87968-817-3). Gordon Pr.

--Convictions & Controversies. facs. ed. LC 74-121460. (Essay Index Reprint Ser). 1935. 19.00 (ISBN 0-8369-1704-9). Ayer Co Pubs.

--The Dead Valley. (H. P. Lovecraft's Favorite Horror Stories Ser.). 16p. (Orig.). 1984. pap. 1.50 (ISBN 0-318-04711-X). Necronomicon.

--Impressions of Japanese Architecture & the Allied Arts. LC 81-52937. (Illus.). 304p. 1982. 11.00 (ISBN 0-8048-1438-4). C E Tuttle.

--Ministry of Art. facs. ed. LC 67-30203. (Essay Index Reprint Ser). 1914. 17.00 (ISBN 0-8369-0347-1). Ayer Co Pubs.

--Walled Towns. 59.95 (ISBN 0-8490-1271-6). Gordon Pr.

Cram, Ralph A., et al. Six Lectures on Architecture. facs. ed. LC 68-57314. (Essay Index Reprint Ser). 1917. 18.00 (ISBN 0-8369-0348-X). Ayer Co Pubs.

Cram, Thomas J. Topographical Memoir. 126p. 1978. 12.00 (ISBN 0-87770-193-8). Ye Galleon.

Cram, W. Bartlett. Picture History of New England Passenger Vessels. LC 80-67991. (Illus.). 424p. 1981. 35.00 (ISBN 0-686-30159-5). Burntcoat Corp.

--Picture History of New England Passenger Vessels. LC 80-67991. (Illus.). 414p. 1980. 35.00 (ISBN 0-917012-27-5). Burntcoat Corp.

Cram, W. J., et al, eds. Membrane Transport in Plants. Sigler, K. 560p. 1984. 44.95x (ISBN 0-471-90467-8, Pub. by Wiley-Interscience). Wiley.

Cramb, J. A. Germany & England. 1914. 12.50 (ISBN 0-8482-3566-5). Norwood Edns.

Crambach, A., jt. ed. see Deyl, Z.

Cramblit, Joella, jt. auth. see Belton, John.

Cramer, C. H. Open Shelves & Open Minds: A History of the Cleveland Public Library. LC 70-170150. (Illus.). 1972. 12.00 (ISBN 0-8295-0219-X). UPB.

Cramer, Chris & Harris, Sim. Hostage. 1984. 30.00x (ISBN 0-906549-25-6, Pub. by J Clare Bks UK); pap. 15.00x (ISBN 0-906549-26-4). State Mutual Bk.

Cramer, D. L. Craniofacial Morphology of Pan Paniscus. Szalay, F. S., ed. (Contributions to Primatology: Vol. 10). (Illus.). 1977. 20.50 (ISBN 3-8055-2391-2). S Karger.

Cramer, Edith. Early American Decoration Made Easy: 18 Full-Size Patterns for Furniture & Trays. (Crafts Ser.). 90p. 1985. pap. 4.50 (ISBN 0-486-24776-7). Dover.

Cramer, Eugene, ed. Victoria: Officium Hebdomadae Sanctae, Pts. 1-4. (Wissenschaftliche Abhandlungen - Musicological Studies Ser.: No. 31). 1982. Pt. 1, 170p. lib. bdg. 30.00 (ISBN 0-931902-04-5); Pt. 2, 270p. lib. bdg. 30.00 (ISBN 0-931902-05-3); Pt. 3, 370p. lib. bdg. 30.00 (ISBN 0-931902-06-1); Pt. 4, 470p. lib. bdg. 30.00 (ISBN 0-931902-07-X). Inst Mediaeval Mus.

Cramer, Frederick, jt. auth. see Donaldson, Ivan.

Cramer, Frederick H. Astrology in Roman Law & Politics. LC 54-6119. (American Philosophical Society, Philadelphia. Memoirs. Ser.: Vol. 37). pap. 75.80 (ISBN 0-317-08263-9, 2000352). Bks Demand UMI.

Cramer, Gail L. & Jensen, Clarence W. Agricultural Economics & Agribusiness. 3rd ed. 441p. 1985. 29.95 (ISBN 0-471-87871-5). Wiley.

--Student Study Guide to Accompany Agricultural Economics & Agribusiness. 3rd ed. 156p. 1985. pap. 10.95 (ISBN 0-471-81074-6). Wiley.

Cramer, Gail L. & Held, Walter G., Jr., eds. Grain Marketing Economics. 343p. 1983. 38.95 (ISBN 0-471-88894-X). Wiley.

Cramer, H. Mathematical Methods of Statistics. (Mathematical Ser.: Vol. 9). 1946. 39.00 (ISBN 0-691-08004-6). Princeton U Pr.

Cramer, Harald. Structural & Statistical Problems for a Class of Stochastic Processes. LC 74-160260. (S. S. Wilks Memorial Lecture Ser.). 1971. pap. 11.50x (ISBN 0-691-08099-2). Princeton U Pr.

Cramer, Harold. Elements of Probability Theory & Some of Its Applications. 2nd ed. LC 73-90331. 282p. 1973. pap. text ed. 12.50 (ISBN 0-88275-144-1). Krieger.

--Random Variables & Probability Distribution. 3rd ed. (Cambridge Tracts in Mathematics & Mathematical Physics). 1970. 29.95 (ISBN 0-521-07685-4). Cambridge U Pr.

Cramer, Hinrich & Schultz, Joachim. Cyclic Three Prime, Five Prime -Nucleotides: Mechanisms of Action. LC 76-45361. 554p. 1977. 91.95 (ISBN 0-471-99456-1, Pub. by Wiley-Interscience). Wiley.

Cramer, J. A. A Geographical & Historical Description of Ancient Greece, 3 vols. LC 77-6974. 1977. Repr. of 1828 ed. lib. bdg. 95.00 set (ISBN 0-89341-211-2). Longwood Pub Group.

Cramer, J. A., tr. see Nucius, Nicander.

Cramer, J. B. Fifty Selected Piano Studies. Von Bulow, Hans, ed. (Carl Fischer Music Library: No. 522). 53p. 1908. pap. 1.00 (ISBN 0-8258-0133-8). Fischer Inc NY.

--Fifty Selected Studies for Piano. Von Bulow, Hans, ed. (Carl Fischer Music Library: No. 525). 116p. 1946. pap. 10.00 (ISBN 0-8258-0138-9, L 525). Fischer Inc NY.

Cramer, J. Grant, tr. see Grundtvig, Sven.

Cramer, J. Grant, tr. see Grundtvig, Svendt.

Cramer, J. S. Empirical Econometrics. 277p. 1971. pap. 36.25 (ISBN 0-7204-3037-2, North-Holland). Elsevier.

Cramer, James. Uniforms of the World's Police: With Brief Data on Organizations, Systems, & Weapons. (Illus.). 216p. 1968. photocopy ed. 25.75x (ISBN 0-398-00355-6). C C Thomas.

Cramer, James A., ed. Courts & Judges. LC 81-5611. (Sage Criminal Justice System Annuals Ser.: Vol. 15). (Illus.). 280p. 1981. pap. 14.00 (ISBN 0-8039-1641-8); 28.00 (ISBN 0-8039-1640-X). Sage.

--Preventing Crime. LC 78-8400. (Criminal Justice System Annuals Ser.: Vol. 10). 225p. 1978. 28.00 (ISBN 0-8039-1047-9); pap. 14.00 (ISBN 0-8039-1048-7). Sage.

Cramer, James A., jt. ed. see McDonald, William F.

Cramer, Joe J., Jr., jt. auth. see Nelson, G. Kenneth.

Cramer, John B. Selected Works. (The London Pianoforte School 1770-1860 Ser.). 240p. 1984. lib. bdg. 66.00 (ISBN 0-8240-6159-4). Garland Pub.

Cramer, Kenneth R. & Pai, Shi I. Magnetofluid Dynamics for Engineers & Applied Physicists. (Illus.). 360p. 1973. text ed. 45.00 (ISBN 0-07-013425-1). McGraw.

Cramer, Lynne C. & Sullivan, Roy F. Audiological Evaluation & Aural Rehabilitation of the Deaf-Blind Adult. 240p. 1979. 7.00 (ISBN 0-318-17871-0). H Keller Natl Ctr.

Cramer, Malinda E. Divine Science & Healing. 1974. 6.95 (ISBN 0-686-24349-8); pap. 4.50 (ISBN 0-686-24350-1). Divine Sci Fed.

Cramer, Owen, et al, eds. see Rivers, Gloria.

Cramer, Patricia, jt. auth. see Bollinger, Theresa.

Cramer, Phebe. Word Association. LC 68-14652. 1968. 48.00 (ISBN 0-12-196450-7). Acad Pr.

Cramer, Quentin. Medical Tips for the Pre-Retiree & Retiree. LC 80-53784. 171p. 1982. 9.95 (ISBN 0-533-04884-2). Vantage.

Cramer, R. H., tr. see Ferrari, Carlo & Tricomi, Francesco.

Cramer, Raymond L. Psicologia de Jesus y la Salud Mental. Vargas, Carlos A., tr. from Eng. LC 76-16438. 191p. (Span.). 1976. pap. 4.75 (ISBN 0-89922-074-6). Edit Caribe.

--Psychology of Jesus & Mental Health. pap. 6.95 (ISBN 0-310-22721-6, Pub. by Cowman). Zondervan.

Cramer, Robert F. Hunger Fighter in Burma: The Story of Brayton Case. (Orig.). 1968. pap. 0.95 (ISBN 0-377-84111-0). Friend Pr.

Cramer, Ronald, jt. auth. see Stauffer, Russell G.

Cramer, Rose F. Wayne County, Missouri. (Illus.). 734p. 1972. 11.00 (ISBN 0-911208-22-4). Ramfre.

Cramer, Stanley H., jt. auth. see Herr, Edwin L.

Cramer, Steven A. Great Shall Be Your Joy. 228p. 1984. 8.95 (ISBN 0-934126-48-8). Randall Bk Co.

--The Worth of a Soul. 127p. 1983. 7.95 (ISBN 0-934126-29-1). Randall Bk Co.

Cramer, Thomas, tr. see Hartman, Von Aue.

Cramer, William D., jt. auth. see Erickson, Jonathan.

Cramers, C. A., ed. see International Symposium, 3rd, Amsterdam, Sept. 1976.

Cramlet, Ross C. Woodturning Visualized. rev ed. 1973. pap. 10.00 (ISBN 0-02-813770-1). Glencoe.

--Woodwork Visualized. rev. ed. (Illus., Orig.). 1967. pap. text ed. 10.00 (ISBN 0-02-813790-6). Glencoe.

Cramm, R. H. & Sibbach, W. R., eds. Coextrusion Coating & Film Fabrication. (Illus.). 1983. 54.95 (ISBN 0-89852-412-1). TAPPI.

Crammatte, Alan B. Deaf Persons in Professional Employment. 208p. 1967. 19.50x (ISBN 0-398-00356-4). C C Thomas.

Crammer, David J. & Woolston, Valerie A. Southern Africa. LC 80-14066. (World Education Ser.). (Illus.). 256p. (Orig.). 1980. pap. text ed. 6.00 (ISBN 0-910054-58-4). Am Assn Coll Registrars.

Cramond, Mike. Killer Bears. (Illus.). 224p. 1981. 7.95 (ISBN 0-684-17285-2, ScribT). Scribner.

Cramp, D. G. Quantitative Approaches to Metabolism: The Role of Tracers & Models in Clinical Medicine. LC 81-21992. 390p. 1982. 64.95 (ISBN 0-471-10172-9, Pub. by Wiley-Interscience). Wiley.

Cramp, D. G., jt. ed. see Carson, E. R.

Cramp, Rosemary. Corpus Anglo-Saxon Stone Sculpture. (Illus.). 1985. 155.00x (ISBN 0-19-726012-8). Oxford U Pr.

Cramp, Stanley, ed. Handbook of the Birds of Europe, the Middle East, & North Africa: The Birds of the Western Palearctic, Vol. 3: Waders to Gulls. (Illus.). 1983. 98.00x (ISBN 0-19-857506-8). Oxford U Pr.

Cramp, Stanley, et al, eds. Handbook of the Birds of Europe, the Middle East & North Africa: The Birds of Western Palearctic, Vol. 2, Hawks to Buzzards. (Illus.). 1980. text ed. 98.00x (ISBN 0-19-857505-X). Oxford U Pr.

--Handbook of the Birds of Europe, the Middle East, & North Africa: The Birds of the Western Palearctic, Vol. 1, Ostrich to Ducks. (Illus.). 1977. 98.00x (ISBN 0-19-857358-8). Oxford U Pr.

Crampin, M., jt. auth. see Pirani, F. A.

Crampton Associates, ed. Airport Transit Guide. (Illus.). 64p. Date not set. pap. price not set. Crampton Assoc.

Crampton, Beecher. Grasses in California. (California Natural History Guides Ser.). (Illus., Orig.). 1974. pap. 5.95 (ISBN 0-520-02507-5). U of Cal Pr.

Crampton, C. Gregory. Historical Sites in Cataract & Narrow Canyons & in Glen Canyon to California Bar. (Glen Canyon Ser: No. 24). Repr. of 1964 ed. 28.00 (ISBN 0-404-60672-5). AMS Pr.

--Historical Sites in Glen Canyon, Mouth of Hansen Creek to Mouth of San Juan River. (Glen Canyon Ser: No. 17). Repr. of 1962 ed. 30.00 (ISBN 0-404-60661-X). AMS Pr.

--Historical Sites in Glen Canyon, Mouth of San Juan River to Lees Ferry. (Glen Canyon Ser: No. 12). Repr. of 1960 ed. 30.00 (ISBN 0-404-60646-6). AMS Pr.

--Land of Living Rock: The Grand Canyon & the High Plateaus: Arizona, Utah, Nevada. LC 84-27593. (Illus.). 304p. 1985. pap. 16.95 (ISBN 0-87905-191-4). Gibbs M Smith.

--Outline History of the Glen Canyon Region, 1776-1922. (Glen Canyon Ser: No. 9). Repr. of 1959 ed. 32.50 (ISBN 0-404-60642-3). AMS Pr.

--The San Juan Historical Sites. (Glen Canyon Ser: No. 22). Repr. of 1964 ed. 24.50 (ISBN 0-404-60709-8). AMS Pr.

--Standing Up Country: The Canyonlands of Utah & Arizona. LC 83-18750. (Illus.). 224p. 1983. pap. 12.75 (ISBN 0-87905-081-0, Peregrine Smith). Gibbs M Smith.

--The Zunis of Cibola. LC 77-72586. (Illus.). 1978. 19.95 (ISBN 0-87480-120-6). U of Utah Pr.

Crampton, C. Gregory, jt. auth. see Rusho, W. L.

Crampton, C. Gregory, ed. The Mariposa Indian War, 1850-1851: Diaries of Robert Eccleston - the California Gold Rush, Yosemite, & the High Sierra. LC 58-62761. vii, 168p. 1975. Repr. of 1957 ed. 14.95 (ISBN 0-87480-024-2). U of Utah Pr.

Crampton, C. Gregory, ed. see Stanton, Robert B.

Crampton, Charles. Canework. (Illus.). xxxx, 142p. 1979. 10.50 (ISBN 0-7134-4972-1, Pub. by Batsford England). David & Charles.

--Canework. (Illus.). 142p. 1984. 10.95 (ISBN 0-85219-131-6, Pub. by Batsford England). David & Charles.

Crampton, E. P. Christianity in South-Western Nigeria. 256p. pap. 30.00x (ISBN 0-225-66312-0, Pub. by G Chapman England). State Mutual Bk.

Crampton, E. W. & Harris, L. E. Applied Animal Nutrition: The Use of Feedstuffs in the Formulation of Livestock Rations. 2nd ed. LC 68-10996. (Animal Science Ser.). (Illus.). 753p. 1969. text ed. 35.95 (ISBN 0-7167-0814-0). W H Freeman.

Crampton, Esme. A Handbook of the Theatre. 2nd ed. 264p. (Orig.). 1973. pap. text ed. 12.00x (ISBN 0-435-18185-8). Heinemann Ed.

Crampton, Frank A. Deep Enough: A Working Stiff in the Western Mine Camps. LC 81-43639. (Illus.). 304p. 1982. Repr. of 1956 ed. 18.95 (ISBN 0-8061-1716-8). U of Okla Pr.

Crampton, Georgia R. The Condition of Creatures: Suffering & Action in Chaucer & Spenser. LC 73-93281. pap. 54.50 (ISBN 0-317-09682-6, 2021992). Bks Demand UMI.

Crampton, Luke, jt. auth. see Rees, Dafyyd.

Crampton, Patricia, abridged by see Masefield, John.

Crampton, Patricia, tr. see Bomans, Godfried.

Crampton, Patricia, tr. see Gyllenskold, Karin.

Crampton, Patricia, tr. see Hildesheimer, Wolfgang.

Crampton, Patricia, tr. see Kooiker, Leonie.

Crampton, Patricia, tr. see Valencak, Hannelore.

Crampton, Richard. The Hollow Detente: Anglo-German Relations in the Balkans, 1911-1914. (Illus.). 250p. 1980. text ed. 19.25x (ISBN 0-391-02159-1). Humanities.

Crampton, Richard J. Bulgaria, Eighteen Seventy-Eight to Nineteen Eighteen: A History. (East European Monographs: No. 138). 580p. 1983. 45.00 (ISBN 0-88033-029-5). East Eur Quarterly.

Cramsie, Hilde F. Teatro y Censura en la Espana Franquista. LC 83-49363. (American University Studies II - Romance Languages & Literature: Vol. 9). 213p. 1985. text ed. 25.60 (ISBN 0-8204-0092-0). P Lang Pubs.

Cramton, Roger & Sedler, Robert. Conflict of Laws. (Sum & Substance Ser.). 1979. 10.95 (ISBN 0-686-23340-9). Josephson-Kluwer Legal Educ Ctrs.

Cramton, Roger C., et al. Conflict of Laws, Cases, Comments, Questions. 3rd ed. LC 81-7405. (American Casebook Ser.). 1026p. 1981. text ed. 27.95 (ISBN 0-314-59493-0). West Pub.

Cran, James A. Spare Parts Inc. LC 85-50729. 200p. 1985. 19.95 (ISBN 0-913495-02-6); pap. 9.95 (ISBN 0-913495-03-4). Taurus Pub Co.

--The Two Million Dollar Hit. 232p. (Orig.). 1983. 19.95x (ISBN 0-913495-00-X); pap. 9.95x (ISBN 0-913495-01-8). Taurus Pub Co.

Cranach, M., et al. Human Ethology. LC 78-27330. (Illus.). 1980. 89.50 (ISBN 0-521-22320-2); pap. 29.95 (ISBN 0-521-29591-2). Cambridge U Pr.

Cranach, M. Von see Von Cranach, M.

Cranach, Mario, ed. Methods of Inference from Animal to Human Behavior: Proceedings of the Conference on the Logic of Inference from Animal to Human Behavior Held in Muren, Switzerland, in March 1973. (Maison Des Sciences Del'homme: Publications No. 3). 1976. 26.80x (ISBN 90-2797-763-1). Mouton.

Cranach, Mario Von see Von Cranach, Mario.

Cranberry, Nola, tr. see Shely, Patricia.

Cranberry, Nola, tr. see Woggon, Guillermo.

Cranch, Christopher P. The Bird & the Bell, with Other Poems. LC 72-4960. (The Romantic Tradition in American Literature Ser.). 344p. 1972. Repr. of 1875 ed. 26.00 (ISBN 0-405-04632-4). Ayer Co Pubs.

--Collected Poems, 1835-1892. DeFalco, Joseph, ed. LC 70-161930. 744p. 1971. 90.00x (ISBN 0-8201-1091-4). Schol Facsimiles.
--The Life & Letters of Christopher Pearse Cranch. LC 72-90096. (Illus.). Repr. of 1917 ed. 23.00 (ISBN 0-404-05641-5). AMS Pr.
Crandall, Arthur G. New England Joke Lore: The Tonic of Yankee Humor. 1979. Repr. of 1922 ed. lib. bdg. 40.00 (ISBN 0-8482-7566-7). Norwood Edns.
Crandall, B. F. & Brazier, A. B, eds. Prevention of Neural Tube Defects: the Role of Alpha-Feto-Protein. (UCLA Forum in Medicinal Sciences: Vol. 20). 1978. 25.00 (ISBN 0-12-195350-5). Acad Pr.
Crandall, B. J. Morphology & Development of Branches in the Leafy Hepaticae. (Illus.). 1970. 28.00 (ISBN 3-7682-5430-5). Lubrecht & Cramer.
Crandall, Coryl, ed. Swetnam, the Woman-Hater: The Controversy & the Play. LC 69-11982. (Illus.). 176p. 1969. 4.95 (ISBN 0-911198-22-9). Purdue U Pr.
Crandall, D. R. & Mullineaux, D. R. Pleistocene Sequence in Southeastern Part of the Puget Sound Lowland, Washington. (Reprint Ser.: No. 2). (Illus.). 14p. 1958. 0.25 (ISBN 0-686-36910-6). Geologic Pubns.
Crandall, Faye E. Into the Copper River Valley. 1983. 9.95 (ISBN 0-8062-2025-2). Carlton.
Crandall, G. Douglas. Selected Exercises for the Biochemistry Laboratory. (Illus.). 104p. 1983. pap. 9.95x (ISBN 0-19-503185-7). Oxford U Pr.
Crandall, Hugh. Grand Teton: The Story Behind the Scenery. LC 78-57539. (Illus.). 1978. lib. bdg. 8.95 (ISBN 0-916122-47-6); pap. 3.75 (ISBN 0-916122-22-0). KC Pubns.
--Shenandoah: The Story Behind the Scenery. LC 74-30797. (Illus.). 1975. 8.95 (ISBN 0-916122-40-9); pap. 3.75 (ISBN 0-916122-15-8). KC Pubns.
--Yellowstone: The Story Behind the Scenery. LC 76-57453. (Illus.). 1977. 8.95 (ISBN 0-916122-46-8); pap. 3.75 (ISBN 0-916122-21-2). KC Pubns.
Crandall, James E. Theory & Measurement of Social Interest. 224p. 1981. 26.00x (ISBN 0-231-05256-1). Columbia U Pr.
Crandall, Jo Ann. Adult Vocational ESL. (Language in Education Ser.: No. 22). 51p. 1979. pap. 5.95 (ISBN 0-15-599054-3). Ctr Appl Ling.
Crandall, Jo Ann, et al. Teaching the Spanish-Speaking Child: A Practical Guide. 74p. (Orig.). 1981. pap. 6.50x (ISBN 0-15-599055-1). Ctr Appl Ling.
Crandall, Katherine. The Fine Old Town of Stonington. 1975. pap. 5.00 (ISBN 0-910258-03-1). Book & Tackle.
Crandall, Lee S. Management of Wild Mammals in Captivity. LC 64-10498. (Illus.). 1964. 40.00x (ISBN 0-226-11758-8). U of Chicago Pr.
Crandall, Michael G., ed. Nonlinear Evolution Equations. (MEC Seminars & Symposia: No. 40). 1978. 15.50 (ISBN 0-12-195250-9). Acad Pr.
Crandall, N. Emily Bronte, a Psychological Portrait. Repr. of 1957 ed. 28.00 (ISBN 0-527-20400-5). Kraus Repr.
Crandall, Ralph J., jt. auth. see Taylor, Robert M.
Crandall, Ralph J., ed. Genealogical Research in New England. LC 83-82075. 190p. 1984. 17.50 (ISBN 0-8063-1050-2). Genealog Pub.
Crandall, Richard C. Gerontology: A Behavioral Science Approach. LC 79-25622. (Illus.). 560p. 1980. text ed. 23.95 (ISBN 0-394-34833-8, RanC). Random.
Crandall, Richard E. Pascal Applications for the Sciences. LC 82-24832. (Self-Teaching Guides). 224p. 1983. pap. text ed. 16.95 (ISBN 0-471-87242-3, 1-581). Wiley.
Crandall, Rick, jt. auth. see Diener, Edward.
Crandall, Robert. Ministry to Persons: Organization & Administration. (Illus.). 96p. (Orig.). 1981. pap. 3.50 (ISBN 0-89367-070-7). Light & Life.
Crandall, Robert W. Controlling Industrial Pollution: The Economics & Politics of Clean Air. LC 82-45982. 220p. 1983. 26.95 (ISBN 0-8157-1604-4); pap. 9.95 (ISBN 0-8157-1603-6). Brookings.
--The U. S. Steel Industry in Recurrent Crisis: Policy Options in a Competitive World. LC 81-4642. 200p. 1981. 22.95 (ISBN 0-8157-1602-8); pap. 8.95 (ISBN 0-8157-1601-X). Brookings.
Crandall, Robert W. & Lave, Lester B., eds. Scientific Basis of Health & Safety Regulation. (Studies in the Regulation of Economic Activity). 1981. 31.95 (ISBN 0-8157-1600-1); pap. 11.95 (ISBN 0-8157-1599-4). Brookings.
Crandall, Ronald & Sells, Ray. There's New Life in the Small Congregation: Why It Happens & How. LC 83-71697. 120p. (Orig.). 1983. pap. 7.50 (ISBN 0-88177-001-9, DR001B). Discipleship Res.
Crandall, Ruth. Buzzy Bee Storybook. (A Happy Day Bk.). (Illus.). 24p. (gr. 1-3). 1980. 1.39 (ISBN 0-87239-409-3, 3641). Standard Pub.
Crandall, Samuel B. Treaties, Their Making & Enforcement. LC 74-76672. (Columbia University Studies in the Social Sciences: No. 54). Repr. of 1904 ed. 19.50 (ISBN 0-404-51054-X). AMS Pr.
Crandall, Stephen H. Engineering Analysis. LC 82-20335. 428p. 1983. Repr. of 1956 ed. lib. bdg. 28.50 (ISBN 0-89874-577-2). Krieger.
Crandall, Stephen H. & Karnopp, Dean C. Dynamics of Mechanical & Electromechanical Systems. LC 82-9890. 466p. 1982. Repr. of 1968 ed. lib. bdg. 36.00 (ISBN 0-89874-529-2). Krieger.
Crandall, Stephen H. & Mark, W. D. Random Vibration in Mechanical Systems. 1963. 39.00 (ISBN 0-12-196750-6). Acad Pr.
Crandall, Stephen H., et al. Introduction to the Mechanics of Solids. 2nd ed. (Illus.). 640p. 1972. text ed. 45.00 (ISBN 0-07-013436-7). McGraw.
--An Introduction to the Mechanics of Solids: SI Units. 2nd ed. (Illus.). 1978. text ed. 45.00 (ISBN 0-07-013441-3). McGraw.
Crandall-Stotler, Barbara & Jacobson, Katherine, eds. Bios: Process & Diversity. 1983. wire coil 14.95 (ISBN 0-8403-3125-8). Kendall-Hunt.
Crandell, Clifton E., ed. Comprehensive Care in Dentistry, Vol. 3. LC 78-16967. (Postgraduate Dental Handbook Ser.). 170p. 1979. 20.50 (ISBN 0-88416-164-1). PSG Pub Co.
Crane. The Red Badge of Courage. (American Classics Ser.). (gr. 9-12). 1977. pap. text ed. 3.99 (ISBN 0-88343-417-2); tchrs'. manual 3.50 (ISBN 0-88343-418-0); cassettes 52.00 (ISBN 0-88343-428-8). McDougal-Littell.
Crane, et al. An Introduction to Linguistics. 320p. (Orig.). 1981. pap. 15.95 (ISBN 0-316-16015-6). Little.
Crane, Alan P. Corrosion of Reinforcement in Concrete Construction. LC 83-10796. (Engineering Science Ser.). 432p. 1983. 89.95x (ISBN 0-470-27477-8). Halsted Pr.
Crane, Arthur G. Education for the Disabled in War & Industry: Army Hospital Schools. LC 70-176678. (Columbia University. Teachers College. Contributions to Education: No. 110). Repr. of 1921 ed. 22.50 (ISBN 0-404-55110-6). AMS Pr.
Crane, Barbara. ES 1 Skillbooklet. (Crane Reading System-English Ser.). (Illus.). (gr. k-2). 1982. pap. text ed. 17.02 per 10 (ISBN 0-89075-038-6). Crane Pub Co.
--A Head Start Through Reading. (Crane Reading System-English Ser.). (Illus.). (gr. k-2). 1977. pap. text ed. 26.55 (ISBN 0-89075-135-8). Crane Pub Co.
Crane, Barbara J. Apple & the Ax. (Crane Reading System-English Ser.). (Illus.). (gr. k-2). 1977. pap. text ed. 4.09 (ISBN 0-89075-097-1). Crane Pub Co.
--As I Skillbooklet. (Crane Reading System-English Ser.). (Illus.). (gr. k-2). 1977. pap. text ed. 17.02 per 10 (ISBN 0-89075-027-0). Crane Pub Co.
--AS 2 Skillbooklet. (Crane Reading System - English Ser.). (Illus.). (gr. k-2). 1982. pap. text ed. 17.02 per 10 (ISBN 0-89075-029-7). Crane Pub Co.
--The Baby Jay. (Crane Reading System-Eng. Ser.). (Illus.). (gr. k-2). 1977. pap. 3.86 (ISBN 0-89075-095-5). Crane Pub Co.
--The Bee Book. (Crane Reading System-English Ser.). (Illus.). (gr. k-2). 1977. pap. text ed. 3.86 (ISBN 0-89075-094-7). Crane Pub Co.
--BS Skillbooklet, No. I. (Crane Reading System-Eng. Ser.). (Illus.). (gr. k-2). 1982. pap. text ed. 17.02 per 10 (ISBN 0-89075-031-9). Crane Pub Co.
--Crane Reading System, Practice Bks, A-J. Incl. Practice Book A (ISBN 0-89075-052-1); Practice Book B (ISBN 0-89075-054-8); Practice Book C (ISBN 0-89075-055-6); Practice Book D (ISBN 0-89075-056-4); Practice Book E (ISBN 0-89075-057-2); Practice Book F (ISBN 0-89075-058-0); Practice Book G (ISBN 0-89075-059-9); Practice Book H (ISBN 0-89075-060-2); Practice Book I (ISBN 0-89075-061-0); Practice Book J (ISBN 0-89075-062-9). (Illus.). (gr. k-2). 1977. pap. text ed. 3.53 ea. A-E; pap. 3.71 ea. F-J. Crane Pub Co.
--Crane Reading System in Spanish, Levels A-E. Wasser, Lyneil L. & Gallegos, Louisa M., eds. Lasarte, Francisco, tr. Incl. Level A. Libro De Lectura. pap. 3.95 (ISBN 0-89075-163-3); Libro De Ejercicios. pap. 3.59 (ISBN 0-89075-158-7); Level B. Libro De Lectura. pap. 3.95 (ISBN 0-89075-164-1); Libro De Ejercicios. pap. 3.59 (ISBN 0-89075-159-5); Level C. Libro De Lectura. pap. 3.95 (ISBN 0-89075-166-8); Libro De Ejercicios. pap. 3.59 (ISBN 0-89075-160-9); Level D. Libro De Lectura. pap. 3.95 (ISBN 0-89075-167-6); Libro De Ejercicios. pap. 3.59 (ISBN 0-89075-161-7); Level E. Libro De Lectura. pap. 3.95 (ISBN 0-89075-168-4); Libro De Ejercicios. pap. 3.59 (ISBN 0-89075-162-5). (Illus.). (gr. k-6). 1978. pap. levels A-E guidebook to system 26.73 (ISBN 0-89075-169-2). Crane Pub Co.
--Crane Reading System in Spanish: Libros de trabajo, Levels A-E. Incl. Level A-1 (ISBN 0-89075-152-8); Level A-2 (ISBN 0-89075-153-6); Level B-1 (ISBN 0-89075-154-4); Level C-1 (ISBN 0-89075-155-2); Level D-1 (ISBN 0-89075-156-0); Level E-1 (ISBN 0-89075-157-9). (Illus.). (gr. k-2). 1978. per 10 17.25 (ISBN 0-686-67205-4). Crane Pub Co.
--CS 1 Skillbooklet. (Crane Reading System - English Ser.). (Illus.). (gr. k-2). 1981. pap. text ed. 17.02 per 10 (ISBN 0-89075-033-5). Crane Pub Co.
--DS 1 Skill booklet. (Crane Reading System - English Ser.). (Illus.). (gr. k-2). 1982. pap. text ed. 17.02 per 10 (ISBN 0-89075-035-1). Crane Pub Co.
--GS 1 Skill Booklet. (Crane Reading System - English Ser.). (Illus.). (gr. k-2). 1981. pap. text ed. 17.02 per 10 (ISBN 0-89075-042-4). Crane Pub Co.
--I'm Late. (Crane Reading System-English Ser.). (Illus.). (gr. k-2). 1977. pap. text ed. 4.09 (ISBN 0-89075-099-8). Crane Pub Co.
--Me. (Crane Reading System-English Ser.). (gr. k-2). 1977. pap. text ed. 3.86 (ISBN 0-89075-092-0). Crane Pub Co.
--My New Friends. (Crane Reading System-English Ser.). (gr. k-2). 1977. pap. text ed. 4.09 (ISBN 0-89075-102-1). Crane Pub Co.
--Only for a Day. (Crane Reading System-English Ser.). (Illus.). (gr. k-2). 1977. pap. text ed. 4.09 (ISBN 0-89075-101-3). Crane Pub Co.
--Over the Top. (Crane Reading System - English Ser.). (Illus.). (gr. k-2). 1977. pap. text ed. 4.09 (ISBN 0-89075-100-5). Crane Pub Co.
--Playmates. (Crane Reading System-English Ser.). (Illus.). (gr. k-2). 1977. pap. text ed. 3.86 (ISBN 0-89075-096-3). Crane Pub Co.
--The Queen & I. (Crane Reading System-English Ser.). (Illus.). (gr. k-2). 1977. pap. text ed. 3.86 (ISBN 0-89075-093-9). Crane Pub Co.
Crane, Basil K. Dust from an Alkali Flat: A Forest Ranger Remembers Central Nevada. LC 83-27330. (Bristlecone Paperback Ser.). (Illus.). 148p. 1984. pap. 9.50 (ISBN 0-87417-085-0). U of Nev Pr.
Crane, Bob, jt. auth. see Lenett, Robin.
Crane, Bonnie L. Blanche Ames: Artist & Activist. (Illus.). 40p. (Orig.). 1982. pap. 4.95 (ISBN 0-934358-10-9). Brockton Art Fuller.
Crane, Carla, jt. auth. see Steller, Joseph D., Jr.
Crane, Carla S., ed. Energy-Efficient Community Development Techniques. Steller, Joseph D., Jr. LC 81-51163. 170p. 1981. pap. 19.00 (ISBN 0-87420-598-0). Urban Land.
Crane, Caroline. Someone at the Door. 196p. 1985. 13.95 (ISBN 0-396-08601-2). Dodd.
--Something Evil. LC 84-8171. 224p. 1984. 12.95 (ISBN 0-396-08419-2). Dodd.
--The Third Passenger. LC 82-19923. 1983. 10.95 (ISBN 0-396-08132-0). Dodd.
--Trick or Treat. 1983. 11.95 (ISBN 0-396-08217-3). Dodd.
--Woman Vanishes. 215p. 1984. 12.95 (ISBN 0-396-08310-2). Dodd.
Crane, Catherine. What Do You Say to a Naked Room? (Illus.). 1979. 29.95 (ISBN 0-385-27121-2, Dial); pap. 14.95 (ISBN 0-385-27122-0). Doubleday.
Crane, Catherine C. Personal Places. (Illus.). 144p. 1982. 25.00 (ISBN 0-8230-7422-6, Witney Lib); pap. 12.95 (ISBN 0-8230-7423-4). Watson-Guptill.
Crane, Charles. Bible & Mormon Scriptures Compared. 4th ed. LC 83-72713. (Illus.). 1976. pap. 2.95 (ISBN 0-89900-100-9). College Pr Pub.
Crane, Chilton & Warren, Richard. Procedures in Vascular Surgery. 2nd ed. LC 75-22597. 1976. text ed. 42.50 (ISBN 0-316-16014-8). Little.
Crane, Clarkson. The Western Shore. LC 84-27669. 320p. 1985. pap. 10.95 (ISBN 0-87905-192-2). Gibbs M Smith.
Crane, Dale. Aircraft Corrosion Control. (AMP Training Ser.). (Illus.). 48p. 1979. pap. text ed. 3.95 (ISBN 0-89100-111-5). Aviation Maintenance.
--Aircraft Fabric Covering. (Aviation Maintenance Training Course Ser.). (Illus.). 54p. 1978. pap. 4.95 (ISBN 0-89100-077-1, EA-ADF). Aviation Maintenance.
--Aircraft Fuel Metering Systems. (Aviation Maintenance Training Course Ser.). (Illus.). 69p. 1975. pap. 5.95 (ISBN 0-89100-057-7, EA-FMS). Aviation Maintenance.
--Aircraft Reciprocating Engines. (Illus.). 113p. 1979. pap. 5.95 (ISBN 0-89100-075-5, EA-ARE). Aviation Maint.
--Aircraft Sheet Metal Construction & Repair. (Aviation Technician Training Ser.). (Illus.). 88p. 1978. pap. 5.95 (ISBN 0-89100-069-0, EA-SMF). Aviation Maintenance.
--Aircraft Tires & Tubes. 2nd. ed. (Aviation Technician Training Ser.). (Illus.). 46p. 1980. pap. text ed. 4.95 (ISBN 0-89100-178-6, EA-ATT-2). Aviation Maintenance.
--Aircraft Wheels, Brakes & Antiskid Systems. (Aviation Technician Training Ser.). (Illus.). 61p. 1979. pap. text ed. 5.95 (ISBN 0-89100-099-2, EA-AWB). Aviation Maintenance.
--Applied Science for the Aviation Technician. (Illus.). 182p. 1978. pap. 8.95 (ISBN 0-89100-085-2, EA-AS). Aviation Maint.
--Basic Electricity. (Aviation Techinican Training Ser.). (Illus.). 55p. 1975. pap. text ed. 5.95 (ISBN 0-89100-055-0, EA-BE-1). Aviation Maint.
--ITP Airframe Textbook. 679p. (Orig.). 1982. pap. 19.95 (ISBN 0-89100-248-0, ITP-AB); wkbk. 8.95 (ISBN 0-89100-249-9, ITP-AW-B); study guide 6.95 (ISBN 0-89100-244-8, ITP-ASG-B). Aviation Maintenance.
--ITP General Textbook. 542p. (Orig.). 1981. pap. 19.95 (ISBN 0-89100-241-3, ITP-GB); wkbk. 8.95 (ISBN 0-89100-242-1, ITP-GW-B); study guide 6.95 (ISBN 0-89100-201-4, ITP-GSG-B). Aviation Maintenance.
--Private Pilot: Airplane. (A Capstan Guide, Fast-Track Method Ser.). (Illus.). 176p. (Orig.). 1985. pap. text ed. 8.95 (ISBN 0-914565-06-0). Capstan Pubns.
--So You Think You Know...? Quiz Book. (Aviation Training Ser.). (Illus.). 297p. 1980. pap. 10.95 (ISBN 0-89100-071-2, EA-QB). Aviation Maintenance.
--Technical Instruction. 209p. 1981. pap. text ed. 12.95 (ISBN 0-89100-183-2, EA-183-2). Aviation Maintenance.
Crane, Dale & Carlson, Neal. Aircraft Painting & Finishing. 2nd. ed. (Aviation Maintenance Training Course Ser.). (Illus.). 67p. 1980. pap. 5.95 (ISBN 0-89100-152-2, EA-AP-2). Aviation Maintenance.
Crane, Dale & Scheppler, Robert. Aircraft Oxygen Systems. (AMP Training Ser.). (Illus.). 1975. pap. text ed. 3.95 (ISBN 0-89100-056-9, EA-AOS-1). Aviation Maintenance.
Crane, Dale, jt. auth. see Aviation Maintenance Publishers &.
Crane, Dale, ed. Aircraft Air Conditioning Systems: Vapor Cycle. 2nd. ed. (Aviation Technician Training Ser.). (Illus.). 25p. 1975. pap. 3.95 (ISBN 0-89100-051-8, EA-AAC-1). Aviation Maint.
--Basic Electronics & Radio Installation. (Aviation Technician Training Ser.). 77p. 1977. pap. 5.95 (ISBN 0-89100-064-X, EA-BEM). Aviation Maint.
--Capstan Encyclopedic Dictionary of Technical Terms. (ABC (A Basic Course) Ser.). (Illus., Orig.). 1984. pap. 29.95 (ISBN 0-914565-02-8). Capstan Pubns.
Crane, Dale, ed. see Aviation Maintenance Foundation.
Crane, Dale, ed. see Aviation Maintenance Publishers.
Crane, Dale, jt. ed. see Jones, David.
Crane, Dale, et al. ITP Powerplant Textbook. 563p. (Orig.). 1983. pap. 19.95 (ISBN 0-89100-251-0, ITP-P); wkbk. 8.95 (ISBN 0-89100-252-9, ITP-PW); study guide 6.95 (ISBN 0-89100-253-7, ITP-PSG). Aviation Maintenance.
--Aircraft Technical Dictionary. 2nd ed. (Aviation Maintenance Training Course Ser.). 262p. 1980. pap. 5.95 (ISBN 0-89100-124-7, EA-ATD-2). Aviation Maintenance.
Crane, Debra J. & Berson, Misha, eds. Young Stages: A Guide to Theatre & Dance for Youth in the San Francisco Bay Area. LC 82-51320. (Illus.). 72p. (Orig.). 1982. pap. 5.00 (ISBN 0-9605896-1-9). Theatre Ctr Bay.
Crane, Diana. Invisible Colleges: Diffusion of Knowledge in Scientific Communities. LC 77-182088. 1972. 10.50x (ISBN 0-226-11857-6). U of Chicago Pr.
--The Sanctity of Social Life: Physicians' Treatment of Critically Ill Patients. LC 74-15510. 186p. 1975. 14.95x (ISBN 0-87154-209-9). Russell Sage.
Crane, Diane. The Sanctity of Social Life: Physician's Treatment of Critically Ill Patients. LC 74-15510. (Illus.). 286p. 1977. pap. text ed. 8.95x (ISBN 0-87855-648-6). Transaction Bks.
Crane, Donald P. Personnel: The Management of Human Resources. 3rd ed. LC 81-19295. 752p. 1982. text ed. write for info. (ISBN 0-534-01070-9). Kent Pub Co.
Crane, Donald P. & Jones, William A., Jr. The Public Manager's Guide. 288p. 1982. text ed. 20.00 (ISBN 0-87179-361-X); pap. 15.00 (ISBN 0-87179-375-X). BNA.
Crane, Dougall. Johannes Secundus: His Life, Work, & Influence on English Literature. 1931. pap. 8.00 (ISBN 0-384-10100-3). Johnson Repr.
Crane, Dwight B., jt. auth. see Bradley, Stephen P.
Crane, Dwight B., ed. Financial Management. 510p. 1983. 24.95 (ISBN 0-317-12396-3, 498). Wiley.
Crane, Edgar. Marketing Communications. 2nd ed. LC 72-4505. (Marketing Ser). Repr. of 1972 ed. 127.50 (ISBN 0-8357-9929-8, 2013116). Bks Demand UMI.
Crane, Edward H., jt. ed. see Boaz, David.
Crane, Elaine F. A Dependent People: Newport, Rhode Island, in the Revolutionary Era. (Illus.). 300p. 1985. 40.00 (ISBN 0-8232-1111-8). Fordham.
Crane, Eva. The Archaelogy of Beekeeping. LC 82-74021. (Illus.). 320p. 1983. 39.50x (ISBN 0-8014-1609-4). Cornell U Pr.
Crane, Eva & Townsend, G. F. Index to Agricultural Abstracts Nineteen Fifty to Nineteen Seventy-Two. 1824p. 1976. 113.00x (ISBN 0-686-78860-5, Pub. by Intl Bee Res England). State Mutual Bk.
Crane, F. A., jt. auth. see Charles, J. A.
Crane, Frederick. Extant Medieval Musical Instruments: A Provisional Catalogue by Types. LC 72-185993. (Illus.). 120p. 1972. text ed. 10.00x (ISBN 0-87745-022-6). U of Iowa Pr.
--Materials for the Study of the 15th-Century Basse Danse. (Wissenschaftliche Abhandlungen-Musicological Studies: Vol. 16). 128p. 1970. lib. bdg. 30.00 (ISBN 0-912024-86-0). Inst Mediaeval Mus.
Crane, Frederick G. Automobile Insurance Rate Regulation. 1962. 5.00x (ISBN 0-87776-105-1, R105). Ohio St U Admin Sci.
--Insurance Principles & Practices. 2nd ed. LC 83-17054. 550p. 1984. text ed. 31.95 (ISBN 0-471-87629-1); write for info. tchrs ed. (ISBN 0-471-88122-8). Wiley.

Crane, George W. Doctor Crane's Radio Talks. pap. 3.00 (ISBN 0-910748-05-5). Hopkins.
--Guidebook for Counseling: How to Cash in on Your Worries. LC 56-8620. (Illus.). 4.95 (ISBN 0-910748-02-0). Hopkins.
Crane, George W., et al. Psychology Applied. LC 60-5016. (Illus.). 846p. 16.95x (ISBN 0-910748-03-9). Hopkins.
Crane, Gerald C. Law Library Fund Raising: A Primer. (Law Library Information Reports Ser.: Vol. 4). 85p. 1983. pap. 100.00 loose leaf (ISBN 0-87802-079-9). Glanville.
Crane, H., ed. International Cycling Guide: 1982. 1982. 50.00 (ISBN 0-686-45843-5, Pub. by Selpress Bks England). State Mutual Bk.
Crane, H. W. see Wooley, Henry T.
Crane, Harold S., jt. auth. see Durrant, Stephen D.
Crane, Hart. Bridge. new ed. LC 72-131277. 1970. pap. 4.95 (ISBN 0-87140-225-4). Liveright.
--Complete Poems & Selected Letters & Prose of Hart Crane. (Anchor Literary Library). 1966. pap. 5.95 (ISBN 0-385-01531-3, Anch). Doubleday.
--Complete Poems & Selected Letters & Prose of Hart Crane. Weber, B., ed. (Black and Gold Lib). 1946. 19.95 (ISBN 0-87140-959-3). Liveright.
--White Buildings. 1972. pap. 3.95 (ISBN 0-87140-272-6). Liveright.
Crane, Helen E. Humanisme Dans L'oeuvre De Saint Exupery. 347p. (Fr). 1957. 5.00 (ISBN 0-911536-09-4). Trinity U Pr.
Crane, Henry H. Achieving an All-in Victory. Moorehead, Kent D., ed. 1977. pap. 4.50 (ISBN 0-89536-308-9). CSS of Ohio.
Crane, Hewitt D. The New Social Marketplace: Notes on Effecting Social Change in America's Third Century. LC 80-11674. (Communication & Information Science Ser.). (Illus.). 112p. 1980. text ed. 22.50 (ISBN 0-89391-063-5). Ablex Pub.
Crane, Irving & Sullivan, George. Pocket Billiards. 1965. pap. 2.50 (ISBN 0-346-12359-3). Cornerstone.
Crane, J. D. El Espiritu Santo en la Experiencia del Cristiano. De Lerin, Olivia, tr. Orig. Title: The Christian's Esperience of the Holy Spirit. 128p. 1982. Repr. of 1979 ed. 5.95 (ISBN 0-311-09093-1). Casa Bautista.
--Manual Para Predicadores Laicos. 122p. 1982. pap. 2.10 (ISBN 0-311-42039-7). Casa Bautista.
Crane, J. R. Fighting Yankees & Other Yarns. LC 67-16828. (Illus.). 1973. pap. 3.95 (ISBN 0-87027-137-7). Cumberland Pr.
Crane, James & Estudios, Guias de. Guia de Estudios Sobre Manual Para Predicadores Laicos. 88p. 1982. pap. 3.50 (ISBN 0-311-43502-5). Casa Bautista.
Crane, James D. El Sermon Eficaz. 308p. 1983. pap. 4.50 (ISBN 0-311-07606-8). Casa Bautista.
Crane, James D. & Diaz, Jorge E. Lecciones Para Nuevos Creyentes Student. 64p. 1981. pap. 1.65 (ISBN 0-311-13835-7); teacher ed. 2.95 (ISBN 0-311-13838-1). Casa Bautista.
Crane, Joan. Willa Cather: A Bibliography. LC 81-23134. xxviii, 412p. 1982. 35.00x (ISBN 0-8032-1415-4). U of Nebr Pr.
Crane, Joan St. C., compiled by. Carl Sandburg, Philip Green Wright, & the Asgard Press, 1900-1910: A Descriptive Catalogue of Early Books, Manuscripts, & Letters in the Clifton Waller Barrett Library, University of Virginia. LC 75-6824. (Illus.). xvi, 132p. 1975. 17.50x (ISBN 0-8139-0565-6). U Pr of Va.
--Robert Frost: A Descriptive Catalogue of Books & Manuscripts in the Clifton Waller Barrett Library, University of Virginia. LC 73-89904. (Illus.). xxvi, 280p. 1974. 17.50x (ISBN 0-8139-0509-5). U Pr of Va.
Crane, Jocelyn. Fiddler Crabs of the World: Ocypodidae - Genus UCA. LC 70-166366. 660p. 1975. 105.00x (ISBN 0-691-08102-6). Princeton U Pr.
Crane, John. Laboratory Experiments for Microprocessor Systems. (Illus.). 192p. 1980. pap. text ed. 21.95 (ISBN 0-13-519694-9). P-H.
Crane, John A. The Evaluation of Social Policies. (International Series in Social Welfare). 1982. lib. bdg. 27.00 (ISBN 0-89838-075-8). Kluwer-Nijhoff.
Crane, John K. The Root of All Evil: The Thematic Unity of William Styron's Fiction. 1985. 17.95x (ISBN 0-87249-447-0). U of SC Pr.
Crane, John R., ed. see Zucconi, Paul J., et al.
Crane, Julia & Angrosino, Michael. Field Project in Anthropology: A Student Handbook. 2nd ed. (Illus.). 207p. (Orig.). 1984. pap. 7.95x (ISBN 0-88133-078-7). Waveland Pr.
Crane, Keith, tr. see Pecsi, Kalman.
Crane, Lawrence, jt. auth. see McCormack, P. D.
Crane, Leah. Dark Ecstasy. (Superromances Ser.). 384p. 1983. pap. 2.95 (ISBN 0-373-70066-0, Pub. by Worldwide). Harlequin Bks.
Crane, Louise. Land & People of the Congo. LC 79-141447. (Portraits of the Nations Series). (Illus.). 144p. (gr. 7-9). 1971. PLB 10.89 (ISBN 0-397-31172-9). Lipp Jr Bks.
Crane, Lucy, tr. see Grimm, Jakob & Grimm, Wilhelm.
Crane, Lucy, tr. see Grimm, Wilhelm K. & Grimm, Jacob.
Crane, Mary. Rape: Avoidance & Resistance, A Nonviolent Approach. (Orig.). 1982. pap. 3.50 (ISBN 0-940460-04-1). Peace & Gladness.
Crane, Meg. Insanity Claus. (Orig.). 1984. pap. 3.95 (ISBN 0-671-52623-5, Long Shadow Bks). PB.
Crane, Michael, jt. ed. see Stofflet, Mary.
Crane, Milton, ed. Fifty Great American Short Stories. (Orig.). (gr. 9 up). pap. 3.95 (ISBN 0-553-24795-6). Bantam.
--Fifty Great Short Stories. (gr. 9 up). pap. 3.95 (ISBN 0-553-25482-0); tchr's guide avail. Bantam.
--Shakespeare's Art. 210p. 1973. 11.00x (ISBN 0-226-11835-5). U of Chicago Pr.
Crane, Milton, ed. see Shakespeare, William.
Crane, Moira. The Life of Lucy Fern, Pt. 1. (Literacy Volunteers of America Readers Ser.). 48p. (Orig.). 1983. pap. 2.46 (ISBN 0-8428-9600-7). Cambridge Bk.
--The Life of Lucy Fern, Pt. 2. (Literacy Volunteers of America Readers Ser.). 48p. (Orig.). 1983. pap. 2.46 (ISBN 0-8428-9601-5). Cambridge Bk.
Crane, Nathalia C. Janitor's Boy & Other Poems. LC 76-9892. (Children's Literature Reprint Ser.). (gr. 3-5). 1976. 15.00x (ISBN 0-8486-0003-7). Core Collection.
Crane, Nicholas. Cycling in Eurpoe. (Illus.). 320p. 12.95 (ISBN 0-317-30369-4, P977). Haynes Pubns.
--International Cycling Guide: 1983. (International Cycling Guide Ser.). (Illus.). 336p. 1983. pap. 9.95 (ISBN 0-900730-11-0). NY Zoetrope.
Crane, Nicholas & Gausden, Christa. The CTC Route Guide to Cycling in Britain & Ireland. (Illus.). 432p. 15.95 (ISBN 0-902280-64-3, P964). Haynes Pubns.
Crane, Nicholas, ed. International Cycling Guide: 1984. (International Guide Ser.). (Illus.). 288p. (Orig.). 1984. pap. 11.95 (ISBN 0-900730-12-9, Pub. by Tantivy). NY Zoetrope.
--International Cycling Guide 1985-1986. (Tantivy Ser.). (Illus.). 264p. (Orig.). 1985. pap. 12.95 (ISBN 0-900730-19-6, Pub. by Tantivy). NY Zoetrope.
Crane, Nick & Crane, Richard. Bicycles up Kilimanjaro. (Illus.). 160p. 1986. 13.95 (ISBN 0-946609-27-6, Pub. by Oxford Ill Pr). Interbook.
Crane, Philip, jt. auth. see Bush, George.
Crane, Philip M. Democrat's Dilemma: How the Liberal Left Captured the Democratic Party. LC 64-14592. 1964. pap. 1.50 (ISBN 0-911956-08-5). Constructive Action.
--The Sum of Good Government. LC 76-43560. 210p. 1976. pap. 1.95 (ISBN 0-916054-07-1, Dist. by Kampmann). Green Hill.
--Surrender in Panama: The Case Against the Treaty. LC 77-93941. 180p. 1978. 7.95 (ISBN 0-916054-57-8, Dist. by Kampmann). Green Hill.
Crane, Philip M., ed. Liberal Cliches & Conservative Solutions. 161p. 1984. pap. 3.95 (ISBN 0-89803-147-8). Green Hill.
Crane, R. S. Critical & Historical Principles of Literary History. LC 75-159832. 1971. pap. 1.75x (ISBN 0-226-11826-6, P442, Phoen). U of Chicago Pr.
Crane, R. S. & Kaye, F. B. A Census of British Newspapers & Periodicals, 1620-1800. vi, 205p. 1979. Repr. of 1927 ed. 25.00 (ISBN 0-900470-49-6). Oak Knoll.
--Census of British Newspapers & Periodicals, 1620-1800. 20.00x (ISBN 0-87556-060-1). Saifer.
Crane, R. T. The Utility of All Kinds of Higher Schooling. 1979. Repr. of 1909 ed. lib. bdg. 30.00 (ISBN 0-8492-4028-X). R West.
Crane, Rhonda J. The Politics of International Standards: France & the Color TV War. LC 79-4231. (Communication & Information Science Ser.). 1979. 22.50x (ISBN 0-89391-019-8). Ablex Pub.
Crane, Richard, jt. auth. see Crane, Nick.
Crane, Robert D., jt. auth. see Fryer, Christopher.
Crane, Robert I. A History of South Asia. LC 73-78930. (AHA Pamphlets: No. 513). 80p. (Orig.). 1973. pap. text ed. 1.50 (ISBN 0-87229-014-X). Am Hist Assn.
Crane, Robert I., ed. Aspects of Political Mobilization in South Asia. LC 76-5434. (Foreign & Comparative Studies Program, South Asian Ser.: No. 1). 1976. pap. text ed. 6.00x (ISBN 0-915984-75-X). Syracuse U Foreign Comp.
Crane, Robert I. & Spangenberg, Bradford, eds. Language & Society in Modern India: Essays in Honor of Professor Robert O. Swan. 1981. 12.00x (ISBN 0-8364-0788-1). South Asia Bks.
Crane, Robert I., jt. ed. see Barrier, N. G.
Crane, Robert T. The State in Constitutional & International Law. LC 78-63921. (Johns Hopkins University. Studies in the Social Sciences. Twenty-Fifth Ser. 1907: 6-7). Repr. of 1907 ed. 13.50 (ISBN 0-404-61172-9). AMS Pr.
Crane, Ronald S. The Language of Criticism & the Structure of Poetry. (University of Toronto, Alexander Foundation, the Alexander Lectures: 1951-52). pap. write for info. Bks Demand UMI.
--The Vogue of Medieval Chivalric Romance During the English Renaissance. LC 72-192915. Repr. of 1919 ed. lib. bdg. 10.00 (ISBN 0-8414-1131-X). Folcroft.
Crane, Ronald S., jt. auth. see Bryan, William F.
Crane, Ronald S., ed. see Goldsmith, Oliver.
Crane, Ronald S., et al. A Census of British Newspapers & Periodicals: 1620-1800. (University of North Carolina Studies in Philology: Vol. 24, No. 1). 205p. pap. 15.00 (ISBN 0-384-10103-8). Johnson Repr.
Crane, Ronald S., et al, eds. Critics & Criticism: Ancient & Modern. abr ed. LC 52-7330. 1957. pap. 6.00x (ISBN 0-226-11793-6, P15, Phoen). U of Chicago Pr.
Crane, Ronald S., et alcompiled by. English Literature, Sixteen Sixty to Eighteen Hundred: A Bibliography of Modern Studies (Volume 2 1939-1950) LC 73-19999. 715p. 1974. Repr. of 1952 ed. 25.00x (ISBN 0-87752-163-8). Gordian.
Crane, Ruth & Goad, Marcine H. Self-Evaluation Career Guide. LC 78-1362. 79p. 1978. pap. 3.50 (ISBN 0-87576-067-8). Pilot Bks.
Crane, Santiago D., tr. see Blackwood, A. W.
Crane, Stephan see Throp, Willard.
Crane, Stephen. Black Riders & Other Lines. LC 74-3127. 1896. lib. bdg. 25.00 (ISBN 0-8414-3614-2). Folcroft.
--The Blue Hotel & Other Stories. Orig. Title: Maggie & Other Stories. 1982. pap. 4.95 (ISBN 0-671-46036-6). WSP.
--Bride Comes to Yellow Sky. (Classic Short Stories Ser.). (Illus.). 40p. (gr. 6-12). 1982. PLB 8.95 (ISBN 0-87191-827-7). Creative Ed.
--The Complete Poems of Stephen Crane. Katz, Joseph, ed. & intro. by. 191p. 1972. pap. 7.95 (ISBN 0-8014-9130-4, CP130). Cornell U Pr.
--Great Short Works of Stephen Crane: Red Badge of Courage, Monster, Maggie, Open Boat, Blue Hotel, Bride Comes to Yellow Sky & Other Works. rev ed. Colvert, J., ed. pap. 3.80i (ISBN 0-06-083032-8, P3032, PL). Har-Row.
--Little Regiment: And Other Episodes of the American Civil War. facsimile ed. LC 70-150471. (Short Story Index Reprint Ser.). Repr. of 1896 ed. 12.50 (ISBN 0-8369-3811-9). Ayer Co Pubs.
--The Little Regiment: And Other Episodes of the American Civil War. 150p. 1983. Repr. of 1897 ed. lib. bdg. 40.00 (ISBN 0-8495-0968-8). Arden Lib.
--Maggie: A Girl of the Streets. 1978. pap. 2.25 (ISBN 0-449-30854-5, Prem). Fawcett.
--Maggie, a Girl of the Streets: A Story of New York. LC 66-20867. 1978. Repr. of 1893 ed. 35.00x (ISBN 0-8201-1268-2). Schol Facsimiles.
--Maggie: A Girl of the Streets (Eighteen Ninety-Three) Gullason, Thomas A., ed. (Norton Critical Edition). 1980. 20.95x (ISBN 0-393-01222-0); pap. 5.95x (ISBN 0-393-95024-7). Norton.
--Maggie & Other Stories. (Classics Ser.). (gr. 11 up). pap. 2.50 (ISBN 0-8049-0166-X, CL-166). Airmont.
--Maggie & Other Stories. 17.95 (ISBN 0-88411-572-0, Pub. by Aeonian Pr). Amereon Ltd.
--Men, Women & Boats. facsimile ed. LC 70-113652. (Short Story Index Reprint Ser.). 1921. 19.00 (ISBN 0-8369-3381-8). Ayer Co Pubs.
--The Open Boat. (Creative's Classic Ser.). (Illus.). 64p. (gr. 6-12). 1982. lib. bdg. 8.95 (ISBN 0-87191-826-9). Creative Ed.
--Open Boat, & Other Tales of Adventure. LC 6-30865. 1898. 39.00x (ISBN 0-403-00012-2). Scholarly.
--The Portable Stephen Crane. Katz, Joseph, ed. (Viking Portable Library: No. 68). 1977. pap. 7.95 (ISBN 0-14-015068-4). Penguin.
--Prose & Poetry. Levenson, J. C., ed. LC 83-19908. 1450p. 1984. 27.50 (ISBN 0-940450-17-8, Pub. by Library of America). Literary Classics.
--Red Badge of Courage. (Classics Ser). (gr. 7 up). 1964. pap. 1.50 (ISBN 0-8049-0003-5, CL-3). Airmont.
--Red Badge of Courage. (Literature Ser). (gr. 7-12). 1969. pap. text ed. 4.83 (ISBN 0-87720-712-7). AMSCO Sch.
--The Red Badge of Courage. 1979. pap. 1.25 (ISBN 0-89598-016-9). Andor Pub.
--The Red Badge of Courage. (Bantam Classics Ser.). 149p. (Orig.). (gr. 7-12). 1981. pap. 1.50 (ISBN 0-553-21011-4). Bantam.
--The Red Badge of Courage. LC 69-13318. (Merrill Standard Ser). 1975. 6.00 (ISBN 0-910294-29-1); pap. 4.00 (ISBN 0-910294-30-5). Brown Bk.
--Red Badge of Courage. LC 42-36053. 1942. 6.95 (ISBN 0-394-60493-8); pap. 3.75 (ISBN 0-394-30945-6). Modern Lib.
--Red Badge of Courage. (Modern Library College Editions). 1951. pap. 3.75 (ISBN 0-394-30945-6, T45, RanC). Random.
--The Red Badge of Courage. Shapiro, Irwin, ed. LC 73-75464. (Now Age Illustrated Ser.). (Illus.). 64p. (Orig.). (gr. 5-10). 1973. 5.00 (ISBN 0-88301-214-6); pap. 1.95 (ISBN 0-88301-101-8). Pendulum Pr.
--The Red Badge of Courage. Wright, Betty R., adapted by. LC 81-2611. (Raintree Short Classics). (Illus.). 48p. (gr. 4 up). 1981. PLB 15.15 (ISBN 0-8172-1670-7). Raintree Pubs.
--The Red Badge of Courage. rev. ed. Dixson, Robert J., ed. (American Classics Ser.: Bk. 10). (gr. 9 up). 1974. pap. text ed. 3.80 (ISBN 0-88345-206-5, 18129); cassettes 45.00 (ISBN 0-685-38931-6, 58235). Regents Pub.
--Red Badge of Courage. (gr. 7-12). 1972. pap. 1.95 (ISBN 0-590-02117-6). Scholastic Inc.
--Red Badge of Courage. LC 67-26616. 1967. Repr. of 1894 ed. 25.00x (ISBN 0-8201-1010-8). Schol Facsimiles.
--The Red Badge of Courage. Shefter, Harry, ed. (Enriched Classics Edition Ser.). 224p. pap. 2.95 (ISBN 0-671-50132-1). WSP.
--The Red Badge of Courage. Wright, Betty R., adapted by. LC 81-2611. (Raintree Short Classics Ser.). (Illus.). 48p. (gr. 4-12). 1983. pap. 9.27 (ISBN 0-8172-2019-4). Raintree Pubs.
--The Red Badge of Courage. 134p. 1983. pap. text ed. 3.95x (ISBN 0-460-01309-2, Pub. by Evman England). Biblio Dist.
--The Red Badge of Courage. Binder, Henry, ed. 192p. 1983. pap. 6.95 (ISBN 0-380-64113-5, 64113). Avon.
--The Red Badge of Courage. LC 82-82814. (Illus.). 176p. 1982. 12.95 (ISBN 0-89577-155-1). RD Assn.
--The Red Badge of Courage. 9.95 (ISBN 0-89190-118-3, Pub. by Am Repr). Amereon Ltd.
--Red Badge of Courage: An Annotated Text with Critical Essays. rev. ed. (Norton Critical Editors Ser.). 1976. pap. 4.95x (ISBN 0-393-09182-1, NortonC). Norton.
--The Red Badge of Courage: An Episode of the American Civil War. Binder, Henry, ed. 1982. 14.95 (ISBN 0-393-01345-6). Norton.
--The Red Badge of Courage & Other Favorites. LC 80-54131. (Silver Classics Ser.). 288p. (gr. 6 up). 1985. pap. 3.67 (ISBN 0-382-09990-7). Silver.
--Red Badge of Courage & Other Stories. (Great Il. Classics). (gr. 9 up). 1979. 8.95 (ISBN 0-396-07755-2). Dodd.
--Red Badge of Courage & Other Writings. Chase, Richard, ed. (YA) (gr. 9 up). 1960. pap. 5.95 (ISBN 0-395-05143-6, RivEd). HM.
--Red Badge of Courage & Selected Prose & Poetry. 3rd ed. Gibson, William M., ed. LC 69-10874. (Rinehart Editions). 1969. pap. text ed. 12.95 (ISBN 0-03-073360-X, HoltC). HR&W.
--Red Badge of Courage & Selected Stories. (RL 7). 1952. pap. 1.50 (ISBN 0-451-51592-7, CW1592, Sig Classics). NAL.
--Red Badge of Courage, with Reader's Guide. (AMSCO Literature Program). (gr. 9-12). 1971. pap. text ed. 5.75 (ISBN 0-87720-811-5); tchrs. ed. 3.65 (ISBN 0-87720-911-1). AMSCO Sch.
--Stephen Crane: An Exhibition of His Writings Held at the Columbia University Libraries: 1871-1900. (Illus.). 1956. 5.00x (ISBN 0-686-00800-6). O'Brien.
--Stephen Crane: An Omnibus. Stallman, Robert W., ed. 1952. 12.95 (ISBN 0-394-42070-5). Knopf.
--Stories & Tales. Stallman, Robert W., ed. 1955. pap. 2.95 (ISBN 0-394-70010-4, Vin, V10). Random.
--Whilomville Stories. 1972. Repr. of 1900 ed. lib. bdg. 18.00 (ISBN 0-8422-8032-4). Irvington.
--Whilomville Stories. LC 5011. 1900. 16.00x (ISBN 0-403-00013-0). Scholarly.
--Works of Stephen Crane: Vol. 1. Bowery Tales. Bowers, Fredson, ed. Incl. Maggie; George's Mother. LC 68-8536. (Illus.). 184p. 1969. 25.00x (ISBN 0-8139-0258-4). U Pr of Va.
--The Works of Stephen Crane: Vol. 10: Poems & Literary Remains. Bowers, Fredson, ed. LC 68-8536. 1975. 20.00x (ISBN 0-8139-0610-5). U Pr of Va.
--Works of Stephen Crane, Vol. 2: The Red Badge of Courage. Bowers, Fredson, ed. LC 68-8536. 1975. 25.00x (ISBN 0-8139-0514-1). U Pr of Va.
--The Works of Stephen Crane, Vol. 3. Bowers, Fredson, ed. Bd. with The Third Violet; Active Service. LC 68-8536. 492p. 1976. 25.00x (ISBN 0-8139-0666-0). U Pr of Va.
--Works of Stephen Crane: Vol. 4, The O'Ruddy. Bowers, Fredson, ed. LC 68-8536. (Illus.). 362p. 1971. 25.00x (ISBN 0-8139-0341-6). U Pr of Va.
--Works of Stephen Crane: Vol. 5, Tales of Adventure. Bowers, Fredson, ed. LC 68-8536. (Illus.). 242p. 1970. 25.00x (ISBN 0-8139-0302-5). U Pr of Va.
--Works of Stephen Crane: Vol. 6, Tales of War. Bowers, Fredson, ed. LC 68-8536. (Illus.). 320p. 1970. 30.00x (ISBN 0-8139-0294-0). U Pr of Va.
--Works of Stephen Crane: Vol. 7, Tales of Whilomville. Bowers, Fredson, ed. Incl. The Monster; His New Mittens. LC 68-8536. (Illus.). 277p. 1969. 25.00x (ISBN 0-8139-0259-2). U Pr of Va.
--Works of Stephen Crane, Vol. 8: Tales, Sketches, & Reports. Bowers, Fredson, ed. LC 68-8536. (Illus.). 1183p. 1973. 45.00x (ISBN 0-8139-0405-6). U Pr of Va.
--Works of Stephen Crane, Vol. 9, Reports of War. Bowers, Fredson, ed. LC 68-8536. (Illus.). 678p. 1971. 35.00x (ISBN 0-8139-0342-4). U Pr of Va.
--Wounds in the Rain. LC 72-3294. (Short Story Index Reprint Ser). 1972. Repr. of 1900 ed. 24.50 (ISBN 0-8369-4145-4). Ayer Co Pubs.
--Wounds in the Rain: A Collection of Stories Relating to the Spanish-American War of 1898. 347p. 1983. Repr. of 1905 ed. lib. bdg. 40.00 (ISBN 0-89987-146-1). Darby Bks.
Crane, Stephen & Barr, Robert. The O'Ruddy, a Romance. 356p. 1983. Repr. of 1903 ed. lib. bdg. 40.00 (ISBN 0-8495-0967-X). Arden Lib.
--The O'Ruddy, a Romance. 356p. 1983. Repr. of 1903 ed. lib. bdg. 40.00 (ISBN 0-89987-147-X). Darby Bks.
Crane, Stephen, Jr. The Red Badge of Courage: An Episode of the American Civil War. (Penguin American Library). 162p. 1983. pap. 2.95 (ISBN 0-14-039021-9). Penguin.
Crane, T. F. Italian Popular Tales. 59.95 (ISBN 0-8490-0428-4). Gordon Pr.

Crane, Teresa. Molly. 537p. 1982. 16.95 (ISBN 0-698-11072-2, Coward). Putnam Pub Group.

Crane, Theodore R., ed. Colleges & the Public Seventeen Eighty-Seven to Eighteen Sixty-Two. LC 63-9583. (Classics in Education Ser.). (Orig.). 1963. text ed. 10.00 (ISBN 0-8077-1200-0); pap. text ed. 5.00x (ISBN 0-8077-1197-7). Tchrs Coll.

Crane, Thomas E. The Message of St. John: The Spiritual Teachings of the Beloved Disciple. LC 80-11779. 184p. (Orig.). 1980. pap. 5.95 (ISBN 0-8189-0402-X). Alba.

--Patterns in Biblical Spirituality. Date not set. cancelled (ISBN 0-87193-144-3). Dimension Bks.

--The Synoptics: Mark, Matthew & Luke Interpret the Gospel. 240p. 1982. 40.00x (ISBN 0-7220-8711-X, Pub. by Sheed & Ward UK). State Mutual Bk.

Crane, Thomas F. The Exempla or Illustrative Stories from the Sermones: Vulgares off Jacques de Vitry. (Folk-Lore Society, London, Ser.: Vol. 26). pap. 35.00 (ISBN 0-317-16257-8). Kraus Repr.

--Italian Popular Tales. LC 68-21762. 424p. 1968. Repr. of 1885 ed. 37.00x (ISBN 0-8103-3462-3). Gale.

--Italian Popular Tales. 1976. lib. bdg. 59.95 (ISBN 0-8490-2088-3). Gordon Pr.

Crane, Thomas F., ed. see Jacobus De Vitriaco.

Crane, Tim, jt. auth. see Bannister, Hank.

Crane, Verner. The Southern Frontier, Sixteen Seventy to Seventeen Thirty-Two. LC 76-54227. 1977. Repr. of 1956 ed. lib. bdg. 22.50x (ISBN 0-8371-9336-2, CRSF). Greenwood.

Crane, Verner W. Benjamin Franklin & a Rising People. (Library of American Biography). 219p. 1962. pap. text ed. 6.95 (ISBN 0-316-16012-1). Little.

--The Southern Frontier, 1670-1732. 384p. 1982. pap. text ed. 7.95x (ISBN 0-393-00948-3). Norton.

Crane, Verner W., ed. see Franklin, Benjamin.

Crane, Walter. An Alphabet of Old Friends & the Absurd ABC. (Illus.). 1981. 12.95 (ISBN 0-500-01260-1). Thames Hudson.

--Artist's Reminiscences. LC 68-21763. (Illus.). 540p. 1968. Repr. of 1907 ed. 40.00x (ISBN 0-8103-3522-0). Gale.

--Beauty & the Beast & Other Tales. LC 82-80982. (Illus.). 1982. 12.95 (ISBN 0-500-01285-7). Thames Hudson.

--Flora's Feast: A Masque of Flowers. (Facsimile Classics Ser.). (Illus.). 44p. 1981. 10.95 (ISBN 0-8317-7925-X, Rutledge Pr). Smith Pubs.

--The Frog Prince: And Other Stories. (Facsimile Classics Ser.). (Illus.). 40p. 1981. 10.95 (ISBN 0-8317-3665-8, Rutledge Pr). Smith Pubs.

--Of the Decorative Illustration of Books Old & New. LC 68-30611. 356p. 1968. Repr. of 1905 ed. 48.00x (ISBN 0-8103-3299-X). Gale.

--William Morris & His Work. 1911. lib. bdg. 8.50 (ISBN 0-8414-3544-8). Folcroft.

--William Morris to Whistler. 1978. Repr. lib. bdg. 25.00 (ISBN 0-8495-0836-3). Arden Lib.

--William Morris to Whistler. LC 73-19972. 1911. lib. bdg. 25.00 (ISBN 0-8414-3534-0). Folcroft.

Crane, Warren E. Totem Tales. 106p. pap. 7.95 (ISBN 0-8466-0119-2, S119). Shorey.

Crane, William B. Encore. LC 83-2629. 216p. (gr. 4-8). 1983. 11.95 (ISBN 0-689-30982-1). Atheneum.

Crane, William C. Life & Select Literary Remains of Sam Houston of Texas, 2 vols in 1. LC 74-38348. (Select Bibliographies Reprint Ser.). Repr. of 1884 ed. 34.50 (ISBN 0-8369-6765-8). Ayer Co Pubs.

Cranefield, Paul F., ed. Two Great Scientists of the Nineteenth Century: Correspondence of Emil Du Bois-Reymond & Carl Ludwig. Ayed, Sabine L., tr. from Ger. LC 79-24140. 204p. 1982. text ed. 17.50x (ISBN 0-8018-2351-X). Johns Hopkins.

Cranefield, Paul F. & Hoffman, Brian F., eds. Paired Pulse Stimulation of the Heart. (Illus.). 224p. 1968. 7.50x (ISBN 0-87470-009-4). Rockefeller.

Craner, Max & Muns, Ron. Hey, Wait for Me... I'm Your Leader. 150p. 1982. 5.50 (ISBN 0-88290-206-7, 2049). Horizon Utah.

Craney, Jan & Caldwell, Esther, eds. The True Life Story of... 144p. 1982. text ed. 18.50 (ISBN 0-7022-1530-9); pap. 9.50 (ISBN 0-7022-1531-7). U of Queensland Pr.

Cranfield, C. E. Commentary on Romans. abr. ed. 320p. 1985. pap. 10.95 (ISBN 0-8028-0012-2). Eerdmans.

Cranfield Fluidics Conference, 1st. Proceedings. 1965. 29.00x (ISBN 0-686-71058-4). BHRA Fluid.

Cranfield Fluidics Conference, 2nd. Proceedings. 1967. text ed. 36.00x (ISBN 0-685-85166-4, Dist. by Air Science Co.). BHRA Fluid.

Cranfield Fluidics Conference, 3rd. Proceedings. 1968. text ed. 47.00x (ISBN 0-900983-01-9, Dist. by Air Science Co.). BHRA Fluid.

Cranfield Fluidics Conference, 4th. Proceedings. 1970. text ed. 54.00x (ISBN 0-900983-08-6, Dist. by Air Science Co.). BHRA Fluid.

Cranfield Fluidics Conference, 5th. Proceedings. 1972. text ed. 54.00x (ISBN 0-900983-24-8, Dist. by Air Science Co.). BHRA Fluid.

Cranfield Fluidics Conference, 6th. Proceedings. 1974. 40.00x (ISBN 0-686-71057-6). BHRA Fluid.

Cranfield Fluidics Conference, 7th. Proceedings. 1977. 51.00x (ISBN 0-900983-50-7). BHRA Fluid.

Cranfield, Geoffrey A. The Development of the Provincial Newspaper, 1700-1760. LC 77-16348. (Illus.). 1978. Repr. of 1962 ed. lib. bdg. 24.75x (ISBN 0-313-20017-3, CRDP). Greenwood.

--The Press & Society: From Caxton to Northcliffe. LC 77-21904. (Themes in British Social History). 1978. text ed. 22.00x (ISBN 0-582-48983-0). Longman.

Cranfill, Thomas M. & Clark, Robert L., Jr. Anatomy of the Turn of the Screw. LC 78-159037. 1971. Repr. of 1965 ed. text ed. 12.50x (ISBN 0-87752-151-4). Gordian.

Cranfill, Thomas M., ed. The Muse in Mexico: A Mid-Century Miscellany. (Illus.). 182p. 1959. 12.50 (ISBN 0-292-73310-0). U of Tex Pr.

Cranford, Carolyn E., ed. see American Automobile Association.

Cranford, Peter G. But for the Grace of God. (Illus.). 200p. 1982. pap. 8.95 (ISBN 0-9605822-1-5). Great Pyramid.

--How to Be Your Own Psychologist: The Art of Irresistible Influence--Compossibility! 223p. 1981. 14.95 (ISBN 0-9605822-0-7). Great Pyramid.

Cranford, Ronald E. & Doudera, A. Edward, eds. Institutional Ethics Committees & Health Care Decision Making. LC 84-14640. (Illus.). 426p. 1984. text ed. 28.00 (ISBN 0-914904-98-1, 00796). Health Admin Pr.

Crangle, D. J. The Magnetic Properties of Solids. (Structures & Properties of Solids Ser.). 192p. 1977. pap. text ed. 17.50 (ISBN 0-7131-2574-8). E Arnold.

Cranham, Gerry, jt. auth. see Scott, Brough.

Cranin, A. Norman. Oral Implantology. (Illus.). 384p. 1970. photocopy ed. 49.75x (ISBN 0-398-00357-2). C C Thomas.

Crank, D. H., et al. Methods of Teaching Shorthand & Transcription. 1982. 24.60 (ISBN 0-07-013465-0). McGraw.

Crank, J. The Mathematics of Diffusion. 2nd ed. (Illus.). 1975. pap. 26.95x (ISBN 0-19-853411-6). Oxford U Pr.

Crank, John. Free & Moving Boundary Problems. (Illus.). 1984. 64.00x (ISBN 0-19-853357-8). Oxford U Pr.

Crank, John & Park, Geoffrey S., eds. Diffusion in Polymers. 1968. 86.00 (ISBN 0-12-197050-7). Acad Pr.

Crankshaw, Edward. Bismarck. LC 80-29171. (Illus.). 480p. 1981. 19.95 (ISBN 0-670-16982-X). Viking.

--Bismarck. 1983. pap. 7.95 (ISBN 0-14-006344-7). Penguin.

--The Fall of the House of Habsburg. 1983. pap. 7.95 (ISBN 0-14-006459-1). Penguin.

--The Forsaken Idea: A Study of Viscount Milner. LC 73-17918. 178p. 1974. Repr. of 1952 ed. lib. bdg. 15.00x (ISBN 0-8371-7278-0, CRFI). Greenwood.

--Gestapo: Instrument of Tyranny. LC 79-21687. Repr. of 1956 ed. 16.95 (ISBN 0-89201-086-X). Zenger Pub.

--Memoir. 1985. write for info. (ISBN 0-670-80405-3). Viking.

--New Cold War: Moscow Vs. Peking. facs. ed. LC 79-133518. (Select Bibliographies Reprint Ser). 1963. 15.00 (ISBN 0-8369-5550-1). Ayer Co Pubs.

--Putting up with the Russians. (Nonfiction Ser.). 1985. pap. price not set. Penguin.

--Putting up with the Russians: Commentary & Criticism, 1947-84. 288p. 1984. 17.95 (ISBN 0-670-58330-8, E Sifton Bks). Viking.

--The Shadow of the Winter Palace. 1978. pap. 5.95 (ISBN 0-14-004622-4). Penguin.

Crankshaw, Edward, ed. see Aksakov, Sergei.

Cranley, John J. Vascular Surgery, Vol. 2: Peripheral Venous Diseases. (Illus.). 1975. 62.50x (ISBN 0-06-140666-X, Harper Medical). Lippincott.

Cranley, Mecca, jt. auth. see Ziegel, Erna.

Cranmer, Arthur. The Art of Singing. 90p. 1974. 9.95 (ISBN 0-234-77397-9). Dufour.

Cranmer, Don. Collector's Encyclopedia, Toys: Banks, with Prices. 112p. 1985. pap. 10.95 (ISBN 0-89145-256-7). Wallace-Homestead.

Cranmer, H. Jerome. The New Jersey Canals: State Policy & Private Enterprise, 1820-1832. LC 77-14768. (Dissertations in American Economic History Ser.). 1978. 34.50 (ISBN 0-405-11030-8). Ayer Co Pubs.

Cranmer, John L. Basic Drilling Engineering Manual. LC 82-12322. 160p. 1982. 64.95x (ISBN 0-87814-199-5, P-4312). Pennwell Bks.

--Basic Pipeline Engineering Manual. 240p. 1983. 64.95 (ISBN 0-87814-244-4). Pennwell Bks.

Cranmer, John L., Jr. BASIC Reservoir Engineering Manual. 232p. 1982. 64.95x (ISBN 0-87814-196-0, P-4310). Pennwell Bks.

Cranmer, Kathryn. Passionate Enemies. (Harlequin Presents Ser.). 1982. pap. 1.75 (ISBN 0-373-02516-5). Harlequin Bks.

Cranmer, Thomas. Miscellaneous Writings & Letters of Thomas Cranmer, Archbishop of Canterbury, Martyr, 1556. 1846. 51.00 (ISBN 0-384-10110-0). Johnson Repr.

--Writings & Disputations of Thomas Cranmer, Archbishop of Canterbury, Martyr. 1844. 41.00 (ISBN 0-384-10120-8). Johnson Repr.

Cranmer-Byng, J. L., ed. Chinese Buddhist Verse. Robinson, Richard H., tr. from Chinese. LC 79-8725. 1980. Repr. of 1954 ed. lib. bdg. 18.75x (ISBN 0-313-22168-5, ROCB). Greenwood.

Cranmer-Byng, J. L., ed. see Murray, Margaret A.

Cranmer-Byng, L. The Vision of Asia: An Interpretation of Chinese Art & Culture. 1979. Repr. of 1933 ed. lib. bdg. 30.00 (ISBN 0-8492-4025-5). R West.

Cranmer-Byng, L., ed. see Cohen, A.

Cranmer-Byng, Launcelot A. A Lute of Jade: Selections from the Classical Poets of China. LC 77-26072. 1978. Repr. of 1959 ed. lib. bdg. 18.75x (ISBN 0-313-20080-7, CBLJ). Greenwood.

Cranna, Ian, ed. The Rock Yearbook, 1986. (Illus.). 224p. 1985. 24.95 (ISBN 0-312-68792-3); pap. 13.95 (ISBN 0-312-68789-3). St Martin.

Crano, William D. & Messe, Lawrence A. Social Psychology: Principles & Themes of Interpersonal Behavior. 1982. 26.95x (ISBN 0-256-02403-0). Dorsey.

Cranor, Henry D. Marriage Licenses of Caroline County, Maryland, 1774-1815. LC 75-986. 62p. 1975. pap. 5.00 (ISBN 0-8063-0667-X). Genealog Pub.

Cranor, Phoebe. Is Anybody Listening When I Pray? LC 79-27475. 112p. (Orig.). 1980. pap. 3.95 (ISBN 0-87123-200-6, 210200). Bethany Hse.

--Why Did God Let Grandpa Die? LC 76-17737. 128p. 1976. pap. 3.50 (ISBN 0-87123-603-6, 200603). Bethany Hse.

--Why Doesn't God Do Something? LC 78-118. 144p. (YA) 1978. pap. 2.95 (ISBN 0-87123-605-2, 200605). Bethany Hse.

Cranshaw, T. E., et al. Mossbauer Spectroscopy & Its Applications. (Illus.). 120p. Date not set. price not set (ISBN 0-521-30482-2); pap. price not set (ISBN 0-521-31521-2). Cambridge U Pr.

Cranson, K. R. Crater Lake Gem of the Cascades. 2nd ed. LC 82-81993. 111p. 1982. pap. 5.95 (ISBN 0-8323-0426-3). Binford.

Cranston, Edwin A. The Izumi Shikibu Diary: A Romance of the Heian Court. Shikibu, Izumi, ed. LC 69-13766. (Harvard-Yenching Institute Monograph Ser.: No. 19). 1969. 20.00x (ISBN 0-674-46985-2). Harvard U Pr.

Cranston, Maurice. Jean Jacques: The Early Life & Work of Jean-Jacques Rosseau, 1712-1754. (Illus.). 382p. 1983. 22.45 (ISBN 0-393-01744-3). Norton.

--John Locke: A Biography. Mayer, J. P., ed. LC 78-67349. (European Political Thought Ser.). 1979. Repr. of 1957 ed. lib. bdg. 34.50x (ISBN 0-405-11690-X). Ayer Co Pubs.

--What Are Human Rights? LC 73-4849. 171p. 1973. 7.95 (ISBN 0-8008-8148-6). Taplinger.

--What Are Human Rights? LC 73-4849. 1978. pap. 4.95 (ISBN 0-8008-8149-4). Taplinger.

Cranston, Maurice & Mair, Peter. Ideology & Politics. 168p. 1981. 26.00 (ISBN 90-286-0770-6). Sijthoff & Noordhoff.

Cranston, Maurice, tr. see Hartnack, Justus.

Cranston, Maurice, tr. see Rousseau, Jean-Jacques.

Cranston, Ross. Consumers & the Law. 2nd ed. (Law in Context Ser.). xxxvi, 503p. 1984. 38.50 (ISBN 0-297-78272-X, Pub. by Weidenfeld & Nicolson England). Rothman.

--Legal Foundations of the Welfare State. (Law in Context Ser.). (Illus.). xxxiv, 453p. 1985. 26.00x (ISBN 0-297-78487-0, Pub. by Weidenfeld & Nicolson England). Rothman.

--Regulating Business: Law & Consumer Agencies. (Oxford Socio-Legal Studies Ser.). 1979. text ed. 28.00x (ISBN 0-333-23890-7). Humanities.

Cranston, Ruth. World Faith. facs. ed. LC 68-58782. (Essay Index Reprint Ser). 1949. 15.00 (ISBN 0-8369-0108-8). Ayer Co Pubs.

Cranston, S. L., jt. auth. see Head, Joseph.

Cranston, Sylvia & Williams, Carey. Reincarnation: A New Horizon in Science, Religion & Society. 1984. 16.95 (ISBN 0-517-55496-8, Harmony). Crown.

Cranston-Bennett, Mary E., ed. see Miller, Dorothy.

Cranstoon, James, ed. see Scott, Alexander.

Cranstoun, James. Satirical Poems of the Time of the Reformation, 2 Vols. LC 71-144550. Repr. of 1893 ed. Set. 74.50 (ISBN 0-404-08629-2). AMS Pr.

Crant, Phillip, tr. see Bazin, Herve.

Cranton, Elmer & Brecher, Arline. Bypassing Bypass: The New Technique of Chelation Therapy. LC 83-40367. 240p. 1984. 16.95 (ISBN 0-8128-2950-6). Stein & Day.

Cranton, Elmer M., jt. auth. see Passwater, Richard A.

Cranwell, John P. Spoilers of the Sea. facsimile ed. LC 78-93331. (Essay Index Reprint Ser.). 1941. 27.50 (ISBN 0-8369-1563-1). Ayer Co Pubs.

Cranz, Edward F. The Publishing History of the Aristotle: Commentaries of Thomas Aquinas. 36p. 1978. pap. 5.00 (ISBN 0-8232-0090-6). Fordham.

Cranz, F. Edward, ed. Catalogus Translationum et Commentariorum: Mediaeval & Renaissance Latin Translation & Commentaries, Vol. 3. 481p. 1976. pap. 41.95x (ISBN 0-8132-0540-9). Cath U Pr.

--Catalogus Translationum et Commentariorum: Mediaeval & Renaissance Latin Translations & Commentaries, Annotated Lists & Guides, Vol. 4. LC 60-4006. 524p. 1980. 66.95x (ISBN 0-8132-0547-6). Cath U Pr.

Cranz, F. Edward & Kristeller, Paul O., eds. Catalogus Translations & Commentariorum: Medieval & Renaissance Latin Translations & Commentaries, Vol. 5. 448p. 1984. 66.95X (ISBN 0-8132-0580-8). Cath U Pr.

--Catalogus Translationum Et Commentariorum: Mediaeval & Renaissance Latin Translations & Commentaries, Vol. VI. 1986. price not set (ISBN 0-8132-0618-9). Cath U Pr.

Cranz, Galen. The Politics of Park Design: A History of Urban Parks in America. (Illus.). 352p. 1982. 32.50x (ISBN 0-262-03080-5). MIT Pr.

Crapanzano, Vincent. The Hamadsha: A Study in Moroccan Ethnopsychiatry. LC 72-75529. 1973. 36.50x (ISBN 0-520-02241-6); pap. 8.95x (ISBN 0-520-04510-6). U of Cal Pr.

--Portrait of a Moroccan. 1985. pap. 8.95 (ISBN 0-226-11871-1). U of Chicago Pr.

--Tuhami: Portrait of a Moroccan. LC 79-24550. xvi, 188p. 1985. lib. bdg. 17.50x (ISBN 0-226-11870-3); pap. 8.95 (ISBN 0-226-11871-1). U of Chicago Pr.

--Waiting: The Whites of South Africa. LC 83-42752. 358p. 1985. 19.45 (ISBN 0-394-50986-2). Random.

Crapanzano, Vincent & Garrison, Vivian, eds. Case Studies in Spirit Possession. LC 76-26653. (Contemporary Religious Movements Ser.). pap. 118.30 (ISBN 0-317-08510-7, 2055396). Bks Demand UMI.

Crape, James R. Engineering Career Package. (Illus.). 304p. 1982. pap. 23.00x (ISBN 0-916367-02-9, ECP-23). J R C Pub.

--Power Plant Engineering Opportunities. LC 82-61199. (Illus.). 52p. (Orig.). 1982. pap. 4.95 (ISBN 0-916367-01-0). J R C Pub.

--Steam & Diesel Power Plant Operators Examinations. 2nd ed. LC 82-2198. (Illus.). 252p. 1982. pap. 21.95x (ISBN 0-916367-00-2, CU47-SD2). J R C Pub.

Crape, Marie, ed. see League of Women Voters of Pennsylvania.

Crapo, Henry H. & Rota, Gian-Carlo. On the Foundations of Combinatorial Theory: Combinatorial Geometries. 1970. pap. 10.00x (ISBN 0-262-53016-3). MIT Pr.

Crapo, Lawrence. The Messengers of Life. 200p. 1985. 21.95 (ISBN 0-7167-1757-3); pap. 11.95 (ISBN 0-7167-1753-0). W H Freeman.

Crapo, Lawrence M., jt. auth. see Fries, James F.

Crapol, Edward P. America for Americans: Economic Nationalism & Anglophobia in the Late Nineteenth Century. LC 71-176287. (Contributions in American History Ser.: No. 28). 248p. 1973. lib. bdg. 29.95 (ISBN 0-8371-6273-4, CRA/). Greenwood.

Crapper. Introduction to Waterwaves. (Mathematics & Its Applications Ser.). 224p. 1984. 54.95 (ISBN 0-470-20122-3). Wiley.

Crapps, Robert W., et al. Introduction to the New Testament. 566p. 1969. text ed. 30.95 (ISBN 0-394-34415-4, RandC). Random.

Crapsey, Adelaide. A Study in English Metrics. LC 77-6978. 1977. Repr. of 1918 ed. lib. bdg. 10.00 (ISBN 0-89341-169-8). Longwood Pub Group.

--A Study in English Metrics. 1918. Repr. 10.00 (ISBN 0-8274-3547-9). R West.

Crapsey, Edward. Nether Side of New York. LC 69-14919. (Criminology, Law Enforcement, & Social Problems Ser.: No. 46). 1969. Repr. of 1872 ed. 12.00x (ISBN 0-87585-046-4). Patterson Smith.

Crary, Catherine S., ed. Dear Belle: Letters from a Cadet & Officer to His Sweetheart, 1858-1865. LC 65-14052. (Illus.). 1965. 18.50x (ISBN 0-8195-3052-2). Wesleyan U Pr.

Crary, David T. & Pfahl, John K. Personal Finance. 7th ed. LC 79-27578. (Illus.). pap. 16.00 (ISBN 0-317-09664-8, 2021501). Bks Demand UMI.

Crary, David T., et al. Personal Finance. 7th ed. LC 79-27578. 208p. 1980. pap. 16.95x (ISBN 0-471-07802-6). Wiley.

Crary, Elizabeth. I Can't Wait. LC 82-6277. (Children's Problem Solving Bks.). (Illus.). 32p. (Orig.). (ps-2). 1982. PLB 9.95 (ISBN 0-9602862-6-8); pap. 3.95 (ISBN 0-9602862-3-3). Parenting Pr.

--I Want It. LC 82-2129. (Children's Problem Solving Bks.). (Illus.). 32p. (Orig.). (ps-2). 1982. PLB 9.95 (ISBN 0-9602862-5-X); pap. 3.95 (ISBN 0-9602862-2-5). Parenting Pr.

--I Want to Play. LC 82-3610. (Children's Problem Solving Bks.). (Illus.). 32p. (Orig.). (ps-2). 1982. PLB 9.95 (ISBN 0-9602862-7-6); pap. 3.95 (ISBN 0-9602862-4-1). Parenting Pr.

--I'm Lost. LC 84-62128. (Childrens Problem Solving Bks.). (Illus.). 32p. (Orig.). (ps-2). 1985. PLB 9.95 (ISBN 0-943990-08-4); pap. 3.95 (ISBN 0-943990-09-2). Parenting Pr.

--Kids Can Cooperate. LC 84-60587. (Illus.). 112p. 1984. lib. bdg. 12.95 (ISBN 0-943990-05-X); pap. 7.95 (ISBN 0-943990-04-1). Parenting Pr.

--My Name Is Not Dummy. (Children's Problem Solving Bks.). (Illus.). 32p. (Orig.). (ps-2). 1983. PLB 9.95 (ISBN 0-9602862-9-2); pap. 3.95 (ISBN 0-9602862-8-4). Parenting Pr.

--Without Spanking or Spoiling: A Practical Approach to Toddler & Preschool Guidance. LC 79-18253. (Illus.). 104p. (Orig.). 1979. pap. 7.95 (ISBN 0-9602862-0-9); write for info leaders' guide (ISBN 0-9602862-1-7). Parenting Pr.

Crary, John. Reminiscences of the Old South from 1834 to 1866. Weller, May, ed. Regina M. (Southern History & Genealogy Ser.: Vol. I). (Illus.). ixii, 164p. 1985. 17.95x (ISBN 0-933776-21-7). Perdido Bay.

Crary, Jonathan & Levin, Kim. Eleanor Antin: The Angel of Mercy. (Illus.). 28p. 1977. pap. 4.50x (ISBN 0-934418-02-0). La Jolla Mus Contemp Art.
Crary, Michael A., ed. Phonological Intervention: Concepts & Procedures. LC 81-21706. (Illus.). 128p. 1982. pap. 15.00 (ISBN 0-933014-73-2). College-Hill.
Crary, Robert W., jt. auth. see Lorr, Regina E.
Crase, Douglas. The Revisionist. 96p. 1981. 10.95 (ISBN 0-316-16062-8); pap. 5.95 (ISBN 0-316-16060-1). Little.
Craseman, Bernard, ed. Atomic Inner-Shell Processes, 2 vols. Incl. Vol. 1. Production & Decay of Inner-Shell Vacancies. 1975. 80.00 (ISBN 0-12-196901-0); Vol. 2. Experimental Approaches & Applications. 1975. 66.00 (ISBN 0-12-196902-9). Acad Pr.
Crasemann, B., jt. auth. see Powell, John L.
Crasemann, Bernard, ed. X-Ray & Atomic Inner-Shell Physics, 1982. LC 82-74075. (AIP Conf. Proc. Ser.: No. 94). 802p. 1982. lib. bdg. 44.50 (ISBN 0-88318-193-2). Am Inst Physics.
Crashaw, Richard. The Complete Poetry of Richard Crashaw. Williams, George W., ed. (Illus.). 736p. 1974. pap. 5.95x (ISBN 0-393-00728-6, Norton Lib). Norton.
--The Complete Works of Richard Crashaw, 2 vols. LC 73-21062. (Fuller Worthies' Library). (Illus.). Repr. of 1873 ed. Set. 100.00 (ISBN 0-404-11479-2). AMS Pr.
--The Poems of Richard Crashaw. Tutin, J. R., ed. 1977. Repr. lib. bdg. 20.00 (ISBN 0-8414-1822-5). Folcroft.
--The Religious Poems of Richard Crashaw. Shepherd, R. Eric, ed. 1914. lib. bdg. 20.00 (ISBN 0-8414-2407-1). Folcroft.
Crashaw, W., tr. see Balbani, Niccolo.
Crashaw, William. The Sermon Preached at the Cross, February 14, 1607. Repr. of 1608 ed. 27.00 (ISBN 0-384-10125-9). Johnson Repr.
Crasilneck, Harold B. & Hall, James A. Clinical Hypnosis: Principles & Applications. LC 75-23325. (Illus.). 364p. 1975. 39.00 (ISBN 0-8089-0907-X, 790935). Grune.
--Clinical Hypnosis: Principles & Applications. 2nd ed. 496p. 1985. 29.50 (ISBN 0-8089-1681-5, 790934). Grune.
Craske, Margaret. The Dance of Love: My Life with Meher Baba. LC 80-53859. 180p. (Orig.). 1980. pap. 6.95 (ISBN 0-913078-40-9). Sheriar Pr.
Crass, Maurice, 3rd, ed. Vascular Smooth Muscle: Metabolic Ionic & Contractile Mechanisms. Barnes, Charles. (Research Topics in Physiology Ser.). 1982. 37.50 (ISBN 0-12-195220-7). Acad Pr.
Crass, Philip. The Wallace Factor. (Orig.). 1976. pap. 1.95 (ISBN 0-532-19108-0). Woodhill.
Craster, H. H., ed. see Halifax, Edward F.
Cratch, Stephen C. & Johansson, Anders B. The Hindu Vedic Master Operations Guide: Astrological Software for the IBM PC. Johansson, Lilian M., ed. (Illus.). 200p. (Orig.). 1985. 30.00 (ISBN 0-914725-12-2); pap. 18.00 (ISBN 0-914725-10-6); spiral 24.00 (ISBN 0-914725-11-4). Astro Dynasty Pub Hse.
Crater, Don R. Cone Crafting. (Illus.). 52p. (Orig.). 1980. pap. 6.95 (ISBN 0-940654-00-8). Tribune Pub.
--The Dried Guide. LC 81-52464. (Illus.). 56p. (Orig.). 1981. pap. 7.95 (ISBN 0-940654-01-6). Tribune Pub.
Crater, Flora. Woman Activist Guide for Women Candidates. rev. ed. 1978. pap. 1.00 (ISBN 0-917560-11-6). Woman Activist.
--The Woman Activist Guide to Lobbying, 1977. rev. ed. 1977. pap. 1.00 (ISBN 0-917560-08-6). Woman Activist.
--Woman Activist Guide to Precinct Politics. 2nd ed. 1979. pap. 2.00 (ISBN 0-917560-13-2). Woman Activist.
Crater, Flora, et al. The Almanac of Virginia Politics: 1977. Incl. Almanac of Virginia Politics: 1978 Supplement. Crater, Flora et al. (Illus.). 1978. pap. 2.00 (ISBN 0-917560-09-4); Almanac of Virginia Politics: 1979. 2nd. ed. Crater, Flora et al. 1979. pap. 5.95 (ISBN 0-917560-13-2, 78-6331); Almanac of Virginia Politics: 1980 Supplement. Crater, Flora. (Illus.). pap. 3.95 (ISBN 0-917560-13-2); Almanac of Virginia Politics: 1981. 3rd. ed. Crater, Flora et al. (Illus.). 1981. pap. 7.95 (ISBN 0-917560-16-7, 80-71076); Almanac of Virginia Politics: 1982 Supplement. Crater, Flora et al. (Illus.). 1982. pap. 4.95 (ISBN 0-917560-17-5); Almanac of Virginia Politics: 1983 Edition. Crater, Flora at al. (Illus.). 1983. pap. 9.95 (ISBN 0-917560-18-3); Almanac of Virginia Politics: 1985 Edition. Crater, Flora & Williams, Greg. 16.95 (ISBN 0-917560-20-5). LC 76-24321. (Illus.). 1977. pap. 3.95 (ISBN 0-917560-07-8). Woman Activist.
Crater, Flora at al. see Crater, Flora, et al.
Crater, Flora et al. see Crater, Flora, et al.
Crater, Mildred, ed. see Lohr, Andrew.
Craterus. The Fragments from His Collection of Athenian Decrees: De Crateri Psephismaton Synagoge et de Locis Aliquot Plutarchi Ex Ea Petitis. 1979. 15.00 (ISBN 0-89005-208-5). Ares.
Craton, Michael. Roots & Branches: Current Directions in Slave Studies. LC 79-22464. 304p. 1980. 48.00 (ISBN 0-08-025367-9). Pergamon.
--Testing the Chains: Resistance to Slavery in the British West Indies. LC 82-71600. (Illus.). 389p. 1982. 32.50x (ISBN 0-8014-1252-8). Cornell U Pr.
Craton, Michael M. Searching for the Invisible Man: Slaves & Plantation Life in Jamaica. LC 76-48281. 1978. 35.00x (ISBN 0-674-79629-2). Harvard U Pr.
Cratt, Bryant J. Active Learning: Games to Enhance Academic Abilities. 2nd ed. (Illus.). 176p. 1985. pap. text ed. 18.95 (ISBN 0-13-003468-1). P-H.
Cratty, B. Teaching Motor Skills. (Man in Action Ser.). (Illus.). 1973. pap. text ed. 14.95 (ISBN 0-13-893958-6). P-H.
Cratty, Bryant J. Active Learning: Games to Enhance Academic Abilities. (Physical Education Ser). (Illus.). 1971. pap. text ed. 14.95 (ISBN 0-13-003491-6). P-H.
--Adapted Physical Education for Handicapped Children & Youth. (Illus.). 552p. 1980. text ed. 28.95 (ISBN 0-89108-097-X). Love Pub Co.
--Developmental Games for Physically Handicapped Children. 1969. pap. text ed. 3.95 (ISBN 0-917962-17-6). Peek Pubns.
--Motor Activity & the Education of Retardates. LC 73-23008. (Lea & Febiger Health, Physical Education & Recreation Ser.). (Illus.). Repr. of 1972 ed. 78.00 (ISBN 0-8357-9411-3, 2014537). Bks Demand UMI.
--Movement Behavior & Motor Learning. 3rd ed. LC 73-1938. (Health & Physical Education & Recreation Ser.). (Illus.). 512p. 1973. text ed. 11.50 (ISBN 0-8121-0425-0). Lea & Febiger.
--Perceptual-Motor Behavior & Educational Processes. (Illus.). 284p. 1971. 25.50x (ISBN 0-398-00359-9). C C Thomas.
--Psychological Preparation & Athletic Excellence. 200p. 1984. 16.95 (ISBN 0-932392-17-2); pap. 10.95 (ISBN 0-932392-12-1). Mouvement Pubns.
--Psychology in Contemporary Sport: Guidelines for Coaches & Athletes. LC 82-11229. (Illus.). 352p. 1983. 25.95 (ISBN 0-13-734129-6). P-H.
--Remedial Motor Activity for Children. LC 74-26973. (Illus.). 327p. 1975. text ed. 13.50 (ISBN 0-8121-0513-3). Lea & Febiger.
--Social Psychology in Athletics. (Illus.). 320p. 1981. text ed. 25.95 (ISBN 0-13-817650-7). P-H.
Cratty, Bryant J. & Hanin, Yuri L. The Athlete in the Sports Team. 231p. 1980. text ed. 14.95 (ISBN 0-89108-099-6). Love Pub Co.
Cratty, Bryant J. & Hutton, Robert S. Experiments in Movement Behavior & Motor Learning. LC 72-85840. (Illus.). 1969. pap. 42.40 (ISBN 0-317-08090-3, 2014538). Bks Demand UMI.
Cratty, Bryant J. & Martin, Margaret M. Perceptual-Motor Efficiency in Children: The Measurement & Improvement of Movement Attributes. LC 69-15646. (Health Education, Physical Education & Recreation Ser.). pap. 59.80 (ISBN 0-317-09377-0, 2003763). Bks Demand UMI.
Cratty, Bryant J. & Piggot, Rob. Student Projects in Sport Psychology. 1984. pap. 9.95 (ISBN 0-932392-15-6). Mouvement Pubns.
Cratty, Bryant J. & Sams, Theressa A. The Body-Image of Blind Children. 72p. 1968. 6.00 (ISBN 0-89128-014-6, PAMR014). Am Foun Blind.
Cratty, Bryant J., et al. Movement Activities, Motor Ability & the Education of Children. (Illus.). 192p. 1970. 19.75x (ISBN 0-398-00360-2). C C Thomas.
Cratty, Bryant S. Perceptual & Motor Development in Infants & Young Children. 2nd ed. 1979. 24.95 (ISBN 0-13-657023-2). P-H.
Crauder, Renee C. & Etter-Lewis, Gwendolyn E. A Short Course in Remedial English Composition. 1977. pap. 3.95x (ISBN 0-8134-1938-7, 1938); instructor's manual 1.00 (ISBN 0-8134-1939-5, 1939). Interstate.
Crauford, Emma, tr. see Marcel, Gabriel.
Crauford, Lane. Acting: Its Theory & Practice. LC 75-84510. 1930. 20.00 (ISBN 0-405-08400-5, Blom Pubns). Ayer Co Pubs.
Craufurd, Emma, tr. see Walter, Gerard.
Craun, Joan, ed. see Meyer, Barbara.
Crauzat, de see De Crauzat, E.
Cravalho, Ernest G. & Smith, Joseph L., Jr. Engineering Thermodynamics. 560p. 1981. text ed. 36.95 (ISBN 0-273-01604-0). Pitman Pub MA.
Cravalho, Ernest G. see McNeil, Barbara J.
Crave, Michael R., jt. auth. see Twarog, Katherine J.
Craven, Avery. Coming of the Civil War. 2nd ed. LC 57-8572. 1966. pap. 4.50x (ISBN 0-226-11894-0, P210, Phoen). U of Chicago Pr.
Craven, Avery O. Civil War in the Making, 1815-1860. LC 59-7943. (Walter Lynwood Fleming Lectures). xiv, 116p. 1968. pap. text ed. 5.95x (ISBN 0-8071-0131-1). La State U Pr.
--Edmund Ruffin, Southerner: A Study in Secession. LC 64-11059. x, 284p. 1966. pap. text ed. 8.95x (ISBN 0-8071-0104-4). La State U Pr.
--Growth of Southern Nationalism, 1848-1861. LC 53-11470. (History of the South, Vol. 6). (Illus.). x, 434p. 1953. 27.50x (ISBN 0-8071-0006-4). La State U Pr.
--An Historian & the Civil War. LC 64-15802. (Phoenix Bks.). pap. 59.80 (ISBN 0-317-10813-1, 2020049). Bks Demand UMI.
--Rachel of Old Louisiana. LC 74-15921. (Illus.). xiv, 122p. 1975. 14.95 (ISBN 0-8071-0095-1). La State U Pr.
--The Repressible Conflict, 1830-1861. LC 83-45425. Repr. of 1939 ed. 19.00 (ISBN 0-404-20070-2). AMS Pr.
--Soil Exhaustion As a Factor in the Agricultural History of Virginia and Maryland, 1606-1860. 1926. 11.50 (ISBN 0-8446-1136-0). Peter Smith.
Craven, B. D. Functions of Several Variables. 144p. 1981. 23.00x (ISBN 0-412-23330-4, NO. 6607, Pub by Chapman & Hall England); pap. 9.95x (ISBN 0-412-23340-1, NO. 6606). Methuen Inc.
--Mathematical Programming & Control Theory. (Mathematics Ser.). 1978. pap. 15.95 (ISBN 0-412-15500-1, NO. 6070, Pub. by Chapman & Hall). Methuen Inc.
Craven, Bruce D. Lebesque Measure & Integral. LC 81-12151. 224p. 1982. text ed. 39.95 (ISBN 0-273-01754-3). Pitman Pub MA.
Craven, Darce. A Guide to District Nurses. Reverby, Susan, ed. LC 83-49139. (The History of American Nursing Ser.). 136p. 1984. Repr. of 1889 ed. lib. bdg. 25.00 (ISBN 0-8240-6508-5). Garland Pub.
Craven, Elizabeth. Journey Through the Crimea to Constantinople in a Series of Letters. LC 73-115525. (Russia Observed, Series I). 1970. Repr. of 1789 ed. 23.50 (ISBN 0-405-03018-5). Ayer Co Pubs.
Craven, George M. How Photography Works. (Illus.). 150p. 1986. pap. text ed. 12.95 (ISBN 0-13-400789-1). P-H.
--Object & Image. 2nd ed. 400p. 1982. 29.95 (ISBN 0-13-628966-5). P-H.
Craven, Henry & Barfield, John. English-Congo & Congo-English Dictionary. facs. ed. LC 75-157365. (Black Heritage Library Collection). (Eng. & Congo.). 1883. 19.75 (ISBN 0-8369-8803-5). Ayer Co Pubs.
Craven, J., jt. auth. see Cleaveland, A.
Craven, J. L., jt. auth. see Lumley, J. S.
Craven, J. L., jt. ed. see Lumley, J. S.
Craven, John. Distribution of the Product. (Studies in Economics). (Illus., Orig.). 1979. text ed. 28.50x (ISBN 0-04-339014-5). Allen Unwin.
--Introduction to Economics: An Integrated Approach to Fundamental Principles. 450p. 1984. 39.95x (ISBN 0-631-13636-3); pap. 19.95x (ISBN 0-631-13637-1). Basil Blackwell.
Craven, John P. The Management of Pacific Marine Resources: Present Problems & Future Trends. (Illus.). 96p. 1982. lib. bdg. 14.00x (ISBN 0-86531-424-1). Westview.
Craven, John V. Industrial Organization, Anti-Trust & Public Policy. (Middlebury College Conference Series in Economic Issues). 1982. lib. bdg. 25.00 (ISBN 0-89838-103-7). Kluwer-Nijhoff.
Craven, Ken. Ride It: The Complete Book of Motorcycle Touring. (Drive it! Ride it! Ser.). 134p. 9.95 (ISBN 0-85429-223-3). Haynes Pubns.
Craven, Linda. Stepfamilies: New Patterns of Harmony. LC 82-60652. (Teen Survival Library). (Illus.). 192p. (gr. 7 up). 1982. 9.79; pap. 4.95 (ISBN 0-671-49486-4). Messner.
Craven, Margaret. Again Calls the Owl. 1981. pap. 3.50 (ISBN 0-440-30074-6). Dell.
--The Home Front. 432p. 1982. pap. 3.95 (ISBN 0-440-13517-6). Dell.
--The Home Front. (General Ser.). 1981. lib. bdg. 17.95 (ISBN 0-8161-3267-4, Large Print Bks). G K Hall.
--I Heard the Owl Call My Name. 160p. (gr. 7 up). 1974. pap. 2.50 (ISBN 0-440-34369-0, LE). Dell.
--I Heard the Owl Call My Name. LC 73-10800. (Illus.). 144p. 1973. 11.95 (ISBN 0-385-02586-6). Doubleday.
--Walk Gently This Good Earth. 192p. (gr. 7 up). 1979. pap. 2.25 (ISBN 0-440-39484-8). Dell.
Craven, Martin A. The Carlos Confessions. 1978. pap. 2.25 (ISBN 0-532-22143-5). Woodhill.
Craven, Paul. An Impartial Umpire: Industrial Relations & the Canadian State, 1900-1911. (The State & Economic Life Ser.). 560p. 1980. 27.50x (ISBN 0-8020-5505-2). U of Toronto Pr.
Craven, Paul J., Jr., jt. auth. see Baker, Robert A.
Craven, Robert R. Guide to Fishing: Westchester & Putnam Counties. 96p. 1982. pap. 4.95 (ISBN 0-686-35793-0). Outdoor Pubns.
Craven, Robert R., compiled by. Billiards, Bowling, Table Tennis, Pinball & Video Games: A Bibliographic Guide. LC 82-21077. xvi, 163p. 1983. lib. bdg. 29.95 (ISBN 0-313-23462-0, CBB/). Greenwood.
Craven, Roy C. Concise History of Indian Art. (Illus.). 252p. 1985. pap. 9.95 (ISBN 0-500-20146-3). Thames Hudson.
Craven, Roy C., Jr. Ceremonial Centers of the Maya. LC 74-2016. (Illus.). 152p. 1974. 20.00 (ISBN 0-8130-0447-0). U Presses Fla.
--Indian Sculpture in the John & Mable Ringling Museum of Art. LC 61-63517. (University of Florida Humanities Monographs: No. 6). (Illus.). 1961. pap. 3.50 (ISBN 0-8130-0050-5). U Presses Fla.
Craven, Rulon G. The Effective Missionary. LC 82-1471. 106p. 1982. 6.95 (ISBN 0-87747-898-8). Deseret Bk.
Craven, Sara. A Bad Enemy. (Harlequin Presents Ser.). 192p. 1983. pap. 1.95 (ISBN 0-373-10647-5). Harlequin Bks.
--Counterfeit Bride. (Harlequin Presents Ser.). 192p. 1983. pap. 1.75 (ISBN 0-373-10561-4). Harlequin Bks.
--Dark Summer Dawn. (Harlequin Presents Ser.). 192p. 1982. pap. 1.75 (ISBN 0-373-10487-1). Harlequin Bks.
--Les Oiseaux de Jais. (Harlequin Romantique Ser.). 192p. 1983. pap. 1.95 (ISBN 0-373-41204-5). Harlequin Bks.
--Pagan Adversary. (Harlequin Presents Ser.). 192p. 1983. pap. 1.95 (ISBN 0-373-10616-5). Harlequin Bks.
--La Pierre Des Voeux. (Harlequin Collection Ser.). 192p. 1983. pap. 1.95 (ISBN 0-373-49337-1). Harlequin Bks.
--Sup with the Devil. (Harlequin Presents Ser.). 192p. 1983. pap. 1.95 (ISBN 0-373-10599-1). Harlequin Bks.
--Unguarded Moment. (Harlequin Presents Ser.). 1982. pap. 1.75 (ISBN 0-373-10551-7). Harlequin Bks.
Craven, Thomas. Modern Art: The Men, the Movements, the Meaning. LC 40-7043. 1940. Repr. 49.00x (ISBN 0-403-03081-1). Somerset Pub.
Craven, Toni. Artistry & Faith in the Book of Judith. LC 82-25000. (Society of Biblical Literature Dissertation Ser.). 150p. 1983. pap. 11.25 (ISBN 0-89130-612-9, 06 01 70). Scholars Pr GA.
Craven, Wayne. Sculpture in America. 2nd ed. LC 82-40439. (Illus.). 808p. 1983. 50.00 (ISBN 0-87413-225-8). U Delaware Pr.
--Sculpture in America. 2nd. ed. LC 82-40439. (Illus.). 808p. 1983. 50.00 (ISBN 0-8453-4776-4). Cornwall Bks.
Craven, Wesley F. The Colonies in Transition, 1660-1713. (New American Nation Ser). 1968. 22.07xi (ISBN 0-06-010913-0, HarpT). Har-Row.
--Dissolution of the Virginia Company: The Failure of a Colonial Experiment. 1964. 11.50 (ISBN 0-8446-1137-9). Peter Smith.
--The Legend of the Founding Fathers. LC 82-25241. (New York University, Stokes Foundation, Anson G. Phelps Lectureship on Early American History Ser.). vii, 222p. 1983. Repr. of 1956 ed. lib. bdg. 27.50x (ISBN 0-313-23840-5, CRLE). Greenwood.
--Southern Colonies in the Seventeenth Century, 1607-1689. LC 49-3595. (History of the South Ser.: Vol. 1). (Illus.). xvi, 452p. 1949. 27.50x (ISBN 0-8071-0001-3); pap. text ed. 8.95x (ISBN 0-8071-0011-0). La State U Pr.
Craven, Wesley F. & Cate, James L. The Army Air Forces in World War II, 7 vols. Gilbert, James, ed. LC 79-7244. (Flight: Its First Seventy-Five Years Ser.). (Illus.). 1979. Repr. of 1948 ed. Set. lib. bdg. 294.00x (ISBN 0-405-12135-0); lib. bdg. 42.00x ea. Vol. 1 (ISBN 0-405-12136-9). Vol. 2 (ISBN 0-405-12137-7). Vol. 3 (ISBN 0-405-12138-5). Vol. 4. Vol. 5. Vol. 6 (ISBN 0-405-12141-5). Vol. 7 (ISBN 0-405-12142-3). Ayer Co Pubs.
Craven, Wesley F., jt. auth. see United States Air Force Historical Division Staff.
Craven, Wesley F. & Cate, James L., eds. Europe-Argument to V-E Day: January 1944 to May 1945, Vol. 3. (The Army Air Force in World War II Ser.). (Illus.). 938p. 1984. Repr. of 1951 ed. write for info. (ISBN 0-912799-05-6). Off Air Force.
--Europe-Torch to Pointblank: August 1942 to December 1942, Vol. 2. (The Army Air Forces in World War II Ser.). (Illus.). 897p. Repr. of 1949 ed. write for info. (ISBN 0-912799-04-8). Off Air Force.
--Men & Planes, Vol. 6. (The Army Air Forces in World War II Ser.). (Illus.). 807p. 1983. Repr. of 1955 ed. write for info. Off Air Force.
--The Pacific - Guadacanal to Saigon: August 1942 to July 1944, Vol. 4. (The Army Air Force in World War II Ser.). (Illus.). 825p. 1983. Repr. of 1950 ed. write for info. (ISBN 0-912799-06-4). Off Air Force.
--The Pacific-Matterhorn to Nagasaki: June 1944 to August 1945, Vol. 5. (The Army Air Forces in World War II Ser.). (Illus.). 878p. 1983. Repr. of 1953 ed. write for info. (ISBN 0-912799-07-2). Off Air Force.
--Plans & Early Operations: January 1939 to August 1942, Vol. 1. 2nd ed. (The Army Air Forces in World War II Ser.). (Illus.). 788p. 1983. Repr. of 1948 ed. write for info. (ISBN 0-912799-01-3). Off Air Force.
--Services Around the World, Vol. 7. (The Army Air Forces in World War II Ser.). (Illus.). 667p. 1983. Repr. of 1958 ed. write for info. (ISBN 0-912799-09-9). Off Air Force.
Cravens, David M. Strategic Marketing. 1982. 28.95x (ISBN 0-256-02645-9). Irwin.
Cravens, David W. The Sales Manager's Book of Marketing Planning. LC 83-70858. 225p. 1983. 22.95 (ISBN 0-87094-419-3). Dow Jones-Irwin.
Cravens, David W. & Hills, Gerald E. Marketing Decision Making. rev. ed. 1980. 29.95x (ISBN 0-256-02348-4). Irwin.
Cravens, David W. & Lamb, Charles W., Jr. Strategic Marketing Cases & Applications. 1983. 28.95x (ISBN 0-256-02936-9). Irwin.
Cravens, Gwyneth. Love & Work. LC 81-13650. 352p. 1982. 13.50 (ISBN 0-394-52184-6). Knopf.
--Love & Work. 368p. 1983. pap. 2.95 (ISBN 0-449-20047-7, Crest). Fawcett.

Cravens, Hamilton. Triumph of Evolution: American Scientists & the Heredity-Environment Controversy, 1900-1941. LC 77-20570. (Illus.). 1978. 26.00x (ISBN 0-8122-7744-9). U of Pa Pr.

Cravens, Hamilton, ed. Ideas in America's Cultures. (Illus.). 200p. 1982. text ed. 15.95x (ISBN 0-8138-0081-1). Iowa St U Pr.

Cravens, Sydney P., jt. ed. see Aycock, Wendell M.

Craver, Clara D., ed. Polymer Characterization: Interdisciplinary Approaches. LC 70-163285. 279p. 1971. 39.50x (ISBN 0-306-30545-3, Plenum Pr). Plenum Pub.

--Polymer Characterization, Spectroscopic, Chromatographic, & Physical Instrumental Methods. LC 82-24496. (Advances in Chemistry Ser.: No. 203). 791p. 1983. lib. bdg. 69.95 (ISBN 0-8412-0700-3). Am Chemical.

Craver, Elena B. The Bulgarian Longevity: Clues to a Long Life. 110p. 1982. 6.50 (ISBN 0-682-49894-7). Exposition Pr FL.

Craver, John. Graph Paper from Your Copier. LC 80-80170. (Illus.). 232p. 1980. pap. 12.95 (ISBN 0-89586-045-7). H P Bks.

--VisiCalc for Apple II, II Plus, & IIe. (Illus.). 192p. 1983. 14.95 (ISBN 0-89586-274-3). H P Bks.

Craver, Rebecca. Impact of Intimacy: Mexican-Anglo Intermarriage in New Mexico 1821-1846, No. 66. (Southwestern Studies Ser.). 1982. 10.00 (ISBN 0-87404-125-2); pap. 4.00. Tex Western.

Craver, Sam, jt. auth. see Ozmon, Howard.

Craver, Samuel, jt. auth. see Ozmon, Howard.

Cravey, R. H., jt. auth. see Gottschalk, L. A.

Cravey, Robert H. & Baselt, Randall C., eds. Introduction to Forensic Toxicology. LC 79-56929. (Illus.). 300p. 1981. text ed. 48.00 (ISBN 0-931890-06-3). Biomed Pubns.

Cravey, Robin. Diverging. (Illus.). 64p. (Orig.). 1983. pap. 5.00 (ISBN 0-912973-00-5). Tilted Planet.

--Diverging: Poems by Robin Cravey. LC 83-5029. (Illus.). 64p. (Orig.). 1984. 12.00 (ISBN 0-912973-03-X); pap. 5.00 (ISBN 0-912973-00-5). Tilted Planet.

Cravey, Robin, ed. Tilted Planet Tales. LC 84-2536. (Illus.). 138p. (Orig.). 1984. 15.00 (ISBN 0-912973-02-1); pap. 6.00 (ISBN 0-912973-01-3). Tilted Planet.

Craw, Julia & French, Bernada. Family Fun with Rocks. pap. 1.00 (ISBN 0-910652-16-3). Gembooks.

Crawford. Evacuation of Americans from Beirut. (Arab Background Ser.). 1972. pap. 3.95x (ISBN 0-86685-009-0). Intl Bk Ctr.

--Marine & Offshore Pumping & Piping Systems. 1981. text ed. 54.95 (ISBN 0-408-00548-3). Butterworth.

Crawford & Taylor. The History of Music, Vol. 3. Date not set. 6.85 (ISBN 0-317-20163-8). Campus.

Crawford, et al. Microcomputer Keyboarding-Formatting Applications. 1985. text ed. price not set wkbk. & diskettes (ISBN 0-538-26100-5, Z10). SW Pub.

--Microcomputer Keyboarding-Formatting Applications. 1986. pap. text ed. price not set (ISBN 0-538-21100-8, U10). SW Pub.

--The History of Music, Vol. 1. Date not set. 2.90 (ISBN 0-317-20157-3). Campus.

--The History of Music, Vol. 2. Date not set. 4.50 (ISBN 0-317-20161-1). Campus.

Crawford, A. Berry & Peterson, Dean F. Environmental Management in the Colorado River Basin. LC 74-121364. 313p. 1974. pap. 8.00 (ISBN 0-87421-068-2). Utah St U Pr.

Crawford, A. Berry, jt. ed. see Peterson, Dean F.

Crawford, Alan. C. R. Ashbee. LC 85-40459. (Illus.). 416p. 1985. 45.00x (ISBN 0-300-03467-9). Yale U Pr.

--Thunder on the Right: The "New Right" & the Politics of Resentment. 1981. pap. 3.95 (ISBN 0-394-74862-X). Pantheon.

--Thunder on the Right: The "New Right" & the Politcs of Resentment. 1980. 13.95 (ISBN 0-394-50663-4). Pantheon.

Crawford, Albert B. Incentives to Study: A Survey of Student Opinions. 1929. 59.50x (ISBN 0-685-69804-1). Elliots Bks.

Crawford, Albert B. & Burnham, Paul S. Forecasting College Achievement: A Survey of Aptitude Tests for Higher Education, Part I., General Considerations in the Measurement of Academic Progress. 1946. 49.50x (ISBN 0-686-51387-8). Elliots Bks.

Crawford, Albert G. & Monson, Rela G. Academy & Community: A Study of the Jewish Identity & Involvement of Professors. LC 80-68432. 40p. 1980. pap. 2.00. Am Jewish Comm.

Crawford, Alice O. Please Say Yes. (Sweet Dreams Ser.: No. 59). 128p. (Orig.). (gr. 6-8). 1984. pap. text ed. 2.25 (ISBN 0-553-24096-X). Bantam.

Crawford, Andy. Mules Go to War. (Illus.). 87p. pap. 8.00 (ISBN 0-318-12507-2). Am Donkey.

Crawford, Ann. This Is No Place for a Nervous Person. (Illus., Orig.). pap. 5.00x (ISBN 0-915494-12-4). Fibonacci Corp.

Crawford, Ann, jt. auth. see Crawford, William.

Crawford, Anne, ed. Europa Biographical Dictionary of British Women. 424p. 1983. 55.00x (ISBN 0-905118-77-4, Pub. by Europa England). Gale.

Crawford, Anne, et al, eds. Europa Biographical Dictionary of British Women: Over 1000 Notable Women from Britain's Past. 436p. 1984. 55.00x (ISBN 0-8103-1789-3). Gale.

Crawford, Annie L. & Kilander, Viginia C. Psychiatric Nursing & Mental Health Nursing: A Basic Manual. 6th ed. LC 84-11423. 194p. 1984. pap. text ed. 11.95 (ISBN 0-8036-2113-2). Davis Co.

Crawford, Anthony R., ed. Posters of World War I & World War II in George C. Marshall Research Foundation. LC 79-9852. (Illus.). xi, 128p. 1979. 9.95x (ISBN 0-8139-0778-0). U Pr of Va.

Crawford, Arch. A Doll Named Moses. 424p. 1982. 15.00 (ISBN 0-682-49729-0). Exposition Pr FL.

Crawford, Arthur W. Monetary Management Under the New Deal. LC 70-173988. (FDR & the Era of the New Deal Ser.). 380p. 1972. Repr. of 1940 ed. lib. bdg. 49.50 (ISBN 0-306-70374-2). Da Capo.

Crawford, B. J. A Little Help from a Friend. 48p. (Orig.). 1982. pap. 7.50 (ISBN 0-911535-00-4). B J Serv.

Crawford, Bartholow V., ed. Henry David Thoreau: Representative Selections. 1978. Repr. of 1934 ed. lib. bdg. 45.00 (ISBN 0-8495-5117-X). Arden Lib.

Crawford, Benny. Book for Every Body. LC 78-55792. 240p. 1979. pap. 7.95 (ISBN 0-89037-132-6). Anderson World.

Crawford, Bill, jt. auth. see Wray, Bill.

Crawford, C. Land of the Montezumas. 1976. lib. bdg. 59.95 (ISBN 0-8490-2126-X). Gordon Pr.

Crawford, C. C. The Eternal Spirit: His Person & Powers. (The Bible Study Textbook Ser.). 1973. 14.30 (ISBN 0-89900-050-9). College Pr Pub.

--Genesis, Vol. II. (The Bible Study Textbook Ser.). 1968. 15.90 (ISBN 0-89900-003-7). College Pr Pub.

--Genesis, Vol. III. (The Bible Study Textbook Ser.). (Illus.). 1970. 14.30 (ISBN 0-89900-004-5). College Pr Pub.

--Survey Course in Christian Doctrine, Vols. III & IV. LC 71-1388. (The Bible Study Textbook Ser.). 1964. 13.80 (ISBN 0-89900-054-1). College Pr Pub.

--What the Bible Says about Faith. LC 82-72621. (What the Bible Says Ser.). 380p. 1982. 13.50 (ISBN 0-89900-089-4). College Pr Pub.

Crawford, C. Merle. New Products Management. 1983. 32.95x (ISBN 0-256-02845-1). Irwin.

Crawford, Chares. The Marlowe Concordance: 3 pts., A-Goods, 1911-13 with: Pt,.4 Goodwill-Lake, Materials for the Study of the Old English Drama Ser. 1: V, 34-Ser. 2: vol. 2. pap. 107.00 (ISBN 0-317-16427-9). Kraus Repr.

Crawford, Charles. Collectanea First Series: Richard Barfield, Marlowe, Shakespeare, Ben Jonson, John Webster, Sir Philip Sydney, Edmund Spenser. 1973. Repr. of 1906 ed. 40.00 (ISBN 0-8274-1519-2). R West.

--Collectanea Second Series: Montaigne, Webster, Marston, Donne. 1973. Repr. of 1907 ed. 40.00 (ISBN 0-8274-1776-4). R West.

--Leader: Letter Perfect. (gr. 4-6). 1984. pap. 1.95 (ISBN 0-671-43535-3). PB.

--Letter Perfect. (gr. 7-9). 1979. pap. 1.50 (ISBN 0-671-29945-X). Archway.

Crawford, Charles, ed. A Concordance to the Works of Thomas Kyd: Materials for the Study of Old English Drama, Ser. 1: vol. 15, 3 pts. pap. 120.00 (ISBN 0-317-16424-4). Kraus Repr.

Crawford, Charles P. Letter Perfect. (gr. 7 up). 1977. 9.95 (ISBN 0-525-33635-4). Dutton.

--Letter Perfect. 176p. (gr. 7-10). 1984. pap. text ed. 1.95 (ISBN 0-671-43535-3). Archway.

Crawford, Charles W. Yesterday's Memphis. LC 76-10384. (Historic Cities Ser: No. 25). (Illus.). 160p. 1976. 9.95 (ISBN 0-912458-69-0). E A Seemann.

Crawford, Charles W., ed. Memphis Memories: Thirty-Two Historic Postcards. LC 83-1202. (Illus.). 16p. 1983. pap. 3.95 (ISBN 0-87049-382-5). U of Tenn Pr.

Crawford, Charles W., ed. see Broer, Jill S., et al.

Crawford, Charles W., ed. see Holt, Edgar A.

Crawford, Charles W., ed. see Livingood, James W.

Crawford, Charles W., ed. see Mason, Robert L.

Crawford, Chris. The Art of Computer Game Design: Reflections of a Master Game Designer. 120p. (Orig.). 1984. pap. 14.95 (ISBN 0-07-881117-1, 117-1). Osborne-McGraw.

Crawford, Christina. Mommie Dearest. 352p. 1984. pap. 3.95 (ISBN 0-425-07289-4). Berkley Pub.

--Mommie Dearest. LC 78-14977. (Illus.). 1978. 9.95 (ISBN 0-688-03386-5). Morrow.

Crawford, Claud C. The End of the Rope. rev. ed. LC 85-90684. 96p. 1985. pap. 5.95 (ISBN 0-933697-00-7). Claud Crawford.

--Giants, Lovers, & Seekers. 96p. (Orig.). 1983. pap. 5.95 (ISBN 0-933697-02-3). Claud Crawford.

--Integrity: The Other Side of Mental Health. 104p. (Orig.). 1984. pap. 5.95 (ISBN 0-933697-01-5). Claud Crawford.

--Sometimes Giant. 96p. (Orig.). 1984. pap. text ed. 5.95 (ISBN 0-933697-03-1). Claud Crawford.

Crawford, Clifford C. Biology of Desert Invertebrates. (Illus.). 314p. 1981. 42.00 (ISBN 0-387-10807-6). Springer Verlag.

Crawford, D. The City of London: Its Architectural Heritage. 1977. soft cover 25.00 (ISBN 0-85941-043-9); cased 40.00 (ISBN 0-85941-049-8). State Mutual Bk.

Crawford, D. F., jt. auth. see Messel, H.

Crawford, D. G. The Study of English. 1928. 15.00 (ISBN 0-8274-3549-5). R West.

Crawford, D. H., ed. Beowulf. (Medieval Library). Repr. of 1926 ed. 17.50 (ISBN 0-8154-0055-1). Cooper Sq.

Crawford, Dan R. Evangelife: A Guide to Life-Style Evangelism. LC 84-1805. 1984. pap. 4.95 (ISBN 0-8054-6247-3). Broadman.

--Single Adults: Resource & Recipients for Revival. 1985. pap. 5.95 (ISBN 0-8054-3236-1). Broadman.

Crawford, Daniel. Thinking Black: Twenty-Two Years Without a Break in the Long Grass of Central Africa. Repr. of 1913 ed. 24.75x (ISBN 0-8371-1752-6, CRT&). Greenwood.

Crawford, David & Crawford, Leona. Missionary Adventures in the South Pacific. LC 67-15137. 1967. 5.50 (ISBN 0-8048-0403-6). C E Tuttle.

Crawford, David A. Evolution of Italian Sculpture. LC 72-81977. xiv, 348p. 1974. Repr. of 1909 ed. 32.00 (ISBN 0-8337-0730-2). B Franklin.

Crawford, David L., et al, eds. Symposium on Support & Testing of Large Astronomical Mirrors: Proceedings Held in Tuscon, Arizona, December 4-6, 1966. (Arizona University, Optical Sciences Center, Technical Report: Vol. 30). pap. 63.00 (ISBN 0-317-28566-1, 2055253). Bks Demand UMI.

Crawford, Diane. Savage Eden. (Second Chance at Love Ser.: No. 79). 1982. pap. 1.75 (ISBN 0-515-06690-7). Jove Pubns.

--Season of Marriage, No. 158. 192p. 1983. pap. 1.95 (ISBN 0-515-07246-X). Jove Pubns.

Crawford, Donald R. Practical Guide to Airplane Performance & Design. (Illus.). 1979. pap. 18.95 (ISBN 0-911721-54-1, Pub. by D R Crawford). Aviation.

--A Practical Guide to Airplane Performance & Design. rev. ed. (Illus.). 222p. 1981. pap. 18.95 (ISBN 0-9603934-0-4). Crawford Aviation.

Crawford, Donald W. Kant's Aesthetic Theory. LC 73-15259. pap. 50.00 (ISBN 0-317-12976-7, 2017819). Bks Demand UMI.

Crawford, Dorothy J. Kerkeosiris: An Egyptian Village in the Ptolemaic Period. LC 70-96083. (Classical Studies). (Illus.). 1971. 39.50 (ISBN 0-521-07607-2). Cambridge U Pr.

Crawford, E., jt. ed. see Bernhard, C. G.

Crawford, E. David & Borden, Thomas A., eds. Genitourinary Cancer Surgery. LC 81-23624. (Illus.). 575p. 1982. text ed. 98.50 (ISBN 0-8121-0812-4). Lea & Febiger.

Crawford, E. Stanley, ed. Diseases of the Aorta: Including an Atlas of Angiographic Pathology & Surgical Technique. Crawford, John L. (Illus.). 400p. 1984. lib. bdg. 135.00 (ISBN 0-683-02235-0). Williams & Wilkins.

Crawford, Edna, tr. see Fukai, Shinji.

Crawford, Elisabeth. The Beginnings of the Nobel Institution: The Science Prizes 1901-1950. 300p. 1984. 34.50 (ISBN 0-521-26584-3). Cambridge U Pr.

Crawford, Elisabeth D., tr. see Brothers Grimm.

Crawford, Elisabeth T. The Sociology of the Social Sciences: A Trend Report & Bibliography. (Current Sociology-la Sociologie Contemporaine: No. 19-2). 1973. pap. 8.40x (ISBN 90-2797-655-4). Mouton.

Crawford, Elizabeth, tr. see Koci, Marta.

Crawford, Elizabeth D., jt. ed. see De Montreville, Doris.

Crawford, Elizabeth D., tr. from Ger. The Seven Ravens: The Brothers Grimm. LC 80-25365. Orig. Title: Die Sieben Raven. (Illus.). 24p. (gr. k-3). 1981. 11.25 (ISBN 0-688-00371-0); PLB 11.88 (ISBN 0-688-00372-9). Morrow.

Crawford, Elizabeth D., tr. see Brothers Grimm.

Crawford, Elizabeth d., tr. see Brothers Grimm.

Crawford, Elizabeth D., tr. see Brothers Grimm.

Crawford, Ellen. Why Me? 156p. (gr. 5 up). 1985. 12.95 (ISBN 0-316-15326-5). Little.

Crawford, Emmanuel J. Oil & the Changed Structure of the World at the Beginning of the Twenty-First Century. 1980. 74.75x (ISBN 0-930008-49-9). Inst Econ Pol.

Crawford, Evelyn M. Personal Data Directory. 56p. (Orig.). 1982. pap. 5.95 (ISBN 0-9608966-0-0). Quality Serv.

Crawford, F. Marion. Nightmare Ship. LC 81-21805. (Illus.). 32p. (gr. 5-10). 1982. PLB 9.79 (ISBN 0-89375-632-6); pap. text ed. 2.50 (ISBN 0-89375-633-4). Troll Assocs.

Crawford, F. S., ed. see Averroes.

Crawford, Finla G. Continuing Education. 1958. 2.50 (ISBN 0-87060-087-7, PUC 7). Syracuse U Cont Ed.

Crawford, Francis M. American Politician. LC 73-111088. (BCL Ser. I). Repr. of 1893 ed. 9.00 (ISBN 0-404-01828-9). AMS Pr.

--American Politician. LC 32-33609. 1893. 8.00x (ISBN 0-403-00034-3). Scholarly.

--Katharine Lauderdale, 2 Vols. LC 6-30895. 1968. Repr. of 1894 ed. Set. 49.00x (ISBN 0-403-00099-8). Scholarly.

--Marzio's Crucifix. LC 79-80626. (BCL Ser. I). Repr. of 1887 ed. 11.00 (ISBN 0-404-01829-7). AMS Pr.

--Marzio's Crucifix. LC 4-15090. 1887. 9.00x (ISBN 0-403-00014-9). Scholarly.

--Mister Isaacs. LC 71-92607. (BCL Ser. I). 1969. Repr. of 1882 ed. 12.50 (ISBN 0-404-01835-1). AMS Pr.

--Mister Isaacs: A Tale of Modern India. 1882. 9.00x (ISBN 0-403-00015-7). Scholarly.

--Novel: What It Is. LC 73-98831. Repr. of 1893 ed. lib. bdg. 18.75x (ISBN 0-8371-2924-9, CRTN). Greenwood.

--The Novel: What It Is. LC 76-104434. lib. bdg. 12.75 (ISBN 0-8398-0280-3); pap. text ed. 6.25x (ISBN 0-89197-869-0). Irvington.

--The Rulers of the South, 2 vols. Set. 250.00 (ISBN 0-8490-0979-0). Gordon Pr.

--With the Immortals. Reginald, R. & Menville, Douglas, eds. LC 75-46264. (Supernatural & Occult Fiction Ser.). 1976. Repr. of 1888 ed. lib. bdg. 23.50x (ISBN 0-405-08122-7). Ayer Co Pubs.

--Zoroaster. LC 74-126704. (BCL Ser. I). Repr. of 1885 ed. 12.50 (ISBN 0-404-01836-X). AMS Pr.

--Zoroaster. LC 6-30882. 1885. 11.00x (ISBN 0-403-00100-5). Scholarly.

Crawford, Francis Marion. Novel, What It Is. facs. ed. LC 79-75506. (Select Bibliographies Reprint Ser). 1893. 14.50 (ISBN 0-8369-5003-8). Ayer Co Pubs.

Crawford, Fred A. & Pass, Harvey I. Surgical Management of Acquired Heart Disease. 306p. 1985. 45.00 (ISBN 0-87527-338-6). Green.

Crawford, Fred D. H. M. Tomlinson. (English Authors Ser.). 1981. lib. bdg. 15.95 (ISBN 0-8057-6800-9, Twayne). G K Hall.

--Mixing Memory & Desire: The Waste Land & Modern British Novels. LC 82-477. 170p. 1982. 22.50x (ISBN 0-271-00308-1). Pa St U Pr.

Crawford, Fred L. Career Planning for the Blind: A Manual for Students & Teachers. 189p. 1966. 3.95 (ISBN 0-374-11905-8). FS&G.

Crawford, Fred R. Civil Aggression & Urban Disorders. 1967. pap. 1.00 (ISBN 0-89937-024-1). Ctr Res Soc Chg.

Crawford, Fred R., ed. American Government: Two Hundred Years of Change. LC 76-7731. 1976. pap. 5.00 (ISBN 0-89937-006-3). Ctr Res Soc Chg.

--A Decade of Sociological Challenges. LC 75-7545. 1975. pap. 1.00 (ISBN 0-89937-013-6). Ctr Res Soc Chg.

--Exploring Mental Health Parameters, Vol. III. LC 80-67929. (Orig.). 1980. pap. 8.00 (ISBN 0-89937-030-6). Ctr Res Soc Chg.

--Violence & Dissent in Urban America. 1970. pap. 2.00 (ISBN 0-89937-022-5, Southern Newspapers Publishers Association Foundation). Ctr Res Soc Chg.

Crawford, Fred R., intro. by see Seventy First Infantry Division, U.S. Army.

Crawford, Fred R., et al. Certain Reactions by the Atlanta Public to the Death of the Rev. Dr. Martin Luther King Jr. LC 73-85669. 1969. pap. 3.00 (ISBN 0-89937-023-3). Ctr Res Soc Chg.

Crawford, Frederick. Hans Christian Andersen's Correspondence with the Late Grand-Duke of Saxe-Weimar, Charles Dickens, Etc. 1979. Repr. lib. bdg. 45.00 (ISBN 0-8495-0944-0). Arden Lib.

Crawford, G. E., jt. auth. see Birnbaum, S. L.

Crawford, Gary W. Paleoethnobotany of the Kameda Peninsula Jomon. (Anthropological Papers: No. 73). (Illus.). 200p. 1983. pap. 8.00x (ISBN 0-932206-95-6). U Mich Mus Anthro.

Crawford, Gary W., ed. Bibliography of Gothic Studies, 1980. (Gothic Chapbooks Ser.: No. 1). (Orig.). 1983. pap. text ed. 2.00 (ISBN 0-913045-00-4). Gothic Pr.

--Bibliography of Gothic Studies, 1981. (Gothic Chapbooks: No. 2). 50p. (Orig.). 1985. pap. text ed. cancelled (ISBN 0-913045-03-9). Gothic Pr.

--Gothic. 150p. 1984. lib. bdg. 25.00 (ISBN 0-913045-02-0). Gothic Pr.

Crawford, George W. Prince Hall & His Followers. LC 74-144591. Repr. of 1914 ed. 16.00 (ISBN 0-404-00145-9). AMS Pr.

Crawford, H. S. Irish Carved Ornament (from Monuments of the Christian Period) 2nd ed. (Illus.). 144p. 1980. pap. 7.50 (ISBN 0-85342-632-5, Pub. by Mercier Pr Ireland). Irish Bk Ctr.

Crawford, H. W. & McDowell, Milton C. Math Workbook for Foodservice-Lodging. 240p. 1980. pap. 14.95 (ISBN 0-8436-2197-4). Van Nos Reinhold.

Crawford, H. Warren & Rodgers, John F. Maryland Supplement for Modern Real Estate Practice. 3rd ed. LC 82-22223. 152p. (Orig.). 1982. pap. text ed. 8.95 (ISBN 0-88462-267-3, 1510-08, Real Estate Ed). Longman USA.

--Maryland Supplement for Modern Real Estate Practice. 4th ed. LC 84-27749. 192p. (Orig.). 1985. pap. text ed. 9.95 (ISBN 0-88462-511-7, 1510-08, Real Estate Ed). Longman USA.

Crawford, Harold B., ed. see Transamerica Delaval Inc.

Crawford, Harriet, ed. Subterranean Britain. LC 79-16858. 1979. 22.50x (ISBN 0-312-77477-X). St Martin.

Crawford, Hick, jt. auth. see Lowe, Julian.

Crawford, Hollie & McDowell, Milton C. Metric Workbook for Food Service & Lodging. LC 76-22181. 224p. 1976. pap. 12.95 (ISBN 0-8436-2103-6). Van Nos Reinhold.

Crawford, Irene. Aids to Independence: A Guide to Products for the Disabled & Elderly. (Illus.). 120p. (Orig.). 1985. pap. 11.95 (ISBN 0-88908-608-7, 9536, Pub. by Intl Self-Counsel Pr). TAB Bks.

Crawford, J. Risks & Labour. (Perinatal Practice Ser.). 43.50 (ISBN 0-471-90371-X). Wiley.

Crawford, J. F. & Smith, P. G. Landfill Technology. (Illus.). 192p. 1985. pap. text ed. 29.95 (ISBN 0-408-01407-5). Butterworth.

Crawford, J. H., Jr., et al, eds. Defect Properties & Processing of High-Technology Nonmetallic Materials: Proceedings of the Symposium on Defect Properties & Processing of High-Tecnology Nonmetalic Materials, Boston, MA, Nov. 14-17, 1983. (Materials Research Society Symposia Proceedings Ser.: Vol. 24). 494p. 1984. 80.00 (ISBN 0-444-00904-3, North Holland). Elsevier.

Crawford, J. R. Lovely Peggy: A Play in Three Acts Based on the Love Romance of Margaret Woffington & David Garrick. 1911. 24.50x (ISBN 0-686-51412-2). Elliots Bks.

Crawford, J. S. Obstetric Analgesia & Anaesthesia. 2nd ed. (Current Reviews in OB-GYN Ser.: Vol.1). 169p. 1984. pap. 16.00 (ISBN 0-443-03249-1). Churchill.

Crawford, J. S., et al, eds. Obstetric Clinical Care. 418p. 1980. 73.75 (ISBN 0-444-80211-8, Biomedical Pr). Elsevier.

Crawford, J. Wickersham. Spanish Pastoral Drama. LC 74-4111. 1915. lib. bdg. 22.50 (ISBN 0-8414-3610-X). Folcroft.

Crawford, Jack & Stancavage, Fran. Facilitator's Handbook of Alcholism Counciling: A Comprehensive Training Course. 1981. 42.00 (ISBN 0-8240-7190-5). Garland Pub.

Crawford, Jack R. What to Read in English Literature. 388p. Repr. of 1928 ed. lib. bdg. 40.00 (ISBN 0-918377-49-8). Russell Pr.

Crawford, James. Australian Courts of Law. 1982. 45.00x (ISBN 0-19-554344-0). Oxford U Pr.

--Cocopa Texts. LC 81-24046. (University of California Publications in Linguistics Ser.: Vol. 100). 1983. pap. text ed. 35.00x (ISBN 0-520-09652-5). U of Cal Pr.

--The Creation of States in International Law. 1979. 58.00x (ISBN 0-19-825347-8). Oxford U Pr.

Crawford, James H. & Slifkin, Lawrence M., eds. Point Defects in Solids, 3 vols. Incl. Vol. 1, General & Ionic Crystals. 556p. 1972. 75.00x (ISBN 0-306-37511-7); Vol. 2, Semiconductor & Molecular Crystals. 480p. 1975. 75.00 (ISBN 0-306-37512-5); Vol. 3, Defects in Metals. 1978. 37.50x (ISBN 0-306-37513-3). LC 72-183562. (Illus., Plenum Pr). Plenum Pub.

Crawford, James L. Bibliography of Royal Proclamations of the Tudor & Stuart Sovereigns & of Others Published Under Authority, Fourteen Eighty-Five to Seventeen Fourteen, 3 vols. in 2. LC 68-1518. 661p. 1910-13. Repr. 153.00 (ISBN 0-8337-0724-8). B Franklin.

--Bibliotheca Lindesiana: Catalogue of a Collection of English Ballads of the 17th & 18th Centuries, 2 Vols. 1963. Repr. of 1890 ed. 71.50 (ISBN 0-8337-0728-0). B Franklin.

--Catalogue of a Collection of 1500 Tracts by Martin Luther & His Contemporaries, 1511-1598. 1965. Repr. of 1903 ed. 32.00 (ISBN 0-8337-1001-X). B Franklin.

--Catalogue of English Broadsides, 1505-1897. 1965. Repr. of 1898 ed. 53.50 (ISBN 0-8337-0729-9). B Franklin.

--Handlist of Proclamations Issued by Royal & Other Constitutional Authorities 1714-1910. 1966. Repr. of 1910 ed. 89.00 (ISBN 0-8337-0721-3). B Franklin.

Crawford, James M. The Mobilian Trade Language. LC 78-13149. pap. 37.50 (ISBN 0-317-20138-7, 2023167). Bks Demand UMI.

--Studies in Southeastern Indian Languages. 464p. 1975. 25.00 (ISBN 0-87797-112-9). Cherokee.

Crawford, Jane D. The Premedical Planning Guide to Allopathic, Osteopathic & Podiatric Medical Schools. 250p. (Orig.). 1985. pap. 12.50 (ISBN 0-941406-06-7). Betz Pub Co Inc.

Crawford, Jay B. Credit Mobilier of America. LC 75-155099. Repr. of 1880 ed. 11.50 (ISBN 0-404-01837-8). AMS Pr.

--Credit Mobilier of America: Its Origin & History, Its Work of Constructing the Union Pacific Railroad & the Relation of Congress Therewith. LC 69-13868. Repr. of 1880 ed. lib. bdg. 15.00x (ISBN 0-8371-0364-9, CRCM). Greenwood.

Crawford, Jerry L. Acting: In Person & In Style. 3rd ed. 554p. 1983. pap. text ed. write for info. (ISBN 0-697-04234-0). Wm C Brown.

Crawford, Joe, ed. Black Photographers Annual, Vol. 2. annual (Illus.). 150p. (Orig.). 1974. 7.95 (ISBN 0-913564-02-8). Another View.

--Black Photographers Annual, Vol. 4. LC 72-96849. 1980. 12.95 (ISBN 0-913564-06-0); pap. 8.95 (ISBN 0-913564-07-9). Another View.

Crawford, Joe V., jt. auth. see Arnbal, Carl A.

Crawford, John. Baboon Dooley, Rock Critic: All the Baboons You Can Eat. (Illus.). cancelled. Open Bks & Recs.

--Romantic Criticism of Shakespearean Drama. (Salzberg Studies in English Literature: Romantic Reassessment Ser.: No. 79). 1978. pap. text ed. 25.50x (ISBN 0-391-01352-1). Humanities.

Crawford, John, jt. auth. see Le Sueur, Meridel.

Crawford, John & Morin, J. Donald, eds. The Eye in Childhood. 1983. 83.50 (ISBN 0-8089-1503-7, 790936). Grune.

Crawford, John & Okita, Saburo, eds. Australia & Japan: Issues in the Economic Relationship. (Australia-Japan Economic Relations Research Project Monograph: No. 2). (Illus.). 140p. 1980. pap. text ed. 3.80 (ISBN 0-9596197-1-2). Australia N U P.

Crawford, John C. Totontepec Mixe Phonotagmemics. (Publications in Linguistics & Related Fields Ser.: No. 8). 197p. 1963. pap. 3.00 (ISBN 0-88312-408-4); microfiche 3.00 (ISBN 0-88312-313-4). Summer Inst Ling.

Crawford, John C., tr. see Hahl-Koch, Jelena.

Crawford, John G., et al. Wartime Agriculture in Australia & New Zealand, 1939-50. (Illus.). 1954. 30.00x (ISBN 0-8047-0455-4). Stanford U Pr.

Crawford, John J. History of the Indian Archipelago, 3 vols. (Illus.). 1967. Repr. 145.00x (ISBN 0-7146-1157-3, F Cass Co). Biblio Dist.

--History of the Indian Archipelago, 3 Vols. LC 68-89362. Repr. of 1820 ed. 125.00x (ISBN 0-678-05164-X). Kelley.

Crawford, John L. see Crawford, E. Stanley.

Crawford, John R. How to Be a Consistent Winner in the Most Popular Card Games. pap. 2.95 (ISBN 0-385-09687-9, C180, Dolp). Doubleday.

Crawford, John R., jt. auth. see Jacoby, Oswald.

Crawford, John R., ed. see Jacoby, Oswald.

Crawford, John S. Wolves, Bears & Bighorns: Wilderness Observations & Experiences of a Professional Outdoorsman. LC 80-22007. (Illus.). 192p. 1980. 25.00 (ISBN 0-88240-146-7); pap. 19.00 (ISBN 0-88240-144-0). Alaska Northwest.

Crawford, John T., III & Hustrulid, William A., eds. Open Pit Mine Planning & Design. LC 79-52269. (Illus.). 367p. 1979. text ed. 30.00x (ISBN 0-89520-253-0). Soc Mining Eng.

Crawford, John W. Early Shakespearean Actresses. LC 84-47691. (American University Studies IV (English Language & Literature): Vol. 8). 205p. (Orig.). 1984. text ed. 25.00 (ISBN 0-8204-0099-8). P Lang Pubs.

--Steps to Success: A Study Skills Handbook. rev. ed. 1981. pap. text ed. 6.95 (ISBN 0-8403-2508-8, 40250801). Kendall-Hunt.

Crawford, Joseph H., et al. Three Hundred Thirty Three: A Bibliography of the Science Fantasy Novel. LC 74-15959. (Science Fiction Ser). 82p. 1965. Repr. 14.00x (ISBN 0-405-06324-5). Ayer Co Pubs.

Crawford, Karen. Straight from the Heart. (Caprice Romance Ser.: No. 60). 144p. 1985. pap. 2.25 (ISBN 0-441-79021-6, Pub. by Tempo). Ace Bks.

Crawford, Kenneth & Simmons, Paul. Growing up with Sex. (Sexuality in Christian Living Ser). 80p. (gr. 7-9). 1973. pap. 6.95 (ISBN 0-8054-5312-1). Broadman.

Crawford, Kenneth, jt. auth. see Simmons, Paul D.

Crawford, Kenneth G. The Pressure Boys: The Inside Story of Lobbying in America. LC 73-19139. (Politics & People Ser.). 320p. 1974. Repr. 21.00x (ISBN 0-405-05864-0). Ayer Co Pubs.

Crawford, L. D., jt. auth. see Carne, P. B.

Crawford, Lela Ann, jt. auth. see Crawford, William R.

Crawford, Leona, jt. auth. see Crawford, David.

Crawford, Lester M., jt. auth. see Soave, Orland.

Crawford, Lewis. The Medora Deadwood Stageline. (Shorey Historical Ser.). 26p. pap. 3.00 (ISBN 0-8466-0036-6, S36). Shorey.

Crawford, Linda. Ghost of a Chance. 1985. 15.95 (ISBN 0-87795-677-4). Arbor Hse.

--Something to Make Us Happy. 1979. pap. 2.25 (ISBN 0-345-28433-X). Ballantine.

Crawford, Lloyd V. Pediatric Allergic Diseases - Focus on Clinical Diagnosis. 2nd ed. 1982. 35.00 (ISBN 0-87488-826-3). Med Exam.

Crawford, Lloyd V., jt. auth. see Lieberman, Phillip.

Crawford, Lucy. Supervisory Skills in Marketing. Dorr, Eugene, ed. (Occupational Manuals & Projects in Marketing Ser.). (Illus.). (gr. 9-10). 1977. pap. text ed. 8.60 (ISBN 0-07-013471-5). McGraw.

Crawford, Lucy & Lynch, Richard. Finance & Credit. (Career Competencies in Marketing). (Illus.). (gr. 11-12). 1978. pap. text ed. 8.68 (ISBN 0-07-013481-2). McGraw.

Crawford, M. A., tr. see De Balzac, Honore.

Crawford, M. V., tr. see Kurth, Godefried J.

Crawford, Mabel S. Life in Tuscany. LC 77-87713. Repr. of 1859 ed. 26.50 (ISBN 0-404-16514-1). AMS Pr.

Crawford, Malcolm & Poole, James, eds. Ten Years of Multinational Business. (Economist Intelligence Ser.). 184p. 1982. 29.95x (ISBN 0-89011-580-X). Ballinger Pub.

Crawford, Marion. Elizabeth the Queen: The Story of Britain's New Sovereign. LC 74-97380. Repr. of 1952 ed. lib. bdg. 15.00x (ISBN 0-8371-3739-X, CREQ). Greenwood.

Crawford, Marion A., tr. see Balzac, Honore De.

Crawford, Marion A., tr. see De Balzac, Honore.

Crawford, Marjorie F. KinderArt Drawing. (Illus.). 57p. 1982. 7.00 (ISBN 0-9610102-0-7). Edutech.

Crawford, Marshal A., jt. auth. see Grauer, Robert T.

Crawford, Marshall, jt. auth. see Grauer, Robert T.

Crawford, Marshall A., jt. auth. see Grauer, Robert G.

Crawford, Mary C. Goethe & His Woman Friends. LC 72-1563. (Studies in German Literature, No. 13). (Illus.). 1972. Repr. of 1911 ed. lib. bdg. 72.95x (ISBN 0-8383-1448-1). Haskell.

--Little Pilgrimages Among Old New England Inns: Being an Account of Little Journeys to Various Quaint Inns & Hostelries of Colonial New England. LC 76-107629. (Illus.). 400p. 1970. Repr. of 1907 ed. 40.00x (ISBN 0-8103-3536-0). Gale.

--Romance of the American Theatre. LC 70-144957. 1971. Repr. of 1940 ed. 59.00x (ISBN 0-403-00909-X). Scholarly.

--Romantic Days in Old Boston. 1973. Repr. of 1910 ed. 30.00 (ISBN 0-8274-1518-4). R West.

Crawford, Mary M. Student Folkways & Spending at Indiana University, 1940-1941. LC 68-58563. (Columbia University. Studies in the Social Sciences: No. 499). Repr. of 1943 ed. 21.00 (ISBN 0-404-51499-5). AMS Pr.

Crawford, Max. The Backslider. 271p. 1976. 8.95 (ISBN 0-374-10800-5). FS&G.

--Lords of the Plain. LC 84-45054. 352p. 1985. 14.95 (ISBN 0-689-11475-3). Atheneum.

--Waltz Across Texas. 1978. pap. 1.95 (ISBN 0-380-01856-X, 36533). Avon.

--Waltz Across Texas. LC 74-26604. 393p. 1975. 8.95 (ISBN 0-374-28628-0). FS&G.

Crawford, Medorem. Journal of Medorem Crawford. 26p. 1967. Repr. of 1897 ed. pap. 3.00 (ISBN 0-87770-041-9). Ye Galleon.

Crawford, Meodrem. Journal of Meodrem Crawford. facs. ed. (Shorey Historical Ser.). 26p. pap. 2.95 (ISBN 0-8466-0141-9, S141). Shorey.

Crawford, Michael. Ancient Greece & Rome. (Sources of History Ser.). 238p. 1984. 37.50 (ISBN 0-521-24782-9); pap. 13.95 (ISBN 0-521-28958-0). Cambridge U Pr.

--Coinage & Money under the Roman Republic. Date not set. price not set. U of Cal Pr.

--The Roman Republic. LC 81-20047. (Illus.). 224p. 1982. pap. text ed. 6.95x (ISBN 0-674-77931-2). Harvard U Pr.

--Roman Republican Coinage. LC 77-164450. (Illus.). 750p. 1975. 275.00 (ISBN 0-521-07492-4). Cambridge U Pr.

Crawford, Michael, jt. auth. see Beard, Mary.

Crawford, Michael, jt. auth. see Kays, William M.

Crawford, Michael & Whitehead, David, eds. Archaic & Classical Greece: A Selection of Ancient Sources in Translation. LC 82-4355. 700p. 1983. 72.50 (ISBN 0-521-22775-5); pap. 19.95 (ISBN 0-521-29638-2). Cambridge U Pr.

Crawford, Michael H., ed. Black Caribs: A Case Study in Biocultural Adaptation, Vol. 3. (Current Developments in Anthropological Genetics: Vol. 3). 414p. 1984. 59.50x (ISBN 0-306-41308-6, Plenum Pr). Plenum Pub.

Crawford, Michael H. & Mielke, James H., eds. Current Developments in Anthropological Genetics, Vol. 2: Ecology & Population Structure. LC 79-24900. (Illus.). 520p. 1982. text ed. 59.50x (ISBN 0-306-40842-2, Plenum Pr). Plenum Pub.

Crawford, Michael H., jt. ed. see Mielke, James H.

Crawford, Morris H., jt. auth. see Hartland-Thunberg, Penelope.

Crawford, Nelson A. The Ethics of Journalism. (American Studies). 1969. Repr. of 1924 ed. 24.00 (ISBN 0-384-10130-5). Johnson Repr.

--Ethics of Journalism. LC 71-131676. 1970. Repr. of 1929 ed. 14.00x (ISBN 0-403-00563-9). Scholarly.

--We Liberals. facs. ed. LC 68-22908. (Essay Index Reprint Ser.). 1936. 15.00 (ISBN 0-8369-0349-8). Ayer Co Pubs.

Crawford, Nick, jt. ed. see Lowe, Julian.

Crawford, O. William & Gautot, Henri J., eds. X-Ray Technology Examination Review Book, Vol. 2. 3rd ed. 1973. pap. 13.25 (ISBN 0-87488-442-X). Med Exam.

Crawford, Oliver. Done This Day: The European Idea in Action. LC 74-102067. 1970. 13.50 (ISBN 0-8008-2266-8). Taplinger.

--The Execution. 288p. 1985. pap. 3.50 (ISBN 0-446-31334-3). Warner Bks.

Crawford, Osbert G. The Fung Kingdom of Sennar: With a Geographical Account of the Middle Nile Region. LC 74-15021. (Illus.). Repr. of 1951 ed. 55.00 (ISBN 0-404-12019-9). AMS Pr.

Crawford, Oswald. Lyrical Verse from Elizabeth to Victoria. 1977. Repr. of 1896 ed. lib. bdg. 25.00 (ISBN 0-8482-0475-1). Norwood Edns.

Crawford, Patricia. Denzil Holles, Fifteen Ninety-Eight to Sixteen Eighty: A Study of His Political Career. 1982. 60.00X (ISBN 0-901050-52-0, 07550042, Pub. by Royal Hist Soc England). State Mutual Bk.

--Denzil Holles, 1598-1980: Study of His Political Career. (Royal Historical Society - Studies in History Ser.: Vol. 16). 243p. 1979. text ed. 39.50x (ISBN 0-901050-52-0, Pub. by Swiftbks England). Humanities.

Crawford, Patricia, ed. Exploring Women's Past. 224p. 1985. pap. text ed. 12.50x (ISBN 0-86861-604-4). Allen Unwin.

Crawford, Peter, jt. auth. see Allaby, Michael.

Crawford, Petrina. Seed of Evil. 1976. pap. 1.25 (ISBN 0-685-73459-5, LB410, Leisure Bks). Dorchester Pub Co.

Crawford, Quantz. Methods of Psychic Development. LC 82-83876. 1983. pap. 5.95 (ISBN 0-87728-545-4). Weiser.

Crawford, R. J. Plastics Engineering. (Illus.). 360p. 1981. pap. 28.00 (ISBN 0-08-026263-5). Pergamon.

Crawford, R. M. A Bit of a Rebel: The Life & Work of George Arnold Wood (1865-1928) (Illus.). 368p. 1976. 33.00x (ISBN 0-424-00005-9, Pub by Sydney U Pr). Intl Spec Bk.

Crawford, Ralston. Music in the Street: Photographs of New Orleans by Ralston Crawford. LC 83-80537. (Illus.). xii, 36p. (Orig.). 1983. pap. 10.00x (ISBN 0-917860-14-4). Historic New Orleans.

Crawford, Richard. American Studies & American Musicology: A Point of View & a Case in Point. LC 75-874. (I.S.A.M. Monographs: No. 4). 34p. 1975. pap. 3.00 (ISBN 0-914678-03-5). Inst Am Music.

--A Historian's Introduction to Early American Music. (Illus.). 1980. pap. 4.00 (ISBN 0-912296-44-5, Dist. by U Pr of Va). Am Antiquarian.

--Studying American Music. (I. S. A. M. Special Publications Ser.: No. 3). (Orig.). 1985. pap. write for info (ISBN 0-914678-25-6). Inst Am Music.

Crawford, Richard, jt. auth. see McKay, David.

Crawford, Richard, ed. see Billings, William.

Crawford, Richard L. Andrew Law, American Psalmodist. (Music Ser.). (Illus.). xix, 424p. 1981. Repr. of 1968 ed. lib. bdg. 37.50 (ISBN 0-306-76090-8). Da Capo.

Crawford, Richard P. & Hidalgo, Richard J., eds. Bovine Brucellosis: An International Symposium. LC 76-51649. (Illus.). 448p. 1977. 12.50x (ISBN 0-89096-032-1). Tex A&M Univ Pr.

Crawford, Robert. In Art We Trust: Boards of Trustees in the Performing Arts. 88p. 1982. 12.95x (ISBN 0-9602942-3-6). Drama Bk.

Crawford, Robert P. Direct Creativity. Repr. of 1964 ed. flexible cover 8.00 (ISBN 0-87034-009-3). Fraser Pub Co.

--The Techniques of Creative Thinking. 1964. Repr. of 1954 ed. flexible cover 10.00 (ISBN 0-87034-010-7). Fraser Pub Co.

--Think for Yourself. 1979. Repr. of 1937 ed. 10.00 (ISBN 0-87034-011-5). Fraser Pub Co.

Crawford, Robert W., ed. see Board Members & Managing Directors of Theatre Companies, Dance Companies, Operas & Orchestras.

Crawford, Ronald L. Images of Transcience in the Poems & Ballads of Friedrich Schiller. (European University Studies: Series 1, German Language & Literature: Vol. 195). 112p. 1977. pap. 13.05 (ISBN 3-261-02944-7). P Lang Pubs.

--Lignin Biodegradation & Transformation. LC 80-39557. 154p. 1981. 37.50x (ISBN 0-471-05743-6, Pub. by Wiley-Interscience). Wiley.

--Readings in Scientific German. LC 83-4860. (American University Studies VI: Foreign Language Instruction): Vol. 1). 126p. 1983. pap. text ed. 11.05 (ISBN 0-8204-0031-9). P Lang Pubs.

Crawford, Ronald L. & Hanson, R. S., eds. Microbial Growth on C. Compounds: Proceedings of the 4th International Symposium. 343p. 1984. 47.00 (ISBN 0-914826-59-X). Am Soc Microbio.

Crawford, Rudd A., Jr. & Copp, David H. Introduction to Computer Programming. 1969. pap. 8.88 (ISBN 0-395-02252-5). HM.

Crawford, S. Cromwell. The Evolution of Hindu Ethical Ideals. (Asian Studies at Hawaii: No. 28). 197p. 1982. pap. text ed. 14.00x (ISBN 0-8248-0782-0). UH Pr.

Crawford, S. J. The Old English Heptateuch, Ms Cott. (EEETS OS Ser.: Vol. 148). Repr. of 1921 ed. 29.00 (ISBN 0-317-15667-5). Kraus Repr.

Crawford, S. J., ed. Byrhtferth's Manual. (EETS OS Ser.: Vol. 177). Repr. of 1928 ed. 25.00 (ISBN 0-317-15669-1). Kraus Repr.

Crawford, Shirley O. Is God Dead Within You? 112p. 1981. 6.50 (ISBN 0-682-49789-4). Exposition Pr FL.

Crawford, Stacy. The Eve Principle: The Story of a Truly Unique Transsexual. LC 84-90083. 98p. 1985. 9.95 (ISBN 0-533-06153-9). Vantage.

Crawford, Susan, jt. ed. see Rees, Alan M.

Crawford, T. Basic Computing: A Complete Course. 393p. 16.25 (ISBN 0-07-548076-X). McGraw.

Crawford, T., ed. see Woolf, Neville.

Crawford, T. James, et al. Basic Information Keyboarding Skills. 1982. text ed. 7.10 (ISBN 0-538-26010-6, Z01). SW Pub.

--Basic Keyboarding & Typewriting Applications. 1983. 7.35 (ISBN 0-538-20370-6, T37). SW Pub.

--Century Twenty-One Typewriting. (gr. 9-12). 1982. text ed. 14.85 (ISBN 0-538-20500-8, T50). SW Pub.

--Computer Keyboarding: An Elementary Course. (gr. 9-12). 1985. 8.95 (ISBN 0-538-26300-8, Z30). SW Pub.

Crawford, Tad. Legal Guide for the Visual Artist. 1979. pap. 6.95 (ISBN 0-8015-4472-6, Hawthorn). Dutton.

--Legal Guide for the Visual Artist. 208p. 1985. pap. 16.95 (ISBN 0-942604-08-3). Madison Square.

Crawford, Tad & Kopelman, Arie. Selling Your Graphic Design & Illustration. 272p. 1981. 14.95 (ISBN 0-312-71252-9). St Martin.

Crawford, Tad & Mellon, Susan. The Artist-Gallery Partnership: A Practical Guide to Consignment. LC 80-28108. 76p. (Orig.). 1981. pap. 5.95 (ISBN 0-915400-26-X). Am Council Arts.

Crawford, Tad, jt. auth. see Kopelman, Arie.

Crawford, Ted. The Writer's Legal Guide. LC 76-56516. 1979. pap. 5.95 (ISBN 0-8015-8938-X, Hawthorn). Dutton.

Crawford, Terry & Bertucci, Bob. Winning Track & Field Drills for Women. LC 81-85973. (Illus.). 160p. 1985. pap. 9.95 (ISBN 0-88011-024-4). Leisure Pr.

Crawford, Thomas. Burns: A Study of the Poems & Songs. 1960. 30.00x (ISBN 0-8047-0055-9); pap. 8.95 (ISBN 0-8047-0056-7, SP18). Stanford U Pr.

--Edinburgh Review & Romantic Poetry 1802-1829. 1971. Repr. of 1955 ed. lib. bdg. 8.50 (ISBN 0-8414-2408-X). Folcroft.

--Pig Who Saved the Day. (Illus.). (gr. 3-4). 1972. pap. 1.50 (ISBN 0-89375-049-2). Troll Assocs.

--Rooster Who Refused to Crow. (Illus.). (gr. 3-4). 1972. pap. 1.50 (ISBN 0-89375-050-6). Troll Assocs.

--Society & the Lyric: A Study of the Song Culture of Eighteenth-Century Scotland. 208p. 1980. 13.50x (ISBN 0-7073-0227-7, Pub. by Scottish Academic Pr). Columbia U Pr.

--Walter Scott. Daiches, David, ed. (Scottish Writers Ser.). 130p. (Orig.). 1983. pap. text ed. 6.50x (ISBN 0-7073-0305-2, Pub. by Scottish Academic Pr Scotland). Columbia U Pr.

Crawford, Thomas, ed. see Scott, Sir Walter.

Crawford, Thomas, et al, eds. Longer Scottish Poems, Vol. II. 400p. 1985. 40.00x (ISBN 0-7073-0329-X, Pub. by Scottish Academic Pr Scotland). Columbia U Pr.

Crawford, Tom. I Want to Say Listen. 1979. saddlestitched in wrappers 2.50 (ISBN 0-686-57433-8, Pub. by Ironwood Pr). Small Pr Dist.

Crawford, Vaughn E. Sumerian Economic Texts from the First Dynasty of Isin. LC 78-63528. (Babylonian Inscriptions in the Collection of James B. Nies: No. 9). Repr. of 1954 ed. 38.00 (ISBN 0-404-60139-1). AMS Pr.

Crawford, Vincent P. Essays in Economic Theory. LC 80-8621. (Outstanding Dissertations in Economics Ser.). 90p. 1983. lib. bdg. 19.00 (ISBN 0-8240-4178-X). Garland Pub.

Crawford, Virginia M. Studies in Foreign Literature. LC 70-103221. 1970. Repr. of 1899 ed. 23.50x (ISBN 0-8046-0858-X, Pub. by Kennikat). Assoc Faculty Pr.

--Studies in Foreign Literature: (Daudet, Huysmans, Verhaeren, Maeterlinck, & D'annunzio) 1908. Repr. 20.00 (ISBN 0-8274-3535-5). R West.

Crawford, W. Rex, tr. see Vasconcelos, Jose.

Crawford, Walt. MARC for Library Use: Understanding the USMARC Formats. LC 84-23376. (Professional Librarian Ser.). 222p. 1984. 36.50 (ISBN 0-86729-120-6); pap. 28.50 (ISBN 0-86729-119-2, 240-BW). Knowledge Indus.

Crawford, Walter B., ed. Reading Coleridge: Approaches & Applications. LC 79-7616. 280p. 1979. 27.50x (ISBN 0-8014-1219-6). Cornell U Pr.

Crawford, Walter B., et al. Samuel Taylor Coleridge: An Annotated Bibliography of Criticism & Scholarship, 1900-1939 (with Additional Entries for 1795-1899, Vol. II. 1983. lib. bdg. 59.50 (ISBN 0-8161-7866-6, Hall Reference). G K Hall.

Crawford, William. Boatowner's Legal Guide. LC 74-33189. (Illus.). 100p. 1975. pap. 5.95 (ISBN 0-87799-050-6). Aztex.

--The Bronc Rider. LC 77-80453. 1977. Repr. of 1965 ed. 9.95 (ISBN 0-916546-04-7). Racz Pub.

--The Keepers of Light: A History & Working Guide to Early Photographic Processes. LC 79-88815. 324p. 1979. pap. 24.95 (ISBN 0-87100-158-6, 2158). Morgan.

--Report on the Penitentiaries of the United States. LC 69-16235. (Criminology, Law Enforcement, & Social Problems Ser.: No. 97). 1969. Repr. of 1835 ed. 45.00x (ISBN 0-87585-097-9). Patterson Smith.

Crawford, William & Crawford, Ann. Military Living's Military Space-A: Air Opportunities Around the World. (Illus.). 360p. (Orig.). 1983. pap. 9.95 (ISBN 0-914862-04-9, VC333.C73). Military Marketing.

Crawford, William & Pootaraksa, Kamolmal. Thai Home Cooking from Kamolmal's Kitchen. 315p. 1985. 16.95 (ISBN 0-453-00493-8). NAL.

Crawford, William E., ed. Louisiana Code of Civil Procedure: As Amended Through the 1983 Regular Session of the Legislature. LC 84-131708. 1983. pap. 24.00 (ISBN 0-317-13475-2). West Pub.

Crawford, William P. Mariner's Celestial Navigation. (Illus.). 1979. 19.95 (ISBN 0-393-60003-3). Norton.

--Mariner's Rules of the Road. (Illus.). 1984. 24.95 (ISBN 0-393-03287-6). Norton.

--Mariner's Weather. (Illus.). 1979. 22.95 (ISBN 0-393-03221-3). Norton.

--Sea Marine Atlas: Southern California. rev. ed. (Illus.). 1979. pap. 19.95 (ISBN 0-393-03219-1). Norton.

Crawford, William R. Bibliography of Chaucer, 1954-1963. LC 66-29836. (Publications in Language & Literature: No. 17). 188p. 1967. 25.00x (ISBN 0-295-74027-2). U of Wash Pr.

Crawford, William R. & Crawford, Lela Ann. Military Living's Military Camping & Rec Areas Around the World. LC 83-17363. (Illus.). 168p. 1983. pap. 6.95 (ISBN 0-914862-05-7). Military Marketing.

Crawford, Williame & Kerstrat, Francoise. New Code of Civil Procedure in France, Bk. 1. De Grivart, tr. from Fr. LC 77-25936. 214p. 1978. 32.50 (ISBN 0-379-20266-2). Oceana.

Crawford, Zelte. Skin Color, Race, & Self-Image: An Exploratory Study of a Group of High School Youths. LC 79-65270. 135p. 1979. perfect bdg. 10.00 (ISBN 0-88247-580-0). R & E Pubs.

Crawford Flitch, J. E., tr. see Duret, Theodore.

Crawfrod, Isabella. Collected Poems. LC 72-91689. (Literature of Canada Ser.). pap. 88.00 (ISBN 0-317-26928-3, 2023607). Bks Demand UMI.

Crawfurd, Oswald. Four Poets: Poems from Wordsworth, Coleridge, Shelley & Keats. 1977. Repr. of 1897 ed. 15.00 (ISBN 0-89984-172-4). Century Bookbindery.

Crawfurd, Raymond H. The King's Evil. LC 75-23701. Repr. of 1911 ed. 21.50 (ISBN 0-404-13251-0). AMS Pr.

Crawhall, Joseph. Quaint Cuts in the Chap Book Style. 88p. 1974. Repr. of 1889 ed. 5.95 (ISBN 0-486-23020-1). Dover.

--Quaint Cuts in the Chap Book Style. Menten, Theodore, ed. (Illus.). 9.00 (ISBN 0-8446-5020-X). Peter Smith.

Crawley, Aileen. The Shadow of God. 320p. 1983. 13.95 (ISBN 0-312-71406-8). St Martin.

Crawley, Alfred E. Studies of Savages & Sex. Besterman, Theodore, ed. (Landmarks in Anthropology Ser). 1969. Repr. of 1929 ed. 16.00 (ISBN 0-384-10140-2). Johnson Repr.

Crawley, Brian E., jt. ed. see Feldman, Stanley A.

Crawley, Derek. Character in Relation to Action in the Tragedies of George Chapman. (Salzburg Studies in English Literature, Jacobean Drama Studies: No. 16). 202p. 1974. pap. text ed. 25.50x (ISBN 0-391-01353-X). Humanities.

Crawley, Eduardo. Dictators Never Die: Nicaragua & the Somoza Dynasty. LC 78-31151. 1979. 20.00 (ISBN 0-312-20007-2). St Martin.

--A House Divided: Argentina, 1880-1980. LC 84-17697. (Illus.). 472p. 1984. 35.00 (ISBN 0-312-39254-0). St Martin.

--Nicaragua in Perspective. 224p. 1984. pap. 8.95 (ISBN 0-312-57248-4). St Martin.

Crawley, Ernest. The Mystic Rose: A Study of Primitive & Primitive Thought in Its Bearing on Marriage. 1932. 35.00 (ISBN 0-8482-3587-8). Norwood Edns.

--The Mystic Rose: A Study of Primitive Marriage and of Primitive Thought in Its Bearing on Marriage, 2 vols. Besterman, Theodore, ed. 1978. Repr. of 1927 ed. lib. bdg. 50.00 (ISBN 0-8495-0718-9). Arden Lib.

--Mystic Rose: A Study of Primitive Marriage & of Primitive Thought in Its Bearing on Marriage, 2 Vols. rev. & enl. ed. Besterman, Theodore, ed. LC 72-164193. 772p. 1971. Repr. of 1927 ed. 47.00x (ISBN 0-8103-3781-9). Gale.

--Studies of Savages & Sex. facs. ed. Besterman, Theodore, ed. LC 77-102231. (Select Bibliographies Reprint Ser). 1929. 26.50 (ISBN 0-8369-5116-6). Ayer Co Pubs.

Crawley, G. M. see Austin, S. M.

Crawley, Geoffrey & Tait, Anna, eds. British Journal of Photography Annual 1986. (Illus.). 222p. (Orig.). 1985. pap. 18.95 (ISBN 0-317-19740-1, Pub. by Henry Greenwood England). Writers Digest.

Crawley, Gerald M. Energy. (Illus.). 320p. 1975. text ed. write for info. (ISBN 0-02-325580-3, 32558). Macmillan.

Crawley, Lawrence, et al. Reproduction, Sex, & Preparation for Marriage. 2nd ed. (Illus.). 256p. 1973. pap. 18.95 (ISBN 0-13-773937-0). P-H.

Crawley, Michael J. Herbivory: The Dynamics of Animal Plant Interactions. LC 82-45903. (Studies in Ecology: Vol. 10). 420p. 1983. text ed. 45.00x (ISBN 0-520-05042-8). U of Cal Pr.

Crawley, Richard, tr. see Thucydides.

Crawley, Stanley W., et al. Steel Buildings: Analysis & Design. 3rd ed. 672p. 1984. text ed. 39.95 (ISBN 0-471-86414-5); write for info. solution (ISBN 0-471-89130-4). Wiley.

Crawley, Tony. Bebe: The Films of Brigitte Bardot. (Illus.). 1977. 14.95 (ISBN 0-8065-0609-1); pap. 6.95 (ISBN 0-685-80816-5). Citadel Pr.

--The Films of Sophia Loren. 256p. 1976. 14.00 (ISBN 0-8065-0512-5). Citadel Pr.

--The Films of Sophia Loren. (Illus.). pap. 7.95 (ISBN 0-8065-0700-4). Citadel Pr.

--Screen Dreams: The Hollywood Pinup. (Illus.). 160p. (Orig.). 1982. pap. 9.95 (ISBN 0-933328-40-0). Delilah Bks.

--The Steven Spielberg Story. LC 83-61198. (Illus.). 144p. 1983. pap. 5.70 (ISBN 0-688-02510-2, Quill NY). Morrow.

Crawley, William B. Bill Tuck: A Political Life in Harry Bird's Virginia. LC 78-16751. pap. 73.30 (ISBN 0-317-30478-X, 2024817). Bks Demand UMI.

Crawley, Winston. Global Mission. 1985. 11.95 (ISBN 0-8054-6340-2). Broadman.

Crawley, Winston & Miller, Charles. A Structured Approach to FORTRAN. 1982. text ed. 25.95 (ISBN 0-8359-7092-2); pap. text ed. 19.95 (ISBN 0-8359-7091-4); instrs'. manual avail. free (ISBN 0-8359-7093-0). Reston.

Crawley-Boevey, Mateo. Jesus King of Love. 1978. 5.50 (ISBN 0-8198-0521-1); pap. 3.95 (ISBN 0-8198-0522-X). Dghtrs St Paul.

--Jesus Rey De Amor. (Span.). 1980. pap. 3.95 (ISBN 0-8198-3909-4). Dghtrs St Paul.

--Meditaciones. (Span.). 1978. plastic bdg. 2.00 (ISBN 0-8198-4706-2). Dghtrs St Paul.

Crawshaw, Alwyn. How to Paint Boats & Harbors. (Illus.). 64p. 1983. pap. 6.95 (ISBN 0-89586-266-2). H P Bks.

--How to Paint Landscapes. (Illus.). 64p. 1983. pap. 6.95 (ISBN 0-89586-267-0). H P Bks.

--How To Paint with Acrylics. 64p. 1982. pap. 6.95 (ISBN 0-89586-158-5). H P Bks.

--How To Paint with Watercolors. 64p. 1982. pap. 6.95 (ISBN 0-89586-157-7). H P Bks.

Crawshaw, G. H. & Ince, J. Textile Floorcoverings. 84p. 1977. 70.00x (ISBN 0-686-63800-X). State Mutual Bk.

Crawshaw, Nancy. The Cyprus Revolt: An Account of the Struugle for Union with Greece. (Illus.). 1978. text ed. 35.00x (ISBN 0-04-940053-3). Allen Unwin.

Crawshaw, W. H. The Interpretation of Literature. 1973. Repr. of 1902 ed. 15.00 (ISBN 0-8274-1521-4). R West.

Crawshay-William, Rupert. Comforts of Unreason: A Study of the Motives Behind Irrational Thought. LC 71-98217. Repr. of 1947 ed. lib. bdg. 18.75x (ISBN 0-8371-3398-X, CRUN). Greenwood.

Craxford, S. R., jt. ed. see Suess, M. J.

Cray-Andrews, Martha, jt. auth. see Baum, Susan E.

Craycroft, Robert & Fazio, Michael, eds. Change & Tradition in the American Small Town. LC 83-14638. (Small Town Ser.). 136p. 1983. pap. text ed. 7.50x (ISBN 0-87805-194-5). U Pr of Miss.

Crayder, Dorothy. The Joker & the Swan. LC 80-8722. (Illus.). 128p. (gr. 3-6). 1981. HarpJ.

--The Riddles of Mermaid House. LC 77-2863. (Illus.). 192p. (gr. 3-7). 1977. 7.95 (ISBN 0-689-30579-6). Atheneum.

--She, the Adventuress. LC 72-86931. (Illus.). 192p. (gr. 3-7). 1973. pap. 1.95 (ISBN 0-689-70457-7, A-86, Aladdin). Atheneum.

C. Raymond Van Dusen. Self-Publishing: How to Cash in on Your Writing Ability Now. (Royal Court Reports Ser.: No. 3). (Illus.). 67p. (Orig.). 1982. pap. 3.95 (ISBN 0-941354-02-4). Royal Court.

Craypo, Charles. The Impact on Organized Labor of Changing Corporate Structure & Technology. 112p. 1979. pap. text ed. 5.00 (ISBN 0-87855-766-0). Transaction Bks.

Crayson, Suzanne. Plants from Plants: How to Grow New Houseplants for Next to Nothing. LC 76-12559. (Illus.). 1976. pap. 6.95i (ISBN 0-397-01127-X, LP-107). Har-Row.

Crayton, Spurgeon E. Screams of Protest. (Illus.). 1982. 10.00 (ISBN 0-8315-0188-X). Speller.

Craz, Albert G. & Mavragis, Edward P. Writing: The Business Letter. (Writing Ser.). 68p. 1981. wkbk. 3.95 (ISBN 0-9602800-1-4). Comp Pr.

--Writing: The Composition. (Writing Ser.). 66p. 1981. wkbk. 3.95 (ISBN 0-9602800-3-0). Comp Pr.

--Writing: The Report. (Writing Ser.). 66p. 1981. wkbk. 3.95 (ISBN 0-9602800-2-2). Comp Pr.

Craze, John. The Companies Act Nineteen Eighty: An Analysis. 1980. 35.00x (ISBN 0-686-92048-1, Pub. by Jordan & Sons England). State Mutual Bk.

Craze, Michael. The Life & Lyrics of Andrew Marvell. 333p. 1979. text ed. 28.50x (ISBN 0-06-491309-0). B&N Imports.

Craze, Tony, et al. Shona, Lunch Girls, the Shelter: The 1983 Verity Bargate Award Winning Short Plays. 128p. pap. 6.95 (ISBN 0-413-53850-8, NO. 3939). Methuen Inc.

Crazzolara, J. P. Zur Gesellschaft & Religion der Nueer. 1953. 46.00 (ISBN 0-384-10150-X). Johnson Repr.

CRC Education Department Staff. Into His Presence: Leader's Guide. (Orig.). 1985. pap. text ed. 3.35 (ISBN 0-930265-08-4). Bd of Pubns CRC.

CRDI, Ottawa. Etat Nutritionnel de la Population Rurale du Sahel: Rapport d'un Groupe de Travail, Paris (France) 28-29 Avril 1980. 96p. 1981. pap. 6.00 (IDRC). Unipub.

--Les Priorities de la Recherche sur la Politique Scientifique et Technique en Africque: Compte Rendu du Colloque tenu a l'Universite d'Ife (Nigeria) du 3-6 Decembre 1979. 32p. 1981. pap. 5.00 (ISBN 0-88936-280-7, IDRC). Unipub.

Creager, Clara. All about Weaving: A Comprehensive Guide to the Craft. LC 78-22311. (Illus.). 412p. 1984. 25.00 (ISBN 0-385-13164-X). Doubleday.

--Weaving: A Creative Approach for Beginners. LC 73-16503. (Illus.). 192p. 1974. pap. 8.95 (ISBN 0-385-02901-2). Doubleday.

Creager, Clifford, jt. auth. see Kovacik, Robert T.

Creager, Joan. Human Anatomy & Physiology. 852p. 1982. text ed. write for info. (ISBN 0-534-01033-4). Wadsworth Pub.

Creager, Maureen, ed. see Walker, Morton.

Creager, William P., et al. Engineering for Dams: Concrete Dams, Vol. II. pap. 104.00 (ISBN 0-317-10812-3, 2012625). Bks Demand UMI.

Creagh, Leta. Products. 1982. 8.95 (ISBN 0-533-05063-4). Vantage.

Creagh, Patrick. The Lament of the Border-Guard. 63p. 1980. pap. text ed. 8.45x (ISBN 0-85635-314-0, Pub. by Carcanet New Pr England). Humanities.

Creagh, Patrick, tr. see Leopardi, Giacomo.

Creagh, Shelby, jt. auth. see Perry, Christopher.

Creagh-Osborne, Richard. This Is Racing. (Illus.). 179p. 1977. 19.95 (ISBN 0-914814-07-9). Sail Bks.

--This Is Sailing. 232p. 1982. 55.00x (ISBN 0-333-32092-1, Pub. by Nautical England). State Mutual Bk.

--This Is Sailing. LC 84-62460. 1985. 17.95 (ISBN 0-688-05429-3, Pub. by Hearst Marine Bks). Morrow.

Creal, Margaret. The Man Who Sold Prayers. (Bessie Bks.). 192p. 1983. 13.41i (ISBN 0-06-039017-4, HarpT). Har-Row.

Crealock, Henry H. Deer Stalking in the Highlands of Scotland. 1982. 500.00x (ISBN 0-686-94026-1, Pub. by A Atha Pub). State Mutual Bk.

Creamer, Daniel. Capital Expansion & Capacity in Postwar Manufacturing. LC 77-10056. (The Conference Board Studies in Business: No. 72). (Illus.). 1977. Repr. of 1961 ed. lib. bdg. 15.00x (ISBN 0-8371-9775-9, CRCE). Greenwood.

--Personal Income During Business Cycles. LC 84-10763. xxx, 166p. 1984. Repr. of 1956 ed. lib. bdg. 35.00x (ISBN 0-313-24421-9, CRPI). Greenwood.

Creamer, Daniel & Coulter, Charles W. Labor & the Shut-Down of the Amoskeag Textile Mills: WPA, National Research Report No. L-5. LC 78-156410. (American Labor Ser., No. 2). (Illus.). 1971. Repr. of 1939 ed. 22.00 (ISBN 0-405-02919-5). Ayer Co Pubs.

Creamer, Daniel, et al. Overseas Research & Development by United States Multinationals, 1966-1975: Estimates of Expenditures & a Statistical Profile. LC 76-8343. (Report Ser.: No. 685). (Illus.). 130p. 1976. pap. 15.00 (ISBN 0-8237-0119-0); pap. 5.00 member. Conference Bd.

Creamer, J. Shane. The Law of Arrest. 3rd ed. LC 79-64589. 653p. 1980. pap. text ed. 22.95 (ISBN 0-03-054896-9, HoltC). HR&W.

Creamer, Lex, jt. auth. see Espy, Hilda C.

Creamer, Lyle R. Computer Applications in Psychology. 1984. velo plastic Bdg. 17.50 (ISBN 0-318-02994-4). L R Creamer.

Creamer, Robert. Babe. (Autographed Sports Classics Ser.). 1981. Repr. of 1974 ed. 17.95 (ISBN 0-941372-02-2). Holtzman Pr.

Creamer, Robert H. Machine Design: Mechanical Engineering Technology. 3rd ed. LC 83-2567. 540p. 1983. 33.95 (ISBN 0-201-11280-9); instr's guide 2.00 (ISBN 0-201-11281-7). Addison-Wesley.

Creamer, Robert W. Babe: The Legend Comes to Life. (Penguin Sports Library). 1983. pap. 6.95 (ISBN 0-14-006859-7). Penguin.

--Stengel: His Life & Times. (Illus.). 336p. 1984. 16.95 (ISBN 0-671-22489-1). S&S.

--Stengel: His Life & Times. 352p. 1985. pap. 8.95 (ISBN 0-440-57829-9, Dell Trade Pbks). Dell.

Crean, David & Ebbeson, Eric, eds. Living Simply: An Examination of Christian Lifestyles. 128p. (Orig.). 1981. pap. 5.95 (ISBN 0-8164-2340-7, Pub. by Seabury). Winston Pr.

Crean, John E., jt. auth. see Briggs, Jeanine.

Crean, John E., et al. Deutsche Sprach und Landeskunde. 2nd ed. 1985. text ed. 27.95 (ISBN 0-394-33675-5, RanC); wkbk. 10.00 (ISBN 0-394-33677-1); lab. manual 10.00 (ISBN 0-394-33678-X); tape program 200.00 (ISBN 0-394-33681-X). Random.

--Deutsche Sprach und Landeskunde. Incl. Ratyck, Joanna. wkbk. 9.00 (ISBN 0-394-32649-0); Crean, John E. lab manual 9.00 (ISBN 0-394-32650-4). 608p. 1981. text ed. 25.00 (ISBN 0-394-32648-2, RanC). Random.

Crease, J., et al, eds. Essays on Oceanography: A Tribute to John Swallow. (Illus.). 578p. 1984. 162.00 (ISBN 0-08-032339-1). Pergamon.

Crease, R., tr. see Taminiaux, J.

Crease, Robert. Vico in English: A Bibliography of Writings by & About Giambattista Vico (1668-1744) (Vichian Studies: No. 1). 1978. text ed. 8.00x (ISBN 0-391-00912-5). Humanities.

Crease, Robert, ed. see Heidigger, Martin.

Creasey, John. The Baron & the Unfinished Portrait. 190p. 1983. pap. 2.95 (ISBN 0-8027-3002-7). Walker & Co.

--The Baron Goes Fast. 192p. 1975. pap. 1.25 (ISBN 0-532-12358-1). Woodhill.

--The Baron in France. 190p. 1983. pap. 2.95 (ISBN 0-8027-3001-9). Walker & Co.

--Baron on Board. (Walker British Paperback Mysteries Ser.). 192p. (Orig.). 1985. pap. 2.95 (ISBN 0-8027-3110-4). Walker & Co.

--Help from the Baron. 188p. 1983. pap. 2.95 (ISBN 0-8027-3000-0). Walker & Co.

--Hide the Baron. (Walker British Paperback Mysteries Ser.). 192p. 1985. pap. 2.95 (ISBN 0-8027-3131-7). Walker & Co.

--Last Laugh for the Baron. LC 74-161111. (British Mystery Ser.). 175p. 1983. pap. 2.95 (ISBN 0-8027-3053-1). Walker & Co.

--Prophet of Fire. 1982. 15.00x (ISBN 0-86025-177-2, Pub. by Ian Henry Pubns England). State Mutual Bk.

--The Toff & the Fallen Angels. 192p. 1983. pap. 2.95 (ISBN 0-8027-3004-3). Walker & Co.

--The Toff & the Runaway Bride. 192p. 1982. 20.00x (ISBN 0-7278-0564-9, Pub. by Severn Hse). State Mutual Bk.

--Trap the Baron. (British Mysteries Ser.). 1983. pap. 2.95 (ISBN 0-8027-3034-5). Walker & Co.

Creasey, John & Ward, Sadie. The Countryside Between the Wars Nineteen Eighteen to Nineteen Forty. (Illus.). 144p. 1984. 18.95 (ISBN 0-7134-1186-4, Pub. by Batsford England). David & Charles.

Creasey, John see Hunt, Kyle, pseud.

Creasey, John see also Marric, J. J.

Creasey, M. G. In-Plant Colour Processing & Printing for the Professional Photographer. 183p. pap. 12.95 (ISBN 0-317-11638-X, 3500, Pub. by Fountain). Morgan.

Creasey, William A. Cancer: An Introduction. (Illus.). 1981. text ed. 25.95x (ISBN 0-19-502951-8); pap. text ed. 15.95x (ISBN 0-19-502952-6). Oxford U Pr.

--Diet & Cancer. LC 84-21845. (Illus.). 221p. 1985. pap. 14.50 (ISBN 0-8121-0975-9). Lea & Febiger.

--Drug Disposition in Humans: The Basis of Clinical Pharmacology. (Illus.). 1979. pap. text ed. 15.95x (ISBN 0-19-502461-3). Oxford U Pr.

Creasman, William T., jt. auth. see DiSaia, Philip J.

Creasy, Donica S., et al. Women & Other Mystical Creatures. (Illus.). 104p. (Orig.). 1983. pap. write for info. (ISBN 0-912919-02-7, B300). Pathway AL.

Creasy, Donna N. Food Careers. (Home Economics Careers Ser.). (gr. 10-12). 1977. pap. 8.68 (ISBN 0-13-392704-0). P-H.

Creasy, Leroy L. & Hrazdina, Geza, eds. Cellular & Subcellular Localization in Plant Metabolism. LC 82-7560. (Recent Advances in Phytochemistry Ser.: Vol. 16). 288p. 1982. 39.50x (ISBN 0-306-41023-0, Plenum Pr). Plenum Pub.

Creasy, Q. R. Quick Reduction of Costs. 180p. 1971. 10.00 (ISBN 0-318-16544-9, A1001); members 9.00 (ISBN 0-318-16545-7). Soc Am Value E.

Creasy, Robert K. & Resnik, Robert. Maternal-Fetal Medicine: Principles & Practice. (Illus.). 1000p. 1984. write for info. (ISBN 0-7216-2749-8). Saunders.

Creasy, Robert K., jt. auth. see Hales, Dianne.

Creasy, Rosalind. The Complete Book of Edible Landscaping: Home Landscaping with Food-Bearing Plants & Resource-Saving Techniques. LC 81-14465. (Illus.). 400p. (Orig.). 1982. 25.00 (ISBN 0-87156-249-9); pap. 14.95 (ISBN 0-87156-278-2). Sierra.

Creasy, Rosalind & Marcie. Earthly Delights. LC 84-23517. (Illus.). 208p. (Orig.). 1985. 19.95 (ISBN 0-87156-841-1). Sierra.

Creative Concepts. American Rock & Roll: The Big Hits of the Late 50's & Early 60's, 6 vols. (Illus., Orig.). 1982. Vol. 1. pap. 9.95 (ISBN 0-486-24317-6); Vol. 2. pap. 9.95 (ISBN 0-486-24318-4); Vol. 3. pap. 8.95 (ISBN 0-486-24319-2); Vol. 4. pap. 8.95 (ISBN 0-486-24320-6); Vol. 5. pap. 8.95 (ISBN 0-486-24321-4); Vol. 6. pap. 9.95 (ISBN 0-486-24678-7). Dover.

--Bluegrass Complete: Complete Words, Music & Guitar Chords for Eighty-Nine Songs. (Illus.). 192p. (Orig.). pap. 9.95 (ISBN 0-486-24503-9). Dover.

Creative Editors. How to Have Fun with a Vegetable Garden. LC 74-12297. (Creative Craft Bks.). (Illus.). 32p. (gr. 2-6). 1974. PLB 7.95 (ISBN 0-87191-363-1). Creative Ed.

Creative Educational Society Editors. How to Have Fun Making Breakfast. LC 73-18257. (Creative Craft Bks.). (Illus.). 32p. (gr. 2-5). 1973. PLB 7.95 (ISBN 0-87191-291-0). Creative Ed.

--How to Have Fun with an Indoor Garden. LC 73-18258. (Creative Craft Bks.). (Illus.). 32p. (gr. 2-5). 1973. PLB 7.95 (ISBN 0-87191-297-X). Creative Ed.

--How to Have Fun with Macrame. LC 73-19667. (Creative Craft Bks.). (Illus.). 32p. (gr. 2-5). 1973. PLB 7.95 (ISBN 0-87191-290-2). Creative Ed.

Creative Homeowner Press Editors. Design, Remodel, & Build Your Bathroom. rev ed. Horowitz, Shirley & Hedden, Jay, eds. LC 80-67154. (Illus.). 160p. 1983. 19.95 (ISBN 0-932944-59-0); pap. 6.95 (ISBN 0-932944-58-2). Creative Homeowner.

Creative Programming Inc. Creative Programming for Young Minds: Atari, 5 vols. (Creative Programming Ser.). 65p. (gr. 4 up). 1983. 9.95 ea. Vol. I (ISBN 0-912079-75-4, 611). Vol. II (ISBN 0-912079-76-2, 612). Vol. III (ISBN 0-912079-77-0, 613). Vol. IV (ISBN 0-912079-78-9, 614). Vol. V (ISBN 0-912079-79-7, 615). Creat Prog Inc.

--Creative Programming for Young Minds: PET, 7 vols. (Creative Programming Ser.). 65p. (gr. 4 up). 9.95 ea. Vol. I (ISBN 0-912079-61-4, 311). Vol. II (ISBN 0-912079-62-2, 312). Vol. III (ISBN 0-912079-63-0, 313). Vol. IV (ISBN 0-912079-64-9, 314). Vol. V (ISBN 0-912079-65-7, 315). Vol. VI (ISBN 0-912079-66-5, 316). Vol. VII (ISBN 0-912079-67-3, 317). Creat Prog Inc.

--Creative Programming for Young Minds: TI 99-4A, 7 vols. (Creative Programming Ser.). 65p. (gr. 4 up). 9.95 ea. Vol. I (ISBN 0-912079-68-1, 411). Vol. II (ISBN 0-912079-69-X, 412). Vol. III (ISBN 0-912079-70-3, 413). Vol. IV (ISBN 0-912079-71-1, 414). Vol. V (ISBN 0-912079-72-X, 415). Vol. VI (ISBN 0-912079-73-8, 416). Vol. VII (ISBN 0-912079-74-6, 417). Creat Prog Inc.

--Creative Programming for Young Minds: VIC-20, 2 vols. 65p. (gr. 4 up). 1983. 9.95 ea. Vol. I (ISBN 0-912079-81-9, 711). Vol. II (ISBN 0-912079-80-0, 712). Creat Prog Inc.

Creative Programming Inc., Staff. Creative Programming: All Stars Level II. rev. ed. (All Stars Ser.). (Illus.). 41p. 1983. wkbk. 9.95 (ISBN 0-912079-06-1, 1002). Creat Prog Inc.

--Creative Programming: All Stars Level III. (All Stars Ser.). (Illus.). 40p. 1983. pap. 9.95 (ISBN 0-912079-07-X, 1003). Creat Prog Inc.

--Creative Programming: Apple II, IIe, Vol. III. rev. ed. 77p. (gr. 4 up). 1983. spiral wkbk. 9.95 (ISBN 0-912079-05-3, 203). Creat Prog Inc.

--Creative Programming: Apple II, IIe, Vol. IV. rev. ed. 80p. 1983. spiral wkbk. 9.95 (ISBN 0-912079-11-8, 204). Creat Prog Inc.

--Creative Programming: Apple II, IIe, Vol. I. (Illus.). 74p. 1983. spiral wkbk 9.95 (ISBN 0-912079-02-9). Creat Prog Inc.

--Creative Programming: Apple II, IIe, Vol. II. 66p. (gr. 4 up). 1983. spiral wkbk. 9.95 (ISBN 0-912079-21-5, 202). Creat Prog Inc.

--Creative Programming: Commodore 64, Vol. II. (Illus.). 75p. (Orig.). (gr. 4 up). 1983. spiral 9.95 (ISBN 0-912079-14-2, 902). Creat Prog Inc.

--Creative Programming: Commodore 64, Vol. III. 80p. (Orig.). (gr. 4 up). 1983. 9.95 (ISBN 0-912079-15-0). Creat Prog Inc.

--Creative Programming: Commodore 64, Vol. I. (Illus.). 75p. (Orig.). (gr. 4 up). 1983. spiral wkbk. 9.95 (ISBN 0-912079-13-4, 901). Creat Prog Inc.

--Creative Programming: Teacher Resource Book, Apple II, IIe. 130p. (Orig.). 1983. 19.95 (ISBN 0-912079-09-6, 299). Creat Prog Inc.

--Creative Programming: Teacher Resource Book, Commodore 64. 130p. 1983. pap. 19.95 (ISBN 0-912079-23-1). Creat Prog Inc.

--Creative Programming: Texas Instruments Professional, Vol. I. 75p. (Orig.). 1983. wkbk. 9.95 (ISBN 0-912079-10-X, 501). Creat Prog Inc.

--Creative Programming: TRS-80, Vol. IV. rev. ed. 1983. spiral 9.95 (ISBN 0-912079-12-6, 104). Creat Prog Inc.

--Creative Programming: TRS-80 Model III, Vol. I. 74p. 1983. spiral wkbk. 9.95 (ISBN 0-912079-00-2, 101). Creat Prog Inc.

--Creative Programming: TRS-80 Model III, Vol. III. rev. ed. 84p. (gr. 4 up). 1983. spiral wkbk. 9.95 (ISBN 0-912079-04-5, 103). Creat Prog Inc.

--Creative Programming: TRS-80, Teacher's Resource Book. 130p. 1983. 19.95 (ISBN 0-912079-08-8, 199). Creat Prog Inc.

Creative Programming Inc. Staff. Programacion Creativa para Mentes Jovenes: Apple, Vols. I & II. Whittenburg, Luz, tr. 104p. (Span.). (gr. 4 up). 9.95 ea. Vol. I (ISBN 0-912079-19-3). Vol. II (ISBN 0-912079-18-5). Creat Prog Inc.

--Programacion Creativa Para Mentes Jovenes: TRS-80, Vol. II. Whittenburg, Luz, tr. 104p. (Span.). (gr. 4 up). pap. 9.95 (ISBN 0-912079-17-7). Creat Prog Inc.

--Programacion Creativa para Mentes Jovenes: TRS-80, Vol. I. Whittenburg, Luz, tr. 104p. (Spanish.). (gr. 4 up). pap. 9.95 (ISBN 0-912079-16-9). Creat Prog Inc.

Creative Sales. Avis City Road Atlas. 7.95 (ISBN 0-385-27010-0, Dial). Doubleday.

Creative Sales Corporation. City Map Atlas & Guide. 1978. 7.95 (ISBN 0-933162-00-6). Creative Sales.

Creaton, David. The Beasts of My Fields. 1978. pap. 1.95 (ISBN 0-380-38497-3, 38497). Avon.

Creaturo, Barbara. Cosmo Quiz Book. 1981. pap. 2.95 (ISBN 0-671-42040-2). PB.

Creaturo, Barbara, ed. Cosmo Quiz Book. 160p. 1980. 8.95 (ISBN 0-87851-113-X). Hearst Bks.

--The New Cosmo Quiz Book. LC 84-9136. (Illus.). 160p. 1984. pap. 5.95 (ISBN 0-688-03954-5, Hearst Bk). Morrow.

Crebillon, Claude see Voltaire, Francois.

Crebillon, Claude P. The Wayward Head & Heart. Bray, Barbara, tr. LC 78-16439. 1978. Repr. of 1963 ed. lib. bdg. 24.75x (ISBN 0-313-20578-7, CRWH). Greenwood.

Crebillon, M. De see De Crebillon, M.

Crecelius, Daniel. The Roots of Modern Egypt: A Study of the Regimes of Ali Bey al-Kabir & Muhammad Bey Abu al-Dhahab, 1760-1775. LC 81-65972. (Middle Eastern History Studies: No. 6). 300p. 1982. 28.00x (ISBN 0-88297-029-1). Bibliotheca.

Crecfroft, D., jt. ed. see Hunter, J. J.

Crecine, John P., ed. Financing the Metropolis: Public Policy in Urban Economies. LC 72-103479. (Urban Affairs Annual Reviews: Vol. 4). pap. 158.00 (ISBN 0-317-29597-7, 2021884). Bks Demand UMI.

--The New Educational Programs in Public Policy, the First Decade. (Public Policy & Government Organizations: Supplement No. 1). 275p. 1981. 42.50 (ISBN 0-686-73775-X). Jai Pr.

--Public Policy & Government Organization, Vol. 1. 350p. 1981. 42.50 (ISBN 0-89232-044-3). Jai Pr.

--Public Policy & Government Organization, Vol. 2. 350p. 1981. 42.50 (ISBN 0-89232-210-1). Jai Pr.

--Public Policy & Government Organization: Command, Control, & Communications in Competing Military Organizations, Vol. 3. 300p. 1983. 42.50 (ISBN 0-89232-216-0). Jai Pr.

Crecraft, Earl W. Freedom of the Seas. facsimile ed. LC 70-102232. (Select Bibliographies Reprint Ser.). 1935. 26.50 (ISBN 0-8369-5117-4). Ayer Co Pubs.

Crede, Charles E., jt. auth. see Harris, Cyril M.

Credland, Arthur G. Whales & Whaling. (Shire Album Ser.: No. 89). (Illus.). 32p. 1983. pap. 2.95 (ISBN 0-85263-597-4, Pub. by Shire Pubns England). Seven Hills Bks.

Credle, Ellis. Down, Down the Mountain. (Illus.). (gr. k-3). 1934. 8.25 (ISBN 0-525-66020-8, 0801-240). Lodestar Bks.

Cree, A. Cree's Dictionary of Latin Quotations. LC 78-51482. (Eng. & Lat.). 1979. 16.00 (ISBN 0-912728-12-4). Newbury Bks.

Cree, John. All about Training the Family Dog. (All About Ser.). (Illus.). 160p. 1985. 14.95 (ISBN 0-7207-1529-6, Pub. by Michael Joseph). Merrimack Pub Cir.

--Training the Alsatian. (Illus.). 160p. 1978. 13.95 (ISBN 0-7207-0993-8, Pub. by Michael Joseph). Merrimack Pub Cir.

--Training the German Shepherd Dog. (Illus.). 208p. 1984. 14.95 (ISBN 0-7207-1520-2, Pub. by Michael Joseph). Merrimack Pub Cir.

Creech, Margaret. Three Centuries of Poor Law Administration: A Study of Legislation in Rhode Island. 19.00 (ISBN 0-405-19031-X). Ayer Co Pubs.

Creech, Nancy. Cooking for Someone Special...Yourself. LC 84-48380. 208p. 1985. pap. 7.95 (ISBN 0-88266-375-5). Garden Way Pub.

Creech, William. Letters, Addressed to Sir John Sinclair, Bart. LC 78-67652. (Scottish Enlightenment Ser.). Repr. of 1793 ed. 18.50 (ISBN 0-404-17187-7). AMS Pr.

Creecy, James R. Scenes in The South, & Other Miscellaneous Pieces. 18.00 (ISBN 0-8369-9186-9, 9055). Ayer Co Pubs.

Creed, Barbara B. Erisa Compliance: Reporting & Disclosure. LC 81-81269. 477p. 1981. text ed. 45.00 (ISBN 0-686-73149-2, J1-1435). PLI.

Creed, Charles. The Art of the Affair. 80p. (Orig.). 1980. pap. 3.95 (ISBN 0-933180-10-1). Ellis Pr.

--Jubilee College State Park: Retrospective by Way of Explanation. 20p. 1980. pap. 2.50 (ISBN 0-933180-11-X). Spoon Riv Poetry.

Creed, J. L., ed. Lactantius: De Mortibus Persecutorm. (Oxford Early Christian Texts Ser.). 1985. 24.95x (ISBN 0-19-826813-0). Oxford U Pr.

Creed, Lisa, ed. The House Within Me: An Anthology of Poems by Children from Little River School. 64p. (Orig.). (ps). 1981. pap. 4.00 (ISBN 0-932112-10-2). Carolina Wren.

Creed, R. S., et al. Reflex Activity of the Spinal Cord. (Illus.). 1972. 32.50x (ISBN 0-19-857355-3). Oxford U Pr.

Creed, Robert, ed. Ecological Genetics & Evolution: Essays in Honor of E. B. Ford. 391p. 1971. 32.50x (ISBN 0-306-50020-5, Plenum Pr). Plenum Pub.

Creed, Roscoe R. PBY: The Cataline Flying Boat. (Illus.). 352p. 1985. 21.95 (ISBN 0-87021-526-4). Naval Inst Pr.

Creedon, John J. Some Uses of Life Insurance in Estate Planning: No. B300. 95p. 1974. pap. 2.31 (ISBN 0-317-30857-2). Am Law Inst.

--Some Vises of Life Insurance in Estate Planning. 95p. 1974. pap. 2.31 (ISBN 0-317-32262-1, B300). Am Law Inst.

Creedon, John J. & Lewis, James B. Life Insurance in Estate Planning, No. B304. 70p. 1974. pap. 15.00 (ISBN 0-317-30855-6). Am Law Inst.

Creedy, J. & O'Brien, D. P. Economic Analysis in Historical Perspective. (Advanced Economics Texts Ser.). 224p. 1984. text ed. 59.95 (ISBN 0-408-11430-4). Butterworth.

Creedy, John. A Laboratory Manual for Schools & Colleges. (Illus.). 1977. text ed. 34.00x (ISBN 0-435-57130-3). Heinemann Ed.

--State Pensions in Britain. LC 81-15507. (National Institute of Economic & Social Research Occasional Papers Ser.: No. 33). (Illus.). 1982. 22.95 (ISBN 0-521-24519-2). Cambridge U Pr.

Creedy, John & Disney, Richard. Social Insurance in Transition. (Illus.). 208p. (Orig.). 1985. 26.00 (ISBN 0-19-877228-9); pap. 11.95 (ISBN 0-19-877227-0). Oxford U Pr.

Creedy, Judith & Wall, Norbert. Real Estate Investment by Objective. LC 79-14085. (Illus.). 416p. 1979. 29.95 (ISBN 0-07-013495-2). McGraw.

Creedy, Thomas. Economics of Labor. 1982. pap. text ed. 19.95 (ISBN 0-408-10826-6). Butterworth.

Creeff, K., ed. Cardiac Glycosides, Pt. 1: Experimental Pharmacology of Cardiac Glycosides. (Handbook of Experimental Pharmacology: Vol. 56-1). (Illus.). 682p. 1981. 197.00 (ISBN 0-387-10917-X). Springer Verlag.

Creegan, Charles C. & Goodnow, Josephine A. Great Missionaries of the Church. facsimile ed. LC 73-37522. (Essay Index Reprint Ser). Repr. of 1895 ed. 24.50 (ISBN 0-8369-2541-6). Ayer Co Pubs.

Creegan, Robert F. The Magic of Truth. 104p. 1980. 5.95 (ISBN 0-8059-2719-0). Dorrance.

Creek, Eddie J., jt. auth. see Smith, J. Richard.

Creekmore, Anna M. & Pokornow, Ila M., eds. Textile History: Readings. LC 81-40873. (Illus.). 342p. (Orig.). 1982. lib. bdg. 39.25 (ISBN 0-8191-2197-5); pap. text ed. 16.75 (ISBN 0-8191-2198-3). U Pr of Amer.

Creekmore, Betsey B. Knoxville. 3rd ed. LC 66-21195. (Illus.). 344p. 1976. 12.95 (ISBN 0-87049-204-7). U of Tenn Pr.

Creekmore, Donna. The Difficult Miss Livingston. (Candlelight Regency Ser.: No. 706). (Orig.). 1982. pap. 1.95 (ISBN 0-440-12164-7). Dell.

--The Silver Shroud. 1978. pap. 1.75 (ISBN 0-532-17198-5). Woodhill.

Creekmore, Hubert, ed. Lyrics of the Middle Ages. LC 69-13869. Repr. of 1959 ed. lib. bdg. 19.75x (ISBN 0-8371-0365-7, CRLM). Greenwood.

Creekmore, Wayne. Through the Micromaze: A Visual Guide from Ashton-Tate. (Through the Micromaze Ser.: Vol. 1). 250p. 1983. pap. 9.95 (ISBN 0-912677-02-3). Ashton-Tate Bks.

Creekmore, Wayne & Behasa, Stephanie. Through the Micromaze: A Visual Guide to Getting Organized. (Through the Micromaze Ser.: Vol. 2). 64p. 1984. pap. 9.95 (ISBN 0-912677-18-X). Ashton-Tate Bks.

Creel, Austin. Dharma in Hindu Ethics. 1978. 11.00x (ISBN 0-88386-999-3). South Asia Bks.

Creel, Catherine. Breathless Passion. (Orig.). 1983. pap. 3.50 (ISBN 0-8217-1204-7). Zebra.

--Texas Bride. (Orig.). 1982. pap. 3.50 (ISBN 0-8217-1050-8). Zebra.

--Texas Flame. 1981. pap. 2.75 (ISBN 0-89083-797-X). Zebra.

--Texas Torment. 1985. pap. 3.95 (ISBN 0-8217-1622-0). Zebra.

--The Yankee & the Belle. 1979. pap. 2.25 (ISBN 0-505-51432-X, Pub. by Tower Bks). Dorchester Pub Co.

--The Yankee & the Belle. 320p. 1984. pap. 3.25 (ISBN 0-8439-2102-1). Dorchester Pub Co.

Creel, G. Mexico: The People Next Door. 1976. lib. bdg. 59.95 (ISBN 0-8490-2251-7). Gordon Pr.

Creel, George. How We Advertised America. LC 72-4664. (International Propaganda & Communications Ser.). (Illus.). 467p. 1972. Repr. of 1920 ed. 32.00 (ISBN 0-405-04745-2). Ayer Co Pubs.

--Sons of the Eagle. facs. ed. LC 79-117778. (Essay Index Reprint Ser). 1927. 21.50 (ISBN 0-8369-1797-9). Ayer Co Pubs.

Creel, George, jt. auth. see Sisson, Edgar.

Creel, George H., jt. auth. see Rice, James A.

Creel, Henry L. Cooking for One Is Fun. LC 75-37370. 224p. 1976. 13.95 (ISBN 0-8129-0632-2). Times Bks.

Creel, Herlee G., et al. Literary Chinese by the Inductive Method, 3 vols. Incl. Vol. 1. Hsiao Ching. rev ed. LC 48-8466. 1948. Repr. pap. 8.50x (ISBN 0-226-12034-1); Vol. 2. Selections from the Lun Yu. LC 38-1458. 1939. 14.00x (ISBN 0-226-12032-5); Vol 3. The Mencius. LC 38-1458. 1952. 14.00x (ISBN 0-226-12033-3). U of Chicago Pr.

Creel, Herrlee G. Birth of China. LC 54-5633. (Illus.). 1954. pap. 7.95 (ISBN 0-8044-6093-0). Ungar.

--Chinese Thought from Confucius to Mao Tse-Tung. LC 53-10054. 1971. pap. 7.95 (ISBN 0-226-12030-9, P394, Phoen). U of Chicago Pr.

--Confucius, the Man & the Myth. LC 72-7816. 363p. 1973. Repr. of 1949 ed. lib. bdg. 23.00x (ISBN 0-8371-6531-8, CRCO). Greenwood.

--Origins of Statecraft in China: The Western Chou Empire, Vol. 1. LC 73-110072. (Illus.). xiv, 560p. 1970. 25.00x (ISBN 0-226-12043-0); pap. 9.95x (ISBN 0-226-12044-9). U of Chicago Pr.

--Shen Pu-Hai: A Chinese Political Philosopher of the Fourth Century, B. C. LC 73-77130. x, 446p. 1975. text ed. 20.00x (ISBN 0-226-12027-9). U of Chicago Pr.

--Sinism: Study of the Evolution of the Chinese World View. LC 74-2904. (China Studies: from Confucius to Mao Ser). 127p. 1975. Repr. of 1929 ed. 17.60 (ISBN 0-88355-165-9). Hyperion Conn.

--Studies in Early Chinese Culture. LC 78-14504. (Perspectives in Asian History Ser.: No. 3). 1979. Repr. of 1937 ed. lib. bdg. 25.00x (ISBN 0-87991-601-X). Porcupine Pr.

--What Is Taoism? And Other Studies in Chinese Cultural History. LC 77-102905. (Midway Reprint Ser.). viii, 192p. 1982. pap. text ed. 11.00x (ISBN 0-226-12047-3). U of Chicago Pr.

Creel, Richard. Religion & Doubt: Toward a Faith of Your Own. 1977. 13.95 (ISBN 0-13-771931-0). P-H.

Creel, Richard E. Divine Impassibility: An Essay in Philosophical Theology. 300p. Date not set. price not set (ISBN 0-521-30317-6). Cambridge U Pr.

Creeley, Robert. A Calendar: Twelve Poems. (Morning Coffee Chapbook Ser.). (Illus.). 30p. 1984. pap. 10.00 (ISBN 0-915124-99-8). Coffee Hse.

--The Collected Poems of Robert Creeley. LC 81-19668. 576p. 1983. 28.50 (ISBN 0-520-04243-3). U of Cal Pr.

--The Collected Prose of Robert Creeley. 518p. 1984. 26.00 (ISBN 0-7145-2792-0, Dist. by Scribner); signed ed. 26.00 (ISBN 0-7145-2815-3, Dist. by Scribner). M Boyars.

--Echoes. LC 81-23284. 20p. (Orig.). 1982. signed 50.00 (ISBN 0-915124-58-0, Pub. by Toothpaste); pap. 6.00 (ISBN 0-915124-59-9). Coffee Hse.

--The Gold Diggers. 160p. 1980. pap. 6.95 (ISBN 0-7145-0256-1, Dist by Scribner). M Boyars.

--Hello. 1976. pap. 5.00 (ISBN 0-685-79279-X). Small Pr Dist.

--Hello: A Journal, Feb. 29-May 3,1976. LC 77-14240. 1978. 7.50 (ISBN 0-8112-0674-2); pap. 2.95 (ISBN 0-8112-0675-0, NDP451). New Directions.

--The Island. 192p. 1980. pap. 6.95 (ISBN 0-7145-0305-3, Dist by Scribner). M Boyars.
--Later. LC 79-15600. 1979. pap. 4.95 (ISBN 0-8112-0736-6, NDP488). New Directions.
--Mabel: A Story. 176p. 1979. 11.95 (ISBN 0-7145-2505-7, Dist by Scribner). M Boyars.
--Mirrors. LC 83-8032. 96p. (Orig.). 1983. pap. 6.95 (ISBN 0-8112-0877-X, NDP559). New Directions.
--Quick Graph: Collected Notes & Essays. Allen, Donald, ed. LC 67-30650. (Writing Ser.: No. 22). 374p. (Orig.). 1970. 10.00 (ISBN 0-87704-010-9). Four Seasons Foun.
--Selected Poems. LC 76-10608. 1976. pap. 8.95 (ISBN 0-684-14810-2, SL688, ScribT). Scribner.
--Thirty Things. (Illus.). 74p. (Orig.). 1976. pap. 10.00 (ISBN 0-87685-208-8). Black Sparrow.
--Was That a Real Poem & Other Essays. Allen, Donald, ed. LC 78-16254. (Writing: 39). 150p. 1979. pap. 5.00 (ISBN 0-87704-042-7). Four Seasons Foun.
Creeley, Robert, jt. auth. see Olson, Charles.
Creeley, Robert, jt. auth. see Paul, Sherman.
Creeley, Robert, ed. see Olson, Charles.
Creeley, Robert, jt. auth. see Olson, Charles.
Creelman, W. G., jt. auth. see Gardner, A. C.
Creemers, B. & Verloop, N., eds. Educational Evaluation in the Netherlands. 100p. 1985. pap. 30.00 (ISBN 0-08-032340-5). Pergamon.
Creer, K. M., ed. see Royal Society Discussion Meeting, January 27-28, 1982, Proceedings.
Creer, K. M., et al, eds. Geomagnetism of Baked Clays & Recent Sediments. 324p. 1983. 53.25 (ISBN 0-444-42231-5, I-268-83). Elsevier.
Creer, Leland H. Mormon Towns in the Region of the Colorado. Incl. The Activities of Jacob Hamblin in the Region of the Colorado. (Glen Canyon Ser.: Nos. 3-4). Repr. of 1958 ed. 20.00 (ISBN 0-404-60633-4). AMS Pr.
Creer, Thomas L. Asthma Therapy: A Behavioral Health Care System for Respiratory Disorders. LC 79-19834. (Behavior Therapy & Behavioral Medicine: Vol. 5). 1979. text ed. 26.95 (ISBN 0-8261-2500-X). Springer Pub.
Creer, Thomas L., jt. auth. see Holyrod, Kenneth A.
Crees, J. George Meredith. LC 67-30812. (Studies in Fiction, No. 34). 1969. Repr. of 1918 ed. lib. bdg. 49.95x (ISBN 0-8383-0712-4). Haskell.
--Meredith Revisited & Other Essays. LC 67-30813. (Studies in Fiction, No. 34). 1969. Repr. of 1921 ed. lib. bdg. 49.95x (ISBN 0-8383-0713-2). Haskell.
Crees, J. H. George Meredith. 238p. 1980. lib. bdg. 20.00 (ISBN 0-8495-0786-3). Arden Lib.
--George Meredith. 238p. 1981. Repr. of 1918 ed. lib. bdg. 25.00 (ISBN 0-89984-114-7). Century Bookbindery.
Creese, Ian, ed. Stimulants: Neurochemical, Behavioral, & Clinical Perspectives. (Central Nervous System Pharmacology Ser.). 360p. 1983. text ed. 54.50 (ISBN 0-89004-895-9). Raven.
Creese, Raymond, ed. see Unwin, Raymond.
Creese, T. M., jt. auth. see Aronszajn, N.
Creese, Thomas M. & Haralick, Robert M. Differential Equations for Engineers. 1978. text ed. 37.95 (ISBN 0-07-013510-X). McGraw.
Creese, Walter L. The Crowning of the American Landscape: Eight Great Spaces & Their Buildings. (Illus.). 320p. 1985. text ed. 55.00x (ISBN 0-691-04029-X). Princeton U Pr.
Creeth, Edmund. Mankynde in Shakespeare. LC 74-15204. 200p. 1976. 18.00x (ISBN 0-8203-0373-9). U of Ga Pr.
Creff, Albert & Wernick, Robert. The Maximum Performance Sports Diet. 1983. pap. 2.95 (ISBN 0-8217-1180-6). Zebra.
Cregan, Ailsa, jt. auth. see Jones, Philip R.
Creger, Ralph & Combs, Barry. Train Power. 1981. pap. 10.00 (ISBN 0-8309-0325-9). Ind Pr MO.
Creger, W. P., et al, eds. Annual Review of Medicine, Vol. 24. LC 51-1659. (Illus.). 1973. text ed. 20.00 (ISBN 0-8243-0524-8). Annual Reviews.
--Annual Review of Medicine, Vol. 25. LC 51-1659. (Illus.). 1974. text ed. 20.00 (ISBN 0-8243-0525-6). Annual Reviews.
--Annual Review of Medicine: Selected Topics in the Clinical Sciences, Vol. 33. LC 51-1659. (Illus.). 1982. text ed. 22.00 (ISBN 0-8243-0533-7). Annual Reviews.
--Annual Review of Medicine: Selected Topics in the Clinical Sciences, Vol. 34. LC 51-1659. (Illus.). 1983. text ed. 27.00 (ISBN 0-8243-0534-5). Annual Reviews.
--Annual Review of Medicine: Selected Topics in the Clinical Sciences, Vol. 26. LC 51-1659. (Illus.). 1975. text ed. 20.00 (ISBN 0-8243-0526-4). Annual Reviews.
--Annual Review of Medicine: Selected Topics in the Clinical Sciences, Vol. 32. LC 51-1659. (Illus.). 1981. text ed. 20.00 (ISBN 0-8243-0532-9). Annual Reviews.
Creger, William P., et al, eds. Annual Review of Medicine: Selected Topics in the Clinical Sciences, Vol. 27. LC 51-1659. (Illus.). 1976. text ed. 20.00 (ISBN 0-8243-0527-2). Annual Reviews.
--Annual Review of Medicine: Selected Topics in the Clinical Sciences, Vol. 28. LC 51-1659. (Illus.). 1977. text ed. 20.00 (ISBN 0-8243-0528-0). Annual Reviews.
--Annual Review of Medicine: Selected Topics in the Clinical Sciences, Vol. 29. LC 51-1659. (Illus.). 1978. text ed. 20.00 (ISBN 0-8243-0529-9). Annual Reviews.
--Annual Review of Medicine: Selected Topics in the Clinical Sciences, Vol. 30. LC 51-1659. (Illus.). 1979. text ed. 20.00 (ISBN 0-8243-0530-2). Annual Reviews.
--Annual Review of Medicine: Selected Topics in the Clinical Sciences, Vol. 31. LC 51-1659. (Illus.). 1980. text ed. 20.00 (ISBN 0-8243-0531-0). Annual Reviews.
--Annual Review of Medicine: Selected Topics in the Clinical Sciences, Vol. 36. LC 51-1659. (Illus.). 658p. 1985. text ed. 27.00 (ISBN 0-8243-0536-1). Annual Reviews.
Cregier, Don M. Bounder from Wales: Lloyd George's Career Before the First World War. LC 76-4894. 328p. 1976. 22.00x (ISBN 0-8262-0203-9). U of Mo Pr.
--The Decline of the British Liberal Party: Why & How. (Illus., Orig.). 1985. write for info. Lorrah & Hitchcock.
Crehan, Stewart. Blake in Context. 365p. 1984. text ed. 48.00x (ISBN 0-391-02855-3, Pub. by Gill & Macmillan Ireland). Humanities.
Creigh, Dorothy W. Adams County, 2 vols. Incl. A Story of the Great Plains. 1972. 25.00 (ISBN 0-934858-00-4); The People. 1971. 10.00 (ISBN 0-934858-01-2). LC 73-176266. (Illus.). Set. 32.50 (ISBN 0-934858-02-0). Adams County.
--Nebraska: A History. (States & the Nation Ser.). (Illus.). 1977. 14.95 (ISBN 0-393-05598-1, Co-Pub. by Aaslh). Norton.
--A Primer for Local Historical Societies. LC 76-231. 153p. 1976. pap. 8.95 (ISBN 0-910050-20-1). AASLH Pr.
--Tales from the Prairie, 3 vols. Incl. Vol. 1. 1970; Vol. 2. 1973; Vol. 3. 1976. pap. 5.95 (ISBN 0-934858-05-5); Vol. 4. 1979. pap. 9.95 (ISBN 0-934858-06-3). LC 74-157038. (Illus.). Set. pap. 6.95 (ISBN 0-934858-09-8); pap. 5.95; pap. 9.95. Adams County.
--Tales from the Prairie, Vol. 5. write for info. (ISBN 0-934858-10-1). Adams County.
Creigh, S. W., jt. ed. see Evans, Eric W.
Creighton. Proteins. LC 83-19541. (Illus.). 515p. 1984. 36.95 (ISBN 0-7167-1566-X). W H Freeman.
Creighton, Andrew J., ed. see Ellebaut.
Creighton, C. History of Epidemics in Britain, 2 vols. 2nd rev ed. (Illus.). 95.00x set (ISBN 0-7146-1294-4, F Cass Co). Biblio Dist.
Creighton, D. G. Harold Adams Innis: Portrait of a Scholar. LC 58-854. 1978. pap. 7.95 (ISBN 0-8020-6329-2). U of Toronto Pr.
Creighton, Donald G. The Road to Confederation: The Emergence of Canada, 1863-1867. LC 75-27652. (Illus.). 1976. Repr. of 1965 ed. lib. bdg. 27.25x (ISBN 0-8371-8435-5, CRRC). Greenwood.
Creighton, Douglas G. Jacques-Francois Deluc of Geneva & His Friendship with Jean-Jacques Rousseau. LC 82-5332. (Romance Monographs: No. 42). 128p. 1983. 14.00x (ISBN 84-499-5926-8). Romance.
Creighton, Gilbert. Seventeenth Century Paintings from the Low Countries. (Illus.). 1966. 8.50 (ISBN 0-8079-0117-2). October.
Creighton, H. C., tr. see Smirnov, A., et al.
Creighton, Helen. Law Every Nurse Should Know. 4th ed. 480p. 1981. text ed. 17.95 (ISBN 0-7216-2753-6). Saunders.
--Songs & Ballads from Nova Scotia. 11.25 (ISBN 0-8446-1920-5). Peter Smith.
--Songs of Nova Scotia. 1968. Dover.
Creighton, Helen & Peacock, Kenneth. Folksongs from Southern New Brunswick. (Illus.). 1971. pap. 8.50X (ISBN 0-660-00045-8, 56348-0, Pub. by Natl Mus Canada). U of Chicago Pr.
Creighton, J., tr. see Wundt, Wilhelm M.
Creighton, James E. Studies in Speculative Philosophy. Stuart, H. R., ed. 1925. 23.00 (ISBN 0-527-20500-1). Kraus Repr.
--Studies in Speculative Philosophy. 290p. 1982. Repr. of 1925 ed. lib. bdg. 35.00 (ISBN 0-89987-134-8). Darby Bks.
Creighton, James L. The Public Involvement Manual. LC 81-66306. (Illus.). 344p. 1981. text ed. 24.00x (ISBN 0-89011-557-5). Abt Bks.
--The Public Involvement Manual. 344p. 1984. Repr. of 1981 ed. lib. bdg. 36.50 (ISBN 0-8191-4097-X). U Pr of Amer.
Creighton, Jane. Ceres in an Open Field. LC 79-26248. (Illus.). 80p. 1980. pap. 3.50 (ISBN 0-918314-12-7). Out & Out.
Creighton, Joanne V. Joyce Carol Oates. (United States Authors Ser.). 1979. lib. bdg. 13.50 (ISBN 0-8057-7212-X, Twayne). G K Hall.
--Margaret Drabble. (Contemporary Writers Ser.). 127p. 1985. pap. 4.95 (ISBN 0-416-38390-4, 9469). Methuen Inc.
--William Faulkner's Craft of Revision: The Snopes Trilogy, the Unvanquished & Go Down Moses. LC 76-51441. 192p. 1977. text ed. 12.95x (ISBN 0-685-76208-4). Wayne St U Pr.
Creighton, John. Complete Guide to the Volvo 1800 Series. (Complete Guide Ser.). (Illus.). 96p. 1982. 14.95 (ISBN 0-901564-56-7, Pub. by Dalton England). Motorbooks Intl.
Creighton, L., ed. see Creighton, Mandell.
Creighton, M., ed. Epochs of English History. 738p. 1981. Repr. of 1889 ed. lib. bdg. 85.00 (ISBN 0-8495-0861-4). Arden Lib.
Creighton, Mandell. The Age of Elizabeth. 1898. 10.00 (ISBN 0-8482-7255-2). Norwood Edns.
--Cardinal Wolsey. 226p. 1982. Repr. of 1888 ed. lib. bdg. 35.00 (ISBN 0-8495-0878-9). Arden Lib.
--Historical Lectures & Addresses. facs. ed. Creighton, L., ed. LC 67-26730. (Essay Index Reprint Ser). 1904. 20.00 (ISBN 0-8369-0350-1). Ayer Co Pubs.
--History of the Papacy from the Great Schism to the Sack of Rome, 6 Vols. rev. ed. LC 74-77897. Repr. of 1897 ed. Set. 165.00 (ISBN 0-404-01870-X); 27.50 ea. AMS Pr.
Creighton, Margaret S. Dogwatch & Liberty Days: Seafaring Life in the Nineteenth Century. LC 73-1982. (Illus.). 85p. 1982. 25.00 (ISBN 0-87577-070-3); pap. 14.95. Peabody Mus Salem.
Creighton, Sue, ed. Capitol Cookbook. 1973. 6.95 (ISBN 0-87244-034-6). Texian.
Creighton, Susan. A Hug from the Heart. (Hugga Bunch Ser.). (ps-3). 1985. 3.50 (ISBN 0-910313-92-X). Parker Bro.
--Huggins & Kisses. (Illus.). 40p. (ps). 1985. 4.00 (ISBN 0-910313-94-6). Parker Bro.
--Hugs from the Heart. (Hugga Bunch Ser.). (Illus.). 32p. (ps-3). 1985. pap. 0.99 (ISBN 0-87372-005-9). Parker Bro.
Creighton, Thomas H. The Lands of Hawaii: Their Use & Misuse. LC 77-16124. 430p. 1978. text ed. 17.50x (ISBN 0-8248-0482-1). UH Pr.
Creighton, Thomas H., ed. Building for Modern Man. facs. ed. LC 74-80385. (Essay Index Reprint Ser). 1949. 17.50 (ISBN 0-8369-1029-X). Ayer Co Pubs.
Creighton, Thomas R. Southern Rhodesia & the Central African Federation. LC 75-32456. (Illus.). 1976. Repr. of 1961 ed. lib. bdg. 18.50x (ISBN 0-8371-8543-2, CRSR). Greenwood.
Creighton, W., ed. see Wieman, Henry Nelson.
Creighton, W. B. Working Women & the Law. (Studies in Labour & Social Law: Vol. 3). 304p. 1979. 35.00x (ISBN 0-7201-0552-8). Mansell.
Creighton, Warren S. The Contributions of Mussolini to the Civilization of Mankind. (Illus.). 137p. 1981. 61.55 (ISBN 0-89266-282-4). Am Classical Coll Pr.
--The Contributions of Mussolini to the Civilization of Mankind. (Illus.). 115p. 1983. 75.45x (ISBN 0-86722-038-4). Inst Econ Pol.
Creishton, H. Campbell, tr. see Rezanov, I. A.
Creizenach, W. English Drama in the Age of Shakespeare. LC 65-15873. (Studies in Drama, No. 39). 1969. Repr. of 1916 ed. lib. bdg. 49.95x (ISBN 0-8383-0533-4). Haskell.
Creizenach, Wilhelm. English Drama in the Age of Shakespeare. 1916. lib. bdg. 45.00 (ISBN 0-8414-2410-1). Folcroft.
--Geschichte des Neureren Dramas, 3 Vols. LC 64-14696. Repr. of 1911 ed. Set. 130.00 (ISBN 0-405-08402-1, Pub. by Blom); 44.00 ea. Vol. 1 (ISBN 0-405-08403-X). Vol. 2 (ISBN 0-405-08404-8). Vol. 3 (ISBN 0-405-08405-6). Ayer Co Pubs.
Crelin, Edmund S. Functional Anatomy of the Newborn. LC 72-91292. (Illus.). 96p. 1973. 24.50x (ISBN 0-300-01632-8). Yale U Pr.
Crelinsten, Dorothy R., tr. see Cusson, Maurice.
Crellin, John K. Medical Care in Pioneer Illinois. LC 82-81512. (Southern Illinois University Medical Humanities Ser.). (Illus.). 128p. 1982. 15.95 (ISBN 0-686-35864-3). Pearson Museum.
Crelling, John C., jt. auth. see Winans, Randall E.
Cremades, Bernardo Maria. Spanish Business Law. LC 85-5619. Date not set. price not set (ISBN 9-06-544220-0, Pub. by Kluwer Law & Taxation). Kluwer Academic.
Cremaschi, Gabriella. Abraham Lincoln. LC 84-51620. (Why They Became Famous Ser.). (Illus.). 64p. (gr. 5 up). 1985. 12.96 (ISBN 0-382-06855-6); pap. 6.95 (ISBN 0-382-06985-4). Silver.
--Albert Schweitzer. LC 84-40404. (Why They Became Famous Ser.). (Illus.). 64p. (gr. 5 up). 1985. 12.96 (ISBN 0-382-06856-4); pap. 6.95 (ISBN 0-382-06986-2). Silver.
Creme, Benjamin. Messages from Maitreya the Christ, Vol. II. 86p. 1985. pap. 3.50 (ISBN 0-936604-05-0). Tara Ctr.
--Messages from Maitreya the Christ, Vol. 1. LC 80-52483. 209p. 1980. pap. 5.00 (ISBN 0-936604-01-8). Tara Ctr.
--The Reappearance of the Christ & the Masters of Wisdom. LC 80-50639. 253p. 1980. pap. 6.00 (ISBN 0-936604-00-X). Tara Ctr.
--Transmission: A Meditation for the New Age. 83p. 1984. pap. 3.50 (ISBN 0-936604-02-6). Tara Ctr.
Cremeans, Charles D. The Reception of Calvinistic Thought in England. LC 83-45578. Date not set. Repr. of 1949 ed. 22.00 (ISBN 0-404-19896-1). AMS Pr.
Cremer, Charles F., jt. auth. see Yoakam, Richard D.
Cremer, Hans-Diedrich, jt. auth. see Blohm, Hannelore.
Cremer, L. & Heckl, M. Structure-Borne Sound: Structural Vibrations & Sound Radiation at Audio Frequencies. rev. ed. Ungar, E. E., tr. from Ger. LC 72-95350. (Illus.). xvi, 528p. 1973. 72.00 (ISBN 0-387-06002-2). Springer-Verlag.
Cremer, L., et al, eds. Principles & Applications of Room Acoustics, Vols. 1 & 2. Shultz, T. J., tr. (Illus.). 1982. Vol. 1: Geometrical, Statistical & Psychological Room Acoustics. 89.00 (ISBN 0-85334-113-3, Pub. by Elsevier Applied Sci England); Vol. 2: Wave Theoretical Room Acoustics. 66.75 (ISBN 0-85334-114-1). Elsevier.
Cremer, Lothar. The Physics of the Violin. Allen, John S., tr. from Ger. 472p. 1984. text ed. 37.50x (ISBN 0-262-03102-7). MIT Pr.
Cremer, Marion, jt. auth. see Warfel, M. C.
Cremer, Peter. U-Boat Commander. 288p. 1984. 14.95 (ISBN 0-87021-969-3). Naval Inst Pr.
Cremers, A. B. & Kriegel, H. P., eds. Theoretical Computer Science: Proceedings, Dortmund, FRG, 1983. (Lecture Notes in Computer Science Ser.: Vol. 145). 367p. 1983. pap. 18.50 (ISBN 0-387-11973-6). Springer-Verlag.
Cremin, B. J. & Beighton, P. Bone Dysplasias of Infancy: A Radiological Atlas. (Illus.). 1978. 51.00 (ISBN 0-387-08816-4). Springer-Verlag.
Cremin, B. J., jt. auth. see Aaronson, Ian A.
Cremin, B. J., jt. auth. see Beighton, P.
Cremin, Lawrence. The Genius of American Education. LC 65-28146. (Horace Mann Lecture: 1965). pap. 33.00 (ISBN 0-317-26788-4, 2024330). Bks Demand UMI.
Cremin, Lawrence A. American Education: The Colonial Experience, 1607-1783. LC 1-9140. 688p. 1972. pap. 11.95 (ISBN 0-06-131670-9, TB 1670, Torch). Har-Row.
--American Education: The National Experience, 1783-1876, Vol. II. LC 79-3387. 624p. 1982. pap. 11.06i (ISBN 0-06-090921-8, CN 921, CN). Har-Row.
--American Education: The National Experience, 1783-1896. LC 79-3387. 1980. 29.95i (ISBN 0-06-010912-2, HarpT). Har-Row.
--Public Education. LC 75-36376. 1979. 8.95 (ISBN 0-465-06775-1); pap. 5.95x (ISBN 0-465-06771-9, TB-5071). Basic.
--Traditions of American Education. LC 76-43456. 1979. 9.95x (ISBN 0-465-08685-3, CN-5040); pap. 4.95x (TB-5057). Basic.
--Transformation of the School: Progressivism in American Education, 1876-1957. 1964. pap. 5.95 (ISBN 0-394-70519-X, V519, Vin). Random.
--The Wonderful World of Ellwood Patterson Cubberley: An Essay on the Historiography of American Education. LC 65-20759. (Orig.). 1965. text ed. 5.50x (ISBN 0-8077-1215-9); pap. text ed. 3.25x (ISBN 0-8077-1212-4). Tchrs Coll.
Cremin, Lawrence A., ed. Republic & the School: Horace Mann on the Education of Free Men. 7th ed. LC 57-9102. (Classics in Education Ser.). (Orig.). 1957. pap. text ed. 4.50x (ISBN 0-8077-1206-X). Tchrs Coll.
Cremin, Lawrence A. & Barnard, Frederick A., eds. American Education: Its Men, Ideas, & Institutions, Series 1-2, 92 vols. 1972. Set. 984.00 (ISBN 0-405-01497-X). Ayer Co Pubs.
Cremin, Lawrence A., ed. see American Unitarian Association.
Cremin, Lawrence A., ed. see Campbell, Thomas M.
Cremins, James J. Legal & Political Issues in Special Education. (Illus.). 134p. 1983. 25.75x (ISBN 0-398-04878-9). C C Thomas.
Cremins, Robert. My Animal ABC. (Illus.). (ps-1). 1983. pap. 1.98 (ISBN 0-517-55099-7). Crown.
--My Animal Mother Goose. (ps-1). 1983. pap. 1.98 (ISBN 0-517-55098-9). Crown.
Cremlyn, R. Pesticides: Preparation & Mode of Action. LC 77-28590. 1978. 57.95 (ISBN 0-471-99631-9, Pub. by Wiley-Interscience); pap. 28.95 (ISBN 0-471-27669-3). Wiley.
Cremmins, Edward T. The Art of Abstracting. (Professional Writing Ser.). (Illus.). 150p. 1982. pap. 14.00 (ISBN 0-89495-015-0). ISI Pr.
Cremona, J. A. Barron's Card Guide to French Grammar. 1963. pap. text ed. 1.75 (ISBN 0-8120-5042-8). Barron.
Cremona, Joseph. Buongiorno Italia! (Illus.). 304p. (Ital.). 1982. pap. text ed. 9.95 (ISBN 0-563-16479-4, 55261, Pub. by British Broadcasting Corp England). EMC.
Cremonesi, Gilles, tr. see Thalmann, Rita & Feinermann, Emmanuel.
Cremony, John C. Life among the Apaches. LC 82-16106. 322p. 1983. pap. 6.50 (ISBN 0-8032-6312-0, BB 828, Bison). U of Nebr Pr.
Cren, E. D. Le see Le Cren, E. D. & Lowe-McConnell, R. H.
Crena De Iongh, Daniel. Byzantine Aspects of Italy. LC 67-19211. (Illus.). 1967. 7.50 (ISBN 0-393-04134-4). Norton.
Crener, Maxime A., jt. auth. see Overgaard, Herman O.
Crenner, James. My Hat Flies on Again. LC 79-25793. 62p. (Orig.). 1980. pap. 4.50 (ISBN 0-934332-23-1). L'Epervier Pr.
Crenshaw. Bedside Manners. 336p. 1983. 14.95 (ISBN 0-07-013581-9). McGraw.
--Belvedere: All Dogs Must Be on a Leash, No. 2. pap. 2.50 (ISBN 0-317-31683-4). Tor Bks.
--Belvedere: Best of Friends, No. 1. pap. 2.50 (ISBN 0-317-31682-6). Tor Bks.
--Belvedere: Don't Push Your Luck, No. 6. pap. 2.50 (ISBN 0-317-31685-0). Tor Bks.
Crenshaw, A. H., jt. auth. see Edmonson, A. S.

Crenshaw, Floyd D. & Flanders, John A., eds. Christian Values & the Academic Disciplines. 224p. (Orig.). 1985. lib. bdg. 20.75 (ISBN 0-8191-4306-5); pap. text ed. 11.50 (ISBN 0-8191-4307-3). U Pr of Amer.
Crenshaw, George. Belvedere. 256p. (Orig.). 1982. pap. 2.50 (ISBN 0-523-49004-6). Pinnacle Bks.
--Belvedere II. 256p. (Orig.). 1982. pap. 2.50 (ISBN 0-523-49020-8). Pinnacle Bks.
--Belvedere III. 256p. 1983. pap. 2.50 (ISBN 0-523-49027-5). Pinnacle Bks.
--Belvedere IV. 256p. (Orig.). 1983. pap. 2.50 (ISBN 0-523-49082-8, Pinnacle Bks). Tor Bks.
--Belvedere: Now Just One Minute, No. 3. 1985. pap. 2.50 (ISBN 0-317-31434-3). Tor Bks.
--Belvedere V. 256p. 1984. pap. 2.50 (ISBN 0-8125-6220-8). Tor Bks.
--The Best of Friends. (Belvedere Ser.: No. 1). 256p. 1985. pap. 2.50 (ISBN 0-8125-6201-1). Tor Bks.
--Don't Push Your Luck. (Belvedere Ser.: No. 6). 256p. (Orig.). 1984. pap. 2.50 (ISBN 0-8125-6222-4). Tor Bks.
Crenshaw, J. L. & Crenshaw, Willis. Essays on Old Testament Ethics: J. P. Hyatt in Memoriam. 1974. 35.00x (ISBN 0-87068-233-4). Ktav.
Crenshaw, James. Gerhard von Rad. (Makers of the Modern Theological Mind Ser.). 1978. 7.95 (ISBN 0-8499-0112-X). Word Bks.
--Telephone Between Worlds. 1977. Repr. of 1950 ed. 6.95 (ISBN 0-87516-017-4). De Vorss.
Crenshaw, James L. Hymnic Affirmation of Divine Justice. LC 75-22349. (Society of Biblical Literature. Dissertation Ser.: No. 24). Repr. of 1975 ed. 36.10 (ISBN 0-8357-9571-3, 2017523). Bks Demand UMI.
--Old Testament Wisdom: An Introduction. LC 80-82183. 262p. 1981. 16.95 (ISBN 0-8042-0143-9); pap. 11.95 (ISBN 0-8042-0142-0). John Knox.
--Prophetic Conflict: Its Effect Upon Israelite Religion. (Beiheft 124 zur Zeitschrift fuer die alttestamentliche Wissenschaft). 1971. 25.20x (ISBN 3-11-003363-1, 3-11-003363-1). De Gruyter.
--Samson: A Secret Betrayed, A Vow Ignored. LC 77-15748. 173p. 1981. text ed. 9.95x (ISBN 0-86554-042-X). Mercer Univ Pr.
--Story & Faith: A Guide to the Old Testament. 539p. 1986. text ed. price not set (ISBN 0-02-325600-1). Macmillan.
--Studies in Ancient Israelite Wisdom. 1974. 59.50x (ISBN 0-87068-255-5). Ktav.
--A Whirlpool of Torment: The Oppressive Presence of God in Ancient Israel. LC 83-18479. (Overtures to Biblical Theology Ser.). 144p. 1984. pap. 7.95 (ISBN 0-8006-1536-0, 1-1536). Fortress.
Crenshaw, James L. & Sandmel, Samuel. The Divine Helmsman: Studies on God's Control of Human Events. 1979. 35.00x (ISBN 0-87068-700-X). Ktav.
Crenshaw, James L., ed. Theodicy in the Old Testament. LC 83-8885. (Issues in Religion & Theology Ser.). 176p. 1983. pap. 6.95 (ISBN 0-8006-1764-9). Fortress.
Crenshaw, Martha, ed. Terrorism, Legitimacy, & Power: The Consequences of Political Violence. Dror, Yehezkel & O'Brien, Conor C. 228p. 1982. 17.95 (ISBN 0-8195-5081-7). Wesleyan U Pr.
Crenshaw, Mary A. The End of the Rainbow. 273p. 1981. 12.95 (ISBN 0-02-528810-5). Macmillan.
--Natural Way to Super Beauty. 1981. pap. 4.50 (ISBN 0-440-16061-8). Dell.
--Shape Up for Super Sex. 1981. pap. 3.50 (ISBN 0-440-17895-9). Dell.
--The Super Foods Diet. 256p. 1983. 12.95 (ISBN 0-02-528820-2). Macmillan.
Crenshaw, O. Slave States in the Presidential Election of 1860. 12.00 (ISBN 0-8446-1138-7). Peter Smith.
Crenshaw, Ollinger. The Slave States in the Presidential Election of 1860. LC 78-64199. (Johns Hopkins University. Studies in the Social Sciences. Sixty-Third Ser. 1945: 3). Repr. of 1945 ed. 11.50 (ISBN 0-404-61305-5). AMS Pr.
Crenshaw, R. S., Jr. Naval Shiphandling. 4th ed. LC 74-26360. (Illus.). 496p. 1975. 19.95x (ISBN 0-87021-474-8). Naval Inst Pr.
--Naval Shiphandling. 4th ed. 496p. 1975. 19.95 (ISBN 0-87021-474-8); bulk rates avail. Naval Inst Pr.
Crenshaw, Roger, jt. auth. see Crenshaw, Theresa.
Crenshaw, Theresa & Crenshaw, Roger. Expressing Your Feelings: The Key to an Intimate Relationship. 240p. (Orig.). (gr. 11-12). 1982. pap. 14.95 (ISBN 0-8290-0252-9). Irvington.
Crenshaw, Troy C. Texas Blackland Heritage. 15.00 (ISBN 0-87244-068-0). Texian.
Crenshaw, Willis, jt. auth. see Crenshaw, J. L.
Crenson, Matthew A. The Federal Machine: Beginnings of Bureaucracy in Jacksonian America. LC 74-6818. (Illus.). 205p. 1975. 19.50x (ISBN 0-8018-1586-X). Johns Hopkins.
--Neighborhood Politics. (Illus.). 384p. 1983. text ed. 22.50x (ISBN 0-674-60785-6). Harvard U Pr.
Creore, JoAnn, jt. auth. see Anderson, James M.
Crepaldi, G., et al, eds. Diabetes, Obesity & Hyperlipidemias. 1979. 65.00 (ISBN 0-12-197035-3). Acad Pr.
Crepaldi, Gaetano, et al, eds. Arteriosclerotic Brain Disease. 286p. 1983. text ed. 59.50 (ISBN 0-89004-886-X). Raven.
--Diabetes Obesity & Hyperlipidemias, No. II. 1983. 47.00 (ISBN 0-12-195480-3). Acad Pr.
Crepax, Guido. Illustrated Emanuelle: Based on the Novel by Emmanuelle Arsan. 144p. 1980. pap. 9.95 (ISBN 0-8021-4316-4, E765, Ever). Grove.
Crepax, Guido, illus. The Illustrated Justine: Based on the Novel by the Marquis De Sade. (Illus.). 160p. 1981. pap. 12.50 (ISBN 0-8021-4358-X, E798, Ever). Grove.
Crepeau, Betty. Activities Programming Recreation: An Activities Handbook-the Technique. (Serving the Elderly Ser.: Pt. 5). 1980. 11.50 (ISBN 0-89634-010-4, 047). New England Geron.
Crepeau, Georges. Belanger: Ou l'Histoire d'un Crime. (Novels by Franco-Americans in New England 1850-1940 Ser.). 49p. (Orig., Fr.). (gr. 10 up). 1979. pap. 4.50 (ISBN 0-911409-14-9). Natl Mat Dev.
Crepeau, Richard C. Baseball: America's Diamond Mind, 1919-1941. LC 79-16237. (Illus.). xii, 228p. 1980. 15.00 (ISBN 0-8130-0645-7). U Presses Fla.
Crepin, F. Primitiae Monographiae Rosarum: Meteriaux Pour Servir a L'Histoire Des Roses, 6 pts. in 1 vol. 1972. Repr. of 1882 ed. 35.00 (ISBN 3-7682-0759-5). Lubrecht & Cramer.
Crepon, P. Dictionnaire Pratique de l'Acupuncture et de l'Acupressure. 186p. (Fr.). 1980. pap. 33.50 (ISBN 0-686-92567-X, M-8979). French & Eur.
Crepps, John E., jt. ed. see Mason, Robert M.
Creps, David B. Randy Roy Persnazznur. LC 80-51270. (Orig.). 1980. pap. 4.95 (ISBN 0-930830-32-6). Great Basin.
Cresap, et al. Teacher Incentives. Koerner, Thomas F., ed. 56p. (Orig.). pap. text ed. 5.00 (ISBN 0-88210-160-9, NASSP). Natl Assn Principals.
Crescenti, Peter & Columbe, Bob. The Official Honeymooners Treasury. (Illus.). 1985. pap. 9.95 (ISBN 0-399-51201-2, Perigee). Putnam Pub Group.
--The Official Honeymooners Treasury. 320p. 1985. pap. 9.95 (ISBN 0-399-51200-4). Putnam Pub Group.
Crescenzi, V., et al, eds. New Developments in Industrial Polysaccharides. 396p. 1985. text ed. 58.00 (ISBN 2-88124-032-1). Gordon.
Cresci, Giovan F. Renaissance Alphabet: Il perfetto scrittore, parte seconda. LC 77-121765. (Illus.). 74p. 1971. 20.00x (ISBN 0-299-05761-5). U of Wis Pr.
Cresci, Martha W. Complete Book of Model Business Letters. 298p. 1976. 16.95 (ISBN 0-13-157438-8); pap. 4.95 (ISBN 0-13-157412-4). P-H.
Cresciani, Gianfranco. Fascism, Anti-Fascism & Italians in Australia: 1922-1945. LC 78-73567. (Illus.). 262p. 1981. text ed. 19.50 (ISBN 0-7081-1158-0, 0094, Pub. by ANUP Australia). Australia N U P.
Crescimanno, Russell. Culture, Consciousness, & Beyond: An Introduction. LC 82-17425. 102p. (Orig.). lib. bdg. 21.50 (ISBN 0-8191-2811-2); pap. text ed. 9.00 (ISBN 0-8191-2812-0). U Pr of Amer.
Crescimbeni, Joseph. Arithmetic Enrichment Activities for Elementary School Children. 1965. 14.95x (ISBN 0-13-046177-6, Parker). P-H.
--Language Enrichment Activities for the Elementary School. (Illus.). 1979. 15.95x (ISBN 0-13-522987-1, Parker). P-H.
--Science Enrichment Activities for the Elementary School. LC 80-28026. 272p. 1981. 24.95x (ISBN 0-13-794693-7, Parker). P-H.
Creso, Irene, ed. Vascular Plants of Western Washington. LC 84-72043. (Illus.). 520p. (Orig.). 1984. pap. 14.95 (ISBN 0-9613916-0-X). Creso.
Crespi, Francesca, illus. A Treasure Box of Fairy Tales: Hansel & Gretel, Rapunzel, Jack & the Beanstalk, & Aladdin. (Illus.). 1984. four bks boxed 8.95 (ISBN 0-8037-0079-2, 0869-260). Dial Bks Young.
Crespi, R. S. Patenting in the Biological Sciences: A Practical Guide for Research Scientists in Biotechnology & the Pharmaceutical & Agrochemical Industries. LC 81-19771. 211p. 1982. 39.95 (ISBN 0-471-10151-6, Pub. by Wiley-Interscience). Wiley.
Crespin, Vick S., et al. Walker's Manual for Construction Cost Estimating. Frank R. Walker Company, ed. (Illus.). 128p. 1981. pap. 12.95 (ISBN 0-911592-85-7). F R Walker.
Crespo, Angel. Juan Ramon Jimenez y la Pintura. (UPREX, Humanidades: No. 26). (Illus.). pap. 1.85 (ISBN 0-8477-0026-7). U of PR Pr.
Crespo, Angel, tr. see Dante Alighieri.
Crespo, Angel, tr. see Gomez Bedate, Pilar.
Crespo, Orestes I. & Louque, Patricia. Parent Involvement in the Education of Minority Language Children: A Resource Handbook. 89p. 1984. 7.40 (ISBN 0-89763-104-8). Natl Clearinghse Bilingual Ed.
Crespo, Patria C. De see Falcon, Luis N. & De Crespo, Patria C.
Crespo, Rafael. Come Yo Te Amo. (Romance Real Ser.). 192p. (Span.). 1981. pap. 1.50 (ISBN 0-88025-003-8). Roca Pub.
--Siempre Junto a Ti. (Romance Real). 192p. (Span.). 1981. pap. 1.50 (ISBN 0-88025-004-6). Roca Pub.
Cress, Donald A., jt. ed. see Cress, Elizabeth J.
Cress, Donald A., ed. & tr. see Descartes, Rene.
Cress, Donald A., tr. see Descartes, Rene.
Cress, Donald A., tr. see Rousseau, Jean-Jacques.
Cress, Elizabeth J. & Cress, Donald A., eds. A Guide to Rare & Out-Of-Print Books in the Vatican Film Library: An Author List. LC 85-9085. 280p. 1985. lib. bdg. 24.75 (ISBN 0-8191-4726-5). U Pr of Amer.
Cress, Lawrence D. Citizens in Arms: The Army & Militia in American Society to the War of 1812. LC 81-15945. (Studies on Armed Forces & Society Ser.). xiv, 238p. 1982. 22.50x (ISBN 0-8078-1508-X). U of NC Pr.
Cress, Mary. Automation. (Science Ser.). 24p. (gr. 6 up). 1977. wkbk. 5.00 (ISBN 0-8209-0153-9, S-15). ESP.
Cress, P., et al. FORTRAN IV with WATFOR & WATFIV. 1970. ref. ed. 22.95 (ISBN 0-13-329433-1). P-H.
--Structured FORTRAN with WATFIV-S. 1980. pap. 22.95 (ISBN 0-13-854752-1). P-H.
Cress, Sheila S., jt. auth. see Loxley, Cynthia M.
Cresser, M. S., jt. auth. see Chalmers, R. A.
Cresser, Malcolm S., jt. auth. see Marr, Ian.
Cressey, Donald, jt. auth. see Coleman, James.
Cressey, Donald R. Other People's Money: A Study in the Social Psychology of Embezzlement. LC 73-7907. (Criminology, Law Enforcement, & Social Problems Ser.: No. 202). 204p. 1973. Repr. of 1953 ed. lib. bdg. 15.00x (ISBN 0-87585-202-5). Patterson Smith.
Cressey, Donald R., jt. auth. see Rosett, Arthur.
Cressey, George B. Soviet Potentials: A Geographic Appraisal. LC 62-8478. (Illus.). 1962. pap. 5.95x (ISBN 0-8156-2034-9). Syracuse U Pr.
Cressey, James. Fourteen Rats & a Rat Catcher. LC 77-4759. (Illus.). (ps-2). 1977. PLB 6.95 (ISBN 0-13-329920-1). P-H.
Cressey, Paul G. The Taxi-Dance Hall. LC 77-180706. Repr. of 1932 ed. 14.50 (ISBN 0-404-01839-4). AMS Pr.
--Taxi-Dance Hall: A Sociological Study in Commercialized Recreation & City Life. LC 69-16236. (Criminology, Law Enforcement, & Social Problems Ser.: No. 76). (Illus., With intro. essay added). 1969. Repr. of 1932 ed. 12.50x (ISBN 0-87585-076-6). Patterson Smith.
Cressey, Roger F. Parasitic Copepods from the Gulf of Mexico & Caribbean Sea. LC 81-9055. (Smithsonian Contributions to Zoology: No. 389). pap. 20.00 (ISBN 0-317-29739-2, 2022199). Bks Demand UMI.
Cressey, William W. Spanish Phonology & Morphology: A Generative View. LC 78-23327. 169p. 1978. pap. text ed. 7.95 (ISBN 0-87840-045-1). Georgetown U Pr.
Cressey, William W. & Borsoi, Edward E. Tertulia: Conversacion, Composicion & Repaso Gramatical. (Span.). 1972. pap. text ed. 16.95 (ISBN 0-13-906826-0). P-H.
Cressey, William W. & Napoli, Donna J., eds. Linguistic Symposium on Romance Languages, No. 9. (Orig.). 1981. pap. text ed. 14.95 (ISBN 0-87840-081-8). Georgetown U Pr.
Cressman, Luther S. Prehistory of the Far West: Homes of Vanished Peoples. LC 75-30153. (Illus.). 1977. 19.95 (ISBN 0-87480-113-3). U of Utah Pr.
--The Sandal & the Cave: The Indians of Oregon. LC 81-915. (Oregon State Monographs--Studies in History: No. 8). (Illus.). 96p. 1981. pap. 5.00 (ISBN 0-87071-078-8). Oreg St U Pr.
Cresson, H. T. Report Upon Pile-Structures in Naaman's Creek, Near Claymont, Delaware. (Harvard University Peabody Museum of Archaeology & Ethnology Papers Ser: HU. PMP Vol. 1, No. 4). pap. 14.00 (ISBN 0-527-01186-X). Kraus Repr.
Cresson, Warder. The Key of David: David the True Messiah. Davis, Moshe, ed. LC 77-70671. (America & the Holy Land Ser.). (Illus.). 1977. Repr. of 1852 ed. lib. bdg. 26.50x (ISBN 0-405-10239-9). Ayer Co Pubs.
Cresson, William P. The Cossacks: Their History & Country. LC 77-87541. Repr. of 1919 ed. 29.50 (ISBN 0-404-16608-3). AMS Pr.
--James Monroe. LC 75-124098. xiv, 577p. 1971. Repr. of 1946 ed. 32.00 (ISBN 0-208-01089-0, Archon). Shoe String.
Cresswell, Anthony M. & Murphy, Michael J. Teachers, Unions, & Collective Bargaining in Public Education. LC 79-91436. 350p. 1980. 26.75x (ISBN 0-8211-0229-X); text ed. 24.50x ten or more copies. McCutchan.
Cresswell, Anthony M. & Murphy, Michael J., eds. Education & Collective Bargaining: Readings in Policy & Research. LC 76-46121. 1977. 25.50x (ISBN 0-8211-0227-3); text ed. 22.75x 10 or more copies. McCutchan.
Cresswell, Don. The Laughable, Loveable, Little Give-Me-As-a-Gift Book, No. 2. (Illus.). 24p. (Orig.). 1984. pap. 2.95 saddle stitch (ISBN 0-930943-01-5). Cresswell Ent.
Cresswell, Helen. Absolute Zero: Being the Second Part of the Bagthorpe Saga. 174p. (gr. 3 up). 1979. pap. 1.75 (ISBN 0-380-45906-X, 45906-X, Camelot). Avon.
--Absolute Zero: Being the Second Part of the Bagthorpe Saga. LC 77-12675. 180p. (gr. 5 up). 1978. 9.95 (ISBN 0-02-725550-6, 72555). Macmillan.
--Bagthorpes Abroad: Being the Fifth Part of The Bagthorpe Saga. LC 84-7125. 204p. (gr. 5-9). 1984. 10.95 (ISBN 0-02-725390-2). Macmillan.
--Bagthorpes Haunted: Being the Sixth Part of the Bagthorpe Saga. (The Bagthorpe Saga Ser.). (Illus.). 192p. (gr. 5-9). 1985. PLB 11.95 (ISBN 0-02-725380-5). Macmillan.
--Bagthorpes Unlimited: Being the Third Part of the Bagthorpe Saga. 182p. 1980. pap. 1.75 (ISBN 0-380-49296-2, 49296-2, Camelot). Avon.
--The Bagthorpes vs the World: Being the Fourth Part of the Bagthorpe Saga. (Illus.). 196p. (gr. 1 up). 1980. pap. 1.95 (ISBN 0-380-51102-9, 51102-9, Camelot). Avon.
--Bagthorpes vs the World: Being the Fourth Part of the Bagthorpe Saga. LC 79-13260. 204p. (gr. 5 up). 1979. 9.95 (ISBN 0-02-725420-8). Macmillan.
--The Beachcombers. LC 72-57348. 144p. (gr. 5 up). 1972. 9.95 (ISBN 0-02-725470-4). Macmillan.
--Dear Shrink. LC 82-7728. 204p. (gr. 7 up). 1982. 9.95 (ISBN 0-02-725560-3). Macmillan.
--A Game of Catch. LC 76-46991. (Illus.). 48p. (gr. 3-6). 1977. 10.95 (ISBN 0-02-725440-2, 72544). Macmillan.
--Night Watchmen. LC 77-120717. (Illus.). 122p. (gr. 4-6). 1970. 9.95 (ISBN 0-02-725480-1). Macmillan.
--Ordinary Jack. (gr. 1-4). 1979. pap. 1.50 (ISBN 0-380-43349-4, 43349-4, Camelot). Avon.
--Ordinary Jack: Being the First Part of the Bagthorpe Saga. LC 77-5146. 192p. (gr. 5 up). 1977. 9.95 (ISBN 0-02-725540-9, 72554). Macmillan.
--The Piemakers. LC 80-14435. (Illus.). 128p. (gr. 3-7). 1980. 9.95x (ISBN 0-02-725410-0). Macmillan.
--The Secret World of Polly Flint. LC 83-24861. (Illus.). 176p. (gr. 4-7). 1984. 10.95 (ISBN 0-02-725400-3). Macmillan.
--Secret World of Polly Flint. (Illus.). 178p. (gr. 4-6). 1985. pap. 3.50 (ISBN 0-14-031542-X, Puffin). Penguin.
--Up the Pier. LC 79-178598. (Illus.). 144p. (gr. 5-7). 1972. 9.95 (ISBN 0-02-725490-9). Macmillan.
--The Winter of the Birds. LC 75-34278. 256p. (gr. 7 up). 1976. 10.95 (ISBN 0-02-725510-7, 72551). Macmillan.
Cresswell, Henry, jt. auth. see Colles, W. Morris.
Cresswell, Henry, jt. auth. see Colles, William M.
Cresswell, Jasmine. The Danewood Legacy. (Coventry Romance Ser.: No. 188). 224p. 1982. pap. 1.50 (ISBN 0-449-50290-2, Coventry). Fawcett.
--Lord Carrisford's Mistress. (Coventry Romance Ser.: No. 199). 192p. 1982. pap. 1.50 (ISBN 0-449-50303-8, Coventry). Fawcett.
--The Reluctant Viscountess. 192p. 1982. pap. 1.50 (ISBN 0-449-50313-5, Coventry). Fawcett.
Cresswell, John & Hartley, John. Teach Yourself Esperanto. (Teach Yourself Ser.). pap. 5.95 (ISBN 0-679-10167-5). McKay.
Cresswell, M. J. Die Sprachen der Logik und Die Logik der Sprache. (Grundlagen der Kommunikation De Gruyter Studienbuch). 1979. 14.40x (ISBN 3-11-004923-6). De Gruyter.
--Structured Meanings: The Semantics of Propositional Attitudes. 1985. 19.95x (ISBN 0-262-03108-6). MIT Pr.
Cresswell, M. J., jt. auth. see Hughes, G. E.
Cresswell, Maxwell J., jt. auth. see Hughes, George E.
Cresswell, Nicholas. Journal of Nicholas Cresswell, 1774-1777. LC 68-26265. 1968. Repr. of 1924 ed. 21.00x (ISBN 0-8046-0092-9, Pub. by Kennikat). Assoc Faculty Pr.
Cresswell, O. D. Chinese Cash. (Illus.). 1980. Repr. of 1915 ed. softcover 10.00 (ISBN 0-915262-41-X). S J Durst.
Cresswell, R. W., jt. auth. see Young, A. P.
Cresswell, Rachel L., jt. auth. see Fry, Elizabeth.
Cresswell, Roy, ed. Passenger Transport & the Environment: The Integration of Public Transport with the Urban Environment. (Illus.). 1977. 49.95x (ISBN 0-249-44153-5). Intl Ideas.
Cressy, David. Education in Tudor & Stuart England. LC 75-32933. 160p. 1976. 22.50 (ISBN 0-312-23730-8). St Martin.
--Literacy & the Social Order. (Illus.). 250p. 1980. 32.50 (ISBN 0-521-22514-0). Cambridge U Pr.
Crestol, Jack & Schneider, Herman M. Tax Planning for Investors: The Eighties Guide to Securities & Commodities Investments & Tax Shelters, 1985. LC 84-73045. 1984. 25.00 (ISBN 0-87094-632-3). Dow Jones-Irwin.
--Tax Planning for Investors: The 1982 Guide to Securities, Investments, & Tax Shelters. LC 82-71350. 175p. 1982. 19.95 (ISBN 0-87094-298-0). Dow Jones-Irwin.
Crestol, Jack, jt. auth. see McQueen, C. Richard.
Crestol, Jack, et al. The Consolidated Tax Return, Principles, Practices, Planning: Annual Supplement. 3rd. ed. 1980. post binder 75.00 (ISBN 0-88262-401-6). Warren.
Creston, Dormer. Andromeda in Wimpole Street. 1973. Repr. of 1929 ed. 25.00 (ISBN 0-8274-0700-9). R West.
Creswell, jt. auth. see Grove.
Creswell, Clifford J., et al. Spectral Analysis of Organic Compounds: An Introductory Programmed Text. 2nd ed. LC 72-77099. 1972. pap. 14.95x (ISBN 0-8087-0335-8). Burgess.
Creswell, John. British Admirals of the Eighteenth Century: Tactics in Battle. 263p. 1972. 18.50 (ISBN 0-208-01223-0, Archon). Shoe String.

--Generals & Admirals: The Story of Amphibious Command. LC 75-8486. (Illus.). 1976. Repr. of 1952 ed. lib. bdg. 19.75x (ISBN 0-8371-8151-8, CRGAD). Greenwood.

Creswell, K. Short Account of Early Muslim Architecture. 1968. 18.00x (ISBN 0-86685-010-4). Intl Bk Ctr.

Creswell, K. A. A Bibliography of the Architecture, Arts & Crafts of Islam. 2nd ed. 120.00 (ISBN 0-89410-306-7, Pub. by FP Van Eck Liechtenstein). Three Continents.

--Early Muslim Architecture: Umayyads, Early 'Abbasids, & Tulunids, 2 vols. in 3 pts. LC 75-11057. 1978. Repr. of 1932 ed. lib. bdg. 375.00 (ISBN 0-87817-176-2). Hacker.

--Muslim Architecture of Egypt, 2 vols. LC 75-11056. (Illus.). 1978. Repr. of 1952 ed. lib. bdg. 350.00 (ISBN 0-87817-175-4). Hacker.

Creswell, Mike. Your God, My God. Pennington, Celeste, ed. (Human Touch-Photo Text Ser.). 172p. 1980. 7.95 (ISBN 0-937170-22-4). Home Mission.

Creswell, Thomas J., jt. auth. see McDavid, Virginia.

Creswell, William H., Jr., jt. auth. see Anderson, Carl L.

Creswick, Alice M. The Red Book of Fruit Jars Number Three. 224p. 13.75 (ISBN 0-318-14894-3, A159). Midwest Old Settlers.

Creswick, Paul. Robin Hood. 362p. 1984. 18.95 (ISBN 0-684-18162-2, ScribJ); deluxe edition 75.00 (ISBN 0-684-18180-0). Scribner.

Cretcher, Dorothy. Steering Clear: Helping Your Child Through the High-Risk Drug Years. 112p. (Orig.). 1982. pap. 4.95 (ISBN 0-86683-689-6). Winston Pr.

Crete, Liliane. Daily Life in Louisiana, 1815-1830. Gregory, Patrick, tr. from Fr. LC 81-8315. (Illus.). xii, 308p. 1981. 30.00x (ISBN 0-8071-0887-1). La State U Pr.

Creteau, Paul G. Principles of Real Estate Law. LC 76-52549. (Illus.). 1977. 19.00 (ISBN 0-9603372-0-2). Castle Pub Co.

--Real Estate Appraising (Step-by-Step) 2nd ed. LC 73-90006. 1974. 15.00 (ISBN 0-9603372-1-0). Castle Pub Co.

Creth, Sheila. Time Management & Conducting Effective Meetings. 53p. 15.00 (ISBN 0-8389-6748-5); members 10.00 (ISBN 0-317-36637-8). Assn Coll & Res Libs.

Creth, Sheila & Duda, Frederick, eds. Personnel Administration in Libraries. 333p. 1981. 29.95x (ISBN 0-918212-25-1). Neal-Schuman.

Cretien, Paul. Financial Management Using Lotus 1-2-3. 1985. 18.95 (ISBN 0-03-003104-4). CBS Ed.

Cretien, Troyes de see De Troyes, Chretien.

Cretser, Gary A. & Leon, Joseph J., eds. Intermarriage in the United States. LC 82-6213. (Marriage & Family Review Ser.: Vol. 5, No. 1). 111p. 1982. text ed. 20.00 (ISBN 0-917724-60-7, B60); pap. text ed. 9.95 (ISBN 0-917724-83-6). Haworth Pr.

Cretti, Luciano & Bosisio, Gina B. House Plants: A Color Guide. (Color Guides Ser.). (Illus.). 196p. 1984. 12.95 (ISBN 0-88254-922-7). Hippocrene Bks.

Creupelandt, H. C., jt. auth. see Abbott, J. C.

Creutz, E. see Fluegge, S.

Creutz, Michael. Quarks, Gluons & Lattices. LC 83-2089. (Cambridge Monographs on Mathematical Physics). 175p. 1984. 34.50 (ISBN 0-521-24405-6). Cambridge U Pr.

--Quarks, Gluons & Lattices. (Monographs on Mathematical Physics). (Illus.). 175p. 1985. pap. 12.95 (ISBN 0-521-31535-2). Cambridge U Pr.

Creutzberg, Gilbert. Ride the Forbidden Horse. 64p. 1984. pap. 4.75x (ISBN 0-89962-344-1). Todd & Honeywell.

Creutzberg, P. Changing Economy in Indonesia: A Selection of Statistical Source Material from the Early 19th Century up to 1940, Volume 5 - National Income. (Illus.). 133p. 1980. pap. 21.00 (ISBN 90-247-2194-6, Pub. by Martinus Nijhoff Netherlands). Kluwer Academic.

Creutzfeld, O., ed. Apperent & Intrinsic Organization of Laminated Structures in the Brain. (Experimental Brain Research, Suppl. 1). (Illus.). 1977. soft cover 34.30 (ISBN 0-387-07923-8). Springer-Verlag.

Creutzfeld, O., et al, eds. Sensory Motor Integration in the Nervous System. (Experimental Brain Research: Supplementum 9). (Illus.). 490p. 1984. 59.00 (ISBN 0-387-13680-0). Springer-Verlag.

Creutzfeldt, O., ed. Hearing Mechanisms & Speech. (Experimental Brain Research Supplementum Ser.: No. 2). (Illus.). 1979. pap. 27.20 (ISBN 0-387-09655-8). Springer-Verlag.

Creutzfeldt, W., ed. Acarbose: Proceedings of the International Symposium on Acarbose Effects on Carbohydrate & Fat Metabolism, First, Montreux, October 8-10, 1981. (International Congress Ser.: No. 594). 588p. 1982. 81.00 (ISBN 0-444-90283-X, I-278-82, Excerpta Medica). Elsevier.

--The Entero-Insular Axis. (Frontiers of Hormone Research: Vol. 7). (Illus.). x, 310p. 1980. 49.00 (ISBN 3-8055-0795-X). S Karger.

Creutzfeldt, Werner & Flosch, Doz U. Delaying Absorption as a Therapeutic Principle in Metabolic Disease. (Illus.). 159p. 1983. text ed. 27.00 (ISBN 0-86577-158-8). Thieme Stratton.

Creux, Francois Du see Du Creux, Francois.

Creuzer, Georg F. Symbolik und Mythologie der Alten Volker Besonders der Griechen, 6 vols. Bolle, Kees W., ed. LC 77-79119. (Mythology Ser.). (Illus., Ger.). 1978. Repr. of 1823 ed. lib. bdg. 325.00x (ISBN 0-405-10531-2). Ayer Co Pubs.

Crevea, Rafael Altamira Y see Altamira Y Crevea, Rafael.

Crevecoeur, J. Hector De see De Crevecoeur, J. Hector.

Crevecoeur, J. Hector St. John De see St. John de Crevecoeur, J. Hector.

Crevecoeur, St. John De see De Crevecoeur, St. John.

Crevel, Rene. Babylon: A Novel. Boyle, Kay, tr. (Illus.). 176p. 1985. 15.50 (ISBN 0-86547-191-6). N Point Pr.

Creveld, Marijke. Epilithic Lichen Communities in the Alpine Zone of Southern Norway. (Bibliotheca Lichenologica: Vol. 17). (Illus.). 288p. 1981. text ed. 35.00x (ISBN 3-7682-1313-7). Lubrecht & Cramer.

Creveld, Martin L. Van see Van Creveld, Martin L.

Creveld, Martin van see Van Creveld, Martin.

Creviston. Contemporary Personal Finance. 1985. 30.01 (ISBN 0-205-08366-8, 108366). Allyn.

Crew, David F. Town in the Ruhr. LC 78-31526. (Social History of Bochum, 1860-1914). 352p. 1979. 29.00x (ISBN 0-231-04300-7). Columbia U Pr.

Crew, Henry, tr. from Latin. The Photismi De Lumine of Maurolycus: A Chapter in Late Medieval Optics. 1940. 12.50x (ISBN 0-686-30225-7). R S Barnes.

Crew, Henry, tr. see Galilei, Galileo.

Crew, Louie. Sunspots. 1st ed. LC 76-20917. 59p. 1976. pap. 3.00x (ISBN 0-916418-06-5). Lotus.

Crew, Louie, ed. The Gay Academic. LC 75-37780. 1978. 15.00 (ISBN 0-88280-036-1). ETC Pubns.

Crew, Michael A. & Kleindorfer, Paul R. Public Utility Economics. LC 78-24611. 1979. 25.00x (ISBN 0-312-65569-X). St Martin.

Crew, Michael A. & Young, Alistair. Paying By Degrees. (Institute of Economic Affairs, Hobart Papers Ser.: No. 75). pap. 4.25 technical (ISBN 0-255-36102-5). Transatlantic.

Crew, Michael A., ed. Analyzing the Impact of Regulatory Change in Public Utilities. LC 83-48674. 208p. 1984. 24.00x (ISBN 0-669-07341-5). Lexington Bks.

--Problems in Public-Utility Economics & Regulation. 192p. 1979. 22.50x (ISBN 0-669-02775-8). Lexington Bks.

--Regulatory Reform & Public Utilities. LC 81-47749. 288p. 1982. 31.50x (ISBN 0-669-04834-8). Lexington Bks.

Crew, P. Mack. Calvinist Preaching & Iconoclasm in the Netherlands, 1544-1569. LC 77-77013. (Studies in Early Modern History). 1978. 37.50 (ISBN 0-521-21739-3). Cambridge U Pr.

Crewdson, John. The Tarnished Door. LC 82-40367. 354p. 1983. 17.95 (ISBN 0-8129-1042-7). Times Bks.

Crewe, Albert V. & Katz, Joseph J. Nuclear Research U. S. A. Knowledge for the Future. (Illus.). 10.00 (ISBN 0-8446-0564-6). Peter Smith.

Crewe, Charles W. Un Vistazo a la Recaida. 12p. 1983. pap. 0.70 (ISBN 0-89486-197-2). Hazelden.

Crewe, Ivor & Fox, Anthony. British Parliamentary Constituencies. 400p. (Orig.). 1984. 54.00 (ISBN 0-571-13236-7); pap. cancelled. Faber & Faber.

Crewe, Ivor, jt. auth. see Sarlvik, Bo.

Crewe, Ivor & Denver, D. T., eds. Electoral Change in Western Democracies: Patterns & Sources of Electoral Volatility. LC 84-40369. 320p. 1985. 29.95 (ISBN 0-312-24098-8). St Martin.

Crewe, Jonathan. Unredeemed Rhetoric: Thomas Nashe & the Scandal of Authorship. LC 82-6554. 144p. 1982. text ed. 15.00x (ISBN 0-8018-2848-1). Johns Hopkins.

Crewe, Jonathan, ed. Stephen Batman's the Doome Warnein All Men to Judgement. Facsimilie ed. (The Renaissance Imagination Ser.). Repr. of 1581 ed. 66.00 (ISBN 0-8240-5461-X). Garland Pub.

Crewe, Nancy M. & Athelstan, Gary T. Functional Assessment Inventory Manual. rev. ed. (Illus.). 96p. 1984. pap. 10.00x (ISBN 0-916671-53-4). Material Dev.

Crewe, Nancy M. & Zola, Irving K. Independent Living for Physically Disabled People: Developing, Implementing & Evaluating Self-Help Rehabilitation Programs. LC 82-48067. (Social & Behavioral Science Ser.). 1983. text ed. 23.95x (ISBN 0-87589-556-5). Jossey-Bass.

Crewe, Quentin. In Search of the Sahara. (Illus.). 272p. 1984. 24.95 (ISBN 0-02-528890-3). Macmillan.

Crewe, Sarah. Golden Illusions. (Second Chance at Love Ser.: No. 135). 192p. 1983. pap. 1.95 (ISBN 0-515-07223-0). Jove Pubns.

--Night Flame. (Second Chance at Love Ser.: No. 195). 192p. 1984. pap. 1.95 (ISBN 0-515-07811-5). Jove Pubns.

--Seaflame. (Second Chance at Love Ser.: No. 233). 192p. 1984. pap. 1.95 (ISBN 0-515-08207-4). Jove Pubns.

--Windflame. (Second Chance at Love: No. 281). 192p. 1985. pap. 2.25 (ISBN 0-425-08462-0). Berkley Pub.

Crewe, Sarah, jt. auth. see Sweeney, Patrick.

Crews, Clyde. English Catholic Modernism: Maude Petre's Way of Faith. LC 83-50747. 156p. 1984. text ed. 16.95x (ISBN 0-268-00912-0, 85-09127). U of Notre Dame Pr.

Crews, Clyde F. Fundamental Things Apply: Reflecting on Christian Basics. LC 83-71005. 104p. (Orig.). 1983. pap. 3.95 (ISBN 0-87793-272-7). Ave Maria.

Crews, Donald. Bicycle Race. LC 84-27912. (Illus.). 24p. (ps-1). 1985. 11.75 (ISBN 0-688-05171-5); lib. bdg. 11.88 (ISBN 0-688-05172-3). Greenwillow.

--Carousel. LC 82-3062. (Illus.). 32p. (ps-1). 1982. 10.75 (ISBN 0-688-00908-5); PLB 10.88 (ISBN 0-688-00909-3). Greenwillow.

--Freight Train. LC 78-2303. (Illus.). 32p. (gr. k-3). 1978. 11.75 (ISBN 0-688-80165-X); PLB 11.88 (ISBN 0-688-84165-1). Greenwillow.

--Freight Train. (Illus.). 24p. (ps-k). 1985. pap. 3.95 (ISBN 0-14-050480-X, Puffin). Penguin.

--Harbor. LC 81-6607. (Illus.). 32p. (ps-1). 1982. 11.75 (ISBN 0-688-00861-5); PLB 11.88 (ISBN 0-688-00862-3). Greenwillow.

--Light. LC 80-20273. (Illus.). 32p. (ps-1). 1981. 10.25 (ISBN 0-688-00303-6); PLB 10.88 (ISBN 0-688-00310-9). Greenwillow.

--Parade. LC 82-20927. (Illus.). 32p. (gr. k-3). 1983. 10.25 (ISBN 0-688-01995-1); PLB 10.88 (ISBN 0-688-01996-X). Greenwillow.

--School Bus. LC 83-18681. (Illus.). 32p. (gr. k-3). 1984. 10.88 (ISBN 0-688-02807-1); PLB 9.55 (ISBN 0-688-02808-X). Greenwillow.

--School Bus. LC 85-576. (Illus.). 32p. (ps-1). 1985. pap. 3.95 (ISBN 0-14-050549-0, Puffin). Penguin.

--Truck. LC 79-19031. (Illus.). 32p. (ps-2). 1980. 10.95 (ISBN 0-688-80244-3); PLB 10.88 (ISBN 0-688-84244-5). Greenwillow.

--Truck. LC 84-18137. (Illus.). 32p. (ps). 1985. 3.95 (ISBN 0-14-050506-7, Puffin). Penguin.

--We Read: A to Z. LC 83-25453. (Illus.). 64p. (ps-1). 1984. 11.50 (ISBN 0-688-03843-3); PLB 10.51 (ISBN 0-688-03844-1). Greenwillow.

Crews, Donald, illus. Truck. (gr. k-3). 1981. sound filmstrip inc. 22.95 (ISBN 0-941078-00-0). Live Oak Media.

Crews, Federick & Schor, Sandra. The Borzoi Handbook for Writers. 540p. 1985. text ed. 12.95 (ISBN 0-394-35501-6, FOS, RanC). Random.

Crews, Frederick. Out of My System: Psychoanalysis, Ideology, & Critical Method. 1975. 22.50x (ISBN 0-19-501947-4). Oxford U Pr.

--The Random House Handbook. 4th ed. 1983. text ed. 15.95 (ISBN 0-394-32395-5, RanC). Random.

--The Random House Reader. 432p. 1981. pap. text ed. 10.00 (ISBN 0-394-32268-1, RanC). Random.

Crews, Frederick C. Pooh Perplex: A Freshman Casebook. (Illus.). 1965. pap. 5.95 (ISBN 0-525-47160-X, 0578-170). Dutton.

Crews, Frederick C., ed. see Hawthorne, Nathaniel.

Crews, Harry. Blood & Grits. LC 78-54605. 1979. 12.45i (ISBN 0-06-010933-5, HarpT). Har-Row.

--Car. LC 83-4462. 156p. 1983. pap. 4.70 (ISBN 0-688-02145-X, Quill NY). Morrow.

--A Childhood: The Biography of a Place. LC 78-54677. 1978. 11.49i (ISBN 0-06-010932-7, HarpT). Har-Row.

--A Childhood: The Biography of a Place. LC 83-4460. 180p. 1983. pap. 5.70 (ISBN 0-688-02398-3, Quill NY). Morrow.

--Florida Frenzy. LC 82-1997. vii, 138p. 1982. pap. 7.00 (ISBN 0-8130-0726-7). U Presses Fla.

--Karate Is a Thing of the Spirit. LC 82-4461. 228p. 1983. pap. 5.70 (ISBN 0-688-02372-X, Quill NY). Morrow.

--Two. 40p. 1984. deluxe ed. 50.00 Signed Ed. (ISBN 0-935716-32-7). Lord John.

Crews, Judson. The Clock of Moss. Berge, Carol & Boyer, Dale, eds. LC 82-73828. (Ahsahta Press Modern & Contemporary Poetry of the West Ser.). 60p. (Orig.). 1983. pap. 3.00 (ISBN 0-916272-21-4). Ahsahta Pr.

--If I: Seventy-Nine Poems. 40p. 1981. 2.50 (ISBN 0-935390-06-5). Wormwood Rev.

--Nations & People. LC 76-50426. 1977. pap. text ed. 1.25x (ISBN 0-916156-19-2). Cherry Valley.

--Nolo Contendere. Whitebird, J., ed. LC 78-73263. 1978. 6.50 (ISBN 0-930324-08-0); pap. 4.00 (ISBN 0-930324-09-9). Wings Pr.

--The Noose - a Retrospective: Four Decades. Goodell, Larry & Brandi, John, eds. (Illus., Orig.). 1980. pap. 4.00 (ISBN 0-915008-16-5). Small Pr Dist.

Crews, Judson, ed. see Greasybear, Charley J.

Crews, Kenneth D. Edward S. Corwin & the American Constitution: A Bibliographical Analysis. LC 84-19185. (Bibliographies & Indexes in Law & Political Science Ser.: No. 2). (Illus.). xiv, 226p. 1985. lib. bdg. 35.00 (ISBN 0-313-24233-X, CRE/). Greenwood.

Crews, William. Four Causes of Reality. LC 69-14354. 1969. 5.50 (ISBN 0-8022-2268-4). Philos Lib.

Crewther, W. G., ed. Fibrous Proteins. 414p. 1968. 55.00x (ISBN 0-306-30665-4, Plenum Pr). Plenum Pub.

Creyke, W. E., et al. Design with Non-Ductile Materials. (Illus.). xix, 294p. 1982. 55.50 (ISBN 0-85334-149-4, I-359-82, Pub. by Elsevier Applied Sci England). Elsevier.

Cribb, A. B. & Cribb, J. W. Plant Life of the Great Barrier Reef & Adjacent Shores. LC 84-3704. (Illus.). 294p. 1985. text ed. 25.00x (ISBN 0-7022-1984-3). U of Queensland Pr.

--Useful Wild Plants in Australia. (Illus.). 269p. 17.50x (ISBN 0-00-216441-8, Pub. by W Collins Australia); pap. 8.95x. Intl Spec Bk.

--Wild Food in Australia. 1980. pap. 6.50x (ISBN 0-00-634436-4, Pub. by W Collins Australia). Intl Spec Bk.

Cribb, A. B., jt. auth. see Cribb, J. W.

Cribb, C. C. Armageddon-Dead Ahead. LC 77-70212. pap. 2.95 (ISBN 0-932046-03-7). Manhattan Ltd NC.

--The Coming Kingdom. LC 77-70213. pap. 2.95 (ISBN 0-932046-04-5). Manhattan Ltd NC.

--The Devil's Empire. LC 77-70211. pap. 2.95 (ISBN 0-932046-02-9). Manhattan Ltd NC.

--Digging Diamonds Daily. LC 77-70215. Set. (ISBN 0-932046-09-6); Vol. 1. 12.95 (ISBN 0-932046-07-X); Vol. 2. 12.95 (ISBN 0-932046-08-8). Manhattan Ltd NC.

--Flying High Against the Sky: If God Has It I Want It! LC 79-84881. Date not set. pap. 2.95 (ISBN 0-932046-16-9). Manhattan Ltd NC.

--From Now till Eternity. LC 76-21571. 12.95 (ISBN 0-932046-00-2). Manhattan Ltd NC.

--Getting Ready for Heaven. LC 78-60614. (If God Has It I Want It!). 1979. pap. 2.95 (ISBN 0-685-96444-2). Manhattan Ltd NC.

--Getting Ready for the Coming Rapture. LC 79-88232. (If God Has It I Want It! Ser.). Date not set. pap. 2.95 (ISBN 0-932046-19-3). Manhattan Ltd NC.

--Getting Your Share of the Spirit's Outpouring. LC 79-88229. (If God Has It I Want It! Ser.). Date not set. pap. 2.95 (ISBN 0-932046-17-7). Manhattan Ltd NC.

--The Horrified & the Glorified. LC 77-70214. pap. 2.95 (ISBN 0-932046-05-3). Manhattan Ltd NC.

--Man's Earth-Lease Is About to Expire. LC 77-70210. pap. 2.95 (ISBN 0-932046-01-0). Manhattan Ltd NC.

--Moving the Hand That Moves the World. LC 79-88930. (If God Has It I Want It! Ser.). Date not set. pap. 2.95 (ISBN 0-932046-18-5). Manhattan Ltd NC.

--Spinning Straw into Gold. LC 79-84880. (If God Has It I Want It!). pap. 2.95 (ISBN 0-932046-15-0). Manhattan Ltd NC.

--Staking Your Claim on Healing. LC 79-83919. (If God Has It I Want It!). 1979. pap. 2.95 (ISBN 0-932046-14-2). Manhattan Ltd NC.

Cribb, J. W. & Cribb, A. B. Wild Medicine in Australia. (Illus.). 228p. 1982. (Pub. by W Collins Australia); pap. text ed. 6.95x (ISBN 0-00-216446-9). Intl Spec Bk.

Cribb, J. W., jt. auth. see Cribb, A. B.

Cribb, James & Cousteau, Jacques. Marine Life of the Caribbean. (Illus.). 1984. 15.95 (ISBN 0-19-540616-8). Skyline Press.

Cribb, James A. Treasures of the Sea: Marine Life of the Pacific Northwest. (Illus.). 1983. 24.95 (ISBN 0-19-540418-1). Oxford U Pr.

Cribb, Larry. How You Can Make Twenty-Five Thousand Dollars a Year with Your Camera: No Matter Where You Live. LC 81-11589. (Illus.). 194p. 1981. 14.95 (ISBN 0-89879-059-X); pap. 9.95 (ISBN 0-89879-060-3). Writers Digest.

Cribben, Larry D. & Ungar, Irwin A. River Birch (Betula nigra L.) Communities of Southeastern Ohio. 1974. 2.00 (ISBN 0-86727-076-4). Ohio Bio Survey.

Cribbet, John E. & Johnson, Corwin W. Property, Cases & Materials On. 5th ed. LC 84-4137. (University Casebook Ser.). 1626p. 1984. text ed. 31.00 (ISBN 0-88277-171-X). Foundation Pr.

Cribbin, J. Leadership. 1982. 15.95 (ISBN 0-8144-5726-6). AMACOM.

Cribbin, James, jt. auth. see Hanan, Mack.

Cribbin, James J. Effective Managerial Leadership. (AMACOM Executive Books). 1978. pap. 4.95 (ISBN 0-8144-7504-3). AMACOM.

--Effective Managerial Leadership. LC 71-166554. pap. 43.00 (ISBN 0-317-19943-9, 2023564). Bks Demand UMI.

--Leadership: Strategies for Organizational Effectiveness. 304p. 1982. 15.95 (ISBN 0-8144-5726-6). AMACOM.

--Leadership: Your Competitive Edge. LC 81-12722. 304p. pap. 9.95 (ISBN 0-8144-7619-8). AMACOM.

Crichfield, Grant. Three Novels of Madame De Duras: Ourika, Edouard, Olivier. (De Proprietatibus Litterarum, Series Practica: No. 114). 67p. (Orig.). 1975. pap. text ed. 11.20x (ISBN 90-2793-316-2). Mouton.

Crichlow, Henry B. Modern Reservoir Engineering: A Simulation Approach. (Illus.). 1977. 43.95 (ISBN 0-13-597468-2). P-H.

Crichton, Alexander. An Inquiry into the Nature & Origin of Mental Derangement, 2 vols. in 1. LC 75-14763. (Language, Man & Society). Repr. of 1798 ed. 47.50 (ISBN 0-404-08212-2). AMS Pr.

Crichton, Anne. Health Policy Making: Fundamental Issues in the United States, Canada, Great Britain, Australia. LC 80-19194. (Illus.). 438p. 1981. text ed. 40.00 (ISBN 0-914904-44-2). Health Admin Pr.

Crichton, J. M., jt. auth. see Howells, W. W.

Crichton, Kyle S. Law & Order LTD: The Rousing Life of Elfego Baca of New Mexico. LC 73-14200. (The Mexican American Ser.). (Illus.). 258p. 1974. Repr. 19.00x (ISBN 0-405-05674-5). Ayer Co Pubs.

Crichton, M. Ian, ed. Proceedings of the Second International Symposium on Trichoptera. 1978. lib. bdg. 60.50 (ISBN 90-6193-548-2, Pub. by Junk Pubs Netherlands). Kluwer Academic.

Crichton, Michael. The Andromeda Strain. 304p. (gr. 9 up). 1981. pap. 3.95 (ISBN 0-440-10199-9). Dell.

--Andromeda Strain. 1969. 15.95 (ISBN 0-394-41525-6). Knopf.

--Congo. 1981. pap. 3.95 (ISBN 0-380-56176-X, 69682-7). Avon.

--Congo. (General Ser.). 1981. lib. bdg. 14.95 (ISBN 0-8161-3202-X, Large Print Bks). G K Hall.

--Congo. LC 80-7972. 352p. 1980. 10.95 (ISBN 0-394-51392-4). Knopf.

--Electronic Life. 256p. 1984. pap. 3.95 (ISBN 0-345-31739-4). Ballantine.

--Electronic Life: How to Think about Computers. LC 83-48022. 1983. 12.95 (ISBN 0-394-53406-9). Knopf.

--Five Patients. 224p. 1981. pap. 2.95 (ISBN 0-380-57364-4, 62919-4). Avon.

--The Great Train Robbery. 1975. 13.95 (ISBN 0-394-49401-6). Knopf.

--Jasper Johns. LC 77-78150. (Illus.). 1977. 45.00 (ISBN 0-8109-1161-2). Abrams.

--The Terminal Man. (YA) 1972. 13.50 (ISBN 0-394-44768-9). Knopf.

--The Terminal Man. 320p. 1982. pap. 2.95 (ISBN 0-380-56960-4, 68734-8). Avon.

Crichton, Ronald. Falla. LC 81-71303. (BBC Music Guides Ser.). 104p. (Orig.). 1983. pap. 5.95 (ISBN 0-295-95926-6). U of Wash Pr.

Crichton, Whitcomb. Practical Course in Modern Locksmithing. 222p. 1943. 16.95 (ISBN 0-911012-06-0). Nelson-Hall.

Crichton-Browne, James. Burns from a New Point of View. Repr. of 1937 ed. 9.50 (ISBN 0-8414-2412-8). Folcroft.

--Burns from a New Point of View. LC 74-103178. 1970. Repr. of 1937 ed. 19.00x (ISBN 0-8046-0815-6, Pub. by Kennikat). Assoc Faculty Pr.

--Victorian Jottings. (Victorian Age Ser). 1926. Repr. 15.00 (ISBN 0-8482-7585-3). Norwood Edns.

Crichton-Browne, James & Carlyle, Alexander. The Nemesis of Froude. 1973. Repr. of 1903 ed. 20.00 (ISBN 0-8274-1764-0). R West.

Crichton-Smith, I. Selected Poems. LC 74-135657. 1971. 12.95 (ISBN 0-8023-1160-1). Dufour.

Crichton-Stuart, John P., tr. see Coptic Church.

Crick, jt. auth. see Dupuy.

Crick, Bernard. The American Science of Politics: Its Origin & Conditions. LC 82-15829. xv, 252p. 1982. lib. bdg. 35.00x (ISBN 0-313-23696-8, CRAS). Greenwood.

--George Orwell: A Life. (Illus.). 1981. 17.95 (ISBN 0-316-16112-8, Pub. by Atlantic Monthly Pr). Little.

--George Orwell: Crick. (Illus.). 474p. 1982. pap. 8.95 (ISBN 0-14-005856-7). Penguin.

--In Defence of Politics. rev. ed. LC 72-86545. 1972. pap. 7.00x (ISBN 0-226-12065-1, P492, Phoen). U of Chicago Pr.

--In Defense of Politics. 2nd ed. LC 72-86545. 1973. 15.00x (ISBN 0-226-12064-3). U of Chicago Pr.

--In Defense of Politics. rev. ed. 256p. 1983. pap. 5.95 (ISBN 0-14-020655-8, Pelican). Penguin.

Crick, Bernard & Heater, Derek. Essays on Political Education. 202p. 1977. 28.00x (ISBN 0-905273-04-4, Pub. by Falmer Pr); pap. 14.00x (ISBN 0-905273-03-6, Pub. by Falmer Pr). Taylor & Francis.

Crick, Bernard, ed. Unemployment. 151p. 1981. pap. 5.95x (ISBN 0-416-32470-3, NO. 3539). Methuen Inc.

Crick, Bernard & Heater, Derek, eds. Political Realities. write for info. Longman.

Crick, Bernard, ed. see Machiavelli, Niccolo.

Crick, Bernard, jt. ed. see Robson, William A.

Crick, Bernard, ed. see Sharp, Ronald A.

Crick, Brian & Ferns, John, eds. George Whalley: Studies in Literature & the Humanities. 200p. Date not set. 27.50x (ISBN 0-7735-0535-0). McGill-Queens U Pr.

Crick, Francis. Life Itself. 1982. pap. 6.95 (ISBN 0-671-25563-0, Touchstone Bks). S&S.

--Of Molecules & Men. LC 66-26994. (Jesse & John Danz Lecture Ser.). 118p. 1967. pap. 5.95x (ISBN 0-295-97869-4, WP-26). U of Wash Pr.

Crick, Joe E. & Stolurow, Lawrence M. The Use of Computers in High Schools. LC 74-121200. 172p. 1965. 25.00 (ISBN 0-403-04492-8). Scholarly.

Crick, Michael. Militant. 200p. (Orig.). 1984. pap. 9.95 (ISBN 0-571-13256-1). Faber & Faber.

Crick, Paul A. Living Abroad & Sailing. 128p. 1981. 8.00 (ISBN 0-682-49808-4, Banner). Exposition Pr FL.

Crick, Ronald P., jt. auth. see Leychecker, Wolfgang.

Cricket Magazine Editors, jt. auth. see Leonard, Marcia.

Cricket Magazine Editors, jt. auth. see Leverich, Kathleen.

Cricket Magazine Editors, jt. auth. see Watson, Pauline.

Crickmay, Anthony. Dancers. LC 81-48551. (Illus.). 128p. 1982. 50.00 (ISBN 0-688-01239-6). Morrow.

Crickmay, Marie C. Help the Stroke Patient to Talk. (Illus.). 132p. 1977. pap. 11.75x (ISBN 0-398-03593-8). C C Thomas.

--Speech Therapy & the Bobath Approach to Cerebral Palsy. (Illus.). 192p. 1981. 22.75x (ISBN 0-398-00362-9). C C Thomas.

Crickmer, D. F. & Zegeer, D. A., eds. Elements of Practical Coal Mining. 2nd ed. LC 79-57346. (Illus.). 847p. 1981. 44.00x (ISBN 0-89520-270-0). Soc Mining Eng.

Criddle, Byron, jt. auth. see Bell, David S.

Criddle, W. J. & Ellis, G. P. Spectral & Chemical Characterization of Organic Compounds: A Laboratory Handbook. 2nd ed. LC 80-40497. 115p. 1980. 45.95x (ISBN 0-471-27813-0, Pub. by Wiley-Interscience); pap. 21.95 (ISBN 0-471-27812-2). Wiley.

Criden, Yosef & Gelb, Saadia. The Kibbutz Experience: Dialogue in Kfar Blum. LC 75-36487. 1976. pap. 5.50 (ISBN 0-8052-0511-X). Schocken.

Crider, A. Schizophrenia: A Biophysical Perspective. 224p. 1979. 29.95x (ISBN 0-89859-465-0). L Erlbaum Assocs.

Crider, Allen B., ed. Mass Market Publishing in America. 1982. lib. bdg. 36.50 (ISBN 0-8161-8590-5, Hall Reference). G K Hall.

Crider, Andrew B., et al. Psychology. 1983. text ed. 28.95x (ISBN 0-673-15316-9); study Guide 10.95 (ISBN 0-673-15337-1). Scott F.

--Psychology. 2nd ed. 1985. 28.95x (ISBN 0-673-18217-7). Scott F.

Crider, Bill, ed. see Computer Skill Builders Editors.

Crider, Charles C. & Kistler, Robert C. The Seventh-Day Adventist Family: An Empirical Study. 296p. 1979. pap. 3.95 (ISBN 0-943872-77-4). Andrews Univ Pr.

Crider, Janet. Word for Word: A Comparative Guide to Word Processing Software. 250p. (Orig.). 1984. pap. 16.95 (ISBN 0-88134-154-1, 154-1). Osborne-McGraw.

Crider, Janet & Wagner, Camen. CAI Guide to Courseware Languages. (Illus.). 288p. 1985. pap. cancelled (ISBN 0-88056-316-8). Dilithium Pr.

Crider, Virginia. Allegheny Gospel Trails. (Illus.). 1971. 7.50 (ISBN 0-87813-502-2). Christian Light.

--Answering the Cry. (Northland Ser.). 1976. pap. 2.50 (ISBN 0-87813-510-3). Christian Light.

--Cry of the Northland. (Northland Ser). 1973. pap. 2.50 (ISBN 0-87813-505-7). Christian Light.

--The Lost God. 1968. pap. 1.10 (ISBN 0-686-05590-X). Rod & Staff.

Cridisque, L. Videos. 1977. pap. 1.50 (ISBN 0-686-20611-8). Ghost Dance.

Cridland, Nancy C., jt. auth. see Wiltz, John E.

Criel, Geert, jt. auth. see Lutsenburg Maas, Jacob van.

Criep, Leo H. Allergy & Clinical Immunology: With Addenda. LC 76-14352. (Illus.). 672p. 1976. 99.50 (ISBN 0-8089-0823-5, 790942). Grune.

--Clinical Immunology & Allergy. 2nd ed. LC 68-20165. (Illus.). 976p. 1969. 115.00 (ISBN 0-8089-0105-2, 790940). Grune.

Crigelionis, B., ed. Stochastic Differential Systems; Filtering & Control: Proceedings. (Lecture Notes in Control & Information Sciences Ser.: Vol. 25). 362p. 1981. pap. 26.00 (ISBN 0-387-10498-4). Springer-Verlag.

Crighton, D. B., ed. Immunological Aspects of Reproduction in Mammals. (Nottingham Easter School Ser.: No. 38). 448p. 1984. text ed. 135.00 (ISBN 0-408-10865-7). Butterworth.

Crighton, Richard. The Million Dollar Lift. 288p. 1981. pap. 2.50 (ISBN 0-380-76604-3, 76604). Avon.

Crigorieff, R. D., jt. ed. see Alefeld, G.

Crihfield, Liza. Ko-Uta: Little Songs of the Geisha World. LC 78-66085. (Illus.). 1979. 8.50 (ISBN 0-8048-1292-6). C E Tuttle.

Crikshank, G. Grimm's Fairy Tales. (Illus.). (gr. 7 up). 1950. pap. 2.95 (ISBN 0-14-030052-X, Puffin). Penguin.

Crile, George. The Phenomena of Life: A Radio-Electric Interpretation. Rowland, Amy, ed. 377p. Repr. of 1936 ed. lib. bdg. 60.00 (ISBN 0-89984-026-4). Century Bookbindery.

--The Phenomena of Life: A Radio-Electric Interpretation. Rowland, Amy, ed. (Illus.). 379p. 1985. Repr. of 1936 ed. lib. bdg. 50.00 (ISBN 0-89987-193-3). Darby Bks.

Crile, George & Lower, William E. Anoci-Association. 1914. 25.00 (ISBN 0-8274-4195-9). R West.

Crile, George W. Bipolar Theory of Living Processes. 2nd ed. 1981. Repr. of 1955 ed. 18.95x (ISBN 0-686-76728-4). B Of A.

Crile, George W. & Rowland, Amy F. A Mechanistic View of War & Peace. 1978. Repr. of 1915 ed. lib. bdg. 20.00 (ISBN 0-8492-3845-5). R West.

Criley, J. Michael, jt. ed. see French, William J.

Crilley, Raymond E. & Burkholder, Charles E. Collecting Model Farm Toys of the World. LC 78-55487. (Illus.). 1984. pap. 17.95 (ISBN 0-89404-011-1). Aztex.

--International Directory of Model Farm Tractors. (Illus.). 356p. 1985. pap. 29.95 (ISBN 0-88740-030-2). Schiffer.

Crilly, Eileen & Morris, Stephanie. Get Ready, Set, Grow. LC 84-60318. 1984. pap. 8.95 (ISBN 0-8224-4337-6). Pitman Learning.

Crilly, Eugene R. Material & Process Applications: Land, Sea, Air, Space. (The Science of Advanced Materials & Process Engineering Ser.). 1981. 55.00 (ISBN 0-938994-18-2). Soc Adv Material.

Crilly, Howard M. The Night the Opera House Burned: A Tale of Three Cities. 208p. 1984. 8.95 (ISBN 0-8059-2937-1). Dorrance.

Crilly, Oliver, jt. auth. see Gallagher, Chuck.

Crim, John W. Compensating Non-Supervisory Professional Employees. Dufey, Gunther, ed. LC 78-24418. (Research for Business Decisions Ser.: No. 8). 134p. 1978. 39.95 (ISBN 0-8357-0964-7). UMI Res Pr.

Crim, Keith, tr. see Pannenberg, Wolfhart.

Crim, Keith, tr. see Westermann, Claus.

Crim, Keith, et al, eds. Abingdon Dictionary of Living Religions. LC 81-1465. 864p. 1981. 39.95 (ISBN 0-687-00409-8). Abingdon.

Crim, Keith R., jt. ed. see Buttrick, George A.

Crim, Keith R., tr. see Gese, Hartmut.

Crim, Keith R., tr. see Wolff, Hans W.

Crim, Keith R., et al, eds. The Interpreter's Dictionary of the Bible, Supplementary Volume. LC 62-9387. (Illus.). 1976. 22.95 (ISBN 0-687-19269-2). Abingdon.

Crim, Kerth, tr. see Pannenberg, Wolfhart.

Crim, Lottie R. Come Care with Me. LC 82-73369. (Illus.). 1983. pap. 4.50 (ISBN 0-8054-5431-4). Broadman.

Crime & Justice History Group. Criminal Justice History: An International Annual, Vol. I. (Illus.). 294p. 1980. 24.00 (ISBN 0-686-92362-6). Meckler Pub.

Crime & Justice History Group, ed. Criminal Justice History: An International Annual, Vol. 2. (Illus.). 210p. 1981. 24.00 (ISBN 0-686-98515-X). Meckler Pub.

Crimes, T. P. & Harper, J. C. Trace Fossils Two: Geological Journal Special Issue, Vol. 9. (Liverpool Geological Society & the Manchester Geological Association Ser.). 360p. 1977. 94.95 (ISBN 0-471-27756-8, Pub. by Wiley-Interscience). Wiley.

Criminal Justice Section Members. Criminal Appeals Primer. 27p. 1984. pap. 16.50. Amer Bar Assn.

--Limited Waiver of Attorney-Client Privilege & Work-Product Doctrine in Internal Corporate Investigations: An Emerging Corporate "Self Evaluative" Privilege. 56p. 1983. 2.00 (ISBN 0-317-16878-9). Amer Bar Assn.

Criminal Justice Training Commission Staff & Butterworth Staff. Strategies & Techniques in Criminal Defense. 2nd ed. 498p. 1983. looseleaf 95.00 (ISBN 0-409-20335-1). Butterworth Legal Pubs.

Criminal Law Reporter Editorial Staff. The Criminal Law Reporter Cumulative Digest & Index, 2 Vols. 3325p. 1982. Set. 150.00 (ISBN 0-317-10346-6). BNA.

Criminal Law Seminar (Maine State Bar Association) & University of Maine School of Law. Recent Developments in Criminal Law Materials for the Continuing Legal Education. LC 84-116496. Date not set. price not set. Maine St Bar.

Criminal Practice Institute & Carlin, Mark S. Trial Manual. LC 83-120887. Date not set. price not set. DC Bar Assn.

Criminale, William O., Jr., jt. auth. see Betchov, Robert.

Criminological Colloquium. Trends in Crime: Comparative Studies & Technical Problems: Reports Presented to the Fifth Criminological Colloquium. Council of Europe, Directorate of Legal affairs. LC 84-210031. (Collected Studies in Criminological Research: Vol. 20). 119p. Date not set. price not set (ISBN 9-287-10211-2). CE Crime Pubns.

Crimmins, C. E. Entre Chic: The Mega-Guide to Entrepreneurial Excellence. 150p. 1985. pap. 6.95 (ISBN 0-8144-7635-X). Amacom.

--Y. A. P. The Official Young Aspiring Professional's Fast-Track Handbook. LC 83-16072. (Illus.). 128p. (Orig.). 1983. lib. bdg. 12.90 (ISBN 0-89471-244-6); pap. 4.95 (ISBN 0-89471-243-8). Running Pr.

Crimmins, Eileen M., jt. auth. see Easterlin, Richard A.

Crimmins, James C. & Keil, Mary. Enterprise in the Nonprofit Sector. LC 83-60521. 141p. (Orig.). 1983. pap. 7.00 (ISBN 0-941182-03-7). Am Council Arts.

Crimmins, John J., jt. auth. see Hugard, Jean.

Crimmins, Sheila, jt. auth. see Souweine, Judith.

Crimmins, Timothy, jt. ed. see Shumsky, Neil L.

Crimp, Bryan. The Record Year-One. 541p. 1979. 55.00x (ISBN 0-7156-1364-2, Pub. by Duckworth England). Biblio Dist.

Crimp, Douglas, jt. auth. see Marincola, Paula.

Crimson, Fred. U. S. Military Wheeled Vehicles. (Illus.). 472p. 38.95 (ISBN 0-317-11556-1). Diamond Farm Bk.

Criner, E. Successful Cost Reduction for Engineers & Managers. 1983. 29.95 (ISBN 0-442-21579-7). Van Nos Reinhold.

Crinion, Gregory P., ed. Transnational Dispute Resolution, 1984. (Wisconsin International Law Journal Ser.). 300p. (Orig.). 1985. pap. text ed. 8.00 (ISBN 0-933431-02-3). U Wisc Law Madison.

Crinita, Joey. The Medium Touch: A New Approach to Mediumship. Horwege, Richard A., ed. LC 81-19592. (Orig.). 1982. pap. 6.95 (ISBN 0-89865-176-X). Donning Co.

Crinklaw, Frances & Frizzi, Richard J. Teaching Consonant Blends & Digraphs in Context. (Word Analysis Library Ser.). (Illus.). 1980. spiral bdg. 15.50x (ISBN 0-87628-958-8, C-9588-9); dup masters 17.50x (ISBN 0-87628-959-6, C-9596-2). Ctr Appl Res.

--Teaching Consonants in Context. (Word Analysis Library). (Illus.). 1980. spiral bdg. 15.50x (ISBN 0-87628-956-1, C-9561-6); dup masters 17.50x (ISBN 0-87628-965-0, C-9650-7). Ctr Appl Res.

--Teaching Vowels & Vowel Digraphs in Context. (Word Analysis Library Ser.). (Illus.). 1980. spiral bdg. 15.50x (ISBN 0-87628-966-9, C-9669-7); dup. masters 17.50x (ISBN 0-87628-963-4, C-9634-1). Ctr Appl Res.

Crinkley, Richmond. Walter Pater: Humanist. LC 70-119811. 200p. 1970. 18.00x (ISBN 0-8131-1221-4). U Pr of Ky.

Crinkley, Robert. Your Manufacturing Company: How to Start It, How to Manage It. LC 81-20801. (Illus.). 256p. 1982. 29.95 (ISBN 0-07-013680-7). McGraw.

Crinzi, Debbie. Principles of Discipleship. 102p. 1984. pap. text ed. 5.00 (ISBN 0-8309-0394-1). Herald Hse.

Cripe, Helen. Thomas Jefferson & Music. LC 73-81099. (Thomas Jefferson Memorial Foundation Series). (Illus.). viii, 157p. 1974. 7.50x (ISBN 0-8139-0504-4); pap. 3.95x (ISBN 0-8139-0547-8). U Pr of Va.

Cripe, Helen & Campbell, Diane. American Manuscripts, 1763-1815: An Index to Documents Described in Auction Records & Dealers' Catalogs. LC 77-2525. 1977. 110.00 (ISBN 0-8420-2122-1). Scholarly Res Inc.

Crippa, Erminio. Men in Black. 1955. 1.50 (ISBN 0-8198-0506-8). Dghtrs St Paul.

Crippen, Cynthia, jt. ed. see Reno, Edward A., Jr.

Crippen, Dan. Managing County Money: A Cash Flow Problem. 1975. write for info. U of SD Gov Res Bur.

Crippen, G. M. Distance Geometry & Conformational Calculations. LC 80-42044. (Chemometrics Research Studies). 58p. 1981. 34.95 (ISBN 0-471-27991-9, Pub. by Research Studies Pr). Wiley.

Crippen, John K. Successful Direct-Mail Methods. LC 84-46056. 348p. 1985. lib. bdg. 40.00 (ISBN 0-8240-6750-9). Garland Pub.

Crippen, Lee F. Simon Cameron: Ante Bellum Years. LC 76-168674. (American Scene Ser). 1972. Repr. of 1942 ed. lib. bdg. 39.50 (ISBN 0-306-70362-9). Da Capo.

Crippen, Raymond C. GC-LC, Instruments, Derivatives in Identifying Pollutants & Unknowns. (Illus.). 452p. 1983. 83.00 (ISBN 0-08-027185-5). Pergamon.

--The Waste of Money. LC 76-8794. 1977. 19.95 (ISBN 0-87949-079-9). Ashley Bks.

Crippen, Thomas G. Christmas & Christmas Lore. LC 69-16067. (Illus.). 256p. 1972. Repr. of 1923 ed. 48.00x (ISBN 0-8103-3029-6). Gale.

--Christmas & Christmas Lore. 1976. lib. bdg. 59.95 (ISBN 0-8490-1617-7). Gordon Pr.

Crippen, Waldo. The Kansas Pacific Railroad: A Cross Section of an Age of Railroad Building. Bruchey, Stuart, ed. LC 80-1278. (Railroads Ser.). 1981. lib. bdg. 12.00x (ISBN 0-405-13753-2). Ayer Co Pubs.

--The Kansas Pacific Railroad: A Cross Section of an Age of Railroad Building. 12.00 (ISBN 0-405-13753-2). Ayer Co Pubs.

Cripps, Ann, ed. Countryman Rescuing the Past. (Countryman Ser.). (Illus.). 1975. 5.50 (ISBN 0-7153-6071-X). David & Charles.

Cripps, Arthur S. Africa for Africans. LC 79-98716. (Illus.). Repr. of 1927 ed. 17.50x (ISBN 0-8371-2764-5, CRB&, Pub. by Negro U Pr). Greenwood.

Cripps, E. L. Regional Science: New Concepts & Old Problems. (London Papers in Regional Science). 210p. 1980. pap. text ed. 15.50x (ISBN 0-85086-048-2, ?NO. 2958, Pub. by Pion England). Methuen Inc.

Cripps, E. L., ed. Space-Time Concepts in Urban & Regional Models. (London Papers in Regional Science). 238p. 1974. pap. 15.50x (ISBN 0-85086-044-X, NO.2955, Pub. by Pion England). Methuen Inc.

Cripps, Elizabeth A., ed. see Kingsley, Charles.

Cripps, Francis, jt. auth. see Godley, Wynne.

Cripps, Louise L. Human Rights in a United States Colony. 192p. 1982. 19.95 (ISBN 0-87073-588-8); pap. 9.95 (ISBN 0-87073-589-6). Schenkman Bks Inc.

--The Spanish Caribbean: From Columbus to Castro. 1979. lib. bdg. 21.00 (ISBN 0-8161-9003-8, Univ Bks). G K Hall.

Cripps, Martin. An Introduction to Computer Hardware. 1978. text ed. 24.95 (ISBN 0-316-16114-4). Little.

Cripps, Richard S. Amos. 1981. lib. bdg. 13.50 (ISBN 0-86524-081-7, 3001). Klock & Klock.

Cripps, S. Peridontal Disease: Recognition, Interception & Perception. 1984. text ed. 78.00 (ISBN 0-86715-118-8). Quint Pub Co.

Cripps, T. F. & Tarling, R. J. Growth in Advanced Captialist Economies, 1950-1970. LC 73-84317. (University of Cambridge, Dept. of Applied Economics, Occasional Paper: 40). pap. 20.00 (ISBN 0-317-26016-2, 2024429). Bks Demand UMI.

Cripps, Thomas. Black Film As Genre. LC 77-23630. (Midland Bks.: No. 227). (Illus.). 192p. 1978. 12.50x (ISBN 0-253-37502-9). Ind U Pr.
--Black Film As Genre. LC 77-23630. pap. 48.00 (ISBN 0-317-27934-3, 2056029). Bks Demand UMI.
--Slow Fade to Black: The Negro in American Film, 1900-1942. (Illus.). 1977. pap. 9.95 (ISBN 0-19-502130-4, 484, GB). Oxford U Pr.
Cripps, Thomas & Balio, Tino, eds. The Green Pastures. LC 79-3959. (Wisconsin-Warner Bros. Screenplay Ser.). (Illus.). 1979. 17.50x (ISBN 0-299-07920-1); pap. 6.95 (ISBN 0-299-07924-4). U of Wis Pr.
Cripps, W. Old French Silver Marks. LC 73-78444. (Illus.). 1972. Repr. of 1880 ed. 10.00 (ISBN 0-912728-01-9). Newbury Bks.
Cripps, Yvonne M. Controlling Technology: Genetic Engineering & the Law. LC 80-13754. 170p. 1980. 32.95x (ISBN 0-03-056806-4). Praeger.
Cripps-Day, Francis H. The History of Tournament in England & in France. LC 78-63490. (Illus.). 264p. Repr. of 1918 ed. 36.50 (ISBN 0-404-17138-9). AMS Pr.
Cripwell, Kenneth. Language. Yapp, Malcolm, et al, eds. (World History Ser.). (Illus.). (gr. 10). 1980. lib. bdg. 6.95 (ISBN 0-89908-146-0); pap. text ed. 2.45 (ISBN 0-89908-121-5). Greenhaven.
Criqui, Michael J., jt. ed. see Kaplan, Robert M.
Crisafulli, Alessandro S., ed. Linguistic & Literary Studies in Honor of Helmut A. Hatzfeld. 410p. 1964. 26.95x (ISBN 0-8132-0333-3). Cath U Pr.
Crisci, Elizabeth. Ninety-Nine Fun Ideas for Teaching Bible Verses. (Illus.). 112p. 1985. pap. 3.95 (ISBN 0-87239-869-2, 3072). Standard Pub.
--What Do You Do with Joe? Problem Pupils & Tactful Teachers. LC 81-50236. (Illus.). 64p. (Orig.). 1981. pap. 2.95 (ISBN 0-87239-414-X, 3650). Standard Pub.
Criscoe, Betty L. & Gee, Thomas C. Content Reading: A Diagnostic Prescriptive Approach. (Illus.). 384p. 1984. 26.95 (ISBN 0-13-171389-2). P-H.
Criscuolo, Nicholas P. Look It up! One Hundred & One Dictionary Activities to Develop Word Skills. LC 78-75217. 1979. pap. 5.50 (ISBN 0-8224-4330-9). Pitman Learning.
--One Hundred Individualized Activities for Reading. 1974. pap. 4.95 (ISBN 0-8224-5065-8). Pitman Learning.
--One Hundred Twenty-Five Motivators for Reading. LC 77-83523. 1978. pap. 5.25 (ISBN 0-8224-5069-0). Pitman Learning.
Crisi, J. Bruce. When the Family Hurts. 1982. pap. 5.95 (ISBN 0-8423-7996-7). Tyndale.
Crisler, Janet, jt. auth. see Kinard, Malvina.
Crisler, Lois. Arctic Wild. LC 73-4073. (Illus.). 320p. (Memorial ed.). (YA) 1973. 12.45i (ISBN 0-06-010917-3, HarpT). Har-Row.
Crisman, Ruth. The Mississippi. (First Books). (Illus.). 72p. 1984. lib. bdg. 8.90 (ISBN 0-531-04826-8). Watts.
Crismon, Major F. U. S. Military Wheeled Vehicles. Dammann, George H., ed. LC 82-73699. (Automotive Ser.). 472p. 1983. 34.95 (ISBN 0-912612-21-5). Crestline.
Crisp, A. H. Anorexia Nervosa: Let Me Be. LC 78-42826. 1982. 18.50 (ISBN 0-8089-1303-4, 790941). Grune.
Crisp, Arthur H. & Stonehill, Edward. Sleep, Nutrition & Mood. LC 75-16121. 173p. 1976. 48.95 (ISBN 0-471-18688-0, Pub. by Wiley-Interscience). Wiley.
Crisp, Carl E., jt. auth. see Crafts, Alden S.
Crisp, Clement & Clarke, Mary. Ballet Goer's Guide. LC 81-47496. (Illus.). 352p. 1981. 22.50 (ISBN 0-394-51307-X). Knopf.
Crisp, Clement, jt. auth. see Clarke, Mary.
Crisp, D. J., ed. see European Marine Biology Symposium Staff.
Crisp, Frank. Mediaeval Gardens. LC 67-4273. (Illus.). 1979. lib. bdg. 75.00 (ISBN 0-87817-007-3). Hacker.
Crisp, H. & Rudduck, L. The Mothering Years: The Story of the Canberra Mothercraft Society 1926-79. (Illus.). 112p. (Orig.). 1980. pap. text ed. 4.95 (ISBN 0-9595400-0-8, 0584). Australia N U P.
Crisp, Jeff. The Story of an African Working Class: Ghanaian Miners' Struggles 1870-1980. (Africa Ser.). (Illus.). 218p. 1984. 26.25x (ISBN 0-86232-378-9, Pub. by Zed Pr England); pap. 10.25 (ISBN 0-86232-150-6, Pub. by Zed Pr England). Biblio Dist.
Crisp, Jerry, tr. see Vesaas, Tarjei.
Crisp, N. J. The Brink. 1983. pap. 3.50 (ISBN 0-671-45605-9). PB.
--Yesterday's Gone. LC 83-47879. 324p. 1983. 16.95 (ISBN 0-670-79389-2). Viking.
Crisp, Quentin. How to Become a Virgin. 192p. 1982. pap. 6.95 (ISBN 0-312-39544-2). St Martin.
--The Naked Civil Servant. 1983. pap. 6.95 (ISBN 0-452-25413-2, 25413, Plume). NAL.
Crisp, Quentin & Kettelhack, Guy. The Wit & Wisdom of Quentin Crisp. LC 84-47617. 120p. 1984. pap. 8.61i (ISBN 0-06-091178-6, CN 1178, CN). Har-Row.
Crisp, S., jt. auth. see Wilson, A. D.
Crisp, Tony. Do You Dream: How to Gain Insight into Your Dreams. 1972. pap. 9.95 (ISBN 0-525-47326-2, 0966-290). Dutton.
Crisp, William. Spytrap. 200p. 1983. 12.45 (ISBN 0-394-52971-5). Pantheon.
Crisp, Wynnlee. Development & Use of the Outdoor Classroom: An Annotated Bibliography. LC 75-15537. 145p. 1975. 16.50 (ISBN 0-8108-0831-5). Scarecrow.
Crispen, R. G. Cancer: Etiology & Prevention. 448p. 1983. 77.75 (ISBN 0-444-00785-7, Biomedical Pr). Elsevier.
Crispen, R. G., ed. Neoplasm Immunity. (Developments in Cancer Research Ser.: Vol. 3). 572p. 1980. 88.75 (ISBN 0-444-00433-5, Biomedical Pr). Elsevier.
--Tumor Progression. (Developments in Cancer Research Ser.: Vol. 2). 388p. 1980. 65.00 (ISBN 0-444-80133-2, Biomedical Pr). Elsevier.
Crispen, Ray, ed. see Symposium, Chicago, 1973.
Crispen, Ray G., ed. Cancer Immunology: Experimental & Clinical. new ed. LC 79-2910. (Illus.). 1979. lib. bdg. 42.00 (ISBN 0-89500-016-4). Sci Pr.
Crispen, Ray G., ed. see Annual Chicago Symposium on Neoplasm Immunity, 2nd, Chicago, 1974.
Crispen, Ray G., ed. see Annual Chicago Symposium, 4th Chicago, 1975.
Crispens, Charles G., Jr. Handbook on the Laboratory Mouse. 278p. 1975. pap. 14.75x spiral (ISBN 0-398-03403-6). C C Thomas.
--The Vertebrates: Their Forms & Functions. (Illus.). 224p. 1978. 23.50x (ISBN 0-398-03721-3). C C Thomas.
Crispin, A. C. Sylvester. 256p. (Orig.). 1985. pap. 2.95 (ISBN 0-8125-8173-3). Tor Bks.
--V. 288p. (Orig.). 1984. pap. 2.95 (ISBN 0-523-42237-7). Pinnacle Bks.
--V. 1984. lib. bdg. 13.95 (ISBN 0-8398-2840-3, Gregg). G K Hall.
--Yesterday's Son. (Star Trek Ser.). (Orig.). 1983. pap. 2.95 (ISBN 0-671-47315-8, Timescape). PB.
--Yesterday's Son. (Star Trek Ser.). 1984. lib. bdg. 10.95 (ISBN 0-8398-2830-6, Gregg). G K Hall.
Crispin, A. C. & Weinstein, Howard. V: East Coast Crisis. 1984. lib. bdg. 12.95 (ISBN 0-8398-2841-1, Gregg). G K Hall.
Crispin, A. C., jt. auth. see Norton, Andre.
Crispin, A. C., jt. auth. see Weinstein, Howard.
Crispin, Edmund. Beware of the Trains. 1981. pap. 3.95 (ISBN 0-14-005834-6). Penguin.
--Buried for Pleasure. 191p. Repr. of 1948 ed. lib. bdg. 13.95x (ISBN 0-89190-691-6, Pub. by River City Pr). Amereon Ltd.
--Buried for Pleasure. Barzum, Jacques & Taylor, Wendell H., eds. LC 75-44967. (Crime Fiction Ser). 1976. Repr. of 1949 ed. lib. bdg. 21.00 (ISBN 0-8240-2362-5). Garland Pub.
--Buried for Pleasure. LC 49-8208. 1980. pap. 3.37i (ISBN 0-06-080506-4, P 506, PL). Har-Row.
--The Case of the Gilded Fly. 1980. pap. 2.50 (ISBN 0-380-50187-2, 63552-6). Avon.
--Fen Country. 176p. 1980. 9.95 (ISBN 0-8027-5424-4). Walker & Co.
--Fen Country. 11.95 (ISBN 0-89190-694-0, Pub. by Am Repr). Amereon Ltd.
--Fen Country: Twenty-Six Stories. (Crime Ser.). 160p. 1981. pap. 3.95 (ISBN 0-14-005946-6). Penguin.
--Frequent Hearses. 1982. pap. 2.95 (ISBN 0-14-006325-0). Penguin.
--The Glimpses of the Moon. 1979. pap. 3.50 (ISBN 0-380-45062-3, 69021-7). Avon.
--Glimpses of the Moon. 1978. 8.95 (ISBN 0-8027-5391-4). Walker & Co.
--Glimpses of the Moon. 16.95 (ISBN 0-89190-107-8, Pub. by Am Repr). Amereon Ltd.
--Holy Disorders. (General Ser.). 1980. lib. bdg. 13.95 (ISBN 0-8161-3111-2, Large Print Bks). G K Hall.
--The Long Divorce. (Penguin Crime Monthly Ser.). 256p. 1981. pap. 3.50 (ISBN 0-14-001304-0). Penguin.
--Love Lies Bleeding. (Crime Monthly Ser.). 1982. pap. 3.50 (ISBN 0-14-000974-4). Penguin.
--Love Lies Bleeding. LC 81-511701. 1981. 9.95 (ISBN 0-8027-5444-9). Walker & Co.
--The Moving Toy Shop. 13.95 (ISBN 0-8488-0104-0, Pub. by Amereon Hse). Amereon Ltd.
--The Moving Toyship. LC 80-54479. 1981. 9.95 (ISBN 0-8027-5434-1). Walker & Co.
--The Moving Toyshop. 1977. pap. 3.50 (ISBN 0-14-001315-6). Penguin.
--Swan Song. 192p. Repr. of 1947 ed. lib. bdg. 13.95 (ISBN 0-89190-692-4, Pub. by River City Pr). Amereon Ltd.
--Swan Song. 192p. 1981. pap. 2.95 (ISBN 0-380-55145-4, 70020). Avon.
--Swan Song. 208p. 1980. 9.95 (ISBN 0-8027-5420-1). Walker & Co.
Crispin, Elmund. Love Lies Bleeding. 13.95 (ISBN 0-89190-693-2, Pub. by Am Repr). Amereon Ltd.
Crispin, J. W., Jr. & Siegel, K. M., eds. Methods of Radar Cross Section Analysis. (Electrical Science Ser). 1968. 90.00 (ISBN 0-12-197750-1). Acad Pr.
Crispin, John & Crispin, Ruth. Progress in Spanish. 2nd ed. LC 77-18684. 1978. text ed. 19.00 (ISBN 0-394-33399-3, RanC); wkbk. 6.95 (ISBN 0-394-33400-0). Random.
Crispin, Ruth, jt. auth. see Crispin, John.
Crispino, James A. The Assimilation of Ethnic Groups: The Italian Case. LC 80-69267. 205p. 1980. text ed. 14.95x (ISBN 0-913256-39-0). Ctr Migration.
Crispo, Andrew J. Hubert Long-Selected Works, Nineteen Fifty-Eight to Nineteen Eighty. (Illus.). 60p. (Orig.). 1980. pap. 10.00 (ISBN 0-937014-00-1). Crispo Gallery.
Crispo, Dorothy. The Story of Our Fruits & Vegetables. pap. 4.95 (ISBN 0-8159-6826-4). Devin.
Crispo, John H. G. The Role of International Unionism in Canada. (Illus.). 59p. 1967. 1.50 (ISBN 0-88806-085-8). Inst C D Howe.
Criss, Wayne E., jt. ed. see Morris, Harold P.
Criss, Wayne E., jt. ed. see Sharma, Rameshwar K.
Crissey, Clair M. Layman's Bible Book Commentary: Matthew, Vol. 15. LC 79-56691. 1981. 5.75 (ISBN 0-8054-1185-2). Broadman.
Crissey, Harrington E., Jr. Athletes Away. (Illus.). 75p. (Orig.). 1984. pap. 4.00 (ISBN 0-9608878-3-0). H E Crissey.
--Teenagers, Graybeards & 4-F's. Incl. Vol. 1. The National League. (Illus.). 150p. 1981; Vol. 2. The American League. (Illus.). 179p. 1982. pap. 11.00 (ISBN 0-9608878-1-4). H E Crissey.
Crissey, John T. & Parish, Lawrence C. The Dermatology & Syphilology of the Nineteenth Century. LC 81-1954. 488p. 1981. 59.00x (ISBN 0-03-059459-6). Praeger.
Crissey, John T., jt. auth. see Shelley, Walter B.
Crissman, Jack K., jt. auth. see Lenox, Ronald S.
Crissman, Randy D., jt. ed. see Caldwell, Stan R.
Crissman, Susan & Weintraut, Steven. Collegiate Guide to the Macintosh. trade ed. (Micropower Ser.). 208p. 1985. pap. cancelled (ISBN 0-697-00740-5). Wm C Brown.
Crissy, W. J., et al. Selling: The Personal Force in Marketing. LC 76-45848. (Marketing Ser.). 491p. 1977. text ed. 37.50 (ISBN 0-471-18757-7). Wiley.
Crissy, William J., et al. Effective Selling: A Short Course for Professionals. LC 76-45818. 338p. 1977. 24.95 (ISBN 0-471-01924-0). Krieger.
Crist, jt. auth. see Krause.
Crist, Ed, jt. auth. see Krause, John.
Crist, Evamae B. Take This House. (Illus.). 129p. 1977. pap. 2.25 (ISBN 0-8361-1817-0). Herald Pr.
Crist, Judith. Take Twenty-Two: Moviemakers on Moviemaking. LC 83-47934. 496p. 1984. 25.00 (ISBN 0-670-49185-3). Viking.
Crist, Larry, et al, trs. see Greimas, A. J. & Courtes, J.
Crist, Linda L., ed. see Davis, Jefferson.
Crist, Lyle M. Runaways. (Illus.). 1976. pap. text ed. 3.00 (ISBN 0-914720-06-6). Pale Horse.
Crist, Lynda L. & Seaton Dix, Mary, eds. The Papers of Jefferson Davis: Eighteen Fifty-Three to Eighteen Fifty-Five, Vol. 5. (Illus.). 592p. 1985. text ed. 37.50 (ISBN 0-8071-1240-2). La State U Pr.
Crist, Meredith S. & Laffer, Arthur, eds. Future American Energy Policy. LC 80-8992. 176p. 1982. 24.00x (ISBN 0-669-04489-X). Lexington Bks.
Crist, Nola P. Mother Cee. 1985. 8.95 (ISBN 0-533-06588-7). Vantage.
Crist, Patricia A. Perspectives in Practice: Issues in Clinical Education. LC 85-61756. (Current Practice Ser.). 124p. 1985. pap. text ed. 14.50 (ISBN 0-943432-51-0). Slack Inc.
Crist, Raymond E., jt. ed. see Hopkins, Edward A.
Crist, Raymond F., jt. auth. see Burrill, Harry.
Crist, Vonnie, jt. ed. see Keenan, Jean.
Cristel, Francine. Skipping a Grade Can Be Fun. 1984. 5.00 (ISBN 0-89824-037-9). Trillium Pr.
Cristenson, Larry. The Renewed Mind. LC 74-12770. 144p. (Orig.). 1974. pap. 4.95 (ISBN 0-87123-479-3, 210479). Bethany Hse.
Cristescu, Aurelia & United Nations, Sub-Commission on Prevention of Discrimination & Protection of Minorities. The Right to Self-Determination: Historical & Current Development on the Basis of United Nations Instruments. LC 82-101999. (Illus.). iiii, 125p. Date not set. price not set. UN.
Cristescu, Cornelia & Klepczynski, W. J., eds. Asteroids, Comets, Meteoric Matter: Proceedings. (Illus.). 333p. 1975. text ed. 60.00x (ISBN 0-87936-008-9). Scholium Intl.
Cristescu, R. Ordered Vector Spaces & Linear Operations. 1976. 42.00 (ISBN 0-9961002-5-3, Pub. by Abacus England). Heyden.
Cristescu, Romulus & Marinescu, Gheorgha. Applications of the Theory of Distributions. Teleman, Silviu, tr. from Romanian. LC 72-9080. pap. 56.80 (ISBN 0-317-09168-9, 2016146). Bks Demand UMI.
Cristiani, Leon. A Cross for Napoleon. 1980. 4.00 (ISBN 0-8198-1404-0); pap. 2.00 (ISBN 0-8198-1405-9). Dghtrs St Paul.
--Evidence of Satan in the Modern World. Rowland, Cynthia, tr. from Fr. (Eng.). 1977. pap. 5.50 (ISBN 0-89555-032-6). TAN Bks Pubs.
--Saint Bernadette. LC 65-15727. (Illus.). 181p. 1981. pap. 3.95 (ISBN 0-8189-0421-6). Alba.
--St. Bernard of Clairvaux. 1977. 3.95 (ISBN 0-8198-0463-0); pap. 2.95 (ISBN 0-8198-0464-9). Dghtrs St Paul.
--St. Joan of Arc, Virgin-Soldier. 1977. 3.95 (ISBN 0-8198-0465-7); pap. 2.95 (ISBN 0-8198-0466-5). Dghtrs St Paul.
--St. Margaret Mary Alacoque. 1976. 5.00 (ISBN 0-8198-0456-8). Dghtrs St Paul.
Cristiani, Theresa S., jt. auth. see George, Rickey L.
Cristiani, Therese S., jt. auth. see George, Rickey L.
Cristini, Ermanno & Puricelli, Luigi. Cristini-Puricelli Nature Set. Saunders, Robert, ed. (Illus.). (ps up). 1985. 12.95 (ISBN 0-88708-010-3, Pub. by Picture Bk Studio USA). Neugebauer Pr.
--In My Garden. Orig. Title: Falter, Blumen, Tierre und Ich. (Illus.). 28p. 9.95 (ISBN 0-907234-05-4, Pub. by Picture Bk Studio USA). Neugebauer Pr.
--In My Garden. Saunders, Robert, ed. LC 85-9402. (Illus.). 28p. (ps up). 1985. pap. 4.50 (ISBN 0-88708-007-3, Pub. by Picture Bk Studio USA). Neugebauer Pr.
--In the Pond. LC 84-972. (Illus.). 28p. 1984. 9.95 (ISBN 0-907234-43-7, Pub. by Picture Bk Studio USA). Neugebauer Pr.
--In the Pond. Saunders, Robert, ed. (Illus.). 28p. (ps up). 1985. pap. 4.50 (ISBN 0-88708-009-X, Pub. by Picture Bk Studio USA). Neugebauer Pr.
--In the Woods. Saunders, Robert, ed. (Illus.). 28p. (ps up). 1985. pap. 4.50 (ISBN 0-88708-008-1, Pub. by Picture Bk Studio USA). Neugebauer Pr.
Cristini, Ermanno & Puricelli, Luigi, illus. In the Woods. LC 83-8153. (Illus.). 28p. (ps). 1983. 9.95 (ISBN 0-907234-31-3, Pub. by Picture Bk Studio USA). Neugebauer Pr.
Cristofalo, V. J., jt. auth. see Holeckova, E.
Cristofalo, V. J. & Holeckova, E., eds. Cell Impairment in Aging & Development. LC 75-1310. (Advances in Experimental Medicine & Biology Ser.: Vol. 53). 572p. 1975. 72.50x (ISBN 0-306-39053-1, Plenum Pr). Plenum Pub.
Cristofalo, V. J., et al, eds. Explorations in Aging. LC 75-20442. (Advances in Experimental Medicine & Biology Ser.: Vol. 61). 316p. 1975. 39.50x (ISBN 0-306-39061-2, Plenum Pr). Plenum Pub.
Cristofalo, Vincent J., et al. Altered Endocrine Status During Aging. LC 84-7867. (Modern Aging Research Ser.: Vol. 6). 276p. 1984. 44.00 (ISBN 0-8451-2306-8). A R Liss.
Cristofar, Leo, jt. ed. see Dorfman, Wilfred.
Cristofaro, Cris & Cotler, Joanna. The Rotating Spaghetti Fork & Other Items You Can't Live Without. (Illus.). 80p. (Orig.). 1985. pap. 4.95 (ISBN 0-399-51127-X, Perigee). Putnam Pub Group.
Cristofer, Michael. The Shadow Box. LC 77-21670. 1977. 8.95 (ISBN 0-910482-90-X). Drama Bk.
Cristoforo, R. J. The Complete Book of Stationary Power Tool Techniques. (Popular Science Ser.). (Illus.). 480p. 1985. 31.95 (ISBN 0-317-31387-8). Rodale Pr Inc.
Cristoforo, R. J. De see De Cristoforo, R. J.
Cristol, A. Solid State Video Cameras. (EPO Applied Technology Ser.: Vol. 7). 250p. 1986. 62.50 (ISBN 0-08-030579-2). Pergamon.
Cristos, Serena, et al. Medicine, Psychology & Science in Automobile Driving. LC 83-45544. 140p. 1984. 29.95 (ISBN 0-88164-110-3); pap. 21.95 (ISBN 0-88164-111-1). ABBE Pubs Assn.
Cristy, Ann. Enthralled. (Second Chance at Love Ser.: No. 103). 1983. pap. 1.75 (ISBN 0-515-06867-5). Jove Pubns.
--Homecoming. (To Have & to Hold Ser.: No. 24). 192p. 1984. pap. 1.95 (ISBN 0-515-07826-3). Jove Pubns.
--No Gentle Possession. 192p. 1984. pap. 1.95 (ISBN 0-515-07581-7). Jove Pubns.
--Torn Asunder. (Second Chance at Love Ser.: No. 60). 192p. 1982. pap. 1.75 (ISBN 0-515-06660-5). Jove Pubns.
--Tread Softly, No. 3. 192p. 1983. pap. 1.95 (ISBN 0-515-06930-2). Jove Pubns.
Criswell, Ann. Dining In-Houston, Vol. II. (Dining in Ser.). 200p. 1980. pap. 7.95 (ISBN 0-89716-065-7). Peanut Butter.
Criswell, Carl S. Autumn Totem: A Book of Lyrics. LC 76-1915. 80p. 1976. 5.00 (ISBN 0-8233-0249-0). Golden Quill.
--The Mountains of the Frontier. 1978. 5.00 (ISBN 0-8233-0288-1). Golden Quill.
--Shadow & Sheen. 1983. 5.50 (ISBN 0-8233-0360-8). Golden Quill.
--The Still House of Time. 1980. 5.50 (ISBN 0-8233-0325-X). Golden Quill.
Criswell, Charles. Nobody Knows What the Stork Will Bring. 1958. 7.95 (ISBN 0-8392-1076-0). Astor-Honor.
Criswell, Cleta. Group Feeding: Quality Recipes & Diet Modification. LC 83-61165. 1983. 19.50x (ISBN 0-89313-038-9). G F Stickley Co.
Criswell, E. H; see King, A. T.
Criswell, Joan, et al, eds. Mathematical Methods in Small Group Processes. 1962. 27.50x (ISBN 0-8047-0116-4). Stanford U Pr.
Criswell, John W. Planned Maintenance for Productivity & Energy Conservation. (Illus.). 250p. 1983. text ed. 36.00 (ISBN 0-915586-71-1). Fairmont Pr.
Criswell, Robert. Uncle Tom's Cabin Contrasted with Buckingham Hall, the Planter's Home. LC 72-950. Repr. of 1852 ed. 15.00 (ISBN 0-404-00254-4). AMS Pr.
Criswell, Susie G. Nature with Art: Classroom & Outdoor Art Activities with Natural History. (Illus.). 160p. 1985. 17.95 (ISBN 0-13-610312-X); pap. 9.95 (ISBN 0-13-610304-9). P-H.

Criswell, W. A. Abiding Hope. 320p. 1981. 10.95 (ISBN 0-310-43840-3). Zondervan.
--Acts: An Exposition. 948p. 1983. Repr. 19.95 (ISBN 0-310-44150-1). Zondervan.
--The Baptism, Filling & Gifts of the Holy Spirit. 192p. 1973. pap. 4.95 (ISBN 0-310-22751-8). Zondervan.
--Criswell's Guidebook for Pastors. LC 79-7735. 1980. 12.95 (ISBN 0-8054-2536-5). Broadman.
--Ephesians: An Exposition. 308p. 1981. pap. 6.95 (ISBN 0-310-22781-X). Zondervan.
--Exposition of Galatians. 160p. 1980. pap. 5.95 (ISBN 0-310-22791-7). Zondervan.
--Expository Sermons on Revelation, 5 Vols. in 1. 1961-66. 24.95 (ISBN 0-310-22840-9). Zondervan.
--Expository Sermons on the Book of Daniel. 651p. 16.95 (ISBN 0-310-22800-X, Pub. by Minister Res Lib). Zondervan.
--Great Doctrines of the Bible, Vol. 1. 144p. 1982. 7.95 (ISBN 0-310-43850-0). Zondervan.
--Great Doctrines of the Bible, Vols. 1, 2, 3, & 4. 192p. 1982. Repr. 33.80 (ISBN 0-310-43868-3). Zondervan.
--Great Doctrines of the Bible, Vol. 2. 192p. 1982. 9.95 (ISBN 0-310-43860-8). Zondervan.
--Great Doctrines of the Bible, Vol. 5. 144p. 1985. 9.95 (ISBN 0-310-43930-2, Pub. by Minister Res Lib). Zondervan.
--Great Doctrines of the Bible: Ecclesiology. (Vol. 3). 128p. 1983. 8.95 (ISBN 0-310-43900-0). Zondervan.
--Great Doctrines of the Bible, Vol. 4: Pneumatology. 112p. 1984. 7.95 (ISBN 0-310-43910-8, 11662, Pub. by Minister Res Lib). Zondervan.
--Isaiah: An Exposition. (Expository Sermons of Dr. Criswell Ser.). 320p. 1982. pap. 8.95 (ISBN 0-310-22871-9). Zondervan.
--What a Savior! LC 77-82399. 1978. 7.50 (ISBN 0-8054-5155-2). Broadman.
--What to Do until Jesus Comes Back. LC 75-8327. 154p. 1976. 4.95 (ISBN 0-8054-5555-8). Broadman.
--Why I Preach That the Bible Is Literally True. LC 69-13142. 1969. pap. 3.95 (ISBN 0-8054-5536-1). Broadman.
--With a Bible in My Hand. LC 78-69708. 1978. 8.50 (ISBN 0-8054-1520-3). Broadman.
Critchell, Laurence. Four Stars of Hell. (Airborne Ser.: No. 13). (Illus.). 368p. 1982. Repr. of 1947 ed. 18.95 (ISBN 0-89839-059-1). Battery Pr.
Critcher, Chas, jt. auth. see Clarke, John.
Critcher, Harold & Critcher, June, eds. Why We Are Happily Married. 1979. pap. 3.95 (ISBN 0-89265-054-0). Randall Hse.
Critcher, June, jt. ed. see Critcher, Harold.
Critchfield, Howard J. General Climatology. 4th ed. (Illus.). 464p. 1983. text ed. 33.95 (ISBN 0-13-349217-6). P-H.
Critchfield, Jim & Hopkins, Jerry. You Were Born on a Rotten Day. LC 67-20351. Orig. Title: Horoscope. (Illus.). 1969. pap. 2.50 (ISBN 0-8431-0071-0). Price Stern.
Critchfield, M., jt. auth. see Dwyer, T.
Critchfield, Margot & Dwyer, Thomas. Pocket Guide to Microsoft BASIC. (Micro Computer Ser.). 1983. pap. 6.95 (ISBN 0-201-10364-8). Addison-Wesley.
Critchfield, Margot, jt. auth. see Dwyer, Thomas.
Critchfield, Margot, jt. auth. see Dwyer, Thomas A.
Critchfield, Margot A., jt. auth. see Dwyer, Thomas A.
Critchfield, Richard. The Golden Bowl be Broken: Peasant Life in Four Cultures. LC 73-77855. pap. 80.00 (ISBN 0-317-27933-5, 2056030). Bks Demand UMI.
--Shahhat: An Egyptian. 1978. 19.95x (ISBN 0-8156-2202-3). Syracuse U Pr.
--Shahhat: An Egyptian. LC 78-11945. (Contemporary Issues in the Middle East Ser.). (Illus.). 264p. 1984. pap. text ed. 9.95x (ISBN 0-8156-0151-4). Syracuse U Pr.
--Villages. LC 80-1721. (Illus.). 408p. 1983. pap. 10.95 (ISBN 0-385-18375-5, Anch). Doubleday.
Critchley, Deanne L. & Mauring, Judith T., eds. The Psychiatric Mental Health Clinical Specialist: Theory, Research, & Practice. LC 84-19509. 600p. 1985. text ed. 26.95 (ISBN 0-471-87506-6, Pub. by Wiley Med). Wiley.
Critchley, Edmund. Speech Origins & Development. (Illus.). 152p. 1967. 14.75x (ISBN 0-398-00364-5). C C Thomas.
Critchley, Eileen A., jt. auth. see Critchley, Macdonald.
Critchley, J., jt. auth. see Cartwright, J.
Critchley, J. P., et al, eds. Heat-Resistant Polymers: Technologically Useful Materials. 448p. 1983. 65.00x (ISBN 0-306-41058-3, Plenum Pr). Plenum Pub.
Critchley, John. Feudalism. 1977. text ed. 22.50x (ISBN 0-04-909009-7); pap. text ed. 8.95x (ISBN 0-04-909010-0). Allen Unwin.
Critchley, Julian. The North Atlantic Alliance & the Soviet Union in the Nineteen Eighties. 210p. 1982. text ed. 30.50x (ISBN 0-333-29469-6, Pub. by Macmillan England). Humanities.
--Warning & Response. LC 78-8810. 144p. 1978. 19.50x (ISBN 0-8448-1362-1). Crane-Russak Co.
Critchley, Macdonald. The Citadel of the Senses. (Illus.). 375p. 1985. text ed. 35.00 (ISBN 0-88167-105-3). Raven.
--The Divine Banquet of the Brain. LC 78-24621. 279p. 1979. text ed. 25.50 (ISBN 0-89004-348-5). Raven.
--Language of Gesture. LC 72-191591. 1939. lib. bdg. 20.00 (ISBN 0-8414-2414-4). Folcroft.
--Language of Gesture. LC 74-122981. (Studies in Language, No. 41). 1970. Repr. of 1939 ed. lib. bdg. write for info. (ISBN 0-8383-1113-X). Haskell.
--Mirror Writing. LC 78-72793. Repr. of 1928 ed. 17.50 (ISBN 0-404-60857-4). AMS Pr.
Critchley, McDonald. Parietal Lobes. (Illus.). 1966. Repr. of 1953 ed. 52.95x (ISBN 0-02-843300-9). Hafner.
Critchley, Macdonald & Critchley, Eileen A. Dyslexia Defined. (Illus.). 172p. 1978. 17.00x (ISBN 0-398-03885-6). C C Thomas.
Critchley, Macdonald & Henson, R. A. Music & the Brain: Studies in the Neurology of Music. (Illus.). 476p. 1977. 37.50x (ISBN 0-398-03653-5). C C Thomas.
Critchley, Macdonald, ed. Butterworths Medical Dictionary. 2nd ed. LC 77-30154. 1978. 29.95 (ISBN 0-407-00061-5). Butterworth.
Critchlow, Arthur J. Introduction to Robotics. 550p. 1986. text ed. price not set lab manual & instrs.' manual (ISBN 0-02-325590-0). Macmillan.
Critchlow, Donald T. The Brookings Institution, Nineteen Sixteen to Nineteen Fifty-Two: Expertise & the Public Interest in a Democratic Society. LC 84-20699. (Illus.). 247p. 1985. 23.00 (ISBN 0-87580-103-X). N Ill U Pr.
Critchlow, Donald T., ed. Socialism in the Hearthland: The Midwestern Experience, Nineteen Hundred to Nineteen Twenty-Five. LC 85-40602. 224p. 1986. text ed. 21.95x (ISBN 0-268-01719-0, 85-17195, Dist. by Har-Row). U of Notre Dame Pr.
Critchlow, F. L., tr. see Desclot, Bernardo.
Critchlow, Keith. Islamic Patterns. LC 82-74543. (Illus.). 192p. 1984. pap. 12.95f (ISBN 0-500-27071-6). Thames Hudson.
--Order in Space: A Design Source Book. LC 73-120105. (Illus.). 1970. spiral bdg. 12.95 (ISBN 0-670-52830-7, Studio). Viking.
Crite, Allan R. Towards a Rediscovery of the Cultural Heritage of the United States. 23p. (Orig.). 1968. pap. 1.00 (ISBN 0-934552-24-X). Boston Athenaeum.
Crites, J. O. Vocational Psychology. 1969. text ed. 44.95 (ISBN 0-07-013780-3). McGraw.
Crites, John O. Career Counseling: Models, Methods & Materials. (Illus.). 240p. 1981. text ed. 24.95x (ISBN 0-07-013781-1). McGraw.
Crites, Laura, jt. ed. see Hepperle, Winifred L.
Crites, Ronald W., jt. auth. see Reed, Sherwood C.
Critescu, N. & Suliciu, I. Viscoplasticity. 1982. lib. bdg. 64.40 (ISBN 90-247-2592-5, Pub. by Martinus Nijhoff Netherlands). Kluwer Academic.
Critical Mass Energy Project. Tube Leaks: A Consumer's & Worker's Guide to Steam Generator Problems at Nuclear Power Plants. Udell, Richard, ed. (Illus.). 64p. 1982. saddle-stitched 3.50 (ISBN 0-937188-21-2). Pub Citizen Inc.
Critical Mass Energy Project Staff, jt. auth. see Clewett, John.
Critser, James R., Jr. Air Pollution Control: Internal Combustion Engines - Exhaust Treatment 1976. (Ser. 4IC-76). 1977. 115.00 (ISBN 0-914428-40-3). Lexington Data.
--Air Pollution Control-Processes, Equipment, Instrumentation. Incl. Indexes & Abstracts 1967-1971. 310.00 (ISBN 0-914428-08-X, 4-6771B). (Ser. 4-67713). Lexington Data Inc.
--Antioxidants & Stabilizers for Polymers. Incl. Indexes & Abstracts 1967-1971. 315.00 (ISBN 0-914428-06-3). (Ser. 3-6771B). 1972. Lexington Data Inc.
--Antioxidants & Stabilizers for Polymers. (Ser. 3-72). 185p. 1973. 115.00 (ISBN 0-914428-12-8). Lexington Data.
--Antioxidants & Stabilizers for Polymers. (Ser. 3-73). 136p. 1974. 115.00 (ISBN 0-914428-19-5). Lexington Data.
--Antioxidants & Stabilizers for Polymers. (Ser. 3-74). 1975. 120.00 (ISBN 0-914428-24-1). Lexington Data.
--Antioxidants & Stabilizers for Polymers. (Ser. 3-75). 1976. 120.00 (ISBN 0-914428-34-9). Lexington Data.
--Antioxidants & Stabilizers for Polymers. (Ser. 3-76). 1977. 125.00 (ISBN 0-914428-50-0). Lexington Data.
--Biotechnical Engineering: Equipment & Processes. (Ser. 14-81). 1982. 210.00 (ISBN 0-914428-92-6). Lexington Data.
--Biotechnical Engineering: Equipment & Processes. (Ser.14-82). 267p. 1983. 210.00 (ISBN 0-88178-011-1). Lexington Data.
--Biotechnical Engineering: Equipment & Processes. (Ser. 14-83). 318p. 1984. 210.00 (ISBN 0-88178-012-X). Lexington Data.
--Biotechnical Engineering: Equipment & Processes. (Series 14-84). 293p. 1985. 210.00 (ISBN 0-88178-023-5). Lexington Data.
--Blood Technology. (Ser. 10BT-81). 1982. 100.00 (ISBN 0-914428-90-X). Lexington Data.
--Blood Technology. (Ser. 10BT-79). 101p. 1980. 90.00 (ISBN 0-914428-75-6). Lexington Data.
--Blood Technology. (Ser.10BT-82). 1983. 100.00 (ISBN 0-88178-004-9). Lexington Data.
--Blood Technology. (Ser. 10BT-80). 1981. 100.00 (ISBN 0-914428-84-5). Lexington Data.
--Blood Technology. (Series 10BT-83). 176p. 1984. 100.00 (ISBN 0-88178-015-4). Lexington Data.
--Blood Technology. (Series 10BT-84). 1985. 100.00 (ISBN 0-88178-052-9). Lexington Data.
--Cancer: Diagnosis & Therapy. (Ser. 10CDT-81). 1982. 80.00 (ISBN 0-914428-93-4). Lexington Data.
--Cancer: Diagnosis & Therapy. (Ser. 10CDT - 80). 1981. 80.00 (ISBN 0-914428-77-2). Lexington Data.
--Cancer: Diagnosis & Therapy. (Series 10CDT-79). 72p. 1980. 70.00 (ISBN 0-914428-64-0). Lexington Data.
--Cancer: Diagnosis & Therapy. (Ser.10CDT-82). 1983. 80.00 (ISBN 0-88178-005-7). Lexington Data.
--Cancer: Diagnosis & Therapy. (Ser. 10CDT-83). 126p. 1984. 80.00 (ISBN 0-88178-016-2). Lexington Data.
--Cancer: Diagnosis & Therapy. (Ser. 10CDT-84). 1985. 90.00 (ISBN 0-88178-053-7). Lexington Data.
--Cardiac Technology. (Ser. 10CT-81). 123p. 1982. 100.00 (ISBN 0-914428-95-0). Lexington Data.
--Cardiac Technology. (Ser. 10CT-80). 1981. 90.00 (ISBN 0-914428-81-0). Lexington Data.
--Cardiac Technology. (Ser. 10CT-83), 99p. 1984. 100.00 (ISBN 0-88178-021-9). Lexington Data.
--Cardiac Technology. (Ser. 10CT-82). 100p. 1983. 100.00 (ISBN 0-88178-010-3). Lexington Data.
--Clinical Assays. (Ser. 10CA-81). 1982. 100.00 (ISBN 0-914428-88-8). Lexington Data.
--Clinical Assays. (Ser. 10CA 80). 1981. 100.00 (ISBN 0-914428-78-0). Lexington Data.
--Clinical Assays. (Ser. 10CA-79). 122p. 1980. 90.00 (ISBN 0-914428-65-9). Lexington Data.
--Clinical Assays. (Ser.10CA-82). 1983. 100.00 (ISBN 0-88178-003-0). Lexington Data.
--Clinical Assays. (Ser. 10CA-83). 200p. 1984. 100.00 (ISBN 0-88178-014-6). Lexington Data.
--Clinical Assays Series, No. 10CA-84. 1985. 100.00 (ISBN 0-88178-051-0). Lexington Data.
--Energy Systems: Solar, Water, Wind, Geothermal. (Series 11-80). 1982. 150.00 (ISBN 0-914428-83-7). Lexington Data.
--Energy Systems: Solar, Wind, Water, Geothermal. (Ser. 11-78). 1979. 135.00 (ISBN 0-914428-58-6). Lexington Data.
--Energy Systems: Solar, Wind, Water, Geothermal. (Ser. 11-79). 1981. 140.00 (ISBN 0-914428-70-5). Lexington Data.
--Energy Systems: Solar, Wind, Water, Geothermal. (Ser. 11-77). 1978. 130.00 (ISBN 0-914428-47-0). Lexington Data.
--Energy Systems: Solar, Wind, Water, Geothermal. (Ser. 11-82). 1983. 150.00 (ISBN 0-88178-001-4). Lexington Data.
--Energy Systems: Solar, Wind, Water Geothermal. (Ser.11-81). 204p. 1983. 150.00 (ISBN 0-88178-000-6). Lexington Data.
--Flame Retardants for Plastics, Rubber & Textiles: Including Indexes & Abstracts 1967 to 1971. Incl. 315.00 (ISBN 0-914428-03-9). (Ser. 2-6771b). 1971. Lexington Data.
--Flame Retardants for Plastics, Rubber & Textiles (July 1971-June 1972) (Ser. 2-7172). 107p. 1972. 110.00 (ISBN 0-914428-11-X). Lexington Data Inc.
--Flame, Retardants for Plastics, Rubber, Textiles & Paper (July 1978-June 1979) (Ser. 2-7879). 1979. 123.00 (ISBN 0-914428-61-6). Lexington Data.
--Flame Retardants for Plastics, Rubber Textiles & Paper (July 1972-June 1973) (Ser. 2-7273). 112p. 1973. 110.00 (ISBN 0-914428-14-4). Lexington Data.
--Flame Retardants for Plastics, Rubber, Textiles & Paper (July 1973-June 1974) (Ser. 2-7374). 1974. 123.00 (ISBN 0-914428-22-5). Lexington Data.
--Flame Retardants for Plastics, Rubber, Textiles & Paper (July 1974-June 1975) (Ser. 2-7475). 1975. 123.00 (ISBN 0-914428-30-6). Lexington Data.
--Flame Retardants for Plastics, Rubber, Textiles & Paper (July 1975-June 1976) (Ser. 2 - 7576). 1976. 123.00 (ISBN 0-914428-37-3). Lexington Data.
--Flame Retardants for Plastics, Rubber, Textiles & Paper (July 1976-June 1977) (Ser. 2-7677). 1977. 123.00 (ISBN 0-914428-49-7). Lexington Data.
--Flame Retardants for Plastics, Rubber, Textiles & Paper (July 1977-June 1978) (Ser. 2-7778). 1978. 123.00 (ISBN 0-914428-55-1). Lexington Data.
--Flame Retardants for Plastics, Rubber, Textiles & Paper (July 1979-June 1980) (Ser. 2-7980). 136p. 1980. refer. 130.00 (ISBN 0-914428-73-X). Lexington Data.
--Flame Retardants for Plastics, Rubber, Textiles & Paper (July 1980-June 1981) (Ser. 2-8081). 152p. 130.00 (ISBN 0-914428-82-9). Lexington Data.
--Free Radical Initiators (Oct. 1970-Dec. 1971) (Ser. 1-7071). 1974. 105.00 (ISBN 0-914428-21-7). Lexington Data.
--Free Radical Initiators: 1953-1970, Ser. 1B. Incl. Indexes Plus Abstracts & a Survey of the U.S. Market. 247p. 575.00 (ISBN 0-914428-00-4). 1971. Lexington Data Inc.
--Free Radical Initiators (1972) (Ser. 1-72). 1975. 55.00 (ISBN 0-914428-27-6). Lexington Data.
--Free Radical Initiators (1973) (Ser. No. 1-73). 86p. 1975. 55.00 (ISBN 0-914428-31-4). Lexington Data.
--Herbicides. (Ser. 12-77). 1978. 80.00 (ISBN 0-914428-48-9). Lexington Data.
--Ion Exchange-Chromatography: Processes & Equipment, 1973. (Ser. 7-73). 1974. 115.00 (ISBN 0-914428-23-3). Lexington Data.
--Knitting Machinery (1975) (Ser. 9-75). 1976. 75.00 (ISBN 0-914428-39-X). Lexington Data.
--Laser Manufacture & Technology 1974. (Ser. 6-74). 1975. 250.00 (ISBN 0-914428-26-8). Lexington Data.
--Lasers: Equipment & Applications, 2 pts. Incl. No. 6AC-76. Part I-Apparatus & Components. 145.00 (ISBN 0-914428-42-X); No. 6AP-76. Part II-Applications. 130.00 (ISBN 0-914428-43-8). 1977. Set. 275.00 (ISBN 0-914428-53-5). Lexington Data.
--Lasers: Equipment & Applications, 2 pts. Incl. Pt. I. Apparatus & Components. (No. 6AC-77) (ISBN 0-914428-44-6); Pt. II. Applications. (No. 6AP-77) (ISBN 0-914428-45-4). (No. 6-77). 1978. Set. 290.00 (ISBN 0-914428-56-X). Lexington Data.
--Lasers: Equipment & Applications. (Ser. 6-79). 1985. 315.00 (ISBN 0-88178-059-6). Lexington Data.
--Lasers: Equipment & Applications. (Ser. 6-78). 1984. 305.00 (ISBN 0-88178-058-8). Lexington Data.
--Lasers: Equipment & Applications. (Ser. 6-80). 397p. 1985. 325.00 (ISBN 0-88178-022-7). Lexington Data.
--Lasers: Equipment & Applications (1975) (Ser. No. 6-75). 1976. 275.00 (ISBN 0-914428-32-2). Lexington Data.
--Medical Diagnostic Apparatus-Systems. (Ser. 10DAS-81). 1982. 100.00 (ISBN 0-914428-89-6). Lexington Data.
--Medical Diagnostic Apparatus-Systems. (Ser. 10DAS-79). 142p. 1980. 90.00 (ISBN 0-914428-66-7). Lexington Data.
--Medical Diagnostic Apparatus-Systems. (Ser. 10 DAS-82). 1983. 100.00 (ISBN 0-88178-006-5). Lexington Data.
--Medical Diagnostic Apparatus-Systems. (Ser. 10 DAS-80). 1981. 100.00 (ISBN 0-914428-80-2). Lexington Data.
--Medical Diagnostic Apparatus-Systems. (Ser. 10DAS-83). 186p. 1984. 100.00 (ISBN 0-88178-017-0). Lexington Data.
--Medical Diagnostic Apparatus-Systems. (Ser. 10DAS-84). 1985. 100.00 (ISBN 0-88178-054-5). Lexington Data.
--Medical Technology: Advanced Medical Apparatus-Systems. (Ser. 10 AMA-78). 1980. 370.00 (ISBN 0-914428-59-4). Lexington Data.
--Medical Technology: Advanced Medical Apparatus-Systems. (Ser 10AMA-77). 1978. 360.00 (ISBN 0-914428-46-2). Lexington Data.
--Medical Technology: Electrical-Electronic Apparatus 1976. (Ser. 10 - 76). 1977. 250.00 (ISBN 0-914428-41-1). Lexington Data.
Critser, James R, Jr. Medical Therapeutic Apparatus-Systems. (Ser. 10TAS-80). 138p. 1981. 80.00 (ISBN 0-914428-91-8). Lexington Data.
Critser, James R., Jr. Medical Therapeutic Apparatus-Systems. (Ser. 10TAS-79). 1981. 70.00 (ISBN 0-914428-69-1). Lexington Data.
--Medical Therapeutic Apparatus Systems. (Ser. 10TAS-81). 131p. 1982. 80.00 (ISBN 0-914428-98-5). Lexington Data.
--Medical Therapeutic Apparatus-Systems. (Ser. 10TAS-82). 1983. 80.00 (ISBN 0-88178-009-X). Lexington Data.
--Medical Therapeutic Apparatus-Systems. (Series 10TAS-83). 115p. 1984. 80.00 (ISBN 0-88178-019-7). Lexington Data.
--Membrane Separation Processes. (Series 5-80). 221p. 1981. 135.00 (ISBN 0-914428-76-4). Lexington Data.
--Membrane Separation Processes. (Series 5-81). 1982. 135.00 (ISBN 0-914428-87-X). Lexington Data.
--Membrane Separation Processes. Incl. Index & Abstracts 1967-1971. 320.00 (ISBN 0-914428-10-1). (No.5-6771). 1972. Lexington Data Inc.
--Membrane Separation Processes. (Ser. 5-79). 1980. 130.00 (ISBN 0-914428-72-1). Lexington Data.
--Membrane Separation Processes. (Ser. 5-78). 1979. 130.00 (ISBN 0-914428-60-8). Lexington Data.
--Membrane Separation Processes. (Ser. 5-77). 1978. 124.00 (ISBN 0-914428-54-3). Lexington Data.
--Membrane Separation Processes. (Ser. 5-72). 120p. 1973. 110.00 (ISBN 0-914428-13-6). Lexington Data.
--Membrane Separation Processes. (Ser. 5-73). 1974. 110.00 (ISBN 0-914428-20-9). Lexington Data.
--Membrane Separation Processes. (Ser. 5-74). 1975. 124.00 (ISBN 0-914428-25-X). Lexington Data.
--Membrane Separation Processes. (Ser. No. 5-75). 1976. 124.00 (ISBN 0-914428-33-0). Lexington Data.
--Membrane Separation Processes. (Ser. (5-76)). 1977. 124.00 (ISBN 0-914428-51-9). Lexington Data.
--Membrane Separation Processes. (Ser.5-82). 1983. 135.00 (ISBN 0-88178-002-2). Lexington Data.

--Membrane Separation Processes. (Ser. 5-83). 160p. 1984. 135.00 (ISBN 0-88178-013-8). Lexington Data.
--Membrane Separation Processes. (Ser. 5-84). 197p. 1985. 140.00 (ISBN 0-88178-050-2). Lexington Data.
--Organophosphorus Compounds: Preparations & Applications, 1973. (Ser. 8-73). 1974. 200.00 (ISBN 0-914428-28-4). Lexington Data.
--Organophosphorus Compounds: Preparations & Applications, 1974. (Ser. 8-74). 1975. 210.00 (ISBN 0-914428-29-2). Lexington Data.
--Organophosphorus Compounds: Preparations & Applications, 1975. (Ser. 8-75). 1976. 220.00. Lexington Data.
--Organophosphorus Compounds: Preparations & Applications (1976) (Ser. 8-76). 1977. 230.00 (ISBN 0-914428-52-7). Lexington Data.
--Pesticides. (Ser. 13-78). 1979. 195.00 (ISBN 0-914428-63-2). Lexington Data.
--Prostheses & Contact Lens. (Ser. 10PC-79). 1981. refer. 70.00 (ISBN 0-914428-67-5). Lexington Data.
--Prostheses & Contact Lenses. (Series 10PC-80). 1981. 80.00 (ISBN 0-914428-85-3). Lexington Data.
--Prostheses & Contact Lenses. (Ser. 10PC-81). 126p. 1982. 80.00 (ISBN 0-914428-96-9). Lexington Data.
--Prostheses & Contact Lenses. (Series 10PC-83). 101p. 1984. 80.00 (ISBN 0-88178-020-0). Lexington Data.
--Prostheses & Contact Lenses. (Ser. 10PC-82). 106p. 1983. 80.00 (ISBN 0-88178-008-1). Lexington Data.
--Proteins-Peptides: Preparations & Applications. (Ser. 15-84). 182p. 1985. 125.00 (ISBN 0-88178-024-3). Lexington Data.
--Radiological Equipment. (Ser. 10R-80). 1981. 80.00 (ISBN 0-914428-86-1). Lexington Data.
--Radiological Equipment. (Ser. 10R-79). 1980. 70.00 (ISBN 0-914428-68-3). Lexington Data.
--Radiological Equipment. (Ser. 10R-81). 115p. 1982. 80.00 (ISBN 0-914428-97-7). Lexington Data.
--Radiological Equipment. (Ser. 10R-82). 1983. 80.00 (ISBN 0-88178-007-3). Lexington Data.
--Radiological Equipment. (Ser. 10R-83). 88p. 1984. 80.00 (ISBN 0-88178-018-9). Lexington Data.
--Radiological Equipment. (Ser. 10R-84). 1984. 90.00 (ISBN 0-88178-055-3). Lexington Data.

Crittall, Elizabeth, ed. Victoria History of the Counties of England: Wiltshire, Vol. 9. (Illus.). 1970. 27.25x (ISBN 0-19-722736-8). Oxford U Pr.

Crittenden, Alan. How to Adjust to Adjustable Home Mortgages. 46p. (Orig.). 1981. pap. 4.00 (ISBN 0-917982-25-8). Cougar Bks.

Crittenden, Alan, ed. The Almanac of Investments. LC 83-5168. (Illus.). 514p. 1984. 12.95 (ISBN 0-913153-03-6). Crittenden.
--Hidden Treasures. LC 85-50537. (Illus.). 550p. 1985. pap. 7.95 (ISBN 0-913153-04-4, Pub. by Union Square Bks). Crittenden.

Crittenden, Alan & Goodwin, Sandra, eds. The Hidden Treasures Directory of Dealers & Auction Houses. 1000p. Date not set. 95.00 (ISBN 0-913153-05-2). Crittenden.

Crittenden Editors. The Best of Crittenden's Meet the Lenders: 1985. (Illus.). 160p. (Orig.). 1985. pap. 57.00 (ISBN 0-913153-06-0). Crittenden.

Crittenden, Faith J. Discharge Planning for Health Care Facilities. LC 81-12894. 224p. 1982. pap. text ed. 29.95 (ISBN 0-89303-210-7). Brady Comm.

Crittenden, H. Temple. Comp'ny. 1967. 12.50 (ISBN 0-87012-061-1). McClain.
--Maine Scenic Route. 1966. 12.50 (ISBN 0-87012-060-3). McClain.

Crittenden, John A. Parties & Elections in the United States. (Illus.). 464p. 1982. 27.95 (ISBN 0-13-650903-7). P-H.

Crittenden, Mabel & Telfer, Dorothy. Wildflowers of the West. LC 75-9076. (Illus.). 1975. pap. 9.95 (ISBN 0-89087-069-1). Celestial Arts.

Crittenden, Max D., Jr., et al. Cordilleran Metamorphic Core Complexes. LC 80-67489. (Memoir: No. 153). 1980. 27.00 (ISBN 0-8137-1153-3). Geol Soc.

Crittenden, Penelope, jt. auth. see North, Barbara.

Crittenden, Penelope, jt. auth. see North, Barbara B.

Crittenden, Penelope P., jt. auth. see North, Barbara A.

Crittenden, Roger. The Thames & Hudson Manual of Film Editing. (Illus.). 1982. 18.95 (ISBN 0-500-67023-4); pap. 10.95f (ISBN 0-500-68023-X). Thames Hudson.

Crittenden, V. A Bibliography of the First Fleet. LC 81-69215. 359p. (Orig.). 1982. pap. text ed. 10.95 (ISBN 0-7081-1174-2, Pub. by ANUP Australia). Australia N U P.

Crivellari, Lucio, jt. ed. see Beckman, John E.

Crix, Frederick C. Reprographic Management Handbook. 2nd ed. 332p. 1979. text ed. 36.75x (ISBN 0-220-67010-2, Pub. by Busn Bks England). Brookfield Pub Co.

CRM Books. Readings in Psychology Today. 4th ed. 1978. pap. text ed. 9.95 (ISBN 0-394-32244-4, RanC). Random.

Cro, Stelio. Realidad y Utopia en el Descubrimiento y Conquista de la America Hispana, 1492-1682. (Span.). 1984. 20.50x (ISBN 0-936968-07-9). Intl Bk Ctr.

Croall, James. Disaster at Sea. 1981. pap. 2.75 (ISBN 0-8128-7043-3). Stein & Day.

Croall, Jonathan. Neill of Summerhill: The Permanent Rebel. (Illus.). 428p. 1983. 19.50 (ISBN 0-394-51403-3). Pantheon.

Croall, Jonathan, ed. see Neill, A. S.

Croall, Stephen. Ecology for Beginners. (Illus.). 1981. pap. 3.95 (ISBN 0-394-74872-7). Pantheon.

Croasdale, Hannah & Bicudo, Carlos E. A Synopsis of North American Desmids Part II: Desmidiaceae: Placodermae Section 5. The Filamentous Genera. LC 70-183418. (Illus.). vi, 117p. 1983. 26.50x (ISBN 0-8032-3661-1). U of Nebr Pr.

Croasdale, Hannah T., jt. auth. see Prescott, G. W.

Croat, Thomas B. Flora of Barro Colorado Island. LC 76-23371. (Illus.). 953p. 1978. 60.00x (ISBN 0-8047-0950-5). Stanford U Pr.

Croatto, J. Severino. Exodus: A Hermeneutics of Freedom. LC 80-26148. 112p. (Orig.). 1981. pap. 4.95 (ISBN 0-88344-111-X). Orbis Bks.

Crobsy, Nina E. & Marten, Elizabeth H. Don't Teach Let Me Learn: About Pirates, Kings & Things, From Girls to Women, Famous Women. (The Don't Teach! Let Me Learn Ser.). (Illus.). 72p. (gr. 3-10). 1983. pap. 5.95 teacher enrichment book (ISBN 0-88047-031-3, 8314). DOK Pubs.

Croce, Arlene. Afterimages. LC 78-4592. 1977. 12.95 (ISBN 0-394-41093-9, Vin). Random.
--The Fred Astaire & Ginger Rogers Book. (Illus.). 1978. pap. 7.95 (ISBN 0-394-72476-3, Vin). Random.
--Going to the Dance. LC 81-48110. 1982. 20.00 (ISBN 0-394-52441-1); pap. 8.95 (ISBN 0-394-70826-1). Knopf.

Croce, Benedetto. Aesthetic. Ainslie, Douglas, tr. LC 78-58500. 544p. 1978. pap. 9.95 (ISBN 0-87923-255-2, Nonpareil Bk.). Godine.
--Autobiography. facsimile ed. Collingwood, R. G., tr. LC 79-114871. (Select Bibliographies Reprint Ser.). 1927. 13.00 (ISBN 0-8369-5276-6). Ayer Co Pubs.
--Benedetto Croce's Poetry & Literature: An Introduction to the Criticism & History. Gullace, Giovanni, tr. from Ital. & intro. by. LC 80-19511. 272p. 1981. 24.95x (ISBN 0-8093-0982-3). S Ill U Pr.
--Ce qui est vivant et Ce qui est morte De la philosophie De Hegel: Etude Critique Suivie d,un Essai De Bibliographie Hegelienne. Buriot, Henri, tr. from Ital. (Reprints in Philosophy Ser.). (Fr.). Repr. of 1910 ed. lib. bdg. 40.00x (ISBN 0-697-00051-6). Irvington.
--Conduct of Life. facs. ed. Livingston, A., tr. LC 67-30204. (Essay Index Reprint Ser). 1924. 18.00 (ISBN 0-8369-0351-X). Ayer Co Pubs.
--Croce, the King & the Allies. LC 78-63660. (Studies in Fascism: Ideology & Practice). Repr. of 1950 ed. 22.00 (ISBN 0-404-16916-3). AMS Pr.
--Defence of Poetry. LC 72-10862. 1933. lib. bdg. 8.50 (ISBN 0-8414-0766-5). Folcroft.
--Essays on Marx & Russia. DeGennaro, Angelo A., tr. LC 66-17538. (Milestones of Thought Ser.). 1966. pap. 3.95 (ISBN 0-8044-6098-1). Ungar.
--The Essence of Aesthetic. LC 73-12554. 1921. lib. bdg. 16.50 (ISBN 0-8414-3439-5). Folcroft.
--European Literature in the Nineteenth Century. LC 67-30822. (Studies in Comparative Literature, No. 35). 1969. Repr. of 1924 ed. lib. bdg. 49.95 (ISBN 0-8383-0735-3). Haskell.
--Goethe. LC 78-103179. 1970. Repr. of 1923 ed. 19.50x (ISBN 0-8046-0816-4, Pub. by Kennikat). Assoc Faculty Pr.
--Guide to Aesthetics. Romanell, Patrick, tr. 120p. 1984. pap. text ed. 5.00 (ISBN 0-8191-3313-2). U Pr of Amer.
--Historical Materialism & the Economics of Karl Marx. LC 78-66239. (Social Science Classics). 225p. 1981. 29.95 (ISBN 0-87855-313-4); pap. text ed. 9.95 (ISBN 0-87855-695-8). Transaction Bks.
--Historical Materialism of the Economics of Karl Marx. 188p. 1966. Repr. of 1914 ed. 28.50x (ISBN 0-7146-1218-9, BHA-01218, F Cass Co). Biblio Dist.
--History As the Story of Liberty. 320p. 1984. pap. text ed. 13.50 (ISBN 0-8191-3312-4). U Pr of Amer.
--History: Its Theory & Practice. Ainslie, Douglas, tr. LC 60-14177. 1960. Repr. of 1920 ed. 16.00x (ISBN 0-8462-0160-7). Russell.
--The History of the Kingdom of Naples. Hughes, H. Stuart, ed. Frenaye, Frances, tr. from Ital. LC 71-113253. (Classic European Historians Ser.). xxiv, 260p. 1972. pap. 2.95x (ISBN 0-226-12081-3, P377, Phoen). U of Chicago Pr.
--The History of the Theory of the Beautiful. (Illus.). 131p. 1984. 117.85x (ISBN 0-86650-109-6). Gloucester Art.
--My Philosophy & Other Essays on the Moral & Political Problems of Our Time. Caritt, E. F., tr. LC 75-41068. (BCL Ser. II). Repr. of 1949 ed. 18.75 (ISBN 0-404-14526-4). AMS Pr.
--The Mystery of the Two Personalities in Shakespeare's Tragedies of Love & Death, 2 vols, Vols. 1 & 2. (Illus.). 257p. 157.75 (ISBN 0-89266-473-8). Am Classical Coll Pr.
--The Philosophy of History. (Illus.). 123p. 1983. 89.75 (ISBN 0-89901-128-4). Found Class Reprints.
--The Philosophy of Politics. (Most Meaningful Classics in World Literature Ser.). (Illus.). 127p. 1983. 77.85x (ISBN 0-89266-422-3). Am Classical Coll Pr.
--Philosophy of the Practical. Ainslie, Douglas, tr. LC 66-30790. 1913. 15.00x (ISBN 0-8196-0192-6). Biblo.
--The Poetry of Dante. 319p. Repr. of 1922 ed. 10.00x (ISBN 0-911858-12-1). Appel.
--The Problem of the Irrational in History. 180p. 1985. 93.45 (ISBN 0-89920-082-6). Am Inst Psych.
--Sentiment & Romance in the Poetry by Shakespeare. 139p. 1983. 89.85x (ISBN 0-89266-414-2). Am Classical Coll Pr.
--The Theory of Harmony in the Romantic Poetry by Ludovico Ariosto. (Illus.). 111p. 1983. 88.45x (ISBN 0-89266-413-4). Am Classical Coll Pr.
--The Theory of Intuition & Expression in Art. (Illus.). 142p. 1983. 83.55x (ISBN 0-86650-070-7). Gloucester Art.
--What Is Living & What Is Dead in the Philosophy of Hegel. LC 83-48504. (The Philosophy of Hegel Ser.). 245p. 1984. lib. bdg. 30.00 (ISBN 0-8240-5627-2). Garland Pub.
--What Is Living & What Is Dead of the Philosophy of Hegel. Ainslie, Douglas, tr. from Ital. 268p. 1985. pap. text ed. 10.25 (ISBN 0-8191-4279-4). U Pr of Amer.

Croce, Benedetto, tr. see Basile, Giovanni B.

Croce, Benetto. Croce's Aesthetic. LC 74-28385. 1919. 8.50 (ISBN 0-8414-3301-1). Folcroft.

Croce, Pat. The Baseball Player's Guide to Sports Medicine. LC 82-83936. (Illus.). 160p. (Orig.). 1984. pap. 9.95 (ISBN 0-88011-104-6). Leisure Pr.
--Stretching for Athletics. Rev. ed. LC 83-80859. (Illus.). 208p. 1984. pap. 7.95 (ISBN 0-88011-119-4). Leisure Pr.
--The Tennis Player's Guide to Sports Medicine. LC 83-80729. (Illus.). 176p. (Orig.). 1984. pap. 9.95 (ISBN 0-88011-155-0). Leisure Pr.
--The Young Athlete's Guide to Stretching. LC 83-80703. (Illus.). 144p. (Orig.). 1984. pap. 7.95 (ISBN 0-88011-205-0). Leisure Pr.

Croce, Pat & Cooper, Bruce C. Conditioning for Ice Hockey Year-Round. LC 82-83917. (Illus.). 176p. (Orig.). 1983. pap. 9.95 (ISBN 0-88011-090-2). Leisure Pr.

Crocetti, Gino. Graduate Record Examination General (Aptitude) Test: (GRE) LC 82-18475. 448p. (Orig.). 1983. pap. 7.95 (ISBN 0-668-05479-4, 5479). Arco.

Crocetti, Gino & Clarke, B. M. Law School Admission Test: Preparation for the New Test. LC 82-1825. 416p. (Orig.). 1982. pap. 7.95 (ISBN 0-668-05427-1, 5427). Arco.

Crocetti, Gino & Stella, Frank. What's for Dinner Tomorrow? Corporate Views of New Food Products. LC 79-93419. 1979. pap. 3.95 (ISBN 0-918780-15-2). INFORM.

Crocetti, Gino, et al. Graduate Management Admission Test (GMAT) 2nd ed. 464p. (Orig.). 1984. pap. 8.95 (ISBN 0-668-06169-3, 6169-3). Arco.

Crocetti, Guido M., et al. Contemporary Attitudes Toward Mental Illness. LC 73-80071. (Contemporary Community Health Ser.). Repr. of 1974 ed. 65.50 (ISBN 0-8357-9752-X, 2017864). Bks Demand UMI.

Crochet, M. J. Numerical Simulation of Non-Newtonian Flow. (Rheology Ser.: Vol. 1). 1984. 65.50 (ISBN 0-444-42291-9). Elsevier.

Crochiere, Ronald E. & Rabiner, Lawrence R. Multirate Digital Signal Processing. (Illus.). 336p. 1983. 33.95 (ISBN 0-13-605162-6). P-H.

Crociata, Francis, jt. auth. see Ouzer, Louis.

Crock, Clement H. No Cross No Crown. 1974. Repr. 3.00 (ISBN 0-8198-0510-6). Dghtrs St Paul.

Crock, H. V. Practice of Spinal Surgery. (Illus.). 340p. 1983. 97.00 (ISBN 0-387-81738-7). Springer-Verlag.

Crock, H. V. & Yoshizaua, H. The Blood Supply of the Vertebral Column & Spinal Cord in Man. LC 76-40960. 1977. 63.00 (ISBN 0-387-81402-7). Springer-Verlag.

Crockard, Alan, jt. ed. see Odling-Smee, William.

Crocker, A. C. Predicting Teaching Success. 14.00x (ISBN 0-85633-037-X, Pub. by NFER Nelson). Taylor & Francis.
--Statistics for the Teacher. 160p. 1981. 10.00x (ISBN 0-85633-220-8, Pub. by NFER Nelson UK). Taylor & Francis.

Crocker, Betty. Betty Crocker's Buffets: Menus, Recipes & Planning Tips for Easy & Successful Home Entertaining. LC 84-42536. (Illus.). 192p. 1984. 13.45 (ISBN 0-394-53592-8). Random.
--Betty Crocker's Chocolate Cookbook. (Illus.). 1985. 12.45 (ISBN 0-394-53594-4). Random.
--Betty Crocker's Deluxe Wedding Plan Book. 1979. 6.95 (ISBN 0-307-09553-3, Golden Pr). Western Pub.

Crocker, Bosworth. Humble Folk. LC 77-94338. (One-Act Plays in Reprint Ser.). 1978. Repr. of 1923 ed. 18.50x (ISBN 0-8486-2036-4). Core Collection.

Crocker, Chester A., jt. ed. see Bissel, Richard E.

Crocker, Chris. Cyndi Lauper. Arico, Diane, ed. (Illus.). 64p. (gr. 3-7). 1985. pap. 3.50 (ISBN 0-671-55475-1). Wanderer Bks.
--Wham! Arico, Diane, ed. (Hot Rock Ser.). (Illus.). 64p. (gr. 3-7). 1985. lib. bdg. 8.79 (ISBN 0-671-60374-4); pap. 3.50. Wanderer Bks.
--Wham. (Illus.). 64p. (gr. 3-7). 1985. 8.79 (ISBN 0-671-60374-4); pap. 3.95 (ISBN 0-671-60281-0). Messner.

Crocker, Chris, ed. see Brickner, Dave, et al.

Crocker, Chris, ed. see Glau, Gregory R., et al.

Crocker, Chris, ed. see Vick, Bill, et al.

Crocker, Chris, et al, eds. see Young, George & Stark, Peter.

Crocker, David. Praxis & Democratic Socialism: The Critical Social Theory of Markovic & Stojanovic. 335p. 1983. text ed. 20.45x (ISBN 0-391-02610-0, Pub. by Harvester England). Humanities.

Crocker, Dean, jt. auth. see Young, J. A.

Crocker, Deborah, jt. auth. see Esquire Magazine Editors.

Crocker, Diane. The Snuggle Book. (Illus.). 144p. 1985. 10.95 (ISBN 0-943084-30-X); pap. 6.95 (ISBN 0-943084-31-8). Contemp Bks.
--The Snuggle Book: The Fine Art of Snuggling. (Illus.). 144p. 1985. 10.95 (ISBN 0-943084-30-X); pap. 6.95 (ISBN 0-943084-31-8). Turnbull & Willoughby.

Crocker, Diane S. How to Design & Build Storage Projects. Smith, Sally W., ed. LC 82-63126. (Illus.). 96p. (Orig.). 1983. pap. 5.95 (ISBN 0-89721-017-4). Ortho.

Crocker, E., jt. auth. see Kramsch, C.

Crocker, George N. Roosevelt's Road to Russia. LC 74-26540. (FDR & the Era of the New Deal Ser.). (Illus.). xvii, 312p. 1975. Repr. of 1959 ed. lib. bdg. 39.50 (ISBN 0-306-70714-4). Da Capo.

Crocker, Helen B. The Green River of Kentucky. LC 76-4433. (Kentucky Bicentennial Bookshelf Ser.). (Illus.). 120p. 1976. 6.95 (ISBN 0-8131-0226-X). U Pr of Ky.

Crocker, Herbert L., jt. auth. see Ciabotti, Patricia A.

Crocker, J. Christopher. Vital Souls: Bororo Cosmology, Natural Symbolism, & Shamanism. 200p. Date not set. 29.95 (ISBN 0-317-27477-5). U of Ariz Pr.
--Vitals Souls: Bororo Cosology, Natural Symbolism & Shamanism. LC 85-1003. (Anthropology of Form & Meaning Ser.). 1985. 29.95x (ISBN 0-8165-0877-1). U of Ariz Pr.

Crocker, J. Christopher, jt. ed. see Sapir, J. David.

Crocker, Joanne, jt. auth. see Methven, Barbara.

Crocker, John. Bermuda, Bahamas, Hispanola, Puerto Rico & the Virgin Islands. 15.00x (ISBN 0-87556-062-8). Saifer.

Crocker, John F. Reye's Syndrome II. 512p. 1979. 54.50 (ISBN 0-8089-1178-3, 790946). Grune.

Crocker, John R. The Student Guide to Catholic Colleges & Universities. LC 82-48923. 468p. (Orig.). 1983. pap. 9.57 (ISBN 0-06-061602-4, RD/459, HarpR). Har-Row.

Crocker, Jong & Crocker, Wilson. Reading & Following Recipes. (Illus.). 80p. 1985. 14.95 (ISBN 0-88102-036-2). Janus Bks.

Crocker, Lawrence H. Positive Liberty: An Essay in Normative Political Philosophy. (Melbourne International Philosophy Ser.: Vol. 7). 156p. 1980. lib. bdg. 29.00 (ISBN 90-247-2291-8, Pub. by Martinus Nijhoff Netherlands). Kluwer Academic.

Crocker, Lawrence P. The Army Officer's Guide. 42nd ed. (Illus.). 576p. 1983. pap. 14.95 (ISBN 0-8117-2133-7). Stackpole.
--The Army Officer's Guide. rev., 43rd ed. Senko, Peggy, ed. (Illus.). 576p. 1985. pap. 14.95 (ISBN 0-8117-2166-3). Stackpole.

Crocker, Lester G. An Age of Crisis: Man & World in Eighteenth Century French Thought. LC 59-14233. (Goucher College Ser.). Repr. of 1959 ed. 129.00 (ISBN 0-8357-9260-9, 2011983). Bks Demand UMI.
--Diderot's Chaotic Order: Approach to Synthesis. LC 73-16756. 188p. 1974. 22.50 (ISBN 0-691-07199-3). Princeton U Pr.

Crocker, Lester G., ed. see Rousseau, Jean-Jacques.

Crocker, Lester G., jt. ed. see Seibert, Louise C.

Crocker, Lester G., ed. see Voltaire.

Crocker, Lionel. An Analysis of Lincoln & Douglas As Public Speakers & Debaters. (Illus.). 568p. 1968. 54.50x (ISBN 0-398-00366-1). C C Thomas.
--Harry Emerson Fosdick's Art of Preaching: An Anthology. 296p. 1971. 19.75x (ISBN 0-398-00368-8). C C Thomas.

Crocker, Lionel & Carmack, Paul A. Readings in Rhetoric. 616p. 1965. 50.75x (ISBN 0-398-00368-8). C C Thomas.

Crocker, M. J. & Kessler, F. M., eds. Noise & Noise Control, Vol. II. 312p. 1982. 90.00 (ISBN 0-8493-5094-8). CRC Pr.

Crocker, Malcolm J. Noise Control. 416p. 1984. 64.50 (ISBN 0-442-21749-8). Van Nos Reinhold.

Crocker, Malcolm J. & Price, A. J. Noise & Noise Control, Vol. I. new ed. (Uniscience Ser.). 299p. 1975. 56.00 (ISBN 0-87819-064-3). CRC Pr.

Crocker, Mary W. Historic Architecture in Mississippi. 3rd ed. LC 72-92483. (Illus.). 256p. 1977-1982. 17.50 (ISBN 0-87805-022-1). U Pr of Miss.

Crocker, Mel. PBY-the Beloved Cat: The Navy's Astonishing Fighter Bomber of WWII. 1983. 35.00 (ISBN 0-917734-09-2). Monitor.

Crocker, Olga, et al. Quality Circles: A Guide to Participation & Productivity. Date not set. price not set. Facts on File.

Crocker, Richard L. The Early Medieval Sequence. LC 74-84143. 1977. 65.00x (ISBN 0-520-02847-3). U of Cal Pr.

Crocker, Ruth, jt. ed. see Altman, Marjorie.

Crocker, Sabin. Piping Handbook. 5th ed. King, R. C., ed. 1967. 79.50 (ISBN 0-07-013841-9). McGraw.

Crocker, Samuel. That Island: A Political Romance. LC 76-42807. Repr. of 1892 ed. 15.50 (ISBN 0-404-60065-4). AMS Pr.

Crocker, Sturgis. Sam Crockers Boats: A Design Catalog. LC 84-48687. (Illus.). 256p. 1985. 32.50 (ISBN 0-87742-195-1). Intl Marine.

Crocker, Thomas D. & Teasley, John I., eds. Economic Perspectives on Acid Deposition Control. (Acid Percipitation Ser.: Vol. 8). 208p. 1984. text ed. 32.50 (ISBN 0-250-40573-3). Butterworth.

Crocker, Walter. Nigeria: A Critique of British Colonial Administration. 1976. lib. bdg. 59.95 (ISBN 0-8490-2345-9). Gordon Pr.

Crocker, Walter R. Nigeria: A Critique of British Colonial Administration. facsimile ed. LC 76-160964. (Select Bibliographies Reprint Ser). Repr. of 1936 ed. 22.00 (ISBN 0-8369-5832-2). Ayer Co Pubs.

Crocker, Wilson, jt. auth. see Crocker, Jong.

Crocket, Dresda, jt. auth. see Cox, Michael.

Crockett, A. International Money Issues. 1980. pap. 17.95 (ISBN 0-442-30716-0). Van Nos Reinhold.

--Money Theory Policy & Institutions. 2nd ed. 1973. 32.50 (ISBN 0-442-30735-7). Van Nos Reinhold.

Crockett, Albert S. Peacocks on Parade: A Narrative of a Unique Period in American Social History & Its Most Colorful Figures. facsimile ed. LC 75-1836. (Leisure Class in America Ser.). (Illus.). 1975. Repr. of 1931 ed. 22.00x (ISBN 0-405-06905-7). Ayer Co Pubs.

Crockett, Andrew D. International Money: Issues & Analysis. 1978. 39.00 (ISBN 0-12-195750-0). Acad Pr.

Crockett, Arthur. Miracle a Minute. (Illus.). 72p. 1982. 8.95 (ISBN 0-938294-11-3). Global Comm.

--Three Secret Prophecies of Fatima Revealed. (Illus.). 72p. 1982. pap. 8.95 (ISBN 0-938294-13-X). Global Comm.

Crockett, Barry G. & Crockett, Lynette B. Seventy-Two-Hour Family Emergency Preparedeness Checklist: Prepare Every Needful Thing. 2nd rev. ed. LC 83-73117. (Illus.). 61p. 1983. pap. 4.95 (ISBN 0-915131-06-4). Crockett Pub Co.

Crockett, Candace, jt. auth. see Chamberlain, Marcia.

Crockett, David. The Autobiography of David Crockett. LC 80-2887. (BCL Ser.: No. I & II). pap. text ed. 42.50 (ISBN 0-404-18059-0). AMS Pr.

--A Narrative of the Life of David Crockett. Arpad, Joseph J., ed. 1972. 7.95x (ISBN 0-8084-0020-7); pap. 4.95x (ISBN 0-8084-0021-5). New Coll U Pr.

--A Narrative of the Life of David Crockett. 1977. Repr. 59.00x (ISBN 0-403-07781-8). Scholarly.

--Narrative of the Life of David Crockett of the State of Tennessee. LC 72-177358. (Tennesseana Editions Ser.). 282p. 1973. 12.95 (ISBN 0-87049-119-9). U of Tenn Pr.

--Sketches & Eccentricities of Colonel David Crockett of West Tennessee. LC 74-15735. (Popular Culture in America Ser.). 214p. 1975. Repr. of 1833 ed. 20.00x (ISBN 0-405-06370-9). Ayer Co Pubs.

Crockett, Desda. Salads. (Best of Vegetarian Cooking Ser.). 128p. 1983. pap. 3.95 (ISBN 0-7225-0764-X). Thorsons Pubs.

Crockett, Dina B., tr. see Apresjan, Ju. D.

Crockett, Edward S., jt. auth. see Culliney, John L.

Crockett, Eleanor E. Fifty-Three Ford. 1979. pap. 2.50 (ISBN 0-930324-14-5). Wings Pr.

Crockett, Fred E. Special Fleet: The History of the Presidential Yachts. LC 84-51558. (Illus.). 112p. (Orig.). 1985. pap. 8.95 (ISBN 0-89272-171-5). Down East.

Crockett, H. Dale. Focus on Watergate: An Examination of the Moral Dilemma of Watergate in the Light of Civil Religion. LC 81-16952. 126p. 1982. 10.95x (ISBN 0-86554-017-9). Mercer Univ Pr.

Crockett, Harry J., Jr. & Schulman, Jerome L., eds. Achievement among Minority Americans: A Conference Report. 148p. 1972. text ed. 11.25x (ISBN 0-87073-658-2). Schenkman Bks Inc.

Crockett, J. S. For Those Who Sell. 1979. pap. 2.95 (ISBN 0-346-12408-5). Cornerstone.

--For Those Who Sell (& Who the Hell Doesn't?!) LC 74-84339. 1974. 9.95 (ISBN 0-87863-077-5). Farnswth Pub.

Crockett, J. S. Dave see Crockett, J. S.

Crockett, James. Crockett's Victory Garden. (Illus.). 1977. 27.50 (ISBN 0-316-16120-9); pap. 16.45i (ISBN 0-316-16121-7). Little.

Crockett, James E. Your Heart: In Sickness & in Health. (Illus.). 176p. (Orig.). 1984. pap. 10.00 (ISBN 0-9611980-0-1). Eucalyptus Pr.

Crockett, James R., jt. auth. see Casler, Darwin J.

Crockett, James U. Crockett's Flower Garden. 1981. 27.50 (ISBN 0-316-16132-2); pap. 16.45 (ISBN 0-316-16133-0). Little.

--Crockett's Indoor Garden. LC 78-8939. 1978. 27.50 (ISBN 0-316-16124-1); pap. 16.45 (ISBN 0-316-16126-8). Little.

Crockett, Jim, ed. The Guitar Player Book. rev. ed. LC 79-2350. (Illus.). 416p. 1979. pap. 9.95 (ISBN 0-394-17169-1, E739, Ever). Grove.

Crockett, John C. From the Bottom of the Tennie Ladder. (Illus.). 1982. 7.95 (ISBN 0-533-05195-9). Vantage.

Crockett, Joseph P. Federal Tax System of the United States: A Survey of Law & Administration. LC 72-100154. xxii, 288p. Repr. of 1955 ed. lib. bdg. 15.00x (ISBN 0-8371-3681-4, CRTS). Greenwood.

Crockett, Lynette B., jt. auth. see Crockett, Barry G.

Crockett, Maline. More Stories to See & Share. (Illus.). 64p. 1981. pap. 3.95 (ISBN 0-87747-886-4). Deseret Bk.

Crockett, Maline C. Stories to See & Share. 80p. 1980. pap. 3.95 (ISBN 0-87747-828-7). Deseret Bk.

Crockett, Mary. Roads & Traveling. (Illus.). (gr. 4 up). 9.50x (ISBN 0-392-04439-0, LTB). Sportshelf.

Crockett, Mary E. Church Laces-Creative Crocheting. (Illus.). 125p. 1979. 9.00 (ISBN 0-8187-0037-8). Harlo Pr.

Crockett, Norman L. The Woolen Industry of the Midwest. LC 75-111505. (Illus.). 176p. 1970. 16.00x (ISBN 0-8131-1195-1). U Pr of Ky.

Crockett, Norman L. & Snell, Ronald K., eds. A New Order in the World: Readings in American History, 1607-1861. LC 72-9271. 302p. 1973. pap. 10.95x (ISBN 0-8061-1103-8). U of Okla Pr.

Crockett, Richard F. Angels Twelve. LC 84-90388. 1984. 15.00 (ISBN 0-87212-183-6). Libra.

Crockett, Richard H. & Horsch, James E. Jesus Life Songbook. 134p. 1975. pap. 3.95. Herald Pr.

Crockett, Richard H. & Horsch, James E., eds. Jesus Life Songbook. 134p. 1975. pap. 3.95 (ISBN 0-8361-2785-4). Herald Pr.

Crockett, S. R. Bog-Myrtle & Peat: Being Tales, Chiefly of Galloway. 389p. 1982. Repr. of 1895 ed. lib. bdg. 30.00 (ISBN 0-89987-122-4). Darby Bks.

Crockett, S. R., et al. Tales of Our Coast. LC 70-116966. (Short Story Index Reprint Ser). (Illus.). 1896. 17.00 (ISBN 0-8369-3470-9). Ayer Co Pubs.

Crockett, Samuel R. Adventurer in Spain. facsimile ed. LC 70-106282. (Short Story Index Reprint Ser.). 1903. 19.00 (ISBN 0-8369-3319-2). Ayer Co Pubs.

--Bog-Myrtle & Peat: Being Tales Chiefly of Galloway. LC 72-5909. (Short Story Index Reprint Ser.). Repr. of 1895 ed. 25.50 (ISBN 0-8369-4206-X). Ayer Co Pubs.

--Love Idylls. LC 73-130055. (Short Story Index Reprint Ser). 1901. 18.00 (ISBN 0-8369-3572-1). Ayer Co Pubs.

--Stickit Minister, & Some Common Men. facsimile 2nd ed. LC 72-163023. (Short Story Index Reprint Ser.). Repr. of 1893 ed. 18.00 (ISBN 0-8369-3937-9). Ayer Co Pubs.

Crockett, W. David. Promotion & Publicity for Churches. LC 74-80382. 48p. (Orig.). 1974. pap. 3.95 (ISBN 0-8192-1181-8). Morehouse.

Crockett, W. E. Chemical Engineering Review for PE Exam. 225p. 1985. 29.50 (ISBN 0-471-87874-X). Wiley.

Crockett, W. S. The Scott Country. 1902. lib. bdg. 30.00 (ISBN 0-8414-9144-5). Folcroft.

--The Scott Originals. 1973. Repr. of 1912 ed. 25.00 (ISBN 0-8274-1765-9). R West.

Crockett, W. S. & Caw, James I. Sir Walter Scott. LC 72-12503. 1972. Repr. of 1903 ed. lib. bdg. 10.00 (ISBN 0-8414-0931-5). Folcroft.

Crockett, William D. Harmony of Samuel, Kings & Chronicles. 1951. 12.95 (ISBN 0-8010-2326-2). Baker Bk.

Crockett, William J. A Case Study in Organizational Development: A Major U. S. Government Agency. 50p. 1984. pap. text ed. 30.00 (ISBN 0-934383-02-2). Pride Prods.

--Fiftieth Anniversary "Voices from the Heart". 11p. 1985. pap. text ed. 3.00 (ISBN 0-934383-01-4). Pride Prods.

--Love-Voices from the Heart. 15p. 1985. pap. text ed. 3.00 (ISBN 0-934383-03-0). Pride Prods.

--Personal Excellence. 400p. (Orig.). 1984. pap. text ed. 1000.00 (ISBN 0-934383-00-6). Pride Prods.

Crockett, William S. Footsteps of Scott. LC 74-14837. 1974. Repr. of 1909 ed. lib. bdg. 20.00 (ISBN 0-8414-3607-X). Folcroft.

Crockford, H. D., et al. Laboratory Manual of Physical Chemistry. 2nd ed. 352p. 1976. text ed. 25.50 (ISBN 0-471-18844-1). Wiley.

Crockford, Neil. An Introduction to Risk Management. 110p. 1980. 17.95 (ISBN 0-85941-116-8). Woodhead-Faulkner.

Crockwell, J. H. Pictures & Biographies of Brigham Young & His Wives. 1980. lib. bdg. 59.95 (ISBN 0-8490-3158-3). Gordon Pr.

Crocome, Marjorie, et al. LALI: A Pacific Anthology. Wendt, Albert, ed. (Pacific Paperbacks Ser.). (Illus.). 303p. (gr. 10-12). 1980. pap. 14.00 (ISBN 0-582-71772-8, Pub. by Longman Paul New Zealand). Three Continents.

Croel, Thomas E. Maggie, Medworth & Me: How to Cook for Pets. 84p. 1984. write for info. G Whittell Mem.

Croes, Martin & McNicoll, Andre. Marijuana Reappraised: Two Personal Accounts. LC 77-15695. 20p. 1977. pap. 1.00 (ISBN 0-913098-08-6). Myrin Institute.

Crofford, Emily. A Matter of Pride. LC 81-387. (Illus.). 48p. (gr. 3-6). 1981. PLB 8.95g (ISBN 0-87614-171-8, AACR2). Carolrhoda Bks.

--Stories from the Blue Road. LC 81-21229. (Illus.). 168p. (gr. 3-7). 1982. PLB 8.95g (ISBN 0-87614-189-0). Carolrhoda Bks.

Croffut, W. A., ed. see Hitchcock, Ethan A.

Croffut, William A. American Procession, Eighteen Fifty-Five to Nineteen Fourteen. facs. ed. LC 68-20293. (Essay Index Reprint Ser). 1931. 20.00 (ISBN 0-8369-0352-8). Ayer Co Pubs.

--The Vanderbilts & the Story of their Fortune. facsimile ed. LC 75-1837. (Leisure Class in America Ser.). (Illus.). 1975. Repr. of 1886 ed. 20.00x (ISBN 0-405-06906-5). Ayer Co Pubs.

Croft, A. J. Cryogenic Laboratory Equipment. LC 65-11337. (International Cryogenics Monographs Ser.). 182p. 1969. 39.50x (ISBN 0-306-30253-5, Plenum Pr). Plenum Pub.

Croft, B. A., jt. auth. see Welch, S. M.

Croft, B. A. & Hoyt, S. C., eds. Integrated Management of Insect Pests of Pome & Stone Fruit. LC 82-13659. (Environmental Science & Technology Texts & Monographs). 454p. 1983. 52.50x (ISBN 0-471-05334-1, Pub. by Wiley-Interscience). Wiley.

Croft, Barbara L. The Checklist Kit for Resume Writing & Job Application Letters. 16p. 1982. 3.50 (ISBN 0-9609580-0-2). Different Drum.

Croft, Barbara Y., jt. ed. see Price, Ronald R.

Croft, Brian, jt. auth. see Dover, Michael.

Croft, David. Applied Statistics for Management Studies. 3rd ed. (Illus.). 304p. (Orig.). 1983. pap. text ed. 19.95x (ISBN 0-7121-0182-9, Pub. by Macdonald & Evans England). Trans-Atlantic.

Croft, Doreen & Hess, Robert D. Activities Handbook for Teachers of Young Children. 3rd ed. LC 79-90365. 1980. pap. text ed. 15.50 (ISBN 0-395-28698-0). HM.

Croft, Doreen J. Parents & Teachers: A Resource Book for Home, School & Community Relations. 1979. pap. text ed. write for info. (ISBN 0-534-00610-8). Wadsworth Pub.

Croft, Doreen J. & Hess, Robert D. An Activities Handbook for Teachers of Young Children. 4th ed. LC 84-82414. 384p. 1984. pap. write for info (ISBN 0-395-35762-4). HM.

Croft, Doreen J., jt. auth. see Hess, Robert.

Croft, H. & Guy, R. K. Unsolved Problems in Intuitive Mathematics: Unsolved Problems in Number Theory, Vol. 1. (Problem Books in Mathematics Ser.). (Illus.). 160p. 1981. 22.00 (ISBN 0-387-90593-6). Springer Verlag.

Croft, Herbert S., ed. see Elyot, Thomas.

Croft, J. R. & Kanis, A. Handbooks of the Flora of Papua New Guinea, Vol. II. (Illus.). 276p. 1982. text ed. 37.95x (ISBN 0-522-84204-6, Pub. by Melbourne U Pr Australia). Intl Spec Bk.

Croft, John. Natural Relief from Arthritis. 1981. 29.95x (ISBN 0-317-07277-3, Regent House). B of A.

Croft, K. Science Readings for Students of English As a Second Language, with Exercises for Vocabulary Development. 1968. 2.75 (ISBN 0-07-013883-4). McGraw.

Croft, Karen. Good for Me Cookbook. (Illus.). (gr. k-5). pap. 1.95 (ISBN 0-88247-177-5). R & E Pubs.

Croft, Kenneth. A Practice Book on English Stress & Intonation. 81p. 1961. pap. 5.50 (ISBN 0-87789-013-7); cassette tapes 90.00 (ISBN 0-87789-125-7). Eng Language.

--Reading & Word Study: For Students of English As a Second Language. (Illus.). 1969. pap. text ed. 14.95 (ISBN 0-13-756742-1). P-H.

--Readings on English As a Second Language: For Teachers & Teacher Trainees. 1980. 19.95 (ISBN 0-316-16137-3). Little.

Croft, L. R. Handbook of Protein Sequence Analysis: A Compilation of Amino Acid Sequences of Proteins. LC 79-41487. 644p. 1980. 137.95 (ISBN 0-471-27703-7). Wiley.

--Introduction to Protein Sequence Analysis. LC 79-41488. 157p. 1980. pap. 21.95 (ISBN 0-471-27710-X). Wiley.

Croft, Mary K., jt. auth. see Steward, Joyce S.

Croft, P. J., ed. The Poems of Robert Sidney, Edited from the Poet's Autograph Notebook with Introduction & Commentary. 1984. 67.00x (ISBN 0-19-812726-X). Oxford U Pr.

Croft, Pauline. The Spanish Company. 1973. 50.00x (ISBN 0-686-96611-2, Pub by London Rec Soc England). State Mutual Bk.

Croft, Terrell, et al. American Electrician's Handbook. 10th ed. 1664p. 1980. 53.95 (ISBN 0-07-013931-8). McGraw.

Croft, William. The Symphony & Overture in Great Britain. Barrys, Brook & Platt, Richard, eds. LC 83-20758. (The Symphony Ser.). 1984. lib. bdg. 90.00 (ISBN 0-8240-3840-1). Garland Pub.

Croft-Cooke, R. St. George for England. 1968. Repr. of 1966 ed. text ed. 11.00x (ISBN 0-317-13479-5, Pub. by C Woolf UK). Humanities.

Croft-Cooke, Rupert. Rudyard Kipling. LC 74-7100. (English Biography Ser., No. 31). 1974. lib. bdg. 31.95x (ISBN 0-8383-1856-8). Haskell.

Croft-Cooke, Rupert see Bruce, Leo, pseud.

Crofton, Ian & Fraser, Donald. A Dictionary of Musical Quotations. 192p. 1985. 14.95 (ISBN 0-02-906530-5, Pub by Schimer Book). MacMillan.

Crofton, Ian & Fraser, Donald, eds. A Dictionary of Musical Quotations. 162p. 1985. 14.95 (ISBN 0-317-28399-5). Schirmer Bks.

Crofton, John & Douglas, Andrew. Respiratory Diseases. 3rd ed. (Illus.). 836p. 1981. 72.50 (ISBN 0-8016-1142-3, Blackwell). Mosby.

Crofts, Ellen. Chapters in the History of English Literature, from 1509 to the Close of the Elizabethan Period. 1979. Repr. of 1884 ed. lib. bdg. 25.00 (ISBN 0-8495-0949-1). Arden Lib.

Crofts, Freeman W. The Cask. lib. bdg. 12.95x (ISBN 0-89966-245-5). Buccaneer Bks.

--The Cask: A Classic Detective Novel. 320p. 1977. pap. 5.95 (ISBN 0-486-23457-6). Dover.

--The Cheyne Mystery. 15.95 (ISBN 0-88411-070-2, Pub. by Aeonian Pr). Amereon Ltd.

--Mystery in the English Channel. 320p. 1977. Repr. lib. bdg. 14.95x (ISBN 0-89966-273-0). Buccaneer Bks.

--The Pit-Prop Syndicate. (Crime Ser.). 1978. pap. 3.95 (ISBN 0-14-000512-9). Penguin.

--Sir John Magill's Last Journey. Incl. Vols. 1-3. 72p. 1972-75. Repr. avail. (0039); Vols. 4-7. 120p. 1975-79 (0050). 301p. 1977. Repr. lib. bdg. 13.95x (ISBN 0-89966-274-9). Buccaneer Bks.

Crofts, I. Wordsworth & the Seventeenth Century. LC 74-28470. lib. bdg. 6.00 (ISBN 0-8414-3501-4). Folcroft.

Crofts, J. E., jt. auth. see Rouland, David.

Crofts, John E. Shakespeare & the Post Horses: A New Study of the Merry Wives of Windsor. LC 78-153313. Repr. of 1937 ed. 19.00 (ISBN 0-404-01856-4). AMS Pr.

Crofts, Trudy. The Hunter & the Quail. (Jataka Tales for Children Ser.). (Illus.). 24p. (gr. 1-6). 1977. pap. 4.95 (ISBN 0-913546-30-5). Dharma Pub.

Crofut, Doris. By Faith Alone: A Novel of the Huguenot Settlement at New Paltz, New York. LC 72-77198. 147p. 1972. 11.95 (ISBN 0-912526-02-5). Lib Res.

Crofutt, George A. Crofutt's Grip - Sack Guide of Colorado. rev. ed. Rizzari, Francis, et al, eds. (Illus.). 1981. pap. 12.95 (ISBN 0-933472-56-0). Johnson Bks.

Croger, T. R. Notes on Conductors & Conducting. 1976. lib. bdg. 29.00 (ISBN 0-403-03785-9). Scholarly.

Croghan, Anthony. Code for Cataloging Non Book Media. (Orig.). 1972. pap. 8.50x (ISBN 0-9501212-4-X). J Norton Pubs.

--Manual & Code of Rules for Simple Cataloging. 2nd ed. 1974. pap. 6.95x plus 24 audio cassettes (ISBN 0-9501212-6-6). J Norton Pubs.

Croghan, George. Army Life on the Western Frontier: Selections From the Official Reports Made Between 1826 & 1945. 1st ed. Prucha, Francis P., ed. LC 58-11600. (Illus.). pap. 58.00 (ISBN 0-317-08318-X, 2004767). Bks Demand UMI.

Croghan, Martin J. & Croghan, Penelope P. Ideological Training in Communist Education. LC 79-47986. 209p. 1980. text ed. 22.75 (ISBN 0-8191-0992-4); pap. text ed. 12.00 (ISBN 0-8191-0993-2). U Pr of Amer.

--Role Models & Readers: A Sociological Analysis. LC 79-5430. 1980. pap. 10.75 (ISBN 0-8191-0879-0). U Pr of Amer.

Croghan, Penelope P., jt. auth. see Croghan, Martin J.

Croghan, Tonita, jt. auth. see Brace, Betty L.

Crogman, W. H., jt. auth. see Gibson, J. W.

Crogman, William H. Talks for the Times. facs. ed. LC 78-152919. (Black Heritage Library Collection Ser). 1896. 20.25 (ISBN 0-8369-8763-2). Ayer Co Pubs.

Crogman, William H., jt. auth. see Kletzing, Henry F.

Crogman, William H., jt. auth. see Nichols, J. L.

Croinin, D. O., jt. auth. see Dillon, Myles.

Croisdale, D. W., et al, eds. Computerized Braille Production: Today & Tomorrow. 422p. 1983. pap. 19.50 (ISBN 0-387-12057-2). Springer-Verlag.

Croiset, Alfred & Croiset, Maurice. Abridged History of Greek Literature. Heffelbower, G. F., tr. LC 78-131510. Repr. of 1904 ed. 32.50 (ISBN 0-404-01857-2). AMS Pr.

Croiset, Maurice. Aristophanes & the Political Parties at Athens. Loeb, James, tr. LC 72-7886. (Greek History Ser). Repr. of 1909 ed. 15.00 (ISBN 0-405-04780-0). Ayer Co Pubs.

Croiset, Maurice, jt. auth. see Croiset, Alfred.

Croissant, DeWitt C. Studies in the Work of Colley Cibber. (English Literature Ser., No. 33). 1970. pap. 27.95x (ISBN 0-8383-0088-X). Haskell.

Croix, Don La see Kaufman, Peter B. & La Croix, Don.

Croix, Grethe La see La Croix, Grethe & Pesch, Imelda M.

Croix, Rick C. de see De Croix, Rick C.

Croizat, Victor. Brown Water Navy: The River & Coastal War in Indo-China & Vietnam 1948-1972. (Illus.). 160p. 1985. 17.95 (ISBN 0-7137-1272-4, Pub. by Blandford Pr England). Sterling.

Croizier, Ralph C. Koxinga & Chinese Nationalism: History, Myth & the Hero. (East Asian Monographs Ser: No. 66). 150p. 1977. pap. 11.00x (ISBN 0-674-50566-2). Harvard U Pr.

Croke & Emmett, eds. History & Historians in Late Antiquity. 184p. 1984. o. s. i. 25.00 (ISBN 0-08-029840-0). Pergamon.

Croke, B. F. & Harris, J. D. Religious Conflict in Fourth Century Rome. (Sources in Ancient History Ser.). 139p. (Orig.). 1982. pap. 21.00x (ISBN 0-424-00091-1, Pub. by Sydney U Pr Australia). Intl Spec Bk.

Croke, Katherine B. & Fairchild, Betty J. Let's Play Games! 62p. 1978. 1-9 copies 1.25 ea. (E-60); 10-99 copies 1.15 ea.; 100 copies or more 1.00 ea. Natl Easter Seal.

Croker, J. W., jt. auth. see Scott, W.

Croker, John W. The Correspondence & Diaries of the Late Right Honourable John Wilson Croker, LL.D., FR.S. Secretary to the Admiralty from 1809-1830, 2 vols. Jennings, Louis J., ed. 1978. Repr. of 1884 ed. lib. bdg. 45.00 set (ISBN 0-8492-3961-3). R West.

--Croker Papers, 3 Vols. rev. ed. 2nd ed. Jennings, L. J., ed. LC 77-154125. Repr. of 1885 ed. Set. 125.00 (ISBN 0-404-01880-7). Vol. 1 (ISBN 0-404-01881-5). Vol. 2 (ISBN 0-404-01882-3). Vol. 3 (ISBN 0-404-01883-1). AMS Pr.

--Essays on the Early Period of the French Revolution. LC 78-114146. Repr. of 1857 ed. 34.50 (ISBN 0-404-01858-0). AMS Pr.

Croker, John W., et al, eds. see Pope, Alexander.

Croker, T. Crofton. Irish Folk Stories for Children. (Illus.). 90p. (gr. 6 up). 1983. pap. 3.95 (ISBN 0-85342-690-2, Pub. by Mercier Pr Ireland). Irish Bk Ctr.

Croker, Thomas. Researches in the South of Ireland: A Source Book of Irish Folk Tradition. 1969. Repr. of 1824 ed. 30.00x (ISBN 0-7165-0077-9, BBA 02154, Pub. by Irish Academic Pr Ireland). Biblio Dist.

Croker, Thomas C. Fairy Legends & Traditions of the South of Ireland. LC 82-5885. 1983. 60.00x (ISBN 0-8201-1380-8). Schol Facsimiles.

Croker, Thomas C., ed. Narratives Illustrative of the Contests in Ireland in 1641 & 1690. (Camden Society, London. Publications. First Ser.: No. 14). Repr. of 1841 ed. 24.00 (ISBN 0-404-50114-1). AMS Pr.

--Narratives Illustrative of the Contests in Ireland in 1641 & 1690. 1841. 24.00 (ISBN 0-384-10190-9). Johnson Repr.

--Popular Songs, Illustrative of the French Invasions of Ireland. Repr. of 1845 ed. 32.00 (ISBN 0-384-10205-0). Johnson Repr.

Crokett, Christina. To Touch a Dream. (Super Romances Ser.). 384p. 1983. pap. 2.95 (ISBN 0-373-70055-5, Pub. by Worldwide). Harlequin Bks.

Crolier, M. J. & Bingham, J. W. Geology of Parts of Grant, Adams, & Franklin Counties, East-Central Washington. (Illus.). 91p. 1978. 1.50 (ISBN 0-686-34720-X). Geologic Pubns.

Croll, Carolyn. Too Many Babas. LC 78-22474. (I Can Read Bk.). (Illus.). 64p. (gr. k-3). 1979. PLB 9.89 (ISBN 0-06-021384-1). HarpJ.

Croll, Elisabeth. Chinese Women since Mao. LC 83-16624. 144p. 1984. pap. 11.95 (ISBN 0-87332-267-3). M E Sharpe.

--The Family Rice Bowl: Food & Domestic Economy in China. (Illus.). 394p. 1983. 29.50x (ISBN 0-86232-124-7, Pub. by Zed Pr England); 10.75 (ISBN 0-86232-125-5). Biblio Dist.

--The Politics of Marriage in Contemporary China. LC 80-40586. (Contemporary China Institute Publications Ser.). (Illus.). 224p. 1981. 44.50 (ISBN 0-521-23345-3). Cambridge U Pr.

--Women in Post-Mao China. 144p. 1984. cancelled (ISBN 0-86232-173-5, Pub. by Zed Pr England); pap. cancelled (ISBN 0-86232-174-3, Pub. by Zed Pr England). Biblio Dist.

Croll, Elisabeth, et al, eds. China's One-Child Family Policy. LC 84-26756. 256p. 1985. 27.50 (ISBN 0-312-13356-1). St Martin.

Croll, Elisabeth J. Feminism & Socialism in China. 1978. 27.50 (ISBN 0-7100-8816-7). Routledge & Kegan.

Croll, Elizabeth F. Women in Rural Development: The People's Republic of China. 61p. (Second Impression, 1980). 1983. pap. 8.55 (ISBN 92-2-102054-1, ILO269, ILO). Unipub.

Croll, N. A., ed. The Organisation of Nematodes. 1977. 69.00 (ISBN 0-12-196850-2). Acad Pr.

Croll, Neil A. Parasitism & Other Associations. (Illus.). 115p. 1973. 14.00x (ISBN 0-8464-0702-7). Beekman Pubs.

Croll, Neil A. & Matthews, Bernard E. Biology of Nematodes. LC 75-505520. (Tertiary Level Biology Ser.). 201p. 1977. Repr. 26.95x (ISBN 0-470-99028-7). Halsted Pr.

Croll, Neil A. & Cross, John H., eds. Human Ecology & Infectious Diseases. 1983. 49.50 (ISBN 0-12-196880-4). Acad Pr.

Croll, Paul & Moses, Diana. One in Five: The Assessment & Incidence of Special Educational Needs. (Special Needs in Education Ser.). 192p. 1985. 24.95x (ISBN 0-7102-0322-5). Routledge & Kegan.

Croll, R. D. & Doery, A. C. Successful Conferences. 38p. 1983. pap. 2.50x (ISBN 0-643-00371-1, Pub. by CSIRO Australia). Intl Spec Bk.

Croly, David G. Miscegenation. LC 70-104435. Repr. of 1864 ed. lib. bdg. 29.00 (ISBN 0-8398-0281-1). Irvington.

Croly, Herbert. The Promise of American Life. (American Reform in the 20th Century Ser.). 468p. 1986. Repr. of 1914 ed. lib. bdg. 49.50 (ISBN 0-306-76277-3). Da Capo.

Croly, Herbert D. Willard Straight. 44.00 (ISBN 0-8369-7107-8, 7941). Ayer Co Pubs.

Croly, Jane, jt. auth. see Fairfield, Francis G.

Crom, Scott. Obstacles to Mystical Experience. 1983. pap. 5.00x (ISBN 0-87574-132-0, 132). Pendle Hill.

--On Being Real. LC 67-29811. (Orig.). 1967. pap. 5.00x (ISBN 0-87574-155-X, 155). Pendle Hill.

--Quaker Worship & Techniques of Meditation. 1983. pap. 5.00x (ISBN 0-87574-195-9, 195). Pendle Hill.

Crom, Theodore R. Art of Time. 54p. 1984. pap. 7.50 (ISBN 0-8130-0813-1). U Presses Fla.

Cromack, Celeste, ed. see Hunt, Tamara.

Cromack, Celeste, ed. see Renfro, Nancy.

Croman, Dorothy Y. Danger in Sagebrush Country. (Outlands Adventure Ser.). 144p. (gr. 4-7). 1984. 2.95 (ISBN 0-8423-0514-9). Tyndale.

--The Mystery of Steamboat Rock. (Outlands Adventure Ser.). 208p. (gr. 4-7). 1984. pap. 2.95 (ISBN 0-8423-4671-6). Tyndale.

--Trouble on the Blue Fox Island. (Outlands Adventure Ser.). 176p. (gr. 4-7). 1985. 3.50 (ISBN 0-8423-7345-4). Tyndale.

Croman, Natalie. John Galsworthy: A Study in Continuity & Contrast. LC 72-194104. 1933. lib. bdg. 15.00 (ISBN 0-8414-2416-0). Folcroft.

Cromartie, Bill. Braggin' Rights: A Game by Game History of the Alabama-Auburn Football Rivalry 1893 to 1981. LC 82-82118. (Great Rivalry Ser.). (Illus.). 400p. 1982. pap. 9.95 (ISBN 0-88011-070-8). Leisure Pr.

--There Goes Herschel: Countdown to the Pros. LC 83-80722. (Illus.). 224p. (Orig.). 1983. pap. 11.95 (ISBN 0-88011-159-3). Leisure Pr.

Cromartie, Bill, jt. auth. see Peterson, James A.

Crombag, H. F., jt. auth. see Chang, T. M.

Crombag, H. G. & De Gruijter, D. N., eds. Contemporary Issues in Educational Testing. (Psychological Studies: No. 9). (Illus.). 1974. text ed. 24.80x (ISBN 90-2797-521-3). Mouton.

Crombie, A. C. Augustine to Galileo. (Illus.). 1979. text ed. 25.00x (ISBN 0-674-05273-0). Harvard U Pr.

Crombie, David. The Synthesizer & Electronic Keyboard Handbook. LC 84-47863. (Illus.). 1984. 25.00 (ISBN 0-394-54084-0); pap. 13.95 (ISBN 0-394-72711-8). Knopf.

Crombie, I. M. An Examination of Plato's Doctrines, 2 vols. Incl. Vol. 1. Plato on Man & Society. 1962. text ed. 36.50x (ISBN 0-7100-3608-6); Vol. 2. Plato on Knowledge & Reality. 1963. text ed. 41.00x (ISBN 0-391-01053-0). (International Library of Philosophy & Scientific Method). Set. text ed. 41.00x (ISBN 0-391-01053-0). Humanities.

--Plato: The Midwife's Apprentice. LC 81-6812. viii, 195p. 1981. Repr. of 1965 ed. lib. bdg. 19.75x (ISBN 0-313-23243-1, CRPL). Greenwood.

Crombie, J. W. The Poets & Peoples of Foreign Lands. 1979. Repr. of 1890 ed. lib. bdg. 25.00 (ISBN 0-8482-7567-5). Norwood Edns.

Crombie, Lance. Making Alcohol Fuel: Recipe & Procedure. (Illus., Orig.). 1979. pap. 8.00 (ISBN 0-936222-00-X). Rutan Pub.

Crombie, Mildred. Reflections Then & Now. Perry, Marion, ed. LC 81-52041. (Illus.). 55p. (Orig.). 1981. pap. 4.95 (ISBN 0-938838-07-5). Textile Bridge.

Cromblehome, Roger, jt. auth. see Kirtland, Terry.

Cromelin, Paul L. Bridge Is Beautiful. 1979. 10.95 (ISBN 0-671-96044-X); pap. 4.95 (ISBN 0-346-12420-4). Cornerstone.

Cromer, A. Physics in Science & Industry. 1980. text ed. 34.95 (ISBN 0-07-014437-0). McGraw.

Cromer, Alan. Experiments in Physics. 192p. 1981. pap. text ed. 10.95 (ISBN 0-8403-2804-4, 40280401). Kendall-Hunt.

--Physics for the Life Sciences. 2nd ed. (Illus.). 1976. text ed. 32.95 (ISBN 0-07-014434-6). McGraw.

Cromer, Evelyn B. Political & Literary Essays: 1st Series. facs. ed. LC 68-8453. (Essay Index Reprint Ser). 1913. 23.75 (ISBN 0-8369-1058-3). Ayer Co Pubs.

--Political & Literary Essays: 2nd Series. facsimile ed. LC 73-108636. (Essay Index Reprint Ser.). 1914. 20.00 (ISBN 0-8369-1564-X). Ayer Co Pubs.

--Political & Literary Essays: 3rd Series. facsimile ed. LC 74-107690. (Essay Index Reprint Ser.). 1916. 21.50 (ISBN 0-8369-1494-5). Ayer Co Pubs.

Cromer, John, jt. ed. see Bullen, Keith.

Cromer, Peggy, ed. see Zalm, Bill V.

Cromett, Michael F. & Gaut, Gregory A. Criminals Appeals: Effective Practice & Procedure. (Minnesota Criminal Law Ser.). 1984. looseleaf 65.00 (ISBN 0-86678-357-1). Butterworth MN.

Cromie, Alice. Restored America: A Tour Guide. 1984. 6.98 (ISBN 0-517-42609-9, AM Legacy Pr.). Crown.

--Tour Guide to the Old West. 1982. pap. 9.95 (ISBN 0-8129-6323-7). Times Bks.

Cromie, Henry. Notes & Corrections for the Ryme-Index. 1875. 15.00 (ISBN 0-8274-3047-7). R West.

Cromie, Marguerite. Children Sing. 1975. pap. 1.25 (ISBN 0-8198-0390-1). Dghtrs St Paul.

Cromie, Richard M. Christ Will See You Through. 60p. (Orig.). 1985. pap. 1.00 (ISBN 0-914733-04-4). Desert Min.

--How to Live with Cancer. LC 84-72666. pap. 1.00 (ISBN 0-914733-01-X). Desert Min.

--Sometime Before the Dawn. 111p. (Orig.). 1982. 10.95 (ISBN 0-317-14978-4); pap. 6.95 (ISBN 0-317-14979-2). Desert Min.

Cromie, Richard M., jt. auth. see Davis, Warren B.

Cromie, Robert. Chicago. LC 80-17624. (Illus.). 128p. 1980. 35.00 (ISBN 0-528-81102-9). Rand.

--Chicago in Color. (Profiles of America Ser.). 1969. 8.95 (ISBN 0-8038-1203-5). Hastings.

--A Short History of Chicago. (Short History Ser.). (Illus.). 160p. (Orig.). 1984. pap. 9.95 (ISBN 0-938530-28-3). Lexikos.

Cromie, Robert & Warne, F. A. A Plunge into Space. LC 75-28853. (Classics of Science Fiction Ser.). (Illus.). 240p. 1976. 13.50 (ISBN 0-88355-367-8); pap. 4.50 (ISBN 0-88355-452-6). Hyperion Conn.

Cromie, William. Skylab: The Story of Man's First Station in Space. LC 74-25983. (Illus.). 192p. (gr. 7 up). 1976. 10.95 (ISBN 0-679-20300-1). McKay.

Cromie, William J. Steven & the Green Turtle. LC 77-85040. (Science I Can Read Bk.). (Illus.). 64p. (gr. k-3). 1970. PLB 9.89 (ISBN 0-06-021374-4). HarpJ.

Crommelin, M., jt. auth. see Saunders, C.

Crommelinck, M., jt. auth. see Roucoux, A.

Crompsey, Bob. The Scottish Footballer. 77p. 1981. 10.00x (ISBN 0-85158-128-5, Pub. by Blackwood & Sons England). State Mutual Bk.

Crompton, A. C., jt. auth. see Langley, F. A.

Crompton, Alastair. The Craft of Copywriting: How to Write Great Copy That Sells. (Illus.). 185p. 1982. 14.95 (ISBN 0-13-188409-3); pap. 7.95 (ISBN 0-13-188391-7). P-H.

Crompton, Anne. The Untamed. 256p. (Orig.). 1981. pap. 2.75 (ISBN 0-523-41151-0). Pinnacle Bks.

Crompton, Anne E. The Ice Trail. 128p. (gr. 3-7). 1980. 9.50 (ISBN 0-416-30691-8, NO. 0191). Methuen Inc.

--The Lifting Stone. LC 77-10607. (Illus.). 40p. (ps-3). 1978. reinforced bdg. 7.95 (ISBN 0-8234-0325-4). Holiday.

--Queen of Swords. LC 79-26496. 1980. 8.95 (ISBN 0-416-30611-X, NO. 0165). Methuen Inc.

--The Rain-Cloud Pony. LC 76-47545. (Illus.). 128p. (gr. 3-6). 1977. 5.95 (ISBN 0-8234-0295-9). Holiday.

--The Sorcerer. LC 82-61042. 176p. 1982. Repr. of 1971 ed. 16.95 (ISBN 0-933256-36-1). Second Chance.

--A Woman's Place. (Illus.). 224p. 1980. pap. 2.25 (ISBN 0-345-28790-8). Ballantine.

Crompton, Anne Eliot. The Winter Wife. (Illus.). 48p. 1975. 8.95g (ISBN 0-316-16143-8, Pub. by Atlantic Monthly Pr). Little.

Crompton, D. W. Parasitic Worms. LC 79-20223. (Wykeham Science Ser.: No. 57). 207p. 1980. pap. 15.95x (ISBN 0-8448-1342-7). Crane-Russak Co.

Crompton, D. W. & Joyner, S. M. Parasitic Worms. 208p. 1980. pap. cancelled (ISBN 0-85109-830-4). Taylor & Francis.

Crompton, D. W. & Newton, B. A., eds. Trends & Perspectives in Parasitology, No. 1. LC 80-42159. (Illus.). 150p. 1981. 29.95 (ISBN 0-521-23821-8); pap. 11.95 (ISBN 0-521-28242-X). Cambridge U Pr.

--Trends & Perspectives in Parasitology, No. 2. LC 80-42159. (Illus.). 91p. 1982. 21.95 (ISBN 0-521-24830-2); pap. 8.95 (ISBN 0-521-28989-0). Cambridge U Pr.

Crompton, D. W. & Nickol, B. B., eds. Biology of Acanthocephala. (Illus.). 512p. Date not set. 89.50 (ISBN 0-521-24674-1). Cambridge U Pr.

Crompton, Don. A View from the Spire: William Golding's Later Novels. 208p. 1985. 24.95 (ISBN 0-631-13826-9). Basil Blackwell.

Crompton, John, jt. auth. see National Park Service Staff.

Crompton, John L., jt. auth. see Howard, Dennis R.

Crompton, Louis. Byron & Greek Love: Homophobia in Nineteenth Century England. LC 84-16463. 424p. 1985. 24.95 (ISBN 0-520-05172-6). U of Cal Pr.

--Shaw the Dramatist. LC 69-11202. xii, 261p. 1969. 19.95x (ISBN 0-8032-0031-5). U of Nebr Pr.

Crompton, Louis, ed. Charles Dickens: Great Expectations. 567p. 1964. pap. text ed. write for info. (ISBN 0-02-325710-5). Macmillan.

Crompton, Louis, ed. see Dickens, Charles.

Crompton, Louis, ed. see Shaw, Bernard.

Crompton, Margaret. Adolescents & Social Workers. Davies, Martin, ed. (Community Care Practice Handbook Ser.). vi, 91p. (Orig.). 1983. pap. text ed. 8.50x (ISBN 0-435-82189-X). Gower Pub Co.

--The House Where Jack Lives. (Illus.). 30p. (ps-1). 1980. 4.95 (ISBN 0-370-30027-0, Pub. by the Bodley Head). Merrimack Pub Cir.

--Passionate Search: A Life of Charlotte Bronte. 252p. 1982. Repr. of 1955 ed. lib. bdg. 40.00 (ISBN 0-89984-121-X). Century Bookbindery.

--Respecting Children: Social Work with Young People. LC 80-5820. (Illus.). 246p. 1980. 25.00 (ISBN 0-8039-1544-6); pap. 12.50 (ISBN 0-8039-1545-4). Sage.

Crompton, Paul H. Karate Training Methods. 1984. 22.00x (ISBN 0-901764-67-1, Pub. by P H Crompton Ltd UK). State Mutual Bk.

Crompton, R. W., jt. auth. see Huxley, L. G.

Crompton, Richard. The Mansion of Magnanimitie: Wherein Is Shewed the Acts of Sundrie English Kings. LC 74-28841. (No. 722). 1975. Repr. of 1599 ed. 9.50 (ISBN 90-221-0722-1). Walter J Johnson.

--Star-Chamber Cases, Shewing What Causes Properly Belong to the Cognizance of That Court. LC 74-28842. (English Experience Ser.: No. 723). 1975. Repr. of 1630 ed. 6.00 (ISBN 90-221-0723-X). Walter J Johnson.

Crompton, Rosemary & Gubbay, Jon. Economy & the Class Structure. LC 77-26302. 1978. 25.00x (ISBN 0-312-23676-X). St Martin.

Crompton, Rosemary & Jones, Gareth. White Collar Proletariat: Deskilling & Gender in Clerical Work. 360p. 1984. 34.95 (ISBN 0-87722-356-4). Temple U Pr.

Crompton, Rosemary, jt. auth. see Wedderburn, Dorothy.

Crompton, T., illus. The Good Samaritan: Retold by Catherine Storr. (People of the Bible Ser.). (Illus.). 32p. 1984. 10.65 (ISBN 0-8172-1988-9, Raintree Childrens Books Belitha Press Ltd. - London). Raintree Pubs.

Crompton, T. R. The Analysis of Plastics. (Series in Analytical Chemistry: Vol. 8). (Illus.). 452p. 1984. 54.00 (ISBN 0-08-026251-1). Pergamon.

--Chemical Analysis of Additives in Plastics. 2nd ed. 1977. text ed. 62.00 (ISBN 0-08-020497-X). Pergamon.

--Chemical Analysis of Organometallic Compounds, 5 vols. (Analysis of Organic Materials Ser). Vol. 1, 1974. 49.00 (ISBN 0-12-197301-8); Vol. 2, 1975. 39.00 (ISBN 0-12-197302-6); Vol. 4, 1975. 55.00 (ISBN 0-12-197304-2); Vol. 5, 1978. 85.00 (ISBN 0-12-197305-0). Acad Pr.

--Determination of Organic Substances in Water, 2 vols. 1985. Vol. 1. 85.00 (ISBN 0-471-90468-6); Vol. 2. write for info. (ISBN 0-471-90469-4). Wiley.

--Gas Chromatography of Organometallic Compounds. LC 82-523. 600p. 1982. 85.00x (ISBN 0-306-40987-9, Plenum Pr). Plenum Pub.

--Small Batteries: Primary Cells, Vol. 2. LC 81-11495. 240p. 1983. Repr. 69.95x (ISBN 0-470-27356-9). Halsted Pr.

--Small Batteries: Secondary Cells, Vol. 1. LC 81-6990. 226p. 1982. Repr. 74.95x (ISBN 0-470-27267-8). Halsted Pr.

Cromwall, Liz & Hibner, Dixie. Finger Frolics: Fingerplays for Young Children. rev. ed. 1983. pap. 8.95 (ISBN 0-933212-10-0). Partner Pr.

Cromwell, Ellen. Early Reading Through Experience: Feathers in My Cap. LC 80-14498. 1980. pap. 9.95 (ISBN 0-87491-296-2). Acropolis.

Cromwell, Florence, ed. Occupational Therapy Assessment As the Keystone to Treatment Planning. LC 84-697. (Occupational Therapy in Health Care Ser.: Vol. 1, No. 2). 124p. 1984. text ed. 19.95 (ISBN 0-86656-305-9). Haworth Pr.

Cromwell, Florence S., ed. The Changing Roles of Occupational Therapists in the 1980s. LC 83-22818. (Occupational Therapy in Health Care Ser.: Vol. 1, No. 1). 99p. 1984. text ed. 19.95 (ISBN 0-86656-294-X, B294). Haworth Pr.

--Occupational Therapy & Adolescents with Disability. (Occupational Therapy in Health Care Ser.: Vol. 2, No. 3). 160p. 1985. text ed. 24.95 (ISBN 0-86656-447-0); pap. text ed. 16.95 (ISBN 0-86656-455-1). Haworth Pr.

--Occupational Therapy & the Patient with Pain. LC 84-10496. (Occupational Therapy in Health Care Ser.: Vol. 1, No. 3). 114p. 1984. text ed. 22.95 (ISBN 0-86656-306-7, B306); pap. text ed. 14.95 (ISBN 0-86656-453-5). Haworth Pr.

--Occupational Therapy Strategies & Adaptations for Independent Daily Living. LC 84-19157. (Occupational Therapy in Health Care Ser.: Vol. 1, No. 4). 200p. 1985. text ed. 22.95 (ISBN 0-86656-350-4); 17.95 (ISBN 0-86656-380-6). Haworth Pr.

--Private Practice in Occupational Therapy. LC 85-5513. (Occupational Therapy in Health Care: Vol. 2, No. 2). 152p. 1985. text ed. 22.95 (ISBN 0-86656-411-X); pap. text ed. 14.95 (ISBN 0-86656-412-8). Haworth Pr.

--The Roles of Occupational Therapists in Continuity of Care. LC 85-899. (Occupational Therapy in Health Care Ser.: Vol. 2, No. 1). 176p. 1985. text ed. 22.95 (ISBN 0-86656-392-X); pap. text ed. 17.95 (ISBN 0-86656-393-8). Haworth Pr.

--Work-Related Programs in Occupational Therapy. (Occupational Therapy in Health Care: Vol. 2, No. 4). 136p. 1985. 22.95 (ISBN 0-86656-487-X); pap. text ed. 14.95 (ISBN 0-86656-519-1). Haworth Pr.

Cromwell, Giles. The Virginia Manufactory of Arms. LC 74-8802. 1975. 20.00 (ISBN 0-8139-0573-7). U Pr of Va.

Cromwell, Jerry, et al. A Study of Administrative Costs in Physicians' Offices Under Medicaid. 1977. pap. 38.60 (ISBN 0-89011-508-7, HMD-144). Abt Bks.

Cromwell, John W. The Negro in American History: Men & Women Eminent in the Evolution of the American of African Descent. (Basic Afro-American Reprint Library). 1969. Repr. of 1914 ed. 18.00 (ISBN 0-384-10215-8). Johnson Repr.

Cromwell, Leslie & Arditti, M. Medical Instrumentation for Health Care. (Illus.). 1976. Ref. Ed. 32.95 (ISBN 0-13-572602-6). P-H.

Cromwell, Leslie, et al. Biomedical Instrumentation & Measurements. 2nd ed. (Illus.). 1980. text ed. 31.95 (ISBN 0-13-076448-5). P-H.

Cromwell, Liz & Hibner, Dixie. Explore & Create: Activities for Young Children: Art, Games, Cooking, Science, & Math. (Orig.). 1979. pap. 14.95 (ISBN 0-933212-12-7, Dist. by Gryphon House). Partner Pr.

Cromwell, Marie. Sour Grapes. 1984. 6.95 (ISBN 0-533-06038-9). Vantage.

Cromwell, Otelia. Lucretia Mott. LC 79-139913. (Illus.). 1971. Repr. of 1958 ed. 14.00x (ISBN 0-8462-1579-9). Russell.

--Thomas Heywood: A Study in the Elizabethan Drama of Everyday Life. LC 69-15681. (Yale Studies in English Ser.: No. 78). viii, 227p. 1969. Repr. of 1928 ed. 17.50 (ISBN 0-208-00767-9, Archon). Shoe String.

Cromwell, Paul F., Jr., jt. auth. see Killinger, George G.

Cromwell, Paul F., Jr., ed. Jails & Justice. (Illus.). 336p. 1975. 24.50x (ISBN 0-398-03144-4). C C Thomas.

Cromwell, Paul F., Jr., et al. Introduction to Juvenile Delinquency: Text & Readings. (Criminal Justice Ser.). 1978. pap. text ed. 19.95 (ISBN 0-8299-0153-1). West Pub.

--Probation & Parole in the Criminal Justice System. 2nd ed. (Illus.). 460p. 1985. text ed. 19.95 (ISBN 0-314-85256-5). West Pub.

Cromwell, Ronald, et al. The Kvebaek Family Sculpture Technique: A Diagnostic & Research Tool in Family Therapy. 39p. 1980. pap. 3.95 (ISBN 0-932930-30-1). Pilgrimage Inc.

Cromwell, V., et al. Aspects of Government in Nineteenth Century Britain. (Government & Society in 19th Century Britain Ser.). 144p. 1978. 20.00x (ISBN 0-7165-2212-8, BBA 02033, Pub. by Irish Academic Pr Ireland). Biblio Dist.

Cron, Leslie Le see LeCron, Leslie & Bordeaux, Jean.

Cron, Leslie M. Le see LeCron, Leslie M.

Cronan, David S. Underwater Minerals. (Ocean Science Resources & Technology Ser.). 1980. 65.00 (ISBN 0-12-197480-4). Acad Pr.

Cronan, Marion & Atwood, June. First Foods. rev. ed. (gr. 7-9). 1976. text ed. 17.32 (ISBN 0-02-663820-7); tchr's guide 2.00 (ISBN 0-02-663830-4). Bennett IL.

Cronau, Rudolf. German Achievements in America. 59.95 (ISBN 0-8490-0225-7). Gordon Pr.

--Three Centuries of German Life in America. 59.95 (ISBN 0-8490-1210-4). Gordon Pr.

Cronbach, Abraham. The Quest for Peace. LC 79-137533. (Peace Movement in America Ser). ix, 223p. 1972. Repr. of 1937 ed. lib. bdg. 16.95x (ISBN 0-89198-061-X). Ozer.

--Stories Made of Bible Stories. 1961. 13.95x (ISBN 0-8084-0386-9). New Coll U Pr.

Cronbach, L. J. & Drenth, P. J. Mental Tests & Cultural Adaptation. LC 72-79985. (Psychology Ser.). 1972. pap. text ed. 21.60 (ISBN 0-686-22640-2). Mouton.

Cronbach, Lee J. Designing Evaluations of Educational & Social Programs. LC 81-48664. (Social & Behavioral Science Ser.). 1982. text ed. 21.95x (ISBN 0-87589-525-5). Jossey-Bass.

--Educational Psychology. 3rd ed. 875p. 1977. text ed. 22.95 (ISBN 0-15-520883-7, HC); instr's. manual with test questions avail. (ISBN 0-15-520885-3); study guide by B. Goodson 7.95 (ISBN 0-15-520886-1). HarBraceJ.

--Essentials of Psychological Testing. 4th ed. 630p. 1984. text ed. 28.95 scp (ISBN 0-06-041419-7, HarpC); instr's. manual 3.00 (ISBN 0-06-361422-7). Har-Row.

Cronbach, Lee J. & Snow, Richard E. Aptitudes & Instructional Methods: A Handbook for Research on Interactions. LC 76-5510. (Illus.). 1981. 47.50x (ISBN 0-8290-0102-6); pap. text ed. 19.50x (ISBN 0-8290-0103-4). Irvington.

Cronbach, Lee J., et al. Toward Reform of Program Evaluation: Aims, Methods, & Institutonal Arrangements. LC 80-8013. (Social & Behavioral Science & Higher Education Ser.). 1980. text ed. 22.95x (ISBN 0-87589-471-2). Jossey-Bass.

Crondahl, J. IBM Displaywriter User's Guide. LC 83-9940. (Illus.). 1983. pap. 14.95 (ISBN 0-89303-538-6). Brady Comm.

Crondahl, Judy R. IBM Displaywriter User's Guide. 2nd ed. (Illus.). 252p. 1985. pap. 16.95 (ISBN 0-89303-608-0). Brady Comm.

Crone, Alla. East Lies the Sun. (Orig.). 1982. pap. 3.50 (ISBN 0-440-12229-5). Dell.

--Legacy of Amber. (Orig.). 1985. pap. 3.95 (ISBN 0-440-14728-X). Dell.

--North of the Moon. (Orig.). 1984. pap. 3.95 (ISBN 0-440-16572-5). Dell.

--Winds over Manchuria. (Orig.). 1983. pap. 3.50 (ISBN 0-440-18853-9). Dell.

Crone, C. Z., ed. see Symposium on the Transfer of Molecules & Ions Between Capillary Blood & Tissue - Alfred Benzon Symposium 2.

Crone, Donald K. The ASEAN States: Coping with Dependence. LC 83-2433. 240p. 1983. 29.95x (ISBN 0-03-062911-X). Praeger.

Crone, G. R. Background to Political Geography. LC 69-14376. (Illus.). 1970. 13.95 (ISBN 0-8023-1202-0). Dufour.

Crone, G. R., ed. The Voyages of Cadamosto. (Hakluyt Society Works Series II: Vol. 80). (Illus.). Repr. of 1937 ed. 25.00 (ISBN 0-317-15629-2). Kraus Repr.

Crone, J. Magnetic Healer's Guide. 1981. pap. 15.95x (ISBN 0-317-07276-5, Regent House). B of A.

Crone, Marie-Luise. Untersuchungen Zur Reichskirchenpolitik Lothars III, 1125-1137: Zwischen Reichskirchlicher Tradition Und Reformkurie. (European University Studies: No.3, Vol. 170). 398p. 1982. 40.55 (ISBN 3-8204-7019-0). P Lang Pubs.

Crone, Moira. The Winnebago Mysteries. LC 81-71642. 128p. 1982. 10.95 (ISBN 0-914590-68-5); pap. 5.95 (ISBN 0-914590-69-3). Fiction Coll.

Crone, Patricia. Slaves on Horses. LC 79-50234. 1980. 49.50 (ISBN 0-521-22961-8). Cambridge U Pr.

Crone, Patricia & Cook, M. Hagarism: The Making of the Islamic World. LC 75-41714. 1980. pap. 14.95 (ISBN 0-521-29754-0). Cambridge U Pr.

--Hagarism: The Making of the Islamic World. LC 75-41714. 268p. 1977. 37.50 (ISBN 0-521-21133-6). Cambridge U Pr.

Crone, Rainer F. Numerals: Nineteen Twenty-Four to Nineteen Seventy-Seven. (Illus.). 84p. 1978. pap. 12.50x (ISBN 0-317-12098-0). U Pr of New Eng.

Crone, Robert A. Diplopia. 488p. 1974. 164.00 (ISBN 0-444-16000-0, Excerpta Medica). Elsevier.

Crone, Ruth, jt. auth. see Brown, Marion M.

Cronen, Vernon E., jt. auth. see Pearce, W. Barnett.

Cronenberger, J. Helen, et al. The Apple II in the Clinical Laboratory. 225p. 1984. spiral bdg. 22.50 (ISBN 0-316-15748-1). Little.

Croner, Fritz. Soziologie der Angestellten: Sociology of the White Collar. LC 74-25744. (European Sociology Ser.). 312p. 1975. Repr. 23.50x (ISBN 0-405-06499-3). Ayer Co Pubs.

Croner, Helga. More Stepping Stones to Jewish Christian Relations. (Stimulus Bk.). 240p. (Orig.). 1985. pap. 7.95 (ISBN 0-8091-2708-3). Paulist Pr.

--Stepping Stones to Further Jewish-Christian Relations: An Unabridged Collection of Christian Documents. 157p. pap. 10.00 (ISBN 0-686-95183-2). ADL.

Croner, Helga, ed. Issues in the Jewish Christian Dialogue. LC 79-88933. 200p. 1979. pap. 7.95 (ISBN 0-8091-2238-3). Paulist Pr.

Croner, Helga & Klenicki, Leon, eds. Issues in the Jewish-Christian Dialogue: Jewish Perspectives on Covenant Mission & Witness. 190p. 7.95 (ISBN 0-686-95172-7). ADL.

Croner, Helga, jt. ed. see Cohen, Martin A.

Croner, Helga, tr. see Thoma, Clemens.

Croner, John A. The Basque & the Boy. LC 80-15675. 1982. 14.95 (ISBN 0-87949-176-0). Ashley Bks.

Croney, Claude & Movalli, Charles. Croney on Watercolor. LC 81-18961. 144p. 1982. pap. 14.95 (ISBN 0-89134-041-6). North Light Pub.

Croney, Claude, jt. auth. see Blake, Wendon.

Croney, John. Drawing by Sea & River. LC 84-25503. (Illus.). 144p. 1984. 14.95 (ISBN 0-89134-104-8). North Light Pub.

Cronhelm, Frederick W. Double Entry by Single: A New Method of Book-Keeping. Brief, Richard P., ed. LC 77-87267. (Development of Contemporary Accounting Thought Ser). 1978. Repr. of 1818 ed. lib. bdg. 34.50x (ISBN 0-405-10896-6). Ayer Co Pubs.

Cronhjort, B., ed. see IFAC-IFIP Workshop, Mariehamn-Aland, Finland, 1978.

Cronin. Mathematics of Cell Electrophysiology. (Lecture Notes in Pure & Applied Mathematics Ser.: Vol. 63). 144p. 1981. 29.75 (ISBN 0-8247-1157-2). Dekker.

Cronin, A. J. Adventures in Two Worlds. 1956. 7.95 (ISBN 0-316-16155-1). Little.

--Beyond This Place. 320p. 1984. 16.45i (ISBN 0-316-16195-0); pap. 6.70 (ISBN 0-316-16192-6). Little.

--The Citadel. 1937. 16.45 (ISBN 0-316-16158-6); pap. 6.70i (ISBN 0-316-16183-7). Little.

--Grand Canary. 1933. 14.95 (ISBN 0-575-01607-8, Pub. by Gollancz England). David & Charles.

--The Green Years. 1949. 14.95 (ISBN 0-575-00479-7, Pub. by Gollancz England). David & Charles.

--The Green Years. 1978. pap. 1.95 (ISBN 0-671-82101-6). PB.

--The Green Years. LC 84-80912. 320p. 1984. 16.45i (ISBN 0-316-16193-4); pap. 6.70i. Little.

--The Keys of the Kingdom. 1979. Repr. lib. bdg. 17.95x (ISBN 0-89966-431-8). Buccaneer Bks.

--The Keys of the Kingdom. 352p. 1984. 16.45i (ISBN 0-316-16189-6); pap. 6.70i (ISBN 0-316-16184-5). Little.

--Shannon's Way. 320p. 16.45i (ISBN 0-316-16191-8); pap. 6.70i (ISBN 0-316-16185-3). Little.

--A Song of Sixpence. 14.95 (ISBN 0-89190-218-X, Pub. by Am Repr). Amereon Ltd.

--Three Loves. 256p. 1932. 12.95 (ISBN 0-575-00069-4, Pub. by Gollancz England). David & Charles.

Cronin, A. J., et al. Great Unsolved Crimes. LC 74-10424. (Classics of Crime &Criminology Ser.). (Illus.). 351p. 1975. Repr. of 1935 ed. 19.50 (ISBN 0-88355-191-8). Hyperion Conn.

Cronin, Anthony. Forty-One Sonnet-Poems Eighty-Two. 47p. 1981. pap. 4.95 (ISBN 0-906897-28-9). Dufour.

--Heritage Now: Irish Literature in the English Language. 215p. 1983. 17.95x (ISBN 0-312-36993-X). St Martin.

--An Irish Eye. 160p. 1985. pap. 6.95 (ISBN 0-86322-055-X, Pub. by Brandon Bks). Longwood Pub Group.

--The Life of Riley. 222p. 1983. 12.95 (ISBN 0-86322-010-X, Pub. by Brandon Bks); pap. 5.95 (ISBN 0-86322-037-1). Longwood Pub Group.

--New & Selected Poems. 128p. 1982. pap. text ed. 11.00x (ISBN 0-85635-367-1, 40680, Pub. by Carcanet New Pr England). Humanities.

--R. M. S. Titanic. (Raven Long Poems Ser.). 1981. 8.95 (ISBN 0-906897-31-9). Dufour.

--Reductionist Poem. 39p. 1980. pap. 4.95 (ISBN 0-906897-12-2). Dufour.

Cronin, Blaise. Direct Mail Advertising & Public Library Use. (R&D Report: No. 5539). (Illus.). 57p. (Orig.). 1980. pap. 12.00 (ISBN 0-905984-58-7, Pub. by British Lib). Longwood Pub Group.

Cronin, Constance. Sting of Change: Sicilians in Sicily & Australia. LC 70-112707. 1970. 20.00x (ISBN 0-226-12110-0). U of Chicago Pr.

Cronin, Denis. Anxiety, Depression & Phobias: How to Understand & Deal with Them. 129p. 1981. 10.95 (ISBN 0-13-038638-3); pap. 4.95 (ISBN 0-13-038620-0). P-H.

Cronin, Etain. Contact Dermatitis. (Illus.). 960p. 1980. text ed. 69.00 (ISBN 0-443-02014-0). Churchill.

Cronin, F. Patrick, ed. see National Conference on Vocational Education in Corrections, 1977.

Cronin, Gaynell. Sunday Throughout the Week. LC 81-68992. (Illus.). 176p. (Orig.). 1981. pap. 5.95 (ISBN 0-87793-241-7). Ave Maria.

Cronin, Gaynell & Cronin, Jim. Celebrations. 1980. pap. 7.55 (ISBN 0-88479-031-2). Arena Lettres.

--The Mass: Great Common Prayer. 1977. pap. 7.55 (ISBN 0-88479-006-1). Arena Lettres.

--Prayer. 1980. pap. 7.55 (ISBN 0-88479-032-0). Arena Lettres.

Cronin, Gaynell & Gaynell, Jim. The Rosary. 1978. 7.55 (ISBN 0-88479-018-5). Arena Lettres.

Cronin, Gaynell B. Activities for the Christian Family Handbook (Paths of Life) LC 79-92007. 1980. 2.45 (ISBN 0-8091-2269-3). Paulist Pr.

--Holy Days & Holidays: Prayer Celebrations with Children. rev. ed. 1985. pap. 7.95 (ISBN 0-86683-226-2). Winston Pr.

Cronin, Godfrey E. & Young, William M. Four Hundred Navels: The Future of School Health in America. LC 78-59711. 121p. 1979. pap. 5.00 (ISBN 0-87367-766-8). Phi Delta Kappa.

--Four Hundred Navels: The Future of School Health in America. 150p. 1978. 5.00 (ISBN 0-87367-766-8); members 4.00 (ISBN 0-317-35561-9). Phi Delta Kappa.

Cronin, Grover. Monarch Notes on Fielding's Tom Jones. (Orig.). pap. 2.95 (ISBN 0-671-00614-2). Monarch Pr.

Cronin, Harry C. Eugene O'Neill, Irish & American: A Study in Cultural Context. LC 76-6331. (Irish Americans Ser). 1976. 15.00 (ISBN 0-405-09327-6). Ayer Co Pubs.

Cronin, Isaac. The International Squid Cookbook. (Illus.). 96p. 1981. pap. 7.95 (ISBN 0-943186-07-2, 0-671-55807-2). Aris Bks Harris.

Cronin, Isaac, et al. The California Seafood Cookbook: A Cook's Guide to the Fish & Shellfish of California, the Pacific Coast & Beyond. LC 82-24450. (Illus.). 288p. 1983. 20.00 (ISBN 0-943186-04-8, 0-671-55802-1); pap. 12.95 (ISBN 0-943186-03-X, 0-671-55839-0). Aris Bks Harris.

Cronin, Issac & Pallais, Rafael. Champagne! (Orig.). 1984. pap. 5.95 (ISBN 0-671-52733-9, Long Shadow Bks). PB.

Cronin, J. Differential Equations: Pure & Applied Math, Vol. 54. 392p. 1980. 39.75 (ISBN 0-8247-6819-1). Dekker.

--Gerald Griffin: A Critical Biography 1803-1840. LC 77-80831. (Illus.). 1978. 29.95 (ISBN 0-521-21800-4). Cambridge U Pr.

Cronin, James E. Industrial Conflict in Modern Britain. 242p. 1979. 25.00x (ISBN 0-8476-6188-1). Rowman.

--Labour & Society in Britain 1918-1979. 240p. 1984. 22.00x (ISBN 0-8052-3930-8). Schocken.

Cronin, James E., ed. The Diary of Elihu Hubbard Smith (1771-1798) LC 72-83462. (Memoirs Ser.: Vol. 95). (Illus.). 1973. 20.00 (ISBN 0-87169-095-0). Am Philos.

Cronin, James E. & Schneer, Jonathan, eds. Social Conflict & the Political Order in Modern Britain. 256p. 1982. 25.00 (ISBN 0-8135-0956-4). Rutgers U Pr.

Cronin, James E. & Sirianni, Carmen, eds. Work, Community & Power: The Experience of Labor in Europe & America, 1900-1925. 306p. 1983. 29.95 (ISBN 0-87722-308-4); pap. text ed. 12.95 (ISBN 0-87722-309-2). Temple U Pr.

Cronin, James E., ed. see Smith, Elihu H.

Cronin, Jane. Fixed Points & Topological Degree in Nonlinear Analysis. LC 63-21550. (Mathematical Surveys Ser.: Vol. 11). 198p. 1982. pap. 30.00 (ISBN 0-8218-1511-3, SURV-11). Am Math.

Cronin, Jeremiah A., et al. University of Chicago Graduate Problems in Physics with Solutions. 1979. pap. 9.00x (ISBN 0-226-12109-7, P809, Phoen). U of Chicago Pr.

Cronin, Jim, jt. auth. see Cronin, Gaynell.

Cronin, John. The Anglo-Irish Novel: The Nineteenth Century, Vol. 1. 157p. 1980. 24.50x (ISBN 0-389-20014-X). B&N Imports.

--Somerville & Ross. LC 78-126031. (Irish Writers Ser.). 111p. 1972. 4.50 (ISBN 0-8387-7767-8); pap. 1.95 (ISBN 0-8387-7698-1). Bucknell U Pr.

Cronin, John W., jt. auth. see Wise, W. Harvey, Jr.

Cronin, Joseph M. The Control of Urban Schools: Perspective on the Power of Educational Reformers. LC 72-78608. 288p. 1973. 12.95 (ISBN 0-02-906910-6). Free Pr.

Cronin, Kathleen M., jt. auth. see Lane, Gere H.

Cronin, Kathryn. Colonial Casualties: Chinese in Early Victoria. (Illus.). 175p. 1983. 17.95x (ISBN 0-522-84221-6, Pub. by Melbourne U Pr Australia). Intl Spec Bk.

Cronin, L. Eugene, ed. Estuarine Research, 2 vols. Incl. Vol 1. Chemistry & Biology. 70.50 (ISBN 0-12-197501-0); Vol 2. Geology & Engineering. 71.00 (ISBN 0-12-197502-9). 1975. Acad Pr.

Cronin, L. Eugene, jt. ed. see Neilson, Bruce J.

Cronin, Morton J. Vocabulary One Thousand: With Words in Context. 2nd ed. 180p. 1981. pap. text ed. 10.95 (ISBN 0-15-594987-X, HC); test booklet avail. (ISBN 0-15-594988-8). HarBraceJ.

Cronin, Ned J., ed. EIS Annual Review, Vol. 1. LC 78-73101. (Illus.). xii, 397p. 1978. text ed. 25.00 (ISBN 0-87815-024-2). Info Resources.

Cronin, Richard. Shelley's Poetic Thoughts. 1981. 25.00 (ISBN 0-312-71664-8). St Martin.

Cronin, Sean. Irish Nationalism: A History of Its Roots & Ideology. 394p. 1981. 17.50 (ISBN 0-8264-0062-0). Continuum.

--Irish Nationalism: A History of Its Roots & Ideology. 391p. 1980. pap. 9.50 (ISBN 0-906187-35-4). Univ Press.

--Protest in Arms: The Young Ireland Rebellion of July-August 1848. 200p. 1985. cancelled 25.00 (ISBN 0-906187-58-3, Pub. by Univ Pr of Ireland). Longwood Pub Group.

Cronin, T. M., jt. auth. see Barnett, S.

Cronin, Thomas E. Rethinking the Presidency. 1982. 12.95 (ISBN 0-316-16151-9). Little.

--The State of the Presidency. 2nd ed. 1980. pap. text ed. 12.95 (ISBN 0-316-16179-9). Little.

Cronin, Thomas E., et al. U. S. v. Crime in the Streets. LC 80-8842. (Illus.). 224p. 1981. 20.00x (ISBN 0-253-19017-7). Ind U Pr.

Cronin, Unter M., ed. see Simon, Elisabeth.

Cronin, Vincent. Mary Portrayed. 12.50 (ISBN 0-87505-213-4). Borden.

--The View from Planet Earth: Man Looks at the Cosmos. LC 81-4056. (Illus.). 352p. 1981. 15.00 (ISBN 0-688-00642-6). Morrow.

--The View from Planet Earth: Man Looks at the Cosmos. LC 82-16654. (Illus.). 384p. 1983. pap. 6.70 (ISBN 0-688-01479-8, Quill NY). Morrow.

Cronin, Vincent, ed. Essays by Divers Hands: Innovation in Contemporary Literature. (Being the Transactions of a Royal Society of Literature, New Ser.: Vol. XL). 162p. 1979. 21.50x (ISBN 0-8476-3043-9). Rowman.

Cronise, Florence M. & Ward, Henry W. Cunnie Rabbit, Mr. Spider & Other Beef: West African Folk Tales. LC 72-99363. 1969. Repr. of 1903 ed. lib. bdg. 16.50 (ISBN 0-8411-0034-9). Metro Bks.

Cronje, Gillian & Cronje, Suzanne. The Workers of Namibia. 134p. 1979. 4.50 (ISBN 0-317-36667-X). Africa Fund.

Cronje, Suzanne, jt. auth. see Cronje, Gillian.

Cronk, Elsie, jt. auth. see Saunders, Virginia.

Cronk, George. The Message of the Bible: An Orthodox Christian Perspective. LC 82-7355. 293p. (Orig.). 1982. pap. 8.95 (ISBN 0-913836-94-X). St Vladimirs.

Cronk, Loren, ed. Guide to Natural Food Restaurants. 3rd ed. LC 83-51080. Orig. Title: Annual Directory of Vegetarian Restaurants. 209p. 1984. pap. 8.95 (ISBN 0-938962-02-7). Daystar Pub Co.

Cronk, Loren K. Guide to Natural Food Restaurants. LC 85-10983. 208p. 1985. Repr. of 1983 ed. lib. bdg. 19.95x (ISBN 0-89370-880-1). Borgo Pr.

Cronk, Louise H., jt. auth. see Handy, Ralph S.

Cronk, Shanler D., et al, eds. Criminal Justice in Rural America. 255p. 1982. 3.00 (ISBN 0-318-01084-4). U of Tenn Sch.

--Juvenile Justice in Rural America. 255p. 3.00 (ISBN 0-686-40935-3). U of Tenn Sch.

Cronkhite, Bernice, ed. Handbook for College Teachers: An Informal Guide. LC 71-94581. Repr. of 1950 ed. lib. bdg. 15.00x (ISBN 0-8371-2549-9, CRHC). Greenwood.

Cronkhite, Gary. Public Speaking & Critical Listening. LC 77-87452. 1978. 26.95 (ISBN 0-8053-1901-8). Benjamin-Cummings.

Cronkite, E. P. & Carstens, A. L. Diffusion Chamber Culture: Hemopoiesis, Cloning of Tumors, Cytogenetic & Carinogenic Assays. (Illus.). 270p. 1980. pap. 51.00 (ISBN 0-387-10064-4). Springer-Verlag.

Cronkite, Eugene D. & Berliner, Robert W. Blood & Lymph & the Excretion of Urine. LC 72-85159. 84p. 1973. pap. 9.50 (ISBN 0-686-86249-X). Krieger.

Cronkite, Kathy. On the Edge of the Spotlight. 320p. 1982. pap. 3.50 (ISBN 0-446-80944-6). Warner Bks.

Cronkite, Walter. Challenges of Change. 1971. pap. 7.50 (ISBN 0-685-57334-6). Pub Aff Pr.

Cronley, Jay. Cheap Shot. LC 83-45499. 256p. 1984. 13.95 (ISBN 0-689-11445-1). Atheneum.

--Funny Farm. LC 85-47599. 256p. 1985. 14.95 (ISBN 0-689-11609-8). Atheneum.

--Funny Farm: A Sweeping Epic of the Sticks. 256p. 1985. 14.95 (ISBN 0-689-11609-8). Atheneum.

Cronne, H. A., et al, eds. Essays in British & Irish History in Honour of James Eadie Todd. 1977. Repr. of 1949 ed. lib. bdg. 25.00 (ISBN 0-8495-0711-1). Arden Lib.

--Essays in British & Irish History in Honour of James Eadie Todd. Quinn, D. B. 1977. Repr. of 1949 ed. lib. bdg. 30.00 (ISBN 0-8482-3478-2). Norwood Edns.

Cronon, E. David. Black Moses: The Story of Marcus Garvey & the Universal Negro Improvement Association. 2nd ed. (Illus.). 302p. 1969. pap. 8.50x (ISBN 0-299-01214-X). U of Wis Pr.

--Josephus Daniels in Mexico. (Illus.). 384p. 1960. 17.50x (ISBN 0-299-02061-4); pap. 6.95x (ISBN 0-299-02064-9). U of Wis Pr.

Cronon, E. David & Rosenof, Theodore D.compiled by. The Second World War & the Atomic Age, 1940-1973. LC 74-28589. (Goldentree Bibliographies in American History Ser). (Orig.). 1975. pap. 14.95x (ISBN 0-88295-538-1). Harlan Davidson.

Cronon, William. Changes in the Land: Indians, Colonists, & the Ecology of New England. (American Century Ser.). (Illus.). 242p. 1983. 15.95 (ISBN 0-8090-3405-0); pap. 6.95 (ISBN 0-8090-0158-6). Hill & Wang.

Cronquist, A., et al. Intermountain Flora: Vascular Plants of the Intermountain West, U.S.A. - the Monocotyledons, Vol. 6. LC 73-134298. 1977. 67.50x (ISBN 0-231-04120-9). Columbia U Pr.

Cronquist, Arthur. Basic Botany. 2nd ed. 662p. 1981. text ed. 28.95 scp (ISBN 0-06-041429-4, HarpC). Har-Row.

--How to Know the Seed Plants. (Pictured Key Nature Ser.). 250p. 1979. wire coil (ISBN 0-697-04761-X). Wm C Brown.

--An Integrated System of Classification of Flowering Plants. LC 80-39556. (Illus.). 1152p. 1981. 132.00x (ISBN 0-231-03880-1). Columbia U Pr.

--Vascular Flora of the Southeastern United States: Vol. 1-Asteraceae. Radford, Albert E., ed. LC 79-769. xv, 261p. 1980. 25.00x (ISBN 0-8078-1362-1). U of NC Pr.

Cronquist, Arthur, jt. auth. see Gleason, Henry A.

Cronquist, Arthur, jt. auth. see Hitchcock, C. Leo.

Cronquist, Arthur, et al. Composite. LC 78-17496. (North American Flora Ser. II: Pt. 10). 1978. pap. 25.00x (ISBN 0-89327-191-8). NY Botanical.

Cronquist, Neil R., jt. auth. see Chingos, Peter T.

Cronstrom, C., ed. Topics in Theoretical Physics, Vol. 1. (Liperi Summer School of Theoretical Physics Ser.). 318p. 1969. 80.95 (ISBN 0-677-13180-1). Gordon.

Cronwright-Schreiner, S. C., jt. auth. see Findlay, Frederick R. N.

Cronwright-Schreiner, Samuel. The Life of Olive Schreiner. LC 72-2122. (Studies in Women's Rights, No. 51). (Illus.). 1972. Repr. of 1924 ed. lib. bdg. 59.95x (ISBN 0-8383-1461-9). Haskell.

Cronyn, George W., ed. American Indian Poetry: An Anthology of Songs & Chants. LC 73-133483. 1970. pap. 5.95 (ISBN 0-87140-226-2). Liveright.

Croog, Sydney & Levine, Sol. The Heart Patient Recovers. LC 77-608112. 432p. 1977. text ed. 29.95 (ISBN 0-87705-247-6). Human Sci Pr.

Croog, Sydney H. & Levine, Sol. Life after a Heart Attack: Social & Psychological Factors Eight Years Later. LC 81-6702. 328p. 1982. 29.95 (ISBN 0-89885-071-1). Human Sci Pr.

Crook, B. M., tr. see UNESCO Colloqium, 10th Anniversary of the Death of Albert Einstein & Teilhard De Charden.

Crook, B. M., tr. see Weltner, K.

Crook, Beverly C. Fair Annie of Old Mule Hollow. (YA) (gr. 7 up). 1980. pap. 1.95 (ISBN 0-380-49007-2, 49007-2). Avon.

--Fair Annie of Old Mule Hollow. (gr. 6 up). 1978. 7.95 (ISBN 0-07-014487-7). McGraw.

--Invite a Bird to Dinner: Simple Feeders You Can Make. LC 78-8657. (Illus.). (gr. 3-7). 1978. 10.00 (ISBN 0-688-41849-X); PLB 10.88 (ISBN 0-688-51849-4). Lothrop.

Crook, D. P. Benjamin Kidd: Portrait of a Social Darwinist. LC 83-19009. 280p. 1984. 54.50 (ISBN 0-521-25804-9). Cambridge U Pr.

Crook, David P. American Democracy in English Politics. 1965. text ed. 7.25x (ISBN 0-19-821338-7). Oxford U Pr.

--Diplomacy During the American Civil War. 209p. 1975. pap. text ed. 8.95 (ISBN 0-394-34170-8, RanC). Random.

Crook, E. J., tr. see Jordan, Richard.

Crook, Eugene J., ed. Fearful Symmetry: Doubles & Doubling in Literature & Film; Selected Papers from the 5th Annual Florida State University Conference on Literature & Film. LC 81-19684. x, 175p. (Orig.). 1981. pap. 8.00 (ISBN 0-8130-0723-2). U Presses Fla.

Crook, Gillian, ed. Man in the Centre: Proceedings of a Symposium, Alice Springs, 3-5 April 1979. (Illus.). viii, 232p. (Orig.). 1983. pap. text ed. 8.60x (ISBN 0-643-03508-7, Pub by CSIRO). Intl Spec Bk.

Crook, Guy & Heinstein, Martin. The Older Worker in Industry. Stein, Leon, ed. LC 79-8664. (Growing Old Ser.). (Illus.). 1980. Repr. of 1958 ed. lib. bdg. 14.00x (ISBN 0-405-12782-0). Ayer Co Pubs.

Crook, H. Clifford. Campanulas. LC 76-46559. (Illus.). 1977. Repr. of 1951 ed. 12.50 (ISBN 0-913728-18-7). Theophrastus.

Crook, J., jt. auth. see Reekie, W.

Crook, J. A. Law & Life of Rome: Ninety B. C. to A. D. Two Hundred & Twelve. LC 67-20633. 352p. 1984. pap. 10.95x (ISBN 0-8014-9273-4). Cornell U Pr.

Crook, J. Mordaunt. William Burges & the High Victorian Dream. LC 81-1592. (Illus.). 632p. 1981. 60.00x (ISBN 0-226-12117-8). U of Chicago Pr.

Crook, J. Mordaunt & Lennox-Boyd, C. Axel Haig & the Victorian Vision of the Middle Ages. (Genius of Architecture Ser.: No. 3). (Illus.). 120p. 1984. text ed. 19.95x (ISBN 0-04-720029-4); pap. 9.95 (ISBN 0-04-720030-8). Allen Unwin.

Crook, James W. German Wage Theories: A History of Their Development. LC 72-77989. (Columbia University. Studies in the Social Sciences: No. 24). 1968. Repr. of 1898 ed. 16.50 (ISBN 0-404-51024-8). AMS Pr.

Crook, John A. Consilium Principis: Imperial Councils & Counsellors from Augustus to Diocletian. LC 75-7309. (Roman History Ser.). 1975. Repr. 20.00x (ISBN 0-405-07191-4). Ayer Co Pubs.

Crook, John H. The Evolution of Human Consciousness. (Illus.). 1980. 42.00x (ISBN 0-19-857174-7); pap. 16.95x (ISBN 0-19-857187-9). Oxford U Pr.

Crook, John H., jt. ed. see Michael, Richard P.

Crook, M. A., ed. see Symposium on Liquid Scintillation Counting.

Crook, Michael, tr. see Van Buren, Ariane & Pyle, Leo.

Crook, Roger H. An Open Book to the Christian Divorcee. LC 73-87064. pap. 4.95 (ISBN 0-8054-5217-6). Broadman.

--Our Heritage & Our Hope: A History of Pullen Memorial Baptist Church 1884-1984. (Illus.). 252p. 1985. 10.00 (ISBN 0-9614485-0-4). Pullen Mem Baptist.

Crook, Welton J. Abacus Arithmetic. LC 58-7709. (Illus.). 1958. pap. 2.95 (ISBN 0-87015-078-2). Pacific Bks.

Crook, William. You & Allergy. 1981. pap. 4.95x (ISBN 0-317-07278-1, Regent House). B of A.

Crook, William G. Are You Allergic? rev. ed. 1978. pap. 6.95 (ISBN 0-933478-02-X). Future Health.

--Can Your Child Read? Is He Hyperactive? rev. ed. 1977. pap. 6.95 (ISBN 0-933478-01-1). Future Health.

--Tracking Down Hidden Food Allergy. 2nd ed. (Illus.). 104p. (Orig.). 1980. pap. 6.95 (ISBN 0-933478-05-4). Future Health.

--The Yeast Connection: A Medical Breakthrough. LC 83-62508. (Illus.). 296p. 1984. 15.95 (ISBN 0-933478-06-2). Future Health.

--The Yeast Connection: A Medical Breakthrough. LC 83-62508. (Illus.). 304p. 1985. 15.95 (ISBN 0-933478-10-0). Future Health.

Crookall, J. R., ed. Electromachining: Proceedings of the Seventh International Symposium, Birmingham, UK, April 1983. iv, 478p. 1983. 76.75 (ISBN 0-444-86665-5, I-278-83, North-Holland). Elsevier.

Crookall, Philip. Computer Programming for Real Beginners: Simplified & Self-Taught. LC 84-12292. 96p. 1984. pap. 5.95 (ISBN 0-668-06130-8, 6130-8). Arco.

Crookall, R. Interpretation of Cosmic & Mystical Experiences. 187p. 1969. 11.95 (ISBN 0-227-67729-3). Attic Pr.

--Intimations of Immortality. 157p. 1965. 11.95 (ISBN 0-227-67662-9). Attic Pr.

--Supreme Adventure: Analyses of Psychic Communication. rev. ed. 288p. 1975. 17.95 (ISBN 0-227-67606-8). Attic Pr.

Crookall, Robert. Case-Book of Astral Projection, 545-746. 160p. 1980. pap. 3.95 (ISBN 0-8065-0730-6). Citadel Pr.

--Casebook of Astral Projection, 546-746. 1972. 7.95 (ISBN 0-8216-0061-3). Univ Bks.

--Out-of-the Body Experiences: A Fourth Analysis. 1977. pap. 4.95 (ISBN 0-8065-0610-5). Citadel Pr.

--Psychic Breathing. LC 85-11042. 96p. 1985. Repr. lib. bdg. 16.95x (ISBN 0-89370-680-9). Borgo Pr.

--Psychic Breathing. 96p. 1985. pap. 6.95 (ISBN 0-87877-080-1). Newcastle Pub.

--The Study & Practice of Astral Projection. 1977. pap. 3.95 (ISBN 0-8065-0547-8). Citadel Pr.

--Study & Practice of Astral Projection. 1966. 7.50 (ISBN 0-8216-0154-7). Univ Bks.

--The Techniques of Astral Projection. 112p. 1975. pap. 6.95 (ISBN 0-85030-261-7). Weiser.

Crooke, H., tr. see Pare, Ambroise.

Crooke, John. Better Tennis. (Better Ser.). (Illus.). (gr. 7 up). 17.95x (ISBN 0-7182-1465-X, SpS). Sportshelf.

--Better Tennis. (Illus.). 192p. 1984. 13.95 (ISBN 0-7182-1465-X, Pub. by Kaye & Ward). David & Charles.

Crooke, S. T. & Prestayko, A. W., eds. Cancer & Chemotherapy: Antineoplastic Agents, Vol. 3. LC 79-8536. 1981. 55.00 (ISBN 0-12-197803-6). Acad Pr.

Crooke, Stanley T. & Bradner, W. T. Bleomycin: A Review. 20.00 (ISBN 0-915340-05-4). PJD Pubns.

Crooke, Stanley T. & Prestayko, Archie W. Cancer & Chemotherapy: Introduction to Clinical Oncology, Vol. 2. LC 79-8536. 1981. 55.00 (ISBN 0-12-197802-8). Acad Pr.

Crooke, Stanley T. & Reich, Steven D., eds. Anthracyclines: Current Status & New Developments. 1980. 44.50 (ISBN 0-12-197780-3). Acad Pr.

Crooke, Stanley T., jt. ed. see Poste, George.

Crooke, W., ed. see Tavernier, J. B.

Crooke, William, ed. see Fryer, John.

Crookenden, Julia, tr. see Khazanov, A. M.

Crookenden, Napier. Drop Zone Normandy. LC 75-38402. 1976. 12.50 (ISBN 0-684-14595-2, ScribT). Scribner.

Crooker, Barbara, jt. auth. see Machan Aal, Katharyn.

Crooker, T. W. & Leis, B. N., eds. Corrosion Fatigue: Mechanics, Metallurgy, Electrochemistry, & Engineering. LC 82-83519. (Special Technical Publications Ser.: No. 801). 522p. 1983. text ed. 62.00 (ISBN 0-8031-0245-3, 04-801000-30). ASTM.

Crooker, T. W., jt. ed. see Gallagher, J. P.

Crookes, R. J., jt. ed. see Thring, M. W.

Crookes, William. Researches in Spiritualism. (Illus.). 112p. 1984. Repr. of 1880 ed. photocopy 8.95 (ISBN 0-915554-18-6). Sourcebook.

--The Wheat Problem. LC 75-27633. (World Food Supply Ser.). (Illus.). 1976. Repr. of 1900 ed. 23.50x (ISBN 0-405-07775-0). Ayer Co Pubs.

Crooks, jt. auth. see Downs, Eliza.

Crooks, J. Drugs & the Elderly. 320p. 1979. text ed. 50.00 (ISBN 0-8391-1438-9). Univ Park.

Crooks, J. E. The Spectrum in Chemistry. 1978. pap. 23.50 (ISBN 0-12-195552-4). Acad Pr.

Crooks, J. J. History of the Colony of Sierra Leone, Western Africa. 376p. 1972. Repr. of 1903 ed. 30.00x (ISBN 0-7146-1646-X, BHA-01646, F Cass Co). Biblio Dist.

--Records Relating to the Gold Coast Settlements from 1750 to 1874. 576p. 1973. Repr. of 1923 ed. 38.00x (ISBN 0-7146-1647-8, BHA-01647, F Cass Co). Biblio Dist.

Crooks, James B. Politics & Progress: The Rise of Urban Progressivism in Baltimore, 1895 to 1911. LC 68-21805. pap. 68.30 (ISBN 0-317-30010-5, 2051877). Bks Demand UMI.

Crooks, John J. A History of the Colony of Sierra Leone, Western Africa. LC 76-99364. (Illus.). xiv, 375p. 1972. Repr. of 1903 ed. lib. bdg. 20.00 (ISBN 0-8411-0035-7). Metro Bks.

Crooks, Robert & Baur, Karla. Our Sexuality. 2nd ed. 1983. 27.95 (ISBN 0-8053-1914-X); study guide 8.95 (ISBN 0-8053-1915-8); instr's guide 6.95 (ISBN 0-8053-1916-6); slide package 50.00 (ISBN 0-8053-1918-2). Benjamin-Cummings.

Crooks, Thomas C. & Hancock, Harry L. Basic Technical Mathematics. 1969. text ed. write for info. (ISBN 0-02-325640-0, 32564). Macmillan.

Crooks, Valerie C., jt. ed. see Abrahams, Joel P.

Crookse, Mark. Achieving Wellness Through Risk Taking: The End of Boredom. (Illus.). 208p. 1985. 15.00 (ISBN 0-682-40249-4). Exposition Pr FL.

Crookshank, Anne. Irish Sculpture from Sixteen Hundred to the Present. (Aspects of Ireland Ser.: Vol. 9). (Illus.). 80p. (Orig.). 1984. pap. 7.95 (ISBN 0-906404-18-5, Pub. by Dept Foreign Ireland). Irish Bks Media.

--The Painters of Ireland: 1600-1920. (Illus.). 304p. 1979. 45.00 (ISBN 0-214-20678-5, Pub. by G Malik Bk Pubs). Eastview.

Crookshank, Anne O. Irish Art from Sixteen Hundred. (Aspects of Ireland Ser.: Vol. 4). (Illus.). 80p. 1979. pap. 5.95 (ISBN 0-906404-04-5, Pub. by Dept Foreign Ireland). Irish Bks Media.

Crookshank, Edgar M. History & Pathology of Vaccination, 2 vols. LC 75-23702. Repr. of 1889 ed. 105.00 set (ISBN 0-404-13330-4). AMS Pr.

Crookston, Peter, ed. The Ages of Britain. LC 83-61036. (Illus.). 224p. 1983. 19.95 (ISBN 0-312-01401-5). St Martin.

--Village England. (Illus.). 256p. 1980. 16.95 (ISBN 0-09-142320-1, NO. 0216, Pub. by Hutchinson England). Methuen Inc.

Crools, J. Mordaunt, ed. see Eastlake, Charles.

Croom, Emily A. Unpuzzling Your Past: A Basic Guide to Genealogy. LC 82-24514. (Illus.). 128p. 1983. pap. 7.95 (ISBN 0-932620-21-3). Betterway Pubns.

Croom, George E., Jr. & Van Der Wal, John. Now You Can Profit from Inflation. 264p. 1981. 14.95 (ISBN 0-442-25397-4). Van Nos Reinhold.

Croome, Angela. Hovercraft. (Illus.). (gr. 5 up). 1962. 7.95 (ISBN 0-8392-3008-7). Astor-Honor.

Croome, D. J. & Roberts, B. M. Air Conditioning & Ventilation of Buildings, Vol. 1. 2nd ed. LC 79-40965. (International Ser. in Heating, Ventilation & Refrigeration: Vol. 14). (Illus.). 575p. 1981. text ed. 66.00 (ISBN 0-08-024779-2). Pergamon.

Croome, D. J. & Sherratt, A. F., eds. Condensation in Buildings. (Illus.). 271p. 1972. 39.00 (ISBN 0-85334-548-1, Pub. by Elsevier Applied Sci England). Elsevier.

Croome, D. J. & Sherratt, A. F. C., eds. Quality & Total Cost in Buildings & Services Design. 1978. text ed. 40.00x (ISBN 0-904406-40-7). Longman.

Croome-Gale, Derek J. Noise, Buildings, & People. LC 73-7982. 500p. 1977. pap. text ed. 50.00 (ISBN 0-08-019816-3). Pergamon.

Croonenburg, Englebert J. Van see Van Croonenburg, Englebert J.

Crop, Sheldon. Local Area Networks for the IBM PC XT. 225p. 1984. pap. 14.95 (ISBN 0-89588-243-4). SYBEX.

--Office Efficiency with Personal Computers. 175p. 1984. pap. cancelled (ISBN 0-89588-165-9). SYBEX.

Crop, Sheldon & Mosher, Doug. Portable Computers. LC 83-50713. (Illus.). 112p. pap. cancelled (ISBN 0-89588-144-6). SYBEX.

Cropley, A. J. The Education of Immigrant Children: A Social-Psychological Introduction. 216p. 1984. 32.00x (ISBN 0-7099-0788-5, Pub. by Salem Acad). Merrimack Pub Cir.

--Towards a System of Lifelong Education: Some Practical Considerations. LC 80-40417. (Advances in Lifelong Education Ser.: Vol. 7). (Illus.). 234p. 1980. pap. 12.25 (ISBN 0-08-026067-5). Pergamon.

Cropley, A. J., ed. & contrib. by. Lifelong Education: A Stocktaking. (UIE Monographs: Unesco Institute for Education: No. 8). 115p. 1979. pap. 5.50 (ISBN 92-820-1021-X, U897, UNESCO). Unipub.

Cropley, Arthur J., jt. auth. see Knapper, Christopher K.

Cropper, Elizabeth. The Ideal of Painting: Pietro Testa's Dusseldorf Notebook. LC 83-42595. (Illus.). 400p. 1984. 80.00x (ISBN 0-691-04021-4). Princeton U Pr.

Cropper, Margaret. Flame Touches Flame: George Herbert, Nicholas Ferrar, Henry Vaughan, Jeremy Taylor, Margaret Godolphin, Thomas Ken. 1973. Repr. of 1951 ed. 20.00 (ISBN 0-8274-1522-2). R West.

Cropper, Mariam. South Carolina Water Ways. LC 77-86081. lib. bdg. 10.00 (ISBN 0-89593-133-8). Accelerated Index.

Cropper, William H. Quantum Physicists & an Introduction to Their Physics. (Illus.). 270p. 1970. pap. 9.95x (ISBN 0-19-500861-8). Oxford U Pr.

Cropsey, Joseph. Political Philosophy & the Issues of Politics. LC 76-22960. 1977. lib. bdg. 22.00x (ISBN 0-226-12123-2). U of Chicago Pr.

--Political Philosophy & the Issues of Politics. LC 76-22960. 1980. pap. 7.50x (ISBN 0-226-12124-0, 864, Phoen). U of Chicago Pr.

--Polity & Economy: An Interpretation of the Principles of Adam Smith. Archival ed. LC 76-56126. 1977. Repr. of 1957 ed. lib. bdg. 35.00x (ISBN 0-8371-9418-0, CRPE). Greenwood.

Cropsey, Joseph, jt. auth. see Strauss, Leo.

Cropsey, Joseph, ed. see Hobbes, Thomas.

Cros, Charles & Corbiere, Tristan. Oeuvres Completes. 1512p. 41.50 (ISBN 0-686-56491-X). French & Eur.

Crosbie, A. L., ed. Aerothermodynamics & Planetary Entry. (Illus.). 441p. 55.00 (ISBN 0-915928-52-3, PAAS77); 35.00 (ISBN 0-317-32129-3). AIAA.

Crosbie, John S. Crosbie's Book of Punned Haiku. LC 79-64788. (Illus.). 64p. 1979. pap. 2.95 (ISBN 0-89480-110-4, 295). Workman Pub.

Crosbie, Michael J. The Jersey Devil Design-Build Book. LC 84-26367. 1985. 16.95 (ISBN 0-87905-188-4). Gibbs M Smith.

Crosbie, Paddy. Your Dinner's Poured out. (Illus.). 224p. 1982. 13.95 (ISBN 0-905140-92-3, Pub. by O'Brien Pr Ireland); pap. 5.95 (ISBN 0-86278-032-2). Irish Bks Media.

Crosbie, Robert. Answers to Questions on the Ocean of Theosophy. 249p. 1933. 5.00 (ISBN 0-938998-12-9). Theosophy.

--The Friendly Philosopher. (Illus.). vii, 415p. 1934. Repr. 6.00 (ISBN 0-938998-13-7). Theosophy.

Crosbie, Robert, jt. auth. see Judge, William Q.

Crosbie, Sylvia K. A Tacit Alliance: France & Israel from the Suez to the Six-Day War. (Studies of the Middle East Institute, Columbia University). 304p. 1974. 31.50x (ISBN 0-691-07557-3). Princeton U Pr.

Crosby. Art of Holding the Violin & Bow As Exemplified by Ole Bull. Repr. lib. bdg. 19.00 (ISBN 0-403-03869-3). Scholarly.

--Illusion & Disillusion: The Self in Love & Marriage. 3rd ed. 1984. write for info. (ISBN 0-317-13036-6). Wadsworth Pub.

Crosby, et al. Building College Spelling Skills. 192p. (Orig.). 1981. pap. text ed. 10.95 (ISBN 0-316-16186-1); tchr's. manual avail. (ISBN 0-316-16188-8). Little.

Crosby, A. B., jt. auth. see Bull, Sara.

Crosby, Alexander. Old Greenwood: Pathfinder of the West. LC 67-26263. (Illus.). (gr. 5-10). 1968. 3.95 (ISBN 0-934612-00-5). Talisman.

Crosby, Alexander L. Pond Life. LC 64-12627. (Junior Science Bks.). (Illus.). (gr. 2-5). 1964. PLB 7.47 (ISBN 0-8116-6169-5). Garrard.

--The Rimac: River of Peru. LC 67-10021. (Illus.). (gr. 5). 1965. PLB 4.47 (ISBN 0-8116-6366-3). Garrard.

--Tarantulas. LC 80-7672. (Illus.). 64p. (gr. 3-7). 1981. 8.50 (ISBN 0-8027-6393-6); PLB 8.85 (ISBN 0-8027-6394-4). Walker & Co.

--The World of Rockets. (Gateway Ser: No. 13). (gr. 3-6). 1965. PLB 5.99 (ISBN 0-394-90113-4, BYR). Random.

Crosby, Alfred W., Jr. America, Russia, Hemp, & Napoleon: American Trade with Russia & the Baltic, 1783-1812. LC 65-18735. 1965. 6.50 (ISBN 0-8142-0041-9). Ohio St U Pr.
--The Columbian Exchange: Biological and Cultural Consequences of 1492. LC 73-140916. (Contributions in American Studies: No. 2). 268p. 1972. lib. bdg. 29.95 (ISBN 0-8371-5821-4, CCE/); pap. 29.95 (ISBN 0-8371-7228-4). Greenwood.
--Epidemic & Peace, Nineteen Eighteen. LC 75-23861. (Illus.). 337p. 1976. lib. bdg. 35.00 (ISBN 0-8371-8376-6, CPD/). Greenwood.
Crosby, Allan J. & Bruce, John, eds. Accounts & Papers Relating to Mary Queen of Scots. (Camden Society, London. Publications. First Ser.: No. 93). Repr. of 1867 ed. 19.00 (ISBN 0-404-50193-1). AMS Pr.
Crosby, Allen J., ed. Accounts & Papers Relating to Mary Queen of Scots. 1967. Repr. of 1867 ed. 19.00 (ISBN 0-384-10235-2). Johnson Repr.
Crosby, Benjamin, jt. auth. see Lindenberg, Marc.
Crosby, C. E., jt. auth. see Plog, H.
Crosby, Caresse. The Passionate Years. LC 78-31388. (Neglected Books of the Twentieth Century). (Illus.). 1979. pap. 6.95 (ISBN 0-912946-66-0). Ecco Pr.
Crosby, Chester A., jt. auth. see Chesbro, Paul L.
Crosby County Historical Commission. A History of Crosby County, Eighteen Seventy-Six to Nineteen Seventy-Seven. 1978. 71.43x (ISBN 0-686-31815-3). Crosby County.
Crosby County Pioneer Memorial Staff. Gone but Not Forgotten: Cemetery Survey of Crosby County, Texas. 1983. 20.00x; pap. 15.00x (ISBN 0-9606940-4-8). Crosby County.
Crosby, Cynthia A. Historical Dictionary of Malawi. LC 80-18. (African Historical Dictionaries Ser.: No. 25). 280p. 1980. lib. bdg. 20.00 (ISBN 0-8108-1287-8). Scarecrow.
Crosby, Donald A. Horace Bushnell's Theory of Language: In the Context of Other Nineteenth-Century Philosophies of Language. (Studies in Philosophy: No. 22). 300p. 1975. text ed. 33.60x (ISBN 90-2793-044-9). Mouton.
--Interpretive Theories of Religion. (Religion & Reason Ser.: No.20). 336p. 1981. 26.00x (ISBN 90-279-3039-2). Mouton.
Crosby, Donald F. God, Church, & Flag: Senator Joseph R. McCarthy & the Catholic Church, 1950-1957. LC 77-14064. xv, 307p. 1978. 25.00 (ISBN 0-8078-1312-5). U of NC Pr.
Crosby, Donald G., ed. Natural Pest Control Agents. LC 66-22355. (Advances in Chemistry Ser.: No. 53). 1966. 15.95 (ISBN 0-8412-0054-8). Am Chemical.
Crosby, Donald G., jt. ed. see Jacobson, Martin.
Crosby, Donald H. & Schoolfield, George C., eds. Studies in the German Drama: A Festschrift in Honor of Walter Silz. (Studies in the Germanic Languages & Literatures Ser.: No. 76). xxiv, 252p. 1974. 22.50 (ISBN 0-8078-8076-0). U of NC Pr.
Crosby, Edward, et al, eds. The African Experience in Community Development: The Continuing Struggle in Africa & the Americas, Vol. 1. 420p. (Orig.). 1981. pap. text ed. 18.95x (ISBN 0-89894-025-7). Advocate Pub Group.
Crosby, Elizabeth C., et al, eds. Comparative Correlative Neuroanatomy of the Vertebrate Telencephalon. Carey, Joshua. (Illus.). 1982. text ed. write for info. (ISBN 0-02-325690-7). Macmillan.
Crosby, Ernest. Collected Poems, 4 vols. 400.00 (ISBN 0-87968-882-3). Gordon Pr.
--Edward Carpenter: Poet & Prophet. 59.95 (ISBN 0-8490-0095-5). Gordon Pr.
--Garrison the Non-Resistant. LC 72-137534. (Peace Movement in America Ser.). 141p. 1972. Repr. of 1905 ed. lib. bdg. 11.95x (ISBN 0-89198-062-8). Ozer.
Crosby, Ernest H. Captain Jinks, Hero. LC 68-57519. (The Muckrakers Ser.). Repr. of 1902 ed. lib. bdg. 18.75 (ISBN 0-8398-0282-X). Irvington.
--Edward Carpenter: Poet & Prophet. LC 74-8994. 1905. 7.50 (ISBN 0-8414-3358-5). Folcroft.
--Tolstoy & His Message. 93p. 1980. Repr. of 1903 ed. lib. bdg. 12.50 (ISBN 0-8414-3031-4). Folcroft.
--Tolstoy & His Message. 1906. 15.00 (ISBN 0-8274-3636-X). R West.
Crosby, Everett U. & Webb, Charles R., Jr., eds. The Past As Prologue: Sources & Studies in European Civilization, 2 vols. LC 70-166559. (Illus.). 1973. Vol. 1. pap. text ed. 7.95x (ISBN 0-89197-331-1); Vol. 2. pap. text ed. 7.95x (ISBN 0-89197-332-X). Set. Irvington.
Crosby, Everett U., et al. Medieval Studies: A Bibliographical Guide. LC 83-48259. (Reference Library of the Humanities: Vol. 427). 1156p. 1984. 109.00 (ISBN 0-8240-9107-8). Garland Pub.
Crosby, Fanny J. Fanny Crosby Speaks Again. Hustad, Donald P., ed. LC 77-75907. (Illus.). 1977. pap. 2.50 (ISBN 0-916642-08-9). Hope Pub.
Crosby, Faye J. Relative Deprivation & Working Women. (Illus.). 1982. text ed. 22.95x (ISBN 0-19-503146-6); pap. text ed. 9.95x (ISBN 0-19-503147-4). Oxford U Pr.
Crosby, Gary & Firestone, Ross. Going My Own Way. 304p. 1984. pap. 3.50 (ISBN 0-449-20544-4, Crest). Fawcett.
Crosby, Gerda R. Disarmament & Peace in British Politics, 1914-1919. LC 57-8623. (Historical Monographs Ser: No. 32). 1957. 14.00x (ISBN 0-674-21150-2). Harvard U Pr.
Crosby, Harold E., jt. auth. see Edgerly, George A.
Crosby, Harriett, ed. see Hart, David.
Crosby, Harry. The Cave Paintings of Baja California. Rev. ed. LC 83-26220. (Illus.). 200p. 1984. 27.50 (ISBN 0-913938-27-0). Copley Bks.
--Shadows of the Sun: The Diaries of Harry Crosby. Germain, Edward, ed. 300p. (Orig.). 1977. 14.00 (ISBN 0-87685-304-1); pap. 8.50 (ISBN 0-87685-303-3). Black Sparrow.
Crosby, Harry H., jt. ed. see Bond, George R.
Crosby, Harry W. Last of the Californios. Pourade, Richard F., ed. LC 81-68663. (Illus.). 206p. 1981. 22.50 (ISBN 0-913938-23-8). Copley Bks.
Crosby, Jack L. Computer Simulation in Genetics. LC 72-5715. pap. 122.30 (ISBN 0-317-28345-6, 2016182). Bks Demand UMI.
Crosby, John. Dear Judgement. 1979. pap. 2.50 (ISBN 0-671-82572-0). PB.
--Men in Arms. LC 82-40168. 256p. 1983. 14.95 (ISBN 0-8128-2885-2). Stein & Day.
--Men in Arms. 304p. 1985. pap. 3.50 (ISBN 0-8128-8086-2). Stein & Day.
--Party of the Year. LC 78-24694. 1979. 9.95 (ISBN 0-8128-2606-X). Stein & Day.
--Penelope Now. 256p. 1984. pap. 3.95 (ISBN 0-8128-8034-X). Stein & Day.
--Take No Prisoners. 320p. (Orig.). 1985. pap. 3.95 (ISBN 0-446-32777-8). Warner Bks.
Crosby, John, ed. see Reinach, Adolf, et al.
Crosby, John, et al. Metaphysics. Marshner, William, tr. from Ger. (Aletheia-an International Journal of Philosophy: Vol. 1, Pt. 2). 251p. (Orig.). 1981. pap. 18.95 (ISBN 0-86663-784-2); with subscription 15.95 (ISBN 0-86663-782-6). Ide Hse.
Crosby, John A., tr. see Godfrey, W. Earl.
Crosby, John F. Reply to Myth: Perspectives on Intimacy. 669p. Date not set. pap. 16.95 (ISBN 0-471-81541-1). Wiley.
--Sexual Autonomy: Toward a Humanistic Ethic. (Illus.). 152p. 1981. 15.75x (ISBN 0-398-04521-6). C C Thomas.
Crosby, John F., jt. auth. see Williams, Carl E.
Crosby, Josiah. Siam: The Crossroads. LC 72-179186. Repr. of 1945 ed. 17.50 (ISBN 0-404-54817-2). AMS Pr.
Crosby, Kathryn. My Life with Bing. LC 82-74361. (Illus.). 358p. 1983. 29.95 (ISBN 0-938728-01-6). Collage Inc.
Crosby, Lamar H., Jr. The Vice of Verse & Other Slanderous Rhymes Concerning Famous Philosophers. Bell, Harrison B., ed. (Illus.). 96p. (Orig.). 1984. pap. 9.95 (ISBN 0-916153-00-2). Ten-Thirty Pr.
Crosby, Laura S. Art: Ideas for Elementary Classroom Teachers; Bulletin Board Suggestions; Patterns; Ideas for Holidays. (Illus.). 1985. pap. 18.00x spiral bound (ISBN 0-915114-04-6). Lewis-Sloan.
Crosby, Margaret. Violin Obligato & Other Studies. facsimile ed. LC 74-106283. (Short Story Index Reprint Ser.). 1891. 19.00 (ISBN 0-8369-3320-6). Ayer Co Pubs.
Crosby, Marilyn. Doomsday Journal Skillbuilders: 1982. Incl. Fireball. pap. 6.60 (ISBN 0-8224-1939-4); Final Warning. pap. 6.60 (ISBN 0-8224-1940-8); The Seep. pap. 6.60 (ISBN 0-8224-1941-6); Bedford Fever. pap. 6.60 (ISBN 0-8224-1942-4); Lost Valley. pap. 6.60 (ISBN 0-8224-1943-2); Comet! pap. 6.60 (ISBN 0-8224-1944-0). 1983. Set. pap. 31.68 pkg. of 10, each of 6 titles (ISBN 0-8224-1938-6). Pitman Learning.
Crosby, Michael H. The Spirituality of the Beatitudes: Matthew's Challenge for First World Christians. LC 80-24755. 256p. (Orig.). 1981. pap. 7.95 (ISBN 0-88344-465-8). Orbis Bks.
--Thy Will Be Done: Praying the Our Father As Subversive Activity. LC 77-5118. 262p. (Orig.). 1977. pap. 6.95 (ISBN 0-88344-497-6). Orbis Bks.
Crosby, N. T. Food Packaging Materials: Aspects of Analysis & Migration of Contaminants. (Illus.). 190p. 1981. 33.50 (ISBN 0-85334-926-6, Pub. by Elsevier Applied Sci England). Elsevier.
Crosby, Nina. Tomorrow's Decisions Today: The Corporation. 51p. (Orig.). 1979. pap. text ed. 5.95 (ISBN 0-914634-72-0, 7910). DOK Pubs.
Crosby, Nina & Marten, Elizabeth. Building Blocks for Academic Growth-Circus. (Building Blocks Ser.). (Illus.). 68p. (Orig.). 1983. pap. text ed. 4.95 teacher enrichment (ISBN 0-88047-022-4). DOK Pubs.
--Building Blocks for Academic Growth: Insects. (Building Blocks Ser.). (Illus.). 68p. (Orig.). (gr. 1-5). 1983. pap. text ed. 5.95 (ISBN 0-88047-023-2, 8308). DOK Pubs.
--Building Blocks for Academic Growth: Lucky Legends. (Building Blocks Ser.). (Illus.). 68p. (Orig.). (gr. 1-5). 1983. pap. text ed. 5.95 (ISBN 0-88047-024-0, 8309). DOK Pubs.
--Discovering Geology. (The Discovering Series). (Illus.). 72p. (gr. 3-12). 1982. tchr's manual 4.95 (ISBN 0-88047-003-8, 8203). DOK Pubs.
Crosby, Nina & Marten, Elizabeth H. Don't Teach Let Me Learn About Art, Poetry, Shakespeare & Music. (Illus.). 72p. 1979. pap. 5.95 tchr's enrichment manual (ISBN 0-914634-68-2). DOK Pubs.
Crosby, Nina, jt. auth. see Marten, Elizabeth.
Crosby, Nina E. & Marten, Elizabeth H. Discovering Philosophy. (Illus.). 72p. (Orig.). 1980. pap. 5.95 (ISBN 0-914634-81-X). DOK Pubs.
--Discovering Psychology. (Illus.). 86p. (Orig.). 1981. pap. text ed. 5.95 (ISBN 0-914634-94-1). DOK Pubs.
--Don't Teach Let Me Learn: A "How to" Guide for Managing an Individualized Learning Environment. (Illus.). 56p. (Orig.). 1980. pap. text ed. 4.95 (ISBN 0-914634-82-8). DOK Pubs.
--Don't Teach Let Me Learn About Aerodynamics, Robots & Computers, Science Fiction & Astronomy. (Illus.). 80p. (Orig.). (gr. 3-10). 1979. pap. 5.95 (ISBN 0-914634-60-7, 7902). DOK Pubs.
--Don't Teach Let Me Learn About Arachnids, Frogs, & Toads, the Animal Kingdom, Fish & Undersea Life. (Illus.). 88p. 1981. pap. 5.95 tchr's enrichment manual (ISBN 0-914634-97-6). DOK Pubs.
--Don't Teach Let Me Learn About Architecture, Chefs, Cooking, & Foods. Zilliox, tr. (Illus.). 72p. (Orig.). 1981. pap. 5.95 tchr's enrichment manual (ISBN 0-914634-98-4). DOK Pubs.
--Don't Teach! Let Me Learn about Fantasy, Magic, Monkeys & Monsters. (The Don't Teach! Let Me Learn Ser.). (Illus.). 72p. (Orig.). 1984. 5.95 (ISBN 0-88047-045-3, 8410). DOK Pubs.
--Don't Teach Let Me Learn: About Horses, Veterinary Medicine, Agribusiness, Forestry. (The Don't Teach! Let Me Learn Ser.). (Illus.). 72p. (gr. 3-6). 1982. 5.95 (ISBN 0-88047-007-0, 8202). DOK Pubs.
--Don't Teach Let Me Learn: About Mysteries, Mythology, Fairy Tales, Fables, Legends, the Supernatural. (The Don't Teach! Let Me Learn Ser.). (Illus.). 72p. (gr. 3-6). 1978. 5.95 (ISBN 0-88047-006-2, 8209). DOK Pubs.
--Don't Teach Let Me Learn: About Nutrition, Chemistry, Medicine, Nursing. (The Don't Teach! Let Me Learn Ser.). (Illus.). 72p. (gr. 3-6). 1983. 5.95 (ISBN 0-88047-030-5, 8313). DOK Pubs.
--Don't Teach Let Me Learn: About Opera, Ballet, American Theatre, Cinema. (The Don't Teach Let Me Learn Ser.). (Illus.). 72p. (gr. 3-6). 1983. 5.95 (ISBN 0-88047-008-9, 8210). DOK Pubs.
--Don't Teach Let Me Learn about Presidents, of the U.S. People, Genealogy, Immigrants. (Illus.). 80p. (Orig.). 1979. pap. 5.95 tchr's enrichment manual (ISBN 0-914634-67-4). DOK Pubs.
--Don't Teach Let Me Learn About Tear-Jerkers, Humor, Cartoons & Comics, the Newspaper. (Illus.). 88p. (Orig.). 1979. pap. 5.95 (ISBN 0-914634-61-5). DOK Pubs.
--Don't Teach Let Me Learn: About the F.B.I., Firefighters, Felines, Futures. (The Don't Teach! Let Me Learn Ser.). (Illus.). 72p. (gr. 3-6). 1983. teacher enrichment book 5.95 (ISBN 0-88047-029-1, 8312). DOK Pubs.
--Don't Teach! Let Me Learn about World War II, Adventure, Dreams & Superstition. (The Don't Teach! Let Me Learn Ser.). (Illus.). 72p. (Orig.). (gr. 3-10). 1984. 5.95 (ISBN 0-88047-044-5, 8411). DOK Pubs.
--Know Your State. (Illus.). 32p. (Orig.). (gr. 4-7). 1984. pap. 3.95 (ISBN 0-88047-036-4, 8401). DOK Pubs.
Crosby, Percy L. Skippy. Blackbeard, Bill, ed. LC 76-53037. (Classic American Comic Strips). 1977. 16.95 (ISBN 0-88355-629-4); pap. 10.00 (ISBN 0-88355-628-6). Hyperion Conn.
Crosby, Philip B. The Art of Getting Your Own Sweet Way. 2nd ed. (Illus.). 240p. 1981. 18.95 (ISBN 0-07-014515-6). McGraw.
--The Art of Getting Your Own Sweet Way. 2nd ed. 240p. 1982. pap. 5.95 (ISBN 0-07-014527-X). McGraw.
--Quality Is Free: The Art of Making Quality Free. 1979. 24.95 (ISBN 0-07-014512-1). McGraw.
--Quality Is Free: The Art of Making Quality Certain. 1980. pap. 3.95 (ISBN 0-451-62247-2, ME2247, Ment). NAL.
--Quality Without Tears: The Art of Hassle-Free Management. 192p. 1984. 19.95 (ISBN 0-07-014530-X). McGraw.
--Quality Without Tears: The Art of Hassle-Free Management. 1985. pap. 8.95 (ISBN 0-452-25658-5, Plume). NAL.
Crosby, Phoebe. Stars. LC 60-9233. (Junior Science Ser.). (Illus.). (gr. 2-5). 1960. PLB 7.47 (ISBN 0-8116-6153-9). Garrard.
Crosby, R. M. & Liston, R. A. The Waysiders: Reading & the Dyslexic Child. LC 76-12222. (John Day Bk.). 1976. 11.49 (ISBN 0-381-98290-4). T Y Crowell.
Crosby, Robert W., ed. Cities & Regions As Nonlinear Decision Systems. (AAAS Selected Symposium: No. 77). 200p. 1983. 28.00x (ISBN 0-86531-530-2). Westview.
Crosby, Ruth. From an Old Leather Trunk. (Illus.). 192p. 1974. 6.95 (ISBN 0-8158-0318-4). Chris Mass.
--I Was a Summer Boarder. 1966. 6.95 (ISBN 0-8158-0080-0). Chris Mass.
Crosby, S. S. Early Coins of America. LC 83-71431. 1984. Repr. of 1875 ed. lib. bdg. 45.00 (ISBN 0-942666-24-0). S J Durst.
Crosby, Sumner M. The Apostle Bas-Relief at Saint-Denis. LC 71-179471. (Yale Publications in the History of Art Ser.: No. 21). (Illus.). pap. 56.00 (ISBN 0-317-10455-1, 2021993). Bks Demand UMI.
Crosby, Sumner M., et al. The Royal Abbey of Saint-Denis in the Time of Abbot Suger (1122-1151) Shultz, Ellen, ed. LC 80-28849. (Illus.). 128p. 1981. pap. 12.95 (ISBN 0-87099-261-9). Metro Mus Art.
Crosby, Sylvester S. The Early Coins of America. LC 77-189168. (Illus.). 432p. 1974. 60.00x (ISBN 0-88000-035-X). Quarterman.
--Early Coins of America. rev. ed. LC 77-189168. 1983. 45.00x (ISBN 0-88000-138-0). Quarterman.
--Early Coins of America & the Laws Governing Their Issue. LC 70-118743. (Research & Source Works: No. 544). 1970. Repr. of 1875 ed. lib. bdg. 26.50 (ISBN 0-8337-0737-X). B Franklin.
Crosby, Thomas. History of the English Baptists: 1740 Ed, 4 vols. in 2 vols. Set. 45.00 (ISBN 0-686-12405-7). Church History.
Crosby, Tony. An Austin Sketchbook. (Illus.). 1978. 12.50 (ISBN 0-88426-053-4). Encino Pr.
Crosby, Travis L. Sir Robert Peel's Administration, 1841-46. (Elections & Administrations Ser.). 190p. 1976. 17.50 (ISBN 0-208-01517-5, Archon). Shoe String.
Crosby, William F. Boat Sailing: A Primer for the Beginner. 1977. lib. bdg. 69.95 (ISBN 0-8490-1517-0). Gordon Pr.
Crose, Lester A. Passport for a Reformation. 1981. pap. 7.95 (ISBN 0-87162-242-4, D6100). Warner Pr.
Crosher, Judith. The Aztecs. (Peoples of the Past Ser.). 80p. (gr. 4 up). 1985. pap. 5.75 (ISBN 0-382-06918-8). Silver.
--The Greeks. (Peoples of the Past Ser.). 80p. (gr. 4 up). 1985. pap. 5.75 (ISBN 0-382-06913-7). Silver.
Crosher, Judith & Strongman, Harry. The Greeks. LC 77-86190. (Peoples of the Past Ser.). (Illus.). 64p. (gr. 6 up). 1977. PLB 12.68 (ISBN 0-382-06119-5). Silver.
Crosher, Judith, et al. The Aztecs. LC 77-86189. (Peoples of the Past Ser.). (Illus.). 1977. PLB 13.72 (ISBN 0-382-06123-3). Silver.
Crosier, Barney. Vermont Blood. 128p. 1980. pap. 5.95 (ISBN 0-9603900-6-5). Lanser Pr.
Crosier, Keith, jt. auth. see Bowey, Angela.
Crosignani, Bruce, et al. Guiding, Diffraction & Confinement of Optical Radiation. Date not set. price not set (ISBN 0-12-199070-2). Acad Pr.
Crosignani, Bruno & Di Porto, Paolo. Statistical Properties of Scattered Light. (Quantum Electronics Ser.). 1975. 59.50 (ISBN 0-12-199050-8). Acad Pr.
Crosignani, P. G. & Robyn, C. Prolactin & Human Reproduction. 1977. 57.50 (ISBN 0-12-198345-5). Acad Pr.
Crosignani, P. G. & James, V. H., eds. Recent Progress in Reproductive Endocrinology. 1975. 119.00 (ISBN 0-12-198360-9). Acad Pr.
Crosignani, P. G. & Mishell, D., eds. Ovulation in the Human. (Serono Symposium: No. 8). 1977. 59.50 (ISBN 0-12-198340-4). Acad Pr.
Crosignani, P. G. & Rubin, B., eds. Microsurgery in Female Infertility. (Proceedings of the Serono Clinical Colloquia on Reproduction Ser.: No. 1). 142p. 1980. 31.00 (ISBN 0-8089-1258-5, 790948). Grune.
Crosignani, P. G. & Rubin, B. L., eds. Genetic Control of Gamete Production & Function. LC 82-71233. (Serono Clinical Colloquia on Reproduction Ser.: No. 3). 1982. 42.00 (ISBN 0-8089-1505-3, 790947). Grune.
Crosignani, P. G. & Rubin, Betty, eds. Endocrinology of Human Infertility: New Aspects. (Serono Clinical Colloquia on Reproduction Ser.: No. 2). 456p. 1981. 73.00 (ISBN 0-8089-1393-X, 790949). Grune.
Crosignani, P. G., jt. ed. see Albertini, A.
Crosignani, Pier G. & Pardi, Giorgio, eds. Fetal Evaluation During Pregnancy & Labor: Experimental & Clinical Aspects. 307p. 1972. 68.00 (ISBN 0-12-198350-1). Acad Pr.
Croskery, Beverly F. Death Education: Attitudes of Teachers, School Board Members & Clergy. LC 78-68458. 1979. perfect bdg. 9.95 (ISBN 0-88247-559-2). R & E Pubs.
Croskery, Sidney E. Whilst I Remember. 196p. 1983. pap. 13.95 (ISBN 0-85640-260-5, Pub. by Blackstaff Pr). Irish Bks Media.
Crosland, Andrew, compiled by. Concordance to F. Scott Fitzgerald's the Great Gatsby. LC 74-11607. (A Bruccoli Clark Book). (Illus.). 425p. 1975. 75.00x (ISBN 0-8103-1005-8). Gale.
--Concordance to the Complete Poetry of Stephen Crane. LC 74-30426. (A Bruccoli Clark Book). 210p. 1975. 85.00x (ISBN 0-8103-1006-6). Gale.
Crosland, Anthony. The Future of Socialism. 384p. 1981. 40.00x (ISBN 0-224-01888-4, Pub. by Cape England). State Mutual Bk.
Crosland, Charles A. The Future of Socialism. LC 77-4064. 1977. Repr. of 1964 ed. lib. bdg. 26.75x (ISBN 0-8371-9586-1, CRF). Greenwood.
Crosland, Jessie. Old French Epic. LC 73-117589. (Studies in French Literature, No. 45). 1970. Repr. of 1951 ed. lib. bdg. 49.95x (ISBN 0-8383-1022-2). Haskell.

Cross, James A. Answers from the Word. 1974. pap. 2.95 (ISBN 0-87148-012-3). Pathway Pr.

--The Glorious Gospel. 1956. 4.25 (ISBN 0-87148-350-5). Pathway Pr.

--A Study of the Holy Ghost. 1973. pap. 4.25 (ISBN 0-87148-006-9). Pathway Pr.

Cross, James A., ed. Un Estudio del Espiritu Santo. 182p. (Span.). 1980. pap. 4.95 (ISBN 0-87148-883-3). Pathway Pr.

Cross, James E. Conflict in the Shadows. LC 75-17468. 180p. 1975. Repr. of 1963 ed. lib. bdg. 18.75x (ISBN 0-8371-8305-7, CRCS). Greenwood.

Cross, James E. & Hill, Thomas D., eds. The Prose Solomon & Saturn; & Adrian & Ritheus. (McMaster Old English & Texts Ser.). 1982. 35.00x (ISBN 0-8020-5472-2); pap. 12.50 (ISBN 0-8020-6509-0). U of Toronto Pr.

Cross, Jean & Farrer, Donald. Dust Explosions. LC 82-7499. 259p. 1982. text ed. 37.50 (ISBN 0-306-40871-6, Plenum Pr). Plenum Pub.

Cross, Jeanne. Simple Printing Methods. LC 72-39812. (Illus.). 48p. (gr. 6 up). 1972. 10.95 (ISBN 0-87599-192-0). S G Phillips.

Cross, Jeff, ed. see European Syndicate of Soccer Experts.

Cross, Jennifer. The Supermarket Trap: The Consumer & the Food Industry. Rev., Bk. 1 ed. LC 75-10806. pap. 79.50 (ISBN 0-317-27929-7, 2056031). Bks Demand UMI.

Cross, Jerry & Cross, Pauline. Knowing Yourself Inside-Out for Self Direction. (Illus.). 259p. 1983. pap. 9.95 (ISBN 0-9610820-1-1). Crystal Pubns.

Cross, John & Guyer, Mel. Social Traps. (Illus.). 1980. pap. 7.50 (ISBN 0-472-06315-4). U of Mich Pr.

Cross, John, jt. auth. see Galliher, John.

Cross, John C., jt. auth. see Harney, Malachi L.

Cross, John G. A Theory of Adaptive Economic Behaviour. LC 83-7563. 199p. 1983. 39.50 (ISBN 0-521-25110-9). Cambridge U Pr.

Cross, John H., jt. ed. see Croll, Neil A.

Cross, John K. Best Black Magic Stories. Repr. of 1960 ed. 20.00 (ISBN 0-89987-131-3). Darby Bks.

--The Children's Omnibus. 15.00 (ISBN 0-686-18158-1). Havertown Bks.

Cross, John S. The Gloster Fancy Canary. (Illus.). 200p. 1980. 13.50 (ISBN 0-904558-42-8). Saiga.

Cross, K. Patricia. Accent on Learning: Improving Instruction & Reshaping the Curriculum. LC 75-24003. (Higher Education Ser.). (Illus.). 320p. 1976. 19.95x (ISBN 0-87589-269-8). Jossey-Bass.

--Adults As Learners: Increasing Participation & Facilitating Learning. LC 80-26985. (Higher Education Ser.). 1981. text ed. 17.95x (ISBN 0-87589-491-7). Jossey-Bass.

--Beyond the Open Door: New Students to Higher Education. LC 77-170212. (Higher Education Ser.). 1971. 19.95x (ISBN 0-87589-111-X). Jossey-Bass.

--The Missing Link: Connecting Adult Learners to Learning Resources. 80p. 1978. pap. 4.50 (ISBN 0-87447-062-5, 237402). College Bd.

Cross, K. Patricia & McCartan, Anne-Marie. Adult Learning: State Policies & Institutional Practices. Fife, Jonathan D., ed. & frwd. by. LC 84-221532. (ASHE-ERIC Higher Education Research Report Ser.: No. 1, 1984). (Illus.). 162p. (Orig.). 1984. pap. 7.50 (ISBN 0-913317-10-1). Assn Study Higher Educ.

Cross, K. Patricia, jt. ed. see Gould, Samuel B.

Cross, K. Patricia, et al. Planning Non-Traditional Programs: An Analysis of the Issues for Postsecondary Education. LC 73-18505. (Higher Education Ser). 1974. 19.95x (ISBN 0-87589-217-5). Jossey-Bass.

Cross, L., et al. Readings in Sociology. 1969. pap. text ed. 7.25x (ISBN 0-8290-1181-1). Irvington.

Cross, L. S. Paul's Letters Made Easy for Devotions. 120p. (Orig.). 1982. pap. 4.95 (ISBN 0-89221-090-7, Pub by SonLife). New Leaf.

Cross, Larry R., jt. ed. see Owen, Wyn F.

Cross, Laurella B. Jenny's New Game: How to Protect Children Against Kidnapping & Assault. rev., 3rd ed. 298p. (Orig.). 1984. pap. 8.95 (ISBN 0-9612806-0-3). L B Cross.

Cross, Lawrence, jt. auth. see Savells, Jerald.

Cross, Lee & Goin, Kenneth, eds. Identifying Handicapped Children. LC 76-52246. (First Chance Ser.). 1984. pap. 9.95 (ISBN 0-8027-7264-1). Walker & Co.

Cross, Lee, jt. ed. see Ellis, Norman E.

Cross, Lee M. Morgan County Tennessee Eighteen-Fifty Census. Spurling, Larry R., ed. iii, 75p. 1985. pap. 11.50 (ISBN 0-917890-53-1). Heritage Bk.

Cross, Leland L., et al, eds. see Becker, Elle F.

Cross, Lowell M. A Bibliography of Electronic Music. LC 67-2573. pap. 34.00 (ISBN 0-317-09917-5, 2014178). Bks Demand UMI.

Cross, Luther. Object Lessons for Children. (Object Lesson Ser). (Illus., Orig.). (gr. 2-5). 1967. pap. 3.95 (ISBN 0-8010-2315-7). Baker Bk.

Cross, Luther S. Easy Object Stories. 114p. 1984. pap. 3.95 (ISBN 0-8010-2502-8). Baker Bk.

--Growing in Faith: Devotions for Parent-Child Interaction. 32p. (Orig.). 1984. pap. 2.25 (ISBN 0-8066-2070-6, 23-1606). Augsburg.

--Story Sermons for Children. (Object Lesson Ser.). (Orig.). 1966. pap. 3.50 (ISBN 0-8010-2328-9). Baker Bk.

Cross, M. & Moscardini, A. O. Learning the Art of Mathematical Modelling. (Mathematics & Its Applications Ser.). 1985. 34.95 (ISBN 0-470-20168-1); pap. 15.95 (ISBN 0-470-20169-X). Halsted Pr.

Cross, Malcolm. Urbanization & Urban Growth in the Caribbean. LC 78-67307. (Urbanization in Developing Countries Ser.). pap. 46.50 (ISBN 0-317-26045-6, 2024438). Bks Demand UMI.

Cross, Marion E. see Eliot, George, pseud.

Cross, Michael. New Firm Formation & Regional Development. 354p. 1981. text ed. 44.50x (ISBN 0-566-00372-4). Gower Pub Co.

--U. S. Corporate Personnel Reduction Policies. 144p. 1981. text ed. 35.50x (ISBN 0-566-00501-8). Gower Pub Co.

Cross, Michael, ed. Grow Your Own Energy. (New Scientist Guides Ser.). (Illus.). 256p. 1984. 24.95 (ISBN 0-85520-731-0); pap. 8.95x (ISBN 0-85520-730-2). Basil Blackwell.

--Managing Workforce Reduction: An International Survey. LC 84-18088. 224p. 1985. 26.95 (ISBN 0-03-002654-7). Praeger.

Cross, Mike. Wind Power. (Energy Today Ser.). (Illus.). 32p. (gr. 1-6). 1985. PLB 9.40 (ISBN 0-531-17007-1, Gloucester Pr). Watts.

Cross, Milton. New Milton Cross' Complete Stories of the Great Operas. rev. ed. 1955. 17.95 (ISBN 0-385-04324-4). Doubleday.

Cross, Milton & Ewen, David. Milton Cross New Encyclopedia of the Great Composers & Their Music, 2 vols. LC 70-87097. two-volume, boxed set 39.95 (ISBN 0-385-03635-3). Doubleday.

Cross, Milton & Kohrs, Karl. The New Milton Cross More Stories of the Great Operas. LC 79-8023. 816p. 1980. 19.95 (ISBN 0-385-14776-7). Doubleday.

Cross, N. The Automated Architect. (Research in Planning & Design Ser.). 178p. 1977. text ed. 18.95x (ISBN 0-85086-057-1, NO.2934, Pub. by Pion England). Methuen Inc.

Cross, N. J., jt. auth. see Allen, G. R.

Cross, Nigel. The Common Writer: Life in Nineteenth-Century Grub Street. 250p. Date not set. price not set (ISBN 0-521-24564-8). Cambridge U Pr.

--Design Methodology. LC 84-7433. 1984. 49.95x (ISBN 0-471-10248-2). Wiley.

Cross, Osborne. Report in the Form of a Journal, the March of the Regiment of Mounted Riflemen to Oregon in 1849. 1967. Repr. of 1851 ed. 16.95 (ISBN 0-87770-008-7). Ye Galleon.

Cross, Paul, et al. Bedford County. (Tennessee County History Ser.). (Illus.). 144p. Date not set. 12.50x (ISBN 0-87870-100-1). Memphis St Univ.

Cross, Pauline, jt. auth. see Cross, Jerry.

Cross, Peter. Trouble for Trumpets. LC 83-43115. (Illus.). (gr. 3 up). 1985. 9.95 (ISBN 0-394-86513-8, BYR); PLB 8.99 (ISBN 0-394-96513-2). Random.

Cross, R. C. & Woozley, A. D. Plato's Republic: A Philosophical Commentary. new ed. 1979. pap. text ed. 11.95 (ISBN 0-312-61508-6). St Martin.

Cross, R. J. & Mingos, D. M. Organometallic Compounds of Nickel, Palladium, Copper, Silver, & Gold. (Chemistry Sourcebooks Ser.). 346p. 40.00 (ISBN 0-412-26850-7, Pub. by Chapman & Hall). Methuen Inc.

Cross, R. Nicol. Socrates. facs. ed. LC 70-130546. (Select Bibliographies Reprint Ser). 1914. 20.00 (ISBN 0-8369-5519-6). Ayer Co Pubs.

Cross, Ralph. Denton's Army. 1979. pap. 1.75 (ISBN 0-505-51388-9, Pub. by Tower Bks). Dorchester Pub Co.

--Denton's Army. 208p. 1983. pap. 2.25 (ISBN 0-8439-2060-2, Leisure Bks). Dorchester Pub Co.

--Key to Murder. (Orig.). 1980. pap. 1.95 (ISBN 0-505-51487-7, Pub. by Tower Bks). Dorchester Pub Co.

Cross, Ralph D. & Wales, Robert W., eds. Atlas of Mississippi. LC 74-78569. (Illus.). 1974. 5.00x (ISBN 0-87805-061-2). U Pr of Miss.

Cross, Randy K., ed. see Stribling, Thomas S.

Cross, Reuben. The Completest Fly Tier. (Illus.). 224p. 1971. 7.95 (ISBN 0-88395-008-1). Freshet Pr.

Cross, Richard F. Bank Security Desk Reference: Annual Supplement. 1st ed. LC 81-69999. 1981. Supplement issued anually. 54.00 (ISBN 0-88262-632-9). Warren.

Cross, Richard K. Malcolm Lowry: A Preface to His Fiction. LC 79-16091. 1980. 12.50x (ISBN 0-226-12125-9); pap. 5.95 (ISBN 0-226-12126-7). U of Chicago Pr.

Cross, Robert & Cross, Sue. Focus on Team Teaching. Romano, Louis G., ed. (Illus.). 24p. 1983. pap. text ed. 2.50 (ISBN 0-918449-02-2). MI Middle Educ.

Cross, Robert A. Emergence of Liberal Catholicism in America. LC 58-5593. 1958. 22.50x (ISBN 0-674-24800-7). Harvard U Pr.

Cross, Robert B., tr. see Rigaud, Milo.

Cross, Robert D., ed. The Church & the City: 1865-1910. LC 66-17273. 1967. 37.50x (ISBN 0-672-50994-6). Irvington.

Cross, Robert R., jt. auth. see Dornette, W. Stuart.

Cross, Robin. The Hollywood History of World War II. (Illus.). 64p. 1984. pap. 7.95 (ISBN 0-312-38841-1). St Martin.

Cross, Roger. The Yorkshire Ripper. (Illus.). 255p. 1981. pap. 2.95 (ISBN 0-440-19802-X). Dell.

Cross, Roy, jt. auth. see Green, William.

Cross, Rupert. Precedent in English Law. 3rd. ed. 1977. pap. text ed. 13.95x (ISBN 0-19-876073-6). Oxford U Pr.

Cross, Ruth. Soldier of Good Fortune. 1936. 10.00 (ISBN 0-88289-287-8). Pelican.

Cross, Samuel H. Mediaeval Russian Churches. 1949. 10.00x (ISBN 0-910956-27-8). Medieval Acad.

Cross, Samuel H., ed. Russian Primary Chronicle: Laurentian Text. Sherbowitz-Wetzor, O. P., tr. LC 53-10264. 1968. Repr. of 1953 ed. 10.00x (ISBN 0-910956-34-0). Medieval Acad.

Cross, Samuel H., ed. see Pushkin, Alexander S.

Cross, Sue, jt. auth. see Cross, Robert.

Cross, T. B., jt. auth. see Blanking-Clark, T.

Cross, T. P., jt. auth. see Nitze, W. A.

Cross, Theodore. The Black Power Imperative: Racial Inequality & the Politics of Nonviolence. LC 84-80109. 907p. 1984. 19.95 (ISBN 0-916631-00-1). Faulkner Bks.

Cross, Thomas B. Centrex: Strategic Outlook. (Illus.). 140p. 1984. Binder 2500.00 (ISBN 0-923426-02-7). Cross Info.

--Intelligent Buildings & Information Systems. (Illus.). 300p. 1984. binder 970.00 (ISBN 0-923426-03-5). Cross Info.

--Strategies for Telecommunications Management. 320p. 1984. Binder 850.00 (ISBN 0-923426-01-9). Cross Info.

--Telecommunications Outlook. (Illus.). 300p. 1985. 1300.00 (ISBN 0-923426-04-3). Cross Info.

Cross, Thomas B. & Raizman, Marjorie B. Networking: An Electronic Mail Handbook. 1985. pap. 18.95 (ISBN 0-673-18008-5). Scott F.

Cross, Thomas B., jt. auth. see Gouin, Michelle D.

Cross, Thomas B., jt. auth. see Kelleher, Kathleen.

Cross, Thomas B., jt. auth. see Weidlein, James R.

Cross, Tim, jt. auth. see Lane, Ron.

Cross, Tim L., jt. auth. see Lane, Ronald J.

Cross, Tim L., jt. auth. see Lane, Ronald L.

Cross, Tom P. Harper & Bard. 1978. Repr. of 1931 ed. lib. bdg. 15.00 (ISBN 0-8492-3951-6). R West.

--Harper & the Bard: The Beauties of Irish Literature. 59.95 (ISBN 0-8490-0282-6). Gordon Pr.

--Witchcraft in North Carolina. 70p. 1980. Repr. of 1919 ed. lib. bdg. 15.00 (ISBN 0-8414-9992-6). Folcroft.

Cross, Tom P. & Nitze, William N. Lancelot & Guinevere: A Study of the Origins of Courtly Love. LC 79-91348. 1970. Repr. of 1922 ed. 9.00x (ISBN 0-87753-010-6). Phaeton.

Cross, Tom P. & Slover, Clark H., eds. Ancient Irish Tales. (Illus.). 615p. 1969. Repr. of 1936 ed. 23.50x (ISBN 0-06-480177-2). B&N Imports.

Cross, Tony, jt. auth. see Kilvington, Russel.

Cross, W. & Florio, C. You Are Never Too Old to Learn. 1978. pap. 12.95 (ISBN 0-07-014514-8). McGraw.

Cross, W. L. Four Contemporary Novelists. LC 70-136401. (BBcL Ser. I). Repr. of 1930 ed. 12.50 (ISBN 0-404-01867-X). AMS Pr.

Cross, Whitney R. The Burned-Over District: The Social & Intellectual History of Enthusiastic Religion in Western New York, 1800-1850. LC 81-2636. xii, 383p. 1981. Repr. of 1950 ed. lib. bdg. 31.50x (ISBN 0-374-91932-1). Octagon.

--The Burned-Over District: The Social & Intellectual History of Enthusiastic Religion in Western New York, 1800-1850. 400p. 1982. pap. 9.95x (ISBN 0-8014-9232-7). Cornell U Pr.

Cross, Wilbur. Brazil. LC 84-7602. (Enchantment of the World Ser.). (Illus.). 128p. (gr. 5-9). 1984. lib. bdg. 19.95 (ISBN 0-516-02753-0). Childrens.

--Coal. LC 83-7590. (Science & Technology Ser.). (Illus.). 100p. (gr. 5 up). 1983. PLB 14.00 (ISBN 0-516-00508-1). Childrens.

--Egypt. LC 82-9465. (Enchantment of the World). (Illus.). (gr. 5-9). 1982. PLB 19.95 (ISBN 0-516-02762-X). Childrens.

--Kids & Booze: What You Must Know to Help Them. 1979. pap. 5.95 (ISBN 0-87690-314-6, 0578-170). Dutton.

--Petroleum. (Science & Technology Ser.). (Illus.). 100p. (gr. 5 up). 1983. PLB 14.00 (ISBN 0-516-00509-X). Childrens.

--Samuel S. Stratton: A Story of Political Gumption. (Future Maker Ser). (Illus.). 1964. 3.95 (ISBN 0-685-11981-5). Heineman.

--Solar Energy. LC 84-23243. (Science & Technology Ser.). (Illus.). (gr. 5 up). 1984. lib. bdg. 14.00 (ISBN 0-516-00511-1). Childrens.

--Space Shuttle. (Illus.). 100p. (gr. 3 up). 1985. 4.95 (ISBN 0-516-40513-6). Childrens.

Cross, Wilbur, jt. auth. see Pace, Nicholas A.

Cross, Wilbur, ed. see Yale Review.

Cross, Wilbur L. The Development of the English Novel. 1930. 30.00 (ISBN 0-8495-6276-7). Arden Lib.

--Development of the English Novel. LC 78-90494. Repr. of 1899 ed. lib. bdg. 18.75x (ISBN 0-8371-2204-X, CREN). Greenwood.

--Four Contemporary Novelists. facs. ed. LC 67-22087. (Essay Index Reprint Ser.). 1930. 17.00 (ISBN 0-8369-0353-6). Ayer Co Pubs.

--History of Henry Fielding, 3 Vols. LC 64-10385. (Illus.). 1963. Repr. of 1918 ed. Set. 60.00x (ISBN 0-8462-0403-7). Russell.

--The Modern English Novel. 1928. 29.50x (ISBN 0-686-51417-3). Elliots Bks.

--The Modern English Novel: An Address Before the American Academy of Arts & Letters. 9.00 (ISBN 0-8369-6927-8, 7808). Ayer Co Pubs.

Cross, Wilbur L., ed. see Sterne, Laurence.

Crossan, Bettie. Beware! Be Wise. 130p. (Orig.). 1984. pap. 2.95 (ISBN 0-87508-148-7). Chr Lit.

Crossan, Gregory D. A Relish for Eternity: The Process of Divinization in the Poetry of John Clare. (Salzburg Studies in English Literature, Romantic Reassessment: No. 53). 291p. 1976. pap. text ed. 25.50x (ISBN 0-391-01354-8). Humanities.

Crossan, John. In Parables. LC 73-7067. 160p. 1973. 12.95xi (ISBN 0-06-061606-7, HarpR). Har-Row.

Crossan, John D. Cliffs of Fall: Paradox & Polyvalence in the Parables of Jesus. 128p. 1980. 9.95 (ISBN 0-8164-0113-6, Pub. by Seabury). Winston Pr.

--The Dark Interval: Towards a Theology of Story. 1975. pap. cancelled (ISBN 0-913592-52-8). Argus Comm.

--Finding Is the First Act. 141p. 1979. pap. 8.25 (ISBN 0-317-35691-7, 06-06-09); pap. 5.50 members (ISBN 0-317-35692-5). Scholars Pr GA.

--Four Other Gospels: Shadows on the Contour of the Canon. 208p. (Orig.). 1985. 15.95 (ISBN 0-86683-959-3, Pub. by Seabury). Winston Pr.

--A Fragile Craft: The Work of Amos Niven Wilder. Richards, Kent, ed. LC 80-19755. 1981. pap. 8.95 (ISBN 0-89130-424-X, 06 11 03). Scholars Pr GA.

--In Fragments: The Aphorisms of Jesus. LC 83-47719. 384p. 1983. 23.99i (ISBN 0-06-061608-3, HarpR). Har-Row.

--In Parables: The Challenge of the Historical Jesus. LC 73-7067. 141p. 1985. pap. 9.95 (ISBN 0-06-061609-1, HarpR). Har-Row.

Crossan, John D., ed. Semeia Nineteen: The Book of Job & Ricoeur's Hermeneutics. (Semeia Ser.). pap. 9.95 (ISBN 0-686-96266-4, 06 20 19). Scholars Pr GA.

--Semeia Ten: Narrative Syntax: Traditions & Reviews. (Semeia Ser.). pap. 9.95 (ISBN 0-686-96237-0, 06 20 10). Scholars Pr GA.

Crossan, John Dominic. Finding Is the First Act: Trove Folktales & Jesus' Treasures Parable. pap. 4.95 (ISBN 0-317-31444-0). Fortress.

Crossan, John Dominic, ed. Narrative Syntax. 156p. 1978. pap. 9.95 (ISBN 0-317-35705-0, 06-20-10); pap. 6.95 members (ISBN 0-317-35706-9). Scholars Pr GA.

Crossan, Richard M. & Nance, Harold W. Master Standard Data: The Economic Approach to Work, Measurement. rev. ed. LC 80-11165. 268p. 1980. Repr. of 1972 ed. lib. bdg. 18.50 (ISBN 0-89874-133-5). Krieger.

Crossant, Jeanne. Aristote et les Mysteres. Vlastos, Gregory, ed. LC 78-15863. (Morals & Law in Ancient Greece Ser.). (Fr. & Ger.). 1979. Repr. of 1932 ed. lib. bdg. 19.00x (ISBN 0-405-11534-2). Ayer Co Pubs.

Crosse, Howard & Hempel, Goerge. Management Policies for Commercial Banks. 3rd ed. (Illus.). 1980. text ed. 31.95 (ISBN 0-13-549030-8). P-H.

Crossen, Forest. Golden Mirage. 1982. 9.95 (ISBN 0-913730-03-3). Robinson Pr.

--Switzerland Trail of America. 1978. 44.75 (ISBN 0-913730-23-8). Robinson Pr.

--Western Yesterdays, 12 Vols. 1972. 44.95 set (ISBN 0-913730-09-2). Robinson Pr.

Crosser, Paul F. A Prolegomena to All Future Metaeconomics. LC 72-13845. 240p. 1974. 10.00 (ISBN 0-87527-099-9). Fireside Bks.

Crosser, Paul K. Prolegomena to All Future Metaeconomics: Formation & Deformation of Economic Thought. LC 72-13845. (Illus.). 240p. 1974. 10.00x (ISBN 0-87527-099-9). Green.

Crossett, John M., jt. tr. see Arieti, James A.

Crossette, Barbara & Lowe, Wendy, eds. America's Wonderful Little Hotels & Inns 1985: Eastern Region. 5th ed. 394p. 1985. pap. 10.95 (ISBN 0-312-92010-5). Congdon & Weed.

--America's Wonderful Little Hotels & Inns 1985: Western Region. 224p. 1985. pap. 8.95 (ISBN 0-312-92011-3). Congdon & Weed.

Crossfield, A. Scott & Blair, Clay, Jr. Always Another Dawn: The Story of a Rocket Test Pilot. LC 73-169413. (Literature & History of Aviation Ser). 1972. Repr. of 1960 ed. 31.00 (ISBN 0-405-03758-9). Ayer Co Pubs.

Crossfield, R. C. Book of Onias. LC 70-86503. 1969. 5.00 (ISBN 0-8022-2290-0). Philos Lib.

Crossgrove, Hannelore & Crossgrove, William C. Graded German Reader. 2nd ed. 1978. pap. text ed. 8.95x (ISBN 0-669-01533-4). Heath.

Crossgrove, William C., jt. auth. see Crossgrove, Hannelore.

Crossick, Geoffrey. An Artisan Elite in Victorian Society: Kentish London 1840-1880. 306p. 1978. 24.50x (ISBN 0-8476-6098-2). Rowman.

Crossick, Geoffrey, ed. The Lower-Middle Class in Britain, 1870-1914. LC 76-25410. 1977. 25.00x (ISBN 0-312-49980-9). St Martin.

--Shopkeepers & Master Artisans in Nineteenth-Century Europe. 304p. 1984. 35.00 (ISBN 0-416-35660-5, NO. 4153). Methuen Inc.

Crossin, John W. What Are They Saying about Virtue. (WATSA Ser.). pap. 4.95 (ISBN 0-8091-2674-5). Paulist Pr.

Crossing, William. Crossing's Guide to Dartmoor. 2nd ed. (Illus.). 529p. 1965. 13.50 (ISBN 0-7153-4017-4, Pub. by Batsford, England). David & Charles.

Crouch. Rainbow Warrior's Bridge. 8.95 (ISBN 0-7207-1296-3, Pub. by Michael Joseph). Merrimack Pub Cir.

Crouch, A. Mr. G. B. Shaw: A Sketch. LC 75-17983. 1975. Repr. of 1932 ed. lib. bdg. 10.00 (ISBN 0-8414-3625-8). Folcroft.

Crouch, Ben M. The Keepers: Prison Guards & Contemporary Corrections. 368p. 1980. 36.75x (ISBN 0-398-03970-4). C C Thomas.

Crouch, Bill, Jr., jt. auth. see Kelley, Walt Mrs.

Crouch, Bill, Jr., jt. ed. see Kelly.

Crouch, Brodie. Beneath Stars of Hope. pap. 3.50 (ISBN 0-89315-001-0). Lambert Bk.

--The Myth of Mormon Inspiration. 7.50 (ISBN 0-89315-158-0). Lambert Bk.

--Study of Minor Prophets. pap. 2.50 (ISBN 0-89315-291-9). Lambert Bk.

Crouch, Bruce R. & Chamala, Shankarish. Extension Education & Rural Development, Vol. 1: International Experience in Communication & Innovation. LC 79-41221. 371p. 1981. 71.95x (ISBN 0-471-27829-7, Pub. by Wiley-Interscience). Wiley.

Crouch, Bruce R. & Chamala, Shankarish, eds. Extension Education & Rural Development, Vol. 2: International Experience in Strategies for Planned Change. LC 79-41221. 325p. 1981. 59.95x (ISBN 0-471-27675-8, Pub. by Wiley-Interscience). Wiley.

Crouch, Charles E. Principles of New Testament Christianity. 1985. pap. 5.50 (ISBN 0-89137-546-5). Quality Pubns.

Crouch, Colin. Class Conflict & the Industrial Relations Crisis. 1977. text ed. 34.00x (ISBN 0-435-82250-0). Gower Pub Co.

--The Politics of Industrial Relations. (Political Issues of Modern Britain Ser.). 1979. text ed. 25.75x (ISBN 0-391-01163-4). Humanities.

Crouch, Colin, ed. British Political Sociology Yearbook: Participation in Politics, Vol. 3. 282p. 1977. 37.00x (ISBN 0-85664-242-8, Pub. by Croom Helm Ltd). Longwood Pub Group.

Crouch, Colin & Heller, Frank A., eds. International Yearbook of Organizational Democracy for the Study of Participation, Co-Operation & Power, Vol. 1: Organizational Democracy & Political Processes Power-Organizational Democracy & Political Processes. 660p. 1983. 69.95x (ISBN 0-471-90089-3, Pub. by Wiley-Interscience). Wiley.

Crouch, Colin & Pizzorno, Alessandro, eds. The Resurgence of Class Conflict in Western Europe Since 1968, 2 vols. Incl. Vol. 1. text ed. 49.50x (ISBN 0-8419-0355-7); Vol. 2. text ed. 49.50x (ISBN 0-8419-0356-5). LC 77-16076. 1978. Holmes & Meier.

Crouch, D. History of Architecture. 384p. 1984. 24.95 (ISBN 0-07-014531-8); pap. 19.95 (ISBN 0-07-014524-5). McGraw.

Crouch, Daniel J. Archaelogical Investigations of the Kiowa & Comanche Indian Agency Commissaries 34-Cm 232. (Contributions of the Museum of the Great Plains Ser.: No. 7). (Illus.). 1978. pap. 11.30 (ISBN 0-685-91362-7). Mus Great Plains.

Crouch, Dora P., et al. Spanish City Planning in North America. (Illus.). 304p. 1982. 40.00x (ISBN 0-262-03081-0). MIT Pr.

Crouch, Dorothy. Entertaining Without Alcohol: For Those Who Abstain. 166p. 1985. 14.95 (ISBN 0-87491-794-8); pap. 8.95 (ISBN 0-87491-795-6). Acropolis.

Crouch, Edmond, jt. auth. see Wilson, Richard.

Crouch, Harold. The Army & Politics in Indonesia. LC 77-90901. 376p. 1978. 34.95x (ISBN 0-8014-1155-6). Cornell U Pr.

--Domestic Political Structures & Regional Economic Co-Operation. 101p. 1985. pap. text ed. 17.50 (ISBN 9971-902-80-X, Pub. by Inst Southeast Asian Stud). Gower Pub Co.

--Malaysia's Nineteen Eighty-Two General Election. 72p. (Orig.). 1982. pap. text ed. 7.50x (ISBN 9971-902-45-1, Pub. by Inst Southeast Asian Stud). Gower Pub Co.

Crouch, Harold & Hing, Lee K. Malaysian Politics & the 1978 Election. (Illus.). 1980. text ed. 39.95x (ISBN 0-19-580464-3). Oxford U Pr.

Crouch, Holmes F. Nuclear Ship Propulsion. LC 59-13449. (Illus.). 369p. 1960. 20.00x (ISBN 0-87033-071-3). Cornell Maritime.

Crouch, Howard E. & Augustine, Mary. After Damien: Dutton, Yankee Soldier at Molokai. LC 81-67534. (Illus.). 144p. (Orig.). 1981. pap. 5.95 (ISBN 0-9606330-0-6). Damien-Dutton Soc.

Crouch, Isabel, jt. auth. see Dubois, Betty L.

Crouch, James & Carr, Micheline. Anatomy & Physiology: A Laboratory Manual. LC 76-56507. (Illus.). 369p. 1977. spiral bdg. 18.95 (ISBN 0-87484-356-1). Mayfield Pub.

Crouch, James E. Essential Human Anatomy: A Text-Atlas. LC 80-20699. (Illus.). 562p. 1982. text ed. 23.50 (ISBN 0-8121-0755-1). Lea & Febiger.

--Functional Human Anatomy. 4th ed. LC 83-24862. (Illus.). 645p. 1985. text ed. 32.50 (ISBN 0-8121-0930-9). Lea & Febiger.

--Introduction to Human Anatomy. 6th ed. (Illus.). 266p. 1973. spiral 14.95 (ISBN 0-87484-540-8). Mayfield Pub.

--Text-Atlas of Cat Anatomy. LC 68-25206. pap. 103.80 (ISBN 0-317-27963-7, 2056016). Bks Demand UMI.

Crouch, Marcus. Discovering Walks in West Kent. (Discovering Ser.: No. 239). (Illus.). 1983. pap. 3.95 (ISBN 0-85263-418-8, Pub. by Shire Pubns England). Seven Hills Bks.

--The Ivory City: And Other Stories from India & Pakistan. (Illus.). 192p. (gr. 3-7). 1981. 11.95 (ISBN 0-7207-1188-6, Pub. by Michael Joseph). Merrimack Pub Cir.

--The Nesbit Tradition: Children's Novels 1945-1972. (Illus.). 239p. 1972. 13.75x (ISBN 0-87471-146-0). Rowman.

--Rich Man, Poor Man, Beggarman, Thief. (Illus.). 168p. (gr. 5-8). 1985. 13.95 (ISBN 0-19-278111-1, Pub. by Oxford U Pr Childrens). Merrimack Pub Cir.

--The Whole World Storybook. (Illus.). 160p. (gr. k-4). 1983. text ed. 13.95 (ISBN 0-19-278103-0, Pub. by Oxford U Pr Childrens). Merrimack Pub Cir.

Crouch, Margaret, ed. Renewable Energy Dictionary. 500p. 1982. 27.50 (ISBN 0-86619-161-5, 11073-BK). Vols Tech Asst.

--Six Simple Pumps. 94p. 1983. 7.65 (ISBN 0-86619-166-6, E-11075). Vols Tech Asst.

Crouch, Martin & Porter, Robert. Understanding Soviet Politics Through Literature. 300p. 1984. text ed. 27.50x (ISBN 0-04-320155-5); pap. text ed. 9.95x (ISBN 0-04-320158-X). Allen Unwin.

Crouch, Milton & Raum, Hans, eds. Directory of State & Local History Periodicals. LC 77-4396. 136p. 1977. pap. 7.00x (ISBN 0-8389-0246-4). ALA.

Crouch, Owen. Expository Preaching & Teaching-Hebrews. LC 83-71985. 454p. (Orig.). 1983. pap. 9.95 (ISBN 0-89900-197-1). College Pr Pub.

--What the Bible Says about the Bible. LC 81-65515. (What the Bible Says Ser.). 370p. 1981. 13.50 (ISBN 0-89900-082-7). College Pr Pub.

Crouch, Richard E. Interstate Custody Litigation: A Guide to Use & Court Interpretation of the Uniform Child Custody Jurisdiction Act. LC 81-6082. 148p. 1981. pap. text ed. 12.50 (ISBN 0-87179-357-1). BNA.

Crouch, Robert L. Human Behavior: An Economic Approach. LC 78-10391. (Illus.). 1979. pap. text ed. write for info. (ISBN 0-87872-205-X). Wadsworth Pub.

Crouch., S. L. & Starfield, A. M. Boundary Element Methods in Solid Mechanics. (Illus.). 1983. 35.00x (ISBN 0-04-620010-X). Allen Unwin.

Crouch, Sarah, jt. auth. see Boswell, Jeanetta.

Crouch, Steve. Fog & Sun, Sea & Stone: The Monterey Coast. LC 80-66365. (Illus.). 160p. 1980. 26.50 (ISBN 0-912856-61-0). Graphic Arts Ctr.

Crouch, Steven L., ed. see Symposium on Rock Mechanics(16th, 1975, University of Minnesota).

Crouch, Sunny. Marketing Research for Managers. (Illus.). 336p. 1985. pap. 17.50 (ISBN 0-434-90282-9, Pub. by W Heinemann Ltd). David & Charles.

Crouch, T. Matrix Methods Applied to Engineering Rigid Body Mechanics. LC 80-41186. 385p. 1980. 54.00 (ISBN 0-08-024245-6); pap. 19.75 (ISBN 0-08-024246-4). Pergamon.

Crouch, Thomas. The Giant Leap: A Chronology of Ohio Aerospace Events & Personalities, 1915-1969. (Illus.). 77p. 1971. pap. 0.50 (ISBN 0-318-00826-2). Ohio Hist Soc.

Crouch, Tim & Dessem, Ralph. Hunger Workbook. (Orig.). 1977. pap. text ed. 4.25 (ISBN 0-89536-099-3). CSS of Ohio.

Crouch, Tom D. Bleriot XI: The Story of a Classic Airplane. LC 81-607931. (Famous Aircraft of the National Air & Space Museum Ser.). (Illus.). 144p. (Orig.). 1982. pap. 8.95 (ISBN 0-87474-345-1). Smithsonian.

--A Dream of Wings: Americans & the Airplane, Eighteen Seventy-Five to Nineteen Hundred Five. (Illus.). 1981. 15.95 (ISBN 0-393-01385-5). Norton.

--The Eagle Aloft: Two Centuries of the Balloon in America. LC 83-17079. (Illus.). 770p. 1983. text ed. 49.50 (ISBN 0-87474-346-X). Smithsonian.

Crouch, Tom D., ed. Charles A. Lindbergh: An American Life. LC 77-14537. (Illus.). 128p. 1977. 10.95 (ISBN 0-87474-342-7); pap. 6.50 (ISBN 0-87474-343-5). Smithsonian.

Crouch, Tom D., jt. ed. see Hallion, Richard P.

Crouch, W. W. Guide for Modern Personnel Commissions. 1973. 7.00 (ISBN 0-87373-059-3). Intl Personnel Mgmt.

--Science & the Bible in a Troubled World. LC 84-90294. 102p. 1985. 8.95 (ISBN 0-317-28937-3). Vantage.

Crouch, Winston W. Organized Civil Servants: Public Employer-Employee Relations in California. LC 77-91767. 1978. 35.00x (ISBN 0-520-03626-3). U of Cal Pr.

Crouch, Winston W., et al. California Government & Politics. 7th ed. (Illus.). 288p. 1981. pap. 15.95 (ISBN 0-13-112433-1). P-H.

Croucher, J. H. & Le Gray, Gustave. Plain Directions for Obtaining Photographic Pictures by the Calotype & Energiatype, Also Upon Albumenized Paper & Glass, by Collodion & Albumen, Etc., Etc, Pts. 1-3. LC 72-9191. (The Literature of Photography Ser.). Repr. of 1853 ed. 23.50 (ISBN 0-405-04901-3). Ayer Co Pubs.

Croucher, John S. Operations Research: A First Course. (Illus.). 320p. 1980. 32.00 (ISBN 0-08-024798-9); pap. 14.85 (ISBN 0-08-024797-0). Pergamon.

Croucher, Melvin D., jt. ed. see Hair, Michael.

Croucher, Michael & Reid, Howard. The Fighting Arts. (Illus.). 1983. 19.95 (ISBN 0-671-47158-9); pap. 12.95 (ISBN 0-671-47273-9). S&S.

Croucher, Norman. A Man & His Mountains. (Illus.). 196p. 1985. 18.95 (ISBN 0-7182-2000-5, Pub. by Kaye & Ward). David & Charles.

--Outdoor Pursuits for Disabled People. 180p. 1981. pap. 9.50 (ISBN 0-85941-186-9). Woodhead-Faulkner.

Croucher, Richard. Engineers at War Nineteen Thirty-Nine to Nineteen Forty-Five. (Illus.). 400p. 1982. pap. 13.95 (ISBN 0-85036-271-7); 30.00 (ISBN 0-85036-270-9). Dufour.

Croucher, Robert M. The Observer's Book of Motorcycles. (Illus.). 192p. 1976. 4.95 (ISBN 0-7232-1572-3, Pub. by Warne Pubs England). Motorbooks Intl.

Croucher, Ronald & Woolley, Alan R. Fossils, Minerals & Rocks: Collection & Preservation. LC 82-1282. (Illus.). 64p. 1982. 7.95 (ISBN 0-521-24736-5, Copublished with the British Museum). Cambridge U Pr.

Croucher, Trevor. Discography of Early Music. 500p. 1981. 50.00x (ISBN 0-85365-613-4, Pub. by Lib Assn England). State Mutual Bk.

--Early Music Discography, 2 vols. 582p. (Orig.). 1981. Set. pap. text ed. 67.50 (ISBN 0-89774-018-1). Oryx Pr.

Crouchett, Lawrence P. William Byron Rumford: The Life & Public Services of a California Legislator. LC 83-20653. (A Gossypium Bk.). (Illus.). 152p. 1984. 14.95 (ISBN 0-910823-01-4). Downey PLace.

Crouchett, Lorraine J. Filipinos in California: From the Days of the Galleons to the Present. LC 82-73374. (Illus.). 154p. 1983. 11.95 (ISBN 0-910823-00-6). Downey Place.

Crouchley, Arthur Edwin. Investment of Foreign Capital in Egyptian Companies & Public Debt. Wilkins, Mira, ed. LC 76-29989. (European Business Ser.). 1977. Repr. of 1936 ed. lib. bdg. 18.00x (ISBN 0-405-09721-2). Ayer Co Pubs.

Crough-Osborne, Richard. This Is Racing. 152p. 1982. 35.00x (ISBN 0-333-32089-1, Pub. by Nautical England). State Mutual Bk.

Crounse, Helen W., pseud. What Is Wrong with the Truth? 1971. 13.95x (ISBN 0-8084-0357-5). New Coll U Pr.

Crounse, Robert G., jt. ed. see Brown, A. C.

Crouse & Maple. Button Classics. LC 77-121197. 17.50 (ISBN 0-87282-019-X). CHB-ALF.

Crouse, Betty, tr. see Jonas, Ilsedore B.

Crouse, David B., jt. auth. see Eldred, Nelson R.

Crouse, David B, jt. auth. see Reed, Robert F.

Crouse, Maurice. The Public Treasury of Colonial South Carolina. LC 76-56125. (Tricentennial Studies Ser.: No. 10). xvi, 142p. 1977. 19.95x (ISBN 0-87249-255-9). U of SC Pr.

Crouse, Nellis M. French Pioneers in the West Indies, 1624-1664. 1972. lib. bdg. 20.00x (ISBN 0-374-91937-2). Octagon.

--French Struggle for the West Indies, 1665-1713. 1966. lib. bdg. 20.50x (ISBN 0-374-91938-0). Octagon.

--Lemoyne D'Iberville: Soldier of New France. LC 71-15904. 1972. Repr. of 1954 ed. 25.00x (ISBN 0-8046-1677-9, Pub. by Kennikat). Assoc Faculty Pr.

Crouse, R. L. Preparing & Conducting a V.E. Training Seminar. 63p. pap. 10.25 (ISBN 0-318-16540-6, B1012); pap. 9.25 members (ISBN 0-318-16541-4). Soc Am Value E.

Crouse, Russell see Mersand, Joseph E.

Crouse, Timothy. The Boys on the Bus: Riding with the Campaign Press Corps. 1976. pap. 2.95 (ISBN 0-345-29338-X). Ballantine.

Crouse, W. H. Automotive Electronics & Electrical Equipment. 10th ed. 368p. 1985. price not set (ISBN 0-07-014895-3). McGraw.

Crouse, W. H. & Anglin, D. L. Automotive Air Conditioning. 2nd ed. LC 82-4682. 304p. 1983. text ed. 21.10x (ISBN 0-07-014857-0). McGraw.

--Automotive Body Repair & Refinishing. 2nd ed. 400p. 1985. 28.95 (ISBN 0-07-014867-8); wkbk. 12.00 (ISBN 0-07-014868-6). McGraw.

--Automotive Mechanics. 9th ed. 672p. 1984. 26.70 (ISBN 0-07-014860-0); 11.95 (ISBN 0-07-014871-6). McGraw.

--Automotive Tune-Up. 2nd ed. LC 82-7320. (Automotive Technology Ser.). 1983. text ed. 21.60 (ISBN 0-07-014836-8). McGraw.

Crouse, William H. Automotive Electronics & Electrical Equipment. 9th ed. LC 79-24438. (Illus.). 1980. pap. text ed. 22.85 (ISBN 0-07-014831-7). McGraw.

--Automotive Mechanics. 8th ed. LC 79-12845. (Illus.). 1980. text ed. 26.70 (ISBN 0-07-014820-1). McGraw.

--Automotive Service Business: Operation & Management. LC 72-666. 1972. pap. text ed. 21.60 (ISBN 0-07-014605-5). McGraw.

--Car Troubles: Causes & Cures. (Illus.). 144p. pap. 5.95 (ISBN 0-911709-00-2). W Kaufmann.

--Small Engines: Operation & Maintenance. (Automotive Technology Ser.). (Illus.). 448p. 1973. pap. text ed. 22.85 (ISBN 0-07-014691-8). McGraw.

Crouse, William H. & Anglin, D. L. Automotive Engine Design. 1970. text ed. 21.60 (ISBN 0-07-014671-3). McGraw.

--Automotive Mechanics. 7th ed. (Illus.). 640p. (gr. 11-12). 1975. text ed. 29.20 (ISBN 0-07-014535-0). McGraw.

Crouse, William H. & Anglin, Don L. Auto Shop Workbook. 256p. 1984. 12.15 (ISBN 0-07-014572-5). McGraw.

Crouse, William H. & Anglin, Donald L. The Auto Book. 2nd ed. (Illus.). 1978. text ed. 28.20 (ISBN 0-07-014560-1). McGraw.

--The Auto Book. 3rd ed. LC 83-16206. 640p. 1983. 28.20 (ISBN 0-07-014571-7); study guide 12.15 (ISBN 0-07-014573-3). McGraw.

--Automotive Automatic Transmissions. 6th ed. LC 81-14262. (Illus.). 304p. 1983. pap. 20.05 (ISBN 0-07-014771-X). McGraw.

--Automotive Body Repair & Refinishing. (Illus.). 1980. text ed. 29.95 (ISBN 0-07-014791-4). McGraw.

--Automotive Brakes, Suspension & Steering. 6th ed. LC 82-17187. (Automotive Technology Ser.). 1983. 21.60 (ISBN 0-07-014828-7). McGraw.

--Automotive Chassis & Body. 5th ed. (Automotive Technology Ser.). (Illus.). 416p. 1975. soft cover 21.60 (ISBN 0-07-014653-5). McGraw.

--Automotive Emission Control. 3rd ed. LC 83-1015. (Automotive Technology Ser.). 288p. 1983. pap. text ed. 21.10 (ISBN 0-07-014816-3). McGraw.

--Automotive Engines. 5th ed. (Automotive Technology Ser.). 1975. 22.60 (ISBN 0-07-014602-0). McGraw.

--Automotive Engines. 6th ed. (Illus.). 96p. 1980. 22.60 (ISBN 0-07-014825-2). McGraw.

--Automotive Fuel, Lubricating & Cooling Systems. 6th ed. Gilmore, D. E., ed. (Illus.). 352p. 1980. pap. text ed. 21.10 (ISBN 0-07-014862-7). McGraw.

--Automotive Manual Transmissions & Power Trains. 6th ed. LC 81-17206. (Illus.). 352p. 1983. pap. text ed. 20.05 (ISBN 0-07-014776-0). McGraw.

--Automotive Technician's Handbook. (Illus.). 1979. 36.50 (ISBN 0-07-014751-5). McGraw.

--Automotive Tools, Fasteners, & Measurements: A Text-Workbook. (Automotive Technology Ser.). (Illus.). (gr. 9-12). 1977. 14.15 (ISBN 0-07-014630-6). McGraw.

--Motor Vehicle Inspection. (Illus.). 1978. 35.05 (ISBN 0-07-014813-9). McGraw.

--Motorcycle Mechanics. LC 81-217. (Illus.). 384p. 1982. pap. text ed. 24.40 (ISBN 0-07-014781-7). McGraw.

--Small Engine Mechanics. 2nd ed. LC 79-4658. (Illus.). 1979. pap. text ed. 22.85 (ISBN 0-07-014795-7). McGraw.

Crousel, R. L. How to Plan & Organize a V.E. Seminar. 55p. pap. 10.25 (ISBN 0-318-16538-4, B1011); pap. 9.25 members (ISBN 0-318-16539-2). Soc Am Value E.

Crouser, R. L. It's Unlucky to Be Behind at the End of the Game: And Other Great Sports Retorts. LC 82-22915. (Illus.). 160p. 1983. 11.95 (ISBN 0-688-01968-4). Morrow.

--It's Unlucky to Be Behind at the End of the Game & Other Great Sports Retorts. LC 82-23094. (Illus.). 160p. (Orig.). 1983. pap. 4.70 (ISBN 0-688-01970-6, Quill NY). Morrow.

Croushore, James H., ed. see De Forest, John W.

Crout, D. H. Chemistry of Natural Products. Date not set. 35.00 (ISBN 0-87735-213-5). Freeman Cooper.

Crout, D. H., jt. auth. see Geissman, T. A.

Crout, George C. Butler County: An Illustrated History. (Illus.). 128p. 1984. 19.95 (ISBN 0-89781-067-8). Windsor Pubns Inc.

Crout, Robert R., jt. auth. see Heggoy, Alf A.

Crout, Robert R., jt. ed. see Idzerda, Stanley J.

Croutch, Albert. Housing Migratory Agricultural Workers in California, 1913-1948. LC 74-31764. 1975. soft bdg. 11.00 (ISBN 0-88247-331-X). R & E Pubs.

Crouter, George. Colorado's Highest: The Majestic Fourteeners. Skiff, Carl & Collman, Russ, eds. (Illus.). 144p. 1977. 16.50 (ISBN 0-913582-22-0). Sundance.

Crouter, Natalie. Forbidden Diary: A Record of Wartime Internment, 1941-1945. Bloom, Lynn Z., ed. (American Woman's Diary Ser.: No. 2). 1980. 21.95 (ISBN 0-89102-105-1). B Franklin.

Crouthamel, James L. James Watson Webb: A Biography. LC 70-82536. 1969. 18.00x (ISBN 0-8195-4005-6). Wesleyan U Pr.

Crouthamel, William & Sarupu, Allen, eds. Animal Models for Oral Drug Delivery in Man: In Situ & In Vivo Approaches. 192p. 1983. text ed. 54.00 (ISBN 0-917330-49-8). Am Pharm Assn.

Crouthers, David D. Flags of American History. LC 77-26205. (Profile Ser.). (gr. 6 up). 1973. 6.95 (ISBN 0-8437-3080-3). Hammond Inc.

Crouwel, J., jt. auth. see Littauer, M.

Crouzet, ed. see Stendhal.

Crouzet, Francois. The First Industrialists: The Problem of Origins. (Illus.). 212p. 1985. 37.50 (ISBN 0-521-26242-9). Cambridge U Pr.

--The Victorian Economy. Forster, A. S., tr. 400p. 1982. 36.00x (ISBN 0-231-05542-0); pap. 16.00x (ISBN 0-231-05543-9). Columbia U Pr.
Crovello, Theodore J., et al. The Vascular Plants of Indiana: A Computer Based Checklist. LC 83-10024. 160p. 1983. text ed. 15.00x (ISBN 0-268-01923-1, 85-19233). U of Notre Dame Pr.
Crovitz, Elaine & Buford, Elizabeth. Courage Knows No Sex. 1978. 8.95 (ISBN 0-8158-0363-X). Chris Mass.
Crow, Aileen, jt. auth. see Dell, Cecily.
Crow, Alice. Educational Psychology. rev. ed. (Quality Paperback: No. 53). (Orig.). 1972. pap. 3.95 (ISBN 0-8226-0053-6). Littlefield.
Crow, Alice, jt. auth. see Crow, Lester D.
Crow, Ben, et al. Third World Atlas. 76p. 1984. 35.00x (ISBN 0-335-15015-2, Pub. by Open Univ Pr); pap. 15.00x (ISBN 0-335-10259-X, Pub. by Open Univ Pr). Taylor & Francis.
Crow, C. Paul Valery & Maxwell's Demon: Natural Order & Human Possibility. (Occasional Papers in Modern Languages: No. 8). 83p. 1972. pap. text ed. 4.75x (ISBN 0-900480-26-2, Pub. by U Hull England). Humanities.
Crow, Carl. Great American Customer. facs. ed. LC 77-111823. (Essay Index Reprint Ser). 1943. 20.00 (ISBN 0-8369-1645-X). Ayer Co Pubs.
--He Opened the Door of Japan. LC 74-5552. (Illus.). 275p. 1974. Repr. of 1939 ed. lib. bdg. 22.50x (ISBN 0-8371-7512-7, CROD). Greenwood.
Crow, Charles L. Janet Lewis. LC 80-69012. (Western Writers Ser.: no. 41). (Illus.). 48p. (Orig.). 1980. pap. 2.00x (ISBN 0-88430-065-X). Boise St Univ.
Crow, Charles L., jt. ed. see Kerr, Howard.
Crow, Charles S. Evaluation of English Literature in the High School. LC 74-176679. (Columbia University. Teachers College. Contributions to Education Ser.: No. 141). Repr. of 1924 ed. 22.50 (ISBN 0-404-55141-6). AMS Pr.
Crow, Christine. Paul Valery & the Poetry of Voice. LC 81-10069. (Major European Authors Ser.). 1982. 54.50 (ISBN 0-521-24182-0). Cambridge U Pr.
Crow, D. E. & Miller, J. A., eds. Nonsteady Fluid Dynamics: Presented at the Winter Annual Meeting of the American Society of Mechanical Engineers, San Francisco, California, Dec. 10-15, 1978. LC 78-59889. pap. 64.50 (ISBN 0-317-08551-4, 2011590). Bks Demand UMI.
Crow, D. R. Principles & Applications of Electrochemistry. 2nd ed. LC 79-75. (Chemistry Textbook Ser.). 238p. 1979. pap. 14.95x (ISBN 0-412-16020-X, NO. 6071, Pub. by Chapman & Hall England). Methuen Inc.
Crow, Donna F. The Desires of Your Heart. Severance, Anne, ed. 1985. pap. 2.50 (ISBN 0-310-46702-0, Pub. by Serenade-Serenata). Zondervan.
--The Frantic Mother Cookbook. LC 82-81918. (Orig.). 1982. pap. 4.95 (ISBN 0-89081-356-6). Harvest Hse.
--Greengold Autumn. (Serenade Serenata Ser.: No. 11). 192p. (Orig.). 1984. pap. 1.95 (ISBN 0-310-46572-9). Zondervan.
--Mr. X's Golden Scheme. (Making Choices Ser.). (Illus.). 124p. (gr. 4-8). 1985. pap. 2.50 (ISBN 0-89191-953-8, 59535, Chariot Bks). Cook.
--Professor Q's Mysterious Machine. (Making Choices Ser.: No. 3). (gr. 3-8). 1983. pap. 2.50 (ISBN 0-89191-562-1). Cook.
Crow, Duncan, ed. Modern Battle Tanks. LC 78-4192. (Illus.). 1978. pap. 7.95 (ISBN 0-668-04650-3). Arco.
Crow, Edwin L., et al. Statistics Manual. (Illus.). 1955. pap. 6.00 (ISBN 0-486-60599-X). Dover.
Crow, G. D., jt. auth. see Crow, John A.
Crow, Gary A. Children at Risk: A Handbook of the Signs & Symptoms of Early Childhood Difficulties. LC 77-87859. 1978. 12.95 (ISBN 0-8052-3675-9). Schocken.
--Children at Risk: Handbook of the Signs & Symptoms of Early Childhood Disabilities. LC 77-87859. 288p. 1980. pap. 6.95 (ISBN 0-8052-0655-8). Schocken.
Crow, Gerald. Ruskin. LC 73-19678. (Great Lives Ser.). 1936. lib. bdg. 12.50 (ISBN 0-8414-3530-8). Folcroft.
Crow, Gerald H. William Morris, Designer. LC 75-28168. 1975. Repr. of 1934 ed. lib. bdg. 30.00 (ISBN 0-8414-3469-7). Folcroft.
--William Morris: Designer. 120p. 1980. Repr. of 1934 ed. lib. bdg. 25.00 (ISBN 0-8492-3970-2). R West.
Crow, Harte C., jt. auth. see Bartrum, Royal J., Jr.
Crow, Hugh C. Memoirs of the Late Captain Hugh Crow of Liverpool. (Illus.). 316p. 1970. Repr. of 1830 ed. 35.00x (ISBN 0-7146-1801-2, F Cass Co). Biblio Dist.
Crow, Jack E., et al, eds. Crystalline Electric Field & Structural Effects in f-Electron Systems. LC 80-12454. 650p. 1980. 89.50x (ISBN 0-306-40443-5, Plenum Pr). Plenum Pub.
Crow, James F. Genetics Notes: An Introduction to Genetics. 8th ed. 303p. 1983. pap. text ed. 12.95x (ISBN 0-8087-4805-X). Burgess.
--How Well Can We Assess Genetic Risk? Not Very. 1981. 9.00 (ISBN 0-913392-56-1). NCRP Pubns.
Crow, James F. & Denniston, Carter. Genetic Distance. LC 74-23683. 203p. 1974. 35.00x (ISBN 0-306-30827-4, Plenum Pr). Plenum Pub.
Crow, James F. & Kimura, Motoo. An Introduction to Population Genetics Theory. LC 78-103913. 1970. text ed. 21.95x (ISBN 0-8087-2901-2). Burgess.
Crow, James T. New Baja Handbook. rev. ed. LC 73-81325. (Illus.). 1974. enlarged ed. 3.95 (ISBN 0-393-60005-X). Norton.
Crow, James T. & Warren, Cameron A. Four Wheel Drive Handbook. (Illus.). 96p. 1976. Repr. 3.95. Norton.
Crow, Jeffrey J. & Durden, Robert F. Maverick Republican in the Old North State: A Political Biography of Daniel L. Russell. LC 77-3657. (Southern Biography Ser.). xx, 202p. 1977. 22.50x (ISBN 0-8071-0291-1). La State U Pr.
Crow, Jeffrey J. & Hatley, Flora J., eds. Black Americans in North Carolina & the South. LC 83-21762. (Illus.). 210p. 1984. 19.95 (ISBN 0-8078-1593-4). U of NC Pr.
Crow, Jeffrey J. & Tise, Larry E., eds. The Southern Experience in the American Revolution. LC 77-21519. xvii, 310p. 1979. 27.50 (ISBN 0-8078-1313-3); pap. 8.00x (ISBN 0-8078-4059-9). U of NC Pr.
--Writing North Carolina History. LC 79-439. xviii, 249p. 1979. 22.00 (ISBN 0-8078-1369-9). U of NC Pr.
Crow, John & Wilson, F. P., eds. Jacob & Esau. LC 82-45707. (Malone Society Reprint Ser.: No. 104). Repr. of 1956 ed. 40.00 (ISBN 0-404-63105-3). AMS Pr.
Crow, John A. The Epic of Latin America. LC 78-62860. 1000p. 1980. 46.50x (ISBN 0-520-04107-0); pap. 14.95 (ISBN 0-520-03776-6, CAL. NO. 458). U of Cal Pr.
--Se Habla Espanol. 1979. text ed. 21.95 scp (ISBN 0-06-041434-0, HarpC); scp tapes 250.00 (ISBN 0-06-047489-0); instructor's manual avail. (ISBN 0-06-361450-2); scp student wkbk. 10.50 (ISBN 0-06-041435-9). Har-Row.
--Spain: The Root & the Flower. 3rd rev. expurgated ed. LC 84-8652. 1985. 18.50x (ISBN 0-520-05123-8); pap. 9.95 (ISBN 0-520-05133-5, CAL 795). U of Cal Pr.
Crow, John A. & Crow, G. D. Panorama de las Americas. 5th ed. (Span.). 1980. pap. text ed. 15.95 (ISBN 0-03-050561-5). HR&W.
Crow, John A. & Dudley, Edward. El Cuento. 2nd ed. LC 83-1644. (Span.). 1984. text ed. 16.95 (ISBN 0-03-063393-1, HoltC). HR&W.
Crow, John A., ed. An Anthology of Spanish Poetry: From the Beginnings to the Present Day, Including Both Spain & Spanish America. LC 79-4619. 240p. 1979. text ed. 25.00x (ISBN 0-8071-0482-5); pap. text ed. 8.95x (ISBN 0-8071-0483-3). La State U Pr.
Crow, John E. Mexican Americans in Contemporary Arizona: A Social & Demographic View. LC 75-1813. 1975. soft bdg 10.95 (ISBN 0-88247-353-0). R & E Pubs.
Crow, John T. Vocabulary for Advanced Reading Comprehension: The Keyword Approach. (Illus.). 288p. 1986. pap. text ed. 10.95 (ISBN 0-13-942988-3). P H.
Crow, John T. & Strickland, Nancy. Communication Skillbook 2: Growing with English. (Communication Skillbooks). 1979. 3.95 (ISBN 0-88499-222-5). Inst Mod Lang.
Crow, Judson O. McDowell County North Carolina Land Entry Abstracts: 1843-1869, Vol. 1. LC 82-20499. 504p. 1983. pap. 20.00 (ISBN 0-87152-365-5). Reprint.
Crow, Lawrence. The Third Old House Catalog. 224p. 1982. 9.95 (ISBN 0-02-080050-9). Macmillan.
Crow, Lester C. Introduction to Guidance: Basic Principles & Practices. 2nd ed. 464p. 1960. 20.50 (ISBN 0-442-21291-7, Pub. by Van Nos Reinhold). Krieger.
Crow, Lester D. Introduction to Education. 320p. 1974. 9.75 (ISBN 0-8158-0320-6). Chris Mass.
Crow, Lester D. & Crow, Alice. How to Study. 1963. pap. 3.95 (ISBN 0-02-013500-9, Collier). Macmillan.
--Human Development & Learning. Rev. ed. LC 74-26685. 590p. 1975. Repr. of 1965 ed. 29.50 (ISBN 0-88275-252-9). Krieger.
--Our Teen-Age Boys & Girls. facs. ed. LC 68-58783. (Essay Index Reprint Ser). 1945. 18.50 (ISBN 0-8369-1030-3). Ayer Co Pubs.
--Outline of General Psychology. rev. ed. (Quality Paperback Ser: No. 28). (Orig.). 1976. pap. 5.95 (ISBN 0-8226-0028-5). Littlefield.
Crow, Lester D. & Graham, Thomas F. Human Development & Adjustment. (Quality Paperback Ser.: No. 258). (Orig.). 1973. pap. 3.95 (ISBN 0-8226-0258-X). Littlefield.
Crow, Majorie. Pharmacology for the Elderly: A Nurse's Guide to Quality Care. (Nursing Education Ser.). 1984. pap. text ed. 16.95x (ISBN 0-8077-2752-0). Tchrs Coll.
Crow, Marjorie & Lounsbury, Patricia F. Practice Tests for the L. P. N. LC 80-39735. 112p. (Orig.). 1981. pap. text ed. 7.50x (ISBN 0-668-05189-2, 5189). Arco.
Crow, Marjorie R. Practice Tests for the L. P. N. 112p. 1981. pap. 10.95 (ISBN 0-317-17132-1). ACC.
Crow, Mark A., jt. auth. see Danskin, David G.
Crow, Martha F. The American Country Girl. LC 74-3936. (Women in America Ser). (Illus.). 398p. 1974. Repr. of 1915 ed. 31.00x (ISBN 0-405-06083-1). Ayer Co Pubs.
--Christ in the Poetry of Today: An Anthology from American Poets. 1978. Repr. of 1917 ed. lib. bdg. 25.00 (ISBN 0-8495-0912-2). Arden Lib.
--Elizabethan Sonnet - Cycles, 4 Vols. LC 69-19815. Repr. of 1898 ed. Set. 62.50 (ISBN 0-404-01890-4). AMS Pr.
--English Sonnet Cycles, 4 vols. 450.00 (ISBN 0-8490-0118-8). Gordon Pr.
Crow, Mary. The Business of Literature. (Illus.). 24p. 1981. 25.00 (ISBN 0-939622-15-7); pap. 5.00 (ISBN 0-939622-16-5). Four Zoas Night.
--Going Home. 1979. pap. 2.00 (ISBN 0-89924-019-4). Lynx Hse.
Crow, Mary, ed. Woman Who Has Sprouted Wings: Poems by Contemporary Latin American Women Poets. Felstiner, John & Walsh, Donald, trs. LC 84-5672. 1984. pap. 12.95 (ISBN 0-935480-14-5). Lat Am Lit Rev Pr.
Crow, Michael M., ed. High Sulfur Coal Exports: An International Analysis. LC 83-4657. 256p. 1983. 30.00x (ISBN 0-8093-1122-4). S Ill U Pr.
Crow, Paul A., Jr. Christian Unity: Matrix for Mission. (Orig.). 1982. pap. 4.95 (ISBN 0-377-00115-5). Friend Pr.
Crow, R., et al, eds. Experiments with Normal & Transformed Cells. 175p. 1979. lab manual 23.00x (ISBN 0-87969-123-9). Cold Spring Harbor.
Crow, Ron, jt. auth. see Glass, Dick.
Crow, Ruth & McCarthy, Ginny, eds. Teenage Women in the Juvenile Justice System: Changing Values. 169p. (Orig.). 1979. pap. 6.00 (ISBN 0-9608696-1-1). New Dir Young Women.
Crow, Susan H. Cabo San Lucas. (Illus.). 112p. (Orig.). 1984. pap. 8.95 (ISBN 0-912457-00-7). Graphic Image.
Crow, T. J. Disorders of Neurohumoural Transmission. 1983. 65.00 (ISBN 0-12-195980-5). Acad Pr.
Crow, Thomas E. Painters & Public Life in Eighteenth-Century Paris. LC 85-5375. (Illus.). 292p. 1985. 40.00x (ISBN 0-300-03354-0). Yale U Pr.
Crow, Todd, ed. Bartok Studies. LC 76-257. (Detroit Reprints in Music). 1976. 15.00 (ISBN 0-911772-78-2). Info Coord.
Crow, W. B. Occult Properties of Herbs & Plants. (Paths to Inner Power Ser). 1971. pap. 2.50 (ISBN 0-85030-196-3). Weiser.
--Precious Stones: Their Occult Power. (Paths to Inner Power Ser). 1972. pap. 2.50 (ISBN 0-85030-206-4). Weiser.
--Witchcraft, Magic & Occultism. pap. 5.00 (ISBN 0-87980-173-5). Wilshire.
Crow, Wendell C. Communication Graphics. (Illus.). 336p. 1986. text ed. 26.95 (ISBN 0-13-153792-X). P-H.
Crowder, Anne S., jt. auth. see Skydell, Barbara.
Crowder, Billy L., ed. Ion Implantation in Semiconductors & Other Materials. LC 73-14789. (IBM Research Symposia Ser.). 654p. 1973. 85.00x (ISBN 0-306-30756-1, Plenum Pr). Plenum Pub.
Crowder, C. M., ed. English Society & Government in the Fifteenth Century. LC 68-79460. (Selections from History Today Ser.,No. 2). (Illus.). 1967. 7.95; pap. 5.95 (ISBN 0-05-000809-9). Dufour.
Crowder, David L. Tendoy, Chief of the Lemhis. LC 75-76336. (Illus., Orig.). (gr. 5-9). 1969. pap. 2.75 (ISBN 0-87004-129-0). Caxton.
Crowder, Jennie, jt. auth. see Vinroot, Sally.
Crowder, Ken. The Iron Web. 192p. 1985. 14.95 (ISBN 0-8027-0846-3). Walker & Co.
Crowder, L. V. & Chheda, H. R. Tropical Grassland Husbandry. Wrigley, G., ed. (Tropical Agriculture Ser.). (Illus.). 562p. 1983. text ed. 60.00x (ISBN 0-582-46677-6). Longman.
Crowder, M., ed. see Tarikh.
Crowder, Michael. The Story of Nigeria. 4th ed. 432p. 1978. pap. 9.95 (ISBN 0-571-04947-8). Faber & Faber.
--West Africa: An Introduction to Its History. (Illus.). 1977. pap. text ed. 8.95x (ISBN 0-582-60003-0). Longman.
--West Africa under Colonial Rule. LC 68-27618. 1968. pap. 16.95 (ISBN 0-8101-0654-X). Northwestern U Pr.
Crowder, Michael, ed. The Cambridge History of Africa: 1940-1975, Vol. 8. (Illus.). 800p. 1985. 84.50 (ISBN 0-521-22409-8). Cambridge U Pr.
--West African Resistance: The Military Response to Colonial Occupation. LC 73-127106. (Illus.). 314p. 1971. text ed. 35.00x (ISBN 0-8419-0049-3, Africana). Holmes & Meier.
Crowder, Michael, jt. ed. see Ajayi, J. F.
Crowder, Michael, jt. ed. see Oliver, Roland.
Crowder, Richard. Carl Sandburg. (United States Authors Ser.). 1963. lib. bdg. 13.50 (ISBN 0-8057-0648-8, Twayne). G K Hall.
Crowder, Robert G. Principles of Learning & Memory. 544p. 1976. text ed. 29.95x (ISBN 0-89859-115-5). L Erlbaum Assocs.
--The Psychology of Reading. (Illus.). 1982. pap. text ed. 9.95x (ISBN 0-19-503139-3). Oxford U Pr.
Crowder, Vera. Salem Methodism. LC 85-71208. 236p. 1985. 25.00 (ISBN 0-89227-110-8). Commonwealth Pr.
Crowder, Vernon & Jolly, Sonny. Activities for Physical Education. (Illus.). 249p. 1983. pap. text ed. 14.95x (ISBN 0-88136-006-6). Jostens.
--Concepts of Physical Education. (Illus., Orig.). pap. text ed. 8.95 (ISBN 0-88136-002-3). Jostens.
Crowder, William. Seashore Life Between the Tides. LC 75-16036. Orig. Title: Between the Tides. (Illus.). 512p. 1975. pap. 7.50 (ISBN 0-486-23221-2). Dover.
--Seashore Life Between the Tides. (Illus.). 12.00 (ISBN 0-8446-5173-7). Peter Smith.
Crowdis, David G. & Wheeler, Brandon W. Precalculus Mathematics. 1976. text ed. write for info. (ISBN 0-02-472030-5). Macmillan.
Crowdis, David G., et al. Concepts of Calculus with Applications to Business & Economics. 1975. text ed. write for info. (ISBN 0-02-473010-6); tchrs' manual free (ISBN 0-02-473020-3). Macmillan.
Crowe & Bowen. With Tails We Win. (Illus.). 1954. pap. 2.00 (ISBN 0-9600102-5-4). Shields.
Crowe & Laseau. Visual Notes for Architects & Designers. 1984. 24.95 (ISBN 0-442-29335-6). Van Nos Reinhold.
Crowe, A. & Crowe, A. Mathematics for Biologists. 1969. 27.50 (ISBN 0-12-198250-5). Acad Pr.
Crowe, Alfred. A Guide to Autogyros. (Illus.). 64p. pap. cancelled (ISBN 0-933078-08-0). Aviation.
Crowe, Andrew. A Field Guide to the Native Edible Plants of New Zealand. (Illus.). 196p. 1983. 19.95x (ISBN 0-00-216983-5, Pub. by W Collins New Zealand). Intl Spec Bk.
Crowe, Brenda. The Playgroup Movement. LC 73-80534. 1973. 8.50x (ISBN 0-8052-3522-1). Schocken.
Crowe, Catherine S. The Night Side of Nature, 2 vols. LC 76-18829. 1976. Repr. of 1848 ed. lib. bdg. 75.00 (ISBN 0-8414-3623-1). Folcroft.
--Susan Hopley: Or, the Adventures of a Maidservant, 3 vols. in 2. LC 79-8258. Repr. of 1841 ed. Set. 84.50 (ISBN 0-404-61836-7). Vol. 1 (ISBN 0-404-61837-5). Vol. 2. AMS Pr.
Crowe, Cecily. Bloodrose House. 192p. 1985. 11.95 (ISBN 0-312-08483-8). St Martin.
Crowe, Clayton T., jt. auth. see Roberson, John A.
Crowe, D. G., jt. auth. see Dereniak, E. L.
Crowe, Diana B. How to Talk Money. 144p. 1984. pap. 7.95 (ISBN 0-345-31709-2). Ballantine.
Crowe, Dianna B. How to Talk Money. 144p. (Orig.). 1984. pap. 7.95 (ISBN 0-911818-57-X). World Almanac.
Crowe, Eyre. Thackeray's Haunts & Homes. LC 74-2069. 1897. lib. bdg. 15.00 (ISBN 0-8414-3542-1). Folcroft.
Crowe, Frank W., et al. A Clinical, Pathological & Genetic Study of Multiple Neurofibromatosis. (Illus.). 192p. 1956. photocopy ed. 19.75x (ISBN 0-398-00370-X). C C Thomas.
Crowe, Frederick E. The Lonergan Enterprise. LC 80-51569. 120p. (Orig.). 1980. pap. 6.00 (ISBN 0-936384-02-6). Cowley Pubns.
--Method in Theology: An Organon for Our Time. LC 80-81015. (Pere Marquette Ser.). 68p. 1980. 7.95 (ISBN 0-87462-519-X). Marquette.
Crowe, Frederick E., ed. A Third Collection: Papers by Bernard J. F. Longergan, S. J. LC 84-61028. 272p. 1985. pap. 9.95 (ISBN 0-8091-2650-8). Paulist Pr.
Crowe, Gregory D., jt. auth. see Crowe, Patrick H.
Crowe, James W., jt. auth. see Brennan, William T.
Crowe, Jaon M. & Douglas, Hugh M. Effective Loss Prevention (IS178) 1981. 75.00x (ISBN 0-686-45779-X, Pub. by RoSPA Can Hse England). State Mutual Bk.
Crowe, Jerome. The Acts. Harrington, Wilfrid & Senior, Donald, eds. (New Testament Message Ser.: Vol. 8). 204p. 1980. 12.95 (ISBN 0-89453-196-4); pap. 8.95 (ISBN 0-89453-131-X). M Glazier.
Crowe, John. A Touch of Darkness. 192p. 1974. pap. 1.25 (ISBN 0-532-12229-1). Woodhill.
Crowe, John H. & Clegg, James S., eds. Anhydrobiosis. LC 73-12354. (Benchmark Papers in Biological Concepts Ser.: Vol. 2). 477p. 1973. 55.00 (ISBN 0-87933-039-2). Van Nos Reinhold.
--Dry Biological Systems. 1978. 44.00 (ISBN 0-12-198080-4). Acad Pr.
Crowe, Joseph A. Handbook of Painting: German, Flemish, & Dutch Schools, 2 vols. LC 70-145126. (Illus.). 1972. Repr. of 1898 ed. 65.00 (ISBN 0-403-01059-4). Scholarly.
--Raphael, His Life & Works. LC 72-2584. (Select Bibliographies Reprint Ser). 1972. Repr. of 1885 ed. 48.00 (ISBN 0-8369-6852-2). Ayer Co Pubs.
Crowe, Joseph A. & Cavalcaselle, Giovanni B. History of Painting in Italy, Umbria, Florence, Siena: From the 2nd to the 16th Century, 6 Vols. LC 70-154118. (Illus.). Repr. of 1914 ed. Set. 245.00 (ISBN 0-404-01920-X). AMS Pr.
--A History of Painting in North Italy, 3 vols. LC 76-22574. (Illus.). Repr. of 1912 ed. 145.00 set (ISBN 0-404-09290-X). AMS Pr.
Crowe, Keith J. A History of the Original Peoples of Northern Canada. (Illus.). 172p. 1974. pap. 6.95 (ISBN 0-7735-0220-3). McGill-Queens U Pr.
Crowe, Kenneth, et al, eds. Exotic Atoms, 1979: Fundamental Interactions & Structure of Matter. LC 79-23072. (Ettore Majorana International Science Ser., Physical Science: Vol. 4). 410p. 1980. 65.00x (ISBN 0-306-40322-6, Plenum Pr). Plenum Pub.

Crowe, Linda, jt. ed. see Kronus, Carol L.
Crowe, Michael J. History of Vector Analysis: Evolution of the Idea of a Vectoral System. 1967. 24.95x (ISBN 0-268-00118-9). U of Notre Dame Pr.
--A History of Vector Analysis: The Evolution of the Idea of a Vectorial System. 278p. 1985. pap. 6.50 (ISBN 0-486-64955-5). Dover.
Crowe, Michael R. & Adams, Kay A. The Current Status of Assessing Experiential Education Programs. 100p. 1979. 6.25 (ISBN 0-318-15439-0, IN 163). Natl Ctr Res Voc Ed.
Crowe, Michael R. & Beckman, Carol A., eds. Perspectives on Investigating the Consequences of Experiential Education. 102p. 1979. 6.25 (ISBN 0-318-15533-8, IN 164). Natl Ctr Res Voc Ed.
Crowe, P. R. Concepts in Climatology. LC 77-174727. 355p. 1972. 37.50 (ISBN 0-312-16065-8). St Martin.
Crowe, Patrick H. Teacher Survival Handbook. LC 82-60573. 125p. (Orig.). 1983. pap. 8.95 (ISBN 0-88247-680-7). R & E Pubs.
Crowe, Patrick H. & Crowe, Gregory D. Money-Grubbing: A Student's Guide to Part-time Jobs & Self-Run Businesses. 150p. 1983. pap. 5.95 (ISBN 0-914091-29-8). Chicago Review.
Crowe, Peggy, ed. see Martinek, Thomas A.
Crowe, Percy R. Concepts in Climatology. LC 72-176213. (Geographies for Advanced Study Ser.). pap. 152.30 (ISBN 0-317-08860-2, 2019601). Bks Demand UMI.
Crowe, Richard C. Against All Enemies Foreign & Domestic. 1981. 10.00 (ISBN 0-533-04832-X). Vantage.
Crowe, Robert L. Clyde Monster. (Illus.). (ps-3). 1976. 10.95 (ISBN 0-525-28025-1, 01063-320). Dutton.
--Tyler Toad & the Thunder. LC 80-347. (Illus.). 32p. (ps-1). 1980. 10.25 (ISBN 0-525-41795-8, 0995-300). Dutton.
Crowe, Ronald. Two in the Bush. 157p. (Orig.). 1984. pap. 4.00 (ISBN 0-9603640-3-X). Sundog Pr.
Crowe, Samuel J. Halsted of Johns Hopkins: The Man & His Men. (Illus.). 268p. 1957. 28.50x (ISBN 0-398-00371-8). C C Thomas.
Crowe, Steve. Satellite Television & Your Backyard Dish. Krieger, Robin, ed. LC 81-90593. (Illus.). 200p. (Orig.). 1982. 20.00 (ISBN 0-910419-00-0); pap. 15.00 (ISBN 0-910419-01-9); trade special 15.00 (ISBN 0-910419-02-7). Satellite.
Crowe, Sybil E. Berlin West African Conference, 1884-1885. Repr. of 1942 ed. 29.75x (ISBN 0-8371-3287-8, CRC&, Pub. by Negro U Pr). Greenwood.
Crowe, Sylvia. Garden Design. (Illus.). 224p. 1981. 50.00x (ISBN 0-906527-05-8). Intl Ideas.
Crowe, W. Houghton. The Brontes of Ballynaskeagh. 180p. 10.00 (ISBN 0-85221-100-7). Dufour.
Crowe, Walter C., et al. Principles & Methods of Adapted Physical Education & Recreation. 4th ed. LC 81-1004. (Illus.). 524p. 1981. text ed. 23.95 (ISBN 0-8016-0327-7). Mosby.
Crowe-Carraco, Carol. Big Sandy. LC 78-58126. (Kentucky Bicentennial Bookshelf Ser.). (Illus.). 152p. 1979. 6.95 (ISBN 0-8131-0234-0). U Pr of Ky.
Crowell, Benedict & Wilson, Robert F. The Armies of Industry: Our Nation's Manufacture of Munitions for a World in Arms, 1917-1918, 2 vols. in one. LC 74-75235. (The United States in World War 1 Ser). (Illus.). xxviii, 738p. 1974. Repr. lib. bdg. 49.95x (ISBN 0-89198-101-2). Ozer.
--Demobilization: Our Industrial & Military Demobilization After the Armistice, 1918-1920. LC 74-75236. (The United States in World War 1 Ser). (Illus.). xvi, 333p. 1974. Repr. of 1921 ed. lib. bdg. 22.95x (ISBN 0-89198-102-0). Ozer.
--The Giant Hand: Our Mobilization & Control of Industry & Natural Resources, 1917-1918. LC 74-75237. (The United States in World War 1 Ser). (Illus.). xxx, 191p. 1974. Repr. of 1921 ed. lib. bdg. 18.95x (ISBN 0-89198-099-7). Ozer.
--The Road to France: The Transportation of Troops & Military Supplies, 1917-1918, 2 vols. in one. LC 74-75238. (The United States in World War 1 Ser). (Illus.). xv, 675p. 1974. Repr. of 1921 ed. lib. bdg. 42.95x (ISBN 0-89198-100-4). Ozer.
Crowell, E. B. Buddhist Mahayana Texts. lib. bdg. 79.95 (ISBN 0-87968-499-2). Krishna Pr.
Crowell, H. R. & Fox, H. R. Introduction to Know Theory. 4th ed. LC 77-22776. (Graduate Texts in Mathematics: Vol. 57). (Illus.). 1977. Repr. of 1963 ed. 29.80 (ISBN 0-387-90272-4). Springer-Verlag.
Crowell, Ivan H. Chip Carving Patterns & Designs. LC 77-78511. (Illus.). 1978. pap. 2.75 (ISBN 0-486-23532-7). Dover.
--Chip Carving Patterns & Designs. LC 77-78511. 1977. lib. bdg. 10.50x (ISBN 0-88307-592-X). Gannon.
Crowell, Laura E., jt. auth. see Scheidel, Thomas M.
Crowell, Laura I. Speaking His Peace. 160p. 1985. pap. 8.95 (ISBN 0-8192-1359-4). Morehouse.
Crowell, Lynda & Mariotti, Maryanne. The Parents' Guide to Austin, 1981. rev. ed. (Illus.). 176p. 1981. pap. 5.95 (ISBN 0-938934-00-7). C&M Pubns.
--The Parent's Guide to Austin, 1982-83. (Illus.). 208p. 1982. pap. 5.95 (ISBN 0-938934-02-3). C&M Pubns.
Crowell, Lynda, ed. see Nelson, David & Vlerebome, Peggy.
Crowell, Marnie R. North to the St. Lawrence. LC 75-22513. (Illus.). 100p. (Orig.). 1975. pap. 3.50 (ISBN 0-916136-01-9). Raquette Pr.
Crowell, Michael. The Precinct Manual: 1984. 57p. 1984. 2.50 (ISBN 0-686-39448-8). U of NC Inst Gov.
--Search Warrants in North Carolina. 118p. 1976. 2.00 (ISBN 0-686-39458-5). U of NC Inst Gov.
Crowell, Michael & Heath, Milton S., Jr. The General Assembly of North Carolina: A Handbook for Legislators. 4th ed. (Law & Government Ser.). 1981. 1979 suppl. 2.50 (ISBN 0-686-28571-9). U of NC Inst Gov.
Crowell, Michael, jt. auth. see University of North Carolina at Chapel Hill, Institute of Government Staff.
Crowell, Michael, jt. auth. see University of North Carolina at Chapel Hill, Institute of Government.
Crowell, Michael, ed. State of North Carolina Extradition Manual. 55p. 1980. 5.00 (ISBN 0-686-39459-3). U of NC Inst Gov.
Crowell, Michael G., jt. auth. see Hook, Julius N.
Crowell, Muriel B. The Fine Art of Needlepoint. (Illus.). 128p. 1973. 10.95i (ISBN 0-690-29799-8). T Y Crowell.
Crowell, Norton B. Triple Soul: Browning's Theory of Knowledge. 235p. 1963. text ed. 29.50x (ISBN 0-8290-0228-6). Irvington.
Crowell, Pattie & Stanford, Ann. Critical Essays on Anne Bradstreet. (Critical Essays on American Literature Ser.). 1983. lib. bdg. 44.50 (ISBN 0-8161-8643-X). G K Hall.
Crowell, Pers. King Moo, the Wordmaker. LC 75-21133. (Illus.). (gr. 1-3). 1976. 5.95 (ISBN 0-87004-253-X). Caxton.
Crowell, Richard H. & Slesnick, William E. Calculus with Analytic Geometry. (Illus.). 1968. 26.95x (ISBN 0-393-09782-X). Norton.
Crowell, Robert L. The Lore & Legends of Flowers. LC 79-7829. (Illus.). 88p. (YA) (gr. 7 up). 1982. 13.94i (ISBN 0-690-03991-3); PLB 13.89g (ISBN 0-690-04035-0). Crowell Jr Bks.
Crowell, Sidney R., jt. auth. see Lomax, Alan.
Crowell, Thomas L. Index to Modern English. (Illus.). 1964. pap. 7.95 (ISBN 0-07-014734-5). McGraw.
--Modern English Essays. (Saxon Series in English As a Second Language). 1964. 3.95 (ISBN 0-07-014733-7). McGraw.
--Modern Spoken English. (Saxon Series in English As a Second Language). 1961. 4.25 (ISBN 0-07-014730-2). McGraw.
Crowell, W., ed. Portability of Numerical Software: Proceedings. LC 77-13623. (Lecture Notes in Computer Science: Vol. 57). 1977. pap. text ed. 28.00 (ISBN 0-387-08446-0). Springer-Verlag.
Crowest, F. J. Cherubini. 1976. Repr. of 1890 ed. lib. bdg. 29.00x (ISBN 0-403-03761-1). Scholarly.
Crowest, Frederick. Great Tone-Poets: Being Short Memoirs of the Greater Musical Composers. facsimile ed. LC 70-38711. (Essay Index Reprint Ser). Repr. of 1874 ed. 25.50 (ISBN 0-8369-2641-2). Ayer Co Pubs.
--Story of British Music from the Earliest Times to the Tudor Period. 404p. 1984. pap. cancelled (ISBN 0-89341-525-1). Longwood Pub Group.
Crowest, Frederick J. Beethoven. LC 77-6177. 1977. Repr. of 1921 ed. lib. bdg. 35.00 (ISBN 0-89341-128-0). Longwood Pub Group.
--The Great Tone Poets. LC 77-94566. 1978. Repr. of 1874 ed. lib. bdg. 40.00 (ISBN 0-89341-404-2). Longwood Pub Group.
--The Story of British Music: From the Earliest Times to the Tudor Period. LC 76-22328. (Illus.). 1976. Repr. of 1896 ed. lib. bdg. 40.00 (ISBN 0-89341-024-1). Longwood Pub Group.
--The Story of the Art of Music. 1979. Repr. of 1904 ed. lib. bdg. 25.00 (ISBN 0-8495-0921-1). Arden Lib.
--Verdi: Man & Musician. LC 74-24065. Repr. of 1897 ed. 21.00 (ISBN 0-404-12890-4). AMS Pr.
Crowfoot, Grace M. & Roth, H. Ling. Handspinning & Wool Combing. (Illus.). Repr. 5.95 (ISBN 0-686-09824-2). Robin & Russ.
Crowfoot, J. W. Early Churches in Palestine. (British Academy, London, Schweich Lectures on Biblical Archaeology Series, 1937). pap. 28.00 (ISBN 0-317-15887-2). Kraus Repr.
Crowfoot, James, et al. Action for Educational Equity: A Guide for Parents & Members of Community Groups. 184p. (Orig.). 1982. pap. text ed. 9.00 (ISBN 0-917754-19-0). Inst Responsive.
Crowfoot, James E., jt. auth. see Lesnick, Michael T.
Crowfoot, John, tr. see Petrovsky, A.
Crowhurst, Eric. Acol in Competition. 384p. 1981. 24.95 (ISBN 0-7207-1273-4, Pub. by Michael Joseph). Merrimack Pub Cir.
--ACOL in Competition. 385p. 1984. pap. 13.95 (ISBN 0-7207-1525-3, Pub. by Michael Joseph). Merrimack Pub Cir.
Crowhurst, Les & Burton, Peter. Small Offset: Preparation & Press. (Illus.). 172p. 1982. avail. (ISBN 0-88362-044-8, 1517). Graphic Arts Tech Found.
Crowhurst, Norman. Basic Mathematics, 2 vols. (Illus., Orig.). (gr. 9 up). 1961. Vol. 1 Arithmetic. pap. 7.65 (ISBN 0-8104-0447-8); Vol. 2 Integrated Algebra, Geometry & Calculus. pap. 7.65 (ISBN 0-8104-0448-6); Vol. 1. exam set 0.50 (ISBN 0-8104-0567-9); Vol. 2. exam set 0.50 (ISBN 0-8104-0568-7). Hayden.
Crowhurst, Norman E. Problem Solving Arts: Part Three Syllabus. 1978. pap. text ed. 10.45 (ISBN 0-89420-040-2, 256130); cassette recordings 196.20 (ISBN 0-89420-177-8, 256090). Natl Book.
Crowhurst, Norman H. Basic Electronics Course. LC 75-178692. 1972. pap. 13.95 (ISBN 0-8306-1588-1, 588). TAB Bks.
--Basic Electronics: Syllabus. 1974. pap. text ed. 8.45 (ISBN 0-89420-072-0, 250111); cassette recordings 149.75 (ISBN 0-89420-126-3, 250000). Natl Book.
--English: Syllabus. 138p. 1974. pap. text ed. 7.65 (ISBN 0-89420-073-9, 171050); cassette recordings 135.90 (ISBN 0-89420-145-X, 171000). Natl Book.
--Introductory Physics: Syllabus. 1974. pap. text ed. 9.35 (ISBN 0-89420-084-4, 230330); cassette recordings 164.70 (ISBN 0-89420-158-1, 230000). Natl Book.
--Problem Solving Arts: Part One Syllabus. 1976. pap. text ed. 9.95 (ISBN 0-89420-085-2, 256040); cassette recordings 227.10 (ISBN 0-89420-175-1, 256000). Natl Book.
--Problem Solving Arts: Part Two Syllabus. 1977. pap. text ed. 10.25 (ISBN 0-89420-029-1); cassette recordings 195.80 (ISBN 0-89420-176-X, 256050). Natl Book.
--Statistics. 110p. (Orig.). 1981. pap. text ed. 10.45 (ISBN 0-89420-111-5, 413040); cassette recordings 103.95 (ISBN 0-89420-202-2, 413000). Natl Book.
--Taking the Mysticism from Mathematics. 2nd ed. 178p. (Orig.). 1981. pap. 7.65 (ISBN 0-89420-223-5, 297020). Natl Book.
Crowhurst-Lennard, Suzanne H. & Lennard, Henry L. Public Life in Urban Places. LC 83-83342. 80p. (Orig.). 1984. pap. 8.95 (ISBN 0-935824-03-0). Gondolier.
Crowin, T. M. Elementary Calculus. (Mathematical Topics for Engineering & Science Students Ser.). (Illus.). 1976. 18.50x (ISBN 0-8464-0365-X); pap. 12.50x (ISBN 0-686-77141-9). Beekman Pubs.
Crowl, jt. auth. see Isely.
Crowl, James W. Angels in Stalin's Paradise: Western Reporters in Soviet Russia, 1917 to 1937, a Case Study of Louise Fischer & Walter Duranty. LC 81-40058. (Illus.). 232p. 1982. lib. bdg. 24.75 (ISBN 0-8191-2185-1); pap. text ed. 12.25 (ISBN 0-8191-2186-X). U Pr of Amer.
Crowl, Philip A. The Intelligent Traveller's Guide to Historic Britain. LC 81-19469. (Illus.). 832p. 1983. 39.95; pap. 19.95. Congdon & Weed.
Crowl, Phillip. The Intelligent Traveller's Guide to Historic Britain. (Illus.). 600p. 1982. 39.95 (ISBN 0-312-92337-6); pap. 19.95 (ISBN 0-312-92338-4). St Martin.
Crowl, Phillip see Radoff, Morris L., et al.
Crowl, Phillip A. Maryland During & After the Revolution: A Political & Economic Study. LC 78-64189. (Johns Hopkins University. Studies in the Social Sciences. Sixty-First Ser. 1943: 1). Repr. of 1943 ed. 18.50 (ISBN 0-404-61296-2). AMS Pr.
Crowl, Thomas K. Fundamentals of Research: A Practical Guide for Educators & Special Educators. (Illus.). 275p. 1986. text ed. 26.95x (ISBN 0-942280-13-X). Pub Horizons.
Crowle, Alfred J. Immunodiffusion. 2nd ed. 1973. 76.50 (ISBN 0-12-198156-8). Acad Pr.
Crowley. I Could Talk Old-Story Good. (California Library Reprint Ser.: No. 124). 1983. Repr. text ed. 25.00x (ISBN 0-520-05083-5). U of Cal Pr.
--Syllabus of Visual Aids in Pathology. 1972. 251.50 (ISBN 0-8151-2032-X). Year Bk Med.
Crowley, jt. auth. see Trilling.
Crowley, A, jt. auth. see Yuen, Ko.
Crowley, Aleister. A. H. A. LC 83-82342. 80p. 1983. pap. 4.95 (ISBN 0-941404-29-3). Falcon Pr Az.
--Ahab & Other Poems. 1973. lib. bdg. 79.95 (ISBN 0-87968-221-3). Krishna Pr.
--The Argonauts. 1973. lib. bdg. 79.95 (ISBN 0-87968-222-1). Krishna Pr.
--The Banned Lecture. 1981. Repr. of 1930 ed. pap. 3.50 (ISBN 0-935458-99-9). Thirteenth Hse.
--Book Four. 1973. lib. bdg. 79.95 (ISBN 0-87968-114-4). Krishna Pr.
--Book Four. LC 70-146544. 128p. 1980. pap. 6.95 (ISBN 0-87728-513-6). Weiser.
--The Book of Lies. 1973. lib. bdg. 79.95 (ISBN 0-87968-115-2). Krishna Pr.
--Book of Lies. LC 79-16636. (Illus.). 186p. (Orig.). 1981. pap. 7.95 (ISBN 0-87728-516-0). Weiser.
--Book of the Law. 128p. 1976. pap. 4.50 (ISBN 0-87728-334-6). Weiser.
--Book of the Law: Technically Called Liber AL vel Legis - Sub Figura CCXX As Delivered by XCIII 418 to DCLXVI. LC 72-96601. 1983. 9.00x (ISBN 0-913576-27-1); deluxe ed. 35.00x leather (ISBN 0-913576-28-X). Thelema Pubns.
--The Book of Thoth. LC 79-16399. (Illus.). 287p. 1977. pap. 8.95 (ISBN 0-913866-12-1). US Games Syst.
--The Book of Thoth. LC 79-16399. (Illus.). 287p. (Orig.). 1974. pap. 8.95 (ISBN 0-87728-268-4). Weiser.
--Clouds Without Water. 1973. lib. bdg. 59.95 (ISBN 0-87968-111-X). Krishna Pr.
--Clouds Without Water. 139p. 1973. Repr. 3.50 (ISBN 0-911662-50-2). Yoga.
--The Collected Works of Aleister Crowley, 3 vols. 1974. lib. bdg. 300.00 (ISBN 0-87968-130-6). Krishna Pr.
--Collected Works of Aleister Crowley, 3 vols. 1974. Repr. 8.00 ea.; Vol. 1 269p. (ISBN 0-911662-51-0); Vol. 2 282p. (ISBN 0-911662-52-9); Vol. 3 248p. (ISBN 0-911662-53-7). Yoga.
--The Collected Writings of Aleister Crowley, 3 vols. 1973. 300.00 (ISBN 0-87968-130-6). Gordon Pr.
--Creed of the Thelemites. 1973. lib. bdg. 79.95 (ISBN 0-87968-500-X). Krishna Pr.
--Diary of a Drug Fiend. 1973. lib. bdg. 79.95 (ISBN 0-87968-110-1). Krishna Pr.
--Diary of a Drug Fiend. LC 79-142495. 1970. pap. 5.95 (ISBN 0-87728-146-7). Weiser.
--Dream of Scipio. 1973. lib. bdg. 79.95 (ISBN 0-87968-501-8). Krishna Pr.
--Eight Lectures on Yoga. 1972. pap. 2.95 (ISBN 0-87728-122-X). Weiser.
--Eight Lectures on Yoga. 80p. 1985. pap. 5.95 (ISBN 0-941404-36-6). Falcon Pr AZ.
--Equinox of the Gods. 1973. lib. bdg. 79.95 (ISBN 0-87968-157-8). Krishna Pr.
--The Equinox: Vols. 1-10. LC 72-77558. 1972. Set. 250.00 (ISBN 0-87728-206-4). Weiser.
--The High History of Good Sir Palamedes. 1973. lib. bdg. 79.95 (ISBN 0-87968-503-4). Krishna Pr.
--The Holy Books of Thelema. rev. ed. LC 82-50829. 1983. cloth 17.50 (ISBN 0-87728-579-9). Weiser.
--In Residence. 1973. lib. bdg. 79.95 (ISBN 0-87968-504-2). Krishna Pr.
--Jepthah & Other Mysteries. 1973. lib. bdg. 79.95 (ISBN 0-87968-217-5). Krishna Pr.
--Konx Om Pax. 108p. 1973. Repr. 3.50 (ISBN 0-911662-49-9). Yoga.
Crowley, Aleister, pseud. Liber XXI, Khing Kang King - The Classic of Purity. LC 73-11427. (Illus.). 14.95x (ISBN 0-913576-16-6). Thelema Pubns.
Crowley, Aleister. The Magical Record of the Beast 666. Symonds, John & Grant, Kenneth, eds. 326p. 1979. 40.50 (ISBN 0-7156-0636-0, Pub. by Duckworth England); limited ed. slipcased signed ed. 95.00 (ISBN 0-686-37758-3, BPX 02623). Biblio Dist.
--The Magical Record of the Beast 666. Symonds, John & Grant, Kenneth, eds. 326p. 1972. pap. 14.95 (ISBN 0-7156-0636-0). US Games Syst.
--Magick. pap. 6.50x (ISBN 0-685-22024-9). Wehman.
--Magick. Symonds, John & Grant, Kenneth, eds. LC 74-24002. (Illus.). 511p. 1974. Repr. of 1973 ed. 25.00 (ISBN 0-87728-254-4). Weiser.
--Magick in Theory & Practice. (Illus.). 480p. 1976. pap. 6.50 (ISBN 0-486-23295-6). Dover.
--Magick in Theory & Practice. 1973. lib. bdg. 100.00 (ISBN 0-87968-128-4). Krishna Pr.
--Magick, in Theory & Practice. 14.25 (ISBN 0-8446-5476-0). Peter Smith.
--Magick Without Tears. 3rd ed. Regardie, Israel, ed. LC 82-83310. 560p. 1982. collector's ed. 49.94 (ISBN 0-941404-16-1); pap. 13.95 (ISBN 0-941404-17-X). Falcon Pr Az.
--Moonchild. LC 72-142496. 1970. pap. 6.95 (ISBN 0-87728-147-5). Weiser.
--Olla: An Anthology of Sixty Years Song. 1973. lib. bdg. 79.95 (ISBN 0-87968-505-0). Krishna Pr.
--One Star in Sight. 1973. lib. bdg. 59.95 (ISBN 0-87968-506-9). Krishna Pr.
--Orpheus. 1973. lib. bdg. 79.95 (ISBN 0-87968-176-4). Krishna Pr.
--Seven Seven Seven: A Study of the Kabbalah. 1973. lib. bdg. 80.00 (ISBN 0-87968-105-5). Krishna Pr.
--Seven Seven Seven & Other Quabilistic Writings. rev. ed. LC 73-80056. 274p. 1970. 12.50 (ISBN 0-87728-222-6). Weiser.
--Songs of the Spirit. 1973. lib. bdg. 79.95 (ISBN 0-87968-220-5). Krishna Pr.
--The Soul of Osiris. 1973. lib. bdg. 79.95 (ISBN 0-87968-177-2). Krishna Pr.
--The Soul of the Desert. LC 74-10890. 1976. 9.00x (ISBN 0-913576-08-5). Thelema Pubns.
--The Star & the Garter. 1973. lib. bdg. 79.95 (ISBN 0-87968-175-6). Krishna Pr.
--The Stratagem & Other Stories. facsimile ed. LC 74-167446. (Short Story Index Reprint Ser.). Repr. of 1929 ed. 11.00 (ISBN 0-8369-3972-7). Ayer Co Pubs.
--The Stratagem & Other Stories. 1973. lib. bdg. 79.95 (ISBN 0-87968-117-9). Krishna Pr.
--Tale of Archais. 1973. lib. bdg. 79.95 (ISBN 0-87968-218-3). Krishna Pr.
--Tannhauser: A Story of All Time. 1973. lib. bdg. 79.95 (ISBN 0-87968-215-9). Krishna Pr.
--Tarot Divination. 68p. 1976. pap. 2.00 (ISBN 0-87728-347-8). Weiser.
--The Thoth Deck. 12.00 (ISBN 0-685-47277-9). Weiser.
--Vision & the Voice. 1972. pap. 7.50 (ISBN 0-87913-001-6). Weiser.
--The Whirlpool. 1973. lib. bdg. 79.95 (ISBN 0-87968-507-7). Krishna Pr.
--The World's Tragedy. Regardie, Israel, ed. Date not set. pap. price not set (ISBN 0-941404-18-8). Falcon Pr Az.
Crowley, Aleister & Aiwass. Liber AL vel Legis, The Book of the Law. 1980. 15.00 (ISBN 0-933454-03-1). O T O.

Crowley, Aleister & Motta, Marcelo. Equinox: Sex & Religion, Vol. 5. (No. 4). 1981. 44.00 (ISBN 0-933454-04-X, Pub. by Thelema Pub). O T O.
--Equinox: The Chinese Texts of Mapick & Mysticism, Vol. 5. (No. 3). 1980. 44.00 (ISBN 0-933454-02-3, Pub. by Thelema Pub). O T O.
--Ofiflamme: The Law, Vol. 6. (No. 4). Date not set. 11.00 (ISBN 0-913735-04-3, Pub by OTO). O T O.
--Oriflamme: Magick & Mysticism, Vol. VI, No. 2. 1982. 15.00 (ISBN 0-933454-06-6). O T O.
--Oriflamme, Vol. VI, No. 1: Yoga & Magick. 1984. 8.00 (ISBN 0-913735-02-7). O T O.
--Oriflamme Vol. VI, No. 3: Magick without Tears Unexpurgated Commented, Pt. 1. 645p. 1983. pap. 25.00 (ISBN 0-913735-00-0). O T O.
--Oriflamme Vol. VI, No. 4: Magick Without Tears Unexpurgated Commented, Pt. II. rev. ed. 1984. 25.00 (ISBN 0-913735-01-9). O T O.
--Oriflamme, Vol. VI, No. 5: Thelemic Magick, Being Book Four Commented, Part III, Vol. 6. 1985. 25.00 (ISBN 0-913735-03-5). O T O.
Crowley, Aleister & Motta, Marcelo R. Equinox, Vol. 5, No. 2. LC 78-68846. 1979. o.s.i 44.00 (ISBN 0-933454-00-7, Pub. by Thelema Publishing Company); deluxe ed. 93.00 limited (ISBN 0-933454-01-5). O T O.
Crowley, Aleister see Kerval, Alastor de, pseud.
Crowley, Arthur. Bonzo Beaver. (Illus.). 32p. (gr. k-3). 1980. PLB 7.95 (ISBN 0-395-29081-3). HM.
Crowley, C. George. A Dental Bibliography: 1536-1885. 59.95 (ISBN 0-8490-0018-1). Gordon Pr.
Crowley, C. J. Persisting Latinisms in 'El Poema De Mio Cid' & Other Selected Old Spanish Literary Works. (LD Ser.). 1952. pap. 16.00 (ISBN 0-527-00794-3). Kraus Repr.
Crowley, Carleen. All about Clothes. (Gregg-McGraw-Hill Series for Independent Living). 1978. pap. text ed. 9.60 (ISBN 0-07-014765-5). McGraw.
Crowley, D. A., ed. A History of Wiltshire, Vol. 12. (The Victoria History of the Counties of England Ser.). (Illus.). 1983. 150.00x (ISBN 0-19-722759-7). Oxford U Pr.
--Victoria History of the Counties of England: Wiltshire - Downton Hundred, Elstub & Everleigh Hundred, Vol. 11. (Illus.). 1980. 139.00x (ISBN 0-19-722751-1). Oxford U Pr.
Crowley, D. J. Understanding Communication: The Signifying Web. (Communication & the Human Condition Ser.). 211p. 1983. 37.50 (ISBN 0-677-05920-5). Gordon.
Crowley, Dale. Soon Coming of Our Lord. 1958. pap. 2.95 (ISBN 0-87213-091-6). Loizeaux.
Crowley, Edward J. Lamentations, Baruch, Sophonia, Nahum, Habacuc. (Bible Ser.). pap. 1.00 (ISBN 0-8091-5078-6). Paulist Pr.
Crowley, Elaine. Kilgoran. LC 84-13716. 360p. 1985. 16.95 (ISBN 0-385-19744-6). Doubleday.
Crowley, Ellen T., ed. Acronyms, Initialisms, & Abbreviations Dictionary, 2 pts, Vol. 1. 9th ed. LC 78-18362. 2048p. 1984. 150.00x (ISBN 0-8103-0511-9). Gale.
--International Acronyms, Initialisms, & Abbreviations Dictionary: A Guide to International Acronymns, Initialisms, Abbreviations, Alphabetic Symbols, Contractions, & Similar Condensed Appellations in All Fields. 950p. 1984. 140.00x (ISBN 0-8103-0509-7). Gale.
Crowley, Ellen T. & Sheppard, Helen, eds. Acronyms, Initialisms, & Abbreviations Dictionary: Vol. 2, New Acronyms, Initialisms, & Abbreviations. 9th ed. pap. Gale.
--Acronyms, Initialisms, & Abbreviations Dictionary: Vol. 3, Reverse Acronyms, Initialisms, & Abbreviations Dictionary, 2 pts. 9th ed. 2000p. 1984. 180.00x (ISBN 0-8103-0512-7). Gale.
Crowley, Flor. In West Cork Long Ago. 127p. (Orig.). pap. 4.95 (ISBN 0-85342-600-7, Co-dist. by Irish Bks Media). Irish Bk Ctr.
Crowley, Frank, ed. A New History of Australia. LC 78-14279. 639p. 1975. text ed. 42.50x (ISBN 0-8419-6100-X). Holmes & Meier.
Crowley, George D. & Manning, Richard L. Criminal Tax Fraud: Representing the Taxpayer Before Trial. 1976. text ed. 30.00 (ISBN 0-685-85367-5, J1-1409). PLI.
Crowley, Gerald & Lieba Inc. Staff. Fine Art of Garnishing. (Illus.). 104p. (Orig.). 1981. pap. text ed. write for info. (ISBN 0-941076-00-8). Lieba Inc.
Crowley, J. Donald, ed. Hawthorne: The Critical Heritage. 1971. 36.00x (ISBN 0-7100-6886-7). Routledge & Kegan.
Crowley, J. Donald, ed. see Defoe, Daniel.
Crowley, J. Donald, ed. see James, Henry.
Crowley, J. Donald, jt. ed. see Sattelmeyer, Robert.
Crowley, J. E. This Sheba, Self: The Conceptualization of Economic Life in Eighteenth-Century America. LC 73-19334. (Studies in Historical & Political Science, 92nd Ser: Ninety-Second Series (1974)). 174p. 1974. 16.00x (ISBN 0-8018-1579-7). Johns Hopkins.
Crowley, J. S. & Zimmerman, L. Z. Practical Passive Solar Design: A Guide to Homebuilding & Land Development. 256p. 1983. 37.95 (ISBN 0-07-014769-8). McGraw.
Crowley, James B., tr. see Morley, James W.
Crowley, James F. Alliance for Change: A Plan for Community Action on Adolescent Drug Abuse. LC 84-71356. (Illus.). 226p. (Orig.). 1984. pap. 8.95 (ISBN 0-9613416-0-2). Comm Intervention.
Crowley, John, et al, eds. Survival Analysis. LC 82-84316. (Institute of Mathematical Statistics Lecture Notes-Monograph Ser.: Vol. 2). x, 302p. (Orig.). 1982. pap. text ed. 25.00 (ISBN 0-940600-02-1). Inst Math.
Crowley, John W. The Black Heart's Truth: The Early Career of W. D. Howells. LC 84-20908. 367p. 1985. 19.95x (ISBN 0-8078-1632-9). U of NC Pr.
Crowley, Leonard V. Introduction to Human Disease. LC 82-19960. 700p. 1983. text ed. 23.75 pub net (ISBN 0-534-01264-7). BrookS-Cole.
--Introductory Concepts in Anatomy & Physiology. LC 76-2249. (Illus.). Repr. of 1976 ed. 115.50 (ISBN 0-8357-9612-4, 2015077). Bks Demand UMI.
Crowley, Mary. String of Pearls. 160p. 1985. 9.95 (ISBN 0-8499-0499-4, 0499-4). Word Bks.
Crowley, Mary C. Mary C. Crowley's Decorate Your Home with Love. (Illus.). 160p. 1985. 16.95 (ISBN 0-8007-1454-7). Revell.
--A Pocketful of Hope. 352p. 1981. 9.50 (ISBN 0-8007-1272-2). Revell.
--Women Who Win. (Illus.). 160p. 1979. 9.95 (ISBN 0-8007-0993-4). Revell.
--You Can Too. 128p. 1980. pap. 4.95 (ISBN 0-8007-5028-4, Power Bks). Revell.
Crowley, Maureen, ed. Energy: Sources of Print & Nonprint Materials. LC 79-26574. (Neal-Schuman Sourcebook Ser.). 341p. 1980. 35.00 (ISBN 0-918212-16-2). Neal-Schuman.
Crowley, Merrily F., jt. auth. see Suitor, Carol J.
Crowley, Richard. The Way to Wealth, Wherein Is Plainly Taught a Remedy for Sedicion. LC 74-28843. (English Experience Ser.: No. 724). 1975. Repr. of 1550 ed. 3.50 (ISBN 90-221-0724-8). Walter J Johnson.
Crowley, Robert. The IBM PC: VisiCalc. 256p. 1984. pap. 20.45 (ISBN 0-03-062634-X); pap. 40.45 with diskette (ISBN 0-03-063982-4). HR&W.
--The Select Works of Robert Crowley, Printer, Archdeacon of Hereford, Vicar of St. Lawrence, Jewry. Cowper, J. M., ed. (EETS, ES Ser.: No. 15). Repr. of 1872 ed. 17.00 (ISBN 0-527-00230-5). Kraus Repr.
--Using the IBM PC: PFS Files-PFS Report. 1984. 19.95 (ISBN 0-03-063994-8). HR&W.
--Using the IBM Personal Computer: PFS File-Report. 1984. 18.45 (ISBN 0-03-069399-3). HR&W.
Crowley, Robert T., jt. auth. see Corson, William R.
Crowley, Ruth A. Charles de Villers. (Stanford German Studies: Vol. 14). 175p. 1978. pap. 20.20 (ISBN 3-261-03060-7). P Lang Pubs.
Crowley, Ruth A., tr. see Ingarden, Roman.
Crowley, Sharon, ed. Speech & Drama in the English Class. 89p. 1978. 6.00 (ISBN 0-8141-4634-1). NCTE.
--The Teaching of Composition. 115p. (Reprinted from Oct. 1976 Arizona English Bulletin). 5.25 (ISBN 0-317-35332-2, 50608); members 3.75 (ISBN 0-317-35333-0). NCTE.
Crowley, T. The Middle Clarence Dialects of Bandjalang. (AIAS Research & Regional Ser.: No. 12). 1978. pap. text ed. 19.75x (ISBN 0-391-00944-3). Humanities.
Crowley, T. E. Beam Engines. 1982 ed. (Albums Ser.: No. 15). (Illus.). 32p. pap. 2.95 (ISBN 0-85263-595-8, Pub. by Shire Pubns England). Seven Hills Bks.
--Discovering Mechanical Music. (Discovering Ser.: No. 200). (Illus.). 48p. (Orig.). 1983. pap. 3.50 (ISBN 0-85263-371-8, Pub. by Shire Pubns England). Seven Hills Bks.
--Discovering Old Bicycles. 2.50 (ISBN 0-913714-19-4). Legacy Bks.
--Discovering Old Motor Cycles. (Discovering Ser.: No. 160). (Illus.). 55p. (Orig.). 1983. pap. 3.95 (ISBN 0-85263-557-5, Pub. by Shire Pubns England). Seven Hills Bks.
Crowley, Thomas H. Understanding Computers. (Orig.). (YA) (gr. 9-12). 1967. pap. 4.95 (ISBN 0-07-014761-2). McGraw.
Crowley, William, ed. Rushton's Rowboats & Canoes, 1903. LC 82-48169. (Illus.). 128p. 1983. pap. 8.95 (ISBN 0-87742-164-1). Intl Marine.
Crowley, William J. Grow with Strong Words. 96p. (Orig.). (gr. 2). 1985. pap. 8.50 (ISBN 0-682-40269-9). Exposition Pr FL.
Crowmarsh, P. First Steps to Astrology. (Paths to Inner Power Ser.). pap. 2.75 (ISBN 0-85030-391-5). Weiser.
Crown, et al. Abstract Algebra. (Pure & Applied Mathematics Ser.). 488p. 1986. price not set (ISBN 0-8247-7456-6). Dekker.
Crown, Alan D. A Bibliography of the Samaritans. LC 84-1386. (ATLA Bibliography Ser.: No. 10). 212p. 1984. 17.50 (ISBN 0-8108-1693-8). Scarecrow.
Crown, David A. Forensic Examination of Paints & Pigments. 276p. 1968. 24.75x (ISBN 0-398-00372-6). C C Thomas.
Crown, Fenya. How to Recycle Old Clothes into New Fashions. LC 77-4819. (Illus.). 1977. 8.95 (ISBN 0-13-430819-0). P-H.
Crown, Francis J., Jr. Surveys of the Confederate Postmasters' Provisionals. lib. bdg. 100.00x (ISBN 0-88000-124-0). Quarterman.
Crown, Francis J., Jr., ed. Confederate Postal History. LC 75-39499. (Illus.). 1976. 30.00x (ISBN 0-88000-077-5). Quarterman.
Crown, Gerald H. One Hundred One Pretentious Hors D'Oeuvres. LC 83-15385. (Illus.). 120p. 1983. pap. 5.95 (ISBN 0-914091-36-0). Chicago Review.
Crown, J. C., jt. auth. see Bittinger, M. L.
Crown, J. Conrad & Bittinger, Marvin L. Finite Mathematics: A Modeling Approach. 2nd ed. LC 80-19472. (Mathematics Ser.). (Illus.). 480p. 1981. text ed. 29.95 (ISBN 0-201-03145-0); instrs' manual 3.50 (ISBN 0-201-03146-9). Addison-Wesley.
Crown, J. Conrad, jt. auth. see Bittinger, Marvin L.
Crown, P. Retail Merchandising. LC 65-22172. (Business Almanac Ser.: No. 3). 92p. 1966. 5.95 (ISBN 0-379-11203-5). Oceana.
Crown, Patricia. Drawings by E. F. Burney. LC 82-21300. (Illus.). 80p. 1982. pap. 7.50 (ISBN 0-87328-124-1). Huntington Lib.
Crown, Paul. Legal Protection for the Consumer. 2nd ed. 94p. 1978. 5.95 (ISBN 0-317-30258-2). Oceana.
--What You Should Know about Building Your Mailing Lists. LC 72-13927. (Business Almanac Ser.: No. 20). 121p. 1973. 5.95 (ISBN 0-379-11220-5). Oceana.
Crown, S. Essential Principles of Psychiatry. LC 72-128608. 307p. 1970. text ed. 20.50 (ISBN 0-911216-16-2). Raven.
Crown, Sidney. Practical Psychiatry, Vol. 1. 320p. 1981. 100.00x (ISBN 0-7198-2526-1, Pub. by Northwood Bks). State Mutual Bk.
--Psychosexual Problems: Psychotherapy, Counseling & Behavioral Modifications. 480p. 1977. 40.00 (ISBN 0-8089-0953-3, 790950). Grune.
Crown, Sidney, ed. Contemporary Psychiatry. 1984. pap. 39.95 (ISBN 0-407-00293-6). Butterworth.
Crown, W. The Heritage of Buddhist Poetry. 1985. 6.95 (ISBN 0-533-06003-6). Vantage.
Crowne, D. P. The Experimental Study of Personality. 272p. 1979. 29.95x (ISBN 0-89859-410-3). L Erlbaum Assocs.
Crowne, Douglas P. & Marlowe, David. The Approval Motive: Studies in Evaluative Dependence. LC 80-475. (Illus.). xii, 233p. 1980. Repr. of 1964 ed. lib. bdg. 27.50x (ISBN 0-313-22365-3, CRAM). Greenwood.
Crowne, John. City Politigues. Wilson, John H., ed. LC 67-12641. (Regents Restoration Drama Ser). xx, 159p. 1967. 15.50x (ISBN 0-8032-0355-1); pap. 3.95x (ISBN 0-8032-5355-9, BB 262, Bison). U of Nebr Pr.
--Dramatic Works of John Crowne, 4 Vols. Maidment, James & Logan, W. H., eds. LC 67-18423. 1967. Repr. of 1874 ed. Set. 110.00 (ISBN 0-405-08407-2, Blom Pubns); 27.50 ea. Vol. 1 (ISBN 0-405-08408-0). Vol. 2 (ISBN 0-405-08409-9). Vol. 3 (ISBN 0-405-08410-2). Vol. 4 (ISBN 0-405-08411-0). Ayer Co Pubs.
--The Dramatic Works of John Crowne, 4 vols. 1873. 350.00 set (ISBN 0-932062-40-7). Sharon Hill.
Crowne, William. A True Relation of All the Remarkable Places Observed in the Travels of Thomas Lord Howard. LC 77-171742. (English Experience Ser.: No. 357). 1971. Repr. of 1637 ed. 11.50 (ISBN 90-221-0357-9). Walter J Johnson.
Crownhart-Vaughan, E. A., jt. tr. see Dmytryshyn, Basil.
Crownhart-Vaughan, E. A., tr. see Golovin, Pavel N.
Crownhart-Vaughan, E. A., tr. see Khlebnikov, Kyrill T.
Crownhart-Vaughan, E. A., tr. see Krasheninnikov, Stepan P.
Crownhart-Vaughan, E. A. P., tr. see Golovin, Pavel N.
Crownhart-Vaughan, E. A. P., tr. see Krasheninnikov, Stepan P.
Crownhart-Vaughn, E. A., ed. see Golovin, Pavel N.
Crowningshield, Gerald & Gorman, Kenneth A. Cost Accounting: Principles & Managerial Applications. 4th ed. LC 78-69551. (Illus.). 1979. text ed. 31.50 (ISBN 0-395-26797-8); instr's. manual 4.75 (ISBN 0-395-26798-6). HM.
Crowninshield, Francis W. Manners for the Metropolis: An Entrance Key to the Fantastic Life of the 400. facsimile ed. LC 75-1838. (Leisure Class in America Ser.). (Illus.). 1975. Repr. of 1909 ed. 14.00x (ISBN 0-405-06907-3). Ayer Co Pubs.
Crownover, Richard. Erotic Mexico: A Travellers Unofficial Guide. 1975. pap. 2.00 (ISBN 0-914778-11-0). Phoenix Bks.
--Lover's Language Guide to Japan. 1976. pap. 3.00 (ISBN 0-914778-17-X). Phoenix Bks.
--Sensual Yoga: For Men & Women. 1976. pap. 1.50 (ISBN 0-914778-13-7). Phoenix Bks.
Crowquill, Alfred. The Laughing Philosopher. Repr. of 1889 ed. 15.00 (ISBN 0-8274-4155-X). R West.
Crowquill, Alfred, ed. The Laughing Philosopher. 329p. 1980. Repr. of 1899 ed. lib. bdg. 40.00 (ISBN 0-89760-123-8). Telegraph Bks.
Crowson, Angelina A. Head Injuries: Medical Subject Analysis & Research Guide with Bibliography. LC 84-45740. 150p. 1985. 29.95 (ISBN 0-88164-258-4); pap. 21.95 (ISBN 0-88164-259-2). ABBE Pubs Assn.
Crowson, Elmer T. Life As Revealed Through Early American Court Records, Including the Story of Col. John Custis of Arlington, Queen's Creek & Williamsburg. (Illus.). 1981. 17.50 (ISBN 0-89308-146-9). Southern Hist Pr.
Crowson, Milton. The Epistle to the Hebrews. 1974. pap. 3.95 (ISBN 0-89265-021-4). Randall Hse.
Crowson, Milton, jt. auth. see Fry, Malcolm C.
Crowson, P. C. & Richards, B. A. Economics for Managers. 2nd ed. (Illus.). 248p. 1978. pap. 19.95x (ISBN 0-7131-3397-X). Intl Ideas.
Crowson, P. S. Tudor Foreign Policy. LC 73-81733. 288p. 1973. 25.00 (ISBN 0-312-82285-5). St Martin.
Crowson, Paul. Animals in Focus: The Business Life of a Natural History Film Unit. (Illus.). 160p. 1981. 19.75 (ISBN 0-904573-34-6); pap. 9.95 (ISBN 0-904573-59-1). Caliban Bks.
Crowson, Phillip. Minerals Handbook: 1982-83. 144p. text ed. 32.95 (ISBN 0-442-21504-5). Van Nos Reinhold.
--Minerals Handbook: 1984-85. (Illus.). 304p. 1985. 49.95x (ISBN 0-87201-566-1). Gulf Pub.
Crowson, R. A., ed. The Biology of Coleoptera. LC 77-71815. 1981. 139.50 (ISBN 0-12-196050-1). Acad Pr.
Crowther, Arnold & Crowther, Patricia. The Secrets of Ancient Witchcraft. Bd. with The Witches Tarot. 1974. 7.95 (ISBN 0-8216-0221-7). Univ Bks.
Crowther, Betty, jt. auth. see Bates, William.
Crowther, Bosley. The Lion's Share: The Story of an Entertainment Empire. LC 82-49221. (Cinema Classics Ser.). 325p. 1984. lib. bdg. 38.00 (ISBN 0-8240-5756-2). Garland Pub.
Crowther, Bruce. Robert Mitchum. (Illus.). 128p. 1984. 18.95 (ISBN 0-86276-059-3); pap. 11.95 (ISBN 0-86276-058-5). Proteus Pub NY.
--Robert Redford. (Film Stars Ser.). (Illus.). 96p. 1985. 8.95 (ISBN 0-87052-119-5). Hippocrene Bks.
Crowther, Don K. Programming for Profit: How to Write & Sell Computer Programs. 272p. 1984. pap. text ed. 14.95 (ISBN 0-88190-342-6). Datamost.
Crowther, Duane S. Atlas & Outline of the Acts of the Apostles. LC 83-80528. 1983. pap. 6.95 (ISBN 0-88290-219-9). Horizon-Utah.
--Atlas & Outline of the Life of Christ. LC 83-82414. 120p. (Orig.). 1983. pap. 6.95 (ISBN 0-88290-207-5). Horizon Utah.
--Come unto Christ. LC 70-173393. (Scripture Guide Ser.). 1971. pap. 5.95 (ISBN 0-88290-007-2). Horizon Utah.
--Family Ancestral Record: Adult Genealogy Starter Kit. LC 78-52113. 1978. 5.50 (ISBN 0-88290-088-9). Horizon Utah.
--Gifts of the Spirit. LC 65-29176. 352p. 1983. 8.95 (ISBN 0-88290-210-5). Horizon Utah.
--God & His Church. LC 76-173392. (Scripture Guide Ser.). 1971. pap. 5.95 (ISBN 0-88290-006-4). Horizon Utah.
--A Guide to Effective Scripture Study. LC 75-5321. (Scripture Guide Ser). 1975. pap. 4.95 (ISBN 0-88290-004-8). Horizon Utah.
--My Family Heritage: Youth Genealogy Starter Kit. LC 78-52120. 1981. 5.95 (ISBN 0-88290-087-0). Horizon Utah.
--The Patriarchs & the Law. LC 81-8055. 400p. 1981. write for info. (ISBN 0-88290-178-8, 1056). Horizon Utah.
--The Plan of Salvation & the Future in Prophecy. LC 72-173391. (Scripture Guide Ser.). 1971. pap. 5.95 (ISBN 0-88290-005-6). Horizon Utah.
--The Prophecies of Joseph Smith. LC 83-80664. 413p. 1873. 9.95 (ISBN 0-88290-221-0). Horizon-Utah.
--Prophetic Warnings to Modern America. LC 77-87431. 415p. 1977. 10.95 (ISBN 0-88290-016-1). Horizon Utah.
--Prophets & Prophecies of the Old Testament. 2nd ed. LC 66-25508. (Comprehensive Bible Ser.). (Illus.). 644p. 1973. Repr. of 1967 ed. 10.95 (ISBN 0-88290-022-6). Horizon Utah.
--Reading Guide to the Book of Mormon: A Simplified Program Featuring Brief Outlines & Doctrinal Summaries. LC 75-5322. 1975. 7.50 (ISBN 0-88290-045-5). Horizon Utah.
--Teaching Choral Concepts: Simple Lesson Plans & Teaching Aids for in -Rehearsal Choir Instruction. LC 79-89356. (Illus.). 1979. 18.95 (ISBN 0-88290-119-2). Horizon Utah.
--This Is My Life: Personal History Guide. LC 78-52406. 1979. 5.95 (ISBN 0-88290-089-7). Horizon Utah.
--La Vida Sempiterna. DeHoyos, R., tr. from Eng. LC 81-80953. 390p. (Span.). 1982. pap. 8.95 (ISBN 0-88290-185-0, 4802). Horizon Utah.
Crowther, Duane S. & Crowther, Jean D., eds. The Joy of Being a Woman: Guidance for Meaningful Living by Outstanding LDS Women. LC 72-88910. 1972. 8.95 (ISBN 0-88290-015-3). Horizon Utah.
Crowther, Geoff. Korea-a Travel Survival Kit. (Lonely Planet Travel Ser.). (Illus.). 160p. (Orig.). 1983. pap. 6.95 (ISBN 0-88254-673-2, Pub. by Lonely Planet Australia). Hippocrene Bks.

Crowther, Geoff & Wheeler, Tony. Malaysia, Singapore & Brunei. (Lonely Planet Travel Ser.). (Illus.). 200p. (Orig.). 1982. pap. 7.95 (ISBN 0-908086-31-8, Pub. by Lonely Planet Australia). Hippocrene Bks.

Crowther, Geoffrey, jt. auth. see Layton, Walter T.

Crowther, Greg. Africa on a Shoestring. 2nd ed. (Travel Paperbacks Ser.). 368p. 1983. pap. 12.95 (ISBN 0-908086-19-9, Pub. by Lonely Planet Australia). Hippocrene Bks.

Crowther, J. R., jt. auth. see Wardley, R. C.

Crowther, James G. Famous American Men of Science. facs. ed. LC 69-18925. (Essay Index Reprint Ser). 1937. 27.50 (ISBN 0-8369-0040-5). Ayer Co Pubs.

--Founders of British Science: John Wilkins, Robert Boyle, John Ray, Christopher Wren, Robert Hooke, Isaac Newton. LC 82-2954. (Illus.). xii, 296p. 1982. Repr. of 1960 ed. lib. bdg. 42.50x (ISBN 0-313-23540-6, CRFO). GreenWood.

Crowther, Jean D. Book of Mormon Puzzles & Pictures for Young Latter-Day Saints. LC 77-74495. (Books for LDS Children). (Illus.). (gr. 3 up). 1977. pap. 4.95 (ISBN 0-88290-080-3). Horizon Utah.

--Growing Up in the Church: Gospel Principles & Practices for Children. rev. ed. LC 67-25433. (Illus.). 84p. (gr. 2-6). 1973. Repr. of 1965 ed. 5.95 (ISBN 0-88290-024-2). Horizon Utah.

--A Mother's Prayer. 1978. pap. 0.95 (ISBN 0-88290-099-4). Horizon Utah.

--Pedigree Patterns. 24p. (Orig.). 1981. pap. 4.95 (ISBN 0-88290-195-8, 2880). Horizon Utah.

--What Do I Do Now, Mom? LC 80-82257. (Illus.). 86p. (gr. 9-12). 1980. 6.95 (ISBN 0-88290-134-6). Horizon Utah.

Crowther, Jean D., jt. ed. see Crowther, Duane S.

Crowther, Jonathan. Advanced Crosswords, for Learners of English as a Foreign Language. (Orig.). 1981. pap. 3.25x (ISBN 0-19-581752-4). Oxford U Pr.

--Elementary Crosswords. (Illus.). 1981. pap. 3.25x (ISBN 0-19-581750-8). Oxford U Pr.

--Intermediate Crosswords, for Learners of English as a Foreign Language. 1980. pap. 3.25x (ISBN 0-19-581751-6). Oxford U Pr.

--Introductory Crosswords. (Illus.). 1981. pap. text ed. 3.25x (ISBN 0-19-581749-4). Oxford U Pr.

Crowther, M. A. Church Embattled: Religious Controversey in Mid-Victorian England. (Library of Politics & Society Ser.). 272p. 1970. 19.50 (ISBN 0-208-01091-2, Archon). Shoe String.

Crowther, M A. The Workhouse System, 1834-1929: The History of an English Social Institution. LC 81-11581. 300p. 1982. 26.00x (ISBN 0-8203-0594-4). U of Ga Pr.

Crowther, Patricia. Lid off the Cauldron. LC 84-52290. (Illus.). 166p. (Orig.). 1985. pap. 6.95 (ISBN 0-87728-629-9). Weiser.

Crowther, Patricia, jt. auth. see Crowther, Arnold.

Crowther, Patricia P., et al. The Grand Kentucky Junction: Memoirs. Watson, Richard A. & Brucker, Roger W., eds. LC 83-26170. 96p. (Orig.). 1984. pap. 10.00x (ISBN 0-939748-08-8). Cave Bks MO.

Crowther, Richard L. Affordable Passive Solar Homes. 188p. 1983. 24.00x (ISBN 0-89553-129-1). Am Solar Energy.

--Affordable Passive Solar Homes. LC 84-5404. (Illus.). 192p. (Orig.). 1984. pap. 24.00 (ISBN 0-916653-00-5, 65300). Sci Tech.

Crowther, Robert. Jungle Jumble. (Illus.). 32p. (ps-1). 1983. 5.95 (ISBN 0-670-41076-4). Viking.

--The Most Amazing Hide-&-Seek Alphabet Book. LC 77-79334. (Illus.). (ps-1). 1978. 11.95 (ISBN 0-670-48996-4, Co-Pub by Kestrel Bks). Viking.

--The Most Amazing Hide & Seek Counting Book. (Illus.). 14p. 1981. 11.95 (ISBN 0-670-48997-2). Viking.

--Most Amazing Hide & Seek: Opposites. LC 85-42757. 12p. (ps-3). 1985. 11.95 (ISBN 0-670-80121-6). Viking.

Crowther, Rodney G. Surname Index to Sixty-Five Volumes of Colonial & Revolutionary Pedigrees. 143p. 17.25 (ISBN 0-915156-27-X). Natl Genealogical.

Crowther, S. J. & Fawcett, Marion. Science & Medicine to Eighteen-Seventy: Pamphlets in the Library. 200p. 1968. 2.00 (ISBN 0-317-33133-7, NO.1). Am Philos.

Crowther, Samuel. Journal of an Expedition Up the Niger & Tshadda Rivers Undertaken by MacGregor Laird..in 1854. 248p. 1970. Repr. of 1855 ed. 37.50x (ISBN 0-7146-1866-7, F Cass Co). Biblio Dist.

--The Romance & Rise of the American Tropics. Bruchey, Stuart & Bruchey, Eleanor, eds. LC 76-4999. (American Business Abroad Ser.). (Illus.). 1976. Repr. of 1929 ed. lib. bdg. 43.00 (ISBN 0-405-09268-7). Ayer Co Pubs.

Crowther, Samuel, jt. auth. see Ford, Henry.

Crowther, Samuel, jt. auth. see Schon, James F.

Crowther-Hunt, Norman. Two Early Political Associations: The Quakers & the Dissenting Deputies in the Age of Sir Robert Walpole. LC 78-23805. 1979. Repr. of 1961 ed. lib. bdg. 24.75x (ISBN 0-313-21036-5, HUTW). Greenwood.

Croxall, Harold E. & Smith, Lionel P. The Fight for Food: Factors Limiting Agricultural Production. 232p. 1984. text ed. 25.00 (ISBN 0-04-630011-2); pap. text ed. 7.95 (ISBN 0-04-630012-0). Allen Unwin.

Croxford, Leslie. Solomon's Folly. LC 75-1458. 1978. 8.95 (ISBN 0-8149-0763-6). Vanguard.

--Solomon's Folly. LC 83-9199. (Phoenix Fiction Ser.). 208p. 1984. pap. 6.95 (ISBN 0-226-12149-6). U of Chicago Pr.

Croxton, Anthony H. Railways of Zimbabwe. (Illus.). 316p. 1982. 22.50 (ISBN 0-7153-8130-X). David & Charles.

Croxton, Clive A. Russian for the Scientist & Mathematician. LC 83-10209. 210p. 1984. 34.95x (ISBN 0-471-90260-8, Pub. by Wiley-Interscience). Wiley.

--Statistical Mechanics of the Liquid Surface. LC 79-40819. 345p. 1980. 89.95 (ISBN 0-471-27663-4, Pub. by Wiley-Interscience). Wiley.

Croxton, Frederick E. Elementary Statistics: With Applications in Medicine & the Biological Sciences. (Illus.). 1953. pap. 6.95 (ISBN 0-486-60506-X). Dover.

Croxton, P. C., et al. Structures & Materials: A Programmed Approach. (Illus.). 300p. 1974. text ed. 18.50x (ISBN 0-8464-0890-2). Beekman Pubs.

Croy, D. E. & Dougherty, D. A. Handbook of Thermal Insulation Applications. LC 83-22118. (Energy Technology Review Ser.: No.89). (Illus.). 392p. 1984. 45.00 (ISBN 0-8155-0968-5). Noyes.

Croy, Genevieve, pseud. Corporations, l'Industrie et le Commerce a Chartres du Onzieme Siecle a la Revolution. LC 68-56768. (Research & Source Works Ser: No. 253). (Illus., Fr). 1968. Repr. of 1917 ed. 32.50 (ISBN 0-8337-0004-9). B Franklin.

Croy, Homer. How Motion Pictures Are Made. Jowett, Garth S., ed. LC 77-11373. (Aspects of Film Ser.). (Illus.). 1978. Repr. of 1918 ed. lib. bdg. 23.50x (ISBN 0-405-11129-0). Ayer Co Pubs.

Croydon, E. A. P. & Michel, M. F., eds. Augmentin. (Current Clinical Practice Ser.: Vol. 4). 366p. 1983. 110.75 (ISBN 0-444-90321-6, I-242-83). Elsevier.

Croydon, Michael, compiled by see Jeong, Tung Hon.

Croydon, W. F. & Parker, E. H. Dielectric Films on Gallium Arsenide, Vol.1. (Electrocomponent Science Monographs). 160p. 1981. 23.00 (ISBN 0-677-05710-5). Gordon.

Crozel, H. Bibliographie Critique d'Origene: Supplement, No. I. 1983. 73.00 (ISBN 90-247-2704-9, Pub. by Martinus Nijhoff Netherlands). Kluwer Academic.

Crozet, Felix. Revue de la Musique Dramatique en France. Bd. with Supplement a la Revue de la Musique Dramatique en France. LC 80-2270. 1981. Repr. of 1866 ed. 48.50 (ISBN 0-404-18833-8). AMS Pr.

Crozier. Portrait of Robin Crozier. pap. 4.50x (ISBN 0-89955-358-3, Pub. by Ceolfrith Pr England). Intl Spec Bk.

Crozier, Alan. Biochemistry & Physiology of Gibberellins, 2 vols. LC 83-13862. 576p. 1983. Vol. 1. 62.50 (ISBN 0-03-059054-X); Vol. 2. 59.50x (ISBN 0-03-059056-6). Praeger.

Crozier, Alan & Hillman, John R., eds. The Biosynthesis & Metabolism of Plant Hormones. (Society for Experimental Biology Seminar Ser.: No. 23). 300p. 1985. 29.95 (ISBN 0-521-26424-3). Cambridge U Pr.

Crozier, Alice. Novels of Harriet Beecher Stowe. LC 73-83010. 1969. Repr. of 1896 ed. 22.50x (ISBN 0-19-500521-X). Oxford U Pr.

Crozier, Andrew. All Where Each Is. 320p. (Orig.). 1985. 26.00 (ISBN 0-907954-02-2, Pub. by Allardyce & Barnett). Small Pr Dist.

--All Where Each Is. (Agneau 2 Paperbook Ser.: 2). 320p. (Orig.). 1985. pap. 15.00 (ISBN 0-907954-03-0, Pub. by Allardyce & Barnett). Small Pr Dist.

--High Zero. (Orig.). 1978. pap. 4.00 (ISBN 0-685-99427-9, Pub. by St Edns). Small Pr Dist.

Crozier, Brian. The Minimum State: Beyond Party Politics. 1979. 27.00 (ISBN 0-241-10242-1, Pub. by Hamish Hamilton England). David & Charles.

--Struggle for the Third World. LC 66-18563. 1966. 7.95 (ISBN 0-8023-1035-4). Dufour.

Crozier, Brian, ed. Annual of Power & Conflict, 1978-79. 8th ed. LC 77-370326. 502p. 1979. 40.00x (ISBN 0-8002-2220-2). Intl Pubns Serv.

--Annual of Power & Conflict, 1979-80: A Survey of Political Violence & International Influence. 9th ed. LC 77-370326. 510p. 1980. 65.00x (ISBN 0-8002-2671-2). Intl Pubns Serv.

Crozier, Brian, ed. see Gladwyn, Hubert M.

Crozier, Brian, et al. This War Called Peace. LC 84-24137. 315p. 1985. 17.95 (ISBN 0-87663-463-3). Universe.

Crozier, Emmet. American Reporters on the Western Front, 1914 to 1918. LC 80-19400. (Illus.). xii, 299p. 1980. Repr. of 1959 ed. lib. bdg. 32.50x (ISBN 0-313-22655-5, CRAR). Greenwood.

Crozier, Michel. Bureaucratic Phenomenon. LC 63-20916. 1967. pap. 10.00x (ISBN 0-226-12166-6, P280, Phoen). U of Chicago Pr.

--A Strategies for Change: The Future of French Society. Beer, William, tr. from Fr. (Organization Studies). 1982. 24.75x (ISBN 0-262-03082-9). MIT Pr.

--The Trouble with America. Heinegg, Peter, tr. from Fr. LC 84-2549. 200p. 1984. 19.95 (ISBN 0-520-04978-0). U of Cal Pr.

--World of the Office Worker. Landau, David, tr. from Fr. LC 76-141150. (Studies in Urban Society Ser.). 1971. 22.00x (ISBN 0-226-12167-4). U of Chicago Pr.

Crozier, Michel & Friedberg, Erhard. Actors & Systems: The Politics of Collective Action. Goldhammer, Arthur, tr. LC 80-13803. 272p. 1980. lib. bdg. 30.00x (ISBN 0-226-12183-6). U of Chicago Pr.

Crozier, Michel, et al. The Crisis of Democracy: Report on the Governability of Democracies to the Trilateral Commission. LC 75-27167. 1975. pap. 10.00x (ISBN 0-8147-1365-3). NYU Pr.

--The Crisis of Democracy. 1975. 15.00 (ISBN 0-318-02780-1); pap. 4.95 (ISBN 0-318-02781-X). Trilateral Comm.

Crozier, Patrick. Electronic Instruments & Measurements. 383p. 1985. text ed. 24.00 (ISBN 0-534-04311-9). Breton Pubs.

--Introduction to Electronics. 1983. write for info. (ISBN 0-686-92674-9, Breton Pubs). Wadsworth Pub.

Crozier, Robin & Bennett, John M. Meat Click. 1980. 2.00 (ISBN 0-935350-02-0). Luna Bisonte.

Crozier, Ruth, jt. ed. see Lepow, Irwin H.

Crozier, S. Neal. Archaeological Excavations at Kamehameha III Road, North Kona, Island of Hawaii-Phase II. (Departmental Report: No. 71-5). 30p. 1981. pap. 2.00 (ISBN 0-910240-78-7). Bishop Mus.

Crozier, S. Neal, jt. auth. see Kelly, Marion.

Crozier, W. R. & Chapman, A. J., eds. Cognitive Processes in the Perception of Art. (Advances in Psychology Ser.: Vol. 19). 448p. 1984. 52.00 (ISBN 0-444-87501-8, I-239-84). Elsevier.

Crozier, William A. Virginia County Records, 6 vols. Incl. Vol. 1. Spotsylvania County, 1721-1800. 576p. 1978. Repr. of 1905 ed. 25.00 (ISBN 0-8063-0468-5); Vol. 2. Virginia Colonial Militia, 1651-1776. 144p. 1982. Repr. of 1905 ed. 12.50 (ISBN 0-8063-0084-1); Vol. 3. Williamsburg Wills. 77p. 1973. Repr. of 1906 ed. 9.50 (ISBN 0-8063-0086-8); Vol. 4. Early Virginia Marriages. 155p. 1982. Repr. of 1907 ed. 12.50 (ISBN 0-8063-0568-1); Vol. 5. Virginia Heraldica. 116p. 1978. Repr. of 1908 ed. 12.50 (ISBN 0-8063-0085-X); Vol. 6. Miscellaneous County Records. 1971. Repr. of 1909 ed. 15.00 (ISBN 0-8063-0469-3); Vol. 7. Miscellaneous County Records. 1971. Repr. of 1910 ed. 12.50 (ISBN 0-8063-0470-7); Vol. 8. A Key to Southern Pedigrees. 80p. 1978. Repr. of 1911 ed. 9.50 (ISBN 0-8063-0471-5); Vol. 9. Miscellaneous County Records. 1971. Repr. of 1911 ed. 10.00 (ISBN 0-8063-0472-3); Vol. 10. Miscellaneous County Records. 95p. 1971. Repr. of 1912 ed. 12.00 (ISBN 0-8063-0473-1); New Ser., Vol. 1. Westmoreland County. 1971. Repr. of 1913 ed. 10.00 (ISBN 0-8063-0474-X). LC 67-29835. Genealog Pub.

Crozier, William A., ed. see Virginia County Records.

Crozy, Alan, tr. see Mishustin, E. N. & Shil'nikova, V. K.

Crss, Wilbur. Kids & Booze: What You Must Know to Help Them. 180p. 1979. 0.95 (ISBN 0-318-15337-8); pap. 4.95 (ISBN 0-318-15338-6). Natl Coun Alcoholism.

Cru, R. Loyalty. Diderot As a Disciple of English Thought. LC 13-16145. (Columbia University. Studies in Romance Philology & Literature: No. 13). Repr. of 1925 ed. 33.75 (ISBN 0-404-50613-5). AMS Pr.

Cruce, Emeric. New Cyneas. LC 75-147415. (Library of War & Peace; Proposals for Peace: a History). lib. bdg. 46.00 (ISBN 0-8240-0213-X). Garland Pub.

Cruden, Alexander. Cruden's Compact Concordance. 1968. 9.95 (ISBN 0-310-22910-3). Zondervan.

--Cruden's Complete Concordance. 1949. 13.95 (ISBN 0-310-22920-0). Zondervan.

--Cruden's Complete Concordance. 1976. pap. 8.95 (ISBN 0-310-22921-9). Zondervan.

--Cruden's Concordance. 1982. pap. 3.95 (ISBN 0-515-06741-5). Jove Pubns.

--Cruden's Concordance. 1872. 15.00 (ISBN 0-7232-0260-5). Warne.

--Cruden's Concordance. Eadie, ed. 1982. pap. 7.95 (ISBN 0-89081-362-0). Harvest Hse.

--Cruden's Concordance: Handy Reference Edition. (Baker's Paperback Reference Library). 344p. 1982. pap. 6.95 (ISBN 0-8010-2478-1). Baker Bk.

--Cruden's Concordance to the Old & New Testaments. unabridged ed. 720p. 17.95 (ISBN 0-8007-0058-9); pap. 3.95 (ISBN 0-8007-8055-8, Spire Bks). Revell.

--Cruden's Handy Concordance. pap. 2.95 (ISBN 0-310-22931-6). Zondervan.

--Cruden's Pocket Dictionary of Bible Terms. (Direction Bks). 1976. pap. 6.95 (ISBN 0-8010-2380-7). Baker Bk.

--Cruden's Unabridged Concordance. 17.95 (ISBN 0-8010-2316-5). Baker Bk.

--Cruden's Unabridged Concordance. LC 54-11084. 17.95 (ISBN 0-8054-1123-2). Broadman.

Cruden, Robert. James Ford Rhodes: The Man, the Historian & His Work. LC 79-28196. xiii, 290p. 1980. Repr. of 1961 ed. lib. bdg. 32.50x (ISBN 0-313-22255-X, CRJF). Greenwood.

--Many & One: A Social History of the United States. (Illus.). 1980. text ed. 24.95 (ISBN 0-13-555714-3). P-H.

Cruden, Stewart. Scottish Mediaeval Churches. 400p. 1985. text ed. 57.00x (ISBN 0-85976-104-5, Pub. by John Donald Scotland). Humanities.

Crudi & Larkin. Core Curriculum for Intravenous Nursing. 1984. 24.95 (ISBN 0-397-54516-9, Lippincott Nursing). Lippincott.

Crue, Benjamin L., Jr. Pain & Suffering: Selected Aspects. (Illus.). 224p. 1970. photocopy ed. 19.75x (ISBN 0-398-00374-2). C C Thomas.

Crue, Benjamin L., Jr., ed. Pain: Research & Treatment. (City of Hope Symposium Ser.). 1975. 70.00 (ISBN 0-12-198950-X). Acad Pr.

Crueger, Anneliese, jt. auth. see Crueger, Wulf.

Crueger, Wulf & Crueger, Anneliese. Biotechnology: A Textbook of Industrial Microbiology. Science Tech Inc., tr. from Ger. LC 84-1340. (Illus.). 350p. 1984. text ed. 30.00x (ISBN 0-87893-126-0). Sinauer Assoc.

Cruess, Alan, jt. auth. see Schachat, Andrew.

Cruess, Richard L., ed. Musculoskeletal System: Embryology, Biochemistry & Physiology. (Illus.). 424p. 1982. 75.00 (ISBN 0-443-08108-5). Churchill.

Cruess, Richard L. & Mitchell, Nelson S., eds. Surgical Management of Degenerative Arthritis of the Lower Limb. LC 75-20440. (Illus.). Repr. of 1975 ed. 62.00 (ISBN 0-8357-9421-0, 2014539). Bks Demand UMI.

Cruess, Richard L. & Rennie, William R., eds. Adult Orthopaedics, 2 vols. (Illus.). 1566p. 1984. text ed. 149.00 (ISBN 0-443-08107-7). Churchill.

Cruetz, W. New Light on the Protocols of Zion. 1982. lib. bdg. 69.95 (ISBN 0-87700-366-1). Revisionist Pr.

Crugnola, Aldo M., jt. ed. see Deanin, Rudolph D.

Cruickshank, A. A., jt. auth. see Kubalkova, V.

Cruickshank, A. B., ed. Where Town Meets Country: Problems of Peri-Urban Areas of Scotland, Royal Scottish Geographical Society Symposium May 1981. (Illus.). 140p. 1982. 17.00 (ISBN 0-08-028442-6, R130); 11.75 (ISBN 0-08-028443-4, R145). Pergamon.

Cruickshank, A. H. Ben Jonson. LC 74-3255. 1912. lib. bdg. 8.50 (ISBN 0-8414-3608-8). Folcroft.

Cruickshank, Albert, jt. auth. see Kubalkova, Vendulka.

Cruickshank, Allan D. Cruickshank's Photographs of Birds of America. LC 77-70078. (Illus.). 1977. pap. 7.95 (ISBN 0-486-23497-5). Dover.

--Cruikshank's Photographs of Birds of America. (Illus.). 16.50 (ISBN 0-8446-5567-8). Peter Smith.

Cruickshank, Allan D. & Cruickshank, Helen. One Thousand & One Questions Answered About Birds. LC 75-41881. (The One Thousand & One Questions Ser.). (Illus.). 320p. 1976. pap. 4.95 (ISBN 0-486-23315-4). Dover.

Cruickshank, Allan D. & Cruickshank, Helen G. One-Thousand One Questions Answered About Birds. 14.50 (ISBN 0-8446-5483-3). Peter Smith.

Cruickshank, Bruce. Eighteen Years on the Gold Coast of Africa, 2 vols. 1966. Repr. of 1853 ed. 75.00x set (ISBN 0-7146-1802-0, BHA-01802, F Cass Co). Biblio Dist.

Cruickshank, Charles. Deception in World War II. (Illus.). 1979. 19.95x (ISBN 0-19-215849-X). Oxford U Pr.

--Greece, Nineteen Forty to Nineteen Forty-One. Frankland, Noble & Dowling, Christopher, eds. LC 79-52239. (The Politics & Strategy of the Second World War). 206p. 1979. 18.50 (ISBN 0-87413-159-6). U Delaware Pr.

--SOE in the Far East. (Illus.). 1984. 25.00 (ISBN 0-19-215873-2). Oxford U Pr.

Cruickshank, Don, ed. see Wilson, Edward M.

Cruickshank, Don W., jt. auth. see Wilson, Edward M.

Cruickshank, Donald R. Models for the Preparation of America's Teachers. LC 84-6216. 132p. 1985. pap. text ed. 3.50 (ISBN 0-87367-430-8). Phi Delta Kappa.

Cruickshank, Douglas & Messinger, Evelyn. The Cosmic Klondike: Being a Layman's Guide for the Gaining of Access to the National & International Telecommunications Satellite Systems. 350p. 1986. 18.95 (ISBN 0-917320-02-6); pap. 12.95 (ISBN 0-917320-03-4). Mho & Mho.

Cruickshank, Helen, jt. auth. see Cruickshank, Allan D.

Cruickshank, Helen G., jt. auth. see Cruickshank, Allan D.

Cruickshank, Helen G., ed. John & William Bartram's America. (American Naturalists Ser.). (Illus.). 14.95 (ISBN 0-8159-5101-9). Devin.

Cruickshank, J. M., et al, eds. Atenolol & Renal Function. (Royal Society of Medicine International Congress & Symposium Ser.: No. 19). 112p. 1980. pap. 20.50 (ISBN 0-8089-1237-2, 790952). Grune.

Cruickshank, James. Soil Geography. (Illus.). 265p. pap. 8.95 (ISBN 0-7153-5847-2). David & Charles.

Cruickshank, John. Albert Camus & the Literature of Revolt. LC 78-16380. 1978. Repr. of 1959 ed. lib. bdg. 42.50 (ISBN 0-313-20580-9, CRAC). Greenwood.

--Aspects of the Modern European Mind. LC 75-422041. (Problems & Perspectives in History Ser.). pap. 53.00 (ISBN 0-317-08919-6, 2006381). Bks Demand UMI.

--Variations on Catastrophe: Some French Responses to the Great War. 1982. 34.95x (ISBN 0-19-212599-0). Oxford U Pr.

Cruickshank, John, ed. The Novelist As Philosopher: Studies in French Fiction, Nineteen Thirty-Five to Nineteen Sixty. LC 77-28882. 257p. 1978. Repr. of 1962 ed. lib. bdg. 24.75x (ISBN 0-313-20271-0, CRNP). Greenwood.

Cruickshank, Marjorie. Children & Industry. 189p. 1981. text ed. 15.50x (ISBN 0-7190-0809-3, Pub. by Manchester England). Humanities.

Cruickshank, R., et al. Role of Immunization in Communicable Disease Control. (Public Health Papers Ser: No. 8). 118p. (Eng, Fr, Rus, & Span.). 1961. pap. 2.00 (ISBN 92-4-130008-6). World Health.

Cruickshank, William. A Teaching Method for Brain-Injured & Hyperactive Children: A Demonstration-Pilot Study. LC 81-6255. (Syracuse University Special Education & Rehabilitation Monograph: No. 6). (Illus.). xxi, 576p. 1981. Repr. of 1961 ed. lib. bdg. 45.00x (ISBN 0-313-23071-4, CRTC). Greenwood.

Cruickshank, William M. Concepts in Learning Disabilities: Selected Writings, Vol. 2. LC 80-29024. 296p. 1981. text ed. 20.00x (ISBN 0-8156-2239-2). Syracuse U Pr.

--Concepts in Special Education: Selected Writings, Vol. 1. LC 80-29024. 392p. 1981. text ed. 25.00x (ISBN 0-8156-2238-4). Syracuse U Pr.

Cruickshank, William M., ed. Approaches to Learning: The Best of ACLD, Vol. 1. (Illus.). 240p. 1980. pap. 11.95x (ISBN 0-8156-2203-1). Syracuse U Pr.

--Cerebral Palsy: A Developmental Disability. rev. 3rd ed. LC 75-34275. 1976. text ed. 26.00x (ISBN 0-8156-2168-X). Syracuse U Pr.

--Learning Disabilities in Home, School, & Community. 1979. pap. 8.95x (ISBN 0-8156-2208-2). Syracuse U Pr.

--Teacher of Brain Injured Children: A Discussion of the Bases for Competency. LC 66-20050. (Special Education & Rehabilitation Monograph: No. 7). 1966. 10.95x (ISBN 0-8156-2096-9). Syracuse U Pr.

Cruickshank, William M. & Hallahan, Daniel P., eds. Perceptual & Learning Disabilities in Children. Incl. Vol. 1. Psychoeducational Practices. LC 74-24303. 496p. 28.00x (ISBN 0-8156-2165-5); Vol. 2. Research & Theory. LC 74-24303. 498p. 32.00x (ISBN 0-8156-2166-3). (Illus.). 1975. Syracuse U Pr.

Cruickshank, William M. & Kliebhan, Joanne M., eds. Early Adolescence to Early Adulthood: The Best of ALCD, Vol. 5. LC 83-17968. (The Best of ACLD Ser.). (Illus.). 208p. 1983. pap. text ed. 12.95x (ISBN 0-8156-2301-1). Syracuse U Pr.

Cruickshank, William M. & Lerner, Janet, eds. Coming of Age: Vol. 3: The Best of ACLD. LC 81-21404. 1982. pap. 12.95x (ISBN 0-8156-2258-9). Syracuse U Pr.

Cruickshank, William M. & Silver, Archie A., eds. Bridges to Tomorrow: The Best of ACLD, Vol. 2. 1981. pap. 11.95x (ISBN 0-8156-2237-6). Syracuse U Pr.

Cruickshank, William M. & Tash, Eli, eds. Academics & Beyond: The Best of ACLD, Vol. 4. (The Best of ACLD Ser.). 256p. pap. text ed. 13.95X (ISBN 0-8156-2272-4). Syracuse U Pr.

Cruickshank, William M., et al. Misfits in the Public Schools. LC 69-13137. 1969. 10.00x (ISBN 0-8156-2130-2). Syracuse U Pr.

--Preparation of Teachers of Brain-Injured Children. LC 68-31430. (Special Education & Rehabilitation Monograph: No. 8). (Illus.). 1968. 8.00x (ISBN 0-8156-2123-X). Syracuse U Pr.

--Learning Disabilities: The Struggle from Adolescence Toward Adulthood. (Illus.). 304p. 1980. pap. 9.95x (ISBN 0-8156-2221-X). Syracuse U Pr.

Cruickshanks, Eveline. Political Untouchables: The Tories & the '45. LC 79-10340. (Illus.). 166p. 1979. text ed. 32.50x (ISBN 0-8419-0511-8). Holmes & Meier.

Cruickshanks, Eveline, ed. Ideology & Conspiracy: Aspects of Jacobitism 1689-1759. 231p. 1982. text ed. 32.00x (ISBN 0-85976-084-7, 40740, Pub. by John Donald Scotland). Humanities.

--Parliamentary History: A Yearbook, 3 vols. 1984. Vol. 1, 281 p. 22.50 (ISBN 0-312-59720-7); Vol. 2, 256 p. 22.50 (ISBN 0-312-59721-5); Vol. 3, 252 p. 22.50 (ISBN 0-312-59722-3). St Martin.

Cruikshank, Dale P., jt. ed. see Chapman, Clark R.

Cruikshank, Donald R., ed. Teaching Is Tough. (Applied Education Ser.). (Illus.). 368p. 1980. text ed. 14.95 (ISBN 0-13-893495-9, Spec); pap. 6.95 (ISBN 0-13-893487-8). P-H.

Cruikshank, Eleanor P. French-English Instant Vocabulary. 88p. (Fr. & Eng.). 1980. pap. 4.00 (ISBN 0-9605284-0-7). Cruikshank.

Cruikshank, Ernest A., ed. Documentary History of the Campaign Upon the Niagara Frontier, 1812-1814, 4 Vols. LC 74-146387. (First American Frontier Ser). (Illus.). 1971. Repr. of 1909 ed. 170.00 (ISBN 0-405-02838-5). Ayer Co Pubs.

--Documents Relating to the Invasion of Canada & the Surrender of Detroit, 1812. LC 70-146386. (First American Frontier Ser). (Illus.). 1971. Repr. of 1912 ed. 18.00 (ISBN 0-405-02837-7). Ayer Co Pubs.

Cruikshank, George. Cruikshank Prints for Hand Coloring. pap. 6.95 (ISBN 0-486-23684-6). Dover.

--Graphic Works of George Cruikshank. Vogler, Richard A., ed. (Pictorial Archive Ser.). (Illus.). 1980. pap. 7.95 (ISBN 0-486-23438-X). Dover.

--Graphic Works of George Cruikshank. 19.00 (ISBN 0-8446-5747-6). Peter Smith.

--The Tragical Comedy or Comical Tragedy of Punch & Judy. (Illus.). 1976. pap. 2.25 (ISBN 0-7100-8199-5). Routledge & Kegan.

Cruikshank, George, illus. Punch & Judy. LC 70-174866. Repr. of 1929 ed. 17.00 (ISBN 0-405-09123-0, Blom Pubns). Ayer Co Pubs.

Cruikshank, Margaret. The Lesbian Path. 1980. pap. 6.95 (ISBN 0-912216-20-4). Angel Pr.

--New Lesbian Writing. LC 83-22603. 220p. 1984. pap. 7.95 (ISBN 0-912516-81-X). Grey Fox.

Cruikshank, Margaret, ed. Lesbian Studies: Present & Future. 286p. pap. 9.95 (ISBN 0-935312-07-2). Feminist Pr.

Cruikshank, Margaret L., ed. The Lesbian Path. rev. ed. LC 85-12519. 200p. 1985. pap. 8.95 (ISBN 0-912516-96-8). Grey Fox.

Cruikshank, R. J. Charles Dickens & Early Victorian England. 1949. 40.00 (ISBN 0-8274-2035-8). R West.

Cruikshank, Robert J. The Humour of Dickens. LC 75-33282. 1975. lib. bdg. 12.50 (ISBN 0-8414-3477-8). Folcroft.

Cruikshank, W. Psychology of Exceptional Children & Youth. 4th ed. 1980. 33.95 (ISBN 0-13-733808-2). P-H.

Cruikshank, Warren L., jt. auth. see Burke, John D.

Cruise, et al. A Resource Guide for Introductory Statistics. 356p. 1984. pap. text ed. 24.95 (ISBN 0-8403-3361-7). Kendall-Hunt.

Cruise, Ben, compiled by. My Book of Poems. (Little Golden Book Special Editions). (Illus.). 32p. (ps-2). 1985. 4.95 (ISBN 0-307-11634-4, 11634, Pub. by Golden Bks). Western Pub.

Cruise, Boyd. Boyd Cruise. LC 76-24712. (Illus.). 72p. 1976. 20.00x (ISBN 0-917860-01-2). Historic New Orleans.

--Index to the Louisiana Historical Quarterly, Vol. 1-33. 1956. slip case 50.00 (ISBN 0-911116-05-2). Pelican.

Cruise, Boyd & Harton, Merle. Signor Faranta's Iron Theatre. LC 82-83592. (Illus.). 150p. 1982. 15.95x (ISBN 0-917860-13-6). Historic New Orleans.

Cruise, Edwina, tr. see Bitsilli, Peter.

Cruise, Edwina, tr. see Chudakov, A. P.

Cruise, James, jt. auth. see Kenney, Stanley.

Cruise, Robert J., jt. auth. see Blitchington, Peter.

Cruit, Robert L., jt. auth. see Cruit, Ronald L.

Cruit, Ron. One Hundred Seventy-Five Ways to Win a Free Drink: The Complete Book of Bar Bets. 160p. 1985. pap. 6.95 (ISBN 0-396-08586-5). Dodd.

Cruit, Ronald L. Intruder in Your Home. 277p. 1984. 17.95 (ISBN 0-8128-2900-X); pap. 3.95 (ISBN 0-8128-8091-9). Stein & Day.

--Intruder in Your Home: How to Defend Yourself Legally With A Firearm. LC 82-42727. 288p. 1983. 17.95 (ISBN 0-8128-2900-X). Stein & Day.

Cruit, Ronald L. & Cruit, Robert L. Survive the Coming Nuclear War: How to Do It. LC 81-48445. (Illus.). 208p. 1982. 16.95 (ISBN 0-8128-2849-6). Stein & Day.

--Survive the Coming Nuclear War: How to Do It. LC 81-48445. (Illus.). 208p. 1984. pap. 8.95 (ISBN 0-8128-6222-8). Stein & Day.

Crul, J., jt. ed. see Vickers, M. D.

Crum, H. A. Sphagnophyta. (North American Flora Series II: Pt. II). 1984. 25.00x (ISBN 0-89327-252-3). NY Botanical.

Crum, Howard A. & Anderson, Lewis E. Mosses of Eastern North America, 2 Vols. LC 79-24789. (Illus.). 576p. 1981. Set. 100.00x (ISBN 0-231-04516-6). Columbia U Pr.

Crum, Howard A., jt. auth. see Steere, William C.

Crum, Jesse K. The Art of Inner Listening. LC 74-21643. (Orig.). 1975. pap. 2.25 (ISBN 0-8356-0303-2, Quest). Theos Pub Hse.

Crum, Lawrence L. Electronic Funds Transference in Texas: The Stage of Its Development & Outlook for the 1980's. (Research Monograph Ser.: 1979-2). 45p. (Orig.). 1980. pap. 5.00 (ISBN 0-87755-240-1). Bureau Busn UT.

--Time Deposits in Present Day Commercial Banking. LC 64-63739. (University of Florida Social Sciences Monographs: No. 20). 1963. pap. 3.50 (ISBN 0-8130-0051-3). U Presses FLA.

Crum, Lawrence L., jt. auth. see Grant, Joseph M.

Crum, Margaret, ed. First-Line Index of English Poetry, 1500-1800, in Manuscripts of the Bodleian Library, Oxford, 2 vols. xi, 1257p. 1969. Set. 75.00x (ISBN 0-87352-018-1, Z6). Modern Lang.

Crum, Mary A. Devotions for Young Mothers. 96p. 1986. price not set. Baker Bk.

Crum, Mason. Gullah: Negro Life in the Carolina Sea Islands. LC 68-28592. Repr. of 1940 ed. 18.75x (ISBN 0-8371-0897-7, CRG&, Pub. by Negro U Pr). Greenwood.

Crum, Milton. Manual on Preaching. LC 77-79775. 1977. text ed. 8.95 (ISBN 0-8170-0744-X). Judson.

Crum, Milton, Jr., jt. auth. see Reid, Richard.

Crum, R. L., jt. auth. see Derkinderen, F.

Crum, Ralph B. Scientific Thought in Poetry. LC 31-29142. Repr. of 1931 ed. 16.50 (ISBN 0-404-01868-8). AMS Pr.

Crum, Robert P. Research & Publication in Value Added Taxation: A Comprehensive Background & Compilation. (Public Administration Series Bibliography P-1587). 76p. 1984. pap. 11.25 (ISBN 0-89028-217-X). Vance Biblios.

Crum, Robert P., jt. auth. see Namazi, Mohammad.

Crum, Roy L., jt. auth. see Derkinderen, Frans G.

Crum, Roy L. & Derkinderen, Frans G., eds. Capital Budgeting Under Conditions of Uncertainty. (Nijenrode Studies in Business: Vol. 5). 240p. 1980. lib. bdg. 20.00 (ISBN 0-89838-045-6, Pub. by Martinus Nijhoff Netherlands). Kluwer Academic.

Crum, Walter E., ed. Coptic Dictionary. 1939. Repr. of 1962 ed. 98.00x (ISBN 0-19-864404-3). Oxford U Pr.

Crumb, Charles V. Training People Effectively. (Lefax Data Bks.: No. 660). pap. 3.00 (ISBN 0-685-52794-8). LeFax.

Crumb, Dana & Cohen, Sherry. Eat It: A Cookbook. pap. 2.95 (ISBN 0-88388-019-9). Bellerophon Bks.

Crumb, Lawrence N. Historic Preservation in the Pacific Northwest: A Bibliography of Sources, 1947-1978. (CPL Bibliographies: No. 11). 63p. 1979. pap. 7.00 (ISBN 0-86602-011-X). CPL Biblios.

--Historic Preservation in the Pacific Northwest: A Bibliography of Sources, 1947-1978. (CCPL Bibliographies Ser.: No. 11). 63p. 7.00 (ISBN 0-86602-011-X). Coun Plan Librarians.

Crumb, Robert, jt. auth. see Fiene, Donald M.

Crumbaugh, James C. Everything to Gain: A Guide to Self-Fulfillment Through Logoanalysis. LC 72-80164. 1973. 17.95 (ISBN 0-911012-14-1). Nelson-Hall.

Crumbaugh, James C., et al. Logotherapy: New Help for Problem Drinkers. LC 79-18635. 176p. 1981. 17.95x (ISBN 0-88229-421-0). Nelson-Hall.

Crumbaugh, Lee. How to Use Multiplan. Rinehart, Janice S., ed. (Illus.). 70p. (gr. 7 up). 1983. wkbk. & tapes 75.00 (ISBN 0-318-01205-7). Flip Track.

Crumbaugh, Lee F. How to Use VisiCalc. (Illus.). 55p. (gr. 7 up). 1983. wkbk. & tapes 75.00 (ISBN 0-318-01219-7). Flip Track.

Crumbaugh, Lee F. & August, B. Alan. How to Use SuperCalc. (Illus.). 54p. (gr. 7 up). 1983. wkbk. & tapes 75.00 (ISBN 0-318-01218-9). Flip Track.

Crumbley, jt. auth. see McCarthy.

Crumbley, D. L., jt. auth. see Milam, Edward.

Crumbley, D. Larry. A Practical Guide to Preparing a Federal Estate Tax Return. 7th ed. 1980. pap. 11.50 1983 supplement (ISBN 0-88450-057-8, 1703-B). Lawyers & Judges.

--A Practical Guide to Preparing a Federal Gift Tax Return. 5th ed. 1980. pap. text ed. 11.50 1983 supplement (ISBN 0-88450-058-6, 1705-B). Lawyers & Judges.

--Readings in Selected Tax Problems of the Oil Industry. 280p. 1982. 15.95x (ISBN 0-87814-201-0). Pennwell Bks.

Crumbley, D. Larry & Davis, P. Michael. Organizing, Operating & Terminating Subchapter S Corporations, Law, Taxation & Accounting. rev. ed. 1980. text ed. 40.00 1983 supplement (ISBN 0-88450-063-2, 1711-B). Lawyers & Judges.

Crumbley, D. Larry & Grossman, Steven D. Readings in Oil Industry Accounting. 238p. 1980. 15.95x (ISBN 0-87814-123-5). Pennwell Bks.

Crumbley, D. Larry & Milam, Edward E. Estate Planning: A Guide for Advisors & Their Clients. 200p. 1985. 19.95 (ISBN 0-87094-686-2). Dow Jones-Irwin.

--Estate Planning in the Eighties. Rev. ed. LC 82-16314. pap. 60.00 (ISBN 0-317-19934-X, 2023573). Bks DEmand UMI.

Crumbley, D. Larry & Reese, Craig E. Readings in the Crude Oil Windfall Profit Tax. 375p. 1982. 15.95x (ISBN 0-87814-185-5). Pennwell Bks.

Crumbley, D. Larry, jt. auth. see McCarthy, Clarence.

Crumbley, D. Larry, jt. auth. see Milam, Edward E.

Crumbley, Larry & Curtis, Jerry. Donate Less to the I.R.S: The Antique Collector's & Seller's Tax Reduction Guide. LC 81-21806. 136p. 1981. pap. 6.95 (ISBN 0-911572-23-6). Vestal.

Crumbo, Kim. A River Runner's Guide to the History of the Grand Canyon. (Illus.). 96p. (Orig.). 1981. pap. 4.95 (ISBN 0-933472-61-7). Johnson Bks.

Crume, Marion, ed. The World of Paul Crume. 320p. 1980. 17.50 (ISBN 0-87074-176-4). SMU Press.

Crume, Vic. Billion Dollar Hobo. (gr. 4-6). 1979. pap. 1.95 (ISBN 0-590-05442-2). Scholastic Inc.

--Ghost That Came Alive. (gr. 4-6). 1976. pap. 1.95 (ISBN 0-590-09912-4). Scholastic Inc.

--Herbie Goes to Monte Carlo. (gr. 7-9). 1977. pap. 1.95 (ISBN 0-590-10402-0). Scholastic Inc.

--The Mystery in Dracula's Castle. (gr. 4-6). 1974. pap. 1.95 (ISBN 0-590-06859-8). Scholastic Inc.

--The Shaggy D.A. 1981. pap. 1.75 (ISBN 0-449-13642-6, GM). Fawcett.

Crumeyrolle, A. & Grifone, J., eds. Symplectic Geometry. (Research Notes in Mathematics Ser.: No. 80). 280p. 1983. pap. text ed. 23.95 (ISBN 0-273-08575-1). Pitman Pub MA.

Crumley, James. Dancing Bear. 256p. 1983. 12.95 (ISBN 0-394-52195-1). Random.

--Dancing Bear. LC 84-40008. (Vintage Contemporaries Ser.). 240p. 1984. pap. 5.95 (ISBN 0-394-72576-X, Vin). Random.

--The Last Good Kiss. 1983. pap. 3.50 (ISBN 0-671-49889-4). PB.

--The Muddy Fork. 30p. 1984. Limited signed ed. 50.00 (ISBN 0-935716-26-2). Lord John.

Crumm, Ronald J., jt. auth. see Graves, Phillip E.

Crummel, Alex. Africa & America. facs. ed. LC 72-79009. (Black Heritage Library Collection Ser). 1891. 20.25 (ISBN 0-8369-8550-8). Ayer Co Pubs.

Crummell, Alexander. Africa & America: Addresses & Discourses. LC 70-77198. Repr. of 1891 ed. 20.50x (ISBN 0-8371-1291-5, CRA&, Pub. by Negro U Pr). Greenwood.

--Africa & America: Addresses & Discourses. 1977. Repr. 18.00x (ISBN 0-403-07784-2). Scholarly.

--Future of Africa. LC 78-79770. Repr. of 1862 ed. 22.50x (ISBN 0-8371-0972-8, CRF&, Pub. by Negro U Pr). Greenwood.

--Future of Africa. LC 79-92424. 1862. 19.00x (ISBN 0-403-00156-0). Scholarly.

Crummer, Roy E., jt. auth. see Plane, Donald R.

Crummett, P. Button Guide Books, 2 bks. LC 69-20804. 10.00 set; Bk. 1, 1969. (ISBN 0-87282-104-8); Bk. 2, 1972. CHB-ALF.

Crummey, Donald & Stewart, C. C., eds. Modes of Production in Africa: The Precolonial Era. LC 81-1433. (Sage Series on African Modernization & Development: Vol. 5). (Illus.). 256p. 1981. 29.95 (ISBN 0-8039-1133-5); pap. 14.95 (ISBN 0-8039-1134-3). Sage.

Crummey, Robert O. Aristocrats & Servitors: The Boyer Elite in Russia, 1613-1689. LC 83-3064. (Illus.). 288p. 1983. 30.00x (ISBN 0-691-05389-8). Princeton U Pr.

--Old Believers & the World of Antichrist: The Vyg Community & the Russian State, 1694-1855. LC 79-98121. (Illus.). 278p. 1970. 30.00x (ISBN 0-299-05560-4). U of Wis Pr.

Crummey, Robert O., jt. ed. see Berry, Lloyd E.

Crummy, Philip. Aspects of Anglo-Saxon & Norman Colchester. (CBA Research Reports Ser.: No. 39). 100p. 1981. pap. text ed. 33.45x (ISBN 0-906780-06-3, Pub. by Coun Brit Archaeology). Humanities.

Crump, Arthur. The Theory of Stock Speculation. LC 83-80982. 1983. pap. 8.00 (ISBN 0-87034-068-9). Fraser Pub Co.

Crump, C. G. & Jacob, E. F., eds. Legacy of the Middle Ages. (Legacy Ser.). (Illus.). 1926. 32.50x (ISBN 0-19-821907-5). Oxford U Pr.

Crump, Charles G. History & Historical Research. LC 72-21805. 1974. Repr. of 1928 ed. lib. bdg. 20.50 (ISBN 0-8337-5041-0). B Franklin.

Crump, Charles G., ed. see Landor, Walter S.

Crump, Claudia. Indiana Studies Program: Activity Manual. Combs, Eunice A., ed. (Illus.). 201p. (gr. 4). 1983. duplicating masters 49.00 (ISBN 0-943068-77-0); tchr's guide, 42p. 5.00 (ISBN 0-943068-78-9). Graphic Learning.

Crump, Claudia & Dunfee, Maxine. Teaching for Social Values in Social Studies. Markun, Patricia M., ed. LC 74-78766. 1977. pap. 2.75x (ISBN 0-87173-009-X). ACEI.

Crump, David & Berman, Jeffery B. The Story of a Civil Suit: Dominquez v. Scott's Food Stores. 117p. (Orig.). 1983. pap. text ed. 11.25x (ISBN 0-916081-01-X). J Marshall Pub Co.

Crump, David & Curtis, J. Jerome, Jr. The Anatomy of a Real Property Transaction. 104p. (Orig.). 1984. pap. text ed. 11.25x (ISBN 0-916081-02-8). J Marshall Pub Co.

Crump, David & Mertens, William J. The Story of a Criminal Case: The State v. Albert Delman Greene. 154p. (Orig.). 1984. pap. text ed. 11.95x (ISBN 0-916081-00-1). J Marshall Pub Co.

Crump, David, jt. auth. see Dorsaneo, William V.

Crump, Donald J. Creatures Small & Furry. LC 83-13456. (Books for Young Explorers, Set 10). 32p. (ps-3). 1983. of 4 10.95 set (ISBN 0-87044-486-7); lib. bdg. 12.95 (ISBN 0-87044-491-3). Natl Geog.

Crump, Donald J., ed. Alaska's Magnificent Parklands. (Special Publications, Ser. 18). 200p. 1984. 6.95 (ISBN 0-87044-442-5); lib. bdg. 8.50 (ISBN 0-87044-447-6). Natl Geog.

--Amazing Animals of Australia. (Books for World Explorers, Series 6: No. 2). (Illus.). 104p. 1985. lib. bdg. 8.50 (ISBN 0-87044-520-0). Natl Geog.

--America's Hidden Corners. LC 82-47844. (Special Publications, Ser. 18). 200p. 1983. 6.95 (ISBN 0-87044-441-7); lib. bdg. 8.50 (ISBN 0-87044-446-8). Natl Geog.

--America's Seashore Wonderlands. (Special Publications, Series 20: No. 2). (Illus.). 1985. 7.95 (ISBN 0-87044-543-X); lib. bdg. 8.50 (ISBN 0-87044-548-0). Natl Geog.

--America's Wild & Scenic Rivers. LC 83-47843. (Special Publications, Ser. 18). 200p. 1983. 6.95 (ISBN 0-87044-440-9); lib. bdg. 8.50 (ISBN 0-87044-445-X). Natl Geog.

--America's Wild Woodlands. (Special Publications Ser.: No. 20, no. 1). (Illus.). 200p. 1985. 7.95 (ISBN 0-87044-542-1); lib. bdg. 8.50 (ISBN 0-87044-547-2). Natl Geog.

--Blue Horizons: Paradise Isles of the Pacific. (Special Publications, Series 20: No. 3). (Illus.). 1985. 7.95 (ISBN 0-87044-544-8); lib. bdg. 8.50 (ISBN 0-87044-549-9). Natl Geog.

--Canada's Wilderness Lands. LC 81-48074. 200p. 1982. 6.95 (ISBN 0-87044-413-1); lib. bdg. 8.50 (ISBN 0-87044-418-2). Natl Geog.

--Exploring America's Scenic Highways. (Special Publications Series 19: No. 4). (Illus.). 200p. 1985. 6.95 (ISBN 0-87044-479-4); lib. bdg. 8.50 (ISBN 0-87044-484-0). Natl Geog.
--Exploring America's Valleys: From Shenandoah to the Rio Grande. (Special Publications Ser.: No. 19). 200p. 1984. 6.95 (ISBN 0-87044-476-X); PLB 8.50 (ISBN 0-87044-481-6). Natl Geog.
--Giants from the Past. LC 81-47893. (Books for World Explorers: No. IV). 104p. (gr. 3-8). 1983. 6.95 (ISBN 0-87044-424-7); PLB 8.50 (ISBN 0-87044-429-8). Natl Geog.
--How Animals Behave. (Books for World Explorers Ser.: No. 5). (Illus.). 104p. (gr. 3-8). 1984. 6.95 (ISBN 0-87044-500-6); PLB 8.50 (ISBN 0-87044-505-7). Natl Geog.
--How Things Work. LC 81-47894. (Books for Young Explorers, Ser. 4). (Illus.). 104p. (gr. 7 up). 1983. 6.95 (ISBN 0-87044-425-5); PLB 8.50 (ISBN 0-87044-430-1). Natl Geog.
--Nature's World of Wonders. LC 82-47842. (Special Publications, Ser. 18). 200p. 1983. 6.95 (ISBN 0-87044-439-5); lib. bdg. 8.50 (ISBN 0-87044-444-1). Natl Geog.
--On the Brink of Tomorrow: Frontiers of Science. LC 81-48075. (Special Publications Ser.: No. XVII). 200p. 1982. PLB 8.50 (ISBN 0-87044-419-0). Natl Geog.
--Preserving America's Past. LC 81-48076. (Special Publications Ser.: No. 17). 200p. 1983. 6.95 (ISBN 0-87044-415-8); lib. bdg. 8.50 (ISBN 0-87044-420-4). Natl Geog.
--Secret Corners of the World. LC 81-48073. 200p. 1982. 6.95 (ISBN 0-87044-412-3); lib. bdg. 8.50. Natl Geog.
--Secrets of Animal Survival. LC 81-47895. (Books for World Explorers, Ser. 4). (Illus.). 104p. (gr. 3 up). 1983. 6.95 (ISBN 0-87044-426-3); PLB 8.50 (ISBN 0-87044-431-X). Natl Geog.
--Small Inventions That Make a Big Difference. LC 83-23770. (Books for World Explorers, Ser. 5). 104p. (gr. 3-8). 1984. 6.95 (ISBN 0-87044-498-0); PLB 8.50 (ISBN 0-87044-503-0, 00503). Natl Geog.
--Your Wonderful Body. LC 81-47892. (Books for World Explorers: Series 4). 104p. (gr. 4-8). 1982. 6.95 (ISBN 0-87044-423-9); PLB 8.50 (ISBN 0-87044-428-X). Natl Geog.
Crump, Donald J., ed. see Amos, William H.
Crump, Donald J., ed. see Eugene, Toni.
Crump, Donald J., ed. see Fisher, Ronald M.
Crump, Donald J., ed. see McCauley, Jane R.
Crump, Donald J., ed. see McGrath, Susan.
Crump, Donald J., ed. see Martin, Paul D.
Crump, Donald J., ed. see O'Neill, Catherine.
Crump, Donald J., ed. see Rinard, Judith E.
Crump, Donald J., ed. see Urquhart, Jennifer C.
Crump, Donald J., ed. see Venino, Suzanne.
Crump, Donald J., ed. see Winston, Peggy D.
Crump, Elaine C. Chinaberry Beads. LC 78-21581. (Illus., Fr. & Eng.). pap. 3.95 (ISBN 0-88289-228-2). Pelican.
Crump, Fred, Jr. Missy & the Duke: Missy y el Duque. Woyde, Horst, tr. (Eng. & Span.). (gr. 3-7). 1977. 7.50 (ISBN 0-87917-058-1). Ethridge.
--Ringo the Raccoon. (ps-3). 1983. pap. 7.95 (ISBN 0-516-09117-4). Childrens.
Crump, G. B. The Novels of Wright Morris: A Critical Interpretation. LC 77-15796. viii, 258p. 1978. 19.95x (ISBN 0-8032-0962-2). U of Nebr Pr.
Crump, G. B., ed. Petroanalysis 81: Advances in Analytical Chemistry in the Petroleum Industry. Proceedings of the Institute of Petroleum (IP) 456p. 1983. 89.95 (ISBN 0-471-26217-X, Pub. by Wiley Interscience). Wiley.
Crump, Galbraith M. The Mystical Design of "Paradise Lost". 194p. 1975. 18.00 (ISBN 0-8387-1519-2). Bucknell U Pr.
Crump, Galbraith M., ed. Poems on Affairs of State: Augustan Satirical Verse 1660-1714, Vol. 4 1685-1688. LC 63-7938. (Illus.). 1968. 52.00x (ISBN 0-300-00389-7). Yale U Pr.
Crump, Geoffrey H. A Guide to the Study of Shakespeare's Plays. LC 72-13512. 1973. lib. bdg. 15.00 (ISBN 0-8414-1184-0). Folcroft.
--Selections from English Dramatists. 1978. Repr. of 1927 ed. lib. bdg. 27.00 (ISBN 0-8495-0848-7). Arden Lib.
--Speaking Poetry. LC 76-23449. 1976. Repr. of 1953 ed. lib. bdg. 20.00 (ISBN 0-8414-3596-0). Folcroft.
Crump, I. A. Australian Scientific Societies & Professional Associations. 226p. 1981. 30.00x (ISBN 0-643-00282-0, Pub. by CSIRO Australia). State Mutual Bk.
--Australian Scientific Societies & Professional Associations. (3 microfiches). 1978. pap. 13.75 (ISBN 0-686-71823-2, C034, CSIRO). Unipub.
--Scientific & Technical Research Centres in Australia. 1228p. 1982. 40.00x (ISBN 0-643-02820-X, Pub. by CSIRO Australia). State Mutual Bk.
--Scientific & Technical Research Centres in Australia. 224p. 1981. pap. 9.00 (ISBN 0-686-71844-5, C036, CSIRO). Unipub.
Crump, Ian A., ed. Scientific & Technical Research Centres in Australia. new ed. 1977. 11.00x (ISBN 0-643-00145-X, Pub. by CSIRO); pap. 7.25x (ISBN 0-643-00140-9, Pub. by CSIRO). Intl Spec Bk.
Crump, Irving. Our Merchant Marine Academy, Kings Point. LC 74-5553. (Illus.). 236p. 1975. Repr. of 1958 ed. lib. bdg. 22.50x (ISBN 0-8371-7511-9, CRMA). Greenwood.
--Our United States Coast Guard Academy. LC 74-5554. (Illus.). 241p. 1975. Repr. of 1961 ed. lib. bdg. 24.75x (ISBN 0-8371-7510-0, CRCG). Greenwood.
Crump, J. I. Chinese Theater in the Days of Kublai Khan. LC 79-20046. 429p. 1980. 29.95x (ISBN 0-8165-0697-3); pap. text ed. 14.95x (ISBN 0-8165-0656-6). U of Ariz Pr.
--Songs from Xanadu: Studies in Mongrol-Dynasty Song-Poetry (San-ch'u) LC 83-7809. (Michigan Monographs in Chinese Studies: No. 47). (Illus.). xi, 232p. (Orig.). 1983. pap. 10.00 (ISBN 0-89264-047-2). U of Mich Ctr Chinese.
Crump, J. I., jt. auth. see Fidler, Sharon J.
Crump, J. I., ed. Chinese & Japanese Music-Dramas. Malm, William P. (Michigan Monographs in Chinese Studies: No. 19). (Illus.). 255p. 1975. pap. 6.00 (ISBN 0-89264-019-7). U of Mich Ctr Chinese.
Crump, J. I., Jr., ed. Selections from the Shui-Hu Chuan. 1.75 (ISBN 0-88710-085-6); tapes avail. (ISBN 0-88710-086-4). Far Eastern Pubns.
Crump, James I. Intrigues: Studies of the Chan-kuo tse. LC 64-17440. pap. 56.00 (ISBN 0-317-08147-0, 2050828). Bks Demand UMI.
Crump, John. The Origins of Socialist Thought in Japan. LC 82-23075. 415p. 1984. 30.00x (ISBN 0-312-58872-0). St Martin.
Crump, Martha L. Reproductive Strategies in a Tropical Anuran Community. (Miscellaneous Publications Ser.: No. 61). 68p. 1974. pap. 3.75 (ISBN 0-686-79838-4). U of KS Mus Nat Hist.
Crump, Martha L., jt. auth. see Duellman, William E.
Crump, Mary M. The Epyllion from Theocritus to Ovid. Commager, Steele, ed. LC 77-70761. (Latin Poetry Ser.). 1978. lib. bdg. 39.00 (ISBN 0-8240-2966-6). Garland Pub.
Crump, R. W. Charlotte & Emily Bronte, 1846-1915: A Reference Guide. 1982. lib. bdg. 29.00 (ISBN 0-8161-7953-0, Hall Reference). G K Hall.
Crump, R. W., ed. see Rossetti, Christina.
Crump, R. W., ed. see Rossetti, Christina G.
Crump, Ralph W., ed. The Design Connection: Energy & Technology in Architecture. Harms, Martin J. (Preston Thomas Memorial Series in Architecture). 144p. 1981. 23.95 (ISBN 0-442-23125-3). Van Nos Reinhold.
Crump, Rebbecca. Charlotte & Emily Bronte, 1916-1954: A Reference Guide. 1985. lib. bdg. 32.00 (ISBN 0-8161-8672-3). G K Hall.
Crump, Rebecca W. Christina Rossetti: A Reference Guide. (General Ser.). 1976. lib. bdg. 22.00 (ISBN 0-8161-7847-X, Hall Reference). G K Hall.
Crump, Richard. Maserati Road Cars 1946-1979. (Illus.). 229p. 1979. 35.00 (ISBN 0-914822-26-8). Barnes Pub.
Crump, Richard & Box, Rob de la. Maserati: Sports Racing & GT Cars from 1926. (Illus.). 28.95 (ISBN 0-85429-302-7, F302). Haynes Pubns.
Crump, Richard & Box, Robert D. Lamborghini: The Cars from Sant'agata Bolognese. (Illus.). 208p. 1981. 29.95 (ISBN 0-85045-408-5, Pub. by Osprey England). Motorbooks Intl.
Crump, Richard & Rive Box, Bob De La. Automotive Art of Bertone. 168p. 24.95 (ISBN 0-85429-349-3, F349). Haynes Pubns.
Crump, Richard, jt. auth. see De La Rive Box, Rob.
Crump, Spencer. Fundamentals of Journalism. (Illus.). 224p. 1974. text ed. 25.15 (ISBN 0-07-014835-X). McGraw.
--Henry Huntington the Pacific Electric: A Pictorial Album. 2nd revised ed. 10.00 (ISBN 0-87046-048-X, Pub. by Trans-Anglo). Interurban.
--Rail Car, Locomotive & Trolley Builders: An All-Time Directory. Date not set. write for info. (ISBN 0-87046-032-3, Pub. by Trans-Anglo). Interurban.
--Ride the Big Red Cars: How Trolleys Helped Build Southern California. 5th rev. ed. LC 77-72017. (Illus.). 24.95 (ISBN 0-87046-047-1, Pub. by Trans-Anglo). Interurban.
Crump, Thomas. The Phenomenon of Money. (The Library of Man). 304p. 1981. 40.00x (ISBN 0-7100-0856-2). Routledge & Kegan.
Crump, William B., ed. The Leeds Woollen Industry, 1780-1820. (Illus.). 1931. pap. 34.00 (ISBN 0-384-10265-4). Johnson Repr.
Crumpacker, Emily & Flesher, Vivienne. Seasonal Gifts from the Kitchen. LC 83-61796. 96p. 1983. 10.95 (ISBN 0-688-02569-2). Morrow.
Crumpacker, Emily, jt. auth. see Logan, Muriel B.
Crumpacker, Laurie, ed. see Burr, Esther E.
Crumpe, Samuel. Essay on the Best Means of Providing Employment for the People. 2nd. ed. LC 67-29499. Repr. of 1795 ed. 37.50x (ISBN 0-678-00410-2). Kelley.
Crumpler, Fred G. & Wake Forest University Continuing Legal Education. North Carolina Criminal Cases Manual. LC 84-235198. (Illus.). 1984. write for info. U Wake Forest.
Crumpler, Gus H. Under the Burmese Pagoda. 1975. 10.00 (ISBN 0-9606378-9-3). G H Crumpler.
Crumpton, M. J., jt. ed. see Garland, P. B.
Crumrime, Jeffery C., ed. see Magic Valley Rehabilitation Services, Inc.
Crumrine, Boyd. Virginia Court Records in Southwestern Pennsylvania: Records of the District of West Augusta & Ohio & Yohogania Counties, Virginia, 1775-1780. LC 74-7238. (Illus.). 542p. 1981. Repr. of 1902 ed. 25.00 (ISBN 0-8063-0624-6). Genealog Pub.
Crumrine, Lynne S. The Phonology of Arizona Yaqui: With Texts. LC 61-64124. (University of Arizona, Anthropological Papers: No. 5). pap. 20.00 (ISBN 0-317-28630-7, 2055379). Bks Demand UMI.
Crumrine, N. Ross. The Mayo Indians of Sonora: A People Who Refuse to Die. LC 76-8563. 167p. 1977. 12.50x (ISBN 0-8165-0605-1); pap. text ed. 5.95x (ISBN 0-8165-0473-3). U of Ariz Pr.
Crunden, Robert, ed. Traffic of Ideas Between India & America. 1985. 37.50x (ISBN 0-8364-1317-2, Pub. by Chanakya). South Asia Bks.
Crunden, Robert M. Ministers of Reform: The Progressives' Achievement in American Civilization, 1889-1920. LC 82-70848. 1982. 17.95 (ISBN 0-465-04631-2). Basic.
--Ministers of Reform: The Progressives' Achievement in American Civilization, 1889-1920. 320p. 1985. pap. 10.95x (ISBN 0-252-01167-8). U of Ill Pr.
--New Perspectives on America & South Asia. 1984. 18.50x (ISBN 0-8364-1235-4, Pub. by Chanakya India). South Asia Bks.
Crunden, Robert M., ed. The Superfluous Men: Conservative Critics of American Culture, 1900-1945. 309p. 1977. 14.95 (ISBN 0-292-77527-X). U of Tex Pr.
Crunkilton, John R. & Krebs, Al H. Teaching Agriculture Through Problem Solving. 3rd ed. 1981. text ed. 13.50x (ISBN 0-8134-2199-3). Interstate.
Crunkilton, John R., jt. auth. see Finch, Curtis R.
Crunlan, Stephen A. & Lambrides, Daniel H. Healing Relationships: A Christian's Manual of Lay Counseling. LC 83-70103. 325p. 1984. 6.45 (ISBN 0-87509-329-9); pap. 2.95 (ISBN 0-87509-354-X). Chr Pubns.
Cruse, Amy. After the Victorians. LC 76-158495. 1971. Repr. of 1938 ed. 39.00x (ISBN 0-403-01315-1). Scholarly.
--Elizabethan Lyrists & Their Poetry. LC 76-120974. (Poetry & Life Ser.). Repr. of 1913 ed. 7.25 (ISBN 0-404-52507-5). AMS Pr.
--Elizabethan Lyrists & Their Poetry. LC 72-194435. 1972. lib. bdg. 10.00 (ISBN 0-8414-2421-7). Folcroft.
--English Literature Through the Ages: Beowulf to Stevenson. 1973. lib. bdg. 15.00 (ISBN 0-8414-2422-5). Folcroft.
--English Literature Through the Ages: Beowulf to Stevenson. 592p. 1982. Repr. lib. bdg. 45.00 (ISBN 0-89984-120-1). Century Bookbindery.
--Englishman & His Books in the Early Nineteenth Century. LC 68-20218. (Illus.). 1968. Repr. of 1930 ed. 20.00 (ISBN 0-405-08412-9, Blom Pubns). Ayer Co Pubs.
--The Englishman & His Books in the Early Nineteenth Century. 1973. lib. bdg. 20.00 (ISBN 0-8414-2423-3). Folcroft.
--The Golden Road in English Literature: From Beowulf to Bernard Shaw. 669p. 1982. Repr. lib. bdg. 45.00 (ISBN 0-89984-119-8). Century Bookbindery.
--Robert Louis Stevenson. LC 73-12592. 1915. lib. bdg. 17.50 (ISBN 0-8414-3447-6). Folcroft.
--Sir Walter Scott. 1973. Repr. of 1915 ed. 20.00 (ISBN 0-8274-1766-7). R West.
--Stories from George Eliot. 1913. 20.00 (ISBN 0-8274-3510-X). R West.
Cruse, Harold. The Crisis of the Negro Intellectual: A Historical Analysis of the Failure of Black Leadership. LC 84-60452. 696p. 1984. pap. 10.95 (ISBN 0-688-03886-7, Quill NY). Morrow.
Cruse, J. M. & Lewis, R. E., eds. Autoimmunity: Basic Concepts & Systemic & Selected Organ-Specific Diseases. (Concepts in Immunopathology: Vol. 1). (Illus.). viii, 362p. 1985. 84.25 (ISBN 3-8055-3908-8). S Karger.
--Immunoregulation & Autoimmunity. (Concepts in Immunopathology: Vol. 3). (Illus.). x, 278p. 1985. 63.50 (ISBN 3-8055-4076-0). S Karger.
--Organ Based Autoimmune Diseases. (Concepts in Immunopathology: Vol. 2). (Illus.). x, 278p. 1985. 63.50 (ISBN 3-8055-3929-0). S Karger.
Cruse, J. M. & Lewis, R. E., Jr., eds. The Year in Immunology, 1984-85. (The Year in Immunology Ser.: Vol. 1). (Illus.). vi, 234p. 1985. 67.25 (ISBN 3-8055-4025-6). S Karger.
Cruse, J. M. & Schwartz, L. M., eds. The Year in Immunology, 1983. (Journal: Survey of Immunologic Research: Vol. 3, No. 2-3). (Illus.). 156p. 1984. pap. 34.25 (ISBN 3-8055-3881-2). S Karger.
Cruse, Joanna S. The Money Puzzle: The World of Macroeconomics, Study Guide (Telecourse Developed by Miami-Dade Community College) 543p. 1983. pap. text ed. 16.50 scp (ISBN 0-06-043273-X, HarpC); instr's Manual avail. (ISBN 0-06-363265-9). Har-Row.
Cruse, Larry & Warren, Sylvia B., eds. Microcartography: Applications for Archives & Libraries. 1982 ed. LC 81-19718. (Western Association of Map Libraries, Occasional Paper: No. 6). (Illus.). 212p. 1981. pap. 20.00 (ISBN 0-939112-07-8). Western Assn Map.
Cruse, T. A., ed. Fatigue Life Technology, Bk No. H00096. Gallagher, J. P. pap. text ed. 18.00 (ISBN 0-685-79860-7). ASME.
Cruse, T. A. & Rizzo, F. J., eds. Boundary-Integral Equation Method: Computational Applications in Applied Mechanics AMD, Vol. 11. 148p. 1975. pap. text ed. 14.00 (ISBN 0-685-78341-3, I00089). ASME.
Cruse, T. A., ed. see American Society of Mechanical Engineers.
Cruse, Thomas A. & Griffin, Donald S., eds. Three-Dimensional Continuum Computer Programs for Structural Analysis: Presented at the Winter Annual Meeting of the American Society of Mechanical Engineers, New York, NY, November 26-30, 1972. LC 72-92593. pap. 20.00 (ISBN 0-317-10641-4, 2022061). Bks Demand UMI.
Crusius, Vera C. Quantity Food Management: Principles & Applications. (Orig.). 1981. pap. text ed. 14.95x (ISBN 0-8087-2966-7). Burgess.
Cruso, H. A. Sir Walter Raleigh. 1973. Repr. of 1907 ed. 25.00 (ISBN 0-8274-1789-6). R West.
Cruso, John. Militarie Instructions for the Cavallrie. LC 68-54631. (English Experience Ser.: No. 55). 108p. 1968. Repr. of 1632 ed. 25.00 (ISBN 90-221-0055-3). Walter J Johnson.
Crussard, Claude. Un Musicien francais oublie, Marc-Antoine Charpentier, 1634-1704. LC 76-43912. (Music & Theatre in France in the 17th & 18th Centuries). Repr. of 1945 ed. 16.50 (ISBN 0-404-60155-3). AMS Pr.
Crussell, Leah A., ed. Three Hundred Sixty-Five Devotions. large print ed. 384p. 1985. 5.95 (ISBN 0-87239-852-8, 4086); pocket ed. 3.95 (ISBN 0-87239-851-X). Standard Pub.
Crusswell, Helen. Baythorpus Unlimited. 1978. 9.95 (ISBN 0-317-12068-9). Macmillan.
Crutch, Denis. The Lewis Carroll Handbook. rev. ed. (Illus.). xix, 340p. 37.50 (ISBN 0-208-01780-1, Archon). Shoe String.
Crutcher, Chris. Running Loose. LC 82-20935. 160p. (YA) (gr. 10 up). 1983. reinforced bdg. 10.25 (ISBN 0-688-02002-X). Greenwillow.
--Running Loose. (gr. k-12). 1986. pap. 2.75 (ISBN 0-440-97570-0, LFL). Dell.
Crutcher, Ernest R., jt. auth. see Beeson, Richard D.
Crutcher, Roberta. Personality & Reason. 1979. Repr. of 1931 ed. lib. bdg. 40.00 (ISBN 0-8495-0917-3). Arden Lib.
Crutchfield, Carolyn A. & Barns, Marylon R. Neurophysiological Basis of Patient Treatment: Peripheral Receptors & Muscle Control, Vol. III. (Illus.). 1984. pap. 17.00x (ISBN 0-936030-03-8). Stokesville Pub.
Crutchfield, Carolyn A., jt. auth. see Barnes, Marylou R.
Crutchfield, James, jt. ed. see Brown, Gardner M., Jr.
Crutchfield, James A. A Heritage of Grandeur. (Illus.). 120p. 1981. 29.95 (ISBN 0-686-46061-8). Carnton Assn.
--Timeless Tennesseans. (Illus.). 200p. 1983. 19.95 (ISBN 0-87397-186-8). Strode.
Crutchfield, James A. & Lawson, Rowena. West African Marine Fisheries: Alternatives for Management. LC 73-10843. (Program of International Studies of Fishery Arrangements Ser.: No. 3). pap. 20.00 (ISBN 0-317-28865-2, 2020960). Bks Demand UMI.
Crutchfield, James A. & Pontecorvo, Giulio. The Pacific Salmon Fisheries: A Study of Irrational Conservation. LC 72-75180. (Resources for the Future Ser). (Illus.). 220p. 1969. 14.00x (ISBN 0-8018-1025-6). Johns Hopkins.
--The Pacific Salmon Fisheries: A Study of Irrational Conservation. 232p. 1969. 14.00 (ISBN 0-8018-1025-6). Resources Future.
Crutchfield, Richard & Krech, David. Psychology: A Basic Course. 1976. text ed. 17.95 (ISBN 0-394-31908-7, KnopfC); tchr's. manual o.p. avail. (ISBN 0-394-31173-6); wkbk. o.p. 6.95 (ISBN 0-394-31174-4). Knopf.
Crutchfield, Richard, jt. auth. see Krech, David.
Crutchley, Brooke, ed. see Morison, Stanley.
Crutsinger, George M. Survey Study of Teacher Training in Texas, & a Suggested Program. LC 79-176680. (Columbia University. Teachers College. Contributions to Education: No. 537). Repr. of 1933 ed. 22.50 (ISBN 0-404-55537-3). AMS Pr.
Cruttenden, Alan. Language in Infancy & Childhood: A Linguistic Introduction to Language Acquisition. LC 78-22106. 1979. 25.00 (ISBN 0-312-46606-4). St Martin.
Cruttwell, Charles R. A History of the Great War: 1914-1918. (Illus.). 655p. 1983. pap. 10.95 (ISBN 0-586-08398-7, Pub. by Granada England). Academy Chi Pubs.
Cruttwell, Charles T. A History of Roman Literature: From the Earliest Period to the Death of Marcus Aurelius. 1898. 25.00 (ISBN 0-8274-3943-1). R West.
--Literary History of Early Christianity, 2 Vols. LC 76-129369. Repr. of 1893 ed. 65.00 (ISBN 0-404-01877-7). AMS Pr.
Cruttwell, Maud. Donatello. facsimile ed. LC 71-37334. (Select Bibliographies Reprint Ser). (Illus.). Repr. of 1911 ed. 35.00 (ISBN 0-8369-6681-3). Ayer Co Pubs.
--Luca Signorelli. LC 75-131677. (Illus.). xi, 144p. 1972. Repr. of 1907 ed. 19.00 (ISBN 0-403-00912-X). Scholarly.

Cruttwell, Patrick. The Shakespearean Moment & Its Place in the Poetry of the Seventeenth Century. LC 55-541. 262p. 1954. 29.00x (ISBN 0-231-02082-1). Columbia U Pr.
Cruttwell, Patrick, ed. see Johnson, Samuel.
Cruttwell, Robert W. Virgil's Mind at Work. LC 68-58959. Repr. of 1947 ed. 20.00 (ISBN 0-8154-0270-8). Cooper Sq.
--Virgil's Mind at Work: An Analysis of the Symbolism of the Aeneid. LC 78-114505. 1971. Repr. of 1946 ed. lib. bdg. 18.75x (ISBN 0-8371-4733-6, CRVM). Greenwood.
Crutwell, Maud. Luca & Andrea Della Robbia. LC 79-155625. (Illus.). Repr. of 1902 ed. 29.50 (ISBN 0-404-01869-6). AMS Pr.
Cruysberg, J. R., jt. ed. see Deutman, A. F.
Cruz, Daniel da see Da Cruz, Daniel.
Cruz, Emmanuel M., ed. see Hopkins, Kevin D.
Cruz, F. De La see De La Cruz, F. & LaVeck, G. D.
Cruz, Felix de la, jt. ed. see Lubs, Herbert.
Cruz, Felix F. De La see Davidson, Richard L. & De La Cruz, Felix F.
Cruz, Felix F. de la see De la Cruz, Felix F.
Cruz, Gilbert R. & Irby, James A. Texas Bibliography. 1982. 15.95 (ISBN 0-89015-307-8). Eakin Pubns.
Cruz, Guillermo F., ed. see De Bibar, Geronimo.
Cruz, Isagani R. Beyond Futility: The Filipino as Critic. vii, 96p. (Orig.). 1984. pap. 7.50x (ISBN 0-318-01389-4, Pub. by New Day Philippines). Cellar.
Cruz, J. B., Jr., ed. System Sensitivity Analysis. LC 72-93263. (Benchmark Papers in Electrical Engineering & Computer Science Ser: Vol. 1). 428p. 1973. 55.95 (ISBN 0-87933-020-1). Van Nos Reinhold.
Cruz, Joan C. Desires of Thy Heart. Keith, Judith, ed. LC 76-39600. 1977. 8.95 (ISBN 0-913024-10-4). Tandem Pr.
--The Incorruptibles. LC 77-93992. (Illus.). 1977. pap. 8.00 (ISBN 0-89555-066-0). TAN Bks Pubs.
--Relics. LC 84-60744. (Illus.). 352p. 1984. pap. 10.95 (ISBN 0-87973-701-8, 701). Our Sunday Visitor.
Cruz, Jose B. & Van Valkenburg, M. E. Signals in Linear Circuits. 480p. 1974. text ed. 37.95 (ISBN 0-395-16971-2); instr's. manual 11.50 (ISBN 0-395-17838-X). HM.
Cruz, Jose B., Jr., ed. Advances in Control Systems: Theory & Application. 1983. 45.00 (ISBN 0-89232-411-2). Jai Pr.
--Advances in Large Scale Systems: Theory & Applications, Vol. 1. 1984. 45.00 (ISBN 0-89232-252-7). Jai Pr.
Cruz, Lopez. La Musica Folklorica De Puerto Rico. 1967. 19.95 (ISBN 0-87751-008-3, Pub by Troutman Press). E Torres & Sons.
Cruz, Luis O. Introduction to Projective Cognition. LC 83-26278. 126p. 1985. 13.50 (ISBN 0-8022-2448-2). Philos Lib.
Cruz, M. & Ignashev, S. P. Tagalog-Russian Dictionary. 388p. (Tagalog & Rus.). 1959. leatherette 4.75 (ISBN 0-686-92479-7, M-9052). French & Eur.
Cruz, Manny & Symington, Nikki. Alice Barnes: American Activist. Kern, Ann T., ed. LC 82-74177. (Illus.). 52p. (Orig.). 1982. pap. 7.50 (ISBN 0-911719-00-8). Connections CA.
Cruz, Manuel & Cruz, Ruth. A Chicano Christmas Story. LC 80-69444. (Illus.). 48p. (Orig., Span.). (ps-5). 1981. pap. text ed. 3.95 (ISBN 0-86624-000-4, RM7). Bilingual Ed Serv.
Cruz, MaryCarmen E., jt. auth. see Gonzalez, RoseAnn D.
Cruz, Mercedes Santa see Santa Cruz, Mercedes.
Cruz, Nicky. Run Baby Run: The Story of a Gang-Lord Turned Crusader. LC 68-23446. 240p. 1968. pap. 2.95 (ISBN 0-912106-58-1, Pub. by Logos). Bridge Pub.
Cruz, Nicky & Buckingham, Jamie. Run Baby Run. (gr. 9-12). 1984. pap. 2.95 (ISBN 0-515-08193-0). Jove Pubns.
Cruz, Rodolfo A. Instrucciones Practicas para Nuevos Creyentes. LC 77-71308. 78p. (Orig., Span.). 1970. pap. text ed. 2.00 (ISBN 0-89922-002-9). Edit Caribe.
Cruz, Rosa M., jt. ed. see Sanchez, Rosaura.
Cruz, Ruperto Vazquez. Estadistica Elemental: Primera Part. 7th ed. pap. 4.50 (ISBN 0-8477-2619-3). U of PR Pr.
Cruz, Ruth, jt. auth. see Cruz, Manuel.
Cruz, Sov J. de La see De La Cruz, Sov J.
Cruz, Victor H. By Lingual Wholes. 1982. pap. 5.95x (ISBN 0-917672-19-4); lib. bdg. 15.00x (ISBN 0-917672-20-8). Momos.
Cruz Aymes, Maria de la see De la Cruz Aymes, Maria & Buckley, Francis J.
Cruzic, Kathleen. Disabled? Yes, Defeated? No! Resources for the Disabled & Their Families, Friends, Teachers & Therapists. (Illus.). 240p. 1982. 12.95 (ISBN 0-13-215681-4); pap. 6.95 (ISBN 0-13-215673-3). P-H.
Cruz Monclava, Lidio. Historia De Puerto Rico: Siglo XIX, 6 vols. Set. pap. 60.00 (ISBN 0-8477-0801-2). U of PR Pr.
--Historia Del Ano 1887. 3rd ed. pap. 3.10 (ISBN 0-8477-0809-8). U of PR Pr.
Cruz Monclava, Lidio, jt. auth. see Bothwell, Reece B.
Cruz-Uribe, Eugene. Saite & Persian Demotic Cattle Documents: A Study in Legal Forms & Principles in Ancient Egypt. (American Studies in Papyrology: Vol. 26). write for info. Amer Bar Assn.
Cruz-Uribe, Kathryn, jt. auth. see Klein, Richard G.
Cryan, John & Surbeck, Elaine. Early Childhood Education: Foundations for Lifelong Learning. LC 79-66528. (Fastback Ser.: No. 133). 62p. (Orig.). 1979. pap. 0.75 (ISBN 0-87367-133-3). Phi Delta Kappa.
Crye, Stephen. Joyride. 288p. (Orig.). 1983. pap. 2.95 (ISBN 0-523-41864-7). Pinnacle Bks.
Cryer, A. Biochemical Interactions at the Endothelium. 1983. 106.50 (ISBN 0-444-80478-1, I-007-83). Elsevier.
Cryer, A. & Van, R. L. New Perspectives in Adipose Tissue-Structure, Function & Development. (Illus.). 480p. 1985. text ed. 94.95 (ISBN 0-408-10857-6). Butterworth.
Cryer, Colin W. Numerical Functional Analysis. (Monographs on Numerical Analysis). 1982. 39.00x (ISBN 0-19-853410-8). Oxford U Pr.
Cryer, James, tr. see Li Ch'ing Chao.
Cryer, Neil. Graphics on the BBC Microcomputer. 16.95 (ISBN 0-13-363283-0); disk 12.95 (ISBN 0-13-363242-3). P-H.
Cryer, Neil & Cryer, Pat. BASIC Programming on the BBC Microcomputer. xii, 195p. 1983. 16.95 (ISBN 0-13-066407-3); pap. 11.95. P-H.
--Pocket Guide: Programming for the BBC Micro. (Pitman Programming Pocket Guide Ser.). 64p. (Orig.). 1984. pap. 6.95 (ISBN 0-273-01979-1). Pitman Pub MA.
Cryer, Pat, jt. auth. see Cryer, Neil.
Cryer, Pat, ed. Training Activities for Teachers in Higher Education, Vol. 1. 64p. 1982. 30.00 (ISBN 0-8002-3877-X). Taylor & Francis.
Cryer, Philip E. Diagnostic Endocrinology. 2nd ed. (Illus.). 1979. text ed. 24.95x (ISBN 0-19-502525-3); pap. text ed. 12.95x (ISBN 0-19-502526-1). Oxford U Pr.
Crying Wind Stafford. Crying Wind. LC 80-3843. 192p. 1981. pap. 2.95 (ISBN 0-89081-263-2). Harvest Hse.
Crying Wind. My Searching Heart. LC 80-83846. 242p. 1981. pap. 5.95 (ISBN 0-89081-262-4). Harvest Hse.
Cryle, P. M. The Thematics of Commitment: The Tower & the Plain. LC 84-42590. 456p. 1984. text ed. 40.00x (ISBN 0-691-06610-8). Princeton U Pr.
Crymes, Ruth. Some Systems of Substitution Correlations in Modern American English: With Implications for the Teaching of English As a Second Language. (Janua Linguarum, Ser. Major: No. 23). 1968. text ed. 22.40x (ISBN 90-2790-614-9). Mouton.
Crymes, Ruth, jt. ed. see Alatis, James E.
Crymes, Ruth, et al. Developing Fluency in English: With Sentence-Combining Practice in Nominalization. (Illus.). 256p. 1974. pap. text ed. 12.95 (ISBN 0-13-204826-4). P-H.
Crynes, B. L., ed. Heterogeneous Catalysis. LC 80-25535. (AIChEMI Modular Instruction E-Ser.: Vol. 3). 70p. 1982. pap. 30.00 (ISBN 0-8169-0212-7); pap. 15.00 members (ISBN 0-317-03790-0). Am Inst Chem Eng.
Crynes, B. L. & Fogler, H. S., eds. Rate of Reaction, Sensitivity & Chemical Equilibrium. LC 80-25535. (AIChEMI Modular Instruction B. Ser.). 56p. 1981. pap. 30.00 (ISBN 0-8169-0180-5); pap. 15.00 members (ISBN 0-317-03844-3). Am Inst Chem Eng.
--Reactor Stability: Sensitivity & Mixing Effects. LC 80-25535. (Alchemi Series E: Kinetics). 98p. 1984. pap. 30.00 (ISBN 0-8169-0239-9); pap. 15.00 members (ISBN 0-317-17543-2). Am Inst Chem Eng.
--Reactors & Rate Data. LC 80-24435. (AIChEMI Modular Instruction E. Ser.: Vol. 2). 94p. 1981. pap. 30.00 (ISBN 0-8169-0180-5, J-11); pap. 15.00 members (ISBN 0-317-03846-X). Am Inst Chem Eng.
Crynes, Billy L. Chemical Reactions As a Means of Separation. (Chemical Processing & Engineering Ser.: Vol. 11). 1977. 65.00 (ISBN 0-8247-6374-2). Dekker.
Crynes, Billy L., jt. ed. see Albright, Lyle F.
Cryogenic Society of America, LNG Terminals & Safety Symposium. Applications of Cryogenic Technology: Proceedings, Vol. 9. Petsinger, Robert E. & Vance, Robert W., eds. LC 68-57815. 1979. 45.00x (ISBN 0-87936-014-3). Scholium Intl.
Cryogenics Committee of the BCC. Vacuum Insulated Cryogenic Pipe. 20p. 1981. 11.00x (ISBN 0-85295-066-7, Pub. by Inst Chem Eng England). State Mutual Bk.
Crypton. Timid Virgins Make Dull Company & Other Puzzles, Pitfalls & Paradoxes. (Penguin Nonfiction Ser.). 208p. 1985. pap. 5.95 (ISBN 0-317-19377-5). Penguin.
Crypton, jt. auth. see Museum of Science & Industry.
Crypton, Dr. Timid Virgins Make Dull Company & Other Puzzles, Pitfalls & Paradoxes. (Illus.). 192p. 1984. 14.95 (ISBN 0-670-71575-1). Viking.
Crystal. Linguistic Controversies. (Illus.). 288p. 1982. text ed. 44.95 (ISBN 0-7131-6349-6). Univ Park.
Crystal, D. Prosodic Systems & Intonation in English. LC 69-13792. (Cambridge Studies in Linguistics: No. 1). (Illus.). 1969. 57.50 (ISBN 0-521-07387-1); pap. 21.95 (ISBN 0-521-29058-9). Cambridge U Pr.
Crystal, D. J., jt. auth. see Bolton, W. F.
Crystal, David. Child Language, Learning & Linguistics. 114p. 1976. pap. text ed. 11.95 (ISBN 0-7131-5891-3). E Arnold.
--Clinical Linguistics. (Disorders of Human Communication Ser.: Vol. 3). (Illus.). 250p. 1981. 32.00 (ISBN 0-387-81622-4). Springer-Verlag.
--Directions in Applied Linguistics. LC 81-66371. (Applied Language Studies). 1981. 36.00 (ISBN 0-12-198420-6). Acad Pr.
--The English Tone of Voice: Essays in Intonation, Prosody & Paralanguage. LC 76-5970. (Illus.). 200p. 1976. 25.00x (ISBN 0-312-25550-0). St Martin.
--Linguistic Encounters with Language Handicap. 184p. 1985. 24.95x (ISBN 0-631-13869-2). Basil Blackwell.
--Profiling Linguistic Disability. 224p. 1982. pap. text ed. 19.95 (ISBN 0-7131-6354-2). E Arnold.
Crystal, David & Quirk, Randolph. Systems of Prosodic & Paralinguistic Features in English. (Janua Linguarum, Ser. Minor: No. 39). (Orig.). 1964. pap. text ed. 14.00x (ISBN 90-2790-574-6). Mouton.
Crystal, David, ed. Linguistic Controversies. 256p. 1982. text ed. 49.50 (ISBN 0-7131-6349-6). E Arnold.
Crystal, David, ed. see Barber, Charles.
Crystal, David, ed. see Blake, N. F.
Crystal, David, ed. see Brook, G. L.
Crystal, David, ed. see Chang, R. & Chang, M. S.
Crystal, David, ed. see Chapman, Raymond.
Crystal, David, ed. see Elliott, Ralph W.
Crystal, David, ed. see Partridge, Eric.
Crystal, David, eds. see Perera, Katharine.
Crystal, David, ed. see Phillipps, K. C.
Crystal, David, ed. see Todd, Loreto.
Crystal, Graef S. Questions & Answers on Executive Compensation: How to Get What You're Worth. LC 84-11630. 196p. 1984. 27.50 (ISBN 0-13-748476-3, Busn); pap. 9.95 (ISBN 0-13-748468-2). P-H.
Crystal, John C. & Bolles, Richard N. Where Do I Go from Here with My Life? LC 78-61867. (Illus.). 1980. pap. 9.95 (ISBN 0-89815-084-1). Ten Speed Pr.
Crystal, M., jt. auth. see Totty, P.
Crystal, Michael & Higham, John, eds. Loose on Liquidators: The Role of a Liquidator in a Voluntary Winding-up. 2nd ed. 1981. 90.00x (ISBN 0-85308-064-X, Pub. by Jordan & Sons UK). State Mutual Bk.
Crystal, Michael R., jt. auth. see Carris, Joan D.
Crystal, Stephen. America's Old Age Crisis: Public Policy & the Two Worlds of Aging. LC 82-70849. 1982. 16.50 (ISBN 0-465-00124-6). Basic.
--America's Old Age Crisis: Public Policy & the Two Worlds of Aging. LC 82-70849. 232p. 1984. pap. 6.95 (ISBN 0-465-00125-4, CN 5119). Basic.
CSAA. When Children Ask about Sex. 42p. 1974. pap. 1.50 (ISBN 0-87183-243-7). Jewish Bd Family.
--You, Your Child & Drugs. 1971. pap. 1.75 (ISBN 0-87183-238-0). Jewish Bd Family.
CSAAT. What to Tell Your Child about Sex. rev. ed. 1974. 5.70 (ISBN 0-87183-241-0). Jewish Bd Family.
Csaba, G. The Ontogeny & Phylogeny of Hormone Receptors, Vol. 15. (Monographs in Developmental Biology: Vol. 15). (Illus.). xii, 172p. 1981. 61.50 (ISBN 3-8055-2174-X). S Karger.
Csaba, L., et al, eds. Networks from the User's Point of View. 664p. 1981. 89.50 (ISBN 0-444-86291-9, North-Holland). Elsevier.
Csakany, B. & Schmidt, J. Contributions to Universal Algebra. (Colloquia Mathematica Ser.: Vol. 17). 608p. 1978. 119.25 (ISBN 0-7204-0725-7, North-Holland). Elsevier.
Csakany, B. & Rosenberg, I., eds. Finite Algebra & Multiple-Valued Logic. (Colloquia Mathematica Societatis Janos Bolyai: Vol. 28). 880p. 1982. 127.75 (ISBN 0-444-85439-8, North-Holland). Elsevier.
Csakany, B., et al, eds. Universal Algebra. (Colloquia Mathematica Societatis Janos Bolyai: Vol. 29). 804p. 1982. 138.50 (ISBN 0-444-85405-3, North-Holland). Elsevier.
Csaki. State-Space Methods for Control Systems. 1976. 46.00 (ISBN 0-9960005-1-8, Pub. by Akademiai Kaido Hungary). Heyden.
Csaki, C. Simulation & Systems Analysis in Agriculture. (Developments in Agricultural Engineering Ser.: Vol. 2). 1985. 55.75 (ISBN 0-444-99622-2). Elsevier.
Csaki, F. & Anszky, K. Power Electronics. 1980. Repr. of 1975 ed. 50.50 (ISBN 0-9960004-9-6, Pub. by Akademiai Kaido Hungary). Heyden.
Csaki, Frigyes, et al. Power Electronics. rev. ed. Balkay, B., tr. (Illus.). 1980. 50.50 (ISBN 0-9960004-9-6, Pub. by Akademiai Kaido Hungary). Heyden.
Csaki, Luciana C. & Nowakowska, Marie S. Biographical Dictionary of Women Writers in Romance Languages. 150p. 1985. lib. bdg. 20.00 (ISBN 0-8240-8726-7). Garland Pub.
Csaky, T. Z. & Barnes, B. A. Cutting's Handbook of Pharmacology. 7th ed. (Illus.). 768p. 1984. pap. 29.95x (ISBN 0-8385-1418-9). ACC.
Csaky, T. Z., ed. Intestinal Absorption & Malabsorption. LC 74-80532. 318p. 1975. 35.50 (ISBN 0-89004-020-6). Raven.
--Pharmacology of Intestinal Permeation I. (Handbook of Experimental Pharmacology Ser.: Vol. 70, Pt. 1). (Illus.). 800p. 1984. 217.00 (ISBN 0-387-13100-0). Springer-Verlag.
--Pharmacology of Intestinal Permeation 2. (Handbook of Experimental Pharmacology Ser.: Vol. 70, Pt. 2). (Illus.). 640p. 1984. 188.00 (ISBN 0-387-13101-9). Springer Verlag.
Csaky, T. Z. & Gordon, H. A., eds. Aging of the Digestive System. (Aging Ser.). Date not set. write for info. (ISBN 0-89004-310-8, 404). Raven.
Csanady, G. T. Circulation in the Coastal Ocean. 1982. 52.50 (ISBN 90-277-1400-2, Pub. by Reidel Holland). Kluwer Academic.
--Turbulent Diffusion in the Environment. LC 72-92527. (Geophysics & Astrophysics Monographs: No. 3). (Illus.). 248p. 1973. lib. bdg. 37.00 (ISBN 90-277-0260-3); pap. text ed. 21.00 (ISBN 90-277-0261-6). Kluwer Academic.
Csanyi. General Theory of Evolution. (Studia Biologica Academiae Scientiarum Hungaricae: Vol. 18). 1982. 16.00 (ISBN 0-9960072-7-X, Pub. by Akademiai Kaido Hungary). Heyden.
Csaszar, A. General Topology. Cohn, P. M., ed. 1978. 60.00 (ISBN 0-9960018-2-4, Pub. by A Hilger England). Heyden.
--Topology, 2 vols. (Colloquia Mathematica Societatis Janos Bolyai: Vol. 23). 1260p. 1980. Set. 149.00 (ISBN 0-444-85406-1, North-Holland). Elsevier.
Csath, Geza. The Magician's Garden & Other Stories. Kessler, Joscha & Rogers, Charlotte, trs. from Hungarian. (Illus.). 1980. 21.00x (ISBN 0-231-04732-0). Columbia U Pr.
--Opium & Other Stories. 208p. 1983. pap. 4.95 (ISBN 0-14-006689-6). Penguin.
Cscapes. C Library Reference for UNIX. rev. ed. 16p. 1983. 4.00 (ISBN 0-916151-00-X). Specialized Sys.
CSE Microelectronics Group. Microelectronics: Capitalist Technology & the Working Class. 152p. 1981. 29.00x (ISBN 0-906336-16-3, Pub. by CSE Bks England). State Mutual Bk.
Csepinszky, A., ed. Input-Output Techniques. 1976. 29.00 (ISBN 0-9960004-7-X, Pub. by Akademiai Kaido Hungary). Heyden.
Cserr, Helen F., et al, eds. see Symposium Held at the Mount Desert Island Biological Laboratory, Salisbury Cove, Maine, Sept. 1974.
Csete, Marie, jt. auth. see Rippe, James.
Csettkey, Laszlo. Az 1944 Oktoberi Esemenyek Es Az Osszeomlas Eloestejen. LC 81-50628. 125p. (Orig., Hungarian.). 1981. pap. write for info. (ISBN 0-935484-08-6). Universe Pub Co.
Csiba, E. Leathercraft. (Illus.). 8.50 (ISBN 963-13-4641-2). Newbury Bks.
Csicsery-Ronay, Istvan. Salata Kalman: Dokumentumdrama. LC 84-60250. 91p. (Hung.). 1984. 8.00 (ISBN 0-911050-55-8); pap. 6.00 (ISBN 0-911050-54-X). Occidental.
Csida, Joseph. The Magic Ground. 320p. 1981. pap. 3.50 (ISBN 0-671-83135-6). PB.
--The Music-Record Career Handbook. rev. ed. 360p. 1980. 16.95 (ISBN 0-8230-7581-8, Billboard Bks). Watson-Guptill.
--Remember This House. 576p. (Orig.). 1985. pap. 3.95 (ISBN 0-553-22844-7). Bantam.
--Unknown Shores: The Saga of the Steeles, Vol. II. (Richard Galen Bks.). (Orig.). 1981. pap. 3.50 (ISBN 0-671-83136-4). PB.
Csikos-Nagy, B. Towards a New Price Revolution. 1981. 40.00x (ISBN 0-569-08548-9, Pub. by Collet's). State Mutual Bk.
Csikos-Nagy, Bela. Pricing in Hungary. (Institute of Economic Affairs, Occasional Papers Ser.: No. 19). pap. 2.50 technical (ISBN 0-255-69617-5). Transatlantic.
--Socialist Economic Policy. LC 72-90020. 1979. 26.00 (ISBN 0-312-73745-9). St Martin.
Csikos-Nagy, Bela, et al, eds. The Economics of Relative Prices. LC 83-40163. 350p. 1984. 35.00 (ISBN 0-312-23442-2). St Martin.
Csikszentmihalyi, Mihaly. Beyond Boredom & Anxiety: The Experience of Play in Work & Games. LC 75-21751. (Social & Behavioral Science Ser.). (Illus.). 1975. 19.95x (ISBN 0-87589-261-2). Jossey-Bass.
Csikszentmihalyi, Mihaly & Larson, Reed. Being Adolescent: Conflict & Growth in the Teenage Years. LC 83-45253. 332p. 1984. 21.95 (ISBN 0-465-00646-9). Basic.
Csikszentmihalyi, Mihaly, jt. auth. see Getzels, Jacob W.
Csikszentmihalyi, Mihalyi & Rochberg-Halton, Eugene. The Meaning of Things: Symbols in the Development of the Self. LC 81-1443. 256p. 1981. 44.50 (ISBN 0-521-23919-2); pap. 15.95 (ISBN 0-521-28774-X). Cambridge U Pr.
Csillik, B., ed. see International Society for Neurovegatative Research-Tinany-1972.
CSIRO. Insects of Australia. 1973. Repr. 55.00x (ISBN 0-522-83837-5, Pub by Melbourne U Pr Australia). Intl Spec Bk.

Csiszar, I. & Elias, P. Topics in Information Theory. (Colloquia Mathematica Societatis Janos Bolyai Ser.: Vol. 16). 592p. 1977. 106.50 (ISBN 0-7204-0699-4, North Holland). Elsevier.

Csiszar, I., ed. see CISM (International Center for Mechanical Sciences), Dept. of Automation & Information, 1970.

Csiszar, I., ed. see CISM (International Center for Mechanical Sciences), Dept. of Automation & Information.

Csiszar, Imre & Korner, Janos. Information Theory: Coding Theorems for Discrete Memoryless Systems. (Probability and Mathematical Statistics Ser.). 1982. 64.00 (ISBN 0-12-198450-8). Acad Pr.

Csizinsky, A. Vimlati, jt. auth. see Old, Leila S.

Csizmadia, I. G. Molecular Structure & Conformation: Recent Advances. (Progress in Theoretical Organic Chemistry Ser.: Vol. 3). 344p. 1982. 93.75 (ISBN 0-444-42089-4, I-260-82). Elsevier.

Csizmadia, I. G., ed. Applications of MO Theory in Organic Chemistry. (Progress in Theoretical Organic Chemistry Ser.: Vol. 2). 626p. 1977. 106.50 (ISBN 0-444-41565-3). Elsevier.

Csokits, Janos, tr. see Pilinszky, Janos.

Csoma, Sandor K. The Life & Teachings of Buddha. LC 78-72399. Repr. of 1957 ed. 21.50 (ISBN 0-404-17258-X). AMS Pr.

--Tibetan Studies: Being a Reprint of the Articles Contributed to the Journal of the Asiatic Society of Bengal. Denilson, E., ed. LC 78-72400. Repr. of 1912 ed. 27.50 (ISBN 0-404-17259-8). AMS Pr.

Csoma de Koros, Alexander. A Dictionary of Tibetan & English. 351p. (Tibetan & Eng.). 1978. Repr. of 1834 ed. 55.00 (ISBN 0-89684-107-3, Pub. by Cosmo Pubns India). Orient Bk Dist.

--Tibetan-English Dictionary, 4 vols. Incl. Vol. 1. Essay towards a Dictionary Tibetan English. 392p. text ed. 48.00x (ISBN 963-05-3819-9); Vol. 2. A Grammar of the Tibetan Language. 244p. text ed. 35.50x (ISBN 963-05-3820-2); Vol. 3. Sanskrit Tibetan-English Vocabulary. 390p. text ed. 53.50x (ISBN 963-05-3821-0); Vol. 4. Tibetan Studies. 459p. text ed. 62.00x (ISBN 963-05-3822-9). (Collected Works of Csomo de Koros). 1984. Repr. Set. text ed. 165.50x (ISBN 0-317-07225-0, Pub. by Kultura Hungary). Humanities.

Csomos, G. Clinical Hepatology: History-Present State-Outlook. (Illus.). 430p. 1983. 48.00 (ISBN 0-387-11838-1). Springer-Verlag.

Csoori, Sandor. Memory of Snow. Kolumban, Nicholas, tr. from Hungarian. (Translation Ser.). (Illus.). 72p. 1983. 22.50 (ISBN 0-915778-53-X); pap. 8.50 (ISBN 0-915778-52-1); deluxe ed. 125.00 (ISBN 0-915778-54-8). Penmaen Pr.

Csorba, Illes P. Image Tubes. LC 83-51122. 45.00 (ISBN 0-672-22023-7, 21984). Sams.

Csorgo, M. & Revesz, P. Strong Aproximations in Probability & Statistics. LC 79-57112. (Probability & Mathematical Statistics Ser.). 1981. 44.50 (ISBN 0-12-198540-7). Acad Pr.

Csorgo, M., et al, eds. Statistics & Related Topics: Proceedings Conference, Ottawa, Canada, May, 1980. 388p. 1981. 53.25 (ISBN 0-444-86293-5, North-Holland). Elsevier.

Csorgo, Miklos. Quantile Processes with Statistical Applications. LC 83-60222. (CBMS-NSF Regional Conference Ser.: No. 42). xiii, 156p. 1983. pap. text ed. 17.50 (ISBN 0-89871-185-1). Soc Indus-Appl Math.

Csorna, S. E., jt. ed. see Panvini, R. S.

CSPI Staff. The Midget Encyclopedia of Food & Nutrition. 1978. pap. 0.50 (ISBN 0-89329-008-4). Ctr Sci Public.

Csuti, Blair. Type Specimens of Recent Mammals in the Museum of Vertebrate Zoology, University of California, Berkeley. (U. C. Publications in Zoology Ser.: Vol. 114). 80p. 1981. 13.50x (ISBN 0-520-09622-3). U of Cal Pr.

Cua, A. S. Dimensions of Moral Creativity: Paradigms, Principles, & Ideals. LC 77-16169. 1978. 22.50x (ISBN 0-271-00540-8). Pa St U Pr.

--Ethical Argumentation: A Study of Hsun Tzu's Moral Epistemology. LC 84-24016. 288p. 1985. text ed. 23.50x (ISBN 0-8248-0942-4). UH Pr.

--The Unity of Knowledge & Action: A Study in Wang Yang-Ming's Moral Psychology. LC 81-23060. 147p. 1982. text ed. 12.95x (ISBN 0-8248-0786-3). UH Pr.

Cuadra, Carlos, et al, eds. Annual Review of Information Science & Technology, Vol. 10. LC 66-25096. 1975. 27.50 (ISBN 0-87715-210-1). Am Soc Info Sci.

Cuadra, Carlos A., ed. The Annual Review of Information Science & Technology, 1968, Vol. 3. LC 66-25096. (Illus.). 457p. 1968. 45.00 (ISBN 0-685-94669-X, 315-BW). Knowledge Indus.

Cuadra, Carlos A. & Luke, Ann W., eds. The Annual Review of Information Science & Technology, 1969, Vol. 4. LC 66-25096. 547p. 1969. 45.00 (ISBN 0-85229-147-7, 314-BW). Knowledge Indus.

--The Annual Review of Information Science & Technology, 1970, Vol. 5. LC 66-25096. 468p. 1970. 45.00 (ISBN 0-85229-156-6, 313-BW). Knowledge Indus.

--The Annual Review of Information Science & Technology, 1972, Vol. 7. LC 66-25096. (Illus.). 606p. 1972. 45.00 (ISBN 0-87715-206-3, 312-BW). Knowledge Indus.

--The Annual Review of Information Science & Technology, 1973, Vol. 8. LC 66-25096. 411p. 1973. 45.00 (ISBN 0-87715-208-X, 311-BW). Knowledge Indus.

--The Annual Review of Information Science & Technology, 1974, Vol. 9. LC 66-25096. (Illus.). 457p. 1974. 45.00 (ISBN 0-87715-209-8, 310-BW). Knowledge Indus.

--The Annual Review of Information Science & Technology, 1975, Vol. 10. LC 66-25096. 476p. 1975. 45.00 (ISBN 0-87715-210-1, 309-BW). Knowledge Indus.

Cuadra, Hector, jt. ed. see Lozoya, Jorge A.

Cuadra, Pablo A. The Jaguar & the Moon. Merton, Thomas, tr. from Span. LC 74-82760. (Keepsake Ser: Vol. 5). (Illus.). 1974. 10.00 (ISBN 0-87775-060-2); pap. 5.00 (ISBN 0-87775-064-5). Unicorn Pr.

--Songs of Cifar & the Sweet Sea. Schulman, Grace & De Zavala, Ann M., trs. from Sp. (A Center for Inter-American Relations Book). 144p. 1979. 21.00x (ISBN 0-231-04772-X); pap. 11.00x (ISBN 0-231-04773-8). Columbia U Pr.

Cua-Lim, Felicidad, et al. Asthma Research: Clinical Studies. 204p. 1974. text ed. 29.00x (ISBN 0-8422-7172-4). Irvington.

Cuaron, Alicia V., et al. Adelante, Mujer Hispana: A Conference Model for Hispanic Women. 1980. pap. 9.00 (ISBN 0-931738-09-1). Info Systems.

Cuartas, Augusto, jt. auth. see Santamarie, Andres.

Cuatrecasas, Jose. Brunelliaceae. (Flora Neotropica Monograph: No. 2). 1984. Repr. of 1970 ed. 15.00x (ISBN 0-89327-263-9). NY Botanical.

Cuatrecasas, P. & Greaves, M. F., eds. Receptors & Recognition, Series A, 6 vols. Incl. Vol. 1. (No. 6072). 175p. 1976 (ISBN 0-412-13800-X); Vol. 2. 229p. 1976 (ISBN 0-412-13810-7, NO. 6073); Vol. 3. 166p. 1977 (ISBN 0-412-14310-0, NO. 6074); Vol. 4. 258p. 1977 (ISBN 0-412-14330-5, NO. 6075); Vol. 5. 212p. 1978 (ISBN 0-412-15270-3, NO. 6076); Vol. 6. 199p. 1978 (ISBN 0-412-15290-8, NO. 6077). 85.20 set (ISBN 0-412-15950-3, NO. 6878, Pub. by Chapman & Hall England); 15.95 ea. Methuen Inc.

Cuatrecasas, P. & Jacobs, S., eds. Membrane Receptors. (Receptors & Recognition Ser. B: Vol. 11). 1981. 49.95x (ISBN 0-412-21740-6, NO. 2156, Pub. by Chapman & Hall). Methuen Inc.

Cuban, Larry. Teachers & Machines: The Classroom Use of Technology. 112p. 1985. pap. text ed. 8.95x (ISBN 0-8077-2792-X). Tchrs Coll.

--To Make a Difference: Teaching in the Inner City. LC 74-102197. 1970. pap. text ed. 4.95 (ISBN 0-02-906890-8). Free Pr.

--Urban School Chiefs Under Fire. LC 75-19509. (Illus.). 272p. 1976. 16.00x (ISBN 0-226-12314-6). U of Chicago Pr.

Cuban National Planning Council, et al. The Cuban Minority in the U. S. The Preliminary & Final Reports on Need Identification & Program Evaluation, 2 vols. Set. 75.00 (ISBN 0-405-13199-2). Ayer Co Pubs.

Cubarikov, V. N. see Steklov Institute of Mathematics.

Cubas, Antonio G. The Republic of Mexico in Eighteen Seventy-Six: A Political & Ethnological Division of the Population, Character, Habits, Costumes & Vocations of Its Inhabitants. (Mexico Ser.). 1979. lib. bdg. 59.95 (ISBN 0-8490-2997-X). Gordon Pr.

Cubberley, Ellwood P. School Funds & Their Apportionment, a Consideration of the Subject with Reference to a More General Equalization of Both the Burdens & the Advantages of Education. LC 72-176681. (Columbia University. Teachers College. Contributions to Education: No. 2). Repr. of 1906 ed. 22.50 (ISBN 0-404-55002-9). AMS Pr.

--Syllabus of Lectures on the History of Education with Selected Bibliographies & Suggested Readings. 2nd ed. (Illus.). 360p. 1971. Repr. of 1904 ed. 22.50x (ISBN 0-87471-010-3). Rowman.

Cubberley, Ellwood P., ed. Readings in Public Education in the United States: A Collection of Sources & Readings to Illustrate the History of Educational Practice & Progress in the United States. LC 79-104258. Repr. of 1934 ed. lib. bdg. 24.50x (ISBN 0-8371-3912-0, CUPE). Greenwood.

Cubberley, Ellwood P., ed. see Chapman, J. C., et al.

Cubberley, William. The Commodity Market Today. 62p. (Orig.). 1979. pap. 11.00x (ISBN 0-686-37422-3). Future Pub FL.

Cubberly, Ray E. The Role of Fouche During the Hundred Days. LC 78-626285. 1969. 3.50 (ISBN 0-87020-136-0, Logmark Eds). State Hist Soc Wis.

Cubbon, A. M. Crossses of the Isle of Man. pap. 4.95. British AM Bks.

--Prehistoric Sites in the Isle of Man. pap. 3.95 (ISBN 0-686-10856-6). British Am Bks.

Cube, Hans L. von see Von Cube, Hans L. & Staimle, Fritz.

Cube, R. Empty Cornucopia. 1984. 14.95 (ISBN 0-533-06084-2). Vantage.

Cubeddu, R. & Andreoni, A., eds. Porphyrins in Tumor Phototherapy. 450p. 1984. 67.50x (ISBN 0-306-41630-1, Plenum Pr). Plenum Pub.

Cubenas, Jose A. Spanish & Hispanic Presence in Florida from the Discovery to the Bicentennial. 1979. pap. 4.00 (ISBN 84-499-2888-5). Edit Mensaje.

Cubine-Apple, Nancycaroline B., ed. see Kolbaska, John.

Cubine-Apple, Nancycaroline B., ed. see Stach, Alex G.

Cubit, Harry. Electrical Construction Cost Estimating. (Illus.). 320p. 1981. 39.95 (ISBN 0-07-014885-6). McGraw.

Cubitt, jt. auth. see British Horse Society & Pony Club.

Cubitt, Heather. Luther & the Reformation. Reeves, Marjorie, ed. (Then & There Ser.). (Illus.). 96p. (gr. 7-12). 1976. pap. text ed. 3.75 (ISBN 0-582-20542-5). Longman.

--Russia under the Last Tsar. Reeves, Marjorie, ed. (Then & There Ser.). (Illus.). 96p. (Orig.). (gr. 7-12). 1980. pap. text ed. 3.40 (ISBN 0-582-22141-2). Longman.

--Spain & Her Empire Under Philip II. Reeves, Marjorie, ed. (Then & There Ser.). (Illus.). 96p. (Orig.). (gr. 7-12). 1976. pap. text ed. 3.40 (ISBN 0-582-20434-8). Longman.

Cubitt, J. M., ed. Mathematical Models in the Earth Sciences: Proceedings of the 7th Geochautauqua, Syracuse University, Oct. 1978. 90p. 1980. pap. 45.00 (ISBN 0-08-025305-9). Pergamon.

Cubitt, J. M. & Henley, S., eds. Statistical Analysis in Geology. LC 78-17368. (Benchmark Papers in Geology: Vol. 37). 340p. 1978. 54.95 (ISBN 0-87933-335-9). Van Nos Reinhold.

Cubitt, J. M. & Reyment, R. A., eds. Quantitative Stratigraphic Correlation. LC 81-21926. (International Geological Correlation Programme Ser.). 301p. 1982. 59.95 (ISBN 0-471-10171-0, Pub. by Wiley-Interscience). Wiley.

Cubitt, John M. & Burek, Cynthia V. A Bibliography of Electron Spin Resonance Applications in the Earth Sciences. (Bibliography Ser.). 1980. 10.00x (ISBN 0-686-27378-8, Pub. by GEO Abstracts England). State Mutual Bk.

Cuca, Roberto. Family Planning Programs: An Evaluation of Experience. (Working Paper: No. 345). xii, 134p. 1979. 5.00 (ISBN 0-686-36195-4, WP-0345). World Bank.

Cuca, Roberto & Pierce, Catherine S. Experiments in Family Planning: Lessons from the Developing World. (World Bank Ser.). 280p. 1978. text ed. 25.00x (ISBN 0-8018-2013-8); pap. text ed. 9.95x (ISBN 0-8018-2014-6). Johns Hopkins.

Cucari, Attilio, jt. auth. see Angelucci, Enzo.

Cucchiella, S. Baltimore Deco. (Illus.). 64p. (Orig.). 1984. pap. 8.95 (ISBN 0-940776-16-2). Maclay Assoc.

Cucco, Ulisse, jt. auth. see Joseph, Lou.

Cuchi, Jose C. Un Problema En America: The American Problem, Spanish Text. LC 74-14227. (The Puerto Rican Experience Ser.). (Illus.). 246p. 1975. Repr. 18.00x (ISBN 0-405-06217-6). Ayer Co Pubs.

Cucin, Robert L. Keeping Face: A Plastic Surgeon's Guide to Preserving & Improving Nature's Gifts. (Illus.). 183p. 1985. 22.50 (ISBN 0-9608304-2-1). Rocin.

--Kindest Cut. (Illus.). 193p. 1985. 15.95 (ISBN 0-9608304-0-5). Rocin.

Cucksey, J. & Medland, D. The Unlisted Securities Market. (Waterlow Executive Bulletins Ser.). 72p. 1984. pap. 11.15 (ISBN 0-08-039197-4). Pergamon.

Cucuel, G. La Poupliniere et la Musique de Chambre Au XVIII Siecle. LC 70-158961. (Music Ser). (Fr.). 1971. Repr. of 1913 ed. lib. bdg. 49.50 (ISBN 0-306-70186-3). Da Capo.

Cucuel, Georges. Les Createurs de l'Opera-Comique Francais. LC 80-2271. Repr. of 1914 ed. 29.50 (ISBN 0-404-18834-6). AMS Pr.

Cucumber Group. Why Cucumbers Are Better Than Men. LC 82-24194. (Illus.). 32p. 1983. pap. 2.95 (ISBN 0-87131-399-5). M Evans.

Cudahy, Brian. Destination Loop. LC 82-11953. 1982. 16.95 (ISBN 0-8289-0480-4). Greene.

Cudahy, Brian J. Under the Sidewalks of New York: The Story of the Greatest Subway System in the World. LC 79-15221. (Illus.). 1979. 16.95 (ISBN 0-8289-0352-2). Greene.

Cudahy, Sheila. The Bristle Cone Pine & Other Poems. 61p. 1976. 5.95 (ISBN 0-15-114185-1). HarBraceJ.

Cudakov, N. G., et al. Number Theory & Analysis. (Translations Ser.: No. 1, Vol. 2). 1970. Repr. of 1962 ed. 32.00 (ISBN 0-8218-1602-0, TRANS-1-2). Am Math.

Cudd, Kermit G., jt. auth. see Ettkin, Lawrence P.

Cuddihy, Michael. Celebrations. 28p. 1980. pap. 8.00 (ISBN 0-914742-52-3). Copper Canyon.

Cuddihy, William. Agricultural Price Management in Egypt. (Working Paper: No. 388). x, 164p. 1980. 5.00 (ISBN 0-686-36062-1, WP-0388). World Bank.

Cuddington, John T., et al. Disequilibrium Macroeconomics in Open Economies. 272p. 1984. 34.95x (ISBN 0-631-13532-4). Basil Blackwell.

Cuddon, J. A. Dictionary of Literary Terms. 1982. pap. 8.95 (ISBN 0-14-051112-1). Penguin.

--Yugoslavia. (Companion Guides Ser.). (Illus.). 1984. pap. 16.95 (ISBN 0-13-154824-7) (ISBN 0-13-154816-6). P-H.

Cuddon, J. A., ed. The Penguin Book of Ghost Stories. (Penguin Fiction Ser.). 512p. 1985. pap. 6.95 (ISBN 0-14-006800-7). Penguin.

--The Penguin Book of Horror Stories. (Penguin Fiction Ser.). 560p. 1985. pap. 6.95 (ISBN 0-14-006799-X). Penguin.

Cuddy, Dennis L. Contemporary American Immigration: Interpretive Essays (European & Non-European, 2 vols. (Immigrant Heritage of America Ser.). 1982. Non-european. 18.50 (ISBN 0-8057-8420-9, Twayne); European. 18.50 (ISBN 0-8057-8421-7); lib. bdg. 31.50 (ISBN 0-8057-8422-5). G K Hall.

--Contemporary Australian-American Relations. LC 80-65615. 155p. 1981. perfect bdg. 12.95 (ISBN 0-86548-027-3). R & E Pubs.

--The Yanks Are Coming: American Immigration to Australia. LC 77-79060. 1977. 11.95 (ISBN 0-88247-459-6). R & E Pubs.

Cuddy, Jack, ed. see Dempsey, Jack.

Cuddy, Joseph E. Irish-America & National Isolationism: 1914-1920. LC 76-6332. (Irish Americans Ser.). 1976. 22.00 (ISBN 0-405-09328-4). Ayer Co Pubs.

Cude, Wilfred. A Due Sense of Differences: An Evaluative Approach to Canadian Literature. LC 80-67244. 237p. lib. bdg. 22.75 (ISBN 0-8191-1206-2); pap. text ed. 12.00 (ISBN 0-8191-1207-0). U Pr of Amer.

Cudia, S. J., jt. auth. see Benton, Allen H.

Cudinach, Salvidor, ed. & tr. see Piarist Fathers.

Cudjoe, Selwyn R. Movement of the People. 224p. (Orig.). 1983. text ed. 18.95 (ISBN 0-686-39680-4); pap. text ed. 8.95 (ISBN 0-911565-22-1). Calaloux Pubns.

--Resistance & Caribbean Literature. LC 76-25616. xii, 319p. 1981. 20.00x (ISBN 0-8214-0353-2, 82-82451); pap. 8.95x (ISBN 0-8214-0573-X, 82-82469). Ohio U Pr.

Cudkowicz, Leon. The Human Bronchial Circulation in Health & Disease. LC 68-30266. 440p. 1968. 26.50 (ISBN 0-683-02210-5, Pub. by Williams & Wilkins). Krieger.

Cudkowitz, Gustavo, et al, eds. Natural Resistance Systems Against Foreign Cells, Tumors & Microbes. (Perspectives in Immunology Ser.: Vol. 7). 1978. 43.00 (ISBN 0-12-199735-9). Acad Pr.

Cudlip, David R. Comprador. 416p. 1984. 16.95 (ISBN 0-525-24230-9, 01646-490). Dutton.

--Comprador. 432p. 1985. pap. 3.95 (ISBN 0-380-69908-7). Avon.

Cudlipp, Edythe. Adenauer. (World Leaders: Past & Present Ser.). (Illus.). 112p. 1985. lib. bdg. 15.95x (ISBN 0-87754-582-0). Chelsea Hse.

Cudsi, Alex & Dessouki, Ali E. Hillal, eds. Islam & Power in the Contemporary Muslim World. LC 81-47608. 208p. 1981. text ed. 20.00x (ISBN 0-8018-2697-7). Johns Hopkins.

Cudworth, Marsha & Michaels, Howard. Victorian Holidays: A Guide to Guesthouses, Bed & Breakfast Inns & Restaurants of Cape May, N. J. 2nd, rev. & enlarged ed. LC 82-83816. 125p. (Orig.). pap. 7.95 (ISBN 0-9608554-1-6, Pub. by Lady Raspberry). Bric-A-Brac.

Cudworth, Ralph. A Treatise Concerning Eternal & Immutable Morality. Wellek, Rene, ed. LC 75-11214. (British Philosophers & Theologians of the 17th & 18th Centuries Ser.: Vol. 17). 1976. Repr. of 1731 ed. lib. bdg. 51.00 (ISBN 0-8240-1768-4). Garland Pub.

--True Intellectual System of the Universe. Repr. of 1678 ed. 211.00 (ISBN 3-7728-0103-X). Adlers Foreign Bks.

--The True Intellectual System of the Universe, 2 vols. Wellek, Rene, ed. LC 75-11213. (British Philosophers & Theologians of the 17th & 18th Centuries Ser.: Vol. 16). 1978. Repr. of 1678 ed. Set. lib. bdg. 101.00 (ISBN 0-8240-1767-6). Garland Pub.

Cue Canovas, Agustin. Los Estados Unidos y el Mexico Olvidado. Cortes, Carlos E., ed. LC 76-5224. (Chicano Heritage Ser.). (Span.). 1976. Repr. of 1970 ed. 14.00x (ISBN 0-405-09498-1). Ayer Co Pubs.

Cuelho, Art. Last Foot of Shade. 36p. (Orig.). 1975. pap. 3.00 (ISBN 0-914974-05-X). Holmgangers.

Cuellar, Gabriel. Fancy Programming in Applesoft. 1983. 16.95 (ISBN 0-8359-1856-4); incl. disk 30.00 (ISBN 0-8359-1858-0). Reston.

--Fancy Programming in IBM PC BASIC. 17.95 (ISBN 0-8359-1860-2); incl. disk 29.95 (ISBN 0-8359-1854-8). Reston.

--Games for the IBM-PC. 1984. 19.95 (ISBN 0-8359-2420-3). Reston.

--Graphics Made Easy for the IBM PC & PC XT. (Illus.). 442p. 18.95 (ISBN 0-317-12839-6). P-H.

--Graphics Made Easy for the IBM PC or PC XT. (Illus.). 1984. pap. 18.95 (ISBN 0-8359-2569-2). Reston.

Cuellar, Javier Perez de. United Nations Action in the Field of Human Rights. 389p. 1985. pap. 37.00 (UN83/14/2, UN). Unipub.

Cuello, A. C., ed. Brain Microdissection Techniques. (IBRO Handbook Ser.: Methods in the Neurosciences). 186p. 1983. 53.95 (ISBN 0-471-10523-6, Pub. by Wiley-Interscience); pap. 24.95 (ISBN 0-471-90019-2, Pub. by Wiley-Interscience). Wiley.

--Immunohistochemistry. (IBRO Handbook Ser.: Methods in the Neurosciences). 501p. 1983. 95.00 (ISBN 0-471-10245-8, Pub. by Wiley-Interscience); pap. 39.95 498p (ISBN 0-471-90052-4). Wiley.

Cuenca, Alfredo O., Jr. Second Selected Poems. 84p. (Orig.). 1982. pap. 6.00x (ISBN 0-686-37567-X, Pub. by New Day Philippines). Cellar.

Cueni, R. Robert. It Was a Day Like This. (Orig.). 1977. pap. 2.25 (ISBN 0-89536-111-6). CSS of Ohio.

Cuenod, M. & Durling, A. Discrete-Time Approach for System Analysis. (Electrical Science Ser.). 1969. 60.00 (ISBN 0-12-198550-4). Acad Pr.

Cuenod, M., et al, eds. see International Symposium, Switzerland, Sept. 1978.

Cuenod, M. A., ed. see IFAC Symposium, Zurich, Switzerland, 29-31 Aug. 1979.

Cuesta, Benedicto. El Paisano: Nuevo Mexico: Vida y Dilema. 1976. pap. 4.95 (ISBN 0-913270-59-8). Sunstone Pr.

Cuesta, Felip Arroyo De La see Arroyo De La Cuesta, Felipe.

Cuesta Mendoza, Antonio. Historia de la educacion en Puerto Rico (1512-1826) LC 73-3581. (Catholic University of America. Studies in American Church History: No. 27). Repr. of 1937 ed. 26.00 (ISBN 0-404-57777-6). AMS Pr.

Cueto-Rua, Julio C. Judicial Methods of Interpretation of the Law. 508p. 1981. 30.00 (ISBN 0-940448-08-4). LSU Paul M Hebert Law Cen Pub Inst.

Cueva, Agustin. The Process of Political Domination in Ecuador. Salti, Danielle, tr. LC 79-809. 109p. 1981. 19.95 (ISBN 0-87855-338-X). Transaction Bks.

Cuff, Barry. Damned Spot. 1969. pap. 0.95 (ISBN 0-87067-172-3, BH172). Holloway.

--Right Fuse. (Orig.). 1969. pap. 0.95 (ISBN 0-87067-179-0, BH179). Holloway.

Cuff, David J. & Mattson, Mark T. Thematic Maps. (Illus.). 176p. 1982. 14.95x (ISBN 0-416-60221-5, NO. 2893); tchr's. manual 2.95 (ISBN 0-416-34320-1, NO. 3731). Methuen Inc.

Cuff, David J. & Young, William J. The United States Energy Atlas. (Illus.). 1980. 85.00 (ISBN 0-02-691250-3). Free Pr.

Cuff, E. C. & Payne, G. C., eds. Crisis in the Curriculum. LC 84-29202. 248p. 1985. 31.00 (ISBN 0-7099-3421-1, Pub. by Croom Helm Ltd). Longwood Pub Group.

--Perspectives in Sociology. 2nd ed. 1983. pap. text ed. 7.95x (ISBN 0-04-301157-8). Allen Unwin.

Cuff, E. C., jt. ed. see Payne, G. C.

Cuff, P. J., tr. see Gabba, Emilio.

Cuff, Penelope, jt. auth. see Page, Clint.

Cuff, Penelope, jt. ed. see Page, Clint.

Cuff, Robert D. The War Industries Board: Business-Government Relations during World War 1. LC 72-4002. 320p. 1973. 30.00x (ISBN 0-8018-1360-3). Johns Hopkins.

Cuff, W. R. & Tomczak, M., Jr., eds. Synthesis & Modeling of Inermitent Estuaries. (Lecture Notes on Coastal and Estuarine Studies Ser.: Vol. 3). 302p. 1983. pap. 24.00 (ISBN 0-387-12681-3). Springer Verlag.

Cuffee. Lords of the Soil. 15.00 (ISBN 0-911660-24-0). Yankee Peddler.

Cuffee, James W. Spiritual Automobile. Knickerbocker, Charles, ed. 44p. 1980. 4.75 (ISBN 0-682-48997-2). Exposition Pr FL.

Cufley, C. F. Ocean Freights & Chartering. rev. ed. (Illus.). 1980. 55.00 (ISBN 0-686-77963-0). Heinman.

--Ocean Freights & Chartering. (Illus.). 562p. 1980. Repr. of 1964 ed. 35.00x (ISBN 0-246-11383-9). Sheridan.

Cugat, X. Rumba Is My Life. (Ballroom Dance Ser.). 1985. lib. bdg. 79.95 (ISBN 0-87700-848-5). Revisionist Pr.

Cugiani, M., jt. auth. see Archetti, F.

Cugno, Alain. St. John of the Cross: Reflections on Mystical Experience. Wall, Barbara, tr. Orig. Title: Saint Jean De la Croix. (Illus.). 192p. 1982. pap. 13.95 (ISBN 0-8164-0132-2, Pub. by Seabury). Winston Pr.

Cugy, Andre & Page, Kogan. Industrial Robot Specifications. Ioannou, Adrian, ed. LC 84-14660. 367p. 1984. text ed. 175.00 (ISBN 0-8144-7628-7). Amacom.

Cuinat, R., et al. Ecological Diagnosis in Salmonid Streams: Method & Example. (European Inland Fisheries Advisory Commission (EIFAC): Technical Papers: No. 22). 135p. (Eng. & Fr., 2nd Printing 1976). 1975. pap. 9.00 (ISBN 92-5-102074-4, F762, FAO). Unipub.

Cuisance, P. & Seabrook, P. Arbustes d'ornement. (Collection "Flore"). (Illus.). 144p. (Fr.). 1970. 15.95x (ISBN 2-03-074705-X). Larousse.

Cuisenier. Jules Romain, L'unanimisme et les Hommes de Bonne Volonte. 10.50 (ISBN 0-685-37080-1). French & Eur.

Cuisenier, J. The Family Life Cycle in European Societies. (New Babylon Studies in the Social Sciences: No. 28). 1977. 32.80x (ISBN 90-279-7822-0). Mouton.

Cuisenier, Jean. Economie et Parente: Leurs Affinites de Structure dans le Domaine Turc et dans le Domaine Arabe. (Le Monde d'Outre-Mer Passe & Present, Etudes: No. 60). (Illus.). 1975. pap. 57.60x (ISBN 90-2797-675-9). Mouton.

Cuisenier, Jean, ed. Europe As a Cultural Area. (World Anthropology Ser.). 1979. text ed. 23.20x (ISBN 90-279-7790-9). Mouton.

Cuisin, Michael. The Frozen North. LC 83-5219. (Nature's Hidden World Ser.). 48p. (gr. 2 up). 1984. 12.68 (ISBN 0-382-06711-8). Silver.

Cuisin, Michel. Animals of the African Plains. LC 80-53904. (Nature's Hidden World Ser.). 48p. (gr. 2 up). 12.68 (ISBN 0-382-06454-2). Silver.

--Birds of Prey. LC 80-53901. (Nature's Hidden World Ser.). 48p. (gr. 2 up). 12.68 (ISBN 0-382-06455-0). Silver.

--Dictionnaire oiseaux. (Illus., Fr.). pap. 8.50 (ISBN 0-685-13879-8, 3729). Larousse.

--The Frozen North. LC 83-5219. (Nature's Hidden World Ser.). (Illus.). 48p. (gr. 3 up). 1985. pap. 4.75 (ISBN 0-382-09148-5). Silver.

--Lakes & Rivers. LC 80-53906. (Nature's Hidden World Ser.). 48p. (gr. 2 up). 12.68 (ISBN 0-382-06452-6). Silver.

--Mountain Animals. LC 80-53905. (Nature's Hidden World Ser.). 48p. (gr. 2 up). PLB 12.68 (ISBN 0-382-06452-6). Silver.

--Prehistoric Life. LC 80-53903. (Nature's Hidden World Ser.). 48p. (gr. 2 up). 12.68 (ISBN 0-382-06453-4). Silver.

--Woods & Forests. LC 80-53902. (Nature's Hidden World Ser.). 48p. (gr. 2 up). 12.68. Silver.

Cuisinier, Jeanne. Danses magiques de Kelantan. LC 77-87024. 1977. Repr. of 1936 ed. 27.00 (ISBN 0-404-16809-4). AMS Pr.

Cuison, Mejia C., jt. auth. see Kim, Hyung-Chan.

Cukierman, Alex. Inflation, Stagflation, Relative Prices & Relative Prices & Imperfect Information. (Illus.). 224p. 1984. 32.50 (ISBN 0-521-25630-5). Cambridge U Pr.

Cukor, George. What Price Hollywood? (RKO Classic Screenplay Ser.). 1984. o. s. i. 14.95 (ISBN 0-8044-2149-8); pap. 8.95 (ISBN 0-8044-6094-9). Ungar.

Cukor, Gyorgy. Strategies of Industrialisation in the Developing Countries. LC 73-89996. 288p. 1974. 26.00 (ISBN 0-312-76440-5). St Martin.

Cukwurah, A. O. The Settlement of Boundary Disputes in International Law. 320p. 1967. 10.00 (ISBN 0-317-30232-9). Oceana.

Culanovski, I. V., et al. Twenty-Five Papers on Statistics & Probability. LC 61-9803. (Selected Translations in Mathematical Statistics & Probability Ser.: Vol. 1). 1961. 37.00 (ISBN 0-8218-1451-6, STAPRO-1). Am Math.

Culberson, Chicita F. Chemical & Botanical Guide to Lichen Products. 1979. pap. text ed. 31.50 (ISBN 3-87429-165-0). Lubrecht & Cramer.

Culberson, W. L., ed. see Tuckerman, E.

Culbert, David, ed. Mission to Moscow. (Wisconsin-Warner Bros. Screenplay Ser.). (Illus.). 280p. 1980. 17.50x (ISBN 0-299-08380-2); pap. 6.95 (ISBN 0-299-08384-5). U of Wis Pr.

Culbert, David H. News for Everyman: Radio & Foreign Affairs in Thirties America. LC 75-23862. 238p. 1976. lib. bdg. 29.95 (ISBN 0-8371-8260-3, CRC/). Greenwood.

Culbert, M., jt. auth. see Bradford, R.

Culbert, Michael. Freedom from Cancer. 238p. 2.95 (ISBN 0-318-15659-8). Natl Health Fed.

--What the Medical Establishment Won't Tell You That Could Save Your Life. 1983. 7.95x. Cancer Control Soc.

Culbert, Michael, jt. auth. see Harper, Harold.

Culbert, Michael L. What the Medical Establishment Won't Tell You That Could SAVE YOUR LIFE! Friedman, Robert S., ed. LC 82-9607. 300p. (Orig.). 1983. pap. 7.95 (ISBN 0-89865-256-1). Donning Co.

Culbert, Mike. Freedom from Cancer. 2.95 (ISBN 0-89245-007-X). Cancer Control Soc.

--Vitamin B17, the Fight for Laetrile. 8.95 (ISBN 0-87000-279-1). Cancer Control Soc.

Culbert, Samuel & McDonough, John J. Radical Mangement: Power Politics & the Pursuit of Trust. 240p. 1985. 17.95 (ISBN 0-02-905940-2). Free Pr.

Culbert, Samuel A. & McDonough, John J. The Invisible War: Pursuing Self-Interests at Work. LC 79-18682. 226p. 1980. 21.95 (ISBN 0-471-05855-6, Pub. by Wiley-Interscience). Wiley.

--Radical Management: Power-Politics & the Pursuit of Trust. 240p. 17.95 (ISBN 0-02-905940-2). Free Pr.

--Radical Management: Power Politics & the Pursuit of Trust. 240p. 1985. 17.26x (ISBN 0-02-905940-2). Free Pr.

Culbert, T. Patrick. Lost Civilization: The Story of the Classic Maya. (Longacre Ser.). (Illus.). 1974. pap. text ed. 11.50 scp (ISBN 0-06-041448-0, HarpC). Har-Row.

Culbert, T. Patrick, jt. auth. see Schusky, Ernest.

Culbert, T. Patrick, ed. The Classic Maya Collapse. 2nd ed. LC 72-94657. (Illus.). 560p. 1984. pap. 14.95x (ISBN 0-8263-0724-8). U of NM Pr.

Culbertson, Alan N. & Kenney, D. E. Contract Administration Manual for the Design Professional: How to Establish, Systematize, & Monitor Construction Contract Controls. (Illus.). 320p. 1983. 346.50 (ISBN 0-07-014894-5). McGraw.

Culbertson, B. M., jt. auth. see Trivedi, B. C.

Culbertson, Bill M. & Pittman, C. U., Jr., eds. New Monomers & Polymers. 450p. 1983. 59.50x (ISBN 0-306-41477-5, Plenum Pr). Plenum Pub.

Culbertson, Charles V. Managing Your Safety Manager. 48p. 1981. 5.50 (ISBN 0-937802-01-8). Risk Mgmt Soc.

Culbertson, J. M., jt. ed. see Smith, W. L.

Culbertson, Jack A. & Henson, Curtis. Performance Objectives for School Principals. LC 74-75367. 1974. 22.25x (ISBN 0-8211-0223-0); text ed. 19.75x 10 or more copies. McCutchan.

Culbertson, James T. Consciousness: Natural & Artifical. LC 81-81617. 1983. 13.95 (ISBN 0-87212-152-6). Libra.

--The Minds of Robots: Sense Data, Memory Images & Behavior in Conscious Automata. LC 63-7256. (Illus.). Repr. of 1963 ed. 120.00 (ISBN 0-8357-9690-6, 2011734). Bks Demand UMI.

--Sensations, Memories & the Flow of Time: A Theory of Subjective States - Reductive Materialism Using a Spacetime Analysis. LC 75-30170. (Illus.). 1976. 8.00x (ISBN 0-916298-01-9). Cromwel.

Culbertson, John M. Competition-Constructive & Destructive. 44p. (Orig.). 1985. pap. 2.95 (ISBN 0-918357-05-5); pap. text ed. 2.20x (ISBN 0-918357-06-3). Twen Fir Pr.

--The Dangers of Free Trade. 44p. 1985. pap. 2.95 (ISBN 0-918357-03-9); pap. text ed. 2.20x (ISBN 0-918357-04-7). Twen Fir Pr.

--International Trade & the Future of the West. LC 84-8699. (Illus.). 242p. 1984. 17.95 (ISBN 0-918357-00-4). Twen Fir Pr.

--International Trade & the Future of the West. LC 84-8699. (Illus.). 242p. 1985. pap. 8.95 (ISBN 0-918357-01-2); pap. text ed. 6.70x (ISBN 0-918357-02-0). Twen Fir Pr.

Culbertson, Joseph. Indian Scout: Memoirs Eighteen Seventy-Six to Eighteen Ninety-Five. rev. ed. Trout, M. D., ed. LC 84-50262. Orig. Title: Joseph Culbertson-Boy Scout. (Illus.). 181p. 1985. pap. 16.95 (ISBN 0-317-13520-1). Van Allen Pub.

Culbertson, Paul. Living Portraits from the Old Testament. 1978. pap. 2.95 (ISBN 0-8341-0507-1). Beacon Hill.

Culbertson, Robert G. Order under Law: Readings in Criminal Justice. 2nd ed. 276p. 1984. pap. text ed. 8.95x (ISBN 0-88133-094-9). Waveland Pr.

Culbertson, Robert G., jt. ed. see Weisheit, Ralph A.

Culbertson, Ron, jt. auth. see Goldberg, Harry.

Culbertson, Stuart A., jt. auth. see Ferster, Charles.

Culbertson, William. God's Provision for Holy Living. (Moody Classics Ser.). 1984. pap. 3.95 (ISBN 0-8024-3043-0). Moody.

Culbertson, William P., Jr., jt. ed. see Breit, William.

Culbertson, William S. Alexander Hamilton: An Essay. 1916. 29.50x (ISBN 0-686-50039-3). Elliots Bks.

Culbreath, Myrna & Marshak, Sondra. Star Trek: The New Voyages. 256p. (gr. 6-12). 1976. pap. 2.95 (ISBN 0-553-24636-4, 12753-5). Bantam.

Culbreath, Myrna, jt. auth. see Marshak, Sondra.

Culbreath, Myrna, jt. ed. see Marshak, Sondra.

Cule, John. A Doctor for the People: Two Thousand Years of General Practice in Britain. 160p. 1980. 50.00x (ISBN 0-906141-29-X, Pub. by MTO Pr). State Mutual Bk.

--A Doctor for the People: 2000 Years of General Practice in Britain. (Illus.). 1981. PLB 39.00 (ISBN 0-906141-29-X, Pub. by Update Pubns England). Kluwer Academic.

Culhane, John. Special Effects in the Movies: How They Do It. 192p. 1981. pap. 9.95 (ISBN 0-345-28606-5). Ballantine.

--Walt Disney's Fantasia. LC 82-24303. (Illus.). 240p. 1983. 35.00 (ISBN 0-8109-0822-0). Abrams.

Culhane, P. T., jt. auth. see O'Toole, L. M.

Culhane, Paul J. Public Lands Politics: Interest Group Influence on the Forest Service & the Bureau of Land Management. LC 80-8776. (Resources for the Future Ser.). (Illus.). 416p. 1981. text ed. 32.50x (ISBN 0-8018-2598-9); pap. text ed. 11.95x (ISBN 0-8018-2599-7). Johns Hopkins.

Culhane, Paul J. & Friesema, H. Paul. Forecasts & Environmental Decision Making: The Content & Accuracy of Environmental Impact Statements. (Social Impact Assessment Ser.: No. 11). 250p. 1985. pap. 21.50x (ISBN 0-8133-0154-8). Westview.

Culhane, T., jt. auth. see Chartier, J. P.

Culhane, Terry. Russian Language & People. (Illus.). 192p. 1980. pap. text ed. 11.95 (ISBN 0-563-16303-8, 65255, British Broadcasting Corp England). EMC.

Culi, Yaakov. The Torah Anthology: Mem Lo'ez, 9 vols. Kaplan, Aryeh, tr. Incl. Vol. 1. Beginnings: From Creation Until Abraham. 540p. 14.95 (ISBN 0-940118-01-7); Vol. 2. The Patriarchs: From Abraham Until Jacob. 600p. 15.95 (ISBN 0-940118-02-5); Vol. 3. The Twelve Tribes: From Jacob Until Joseph. 708p; Vol. 4. Israel in Egypt: Subjugation & Prelude to the Exodus. 280p. 12.95 (ISBN 0-940118-04-1); Vol. 5. Redemption: The Exodus from Egypt. 436p. 15.95 (ISBN 0-940118-05-X); Vol. 6. The Ten Commandments: Revelation at Sinai. 534p. 16.95 (ISBN 0-940118-06-8); Vol. 7. The Law: The First Codification. 363p. 13.95 (ISBN 0-940118-07-6); Vol. 8. Acceptance: Establishing the Covenant. 250p. 12.95 (ISBN 0-940118-08-4); Vol. 9. The Tabernacle: Plans for the Sanctuary. 413p. 15.95 (ISBN 0-940118-09-2). (MeAm Lo'ez Ser.). (Illus.). 1977-1980. Maznaim.

Culianu, Ioan P. Psychanodia I: A Survey of the Evidence Concerning the Ascension of the Soul & its Relevance. (Etudes Prelimminaires aux Religions Orientales dans l'Empire Romain Ser.: No. 99). 81p. 1983. pap. text ed. 17.25x (ISBN 90-04-06903-8, Pub. by Brill Holland). Humanities.

Culicover, Peter W. Syntax. 2nd ed. 356p. 1982. 29.50 (ISBN 0-12-199256-X). Acad Pr.

--Syntax: Internatonal Edition. 1977. 13.50 (ISBN 0-12-199230-6). Acad Pr.

Culicover, Peter W. & Wilkins, Wendy K. Locality in Linguistic Theory. 1984. 44.50 (ISBN 0-12-199280-2). Acad Pr.

Culicover, Peter W., jt. auth. see Wexler, Kenneth.

Culin, Charlotte. Cages of Glass, Flowers of Time. LC 79-14460. 312p. (YA) (gr. 7-9). 1979. 10.95 (ISBN 0-02-725450-X). Bradbury Pr.

--Cages of Glass, Flowers of Time. 288p. (YA) (gr. 7 up). 1982. pap. 2.75 (ISBN 0-440-91319-5, LFL). Dell.

Culin, Robert S. Games of the North American Indians. LC 73-8094. (Illus.). Repr. of 1907 ed. 85.00 (ISBN 0-404-11201-3). AMS Pr.

Culin, Stewart. Chess & Playing-Cards. LC 75-35065. (Studies in Play & Games). (Illus.). 1976. Repr. 31.00x (ISBN 0-405-07916-8). Ayer Co Pubs.

--Chinese Games with Dice & Dominoes. (Shorey Lost Arts Ser.). (Illus.). 74p. pap. 5.95 (ISBN 0-8466-6017-2, U17). Shorey.

--Games of the North American Indians. LC 74-12653. (Illus.). 864p. 1975. Repr. of 1907 ed. 14.95 (ISBN 0-486-23125-9). Dover.

Culinary Arts Inst., jt. auth. see Spitler, Sue.

Culinary Arts Institute. The Book of Pies & Pastries. (Adventures in Cooking Ser.). (Illus.). 80p. 1985. pap. 3.95 (ISBN 0-8326-0674-X, 2543). Delair.

--Chicken, 3 Vols. (The Good Eating Ser.). (Illus.). 112p. pap. 4.95 (ISBN 0-8326-0665-0, 1801). Delair.

--Christmas Favorites. (Adventures in Cooking Ser.). (Illus.). 8p. pap. 3.95 (ISBN 0-8326-0639-1, 2532). Delair.

--Classic Cake Recipes. (Adventures in Cooking Ser.). (Illus.). pap. 3.95 (ISBN 0-8326-0675-8, 2544). Delair.

--Cooking for Christmas. (Adventures in Cooking Ser.). (Illus.). pap. 3.95 (ISBN 0-8326-0640-5, 2533). Delair.

--Cooking with Cheese. (Adventures in Cooking Ser.). (Illus.). pap. 3.95 (ISBN 0-8326-0632-4, 2531). Delair.

--Creative Leftover Cookery. (Adventures in Cooking Ser.). (Illus.). 80p. 1985. pap. 3.95 (ISBN 0-8326-0673-1, 2542). Delair.

--The Culinary Arts Institute Christmas Cookbook. (Illus.). 192p. 12.95 (ISBN 0-8326-0635-9, 1135). Delair.

--Fish & Shellfish. (The Good Eating Ser.). (Illus.). 112p. pap. 4.95 (ISBN 0-8326-0666-9, 1802). Delair.

--The Fish & Shellfish Cookbook. (Adventures in Cooking Ser.). (Illus.). pap. 3.95 (ISBN 0-8326-0669-3, 2538). Delair.

--German & Viennese Cooking. (Adventures in Cooking Ser.). (Illus.). pap. 3.95 (ISBN 0-8326-0626-X, 2524). Delair.

--The Holiday Cookbook. (Adventures in Cooking Ser.). (Illus.). pap. 3.95 (ISBN 0-8326-0629-4, 2527). Delair.

--How to Make Candy. (Adventures in Cooking Ser.). (Illus.). pap. 3.95 (ISBN 0-8326-0637-5, 2534). Delair.

--Hungarian Cookbook. (Adventures in Cooking Ser.). (Illus.). pap. 3.95 (ISBN 0-8326-0627-8, 2525). Delair.

--Kitchen Treasury. (Illus.). 800p. 19.95 (ISBN 0-8326-0636-7, 1140). Delair.

--The Meat Cookbook. (Adventures in Cooking Ser.). (Illus.). 80p. 1985. pap. 3.95 (ISBN 0-8326-0667-7, 2536). Delair.

--One Thousand & One Kitchen Favorites. (Illus.). 400p. 12.95 (ISBN 0-317-06818-0, 1125). Delair.

--The Poultry Cookbook. (Adventures in Cooking Ser.). (Illus.). 80p. 1984. pap. 3.95 (ISBN 0-8326-0668-5, 2537). Delair.

--Quick Dishes for the Woman in a Hurry. (Adventures in Cooking Ser.). (Illus.). pap. 3.95 (ISBN 0-8326-0631-6, 2529). Delair.

--The Salad Book. (Adventures in Cooking Ser.). (Illus.). pap. 3.95 (ISBN 0-8326-0628-6, 2526). Delair.

--The Sandwich Book. (Adventures in Cooking Ser.). (Illus.). 80p. 1985. pap. 3.95 (ISBN 0-8326-0671-5, 2540). Delair.

--Scandinavian Cookbook. (Adventures in Cooking Ser.). (Illus.). pap. 3.95 (ISBN 0-8326-0633-2, 2530). Delair.

--Snacks for All Occasions. (Adventures in Cooking Ser.). (Illus.). 80p. 1984. pap. 3.95 (ISBN 0-8326-0672-3, 2541). Delair.

--Tofu, American Style. (Adventures in Cooking Ser.). (Illus.). 80p. 1985. pap. 3.95 (ISBN 0-8326-0676-6, 2545). Delair.

--Vegetables. (The Good Eating Ser.). (Illus.). 112p. pap. 4.95 (ISBN 0-8326-0664-2, 1800). Delair.

--Vegetables from Artichokes to Zucchini. (Adventures in Cooking Ser.). (Illus.). 80p. 1984. pap. 3.95 (ISBN 0-8326-0670-7, 2539). Delair.

Culinary Arts Institute, jt. auth. see Time-Life Books.

Culinary Arts Institute, ed. Nutrition Cookbook. LC 77-73012. (Adventures in Cooking Ser.). (Illus.). 1978. pap. 3.95 (ISBN 0-8326-0572-7, 2514). Delair.
Culinary Arts Institute, tr. see Goock, Roland.
Culinary Arts Institute Staff, ed. The Budget Cookbook. LC 76-3308. (Adventures in Cooking Ser.). (Illus.). 1976. pap. 3.95 (ISBN 0-8326-0550-6, 2505). Delair.
Culinary Arts Institute Staff. The Culinary Arts Institute French Cookbook. (Illus.). 192p. 1983. spiral binding 7.95 (ISBN 0-671-47238-0, Fireside). S&S.
--Wok, Fondue, & Chafing Dish. LC 78-54625. (Adventures in Cooking Ser.). (Illus.). 1980. pap. 3.95 (ISBN 0-8326-0605-7, 2518). Delair.
Culinary Arts Institute Staff, jt. auth. see Carter, Linda.
Culinary Arts Institute Staff, jt. auth. see Hamelecourt, Juliette.
Culinary Arts Institute Staff, jt. auth. see Johnson, Jackie.
Culinary Arts Institute Staff, jt. auth. see Magida, Phylis.
Culinary Arts Institute Staff, jt. auth. see Phillips, Margot.
Culinary Arts Institute Staff, jt. auth. see Stover, Annette A.
Culinary Arts Institute Staff, ed. Bread & Soup Cookbook. LC 76-26728. (Adventures in Cooking Ser.). (Illus.). 1976. pap. 3.95 (ISBN 0-686-96700-3, 2510). Delair.
--The Cookie Jar. LC 76-41576. (Adventures in Cooking Ser.). (Illus.). 1978. pap. 3.95 (ISBN 0-8326-0563-8, 2511). Delair.
--Crockery Cooking. LC 76-10107. (Adventures in Cooking Ser.). (Illus.). 1978. pap. 3.95 (ISBN 0-8326-0551-4, 2506). Delair.
--The Dessert Book. LC 77-80563. (Adventures in Cooking Ser.). (Illus.). 1978. pap. 3.95 (ISBN 0-8326-0601-4, 2515). Delair.
--Italian Cookbook. LC 77-72330. (Adventures in Cooking Ser.). (Illus.). 1977. pap. 3.95 (ISBN 0-8326-0570-0, 2509). Delair.
--Mexican Cookbook. LC 76-45600. (Adventures in Cooking Ser.). (Illus.). 1976. pap. 3.95 (ISBN 0-8326-0564-6, 2507). Delair.
--Microwave Cooking. LC 76-53103. (Adventures in Cooking Ser.). (Illus.). 1977. pap. 3.95 (ISBN 0-8326-0568-9, 2513). Delair.
--The New World Encyclopedia of Cooking. rev. ed. LC 72-5575. (Illus.). 848p. 1980. 17.95 (ISBN 0-8326-0540-9, 1403-N). Delair.
--Polish Cookbook. LC 76-14648. (Adventures in Cooking Ser.). (Illus.). 1976. pap. 3.95 (ISBN 0-8326-0552-2, 2508). Delair.
Culinary Arts Institute Staff & MacDonald, Barbara, eds. Parties for All Seasons. LC 75-34804. (Adventures in Cooking Ser.). (Illus.). 1976. pap. 3.95 (ISBN 0-8326-0558-1, 2504). Delair.
Culinary Arts Institute Staff, jt. ed. see De Proft, Melanie.
Culinary Arts Institute Staff, jt. ed. see MacDonald, Barbara.
Culinary Arts Institute Staff, jt. ed. see Munson, Dee.
Culinary Arts Intstitute Staff, jt. ed. see MacDonald, Barbara.
Culinary Institute of America. The Professional Chef. 5th ed. Folsom, Le Roi A., ed. 608p. 1986. text ed. cancelled (ISBN 0-8436-2201-6). Van Nos Reinhold.
--The Professional Chef's Knife. LC 77-26689. (Illus.). 64p. 1978. pap. 9.95 (ISBN 0-8436-2125-7). Van Nos Reinhold.
Culkin, David F. & Kirsch, Sondra L. Managing Human Resources in Recreation, Parks & Leisure Services. 596p. 1986. pap. text ed. price not set (ISBN 0-02-326320-2). Macmillan.
Cull, John C., jt. auth. see Hardy, Richard G.
Cull, John G. & Golden, Larry B. Psychotherapeutic Techniques in School Psychology. 266p. 1984. 19.75x (ISBN 0-398-04927-0). C C Thomas.
Cull, John G., jt. auth. see Hardy, Richard E.
Cull, John G. & Hardy, Richard, eds. Problems of Disadvantaged & Deprived Youth. 272p. 1975. 29.75x (ISBN 0-398-03171-1). C C Thomas.
Cull, John G. & Hardy, Richard E., eds. Alcohol Abuse & Rehabilitation Approaches. 220p. 1974. 28.50x (ISBN 0-398-03017-0). C C Thomas.
--Behavior Modification in Rehabilitation Settings: Applied Principles. (Illus.). 272p. 1974. 32.50x (ISBN 0-398-03131-2). C C Thomas.
--Career Guidance for Black Adolescents: A Guide to Selected Professional Occupations. 176p. 1975. 17.50x (ISBN 0-398-03119-3). C C Thomas.
--Considerations in Rehabilitation Facility Development. (Illus.). 232p. 1977. 31.50x (ISBN 0-398-03347-1). C C Thomas.
--Fundamentals of Criminal Behavior & Correctional Systems. (Illus.). 364p. 1973. 39.75x (ISBN 0-398-02637-8). C C Thomas.
--Organization & Administration of Drug Abuse Treatment Programs. (Illus.). 360p. 1974. 27.50x (ISBN 0-398-03113-4). C C Thomas.
--Physical Medicine & Rehabilitation Approaches in Spinal Cord Injury. (Illus.). 336p. 1977. 40.50x (ISBN 0-398-03609-8). C C Thomas.
--Problems of Runaway Youth. (Illus.). 184p. 1976. spiral 25.50x (ISBN 0-398-03425-7). C C Thomas.
--Rehabilitation Facility Approaches in Severe Disabilities. (Illus.). 352p. 1975. 31.50x (ISBN 0-398-03324-2). C C Thomas.
--Understanding Disability for Social & Rehabilitation Services. (Illus.). 220p. 1973. 18.75x (ISBN 0-398-02889-3). C C Thomas.
--Vocational Rehabilitation: Profession & Process. (Illus.). 576p. 1977. 50.75x (ISBN 0-398-02266-6). C C Thomas.
Cull, John G., jt. ed. see Hardy, Richard E.
Culleeney, Maureen A. WordStar Simplified: Mastering the Essentials. (Illus.). 256p. 1985. pap. 16.95 (ISBN 0-13-963596-3). P-H.
Cullen, A. L., ed. Microwave Measurements: Proceedings, Institution of Electrical Engineers Special Issue, Part H, Vol. 127, No. 2. 50p. 27.00 (ISBN 0-317-34293-2). Inst Elect Eng.
Cullen, Alex. Adventures in Socialism. LC 68-55519. Repr. of 1910 ed. 27.50x (ISBN 0-678-00804-3). Kelley.
--Adventures in Socialism New Lanark Establishment & Orbiston Community. LC 70-134404. Repr. of 1910 ed. 11.00 (ISBN 0-404-08448-6). AMS Pr.
Cullen, Allen. Stirrings in Sheffield on Saturday Night. 1981. pap. 4.95 (ISBN 0-413-31340-9, NO.6475). Methuen Inc.
Cullen, C., et al. Fundamentals of Math, Vols. 1 & 2. (gr. 9-12). 1982. text ed. 18.95 ea. Vol. 1 (ISBN 0-8120-5469-5). Vol. 2 (ISBN 0-8120-5470-9). pap. text ed. 11.95 ea. Vol. 1 (ISBN 0-8120-2501-6). Vol. 2 (ISBN 0-8120-2508-3). Barron.
Cullen, Catherine, tr. see Favret-Saada, Jeanne.
Cullen, Charles G. Linear Algebra & Differential Equations. 1979. write for info. (ISBN 0-87150-262-3, PWS 2131, Prindle). PWS Pubs.
--Math for Biosciences. 800p. 1983. text ed. write for info. (ISBN 0-87150-352-2, 2761, Prindle). PWS Pubs.
Cullen, Charles T. & Johnson, Herbert A., eds. The Papers of John Marshall, Vol. 2: Correspondence & Papers, July 1788-Dec. 1795; Account Book, July 1788-Dec. 1795. LC 74-9575. (Institute of Early American History & Culture Ser.). xxxvi, 547p. 1977. 30.00 (ISBN 0-8078-1302-8). U of NC Pr.
Cullen, Charles T. & Tobias, Leslie, eds. The Papers of John Marshall: Correspondence & Papers, January 1799-October 1800, Vol. IV. LC 74-9575. (Institute of Early American History & Culture Ser.). xxxii, 365p. 1984. 35.00 (ISBN 0-8078-1586-1). U of NC Pr.
Cullen, Charles T., ed. see Jefferson, Thomas.
Cullen, Charles T., jt. ed. see Stinchcombe, William C.
Cullen, Countee. Color. LC 70-101515. (American Negro: His History & Literature, Ser. No. 3). 1970. Repr. of 1925 ed. 14.00 (ISBN 0-405-01919-X). Ayer Co Pubs.
--On These I Stand. LC 47-30109. 1947. 10.95i (ISBN 0-06-010925-4, HarpT). Har-Row.
--One Way to Heaven. LC 73-18572. Repr. of 1932 ed. 19.00 (ISBN 0-404-11383-4). AMS Pr.
Cullen, Countee, ed. Caroling Dusk: An Anthology of Verse by Negro Poets. LC 73-18651. 1955. text ed. 29.00x (ISBN 0-686-66924-X). Irvington.
Cullen, D. J., jt. auth. see Cook, T. M.
Cullen, David J. Historical Northern California. LC 84-62823. (Mother Lode Ser.: No. 2). 85p. 19.00 (ISBN 0-934827-00-1). Heritage Map Co.
Cullen, Donald E. National Emergency Strikes. LC 68-66472. (ILR Paperback Ser.: No. 7). 144p. 1968. pap. 3.00 (ISBN 0-87546-032-1). ILR Pr.
Cullen, Francis T. Rethinking Crime & Deviance Theory: The Emergence of a Structuring Tradition. LC 83-17796. 190p. 1984. text ed. 27.50x (ISBN 0-86598-073-X). Rowman & Allanheld.
Cullen, Francis T. & Gilbert, Karen E. Reaffirming Rehabilitation. 315p. (Orig.). 1982. pap. text ed. 15.95 (ISBN 0-87084-175-0). Anderson Pub Co.
Cullen, Frank, jt. auth. see Cullen, Mary Anne.
Cullen, G. W. & Wang, C. C., eds. Heteroepitaxial Semiconductors for Electronic Devices. LC 77-21749. (Illus.). 1978. 98.00 (ISBN 0-387-90285-6). Springer-Verlag.
Cullen, Gordon. Concise Townscape. (Illus.). 1961. pap. 10.95 (ISBN 0-442-21770-6). Van Nos Reinhold.
Cullen, I. see Diamond, Donald R. & McLoughlin, J. B.
Cullen, I. G., ed. Analysis & Decision in Regional Policy. (London Papers in Regional Science). 232p. 1979. 19.50x (ISBN 0-85086-070-9, NO.2936, Pub. by Pion England). Methuen Inc.
Cullen, Ian. Applied Urban Analysis: A Critique & Synthesis. (Orig.). 1985. 27.00x (ISBN 0-416-36430-6, 4082); pap. 12.95x (ISBN 0-416-36440-3, 4083). Methuen Inc.
Cullen, J., jt. auth. see Davis, P. H.
Cullen, J., ed. Experimental Behavior: A Basis for the Study of Mental Disturbance. (Illus.). 464p. 1974. 25.00x (ISBN 0-7165-2231-4, Pub by Irish Academic Pr). Biblio Dist.
Cullen, J., et al, eds. Breakdown in Human Adaptation to 'Stress' Towards a Multidisciplinary Approach, 2 Vols. 1983. lib. bdg. 144.00 (ISBN 0-89838-607-1, Pub. by Martinus Nijhoff Netherlands). Kluwer Academic.
Cullen, Jim. Achieving Electrical Independence. Wolf, Ray, ed. (Illus.). 288p. 1985. 21.95 (ISBN 0-87857-587-1); pap. 14.95 (ISBN 0-87857-588-X). Rodale Pr Inc.
Cullen, John B. Structure of Professionalism. (Illus.). 1979. text ed. 17.50 (ISBN 0-89433-084-5). Petrocelli.
Cullen, John B. & Watkins, Floyd C. Old Times in the Faulkner Country. LC 61-1874. xvi, 132p. 1975. 14.95 (ISBN 0-8071-0099-4). La State U Pr.
Cullen, John B., jt. auth. see Carter, Nancy M.
Cullen, John T. How to Balance Your Checkbook. 50p. (Orig.). (gr. 7-12). 1983. pap. text ed. 1.95 (ISBN 0-913819-00-X). Start Now Pr.
Cullen, Joseph, ed. Legacies in the Study of Behavior: The Wisdom & Experience of Many. (Illus.). 288p. 1975. 29.00x (ISBN 0-398-03147-9). C C Thomas.
Cullen, L. M. Anglo-Irish Trade Sixteen Hundred Sixty to Eighteen Hundred. LC 68-56548. 1968. 27.50x (ISBN 0-678-06757-0). Kelley.
--Economic History of Ireland since 1660. pap. 14.95 (ISBN 0-7134-1382-4, Pub. by Batsford England). David & Charles.
--The Emergence of Modern Ireland 1600-1900. LC 81-6548. 292p. 1981. 37.50x (ISBN 0-8419-0727-7). Holmes & Meier.
--Life in Ireland. 1979. pap. 14.95 (ISBN 0-7134-1449-9, Pub. by Batsford England). David & Charles.
Cullen, Louis & Smout, T. C. Comparative Aspects of Irish & Scottish Economic & Social Development 1600-1900. 260p. 1982. 50.00x (ISBN 0-85976-017-0, Pub. by Donald Pubs Scotland). State Mutual Bk.
Cullen, M. O. How to Carve Meat, Game & Poultry. 224p. 1976. pap. 3.50 (ISBN 0-486-23313-8). Dover.
--How to Carve Meat, Game & Poultry. 12.50 (ISBN 0-8446-5480-9). Peter Smith.
Cullen, Mary Anne & Cullen, Frank. The Eighty Proof Cookbook: An Introduction to Cooking with High Sprits. 192p. pap. 69.50 prepack (ISBN 0-312-24054-6). St Martin.
Cullen, Matthew & Woolrey, Sharon. World Congress on Land Policy: Nineteen Eighty Proceedings. LC 81-47762. 544p. 1982. 38.00x (ISBN 0-686-98362-9). Lexington Bks.
Cullen, Maurice R. Battle Road: Birthplace of the American Revolution. LC 72-111381. (Illus.). 1970. pap. 3.95 (ISBN 0-85699-012-4). Chatham Pr.
Cullen, Maurice R., Jr. Mass Media & the First Amendment: An Introduction to the Issues, Problems, & Practices. 480p. 1981. pap. text ed. write for info. (ISBN 0-697-04344-4); write for info. instr's. manual (ISBN 0-697-04346-0). Wm C Brown.
Cullen, Patrick & Roche, Thomas P., Jr., eds. Spenser Studies: A Renaissance Poetry Annual, Vol. II. (Spenser Studies). (Illus.). 255p. 1981. cancelled (ISBN 0-8229-3433-7). U of Pittsburgh Pr.
--Spenser Studies: A Renaissance Poetry Annual, Vol. I. (Spenser Studies). (Illus.). 1980. cancelled (ISBN 0-8229-3408-6). U of Pittsburgh Pr.
--Spenser Studies: A Renaissance Poetry Annual, Vol. III. (Spenser Studies). 209p. 1982. cancelled (ISBN 0-8229-3457-4). U of Pittsburgh Pr.
--Spenser Studies: A Renaissance Poetry Annual, Vol. IV. 187p. 1983. cancelled. U of Pittsburgh Pr.
--Spenser Studies: A Renaissance Poetry Annual, 5 Vols. 250p. 1985. Vol. 5. 34.50 (ISBN 0-404-19205-X); Set. 172.00 (ISBN 0-404-19200-9). AMS Pr.
--Spenser Studies: A Renaissance Poetry Annual, Vols. 1-5. 184p. 1984. Set. 172.50 (ISBN 0-404-19200-9); Vol. 1, 1980. 34.50 (ISBN 0-404-19201-7); Vol. 2, 1981. 34.50 (ISBN 0-404-19202-5); Vol. 3, 1982. 34.50 (ISBN 0-404-19203-3); Vol. 4, 1983. 34.50 (ISBN 0-404-19204-1). Vol. 5 (ISBN 0-404-19205-X). AMS Pr.
Cullen, Patrick R. Greyhound Racing's Precision Players. (Orig.). 1980. pap. 5.95 (ISBN 0-686-31807-2). Precision Pub Co.
Cullen, Patsy & Kirby, John. Design & Production of Media Presentations for Libraries. 200p. 1985. text ed. price not set (ISBN 0-566-03548-0). Gower Pub Co.
Cullen, Rosemary, ed. see Daley, Augustin.
Cullen, Rosemary, ed. see Gillette, William H.
Cullen, Stuart C. & Larson, C. Philip. Essentials of Anesthetic Practice. (Illus.). 358p. 1974. 41.50 (ISBN 0-8151-2052-4). Year Bk Med.
Cullen, Sue, jt. ed. see Adams, Ruth.
Cullen, Susan E., jt. ed. see Pierce, Carl W.
Cullen, T. R. The Ego & the Machine. 3rd ed. 2.00 (ISBN 0-930768-00-0). Gottlieb & Allen.
Cullen, Timothy, tr. see Averoff-Tossizza, Evangelos.
Cullen, Timothy, tr. see Frantzeskakis, Ion F.
Cullen, W. R., jt. auth. see Addison, A. W.
Cullen, William. First Lines for the Practice of Physic. Bd. with Physiology; or, an Attempt to Explain the Functions & Laws of the Nervous System. Peart, E. (Contributions to the History of Psychology Ser., Vol. XII, Pt. A: Orientations). 1985. Repr. of 1822 ed. 30.00 (ISBN 0-89093-314-6). U Pubns Amer.
Cullen-Tanaka, Janet. Fire Mountain. 288p. (Orig.). 1980. pap. 2.50 (ISBN 0-89083-646-9). Zebra.
Culler, A. D., ed. see Arnold, Matthew.
Culler, A. D., ed. see Newman, Cardinal John H.
Culler, Arthur D. Imaginative Reason: The Poetry of Matthew Arnold. LC 76-42264. (Illus.). 1976. Repr. of 1966 ed. lib. bdg. 27.50x (ISBN 0-8371-8979-9, CUIR). Greenwood.
--The Imperial Intellect. LC 55-8700. Repr. of 1955 ed. lib. bdg. 17.25x (ISBN 0-8371-7683-2, CUII). Greenwood.
Culler, Jonathan. Flaubert: The Uses of Uncertainty. rev. ed. LC 84-21499. 272p. (Orig.). 1985. pap. text ed. 12.95x (ISBN 0-8014-9305-6). Cornell U Pr.
--On Deconstruction: Literary Theory in the 1970's. LC 82-7414. 312p. 1982. 24.95x (ISBN 0-8014-1322-2); pap. 8.95x (ISBN 0-8014-9201-7). Cornell U Pr.
--The Pursuit of Signs: Semiotics, Literature, Deconstruction. LC 80-70539. 224p. 1981. 19.95x (ISBN 0-8014-1417-2); pap. 8.95x (ISBN 0-8014-9224-6). Cornell U Pr.
--Roland Barthes. 1983. 19.95x (ISBN 0-19-520420-4); pap. 5.95 (ISBN 0-19-520421-2, GB738). Oxford U Pr.
--Structuralist Poetics: Structuralism, Linguistics & the Study of Literature. LC 74-11608. 316p. 1976. pap. 8.95x (ISBN 0-8014-9155-X). Cornell U Pr.
Culler, Jonathan D., ed. The Harvard Advocate Centennial Anthology. 512p. 1966. 19.25 (ISBN 0-87073-120-3). Schenkman Bks Inc.
Culler, R. D. Boats, Oars, & Rowing. LC 77-85408. pap. 39.80 (ISBN 0-317-27608-5, 2025069). Bks Demand UMI.
--Skiffs & Schooners. LC 74-17905. pap. 51.80 (ISBN 0-317-27637-9, 2025076). Bks Demand UMI.
Culler, Ted. Articulation Disorders: A Basic Guide to Intervention in the Schools. LC 84-13347. 120p. (Orig.). 1984. pap. 12.00 (ISBN 0-89079-078-7). Pro Ed.
Culleton, R. Gerald. The Prophets & Our Times. 1974. pap. 6.00 (ISBN 0-89555-050-4). TAN Bks Pubs.
--The Reign of AntiChrist. 1974. pap. 6.00 (ISBN 0-89555-047-4). TAN Bks Pubs.
Culley, James, jt. auth. see Lazer, William.
Culley, John H. Cattle, Horses & Men of the Western Range. LC 84-2769. (Illus.). 337p. 1984. 25.00x (ISBN 0-8165-0891-7); pap. 11.50 (ISBN 0-8165-0865-8). U of Ariz Pr.
Culley, Margaret, ed. see Chopin, Kate.
Culley, Margo, intro. by. A Day at a Time: Being the Diary Literature of American Women from 1764 to the Present. 400p. (Orig.). 1985. text ed. 29.95 (ISBN 0-935312-50-1); pap. text ed. 12.95 (ISBN 0-935312-51-X). Feminist Pr.
Culley, Margo, ed. A Day at a Time: Being the Diary Literature of American Women from 1766 to the Present. 400p. 1985. 29.95 (ISBN 0-935312-50-1); pap. 12.95 (ISBN 0-935312-51-X). Feminist Pr.
Culley, Margo & Portuges, Catherine, eds. Gendered Subjects: The Dynamics of Feminist Teaching. 128p. 1985. 24.95x (ISBN 0-7102-0608-9); pap. 12.95 (ISBN 0-7100-9907-X). Routledge & Kegan.
Culley, Margo, jt. ed. see Hoffman, Leonore.
Culley, Robert C., ed. Semeia Five: Oral Tradition & Old Testament Studies. 163p. 1976. pap. 9.95 (ISBN 0-317-35721-2); pap. 6.95 members (ISBN 0-317-35722-0). Scholars Pr GA.
--Semeia Three: Classical Hebrew Narrative. 135p. 1975. pap. 9.95 (ISBN 0-317-35730-1, 06-20-03). Scholars Pr GA.
Culley, Robert C. & Overholt, Thomas W., eds. Semeia Twenty-One: Anthropological Perspectives on Old Testament Prophecy. pap. 9.95 (ISBN 0-686-96279-6, 06 20 21). Scholars Pr GA.
Culley, Thomas D. Jesuits & Music. 401p. 1970. 29.00 (ISBN 88-7041-582-1). Jesuit Hist.
Culley, Thomas R., jt. auth. see Hansen, David A.
Culley, W. T. Caxton Eneydos. (EETS ES Ser.: Vol. 57). Repr. 20.00 (ISBN 0-317-15674-8). Kraus Repr.
Culliford, Pierre see Delporte, pseud.
Culliford, Pierre see Peyo, pseud.
Culligan, Emmett. Fatima Secret. 1975. pap. 1.50 (ISBN 0-89555-052-0). TAN Bks Pubs.
Culligan, Emmett J. The Last World War & the End of Time. (Illus.). 210p. 1981. pap. 6.00 (ISBN 0-89555-034-2). TAN Bks Pubs.
Culligan, Matthew J. Getting Back to the Basics of Selling. 128p. 1981. 9.95 (ISBN 0-517-54412-1). Crown.
Culligan, Matthew J. & Greene, Dolph. Getting Back to the Basics of Public Relations & Publicity. 128p. 1982. 10.95 (ISBN 0-517-54722-8). Crown.
Culligan, Matthew J. & Sedlacek, Keith. How to Avoid Stress Before It Kills You. 8.95 (ISBN 0-517-30556-9). Crown.
Culligan, Matthew J., et al. Back to Basics Management: The Lost Craft of Leadership. LC 82-18196. (Illus.). 192p. 1983. 14.95 (ISBN 0-87196-755-3). Facts on File.
Culligan, Pat, jt. auth. see Brown, Vera.
Cullin, William H. How to Conduct Foreign Military Sales: FY 1985-86 Update. 150p. text ed. 40.00 (ISBN 0-87179-484-5). BNA.
--How to Conduct Foreign Military Sales: The United States Guide (with FY84-85 update) LC 82-1228. 516p. loose-leaf 120.00 (ISBN 0-87179-379-2); update alone 40.00 (ISBN 0-87179-447-0). BNA.
Cullinan, Angeline M., jt. auth. see Cullinan, John E.
Cullinan, Bernice E., ed. Literature & Young Children. Carmichael, Carolyn W. LC 77-4870. 173p. (Orig.). 1977. pap. 11.25 (ISBN 0-8141-2972-2). NCTE.

Cullinan, Bernice E., et al. Literature & the Child. 594p. 1981. text ed. 24.95 (ISBN 0-15-551110-6, HC). HarBraceJ.

Cullinan, Elizabeth. Yellow Roses. 1977. 11.95 (ISBN 0-670-79387-6). Viking.

Cullinan, John E. & Cullinan, Angeline M. Illustrated Guide to X-Ray Technics. 2nd ed. (Illus.). 179p. 1980. text ed. 36.50 (ISBN 0-397-50425-X, 65-05705, Lippincott Medical). Lippincott.

Cullinan, Justine, jt. ed. see Boland, Bill M.

Cullinan, Mary. Susan Ferrier. (English Authors Ser.: No. 392). 1984. lib. bdg. 18.95 (ISBN 0-8057-6878-5, Twayne). G K Hall.

Cullinan, Thomas. The Beseiged. 1973. pap. 1.25 (ISBN 0-380-01049-6, 15453). Avon.

Culliney, John L. The Forests of the Sea: Life & Death on the Continental Shelf. LC 76-21296. (Illus.). 300p. 1977. 9.95 (ISBN 0-87156-181-6). Sierra.

Culliney, John L. & Crockett, Edward S. Exploring Underwater: The Sierra Club Guide to Scuba & Snorkeling. LC 79-21944. (Outdoor Activities Guides Ser.). (Illus.). 352p. 1980. pap. 8.95 (ISBN 0-87156-270-7). Sierra.

Culling, C. F., et al. Cellular Pathology Technique. 4th ed. 1985. text ed. 59.95 (ISBN 0-407-72903-8). Butterworth.

Culling, L. T. Incredible I Ching. LC 79-18011. 64p. 1969. pap. 2.95 (ISBN 0-87728-054-1). Weiser.

Culling, Louis T. Occult Renaissance Nineteen Seventy-Two to Two Thousand Eight. (Illus.). 1972. pap. 1.00 (ISBN 0-87542-133-4). Llewellyn Pubns.

--The Pristine Yi King. Patterson, Thaynne W., ed. LC 84-48090. (Practical Magick Ser.). (Illus.). 160p. (Orig.). 1986. pap. 7.95 (ISBN 0-87542-107-5, L-107). Llewellyn Pubns.

Cullingan, Kevin, intro. by. Spiritual Direction: Contemporary Readings. 237p. (Orig.). 1983. pap. 5.95 (ISBN 0-914544-43-8). Living Flame Pr.

Cullingford, Cedric. Children & Television. 264p. 1984. 22.50 (ISBN 0-312-13235-2). St Martin.

Cullingford, Elizabeth. Yeats, Ireland & Facism. LC 80-12734. (The Gotham Library). 256p. 1981. 32.50x (ISBN 0-8147-1380-7). NYU Pr.

Cullingford, R. A., et al. Timescales in Geomorphology. LC 79-40517. 360p. 1980. 103.95 (ISBN 0-471-27600-6, Pub. by Wiley-Interscience). Wiley.

Cullingford, Richard E. Natural Language Processing: A Knowledge Engineering Approach. (Computer Science Ser.). 400p. 1985. 29.95x (ISBN 0-8476-7358-8). Rowman & Allanheld.

Cullingworth, J. B. Essays on Housing Policy: The British Scene. 1979. text ed. 25.00x (ISBN 0-04-350054-4); pap. text ed. 12.50x (ISBN 0-04-350055-2). Allen Unwin.

--Town & Country Planning in Britain. 8th ed. (The New Local Government Ser.: No. 8). 400p. 1982. text ed. 28.50x (ISBN 0-04-711010-4); pap. 14.95x (ISBN 0-04-711011-2). Allen Unwin.

--Town & Country Planning in Britain. 9th ed. (New Local Government Ser.: No. 8). 430p. 1985. pap. text ed. 14.95x (ISBN 0-04-711013-9). Allen Unwin.

Cullinhan, Douglas & Epstein, Michael. Behavior Disorders of Children & Adolescents. (Illus.). 384p. 1983. 26.95 (ISBN 0-13-072041-0). P-H.

Cullins, Laura, jt. auth. see Cullins, Warren.

Cullins, Warren & Cullins, Laura. Zeballos, Its Gold Its People Yesterday & Today: An Historical Documentation. (Orig.). 1982. pap. 7.75 (ISBN 0-9608386-0-0). Cullins.

Cullis, A. G., ed. Microscopy of Semiconducting Materials 1983, (Institute of Physics Conference Ser.: No. 67). 500p. 1983. 55.00 (ISBN 0-9960040-3-3, Pub. by A Hilger England). Heyden.

Cullis, A. G. & Joy, D. C., eds. Microscopy of Semiconducting Materials, 1981. 464p. 1981. 95.00x (ISBN 0-85498-151-9, Pub. by A Hilger). State Mutual Bk.

Cullis, C. A., jt. ed. see Jordan, E. G.

Cullis, C. F. & Hirschler, M. The Combustion of Organic Polymers. (International Series of Monographs on Chemistry). (Illus.). 1981. text ed. 85.00x (ISBN 0-19-851351-8). Oxford U Pr.

Cullis, C. F. & Firth, J. G., eds. Detection & Measurement of Hazardous Gases. LC 81-2785. 1981. text ed. 35.00x (ISBN 0-435-71030-3). Heinemann Ed.

Cullis, J. G., et al. The Economics of Outpatient Clinic Location. 224p. 1981. text ed. 42.75x (ISBN 0-566-00303-1). Gower Pub Co.

Cullis, John G. & West, Peter A. The Economics of Health: An Introducton. LC 79-50451. 1979. 30.00x (ISBN 0-8147-1377-7). NYU Pr.

Cullison, Arthur E. Feeds & Feeding. 3rd ed. 600p. 1981. text ed. 24.95 (ISBN 0-8359-1905-6); instr's manual free (ISBN 0-8359-1906-4). Reston.

Cullison, William R., III. Architecture in Louisiana: A Documentary History, Selected Drawings, Photographs & Other Pelican State Building Records. (Illus.). 100p. 1983. pap. 7.50 (ISBN 0-9603212-6-8). Tulane U Ctr Lat.

Culliton, Joseph T. Non-Violence-Central to Christian Spirituality: Perspectives from Scriptures to the Present. LC 82-7964. (Toronto Studies in Theology: Vol. 8). 312p. 1982. 49.95x (ISBN 0-88946-964-4). E Mellen.

--Obedience-Gateway to Freedom. LC 78-71962. 1978. pap. 3.95 (ISBN 0-88270-352-8, Pub. by Logos). Bridge Pub.

--Personal Presence: Its Effects on Honesty & Truthfulness. LC 85-6218. 202p. (Orig.). 1985. 22.00 (ISBN 0-8191-4661-7); pap. text ed. 10.75 (ISBN 0-8191-4662-5). U Pr of Amer.

--A Processive World View for Pragmatic Christians. LC 75-3781. 312p. 1975. 12.50 (ISBN 0-8022-2170-X). Philos Lib.

Cullity, B. D. Elements of X-Ray Diffraction. 2nd ed. LC 77-73950. (Illus.). 1978. text ed. 36.95 (ISBN 0-201-01174-3). Addison-Wesley.

Cullity, Berrard D. Introduction to Magnetic Materials. LC 71-159665. 1972. text ed. 41.95 (ISBN 0-201-01218-9). Addison-Wesley.

Cullity, Maurice. The History of Dairying in Western Australia. 488p. 1980. 35.00x (ISBN 0-85564-177-0, Pub. by U of West Australia Pr Australia). Intl Spec Bk.

Cullman, Elissa, jt. auth. see Brant, Sandra.

Cullman, Oscar. Christ & Time: The Primitive Christian Conception of Time & History. 1977. lib. bdg. 59.95 (ISBN 0-8490-1614-2). Gordon Pr.

Cullmann, Oscar. Baptism in the New Testament. LC 78-6937. 84p. 1978. pap. 5.95 (ISBN 0-664-24219-7). Westminster.

--The Christology of the New Testament. rev. ed. Guthrie, Shirley C. & Hall, Charles A. M., trs. LC 59-10178. 364p. 1980. pap. 11.95 (ISBN 0-664-24351-7). Westminster.

--Early Christian Worship. LC 78-6636. 126p. 1978. pap. 6.65 (ISBN 0-664-24220-0). Westminster.

--New Testament: An Introduction for the General Reader. LC 68-12796. 138p. 1968. pap. 4.95 (ISBN 0-664-24817-9). Westminster.

Cullmann, Oscar & Leenhardt, Franz J. Essays on the Lord's Supper. LC 58-8979. 1958. pap. 4.95 (ISBN 0-8042-3748-4). John Knox.

Cullom, Shelby. Fifty Years of Public Service: Personal Recollections of Shelby M. Cullom. LC 75-87504. (American Public Figures Ser.). 1969. Repr. of 1911 ed. lib. bdg. 55.00 (ISBN 0-306-71410-8). Da Capo.

Cullop, Charles P. Confederate Propaganda in Europe, 1861-1865. LC 69-12937. 1969. 9.95x (ISBN 0-87024-106-0). U of Miami Pr.

Cullop, Floyd G. Constitution of the United States: An Introduction. (Education Ser). (Orig.). 1969. pap. 2.95 (ISBN 0-451-62431-9, ME2318, Ment). NAL.

Cullum. Handbook of Engineering Design. Date not set. text ed. cancelled (ISBN 0-408-00558-0). Butterworth.

Cullum, Jane K. & Willoughby, Ralph A. Lanczos Algorithms for Large Symmetric Eigenvalue Computations (Vol. 1, Theory) (Progress in Scientific Computing: Vol. 3). 287p. 1985. text ed. 29.95x (ISBN 0-8176-3058-9). Birkhauser.

--Lanczos Algorithms for Large Symmetric Eigenvalue Computations (Vol. 2, Programs) (Progress in Scientific Computing Ser.: Vol. 4). 1985. text ed. 49.95x (ISBN 0-8176-3295-6). Birkhauser.

Cullumber, Norman. Please Lead Us in Prayer: Practical Aids for Church Enrichment. (P. A. C. E. Ser.). 96p. (Orig.). 1980. pap. 4.95 (ISBN 0-8272-2928-3). CBP.

Cullup, Michael. Reading Geographies. 96p. 1982. pap. text ed. 7.50x (ISBN 0-85635-429-5, 51124, Pub. by Carcanet Pr England). Humanities.

Cullup, Michael, ed. The Stomach & His Friends & Other Stories. (Heinemann Secondary Readers Ser.). 1973. pap. text ed. 3.00x (ISBN 0-435-92510-5). Heinemann Ed.

Cullwick, Hannah. The Diaries of Hannah Cullwick, Victorian Maidservant. Stanley, Liz, ed. LC 84-11638. (Illus.). 385p. 1984. 25.00 (ISBN 0-8135-1070-8); pap. 10.95 (ISBN 0-8135-1071-6). Rutgers U Pr.

Cully, Iris V. Christian Child Development. LC 78-19507. 176p. 1983. pap. 6.68i (ISBN 0-06-061654-7, RD/453, HarpR). Har-Row.

--Education for Spiritual Growth. LC 83-48464. 192p. 1984. 13.41 (ISBN 0-06-061655-5, HarpR). Har-Row.

--Planning & Selecting Curriculum for Christian Education. 128p. 1983. pap. 8.95 (ISBN 0-8170-0987-6). Judson.

--We Give Thanks. (Illus., Orig.). 1976. pap. text ed. 1.95x (ISBN 0-8192-4070-2); tchr's. ed. 4.50x (ISBN 0-8192-4069-9); guidebk. for parents 1.95x (ISBN 0-8192-4071-0). Morehouse.

Cully, Iris V. & Cully, Kendig B. A Guide to Biblical Resources. LC 81-80625. 160p. (Orig.). 1981. pap. 7.95 (ISBN 0-8192-1286-5). Morehouse.

Cully, Iris V. & Cully, Kendig B., eds. Process & Relationship: Issues in Theology, Philosophy, & Religious Education. LC 77-18760. 139p. (Orig.). 1978. pap. 8.95 (ISBN 0-89135-012-8). Religious Educ.

Cully, Kendig B., jt. auth. see Cully, Iris V.

Cully, Kendig B., ed. Confirmation Re-Examined. LC 82-81428. 144p. (Orig.). 1982. pap. 7.95 (ISBN 0-8192-1304-7). Morehouse.

Cully, Kendig B., jt. ed. see Cully, Iris V.

Culman, L. Cultural Revolution in the Provinces. LC 77-162858. (East Asian Monographs Ser: No. 42). 1971. pap. 11.00x (ISBN 0-674-17985-4). Harvard U Pr.

Culmer, Jack, ed. A Book of Bahamian Verse. 1977. lib. bdg. 59.95 (ISBN 0-8490-1529-4). Gordon Pr.

Culmsee, Carlton. Shapes for the Deep Unrest. 22p. 1970. pap. 3.00 (ISBN 0-87421-038-0). Utah St U Pr.

Culmsee, Carlton, jt. auth. see Nielsen, Veneta L.

Culotta, W., et al, eds. Local Area Networks: Proceedings of the LACASIS Seminar, Los Angeles, 1984. (Illus.). 174p. 1985. pap. text ed. 28.50x (ISBN 0-913203-12-2). Pacific Info.

Culp. Surgical Urology. 5th ed. 1985. 69.95 (ISBN 0-8151-2070-2). Year Bk Med.

Culp, Archie W. Principles of Energy Conversion. (Illus.). 1979. text ed. 42.00 (ISBN 0-07-014892-9). McGraw.

Culp, D. W., ed. Twentieth Century Negro Literature. LC 69-18586. (American Negro: His History & Literature Ser., No. 2). 1969. Repr. of 1902 ed. 23.00 (ISBN 0-405-01856-8). Ayer Co Pubs.

Culp, Daniel W., ed. Twentieth Century Negro Literature. facs. ed. LC 73-89416. (Black Heritage Library Collection Ser). 1902. 24.00 (ISBN 0-8369-8551-6). Ayer Co Pubs.

Culp, David A., jt. auth. see Flocks, R. H.

Culp, David A. & Loening, Stefan A., eds. Genitourinary Oncology. LC 83-19583. (Illus.). 632p. 1985. text ed. 102.00 (ISBN 0-8121-0914-7). Lea & Febiger.

Culp, Edwin D. Oregon, the Way It Was. LC 81-1266. (Illus.). 235p. 1981. pap. 14.95 (ISBN 0-87004-285-8). Caxton.

Culp, George & Nickles, Herbert. An Apple for the Teacher: Fundamentals of Instructional Computing. 225p. 1983. pap. write for info. Wadsworth Pub.

--Instructional Computing Fundamentals for IBM Microcomputers. LC 84-7661. (Computer Science Ser.). 320p. 1984. pap. text ed. 15.00 pub net (ISBN 0-534-03364-4). Brooks-Cole.

Culp, George & Nickles, Herbert N. An Apple for the Teacher: Fundamentals of Instructional Computing. 256p. 1983. pap. text ed. 14.00 pub net (ISBN 0-534-01378-3, 82-24506). Brooks-Cole.

Culp, George, jt. auth. see Nickles, Herbert.

Culp, George H. & Nickles, Herbert L. An Apple for the Teacher: Fundamentals of Instructional Computing. 2nd ed. 275p. 1985. pap. 20.25 (ISBN 0-534-05832-9). Brooks-Cole.

Culp, George H., jt. auth. see Nickles, Herbert.

Culp, Gordon, ed. Trihalomethane Reduction in Drinking Water: Technologies, Costs, Effectiveness, Monitoring, Compliance. LC 84-14906. (Pollution Technology Review Ser.: No. 114). (Illus.). 251p. 1985. 42.00 (ISBN 0-8155-1002-0). Noyes.

Culp, Gordon, et al. Wastewater Reuse & Recycling Technology. LC 80-21778. (Pollution Technology Review Ser.: 72). (Illus.). 838p. 1981. 48.00 (ISBN 0-8155-0829-8). Noyes.

Culp, Mary B. & Spann, Sylvia. Me? Teach Reading? LC 79-4309. 1979. pap. 12.95 (ISBN 0-673-16397-0). Scott F.

Culp, Rober D., et al, eds. Guidance & Control 1985: Feb. 2-6, 1985, Keystone, CO. LC 57-43769. (Advances in the Asronautical Sciences Ser.: Vol. 57). (Illus.). 618p. (Orig.). 1985. lib. bdg. 65.00 (ISBN 0-87703-211-4, Pub By Am Astro Soc); pap. text ed. 50.00 (ISBN 0-87703-212-2). Univelt Inc.

Culp, Robert D., ed. Guidance & Control, 1979. LC 57-43769. (Advances in the Astronautical Sciences Ser.: Vol. 39). (Illus.). 429p. lib. bdg. 45.00x (ISBN 0-87703-100-2, Pub. by Am Astronaut); microfiche suppl. 5.00x (ISBN 0-87703-128-2). Univelt Inc.

Culp, Robert D. & Bauman, Edward J., eds. Guidance & Control: 1982. LC 57-43769. (Advances in the Astronautical Sciences Ser.: Vol. 48). (Illus.). 558p. (Orig.). 1982. lib. bdg. 65.00x (ISBN 0-87703-170-3, Pub. by Am Astronaut); pap. text ed. 50.00x (ISBN 0-87703-171-1). Univelt Inc.

Culp, Robert D. & Stafford, Parker S., eds. Guidance & Control 1984. LC 57-43769. (Advances in the Astronautical Sciences Ser.: Vol. 55). 500p. (Orig.). 1984. lib. bdg. 60.00x (ISBN 0-87703-199-1, Pub. by Am Astro Soc); pap. text ed. 50.00 (ISBN 0-87703-200-9); microfiche suppl. 15.00x (ISBN 0-87703-201-7). Univelt Inc.

Culp, Russell L. & Wesner, George M. Handbook of Advanced Wastewater Treatment. 2nd ed. 1978. 42.50 (ISBN 0-442-21784-6). Van Nos Reinhold.

Culp, Wesner, Clup, Inc., jt. auth. see Owen, William F.

Culp, William J. & Ochoa, Jose, eds. Abnormal Nerves & Muscles As Impulse Generators. (Illus.). 1982. text ed. 65.00x (ISBN 0-19-502936-4). Oxford U Pr.

Culpeper, Nicholas. Complete Herbal. (Illus.). 1960. 14.95x (ISBN 0-685-21926-7). Wehman.

--Culpeper's Color Herbal. (Illus.). 224p. (Orig.). 1983. pap. 12.95 (ISBN 0-8069-7690-X). Sterling.

--Culpeper's Herbal Remedies. pap. 3.00 (ISBN 0-87980-025-9). Wilshire.

Culpeper, Thomas. A Tract Against Usurie. LC 74-80170. (English Experience Ser.: No. 649). 22p. 1974. Repr. of 1621 ed. 3.50 (ISBN 90-221-0649-7). Walter J Johnson.

Culpepper, jt. auth. see Miller.

Culpepper, Fred, jt. auth. see Miller, Rex.

Culpepper, Fred W., Jr., jt. auth. see Miller, Rex.

Culpepper, Pat & Heard, Robert. Goal Line. LC 84-82423. (Illus.). 187p. 1984. 16.95 (ISBN 0-937642-02-9). Honey Hill.

Culpepper, R. Alan. Anatomy of the Fourth Gospel: A Study in Literary Design. LC 82-16302. (Foundations & Facets Ser.). 256p. 1983. 19.95 (ISBN 0-8006-2102-6, 1-2102). Fortress.

--The Johannine School: An Evaluation of the Johannine-School Hypothesis Based on an Investigation of the Nature of Ancient Schools. LC 75-34235. (Society of Biblical Literature. Dissertation Ser.: No. 26). Repr. of 1975 ed. 62.40 (ISBN 0-8357-9576-4, 2017525). Bks Demand UMI.

Culpepper, R. Alan, ed. see Hayes, John.

Culpepper, Robert H. God's Calling: A Missionary Autobiography. LC 80-68643. 1981. 6.95 (ISBN 0-8054-6323-2). Broadman.

Culpin, Claude. Farm Machinery. 9th ed. (Illus.). 416p. 1977. 36.95x (ISBN 0-8464-0403-6); 19.95. Beekman Pubs.

--Farm Machinery. 10th ed. (Illus.). 464p. 1981. pap. text ed. 24.50x (ISBN 0-246-11539-4, Pub. by Granada England). Brookfield Pub Co.

--Farm Machinery. 10th ed. 464p. 1981. 42.00x (ISBN 0-246-11539-4, Pub. by Granada England); pap. 25.00x (ISBN 0-246-11585-8, Pub. by Granada England). Sheridan.

--Profitable Farm Mechanization. 3rd ed. (Illus.). 336p. 1975. text ed. 24.95x (ISBN 0-8464-0037-5). Beekman Pubs.

--Profitable Farm Mechanization. 3rd ed. 320p. 1975. 25.00x (ISBN 0-246-11571-8, Pub. by Granada England). Sheridan.

Culshaw, John. The Concerto. LC 78-60138. (The World of Music). (Illus.). 1979. Repr. of 1949 ed. lib. bdg. 24.75x (ISBN 0-313-20547-7, CUCO). Greenwood.

--Putting the Record Straight: The Autobiography of John Culshaw. LC 81-52555. 352p. 1982. 17.50 (ISBN 0-670-58326-X). Viking.

Culton, Martha. This Is That. (Illus.). 1983. 6.95 (ISBN 0-533-05647-0). Vantage.

Cultra, Quen. Queequeg's Odyssey. LC 77-10366. (Illus.). 1977. 10.00 (ISBN 0-914090-38-0). Chicago Review.

Cultural & Social Centre, Asian & Pacific Council, compiled by. Asian & Pacific Short Stories. LC 73-93869. 1974. 6.75 (ISBN 0-8048-1125-3). C E Tuttle.

Cultural Assistance Center. Partners: A Practical Guide to Corporate Support of the Arts. 112p. pap. 8.95 (ISBN 0-317-36355-7, NO. 417). Am Council Arts.

--Public & Private Support for the Arts in New York City: A Review with Recommendations for Improvement in the 80's. LC 80-65497. 160p. (Orig.). 1980. pap. 6.50x (ISBN 0-89062-098-9, Pub. by Cultural Assist). Pub Ctr Cult Res.

Cultural Assistance Center, ed. America's Stake in New York City Arts & Culture. LC 78-56952. (Illus.). 72p. 1978. pap. 4.50x (ISBN 0-89062-030-X, Pub. by Cultural Assistance Center). Pub Ctr Cult Res.

Cultural Assistance Center Staff. A Guide to New York City Museums. 2nd ed. (Illus.). 64p. 1983. pap. 1.50 (ISBN 0-486-24454-7). Dover.

Cultural Correspondence Staff. We Will Not Be Disappeared: A Directory of Arts Activism. (Illus.). 160p. 1984. 15.00x (ISBN 0-941702-09-X); pap. 5.00 (ISBN 0-941702-10-3). Lake View Pr.

Cultural Relics Administration Committee, Tibet Autonomous Region. The Potala Palace of Tibet. (Illus.). 128p. 1983. 25.00 (ISBN 0-917056-36-1, Pub by Joint Pub Co HK). Cheng & Tsui.

Cultural Services Inc. Staff. Arts & Sports U. S. A. (Orig.). 1985. 35.00 (ISBN 0-913169-00-5, Dist. Oryx Press). Cultural Serv.

Culturgrames. The Notion Around Us. LC 85-70540. 210p. (Orig.). 1985. pap. 15.00 (ISBN 0-912048-37-9). Garrett Pk.

Culver, Bruce & Murphy, Bill. Panzer Colors. (Illus.). 96p. 1984. pap. 6.95 (ISBN 0-89747-057-5, 6251). Squad Sig Pubns.

Culver, Carmen M. & Hoban, Gary J. Power to Change: Issues for the Innovative Educator. Goodlad, John I., ed. (IDEA Reports on Schooling). (Illus.). 380p. 1973. text ed. 19.95 (ISBN 0-07-014890-2). McGraw.

Culver, Charles M. & Gert, Bernard. Philosophy in Medicine: Conceptual & Ethical Issues in Medicine & Psychiatry. 1982. PLB 21.95x (ISBN 0-19-502979-8); pap. text ed. 10.95x (ISBN 0-19-502980-1). Oxford U Pr.

Culver, David C. Cave Life: Evolution & Ecology. (Illus.). 208p. 1982. text ed. 25.00x (ISBN 0-674-10435-8). Harvard U Pr.

Culver, Dorothy C. Bibliography of Crime & Criminal Justice: Nineteen Twenty-Seven to Nineteen Thirty-One. LC 69-16228. (Criminology, Law Enforcement, & Social Problems Ser.: No. 99). 1969. Repr. of 1934 ed. 24.00x (ISBN 0-87585-099-5). Patterson Smith.

Culver, Dorothy C., ed. Bibliography of Crime & Criminal Justice: Nineteen Thirty-Two to Nineteen Thirty-Seven. LC 69-16227. (Criminology, Law Enforcement, & Social Problems Ser.: No. 100). 1969. Repr. of 1939 ed. 24.00x (ISBN 0-87585-100-2). Patterson Smith.

Culver, Henry H., Jr. IFR Pocket Simulator Procedures. 3rd ed. LC 76-27149. (Illus.). 1982. spiral bdg. 19.95 (ISBN 0-9601062-1-9, Pub. by FIP). Aviation.

Culver, John H. & Syer, John C. Power & Politics in California. 2nd ed. LC 83-21636. 319p. 1984. pap. 14.95 (ISBN 0-471-89334-X). Wiley.

Culver, Louisa C. Peggy & Her Boyfriend: A True Love Story. (Illus.). 61p. 1979. pap. 2.50 (ISBN 0-682-49251-5). Exposition Pr FL.

--Peggy & Pete: A Story of Lasting Love & Success. 224p. 1979. 7.50 (ISBN 0-682-49252-3). Exposition Pr FL.

Culver, Perry J., jt. ed. see Page, Lot B.

Culver, R. B. & Ianna, P. A. The Gemini Syndrome: A Scientific Evaluation of Astrology. LC 84-42791. (Science & the Paranormal Ser.). (Illus.). 216p. 1984. 18.95 (ISBN 0-87975-286-6); pap. 11.95 (ISBN 0-87975-264-5). Prometheus Bks.

Culver, Raymond B. Horace Mann & Religion in the Massachusetts Public Schools. LC 72-89168. (American Education: Its Men, Institutions & Ideas, Ser. 1). 1969. Repr. of 1929 ed. 17.00 (ISBN 0-405-01406-6). Ayer Co Pubs.

Culver, Robert D. A Greater Commission: A Theology of World Missions. (Orig.). 1984. pap. text ed. 9.95 (ISBN 0-8024-3302-2). Moody.

--The Histories & Prophecies of Daniel. 192p. (Orig.). 1980. pap. 4.95 (ISBN 0-88469-131-4). BMH Bks.

--Life of Christ. LC 76-17967. 272p. 1976. pap. 9.95 (ISBN 0-8010-2498-6). Baker Bk.

--The Peacemongers. Carpenter, Mark, ed. 160p. 1985. pap. 5.95 (ISBN 0-8423-4789-5). Tyndale.

Culver, Robert D., jt. auth. see Perry, Lloyd M.

Culver, Roger B. Astronomy. (Illus.). 1979. pap. 4.95 (ISBN 0-06-460158-7, CO 158, COS). B&N NY.

--Introduction to Experimental Astronomy. 2nd ed. (Illus.). 208p. 1983. pap. text ed. 9.95x (ISBN 0-7167-1495-7). W H Freeman.

--Sun-Sign Sunset: A Statistical Investigation of the Claims of Sun-Sign Astrology. (The Astronomy Quarterly Library: Vol. 5). 1983. pap. 9.95 (ISBN 0-912918-00-4). Pachart Pub Hse.

Culver, Roger B. & Ianna, Phillip A. The Gemini Syndrome: Star Wars of the Oldest Kind. (The Astronomy Quarterly Library: Vol. 1). 225p. 1979. 11.95 (ISBN 0-912918-17-9, 0017). Pachart Pub Hse.

Culver, Ruth. How to Hold a Quilt Show: A Practical Guide. (Illus.). 176p. (Orig.). 1984. pap. 17.95 (ISBN 0-9615155-0-3). Culver Pubns.

Culver, Sylvia A. Keep the River Flowing. 92p. 1979. pap. 2.50 (ISBN 0-8341-0592-6). Beacon Hill.

Culver, Timothy. Ex Officio. LC 70-106590. 512p. 1970. 6.95 (ISBN 0-87131-006-6). M Evans.

Culver, Vivian M. Modern Bedside Nursing. 8th ed. LC 73-88258. (Illus.). 862p. 1974. text ed. 21.50 (ISBN 0-7216-2782-X). Saunders.

Culver, William, jt. ed. see Greaves, Thomas.

Culverwel, Nathanael. An Elegant & Learned Discourse on the Light of Nature, 1652: Nathanael Culverwel (1618-1651) Wellek, Rene, ed. Bd. with Spiritual Opticks. LC 75-11215. (British Philosophers & Theologians of the 17th & 18th Centuries Ser.). 456p. 1978. lib. bdg. 51.00 (ISBN 0-8240-1769-2). Garland Pub.

Culverwell, Geoffrey, tr. see Porzio, Domenico, et al.

Culverwell, Geoffrey, tr. see Stang, Ragna.

Culverwell, J. P., ed. see Faucher, L.

Culwick, Arthur T. & Culwick, G. M. Ubena of the Rivers. LC 76-44707. Repr. of 1935 ed. 42.50 (ISBN 0-404-15883-8). AMS Pr.

Culwick, G. M., jt. auth. see Culwick, Arthur T.

Culyer, A. J. Measuring Health: Lessons for Ontario. (Ontario Economic Council Research Studies). 1978. pap. 12.50 (ISBN 0-8020-3354-7). U of Toronto Pr.

--Need & the National Health Service: Economics & Social Choice. 163p. 1976. 13.50x (ISBN 0-87471-896-1). Rowman.

--The Political Economy of Social Policy. 1980. 32.50 (ISBN 0-312-62242-2). St Martin.

Culyer, A. J., jt. auth. see Cooper, M.

Culyer, A. J., ed. Economic Policies & Social Goals: Aspects of Public Choice. LC 74-23031. 308p. 1975. 35.00 (ISBN 0-312-23450-3). St Martin.

--Health Indicators. LC 83-4271. 223p. 1983. 32.50x (ISBN 0-312-36530-6). St Martin.

Culyer, A. J. & Horisberger, B, eds. Economic & Medical Evaluation of Health Care Technologies. (Illus.). 415p. 1983. 22.00 (ISBN 0-387-12987-1). Springer Verlag.

Culyer, A. J., jt. ed. see Terny, Guy.

Culyer, A. J., et al, eds. An Annotated Bibliography of Health Economics: English Language Sources. LC 77-79018. 1977. 45.00x (ISBN 0-312-03873-9). St Martin.

Cumba, Ana M. The World of Miss Universe. LC 75-26269. (Illus.). 270p. 1976. 9.95 (ISBN 0-87141-053-2). Manyland.

Cumberland, Charles C. Mexican Revolution. Incl. Genesis under Madero. 308p. 1974. Repr. of 1952 ed. pap. 8.95x (ISBN 0-292-75017-X); The Constitutionalist Years. LC 74-38506. (Illus.). 469p. 1972. 22.50x (ISBN 0-292-75000-5); pap. 10.95 (ISBN 0-292-75016-1). (Illus.). pap. U of Tex Pr.

--Mexican Revolution, Genesis Under Madero. LC 71-90495. Repr. of 1952 ed. lib. bdg. 19.25x (ISBN 0-8371-2126-4, CUMR). Greenwood.

--Mexico: The Struggle for Modernity. LC 68-15891. (Latin American Histories Ser.). (Orig.). 1968. pap. 9.95x (ISBN 0-19-500766-2). Oxford U Pr.

--The United States-Mexican Border: A Selective Guide to the Literature of the Region. 1960. pap. 17.00 (ISBN 0-384-10360-X). Johnson Repr.

Cumberland, David. Death & Justice Frescoes. new ed. (Illus.). 96p. (Orig.). 1972. 7.00 (ISBN 0-912846-26-7); pap. 2.95 (ISBN 0-912846-27-5). Bookstore Pr.

Cumberland, Gerald. Set Down in Malice: A Book of Reminiscences. 1909. 20.00 (ISBN 0-932062-39-3). Sharon Hill.

--Written in Friendship: A Book of Reminiscences. 1923. 25.00 (ISBN 0-932062-38-5). Sharon Hill.

Cumberland, John H. Regional Development: Experiences & Prospects in the United States of America. 170p. 1971. text ed. 13.00x (ISBN 90-2797-266-4). Mouton.

Cumberland, John H., et al, eds. Economics of Managing Chlorofluorocarbons: Stratospheric Ozone & Climate Issues. LC 82-11279. (Resources for the Future Ser.). 536p. 1982. text ed. 28.00x (ISBN 0-8018-2963-1). Johns Hopkins.

Cumberland, Richard. Memoirs. Flanders, Henry, ed. LC 72-91487. 1856. 27.50 (ISBN 0-405-08413-7, Blom Pubns). Ayer Co Pubs.

--The Plays of Richard Cumberland: Eighteenth Century English Drama Ser, 3 Vols. Borkat, Roberta F., ed. LC 78-66651. lib. bdg. 436.00 (ISBN 0-8240-3587-9). Garland Pub.

Cumberland, Stuart. A Thought-Reader's Thoughts: Being the Impressions & Confessions of Stuart Cumberland. LC 75-7373. (Perspectives in Psychical Research Ser.). 1975. Repr. of 1888 ed. 25.50x (ISBN 0-405-07024-1). Ayer Co Pubs.

Cumberland, William H. Wallace M. Short: Iowa Rebel. 178p. 1983. pap. text ed. 14.95x (ISBN 0-8138-1646-7). Iowa St U Pr.

Cumberlege, Marcus. Firelines. 1977. sewn in wrappers 4.95 (ISBN 0-685-04170-0, Pub. by Anvil Pr). Small Pr Dist.

--Running Toward a New Life. 1972. 5.95 (ISBN 0-685-27677-5, Pub. by Anvil Pr); signed ltd. ed. 15.00 (ISBN 0-685-27678-3). Small Pr Dist.

Cumbers, Frank, jt. auth. see Meyer, F. B.

Cumbey, Constance. The Hidden Dangers of the Rainbow: The New Age Movement & Our Coming Age of Barbarism. LC 83-80044. 271p. (Orig.). 1983. pap. 5.95 (ISBN 0-910311-03-X). Huntington Hse Inc.

Cumbler, John T. A Moral Response to Industrialism: The Lectures of Reverend Cook in Lynn, Massachusetts. LC 81-9338. (American Social History Ser.). 180p. 1982. 34.50x (ISBN 0-87395-558-7); pap. 12.95x (ISBN 0-87395-559-5). State U NY Pr.

--Working-Class Community in Industrial America: Work, Leisure, & Struggle in Two Industrial Cities, 1880-1930. LC 78-57768. (Contributions in Labor History: No. 8). 1979. lib. bdg. 29.95 (ISBN 0-313-20615-5, CWC/). Greenwood.

Cumbow, Robert C. Pardon Me, Roy, & Other Groaners. 128p. (Orig.). 1983. pap. 1.95 (ISBN 0-523-42040-4). Pinnacle Bks.

Cument, Carlos E. & Burns, Barbara J. Practical Psychiatry for the Health Professional. LC 84-4926. (Illus.). 223p. text ed. 27.50 (ISBN 0-89335-198-9). SP Med & Sci Bks.

Cument, E E. Exporters' Encyclopaedia, 1985-86. (Illus.). 1800p. 1985. 365.00 (ISBN 0-918257-09-3). Dun's Mktg.

Cumerford, William R. Fund Raising: A Professional Guide. LC 77-93555. 1978. 29.95 (ISBN 0-918214-02-5). F E Peters.

Cumine, Earl. Shringar: The Golden Book of Indian Hair Styles. (Illus.). 1975. pap. 2.50 English, Urdu, & Tamil (ISBN 0-88253-454-8). Ind-US Inc.

Cuming, G. J., ed. see Church of England.

Cuming, G. J., jt. ed. see Jasper, R. C.

Cuming, Geoffrey. A History of Anglican Liturgy. (Illus.). 450p. 1980. Repr. of 1969 ed. text ed. 42.50x (ISBN 0-333-30661-9). Humanities.

Cuming, Maurice. Theory & Practice of Personnel Management. 2nd ed. 1975. pap. 23.95x (ISBN 0-434-90290-X). Intl Ideas.

Cuming, Maurice W. Personnel Management in the National Health Service. 1978. pap. 16.95 (ISBN 0-434-90291-8, Pub. by W Heinemann Ltd). David & Charles.

Cuming, Pamela. The Power Handbook: A Strategic Guide to Personal & Organizational Effectiveness. LC 80-14039. 336p. 1980. pap. 15.95 (ISBN 0-8436-0778-5). Van Nos Reinhold.

Cumings, Art. There's a Monster Eating My House. LC 80-25378. (Illus.). 48p. (ps-3). 1981. 5.95 (ISBN 0-8193-1053-0). Parents.

Cumings, Bruce. The Origins of the Korean War: Liberation & the Emergence of Separate Regimes, 1945-1947. LC 80-8543. (Illus.). 552p. 1981. 48.00x (ISBN 0-691-09383-0); pap. 19.50x LPE (ISBN 0-691-10113-2). Princeton U Pr.

--The Two Koreas. LC 84-81643. (Headline Ser.: 269). (Illus.). 80p. 1984. 3.00 (ISBN 0-87124-092-0). Foreign Policy.

Cumings, Bruce, ed. Child of Conflict: The Korean-American Relationship 1945-1953. LC 82-48871. (Publications on Asia of the School of International Studies: No. 37). 352p. 1983. 25.00x (ISBN 0-295-95995-9). U of Wash Pr.

Cumings, J. N., ed. Biochemical Aspects of Nervous Diseases. LC 70-178775. 274p. 1972. 35.00x (ISBN 0-306-30564-X, Plenum Pr). Plenum Pub.

Cummin, Katharine H. Radnor: A Rare & Pleasing Thing. LC 76-56871. (Illus.). 1978. 19.75 (ISBN 0-913896-11-X). Owlswick Pr.

Cummin, Katherine H. Connecticut Militia General: Gold Selleck Silliman. LC 79-57128. (Connecticut Bicentennial Ser.: Vol. XXXV). 1980. write for info. (ISBN 0-918676-21-5). Conn Hist Com.

Cumming, A. P., jt. auth. see Wright, P.

Cumming, Anne. Sensuality: Captured by the Great Photographers of the World. (Illus.). 112p. (Orig.). 1983. pap. 12.95 (ISBN 0-933328-82-6). Delilah Bks.

Cumming, B. Egyptian Historical Records of the Late Eighteenth Dynasty, Fac. II. 240p. 1984. pap. text ed. 14.50x (ISBN 0-85668-272-1, Pub. by Aris & Phillips England). Humanities.

Cumming, Barbara. Egyptian Historical Records of the Later Eighteenth Dynasty, Fascicle III. 361p. 1984. pap. text ed. 13.00x (ISBN 0-85668-284-5, Pub. by Aris & Phillips England). Humanities.

--Egyptian Historical Records of the Late Eighteenth Dynasty, Fac. I. 180p. 1982. pap. text ed. 14.50x (ISBN 0-85668-218-7, Pub. by Aris & Phillips England). Humanities.

Cumming, C. E., et al. Making the Change. (SCRE Publications Ser.). 48p. 1981. text ed. 12.75x (ISBN 0-901116-78-5, Pub. by Scottish Coun England); pap. text ed. 6.75x (ISBN 0-901116-79-3, Pub. by Scottish Coun England). Humanities.

Cumming, Candy. Sex & Your Diet. LC 83-80738. (Illus.). 176p. (Orig.). 1985. pap. 8.95 (ISBN 0-88011-166-6). Leisure Pr.

Cumming, Candy & Newman, Vicky. Eater's Guide: Nutrition Basics for Busy People. (Illus.). 192p. 1981. 12.95 (ISBN 0-13-223057-7); pap. 6.95 (ISBN 0-13-223040-2). P-H.

Cumming, Caroline K. & Petit, Walter W., eds. Russian-American Relations, March 1917-March 1920. LC 75-39049. (Russian Studies: Perspectives on the Revolution Ser). xxviii, 375p. 1976. Repr. of 1920 ed. 30.25 (ISBN 0-88355-428-3). Hyperion Conn.

Cumming, Charles G. Assyrian & Hebrew Hymns of Praise. LC 34-3318. (Columbia University. Oriental Studies: No. 12). Repr. of 1934 ed. 16.50 (ISBN 0-404-50502-3). AMS Pr.

Cumming, Diane, tr. see Michaelle.

Cumming, Doug, jt. auth. see Cumming, Joe.

Cumming, Elaine & Henry, William E. Growing Old: The Process of Disengagement. Kastenbaum, Robert, ed. LC 78-22197. (Aging & Old Age Ser.). (Illus.). 1979. Repr. of 1961 ed. lib. bdg. 25.50x (ISBN 0-405-11814-7). Ayer Co Pubs.

Cumming, Elaine, jt. auth. see Cumming, John.

Cumming, G. & Bonsignore, G., eds. Pulmonary Circulation in Health & Disease. LC 80-20154. (Ettore Majorana International Sciences Ser.--Life Sciences: Vol. 3). 451p. 1980. 59.50x (ISBN 0-306-40473-7, Plenum Pr). Plenum Pub.

--Smoking & the Lung. (Ettore Majorana International Science Series, Life Sciences: Vol. 17). 520p. 1985. 82.50x (ISBN 0-306-41828-2, Plenum Pr). Plenum Pub.

Cumming, G., jt. ed. see Bonsignore, G.

Cumming, Gordon & Bonsignore, Giovanni, eds. Cellular Biology of the Lung. LC 81-23407. (Ettore Majorana International Science Ser., Life Sciences: Vol. 10). 496p. 1982. text ed. 65.00 (ISBN 0-306-40910-0, Plenum Pr). Plenum Pub.

--Drugs & the Lung. (Ettore Majorana International Science Ser.: Life Sciences). 294p. 1984. 49.50x (ISBN 0-306-41600-X, Plenum Pr). Plenum Pub.

Cumming, Henry H. Franco-British Rivalry in the Post-War Near East: The Decline of French Influence. LC 79-2854. (Illus.). 229p. 1981. Repr. of 1938 ed. 21.50 (ISBN 0-8305-0029-4). Hyperion Conn.

Cumming, Ian. James Mill on Education. 1959. 17.50 (ISBN 0-932062-37-7). Sharon Hill.

--James Mills on Education. 1978. Repr. of 1959 ed. lib. bdg. 10.00 (ISBN 0-8492-3962-1). R West.

Cumming, James see Bates, Martin & Dudley-Evans, Tony.

Cumming, James C. Making Fashion & Textile Publicity Work. LC 74-135630. 148p. 1971. 5.95 (ISBN 0-87005-093-1). Fairchild.

Cumming, James T. & Moll, Hans G. And, God, What About...? 1980. 4.50 (ISBN 0-570-03806-5, 12-2915). Concordia.

--Hey God, What About...? (Illus.). 1977. pap. 4.50 (ISBN 0-570-03758-1, 12-2666). Concordia.

Cumming, Joe & Cumming, Doug. The Family Secret. LC 82-83143. (Illus.). 76p. 1982. 8.95 (ISBN 0-931948-40-1). Peachtree Pubs.

Cumming, John. Contribution Towards a Bibliography Dealing with Crime & Cognate Subjects. 3rd ed. LC 71-108220. (Criminology, Law Enforcement, & Social Problems Ser.: No. 103). 1970. Repr. of 1935 ed. 12.00x (ISBN 0-87585-103-7). Patterson Smith.

Cumming, John & Cumming, Elaine. Ego & Milieu: Theory & Practice of Environmental Therapy. LC 62-18829. 300p. 1962. lib. bdg. 26.95x (ISBN 0-202-26088-7); pap. text ed. 13.95 (ISBN 0-202-26044-5). Aldine Pub.

Cumming, John & Burns, Paul, eds. Prayers for Our Times. 144p. 1983. 10.95 (ISBN 0-8245-0071-7); pap. 6.95 (ISBN 0-8245-0107-1). Crossroad NY.

Cumming, John, tr. see Horkheimer, Max & Adorno, Theodor W.

Cumming, Patricia. Afterwards. LC 73-94068. 64p. 1974. pap. 6.95 (ISBN 0-914086-02-2). Alicejamesbooks.

--Letter from an Outlying Province. LC 76-19884. 80p. 1976. pap. 6.95 (ISBN 0-914086-14-6). Alicejamesbooks.

Cumming, Robert. Equilibrium & the Rotary Disc. (Illus.). 32p. 1980. pap. 4.50 (ISBN 0-933442-03-3). Dianas Bimonthly.

--Just Look: A Book About Paintings. LC 79-9315. (Illus.). (gr. 4 up). 1980. 12.95 (ISBN 0-684-16339-X, ScribJ). Scribner.

Cumming, Robert D. Human Nature & History: A Study of the Development of Liberal Political Thought, 2 Vols. LC 68-54081. 1969. Set. 45.00x (ISBN 0-226-12364-2). U of Chicago Pr.

--The Philosophy of Jean-Paul Sartre. 1972. pap. 4.95 (ISBN 0-394-71808-9, V808, Vin). Random.

--Starting Point: An Introduction to the Dialectic of Existence. LC 78-16317. 1979. lib. bdg. 40.00x (ISBN 0-226-12347-2). U of Chicago Pr.

Cumming, Robert E., ed. Christie's Guide to Collecting. (Illus.). 208p. 1984. 15.95 (ISBN 0-13-133620-7). P-H.

Cumming, Robert G. Casebook of Psychiatric Emergencies: The "On Call" Dilemma. 150p. 1983. text ed. 18.00 (ISBN 0-8391-1811-2, 19283). Univ Park.

Cumming, Valerie. Exploring Costume History. (Illus.). 72p. 1981. 14.95 (ISBN 0-7134-1829-X, Pub. by Batsford England). David & Charles.

--Gloves. (Illus.). 96p. 1982. text ed. 13.95x (ISBN 0-7134-1008-6). Drama Bk.

--A Visual History of Costume: The Seventeenth Century. LC 83-14120. (Visual History of Costume Ser.). (Illus.). 152p. 1984. text ed. 17.95x (ISBN 0-89676-078-2). Drama Bk.

Cumming, W. P., ed. The Revelations of Saint Birgitta. (EETS, OS Ser.: No. 178). Repr. of 1929 ed. 38.00 (ISBN 0-527-00175-9). Kraus Repr.

Cumming, William. Sketchbook: A Memoir of the 1930s & the Northwest School. LC 84-40324. (Illus.). 288p. 1984. 16.95 (ISBN 0-295-96156-2). U of Wash Pr.

Cumming, William K. Follow ME. 6.95 (ISBN 0-917920-01-5); pap. 1.95 (ISBN 0-917920-00-7). Mustardseed.

Cumming, William P. British Maps of Colonial America. LC 73-84190. pap. 31.50 (ISBN 0-317-28258-1, 2024089). Bks Demand UMI.

--North Carolina in Maps. 36p. 1966. of 15 maps with booklet 15.00 set (ISBN 0-86526-137-7). NC Archives.

Cummings. Make Your Own Robots. 1981. 8.95 (ISBN 0-679-20686-8). McKay.

--Men in the Sunlight of the Word. pap. 5.95 (ISBN 0-686-27771-6). Schmul Pub Co.

Cummings & Nelson. Beginning Assessment Test for Reading. 1975. 66.60i (ISBN 0-397-43662-9). Har-Row.

Cummings, A. L. & Fales, D. A., Jr. The Crowninshield-Bentley House. LC 76-16905. (Historic House Booklet Ser.: No. 2). 1976. 2.00 (ISBN 0-88389-060-7). Essex Inst.

Cummings, Abbot L., ed. Architecture in Colonial Massachusetts: A Conference Held by the Colonial Society of Massachusetts, September 19 & 20, 1974. LC 79-51657. 1979. 30.00x (ISBN 0-8139-0855-8, Colonial Soc MA). U Pr of Va.

Cummings, Abbot L., ed. see Colonial Society of Massachusetts.

Cummings, Abbott L. The Framed Houses of Massachusetts Bay, 1625-1725. LC 78-8390. (Illus.). 280p. 1982. 40.00x (ISBN 0-674-31680-0, Belknap Pr); pap. 12.95 (ISBN 0-674-31681-9, Belknap Pr). Harvard U Pr.

Cummings, Al & Cummings, Jo B. Gunkholing in the San Juans. 240p. (Orig.). 1984. pap. 7.17 (ISBN 0-931923-00-X). Nor'Westing.

Cummings, Bart. Benevolent Dictators. LC 83-72178. 400p. 1984. 24.95 (ISBN 0-87251-091-3). Crain Bks.

Cummings, Bernice & Schuck, Victoria. Women Organizing: An Anthology. LC 79-18956. 422p. 1979. 25.00 (ISBN 0-8108-1245-2). Scarecrow.

Cummings, Betty S. Hew Against the Grain. LC 76-25593. 180p. (gr. 6-9). 1977. 6.95 (ISBN 0-689-30551-6). Atheneum.

--Say These Names (Remember Them) LC 84-11422. 300p. 1984. 14.95 (ISBN 0-910923-15-9). Pineapple Pr.

Cummings, Bill. Valentines to Make Yourself. (Illus.). 24p. (YA) 1985. pap. 2.25 (ISBN 0-590-30886-6). Scholastic Inc.

Cummings, Brian, jt. auth. see Smith, Leslie.

Cummings, Bryan J., jt. auth. see Pollack, Lawrence.

Cummings, C. E. Studies in Educational Costs. 1972. 15.00x (ISBN 0-7073-0197-1, Pub. by Scottish Academic Pr Scotland). Columbia U Pr.

Cummings, Calvin K. Confessing Christ. 3rd, rev. ed. (Orig.). 1977. pap. 1.45 (ISBN 0-934688-04-4). Great Comm Pubns.

Cummings, Calvin R., ed. Underwater Archaeology: The Proceedings of the Eleventh Conference on Underwater Archaeology. (Illus.). 200p. (Orig.). 1982. pap. text ed. 14.00x (ISBN 0-910651-03-5). Fathom Eight.

Cummings, Catherine M. & Smith, B. R. Speech One Hundred & Three Handbook. rev. ed. 1985. pap. text ed. write for info. (ISBN 0-89917-449-3). Tichenor Pub.

Cummings, Charles. Monastic Practices. pap. 7.95 (ISBN 0-317-14119-8). Cistercian Pubns.

--The Mystery of the Ordinary: Discovering the Richness of Everyday Experiences. LC 81-47846. 144p. 1982. 9.57i (ISBN 0-06-061652-0, HarpR). Har-Row.

--Spirituality & the Desert Experience. Date not set. cancelled (ISBN 0-87193-166-4). Dimension Bks.

Cummings, Charles M. Yankee Quaker Confederate General: The Curious Career of Bushrod Rust Johnson. LC 76-118805. (Illus.). 417p. 1971. 28.50 (ISBN 0-8386-7706-1). Fairleigh Dickinson.

Cummings, Charles W., et al. Atlas of Laryngeal Surgery. (Illus.). 448p. 1984. casebound 94.95 (ISBN 0-8016-1181-4). Mosby.

Cummings, Clarence A. The Illustrated History of Italian Architecture, 2 Vols. (Illus.). 317p. 1984. 157.45 (ISBN 0-86650-126-6). Gloucester Art.

Cummings, Connie. Solar Returns. 110p. 1981. 7.00 (ISBN 0-86690-006-3, 1048-01). Am Fed Astrologers.

Cummings, D., tr. see Makrakis, Apostolos.

Cummings, D., tr. see Philaretos, S. D.

Cummings, D., tr. see Philaretos, Sotirios D.

Cummings, Darold B. & Johnson, Gary. What Not to Name Your Baby. (Illus.). 64p. (Orig.). 1982. pap. 2.95 (ISBN 0-914743-01-5). Matrix Design Pubns.

Cummings, David, jt. auth. see Pipkin, Bernard.

Cummings, David, ed. The Basis for a Christian School. 1982. pap. 4.50 (ISBN 0-87552-158-4). Presby & Reformed.

--The Purpose of a Christian School. 1979. kivar 4.50 (ISBN 0-87552-157-6). Presby & Reformed.

Cummings, Davie L. Ain't No Melody Like the Tune. LC 75-12141. (Illus., Orig.). 1975. pap. text ed. 1.95x (ISBN 0-915660-01-6). Vital Pr.

--Inside the Storm. LC 78-64534. (Illus., Orig.). 1979. pap. text ed. 2.00 (ISBN 0-915660-02-4). Vital Pr.

Cummings, Denver, tr. see Agapius, et al.

Cummings, Denver, tr. see Livadeas, Themistocles & Charitos, Minas.

Cummings, Denver, tr. see Makrakis, Apostolos.

Cummings, Des, Jr., jt. auth. see Dudley, Roger L.

Cummings, Donald J., et al, eds. Extra Chromosomal DNA: Icn-Ucla Symposia on Molecular & Cellular Biology, Vol. XV. LC 79-26592. 1979. 49.50 (ISBN 0-12-198780-9). Acad Pr.

Cummings, Donald W. & Herum, John, eds. Tempo: Life, Work & Leisure. (Illus.). 336p. 1974. pap. text ed. 16.50 (ISBN 0-395-17839-8); instr's. guide 3.00 (ISBN 0-395-17867-3). HM.

Cummings, E. E. Complete Poems, Nineteen Thirteen to Nineteen Sixty-Two. LC 72-78457. 1972. 22.95 (ISBN 0-15-121060-8). HarBraceJ.

--Complete Poems, Nineteen-Thirteen to Nineteen Sixty-Two. LC 80-14213. 1980. pap. 12.95 (ISBN 0-15-621062-2, Harv). HarBraceJ.

--E. E. Cummings: A Selection of Poems. LC 65-24992. (Orig.). 1965. pap. 3.95 (ISBN 0-15-680675-4, Harv). HarBraceJ.

--The Enormous Room. rev. ed. Firmage, George J., ed. (Illus.). 1978. 12.95 (ISBN 0-87140-630-6); pap. 5.95 (ISBN 0-87140-119-3). Liveright.

--The Enormous Room. LC 34-2154. 1934. 5.95 (ISBN 0-394-60427-X). Modern Lib.

--Fairy Tales. 1965. 6.95 (ISBN 0-15-227080-9, HJ). HarBraceJ.

--Fairy Tales. LC 75-8515. (Illus.). 39p. (gr. 2-3). 1975. pap. 2.95 (ISBN 0-15-629895-3, VoyB). HarBraceJ.

--Him. 1972. pap. 3.25 (ISBN 0-553-22806-4). Bantam.

--Him. new ed. LC 76-131278. (Orig.). 1970. pap. 4.95 (ISBN 0-87140-224-6). Liveright.

--Hist Whist & Other Poems for Children. Firmage, George J., ed. (Illus.). (gr. 3 up). 1983. 10.95 (ISBN 0-87140-640-3). Liveright.

--I: Six Non Lectures. LC 53-10472. (Charles Eliot Norton Lectures Ser: 1952-1953). 1953. pap. 3.95 (ISBN 0-674-44010-2). Harvard U Pr.

--Is Five. new ed. LC 76-114376. 1970. 6.00 (ISBN 0-87140-549-0); pap. 3.95 (ISBN 0-87140-202-5). Liveright.

--Is Five... Firmage, George J., ed. 1985. 14.95 (ISBN 0-87140-648-9); pap. 6.95 (ISBN 0-87140-136-3). Liveright.

--Ninety-Five Poems. LC 58-10909. 1971. pap. 3.95 (ISBN 0-15-665950-6, Harv). HarBraceJ.

--No Thanks. Firmage, James, ed. 1978. 9.95 (ISBN 0-87140-631-4); pap. 3.95 (ISBN 0-87140-120-7). Liveright.

--One Hundred Selected Poems. (Orig.). (YA) (gr. 9 up). 1959. pap. 2.95 (ISBN 0-394-17219-1, E190, Ever). Grove.

--One Times One. LC 54-10935. 55p. 1972. pap. 2.95 (ISBN 0-15-668800-X, Harv). HarBraceJ.

--Seventy-Three Poems. LC 63-20271. 1971. pap. 2.95 (ISBN 0-15-680676-2, Harv). HarBraceJ.

--Tulips & Chimneys. Firmage, George J., ed. 1976. 10.00 (ISBN 0-87140-622-5); pap. 7.95 (ISBN 0-87140-112-6). Liveright.

--Viva. LC 70-131279. 1970. 6.00 (ISBN 0-87140-528-8); pap. 2.95 (ISBN 0-87140-223-8). Liveright.

--W (Viva) rev. ed. Firmage, George James, ed. (Transcript Edition Ser.). 1979. 9.95 (ISBN 0-87140-636-5); pap. 3.95 (ISBN 0-87140-125-8). Liveright.

--Xaipe. Firmage, George J., ed. 1979. 9.95 (ISBN 0-87140-633-0); pap. 3.95 (ISBN 0-87140-121-5). Liveright.

Cummings, Edward E. Anthropos. LC 76-47444. 1976. Repr. of 1930 ed. lib. bdg. 10.00 (ISBN 0-8414-3479-4). Folcroft.

--Anthropos: The Future of Art. 1979. Repr. of 1944 ed. lib. bdg. 10.00 (ISBN 0-8492-3857-9). R West.

Cummings, F. Jay. The Future of Commercial Banking: Proceedings of the 1982 Political Economy Research Institute Conference on Banking & Financial Institutions. Jones, Deborah G., ed. (Illus.). 146p. (Orig.). 1983. lib. bdg. 25.50 (ISBN 0-8191-3293-4); pap. text ed. 12.25 (ISBN 0-8191-3294-2). U Pr of Amer.

Cummings, Frank. Capitol Hill Manual. 2nd ed. LC 83-21048. 338p. 1984. pap. 25.00 (ISBN 0-87179-355-5). BNA.

Cummings, Frank & Barry, Michael P. Federal Labor Laws: No. B363. (Rules for Operation of Qualified Plans). 27p. 1978. pap. 6.00 (ISBN 0-317-31182-4). Am Law Inst.

Cummings, Gordon, et al. Soft Tissue Changes in Contractures, Vol. 1. (Orthopedic Physical Therapy Ser.). (Illus.). 1983. pap. 12.75x (ISBN 0-936030-02-X). Stokesville Pub.

Cummings, H. Wayland & Somervill, Charles E., Jr. Overcoming Communication Barriers in the Church. 176p. 1981. pap. 8.95 (ISBN 0-8170-0924-8). Judson.

Cummings, H. Wayland, et al. Managing Communication in Organizations: An Introduction. 361p. 1982. pap. text ed. 18.95x (ISBN 0-89787-314-9). Gorsuch Scarisbrick.

Cummings, Harold J. Prescription for Tomorrow. Rev. ed. LC 80-25723. 112p. 1982. 6.95 (ISBN 0-87863-034-1). Farnswth Pub.

Cummings, Homer & McFarland, Carl. Federal Justice. LC 76-109552. (American Constitutional & Legal History Ser). 1970. Repr. of 1937 ed. lib. bdg. 59.50 (ISBN 0-306-71906-1). Da Capo.

Cummings, Hubertis. Indebtedness of Chaucer's Works to the Italian Works of Boccaccio. LC 65-21098. (Studies in Comparative Literature, No. 35). 1969. Repr. of 1916 ed. lib. bdg. 39.95x (ISBN 0-8383-0534-2). Haskell.

Cummings, Hubertis M. Indebtedness of Chaucer's Work to the Italian Works of Boccaccio. LC 67-30901. 1967. Repr. of 1916 ed. 10.00 (ISBN 0-87753-011-4). Phaeton.

--The Indebtedness of Chaucer's Works to the Italian Boccaccio. 1973. lib. bdg. 20.00 (ISBN 0-8414-2428-4). Folcroft.

Cummings, J. Railway Motor Buses & Bus Services in the British Isles, Vol. 1: 1902-1933. 136p. 1982. 30.00x (ISBN 0-86093-011-4, Pub. by ORPC Ltd UK). State Mutual Bk.

--Railway Motor Buses & Bus Services in the British Isles, Vol. 2: 1902-1933. 188p. 1982. 32.00x (ISBN 0-86093-050-5, Pub. by ORPC Ltd UK). State Mutual Bk.

Cummings, J. T. & Moll, H. Prayers for College Students. LC 12-2962. 1982. pap. 4.95 (ISBN 0-570-03869-3). Concordia.

Cummings, Jack. Complete Guide to Real Estate Financing. (Illus.). 1978. 29.95 (ISBN 0-13-160481-3, Busn). P-H.

--Dead Man's Medal. LC 83-42847. (Western Ser.). 192p. 1984. 12.95 (ISBN 0-8027-4028-6). Walker & Co.

--Lauderdale Run. 1979. pap. 1.75 (ISBN 0-532-17208-6). Woodhill.

--Lynch's Revenge. 192p. 1985. 13.95 (ISBN 0-8027-4045-6). Walker & Co.

--One Thousand Dollars Down Can Make You Rich: Tactics for Real Estate Investors. 320p. 24.95 (ISBN 0-317-18450-4); pap. 8.95 (ISBN 0-317-18451-2). P-H.

--Sergeant Gringo. 192p. 1984. 12.95 (ISBN 0-8027-4044-8). Walker & Co.

--Successful Real Estate Investing for the Single Person. LC 81-83486. 368p. 1982. pap. 3.95 (ISBN 0-86721-035-4). Jove Pubns.

Cummings, James E. A Handbook on the Holy Spirit. LC 77-79551. 208p. 1977. pap. 3.95 (ISBN 0-87123-541-2, 200541). Bethany Hse.

Cummings, Jean. Alias the Buffalo Doctor. LC 80-81714. (Illus.). 272p. 1980. 11.95 (ISBN 0-8187-0039-4). Harlo Pr.

--They Call Him the Buffalo Doctor. LC 73-147172. 320p. 1980. Repr. of 1971 ed. 7.00 (ISBN 0-8187-0035-1). Harlo Pr.

Cummings, Jeffrey. Clinical Neurology & Neuropsychiatry. 272p. 1985. 44.50 (ISBN 0-8089-1722-6, 790955). Grune.

Cummings, Jeffrey L. & Benson, D. Frank. Dementia: A Clinical Approach. 406p. 1983. text ed. 34.95 (ISBN 0-409-95044-0). Butterworth.

Cummings, Jo B., jt. auth. see Cummings, Al.

Cummings, Joe. Thailand: A Travel Survival Kit. (Lonely Planet Travel Ser.). (Illus.). 144p. (Orig.). 1982. 30.00 (ISBN 0-88254-672-4, Pub. by Lonely Planet Australia). State Mutual Bk.

--Thailand Phrasebook. 1984. 2.25 (ISBN 0-317-14113-9, Pub. by Lonely Planet Australia). Hippocrene Bks.

Cummings, John. Deuteronomy. 1982. lib. bdg. 16.00 (ISBN 0-86524-085-X, 0501). Klock & Klock.

--Negro Population in the United States, 1790-1915. LC 68-28992. (American Negro: His History & Literature Ser., No. 1). 1968. Repr. of 1918 ed. 29.00 (ISBN 0-405-01811-8). Ayer Co Pubs.

Cummings, John & Burns, Paul, eds. The Church Now. 235p. 1980. 15.00x (ISBN 0-7171-1082-6, Pub. by Gill & Macmillan Ireland). State Mutual Bk.

Cummings, John T., jt. auth. see Askari, Hossein.

Cummings, Kathleen R. Architectural Records in Chicago. (Illus.). 92p. 1981. pap. 12.95 (ISBN 0-86559-052-4). Art Inst Chi.

Cummings, L. L. Improving Human Resource Effectiveness: An Annotated Bibliography of Behavioral Science Contributions. LC 81-52318. 348p. 1982. 27.50 (ISBN 0-939900-03-3). Am Soc Personnel.

Cummings, L. L. & Dunham, Randall B. Introduction to Organizational Behavior: Text & Readings. 1980. pap. 19.95x (ISBN 0-256-02043-4). Irwin.

Cummings, L. L. & Frost, Peter. Publishing in the Organizational Sciences. 1985. 10.00x (ISBN 0-317-19954-4). Irwin.

Cummings, L. L. & Staw, B. Research in Organizational Behavior, Vol. 7. 57.50 (ISBN 0-89232-497-X). Jai Pr.

Cummings, L. L., jt. auth. see Harnett, D. L.

Cummings, L. L., jt. auth. see Scott, William E.

Cummings, L. L., ed. Research in Organizational Behavior, Vol. 5. 350p. 1983. 45.00 (ISBN 0-89232-271-3). Jai Pr.

Cummings, L. L. & Staw, Barry, eds. Research in Organizational Behavior, Vol. 3. 356p. 1981. 42.50 (ISBN 0-89232-151-2). Jai Pr.

Cummings, L. L., jt. ed. see Staw, Barry.

Cummings, Larry, ed. Combinatorics on Words: Progress & Perspectives (Symposium) 1983. 37.00 (ISBN 0-12-198820-1). Acad Pr.

Cummings, Larry L., jt. ed. see Staw, Barry M.

Cummings, M. & Simmons, R. The Language of Literature: A Stylistic Introduction to the Study of Literature. (Language Teaching Methodology Ser.). (Illus.). 192p. 1983. pap. 12.00 (ISBN 0-08-028629-1). Pergamon.

Cummings, Marcus F. & Miller, Charles C. Victorian Architectural Details: Two Pattern Books by Cummings & Miller. (The Athenaeum Library of Nineteenth Century America). (Illus.). 1978. pap. text ed. 18.00 (ISBN 0-89257-022-9). Am Life Foun.

Cummings, Marlene. Individual Differences: A Program for Elementary School Age Children. 588p. (gr. 1-6). 12.50 (ISBN 0-686-74870-0). ADL.

Cummings, Marlene A., et al, eds. Individual Differences: An Experience in Human Relations for Children. 588p. 12.50 (ISBN 0-686-74912-X). ADL.

Cummings, Mary. Lives of the Buddha in the Art & Literature of Asia. LC 80-67341. (Michigan Papers on South & Southeast Asia: No. 20). (Illus.). xiii, 225p. 1982. 17.25x (ISBN 0-89148-022-6); pap. 9.00x (ISBN 0-89148-023-4). Ctr S&SE Asian.

Cummings, Mary L., ed. Full Circle: Stories of Mennonite Women. LC 78-66879. 1978. pap. 5.25 (ISBN 0-87303-014-1). Faith & Life.

Cummings, Michael R., jt. auth. see Klug, William S.

Cummings, Michel R. Mongrel Harmony: Poems, 1976-1980. (Beacon Presse Poetry Ser.: No. 2). 42p. (Orig.). 1980. pap. 1.95 (ISBN 0-935954-05-8). Gormezano Ref.

Cummings, Milton C., Jr. & Wise, David. Democracy under Pressure: An Introduction to the American Political System. 4th ed. 689p. 1981. text ed. 23.95 (ISBN 0-15-517343-X, HC); study guide 8.95 (ISBN 0-15-517344-8); price not set tests avail. HarBraceJ.

--Democracy under Pressure: An Introduction to the American Political System. 5th ed. 1985. text ed. write for info. (ISBN 0-15-517346-4, HC); study guide avail. (ISBN 0-15-517347-2); tests avail. (ISBN 0-15-517348-0). HarBraceJ.

Cummings, Monette. The Beauty's Daughter. 192p. 1985. 13.95 (ISBN 0-8027-0852-8). Walker & Co.

--Don't Wager on Love. (Orig.). 1981. pap. 1.95 (ISBN 0-8439-8041-9, Tiara Bks). Dorchester Pub Co.

--Guardian Devil. (Orig.). 1981. pap. 1.75 (ISBN 0-8439-8020-6, Tiara Bks). Dorchester Pub Co.

--Lady Sheila's Groom. LC 83-40427. 192p. 1984. 12.95 (ISBN 0-8027-0759-9). Walker & Co.

--The Scandalous Widow. 192p. (Orig.). 1982. pap. 2.25 (ISBN 0-8439-1102-6, Leisure Bks). Dorchester Pub Co.

--See No Love. LC 82-63201. 192p. 1983. 12.95 (ISBN 0-8027-0738-6). Walker & Co.

Cummings, Nancy B. & Klahr, Saulo, eds. Chronic Renal Disease: Causes, Complications & Treatment. 624p. 1985. 75.00x (ISBN 0-306-41764-2, Plenum Pr). Plenum Pub.

Cummings, Nancy B. & Michael, Alfred F., eds. Immune Mechanisms in Renal Disease. 596p. 1983. 65.00x (ISBN 0-306-40948-8, Plenum Pr). Plenum Pub.

Cummings, O. R. Berkshire Street Railway. (Transportation Bulletin: No. 79). (Illus.). 1972. 7.50 (ISBN 0-910506-15-9). De Vito.

--Street Cars of Boston: Closed Horse & Electric Cars to 1900, Vol. 1. (Illus.). 92p. (Orig.). 1973. pap. 6.00 (ISBN 0-911940-18-9). Cox.

--Street Cars of Boston, Vol. 6: Birneys, Type 5, Semiconvertibles, Parlor, Private, & Mail Cars. (Illus.). 84p. (Orig.). 1980. pap. 9.00 (ISBN 0-911940-34-0). Cox.

--Trolleys to Augusta, Maine. (Transportation Bulletin: No. 76). (Illus.). 1969. 5.00 (ISBN 0-910506-03-5). De Vito.

Cummings, P. Howard & Porter, Stephen R. Quick Reference of Common Emergency Drugs. LC 83-10386. 421p. 1983. pap. 14.50x (ISBN 0-471-87703-4, Pub. by Wiley Med). Wiley.

Cummings, Parke & Lapin, Nora. Fairfield County: An Insider's Guide. LC 75-8337. 288p. 1975. pap. 3.95 (ISBN 0-88208-055-5). Lawrence Hill.

Cummings, Pat. Jimmy Lee Did It. LC 84-21322. (Illus.). (ps-1). 1985. 11.75 (ISBN 0-688-04632-0); PLB 11.88 (ISBN 0-688-04633-9). Lothrop.

Cummings, Patrick E. Poems for the Woman I Love 1974-79. 33p. 1984. 5.95 (ISBN 0-533-05969-0). Vantage.

Cummings, Paul. Artists in Their Own Words. (Illus.). 316p. 1982. pap. 7.95 (ISBN 0-312-05513-7). St Martin.

--Twentieth-Century American Drawings: The Figure in Context. John, Angela G. & Grove, Migs, eds. (Illus.). 144p. 1984. pap. 16.00 (ISBN 0-88397-077-5). Intl Exhibit Foun.

Cummings, Paul, jt. auth. see Bame, E. Allen.

Cummings, Paul, compiled by. Dictionary of Contemporary American Artists. 4th ed. (Illus.). 640p. 1982. 50.00x (ISBN 0-312-20097-8). St Martin.

Cummings, Paul, et al. Willem de Kooning: Drawings-Paintings-Sculpture, A Whitney Museum Book. (Illus.). 1984. 45.00 (ISBN 0-393-01840-7). Norton.

Cummings, Peter. Bicycle Consciousness. LC 79-51321. 1979. 4.00 (ISBN 0-912678-40-2). Greenfld Rev Pr.

Cummings, R. D., tr. see Plato.

Cummings, Ralph W., Jr., jt. auth. see Wortman, Sterling.

Cummings, Ray. Girl in the Golden Atom. LC 73-13251. (Classics of Science Fiction Ser.). (Illus.). 357p. 1973. 12.50 (ISBN 0-88355-107-1); pap. 10.00 (ISBN 0-88355-136-5). Hyperion Conn.

--The Man Who Mastered Time. LC 74-15960. (Science Fiction Ser). 362p. 1975. Repr. of 1929 ed. 26.50x (ISBN 0-405-06284-2). Ayer Co Pubs.

--Tarrano the Conqueror. Del Ray, Lester, ed. LC 75-400. (Library of Science Fiction). 1975. lib. bdg. 21.00 (ISBN 0-8240-1406-5). Garland Pub.

Cummings, Raymond. Girl in the Golden Atom. 1976. lib. bdg. 12.95x (ISBN 0-89968-175-1). Lightyear.

Cummings, Rhoda W. & Maddux, Cleborne D. Parenting the Learning Disabled: A Realistic Approach. 150p. 1985. 19.75x (ISBN 0-398-05151-8). C C Thomas.

Cummings, Richard. Be Your Own Detective. (YA) 1980. 7.95 (ISBN 0-679-20682-5). McKay.

--Contemporary Selling. 1979. 27.50 (ISBN 0-395-30584-5); Instr's. manual 1.10 (ISBN 0-395-30585-3). HM.

--Make Your Own Model Forts & Castles. (Illus.). (gr. 6 up). 1977. 8.95 (ISBN 0-679-20400-8). McKay.

--The Pied Piper: Allard K. Lowenstein & the Liberal Dream. LC 83-49377. 416p. 1984. 19.95 (ISBN 0-394-53848-X, GP 895). Grove.

--Proposition Fourteen: A Secessionist Remedy. LC 80-8917. 128p. (Orig.). 1981. pap. 3.95 (ISBN 0-394-17890-4, E776, BC). Grove.

--Proposition Fourteen: A Secessionist Remedy. LC 80-80357. 128p. 1980. 11.95 (ISBN 0-932966-09-8); pap. 7.50 (ISBN 0-932966-16-0). Permanent Pr.

Cummings, Richard L. & Lemke, Donald A. Educational Innovations in Latin America. LC 73-390. 1973. 20.00 (ISBN 0-8108-0585-5). Scarecrow.

Cummings, Richard O. American & His Food: A History of Food Habits in the United States. LC 74-112536. (Rise of Urban America). (Illus.). 1970. Repr. of 1940 ed. 21.00 (ISBN 0-405-02445-2). Ayer Co Pubs.

Cummings, Robert. Just Imagine: 82-60036. (Illus.). 64p. (gr. 4 up). 1982. 12.95 (ISBN 0-684-17762-5, ScribT). Scribner.

Cummings, Robert D., jt. auth. see Church, F. J.

Cummings, Robert J., jt. auth. see Browne, Robert S.

Cummings, Robert W. Unto You Is the Promise. pap. 0.79 (ISBN 0-88243-750-X, 02-0750). Gospel Pub.

Cummings, Ronald G. Interbasin Water Transfers: A Case Study in Mexico. LC 74-6819. pap. 31.80 (ISBN 0-317-26457-5, 2023793). Bks Demand UMI.

--Water Resource Management in Northern Mexico. LC 72-3612. pap. 20.00 (ISBN 0-317-26458-3, 2023794). Bks Demand UMI.

Cummings, Ronald G., et al, eds. Valuing Public Goods: An Assessment of the Contingent Valuation Method. LC 85-14298. (Illus.). 304p. 1985. 54.50x (ISBN 0-8476-7448-7). Rowman.

Cummings, Scott. Immigrant Minorities & the Urban Working Class: The Ambiguous Political Legacy. LC 83-17243. (National University Publications Ser.). 151p. 1983. 16.00x (ISBN 0-8046-9338-2). Assoc Faculty Pr.

Cummings, Scott, ed. Self-Help in Urban America: Patterns of Minority Business Enterprise. (National University Publications, Interdisciplinary Urban Ser.). 1980. 23.95x (ISBN 0-8046-9251-3, Pub. by Kennikat). Assoc Faculty Pr.

Cummings, Stephen & Ullman, Dana. Everybody's Guide to Homeopathic Medicines. 324p. 1984. 15.95; pap. 9.95 (ISBN 0-87477-324-5). J P Tarcher.

Cummings, Thomas, jt. auth. see Huse, Edgar F.

Cummings, Thomas G. & Molloy, Edmond S. Improving Productivity & the Quality of Work Life. LC 76-24348. (Praeger Special Studies). 328p. 1977. pap. 19.95 (ISBN 0-03-022601-5). Praeger.

Cummings, Thomas G. & Srivastva, Suresh. Management of Work: A Socio-Technical Systems Approach. LC 76-47659. 247p. 1977. pap. 14.95 (ISBN 0-88390-166-8). Univ Assocs.

Cummings, Thomas G., jt. auth. see Glassman, Alan M.

Cummings, Thomas G., ed. Systems Theory for Organization Development. LC 79-42906. (Individuals, Groups & Organizations Ser.). 362p. 1980. 57.95 (ISBN 0-471-27691-X, Pub. by Wiley-Interscience). Wiley.

Cummings, Thomas S. Historic Annals of the National Academy of Design. LC 71-87503. (Library of American Art). 1969. Repr. of 1865 ed. lib. bdg. 42.50 (ISBN 0-306-71411-6). Da Capo.

Cummings, Violet. Has Anybody Really Seen Noah's Ark? 416p. 1982. pap. 8.95 (ISBN 0-89051-086-5). Master Bks.

Cummings, William, ed. Scott Standard Postage Catalogue, 1985, Vol. I. (Illus.). 1000p. 1984. 20.00 (ISBN 0-89487-062-9). Scott Pub Co.

--Scott Standard Postage Stamp Catalogue, 1985, Vol. IV. (Illus.). 1000p. 1984. pap. 20.00 (ISBN 0-89487-065-3). Scott Pub Co.

--Scott Standard Postage Stamp Catalogue, 1985, Vol. III. (Illus.). 1000p. 1984. pap. 20.00 (ISBN 0-89487-064-5). Scott Pub Co.

--Scott Standard Postage Stamp Catalogue, 1985, Vol. II. (Illus.). 1000p. 1984. pap. 20.00 (ISBN 0-89487-063-7). Scott Pub Co.

Cummings, William, et al, eds. Scott Specialized Catalogue of United States Postage Stamps, 1985. (Illus.). 1000p. 1984. pap. 20.00 (ISBN 0-89487-066-1). Scott Pub Co.

Cummings, William A. Italian Southern & Sicilian Architecture. (Illus.). 147p. 1984. 88.75x (ISBN 0-86650-091-X). Gloucester Art.

Cummings, William H. Purcell. LC 68-25285. (Studies in Drama, No. 39). 1969. Repr. of 1881 ed. lib. bdg. 49.95x (ISBN 0-8383-0285-8). Haskell.

Cummings, William K. Education & Equality in Japan. LC 79-3199. 1980. 30.00 (ISBN 0-691-09385-7); pap. 15.50 ltd. ed. (ISBN 0-691-10088-8). Princeton U Pr.

Cummings, William K., et al. Changes in the Japanese University: A Comparative Perspective. LC 78-19787. 288p. 1979. 39.95x (ISBN 0-03-045546-4). Praeger.

Cummings, William W. & Weinfeld, Barbara A., eds. Scott Standard Postage Stamp Catalogue: 1984, Vol. II. (Illus.). 1100p. 1983. softcover 20.00 (ISBN 0-89487-054-8). Scott Pub Co.

Cummings, William W. & Weinfield, Barbara, eds. Scott Specialized Catalogue of United States Stamps, 1984. (Illus.). 900p. 1983. pap. 20.00 (ISBN 0-89487-057-2). Scott Pub Co.

Cummings, William W. & Weinfield, Barbara A., eds. Scott Standard Postage Stamp Catalogue: 1984, Vol. I. (Illus.). 900p. 1983. softcover 20.00 (ISBN 0-89487-053-X). Scott Pub Co.

--Scott Standard Postage Stamp Catalogue 1984, Vol. IV. (Illus.). 1000p. 1983. softcover 20.00 (ISBN 0-89487-056-4). Scott Pub Co.

--Scott Standard Postage Stamp Catalogue 1984, Vol. III. (Illus.). 1983. softcover 20.00 (ISBN 0-89487-055-6). Scott Pub Co.

Cummings-Wing, Julia. Speak for Yourself: An Integrated Method of Voice & Speech Training. LC 83-26862. (Illus.). 272p. 1984. lib. bdg. 24.95x (ISBN 0-8304-1024-4); pap. text ed. 11.95x (ISBN 0-88229-827-5). Nelson-Hall.

Cummins, C. Lyle, et al. A History of the Automotive Internal Combustion Engine. 56p. 1976. 12.00 (ISBN 0-89883-183-0, SP-409). Soc Auto Engineers.

Cummins, C. Lyle, Jr. Internal Fire: The Internal Combustion Engine, 1673-1900. LC 75-40701. (Illus.). 1976. 20.00x (ISBN 0-917308-01-8). Carnot Pr.

Cummins, D. Duane. A Handbook for Today's Disciples in the Christian Church: Disciples of Christ. LC 81-10029. 64p. (Orig.). 1981. pap. 1.95 (ISBN 0-8272-1419-7, 10H1309). CBP.

--Un Manual Para los Discipulos de Hoy. Delgado, Conchita & Sanchez, Zayda N., trs. from Eng. (Illus.). 64p. (Orig., Span.). 1983. pap. 2.25 (ISBN 0-8272-2316-1). CBP.

--William Robinson Leigh: Western Artist. LC 79-6707. (Gilcrease-Oklahoma Series on Western Art & Artists: Vol. 2). (Illus.). 200p. 1980. 27.95 (ISBN 0-8061-1628-5). U of Okla Pr.

Cummins, D. Duane & White, William G. American Foreign Policy. (Inquiries into American History Ser.). (gr. 11-12). 1980. pap. 6.00 (ISBN 0-02-652860-6, 64115); tchrs' ed. o.p. 5.28 (ISBN 0-02-641160-1, 64116). Glencoe.

--The American Frontier. rev. ed. (Inquiries into American History Ser.). (gr. 11-12). 1980. pap. text ed. 6.00 (ISBN 0-02-652700-6, 64122); tchr's. ed. o.p. 5.28 (ISBN 0-02-641250-0, 64125). Glencoe.

--The American Revolution. rev. ed. (Inquiries into American History Ser.). (gr. 11-12). 1980. pap. text ed. 6.00 (ISBN 0-02-641280-2, 64128); tchr's ed. o.p. 5.28 (ISBN 0-02-641330-2, 64133). Glencoe.

--Contrasting Decades: The Nineteen Twenties & Nineteen Thirties. (Inquiries into American History Ser.). (gr. 11-12). 1980. pap. 6.00 (ISBN 0-02-652900-9, 64135); tchrs' ed. o.p. 5.28 (ISBN 0-02-641360-4, 64136). Glencoe.

--The Federal Period. (Inquiries into American History Ser). (gr. 11-12). 1973. pap. 6.00 (ISBN 0-02-652620-4, 64142); tchrs' manual o.p. 2.68 (ISBN 0-685-03317-1, 64143). Glencoe.

--Industrialism: The American Experience. (Inquiries into American History Ser.). (gr. 11-12). 1980. pap. text ed. 6.00 (ISBN 0-02-652820-7, 64146); tchr's ed. o.p. 5.28 (ISBN 0-02-641470-8, 64147). Glencoe.

--Our Colonial History: Plymouth & Jamestown. (Inquiries into American History Ser). (gr. 11-12). 1980. pap. 6.00 (ISBN 0-02-652500-3, 64154); tchrs' ed. o.p. 5.28 (ISBN 0-02-641550-X, 64155). Glencoe.

Cummins, D. Duane & Hohweiler, Daryl, eds. An Enlisted Soldier's View of the Civil War: The Wartime Papers of Joseph R. Ward, Jr. (Illus.). 292p. (Orig.). 1981. pap. 7.50x (ISBN 0-9605732-0-8). Belle Pubns.

Cummins, Duane D. & White, William G. Origins of the Civil War. (Inquiries into American History Ser.). (gr. 11-12). 1980. pap. 6.00 (ISBN 0-02-652740-5, 64150); tchrs' ed. o.p. 5.28 (ISBN 0-02-641510-0, 64151). Glencoe.

Cummins, G. B. & Hiratsuka, Y. Illustrated Genera of Rust Fungi. rev. ed. LC 83-72397. (Illus.). 152p. 1983. spiral bound 16.00 (ISBN 0-89054-058-6). Am Phytopathol Soc.

Cummins, George B. Rust Fungi on Legumes & Composites in North America. LC 78-60541. 426p. 1978. pap. 14.95x (ISBN 0-8165-0653-1). U of Ariz Pr.

Cummins, H. Z., jt. auth. see Williamson, S. J.

Cummins, H. Z. & Levanyuk, A. P., eds. Light Scattering Near Phase Transitions. (Modern Problems in Condensed Matter Science Ser.: Vol. 5). 660p. 1984. 129.00 (ISBN 0-444-86466-0, North-Holland). Elsevier.

Cummins, H. Z. & Pike, E. R., eds. Photon Correlation & Light Beating Spectroscopy. LC 74-938. (NATO ASI Series B, Physics: Vol. 3). 584p. 1974. 89.50x (ISBN 0-306-35703-8, Plenum Pr). Plenum Pub.

--Photon Correlation Spectroscopy & Velocimetry. LC 77-3154. (NATO ASI Series B, Physics: Vol. 23). 589p. 1977. 89.50 (ISBN 0-306-35723-2, Plenum Pr). Plenum Pub.

Cummins, Harold. Dermatoglyphics in Indians of Southern Mexico & Central America: Santa Eulalia, Tzeltal, Lacondon & Maya. (Middle American Research Series Publication: No. 4). pap. 20.00 (ISBN 0-317-28692-7, 2051616). Bks Demand UMI.

Cummins, J. David. Development of Life Insurance Surrender Values in the United States. LC 73-87483. (S. S. Huebner Foundation Monographs: No. 2). 81p. 1973. pap. 9.00 (ISBN 0-918930-02-2). Huebner Foun Insur.

--Investment Activities of Life Insurance Companies. 1977. 19.00x (ISBN 0-256-01974-6). Irwin.

--Strategic Planning & Modeling in Property-Liability Insurance. 1984. lib. bdg. 47.50 (ISBN 0-89838-159-2). Kluwer Nijhoff.

Cummins, J. David & Smith, Barry D. Risk Classification in Life Insurance. 1982. lib. bdg. 45.00 (ISBN 0-89838-114-2). Kluwer-Nijhoff.

Cummins, J. G. The Spanish Traditional Lyric. LC 76-1222. 1977. pap. 10.25 (ISBN 0-08-018116-3). Pergamon.

Cummins, J. S. Sucesos de las Islas Filipinos, by Atonio Marga, 1609. 348p. 1971. 40.00x (ISBN 0-686-79460-5, Pub. by Hakluyt Soc England). State Mutual Bk.

Cummins, Jack, jt. auth. see Wartell, Michael.

Cummins, Jacqueline. End of Innocence. 1961. 9.95 (ISBN 0-8392-1028-0). Astor-Honor.

Cummins, Jerry, et al. Programming in BASIC. 1983. 13.20 (ISBN 0-675-05650-0). Merrill.

Cummins, Kenneth L., ed. see Proceedings of a Workshop, Palo Alto, California, July 1979, et al.

Cummins, Kenneth W., jt. auth. see Merritt, Ricard W.

Cummins, Light T. & Jeansonne, Glen, eds. A Guide to the History of Louisiana. LC 82-6108. (Reference Guides to State History & Research Ser.). xi, 297p. 1982. lib. bdg. 35.00 (ISBN 0-313-22959-7, JLO/). Greenwood.

Cummins, Louise. The Decennial Dilemma: Redistricting. (Illus.). 1984. pap. text ed. 1.25 (ISBN 0-915757-02-8). League Women Voters TX.

Cummins, Marcey, ed. Four Corners Explorer. 32p. pap. write for info. Four Corners.

Cummins, Maria. The Lamplighter. 1972. Repr. of 1854 ed. 19.50 (ISBN 0-8422-8031-6). Irvington.

--The Lamplighter. 1981. Repr. lib. bdg. 30.00 (ISBN 0-686-71927-1). Scholarly.

Cummins, Martha H. & Slade, Carole. Writing the Research Paper: A Guide & Sourcebook. LC 78-69613. (Illus.). 1979. pap. text ed. 14.50 (ISBN 0-395-27259-9); instr's manual 0.50 (ISBN 0-395-27260-2). HM.

Cummins, Mary Ann, jt. auth. see Burnett, Millie.

Cummins, P. D., tr. see Del Boca, Angelo.

Cummins, Patricia. Commercial French. (Illus.). 320p. 1982. 24.95 (ISBN 0-13-152710-X). P-H.

Cummins, Patricia W. Literary & Historical Perspectives of the Middle Ages. 232p. 1982. 8.00 (ISBN 0-937058-15-7). West Va U Pr.

Cummins, Robert. Friendship. 1972. pap. 3.95 (ISBN 0-88489-034-1). St Marys.

--The Nature of Psychological Explanation. (Illus.). 256p. 1985. text ed. 22.50x (ISBN 0-262-03094-2); pap. 8.95 (ISBN 0-262-53065-1). MIT Pr.

Cummins, Robert A. Improvement & Distribution of Practice. LC 76-176682. (Columbia University. Teachers College. Contributions to Education: No. 97). Repr. of 1919 ed. 22.50 (ISBN 0-404-55097-5). AMS Pr.

Cummins, Roger W. Humorous but Wholesome: A History of Palmer Cox & the Brownies, 1974. LC 72-97477. pap. 18.00 (ISBN 0-87282-020-3). CHB-ALF.

Cummins, Thomas J., jt. ed. see Dunphy, Thomas.

Cummins, Virginia R. Rookwood Pottery Potpourri. LC 79-92591. (Illus.). 144p. (Orig.). 1980. pap. 26.00 (ISBN 0-9603818-0-5). C R Leonard & Assocs.

Cummins, W. A., jt. ed. see Clough, T. H.

Cummins, Walter. Where We Live. (Short Stories Ser.: Vol. 2). 94p. (Orig.). 1983. pap. text ed. 6.50 (ISBN 0-89924-037-2). Lynx Hse.

Cummins, Walter J. Demonstrating God's Power. LC 85-50446. 1985. 6.95 (ISBN 0-910068-60-7). Am Christian.

Cummins, William H. The Great Italian Villas of the Renaissance. (The Masters of World Architecture Library). (Illus.). 148p. 1982. Repr. of 1908 ed. 137.85 (ISBN 0-686-83080-6). Found Class Reprints.

Cumnock, Frances, ed. Catalog of the Salem Congregation Music. (Illus.). 682p. 31.50 (ISBN 0-8078-1398-2). Moravian Music.

--Catalogue of the Salem Congregation Music. (Illus.). 682p. 31.50 (ISBN 0-8078-1398-2). Moravian Music.

Cumont, F. Etudes Syriennes. (Illus.). xii, 379p. (Fr.). Repr. of 1917 ed. lib. bdg. 60.00x (ISBN 0-89241-192-9). Caratzas.

Cumont, Franz. Astrology & Religion among the Greeks & Romans. 1912. pap. 3.50 (ISBN 0-486-20581-9). Dover.

--Astrology & Religion among the Greeks & Romans. 12.75 (ISBN 0-8446-1927-2). Peter Smith.

--The Mysteries of Mithra. 2nd ed. McCormack, Thomas J., tr. (Illus., Fr). 1911. pap. 5.95 (ISBN 0-486-20323-9). Dover.

--Mysteries of Mithra. (Illus.). 13.50 (ISBN 0-8446-1926-4). Peter Smith.

--Oriental Religions in Roman Paganism. 1911. pap. 5.95 (ISBN 0-486-20321-2). Dover.

--Oriental Religions in Roman Paganism. 14.00 (ISBN 0-8446-1925-6). Peter Smith.

--Recherches sur le Symbolisme Funeraire des Romains. facsimile ed. LC 75-10632. (Ancient Religion & Mythology Ser.). (Illus., Fr.). 1976. Repr. of 1942 ed. 57.50x (ISBN 0-405-07007-1). Ayer Co Pubs.

Cumont, Franz, jt. auth. see Bidez, Joseph.

Cumoutier, G. Les Chants et les traditions populaires des Annamites. LC 78-20123. (Collection de contes et de chansons populaires: Vol. 15). Repr. of 1890 ed. 21.50 (ISBN 0-404-60365-3). AMS Pr.

Cumper, G. E. Determinants of Health Levels in Developing Countries. LC 83-13906. (Tropical Medicine Research Studies Ser.: 1-520). 150p. 1984. 38.00x (ISBN 0-471-90268-3, Pub by Res Stud Pr). Wiley.

Cumper, G. E., ed. The Economy of the West Indies. LC 73-19112. 273p. 1975. Repr. of 1960 ed. lib. bdg. 18.25x (ISBN 0-8371-7300-0, CUEW). Greenwood.

Cumpiano, W. Guitar Tradition & Technolgy. 1986. cancelled (ISBN 0-442-26845-9). Van Nos Reinhold.

Cumpston, I. M. Indians Overseas in British Territories: 1839-1854. 198p. 1969. Repr. of 1953 ed. 17.95x (ISBN 0-8464-0506-7). Beekman Pubs.

Cumpston, I. M., ed. The Growth of the British Commonwealth: 1880-1932. (Documents of Modern History Ser.). 192p. 1973. 20.00 (ISBN 0-312-35140-2). St Martin.

Cumpsty, Denise. Book of the Netherland Dwarf. 186p. 1984. 13.50 (ISBN 0-904558-45-2). Saiga.

Cunanan, Augustina S., jt. auth. see Cabrera, Neonetta C.

Cunard, Nancy. Grand Man: Memories of Norman Douglas. 1979. Repr. of 1954 ed. lib. bdg. 25.00 (ISBN 0-8495-0940-8). Arden Lib.

--Grand Man: Memories of Norman Douglas. 317p. 1981. Repr. of 1954 ed. lib. bdg. 30.00 (ISBN 0-89760-122-X). Telegraph Bks.

Cunard, Nancy, ed. Negro: An Anthology Collected & Edited by Nancy Cunard. LC 76-76599. (Illus.). 492p. 1970. 50.00 (ISBN 0-8044-1210-3). Ungar.

Cunard, Nancy & Ford, Hugh, eds. Negro: An Anthology. (Illus.). 496p. 1984. pap. 19.95 (ISBN 0-8044-6095-7). Ungar.

Cundall, A. E. Genesis & Exodus. (Bible Study Commentaries Ser.). 126p. 1980. pap. 4.50 (ISBN 0-87508-150-9). Chr Lit.

Cundall, Alan W., jt. auth. see Kelley, Bruce K.

Cundall, Arthur E. & Morris, Leon. Judges & Ruth. LC 68-31426. (Tyndale Old Testament Commentary Ser). (Illus.). 1968. 10.95 (ISBN 0-87784-896-3); pap. 6.95 (ISBN 0-87784-257-4). Inter-Varsity.

Cundall, Frank. Bibliographia Jamaicensis. LC 70-168276. (Bibliography & Reference Ser: No. 433). 1971. Repr. of 1902 ed. lib. bdg. 16.50 (ISBN 0-8337-0739-6). B Franklin.

--Bibliography of the West Indies (Excluding Jamaica) 1971. Repr. of 1909 ed. 17.00 (ISBN 0-384-10364-2). Johnson Repr.

Cundall, Joseph. Brief History of Wood-Engraving from Its Invention. LC 77-94569. 1979. Repr. of 1895 ed. lib. bdg. 25.00 (ISBN 0-89341-234-1). Longwood Pub Group.

--The Life & Genius of Rembrandt. LC 77-94567. 1979. Repr. of 1867 ed. lib. bdg. 30.00 (ISBN 0-89341-235-X). Longwood Pub Group.

--On Bookbindings, Ancient & Modern. LC 77-94568. 1979. Repr. of 1881 ed. lib. bdg. 20.00 (ISBN 0-89341-236-8). Longwood Pub Group.

Cundall, R. B. & Gilbert, A. Photochemistry. (Studies in Modern Chemistry Ser.). 220p. 1970. 19.50x (ISBN 0-306-50009-4, Plenum Pr). Plenum Pub.

Cundall, R. B., jt. ed. see Jennings, K. R.

Cundall, R. B., et al, eds. Time-Resolved Fluorescence Spectroscopy in Biochemistry & Biology. (NATO ASI Series A, Life Sciences: Vol. 69). 800p. 1983. 110.00x (ISBN 0-306-41476-7, Plenum Pr). Plenum Pub.

Cundell, John & King, Jim. Introducing Model Marine Steam. (Illus.). 112p. (Orig.). 1983. pap. 11.95 (ISBN 0-85242-814-6, Pub. by Argus). Aztex.

Cundick, Robert, ed. A First Album for Church Organists. (Illus.). 64p. 1967. pap. 7.95 (ISBN 0-8258-0227-X, 0-4655). Fischer Inc NY.

Cundiff, David E. & Brynteson, Paul. Health Fitness: Guide to a Life Style. (Illus.). 1979. pap. text ed. 14.95 (ISBN 0-8403-2016-7, 40201605). Kendall-Hunt.

Cundiff, Ed, et al. Fundamentals of Modern Marketing. 4th ed. (Illus.). 432p. 1985. text ed. 28.95 (ISBN 0-13-341439-6). P-H.

Cundiff, Edward W. & Hilger, Marye T. International Marketing. (Illus.). 544p. 1984. text ed. 27.95 (ISBN 0-13-473158-1). P-H.

Cundiff, Edward W. & Still, Richard R. Basic Marketing: Concepts, Decisions & Strategies. 2nd ed. LC 79-138478. 1971. ref. ed. o.p. 24.95 (ISBN 0-13-062638-4); study guide 4.95 (ISBN 0-13-062620-1). P-H.

Cundiff, Edward W., jt. auth. see Still, Richard R.

Cundiff, Edward W. & Leonard, Edgar W., eds. Readings in Sales Management. 141p. 1981. 18.00 (ISBN 0-318-12858-6); members 12.00 (ISBN 0-318-12859-4). Am Mktg NJ.

Cundiff, Edward W., et al. Fundamentals of Modern Marketing. 3rd ed. 1980. text ed. 28.95 (ISBN 0-13-341388-8). P-H.

Cundiff, M. Kinesics: The Power of Silent Command. 1972. 4.95 (ISBN 0-13-516245-9, Parker). P-H.

Cundy, et al. Infection Control in Health Care Facilities. (Illus.). 232p. 1977. text ed. 27.00 (ISBN 0-8391-1158-4). Univ Park.

Cundy, Henry M. & Rollett, A. P. Mathematical Models. 2nd ed. (Illus.). 1961. 16.95 (ISBN 0-19-832504-5). Oxford U Pr.

Cundy, Ian. Ephesians-Thessalonians. 1981. pap. 4.50 (ISBN 0-87508-173-8). Chr Lit.

Cundy, Martyn. The Caribbean Mathematics Project: Training the Teacher as the Agent of Reform. (Experiments & Innovations in Education Ser.: No. 32). 72p. 1977. pap. 5.00 (ISBN 92-3-101503-6, U760, UNESCO). Unipub.

Cundy, Percival, tr. see Ukrainka, Lesia.

Cundy, Percival, tr. see Ukrainka, Lesya.

Cuneo, Henry M. & Rand, Carl W. Brain Tumors of Childhood. (Illus.). 236p. 1952. photocopy ed. 25.50x (ISBN 0-398-04235-7). C C Thomas.

Cuneo, Terence. The Railway Painting of Terence Cuneo. (Illus.). 130p. 1984. 27.50 (ISBN 0-904568-43-1, Pub. by New Cavendish, England). Schiffer.

Cuney-Hare, Maud. Negro Musicians & Their Music. LC 74-4108. (Music Reprint Ser.). 1974. Repr. of 1936 ed. 42.50 (ISBN 0-306-70652-0). Da Capo.

Cunff, Madeleine Le. Sur le Vif. LC 77-10091. (Illus., Fr.). 1977. pap. text ed. 7.95 (ISBN 0-88436-454-2, 40254). EMC.

Cunge, J. A. & Holley, F. M. Practical Aspects of Computational River Hydraulics. LC 79-25810. (Water Resources Engineering Ser.). 420p. 1981. text ed. 82.95 (ISBN 0-273-08442-9). Pitman Pub MA.

Cunge, J. A., jt. auth. see Abbott, M. B.

Cunge, J. A., ed. see Benque, J. P., et al.

Cunha. Infectious Disease in the Elderly. 1986. price not set (ISBN 0-88416-475-6). PSG Pub Co.

Cunha, ed. Swine Feeding & Nutrition. (Animal Feeding & Nutrition Ser). 1977. 33.00 (ISBN 0-12-196550-3). Acad Pr.

Cunha, Burke A., jt. ed. see Ristuccia, Angela M.

Cunha, Deborah, ed. Public Welfare Directory, 1980-1981. LC 41-4981. 1980. pap. 35.00x (ISBN 0-910106-11-8). Am Pub Welfare.

Cunha, Dorothy G., jt. auth. see Cunha, George M.

Cunha, George M. & Cunha, Dorothy G. Conservation of Library Materials: A Manual & Bibliography on the Care, Repair, & Restoration of Library Materials, 2 vols. 2nd ed. LC 77-163871. Vol. 1, 1971. 406p. 25.00 (ISBN 0-8108-0427-1); Vol. 2, 1972. 428p. 25.00 (ISBN 0-8108-0525-1); 42.50 set. Scarecrow.

--Library & Archives Conservation: 1980's & Beyond, 2 Vols. LC 82-10806. 1983. Vol. I, 220 p. 16.00 (ISBN 0-8108-1587-7); Vol. II Bibliography, 425 p. 28.50 (ISBN 0-8108-1604-0); 39.50 set. Scarecrow.

Cunha, L. V. da see Yevjevich, Vujica.

Cunha, Luis V., et al. Management & Law for Water Resources. LC 77-7611. 1977. 32.00 (ISBN 0-918334-20-9). WRP.

Cunha, M. Rachel, et al. The Portuguese in Rhode Island: A Histroy. Conley, Patrick T., ed. (Rhode Island Ethnic Heritage Ser.). (Illus.). 33p. (Orig.). 1985. pap. 2.75 (ISBN 0-917012-72-0). RI Pubns Soc.

Cunha, Tony J. Horse Feeding & Nutrition. LC 80-531. (Animal Feeding & Nutrition Ser.). 1980. 33.00 (ISBN 0-12-196560-0). Acad Pr.

Cunha-Vaz, Jose G., ed. The Blood-Retinal Barriers. LC 80-10517. (NATO ASI Series A, Life Sciences: Vol. 32). 405p. 1980. 52.50x (ISBN 0-306-40430-3, Plenum Pr). Plenum Pub.

Cuniberti, John M. The Birth of a Nation: A Formal Shot-by-Shot Analysis Together with Microfiche. (Illus.). 232p. 1979. 285.00 (ISBN 0-89235-016-4). Res Pubns Conn.

Cuningham, Charles E. Timothy Dwight, 1752-1817: A Biography. LC 75-41069. Repr. of 1942 ed. 21.50 (ISBN 0-404-14746-1). AMS Pr.

Cuningham, William. The Cosmographical Glasse, Conteinyng the Principles of Cosmographie, Etc. LC 68-54632. (English Experience Ser.: No. 44). 1968. Repr. of 1559 ed. 49.00 (ISBN 90-221-0044-8). Walter J Johnson.

Cunliffe, B. W. Danebury, An Iron Age Hillfort in Hampshire, 2 vols. (CBA Research Reports Ser.: No. 52). 400p. 1984. Set. pap. text ed. 84.50x (ISBN 0-906780-27-6). Vol. 1 (ISBN 0-906780-28-4). Vol. 2 (ISBN 0-906780-29-2). Humanities.

Cunliffe, B. W. & Fulford, M. G., eds. Corpus Signorum Imperii Romani, Great Britain: Vol. 1, Fascicle 2, Bath & the Rest of Wesswex. (British Academy). (Illus.). 1982. 98.00x (ISBN 0-19-726004-7). Oxford U Pr.

Cunliffe, Barry. Danebury: Anatomy of an Iron Age Hillfort. 192p. 1985. 24.00 (ISBN 0-7134-0998-3, NO. 9351). Methuen Inc.

--Roman Bath Discovered. rev. ed. 256p. 1984. 30.00x (ISBN 0-7102-0196-6). Routledge & Kegan.

Cunliffe, Barry, ed. Coinage & Society in Britain & Gaul: Some Current Problems. (CBA Research Reports Ser.: No. 38). 100p. 1981. pap. text ed. 26.45x (ISBN 0-906780-04-7, Pub. by Coun Brit Archaeology). Humanities.

Cunliffe, BArry W. Roman Bath. LC 72-856399. (Society of Antiquaries of London, Research Committee, Reports: No. 24). pap. 91.00 (ISBN 0-317-28840-7, 2020785). Bks Demand UMI.

Cunliffe, Corinna. Hand of Fortune. 1985. pap. 2.50 (ISBN 0-451-13763-9, Sig). NAL.

Cunliffe, Frederick & Piazza, Peter B. Criminalistics & Scientific Investigation. (Ser. in Criminal Justice). (Illus.). 1980. text ed. 27.95 (ISBN 0-13-193284-5). P-H.

Cunliffe, J. W. English Literature: During the Last Half Century. 1977. Repr. of 1919 ed. lib. bdg. 15.00 (ISBN 0-8495-0713-8). Arden Lib.

--English Literature During the Last Half-Century. 2nd, rev. & enl. ed. 357p. 1981. Repr. of 1923 ed. lib. bdg. 30.00 (ISBN 0-8492-4075-1). R West.

--English Literature in the Twentieth Century. 341p. Repr. of 1934 ed. lib. bdg. 75.00 (ISBN 0-8492-4101-4). R West.

--Influence of Seneca on Elizabethan Tragedy. 69.95 (ISBN 0-87968-079-2). Gordon Pr.

Cunliffe, J. W., jt. auth. see Bacourt, Pierre de.

Cunliffe, John. Riddles & Rhymes & Rigmaroles. 80p. (gr. 1-5). 1982. 10.95 (ISBN 0-233-96306-5). Andre Deutsch.

Cunliffe, John W. Century Readings in European Literature: Medieval & Modern. 543p. 1983. Repr. of 1925 ed. lib. bdg. 50.00 (ISBN 0-89984-124-4). Century Bookbindery.

--English Literature During the Last Half-Century. 2nd rev. & enl. facsimile ed. LC 70-156636. (Essay Index Reprint Ser.). Repr. of 1923 ed. 21.00 (ISBN 0-8369-2276-X). Ayer Co Pubs.

--English Literature in the Twentieth Century. facs. ed. LC 67-23199. (Essay Index Reprint Ser). 1933. 19.00 (ISBN 0-8369-0355-2). Ayer Co Pubs.

--Influence of Seneca on Elizabethan Tragedy. 155p. 1965. Repr. of 1893 ed. 16.50 (ISBN 0-208-00038-0, Archon). Shoe String.

--Leaders of the Victorian Revolution. LC 69-1648. Repr. of 1934 ed. 25.50x (ISBN 0-8046-0521-1, Pub. by Kennikat). Assoc Faculty Pr.

Cunliffe, John W., ed. Early English Classical Tragedies. 1971. Repr. of 1912 ed. 59.00x (ISBN 0-403-00913-8). Scholarly.

--Poems of the Great War. facsimile ed. LC 72-160904. (Granger Index Reprint Ser.). Repr. of 1916 ed. 19.00 (ISBN 0-8369-6267-2). Ayer Co Pubs.

Cunliffe, John W., et al, eds. Century Readings in English Literature. 5th ed. 1955. 64.50x (ISBN 0-89197-068-1). Irvington.

Cunliffe, Keith. Index to the Archives of Macmillan & Company 1854-1924. (Illus.). 120p. 1985. lib. bdg. 70.00 (ISBN 0-317-14569-X). Chadwyck-Healey.

Cunliffe, Lesley, jt. auth. see Brown, Craig.

Cunliffe, Marcus. Chattel Slavery & Wage Slavery: The Anglo-American Context, 1830-1860. LC 78-27195. (Mercer University Lamar Memorial Lectures: No. 22). 150p. 1979. 12.00x (ISBN 0-8203-0471-9). U of Ga Pr.

--George Washington: Man & Monument. rev. ed. 1984. pap. 3.50 (ISBN 0-451-62342-8, ME2342, Ment). NAL.

--The Literature of the United States. 4th, rev. ed. 414p. 1985. pap. 6.95 (ISBN 0-14-022514-5). Penguin.

--Nation Takes Shape: Seventeen Eighty-Nine - Eighteen Thirty-Seven. LC 59-5770. (Chicago History of American Civilization Ser). 1960. pap. 8.00x (ISBN 0-226-12667-6, CHAC3). U of Chicago Pr.

Cunliffe, Marcus & Winks, Robin W., eds. Pastmasters: Some Essays on American Historians. LC 78-27918. 1979. Repr. of 1969 ed. lib. bdg. 32.50x (ISBN 0-313-20938-3, CUPA). Greenwood.

Cunliffe, Marcus, ed. see Weems, Mason L.

Cunliffe, Richard J. A Lexicon of the Homeric Dialect. 456p. 1977. pap. 14.95x (ISBN 0-8061-1430-4). U of Okla Pr.

--A New Shakespearean Dictionary. LC 76-39872. Repr. of 1910 ed. 24.00 (ISBN 0-404-01377-5). AMS Pr.

--New Shakespearean Dictionary. LC 72-194980. 1922. lib. bdg. 38.50 (ISBN 0-8414-2431-4). Folcroft.

--A New Shakespearean Dictionary. 1977. lib. bdg. 69.95 (ISBN 0-8490-2340-8). Gordon Pr.

Cunliffe, W. J. & Cotterill, J. A. The Acnes: Clinical Features, Pathogenesis & Treatment. LC 75-21145. (Major Problems in Dermatology Ser.: Vol. 6). (Illus.). 306p. 1975. 15.00 (ISBN 0-7216-2785-4). Saunders.

Cunliffe, W. J. & Miller, A., eds. Retinoid Therapy: A Review of Clinical & Laboratory Research. 376p. 1983. text ed. 49.00 (ISBN 0-85200-740-X, Pub. by MTP Pr England). Kluwer Academic.

Cunliffe-Jones, H., ed. Book of Jeremiah. 1961. 8.95 (ISBN 0-02-529260-9). Macmillan.

Cunliffe-Jones, Hubert & Drewery, Benjamin, eds. A History of Christian Doctrine. LC 79-21689. 616p. 1980. 29.95 (ISBN 0-8006-0626-4, 1-626). Fortress.

Cunnard, Nancy. Negro Anthology. LC 69-16589. (Illus.). Repr. of 1934 ed. 110.00 (ISBN 0-8371-1952-9, CUN&, Pub. by Negro U Pr). Greenwood.

Cunneen, Christopher. Kings' Men: Australian Governors-General from Hopetoun to Isaacs. (Illus.). 200p. 1984. text ed. 28.50x (ISBN 0-86861-238-3). Allen Unwin.

Cunniff, Lois. The Book of Fees: What You'll Pay the Pros to Do What You Can't, Won't or Dare Not Do Yourself. LC 84-9042. 256p. 1984. 12.95 (ISBN 0-688-03275-3). Morrow.

Cunniff, Patrick, jt. auth. see Anand, Davinder K.

Cunniff, Patrick F., jt. auth. see Anand, Davinder K.

Cunniff, Roger, ed. see Pacific Coast Council on Latin American Studies.

Cunnigham, J. D. History of the Sikhs. 452p. 1981. 125.00x (ISBN 0-686-78865-6, Pub. by Chand & Co India). State Mutual Bk.

Cunningham. Cunningham's Manual of Practical Anatomy: Vol. 1, Upper & Lower Limbs, 3 vols. 14th ed. Romanes, G. J., ed. (Illus.). 1976. pap. text ed. 13.95x (ISBN 0-19-263129-2). Oxford U Pr.

--Cunningham's Manual of Practical Anatomy: Vol. 2 Thorax & Abdomen. 14th ed. Romanes, G. J., ed. (Illus.). 1977. pap. text ed. 13.95x (ISBN 0-19-263135-7). Oxford U Pr.

--Cunningham's Manual of Practical Anatomy: Vol. 3 Head & Neck & Brain. 14th ed. Romanes, G. J., ed. (Illus.). 1979. 13.95x (ISBN 0-19-263205-1). Oxford U Pr.

--Cunningham's Textbook of Anatomy. 12th ed. Romanes, G. J., ed. (Illus.). 1981. text ed. 43.50x (ISBN 0-19-263134-9). Oxford U Pr.

Cunningham, A. J., ed. The Generation of Antibody Diversity: A New Look. 1976. 40.00 (ISBN 0-12-199850-9). Acad Pr.

Cunningham, Agnes. The Bishop in the Church: Patristic Texts on the Role of the Episkopos. (Theology & Life Ser.: Vol. 13). 1985. pap. 4.95 (ISBN 0-89453-469-6). M Glazier.

--The Early Church & the State. LC 81-70666. (Sources of Early Christian Thought Ser.). 128p. 1982. pap. 6.95 (ISBN 0-8006-1413-5, 1-1413). Fortress.

--Prayer: Personal & Liturgical. (Message of the Fathers of the Church Ser.: Vol. 16). 1985. 10.95 (ISBN 0-89453-356-8); pap. 7.95 (ISBN 0-89453-327-4). M Glazier.

Cunningham, Alastair J., jt. ed. see Sercarz, Eli E.

Cunningham, Alexander. The Bhilsa Topes; or Buddhist Monuments of Central India. LC 78-72401. Repr. of 1854 ed. 47.50 (ISBN 0-404-17263-6). AMS Pr.

--Mahabohdi, or the Great Buddhist Temple Under the Bohdl Tree at Buddha-Gaya. LC 78-72402. Repr. of 1892 ed. 28.00 (ISBN 0-404-17264-4). AMS Pr.

Cunningham, Allan. Life & Land of Burns. LC 76-144554. Repr. of 1841 ed. 24.00 (ISBN 0-404-08512-1). AMS Pr.

--The Life of Robert Burns. 1973. Repr. of 1834 ed. 16.50 (ISBN 0-8274-1768-3). R West.

--The Songs of Scotland, Ancient & Modern, 4 vols. LC 75-144551. Repr. of 1825 ed. Set. 135.00 (ISBN 0-404-08640-3); 33.75 ea. Vol. 1 (ISBN 0-404-08641-1). Vol. 2 (ISBN 0-404-08642-X). Vol. 3 (ISBN 0-404-08643-8). Vol. 4 (ISBN 0-404-08644-6). AMS Pr.

Cunningham, Allan & Burns, Robert. Remarks on Scottish Songs & Ballads, Ancient & Modern: With Anecdotes of Their Authors. 384p. 1982. Repr. of 1841 ed. lib. bdg. 100.00 (ISBN 0-8495-0607-7). Arden Lib.

Cunningham, Ann Marie & Fitzpatrick, Mariana, eds. Future Fire: Weapons for the Apocalypse. LC 82-17381. 274p. 1983. pap. 8.95 (ISBN 0-446-37031-2). Warner Bks.

Cunningham, Anne R., ed. see Rowe, John.

Cunningham, B., jt. auth. see Cunningham Grahame, R. B.

Cunningham, Beryl M. & Holtrop, Wm. Woodshop Tool Maintenance. rev. ed. (Illus.). 296p. 1974. pap. text ed. 23.48 (ISBN 0-02-666280-9). Bennett IL.

Cunningham, Bess V. The Prognostic Value of a Primary Group Test: A Study of Intelligence & Relative Achievement in the First Grade. LC 70-176683. (Columbia University. Teachers College. Contributions to Education: No. 139). Repr. of 1923 ed. 22.50 (ISBN 0-404-55139-4). AMS Pr.

Cunningham, Bill. Flames in the Wind. (Illus.). 113p. (gr. 7-12). pap. 9.95 (ISBN 0-913383-01-5). McClanahan Pub.

--On Bended Knees: The Night Rider Story. LC 83-60651. (Illus.). 256p. (gr. 7-12). 1983. 15.95 (ISBN 0-913383-00-7). McClanahan Pub.

Cunningham, Bronnie. Best Book of Riddles, Puns & Jokes. LC 78-1238. 128p. 1979. 7.95 (ISBN 0-385-12982-3). Doubleday.

Cunningham, C. M. & Drury, P. J. Post-Medieval Sites & Their Pottery: Moulsham Street, Chelmsford. (CBA Research Reports: No. 54). (Illus.). 80p. 1985. pap. text ed. 24.75x (ISBN 0-906780-41-1, Pub. by Coun Brit Archaeology). Humanities.

Cunningham, Carl L., jt. auth. see Fox, Richard H.

Cunningham, Caroline, tr. see Asch, Sholem.

Cunningham, Carolyn, compiled by. Montana Weather. (Illus.). 156p. 1982. pap. 6.95 (ISBN 0-938314-03-3). MT Mag.

Cunningham, Cathy. Curse of Valkyrie House. 176p. 1981. pap. 1.95 (ISBN 0-8439-0970-6, Leisure Bks). Dorchester Pub Co.

Cunningham, Charles. Germany Today & Tomorrow. LC 70-180396. Repr. of 1936 ed. 29.50 (ISBN 0-404-56117-9). AMS Pr.

Cunningham, Charles H. Audiencia in the Spanish Colonies As Illustrated by the Audiencia in Manila, 1583-1800. LC 72-131250. 1971. Repr. of 1919 ed. text ed. 15.00x (ISBN 0-87752-130-1). Gordian.

Cunningham, Chet. Aztec Gold. (Jim Steele Ser.: No. 6). (Orig.). 1981. pap. 1.95 (ISBN 0-505-51690-X, Pub. by Tower Bks). Dorchester Pub Co.

--Bloody Gold. 1980. pap. 1.75 (ISBN 0-505-51492-3, Pub. by Tower Bks). Dorchester Pub Co.

--Cheyenne Payoff. 368p. (Orig.). 1981. pap. 2.25 (ISBN 0-440-01269-4). Dell.

--Devil's Gold. (Orig.). 1980. pap. 1.75 (ISBN 0-505-51510-5, Pub. by Tower Bks). Dorchester Pub Co.

--Die of Gold. 1980. pap. 1.50 (ISBN 0-505-51471-0, Pub. by Tower Bks). Dorchester Pub Co.

--The Frisco Lady. (Pinkerton Agent Brad Spear Ser.: No. 4). 320p. (Orig.). 1981. pap. 2.25 (ISBN 0-440-02583-4, Banbury). Dell.

--The Gold & the Glory. 1977. pap. 1.75 (ISBN 0-8439-0450-X, Leisure Bks). Dorchester Pub Co.

--Gold Train. (Jim Steel Ser.: No. 5). (Orig.). 1981. pap. 1.75 (ISBN 0-505-51615-2, Pub. by Tower Bks). Dorchester Pub Co.

--The Gold Wagon. 1980. pap. 1.50 (ISBN 0-505-51460-5, Pub. by Tower Bks). Dorchester Pub Co.

--The Painted Women. (Pinkerton Agent Brad Spear Ser.: No. 5). 320p. (Orig.). 1981. pap. 2.25 (ISBN 0-440-06800-2, Banbury). Dell.

--The Patriots. 720p. (Orig.). 1982. pap. 3.95 (ISBN 0-505-51835-X, Pub. by Tower Bks). Dorchester Pub Co.

--The Power & the Prize. 1977. pap. 1.95 (ISBN 0-8439-0483-6, Leisure Bks). Dorchester Pub Co.

--Rainbow Saga. 1979. pap. 1.95 (ISBN 0-8439-0622-7, Leisure Bks). Dorchester Pub Co.

--Seeds of Rebellion. (Patriots Bicentennial Ser.). 1977. pap. 1.75 (ISBN 0-505-51129-0, Pub. by Tower Bks). Dorchester Pub Co.

--The Silver Mistress. (Pinkerton Agent Brad Spear Ser.: No. 2). 352p. (Orig.). 1981. pap. 2.25 (ISBN 0-440-07940-3, Banbury). Dell.

--This Splendid Land. 1979. pap. 1.95 (ISBN 0-8439-0638-3, Leisure Bks). Dorchester Pub Co.

--Tuscon Temptress. (Agent Brad Spear Ser.: No. 3). (Orig.). 1981. pap. 2.25 (ISBN 0-440-09140-3, Banbury). Dell.

--Two Hundred & Twenty-Two Ways to Save Gas: And Get the Best Possible Mileage. LC 80-26423. (Illus.). 96p. 1981. 10.95 (ISBN 0-13-935221-X); pap. 3.95 (ISBN 0-13-935213-9). P-H.

Cunningham, Cliff. Down's Syndrome: An Introduction for Parents. 187p. 1982. 12.95 (ISBN 0-285-64931-0, Pub. by Souvenir Pr). Brookline Book.

Cunningham, Cliff & Sloper, Patricia. Helping Your Exceptional Baby: A Practical & Honest Approach to Raising a Mentally Handicapped Baby. (Illus.). 1981. 6.95 (ISBN 0-394-73867-5). Pantheon.

--Helping Your Handicapped Baby. 336p. 1979. 24.00x (ISBN 0-285-64866-7, Pub. by Souvenir Pr). State Mutual Bk.

Cunningham, Colin. Building for the Victorians. (Cambridge Introduction to the History of Mankind Ser.). (Illus.). 48p. Date not set. pap. price not set (ISBN 0-521-23314-3). Cambridge U Pr.

Cunningham, Dale S., tr. see Pfluger, A.

Cunningham, Dennis, et al. Control of Cellular Division & Development, 2 pts. LC 81-8434. (Progress in Clinical & Biological Research Ser.: Vol. 66). 1981. Pt. A, 636p. 72.00 (ISBN 0-8451-0156-0); Pt. B, 458p. 66.00 (ISBN 0-8451-0157-9). Set (ISBN 0-8451-0066-1). A R Liss.

Cunningham, Dixon C., et al. Cases on Financial Institutions. LC 77-90644. (Finance Ser.). 510p. 1979. text ed. 33.95 (ISBN 0-471-84156-0, Pub. by Grid). Wiley.

Cunningham, Don R., jt. auth. see Heighton, Elizabeth J.

Cunningham, Donald H., jt. auth. see Pearsall, Thomas E.

Cunningham, Donald H., jt. auth. see Sparrow, W. Keats.

Cunningham, Donald H., ed. A Reading Approach to Professional Police Writing. (Illus.). 152p. 1972. photocopy ed. 14.50x (ISBN 0-398-02503-7). C C Thomas.

Cunningham, Donna. An Astrological Guide to Self-Awareness. LC 78-57820. 1978. pap. 6.95 (ISBN 0-916360-09-1). CRCS Pubns NV.

--Being a Lunar Type in a Solar World. LC 82-50534. 334p. 1982. pap. 9.95 (ISBN 0-87728-522-5). Weiser.

Cunningham, E. V. The Case of the Angry Actress. 192p. 1984. pap. 2.95 (ISBN 0-440-11093-9). Dell.

--The Case of the Kidnapped Angel. (Nightingale Ser.). 1983. pap. 7.95 (ISBN 0-8161-3471-5, Large Print Bks). G K Hall.

--The Case of the Kidnapped Angel. (Masao Masuto Mystery Ser.: No. 5). 192p. 1983. pap. 2.95 (ISBN 0-440-11224-9). Dell.

--The Case of the Kidnapped Angel: A Masao Masuto Mystery. 192p. 1982. 12.95 (ISBN 0-385-28118-8). Delacorte.

--The Case of the Murdered MacKenzie. LC 83-27220. (A Masao Masuto Mystery Ser.). 192p. 1984. 11.95 (ISBN 0-385-29337-2). Delacorte.

--The Case of the Murdered MacKenzie. (Nightingale Large Print Ser.). 1985. pap. 9.95 (ISBN 0-8161-3771-4, Large Print Bks). G K Hall.

--The Case of the Murdered Mackenzie. 1985. pap. 2.95 (ISBN 0-440-11223-0). Dell.

--The Case of the One-Penny Orange. (General Ser.). 1982. lib. bdg. 11.95 (ISBN 0-8161-3334-4, Large Print Bks). G K Hall.

--The Case of the One-Penny Orange. LC 81-80704. (A Masao Masuto Mystery Ser.). 176p. (Orig.). 1982. pap. 3.50 (ISBN 0-03-059858-3, Owl Bks). HR&W.

--The Case of the Poisoned Eclairs. 1980. pap. 2.25 (ISBN 0-440-11256-7). Dell.

--The Case of the Poisoned Eclairs. (Nightingale Ser.). 1982. pap. 9.95 (ISBN 0-8161-3333-6, Large Print Bks). G K Hall.

--The Case of the Russian Diplomat. LC 81-80705. (A Masao Masuto Mystery Ser.). 176p. 1982. pap. 3.50 (ISBN 0-03-059857-5, Owl Bks). HR&W.

--The Case of the Sliding Pool. (Nightingale Ser.). 1982. pap. 9.95 (ISBN 0-8161-3348-4, Large Print Bks). G K Hall.

--The Case of the Sliding Pool. 1983. pap. 2.95 (ISBN 0-440-12092-6). Dell.

--The Wabash Factor. 1986. 14.95 (ISBN 0-318-11917-X). Delacorte.

Cunningham, Earlene B. Biochemistry: Mechanisms of Metabolism. (Illus.). 1977. text ed. 42.95 (ISBN 0-07-014927-5). McGraw.

Cunningham, Edward G., jt. auth. see Bux, William E.

Cunningham, Eileen R. Classification for Medical Literature. rev. ed. 5th ed. LC 67-17562. 1967. 12.95x (ISBN 0-8265-1097-3). Vanderbilt U Pr.

Cunningham, Eileen S. Lower Illinois Valley, Greene County 1821, Containment: Morgan to 1823, Scott to 1823, Macoupin to 1829, Jersey to 1839. 1980. 98.40 (ISBN 0-686-29479-3, AU00128); pap. 88.40 (ISBN 0-686-29480-7). E S Cunningham.

--Lower Illinois Valley Limestone Houses. 1976. pap. 3.00 (ISBN 0-686-31826-9) (ISBN 0-686-29476-9). E S Cunningham.

Cunningham, Eileen S., ed. Old Settlers Association of Greene County, Illinois: Coda of the Deep Snow of 1830. 1976. 17.00 (ISBN 0-686-29477-7, AU00122); pap. 12.00 (ISBN 0-686-29478-5). E S Cunningham.

Cunningham, Eugene. Triggernometry. LC 41-1849. (Illus.). 1941. 12.95 (ISBN 0-87004-032-4). Caxton.

Cunningham, Eugene, ed. see Poe, Sophie A.

Cunningham, Everett W., jt. auth. see Jewell, Malcolm E.

Cunningham, Francis, ed. Images of Women in Mission: Resource Guide & National Directory of Catholic Church Vocations for Women. 192p. 1981. pap. 5.95 (ISBN 0-8091-2350-9). Paulist Pr.

Cunningham, Frank. James David Forbes: Pioneer Scottish Glaciologist. 475p. 1983. 60.00x (ISBN 0-7073-0320-6, Pub. by Scottish Academic Pr Scotland). Columbia U Pr.

Cunningham, Frank E., jt. auth. see Suderman, Darrel R.

Cunningham, G. The Management of Aid Agencies. 220p. 1975. 22.50 (ISBN 0-85664-029-8). Croom Helm.

Cunningham, G. E., jt. auth. see Wade, James E.

Cunningham, G. F., jt. auth. see Burton, S. M.

Cunningham, G. H. The Gasteromycetes of Australia & New Zealand. (Bibliotheca Mycologica 67). 1979. Repr. of 1942 ed. lib. bdg. 28.00 (ISBN 3-7682-1231-9). Lubrecht & Cramer.

Cunningham, G. R., et al, eds. Regulation of Male Fertility. (Clinics in Andrology Ser.: No. 5). (Illus.). 245p. 1981. PLB 68.50 (ISBN 90-247-2373-6, Pub. by Martinus Nijhoff Netherlands). Kluwer Academic.

Cunningham, Gail. The New Woman & the Victorian Novel. LC 78-6179. 1978. text ed. 28.50x (ISBN 0-06-491347-3). B&N Imports.

Cunningham, Gary L., jt. auth. see Hoy, Marjorie A.

Cunningham, Gary M. An Accounting Research Framework for Multinational Enterprises. Dufey, Gunter, ed. LC 78-24444. (Research for Business Decisions Ser.: No. 5). 220p. 1978. 44.95 (ISBN 0-8357-0968-X). UMI Res Pr.

Cunningham, Gary M., et al. Accounting for Shareholders' Equity by Texas Corporations. (Studies in Accounting: No. 8). 1978. pap. 5.00 (ISBN 0-87755-233-9). Bureau Busn UT.

Cunningham, Genevieve. Aftermath. LC 79-55687. 303p. (Orig.). pap. 3.95x (ISBN 0-935774-01-7). Elgen Pub Co.

Cunningham, George K. Measurement & Evalaution in Education. 899p. 1986. text ed. price not set (ISBN 0-02-326330-X). Macmillan.

Cunningham, Gerry & Hansson, Margaret. Light Weight Camping Equipment & How to Make It. rev. ed. (Illus.). 160p. 1976. encore ed 5.95 (ISBN 0-684-14261-9, ScribT); (ScribT). Scribner.

Cunningham, Glenn & Sand, George. Never Quit. 144p. (gr. 6 up). 1981. PLB 7.95 (ISBN 0-310-60210-6, Pub by Chosen Bks). Zondervan.

Cunningham, Gustavus W. Five Lectures on the Problem of the Mind. LC 75-3007. (Philosophy in America Ser.). Repr. of 1925 ed. 17.50 (ISBN 0-404-59123-X). AMS Pr.

--Idealistic Argument in Recent British & American Philosophy. facs. ed. LC 67-23200. (Essay Index Reprint Ser). 1933. 27.50 (ISBN 0-8369-0356-0). Ayer Co Pubs.

--Idealistic Argument in Recent British & American Philosophy. LC 76-98750. Repr. of 1933 ed. lib. bdg. 21.00x (ISBN 0-8371-2833-1, CUBA). Greenwood.

--Thought & Reality in Hegel's System. LC 83-48505. (The Philosophy of Hegel Ser.). 151p. 1984. lib. bdg. 25.00 (ISBN 0-8240-5628-0). Garland Pub.

Cunningham, H. H. Doctors in Gray: The Confederate Medical Service. (Illus.). 13.75 (ISBN 0-8446-0566-2). Peter Smith.

Cunningham, Harry A. Material Facilities Needed in the Training of Intermediate Grade Teachers in Science. LC 73-176684. (Columbia University. Teachers College. Contributions to Education Ser.: No. 812). Repr. of 1940 ed. 22.50 (ISBN 0-404-55812-7). AMS Pr.

Cunningham, Hugh. Leisure in the Industrial Revolution Seventeen Eighty to Eighteen Eighty. LC 80-13354. 1980. 26.00 (ISBN 0-312-47894-1). St Martin.

--The Volunteer Force: A Social & Political History, 1859-1908. (Illus.). 168p. 1975. 16.50 (ISBN 0-208-01569-8, Archon). Shoe String.

Cunningham, I. C., jt. ed. see Pearsall, Derek.

Cunningham, Imogen. After Ninety. LC 77-73306. (Illus.). 112p. 1977. 20.00x (ISBN 0-295-95559-7); pap. 14.95x (ISBN 0-295-95673-9). U of Wash Pr.

--Imogen Cunningham: Photographs. LC 71-117733. (Illus.). 128p. 1970. pap. 14.95 (ISBN 0-295-95452-3). U of Wash Pr.

--Imogen! Imogen Cunningham Photographs 1910-1973. LC 74-2490. (Index of Art in the Pacific Northwest Ser.: No. 7). (Illus.). 112p. 1974. 25.00 (ISBN 0-295-95332-2); pap. 12.50 (ISBN 0-295-95333-0). U of Wash Pr.

Cunningham, Ineke. Modernity & Academic Performance: A Study of Students in a Puerto Rican High School. 4.35 (ISBN 0-8477-2705-X); pap. 3.10 (ISBN 0-8477-2706-8). U of PR Pr.

Cunningham, Isabel S. Frank N. Meyer: Plant Hunter in Asia. (Illus.). 318p. 1984. 29.95 (ISBN 0-8138-1148-1). Iowa St U Pr.

Cunningham, Isabella C., jt. auth. see Cunningham, William H.

Cunningham, Isabella C., et al. Social Class & Consumption: Behavior in San Paulo, Brazil. Moore, Russell M., ed. (Studies in Marketing: No. 23). 1976. pap. 4.00 (ISBN 0-87755-258-4). Bureau Busn UT.

Cunningham, J., jt. auth. see Williams, D. F.

Cunningham, J. O. The History of Champaign County. Schlipf, Frederick A., ed. LC 84-72777. (Champaign County Historical Archives Historical Publications Ser.: No. 7). (Illus.). 538p. 1984. Repr. of 1905 ed. 34.00x (ISBN 0-9609646-2-2). Champaign County.

Cunningham, J. Patrick, ed. Who Owns What in World Banking, 1980-81. 304p. 1980. pap. 142.50 (ISBN 0-902998-37-4). Intl Pubns Serv.

Cunningham, J. S. Where Are They? The After-Life of a Figure of Speech. 1981. 20.00x (ISBN 0-85672-205-7, Pub. by Brit Acad England). State Mutual Bk.

Cunningham, J. S., ed. see Marlowe, Christopher.

Cunningham, J. S., ed. see Pope, Alexander.

Cunningham, J. V. Collected Essays of J. V. Cunningham. LC 75-21800. xii, 463p. 1977. o.p 20.00 (ISBN 0-8040-0670-9, 82-73682, Pub. by Swallow); pap. 10.95 (ISBN 0-8040-0671-7, 82-73690, Pub. by Swallow). Ohio U Pr.

--Collected Poems & Epigrams. LC 71-132578. 142p. 1971. pap. 9.95 (ISBN 0-8040-0517-6, 82-72551, Pub. by Swallow). Ohio U Pr.

--Exclusions of a Rhyme: Poems & Epigrams. LC 60-8072. 120p. (Orig.). 1960. (Pub. by Swallow); pap. 6.95 (ISBN 0-8040-0102-2, 82-74235, Pub. by SWallow). Ohio U Pr.

--Journal of John Cardan. LC 64-16116. 56p. 1964. 2.95x (ISBN 0-8040-0173-1, 82-71108, Pub. by Swallow). Ohio U Pr.

--Let Thy Words Be Few. 24p. (Orig.). 1985. pap. price not set (ISBN 0-936576-11-1). Symposium Pr.

--Woe or Wonder: The Emotional Effect of Shakespearean Tragedy. 134p. 1964. pap. 5.00x (ISBN 0-8040-0323-8, 82-72296, Pub by Swallow). Ohio U Pr.

Cunningham, J. V., ed. The Problem of Style. 300p. Date not set. pap. cancelled (ISBN 0-941324-03-6). Van Vactor & Goodheart.

Cunningham, James. A Vanquished Hope: The Church in Russia on the Eve of the Revolution. 1981. pap. 40.00x (ISBN 0-913836-70-2, Pub. by Mowbray England). State Mutual Bk.

Cunningham, James & Cunningham, Partricia. Reading in Elementary Classrooms: Strategies & Observations. LC 82-7814. 512p. 1982. text ed. 21.95x (ISBN 0-582-28390-6). Longman.

Cunningham, James F. Uganda & Its Peoples. LC 73-88427. (Illus.). Repr. of 1905 ed. 43.00x (ISBN 0-8371-1831-X, CUU&). Greenwood.

--Uganda & Its Peoples: Notes on the Protectorate of Uganda, Especially the Anthropology & Ethnology of Its Indigenous Races. LC 70-99365. 1969. Repr. of 1905 ed. lib. bdg. 20.00 (ISBN 0-8411-0036-5). Metro Bks.

Cunningham, James V. & Kotler, Milton. Building Neighborhood Organizations. LC 83-1182. 224p. 1983. text ed. 15.95x (ISBN 0-268-00668-7, 85-06685); pap. text ed. 7.95x (ISBN 0-268-00669-5, 85-06693). U of Notre Dame Pr.

Cunningham, James W. A Vanquished Hope: The Movement for Church Renewal in Russia, 1905-1906. LC 81-9077. 384p. 1981. pap. text ed. 9.95 (ISBN 0-913836-70-2). St Vladimirs.

Cunningham, Jere. The Abyss. 1982. 13.95 (ISBN 0-671-61020-1, Wyndham Bks). S&S.

--Love Object. 198p. 1985. 12.50 (ISBN 0-910489-03-3). Scream Pr.

Cunningham, Jo. The Autumn Leaf Story. (Illus.). pap. 6.50 (ISBN 0-686-51517-X, 99073); price guide 2.50 (ISBN 0-686-51518-8, 99074). Wallace-Homestead.

Cunningham, John. New Jersey, A Scenic Discovery. Patrick, James B., ed. (A Scenic Discovery Ser.). (Illus.). 120p. 1981. 27.50 (ISBN 0-89909-049-4). Foremost Pubs.

--The Poetics of Byron's Comedy in Don Juan. (Salzburg - Romantic Reassessment Ser.: No. 106). 242p. 1982. pap. text ed. 25.50x (ISBN 0-391-02778-6, Pub. by Salzburg Austria). Humanities.

Cunningham, John, jt. auth. see Hanckel, Frances.

Cunningham, John, ed. Who Owns What in World Banking, 1981-82. 288p. (Orig.). 1981. pap. 105.00x (ISBN 0-902998-46-3). Intl Pubns Serv.

Cunningham, John D. Human Biology. 449p. 1983. text ed. 27.50 scp (ISBN 0-06-041451-0, HarpC); instr's. manual avail.; test bank avail. (ISBN 0-06-361454-5). Har-Row.

Cunningham, John E. Building & Installing Electronic Intrusion Alarms. 3rd ed. LC 82-50021. 160p. 1982. pap. 10.95 (ISBN 0-672-21954-9). Sams.

--Cable Television. 2nd ed. LC 80-52937. 392p. 1980. pap. 13.95 (ISBN 0-672-21755-4). Sams.

--Security Electronics. 3rd ed. LC 82-51040. 264p. 1983. pap. 13.95 (ISBN 0-672-21953-0). Sams.

Cunningham, John E. & Horn, Delton T. Handbook of Remote Control & Automation Techniques. 2nd ed. (Illus.). 350p. 1984. 21.95 (ISBN 0-8306-0777-3); pap. 13.95 (ISBN 0-8306-1777-9, 1777). TAB Bks.

Cunningham, John J. Contemporary Clinical Nutrition: A Conspectus. 400p. 1985. pap. text ed. 19.95 (ISBN 0-89313-068-0). G F Stickley Co.

--Introduction to Nutritional Physiology. (Illus.). 400p. 1983. 22.95x (ISBN 0-89313-031-1); text ed. 22.95x (ISBN 0-686-38084-3). G F Stickley.

Cunningham, John J., ed. Controversies in Clinical Nutrition. LC 80-50827. (Illus.). 240p. 1980. pap. 15.95x (ISBN 0-89313-021-4). G F Stickley Co.

Cunningham, John M. High Noon: A Screen Adaptation, Directed by Fred Zinneman. Garrett, George P., et al, eds. LC 71-135273. (Film Scripts Ser.). 1971. pap. text ed. 12.95x (ISBN 0-89197-788-0). Irvington.

Cunningham, John R., jt. auth. see Johns, Harold E.

Cunningham, John T. This Is New Jersey. 3rd ed. 1978. 20.00 (ISBN 0-8135-0859-2); pap. 12.95 (ISBN 0-8135-0862-2). Rutgers U Pr.

Cunningham, John T., intro. by. Murder Did Pay: Nineteenth Century New Jersey Murders. (New Jersey Historical Classics). (Illus.). 193p. 1981. text ed. 12.95 (ISBN 0-911020-04-7). NJ Hist Soc.

Cunningham, JoLynn & Miller, Sandra W. Child Passenger Safety: A Family Affair. 1979. 2.00 (ISBN 0-686-26995-0, A261-08440). Home Econ Educ.

Cunningham, Joseph F., jt. auth. see Strauz, John X.

Cunningham, Joyce I. & Wilson, W. D. A Concordance to Andre Gide's la Symphonie Pastorale. LC 78-19620. (Reference Library of the Humanities: Vol. 124). 1979. lib. bdg. 48.00 (ISBN 0-8240-9754-8). Garland Pub.

Cunningham, Julia. Burnish Me Bright. 96p. (gr. k-6). 1980. pap. 1.25 (ISBN 0-440-40870-9, YB). Dell.

--Come to the Edge. (Illus.). 88p. (gr. 7 up). 1978. pap. 1.95 (ISBN 0-380-40337-4, 60517-1, Camelot). Avon.

--Dear Rat. (Illus.). 130p. (gr. 2-5). 1976. pap. 1.95 (ISBN 0-380-00908-0, 58644-4, Camelot). Avon.

--Dorp Dead. (Illus.). 92p. (gr. 3-7). 1974. pap. 2.25 (ISBN 0-380-00709-6, 65953-0, Camelot). Avon.

--Far in the Day. (gr. k-6). 1980. pap. 1.50 (ISBN 0-440-43185-9, YB). Dell.

--Far in the Day. (Illus.). (gr. 5-9). 1972. PLB 6.99 (ISBN 0-394-92385-5). Pantheon.

--Flight of the Sparrow. 128p. (YA) 1982. pap. 1.95 (ISBN 0-380-57653-8, 57653-8, Camelot). Avon.

--Flight of the Sparrow. LC 80-12788. 144p. (gr. 5-9). 1980. 6.95 (ISBN 0-394-84501-3); PLB 6.99 (ISBN 0-394-94501-8). Pantheon.

--Macaroon. 1978. pap. 1.50 (ISBN 0-440-45206-6, YB). Dell.

--Maybe, a Mole. 96p. (gr. 3-7). 1975. pap. 0.95 (ISBN 0-440-45562-6, YB). Dell.

--Maybe, a Mole. LC 74-155. (Illus.). 96p. (gr. 2-5). 1974. PLB 6.99 (ISBN 0-394-92929-2). Pantheon.

--A Mouse Called Junction. LC 79-9927. (Illus.). 32p. (gr. k-3). 1980. 7.95 (ISBN 0-394-84112-3); PLB 7.99 (ISBN 0-394-94112-8). Pantheon.

--The Silent Voice. 176p. (gr. 5-9). 1981. 11.95 (ISBN 0-525-39295-5, 01160-350, Unicorn bk). Dutton.

--The Silent Voice. 160p. (gr. 4-7). 1983. pap. 2.50 (ISBN 0-440-48404-9, YB). Dell.

--Tuppenny. 96p. (gr. 4-7). 1981. pap. 1.95 (ISBN 0-380-55582-4, 55582-4, Camelot). Avon.

--Wolf Roland. LC 82-19068. 96p. (gr. 5 up). 1983. 9.95 (ISBN 0-394-85892-1); PLB 9.99 (ISBN 0-394-95892-6). Pantheon.

Cunningham, Julie, ed. see Vander Vlist, Abraham.

Cunningham, Kenneth S. The Measurement of Early Levels of Intelligence. LC 72-176701. (Columbia University. Teachers College. Contributions to Education Ser.: No. 259). Repr. of 1927 ed. 22.50 (ISBN 0-404-55259-5). AMS Pr.

Cunningham, Kevin, ed. see Sargeson, Frank.

Cunningham, Lawrence. Catholic Heritage. 240p. 1985. pap. 9.95 (ISBN 0-8245-0685-5). Crossroad NY.

--Saint Francis of Assisi. LC 81-47419. (Illus.). 128p. 1981. net 5.00 (ISBN 0-06-061651-2, HarpR). Har-Row.

Cunningham, Lawrence & Reich, John. Culture & Values: A Survey of the Western Humanities, 2 vols. 1982. Vol. 1. pap. text ed. 22.95 (ISBN 0-03-054001-1); Vol. 2. pap. text ed. 22.95 (ISBN 0-03-054011-9). HR&W.

Cunningham, Lawrence, ed. Mother of God. LC 82-47741. 132p. 1982. 4.50 (ISBN 0-686-97232-5, HarpR). Har-Row.

Cunningham, Lawrence S. The Catholic Heritage: Martyrs, Ascetics, Pilgrims, Warriors, Mystics, Theologians, Artists, Humanists, Activists, Outsiders & Saints. 256p. 1983. 14.95 (ISBN 0-8245-0592-1). Crossroad NY.

Cunningham, Lawrence S., tr. see Bonaventure, St.

Cunningham, Leon, jt. ed. see Colowick, Sidney.

Cunningham, Les. Hypnosport. (Illus.). 180p. (Orig.). 1981. pap. 6.95 (ISBN 0-930298-09-8). Westwood Pub Co.

Cunningham, Loren & Rogers, Janice. Is That Really You, God? 160p. 1984. pap. 5.95 (ISBN 0-310-60711-6, Pub by Chosen Bks). Zondervan.

Cunningham, Louis & Peters, Herman J. Counseling Theories: A Selective Examination for School Counselors. LC 72-83704. 1973. text ed. 19.95 (ISBN 0-675-09066-0). Merrill.

Cunningham, Louisa. The Spirit of Place: Japanese Paintings of the Sixteenth through Nineteenth Centuries. Neill, Peter, ed. (Illus.). 80p. (Orig.). 1984. pap. 6.95x (ISBN 0-89467-030-1). Yale Art Gallery.

Cunningham, Luverne, et al, eds. Educational Administration: The Developing Decades. LC 76-27956. 1977. 27.25x (ISBN 0-8211-0226-5); text ed. 24.75x 10 or more copies. McCutchan.

Cunningham, M. C. & Kenneth, A. G. Flora of Kintyre. 89p. 50.00x (ISBN 0-7158-1340-4, Pub. by EP Pub England). State Mutual Bk.

Cunningham, Maggi. Little Turtle. LC 77-16764. (Story of an American Indian Ser.). (Illus.). (gr. 5 up). 1978. PLB 7.95 (ISBN 0-87518-158-9). Dillon.

Cunningham, Marion. The Fannie Farmer Baking Book. LC 84-47862. (Illus.). 1984. 16.95 (ISBN 0-394-53332-1). Knopf.

Cunningham, Marion, rev. by. Fannie Farmer Cookbook. LC 79-2097. (Illus.). 1979. 16.95 (ISBN 0-394-40650-8). Knopf.

Cunningham, Marion & Laber, Jeri, eds. The Fannie Farmer Large Print Cookbook. (Reference Ser.). 1985. lib. bdg. 16.95 (ISBN 0-8161-3726-9, Large Print Bks); pap. 10.95 (ISBN 0-8161-3817-6). G K Hall.

Cunningham, Mary. Powerplay. 352p. 1985. pap. 3.95 (ISBN 0-449-12829-6, GM). Fawcett.

Cunningham, Mary & Schumer, Fran. Powerplay: What Really Happened at Bendix. 320p. 1984. 15.95 (ISBN 0-671-47563-0, Linden Pr). S&S.

Cunningham, Mary S. The Woman's Club of EL Paso: Its First Thirty Years. 1978. 10.00 (ISBN 0-87404-061-2). Tex Western.

Cunningham, Maureen A., jt. auth. see Neumann, Peter H.

Cunningham, Merce & Lesschaeve, Jacqueline. The Dancer & the Dance: Merce Cunningham in Conversation with Jacqueline Lesschaeve. Nathan, Henry, ed. (Illus.). 224p. 1985. 27.50 (ISBN 0-7145-2809-9, Dist. by Scribner). M Boyars.

Cunningham, Michael. Golden States. 1984. 12.95 (ISBN 0-517-55279-5). Crown.

--Intelligence: Its Organization & Development. 1972. 37.50 (ISBN 0-12-199150-4). Acad Pr.

Cunningham, Michael, jt. auth. see Denson, Wil.

Cunningham, Nella, ed. see Cotera, Martha P.

Cunningham, Noble E., Jr. The Image of Thomas Jefferson in the Public Eye: Portraits for the People, 1800-1809. LC 80-22757. (Illus.). 1981. 14.95x (ISBN 0-8139-0821-3). U Pr of Va.

--The Jeffersonian Republicans: The Formation of a Party Organization, 1789-1801. (Institute of Early American History & Culture Ser.). xiii, 279p. 1957. 25.00 (ISBN 0-8078-0730-3). U of NC Pr.

--The Process of Government Under Jefferson. LC 77-85535. (Illus.). 1978. 37.50 (ISBN 0-691-04651-4). Princeton U Pr.

Cunningham, Noble E., Jr., ed. Early Republic: 1789-1828. LC 68-65040. (Documentary History of the United States Ser). xii, 274p. 1968. 19.95x (ISBN 0-87249-120-X). U of SC Pr.

Cunningham, Olshfski. Management Turnover in Tennessee Government. 93p. 1985. pap. text ed. 5.00 (ISBN 0-914079-12-3). Bureau Pub Admin U Tenn.

Cunningham, P. & Halliwell, J. O., eds. Revels & Jests: Extracts from the Accounts of the Revels at Court in the Reigns of Queen Elizabeth & King James I. Bd. with Tarlton's Jests & News Out of Purgatory. (Shakespeare Society of London: Vol. 13). pap. 42.80 (ISBN 0-317-16540-2). Kraus Repr.

Cunningham, P. J., jt. auth. see Riley, P. A.

Cunningham, Partricia, jt. auth. see Cunningham, James.

Cunningham, Patricia M., et al. Classroom Reading Instruction, K-5: Alternative Approaches. 210p. 1977. pap. text ed. 12.95 (ISBN 0-669-00324-7). Heath.

Cunningham, Paula, ed. Sample West Kentucky. LC 85-60764. (Illus.). 112p. 1985. pap. 7.95 (ISBN 0-913383-03-1). McClanahan Pub.

Cunningham, Peter. The Cunningham Rags-to-Riches Financial Recovery System. LC 83-70248. 75p. 1983. pap. 29.50 (ISBN 0-911659-02-1). Cunningham Pub Co.

--Extracts from the Accounts of the Revels at Court, in the Reigns of Queen Elizabeth & King James One. LC 74-127902. Repr. of 1842 ed. 21.50 (ISBN 0-404-01885-8). AMS Pr.

--How to Average One Thousand a Week (or more) in Super-Successful Service Business. LC 83-70032. (Illus.). 100p. 1983. pap. text ed. 10.00 (ISBN 0-911659-00-5). Cunningham Pub Co.
--How to Recognize Super-Successful Products & Services Destined for Million Dollar Success. LC 83-70031. (Illus.). 50p. 1983. pap. text ed. 15.00 (ISBN 0-911659-01-3). Cunningham Pub Co.
Cunningham, Philip, ed. see Vander Vlist, Abraham.
Cunningham, Phyllis F. My Godmother: Theodate Pope Riddle & Reminiscences of Creativity. LC 83-12202. 96p. 1983. 10.95 (ISBN 0-914016-97-0). Phoenix Pub.
Cunningham, Randy, et al. Fox Two! America's First Ace in Vietnam. (Illus.). 160p. 1984. pap. 8.95 (ISBN 0-912173-01-7). Champlin Museum.
Cunningham, Raymond J., ed. see Mather, Cotton.
Cunningham, Richard, tr. see Bombal, Maria L.
Cunningham, Richard B. The Christian Faith & Its Contemporary Rivals. LC 81-65821. Date not set. pap. 6.50 (ISBN 0-8054-6705-X). Broadman.
--Creative Stewardship. LC 79-973. (Creative Leadership Ser.). 1979. 6.50 (ISBN 0-687-09844-0). Abingdon.
Cunningham, Richard G. Annotated Bibliography of the Work of the Canon Law Society of America 1965-1980. 121p. (Orig.). 1982. pap. 4.50 (ISBN 0-943616-06-9). Canon Law Soc.
Cunningham, Robert, jt. auth. see Patchin, Robert I.
Cunningham, Robert, tr. see Boros, Ladislaus.
Cunningham, Robert, tr. see Ratzinger, Joseph Cardinal.
Cunningham, Robert, tr. see Schneider, Reinhold.
Cunningham, Robert C. Filled with the Spirit. LC 73-190446. 48p. 1972. pap. 0.75 (ISBN 0-88243-712-7, 02-0712). Gospel Pub.
--Getting Together with Luke & Acts. 47p. 1972. pap. 0.50 (ISBN 0-88243-930-8, 02-0930). Gospel Pub.
Cunningham, Robert E. Stillwater Through the Years. LC 79-89768. (Illus.). 1980. Repr. of 1974 ed. text ed. 14.95x (ISBN 0-934188-05-X). Evans Pubns.
--Stillwater Where Oklahoma Began. LC 79-89767. (Illus.). 1979. Repr. of 1969 ed. text ed. 14.95x (ISBN 0-934188-04-1). Evans Pubns.
Cunningham, Robert H., ed. Amusing Prose Chap-Books. Repr. of 1889 ed. 25.00 (ISBN 0-8274-4156-8). R West.
--Amusing Prose Chap-Books: Chiefly of Last Century. 1978. Repr. lib. bdg. 50.00 (ISBN 0-8495-0758-8). Arden Lib.
Cunningham, Robert J., tr. see Ratzinger, Joseph C.
Cunningham, Robert L., ed. Liberty & the Rule of Law. LC 78-6372. (Texas a & M Univ. Economic Ser.: No. 3). (Illus.). 496p. 1979. 28.50x (ISBN 0-89096-056-9). Tex A&M Univ Pr.
Cunningham, Robert M., Jr. Asking & Giving: A Report on Hospital Philanthropy. LC 85-11054. 148p. (Orig.). 1980. pap. 18.75 (ISBN 0-939450-66-6, AHA-064130). AHPI.
--Governing Hospitals: Trustees in the Competitive Environment. rev. ed. 236p. 1985. pap. 25.00 (ISBN 0-939450-56-9, 196112). Am Hospital.
--Governing Hospitals: Trustees in the Competitive Environment. 236p. 1985. pap. 25.00 (ISBN 0-939450-56-9, 196112). AHPI.
--The Healing Mission & the Business Ethic. LC 81-84917. 305p. 1982. 23.95 (ISBN 0-931028-21-3). Pluribus Pr.
--Wellness at Work. LC 81-15500. 137p. 1982. pap. text ed. 7.95 (ISBN 0-914818-08-2, Inquiry Bk). Blue Cross & Shield.
Cunningham, Robert S. Halos & Pitchforks: Philosophical Ramblings of a Wandering Physician. 1984. 8.95 (ISBN 0-533-05614-4). Vantage.
--Love Poems. (Poetry for Today Ser.: Vol. 2). 50p. 1975. 5.00 (ISBN 0-87881-024-2). Mojave Bks.
--Rationale. (Poetry for Today Ser.: Vol. 1). 80p. 1974. 6.50 (ISBN 0-87881-013-7). Mojave Bks.
--Rippling Rhymes & Fairy Tales. (Poetry for Today Ser.: Vol. 3). x, 52p. 1975. 5.50 (ISBN 0-87881-030-7). Mojave Bks.
Cunningham, Roberto E. & Williams, R. J. Diffusion in Gases & Porous Media. LC 79-12120. 298p. 1980. 45.00x (ISBN 0-306-40537-7, Plenum Pr). Plenum Pub.
Cunningham, Roger A., jt. auth. see Mandelker, Daniel R.
Cunningham, Roger A., et al. The Law of Property, Lawyer's Edition. LC 83-19850. (Hornbook Series Lawyer's Edition). 1070p. 1984. text ed. 37.95 (ISBN 0-314-76525-5). West Pub.
Cunningham, Roger A., et al, eds. The Law of Property: Student Ed. LC 83-21596. (Hornbook Ser.). 916p. 1984. text ed. 23.95 (ISBN 0-314-76524-7). West Pub.
Cunningham, Rupert C., tr. see Roussel, Raymond.
Cunningham, S. Language & the Phenomenological Reductions of E. Husserl. (Phaenomenologica Ser: No. 70). 1976. pap. 18.50 (ISBN 90-247-1823-6, Pub. by Martinus Nijhoff Netherlands). Kluwer Academic.
Cunningham, S. A., ed. Confederate Veteran, 40 vols. (Illus.). 20000p. 1985. Repr. of 1893 ed. 1000.00 (ISBN 0-916107-14-0). Broadfoot.
Cunningham, Sarah C. Beyond the Flames. 320p. (Orig.). 1985. pap. 10.00 (ISBN 0-914339-06-0). P E Randall Pub.
Cunningham, Scott. Bibliography of the Writings of Carl Van Vechten. LC 72-186832. 1924. lib. bdg. 15.00 (ISBN 0-8414-0575-1). Folcroft.
--Cunningham's Encyclopedia of Magical Herbs. Buske, Terry, ed. LC 84-48091. (Practical Magick Ser.). (Illus.). 333p. (Orig.). 1985. pap. 12.95 (ISBN 0-87542-122-9, L-122). Llewellyn Pubns.
--Earth Power: Techniques of Natural Magic. 3rd ed. Weschcke, Carl L., ed. LC 83-81244. (Practical Magick Ser.). (Illus.). 250p. 1985. pap. 6.95 (ISBN 0-87542-121-0, L-121). Llewellyn Pubns.
--Magical Herbalism. 1981. pap. 24.95 (ISBN 0-317-07271-4, Regent House). B of A.
--Magical Herbalism: The Secret Craft of the Wise. 4th ed. LC 83-80172. 1984. 7.95 (ISBN 0-87542-120-2). Llewellyn Pubns.
Cunningham, Simon. The Copper Industry in Zambia: Foreign Mining Companies in a Developing Country. 366p. 1981. 49.95 (ISBN 0-03-059698-X). HR&W.
Cunningham, Susan, jt. auth. see Swenson, Gwen.
Cunningham, Thomas J., Jr., jt. auth. see Ellis, William D.
Cunningham, Valentine. Everywhere Spoken Against: Dissent in the Victorian Novel. 1975. 29.95x (ISBN 0-19-812066-4). Oxford U Pr.
Cunningham, W. J. Agony at Galloway: One Church's Struggle with Social Change. LC 79-56698. 1980. 3.95 (ISBN 0-87805-117-1). U Pr of Miss.
Cunningham, W. Patrick, ed. The Music Locator. 1976. pap. 21.95 (ISBN 0-89390-001-X). Resource Pubns.
Cunningham, Walker. The Keyboard Music of John Bull. Buelow, George, ed. LC 84-59. (Studies in Musicology: No. 71). 274p. 1984. 44.95 (ISBN 0-8357-1466-7). UMI Res Pr.
Cunningham, William. Alien Immigrants to England. 2nd ed. (Illus.). 286p. 1969. Repr. of 1897 ed. 29.50x (ISBN 0-7146-1295-2, F Cass Co). Biblio Dist.
--Alien Immigrants to England. LC 72-94541. (Illus.). Repr. of 1897 ed. lib. bdg. 27.50x (ISBN 0-678-05098-8). Kelley.
--The Growth of English Industry & Commerce, 3 vols. in 2. Incl. Vol. 1. Early & Middle Ages. 5th ed; Vol. 2. Modern Times: the Mercantile System. 4th ed; Vol. 3. Modern Times: Laissez Faire. 4th ed. LC 66-21667. Repr. of 1907 ed. Set. 95.00x (ISBN 0-678-00288-6). Kelley.
--Growth of the English Industry & Commerce, 2 vols. 5th ed. 1968. Repr. of 1910 ed. Set. 95.00x (ISBN 0-7146-1296-0, BHA-01296, F Cass Co). Biblio Dist.
--Historical Theology, 2 vols. 1979. Set. 35.95 (ISBN 0-85151-058-2); Vol. 1. (ISBN 0-85151-286-0); Vol. 2. (ISBN 0-85151-287-9). Banner of Truth.
--Reformers & the Theology of Reformation. 1979. 17.95 (ISBN 0-85151-013-2). Banner of Truth.
--Systematic Planning for Educational Change. LC 81-84692. 323p. 1982. text ed. 20.95 (ISBN 0-87484-551-3). Mayfield Pub.
Cunningham, William B., ed. Canada, the Commonwealth & the Common Market: A Report of the 1962 Summer Institute, Mount Allison University. LC 63-25277. pap. 37.50 (ISBN 0-317-20724-5, 2023825). Bks Demand UMI.
Cunningham, William H. Segmentation in the United States Compact-Car Market. (Studies in Marketing: No. 16). 1972. pap. 4.00 (ISBN 0-87755-162-6). Bureau Busn UT.
Cunningham, William H. & Cunningham, Isabella C. Marketing: A Managerial Approach. 1981. text ed. 22.95 (ISBN 0-538-19100-7, S10). SW Pub.
Cunningham, William H., et al. Introduction to Business. 1984. text ed. 23.95 (ISBN 0-538-07900-2, G90). SW Pub.
Cunninghame Graham, R. B. Mogreb-El-Acksa: A Journey in Morocco. LC 83-63446. xv, 358p. 1985. pap. 10.95 (ISBN 0-910395-10-1). Marlboro Pr.
Cunninghame-Graham, Robert B. Brazilian Mystic. facs. ed. LC 70-146856. (Select Bibliographies Reprint Ser.). 1920. 19.00 (ISBN 0-8369-5623-0). Ayer Co Pubs.
--Jose Antonio Paez. facsimile ed. LC 73-146857. (Select Bibliographies Reprint Ser). Repr. of 1929 ed. 25.50 (ISBN 0-8369-5624-9). Ayer Co Pubs.
--Writ in Sand. facs. ed. LC 69-17571. (Essay Index Reprint Ser). 1932. 17.00 (ISBN 0-8369-0068-5). Ayer Co Pubs.
Cunninghame-Green, R. A. Minimax Algebra. LC 79-1314. (Lecture Notes in Economics & Mathematical Systems: Vol. 166). 1979. pap. 19.00 (ISBN 0-387-09113-0). Springer-Verlag.
Cunningham Graham, R. B. & Carpenter, Edward. With the Northwest Wind. 59.95 (ISBN 0-8490-1312-7). Gordon Pr.
Cunningham Grahame, R. B. & Cunningham, B. Vanished Arcadia. 1973. 59.95 (ISBN 0-8490-1254-6). Gordon Pr.
Cunningsworth, Alan. Evaluating & Selecting EFL Teaching Materials. vi, 106p. (Orig.). 1984. pap. text ed. 12.00x (ISBN 0-435-28006-6). Heinemann Ed.
Cunnington, C. W. The History of Underclothes. 1976. lib. bdg. 75.00 (ISBN 0-8490-2011-5). Gordon Pr.
--Why Women Wear Clothes. 1979. lib. bdg. 75.00 (ISBN 0-8490-2821-3). Gordon Pr.
Cunnington, C. Willet & Cunnington, Phillis. The History of Underclothes. rev. ed. Mansfield, A. D. & Mansfield, Valerie, eds. (Illus.). 208p. 1982. 28.95 (ISBN 0-571-11747-3). Faber & Faber.
Cunnington, C. Willett & Cunnington, Phillis. Handbook of English Costume in the Eighteenth-Century. rev. ed. (Illus.). 1972. 15.00 (ISBN 0-8238-0128-4). Plays.
--Handbook of English Costume in the Nineteenth-Century. 1970. 15.95 (ISBN 0-8238-0080-6). Plays.
--Handbook of English Costume in the Sixteenth-Century. rev. ed. enl. ed. (Illus.). 1970. 15.00 (ISBN 0-8238-0081-4). Plays.
--Handbook of English Costume in the Seventeenth-Century. rev. ed. LC 78-189282. (Handbook of Costume Ser.). 1973. 15.00 (ISBN 0-8238-0135-7). Plays.
Cunnington, Cecil W. Feminine Attitudes in the Nineteenth Century. LC 72-2089. (English Literature Ser., No. 33). 1972. Repr. of 1935 ed. lib. bdg. 49.95x (ISBN 0-8383-1483-X). Haskell.
Cunnington, E. E. Chess for Beginners. 1.00 (ISBN 0-685-02609-4, 00545181). Stein Pub.
Cunnington, P. Children's Costume in England. 1972. text ed. 18.75x (ISBN 0-7136-0371-2). Humanities.
--Costume for Births, Marriages & Deaths. 1978. Repr. of 1972 ed. text ed. 23.25x (ISBN 0-7136-1192-8). Humanities.
Cunnington, Phillis. Costume. (Junior Reference Bks.). (Illus.). (gr. 6up). 1970. 8.95 (ISBN 0-7136-0104-3). Dufour.
Cunnington, Phillis & Lucas, Catherine. Charity Costumes: Of Children, Scholars, Almsfolk, Pensioners. (Illus.). 331p. 1978. 30.00x (ISBN 0-06-491346-5). B&N Imports.
--Costume of Household Servants: From the Middle Ages to 1900. (Illus.). 165p. 1974. 28.50x (ISBN 0-06-491342-2). B&N Imports.
Cunnington, Phillis, jt. auth. see Cunnington, C. Willet.
Cunnington, Phillis, jt. auth. see Cunnington, C. Willett.
Cunnison, J., jt. auth. see Scott, William R.
Cuno, James B., jt. auth. see Wasserman, Jeanne L.
Cuntz, Otto. Die Geographie Des Ptolemaeus: Galliae, Germania, Raetia, Noricum, Pannoniae, Illyricum, Italia. LC 75-7310. (Roman History Ser.). 1975. Repr. 19.00x (ISBN 0-405-07192-2). Ayer Co Pubs.
Cuny, Frederick C. Disasters & Development. (Illus.). 278p. 1983. 29.95x (ISBN 0-19-503292-6); pap. 17.95x (ISBN 0-19-503293-4). Oxford U Pr.
Cuny, Hubert, jt. auth. see Sirjean, Gaston.
Cuny, L. Role De Dupont De Nemours En Matiere Fiscale a l'Assemblee Constituante. LC 74-132533. (Research & Source Works Ser.: No. 823). (Fr). 1971. Repr. of 1909 ed. lib. bdg. 22.50 (ISBN 0-8337-0741-8). B Franklin.
Cunynghame, Arthur. The Opium War: Being Recollections of Service in China. LC 72-79815. (China Library Ser.). 1972. Repr. of 1845 ed. lib. bdg. 27.00 (ISBN 0-8420-1359-8). Scholarly Res Inc.
Cunynghame, Henry H. Time & Clocks: A Description of Ancient & Modern Methods of Measuring Time. LC 77-78127. (Illus.). 208p. 1970. Repr. of 1906 ed. 35.00x (ISBN 0-8103-3576-X). Gale.
Cuomo, George. Geronimo & the Girl Next Door. LC 81-670248. 1973. 1.00 (ISBN 0-933532-16-4). BkMk.
Cuomo, Mario. Forest Hills Diary: The Crisis of Low-Income Housing. LC 83-48042. 1983. pap. 4.95 (ISBN 0-394-72173-X, Vin). Random.
Cuomo, Mario M. Diaries of Mario M. Cuomo: The Campaign for Governor. LC 83-43200. (Illus.). 484p. 1984. 19.95 (ISBN 0-394-53695-9). Random.
Cuong, Nguyen. Simple Vietnamese for Americans. 12.50 (ISBN 0-87559-169-8). Shalom.
Cuoq, Jean A. Etudes Philologiques Sur Quelques Langues Sauvages De l'Amerique. 1866. 17.00 (ISBN 0-384-10370-7). Johnson Repr.
--Etudes Philologiques Sur Quelques Langues Sauvages De L'Amerique (Montreal, 1866) (Canadiana Avant 1867: No. 9). 1966. 15.60x (ISBN 90-2796-328-2). Mouton.
Cupach, William R., jt. auth. see Spitzberg, Brian H.
Cupich, Anne M. Steve Oh Steve! 1985. 6.75 (ISBN 0-8062-2436-3). Carlton.
Cupit, John T. Brief History of Vernon Parish, Louisiana. 1963. 12.50 (ISBN 0-685-08150-8). Claitors.
Cupitt, Don. Taking Leave of God. 192p. 1981. 9.95 (ISBN 0-8245-0045-8). Crossroad NY.
Cuplan. Classified Directory of Artists's Signatures, Symbols, & Monograms. 1982. 225.00. Apollo.
CUPM. Recommendations for a General Mathematical Sciences Program. LC 81-83644. 1981. pap. 3.50 (ISBN 0-88385-437-6). Math Assn.
Cupo, Hortense. The Missing Arrow. 144p. 1984. pap. 10.95 (ISBN 0-8059-2921-5). Dorrance.
Cupo, Joe. Weather: Records, Patterns & Phenomena. Monegain, Bernie, ed. (Maine Geographic Ser.). (Illus.). 48p. 1983. pap. 2.95 (ISBN 0-89933-067-3). DeLorme Pub.
Cupp, Easter E. Marine Plankton Diatoms of the West Coast of North America. 1977. pap. text ed. 33.60x (ISBN 3-87429-125-1). Lubrecht & Cramer.
Cupper, Jack & Cupper, Lindsay. Hawks in Focus: A Study of Australia's Birds of Prey. (Illus.). 208p. 1982. 30.00 (ISBN 0-686-97177-9). Buteo.
Cupper, Lindsay, jt. auth. see Cupper, Jack.
Cuppleditch, David. Phil May: The Artist & His Wit. (Illus.). 127p. 1982. 27.50 (ISBN 0-8390-0292-0). Abner Schram Ltd.
Cupps, P. T., jt. ed. see Cole, H. H.
Cupps, Thomas R. & Fauci, Anthony S. The Vasculitides. (Major Problems in Internal Medicine: No.21). 1981. pap. 34.00 (ISBN 0-7216-2794-3). Saunders.
Cuppy, Will. Decline & Fall of Practically Everybody. LC 83-48892. 256p. 1984. pap. 8.95 (ISBN 0-87923-514-4). Godine.
--How to Attract the Wombat. LC 82-20072. (Illus.). 192p. 1949. pap. 6.95 (ISBN 0-226-12828-8). U of Chicago Pr.
--How to Become Extinct. LC 82-17649. (Illus.). 114p. 1941. pap. 5.95 (ISBN 0-226-12826-1). U of Chicago Pr.
--How to Tell Your Friends from the Apes. (Illus.). 1985. pap. 4.95 (ISBN 0-87140-134-7). Liveright.
Curatorial Staff, Metropolitan Museum of Art. Metropolitan Museum of Art: Notable Acquisitions, 1965-1975. LC 75-31761. (Illus.). 304p. 1975. pap. 4.95 (ISBN 0-87099-141-8). Metro Mus Art.
Curators of the Castle Museum. The Yorke Story. 23p. 1984. 30.00x (ISBN 0-317-07157-2, Pub. by Castle Mus UK). State Mutual Bk.
Curb, Rosemary & Manahan, Nancy, eds. Lesbian Nuns: Breaking Silence. 432p. 1985. 16.95 (ISBN 0-930044-63-0); pap. 9.95 (ISBN 0-930044-62-2). Naiad Pr.
Curby, Vicki M. Women Administrators in Higher Education: Their Geographic Mobility. 1980. 5.00 (ISBN 0-317-01239-8); members 4.00 (ISBN 0-317-01240-1). Natl Assn Women.
Curby, William A., jt. auth. see Gall, Lorraine S.
Curchack, Norma & Parzych, Patricia A. Secretarial Training for the Changing Office. (Illus., Orig.). 1977. pap. text ed. 13.95 (ISBN 0-15-579280-6, HC); instr's manual avail. (ISBN 0-15-579281-4). HarBraceJ.
Curchak, Norma, et al. Legal Typewriting. 2nd ed. (Illus.). 1980. pap. text ed. 13.15 (ISBN 0-07-014940-2). McGraw.
Curcic, Slobodan. Art & Architecture in the Balkans: An Annotated Bibliography. 448p. 1984. lib. bdg. 65.00 (ISBN 0-8161-8326-0, Hall Reference). G K Hall.
--Gracanica: King Milutin's Church & Its Place in Late Byzantine Architecture. LC 79-11984. (Illus.). 1980. 34.95x (ISBN 0-271-00218-2). Pa St U Pr.
Curcio, Louis L. & Galanti, Marie E. Nouveau Visage Du Monde Francais. 2nd ed. 203p. 1981. 17.50 (ISBN 0-395-30978-6). HM.
Curcio, Louise. The Musician's Handbook. 1968. pap. 1.50 (ISBN 0-915282-03-8). J Patelson Mus.
Curcio, Michele. Dictionnaire de l'Astrologie. 292p. (Fr.). 1976. pap. 9.95 (ISBN 0-686-56829-X, M-6607). French & Eur.
Curcio, Robert A. di see Di Curcio, Robert A.
Curds, C. R. Ecological Aspects of Used Water Treatment, 2 vols, Vols. 2 & 3. Hawkes, H. A., ed. 1983. 60.00 ea. (ISBN 0-12-199503-8). Acad Pr.
Curds, C. R. & Hawkes, H. A., eds. Ecological Aspects of Used Water Treatment, Vol. 1. 1976. 66.00 (ISBN 0-12-199501-1). Acad Pr.
Curds, Colin, et al. British & Other Freshwater Ciliated Protozoa: Part 2. LC 81-15541. (Synopses of the British Fauna Ser.: No. 23). 400p. 1983. 72.50 (ISBN 0-521-25033-1). Cambridge U Pr.
Curds, Colin R. British & Other Freshwater Ciliated Protozoa: Part 1. LC 81-15541. (Synopses of the British Fauna Ser.: No. 22). 150p. 1982. 59.50 (ISBN 0-521-24257-6). Cambridge U Pr.
Cure, Karen, et al. An Old-Fashioned Christmas: American Holiday Traditions. (Illus.). 160p. 1984. 22.50 (ISBN 0-8109-1816-1). Abrams.
Curelaru, M., jt. auth. see Eisenstadt, S. N.
Curet, Bernard. Our Pride: Pointe Coupee. Woolfolk, Doug, ed. (Illus.). 112p. 1981. 12.50 (ISBN 0-86518-020-2). Moran Pub Corp.
Curet, Miriam De Anda De see Curet de De Anda, Miriam.
Curet De Anda, Miriam. El Sistema Expresivo De Ricardo Guiraldes. LC 76-8166. (Coleccion Mente y Palabra). 383p. (Orig., Span.). 1976. 6.25 (ISBN 0-8477-0532-3); pap. 5.00 (ISBN 0-8477-0533-1). U of PR Pr.
Curet de De Anda, Miriam. Le Poesia De Jose Gautier Benitez. LC 80-17629. (Coleccion Mente y Palabra Ser.). (Illus.). 232p. 1980. 6.25 (ISBN 0-8477-0570-6); pap. 5.00 (ISBN 0-8477-0571-4). U of PR Pr.
Cureton, E. E. & D'Agostino, R. B. Factor Analysis: An Applied Approach. (Illus.). 480p. 1983. text ed. 39.95x (ISBN 0-89859-048-5). L Erlbaum Assocs.
Cureton, T. K. Physical Fitness Workbook for Adults. 1970. 10.00x (ISBN 0-87563-039-1). Stipes.
Cureton, T. K., et al. Endurance of Young Men, Analysis of Endurance Exercises & Methods of Evaluating Motor Fitness. (SRCD M Ser.). 1945. 24.00 (ISBN 0-527-01534-2). Kraus Repr.
Cureton, Thomas K. Physiological Effects of Exercise Programs on Adults. (Illus.). 228p. 1971. photocopy ed. 23.00x (ISBN 0-398-00377-7). C C Thomas.

--The Physiological Effects of Wheat Germ Oil on Humans in Exercise: Forty-Two Physical Training Programs Utilizing 894 Humans. (Illus.). 552p. 1972. 47.50x (ISBN 0-398-02270-4). C C Thomas.

Cureton, William, ed. Spicilegium Syriacum: Containing Remains of Bardesan, Meliton, Ambrose & Mara Bar Serapion, 1855. 1965. 10.00x (ISBN 0-8401-0493-6). A R Allenson.

Curfman, F. L. Automotive Radiator Construction & Restoration for Antique & Classic. LC 76-6299. Orig. Title: Manual of Automotive Radiator Construction & Repair. (Illus.). 1976. Repr. of 1921 ed. 15.00 (ISBN 0-911160-00-0). Post-Era.

Curhan, Joan P., jt. auth. see Vaupel, James W.

Curhan, Joan P., et al. Tracing the Multinationals: A Sourcebook on U. S. - Based Enterprise. LC 77-9979. 456p. 1977. prof ref 40.00x (ISBN 0-88410-655-1). Ballinger Pub.

Curi, K. Treatment & Disposal of Liquid & Solid Industrial Wastes: Proceedings of the Third Turkish-German Environmental Engineering Symposium, Istanbul, July 1979. LC 80-40993. (Illus.). 515p. 1980. 96.00 (ISBN 0-08-023999-4). Pergamon.

Curi, K., ed. Theory & Practice of Biological Wastewater Treatment. Eckenfelder, W. Wesley. (NATO, Advanced Study Institute Series Applied Science: No. 35). 548p. 1980. 49.50x (ISBN 90-286-0510-X). Sijthoff & Noordhoff.

Curi, Kriton. Appropriate Waste Management for Developing Countries: Proceedings of the First International Symposium on Environmental Technology for Developing Countries held in Istanbul, Turkey, July 7-14, 1982. 690p. 1985. 95.00x (ISBN 0-306-41909-2, Plenum Pr). Plenum Pub.

Curie, Barbara. Buzzy Bee Goes to School. LC 82-62729. (Happy Day Bks.). (Illus.). 24p. (ps-2). 1983. 1.39 (ISBN 0-87239-633-9, 3553). Standard Pub.

--Buzzy Bee Says "Bee Happy". (A Happy Day Bk.). (Illus.). 24p. (gr. k-3). 1979. 1.39 (ISBN 0-87239-355-0, 3625). Standard Pub.

Curie, Eve. Madame Curie: A Biography. Sheean, Vincent, tr. 412p. 1984. Repr. of 1938 ed. lib. bdg. 28.00 (ISBN 0-918377-11-0). Russell Pr.

--Madame Curie: A Biography. Sheean, Vincent, tr. 412p. Date not set. Repr. of 1943 ed. text ed. 25.00 (ISBN 0-8482-3600-9). Norwood Edns.

Curie, Marie. Radioactive Substances. 1983. pap. 4.95 (ISBN 0-8022-2433-4). Philos Lib.

--Radioactive Substances: A Translation from the French of the Classical Thesis Presented to the Faculty of Sciences in Paris. LC 79-139128. (Illus.). 1971. Repr. of 1961 ed. lib. bdg. 18.75x (ISBN 0-8371-5744-7, CURS). Greenwood.

Curiel, D., et al. Trends in the Study of Morbidity & Mortality. (Public Health Paper Ser: No. 27). 196p. (Eng, Fr, Rus, & Span.). 1965. pap. 3.60 (ISBN 92-4-130027-2). World Health.

Curio, Augustine. A Notable History of the Saracens. Newton, Thomas, ed. LC 77-6870. (English Experience Ser.: No. 863). 1977. Repr. of 1575 ed. lib. bdg. 29.00 (ISBN 90-221-0863-5). Walter J Johnson.

Curio, E. The Ethnology of Predation. (Illus.). 1976. 45.00 (ISBN 0-387-07720-0). Springer-Verlag.

Curjel, C. R., jt. auth. see Arkowitz, M.

Curl, Beverly A., jt. auth. see Pace, Denny F.

Curl, Clifford D., jt. auth. see Teffinger, Donald J.

Curl, Clifford D., jt. auth. see Treffinger, Donald J.

Curl, David H. Photocommunication: A Guide to Creative Photography. (Illus.). 1979. pap. text ed. write for info. (ISBN 0-02-326350-4). Macmillan.

--Photocommunication: A Guide to Creative Photography. rev. ed. LC 76-19049. (Illus.). 320p. (Orig.). 1984. pap. 16.95 (ISBN 0-88196-000-4). Oak Woods Media.

Curl, Donald W. Mizner's Florida: American Resort Architecture. LC 83-22205. (American Monograph Newhouse Ser.). (Illus.). 250p. 1984. 30.00x (ISBN 0-262-03104-3). MIT Pr.

--Murat Halstead & the Cincinnati Commercial. LC 80-12046. (Illus.). ix, 186p. 1980. 17.50 (ISBN 0-8130-0669-4). U Presses Fla.

Curl, Donald W., ed. see Pierce, Charles W.

Curl, James S. A Celebration of Death. 1980. 35.00 (ISBN 0-684-16613-5). Scribner.

--The Egyptian Revival. (Illus.). 256p. 1982. 50.00 (ISBN 0-04-724001-6). Allen Unwin.

--The Victorian Celebration of Death: The Architecture & Planning of the 19th-Century Necropolis. LC 70-184048. 222p. 1972. 35.00x (ISBN 0-8103-2000-2). Gale.

Curl, John. A History of Work Cooperation in America. 58p. 1980. 3.75 (ISBN 0-318-15072-7, Published by The Homeward Press). NASCO.

--History of Work Cooperation in America: Cooperatives, Cooperative Movements, Collectivity & Communalism from Early America to the Present. LC 80-84234. (Illus.). 64p. (Orig.). 1980. pap. 3.75 (ISBN 0-938392-00-X). Homeward Pr.

--Tidal News. 108p. (Orig.). 1982. pap. 5.00 (ISBN 0-938392-02-6). Homeward Pr.

Curl, John, et al. History of Collectivity in the San Francisco Bay Area. (Illus.). 64p. (Orig.). 1982. pap. 3.75 (ISBN 0-938392-01-8). Homeward Pr.

Curl, Michael. The Anagram Dictionary. 288p. 1982. 30.00x (ISBN 0-7091-9674-1, Pub. by Robert Hale England). State Mutual Bk.

Curl, Vega. Pasteboard Masks: Fact As Spiritual Symbol in the Novels of Hawthorne & Melville. LC 72-193943. 1931. lib. bdg. 10.00 (ISBN 0-8414-2432-2). Folcroft.

Curland, David. Beauty & the Beast. (A Language-Film Study Guide Ser.). 52p. (Orig.). (gr. 9-12). 1984. pap. text ed. 4.95x (ISBN 0-913349-02-X). Public Media Inc.

Curland, David, ed. The Green Wall. (A Language Film Study Guide). 42p. 1983. pap. text ed. 4.95 (ISBN 0-913349-01-1). Public Media Inc.

Curle, Adam. Educational Planning: The Adviser's Role. (Fundamentals of Educational Planning: No. 8). 28p. (2nd Printing 1971). 1968. pap. 5.00 (ISBN 92-803-1023-2, U207, UNESCO). Unipub.

--Planning for Education in Pakistan: A Personal Case Study. LC 66-14440. (Illus.). 1966. 15.00x (ISBN 0-674-67100-7). Harvard U Pr.

--The Professional Identity of the Educational Planner. (Fundamentals of Educational Planning: No. 11). 49p. (Orig.). 1969. pap. 5.25 (ISBN 92-803-1030-5, U494, UNESCO). Unipub.

--True Justice: Quaker Peace Makers & Peace Making. 106p. 1981. pap. 25.00x (ISBN 0-85245-156-3, Pub. by Quaker Hme Serv England). State Mutual Bk.

Curle, Adam, jt. auth. see O'Connell, James.

Curle, R. H. Aspects of George Meredith. LC 71-176496. (English Biography Ser., No. 31). 1972. Repr. of 1908 ed. lib. bdg. 52.95x (ISBN 0-8383-1363-9). Haskell.

Curle, Richard. Caravansary & Conversation. facs. ed. LC 73-134070. (Essay Index Reprint Ser). 1937. 19.00 (ISBN 0-8369-2151-8). Ayer Co Pubs.

--Into the East. Repr. of 1923 ed. 30.00 (ISBN 0-8482-3571-1). Norwood Edns.

--Into the East: Notes on Burma & Malaya. Repr. of 1923 ed. 20.00 (ISBN 0-686-19872-7). Ridgeway Bks.

--Joseph Conrad Korzeniowski: Essays & Studies. LC 74-3181. 1958. 20.00 (ISBN 0-8414-3616-9). Folcroft.

--Joseph Conrad: The History of His Books. LC 74-3181. lib. bdg. 10.00. Folcroft.

--Letters of Joseph Conrad to Richard Curle. LC 73-14720. 1928. lib. bdg. 20.00 (ISBN 0-8414-3470-0). Folcroft.

--Life Is a Dream. facsimile ed. LC 78-106284. (Short Story Index Reprint Ser.). 1914. 19.00 (ISBN 0-8369-3321-4). Ayer Co Pubs.

--Robert Browning & Julia Wedgwood: A Broken Friendship As Revealed in Their Letters. 1973. Repr. of 1937 ed. 25.00 (ISBN 0-8274-1770-5). R West.

Curle, Richard, ed. Notes by Joseph Conrad Written in a Set of His First Editions in the Possession of Richard Curle. LC 74-7461. 1925. lib. bdg. 10.00 (ISBN 0-8414-3648-7). Folcroft.

Curle, Richard H. Aspects of George Meredith. LC 72-91349. 1970. Repr. of 1908 ed. 10.00x (ISBN 0-87753-012-2). Phaeton.

Curlee, Ernie J. The Complete Book of Competition Treasure Hunting: How to Win, How to Sponsor. Nelson, Bettye, ed. LC 79-65312. (Guidebook Ser.). (Illus.). 88p. (Orig.). 1979. pap. 5.95 (ISBN 0-915920-34-4). Ram Pub.

Curlee, Richard F. & Perkins, William H., eds. Nature & Treatment of Stuttering: New Directions. LC 83-26337. (Illus.). 506p. 1984. 29.50 (ISBN 0-933014-71-6). College-Hill.

Curlee-Salisbury, Joan. When the Woman You Love Is an Alcoholic. LC 78-73017. (When Bk). (Illus.). 1978. pap. 2.45 (ISBN 0-87029-143-2, 20229-1). Abbey.

--When the Woman You Love is an Alcoholic. 96p. 1979. 1.95 (ISBN 0-318-15359-9). Natl Coun Alcoholism.

Curless, Todd. Turbochargers: Theory, Installation, Maintenance & Repair. LC 84-16425. (Illus.). 176p. (Orig.). 1984. pap. 11.95 (ISBN 0-8306-0211-9, 2111). TAB Bks.

Curley & Rose. The Nursing Process: A Self Learning Module. 138p. 1983. 8.95 (ISBN 0-683-09538-2). Williams & Wilkins.

Curley, Arthur & Broderick, Dorothy. Building Library Collections. 6th ed. LC 84-23665. 350p. 1985. 18.75 (ISBN 0-8108-1776-4). Scarecrow.

Curley, Arthur & Varlejs, Jana. Akers' Simple Library Cataloging. 7th, completely rev. ed. LC 76-26897. 1984. 16.50 (ISBN 0-8108-0978-8). Scarecrow.

Curley, Daniel. Ann's Spring. LC 76-30652. (Illus.). (gr. 3-7). 1977. Crowell Jr Bks.

--Billy Beg & the Bull. LC 77-11551. (Illus.). (gr. 4-6). 1978. 6.95i (ISBN 0-690-03808-9). Crowell Jr Bks.

--In the Hands of Our Enemies Stories. LC 78-135473. 1970. 5.95 (ISBN 0-252-00141-9). U of Ill Pr.

--Living with Snakes. LC 84-22773. 144p. 1985. 13.95 (ISBN 0-8203-0767-X). U of Ga Pr.

--Love in the Winter. LC 76-7541. (Illinois Short Fiction Ser). 118p. 1976. 11.95x (ISBN 0-252-00551-1); pap. 5.95 (ISBN 0-252-00578-3). U of Ill Pr.

Curley, Daniel, et al, eds. Accent: An Anthology, 1940-60. LC 73-76274. 519p. 1973. 22.50x (ISBN 0-252-00349-7). U of Ill Pr.

Curley, Dorothy. Community Service: Innovations in Outreach at the Brooklyn Public Library. LC 77-137361. (Public Library Reporter Ser.: No. 16). pap. 20.00 (ISBN 0-317-26588-1, 2024193). Bks Demand UMI.

Curley, Dorothy N., et al, eds. Modern American Literature, 3 Vols. 4th enl. ed. LC 76-76599. (Library of Literary Criticism Ser.). (gr. 9-12). 1969. text ed. 165.00 (ISBN 0-8044-3046-2). Ungar.

Curley, E. M. Descartes Against the Skeptics. LC 77-14366. 1978. 17.50x (ISBN 0-674-19826-3). Harvard U Pr.

Curley, Ed. Church Feasts & Celebrations. (gr. 1-3). 1983. 9.95 (ISBN 0-89837-085-X, Pub. by Pflaum Pr). Peter Li.

--The Mass for Young Catholics. (gr. 1-3). 1978. 9.95 (ISBN 0-686-89575-4, Pub. by Pflaum Pr). Peter Li.

--Morals, Value, & Motivation: Ethics for Today. (gr. 9-12). 1978. 9.95 (ISBN 0-89837-039-6, Pub. by Pflaum Pr). Peter Li.

--Saints for Young Christians. (gr. 4-6). 1983. 9.95 (ISBN 0-89837-088-4, Pub. by Pflaum Pr). Peter Li.

--The Spiritual & Corporal Works of Mercy. (gr. 4-6). 1982. 9.95 (ISBN 0-89837-025-6, Pub. by Pflaum Pr). Peter Li.

Curley, Edwin, ed. see Spinoza, Baruch.

Curley, James M. I'd Do It Again: A Record of All My Uproarious Years. LC 76-6333. (Irish Americans Ser). (Illus.). 1976. Repr. of 1957 ed. 32.00 (ISBN 0-405-09329-2). Ayer Co Pubs.

Curley, Jayme, et al. The Balancing Act II: A Career & a Family. rev. ed. LC 81-38524. 300p. 1981. pap. 8.95 (ISBN 0-914091-08-5). Chicago Review.

Curley, Kathleen F. Word Processing: First Step to the Office of the Future. 174p. 1983. 31.95 (ISBN 0-03-062909-8). Praeger.

Curley, Lois, jt. ed. see Hestenes, Roberta.

Curley, Marie T. The Buckram Syndrome: A Critical Essay on Paperbacks in Public Libraries of the United States. LC 68-31033. (Public Library Reporter Ser.: NO. 13). pap. 20.00 (ISBN 0-317-26291-2, 2024258). Bks Demand UMI.

Curley, Martha A. Pediatric Cardiac Dysrhythmias. (Illus.). 224p. 1985. pap. text ed. 17.95 (ISBN 0-89303-758-3). Brady Comm.

Curley, Maureen. First Prayers for Young Catholics. (Children of the Kingdom Activities Ser.). (gr. 1-4). 1978. 9.95 (ISBN 0-89837-008-6, Pub. by Pflaum Pr). Peter Li.

--God's Early Helpers. (gr. 4-7). 1974. 9.95 (ISBN 0-89837-018-3, Pub. by Pflaum Pr). Peter Li.

--The Sacraments. (Children of the Kingdom Activities Ser.). (gr. 4-7). 1975. 9.95 (ISBN 0-89837-019-1, Pub. by Pflaum Pr). Peter Li.

--The Ten Commandments. (Children of the Kingdom Activities Ser.). (gr. 4-7). 1976. 9.95 (ISBN 0-89837-015-9, Pub. by Pflaum Pr). Peter Li.

Curley, Michael J. Church & State in the Spanish Floridas (1783-1822) LC 73-3584. (Catholic University of America. Studies in American Church History: No. 30). Repr. of 1940 ed. 36.00 (ISBN 0-404-57780-6). AMS Pr.

Curley, Michael J., tr. from Lat. Physiologus. (Illus.). 136p. 1979. text ed. 12.95 (ISBN 0-292-76456-1). U of Tex Pr.

Curley, Richard T. Elders, Shades, & Women: Ceremonial Change in Lango, Uganda. LC 70-634788. 1973. 29.50x (ISBN 0-520-02149-5). U of Cal Pr.

Curley, Rosemarie C. The Nursing Process: A Self-Directed Manual. 272p. (Orig.). 1983. pap. 8.95 (ISBN 0-935236-28-7). Nurseco.

Curley, Thomas M. Samuel Johnson & the Age of Travel. LC 74-30677. 304p. 1976. 25.00x (ISBN 0-8203-0380-1). U of Ga Pr.

Curley, Thomas M., ed. A Course of Lectures on the English Law Delivered at the University of Oxford 1767-1773 by Sir Robert Chambers, Second Vinerian Professor of English Law, 2 vols, Vol. II. LC 84-40493. 700p. 1985. Set. text ed. 60.00x (ISBN 0-299-10012-X). U of Wis Pr.

Curlin, Vashti, jt. auth. see Allen, Hattie L.

Curling, B. C. The History of the Institute of Marine Engineers. 242p. 1961. 3.00x (ISBN 0-900976-92-6, Pub. by Inst Marine Eng). Intl Spec Bk.

Curling, J. M. Methods of Plasma Protein Fractionation. 1980. 59.50 (ISBN 0-12-199550-X). Acad Pr.

Curling, Jonathan. Edward Wortley Montagu Seventeen Thirteen to Seventeen Seventy-Six: The Man in the Iron Wig. 1954. Repr. 25.00 (ISBN 0-8274-2227-X). R West.

Curme, G. O. A Grammar of the German Language. 1980. Repr. of 1905 ed. lib. bdg. 50.00 (ISBN 0-89760-112-2). Telegraph Bks.

Curme, George O. English Grammar. (Orig.). 1947. pap. 4.76i (ISBN 0-06-460061-0, CO 61, COS). B&N NY.

--A Grammar of the English Language. 1983. 40.00 set (ISBN 0-930454-03-0). Verbatim Bks.

--A Grammar of the English Language: Parts of Speech, Vol. 1. LC 77-87423. 400p. 1983. 20.00 (ISBN 0-930454-02-2). Verbatim Bks.

--A Grammar of the English Language: Syntax, Vol. 2. LC 77-87422. 640p. 1983. 20.00 (ISBN 0-930454-01-4). Verbatim Bks.

--A Grammar of the German Language, 2 vols. Set. 250.00 (ISBN 0-87968-213-2). Gordon Pr.

--Grammar of the German Language. 2nd ed. 1952. 30.00 (ISBN 0-8044-0113-6). Ungar.

C.U.R.N. Project, Michigan Nurses Association. Clean Intermittent Catherization. Reynolds, Margaret A., ed. (Using Research to Improve Nursing Practice Ser.). 112p. 1982. 15.00 (ISBN 0-8089-1463-4, 792071). Grune.

--Intravenous Cannula Change. Haller, Karen B., ed. (Using Research to Improve Nursing Practice Ser.: Vol. IX). (Illus.). 112p. 1981. pap. 16.00 (ISBN 0-8089-1389-1, 792064). Grune.

--Pain: Deliberative Nursing Interventions. (Using Research to Improve Nursing Practice Ser.: Vol. V). 160p. 1981. pap. 16.00 (ISBN 0-8089-1401-4, 792069). Grune.

--Structured Preoperative Teaching. (Using Research to Improve Clinical Practice Ser.: Vol. I). (Illus.). 165p. 1980. pap. 13.50 (ISBN 0-8089-1311-5, 792065). Grune.

Curnock, Kathleen & Hardiker, Pauline. Towards Practice Theory: Skills & Methods in Social Assessments. (Library of Social Work). (Illus.). 1979. pap. 12.95x (ISBN 0-7100-0339-0). Routledge & Kegan.

Curnonsky. Cuisine et vins de France. new ed. (Illus., Fr.). 53.75x (ISBN 0-685-13844-5, 3975). Larousse.

Curnou, Susan, jt. auth. see Curnow, Ray.

Curnow, R. C., jt. auth. see Barron, Iann.

Curnow, R. N., jt. auth. see Mead, R.

Curnow, Ray & Curnou, Susan. Games, Graphics & Sound. (Clear & Simple Home Computer Ser.: Vol III). (Illus.). 128p. 1984. 9.95 (ISBN 0-671-49444-9, Fireside). S&S.

Curnow, Ray & Curran, Susan. First Steps in BASIC. (The Clear & Simple Home Computer Ser.: Vol. II). (Illus.). 192p. 1983. pap. 9.95 (ISBN 0-671-49443-0, Fireside). S&S.

--Learning with Your Home Computer. (Clear & Simple Home Computer Ser.: Vol. IV). (Illus.). 128p. 1984. 9.95 (ISBN 0-671-49445-7, Fireside). S&S.

Curnow, Ray, jt. auth. see Barron, Iann.

Curnow, Ray, jt. auth. see Curran, Susan.

Curnow, Wystan, jt. auth. see Allen, Jim.

Curnow, Wystan, ed. Essays on New Zealand Literature. 192p. (Orig.). 1983. pap. text ed. 9.95 (ISBN 0-435-18195-5, Pub. by Heinemann Pub New Zealand). Intl Spec Bk.

Curns, Eileen. Negatives to Positives. (Illus.). 39p. 1982. 8.00 (ISBN 0-317-27359-0). Accord Il.

Curns, Eileen, et al. Pathways to People. 2nd Rev. ed. 73p. 1978. 15.00 (ISBN 0-942968-00-X). Accord Il.

Curns, Elleen B. Stress. 3rd ed. 34p. 1981. write for info. ACCORD IL.

Curoe, Philip R. Educational Attitudes & Policies of Organized Labor in the United States. LC 76-176702. (Columbia University. Teachers College. Contributions to Education: No. 201). Repr. of 1926 ed. 22.50 (ISBN 0-404-55201-3). AMS Pr.

--Educational Attitudes & Policies of Organized Labor in the United States. LC 76-89169. (American Education: Its Men, Institutions & Ideas, Ser. 1). 1969. Repr. of 1926 ed. 16.00 (ISBN 0-405-01407-4). Ayer Co Pubs.

Curr, John. Coal Viewer & Engine Builder's Practical Companion. 2nd ed. 96p. 1970. Repr. of 1797 ed. 28.50x (ISBN 0-7146-2429-2, F Cass Co). Biblio Dist.

--Coal Viewer & Engine Builder's Practical Companion. LC 74-96376. (Illus.). Repr. of 1797 ed. lib. bdg. 22.50x (ISBN 0-678-05104-6). Kelley.

Curr, Rosemary, jt. auth. see Cutts, Paddy.

Currall, H. F. J., ed. Phonograph Record Libraries. 2nd ed. xiv, 303p. 1970. 22.50 (ISBN 0-208-00381-9, Archon). Shoe String.

Curran, et al. Tax Planning Forms for Business & Individuals. 1985. 64.00 (ISBN 0-88712-284-1). Warren.

Curran, Barbara A. The Legal Needs of the Public: The Final Report of a National Survey. Sikes, Bette, ed. 418p. 1977. 25.00 (ISBN 0-910058-82-2, 765-0017). Am Bar Foun.

--Trends in Consumer Credit Legislation. LC 65-17284. (Illus.). pap. 101.50 (ISBN 0-317-09650-8, 2020192). Bks Demand UMI.

Curran, Barbara A. & Rosich, Katherine J. Data Manual for the Survey of the Legal Needs of the Public. Sikes, Bette, ed. 398p. 1980. 100.00 (ISBN 0-910058-83-0). Am Bar Foun.

Curran, C. P. Dublin Decorative Plasterwork of the Seventeenth & Eighteenth Centuries. 298p. 1967. 50.00x (ISBN 0-85458-000-X, Pub. by Academy Editions England). State Mutual Bk.

Curran, Charles. Moral Theology: A Continuing Journey. LC 81-23160. 238p. 1982. text ed. 17.95 (ISBN 0-268-01350-0); pap. text ed. 7.95 (ISBN 0-268-01351-9). U of Notre Dame Pr.

Curran, Charles C., ed. see American Library Association, Library Research Round Table.

Curran, Charles E. American Catholic Social Ethics: Twentieth Century Approaches. LC 82-4829. 336p. 1982. 24.95 (ISBN 0-268-00603-2). U of Notre Dame Pr.

--American Catholic Social Ethics: Twentieth-Century Approaches. LC 82-4829. 353p. 1984. text ed. 9.95 (ISBN 0-268-00609-1, 85-06099). U of Notre Dame Pr.

--Catholic Moral Theology in Dialogue. LC 76-14906. 1976. text ed. 18.95x (ISBN 0-268-00716-0); pap. 5.95 (ISBN 0-268-00717-9). U of Notre Dame Pr.

--Critical Concerns in Moral Theology. LC 83-40593. 288p. 1984. text ed. 16.95 (ISBN 0-268-00747-0, 85-07477). U of Notre Dame Pr.

--Directions in Catholic Social Ethics. LC 84-28079. 304p. (Orig.). 1985. pap. text ed. 8.95 (ISBN 0-268-00853-1, 85-08533). U of Notre Dame Pr.

--Directions in Fundamental Moral Theology. LC 85-2543. 304p. 1985. pap. text ed. 8.95x (ISBN 0-268-00854-X, 85-08541, Dist. by Har-Row). U of Notre Dame Pr.

--Issues in Sexual & Medical Ethics. LC 77-89767. 1979. pap. 6.95 (ISBN 0-268-01142-7). U of Notre Dame Pr.

--Issues in Sexual & Medical Ethics. LC 77-89767. 1978. text ed. 18.95x (ISBN 0-268-01141-9). U of Notre Dame Pr.

--New Perspectives in Moral Theology. LC 76-13206. 293p. 1976. text ed. 18.95 (ISBN 0-268-01449-3); pap. 6.95 (ISBN 0-268-01450-7). U of Notre Dame Pr.

--Transition & Tradition in Moral Theology. LC 78-20877. 272p. 1980. pap. text ed. 6.95 (ISBN 0-268-01838-3). U of Notre Dame Pr.

--Transition & Tradition in Moral Theology. LC 78-20877. 1979. text ed. 18.95x (ISBN 0-268-01837-5, Dist. by Har Row). U of Notre Dame Pr.

Curran, Charles E. & McCormick, Richard. Readings in Moral Theology: No. 1, Moral Norms & Catholic Tradition. LC 79-84237. 1979. pap. 7.95 (ISBN 0-8091-2203-0). Paulist Pr.

Curran, Charles E. & McCormick, Richard A. Readings in Moral Theology: The Use of Scripture in Moral Theology. 1984. pap. 9.95 (ISBN 0-8091-2563-3). Paulist Pr.

Curran, Charles E., ed. Absolutes in Moral Theology? LC 75-3988. 320p. 1976. Repr. of 1968 ed. lib. bdg. 25.00x (ISBN 0-8371-7450-3, CUMT). Greenwood.

Curran, Charles E. & McCormick, Richard A., eds. Readings in Moral Theology, No. 2: The Distinctiveness of Christian Ethics. LC 79-84237. 360p. 1980. pap. 5.95 (ISBN 0-8091-2303-7). Paulist Pr.

--Readings in Moral Theology: The Magisterium & Morality, No. 3. LC 81-82436. (Orig.). 1981. pap. 7.95 (ISBN 0-8091-2407-6). Paulist Pr.

Curran, David F. The Ginseng Disease & Pest Reference Guide. Curran, Patricia A., ed. (Illus.). 152p. (Orig.). 1985. spiral 60.00 (ISBN 0-318-04401-3). D F Curran Prods.

--A Pilgrimage: Visiting Richard Brautigan, August, 1982. Curran, Patricia A., ed. (Illus.). 50p. (Orig.). 1985. pap. 6.00 (ISBN 0-318-04402-1). D F Curran Prods.

Curran, David F. & Curran, Patricia A. The Complete Ginseng Grower's Manual. LC 83-70439. (Illus.). 148p. (Orig.). 1983. pap. 50.00. D F Curran Prods.

Curran, Dolores. Family: A Church Challenge for the 80's. (Orig.). 1980. pap. 3.50 (ISBN 0-86683-640-3). Winston Pr.

--Family Prayer. rev. ed. 136p. (Orig.). 1983. pap. text ed. 5.95 (ISBN 0-86716-014-4). St Anthony Mess Pr.

--In the Beginning There Were the Parents: Discussion Guide. 1980. pap. 2.95 (ISBN 0-03-056978-8). Winston Pr.

--In the Beginning There Were the Parents. 1978. pap. 4.95 (ISBN 0-03-042766-5). Winston Pr.

--Traits of a Healthy Family. 336p. 1984. pap. 3.50 (ISBN 0-345-31750-5). Ballantine.

--Traits of a Healthy Family: Fifteen Traits Commonly Found in Healthy Families by Those Who Work With Them. LC 82-70489. 300p. 1983. 14.95 (ISBN 0-86683-643-8). Winston Pr.

--Traits of a Healthy Family: Fifteen Traits Commonly Found in Healthy Families by Those Who Work with Them. 1984. pap. 7.95 (ISBN 0-86683-815-5, 8444). Winston Pr.

--Who, Me Teach My Child Religion? rev. ed. 156p. 1981. pap. 6.95. Winston Pr.

Curran, Donald J. Metropolitan Financing: The Milwaukee Experience, 1920-1970. LC 72-7984. 182p. 1973. 27.50x (ISBN 0-299-06290-2). U of Wis Pr.

Curran, Donald J., ed. see Groves, Harold M.

Curran, Douglas. In Advance of the Landing. (Illus.). 144p. 1985. pap. 16.95 (ISBN 0-89659-523-4). Abbeville Pr.

Curran, Eileen. Bird's Nests. LC 84-8658. (Illus.). 32p. (gr. k-2). 1985. PLB 9.89 (ISBN 0-8167-0341-8); pap. text ed. 2.50 (ISBN 0-8167-0342-6). Troll Assocs.

--Easter Parade. LC 84-8630. (Giant First Start Reader Ser.). (Illus.). 32p. (gr. k-2). 1985. PLB 9.89 (ISBN 0-8167-0353-1); pap. text ed. 2.50 (ISBN 0-8167-0433-3). Troll Assocs.

--Hello, Farm Animals. LC 84-8657. (Illus.). 32p. (gr. k-2). 1985. PLB 9.89 (ISBN 0-8167-0345-0); pap. text ed. 2.50 (ISBN 0-8167-0346-9). Troll Assocs.

--Home for a Dinosaur. LC 84-8627. (Giant First-Start Readers Ser.). (Illus.). 32p. (gr. k-2). 1985. lib. bdg. 9.89 (ISBN 0-8167-0351-5); pap. text ed. 2.50 (ISBN 0-8167-0431-7). Troll Assocs.

--Life in the Forest. LC 84-16455. (Illus.). 32p. (gr. k-2). 1985. PLB 9.89 (ISBN 0-8167-0446-5); pap. text ed. 2.50 (ISBN 0-8167-0447-3). Troll Assocs.

--Life in the Meadow. LC 84-12384. (Illus.). 32p. (gr. k-2). 1985. PLB 9.89 (ISBN 0-8167-0343-4); pap. text ed. 2.50 (ISBN 0-8167-0344-2). Troll Assocs.

--Life in the Pond. LC 84-16285. (Illus.). 32p. (gr. k-2). 1985. lib. bdg. 9.89 (ISBN 0-8167-0452-X); pap. text ed. 2.50 (ISBN 0-8167-0453-8). Troll Assocs.

--Life in the Sea. LC 84-16190. (Illus.). 32p. (gr. k-2). 1985. lib. bdg. 9.89 (ISBN 0-8167-0448-1); pap. text ed. 2.50 (ISBN 0-8167-0449-X). Troll Assocs.

--Little Christmas Elf. LC 84-8628. (Giant First Start Reader Ser.). (Illus.). 32p. (gr. k-2). 1985. PLB 9.89 (ISBN 0-8167-0352-3); pap. text ed. 2.50 (ISBN 0-8167-0432-5). Troll Assocs.

--Look at a Tree. LC 84-8843. (Illus.). 32p. (gr. k-2). 1985. PLB 9.89 (ISBN 0-8167-0349-3); pap. text ed. 2.50 (ISBN 0-8167-0350-7). Troll Assocs.

--Mountains & Volcanoes. LC 84-8638. (Illus.). 32p. (gr. k-2). 1985. PLB 9.89 (ISBN 0-8167-0347-7); pap. text ed. 2.50 (ISBN 0-8167-0348-5). Troll Assocs.

Curran, Francis X. Catholics in Colonial Law. 1963. 2.95 (ISBN 0-8294-0016-8). Loyola.

--The Return of the Jesuits. LC 66-29559. 1966. 3.00 (ISBN 0-8294-0018-4). Loyola.

Curran, Harold. Fearful Crossing: The Central Overland Trail Through Nevada. (Illus.). 212p. (Orig.). 1982. pap. 12.00 (ISBN 0-930830-09-1). Great Basin.

Curran, James, ed. The British Press: A Manifesto. (Communications & Culture Ser.). 1978. text ed. 33.00x (ISBN 0-333-23459-6). Humanities.

--The Future of the Left. (Polity Press Bk.). 352p. 1985. 29.95x (ISBN 0-7456-0003-4); pap. 9.95x (ISBN 0-7456-0004-2). Basil Blackwell.

Curran, James & Porter, Vincent, eds. British Cinema History. LC 83-11932. 452p. 1983. 32.50x (ISBN 0-389-20417-X, 07303). B&N Imports.

Curran, James, et al, eds. Mass Communication & Society. LC 78-68700. 478p. 1979. pap. 14.50 (ISBN 0-8039-1193-9). Sage.

Curran, James P. & Monti, Peter, eds. Social Skills Training: A Practical Handbook for Assessment & Treatment. LC 81-6374. 447p. 1982. 35.00 (ISBN 0-89862-610-2, 2610). Guilford Pr.

Curran, James T., et al, eds. Police & Law Enforcement, Nineteen Seventy-Three to Nineteen Eighty-One, 3 vols. LC 73-7210. (Orig.). 1973. Set. lib. bdg. 142.50 (ISBN 0-404-19542-3); Vol. 1. lib. bdg. 47.50 (ISBN 0-404-11200-5); Vol. 2. lib. bdg. 47.50 (ISBN 0-404-11205-6); Vol. 3. 47.50 (ISBN 0-404-11207-2); Vol. 1. pap. 8.95 (ISBN 0-404-11204-8); Vol. 2. pap. 9.95 (ISBN 0-404-11206-4). AMS Pr.

Curran, Jeanne & Telesky, Carol. Up the Job Market: Finding Your Way. 175p. 1980. 9.00 (ISBN 0-317-33288-0). Am Sociological.

Curran, John P. Primer of Sports Injuries. (Illus.). 112p. 1968. photocopy ed. 11.75x (ISBN 0-398-00378-5). C C Thomas.

Curran, John S., jt. auth. see Curran, Samuel C.

Curran, Joseph. Introductory Sociology. LC 76-30856. 1977. 20.95 (ISBN 0-07-014947-X). McGraw.

Curran, Joseph M. The Birth of the Irish Free State, 1921-1923. LC 79-4088. 400p. 1980. 25.00 (ISBN 0-8173-0013-9). U of Ala Pr.

Curran, June. Drawing Home Plans: A Simplified Drafting System for Planning & Design. Giumarra, Nancy & Weine, Ruth, eds. LC 78-72188. (Illus.). 1979. 24.95 (ISBN 0-932370-01-2); pap. 14.95 (ISBN 0-932370-02-0). Brooks Pub Co.

--Drawing Home Plans: A Simplified Drafting System for Planning & Design. LC 78-72188. (Illus.). 241p. 24.95x (ISBN 0-932370-01-2); pap. 14.95 (ISBN 0-932370-02-0). W Kaufmann.

--Profile Your Lifestyle: Questions to Ask Yourself Before Building, Buying or Remodeling a Home. Wilbur, Shay & Weine, Ruth, eds. LC 78-72187. 1979. pap. 7.95 (ISBN 0-932370-00-4). Brooks Pub Co.

--Profile Your Lifestyle: Questions to Ask Yourself Before Building, Buying, or Remodeling. LC 78-72187. 159p. 1979. pap. 7.95 (ISBN 0-932370-00-4). W Kaufmann.

Curran, Michael. The Antiphonary of Bangor. 200p. 1983. 50.00x (ISBN 0-7165-0338-7, BBA 05250, Pub. by Irish Academic Pr Ireland). Biblio Dist.

Curran, Michael, jt. auth. see MacKenzie, David.

Curran, Mona. Collecting Antique Jewelry. (Illus.). 10.95 (ISBN 0-87523-149-7). Emerson.

--Treasury of Jewels & Gems. (Illus.). 1962. 11.95 (ISBN 0-87523-139-X). Emerson.

Curran, P. F., jt. auth. see Katchalsky, Aharon.

Curran, Patricia A., jt. auth. see Curran, David F.

Curran, Patricia A., ed. see Curran, David F.

Curran, Paul. Principles of Remote Sensing. (Illus.). 260p. 1984. text ed. 24.95 (ISBN 0-582-30097-5). Longman.

Curran, R. C. Atlas de Histopatologia. 96p. (Span.). 1979. write for info. (S-37588). French & Eur.

--Color Atlas of Histopathology. 2nd ed. (Illus.). 1972. text ed. 39.50x (ISBN 0-19-519151-X). Oxford U Pr.

--Color Atlas of Histopathology. 3rd ed. (Oxford Color Atlases of Pathology Ser.). (Illus.). 300p. 1985. 37.50 (ISBN 0-19-921058-6). Oxford U Pr.

Curran, R. C. & Jones, E. L. Atlas de Patologia Macroscopica. 148p. (Spanish.). 1978. write for info. (S-37589). French & Eur.

--Gross Pathology: A Color Atlas. (Illus.). 1974. text ed. 39.50x (ISBN 0-19-519797-6). Oxford U Pr.

Curran, R. M., ed. Creep-fatique Interaction, 1976 ASME-EPC Symposium: Presented at the Winter Meeting of the ASME, New York, N. Y. December 5-10, 1976. LC 76-28849. pap. 109.50 (ISBN 0-317-08007-5, 2016816). Bks Demand UMI.

Curran, Raymond J. Architecture & the Urban Experience. 240p. 1983. 32.50 (ISBN 0-442-21208-9). Van Nos Reinhold.

Curran, Ronald, ed. The Weird Gathering & Other Tales. 1979. pap. 2.50 (ISBN 0-449-23994-2, Crest). Fawcett.

Curran, Samuel C. & Curran, John S. Energy & Human Needs. LC 79-16728. 330p. 1979. 32.95x (ISBN 0-470-26818-2). Halsted Pr.

Curran, Stuart. Shelley's Annus Mirabilis: The Maturing of an Epic Vision. LC 74-20037. (Illus.). 225p. 1975. 14.50 (ISBN 0-87328-064-4). Huntington Lib.

--Shelley's Cenci Scorpions Ringed with Fire. LC 71-120753. (Illus.). 1970. 31.00x (ISBN 0-691-06196-3). Princeton U Pr.

Curran, Stuart, ed. Le Bossu & Voltaire on the Epic: Rene le Bossu, Treatise of the Epic Poem, 1695 & Voltaire, Essay on Epic Poetry, 1727. LC 73-133363. 1970. 50.00x (ISBN 0-8201-1086-8). Schol Facsimiles.

Curran, Stuart & Wittreich, Joseph A., Jr., eds. Blake's Sublime Allegory: Essays on the "Four Zoas," "Milton," & "Jerusalem". LC 72-1377. (Illus.). 404p. 1973. 32.50x (ISBN 0-299-06180-9). U of Wis Pr.

Curran, Susan. Get More from the Epson Printer. (Illus.). 160p. (Orig.). 1985. pap. 15.95 (ISBN 0-00-383001-2, Pub. by Collins England). Sheridan.

--New Technology & Insurance. 1981. 50.00x (ISBN 0-686-97106-X, Pub. by Fourmat England). State Mutual Bk.

Curran, Susan & Curnow, Ray. Overcoming Computer Illiteracy: A Friendly Introduction to Computers. (Illus.). 448p. 1984. pap. 12.95 (ISBN 0-14-007159-8). Penguin.

Curran, Susan & Mitchell, Horace. Office Automation: An Essential Management Strategy. 225p. 1982. pap. 16.00x (ISBN 0-8448-1487-3). Crane-Russak Co.

Curran, Susan & Norman, Margaret. Business Applications on the BBC Micro. (Illus.). 218p. (Orig.). 1984. pap. 15.95 (ISBN 0-246-12530-6, Pub. by Granada England). Sheridan.

Curran, Susan, jt. auth. see Curnow, Ray.

Curran, Susan, jt. auth. see Pask, Gordon.

Curran, Thomas J., jt. auth. see Coppa, Frank J.

Curran, Trisha. A New Note on the Film. Jowett, Garth S., ed. LC 79-6671. (Dissertations on Film, 1980 Ser.). 1980. lib. bdg. 17.00x (ISBN 0-405-12905-X). Ayer Co Pubs.

Curran, Valerie. Nigerian Children: Developmental Perspectives. 224p. 1984. pap. 25.95X (ISBN 0-7100-9515-5). Routledge & Kegan.

Curran, Valerie & Golombok, Susan. Pill Popping: How You Can Get Clear. 176p. (Orig.). 1985. pap. 6.95 (ISBN 0-571-13508-0). Faber & Faber.

Curran, William. Beautiful Wisconsin. LC 79-777. 72p. 1984. 12.95 (ISBN 0-915796-63-5); pap. 7.95 (ISBN 0-89802-424-2). Beautiful Am.

--Mitts: A Celebration of the Art of Fielding. LC 85-2897. (Illus.). 224p. 1985. 15.95 (ISBN 0-688-04489-1). Morrow.

Curran, William & Shapiro, E. Donald. Law, Medicine & Forensic Science. 3rd ed. LC 81-81207. 1181p. 1982. text ed. 33.00 (ISBN 0-316-16510-7). Little.

Curran, William C. Beautiful Los Angeles. LC 79-12045. 72p. 1979. 12.95 (ISBN 0-89802-056-5); pap. 6.95 (ISBN 0-89802-055-7). Beautiful Am.

--Beautiful Washington D. C. 2nd ed. LC 79-17658. (Illus.). 72p. 1984. 12.95 (ISBN 0-89802-010-7); pap. 7.95 (ISBN 0-89802-009-3). Beautiful Am.

Curran, William J., et al. Modern Legal Medicine, Psychiatry & Forensic Science. LC 79-19477. (Illus.). 1310p. 1980. text ed. 99.50x (ISBN 0-8036-2292-9). Davis Co.

--Electrical Safety & Hazards in Hospitals. 205p. 1974. text ed. 19.50x (ISBN 0-8422-7135-X). Irvington.

Currat, Nancy, jt. auth. see Giese, Elizabeth A.

Currell, David. Learning with Puppets. 208p. 1980. 15.95 (ISBN 0-8238-0250-7). Plays.

Currell, Melville E. Political Woman. 201p. 1974. 16.50x (ISBN 0-87471-564-4). Rowman.

Currell, R. G. & Hurlbut, E. P. The Ruler of the Kings on the Earth: A Clear Look at Amillennialism for the Lay Person. 126p. 1983. pap. 4.95 (ISBN 0-87552-211-4). Presby & Reformed.

Curren, Anna M. Clinical Nursing Skills. (Illus.). 370p. 1983. pap. text ed. 22.95 (ISBN 0-918082-02-1). Wallcur Inc.

Curren, Anna M. & Munday, Laurie D. Math for Meds: A Programmed Text. 4th ed. LC 76-43259. (Illus.). 120p. 1984. pap. text ed. 13.95 (ISBN 0-918082-03-X). Wallcur Inc.

Curren, Art. Kitbashing Model Railroad Structures. (Illus., Orig.). 1985. pap. price not set (ISBN 0-89024-059-0). Kalmbach.

Curren, Mary T., et al, eds. Advances in Consumer Research: Index for Volumes 7-11 (1980-1984) 89p. pap. 8.00 (ISBN 0-915552-12-4). Assn Consumer Res.

Current Biography Staff, jt. auth. see Moritz, Charles.

Current Digest of the Soviet Press Staff, tr. see Ehlers, Robert, et al.

Current Digest of the Soviet Press Staff, tr. see Ehlers, Robert & Bessel, Richard.

Current Digest of the Soviet Press Staff, tr. see Gruliow, Leo.

Current Digest of the Soviet Press Staff, tr. see Gruliow, Leo & Gruliow, Rebecca.

Current Digest of the Soviet Press Staff, tr. see Gruliow, Leo & Neuweld, Mark.

Current Digest of the Soviet Press Staff, tr. see Saikowski, Charlotte, et al.

Current Documents & Information Staff. African Newspaper Index, Vol. 1, No. 2. Nyang, Elizabeth T., ed. 73p. 1982. 15.00 (ISBN 0-686-35976-3). Current Documents.

Current, Marion E. Looking at Each Other. (Illus.). 96p. 1983. pap. 4.55 (ISBN 0-8048-1415-5, Pub. by Seoul Intl Publishing House). C E Tuttle.

Current, Richard, et al. Current History of the United States. 2nd ed. 1048p. 1985. text ed. 27.95 (ISBN 0-394-34023-X, KnopfC); Vol. 1. pap. text ed. 17.95 (ISBN 0-394-34021-3); Vol. 2. pap. text ed. 17.95 (ISBN 0-394-34022-1). Knopf.

Current, Richard M., et al. Essentials of American History, 2 vols. 4th ed. 1986. pap. text ed. 10.95 ea. Vol 1: To 1877 (ISBN 0-394-35478-8). Vol. 2: Since 1865 (ISBN 0-394-35479-6). Set of 2 vols. pap. text ed. 16.95. Knopf.

Current, Richard N. Daniel Webster & the Rise of National Conservatism. (The Library of American Biography). 215p. 1962. pap. text ed. 6.95 (ISBN 0-316-16515-8). Little.

--History of Wisconsin Vol. 2: The Civil War Era, 1848-1873. LC 72-12941. (History of Wisconsin Ser.). (Illus.). 659p. 1976. 25.00 (ISBN 0-87020-160-3). State Hist Soc Wis.

--Lincoln & the First Shot. (Critical Periods of History Ser). (Orig.). 1963. pap. text ed. 7.80 scp (ISBN 0-397-47044-4, HarpC). Har-Row.

--The Lincoln Nobody Knows. LC 80-16138. x, 314p. 1980. Repr. of 1958 ed. lib. bdg. 27.50x (ISBN 0-313-22450-1, CULN). Greenwood.

--The Lincoln Nobody Knows. (American Century Ser.). 314p. 1963. pap. 6.95 (ISBN 0-8090-0059-8). Hill & Wang.

--Northernizing the South. LC 82-23804. (Mercer University Lamar Memorial Lecture Ser.: No. 26). 160p. 1983. 12.50x (ISBN 0-8203-0666-5). U of Ga Pr.

--Old Thad Stevens: A Story of Ambition. LC 80-15189. (Illus.). v, 344p. 1980. Repr. of 1942 ed. lib. bdg. 32.50x (ISBN 0-313-22569-9, CUOT). Greenwood.

--The Political Thought of Abraham Lincoln. LC 67-30069. 1967. pap. write for info. (ISBN 0-02-326420-9, AHS46). Macmillan.

--Secretary Stimson: A Study in Statecraft. xxv, 272p. 1970. Repr. of 1954 ed. 21.00 (ISBN 0-208-00966-3, Archon). Shoe String.

--Speaking of Abraham Lincoln: The Man & His Meaning for Our Times. LC 83-3568. 208p. 1983. 17.50 (ISBN 0-252-01056-6). U of Ill Pr.

--Wisconsin: A History. LC 77-2176. (States & the Nation Ser.). (Illus.). 1977. 14.95 (ISBN 0-393-05624-4, Co-Pub by AASLH). Norton.

Current, Richard N. & Goodwin, Gerald. Current History of the United States. 1980. text ed. 23.00 (ISBN 0-394-32338-6, KnopfC). Knopf.

Current, Richard N. & Williams, T. Harry. American History: A Survey, 2 vols. 6th ed. 1000p. 1983. text ed. 27.00 (ISBN 0-394-33043-9, KnopfC); Vol. 1. pap. text ed. 17.00 (ISBN 0-394-33079-X); Vol. 2. pap. text ed. 17.00 (ISBN 0-394-33080-3); wkbk. 7.00 (ISBN 0-394-33222-9). Knopf.

Current, Richard N., ed. Reconstruction in Retrospect: Views from the Turn of the Century. LC 77-80044. xxii, 166p. 1969. 17.50x (ISBN 0-8071-0850-2); pap. text ed. 4.95x (ISBN 0-8071-0140-0). La State U Pr.

--Sections & Politics: Selected Essays by William B. Hesseltine. LC 68-65095. 150p. 1968. 7.50 (ISBN 0-87020-027-5). State Hist Soc Wis.

Current, Richard N., ed. see Hood, John B.

Current, Richard N., ed. see Lincoln, Abraham.

Current, Richard N., et al. American History Two. 6th ed. 1983. study guide 7.00 (ISBN 0-394-33223-7, KnopfC). Knopf.

--Essentials of American History. 3rd ed. 1979. pap. text ed. 13.00 (ISBN 0-394-32337-8, KnopfC). Knopf.

--History of the United States, Vol. 1, To 1877, Vol. 2, Since 1865. 3rd ed. (Illus.). 1983. Vol. 1. text ed. 17.00 (ISBN 0-394-33079-X, KnopfC); Vol. 2. 17.00 (ISBN 0-394-33080-3). Knopf.

--Essentials of American History, 2 vols. 3rd ed. 1980. pap. text ed. 8.95 ea. Vol. 1, To 1877, 208p (ISBN 0-394-32429-3). Vol. 2, Since 1865, 200p (ISBN 0-394-32430-7). Knopf.

--The Essentials of American History, 2 vols. 1977. pap. text ed. 8.95 ea. (KnopfC). Knopf.

Current, Richard N., et al, eds. Words That Made American History: From Colonial Times to the 1870's, Vol. I. 3rd abridged & Updated ed. 1978. pap. 14.95 (ISBN 0-316-16517-4). Little.

--Words That Made American History since the Civil War: Abridged & Updated, Vol. 2. 3rd ed. Garraty, John A. & Weinberg, Julius. 605p. 1978. pap. 13.95 (ISBN 0-316-16518-2). Little.

Current Staff of the Soviet Press Staff, tr. see Ehlers, Robert & Bessel, Richard.

Current-Garcia, Eugene. The American Short Story Before Eighteen Fifty: A Critical History. (Twayne Short Story Ser.). 1985. lib. bdg. 17.95 (ISBN 0-8057-9359-3, Twayne). G K Hall.

--O. Henry. (United States Authors Ser.). 1972. lib. bdg. 13.50 (ISBN 0-8057-0368-3, Twayne). G K Hall.

Current-Garcia, Eugene & Patrick, Walton R. American Short Stories. 4th ed. 1982. pap. text ed. 15.00x (ISBN 0-673-15570-6). Scott F.

--What Is the Short Story? Studies in the Development of a Literary Form. 1974. pap. 13.05x (ISBN 0-673-07886-8). Scott F.

Currer, Caroline & Stacey, Margaret, eds. Concepts of Health, Illness & Disease: A Comparative Perspective. 256p. 1985. 27.00 (ISBN 0-907582-18-4, Pub. by Berg Pubs); pap. 9.95 (ISBN 0-907582-19-2). Longwood Pub Group.

Currer-Briggs, Noel. The Carters of Virginia: Their English Ancestry. 120p. 1979. 23.75x (ISBN 0-8476-2403-X). Rowman.

--The Carters of Virginia: Their English Ancestry. 1979. 39.00x (ISBN 0-85033-307-5, Pub. by Phillimore England). State Mutual Bk.

--Colonial Settlers & English Adventurers. LC 70-177281. 393p. 1971. 22.50 (ISBN 0-8063-0488-X). Genealog Pub.

--English Adventurers & Virginian Settlers. 837p. 1980. Repr. of 1869 ed. 30.00 (ISBN 0-8063-0488-X). Genealog Pub.

--Worldwide Family History. 200p. 1982. 19.95x (ISBN 0-7100-0934-8). Routledge & Kegan.

Curreri, Joseph. Virginia's Natural Bridge. (Illus.). 32p. 1984. 18.00 (ISBN 0-88014-054-2). Mosaic Pr OH.

Currey, Bruce & Hugo, Graeme, eds. Famine As a Geographical Phenomenon. 1984. lib. bdg. 37.00 (ISBN 90-277-1762-1, Pub. by Reidel Holland). Kluwer Academic.

Currey, C. Brothers Bent. 1968. pap. 18.00x (ISBN 0-424-05700-X, Pub. by Sydney U Pr). Intl Spec Bk.

Currey, Cecil B. Follow Me & Die: The Destruction of an American Division in World War II. LC 82-48509. (Illus.). 320p. 1984. 18.95 (ISBN 0-8128-2892-5); pap. 3.95 (ISBN 0-8128-8121-4). Stein & Day.

--Reason & Revelation: John Duns Scotus on Natural Theology. LC 77-9614. (Synthesis Ser.). 1977. pap. 0.75 (ISBN 0-8199-0717-0). Franciscan Herald.

--Road to Revolution: Benjamin Franklin in England 1765-1775. (Illus.). 13.25 (ISBN 0-8446-1931-0). Peter Smith.

Currey, H. L., et al, eds. Masson & Curey's Clinical Rheumatology. 3rd ed. (Illus.). 372p. 1981. text ed. 43.50 (ISBN 0-397-58272-2, 65-72796, Lippincott Medical). Lippincott.

Currey, J. D., jt. ed. see Vincent, J. F.

Currey, John. The Mechanical Adaptations of Bones. LC 84-42591. (Illus.). 360p. 1984. text ed. 37.50x (ISBN 0-691-08342-8). Princeton U Pr.

Currey, L. W. Science Fiction & Fantasy Authors: A Bibliography of First Printings of Their Fiction & Selected Nonfiction. LC 79-18217. 571p. 1979. 68.50 (ISBN 0-8161-8242-6). Ultramarine Pub.

Currey, L. W. & Reginald, R. Science Fiction & Fantasy Reference Guide: An Annotated History of Critical & Biographical Works. LC 80-22715. (Borgo Reference Library: Vol. 4). 96p. (Orig.). 1986. lib. bdg. 19.95x (ISBN 0-89370-145-9); pap. text ed. 9.95x (ISBN 0-89370-245-5). Borgo Pr.

Currey, L. W., jt. auth. see Reginald, R.

Currey, Muriel, tr. see Badoglio, Pietro.

Currey, R. N., tr. Formal Spring. facsimile ed. LC 76-80372. (Granger Index Reprint Ser). 1950. 15.00 (ISBN 0-8369-6054-8). Ayer Co Pubs.

Currey, Richard. Crossing Over: A Vietnam Journal. 64p. (Orig.). 1980. 8.95 (ISBN 0-918222-21-4); pap. 3.95 (ISBN 0-918222-22-2). Apple-Wood.

Curriculium Adaption Network for Bilingual Bicultural Education. ESL Reader: Un Nino Llamado Manuel. Quinones, Nathan, ed. LC 76-6000. (Sp.). 1976. pap. 2.95 (ISBN 0-8120-0700-X). Barron.

Curriculm Development Unit Dublin Vocation Ed. Comm., jt. ed. see McMahon, Agnes.

Curriculum Development Unit. Dublin Divided City: Portrait of Dublin 1913. 1978. text ed. 11.00x (ISBN 0-905140-50-8). Humanities.

--Families & Friends. (Illus.). 96p. (gr. 3 up). 1978. pap. 5.25 (ISBN 0-905140-58-3, Pub. by O'Brien Pr Ireland). Irish Bks Media.

--Heroic Tales From the Ulster Cycle. (Illus.). 136p. (gr. 3 up). 1982. pap. 5.25 (ISBN 0-86278-020-9, Pub. by O'Brien Pr Ireland). Irish Bks Media.

Curriculum Development Unit, ed. Dublin Nineteen Thirteen. (Illus.). 112p. 1982. 9.95 (ISBN 0-905140-50-8, Pub. by O'Brien Pr Ireland); pap. 6.95 (ISBN 0-86278-023-3, Pub. by O'Brien Pr Ireland). Irish Bks Media.

--Field & Shore: Daily Life & Taditions, Aran Islands 1900. (Illus.). 83p. (Orig.). 1982. pap. 4.95 (ISBN 0-905140-13-3, Pub. by O'Brien Pr Ireland). Irish Bks Media.

--Island Stories. (Illus.). 80p. (gr. 5 up). 1982. pap. 4.95 (ISBN 0-905140-22-2, Pub. by O'Brien Pr Ireland). Irish Bks Media.

--Urban Ireland: Development of Towns & Villages. (Illus.). 128p. 1982. 14.95 (ISBN 0-86278-017-9, XPub. by O'Brien Pr Ireland); pap. 6.95 (ISBN 0-86278-018-7, Pub. by O'Brien Pr Ireland). Irish Bks Media.

--Viking Settlement to Medieval Dublin. (Illus.). 104p. 1979. 12.95 (ISBN 0-905140-48-6, Pub. by O'Brien Pr Ireland). Irish Bks Media.

--The World of Stone: Life, Folklore & Legends of Aran - Island Life Ser, Bk. 1. (Illus.). 1977. pap. 4.95 (ISBN 0-905140-12-5). Irish Bk Ctr.

--A World of Stone: Life, Folklore & Legends of the Aran Islands. (Illus.). 80p. (Orig.). 1982. pap. 4.50 (ISBN 0-905140-15-X, Pub. by O'Brien Pr Ireland). Irish Bks Media.

Curriculum Guide Rewrite Committee. Teaching about Drugs: A Curriculum Guide, K-12. 3rd ed. 205p. 1985. 13.95 (ISBN 0-317-37219-X). Am Sch Health.

Curriculum Information Center, compiled by. Microcomputers in Schools, 1984-85. rev. ed. 100p. (Orig.). 1985. pap. 50.00 (ISBN 0-89770-338-3). Market Data Ret.

Curriculum Theory Conference, University of Wisconsin, Milwaukee, November 11-14, 1976. Curriculum Theory: Proceedings. Molnar, Alex & Zahorik, John A., eds. LC 77-86522. 1977. pap. text ed. 7.00 (ISBN 0-87120-086-4, 611-77112). Assn Supervision.

Currie, Angela, jt. auth. see Currie, Graham.

Currie, B. & Sharpe, R. A. Design of Structural Elements Level IV. (Illus.). 176p. 1984. pap. text ed. 23.95x (ISBN 0-7121-0443-7). Trans-Atlantic.

--Structural Detailing. (Illus.). 160p. pap. text ed. 18.50x (ISBN 0-7121-1985-X). Trans-Atlantic.

Currie, Barbara. Pioneers in the American West, 1780-1840. Reeves, Marjorie, ed. (Then & There Ser.). (Illus.). 92p. (Orig.). (gr. 7-12). 1969. pap. text ed. 3.75 (ISBN 0-582-20454-2). Longman.

--Railroads & Cowboys in the American West. Reeves, Marjorie, ed. (Then & There Ser.). (Illus.). 112p. (Orig.). (gr. 7-12). 1974. pap. text ed. 3.75 (ISBN 0-582-20533-6). Longman.

Currie, Brainerd. Selected Essays on the Conflict of Laws. LC 63-17326. pap. 160.00 (ISBN 0-317-28857-1, 2017896). Bks Demand UMI.

Currie, D., et al, eds. Macroeconomic Analysis: Essays in Macroeconomics & Econometrics. (Illus.). 491p. 1981. 44.00 (ISBN 0-7099-0311-1, Pub. by Croom Helm Ltd). Longwood Pub Group.

--Microeconomic Analysis: Essays in Microeconomics & Economic Development. 495p. 1981. 44.00 (ISBN 0-7099-0709-5, Pub. by Croom Helm Ltd). Longwood Pub Group.

Currie, David. Air Pollution: Federal Law & Analysis. LC 81-21566. 930p. 1982. 95.00 (ISBN 0-317-11928-1). Callaghan.

Currie, David M. Come, Let Us Worship God: A Handbook of Prayers for Leaders of Worship. LC 77-6808. 132p. 1977. softcover 4.25 (ISBN 0-664-24757-1). Westminster.

Currie, David P. The Constitution in the Supreme Court: The First Hundred Years, 1789-1888. LC 85-1205. 472p. 1985. lib. bdg. 45.00x (ISBN 0-226-13108-4). U of Chicago Pr.

--Federal Courts Cases & Materials. 3rd ed. 1042p. 1982. 25.95. West Pub.

--Federal Jurisdiction. 2nd ed. LC 81-2051. (Nutshell Ser.). 258p. 1981. pap. text ed. 7.95 (ISBN 0-314-58807-8). West Pub.

--OSHA. 54p. (Reprinted from 1976 ABF Res. J., No.4). 1976. 2.50 (ISBN 0-317-33349-6). Am Bar Foun.

Currie, David P., ed. Federalism & the New Nations of Africa. LC 64-23421. pap. 112.00 (ISBN 0-317-09606-0, 2020050). Bks Demand UMI.

Currie, David R. On the Way! LC 81-69403. 1982. pap. 3.95 (ISBN 0-8054-5336-9, 4253-36). Broadman.

Currie, Donald J. Abdominal Pain. (Illus.). 1979. text ed. 21.95 (ISBN 0-07-014942-9). McGraw.

Currie, Donald J. & Smialowski, Arthur. Photographic Illustration for Medical Writing. (Illus.). 132p. 1962. photocopy ed. 15.75x (ISBN 0-398-00379-3). C C Thomas.

Currie, Donald J., jt. auth. see Smialowski, Arthur.

Currie, Dorothy H. How to Organize a Children's Library. LC 65-14215. 184p. 1965. 10.00 (ISBN 0-379-00233-7). Oceana.

Currie, Elliot. Crime & Community: Understanding Criminal Violence. LC 85-6300. 273p. 1985. 19.95 (ISBN 0-394-53219-8). Pantheon.

Currie, Elliot, et al. America's Problems: Social Issues & Public Policy. 1984. 25.95 (ISBN 0-316-16534-4) (ISBN 0-316-16535-2). Little.

Currie, Elliott, jt. auth. see Skolnick, Jerome H.

Currie, G., ed. see Lakatos, Imre.

Currie, George & Graham, J. Origines of CSIRO. 216p. 1981. 29.00x (ISBN 0-643-02754-8, Pub. by CSIRO Australia). State Mutual Bk.

Currie, Graham & Currie, Angela. Cancer: The Biology of Malignant Disease. 144p. 1983. pap. text ed. 16.50 (ISBN 0-7131-4400-9). E Arnold.

Currie, Gregory. Frege: An Introduction to His Philosophy. LC 81-22880. 224p. 1982. text ed. 29.50x (ISBN 0-389-20268-1). B&N Imports.

Currie, Gregory & Musgrave, Alan, eds. Popper & the Human Sciences. 1985. lib. bdg. 41.50 (ISBN 90-247-2998-X, Pub. by Martinus Nijhoff Netherlands); pap. text ed. 14.95 (ISBN 90-247-3141-0, Pub. by Martinus Nijhoff Netherlands). Kluwer Academic.

Currie, H. M. Silver Latin Epic. (Orig.). 1985. pap. 7.50 (ISBN 0-86516-125-9). Bolchazy-Carducci.

Currie, H. MacL. Silver Latin Epic: An Approach. 140p. 1981. 29.00x (ISBN 0-906515-37-8, Pub. by Bristol Classical Pr). State Mutual Bk.

Currie, Hector. Cinema Drama Schema: Eastern Metaphysic in Western Art. LC 84-20771. 192p. 1985. 14.95 (ISBN 0-8022-2461-X). Philos Lib.

Currie, I. G., ed. Fundamental Mechanics of Fluids. 480p. 1974. text ed. 49.00 (ISBN 0-07-014950-X). McGraw.

Currie, J. M. The Economic Theory of Agricultural Land Tenure. LC 80-41114. (Illus.). 1981. 37.50 (ISBN 0-521-23634-7). Cambridge U Pr.

Currie, Janice K., jt. auth. see Heyneman, Stephen P.

Currie, Jean. The Travellers' Guide to Rhodes. rev. ed. (Illus.). 1981. pap. 9.95 (ISBN 0-224-01927-9, Pub. by Jonathan Cape). Merrimack Pub Cir.

Currie, John M. & British Columbia Institute of Technology. Unit Operations in Mineral Processing. 340p. 1978. Repr. of 1973 ed. 7.20 (ISBN 0-918062-13-6). Colo Sch Mines.

Currie, Kit, jt. auth. see Evelyn, John.

Currie, Lauchlin. The Role of Economic Advisors in Developing Countries. LC 81-6623. (Contributions in Economics & Economic History Ser.: No. 44). (Illus.). 288p. 1981. 29.95 (ISBN 0-313-23064-1, CUE/). Greenwood.

--Taming the Megalopolis: A Design for Urban Growth. 1976. 11.25 (ISBN 0-08-021397-9). Pergamon.

Currie, Laurence. The Baton in the Knapsack. 224p. 1980. Repr. lib. bdg. 25.00 (ISBN 0-8495-0850-9). Arden Lib.

Currie, Lloyd A., ed. Nuclear & Chemical Dating Techniques. LC 81-20649. (ACS Symposium Ser.: No. 176). 1982. 54.95 (ISBN 0-8412-0669-4). Am Chemical.

Currie, Nicholas C. Techniques of Radar Reflectivity Measurement. LC 83-72777. (Radar Ser.). (Illus.). 500p. 1983. 72.00 (ISBN 0-89006-131-9). Artech Hse.

Currie, Robert. Industrial Politics. LC 78-40480. 1979. 38.50x (ISBN 0-19-827419-X). Oxford U Pr.

Currie, Robert, et al. Churches & Churchgoers: Patterns of Church Growth in the British Isles since 1700. (Illus.). 1978. 42.00x (ISBN 0-19-827218-9). Oxford U Pr.

Currie, Russel M. Work Study. pap. 26.95x (ISBN 0-273-00959-1). Sportshelf.

Currie, S., jt. auth. see Behan, P. O.

Currie, Steven. Understanding & Using dBASE III on the IBM PC. 1985. FPT 15.95. CBS Ed.

Currie, Steven, jt. auth. see Smolin, C. R.

Currie, Thomas W., Jr. Austin Presbyterian Theological Seminary: A Seventy-Fifth Anniversary History. LC 77-89961. 285p. 1978. 12.00 (ISBN 0-911536-71-X). Trinity U Pr.

Currie, W. B. Days & Nights of Game Fishing: A Book of Places, Experiences, Discussion & Atmosphere on the Catching of Trout, Sea Trout & Salmon. (Illus.). 240p. 1984. 15.95 (ISBN 0-04-799024-4). Allen Unwin.

Currie, William. An Historical Account of the Climates & Diseases of the U. S. A. & of the Remedies & Methods of Treatment. LC 70-180570. (Medicine & Society in America Ser). 428p. 1972. Repr. of 1792 ed. 23.00 (ISBN 0-405-03945-X). Ayer Co Pubs.

Currie, Winifred. Creative Classroom Communications. 126p. 1972. pap. 1.25 (ISBN 0-88243-507-8, 02-0507). Gospel Pub.

Currier, Chet, jt. auth. see Associated Press.

Currier, Dean P. Elements of Research in Physical Therapy. 2nd ed. 360p. 1984. lib. bdg. 23.95 (ISBN 0-683-02247-4). Williams & Wilkins.

Currier, Don, ed. see McGuire, Mike.

Currier, E. M. E. A. Silvermarks, Sixteen Ninety to Eighteen Forty. LC 78-96937. 15.00 (ISBN 0-87282-021-1). CHB-ALF.

Currier, Ernest M. Marks of Early American Silversmiths. limited ed. LC 74-111387. (Illus.). 192p. 1970. deluxe ed. 50.00x (ISBN 0-9600266-1-4). R A Green.

Currier, F., tr. see Gail, Otto W.

Currier, John J. History of Newburyport, Massachusetts, 2 vols. LC 77-88166. (Illus.). Repr. of 1905 ed. Set 45.00; Vol. 1, 1977. 0.00 (ISBN 0-912274-70-0); Vol. 2, 1978. 0.00 (ISBN 0-912274-97-2). NH Pub Co.

Currier, Philip J. Currier Family Records of U. S. A. & Canada, 3 Vols. LC 84-71210. 1300p. 1984. Set. lib. bdg. 90.00 (ISBN 0-9613636-0-6); Vol. I: Descendants of Richard Currier (1616-1686-7) of Salisbury & Amesbury Mass. lib. bdg. 45.00 (ISBN 0-9613636-1-4); Vol. II. lib. bdg. 35.00 (ISBN 0-9613636-2-2); Vol. III. lib. bdg. 20.00 (ISBN 0-9613636-3-0). P J Currier.

Currier, Richard L., ed. see Meshorer, Ya'akov.

Currier, Richard L., jt. auth. see Hoebel, Adamson.

Currier, Robert D., jt. auth. see Haerer, Armin.

Currier, Thomas F. A Bibliography of Oliver Wendell Holmes. Tilton, Eleanor M., ed. LC 53-11420. pap. 160.00 (ISBN 0-317-10318-0, 2050257). Bks Demand UMI.

Currimbhoy, Asif. Darjeeling Tea? (Writers Workshop Bluebird Ser.). 64p. 1975. 8.00 (ISBN 0-88253-522-6); pap. text ed. 4.80 (ISBN 0-88253-521-8). Ind-US Inc.

--The Dissident M. L. A. (Bluebird Bk.). 56p. 1975. pap. 4.80 (ISBN 0-88253-842-X). Ind-US Inc.

--An Experiment with Truth. (Writers Workshop Bluebird Book Ser.). 62p. 1975. pap. text ed. 4.80 (ISBN 0-88253-537-4). Ind-US Inc.

--Goa. (Writers Workshop Bluebird Book Ser.). 82p. 1975. pap. text ed. 4.80 (ISBN 0-88253-549-8). Ind-US Inc.

--Inquilab. 1970. 10.00 (ISBN 0-89253-784-1); pap. text ed. 4.80 (ISBN 0-88253-807-1). Ind-US Inc.

--The Miracle Seed. (Writers Workshop Bluebird Ser.). 38p. 1975. pap. text ed. 4.80 (ISBN 0-88253-575-7). Ind-US Inc.

--Om Mane Padme Hum! Hail to the Jewel in the Lotus. (Bluebird Ser.). 67p. 1975. 12.00 (ISBN 0-88253-594-3); pap. text ed. 4.80 (ISBN 0-88253-593-5). Ind-US Inc.

--Sonar Bangla. 1972. pap. text ed. 4.80 (ISBN 0-88253-764-4). Ind-US Inc.

--This Alien...Native Land. 12.00 (ISBN 0-89253-796-5); flexible cloth 6.75 (ISBN 0-89253-527-X). Ind-US Inc.

Currimbhoy, Nayana. Indira Gandhi. (Impact Biography Ser.). (Illus.). 128p. (gr. 7 up). 1985. PLB 9.90 (ISBN 0-531-10064-2). Watts.

Currin, Beverly M. The Hope That Never Disappoints. 128p. (Orig.). 1983. pap. 8.75 (ISBN 0-687-17415-5). Abingdon.

Curry & Sykes. Conduct of Meetings. 197p. 1981. 30.00x (ISBN 0-85308-037-2, Pub. by Jordan & Sons England). State Mutual Bk.

Curry, et al. Twenty Years of Community Medicine: A Hunterdon Medical Center Symposium. LC 74-80237. (Illus.). 192p. 1974. 15.00 (ISBN 0-914366-01-7). Columbia Pub.

Curry, A. S., ed. & intro. by. Analytical Methods in Human Toxicology, Part 1. (Illus.). 319p. 1985. 59.00 (ISBN 0-89573-416-8). VCH Pubs.

Curry, Alan. Poison Detection in Human Organs. 3rd ed. (Illus.). 376p. 1976. 34.50x (ISBN 0-398-03433-8). C C Thomas.

Curry, Allen D. Leader's Guide for John W. Sanderson's "The Fruit of the Spirit". A Teaching Manual for Use in Adult Study Groups. (Orig.). 1978. pap. 2.95 (ISBN 0-934688-07-9). Great Comm Pubns.

Curry, Ann. Teaching About the Other Americans: Minorities in United States History. 8.95 (ISBN 0-86548-028-1). R & E Pubs.

Curry, Barbara. Model Aircraft. (First Bks.). (Illus.). (gr. 4 up). 1979. PLB 8.90 s&l (ISBN 0-531-02260-9). Watts.

--Model Historical Aircraft. LC 82-4779. (First Bks.). (Illus.). 72p. (gr. 4 up). 1982. PLB 8.90 (ISBN 0-531-04465-3). Watts.

Curry, Charles E. Black America: Make Yourself Wealthy. Date not set. pap. 7.00 (ISBN 0-917885-00-7). Black Am Pubns.

Curry, David. Contending to Be the Dream. (Illus.). 1979. pap. 3.00 (ISBN 0-685-96085-4). New Rivers Pr.

--Sunshine Patriots: Punishment & the Vietnam Offender. LC 81-40450. 192p. 1985. 14.95 (ISBN 0-268-01706-9). U of Notre Dame Pr.

Curry, David P. James McNeil Whistler at the Freer Gallery of Art. (Illus.). 320p. (Orig.). 1984. pap. 30.00 (ISBN 0-934686-53-X). Freer.

--James McNeill Whistler. LC 83-25525. (Freer Gallery Bk.). (Illus.). 1984. 50.00 (ISBN 0-393-01847-4). Norton.

Curry, Dean C., ed. Evangelicals & the Bishops' Pastoral Letter. LC 84-4005. 254p. (Orig.). 1984. pap. 10.95 (ISBN 0-8028-1985-0). Eerdmans.

Curry, Dudley & Frame, Robert. Accounting Principles: A Multimedia Program. LC 72-95544. 1973. Modules 1-15. pap. text ed. 23.95 add. suppl. may be obtained from Publisher (ISBN 0-675-08992-1). Merrill.

Curry, Dudley, jt. auth. see Frame, Robert.

Curry, Dudley W. Introduction to Management Accounting. 6th ed. (Illus.). 208p. 1984. student guide 13.95 (ISBN 0-13-487851-5). P-H.

Curry, E. R. Hoover's Dominican Diplomacy & the Origins of the Good Neighbor Policy. Freidel, Frank, ed. LC 78-62379. (Modern American History Ser.: Vol. 5). 1979. lib. bdg. 36.00 (ISBN 0-8240-3629-8). Garland Pub.

Curry, Elissa. Black Lace & Pearls. (Second Chance at Love Ser.: No. 213). 192p. 1984. pap. 1.95 (ISBN 0-515-07961-8). Jove Pubns.

--Dating Games. (Second Chance at Love Ser.: No. 227). 192p. 1984. pap. 1.95 (ISBN 0-515-08201-5). Jove Pubns.
--Gentleman At Heart. (Second Chance At Love Ser.: No. 263). 192p. 1985. pap. 1.95 (ISBN 0-425-08151-6). Berkley Pub.
--Kiss Me Cait. (To Have & to Hold Ser.: No. 23). 192p. 1984. pap. 1.95 (ISBN 0-515-07825-5). Jove Pubns.
--Lady Be Good. (Second Chance at Love Ser.: No. 247). 192p. 1985. pap. 2.95 (ISBN 0-425-07774-8). Jove Pubns.
--Lady with a Past. (Second Chance at Love Ser.: No. 193). 192p. 1984. pap. 1.95 (ISBN 0-515-07809-3). Jove Pubns.
--Playing for Keeps. (To Have & to Hold Ser.: No. 18). 192p. 1984. pap. 1.95 (ISBN 0-515-06945-0). Jove Pubns.
--Sophisticated Lady. (Second Chance At Love Ser.: No. 287). 192p. 1985. pap. 2.25 (ISBN 0-425-08509-0). Berkley Pub.
--Trial By Desire. 192p. 1984. pap. 1.95 (ISBN 0-515-07589-2). Jove Pubns.
--Winter Wildfire. (Second Chance at Love Ser.: No. 178). 192p. 1984. pap. 1.95 (ISBN 0-515-07593-0). Jove Pubns.
Curry, Estell H., jt. auth. see Silvius, George H.
Curry Foundation & Nichols, William P. Agriculture, Stability & Growth: Towards a Cooperative Approach. LC 84-16858. 240p. 1984. text ed. 22.50x (ISBN 0-8046-9383-8, 9383, Natl U). Assoc Faculty Pr.
Curry, Gene. Ace in the Hole. (Saddler Ser.: No. 6). (Orig.). 1981. pap. 1.95 (ISBN 0-505-51666-7, Pub. by Tower Bks). Dorchester Pub Co.
--Colorado Crossing. (Jim Saddler Ser.: No. 3). 1979. pap. 1.75 (ISBN 0-505-51418-4, Pub. by Tower Bks). Dorchester Pub Co.
--A Dirty Way to Die. (Saddler Ser.: No. 1). 1979. pap. 1.75 (ISBN 0-505-51398-6, Pub. by Tower Bks). Dorchester Pub Co.
--Hot As a Pistol. (Saddler Ser.: No. 4). (Orig.). 1980. pap. text ed. 1.75 (ISBN 0-505-51552-0, Pub. by Tower Bks). Dorchester Pub Co.
--Wild, Wild Women. (Saddler Ser.: No. 5). (Orig.). 1980. pap. 1.75 (ISBN 0-686-86792-0, Pub. by Tower Bks). Dorchester Pub Co.
--Wildcat Woman. (Saddler Ser.: No. 2). 1979. pap. 1.75 (ISBN 0-505-51407-9, Pub. by Tower Bks). Dorchester Pub Co.
--Yukon Ride. (Saddler Ser.: No. 7). 192p. (Orig.). 1981. pap. 2.25 (ISBN 0-505-51734-5, Pub. by Tower Bks). Dorchester Pub Co.
Curry, George, jt. auth. see Walker, Richard L.
Curry, George J., et al. Profiles in Trauma. (Illus.). 288p. 1969. photocopy ed. 24.50x (ISBN 0-398-00382-3). C C Thomas.
Curry, Guy L. & Feldman, Richard M. Mathematical Foundations of Population Dynamics. LC 85-40054. (TEES Monograph Ser.: No. 3). 284p. 1985. lib. bdg. 46.50 (ISBN 0-89096-256-1). Tex A&M Univ Pr.
Curry, Haskell B. Foundations of Mathematical Logic. 2nd ed. 1977. pap. 7.95 (ISBN 0-486-63462-0). Dover.
--Theory of Formal Deducibility. (Orig.). 1957. pap. 2.25x (ISBN 0-268-00274-6). U of Notre Dame Pr.
Curry, Hayden & Clifford, Denis. A Legal Guide for Lesbian & Gay Couples. 3rd ed. Warner, Ralph, ed. LC 80-18278. (Illus.). 272p. 1985. pap. 17.95 (ISBN 0-87337-004-X). Nolo Pr.
Curry, Herbert F., jt. auth. see Pollitt, Ronald.
Curry, J. E. & King, Glen D. Race Tensions & the Police. 152p. 1962. 14.75x (ISBN 0-398-00383-1). C C Thomas.
Curry, Jabez L. Brief Sketch of George Peabody, & a History of the Peabody Education Fund Through Thirty Years. LC 79-75530. (Illus.). Repr. of 1898 ed. 17.50x (ISBN 0-8371-1097-1, CUG&, Pub. by Negro U Pr). Greenwood.
Curry, Jane. The River's in My Blood: Riverboat Pilots Tell Their Stories. LC 82-11068. xx, 288p. 1983. 17.50 (ISBN 0-8032-1416-2). U of Nebr Pr.
--The River's in My Blood: Riverboat Pilots Tell Their Stories. LC 82-11068. (Illus.). xx, 298p. 1985. pap. 7.95 (ISBN 0-8032-6316-3, BB-916, Bison). U of Nebr Pr.
Curry, Jane, ed. see Holley, Marietta.
Curry, Jane L. The Bassumtyte Treasure. LC 77-14381. 136p. (gr. 4-7). 1978. 9.95 (ISBN 0-689-50100-5, McElderry Bk). Atheneum.
--The Black Book of Polish Censorship. LC 83-47813. 1984. 8.95 (ISBN 0-394-71734-1, Vin). Random.
--The Great Flood Mystery. LC 85-1322. 180p. (gr. 3-6). 1985. 12.95 (ISBN 0-689-50306-7, McElderry Bk). Atheneum.
--The Lost Farm. LC 73-85320. (Illus.). 138p. (gr. 3-7). 1974. 5.95 (ISBN 0-689-30427-7, McElderry Bk). Atheneum.
--Over the Sea's Edge. LC 70-152693. (Illus.). 182p. (gr. 4-6). 1971. 5.25 (ISBN 0-15-259010-2, HJ). HarBraceJ.
--Poor Tom's Ghost. LC 76-28468. 192p. (gr. 5-9). 1977. 8.95 (ISBN 0-689-50072-6, McElderry Bk). Atheneum.
--Press Control Around the World. LC 82-9837. 304p. 1982. 33.95 (ISBN 0-03-059869-9). Praeger.
--Shadow Dancers. LC 83-3733. 204p. (gr. 7 up). 1983. 10.95 (ISBN 0-689-50276-1, Argo). Atheneum.
--The Wolves of Aam. LC 80-24370. 204p. (gr. 7 up). 1981. 9.95 (ISBN 0-689-50173-0, Argo). Atheneum.
Curry, Jane L., ed. & tr. The Black Book of Polish Censorship: A Rand Corporation Research Study. 1984. 24.95 (ISBN 0-394-53291-0). Random.
Curry, Jane L., ed. Dissent in Eastern Europe. LC 83-2168. 240p. 1983. 31.95x (ISBN 0-03-062368-5). Praeger.
Curry, Jennifer. The Winemaker's Reference Book. (Illus.). 224p. 1985. 22.00 (ISBN 0-7153-8308-6). David & Charles.
Curry, Jess, Jr. & Bonner, David. How to Find & Buy Good Software: A Guide for Business & Professional People. (Illus.). 176p. 1983. 17.95 (ISBN 0-13-406660-X); pap. 8.95 (ISBN 0-13-406652-9). P-H.
Curry, Jess W., Jr. & Bonner, David M., eds. Up & Running: The Small Business Computer Implementation Cookbook. (Illus.). 150p. 1984. 17.95 (ISBN 0-13-937723-9); pap. 9.95 (ISBN 0-13-937715-8). P-H.
Curry, Jesse W., Jr., jt. auth. see Christie, Linda G.
Curry, John. Animal Skeletons. (Studies in Biology: No. 21). 56p. 1978. pap. text ed. 8.95 (ISBN 0-7131-2282-X). E Arnold.
Curry, Judith B. & Peppe, Kathryn K., eds. Mental Retardation: Nursing Approaches to Care. LC 77-26307. 246p. 1978. pap. text ed. 14.95 (ISBN 0-8016-1196-2). Mosby.
Curry, Kenneth. The Contributions of Robert Southey to the Morning Post. LC 82-15927. 224p. 1984. text ed. 19.75x (ISBN 0-8173-0139-9). U of Ala Pr.
--Sir Walter Scott's Edinburgh Annual Register. LC 77-8136. 1977. 18.95x (ISBN 0-87049-208-X). U of Tenn Pr.
Curry, Leah J. & Rood, Larry A. Head Start Parent Handbook. rev. ed. 1978. pap. 1.95x (ISBN 0-87659-600-6). Gryphon Hse.
Curry, Leonard, jt. auth. see MacMahon, Edward.
Curry, Leonard P. The Free Black in Urban America, 1800-1850: The Shadow of the Dream. LC 80-27811. (Illus.). 416p. 1981. lib. bdg. 30.00x (ISBN 0-226-13124-6). U of Chicago Pr.
Curry, Mary Margaret. The World of Mexican Cooking. pap. 4.95 (ISBN 0-8402-1191-0). Corona Pub.
Curry, Nancy L. Fencing. LC 82-83919. (Illus.). 144p. (Orig.). 1983. pap. 9.95 (ISBN 0-918438-99-3). Leisure Pr.
Curry, Neil, tr. see Euripides.
Curry, Nigel, jt. ed. see Blunden, John.
Curry, Peggy S. So Far from Spring. LC 83-21179. 344p. 1984. 16.95 (ISBN 0-87108-661-1); pap. 9.95 (ISBN 0-87108-677-8). Pruett.
--Summer Range. 52p. (Orig.). 1981. 10.00 (ISBN 0-937160-05-9); pap. 5.00 (ISBN 0-937160-04-0). Dooryard.
Curry, Peter. A B C. 32p. (ps-2). 1983. 3.95 (ISBN 0-8431-0782-0). Price Stern.
--Animals. (Peter Curry Bks.). (Illus.). 32p. 1984. 3.95 (ISBN 0-8431-0924-6). Price Stern.
--Clothes. (Peter Curry Board Bks.). 12p. (Orig.). 1984. 1.95 (ISBN 0-8431-1045-7). Price Stern.
--Colors. 32p. (ps-2). 1983. 3.95 (ISBN 0-8431-0781-2). Price Stern.
--The Good Night Book. (Peter Curry Board Bks.). 12p. 1984. 3.95 (ISBN 0-8431-1049-X). Price Stern.
--I Can Hear. (Peter Curry Bks.). (Illus.). 32p. 1984. 3.95 (ISBN 0-8431-0948-3). Price Stern.
--I Can See. (Peter Curry Bks.). (Illus.). 32p. 1984. 3.95 (ISBN 0-8431-0947-5). Price Stern.
--Indoors. (Peter Curry Board Bks.). 12p. 1984. 1.95 (ISBN 0-8431-1046-5). Price Stern.
--One, Two, Three. 32p. (ps-2). 1983. 3.95 (ISBN 0-8431-0783-9). Price Stern.
--Outside. (Peter Curry Board Bks.). 12p. (Orig.). 1984. pap. 1.95 (ISBN 0-8431-1047-3). Price Stern.
--Play. (Peter Curry Board Bks.). 12p. 1.95 (ISBN 0-8431-1044-9). Price Stern.
--Shapes. 32p. (ps-2). 1983. 3.95 (ISBN 0-8431-0784-7). Price Stern.
--Trucks, Trains, Boats, Planes. (Peter Curry Bks.). (Illus.). 32p. 1984. 3.95 (ISBN 0-8431-0923-8). Price Stern.
--You & Me-Me. (Peter Curry Board Bks.). 12p. (Orig.). 1984. 3.95 (ISBN 0-8431-1048-1). Price Stern.
Curry, R. N. Fundamentals of Natural Gas Conditioning. 118p. 1981. 39.95x (ISBN 0-87814-162-6). Pennwell Bks.
Curry, Richard O. & Cowden, Joanna D., eds. Slavery in America: Theodore Weld's American Slavery As It Is. LC 71-174160. (Primary Sources in American History Ser.). 1972. text ed. 12.95x (ISBN 0-88295-780-5); pap. text ed. 6.95x (ISBN 0-88295-781-3). Harlan Davidson.
Curry, Robert. Bahamian Lore. 1976. lib. bdg. 69.95 (ISBN 0-8490-1378-X). Gordon Pr.
--Training for Trainers: The Technique. (Serving the Elderly Ser.: Pt. 6). 1979. pap. text ed. 11.00 (ISBN 0-89634-008-2, 048). New England Geron.
Curry, Robert L., Jr., jt. auth. see Rothchild, Donald.
Curry, Roy W. Woodrow Wilson & Far Eastern Policy, 1913-1921. 1968. lib. bdg. 29.00x (ISBN 0-374-91957-7). Octagon.
Curry, S. E. Vocal & Literary Interpretation of the Bible. 1979. Repr. of 1903 ed. 30.00 (ISBN 0-8414-9988-8). Folcroft.
Curry, S. S. Browning & the Dramatic Monologue. LC 65-26455. (Studies in Browning, No. 4). 1969. Repr. of 1908 ed. lib. bdg. 75.00x (ISBN 0-8383-0535-0). Haskell.
--Vocal & Literary Interpretation of the Bible. 1909. 22.50 (ISBN 0-8274-3677-7). R West.
Curry, Stephen H. Drug Disposition & Pharmacokinetics. 3rd ed. (Illus.). 344p. 1981. pap. text ed. 37.00 (ISBN 0-632-00639-0, B-1126-1). Mosby.
Curry, Stephen H. & Whelpton, Robin. Manual of Laboratory Pharmacokinetics: Experiments in Biopharmaceutics, Biochemical Pharmacology, & Pharmacokinetics with a Consideration of Relevant Instrumental & Chromatographic Techniques. LC 82-2643. 189p. 1983. 24.95 (ISBN 0-471-10247-4, Pub. by Wiley-Interscience). Wiley.
Curry, Susan & Rich, Susan, eds. Kline Guide to the Chemical Industry. 4th ed. (Illus.). 590p. 1980. pap. 147.00 (ISBN 0-917148-13-4). Kline.
Curry, Thomas S., III, et al. Christensen's Introduction to the Physics of Diagnostic Radiology. 3rd ed. LC 84-3951. (Illus.). 515p. 1984. text ed. 30.00 (ISBN 0-8121-0918-X). Lea & Febiger.
Curry, Timothy & Jiobu, Robert. Sports: A Social Perspective. (Illus.). 288p. 1984. 21.95 (ISBN 0-13-837823-1). P-H.
Curry, Timothy J. & Clarke, Alfred C. Introducing Visual Sociology. (Illus.). 1983. pap. text ed. 9.95 (ISBN 0-8403-3082-0, 403-88201). Kendall-Hunt.
Curry, W. H. Sun Rising on the West: The Saga of Henry Clay & Elizabeth Smith. 1979. 20.00x (ISBN 0-686-31817-X). Crosby County.
Curry, W. Lawrence, ed. Anthems for the Junior Choir, 5 bks. 1.50 ea. Westminster.
--Service Music for the Adult Choir. 3.50 ea. (ISBN 0-664-10059-7). Westminster.
--Songs & Hymns for Primary Children. (gr. 1-3). 1978. softcover 3.95 (ISBN 0-664-10117-8). Westminster.
Curry, Walter C. Demonic Metaphysics of Macbeth. (Studies in Shakespeare, No. 24). 1970. pap. 40.00x (ISBN 0-8383-0020-0). Haskell.
--Middle English Ideal of Personal Beauty, As Found in the Metrical Romances, Chronicles & Legends of the Thirteenth, Fourteenth & Fifteenth Centuries. LC 77-25152. 1916. lib. bdg. 10.00 (ISBN 0-8414-0905-6). Folcroft.
--Middle English Ideal of Personal Beauty. LC 70-180443. Repr. of 1916 ed. 11.50 (ISBN 0-404-01886-6). AMS Pr.
--Milton's Ontology, Cosmogony & Physics. LC 57-5833. (Illus.). 226p. 1957. pap. 6.00x (ISBN 0-8131-0102-6). U Pr of Ky.
--Shakespeare's Philosophical Patterns. 12.50 (ISBN 0-8446-0567-0). Peter Smith.
Curry-Lindahl, Kai. Bird Migration in Africa, Vol. I. LC 80-40245. 1982. 99.50 (ISBN 0-12-200101-X). Acad Pr.
--Report to the Government of Liberia on Conservation Management & Utilization of Wildlife Resources. (Illus.). 31p. 1969. pap. 8.00 (ISBN 2-88032-044-5, IUCN61, IUCN). Unipub.
--Wildlife of the Prairies & Plains. LC 80-27927. (Wildlife Habitat Ser.). (Illus.). 232p. 1981. 19.95 (ISBN 0-8109-1766-1). Abrams.
Curry Woods, Marjorie, ed. An Early Commentary on the Poetria Nova of Geoffrey of Vinsauf. LC 83-48228. (Medieval Studies Ser.). 500p. 1985. lib. bdg. 66.00 (ISBN 0-8240-9435-2). Garland Pub.
Curson, Julie P. A Guide's Guide to Philadelphia. 4th rev. ed. LC 81-67768. (Illus.). 496p. (Orig.). 1982. pap. text ed. 6.95 (ISBN 0-913694-04-5). Curson Hse.
Curt, E., ed. see Wohlstein, Herman.
Curtain, Mary. Armond & the First Christmas. (Arch Bk.: No. 16). (Illus.). 1979. 0.99 (ISBN 0-570-06129-6, 59-1247). Concordia.
Curtain, R. F., ed. see Control Theory Centre Symposium, University of Warwick, 1972.
Curtain, Ruth & Pritchard, A. J., eds. Functional Analysis in Modern Applied Mathematics. 1977. 59.50 (ISBN 0-12-196250-4). Acad Pr.
Curtas, Ted. Tears of Joy. 3.95 (ISBN 0-686-12741-2); pap. 3.95 (ISBN 0-686-12742-0). Grace Pub Co.
Curtayne, Alice. Recall to Dante. LC 77-101025. 1969. Repr. of 1932 ed. 19.50x (ISBN 0-8046-0692-7, Pub. by Kennikat). Assoc Faculty Pr.
--St. Catherine of Siena. LC 80-53745. 1980. pap. 7.50 (ISBN 0-89555-162-4). Tan Bks Pubs.
Curteis, A., jt. auth. see Given-Wilson, C.
Curthoys, Ann & Merritt, John, eds. Australia's First Cold War. 280p. 1985. text ed. 27.50x (ISBN 0-86861-465-3); pap. text ed. 13.50x (ISBN 0-86861-473-4). Allen Unwin.
Curthoys, J. S., jt. ed. see Atrens, D. M.
Curti, Carlos. Skouras, King of Fox Studios. (Orig.). 1967. pap. 0.95 (ISBN 0-87067-141-3, BH141). Holloway.
Curti, Merle. American Paradox: The Conflict of Thought & Action. LC 72-11304. 116p. 1973. Repr. of 1956 ed. lib. bdg. 15.00x (ISBN 0-8371-6647-0, CUAP). Greenwood.
--American Philanthropy Abroad: A History. 1963. 42.50 (ISBN 0-8135-0422-8). Rutgers U Pr.
--Growth of American Thought. 3rd ed. LC 81-3433. 949p. 1981. pap. 19.95 (ISBN 0-87855-879-9). Transaction Bks.
--Human Nature in American Thought: A History. LC 79-3965. 472p. 1980. 35.00x (ISBN 0-299-07970-8). U of Wis Pr.
--The Making of an American Community: A Case Study of Democracy in a Frontier County. 1959. 32.50x (ISBN 0-8047-0534-8). Stanford U Pr.
--The Nineteen Twenties in Historical Perpective. (Cotton Memorial Papers). pap. 3.00 (ISBN 0-87404-076-0). Tex Western.
--Probing Our Past. 1959. 12.00 (ISBN 0-8446-1140-9). Peter Smith.
--Social Ideas of American Educators. (Quality Paperback Ser.: No. 105). 613p. 1978. pap. 6.95 (ISBN 0-8226-0105-2). Littlefield.
Curti, Merle E. American Peace Crusade, Eighteen Fifteen to Eighteen Sixty. 1965. lib. bdg. 18.50x (ISBN 0-374-91976-3). Octagon.
--Bryan & World Peace. LC 77-147453. (Library of War & Peace; Peace Leaders: Biographies & Memoirs). lib. bdg. 46.00 (ISBN 0-8240-0247-4). Garland Pub.
--Bryan & World Peace. 1969. lib. bdg. 17.00x (ISBN 0-374-91996-8). Octagon.
--The Learned Blacksmith: The Letters & Journals of Elihu Burritt. LC 70-137536. (Peace Movement in America Ser). ix, 241p. 1972. Repr. of 1937 ed. lib. bdg. 16.95x (ISBN 0-89198-063-6). Ozer.
--Peace or War: The American Struggle 1635-1936. 1959. Repr. of 1936 ed. 15.00x (ISBN 0-910324-03-4). Canner.
--Peace or War: The American Struggle, 1636-1936. LC 70-143428. (Peace Movement in America Ser.). 374p. 1972. Repr. of 1936 ed. lib. bdg. 20.95x (ISBN 0-89198-064-4). Ozer.
Curti, Merle E. & Birr, Kendall. Prelude to Point Four: American Technical Missions Overseas 1838 to 1938. LC 78-4874. 284p. 1978. Repr. of 1954 ed. lib. bdg. 21.25x (ISBN 0-313-20397-0, CUPP). Greenwood.
Curti, Merle E., jt. auth. see Burritt, Elihu.
Curti, Merle E., ed. Learned Blacksmith: The Letters & Journals of Elihu Burritt. Bd. with Congress of Nations: Addresses at the International Peace Congresses at Brussels (1848), Paris (1849), & Frankfort (1850) Burritt, Elihu. LC 72-147721. (Library of War & Peace; Peace Leaders: Biographies & Memoirs). 1972. lib. bdg. 46.00 (ISBN 0-8240-0248-2). Garland Pub.
Curti, Merle E., et al. History of American Civilization. facs. ed. LC 68-29199. (Essay Index Reprint Ser.). 1953. 39.00 (ISBN 0-8369-1031-1). Ayer Co Pubs.
Curtice, David & James Patton Systems Control, Inc. Handbook of the Operation of Small Wind Turbines on a Utility Distribution System. 2nd ed. (Illus.). 192p. 1984. pap. text ed. 49.50 (ISBN 0-88016-009-8). Windbks.
Curtice, Harlow H. & Finney, Frederick M. Development & Growth of the General Motors Corporation: An Economic Analysis, 1908-1955. 1979. 8.95 (ISBN 0-89421-006-8). Challenge Pr.
Curtice, Randolph. The Age of Curiosity: Especially for Grandmothers. (Illus.). 1978. 7.50 (ISBN 0-9601722-0-3). North Lake Prod.
Curtice, Robert M. Access Mechanisms & Data Structure Support in Data Base Management Systems. (Data Base Monograph: No. 1). 1975. pap. 15.00 (ISBN 0-89435-017-X). QED Info Sci.
--Planning for Data Base Systems. (Data Base Monograph: No. 2). 1976. pap. 15.00 (ISBN 0-89435-018-8). QED Info Sci.
Curtice, Robert M. & Jones, Paul E., Jr. Logical Data Base Design. (Van Nos Reinhold Data Processing Ser.). 272p. 1982. 34.50 (ISBN 0-442-24501-7). Van Nos Reinhold.
Curtice, Robert M., ed. see Carroll, John M.
Curtice, Robert M., ed. see Chen, Peter.
Curtice, Robert M., ed. see Jones, Paul E., Jr.
Curties, T. J. The Monk of Udolpho: A Romance. Varma, Sir Devendra P., ed. LC 77-2037. (Gothic Novels III). 1977. lib. bdg. 92.50x (ISBN 0-405-10136-8). Ayer Co Pubs.
Curtin & London Editors. The Book of 35mm Photography: A Complete Guide for Creative Photographers. (Illus.). 176p. 1983. pap. 15.95 (ISBN 0-930764-41-2). Curtin & London.
Curtin, Bernadette M., jt. auth. see Hecklinger, Fred J.
Curtin, Brain J. The Myopias: Basic Science & Clinical Managemant. (Illus.). 500p. 1985. text ed. write for info. (ISBN 0-06-140672-4, Harper Medical). Lippincott.
Curtin, Deane W. The Aesthetic Dimension of Science. LC 81-19243. 1982. 12.50 (ISBN 0-8022-2393-1). Philos Lib.
Curtin, Dennis. Into Your Darkroom: Step-by-Step. (Illus.). 96p. (Orig.). 1981. pap. 12.95 (ISBN 0-930764-24-2). Curtin & London.
--Your Automatic Camera. (Your Automatic Camera Ser.). (Illus.). 128p. (Orig.). 1980. pap. 6.95 (ISBN 0-930764-17-X). Curtin & London.
Curtin, Dennis & Alves, Jeff. Controlling Financial Performance for Higher Profits: An Apple Business User's Guide. 160p. 1983. pap. 14.95 (ISBN 0-930764-58-7). Van Nos Reinhold.

--Controlling Financial Performance for Higher Profits: An IBM-PC Business User's Guide. 160p. 1983. pap. 14.95 (ISBN 0-930764-57-9); software disk 29.95 (ISBN 0-930764-68-4); bk. & disk 39.95 (ISBN 0-930764-78-1). Van Nos Reinhold.

Curtin, Dennis & Alves, Jefffey. Controlling Financial Performance: Apple Business Users Guide. (Illus.). 224p. (Orig.). 1983. pap. 15.50. Curtin & London.

Curtin, Dennis & Alves, Jeffrey. Controlling Financial Performance: An IBM-PC Business Users Guide. (Illus.). 160p. (Orig.). 1983. pap. 15.50 (ISBN 0-930764-57-9). Curtin & London.

Curtin, Dennis & DeMaio, Joe. The Darkroom Handbook: A Complete Guide to the Best Design, Construction & Equipment. (Illus.). 1979. 17.95 (ISBN 0-930764-08-0); pap. 12.95 (ISBN 0-930764-06-4). Curtin & London.

Curtin, Dennis & London, Barbara. What Are You Doing Wrong with Your Automatic Camera. (Your Automatic Camera Ser.). (Illus.). 144p. (Orig.). 1980. pap. 6.95 (ISBN 0-930764-20-X). Curtin & London.

Curtin, Dennis, jt. auth. see Alves, Jeff.

Curtin, Dennis, jt. auth. see Osgood, William.

Curtin, Dennis, et al. Controlling Financial Performance: A 1-2-3 Business User's Guide. 1983. 16.95 (ISBN 0-930764-73-0). Van Nos Reinhold.

Curtin, Dennis, jt. auth. see Alves, Jeffrey.

Curtin, Dennis P. Manager's Guide to Framework: An Illustrated Short Course. 160p. 1985. pap. 18.95 (ISBN 0-13-550070-2). P-H.

--Manager's Guide to Symphony: An Illustrated Short Course. 160p. 1985. pap. 18.95 (ISBN 0-13-550047-8). P-H.

--The WordStar Handbook. (Illus.). 160p. (Orig.). 1983. pap. 16.50 (ISBN 0-930764-64-1). Curtin & London.

--The WordStar Handbook. 1984. pap. 15.95 (Co-published by Curtin & London). Van Nos Reinhold.

Curtin, Dennis P. & Osgood, William R. Preparing Your Business Budget with Symphony. (Illus.). 160p. 1985. pap. 21.95 (ISBN 0-13-698804-0). P-H.

Curtin, Dennis P., jt. auth. see Alves, Jeffrey R.

Curtin, Dennis P., jt. auth. see Molloy, James F.

Curtin, Dennis P., jt. auth. see Molloy, James F., Jr.

Curtin, Dennis P., jt. auth. see Osgood, William R.

Curtin, Dennis P., jt. auth. see Robbins, Jane E.

Curtin, Dennis P., et al. Controlling Financial Performance: A 1-2-3 Business User's Guide. (Illus.). 176p. (Orig.). 1983. pap. 17.50 (ISBN 0-930764-73-0). Curtin & London.

--Controlling Financial Performance for Higher Profits: A Multiplan Business User's Guide. (Illus.). 176p. 1984. pap. 19.50 (ISBN 0-930764-87-0); disk 29.95. Van Nos Reinhold.

Curtin, Dennis P., jt. auth. see Alves, Jeffrey R.

Curtin, Jeremiah. Journey in Southern Siberia: The Mongols, Their Religion & Their Myths. LC 77-115526. (Russia Observed Ser). (Illus.). 1971. Repr. of 1909 ed. 24.50 (ISBN 0-405-03079-7). Ayer Co Pubs.

--The Mongols: A History. LC 72-6183. 426p. 1973. Repr. of 1908 ed. lib. bdg. 26.75x (ISBN 0-8371-5445-6, CUMO). Greenwood.

--Myths & Folk-Lore of Ireland. 1976. Repr. 18.00x (ISBN 0-7158-1090-1). Charles River Bks.

--Myths & Folk Tales of Ireland. LC 69-18206. 256p. 1975. pap. 4.50 (ISBN 0-486-22430-9). Dover.

--Myths & Folk-Tales of the Russians, Western Slavs, & Magyars. LC 74-160611. Repr. of 1890 ed. 31.00 (ISBN 0-405-08414-5, Blom Pubns). Ayer Co Pubs.

--Myths & Folktales of the Russians, Western Slavs, & Magyars. 1977. lib. bdg. 59.95 (ISBN 0-8490-2326-2). Gordon Pr.

--Myths of the Modocs: Indian Legends from the Northwest. LC 74-170711. Repr. of 1912 ed. 20.00 (ISBN 0-405-08415-3, Blom Pubns). Ayer Co Pubs.

--Tales of the Fairies & the Ghost-World. LC 75-152760. Repr. of 1895 ed. 20.00 (ISBN 0-405-08416-1, Blom Pubns). Ayer Co Pubs.

Curtin, Jeremiah, tr. see Sienkiewicz, Henryk.

Curtin, Kaier. We Can Always Call Them Bulgarians. (Illus.). 280p. 1986. 13.95 (ISBN 0-932870-36-8). Alyson Pubns.

Curtin, Katie. Women in China. LC 74-14166. 96p. 1975. 12.00 (ISBN 0-87348-404-5); pap. 2.95 (ISBN 0-87348-405-3). Path Pr NY.

Curtin, L. S. By the Prophet of the Earth: Ethnobotany of the Pima. LC 83-24334. (Illus.). 156p. 1984. pap. 6.95 (ISBN 0-8165-0854-2). U of Ariz Pr.

Curtin, Leah & Flaherty, M. Josephine. Nursing Ethics: Theories & Pragmatics. LC 81-17962. (Illus.). 378p. 1981. pap. text ed. 16.95 (ISBN 0-89303-053-8). Brady Comm.

Curtin, Leslie. Status of Women: A Comparative Analysis of Twenty Developing Countries. 60p. 1982. avail. Population Ref.

Curtin, Marilyn & Hall, Mary B. Scientific Dressing: Your Precise Image. (Illus.). 104p. (Orig.). 1985. pap. 9.95 (ISBN 0-9615141-9-1). Ro-Lyn Ind.

Curtin, Mary E., ed. Symposium on Love. LC 73-10475. 244p. 1973. text ed. 26.95 (ISBN 0-87705-116-X). Human Sci Pr.

Curtin, Michael. The Replay. LC 81-15536. 271p. 1982. 9.95 (ISBN 0-8076-1027-5). Braziller.

Curtin, Philip, jt. auth. see Bohannan, Paul.

Curtin, Philip, et al. African History. 1978. pap. text ed. 16.95 (ISBN 0-316-16542-5). Little.

Curtin, Philip D. Atlantic Slave Trade: A Census. 358p. 1969. pap. 11.95x (ISBN 0-299-05404-7). U of Wis Pr.

--Cross-Cultural Trade in World History. LC 83-23202. (Studies in Comparative World History). 352p. 1984. 34.50 (ISBN 0-521-26319-0); pap. 9.95 (ISBN 0-521-26931-8). Cambridge U Pr.

--Cross-Cultural Trade in World History. 304p. 1984. 34.50 (ISBN 0-521-26319-0); pap. 9.95 (ISBN 0-521-26931-8). Cambridge U Pr.

--Economic Change in Precolonial Africa: Senegambia in the Era of the Slave Trade, 2 vols. LC 74-5899. (Illus.). 1975. Vol. 1, 394p. 35.00x (ISBN 0-299-06640-1); Supplementary Evidence, 164p. 35.00x (ISBN 0-299-06650-9). U of Wis Pr.

--Image of Africa: British Ideas & Action, 1780-1850, 2 vols. in 1. (Illus.). 1964. 37.50x (ISBN 0-299-03020-2); Vol. 1, 302p. pap. 9.95x (ISBN 0-299-83025-X); Vol. 2, 248p. pap. 9.95x (ISBN 0-299-83026-8). U of Wis Pr.

--Precolonial African History. LC 73-93606. (AHA Pamphlets: No. 501). (Illus.). 60p. 1974. pap. text ed. 1.50 (ISBN 0-87229-017-4). Am Hist Assn.

--Two Jamaicas: The Role of Ideas in a Tropical Colony, 1830-1865. LC 69-10082. (Illus.). 1968. Repr. of 1955 ed. lib. bdg. 22.75 (ISBN 0-8371-0055-0, CUTJ). Greenwood.

Curtin, Philip D., ed. Africa & the West: Intellectual Responses to European Culture. LC 77-176409. 272p. 1972. 30.00x (ISBN 0-299-06121-3); pap. 13.50x (ISBN 0-299-06124-8). U of Wis Pr.

--Africa Remembered: Narratives by West Africans from the Era of the Slave Trade. (Illus.). 1967. 25.00x (ISBN 0-299-04281-2); pap. 13.50x (ISBN 0-299-04284-7). U of Wis Pr.

Curtin, Richard. Running Your Own Show: Mastering the Basics of Small Business. 1983. pap. 4.50 (ISBN 0-451-62400-9, Ment). NAL.

Curtin, Richard T. Running Your Own Show: Mastering the Basics of Small Business. LC 81-14746. (Wiley Series on Small Business Management). 226p. 1982. 17.95 (ISBN 0-471-86074-3, Pub. by Ronald Pr). Wiley.

Curtin, Richard T., ed. Surveys of Consumers, 1974-75: Contributions to Behavioral Economics. LC 72-619718. 336p. 1976. 16.00x (ISBN 0-87944-209-3). Inst Soc Res.

Curtin, Rosalie, et al. R. C. I. A. A Practical Approach to Christian Initiation. 136p. (Orig.). 1981. pap. 10.95 (ISBN 0-697-01759-1). Wm C Brown.

Curtin, Sharon R. Nobody Ever Died of Old Age. LC 72-6157. 1973. (Pub. by Atlantic Monthly Pr); pap. 7.70i (ISBN 0-316-16547-6, Pub by Atlantic Monthly Pr.). Little.

Curtin, Timothy & Murray, David. Economic Sanctions & Rhodesia. (Institute of Economic Affairs, Research Monographs: No. 12). 1968. pap. 2.50 technical (ISBN 0-685-20574-6). Transatlantic.

Curtin, W. G. Structural Masonry Detailing. (Illus.). 256p. 1984. text ed. 59.00x (ISBN 0-246-11850-4, Pub. by Granada England). Sheridan.

Curtin, W. G., et al. Structural Masonry Designer's Manual. (Illus.). 448p. 1982. text ed. 85.00x (ISBN 0-246-11208-5). Sheridan.

Curtin, William M., ed. see Cather, Willa.

Curtis. Invasion of the Brain Sharpeners. LC 80-21434. (Capers Ser.). (Illus.). 128p. (gr. 3-6). 1981. PLB 1.95 (ISBN 0-394-84676-1); pap. 4.99 (ISBN 0-394-94676-6). Knopf.

--Sweelinck's Keyboard Music. (Publications of Sir Thomas Browne Institute: No. 4). 1972. lib. bdg. 23.00 (ISBN 90-6021-062-X, Pub. by Leiden Univ. Holland). Kluwer Academic.

Curtis, et al. Educational Resources Management System. 3.75 (ISBN 0-685-57172-6). Assn Sch Busn.

Curtis, A. S. Cell Surface: Its Molecular Role in Morphogenesis. 1967. 76.50 (ISBN 0-12-199650-6). Acad Pr.

Curtis, A. S., ed. Cell-Cell Recognition. LC 77-28646. (Society for Experimental Biology: Symposia No. 32). (Illus.). 1978. 82.50 (ISBN 0-521-22020-3). Cambridge U Pr.

Curtis, A. S. & Pitts, J. D., eds. Cell Adhesion & Motility. LC 79-53315. (British Society for Cell Biology Symposium Ser.: No. 3). 1980. 110.00 (ISBN 0-521-22936-7). Cambridge U Pr.

Curtis, Alan R. Practical Math for Business. 3d ed. LC 82-84521. 368p. 1983. 22.95 (ISBN 0-395-32698-2); instr's. annotated ed. 23.95 (ISBN 0-395-32699-0). HM.

Curtis, Albert B. White Pines & Fires: Cooperative Forestry in Idaho. LC 82-84295. (Gem Books-Historical). (Illus.). 200p. 1983. 19.95 (ISBN 0-89301-090-1). U Pr of Idaho.

Curtis, Anthony. The Lyle Official Antiques Review. (Illus.). 672p. 1985. pap. 10.95 (ISBN 0-399-51179-2, Lyle). Putnam Pub Group.

Curtis, Anthony, compiled by. Antiques & Their Values. Incl. China (ISBN 0-698-11121-4); Furniture (ISBN 0-698-11159-1); Glass (ISBN 0-698-11158-3); Silver (ISBN 0-698-11160-5). 1982. pap. 5.95 ea. (Coward). Putnam Pub Group.

--The Lyle Official Antiques Review, 1985. (Illus.). 672p. 1984. pap. 9.95 (ISBN 0-399-51088-5, Perigee). Putnam Pub Group.

Curtis, Anthony, ed. see James, Henry.

Curtis, Arthur F. A Treatise on the Law of Arson. lxviii, 689p. 1936. lib. bdg. 38.50 (ISBN 0-89941-371-4). W S Hein.

Curtis, Audrey. A Curriculum for the Pre-School Child. 192p. 1985. pap. 14.00x (ISBN 0-7005-0640-3, Pub. by NFER Nelson UK). Taylor & Francis.

Curtis, Audrey & Blatchford, Peter. Meeting the Needs of Socially Handicapped Children: The Background of "My World". 128p. 1981. 16.00x (ISBN 0-85633-227-5, Pub. by NFER Nelson UK). Taylor & Francis.

Curtis, Audrey & Hill, Sheelagh. My World: A Handbook of Ideas. 158p. 1978. 11.00 (ISBN 0-85633-156-2, Pub. by NFER Nelson UK). Taylor & Francis.

Curtis, Benjamin R. A Memoir of Benjamin Robbins Curtis, 2 Vols. LC 77-75298. (The American Scene Ser.). 1970. Repr. of 1879 ed. 115.00 (ISBN 0-306-71267-9). Da Capo.

Curtis, Bill. Human Factors in Software Development. (Tutorial Texts Ser.). 641p. 1981. 36.00 (ISBN 0-8186-0390-9, Q390). IEEE Comp Soc.

--Tutorial: Human Factors in Software Development. 2nd ed. 780p. 1985. 48.00 (ISBN 0-8186-0577-4); prepub. 32.00 (ISBN 0-317-31801-2). IEEE Comp Soc.

Curtis, Bob. Food Service Security: Internal Control. LC 75-33513. 256p. 1975. 21.95 (ISBN 0-86730-214-3). Lebhar Friedman.

--Security Control: External Theft. LC 76-163714. (Security Control Ser.). 1971. 21.95 (ISBN 0-86730-504-5). Lebhar Friedman.

--Security Control: Internal Theft. LC 72-90623. (Security Control Ser.). 1973. 21.95 (ISBN 0-86730-503-7). Lebhar Friedman.

Curtis, Brian. Life of the Fish: His Manners & Morals. (Illus.). 12.75 (ISBN 0-8446-1933-7). Peter Smith.

--Life Story of the Fish. 2nd ed. 1949. pap. 5.95 (ISBN 0-486-20929-6). Dover.

Curtis, Brian A., et al. An Introduction to the Neurosciences. LC 74-145556. (Illus.). 830p. 1972. 27.50 (ISBN 0-7216-2810-9). Saunders.

Curtis, Bruce. William Graham Sumner. (United States Authors Ser.). 1981. lib. bdg. 13.50 (ISBN 0-8057-7324-X, Twayne). G K Hall.

Curtis, C. J. Task of Philosophical Theology. LC 67-17634. 1968. 4.50 (ISBN 0-8022-0328-0). Philos Lib.

Curtis, C. Michael, ed. see Burke, Alan D.

Curtis, C. W. Linear Algebra: An Introductory Approach. (Undergraduate Texts in Mathematics Ser.). (Illus.). 340p. 1984. 24.00 (ISBN 0-387-90992-3). Springer-Verlag.

Curtis, Carl T. & Courtemanche, Regis. Forty Years Against the Tide: A Washington Memoir. 350p. 1985. 18.95 (ISBN 0-89526-590-7). Regnery-Gateway.

Curtis, Carolyn, ed. Before the Rainbow: What We Know about Acid Rain. (Decisionmakers Bookshelf Ser.: Vol. 9). (Illus.). 102p. (Orig.). 1980. pap. 2.50 (ISBN 0-931032-09-1). Edison Electric.

Curtis, Charles, et al. Perspectives on God: Sociological, Theological & Philosophical. LC 78-62943. 1978. pap. text ed. 11.25 (ISBN 0-8191-0605-4). U Pr of Amer.

Curtis, Charles H. & Gibson, W. The Book of Topiary. LC 84-50509. (Illus.). 160p. 1985. pap. 6.50 (ISBN 0-8048-1491-0). C E Tuttle.

Curtis, Charles K., jt. auth. see Shaver, James K.

Curtis, Charles P. The Modern Prudent Investor - What the General Practitioner Should Know About Investments: No. B236. 145p. 1961. pap. 2.64 (ISBN 0-317-30825-4). Am Law Inst.

Curtis, Charles P., Jr. & Greenslet, Ferris. The Practical Cogitator: The Thinker's Anthology. 1983. pap. 8.95 (ISBN 0-395-34635-5); pap. 53.70 6-copy prepack (ISBN 0-395-34931-1). HM.

Curtis, Charles W. & Reiner, Irving. Methods of Representation Theory: With Applications to Finite Groups & Orders, Vol. I. LC 81-7416. (Pure & Applied Mathematics: Wiley-Interscience Series of Tests, Monographs & Tracts). 819p. 1981. 69.50x (ISBN 0-471-18994-4, Pub. by Wiley-Interscience). Wiley.

--Representation Theory of Finite Groups & Associative Algebras. LC 62-16994. (Pure & Applied Mathematics Ser.). 685p. 1962. 69.50 (ISBN 0-470-18975-4, Pub. by Wiley-Interscience). Wiley.

Curtis, Chris & Post, Don. Be Your Own Chimney Sweep. LC 79-12608. (Illus.). 1979. pap. 5.95 (ISBN 0-88266-157-4). Garden Way Pub.

Curtis, Christopher, et al. Whole-Body Autoradiography. (Biological Techniques Ser.). 1981. 35.00 (ISBN 0-12-199660-3). Acad Pr.

Curtis, D. Progress & Eternal Recurrence in the Work of Gabriel Naude. (Occasional Papers in Modern Languages: No. 4). 53p. 1967. pap. text ed. 5.75x (ISBN 0-317-13264-4, Pub. by U Hull England). Humanities.

Curtis, D. R. & McIntyre, A. K., eds. Studies in Physiology Presented to John C. Eccles. (Illus.). 1965. 25.00 (ISBN 0-387-03411-0). Springer-Verlag.

Curtis, D. R., jt. ed. see Simpson, Lance.

Curtis, Dan B. & Brewer, Robert S. Speaking As a Farmer: Winning FFA Speeches, Principles of Speech Preparation & Presentation. 256p. 1980. pap. text ed. 10.95 (ISBN 0-8403-2248-8). Kendall-Hunt.

Curtis, David. Learn While You Sleep. 2nd ed. LC 60-15692. 1964. 5.00 (ISBN 0-87212-007-4); pap. 2.95 (ISBN 0-87212-008-2). Libra.

Curtis, David A. Strategic Planning for Smaller Business: Improving Corporate Performance & Personal Reward. LC 82-48171. 224p. 1983. 22.00 (ISBN 0-669-06011-9); pap. 11.00x (ISBN 0-669-09815-9). Lexington Bks.

Curtis, David B., jt. auth. see Shewchun, John S.

Curtis, Denis, et al. Dead Martyrs & Living Heroes. LC 83-61651. 260p. 13.95 (ISBN 0-88400-097-4). Shengold.

Curtis, Don B., jt. auth. see Brewer, Robert S.

Curtis, Donald. The Christ-Based Teachings. LC 75-40657. 1976. 4.95 (ISBN 0-87159-016-6). Unity School.

--Daily Power for Joyful Living. 1975. pap. 5.00 (ISBN 0-87980-300-2). Wilshire.

--How to Be Great. 1985. pap. 5.00 (ISBN 0-87980-410-6). Wilshire.

--Human Problems & How to Solve Them. 1975. pap. 5.00 (ISBN 0-87980-298-7). Wilshire.

--Science of Mind in Daily Living. 1975. pap. 5.00 (ISBN 0-87980-299-5). Wilshire.

--The Way of the Christ. 1974. 4.95 (ISBN 0-87159-169-3). Unity School.

--Your Thoughts Can Change Your Life. pap. 5.00 (ISBN 0-87980-179-4). Wilshire.

Curtis, Donald A. Fantasy on Sunset Mountain. LC 82-74122. 44p. (Orig.). (gr. 3-12). 1982. pap. 3.50 (ISBN 0-9610284-0-8). D A Curtis.

Curtis, Doris M. Sedimentary Processes: Diagenesis. (Society of Economic Paleontologists & Mineralogists, Reprint Ser.: No. 1). pap. 55.50 (ISBN 0-317-27145-8, 2024747). Bks Demand UMI.

Curtis, Doris M., et al. How to (Try to) Find on Oil Field. 94p. 1981. 23.95x (ISBN 0-87814-166-9). Pennwell Bks.

Curtis, Dunn see Bellairs, Ruth, et al.

Curtis, Edith R. Season in Utopia: The Story of Brook Farm. LC 74-102485. 1971. Repr. of 1961 ed. 25.00x (ISBN 0-8462-1510-1). Russell.

Curtis, Edmund. History of Ireland. 6th ed. 1961. pap. 15.95x (ISBN 0-416-67730-4, NO. 2158). Methuen Inc.

--A History of Medieval Ireland from 1086 to 1513. 1976. lib. bdg. 59.95 (ISBN 0-8490-1977-X). Gordon Pr.

--Roger of Sicily & the Normans in Lower Italy, 1016-1154. LC 70-180443. (Heroes of the Nation Ser.). Repr. of 1912 ed. 30.00 (ISBN 0-404-56536-0). AMS Pr.

Curtis, Edmund & McDowell, R. B., eds. Irish Historical Documents. 1977. 41.00x (ISBN 0-416-85930-5, NO.2627). Methuen Inc.

Curtis, Edward E. Organization of the British Army in the American Revolution. LC 73-91297. 1969. Repr. of 1926 ed. 22.50 (ISBN 0-404-01887-4). AMS Pr.

--The Organization of the British Army in the American Revolution. LC 72-131679. 223p. 1972. Repr. of 1926 ed. 39.00 (ISBN 0-403-00566-3). Scholarly.

Curtis, Edward S. In the Land of Head-Hunters. (Illus.). 114p. 1978. 7.95 (ISBN 0-913668-48-6); pap. 3.95 (ISBN 0-913668-47-8). Ten Speed Pr.

--Indian Days of the Long Ago. (Illus.). 1978. 8.95 (ISBN 0-913668-46-X); pap. 5.95 (ISBN 0-913668-45-1). Ten Speed Pr.

--The North American Indian, Being a Series of Volumes Picturing & Describing the Indians of the U. S. & Alaska, 20 Vols., Supplement to Vol. 1-20 in 4 Vols, Vols. 4-8, 10-16, 18, 19. (Reprint, Orig, Pub, 1907-1930). 1970. Set. 1800.00 (ISBN 0-384-10395-2); 85.00 ea.; supplements 95.00 ea. Johnson Repr.

--Selected Writings of Edward S. Curtis. 3rd ed. Gifford, Barry, ed. LC 76-7891. (Illus.). 200p. 1976. pap. 6.95 (ISBN 0-916870-00-6). Creative Arts Bk.

Curtis, Elwood A. A Wet Butt & a Hungry Gut. LC 74-84152. 1974. 3.98 (ISBN 0-910244-81-2). Blair.

Curtis, Emily B. Reflected Glory in a Bottle: Chinese Snuff Bottle Portraits. (Illus.). 128p. 1980. 25.00 (ISBN 0-9605096-0-7, Pub. by). C E Tuttle.

Curtis, Eugene W. The French Assembly of 1848 & American Constitutional Doctrines. 1980. lib. bdg. 27.50x (ISBN 0-374-92011-7). Octagon.

--Saint-Just, Colleague of Robespierre. LC 73-14540. xi, 402p. 1973. Repr. of 1935 ed. lib. bdg. 31.50x (ISBN 0-374-92010-9). Octagon.

Curtis, Francis. The Republican Party: A History of Its Fifty Years Existence, 2 vols. LC 75-41070. (BCL Ser. II). Repr. of 1904 ed. Set. 69.50 (ISBN 0-404-14870-0). AMS Pr.

Curtis, Francis D. Some Values Derived from Extensive Reading of General Science. LC 75-177601. (Columbia University. Teachers College. Contributions to Education: No. 163). Repr. of 1924 ed. 22.50 (ISBN 0-404-55163-7). AMS Pr.

Curtis, G. H., jt. auth. see Williams, Howell.

Curtis, G. H., et al. Effect of Ethane & Propane Extraction on Supply of Natural Gas. 51p. 1973. pap. 5.00 (ISBN 0-318-12603-6, F40102). Am Gas Assn.

Curtis, George T. Constitutional History of the United States: From Their Declaration of Independence to the Close of Their Civil War, 2 vols. (American Constitution & Legal History Ser.). 1100p. 1974. Repr. of 1896 ed. Set. lib. bdg. 145.00 (ISBN 0-306-70611-3). Da Capo.

--Life of James Buchanan, Fifteenth President of the United States, 2 Vols. facs. ed. LC 69-16849. (Select Bibliographies Reprint Ser). 1883. Set. 44.00 (ISBN 0-8369-5004-6); Vol. 2. 22.00 (ISBN 0-8369-9648-8); Vol. 2. 22.00 (ISBN 0-8369-9649-6). Ayer Co Pubs.

Curtis, George W. Ars Reck Vivendi: Being Essays Contributed to "the Easy Chair". LC 72-4608. (Essay Index Reprint Ser.). Repr. of 1897 ed. 14.50 (ISBN 0-8369-2941-1). Ayer Co Pubs.

--Early Letters of George William Curtis to John S. Dwight. Cooke, George W., ed. LC 75-134372. Repr. of 1898 ed. 10.00 (ISBN 0-404-08420-6). AMS Pr.

--Early Letters of George William Curtis to John S. Dwight. LC 72-122647. 1971. Repr. of 1898 ed. 23.00x (ISBN 0-8046-1295-1, Pub. by Kennikat). Assoc Faculty Pr.

--From the Easy Chair, 3 vols. LC 69-13870. 1892-1894. Repr. Set. lib. bdg. 37.50x (ISBN 0-8371-0368-1, CUEC). Greenwood.

--From the Easy Chair. 1973. Repr. of 1893 ed. 10.00 (ISBN 0-8274-1594-X). R West.

--From the Easy Chair: Second Series. 1894. 10.00 (ISBN 0-8274-2382-9). R West.

--From the Easy Chair: Third Series. 1894. 10.00 (ISBN 0-8274-2383-7). R West.

--Literary & Social Essays. LC 67-27589. 1968. Repr. of 1894 ed. 22.50x (ISBN 0-8046-0094-5, Pub. by Kennikat). Assoc Faculty Pr.

--Literary & Social Essays. 1894. 15.00 (ISBN 0-8274-3865-6). R West.

--Our Best Society. 1973. Repr. of 1856 ed. 10.00 (ISBN 0-8274-1593-1). R West.

--Potiphar Papers. LC 72-121280. (BCL Ser. I). Repr. of 1856 ed. 9.50 (ISBN 0-404-01888-2). AMS Pr.

--The Potiphar Papers. 1906. 10.00 (ISBN 0-8274-3192-9). R West.

--Potiphar Papers. LC 4-13872. 1900. 8.00x (ISBN 0-403-00098-X). Scholarly.

--Prue & I. 1904. 10.00 (ISBN 0-8274-3219-4). R West.

--Washington Irving: A Sketch. LC 76-28379. 1976. Repr. of 1901 ed. lib. bdg. 20.00 (ISBN 0-8414-3489-1). Folcroft.

Curtis, George W., ed. The Correspondence of John Lothrop Motley, 2 vols. 1889. Set. 50.00 (ISBN 0-8482-3558-4). Norwood Edns.

Curtis, George W., ed. see Downing, Andrew J.

Curtis, George W., ed. see Motley, John L.

Curtis, Gerald. Election Campaigning Japanese Style. LC 83-81376. 290p. 1984. pap. 5.95 (ISBN 0-87011-630-4). Kodansha.

Curtis, Gerald, jt. auth. see Passin, Herbert.

Curtis, Gerald L. Election Campaigning: Japanese Style. LC 70-154343. (Studies of the East Asian Institute). 275p. 1971. 26.00x (ISBN 0-231-03512-8). Columbia U Pr.

Curtis, Gerald L., jt. auth. see Ushiba, Nobuhiko.

Curtis, Gerald L. & Han, Sung-Joo, eds. The U. S.-South Korean Alliance. LC 82-49205. (Illus.). 256p. 1983. 27.50x (ISBN 0-669-06438-6). Lexington Bks.

Curtis, Helena. Biology. 4th ed. LC 82-83895. (Illus.). 1983. text ed. 35.95x (ISBN 0-87901-186-6); study guide 9.95x (ISBN 0-87901-187-4); lab topics in biology. 13.95x. Worth.

Curtis, Helena & Barnes, Sue N. Invitation to Biology. 4th ed. 1985. text ed. 29.95x (ISBN 0-87901-255-2); study guide 8.95 (ISBN 0-87901-256-0). Worth.

Curtis, Helene & Dudley, Cliff. All That I Have. LC 77-81394. 1979. pap. 2.95 (ISBN 0-89221-044-3). New Leaf.

Curtis, Henry. Beauties of the Rose. facsimile ed. (Illus.). 120p. 1981. 65.00 (ISBN 0-936736-00-3). Sweetbrier.

Curtis, Howard J. Biological Mechanisms of Aging. (Illus.). 148p. 1966. 14.75x (ISBN 0-398-00384-X). C C Thomas.

Curtis, Ian. Long Voyage of War. pap. 4.95 (ISBN 0-7145-0784-9). Riverrun NY.

Curtis, J. & Scott, W. Social Stratification: Canada. 1972. 15.95 (ISBN 0-13-818625-1). P-H.

--Social Stratification: Canada. 2nd ed. 1979. pap. 13.25 (ISBN 0-13-818633-2). P-H.

Curtis, J. A. & Biedenbach, J. M., eds. Educational Telecommunications Delivery Systems. 150p. 1979. 7.00 (ISBN 0-317-33251-1). Am Soc Ag Eng.

Curtis, J. Jerome, Jr., jt. auth. see Crump, David.

Curtis, J. W. The Coinage of Pharaonic Egypt. 1979. 3.00 (ISBN 0-89005-283-2). Ares.

Curtis, Jack. Eagles Over Big Sur. 144p. (Orig.). 1981. pap. 7.95 (ISBN 0-88496-160-5). Capra Pr.

--The Man in Place. (Illus.). 36p. 1982. 35.00x. Turkey Pr.

Curtis, Jack D. & Detert, Richard A. How to Relax: A Holistic Approach to Stress Management. LC 80-84021. 222p. 1981. pap. 9.95 (ISBN 0-87484-527-0). Mayfield Pub.

Curtis, James. Between Flops: A Biography of Preston Sturges. LC 84-7129. (Illus.). 356p. 1984. pap. 9.95 (ISBN 0-87910-027-3). Limelight Edns.

--James Whale. LC 82-5965. (Filmmakers Ser.: No. 1). 267p. 1982. 17.50 (ISBN 0-8108-1561-3). Scarecrow.

--Riding Old Trails. rev. ed. (Illus.). 330p. 1983. 13.95 (ISBN 0-914459-00-7). Rocky Mount CO.

Curtis, James C. Andrew Jackson & the Search for Vindication. (Library of American Biography). 1976. 7.50 (ISBN 0-316-16554-9); pap. text ed. 6.95 (ISBN 0-316-16553-0). Little.

--The Fox at Bay: Martin Van Buren & the Presidency, 1837-1841. LC 72-111507. 248p. 1970. 22.00x (ISBN 0-8131-1214-1). U Pr of Ky.

Curtis, James C. & Gould, Lewis L., eds. The Black Experience in America: Selected Essays. 209p. 1970. pap. 5.95x (ISBN 0-292-70096-2). U of Tex Pr.

Curtis, James F., ed. Processes & Disorders of Human Communication. 1978. text ed. 21.50 scp (ISBN 0-06-041459-6, HarpC). Har-Row.

Curtis, James M. Culture As Polyphony: An Essay on the Nature of Paradigms. LC 77-25242. 224p. 1978. text ed. 17.00x (ISBN 0-8262-0251-9). U of Mo Pr.

--Solzhenitsyn's Traditional Imagination. LC 83-4941. 240p. 1984. 20.00x (ISBN 0-8203-0691-6). U of Ga Pr.

Curtis, James R., jt. auth. see Boswell, Thomas D.

Curtis, Jane & Curtis, Will. Welcome the Birds to Your Home. LC 79-20819. (Illus.). 1980. pap. 5.95 (ISBN 0-8289-0354-9). Greene.

Curtis, Jane, jt. auth. see Curtis, Will.

Curtis, Jane, et al. Green Mountain Adventures: Vermont's Long Trail. 08/1985 ed. LC 85-80828. (Illus.). 96p. 14.95 (ISBN 0-930985-03-6); pap. 9.95 (ISBN 0-930985-02-8). Curtis Lieberman.

--The World of George Perkins Marsh. (Illus.). 128p. 1982. 14.95 (ISBN 0-914378-89-9); pap. 9.95 (ISBN 0-914378-90-2). Countryman.

Curtis, Jane W. & Curtis, Will. Return to These Hills: The Vermont Years of Calvin Coolidge. (Illus.). 96p. 1985. 17.50 (ISBN 0-930985-00-1, Dist. by David & Charles); pap. 9.95 (ISBN 0-930985-01-X, Dist. by David & Charles). Curtis Lieberman.

Curtis, Jared, ed. see Wordsworth, William.

Curtis, Jeffery & Greenway, Ambrose. Soviet Merchant Ships. 5th ed. (Illus.). 264p. 1985. text ed. 20.00 (ISBN 0-85937-324-X, Pub. by K Mason). Sheridan.

Curtis, Jerry, jt. auth. see Crumbley, Larry.

Curtis, Jim, ed. see Walther, Mina.

Curtis, Jody, jt. ed. see Close, Arthur.

Curtis, Jody, jt. ed. see Close, Arthur C.

Curtis, John. Current Resources in Family Therapy. 40p. 1981. pap. 3.95 (ISBN 0-686-33182-6). Pilgrimage Inc.

Curtis, John & Greene, John. Human Sexuality: An Annotated Bibliography. 70p. 1980. softcover 5.95 (ISBN 0-932930-16-6). Pilgrimage Inc.

--Premarital, Marital, & Family Therapy: An Annotated Bibliography. 72p. 1979. pap. 5.95 (ISBN 0-932930-15-8). Pilgrimage Inc.

Curtis, John D. & Detert, Richard A. Learn to Relax: A Fourteen Day Program. LC 83-7661. (Illus.). 112p. (Orig.). 1985. pap. 4.95 (ISBN 0-9611456-0-9). Coulee Pr.

Curtis, John D. & Papenfuss, Richard L. Health Instruction: A Task Approach. LC 79-56570. 1980. pap. text ed. 14.95x (ISBN 0-8087-2914-4). Burgess.

Curtis, John D., et al. Teaching Stress Management & Relaxation Skills: An Instructor's Guide. (Illus.). 280p. 1985. text ed. 26.50 (ISBN 0-9611456-2-5). Coulee Pr.

Curtis, John F., jt. auth. see Jenkins, Michael D.

Curtis, John T. Vegetation of Wisconsin: An Ordination of Plant Communities. (Illus.). 672p. 1959. 27.50 (ISBN 0-299-01940-3). U of Wis Pr.

Curtis, Joseph E., jt. auth. see Kraus, Richard G.

Curtis, Joy, jt. auth. see Benjamin, Martin.

Curtis, Joyce. Pickle-Ball: For Player & Teacher. (Illus.). 112p. 1985. pap. 6.95x. Morton Pub.

Curtis, June. The Gracious Woman: Developing A Servant's Heart Through Hospitality. 176p. (Orig.). 1985. pap. 4.95 (ISBN 0-89081-489-9). Harvest Hse.

Curtis, Kenneth M. & Carroll, John E. Canadian-American Relations: The Promise & the Challange. LC 83-47990. 128p. 1983. 21.50x (ISBN 0-669-06793-8). Lexington Bks.

Curtis, L. G. Papers Relating to the Application of the Principle of Dyarchy to the Government of India. 668p. 1972. Repr. of 1920 ed. 45.00x (ISBN 0-7165-2117-2, Pub. by Irish Academic Pr Ireland). Biblio Dist.

Curtis, L. P., Jr. & Winks, Robin W., eds. The Historian's Workshop: Original Essays by Sixteen Historians. LC 83-49172. (History & Historiography Ser.). 326p. 1985. lib. bdg. 32.00 (ISBN 0-317-14516-9). Garland Pub.

Curtis, L. R., jt. auth. see Barrett, E. C.

Curtis, Laura A. The Elusive Daniel Defoe. (Critical Studies). 216p. 1984. 28.50x (ISBN 0-389-20063-8, 06833). B&N Imports.

Curtis, Laura A., ed. see Defoe, Daniel.

Curtis, Lawrence H. & Tanenhaus, Edward D. Management of Mass Tort Litigation. Practising Law Institute, ed. LC 83-62213. (Litigation & Administrative Practice Ser.). (Illus.). 1056p. 1983. 35.00. PLI.

Curtis, Leonard F., jt. ed. see Barrett, Eric C.

Curtis, Leonard T., jt. auth. see L'Abate, Luciano.

Curtis, Lewis P. Chichester Towers. LC 66-21514. (Illus.). Repr. of 1966 ed. 32.50 (ISBN 0-8357-1319-9, 2013199). Bks Demand UMI.

--The Politics of Laurence Sterne. 1978. Repr. of 1929 ed. lib. bdg. 22.50 (ISBN 0-8495-0742-1). Arden Lib.

--The Politics of Laurence Sterne. LC 73-6822. Repr. of 1929 ed. lib. bdg. 20.00 (ISBN 0-8414-3365-8). Folcroft.

Curtis, Lindsay. Making of a Prophet. 1974. pap. 3.95 (ISBN 0-89036-035-9). Hawkes Pub Inc.

Curtis, Lindsay, et al. Pregnant & Beautiful. 240p. 1985. pap. 8.95 (ISBN 0-89586-366-9). H P Bks.

Curtis, Lindsay R. Cigarrillo: Contaminante, No. 1. 48p. pap. 1.10 (ISBN 0-311-46073-9). Casa Bautista.

--Feminine & Fit. new ed. (Illus.). 128p. (Orig.). 1975. pap. 3.95 (ISBN 0-89036-049-9). Hawkes Pub Inc.

Curtis, Lindsay R. & Coroles, Yvonne. Pregnant & Lovin' It. LC 77-82012. (Illus.). 1977. pap. 6.95 (ISBN 0-912656-82-4). H P Bks.

Curtis, Lindsay R., jt. auth. see Whitehead, Lana E.

Curtis, Lionel. Capital Question of China. LC 76-115200. 1971. Repr. of 1932 ed. 24.50x (ISBN 0-8046-1093-2, Pub. by Kennikat). Assoc Faculty Pr.

Curtis, Liz. Ireland-the Propaganda War: The British Media & the "Battle for Hearts & Minds". 342p. (Orig.). 1983. pap. 8.25 (ISBN 0-86104-757-5). Pluto Pr.

Curtis, Lory V., jt. auth. see Derato, Frank C.

Curtis, Lynn A. Violence, Race, & Culture. 1977. pap. text ed. 8.95x (ISBN 0-669-01066-9). Heath.

Curtis, Lynn A., ed. American Violence & Public Policy: An Update of the National Commission on the Causes & Prevention of Violence. LC 84-40194. 288p. 1985. 23.00X (ISBN 0-300-03231-5). Yale U Pr.

Curtis, M. L. Matrix Groups. 2nd ed. (Universitext Ser.). (Illus.). xiii, 210p. 1984. pap. 19.80 (ISBN 0-387-96074-0). Springer-Verlag.

Curtis, Marcia, jt. auth. see Bechtel, Lenore.

Curtis, Mary E., jt. auth. see Lesgold, Alan M.

Curtis, Michael. Comparative Government & Politics. 2nd ed. (Comparative Government Ser.). 1978. pap. text ed. 12.25 scp (ISBN 0-06-041462-6, HarpC). Har-Row.

--Three Against the Third Republic: Sorel, Barres & Maurras. LC 76-26140. 1976. Repr. of 1959 ed. lib. bdg. 22.50x (ISBN 0-8371-9048-7, CUTR). Greenwood.

--Totalitarianism. LC 78-66238. (Issues in Contemporary Civilization). 128p. 1979. 5.95x (ISBN 0-87855-288-X). Transaction Bks.

--Totalitarianism. LC 78-66238. 128p. pap. 33.50 (ISBN 0-317-27282-9, 2024162). Bks Demand UMI.

Curtis, Michael, ed. Antisemitism in the Contemporary World. 200p. 1985. 28.00x (ISBN 0-8133-0157-2). Westview.

--Great Political Theories, Vol. II. 1976. pap. 4.50 (ISBN 0-380-01235-9, 84251-3, Discus). Avon.

--Great Political Theories, Vol. I. 1980. pap. 4.50 (ISBN 0-380-00785-1, 84244-0, Discus). Avon.

--People & Politics in the Middle East. LC 72-140617. 335p. 1971. 19.95 (ISBN 0-87855-000-3); pap. 9.95x (ISBN 0-87855-500-5). Transaction Bks.

Curtis, Michael & Chertoff, Mordecai S., eds. Israel: Social Structure & Change. LC 73-78696. (Third World Ser). 460p. 1973. pap. 5.95 (ISBN 0-87855-575-7). Transaction Bks.

--Israel: Social Structure & Change. 443p. pap. 4.95 (ISBN 0-686-95160-3). ADL.

Curtis, Michael & Gitelson, Susan A., eds. Israel in the Third World. LC 75-44817. 520p. (Orig.). 1976. 19.95 (ISBN 0-87855-130-1); pap. text ed. 9.95x (ISBN 0-87855-603-6). Transaction Bks.

Curtis, Michael & Neyer, Joseph, eds. The Palestinians: People, History, Politics. new ed. 278p. (Orig.). 1975. 14.95 (ISBN 0-87855-112-3). Transaction Bks.

Curtis, Michael, et al. Introduction to Comparative Government. 512p. 1984. text ed. 25.50 scp (ISBN 0-06-041463-4, HarpC). Har-Row.

Curtis, Michael J. & Zins, Joseph E. The Theory & Practice of School Consultation. (Illus.). 384p. 1981. 40.75x (ISBN 0-398-04171-7). C C Thomas.

Curtis, Michael K., jt. auth. see Johnston, Martha E.

Curtis, Mike. The Savage Women. 1976. pap. 1.50 (ISBN 0-685-72353-4, LB379DK, Leisure Bks). Dorchester Pub Co.

Curtis, Monica, ed. Norway & the War, September 1939-December 1940. 1941. 31.00 (ISBN 0-384-12075-X); pap. 26.00 (ISBN 0-685-13530-6). Johnson Repr.

Curtis, Nancy. Cockatiels. (Orig.). pap. 3.95 (ISBN 0-87666-420-6). TFH Pubns.

Curtis, Natalie. Indians' Book. rev. ed. (Illus.). 1968. pap. 10.00 (ISBN 0-486-21939-9). Dover.

Curtis, Neil. Fossils. LC 83-51439. (Easy-Read Fact Bks.). (Illus.). 32p. (gr. 3-5). 1984. PLB 9.40 (ISBN 0-531-03773-8). Watts.

Curtis, Nelson. Butterflies of Idaho & the Northern Rockies. LC 84-50760. (Northwest Naturalist Ser.). (Illus.). 472p. (Orig.). 1986. pap. 24.95 (ISBN 0-89301-102-9). U Pr of Idaho.

Curtis, O. B. & Nolan, Alan T. History of the Twenty-Fourth Michigan of the Iron Brigade: Known as the Detroit & Wayne County Regiment. 495p. 1984. Repr. of 1891 ed. 35.00 (ISBN 0-913419-07-9). Butternut Pr.

Curtis, Olin A. The Christian Faith. LC 56-9279. 1971. 14.95 (ISBN 0-8254-2310-4). Kregel.

Curtis, P. E. & Courson, R. L. Outline of Soil Fertility. 1981. spiral bdg. 8.80x (ISBN 0-87563-204-1). Stipes.

Curtis, Patricia. All Wild Creatures Welcome: The Story of a Wildlife Rehabilitation Center. (Illus.). 160p. (gr. 5-9). 1985. 13.95 (ISBN 0-525-67164-1, 01354-410). Lodestar Bks.

--Animal Partners: Training Animals to Help People. (Illus.). 144p. (gr. 7 up). 1982. 10.95 (ISBN 0-525-66791-1, 01063-320). Lodestar Bks.

--The Animal Shelter. (Illus.). 160p. (gr. 5-9). 1984. 13.95 (ISBN 0-525-66783-0, 01354-410). Lodestar Bks.

--Cindy, a Hearing Ear Dog. LC 80-24487. (Illus.). (gr. 3-5). 1981. 10.25 (ISBN 0-525-27950-4, 0995-300). Dutton.

--Greff: The Story of a Guide Dog. (Illus.). 64p. (gr. 5-9). 1982. 9.95 (ISBN 0-525-66754-7, 0966-290). Lodestar Bks.

--The Indoor Cat: How to Understand, Enjoy & Care for House Cats. (Illus.). 192p. 1982. pap. 5.95 (ISBN 0-399-50596-2, Perigee). Putnam Pub Group.

Curtis, Paul E., et al. Here's How: On-Job-Training, Agricultural Mechanics. 157p. 1972. pap. text ed. 4.00x (ISBN 0-8134-1433-4, 1433). Interstate.

--Here's How: On-Job-Training, Agricultural Products-Processing, Marketing, & Services. 133p. 1972. pap. text ed. 4.00x (ISBN 0-8134-1434-2, 1434). Interstate.

--Here's How: On-Job-Training, Agricultural Resources & Forestry. 159p. 1972. pap. text ed. 4.00x (ISBN 0-8134-1436-9, 1436). Interstate.

--Here's How: On-Job-Training, Agricultural Supplies & Services. 111p. 1972. pap. text ed. 4.00x (ISBN 0-8134-1432-6, 1432). Interstate.

Curtis, Philip. Invasion from below the Earth. LC 81-101. (A Capers Bk.). (Illus.). 128p. (gr. 3 up). 1981. PLB 4.99 (ISBN 0-394-94895-5); pap. 1.95 (ISBN 0-394-84895-0). Knopf.

--Invasion of the Comet People: A Capers Book. LC 82-9923. (Illus.). 128p. (gr. 3-5). 1983. 1.95 (ISBN 0-394-85490-X); lib. bdg. 5.99 (ISBN 0-394-95490-4). Knopf.

Curtis, Philip C., Jr. Calculus with an Introduction to Vectors. LC 78-25618. 486p. 1979. Repr. of 1972 ed. text ed. 25.50 (ISBN 0-88275-822-5). Krieger.

Curtis, R., tr. see Madelin, Louis.

Curtis, R. J., tr. see Istrati, Panait.

Curtis, R. K. Evolution or Extinction: The Choice Before Us-A Systems Approach to the Study of the Future. 420p. 1982. 55.00 (ISBN 0-08-027933-3); pap. 28.00 (ISBN 0-08-027932-5). Pergamon.

Curtis, Renee L. Le Roman de Tristan en Prose. Incl. Vol. I. (Arthurian Studies: No. XII). 260p. 1985. 29.50 (ISBN 0-85991-181-0); Vol. II. 320p. 29.50 (ISBN 0-85991-182-9); Vol. III. (Arthurian Studies: No. XIV). 288p. 1985. 37.50 (ISBN 0-85991-183-7). (Arthurian Studies, Pub. by Boydell & Brewer). Longwood Pub Group.

--Le Roman de Tristan en Prose, Vol. II. (Arthurian Studies: Vol. XIII). 320p. 1985. 29.50 (ISBN 0-85991-182-9, Pub. by Boydell & Brewer). Longwood Pub Group.

--Tristan Studies. 96p. 1985. 15.00 (ISBN 0-85991-188-8, Pub. by Boydell & Brewer). Longwood Pub Group.

Curtis, Richard. How to Be Your Own Literary Agent: The Business of Getting Your Book Published. 1984. 12.95 (ISBN 0-395-33123-4); pap. 7.95 (ISBN 0-395-36142-7). HM.

--The Story of Elsie & Jane. (Illus.). 32p. (gr. k-3). 1984. laminated boards 6.95 (ISBN 0-370-30505-1, Pub. by the Bodley Head). Merrimack Pub Cir.

--WordStar on the IBM PC. (A BYTE Bk.). 208p. 1984. pap. 11.95 (ISBN 0-07-014978-X). McGraw.

Curtis, Richard, jt. auth. see Touster, Irwin.

Curtis, Richard F., jt. auth. see Borhek, James T.

Curtis, Richard H. After the Hawk. (Skymasters Ser.). 320p. 1982. pap. 3.25 (ISBN 0-440-00286-9, Emerald). Dell.

--The Aviatrix. (Skymasters Ser.: No. 7). 320p. (Orig.). 1983. pap. 3.25 (ISBN 0-440-00333-4, Emerald). Dell.

--Every Man an Eagle. (Skymasters Ser.: No. 8). (Orig.). 1983. pap. 3.25 (ISBN 0-440-02276-2, Emerald). Dell.

Curtis, Robert. On ESP. (Illus.). (gr. 3-7). 1975. pap. 1.50 (ISBN 0-13-634287-6). P-H.

Curtis, Robert H. Questions & Answers about Alcoholism. LC 76-7560. (Illus.). 1976. lib. bdg. 9.95 (ISBN 0-13-748459-3). P H.

--Questions & Answers About Alcoholism. 91p. 1976. 5.95 (ISBN 0-318-15346-7). Natl Coun Alcoholism.

Curtis, S. J. Introductory History of English Education Since 1800. 1981. 24.00x (ISBN 0-7231-0733-5, Pub. by Univ Tutorial England). State Mutual Bk.

Curtis, S. J. & Boultwood, M. E. Short History of Educational Ideas. 1981. 25.00x (ISBN 0-7231-0767-X, Pub. by Univ Tutorial England). State Mutual Bk.

Curtis, Sam. Harsh-Weather Camping: How to Enjoy Backpacking, Canoeing & Bicycling under Any Conditions. LC 83-7240. (Illus.). 224p. 1983. 14.95 (ISBN 0-668-05833-1); pap. 7.95 (ISBN 0-668-05840-4). Arco.

Curtis, Sandra. The Joy of Movement in Early Childhood. LC 81-16520. (Early Childhood Education Ser.). (Illus.). 1982. pap. text ed. 12.95x (ISBN 0-8077-2691-5). Tchrs Coll.

Curtis, Stanley E. Environmental Management in Animal Agriculture. (Illus.). 410p. 1983. pap. text ed. 43.25x (ISBN 0-8138-0556-2). Iowa St U Pr.

Curtis, Stanley J. Education in Britain since 1900. LC 71-104264. Repr. of 1952 ed. lib. bdg. 15.75x (ISBN 0-8371-3913-9, CUEB). Greenwood.

--History of Education in Great Britain. 3rd ed. LC 75-104265. (Illus.). 1971. Repr. of 1953 ed. lib. bdg. 29.75x (ISBN 0-8371-3914-7, CUGB). Greenwood.

Curtis, Susan P. Take-Along Crafts. (Illus.). 72p. (Orig.). 1982. pap. 2.50 (ISBN 0-918178-28-2). Simplicity.

Curtis, T. Dannie Abse. (Writers of Wales Ser.). 132p. 1985. pap. text ed. 8.50x (ISBN 0-7083-0896-1, Pub. by Univ of Wales Pr England). Humanities.

Curtis, Thomas C., jt. auth. see Steele, David H.

Curtis, Thomas E. Aesthetic Education & the Quality of Life. LC 81-82468. (Fastback Ser.: No. 168). 50p. 1981. pap. 0.75 (ISBN 0-87367-168-6). Phi Delta Kappa.

Curtis, Thomas E. & Bidwell, Wilma W. Curriculum & Instruction for Emerging Adolescents. LC 76-9327. (Illus.). 1977. text ed. 18.45 (ISBN 0-201-00902-1). Addison-Wesley.

Curtis, Tony. Letting Go. 57p. 1983. pap. 8.95 (ISBN 0-907476-25-2). Dufour.

--Lyle Official Arms & Armour Review, 1983. (Illus.). 416p. 24.95 (ISBN 0-686-47037-0). Apollo.

Curtis, Tony, ed. The Antiques Collector's Pocketbook. (Illus.). 1978. 6.95 (ISBN 0-902921-03-7). Apollo.

--Bronze. (Illus.). 1978. 2.00 (ISBN 0-902921-40-1). Apollo.

--China. (Illus.). 1978. 2.00 (ISBN 0-902921-43-6). Apollo.

--Furniture. (Illus.). 1978. 2.00 (ISBN 0-902921-46-0). Apollo.

--Glass. (Illus.). 1978. 2.00 (ISBN 0-902921-48-7). Apollo.

--Instruments. (Illus.). 1978. 2.00 (ISBN 0-902921-39-8). Apollo.

--Ivory. Enneking, John J. (Illus.). 1978. 2.00 (ISBN 0-902921-85-1). Apollo.

--Kitchen Equipment. (Illus.). 1978. 2.00 (ISBN 0-902921-41-X). Apollo.

--Lyle Official Antiques Review, 1982. (Illus.). 1980. cancelled 24.95 (ISBN 0-8256-9686-0). Apollo.

--Lyle Official Antiques Review, 1984. (Illus.). 1984. 24.95 (ISBN 0-686-43846-9). Apollo.

--Lyle Official Arms & Armour Review, 1982. (Illus.). 1980. 24.95 (ISBN 0-8256-9687-9). Apollo.

--Lyle Official Books Review, 1982. (Illus.). 1980. cancelled 24.95 (ISBN 0-8256-9685-2). Apollo.

--Militaria. (Illus.). 1978. 2.00 (ISBN 0-902921-49-5). Apollo.

--Musical Instruments. (Illus.). 1978. 2.00 (ISBN 0-902921-50-9). Apollo.

--Oriental Art. (Illus.). 1978. 2.00 (ISBN 0-902921-88-6). Apollo.

--Pewter. (Illus.). 1978. 2.00 (ISBN 0-902921-54-1). Apollo.

--Tables. (Illus.). 1978. 2.00 (ISBN 0-902921-86-X). Apollo.

--Veteran & Vintage Cars. (Illus.). 1978. 2.00 (ISBN 0-902921-53-3). Apollo.

Curtis, Ursula. Widow's Web. LC 56-5742. (Red Badge Mysteries Ser.). 1983. pap. 3.50 (ISBN 0-396-08164-9). Dodd.

Curtis, Virginia, jt. ed. see Bair, Frederick H.

Curtis, W. Robert. Area Based Human Services. 2nd ed. LC 79-18356. (Organizational Development of State Human Services Ser.). (Illus.). 1979. pap. 5.95 (ISBN 0-89995-004-3). Social Matrix.

--Community Human Service Networks: New Roles for Mental Health Workers. 2nd ed. (Community & Neighborhood Development Ser.). 1979. pap. 3.95 (ISBN 0-89995-021-3). Social Matrix.

--The Future Use of Social Networks in Mental Health. LC 79-18997. (The Client As a Social Network Ser.). 1979. pap. 4.95 (ISBN 0-89995-033-7). Social Matrix.

Curtis, W. Robert & Yessian, Mark. Effective Management of Human Services: An Analytic Framework, Pt. I. (Organizational Development of State Human Services Ser.). (Orig.). 1979. pap. 2.95 (ISBN 0-89995-001-9). Social Matrix.

Curtis, W. Robert, jt. auth. see Yessian, Mark.

Curtis, Walt. The Erotic Flying Machine. (Illus.). 80p. (Orig.). 1971. pap. 2.00 (ISBN 0-912874-02-3). Out of the Ashes.

--Mad Bomber's Notebook. (Illus., Orig.). 1974. pap. 0.50 (ISBN 0-912874-10-4). Out of the Ashes.

--Mala Noche. (Illus.). 1977. pap. 0.60 (ISBN 0-685-79529-2). Out of the Ashes.

--Peckerneck Country. 1978. 2.50 (ISBN 0-932191-05-3). Mr Cogito Pr.

--The Sunflower. 1975. pap. 0.75 (ISBN 0-685-65549-0). Out of the Ashes.

Curtis, Wayne C. Microeconomic Concepts for Attorneys: A Reference Guide. LC 83-23051. xvi, 153p. 1984. lib. bdg. 29.95 (ISBN 0-89930-060-X, CMC/, Quorum). Greenwood.

--Statistical Concepts for Attorneys: A Reference Guide. LC 82-24068. xviii, 230p. 1983. lib. bdg. 35.00 (ISBN 0-89930-033-2, CSA/, Quorum). Greenwood.

Curtis, Will & Curtis, Jane. Antique Woodstoves: Artistry in Iron. (Illus.). 64p. 1975. pap. 7.00 (ISBN 0-89166-000-3). Cobblesmith.

Curtis, Will, jt. auth. see Curtis, Jane.

Curtis, Will, ed. The Nature of Things. 312p. 1985. 15.95 (ISBN 0-88150-028-3). Countryman.

Curtis, Will, jt. auth. see Curtis, Jane W.

Curtis, William. Modern Architecture since Nineteen Hundred. 400p. 1983. text ed. 39.95 (ISBN 0-13-586677-4); pap. text ed. 31.95 (ISBN 0-13-586669-3). P-H.

--A Short History of the Browntail Moth. 1969. 40.00x (ISBN 0-317-07175-0, Pub. by FW Classey UK). State Mutual Bk.

Curtis, William, jt. auth. see Sekler, Eduard F.

Curtis, William E. The Capitals of Spanish America. 1976. lib. bdg. 59.95 (ISBN 0-8490-1570-7). Gordon Pr.

--Children of the Sun. LC 74-7946. Repr. of 1883 ed. 15.00 (ISBN 0-404-11833-X). AMS Pr.

Curtis, William J., et al, eds. Insights: Readings in Children's Literture. 74p. 1970. pap. text ed. 4.50x (ISBN 0-686-81284-0). Irvington.

Curtis, William R. Lambeth Conferences: The Solution for Pan-Anglican Organization. LC 68-58565. (Columbia University Studies in the Social Sciences: No. 488). Repr. of 1942 ed. 24.50 (ISBN 0-404-51488-X). AMS Pr.

Curtis, Winifred. The Endemic Flora of Tasmania, 6 vols. 1981. 110.00x ea. (Pub. by RHS Ent England); Set. 550.00x (ISBN 0-686-78774-9). State Mutual Bk.

Curtis-Prior, P. B., ed. Biochemical Pharmacology of Obesity. 472p. 1984. 127.00 (ISBN 0-444-80353-X, I-076-84, Biomedical Pr). Elsevier.

Curtiss Aeroplane & Motor Corp. Curtiss Standard JN-4D Military Tractor (Aircraft) Handbook. Rice, M. S., ed. (Illus.). 1976. pap. 6.95 (ISBN 0-87994-013-1, Pub. by AvPubns). Aviation.

Curtiss, David R. Analytic Functions of a Complex Variable. (Carus Monograph: No. 2). 173p. 1926. 19.50 (ISBN 0-88385-002-8, CAM-02). Math Assn.

Curtiss, Eleanor. For Young Souls. 1941. pap. 1.95 (ISBN 0-87516-303-3). De Vorss.

Curtiss, Ellen T. & Untersee, Philip A. Corporate Responsibilities & Opportunities to 1990. (Arthur D. Little Books). (Illus.). 1979. 32.00x (ISBN 0-669-02848-7). Lexington Bks.

Curtiss, F. H., jt. auth. see Curtiss, H. A.

Curtiss, F. H., jt. auth. see Curtiss, H. H.

Curtiss, F. H., jt. auth. see Curtiss, Harriette A.

Curtiss, F. Homer. Coming World Changes. 136p. 1981. pap. 7.00 (ISBN 0-89540-090-1, SB-090). Sun Pub.

Curtiss, F. Homer, jt. auth. see Curtiss, Harriette A.

Curtiss, George B. Protection & Prosperity: An Account of Tariff Legislation & Its Effect in Europe & America, 2 vols. (The Neglected American Economists Ser.). 1974. Set. lib. bdg. 121.00 (ISBN 0-8240-1032-9); lib. bdg. 50.00 ea. Garland Pub.

Curtiss, H. A. & Curtiss, F. H. Gems of Mysticism. 83p. 4.00 (ISBN 0-89540-143-6, SB-143). Sun Pub.

--Gems of Mysticism. 83p. 1985. pap. 4.00 (ISBN 0-89540-143-6, SB-143). Sun Pub.

--The Key of Destiny. 372p. 1981. pap. 9.00 (ISBN 0-89540-070-7, SB-070). Sun Pub.

--The Key to the Universe. 391p. 1981. pap. 9.50 (ISBN 0-89540-069-3, SB-069). Sun Pub.

--The Message of Aquaria. 487p. 1981. pap. 17.50 (ISBN 0-89540-065-0, SB-065). Sun Pub.

--The Voice of Isis. 472p. 1985. pap. 17.50 (ISBN 0-89540-130-4, SB-130). Sun Pub.

Curtiss, H. C., Jr., jt. auth. see Dowell, E. H.

Curtiss, H. H. & Curtiss, F. H. Inner Radiance. 369p. 1985. pap. 19.00 (ISBN 0-89540-149-5, SB-149). Sun Pub.

Curtiss, Harriete & Homer, F. Potent Prayers. 1976p. pap. 1.00 (ISBN 0-87516-362-9). De Vorss.

Curtiss, Harriette & Homer, F. Four-Fold Health. 1936. 4.95 (ISBN 0-87516-304-1). De Vorss.

--The Truth about Evolution & the Bible. 1928. 5.50 (ISBN 0-87516-308-4). De Vorss.

Curtiss, Harriette A. & Curtiss, F. H. The Key of Destiny. 400p. 1983. pap. 9.95 (ISBN 0-87877-067-4). Newcastle Pub.

Curtiss, Harriette A. & Curtiss, F. Homer. The Key of Destiny. LC 83-21329. 400p. 1983. Repr. lib. bdg. 19.95x (ISBN 0-89370-667-1). Borgo Pr.

--The Key to the Universe. LC 83-22411. 400p. 1983. Repr. lib. bdg. 19.95x (ISBN 0-89370-668-X). Borgo Pr.

Curtiss, Harriette A. & Curtiss, Homer. The Key to the Universe. 400p. 1983. pap. 9.95 (ISBN 0-87877-068-2). Newcastle Pub.

Curtiss, Homer, jt. auth. see Curtiss, Harriette A.

Curtiss, J. H. Introduction to the Theory of Functions of a Complex Variable. (Pure & Applied Mathematics Ser.: Vol. 44). 1978. 29.75 (ISBN 0-8247-6501-X). Dekker.

Curtiss, J. H., ed. see Symposium in Applied Mathematics, Santa Monica Calif, 1953.

Curtiss, John S. An Appraisal of the Protocols of Zion. LC 78-63661. (Studies in Fascism: Ideology & Practice). Repr. of 1942 ed. 12.50 (ISBN 0-404-16924-4). AMS Pr.

--The Russian Church & the Soviet State, 1917-1950. 1953. 11.75 (ISBN 0-8446-1141-7). Peter Smith.

--The Russian Revolutions of 1917. LC 82-15180. 192p. 1982. pap. 7.50 (ISBN 0-89874-499-7). Krieger.

--Russia's Crimean War. LC 76-28915. (Illus.). xii, 597p. 1979. 36.00 (ISBN 0-8223-0374-4). Duke.

Curtiss, John S., ed. Essays in Russian & Soviet History: In Honor of Geroid Tanquary Robinson. LC 62-9706. 345p. 1963. 31.50x (ISBN 0-231-02521-1). Columbia U Pr.

Curtiss, Mina. Bizet & His World. LC 76-55412. 1977. Repr. of 1958 ed. lib. bdg. 34.00x (ISBN 0-8371-9427-X, CUBI). Greenwood.

--Bizet & His World. (Illus.). 511p. 1974. pap. 15.00x (ISBN 0-8443-0085-3). Vienna Hse.

Curtiss, Mina, ed. see Degas, Hilaire G.

Curtiss, Richard D. Thomas E. Williams & the Fine Arts Press. (Illus.). xv, 119p. 1973. 20.00 (ISBN 0-87093-091-5). Dawsons.

Curtiss, Richard D., et al, eds. A Guide for Oral History Programs. 1973. 10.00 (ISBN 0-930046-03-X). CSUF Oral Hist.

Curtiss, Richard H. A Changing Image: American Perceptions of the Arab-Israeli Dispute. LC 83-149825. (Illus.). 216p. 1982. 9.95 (ISBN 0-318-01032-1); text ed. 6.00x (ISBN 0-318-01033-X). Am Educ Trust.

Curtiss, Richard I. Taking Off. Schriver, Peter, ed. 192p. 1981. pap. 1.00 Outlet (ISBN 0-517-53901-2, Harmony). Crown.

Curtiss, Susan R. Genie: A Linguistic Study of a Modern-Day "Wild Child". 1977. 34.50 (ISBN 0-12-196350-0). Acad Pr.

Curtiss, Ursala. Don't Open the Door. 1984. pap. 3.50 (ISBN 0-396-08444-3). Dodd.

Curtiss, Ursula. Death of a Crow. LC 82-19951. 1983. 10.95 (ISBN 0-396-08130-4). Dodd.

--Dog in the Manger. 192p. 1982. 9.95 (ISBN 0-396-08057-X). Dodd.

--The House on Plymouth Street & Other Stories. 224p. 1985. 14.95 (ISBN 0-396-08685-3). Dodd.

--In Cold Pursuit. 1979. pap. 1.95 (ISBN 0-345-28443-7). Ballantine.

Curtiss, Vienna I. Cappy: Rollicking Rancher Atop Arizona's Mighty Rim. LC 79-84471. (Illus.). 1979. 12.00 (ISBN 0-9602742-0-0). Collectors Choice.

--I Should Be Glad to Help You, Madame: Europe Minus One's Wardrobe. LC 79-58850. (Illus.). 1979. 6.00 (ISBN 0-9602742-1-9). Collectors Choice.

--Pageant of Art. LC 77-280. (Illus.). 1979. 27.50 (ISBN 0-9602742-2-7). Collectors Choice.

Curtius, E. R. European Literature & the Latin Middle Ages. Trask, Willard R., tr. LC 52-10619. (Bollingen Ser., Vol. 36). 682p. 1953. pap. 12.95 (ISBN 0-691-01793-X). Princeton U Pr.

Curtius, Ernst R. Essays on European Literature. Kowal, Michael, tr. from Ger. 484p. 1973. 40.00x (ISBN 0-691-06252-8); pap. 20.00 LPE (ISBN 0-691-10010-1). Princeton U Pr.

Curtius, Ernst Robert. Civilization of France: An Introduction. facsimile ed. Wyon, Olive, tr. LC 70-148877. (Select Bibliographies Reprint Ser). Repr. of 1932 ed. 16.00 (ISBN 0-8369-5648-6). Ayer Co Pubs.

Curtius, H. C. & Roth, Marc, eds. Clinical Biochemistry: Principles & Methods, 2 vols. LC 73-84154. 1974. Set. 184.00 (ISBN 3-11-007669-1); pap. 49.50x; Vol. 1. pap. 49.50x (ISBN 3-11-007670-5); Vol. 2. pap. 49.50x (ISBN 3-1100-7669-1). De Gruyter.

Curtius, H. C., et al, eds. Biochemical & Clinical Aspects of Pteridines, Vol. 2 - Cancer, Immunology, Metabolic Diseases: Proceedings, Second Winter Workshop on Pterdines, March 6-9, 1983, St. Christopher, Arlberg, Austria. LC 83-24079. xv, 435p. 1984. 87.00x (ISBN 3-11-009813-X). De Gruyter.

Curtius, H. C., jt. ed. see Wachter, H.

Curtius, Quintus. History of Alexander, 2 vols. (Loeb Classical Library: No. 368-369). 12.50x ea. Vol. 1 (ISBN 0-674-99405-1). Vol. 2 (ISBN 0-674-99407-8). Harvard U Pr.

Curtius Rufus, Quintus. A History of Quintus Curcius, Conteyning the Actes of the Greate Alexander. Brende, J., tr. LC 77-25709. (English Experience Ser.: No. 303). 452p. 1971. Repr. of 1553 ed. 49.00 (ISBN 90-221-0303-X). Walter J Johnson.

Curtler, Hugh. A Theory of Art, Tragedy & Culture: The Philosophy of Eliseo Vivas. (The World of Art Ser.). 224p. 1983. pap. text ed. 7.95 (ISBN 0-930586-15-8). Haven Pubns.

--What is Art? (The World of Art Ser.). (Illus.). 220p. (Orig.). 1983. pap. text ed. 10.50 (ISBN 0-930586-17-4). Haven Pubns.

Curtler, Hugh M. Eliseo Vivas: A Bibliography. LC 80-9013. (American Literature Catolog Ser.). 150p. 1982. lib. bdg. 26.00 (ISBN 0-8240-9300-3). Garland Pub.

--Vivas As Critic: Essays in Poetics & Criticism. LC 82-50419. 274p. 1982. 22.50x (ISBN 0-87875-224-2). Whitston Pub.

Curto, Josephine. How to Become a Single Parent: A Guide for Single People Considering Adoption or Natural Parenthood Alone. 238p. 1983. 14.95 (ISBN 0-13-396192-3); pap. 6.95 (ISBN 0-13-396184-2). P-H.

Curto, Peter. Love: A Poem. 3.75 (ISBN 0-533-01533-2). Vantage.

--Realities. 1983. 5.95 (ISBN 0-533-05454-0). Vantage.

--Whispers from the Woods. 3.75 (ISBN 0-533-00121-8). Vantage.

Curto, Peter T. An American Testament. LC 84-90220. 67p. 1984. 6.95 (ISBN 0-533-06273-X). Vantage.

--The Beethoven Letters to the FBI. 1985. 6.95 (ISBN 0-533-06608-5). Vantage.

Curton, Josephine. Hard Times Notes. (Orig.). 1964. pap. 3.25 (ISBN 0-8220-0578-6). Cliffs.

Curts, Paul. Luther's Variations in Sentence Arrangement From the Modern Literary Usage With Primary Reference to the Position of the Verb. 1910. 39.50x (ISBN 0-686-83611-1). Elliots Bks.

Curts, Paul H., tr. see Hebbel, Friedrich.

Curtze, Maximilian. Urkunden Zur Geschichte der Mathematik Im Mittelalter & der Renaissance. (Bibliotheca Mathematica Teubneriana Ser: No. 45). (Ger). 1969. Repr. of 1902 ed. 45.00 (ISBN 0-384-10402-9). Johnson Repr.

Curval, Philippe. Brave Old World. Cox, Steve, tr. from Fr. 262p. 1983. 13.95 (ISBN 0-8052-8135-5, Pub. by Allison & Busby England). Schocken.

Curvin, Robert & Porter, Bruce. Blackout Looting: New York City, July 13, 1977. LC 78-20817. 240p. 1979. 13.95x (ISBN 0-470-26669-4); pap. text ed. 6.95x (ISBN 0-470-26627-9). Halsted Pr.

--Blackout Looting: New York City, July 13, 1977. 240p. 1979. text ed. 13.95 (ISBN 0-89876-060-7); pap. text ed. 6.95 (ISBN 0-89876-059-3). Gardner Pr.

Curwen, C. A. Taiping Rebel: The Deposition of Li Hsiu-Ch' eng. LC 76-8292. (Cambridge Studies in Chinese History, Literature & Institutions). (Illus.). 1977. 57.50 (ISBN 0-521-21082-8). Cambridge U Pr.

Curwen, H., tr. see Poe, Edgar Allan.

Curwen, Henry. History of Booksellers, the Old & the New. LC 68-19656. (Illus.). 490p. 1968. Repr. of 1873 ed. 37.00x (ISBN 0-8103-3300-7). Gale.

Curwen, Peter J. The UK Publishing Industry. (Illus.). 176p. 1981. 18.00 (ISBN 0-08-024081-X). Pergamon.

Curwen, Samuel. Journal & Letters of Samuel Curwen, an American in England, from 1775-1783. Ward, George A., ed. LC 70-14720. (Era of the American Revolution Ser). 1970. Repr. of 1864 ed. lib. bdg. 85.00 (ISBN 0-306-71923-1). Da Capo.

--Journal & Letters of the Late Samuel Curwen. Ward, G. A., ed. LC 72-1002. Repr. of 1842 ed. 37.50 (ISBN 0-404-01889-0). AMS Pr.

--The Journal of Samuel Curwen, Loyalist, 2 vols. Oliver, Andrew, ed. LC 72-180150. (Illus.). 1972. Set. text ed. 50.00x (ISBN 0-674-48380-4). Harvard U Pr.

Curwin, H. A History of Booksellers. 59.95 (ISBN 0-8490-0318-0). Gordon Pr.

Curwin, Richard & Fuhrmann, Barbara. Discovering Your Teaching Self: Humanistic Approaches to Effective Teaching. LC 74-11371. (Curriculum & Teaching Ser.). (Illus.). 256p. 1975. pap. text ed. 18.95 (ISBN 0-13-216077-3). P-H.

Curwin, Richard & Mendler, Allen. The Discipline Book: A Complete Guide to School & Classroom Management. (Illus.). 1979. pap. 11.95 (ISBN 0-8359-1336-8). Reston.

Curwin, Richard & Timmerman, Tim. Making Evaluation Meaningful. (Mandala Series in Education). 1985. text ed. 16.50x (ISBN 0-8290-0555-2); 9.95 (ISBN 0-8290-1078-5). Irvington.

Curwin, Sandra, jt. ed. see Stanish, William D.

Curwood, James O. Baree, Son of Kazan. Repr. lib. bdg. 15.95 (ISBN 0-88411-858-4, Pub. by Aeonian Pr). Amereon Ltd.

--Courage of Captain Plum. LC 71-144593. (BCL Ser. I). (Illus.). Repr. of 1908 ed. 18.00 (ISBN 0-404-01895-5). AMS Pr.

--Falkner of the Inland Seas. 1976. Repr. of 1931 ed. lib. bdg. 16.95 (ISBN 0-88411-851-7, Pub. by Aeonian Pr). Amereon Ltd.

--The Flaming Forest. 1976. Repr. of 1946 ed. lib. bdg. 16.95 (ISBN 0-88411-852-5, Pub. by Aeonian Pr). Amereon Ltd.

--The Glory of Living. 20.95 (ISBN 0-89190-144-2, Pub. by Am Repr). Amereon Ltd.

--God's Country: The Trail of Happiness. 1976. Repr. of 1921 ed. lib. bdg. 13.95 (ISBN 0-88411-853-3, Pub. by Aeonian Pr). Amereon Ltd.

--The Gold Hunters. 1976. Repr. of 1944 ed. lib. bdg. 17.95 (ISBN 0-88411-854-1, Pub. by Aeonian Pr). Amereon Ltd.

--Kazan. 1976. Repr. of 1914 ed. lib. bdg. 18.95 (ISBN 0-88411-855-X, Pub. by Aeonian Pr). Amereon Ltd.

--Nomads of the North. 1919. 39.00x (ISBN 0-403-00802-6). Scholarly.
--Nomads of the North: A Story of Romance & Adventure under the Open Stars. LC 78-127911. (BCL Ser. I). (Illus.). Repr. of 1919 ed. 17.50 (ISBN 0-404-01896-3). AMS Pr.
--The River's End. 1976. Repr. of 1919 ed. lib. bdg. 16.95x (ISBN 0-88411-856-8, Pub. by Aeonian Pr). Amereon Ltd.
--The Valley of the Silent Men. 1976. Repr. of 1920 ed. lib. bdg. 16.95x (ISBN 0-88411-857-6, Puib. by Aeonian Bks). Amereon Ltd.
Curzio, M. Some Problems of Sylow Type in Locally Finite Groups. 1981. 23.00 (ISBN 0-12-363605-1). Acad Pr.
Curzon, Daniel. Among the Carnivores. Ashton, Sylvia, ed. LC 77-94071. 1979. 14.95 (ISBN 0-87949-124-8). Ashley Bks.
--From Violent Men: A Novel. 248p. (Orig.). 1983. pap. 6.95 (ISBN 0-930650-04-2). D Brown Bks.
--Human Warmth & Other Stories. LC 80-23270. 140p. 1981. pap. 4.95 (ISBN 0-912516-54-2). Grey Fox.
--The Joyful Blue Book of Gracious Gay Etiquette. (Orig.). 1982. pap. 4.95 (ISBN 0-930650-03-4). D Brown Bks.
--The Misadventures of Tim McPick: A Gay Comedy. LC 75-32707. 1980. pap. 4.50 (ISBN 0-930650-02-6). D Brown Bks.
--The Revolt of the Perverts (Gay Short Stories) LC 77-83394. (Orig.). 1978. pap. 4.50 (ISBN 0-930650-01-8). D Brown Bks.
--Something You Do in the Dark. LC 77-150260. 1979. pap. 11.95 (ISBN 0-87949-138-8). Ashley Bks.
--The World Can Break Your Heart. LC 84-19409. 256p. (Orig.). 1985. pap. 6.95 (ISBN 0-915175-07-X). Knights Pr.
Curzon, G., ed. The Biochemistry of Psychiatric Disturbances. LC 80-40498. 144p. 1980. 49.95x (ISBN 0-471-27814-9, Pub. by Wiley-Interscience). Wiley.
Curzon, G., jt. ed. see Tricklebank, M. D.
Curzon, George. Frontiers. LC 76-48338. 1977. Repr. of 1908 ed. lib. bdg. 22.50x (ISBN 0-8371-9316-8, CUFR). Greenwood.
Curzon, George N. Persia & the Persian Question, 2 vols. new ed. 1966. 85.00x set (ISBN 0-7146-1969-8, F Cass Co). Biblio Dist.
--Persia & the Persian Question, 2 vols. 1976. lib. bdg. 200.00 (ISBN 0-8490-2422-6). Gordon Pr.
--Russia in Central Asia in 1889 & the Anglo-Russian Question. new ed. (Illus.). 477p. 1967. 39.50x (ISBN 0-7146-1465-3, F Cass Co). Biblio Dist.
Curzon, L. B. A Dictionary of Law. 2nd ed. 405p. 1983. pap. 19.95x (ISBN 0-7121-0439-9). Trans-Atlantic.
--English Legal History. 2nd ed. 352p. 1979. pap. 15.95x (ISBN 0-7121-0578-6, Pub. by Macdonald & Evans England). Trans-Atlantic.
--Roman Law. 240p. 1974. pap. 16.95x (ISBN 0-7121-1853-5, Pub. by Macdonald & Evans England). Trans-Atlantic.
Curzon, Lucia. The Chadbourne Luck. (Second Chance at Love, Regency Ser.: No. 3). 192p. (Orig.). 1981. pap. 1.75 (ISBN 0-515-05624-3). Jove Pubns.
--The Dashing Guardian. (Second Chance at Love Ser.: No. 123). 192p. 1983. pap. 1.95 (ISBN 0-515-07211-7). Jove Pubns.
--Mourning Bride, No. 57. (Second Chance at Love Ser.). 1982. pap. 1.75 (ISBN 0-515-05625-1). Jove Pubns.
--Queen of Hearts. (Second Chance at Love Ser.: No. 87). 1982. pap. 1.75 (ISBN 0-515-06698-2). Jove Pubns.
Curzon, Martin E. Trace Elements & Dental Disease. (Illus.). 430p. 1983. case bound 38.50 (ISBN 0-7236-7035-8). PSG Pub Co.
Curzon, Robert. Visits to Monasteries in the Levant. 400p. 1983. pap. 11.95 (ISBN 0-686-46958-5, 021260104X). Hippocrene Bks.
--Visits to Monasteries in the Levant. (Travel Classics Ser.). 400p. 1985. lib. bdg. 23.95 (ISBN 0-7126-0104-X, Pub. by Century Pubs UK). Hippocrene Bks.
Curzon, Victoria. The Essentials of Economic Integration. LC 73-88026. 300p. 1974. 27.50 (ISBN 0-312-26425-9). St Martin.
Cusa, Nicolas De see DeCusa, Nicolas.
Cusa, Nicolas De see De Cusa, Nicolas.
Cusa, Noel, ed. Tunnicliffe's Birds: Measured Drawings by C. N. Tunnicliffe. LC 84-81060. (Illus.). 1984. 49.95 (ISBN 0-316-16556-5). Little.
Cusac, Marian H. Narrative Structure in the Novels of Sir Walter Scott. LC 73-80839. (De Proprietatibus Litterarum, Ser. Practica: No. 6). (Orig.). 1969. pap. text ed. 9.60x (ISBN 0-686-22418-3). Mouton.
Cusack & James. Four Winds & a Family. 12.50x (ISBN 0-392-16669-0, ABC). Sportshelf.
Cusack, David F. Revolution & Reaction: The Internal & International Dynamics of Conflict & Confrontation in Chile. (Monograph Series in World Affairs: Vol. 14, 1976-77 Ser., Bk. 3). 146p. (Orig.). 1977. pap. 5.95 (ISBN 0-87940-052-8). Monograph Series.
Cusack, David F., ed. Agroclimate Information for Development: Reviving the Green Revolution. 300p. 1982. hardcover 22.50x (ISBN 0-86531-429-2). Westview.
Cusack, Isabel L. Ivan the Great. LC 77-26593. (Illus.). (gr. 1-4). 1978. Crowell Jr Bks.
Cusack, Michael, jt. auth. see Pirtle, Caleb.
Cusack, Odean & Smith, Elaine, eds. Pets & the Elderly: The Therapeutic Bond. LC 83-26409. (Activities, Adaptation & Aging Ser.: Vol. 4, Nos. 2/3). (Illus.). 257p. 1984. text ed. 19.95 (ISBN 0-86656-259-1, B259). Haworth Pr.
Cusack, Ralph. Cadenza. rev. ed. LC 84-21372. 228p. 1984. 20.00 (ISBN 0-916583-04-X); pap. 4.50 (ISBN 0-916583-05-8). Dalkey Arch.
Cusack, Suzanne B. Women & Relapse. 36p. (Orig.). 1984. pap. 1.50 (ISBN 0-89486-237-5). Hazelden.
Cusatelli, G. Dizionario Garzanti della Lingua Italiana. 1008p. (Ital.). 1979. 19.95 (ISBN 0-686-97335-6, M-9189). French & Eur.
--Dizionario Garzanti della Lingua Italiana. 2008p. (Ital.). 1980. 49.95 (ISBN 0-686-97336-4, M-9190). French & Eur.
Cusatelli, G. & Brunacci, G. Dizionario Garzanti: Francese-Italiano, Italiano-Francese. Salati, U. & Dominicis, F., eds. 2029p. (Fr. & Ital.). 1980. 49.95 (ISBN 0-686-92560-2, M-6143). French & Eur.
Cusatelli, G., ed. Dizionario Garzanti della Lingua Italiana. 968p. (Ital.). write for info. (M-9188). French & Eur.
Cuse, Arthur. Financial Guideline: Divorce. 160p. (Orig.). 1971. pap. 9.95 (ISBN 0-917474-03-1). Guideline Pub.
--How to Make it in Gold & Not Get @#$! (Orig.). 1974. pap. 9.95 (ISBN 0-917474-02-3). Guideline Pub.
Cusens, A. R. & Pama, R. P. Bridge Deck Analysis. LC 74-3726. 278p. 1975. 64.95 (ISBN 0-471-18998-7, Pub. by Wiley-Interscience). Wiley.
Cusens, Anthony R., jt. auth. see Loo, Yew C.
Cushenbery, Donald C. Guide to Meeting Reading Competency Requirements: Effective Diagnosis & Correction of Difficulties. LC 81-9524. 264p. 1981. 17.50x (ISBN 0-13-370353-3, Parker). P-H.
--Improving Reading Skills in the Content Area. 152p. 1985. 19.75x (ISBN 0-398-05099-6). C C Thomas.
--Reading Improvement Through Diagnosis, Remediation & Individualized Instruction. cancelled 12.95 (ISBN 0-13-756536-4, Parker). P-H.
Cushenbery, Donald C. & Gilreath, Kenneth J. Effective Reading Instruction for Slow Learners. 178p. 1972. 19.75x (ISBN 0-398-02543-6). C C Thomas.
Cushenbery, Donald C. & Howell, Helen. Reading & the Gifted Child: A Guide for Teachers. 186p. 1974. 16.50x (ISBN 0-398-03186-X). C C Thomas.
Cushenbery, Donald C. & Meyer, Ronald E. Reading Comprehension Mastery Kits, 6 bks. Incl. Critical Reading (ISBN 0-87628-701-1); Drawing Conclusions (ISBN 0-87628-698-8); Following Directions (ISBN 0-87628-699-6); Locating Hidden Meaning (ISBN 0-87628-700-3); Recognizing Main Ideas (ISBN 0-87628-697-X); Understanding Details (ISBN 0-87628-696-1). 1980. pap. 8.10x ea. Ctr Appl Res.
Cushieri, A. Common Bile Duct Exploration. (Developments in Surgery Ser.). 1984. lib. bdg. 76.50 (ISBN 0-89838-639-X, Pub. by Martinus Nijhoff Netherlands). Kluwer Academic.
Cushieri, A. & Giles, G. R., eds. Essential Surgical Practice. (Illus.). 1296p. 1982. text ed. 68.00 (ISBN 0-7236-0622-6). PSG Pub Co.
Cushing. Quantifier Meanings. (Linguistics Ser.: Vol. 48). 388p. 1982. pap. 44.75 (ISBN 0-444-86445-8, North Holland). Elsevier.
Cushing, Barry E. Accounting Information Systems & Business Organizations. 3rd ed. LC 81-2411. (Accounting Ser.). (Illus.). 808p. 1981. text ed. 36.95 (ISBN 0-201-10111-4); instrs' manual 21.95 (ISBN 0-201-10112-2). Addison-Wesley.
Cushing, Barry E., jt. auth. see Davis, James R.
Cushing, Barry E. & Krogstad, Jack L., eds. Frontiers of Auditing Research. (Studies in Accounting: No. 7). 1977. pap. 7.00 (ISBN 0-87755-267-3). Bureau Busn UT.
Cushing, C. E., Jr., ed. see Symposium on Radioecology, Oregon State University, May 12-14, 1975.
Cushing, Mrs. C. H. & Gray, Mrs. B., eds. The Kansas Home Cook-Book. 5th ed. LC 72-9792. (Cookery Americana Ser). Repr. of 1886 ed. 11.00 (ISBN 0-405-05045-3). Ayer Co Pubs.
Cushing, C. M. Integrodifferential Equations & Delay Models in Population Dynamics. LC 77-17425. (Lecture Notes in Biomathematics: Vol. 20). 1977. pap. text ed. 14.00 (ISBN 0-387-08449-5). Springer-Verlag.
Cushing, Caleb. Treaty of Washington: Its Negotiation, Execution & the Discussions Relating Thereto. facsimile ed. LC 72-114872. (Select Bibliographies Reprint Ser). 1873. 19.00 (ISBN 0-8369-5277-4). Ayer Co Pubs.
Cushing, D. H. Climate & Fisheries. 1983. 49.50 (ISBN 0-12-199720-0). Acad Pr.
--Detection of Fish. 220p. 1973. text ed. 50.00 (ISBN 0-08-017123-0). Pergamon.
--Fisheries Biology: A Study in Population Dynamics. 2nd ed. LC 79-5405. (Illus.). 320p. 1981. 19.95x (ISBN 0-299-08110-9). U of Wis Pr.
--Marine Ecology & Fisheries. LC 74-82218. (Illus.). 228p. 1975. 62.50 (ISBN 0-521-20501-8); pap. 22.95 (ISBN 0-521-09911-0). Cambridge U Pr.
--Science & the Fisheries. (Studies in Biology: No. 85). 64p. 1978. pap. text ed. 9.85 (ISBN 0-7131-2674-4). E Arnold.
Cushing, D. H., intro. by. Key Papers on Fish Population. (Illus.). 426p. (Orig.). 1983. pap. 42.00 (ISBN 0-904147-58-4). IRL Pr.
Cushing, D. H. see Russell, F. S.
Cushing, David H. Recruitment & Parent Stock in Fishes. (Washington Sea Grant). 197p. 1973. pap. 12.50x (ISBN 0-295-95311-X). U of Wash Pr.
Cushing, Frank H. Explorations of Key Dwellers' Remains on the Gulf Coast of Florida. LC 72-5007. (Antiquities of the New World Ser.: Vol. 13). (Illus.). Repr. of 1896 ed. 22.00 (ISBN 0-404-57313-4). AMS Pr.
--My Adventures in Zuni. LC 70-459. (Wild & Woolly West Ser., No. 5). (Illus.). 1967. 8.00 (ISBN 0-910584-80-X); pap. 2.50 (ISBN 0-910584-05-2). Filter.
--Outlines of Zuni Creation Myths. LC 74-7947. Repr. of 1896 ed. 20.00 (ISBN 0-404-11834-8). AMS Pr.
--Zuni Breadstuff. LC 74-7948. Repr. of 1920 ed. 48.50 (ISBN 0-404-11835-6). AMS Pr.
--Zuni Fetishes. LC 66-23329. (Illus.). 1966. pap. 3.00 (ISBN 0-916122-03-4). KC Pubns.
--Zuni Folk Tales. LC 74-7949. Repr. of 1901 ed. 35.50 (ISBN 0-404-11836-4). AMS Pr.
--Zuni Folk Tales. 1977. lib. bdg. 59.95 (ISBN 0-8490-2858-2). Gordon Pr.
--Zuni: Selected Writings of Frank Hamilton Cushing. Green, Jesse, ed. LC 78-14295. (Illus.). xiv, 440p. 1979. 26.50x (ISBN 0-8032-2100-2); pap. 8.50 (ISBN 0-8032-7007-0, BB 779, Bison). U of Nebr Pr.
Cushing, G. F. Hungarian Prose & Verse. (London East European Ser.). 199p. 1956. 25.00 (ISBN 0-485-17501-0, Pub. by Athlone Pr Ltd). Longwood Pub Group.
Cushing, G. F., et al, trs. see Warriner, Doreen.
Cushing, George & Starsmore, Ian. Steam at Thursford. (Illus.). 200p. 1982. 19.95 (ISBN 0-7153-8154-7). David & Charles.
Cushing, George M. Great Buildings & Sights of Boston: A Photographic Guide. Urquhart, Ross, Jr., ed. (Illus.). 160p. 1982. pap. 7.95 (ISBN 0-486-24219-6). Dover.
Cushing, George M., Jr. Great Buildings of Boston. 1983. 15.50 (ISBN 0-8446-5951-7). Peter Smith.
Cushing, Harry A. History of the Transition from Provincial to Commonwealth Government in Massachusetts. LC 78-120212. (Columbia University. Studies in the Social Sciences: No. 17). Repr. of 1896 ed. 21.50 (ISBN 0-404-51017-5). AMS Pr.
--Voting Trusts: A Chapter in Modern Corporate History. LC 27-22631. (Business Enterprises Reprint Ser.). 262p. 1983. Repr. of 1927 ed. lib. bdg. 35.00 (ISBN 0-89941-273-4). W S Hein.
Cushing, Harvey. Intracranial Tumors: Notes Upon a Series of Two Thousand Verified Cases with Surgical-Mortality Percentages Pertaining Thereto. (Illus.). 154p. 1932. photocopy ed. 19.75x (ISBN 0-398-04236-5). C C Thomas.
--Life of Sir William Osler, 2 Vols. (Illus.). 1940. boxed 75.00x (ISBN 0-19-500524-4). Oxford U Pr.
--Papers Relating to the Pituitary Body, Hypothalamus & Parasympathetic Nervous System. (Illus.). 234p. 1932. photocopy ed. 25.75x (ISBN 0-398-04237-3). C C Thomas.
Cushing, Harvey & Bailey, Percival. Tumors Arising from the Blood Vessels of the Brain: Angiomatous Malformations & Hemangioblastomas. (Illus.). 232p. 1928. photocopy ed. 25.50x (ISBN 0-398-04238-1). C C Thomas.
Cushing, Harvey & Eisenhardt, Louise. The Meningiomas: Their Classification, Regional Behaviour, Life History, & Surgical End Results. (Illus.). 802p. 1938. photocopy ed. 75.50x (ISBN 0-398-04239-X). C C Thomas.
Cushing, Harvey, jt. auth. see Bailey, Percival.
Cushing, Harvey W. Consecratio Medici & Other Papers. facsimile ed. LC 70-99688. (Essay Index Reprint Ser.). 1928. 21.00 (ISBN 0-8369-1565-8). Ayer Co Pubs.
Cushing, Helen G. Children's Song Index: An Index to More Than Twenty-Two Thousand Songs in a Hundred Eighty-Nine Collections Comprising Two Hundred Twenty-Two Volumes. 798p. 1936. Repr. 125.00 (ISBN 0-403-01530-8). Scholarly.
Cushing, James S. The Genealogy of the Cushing Family: An Account of the Ancestors & Descendants of Matthew Cushing, Who Came to America in 1638. LC 79-55650. (Illus.). 668p. 1979. Repr. of 1905 ed. 25.00x (ISBN 0-9603588-0-3). H G Cushing.
Cushing, James T., et al, eds. Science & Reality. LC 84-40360. 240p. 1984. text ed. 21.95 (ISBN 0-268-01714-X, 85-17146); pap. text ed. 11.95 (ISBN 0-268-01715-8, 85-17153). U of Notre Dame Pr.
Cushing, John D. Laws of the Pilgrims. 1978. facsimile ed. 8.50 (ISBN 0-940628-00-7). Pilgrim Hall.
Cushing, John D., ed. A Bibliography of the Laws & Resolves of the Massachusetts Bay: 1642-1780. 60.00 (ISBN 0-89453-383-5). M Glazier.
Cushing, John D., compiled by. The First Laws of the Commonwealth of Massachusetts. (Earliest Laws of the Original Thirteen States Ser.). 1981. 48.00 (ISBN 0-89453-212-X). M Glazier.
--The First Laws of the Commonwealth of Pennsylvania. (Earliest Laws of the Original Thirteen States Ser.). 1981. 58.00 (ISBN 0-89453-220-0). M Glazier.
--The First Laws of the State of Connecticut. (Earliest Laws of the Original Thirteen States Ser.). 1981. 56.00 (ISBN 0-89453-219-7). M Glazier.
--The First Laws of the State of Delaware, 4 vols. (Earliest Laws of the Original Thirteen States Ser.). 1981. Set. 132.00 (ISBN 0-89453-216-2). M Glazier.
--The First Laws of the State of Georgia, 2 vols. (Earliest Laws of the Original Thirteen States Ser.). 1981. 49.00 ea.; Set. 98.00 (ISBN 0-89453-218-9). M Glazier.
--The First Laws of the State of Maryland. (Earliest Laws of the Original Thirteen States Ser.). 1981. 49.00 (ISBN 0-89453-213-8). M Glazier.
--The First Laws of the State of New Jersey. (Earliest Laws of the Original Thirteen States Ser.). 1981. 49.00 (ISBN 0-89453-217-0). M Glazier.
--The First Laws of the State of New York. (Earliest Laws of the Original Thirteen States Ser.). 1981. 45.00 (ISBN 0-89453-223-5). M Glazier.
--The First Laws of the State of North Carolina, 2 vols. (Earliest Laws of the Original Thirteen States Ser.). 1981. Set. 96.00 (ISBN 0-89453-222-7). M Glazier.
--The First Laws of the State of Rhode Island, 2 vols. (Earliest Laws of the Original Thirteen States Ser.). 1981. Set. 94.00 (ISBN 0-89453-224-3). M Glazier.
--The First Laws of the State of South Carolina, 2 vols. 1790 ed. (Earliest Laws of the Original Thirteen States Ser.). 1981. Set. (2 vols.) 82.00 (ISBN 0-89453-214-6). M Glazier.
--The First Laws of the State of Virginia. (Earliest Laws of the Original Thirteen States Ser.). 1981. 45.00 (ISBN 0-89453-221-9). M Glazier.
--The First Laws of the State of New Hampshire. (Law Ser.). 1981. 35.00 (ISBN 0-89453-215-4). M Glazier.
Cushing, John D., intro. by. The Laws & Liberties of Massachusetts 1641-1691, 3 vol. facsimile ed. LC 75-24575. 1976. Set. 95.00 (ISBN 0-8420-2074-8). Scholarly Res Inc.
Cushing, Luther S., ed. see Domat, Jean.
Cushing, M. & Wickwar, W. H. Baron D'Holbach. 59.95 (ISBN 0-87968-707-X). Gordon Pr.
Cushing, Marshall. The Story of Our Post Office, 2 vols. 1976. lib. bdg. 200.00 (ISBN 0-8490-1137-X). Gordon Pr.
Cushing, Mary G. Pierre Le Tourneur. LC 8-30946. (Columbia University. Studies in Romance Philology & Literature: No. 8). Repr. of 1908 ed. 22.50 (ISBN 0-404-50608-9). AMS Pr.
Cushing, Mary W. The Rainbow Bridge. Farkas, Andrew, ed. LC 76-29932. (Opera Biographies). (Illus.). 1977. Repr. of 1954 ed. lib. bdg. 30.00x (ISBN 0-405-09674-7). Ayer Co Pubs.
Cushing, Maureen. Nursing Jurisprudence. 1983. text ed. 18.95 (ISBN 0-8359-5037-9). Reston.
Cushing, Max P. Baron d'Holbach: A Study of Eighteenth Century Radicalism in France. LC 76-166444. (Philosophy Monograph: No. 76). 1971. Repr. of 1914 ed. lib. bdg. 16.50 (ISBN 0-8337-4060-1). B Franklin.
Cushing, Richard C. Mission of the Teacher. 1977. 3.00 (ISBN 0-8198-0542-4); pap. 2.00 (ISBN 0-8198-0543-2). Dghtrs St Paul.
--St. Martin de Porres. LC 62-20203. (Illus.). 75p. 1981. 4.00 (ISBN 0-8198-6818-3, STO280); pap. 2.00 (ISBN 0-8198-6819-1). Dghtrs St Paul.
--St. Patrick & the Irish. 1963. 3.50 (ISBN 0-8198-6824-8); pap. 2.00 (ISBN 0-8198-6827-2). Dghtrs St Paul.
Cushing, Richard J. Eternal Thoughts from Christ the Teacher, 2 Vols. 1962. 3.50 ea. Vol. 1 (ISBN 0-8198-0606-4). Vol. 2 (ISBN 0-8198-0607-2). Dghtrs St Paul.
--Meditations for Religious. 1959. 3.00 (ISBN 0-8198-0102-X). Dghtrs St Paul.
--Pope Pius the Twelfth. (Illus., Orig.). 4.00 (ISBN 0-8198-0125-9). Dghtrs St Paul.
Cushing, Thomas, ed. A Genealogical & Biographical History of Allegheny County, Pennsylvania. LC 75-21638. 577p. 1975. Repr. of 1889 ed. 25.00 (ISBN 0-8063-0686-6). Genealog Pub.
Cushing, Thomas, tr. see Cossery, Albert.
Cushing, William. Anonyms: A Dictionary of Revealed Authorship. 1968. Repr. of 1889 ed. 87.00x (ISBN 3-487-02714-3). Adlers Foreign Bks.
--Initials & Pseudonyms: A Dictionary of Literary Disguises, 2 Vols. 1969. Repr. of 1886 ed. Set. 107.50x (ISBN 3-4870-2516-7). Adlers Foreign Bks.
--Initials & Pseudonyms: A Dictionary of Literary Disguises, 2 Vols. 936p. 1982. Repr. of 1888 ed. Set. 85.00x (ISBN 0-8103-3962-5). Gale.

Cushion, J. P. Pocket Book of British Ceramic Marks. 3rd ed. LC 83-16527. (Illus.). 432p. (Orig.). 1984. pap. 8.95 (ISBN 0-571-13108-5). Faber & Faber.
Cushion, J. P. & Honey, W. B. Handbook of Pottery & Porcelain Marks. 4th, rev. ed. (Illus.). 272p. 1980. 30.00 (ISBN 0-571-04922-2). Faber & Faber.
Cushion, John. Continental Porcelain. Rev. ed. (Letts Collectors' Guides). (Illus.). 79p. 1982. 9.95 (ISBN 0-85097-354-6, Pub by C Letts Bks UK). Seven Hills bks.
--English Porcelain. Rev. ed. (Letts Collector's Guides). (Illus.). 72p. 1982. 9.95 (ISBN 0-85097-349-X, Pub by C Letts Bks UK). Seven Hills Bks.
Cushion, John P. Connoisseur Illustrated Guides: Pottery & Porcelain. (Illus.). 1975. pap. 6.45 (ISBN 0-380-01113-1, 26708). Avon.
--Continental China Collecting for Amateurs. 5.95 (ISBN 0-87505-141-3). Borden.
Cushman. Construction Labor Law. (Business Practice Library). Date not set. price not set (ISBN 0-471-82489-5). Wiley.
--Law of Underground Construction. (Trial Practice Library). Date not set. price not set (ISBN 0-471-82488-7). Wiley.
Cushman, Charlotte. Charlotte Cushman: Her Letters & Memories of Her Life. Stebbins, Emma, ed. LC 76-82823. (Illus.). 1972. Repr. of 1879 ed. lib. bdg. 18.00 (ISBN 0-405-08417-X, Blom Pubns). Ayer Co Pubs.
Cushman, Dan. Dan Cushman's Cow-Country Cook Book. LC 67-21434. (Illus.). 1967. 12.50 (ISBN 0-911436-02-2). Stay Away.
--The Girl I Left Behind Me. 230p. Date not set. 13.95 (ISBN 0-8027-4039-1). Walker & Co.
--Montana-the Gold Frontier. LC 73-83492. 15.00 (ISBN 0-911436-03-0). Stay Away.
--The Muskrat Farm. LC 59-6988. 1977. 12.50 (ISBN 0-911436-05-7). Stay Away.
--Plenty of Room & Air. LC 75-20626. 1975. 12.50 (ISBN 0-911436-04-9). Stay Away.
--Rusty Irons. LC 83-40428. 224p. 1984. 12.95 (ISBN 0-8027-4031-6). Walker & Co.
--Rusty Irons. 1985. pap. 2.50 (ISBN 0-345-32697-0). Ballantine.
--Stay Away, Joe. LC 52-12887. 1968. 12.50 (ISBN 0-911436-01-4); pap. 3.75 (ISBN 0-911436-06-5). Stay Away.
Cushman, Donald P. & Cahn, Dudley D., Jr. Communication in Interpersonal Relationships. (Human Communications Processes Ser.). 304p. 1984. 29.50x (ISBN 0-87395-909-4); pap. 9.95x (ISBN 0-87395-910-8). State U NY Pr.
Cushman, Donald P. & McPhee, Robert D., eds. Message-Attitude-Behavior Relationship: Theory, Methodology & Application. LC 80-529. (Human Communications Research Ser.). 1980. 32.00 (ISBN 0-12-199760-X). Acad Pr.
Cushman, Doug. Nasty Kyle the Crocodile. (Illus.). (ps-1). 1983. 5.95 (ISBN 0-448-16592-9, G&D). Putnam Pub Group.
Cushman, Doug, illus. The Pudgy Fingers Counting Book. (Pudgy Board Bks.). (Illus.). 16p. (ps-3). 1983. pap. 2.95 (ISBN 0-448-10202-1, G&D). Putnam Pub Group.
Cushman, Elizabeth, jt. auth. see Conger, Wilda L.
Cushman, Horatio B. History of the Choctaw, Chickasaw & Natchez Indians. Debo, Angie, ed. LC 72-180607. 503p. (Repr. of abr. 1962 ed. of a work first published in 1899). 1972. 23.00x (ISBN 0-8462-1640-X). Russell.
Cushman, J. A. The American Species of Orthophragmina & Lepidocyclina. 1971. Repr. of 1928 ed. 15.60 (ISBN 0-934454-06-X). Lubrecht & Cramer.
--The Foraminifera of the Mint Spring Calcareous Marl Member of the Marianna Limestone. Repr. of 1922 ed. 4.30 (ISBN 0-934454-37-X). Lubrecht & Cramer.
--A Lower Miocene Foraminifera of Florida. Repr. of 1924 ed. 5.85 (ISBN 0-934454-58-2). Lubrecht & Cramer.
--Upper Cretaceous Foraminifera of the Gulf Coastal Region. Repr. of 1946 ed. 21.80 (ISBN 0-934454-79-5). Lubrecht & Cramer.
--Upper Eocene Foraminifera of the Southeastern U. S. Repr. of 1935 ed. 15.20 (ISBN 0-934454-80-9). Lubrecht & Cramer.
Cushman, J. A. & Cahill, E. D. Miocene Foraminifera of the Coastal Plain of the Eastern U.S. Repr. of 1935 ed. 14.80 (ISBN 0-934454-64-7). Lubrecht & Cramer.
Cushman, J. A. & Cooke, C. W. The Foraminifera of the Bryam Calcareous Marl at Byram, Mississippi & the Byram Calcareous Marl at Mississippi. 1971. 8.30 (ISBN 0-934454-36-1). Lubrecht & Cramer.
--The Foraminifera of the Vicksburg Group. Repr. of 1925 ed. 12.35 (ISBN 0-934454-38-8). Lubrecht & Cramer.
Cushman, John H. Command & Control of Theater Forces: Adequacy. LC 85-9077. (Illus.). 250p. 1985. Repr. of 1983 ed. 25.00 (ISBN 0-916159-06-X). AFCEA Intl Pr.
Cushman, Joseph A. Foraminifera: Their Classification & Economic Use. 4th rev. ed. LC 48-9473. (Illus.). 1948. 50.00x (ISBN 0-674-30801-8). Harvard U Pr.
Cushman, Joseph D., Jr. Goodly Heritage, the Episcopal Church in Florida, 1821-1892. LC 65-28693. (Illus.). 1965. 7.50 (ISBN 0-8130-0054-8). U Presses Fla.
--Sound of Bells: The Episcopal Church in South Florida, 1892-1969. LC 75-30946. (Illus.). 1976. 15.00 (ISBN 0-8130-0518-3). U Presses Fla.
Cushman, Joseph D., Jr., ed. see Eppes, Susan B.
Cushman, Kathleen & Miller, Edward, eds. How to Produce a Small Newspaper: A Guide for Independent Journalists. 2nd, rev. ed. (Illus.). 192p. (Orig.). 1983. 12.95 (ISBN 0-916782-40-9); pap. 9.95 (ISBN 0-916782-39-5). Harvard Common Pr.
Cushman, Keith. D. H. Lawrence at Work: The Emergence of the Prussian Officer Stories. LC 77-22149. 1978. 17.50x (ISBN 0-8139-0728-4). U Pr of Va.
Cushman, Keith, jt. ed. see Healey, E. Claire.
Cushman, Kenneth M., ed. Construction Litigation. 825p. 1981. text ed. 50.00 (ISBN 0-686-78756-0, N3-1334). PLI.
Cushman, Kenneth M., jt. ed. see Cushman, Robert F.
Cushman, L. W. Devil & the Vice in the English Democratic Literature Before Shakespeare. 148p. 1970. Repr. of 1900 ed. 26.00x (ISBN 0-7146-2055-6, F Cass Co). Biblio Dist.
Cushman, M. L. Governance of Teacher Education. LC 76-52063. 1977. 24.00x (ISBN 0-8211-0228-1); text ed. 21.50x 10 or more copies. McCutchan.
Cushman, Margery. Farewell to Youth: The Diary of Margery Cushman. De Gravelles, Virginia W., intro. by. LC 82-70968. (Center for Louisiana Studies Special Publications Ser.). 216p. 1982. 5.95 (ISBN 0-940984-02-4). U of SW LA Ctr LA Studies.
Cushman, Nancy. We're a Family, Aren't We? 1979. 8.50 (ISBN 0-686-24268-8). T Weatherby.
Cushman, R. F. & Stover, A. The McGraw-Hill Construction Form Book. 448p. 1983. 39.95 (ISBN 0-07-014995-X). McGraw.
Cushman, Ralph S., compiled by. Pocket Prayer Book: Large-Type Edition. 1977. 5.00x (ISBN 0-8358-0361-9). Upper Room.
Cushman, Robert E. Civil Liberties in the United States. (Cornell Studies in Civil Liberty). 1969. Repr. of 1956 ed. 19.00 (ISBN 0-384-10400-2). Johnson Repr.
--Faith Seeking Understanding: Essays Theological & Critical. LC 80-69402. xvi, 373p. 1981. 25.00 (ISBN 0-8223-0444-9). Duke.
--The Independent Regulatory Commissions. LC 71-159176. xiv, 780p. 1972. Repr. of 1941 ed. lib. bdg. 52.00x (ISBN 0-374-92019-2). Octagon.
--Therapeia: Plato's Conception of Philosophy. LC 76-6518. 1976. Repr. of 1958 ed. lib. bdg. 42.50 (ISBN 0-8371-8879-2, CUTP). Greenwood.
Cushman, Robert F. Cases in Civil Liberties. 3rd ed. 1979. 18.95. P-H.
--Cases in Civil Liberties. 4th ed. LC 84-11468. 1985. pap. text ed. 20.95 (ISBN 0-13-118605-1). P-H.
--Cases in Constitutional Law. 5th ed. 1979. ref. 29.95. P-H.
--Cases in Constitutional Law. 6th ed. 704p. 1984. text ed. 32.95 (ISBN 0-13-118307-9). P-H.
--Leading Constitutional Decisions. 16th ed. 480p. 1982. pap. text ed. 19.95 (ISBN 0-13-527374-9). P-H.
Cushman, Robert F. & Bigda, John P. The McGraw-Hill Construction Business Handbook: A Practical Guide to Accounting, Credit, Finance, Insurance & Law for the Construction Industry. 2nd ed. LC 83-26792. 1088p. 1984. 59.95 (ISBN 0-07-014994-1). McGraw.
Cushman, Robert F. & Perry, Sherryl R. Planning, Financing & Constructing Health Care Facilities. LC 82-16343. 386p. 1982. 42.50 (ISBN 0-89443-839-5). Aspen Systems.
Cushman, Robert F. & Simon, Michael S. Construction Industry Formbook: A Practical Guide to Reviewing & Drafting Forms for the Construction Industry. LC 78-26427. (Construction Law-Land Use Environmental Publications). 350p. 1979. 70.00 (ISBN 0-07-014976-3, Shepards-McGraw). McGraw.
Cushman, Robert F. & Cushman, Kenneth M., eds. Construction Litigation: Representing the Owner. LC 84-3495. (Trial Practice Library Ser.: 1-676). 381p. 1984. 75.00x (ISBN 0-471-89542-3, Pub. by Wiley Law Pubns). Wiley.
Cushman, Robert F. & Morey, Herbert A., eds. A Guide for the Foreign Investor: Doing Business in the USA. LC 83-70854. 525p. 1984. 45.00 (ISBN 0-87094-422-3). Dow Jones-Irwin.
Cushman, Robert F. & Rodin, Neal I., eds. Property Management Handbook: A Practical Guide to Real Estate Management. LC 84-10427. (Real Estate for Professional Practitioners Ser.: 1-242). 480p. 1984. 49.95x (ISBN 0-471-87503-1, Pub. by Ronald Pr). Wiley.
Cushman, Robert F. & Stamm, Charles H., eds. Handling Property & Casualty Claims. 525p. 1984. Annual supplements avail. 75.00 (ISBN 0-471-89541-5). Wiley.
Cushman, Robert F., et al. High Tech Real Estate: Planning, Adapting & Operating Buildings in the Computer & Telecommunications Age. 1985. 50.00 (ISBN 0-87094-611-0). Dow Jones-Irwin.
Cushman, Robert R. & Stamm, Charles H., eds. Handling Fidelity & Surety Claims. LC 84-7546. 450p. 1984. 75.00x (ISBN 0-471-89543-1, Pub. by Wiley Law Pubns). Wiley.
Cushman, Ronald, jt. auth. see Keyes, Ruth.
Cushman, Ronald A. & Daggett, Willard. Retail Merchandising. (Co-Operative Education Workbook Series). 1975. 5.50 (ISBN 0-87005-153-9). Fairchild.
--Supermarket Merchandising. (Co-Operative Education Wkbk. Ser). (gr. 7-12). 1976. text ed. 5.50 (ISBN 0-87005-155-5); tchrs' manual 2.50 (ISBN 0-87005-158-X). Fairchild.
Cushman, Ronald A. & Daggett, Willard R. Business-Office Teacher's Manual. (Cooperative Education Workbook Ser.). 58p. (gr. 7-12). 1976. 2.50 (ISBN 0-87005-157-1). Fairchild.
--Business-Office Workbook. (Co-Operative Education Workbook Ser.). 75p. (gr. 7-12). 1976. 5.50 (ISBN 0-87005-154-7). Fairchild.
--Retail Merchandising Teacher's Manual. (Co-Operative Education Workbook Series). 1975. 2.50 (ISBN 0-87005-156-3). Fairchild.
Cushman, Rudolf E. Peculiar Forms of Ancient Religious Cults. (Illus.). 1980. deluxe ed. 67.50 (ISBN 0-89266-234-4). Am Classical Coll Pr.
Cushman, Stephen. William Carlos Williams & the Meanings of Measure. LC 85-3364. (Yale Studies in English: No. 193). 176p. 1985. 13.50X (ISBN 0-300-03373-7). Yale U Pr.
Cushner, Nicholas P. Farm & Factory: The Jesuits & the Development of Agrarian Capitalism in Colonial Quito. LC 81-13537. 274p. 1982. 49.50x (ISBN 0-87395-570-6); pap. 14.95x (ISBN 0-87395-571-4). State U NY Pr.
--Jesuit Ranches & the Agrarian Development of Colonial Argentina, 1650-1767. 350p. 1982. 49.50x (ISBN 0-87395-707-5); pap. 15.95x (ISBN 0-87395-706-7). State U NY Pr.
--Landed Estates in the Colonial Philippines. LC 75-27615. (Monograph Ser.: No. 20). 146p. 1976. 11.50x (ISBN 0-938692-10-0). Yale U SE Asia.
--Lords of the Land: Sugar, Wine, & Jesuit Estates of Coastal Peru, 1600-1767. 256p. 1980. 49.50x (ISBN 0-87395-438-6); pap. 15.95x (ISBN 0-87395-447-5). State U NY Pr.
Cushnie, G. C., Jr. Removal of Metals from Wastewater: Neutralization & Precipitation. LC 83-22142. (Pollution Technology Review Ser.: No. 107). (Illus.). 232p. 1984. 32.00 (ISBN 0-8155-0976-6). Noyes.
Cushnie, George C., Jr. Electroplating Wastewater Pollution Control Technology. LC 84-22696. (Pollution Technology Review Ser.: No. 115). (Illus.). 239p. 1985. 36.00 (ISBN 0-8155-1017-9). Noyes.
Cushnie, George C., Jr., jt. auth. see Saltzberg, Edward R.
Cushwa, Frank W. An Introduction to Conrad. 1933. 25.00 (ISBN 0-8274-2581-3). R West.
Cusick, Allison W. & Silberhorn, Gene M. The Vascular Plants of Unglaciated Ohio. 1977. 9.00 (ISBN 0-86727-081-0). Ohio Bio Survey.
Cusick, Lois. Waldorf Parenting Handbook: Useful Information on Child Development & Education from Anthroposophical Sources. 2nd, rev. ed. 1985. pap. 9.95 (ISBN 0-916786-75-7). St George Bk Serv.
Cusick, Philip. The Egalitarian Ideal & the American High School. LC 83-1159. (Research on Teaching Monograph). 256p. 1983. 25.00 (ISBN 0-582-29015-5). Longman.
Cusick, Philip A. Inside High School: The Students World. LC 72-90920. 1973. pap. text ed. 15.95 (ISBN 0-03-091488-4, Holtc). HR&W.
Cusick, Richard T. Evil on the Bayou. (Twilight Ser.: No. 21). (Orig.). (gr. 7-12). 1984. pap. 2.25 (ISBN 0-440-92431-6, LFL). Dell.
Cusick, Rick, compiled by see DaBoll, Raymond.
Cusick, Rick, compiled by see Reynolds, Lloyd J.
Cusick, Rick, jt. auth. see Chappell, Warren.
Cusick, Suzanne G. Valerio Dorico: Music Printer in Sixteenth Century Rome. Buelow, George, ed. LC 81-4745. (Studies in Musicology: No. 43). 330p. 1981. 49.95 (ISBN 0-8357-1173-0). UMI Res Pr.
Cusimano, Vincent J. & Halpern, Stephen. Contemporary Issues in Science: Course Manual. 139p. (Orig.). 1982. pap. text ed. 15.95 (ISBN 0-914639-25-0). SI Cont Ed Inc.
--Contemporary Issues in Science: Implementation Manual. 98p. (Orig.). 1982. pap. text ed. 15.95 (ISBN 0-914639-26-9). SI Cont Ed Inc.
Cusine, Douglas J. & Grant, John P., eds. The Impact of Marine Pollution. LC 80-670. 324p. 1980. text ed. 32.50x (ISBN 0-916672-54-9). Allanheld.
Cuskey, Walter R. & Wathey, Richard B. Female Addiction: A Longitudinal Study. LC 80-8338. (Illus.). 192p. 1981. 23.50 (ISBN 0-669-04029-0). Lexington Bks.
Cuskey, Walter R., et al. Drug-Trip Abroad: American Drug-Refugees in Amsterdam & London. LC 73-182497. (Orig.). 1972. 15.00x (ISBN 0-8122-7653-1); pap. 8.95 (ISBN 0-8122-1041-7, Pa Paperbks). U of Pa Pr.
Cuss, Gladys. Hidden Manna Revealed by the Comforter. 200p. 1981. 9.00 (ISBN 0-682-49768-1). Exposition Pr FL.
--I Have Been Before the Judgement Seat of Christ: A Religious Autobiography. 189p. 1980. 7.95 (ISBN 0-682-49521-2). Exposition Pr FL.
Cussans, J. Handbook of Heraldry. 59.95 (ISBN 0-8490-0278-8). Gordon Pr.
Cussen, J., jt. auth. see Dominicis, M. C.
Cussen, Joseph A. World Youth & the Family. 1984. pap. 6.95 (ISBN 0-941850-14-5). Sunday Pubns.
Cussen, June M. Florida Spring: Promises Already Fulfilled. (The Seasons of Florida Ser.). (Illus.). 200p. price not set. Pineapple Pr.
Cusset, Francis. English-French & French-English Technical Dictionary. rev. ed. (Eng. & Fr.). 1967. 28.50 (ISBN 0-8206-0043-1). Chem Pub.
--Vocabulaire Technique Allemand-Francais, Francais-Allemand. 8th ed. 474p. (Fr. & Ger.). 1977. 29.95 (ISBN 0-686-56970-9, M-6097). French & Eur.
--Vocabulaire Technique Anglais-Francais, Francais-Anglais. 9th ed. 434p. (Fr. & Ger.). 1977. 47.50 (ISBN 0-686-56971-7, M-6098). French & Eur.
Cussianovich, Alejandro. Religious Life & the Poor: Liberation Theology Perspectives. Drury, John, tr. from Sp. LC 78-16740. Orig. Title: Desde los Pobres de la Tiera. 168p. (Orig.). 1979. pap. 6.95 (ISBN 0-88344-429-1). Orbis Bks.
Cussler, Clive. Cyclops. 1985. 17.95 (ISBN 0-317-20672-9). S&S.
--Deep Six. 432p. 1984. 18.95 (ISBN 0-671-50373-1). S&S.
--Deep Six. 1985. pap. 4.50 (ISBN 0-671-55797-1). PB.
--Iceberg. 1977. pap. 3.95 (ISBN 0-553-14641-6). Bantam.
--The Mediterranean Caper. 1977. pap. 3.95 (ISBN 0-553-23328-9). Bantam.
--Night Probe! 1984. pap. 3.95 (ISBN 0-553-20663-X). Bantam.
--Night Probe. (General Ser.). 1982. 17.95 (ISBN 0-8161-3346-8, Large Print Bks). G K Hall.
--Pacific Vortex. 346p. 1983. pap. 3.95 (ISBN 0-553-22866-8). Bantam.
--Pacific Vortex. (Large Print Books (General Ser.)). 1985. lib. bdg. 15.95 (ISBN 0-8161-3887-7). G K Hall.
--Raise the Titanic! 384p. 1980. pap. 3.95 (ISBN 0-553-22889-7). Bantam.
--Vixen Zero Three. 1979. pap. 4.50 (ISBN 0-553-25487-1). Bantam.
Cussler, E. L. Diffusion: Mass Transfer in Fluid Systems. LC 83-1905. (Illus.). 400p. 1984. 49.50 (ISBN 0-521-23171-X). Cambridge U Pr.
--Multicomponent Diffusion. (Chemical Engineering Monographs: Vol. 3). 176p. 1976. 51.00 (ISBN 0-444-41326-X). Elsevier.
Cusson, Maurice. Why Delinquency? Crelinsten, Dorothy R., tr. from Fr. 193p. (Orig.). 1983. 20.00x (ISBN 0-8020-2514-5); pap. 8.95 (ISBN 0-8020-6530-9). U of Toronto Pr.
Cust, Anna M. The Ivory Workers of the Middle Ages. LC 70-178523. Repr. of 1902 ed. 21.00 (ISBN 0-404-56537-9). AMS Pr.
Cust, Edward. Lives of the Warriors of the Civil Wars of France & England: Warriors of the Seventeenth Century, 2 vols. facsimile ed. LC 76-38737. (Essay Index Reprint Ser). Repr. of 1867 ed. 40.00 (ISBN 0-8369-2642-0). Ayer Co Pubs.
--Lives of the Warriors of the Thirty Years' War: Warriors of the Seventeenth Century, 2 vols. facsimile ed. LC 75-38742. (Essay Index Reprint Ser). Repr. of 1865 ed. 36.00 (ISBN 0-8369-2643-9). Ayer Co Pubs.
Cust, Katherine I., ed. see Deguilleville, Guillaume de.
Custance, Arthur C. Doorway Papers: Flood; Local or Global, Vol. 9. 312p. 1985. pap. text ed. 9.95 (ISBN 0-310-23041-1, Pub. by Academie Bks). Zondervan.
--Doorway Papers: Indexes of the Doorway Papers, Vol. 10. 256p. 1985. pap. text ed. 9.95 (ISBN 0-310-38651-9, Pub. by Academie Bks). Zondervan.
--Doorway Papers: The Virgin Birth & the Incarnation, Vol. 5. 400p. 1985. pap. text ed. 10.95 (ISBN 0-310-22991-X, Pub. by Academie Bks). Zondervan.
--Evolution of Creation? (The Doorway Papers Ser.: Vol. 4). 340p. 1981. pap. 8.95 (ISBN 0-310-22981-2). Zondervan.
--The Flood: Local or Global? (Doorway Papers Ser.: Vol. 9). 1979. 9.95 (ISBN 0-310-23040-3). Zondervan.
--Genesis & Early Man, Vol II. (The Doorway Papers). 340p. 1981. pap. 8.95 (ISBN 0-310-22961-8). Zondervan.
--Indexes of the Doorway Papers, Vol. 10. 1980. 9.95 (ISBN 0-310-38650-0). Zondervan.
--Man in Adam & in Christ, Vol. 3. 336p. 1975. text ed. 9.95 (ISBN 0-310-23021-7). Zondervan.
--The Mysterious Matter of the Mind. (Christian Free University Curriculum Ser.). 1979. pap. 3.95 (ISBN 0-310-38011-1). Zondervan.
--Noah's Three Sons: Human History in Three Dimensions, Vol. 1. 320p. 1974. 9.95 (ISBN 0-310-22951-0). Zondervan.
--Science & Faith, Vol. 8. 9.95 (ISBN 0-310-23031-4). Zondervan.
--Sovereignty of Grace. 1979. 12.95 (ISBN 0-87552-160-6). Presby & Reformed.
--Time & Eternity & Other Biblical Studies. (The Doorway Papers Ser.: Vol. 6). 240p. 1982. pap. 8.95 (ISBN 0-310-23001-2). Zondervan.
--The Virgin Birth & the Incarnation, Vol. 5. 1976. 12.95 (ISBN 0-310-22990-1). Zondervan.
Custance, David R., jt. auth. see King, Gillian M.
Custance, Reginald. Study of War. LC 76-110929. 1970. Repr. of 1924 ed. 22.50x (ISBN 0-8046-0912-8, Pub. by Kennikat). Assoc Faculty Pr.

Custance, Roger. Winchester College: Sixth-Centenary Essays. (Illus.). 1982. 48.00x (ISBN 0-19-920103-X). Oxford U Pr.

Custer, Dan. The Miracle of Mind Power. 288p. 1983. pap. 5.95 (ISBN 0-13-585414-8, Reward). P-H.

--The Miracle of Mind Power. 263p. 1985. pap. 7.95 (ISBN 0-930298-20-9). Westwood Pub Co.

Custer, Elizabeth. Boots & Saddles. 312p. 1977. Repr. of 1902 ed. lib. bdg. 16.95x (ISBN 0-89966-266-8). Buccaneer Bks.

Custer, Elizabeth B. Boots & Saddles, or Life in Dakota with General Custer. 307p. 1969. Repr. of 1885 ed. 15.00 (ISBN 0-87928-006-9). Corner Hse.

--Boots & Saddles: Or Life in Dakota with General Custer. (Western Frontier Library: No. 17). (Illus.). 13.95 (ISBN 0-8061-0487-2); pap. 7.95 (ISBN 0-8061-1192-5). U of Okla Pr.

--Boots & Saddles or: Life in Dakota with General Custer. 312p. 1977. pap. 7.95. Corner Hse.

--The Kid. (Custer Monograph: No. 2). (Illus.). 47p. 1978. Repr. of 1900 ed. limited ed. 8.00x (ISBN 0-940696-05-3). Monroe County Lib.

--Tenting on the Plains. 403p. 1973. Repr. of 1887 ed. 16.95 (ISBN 0-87928-042-5). Corner Hse.

--Tenting on the Plains. LC 72-145498. (Western Frontier Library: Vols. 46, 47, 48). (Illus.). 1971. boxed set 18.95 (ISBN 0-8061-0943-2). U of Okla Pr.

Custer, George. My Life on the Plains. (The Men Who Made the West Ser.: No. 1). 288p. 1982. pap. 2.50 (ISBN 0-8439-1118-2, Leisure Bks). Dorchester Pub Co.

Custer, George A. My Life on the Plains. 620p. 1974. pap. 5.95 (ISBN 0-8065-0451-X). Citadel Pr.

--My Life on the Plains. Quaife, Milo M., ed. LC 67-2618. (Illus.). xlii, 632p. 1966. pap. 9.95 (ISBN 0-8032-5042-8, BB 328, Bison). U of Nebr Pr.

--My Life on the Plains: Or Personal Experiences with Indians. (Western Frontier Library Ser.: No. 52). 1976. 15.95 (ISBN 0-8061-0523-2); pap. 7.95 (ISBN 0-8061-1357-X). U of Okla Pr.

--Wild Life on the Plains & Horrors of Indian Warfare. LC 79-90403. (Mass Violence in America Ser). Repr. of 1891 ed. 22.50 (ISBN 0-405-01300-0). Ayer Co Pubs.

Custer, Jay F. Delaware Prehistoric Archaeology: An Ecological Approach. (Illus.). 224p. 1984. 28.50 (ISBN 0-87413-233-9). U Delaware Pr.

Custer, Patricia A. Word Processing: Hands-on Exercises. (Illus.). 240p. 1984. pap. text ed. 18.95 (ISBN 0-13-963463-0). P-H.

--Word Processing: The Applications Specialist. (Illus.). 352p. 1986. text ed. 23.95 (ISBN 0-13-963562-9). P-H.

Custer, Robert & Milt, Harry. When Luck Runs Out: Help for Compulsive Gamblers & Their Families. 1985. 16.95. Facts on File.

Custer, Stewart. Does Inspiration Demand Inerrancy? 1968. pap. 3.50 (ISBN 0-934532-07-9). Presby & Reformed.

--The Stars Speak: Astronomy in the Bible. (Illus.). 203p. (Orig.). 1977. pap. 6.95 (ISBN 0-89084-059-8). Bob Jones Univ Pr.

--Tools for Preaching & Teaching the Bible. 240p. (Orig.). 1979. pap. 6.95 (ISBN 0-89084-064-4). Bob Jones Univ Pr.

--A Treasury of New Testament Synonyms. 161p. 1975. 7.95 (ISBN 0-89084-025-3). Bob Jones Univ Pr.

Custine, Marquis De see De Custine, Marquis.

Custis, John P., jt. auth. see DeTalavera, Frances.

Custis, Peter, jt. auth. see Freeman, Thomas.

Custodio, Maurice M., ed. Contemporary Fiction: Today's Outstanding Writers. LC 76-28714. (Illus.). 1976. 10.00x (ISBN 0-914024-26-4); pap. 4.00 (ISBN 0-914024-27-2). SF Arts & Letters.

Custodio, Sidney & Dudley, Cliff. Love-Hungry Priest. LC 82-61308. 192p. (Orig.). 1983. pap. 2.95 (ISBN 0-89221-099-0). New Leaf.

Custred, Glynn, jt. ed. see Orlove, Benjamin S.

Custumbis, Michael M. A Bibliographic Guide to Materials on Greeks in the United States: Nineteen Ninety to Nineteen Sixty-Eight. LC 74-130283. 100p. 1970. 9.95 (ISBN 0-317-34056-5, 0-913256-02-1). Ctr Migration.

Cusumano, Camille. Tofu, Tempeh & Other Soy Delights: Enjoying Traditional Oriental Soyfoods in American-Style Cuisine. (Illus.). 272p. 1984. pap. 12.95 (ISBN 0-87857-489-1, 07-189-1). Rodale Pr Inc.

Cusumano, James A. & Farkas, Adalbert, eds. Catalysis in Coal Conversion. LC 77-25620. 1978. 47.50 (ISBN 0-12-199935-1). Acad Pr.

Cusumano, Michael A. The Japanese Automobile Industry: Technology & Management at Nissan & Toyota. (Harvard East Asian Monographs: No. 122). 400p. 1985. text ed. 25.00x (ISBN 0-674-47255-1, Pub. by Coun East Asian Stud). Harvard U Pr.

Cusumano, Michele. Just As the Boy Dreams of White Thighs under Flowered Skirts. 28p. (Orig.). 1980. pap. 3.00 (ISBN 0-935252-24-X); o. p. 5.00 (ISBN 0-686-63441-1). Street Pr.

Cusworth, D. C. Biochemical Screening in Relation to Mental Retardation. LC 73-129632. 1971. pap. 7.75 (ISBN 0-08-016416-1). Pergamon.

Cutajar, M. Zammit, ed. UNCTAD & the South-North Dialogue: The First Twenty Years. LC 84-6484. 338p. 1985. 39.50 (ISBN 0-08-028144-3, Pub. by Aberdeen Scotland). Pergamon.

Cutbill, J. L. Data Processing in Biology & Geology. (Systematics Association Ser.: Special Vol. 3). 1971. 59.50 (ISBN 0-12-199750-2). Acad Pr.

Cutbirth, Nancy, jt. ed. see Cutts, John P.

Cutchin, D. A. Guide to Public Administration. LC 80-84211. 159p. 1981. pap. text ed. 8.95 (ISBN 0-87581-272-4). Peacock Pubs.

Cutchins, Judy & Johnston, Ginny. Are Those Animals Real? LC 84-1049. (Illus.). 96p. (gr. 2-5). 1984. 11.75 (ISBN 0-688-03879-4, Morrow Junior Books); lib. bdg. 11.88 (ISBN 0-688-03880-8). Morrow.

Cutchins, Judy, jt. auth. see Johnston, Ginny.

Cutcliffe, Stephen H., et al, eds. Technology & Values in American Civilization: A Guide to Information Sources. (American Information Guide Ser.: Vol. 9). 728p. 1980. 60.00x (ISBN 0-8103-1475-4). Gale.

Cutforth, A. E. Methods of Amalgamation. LC 82-48358. (Accountancy in Transition Ser.). 354p. 1982. lib. bdg. 39.00 (ISBN 0-8240-5310-9). Garland Pub.

Cutforth, Arthur E. Audits. LC 82-48357. (Accountancy in Transition Ser.). 164p. 1982. lib. bdg. 22.00 (ISBN 0-8240-5309-5). Garland Pub.

Cuthbert. The Capuchins: A Contribution to the History of the Counter Reformation, 2 vols. 1977. lib. bdg. 250.00 (ISBN 0-8490-1571-5). Gordon Pr.

Cuthbert, jt. ed. see Lamble, J. W.

Cuthbert, A. W., et al, eds. Amiloride & Epithelial Sodium Transport. LC 79-251. (Illus.). 202p. 1979. text ed. 22.50 (ISBN 0-8067-0311-3). Urban & S.

Cuthbert, Arthur A. The Life & World-Work of Thomas Lake Harris, Written from Direct Personal Knowledge. LC 72-2954. Repr. of 1909 ed. 21.50 (ISBN 0-404-10719-2). AMS Pr.

Cuthbert, Clifton. Another Such Victory. LC 74-22777. (Labor Movement in Fiction & Non-Fiction). Repr. of 1937 ed. 21.50 (ISBN 0-404-58417-9). AMS Pr.

Cuthbert, John A. West Virginia Folk Music. 185p. 1982. 10.00 (ISBN 0-937058-12-2). West Va U Pr.

Cuthbert, John A. & Ward, Barry J. Vernacular Architecture in America: A Selective Bibliography. 1984. lib. bdg. 39.95 (ISBN 0-8161-0436-0, Hall Reference). G K Hall.

Cuthbert, Mabel J. How to Know the Fall Flowers. (Pictured Key Nature Ser.). 206p. 1948. wire coil write for info. avail. (ISBN 0-697-04810-1). Wm C Brown.

Cuthbert, Mabel J. & Verhoek, Susan. How to Know the Spring Flowers. 2nd ed. (Pictured Key Nature Ser.). 300p. 1982. write for info. wire coil (ISBN 0-697-04782-2). Wm C Brown.

Cuthbert, Norman, jt. auth. see Isles, Keith S.

Cuthbert, Sheila L. The Irish Harp Book - a Tutor & Companion. 1977. pap. text ed. 27.00 large format limp bdg. (ISBN 0-85342-279-6, Co-dist. by Irish Bks Media). Irish Bk Ctr.

Cuthbert, Thomas R., Jr. Circuit Design Using Personal Computers. LC 82-16015. 494p. 1983. 45.95x (ISBN 0-471-87700-X, Pub. by Wiley-Interscience). Wiley.

Cuthbertson, A., jt. ed. see Kempster, A. J.

Cuthbertson, David. A Tragedy of the Reformation: Being the Authentic Narrative of the History & Burning of the "Christianismi Restitutio", 1953, with a Succinct Account of the Theological Controversy Between Michael Servetus, Its Author, & the Reformer, John Calvin. LC 83-45608. Date not set. Repr. of 1912 ed. 20.00 (ISBN 0-404-19826-0). AMS Pr.

Cuthbertson, Evan J. Tennyson, the Story of His Life. LC 73-14566. Repr. of 1898 ed. lib. bdg. 15.00 (ISBN 0-8414-3472-7). Folcroft.

Cuthbertson, Gilbert M. Political Myth & Epic. xxi, 234p. 1975. 10.00x (ISBN 0-87013-185-0). Mich St U Pr.

--Political Power. LC 68-5794. (Rice University Studies: Vol. 54, No. 1). 72p. 1968. pap. 10.00x (ISBN 0-89263-195-3). Rice Univ.

Cuthbertson, Joanne & Schevill, Susanna. Helping Your Child Sleep Through the Night. LC 84-18807. (Illus.). 264p. 1985. pap. 7.95 (ISBN 0-385-19250-9). Doubleday.

Cuthbertson, John. Complete Glossary to the Poetry & Prose of Robert Burns. 1886. 22.50 (ISBN 0-8337-0747-7). B Franklin.

--Complete Glossary to the Poetry & Prose of Robert Burns. (Illus.). 1886. 33.00 (ISBN 0-384-10410-X). Johnson Repr.

--Register of Marriages & Baptisms Performed by Rev. John Cuthbertson, Covenantor Minister, 1751-1791. Fields, S. Helen, ed. LC 83-81655. (Illus.). 301p. 1983. Repr. of 1934 ed. 20.00 (ISBN 0-8063-1047-2). Genealog Pub.

Cuthbertson, K. Macroeconomic Policy: New Cambridge, Keynesian & Monetarist Controversies. LC 79-12195. (New Studies in Economic). 209p. 1979. 39.95x (ISBN 0-470-26740-2). Halsted Pr.

Cuthbertson, Lulu L., jt. auth. see Cuthbertson, Stuart.

Cuthbertson, Stuart. Italian Verb Wheel. 1937. 3.95x (ISBN 0-669-30221-X). Heath.

Cuthbertson, Stuart & Cuthbertson, Lulu L. French Verb Wheel. 1935. 3.95 (ISBN 0-669-26674-4). Heath.

--German Verb Wheel. 1935. 3.95x (ISBN 0-669-28753-9). Heath.

--Spanish Verb Wheel. 1935. 3.95 (ISBN 0-669-31427-7). Heath.

Cuthbertson, Tom. Anybody's Bike Book. 3rd, rev. ed. (Illus.). 208p. 1984. pap. 6.95 (ISBN 0-89815-124-4). Ten Speed Pr.

--Anybody's Bike Book: The New Revised & Expanded Edition. rev ed. LC 76-29188. (Illus.). 1979. 8.95 (ISBN 0-89815-004-3); pap. 4.95 (ISBN 0-89815-003-5). Ten Speed Pr.

--Anybody's Roller Skating Book. LC 81-50301. (Illus.). (YA) 1981. pap. 4.95 (ISBN 0-89815-040-X). Ten Speed Pr.

--Anybody's Skateboard Book. (Illus.). 144p. (Orig.). 1976. pap. 3.00 (ISBN 0-913668-57-5). Ten Speed Pr.

--Better Bikes: A Manual for an Alternative Mode of Transportation. LC 80-5101. (Illus.). 128p. 1980. 7.95 (ISBN 0-89815-025-6); pap. 4.95 (ISBN 0-89815-024-8). Ten Speed Pr.

--The Bike Bag Book. LC 81-50252. (Illus.). 144p. (Orig.). 1981. pap. 2.95 kivar cover (ISBN 0-89815-039-6). Ten Speed Pr.

--Bike Tripping. rev. ed. 192p. 1984. pap. 5.95 (ISBN 0-89815-123-6). Ten Speed Pr.

Cuthertson, Evan J. Tennyson: The Story of His Life. 1978. lib. bdg. 20.00 (ISBN 0-8495-0745-6). Arden Lib.

Cuti, Nicola, jt. auth. see Byrne, John.

Cutillo, Brian, jt. auth. see Rimpoche, Kunga.

Cutino, Peter & Bledsoe, Dennis, eds. Polo: The Manual for Coach & Player. LC 75-20710. (Illus.). 225p. 1975. pap. 11.45 (ISBN 0-685-56491-6). Swimming.

Cutkomp, Laurence K., jt. auth. see Eesa, Naeem M.

Cutlack, F. M. see Bean, C. E.

Cutland, N. J. Computability: An Introduction to Recursive Function Theory. LC 79-51823. 1980. 62.50 (ISBN 0-521-22384-9); pap. 19.95 (ISBN 0-521-29465-7). Cambridge U Pr.

Cutler & Davis. Detergency, Pt. III. (Surfactant Science Ser.: Vol. 5). 384p. 1981. 55.00 (ISBN 0-8247-6982-1). Dekker.

Cutler & Garcia. The Medical Management of Menopause & Premenopause. LC 65-7966. 1984. 27.50 (ISBN 0-397-50631-7, Lippincott Medical). Lippincott.

Cutler, et al, eds. Correspondence of James Polk, 1842-1843, Vol. 6. LC 75-84005. (Polk Project Ser.). 1983. 32.50x (ISBN 0-8265-1211-9). Vanderbilt U Pr.

Cutler, A. & Nye, D. Justice & Predictability. 192p. 1983. text ed. 36.50x (ISBN 0-333-31515-4, Pub. by Macmillan England). Humanities.

Cutler, A. & Ladd, D. R., eds. Prosody: Models & Measurement. (Springer Series in Language & Communication: Vol. 14). (Illus.). 180p. 1983. 26.00 (ISBN 0-387-12428-4). Springer-Verlag.

Cutler, A. J., jt. ed. see Hart, A. B.

Cutler, Abbot. Eighteen Forty-Three Rebecca Eighteen Forty-Seven. LC 81-50174. (Chapbook Ser.: No. 4). 64p. (Orig.). 1981. pap. 5.95 (ISBN 0-937672-03-3). Rowan Tree.

Cutler, Allan H. & Cutler, Helen E. The Jew As Ally of the Muslim: Medieval Roots of Anti-Semitism. LC 84-40295. 594p. 1985. text ed. 50.00 (ISBN 0-268-01190-7, 85-11909). U of Notre Dame Pr.

Cutler, Ann & McShane, Rudolph, trs. The Trachtenberg Speed System of Basic Mathematics. LC 81-13439. 270p. 1982. Repr. of 1960 ed. lib. bdg. 27.50x (ISBN 0-313-23200-8, CUTS). Greenwood.

Cutler, Anne, ed. Slips of the Tongue & Language Production. 293p. 1982. pap. 16.95 (ISBN 90-279-3120-8). Mouton.

Cutler, Anthony. Transfigurations: Studies in the Dynamics of Byzantine Iconography. LC 75-1482. (Illus.). 226p. 1975. 32.50x (ISBN 0-271-01194-7). Pa St U Pr.

Cutler, Antony, et al. Marx's Capital & Capitalism Today, Vol. 1. 1977. pap. 10.50 (ISBN 0-7100-8746-2). Routledge & Kegan.

Cutler, B. D. & Stiles, Villa. Modern British Authors: Their First Editions. 1978. Repr. of 1930 ed. lib. bdg. 20.00 (ISBN 0-8495-0808-8). Arden Lib.

Cutler, Barbara C. Unraveling the Special Education Maze: An Action Guide for Parents. LC 80-54006. 318p. (Orig.). 1981. pap. text ed. 11.95 (ISBN 0-87822-224-3, 2243). Res Press.

Cutler, Bradley D. Modern British Authors: Their First Editions. LC 73-558. 1930. lib. bdg. 20.00 (ISBN 0-8414-1453-X). Folcroft.

--Sir James Barrie: A Bibliography with Full Collations of the American Unauthorized Editions. 1967. Repr. of 1931 ed. 24.50 (ISBN 0-8337-0748-5). B Franklin.

Cutler, Bruce. Dark Fire. LC 84-73435. 1985. pap. 6.95 (ISBN 0-933532-47-4). BkMk.

--The Doctrine of Selective Depravity. (Inland Seas Ser.: No. 1). 1980. pap. 5.00 (ISBN 0-686-61808-4). Juniper Pr WI.

--The Maker's Name. (W.N.J. Ser.: No. 14). 1980. 10.00 (ISBN 0-686-61805-X); signed ed. 20.00 (ISBN 0-686-61806-8); pap. 6.00 (ISBN 0-686-61807-6). Juniper Pr WI.

Cutler, Bruce S., et al. Manual of Clinical Problems in Surgery: With Annotated Key References. (The Spiral Manual Ser.). 484p. 1984. spiral bdg. 18.95 (ISBN 0-316-16575-1). Little.

Cutler, C. Practice Your BASIC. (Computer & Electronics Ser.). (Illus.). 48p. (gr. 6 up). 1983. 8.95 (ISBN 0-86020-744-7); lib. bdg. 12.95 (ISBN 0-88110-142-7); pap. 5.95 (ISBN 0-86020-743-9). EDC.

Cutler, Carl C. Greyhounds of the Sea. 3rd ed. (Illus.). 667p. 1984. 32.95 (ISBN 0-87021-232-X). Naval Inst Pr.

--Mystic: The Story of a Small New England Seaport. (Illus.). 56p. 1980. pap. 4.00 (ISBN 0-913372-14-5). Mystic Seaport.

Cutler, Carol. Carol Cutler's Great Fast Breads: Popovers to Panettone in Two Hours of Less. 256p. 1985. 13.95 (ISBN 0-89256-272-2). Rawson Assocs.

--Cuisine Rapide: Two Hundred Thirty Recipes. 1983. pap. 3.98 (ISBN 0-517-54901-8, C N Potter). Crown.

--Pate, the New Main Course for the 80's: A Menu Cookbook. (Illus.). 256p. 1983. 14.95 (ISBN 0-89256-232-3). Rawson Assocs.

--Woman's Day Complete Guide to Entertaining. 256p. (Orig.). 1984. pap. 5.95 (ISBN 0-671-44671-1). PB.

Cutler, Charles L. How We Made It to One Hundred: Wisdom from the Super Old. LC 77-87771. 1978. 9.95 (ISBN 0-9601502-1-8). Rockfall Pr.

Cutler, Charles L. see Weaver, Glenn.

Cutler, D. F. see Metcalfe, C. R.

Cutler, David, jt. auth. see Alston, Edith.

Cutler, Donald R., ed. Updating Life & Death: Essays in Ethnics & Medicine. LC 74-89959. (Orig.). 1969. pap. 4.50x (ISBN 0-8070-1581-4, BP333). Beacon Pr.

Cutler, E. F. & Alvin, K. L. The Plant Cuticle. (Linn Soc Symposium Ser.: No. 10). 1982. 90.00 (ISBN 0-12-199920-3). Acad Pr.

Cutler, Ebbitt. I Once Knew an Indian Woman. (Illus.). 72p. (gr. 5 up). Date not set. text ed. 7.95 (ISBN 0-317-27069-9, Dist. by U of Toronto Pr); pap. 4.95 (ISBN 0-88776-068-6). Tundra Bks.

--If I Were a Cat I Would Sit in a Tree. (Illus.). 28p. (gr. k-4). Date not set. text ed. 6.95 (ISBN 0-88776-177-1, Dist. by U of Toronto Bks). Tundra Bks.

Cutler, Ebbitt, tr. see De Pressense, Domitille.

Cutler, Ebbitt, tr. see Morgenstern, Christian.

Cutler, Ebbitt, tr. see Ozawa, Ryokichi.

Cutler, Eliot R., jt. auth. see Reilly, John R.

Cutler, G. Ripley. Of Battles Long Ago: Memoirs of an American Ambulance Driver in World War I. Knickerbocker, Charles H., ed. LC 79-50656. (Illus.). 280p. 1979. 15.00 (ISBN 0-682-49396-1). Exposition Pr FL.

Cutler, Helen E., jt. auth. see Cutler, Allan H.

Cutler, Hugh C. Corn, Cucurbits & Cotton from Glen Canyon. (Glen Canyon Ser: No. 30). Repr. of 1966 ed. 26.00 (ISBN 0-404-60680-6). AMS Pr.

Cutler, Irving. Chicago: Metropolis of the Mid-Continent. 3rd ed. LC 75-40940. (Illus.). 1982. perfect bdg. 11.95 (ISBN 0-8403-2645-9). Kendall-Hunt.

Cutler, Irving, jt. auth. see Jensen, Richard.

Cutler, Ivor. A Flat Man. (Illus.). 1977. signed 15.00 (ISBN 0-685-04171-9, Pub. by Trigram Pr); bound 7.00 (ISBN 0-685-04172-7); sewn in wrappers 4.00 (ISBN 0-685-04173-5). Small Pr Dist.

--Many Flies Have Feathers. 1973. 7.00 (ISBN 0-685-29887-6, Pub. by Trigram Pr); signed ed. 15.00 (ISBN 0-685-29888-4); pap. 4.00 (ISBN 0-685-29889-2). Small Pr Dist.

Cutler, James E. Lynch Law: An Investigation into the History of Lynching in the United States. LC 77-88428. Repr. of 1905 ed. 22.50x (ISBN 0-8371-1821-2, CUL&, Pub. by Negro U Pr). Greenwood.

--Lynch-Law: An Investigation into the History of Lynching in the United States. LC 69-14920. (Criminology, Law Enforcement, & Social Problems Ser.: No. 70). (Illus.). 1969. Repr. of 1905 ed. 11.00x (ISBN 0-87585-070-7). Patterson Smith.

Cutler, Jervis. Topographical Description of the State of Ohio, Indiana Territory, & Louisiana. LC 78-146388. (First American Frontier Ser). (Illus.). 1971. Repr. of 1812 ed. 17.00 (ISBN 0-405-02839-3). Ayer Co Pubs.

Cutler, John. Understanding Aircraft Structures. (Illus.). 170p. 1981. text ed. 30.00x (ISBN 0-246-11310-3, Pub. by Granada). Sheridan.

Cutler, John L. & Thompson, Lawrence S., eds. American Notes & Queries Supplement, Vol. 1. LC 77-93778. (Studies in American & English Literature). 1978. 18.50x (ISBN 0-87875-139-4). Whitston Pub.

Cutler, Julia P. Life & Times of Ephraim Cutler Prepared from His Journals & Correspondence by His Daughter Julia Perkins Cutler with Biographical Sketches of Jervis Cutler & William Parker Cutler. LC 71-146389. (First American Frontier Ser.). (Illus.). 1971. Repr. of 1890 ed. 24.50 (ISBN 0-405-02840-7). Ayer Co Pubs.

Cutler, Julian S. Seasons of Friendship. 1983. 4.95 (ISBN 0-8378-2032-4). Gibson.

Cutler, Kathy. Festive Bread Book. 288p. 1982. 14.95 (ISBN 0-8120-5453-9). Barron.

Cutler, Keir, jt. auth. see Cutler, Mickey.

Cutler, Laurence S. & Cutler, Sherrie S. Recycling Cities for People. 2nd ed. 314p. 1982. pap. 29.95 (ISBN 0-8436-0170-1); 16.95 (ISBN 0-442-21604-1). Van Nos Reinhold.
Cutler, Laurence S., jt. ed. see Dietz, Albert G.
Cutler, Lloyd N. Global Interdependence & the Multinational Firm. LC 78-58094. (Headline Ser.: 239). 1978. pap. 3.00 (ISBN 0-87124-046-7). Foreign Policy.
Cutler, M. E., tr. see Nickl, Peter.
Cutler, Melvin. Liquid Semiconductors. 1977. 49.50 (ISBN 0-12-196650-X). Acad Pr.
Cutler, Merritt. Basic Tennis Illustrated. (Illus.). 111p. 1980. pap. 6.95 (ISBN 0-486-24006-1). Dover.
Cutler, Merritt D. How to Cut Drawings on Scratchboard. (Illus.). 88p. 1960. 10.95 (ISBN 0-8230-2350-8). Watson-Guptill.
Cutler, Michael, ed. see Ninth Goddard Memorial Symposium, Washington, D. C., 1971.
Cutler, Mickey. Great Hockey Masks. (Illus.). 32p. 1983. pap. 7.95 (ISBN 0-88776-152-6). Tundra Bks.
Cutler, Mickey & Cutler, Keir. The Glory Boys. (Illus.). 3.95 (ISBN 0-88776-115-1). Tundra Bks.
Cutler, Neal, ed. Symposium on Aging & Public Policy. (Orig.). 1984. pap. 8.00 (ISBN 0-918592-76-3). Policy Studies.
Cutler, Paul. Problem Solving in Clinical Medicine: From Data to Diagnosis. 2nd ed. 400p. 1985. pap. text ed. 28.00 (ISBN 0-683-02252-0). Williams & Wilkins.
Cutler, Paul H. & Lucas, A. A., eds. Quantum Metrology & Fundamental Physical Constants. (NATO ASI Series B, Physics). 670p. 1983. 95.00x (ISBN 0-306-41372-8, Plenum Pr). Plenum Pub.
Cutler, R., tr. from Rus. see Bakunin, Mikhail.
Cutler, R. B. & Morris, William. Alias Oswald. (Illus.). 218p. 1984. 20.00 (ISBN 0-87867-099-8); pap. 7.95 (ISBN 0-87867-100-5). Ramparts.
Cutler, R. G., ed. Cellular Ageing: Concepts & Mechanisms: Part I: General Concepts. Mechanisms I: Fidelity of Information Flow, 2 pts. (Interdisciplinary Topics on Gerontology: Vol. 9). (Illus.). 150p. 1976. pap. 48.75 (ISBN 3-8055-2283-5). S Karger.
--Cellular Ageing: Concepts & Mechanisms: Part II: Mechanisms II: Translation, Transcription & Structural Properties, 2 pts. (Interdisciplinary Topics in Gerontology: Vol. 10). (Illus.). 150p. 1976. pap. 32.00 (ISBN 3-8055-2284-3). S Karger.
Cutler, Roger L. The Bottom Line: A Practical Guide to Computerized Bookkeeping. Badler, Scott, ed. (Illus.). 240p. (Orig.). 1984. pap. 19.95 (ISBN 0-938408-09-7). Bash Educ Serv.
Cutler, Roland. Firstborn. 1978. pap. 2.75 (ISBN 0-449-14002-4, GM). Fawcett.
--The Gates of Sagittarius. 304p. 1981. pap. 2.75 (ISBN 0-380-56085-2, 56085). Avon.
--The Seventh Sacrament. 352p. (Orig.). 1984. pap. 3.95 (ISBN 0-440-17940-8). Dell.
Cutler, Sherrie S., jt. auth. see Cutler, Laurence S.
Cutler, Stephen J., jt. ed. see Yinger, J. Milton.
Cutler, W. G. & Davis, R. C., eds. Detergency: Theory & Test Methods, Pt. 1. (Surfactant Science Ser.: Vol. 5). 464p. 1972. 85.00 (ISBN 0-8247-1113-0). Dekker.
--Detergency: Theory & Test Methods, Part 2. (Surfactant Science Ser.: Vol. 5). 296p. 1975. 85.00 (ISBN 0-8247-1114-9). Dekker.
Cutler, Wade E. Triple Your Reading Speed. LC 70-93505. (Prog. Bk.). 1970. lib. bdg. 7.50 o. p. (ISBN 0-668-02084-9); pap. 5.00 (ISBN 0-668-02083-0). Arco.
Cutler, Wayne, ed. Correspondence of James K. Polk, Vol. 6: 1842-1843. 1983. 32.50 (ISBN 0-8265-1211-9). U of Ill Pr.
Cutler, Wayne & Harris, Michael H., eds. Justin Winsor: Scholar-Librarian. LC 80-19310. (Heritage of Librarianship: No. 5). 196p. 1980. lib. bdg. 25.00 (ISBN 0-87287-200-9). Libs Unl.
Cutler, Wayne, jt. ed. see Weaver, Herbert.
Cutler, Wayne, et al, eds. Correspondence of James K. Polk 1839-1841. LC 75-84005. (Polk Project Ser.: Vol. 5). 1980. 32.50x (ISBN 0-8265-1208-9). Vanderbilt U Pr.
Cutler, William W., 3rd & Gillette, Howard, Jr., eds. The Divided Metropolis: Social & Spatial Dimensions of Philadelphia, 1800-1975. LC 79-7729. (Contributions in American History: No. 85). (Illus.). 1980. lib. bdg. 29.95 (ISBN 0-313-21351-8, GDM/). Greenwood.
Cutler, Winnifred B., et al. Menopause: A Guide for Women & the Men Who Love Them. (Illus.). 1983. 15.00 (ISBN 0-393-01709-5). Norton.
--Menopause: A Guide for Women & the Men Who Love Them. (Illus.). 272p. 1985. pap. 6.95 (ISBN 0-393-30242-3). Norton.
Cutliff, Lewis D., jt. auth. see Wagoner, John J.
Cutlip, Glen, jt. auth. see Shockley, Robert.
Cutlip, Ralph. Action Stories of Yesterday & Today. (Orig.). (gr. 7-12). 1971. pap. text ed. 6.08 (ISBN 0-87720-351-2). AMSCO Sch.
--Stories from the Four Corners. (gr. 7-12). 1975. pap. text ed. 6.08 (ISBN 0-87720-354-7). AMSCO Sch.
--Stories That Live. (gr. 7-12). 1973. 6.08 (ISBN 0-87720-352-0). AMSCO Sch.
Cutlip, Scott M., ed. Public Relations Bibliography. 2nd ed. 320p. 1965. 20.00x (ISBN 0-299-03510-7). U of Wis Pr.
Cutlip, Scott M., et al. Effective Public Relations. 6th ed. (Illus.). 640p. 1985. text ed. 28.95 (ISBN 0-13-245077-1). P-H.
Cutmore, M. The Watch Collector's Handbook. LC 75-42563. (Illus.). 160p. 1976. 14.50 (ISBN 0-8048-1174-1). C E Tuttle.
Cutmore, Maxwell. The Pocket Watch Handbook. (Illus.). 192p. 1985. 19.95 (ISBN 0-668-06423-4). Arco.
Cutrer, Thomas W. Parnassus on the Mississippi: The Southern Review & the Baton Rouge Literary Community, 1935-1942. LC 83-24913. (Southern Literary Studies). (Illus.). 320p. 1984. text ed. 27.50x (ISBN 0-8071-1143-0). La state U Pr.
Cutright, Paul R. Great Naturalists Explore South America. facs. ed. LC 68-8454. (Essay Index Reprint Ser). 1940. 26.50 (ISBN 0-8369-0357-9). Ayer Co Pubs.
--Theodore Roosevelt: The Making of a Conservationist. LC 84-16205. (Illus.). 304p. 1985. 22.95x (ISBN 0-252-01190-2). U of Ill Pr.
Cutright, Paul R. & Brodhead, Michael J. Elliott Coues: Naturalist & Frontier Historian. LC 80-12424. (Illus.). 510p. 1981. 28.50x (ISBN 0-252-00802-2). U of Ill Pr.
Cutright, W. B. History of Upshur County. 1977. Repr. of 1907 ed. 25.00 (ISBN 0-87012-291-6). McClain.
Cutrubus, C. Nina, jt. ed. see Hamilton, Charles M.
Cutrufelli, Maria R. Women of Africa: Roots of Oppression. Romano, Nicolas, tr. from Italian. LC 83-225772. (Illus.). 192p. 1983. 24.75x (ISBN 0-86232-083-6, 1-102, Pub. by Zed Pr England); pap. 9.25 (ISBN 0-86232-084-4). Biblio Dist.
Cutsforth, Thomas D. The Blind in School & Society: A Psychological Study. 269p. 1951. pap. 6.00 (ISBN 0-89128-011-1, PPP001). Am Foun Blind.
Cutt, Thomas & Nyenhuis, Jacob E., eds. Petronius: Cena Trimalchionis. rev. ed. LC 73-105090. (Classical Text Ser). 132p. (Latin). 1970. pap. text ed. 4.95x (ISBN 0-8143-1410-4). Wayne St U Pr.
--Plautus: Amphitruo. rev. ed. (Classical Text Ser). 225p. (Lat). 1970. pap. text ed. 5.95x (ISBN 0-8143-1411-2). Wayne St U Pr.
Cutten, D. E. Autosuggestion & Hypnotism, 2 vols. (Illus.). 236p. 1985. Set. 147.50 (ISBN 0-89920-093-1). Am Inst Psych.
Cutten, George B. Mind: Its Origin & Goal. Repr. of 1925 ed. 25.00 (ISBN 0-89987-049-X). Darby Bks.
--Mind: Its Origin & Goal. 1925. 24.50x (ISBN 0-685-89766-4). Elliots Bks.
--The Psychology of Alcoholism. Grob, Gerald N., ed. LC 80-1223. (Addiction in America Ser.). 1981. Repr. of 1907 ed. lib. bdg. 32.00x (ISBN 0-405-13579-3). Ayer Co Pubs.
--Silversmiths of Virginia. (Illus.). 1976. Repr. 17.50 (ISBN 0-685-65625-X). Dietz.
--Speaking with Tongues: Historically & Psychologically Considered. 1927. 39.50x (ISBN 0-685-69805-X). Elliots Bks.
Cutter, Bruce. Nectar in a Sieve. (Juniper Bks.: No. 45). 1983. pap. 4.00 (ISBN 0-317-07408-3). Juniper Pr WI.
Cutter, Bruce, ed. Wood & Fiber Science. (Orig.). pap. text ed. 55.00 (ISBN 0-686-40829-2). Soc Wood.
Cutter, C. A. C. A. Cutter's Three-Figure Author Table: Swanson-Swift Revision. 30p. 1969. 16.00 (ISBN 0-87287-209-2). Libs Unl.
--C. A. Cutter's Two-Figure Author Table: Swanson-Swift Revision. 4p. 1969. 11.00 (ISBN 0-87287-208-4). Libs Unl.
Cutter, C. A. & Sanborn. Cutter-Sanborn Three-Figure Author Table: Swanson-Swift Revision. 34p. 1969. 16.00 (ISBN 0-87287-210-6). Libs Unl.
Cutter, Charles & Oppenheim, Micha F. Jewish Reference Sources: A Select, Annotated Bibliographic Guide. LC 82-15434. (Reference Library of Social Science: Vol. 126). 180p. 1985. lib. bdg. 24.00 (ISBN 0-8240-9347-X). Garland Pub.
Cutter, Elizabeth G. Plant Anatomy, Pt. I: Cells & Tissues. 2nd ed. (Illus.). 1978. text ed. 18.95 (ISBN 0-201-01236-7). Addison-Wesley.
Cutter, Fred. Art & the Wish to Die. LC 82-81700. 256p. 1982. text ed. 26.95x (ISBN 0-88229-370-2); pap. text ed. 15.95x (ISBN 0-88229-813-5). Nelson-Hall.
--Coming to Terms with Death: How to Face the Inevitable with Wisdom & Dignity. LC 74-8397. 320p. 1974. 21.95x (ISBN 0-911012-29-X). Nelson-Hall.
Cutter, John. American Vengeance. (The Specialist Ser.: No. 11). 1985. pap. 2.75 (ISBN 0-451-13910-0, Sig). NAL.
--The Beirut Retaliation. (Specialist Ser.: No. 10). 1985. pap. 2.75 (ISBN 0-451-13758-2, Sig). NAL.
--The Big One. (The Specialist Ser.: No. 6). 1984. pap. 2.95 (ISBN 0-451-13272-6, Sig). NAL.
--The Maltese Vengeance. (The Specialist Ser.: No. 5). 1984. pap. 2.25 (ISBN 0-451-13192-4, Sig). NAL.
--Manhattan Revenge. (Specialist Ser.: No. 2). 1984. pap. 2.25 (ISBN 0-451-12800-1, Sig). NAL.
--One-Man Army. (Specialist Ser.: No. 8). 1985. pap. 2.50 (ISBN 0-451-13518-0, Sig). NAL.
--The Psycho Soldiers. (The Specialist Ser.: No. 4). 1984. pap. 2.25 (ISBN 0-451-13105-3, Sig). NAL.
--The Specialist, No. 1: A Talent for Revenge. 1984. pap. 2.25 (ISBN 0-451-12799-4, Sig). NAL.
--Sullivan's Revenge. (The Specialist: No. 3). 1984. pap. 2.25 (ISBN 0-451-13049-9, Sig). NAL.
--The Vendetta. (The Specialist Ser.: No.7). 1985. pap. 2.50 (ISBN 0-451-13403-6, Sig). NAL.
--Vengeance Mountain. (Specialist Ser.: No. 9). 1985. pap. 2.75 (ISBN 0-451-13614-4, Sig). NAL.
Cutter, John M. Cutter's Official Guide to Hot Springs, Arkansas: 1917. (Illus.). 1979. pap. 3.95 (ISBN 0-89646-057-6). Outbooks.
Cutter, Leela. Death of the Party. 208p. 1985. 12.95 (ISBN 0-312-18871-4). St Martin.
--Murder After Tea Time. 154p. 1981. 9.95 (ISBN 0-312-55276-9). St Martin.
--Who Stole Stonehenge? 224p. 1983. 11.95 (ISBN 0-312-87043-4). St Martin.
Cutter, N., jt. auth. see Tatchell.
Cutter, Ralph. Sierra Trout Guide. (Illus.). 120p. (Orig.). 1984. 14.95 (ISBN 0-936608-24-2); pap. 7.95 (ISBN 0-936608-23-4). F Amato Pubns.
Cutter, Susan L., et al. Exploitation, Conservation, Preservation: A Geographic Perspective on Natural Resource Use. LC 84-18298. (Illus.). 468p. 1985. 25.00x (ISBN 0-86598-129-9). Rowman & Allanheld.
Cutter, Tom. Barbary Coast Tong. (Tracker Ser.: No. 6). 144p. 1985. pap. 2.25 (ISBN 0-380-89583-8). Avon.
--The Blue Cut Job. (Tracker Ser.). 192p. 1983. pap. 2.25 (ISBN 0-380-84483-4, 84483). Avon.
--Chinatown Chance. (Tracker Ser.: No. 4). 1983. pap. 2.25 (ISBN 0-380-84988-7, 84988). Avon.
--Huntsville Breakout. (The Tracker Ser.: No. 7). 144p. 1985. pap. 2.25 (ISBN 0-380-89584-6). Avon.
--Lincoln County. (Tracker Ser.: No. 2). 160p. 1983. pap. 2.25 (ISBN 0-380-84152-5, 84152-5). Avon.
--The Oklahoma Score. (The Tracker Ser.: No. 5). 144p. 1985. pap. 2.25 (ISBN 0-380-89531-5). Avon.
--The Winning Hand. (Tracker Ser.). 176p. 1983. pap. 2.25 (ISBN 0-380-83899-0, 83899-0). Avon.
Cutter, William. Life of Israel Putnam. LC 78-120874. (American Bicentennial Ser). 1970. Repr. of 1846 ed. 32.50x (ISBN 0-8046-1267-6, Pub. by Kennikat). Assoc Faculty Pr.
Cutting, C. V, ed. see Long Ashton Research Station Symposium, University of Bristol, Sept. 1971.
Cutting, G. W. Process Audits on Mineral Dressing Processes: Their Generation & Practical Use, 1978. 1981. 69.00x (ISBN 0-686-97143-4, Pub. by W Spring England). State Mutual Bk.
Cutting, James E., jt. ed. see Kavanagh, James F.
Cutting, Jorge. La Salvacion: Su Seguridad, Creteza y Gozo. 2nd ed. Daniel, Roger P., ed. Bautista, Sara, tr. from Eng. (La Serie Diamante). 48p. (Span.). 1982. pap. 0.85 (ISBN 0-942504-05-4). Overcomer Pr.
--La Venida del Senor. 2nd ed. Bennett, Gordon H., ed. Bautista, Sara, tr. from Eng. (La Serie Diamante). 48p. (Span.). 1982. pap. 0.85 (ISBN 0-942504-10-0). Overcomer Pr.
Cutting, Mary S. Little Stories of Courtship. facsimile ed. LC 79-98566. (Short Story Index Reprint Ser.). 1905. 17.00 (ISBN 0-8369-3140-8). Ayer Co Pubs.
--Little Stories of Married Life. facsimile ed. LC 70-152968. (Short Story Index Reprint Ser.). Repr. of 1896 ed. 17.00 (ISBN 0-8369-3796-1). Ayer Co Pubs.
--More Stories of Married Life. facsimile ed. LC 75-37264. (Short Story Index Reprint Ser.). Repr. of 1906 ed. 17.00 (ISBN 0-8369-4075-X). Ayer Co Pubs.
--Refractory Husbands. LC 79-128729. (Short Story Index Reprint Ser). 1913. 14.00 (ISBN 0-8369-3620-5). Ayer Co Pubs.
Cutting, Starr W. Der Conjunctiv Bei Hartmann Von Aue. LC 76-173037. (Chicago. University. Germanic Studies: No. 1). Repr. of 1894 ed. 18.00 (ISBN 0-404-50271-7). AMS Pr.
Cuttino, G. P. English Medieval Diplomacy. LC 84-48297. 160p. 1985. 25.00x (ISBN 0-253-31954-4). Ind U Fr.
Cuttle, Constance, et al. Completely Cheese. LC 77-2818. (Illus.). 1978. 16.95 (ISBN 0-8246-0220-X). Jonathan David.
Cuttler, Charles. D. Northern Painting. LC 68-20103. 1973. pap. text ed. 31.95 (ISBN 0-03-089476-X, HoltC). HR&W.
Cuttler, S. H. The Law of Treason & Treason Trials in Later Medieval France. LC 81-3880. (Cambridge Studies in Medieval Life & Thought: No. 16). 296p. 1982. 54.50 (ISBN 0-521-23968-0). Cambridge U Pr.
Cuttriss, Frank. Romany Life: Experienced & Observed During Many Years of Friendly Intercourse with the Gypsies. LC 75-3453. (Illus.). Repr. of 1915 ed. 34.50 (ISBN 0-404-16887-6). AMS Pr.
Cutts, A. M. Dios y Sus Ayudantes. (Illus.). 48p. (Span.). 1981. pap. 1.10 (ISBN 0-311-38548-6). Casa Bautista.
Cutts, Anson B. Poems of My Youth. 1982. 5.95 (ISBN 0-533-05348-X). Vantage.
Cutts, David. I Can Read About Creatures of the Night. new ed. LC 78-68468. (Illus.). (gr. 2-5). 1979. pap. 1.50 (ISBN 0-89375-202-9). Troll Assocs.
--I Can Read About Reptiles. LC 72-96954. (Illus.). (gr. 2-4). 1973. pap. 1.50 (ISBN 0-89375-058-1). Troll Assocs.
--I Can Read About Thunder & Lightning. new ed. LC 78-66273. (Illus.). (gr. 2-6). 1979. pap. 1.50 (ISBN 0-89375-217-7). Troll Assocs.
--Look-a Butterfly. LC 81-11369. (Now I Know Ser.). (Illus.). 32p. (gr. k-2). 1982. PLB 9.89 (ISBN 0-89375-662-8); pap. 1.25 (ISBN 0-89375-663-6). Troll Assocs.
--More About Dinosaurs. LC 81-11432. (Now I Know Ser.). (Illus.). 32p. (gr. k-2). 1982. PLB 9.89 (ISBN 0-89375-668-7); pap. 1.25 (ISBN 0-89375-669-5). Troll Assocs.
Cutts, David, retold by. Gingerbread Boy. LC 78-18069. (Illus.). 32p. (gr. k-4). 1979. PLB 7.89 (ISBN 0-89375-122-7); pap. 1.95 (ISBN 0-89375-100-6). Troll Assocs.
--House That Jack Built. new ed. LC 78-18951. (Illus.). 32p. (gr. k-4). 1979. PLB 7.89 (ISBN 0-89375-127-8); pap. 1.95 (ISBN 0-89375-105-7). Troll Assocs.
Cutts, Edward L. Parish Priests & Their People in the Middle Ages in England. LC 74-107457. Repr. of 1898 ed. 32.50 (ISBN 0-404-01898-X). Ams Pr.
--Scenes & Characters of the Middle Ages. LC 67-27866. (Social History Reference Ser.). (Illus.). 560p. 1968. Repr. of 1872 ed. 40.00x (ISBN 0-8103-3257-4). Gale.
--Scenes & Characters of the Middle Ages. 1977. lib. bdg. 59.95 (ISBN 0-8490-2569-9). Gordon Pr.
--Scenes & Characters of the Middle Ages. LC 77-23575. 1977. Repr. of 1922 ed. lib. bdg. 45.00 (ISBN 0-89341-160-4). Longwood Pub Group.
--Science & Characters of the Middle Ages. 552p. 1981. Repr. of 1926 ed. lib. bdg. 40.00 (ISBN 0-8495-0876-2). Arden Lib.
Cutts, J. H. Methods in Cell Separation Used in Hematology. 1970. 55.00 (ISBN 0-12-200050-1). Acad Pr.
Cutts, John P. Shattered Glass: A Dramatic Pattern in Shakespeare's Early Plays. LC 68-22253. 154p. 1968. 8.95x (ISBN 0-8143-1358-2). Wayne St U Pr.
Cutts, John P., ed. Seventeenth Century Songs & Lyrics. facsimile ed. LC 70-80373. (Granger Index Reprint Ser). 1959. 21.00 (ISBN 0-8369-6055-6). Ayer Co Pubs.
Cutts, John P. & Cutbirth, Nancy, eds. Love's Changelinges Change. LC 74-84570. (North American Mentor Texts & Studies Ser: No. 2). (Based on Sir Philip Sidney's Arcadia, 1590). 1974. pap. 10.00 (ISBN 0-87423-009-8). Westburg.
Cutts, Paddy & Curr, Rosemary. Creative Techniques in Stage & Theatrical Photography. (Illus.). 168p. 1983. text ed. 15.00x (ISBN 0-7134-0667-4). Drama Bk.
Cutts, Paddy & Payne, Christina. Pedigree Cats & Kittens. LC 83-11938. (Illus.). 64p. (Orig.). 1984. 7.95 (ISBN 0-668-05949-4); pap. 3.95 (ISBN 0-668-05953-2). Arco.
Cutts, Paddy, jt. auth. see Payne, Christian.
Cutts, Simon. Piano Stool: Footnotes. pap. 10.00 (ISBN 0-912330-55-4). Jargon Soc.
--Quelques Pianos. LC 75-37301. 1976. pap. 3.00 (ISBN 0-912330-35-X, Dist. by Inland Bk). Jargon Soc.
Cutul, Ann-Marie, ed. Twentieth-Century European Painting: A Guide to Information Sources. LC 79-24249. (Art & Architecture Information Guide Ser.: Vol. 9). 1980. 60.00x (ISBN 0-8103-1438-X). Gale.
Cuviella, Patrick & Woosley, Hugh. Basic Medical Laboratory Subjects. LC 74-18675. (Allied Health Ser). 1975. pap. 7.20 scp (ISBN 0-672-61383-2). Bobbs.
Cuvier, Georges. The Class Mammalia: The Animal Kingdom Arranged in Conformity with Its Organization by the Baron Cuvier, Vols. 1-5. Sterling, Keir B., ed. LC 77-81117. (Biologists & Their World Ser.). (Illus.). 1978. Repr. of 1827 ed. Set. lib. bdg. 217.00x (ISBN 0-405-10746-3); lib. bdg. 43.40x ea. Vol. 1 (ISBN 0-405-10765-X). Vol. 2 (ISBN 0-405-10766-8). Vol. 3 (ISBN 0-405-10767-6). Vol. 4 (ISBN 0-405-10768-4). Vol. 5 (ISBN 0-405-10769-2). Ayer Co Pubs.
--Essay on the Theory of the Earth: Mineralogical Notes, & an Account of Cuvier's Geological Discoveries. Albritton, Claude C., Jr., ed. Kerr, Robert, tr. LC 77-6517. (History of Geology Ser.). (Illus.). 1978. Repr. of 1817 ed. lib. bdg. 32.00 (ISBN 0-405-10439-1). Ayer Co Pubs.
--Memoirs on Fossil Elephants & on Reconstruction of the Genera Palaeotherium & Anoplotherium. Gould, Stephen J., ed. LC 79-8327. (Illus., Fr.). 1980. Repr. of 1812 ed. lib. bdg. 80.00x (ISBN 0-405-12709-X). Ayer Co Pubs.
Cuvier, Georges B. Animal Kingdom, Arranged After Its Organization: Forming a Natural History of Animals, & an Introduction to Comparative Anatomy. LC 6-14947. (Illus.). 1969. Repr. of 1863 ed. 63.00 (ISBN 0-527-20900-7). Kraus Repr.
Cuvillier, Armand. Diccionario de Filosofia. 228p. (Span.). 1961. 14.95 (ISBN 0-686-56713-7, S-33052). French & Eur.

Cuvillier, Rolande. The Reduction of Working Time: Scope & Implications in Industrialised Market Economies. International Labour Office Staff, ed. 150p. 1984. text ed. 19.95 (ISBN 92-2-103817-3); pap. 14.25 (ISBN 92-2-102702-3). Intl Labour Office.

--The Reduction of Working Time: Scope & Implications in Industrialized Market Economies. 150p. 1985. pap. 14.25 (ISBN 92-2-102702-3, ILO346, ILO). Unipub.

Cuyas, A., ed. New Appleton's Cuyas English-Spanish & Spanish-English Dictionary. 5th ed. (Eng. & Span.). 1972. 21.95 (ISBN 0-13-611749-X); thumb-indexed 20.95 (ISBN 0-13-611756-2). P-H.

Cuyas, Arturo. English-Spanish to Spanish-English Dictionary. rev. ed. 548p. (Span. & Eng.). 1982. pap. 2.50 (ISBN 0-13-615559-6). P-H.

Cuyas Armengol, Arturo. Diccionario de Bolsillo Frances-Espanol, Espagnol-Francais. 670p. (Span. & Fr.). 1971. pap. 3.50 (ISBN 84-7183-048-5, S-50391). French & Eur.

--Diccionario Manual Frances-Espanol, Espagnol-Francais. 36th ed. 830p. (Span. & Fr.). 1977. 5.95 (ISBN 84-7183-047-7, S-50390). French & Eur.

--Diccionario Manual Ingles-Espanol, Spanish-English. 2nd ed. 768p. (Eng. & Span.). 1975. 5.95 (ISBN 84-7183-044-2, S-12389). French & Eur.

--Diccionario Manual Ingles-Espanol, Spanish-English. 35th ed. 768p. (Eng. & Span.). 1978. pap. 4.50 (ISBN 84-7183-005-1, S-12389). French & Eur.

--Gran Diccionario Cuyas Ingles-Espanol, Spanish-English. 6th ed. 1640p. (Eng. & Span.). 1977. 26.95 (ISBN 84-7183-008-6, S-12386). French & Eur.

Cuyler, Lewis. Short Bike Rides in the Berkshires. LC 79-50694. (Illus.). 128p. 1979. pap. 4.95 (ISBN 0-87106-028-0). Globe Pequot.

Cuyler, Louise, ed. see Isaac, Heirich.

Cuyler, Margery. The All-Around Christmas Book. LC 82-3104. (Illus.). 96p. (gr. 2-5). 1982. 11.50 (ISBN 0-03-060387-0); pap. 4.95 (ISBN 0-03-062183-6). HR&W.

--All Around Pumpkin Book. LC 79-4820. (Illus.). (gr. 3-7). 1980. pap. 3.95 (ISBN 0-03-568188-8). HR&W.

--Jewish Holidays. LC 77-10801. (Illus.). (gr. 2-5). 1978. 6.95 (ISBN 0-03-039936-X). HR&W.

--Sir William & the Pumpkin Monster. LC 84-610. (Illus.). (gr. 5-8). 1984. 9.95 (ISBN 0-03-064032-6). HR&W.

--The Trouble with Soap. LC 81-12636. 144p. (gr. 5 up). 1982. 9.95 (ISBN 0-525-45111-0, 0966-290, Unicorn Bk). Dutton.

--The Trouble with Soap. 112p. (gr. 5-8). 1985. pap. 2.25 (ISBN 0-590-32870-0, Apple Paperbacks). Scholastic Inc.

Cuyler, Margery, ed. see Adkins, Jan.

Cuyler, Patricia L. Sumo: History, Rites, Traditions. LC 79-18859. (Illus.). 1979. 16.50 (ISBN 0-8348-0145-0). Weatherhill.

Cuyler, Susanna. Modern Rugmaking & Tapestry Techniques: Speed Hook Tufting, Rya & Double-Time Latch. (Illus.). 120p. (Orig.). 1985. pap. 10.00 (ISBN 0-9612018-1-9). B Rugged.

--Rocks & Rugs: My Summer Vacation. (Illus.). 152p. (Orig.). 1983. pap. 6.00 (ISBN 0-9612018-0-0). B Rugged.

--The Shortest Shorter: A Distillation of the Oxford English Dictionary A - M. (Illus., Orig.). 1985. pap. 5.00 (ISBN 0-9612018-2-7). B Rugged.

Cuyt, A. Pade Approximants for Operators: Theory & Applications. (Lecture Notes in Mathematics Ser.: Vol. 1065). ix, 138p. 1984. pap. 10.50 (ISBN 0-387-13342-9). Springer-Verlag.

Cuyvers, Luc. Ocean Uses & Their Regulation. LC 84-3587. 179p. 1984. 29.95x (ISBN 0-471-88676-9, Pub. by Wiley-Interscience); pap. text ed. 19.95x (ISBN 0-471-88675-0). Wiley.

Cuzin, Jean P., jt. auth. see Laclotte, Michele.

Cuzin, Jean-Pierre, jt. auth. see Laclotte, Michael.

Cuzner, Bernard. A First Book of Metal-Work. 192p. 1980. 11.00x (ISBN 0-905418-54-9, Pub. by Gresham England). State Mutual Bk.

Cuzner, M. L., jt. ed. see Davison, A. N.

Cuzzort, Ray P. & King, Edith W. Twentieth Century Social Thought. 3rd ed. LC 80-10204. 389p. 1980. pap. text ed. 23.95 (ISBN 0-03-052521-7, HoltC). HR&W.

Cvancara, Alan M. A Field Manual for the Amateur Geologist: Tools & Activities for Exploring Our Planet. 240p. 1985. 22.95 (ISBN 0-13-316530-2); pap. 12.95 (ISBN 0-13-316522-1). P-H.

Cvetanovic, Ratimir J. English-Serbocroatian, Serbocroatian-English Dictionary. (Eng. & Serbocroatian.). 24.50 (ISBN 0-87557-074-7, 074-7). Saphrograph.

Cvetkovich, George, et al. Social Psychology. LC 83-10789. 500p. 1984. text ed. 27.95 (ISBN 0-03-063411-3). HR&W.

Cvetlovic, Dragos, et al, eds. Spectra of Graphs: Theory & Applications. LC 79-50490. (Pure & Applied Mathematics Ser.). 1980. 67.50 (ISBN 0-12-195150-2). Acad Pr.

Cvitanovic. Universality in Chaos. 1984. 48.00 (ISBN 0-9903000-1-3, Pub. by A Hilger England). Heyden.

Cwieka, Raymond. Sources of the Polish Tradition, 3 vols. Bd. with Vol. 1. The Great Polish Walking Dance: Polonaise. pap. 15.00 (ISBN 0-317-13909-6); Vol. 2. The Elegant Running-Sliding Dance: Mazur, Maqurka. 1983; Vol. 3. Dance Figures: Historical Contemporary (A Choreographer's Handbook) 1984. Complete 3 vols. set. pap. 35.00 (ISBN 0-317-13907-X); Vols. II & III Bound as a Set. pap. 25.00 (ISBN 0-317-13908-8). R Cwieka.

Cwikel, M. & Peetre, J. Interpolation Spaces & Allied Topics in Analysis: Proceedings of the Conference Held in Lund, Sweden, August 29 - September 1, 1983. (Lecture Notes in Mathematics Ser.: Vol. 1070). iii, 239p. 1984. pap. 13.50 (ISBN 0-387-13363-1). Springer-Verlag.

Cwiklo, William E., ed. Computers in Litigation Support. 353p. Repr. text ed. 25.00 (ISBN 0-89433-086-1). Petrocelli.

CWL. Mail Drops. (Security & Survival Ser.). 48p. (Orig.). 1985. pap. 10.00 (ISBN 0-939856-45-X). Tech Group.

--Urban & Rural Survival: Rural Home Modifications. (Security & Survival Ser.). (Illus.). 60p. (Orig.). 1985. pap. 15.00 (ISBN 0-939856-48-4). Tech Group.

--Urban Survival: Home Modifications. (Security & Survival Ser.). (Illus.). 100p. (Orig.). 1985. pap. 20.00 (ISBN 0-939856-47-6). Tech Group.

--Urban Survival: Vehicles. (Security & Survival Ser.). (Illus.). 48p. (Orig.). 1985. pap. 15.00 (ISBN 0-939856-46-8). Tech Group.

Cy De Cosse Inc. Staff. Clothing Care & Repair. (Singer Sewing Reference Library). (Illus.). 128p. 1985. 17.95 (ISBN 0-86573-205-1). Cy De Cosse.

--Clothing Care & Repair. (Singer Sewing Reference Library). (Illus.). 128p. 1985. pap. 9.95 (ISBN 0-86573-206-X). Cy De Cosse.

--Sewing Essentials. (Singer Sewing Reference Library). (Illus.). 128p. 1984. 17.95 (ISBN 0-86573-201-9). Cy De Cosse.

--Sewing Essentials. (Singer Sewing Reference Library). (Illus.). 128p. 1984. pap. 9.95 (ISBN 0-86573-202-7). Cy De Cosse.

--Sewing for Style. (Singer Sewing Reference Library). (Illus.). 128p. 1985. pap. 9.95 (ISBN 0-86573-208-6). Cy De Cosse.

--Sewing for Style. (Singer Sewing Reference Library). (Illus.). 128p. 1985. 17.95 (ISBN 0-86573-207-8). Cy De Cosse.

--Sewing for the Home. (Singer Sewing Reference Library). (Illus.). 128p. 1984. 17.95 (ISBN 0-86573-203-5); pap. 9.95 (ISBN 0-86573-204-3). Cy De Cosse.

--Sewing Specialty Fabrics. (Singer Sewing Reference Library). (Illus.). 128p. 1985. 17.95 (ISBN 0-86573-209-4); pap. 9.95 (ISBN 0-86573-210-8). Cy De Cosse.

Cy DeCosse, Incorporated Staff, ed. see Sternberg, Dick.

Cyan, Erwin Di see Moser, Robert H. & Di Cyan, Erwin.

Cybertronics International, Inc. Cyber LOGO Turtle: A First Step in Computer Literacy. 1984. manual & disk 55.00 (ISBN 0-8359-1203-5). Reston.

Cyborg Software Systems, Inc., et al. The ZX-80, ZX-81, & Timex-Sinclair 1000 Microcomputers. rev. ed. (Nanos Reference Cards Ser.). (Illus.). 20p. 1982. 5.95 (ISBN 0-915069-13-X). Nanos Sys.

Cyborg Software Systems Incorporate, et al. The CP-M System. (Nanos Reference Cards Ser.). 20p. (Orig.). 1984. pap. 5.95 (ISBN 0-915069-20-2). Nanos Sys.

Cybulski, Jerome S., jt. ed. see Sigmon, Becky A.

Cyca, Robert & Harcombe, Andrew. Exploring Manning Park. 2nd ed. LC 79-13910. (Illus.). 128p. 1979. pap. 6.95 (ISBN 0-916890-76-7). Mountaineers.

Cyert, Richard M. The American Economy, Nineteen Sixty to Two Thousand. LC 82-48600. (Charles C. Moskowitz Memorial Lecture Ser.: Vol. XXLII). 1983. 12.95 (ISBN 0-02-923100-0). Free Pr.

Cyert, Richard M. & DeGroot, Morris H. Bayesian Analysis & Uncertainty in Economic Theory. (Probability & Statistics Ser.). (Illus.). 224p. 1986. 34.95x (ISBN 0-8476-7471-1). Rowman & Allanheld.

Cyert, Richard M. & March, J. G. Behavioral Theory of the Firm. 1963. ref. ed. 30.95 (ISBN 0-13-073304-0). P-H.

Cyert, Richard M., jt. auth. see Argyris, Chris.

Cyert, Richard M., jt. auth. see Cohen, Kalman J.

Cykler, Edmund, jt. auth. see Wold, Milo.

Cykler, Edmund, jt. auth. see Wold, Milo A.

Cylwicki, Albert. If Today You Hear His Voice: Reflections on the Sunday Readings. LC 81-10966. 553p. (Orig.). 1981. pap. 12.95 (ISBN 0-8189-0418-6). Alba.

Cynewulf. The Christ of Cynewulf; a Poem in Three Parts: The Advent, the Ascension, & the Last Judgement. Cook, Albert S., ed. LC 73-178524. Repr. of 1900 ed. 32.50 (ISBN 0-404-56538-7). AMS Pr.

--Christ of Cynewulf: A Poem in Three Parts, the Advent, the Ascension, & the Last Judgment. facsimile ed. Cook, Albert S., ed. LC 74-114906. (Select Bibliographies Reprint Ser). 1900. 25.50 (ISBN 0-8369-5310-X). Ayer Co Pubs.

--Elene. Gradon, P. O., ed. (Old English Ser). 1966. pap. text ed. 4.25x (ISBN 0-89197-573-X). Irvington.

--Elene: An Old English Poem. Kent, Charles W., ed. LC 77-178525. Repr. of 1889 ed. 21.00 (ISBN 0-404-56539-5). AMS Pr.

--Juliana. Woolf, Rosemary, ed. (Old English Ser.). 1966. pap. text ed. 2.95x (ISBN 0-89197-574-8). Irvington.

Cynk, Jerzy B. Polish Aircraft: 1893-1939. (Putnam Aeronautical Bks.). (Illus.). 782p. 1979. 27.95 (ISBN 0-370-00085-4, Pub. by the Bodley Head). Merrimack Pub Cir.

Cynkin, Simme. Occupational Therapy. 1979. 13.95 (ISBN 0-316-16610-3). Little.

Cynn, Hugh H., tr. see Riley, John W., Jr. & Schramm, Wilbur.

Cynthia, Duval & Karcheski, Walter. Medieval & Renaissance Splendor: The Romance of Arts, Armor & Works of Art from the John Woodman Higgins. LC 83-83306. (Illus.). 160p. (Orig.). 1984. pap. 20.00 (ISBN 0-916758-15-X). Ringling Mus Art.

Cypert, Samuel A. Writing Effective Business Letters, Memos, Proposals, & Reports. 320p. 1983. 15.95 (ISBN 0-8092-5605-3); pap. 8.95 (ISBN 0-8092-5604-5). Contemp Bks.

--Writing Effective Business Letters, Memos, Proposals & Reports. 320p. 1984. pap. 9.95 (ISBN 0-8092-5604-5). Contemp Bks.

Cypess, Sandra M., ed. Essays in Romance Languages & Literature Including Latin American. 196p. 1979. Repr. 12.50 (ISBN 0-87291-130-6). Coronado Pr.

Cyporyn, Dennis. Blue Grass Songbook. 224p. 1972. pap. 3.95 (ISBN 0-02-060380-0, Collier). Macmillan.

Cypress, Beulah J. Office Visits for Disease of the Circulatory System: The National Ambulatory Medical Care Survey: United States, 1975-76. Cox, Klaudia, ed. (Ser. 13: No. 40). 1979. pap. text ed. 1.75 (ISBN 0-8406-0155-7). Natl Ctr Health Stats.

Cypress, Beulah K. Medication Therapy in Office Visits for Selected Diagnoses: National Ambulatory Medical Care Survey, United States, 1980. Cox, Klaudia, ed. (Ser. 13: No. 71). 65p. 1982. pap. text ed. 1.85 (ISBN 0-8406-0266-9). Natl Ctr Health Stats.

--The National Ambulatory Medical Care Survey: Office Visits to Internists United States, January-December 1975. Cox, Klaudia, ed. (Series 13: No. 36). 1978. pap. text ed. 1.50 (ISBN 0-8406-0132-8). Natl Ctr Health Stats.

--Office Visits by Women: The National Ambulatory Medical Care Survey, 1977. Shipp, Audrey, ed. (Series 13: No. 40). 1980. pap. text ed. 1.75 (ISBN 0-8406-0182-4). Natl Ctr Health Stats.

--Office Visits for Diseases of the Respiratory System: The National Ambulatory Medical Care Survey, United States 1975-76. Cox, Klaudia, ed. (Ser. 13-42). 1979. pap. text ed. 1.75 (ISBN 0-8406-0160-3). Natl Ctr Health Stats.

--Patterns of Ambulatory Care-General & Family Practice: The National Ambulatory Medical Care Survey. Shipp, Audrey, ed. (Series 13: No. 73). 55p. 1983. pap. 1.95 (ISBN 0-8406-0282-0). Natl Ctr Health Stats.

--Patterns of Ambulatory Care in Obstetrics & Gynecology: The National Ambulatory Medical Care Survey Jan. 1980 to Dec. 1981. Shipp, Audrey, ed. (Series 13, No. 76). 55p. 1984. pap. text ed. 1.94 (ISBN 0-8406-0289-8). Natl Ctr Health Stats.

--Use of Health Services for Disorders of the Female Reproductive System: United States 1977-78. Cox, Klaudia, ed. (Series Thirteen: No. 63). 50p. 1981. pap. 1.75 (ISBN 0-686-79386-2). Natl Ctr Health Stats.

Cypress, Beulah K. & Shipp, Audrey. Patients' Reasons for Visiting Physicians: The National Ambulatory Medical Care Survey, United States, 1977-78, No.56. (Ser.13). 50p. 1981. pap. 1.75 (ISBN 0-686-73364-9). Natl Ctr Health Stats.

Cypress, Beulah K., jt. auth. see Hing, Ester.

Cypress, Beulah K., ed. see Shipp, Audrey.

Cyprian, Saint A Christian Preparation for Death. pap. 1.50 (ISBN 0-686-25548-8). Eastern Orthodox.

Cyprian, St. Complete Letters. LC 65-12906. (Fathers of the Church Ser.: Vol. 51). 352p. 1964. 19.95x (ISBN 0-8132-0051-2). Cath U Pr.

--The Lapsed & the Unity of the Church. pap. 2.95 (ISBN 0-686-05646-9). Eastern Orthodox.

--Life & Works of St. Cyprian of Carthage, 4 vols. Vols. 1, 2, & 4. pap. 1.50 ea.; Vol. 3. pap. 2.95 (ISBN 0-686-05649-3); pap. 6.95 set (ISBN 0-686-05650-7). Eastern Orthodox.

--On Mortality. pap. 1.50 (ISBN 0-686-05658-2). Eastern Orthodox.

--Selected Treatises. LC 77-81349. (Fathers of the Church Ser.: Vol. 36). 372p. 1958. 19.95x (ISBN 0-8132-0036-9). Cath U Pr.

Cyprian, Uzoigwe. The Betrayal. 50p. 1984. 3.00 (ISBN 0-89697-228-3). Intl Univ Pr.

Cyprianus, Gallus. Cypriana Galli Poetae Heptatevchos. (Corpus Scriptorum Ecclesiasticorum Latinorum Ser: Vol. 23). (Lat). 1881. 50.00 (ISBN 0-384-10515-7). Johnson Repr.

Cyprianus, Saint Opera Omnia. (Corpus Scriptorum Ecclesiasticorum Latinorum Ser: Vol. 3). 1868-1871. pap. 131.00 (ISBN 0-384-10518-1). Johnson Repr.

Cyprien, Michael, jt. auth. see Ross, Anne.

Cypser, R. J. Communications Architecture for Distributed Systems. LC 76-52673. (Illus.). 1978. text ed. 38.95 (ISBN 0-201-14458-1). Addison-Wesley.

--Communications Architecture for Distributed Systems. 711p. 1978. 21.95 (ISBN 0-686-98122-7). Telecom Lib.

Cyr & Sobeck. Real Estate Brokerage: A Success Guide. 29.95 (ISBN 0-88462-359-9). Caroline Hse.

Cyr, Arthur. British Foreign Policy & the Atlantic Area: The Techniques of Accommodation. LC 79-4331. 172p. 1979. text ed. 29.50x (ISBN 0-8419-0489-8). Holmes & Meier.

Cyr, Arthur I. Liberal Party Politics in Britain. LC 76-702. 350p. 1977. text ed. 12.95 (ISBN 0-87855-145-X). Transaction Bks.

Cyr, Frank W. Responsibility for Rural-School Administration: Allocation of Responsibilities in the Administration of Schools in Rural Areas. LC 70-176703. (Columbia University. Teachers College. Contributions to Education: No. 579). Repr. of 1933 ed. 22.50 (ISBN 0-404-55579-9). AMS Pr.

Cyr, Frederick. School for Scandal. LC 85-70198. 200p. 1985. pap. 3.95 (ISBN 0-394-62057-7, B-523, BC). Grove.

Cyr, Helen W. A Filmography of the Third World, 1976-1983: An Annotated List of 16mm Films. LC 84-23564. 285p. 1985. 20.00 (ISBN 0-8108-1768-3). Scarecrow.

Cyr, John & Sobeck, Joan M. Real Estate Brokerage: A Success Guide. 336p. 1982. 29.95 (ISBN 0-88462-359-9, 1965-01, Real Estate Ed). Longman USA.

Cyras, A. A. Mathematical Models for the Analysis & Optimization of Elastoplastic Structures. (Series in Civil & Mechanical Engineering: 1-622). 121p. 1983. text ed. 39.95x (ISBN 0-470-20020-0). Halsted Pr.

Cyres, Viscount St. see St. Cyres, Viscount.

Cyriax, G. R., ed. Effective Use of the Fidic Contract & Standard Conditions: A Gower Executive Report. 154p. (Orig.). 1982. pap. text ed. 65.95x (ISBN 0-566-03036-5). Gower Pub Co.

--Liability in Trans-European Road Transport. 90p. 1980. pap. 65.00x (ISBN 0-566-03018-7). Gower Pub Co.

--Negotiating a Shorter Working Week. 88p. (Orig.). 1980. pap. text ed. 69.00x (ISBN 0-566-03007-1). Gower Pub Co.

--Planning Employee Share Schemes. 54p. (Orig.). 1981. pap. text ed. 47.50x (ISBN 0-566-03024-1). Gower Pub Co.

Cyriax, George, ed. Liquidation & Bankruptcy Aspects of Conveyancing. 48p. (Orig.). 1982. pap. text ed. 63.00x (ISBN 0-566-03035-7). Gower Pub Co.

--World Index of Economic Forecasts. 2nd ed. 400p. 1981. 95.00 (ISBN 0-87196-529-1). Facts on File.

--World Index of Economic Forecasts. LC 78-56982. (Praeger Special Studies). 395p. 1978. 275.00 (ISBN 0-03-046216-9). Praeger.

Cyriax, J. Textbook of Orthopaedic Medicine: Diagnosis of Soft Tissue Lesions, Vol. 1. 8th ed. (Illus.). 1982. text ed. 55.00 (ISBN 0-7216-0777-2, Pub. by Bailliere-Tindall). Saunders.

Cyriax, James & Coldham, Margaret. Textbook of Orthopaedic Medicine: Treatment by Manipulation, Massage & Injection, Vol. 2. 11th ed. (Illus.). 290p. Date not set. price not set (Pub. by Bailliere-Tindall). Saunders.

Cyriax, James & Cyriax, Patricia. Illustrated Manual of Orthopedic Medicine. (Illus.). 240p. 1983. text ed. 39.95 (ISBN 0-407-00262-6). Butterworth.

Cyriax, James & Russell, Gillean. Textbook of Orthopaedic Medicine: Treatment by Manipulation, Massage & Injection, Vol. II. 10th ed. (Illus.). 1980. text ed. 52.00 (ISBN 0-7216-0718-7, Pub. by Bailliere-Tindall). Saunders.

Cyriax, Patricia, jt. auth. see Cyriax, James.

Cyrier, Barbara A. A Miracle Strikes. 1985. 6.75 (ISBN 0-8062-2448-7). Carlton.

Cyril Of Jerusalem, St. Catecheses Thirteen-Eighteen & Other Works, Vol. 2. (Fathers of the Church Ser.: Vol. 64). 1970. 14.95x (ISBN 0-8132-0064-4). Cath U Pr.

--Procatechesis, Catacheses One - Twelve. LC 68-55980. (Fathers of the Church Ser.: Vol. 61). 279p. 1969. 15.95x (ISBN 0-8132-0061-X). Cath U Pr.

Cyril Of Jerusalem, Saint St. Cyril of Jerusalem on the Sacraments. 83p. 1977. pap. 3.95 (ISBN 0-913836-39-7). St Vladimirs.

Cyrs, Thomas E., Jr., ed. Handbook for the Design of Instruction in Pharmacy Education. 200p. 1977. 6.50 (ISBN 0-686-83878-5). Am Assn Coll Pharm.

--Handboook for the Design of Instruction in Pharmacy Education. 200p. 6.50 (ISBN 0-937526-06-1). Am Assn Coll Pharm.

Cyrus, Cinda. A Primer of Oilwell Service & Workover. 3rd ed. Gerding, Mildred, ed. (Illus.). 106p. (Orig.). 1979. pap. text ed. 6.50 (ISBN 0-88698-117-4, 3.60030). Petex.

--Well Cementing. Paxson, Jeanette R., ed. (Oil & Gas Production Ser.). (Illus.). 82p. (Orig.). 1983. pap. text ed. 5.00 (ISBN 0-88698-112-3, 3.30610). Petex.

Cyrus, Cinda, ed. see Hosmanek, Max.

Cyrus, Lee. Gypsies & Angels. 113p. 1984. 5.95 (ISBN 0-89697-155-4). Intl Univ Pr.

Cyrus Willaim Rice & Co. Copper in Feedwater to Supercritical Steam Generating Units. 55p. 1965. 8.25 (ISBN 0-317-34503-6, 69). Intl Copper.

Cysarz, Herbert. Sein und Werden, Entwurf Eines Universaltheoretischen Spektrums: Mit Einer Einfuhrung, 1970. LC 70-108599. (Classics in Germanic Literatures and Philosophy Ser). 1970. Repr. of 1948 ed. 25.00 (ISBN 0-384-10525-4). Johnson Repr.

--Weltraetsel Im Wort: Mit Einem Anhang: Zwanzig Jahre Spater, 1970. LC 76-108598. (Classics in Germanic Literatures & Philosophy Ser). 1970. Repr. of 1948 ed. 29.00 (ISBN 0-384-10528-9). Johnson Repr.

Cyster, R., et al. Parental Involvement in Primary Schools. 212p. 1980. 16.00x (ISBN 0-85633-211-9, Pub. by NFER Nelson UK). Taylor & Francis.

Cywinski, Jozef. The Essentials in Pressure Monitoring: Blood & Other Body Fluids. (The Tardieu Ser.: No. 3). (Illus.). 120p. 1980. pap. 20.00 (ISBN 90-247-2385-X, Pub. by Martinus Nijhoff Netherlands). Kluwer Academic.

Cywinski, Ray. Preston Sturges: A Guide to References & Resources. 1984. lib. bdg. 42.00 (ISBN 0-8161-8510-7, Hall Reference). G K Hall.

Cyzevs'Kyj, Dmytro. A History of Ukrainian Literature from the 11th to the End of the 19th Century. Ferguson, D., tr. LC 73-94029. 681p. 1975. pap. text ed. 20.00 (ISBN 0-87287-170-3). Ukrainian Acad.

Cyzyk, Janet. Entering the Reader's World, 3 bks. Mendyk, Dennis, ed. (Adult Literacy Training Ser.). (Illus.). 160p. 1982. pap. 5.13 ea. Bk. 1 (ISBN 0-8428-9503-5). Bk. 2 (ISBN 0-8428-9504-3). Bk. 3 (ISBN 0-8428-9505-1). Cambridge Bk.

Cyzyk, Janet L. Baltimore County Design: Administrator's Manual. Maryland State Dept. of Education, ed. (Correlates Test to Adult Literacy Ser.). (Illus.). 128p. 1982. pap. text ed. 13.26 (ISBN 0-8428-9501-9); student test bklt. 3.33 (ISBN 0-8428-9500-0). Cambridge Bk.

Czaczkes, J. W. & De-Nour, A. Kaplan. Chronic Hemodialysis As a Way of Life. LC 78-3605. 1978. 22.50 (ISBN 0-87630-165-0). Brunner-Mazel.

Czaja, Paul C. Writing with Light: A Simple Workshop in Basic Photography. LC 72-93261. 96p. (gr. 6 up). 1973. 6.95 (ISBN 0-85699-068-X). Chatham Pr.

Czajka, Peter A. & Duffy, James P. Poisoning Emergencies: A Guide for Emergency Medical Personnel. LC 79-20542. 1980. pap. text ed. 12.95 (ISBN 0-8016-1205-5). Mosby.

Czaky, Mick, ed. How Does It Feel? Exploring the World of Your Senses: Exploring the Five Senses. (Illus.). 1979. 3.98 (ISBN 0-517-53829-6); pap. 1.00 (ISBN 0-517-53983-7). Crown.

Czanderna, A. W., ed. Methods of Surface Analysis. (Methods & Phenomena Ser.: Vol. 1). 482p. 1975. 83.00 (ISBN 0-444-41344-8). Elsevier.

Czanderna, A. W. & Wolsky, S. P., eds. Microweighing in Vacuum & Conrolled Environments. (Methods & Phenomena Ser.: Vol. 4). 404p. 1980. 74.50 (ISBN 0-444-41868-7). Elsevier.

Czanderna, A. W., jt. ed. see Lu, C.

Czapla, Cathy Y. Genetic Memories. 12p. 1983. pap. 1.00 (ISBN 0-686-46861-9). Samisdat.

--Heirloom. 16p. 1981. pap. 1.00 (ISBN 0-686-30659-7). Samisdat.

Czaplinski, Rosemary, et al. Self-Assessment of Current Knowledge in Orthopedic & Rehabilitative Nursing. 1979. pap. 13.00 (ISBN 0-87488-230-3). Med Exam.

Czaplinski, Suzanne M. Sexism in Award-Winning Picture Books. (Illus.). 1973. pap. 2.50x (ISBN 0-912786-21-3). Know Inc.

Czarnecki, D. B. & Blinn, D. W. Diatoms of Southwestern U. S. A. Diatoms of Lower Lake Powell & Vicinity, Vol. 1. (Bibliotheca Phycologica: No. 28). 1977. pap. text ed. 12.40 (ISBN 3-7682-1102-9). Lubrecht & Cramer.

--Diatoms of Southwestern USA: Diatoms of the Colorado River in Grand Canyon National Park and Vicinity, Vol. 2. (Illus.). 1978. pap. text ed. 17.50 (ISBN 3-7682-1182-7). Lubrecht & Cramer.

Czarnecki, Jack. Joe's Book of Mushroom Cookery. LC 83-45494. (Illus.). 352p. 1985. 22.95 (ISBN 0-689-11450-8). Atheneum.

Czarnecki, Jan. The Goths in Ancient Poland. LC 74-20750. 1975. 12.50x (ISBN 0-87024-264-4). U of Miami Pr.

Czarnecki, Jan, compiled by. Soviet Union, 1917-1967: An Annotated Bibliography of Soviet Semicentennial Publications in the Collection of the University of Miami at Coral Gables, Florida. LC 74-14893. 1974. 10.00x (ISBN 0-87024-273-3). U of Miami Pr.

Czarnecki, Mark, tr. see Bourassa, Andre G.

Czarniawska, Barbara. Managing General Managers. 190p. 1985. text ed. write for info. (ISBN 0-566-05065-X). Gower Pub Co.

Czarniecki, Anne D., jt. auth. see Cain, Helen.

Czarnowski, M. S. Productive Capacity of Locality As a Function of Soil & Climate with Particular Reference to Forest Land. LC 64-16087. (Louisiana State University Studies, Biological Science Ser.: No. 5). pap. 48.00 (ISBN 0-317-29879-8, 2051878). Bks Demand UMI.

Czarnowski, Stefan. Le Culte Des Heros et Ses Conditions Sociales. LC 74-25745. (European Sociology Ser.). 472p. 1975. Repr. 35.50x (ISBN 0-405-06500-0). Ayer Co Pubs.

Czarra, Fred, ed. Guide to Historical Reading: Non-Fiction. 11th ed. 1983. 20.00 (ISBN 0-916882-03-9). Heldref Pubns.

Czaykowski, Bogdan, tr. see Bialoszewski, Miron.

Czebatul, Anthony A. The Legend of Protogonos. 1984. 7.95 (ISBN 0-533-06148-2). Vantage.

Czech, Annette. Modernizing Your Personnel Management System. 250p. 1985. 85.50 (ISBN 0-86604-189-3); write for info. 3-ring binder. Hamilton Inst.

Czech, Hella, tr. see Penck, Walther.

Czech, Hella, tr. see Portmann, Adolf.

Czech, Michael P. & Kahn, Ron C. Membrane Receptors & Cellular Regulation. LC 85-4573. (UCLA Ser.: Vol. 23). 444p. 1985. 96.00 (ISBN 0-8451-2622-9). A R Liss.

Czech, Michael P., ed. Molecular Basis of Insulin Action. 490p. 1985. 59.50x (ISBN 0-306-41843-6, Plenum Pr). Plenum Pub.

Czechowicz, James, jt. auth. see Newman, Charles M., II.

Czege, A. Wass. Documented Facts & Figures on Transylvania. LC 77-73539. (Illus.). 1977. 5.00 (ISBN 0-87934-041-X). Danubian.

Czege, A. Wass De see De Czege, A. Wass.

Czege, Albert W. De see De Czege, Albert W., et al.

Czeh, C., jt. ed. see Szabo, T.

Czeilel & Tusnady. Aetiological Studies of Isolated Common Congenital Abnormalities in Hungary. 330p. 1984. 34.00 (ISBN 963-05-3223-9, Pub. by Akademiai Kaido Hungary). Heyden.

Czeisler, Charles A. & Guilleminault, Christian, eds. REM Sleep: Its Temporal Distribution. (Sleep Reprint Ser.: Vol. 2, Nos. 3-4, 1980). 126p. 1980. pap. text ed. 18.50 (ISBN 0-89004-527-5). Raven.

Czeisler, Charles A., jt. ed. see Moore-Ede, Martin C.

Czeizing, Lajos. Panoramas of Budapest. (Illus.). pap. 5.00 (ISBN 0-89918-372-7, H 372). Vanous.

Czeizing, Panorama. Budapest. 3rd ed. (Illus.). 1970. 7.50x (ISBN 0-89918-372-7, H-372). Vanous.

Czempiel, E. O., et al, eds. United States Interests & Western Europe: Arms Control, Energy, Trade. 160p. 1981. 15.00 (ISBN 0-317-07425-3). Transnatl Pubs.

Czempiel, Ernst O. Amerikanische Sicherheitssystem, 1945-1949: Studie zur Aussenpolitik der buergerlichen Gesellschaft. (Beitraege zur auswaertigen und internationalen Politik, 1). (Ger). 1966. 39.60 (ISBN 3-11-000527-1). De Gruyter.

Czepiel, John & Backman, Jules. Changing Marketing Strategies in a New Economy. LC 77-11109. (Key Issues Lecture Ser). 1977. pap. 7.87 scp (ISBN 0-672-97199-2). Bobbs.

Czepiel, John A., et al, eds. The Service Encounter. LC 83-49532. (Advances in Retailing Ser.). 352p. 1984. 31.50x (ISBN 0-669-08273-2). Lexington Bks.

Czermak, Herberth. Kafka's Short Stories Notes. 98p. 1973. pap. 3.75 (ISBN 0-8220-0700-2). Cliffs.

--Magic Mountain: Notes. (Orig.). 1969. pap. 3.25 (ISBN 0-8220-0789-4). Cliffs.

--The Trial Notes. (Orig.). 1976. pap. text ed. 2.75 (ISBN 0-8220-1304-5). Cliffs.

Czermak, Johannes, jt. auth. see Weingartner, Paul A.

Czernek, Karen. Chords of Love: A Visual Experience of Art & Soul. (Illus., Orig.). 1984. pap. 10.00 (ISBN 0-933646-23-2). Aries Pr.

Czerni & Skrzynka. Polish-English Dictionary of Science & Technology. 754p. (Pol. & Eng.). 1976. 95.00x (ISBN 0-686-44737-9, Pub. by Collets). State Mutual Bk.

Czerni, et al. Science & Technical English & Polish Dictionary. 1982. 50.00 (ISBN 0-317-18987-5, P536). Vanous.

Czerni, S. & Skrzynska, M. Polish Concise Technology Dictionary: Polish-English. 5th ed. 846p. 1983. 50.00x (ISBN 0-89918-537-1). Vanous.

--Polish Science & Technology Dictionary: English-Polish. 6th ed. 910p. (Pol. & Eng.). 1982. 50.00x (ISBN 0-89918-536-3, P536). Vanous.

Czerni, Sergiusz & Skrzynska, Maria, eds. English-Polish Dictionary of Science & Technology. 5th ed. 1976. 36.00x (ISBN 0-686-23574-6). Intl Learn Syst.

--Polish-English Dictionary of Science & Technology. 3rd ed. (Pol. & Eng.). 1976. 30.00x (ISBN 0-686-19981-2). Intl Learn Syst.

--Polish-English, English-Polish Dictionary of Science & Technology, 2 Vols. rev. & enl. ed. 1755p. Set. 85.00 (ISBN 0-318-04724-1, Pub. by Wydawnictwa Poland). Heinman.

Czerniak, Eli. Reinforced Concrete Columns, 2 vols. Incl. Vol. 1. Working Stress Design for Concrete Columns. (Illus.). 424p. 18.00 (ISBN 0-8044-4166-9); Vol. 2. Working Stress Design Charts for Spiral Columns. (Illus.). 320p. 15.00 (ISBN 0-8044-4167-7). Set. 33.00 (ISBN 0-8044-4165-0). Ungar.

Czerniawski, Adam, tr. see Rozewicz, Tadeusz.

Czernichow, P. & Robinson, A. D., eds. Diabetes Insipidus in Man. (Frontiers of Hormone Research: Vol. 13). (Illus.). x, 326p. 1985. 70.25 (ISBN 3-8055-3921-5). S Karger.

Czernin, W. H. C., jt. auth. see Dipl-Ing, W. H.

Czerny, Carl. The Art of Finger Dexterity for Piano, No. 1. Seifert, Hans T., ed. (Carl Fischer Music Library: No. 390). (Illus.). 1905. pap. 5.00 (ISBN 0-8258-0120-6). Fischer Inc NY.

--Letters to a Young Lady on the Art of Playing the Piano. Hamilton, J. A., tr. LC 77-94570. 1979. Repr. of 1883 ed. lib. bdg. 17.50 (ISBN 0-89341-405-0). Longwood Pub Group.

--On the Proper Performance of All Beethoven's Works for the Piano. Badura-Skoda, Paul, ed. 1970. pap. 19.00 (ISBN 3-7024-0111-3, 47-13340ENJ). Eur-Am Music.

--One Hundred Practical Exercises for Piano, Op. 139. (Carl Fischer Music Library: No. 371). 76p. 1905. pap. 3.00 (ISBN 0-8258-0134-6). Fischer Inc NY.

--Preparatory School of Finger Dexterity for Piano. Seifert, Hans, ed. (Carl Fischer Music Library: No. 482). 1907. pap. 6.00 (ISBN 0-8258-0124-9, L482). Fischer Inc NY.

--School of Practical Composition, 3 vols. (Music Reprint Ser.). 1979. Repr. of 1848 ed. Set. lib. bdg. 95.00 (ISBN 0-306-79595-7). Da Capo.

--School of Velocity for Piano, 2 bks, Op. 299. (Carl Fischer Music Library: Nos. 341 & 399). 1903. Bk. 1. pap. 4.00 (ISBN 0-8258-0109-5, L-339). Fischer Inc NY.

--School of Velocity for Piano, Op. 299, Complete Edition. 101p. 1903. pap. 6.00 (ISBN 0-8258-0108-7, L 338). Fischer Inc NY.

--Thirty New Studies in Technic for Piano, Op. 849. (Carl Fischer Music Library: No. 487). 56p. 1907. pap. 6.00 (ISBN 0-8258-0127-3, L 487). Fischer Inc NY.

Czerny, Carl, ed. see Bach, J. S.

Czerny, Charles C. Letters to a Young Lady on the Art of Playing the Pianoforte. Hamilton, J. A., tr. from Ger. (Music Ser.). vii, 82p. 1982. Repr. lib. bdg. 17.50 (ISBN 0-306-76123-8). Da Capo.

Czerny, Grazyna, tr. see Duleba, Wladyslaw.

Czerny, Robert, tr. see Ricoeur, Paul.

Czerny, Z. Polish Cookbook. (Illus.). 1976. 22.00x (ISBN 0-89918-535-5, P-535). Vanous.

Czerwinski, Barara S. A Manual of Patient Education for Cardiopulmonary Dysfunction. LC 79-21435. (Illus.). 264p. 1980. pap. text ed. 16.95 (ISBN 0-8016-1197-0). Mosby.

Czerwinski, Frank L., jt. auth. see Samaras, Thomas T.

Czerwionka, F. J., et al. Illinois Tax Handbook: 1984 Edition. 250p. 1983. 11.00x (ISBN 0-317-07500-4, 45043-7). P-H.

Czerwionka, Frederick J, et al. Illinois Tax Handbook, 1984. LC 84-111023. 1984. price not set (ISBN 0-13-450437-2). P-H.

Czestochowski, Joseph. The American Landscape Tradition: A Study & Gallery of Paintings. (Illus.). 160p. 1983. pap. 19.75 (ISBN 0-525-47674-1, 01917-580). Dutton.

Czestochowski, Joseph S. John Steuart Curry & Grant Wood: A Portrait of Rural America. LC 80-27349. (Illus.). 224p. 1981. text ed. 34.00x (ISBN 0-8262-0336-1). U of Mo Pr.

--Works of Arthur B. Davies. LC 79-11546. (Illus.). 1979. 75.00 (ISBN 0-226-68946-8, Chicago Visual Lib); 5 colorfiches & 2 b & w fiches incl. U of Chicago Pr.

Czestochowski, Joseph S., ed. The Art of Marvin Cone. (Illus.). 80p. 1985. 22.50 (ISBN 0-525-24300-3, 02184-660); pap. 10.95 (ISBN 0-525-48149-4, 01063-320). Dutton.

--Contemporary Polish Posters in Full Color. LC 78-64945. (Illus.). 1979. pap. 6.95 (ISBN 0-486-23780-X). Dover.

Czestochowski, Joseph S., ed. see Hassam, Childe.

Czichos. Tribology: A Systems Approach to the Science & Technology of Friction, Lubrication & Wear. (Tribology Ser.: Vol. 1). 400p. 1978. 76.50 (ISBN 0-444-41676-5). Elsevier.

Czigany, Lorant. The Oxford History of Hungarian Literature from the Earliest Times to the Present. LC 83-3997. 582p. 1984. 39.95x (ISBN 0-19-815781-9). Oxford U Pr.

Czinkota, Michael & Marciel, Scot, eds. U. S. - Arab Economic Relations: A Time of Transition. LC 85-3614. 368p. 1985. 44.95 (ISBN 0-03-072024-9). Praeger.

Czinkota, Michael R. Export Development Strategies: U. S. Promotional Policy. LC 81-13919. 172p. 1982. 29.95 (ISBN 0-03-059718-8). Praeger.

Czinkota, Michael R., ed. Export Controls: Building Reasonable Commercial Ties with Political Adversaries. LC 84-4735. 232p. 1984. 29.95 (ISBN 0-03-071021-9). Praeger.

--Export Promotion: The Public & Private Sector Interaction. (Illus.). 346p. 1983. 37.95 (ISBN 0-03-062952-7). Praeger.

Czinkota, Michael R, ed. U. S.-Latin American Trade Relations: Issues & Concerns. Colaiacovo, Juan Luis, et al. LC 83-2311. 316p. 1983. 37.95 (ISBN 0-03-062907-1). Praeger.

Czinkota, Michael R. & Tesar, George, eds. Export Management: An International Context. LC 81-17817. 316p. 1982. 37.95 (ISBN 0-03-060331-5). Praeger.

--Export Policy: A Global Assessment. LC 81-17874. 176p. 1982. 29.95 (ISBN 0-03-060377-3). Praeger.

Czitrom, Daniel J. Media & the American Mind: From Morse to McLuhan. LC 81-14810. xiv, 254p. 1982. 19.95x (ISBN 0-8078-1500-4); pap. 7.95x (ISBN 0-8078-4107-2). U of NC Pr.

Czoboly, E., jt. auth. see Sih, G.

Czompo, Andor. Hungarian Dances. 2nd rev. ed. LC 74-11041. (Illus.). 1980. pap. text ed. 5.95 (ISBN 0-935496-01-7). AC Pubns.

Czompo, Andor, jt. auth. see Czompo, Ann I.

Czompo, Andor, ed. see Czompo, Ann I.

Czompo, Ann I. Recreational Jazz Dance. 2nd ed. Czompo, Andor, ed. LC 79-26223. (Illus.). 1979. pap. text ed. 9.95 (ISBN 0-935496-00-9). AC Pubns.

Czompo, Ann I. & Czompo, Andor. Dance Fundamentals. (Illus.). 54p. (Orig.). 1982. pap. text ed. 5.00 (ISBN 0-935496-02-5). AC Pubns.

Czou Jui-Lin, et al. Four Papers on Partial Differential Equations. LC 51-5559. (Translations Ser.: No. 2, Vol. 41). 1964. 26.00 (ISBN 0-8218-1741-8, TRANS 2-41). Am Math.

Czuber, Eman. Wahrscheinlichkeitsrechnung & 'ihre Anwendung Auf Fehlerausgleichung, Statistik & Lebensversicherung, 2 Vols. (Bibliotheca Mathematica Teubneriana Ser.: Nos. 23 & 24). (Ger). 1969. Repr. of 1938 ed. Set. 60.00 (ISBN 0-384-10585-8). Johnson Repr.

Czuckza, G. T., ed. see Pope John Paul II.

Czudnowski, M. Moshe, jt. ed. see Eulau, Heinz.

Czudnowski, Moshe M. & Landau, Jacob M. The Israeli Communist Party. LC 65-19765. (Studies Ser.: No. 9). 1965. pap. 5.95 (ISBN 0-8179-3092-2). Hoover Inst Pr.

Czudnowski, Moshe M., ed. Does Who Governs Matter? LC 82-22495. (International Yearbook for Studies of Leaders & Leadership Ser.). 292p. 1982. 25.00 (ISBN 0-87580-085-8); pap. 12.50 (ISBN 0-87580-529-9). N Ill U Pr.

--Political Elites & Social Change: Studies of Elite Roles & Attitudes. LC 83-2461. (International Yearbook for Studies of Leaders & Leadership Ser.). 255p. 1983. 25.00 (ISBN 0-87580-093-9); pap. 12.50 (ISBN 0-87580-530-2). N Ill U Pr.

D

D. Bradford Barton Ltd., ed. American Flying Boats: A Pictorial Survey. 1981. 25.00x (ISBN 0-686-97136-1, Pub. by D B Barton England). State Mutual Bk.

--Aviation Workhorses Around the World: A Pictorial Survey. 96p. 1981. 25.00x (ISBN 0-85153-304-3, Pub. by D B Barton England). State Mutual Bk.

--British Float Planes: A Pictorial Survey. 96p. 1981. 25.00x (ISBN 0-85153-255-1, Pub. by D B Barton England). State Mutual Bk.

D. C. Cook Editors. Jesus, the Friend of Children. LC 77-72722. (Illus.). (gr. k-3). 1977. 9.95 (ISBN 0-89191-077-8). Cook.

D. J. B. Copp. Register of Consulting Scientists. 6th ed. 100p. 1984. 27.00 (ISBN 0-9903000-0-5, Pub. by A Hilger England). Heyden.

D. L. Foster Book Company Editors, jt. auth. see Foster, Dennis L.

Daae, E. English-Norwegian, Norwegian-English, Lommeordbok. 568p. (Eng. & Norwegian.). 1980. pap. 8.95 (ISBN 82-573-0152-3, M-9462). French & Eur.

--Francais-Norvegien-Francais Lommerorbok. 455p. (Fr. & Norwegian.). 1981. pap. 12.95 (ISBN 82-573-0162-0, M-9461). French & Eur.

Daaku, K. Yeboa. Osei Tutu & the Asante. (African Historical Biographies Ser.). (Illus.). 48p. 1977. pap. text ed. 2.75x (ISBN 0-435-94470-3). Heinemann Ed.

Daalder, Hans. Cabinet Reform in Britain, Nineteen Fourteen to Nineteen Sixty-Three. 1963. 27.50x (ISBN 0-8047-0139-3). Stanford U Pr.

Daalder, Hans & Mair, Peter, eds. Western European Party Systems: Continuity & Change. 466p. 1983. 39.95 (ISBN 0-8039-9769-8). Sage.

Daalder, Hans & Shils, Edward, eds. Universities, Politicians & Bureaucrats: Europe & the United States. LC 81-9936. (Illus.). 700p. 1982. 92.50 (ISBN 0-521-23673-8). Cambridge U Pr.

Daalder, Joost, ed. see Heywood, Jasper.

Daane, James. Freedom of God. 5.95 (ISBN 0-8028-3421-3). Fuller Theol Soc.

--Preaching with Confidence: A Theological Essay on the Power of the Pulpit. 2nd ed. (Orig.). 1980. pap. 4.95 (ISBN 0-8028-1825-0). Eerdmans.

Dabac, Ulatko. Technisches Woerterbuch, 2 vols. (Serbocroation & Ger.). 1969. 112.00 (ISBN 3-7625-0550-0, M-7653, Pub. by Bauverlag). French & Eur.

Dabagh, Thomas S. Legal Research Guide for California Practice. LC 85-60262. (Legal Bibliographic & Research Reprint Ser.: Vol. 5). 66p. 1985. Repr. of 1939 ed. lib. bdg. 27.50 (ISBN 0-89941-398-6). W S Hein.

DaBaghiano, Brenda, retold by. & illus. Jack & the Beanstalk. (Golden Storytime Bks.). (Illus.). 24p. (ps-1). 1982. 1.95 (ISBN 0-307-11951-3, Golden Bks.). Western Pub.

Dabat, Alejandro & Lorenzano, Luis. The Malvinas & the Crisis of Military Rule. 320p. 1984. 25.00 (ISBN 0-8052-7192-9, Pub. by NLB England); pap. 11.95 (ISBN 0-8052-7193-7). Schocken.

D'Abate, Richard. To Keep the House from Falling in. 39p. 1973. 2.95 (ISBN 0-87886-028-2). Ithaca Hse.

Dabberdt, Walter F. The Whole Air Weather Guide. (Illus.). 1976. pap. 3.50 (ISBN 0-686-85668-6, Pub. by Solstice). Aviation.

Dabberdt, Walter F., ed. Atmospheric Dispersion of Hazardous-Toxic Materials from Transport Accidents: Proceedings of a Course, International Center for Transportation Studies, Amalfi, Italy, 20-24 Sept., 1983. 200p. 1985. 52.00 (ISBN 0-444-87518-2, I-244-84). Elsevier.

Dabbs, Jack A. The French Army in Mexico, 1861-67: A Study in Military Government. (Studies in American History: No. 2). (Illus.). 1963. 31.20x (ISBN 90-2790-228-3). Mouton.

--Glossary of Agricultural Terms, English-Bengali. LC 79-626525. (Eng. & Bengali.). 1969. 3.00 (ISBN 0-911494-05-7). Dabbs.

--Short Bengali-English, English-Bengali Dictionary. 3rd ed. LC 78-149931. 5.00 (ISBN 0-911494-01-4). Dabbs.

--Spoken Bengali: Standard, East Bengal. LC 66-63243. 1966. 3.00 (ISBN 0-911494-03-0). Dabbs.

--Word Frequency in Newspaper Bengali. LC 66-64723. 1966. 3.00 (ISBN 0-911494-04-9). Dabbs.

Dabbs, Jack A., jt. tr. see Breitenkamp, Edward C.

Dabcovich, Lydia. Mrs. Huggins & Her Hen Hannah. Durell, Ann, ed. LC 85-4406. (Illus.). 24p. (ps-2). 1985. 10.95 (ISBN 0-525-44203-0). Dutton.

--Sleepy Bear. (Illus.). 32p. (ps-2). 1982. pap. 9.95 (ISBN 0-525-39465-6, 0966-290, Unicorn Bk). Dutton.

D'Abernon, Edgar V. The Eighteenth Decisive Battle of the World: Warsaw, 1920. LC 75-39050. (Russian Studies: Perspectives on the Revolution Ser). (Illus.). 178p. 1977. Repr. of 1931 ed. 19.25 (ISBN 0-88355-429-1). Hyperion-Conn.

D'Abernun Of Fetcham, Pierre. Secre De Secrez. Beckerlegge, Oliver A., ed. 1944. 14.00 (ISBN 0-384-54695-1). Johnson Repr.

Dabezies, Oliver H., Jr., et al, eds. Contact Lenses: The CLAO Guide to Basic Science & Clinical Practice. 848p. 1984. 199.00 (ISBN 0-8089-1642-4, 790957). Grune.

Da Bibiena, Ferdinando G. see Bibiena, Ferdinando G. Da.

Dabiels, Dorothy. Nicola. 1980. pap. 2.50 (ISBN 0-8439-0783-5, Pub. by Nordon Pubns). Dorchester Pub Co.

Dabney, A. L. Thirteen Millionaires. 1979. 8.95 (ISBN 0-686-24145-2). A L Dabney.

Dabney, Charles W. Universal Education in the South, 2 Vols. LC 70-89170. (American Education: Its Men, Institutions & Ideas, Ser. 1). 1969. Repr. of 1936 ed. Set. 55.00 (ISBN 0-405-01408-2). Ayer Co Pubs.

Dabney, Joseph E. Herk: Hero of the Skies. LC 84-14330. 448p. 1984. pap. 14.95 (ISBN 0-89783-028-8). Larlin Corp.

--More Mountain Spirits. LC 85-10932. (Illus.). 208p. 1985. pap. 7.95 (ISBN 0-914875-03-5, 432). Bright Mtn Bks.

--Mountain Spirits. LC 84-17442. (Illus.). 288p. 1985. pap. 7.95 (ISBN 0-914875-02-7, 432). Bright Mtn Bks.

Dabney, Julia P. Musical Basis of Verse. LC 79-119650. (BCL Ser. I). Repr. of 1901 ed. 11.50 (ISBN 0-404-01916-1). AMS Pr.

Dabney, Lancaster E. Claude Billard, Minor French Dramatist of the Early Seventeenth Century. 1973. pap. 14.00 (ISBN 0-384-10641-2). Johnson Repr.

Dabney, Lewis, ed. The Portable Edmund Wilson. (Portable Library Ser.: No. 98). 1983. 18.75 (ISBN 0-670-77078-7). Viking.

Dabney, Lewis M. The Indians of Yoknapatawpha: A Study in Literature & History. LC 73-77659. x, 163p. 1974. 17.50x (ISBN 0-8071-0058-7). La State U Pr.

Dabney, Lewis M., ed. see Wilson, Edmund.

Dabney, Melodye L. Incest Annotated Bibliography. (Illus.). 68p. (Orig.). 1984. pap. text ed. 25.00 (ISBN 0-9614155-0-9). Dabney.

Dabney, Robert L. Dabney Discussions, Vol. 1. 728p. 1982. Repr. of 1891 ed. 16.95 (ISBN 0-85151-348-4). Banner of Truth.

--Dabney Discussions, Vol. 2. (Religious Ser.). 684p. 1982. Repr. of 1891 ed. 16.95 (ISBN 0-85151-349-2). Banner of Truth.

--Dabney Discussions, Vol. 3. (Religious Ser.). 493p. 1982. Repr. of 1892 ed. 14.95 (ISBN 0-85151-350-6). Banner of Truth.

--Defence of Virginia, through Her of the South. LC 69-18976. Repr. of 1867 ed. 22.50 (ISBN 0-8371-1019-X, DAD&, Pub. by Negro U Pr). Greenwood.

--On Preaching. 1979. 10.95 (ISBN 0-85151-290-9). Banner of Truth.

--The Sensualistic Philosophy of the 19th Century. LC 75-3008. Repr. of 1887 ed. 28.00 (ISBN 0-404-59124-8). AMS Pr.

Dabney, Virginia. The Last Review: The Confederate Reunion, Richmond 1932: An Album. (Illus.). 1984. 27.50 (ISBN 0-912697-06-7). Algonquin Bks.

Dabney, Virginius. Below the Potomac. LC 76-86010. (Essay & General Literature Index Reprint Ser). 1969. Repr. of 1942 ed. 26.50x (ISBN 0-8046-0554-8, Pub. by Kennikat). Assoc Faculty Pr.

--The Jefferson Scandals: A Rebuttal. LC 81-1669. (Illus.). 156p. 1981. 8.95 (ISBN 0-396-07964-4). Dodd.

--Liberalism in the South. LC 77-128983. (BCL Ser. II). Repr. of 1932 ed. 49.50 (ISBN 0-404-00146-7). AMS Pr.

--Mr. Jefferson's University: A History. LC 81-3392. (Illus.). 1981. 14.95 (ISBN 0-8139-0904-X). U Pr of Va.

--Virgina: The New Dominion. 2nd ed. LC 83-18232. 629p. 1983. Repr. of 1971 ed. 9.95 (ISBN 0-8139-1015-3). U Pr of VA.

--Virginia: The New Dominion, a History from 1607 to the Present. LC 78-157580. (Illus.). 629p. pap. 9.95. U Pr of Va.

Dabney, Virginius, et al, eds. New Virginia Review Anthology Three. (Illus.). 304p. (Orig.). 1984. 20.00 (ISBN 0-318-01379-7). New VA.

Dabney, Wendell P. Cincinnati's Colored Citizens: Historical, Sociological & Biographical. LC 73-100287. 1867. cancelled (ISBN 0-8371-2917-6, DAC&, Pub. by Negro U Pr). Greenwood.

--Cincinnati's Colored Citizens: Historical, Sociological & Biographical. LC 26-10464. (Basic Afro-American Reprint Library). 1970. Repr. of 1926 ed. 25.00 (ISBN 0-384-10640-4). Johnson Repr.

Dabois, Abee J. State of Christianity in India - During the Early Nineteenth Century. 1977. 11.00x (ISBN 0-686-12059-0). Intl Bk Dist.

DaBoll, Irene B., jt. auth. see DaBoll, Raymond F.

DaBoll, Raymond. With Respect... to RFD: An Appreciation of Raymond Franklin DaBoll & His Contribution to the Letter Arts. Cusick, Rick, compiled by. LC 77-77376. (Illus.). xvi, 142p. 1978. 25.00 (ISBN 0-931474-00-0). TBW Bks.

DaBoll, Raymond F. & DaBoll, Irene B. Recollections of the Lyceum & Chautauqua Circuits Plus Notes on Calligraphy & Scribal Writing. LC 66-19773. (Illus.). 188p. 1974. 16.95 (ISBN 0-87027-107-5). Cumberland Pr.

Daborn, Robert. A Christian Turn'd Turke, ou, the Tragicall Lives & Deaths of Two Famous Pyrates Ward & Dansiker. LC 73-6116. (English Experience Ser.: No. 583). 70p. 1973. Repr. of 1612 ed. 7.00 (ISBN 90-221-0583-0). Walter J Johnson.

Daborne, Robert. The Poor Man's Comfort. LC 82-45704. (Malone Society Reprint Ser.: No. 100). Repr. of 1954 ed. 40.00 (ISBN 0-404-63101-0). AMS Pr.

Dabout, E., ed. Diccionario de Medicina. (Span.). write for info. (S-37586). French & Eur.

Dabovich, Sebastian. Holy Orthodox Church: Its Ritual, Services, & Sacraments. 1898. pap. 2.95 (ISBN 0-686-00253-9). Eastern Orthodox.

--True Church of Christ. pap. 0.25 (ISBN 0-686-11506-6). Eastern Orthodox.

Dabree, Bonamy, ed. see Stanhope, Phillip D.

D'Abrera, Bernard. Butterflies of the Afro-Tropical Region. 613p. 1980. 295.00x (ISBN 0-317-07042-8, Pub. by EW Classey UK). State Mutual Bk.

--Butterflies of the Neotropical Region. 188p. 1981. 370.00x (ISBN 0-317-07048-7, Pub. by EW Classey UK). State Mutual Bk.

--Butterflies of the Oriental Region. 265p. 1982. 370.00x (ISBN 0-317-07049-5, Pub. by EW Classey UK). State Mutual Bk.

Da Brescia, Bonaventura. Brevis Collectio Artis Musicae. Seay, Albert, ed. (Critical Texts Ser.: No. 11). (Illus.). vi, 93p. 1981. pap. text ed. 6.00 (ISBN 0-933894-01-5). Colo Coll Music.

--Regula Musice Plane. (Monuments of Music & Music Literature in Facsimile Series II: Vol. 77). (Illus.). 46p. (It.). 1975. Repr. of 1497 ed. 20.00x (ISBN 0-8450-2277-6). Broude.

Dabringhaus, Erhard. Klaus Barbie: The Shocking Story of How the U. S. Used This Nazi War Criminal as an Intelligence Agent. LC 83-27506. 208p. 1984. 13.95 (ISBN 0-87491-731-X). Acropolis.

D'Abro, A. Evolution of Scientific Thought from Newton to Einstein. 15.50 (ISBN 0-8446-1937-X). Peter Smith.

--The Rise of the New Physics: Its Mathematical & Physical Theories, 2 vols. Orig. Title: The Decline of Mechanism. 14.50 ea (ISBN 0-8446-0569-7); Set. 29.00. Peter Smith.

Dabrowski, Magdalena. Contrast of Form: Geometric Abstract Art 1910-1980. (Illus.). 302p. 45.00 (ISBN 0-87070-287-4); pap. 23.50 (ISBN 0-87070-289-0). Museum Mod Art.

Dabrowski, Richard A. Advanced Designs for the Woodcarver. LC 77-94903. (Illus.). 1979. spiral bdg. 10.95 (ISBN 0-918036-04-6). Woodcraft Supply.

--Designs for the Woodcarver. LC 76-1141. (Illus.). 1982. Repr. of 1976 ed. spiral bdg. 9.95 (ISBN 0-918036-02-X). Woodcraft Supply.

Dabrowski, Roman. Mussolini, Twilight & Fall. LC 78-20460. 1980. Repr. of 1956 ed. 21.00 (ISBN 0-88355-839-4). Hyperion Conn.

Dabscheck, Braham. Arbitrator at Work: Sir William Raymond Kelly & the Regulation of Australian Industrial Relations. (Australian Studies in Industrial Relations). 169p. 1984. pap. text ed. 18.50x (ISBN 0-86861-119-0). Allen Unwin.

Dabuisson, jt. auth. see IFAC Workshop, Compiegne, France, Oct. 1977.

Dabul, Barbara. The Laryngectomee: A Booklet for Family & Friends. 2nd ed. 1984. pap. 0.75x (ISBN 0-8134-2341-4). Interstate.

Dabydeen, Cyril. Still Close to the Island. 111p. 1980. pap. 8.00 (ISBN 0-88970-036-2, Pub. by Commoner's Pub Canada). Three Continents.

Dabydeen, David, ed. The Black Presence in English Literature. LC 85-5119. (Illus.). 1985. 29.00 (ISBN 0-7190-1096-9, Pub. by Manchester Univ Pr); pap. 11.00 (ISBN 0-7190-1808-0, Pub. by Manchester Univ Pr). Longwood Pub Group.

DaCal, Ernesto G. & Ucelay, Margarita. Literature del Siglo XX. 2nd ed. (Span.). 1968. pap. text ed. 27.95 (ISBN 0-03-055585-X). HR&W.

D'Accone, Frank. The History of a Baroque Opera: Allesandro Scarlatti's Gli Equivoci Nel Sembiante. (Monographs in Musicology: No. 3). 200p. 1985. lib. bdg. 36.00 (ISBN 0-918728-21-5). Pendragon NY.

Dace, Letitia & Dace, Wallace. The Theatre Student: Modern Theatre & Drama. LC 72-75221. (Illus.). 200p. (gr. 7-12). 1973. PLB 15.00 (ISBN 0-8239-0265-X). Rosen Group.

Dace, Wallace. Elements in Dramatic Structure. 1972. pap. 7.95 (ISBN 0-686-00365-9). AG Pr.

--Elements of Dramatic Structure. LC 72-81889. 72p. 1972. pap. 2.95 (ISBN 0-686-05609-4). AG Pr.

--National Theaters in the Larger German & Austrian Cities. (Theater Ser.). (Illus.). 240p. 1981. lib. bdg. 35.00 (ISBN 0-8239-0527-6). Rosen Group.

--A Proposal for a National Theater. (YA) 1978. PLB 15.00 (ISBN 0-8239-0422-9). Rosen Group.

--Subsidies for the Theatre: A Study of the Central European System of Financing Drama, Opera & Ballet. LC 72-84841. 188p. 1973. pap. 7.95 (ISBN 0-686-05610-8). AG Pr.

Dace, Wallace, jt. auth. see Dace, Letitia.

Dacey. What's Wrong with Your Life Insurance. 1966. pap. 2.95 (ISBN 0-02-079490-8, Collier). Macmillan.

Dacey, John. Adolescents Today. 3rd ed. 1986. text ed. 23.95 (ISBN 0-673-16669-4). Scott F.

--Where the World Is: Teaching Basic Skills Outdoors. (Illus.). 192p. 1981. pap. 12.95 (ISBN 0-673-16458-6). Scott F.

Dacey, John S. Adolescents Today. 2nd ed. 1982. text ed. 24.95x (ISBN 0-673-16023-8). Scott F.

--Adult Development. 1982. text ed. 23.80x (ISBN 0-673-16021-1). Scott F.

Dacey, Michael F. Status of Pattern Analysis: Identification of Problems in the Statistical Analysis of Spatial Arrangement. (Discussion Paper Ser.: No. 3.). 1963. pap. 5.75 (ISBN 0-686-32171-5). Regional Sci Res Inst.

Dacey, Michael F. & Karaska, Gerald. Some Experimental Evidence of the Perception of Dot Patterns & Two-Dimensional Shapes. (Discussion Paper Ser.: No. 2). 1963. pap. 5.75 (ISBN 0-686-32170-7). Regional Sci Res Inst.

Dacey, Michael F., et al. Christaller Central Place Structures. (Studies in Geography: No. 22). 1977. 5.95x (ISBN 0-8101-0466-0). Northwestern U Pr.

--One-Dimensional Central Place Theory. (Studies in Geography: No. 21). 1974. 5.95x (ISBN 0-8101-0452-0). Northwestern U Pr.

Dacey, Norman F. Democracy in Israel. 74p. 1976. pap. 3.00 (ISBN 0-911038-68-X). Inst Hist Rev.

--Democracy in Israel. 73p. (Orig.). 1976. pap. 2.50 (ISBN 0-911038-68-X, Inst Hist Rev). Noontide.

--Democracy in Israel. 1981. lib. bdg. 59.95 (ISBN 0-686-73182-4). Revisionist Pr.

--How to Avoid Probate! LC 79-24868. pap. 19.95 updated (ISBN 0-517-55150-0). Crown.

Dacey, Philip. The Boy under the Bed. LC 80-8858. (Poetry & Fiction Ser.). 1981. text ed. 12.00x (ISBN 0-8018-2601-2); pap. text ed. 5.95 (ISBN 0-8018-2602-0). Johns Hopkins.

--Fives. 32p. (Orig.). 1984. pap. 3.00 (ISBN 0-933180-63-2). Spoon Riv Poetry.

--Gerard Manley Hopkins Meets Walt Whitman in Heaven & Other Poems. (Illus.). 100p. 1982. signed ed. o.p. 75.00 (ISBN 0-915778-44-0); pap. 8.50 (ISBN 0-915778-45-9). Penmaen Pr.

--How I Escaped from the Labyrinth & Other Poems. LC 76-55069. (Poetry Ser.). 1977. pap. 3.95 (ISBN 0-915604-08-6). Carnegie-Mellon.

Dacey, Ralph G., Jr., et al, eds. Trauma of the Central Nervous System. (Seminars in Neurological Surgery Ser.). (Illus.). 352p. 1985. text ed. 69.50 (ISBN 0-88167-111-8). Raven.

Dach Bern, H. von see Von Dach Bern, H.

D'Achille, Gino, illus. King Solomon's Mines. LC 82-3843. (Step-Up Adventures Ser.: No. 5). (Illus.). 96p. (gr. 2-5). 1982. PLB 4.99 (ISBN 0-394-95275-8); pap. 1.95 (ISBN 0-394-85275-3). Random.

Dachinger, Penny, jt. ed. see Ulman, Elinor.

Dachman, Ken. The Dachman Permanent Weight-Loss Program. LC 82-2233. 1982. 12.50 (ISBN 0-688-01199-3). Morrow.

Dachs. TV Jokes. (gr. 7-12). pap. 1.50 (ISBN 0-590-05402-3). Scholastic Inc.

Dachs, Anthony J. Khama of Botswana. (African Historical Biographies Ser.). pap. text ed. 2.75x (ISBN 0-435-94467-3). Heinemann Ed.

Dachs, David. One Hundred Pop-Rock Stars. (Illus.). 320p. (Orig.). 1981. pap. 1.95 (ISBN 0-590-31366-5). Scholastic Inc.

Dachs, H., ed. Neutron Diffraction. LC 78-2969. (Topics in Current Physics: Vol. 6). (Illus.). 1978. 40.00 (ISBN 0-387-08710-9). Springer-Verlag.

Dachslager, Howard, et al. Learning BASIC Programming: A Systematic Approach. LC 83-2519. 280p. 1983. pap. text ed. 19.00 pub net (ISBN 0-534-01422-4). Brooks-Cole.

--Learning BASIC Programming: A Systematic Approach. 292p. 1983. pap. write for info. Wadsworth Pub.

Dachtler, Doc. Drawknife. LC 83-19942. 1983. 8.00 (ISBN 0-914134-07-8). Sipapu-Konocti Bks.

Dacier, Andre. The Life of Pythagoras. 208p. 1981. cloth 22.50 (ISBN 0-87728-286-2). Weiser.

Dacio, Juan. Diccionario de los Papas. (Span.). 37.50 (ISBN 84-233-0112-5, S-50110). French & Eur.

Dack, G. M. Food Poisoning. rev., enl. ed. LC 55-12510. (Midway Reprint Ser.). xii, 252p. 1982. pap. 12.00x (ISBN 0-226-13381-8). U of Chicago Pr.

Dacke, Christopher. Calcium Regulation in the Sub-Mammalian Vertebrates. 1979. 49.50 (ISBN 0-12-201050-7). Acad Pr.

Dackerman, Gerald, jt. auth. see Sohl, Marcia.

Dackombe, R., jt. auth. see Gardiner, V.

Dacons, J. C., jt. auth. see Philips, J. P.

Dacorogna, B. Weak Continuity & Weak Semicontinuity of Non-Linear Functionals. (Lecture Notes in Mathematics Ser.: Vol. 922). 120p. 1982. pap. 12.00 (ISBN 0-387-11488-2). Springer-Verlag.

Dacos, Nicole. La Decouverte de la Domus Aurea et la Formation des Grotesques a la Renaissance. (Warburg Institute Studies: Vol. 31). 1969. 29.00 (ISBN 0-317-15607-1). Kraus Repr.

Da Costa, Alcino, et al. News Values & Principles of Cross-Cultural Communication. (Reports & Papers on Mass Communication: No. 85). (Illus.). 51p. 1980. pap. 5.00 (ISBN 92-3-101697-0, U975, UNESCO). Unipub.

Da Costa, Emilia Viotti see Viotti da Costa, Emilia.

Da Costa, Francisco, jt. auth. see Mickle, M. M.

DaCosta, Frank. How to Build Your Own Working Robot Pet. (Illus.). 1979. pap. 9.25 (ISBN 0-8306-1141-X, 1141). TAB Bks.

--Writing BASIC Adventure Programs for the TRS-80. LC 82-5945. (Illus.). 228p. 1982. 14.95 (ISBN 0-8306-2422-8, 1422); pap. 10.25 (ISBN 0-8306-1422-2, 1422). TAB Bks.

DaCosta, I. Noble Families among the Sephardic Jews. 1976. lib. bdg. 134.95 (ISBN 0-8490-2349-1). Gordon Pr.

Da Costa, Leon see Costa, Leon Da.

Da Costa, Michael. Finance & Development: The Role of International Commercial Banks in the Third World. (Replica Edition). 120p. 1982. softcover 18.00x (ISBN 0-86531-917-0). Westview.

Dacque, Edgar. Vergleichende Biologische Formenkunde der Fossilen Niederen Tiere: Biological Comparative Morphology of Lower Fossil Animals. Gould, Stephen J., ed. LC 79-8329. (The History of Paleontology Ser.). (Illus., Ger.). 1980. Repr. of 1921 ed. lib. bdg. 74.50x (ISBN 0-405-12710-3). Ayer Co Pubs.

Dacquino, V. T. Kiss the Candy Days Good-Bye. LC 82-70324. 160p. (gr. 4-6). 1982. 11.95 (ISBN 0-385-28532-9). Delacorte.

--Kiss the Candy Days Good-Bye. (gr. 5-9). 1983. pap. 2.25 (ISBN 0-440-44369-5). Dell.

--Kiss the Candy Days Good-Bye. 144p. (gr. 5-9). pap. 2.25 (ISBN 0-440-44369-5, YB). Dell.

Dacre, Charlotte. Confessions of the Nun of St. Omer: A Tale, 2 Vols. LC 76-131314. (Gothic Novels Ser). 1972. Repr. of 1805 ed. Set. 42.00 (ISBN 0-405-00803-1). Ayer Co Pubs.

--The Libertine, 4 vols. LC 73-22761. 997p. 1974. Repr. of 1807 ed. Set. 88.00x (ISBN 0-405-06012-2). Ayer Co Pubs.

--The Passions, 4 vols, Vol. 9. LC 73-22762. (Gothic Novels Ser.). 1974. Repr. of 1811 ed. Set. 88.00x (ISBN 0-405-06013-0). Ayer Co Pubs.

--Zafloya; or the Moor: A Romance of the Fifteenth Century, 3 vols, Vol. 8. LC 73-22763. (Gothic Novels Ser.). 802p. 1974. Repr. of 1806 ed. Set. 86.00x (ISBN 0-405-06014-9). Ayer Co Pubs.

Dacre, J. B. Think Guitar. 103p. Date not set. pap. 3.95 (ISBN 0-900841-56-7, Pub. by Aztex Corp). Argus Bks.

Dacres, Edward see Machiavelli, Niccolo.

Da Cruz, Daniel. The Ayes of Texas. 256p. (Orig.). 1982. pap. 2.25 (ISBN 0-345-29602-8, Del Rey). Ballantine.

Dacruz, J. More about Fatima. De Oca, V. Montes, tr. from Port. 1979. pap. 1.00 (ISBN 0-913382-16-7, 102-95). Prow Bks-Franciscan.

Dacso, Michael M. Restorative Medicine in Geriatrics. (Illus.). 340p. 1963. photocopy ed. 27.50x (ISBN 0-398-00385-8). C C Thomas.

DaCunha, Euclides. Rebellion in the Backlands. Putnam, Samuel, tr. (Illus.). 1957. pap. 9.95 (ISBN 0-226-12444-4, P22, Phoen). U of Chicago Pr.

Da Cunha, L. V., et al see Yevjevich, Vujica.

Dacus, Joseph A. Annals of the Great Strikes in the United States. LC 72-89728. (American Labor, from Conspiracy to Collective Bargaining, Ser. 1). 480p. 1969. Repr. of 1877 ed. 25.50 (ISBN 0-405-02115-1). Ayer Co Pubs.
--Annals of the Great Strikes in the United States: A Reliable History & Graphic Description of the Causes & Thrilling Events of the Labor Strikes & Riots of 1877. LC 68-57902. (Research & Source Works Ser.: No. 306). (Illus.). 1969. Repr. of 1877 ed. 25.50 (ISBN 0-8337-0755-8). B Franklin.
Dacus, Robert H. Reminiscences of Company "H", First Arkansas Mounted Rifles. 47p. 7.50 (ISBN 0-89029-005-9). Pr of Morningside.
Dacy, Joe, II. Hypnosphere. 1983. 9.95 (ISBN 0-533-05282-3). Vantage.
Dada. Beyond the Mind: Conversations on the Deeper Significance of Living. LC 77-85723. (Illus.). 144p. 1978. pap. 9.00 (ISBN 0-930608-01-1). Dada Ctr.
--Towards the Unknown: The Journey into New-Dimensional Consciousness. LC 81-65123. (Illus.). 128p. (Orig.). 1981. pap. 8.00 (ISBN 0-930608-02-X). Dada Ctr.
Dada, Victor B. Choose the Sex of Your Baby: A Psychological Approach. 1983. 7.95 (ISBN 0-533-05256-4). Vantage.
D'Adam, ed. see Diderot, Denis.
Dadant & Sons, ed. The Hive & the Honey Bee. rev. ed. LC 63-15838. (Illus.). 3740p. 1976. 19.95 (ISBN 0-684-14790-4, ScribT). Scribner.
Dadant & Sons Inc. Beekeeping Questions & Answers. LC 77-80061. (Illus.). 1978. 9.50 (ISBN 0-915698-04-8). Dadant & Sons.
Dadant & Sons, Inc. First Lessons in Beekeeping. (Illus.). 128p. 1982. pap. 4.95 (ISBN 0-684-17423-5, ScribT). Scribner.
--The Honey Kitchen. LC 80-66361. (Illus.). 208p. 1980. 9.20 (ISBN 0-915698-06-4). Dadant & Sons.
--The Honey Kitchen: The Best Honey Recipes in the World. (Illus.). 192p. 1982. 12.95 (ISBN 0-684-17489-8, ScribT). Scribner.
Dadant & Sons, Inc., ed. The Hive & the Honey Bee. LC 63-15838. (Illus.). 740p. 1975. 14.52 (ISBN 0-915698-00-5). Dadant & Sons.
Dadant, C. P. First Lessons in Beekeeping. rev. ed. (Illus.). 128p. 1980. 7.95 (ISBN 0-684-16747-6, ScribT). Scribner.
Dadant, C. P., ed. First Lessons in Beekeeping. LC 75-38347. (Illus.). 128p. 1976. 1.92 (ISBN 0-915698-02-1). Dadant & Sons.
Dadayan, V. S. Macroeconomic Models. 208p. 1981. 7.00 (ISBN 0-8285-2271-5, Pub. by Progress Pubs USSR). Imported Pubns.
Dadd, Bill. Great Trans-Continental Railroad Guide. LC 76-155931. (Illus.). 1971. pap. 6.00 (ISBN 0-912382-06-6). Black Letter.
Dadd, Debra L. Nontoxic & Natural. 300p. (Orig.). 1984. pap. 9.95 (ISBN 0-87477-330-X). J P Tarcher.
Dadd, Debra L., et al. Nutritional Analysis System: A Physician's Manual for Evaluation of Therapeutic Diets. 154p. 1982. pap. 19.50x spiral (ISBN 0-398-04681-6). C C Thomas.
Dadd, M. J., jt. ed. see Gill, R. W.
Daddad, Wadi D. Educational & Economic Effects of Promotion & Repetition Practices. (Working Paper: No. 319). 52p. 1979. 3.00 (ISBN 0-686-36054-0, WP-0319). World Bank.
D'Addario, Joseph D. Build It: Out of Sight Sewing Center. 1972. pap. 5.95 (ISBN 0-686-01898-2). Classic Furn Kits.
D'Addetta, Joseph. American Folk Art Designs & Motifs for Artists & Craftspeople. LC 84-6136. 96p. 1984. pap. 4.50 (ISBN 0-486-24717-1). Dover.
--Treasury of Chinese Design Motifs. (Illus.). 108p. pap. 4.50 (ISBN 0-486-24167-X). Dover.
D'Addetta, Joseph, illus. Traditional Japanese Design Motifs. (Pictorial Archive Ser.). (Illus.). 96p. pap. 4.00 (ISBN 0-486-24629-9). Dover.
D'Addio, Janie. Every Woman Can. Cox, Terri, ed. (Illus.). 112p. 1983. pap. 9.95 (ISBN 0-914759-00-0). Preferred Pr.
D'Addio, Janie & Bach, Othello. Monicas Hannukah House. (Illus.). 64p. (gr. 2-8). 1983. 14.95 (ISBN 0-914759-01-9). Preferred Pr.
Daddio, Ralph, jt. ed. see Kennedy, Joan.
Dadds, Audrey. The Shih Tzu. LC 75-13607. (Complete Breed Book Ser). 224p. 1983. 15.95 (ISBN 0-87605-309-6). Howell Bk.
Daddy, Z. P. Chretien Studies. 208p. 1973. 39.00x (ISBN 0-85261-092-0, Pub. by U of Glasgow Pr Scotland). State Mutual Bk.
Daddysman, James W. The Matamoros Trade: Confederate Commerce, Diplomacy, & Intrigue. LC 81-72031. (Illus.). 216p. 1984. 27.50 (ISBN 0-87413-215-0). U Delaware Pr.
D'Adetta, Joseph. Treasury of Chinese Design Motifs. (Illus.). 1982. 13.75 (ISBN 0-8446-5882-0). Peter Smith.
Dadie, Barnard B. Patron de New-York. pap. 6.50 (ISBN 0-685-35940-9). French & Eur.
Dadie, Bernard. Climbie. Chapman, Karen, tr. from Fr. LC 77-161231. 157p. 1971. text ed. 12.50x (ISBN 0-8419-0080-9, Africana); (Africana). Holmes & Meier.
--Mr. Thogo-Gnini. Brewster, Townsend T., tr. from Fr. (Ubu Repertory Theatre Pubications). (Orig.). 1986. pap. text ed. 6.25 (ISBN 0-913745-16-2). Ubu Repertory.
Dadie, Bernard B. Beatrice du Congo. pap. 6.95 (ISBN 0-685-35630-2). French & Eur.
--Hommes de Tous les Continents. pap. 6.95 (ISBN 0-685-35631-0). French & Eur.
--Monsieur Thogo-gnini. pap. 5.95 (ISBN 0-685-33976-9). French & Eur.
--Le Pagne Noir. pap. 4.95 (ISBN 0-685-35935-2). French & Eur.
--Textes. Mercier, R. & Battestini, M., eds. (Classiques du Monde, Litterature Africaine). pap. 2.50 (ISBN 0-685-35632-9). French & Eur.
--La Ville ou Nul ne Meurt. pap. 3.95 (ISBN 0-685-35633-7). French & Eur.
Dadoo, Y. M., et al. South African Communists Speak, 1915-1980. 474p. 1981. pap. 25.00x (ISBN 0-686-83901-3, Pub. by Inkuleko). Imported Pubns.
Dadourian, H. M. Introduction to Analytic Geometry & the Calculus. LC 80-39791. 256p. 1983. Repr. of 1949 ed. bds. 15.00 (ISBN 0-89874-267-6). Krieger.
Dadson, Theresa. Index to the Legion Observer: Volumes Two Through Nine, 1967-1974. 1979. lib. bdg. 36.50 (ISBN 0-8161-8294-9, Hall Reference). G K Hall.
D.A.E. Project University of Washington. D.A.E Project: Instructional Materials for Dental Health Professions, 25 Bks. Incl. Bk. 1. Establish Patient Relationships. 9.95x (ISBN 0-8077-6041-2); Bk. 2. Self-Care One. 7.95x (ISBN 0-8077-6042-0); Vol. 3. Self-Care Two. 7.95x (ISBN 0-8077-6043-9); Vol. 4. Coronal Polish. 9.95x (ISBN 0-8077-6044-7); Vol. 5. Topical Fluoride. 6.95x (ISBN 0-8077-6045-5); Vol. 6. Normal Radiographic Landmarks. 8.95x (ISBN 0-8077-6046-3); Vol. 7. Oral Inspection. 5.95x (ISBN 0-8077-6047-1); Vol. 8. Oral Inspection. 4.95x (ISBN 0-8077-6048-X); Margination: Overhang Removal. 8.95x (ISBN 0-8077-6049-8); Vol. 10. Root Planning. 5.95x (ISBN 0-8077-6050-1); Vol. 11. Take Study Model Impressions. 7.95x (ISBN 0-8077-6051-X); Vol. 12. Pour & Separate Models. 5.95x (ISBN 0-8077-6052-8); Vol. 13. Trim & Finish Models. 4.95x (ISBN 0-8077-6053-6); Vol. 14. Instrument Transfer One. 6.95x (ISBN 0-8077-6054-4); Vol. 15. Instrument Transfer: Restorative. 6.95x (ISBN 0-8077-6055-2); Vol. 16. Instrument Transfer: Endodontics. 4.95x (ISBN 0-8077-6056-0); Vol. 17. Instrument Transfer: Oral Surgery. 6.95x (ISBN 0-8077-6057-9); Vol. 18. Instrument Transfer: Periodontics. 6.95x (ISBN 0-8077-6058-7); Vol. 19. Maintain Operating Field. 6.95x (ISBN 0-8077-6059-5); Vol. 20. Rubber Dam. 8.50x (ISBN 0-8077-6060-9); Vol. 21. Microbiology. 5.95x (ISBN 0-8077-6061-7); Vol. 22. Sterilization & Disinfection. 8.50x (ISBN 0-8077-6062-5); Vol. 23. Dental Handpieces. 4.95x (ISBN 0-8077-6063-3); Vol. 24. Maintain Equipment & Operatory. 9.95x (ISBN 0-8077-6064-1); Vol. 25. Maintain Sterilization & Laboratory Equipment. 6.95x (ISBN 0-8077-6065-X); Faculty Guide & Test Items 9.95x (ISBN 0-8077-6066-8). 1982. Tchrs Coll.
Daehler, David J., ed. English-Chinese Glossary for Elementary Chinese. LC 77-83819. (CT Language Ser.). (Eng. & Chinese.). 1977. pap. 2.95 (ISBN 0-917056-05-1). Cheng & Tsui.
Daehnhardt, Alfred O., ed. Natursagen, 4 vols. 1971. Repr. of 1907 ed. lib. bdg. 110.00 (ISBN 0-8337-0760-4). B Franklin.
Daehnhardt, Rainer & Neal, W. Keith, eds. Espingarda Perfeyta; or the Perfect Gun: Rules for Its Use Together with Necessary Instructions for Its Construction & Precepts for Good Aiming. (Illus.). 480p. 1975. 48.00x (ISBN 0-85667-014-6, Pub by Sotheby Pubns England). Biblio Dist.
Daellenbach, Hans G. & George, John A. Introduction to Operations Research Techniques. 2nd ed. 1983. text ed. 41.43 (ISBN 0-205-07718-8, EDP 107718); answer book (ISBN 0-205-05756-X). Allyn.
Daemmrich, Horst. The Shattered Self: E. T. A. Hoffmann's Tragic Vision. LC 72-11451. 144p. 1973. text ed. 9.95x (ISBN 0-8143-1493-7). Wayne St U Pr.
Daemmrich, Horst S. Wilhelm Raabe. (World Authors Ser.). 1981. lib. bdg. 14.50 (ISBN 0-8057-6436-4, Twayne). G K Hall.
Daemmrich, Horst S. & Haenicke, Diether H., eds. The Challenge of German Literature. LC 75-131425. 434p. 1971. 13.95x (ISBN 0-8143-1435-X). Wayne St U Pr.
Daems, Herman. The Holding Company & Corporate Control. 1978. lib. bdg. 16.00 (ISBN 90-207-0690-X). Kluwer Academic.
Daems, Herman, jt. auth. see Chandler, Alfred D., Jr.
Daems, Herman, jt. ed. see Chandler, Alfred D., Jr.
Daems, W. T., jt. ed. see Carr, Ian.
Daems, W. T., et al, eds. Cell Biological Aspects of Disease: The Plasma Membrane & Lysosomes. (Boerhaave Series for Postgraduate Medical Education: No. 19). 330p. 1981. PLB 68.50 (ISBN 90-6021-466-8, Pub. by Leiden Univ Netherlands). Kluwer Academic.
Daenell, E. Bluetezeit der Deutsche Hanse: Hansische Geschichte Von der Zweiten Haelfte des XIV Bis Zum Letzten Viertel Des XV Jahrhunderts, 2 vols. 1035p. 1973. Repr. of 1906 ed. Set. 110.00x (ISBN 3-11-004562-1). De Gruyter.
Daentl, Donna L., jt. auth. see Symposium, Society of Craniofacial Genetics, 3rd, New York, N.Y.
Daenzer, Bernard J. Fact-Finding Questionnaire for Risk Managers. 50p. 1978. 15.00 (ISBN 0-937802-09-3); members 13.00 (ISBN 0-317-35681-X). Risk Management.
Daenzer, Bernard J. & Feldhaus, William R. Strategies for Insurance Coverages: Continuing Manual. looseleaf 277.00x (ISBN 0-930868-57-9). Merritt Co.
Daes, Erica-Irene A. The Individual's Duties to the Community & the Limitations on Human Rights & Freedom under Article 29 of the Universal Declaration of Human Rights: A Contribution to the Freedom of the Individual under Law: Study. LC 83-238645. 1983. write for info. UN.
--The Individual's Duties to the Community & the Limitations on Human Rights & Freedoms under Article 29 of the Universal Declaration of Human Rights: Special Report of the Sub-commission on Prevention of Discrimination & Protection of Minorities. 214p. 1983. pap. text ed. 21.00 (UN82/14/1, UN). Unipub.
Daesch, Geraldine. Women Who Lived, Cities That Died. (Riverstone International Poetry Chapbook Ser.). 21p. (Orig.). 1985. write for info. (ISBN 0-936600-05-5). Riverstone Foothills.
Daeschner, C. William. Pediatrics: An Approach to Independent Learning. LC 82-8438. 646p. 1983. pap. 27.50x (ISBN 0-471-05992-7, Pub. by Wiley Med). Wiley.
Dae-Sook Suh, jt. auth. see Koo, Youngnok.
Daetz, Pantell, ed. Environmental Modeling: Analysis & Management. LC 73-22191. (Benchmark Papers in Electric Engineering & Computer Science: Vol. 6). 407p. 1974. 57.00 (ISBN 0-87933-082-1); pap. 31.00 (ISBN 0-87933-138-0). Van Nos Reinhold.
Daff, T. Prices in the Market. flexi-cover 2.50 (ISBN 0-08-018125-2). Pergamon.
Daffe, Jerald. Handbook for Special Services. (Orig.). 1977. pap. 4.00 (ISBN 0-89536-097-7). CSS of Ohio.
Dafoe, John W. Canada: An American Nation. LC 71-110739. Repr. of 1935 ed. 12.50 (ISBN 0-404-00616-7). AMS Pr.
--Clifford Sifton in Relation to His Times. facsimile ed. LC 79-157331. (Select Bibliographies Reprint Ser). Repr. of 1931 ed. 32.00 (ISBN 0-8369-5791-1). Ayer Co Pubs.
Da Foligno, Angela. Divine Consolation of the Blessed Angela Da Foligno. Steegman, M. G., tr. LC 66-30731. (Medieval Library). (Illus.). 265p. 1966. Repr. of 1926 ed. 23.50 (ISBN 0-8154-0072-1). Cooper Sq.
Da Fonseca, F. Peixoto. Dictionnaire Bilingue Larousse, Francais-Portugais et Portugais-Francais. (Apollo). (Fr. & Port.). 10.95 (ISBN 2-03-020909-0, 3791). Larousse.
Da Fonseca, Jose see Carolino, Pedro, pseud.
Da Free, John. The Transmission of Doubt. 475p. (Orig.). 1984. pap. 10.95 (ISBN 0-913922-77-3). Dawn Horse Pr.
--What to Remember to Be Happy. (Illus.). pap. 4.95 (ISBN 0-913922-36-6). Dawn Horse Pr.
Da Free John. Compulsory Dancing. LC 80-80912. 1980. pap. 2.95 (ISBN 0-913922-50-1). Dawn Horse Pr.
--Conscious Exercise & the Transcendental Sun. 3rd rev. ed. LC 77-83388. (Illus.). 258p. 1977. 14.95 (ISBN 0-913922-33-1); pap. 8.95 (ISBN 0-913922-30-7). Dawn Horse Pr.
--Easy Death: Talks & Essays on the Inherent & Ultimate Transcendence of Death & Everything Else. 450p. pap. 10.95 (ISBN 0-913922-57-9). Dawn Horse Pr.
--The Eating Gorilla Comes in Peace. LC 75-24582. 1979. 12.95 (ISBN 0-913922-19-6). Dawn Horse Pr.
--Enlightenment of the Whole Body. LC 77-94504. 1978. pap. 12.95 (ISBN 0-913922-35-8). Dawn Horse Pr.
--The Four Fundamental Questions. 2nd ed. LC 79-92923. 1980. pap. 1.95 (ISBN 0-913922-49-8). Dawn Horse Pr.
--Love of the Two-Armed Form. LC 78-57090. 1978. 12.95 (ISBN 0-913922-37-4). Dawn Horse Pr.
--The Way That I Teach. LC 77-94503. 1978. 10.95 (ISBN 0-913922-38-2); pap. 6.95 (ISBN 0-913922-34-X). Dawn Horse Pr.
Daft, R. I. & Becker, S. W. Innovation in Organizations. 27.50 (ISBN 0-444-00286-3, DII/, Pub. by Elsevier). Greenwood.
Daft, R. L. & Becker, S. W. The Innovative Organization: Innovation Adoption in High Schools. 230p. 1978. pap. 18.75 (ISBN 0-444-99039-9, North Holland). Elsevier.
Daft, Richard L. Organization Theory & Design. (Management Ser.). (Illus.). 570p. 1982. text ed. 30.95 (ISBN 0-314-69645-8). West Pub.
--Organization Theory & Design: International Edition. 570p. 1983. pap. text ed. write for info (ISBN 0-314-68855-2). West Pub.
Daft, Richard L. & Dahlen, Kristen M. Organization Theory: Cases & Applications. (West's Series in Management). (Illus.). 400p. 1984. pap. text ed. 19.95 (ISBN 0-314-77876-4); tchrs.' manual avail. (ISBN 0-314-80326-2). West Pub.
Daft, Richard L., jt. auth. see Campbell, John P.
Daftuar, C. Job Attitudes in Indian Management: A Study in Need Deficiencies & Need Importance. 80p. 1982. text ed. 11.25x (ISBN 0-391-02718-2, Pub. by Concept). Humanities.
Da Gama, Bosco, jt. ed. see Phantom, D. S.
Da Gama, Jose B. The Uruguay: A Historical Romance of South America. Garcia, Frederick & Stanton, Edward, eds. Burton, Richard F., tr. LC 81-15920. 270p. (Port.). 1982. 28.50x (ISBN 0-520-04524-6). U of Cal Pr.
Dagan, Avigdor, et al, eds. The Jews of Czechoslovakia, Vol. III. (Illus.). 700p. 1984. 29.95 (ISBN 0-8276-0230-8). Jewish Pubns.
Daganzo, Carlos. Multinomial Probit: The Theory & Its Application to Demand Forecasting. LC 79-51674. (Economic Theory, Econometrics & Mathematical Economics Ser.). 1979. 37.00 (ISBN 0-12-201150-3). Acad Pr.
D'Agapeyeff, A. Expert Systems: Fifth Generation & UK Suppliers. 1983. pap. 12.50x (ISBN 0-85012-389-5). Hayden.
D'Agata, R., et al, eds. Recent Advances in Male Reproduction: Molecular Basis & Clinical Implications. (Serono Symposia Publications from Raven Press Ser.: Vol. 7). (Illus.). 350p. 1983. text ed. 59.50 (ISBN 0-89004-918-1). Raven.
Dage, John H. La see La Dage, John H.
Dagel, John F. Diesel Engine Repair. LC 81-615. 586p. 1982. 31.95x (ISBN 0-471-03542-4); tchrs' manual avail. (ISBN 0-471-86373-4); student wkbk. 9.95 (ISBN 0-471-88449-9). Wiley.
Dagel, Linda, tr. see Hanft, Ethel W. & Manley, Paula J.
Dagel, Linda L., tr. see Hanft, Ethel W.
D'Agenais & Carruthers. Creating Effective Manuals. 1986. text ed. price not set (ISBN 0-538-21200-4, U20). SW Pub.
Dager, Deborah. Heartaches. 224p. (Orig.). (YA) (gr. 9 up). 1983. pap. 1.95 (ISBN 0-449-70042-9, Juniper). Fawcett.
Dagg, A. I. & James, A. Running, Walking & Jumping: The Science of Locomotion. LC 77-15301. (Wykeham Science Ser.: No. 42). 143p. 1977. 14.95x (ISBN 0-8448-1169-6). Crane-Russak Co.
Dagg, A. J. Running, Walking & Jumping: The Science of Locomotion. 143p. 1977. cancelled (ISBN 0-85109-570-4); pap. write for info. Taylor & Francis.
Dagg, Anne I & Foster, J. Bristol. The Giraffe: Its Biology, Behavior, & Ecology. LC 80-21839. 248p. 1982. Repr. of 1976 ed. text ed. 16.50 (ISBN 0-89874-275-7). Krieger.
Dagg, Anne I., jt. auth. see Gauthier-Pilters, Hilde.
Dagg, John L. Manual of Theology... Christian Doctrine... Church Order, 2 vols. in one. Gausted, Edwins., ed. LC 79-52592. (The Baptist Tradition Ser.). 1980. Repr. of 1858 ed. lib. bdg. 57.50x (ISBN 0-405-12459-7). Ayer Co Pubs.
Dagger, A. Multiple Choice Questions in Electrical Principles. (Illus.). 88p. 1981. pap. 16.50x (ISBN 0-7121-1274-X). Trans-Atlantic.
Daggett. Clinical Endocrinology. (Physical Principles in Medicine Ser.). (Illus.). 192p. 1982. pap. text ed. 17.00 (ISBN 0-8391-1752-3). Univ Park.
--Dynamics of Work. (gr. 9-12). 1984. text ed. 12.50 (ISBN 0-538-07580-5, G58). SW Pub.
--Your Future: Plans & Choices. 1986. text ed. 10.50 (ISBN 0-538-16350-X, P35). SW Pub.
Daggett, et al. Computer & Information Technology. 1986. 14.95 (ISBN 0-538-04550-7, D55). SW Pub.
--Technology at Work: A Survey of Technology. 1986. text ed. price not set (ISBN 0-538-16300-3, P30). SW Pub.
Daggett, Emerson. The Sentinel. 12p. (Orig.). 1981. pap. 2.00 (ISBN 0-932942-01-6). Pacific NW Labor.
Daggett, Harriet S., jt. ed. see Charmatz, Jan P.
Daggett, John M., jt. auth. see Hall, Leo D.
Daggett, Lyle. The Act of Resistance & Other Poems. (Shadow Press, U. S. A. Poetry Chapbook Ser.: No. 3). 36p. 1983. pap. 2.00 saddle-stitch (ISBN 0-937724-03-3). Shadow Pr.
Daggett, Mala, ed. see Bloom, Louise, et al.
Daggett, Max. Low Sky, High Sky, Vol. 1. LC 83-62204. 200p. 1984. 12.95 (ISBN 0-913815-00-4). Priority Pr.
Daggett, Max, et al. Bilingual Skills for Commerce & Industry. (Span. & Eng.). 1984. text ed. 14.00 (ISBN 0-538-22990-X, V99). SW Pub.
Daggett, P. R. Practical Medicine. 1976. 25.50 (ISBN 0-8151-2204-7). Year Bk Med.
Daggett, R. M., ed. & illus. see Kalakaua.
Daggett, Stuart. Chapters on the History of the Southern Pacific. LC 66-22621. (Illus.). Repr. of 1922 ed. 37.50x (ISBN 0-678-00181-2). Kelley.
--Principles of Inland Transportation. LC 78-31183. (Illus.). 1979. Repr. of 1955 ed. lib. bdg. 47.50x (ISBN 0-313-20956-1, DAPI). Greenwood.
--Railroad Consolidation West of the Mississippi River. Bruchey, Stuart, ed. LC 80-1302. (Railroads Ser.). (Illus.). 1981. Repr. of 1933 ed. lib. bdg. 12.00x (ISBN 0-405-13771-0). Ayer Co Pubs.
--Railroad Reorganization. 1908. 35.00 (ISBN 0-384-10665-X). Johnson Repr.
--Railroad Reorganization. LC 67-18576. Repr. of 1908 ed. 37.50x (ISBN 0-678-00239-8). Kelley.
Daggett, Willard & Marrazo, Martin J. Solving Problems - Making Decisions. 1983. text ed. 5.45 wkbk. (ISBN 0-538-07600-3, G60). SW Pub.
Daggett, Willard, jt. auth. see Cushman, Ronald A.
Daggett, Willard R., jt. auth. see Cushman, Ronald A.

Daggs, Elisa. All Africa: The Social, Political & Economic Aspects of Each Country & Area. (Illus.). 1970. 32.50 (ISBN 0-8038-0336-2). Hastings.

Daggy, Robert E., ed. see Merton, Thomas.

Dagher, Fuad J., ed. Cutaneous Wounds. (Illus.). 304p. 1985. 38.00 (ISBN 0-87993-215-5). Futura Pub.

Dagher, Joseph P. Technical Communication: A Practical Guide. (Illus.). 1978. pap. text ed. 19.95 (ISBN 0-13-898247-3). P-H.

--Writing a Practical Guide. LC 74-11784. (Illus.). 1976. pap. text ed. 15.95 (ISBN 0-395-18621-8); instr's. manual 1.35 (ISBN 0-395-18803-2). HM.

Dagher, Yusuf. Arabic Dictionary of Pseudonyms & the Writers Who Use Them. (Arabic.). 1982. 16.00x (ISBN 0-86685-300-6). Intl Bk Ctr.

Daghistany, Ann, jt. ed. see Smitten, Jeffrey R.

Daghlian, Philip B., ed. Essays in Eighteenth-Century Biography. LC 68-27341. pap. 35.30 (ISBN 0-317-27814-2, 2056032). Bks Demand UMI.

Daghlian, Philip B., jt. ed. see Jenkinson, Edward B.

Dagion, John, ed. Trash: True Revelations & Strange Happenings, Vol. 1. (Illus.). 192p. (Orig.). 1985. pap. 10.95 (ISBN 0-917342-07-0). Gay Sunshine.

Daglarca, Fazil Husnu. The Bird & I. Barkan, Stanley H., ed. Halman, Talat Sait, tr. (Cross-Cultural Review Chapbook 4: Turkish Poetry 1). 16p. (Turkish & Eng.). 1980. pap. 2.00 (ISBN 0-89304-803-8). Cross Cult.

Dagless, E. L., jt. ed. see Reijns, G. L.

Dagless, Erik, jt. ed. see Aspinall, David.

Dagless, Erik L. & Aspinall, David. Introduction to Microcomputers. LC 81-5437. 233p. 1982. text ed. 22.95 (ISBN 0-914894-25-0). Computer Sci.

Daglio, S. Daniel, tr. see Yates, Kyle M. & Owens, J. J.

Daglish, R. C., ed. see Taube, A. M., et al.

Dagmar, et al, trs. see Tichy, M. & Rakosnik, J.

Dagnal, Cynthia. Starting Your Own Rock Band. (Illus.). 112p. (Orig.). 1983. pap. 5.95 (ISBN 0-8092-5606-1). Contemp Bks.

Dagneau, Jacques. Les Agences Regionales Du Credit Lyonnais: Annees 1870-1914. Bruchey, Stuart, ed. LC 77-81826. (Dissertations in European Economic History Ser.). (Illus., Fr.). 1977. lib. bdg. 59.50x (ISBN 0-405-10778-1). Ayer Co Pubs.

Dagneaux, Christine. Appalachia: A Separate Place - a Unique People. 1981. 15.00 (ISBN 0-87012-340-8). McClain.

Dagnini, Giorgio. Clinical Laparoscopy. (Illus.). xii, 307p. 1980. 135.00 (ISBN 88-212-0746-3, Pub. by Piccin Italy). J K Burgess.

--Clinical Laparoscopy. (Illus.). 307p. 1980. text ed. 108.00 (ISBN 88-212-0746-3). Igaku-Shoin.

Dagnino, Alfonso G. see Alegria, Fernando, et al.

D'Agnostino, Guido, jt. auth. see Covello, Leonard.

D'Agostino, Dennis. This Date in New York Mets History. LC 80-6157. (This Date Ser.). 256p. 1982. pap. 10.95 (ISBN 0-8128-6068-3). Stein & Day.

Dagostino, Frank. Materials of Construction. 1981. text ed. 26.95 (ISBN 0-8359-4286-4). Reston.

--Mechanical & Electrical Systems in Building. 1982. text ed. 28.95 (ISBN 0-8359-4312-7). Reston.

--Mechanical & Electrical Systems in Construction & Architecture. (Illus.). 1978. ref. ed. 29.95 (ISBN 0-87909-511-3); solutions manual avail. (ISBN 0-87909-510-5). Reston.

--Residential Construction Handbook. 1982. text ed. 39.95 (ISBN 0-8359-6650-X). Reston.

Dagostino, Frank R. Contemporary Architectural Drawing: Residential & Commercial. 1977. 23.95 (ISBN 0-87909-132-0). Reston.

--Estimating in Building Construction. 2nd ed. (Illus.). 1978. text ed. 28.95 (ISBN 0-87909-275-0). solutions manual free (ISBN 0-8359-2749-0). Reston.

D'Agostino, Guido. Olives on the Apple Tree. LC 74-17924. (Italian American Experience Ser). 1975. Repr. 19.00x (ISBN 0-405-06397-0). Ayer Co Pubs.

D'Agostino, Joseph D. The Tarot, the Royal Path to Wisdom. 1975. pap. 3.50 (ISBN 0-87728-329-X). Weiser.

D'Agostino, L. V. Our Family. (Illus.). 1973. 6.95x (ISBN 0-9601076-1-4). L V D'Agostino.

D'Agostino, Peter. Alpha, Trans, Chung: A Photographic Model: Semiotics, Film & Interpretation. LC 78-73214. (Illus.). 1978. pap. 7.95 (ISBN 0-917986-09-1). NFS Pr.

--Coming & Going. LC 82-61856. 88p. 1982. pap. 9.95 (ISBN 0-917986-18-0). NFS Pr.

D'Agostino, Peter, ed. Transmission. 336p. (Orig.). 1984. 29.95 (ISBN 0-934378-25-8); pap. 15.95 (ISBN 0-934378-26-6). Tanam Pr.

D'Agostino, Peter, jt. ed. see Thomas, Lew.

D'Agostino, R. B., jt. auth. see Cureton, E. E.

D'Agostino, Ralph B. & Shuman, Larry. Mathematical Modeling: Applications in Emergency Health Services. LC 84-12917. (Emergency Health Services Review Ser.: Vol. 2, Nos. 2-3). 118p. 1984. 17.95 (ISBN 0-86656-373-3). Haworth Pr.

D'Agostino, Robert A. Basic Reading Skills. LC 82-22737. (Arco Pre-GED Study Guides Ser.). 224p. 1983. pap. 6.95 (ISBN 0-668-05457-3, 5457). Arco.

D'Agostino, Robert A., et al. Mastering Reading Comprehension Skills. LC 81-20494. (Illus.). 224p. (Orig.). 1982. pap. 6.95 (ISBN 0-668-05125-6). Arco.

D'Agostino, Rose, ed. see Trollope, Anthony.

Da Grace, John V. Heads of State & Government: A Comprehensive International Historical Directory. 424p. 1985. 60.00x (ISBN 0-8147-1778-0). NYU Pr.

Dagradi, Angelo E. Gastrointestinal Endoscopy Technique & Interpretation. LC 83-10676. (Illus.). 262p. 1983. text ed. 45.00 (ISBN 0-89640-087-5). Igaku-Shoin.

Daguang, Zhou, ed. see Yunfu, Yuan.

Daguillard, Fritz, ed. see Leukocyte Culture Conference, Seventh, Universite Laval, June, 1972.

Dagut, Menachem, tr. see Hacohen, David.

Dahan, Bonnie, ed. see Kan, Johnny & Leong, Charles L.

Dahdah, Antoine. Dictionary of Arabic Grammar, in Charts & Tables. (Illus., Arabic.). 1982. 30.00x (ISBN 0-86685-292-1). Intl Bk Ctr.

Daheim, Mary. Destiny's Pawn. 432p. 1984. pap. 3.50 (ISBN 0-380-86884-9, 86884). Avon.

Daheim, Mary R. Love's Pirate. 592p. 1983. pap. 3.95 (ISBN 0-380-83840-0, 83840-0). Avon.

Dahiya, Bhagwan, ed. Development Planning Models, 2 vols. 800p. 1981. Set. text ed. 57.50x (ISBN 0-391-02646-1, Pub. by Concept India). Humanities.

Dahiya, Bhim S. The Hero in Hemingway, Vol.1. (English Language & Literature Ser.). 225p. 1978. 12.75x (ISBN 0-391-02540-6). Humanities.

Dahiya, S. Bhagwan. Development Planning Models, 2 Vols. (Illus.). 660p. 1983. text ed. 75.00x set (ISBN 0-86590-122-8). Apt Bks.

Dahl. Prolog for Programmers. 1985. pap. price not set (ISBN 0-471-82495-X). Wiley.

Dahl, A. M. Directory of Directors in the City of New York & Tri-State Area. 750p. 1984. 145.00x (ISBN 0-936612-05-3). DODC.

Dahl, Alf A. & Wilson, J. Douglas. Cabinetmaking & Millwork: Tools, Materials, Layout. LC 53-11586. (Books of the Building Trade). pap. 89.80 (ISBN 0-317-09679-6, 2006111). Bks Demand UMI.

Dahl, Anna. Handwork Patterns for the Whole Year. (Illus.). 48p. (Orig.). (gr. 3 up). 1951. pap. 4.50 (ISBN 0-87239-329-1, 2146). Standard Pub.

Dahl, Arlene. Arlene Dahl's Lovescopes. LC 83-6387. 224p. 1983. 15.95 (ISBN 0-672-52770-7). Bobbs.

Dahl, Arthur L., et al. Mark Tobey: Art & Belief. (Illus.). 128p. (Orig.). 1984. 16.95 (ISBN 0-85398-179-5); pap. 8.95 (ISBN 0-85398-180-9). G Ronald Pub.

Dahl, B. Consumer Legislation in Denmark. 1981. 42.50 (ISBN 0-317-12943-0). Van Nos Reinhold.

Dahl, Barbara, jt. auth. see McCubbin, Hamilton I.

Dahl, Basil. To the Toilers & Other Verses. 59.95 (ISBN 0-8490-1217-1). Gordon Pr.

Dahl, Bonnie. The Loran-C Users Guide. (Illus.). 220p. 1985. pap. 19.95 (ISBN 0-932647-00-6, 011-003). Richardsons Marine.

Dahl, Carol A. Demand for Gasoline. LC 80-8623. (Outstanding Dissertations in Economics Ser.). 150p. 1983. lib. bdg. 24.00 (ISBN 0-8240-4180-1). Garland Pub.

Dahl, Christopher. Louis Auchincloss. (Literature & Life). 200p. 1985. 13.95 (ISBN 0-8044-2123-4). Ungar.

Dahl, Cornwall. Consistent Profits in Short Selling Speculation. (Illus.). 267p. 1976. 61.50 (ISBN 0-89266-011-2). Am Classical Coll Pr.

--Consistent Profits in the Stock Market Formula Plans, 2 vols. in one. (Illus.). 85p. 1975. Set. 65.00 (ISBN 0-913314-66-8). Am Classical Coll Pr.

Dahl, Curtis. Robert Montgomery Bird. (Twayne's United States Authors Ser.). 1963. pap. 5.95x (ISBN 0-8084-0267-6, T31, Twayne). New Coll U Pr.

Dahl, Curtis, ed. see Bird, Robert M.

Dahl, Curtis, ed. see Ely, Ben-Ezra S.

Dahl, David L., jt. auth. see Jenkins, Michael D.

Dahl, Deanna, ed. see Stanley, Charles A.

Dahl, Dolores. Make Ready. LC 82-99847. (Illus.). 91p. (Orig.). 1982. pap. 4.95 (ISBN 0-9608960-0-7). Single Vision.

--The Pearl Within the Shell. LC 83-60744. (Illus.). 119p. (Orig.). 1983. pap. 5.95 (ISBN 0-9608960-1-5). Single Vision.

--Where Heavens Hide. LC 84-51375. (Illus.). 48p. (Orig.). 1984. pap. 3.95 (ISBN 0-9608960-2-3). Single Vision.

Dahl, Eilif & Krog, Hildur. Macrolichens of Denmark, Finland, Norway, & Sweden. (Scandinavian University Books). (Illus.). 180p. 1973. 17.00x (ISBN 82-00-02262-5, Dist. by Columbia U Pr). Universitet.

Dahl, Folke. A Bibliography of English Corantos & Periodical Newsbooks 1620-1642. LC 77-6176. 1977. Repr. of 1952 ed. lib. bdg. 30.00 (ISBN 0-89341-158-2). Longwood Pub Group.

Dahl, Fred, jt. auth. see Sippl, Charles.

Dahl, Fred, jt. auth. see Sippl, Charles J.

Dahl, George. Two Children's Stories for Physicians & Other Wise Men. LC 73-80769. (Orig.). 1973. pap. 2.95 (ISBN 0-912922-03-6). U of Minn Bell.

Dahl, Hartvig. Word Frequencies of Spoken American English. LC 80-116646. xii, 348p. 1980. 60.00 (ISBN 0-930454-07-3). Verbatim Bks.

Dahl, Jens P. & Avery, John, eds. Local Destiny Approximations in Quantum Chemistry & Solid-State Physics. 852p. 1984. 125.00x (ISBN 0-306-41667-0, Plenum Pr). Plenum Pub.

Dahl, June W. Footprints: A History of St. Paul Red Cross. (Illus.). 233p. 1981. 10.00 (ISBN 0-9605584-0-3). St Paul Area.

Dahl, Karin, jt. auth. see Smith, Carl B.

Dahl, Linda. Stormy Weather: The Music & Lives of a Century of Jazzwomen. LC 83-19456. (Illus.). 371p. 1984. 19.45 (ISBN 0-394-53555-3); pap. 12.95 (ISBN 0-394-72271-X). Pantheon.

Dahl, M. V. Clinical Immunodermatology. 1981. 36.50 (ISBN 0-8151-2246-2). Year Bk Med.

Dahl, Marit & Tangerud, Hans. Integration of Handicapped Pupils in Compulsory Education in Norway. 150p. (Orig.). 1983. pap. 13.00x (ISBN 82-00-06450-6). Universitet.

Dahl, Mark V. Common Office Dermatology. 192p. 1982. 41.50 (ISBN 0-8089-1497-9, 790965). Grune.

Dahl, Nancy, jt. ed. see Aldous, Joan.

Dahl, Nils A. Jesus in the Memory of the Early Church. LC 76-27072. 1976. pap. 8.95 (ISBN 0-8066-1561-3, 10-3519). Augsburg.

--Studies in Paul. LC 77-84083. 1977. pap. 9.50 (ISBN 0-8066-1608-3, 10-6100). Augsburg.

Dahl, Norman. Small Boat Sailing. (Illus.). 96p. 1980. 10.95 (ISBN 0-7136-1915-5). Transatlantic.

--Yacht Navigator's Handbook. Hooper, Queane, ed. (Illus.). 192p. 1983. Repr. FPT 21.95 (ISBN 0-688-02482-3, Pub. by Hearst Bks). Morrow.

Dahl, Norman C. & Wiesner, Jerome B., eds. World Change & World Security. (MIT Bicentennial Studies Ser.). 1978. 20.00x (ISBN 0-262-04058-1). MIT Pr.

Dahl, Norman O. Practical Reason, Aristotle & Weakness of the Will. LC 83-14845. (Minnesota Publication in the Humanities Ser.). (Illus.). 296p. 1984. 29.50x (ISBN 0-8166-1245-5); pap. 14.95x (ISBN 0-8166-1246-3). U of Minn Pr.

Dahl, Ole-Johan, jt. auth. see Birtwistle, Graham M.

Dahl, Otto C. Early Phonetic & Phonemic Changes in Austronesia. 176p. 1982. 18.00 (ISBN 82-00-09530-4). Universitet.

Dahl, Patricia & Degenhart, Laura. Where to Go with Kids in the Capital District. (Illus.). 50p. (Orig.). 1982. pap. text ed. 2.50 (ISBN 0-9611292-0-4). With Kids.

Dahl, Patrick, jt. ed. see Pence, Richard A.

Dahl, Paul. Introduction to Electron & Ion Optics. 1973. 35.00 (ISBN 0-12-200650-X). Acad Pr.

Dahl, Richard C. & Davis, Robert. Effective Speaking for Lawyers. LC 75-93751. 150p. 1969. lib. bdg. 30.00 (ISBN 0-930342-11-9). W S Hein.

Dahl, Richard C. & Dix, George E., eds. Crime Law & Justice Annual, 1972, Vol. 1. LC 72-79450. 800p. 1973. lib. bdg. 37.50 (ISBN 0-930342-33-X). W S Hein.

Dahl, Richard C. & Whelan, John F., eds. The Military Law Dictionary. LC 60-10208. 224p. 1960. 15.00 (ISBN 0-379-00042-3). Oceana.

Dahl, Roald. The B. F. G. Dahl. 1985. 3.95 (ISBN 0-14-031597-7, Puffin). Penguin.

--The Best of Roald Dahl. 1978. pap. 6.95 (ISBN 0-394-72549-2, Vin). Random.

--The BFG. LC 82-15548. (Illus.). 221p. (ps-3). 1982. 10.95 (ISBN 0-374-30469-6); ltd., slipcased ed. 30.00 (ISBN 0-374-30471-8). FS&G.

--The BFG. LC 85-566. (Illus.). 208p. (gr. 3-7). 1985. pap. 3.95 (ISBN 0-14-031597-7, Puffin). Penguin.

--Boy: Tales of Childhood. LC 84-48462. (Illus.). 176p. 10.95 (ISBN 0-374-37374-4); signed, limited 30.00 (ISBN 0-374-37375-2). FS&G.

--Boy: Tales of Chilhood. 1986. price not set (Puffin). Penguin.

--Charlie & the Chocolate Factory. 176p. (gr. 4-6). 1981. pap. 2.50 (ISBN 0-553-15248-3, Skylark). Bantam.

--Charlie & the Chocolate Factory. (gr. 4-8). 1979. pap. 2.50 (ISBN 0-553-24478-7). Bantam.

--Charlie & the Chocolate Factory. (gr. 1 up). 1964. 9.99 (ISBN 0-394-81011-2); PLB 8.99 (ISBN 0-394-91011-7). Knopf.

--Charlie & the Chocolate Factory: A Play. George, Richard R., adapted by. 320p. (gr. 3-7). 1983. pap. 2.50 (ISBN 0-14-031125-4, Puffin). Penguin.

--Charlie & the Great Glass Elevator. (gr. 4-8). 1977. pap. 2.50 (ISBN 0-553-15315-3, Skylark). Bantam.

--Charlie & the Great Glass Elevator: The Further Adventures of Charlie Bucket & Willie Wonka, the Chocolate-Maker Extraordinaire. (Illus.). (gr. k-7). 1972. 10.95 (ISBN 0-394-82472-5); PLB 10.99 (ISBN 0-394-92472-X). Knopf.

--Danny the Champion of the World. (gr. 5 up). 1978. pap. 2.50 (ISBN 0-553-15289-0, Skylark). Bantam.

--Danny: The Champion of the World. (Illus.). 208p. (gr. 3 up). 1975. PLB 9.99 (ISBN 0-394-93103-3). Knopf.

--Dirty Beasts. LC 82-83905. (Illus.). 32p. (gr. 1 up). 1984. 11.95 (ISBN 0-374-31790-9). FS&G.

--Dirty Beasts. 1986. price not set (Puffin). Penguin.

--The Enormous Crocodile. LC 77-5081. (Illus.). (ps-3). 1978. PLB 4.95 (ISBN 0-394-83594-8); 6.99g (ISBN 0-394-93594-2). Knopf.

--The Enormous Crocodile. (Skylark Ser.). 48p. (Orig.). (gr. 1-3). 1984. pap. text ed. 2.95 (ISBN 0-553-15243-2, Skylark). Bantam.

--Fantastic Mr. Fox. (gr. 4-8). 1978. pap. 2.25 (ISBN 0-553-15155-X, Skylark). Bantam.

--Fantastic Mister Fox. LC 74-118704. (Illus.). (gr. k-3). 1970. PLB 7.99 (ISBN 0-394-90497-4). Knopf.

--George's Marvelous Medicine. LC 81-11811. (Illus.). 96p. (gr. 3-7). 1982. 7.95 (ISBN 0-394-84600-1); PLB 7.99 (ISBN 0-394-94600-6). Knopf.

--The Giraffe & the Pelly & Me. (Illus.). 32p. (gr. 6 up). 1985. 11.95 (ISBN 0-374-32602-9). FS&G.

--James & the Giant Peach. 160p. (gr. 4-6). 1981. pap. 2.95 (ISBN 0-553-15317-X, Skylark). Bantam.

--James & the Giant Peach. (Illus.). (gr. 3 up). 1961. 13.95 (ISBN 0-394-81282-4); PLB 13.99 (ISBN 0-394-91282-9). Knopf.

--James & the Giant Peach: A Play. Dahl, Roald, adapted by. 128p. (gr. 3-7). 1983. pap. 2.50 (ISBN 0-14-031464-4, Puffin). Penguin.

--Kiss, Kiss. 1959. 13.95 (ISBN 0-394-43202-9). Knopf.

--Magic Finger. LC 66-18657. (Illus.). (gr. 1-5). 1966. 10.10i (ISBN 0-06-021381-7); PLB 10.89 (ISBN 0-06-021382-5). HarpJ.

--The Magic Finger. LC 66-18657. (A Trophy Picture Bk.). (Illus.). 48p. (gr. 3-6). 1983. pap. 3.80i (ISBN 0-06-443045-6, Trophy). HarpJ.

--My Uncle Oswald. 208p. 1981. pap. 2.95 (ISBN 0-345-29410-6). Ballantine.

--My Uncle Oswald. LC 79-19811. 1980. 10.00 (ISBN 0-394-51011-9). Knopf.

--Roald Dahl's Revolting Rhymes. LC 82-15263. (Illus.). 48p. 1983. 9.95 (ISBN 0-394-85422-5); lib. bdg. 9.99 (ISBN 0-394-95422-X). Knopf.

--Roald Dahl's Tales of the Unexpected. pap. 4.95 (ISBN 0-394-74081-5, V-81, Vin). Random.

--Switch Bitch. 192p. 1983. pap. 2.50 (ISBN 0-345-30622-8). Ballantine.

--The Twits. 96p. 1982. pap. 2.50 (ISBN 0-553-15343-9). Bantam.

--The Witches. LC 83-14195. (Illus.). 202p. (ps-3). 1983. pap. 10.95 (ISBN 0-374-38457-6); limited ed. 35.00 (ISBN 0-374-38458-4). FS&G.

--The Witches. LC 85-519. (Illus.). 200p. (gr. 3-7). 1985. pap. 3.95 (ISBN 0-14-031730-9, Puffin). Penguin.

--The Wonderful Story of Henry Sugar & Six More. (gr. 4-8). 1979. pap. 2.50 (ISBN 0-553-15264-5, Skylark Bk). Bantam.

Dahl, Roald & Tannen, Mary. The Twits. LC 80-18410. (Illus.). 96p. (ps-5). 1981. 6.95 (ISBN 0-394-84599-4). Knopf.

Dahl, Roald, ed. Roald Dahl's Book of Ghost Stories. 235p. (ps up). 1984. 12.95 (ISBN 0-374-25131-2); pap. 3.95 (ISBN 0-374-51868-8). FS&G.

Dahl, Robert A. After the Revolution: Authority in a Good Society. (Fastback Ser). 1970. pap. 6.95x (ISBN 0-300-01447-3, YF9). Yale U Pr.

--Congress & Foreign Policy. LC 82-25123. x, 305p. 1983. Repr. of 1950 ed. lib. bdg. 35.00x (ISBN 0-313-23788-3, DACF). Greenwood.

--Controlling Nuclear Weapons: Democracy Versus Guardianship. (Frank W. Abrams Lectures Ser.). 128p. 1985. text ed. 14.95 (ISBN 0-317-18287-0); pap. 8.95 (ISBN 0-317-18288-9). Syracuse U Pr.

--Democracy in the United States. 4th ed. 1981. 20.95 (ISBN 0-395-30793-7); Instr's. manual 1.25 (ISBN 0-395-30794-5). HM.

--Dilemmas of Pluralist Democracy: Autonomy vs. Control. LC 81-16111. (Studies in Political Science: Vol. 31). 1982 207p 25.00x (ISBN 0-300-02543-2); pap. 8.95x 1983 243pp. Yale U Pr.

--Modern Political Analysis. 4th ed. 176p. 1984. 19.95 (ISBN 0-13-596973-5); pap. 14.95 (ISBN 0-13-596965-4). P-H.

--Polyarchy: Participation & Opposition. LC 70-140534. 1971. pap. 9.95x (ISBN 0-300-01565-8, Y254). Yale U Pr.

--Preface to Democratic Theory. LC 56-6642. (Walgreen Foundation Lecture Ser). 1963. pap. 6.00x (ISBN 0-226-13426-1, P115, Phoen). U of Chicago Pr.

--A Preface to Economic Democracy. LC 84-8483. 1985. 14.95 (ISBN 0-520-05345-1). U of Cal Pr.

--Who Governs: Democracy & Power in an American City. LC 61-16913. (Studies in Political Science: No. 4). (Illus.). 1961. 33.50x (ISBN 0-300-00395-1); pap. 8.95x (ISBN 0-300-00051-0, Y73). Yale U Pr.

Dahl, Robert A. & Brown, Ralph S., Jr. Domestic Control of Atomic Energy. LC 51-12965. 1951. pap. 2.00 (ISBN 0-527-03298-0). Kraus Repr.

Dahl, Robert A. & Flanigan, William. New Haven Community Study, 1959. 2nd ed. LC 75-38491. 1975. Repr. of 1971 ed. codebk. write for info. (ISBN 0-89138-024-8). ICPSR.

Dahl, Robert A. & Tufte, Edward R. Size & Democracy. LC 72-97200. 148p. 1973. 12.50x (ISBN 0-8047-0834-7); pap. 5.95 (ISBN 0-8047-0889-4, SP137). Stanford U Pr.

Dahl, Robert A., ed. Political Oppositions in Western Democracies. LC 65-22315. pap. 120.00 (ISBN 0-317-09366-5, 2016758). Bks Demand UMI.

--Social Science Research on Business: Product & Potential. LC 60-9783. 185p. 1959. pap. 14.50x (ISBN 0-231-02407-X). Columbia U Pr.

Dahl, Stephanie H., jt. auth. see Modern Bride Editors.

Dahl, V. & Saint-Dizier, P., eds. Natural Language Understanding & Logic Programming. 1985. 44.50 (ISBN 0-444-87714-2). Elsevier.

Dahl, Vladimir I. Dahl's Russian Dictionary, 4 vols. LC 79-40161. (Illus.). 3000p. (Rus.). 1981. Set. 240.00 (ISBN 0-08-023573-5). Pergamon.

Dahl, W. & Lange, K. W., eds. Kinetics of Metallurgical Processes in Steelmaking: Proceedings. (Illus.). x, 584p. 1975. 100.30 (ISBN 0-387-07366-3). Springer-Verlag.

Dahlberg, Albert. Dental Morphology & Evolution. LC 73-158726. 1971. 20.00x (ISBN 0-226-13481-4). U of Chicago Pr.

Dahlberg, Arthur. How to Save Free Enterprise. LC 74-75390. (Illus.). 368p. 1975. 12.95 (ISBN 0-8159-5708-4). Devin.

Dahlberg, Arthur A. Jobs, Machines & Capitalism. LC 70-91296. (BCL Ser. I). Repr. of 1932 ed. 16.50 (ISBN 0-404-01917-X). AMS Pr.

Dahlberg, Arthur O. How to Reduce Interest Rates & Poverty. 150p. 1984. 14.95 (ISBN 0-8159-5718-1). Devin.

Dahlberg, Charles, tr. see De Lorris, Guillaume & De Meun, Jean.

Dahlberg, E. C. Applied Hydrodynamics in Petroleum Exploration. (Illus.). 161p. 1982. pap. 24.00 (ISBN 0-387-90677-0). Springer-Verlag.

Dahlberg, Edward. Because I Was Flesh. LC 64-10079. 1964. 5.95 (ISBN 0-8112-0263-1). New Directions.

--Bottom Dogs. LC 74-22778. (Labor Movement in Fiction & Non-Fcition). Repr. of 1930 ed. 17.50 (ISBN 0-404-58418-7). AMS Pr.

--Can These Bones Live? rev. ed. LC 60-9220. (Illus.). 1960. 6.50 (ISBN 0-8112-0264-X). New Directions.

--Confessions of Edward Dahlberg. LC 74-132367. 1971. 6.50 (ISBN 0-8076-0589-1). Braziller.

--The Edward Dahlberg Reader. Carroll, Paul, ed. LC 67-12371. 1968. pap. 3.25 (ISBN 0-8112-0030-2, NDP246). New Directions.

--Epitaphs of Our Times. LC 66-25400. 1966. 6.95 (ISBN 0-8076-0385-6). Braziller.

--The Flea of Sodom. LC 73-18392. (American Literature, Ser., No. 49). 1974. lib. bdg. 49.95x (ISBN 0-8383-1739-1). Haskell.

--Leafless American. limited ed. (Illus.). 1967. 16.50 (ISBN 0-911796-02-9). Beacham.

--The Sorrows of Priapus: The Poetic Truths of Mind & Body in Myth & Experience. (Illus.). 120p. 1985. pap. 8.95 (ISBN 0-7145-0670-2, Dist. by Scribner). M Boyars.

--Those Who Perish. LC 75-41070. Repr. of 1934 ed. 15.00 (ISBN 0-404-14528-0). AMS Pr.

Dahlberg, Frances, ed. Woman the Gatherer. LC 80-25262. 1983. text ed. 27.50x (ISBN 0-300-02572-6); pap. 8.95x (ISBN 0-300-02989-6, Y-476). Yale U Pr.

Dahlberg, Kenneth & Bennett, John, eds. Improving Natural Resource Management: Approaches to Multidisciplinary Research. (WVST in Natural Resource & Energy Management Ser.). 360p. 1985. pap. text ed. 28.50x (ISBN 0-8133-7079-5). Westview.

Dahlberg, Kenneth A., ed. Beyond the Green Revolution: The Ecology & Politics of Global Agricultural Development. LC 78-11271. (Illus.). 270p. 1979. 25.00x (ISBN 0-306-40120-7, Plenum Pr). Plenum Pub.

--New Directions for Agriculture & Agricultural Research: Neglected Dimensions & Emerging Alternatives. 220p. 1985. 45.00x (ISBN 0-8476-7417-7). Rowman.

Dahlberg, Kenneth A., et al. Environment & the Global Arena: Actors, Values, Policies, & Futures. Harf, James E. & Trout, B. Thomas, eds. (Duke Press Global Issues Ser.). (Illus.). 188p. (Orig.). 1985. pap. text ed. 10.75 (ISBN 0-8223-0621-2). Duke.

Dahle, John, ed. Library of Christian Hymns, 3 vols. in 2. LC 72-1649. Repr. of 1928 ed. 74.50 set (ISBN 0-404-13202-2). AMS Pr.

Dahlem, Ted. How to Make & Mend Cast Nets. pap. 1.95 (ISBN 0-8200-0608-4). Great Outdoors.

--How to Smoke Seafood. pap. 1.95 (ISBN 0-8200-0803-6). Great Outdoors.

Dahlen, Beverly. A Letter at Easter. 1976. sewn in wrappers 3.00 (ISBN 0-685-88990-4). Effies Bks.

Dahlen, Kristen M., jt. auth. see Daft, Richard L.

Dahlgren, Anders C. Planning the Small Public Library Building. LC 85-9079. (LAMA Small Libraries Publications: No. 11). (Illus.). 24p. 1985. pap. text ed. 5.00x (ISBN 0-8389-5652-1). ALA.

Dahlgren, Erik W. Were the Hawaiian Islands Visited by the Spaniards Before Their Discovery by Captain Cook in 1778? LC 75-35187. (Illus.). Repr. of 1916 ed. 43.50 (ISBN 0-404-14216-8). AMS Pr.

Dahlgren, Lars O. Qualitative Differences in Learning As a Function of Content-Oriented Guidance. (Goteburg Studies in Educational Sciences Ser.: No. 15). 172p. 1975. pap. text ed. 8.75x (ISBN 91-7346-013-3). Humanities.

Dahlgren, Madeleine. South-Mountain Magic. 1882. Repr. of 1975 ed. 8.00 (ISBN 0-87012-202-9). McClain.

Dahlgren, R. M. & Clifford, H. T. The Monocotyledon: A Comparative Study. LC 81-67906. (Botanical Systematics Ser.: No. 2). 1982. 98.50 (ISBN 0-12-200680-1). Acad Pr.

Dahlgren, R. M., et al. The Families of the Monocotyledons. 1985. 98.00 (ISBN 0-387-13655-X). Springer-Verlag.

Dahlhaus, Carl. Analysis & Value Judgement. 2nd ed. Levarie, Siegmund, tr. from Ger. (Pendragon Press Monographs in Musicology & Aesthetics in Music Ser.). Orig. Title: Analyse und Werturteil. 150p. 1983. lib. bdg. 42.00 (ISBN 0-918728-20-7). Pendragon NY.

--Between Romanticism & Modernism: Four Studies in the Music of the Later Nineteenth Century. Whittall, Mary, tr. from Ger. LC 78-54793. (California Studies in 19th Century Music). 100p. 1980. 15.50x (ISBN 0-520-03679-4). U of Cal Pr.

--Esthetics of Music. Austin, William, tr. LC 81-10080. 120p. 1982. 29.95 (ISBN 0-521-23508-1); pap. 10.95 (ISBN 0-521-28007-9). Cambridge U Pr.

--Foundations of Music History. Robinson, J. B., tr. LC 82-9591. 200p. 1983. 29.95 (ISBN 0-521-23281-3); pap. 10.95 (ISBN 0-521-29890-3). Cambridge U Pr.

--Realism in Nineteenth Century Music. Whittall, Mary, tr. from Ger. 160p. 1985. 29.95 (ISBN 0-521-26115-5); pap. 9.95 (ISBN 0-521-27841-4). Cambridge U Pr.

--Richard Wagner's Music Dramas. Whittall, Mary, tr. LC 78-68359. 1979. 27.95 (ISBN 0-521-22397-0). Cambridge U Pr.

Dahlhaus, Carl & Eggebrecht, Hans H. Brockhaus Riemann Musiklexikon, Vol. 1, A-K. (Ger.). 1978. write for info. (ISBN 3-7653-0303-8). Eur-Am Music.

Dahlhaus, Carl, jt. auth. see Deathridge, John.

Dahlheim, Werner. Gewalt und Herrschaft das Provinziale Herrschaftssystem der Roemischen Republik. 1977. 53.40x (ISBN 3-11-006973-3). De Gruyter.

Dahlheimer, John C. Mechanical Face Seal Handbook. LC 72-6443. pap. 50.00 (ISBN 0-317-28144-5, 2055746). Bks Demand UMI.

Dahlie, Hallvard, jt. ed. see Chadbourne, Richard.

Dahlie, Jorgen. A Social History of Scandinavian Immigration, Washington State, 1895-1910. LC 80-849. (American Ethnic Groups Ser.). 1981. lib. bdg. 20.00x (ISBN 0-405-13412-6). Ayer Co Pubs.

Dahlin, David C. Bone Tumors: General Aspects & Data on 6,221 Cases. 3rd ed. (Illus.). 464p. 1981. 44.75x (ISBN 0-398-03692-6). C C Thomas.

Dahlin, Donald C. Impact of the Twenty-Sixth Amendment: The Residence Status of College Students. 1972. write for info. U of SD Gov Res Bur.

--Law Enforcement Planning in South Dakota: A First Report. 1970. write for info. U of SD Gov Res Bur.

--Models of Court Management. LC 83-14975. 170p. 1985. 18.00 (ISBN 0-86733-051-1). Assoc Faculty Pr.

--Rural Crime Prevention in South Dakota. LC 84-621635. (Special Project Ser.: No. 47). (Illus.). viii, 193p. 1982. write for info. U of SD Gov Res Bur.

--South Dakota Jails: Current Conditions & Proposed Directions. 1971. write for info. U of SD Gov Res Bur.

Dahlin, Ebba. French & German Public Opinion on Declared War Aims, 1914-1918. LC 73-155602. (Stanford University. Stanford Studies in History, Economics & Political Science). Repr. of 1933 ed. 15.00 (ISBN 0-404-50968-1). AMS Pr.

Dahlin, Therrin C. & Gillum, Gary P. The Catholic Left in Latin America: A Comprehensive Bibliography. 1981. lib. bdg. 36.50 (ISBN 0-8161-8396-1, Hall Reference). G K Hall.

Dahlitz, Julie. Nuclear Arms Control: With Effective International Agreements. 256p. 1984. text ed. 25.00x (ISBN 0-04-341023-5); pap. text ed. 9.95x (ISBN 0-04-341024-3). Allen Unwin.

Dahlke, Arnold E., jt. auth. see LaCharite, Norman.

Dahlke, Paul. Buddhism & Its Place in the Mental Life of Mankind. LC 78-72403. Repr. of 1927 ed. 29.00 (ISBN 0-404-17265-2). AMS Pr.

--Buddhist Essays. Silicara, Bhikkhu, tr. from Ger. LC 78-72404. Repr. of 1908 ed. 37.50 (ISBN 0-404-17266-0). AMS Pr.

--Buddhist Stories. facsimile ed. Silacara, Bhikkhu, tr. LC 71-106285. (Short Story Index Reprint Ser.). 1913. 19.00 (ISBN 0-8369-3322-2). Ayer Co Pubs.

Dahlman, C. J. The Open Field System & Beyond. LC 79-7658. 1980. 32.50 (ISBN 0-521-22881-6). Cambridge U Pr.

Dahlmann, Friedrich C. The Life of Herodotus. Cox, G. Valentine, tr. LC 77-94571. 1979. Repr. of 1845 ed. lib. bdg. 20.00 (ISBN 0-89341-256-2). Longwood Pub Group.

Dahlquist, Allan. Megasthenes & Indian Religion. 1977. 11.50 (ISBN 0-89684-277-0, Pub. by Motilal Banarsidass India). Orient Bk Dist.

Dahlquist, Germund, jt. auth. see Bjorck, Ake.

Dahlquist, Raf, jt. auth. see Dahlquist, Teresa.

Dahlquist, Raf, jt. auth. see Valenti, Teresa.

Dahlquist, Teresa & Dahlquist, Raf. Halley & His Comet. (Polestar, People & Ideas Ser.). (Illus.). 32p. (gr. k-9). 1985. 12.95 (ISBN 0-931087-03-1). Polestar Nexus.

Dahlqvist, Reine. The Keyed Trumpet & Its Greatest Virtuoso: Anton Weidinger. new ed. LC 75-16223. (Brass Research Ser: No. 1). (Illus.). 25p. 1975. pap. 2.50x (ISBN 0-914282-13-1). Brass Pr.

Dahlsgaard, Inga, et al. Women in Denmark: Yesterday & Today. French, Geoffrey, tr. from Danish. Ytting, Karen, ed. (Denmark in Print & Pictures Ser.). (Illus.). 310p. 1980. 16.95 (ISBN 87-7429-036-3, Pub. by Det Danske Selskab Denmark). Nordic Bks.

Dahlstrand, Frederick C. Amos Bronson Alcott: An Intellectual Biography. LC 80-65282. (Illus.). 500p. 1982. 42.50 (ISBN 0-8386-3016-2). Fairleigh Dickinson.

Dahlstrand, Ingemar. Software Portability & Standards. (Computers & Their Applications Ser.: No. 1403). 150p. 1984. 24.95x (ISBN 0-470-20083-9). Halsted Pr.

Dahlstrom, jt. auth. see Bang.

Dahlstrom, jt. auth. see Muus.

Dahlstrom, jt. auth. see Schoitz.

Dahlstrom & Company. Don't Believe Everything You Read. (Illus.). 40p. (Prog. Bk.). 1984. pap. text ed. 2.99 (ISBN 0-940712-29-6). Dahlstrom & Co.

Dahlstrom, C Sandbach see Sandbach-Dahlstrom, C.

Dahlstrom, Carl E. Strindberg's Dramatic Expressionism. LC 64-14697. Repr. of 1930 ed. 26.50 (ISBN 0-405-08426-9, Blom Pubns). Ayer Co Pubs.

Dahlstrom, Daniel O., ed. Practical Reasoning: ACPA Proceedings, 1984, Vol. 58. 250p. 1985. pap. 12.00 (ISBN 0-918090-18-0). Am Cath Philo.

--Realism. (ACPA Proceedings: Vol. 59). 250p. 1985. 15.00 (ISBN 0-918090-19-9). Am Cath Philo.

Dahlstrom, Harry S. The Company Editor: Editing & Proofreading. (Illus.). 128p. (Orig.). 1984. pap. text ed. 3.99 (ISBN 0-940712-11-3, Study Buddy). Dahlstrom & Co.

--Don't Let People Rip You Off. (Illus.). 40p. (Orig., Prog. Bk.). 1984. pap. text ed. 2.99 (ISBN 0-940712-26-1). Dahlstrom & Co.

--Hey, That's Me: The American Teenager. (Illus.). 40p. (Orig.). 1984. pap. text ed. 2.99 (ISBN 0-940712-30-X). Dahlstrom & Co.

--Job Hunting Handbook. (Illus.). 50p. (Orig., Prog. Bk.). 1984. pap. text ed. 2.99 (ISBN 0-940712-09-1, Study Buddy). Dahlstrom & Co.

--Study Skills Handbook. (Illus.). 50p. (Orig., Prog. Bk.). 1984. pap. text ed. 2.99 (ISBN 0-940712-10-5, Study Buddy). Dahlstrom & Co.

Dahlstrom, J. & Ryel, D. Promises to Keep: Reading & Writing About Values. 1977. pap. text ed. 16.95 (ISBN 0-13-731059-5). P-H.

Dahlstrom, Leona, jt. ed. see Dahlstrom, W. Grant.

Dahlstrom, W. Grant & Dahlstrom, Leona, eds. Basic Readings on the MMPI: A New Selection on Personality Measurement. 1980. 29.50x (ISBN 0-8166-0903-9). U of Minn Pr.

Dahlstrom, W. Grant, et al. MMPI Handbook: Clinical Interpretation, Vol. 1. revised ed. LC 74-172933. (Illus.). 1972. 45.00x (ISBN 0-8166-0589-0). U of Minn Pr.

--An MMPI Handbook: Research Applications, Vol. 2. rev. ed. LC 74-26244. 624p. 1975. 45.00x (ISBN 0-8166-0725-7). U of Minn Pr.

Dahl-Wolfe, Louise. Louise Dahl-Wolfe: A Photographer's Handbook. (Illus.). 192p. 1984. 16.95 (ISBN 0-312-49911-6, Pub. by Marek). St Martin.

Dahm, Charles & Ghelardi, Robert. Power & Authority in the Catholic Church: Cardinal Cody in Chicago. LC 81-40453. 334p. 1982. text ed. 22.95 (ISBN 0-268-01546-5). U of Notre Dame Pr.

Dahm, H. Vladimir Solovyev & Max Scheler: A Contribution to History of Phenomenology in Attempt to a Comparing Interpretation. Wright, Kathleen, tr. LC 74-83007. (Sovietica Ser: No. 34). (Illus.). 406p. 1975. lib. bdg. 60.50 (ISBN 90-277-0507-0, Reidel Holland). Kluwer Academic.

Dahm, Thomas E. Van see Van Dahm, Thomas E.

Dahmann, Donald C. Locals & Cosmopolitans: Patterns of Spatial Mobility During the Transition from Youth to Early Adulthood. LC 82-2721. (Research Papers Ser.: No. 204). 1982. pap. 10.00 (ISBN 0-89065-110-8). U Chicago Dept Geog.

Dahme, Lena F. Women in the Life & Art of Conrad Ferdinand Meyer. LC 77-163662. (Columbia University. Germanic Studies, New Ser.: No. 4). Repr. of 1936 ed. 27.00 (ISBN 0-404-50454-X). AMS Pr.

Dahmen, H. D., jt. auth. see Brandt, S.

Dahmer, Sondra & Kahl, Kurt. The Waiter & Waitress Training Manual. 2nd ed. LC 73-83574. 112p. 1982. pap. 12.95 (ISBN 0-8436-2251-2). Van Nos Reinhold.

Dahmke, Mark. Microcomputer Operating Systems. 240p. 1982. pap. 18.95 (ISBN 0-07-015071-0, BYTE Bks). McGraw.

Dahmke, Mark & Ciarcia, S. The Byte Guide to CP-M. 216p. 1983. pap. 16.95 (ISBN 0-07-015072-9, BYTE Bks). McGraw.

Dahms, Alan M. Emotional Intimacy: Overlooked Requirement for Survival. LC 72-78443. (Illus.). 154p. 1972. 6.95 (ISBN 0-87108-184-9). Publishers Consult.

Dahms, Erna M. Zeit und Zeiterlebnis in den Werken Max Frischs: Bedeutung und Technische Darstellung. (Quellen und Forschungen zur Sprach und Kulturgeschichte der Germanischen Voelker). 1976. 30.40 (ISBN 3-11-006679-3). De Gruyter.

Dahmus, Joseph. The Puzzling Gospels. (Basics of Christian Thought: Vol. 3). 1985. 10.95 (ISBN 0-88347-182-5). Thomas More.

--Seven Decisive Battles of the Middle Ages. LC 83-13490. (Illus.). 270p. (Orig.). 1983. lib. bdg. 23.95X (ISBN 0-8304-1030-9). Nelson-Hall.

--Seven Medieval Historians. LC 81-11332. 320p. 1981. text ed. 23.95x (ISBN 0-88229-712-0); pap. 11.95 (ISBN 0-88229-795-3). Nelson-Hall.

--William Courtenay: Archbishop of Canterbury, 1381-1396. LC 66-18194. 1966. 28.75x (ISBN 0-271-73121-4). Pa St U Pr.

Dahmus, Joseph H. Prosecution of John Wyclyf. 167p. 1970. Repr. of 1952 ed. 17.50 (ISBN 0-208-00953-1, Archon). Shoe String.

Dahneke, Barton E. Measurement of Suspended Particles by Quasi-Elastic Light Scattering. 570p. 1983. 48.50 (ISBN 0-471-87289-X, Pub. by Wiley-Interscience). Wiley.

Dahnsen, Alan. Aircraft. LC 77-15092. (Easy-Read Fact Bks.). (Illus.). (gr. 2-4). 1978. 8.60 (ISBN 0-531-01351-0). Watts.

Dahood, Mitchell, ed. Psalms One, One - Fifty. (Anchor Bible Ser.: Vol. 16). 1966. 16.00 (ISBN 0-385-02765-6, Anchor Pr). Doubleday.

--Psalms Three, One Hundred One - One Hundred Fifty. LC 66-11766. (Anchor Bible Ser.: Vol. 17A). 18.00 (ISBN 0-385-00607-1, Anchor Pr). Doubleday.

--Psalms Two, Fifty-One to One Hundred. LC 66-11766. (Anchor Bible Ser.: Vol. 17). 1966. 16.00 (ISBN 0-385-03759-7, Anchor Pr). Doubleday.

Dahood, Roger. The Avowing of King Arthur: A Critical Edition. Edwards, A. S., ed. LC 83-48232. (Medieval Texts Ser.). 250p. 1984. lib. bdg. 26.00 (ISBN 0-8240-9427-1). Garland Pub.

Dahood, Roger, jt. ed. see Ackerman, Robert W.

Dahrendorf, ed. Europe's Economy in Crisis. 274p. 1982. text ed. 24.95x (ISBN 0-8419-0806-0). Holmes & Meier.

Dahrendorf, Ralf. Class & Class Conflict in Industrial Society. 1959. 27.50x (ISBN 0-8047-0560-7); pap. 9.95x (ISBN 0-8047-0561-5). Stanford U Pr.

--Classes & Conflits de Classes Dans la Societe Industrielle. (L' Oeuvre Sociologique: No. 1). 1972. pap. 14.00x (ISBN 90-2797-014-9). Mouton.

--Essays in the Theory of Society. LC 67-26526. 1968. 25.00x (ISBN 0-8047-0286-1); pap. 8.95 (ISBN 0-8047-0288-8, SP98). Stanford U Pr.

--Life Chances: Approaches to Social & Political Theory. LC 79-18685. 1980. lib. bdg. 15.00x (ISBN 0-226-13408-3). U of Chicago Pr.

--Life Changes: Approaches to Social & Political Theory. LC 79-18685. x, 182p. 1981. pap. 5.95x (ISBN 0-226-13443-1). U of Chicago Pr.

--The New Liberty: Survival & Justice in a Changing World. LC 75-186. x, 112p. 1975. 10.00x (ISBN 0-8047-0882-7). Stanford U Pr.

--On Britain. LC 82-60102. 198p. 1982. pap. 6.95x (ISBN 0-226-13410-5). U of Chicago Pr.

--Society & Democracy in Germany. LC 79-15142. 1980. Repr. of 1969 ed. lib. bdg. 37.50x (ISBN 0-313-22027-1, DASO). Greenwood.

--Society & Democracy in Germany. 1979. pap. 7.95x (ISBN 0-393-00953-X). Norton.

Dai, Bingham. Opium Addiction in Chicago. LC 72-124503. (Criminology, Law Enforcement, & Social Problems Ser.: No. 126). (Intro. index added). 1970. 17.00x (ISBN 0-87585-126-6). Patterson Smith.

Daiber, Franklin. Conservation of Tidal Marshes. 1986. price not set (ISBN 0-442-24873-3). Van Nos Reinhold.

Daiber, Franklin C. Animals of the Tidal Marsh. 432p. 1981. 26.95 (ISBN 0-442-24854-7). Van Nos Reinhold.

Daiche, David. Edinburgh. 1979. 25.00 (ISBN 0-241-89878-1, Pub. by Hamish Hamilton England). David & Charles.

Daiches, David. Critical Approaches to Literature. 2nd ed. LC 81-8180. 416p. (Orig.). 1981. pap. text ed. 14.95x (ISBN 0-582-49180-0). Longman.

--D. H. Lawrence. LC 77-1281. 1977. lib. bdg. 9.50 (ISBN 0-8414-3821-8). Folcroft.

--D. H. Lawrence. 240p. 1980. Repr. of 1963 ed. lib. bdg. 10.00 (ISBN 0-8492-4210-X). R West.

--Edinburgh. 272p. 1982. pap. 6.95 (ISBN 0-586-05237-2, Pub. by Granada England). Academy Chi Pubs.

--Glasgow. (Illus.). 256p. 1982. pap. 7.95 (ISBN 0-586-05357-3, Pub. by Granada England). Academy Chi Pubs.

--God & the Poets: The Gifford Lectures, 1983. 1984. 29.95x (ISBN 0-19-812825-8). Oxford U Pr.

--King James Version of the English Bible. vii, 228p. 1968. Repr. of 1941 ed. 18.50 (ISBN 0-208-00493-9, Archon). Shoe String.

--Literature & Gentility in Scotland. 114p. 1982. 14.00x (ISBN 0-85224-438-X, Pub. by Edinburgh U Pr Scotland). Columbia U Pr.

--Literature & Society. LC 74-95422. (Studies in Comparative Literature, No. 35). 1970. Repr. of 1938 ed. lib. bdg. 49.95x (ISBN 0-8383-0970-4). Haskell.

--Milton. (Orig.). 1966. pap. 4.95x (ISBN 0-393-00347-7, Norton Lib). Norton.

--Milton: Paradise Lost. (Studies in English Literature: No. 76). 64p. 1983. pap. text ed. 6.95 (ISBN 0-7131-6389-5). E Arnold.

--New Literary Values. facs. ed. LC 68-54342. (Essay Index Reprint Ser). 1936. 15.00 (ISBN 0-8369-0358-7). Ayer Co Pubs.

--The Novel & the Modern World. rev. ed. LC 60-11134. xii, 220p. 1984. pap. text ed. 9.00x (ISBN 0-226-13470-9, Midway Reprint). U of Chicago Pr.
--The Place of Meaning in Poetry. 80p. 1980. Repr. of 1935 ed. lib. bdg. 15.00 (ISBN 0-8495-1054-6). Arden Lib.
--Poetry & the Modern World. 1978. Repr. of 1940 ed. lib. bdg. 20.00x (ISBN 0-374-92026-5). Octagon.
--The Present Age after Nineteen Twenty. 376p. Date not set. Repr. of 1966 ed. lib. bdg. 40.00 (ISBN 0-89760-221-8). Telegraph Bks.
--Robert Fergusson. (Scottish Writers Ser.). 127p. (Orig.). 1983. pap. 6.50x (ISBN 0-7073-0313-3, Pub. by Scottish Academic Pr Scotland). Columbia U Pr.
--Stevenson & the Art of Fiction. 1980. Repr. of 1951 ed. lib. bdg. 9.50 (ISBN 0-89987-155-0). Darby Bks.
--Stevenson & the Art of Fiction. LC 73-1140. 1951. lib. bdg. 8.50 (ISBN 0-8414-1856-X). Folcroft.
--A Study of Literature for Readers & Critics. LC 71-152593. 240p. 1972. Repr. of 1948 ed. lib. bdg. 27.50x (ISBN 0-8371-6026-X, DARC). Greenwood.
--Two Studies. LC 77-1314. 1977. Repr. of 1958 ed. lib. bdg. 8.50 (ISBN 0-8414-3817-X). Folcroft.
--Two Studies. 32p. 1980. Repr. of 1958 ed. lib. bdg. 10.00 (ISBN 0-8492-4225-8). R West.
--Two Worlds. 1971. 8.50x (ISBN 0-85621-001-3, Pub. by Scottish Academic Pr Scotland). Columbia U Pr.
--Virginia Woolf. LC 78-12655. 1979. Repr. of 1963 ed. lib. bdg. 24.75x (ISBN 0-313-21187-6, DAVW). Greenwood.
--Willa Cather: A Critical Introduction. LC 71-136061. 1971. Repr. of 1951 ed. lib. bdg. 29.75 (ISBN 0-8371-5211-9, DAWC). Greenwood.
Daiches, David & Flower, John. Literary Landscape of the British Isles: A Narrative Atlas. 288p. 1981. pap. 9.95 (ISBN 0-14-005735-8). Penguin.
Daiches, David, jt. auth. see McDonald, Tamas.
Daiches, David, ed. Andrew Fletcher of Saltoun. 192p. 1979. 12.50x (ISBN 0-7073-0242-0, Pub. by Scottish Academic Pr Scotland). Columbia U Pr.
--A Companion to Scottish Culture. (Illus.). 441p. 1982. text ed. 42.50x (ISBN 0-8419-0792-7). Holmes & Meier.
Daiches, David, ed. see Bronte, Emily.
Daiches, David, ed. see Crawford, Thomas.
Daiches, David, ed. see McDiarmid, Matthew P.
Daiches, David, ed. see Shippey, T. A.
Daiches, Sol. People in Distress: A Geographical Perspective on Psychological Wellbeing. LC 81-4308. (Research Papers Ser.: No. 197). (Illus.). 199p. 1981. pap. 10.00 (ISBN 0-89065-104-3). U Chicago Dept Geog.
Daickes, David, intro. by see Stevenson, Robert Louis.
Daifuku, H. Jeddito Two Sixty-Four: A Basket Maker Three, Pueblo One Site in Northeastern Arizona. LC 61-2973. (HU PMP Ser.). 1961. 12.00 (ISBN 0-527-01285-8). Kraus Repr.
Daigh, Ralph. Maybe You Should Write a Book. LC 76-54952. 1977. pap. 3.95 (ISBN 0-13-566372-5). P-H.
--Maybe You Should Write a Book. LC 76-54952. 1977. 8.95 (ISBN 0-13-566380-6). P-H.
Daigle, A., jt. auth. see Maranda, D.
Daigle, Marsha, tr. see Fuchs, Eric.
Daigle, Pierre. The Mark of Mayonette. LC 79-57238. 77p. 1980. 8.95 (ISBN 0-914216-07-4). Acadian Pub.
Daigle, Pierre V. The Echo of Their Cries. 1978. 9.95 (ISBN 0-914216-04-X); pap. 7.95 (ISBN 0-914216-06-6). Acadian Pub.
--Plow, Sword & Prayers. new ed. Sonnier, Hilda, ed. 1978. pap. 5.65 (ISBN 0-914216-05-8). Acadian Pub.
Daigle, Pierre V. & Vidrine, Andrew. All Things Irreverent & Rebellious. (Illus.). 1980. pap. 3.95 (ISBN 0-914216-06-6). Acadian Pub.
Daigneault, Aubert, ed. Studies in Algebraic Logic. LC 74-84580. (Studies in Mathematics: No. 9). 1975. 16.50 (ISBN 0-88385-109-1). Math Assn.
Daigneault, Ernest A., jt. auth. see Brown, R. Don.
Daigon, Arthur, et al. Put It in Writing. 208p. 1978. pap. text ed. 9.95 (ISBN 0-15-573822-4, HC). HarBraceJ.
Daiken, Leslie. Children's Games Throughout the Year. LC 75-35067. (Studies in Play & Games). (Illus.). 1976. Repr. 23.50x (ISBN 0-405-07918-4). Ayer Co Pubs.
Daiker, Donald A., et al. Literature: Options for Reading & Writing. 1120p. 1985. pap. text ed. 21.50 scp (ISBN 0-06-041477-4, HarpC); write for info. instr's. manual (ISBN 0-06-361491-X). Har-Row.
--The Writer's Options: Combining to Composing. 2nd ed. 388p. 1982. pap. text ed. 11.95 scp (ISBN 0-06-041476-6, HarpC); instructors manual avail. (ISBN 0-06-361493-6). Har-Row.
Daiker, Donald A., et al, eds. Sentence Combining: A Rhetorical Perspective. 408p. 1985. 12.95 (ISBN 0-8093-1191-7). S Ill U Pr.
Daikichi, Irokawa. The Culture of the Meiji Period. Jansen, Marius B., ed. LC 84-42889. (Library of Asian Translations). 320p. 1985. text ed. 33.50x (ISBN 0-691-06634-5). Princeton U Pr.
Dail, Shirley M. Jesus Said "Leave Her Alone". (Illus.). 1979. pap. 2.95x (ISBN 0-9602440-0-X). Jesus-First.
Dailey, Charles A. Entrepreneurial Management: Going All Out for Results. LC 75-169017. (Illus.). Repr. of 1971 ed. 55.50 (ISBN 0-8357-9439-3, 2010382). Bks Demand UMI.
Dailey, Charles A. & Madsen, Ann M. How to Evaluate People in Business: The Track-Record Method of Making Correct Judgments. LC 82-16233. 240p. 1983. pap. 10.95 (ISBN 0-07-015087-7). McGraw.
Dailey, Dwight M. Concert Pieces for the Tenor Saxophone. 1983. 7.50 (ISBN 0-685-21777-9). Wahr.
Dailey, E. J. Practical Muskrat Raising. (Illus.). 136p. pap. 3.50 (ISBN 0-936622-17-2). A R Harding Pub.
Dailey, Eva Q. de see Quinones de Dailey, Eva.
Dailey, Janet. L' Aurore au Coeur de la Nuit. (Collection Harlequin Ser.). 192p. 1983. pap. 1.95 (ISBN 0-373-49339-8). Harlequin Bks.
--The Best Way to Lose. (Nightingale Large Print Paperback Books). 1985. pap. 9.95 (ISBN 0-8161-3699-8). G K Hall.
--Bluegrass King. (Nightingale Paperbacks Ser.). 201p. 1984. pap. 9.95 (ISBN 0-8161-3562-2, Large Print Bks). G K Hall.
--Calder Born, Calder Bred. (Orig.). 1983. pap. 6.95 (ISBN 0-671-83610-2). PB.
--Calder Born, Calder Bred. 384p. 1984. pap. 3.95 (ISBN 0-671-50250-6). PB.
--Calder Born, Calder Bred. Large Print ed. LC 83-18056. 769p. 1984. Repr. of 1983 ed. 16.95 (ISBN 0-89621-503-2). Thorndike Pr.
--Dangerous Masquerade. (Nightingale Paperbacks Ser.). 1984. pap. 9.95 (ISBN 0-8161-3563-0, Large Print Bks). G K Hall.
--Fiesta San Antonio. (Nightingale Paperbacks Ser.). 1984. pap. 9.95 (ISBN 0-8161-3561-4, Large Print Bks). G K Hall.
--For Love of God. 1985. pap. 2.95 (ISBN 0-671-55460-3). PB.
--For the Love of God. (Nightingale Paperbacks Ser.). 1984. pap. 9.95 (ISBN 0-8161-3697-1, Large Print Bks). G K Hall.
--Foxfire Light. (Nightingale Ser.). 1983. pap. 9.95 (ISBN 0-8161-3494-4, Large Print Bks). G K Hall.
--Giant of Mesabi. (Premiere Author Editions Ser.). 192p. 1983. pap. 1.95 (ISBN 0-373-80651-5). Harlequin Bks.
--The Glory Game. 1985. 16.95 (ISBN 0-671-55544-8). S&S.
--The Hostage Bride. 1984. pap. 2.95 (ISBN 0-671-53023-2). PB.
--The Lancaster Men. 1984. pap. 2.95 (ISBN 0-671-54383-0). PB.
--L'Epouse De Juin. (Harlequin Romantique). 192p. 1983. pap. 1.95 (ISBN 0-373-41194-4). Harlequin Bks.
--Mistletoe & Holly. (Nightingale Ser.). 190p. 1983. pap. 8.95 (ISBN 0-8161-3543-6, Large Print Bks). G K Hall.
--Night of the Cotillion. (Nightingale Ser.). 203p. 1983. pap. 9.95 (ISBN 0-8161-3560-6, Large Print Bks). G K Hall.
--Night Way. (General Ser.). 1984. lib. bdg. 13.95 (ISBN 0-8161-3632-7, Large Print). G K Hall.
--Nightway. (Orig.). 1985. pap. 3.95 (ISBN 0-671-47980-6). PB.
--The Pride of Hannah Wade. 1985. pap. 3.95 (ISBN 0-671-49801-0). PB.
--En Revant De Maud. (Harlequin Romantique Ser.). 192p. 1983. pap. 1.95 (ISBN 0-373-41229-0). Harlequin Bks.
--Ride the Thunder. 1985. pap. 3.95 (ISBN 0-671-47981-4). PB.
--Ride the Thunder. (General Ser.). 1984. lib. bdg. 13.95 (ISBN 0-8161-3666-1, Large Print Bks). G K Hall.
--The Rogue. 1983. pap. 3.95 (ISBN 0-671-49982-3). PB.
--The Rogue. (Hall Large Print Bk.). 1985. lib. bdg. 13.95 (ISBN 0-8161-3667-X, Large Print Bks); pap. text ed. 9.95 (ISBN 0-8161-3739-0). G K Hall.
--The Second Time. (Silhouette Romances Ser.). 1984. lib. bdg. 8.95 (ISBN 0-8398-2801-2, Gregg). G K Hall.
--Separate Cabins. (Nightingale Paperbacks Ser.). 199p. 1984. pap. 9.95 (ISBN 0-8161-3599-1, Large Print Bks). G K Hall.
--Separate Cabins. (Silhouette Romances Ser.). 1984. lib. bdg. 8.95 (ISBN 0-8398-2800-4, Gregg). G K Hall.
--Silver Wings, Santiago Blue. 480p. 1984. 15.95 (ISBN 0-671-50405-3, Pub. by Poseidon); deluxe ed. 40.00 (ISBN 0-671-50906-3). S&S.
--Silver Wings, Santiago Blue. (General Ser.). 1984. lib. bdg. 15.95 (ISBN 0-8161-3725-0, Large Print Bks); pap. 10.95 (ISBN 0-8161-3762-5). G K Hall.
--Silver Wings, Santiago Blue. 1985. pap. 4.50 (ISBN 0-317-19744-4). PB.
--Stands a Calder Man. (Orig.). 1983. pap. 3.95 (ISBN 0-671-47398-0). PB.
--Stands A Calder Man. Incl. This Calder Range; This Caldor Sky; Calder Born, Calder Bred. boxed set 15.80 (ISBN 0-671-90082-X). PB.
--Terms of Surrender. (Nightingale Ser.). 1985. pap. 9.95 (ISBN 0-8161-3698-X, Large Print Bks). G K Hall.
--Terms of Surrender. 1985. pap. 2.95 (ISBN 0-671-55795-5). PB.
--That Carolina Summer. (Harlequin Presents Ser.). 192p. 1982. pap. 1.75 (ISBN 0-373-10488-X). Harlequin Bks.
--This Calder Range. (Orig.). 1985. pap. 3.95 (ISBN 0-671-83608-0). PB.
--This Calder Range. large print ed. LC 82-19534. 665p. 1983. Repr. of 1982 ed. 15.95 (ISBN 0-89621-420-6). Thorndike Pr.
--This Calder Sky. 1982. pap. 3.95 (ISBN 0-671-46478-7). PB.
--This Calder Sky. large print ed. LC 82-16862. 667p. 1982. Repr. of 1981 ed. 15.95 (ISBN 0-89621-396-X). Thorndike Pr.
--Touch the Wind. 1985. pap. 3.95 (ISBN 0-671-49230-6). PB.
--Touch the Wind. (General Ser.). 1985. lib. bdg. 13.95 (ISBN 0-8161-3812-5, Large Print Bks); pap. 9.95 (ISBN 0-8161-3838-9, Large Print Bks). G K Hall.
--Western Man. (Nightingale Large Print Ser.). 1985. pap. text ed. 9.95 (ISBN 0-8161-3617-3, Large Print Bks). G K Hall.
--Wildcatter's Woman. (Nightingale Ser.). 1982. pap. 8.95 (ISBN 0-8161-3440-5, Large Print Bks). G K Hall.
--With a Little Luck. (Harlequin Presents Ser.). 192p. 1982. pap. 1.75 (ISBN 0-373-10482-0). Harlequin Bks.
Dailey, Robert H. & Callaham, Michael, eds. Controversies in Trauma Management. (Clinics in Emergency Medicine Ser.: Vol. 6). (Illus.). 257p. 1985. text ed. 30.00 (ISBN 0-443-08192-1). Churchill.
Dailey, Stephanie, tr. see Seleskovitch, Danica.
Dailey, Timothy E., jt. auth. see Wickman, Peter M.
Daille, Jean. Exposition of Colossians. 698p. 1983. lib. bdg. 24.95 (ISBN 0-86524-141-4, 5104). Klock & Klock.
Daily, Benjamin W. Ability of High School Pupils to Select Essential Data in Solving Problems. LC 73-176704. (Columbia University. Teachers College. Contributions to Education: No. 190). Repr. of 1925 ed. 22.50 (ISBN 0-404-55190-4). AMS Pr.
Daily, Elaine K. & Schroeder, John S. Hemodynamic Waveforms: Exercises in Identification & Analysis. 1st ed. LC 82-12419. (Illus.). 277p. 1983. pap. text ed. 16.95 (ISBN 0-8016-1212-8). Mosby.
--Techniques in Bedside Hemodynamic Monitoring. 2nd ed. LC 80-16594. (Illus.). 198p. 1980. pap. text ed. 15.95 (ISBN 0-8016-4363-5). Mosby.
Daily, J. W. & Harleman, D. R. Fluid Dynamics. 1966. 29.95 (ISBN 0-201-01421-1). Addison-Wesley.
Daily, James M. Interpersonal Skills for the Manager. LC 82-73405. 275p. 1982. ringed binder 29.95x (ISBN 0-87094-350-2). Dow Jones-Irwin.
Daily, Janet. Touch the Wind. 320p. 1985. Repr. of 1979 ed. deluxe ed. 30.00 (ISBN 0-88733-000-2, Brandywine Bks). Underwood Miller.
Daily, Jay E. The Anatomy of Censorship. (Books in Library & Information Science: Vol. 6). 424p. 1973. 45.00 (ISBN 0-8247-6065-4). Dekker.
--Cataloging Phonerecordings: Problems & Possibilities. (Practical Library & Information Science Ser.: Vol. 1). 192p. 1975. 39.75 (ISBN 0-8247-6196-0). Dekker.
--Organizing Nonprint Materials. LC 72-87849. (Bks. in Library & Information Science: Vol. 3). 200p. 1972. 39.75 (ISBN 0-8247-6044-1). Dekker.
Daily Nonpareil Office. Sketches of Springfield in 1856. (Annual Monograph Ser.). 96p. 1973. pap. 3.00 facsimile reprint (ISBN 0-686-29090-9). Clark County Hist Soc.
Daily Telegraph. Daily Telegraph Crossword. 2nd ed. 1982. pap. 2.95 (ISBN 0-14-005872-9). Penguin.
Daimler, Harriet, pseud. Darling. LC 82-84624. 176p. (Orig.). 1983. pap. 3.50 (ISBN 0-394-62458-0, B489, BC). Grove.
Daimler, Harriet. Innocence. LC 82-84627. 152p. 1983. pap. 3.50 (ISBN 0-394-62436-X, B490, BC). Grove.
--The Woman Thing. LC 83-84628. 192p. 1984. pap. 3.50 (ISBN 0-394-62459-9, B491, BC). Grove.
Daims, Diva & Grimes, Janet. Towards a Feminist Tradition: An Annotated Bibliography of Novels in English by Women, 1891-1920. Robinson, Doris, ed. 1982. lib. bdg. 91.00 (ISBN 0-8240-9523-5). Garland Pub.
Daims, Diva, jt. auth. see Grimes, Janet.
Dain, Norman. Clifford W. Beers: Advocate for the Insane. LC 79-24290. (Contemporary Community Health Ser.). 1980. 26.95 (ISBN 0-8229-3419-1). U of Pittsburgh Pr.
--Concepts of Insanity in the United States, 1789-1865. 1964. 30.00x (ISBN 0-8135-0443-0). Rutgers U Pr.
Dain, Phyllis. The New York Public Library: A History of Its Founding & Early Years. LC 70-163359. (Illus.). 466p. (Orig.). 1972. 21.00 (ISBN 0-87104-131-6). NY Pub Lib.
Dainard, J. A. Editing Correspondence: Papers Given at the Fourteenth Annual Conference on Editorial Problems, University of Toronto, 3-4 November 1978. LC 80-22003. (Conferences on Editorial Problems Ser.). 143p. 1979. lib. bdg. 22.00 (ISBN 0-8240-2429-X). Garland Pub.
Daines, David R. Water Legislation in the Andean Pact Countries. 200p. 1974. 10.00 (ISBN 0-87421-066-6). Utah St U Pr.
Daines, David R. & Falconi, Gonazalo. Legislacion de Aguas en los Paises del Grupo Andino. 200p. (Span.). 1974. pap. 10.00 (ISBN 0-87421-067-4). Utah St U Pr.
Daines, Delva. Reading in the Content Areas: Strategies for Classroom Teachers. 1982. text ed. 13.60x (ISBN 0-673-16025-4). Scott F.
Daines, Derrick. Twenty-six BASIC Programs for Your Micro. LC 82-61971. 176p. 1983. pap. 8.95 (ISBN 0-672-22047-4, 22047). Sams.
Dainora, J., et al. Materials of Construction for Use in an LNG Pipeline. 130p. 1968. 7.00 (ISBN 0-318-12652-4, L40000). Am Gas Assn.
Dainow, Joseph. The Role of Judicial Decisions & Doctrine in Civil Law & in Mixed Jurisdictions. LC 73-90871. xviii, 350p. 1974. 32.50x (ISBN 0-8071-0080-3). La State U Pr.
Dainow, Joseph, ed. Essays on the Civil Law of Obligations. LC 75-96256. xii, 314p. 1969. 27.50x (ISBN 0-8071-0912-6). La State U Pr.
Dains, Joyce, jt. auth. see Thompson, June.
Daintith, J. & Nelson, R. D. The Penguin Dictionary of Mathematics. (Reference Ser.). 304p. 1985. pap. 5.95 (ISBN 0-14-051119-9). Penguin.
Daintith, John. A Dictionary of Physical Sciences. LC 76-41039. (Illus.). 1977. 25.00x (ISBN 0-87663-723-3, Pica Pr). Universe.
Daintith, John, ed. Dictionary of Chemistry. 1982. pap. 5.72i (ISBN 0-06-463559-7, EH-559). Har-Row.
--Dictionary of Chemistry. (Illus.). 240p. 1982. pap. 5.72i (ISBN 0-06-463559-7, EH 559). B&N NY.
--A Dictionary of Physical Sciences. (A Helix Bk.: No. 379). (Illus.). 340p. 1983. pap. 9.95 (ISBN 0-8226-0379-9). Rowman & Allanheld.
--Dictionary of Physics. 216p. 1982. pap. 6.25i (ISBN 0-06-463560-0, EH-560). Har-Row.
--The Facts on File Dictionary of Chemistry. 224p. 1981. 14.95 (ISBN 0-87196-513-5). Facts on File.
--The Facts on File Dictionary of Physics. 248p. 1981. 14.95 (ISBN 0-87196-511-9). Facts on File.
Dainty, J. C. & Shaw, R. Image Science: Principles, Analysis, & Evaluation of Picture-Imaging Processes. 1975. 69.50 (ISBN 0-12-200850-2). Acad Pr.
Dainville, F. Langage des Geographes Termes, Signes, Couleurs des Cartes Anciennes: 1500-1800. 404p. (Fr.). 1964. pap. 49.95 (ISBN 0-686-56973-3, M-6100). French & Eur.
Dair, Carl. Design with Type. LC 66-23932. 1982. pap. 15.95 (ISBN 0-8020-6519-8). U of Toronto Pr.
Dair, Christina. Winning Ways. (Second Chance at Love Ser.: No. 217). 192p. 1984. pap. 1.95 (ISBN 0-515-08073-X). Jove Pubns.
Daires, John L. Man & His Universe. 1937. 15.00 (ISBN 0-686-17421-6). Ridgeway Bks.
Dais, Eugene E., ed. Law & the Ecological Challenge: Amintaphil, Vol. 2. LC 78-61842. xxiv, 265p. 1979. lib. bdg. 35.00 (ISBN 0-930342-66-6). W S Hein.
Daisetz Teitaro Suzuki. Studies in the Lankavatara Sutra. LC 81-12179. 464p. 1981. pap. 15.00 (ISBN 0-87773-754-1, Prajna). Great Eastern.
Daisne, Johan. Filmographic Dictionary of World Literature, 2 vols, Vol.1. (Fr, Flemish & Ger). 1971. Vol. 1. text ed. 82.50x (ISBN 0-391-01585-0); Vol. 2. text ed. 89.50x (ISBN 0-391-01586-9). Humanities.
Daisne, Johan, pseud. The Man Who Had His Hair Cut Short. Sackett, S. J. N, tr. from Flemish. LC 75-5001. 224p. 1976. Repr. of 1965 ed. lib. bdg. 18.75x (ISBN 0-8371-7426-0, THMW). Greenwood.
Daisne, John. Filmographic Dictionary of World Literature: Supplement A-Z, Vol. 3. 1978. text ed. 108.50x (ISBN 0-391-01587-7). Humanities.
Daisy, Carol A., jt. ed. see Laliberte, Elizabeth.
Daitches, David & Flower, John. Literary Landscapes of the British Isles: A Narrative Atlas. (Illus.). 288p. 1978. 14.95 (ISBN 0-87196-305-1). Facts on File.
Daitz, Stephen G. Aristophanes' Birds. (Living Voice & Greek of Latin Literature Ser.). 93p. 1983. bk. plus 2 audio cassettes 29.95x, (ISBN 0-88432-117-7, 23670). J Norton Pubs.
--Euripides' "Hekabe". (Living Voice of Greek & Latin Literature Ser.). 60p. 1981. with 2 cassettes 29.95x (ISBN 0-88432-084-7, S23650). J Norton Pubs.
--Jerusalem Palimpsest of Euripides. facsimile ed. (Illus.). 1970. 42.50x (ISBN 3-11-001193-X). De Gruyter.
--The Pronunciation & Reading of Classical Latin: A Practical Guide. LC 85-740004. 1984. incl. 2 audio cassettes 19.95 (ISBN 0-88432-125-8, 23675, Audio-Forum). J Norton Pubs.
--Pronunciation of Ancient Greek: A Practical Guide. 14p. 1981. with 2 cassettes 19.95x (ISBN 0-88432-083-9, S23660). J Norton Pubs.

--A Recital of Ancient Greek Poetry. (The Living Voice of Greek & Latin Literature Ser.). 52p. 1978. 4 audio cassettes incl. 48.00x (ISBN 0-88432-029-4, 23600). J Norton Pubs.
Daitzman, Reid. Diagnosis & Intervention in Behavior Therapy & Behavioral Medicine, Vol. 2. 1985. text ed. 39.00 (ISBN 0-8261-4042-4). Springer Pub.
Daitzman, Reid J. Modern Modern Times. 75p. 1981. pap. text ed. 2.95 (ISBN 0-938340-01-8). World Univ Pr.
--Renaissance. 75p. 1983. pap. 2.95 (ISBN 0-938340-02-6). World Univ Pr.
Daitzman, Reid J., ed. Diagnosis & Intervention in Behavior Therapy & Behavioral Medicine, Vol. 1. 320p. 1983. text ed. 34.95 (ISBN 0-8261-4040-8). Springer Pub.
Daiute. Computers & Writing. 200p. (Orig.). 1983. pap. 16.95 (ISBN 0-201-10368-0). Addison-Wesley.
Daiute, Robert J. & Gorman, Kenneth A. Library Operations Research: Computer Programming of Circulation. LC 73-20303. 1974. 28.50. Oceana.
Dajani, Burhan. The Palestine Yearbook, 1973. (Arabic.). 1977. 30.00 (ISBN 0-88728-068-4). Inst Palestine.
Dajani, Burhan, ed. The Palestine Yearbook, 1972. (Arabic.). 1977. 30.00 (ISBN 0-88728-067-6). Inst Palestine.
Dajani, M. S., jt. auth. see Daoudi, M. S.
Dajani, Majed. Oil, Money & Politics. LC 83-90900. 1984. 8.95 (ISBN 0-533-05924-0). Vantage.
Dajoz, R. Introduction to Ecology. LC 76-27620. 416p. 1976. pap. 13.50x (ISBN 0-8448-1008-8). Crane-Russak Co.
Dakan, Peggy, jt. auth. see Bruno, Janet.
Dakang, Zuo, jt. ed. see Biswas, Asu K.
Dakas, Chris & Hausman, Carl D. Common Sense Self Defense. (Illus.). 200p. 1984. pap. 8.95 (ISBN 0-89769-080-X, Dist. by Caroline Hse.). Pine Mntn.
Dake, jt. auth. see Will.
Dake, Antonie C. In the Spirit of the Red Banteng: Indonesian Communists Between Moscow & Peking, 1959-1965. (Illus.). 1973. text ed. 35.20x (ISBN 90-2797-183-8). Mouton.
Dake, Donette, jt. auth. see Will, Mimi.
Dake, Henry C. Art of Gem Cutting. 6th ed. pap. 2.50 (ISBN 0-910652-07-4). Gembooks.
Dake, L. P. Fundamentals of Reservoir Engineering. (Developments in Petroleum Science: Vol. 8). 444p. 1979. pap. 34.00 (ISBN 0-444-41830-X). Elsevier.
Dakers, Andrew. Robert Burns: His Life & Genius. LC 72-3378. (English Literature Ser., No. 33). 1972. Repr. of 1923 ed. lib. bdg. 39.95x (ISBN 0-8383-1507-0). Haskell.
Dakers, Caroline. The Blue Plaque Guide to London. (Illus.). 318p. 1982. 17.95 (ISBN 0-393-01528-9). Norton.
Dakers, Elaine K. Titus Oates. LC 71-114506. (Illus.). 1971. Repr. of 1949 ed. lib. bdg. 18.50x (ISBN 0-8371-4783-2, DATO). Greenwood.
Dakhil, Fahd, et al. Housing Problems in Developing Countries: Proceedings of IAHS International Conference 1978, 2 vols. LC 78-65357. 1979. Set, 1563p. 220.95x (ISBN 0-471-27561-1); Vol. 1, 751p. 102.95x (ISBN 0-471-27558-1); Vol. 2, 812p. 109.95x (ISBN 0-471-27559-X, Pub. by Wiley-Interscience). Wiley.
Dakin, Anthony F. The Supreme Fakers of Our Contemporary Civilization & the Moral & Intellectual Degeneration of Mankind. (Illus.). 129p. 1983. 85.75x (ISBN 0-89266-424-X). Am Classical Coll Pr.
Dakin, Arthur. Calvinism. LC 72-153211. 1971. Repr. of 1940 ed. 21.00x (ISBN 0-8046-1521-7, Pub. by Kennikat). Assoc Faculty Pr.
Dakin, Arthur H. Paul Elmer Moore. (Illus.). 1960. 40.00x (ISBN 0-691-06089-4). Princeton U Pr.
Dakin, C., jt. auth. see Archer, M.
Dakin, Douglas. The Greek Struggle for Independence, 1821-1833. LC 72-89798. 1973. 42.50x (ISBN 0-520-02342-0). U of Cal Pr.
--Turgot & the Ancient Regime in France. 1965. lib. bdg. 27.50x (ISBN 0-374-92033-8). Octagon.
Dakin, Douglas, ed. see Forster, Edward S.
Dakin, Edwin F. Mrs. Eddy: The Biography of a Virginal Mind. 13.25 (ISBN 0-8446-0570-0). Peter Smith.
Dakin, H. S. High-Voltage Photography. 3rd ed. LC 74-77233. 1978. pap. 4.95 (ISBN 0-685-82476-4). H S Dakin.
Dakin, J. C. Education in New Zealand. (World Education Ser.). (Illus.). 143p. 1973. 14.50 (ISBN 0-208-01343-1, Archon). Shoe String.
Dakin, John. Feedback from Tomorrow. (Research in Planning & Design Ser.). 492p. 1980. 33.50x (ISBN 0-85086-071-7, NO. 3020, Pub. by Pion England). Methuen Inc.
Dakin, John, ed. see Mullally, Frederick.
Dakin, Susanna. The Perennial Adventure: A Tribute to Alice Eastwood, 1859-1943. 48p. 1954. 2.50 (ISBN 0-940228-09-2). Calif Acad Sci.
Dakin, Susanna B. A Scotch Paisano in Old Los Angeles: Hugo Reid's Life in California, 1832-1852. (Cal Ser.: No. 397). 1979. pap. 3.95 (ISBN 0-520-03717-0). U of Cal Pr.
Dakin, William J. Modern Problems in Biology. 1979. Repr. of 1929 ed. lib. bdg. 12.50 (ISBN 0-8492-4206-1). R West.
Dal, Bjorn. The Butterflies of Northern Europe. Morris, Michael, ed. Littleboy, Roger, tr. (Illus.). 128p. 1982. 13.00 (ISBN 0-7099-0810-5, Pub. by Croom Helm Ltd). Longwood Pub Group.
Dalaba, Oliver V. That None Be Lost. LC 77-74553. (Workers' Training Ser.). 128p. 1977. 1.25 (ISBN 0-88243-621-X, 02-621). Gospel Pub.
Daladier, Edouard. In Defense of France. facsimile ed. LC 74-156637. (Essay Index Reprint Ser). Repr. of 1939 ed. 18.00 (ISBN 0-8369-2352-9). Ayer Co Pubs.
Dalai, Lama. Selected Writings. 1973. lib. bdg. 79.95 (ISBN 0-87968-508-5). Krishna Pr.
Dalai Lama. My Land & My People. (Illus.). 271p. 1983. Repr. of 1962 ed. 6.95 (ISBN 0-9611474-0-7). Potola Corp.
--The Opening of the Wisdom Eye. LC 70-152732. 178p. 1981. pap. 5.75 (ISBN 0-8356-0549-3, Quest). Theos Pub Hse.
Dalai Lama of Tibet. My Land & My People. 3rd ed. (Illus.). 271p. 1983. Repr. of 1962 ed. 6.95. Potala.
Dalai Lama XIV. Kindness, Clarity & Insight. Hopkins, Jeffrey & Napper, Elizabeth, eds. Hopkins, Jeffrey, tr. LC 84-51198. (Illus.). 250p. (Orig.). 1984. pap. 10.95 (ISBN 0-937938-18-1). Snow Lion.
Dalal, jt. auth. see Watkins.
Dalal, C. B., compiled by. Gandhi Nineteen Fifteen to Nineteen Forty-Eight: A Detailed Chronology. 210p. 1971. 12.00x (ISBN 0-8426-0285-2). Verry.
Dalal, C. B., ed. see Desai, Mahadev.
Dalal, Minakshi L. Conflict in Sanskrit Drama. LC 73-904777. 342p. 1973. 15.00xcancelled (ISBN 0-8002-0546-4). Intl Pubns Serv.
Dalal, Nergis. The Inner Door. 144p. 1975. pap. 1.85 (ISBN 0-89253-028-6). Ind-US Inc.
--Yoga for Rejuvenation. 128p. (Orig.). 1984. pap. 6.95 (ISBN 0-7225-0948-0). Thorsons Pubs.
Dalal, Tarla. Indian Vegetarian Cookbook. (Illus.). 128p. 1985. 13.95 (ISBN 0-312-41403-X). St Martin.
Dalal, Tarlal. The Joys of Vegetarian Cooking. 17.00 (ISBN 0-89410-524-8, Pub. by UBSPD India). Three Continents.
Dalal-Clayton, D. B., ed. Black's Agricultural Dictionary. (Illus.). 512p. 1981. 28.50x (ISBN 0-389-20261-4, 07079). B&N Imports.
--Black's Agricultural Dictionary. 500p. 1985. 31.50x (ISBN 0-389-20556-7). B&N Imports.
D'Alamanon, Bertran. Troubadour Bertram D'Alamanon. Repr. of 1902 ed. 25.00 (ISBN 0-384-04080-2). Johnson Repr.
Daland, Robert T. Exploring Brazilian Bureaucracy: Performance & Pathology. LC 80-67246. 455p. 1981. lib. bdg. 30.50 (ISBN 0-8191-1468-5); pap. text ed. 19.00 (ISBN 0-8191-1469-3). U Pr of Amer.
D'Albas, Andrieu. Death of a Navy: Japanese Naval Action in World War II. 1957. 10.50 (ISBN 0-8159-5302-X). Devin.
D'Alberti, Sarah, ed. Tasso: Aminta. 1967. pap. 3.50x (ISBN 0-913298-21-2). S F Vanni.
Dalbey, Alice F. The Visitor's Guide to Point Reyes National Seashore. LC 73-89770. (Orig.). 1974. pap. 4.95 (ISBN 0-85699-098-1). Chatham Pr.
Dalbiez, Roland. Psychoanalytical Method & the Doctrine of Freud, 2 vols. facsimile ed. Lindsay, T. F., tr. from Fr. (Select Bibliographies Reprint Ser). Repr. of 1941 ed. 47.50 (ISBN 0-8369-6715-1). Ayer Co Pubs.
Dalbor, John B. Spanish Pronunciation. 2nd ed. LC 68-13502. 1980. text ed. 24.95 (ISBN 0-03-049056-1, HoltC). HR&W.
Dalbor, John B. & Sturcken, H. Tracy. Spanish in Review. LC 78-27055. 184p. 1979. pap. text ed. 24.00x (ISBN 0-471-03991-8). wkbk. 184 p. 12.00 (ISBN 0-471-03992-6). Wiley.
Dalbor, John B., jt. auth. see Yates, Donald A.
D'Albuquerque, Alfonso. The Commentaries of the Great Alfonso Dalboquerque, Second Viceroy of India, 4 Vols. Birch, Walter D., ed. & tr. from Portuguese. LC 74-134712. (Hakluyt Society Ser). 1970. Repr. of 1883 ed. Set. lib. bdg. 118.00 (ISBN 0-8337-0289-0). B Franklin.
Dalby, David. Black Through White: Patterns of Communication. (Hans Wolff Memorial Lecture Ser.). (Orig.). 1970. pap. text ed. 2.00 (ISBN 0-941934-02-0). Indiana Africa.
Dalby, David, ed. Language & History in Africa: Collected Papers Presented to the London Seminar on Language & History in Africa. 159p. 1970. 28.50x (ISBN 0-7146-2420-9, F Cass Co). Biblio Dist.
Dalby, Gill & Christmas, Liz. Spinning & Dyeing: An Introductory Manual. (Illus.). 135p. 1985. 22.50 (ISBN 0-7153-8515-1); pap. 12.50 (ISBN 0-7153-8675-1). David & Charles.
Dalby, J. Christian Mysticism & the Natural World. 148p. 1960. 7.95 (ISBN 0-227-67433-2). Attic Pr.
Dalby, Joseph, tr. see Grou, Jean-Nicholas.
Dalby, Lisa. Geisha. 1985. pap. 9.95 (ISBN 0-394-72893-9, Vin). Random.
Dalby, Liza, et al. All Japan: The Catalogue of Everything of Japanese. (Illus.). 224p. 1984. pap. 14.95 (ISBN 0-688-02530-7, Quill NY). Morrow.
Dalby, Liza C. Geisha. LC 82-21934. (Illus.). 408p. 1983. 25.00 (ISBN 0-520-04742-7). U of Cal Pr.
D'Alby, Meriel. Another Dimension: Living & the Quality of Being. 1982. 8.95 (ISBN 0-533-05042-1). Vantage.
Dalby, Richard, ed. see Wakefield, H. Russell.
Dalby, Thomas. Historical Account of the Rise & Growth of the West-India Colonies, & of the Great Advantages They Are to England, in Respect to Trade, London, 1690. LC 75-141095. (Research Library of Colonial Americana). 1972. Repr. of 1690 ed. 18.00 (ISBN 0-405-03300-1). Ayer Co Pubs.
Dalche, Jean G. Economie et Societe dans les Pays de la Couronne de Castille. 352p. 1982. 70.00x (ISBN 0-86078-096-1, Pub. by Variorum). State Mutual Bk.
Dalcho, Frederick. An Historical Account of the Protestant Episcopal Church, in South Carolina, from the First Settlement of the Province, to the War of the Revolution. LC 71-38445. (Religion in America, Ser. 2). 180p. 1972. Repr. of 1820 ed. 42.00 (ISBN 0-405-04064-4). Ayer Co Pubs.
Dal Cin, M., jt. ed. see Kramer, P.
Dal Cin, Mario, et al, eds. Fundamental Interactions at High Energy Three: Tracts in Mathematics & Natural Sciences, 5 vols. Incl. Vol. 1. Nonpolynomial Lagrangians Renormalization & Gravity. Salam, Abdus. 156p. 41.75 (ISBN 0-677-12050-8); Vol. 2. Broken Scale Variance & the Light Cone. Gell-Mann, M. & Wilson, K. 158p. 45.25 (ISBN 0-677-12060-5); Vol. 3. Invited Papers. Hamermesh, M. 166p. 44.25 (ISBN 0-677-12070-2); Vol. 4. Troubles in the External Field Problem for Invariant Wave Equations. Wightman, A. S. 76p. 30.25 (ISBN 0-677-12080-X); Vol. 5. Multiperipheral Dynamics. Chew, G. 90p. 30.25 (ISBN 0-677-12090-7). LC 79-85472. (Illus.). 646p. 1971. Set. 169.75 (ISBN 0-677-12100-8). Gordon.
Dal Co, Francesco. Figures of Architecture & Thought: German Architectural Culture 1890-1920. LC 85-42959. (Illus.). 200p. 1985. pap. 25.00 (ISBN 0-8478-0654-5). Rizzoli Intl.
Dal Co, Francesco, jt. auth. see Tafuri, Manfredo.
Dal Co, Francesco, ed. Kevin Roche. LC 85-43064. (Illus.). 320p. 1985. 45.00 (ISBN 0-8478-0680-4); pap. 29.95 (ISBN 0-317-31443-2). Rizzoli Intl.
Dal Co, Francesco & Mazzariol, Giuseppe, eds. Carlo Scarpa: The Complete Works. LC 84-43106. 319p. 1985. pap. 29.95 (ISBN 0-8478-0591-3). Rizzoli Intl.
Dalcourt, Gerard J. The Methods of Ethics. 254p. 1984. lib. bdg. 25.50 (ISBN 0-8191-3549-6); pap. text ed. 13.25 (ISBN 0-8191-3550-X). U Pr of Amer.
Dale. Pharmacy, Law & Ethics. 3rd ed. 604p. 1983. 26.00 (ISBN 0-85369-168-1, Pub. by Pharmaceutical Pr England). Rittenhouse.
Dale & Larsen, Sandy. Mark: Good News for Today. (Carpenter Studyguide). 80p. 1984. member's handbook 1.95 (ISBN 0-87788-540-0); saddle-stitched leader's handbook 2.95 (ISBN 0-87788-541-9). Shaw Pubs.
Dale, A. M. Metrica Analyses of Tragic Choruses-Dactylo-Epitrite. 101p. 1981. 35.00x (ISBN 0-900587-06-7, Pub. by Inst Class Stud England). State Mutual Bk.
--Metrical Analyses of Tragic Choruses: Fascicule 2: Aeolo-Choriambic. (Bulletin Supplement Ser.: No. 21). 155p. 1981. 50.00x (ISBN 0-900587-42-3, Pub. by Inst Class Stud England). State Mutual Bk.
Dale, A. M., ed. see Euripides.
Dale, Alan T. The Bible in the Classroom. 96p. (Orig.). 1973. pap. 4.95 (ISBN 0-8192-1151-6). Morehouse.
--The Crowd Is Waiting. (Rainbow Books, Bible Story Books for Children). 1976. pap. 1.00 (ISBN 0-8192-1208-3). Morehouse.
--I've Found the Sheep. (Rainbow Books, Bible Story Books for Children). 1976. pap. 1.00 (ISBN 0-8192-1206-7). Morehouse.
--Jesus Is Really Alive Again! (Rainbow Books, Bible Story Books for Children). 1976. pap. 1.00 (ISBN 0-8192-1209-1). Morehouse.
--New World. (Illus.). 429p. (Orig.). 1973. pap. 9.95 (ISBN 0-8192-1149-4). Morehouse.
--Paul the Traveler. (Rainbow Books, Bible Story Books for Children). 1976. pap. 1.00 (ISBN 0-8192-1211-3). Morehouse.
--Portrait of Jesus. (Illus.). 1979. 6.95 (ISBN 0-8317-7091-0, Mayflower Bks). Smith Pubs.
--Who's My Friend? (Rainbow Books (Bible Story Books for Children)). 16p. 1978. pap. 1.00 (ISBN 0-8192-1236-9). Morehouse.
--The Winding Quest. (Illus.). 432p. (Orig.). 1973. pap. 9.95 (ISBN 0-8192-1150-8). Morehouse.
--God Cares for Everybody, Everywhere. (Rainbow Books (Bible Story Books for Children)). (Orig.). 1978. pap. 1.00 (ISBN 0-8192-1237-7). Morehouse.
Dale, Alexander. Healthy Hair & Common Sense. 11.95x (ISBN 0-911638-02-4). Cancer Control Soc.
Dale, Alfred G. An Economic Survey Method for Small Areas. (Area Economic Studies: No. 1). 1955. pap. 4.00 (ISBN 0-87755-020-4). Bureau Busn UT.
--Nuclear Power Development in the U. S. to Nineteen Sixty: A New Pattern in Innovation & Technologica Change. Bruchey, Stuart, ed. LC 78-22670. (Energy & the American Economy Ser.). (Illus.). 1979. lib. bdg. 16.00x (ISBN 0-405-11974-7). Ayer Co Pubs.
Dale, Allen. Cracker Barrel Comments. 1981. 10.00 (ISBN 0-87244-065-6). Texian.
Dale, Alzina S. The Outline of Sanity: A Life G. K. Chesterton. 354p. 1982. 18.95 (ISBN 0-8028-3550-3); pap. 12.95 (ISBN 0-8028-1982-6). Eerdmans.
Dale, Alzina S., ed. Love All & Busman's Honeymoon: Two Plays by Dorothy L. Sayers. LC 84-9746. 225p. 1984. 19.95 (ISBN 0-87338-304-4); pap. 7.95 (ISBN 0-87338-325-7). Kent St U Pr.
Dale, Anthony. Historic Preservation in Foreign Countries, Vol.I: France, England, Ireland, the Netherlands, & Denmark. Stipe, Robert E., ed. (Illus.). 153p. (Orig.). 1984. 11.85 (ISBN 0-911697-00-4). US ICOMOS.
Dale, Anthony, tr. see Gochet, Paul.
Dale, Arbie. Biorhythm. (Orig.). 1976. pap. 1.75 (ISBN 0-671-80779-X). PB.
Dale, Arbie M. Change Your Job, Change Your Life. 224p. 1978. pap. 2.50 (ISBN 0-86721-053-2). Jove Pubns.
Dale, Arbie M. & Snow, Leida. Twenty Minutes a Day to a More Powerful Intelligence. 1984. pap. 2.25 (ISBN 0-87216-646-5). Jove Pubns.
Dale, Barbara & Dale, Jim. The Working Woman Book. (Illus.). 128p. (Orig.). 1985. pap. 6.95 (ISBN 0-8362-1254-1). Andrews McMeel Parker.
Dale, Barbara & Roeber, Johanna. The Pregnancy Exercise Book. 1982. pap. 6.95 (ISBN 0-394-71119-X). Pantheon.
Dale, Brian. Fertilization in Animals. (Studies in Biology: No. 157). 64p. 1983. pap. text ed. 8.95 (ISBN 0-7131-2875-5). E Arnold.
Dale, Carrie Kondy, jt. auth. see Dale, Robert D.
Dale, Celia. Act of Love. 1977. pap. 1.75 (ISBN 0-505-51211-4, Pub. by Tower Bks). Dorchester Pub Co.
--Other People. 1977. pap. 1.75 (ISBN 0-8439-0485-2, Leisure Bks). Dorchester Pub Co.
--A Spring of Love. 1977. pap. 1.50 (ISBN 0-8439-0479-8, Leisure Bks). Dorchester Pub Co.
Dale, Charles W. & Oliva, Ralph A. Practical Applications of D. C. Theory. LC 77-84131. (Illus.). 402p. 1977. pap. text ed. 12.00 (ISBN 0-89512-010-0, LCW8162). Tex Instr Inc.
Dale, Charles W., jt. auth. see Oliva, Ralph A.
Dale, D. M. Applied Audiology for Children. 2nd ed. (Illus.). 176p. 1979. photocopy ed. 20.75x (ISBN 0-398-00387-4). C C Thomas.
--Individualised Integration: Studies of Deaf & Partially-Hearing Children & Students in Ordinary Schools & Colleges. 250p. 1984. 28.50 (ISBN 0-398-04842-8). C C Thomas.
--Language Development in Deaf & Partially Hearing Children. (Illus.). 270p. 1975. photocopy ed. 27.50x (ISBN 0-398-03164-9). C C Thomas.
Dale, Daryl, jt. auth. see Kageler, Len.
Dale, Delbert A. Trumpet Technique. (YA) (gr. 9 up). 1965. 8.75 (ISBN 0-19-322128-4). Oxford U Pr.
Dale, Doris C. Bilingual Books in Spanish & English for Children. 175p. 1985. lib. bdg. 23.50 (ISBN 0-87287-477-X). Libs Unl.
Dale, Doris C., ed. Carl H. Milam & the United Nations Library. LC 76-14866. 149p. 1976. 13.00 (ISBN 0-8108-0941-9). Scarecrow.
Dale, Duane & Magnani, David. Beyond Experts: A Guide for Citizen Group Training. 120p. (Citizen Group Training Project). 1979. pap. 6.85 (ISBN 0-318-17174-0, C30). Natl Ctr Cit Involv.
Dale, Duane & Mitiguy, Nancy. Planning for a Change: A Citizen's Guide to Creative Planning & Program Development. LC 79-624733. (Illus., Orig.). 1978. pap. 8.00x (ISBN 0-934210-01-2). Citizen Involve.
--Planning for a Change: A Citizen's Guide to Creative Planning & Program Development. 88p. 1978. pap. 6.85 (ISBN 0-318-17165-1, C26). Natl Ctr Cit Involv.
Dale, Duane, et al. Beyond Experts: A Guide for Citizen Group Training. LC 79-64419. (Orig.). 1979. pap. 8.00x (ISBN 0-934210-07-1). Citizen Involve.
Dale, Duane D. How to Make Citizen Involvement Work: Strategies for Developing Clout. LC 79-624734. (Illus., Orig.). 1978. pap. 8.00x (ISBN 0-934210-04-7). Citizen Involve.
Dale, E. Management: Theory & Practice. 4th ed. (Management Ser.). (Illus.). 1978. text ed. 33.95 (ISBN 0-07-015188-1). McGraw.
Dale, Edgar. Building a Learning Environment. LC 73-185413. (Foundation Monograph Ser). 152p. 1972. 5.50 (ISBN 0-87367-420-0); pap. 3.95 (ISBN 0-87367-403-0). Phi Delta Kappa.
--Building a Learning Environment. 152p. 1972. 5.50 (ISBN 0-87367-420-0); members 5.00 (ISBN 0-317-35549-X); pap. 3.95 (ISBN 0-87367-403-0); pap. 3.50 members (ISBN 0-317-35550-3). Phi Delta Kappa.
--Children's Attendance at Motion Pictures. Bd. with The Emotional Responses of Children to the Motion Picture Situation. Dysinger, Wendell S. & Ruckmick, Christian A.. LC 75-125462. (Literature of Cinema Ser.: Payne Fund Studies). Repr. of 1935 ed. 16.00 (ISBN 0-405-01643-3). Ayer Co Pubs.
--Content of Motion Pictures. LC 77-124026. (Literature of Cinema Ser: Payne Fund Studies of Motion Pictures & Social Values). Repr. of 1935 ed. 17.00 (ISBN 0-405-01644-1). Ayer Co Pubs.

Dalgado, Sebastiano R. Glossario Luso-Asiatico, 2 Vol. (Romanistik in Geschicte und Geggenwart 11). 580p. (Ger.). 1982. Repr. of 1921 ed. lib. bdg. 160.00 (ISBN 3-87118-479-9, Pub. by Helmut Buske Verlag Hamburg). Benjamins North Am.

Dalgarno, George. Works of George Dalgarno of Aberdeen. Maitland, Thomas, ed. LC 74-165338. (Maitland Club, Glasgow. Publications: No. 29). Repr. of 1834 ed. 16.75 (ISBN 0-404-52987-9). AMS Pr.

--Works of George Dalgarno of Aberdeen. Repr. of 1834 ed. 22.00 (ISBN 0-384-10697-8). Johnson Repr.

Dalgish, Gerard M. A Dictionary of Africanisms: Contributions of Sub-Saharan Africa to the English Language. LC 82-9366. xviii, 203p. 1982. lib. bdg. 39.95 (ISBN 0-313-23585-6, DDA/). Greenwood.

Dalgleish, D. Douglas & Schweikart, Larry. Trident. LC 83-16777. (Science & International Affairs Ser.). (Illus.). 384p. 1984. 32.50 (ISBN 0-8093-1126-7). S Ill U Pr.

Dalgleish, Neil. World Survey. (Illus.). 128p. 1976. pap. 7.95 (ISBN 0-7175-0750-5). Dufour.

Dalgliesh, Alice. Bears on Hemlock Mountain. (Illus.). (gr. 1-4). 1952. (ScribJ); pap. 2.95 (ISBN 0-689-70497-6, SL866, ScribJ). Scribner.

--Bears on Hemlock Mountain. LC 52-11023. 1981. pap. 2.95 (ISBN 0-689-70497-6, A-123, Pub. by Aladdin). Atheneum.

--Christmas. (Encore Edition). (Illus.). (gr. 3-7). 1950. reinforced bdg. 2.49 (ISBN 0-684-12667-2, ScribJ). Scribner.

--Courage of Sarah Noble. (Illus.). (gr. 1-4). 1954. reinforced bdg. 6.95 (ISBN 0-684-12795-4, ScribJ); (ScribJ). Scribner.

--Fourth of July Story. (Illus.). (gr. k-4). 1956. reinforced bdg. 12.95 (ISBN 0-684-13164-1, ScribJ); (ScribJ). Scribner.

--Thanksgiving Story. (Illus.). (gr. k-3). 1954. reinforced bdg. o. p. 9.95 (ISBN 0-684-12330-4, ScribJ); pap. 2.95 (ISBN 0-684-16005-6, SL823, ScribJ). Scribner.

--The Thanksgiving Story. (Illus.). 32p. (Orig.). (gr. k-3). 1985. pap. 3.95 (ISBN 0-689-71053-4, A-166, Aladdin). Atheneum.

Dalgliesh, Walter S. Shakespeare's Macbeth. 2nd ed. LC 74-163664. Repr. of 1864 ed. 11.50 (ISBN 0-404-01918-8). AMS Pr.

Dalglish, Doris N. People Called Quakers. facsimile ed. LC 78-90628. (Essay Index Reprint Ser). 1938. 15.00 (ISBN 0-8369-1254-3). Ayer Co Pubs.

Dalglish, Edward H. Layman's Bible Book Commentary: Jeremiah, Lamentations, Vol. 11. LC 81-65801. 1984. 5.75 (ISBN 0-8054-1181-X). Broadman.

Dalglish, Garven. Of This Man: The Biography of William A. Hillenbrand. LC 82-310. (Illus.). 304p. 1982. 15.00 (ISBN 0-914016-86-5). Phoenix Pub.

Dalglish, Jack, ed. Eight Metaphysical Poets. (The Poetry Bookshelf). 1961. pap. text ed. 5.00x (ISBN 0-435-15031-6). Heinemann Ed.

Dali. Dali by Dali. (Illus.). 160p. 1983. 14.95 (ISBN 0-8109-0071-8). Abrams.

Dali, Salvador. Salvador Dali: The Tarot. (Illus.). 130p. pap. 14.95 (ISBN 0-905005-37-6, Pub. by Salem Hse Ltd). Merrimack Pub Cir.

--The Tarot. (Illus.). 176p. 1985. 14.95 (ISBN 0-88162-076-9, Pub. by Salem Hse Ltd); deluxe ed. 2.50 (ISBN 0-88162-102-1). Merrimack Pub Cir.

--The Unspeakable Confessions of Salvador Dali. Parinaud, Andre, as told to. Salemson, Harold J., tr. from Fr. LC 81-11232. Orig. Title: Comment on Devient Dali. (Illus.). 302p. 1981. pap. 6.95 (ISBN 0-688-00010-X, Quill NY). Morrow.

Dali, T., ed. see Al Fateh-IFAC Workshop, 1st, Tripoli, Libya, May 1980 & El Hares, H.

Dalin, Per. Limits to Change? The Complexity of Educational Change. LC 78-2971. 1978. 19.95 (ISBN 0-312-48691-X). St Martin.

Dalin, Per & Rust, Val D. Can Schools Learn? 176p. 1983. 16.00x (ISBN 0-7005-0610-1, Pub. by NFER Nelson UK). Taylor & Francis.

Dalinka, M. K. Arthrography. (Comprehensive Manuals in Radiology). (Illus.). 209p. 1980. 37.50 (ISBN 0-387-90466-2). Springer-Verlag.

Dalis, G. & Strasser, B. Teaching Strategies for Values Awareness & Decision-Making in Health Education. LC 77-82319. 224p. 1977. 12.00 (ISBN 0-913590-46-0). Slack Inc.

Dalis, Gus T., jt. auth. see Fodor, John T.

Dalisi, Riccardo. Gaudi: Furniture & Objects. LC 80-11463. 1980. 19.95 (ISBN 0-8120-5356-7). Barron.

Da Liu. The Tao & Chinese Culture. LC 78-26767. 192p. (Orig.). 1982. pap. 7.95 (ISBN 0-8052-0702-3). Schocken.

--The Tao of Health & Longevity. LC 77-87860. (Illus.). 1978. pap. 4.95 (ISBN 0-8052-0596-9). Schocken.

Dalke, J. David, jt. auth. see Hart, Lois B.

Dall, Carolin H. The College, the Market, & the Court: Woman's Relation to Education, Labor & Law. LC 72-2596. (American Women Ser: Images & Realities). 540p. 1972. Repr. of 1867 ed. 28.00 (ISBN 0-405-04453-4). Ayer Co Pubs.

Dall, Caroline H. Margaret & Her Friends; or, Ten Conversations with Margaret Fuller Upon the Mythology of the Greeks & Its Expression in Art. LC 72-4961. (The Romantic Tradition in American Literature Ser.). 166p. 1972. Repr. of 1895 ed. 18.00 (ISBN 0-405-04633-2). Ayer Co Pubs.

Dall, Caroline W. Alongside. Baxter, Annette K., ed. LC 79-8785. (Signal Lives Ser.). 1980. Repr. of 1900 ed. lib. bdg. 16.00x (ISBN 0-405-12833-9). Ayer Co Pubs.

Dall, Curtis B. FDR: My Exploited Father-in-Law. LC 68-2835. (Illus.). iii, 192p. 1983. pap. 5.00 (ISBN 0-939484-03-X). Inst Hist Rev.

--Israel's Five Trillion Dollar Secret. 1984. lib. bdg. 79.95 (ISBN 0-87700-561-3). Revisionist Pr.

Dall, W. H. History, Geography, Resources, Vol. 2. (HARRIMAN ALASKA EXPEDITION, 1899 Ser.). Repr. of 1902 ed. 51.00 (ISBN 0-527-38162-4). Kraus Repr.

--Land & Fresh Water Mollusks. Bd. with Hydroids. Nutting, C. C. (Harriman Alaska Expedition, 1899). 24.00 (ISBN 0-527-38173-X). Kraus Repr.

Dall, W. H., et al. A Manual of the Recent & Fossil, Marine Pelecypod Mollusks of the Hawaiian Islands. (BMB Ser.). Repr. of 1938 ed. 34.00 (ISBN 0-527-02261-6). Kraus Repr.

Dall, William. Masks, Labrets, & Certain Aboriginal Customs. facs. ed. (Shorey Indian Ser.). 138p. pap. 6.95 (ISBN 0-8466-0123-0, S123). Shorey.

Dall, William H. Alaska & Its Resources. LC 72-125736. (American Environmental Studies). (Illus.). 1970. Repr. of 1870 ed. 36.50 (ISBN 0-405-02661-7). Ayer Co Pubs.

DallaCosta, Mariarosa & James, Selma. The Power of Women & the Subversion of the Community. 80p. 1981. pap. 3.50 (ISBN 0-9502702-4-5). Falling Wall.

Dallapiccola, A. L., jt. auth. see Goswamy, B. N.

Dallapiccola, Anna L., jt. ed. see Isacco, Enrico.

Dallas A & M University Mothers' Club. Hullabaloo in the Kitchen. 384p. 1983. 12.95 (ISBN 0-9612446-0-7). Dallas A & M Moth.

Dallas, Alexander K., tr. see Schmidt, Max.

Dallas, Daniel B. Pressworking Aids for Designers & Diemakers. LC 77-90988. (Manufacturing Data Ser.). 1978. 26.50x (ISBN 0-87263-042-0). SME.

Dallas, Daniel B., ed. Manufacturing Engineering Transactions-1973, Vol. 2. (Illus.). 249p. 1974. text ed. 25.00 (ISBN 0-87263-101-X). SME.

Dallas, E. S. Poetics: An Essay on Poetry. LC 72-13006. 1973. Repr. of 1852 ed. lib. bdg. 35.00 (ISBN 0-8414-1037-2). Folcroft.

Dallas, Eneas S. The Gay Science, 2 vols. (Classics in Art & Literary Criticism, House Ser). 1970. Repr. of 1866 ed. Set. 75.00 (ISBN 0-384-10700-1). Johnson Repr.

--The Gay Science. Freedman, William & Nadel, Ira B., eds. (The Victorian Muse Ser.). 85.00 (ISBN 0-8240-8604-X). Garland Pub.

--Poetics. 294p. 1980. Repr. of 1852 ed. lib. bdg. 30.00 (ISBN 0-8495-1118-6). Arden Lib.

--Poetics: An Essay on Poetry. (Classics in Art & Literary Criticism, House Ser.). Repr. of 1852 ed. 27.00 (ISBN 0-384-11435-0). Johnson Repr.

--Poetics: An Essay on Poetry. (Victoria Muse Ser.). 302p. 1985. lib. bdg. 40.00 (ISBN 0-8240-8603-1). Garland Pub.

Dallas, Francis G. The Papers of Francis Gregory Dallas, United States Navy: Correspondence & Journal, 1837-1859, Naval History Society, VIII. Allen, Gardner W., ed. LC 18-5068. (Illus.). 303p. 1917. 8.00x (ISBN 0-685-73919-8, New-York Historical Soc.). U Pr of Va.

Dallas, Gloden, jt. auth. see Gill, Doug.

Dallas, Gregor. The Imperfect Peasant Economy: The Loire Country, 1800-1914. LC 81-21558. (Illus.). 352p. 1982. 39.50 (ISBN 0-521-24060-3). Cambridge U Pr.

Dallas, Kenmare. Fire-Bird: A Study of D. H. Lawrence. 81p. 1983. Repr. of 1951 ed. lib. bdg. 18.00 (ISBN 0-8492-1498-X). R West.

Dallas, Philip. Italian Wines. 2nd ed. LC 82-24195. (Books on Wine). 336p. 1983. 26.95 (ISBN 0-571-18071-X); pap. 12.95 (ISBN 0-571-11994-8). Faber & Faber.

Dallas, R. C. History of the Maroons, 2 vols. 1968. Repr. of 1803 ed. 85.00x set (ISBN 0-7146-1934-5, F Cass Co). Biblio Dist.

Dallas, Robert C. Recollections of the Life of Lord Byron: From the Year 1808 to the End of 1814. 344p. 1980. Repr. of 1824 ed. lib. bdg. 65.00 (ISBN 0-8495-1057-0). Arden Lib.

--Recollections of the Life of Lord Byron from the Year 1808 to the End of 1814. LC 75-29173. 1975. Repr. of 1824 ed. lib. bdg. 59.00 (ISBN 0-8414-3728-9). Folcroft.

Dallas, Sandra. Cherry Creek Gothic: Victorian Architecture in Denver. LC 70-108801. (Illus.). 1971. 14.95 (ISBN 0-8061-0910-6). U of Okla Pr.

--Colorado Ghost Towns & Mining Camps. LC 84-40685. (Illus.). 264p. (Orig.). 1985. text ed. 24.95 (ISBN 0-8061-1910-1). U of Okla Pr.

--Gaslights & Gingerbread: Colorado's Historic Homes. 3rd, rev. ed. LC 83-18208. (Illus.). xii, 164p. 1984. 15.95 (ISBN 0-8040-0838-8, Swallow); pap. 9.95 (ISBN 0-8040-0839-6). Ohio U Pr.

--No More Than Five in a Bed: Colorado Hotels in the Old Days. (Illus.). 1967. 13.95 (ISBN 0-8061-0742-1). U of Okla Pr.

--No More Than Five in a Bed: Colorado Hotels in the Old Days. LC 67-15587. (Illus.). 224p. 1984. pap. 9.95 (ISBN 0-8061-1871-7). U of Okla Pr.

--Sacred Paint: Ned Jacob. LC 79-1570. (Illus.). 1979. 35.00 (ISBN 0-913504-50-5). Lowell Pr.

Dallas, Susan, ed. Diary of George Mifflin Dallas While United States Minister to Russia, 1837-1839. LC 70-115527. (Russia Observed, Series I). 1970. Repr. of 1892 ed. 14.00 (ISBN 0-405-03019-3). Ayer Co Pubs.

Dallas-Damis, Athena, tr. see Kazantzakis, Nikos.

Dallas-Damis, Athena G. Island of the Winds. 1976. 9.95 (ISBN 0-89241-022-1). Caratzas.

Dallas-Smith, Peter. Trumpets in Grumpetland. LC 84-11491. (Illus.). 32p. (gr. 3 up). 1985. 8.95 (ISBN 0-394-87028-X); PLB 8.99 (ISBN 0-394-97028-4). Random.

Dallavo, William G. The Power Within Henry Washe. (Illus.). 51p. 1983. pap. 6.00 (ISBN 0-942494-74-1). Coleman Pub.

Dall Croubelis, Simoni see Croubelis, Simoni dall, et al.

Dallek, Robert. The American Style of Foreign Policy: Cultural Politics & Foreign Affairs. LC 82-48877. 336p. 1983. 16.95 (ISBN 0-394-51360-6). Knopf.

--Franklin D. Roosevelt & American Foreign Policy, 1932-1945. 1979. 35.00x (ISBN 0-19-502457-5); pap. 12.95 (ISBN 0-19-502894-5, GB628, GB). Oxford U Pr.

--Ronald Reagan: The Politics of Symbolism. 224p. 1984. 16.50 (ISBN 0-674-77940-1). Harvard U Pr.

Dallek, Robert, ed. The Roosevelt Diplomacy & World War II. LC 78-8325. (American Problem Studies). 132p. 1979. pap. text ed. 6.95 (ISBN 0-88275-687-7). Krieger.

D'Allemagne, Henry R. Les Accessoires Du Costume et Du Mobilier, 3 Vols in 2. LC 72-94899. (Illus., Fr). 1970. Repr. of 1928 ed. Set. lib. bdg. 150.00 (ISBN 0-87817-027-8). Hacker.

--Decorative Antique Ironwork: A Pictorial Treasury. Ostoia, Vera K., tr. LC 67-20193. (Illus.). 1968. pap. 11.95 (ISBN 0-486-22082-6). Dover.

--Decorative Antique Ironwork: A Pictorial Treasury. (Illus.). 19.00 (ISBN 0-8446-1939-6). Peter Smith.

Dallemagne, Pierre G., ed. Oceanographic Data Reduction Manual. 296p. 1974. pap. text ed. 16.50x (ISBN 0-8422-0467-9). Irvington.

Dallenbach, F. B., tr. see Dallenbach-Hellweg, G.

Dallenbach-Hellweg, G. Histopathology of the Endometrium. rev., 3rd ed. Dallenbach, F. B., tr. from Ger. (Illus.). 1981. 79.50 (ISBN 0-387-10658-8). Springer-Verlag.

Dallenbach-Hellweg, G., ed. Cervical Cancer. (Current Topics in Pathology Ser.: Vol. 70). (Illus.). 304p. 1981. 71.00 (ISBN 0-387-10941-2). Springer-Verlag.

--Functional Morphologic Changes in Female Sex Organs Induced by Exogenous Hormones. (Illus.). 220p. 1980. 36.00 (ISBN 0-387-09885-2). Springer-Verlag.

D'Allessandro, M. & Bonne, A. Radioactive Waste Disposal into a Plastic Clay Formation: A Site-Specific Exercise of Probabilistic Assessment of Geological Containment. (Radioactive Waste Management Ser.). 150p. 1981. 29.75 (ISBN 3-7186-0084-6). Harwood Academic.

Dallett, Janet, ed. see Zeller, Max.

Dallett, Janett. Midnight's Daughter. LC 82-84563. 80p. 1983. 75.00 (ISBN 0-911783-01-6). Lockhart Pr.

Dalley, A. F., jt. auth. see Magee, D. F.

Dalley, Gardiner F. Swallow Shelter & Associated Sites. (University of Utah Anthropological Papers: No. 96). (Illus.). 1978. pap. 15.00x (ISBN 0-87480-143-5). U of Utah Pr.

Dalley, Gardiner F., jt. auth. see Fry, Gary F.

Dalley, Janet, tr. see Pushkin, Alexander S.

Dalley, Stephanie. Mari & Karana: Two Old Babylonian Cities. 216p. 1984. text ed. 25.95 (ISBN 0-582-78363-1). Longman.

Dalley, Tessa, ed. Art As Therapy: An Introduction to the Use of Art As a Therapeutic Technique. 201p. 1984. 27.00 (ISBN 0-422-78720-5, NO. 9084, Pub. by Tavistock England); pap. 13.95 (ISBN 0-422-78730-2, NO. 9083). Methuen Inc.

Dallimore. Holly Yew & Box. LC 76-10174. (Illus.). 1976. Repr. 15.00 (ISBN 0-913728-12-8). Theophrastus.

Dallimore, Arnold. Forerunner of the Charismatic Movement. (Orig.). 1983. pap. 7.95 (ISBN 0-8024-0286-0). Moody.

--George Whitefield: The Life & Times of the Great Evangelist of the 18th Century Revival, Vol. II. LC 79-67152. 640p. 1980. 22.50 (ISBN 0-89107-168-7, Crossway Bks). Good News.

--George Whitefield: The Life & Times of the Great Evangelist of the 18th Century Revival, Vol. 1. LC 79-67152. 598p. 1980. 22.50 (ISBN 0-89107-167-9, Crossway Bks). Good News.

--Spurgeon. 1984. 11.95 (ISBN 0-8024-0429-4). Moody.

Dallin, Alexander. Black Box: KAL 007 & the Superpowers. LC 84-24151. 180p. 1985. 14.95 (ISBN 0-520-05515-2); pap. 7.95 (ISBN 0-520-05516-0). U of Cal Pr.

--German Rule in Russia, Nineteen Forty-One to Nineteen Forty-Five. LC 80-241. xx, 695p. 1980. Repr. of 1957 ed. lib. bdg. 52.00x (ISBN 0-374-92041-9). Octagon.

--The Soviet Union at the United Nations: An Inquiry into Soviet Motives & Objectives. LC 75-27679. (Illus.). 244p. 1976. Repr. of 1962 ed. lib. bdg. 27.50x (ISBN 0-8371-8454-1, DASU). Greenwood.

Dallin, Alexander & Breslauer, George W. Political Terror in Communist Systems. 1970. 15.00x (ISBN 0-8047-0727-8); pap. 5.95 (ISBN 0-8047-1085-6, SP-4). Stanford U Pr.

Dallin, Alexander, ed. Diversity in International Communism: A Documentary Record 1961-1963. LC 62-21515. 867p. (Orig.). 1963. pap. 32.00x (ISBN 0-231-08611-3). Columbia U Pr.

Dallin, Alexander, compiled by. Soviet Conduct in World Affairs. LC 75-31359. 318p. 1976. Repr. of 1960 ed. lib. bdg. 35.00x (ISBN 0-8371-8511-4, DASCW). Greenwood.

Dallin, Alexander, ed. The Twenty-Fifth Congress of the CPSU: Assessment & Context. LC 77-2445. (Publication Ser: No. 184). (Illus.). 1977. pap. 6.95x (ISBN 0-8179-6842-3). Hoover Inst Pr.

Dallin, David J. Real Soviet Russia. 1947. 29.50x (ISBN 0-685-69807-6). Elliots Bks.

--Russia & Postwar Europe. 1943. 29.50x (ISBN 0-685-69808-4). Elliots Bks.

--Soviet Foreign Policy After Stalin. LC 75-14596. (Illus.). 543p. 1975. Repr. of 1961 ed. lib. bdg. 45.00x (ISBN 0-8371-8223-9, DASF). Greenwood.

--Soviet Russia & the Far East. vi, 398p. 1971. Repr. of 1948 ed. 23.50 (ISBN 0-208-00996-5, Archon). Shoe String.

--Soviet Russia's Foreign Policy, 1939-42. 1942. 49.50x (ISBN 0-685-88556-9). Elliots Bks.

Dallin, Leon. Basic Music Skills: A Supplementary Program for Self-Instruction. 108p. 1971. pap. text ed. write for info. (ISBN 0-697-03464-X). Wm C Brown.

--Foundations in Music Theory. 2nd ed. 1967. pap. write for info. (ISBN 0-534-00659-0). Wadsworth Pub.

--Introduction to Music Reading. (gr. 9-12). 1977. pap. text ed. 4.95 (ISBN 0-87597-113-X, Crescendo). Taplinger.

--Listener's Guide to Musical Understanding. 5th ed. 454p. 1982. pap. text ed. write for info. (ISBN 0-697-03487-9); student wkbk. avail. (ISBN 0-697-03521-2); recordings avail. (ISBN 0-697-03520-4); instructor's manual avail. (ISBN 0-697-03533-6). Wm C Brown.

--Techniques of Twentieth-Century Composition: A Guide to the Materials of Modern Music. 3rd ed. 306p. 1974. text ed. write for info. (ISBN 0-697-03614-6). Wm C Brown.

Dallin, Leon & Dallin, Lynn. Heritage Songster. 2nd ed. 320p. 1980. write for info, plastic comb (ISBN 0-697-03481-X). Wm C Brown.

Dallin, Leon, jt. auth. see Winslow, Robert W.

Dallin, Lynn. Cancer Causes & Natural Controls. LC 82-13765. 374p. 1984. 19.95 (ISBN 0-87949-224-4). Ashley Bks.

--Cancer Causes & Natural Controls. 1983. 19.95x. Cancer Control Soc.

Dallin, Lynn, jt. auth. see Dallin, Leon.

Dallinger, Frederick W. Nominations for Elective Office in the United States. LC 73-19140. (Politics & People Ser.). 304p. 1974. Repr. 21.00x (ISBN 0-405-05865-9). Ayer Co Pubs.

Dallinger, Jane. Grasshoppers. LC 80-27806. (Lerner Natural Science Bks.). (Illus.). (gr. 4-10). 1981. PLB 10.95 (ISBN 0-8225-1455-9). Lerner Pubns.

--Spiders. LC 80-27548. (Lerner Natural Science Bks.). (Illus.). (gr. 4-10). 1981. PLB 9.95 (ISBN 0-8225-1456-7). Lerner Pubns.

Dallinger, Jane & Johnson, Sylvia A. Frogs & Toads. LC 80-27667. (Lerner Natural Science Bks.). (Illus.). (gr. 4-10). 1982. PLB 10.95 (ISBN 0-8225-1454-0). Lerner Pubns.

Dallinger, Jane & Overbeck, Cynthia. Swallowtail Butterflies. LC 82-15294. (Lerner Natural Science Bks.). (Illus.). 48p. (gr. 4-10). 1982. PLB 9.95 (ISBN 0-8225-1465-6). Lerner Pubns.

Dallinger, Nat. Unforgettable Hollywood. LC 82-3479. (Illus.). 1982. 20.00 (ISBN 0-688-01323-6). Morrow.

--Unforgettable Hollywood. LC 83-60483. (Illus.). 256p. 1983. pap. 12.95 (ISBN 0-688-02475-0, Quill NY). Morrow.

Dallington, R., tr. see Colonna, Francesco.

Dallington, Robert. Aphorismes Civil & Militarie: A Briefe Inference Upon Guicciardines Digression, 2 pts. LC 77-6869. (English Experience Ser.: No. 864). 1977. Repr. of 1613 ed. lib. bdg. 58.00 (ISBN 90-221-0864-3). Walter J Johnson.

--A Survey of the Great Dukes State of Tuscany, in 1596. LC 74-80171. (English Experience Ser.: No. 650). 74p. 1974. Repr. of 1605 ed. 8.00 (ISBN 90-221-0650-0). Walter J Johnson.

Dallington, Robert, tr. see Colonna, Francesco.

Dallison, Dennis. Reflections of My Life: The Apology of John the Baptist. Norman, Ruth, ed. 77p. (Orig.). 1982. pap. text ed. 2.50 (ISBN 0-932642-75-6). Unarius.

--Yamamoto Returns: A True Story of Reincarnation. (Illus.). 200p. 1985. pap. 5.95 (ISBN 0-932642-98-5). Unarius.

Dallman, Elaine, et al, eds. Woman Poet - The South. LC 81-69793. (Woman Poet Ser.). (Illus.). 1986. casebound 16.95 (ISBN 0-935634-07-X); pap. text ed. 8.50 (ISBN 0-935634-06-1). Women-in-Lit.

--Woman Poet: The Midwest. LC 81-69793. (Woman Poet Ser.). (Illus.). 1985. casebound 16.95 (ISBN 0-935634-05-3); pap. text ed. 8.50 (ISBN 0-935634-04-5). Women-in-Lit.

--Woman Poet - The East. LC 81-69793. (Woman Poet Ser.). (Illus.). 123p. 1982. casebound 16.95 (ISBN 0-935634-03-7); pap. 8.50 (ISBN 0-935634-02-9). Women-in-Lit.

--Woman Poet - The West. LC 79-55988. (Woman Poet Ser.). (Illus.). 100p. (Orig.). 1980. casebound 16.95 (ISBN 0-935634-01-0); pap. text ed. 8.50 (ISBN 0-935634-00-2). Women-in-Lit.

Dallman, Martha. Teaching the Language Arts in the Elementary School. 3rd ed. 380p. 1976. text ed. write for info. (ISBN 0-697-06158-2). Wm C Brown.

Dallman, Robert E., jt. auth. see Weiss, Robert M.

Dallmann, Martha, et al. The Teaching of Reading. 6th ed. LC 81-20010. 456p. 1982. text ed. 30.95 (ISBN 0-03-059884-2). HR&W.

Dallmayr, Fred R. Language & Politics. LC 83-50744. 255p. 1985. pap. text ed. 9.95 (ISBN 0-317-17261-1, 85-12717). U of Notre Dame Pr.

--Language & Politics: Why Does Language Matter to Political Philosophy? LC 83-50744. (Loyola U. Series in Political Analysis: Vol. VII). 256p. 1983. text ed. 22.95 (ISBN 0-268-01270-9, 85-12709). U of Notre Dame Pr.

--Polis & Praxis: Excercises in Contemporary Political Theory. LC 84-12252. 245p. 1984. 25.00x (ISBN 0-262-04078-6). MIT Pr.

--Twilight of Subjectivity: Contributions to a Post-Individualist Theory of Politics. LC 80-23433. 376p. 1981. lib. bdg. 22.50x (ISBN 0-87023-314-9); pap. text ed. 10.95x (ISBN 0-87023-315-7). U of Mass Pr.

Dallmayr, Fred R. & McCarthy, Thomas A. Understanding & Social Inquiry. LC 76-22404. 1977. text ed. 21.95x (ISBN 0-268-01912-6). U of Notre Dame Pr.

Dallmayr, Fred R. & McCarthy, Thomas A., eds. Understanding & Social Inquiry. LC 76-22404. 1978. pap. 9.95x (ISBN 0-268-01913-4). U of Notre Dame Pr.

Dallmayr, Winfried R., jt. auth. see Rankin, Robert S.

Dallmeyer, Andrew. The Boys in the Backroom. 42p. 1983. pap. 5.95 (ISBN 0-907540-24-4, NO.3988). Methuen Inc.

Dallmeyer, Dorothy S. Early Education of Toddlers. LC 84-73134. 65p. (Orig.). 1984. pap. 4.95 (ISBN 0-916109-01-1). CeMoMedServ.

Dallmeyer, R. David. Physical Geology Laboratory Text & Manual: A Guide for the Study of Earth. 2nd ed. 1978. wire coil bdg. 13.50 (ISBN 0-8403-1231-8). Kendall-Hunt.

D'Allonnes, Olivier R. Musical Variations on Jewish Thought. Greenberg, Judith, tr. LC 83-15640. 169p. 1984. 12.95 (ISBN 0-8076-1091-7). Braziller.

Dallos, Peter. The Auditory Periphery: Biophysics & Physiology. 1973. 78.00 (ISBN 0-12-200750-6). Acad Pr.

Dally, Ann. Inventing Motherhood: The Consequences of an Ideal. LC 82-10517. 360p. 1983. 19.95 (ISBN 0-8052-3830-1). Schocken.

--Inventing Motherhood: The Consequences of an Ideal. 360p. 1985. pap. 9.95 (ISBN 0-8052-0765-1). Schocken.

--Understanding: Coming to Grips with Moments of Inadequacy, Neurosis, Isolation, Depression, Masochism, Frustration. LC 78-66254. 192p. 1983. pap. 6.95 (ISBN 0-8128-6104-3). Stein & Day.

Dally, Emma. Passage of Seasons. 352p. 1984. pap. 3.50 (ISBN 0-671-44309-7). PB.

Dally, James W. & Riley, William F. Experimental Stress Analysis. 2d ed. LC 77-393. (Illus.). 1977. text ed. 43.00x (ISBN 0-07-015204-7). McGraw.

--Instrumentation for Engineering Measurements. 576p. 1984. text ed. 40.45x (ISBN 0-471-04548-9). Wiley.

Dally, John, jt. ed. see Verdon, Timothy G.

Dally, Joseph W. Vital Records of Woodbridge, New Jersey. Orig. Title: Exerted from Woodbridge & Vicinity (1873) 56p. (Orig.). 1983. pap. 4.50 (ISBN 0-912606-14-2). Hunterdon Hse.

Dally, Kathleen L., jt. auth. see Folts, Harold C.

Dally, Peter. Chemotherapy of Psychiatric Disorders. LC 68-31234. 156p. 1968. 29.50x (ISBN 0-306-30365-5, Plenum Pr). Plenum Pub.

--The Fantasy Games. 1976. pap. 1.75 (ISBN 0-380-00658-8, 29769). Avon.

Dally, Peter & Gomez, Joan. Obesity & Anorexia Nervosa: A Question of Shape. 128p. 1980. pap. 6.95 (ISBN 0-571-11472-5). Faber & Faber.

Dally, Peter, pref. by see Erichsen, Ann.

Dalmais. Crazy Animal Stories. 1982. 9.95 (ISBN 0-07-015198-9). McGraw.

Dalmais, Anne M. Doctor Rabbit's New Home. (Illus.). 48p. (gr. k-2). cancelled (ISBN 0-448-14497-2, G&D). Putnam Pub Group.

Dalmais, Anne-Marie. The Elephant's Airplane & Other Machines. LC 83-83274. (Illus.). 48p. (ps-2). 1984. 6.95 (ISBN 0-307-15579-X, Golden Bks). Western Pub.

Dalman, G. Conrad, jt. auth. see Liboff, Richard L.

Dalman, Gustaf. Jesus Christ in the Talmud, Midrash, Zohar, & the Liturgy of the Synagogue. LC 73-2190. (The Jewish People; History, Religion, Literature Ser.). Repr. of 1893 ed. 11.00 (ISBN 0-405-05256-1). Ayer Co Pubs.

Dalman, Gustaf H. Words of Christ. 1981. lib. bdg. 13.50 (ISBN 0-86524-080-9, 9509). Klock & Klock.

Dalmas & Martin. Touch the Stars: Emergence. 2.95 (ISBN 0-317-31909-4). Tor Bks.

Dalmas, John. Homecoming. 256p. (Orig.). 1984. pap. 2.95 (ISBN 0-8125-3471-9). Tor Bks.

--The Scroll of Man. 256p. (Orig.). 1985. pap. 2.95 (ISBN 0-8125-3425-5). Tor Bks.

--Touch the Stars: Emergence. 320p. (Orig.). 1983. pap. 2.95 (ISBN 0-523-48586-7). Pinnacle Bks.

--The Varkaus Conspiracy. 288p. (Orig.). 1983. pap. 2.95 (ISBN 0-523-48567-0). Tor Bks.

--The Yngling. 256p. (Orig.). 1984. pap. 2.95 (ISBN 0-8125-3473-5). Tor Bks.

Dalmases, Candido de. Ignatius of Loyola, Founder of the Jesuits: His Life & Work. Ganss, George E., frwd. by. Aixala, Jerome, tr. from Span. Index. LC 83-80349. (Series II-Scholarly Studies about the Jesuits in English Translations: No. 6). xxii, 362p. 1985. 16.00 (ISBN 0-912422-59-9); pap. 14.00 smyth sewn (ISBN 0-912422-58-0). Inst Jesuit.

Dal Masetto, Antonio. El Ojo de la Perdiz. 214p. (Span.). 1980. pap. 7.00 (ISBN 0-910061-01-7, 1102). Ediciones Norte.

Dal Maso, L. B. Rome of the Caesars. Hollingworth, Michael, tr. (Bonechi Guides Ser.). (Illus.). 128p. 1984. pap. text ed. 11.95 (ISBN 0-88332-336-2, 8273). Larousse.

Dal Maso, Leonardo B. Raphael. Date not set. price not set. Larousse.

Dalmau, Eduardo Martinez see Martinez Dalmau, Eduardo.

Dalmus, John. The Walkaway Clause. 192p. (Orig.). pap. 2.95 (ISBN 0-931773-48-2). Critics Choice Paper.

D'Alonzo, Bruno J. Educating Adolescents with Learning & Behavior Problems. LC 82-16363. 536p. 34.00 (ISBN 0-89443-847-6). Aspen Systems.

D'Alonzo, C. A., jt. auth. see Rogg, S. G.

Dalos, Gyorgy. Nineteen Eighty-Five. Hood, Stuart & Schmidt, Estella, trs. 1984. 12.45 (ISBN 0-394-53780-7); pap. 4.95 (ISBN 0-394-72482-8). Pantheon.

Dalpadado, J. Kinglsey. Reading the Gospels. 1975. pap. 4.00 (ISBN 0-8198-0454-1). Dghtrs St Paul.

Dalpadado, J. Kingsley. Reading the Acts, Epistles & Revelations. 1977. 6.95 (ISBN 0-8198-0450-9); pap. 5.95 (ISBN 0-8198-0451-7). Dghtrs St Paul.

--Reading the Bible. 1973. 5.95 (ISBN 0-8198-0338-3); pap. 4.95 (ISBN 0-8198-0339-1). Dghtrs St Paul.

Dalphin, John R. The Persistence of Social Inequality in America. 154p. 1982. 15.95 (ISBN 0-87073-614-0); pap. 8.95 (ISBN 0-87073-615-9). Schenkman Bks Inc.

Dalpiaz, P., et al, eds. Fundamental Interactions in Low-Energy Systems. (Ettore Majorana International Sciences Series-Physical Science: Vol. 23). 1985. 85.00x (ISBN 0-317-20605-2, Plenum Pr). Plenum Pub.

D'Alpuget, Blanche. Mediator: A Biography of Sir Richard Kirby. 1978. 26.50x (ISBN 0-522-84129-5, Pub. by Melbourne U Pr). Intl Spec Bk.

--Turtle Beach. 288p. 1983. 14.95 (ISBN 0-671-49241-1). S&S.

--Turtle Beach. 256p. 1984. pap. 3.50 (ISBN 0-345-31818-8). Ballantine.

D'Alquen, Richard J. Gothic Ai & Av. LC 72-94440. (Janua Linguarum, Ser. Practica: No. 151). 182p. 1974. pap. text ed. 36.80x (ISBN 0-686-22578-3). Mouton.

Dalquest, Walter W. & Hall, E. Raymond. A New Bat (Genus Myotis) from Mexico. (Museum Ser.: Vol. 1, No. 12). 8p. 1947. pap. 1.25 (ISBN 0-317-04976-3). U of KS Mus Nat Hist.

--Tadarida Femirisacca (Merriam) in Tamaulipas, Mexico. (Museum Ser.: Vol. 1, No. 13). 4p. 1947. pap. 1.25 (ISBN 0-317-04978-X). U of KS Mus Nat Hist.

Dalquest, Walter W. & Horner, Norman V. Mammals of North-Central Texas. (Illus.). 261p. 1984. 15.00 (ISBN 0-915323-01-X). Midwestern St U Pr.

Dalquest, Walter W., jt. auth. see Hall, E. Raymond.

Dalquest, Walter W., jt. auth. see Lowrey, George H., Jr.

Dalrymple, Andrew A. God Bless Us Every One! Being an Imagined Sequel to "A Christmas Carol". (Illus.). 160p. 1985. 10.95 (ISBN 0-312-33027-8). St Martin.

Dalrymple, Byron W. The Complete Book of Deer Hunting. 256p. pap. 8.95 (ISBN 0-88317-050-7). Stoeger Pub Co.

--Deer Hunting with Dalrymple: A Lifetime of Lore on the Whitetail & Mule Deer. LC 83-3891. 256p. 1983. 16.95 (ISBN 0-668-05868-4); pap. 7.95 (ISBN 0-668-05870-6). Arco.

--How to Rig & Fish Natural Baits. (Funk & W Bk.). (Illus.). 1976. pap. 4.50i (ISBN 0-308-10291-6, TYC-T). T Y Crowell.

Dalrymple, D., ed. see Hales, John.

Dalrymple, D. J., jt. auth. see Thompson, D. L.

Dalrymple, Dana & Dalrymple, Helen. Appalachian Trail Guide Southern Pennsylvania to Northern Virginia (Susquehanna River to Shenandoah National Park) 10th rev. ed. (Orig.). 1979. pap. 6.00 (ISBN 0-915746-12-3). Potomac Appalach.

Dalrymple, David, ed. see Bannatyne, George.

Dalrymple, Douglas J. Merchandising Decision Models for Department Stores. LC 66-64599. 1966. pap. 2.00 (ISBN 0-87744-045-X). Mich St U Pr.

--Sales Management: Concepts & Cases. (Wiley Series in Marketing). 485p. 1982. text ed. 33.00x (ISBN 0-471-07867-0); tchrs. manual 16.00 (ISBN 0-471-09963-5). Wiley.

--Sales Management: Concepts & Cases. 2nd ed. 635p. 1985. text ed. 29.95 (ISBN 0-471-87872-3). Halsted Pr.

Dalrymple, Douglas J. & Parsons, Leonard J. Marketing Management: Strategy & Cases. 3rd ed. LC 79-24833. (Wiley Series in Marketing). 821p. 1983. 35.45x (ISBN 0-471-09847-7). Wiley.

Dalrymple, G. Brent & Lanphere, Marvin A. Potassium-Argon Dating: Principles, Techniques & Applications to Geochronology. LC 71-84047. (Geology Ser.). (Illus.). 258p. 1969. text ed. 30.95 (ISBN 0-7167-0241-X). W H Freeman.

Dalrymple, Helen, jt. auth. see Dalrymple, Dana.

Dalrymple, Helen W., jt. auth. see Goodrum, Charles A.

Dalrymple, James, tr. see Leslie, John.

Dalrymple, Jean. From the Last Row. LC 75-17958. (Illus.). 1975. 15.00 (ISBN 0-88371-008-0). J T White.

Dalrymple, John. An Essay Towards a General History of Feudal Property in Great Britain. vii, 332p. 1979. Repr. of 1757 ed. lib. bdg. 35.00x (ISBN 0-8377-0508-8). Rothman.

--Living the Richness of the Cross. LC 83-70945. 128p. (Orig.). 1983. pap. 3.95 (ISBN 0-87793-274-3). Ave Maria.

--Simple Prayer. (Ways of Prayer Ser.: Vol. 9). 118p. 1984. pap. 4.95 (ISBN 0-89453-301-0). M Glazier.

--Toward the Heart of God. 108p. (Orig.). 1981. pap. 3.95 (ISBN 0-86683-602-0). Winston Pr.

Dalrymple, Margaret F., ed. see Fitzpatrick, John.

Dalrymple, Martha, jt. auth. see Goldstone, Harmon H.

Dalrymple, Mason. Human Biology Laboratory Manual. 80p. 1985. pap. text ed. 9.95 (ISBN 0-8403-3530-X). Kendall-Hunt.

Dalrymple, Paul, et al. A Year of Snow Accumulation at Plateau Station; Thermal Properties & Heat Transfer Processes of Low-Temperature Snow; Radiative Heat Transfer; Process in Snow & Ice; Papers 1, 2, 3 & 4: Meteorological Studies at Plateau Station, Antarctica. Businger, Joost A., ed. (Antarctic Research Ser.: Vol. 25). (Illus.). 1977. pap. 13.50 (ISBN 0-87590-125-5). Am Geophysical.

Dalrymple, Robert A., jt. auth. see Dean, Robert G.

Dalrymple, Ron. Are You a Genius? 15p. 1978. pap. 1.00x (ISBN 0-935882-00-6). Celestial Gifts.

--Increase Your Power of Creative Thinking in Eight Days. LC 85-50428. 115p. (Orig.). 1985. pap. write for info. (ISBN 0-912057-41-6, G-652, Dist. on East Coast by Celestial Gifts). AMORC.

--Mind Wars. 175p. 1981. text ed. 12.95x (ISBN 0-935882-02-2). Celestial Gifts.

--Richard the Liar-Hearted. 40p. (Orig.). 1979. pap. 1.45x (ISBN 0-935882-01-4). Celestial Gifts.

Dalsass, Diana. Cashews & Lentils, Apples & Oats. (Illus.). 1981. pap. 7.95 (ISBN 0-8092-5934-6). Contemp Bks.

--The Good Cake Book. (Illus.). 272p. 1982. 12.95 (ISBN 0-453-00432-6, H432). NAL.

--The Good Cake Book. (Illus.). 1983. pap. 6.95 (ISBN 0-452-25449-3, Plume). NAL.

--Miss Mary's Down-Home Cooking: Traditional Recipes from Lynchburg, Tennessee. LC 84-4857. 208p. 1984. 14.95 (ISBN 0-453-00473-3). NAL.

Dalsemer, Robert G. West Virginia Square Dances. (Illus.). 86p. 1982. pap. 8.25 (ISBN 0-917024-06-0). Country Dance & Song.

Dalston, T., et al. Early Forged Stamps Detector. 1979. Repr. of 1863 ed. softcover 7.00 (ISBN 0-686-64444-1); lib. bdg. 15.00 (ISBN 0-915262-39-8). S J Durst.

Dalton. The Alkaloids. (Studies in Organic Chemistry: Vol. 7). 1979. 110.00 (ISBN 0-8247-6788-8). Dekker.

--The Gentlemen in Black. 2nd ed. Reginald, R. & Menville, Douglas, eds. LC 75-46265. (Supernatural & Occult Fiction Ser.). (Illus.). 1976. Repr. of 1831 ed. lib. bdg. 24.50x (ISBN 0-405-08123-5). Ayer Co Pubs.

--The Miracle of Flight. 1977. 16.95 (ISBN 0-07-015207-1). McGraw.

--Premenstrual Syndrome & Progesterone Therapy. 2nd ed. 1984. 27.50 (ISBN 0-8151-2266-7). Year Bk Med.

Dalton, jt. auth. see Bristow.

Dalton, ed. Nightmare USA: What U.S. Government Agencies Have Done to the American Dream. (Illus.). 1978. pap. 6.00 (ISBN 0-915598-23-X). Church of Scient Info.

Dalton, A. E. Brief & to the Point: Suggestions for Preachers. 272p. 1973. Repr. of 1961 ed. 17.95 (ISBN 0-227-67419-7). Attic Pr.

Dalton, A. J. & Haguenau, Francis. Ultrastructure of the Kidney. (Ultrastructure in Biological Systems). 1967. 51.00 (ISBN 0-12-200956-8). Acad Pr.

Dalton, A. J. & Haguenau, F., eds. Ultrastructure of Tumors Induced by Viruses: Charles Oberling Memorial Volume. (Ultrastructure in Biological Systems). 1962. 49.50 (ISBN 0-12-200950-9). Acad Pr.

Dalton, Albert J. & Hagoenau, Francoise. Ultrastructure of Animal Viruses & Bacteriophages: An Atlas. (Ultrastructure in Biological Systems Ser.). 1973. 83.00 (ISBN 0-12-200960-6). Acad Pr.

Dalton, Albert J. & Haguenau, Francoise, eds. Membranes. (Ultrastructure in Biological Systems Ser.). 1968. 47.50 (ISBN 0-12-200940-1). Acad Pr.

--Nucleus. (Ultrastructure in Biological Systems). 1968. 51.00 (ISBN 0-12-200946-0). Acad Pr.

Dalton, Anne. Prince Star. (Illus.). 32p. (gr. k-3). 1985. 10.95 (ISBN 0-7182-2101-X, Pub. by Kaye & Ward). David & Charles.

Dalton, B. War & Politics in New Zealand, 1855-1870. 1967. 22.00x (ISBN 0-424-05250-4, Pub by Sydney U Pr). Intl Spec Bk.

Dalton, B. J., et al, eds. Theory & Applications of Moment Methods in Many-Fermion Systems. LC 80-21054. 520p. 1980. 75.00x (ISBN 0-306-40463-X, Plenum Pr). Plenum Pub.

Dalton, Bill. Indonesia Handbook. rev. 3rd. ed. Deke, Castleman, ed. (Illus.). 600p. (Orig.). pap. 12.95 (ISBN 0-918373-04-2). Moon Pubns CA.

Dalton, Bill, ed. see Pariser, Harry.

Dalton, Bill, ed. see Stanley, David.

Dalton, Bill, ed. see Williams, George J., III.

Dalton, C., jt. ed. see Morel, T.

Dalton, C. W. You're OK-The World's All Wrong. Herschler, Sara & Garland, L. D., eds. LC 84-70707. 560p. 1985. 17.95 (ISBN 0-916969-00-2). Big Blue Bks.

Dalton, Charles, ed. see Symposium of Fluid Mechanics in the Petroleum Industry (1975: Houston, TX).

Dalton, Clive. Introduction to Practical Animal Breeding. 172p. 1980. pap. 15.50x (ISBN 0-246-11351-0, Pub. by Granada England). Sheridan.

Dalton, Clive, jt. auth. see Kilgour, Ron.

Dalton, Cornelius, et al. Leading the Way: A History of the General Court 1629-1980. (Illus.). 528p. 1984. write for info. (ISBN 0-9613915-0-2); pap. 8.95 (ISBN 0-9613915-1-0). Connolly Sec Commonw.

Dalton, Dan R., jt. auth. see Schuler, Randall S.

Dalton, David. James Dean: The Mutant King. (Illus.). 354p. 1983. pap. 8.95 (ISBN 0-312-43959-8). St Martin.

--Organic Chemistry Experiments. 1986. cancelled. Van Nos Reinhold.

--Piece of My Heart: Janis Joplin. (Illus.). 320p. 1984. 13.95 (ISBN 0-933328-90-7). Delilah Bks.

--Rolling Stones: Biography. 1982. pap. 6.95 (ISBN 0-399-41005-8, Perigee). Putnam Pub Group.

--The Rolling Stones in Their Own Words. (Illus.). 128p. 1983. pap. 6.95 (ISBN 0-399-41007-4, Perigee). Putnam Pub Group.

--The Rolling Stones: The First Twenty Years. 25.00 (ISBN 0-394-52427-6); pap. 13.95 (ISBN 0-394-70812-1). Knopf.

Dalton, David & Cayen, Ron. James Dean: American Icon. (Illus.). 283p. 1984. 29.95 (ISBN 0-312-43958-X). St Martin.

Dalton, David & Farren, Mick. Rolling Stones: In Their Own Words. (Illus.). 128p. (Orig.). 1983. pap. 6.95 (ISBN 0-399-41007-4). Delilah Bks.

Dalton, Dennis. Indian Idea of Freedom: Political Thought of Vivekananda, Aurobindo Ghose, Rabindranath Tagore & Mahatma Gandhi. 1982. 22.00x (ISBN 0-8364-0880-2, Pub. by Academic India). South Asia Bks.

Dalton, Dennis, jt. ed. see Wilson, A. Jeyaratnam.

Dalton, E. T. Tribal History of Eastern India. (Illus.). 327p. 1978. Repr. of 1872 ed. 30.00 (ISBN 0-89684-123-5, Pub. by Cosmo Pubns India). Orient Bk Dist.

Dalton, Elizabeth. Unconscious Structure in Dostoevsky's "The Idiot". A Study in Literature & Psychoanalysis. LC 78-70287. 1979. 26.00x (ISBN 0-691-06364-8). Princeton U Pr.

Dalton, Elyse. Mirrors of the Heart. (Adventures in Love Ser.: No. 35). 1982. pap. 1.95 (ISBN 0-451-11875-8, AJ1875, Sig). NAL.

Dalton, G. E. Managing Agricultural Systems. (Illus.). xii, 163p. 1983. 24.00 (ISBN 0-85334-165-6, I-355-82, Pub. by Elsevier Applied Sci England). Elsevier.

Dalton, G. E., ed. Study of Agricultural Systems. (Illus.). 1975. 61.00 (ISBN 0-85334-640-2, Pub. by Elsevier Applied Sci England). Elsevier.

Dalton, Gene W. & Thompson, Paul H. Novations: Strategies for Career Management. 1985. 18.95 (ISBN 0-673-18181-2). Scott F.

Dalton, George. Economic Systems & Society: Capitalism, Communism & the Third World. 1983. 13.75 (ISBN 0-8446-6076-0). Peter Smith.

Dalton, George, ed. Research in Economic Anthropology, Vol. 1. (Orig.). 1978. lib. bdg. 42.50 (ISBN 0-89232-040-0). Jai Pr.

--Research in Economic Anthropology, Vol. 2. 390p. 1979. 42.50 (ISBN 0-89232-085-0). Jai Pr.

--Research in Economic Anthropology, Vol. 3. 400p. (Orig.). 1980. lib. bdg. 42.50 (ISBN 0-89232-114-8). Jai Pr.

--Research in Economic Anthropology, Vol. 4. 375p. 1981. 42.50 (ISBN 0-89232-189-X). Jai Pr.

--Research in Economic Anthropology, Vol. 6. 1984. 42.50 (ISBN 0-89232-357-4). Jai Pr.

--Tribal & Peasant Economies: Readings in Economic Anthropology. (Texas Press Sourcebooks: No. 2). (Illus.). 600p. 1976. pap. 12.95x (ISBN 0-292-78015-X). U of Tex Pr.

Dalton, George, ed. see Murra, John V.
Dalton, Geroge, ed. Research in Economic Anthropology, Vol. 5. 1983. 42.50 (ISBN 0-89232-221-7). Jai Pr.
Dalton, Gleve. An Introduction to Practical Animal Breeding. 162p. 1984. (Pub. by Granada England); pap. text ed. 16.50x (ISBN 0-246-11351-0). Brookfield Pub Co.
Dalton, H. Microbial Growth on C1 Compounds. 320p. 1981. pap. 76.95 (ISBN 0-471-26098-3, Wiley Heyden). Wiley.
Dalton, Henry. Process of Becoming. 1977. 5.00 (ISBN 0-8233-0258-X). Golden Quill.
Dalton, Hugh. Practical Socialism for Britain. 401p. 1985. lib. bdg. 50.00 (ISBN 0-8240-7609-5). Garland Pub.
--Principles of Public Finance. 4th ed. LC 67-27788. 1954. Repr. 25.00x (ISBN 0-678-06512-8). Kelley.
Dalton, J. W. Lifesavers of Cape Cod. (Photos). 1967. pap. 6.95 (ISBN 0-85699-002-7). Chatham Pr.
Dalton, Jenifer. Run on the Wind. 368p. (Orig.). 1983. pap. 3.50 (ISBN 0-440-01977-X, Emerald). Dell.
Dalton, John. The Professional Cosmetologist. 2nd ed. (Illus.). 1979. text ed. 20.95 (ISBN 0-8299-0186-8); pap. text ed. 17.95 (ISBN 0-8299-0231-7); study guide 10.95 (ISBN 0-8299-0280-5). state board review questions 5.95 (ISBN 0-8299-0290-2); answer key to study guide 1.75 (ISBN 0-8299-0264-3). West Pub.
Dalton, John C. John Call Dalton on Experimental Method: An Original Anthology. Cohen, I. Bernard, ed. LC 79-7957. (Three Centuries of Science in America Ser.). 1980. lib. bdg. 17.00x (ISBN 0-405-12538-0). Ayer Co Pubs.
Dalton, John J. The Cattle Mutilators. (Orig.). 1980. pap. 1.95 (ISBN 0-532-23117-1). Woodhill.
--The Vindicator. (Orig.). 1979. pap. 1.95 (ISBN 0-532-19236-2). Woodhill.
Dalton, John R. Basic Clinical Urology. 288p. 1982. text ed. 20.95 (ISBN 0-06-140664-3, 14-06644, Lippincott Medical). Lippincott.
Dalton, John W. The Professional Cosmetologist. 3rd ed. (Illus.). 550p. 1985. text ed. 21.95 (ISBN 0-314-77877-2); pap. text ed. 12.95 (ISBN 0-314-77878-0); answers to State Board Review Questions avail. (ISBN 0-314-77883-7); study guide answers avail. (ISBN 0-314-77881-0); study guide avail. (ISBN 0-314-77879-9). West Pub.
--State Board Review Questions: The Professional Cosmetologist. 3rd ed. 400p. 1984. write for info (ISBN 0-314-77882-9). West Pub.
Dalton, Joseph G. Ascendant Tables. rev. ed. 1975. pap. 2.00 (ISBN 0-88053-751-5). Macoy Pub.
--Dalton's Tables of Houses. rev. ed. 1983. Repr. s.p. 8.95 (ISBN 0-88053-750-7). Macoy Pub.
Dalton, Katharina. Depression After Childbirth: How to Recognize & Treat Postnatal Illness. (Illus.). 1980. pap. 7.95x (ISBN 0-19-286008-9). Oxford U Pr.
--Once a Month. LC 79-88572. 1979. pap. 6.95 (ISBN 0-89793-005-3). Hunter Hse.
--Once a Month. 2nd ed. LC 83-81699. (Illus.). 256p. 1983. pap. 8.45 (ISBN 0-89793-030-4). Hunter Hse.
--Once a Month. 256p. 1985. Repr. lib. bdg. 19.95x (ISBN 0-89370-591-8). Borgo Pr.
Dalton, L. Venezuela. 1976. lib. bdg. 59.95 (ISBN 0-8490-2793-4). Gordon Pr.
Dalton, Lawrence. Those Elegant Rolls-Royce. 350p. 1981. 75.00x (ISBN 0-686-97075-6, Pub. by D Watson England). State Mutual Bk.
Dalton, Lee. Tag. LC 81-82053. 140p. 1982. 6.95 (ISBN 0-88290-193-1, 2020). Horizon Utah.
Dalton, LeRoy C. & Snyder, Henry D. Topics for Mathematics Clubs. 2nd ed. LC 83-8296. 106p. (gr. 8-12). 1983. pap. 4.75 (ISBN 0-87353-208-2). NCTM.
Dalton, Leroy C. & Snyder, Henry D., eds. Topics for Mathematics Clubs. pap. 2.80 (ISBN 0-686-05576-4). Mu Alpha Theta.
Dalton, Lynn G. Psychology of Progression. LC 75-20921. 1981. pap. text ed. 12.95 (ISBN 0-914350-08-0). Vulcan Bks.
Dalton, M., jt. auth. see Wheeler, C. A.
Dalton, Marie, jt. auth. see Wheeler, Carol A.
D'Alton, Martina. Fatal Finish. 200p. 1982. 11.95 (ISBN 0-8027-5472-4). Walker & Co.
Dalton, Michael. The Countrey Justice, Containing the Practise of the Justices of the Peace out of Their Sessions. LC 70-37969. (American Law Ser.: The Formative Years). 406p. 1972. Repr. of 1622 ed. 27.50 (ISBN 0-405-03996-4). Ayer Co Pubs.
--Countrey Justice, Containing the Practise of the Justices of the Peace out of Their Sessions. LC 74-28844. (English Experience Ser.: No. 725). 1975. Repr. of 1618 ed. 42.00 (ISBN 90-221-0725-6). Walter J Johnson.
Dalton, Mike. The North Dakota Joke Book. 160p. 1982. 8.95 (ISBN 0-8184-0336-5). Lyle Stuart.
--The North Dakota Joke Book. (Illus.). 160p. 1983. pap. 2.95 (ISBN 0-515-07357-1). Jove Pubns.
Dalton, Murphy L., Jr. Searching with 1 & 2 Sensor-Location Magnetometers. rev. ed. (One Hundred Forty-Eight Ser.). (Illus.). 144p. pap. text ed. 19.00 (ISBN 0-317-19114-4). M L Dalton Res.
Dalton, Ormonde M., jt. auth. see Read, Charles H.
Dalton, Patricia. Wildflowers of the Northeast in the Audubon Fairchild Garden. LC 79-20296. (Illus.). 1979. pap. 6.95 (ISBN 0-914016-63-6). Phoenix Pub.
Dalton, Patrick J. Land Law. 3rd ed. LC 83-227802. xliii, 377p. cancelled (ISBN 0-273-01858-2). Pitman Pub MA.
Dalton, Peggy, ed. Approaches to the Treatment of Stuttering. (Illus.). 224p. 1983. 29.00 (ISBN 0-7099-0837-7, Pub. by Croom Helm Ltd); pap. 14.75 (ISBN 0-7099-0824-5). Longwood Pub Group.
Dalton, Phyllis I. Library Service to the Deaf & Hearing Impaired. LC 83-43242. 392p. 1985. lib. bdg. 39.50 (ISBN 0-89774-135-8). Oryx Pr.
Dalton, Robert C. Tongues Like As of Fire. 127p. 1945. pap. 1.25 (ISBN 0-88243-619-8, 02-0619). Gospel Pub.
Dalton, Roque. Clandestine Poems. Paschke, Barbara & Weaver, Eric, eds. Hirschman, Jack, tr. from Span. LC 83-51488. Orig. Title: Poemas Clandestinos. 224p. (Orig.). 1984. pap. 7.00 (ISBN 0-942638-07-7, 26L). Solidarity.
--Poems. Schaaf, Richard, tr. from Span. 88p. (Orig.). 1984. 13.50 (ISBN 0-915306-45-X); pap. 7.50 (ISBN 0-915306-43-3). Curbstone.
--Poetry & Militancy in Latin America: Art on the Line, Vol. 1. LC 81-19498. 54p. 1982. pap. 4.00 (ISBN 0-915306-26-3). Curbstone.
Dalton, Roque, et al. Art on the Line: Poetry & Militancy in Latin America. Scully, Arlene & Scully, James, trs. LC 81-19498. (Art on the Line Ser.: No. 1). 53p. (Orig.). 1982. pap. 4.00 (ISBN 0-915306-26-3). Curbstone.
Dalton, Rosemary, jt. auth. see Barrett, Pat.
Dalton, Roy C. The Jesuits' Estates Question, 1760-1888: A Study of the Background for the Agitation of 1889. LC 74-393033. (Canada Studies in History & Government: No. 11). pap. 53.30 (ISBN 0-317-26918-6, 2023608). Bks Demand UMI.
Dalton, Russel J. Citizen Politics: Public Opinion & Political Parties in the United States, United Kingdom, France & West Germany. 288p. 1986. pap. 14.95x (ISBN 0-934540-44-6). Chatham Hse Pubs.
Dalton, Russell J., et al, eds. Electoral Change in Advanced Industrial Democracies: Realignment or Dealignment? LC 84-42592. 528p. 1985. 55.00 (ISBN 0-691-07675-8); 14.50 (ISBN 0-691-10165-5). Princeton U Pr.
Dalton, Stephen. Split Second: The World of High-Speed Photography. (Illus.). 144p. 1985. 17.95 (ISBN 0-88162-063-7, Pub. by Salem Hse Ltd). Merrimack Pub Cir.
Dalton, T. P. Cambrian Companionship. 128p. 45.00x (ISBN 0-86093-344-X, Pub. by ORPC Ltd UK). State Mutual Bk.
Dalton, Thomas C. The State Politics of Judicial & Congressional Reform: Legitimizing Criminal Justice Policies. LC 84-29763. (Contributions in Political Science Ser.: No. 135). (Illus.). 320p. 1985. lib. bdg. 35.00 (ISBN 0-313-24549-5, DSP/). Greenwood.
Dalton, Thomas F. The Effects of Heat & Stress on Cleanup Personnel Working with Hazardous Materials. 1984. 25.00 (ISBN 0-318-01766-0). Spill Control Assn.
Daltrop, Anne. Politics & the European Community. 2nd ed. (Political Realities Ser.). 166p. 1985. pap. text ed. 5.95 (ISBN 0-582-35303-3). Longman.
DaLuz, P. L., jt. ed. see Weil, M. H.
Dalven, Rachel. The Jews of Jannina. 1985. write for info. (ISBN 0-930685-02-4). Cadmus Press.
Dalven, Rae, tr. see Cavafy, C.
Dalven, Rae, tr. see Ritsos, Yannis.
Dalven, Richard. Introduction to Applied Solid State Physics: Topics on the Applications of Semiconductors, Superconductors, & the Nonlinear Optical Properties of Solids. LC 79-21902. (Illus.). 345p. 1980. 29.50x (ISBN 0-306-40385-4, Plenum Pr). Plenum Pub.
Dal Verme, Francesco. Seeing America & Its Great Men: The Journal & Letters of Count Francesco Dal Verme, 1783-1784. Cometti, Elizabeth, ed. LC 69-17333. (Illus.). Repr. of 1969 ed. 37.30 (ISBN 0-8357-9818-6, 2011164). Bks Demand UMI.
D'Alviella, Eugene F. Goblet see Goblet D'Alviella, Eugene F.
D'Alviella, Goblet. The Migration of Symbols. 278p. 45.00x (ISBN 0-85030-204-8, Pub. by Aquarian Pr England). State Mutual Bk.
Dalwood, C., jt. auth. see Biggs, P.
Daly, A. E., jt. auth. see Nieuwenhuysen, J. P.
Daly, Augustin. Under the Gaslight. LC 76-108468. 1971. Repr. of 1895 ed. 19.00x (ISBN 0-403-00428-4). Scholarly.
Daly, B. B. Woods Practical Guide to Fan Engineering. 3rd ed. (Illus.). 376p. 1978. 27.50x (ISBN 0-8002-2238-5). Intl Pubns Serv.
Daly, Barbara J. Intensive Care Nursing. LC 78-78019. (Current Clinical Nursing Ser.). 1979. pap. 20.00 (ISBN 0-87488-575-2). Med Exam.
--Intensive Care Nursing. 2nd ed. (Current Clinical Nursing Ser.). 1984. pap. text ed. write for info. (ISBN 0-87488-533-7). Med Exam.
Daly, Bruce. The Psychological Theory of the Voluptuous Woman. (Illus.). 1978. deluxe ed. 59.75 (ISBN 0-930582-18-7). Gloucester Art.
Daly, C. P. Settlement of the Jews in North America. 59.95 (ISBN 0-8490-1027-6). Gordon Pr.
Daly, Cahal. Morals, Law & Life. 228p. 1966. 5.95 (ISBN 0-933932-08-1). Scepter Pubs.
Daly, Carroll J. Murder from the East: A Race Williams Story. Sparafucile, Tony, intro. by. LC 78-55862. (Library of Crime Classics). 1978. pap. 4.95 (ISBN 0-930330-01-3). Intl Polygonics.
--The Snarl of the Beast. 1981. 14.50 (ISBN 0-8398-2658-3, Gregg). G K Hall.
Daly, Charles P. First Theater in America: When Was the Drama First Introduced in America? LC 71-130092. (Drama Ser.). 1970. Repr. of 1896 ed. lib. bdg. 16.50 (ISBN 0-8337-0763-9). B Franklin.
--First Theatre in America: When Was the Drama First Introducted in America. LC 68-26284. 1968. Repr. of 1896 ed. 19.50x (ISBN 0-8046-0095-3, Pub. by Kennikat). Assoc Faculty Pr.
Daly, D. J. & Globerman, S. Tariff & Science Policies: Applications of a Model of Nationalism. LC 76-24911. (Ontario Economic Council Research Studies). (Illus.). 1976. pap. 7.50 (ISBN 0-8020-3338-5). U of Toronto Pr.
Daly, D. J., ed. International Comparisons of Prices & Output. (Studies in Income & Wealth: No. 37). 427p. 1972. text ed. 26.00 (ISBN 0-87014-244-5, Dist. by Columbia U Pr). Natl Bur Econ Res.
Daly, David A. A Comparison of Exhibition & Distribution Patterns in Three Recent Feature Motion Pictures. abridged ed. Jowett, Garth S., ed. LC 79-6672. (Dissertations on Film, 1980). lib. bdg. 22.00x (ISBN 0-405-12906-8). Ayer Co Pubs.
Daly, Dominic. The Young Douglas Hyde: The Dawn of the Irish Revolution & Renaissance, 1874-1893. 232p. 1974. 15.00x (ISBN 0-87471-478-8). Rowman.
Daly, Dorothy. Italy. LC 79-89187. (A Rand McNally Pocket Guide). (Illus., Orig.). 1980. pap. 3.95 (ISBN 0-528-84291-9). Rand.
Daly, Elisabeth. The Book of the Lion. 160p. (Orig.). 1985. pap. 2.95 (ISBN 0-553-24883-9). Bantam.
Daly, Elizabeth. And Dangerous to Know. 176p. 1984. pap. 2.95 (ISBN 0-553-24616-X). Bantam.
--Any Shape or Form. (Murder Ink Mystery Ser.: No. 27). 1981. pap. 2.25 (ISBN 0-440-10108-5). Dell.
--Arrow Pointing Nowhere. 1983. pap. 3.25 (ISBN 0-440-10021-6). Dell.
--Death & Letters. 1981. pap. 2.25 (ISBN 0-440-11791-7). Dell.
--Death & Letters. Barzun, J. & Taylor, W. H., eds. LC 81-47376. (Crime Fiction 1950-1975 Ser.). 131p. 1982. lib. bdg. 18.00 (ISBN 0-8240-4979-9). Garland Pub.
--The House Without the Door. 192p. 1984. pap. 2.95 (ISBN 0-553-24610-0). Bantam.
--Night Walk. (Murder Ink Ser.: No. 55). 1982. pap. 2.50 (ISBN 0-440-16609-8). Dell.
--Nothing Can Rescue Me. 192p. 1984. pap. 2.95 (ISBN 0-553-24605-4). Bantam.
Daly, F. C. First Rebels: Strictly Confidential Notes on the Growth of the Revolutionary Movements in Bengal. 1983. Repr. of 1911 ed. 16.50 (ISBN 0-8364-0939-6, Pub. by Rddhi India). South Asia Bks.
Daly, Gabriel. Asking the Father: A Study of the Prayer of Petition. (Ways of Prayer Ser.: Vol. 4). 1982. 8.95 (ISBN 0-89453-428-9); pap. 5.95 (ISBN 0-89453-277-4). M Glazier.
--Transcendence & Immanence: A Study in Catholic Modernism & Integralism. 1980. 37.50x (ISBN 0-19-826652-9). Oxford U Pr.
Daly, Herman E. Steady-State Economics: The Economics of Biophysical Equilibrium & Moral Growth. LC 77-8264. (Illus.). 185p. 1977. text ed. 19.95 (ISBN 0-7167-0186-3); pap. text ed. 9.95 (ISBN 0-7167-0185-5). W H Freeman.
--Toward a Steady-State Economy. LC 72-5710. (Illus.). 332p. 1973. pap. text ed. 11.95 (ISBN 0-7167-0793-4). W H Freeman.
Daly, Herman E., ed. Economics, Ecology, Ethics: Essays Toward a Steady-State Economy. LC 79-29712. (Illus.). 372p. 1980. text ed. 23.95 (ISBN 0-7167-1178-8); pap. text ed. 11.95 (ISBN 0-7167-1179-6). W H Freeman.
Daly, Herman E. & Umana, Alvaro F., eds. Energy, Economics, & Environment: Conflicting Views of an Essential Interrelationship. (AAAS Selected Symposium Ser.: No. 64). 200p. 1981. 25.00x (ISBN 0-86531-282-6). Westview.
Daly, Howell V., et al. An Introduction to Insect Biology & Diversity. (Illus.). 1978. text ed. 39.95 (ISBN 0-07-015208-X). McGraw.
Daly, J. P. The Judica Me Deus of Richard Roll. (Salzburg Elizabethan Studies: No. 92). 126p. 1984. pap. text ed. 25.50x (ISBN 0-391-03243-7, Pub. by Salzburg Austria). Humanities.
Daly, James. Cosmic Harmony & Political Thinking in Early Stuart England. (Transactions Ser.: Vol. 69, Pt. 7). 1979. 6.00 (ISBN 0-87169-697-5). Am Philos.
--Sir Robert Filmer & English Political Thought. LC 78-25913. 1979. 30.00x (ISBN 0-8020-5433-1). U of Toronto Pr.
Daly, James J. Cheerful Ascetic, & Other Essays. facs. ed. LC 68-24847. (Essay Index Reprint Ser). 1931. 14.00 (ISBN 0-8369-0359-5). Ayer Co Pubs.
--Road to Peace. facsimile ed. LC 78-107691. (Essay Index Reprint Ser.). 1936. 17.00 (ISBN 0-8369-1495-3). Ayer Co Pubs.
Daly, Jay. Walls. LC 79-2020. (An Ursula Nordstrom Bk.). 224p. (gr. 7 up). 1980. HarpJ.
Daly, John. Cyclic Nucleotides in the Nervous System. LC 76-62999. (Illus.). 415p. 1977. 45.00x (ISBN 0-306-30971-8, Plenum Pr). Plenum Pub.
Daly, John & Donahue, Thomas R. Labor Law Reform. 41p. 1978. pap. 3.75 (ISBN 0-8447-2129-8). Am Enterprise.
Daly, John A. Peg Woffington. LC 70-91489. (Illus.). 1888. 18.00 (ISBN 0-405-08427-7, Pub. by Blom). Ayer Co Pubs.
Daly, John C., et al. Advertising & the Public Interest. LC 76-20380. 1976. pap. 3.75 (ISBN 0-8447-2088-7). Am Enterprise.
--How Long Should They Serve? Limiting Terms for the President & the Congress. 25p. 1980. pap. 3.75 (ISBN 0-8447-2183-2). Am Enterprise.
Daly, John P. A Generative Syntax of Penoles Mixtec. (Publications in Linguistics Ser.: No. 42). 90p. 1973. pap. 4.00x (ISBN 0-88312-052-6); microfiche 1.93x (ISBN 0-88312-452-1). Summer Inst Ling.
Daly, John W., et al, eds. Physiology & Pharmacology of Adenosine Derivatives. (Illus.). 314p. 1983. text ed. 76.00 (ISBN 0-89004-833-9). Raven.
Daly, Jorge L. The Political Economy of Devaluation: The Case of Peru, 1975-1978. (Replica Edition Ser.). 130p. 1983. softcover 17.00x (ISBN 0-86531-964-2). Westview.
Daly, Joseph L. Strategies & Exercise in Law Related Education: A Teacher's Manual for the Student Lawyer: High School Handbook of Minnesota Law. 3rd ed. 394p. 1981. write for info. (ISBN 0-314-64061-4). West Pub.
--The Student Lawyer: High School Handbook of Minnesota Law. 3rd ed. (Illus.). 219p. 1981. pap. text ed. 5.95 (ISBN 0-314-63145-3). West Pub.
Daly, Joseph M. & Deverall, Joseph M., eds. Toxins in Plant Pathogenesis. 1983. 25.00 (ISBN 0-12-200780-8). Acad Pr.
Daly, Katherine M., et al. Nutrition & Eating Problems of Oral & Head-Neck Surgeries: A Guide to Soft & Liquid Meals. (Illus.). 414p. 1985. 38.50x (ISBN 0-398-04914-9). C C Thomas.
Daly, Kathleen N. The Joys of Christmas: A Celebration in Three Dimensions with Special Holiday Centerpiece. (Illus.). 12p. 1985. 17.95 (ISBN 0-02-725610-3). Macmillan.
--The Macmillan Picture Wordbook. LC 82-6619. (Illus.). 80p. (ps-1). 1982. 7.95 (ISBN 0-02-725600-6). Macmillan.
--The Magic of Horses. Offerman, Lynn, ed. 64p. (gr. 3 up). 1985. 9.95 (ISBN 0-671-49771-5, Little Simon). S&S.
--Raggedy Ann & Andy: Based on the Movie. LC 76-47894. (Illus.). 1977. 8.95 (ISBN 0-672-52301-9). Bobbs.
--The Shyest 'Kid in the 'Patch. (Cabbage Patch Kids Ser.). (Illus.). 40p. (gr. 1-5). 1984. 5.95 (ISBN 0-910313-30-X). Parker Bro.
--The Simon & Schuster Question & Answer Book. Barish, Wendy, ed. (Illus.). 320p. (gr. 3 up). 1982. 8.95 (ISBN 0-671-44427-1). Wanderer Bks.
--Strawberry Shortcake & Pets on Parade. (Strawberry Shortcake Ser.). (Illus.). 40p. (ps-3). 1983. cancelled 5.95 (ISBN 0-910313-06-7). Parker Bro.
--Trim-a-Tree Books, 6 bks. (Illus., Orig.). 1984. Set. pap. 4.95 (ISBN 0-590-33411-5). Scholastic Inc.
Daly, Laura. User's Guide. (Literacy Volunteers of America Readers Ser.). (Orig.). 1983. pap. 12.66 (ISBN 0-8428-9625-2). Cambridge Bk.
Daly, Lloyd W. Iohannis Philoponi: De Vocabulis Quae Diversum Signification Exhibent Secundum Differentiam Accentus. LC 81-72156. (Memoirs Ser.: Vol. 151). 1983. 20.00 (ISBN 0-87169-151-5). Am Philos.
Daly, Lowrie J. The Political Theory of John Wyclif. LC 62-20515. (Jesuit Studies). 1962. 4.95 (ISBN 0-8294-0020-9). Loyola.
Daly, M. W. Sudan. (World Bibliographical Ser.: No. 40). 175p. 1983. lib. bdg. 26.75 (ISBN 0-903450-70-4). ABC-Clio.
Daly, Marsha. Sylvester Stallone: An Illustrated Life. (Illus.). 128p. 1984. pap. 9.95 (ISBN 0-312-78180-6). St Martin.
Daly, Martin & Wilson, Margo. Sex, Evolution & Behavior. 2nd ed. 400p. 1983. pap. text ed. write for info. (ISBN 0-87150-767-6, 4511, Pub. by Willard Grant Pr). PWS Pubs.
Daly, Martin, ed. Modernization in the Sudan. 224p. 1985. text ed. 29.50x (ISBN 0-936508-11-6). Barber Pr.
Daly, Mary. Beyond God the Father: Toward a Philosophy of Women's Liberation. 2nd rev. ed. LC 84-45067. 257p. 1985. 18.95 (ISBN 0-8070-1502-4); pap. 8.95 (ISBN 0-8070-1503-2, BP681). Beacon Pr.
--The Church & the Second Sex. rev. ed. LC 85-47519. 240p. 1985. pap. 8.95 (ISBN 0-8070-1101-0, BP 698). Beacon Pr.
--Gyn-Ecology: The Metaethics of Radical Feminism. LC 78-53790. 1979. pap. 9.95 (ISBN 0-8070-1511-3, BP601). Beacon Pr.
--Pure Lust: Elemental Feminist Philosophy. LC 83-71944. 488p. 1984. 18.95 (ISBN 0-8070-1504-0); pap. 11.95 (ISBN 0-8070-1505-9, BP 692). Beacon Pr.
Daly, Maureen. Seventeenth Summer. (gr. 7-9). 1968. pap. 2.50 (ISBN 0-671-44386-0). Archway.
--Seventeenth Summer. 293p. 1981. Repr. PLB 16.95x (ISBN 0-89966-355-9). Buccaneer Bks.

--Seventeenth Summer. 288p. (YA) 1981. Repr. PLB 12.95x (ISBN 0-89967-029-6). Harmony Raine.
--Seventeenth Summer. 272p. (gr. 6 up). 1985. 10.95 (ISBN 0-396-02322-3). Dodd.
Daly, Maxine E., jt. auth. see Parker, Robert P., Jr.
Daly, Muriel D. Ants' Nest. LC 79-37265. (Short Story Index Reprint Ser.). Repr. of 1938 ed. 18.00 (ISBN 0-8369-4076-8). Ayer Co Pubs.
Daly, N. R., ed. Advances in Mass Spectrometry, Vol. 7 In 2 Parts. 1800p. 1978. 435.95 (ISBN 0-471-25657-9, Pub. by Wiley Heyden). Wiley.
Daly, Niki. Ben's Gingerbread Man. LC 85-3327. (Illus.). 24p. (ps-1). 1985. 4.95 (ISBN 0-670-80806-7). Viking.
--Joseph's Other Red Sock. LC 81-66440. (Illus.). 32p. (ps-2). 1982. PLB 10.95 (ISBN 0-689-50216-8, McElderry Bk). Atheneum.
--Monsters Are Like That. LC 85-3328. (Illus.). 24p. (ps-1). 1985. 4.95 (ISBN 0-670-80807-5). Viking.
--Teddy's Ear. (Illus.). 24p. (ps-1). 1985. 4.95 (ISBN 0-670-80808-3). Viking.
--Vim the Rag Mouse. LC 79-63334. (Illus.). 32p. (ps-4). 1979. 9.95 (ISBN 0-689-50141-2, McElderry Bk). Atheneum.
Daly, Peter. The Biotechnology Business: A Strategic Analysis. 150p. 1985. 25.00x (ISBN 0-8476-7460-6). Rowman.
Daly, Peter M. & Lappe, Claus O. Text und Variantenkonkordanz zu Schillers "Kabale und Liebe". 1976. 182.00x (ISBN 3-11-002225-7). De Gruyter.
Daly, Peter M., ed. Andreas Alciatus, 2 vols. (Illus.). 832p. Date not set. The/Latin Emblems, Vol. I, 368 pp. 125.00X (ISBN 0-8020-2425-4). Emblems in Translation, Vol. II, 464 pp. U of Toronto Pr.
--The European Emblem: Towards an Index Emblematicus. 152p. pap. text ed. 12.00 (ISBN 0-88920-090-4, Pub. by Wilfred Laurier U Pr Canada). Humanities.
Daly, Pierrette, tr. see Konnyu, Leslie.
Daly, Reginald A. The Changing World of the Ice Age. 1963. Repr. of 1934 ed. 21.75x (ISBN 0-02-843500-1). Hafner.
--Igneous Rocks & the Depths of the Earth. (Illus.). 1968. Repr. of 1933 ed. 28.50x (ISBN 0-02-843510-9). Hafner.
--Our Mobile Earth. LC 80-2889. (BCL Ser.: I & II). (Illus.). Repr. of 1926 ed. 47.50 (ISBN 0-404-18066-3). AMS Pr.
--Strength & Structure of the Earth. 1969. Repr. of 1940 ed. 24.95x (ISBN 0-02-843520-6). Hafner.
Daly, Reginald D. Changing World of the Ice Age. 1934. 19.50x (ISBN 0-686-83502-6). Elliots Bks.
Daly, Richard R. After Day One: Implementing the Changes in the Library of Congress Cataloging. 28p. (Orig.). 1981. pap. text ed. 4.00x (ISBN 0-8389-0338-X). ALA.
Daly, Richard T. Applications of the Mathematical Theory of Linguistics. (Janua Linguarum Ser. Minor: No. 185). 1974. pap. text ed. 13.20x (ISBN 90-2792-684-0). Mouton.
Daly, Robert. God's Altar: The World & the Flesh in Puritan Poetry. LC 77-76182. 1978. 21.00x (ISBN 0-520-03480-5). U of Cal Pr.
Daly, Robert J. Christian Biblical Ethics. (Orig.). 1984. pap. 9.95 (ISBN 0-8091-2592-7). Paulist Pr.
--Christian Sacrifice: The Judaeo-Christian Background Before Origen. LC 78-12004. (Studies in Christian Antiquity: Vol. 18). 587p. 1978. 26.95x (ISBN 0-8132-0530-1). Cath U Pr.
Daly, Robert J., jt. auth. see Helgeland, John.
Daly, Robert J., tr. see Von Balthasar, Hans U.
Daly, Robert J., et al, eds. Religious Life in the U. S. Church: The New Dialogue. 1984. pap. 10.95 (ISBN 0-8091-2683-4). Paulist Pr.
Daly, Robert W., ed. see Keeler, William F.
Daly, Saralyn R., tr. from Span. see Ruiz, Juan.
Daly, T. A., ed. Little Book of American Humorous Verse. facsimile ed. LC 73-38597. (Granger Index Reprint Ser.). Repr. of 1926 ed. 16.00 (ISBN 0-8369-6329-6). Ayer Co Pubs.
--A Little Book of American Humorous Verse. LC 79-50840. (Granger Poetry Library). 1979. Repr. of 1926 ed. 16.50x (ISBN 0-89609-156-2). Granger Bk.
Daly, Thomas A. Painting Nature's Quiet Places. (Illus.). 144p. 1984. 24.95 (ISBN 0-8230-3724-X). Watson-Guptill.
Daly, Thomas A. & National Soft Drink Association. NSDA Legal Briefing Conference, September 19-21: Proceedings, 1983, Four Seasons Hotel, Washington, D. C. LC 84-225758. write for info. Amer Bar Assn.
Daly, Victor. Not Only War: A Story of Two Great Conflicts. LC 72-126689. Repr. of 1932 ed. 18.50 (ISBN 0-404-00147-5). AMS Pr.
Dalyell, John G. The Darker Superstitions of Scotland. LC 77-26734. 55.00 (ISBN 0-8414-1863-2). Folcroft.
--The Darker Superstitions of Scotland. 700p. 1980. Repr. of 1835 ed. lib. bdg. 75.00 (ISBN 0-8492-4211-8). R West.
--Musical Memoirs of Scotland, with Historical Annotations. LC 74-40186. 1976. Repr. of 1849 ed. lib. bdg. 45.00 (ISBN 0-8414-3811-0). Folcroft.
--Musical Memoirs of Scotland with Historical Annotations. LC 72-6979. 1972. lib. bdg. 37.50 (ISBN 0-88305-152-4). Norwood Edns.
Dalyell, Sir John G. Musical Memoirs of Scotland. 300p. 1980. Repr. of 1849 ed. lib. bdg. 35.00 (ISBN 0-8492-4214-2). R West.
Dalyell, Tam. One Man's Falklands. 144p. 1982. text ed. 12.25x (ISBN 0-900821-65-5). Humanities.
--Thatcher's Torpedo: The Sinking of the Belgrano. 80p. 1983. text ed. 12.25x (ISBN 0-900821-67-1, Pub. by C Woolf UK). Humanities.
Dalzel, Archibald. History of Dahomey, Inland Kingdom of Africa. (Illus.). 230p. 1967. Repr. of 1793 ed. 35.00x (ISBN 0-7146-1141-7, BHA-01141, F Cass Co). Biblio Dist.
Dalzell, George W., jt. auth. see Canfield, George L.
Dalzell, Helen. Not the Marrying Kind. (Harlequin Romances Ser.). 192p. 1983. pap. 1.75 (ISBN 0-373-02570-X). Harlequin Bks.
Dalzell, J. Ralph. Simplified Concrete Masonry Planning & Building. 2nd, rev. ed. Merritt, Frederick S., rev. by. LC 81-385. 398p. 1981. Repr. of 1972 ed. lib. bdg. 19.50 (ISBN 0-89874-278-1). Krieger.
Dalzell, R. & Townsend, G. Masonry Simplified: Tools, Materials, Practices. 3rd ed. (Illus.). 1972. 14.95 (ISBN 0-8269-0627-3). Am Technical.
Dalzell, Ralph J. & Merritt, Frederick. Plan Reading for Home Builders. 2nd ed. LC 82-14057. 186p. 1983. Repr. of 1972 ed. 14.50 (ISBN 0-89874-393-1). Krieger.
Dalzell, Robert F., Jr. Daniel Webster & the Trial of American Nationalism, 1843-1852. 384p. 1975. pap. 4.95x (ISBN 0-393-00782-0, N782, Norton Lib). Norton.
Dalzell, W. R. The Shell Guide to the History of London. (Illus.). 1981. 29.95 (ISBN 0-393-01593-9). Norton.
Dalziel, Allan. Evatt the Enigma: Controverial Australian. 17.50x (ISBN 0-392-07762-0, SpS). Sportshelf.
Dalziel, Ian W. Tectonic Evolution of a Forearc Terrane, South Georgia Ridge, Antarctica. (Special Paper Ser.: No. 200). (Illus.). 1984. 9.00 (ISBN 0-8137-2200-4). Geol Soc.
Dam, B. A. van see Van Dam, B. A.
Dam, Bastiaan A. van. Shakespeare Problems Nearing Solution. LC 77-23096. 1977. Repr. of 1930 ed. lib. bdg. 9.50 (ISBN 0-8414-9188-7). Folcroft.
--Shakespeare Problems Nearing Solution. 17p. 1980. Repr. of 1930 ed. lib. bdg. 10.00 (ISBN 0-8492-4213-4). R West.
Dam, Bastiaan A. Van & Stoffel, Cornelis O. Chapters on English Printing, Prosody & Punctuation, 1550-1700. Repr. of 1902 ed. 9.00 (ISBN 0-404-06751-4). AMS Pr.
Dam, Bastiaan A. Van & Stoffel, Cornelius O. William Shakespeare: Prosody & Text. LC 75-177557. Repr. of 1900 ed. 15.00 (ISBN 0-404-06752-2). AMS Pr.
Dam, Bastiaan A. Van see Dam, Bastiaan A. Van & Stoffel, Cornelis O.
Dam, Bastiaan A. Van see Van Dam, Bastiaan A. & Stoffel, Cornelius O.
Dam, Cees Van see Van Dam, Cees.
Dam, Cees Van see Van Dam, Cees & Stallaert, Luud M.
Dam, Hari N. The Intellectual Odyssey of Walter Lippmann. 1973. 69.95 (ISBN 0-87968-057-1). Gordon Pr.
Dam, Ine Van see Van Dam, Ine.
Dam, Kenneth W. America's Near West: U. S. -Japan Relations in Perspective. 1984. 3.00 (ISBN 0-317-06767-2). Japan Soc.
--The GATT: Law - the International Economic Organization. LC 75-93088. (Midway Reprint Ser.). 1970. pap. text ed. 22.00x (ISBN 0-226-13496-2). U of Chicago Pr.
--Oil Resources: Who Gets What How? LC 75-43239. 1976. lib. bdg. 20.00x (ISBN 0-226-13497-0); pap. 4.95x (ISBN 0-226-13498-9, P 776, Phoen). U of Chicago Pr.
--The Role of Rules in the International Monetary System. LC 76-47303. 1976. pap. 1.50 (ISBN 0-916770-03-6). Law & Econ U Miami.
--The Rules of the Game: Reform & Evolution in the International Monetary System. LC 81-10416. 1982. pap. 12.50x (ISBN 0-226-13500-4). U of Chicago Pr.
Dam, Kenneth W., jt. auth. see Shultz, George P.
Dam, Mogens, et al, eds. see Epilepsy International Symposium, 12th. Copenhagen, Denmark, et al.
Dam, Raymond van see Van Dam, Raymond.
Dam, Rika van see Green, Kenneth C. & Van Dam, Rika.
Dam, Rika van see Green, Kenneth & Van Dam, Rika.
Dam, Theo Van see Van Dam, Theo.
Dam, V. A. van see Van Dam, B. A.
Damachi, U. G., et al, eds. Industrial Relations in Africa. LC 79-12765. 35.00x (ISBN 0-312-41457-9). St Martin.
Damachi, Ukandi G. Nigerian Modernization. LC 75-183394. 160p. 1972. 7.95 (ISBN 0-89388-030-2). Okpaku Communications.
Damachi, Ukandi G. & Diejomaoh, Victor P. Human Resources & African Development. LC 78-19133. (Praeger Special Studies). 400p. 1978. 49.95 (ISBN 0-03-022826-3). Praeger.
Damachi, Ukandi G., jt. auth. see Seibel, Hans D.
Damachi, Ukandi G. & Seibel, Hans D., eds. Management Problems in Africa. 300p. 1985. 32.50 (ISBN 0-312-51235-X). St Martin.
Damain, A. L. & Solomon, N. A., eds. Antibiotics Containing the Beta-Lactam Structure I. (Handbook of Experimental Pharmacology: Vol. 67-I). (Illus.). 362p. 1983. 118.00 (ISBN 0-387-12107-2). Springer-Verlag.
Damali. I Am That We May Be. 1974. pap. 1.50 (ISBN 0-88378-034-8). Third World.
Damani, L. A., jt. ed. see Gorrod, J. W.
Damarin, Suzanne K. & Leitzel, Joan R. Algebra: A Book for Adults. LC 83-7023. 334p. 1984. text ed. 26.95 (ISBN 0-471-86274-6); write for info. tchr's manual (ISBN 0-471-88838-9). Wiley.
Damaris, Gypsy. Pink Hair. 20p. (Orig.). (gr. 1). 1984. pap. 2.35 (ISBN 0-914917-00-5). Folk Life.
Damas, David & Sturtevant, William C., eds. Handbook of North American Indians, Vol. 5: Arctic. LC 77-17162. (Illus.). 862p. 1985. 29.00n (ISBN 0-87474-185-8, DAV5). Smithsonian.
Damascene, John & Oecuminical Synod Seventh. The Icon. Cavarnos, Constantine, tr. from Gr. (Illus.). 11p. 1979. pap. 0.90 (ISBN 0-914744-19-4). Inst Byzantine.
Damascene, John see John Damascene, Saint.
Damask, A. C. Medical Physics, 2 vols. 1978. Vol. 1 Physiological Physics, External Probes. 34.00 (ISBN 0-12-201201-1). Acad Pr.
Damask, A. C. & Dienes, G. J. Point Defects in Metals. 328p. 1963. 76.50 (ISBN 0-677-00190-8). Gordon.
Damask, A. C. & Swenberg, C. E. Medical Physics, Vol. 3. 1984. 69.00 (ISBN 0-12-201203-8). Acad Pr.
Damask, Arthur. Medical Physics: External Senses, Vol. 2. 1981. 32.50 (ISBN 0-12-201202-X). Acad Pr.
Damaskin, Boris B., et al. Adsorption of Organic Compounds on Electrodes. LC 69-17533. 500p. 1971. 69.50x (ISBN 0-306-30432-5, Plenum Pr). Plenum Pub.
D'Amat, Roman, jt. ed. see Prevost, M. M.
Da Mata, F. S. Soya Bean & Weather. (Technical Note Ser.: No. 160). xvi, 64p. 1978. pap. 20.00 (ISBN 92-63-10498-0, W396, WMO). Unipub.
Damato. How to Collect, Refinish & Restore Antique & Country Furniture. (Illus.). 368p. 1982. o.p 19.95 (ISBN 0-8306-0084-1); pap. 12.95 (ISBN 0-8306-1401-X, 1401). TAB Bks.
D'Amato, Albert C. & D'Amato, Miriam F. Discovering Acadia National Park & Mount Desert Island, Maine: 12 Places to Begin. rev. ed. (Illus.). 144p. 1985. pap. 5.95 (ISBN 0-9615276-0-9). Pro Edit Serv.
D'Amato, Alex & D'Amato, Janet. Italian Crafts: Inspirations from Folk Art. LC 76-30523. (Illus.). 160p. 1977. 7.95 (ISBN 0-87131-227-1). M Evans.
--Quillwork: The Craft of Paper Filigree. LC 74-26757. (Illus.). 128p. 1975. 8.95 (ISBN 0-87131-171-2); pap. 4.95 (ISBN 0-87131-177-1). M Evans.
D'Amato, Alex, jt. auth. see D'Amato, Janet.
D'Amato, Anthony. Jurisprudence: A Descriptive & Normative Analysis of Law. LC 83-24964. 1984. lib. bdg. 53.50 (ISBN 90-247-2919-X, Pub. by Martinus Nijhoff Netherlands). Kluwer Academic.
D'Amato, Francesco. Nuclear Cytology in Relation to Development. LC 76-46045. (Developmental & Cell Biology Ser.: No. 6). 1977. 60.00 (ISBN 0-521-21508-0). Cambridge U Pr.
D'Amato, Janet & D'Amato, Alex. American Indian Craft Inspirations. LC 72-83734. (Illus.). 224p. (YA) 1972. 7.95 (ISBN 0-87131-031-7). M Evans.
--Cardboard Carpentry. (Activity Bks). (Illus.). (gr. 2-5). PLB 8.95 (ISBN 0-87460-085-5). Lion Bks.
--Handicrafts for Holidays. (Illus.). (gr. 1-4). 1967. PLB 8.95 (ISBN 0-87460-086-3). Lion Bks.
--Indian Crafts. (Illus.). (gr. 1-4). PLB 8.95 (ISBN 0-87460-088-X). Lion Bks.
--My First Book of Riddles. (ps-1). 1974. 0.99 (ISBN 0-8431-4150-6). Wonder.
D'Amato, Janet, jt. auth. see D'Amato, Alex.
D'Amato, Janet P. Who's a Horn? What's an Antler? Crafts of Bone & Horn. LC 82-2286. 96p. (gr. 4 up). 1982. PLB 9.79 (ISBN 0-671-41975-7). Messner.
D'Amato, Miriam F., jt. auth. see D'Amato, Albert C.
Da Matta, Roberto. A Divided World: Apinaye Social Structure. (Studies in Cultural Anthropology: No. 6). (Illus.). 216p. 1982. text ed. 40.00x (ISBN 0-674-21288-6). Harvard U Pr.
Damazio, Frank. The Making of a Leader. 246p. 1979. pap. 12.95 (ISBN 0-914936-37-9). Bible Temple.
Dambach, John I. Physical Education in Germany. LC 71-176717. (Columbia University. Teachers College. Contributions to Education: No. 731). Repr. of 1937 ed. 22.50 (ISBN 0-404-55731-7). AMS Pr.
D'Amboise, Jaques, et al. Teaching the Magic of Dance. (Illus.). 1983. 17.95 (ISBN 0-671-46077-3); pap. 10.95 (ISBN 0-671-49401-5). S&S.
Dambriunas, L. A. Introduction to Modern Lithuanian. 2nd, rev. ed. 1972. 25.00 (ISBN 0-685-47301-5). Heinman.
Dambriunas, L A. Introduction to Modern Lithuanian. 1982. Set of Four. Cassettes 40.00 (ISBN 0-686-46524-5). Heinman.
Dambroff, Susan. Memory in Bone. (Illus.). 68p. 1984. pap. 8.00 (ISBN 0-9605966-2-3). Black Oyster.
D'Ambrosia, R. & Drez, D. Prevention & Treatment of Running Injuries. LC 81-86239. 204p. 1982. text ed. 39.50 (ISBN 0-913590-86-X). Slack Inc.
D'Ambrosia, Robert D., ed. Musculoskeletal Disorders: Regional Examination & Differential Diagnosis. LC 77-8562. 1977. 58.50i (ISBN 0-397-50373-3, Lippincott Medical). Lippincott.
D'Ambrosie, Charles A., jt. auth. see Archer, Stephen H.
D'Ambrosio, Bobbe, et al. Spell Well. (Makemaster Bk.). 1980. pap. 9.95 (ISBN 0-8224-6455-1). Pitman Learning.
D'Ambrosio, Bruce, jt. auth. see Klemperer, Katharina.
D'Ambrosio, Charles A. Principles of Modern Investments. LC 75-34094. (Illus.). 512p. 1976. text ed. 27.95 (ISBN 0-574-19210-7, 13-2210); instr's guide avail. (ISBN 0-574-19211-5, 13-2211). SRA.
D'Ambrosio, Charles A., jt. auth. see Archer, Stephen N.
D'Ambrosio, Peter, jt. auth. see Kornbluh, Harvey L.
D'ambrosio, Richard. No Language but a Cry. (gr. 9 up). 1971. pap. 2.25 (ISBN 0-440-36457-4, LE). Dell.
Dambry, Patricia, ed. see Hardy, Judith, et al.
Damburg, Robert, ed. Atomic Physics Six. LC 72-176581. 666p. 1979. 92.50x (ISBN 0-306-40217-3, Plenum Pr). Plenum Pub.
Damby, Patricia, ed. see Hardy, Judith & Churchill, James.
Dame, Enid. Confessions. Barkan, Stanley H., ed. (Cross-Cultural Review Chapbook 12: American Poetry 6). 16p. 1980. pap. 2.00 (ISBN 0-89304-811-9). Cross Cult.
Dame, L. Yucatan. 1976. lib. bdg. 59.95 (ISBN 0-8490-2854-X). Gordon Pr.
Dame, Lorin L. & Brooks, Henry. Handbook of the Trees of New England with Ranges Throughout the United States & Canada. (Illus., With a new Table of Changes in Nomenclature). 11.25 (ISBN 0-8446-4533-8). Peter Smith.
Dame, Richard F., ed. Marsh-Estuarine Systems Simulation. LC 78-31554. (Belle W. Baruch Library in Marine Science Ser.). xii, 260p. 1979. lib. bdg. 39.95x (ISBN 0-87249-375-X). U of SC Pr.
D'Amelio, Joseph. Perspective Drawing Handbook. (Illus.). 12.95 (ISBN 0-8148-0236-2). L Amiel Pub.
--Perspective Drawing Handbook. LC 83-12399. (Illus.). 96p. 1984. pap. 10.95 (ISBN 0-442-21828-1). Van Nos Reinhold.
Damer, Eyre. When the Ku Klux Rode. facsimile ed. LC 79-37588. (Black Heritage Library Collection). Repr. of 1912 ed. 13.25 (ISBN 0-8369-8964-3). Ayer Co Pubs.
--When the Ku Klux Rode. LC 70-106882. Repr. of 1912 ed. 10.25x (ISBN 0-8371-3278-9, DAK&). Greenwood.
Damer, T. Edward. Attacking Faulty Reasoning. 1979. pap. text ed. write for info (ISBN 0-534-00750-3). Wadsworth Pub.
Damerau, Frederick J. Markov Models & Linguistic Theory: An Experimental Study of a Model for English. LC 78-135666. (Janua Linguarum, Ser. Minor: No. 95). (Orig.). 1971. pap. text ed. 18.40x (ISBN 90-2791-707-8). Mouton.
Damerell, Edna K. Twice is Nice: Over 600 Fabulous Recipes for Creating Delicious New Meals from Once-Cooked Food. 360p. 1984. pap. 9.95 (ISBN 0-02-009640-2, Collier). Macmillan.
Damerell, Reginald G. Education's Smoking Gun: How Teachers Colleges Have Destroyed Education in America. 256p. 1985. 17.95 (ISBN 0-88191-025-2). Freundlich.
Dameron, J. Lasley. Popular Literature: Poe's Not So Soon Forgotten Lore. Kadis, Averil J., ed. 1980. pap. 2.50 (ISBN 0-910556-16-4). Enoch Pratt.
Dameron, J. Lasley & Cauthen, Irby B., Jr. Edgar Allan Poe: A Bibliography of Criticism, 1827-1967. LC 73-89824. (Bibliographical Society). xvi, 386p. 1974. 25.00x (ISBN 0-8139-0498-6). U Pr of Va.
Dameron, J. Lasley & Mathews, James W., eds. No Fairer Land: Studies in Southern Literature Before 1900. LC 85-51200. vi, 245p. 1985. 22.50 (ISBN 0-87875-305-2). Whitston Pub.
Damerst, William A. Clear Technical Reports. 2nd ed. 325p. 1982. pap. text ed. 15.95 (ISBN 0-15-507692-2, HC). HarBraceJ.
Dames & Moore. Alternative Siting Requirements & Practices for Nuclear Power Plants (AIF NESP 018) (National Environmental Studies Project: NESP Reports). 300p. 1980. 45.00 (ISBN 0-318-13551-5); to NESP sponsors 15.00 (ISBN 0-318-13552-3). Atomic Indus Forum.
--Generic Methodology for Assessment of Radiation Doses from Groundwater Migration of Radionuclides in LWR Wastes in Shallow Land Burial Trenches (AIF-NESP-013) rev. ed. (National Environmental Studies Project-AIF-Inforum: NESP Reports). 207p. 1979. 60.00 (ISBN 0-318-13580-9); to NESP sponsors 20.00 (ISBN 0-318-13581-7). Atomic Indus Forum.
Dames, Mansel L., tr. see Barbosa, Duarte.
Dames, Ralph T. The Winning Option. LC 79-23369. 128p. 1980. 18.95 (ISBN 0-88229-527-6). Nelson-Hall.
Dameshek, William & Dutcher, Raymond M., eds. Perspectives in Leukemia. LC 67-26211. (A Leukemia Society Symposium Ser.). (Illus.). 312p. 1968. 81.00 (ISBN 0-8089-0108-7, 790975). Grune.

Dameton, Joseph, ed. The Professional Counselor: Competencies, Performance Guidelines & Assessment. 102p. 1980. 7.25 (ISBN 0-911547-63-0, 72141W34); members 6.50 (ISBN 0-686-37319-7). Am Assn Coun Dev.

Dametz, Max. John Vanbrughs Leben und Werke. pap. 25.00 (ISBN 0-384-10755-9), Johnson Repr.

Damewood, Glenn, et al. Noise Abatement at Gas Pipelines Installations: Blow-off Noise Suppression & Regulator Valve Noise Generation, Vol. III. 121p. 1961. softcover 5.50 (ISBN 0-318-12661-3, L00280). Am Gas Assn.

Damiamayan, Dikran. Analysis of Aperture Antennas in Inhomogeneous Media. LC 77-141023. 93p. 1969. 17.50 (ISBN 0-403-04493-6). Mgmt Info Serv.

Damian, Peter. Book of Gomorrah: An Eleventh-Century Treaties Against Clerical Homosexual Practices. Payer, Pierre J., tr. 120p. 1982. pap. text ed. 9.75x (ISBN 0-88920-123-4, Pub. by Wilfred Laurier U Pr Canada). Humanities.

Damiani, Anita. Enlightened Observers: British Travellers to the Near East, Seventeen Fifty to Eighteen Fifty. 1979. 18.00x (ISBN 0-8156-6055-3, Am U Beirut). Syracuse U Pr.

Damiani, Bruno M. La Diana of Montemayor as Social & Religious Teaching. LC 83-3608. (Studies in Romance Languages: No. 28). 128p. 1984. 15.00x (ISBN 0-8131-1489-6). U Pr of Ky.

--Montemayor's Diana, Music, & the Visual Arts. 118p. 1983. 11.00x (ISBN 0-942260-28-7). Hispanic Seminary.

Damiani, Bruno M., ed. Renaissance & Golden Age Essays in Honor of D. W. McPheeters. (Span.). 1984. 25.00 (ISBN 0-916379-10-8). Scripta.

Damiani, Bruno M., tr. see Delicado, Francisco.

Damiani, Rodolfo V. The Stock Market Theory of the Circulation of the Classes: How to Apply & Interpret it Properly for the Maximization of Profits. (Illus.). 113p. 1984. 77.45x (ISBN 0-86654-098-9). Inst Econ Finan.

Damiani Van Den Eynde & Odulphi Van Den Eynde, eds. Guidonis de Orchellis Tractatus de Sacramentis Ex Eius Summa de Sacramentis et Officiis Ecclesiae. (Text Ser). 1953. 11.00 (ISBN 0-686-11549-X). Franciscan Inst.

Damian-Knight, Guy. I Ching on Love. 334p. 1985. 12.95 (ISBN 0-7137-1482-4, Pub. by Blandford England); pap. 7.95 (ISBN 0-7137-1516-2). Sterling.

Damico, Alfonso J. Democracy & the Case for Amnesty. LC 75-12502. (University of Florida Social Sciences Monographs: No. 55). 78p. 1975. pap. 3.50 (ISBN 0-8130-0527-2). U Presses Fla.

--Individuality & Community: The Social & Political Thought of John Dewey. LC 78-7335. 1978. 10.50 (ISBN 0-8130-0602-3). U Presses Fla.

D'Amico, Angela S. One Hundred & One Garlic & Oil Nutritious Italian Recipes. Date not set. 6.95 (ISBN 0-8062-2406-1). Carlton.

D'Amico, Ferninando & Valentini, Gabriele. The Messerschmitt 109 in Italian Service, 1943-1945. Dempsey, Raymond J., ed. LC 84-61276. (Illus.). 128p. 1985. 29.95 (ISBN 0-317-19692-8). Monogram Aviation.

D'Amico, G. & Colasanti, G., eds. Advances in Nephrology & Dialysis. (Contributions to Nephrology: Vol. 45). (Illus.). x, 214p. 1985. 55.50 (ISBN 3-8055-3963-0). S Karger.

--Current Studies in Nephrology: Dialysis & Transplantation, Vol. 48. (Contributions to Nephrology Ser.). (Illus.). x, 190p. 1985. 55.50 (ISBN 3-8055-4141-4). S Karger.

D'Amico, G., et al, eds. IGA Mesangial Nephropathy. (Contributions to Nephrology: Vol. 40). (Illus.). x, 310p. 1984. 69.50x (ISBN 3-8055-3877-4). S Karger.

Damico, Helen. Beowulf's Wealhtheow & the Valkyrie Tradition. LC 83-40262. 256p. 1984. text ed. 35.00x (ISBN 0-299-09500-2). U of Wis Pr.

D'Amico, John F. Renaissance Humanism in Papal Rome: Humanists & Churchmen on the Eve of the Reformation. LC 82-49059. (Studies in Historical & Political Science). 352p. 1983. text ed. 28.50x (ISBN 0-8018-2860-0). Johns Hopkins.

D'Amico, M., jt. auth. see Zikmund, W. G.

D'Amico, Michael, jt. auth. see Zikmund, William.

D'Amico, Paul M. Addictions, Cults & Disease: The Final Solution. LC 79-56100. (Illus.). 172p. 1981. 9.95 (ISBN 0-9607270-0-0). D'Amico.

D'Amico, Robert. Marx & Philosophy of Culture. LC 80-24405. (University of Florida Humanities Monograph: No. 50). viii, 108p. (Orig.). 1981. pap. 7.00 (ISBN 0-8130-0689-9). U Presses Fla.

Damien, Yvonne M. & Smith, Margo L., eds. Anthropological Bibliographies: A Selected Guide. vii, 307p. (Orig.). 1981. 22.50 (ISBN 0-913178-63-2). Redgrave Pub Co.

Damino, Robert. Relations: A Handbook for Living. 260p. (Orig.). 1985. pap. 10.95 (ISBN 0-89769-065-6, Dist. by Caroline Hse.). Pine Mntn.

Damion, Vincent E. Handicapping in the Winners Circle. LC 83-50366. (Winning at the Races Ser.). (Illus., Orig.). 1983. pap. text ed. 14.95 (ISBN 0-9611764-0-7). Three D Pub.

Damirus. Der Longobardischen Koenigin Rosemundae, Wahrhaffte Lebens & Liebesgeschicht. 690p. Repr. of 1729 ed. 75.00 (ISBN 0-384-10760-5). Johnson Repr.

Damis, John. Conflict in Northwest Africa: The Western Sahara Dispute. (Publication Ser.: 278). (Illus.). 245p. 1983. 18.95 (ISBN 0-8179-7781-3); pap. text ed. 9.95 (ISBN 0-8179-7782-1). Hoover Inst Pr.

Damisch, Isabel M. Les Images Chez John Webster, Tome 1 & 2. (Salzburg Studies in English Literature: Jacobean Drama Studies: No. 66 & 67). (Fr.). 1977. pap. text ed. 25.50x (ISBN 0-686-76902-3); Tome 1. pap. text ed. (ISBN 0-391-01355-6); Tome 2. pap. text ed. 25.50x (ISBN 0-391-01356-4). Humanities.

Damjan, Mischa. The False Flamingoes. LC 70-105399. (Illus.). 32p. (ps-3). 6.95 (ISBN 0-87592-016-0). Scroll Pr.

Damjanov, Ivan. General Pathology. 2nd ed. (Medical Outline Ser.). 1982. 23.50 (ISBN 0-87488-628-7). Med Exam.

--Ultrastructural Pathology of Human Tumors, Vol. 1. Horrobin, D. F., ed. LC 79-319782. (Annual Research Reviews Ser.). 1979. 24.00 (ISBN 0-88831-045-5). Eden Pr.

--Ultrastructural Pathology of Human Tumors, Vol. 2. Horrobin, D. F., ed. (Annual Research Reviews). 144p. 1980. 24.00 (ISBN 0-88831-082-X). Eden Pr.

Damjanov, Ivan, et al, eds. The Human Teratomas. LC 82-48865. (Contemporary Biomedicine Ser.). 376p. 1983. 49.50 (ISBN 0-89603-040-7). Humana.

Damjanovich. Membrane Dynamics Transport of Normal Tumor Cells of the International Symposium. 1984. text ed. 45.00 (ISBN 0-9910002-3-4, Pub. by Akademiai Kaido Hungary). Heyden.

Damkaer, Carl & Damkaer, David. Henrik Kroeyer's Publications on Pelagic Marine Copepoda (1838-1849) LC 79-51538. (Transactions Ser.: Vol. 69, Pt. 6). 1979. 8.00 (ISBN 0-87169-696-7). Am Philos.

Damkaer, David, jt. auth. see Damkaer, Carl.

Damkohler, E. E. Estero, Florida 1882. LC 67-19575. 1974. pap. 1.00 (ISBN 0-87208-014-5). Island Pr.

Damlamian, A., jt. ed. see Bardos, C.

Damlouji, Namir F. & Feighner, John. Psychiatry Specialty Board Review. 1983. pap. text ed. 27.50 (ISBN 0-87488-312-1). Med Exam.

Damm, Helene Van see Von Damm, Helene.

Damman, Kirk. The Cruise of the Skuld. 224p. (Orig.). 1985. pap. 6.00 (ISBN 0-914752-21-9). Sovereign Pr.

Dammann, Erik. The Future in Our Hands. (Illus.). 1979. 30.00 (ISBN 0-08-024284-7); pap. 11.50 (ISBN 0-08-024283-9). Pergamon.

Dammann, George, jt. auth. see Moloney, James.

Dammann, George, ed. see Shives, Bob & Thompson, Bill.

Dammann, George H. Illustrated History of Ford. (Illus.). 320p. 28.95 (ISBN 0-317-11548-0). Diamond Farm Bk.

--Illustrated History of Ford, 1903-1970. 3rd ed. LC 73-101694. (Automotive Ser.). (Illus.). 320p. 1974. 24.95 (ISBN 0-912612-02-9). Crestline.

--Seventy Years of Buick. rev. ed. LC 72-94176. (Automotive Ser.). (Illus.). 352p. 1975. 24.95 (ISBN 0-912612-04-5). Crestline.

--Seventy Years of Buick. (Illus.). 352p. 28.95 (ISBN 0-317-11547-2). Diamond Farm Bk.

--Seventy Years of Chrysler. LC 74-75795. (Automotive Ser.). (Illus.). 384p. 1974. 29.95 (ISBN 0-912612-06-1). Crestline.

--Seventy Years of Chrysler. (Illus.). 384p. 32.95 (ISBN 0-317-11553-7). Diamond Farm Bk.

--Sixty Years of Chevrolet. 3rd ed. LC 79-186267. (Automotive Ser.). (Illus.). 320p. 1973. 24.95 (ISBN 0-912612-03-7). Crestline.

--Sixty Years of Chevrolet. (Illus.). 320p. 28.95x (ISBN 0-317-11546-4). Diamond Farm Bk.

Dammann, George H., jt. auth. see Moloney, James H.

Dammann, George H., ed. see Butler, Don.

Dammann, George H., ed. see Butler, F. Donald.

Dammann, George H., ed. see Casteele, Dennis.

Dammann, George H., ed. see Crismon, Major F.

Dammann, George H., ed. see Gunnell, John.

Dammann, George H., ed. see McCall, Walter M.

Dammann, George H., ed. see McPherson, Thomas.

Dammann, George H., ed. see Moloney, James.

Dammann, George H., ed. see Norbeck, Jack.

Dammann, George H., ed. see Wagner, James K.

Dammann, George H., ed. see Wendel, Charles H.

Dammann, Gordon. An Encyclopedia of Civil War Medical Instruments & Equipment. (Illus.). 104p. 1983. 7.95 (ISBN 0-933126-32-8). Pictorial Hist.

Dammann, Nancy. A Social History of the Frontier Nursing Service. (Illus.). 179p. (Orig.). 1982. pap. 5.95 (ISBN 0-9609376-0-9). Soc Change Pr.

Dammann, Ulrich, et al, eds. Data Protection Legislation: An International Documentation, Bd. 5. (Kybernetik, Datenverarbeitung, Recht). 203p. 1977. pap. text ed. 21.00x (ISBN 3-7875-3005-3, Pub. by Alfred Metzner Verlag). Rothman.

Damme, Dirk van see Van Damme, Dirk.

Damme, E. van see Van Damme, E.

Dammers, Richard H. Richard Steele. (English Authors Ser.). 1982. lib. bdg. 14.50 (ISBN 0-8057-6837-8, Twayne). G K Hall.

Dammert, Alfredo & Palaniappan, Sethu. Modelling Investments in the World Copper Sector. 128p. 1985. text ed. 20.00x (ISBN 0-292-79026-0). U of Tex Pr.

Damodaran, L., et al. Designing Systems for People. 193p. 1980. pap. 29.50 (ISBN 0-471-89446-X). Wiley.

Damodaran, Leela, et al. Designing Systems for People. (Illus.). 193p. (Orig.). 1980. pap. 35.00x (ISBN 0-85012-242-2). Intl Pubns Serv.

Damon, et al. The Late Fourth Partner. rev. ed. pap. text ed. 5.00 (ISBN 0-88734-201-9). Players Pr.

Damon, Albert. Human Biology & Ecology. LC 77-559. (Illus.). 1977. pap. text ed. 8.95x (ISBN 0-393-09103-1). Norton.

Damon, Albert, et al. Human Body in Equipment Design. LC 65-22067. (Illus.). 1966. 25.00x (ISBN 0-674-41450-0). Harvard U Pr.

Damon, Dave, ed. see Damon, Valerie H.

Damon, Gene, pseud. Lesbiana. LC 76-45683. 1976. 5.00 (ISBN 0-930044-05-3). Naiad Pr.

Damon, James. The Unfolding & Determinacy Theorems for Subgroups of A & K. LC 84-9333. (Memoirs of the American Mathematical Society Ser.: Vol. 306). 90p. 1984. pap. 10.00 (ISBN 0-8218-2306-X). Am Math.

Damon, Lee. Lady Laughing Eyes. 192p. 1984. pap. 1.95 (ISBN 0-515-06943-4). Jove Pubns.

--Laugh with Me, Love with Me. (Second Chance at Love Ser.: No. 120). 192p. 1983. pap. 1.95 (ISBN 0-515-07208-7). Jove Pubns.

Damon, Lorraine, jt. auth. see Naidech, Howard J.

Damon, Phillip. Modes of Analogy in Ancient & Medieval Verse. (California Library Reprint Ser.: No. 33). 1973. 12.00x (ISBN 0-520-02366-8). U of Cal Pr.

Damon, Phillip, ed. Literary Criticism & Historical Understanding: Essays of the English Institute. LC 67-24335. 190p. 1967. 21.00x (ISBN 0-231-03086-X). Columbia U Pr.

Damon, Phillip see Columbia University. English Institute.

Damon, S. Foster. Amy Lowell: A Chronicle. (Illus.). xxi, 773p. 1966. Repr. of 1935 ed. 35.00 (ISBN 0-208-00150-6, Archon). Shoe String.

--A Blake Dictionary: The Ideas & Symbols of William Blake. LC 65-18187. (Illus.). 472p. 1965. 40.00x (ISBN 0-87057-088-9). U Pr of New Eng.

--Heaven & Hell. Brown, Catherine, ed. (Illus., Orig.). 1978. pap. 5.50 (ISBN 0-914278-17-7). Copper Beech.

--A Note on the Discovery of a New Page of Poetry in William Blake's Milton. LC 73-8920. 1925. lib. bdg. 8.50 (ISBN 0-8414-1881-0). Folcroft.

--William Blake: His Philosophy & Symbols. 20.25 (ISBN 0-8446-1145-X). Peter Smith.

Damon, S. Foster & Hillyer, Robert. Eight More Harvard Poets. 1977. Repr. of 1923 ed. 20.00 (ISBN 0-89984-175-9). Century Bookbindery.

Damon, S. Foster & Hillyer, Robert, eds. Eight More Harvard Poets. 1978. Repr. of 1923 ed. lib. bdg. 25.00 (ISBN 0-8495-1024-4). Arden Lib.

Damon, S. Foster, ed. see Blake, William.

Damon, Valerie H. Grindle Lamfoon & the Procurnious Fleekers. Damon, Dave, ed. LC 78-64526. (Illus.). (gr. 1-12). 1979. 12.95 (ISBN 0-932356-05-2); fleeker ed. 14.95 (ISBN 0-932356-06-0). Star Pubns MO.

--Willo Mancifoot (and the Mugga Killa Whomps) Damon, Dave, ed. LC 83-50739. (Illus.). (gr. 2-6). 1985. 14.95 (ISBN 0-932356-07-9); ltd. art ed. 100.00 (ISBN 0-932356-08-7). Star Pubns Mo.

Damon, William. Social & Personality Development: Essays on the Growth of the Child. 504p. 1983. pap. text ed. 14.95x (ISBN 0-393-95307-6). Norton.

--Social & Personality Development: From Infancy Through Adolescence. (Illus.). 1983. pap. text ed. 14.95x (ISBN 0-393-95248-7). Norton.

--The Social World of the Child. LC 77-79480. (Social & Behavioral Science Ser.). 1977. text ed. 21.95x (ISBN 0-87589-339-2). Jossey-Bass.

Damore, Leo. Cache. LC 78-73868. 1979. 8.95 (ISBN 0-87795-222-1). Arbor Hse.

--The Crime of Dorothy Sheridan. LC 77-93047. 1978. 9.95 (ISBN 0-87795-189-6). Arbor Hse.

--In His Garden: The Anatomy of a Murderer. LC 79-54008. (Illus.). 1981. 14.95 (ISBN 0-87795-250-7). Arbor Hse.

Da Mota, A. Teixeira. Some Aspects of Portuguese Colonization & Sea Trade in West Africa in the 15th & 16th Centuries. (Hans Wolff Memorial Lecture Ser.). 29p. (Orig.). 1978. pap. text ed. 2.50 (ISBN 0-941934-22-5). Indiana Africa.

D'Amoto, Richard F., jt. auth. see McGinnis, Michael R.

D'Amour, Fred E., et al, illus. Manual for Laboratory Work in Mammalian Physiology. 3rd ed. LC 65-17285. 1965. spiral bdg. 19.00x (ISBN 0-226-13563-2). U of Chicago Pr.

Damour, Jacques. One Hundred & One Tips & Hints for Your Boat. Howard-Williams, Jeremy, tr. from Fr. (Illus.). 1981. 13.95 (ISBN 0-393-03262-0). Norton.

--One Hundred & One Tips & Hints for Your Sailboat. LC 81-84142. 192p. 1982. pap. 2.95 (ISBN 0-86721-070-2). Jove Pubns.

Damp, Margaret M. Finding Fulfillment in the Manse. 115p. 1978. pap. 2.95 (ISBN 0-8341-0544-6). Beacon Hill.

Damp, Philip. Growing & Showing Dahlias. (Growing & Showing Ser.). (Illus.). 64p. 1985. 9.95 (ISBN 0-7153-8600-X). David & Charles.

Damp, Phillip. Growing Dahlias. (Illus.). 139p. 1982. 12.95 (ISBN 0-917304-43-8). Timber.

Dampier, Joseph H. Workbook on Christian Doctrine. 64p. (Orig.). (gr. 6 up). 1943. pap. 1.95 (ISBN 0-87239-072-1, 3343). Standard Pub.

Dampier, Robert. To the Sandwich Islands on H. M. S. Blonde. Joerger, Pauline K., ed. LC 73-147156. 141p. 1971. text ed. 15.00x (ISBN 0-87022-176-0). UH Pr.

Dampier, William. Voyage to New Holland. 256p. 1982. text ed. 23.00x (ISBN 0-904387-75-5, Pub. by Alan Sutton England); pap. text ed. 11.00x (ISBN 0-86299-006-8). Humanities.

Dampier, William C. History of Science. 1965. pap. 21.95 (ISBN 0-521-09366-X, 366). Cambridge U Pr.

Dampier, William C. & Whetham, Catherine. The Family & the Nation: A Study in the Natural Inheritance & Social Responsibility. Rosenberg, Charles, ed. LC 83-48562. (The History of Hereditarian Thought Ser.). 233p. 1985. Repr. of 1909 ed. lib. bdg. 30.00 (ISBN 0-8240-5831-3). Garland Pub.

Damrell, Joseph. Search for Identity: Youth, Religion, & Culture. LC 78-5887. (Sage Library of Social Research: No. 64). 232p. 24.00 (ISBN 0-8039-0987-X); pap. 14.00 (ISBN 0-8039-0988-8). Sage.

Damrell, Joseph D. Seeking Spiritual Meaning: The World of Vedanta. LC 77-9145. (Sociological Observations Ser.: No. 2). pap. 63.00 (ISBN 0-317-08760-6, 2021885). Bks Demand UMI.

Damren, Betty R., et al. Training Effective Teachers: A Competency-Based Practicum Model for Teachers of Emotionally Disturbed Children. 53p. 1975. pap. text ed. 4.00x (ISBN 0-89039-134-3). Ann Arbor FL.

Damron, O. Rex & O'Neill, Daniel J. An Introduction to Interpersonal & Public Communication. 139p. 1981. pap. text ed. 6.95x (ISBN 0-89641-021-8). American Pr.

Damrosch, Barbara. Theme Gardens. LC 82-60062. (Illus.). 224p. 1982. 22.50 (ISBN 0-89480-218-6, 351); pap. 12.95 (ISBN 0-89480-217-8, 487). Workman Pub.

Damrosch, Leopold, Jr. God's Plot & Man's Stories: Studies in the Fictional Imagination from Milton to Fielding. LC 84-8754. (Illus.). 376p. 1985. lib. bdg. 25.00x (ISBN 0-226-13579-9). U of Chicago Pr.

--Samuel Johnson & the Tragic Sense. LC 72-38514. 284p. 1972. 25.50x (ISBN 0-691-06233-1). Princeton U Pr.

--Symbol & Truth in Blake's Myth. LC 80-7515. (Illus.). 504p. 1980. 38.00x (ISBN 0-691-06433-4); pap. 14.50x o.p (ISBN 0-691-10095-0). Princeton U Pr.

--The Uses of Johnson's Criticism. LC 75-19431. 236p. 1976. 13.95x (ISBN 0-8139-0625-3). U Pr of Va.

Damroth, Marion. Country Dogs & City Cousins: The Care & Loving of All Puppies. LC 80-81371. (Illus.). 125p. write for info. (ISBN 0-937118-01-X). Home Frosted.

Dams, T., et al, eds. Food & Population: Priorities in Decision Making. 208p. 1978. text ed. 37.95x (ISBN 0-566-00250-7). Gower Pub Co.

Damsgaard, Kristen & Fjeld, Jon. In Good Form on the Platform. 120p. 1985. pap. cancelled (ISBN 82-00-07308-4). Universitet.

Damsker, Matt. Rock Voices. 160p. 1980. pap. 5.95 (ISBN 0-312-68791-5). St Martin.

Damste, P. H. & Lerman, J. W. An Introduction to Voice Pathology: Functional & Organic. (Illus.). 120p. 1975. 15.75x (ISBN 0-398-03289-0). C C Thomas.

Damsteegt, P. Gerard. Foundations of the Seventh-Day Adventist Message & Mission. LC 76-56799. pap. 91.00 (ISBN 0-317-30135-7, 2025318). Bks Demand UMI.

D'Amyot, tr. see Plutarque.

Dan, Alice, et al. The Menstrual Cycle: A Synthesis of Interdisciplinary Research, Vol. 1. LC 80-18837. (Illus.). 1980. text ed. 33.00 (ISBN 0-8261-2630-8); text ed. 55.00 vol. 1-2 set. Springer Pub.

Dan, James W. Book of Essex. 132p. 1979. 29.75x (ISBN 0-905858-09-3, Pub. by Egon England). State Mutual Bk.

Dan, Joseph. Gershom Scholem & the Mystical Dimension of Jewish History. 350p. 1985. 35.00x (ISBN 0-8147-1779-9). NYU Pr.

--Jewish Mysticism & Jewish Ethics. LC 85-40358. 158p. 1985. 20.00 (ISBN 0-295-96265-8). U of Wash Pr.

Dan, Joseph, ed. Studies in Jewish Mysticism. 220p. 1981. 25.00 (ISBN 0-915938-03-0, Dist by Ktav). Assn for Jewish Studies.

--The Teachings of Hasidism. (Orig.). 1983. pap. text ed. 9.95x (ISBN 0-87441-346-X). Behrman.

Dan, Joseph & Talmage, Frank, eds. Studies in Jewish Mysticism. 25.00x (ISBN 0-915938-03-0). Ktav.

Dan, Kiley De see Kiley, Dan De.

Dan, S. Nonlinear & Dynamic Programming: An Introduction. LC 75-6503. (Illus.). vii, 164p. (Orig.). 1975. pap. text ed. 20.00 (ISBN 0-387-81289-X). Springer-Verlag.

Dan, Smith, jt. ed. see Kaldor, Mary.

Dan, Uri. The Face of Terror. 1978. pap. 1.75 (ISBN 0-8439-0526-3, Leisure Bks). Dorchester Pub Co.

Dan, Uri & Mann, Peter. Ultimatum: PU 94. 1977. pap. 1.95 (ISBN 0-8439-0523-9, Leisure Bks). Dorchester Pub Co.

Dan, Uri & Radley, Edward. The Eichmann Syndrome. 1977. pap. 1.75 (ISBN 0-8439-0466-6, Leisure Bks). Dorchester Pub Co.

Dan, Urid & Mann, Peter. Carlos Must Die. 1978. pap. 1.95 (ISBN 0-8439-0543-3, Leisure Bks). Dorchester Pub Co.

Dan, Wim van see Van Dam, Wim.

Dana, Alan S., Jr., jt. auth. see Samitz, M. H.

Dana, Barbara. Crazy Eights. LC 77-25645. (gr. 7 up). 1978. 7.95o.p. (ISBN 0-06-021388-4); PLB 10.89 (ISBN 0-06-021389-2). HarpJ.

--Zucchini. LC 80-8448. (A Charlotte Zolotow Bk.). (Illus.). 128p. (gr. 3-5). 1982. 11.06i (ISBN 0-06-021394-9); PLB 10.89g (ISBN 0-06-021395-7). HarpJ.

--Zucchini. (Illus.). 160p. (gr. 3-6). pap. 2.25 (ISBN 0-553-15285-8, Skylark). Bantam.

Dana, Bill. Cowboy-English, English-Cowboy Dictionary. 96p. (Orig.). 1982. pap. 1.95 (ISBN 0-345-30155-2). Ballantine.

Dana, Bill, jt. auth. see Peter, Laurence J.

Dana, Charles A. Art of Newspaper Making. LC 71-125689. (American Journalists Ser.). 1970. Repr. of 1900 ed. 13.00 (ISBN 0-405-01666-2). Ayer Co Pubs.

--Proudhon & His Bank of the People. 59.95 (ISBN 0-8490-0906-5). Gordon Pr.

--Proudhon & His Bank of the People. Avrich, Paul, ed. (YOung America Ser.: No. 1). 80p. lib. bdg. 14.95 (ISBN 0-88286-067-4); pap. 4.95 (ISBN 0-88286-066-6). C H Kerr.

Dana, Charles A., ed. Household Book of Poetry. facs. ed. LC 77-12923. (Granger Index Reprint Ser). 1882. 32.00 (ISBN 0-8369-6163-3). Ayer Co Pubs.

Dana, Charles H. Two Years Before the Mast. (Regents Illustrated Classics Ser.). (gr. 7-12). 1982. pap. text ed. 2.75 (ISBN 0-88345-482-3, 20571). Regents Pub.

Dana, Charles L. The Peaks of Medical History. 2nd ed. LC 75-23703. (Illus.). Repr. of 1928 ed. 27.50 (ISBN 0-404-13255-3). AMS Pr.

Dana, Doris, ed. & tr. Selected Poems of Gabriela Mistral. LC 77-137467. (Hispanic Foundation Ser). (Illus.). 272p. 1971. 22.00x (ISBN 0-8018-1197-X); pap. 7.95x, cobe (ISBN 0-8018-1256-9). Johns Hopkins.

Dana, E. S. & Ford, W. E. Textbook of Mineralogy. 4th ed. 851p. 1932. 51.95x (ISBN 0-471-19305-4). Wiley.

Dana, E. S. & Hurlbut, C. S. Minerals & How to Study Them. 3rd ed. 323p. 1963. pap. 16.50 (ISBN 0-471-19195-7). Wiley.

Dana, Edward S., et al, eds. A Century of Science in America. LC 72-94344. (The American Scientific Community, 1790-1920 Ser.). 1973. Repr. of 1918 ed. lib. bdg. 34.00 (ISBN 0-8420-1654-6). Scholarly Res Inc.

Dana, H. E. Manual de Eclesiologia. Robleto, Adolfo, tr. Orig. Title: A Manual of Ecclesiology. write for info. (ISBN 0-311-17018-8). Casa Bautista.

--El Mundo Del Nuevo Testamento. Villarello, Ildefonso, tr. 288p. 1977. pap. 4.95 (ISBN 0-311-04342-9). Casa Bautista.

Dana, H. E. & Mantey, J. R. Gramatica Griega Del Nuevo Testamento. Robleto, Adolfo & De Clark, Catalina, trs. 1979. pap. 10.50 (ISBN 0-311-42010-9). Casa Bautista.

Dana, H. E. & Mantey, R. Manual Grammar of the Greek New Testament: With Index. 1957. text ed. write for info. (ISBN 0-02-327070-5, 32707). Macmillan.

Dana, J. D., et al. Systems of Minerology, 3 vols. 7th ed. Incl. Vol. 1. Elements, Sulfides, Sulfosalts, Oxides. 7th ed. Dana, James D., et al. 834p. 1944. 85.00 (ISBN 0-471-19239-2); Vol. 2. Halides, Nitrates, Borates, Carbonates, Sulfates, Phosphates, Arsenates, Tungstates, Molybdates. Dana, James D., et al. 1951. 94.95 (ISBN 0-471-19272-4); Vol. 3. System of Mineralogy: Silica Minerals. Dana, James D., et al. 334p. 1962. 60.00 (ISBN 0-471-19287-2). Pub. by Wiley-Interscience). Wiley.

Dana, James. Sutter of California. lib. bdg. 29.00 (ISBN 0-403-08971-9). Scholarly.

Dana, James D., et al see Dana, J. D., et al.

Dana, John C. Libraries: Addresses & Essays. facs. ed. LC 67-22088. (Essay Index Reprint Ser). 1916. 18.00 (ISBN 0-8369-1329-9). Ayer Co Pubs.

--Libraries: Addresses & Essays. LC 67-22088. (Essay Index Reprint Ser.). 299p. 1982. Repr. of 1916 ed. lib. bdg. 17.00 (ISBN 0-8290-0476-9). Irvington.

Dana, Julian. Sacramento, River of Gold. Skinner, Constance L., ed. LC 72-144963. (Illus.). 1971. Repr. of 1939 ed. 29.00x (ISBN 0-403-00932-4). Scholarly.

--Sutter of California: A Biography. LC 74-11308. (Illus.). 423p. 1974. Repr. of 1934 ed. lib. bdg. 24.00x (ISBN 0-8371-7644-1, DASC). Greenwood.

Dana, Katherine. Opportunities in Counseling & Guidance. (VGM Career Bks.). (Illus.). 160p. 1983. 7.95 (ISBN 0-8442-6596-9, 6596-9, Passport Bks.); pap. 5.95 (ISBN 0-8442-6595-0, 6595-0). Natl Textbk.

Dana, Katherine F. Our Phil, & Other Stories. facsimile ed. LC 74-113653. (Short Story Index Reprint Ser.). 1888. 14.00 (ISBN 0-8369-3382-6). Ayer Co Pubs.

Dana, Mark. Lifemating: New Hope for Those Who've Loved & Lost. 1985. 7.75 (ISBN 0-8062-2447-9). Carlton.

Dana, Mitchell. Beware the Smiling Stranger. 1977. pap. 1.25 (ISBN 0-380-00830-0, 30965). Avon.

Dana, Richard. The Seaman's Friend. LC 79-4623. 1979. Repr. of 1841 ed. lib. bdg. 35.00x (ISBN 0-8201-1330-1). Schol Facsimiles.

--Two Years Before the Mast. 1981. Repr. lib. bdg. 18.95x (ISBN 0-89966-426-1). Buccaneer Bks.

Dana, Richard, ed. Readings in Abnormal Behavior: Toward a Sociopsychological Model. 1970. pap. text ed. 9.95x (ISBN 0-8422-0059-2). Irvington.

Dana, Richard H. A Human Science Model for Personality Assessment with Projective Techniques. (Illus.). 528p. 1982. 39.75x (ISBN 0-398-04448-1). C C Thomas.

--Human Services for Cultural Minorities. LC 81-16464. (Illus.). 382p. (Orig.). 1981. 16.00 (ISBN 0-8391-1687-X). Pro Ed.

--The Idle Man. 59.95 (ISBN 0-87968-271-X). Gordon Pr.

--Two Years Before the Mast. (Classics Ser). (gr. 8 up). pap. 1.95 (ISBN 0-8049-0085-X, CL-85). Airmont.

--Two Years Before the Mast. 1972. 12.95x (ISBN 0-460-00588-X, Evman); pap. 3.50x (ISBN 0-460-01588-5, Evman). Biblio Dist.

--Two Years Before the Mast. new & abr. ed. Fago, John N., ed. (Now Age Illustrated III Ser.). (Illus.). (gr. 4-12). 1977. text ed. 5.00 (ISBN 0-88301-282-0); pap. text ed. 1.95 (ISBN 0-88301-270-7). Pendulum Pr.

--Two Years Before the Mast: Abridged & adapted to grade 2 reading level. Hurdy, John M., ed. (Pacemaker Classics Ser.). 1971. pap. 4.92 (ISBN 0-8224-9235-0); tchrs manual free. Pitman Learning.

Dana, Richard H., Jr. Two Years Before the Mast. Date not set. pap. 3.50 (ISBN 0-451-51764-4, CE1764, Sig Classics). NAL.

--Two Years Before the Mast. Philbrick, Thomas, ed. (Pengiun American Library). 1981. pap. 4.95 (ISBN 0-14-039008-1). Penguin.

Dana, Richard T. The Human Machine in Industry. (Management History Ser.: No. 35). 326p. Repr. of 1927 ed. 22.50 (ISBN 0-87960-038-1). Hive Pub.

Dana, Robert. In a Fugitive Season. LC 79-64294. 80p. 1979. 10.95 (ISBN 0-8040-0804-3, 82-75943, Pub. by Swallow); pap. 5.95 (ISBN 0-8040-0805-1, 82-75950, Pub. by Swallow). Ohio U Pr.

--Power of the Visible. LC 79-171877. 71p. 1971. 8.95 (ISBN 0-8040-0551-6, 82-72833, Pub. by Swallow); pap. 4.95 (ISBN 0-8040-0646-6, 82-72841, Pub. by Swallow). Ohio U Pr.

--Some Versions of Silence. (Orig.). 1967. 4.50 (ISBN 0-393-04145-X); pap. 1.95 (ISBN 0-393-04246-4). Norton.

Dana, Robert see Judson, John.

Dana, Samuel T. & Fairfax, Sally K. Forest & Range Policy. 2nd ed. (Illus.). 496p. 1980. text ed. 39.95 (ISBN 0-07-015288-8). McGraw.

Dana, Samuel T. & Krueger, Myron. California Lands. Bruchey, Stuart, ed. LC 78-53561. (Development of Public Lands Law in the U. S. Ser.). (Illus.). 1979. Repr. of 1958 ed. lib. bdg. 24.50x (ISBN 0-405-11374-9). Ayer Co Pubs.

Dana, William F. The Optimism of Ralph Waldo Emerson. LC 76-46925. 1976. Repr. of 1886 ed. lib. bdg. 10.00 (ISBN 0-8414-3806-4). Folcroft.

--The Optimism of Ralph Waldo Emerson. 59.95 (ISBN 0-8490-0771-2). Gordon Pr.

Dana, William S. How to Know the Wild Flowers. rev. ed. Hylander, Clarence J., ed. (Illus.). 1963. pap. 6.00 (ISBN 0-486-20332-8). Dover.

--How to Know Wild Flowers. 14.00 (ISBN 0-8446-1942-6). Peter Smith.

Danachair, Caoimhin O. A Bibliography of Irish Ethnology & Folk Tradition. 2nd ed. 1978. 32.00 (ISBN 0-85342-490-X). Irish Bk Ctr.

Danaher, Brian G. & Lichtenstein, Edward. Become an Ex-Smoker. LC 78-1679. (Self-Management Psychology Ser.). (Illus.). 1978. 11.95 (ISBN 0-13-072249-9, Spec); pap. 5.95 (ISBN 0-13-072231-6, Spec). P-H.

Danaher, Kevin. The Children's Book of Irish Folktales. (Illus.). 108p. (gr. 4 up). 1984. pap. 7.50 (ISBN 0-85342-718-6, Pub. by Mercier Pr Ireland). Irish Bks Media.

--Folktales of the Irish Countryside. 144p. 1982. pap. 4.95 (ISBN 0-85342-056-4, Pub. by Mercier Pr Ireland). Irish Bks Media.

--Gentle Places & Simple Things. 128p. 1981. pap. 4.95 (ISBN 0-85342-053-X, Pub. by Mercier Pr Ireland). Irish Bks Media.

--In Ireland Long Ago. 192p. 1978. pap. 4.95 (ISBN 0-85342-054-8, Pub. by Mercier Pr Ireland). Irish Bks Media.

--In Whose Interest? A Guide to U. S.-South Africa Relations. 280p. 1985. pap. 11.95 (ISBN 0-89758-038-9). Inst Policy Stud.

--Irish Country People. 128p. 1977. pap. 4.95 (ISBN 0-85342-057-2, Pub. by Mercier Pr Ireland). Irish Bks Media.

--The Political Economy of U. S. Policy Toward South Africa. (Westview Special Studies on Africa). 300p. 1985. pap. 19.85x (ISBN 0-8133-0115-7). Westview.

--That's How It Was. 128p. (Orig.). 1984. pap. 6.95 (ISBN 0-85342-714-3, Pub. by Mercier Pr Ireland). Irish Bks Media.

--The Year in Ireland. 2nd ed. (Illus.). 274p. 1985. pap. 10.95 (ISBN 0-937702-03-X). Irish Bk Ctr.

--The Year in Ireland: A Calendar. (Illus.). 1977. pap. 8.50 (ISBN 0-85342-280-X, Co-dist. by Irish Bks Media). Irish Bk Ctr.

Danald, Ruth M., tr. see Ferlosio, Rafael S.

Danandjaja, James. An Annotated Bibliography of Javanese Folklore. (Occasional Papers: No. 9). 194p. 1983. pap. text ed. 11.25 (ISBN 0-8191-3133-4, Co-pub. by Ctr S SE Asia). U Pr of Amer.

Danarto. Abracadabra. Aveling, Harry, tr. (Writing in Asia Ser.). 1978. pap. text ed. 5.00x (ISBN 0-686-60329-X, 00212). Heinemann Ed.

Danbolt, Benny K. Dentistry, Patients & Dentists: Subject Analysis Index with Reference Bibliography. LC 85-47849. 150p. 1985. 29.95 (ISBN 0-88164-372-6); pap. 21.95 (ISBN 0-88164-373-4). ABBE Pubs Assn.

Danbom, David B. The Resisted Revolution: Urban America & the Industrialization of Agriculture, 1900-1930. 1979. text ed. 11.95x (ISBN 0-8138-0945-2). Iowa St U Pr.

Danbrot, Margaret. The Four Day Wonder Diet: Lose 10 Pounds in 4 Days. 1985. 10.95 (ISBN 0-399-13043-8, Putnam). Putnam Pub Group.

Danbury, Hazel. Teaching Practical Social Work. 85p. 1979. pap. text ed. 7.25x (ISBN 0-7199-0953-8, Pub. by Bedford England). Brookfield Pub Co.

Danbury, Iris. Jacaranda Island, Mandolins of Montori & the Silver Stallion. (Harlequin Romances (3-in-1)). 576p. 1983. pap. 3.95 (ISBN 0-373-20075-7). Harlequin Bks.

Danbury, Richard S., III, ed. Dan River Anthology, 1985. 1985. 15.95 (ISBN 0-89754-040-9); pap. 9.95 (ISBN 0-89754-039-5). Dan River Pr.

--Dan River Anthology '84. 1984. 14.95 (ISBN 0-89754-038-7); pap. 9.95 (ISBN 0-89754-037-9). Dan River Pr.

Danby, Hal. Make It Yourself. (Illus.). 127p. 1974. 7.50x (ISBN 0-8464-1187-3). Beekman Pubs.

Danby, Herbert, tr. Mishnah. 1933. 39.95x (ISBN 0-19-815402-X). Oxford U Pr.

Danby, Herbert, tr. see Klausner, Joseph.

Danby, Herbert see Maimonides, Moses.

Danby, J. M. Computer Applications to Differential Equations. 1985. pap. text ed. 17.95 (ISBN 0-8359-0962-X). Reston.

Danby, John F. Shakespeare's Doctrine of Nature: A Study of King Lear. 234p. (Orig.). 1961. pap. 6.95 (ISBN 0-571-06291-1). Faber & Faber.

Danca, Vince. Bunny: A Bio-Discography of Jazz Trumpeter Bunny Berigan. (Illus., Orig.). 1978. pap. 5.50 (ISBN 0-9602390-1-4). V Danca.

Dance, Daryl C. Folklore from Contemporary Jamaicans. LC 84-5061. 272p. 1985. 23.95 (ISBN 0-87049-436-8). U of Tenn Pr.

--Shuckin' & Jivin': Folklore from Contemporary Black Americans. LC 77-23635. (Midland Bks.: No. 265). 416p. 1978. 27.50 (ISBN 0-253-35220-7); pap. 12.50x (ISBN 0-253-20265-5). Ind U Pr.

Dance Educators of America Staff. Thirteen Ballroom Dances. (Ballroom Dance Ser.). 1985. lib. bdg. 74.00 (ISBN 0-87700-846-9). Revisionist Pr.

Dance Educators of America Staff, ed. New Ballroom Syllabus. (Ballroom Dance Ser.). 1985. lib. bdg. 75.00 (ISBN 0-87700-847-7). Revisionist Pr.

Dance, Edward H. History the Betrayer. LC 73-16869. 162p. 1975. Repr. of 1960 ed. lib. bdg. 15.00x (ISBN 0-8371-7237-3, DAHB). Greenwood.

Dance, F. R. Broadcast Training Techniques: Training in Mass Communication. (Illus.). 122p. 1976. pap. 7.50 (ISBN 92-3-101354-8, U59, UNESCO). Unipub.

Dance, Frank E. Human Communication Theory: Comparative Essays. 299p. 1982. text ed. 21.95 scp (ISBN 0-06-041481-2, HarpC). Har-Row.

Dance in Canada Annual Conference, 7th, Waterloo, Ontario, June 27-July 2, 1979. New Directions in Dance: Proceedings. Taplin, ed. (Pergamon International Series on Dance & the Related Arts). (Illus.). 200p. 1979. 39.00 (ISBN 0-08-024773-3). Pergamon.

Dance, Lynn, jt. auth. see Starck, Robert.

Dance Masters of America. Ballroom Teacher Training Manuals. (Ballroom Dance Ser.). 1985. lib. bdg. 76.00 (ISBN 0-87700-845-0). Revisionist Pr.

Dance Notation Bureau Staff, compiled by. Ballet Collection. (Illus.). 32p. (Orig.). 1980. pap. text ed. 8.50 (ISBN 0-932582-25-7). Dance Notation.

Dance Notation Bureau Staff & Cook, Ray, eds. Jazz Dance Collection: Alvin Ailey, Paul Draper, Peter Gennaro, Billie Mahoney. (Illus.). 17p. (Orig.). 1965. pap. text ed. 6.75x (ISBN 0-932582-27-3). Dance Notation.

Dance, Peter, jt. auth. see Abbott, Tucker.

Dance, S. P. The Collector's Encyclopedia of Shells. 2nd ed. 1982. 24.95 (ISBN 0-07-015292-6). McGraw.

Dance, S. Peter. The Art of Natural History: Animal Illustrators & Their Work. LC 78-56076. (Illus.). 224p. 1978. 85.00 (ISBN 0-87951-077-3). Overlook Pr.

--The World's Shells. LC 76-16581. (Illus.). 1976. 12.95 (ISBN 0-07-015291-8). McGraw.

Dance, Stanley. The World of Count Basie. (Quality Paperbacks Ser.). (Illus.). xxii, 399p. 1985. pap. 10.95 (ISBN 0-306-80245-7). Da Capo.

--The World of Duke Ellington. (Quality Paperbacks Ser.). xii, 311p. 1980. pap. 7.95 (ISBN 0-306-80136-1). Da Capo.

--The World of Earl Hines. (Quality Paperbacks Ser.). (Illus.). 334p. 1983. pap. 10.95 (ISBN 0-306-80182-5). Da Capo.

--The World of Swing. LC 79-15249. (Da Capo Quality Paperback Ser.). (Illus.). 436p. 1979. pap. 7.95 (ISBN 0-306-80103-5). Da Capo.

Dance, Stanley, jt. auth. see Barnet, Charlie.

Dance, Stanley, jt. auth. see Ellington, Mercer.

Dance, Stanley, ed. Jazz Era: The Forties. (Roots of Jazz Ser.). 253p. 1983. Repr. of 1961 ed. lib. bdg. 27.50 (ISBN 0-306-76191-2). Da Capo.

Dance Theater Workshop Staff. Poor Dancer's Almanac: A Survival Manual for Choreographers, Managers & Dancers. White, David R. & Levine, Mindy N., eds. LC 83-72080. 320p. (Orig.). 1984. pap. 15.00 (ISBN 0-9611382-0-3). Dance Theater.

Dancer, W. S. & Hardy, A. V. Greater London. (Geography of the British Isles Ser). 1969. text ed. 6.95 (ISBN 0-521-06920-3). Cambridge U Pr.

Dancey, William S. Archaeological Field Methods. LC 80-69485. 186p. (Orig.). 1981. pap. text ed. 12.95x (ISBN 0-8087-0440-0). Burgess.

Danchenko, L. Folk Art from the Ukraine. 264p. 1982. 38.95 (ISBN 0-8285-2340-1, Pub. by Aurora Pubs USSR). Imported Pubns.

Danchik, Kathleen M. Physician Visits, Volume & Interval Since Last Visit, U.S. 1971. LC 72-20716. (Data from the Health Interview Survey Ser. 10: No. 97). 55p. 1975. pap. text ed. 1.50 (ISBN 0-8406-0032-1). Natl Ctr Health Stats.

Danchik, Kathleen M. & Schoenborn, Charlotte A. Highlights: National Survey of Personal Health Practices & Consequences, United States, 1979. Olmsted, Mary, ed. (Series 10: No. 137). 50p. 1981. pap. 1.75 (ISBN 0-8406-0218-9). Natl Ctr Health Stats.

Dancis, J., jt. ed. see Schneider, H.

Danckaerts, Jasper. Diary of Our Second Trip from Holland to New Netherland, Sixteen Eighty-Three. Scott, Kenneth, ed. (Illus.). 62p. 1969. 28.00 (ISBN 0-8398-0352-4). Parnassus Imprints.

--Journal of Jasper Danckaerts, Sixteen Seventy-Nine to Sixteen Eighty. James, Bartleet B. & Jameson, J. Franklin, eds. (Original Narratives). 310p. 1969. Repr. of 1913 ed. 21.50x (ISBN 0-06-480422-4). B&N Imports.

Danckaerts, Jasper & Sluyter, Peter. Journal of a Voyage to New York & a Tour in Several of the American Colonies in Sixteen Seventy-Nine to Sixteen Eighty. Murphy, Henry C., ed. xv, 437p. 1967. Repr. of 1867 ed. 28.00 (ISBN 0-8398-0351-6). Parnassus Imprints.

Danckert, Ludwig. Directory of European Porcelain Marks, Makers & Factories. Kipling, Rita & Raffo, Pietro, trs. 688p. 1981. 150.00x (ISBN 0-7198-0013-7, Pub. by Northwood Bks). State Mutual Bk.

Danckwerts, P. V. Insights into Chemical Engineering: Selected Papers of P. V. Danckwerts. LC 80-42316. (Illus.). 320p. 1981. 57.00 (ISBN 0-08-026250-3). Pergamon.

Dancla, Charles. Six Airs Varies for Violin & Piano, Op. 89. (Carl Fischer Music Library: No.125). 1911. pap. 3.50 (ISBN 0-8258-0027-7, L125). Fischer Inc NY.

Danco, Katharine L. From the Other Side of the Bed: A Woman Looks at Life in the Family Business. LC 81-13032. 1981. 19.95 (ISBN 0-9603614-2-1). Univ Pr Inc.

Danco, Katy. From The Other Side Of The Bed: A Woman Looks At Life in The Family Business. 176p. 1982. 19.95 (ISBN 0-13-331272-0). P-H.

--From the Other Side of the Bed: A Woman Looks at Life in the Family Business. 163p. 19.95 (ISBN 0-9603614-2-1). Ctr Family Busn.

Danco, Leon A. Beyond Survival: A Business Owner's Guide For Success. 208p. 1982. 19.95 (ISBN 0-13-072074-7). P-H.

--Beyond Survival: A Guide for the Business Owner & his Family. 19.95 (ISBN 0-9603614-0-5). Ctr Family Busn.

--Beyond Survival: A Guide for the Business Owner & His Family. LC 74-29583. (Illus.). 1975. 19.95 (ISBN 0-9603614-0-5). Univ Pr Inc.

--Inside the Family Business. 19.95 (ISBN 0-9603614-1-3). Ctr Family Busn.

--Inside the Family Business. LC 80-23512. (N A). 1980. 19.95 (ISBN 0-9603614-1-3). Univ Pr Inc.

--Inside The Family Business. 260p. 1982. 19.95 (ISBN 0-13-467407-3). P-H.

--Outside Directors in the Family Owned Business: Why, When, Who & How. LC 81-12931. 1981. 29.95 (ISBN 0-9603614-3-X). Univ Pr Inc.

--Outside Directors in the Family Owned Business: Why, When, Who & How. 207p. 29.95 (ISBN 0-9603614-3-X). Ctr Family Busn.

Danco, Leon A. & Jonovic, Donald J. Outside Directors in the Family Owned Business. 216p. 1982. 29.95 (ISBN 0-13-645259-0). P-H.

Dancu, Dumitru, jt. auth. see Dancu, Juliana.

Dancu, Juliana & Dancu, Dumitru. Romanian Icons on Glass. LC 82-10846. (Illus.). 176p. 1983. 13.50x (ISBN 0-8143-1711-1). Wayne St U Pr.

Dancy, Harold K. A Manual on Building Construction. rev. ed. (Illus.). 362p. 1977. pap. 11.50x (ISBN 0-903031-08-6, Pub. by Intermediate Tech England); 24.50x (ISBN 0-903031-82-5). Intermediate Tech.

Dancy, J. C. Shorter Books of the Apocrypha: Cambridge Bible Commentary on the New English Bible. LC 72-76358. (Old Testament Ser.). 224p. (Orig.). 1972. pap. 9.95 (ISBN 0-521-09729-0). Cambridge U Pr.

Dancy, R. M. Sense & Contradiction: A Study in Aristotle. LC 75-2184. (Synthese Historical Library: No. 14). xii, 178p. 1975. lib. bdg. 37.00 (ISBN 90-277-0565-8, Pub. by Reidel Holland). Kluwer Academic.

Dancy, T. E. & Robinson, E. L., eds. Flat Rolled Products: Rolling & Treatment. LC 59-14888. (Metallurgical Society Conference Ser.: Vol. 1). pap. 37.30 (ISBN 0-317-10712-7, 2000664). Bks Demand UMI.

Danda, A. K. Family Planning: An Adaptive Strategy. xiii, 138p. 1984. text ed. 27.50x (ISBN 0-86590-286-0, Pub. by Inter India Pubns India). Apt Bks.

Danda, Ajit K. Studies on Rural Development: Experiences & Issues. xii, 96p. 1984. text ed. 18.95x (ISBN 0-86590-389-1, Pub. by Inter Pubns N Delhi). Apt Bks.

Dandamaev, Muhammad A. Slavery in Babylonia. Powell, Marvin A. & Weisberg, David B., eds. Powell, Victoria A., tr. from Rus. LC 84-10225. 836p. 1984. 55.00 (ISBN 0-87580-104-8). N Ill U Pr.

Dandamayev, M. A., ed. Societies & Languages of the Ancient Near East: Studies in Honour of I. M. Diakonoff. 380p. 1982. pap. 60.50x (00308905X, Pub. by Aris & Phillips England) (ISBN 0-85668-205-5). Humanities.

Dande, Leon. Blue Blood. facsimile ed. LC 72-37589. (Black Heritage Library Collection). Repr. of 1877 ed. 37.25 (ISBN 0-8369-8965-1). Ayer Co Pubs.

Dandekar, Hemalata C. Beyond Curry: Quick & Easy Indian Cooking Featuring Cuisine from Maharashtra State. LC 82-74367. (Special Publication Ser.: No. 3). (Illus.). 160p. (Orig.). 1983. pap. 9.95 (ISBN 0-89148-026-9). Ctr S&SE Asian.

Dandekar, Hemalata C., ed. The Planner's Use of Information: Techniques for Collection, Organization & Communication. LC 82-3119. (Environmental Design Ser.: Vol. 2). 224p. 1982. 29.75 (ISBN 0-87933-429-0). Van Nos Reinhold.

Dandekar, Kumudini. Employment Guarantee Scheme: An Employment Opportunity for Women. 76p. (Orig.). 1983. pap. text ed. 4.95x (ISBN 0-86131-433-6, Pub. by Orient Longman Ltd India). Apt Bks.

Dandekar, M. M. & Sharma, N. K. Water Power Engineering. 451p. 1983. pap. text ed. 18.95x (ISBN 0-7069-2362-6, Pub. by Vikas India). Advent NY.

Dandekar, R. N. The Age of Guptas & Other Essays. 1982. 30.00 (ISBN 0-8364-0916-7, Pub. by Ajanta). South Asia Bks.

Dandekar, V. M. The Demand for Food & Conditions Governing Food Aid During Development. (World Food Programme Studies: No. 1). (Orig.). 1965. pap. 4.50 (ISBN 0-685-09376-X, F112, FAO). Unipub.

--Peasant Worker Alliance. (R. C. Dutt Lectures on Political Economy: 1979). 104p. 1981. pap. text ed. 8.95 (ISBN 0-86131-274-0, Pub. by Orient Longman Ltd India). Apt Bks.

--Peasant-Worker Alliance: Its Basis in the Indian Economy, R. C. Dutt Lectures on Political Economy, 1979. 104p. 1981. cloth 20.00x (ISBN 0-686-94093-8, Pub. by Sangam Bks England). State Mutual Bk.

Dandekar, Varsha. Salads of India. LC 83-1776. 90p. 1983. 14.95 (ISBN 0-89594-075-2); pap. 4.95 (ISBN 0-89594-074-4). Crossing Pr.

Dandekar, W. N. Psychological Foundations of Education. 1981. 11.00x (ISBN 0-8364-0723-7, Pub. by Macmillan India). South Asia Bks.

Dandelot, jt. auth. see Dorst.

Dandin. Dandin's Dasha-Kumara-Charita: The Ten Princes. Ryder, Arthur W., tr. from Sanskrit. pap. 62.00 (ISBN 0-317-09902-7, 2012032). Bks Demand UMI.

--Dasakumaracarita: Adventures of the Ten Princes. 568p. (Eng.). 1979. Repr. 15.00 (ISBN 0-89581-313-0). Asian Human Pr.

Dando, M. & Newman, B., eds. Nuclear Deterrence: Implications & Policy Options for the 1980s. 288p. 1982. text ed. 32.00x (ISBN 0-7194-0079-1, Pub by Castle Hse England). Humanities.

D'Andrade, Kendall, jt. ed. see Werhane, Patricia.

Dandre, Victor E. Anna Pavlova in Art & Life. LC 70-180025. (Illus.). Repr. of 1932 ed. 38.50 (ISBN 0-405-08428-5, Blom Pubns). Ayer Co Pubs.

D'Andrea, Jeanne. Ancient Herbs in the J. Paul Getty Museum. LC 82-81306. 87p. 1982. pap. 10.00 (ISBN 0-89236-035-6). J P Getty Mus.

D'Andrea, Jeanne, ed. see Los Angeles County Museum of Art Curatorial Staff.

D'Andrea, Jeanne, ed. see Moorey, P. R., et al.

D'Andrea, Vaneeta M. The French Canadians: In Their Homeland, in America, in Connecticut. (The Peoples of Connecticut Ser.). Date not set. pap. price not set. Thut World Ed Ctr.

D'Andrea, Vincent J. & Salorey, Peter. Peer Counseling: Skills & Perspectives. 1983. pap. 9.95 (ISBN 0-8314-0064-1). Sci & Behavior.

Dandridge, Raymond G. The Poet & Other Poems. LC 73-18573. Repr. of 1920 ed. 11.50 (ISBN 0-404-11384-2). AMS Pr.

Dandy, D. J., jt. ed. see Jackson, Robert W.

Dandy, David J. Arthroscopic Surgery of the Knee. (Illus.). 150p. 1981. text ed. 57.00 (ISBN 0-443-02047-7). Churchill.

--Arthroscopy of the Knee: A Diagnostic Color Atlas. (Illus.). 159p. 1984. 44.00 (ISBN 0-8121-0912-0). Lea & Febiger.

Dandy, J. E., ed. List of British Vascular Plants: Prepared by J. E. Dandy for the British Museum (Natural History) & the Botanical Society of the British Isles. xvi, 176p. 1982. Repr. of 1958 ed. 12.50x (ISBN 0-565-00449-2, Pub. by Brit Mus Nat Hist England). Sabbot-Natural Hist Bks.

--The Sloane Herbarium. rev. ed. (Illus.). 1958. text ed. 40.00x (ISBN 0-565-00105-1, Pub. by Brit Mus Nat Hist). Sabbot-Natural Hist Bks.

Dandy, Walter E. Benign Tumors in the Third Ventricle of the Brain: Diagnosis & Treatment. (Illus.). 1970. Repr. of 1933 ed. 17.50 (ISBN 0-87266-037-0). Argosy.

--Benign Tumors in the Third Ventricle of the Brain: Diagnosis & Treatment. (Illus.). 171p. 1933. photocopy ed. 19.50x (ISBN 0-398-04241-1). C C Thomas.

Dane, Clemence. Tradition & Hugh Walpole. LC 71-113332. 256p. 1973. Repr. of 1930 ed. 24.00x (ISBN 0-8046-1733-3, Pub by Kennikat). Assoc Faculty Pr.

--Tradition & Hugh Walpole: A Critical Appreciation. 1929. Repr. 15.00 (ISBN 0-8482-7754-6). Norwood Edns.

Dane, Clemence, pseud. Women's Side. facs. ed. LC 70-99629. (Essay Index Reprint Ser.). 1927. 17.00 (ISBN 0-8369-1566-6). Ayer Co Pubs.

Dane, Clemence, ed. see Christie, Agatha, et al.

Dane, Clemens, pseud. Broome Stages. LC 83-45693. Repr. of 1931 ed. 57.50 (ISBN 0-404-20009-5). AMS Pr.

Dane, Les. Big League Sales Closing Techniques. LC 78-135891. 1971. 16.95 (ISBN 0-13-076125-7, Parker). P-H.

Dane, P. M. Learning to Use the BBC Microcomputer: A Gower Read-Out Publication. (Learning to Use Computer Ser.). 96p. (Orig.). 1982. pap. text ed. 12.00x (ISBN 0-566-03452-2). Gower Pub Co.

Dane, Peter, jt. auth. see Moore, Robin.

Daneau, Marcel, jt. ed. see Hero, Alfred O., Jr.

Daneault, Roland R. Poetic Meditations. 64p. 1982. 4.00 (ISBN 0-682-49883-1). Exposition Pr FL.

Danecki, Jan, ed. The Transformation in Poland: Project on Goals, Processes and Indicators of Development. 68p. 1982. pap. 5.00 (ISBN 92-808-0343-3, TUNU198, UNU). Unipub.

Daneel, M. L. Old & New in Southern Shona, Independent Churches, Vol. 1: Background & Rise of the Major Movements. (Change & Continuity in Africa Ser). 1971. text ed. 29.60x (ISBN 0-686-22598-8). Mouton.

--Zionism & Faith-Healing in Rhodesia: Aspects of African Independent Churches. V. A. February Communications, tr. from Dutch. (Illus.). 1970. pap. 6.00x (ISBN 90-2796-278-2). Mouton.

Danekar, ed. see Raghavan, V.

Daneke, Gregory A. & Lagassa, George K. Energy Policy & Public Administration. LC 79-3182. 336p. 1980. 33.00x (ISBN 0-669-03395-2). Lexington Bks.

Daneke, Gregory A., jt. auth. see Steiss, Alan W.

Daneke, Gregory A., ed. Energy, Economics & the Environment: Toward a Comprehensive Perspective. LC 81-47690. 304p. 1981. 31.00x (ISBN 0-669-04717-1). Lexington Bks.

Daneke, Gregory A. & Garcia, Margot W., eds. Public Involvement & Social Impact Assessment. (Social Impact Assessment Ser.: No. 9). 300p. 1983. lib. bdg. 26.50x (ISBN 0-86531-624-4). Westview.

Daneker, Gail, jt. auth. see Grossman, Richard.

Daneliuk, Tim & InfoWorld Editors. InfoWorld's Essential Guide to the TRS-80 Models III & IV. (InfoWorld's Essential Guides Ser.). 250p. (Orig.). 1984. pap. 16.95 (ISBN 0-06-669004-8). Har-Row.

Danella, Utta. Those Von Tallien Women. 352p. 1980. pap. 2.75 (ISBN 0-380-47506-5, 47506). Avon.

Danelski, David J. Rights, Liberties, & Ideals: The Contributions of Milton R. Konvitz. viii, 182p. 1983. text ed. 19.50x (ISBN 0-8377-0518-5). Rothman.

--A Supreme Court Justice Is Appointed. LC 80-21229. (Studies in Political Science). x, 242p. 1980. Repr. of 1964 ed. lib. bdg. 27.50x (ISBN 0-313-22652-0, DASJ). Greenwood.

Danelski, David J., ed. see Hughes, Charles E.

Daneman, Meredith. A Chance to Sit Down. 176p. 1981. pap. 2.25 (ISBN 0-380-54163-7, 54163). Avon.

Danenburg, William, et al. Introduction to Wholesale Distribution. 347p. 40.00 (ISBN 0-318-15140-5); NAW commodity line association members 36.00 (ISBN 0-318-15141-3); NAW members 32.00 (ISBN 0-318-15142-1). Natl Assn Wholesale Dists.

Danenburg, William P. & Coakley, Carroll B., eds. Strengthening Distributive Education: Selections from the Papers of L. T. White. LC 74-75417. 1974. pap. text ed. 4.50x (ISBN 0-8134-1639-6, 1639). Interstate.

Danenport, J., jt. auth. see Rankin, J. C.

Daneshyar, M. One-Dimensional Compressible Flow. 1977. text ed. 35.00 (ISBN 0-08-020414-7); pap. text ed. 11.75 (ISBN 0-08-020413-9). Pergamon.

Daner, Francine J. The American Children of Krsna: Case Studies in Cultural Anthropology. LC 75-15616. 1976. pap. text ed. 9.95 (ISBN 0-03-013546-X, HoltC). HR&W.

Daner, Selma, et al. The Passover Feast Two. 1978. 9.75 (ISBN 0-686-27071-1). Am Mizrachi Women.

Danes, B. Shannon, ed. In Vitro Epithelia & Birth Defects. (Alan R. Liss Ser.: Vol. 16, No. 2). 1980. 55.00 (ISBN 0-8451-1036-5). March of Dimes.

Danes, B. Shannon, et al, eds. In Vitro Epithelia & Birth Defects: Proceedings. LC 80-7693. (Birth Defects: Original Article Ser.: Vol. XVI, No. 2). 390p. 1980. 61.00x (ISBN 0-8451-1036-5). A R Liss.

Danes, F., ed. see International Symposium on Functional Sentence Perspective, 1st, Marienbad, Czechoslovakia.

Daneshvari, Abbas, ed. Essays in Islamic Art & Architecture (In Honor of Katharina Otto-Dorn) LC 81-71740. (Islamic Art & Architecture Ser.: Vol. 1). (Illus.). x, 135p. (Orig., Fr.). 1982. 35.00x (ISBN 0-89003-111-8); pap. text ed. 25.00x (ISBN 0-89003-110-X). Undena Pubns.

Danesi. Learning Italian the Fun Way in Fifteen Minutes a Day. (Fun Way Ser.). 128p. 1985. pap. 8.95 (ISBN 0-8120-2854-6). Barron.

Danesi, Anthony & Duplessis, Laura. Film Review for Reel Lovers. LC 83-72882. 69p. 1984. pap. 5.00 (ISBN 0-9613101-0-3). Brownstone Pubns.

Danesi, Marcel, ed. Issues in Language: Studies in Honor of Robert J. Di Pietro Presented to Him by His Students. LC 81-13647. (Edward Sapir Monograph Ser. in Language, Culture, & Cognition: No. 9). viii, 165p. (Orig.). 1981. pap. 8.00x (ISBN 0-933104-13-8). Jupiter Pr.

Danett, Thomas, tr. see Comines, Philippe de.

Daney, Mike. Coaching Kids Teeball. (Illus.). 117p. (Orig.). 1985. pap. 4.00 (ISBN 0-933715-00-5). Am Youth Sports Pub.

Danford, John W. Wittgenstein & Political Philosophy: A Re-Examination of the Foundation of Social Science. LC 78-6716. 1978. lib. bdg. 20.00x (ISBN 0-226-13593-4). U of Chicago Pr.

--Wittgenstein & Political Philosophy: A Re-Examination of the Foundations of Social Science. LC 78-6716. xiv, 166p. 1981. pap. 6.95x (ISBN 0-226-13594-2). U of Chicago Pr.

Danford, Scott, jt. ed. see Seidel, Andrew D.

Danforth, Amy. Animal Fair. (Illus.). 56p. 1983. text ed. 4.25 (ISBN 0-912883-00-6). Cricket Pubns.

Danforth, Art. Dashed Hopes, Broken Dreams. 60p. 1980. 3.75 (ISBN 0-318-15067-0). NASCO.

--A Model Consumer Cooperative Act: Comprehensive Statue. 101p. 1981. deluxe ed. 17.00 (ISBN 0-318-17927-X, G19C). NASCO.

Danforth, Art, jt. auth. see Sekerak, Emil.

Danforth, David N. & Hughey, Michael J. The Complete Guide Pregnancy. (Illus.). 384p. 1983. 24.95 (ISBN 0-8385-1191-0); pap. 17.95 (ISBN 0-8385-1190-2). ACC.

Danforth, David N., ed. Obstetrics & Gynecology. 4th ed. (Illus.). 1200p. 1982. text ed. 65.00 (ISBN 0-06-140696-1, 14-06966, Harper Medical). Lippincott.

Danforth, Edward J. Song of the White-Throat. LC 77-70657. (Illus.). 1977. pap. 5.95 (ISBN 0-9601174-1-5). E J Danforth.

Danforth Foundation & the Ford Foundation, ed. The School & the Democratic Environment. LC 70-111071. 115p. 1970. 21.00x (ISBN 0-231-03427-X). Columbia U Pr.

Danforth, Helen H. A Tale of Two Cabins. (Illus.). 36p. (Orig.). (gr. 7 up). 1985. pap. 4.95 (ISBN 0-9614899-0-1). Pioneer Farm.

Danforth, Loring M. The Death Rituals of Rural Greece. LC 82-47589. (Illus.). 248p. 1982. 37.50 (ISBN 0-691-03132-0); pap. 12.50x (ISBN 0-691-00027-1). Princeton U Pr.

Danforth, William H. I Dare You. 1976. 3.75 (ISBN 0-9602416-0-4). I Dare You.

Danga, F., tr. see Gauze, G. F.

Dange, S. A. Legends in the Mahabharata. 1969. 9.95 (ISBN 0-89684-240-1). Orient Bk Dist.

Dange, S. S. The Bhagavata Purana: Mytho-Social Study. 1984. 28.50x (ISBN 0-8364-1132-3, Pub. by Ajanta). South Asia Bks.

Dangel, Richard E. & Polster, Richard A., eds. Parent Training. LC 82-15508. 557p. 1984. 35.00 (ISBN 0-89862-627-7). Guilford Pr.

D'Angelo, A., jt. ed. see Mannucci, P. M.

D'Angelo, Dorie. Living with Angels. 3rd ed. 1980. pap. 10.00 (ISBN 0-912216-22-0). Angel Pr.

D'Angelo, E., ed. Cuban & North American Marxism. 214p. 1984. pap. text ed. 19.00x (ISBN 0-317-17369-3, Pub. by B R Gruner Netherlands). Humanities.

D'Angelo, E., et al. Contemporary East European Marxism, Vol. 1. (Praxis - Philosophical & Scientific Reprints Ser.: Vol. 6). 302p. 1982. pap. text ed. 25.75x (ISBN 0-391-02651-8). Humanities.

D'Angelo, Edward. Problem of Freedom & Determinism. LC 68-63295. 1968. 9.00x (ISBN 0-8262-7713-6). U of Mo Pr.

--The Teaching of Critical Thinking. (Philosophical Currents Ser: No. 1). 78p. 1971. text ed. 17.75x (ISBN 90-6032-482-X). Humanities.

D'Angelo, Edward, et al. Contemporary East European Marxism, Vol. II. (Praxis: Vol. 7). 275p. 1982. pap. text ed. 28.25x (ISBN 0-391-02788-3). Humanities.

D'Angelo, Frank. Process & Thought in Composition with Handbook. 3rd ed. 1985. text ed. 15.95 (ISBN 0-316-16987-0); tchr's. ed. avail. (ISBN 0-316-16988-9). Little.

D'Angelo, Frank J. A Conceptual Theory of Rhetoric. 1975. text ed. 17.95 (ISBN 0-316-16980-3). Little.

D'Angelo, Gary A., jt. auth. see Stewart, John.

D'Angelo, George V. The United States Immigration Law: A Practical Guide. 100p. (Orig.). 1985. pap. 10.00 (ISBN 0-934001-00-6). Chapel Hill Pr.

D'Angelo, Henry. Microcomputer Structures. 1981. 24.95 (ISBN 0-07-015294-2, BYTE Bks). McGraw.

D'Angelo, James S., jt. auth. see Missonellie, Joseph.

D'Angelo, Lou. How to Be an Italian. LC 67-26535. (Illus.). 1969. 2.95 (ISBN 0-8431-0021-4). Price Stern.

D'Angelo, Louise. Too Busy for God? Think Again! LC 81-52423. 120p. 1981. Repr. of 1975 ed. pap. 2.50 (ISBN 0-89555-166-7). TAN Bks Pubs.

D'Angelo, Mary R. Moses in the Letter to the Hebrews. LC 78-12917. (Society of Biblical Literature, Dissertation Ser.: No. 42). 1979. pap. 9.95 (ISBN 0-89130-333-2). Scholars Pr GA.

D'Angelo, N., ed. see ESRIN-ESLAB Symposium, 2nd Frascati, Italy 23-27, September, 1968.

D'Angelo, Pascal. Son of Italy. LC 74-17925. (Italian American Experience Ser). 200p. 1975. Repr. 14.00x (ISBN 0-405-06398-9). Ayer Co Pubs.

D'Angelo, Rocco, ed. Confrontations with Youth: A Critical Review of Process & Papers from Ohio's Youth Flight Conference. 350p. 1976. pap. 6.95x (ISBN 0-87776-311-9, AA11). Ohio St U Admin Sci.

D'Angelo, Rosemary, jt. auth. see Boykin-Stith, Lorraine.

Danger, Marilyn, ed. Simply Delicious. 3rd ed. 314p. (Orig.). pap. 9.95 (ISBN 0-9608666-0-4). Miriam Hosp.

Dangerfield, George. Awakening of American Nationalism, 1815-1828. (New American Nation Ser.). (Illus.). 1965. 15.00xi (ISBN 0-06-010945-9, HarpT). Har-Row.

--Awakening of American Nationalism, 1815-1828. (New American Nation Ser.). pap. 8.95xi (ISBN 0-06-133061-2, TB3061, Torch). Har-Row.

--The Era of Good Feelings. 11.75 (ISBN 0-8446-4022-0). Peter Smith.

--Strange Death of Liberal England. (Illus.). 400p. 1984. pap. 6.95 (ISBN 0-586-08025-2, Pub. by Granada England). Academy Chi Pubs.

--Strange Death of Liberal England, 1910-1914. (Illus.). 1961. pap. 4.95 (ISBN 0-399-50227-0, Perigee). Putnam Pub Group.

Dangerfield, Rodney. I Don't Get No Respect. rev. ed. (Illus.). 48p. 1982. pap. 1.75 (ISBN 0-8431-0193-8). Price Stern.

Dangerfield, Royden, ed. see Gordon, David R.

Dangerfield, Royden J. In Defense of the Senate. LC 65-20470. (Illus.). 1966. Repr. of 1933 ed. 28.50x (ISBN 0-8046-0097-X, Pub. by Kennikat). Assoc Faculty Pr.

Dangerfield, Royden J., jt. auth. see Ewing, Cortez A.

Dangerfield, Stanley & Howell, Elsworth. Encyclopedie Internationale Des Chiens. 489p. (Fr. & Eng.). 1974. 67.50 (ISBN 0-686-56972-5, M-6099). French & Eur.

Dangerous Goods Panel of Air Avigation Commission of ICAO. Instructions Techniques pour la Securite du Transport Aerien des Marchandises Dangereuses, 1984. (Fr.). 1983. fabric cover 35.00 (ISBN 0-940394-10-3). Intereg.

Dangerous Goods Panel of Air Navigation Commission of ICAO. Instrucciones Technicas para el Transporte sin Riesgos de Mercancias Peligrosas por Via Aerea, 1984. (Sp.). 1983. fabric cover 35.00x (ISBN 0-940394-09-X). Intereg.

--Instrucciones Technicas para el Transporte sin Riegos de Mercancias Peligrosas por via Aerea, 1985. 510p. (Span.). 1984. write for info (ISBN 0-940394-14-6). Intereg.

--Instructions Techniques pour la Securite du Transport Aerien des Marchandises Dangereuses 1985. 510p. (Fr.). 1984. write for info (ISBN 0-940394-15-4). Intereg.

--Technical Instructions for the Safe Transport of Dangerous Goods by Air, 1984. 1983. fabric cover 35.00 (ISBN 0-940394-08-1). Intereg.

--Technical Instructions for the Safe Transport of Dangerous Goods by Air, 1985. 510p. 1984. write for info. (ISBN 0-940394-13-8). Intereg.

Dangerous Goods Panel of Air Navigations Commissions of ICAO. Technical Instructions for the Safe Transport of Dangerous Goods by Air, 1986. 525p. 1985. 37.00 (ISBN 0-940394-18-9). Intereg.

D'Anghiera, Pietro. De Orbe Novo: The Eight Decades of Peter Martyr D'Anghiera, 2 Vols. MacNutt, Francis A., tr. LC 77-135174. (Research & Source Works Ser.: No. 642). (Philosophy & Monograph Ser., No. 44). 1971. Repr. of 1912 ed. lib. bdg. 50.50 (ISBN 0-8337-0073-1). B Franklin.

D'Angio, G. & Evans, A. Bone Tumors & Soft Tissue Carcinoma. (Management of Malignant Disease Ser.). (Illus.). 1985. text ed. 44.50 (ISBN 0-7131-4377-0). E Arnold.

D' Anglure, Ogier. Saint Voyage De Jherusalem Du Seigneur D'Anglure. Bonnardot, F. & Longnon, A., eds. 1878. 28.00 (ISBN 0-384-53028-1); pap. 22.00 (ISBN 0-384-53018-4). Johnson Repr.

Dangoor, Daniella, tr. see Hocquenghem, Guy.

Dangott, Lilliam & Kalish, Richard. A Time to Enjoy: The Pleasures of Aging. (Illus.). 1978. 11.95 (ISBN 0-13-921692-8, Spec); pap. 4.95 (ISBN 0-13-921684-7). P-H.

D'Angouleme, Marguerite. The Heptameron or Tales & Novels of Marguerite, Queen of Navarre. Machen, Arthur, tr. Repr. 40.00 (ISBN 0-8274-2487-6). R West.

D'Angouleme, Marguerite see Marguerite De Navarre, pseud.

Dang-Tan, Chau & Dang-Tan, Hau. How to Automate Your Office. LC 84-45793. 250p. 1985. 85.00 (ISBN 0-8144-5803-3). Amacom.

Dang-Tan, Hau, jt. auth. see Dang-Tan, Chau.

Danguah, J. B. Akan Doctrine of God. 206p. 1968. 30.00x (ISBN 0-7146-1749-0, F Cass Co). Biblio Dist.

Danhauer, Karen E., jt. auth. see Mumford, Amy Ross.

Danhof, Clarence H. Change in Agriculture: The Northern United States, 1820-1870. LC 70-75430. 1969. text ed. 22.50x (ISBN 0-674-10770-5). Harvard U Pr.

--Government Contracting & Technological Change. LC 79-28531. (Illus.). x, 472p. 1980. Repr. of 1968 ed. lib. bdg. 37.50x (ISBN 0-313-22297-5, DAGT). Greenwood.

Danhof, Kenneth & Smith, Carol. Computing System Fundamentals: An Approach Based on Microcomputers. LC 79-14933. 1981. text ed. 31.95 (ISBN 0-201-01298-7); instrs' manual 2.00 (ISBN 0-201-01245-6). Addison-Wesley.

Dani, Ahmad Hasan. Prehistory & Prohistory of Eastern India. 1981. 28.00x (ISBN 0-8364-0734-2, Pub. by Mukhopadhyay). South Asia Bks.

Danials, Vince. Mendoza's Treasure. 1980. pap. 1.75 (ISBN 0-8439-0721-5, Leisure Bks). Dorchester Pub Co.

Daniel. Application of Statistics to Industrial Experiments. 49p. 39.95 (ISBN 0-318-17066-3). Am Soc QC.

--Georgia Criminal Trial Practice. 3rd ed. 1984. incl. latest pocket part supplement 59.95 (ISBN 0-686-90294-7). Harrison Co GA.

--Georgia Criminal Trial Practice Forms. incl. latest pocket part supplement 72.95 (ISBN 0-686-90337-4); separate pocket part supplement, 1984 25.95 (ISBN 0-686-90338-2). Harrison Co GA.

Daniel, A. R. Bakery Materials & Methods. 4th, rev. ed. (Illus.). 464p. 1978. 20.50 (ISBN 0-85334-700-X, Pub. by Elsevier Applied Sci England). Elsevier.

--Bakery Questions Answered. 254p. 1972. 18.50 (ISBN 0-85334-540-6, Pub. by Elsevier Applied Sci England). Elsevier.

--Up-to-Date Confectionery. 4th, rev. ed. (Illus.). 542p. 1978. 27.75 (ISBN 0-85334-791-3, Pub. by Elsevier Applied Sci England). Elsevier.

Daniel, Abraham. Labor Enterprises in Israel: The Cooperative Economy, Vol. 1. 312p. 1976. pap. text ed. 5.95 (ISBN 0-87855-638-9). Transaction Bks.

--Labor Enterprises in Israel: The Institutional Economy, Vol. 2. 232p. 1976. pap. text ed. 4.95 (ISBN 0-87855-639-7). Transaction Bks.

Daniel, Albert R. Baker's Dictionary. 2nd ed. 209p. 1971. 18.50 (ISBN 0-444-20121-1, Pub. by Elsevier Applied Sci England). Elsevier.

Daniel, Ana. Bali: Behind the Mask. LC 79-3481. (Illus.). 224p. 1981. 30.00 (ISBN 0-394-50264-7); pap. 15.00 (ISBN 0-394-73844-6). Knopf.

Daniel, Barlette. I'll Take Manhattan. (Mirrors Ser.). 144p. (gr. 7 up). 1984. pap. 2.25 (ISBN 0-448-47725-4). Putnam Pub Group.

Daniel, Becky. I Can Draw a Circus. (ps-3). 1982. 5.95 (ISBN 0-86653-082-7, GA 428). Good Apple.

Daniel, Becky & Daniel, Charlie. Arithmetrix. (gr. 5-8). 1980. 5.95 (ISBN 0-916456-75-7, GA 188). Good Apple.

--Big Addition Book. (gr. k-3). 1979. 5.95 (ISBN 0-916456-44-7, GA118). Good Apple.

--Big Subtraction Book. (gr. k-3). 1979. 5.95 (ISBN 0-916456-43-9, GA117). Good Apple.

--Comprehension Zoo. (gr. 2-4). 1979. 5.95 (ISBN 0-916456-40-4, GA113). Good Apple.

--The Division Book. (gr. 3-6). 1980. 5.95 (ISBN 0-916456-77-3, GA 190). Good Apple.

--Good Apple & Teacher Helpers. (gr. 3-7). 1981. 9.95 (ISBN 0-86653-047-9, GA 282). Good Apple.

--I Wonder. (gr. k-3). 1980. 4.95 (ISBN 0-916456-82-X, GA 192). Good Apple.

--The Multiplication Book. (gr. 2-6). 1980. 5.95 (ISBN 0-916456-76-5, GA 191). Good Apple.

--Oh, My Word! (gr. 2-6). 1980. 6.95 (ISBN 0-916456-74-9, GA 189). Good Apple.

--Rainbow Factory. (ps-2). 1982. 5.95 (ISBN 0-86653-063-0, GA 427). Good Apple.

--Ready, Set...Read! (ps-5). 1979. 5.95 (ISBN 0-916456-45-5, GA114). Good Apple.

--Rhyming & Reading. (gr. 1-4). 1979. 5.95 (ISBN 0-916456-42-0, GA115). Good Apple.

--Strain Your Brain. (Gifted & Talented Ser.). 48p. (gr. 4-6). 1980. 4.95 (ISBN 0-88160-032-6, LW 217). Learning Wks.

--Thinker Sheets. (gr. 2-6). 1978. 5.95 (ISBN 0-916456-23-4, GA78). Good Apple.

--What's Next? (gr. k-6). 1979. 5.95 (ISBN 0-916456-41-2, GA116). Good Apple.

Daniel, Becky, jt. auth. see Daniel, Charlie.

Daniel, Bradford, ed. Black, White & Gray. LC 72-6796. (Essay Index Reprint Ser). 1972. Repr. of 1964 ed. 19.00 (ISBN 0-8369-7271-6). Ayer Co Pubs.

Daniel, Charles, jt. auth. see Smith, Page.

Daniel, Charles S. Ai: A Social Vision. LC 70-154438. (Utopian Literature Ser). 1971. Repr. of 1892 ed. 24.50 (ISBN 0-405-03521-7). Ayer Co Pubs.

Daniel, Charlie. Teacher Time Savers. (gr. k-3). 1978. 5.95 (ISBN 0-916456-20-X, GA76). Good Apple.

Daniel, Charlie & Daniel, Becky. Freaky Fractions. (gr. 1-5). 1978. 4.95 (ISBN 0-916456-19-6, GA77). Good Apple.

--Going Bananas Over Language Skills. (gr. 2-6). 1978. 5.95 (ISBN 0-916456-22-6, GA83). Good Apple.

--My Very Own Dictionary. (gr. 1-4). 1978. 5.50 (ISBN 0-916456-17-X, GA81). Good Apple.

--Super Spelling Fun. (gr. 2-6). 1978. 5.95 (ISBN 0-916456-31-5, GA82). Good Apple.

--Warm Smiles, Happy Faces. (gr. k-4). 1978. 4.95 (ISBN 0-916456-24-2, GA79). Good Apple.

--Writing about My Feelings. (gr. 1-4). 1978. 5.95 (ISBN 0-916456-18-8, GA80). Good Apple.

Daniel, Charlie, jt. auth. see Daniel, Becky.

Daniel, Clarence. Haunted Derbyshire. (Illus.). 80p. (Orig.). (gr. 6 up). 1975. pap. write for info. (ISBN 0-913714-40-2). Legacy Bks.

Daniel, Cletus E. The ACLU & the Wagner Act: An Inquiry into the Depression-Era Crisis of American Liberalism. LC 80-22450. (Cornell Studies in Industrial & Labor Relations: No. 20). 146p. 1981. pap. 7.95 (ISBN 0-87546-083-6). ILR Pr.

--Bitter Harvest: A History of California Farmworkers, 1870-1941. LC 80-25664. 368p. 1981. 35.00x (ISBN 0-8014-1284-6). Cornell U Pr.

--Bitter Harvest: A History of California Farmworkers, 1870-1941. 348p. 1982. pap. 8.95 (ISBN 0-520-04722-2). U of Cal Pr.

Daniel, Clifton. Lords, Ladies, & Gentlemen: A Memoir. (Illus.). 1984. 17.95 (ISBN 0-87795-598-0). Arbor Hse.

Daniel, Colin. Demon Tree. (Twilight Ser.: No. 9). (YA) (gr. 7-12). 1983. pap. 1.95 (ISBN 0-440-92097-3, LFL). Dell.

Daniel, Cuthbert. Applications of Statistics to Industrial Experimentation. LC 76-2012. (Applied Probability & Statistics Ser.). 294p. 1976. 42.50x (ISBN 0-471-19469-7, Pub. by Wiley-Interscience). Wiley.

Daniel, Cuthbert & Wood, Fred S. Fitting Equations to Data: Computer Analysis of Multifactor Data. 2nd ed. LC 79-11110. (Probability & Mathematical Statistics Ser.: Applied Section). 1980. 38.95 (ISBN 0-471-05370-8, Pub. by Wiley-Interscience). Wiley.

Daniel, David. Ark. LC 84-24763. 320p. 1984. 16.95 (ISBN 0-312-04919-6, Pub. by Marek). St Martin.

Daniel, Donald C., ed. International Perceptions of the Superpower Military Balance. LC 78-19456. 216p. 1978. 38.95 (ISBN 0-03-046471-4). Praeger.

Daniel, Donald C. & Herbig, Katherine L., eds. Strategic Military Deception. LC 81-14364. (Pergamon Policy Studies on Security Affairs). (Illus.). 400p. 1982. 36.00 (ISBN 0-08-027219-3). Pergamon.

Daniel, Donnie L., jt. auth. see Black, Tyrone.

Daniel, Doris T. Pauline & the Peacock. LC 80-50301. (Illus.). 64p. (Orig.). (ps-8). 1980. pap. 4.95 (ISBN 0-936650-00-1). E C Temple.

Daniel, E. E., jt. ed. see Grover, A. K.

Daniel, E. J. Mindsounds. 1981. pap. 2.50 (ISBN 0-89083-731-7). Zebra.

Daniel, E. Randolph. Abbot Joachim Of Fiore Liber De Concordia Noui Ac Veteris Testamenti. 455p. 18.00 (ISBN 0-87169-738-6). Am Philos.

Daniel, E. Valentine. Fluid Signs: Being a Person the Tamil Way. LC 84-163. 215p. 1984. text ed. 29.95x (ISBN 0-520-04725-7). U of Cal Pr.

Daniel, E. Valentine, jt. auth. see Keyes, Charles F.

Daniel, Edwine E. & Paton, David M. Methods in Pharmacology: Smooth Muscle, Vol. 3. (Illus.). 745p. 1975. 75.00x (ISBN 0-306-35263-X, Plenum Pr). Plenum Pub.

Daniel, Eleanor. The ABC's of VBS. LC 83-5049. 96p. (Orig.). 1984. pap. text ed. 3.95 (ISBN 0-87239-705-X, 3201). Standard Pub.

--What the Bible Says about Sexuality Identity. LC 81-71836. (What the Bible Says Ser.). 350p. 1982. 13.50 (ISBN 0-89900-085-1). College Pr Pub.

Daniel, Eleanor, rev. by see Leavitt, Guy P.

Daniel, Eleanor, rev. by see Root, Orrin.

Daniel, Eleanor, et al. Introduction to Christian Education. LC 79-92587. (Bible College Textbooks Ser.). 352p. (Orig.). 1980. pap. text ed. 6.95 (ISBN 0-87239-394-1, 88581). Standard Pub.

Daniel, Elouise. A Treasury of Books for Family Enjoyment: Books for Children from Infancy to Grade 2. (Illus.). 122p. (Orig.). 1983. pap. text ed. 8.95 (ISBN 0-9611370-0-2). Blue Engine.

Daniel, Elton L. The Political & Social History of Khurasan under Abbasid Rule 747-820. LC 79-53302. 1979. 28.00x (ISBN 0-88297-025-9). Bibliotheca.

Daniel, Evelyn H. & Notowitz, Carol I., eds. Media & Microcomputers in the Library: A Selected, Annotated Resource Guide. LC 83-42935. 168p. 1984. lib. bdg. 24.95 (ISBN 0-89774-117-X). Oryx Pr.

Daniel, Frederick S. Richmond Howitzers in the War: Four Years Campaigning with the Army of Northern Virginia. 155p. 1983. Repr. of 1891 ed. 22.50 (ISBN 0-913419-23-0). Butternut Pr.

Daniel, G. A Hundred & Fifty Years of Archaeology. new ed. 1976. 22.50x (ISBN 0-674-42631-2). Harvard U Pr.

Daniel, Gabriel. Histoire de France, Seventeen Fifty-Five, 17 vols. 1981. write for info. (ISBN 0-08-027648-2, HE 101); microfiche 850.00 (ISBN 0-686-79345-5). Pergamon.

Daniel, George. Recollections of Charles Lamb. LC 74-9598. 1927. lib. bdg. 10.00 (ISBN 0-8414-3745-9). Folcroft.

Daniel, George B., ed. see Sartre, Jean-Paul.

Daniel, Glenda. Dune Country: A Guide for Hikers & Naturalists. LC 77-78782. (Illus.). 167p. 1977. pap. 6.95 (ISBN 0-8040-0757-8, 82-74193, Pub. by Swallow). Ohio U Pr.

--Dune Country: A Hiker's Guide to the Indiana Dunes. Rev. ed. LC 84-10366. (Illus.). x, 176p. 1984. pap. 9.95 (ISBN 0-8040-0854-X, Swallow). Ohio U Pr.

Daniel, Glenda & Sullivan, Jerry. A Sierra Club Naturalist's Guide to the North Woods of Michigan, Wisconsin, Minnesota & Southern Ontario. LC 80-28742. (Naturalist's Guide Ser.). (Illus.). 384p. 1981. 24.95 (ISBN 0-87156-248-0); pap. 10.95 (ISBN 0-87156-277-4). Sierra.

Daniel, Glenda, jt. auth. see Sullivan, Jerry.

Daniel, Glyn. Short History of Archaeology. LC 81-50799. (Ancient Peoples & Places Ser.: No. 100). (Illus.). 1981. 19.95 (ISBN 0-500-02101-5). Thames Hudson.

--A Short History of Archaeology. (Ancient Peoples & Places Ser.). (Illus.). 146p. 1983. pap. 8.95f (ISBN 0-500-27305-7). Thames Hudson.

Daniel, Glyn, ed. Towards a History of Archaeology. 192p. 1981. 27.50 (ISBN 0-500-05039-2). Thames Hudson.

Daniel, Glyn, ed. see Guido, Margaret.

Daniel, Glyn, jt. ed. see Paget, R. F.

Daniel, Glyn E. The Megalith Builders of Western Europe. LC 85-2578. (Illus.). 160p. 1985. Repr. of 1963 ed. lib. bdg. 29.75x (ISBN 0-313-24836-2, DAMG). Greenwood.

Daniel, Glyn E., jt. auth. see Piggott, Stuart.

Daniel, H. The Atlantic Tropical Experiment - GATE. (Illus.). 44p. (Orig.). 1974. pap. 6.00 (ISBN 0-685-51933-3, W161, WMO). Unipub.

--WMO: The Achievement & the Challenge. (Illus.). 48p. (Fr. & Span.). 1976. pap. 6.00 (ISBN 92-63-10410-7, W177, WMO). Unipub.

Daniel, Hawthorne. Islands of the East Indies. LC 77-86669. (Illus.). 1977. Repr. of 1944 ed. 22.00 (ISBN 0-404-16703-9). AMS Pr.

Daniel, Howard, ed. see Callot, Jacques.

Daniel, I. M., ed. Composite Materials: Testing & Design (6th Conference)- STP 787. 587p. 1982. 55.00 (ISBN 0-8031-0695-5, 04787000-33). ASTM.

Daniel, J. W., et al. Mercury Poisoning, No. 2. LC 72-13563. (Illus.). 220p. 1972. text ed. 29.50x (ISBN 0-8422-7073-6). Irvington.

Daniel, James & Bruchley, Stuart, eds. Private Investment: The Key to International Industrial Development: a Report of the San Francisco Conference. LC 80-606. (Multinational Corporations Ser.). 1980. Repr. of 1958 ed. lib. bdg. 30.50x (ISBN 0-405-13355-3). Ayer Co Pubs.

Daniel, James W. & Moore, Ramon E. Computation & Theory in Ordinary Differential Equations. LC 71-117611. (Mathematics Ser.). (Illus.). 172p. 1970. text ed. 23.95 (ISBN 0-7167-0440-4). W H Freeman.

Daniel, James W., jt. auth. see Noble, Ben.

Daniel, Joe. Great American Adventure Book: One Hundred Unforgettable Travel Experiences. LC 84-26006. (Illus.). 240p. 1985. pap. 12.95 (ISBN 0-385-27942-6, Dolp). Doubleday.

Daniel, Joe & Britton, Phil. Texas on the Halfshell. LC 81-43408. (Illus.). 240p. 1982. pap. 12.95 (ISBN 0-385-17904-9, Dolp). Doubleday.

Daniel, John. In the Quiet of the Land. 24p. 1982. pap. write for info. (ISBN 0-9605512-1-2). Clearwater OR.

--Play Melancholy Baby. (Orig.). 1986. pap. price not set (ISBN 0-9602676-3-8). Perseverance Pr.

Daniel, John M. Richmond Examiner During the War. LC 76-125690. (American Journalists Ser). 1970. Repr. of 1868 ed. 20.00 (ISBN 0-405-01667-0). Ayer Co Pubs.

Daniel, John W., jt. ed. see Aldrich, Henry.

Daniel, Joseph C., Jr., ed. Methods in Mammalian Embryology. LC 76-116894. (Animal Science Ser.). (Illus.). 532p. 1971. text ed. 47.95 (ISBN 0-7167-0819-1). W H Freeman.

Daniel, Katinka S. Kodaly Approach, Method Book One. 2nd ed. LC 79-53162. 204p. 1979. wire 21.00 (ISBN 0-916656-13-6); materials for transparencies 21.00 (ISBN 0-916656-14-4). Mark Foster Mus.

--Kodaly in Kindergarten: Fifty Lesson Plans, Curriculum, Song Collection. LC 81-68473. (Illus.). 190p. (Orig.). 1981. wire bdg. 18.50 (ISBN 0-916656-15-2, MF-15). Mark Foster Mus.

Daniel, Katinka S., jt. auth. see Zemke, Lorna.

Daniel, Keith W. Francis Poulenc: His Artistic Development & Musical Style. Buelow, George, ed. LC 81-19767. (Studies in Musicology: No. 52). 400p. 1982. 49.95 (ISBN 0-8357-1284-2). UMI Res Pr.

Daniel, Kira. Backyard Tent. (Illus.). 48p. (Orig.). (gr. 1-3). 1986. PLB 8.59 (ISBN 0-8167-0626-3); pap. text ed. 1.95 (ISBN 0-8167-0627-1). Troll Assocs.

--Habits of Rabbits. (Illus.). 48p. (Orig.). (gr. 1-3). 1986. PLB 8.59 (ISBN 0-8167-0632-8); pap. text ed. 1.95 (ISBN 0-8167-0633-6). Troll Assocs.

--The Magic Kite. (Illus.). 48p. (Orig.). (gr. 1-3). 1986. PLB 8.59 (ISBN 0-8167-0614-X); pap. text ed. 1.95 (ISBN 0-8167-0615-8). Troll Assocs.

Daniel, Larry J. Cannoneers in Gray: The Field Artillery of the Army of Tennessee, 1861-1865. LC 83-17899. (Illus.). xii, 229p. 1984. 19.95 (ISBN 0-8173-0203-4). U of Ala Pr.

Daniel, Larry J. & Gunter, Riley W. Confederate Cannon Foundries. Pioneer Press, ed. LC 76-62878. 17.95 (ISBN 0-913150-38-X). Pioneer Pr.

Daniel, Lee. Dragon Mountain. LC 84-90278. 161p. 1985. 11.95 (ISBN 0-533-06317-5). Vantage.

Daniel, Les. The Silver Skull. 240p. 1983. pap. 2.50 (ISBN 0-441-76687-0). Ace Bks.

Daniel, Lois. How to Write Your Own Life Story: A Step by Step Guide for the Non-Professional Writer. rev. ed. LC 80-66753. 216p. 1985. pap. 8.95 (ISBN 0-914091-76-X). Chicago Review.

Daniel, Lusk. O, Rosie. LC 78-23579. (Illus., Orig.). 1979. pap. 5.95x (ISBN 0-914140-04-3). Carpenter Pr.

Daniel, Mark. The Laughing Man. 288p. 1985. 13.95 (ISBN 0-7181-2405-7, Pub by Michael Joseph). Merrimack Pub Cir.

Daniel, Marky. Songs from a Spanish Sierra. (Illus.). 1984. pap. 5.00 (ISBN 0-911287-04-3). Blue Begonia.

Daniel, May. French Drama of the Unspoken. LC 72-191858. 1953. lib. bdg. 20.00 (ISBN 0-8414-2435-7). Folcroft.

Daniel, Megan. Amelia. 1980. pap. 1.75 (ISBN 0-451-09487-5, E9487, Sig). NAL.

--The Reluctant Suitor. (Orig.). 1981. pap. 1.95 (ISBN 0-451-09671-1, J9671, Sig). NAL.

Daniel, Norman. The Arabs & Mediaeval Europe. 2nd ed. (The Arab Background Ser.). (Illus.). 1979. text ed. 25.95x (ISBN 0-582-78088-8). Longman.

Daniel, Norman A. Heroes & Saracens: A Reinterpretation of the Chansons de Geste. 319p. 1983. 28.50 (ISBN 0-85224-430-4, Pub. by Edinburgh U Pr). Columbia U Pr.

--Islam & the West. 26.00x (ISBN 0-85224-109-7, Pub. by Edinburgh U Pr Scotland). Columbia U Pr.

Daniel, Oliver. Stokowski: A Counterpoint of View. LC 82-2443. (Illus.). 1982. 24.95 (ISBN 0-396-07936-9). Dodd.

Daniel, P. Africanisation, Nationalisation & Inequality. LC 78-31563. (DAE-Industrial Relations & Labour Ser.). 1979. 39.50 (ISBN 0-521-22719-4); pap. 19.95 (ISBN 0-521-29623-4). Cambridge U Pr.

Daniel, P. A., ed. Romeo & Juliet: Parallel Texts of the First 2 Quartos; Quarto 1, 1597 & Quarto 2, 1599. Incl. Romeo & Juliet: Reprint of Quarto 1, 1597. Repr. of 1874 ed; Romeo & Juliet: Reprint of Q. 2, 1599. Repr. of 1874 ed; Romeo & Juliet: Revised Edition Quarto 2, 1599. Repr. of 1875 ed. (New Shakespeare Society, London, Ser.: Vol. 2, Nos. 1-4). pap. 47.00 (ISBN 0-317-17890-3). Kraus Repr.

Daniel, P. A., ed. see Brooke, Arthur.

Daniel, Pete. Breaking the Land: The Transformation of Cotton, Tobacco, & Rice Cultures since 1880. LC 84-197. (Illus.). 368p. 1985. 22.50x (ISBN 0-252-01147-3). U of Ill Pr.

--Deep'n As It Come: The 1927 Mississippi River Flood. 1977. pap. 7.95 (ISBN 0-19-502123-1, 480, GB). Oxford U Pr.

Daniel, Pete, ed. see Washington, Booker T.

Daniel, Peter A. Notes & Conjectural Emendations of Certain Doubtful Passages in Shakespeare's Plays. LC 78-163665. Repr. of 1870 ed. 18.00 (ISBN 0-404-01919-6). AMS Pr.

Daniel, R. P. Dating, Marriage, Sex & Divorce. 75p. pap. 3.95 (ISBN 0-88172-147-6). Believers Bkshelf.

--Gospel & the Path of Separation. pap. 3.25 (ISBN 0-88172-016-X). Believers Bkshelf.

--Let's Play Bible Detective. 36p. pap. 2.95 (ISBN 0-88172-017-8). Believers Bkshelf.

--Outline of Booth's Chart of the Ages. pap. 3.25 (ISBN 0-88172-018-6). Believers Bkshelf.

--Outlines for Christian Youth. pap. 5.95 (ISBN 0-88172-019-4). Believers Bkshelf.

--The Tabernacle Talks Today. pap. 5.25 (ISBN 0-88172-020-8). Believers Bkshelf.

Daniel, R. P., ed. see Dennett, E.

Daniel, R. P., ed. see Grant, F. W.
Daniel, R. P., ed. see Hole, F. B.
Daniel, Ralph T. The Anthem in New England Before Eighteen Hundred. (Music Reprint Ser.). 1979. Repr. of 1966 ed. 35.00 (ISBN 0-306-79511-6). Da Capo.
Daniel, Ralph T., jt. ed. see Apel, Willi.
Daniel, Rebecca. Abraham. (Our Greatest Heritage Ser.). (Illus.). 32p. (gr. 7-12). 1983. wkbk. 3.95 (ISBN 0-86653-133-5, SS 802). Good Apple.
--Adam & Eve. (Our Greatest Heritage Ser.). (Illus.). 32p. (gr. 7-12). 1983. wkbk. 3.95 (ISBN 0-86653-131-9, SS 800). Good Apple.
--Daniel. (Our Greatest Heritage Ser.). (Illus.). 32p. (gr. 7-12). 1983. wkbk. 3.95 (ISBN 0-86653-140-8, SS 809). Good Apple.
--David. (Our Greatest Heritage Ser.). (Illus.). (gr. 7-12). 1983. wkbk. 3.95 (ISBN 0-86653-138-6, SS 807). Good Apple.
--Jonah. (Our Greatest Heritage Ser.). (Illus.). 32p. (gr. 7-12). 1983. wkbk. 3.95 (ISBN 0-86653-141-6, SS 810). Good Apple.
--Joseph. (Our Greatest Heritage Ser.). 32p. (gr. 7-12). 1983. wkbk. 3.95 (ISBN 0-86653-134-3, SS 803). Good Apple.
--Joshua. (Our Greatest Heritage Ser.). (Illus.). 32p. (gr. 7-12). 1983. wkbk. 3.95 (ISBN 0-86653-136-X, SS 805). Good Apple.
--Moses. (Our Greatest Heritage Ser.). (Illus.). 32p. (gr. 7-12). 1983. wkbk. 3.95 (ISBN 0-86653-135-1, SS 804). Good Apple.
--Noah. (Our Greatest Heritage Ser.). (Illus.). (gr. 7-12). 1983. wkbk. 3.95 (ISBN 0-86653-132-7, SS 801). Good Apple.
--Samson. (Our Greatest Heritage Ser.). (Illus.). 32p. (gr. 7-12). 1983. wkbk. 3.95 (ISBN 0-86653-137-8, SS 806). Good Apple.
--Solomon. (Our Greatest Heritage Ser.). (Illus.). 32p. (gr. 7-12). 1983. wkbk. 3.95 (ISBN 0-86653-139-4, SS 808). Good Apple.
--Women of the Old Testament. (Our Greatest Heritage Ser.). (Illus.). 32p. (gr. 7-12). 1983. wkbk. 3.95 (ISBN 0-86653-142-4, SS 811). Good Apple.
Daniel, Richard. In Vain. 160p. 1981. pap. 3.95 (ISBN 0-942086-00-7). Custom Hse Pub.
Daniel, Robert L. American Philanthropy in the Near East, 1820-1960. LC 74-81451. xii, 322p. 1970. 15.00x (ISBN 0-8214-0063-0, 82-80695). Ohio U Pr.
Daniel, Robert P. Psychological Study of Delinquent & Non-Delinquent Negro Boys. LC 75-176718. (Columbia University. Teachers College. Contributions to Education: No. 546). Repr. of 1932 ed. 22.50 (ISBN 0-404-55546-2). AMS Pr.
Daniel, Roger P., ed. see Cutting, Jorge.
Daniel, Roger P., ed. see Mackintosh, Carlos H.
Daniel, Rollin K. & Terzls, Julia. Reconstructive Microsurgery. 1977. 75.00 (ISBN 0-316-17255-3). Little.
Daniel, Rollin K., jt. auth. see Regnault, Paule.
Daniel, Ronald S. Human Sexuality-Methods & Materials for the Education, Family Life & Health Professions, Volume One: An Annotated Guide to the Audio-Visuals. LC 79-84564. (Illus.). 1979. lib. bdg. 45.00 (ISBN 0-934016-03-8); pap. 35.00 (ISBN 0-934016-02-X). Heuristicus.
Daniel, Rudolf & Softsync, Inc. Commodore 64 Programming Guide. (Illus.). 325p. 12.95 (ISBN 0-89303-384-7). Brady Comm.
Daniel, Rudolph M. Timex-Sinclair 2068 Programmer's Guide. (Illus.). 176p. pap. cancelled (ISBN 0-89303-897-0). Brady Comm.
Daniel, Samuel. Poems & a Defence of Ryme. Sprague, Arthur C., ed. 1965. pap. 2.95x (ISBN 0-226-13609-4, P200, Phoen). U of Chicago Pr.
--Samuel Daniel's "Musophilus". Himelick, Raymond, tr. LC 65-22373. 107p. 1965. 3.95 (ISBN 0-911198-08-3). Purdue U Pr.
Daniel, Samuel & Lederer, M. The Tragedie of Cleopatra 1611. (Material for the Study of the Old English Drama Series 1: Vol. 31). pap. 11.00 (ISBN 0-317-15144-4). Kraus Repr.
Daniel, Samuel, tr. see Giovio, Paolo.
Daniel, Scott, jt. auth. see Buscaino, Dale.
Daniel, Stephen H. John Toland: His Methods, Manners, & Mind, No. 7. (Studies in the History of Ideas). 256p. 1984. 25.00x (ISBN 0-7735-1007-9). McGill-Queens U Pr.
Daniel, Thomas M, jt. ed. see Green, Gareth M.
Daniel, Timothy M. General License Study Guide. Dunn, Si, ed. 82p. 1982. pap. 6.95 (ISBN 0-88006-017-4, SG7358). Green Pub Inc.
Daniel, Timothy M., ed. Novice License Study Guide. 98p. 1981. pap. 4.95 (ISBN 0-88006-018-2, SG7357). Green Pub Inc.
Daniel, W. T. The History & Origin of Law Reports: England. LC 12-13803. 359p. 1961. Repr. of 1884 ed. lib. bdg. 32.50 (ISBN 0-89941-348-X). W S Hein.
Daniel, W. W. Maternity Rights: The Experience of Women. 119p. 1980. 29.00x (ISBN 0-686-87303-3, Pub. by Policy Studies). State Mutual Bk.
--Wage Determination in Industry. 132p. 1976. 19.00x (ISBN 0-686-87326-2, Pub. by Policy Studies). State Mutual Bk.
Daniel, W. W. & McIntosh, Neil. Right to Manage: A Study of Leadership & Reform in Employee Relations. 192p. 1972. 15.95x (ISBN 0-8464-0798-1). Beekman Pubs.
Daniel, W. W. & Millward, Neil. Workplace Industrial Relations in Britain. (Policy Studies Institute Ser.). xx, 333p. 1983. text ed. 50.00x (ISBN 0-435-83190-9); pap. text ed. 22.00x (ISBN 0-435-83191-7). Gower Pub Co.
Daniel, W. W. & Stilgoe, Elizabeth. Where Are They Now? A Follow-up Study of the Unemployed. 99p. 1977. 25.00x (ISBN 0-686-87339-4, Pub. by Policy Studies). State Mutual Bk.
Daniel, Walter. The Life of Ailred of Rievaulx. Powicke, Maurice, ed. 1978. Repr. of 1950 ed. 23.95x (ISBN 0-19-822256-4). Oxford U Pr.
Daniel, Walter C. Black Journals of the United States. LC 81-13440. (Historical Guides to the World's Periodicals & Newspapers). x, 432p. 1982. lib. bdg. 45.00 (ISBN 0-313-20704-6, DBJ/). Greenwood.
--Images of the Preacher in Afro-American Literature. LC 80-67247. 250p. (Orig.). 1981. lib. bdg. 22.75 (ISBN 0-8191-1662-9); pap. 11.75 (ISBN 0-8191-1663-7). U Pr of Amer.
Daniel, Walter G. Ambrose Caliver: Adult Education & Civil Servant. 1966. 1.40 (ISBN 0-88379-032-7). A A A C E.
--Reading Interests & Needs of Negro College Freshmen Regarding Social Science Materials. LC 79-176719. (Columbia University. Teachers College. Contributions to Education: No. 862). Repr. of 1942 ed. 22.50 (ISBN 0-404-55862-3). AMS Pr.
Daniel, Wanda R. & Dunlap, Howard G. Help with Capitalization, Abbreviations, & Numbers. (gr. 10-12). 1984. pap. text ed. 3.32 (ISBN 0-395-34821-8); tchr's manual 1.00 (ISBN 0-395-34822-6). HM.
Daniel, Wayne W. Applied Nonparametric Statistics. LC 77-74515. (Illus.). 1978. text ed. 32.50 (ISBN 0-395-25795-6); instructors manual 1.50 (ISBN 0-395-25796-4). HM.
--Biostatistics: A Foundation for Analysis in the Health Sciences. 3rd ed. LC 77-28253. (Probability & Mathematical Statistics Ser.). 534p. 1983. text ed. 38.45 (ISBN 0-471-09753-5). Wiley.
--Essentials of Business Statistics. LC 83-80247. 544p. 1983. text ed. 26.95 (ISBN 0-395-34274-0); instr's. manual 2.00 (ISBN 0-395-34275-9); solutions manual 6.95 (ISBN 0-395-34276-7); study guide 11.50 (ISBN 0-395-34277-5). HM.
--Introductory Statistics with Applications. LC 76-10897. (Illus.). 1977. text ed. 30.95 (ISBN 0-395-24430-7); study guide 12.95 (ISBN 0-395-24843-4). HM.
Daniel, Wayne W. & Terrell, James C. Business Statistics: Basic Concepts & Methodology. 3rd ed. LC 82-83254. 832p. 1982. text ed. 29.95 (ISBN 0-395-32601-X); instr's. resource manual 3.50 (ISBN 0-395-32602-8); study guide 12.50 (ISBN 0-395-32603-6); solutions manual 2.00 (ISBN 0-395-32604-4). HM.
Daniel, Wayne W., ed. Collecting Sensitive Data by Randomized Response: An Annotated Bibliography. LC 79-12210. (Research Monograph: No. 85). 1979. spiral bdg. 15.00 (ISBN 0-88406-127-2). Ga St U Busn Pub.
Daniel, William & Fleiszar, Kathleen. Genetics & Variation. (Illus.). 471p. text ed. 21.80 (ISBN 0-87563-220-3). Stipes.
Daniel, William A. Education of Negro Ministers. LC 77-78581. Repr. of 1925 ed. cancelled (ISBN 0-8371-1410-1, DNM&, Pub. by Negro U Pr). Greenwood.
Daniele, Joseph. How to Build Thirty-Five Great Clocks. Schnell, Judith, ed. (Illus.). 172p. 1984. 29.95 (ISBN 0-8117-1816-6). Stackpole.
Daniele, Joseph W. Building Colonial Furnishings, Miniatures, & Folk Art. LC 76-17006. (Illus.). 256p. 1976. 27.95 (ISBN 0-8117-0451-3). Stackpole.
--Building Early American Furniture. LC 74-10953. (Illus.). 256p. 1974. 19.95. Stackpole.
--Building Masterpiece Miniatures. LC 79-10631. (Illus.). 352p. 1981. text ed. 27.95 (ISBN 0-8117-0306-1). Stackpole.
--Building Miniature Furniture. LC 80-22180. (Illus.). 256p. 1981. 26.95 (ISBN 0-8117-1000-9). Stackpole.
--Early American Metal Projects. LC 75-130495. 16.64 (ISBN 0-87345-142-2). McKnight.
--How to Build a Clock-With Thirty Five Plans & Complete Instructions. (Illus.). 224p. 1982. pap. 12.95 (ISBN 0-940166-01-1). Old Main Bks.
Daniele, R. Anthony, jt. auth. see Clair, Bernard E.
Danielian, Noobar R. A. T. & T. The Story of Industrial Conquest. LC 74-7672. (Telecommunication Ser). 486p. 1974. Repr. of 1939 ed. 30.00x (ISBN 0-405-06038-6). Ayer Co Pubs.
Danielian, Ronald L., jt. auth. see Stanley, Timothy W.
Daniell, B. L., jt. auth. see Waldron, M. B.
Daniell, David. Coriolanus in Europe. (Illus.). 172p. 1980. 32.50 (ISBN 0-485-11192-6, Pub. by Athlone Pr Ltd). Longwood Pub Group.
Daniell, David, ed. The Best Short Stories of John Buchan, No. 1. 246p. 1984. pap. 4.95 (ISBN 0-586-05938-5, Pub. by Granada England). Academy Chi Pubs.
--Best Short Stories of John Buchan, No. 2. 272p. 1984. pap. 4.95 (ISBN 0-586-05939-3, Pub. by Granada England). Academy Chi Pubs.
Daniell, David S. Your Body. (Illus.). (gr. 5 up). 2.50 (ISBN 0-7214-0108-2). Merry Thoughts.
Daniell, G. W. Bishop Wilberforce. 1978. Repr. of 1891 ed. lib. bdg. 20.00 (ISBN 0-8482-0607-X). Norwood Edns.
Daniell, Jere R. Colonial New Hampshire - A History. LC 81-6046. (A History of the American Colonies Ser.). 1981. lib. bdg. 35.00 (ISBN 0-527-18715-1). Kraus Intl.
--Experiment in Republicanism: New Hampshire Politics & the American Revolution, 1741-1794. LC 75-122219. 1970. 17.50x (ISBN 0-674-27806-2). Harvard U Pr.
Daniell, Jo, photos by. Thorn Bird Country. (Illus.). 128p. 1983. pap. 12.95 (ISBN 0-446-37573-X). Warner Bks.
Daniell, Rosemary. Fatal Flowers: On Sin, Sex & Suicide in the Deep South. 288p. 1984. pap. 3.95 (ISBN 0-380-54254-4, 65946, Discus). Avon.
--Sleeping with Soldiers: In Search of the Macho Man. LC 84-6701. 288p. 1985. 14.95 (ISBN 0-03-062431-2). HR&W.
Danielle, Timothy T. The Lawyers: The Inns of Court. LC 76-25744. 353p. 1976. 17.50 (ISBN 0-379-00593-X). Oceana.
Danielli, H. C. The Fossil Alga Girvanella Nicholson & Etheridge. 20.00x (ISBN 0-686-78656-4, Pub. by Brit Mus Pubns England). State Mutual Bk.
Danielli, J. F., jt. auth. see Bourne, G. H.
Danielli, J. F., jt. ed. see Bourne, G. H.
Danielli, J. F., jt. ed. see Bourne, Geoffrey.
Danielli, J. F., jt. ed. see Cadenhead, D. A.
Danielli, J. F., ed. see Symposium on Molecular Pharmacology, 3rd, Buffalo 1968, et al.
Danielli, J. F., et al, eds. Recent Progress in Surface & Membrane Science. Incl. Vol. 4. 1971. 73.50 (ISBN 0-12-571804-7); Vol. 5. 1972. 73.50 (ISBN 0-12-571805-5); Vol. 6. 1973. 73.50 (ISBN 0-12-571806-3); Vol. 7. 1973. 73.50 (ISBN 0-12-571807-1); Vol. 8. 1974. 73.50 (ISBN 0-12-571808-X); Vol. 9. 1975. 73.50 (ISBN 0-12-571809-8); Vol. 10. 1976. 78.00 (ISBN 0-12-571810-1); Vol. 11. 1976. 73.50 (ISBN 0-12-571811-X). Orig. Title: Progress in Surface & Membrane Science. Acad Pr.
--Recent Progress in Surface Science, 3 vols. Incl. Vol. 1. 1964. 73.50 (ISBN 0-12-571801-2); Vol. 2. 1964. 83.00 (ISBN 0-12-571802-0); Vol. 3. 1970. 80.50 (ISBN 0-12-571803-9). Acad Pr.
Danielli, James, jt. ed. see Bourne, Geoffrey.
Danielli, James F., ed. International Review of Cytology Supplement: Vol. 15: Aspects of Cell Regulation. 1983. 40.00 (ISBN 0-12-364376-7). Acad Pr.
Danielli, James F. & DiBerardino, Marie, eds. International Review of Cytology: Supplement No. 9 Nuclear Transplantation. LC 74-17773. 1979. 55.00 (ISBN 0-12-364369-4). Acad Pr.
Danielli, James F., jt. ed. see Bourne, Geoffrey H.
Danielli, James F., jt. ed. see Bourne, Geoggrey H.
Danielli, James F., jt. ed. see Bourne, H.
Danielli, James F., jt. ed. see Cadenhead, D. A.
Daniello, Bernardino. L' Espositione di Bernardino Daniello da Lucca sopra la Comedia de Dante. Hollander, Robert, et al, eds. LC 85-40490. (Illus.). 350p. (Ital.). 1985. Repr. of 1568 ed. 32.50x (ISBN 0-87451-348-0). U Pr of New Eng.
Daniells, Lorna. Business Information Sources. LC 74-30517. 1976. 19.95 (ISBN 0-520-02946-1). U of Cal Pr.
Danielopol, D., jt. ed. see Loffler, H.
Danielou, Alain. The Gods of India. 441p. (Orig.). 1985. pap. 16.95. Inner Tradit.
--Ragas of Northern Indian Music. 1981. 30.00x (ISBN 0-8364-0774-1, Pub. by Munshiram). South Asia Bks.
--Shiva & Dionysus. (Illus.). 250p. 1983. pap. 10.00 (ISBN 0-85692-054-1, Pub. by Salem Hse Ltd). Merrimack Pub Cir.
--Shiva & Dionysus. 250p. (Orig.). 1984. pap. 8.95 (ISBN 0-89281-057-2). Inner Tradit.
Danielou, Alain, tr. see Adigal, Ilango.
Danielou, Jea. God's Life in Us. 1.95 (ISBN 0-317-06464-9). Dimension Bks.
Danielou, Jean. Bible & the Liturgy. (Liturgical Studies Ser.: No. 3). 1956. 10.95 (ISBN 0-268-00018-2). U of Notre Dame Pr.
--The Dead Sea Scrolls & Primitive Christianity. Attanasio, Salvator, tr. from Fr. LC 78-21516. 1979. Repr. of 1958 ed. lib. bdg. 22.50x (ISBN 0-313-21144-2, DADE). Greenwood.
--A History of Early Christian Doctrine Before the Council of Nicaea. Baker, John A., tr. Incl. Vol. 1. The Theology of Jewish Christianity. 1977; Vol. 2. Gospel Message & Hellenistic Culture. LC 72-7090. 1973; Vol. 3. The Origins of Latin Christianity. LC 76-44380. 528p. 1977. 27.50 (ISBN 0-664-21064-3). Westminster.
--Lord of History. 1958. 6.75x (ISBN 0-8092-8971-7). Contemp Bks.
--Prayer As a Political Problem. Kirwan, J. R., ed. 1967. 3.50 (ISBN 0-8362-0278-3, Pub. by Sheed). Guild Bks.
--Salvation of the Nations. 1962. pap. 1.25x (ISBN 0-268-00244-4). U of Notre Dame Pr.
Danielou, Jean & Marrou, Henri. Christian Centuries: First Six Hundred Years. LC 78-55069. (Illus.). 610p. 1969. 19.95 (ISBN 0-8091-0275-7). Paulist Pr.
Danielou, Jean, ed. From Glory to Glory: Texts from Gregory of Nyssa's Mystical Writings. LC 79-38. 304p. 1979. pap. 8.95 (ISBN 0-913836-54-0). St Vladimirs.
Danielou, Cardinal Jean. Why the Church? De Lange, Mauarice F., tr. 196p. 1975. 7.50 (ISBN 0-8199-0562-3). Franciscan Herald.
Daniel-Rops, Henri. Daily Life in the Time of Jesus. O'Brian, Patrick, tr. from Fr. (Illus.). 518p. 1981. pap. 8.95 (ISBN 0-89283-085-9). Servant.
Daniel-Rops, Henry. Two Men in Me. facsimile ed. Meynier, Gil, tr. from Fr. LC 76-163024. (Short Story Index Reprint Ser.). Repr. of 1931 ed. 17.00 (ISBN 0-8369-3938-7). Ayer Co Pubs.
Daniels, A. Pat. Bolivar! Gulf Coast Peninsula. (Illus.). 113p. (Orig.). 1985. pap. 8.95 (ISBN 0-9614885-0-6). Penisula TX.
Daniels, Alan & Yeates, Don. Design & Analysis of Software Systems. 257p. 1983. pap. 14.95 (ISBN 0-89433-212-0). Petrocelli.
Daniels, Althea. The Friendship Factor Study Guide. 32p. (Orig.). 1984. pap. 0.95 (ISBN 0-8066-2079-X, 10-2413). Augsburg.
Daniels, Anthony, jt. auth. see Clair, Bernard.
Daniels, Arlene K., jt. ed. see Benet, James.
Daniels, Arlene K., jt. ed. see Kahn-Hut, Rachel.
Daniels, Arthur M. A Journal of Sibley's Indian Expedition During the Summer of 1863 & Record of the Troops Employed. (Illus.). 154p. 1980. Repr. 30.00 (ISBN 0-911506-13-6). Thueson.
Daniels, Aubrey C. & Rosen, Theodore A. Performance Management: Improving Quality & Productivity Through Positive Reinforcement. LC 82-61868. (Illus.). 1983. 24.95 (ISBN 0-937100-01-3). Perf Manage.
Daniels, Barbara. Winter Rose. 1978. pap. 1.95 (ISBN 0-505-51292-0, Pub. by Tower Bks). Dorchester Pub Co.
Daniels, Barry V. Revolution in the Theatre: French Romantic Theories of Drama. LC 83-1705. (Contributions in Drama & Theatre Studies: No. 7). xii, 249p. 1983. lib. bdg. 29.95 (ISBN 0-313-22476-5, DRT/). Greenwood.
Daniels, Belden, jt. auth. see Litvak, Larry.
Daniels, Belinda S., jt. ed. see Davis, Lenwood G.
Daniels, Bennet, jt. auth. see Daniels, Else.
Daniels, Bruce C. The Connecticut Town: Growth & Development, 1635-1790. LC 79-65331. (Illus.). 249p. 1979. 18.50x (ISBN 0-8195-5036-1); pap. 9.95 (ISBN 0-8195-6065-0). Wesleyan U Pr.
--Dissent & Conformity on Narragansett Bay: The Colonial Rhode Island Town. LC 83-23265. (Illus.). 256p. 1984. text ed. 25.00x (ISBN 0-8195-5083-3, 0-8105-5093-3). Wesleyan U Pr.
Daniels, Bruce C. see Weaver, Glenn.
Daniels, Bruce C., ed. Town & County: Essays on the Structure of Local Government in the American Colonies. LC 77-14834. 1978. 22.00x (ISBN 0-8195-5020-5). Wesleyan U Pr.
Daniels, Carlos G., Jr. Life... with No Strings Attached! 155p. 1984. 5.95 (ISBN 0-89697-144-9). Intl Univ Pr.
Daniels, Christian, jt. auth. see Grove, Linda.
Daniels, Cora L. Encyclopedia of Superstitions, Folklore & the Occult Sciences, 3 vols. 300.00 (ISBN 0-8490-0106-4). Gordon Pr.
Daniels, Cora L. & Stevans, C. M., eds. Encyclopedia of Superstitions, Folklore & the Occult Sciences of the World, 3 vols. LC 70-141151. 1971. Repr. of 1903 ed. 107.00x (ISBN 0-8103-3286-8). Gale.
Daniels, D. & Nestel, B., eds. Resource Allocation to Agricultural Research: Proceedings of a Workshop Held in Singapore, 8-10 June 1981. 180p. (Eng. & Fr.). 1981. pap. 12.00 (ISBN 0-88936-314-5, IDRC182, IDRC). Unipub.
Daniels, Dana. For Love or Money. (Second Chance at Love Ser.: No. 230). 192p. 1984. pap. 1.95 (ISBN 0-515-08204-X). Jove Pubns.
--Unspoken Longings. (Second Chance at Love Ser.: No. 302). 192p. 1985. pap. 2.25 (ISBN 0-425-08630-5). Berkley Pub.
Daniels, David. The Golden Age of Contract Bridge. LC 78-25629. (Illus.). 224p. 1982. 15.95 (ISBN 0-8128-2576-4); pap. 7.95 (ISBN 0-8128-6166-3). Stein & Day.
--Orchestral Music: A Handbook. 2nd ed. LC 81-16678. 425p. 1982. 25.00 (ISBN 0-8108-1484-6). Scarecrow.
Daniels, Dewar, jt. auth. see Francis, Thadys J.
Daniels, Diane & Barron, Anne D. The Professional Secretary: Skills & Techniques for Recognition & Success. 224p. 1982. 15.95 (ISBN 0-8144-5599-9); pap. 7.95 (ISBN 0-8144-7576-0). AMACOM.
Daniels, Dorothy. Crisis at Valcour. 1985. pap. 3.75 (ISBN 0-446-30807-2). Warner Bks.
--For Love & Valcour. 480p. 1983. pap. 3.50 (ISBN 0-446-30256-2). Warner Bks.
--Juniper Hill. 1976. pap. 1.50 (ISBN 0-671-80807-9). WSP.
--Monte Carlo. 1981. pap. 2.75 (ISBN 0-8439-0900-5, Leisure Bks). Dorchester Pub Co.
--The Spanish Chapel. (Inflation Fighters Ser.). 192p. 1982. pap. 1.50 (ISBN 0-8439-1066-6, Leisure Bks). Dorchester Pub Co.
--The Spanish Chapel. 1977. pap. text ed. 1.25 (ISBN 0-505-51165-7, BT51165, Pub. by Tower Bks). Dorchester Pub Co.
Daniels, Douglas H. Pioneer Urbanites: A Social & Cultural History of Black San Francisco. 260p. 1980. 32.95 (ISBN 0-87722-169-3). Temple U Pr.

Daniels, Earl, ed. Art of Reading Poetry. facsimile ed. LC 70-103087. (Granger Index Reprint Ser). 1941. 24.00 (ISBN 0-8369-6102-1). Ayer Co Pubs.

Daniels, Elam J. Como Ser Feliz En el Matrimonio. Orig. Title: How to Be Happily Married. 96p. 1981. pap. 2.10 (ISBN 0-311-46066-6). Casa Bautista.

Daniels, Elizabeth A. Jessie White Mario: Risorgimento Revolutionary. LC 78-158178. (Illus.). vii, 199p. 1972. 14.00 (ISBN 0-8214-0103-3, 82-81081). Ohio U Pr.

Daniels, Ellen S. & Porter, Robert, eds. Community Arts Agencies: A Handbook & Guide. (Illus.). 408p. (Orig.). 1978. pap. 7.50 (ISBN 0-915400-08-1). Am Council Arts.

Daniels, Else & Daniels, Bennet. Vacation at Sea: A Travel Guide for Cruises. (Illus.). 1979. pap. 5.95 (ISBN 0-346-12423-9). Cornerstone.

Daniels, F. J. Basic English: Writer's Japanese-English Word Book. (Eng. & Japanese.). 1969. 35.00 (ISBN 0-89346-100-8, Pub. by Hokuseido Pr). Heian Intl.

Daniels, Farrington. Direct Use of the Sun's Energy. 1974. pap. 2.50 (ISBN 0-345-29226-X). Ballantine.

--Direct Use of the Sun's Energy. LC 64-20913. 391p. 1983. pap. text ed. 7.95x (ISBN 0-300-02986-1). Yale U Pr.

Daniels, Farrington, jt. auth. see Alberty, Robert A.

Daniels, Farrington & Duffie, John A., eds. Solar Energy Research. LC 55-6325. pap. 76.50 (ISBN 0-317-10982-0, 2002069). Bks Demand UMI.

Daniels, Farrington & Smith, Thomas M., eds. Challenge of Our Times. LC 70-118510. (Essay & General Literature Index Reprint Ser). 1971. Repr. of 1953 ed. 27.50 (ISBN 0-8046-1405-9, Pub. by Kennikat). Assoc Faculty Pr.

Daniels, Farrington, et al. Experimental Physical Chemistry. 7th ed. 1970. text ed. 40.95 (ISBN 0-07-015339-6). McGraw.

Daniels, Fay. Eyes of the Psychic World. 96p. 1984. 8.95 (ISBN 0-89962-401-4). Todd & Honeywell.

Daniels, Florence M. Why Art? LC 77-28084. (Illus.). 236p. 1978. 22.95x (ISBN 0-88229-173-4). Nelson-Hall.

Daniels, Frank & Johnson, Evelyne. The Sharon First Picture Dictionary. (Illus.). 96p. 1983. 6.95 (ISBN 0-89531-032-5); pap. 2.95 (ISBN 0-89531-082-1). Sharon Pubns.

--The Sharon Picture Word Book. (Illus.). 96p. 1983. 6.95 (ISBN 0-89531-031-7). Sharon Pubns.

Daniels, Frederick H. Mind Stimulative Correlations in Art Education. (Illus.). 110p. 1981. Repr. of 1909 ed. 45.25 (ISBN 0-89901-024-5). Found Class Reprints.

Daniels, G., ed. Artists from the Royal Botanic Gardens, Kew. (Illus.). 1974. pap. 3.00x (ISBN 0-913196-17-7). Hunt Inst Botanical.

--A Linnaean Keepsake. (Illus., Eng. & Lat.). 1973. 13.00x (ISBN 0-913196-15-0). Hunt Inst Botanical.

Daniels, Gail, ed. Cancer, the Moon Child. (Zodiac Ser.). 160p. (Orig.). (gr. 7 up). 1985. pap. 1.95 (ISBN 0-448-47741-6). Putnam Pub Group.

Daniels, Gene & Gagala, Kenneth. Labor Guide to Negotiating Wages & Benefits. 1985. pap. text ed. 16.95 (ISBN 0-8359-3923-5). Reston.

Daniels, Gene, et al. Labor Guide to Local Union Leadership & Administration. 1985. pap. text ed. 18.95 (ISBN 0-8359-3924-3). Reston.

Daniels, George. The Art of Breguet. (Illus.). 412p. 1975. 132.50 (ISBN 0-85667-004-9, Pub. by Sotheby Pubns England). Biblio Dist.

--Home Guide to Plumbing, Heating, & Air Conditioning. 2nd ed. LC 67-10841. (Popular Science Skill Bk). (Illus.). 1976. pap. 3.95i (ISBN 0-06-010957-2, TD-271, HarpT). Har-Row.

--Solar Homes & Sun Heating. LC 74-15818. (Illus.). 176p. 1976. 14.37i (ISBN 0-06-010937-8, HarpT). Har-Row.

--Watchmaking. (Illus.). 440p. 1981. 65.00x (ISBN 0-85667-150-9, Pub. by Sotheby Pubns Englabd). Biblio Dist.

Daniels, George & Markarian, Ohannes. Watches & Clocks in the Sir David Salomons Collection. (Illus.). 318p. 1983. 65.00x (ISBN 0-85667-074-X, Pub. by Sotheby Pubns England). Biblio Dist.

--Watches & Clocks in the Sir David Salomons Collection. (Illus.). 320p. 50.00 (ISBN 0-318-12098-4, Pub. by Sotheby Pubns England). Biblio Dist.

Daniels, George, jt. auth. see Clutton, Cecil.

Daniels, George & Clutton, Cecil, eds. Clocks & Watches: The Collection of the Worshipful Company of Clockmakers. (Illus.). 160p. 1975. 52.50 (ISBN 0-85667-019-7, Pub. by Sotheby Pubns England). Biblio Dist.

Daniels, George H. American Science in the Age of Jackson. LC 67-28710. 282p. 1968. 29.00x (ISBN 0-231-03073-8). Columbia U Pr.

Daniels, George H., ed. Nineteenth-Century American Science: A Reappraisal. LC 79-186547. 292p. 1972. text ed. 17.95x (ISBN 0-8101-0381-8). Northwestern U Pr.

Daniels, George H. & Rose, Mark H., eds. Energy & Transport: Historical Perspectives on Policy Issues. (Sage Focus Editions: Vol. 52). (Illus.). 288p. 1982. 28.00 (ISBN 0-8039-0786-9); pap. 14.00 (ISBN 0-8039-0787-7). Sage.

Daniels, George M. Tanzania: People-Questions. (People & Systems Ser). (Orig.). 1975. pap. 1.75 (ISBN 0-377-00034-5). Friend Pr.

Daniels, George M., ed. Drums of War. LC 73-92611. 1974. 11.95 (ISBN 0-89388-126-0). Okpaku Communications.

Daniels, Gilbert, ed. see Bonar, Ann.

Daniels, Gilbert, ed. see Hine, Jacqui.

Daniels, Gilbert, ed. see Krussmann, Gerd.

Daniels, Gordon, ed. A Guide to the Reports of the United States Strategic Bombing Survey. (RHS Guides & Handbooks Ser.: No. 12). 115p. 1981. pap. 18.00 (ISBN 0-901050-71-7, Pub. by Boydell & Brewer). Longwood Pub Group.

Daniels, Guy & Hedley, Leslie W., eds. Fiction Eighty-Four: A New Anthology of Innovative Writing. 200p. (Orig.). 1985. pap. 8.95 (ISBN 0-933515-05-7). Exile Pr.

--Fiction 83: A New Anthology of Innovative Writing. annual 200p. (Orig.). 1984. pap. 8.95 (ISBN 0-933515-02-2). Exile Pr.

Daniels, Guy, tr. see Amalrik, Andrei.

Daniels, Guy, tr. see Casals, Felipe G.

Daniels, Guy, tr. see Kondratieff, Nikolai.

Daniels, Guy, tr. see Turchin, Valentin.

Daniels, Guy, tr. see Vishnevskaya, Galina.

Daniels, H. K. Home Life in Norway. LC 77-87709. (Illus.). Repr. of 1911 ed. 24.50 (ISBN 0-404-16499-4). AMS Pr.

Daniels, Harold M. What to Do with Sunday Morning. LC 78-21040. 132p. 1979. softcover 4.95 (ISBN 0-664-24237-5). Westminster.

Daniels, Harvey. Printmaking. LC 77-146054. (Illus.). 1972. 25.00 (ISBN 0-670-57757-X, Studio). Viking.

Daniels, Harvey & Zemelman, Steven. A Writing Project: Training Teachers of Composition from Kindergarten to College. LC 85-896. viii, 246p. (Orig.). 1985. pap. text ed. 12.50x (ISBN 0-435-08216-7). Heinemann Ed.

Daniels, Harvey A. Famous Last Words: The American Language Crisis Reconsidered. LC 82-10281. 304p. 1983. 19.95 (ISBN 0-8093-1055-4); pap. 12.95x (ISBN 0-8093-1093-7). S Ill U Pr.

Daniels, J; see Bernard, William S.

Daniels, Jack, et al. Conditioning for Distance Running: The Scientific Aspects. LC 77-22538. (American College of Sports Medicine Ser.). 106p. 1978. pap. 23.75 (ISBN 0-471-19483-2). Wiley.

Daniels, Jack L., jt. auth. see Gutsch, Kenneth U.

Daniels, James M. Oriented Nuclei: Polarized Targets & Beams. (Pure & Applied Physics Ser.: Vol. 20). 1965. 59.50 (ISBN 0-12-202950-X). Acad Pr.

Daniels, James W. Elementary Linear Algebra & Its Applications. (Illus.). 368p. 1981. text ed. 28.95 (ISBN 0-13-258293-7). P-H.

Daniels, Jeff. Citroen SM. (Osprey Auto History Ser.). (Illus.). 136p. 1981. 14.95 (ISBN 0-85045-381-X, Pub. by Osprey England). Motorbooks Intl.

Daniels, Jeremy, jt. auth. see Mignery, Herb.

Daniels, Jerry C., jt. ed. see Ritzmann, Stephan E.

Daniels, Jim. Places Everyone. LC 85-40366. 96p. 1985. 12.50 (ISBN 0-299-10350-1); pap. 6.95 (ISBN 0-299-10354-4). U of Wis Pr.

Daniels, John. In Freedom's Birthplace: A Study of Boston Negroes. LC 69-18575. (American Negro: His History & Literature Ser., No. 2). 1969. Repr. of 1914 ed. 17.00 (ISBN 0-405-01857-6). Ayer Co Pubs.

--In Freedom's Birthplace: A Study of the Boston Negroes. LC 68-55880. (Illus.). Repr. of 1914 ed. cancelled (ISBN 0-8371-0371-1, DAF&, Pub. by Negro U Pr). Greenwood.

--In Freedom's Birthplace: A Study of the Boston Negroes. (Basic Afro-American Reprint Library). 1969. Repr. of 1914 ed. 24.00 (ISBN 0-384-10775-3). Johnson Repr.

Daniels, John D. & Radebaugh, Lee H. International Business Environments & Operations. 4th ed. LC 35-11127. 816p. 1986. text ed. price not set (ISBN 0-201-10713-9). Addison-Wesley.

Daniels, John D., et al. International Business Environments & Operations. 3rd ed. LC 81-170636. (Illus.). 531p. 1982. text ed. 36.95 (ISBN 0-201-10223-4); instr's manual 10.95 (ISBN 0-201-10224-2). Addison-Wesley.

Daniels, Jonathan. Devil's Backbone: The Story of the Natchez Trace. 270p. 1985. pap. 13.95 (ISBN 0-88289-438-2). Pelican.

--The End of Innocence. LC 73-37285. (FDR & the Era of the New Deal Ser.). 351p. 1972. Repr. of 1954 ed. 39.50 (ISBN 0-306-70423-4). Da Capo.

--Frontier on the Potomac. LC 70-37284. (FDR & the Era of the New Deal Ser.). 262p. 1972. Repr. of 1946 ed. lib. bdg. 35.00 (ISBN 0-306-70425-0). Da Capo.

--Prince of Carpetbaggers. LC 74-3742. (Illus.). 319p. 1974. Repr. of 1958 ed. lib. bdg. 22.50x (ISBN 0-8371-7466-X, DAPO). Greenwood.

--A Southerner Discovers the South. LC 68-16228. (The American Scene Ser.). 1970. Repr. of 1938 ed. lib. bdg. 42.50 (ISBN 0-306-71011-0). Da Capo.

Daniels, Josephus. Editor in Politics. LC 74-2839. (Illus.). 644p. 1974. Repr. of 1941 ed. lib. bdg. 42.50x (ISBN 0-8371-7439-2, DAEI). Greenwood.

--Life of Woodrow Wilson, 1856-1924. LC 72-114509. (Illus.). 1971. Repr. of 1924 ed. lib. bdg. 19.75x (ISBN 0-8371-4729-8, DAWW). Greenwood.

--Life of Woodrow Wilson: 1856-1924. 1979. Repr. of 1924 ed. lib. bdg. 20.00 (ISBN 0-8492-4203-7). R West.

--Life of Woodrow Wilson, 1856-1924. LC 70-144965. (Illus.). 1971. Repr. of 1924 ed. 18.00x (ISBN 0-403-00934-0). Scholarly.

--Shirt-Sleeve Diplomat. LC 73-11621. (Illus.). 547p. 1973. Repr. of 1947 ed. lib. bdg. 27.50x (ISBN 0-8371-7082-6, DASD). Greenwood.

--Tar Heel Editor. LC 74-2840. (Illus.). 544p. 1974. Repr. of 1939 ed. lib. bdg. 37.50x (ISBN 0-8371-7440-6, DATH). Greenwood.

--The Wilson Era: Years of Peace, 1910-1917. LC 74-9269. (Illus.). 615p. 1974. Repr. of 1944 ed. lib. bdg. 37.00x (ISBN 0-8371-7634-4, DAYP). Greenwood.

--The Wilson Era: Years of War & After, 1917-1923. LC 74-9271. (Illus.). 654p. 1974. Repr. of 1946 ed. lib. bdg. 34.00x (ISBN 0-8371-7635-2, DAYW). Greenwood.

Daniels, Kate. The White Wave. LC 83-40341. (Pitt Poetry Ser.). 61p. 1984. 12.95x (ISBN 0-8229-3493-0); pap. 6.95 (ISBN 0-8229-5359-5). U of Pittsburgh Pr.

Daniels, Kate, jt. ed. see Jones, Richard.

Daniels, Kay & Murnane, Mary, eds. Uphill All the Way: A Documentary History of Women in Australia. (Illus.). 335p. 1980. 27.95x (ISBN 0-7022-1476-0); pap. text ed. 14.95x (ISBN 0-7022-1345-4). U of Queensland Pr.

Daniels, Keith W. Old-Time Alternate Energy. (Illus.). 160p. 1983. pap. 6.95 (ISBN 0-934646-14-7). TX S & S Pr.

Daniels, Keith W., compiled by. Hand-made Hand Tools, Eighteen Ninety to Nineteen Forty-Eight. (Illus.). 240p. 1979. pap. 9.95 (ISBN 0-937468-01-0). Lost Data.

--Recycling & Repairing, Nineteen Twelve to Nineteen Forty Eight. (Illus.). 290p. (Orig.). 1978. pap. 9.95 (ISBN 0-937468-00-2). Lost Data.

Daniels, Kim. Your Changing Emotions. (Just for You Ser.: No. 2). 128p. (Orig.). 1985. pap. 2.95 (ISBN 0-523-42370-5). Pinnacle Bks.

Daniels, Kristy. The Dancer. 192p. (Orig.). 1984. pap. 2.25 (ISBN 0-345-31601-0). Ballantine.

Daniels, Les. The Black Castle. 240p. 1983. pap. 2.50 (ISBN 0-441-06515-5, Pub. by Ace Science Fiction). Ace Bks.

--Living in Fear: The History of Horror in the Mass Media. (Quality Paperbacks Ser.). (Illus.). 256p. 1983. pap. 12.95 (ISBN 0-306-80193-0). Da Capo.

Daniels, Lloyd K., ed. Vocational Rehabilitation of the Mentally Retarded: A Book of Readings. (Illus.). 648p. 1974. 37.75x (ISBN 0-398-02582-7). C C Thomas.

Daniels, Lucille & Worthingham, Catherine. Muscle Testing: Techniques of Manual Examination. 4th ed. LC 79-67302. (Illus.). 191p. 1980. 14.95 (ISBN 0-7216-2877-X). Saunders.

--Therapeutic Exercise for Body Aligment and Function. 2nd ed. LC 76-27058. (Illus.). 1977. pap. text ed. 13.95 (ISBN 0-7216-2873-7). Saunders.

Daniels, Lynda M., jt. auth. see Kochar, Mahendra S.

Daniels, M. J. & Markham, P. G. Plant & Insect Mycoplasma Techniques. LC 81-13142. 369p. 1982. 54.95x (ISBN 0-470-27262-7). Halsted Pr.

Daniels, M. J. & Markham, P. J., eds. Plant & Insect Mycoplasma Techniques. 368p. 1981. 37.00 (ISBN 0-7099-0272-7, Pub. by Croom Helm Ltd). Longwood Pub Group.

Daniels, M. S., jt. auth. see Haynes, J. H.

Daniels, Madeline. Realistic Leadership: How to Lead Others in Achieving Company & Personal Goals. 160p. 1983. 12.95 (ISBN 0-13-766816-3); pap. 5.95 (ISBN 0-13-766808-2). P-H.

Daniels, Madeline M. Living Your Religion in the Real World. LC 84-18209. 192p. 13.95 (ISBN 0-13-539016-8); pap. 5.95 (ISBN 0-13-539008-7). P-H.

Daniels, Marcus. BSA Unit Singles '58 - '72. new ed. (Owners Workshop Manuals Ser.: No. 127). 1979. 10.50 (ISBN 0-85696-127-2, Pub. by J H Haynes England). Haynes Pubns.

Daniels, Marion L., tr. from Lat. see Bodin, Jean.

Daniels, Martin, jt. auth. see Pemberton, Steven.

Daniels, Mary. Cat Astrology. (Illus.). 1977. pap. 1.75 (ISBN 0-380-01685-0, 33563). Avon.

Daniels, Mary F., jt. ed. see Bowe, Forrest.

Daniels, Mary L., compiled by. Trollope-to-Reader: A Topical Guide to Digressions in the Novels of Anthony Trollope. LC 83-10873. xxi, 393p. 1983. lib. bdg. 45.00 (ISBN 0-313-23877-4, DTR/). Greenwood.

Daniels, May. The French Drama of the Unspoken. LC 77-2374. (Edinburgh University Publications Language & Literature Ser.: No. 3). 1977. Repr. of 1953 ed. 22.50x (ISBN 0-8371-9464-4, DAFD). Greenwood.

Daniels, Megan. The Unlikely Rivals. 1981. pap. 2.25 (ISBN 0-451-11076-5, AE1076, Sig). NAL.

Daniels, Michael. Split in Two. 8.00 (ISBN 0-89253-680-2). Ind-US Inc.

--That Damn Romantic Fool. 14.00 (ISBN 0-89253-624-1); flexible cloth 6.75 (ISBN 0-89253-625-X). Ind-US Inc.

Daniels, Michael, ed Ramps Are Beautiful: The Architecture of Independence. LC 82-70393. (Illus.). 92p. 1982. pap. text ed. 12.00 (ISBN 0-942846-00-1). Center Independent.

Daniels, Michael C. Anything Out of Place Is Dirt. (Writers Workshop Ser.). 106p. 1975. 9.00 (ISBN 0-88253-498-X); pap. text ed. 4.80 (ISBN 0-88253-497-1). Ind-US Inc.

Daniels, Mortimer B. Corporation Financial Statements. Brief, Richard P., ed. LC 80-1484. (Dimensions of Accounting Theory & Practice Ser.). 1981. Repr. of 1934 ed. lib. bdg. 16.00x (ISBN 0-405-13514-9). Ayer Co Pubs.

Daniels, N. C., ed. see Mintz, S., et al.

Daniels, Neil, jt. auth. see Hudson, Anne.

Daniels, Norman. Forever Wynward. (Wynward Ser.: No. 5). 448p. 1984. pap. 3.50 (ISBN 0-446-30532-4). Warner Bks.

--Just Health Care. (Studies in Philosophy & Health Policy). 250p. Date not set. price not set (ISBN 0-521-23608-8); pap. price not set (ISBN 0-521-31794-0). Cambridge U Pr.

--Thomas Reid's Inquiry: The Geometry of Visibles & the Case for Realism. new ed. LC 74-1478. (Illus.). xxix, 147p. 1974. lib. bdg. 14.95 (ISBN 0-89102-029-2). B Franklin.

--Wynward Glory. 1984. pap. 2.95 (ISBN 0-446-90742-1). Warner Bks.

Daniels, P. W. Office Location & the Journey to Work: A Comparative Study of Five Urban Centers. 192p. 1980. text ed. 35.50x (ISBN 0-566-00352-X). Gower Pub Co.

--Service Industries: Growth & Location. 2nd ed. LC 82-4260. (Cambridge Topics in Geography Ser.). (Illus.). 96p. 1982. 14.95 (ISBN 0-521-23730-0). Cambridge U Pr.

--Spatial Patterns of Office Growth & Location. LC 78-8386. 414p. 1979. 63.95 (ISBN 0-471-99675-0). Wiley.

Daniels, P. W. & Warnes, A. M. Movement in Cities. (Spatial Perspectives on Urban Transportation & Travel Ser.). 413p. 1983. pap. 22.00 (ISBN 0-416-35620-6, NO. 3910). Methuen Inc.

Daniels, Pamela & Weingarten, Kathy. Sooner or Later: The Timing of Parenthood in Adult Lives. 384p. 1983. pap. 6.95 (ISBN 0-393-30132-X). Norton.

Daniels, Pamela, jt. ed. see Ruddick, Sara.

Daniels, Pat, ed. see Rice, Dale.

Daniels, Patricia. Aladdin & the Magic Lamp. LC 79-27304. (Raintree Fairy Tales). (Illus.). 24p. (gr. k-3). 1980. PLB 13.31 (ISBN 0-8393-0257-6). Raintree Pubs.

--Aladdin & the Magic Lamp. LC 79-27304. (Fairy Tale Clippers Ser.). (Illus.). 24p. (gr. k-3). 1981. PLB 27.99 incl. cassette (ISBN 0-8172-1832-7); cassette 14.00. Raintree Pubs.

--Ali Baba & the Forty Thieves. LC 79-27042. (Raintree Fairy Tales). (Illus.). 24p. (gr. k-3). 1980. PLB 13.31 (ISBN 0-8393-0255-X). Raintree Pubs.

--Ali Baba & the Forty Thieves. LC 79-27042. (Fairy Tale Clippers Ser.). (Illus.). (gr. k-3). 1981. PLB 27.99 with cassette (ISBN 0-8172-1837-8); cassette only 14.00. Raintree Pubs.

--Beauty & the Beast. LC 79-28433. (Raintree Fairy Tales). (Illus.). 24p. (gr. k-3). 1980. PLB 13.31 (ISBN 0-8393-0258-4). Raintree Pubs.

--Beauty & the Beast. LC 79-28433. (Fairy Tale Clippers Ser.). (Illus.). 24p. (gr. k-3). 1981. PLB 27.99 incl. cassette (ISBN 0-8172-1833-5); cassette 14.00. Raintree Pubs.

--Cinderella. LC 79-28526. (Raintree Fairy Tales). (Illus.). 24p. (gr. k-3). 1980. PLB 13.31 (ISBN 0-8393-0253-3). Raintree Pubs.

--Cinderella. LC 79-28526. (Fairy Tale Clippers Ser.). (Illus.). (gr. k-3). 1981. PLB 27.99 incl. cassette (ISBN 0-8172-1834-3); cassette 14.00. Raintree Pubs.

--Rumpelstiltskin. LC 79-27140. (Raintree Fairy Tales). (Illus.). 24p. (gr. k-3). 1980. PLB 13.31 (ISBN 0-8393-0252-5). Raintree Pubs.

--Rumpelstiltskin. LC 79-27140. (Fairy Tale Clippers Ser.). (Illus.). (gr. k-3). 1981. PLB 27.99 incl. cassette (ISBN 0-8172-1831-9); cassette 14.00. Raintree Pubs.

--Sinbad the Sailor. LC 79-28588. (Raintree Fairy Tales). (Illus.). 24p. (gr. k-3). 1980. PLB 13.31 (ISBN 0-8393-0256-8). Raintree Pubs.

--Sinbad the Sailor. LC 79-28588. (Fairy Tale Clippers Ser.). (Illus.). 24p. (gr. k-4). 1980. PLB 27.99 incl. cassette (ISBN 0-8172-1835-1); cassette 14.00. Raintree Pubs.

--Sleeping Beauty. LC 79-26974. (Raintree Fairy Tales). (Illus.). 24p. (gr. k-3). 1980. PLB 13.31 (ISBN 0-8393-0254-1). Raintree Pubs.

--Sleeping Beauty. LC 79-26974. (Fairy Tale Clippers Ser.). (Illus.). 24p. (gr. k-4). 1980. PLB 27.99 incl. cassette (ISBN 0-8172-1838-6); cassette 14.00. Raintree Pubs.

--Snow White & the Dwarfs. LC 79-28431. (Raintree Fairy Tales). (Illus.). 24p. (gr. k-3). 1980. lib. bdg. 13.31 (ISBN 0-8393-0251-7). Raintree Pubs.

--Snow White & the Dwarfs. LC 79-28431. (Fairy Tale Clippers Ser.). (Illus.). 24p. (gr. k-4). 1980. PLB 27.99 (ISBN 0-8172-1836-X); cassette 14.00. Raintree Pubs.

Daniels, Patricia, ed. Let's Discover, 16 vols. (Illus.). (gr. k-3). 1981. Set. PLB 306.00 (ISBN 0-8172-1782-7); lib. bdg. 19.13 ea. Raintree Pubs.

--Let's Discover Cold-Blooded Animals. LC 80-24150. (Let's Discover Ser.). (Illus.). 80p. (gr. k-3). 1981. PLB 19.13 (ISBN 0-8172-1752-5). Raintree Pubs.

--Let's Discover Flying. LC 80-22964. (Let's Discover Ser.). (Illus.). 80p. (gr. k-3). 1981. PLB 19.13 (ISBN 0-8172-1772-X). Raintree Pubs.

--Let's Discover: Index. LC 80-22978. (Let's Discover Ser.). (Illus.). 80p. (gr. k-3). 1981. PLB 19.13 (ISBN 0-8172-1780-0). Raintree Pubs.
--Let's Discover Land Travel. LC 80-22954. (Let's Discover Ser.). (Illus.). 80p. (gr. k-3). 1981. PLB 19.13 (ISBN 0-8172-1770-3). Raintree Pubs.
--Let's Discover Outer Space. LC 80-22974. (Let's Discover Ser.). (Illus.). 80p. (gr. k-3). 1981. PLB 19.13 (ISBN 0-8172-1762-2). Raintree Pubs.
--Let's Discover People & Customs. LC 80-22960. (Let's Discover Ser.). (Illus.). 80p. (gr. k-3). 1981. PLB 19.13 (ISBN 0-8172-1764-9). Raintree Pubs.
--Let's Discover People of Long Ago. LC 80-22955. (Let's Discover Ser.). (Illus.). 80p. (gr. k-3). 1981. PLB 19.13 (ISBN 0-8172-1778-9). Raintree Pubs.
--Let's Discover Ships & Boats. LC 80-22959. (Let's Discover Ser.). (Illus.). 80p. (gr. k-3). 1981. PLB 19.13 (ISBN 0-8172-1774-6). Raintree Pubs.
--Let's Discover Sport & Entertainment. (Let's Discover Ser.). (Illus.). 80p. (gr. k-3). 1981. PLB 19.13 (ISBN 0-8172-1768-1). Raintree Pubs.
--Let's Discover the Earth. LC 80-22952. (Let's Discover Ser.). (Illus.). 80p. (gr. k-3). 1981. PLB 19.13 (ISBN 0-8172-1760-6). Raintree Pubs.
--Let's Discover the Prehistoric World. LC 80-22949. (Let's Discover Ser.). (Illus.). 80p. (gr. k-3). 1981. PLB 19.13 (ISBN 0-8172-1776-2). Raintree Pubs.
--Let's Discover the Sea. LC 80-22953. (Let's Discover Ser.). (Illus.). 80p. (gr. k-3). 1981. PLB 19.13 (ISBN 0-8172-1758-4). Raintree Pubs.
--Let's Discover the World of Machines. LC 80-22980. (Let's Discover Ser.). (Illus.). 80p. (gr. k-3). 1981. PLB 19.13 (ISBN 0-8172-1756-8). Raintree Pubs.
--Let's Discover What People Do. LC 80-22965. (Let's Discover Ser.). (Illus.). 80p. (gr. k-3). 1981. PLB 19.13 (ISBN 0-8172-1766-5). Raintree Pubs.
--Let's Discover You & Your Body. LC 80-22970. (Let's Discover Ser.). (Illus.). 80p. (gr. k-3). 1981. PLB 19.13 (ISBN 0-8172-1750-9). Raintree Pubs.
Daniels, Patricia, adapted by see Melville, Herman.
Daniels, Patrick. How to Grow Marijuana Hydroponically. (Illus.). 1978. perfect bdg. 5.95 (ISBN 0-686-25126-1). Pacific Pipeline.
Daniels, Paul R. Teaching the Gifted-Learning Disabled Child. LC 82-22775. 232p. 1983. 29.50 (ISBN 0-89443-928-6). Aspen Systems.
Daniels, Peter J. How to Be Happy Though Rich. 128p. 1985. Repr. of 1984 ed. 9.95 (ISBN 0-8007-1435-0). Revell.
Daniels, Peter T., tr. see Bergstrasser, Gotthelf.
Daniels, R. B., et al, eds. Diversity of Soils in the Tropics. (Illus.). 1978. pap. 5.00 (ISBN 0-89118-055-9). Am Soc Agron.
Daniels, R. W. Introduction to Numerical Methods Optimization Techniques. 294p. 1978. 32.50 (ISBN 0-444-00263-4, North-Holland). Elsevier.
Daniels, Richard. Be Dangerous on Rock Guitar. 148p. (Orig.). 1984. pap. wkbk., 6 cassettes, & poster in hardcover box incl. (ISBN 0-89524-264-8). Cherry Lane.
--Blues Guitar Inside & Out. (Illus., Orig.). 1982. pap. 8.95 (ISBN 0-89524-148-X, 9190). Cherry Lane.
--The Heavy Guitar Bible. (Illus.). 104p. (YA) 1979. pap. 10.00 (ISBN 0-89524-066-1, 9105). Cherry Lane.
--Jimi Hendrix: Note for Note. (Orig.). (YA) 1980. pap. 8.95 (ISBN 0-89524-108-0, 5005). Cherry Lane.
Daniels, Robert H., jt. auth. see Anderson, Frederick.
Daniels, Robert H., jt. auth. see Anderson, Frederick R.
Daniels, Robert L. Lawrence Olivier: Theater & Cinema. LC 78-75346. (Illus.). 1980. 19.95 (ISBN 0-498-02287-0). A S Barnes.
Daniels, Robert V. Red October: Bolshevik Revolution of 1917. LC 84-45069. (Illus.). 294p. 1984. 25.00x (ISBN 0-8070-5644-8); pap. 10.95 (ISBN 0-8070-5645-6, BP679). Beacon Pr.
--Russia: The Roots of Confrontation. LC 84-19152. (American Foreign Policy Library). (Illus.). 411p. 1985. 25.00 (ISBN 0-674-77965-7). Harvard U Pr.
--Studying History: How & Why. 3rd ed. LC 80-18406. 128p. 1981. pap. text ed. 13.95 (ISBN 0-13-858738-8). P-H.
Daniels, Robert V., ed. A Documentary History of Communism, 2 vols. rev. ed. Incl. Vol. I, Communism in Russia. 464p. pap. 14.95x (ISBN 0-87451-299-9); Vol. II, Communism & the World. 480p. pap. 14.95x (ISBN 0-87451-300-6). LC 83-40555. 1984. Set. pap. 60.00x (ISBN 0-87451-298-0). U Pr of New Eng.
--Russian Revolution. 1972. pap. 2.95 (ISBN 0-13-784793-9, Spec, Spec). P-H.
--Stalin Revolution: Foundations of Soviet Totalitarianism. 2nd ed. (Problems in European Civilization Ser.). 1972. pap. 5.95 (ISBN 0-669-82495-X). Heath.
Daniels, Robin. Conversations with Menuhin. 1980. 14.95 (ISBN 0-312-16943-4). St Martin.
Daniels, Roger. Anti-Chinese Violence in North America: An Original Anthology. LC 78-54807. (Asian Experience in North America Ser.). 1979. lib. bdg. 17.00x (ISBN 0-405-11263-7). Ayer Co Pubs.
--The Asian Experience in North America Series: Chinese & Japanese, 47 bks. (Illus.). 1979. Repr. lib. bdg. 1162.00x set (ISBN 0-405-11261-0). Ayer Co Pubs.
--The Bonus March: An Episode of the Great Depression. LC 75-133497. (Illus.). 352p. 1971. lib. bdg. 35.00 (ISBN 0-8371-5174-0, DBM/). Greenwood.
--Concentration Camps North America: Japanese in the United States & Canada During World War II. LC 80-19813. 260p. 1981. text ed. 10.50 (ISBN 0-89874-025-8). Krieger.
--The Decision to Relocate the Japanese Americans. 150p. 1985. pap. text ed. price not set (ISBN 0-89874-879-8). Krieger.
--Politics of Prejudice: The Anti-Japanese Movement in California & The Struggle for Japanese Exclusion. LC 62-63248. 1968. pap. text ed. 3.95x (ISBN 0-689-70059-8, 116). Atheneum.
--The Politics of Prejudice: The Anti-Japanese Movement in California & The Struggle for Japanese Exclusion. (California Library Reprint Ser.). 1978. 29.50x (ISBN 0-520-03412-0); pap. 3.45 (ISBN 0-520-03411-2). U of Cal Pr.
Daniels, Roger, jt. auth. see O'Brien, Robert W.
Daniels, Roger, ed. Citizen 13660. LC 78-54830. (Asian Experience in North America Ser.). (Illus.). 1979. Repr. of 1946 ed. lib. bdg. 16.00x (ISBN 0-405-11287-4). Ayer Co Pubs.
--Reports of the Royal Commission on Chinese Immigration. LC 78-54810. (Asian Experience in North America Ser.). 1979. Repr. of 1885 ed. lib. bdg. 47.50x (ISBN 0-405-11267-X). Ayer Co Pubs.
--Three Short Works on Japanese Americans. LC 78-3223. (Asian Experience in North America Ser.). 1978. lib. bdg. 23.00x (ISBN 0-405-11261-0). Ayer Co Pubs.
--Two Monographs on Japanese Canadians. LC 78-3222. (Asian Experience in North America Ser.). 1979. lib. bdg. 14.00x (ISBN 0-405-11304-8). Ayer Co Pubs.
Daniels, Roger, ed. see Andracki, Stanislaw.
Daniels, Roger, ed. see Bell, Reginald.
Daniels, Roger, ed. see California, State Board of Control.
Daniels, Roger, ed. see Canada Department of Labour.
Daniels, Roger, ed. see Canada Royal Commission on Chinese & Japanese Immigration.
Daniels, Roger, ed. see Coman, Katherine & Lind, Andrew W.
Daniels, Roger, ed. see Condit, Ira M.
Daniels, Roger, ed. see Conroy, Hilary.
Daniels, Roger, ed. see Dooner, W. Pierton.
Daniels, Roger, ed. see Flowers, Montaville.
Daniels, Roger, ed. see Gibson, Otis.
Daniels, Roger, ed. see Gulick, Sidney L.
Daniels, Roger, ed. see Hata, Donald T., Jr.
Daniels, Roger, ed. see Irwin, Wallace.
Daniels, Roger, ed. see Japanese General-Consulate.
Daniels, Roger, ed. see Kachi, Teruko O.
Daniels, Roger, ed. see Kawakami, Kiyoshi K.
Daniels, Roger, ed. see Kil Young Zo.
Daniels, Roger, ed. see Kyne, Peter B.
Daniels, Roger, ed. see LaViolette, Forrest E.
Daniels, Roger, ed. see Lee, Rose H.
Daniels, Roger, ed. see McClatchy, Valentine S.
Daniels, Roger, ed. see Matsumoto, Toru.
Daniels, Roger, ed. see Mears, Eliot G.
Daniels, Roger, ed. see Millis, H. A.
Daniels, Roger, ed. see Shapiro, Harry L.
Daniels, Roger, ed. see Steiner, Jesse F.
Daniels, Roger, ed. see Sugimoto, Howard H.
Daniels, Roger, ed. see Sung, Betty L.
Daniels, Roger, ed. see Thompson, Richard A.
Daniels, Roger, ed. see Tien-Lu Li.
Daniels, Roger, ed. see U. S. Department of War.
Daniels, Roger, ed. see U. S. Dept. of State & Morris, Roland.
Daniels, Roger, ed. see U. S. House of Representatives, Select Committee Investigating National Defense Migration.
Daniels, Roger, ed. see U.S. House of Representatives, Committee on Immigration & Naturalization.
Daniels, Roger, ed. see U.S. Senate Joint Special Committee.
Daniels, Roger, ed. see Wong, Franklin E.
Daniels, Roger, ed. see Wynne, Robert E.
Daniels, Roger, ed. see Yatsushiro, Toshio.
Daniels, Roger, ed. see Young, Charles H., et al.
Daniels, Roger, jt. ed. see Yung, Wing.
Daniels, Sarah. Masterpieces. (Methuen Theatrescript Ser.). 1984. pap. 4.95 (ISBN 0-413-55470-8, NO. 4120). Methuen Inc.
Daniels, Shirley. All You Need to Know about Microcomputers: The Small Business Manager's Advisory. LC 79-64577. (Illus.). 144p. 1979. pap. text ed. 7.95x (ISBN 0-89914-003-3). Third Party Pub.
Daniels, Stephen, jt. auth. see Hallman, Robert.
Daniels, Steve & David, Nicholas. The Archaeology Workbook. LC 81-43519. (Illus.). 120p. (Orig.). 1982. pap. 10.95x (ISBN 0-8122-1125-1). U of Pa Pr.
Daniels, Steven. How Two Gerbils, Twenty Goldfish, Two Hundred Games, Two Thousand Books, & I Taught Them How to Read. LC 78-141992. (Illus.). 170p. 1971. pap. 4.95 (ISBN 0-664-24913-2). Westminster.
Daniels, Stuart R. Inelastic Steel Structure. LC 65-25460. pap. 51.30 (ISBN 0-317-10636-8, 2021774). Bks Demand UMI.
Daniels, V. G., jt. auth. see Huang, C. L.
Daniels, V. G., jt. ed. see Huang, C. L.
Daniels, Velma. Kat: The Tale of a Calico Cat. LC 77-13788. (Illus.). (gr. k-7). 1977. 8.95 (ISBN 0-88289-180-4). Pelican.
Daniels, Velma S. Patches of Joy. 1979. 7.95 (ISBN 0-88289-101-4); pap. 5.95 (ISBN 0-88289-232-0). Pelican.
Daniels, Velma S. & King, Peggy E. Fountain of Love. 192p. (Orig.). 1983. pap. 1.95 (ISBN 0-310-50012-5, Serenade-Saga). Zondervan.
Daniels, Victor & Horowitz, Laurence J. Being & Caring: A Psychology for Living. 2nd ed. 371p. 1984. pap. text ed. 15.95 (ISBN 0-87484-544-0). Mayfield Pub.
Daniels, W. H. Dr. Cullis & His Work. Dayton, Donald W., ed. (The Higher Christian Life Ser.). 364p. 1985. 45.00 (ISBN 0-8240-6410-0). Garland Pub.
--Illustrated History of Methodism. 1977. lib. bdg. 75.00 (ISBN 0-8490-2036-0). Gordon Pr.
Daniels, William R. The American Forty-Five & Seventy-Eight RPM Record Dating Guide, 1940-1959. LC 84-22420. (Discographies Ser.: No. 16). xi, 157p. 1985. lib. bdg. 37.50 (ISBN 0-313-24232-1, DRP/). Greenwood.
Daniels, Winthrop M. Essays. 1943. 24.50x (ISBN 0-685-89750-8). Elliots Bks.
--Recollections of Woodrow Wilson. 1944. 29.50x (ISBN 0-685-89776-1). Elliots Bks.
Danielsen, Albert L. The Evolution of OPEC. LC 81-85395. 305p. 1982. 19.95 (ISBN 0-15-129394-5). HarBraceJ.
--Evolution of OPEC. 304p. 1982. pap. text ed. 9.95 (ISBN 0-15-525080-9, HC). HarbraceJ.
Danielsen, John. Winter Hiking & Camping. 3rd. ed. LC 82-11456. (Illus.). 232p. 1982. pap. 8.95 (ISBN 0-935272-20-8). ADK Mtn Club.
Danielsen, Niels. Papers in Theoretical Linguistics. (Current Issues in Linguistic Theory Ser.: No. 23). 250p. 1984. 28.00x (ISBN 90-272-3509-0). Benjamins North Am.
Danielson, Albert L. & Kamerschen, David R., eds. Current Issues in Public-Utility Economics: Essays in Honor of James C. Bonbright. LC 81-48612. 352p. 1983. 35.00 (ISBN 0-669-05440-2). Lexington Bks.
Danielson, Dennis. Milton's Good God: A Study in Literary Theodicy. LC 81-15535. 272p. 1982. 37.50 (ISBN 0-521-23744-0). Cambridge U Pr.
Danielson, Dorothy & Hayden, Rebecca. Using English: Your Second Language. (Illus.). 228p. 1973. pap. text ed. 14.50x (ISBN 0-13-939678-0). P-H.
Danielson, Dorothy, et al. Reading in English: For Students of ESL. 2nd ed. (Illus.). 1980. pap. text ed. 13.95 (ISBN 0-13-753442-6). P-H.
Danielson, Edward E. Missionary Kid, MK. rev. ed. LC 84-12655. (Mission Candidate Aids Ser.). (Illus.). 104p. 1985. pap. 5.95 (ISBN 0-87808-745-1). William Carey Lib.
Danielson, Elena, jt. auth. see Palm, Charles.
Danielson, Eva, jt. auth. see Jonsson, Bengt R.
Danielson, Henry. Arthur Machen: A Bibliography. LC 73-13506. 1923. lib. bdg. 15.00 (ISBN 0-8414-3683-5). Folcroft.
--Arthur Machen: A Bibliography. LC 79-149784. 1971. Repr. of 1923 ed. 35.00x (ISBN 0-8103-3682-0). Gale.
--Bibliographies of Modern Authors. LC 72-6241. 1921. lib. bdg. 25.00 (ISBN 0-8414-0087-3). Folcroft.
--First Editions of the Writings of Thomas Hardy. LC 77-1239. 1916. lib. bdg. 17.50 (ISBN 0-8414-3818-8). Folcroft.
--First Editions of Thomas Hardy. 1977. 16.50 (ISBN 0-685-81154-9). Porter.
Danielson, Larry, ed. Studies in Folklore & Ethnicity. 1978. pap. 8.95x (ISBN 0-914563-00-9). CA Folklore Soc.
Danielson, Michael N. Federal-Metropolitan Politics & the Commuter Crisis. LC 65-16197. (Metropolitan Politcs Ser.). (Illus.). 244p. 1965. 25.00x (ISBN 0-231-02782-6). Columbia U Pr.
--The Politics of Exclusion. LC 76-7609. 443p. 1976. 30.00x (ISBN 0-231-03697-3); pap. 15.00x (ISBN 0-231-08342-4). Columbia U Pr.
Danielson, Michael N. & Doig, Jameson W. New York: The Politics of Urban Regional Development. LC 81-7480. 352p. 1982. 27.50 (ISBN 0-520-04371-5). U of Cal Pr.
--New York: The Politics of Urban Regional Development. (Illus.). 400p. 1983. pap. 9.95 (ISBN 0-520-04551-3). U of Cal Pr.
Danielson, Michael N. & Murphy, Walter F. American Democracy. 10th ed. (Illus.). 608p. 1983. text ed. 19.95x (ISBN 0-8419-0839-7); tchr's. guide avail. Holmes & Meier.
Danielson, P. Children of the Lion. (Children of the Lion Ser.: Bk. 1). 1985. lib. bdg. 12.95 (ISBN 0-8398-2869-1, Gregg). G K Hall.
--The Lion in Egypt. (Children of the Lion Ser.: Bk. 4). 1985. lib. bdg. 12.95 (ISBN 0-8398-2872-1, Gregg). G K Hall.
--The Shepherd Kings. (Children of the Lion Ser.: Bk. 2). 1985. lib. bdg. 13.95 (ISBN 0-8398-2870-5, Gregg). G K Hall.
--Vengeance of the Lion. (Children of the Lion Ser.: Bk. 3). 1985. lib. bdg. 12.95 (ISBN 0-8398-2871-3, Gregg). G K Hall.
Danielson, Peter. Children of the Lion. 480p. (Orig.). 1980. pap. 3.95 (ISBN 0-553-24448-5). Bantam.
--The Shepherd Kings. 448p. (Orig.). 1981. pap. 3.95 (ISBN 0-553-23749-7). Bantam.
--Vengeance of the Lion. 432p. pap. 3.95 (ISBN 0-553-20351-7). Bantam.
Danielson, Roswell S. Cuban Medicine. LC 76-1768. 247p. 1978. 14.95 (ISBN 0-87855-114-X). Transaction Bks.
Danielson, Wayne, jt. auth. see Prejean, Blanche.
Danielsson. Prisma Modern Engelsk-Svensk. 20.00 (ISBN 0-317-19082-2, SW205). Vanous.
Danielsson, Anna, jt. auth. see Smith, Gudmund.
Danielsson, B. Modern English-Swedish Dictionary. 394p. (Eng. & Swedish.). 1980. 19.95 (ISBN 91-518-1296-7, M-9451). French & Eur.
Danielsson, Bror. Engelsk-Svensk Ordbok (Prisma Modern) 3rd. ed. 396p. 1979. text ed. 20.00x (ISBN 91-518-1296-7, SW205); Svensk-engelsk, 4th Ed. 1982. pap. text ed. 20.00x (ISBN 0-8166-1313-3, SW-204). Vanous.
Danielsson, Henry. Arthur Machen: A Bibliography. LC 74-130267. (Reference Ser., No. 44). 1970. Repr. of 1923 ed. lib. bdg. 42.95x (ISBN 0-8383-1174-1). Haskell.
Daniken, Erich Von see Von Daniken, Erich.
Daniken, Erich von see Von Daniken, Erich.
Daniken, Erich Von see Von Daniken, Erich.
Daniker, Relmond Van see McCullers, Levis D. & Van Daniker, Relmond P.
Danikin, Y., jt. auth. see Pshenichny, B.
Danilevskii, J. A. Lappo see Lappo-Danilevskii, J. A.
Danilevskii, Nikolai I. Rossiia I Evropa. 1966. Repr. of 1895 ed. 33.00 (ISBN 0-384-10785-0). Johnson Repr.
Daniljuk, I. I., ed. On Integral Functionals with Variable Domain of Integration. (Proceedings of the Steklov Institute of Mathematics: No. 118). 1976. 39.00 (ISBN 0-8218-3018-X, STEKLO-118). Am Math.
Daniloff, Raymond G. & Schuckers, Gordon H. Physiology of Speech & Hearing: An Introduction. 1980. text ed. 32.95 (ISBN 0-13-674747-7). P-H.
Daniloff, Raymond G., ed. Articulation Assessment & Treatment Issues. LC 83-23179. (Illus.). 310p. 1984. pap. text ed. 27.50 (ISBN 0-933014-09-0). College Hill.
--Speech Science. (Illus.). 275p. 1985. 34.50 (ISBN 0-933014-95-3). College-Hill.
Danilov, A. D. Chemistry of the Ionosphere. LC 68-31236. (Monographs in Geoscience Ser.). 296p. 1970. 32.50x (ISBN 0-306-30357-4, Plenum Pr). Plenum Pub.
Danilov, Dan P. Immigrating to the U. S. A. 4th ed. 208p. 1983. pap. 14.95 (ISBN 0-88908-912-4, 9507, Pub. by Intl Self-Counsel Pr). TAB Bks.
Danilov, Victor J. Science & Technology Centers. (Illus.). 416p. 1982. 50.00x (ISBN 0-262-04068-9). MIT Pr.
Danilova, E. Z., et al. Las Mujeres Sovieticas. 198p. (Span.). 1977. 3.45 (ISBN 0-8285-1483-6, Pub. by Progress Pubs USSR). Imported Pubns.
Danilova, Y. Z., et al. Soviet Women. 184p. 1975. 2.95 (ISBN 0-8285-0290-0, Pub. by Progress Pubs USSR). Imported Pubns.
Danin, D. Probabilities of the Quantum World. Glebov, oles & Kisin, Vitaly, trs. 270p. 1983. 6.95 (ISBN 0-8285-2739-3, Pub. by Mir Pubs USSR). Imported Pubns.
Daninos, Pierre. Les Carnets du Bon Dieu. pap. 3.95 (ISBN 0-685-23923-7, 2181). French & Eur.
--Les Carnets du Major Thompson. 244p. 1968. 3.95 (ISBN 0-686-55561-9). French & Eur.
--Les Carnets Du Major W. Marmaduke Thompson, Decouverte de la France et des Francais. 1960. 11.95 (ISBN 0-685-11065-6). French & Eur.
--Carnets Du Major W. Marmaduke Thompson. (Illus.). 1963. pap. text ed. 7.95x (ISBN 0-521-04767-6). Cambridge U Pr.
--Un Certain Monsieur Blot. 1964. pap. 3.95 (ISBN 0-685-11072-9, 1278). French & Eur.
--Daninoscope. 448p. 1963. 13.95 (ISBN 0-686-55562-7). French & Eur.
--L' Eternal Second. 256p. 1957. 4.95 (ISBN 0-686-55563-5). French & Eur.
--Le Jacassin. 1962. 12.25 (ISBN 0-685-11266-7). French & Eur.
--Ludovic Morateur Ou le Plus Que Parfait. 248p. 1970. 7.95 (ISBN 0-686-55564-3); pap. 2.95 (ISBN 0-686-55565-1). French & Eur.
--Made in France: Recit. 247p. 14.95 (ISBN 0-686-55566-X). French & Eur.
--Le Major Tricolore, Comment Peut-on Etre Francais. 11.50 (ISBN 0-685-37286-3). French & Eur.
--Le Major Tricolore: Redecouverte de la France et des Francais par le Major W. Marmaduke Thompson. (Illus.). 160p. 1971. 3.95 (ISBN 0-686-55567-8). French & Eur.
--Meridiens. 4.95 (ISBN 0-686-55568-6). French & Eur.
--Les Nouveaux Carnets du Major Thompson. 226p. 1973. 13.95 (ISBN 0-686-55569-4). French & Eur.
--Le Pouvoir aux Enfants. 8.95 (ISBN 0-686-55570-8). French & Eur.
--La Premiere Planete a Droite En Sortant Parla Voie Lactee. 1975. 13.95 (ISBN 0-686-55571-6); pap. 3.95 (ISBN 0-686-55572-4). French & Eur.
--Le Pyjama. 1972. 15.95 (ISBN 0-686-55573-2). French & Eur.

--Snobissimo. 256p. 1964. 8.95 (ISBN 0-686-55574-0); pap. 3.95 (ISBN 0-686-55575-9). French & Eur.
--Sonia ou le Dictionnaire des maux Courants. 352p. (Fr.). 1962. 6.95 (ISBN 0-686-55576-7). French & Eur.
--Le Tour du Mond du Rire. 286p. 1963. 8.95 (ISBN 0-686-55577-5). French & Eur.
--Les Touristocrates. 208p. 1974. 14.95 (ISBN 0-686-55578-3); pap. 3.95 (ISBN 0-686-55579-1). French & Eur.
--Tout l'Humour du Monde. 224p. 1958. 5.95 (ISBN 0-686-55580-5). French & Eur.
--Tout Sonia: Avec: Sonia les Autres et Moi, Comment Vivre avec ou sans Sonia. (Illus.). 435p. 1976. 12.95 (ISBN 0-686-55581-3). French & Eur.
--Toutonia. 1956. pap. 2.50 (ISBN 0-685-11567-4, 154). French & Eur.
--Le Trente-Sixieme Dessous. 1974. 3.95 (ISBN 0-686-55582-1). French & Eur.
--Vacances a Tous Prix. 1972. 3.95 (ISBN 0-686-55583-X). French & Eur.
Danis, Jan S. see Viola, Herman J.
Danish, Barbara. Writing As a Second Language. LC 81-5755. (Orig.). 1981. worktext 9.95 (ISBN 0-915924-10-2). Tchrs & Writers Coll.
Danish Handcraft Guild. Contemporary Danish Cross-Stitch Design. (Illus.). 96p. 1982. 16.95 (ISBN 0-8038-1278-7). Hastings.
--Counted Cross-Stitch Designs for Christmas. (Illus.). 1978. pap. 10.95 (ISBN 0-684-15975-9, SL821, ScribT). Scribner.
Danish, Steve, et al. Helping Skills: A Basic Training Program. 2nd ed. 1980. wkbk softcover 119p. 14.95 (ISBN 0-87705-484-3); leaders manual 68 6.95x (ISBN 0-87705-483-5); Set. 14.95x. Human Sci Pr.
Danishefsky, Isidore. Biochemistry for Medical Sciences. 1980. text ed. 31.95 (ISBN 0-316-17198-0). Little.
Danishefsky, Samuel, jt. auth. see Danishefsky, Sarah E.
Danishefsky, Sarah E. & Danishefsky, Samuel. Progress in Total Synthesis. LC 72-150496. 265p. 1971. 25.00x (ISBN 0-306-50001-9, Plenum Pr). Plenum Pub.
Dank, Gloria, jt. auth. see Dank, Milton.
Dank, Gloria R. The Forest of App. LC 83-1627. 160p. (gr. 5-9). 1983. reinforced 10.25 (ISBN 0-688-02315-0). Greenwillow.
--The Forest of App. (gr. 7 up). 1984. 2.25 (ISBN 0-399-21142-X). Putnam Pub Group.
Dank, Milton. Albert Einstein. LC 82-23853. (Impact Biography Ser.). (Illus.). 128p. (gr. 7up). 1983. PLB 9.90 (ISBN 0-531-04587-0). Watts.
--D-Day. LC 84-7326. (Turning Points of World War II Ser.). (Illus.). 106p. 1984. PLB 9.90 (ISBN 0-531-04863-2). Watts.
--The Dangerous Game. 144p. (YA) (gr. 7 up). 1980. pap. 1.75 (ISBN 0-440-91765-4, LFL). Dell.
--Game's End. LC 78-12625. 1979. 8.95i (ISBN 0-397-31821-9). Lipp Jr Bks.
--Game's End. 160p. (gr. 7 up). pap. 1.75 (ISBN 0-440-92797-8, LFL). Dell.
--Khaki Wings. LC 80-65832. 160p. (gr. 8-12). 1980. 10.95 (ISBN 0-385-28523-X). Delacorte.
--Khaki Wings. 160p. (gr. 7 up). 1983. pap. 1.95 (ISBN 0-317-00572-3, LFL). Dell.
Dank, Milton & Dank, Gloria. The Computer Caper. (The Galaxy Gang Mystery Ser.). 128p. (Orig.). (YA) (gr. 5-9). 1983. pap. 2.25 (ISBN 0-440-91139-7, LFL). Dell.
--The Computer Caper. LC 82-19793. (Galaxy Gang Mystery Ser.). 128p. (gr. 4-6). 1983. PLB 12.95 (ISBN 0-385-29296-1). Delacorte.
--The Computer Game Murder: A Galaxy Gang Mystery. LC 85-1650. (Illus.). 128p. (gr. 5-9). 1985. 12.95 (ISBN 0-385-29411-5). Delacorte.
--The Three-D Traitor: A Galaxy Gang Mystery. LC 84-4324. 128p. (gr. 4-6). 1984. 10.95 (ISBN 0-385-29345-3). Delacorte.
--Treasure Code: A Galaxy Gang Mystery. LC 84-15569. 128p. (gr. 4-6). 1985. 11.95 (ISBN 0-385-29370-4). Delacorte.
--A UFO Has Landed. (The Galaxy Gang Mystery Ser.). 128p. (Orig.). (YA) (gr. 5-9). 1983. pap. 2.25 (ISBN 0-440-99160-9, LFL). Dell.
--A UFO Has Landed. (Galaxy Gang Mystery Ser.). 128p. (gr. 4-6). 1983. PLB 13.95 (ISBN 0-385-29297-X). Delacorte.
Dankenbing, William F. The Creation Book. LC 75-39840. (Illus.). 70p. 1976. 5.95 (ISBN 0-685-68397-4); pap. 3.95 (ISBN 0-685-68398-2). Triumph Pub.
Dankenbring, William F. Beyond Star Wars. LC 78-60520. 1978. 10.95 (ISBN 0-917182-07-3). Triumph Pub.
--The First Genesis: A New Case for Creation. LC 75-10841. (Illus.). 408p. 1975. 8.95 (ISBN 0-685-54180-0). Triumph Pub.
--The First Genesis: The Saga of Creation Versus Evolution. new ed. LC 79-65131. (Illus.). 1979. 12.00 (ISBN 0-917182-14-6). Triumph Pub.
--The Keys to Radiant Health. LC 74-19241. 281p. 1974. 7.50 (ISBN 0-685-61404-2). Triumph Pub.
--The Last Days. LC 77-79265. 1977. 11.95 (ISBN 0-917182-05-7). Triumph Pub.
--Your Keys to Radiant Health. LC 74-19241. (Illus.). 288p. 1975. pap. 1.95 (ISBN 0-87983-119-7). Keats.
Danker, Donald F. Wounded Knee Interviews of Eli S. Ricker. (Nebraska History Magazine Reprints: Vol. 62, No. 2). 243p. 1981. 3.50 (ISBN 0-318-17580-0). Nebraska Hist.
Danker, Donald F., ed. see North, Luther.
Danker, Frederick W. Benefactor: Epigraphic Study of a Graeco-Roman & New Testament Semantic Field. LC 81-70419. 1982. 29.95x (ISBN 0-915644-23-1). Clayton Pub Hse.
--Jesus & the New Age According to St. Luke. 1983. pap. text ed. 12.00 (ISBN 0-915644-25-8). Clayton Pub Hse.
--Luke. Krodel, Gerhard, ed. LC 76-5954. (Proclamation Commentaries: the New Testament Witnesses for Preaching Ser.). 128p. 1976. pap. 4.50 (ISBN 0-8006-0583-7, 1-583). Fortress.
--Multipurpose Tools for Bible Study. rev. ed. 1970. pap. 11.95 (ISBN 0-570-03734-4, 12-2638). Concordia.
--No Room in the Brotherhood: The Preus-Otten Purge of Missouri. LC 77-74386. (Illus.). 1977. text ed. 12.95 (ISBN 0-915644-10-X). Clayton Pub Hse.
--Shorter Lexicon of the Greek New Testament. 2nd, rev. ed. Gingrich, F. Wilbur, rev. by. LC 82-10933. 256p. 1983. lib. bdg. 20.00x (ISBN 0-226-13613-2). U of Chicago Pr.
Danker, Frederick W., jt. auth. see Gingrich, Wilbur F.
Danker, Harold, jt. auth. see Steinberg, Richard M.
Dankert, Clyde E., et al, eds. Hours of Work. LC 78-27581. (Industrial Relations Research Association Publication: No. 32). 1979. Repr. of 1965 ed. lib. bdg. 22.50x (ISBN 0-313-20903-0, DAHW). Greenwood.
Dankin, John & Scott, Kristi, eds. The United States Ski Team. LC 83-82974. (Illus.). 160p. 1983. 24.95 (ISBN 0-913927-01-5). Intl Sport Pubns.
Dankleff, Richard. Popcorn Girl. LC 79-17681. 1979. pap. 4.50 (ISBN 0-87071-334-5). Oreg St U Pr.
--Westerns. LC 83-21979. 96p. 1984. pap. 5.95 (ISBN 0-87071-340-X). Oreg St U Pr.
Danko, X., tr. see Eisenstein, Sergei.
Dankoff, Robert, tr. see Yusuf, Khass H.
Danks, Harry. The Viola d'Amore. rev. 2nd ed. LC 79-313933. (Illus.). 128p. 1979. 52.00 (ISBN 0-900998-16-4, Pub. by S Bonner England). Theodore Front.
Danks, Joseph & Pedzek, Kathy. Reading & Understanding. Murray, Frank, ed. (IRA Ser. on the Development of the Reading Process). 81p. (Orig.). 1980. pap. text ed. 4.00 (ISBN 0-87207-526-5, 526). Intl Reading.
Danks, Joseph H., jt. auth. see Glucksberg, Sam.
Danks, Lawrence J. The Complete Job-Hunting Guide for College Students. (Illus.). 156p. 1985. pap. 7.95 (ISBN 0-13-161415-0). P-H.
--Passing the Real Estate Salesperson's Exam. (Illus.). 228p. 1981. text ed. 21.95 (ISBN 0-8359-5469-2). instr's. manual free (ISBN 0-8359-5470-6). Reston.
--Real Estate Advertising. LC 82-18541. (Illus.). 298p. 1983. 24.95 (ISBN 0-88462-420-X, 1929-01, Real Estate Ed). Longman USA.
Danks, Rabindra. Night Fell: Poems & Drawings. (Illus.). 48p. (Orig.). 1975. pap. 2.95 (ISBN 0-915242-06-0). Pygmalion Pr.
--Shadow Boxing. LC 79-90656. (Illus.). 64p. (Orig.). 1979. pap. 5.00 (ISBN 0-89807-025-2). Illuminati.
Danks, S. M., et al. Photosynthetic Systems: Structure, Function & Assembly. 162p. 1984. 32.95 (ISBN 0-471-10250-4). Wiley.
Dankworth, Avril. Jazz: An Introduction to Its Musical Basis. 1968. pap. 7.95x (ISBN 0-19-316501-5). Oxford U Pr.
Danky, James P. & Hady, Maureen B. Native American Press in Wisconsin & the Nation: Proceedings of the Conference on the Native American Press in Wisconsin & the Nation, April 22-23, 1982. LC 82-17634. 197p. 1982. pap. 6.50 (ISBN 0-936442-10-7). U Wis Lib Sch.
Danky, James P., ed. Genealogical Research: An Introduction to the Resources of the State Historical Society of Wisconsin. LC 79-15148. 56p. 1979. pap. 3.00 (ISBN 0-87020-180-8). State Hist Soc Wis.
--Native American Periodicals & Newspapers, 1828-1982: Bibliography, Publishing Record, & Holdings. LC 83-22579. (Illus.). xxxii, 532p. 1984. lib. bdg. 49.95 (ISBN 0-313-23773-5, DNP/). Greenwood.
Danky, James P. & Shore, Elliott, eds. Alternative Materials in Libraries. LC 81-21353. 255p. 1982. 16.00 (ISBN 0-8108-1508-7). Scarecrow.
Danky, James P., ed. see Bass, Clifford W., et al.
Danky, James P., jt. ed. see Berman, Sanford.
Danky, James P., jt. ed. see Hedy, Maureen E.
Danky, James P., et al, ed. Women's History: Resources at the State Historical Society of Wisconsin. 4th, rev., enl. ed. LC 79-17522. 88p. 1982. pap. 3.95 (ISBN 0-87020-189-1). State Hist Soc Wis.
Danley, Jerry J. Useful Science. (Illus.). 1983. pap. 3.25x (ISBN 0-88323-181-6, 216); tchr's key free (ISBN 0-88323-132-8, 222). Richards Pub.
Danloux-Dumesnils, M. The Metric System: A Critical Study of Its Principles & Practice. 162p. 1969. pap. 16.95 (ISBN 0-485-12013-5, Pub. by Athlone Pr Ltd). Longwood Pub Group.
Danly. Emerging Opportunities for Electroorganic Processes. (Special Report Ser.). 216p. 1984. 435.00 (ISBN 0-8247-7148-6). Dekker.
Danly, Robert L. In the Shade of Spring Leaves: The Life & Writings of Higuchi Ichiyo, a Woman of Letters in Meiji Japan. LC 81-50434. 352p. 1981. 28.50x (ISBN 0-300-02614-5). Yale U Pr.
--In the Shade of Spring Leaves: The Life & Writings of Higuchi Ichiyo, a Woman of Letters in Meiji Japan. LC 81-50434. (Illus.). 355p. 1983. pap. text ed. 10.95x (ISBN 0-300-02981-0). Yale U Pr.
Dann, Bucky. Better Children's Sermons: 54 Visual Lessons, Dialogues, & Demonstrations. LC 83-6851. 124p. (Orig.). 1983. pap. 7.95 (ISBN 0-664-24481-5). Westminster.
--Creating Children's Sermons: Fifty-One Visual Lessons. LC 81-10493. 132p. pap. 7.95 (ISBN 0-664-24383-5). Westminster.
Dann, Colin, jt. auth. see Guthrie, Colin.
Dann, David, jt. auth. see Hornsey, Timothy.
Dann, Florence. Write to Read, Level C. (MCP Writing Skillbooster Ser.). (gr. 3). 1978. pap. text ed. 2.40 (ISBN 0-87895-340-X). Modern Curr.
--Write to Read, Level D. (MCP Writing Skillbooster Ser.). 1978. pap. text ed. 2.40 (ISBN 0-87895-410-4). Modern Curr.
--Write to Read, Level E. (MCP Writing Skillbooster Ser.). (gr. 5). 1978. pap. text ed. 2.40 (ISBN 0-87895-510-0). Modern Curr.
--Write to Read, Level F. (MCP Writing Skillbooster Ser.). (gr. 6). 1978. pap. text ed. 2.40 (ISBN 0-87895-610-7). Modern Curr.
Dann, Jack. Bestiary! Dozois, Gardner, ed. 304p. 1985. pap. 2.95 (ISBN 0-441-05506-0). Ace Bks.
--Christs & Other Poems. 1978. 5.00 (ISBN 0-686-21111-1). Bellevue Pr.
--The Man Who Melted. 288p. 1984. 14.95 (ISBN 0-312-94293-1). Bluejay Bks.
--Timetipping. LC 78-20067. (Science Fiction Ser.). 1980. 8.95 (ISBN 0-385-14338-9). Doubleday.
Dann, Jack & Dozois, Gardener. Unicorns! 320p. 1984. pap. 2.95 (ISBN 0-441-85443-5). Ace Bks.
Dann, Jack & Dozois, Gardner. Magicats! 288p. 1984. pap. 2.95 (ISBN 0-441-51530-4). Ace Bks.
Dann, Jack & Zebrowski, George. Faster Than Light. 352p. 1982. pap. 2.95 (ISBN 0-441-22825-9, Pub. by Ace Science Fiction). Ace Bks.
Dann, John C. The Revolution Remembered: Eyewitness Accounts of the War for Independence. LC 79-19254. 1980. 20.00x (ISBN 0-226-13622-1). U of Chicago Pr.
Dann, John D., ed. The Revolution Remembered: Eyewitness Accounts of the War for Independence. LC 79-19254. (Clements Library Bicentennial Studies). (Illus.). xxvi, 446p. 1983. pap. 12.95 (ISBN 0-226-13624-8, Phoen). U of Chicago Pr.
Dann, Kevin T. Twenty-Five Walks in New Jersey. (Illus.). 128p. (Orig.). 1982. pap. 8.95 (ISBN 0-8135-0935-1). Rutgers U Pr.
Dann, Max. Adventures with My Worst Best Friend. (Illus.). 122p. (gr. 3-7). 1984. laminated boards 10.95 (ISBN 0-19-554361-0, Pub. by Oxford U Pr Childrens). Merrimack Pub Cir.
--Bernice Knows Best. (Illus.). 32p. (gr. 1-5). 1984. bds. 9.95 laminated boards (ISBN 0-19-554414-5, Pub. by Oxford U Pr Childrens). Merrimack Pub Cir.
--Ernest Pickle's Remarkable Robot. (Illus.). 136p. (gr. 3-5). 1986. bds. 9.95 (ISBN 0-19-554577-X, Pub. by Oxford U Pr Childrens). Merrimack Pub Cir.
--Going Bananas. (Illus.). 672p. (gr. 3-7). 1985. laminated boards 9.95 (ISBN 0-19-554460-9, Pub. by Oxford U Pr Childrens). Merrimack Pub Cir.
Dann, Max, et al. The All-Amazing Ha Ha Book. 82p. (gr. 3-7). 1985. bds. 9.95 laminated (ISBN 0-19-554581-8, Pub. by Oxford U Pr Childrens). Merrimack Pub Cir.
Dann, Meryl S., jt. auth. see McNulty, Elizabeth G.
Dann, Sam. Goodbye, Karl Erich. 1984. 15.95 (ISBN 0-312-33857-0). St Martin.
Dann, Uriel. Studies in the History of Transjordan. (Special Studies on the Middle East). 130p. 1984. pap. 15.00x (ISBN 0-86531-793-3). Westview.
Danna, Jo. Finding Your Way Through the Adult Education Maze: A Guide for Mature Career Changers. (Illus.). 250p. (Orig.). Date not set. pap. 10.95 (ISBN 0-9610036-2-6). Palomino Pr.
--It's Never Too Late to Start Over. LC 83-63268. (Illus.). 231p. 1984. pap. 10.95x (ISBN 0-9610036-1-8). Palomino Pr.
--Winning the Job Interview Game: Tips for the High-Tech Era. LC 85-61451. (Illus.). 230p. (Orig.). 1986. pap. 9.95 (ISBN 0-9610036-2-6). Palomino Pr.
Danna, Mark, jt. auth. see Poynter, Dan.
Danne, A. H., jt. ed. see Spedding, E. H.
Dannebring, David D. & Starr, Martin K. Management Science: An Introduction. (Quantitative Methods in Management Ser.). 1981. 34.95 (ISBN 0-07-015352-3). McGraw.
Dannecker, Martin. Theories of Homosexuality. 128p. 1981. pap. 3.95 (ISBN 0-907040-05-5). Gay Mens Pr.
--Theories of Homosexuality. 123p. 1981. pap. 3.95 (ISBN 0-907040-05-5, Pub. by GMP England). Alyson Pubns.
Dannen, Donna & Dannen, Kent. Walks with Nature in Rocky Mountain National Park. LC 80-26665. (Illus.). 64p. 1981. pap. 3.95 (ISBN 0-914788-38-8). East Woods.
Dannen, Donna, jt. auth. see Dannen, Kent.
Dannen, Kent & Dannen, Donna. Rocky Mountain National Park Hiking Trails: Including Indian Peaks. 5th ed. LC 81-17337. (Illus.). 288p. 1982. pap. cancelled (ISBN 0-914788-55-8). East Woods.
--Rocky Mountain National Park Hiking Trails: Including Indian Peaks. 6th ed. LC 84-48887. (Illus.). 288p. 1985. pap. 8.95 (ISBN 0-88742-021-4). East Woods.
--Rocky Mountain Wildflowers. LC 81-7439. (Illus.). 64p. (Orig.). 1981. pap. 2.95 (ISBN 0-9606768-0-5). Tundra Pubns.
Dannen, Kent, jt. auth. see Dannen, Donna.
Dannenbauer, Heinrich, jt. auth. see Haller, Johannes.
Dannenbaum, Jed. Drink & Disorder: Temperance Reform in Cincinnati from the Washingtonian Revival to the WCTU. LC 83-3671. 260p. 1984. 22.50x (ISBN 0-252-01055-8). U of Ill Pr.
Dannenbaum, Julie. Fast & Fresh. LC 80-8199. 240p. 1981. 14.37 (ISBN 0-06-010974-2). Har-Row.
--Italian Fast & Fresh: Delicious Italian Meals to Make in Less Than an Hour. LC 83-48969. (Illus.). 256p. 1984. 15.34 (ISBN 0-06-015291-5, HarpT). Har-Row.
--More Fast & Fresh. LC 82-48114. (Illus.). 256p. 1983. 14.37i (ISBN 0-06-015084-X, HarpT). Har-Row.
Dannenberg, William P., et al. Introduction to Wholesale Distribution. (Illus.). 1978. 25.95 (ISBN 0-13-500777-1); stud. ed. o.p. 16.95 (ISBN 0-685-85447-7). P-H.
Dannenfeldt, Karl H. Church of the Renaissance & Reformation. LC 77-98300. (Church in History Ser). 1978. pap. 4.95 (ISBN 0-570-06271-3, 12-2726). Concordia.
--Leonhard Rauwolf: Sixteenth-Century Physician, Botanist, & Traveler. LC 68-15634. (Monographs in the History of Science Ser). (Illus.). 1968. 22.50x (ISBN 0-674-52500-0). Harvard U Pr.
Dannenfeldt, Karl H., ed. The Renaissance. 2nd ed. (Problems in European Civilization Ser). 1974. pap. text ed. 5.95 (ISBN 0-669-90530-5). Heath.
Dannenfelser, Betty A., jt. auth. see Bomberger, Audery S.
Dannenmaier, William. Mental Health: An Overview. LC 77-21959. 244p. 1978. 20.95x (ISBN 0-88229-124-6). Nelson-Hall.
Danner, Douglas. Expert Witness Checklists. LC 82-84686. 1983. 64.50 (ISBN 0-686-40192-1). Lawyers Co-Op.
--Pattern Deposition Checklists. 2nd ed. LC 79-90263. 1984. 77.50 (ISBN 0-318-02978-2). Lawyers Co-Op.
--Pattern Discovery: Automobiles. 2nd ed. LC 84-82253. 1985. 69.50 (ISBN 0-318-04385-8). Lawyers Co-Op.
--Pattern Discovery: Employment Discrimination, Vol. 1. LC 81-82088. 1981. 79.50 (ISBN 0-686-35943-7). Lawyers Co-Op.
--Pattern Discovery: Securities, Vol. 1. LC 81-82088. 1982. 79.50 (ISBN 0-686-37165-8). Lawyers Co-Op.
--Pattern Interrogatories: 1970-73, 5 vols. LC 75-102027. 1970. 320.50 (ISBN 0-686-14526-7). Lawyers Co-Op.
Danner, Henry R. Roman Law Pleading: An Outline of Its Historical Growth & General Principles. 63p. 1983. Repr. of 1912 ed. lib. bdg. 15.00x (ISBN 0-8377-0519-3). Rothman.
Danner, Horace G. Words from the Romance Languages. LC 80-82095. (Clavis Ser.). (Illus.). 232p. 1980. pap. 7.00x (ISBN 0-937600-00-8). Imprimis.
Danner, Margaret. Impressions of African Art Forms. 1950. pap. 2.00 (ISBN 0-685-07546-X). Broadside.
Danner, Peter L. An Ethics for the Affluent. LC 80-5528. 424p. 1980. lib. bdg. 28.25 (ISBN 0-8191-1163-5); pap. text ed. 15.25 (ISBN 0-8191-1164-3). U Pr of Amer.
Danner, Richard. Patterns of Irony in the Fables of La Fontaine. LC 82-85710. 180p. 1985. text ed. 23.95x (ISBN 0-317-20421-1). Ohio U Pr.
Danner, Victor & Thackston, Wheeler. Ibn 'Ata Illah-Kwaja Abdullah Ansari: The Book of Wisdom-Intimate Conversations. LC 78-1022. (Classics of Western Spirituality-Sufi Ser.). 256p. 1978. 11.95 (ISBN 0-8091-0279-X); pap. 7.95 (ISBN 0-8091-2182-4). Paulist Pr.
Danner, Wilbert R. Limestone Resources of Western Washington. (Bulletin Ser.: No. 52). (Illus.). 474p. 1966. 4.50 (ISBN 0-686-34705-6). Geologic Pubns.
Dannhaeuser, Norbert. Contemporary Trade Strategies in the Philippines. 288p. 1983. 30.00 (ISBN 0-8135-0950-5). Rutgers U Pr.
Dannhauser, Werner J. Nietzsche's View of Socrates. LC 73-20797. 283p. 1974. 27.50x (ISBN 0-8014-0827-X). Cornell U Pr.
Dannhauser, Werner J., ed. see Scholem, Gershom.
Danning, Dave, jt. auth. see Bodenheimer, Susanne.
Dannon, Ann. I Am a Woman. facsimile ed. Katz, Jonathan, ed. LC 75-13750. (Homosexuality Ser.). 1975. Repr. of 1959 ed. 14.00x (ISBN 0-405-07406-9). Ayer Co Pubs.
--Journey to a Woman. facsimile ed. Katz, Jonathan, ed. LC 75-13752. (Homosexuality Ser.). 1975. Repr. of 1960 ed. 12.00x (ISBN 0-405-07408-5). Ayer Co Pubs.

--Women in the Shadows. facsimile ed. Katz, Jonathan, ed. LC 75-13751. (Homosexuality Ser.). 1975. Repr. of 1959 ed. 9.00x (ISBN 0-405-07407-7). Ayer Co Pubs.

Dannox, Ann. Odd Girl Out. facsimile ed. Katz, Jonathan, ed. LC 75-13735. (Homosexuality Ser.). 1975. Repr. of 1957 ed. 14.00x (ISBN 0-405-07405-0). Ayer Co Pubs.

Dannreuther, E. see Hadow, William H.

Dannreuther, E., tr. see Wagner, Richard.

Danns, George. Domination & the Power in Guyana: A Study of the Police in a Third World Context. Coser, Lewis, tr. LC 80-19179. 275p. 1982. 29.95 (ISBN 0-87855-418-1). Transaction Bks.

D'Annunzio. Alcyone: A Selection. Woodhouse, J. R., intro. by. (Italian Texts Ser.). 164p. (Ital.). 1978. pap. text ed. 6.95 (ISBN 0-7190-0684-8, Pub. by Manchester Univ Pr). Longwood Pub Group.

D'Annunzio, Gabriele. Daughter of Jorio: A Pastoral Tragedy. Porter, Charlotte, et al, trs. LC 69-10064. Repr. of 1907 ed. lib. bdg. 19.75x (ISBN 0-8371-0005-4, DADJ). Greenwood.

--Francesca da Rimini. Symons, Arthur, tr. (Illus.). 256p. 1983. Repr. of 1902 ed. 79.85 (ISBN 0-89901-126-8). Found Class Reprints.

--Gabriele D'Annunzio: International Naval Disarmament Conference at Washington & Geneva, Nov. 1921-April 1922. 1930. 7.50x (ISBN 0-686-92124-0). S F Vanni.

--La Gioconda. Symons, Arthur, tr. (Illus.). 175p. 1983. Repr. of 1902 ed. 79.95 (ISBN 0-89901-127-6). Found Class Reprints.

--Tales of My Native Town. Mantellini, Rafael, tr. LC 69-10065. Repr. of 1920 ed. lib. bdg. 22.50x (ISBN 0-8371-0056-9, DANT). Greenwood.

Dano, S. Industrial Production Models: A Theoretical Study. (Illus.). 1966. 22.00 (ISBN 0-387-80753-5). Springer-Verlag.

--Linear Programming in Industry, Theory & Applications: An Introduction. rev. ed. LC 73-13172. (Illus.). 180p. 1974. pap. 25.00 (ISBN 0-387-81189-3). Springer-Verlag.

Da Nobrega, J. C. The Perils of Cultism. 1980. 6.00 (ISBN 0-682-49453-4). Exposition Pr FL.

Danoff, Judith, et al. Early Childhood Education. (Illus.). 1977. text ed. 19.95 o. p. (ISBN 0-07-015343-4); pap. text ed. 21.95 (ISBN 0-07-015342-6). McGraw.

Danois, Vivian De see De Danois, Vivian.

Danon, D., ed. Aging: A Challenge to Science & Society--Vol. 1, Biology. (Illus.). 1981. 68.50x (ISBN 0-19-261254-9). Oxford U Pr.

Danon, J. Lectures on the Mossbauer Effect. LC 68-19092. (Documents on Modern Physics Ser.). 150p. (Orig.). 1968. 45.25 (ISBN 0-677-01530-5). Gordon.

Danon, Samuel & Rosenberg, Samuel N., trs. from Fr. Ami & Amile. 1981. 11.95 (ISBN 0-917786-20-3). Summa Pubns.

Danopoulos, Constantine. Warriors & Politicians in Modern Greece. 1985. 34.95x (ISBN 0-89712-144-9); pap. 24.95. Documentary Pubns.

Danos, Joseph R. A Concordance to the "Roman De la Rose of Guillaume De Lorris". (Studies in the Romance Languages & Literatures: No. 156). 307p. 1975. pap. 19.50x (ISBN 0-8078-9156-8). U of NC Pr.

Danos, M. & Gillet, V. Relativistic Bound Hadrons. Date not set. 85.00. Elsevier.

Danos, M., et al. Methods in Relativistic Nuclear Physics. 308p. 1984. 74.00 (ISBN 0-444-86317-6, North-Holland). Elsevier.

Danos, Paul & Imhoff, Eugene A., Jr. Intermediate Accounting. (Illus.). 1088p. 1983. 38.95 (ISBN 0-13-469338-8); practice set 12.95 (ISBN 0-13-469619-0). P-H.

Danos, Paul, jt. auth. see Arnett, Harold.

Danov, Christo. Alttrakien. LC 73-75484. 1976. 80.00x (ISBN 3-11-003434-4). De Gruyter.

Danowski, F. Fishermen's Wives: Coping with an Extraordinary Occupation. (Marine Bulletin Ser.: No. 37). 78p. 1980. 2.00 (ISBN 0-686-36986-6, P862). URI Mas.

D'Ans, J., et al. Densities of Binary Aqueous Systems & Heat Capacities of Liquid Systems. LC 62-53136. (Landolt-Boernstein Group IV: Vol. 1, Pt. B). (Illus.). 1977. 134.40 (ISBN 0-387-08272-7). Springer-Verlag.

Dansereau, Charles F., jt. auth. see Holley, Charles D.

Dansereau, Pierre. Inscape & Landscape: The Human Perception of Environment. LC 75-9990. 118p. 1975. pap. 10.00x (ISBN 0-231-03992-1). Columbia U Pr.

Dansereau, Pierre, ed. Challenge for Survival: Land, Air, & Water for Man in Megalopolis. LC 78-98397. 235p. 1970. 29.00x (ISBN 0-231-03267-6); pap. 15.00x (ISBN 0-231-08638-5). Columbia U Pr.

Dansey, Harry. New Zealand Maori in Colour. LC 70-109418. (Illus.). 1970. 7.75 (ISBN 0-8048-0889-9). C E Tuttle.

--Te Raukura: The Feathers of the Albatross. xvii, 63p. (A Narrative Play in 2 Acts). (gr. 10 up). 1978. pap. 7.00x (ISBN 0-582-71737-X, Pub. by Longman Paul New Zealand). Three Continents.

Dansker, Judy, ed. see King, Kali.

Danskin, David G. & Crow, Mark A. Biofeedback: An Introduction & Guide. LC 80-84020. 116p. (Orig.). 1981. pap. text ed. 7.95 (ISBN 0-87484-530-0). Mayfield Pub.

Danskin, Elizabeth. Women's Gymnastics. (Physical Education Ser.). (Illus.). 120p. (Orig.). (gr. 12). 1983. pap. 14.95 (ISBN 0-88839-045-9). Hancock House.

Danskin, J., tr. see Nikol'skii, S. M.

Danskin, J. M. Theory of Max-Min, & Its Application to Weapons Allocation Problems. (Econometrics & Operation Research: Vol. 5). (Illus.). 1967. 28.00 (ISBN 0-387-03943-0). Springer-Verlag.

Danskin, J. M., tr. see Yushkevich, A. A. & Dynkin, E. B.

Danson, Lawrence. The Harmonies of the Merchant of Venice. LC 77-12008. 1978. 24.50x (ISBN 0-300-02167-4). Yale U Pr.

--Max Beerbohm & The Mirror of the Past. (Illus.). 96p. 1982. 15.00 (ISBN 0-686-97665-7). Princeton Lib.

Danson, Lawrence N. On King Lear. LC 81-47120. 212p. 1981. 19.50x (ISBN 0-691-06477-6). Princeton U Pr.

Danstrup, John. A History of Denmark. Lindberg, Verner, tr. LC 83-45740. Repr. of 1948 ed. 37.50 (ISBN 0-404-20072-9). AMS Pr.

Dante. Dante's Convivio. Ryan, Christopher, tr. from Ital. (Stanford Literature Studies: Vol. 3). 128p. 1986. pap. 20.00 (ISBN 0-915838-47-8). Anma Libri.

--Dante's Inferno. Musa, Mark, tr. LC 70-126214. (Illus.). 320p. 1971. Ind U Pr.

--Dante's "Paradise". Musa, Mark, tr. from Ital. LC 83-48828. (Illus.). 384p. 1984. 32.50x (ISBN 0-253-31619-7). Ind U Pr.

--Dante's Purgatory. Musa, Mark, tr. LC 80-8098. (Illus.). 384p. 1981. 27.50x (ISBN 0-253-17926-2). Ind U Pr.

--Dante's Rime. Diehl, Patrick S., tr. LC 79-83984. (Lockert Library of Poetry in Translation Ser.). 1979. 32.00 (ISBN 0-691-06409-1); pap. 8.95 (ISBN 0-691-01361-6). Princeton U Pr.

--La Divina Comedia. (Biblioteca De Cultura Basica Ser.). 3.75 (ISBN 0-8477-0703-2). U of PR Pr.

--The Divine Comedy. Purgatorio. Mandelbaum, Allen, tr. from Ital. 336p. (Orig.). 1984. pap. text ed. 3.50 (ISBN 0-553-21133-1). Bantam.

--The Divine Comedy, Vol. 1: Inferno. Musa, Mark, tr. (Penguin Classics Ser.). 432p. 1984. pap. 3.50 (ISBN 0-14-044441-6). Penguin.

--The Divine Comedy, Volume II: Purgatory. Musa, Mark, tr. 384p. 1985. pap. 3.95 (ISBN 0-14-044442-4). Penguin.

--The Last James Dean Book. LC 84-60616. (Illus.). 64p. (Orig.). 1984. pap. 12.95 (ISBN 0-688-03927-8, Quill NY). Morrow.

--Literary Criticism of Dante Alighieri. Haller, Robert S., ed. & tr. LC 72-85402. (Regents Critics Ser). l, 192p. 1974. 19.50x (ISBN 0-8032-0467-1); pap. 5.50x (ISBN 0-8032-5469-5, BB 417, Bison). U of Nebr Pr.

--Literature in the Vernacular. Purcell, Sally, tr. 84p. pap. 5.95 (ISBN 0-85635-274-8). Carcanet.

--Oeuvres Completes. 1912p. 46.95 (ISBN 0-686-56492-8). French & Eur.

--On World Government (De Monarchia) Schneider, H. W., tr. LC 57-1099. 1957. pap. 5.44 scp (ISBN 0-672-60176-1, LLA 15). Bobbs.

--Purgatorio: The Divine Comedy of Dante Alighieri. Mandelbaum, Allen, tr. (The California Dante Ser.: Vol. II). (Illus.). 1982. 29.95 (ISBN 0-520-04516-5). U of Cal Pr.

--The Vita Nuova. Martin, Theodore, tr. & intro. by. Martin, Theodore. LC 74-39195. (Select Bibliographies Reprint Ser). Repr. of 1861 ed. 15.00 (ISBN 0-8369-6797-6). Ayer Co Pubs.

--La Vita Nuova. Reynolds, Barbara, tr. (Classics Ser.). 128p. 1969. pap. 3.95 (ISBN 0-14-044216-2). Penguin.

Dante Alighieri. Inferno. Ciardi, John, tr. 1971. pap. 2.50 (ISBN 0-451-61957-9, ME1957, Ment). NAL.

Dante, Alighieri. Monarchy, & Three Political Letters. Nicholl, D. & Hardie, C., trs. LC 78-20461. 1980. Repr. of 1947 ed. text ed. 15.00 (ISBN 0-88355-840-8). Hyperion Conn.

Dante Alighieri. La Vita Nuova. Mathews, J. Chelsey, ed. Emerson, R. W., tr. 1960. 15.00 (ISBN 0-384-10795-8). Johnson Repr.

Dante Committee. Dante: Essays in Commemoration, 1321-1921. LC 74-132438. (Studies in Dante, No. 9). 1970. Repr. of 1921 ed. lib. bdg. 53.95x (ISBN 0-8383-1194-6). Haskell.

Dante, Jim & Diegel, Leo. Nine Bad Shots of Golf & What to Do About Them. 186p. 1961. pap. 4.95 (ISBN 0-346-12327-5). Cornerstone.

Dante, Jim & Elliott, Len. Four Magic Moves of Winning Golf. 192p. 1963. pap. 3.95 (ISBN 0-346-12299-6). Cornerstone.

Dante Society of America, Inc. Dante Studies: With the Annual Report of the Dante Society. Pellegrini, Anthony L., ed. Incl. Vol. 85. Artinian, Robert, et alcontrib. by. vii, 144p. 1967; Vol. 86. Fergusson, Francis, et alcontrib. by. viii, 196p. 1968; Vol. 87. Contini, Gianfranco, et alcontrib. by. viii, 205p. 1969; Vol. 88. Bernardo, Aldo S., et alcontrib. by. viii, 227p. 1970; Vol. 89. Brown, Emerson, Jr., et alcontrib. by. viii, 148p. 1971; Vol. 90. Berk, Philip R., et alcontrib. by. viii, 216p. 1972; Vol. 91. Bergin, Thomas G., et alcontrib. by. 1973; Vol. 92. Barkens, David, et alcontrib. by. 1974; Vol. 93. Mills, Marguerite, et alcontrib. by. 1975; Vol. 94; Vol. 95; Vol. 96; Vol. 97; Vol. 98. LC 15-2183. pap. 15.00x ea. State U NY Pr.

Dante University of America Press, ed. Dante in the Twentieth Century. (Dante Studies: Vol. 1). 1982. 15.00 (ISBN 0-937832-16-2); leather 25.00 (ISBN 0-937832-17-0); leather ltd. ed. 50.00 (ISBN 0-937832-18-9). Branden Pub Co.

Dante Alighieri. The Ardent Love Poetry by Dante Alighieri. Norton, Elliott, tr. (The Most Meaningful Classics in World Culture Ser.). (Illus.). 117p. 1981. 69.45 (ISBN 0-686-69644-1). Am Classical Coll Pr.

--Dante: The Divine Comedy. LC 54-7242. (Rinehart Editions). 1962. pap. text ed. 11.95 (ISBN 0-03-008690-6, HoltC). HR&W.

--La Divina Commedia. Grandgent, C. H. & Singleton, Charles S., eds. LC 72-78429. (Illus.). 988p. 1972. 50.00x (ISBN 0-674-21290-8); pap. 18.00x (ISBN 0-674-21291-6). Harvard U Pr.

--The Divine Comedy. Fletcher, J. B., tr. from Italian. LC 51-9849. 471p. 1951. 35.00x (ISBN 0-231-01806-1). Columbia U Pr.

--The Divine Comedy. Bergin, Thomas G., ed. & tr. LC 55-8964. (Crofts Classics Ser.). 1955. pap. text ed. 7.95x (ISBN 0-88295-028-2). Harlan Davidson.

--The Divine Comedy. Ciardi, John, tr. (Illus.). 1977. 29.95 (ISBN 0-393-04472-6). Norton.

--The Divine Comedy, 3 vols. rev. ed. Sinclair, John D, tr. Incl. Vol. 1. Inferno. 1961. pap. 8.95 (ISBN 0-19-500412-4, GB65); Vol 2. Purgatorio. 1961. pap. 7.95 (ISBN 0-19-500413-2, GB66); Vol. 3. Paradiso. 1961. pap. 7.95 (ISBN 0-19-500414-0, GB67). pap. 9.95 (GB). Oxford U Pr.

--The Divine Comedy, 3 vols. Sayers, Dorothy L., tr. Incl. Vol. 1. Inferno (Hell) 1950. pap. 2.95 (ISBN 0-14-044006-2); Vol. 2. Purgatorio (Purgatory) 1955. pap. 3.95 (ISBN 0-14-044046-1); Vol. 3. Paradiso (Paradise) 1962. pap. 3.95 (ISBN 0-14-044105-0). (Classics Ser.). pap. Penguin.

--The Divine Comedy, 3 vols. Singleton, Charles S., tr. Incl. Vol. 1. Inferno, 2 pts. 1973. 72.50x (ISBN 0-691-09855-7); Vol. 2. Purgatorio, 2 pts. 1232p. 1973. 72.50x (ISBN 0-691-09887-5); Vol. 3. Paradiso, 2 pts. 1975. 72.50x (ISBN 0-691-09888-3). LC 68-57090. (Bollingen Ser.: Vol. 80). (Eng. & It.). 1975. Set. 195.00x (ISBN 0-686-67212-7); Set. pap. 47.50. Princeton U Pr.

--Divine Comedy. 1955. pap. 4.95 (ISBN 0-394-70126-7, V126, Vin). Random.

--The Divine Comedy. Sisson, C. H., tr. from Ital. LC 81-52140. 688p. 1981. 16.95 (ISBN 0-89526-665-2). Regnery Gateway.

--The Divine Comedy. rev. ed. Bickersteth, Geoffrey, tr. from It. 805p. 1972. Repr. of 1965 ed. 22.50x (ISBN 0-87471-295-5). Rowman.

--The Divine Comedy: Purgatorio, Vol. 2. Singleton, Charles S., tr. from Ital. LC 68-57090. (Bollingen Ser.: No. LXXX). (Illus.). 1260p. (Orig.). 1982. pap. 18.50x (ISBN 0-691-01843-X). Princeton U Pr.

--The Divine Comedy: The Inferno, Vol. 1. Singleton, Charles S., tr. from Italian. LC 68-57090. (Bollingen Ser: Lxxx). (Illus.). 1088p. (Bilingual ed.). 1980. pap. 19.50 (ISBN 0-691-01832-4). Princeton U Pr.

--Episodios Famosos de la Divina Comedia (Primera Parte: Infierno) Cordaro, Philip & Ferracane, Gerardo, eds. Crespo, Angel, tr. from Ital. LC 76-8012. (Coleccion Uprex Serie Humanidades: No. 49). (Orig., Span.). 1976. pap. 1.85 (ISBN 0-8477-0049-6). U of PR Pr.

--Il Convivio. Simonelli, Maria, ed. xxv, 254p. 1966. 8.75x (ISBN 0-685-47488-7). Schoenhof.

--The Inferno: The Divine Comedy of Dante Alighieri, a Verse Translation with Introduction. Mandelbaum, Allen, tr. LC 73-94441. (The California Dante Ser.: Vol. I). (Illus.). 336p. 1980. 24.95 (ISBN 0-520-02712-4). U of Cal Pr.

--De Monarchia. LC 74-147412. (Library of War & Peace; Proposals for Peace: a History). lib. bdg. 46.00 (ISBN 0-8240-0210-5). Garland Pub.

--The New Life & the Convivio. Norton, Charles E., tr. 137p. 1985. 88.25 (ISBN 0-89901-219-1). Found Class Reprints.

--Paradise. Bergin, Thomas G., ed. & tr. LC 54-10684. (Crofts Classics Ser.). 1954. pap. text ed. 0.85x (ISBN 0-88295-030-4). Harlan Davidson.

--Paradiso: Third Book of the Divine Comedy. Mandelbaum, Allen, tr. LC 73-94441. (The California Dante Ser.). (Illus.). 320p. 1984. 29.95 (ISBN 0-520-04517-3). U of Cal Pr.

--Portable Dante. rev. ed. Milano, Paolo, ed. (Viking Portable Library: No. 32). 1977. pap. 6.95 (ISBN 0-14-015032-3, P32). Penguin.

--Purgatory. Bergin, Thomas G., ed. & tr. LC 53-6432. (Crofts Classics Ser.). 1953. pap. text ed. 0.85x (ISBN 0-88295-031-2). Harlan Davidson.

--Translation of the Latin Works of Dante Alighieri. LC 69-13874. Repr. of 1904 ed. lib. bdg. 19.75x (ISBN 0-8371-1799-2, DAAT). Greenwood.

--The Trilogy: Or Dante's Three Visions, 3 vols. Thomas, John, tr. 1978. Repr. of 1859 ed. lib. bdg. 100.00 set (ISBN 0-8492-0669-3). R West.

Dantec, Le see Verlaine, Paul.

Danthine, A., jt. ed. see Boutmy, E. J.

Danthine, Andre & Geradin, Michel, eds. Advanced Software in Robotics: Proceedings of an International Meeting, Liege, Belgium, May 1983. x, 370p. 1984. 48.00 (ISBN 0-444-86814-3, I-533-83, North Holland). Elsevier.

Dantis, Hugh De see De Santis, Hugh.

Danto, A. C. Analytical Philosophy of Action. LC 72-91364. 224p. 1973. 37.50 (ISBN 0-521-20120-9). Cambridge U Pr.

Danto, Arthur. Nietzsche as Philosopher. 250p. 1980. pap. 10.00x (ISBN 0-231-05053-4). Columbia U Pr.

Danto, Arthur C. Narration & Knowledge. 400p. 1985. 35.00s (ISBN 0-231-06116-1); pap. 12.50s (ISBN 0-231-06117-X). Columbia U Pr.

--The Transfiguration of the Commonplace: A Philosophy of Art. 222p. 1981. text ed. 17.50x (ISBN 0-674-90345-5). Harvard U Pr.

--The Transfiguration of the Commonplace: A Philosophy of Art. 288p. 1983. pap. text ed. 6.95x (ISBN 0-674-90346-3). Harvard U Pr.

Danto, Bruce L. Jail House Blues. LC 73-79482. 325p. 1973. 8.95 (ISBN 0-914244-01-9). Epic Pubns.

Danto, Bruce L., et al. Suicide & Bereavement. 17.50 (ISBN 0-405-12505-4). Ayer Co Pubs.

Danto, Bruce L., et al, eds. So You Want to See a Psychiatrist? LC 79-23225. 170p. 1980. lib. bdg. 15.00 (ISBN 0-405-12622-0). Ayer Co Pubs.

--The Human Side of Homicide. 336p. 1982. 27.50x (ISBN 0-231-04964-1). Columbia U Pr.

Danto, Eloise. Small Museums of the French Rivers. (Illus.). 104p. (Orig.). 1985. pap. 9.95 (ISBN 0-9615128-0-6). Eldan Pr.

Danton, Annina P. Hebbel's Nibelungen. LC 71-163666. (Columbia University. Germanic Studies, Old Ser.: No. 8). Repr. of 1906 ed. 17.00 (ISBN 0-404-50408-6). AMS Pr.

Danton, George H. The Culture Contacts of the United States & China. LC 74-4380. xiv, 133p. 1974. Repr. of 1931 ed. lib. bdg. 14.50x (ISBN 0-374-92048-6). Octagon.

--Germany Ten Years After. facsimile ed. LC 79-150180. (Select Bibliographies Reprint Ser). Repr. of 1928 ed. 20.00 (ISBN 0-8369-5693-1). Ayer Co Pubs.

--Nature Sense in the Writings of Ludwig Tieck. LC 78-163673. (Columbia University. Germanic Studies, Old Ser.: No. 9). Repr. of 1907 ed. 15.00 (ISBN 0-404-50409-4). AMS Pr.

Danton, Graham. The Theory & Practice of Seamanship. 9th ed. 538p. 1985. 39.95x (ISBN 0-7102-0418-3). Routledge & Kegan.

Danton, Rebecca. French Jade. (Coventry Romance Ser.: No. 177). 224p. 1982. pap. 1.50 (ISBN 0-449-50278-3, Coventry). Fawcett.

--The Highland Brooch. (Orig.). 1980. pap. 1.75 (ISBN 0-449-50022-5, Coventry). Fawcett.

--Star Sapphire. 1979. pap. 1.75 (ISBN 0-449-50058-6, Coventry). Fawcett.

--White Fire. 1982. pap. 2.75 (ISBN 0-449-24477-6, Crest). Fawcett.

D'Antoni, Hector L., jt. auth. see Markgraf, Vera.

D'Antonio, William, jt. auth. see DeFleur, Melvin L.

D'Antonio, William V. & Form, William H. Influentials in Two Border Cities: A Study in Community Decision-Making. 1965. 16.95 (ISBN 0-268-00135-9). U of Notre Dame Pr.

D'Antonio, William V. & Aldous, Joan, eds. Families & Religions: Conflict & Change in Modern Society. 320p. 1983. 29.00 (ISBN 0-8039-2075-X); pap. 14.50 (ISBN 0-8039-2468-2). Sage.

D'Antonio, William V. & Ehrlich, Howard J., eds. Power & Democracy in America. 1961. pap. 5.95x (ISBN 0-268-00368-8). U of Notre Dame Pr.

D'Antonio, William V., ed. see Drucker, Peter F., et al.

Dantyagi, Susheela. Fundamentals of Textiles & Their Care. 4th ed. 1983. pap. 12.95x (ISBN 0-86131-431-X, Pub. by Orient Longman India). Apt Bks.

Dantzig, G. B. & Eaves, B. C., eds. Studies in Optimization. LC 74-21481. (MAA Studies: No. 10). 174p. 1977. 16.50 (ISBN 0-88385-110-5). Math Assn.

Dantzig, G. B., et al, eds. Mathematics of the Decision Sciences: Part 2. Barlow, R. E., Jr. & Chernoff, H. LC 62-21481. 443p. 1970. Repr. of 1968 ed. text ed. 43.00 (ISBN 0-8218-1112-6, LAM 12). Am Math.

Dantzig, George B. Linear Programming & Extensions. (Rand Corporation Research Studies). 1963. 43.00 (ISBN 0-691-08000-3). Princeton U Pr.

Dantzig, J. A. & Berry, J. T., eds. Modeling of Casting & Welding Processess II. LC 84-61174. (Illus.). 458p. 1984. 45.00 (ISBN 0-89520-477-0). Metal Soc.

Dantzig, Tobias. Number: The Language of Science. 4th rev. ed. (Illus.). 340p. 1967. pap. text ed. 10.95x (ISBN 0-02-906990-4). Free Pr.

Dantzler, W. H., ed. Comparative Renal Handling of Solutes & Water. (Journal: Renal Physiology: Vol. 8, No. 4-5, 1985). (Illus.). 100p. 1985. pap. 39.25 (ISBN 3-8055-4147-3). S Karger.

Danusugondo, Purwanto. Bahasa Indonesia for Beginners, Bk. 1. 1966. pap. 15.00x (ISBN 0-424-05280-6, Pub. by Sydney U Pr). Intl Spec Bk.

--Bahasa Indonesia for Beginners, Bk. 2. 2nd ed. 1969. pap. 15.00x (ISBN 0-424-00018-0, Pub. by Sydney U Pr). Intl Spec Bk.

Danvers, Frederick C. Portuguese in India, 2 Vols. 1966. Set. lib. bdg. 72.00x (ISBN 0-374-92052-4). Octagon.

Danvers, Frederik C. Portuguese in India, 2 vols. new ed. (Illus.). 1966. 95.00x set (ISBN 0-7146-2005-X, F Cass Co). Biblio Dist.

Dany, M. & Laloy, J. R. Le Francais de L'Hotellerie et du Tourisme. 186p. (Fr.). 1980. pap. 14.95 (ISBN 0-686-97381-X, M-9311). French & Eur.

Danysh, Joseph. Stop Without Quitting. LC 74-77668. 120p. 1974. pap. 2.00 (ISBN 0-918970-18-0). Intl Gen Semantics.

Danz, Ernst & Menges, Axel. Modern Fireplaces. (Illus.). 1979. 29.95 (ISBN 0-8038-0165-3). Architectural.

--Modern Fireplaces. 140p. 1979. 75.00x (ISBN 0-85670-599-3, Pub. by Academy Editions England). State Mutual Bk.

Danz, Louis. Personal Revolution & Picasso. LC 74-3421. (Studies in Philosophy, No. 40). 1974. lib. bdg. 46.95x (ISBN 0-8383-2066-X). Haskell.

Danz, Thomas, ed. see Janssen, Peter.

Danzer, Hal, jt. auth. see Kass-Annese, Barbara.

Danzer, Hal C., jt. auth. see Kass-Annese, Barbara.

Danzi, J. Thomas. Free Yourself from Digestive Pain: A Guide to Preventing & Curing Your Digestive Illness. (Illus.). 192p. 1984. 16.95 (ISBN 0-13-330671-2); pap. 7.95 (ISBN 0-13-330663-1). P-H.

Danzig, Alan & Schor, Edith. Thesis: Rhetoric of the Essay. 2nd ed. 352p. 1979. pap. text ed. write for info. (ISBN 0-534-00726-0). Wadsworth Pub.

Danzig, Allison & Brandwein, Peter, eds. Sport's Golden Age, a Closeup of the Fabulous Twenties. facs. ed. LC 68-58784. (Essay Index Reprint Ser). 1948. 22.00 (ISBN 0-8369-0013-8). Ayer Co Pubs.

Danzig, Fred, jt. auth. see Klein, Ted.

Danziger, Carl. Unmarried Heterosexual Cohabitation. LC 78-62233. 1978. soft cover 11.00 (ISBN 0-88247-535-5). R & E Pubs.

Danziger, Edmund J., Jr. The Chippewas of Lake Superior. LC 78-58130. (Civilization of the American Indian Ser: No. 148). (Illus.). 1979. 19.95 (ISBN 0-8061-1487-8). U of Okla Pr.

--Indians & Bureaucrats: Administering the Reservation Policy During the Civil War. LC 73-85486. 250p. 1974. 19.95x (ISBN 0-252-00314-4). U of Ill Pr.

Danziger, Howard. Marriage Stinks. (Illus.). 32p. (Orig.). 1982. pap. 1.25 (ISBN 0-88009-024-3). Planet Bks.

--Shrinks & Other Lunatics. (Illus.). 32p. (Orig.). 1982. pap. 1.25 (ISBN 0-88009-020-0). Planet Bks.

Danziger, James N. Making Budgets: Public Resource Allocation. LC 79-2394. (Sage Library of Social Research: No. 63). 255p. 1978. pap. 12.00 (ISBN 0-8039-1010-X). Sage.

Danziger, James N. & Dutton, William H. Computers & Politics. 320p. 1983. 32.00x (ISBN 0-231-04888-2); pap. 16.00x (ISBN 0-231-04889-0). Columbia U Pr.

Danziger, Jeff. The Champlain Monster. (Illus.). 92p. 1983. pap. 5.95 (ISBN 0-933050-17-8). New Eng Pr VT.

--The Complete Reagan Diet. LC 82-61449. (Illus.). 96p. (Orig.). 1982. pap. 2.95 (ISBN 0-688-01908-0, Quill NY). Morrow.

--Danziger's Classic Vermont Cartoons. rev. ed. 64p. 1980. pap. 3.95 (ISBN 0-9603900-1-4). Lanser Pr.

--The Illustrated Unofficial Hunting Rules. (Illus.). 64p. (Orig.). 1983. pap. 3.95 (ISBN 0-933050-18-6). New Eng Pr VT.

--Our Special Catalogue of Replacement Parts for the Human Body. LC 83-61486. (Illus.). 64p. (Orig.). 1983. pap. 5.70 (ISBN 0-688-02506-4, Quill NY). Morrow.

--Out in the Sticks. 2nd ed. (Illus.). 96p. (Orig.). 1983. pap. 4.95 (ISBN 0-317-03268-2). New Eng Pr VT.

--Out in the Sticks. 3rd ed. (Illus.). 96p. (Orig.). 1983. pap. 4.95 (ISBN 0-317-03269-0). New Eng Pr VT.

--Out in the Sticks. 3rd ed. (Illus.). 96p. (Orig.). 1983. pap. 4.95 (ISBN 0-317-03420-0). New Eng Pr VT.

--The Vermont Mind: Collected Vermont Cartoons. (Illus.). 64p. 1979. pap. 3.95 (ISBN 0-9603900-0-6). New Eng Pr VT.

--Vermont Mind II: Completely Undercoated Cartoons. (Illus.). 96p. (Orig.). 1982. pap. 4.95 (ISBN 0-317-03419-7). New Eng Pr VT.

--The Woodfired Automobile. 80p. 1980. pap. 3.95 (ISBN 0-9603900-2-2). New Eng Pr VT.

Danziger, Marlies K. Oliver Goldsmith & Richard Brinsley Sheridan. LC 77-6946. (Literature and Life Ser.). (Illus.). 192p. 1978. 13.95 (ISBN 0-8044-2129-3). Ungar.

Danziger, Marlies K. & Johnson, Wendell S. The Critical Reader: Analyzing & Judging Literature. LC 78-4302. 1978. 11.95 (ISBN 0-8044-2135-8); pap. 4.95 (ISBN 0-8044-6096-5). Ungar.

Danziger, Marlies K. & Johnson, Wendell S., eds. Poetry Anthology. (Orig.). 1967. pap. text ed. 14.00 (ISBN 0-394-30187-0, RanC). Random.

Danziger, Marlies K., ed. see Johnson, Samuel.

Danziger, Paula. Can You Sue Your Parents for Malpractice? LC 78-72856. 266p. (gr. 7 up). 1979. 13.95 (ISBN 0-385-28112-9). Delacorte.

--Can You Sue Your Parents for Malpractice? pap. 2.25 (ISBN 0-686-74495-0, LE). Dell.

--Can You Sue Your Parents for Malpractice? 144p. (YA) (gr. 7 up). 1980. pap. 2.25 (ISBN 0-440-91066-8, LFL). Dell.

--The Cat Ate My Gymsuit. LC 74-5501. 128p. (gr. 7 up). 1974. 12.95 (ISBN 0-385-28183-8); PLB 12.95 (ISBN 0-385-28194-3). Delacorte.

--The Cat Ate My Gymsuit. 128p. (gr. 5 up). 1975. pap. 2.25 (ISBN 0-440-91612-7, LFL). Dell.

--The Cat Ate My Gymsuit. 160p. (gr. 5 up). 1980. pap. 2.50 (ISBN 0-440-41612-4, YB). Dell.

--The Divorce Express. LC 82-70318. 144p. (gr. 7 up). 1982. 12.95 (ISBN 0-385-28217-6). Delacorte.

--The Divorce Express. 160p. (YA) (gr. 7 up). 1983. pap. 2.25 (ISBN 0-440-92062-0, LFL). Dell.

--It's an Aardvark-Eat-Turtle World. LC 84-17645. 144p. (gr. 7 up). 1985. 13.95 (ISBN 0-385-29371-2). Delacorte.

--The Pistachio Prescription. LC 77-86330. 168p. (gr. 7 up). 1978. 12.95 (ISBN 0-385-28784-4). Delacorte.

--The Pistachio Prescription. 160p. (YA) (gr. 5 up). 1978. pap. 2.25 (ISBN 0-440-96895-X, LFL). Dell.

--There's a Bat in Bunk Five. LC 80-64833. 160p. (gr. 7 up). 1980. 13.95 (ISBN 0-385-29013-6); PLB 13.95 (ISBN 0-385-29015-2). Delacorte.

--There's a Bat in Bunk Five. 160p. (gr. 5-9). 1982. pap. 2.50 (ISBN 0-440-98631-1, LE). Dell.

Danziger, Raphael. Abd al-Qadir & the Algerians: Resistance to the French & Internal Consolidation. LC 76-18061. 1977. text ed. 37.50x (ISBN 0-8419-0236-4, Africana). Holmes & Meier.

Danziger, Robert. The Musical Ascent of Herman Being: A How to Novel. LC 84-80486. (Illus.). 100p. 1985. pap. 6.95 (ISBN 0-9613427-4-9). Jordan Pr.

Danziger, Sheldon & Portney, Kent. Symposium on Distributional Impacts of Public Policies. (Orig.). 1984. pap. 8.00 (ISBN 0-918592-68-2). Policy Studies.

Danzin, A. Science & the Second Renaissance of Europe. 1979. pap. text ed. 27.00 (ISBN 0-08-022442-3). Pergamon.

Danzon, Patricia M. Medical Malpractice: Theory, Evidence, & Public Policy. (Illus.). 312p. 1985. text ed. 25.00x (ISBN 0-674-56115-5). Harvard U Pr.

Dao, Lanny V. Mastering the 8088 Microprocessor. LC 84-16419. (Illus.). 304p. (Orig.). 1984. 22.95 (ISBN 0-8306-0888-5, 1888); pap. 15.95 (ISBN 0-8306-1888-0). TAB Bks.

Dao, Thomas L., ed. see International Symposium on Endogenous Factors Inflencing Host-Tumor Balance, 1966.

Dao, Thomas L., ed. see Workshop on Estrogen Target Tissues & Neoplasia.

Dao, Wong Ming. Stone Made Smooth. 1982. pap. 5.95 (ISBN 0-907821-00-6). OMF Bks.

Dao, Wong Ming see Dao, Wong Ming.

Daoud, Hazim S. Flora of Kuwait: Dicotyledoneae, Vol. I. Al-Rawi, Ali, rev. by. (Illus.). 288p. 1985. 75.00x (ISBN 0-7103-0075-1, Kegan Paul). Routledge & Kegan.

Daoud, Hesham O. Daoud's Aviation Dictionary. 1972. pap. 9.95 (ISBN 0-911720-55-3, Pub. by Daouds). Aviation.

Daoud El-Basri, Abdel Gawad. Aspects of Iraqui Cultural Policy. (Studies & Documents on Cultural Policies). (Illus.). 38p. 1980. pap. 5.00 (ISBN 92-3-101745-4, U995, UNESCO). Unipub.

Daoudi, M. S. The Meaning of Kahlil Gibran. 160p. 1982. 9.95 (ISBN 0-8065-0804-3). Citadel Pr.

--The Meaning of Kahlil Gibran. 140p. 1984. pap. 5.95 (ISBN 0-8065-0929-5). Citadel Pr.

Daoudi, M. S. & Dajani, M. S. Economic Diplomacy: The Political Dynamics of Oil Leverage. (A WVSS in International Relations Ser.). 300p. 1985. 30.00x (ISBN 0-8133-0101-7). Westview.

--Economic Sanctions: Ideals & Experience. (International Library of Economics). 244p. 1983. 26.95x (ISBN 0-7100-9583-X). Routledge & Kegan.

Daoust, H., jt. auth. see Stepek, J.

Daoust, Yvette. Roger Planchon: Director & Playwright. (Illus.). 200p. 1981. 47.50 (ISBN 0-521-23414-X). Cambridge U Pr.

Da Parigi, Tomaso, jt. auth. see De Sommevoire, Alexis.

Da Pisa, Guido. Guido da Pisa's Commentary on Dante's Inferno. Cioffari, Vincenzo, ed. & tr. LC 74-11248. xxv, 750p. 1974. 44.50x (ISBN 0-87395-259-6). State U NY Pr.

Dapkus, David, jt. auth. see Mosby, Jack.

Dapkus, F. Statistics One: A Text for Beginners. 1979. pap. text ed. 13.95 (ISBN 0-89669-042-3). Collegium Bk Pubs.

Dapogny, James. Ferdinand "Jelly Roll" Morton: The Collected Piano Music. (Illus.). 576p. (Orig.). 1982. pap. 23.95 (ISBN 0-87474-351-6). Smithsonian.

Da Ponte, Lorenzo. Memoirs of Lorenzo da Ponte. Abbott, Elizabeth, tr. from Ital. (Music Reprint Ser.). (Illus.). 512p. 1985. Repr. of 1929 ed. lib. bdg. 49.50 (ISBN 0-306-76290-0). Da Capo.

--Mozart's Don Giovanni: Complete Italian Libretto. Bleiler, Ellen H., tr. 121p. 1985. pap. 2.95 (ISBN 0-486-24944-1). Dover.

Da Ponte, Lorenzo see Ponte, Lorenzo Da.

Dapper, Gertrude. Canine Genetics. (Other Dogs Bks). (Illus.). 1985. 16.95 (ISBN 0-87714-112-6). Denlingers.

--German Names for German Dogs. LC 78-52184. (Other Dog Bks.). (Illus.). 1980. 11.95 (ISBN 0-87714-066-9). Denlingers.

--Your German Shorthaired Pointer. LC 74-29657. (Your Dog Book Ser.). (Illus.). 1975. 12.95 (ISBN 0-87714-030-8). Denlingers.

Dapper, Olfert. Description De l'Afrique. (Landmarks in Anthropology Ser). 1970. Repr. of 1686 ed. 80.00 (ISBN 0-384-10820-2). Johnson Repr.

--Umbstandliche und Eigentliche Beschreibung Von Africa. (Illus.). 1967. Repr. of 1670 ed. 78.00 (ISBN 0-384-10825-3). Johnson Repr.

Dapples, Edward C. Basic Geology for Science & Engineering. LC 59-5880. 620p. 1973. Repr. of 1959 ed. 29.50 (ISBN 0-88275-106-9). Krieger.

Dapples, Edward C. & Hopkins, M. E., eds. Environments of Coal Deposition. LC 68-58108. (Geological Society of America Special Paper Ser.: No. 114). pap. 60.50 (ISBN 0-317-10260-5, 2007965). Bks Demand UMI.

D'Appolonia, B. L. & Kunerth, W. H. The Farinograph Handbook. 3rd ed. 80p. 1984. 33.50 (ISBN 0-913250-37-6). Am Assn Cereal Chem.

D'Appolonia, Elio, jt. ed. see Pattison, Harry C.

Da Prato, G. Institutiones Mathematicae: Applications Croissantes & Equations d'revolutions dans les Espaces de Banach. 1977. 35.00 (ISBN 0-12-363602-7). Acad Pr.

Da Prato, G., jt. auth. see Barbu, V.

Da Prista, Alexander. Say It in Portuguese. pap. 2.75 (ISBN 0-486-23676-5). Dover.

D'Aprix, Roger. Communicating for Productivity. (Continuing Management Education Ser.). 112p. 1982. 14.37x (ISBN 0-06-041547-9, HarpC). Harper-Row.

Da Providencia, Joo, jt. ed. see Dreizler, Reiner M.

Dapunt, Otto, jt. auth. see Wittliff, James L.

D'Aquili, Eugene G., jt. auth. see Laughlin, Charles D.

D'Aquili, Eugene G., et al. The Spectrum of Ritual. LC 78-19015. (A Biogenetic Structural Analysis). 408p. 1979. 33.50x (ISBN 0-231-04514-X). Columbia U Pr.

Daquine, Sonia. Les Passagers de L'Argonaute. (Collection Colombine). 192p. 1983. pap. 1.95 (ISBN 0-373-48081-4). Harlequin Bks.

--Si Nos Chemins se Croisent. (Collection Colombine Ser.). 192p. 1983. pap. 1.95 (ISBN 0-373-48068-7). Harlequin Bks.

Dar, B. A. Quranic Ethics. pap. 3.50 (ISBN 0-686-18602-8). Kazi Pubns.

--Qur'anic Ethics. 1970. 4.50x (ISBN 0-87902-160-8). Orientalia.

Dar, R. K. Recent Developments in Federal Financial Relations in India. LC 80-66437. (Centre for Research on Federal Financial Relations Research Monograph: No. 35). 90p. 1981. pap. text ed. 8.00 (ISBN 0-908160-73-9, 1130, Pub. by ANUP Australia). Australia N U P.

Dar, S. N. Costumes of India & Pakistan: A Historical & Cultural Study. (Illus.). 244p. 1983. text ed. 60.00x (ISBN 0-86590-191-0, Pub. by Taraporevala India). Apt Bks.

Dar Systems International Staff, ed. see Seiden, Eric A.

DAR Systems International Staff, ed. see Seiden, Eric A.

DAR Systems International Staff, ed. see Seiden, Eric A., et al.

Dar Systems International Staff, ed. see Seiden, Eric A. & Parisse, David A.

DAR Systems In'tl Staff, ed. LBASIC Reference Manual. 2nd ed. Seiden, Eric A. & Parrise, David A. 100p. (Orig.). 1985. incl. software for Apple Computer 99.95 (ISBN 0-916163-70-9); pap. 24.95 (ISBN 0-916163-71-7). Dar Syst.

Dar Systems Staff, ed. see Seiden, Eric A.

D.A.R. Thronateeska Chapter, compiled by. History & Reminiscences of Dougherty County Georgia. LC 78-12903. 1978. Repr. of 1924 ed. 15.00 (ISBN 0-87152-282-9). Reprint.

Daraca, Jerry R. Conga Drumming: Disco, Soul, Reggae, Rock with Conga Drumming: the Demonstration Recording. LC 79-19350. (Illus.). 72p. 1980. spiral bdg. & cassette 15.00 (ISBN 0-918628-21-0); cassette alone 10.00 (ISBN 0-918628-06-7). Congeros Pubns.

--Conga Drumming: Instructor's Edition. Haldeman, Marian, ed. LC 79-19350. (Illus.). 83p. 1982. 3-ring binder & cassette 25.00 (ISBN 0-918628-23-7, C311-1). Congeros Pubns.

Darack, Arthur. The Guide to Home Appliance Repair. (Illus., Orig.). 1979. pap. 8.95 (ISBN 0-07-015360-4). McGraw.

--How to Repair & Care for Small Home Appliances. LC 82-25084. (Illus.). 184p. 1983. 22.95 (ISBN 0-13-430835-2); pap. 12.95 (ISBN 0-13-430827-1). P-H.

--Outdoor Power Equipment: How It Works, How to Fix It. LC 77-70404. 1977. pap. 4.95 (ISBN 0-8128-2276-5). Stein & Day.

Darack, Arthur & Consumer Group, Inc. Used Cars: How to Avoid Highway Robbery. (Illus.). 240p. 1983. 18.95 (ISBN 0-13-940056-7); pap. 8.95 (ISBN 0-13-940049-4). P-H.

Darack, Arthur & Consumer Group, Inc. Staff. Small Engine Maintenance & Repair for Outdoor Power Equipment. (Illus.). 192p. 1984. 18.95 (ISBN 0-13-813148-1); pap. 9.95 (ISBN 0-13-813130-9). P-H.

Darahan, Iurii. Sahaidak: Virshi, 1922-1924. LC 75-546612. (Ukrai.). 1965. pap. 5.00 (ISBN 0-918884-16-0). Slavia Lib.

Daraul, Arkon. History of Secret Societies. 256p. 1983. pap. 5.95 (ISBN 0-8065-0857-4). Citadel Pr.

--Secret Societies. 1983. Repr. of 1961 ed. 14.95 (ISBN 0-86304-024-1, Pub. by Octagon Pr England). Ins Study Human.

Da Ravenna, Giovanni. Dragmalogia de Elgibili Vite Genere, by Giovanni di Conversino da Ravenna. Eaker, Helen L., ed. LC 79-2342. (Bucknell Renaissance Texts in Translation Ser.). 291p. (Eng. & Latin.). 1980. 28.50 (ISBN 0-8387-1897-3). Bucknell U Pr.

Darazs, Arpad & Jay, Stephen. Sight & Sound: Students' Manual. LC 64-25360. (gr. 3-6). 1965. pap. text ed. 5.00 (ISBN 0-913932-03-5). Boosey & Hawkes.

--Sight & Sound: Teachers' Manual. LC 64-25360. 1965. 7.50 (ISBN 0-913932-02-7). Boosey & Hawkes.

Darbari, J. & Darbari, R. Commonwealth & Nehru. 284p. 1985. text ed. 13.50x (ISBN 0-391-03130-9, Pub. by Vision Bks India). Humanities.

Darbari, R., jt. auth. see Darbari, J.

Darbel, Alain & Schnapper, Dominique. Morphologie De la Haute Administration Francaise, 2 tomes. Incl. Tome 1. Les Agents Du Systeme Administratif. (No. 6). 1969. pap. 10.40x (ISBN 90-2796-256-1); Tome 2. Le Systeme Administratif. (No. 9). 1973. pap. 17.20x (ISBN 0-686-22175-3). (Cahiers Du Centre De Sociologie Europeenne). pap. Mouton.

Darbelnet, J. L. Pensee et Structure. 2nd ed. LC 68-19906. 275p. (Fr.). 1977. deluxe ed. price not set (ISBN 0-02-327510-3, Pub. by Scribner). Macmillan.

Darbey, Jill, jt. auth. see Welles, Sigourney.

Darbey, Jill, jt. auth. see Wells, Sigourney.

Darbishire, tr. see De Vries, H.

Darbishire, H., ed. De Quincey's Literary Criticism. LC 73-15652. 1909. lib. bdg. 20.00 (ISBN 0-8414-3687-8). Folcroft.

Darbishire, Helen. Milton's Paradise Lost. LC 74-3031. 1951. lib. bdg. 12.50 (ISBN 0-8414-3750-5). Folcroft.

--The Poet Wordsworth. LC 79-14336. 182p. 1980. Repr. of 1965 ed. lib. bdg. 27.50x (ISBN 0-313-21483-2, DAWO). Greenwood.

--The Ruined Cottage & Excursion, in Essays Presented to Sir H. Milford. 1948. Repr. 15.00 (ISBN 0-8274-3312-3). R West.

Darbishire, Helen, ed. Early Lives of Milton. LC 77-144967. (Illus.). 1971. Repr. of 1932 ed. 49.00x (ISBN 0-403-00935-9). Scholarly.

Darbishire, Helen, ed. see Milton, John.

Darbishire, Helen, ed. see Wordsworth, William.

D'Arblay, Frances. Doctor Johnson & Fanny Burney. LC 70-98806. Repr. of 1911 ed. lib. bdg. 22.50x (ISBN 0-8371-3067-0, ARJF). Greenwood.

Darbonne, Rodger. Complete Essay of Basic English Grammar. (Illus.). 1967. pap. 4.00 (ISBN 0-911756-02-7, Neptune Bks). Tail Feather.

Darboux, Gaston. Theorie Generale Des Surfaces, 4 Vols. 2nd ed. LC 67-16997. (Fr). 1968. Set. 85.00 (ISBN 0-8284-0216-7). Chelsea Pub.

Darbre, A. & Waterfield, M. D. Practical Protein Biochemistry: A Handbook. 1985. write for info. (ISBN 0-471-90673-5). Wiley.

Darby & Joan. Our Unseen Guest. pap. 5.95 (ISBN 0-87505-091-3). Borden.

Darby Books Staff, tr. Letters from Percy Bysshe Shelley to William Godwin, 2 vols. 1983. Repr. of 1891 ed. Set. lib. bdg. 150.00 (ISBN 0-89987-322-7). Vol.1 110pgs. Vol.2 107pgs. Darby Bks.

Darby, Charles. Drawing Your Pets. (Illus.). 80p. 1982. pap. 2.75 (ISBN 0-86230-043-6). Triplegate.

Darby, D. J. Financing of Industry & Trade. 1970. 18.00x (ISBN 0-8464-0412-5); pap. 9.95x (ISBN 0-8464-0413-3). Beekman Pubs.

Darby, Daniel R., jt. auth. see Steffy, Wilbert.

Darby, David, jt. auth. see Ojakangas, Richard.

Darby, David G. Real Estate for Income & Profit: How You Can Stop Working for a Living & Make Living Work for You. LC 74-84503. (Illus.). 203p. (Orig.). 1974. pap. 14.95 (ISBN 0-915512-01-7). M-L Pub.

Darby, Elisabeth & Smith, Nicola. The Cult of the Prince Consort. LC 83-42869. (Illus.). 128p. 1983. 21.50x (ISBN 0-300-03015-0). Yale U Pr.

Darby, H. C. The Changing Fenland. LC 82-12922. (Illus.). 288p. 1983. 52.50 (ISBN 0-521-24606-7). Cambridge U Pr.

Darby, H. C., jt. auth. see Fullard, Harold.

Darby, H. C., ed. Domesday England. LC 76-11485. (The Domesday Geography of England Ser.). (Illus.). 1977. 87.50 (ISBN 0-521-21307-X). Cambridge U Pr.

--A New Historical Geography of England After 1600. LC 76-26029. 1978. 72.50 (ISBN 0-521-22123-4). Cambridge U Pr.
--A New Historical Geography of England Before 1600. LC 76-26141. 1978. 62.50 (ISBN 0-521-22122-6); pap. 24.95 (ISBN 0-521-29144-5). Cambridge U Pr.
Darby, H. C. & Maxwell, L. S., eds. The Domesday Geography of Northern England. (Domesday Geography of England). (Illus.). 1978. 105.00 (ISBN 0-521-04773-0). Cambridge U Pr.
Darby, H. C. & Terrett, I. B., eds. The Domesday Geography of Midland England. LC 78-134626. pap. 127.00 (ISBN 0-317-28397-9, 2022445). Bks Demand UMI.
Darby, Henry C. Mediaeval Cambridgeshire. (Cambridge Town, Gown & County Ser.: Vol. 15). (Illus.). 1977. pap. 4.25 (ISBN 0-900891-11-4). Oleander Pr.
Darby, J. B., jt. ed. see Freeman, A. J.
Darby, J. N. The Collected Writings, 35 vols. Set. 125.00 (ISBN 0-88172-055-0); 4.00 ea. Believers Bkshelf.
--Letters of J. N. Darby, 3 vols. Set. 18.95 (ISBN 0-88172-061-5); 6.95 ea. Believers Bkshelf.
--Notes & Comments on Scripture, 7 vols. Set. 30.00 (ISBN 0-88172-068-2); 4.95 ea. Believers Bkshelf.
--Notes & Jottings on Scripture. 5.95 (ISBN 0-88172-069-0). Believers Bkshelf.
--Synopsis of the Books of the Bible, 5 vols. Set. 27.50 (ISBN 0-88172-070-4). Believers Bkshelf.
Darby, John. Dressed to Kill: Cartoonists & the Northern Ireland Conflict. (Illus.). 132p. 1983. pap. 9.95 (ISBN 0-904651-91-6, Pub. by Appletree Pr). Irish Bks Media.
--Hell on Hill. (McLeane's Rangers Ser.: No. 3). 1984. pap. 2.50 (ISBN 0-8217-1343-4). Zebra.
--Target Rabaul. (McLeane's Rangers Ser.: No. 2). 1983. pap. 2.50 (ISBN 0-8217-1271-3). Zebra.
Darby, John & Williamson, Arthur. Violence & the Social Services in Northern Ireland. (Studies in Social Policy & Welfare). 1978. text ed. 24.00x (ISBN 0-435-82261-6). Gower Pub Co.
Darby, John, ed. Northern Ireland: The Background to the Conflict. LC 83-4114. (Irish Studies). 176p. 1983. text ed. 32.00x (ISBN 0-8156-2298-8). Syracuse U Pr.
Darby, John F. Personal Recollections of Many Prominent People Whom I Have Known. facsimile ed. LC 75-94. (Mid-American Frontier Ser.). 1975. Repr. of 1880 ed. 36.50x (ISBN 0-405-06860-3). Ayer Co Pubs.
Darby, John J., ed. Speech Evaluation in Psychiatry. (Illus.). 416p. 1980. 46.00 (ISBN 0-8089-1315-8, 790977). Grune.
Darby, John, Jr., ed. Speech & Language: Childhood Disorders. 1985. write for info (ISBN 0-8089-1720-X, 790979). Grune.
--Speech & Language Evaluation in Neurology: Adult Disorders. 1985. write for info (ISBN 0-8089-1719-6, 790976). Grune.
Darby, John K. Speech Evaluation in Medicine. 464p. 1981. 45.00 (ISBN 0-8089-1359-X, 790978). Grune.
Darby, Joseph J., tr. from Ger. Alternative Draft of a Penal Code for the Federal Republic of Germany. (American Ser. of Foreign Penal Codes: Vol. 21). xvi, 157p. 1977. text ed. 17.50x (ISBN 0-8377-0041-8). Rothman.
Darby, Joseph R., jt. auth. see Sears, J. Kern.
Darby, Ken. The Brownstone House of Nero Wolfe. 192p. 1983. 14.45i (ISBN 0-316-17280-4). Little.
Darby, Michael. John Pollard Seddon. (Illus.). 176p. 24.95 (ISBN 0-905209-41-9, Pub. by Victoria & Albert Mus UK). Faber & Faber.
Darby, Michael, et al. The Victoria & Albert Museum: England's Treasury of the World's Finest Decorative Arts. LC 83-3544. (Illus.). 384p. 1983. 40.00 (ISBN 0-670-74590-1, Studio). Viking.
Darby, Michael R. Effects of Social Security on Income & the Capital Stock. 1979. pap. 4.25 (ISBN 0-8447-3329-6). Am Enterprise.
--Labor Force, Employment & Productivity in Historical Perspective. (Monograph & Research Ser.: No. 37). 151p. 1984. 7.00 (ISBN 0-89215-121-8). U Cal LA Indus Rel.
Darby, Michael R. & Melvin, Michael T. Intermediate Macroeconomics. 1985. text ed. 28.95x (ISBN 0-673-15999-X). Scott F.
Darby, Michael R., et al. The International Transmission of Inflation. LC 83-5785. (National Bureau of Economic Research Monograph). (Illus.). 727p. 1984. lib. bdg. 69.00x (ISBN 0-226-13641-8). U of Chicago Pr.
--The International Transmission of Inflation. LC 83-5785. (National Bureau of Economic Research-Monograph). (Illus.). xvi, 728p. 1985. text ed. 22.50x (ISBN 0-226-13642-6). U of Chicago Pr.
Darby, Padraig L., et al. Anorexia Nervosa: Recent Developments in Research. LC 82-17990. (Neurology & Neurobiology: Vol. 3). 472p. 1983. 96.00 (ISBN 0-8451-2702-0). A R Liss.
Darby, Paul H., jt. auth. see Bauer, Royal D.
Darby, Ronald. Viscoelastic Fluids: An Introduction to Properties & Behavior. (Chemical Processing & Engineering Ser.: Vol. 9). 1976. pap. 99.75 (ISBN 0-8247-7128-1). Dekker.
Darby, Tom. The Feast: Meditations on Politics & Time. 256p. 1982. 30.00x (ISBN 0-8020-5578-8). U of Toronto Pr.
Darby, W. J., ed. Food: the Gift of Osiris. 1977. Vol. 1. 69.50 (ISBN 0-12-203401-5); Vol.2. 69.50 (ISBN 0-12-203402-3). Acad Pr.
Darby, W. J., et al, eds. Annual Review of Nutrition, Vol. 1. (Illus.). 1981. text ed. 20.00 (ISBN 0-8243-2801-9). Annual Reviews.
--Annual Review of Nutrition, Vol. 2. (Illus.). 1982. text ed. 22.00 (ISBN 0-8243-2802-7). Annual Reviews.
--Annual Review of Nutrition, Vol. 3. (Illus.). 1983. 27.00 (ISBN 0-8243-2803-5). Annual Reviews.
Darby, William. A Tour from the City of New York to Detroit in the Michigan Territory, Made Between the Second of May & the 22nd of September, 1818, Etc. 1977. Repr. 49.00x (ISBN 0-403-07894-6). Scholarly.
Darby, William J., jt. auth. see Patwardhan, Vinayak N.
Darby, William J., et al, eds. Annual Review of Nutrition, Vol. 4. (Illus.). 610p. 1984. text ed. 27.00 (ISBN 0-8243-2804-3). Annual Reviews.
Darby, William O. & Baumer, William H. We Led the Way. 240p. 1985. pap. 3.50 (ISBN 0-515-08253-8). Jove Pubns.
Darbyshire, Alfred. Art of the Victorian Stage. LC 76-91898. 1907. 18.00 (ISBN 0-405-08429-3, Pub. by Blom). Ayer Co Pubs.
Darbyshire, J. F., jt. ed. see Tinsley, J.
D'Arcais, G. B., jt. auth. see Levelt, W. J.
D'Arcangelo, B. F., et al. Mathematics for Plumbers & Pipe Fitters. 3rd rev. ed. (Applied Mathematics Ser.). (Illus.). 244p. 1982. pap. text ed. 10.20 (ISBN 0-8273-1291-1); instr's. guide 4.20 (ISBN 0-8273-1292-X). Delmar.
D'Arcangelo, Bartholomew, et al. Blueprint Reading for Plumbers: Residential & Commercial. rev. ed. LC 78-24844. (Blueprint Reading Ser.). (gr. 7). 1980. pap. text ed. 14.80 (ISBN 0-8273-1367-5); instr's. guide 4.80 (ISBN 0-8273-1368-3). Delmar.
Darch, Colin, ed. Africa Index to Continental Periodical Literature: Covering 1979-1980, Vols. 4 & 5. 375p. 1983. lib. bdg. 62.00 (ISBN 0-905450-09-4). K G Saur.
--Africa Index to Continental Periodical Literature: 1981, Vol. 6. 240p. 1985. lib. bdg. 40.00 (ISBN 3-598-21823-0). K G Saur.
Darch, Colin, compiled by. Tanzania. (World Bibliographical Ser.: No. 54). 318p. 1985. lib. bdg. 48.50 (ISBN 0-903450-91-7, Pub. by Clio Press England). ABC-Clio.
D'Arco, John A., Jr. The Product of My Thought. LC 82-91042. 54p. 1983. 7.95 (ISBN 0-533-05590-3). Vantage.
D'Arcy & Griffin. Drug Induced Emergencies. 398p. 1980. pap. 26.00 (ISBN 0-7236-0522-X). PSG Pub Co.
D'Arcy, Barbara. Bloomingdale's Book of Home Decorating. LC 73-4064. (Illus.). 264p. 1973. 15.95i (ISBN 0-06-010948-3, HarpT). Har-Row.
Darcy, C. P. The Encouragement of the Fine Arts in Lancashire, 1760-1860. 1977. 22.00 (ISBN 0-7190-1330-5, Pub. by Manchester Univ Pr). Longwood Pub Group.
Darcy, Clare. Allegra. 1976. pap. 1.95 (ISBN 0-451-09611-8, J9611, Sig). NAL.
--Caroline & Julia. LC 81-51969. 192p. 1982. 10.95 (ISBN 0-8027-0694-0). Walker & Co.
--Caroline & Julia. 224p. 1983. pap. 2.50 (ISBN 0-451-12008-6, AE2008, Sig). NAL.
--Cecily. 1984. Repr. of 1972 ed. cancelled (ISBN 0-8027-0381-X); pap. 5.95 (ISBN 0-8027-7274-9). Walker & Co.
--A Clare Darcy Trilogy. 1979. 14.95 (ISBN 0-8027-0627-4). Walker & Co.
--Cressida. 1978. pap. 1.75 (ISBN 0-451-08287-7, E8287, Sig). NAL.
--Cressida. LC 77-73662. 1977. 8.95 (ISBN 0-8027-0575-8). Walker & Co.
--Elyza. (YA) (RL 9). 1977. pap. 2.25 (ISBN 0-451-11023-4, AE1023, Sig). NAL.
--Elyza. LC 75-36245. 288p. 1976. 8.95 (ISBN 0-8027-0516-2). Walker & Co.
--Eugenia. (YA) (RL 9). 1978. pap. 2.50 (ISBN 0-451-11274-1, AE1274, Sig). NAL.
--Georgina. 274p. 1984. Repr. of 1971 ed. cancelled (ISBN 0-8027-0348-8); pap. 5.95 (ISBN 0-8027-7278-1). Walker & Co.
--Lady Pamela. 1977. pap. 2.25 (ISBN 0-451-09900-1, E9900, Sig). NAL.
--Letty. 1981. pap. 2.25 (ISBN 0-451-09810-2, E9810, Sig). NAL.
--Lydia, or Love in Town. 256p. 1974. pap. 1.75 (ISBN 0-451-08272-9, E8272, Sig). NAL.
--Regina. 1978. pap. 2.50 (ISBN 0-451-11113-3, AE1113, Sig). NAL.
--Rolande. 1979. pap. 1.95 (ISBN 0-451-08552-3, J8552, Sig). NAL.
--Rolande. LC 77-85242. 1978. 8.95 (ISBN 0-8027-0588-X). Walker & Co.
--Victoire. LC 73-90389. 288p. 1974. 7.95 (ISBN 0-8027-0443-3). Walker & Co.
D'Arcy, Eithene. Irish Crochet Lace. (Illus.). 64p. 1985. pap. 11.95 (ISBN 0-85219-615-6, Pub. by Batsford England). David & Charles.
D'Arcy, Ella. Modern Instances. LC 82-49094. (Degeneration & Regeneration Ser.). 250p. 1984. lib. bdg. 30.00 (ISBN 0-8240-5552-7). Garland Pub.
--Monochromes. Fletcher, Ian & Stokes, John, eds. LC 76-20056. (Decadent Consciousness Ser.). 1978. lib. bdg. 46.00 (ISBN 0-8240-2754-X). Garland Pub.
D'Arcy, Ella, tr. see Maurois, Andre.
Darcy, Emma. Twisting Shadows. (Harlequin Presents Ser.). 192p. 1983. pap. 1.95 (ISBN 0-373-10648-3). Harlequin Bks.
D'Arcy, G. Minot. Investment Counsel. 1964. 6.95 (ISBN 0-8392-1052-3). Astor-Honor.
D'Arcy, Gordon. Guide to the Birds of Ireland. 176p. Date not set. 15.00 (ISBN 0-88072-030-1, Pub. by Tanager). Longwood Pub Group.
Darcy, Laura, compiled by. The Webster's New World Dictionary of Computer Terms. Date not set. price not set. S&S.
D'Arcy, Margaretta. Tell Them Everything: A Sojourn in the Prison of HM Queen Elizabeth II at Ard Macha (Armagh) 127p. (Orig.). 1981. pap. 3.95 (ISBN 0-86104-349-9). Pluto Pr.
D'Arcy, Margaretta & Arden, John. The Non-Stop Connolly Show, Nos. 1 & 2. (The Non-Stop Connolly Show Ser.). 64p. (Orig.). 1981. Part 1: Boyhood 1868-1889. pap. 5.95 (ISBN 0-904383-80-6, NO. 4123). Part 2: Apprenticeship 1889-1896. Pluto Pr.
--The Non-Stop Connolly Show, No. 4. (Non-Stop Connolly Show Ser.). 87p. (Orig.). 1981. pap. 5.95 (ISBN 0-904383-82-2). Pluto Pr.
--The Non-Stop Connolly Show: Professional 1986-1903, No. 3. (Non-Stop Connolly Show Ser.). 77p. (Orig.). 1981. pap. 5.95 (ISBN 0-904383-81-4, NO. 4141). Pluto Pr.
--The Non-Stop Connolly Show: The Great Lockout, 1910-1914, No. 5. (Non-Stop Connolly Show Ser.). 112p. (Orig.). 1981. pap. 5.95 (ISBN 0-904383-83-0). Pluto Pr.
--The Non-Stop Connolly Show: World War & the Rising, No. 6. (Non-Stop Connolly Show Ser.). 128p. (Orig.). 1981. pap. 5.95 (ISBN 0-904383-84-9, NO. 4144). Pluto Pr.
--Vandaleur's Folly: An Anglo-Irish Melodrama. 96p. 1981. pap. 6.95 (ISBN 0-413-48540-4, NO. 3507). Methuen Inc.
D'Arcy, Margaretta, jt. auth. see Arden, John.
D'Arcy, Martin C. Communism & Christianity. 1957. 10.00 (ISBN 0-8159-5208-2). Devin.
--The Meeting of Love & Knowledge: Perennial Wisdom. LC 78-23621. 1979. Repr. of 1957 ed. lib. bdg. 18.75x (ISBN 0-313-21145-0, DAME). Greenwood.
--The Nature of Belief. facsimile ed. (Select Bibliographies Reprint Ser). Repr. of 1931 ed. 21.00 (ISBN 0-8369-5930-2). Ayer Co Pubs.
--Of God & Man. 1967. pap. 1.25x (ISBN 0-268-00197-9). U of Notre Dame Pr.
--Revelation & Love's Architecture. 90p. 1976. 8.00 (ISBN 0-89182-010-8). Charles River Bks.
--The Sense of History. LC 73-16797. 309p. 1974. Repr. of 1959 ed. lib. bdg. 16.25x (ISBN 0-8371-7230-6, DASE). Greenwood.
D'Arcy, Martin S. The Nature of Belief. LC 72-10693. 236p. 1976. Repr. of 1958 ed. lib. bdg. 18.50x (ISBN 0-8371-6616-0, DANB). Greenwood.
D'Arcy, Mary R. The Saints of Ireland. 241p. 1985. pap. 8.95 (ISBN 0-9614900-0-4). Irish Am Cult.
D'Arcy, P. F. Latrogenic Diseases. 2nd ed. (Illus.). 1979. text ed. 67.50x (ISBN 0-19-264179-4). Oxford U Pr.
D'Arcy, P. F. & Griffin, J. P. Iatrogenic Diseases: Annual Updates. 2nd ed. Incl. Update 1981. (Illus.). 1981. text ed. 69.00x (ISBN 0-19-261263-8); Update 1982. 1982. 69.00x (ISBN 0-19-261356-1); Annual Update. D'Arcy, P. F. & Griffin, J. P., eds. 298p. 1983. 69.00x (ISBN 0-19-261399-5). Oxford U Pr.
D'Arcy, Paula. Song for Sarah: A Young Mother's Journey Through Grief, & Beyond. LC 79-14684. 124p. 1979. 6.95 (ISBN 0-87788-778-0); pap. 2.50 (ISBN 0-87788-780-2). Shaw Pubs.
--Where the Wind Begins: Stories of Hurting People Who Said Yes to Life. 144p. 1985. pap. 5.95 (ISBN 0-87788-925-2). Shaw Pubs.
--Where the Wind Begins: Stories of Hurting People. 144p. 1984. 8.95 (ISBN 0-87788-923-6). Shaw Pubs.
Darcy, Robert L. Some Key Outcomes of Vocational Education: A Report on Evaluation Criteria, Standards & Procedures. 75p. 1980. 4.50 (ISBN 0-318-15565-6, RD192). Natl Ctr Res Voc Ed.
D'Arcy, Susan. The Films of Elizabeth Taylor. Castell, David, ed. (The Films of...Ser.). (Illus.). (gr. 7-12). 1978. Repr. of 1974 ed. PLB 6.95 (ISBN 0-912616-83-0). Greenhaven.
--The Films of Liza Minelli. Castell, David, ed. (The Films of...Ser.). (Illus.). (gr. 7-12). 1978. Repr. of 1973 ed. PLB 6.95 (ISBN 0-912616-82-2). Greenhaven.
D'Arcy, W. G., ed. Solanaceae: Biology & Systematics. (Illus.). 608p. 1985. 60.00x (ISBN 0-231-05780-6). Columbia U Pr.
Darcy-Berube, Francoise & Berube, John-Paul. Come, Let Us Celebrate. 64p. (gr. 2-3). 1984. 3.95 (ISBN 0-7773-8007-2, 8514). Winston Pr.
Dard, R. & Farmer, D. Purchasing in the Construction Industry in Great Britain. 1970. 18.00x (ISBN 0-8464-0771-X). Beekman Pubs.
Darden, Carole, jt. auth. see Darden, Norma Jean.
Darden, Carole, jt. auth. see Jean, Norma.
Darden, Ellington. The Athlete's Guide to Sports Medicine. (Illus.). 1981. pap. 8.95 (ISBN 0-8092-7159-1). Contemp Bks.
--Conditioning for Football. LC 77-76074. (Physical Fitness & Sports Medicine Ser). (Illus.). 1978. pap. 4.95 (ISBN 0-89305-011-3). Anna Pub.
--The Darden Technique For Weight Loss, Body Shaping & Slenderizing. 256p. 1982. 10.95 (ISBN 0-671-44228-7, Fireside). S&S.
--Especially for Women. 2nd ed. LC 82-83949. (Illus.). 224p. 1983. pap. 9.95 (ISBN 0-88011-118-6). Leisure Pr.
--High-Intensity Bodybuilding. 192p. (Orig.). 1984. 11.95 (ISBN 0-399-51103-2, Perigee). Putnam Pub Group.
--How to Lose Body Fat. LC 77-75768. (Physical Fitness & Sports Medicine Ser.). (Illus.). 1977. pap. 4.95 (ISBN 0-89305-012-1). Anna Pub.
--How Your Muscles Work: Featuring Nautilus Training Equipment. Darden, Ellington, ed. LC 77-75757. (Physical Fitness & Sports Medicine Ser.). (Illus.). 1977. pap. 3.95 (ISBN 0-89305-010-5). Anna Pub.
--The Nautilus Advanced Bodybuilding Book. (Illus.). 256p. 1984. pap. 9.95 (ISBN 0-671-49246-2, Fireside). S&S.
--The Nautilus Bodybuilding Book. (Illus.). 256p. 1982. pap. 8.95 (ISBN 0-8092-5815-3). Contemp Bks.
--The Nautilus Book. rev. ed. (Illus.). 288p. 1985. pap. 9.95 (ISBN 0-8092-5416-6); pap. 119.40 12-copy prepack (ISBN 0-8092-5251-1). Contemp Bks.
--The Nautilus Book: An Illustrated Guide to Physical Fitness the Nautilus Way. (Illus.). 1980. 12.95 (ISBN 0-8092-7100-1). Contemp Bks.
--The Nautilus Handbook for Young Athletes. Barish, Wendy, ed. (Illus.). 128p. (Orig.). (gr. 3 up). 1984. pap. 7.95 (ISBN 0-671-49688-3). Wanderer Bks.
--The Nautilus Nutrition Book. (Illus.). 352p. 1981. pap. 9.95 (ISBN 0-8092-5890-0). Contemp Bks.
--The Nautilus Woman: For a Slimmer, Stronger, Sexier Body. (Illus.). 192p. 1983. 8.95 (ISBN 0-671-46126-5, Fireside). S&S.
--No More Fat. (Illus.). 80p. 1983. 5.95 (ISBN 0-671-49245-4, Fireside). S&S.
--Nutrition & Athletic Performance. 1976. pap. 7.95 (ISBN 0-87095-058-4). Borden.
--Nutrition & Athletics Performance. LC 76-10811. 1975. pap. 7.95 (ISBN 0-87095-058-4). Athletic.
--Nutrition for Athletes. LC 77-76070. (Physical Fitness & Sports Medicine Ser.). 1978. pap. 3.95 (ISBN 0-89305-014-8). Anna Pub.
--Olympic Athletes Ask Questions About Exercise & Nutrition. (Physical Fitness & Sports Medicine Ser.). pap. 2.95 (ISBN 0-89305-007-5). Anna Pub.
--Power Racquetball Featuring PST. LC 80-84215. (Illus.). 128p. (Orig.). 1981. pap. text ed. 4.95 (ISBN 0-918438-65-9). Leisure Pr.
--Strength-Training Principles. LC 77-75746. (Physical Fitness & Sports Medicine). (Illus.). 1977. pap. 3.95 (ISBN 0-89305-006-7). Anna Pub.
--The Superfitness Handbook. (Illus.). 1979. 12.95 (ISBN 0-89313-016-8). G F Stickley Co.
--Your Guide to Physical Fitness. (Illus.). 144p. 1982. 10.95 (ISBN 0-89313-053-2). G F Stickley.
Darden, Ellington, jt. auth. see Jones, Terri.
Darden, Ellington, jt. auth. see Pansonby, David.
Darden, Ellington, ed. see Allman, Fred L., Jr.
Darden, Ellington, ed. see Key, James.
Darden, Ellington, ed. see Key, James D.
Darden, Genevieve M., ed. My Dear Husband. LC 80-50605. (Illus.). 96p. 1980. 11.95 (ISBN 0-88492-036-4). W S Sullwold.
Darden, Joe T., ed. The Ghetto: Readings with Interpretations. (National University Publications, Interdisciplinary Urban Ser.). 1981. 19.50x (ISBN 0-8046-9277-7, Pub. by Kennikat). Assoc Faculty Pr.
Darden, Norma Jean & Darden, Carole. Spoonbread & Strawberry Wine: Recipes & Reminiscences of a Family. LC 77-82620. 1978. 15.95 (ISBN 0-385-12468-6, Anchor Pr). Doubleday.
Darden, Robert F. Drawing Power: Knott, Ficklen, & McClanahan, Editorial Cartoonists of the Dallas Morning News. LC 81-86546. (Illus.). 106p. 1983. 19.95 (ISBN 0-918954-37-1). Baylor Univ Pr.
Darden, W. R. & Lusch, R. F., eds. Patronage Behavior & Retail Management. 512p. 1983. 42.00 (ISBN 0-444-00704-0, North-Holland). Elsevier.
Darden, William R., jt. ed. see Lusch, Robert F.
Darden, Wm. R. & Monroe, Kent B., eds. AMA Winter Educators' Conference 1983, Proceedings: Research Methods & Causal Modeling in Marketing. LC 83-3713. (Illus.). 278p. (Orig.). 1983. pap. text ed. 22.00 (ISBN 0-87757-162-7). Am Mktg.
Dardenne, Marilyn. CFE Annual Report: 1983. (Illus.). 25p. (Orig.). Date not set. pap. write for info. (ISBN 0-86599-015-8). Ctr Educ Res.
D'Ardenne, S. R. & Doboson, E. J., eds. Siente Katerine: Re-Edited from Ms Bodley 34 & Other Manuscripts. (Early English Text Soc. Ser. Supplementary Texts). 1981. text ed. 47.50x (ISBN 0-19-722407-5). Oxford U Pr.
Dardess, John. Conquerors & Confucians: Aspects of Political Change in Late Yuan China. LC 72-13308. (Studies in Oriental Culture Ser.). 245p. 1973. 29.00x (ISBN 0-231-03689-2). Columbia U Pr.

Dardess, John W. Confucianism & Autocracy: Professional Elites in the Founding of the Ming Dynasty. LC 82-4822. 400p. 1983. text ed. 38.50x (ISBN 0-520-04659-5); pap. 12.50x (ISBN 0-520-04733-8). U of Cal Pr.

Dardess, Margaret B., jt. ed. see Aoki, Michiko Y.

Dardig, Jill C. & Heward, William L. Sign Here: A Contracting Book for Children & Their Parents. 2nd ed. LC 76-18757. (Illus.). 166p. 1981. pap. 10.00 (ISBN 0-917472-04-7); leader's manual 3.00 (ISBN 0-914474-27-8). F Fournies.

Dardik, H. Arterial Reconstruction in the Lower Extremity. 384p. 1985. price not set (ISBN 0-07-015351-5). McGraw.

Dardik, Irving & Waitley, Denis. Quantum Fitness: Breakthrough to Excellence. 1984. 12.70 (ISBN 0-671-50903-9). PB.

Dardis, Tom. Harold Lloyd: The Man on the Clock. 1983. 19.75 (ISBN 0-670-45227-0). Viking.

--Harold Lloyd: The Man on the Clock. 1984. pap. 10.95 (ISBN 0-14-007555-0). Penguin.

--Keaton: The Man Who Wouldn't Lie Down. (Illus.). 352p. 1980. pap. 4.95 (ISBN 0-14-005701-3). Penguin.

--Some Time in the Sun. 1981. pap. 5.95 (ISBN 0-14-005831-1). Penguin.

Dardjowidjojo, Soenjono. Sentence Patterns of Indonesian. LC 78-6687. (Pali Language Texts: Indonesia). 447p. 1978. pap. text ed. 17.50x (ISBN 0-8248-0418-X). UH Pr.

--Vocabulary Building in Indonesian: An Advanced Reader. LC 82-90652. (Monographs in International Studies, Southeast Asia: No. 64). 660p. 1984. pap. text ed. 18.00x (ISBN 0-89680-118-7, Ohio U Ctr Intl). Ohio U Pr.

Dare, Bernie. Running & Your Body: Applying Physiology to Track Training. (Illus., Orig.). 1980. pap. 8.00 (ISBN 0-911520-92-9). Tafnews.

Dareer, Asma El. Woman, Why Do You Weep? Circumcision & Its Consequences. (Illus.). 144p. 1983. 19.95x (ISBN 0-86232-098-4, Pub. by Zed Pr England); pap. 8.95x (ISBN 0-86232-099-2). Biblio Dist.

Darell-Brown, Susan. The Mississippi. LC 78-62982. (Rivers of the World Ser.). (Illus.). 68p. 1978. PLB 13.96 (ISBN 0-382-06204-3). Silver.

Dar El Mashreq. Arabic-English Students Dictionary. (Arabic & Eng.). 1974. 15.00x (ISBN 2-7214-2107-7). Intl Bk Ctr.

Daremberg, Charles. La Medecine: Histoire & Doctrines. 2nd ed. LC 75-13257. (History of Ideas in Ancient Greece Ser.). (Fr.). 1976. Repr. of 1865 ed. 32.00x (ISBN 0-405-07300-3). Ayer Co Pubs.

Darey-Bembe, Francoise & Bembe, John P. Day by Day with God. 1982. 4.95 (ISBN 0-8215-9908-9). Sadlier.

Darga, Bert. The Executive Sourcebook. (Illus.). 288p. 1985. 17.95 (ISBN 0-671-47772-2). S&S.

Dargan, E. Preston & Weinberg, Bernard. The Evolution of Balzac's "Comedie Humaine". LC 72-91802. 441p. 1973. Repr. of 1942 ed. lib. bdg. 23.50 (ISBN 0-8154-0452-2). Cooper Sq.

Dargan, E. Preston, jt. auth. see Nitze, William A.

Dargan, Edwin C. History of Preaching, 2 Vols. 1965. lib. bdg. 47.00 (ISBN 0-8337-0772-8). B Franklin.

Dargan, Edwin P. The Aesthetic Doctrine of Montesquieu, Its Application in His Writings. (Research & Source Works Ser: No. 181). 1968. Repr. of 1907 ed. 22.50 (ISBN 0-8337-0769-8). B Franklin.

Dargan, James F. My Experiences in Service, or a Nine Months Man. Tanis, Norman E., ed. (American Classics Facsimile Ser.: Pt. I). 416p. 1974. pap. 10.00 (ISBN 0-937048-00-3). CSUN.

Dargan, Joan. Balzac & the Drama of Perspective. LC 85-80419. (French Forum Monographs: No. 60). 175p. 1985. pap. 12.50x (ISBN 0-917058-61-5). French Forum.

Dargan, Marion. Guide to American Biography, 2 vols. in 1. LC 73-13455. 1973. Repr. of 1949 ed. lib. bdg. 24.75x (ISBN 0-8371-7134-2, DAAB). Greenwood.

Dargan, Olive, pseud. Highland Animals. LC 72-6081. (Short Story Index Reprint Ser.). Repr. of 1925 ed. 19.00 (ISBN 0-8369-4207-8). Ayer Co Pubs.

Dargaud, Joseph. The Eucharist in the Life of St. Margaret Mary. pap. 3.50 (ISBN 0-686-74585-X, 101-21). Prow Bks-Franciscan.

D'Argence, Rene. Asian Art: San Francisco Collections. (Great Centers of Art Ser.). (Illus.). 1978. 35.00 (ISBN 0-8390-0199-1, Allanheld & Schram). Abner Schram Ltd.

D'Argencourt, Louise, jt. ed. see Druick, Douglas.

Dargie, E. Mary. Music & Poetry in the Songs of Gustav Mahler. (European University Studies, German Language & Literature: Ser. 1, Vol. 401). 350p. 1981. pap. 34.70 (ISBN 3-261-04864-6). P Lang Pubs.

Dargo, George. Jefferson's Louisiana: Politics & the Clash of Legal Traditions. LC 74-25036. (Studies in Legal History). 272p. 1974. text ed. 17.50x (ISBN 0-674-47370-1). Harvard U Pr.

--Law in the New Republic. LC 82-21224. (Borzoi Books in Law & American Society). 1983. 15.00 (ISBN 0-394-33581-3, KnopfC); pap. 6.95 (ISBN 0-394-33197-4). Knopf.

--Public Power & Privatization: Legal Change in the New Republic. (Law & American Society Ser.). 170p. 1980. pap. text ed. 6.95 (ISBN 0-394-33197-4, RanC). Random.

Dargyay, Eva. Tibetan Village Communities: Structure & Change. 112p. 1982. pap. text ed. 29.50x (ISBN 0-85668-151-2, Pub. by Aris & Phillips England). Humanities.

Dargyay, Eva M. The Rise of Esoteric Buddhism in Tibet. 1977. 14.00 (ISBN 0-8426-0915-6, Pub by Molilal Banarsidass India). Orient Bk Dist.

Darian, Mujana. St. Francis & You. LC 79-88515. (gr. 1-4). 1979. pap. 4.95 (ISBN 0-87973-363-2). Our Sunday Visitor.

Darian, Steven G. English As a Foreign Language: History, Development, & Methods of Teaching. LC 76-177332. 1972. 16.50x (ISBN 0-8061-1005-8). U of Okla Pr.

--The Ganges in Myth & History. LC 77-21374. (Illus.). 236p. 1978. text ed. 12.00x (ISBN 0-8248-0509-7). UH Pr.

D'Ariano, Regina & D'Ariano, Roy. Italo-American Ballads, Poems, Lyrics & Melodies. 1975. 10.00 (ISBN 0-87012-207-X). McClain.

D'Ariano, Roy, jt. auth. see D'Ariano, Regina.

Darian-Smith, Ian. The Nervous System: Section 1, Vol. III: Sensory Processes. 1244p. 1984. 275.00 (ISBN 0-683-01108-1). Waverly Pr.

Darien, Peter. Darien's World: Liveright Edition. (Illus.). 1964. 4.00 (ISBN 0-912156-02-3). Masterwork Pr.

--Darien's World: Oriole Edition, 10 Vols. 1961. 37.00, boxed set (ISBN 0-912156-01-5). Masterwork Pr.

--Ecliptic: College Edition. 1969. pap. 2.00 (ISBN 0-912156-00-7). Masterwork Pr.

Darien-Smith, I., jt. ed. see Goodwin, A. W.

D'Arienzo, Camille, jt. auth. see Willis, Edgar E.

D'Arienzo, Raymond V. & Moracco, John C. Stress in Teaching: A Comparison of Perceived Occupational Stress Factors Between Special Education & Regular Classroom Teachers. 158p. (Orig.). 1982. lib. bdg. 24.00 (ISBN 0-8191-1874-5); pap. text ed. 11.00 (ISBN 0-8191-1875-3). U Pr of Amer.

Da Rif, Andrea. The Blueberry Cake That Little Fox Baked. LC 84-444. (Illus.). 32p. (ps-3). 1984. 10.95 (ISBN 0-689-50307-5, McElderry Bk). Atheneum.

Darilek, Richard E. A Loyal Opposition in Time of War: The Republican Party & the Politics of Foreign Policy from Pearl Harbor to Yalta. LC 75-44655. (Contributions in American History: No.49). 288p. (Orig.). 1976. lib. bdg. 29.95 (ISBN 0-8371-8773-7, DLO/). Greenwood.

DaRin, Doris. Sean O'Casey. LC 75-10107. (Literature and Life Ser.). 228p. 1977. 13.95 (ISBN 0-8044-2136-6). Ungar.

Darin-Drabkin, H. Land Policy & Urban Growth. LC 76-39912. 1977. text ed. 28.00 (ISBN 0-08-020401-5). Pergamon.

Darin-Drabkin, H., jt. auth. see Tuma, Elias H.

Darin-Drabkin, Haim, jt. auth. see Lichfield, Nathaniel.

Daringer, Helen F. Adopted Jane. LC 47-30260. (Illus.). 225p. (gr. 3-7). 1973. pap. 1.25 (ISBN 0-15-602950-2, VoyB). HarBraceJ.

Daringer, Helen F. & Eaton, Anne T., eds. Poet's Craft. LC 72-8284. (Granger Index Reprint Ser). (Illus.). 1972. Repr. of 1935 ed. 21.00 (ISBN 0-8369-6385-7). Ayer Co Pubs.

Dario, Rafaela Contreras de. Short Stories. LC 65-21263. (Hispanic-American Studies Ser: No. 20). (Orig., Span.). 1965. pap. 2.00 (ISBN 0-87024-040-4). U of Miami Pr.

Dario, Rafaela Contreras Del see Dario, Rafaela Contreras de.

Dario, Ruben. Eleven Poems of Ruben Dario: Bilingual Edition. Walsh, Thomas & DeLa Selva, Salomon, trs. 1977. lib. bdg. 59.95 (ISBN 0-8490-1758-0). Gordon Pr.

--El Mundo De los Suenos. (Coleccion Mente y Palabra). 6.25 (ISBN 0-8477-0502-1); pap. 5.00 (ISBN 0-8477-0503-X). U of PR Pr.

Darion, Joe & Wasserman, Dale. Man of La Mancha. 1966. 9.95 (ISBN 0-394-40621-4); pap. 4.95 (ISBN 0-394-40619-2). Random.

Darion, Joe, jt. auth. see Leigh, Mitch.

Darison, W. Phillips, et al. Mass Media: Systems & Effects. 2nd ed. 1982. pap. text ed. 19.95 (ISBN 0-03-052481-4). HR&W.

Darisse, Alan, jt. auth. see Archibald, John.

Darity, Maxine. Dark of the Day. 1978. pap. 1.75 (ISBN 0-532-17188-8). Woodhill.

Darity, William A., Jr. & Horn, Bobbie L. The Loan Pushers. 240p. 1986. professional reference 29.95 (ISBN 0-88730-067-7). Ballinger Pub.

Darity, William, Jr., ed. Labor Economics. 1984. lib. bdg. 39.50 (ISBN 0-89838-086-3). Kluwer Nijhoff.

Darius, Jon. Beyond Vision: One Hundred Historic Scientific Photographs. LC 84-4405. (Illus.). 1984. 29.95 (ISBN 0-19-853245-8). Oxford U Pr.

Darius, Robert G., et al, eds. Gulf Security into the Nineteen Eighties: Perceptual & Strategic Dimensions. (Publication Ser.: No. 291). xii, 134p. 1984. lib. bdg. 21.95 (ISBN 0-8179-7911-5); pap. 10.95 (ISBN 0-8179-7912-3). Hoover Inst Pr.

Dark, Harris E., ed. see Leigh, Bob, et al.

Dark, Harry & Dark, Phyl. The Greatest Ozarks Guidebook. 2nd ed. LC 79-7733. 272p. (Orig.). 1980. pap. 7.95 (ISBN 0-936120-00-2). Greatest Graphics.

Dark, Philip J. An Illustrated Catalogue of Benin Art. 1982. lib. bdg. 68.00 (ISBN 0-8161-0382-8, Hall Library). G K Hall.

Dark, Phyl, jt. auth. see Dark, Harry.

Dark, Robert. Dried Fruit: Natural Goodness All the Year Round. (Natures Way Ser.). 128p. 1983. pap. 1.95 (ISBN 0-7225-0682-1). Thorsons Pubs.

Dark, S. Charles Dickens. LC 75-38650. (Studies in Dickens, No. 52). 1976. lib. bdg. 39.95x (ISBN 0-8383-2113-5). Haskell.

Dark, Sandra. The House on the Prairie. (Orig.). 1979. pap. 2.25 (ISBN 0-532-23318-2). Woodhill.

Dark, Sheila L., jt. auth. see Schultz, Judithm.

Dark, Sidney. Books & the Man. 1973. Repr. of 1921 ed. 15.00 (ISBN 0-8274-1649-0). R West.

--Charles Dickens. 123p. 1980. Repr. of 1919 ed. lib. bdg. 20.00 (ISBN 0-8495-1124-0). Arden Lib.

--Charles Dickens. LC 72-13466. 1973. lib. bdg. 12.50 (ISBN 0-8414-1200-6). Folcroft.

--Five Deans. facsimile ed. LC 71-93332. (Essay Index Reprint Ser.). 1928. 18.00 (ISBN 0-8369-1285-3). Ayer Co Pubs.

--Five Deans: John Colet, John Donne, Jonathan Swift, Arthur Penrhyn Stanley & William Ralph Inge. LC 70-86011. (Essay & General Literature Index Reprint Ser.). 1969. Repr. of 1928 ed. 20.50x (ISBN 0-8046-0555-6, Pub. by Kennikat). Assoc Faculty Pr.

--London Town. 1976. 20.00 (ISBN 0-8495-1131-3). Arden Lib.

--Newman. LC 73-7641. 1934. lib. bdg. 10.00 (ISBN 0-8414-1870-5). Folcroft.

--The Outline of H. G. Wells. LC 74-1050. 1973. Repr. of 1922 ed. lib. bdg. 15.00 (ISBN 0-8414-3719-X). Folcroft.

--Robert Louis Stevenson. LC 76-173849. (English Literature Ser., No. 33). 1971. Repr. of 1924 ed. lib. bdg. 49.95x (ISBN 0-8383-1343-4). Haskell.

--Seven Archbishops. Repr. of 1944 ed. 25.00 (ISBN 0-686-19840-9). Ridgeway Bks.

--Twelve Bad Men. facs. ed. LC 68-54343. (Essay Index Reprint Ser). 1929. 20.00 (ISBN 0-8369-0361-7). Ayer Co Pubs.

--Twelve Masters of English Prose. 1973. 20.00 (ISBN 0-8274-1643-1). R West.

--Twelve More Ladies. facs. ed. LC 70-86744. (Essay Index Reprint Ser). 1932. 18.00 (ISBN 0-8369-1177-6). Ayer Co Pubs.

--Twelve Royal Ladies. facsimile ed. LC 73-99689. (Essay Index Reprint Ser.). 1929. 24.50 (ISBN 0-8369-1459-7). Ayer Co Pubs.

Dark, Sidney & Grey, Rowland. W. S. Gilbert: His Life & Letters. LC 76-177509. (Illus.). Repr. of 1923 ed. 20.00 (ISBN 0-405-08430-7, Blom Pubns). Ayer Co Pubs.

--W. S. Gilbert, His Life & Letters. LC 71-164210. 1971. Repr. of 1923 ed. 40.00x (ISBN 0-8103-3789-4). Gale.

Darke, Jo. Colourful Britain. (Illus.). 80p. 1982. 9.95 (ISBN 0-7134-3821-5, Pub. by Batsford England). David & Charles.

--Colourful Britain. LC 82-78. (Batsford Colour Bks.). (Illus.). 80p. 1984. 9.95 (ISBN 0-7134-3821-5, Pub. by Batsford England). Larousse.

--Cornish Landscapes. (Illus.). 64p. 1983. 12.50 (ISBN 0-7134-4187-9, Pub. by Batsford England). David & Charles.

--Lake District Landscapes. (Illus.). 64p. 1983. 12.50 (ISBN 0-7134-4185-2, Pub. by Batsford England). David & Charles.

--South Coast Landscapes. (Illus.). 64p. 1983. 12.50 (ISBN 0-7134-4189-5, Pub. by Batsford England). David & Charles.

--Yorkshire Landscapes. (Illus.). 64p. 1983. 12.50 (ISBN 0-7134-4183-6, Pub. by Batsford England). David & Charles.

Darke, Nick. The Body. (Royal Shakespeare Company Playtext Ser.). 48p. 1983. pap. 4.95 (ISBN 0-413-53340-9, NO.3902). Methuen Inc.

Darkenwald, Gordon G. & Merriam, Sharan B. Adult Education: Foundations of Practice. 260p. 1982. scp 22.80 (ISBN 0-690-01541-0, HarpC). Har-Row.

Darkenwald, Gordon G., jt. auth. see Beder, Harold W.

Darkenwald, Gordon G. & Knox, Alan B., eds. Meeting Educational Needs of Young Adults. LC 83-82723. (Continuing Education Ser.: No. 21). 1984. pap. text ed. 8.95x (ISBN 0-87589-991-9). Jossey-Bass.

Darker, Rober. Photographic Know-How. (Illus.). 248p. 1980. pap. text ed. 9.95 (ISBN 0-85242-504-X, 3504). Morgan.

Darker, Roger W. Make the Most of Your Pictures. (Photographer's Library Ser.). (Illus.). 168p. 1982. pap. 15.95 (ISBN 0-240-51112-3). Focal Pr.

Darkes, Anna S. How to Make & Use Overhead Transparencies. LC 77-7888. (Illus.). 1977. pap. 3.95 (ISBN 0-8024-3652-8). Moody.

Darkov, A. & Kuznetsov, V. Structural Mechanics. Lachinov, B., tr. (Russian Monographs). 704p. 1969. 186.25 (ISBN 0-677-20830-8). Gordon.

Darkwah, R. H. Menelik of Ethiopia. (African Historical Biographies Ser.). 1972. pap. text ed. 2.75x (ISBN 0-435-94466-5). Heinemann Ed.

Darkwah, R. H. Kofi see Kofi Darkwah, R. H.

Darlaston, Pam, ed. Presents: One Hundred Ideas to Make at Home. (Illus.). 140p. 1982. 19.95 (ISBN 0-7153-8213-6). David & Charles.

Darley, Alex. Passionists of the Southwest: A Revelation of the Penitentes. LC 68-57290. (Beautiful Rio Grande Classics Ser.). 134p. 1983. lib. bdg. 10.00 (ISBN 0-87380-020-6). Rio Grande.

Darley, Frederic L. & Millikan, Clark H., eds. Brain Mechanisms Underlying Speech & Language. LC 67-13316. (Illus.). 272p. 1967. 45.00 (ISBN 0-8089-0111-7, 7909-78). Grune.

Darley, Frederic L., jt. ed. see Keith, Robert L.

Darley, Frederick L. Aphasia. (Illus.). 285p. 1982. 27.95 (ISBN 0-7216-2879-6). Saunders.

Darley, Frederick L., et al. Audio Seminars in Motor Speech Disorders. 1975. pap. 65.00 incl. cassettes (ISBN 0-7216-9892-1). Saunders.

--Motor Speech Disorders. LC 74-25475. (Illus.). 304p. 1975. text ed. 30.00 (ISBN 0-7216-2878-8). Saunders.

Darley, George. George Darley (Seventeen Ninety-Five to Eighteen Forty-Six) Reiman, Donald H., ed. LC 75-31193. (Romantic Context Ser.: Poetry 1789-1830). 1978. lib. bdg. 60.00 (ISBN 0-8240-2144-4). Garland Pub.

Darley, H. C., jt. auth. see Gray, George.

Darley, Henry A. Slaves & Ivory: A Record of Adventure & Exploration in the Unknown Sudan, & Among the Abbyssinia Slave-Raiders. LC 73-99366. (Illus.). xvii, 219p. 1972. Repr. of 1926 ed. lib. bdg. 12.00 (ISBN 0-8411-0037-3). Metro Bks.

--Slaves & Ivory in Abyssinia. LC 77-92741. Repr. of 1935 ed. 19.75x (ISBN 0-8371-1753-4, DAI&). Greenwood.

Darley, John M., jt. auth. see Latane, Bibb.

Darley, John M., et al. Psychology. 2nd ed. (Illus.). 672p. 1984. text ed. 29.95 (ISBN 0-13-733147-9); By Gordon J. Hodge. study guide with practice tests 9.95. P-H.

Darley, Lionel S. Introduction to Bookbinding. (Illus.). 118p. 1977. pap. 7.95 (ISBN 0-571-11082-7). Faber & Faber.

Darley, W. Marshall. Algal Biology: A Physiological Approach. (Illus.). 176p. 1982. pap. text ed. 15.60x (ISBN 0-632-00608-0). Blackwell Pubns.

Darline, R., jt. auth. see Robinson, James H.

Darling. Essentials of Medical Astrology. 12.00 (ISBN 0-86690-004-7). Am Fed Astrologers.

--With Love from Darling's Kitchen. 1982. pap. 9.95 (ISBN 0-930440-17-X). Royal Hse.

Darling, Ada. Antique Jewelry. (Illus.). 200p. 1953. 20.00 (ISBN 0-87282-022-X). CHB-ALF.

Darling, Arthur B. Our Rising Empire 1763-1803. vi, 595p. 1972. Repr. of 1940 ed. 28.00 (ISBN 0-208-01278-8, Archon). Shoe String.

Darling, Bruce, tr. see Tanaka, Ichimatsu.

Darling, Charles W., ed. The New American Songster: Traditional Ballads & Songs of North America. (Illus.). 398p. (Orig.). 1983. lib. bdg. 27.75 (ISBN 0-8191-3396-5); pap. text ed. 14.75 (ISBN 0-8191-3397-3). U Pr of Amer.

Darling, Dale & Van Dyck, Julia. The Airtight Woodstove Cookbook. 128p. (Orig.). 1981. pap. 7.95 (ISBN 0-931790-26-3). Brick Hse Pub.

Darling, David J. Comets, Meteors & Asteroids: Rocks in Space. (Discovering Our Universe Ser.). (Illus.). 64p. (gr. 4 up). 1984. PLB 9.95 (ISBN 0-87518-264-X). Dillon.

--Diana: The People's Princess. (Taking Part Bks.). (Illus.). 72p. (gr. 3 up). 1984. PLB 8.95 (ISBN 0-87518-282-8). Dillon.

--The Galaxies: Cities of Stars. (Discovering Our Universe Ser.). (Illus.). 64p. (gr. 4 up). 1985. PLB 9.95 (ISBN 0-87518-285-2). Dillon.

--The Moon: A Spaceflight Away. (Discovering Our Universe Ser.). (Illus.). 64p. (gr. 4 up). 1984. PLB 9.95 (ISBN 0-87518-262-3). Dillon.

--The New Astronomy: An Ever-Changing Universe. (Discovering Our Universe Ser.). (Illus.). 64p. (gr. 4 up). 1985. PLB 9.95 (ISBN 0-317-13806-5). Dillon.

--Other Worlds: Is There Life Out There? (Discovering Our Universe Ser.). (Illus.). 64p. (gr. 4 up). 1985. PLB 9.95 (ISBN 0-87518-287-9). Dillon.

--The Planets: The Next Frontier. (Discovering Our Universe Ser.). (Illus.). 64p. (gr. 4 up). 1984. PLB 9.95 (ISBN 0-87518-263-1). Dillon.

--The Stars: From Birth to Black Hole. (Discovering Our Universe Ser.). (Illus.). 64p. (gr. 4 up). 1985. PLB 9.95 (ISBN 0-87518-284-4). Dillon.

--The Sun: Our Neighborhood Star. (Discovering Our Universe Ser.). (Illus.). 64p. (gr. 4 up). 1984. PLB 9.95 (ISBN 0-87518-261-5). Dillon.

--The Universe: Past, Present & Future. (Discovering Our Universe Ser.). (Illus.). 64p. (gr. 4 up). 1985. PLB 9.95 (ISBN 0-87518-286-0). Dillon.

--Where Are We Going in Space? (Discovering Our Universe Ser.). (Illus.). 64p. (gr. 4 up). 1984. PLB 9.95 (ISBN 0-87518-265-8). Dillon.

Darling, Donald B. Radiography of Infants & Children: A Problem Oriented Manual of Radiographic & Fluoroscopic Procedures. 3rd ed. (Illus.). 584p. 1979. 76.50x (ISBN 0-398-03740-X). C C Thomas.

Darling, Edward. Three Old Timers of Cape Cod. (Illus.). 1974. 5.00 (ISBN 0-87482-034-0). Wake-Brook.

Darling, Erik & Riker, Tom. Chords for Guitar. LC 79-9702. (Illus.). 1980. pap. 6.95 (ISBN 0-02-870410-X). Schirmer Bks.

Darling, F. F. Naturalist on Rona: Essays of a Biologist in Isolation. LC 42-5414. Repr. of 1939 ed. 12.00 (ISBN 0-527-21400-0). Kraus Repr.

Darling, F. Fraser, jt. auth. see Leopold, A. Starker.

Darling, Frank C. Thailand & the United States. 1965. 12.00 (ISBN 0-8183-0212-7). Pub Aff Pr.

--The Westernization of Asia: A Comparative Political Analysis. 1979. lib. bdg. 23.00 (ISBN 0-8161-9005-4, Univ Bks). G K Hall.
--The Westernization of Asia: A Comparative Political Analysis. 526p. 1980. pap. text ed. 9.95x (ISBN 0-87073-971-9). Schenkman Bks Inc.
Darling, Harold, jt. ed. see Neumeyer, Peter.
Darling, Harold W. Man in His Right Mind. 158p. 1977. pap. 5.95 (ISBN 0-85364-097-1). Attic Pr.
Darling, J., jt. auth. see Rhodius, H.
Darling, J. L. Outclassing the Competition: What You Must Know if You Weren't Born Rich. LC 83-83211. (Illus.). 350p. 1984. 17.95 (ISBN 0-9612414-0-3). Foxcroft Pub.
Darling, J. S., ed. Colonial Keyboard Tunes. LC 80-12691. 24p. 1980. pap. 2.00 (ISBN 0-87935-055-5). Williamsburg.
Darling, James S., ed. A Jefferson Music Book. LC 76-30510. 42p. 1977. pap. 2.95 (ISBN 0-87935-044-X). Williamsburg.
--Little Keyboard Book. LC 71-165364. 16p. 1972. pap. 2.00 (ISBN 0-910412-93-6). Williamsburg.
Darling, James S., ed. see Bremner, Robert.
Darling, Jan. Outclassing the Competition: The Up-&-Comer's Guide to Social Survival. 1985. 14.95 (ISBN 0-312-59127-6). St Martin.
Darling, Jay N. As Ding Saw Hoover. Henry, John M., ed. LC 54-11723. pap. 34.80 (ISBN 0-317-10499-3, 2000454). Bks Demand UMI.
Darling, Joan. Tyler's Folly. (To Have & to Hold Ser.: No. 45). 192p. 1984. pap. 1.95 (ISBN 0-317-13334-9). Jove Pubns.
Darling, Joan, jt. auth. see Shaw, Evelyn.
Darling, John. The Guide to Commodore 64 Software. (Illus.). 160p. (Orig.). 1984. pap. 11.95 (ISBN 0-246-12561-6, Pub. by Granada England). Sheridan.
--Sea Anglers' Guide to Britain & Ireland. 160p. 1982. 60.00x (ISBN 0-7188-2509-8, Pub. by Lutterworth Pr England); pap. 40.00x (ISBN 0-7188-2510-1). State Mutual Bk.
Darling, John R., jt. auth. see Lipson, Harry A.
Darling, Jon, jt. auth. see Darling, Rosalyn B.
Darling, Karen. Weight No More. 120p. 1984. pap. 5.95 (ISBN 0-931432-18-9). Whatever Pub.
Darling, Kathy. Ants Have Pets. LC 77-9079. (For Real Ser.). (Illus.). (gr. 1-6). 1977. PLB 7.47 (ISBN 0-8116-4305-0). Garrard.
--Bug Circus. LC 76-17021. (For Real Bks.). (Illus.). (gr. 2-5). PLB 7.47 (ISBN 0-8116-4301-8). Garrard.
--The Easter Bunny's Secret. LC 78-58521. (Mystery Ser.). (Illus.). (gr. k-3). 1978. PLB 7.59 (ISBN 0-8116-6405-8). Garrard.
--Jack Frost & the Magic Paint Brush. LC 76-14465. (Imagination Ser.). (Illus.). (gr. k-5). 1977. lib. bdg. 7.47 (ISBN 0-8116-4402-2). Garrard.
--The Jelly Bean Contest. LC 72-3450. (Venture Ser.). (Illus.). 64p. (gr. 2). 1972. PLB 7.68 (ISBN 0-8116-6970-X). Garrard.
--Little Bat's Secret. LC 74-8175. (Venture Ser.). (Illus.). 64p. (gr. 2). 1974. PLB 7.68 (ISBN 0-8116-6975-0). Garrard.
--The Mystery in Santa's Toyshop. LC 77-19090. (Mystery Ser.). (Illus.). (gr. k-3). 1978. PLB 7.59 (ISBN 0-8116-6402-3). Garrard.
--Paul & His Little-Big Dog. LC 77-22267. (For Real Ser.). (Illus.). (gr. k-4). 1977. PLB 7.47 (ISBN 0-8116-4307-7). Garrard.
--Pecos Bill Finds a Horse. LC 79-12079. (American Folktales Ser.). (Illus.). (gr. 2-5). 1979. PLB 7.47 (ISBN 0-8116-4047-7). Garrard.
Darling, Kathy & Freed, Debbie. Games Gorillas Play. LC 76-17324. (For Real Bks.). (Illus.). 40p. (gr. k-3). 1976. PLB 7.47 (ISBN 0-8116-4302-6). Garrard.
Darling, Kathy, jt. auth. see Cobb, Vicki.
Darling, Louise, ed. Handbook of Medical Library Practice, Vol. II. 4th ed. 368p. 1983. 27.50 (ISBN 0-912176-14-8); Set. write for info. (ISBN 0-912176-12-1). Med Lib Assn.
--Handbook of Medical Library Practice, Vol. 1. 4th ed. 344p. 1982. 22.50 (ISBN 0-912176-11-3). Med Lib Assn.
Darling, Lowell. One Hand Shaking: A California Campaign Diary. LC 79-3345. 224p. 1980. pap. 5.95 (ISBN --15-668747-X, Harv). HarBraceJ.
Darling, Malcolm L. The Punjab Peasant in Prosperity & Debt. rev. ed. Dewey, Clive, ed. 1978. 14.00x (ISBN 0-8364-0070-4). South Asia Bks.
Darling, Pamela W. & Webster, Duane E. Preservation Planning Program, an Assisted Self-Study Manual for Libraries. 117p. 1982. 15.00 (ISBN 0-318-03507-3); resource notebook 35.00. Assn Res Lib.
Darling, Renny. Beverly Hills Party Planner. (Illus.). 1985. pap. write for info. (ISBN 0-930440-20-X). Royal Hse.
--Cordon Red, White, & Blue: The Great New American Cuisine. (Illus.). 1981. pap. 9.95 (ISBN 0-930440-15-3). Royal Hse.
--Easiest & Best Coffee Cakes & Quick Breads. (Illus.). 1985. pap. 9.95 (ISBN 0-930440-19-6). Royal Hse.
--Great Beginnings & Happy Endings: Hors D'Oeuvres & Desserts for Standing Ovations. (Illus., Orig.). 1979. pap. 9.95 (ISBN 0-930440-11-0). Royal Hse.
--The Joy of Eating: A Simply Delicious Cookbook. LC 76-27499. (Illus.). 1976. pap. 9.95 (ISBN 0-930440-00-5). Royal Hse.
--The Joy of Eating French Food: Great French Dishes Made Easy. 1980. pap. 8.95 (ISBN 0-930440-05-6). Royal Hse.
--The Joy of Entertaining: Renny Darling's Party Planner. LC 78-53363. 1978. 15.95 (ISBN 0-930440-10-2); pap. 9.95 (ISBN 0-930440-08-0). Royal Hse.
--The Love of Eating: Two-Minute Breads & Other Culinary Magic. LC 77-85732. (Illus.). 1977. pap. 9.95 (ISBN 0-930440-01-3). Royal Hse.
--Renny Darling's Diet Gourmet: The Yes, Yes, Yes Cookbook. (Illus.). 1982. pap. 9.95 (ISBN 0-930440-16-1). Royal Hse.
--Renny Darling's Party Planner. (Illus.). 1978. 15.95 (ISBN 0-930440-02-1); pap. 9.95 (ISBN 0-930440-03-X). Royal Hse.
--Selections from "the Joy of Eating". 1978. pap. 2.25 (ISBN 0-930440-07-2). Royal Hse.
--Sugar & Spice & Everything Nice. (Illus.). 1981. pap. 9.95 (ISBN 0-930440-14-5). Royal Hse.
--Sweet Dreams: My Greatest Desserts. (Illus.). 1980. pap. 9.95 (ISBN 0-930440-13-7). Royal Hse.
Darling, Rosalyn B. & Darling, Jon. Children Who Are Different: Meeting the Challenges of Birth Defects in Society. LC 81-18727. 316p. 1982. pap. text ed. 12.95 (ISBN 0-8016-1227-6). Mosby.
Darling, Sharon S. Chicago Ceramics & Glass: An Illustrated History from 1871 to 1933. LC 79-91566. (Illus.). xiv, 222p. 1980. 25.00 (ISBN 0-913820-10-5). Chicago Hist.
--Chicago Ceramics & Glass: An Illustrated History, 1871-1933. LC 79-91566. (Illus.). 240p. 1980. 25.00 (ISBN 0-317-04003-0, 10414-1). U of Chicago pr.
--Chicago Furniture: Art, Craft & Industry 1833-1983. LC 83-25522. (Illus.). 416p. 1984. 50.00 (ISBN 0-393-01818-0). Norton.
Darling, Sharon S. & Casterline, Gail F. Chicago Metalsmiths. (Illus.). 1977. 15.00 (ISBN 0-913820-06-7). Chicago Hist.
--Chicago Metalsmiths. LC 77-76503. (Illus.). 1977. 15.00 (ISBN 0-226-80781-9, 10412-5). U of Chicago Pr.
Darling, Sharon S., jt. auth. see Chicago Historical Society Staff.
Darling, Verah H. & Thorpe, Margaret R. Ophthalmic Nursing. 2nd ed. (Illus.). 200p. 1981. pap. 15.95 (ISBN 0-7216-0821-3, Pub. by Bailliere-Tindall). Saunders.
Darling-Hammond, Linda & Marks, Ellen L. The New Federalism in Education: State Responses to the 1981 Education Consolidation & Improvement Act. LC 83-136421. xvii, 86p. 1983. write for info. (ISBN 0-8330-0491-3). Rand Corp.
Darlington, Beth, ed. The Love Letters of William & Mary Wordsworth. LC 81-67177. (The Cornell Wordsworth Ser.). (Illus.). 248p. 1981. 27.50 (ISBN 0-8014-1261-7). Cornell U Pr.
Darlington, Beth, ed. see Wordsworth, William.
Darlington, C. D. Chromosome Botany & the Origins of Cultivated Plants. rev. ed. 1973. 18.95x (ISBN 0-02-843670-9). Hafner.
--Teaching Genetics. 1965. 7.50 (ISBN 0-8022-0340-X). Philos Lib.
Darlington, C. D. & Lewis, K. R., eds. Chromosomes Today, Vol. 2. LC 65-5655. 275p. 1969. 30.00x (ISBN 0-306-37662-8, Plenum Pr). Plenum Pub.
Darlington, C. LeRoy & Eigenfeld, Neil. The Chemical World: Activities & Explorations. LC 76-4597. (Illus.). 1977. text ed. 20.20 (ISBN 0-395-24070-0); tchr's annotated ed. 24.68 (ISBN 0-395-24071-9). HM.
Darlington, Henry T. Mosses of Michigan. LC 64-25250. (Bulletin Ser.: No. 47). (Illus.). 212p. 1964. text ed. 9.00x (ISBN 0-87737-024-9). Cranbrook.
Darlington, Ida, ed. London Consistory Court Wills, 1492-1547. 1967. 50.00x (ISBN 0-686-96603-1, Pub by London Rec Soc England). State Mutual Bk.
Darlington, Jeanie. Grow Your Own. 1971. pap. 1.75 (ISBN 0-394-71520-9, V520, Dist. by Random). Bookworks.
Darlington, Mansur. BSA Pre-unit Singles '54 - '61. new ed. (Owners Workshop Manuals Ser.: No. 326). 1979. 10.50 (ISBN 0-85696-326-7, Pub. by J H Haynes England). Haynes Pubns.
--Gilera 50: Mopeds '72 Thru '78. (Illus.). pap. 10.50 (ISBN 0-85696-257-0, 257). Haynes Pubns.
--Honda CB CJ 250 & 360 Twins '74 - '78. (Owners Workshop Manuals Ser.: No. 291). 1979. 10.50 (ISBN 0-85696-291-0, Pub. by J H Haynes England). Haynes Pubns.
--Honda NC50 & NA50 Express. (Illus.). pap. 10.50 (ISBN 0-85696-453-0, 453). Haynes Pubns.
--Honda 125 Elsinore & MR175 '73 - '76. (Owners Workshop Manuals Ser.: No. 312). 1979. 10.50 (ISBN 0-85696-312-7, Pub. by J H Haynes England). Haynes Pubns.
--Husqvarna Competition Models '72 - '75. (Owners Workshop Manuals Ser.: No. 221). 1979. 10.50 (ISBN 0-85696-221-X, Pub. by J H Haynes England). Haynes Pubns.
--Moto-Guzzi 750, 850 & 1000 V-Twins '74 - '78. (Owners Workshop Manuals Ser.: No. 339). 1979. 10.50 (ISBN 0-85696-339-9, Pub. by J H Haynes England). Haynes Pubns.
--Mobylette Motobecane Mopeds '66 - '76: '65 Thru '76. (Haynes Owners Workshop Manuals: No. 258). 1976. 10.50 (ISBN 0-85696-258-9, Pub by J H Haynes England). Haynes Pubns.
--Suzuki GS400 & GS425 Twins '77 - '79. pap. 10.50 (ISBN 0-85696-415-8, 415). Haynes Pubns.
--Suzuki GT750 (3-cyl) Models '71 - '77. new ed. (Owners Workshop Manuals Ser.: No. 302). 1979. 10.50 (ISBN 0-85696-302-X, Pub. by J H Haynes England). Haynes Pubns.
--Suzuki Trail Bikes 90 Thru 400cc's '71-'79. new ed. (Owners Workshop Manuals Ser.: No. 218). 1979. 10.50 (ISBN 0-85696-520-0, Pub. by J H Haynes England). Haynes Pubns.
--Yamaha RD400 Twin '76 - '79. (Owners Workshop Manuals Ser.: No. 333). 1977. 10.50 (ISBN 0-85696-548-0, Pub. by J H Haynes England). Haynes Pubns.
--Yamaha Trail Bikes 250, 360 & 400 '68 - '79. new ed. (Owners Workshop Manuals Ser.: No. 263). 1980. 10.50 (ISBN 0-85696-519-7, Pub. by J H Haynes England). Haynes Pubns.
--Yamaha Trail Bikes '72 - '79. (Owners Workshop Manuals Ser.: No. 210). 1981. 10.50 (ISBN 0-85696-661-4, Pub. by J H Haynes England). Haynes Pubns.
--Yamaha XS250, 360 & 400 Twins '77-'79. (Owners Workshop Manual Ser.). 10.50 (ISBN 0-85696-378-X, 378). Haynes Pubns.
--Yamaha XS750 (3-cyl) Models '76 - '81. (Owners Workshop Manuals Ser.: No. 340). 1978. 10.50 (ISBN 0-85696-712-2, Pub. by J H Haynes England). Haynes Pubns.
--Yamaha XT, TT, & SR 500 Singles '75-'79. pap. 10.50 (ISBN 0-85696-342-9, 342). Haynes Pubns.
Darlington, Mansur & Cox, Penny. Honda CX500 V-Twins: '78 on. pap. 10.50 (ISBN 0-85696-713-0, 442). Haynes Pubns.
Darlington, Mansur & Paul, Rik. Suzuki GS550 & GS750 Fours. pap. 10.50 (ISBN 0-85696-946-X, 363). Haynes Pubns.
Darlington, Mansur & Rogers, Chris. Honda GL1000 Gold Wing '75 - '80. (Owners Workshop Manuals Ser.: No. 309). 1981. 10.50 (ISBN 0-85696-710-6, Pub. by J H Haynes England). Haynes Pubns.
Darlington, Mary C., ed. Fort Pitt & Letters from the Frontier. LC 72-106087. (First American Frontier Ser). (Illus.). 1971. Repr. of 1892 ed. 22.00 (ISBN 0-405-02842-3). Ayer Co Pubs.
--History of Col. Henry Bouquet & the Western Frontiers of Pennsylvania, 1747-1764. LC 75-106121. (First American Frontier Ser). (Illus.). 1971. Repr. of 1920 ed. 23.50 (ISBN 0-405-02841-5). Ayer Co Pubs.
Darlington, P. J. Evolution for Naturalists: The Simple Principles & Complex Reality. LC 79-22897. 262p. 1980. 32.50x (ISBN 0-471-04783-X, Pub. by Wiley-Interscience). Wiley.
Darlington, Philip J., Jr. Zoogeography. LC 79-26913. 690p. 1980. Repr. of 1957 ed. lib. bdg. 38.50 (ISBN 0-89874-109-2). Krieger.
Darlington, Richard B. Radicals & Squares: Statistical Methods for the Behavioral Sciences. 1975. 20.00 (ISBN 0-918610-01-X); autotutorial wrkbk. & supplementary chapters 6.25 (ISBN 0-918610-02-8). Logan Hill.
Darlington, Sandy. Buzz: New York in the Fifties. LC 80-69533. 160p. (Orig.). 1981. pap. 3.50 (ISBN 0-9604152-1-1). Arrowhead Pr.
Darlington, Sandy, ed. see De Vegh, Elizabeth.
Darlington, Sandy, ed. see DeVegh, Elizabeth.
Darlington, Sandy, ed. see De Vegh, Elizabeth.
Darlington, Sandy, ed. see Dranow, Ralph.
Darlington, Thomas. The Folk-Speech of South Cheshire. (English Dialect Society Publications Ser.: No. 53). pap. 45.00 (ISBN 0-317-15952-6). Kraus Repr.
Darlington, W. A. J. M. Barrie. LC 73-20391. (English Literature Ser., No. 33). 1974. lib. bdg. 39.95x (ISBN 0-8383-1768-5). Haskell.
--Sheridan. LC 74-7188. (Studies in Drama, No. 39). 1974. lib. bdg. 39.95x (ISBN 0-8383-1926-2). Haskell.
Darlington, William A. Literature in the Theatre, & Other Essays. facs. ed. LC 68-16924. (Essay Index Reprint Ser.). 1925. 17.00 (ISBN 0-8369-0362-5). Ayer Co Pubs.
--Through the Fourth Wall. facs. ed. LC 68-16925. (Essay Index Reprint Ser). 1922. 17.00 (ISBN 0-8369-0363-3). Ayer Co Pubs.
--The World of Gilbert & Sullivan. 21.00 (ISBN 0-8369-5573-0, 6637). Ayer Co Pubs.
Darlington, William M., ed. Christopher Gist's Journals. LC 65-27166. 296p. Repr. of 1893 ed. 19.50 (ISBN 0-405-03671-X). Ayer Co Pubs.
D'Arlon, Ben, jt. auth. see Cagno, Michael.
Darlow, Denys. Musical Instruments. (Junior Ref. Ser). (Illus.). (gr. 6 up). 1980. 8.95 (ISBN 0-7136-2043-9). Dufour.
Darlow, Michael & Hodson, Gillian. Terence Rattigan: The Man & His Work. 25.00 (ISBN 0-7043-2160-2, Pub. by Quartet England). Charles River Bks.
--Terence Rattigan: The Man & His Work. (Illus.). 360p. pap. 12.95 (ISBN 0-7043-3401-1, Pub. by Quartet Bks). Merrimack Pub Cir.
Darmady, E. M. & MacIver, A. Renal Pathology. LC 79-42838. (Postgraduate Pathology Ser.). 560p. 1980. 119.95 (ISBN 0-407-00119-0). Butterworth.
Darmesteter. The Life of Ernest Renan. 1898. Repr. 25.00 (ISBN 0-8274-2884-7). R West.
Darmesteter, Arsene, jt. auth. see Hatzfeld, Adophe.
Darmesteter, J. & Mills, L. H., trs. Zend-Avesta, 3 vols. Repr. 95.00 (ISBN 0-87902-154-3). Orientalia.
Darmesteter, James. English Studies. Darmesteter, Mary, tr. LC 72-3420. (Essay Index Reprint Ser.). Repr. of 1896 ed. 20.00 (ISBN 0-8369-2896-2). Ayer Co Pubs.
--English Studies (the French Revolution & Wordsworth - the Life of George Eliot - George Eliot's Letters - Irish Literature & Ossian) 1896. Repr. 25.00 (ISBN 0-8274-2270-9). R West.
--Selected Essays. facsimile ed. Jastrow, Morris, Jr., ed. LC 70-37149. (Essay Index Reprint Ser). Repr. of 1895 ed. 21.50 (ISBN 0-8369-2492-4). Ayer Co Pubs.
Darmesteter, James & Mills, L. H. The Zend-Avesta, 3 vols. 1974. lib. bdg. 300.00 (ISBN 0-87968-509-3). Krishna Pr.
Darmesteter, James, tr. Zend-Avesta: Selections. 1984. pap. 5.95 (ISBN 0-916411-41-9, Near Eastern). Holmes Pub.
Darmesteter, Mary. Froissart. Poynter, E. Frances, tr. from Fr. 150p. 1983. Repr. of 1895 ed. lib. bdg. 65.00 (ISBN 0-686-47424-4). Century Bookbindery.
--Froissart. Poynter, E. Frances, tr. from French. 150p. 1983. Repr. of 1895 ed. lib. bdg. 50.00 (ISBN 0-89760-147-5). Telegraph Bks.
Darmesteter, Mary, tr. see Darmesteter, James.
D'Arms, John H. Commerce & Social Standing in Ancient Rome. LC 80-25956. (Illus.). 224p. 1981. text ed. 20.00x (ISBN 0-674-14475-9). Harvard U Pr.
D'Arms, John H. & Eadie, John W., eds. Ancient & Modern: Essays in Honor of Gerald F. Else. LC 77-76612. 234p. (Orig.). 1977. pap. 10.00 (ISBN 0-915932-04-0). Trillium Pr.
Darmstadter & Landsberg. Energy Today & Tomorrow: Living with Uncertainty. (Illus.). 240p. 1983. 25.95 (ISBN 0-13-277640-5). P-H.
Darmstadter, Joel. Conserving Energy: Prospects & Opportunities in the New York Region. LC 75-15414. pap. 30.00 (ISBN 0-317-26459-1, 2023795). Bks Demand UMI.
Darmstadter, Joel & Alterman, Jack. How Industrial Societies Use Energy: A Comparative Analysis. 300p. 1977. 22.50 (ISBN 0-8018-2041-3). Resources Future.
Darmstadter, Joel & Teitelbaum, Perry D. Energy in the World Economy: A Statistical Review of Trends in Output Trade & Consumption Since 1925. 888p. 1972. 35.00 (ISBN 0-8018-1282-8). Resources Future.
Darmstadter, Joel, jt. auth. see Lareau, Thomas J.
Darmstadter, Joel, et al. Energy in the World Economy: A Statistical Review of Trends in Output, Trade, & Consumption Since 1925. LC 70-155848. (Resources for the Future Ser). (Illus.). 888p. 1972. 35.00x (ISBN 0-8018-1282-8). Johns Hopkins.
--How Industrial Societies Use Energy: A Comparative Analysis. LC 77-83780. (Resources for the Future Ser.). (Illus.). 300p. 1978. text ed. 22.50x (ISBN 0-8018-2041-3). Johns Hopkins.
--Energy Today & Tomorrow: Living with Uncertainty, A Book From Resources For The Future. 1983. pap. 13.95 (ISBN 0-13-277632-4). P-H.
Darmstadter, Neil. Truck Driver Training Manual. 91p. 1981. pap. text ed. 4.50 (ISBN 0-88711-008-8). Am Trucking Assns.
Darmstaedter, Ludwig. Naturforscher und Erfinder. (Illus.). 1926. 16.00 (ISBN 0-384-10840-7). Johnson Repr.
Darnall, D. W. & Wilkins, R. G., eds. Methods for Determining Metal Ion Environments in Proteins: Structure & Functions of Metalloproteins. (Advances in Inorganic Biochemistry Ser.: Vol. 2). 324p. 1980. 45.50 (ISBN 0-444-00349-5, Biomedical Pr). Elsevier.
Darnall, Jean. Heaven, Here I Come. LC 77-91521. 1978. pap. 2.95 (ISBN 0-88419-148-6). Creation Hse.
Darnall, Margarett J., jt. auth. see Pickens, Buford.
Darnall, William H. The Epson Connection: Apple. (Illus.). 1984. pap. text ed. 16.95 (ISBN 0-8359-1750-9). Reston.
Darnay, Arsen. A Hostage for Hinterland. 256p. 1980. pap. 2.25 (ISBN 0-345-28959-5). Ballantine.
Darnay, Brigitte T., ed. Directory of Special Libraries & Information Centers, Vol. 1: Special Libraries & Information Centers in the United States & Canada, 2 vols. 9th ed. LC 82-6068. 1700p. 1985. Set. 320.00x (ISBN 0-8103-1888-1). Gale.
--Directory of Special Libraries & Information Centers, Vol. 2: Geographic & Personnel Indexes. 9th ed. LC 82-6068. 900p. 1985. 265.00x (ISBN 0-8103-1889-X). Gale.
--National Directory of Newsletters & Reporting Services, Pts. 5-8. 2nd ed. Incl. Pt. 5. 1983; Pt. 6. 1984; Pt. 7. 1984; Pt. 8. 1985. Set. pap. 120.00x (ISBN 0-8103-0677-8). Gale.
--New Special Libraries. 9th ed. (Directory of Special Libraries & Information Centers Ser.: Vol. 3). 500p. 1985. pap. 275.00x (ISBN 0-8103-0281-0). Gale.

--Subject Directory of Special Libraries. 9th ed. Incl. Vol. I. Business & Law Libraries. 145.00x (ISBN 0-8103-1891-1); Vol. II. Education & Information Libraries. 145.00x (ISBN 0-8103-1892-X); Vol. III. Health Sciences Libraries. 145.00x (ISBN 0-8103-1893-8); Vol. IV. Social Sciences & Humanities Libraries. 145.00x (ISBN 0-8103-1894-6); Vol. V. Science & Technology Libraries. 145.00x (ISBN 0-8103-1895-4). 1985. Set. 625.00x (ISBN 0-8103-1890-3). Gale.

Darnbrough, Ann & Kinrade, Derek. Aids for Living. 256p. 1985. 18.00 (ISBN 0-85941-263-6, Pub. by Woodhead-Faulkner); pap. 11.50 (ISBN 0-85941-264-4). Longwood Pub Group.

--Directory for the Disabled: A Handbook of Information & Opportunities for Disabled & Handicapped People. 2nd ed. 208p. 1980. 27.00x (ISBN 0-85941-106-0, Pub. by Woodhead-Faulkner England); pap. 12.00x (ISBN 0-85941-108-7). State Mutual Bk.

--Directory of Sexual Advisory Services (in Great Britain) 128p. 1980. 24.00x (ISBN 0-85941-162-1, Pub. by Woodhead-Faulkner England); pap. 9.00 (ISBN 0-686-69892-4). State Mutual Bk.

--Fund-Raising & Grant-Aid: A Practical & Legal Guide for Charities & Voluntary Organisations. 160p. 1980. 24.00x (ISBN 0-85941-075-7, Pub. by Woodhead-Faulkner England). State Mutual Bk.

Darnbrough, Ann & Kinrade, Derek, eds. Directory for Disabled People: A Handbook of Information & Opportunities for Disabled & Handicapped People. 4th ed. LC 84-19570. 358p. 1985. pap. 16.50 (ISBN 0-85941-255-5, Pub. by Woodhead-Faulkner). Longwood Pub Group.

--The Sex Directory. 224p. 1985. 22.50 (ISBN 0-85941-162-1, Pub. by Woodhead-Faulkner); pap. 15.95 (ISBN 0-85941-163-X). Longwood Pub Group.

Darnell, A. C., jt. auth. see O'Brien, D. P.

Darnell, A. W. Orchids for the Outdoor Garden: A Descriptive List of the World's Orchids for the Use of Amateur Gardeners. LC 76-23979. (Illus.). 512p. 1976. pap. 7.50 (ISBN 0-486-23406-1). Dover.

--Orchids for the Outdoor Garden: A Descriptive List of the World's Orchids for the Use of Amateur Gardeners. 12.00 (ISBN 0-8446-5497-3). Peter Smith.

--Unfamiliar Flowers for Your Garden. (Illus.). 8.25 (ISBN 0-8446-5176-1). Peter Smith.

Darnell, Ermina J. Forks of Elkhorn Church: With Genealogies of Early Members. LC 79-92437. (Illus.). 322p. 1980. Repr. of 1946 ed. 18.50 (ISBN 0-8063-0883-4). Genealog Pub.

Darnell, Frank & Simpson, Patricia. Rural Education: In Pursuit of Excellence. 244p. 1982. pap. 29.95x (ISBN 0-909751-61-7, Pub. by U of W Austral Pr). Intl Spec Bk.

Darnell, J. E., et al. Molecular Cell Biology. (Illus.). 1248p. 1986. text ed. write for info. (ISBN 0-7167-1448-5). W H Freeman.

Darnell, James H. The Deceit of the Evolutionary Theory of Man & of the Universe. (Great Currents of History Library). (Illus.). 137p. 1982. 56.75 (ISBN 0-89266-349-9). Am Classical Coll Pr.

Darnell, Jane R. Euphonic Mnemonics: Rhyming Your Way to an Outstanding Vocabulary. (Orig.). 1983. pap. 3.95 (ISBN 0-671-49171-7). WSP.

Darnell, Rodger O., et al, eds. Alternatives to Prison: Issues & Options, Criminal Justice Prisons. 100p. 1979. pap. 4.95 (ISBN 0-934936-01-3). U of Iowa Sch Soc Wk.

Darnell, W. H. & Barton, P. J. BASIC Kaypro for Kids. (Illus.). 215p. 1984. pap. 16.95 (ISBN 0-8359-0393-1). Reston.

Darner, Kirt I. How to Find Giant Bucks. LaRocco, Rich, ed. LC 84-50216. (Illus.). 283p. (gr. 5 up). 1984. 20.00 (ISBN 0-9614821-0-9). Walsworth's.

Darnovsky, Marcy, jt. auth. see Emerson, Sandra L.

Darnton, Maida C., tr. see Lucas-Dubreton, J.

Darnton, Robert. The Business of Enlightenment: A Publishing History of the Encyclopedie, 1775-1800. LC 78-23826. (Illus.). 1979. 27.50x (ISBN 0-674-08785-2). Harvard U Pr.

--The Great Cat Massacre. 1985. pap. 7.95 (ISBN 0-394-72927-7, Vin). Random.

--The Great Cat Massacre: And Other Episodes in French Cultural History. LC 83-45251. (Illus.). 300p. 1984. 17.95 (ISBN 0-465-02700-8). Basic.

--The Literary Underground of the Old Regime. LC 82-2918. (Illus.). 288p. 1982. 17.50x (ISBN 0-674-53656-8). Harvard U Pr.

--The Literary Underground of the Old Regime. 272p. 1985. pap. 7.95 (ISBN 0-674-53657-6). HArvard U Pr.

--Mesmerism & the End of the Enlightenment in France. LC 68-25607. (Illus.). 1968. 15.00x (ISBN 0-674-56950-4). Harvard U Pr.

Daroczy, Z., jt. auth. see Aczel, J.

Da Rosa, A. M., jt. auth. see Ibarra, F.

Daroy, E. Vallado. Nobody Gathers Seashells & Gunshells Anymore: Sketches of an Island Town. 203p. 1981. pap. 5.75x (ISBN 0-686-32453-6, Pub. by New Day Philippines). Cellar.

Daroy, Esther V. The Drumbeater & Other Stories. 144p. (Orig.). 1982. pap. 5.00 (ISBN 0-686-37579-3, Pub. by New Day Philippines). Cellar.

D'Aroy, Pat, jt. ed. see Barr, Mary.

Darqyay, Eva. The Rise of Esoteric Buddhism in the Tibet. 272p. 1979. pap. 5.95 (ISBN 0-87728-432-6). Weiser.

Darr, A. Method for Zither. 58p. (Ger.). 1950. pap. 8.00 (ISBN 0-8258-0237-7, 0-630). Fischer Inc NY.

Darr, Ann. Cleared for Landing. LC 78-6640. 1978. pap. 5.95 (ISBN 0-931848-01-6). Dryad Pr.

--Riding with the Fireworks. LC 80-70830. 70p. (Orig.). 1981. pap. 6.95 (ISBN 0-914086-33-2). Alicejamesbooks.

Darr, Jack. How to Test Almost Everything Electronic. LC 66-30560. 1967. 10.95 (ISBN 0-8306-2422-8). TAB Bks.

Darr, K., jt. ed. see Rakich, J.

Darr, P., et al. The Demand for Urban Water. (Studies in Applied Regional Science: No. 6). 1976. pap. 15.50 (ISBN 90-207-0647-0, Pub. by Martinus Nijhoff Netherlands). Kluwer Academic.

Darr, Richard K. A History of the Nashua & Lowell Railroad Corporation, 1835-1880. LC 75-41752. (Companies & Men: Business Enterprises in America). (Illus.). 1976. 34.50x (ISBN 0-405-08069-7). Ayer Co Pubs.

Darrach, Brad. Bobby Fischer vs. the Rest of the World. LC 73-81322. 1975. pap. 2.95 (ISBN 0-8128-1850-4). Stein & Day.

Darracott, J., ed. see Fitzwilliam Museum.

Darracott, Joseph, ed. The First World War in Posters: From the Imperial War Museum, London. (Illus.). 14.50 (ISBN 0-8446-5021-8). Peter Smith.

Darracott, Joseph C., ed. The First World War in Posters. (Illus., Orig.). 1974. pap. 7.95 (ISBN 0-486-22979-3). Dover.

Darragh, Colleen. The Pregnancy Day-By-Day Book. (Illus.). 192p. 1983. 9.57 (ISBN 0-06-015152-8, HarpT). Har-Row.

Darragh, Ida & Elwood, Ann. Lamaze Childbirth: A Handbook for Prepared Childbirth. (Illus.). 136p. 1985. pap. 5.95 (ISBN 0-89529-291-2). Avery Pub.

Darrah, D. D. History & Evolution of Freemasonry. 10.95x (ISBN 0-685-21969-0). Wehman.

Darrah, Delmore D. History & Evolution of Freemasonry. (Illus.). 1951. 12.00 (ISBN 0-685-19479-5). Powner.

Darrah, Lawrence B. Food Marketing. LC 74-175620. pap. 98.80 (ISBN 0-317-26267-X, 2055709). Bks Demand UMI.

Darrah, William C. Cartes De Visite in Nineteenth Century Photography. (Illus.). 222p. 1981. 27.00 (ISBN 0-913116-05-X). W. C. Darrah.

--A Critical Review of the Upper Pennsylvanian Floras of the Eastern United States. LC 74-113602. (Illus.). 224p. 1970. 36.00x (ISBN 0-913116-02-5). W C Darrah.

--Pithole: The Vanished City. LC 72-78194. (Illus.). 260p. 1972. 8.50 (ISBN 0-913116-03-3). W C Darrah.

--The World of Stereographs. LC 77-92123. 246p. 1977. 22.50 (ISBN 0-913116-04-1). W C Darrah.

Darrand, Tom C. & Shupe, Anson D. Metaphors of Social Control in a Pentecostal Sect. LC 83-9006. (Studies in Religion & Society: Vol. 6). 232p. 1984. 49.95x (ISBN 0-88946-870-2). E Mellen.

Darras, Jacques. Joseph Conrad & the West: Signs of Empire. 1982. 28.50x (ISBN 0-389-20071-9). B&N Imports.

Darrel, Lance H., jt. auth. see Dever, William G.

Darrell, Bob, ed. see Robertson, Cliff H.

Darrell, Elizabeth. At the Going Down of the Sun. 503p. 1985. 14.95 (ISBN 0-312-05904-3). St Martin.

Darrell, Jesse, tr. see Steiner, Rudolf.

Darrell, Margery, ed. Once Upon a Time: The Fairy-Tale World of Arthur Rackham. (Illus.). 288p. 1972. 17.95 (ISBN 0-670-52574-X, Studio). Viking.

Darrell, Richard W., ed. Viral Diseases of the Eye. LC 84-7897. (Illus.). 341p. 1985. text ed. 46.50 (ISBN 0-8121-0943-0). Lea & Febiger.

Darretta, John. Vittorio de Sica: A Guide to References & Resources. 384p. (gr. 10-12). 1983. lib. bdg. 50.00 (ISBN 0-8161-8468-2, Hall Reference). G K Hall.

Darrid, Bill. Solomon Moon. 448p. 1985. pap. 3.95 (ISBN 0-345-30356-3). Ballantine.

Darroch, Vivian & Silvers, Ronald J. Interpretive Human Studies: An Introduction to Phenomenological Research. LC 82-13636. 276p. 1983. lib. bdg. 26.75 (ISBN 0-8191-2698-5); pap. text ed. 13.00 (ISBN 0-8191-2699-3). U Pr of Amer.

Darrough, Archie. From Me to You. LC 79-64679. 37p. 1982. 4.95 (ISBN 0-533-04316-6). Vantage.

Darrough, Masako N. & Blank, Robert H., eds. Biological Differences & Social Equality: Implications for Social Policy. (Illus.). 272p. 1983. lib. bdg. 29.95 (ISBN 0-313-23022-6, DAS/). Greenwood.

Darrow, Clarence. Crime & Criminals: An Address Delivered to the Prisoners in the Chicago County Jail. LC 73-77548. 48p. 1975. 12.95 (ISBN 0-88286-044-5); pap. 2.00 (ISBN 0-686-77130-3). C H Kerr.

--Crime, Its Cause & Treatment. LC 70-172562. (Criminology, Law Enforcement, & Social Problems Ser.: No. 148). 320p. (Intro. added). 1972. Repr. of 1922 ed. 22.50x (ISBN 0-87585-143-6). Patterson Smith.

--Infidels & Heretics. 69.95 (ISBN 0-87968-240-X). Gordon Pr.

--A Persian Pearl & Other Essays. LC 74-1199. (American Literature Ser., No. 49). 1974. lib. bdg. 75.00x (ISBN 0-8383-1770-7). Haskell.

--Realism in Literature & Art. 59.95 (ISBN 0-8490-0932-4). Gordon Pr.

--Resist Not Evil. LC 78-172567. (Criminology, Law Enforcement & Social Problems Ser.: No. 148). 200p. (With intro. & index added). 1972. lib. bdg. 10.00 (ISBN 0-87585-148-7); pap. 4.00 (ISBN 0-87585-903-8). Patterson Smith.

--The Skeleton in the Closet. 1936. pap. 3.00 (ISBN 0-8283-1438-1). Branden Pub Co.

Darrow, Clarence & Lewis, Arthur. Darrow-Lewis Debate on the Theory of Non-resistance Evil. 26p. pap. cancelled (ISBN 0-911826-48-3). Am Atheist.

Darrow, Clarence see Drummond, Henry.

Darrow, Clarence S. Resist Not Evil. LC 77-137538. (Peace Movement in America Ser). 179p. 1972. Repr. of 1903 ed. lib. bdg. 12.95x (ISBN 0-89198-065-2). Ozer.

--Verdicts Out of Court. Weinberg, Arthur & Weinberg, Lila, eds. (New Reprints in Essay & General Literature Index Ser.). 1975. Repr. of 1963 ed. 31.00 (ISBN 0-518-10198-3, 10198). Ayer Co Pubs.

Darrow, Clarence S. & Lewis, Arthur M. Marx Versus Tolstoy: A Debate. LC 73-137537. (Peace Movement in America Ser). 124p. 1972. Repr. of 1911 ed. lib. bdg. 10.95x (ISBN 0-89198-066-0). Ozer.

Darrow, Frank M. Cybernetics versus Homeostasis. (Illus.). 42p. 1977. pap. 4.00 (ISBN 0-686-82893-3). Darrow.

--Life Styles & Sex. 68p. (Orig.). 1971. pap. text ed. 3.00 (ISBN 0-912636-02-5). Darrow.

--Sex Ethics for Survival. (Illus.). 1968. pap. text ed. 2.00 (ISBN 0-685-08747-6). Darrow.

Darrow, Ken & Pam, Rick. Appropriate Technology Sourcebook, Vol. 1. rev. ed. LC 76-29526. 1981. 10.50 (ISBN 0-917704-12-6); pap. 5.50 (ISBN 0-917704-08-8); vol. 1 & 2 pap set avail. (ISBN 0-917704-09-6); vol. 1 & 2 cloth set avail. (ISBN 0-917704-13-4). Appropriate Techn Proj.

--Appropriate Technology Sourcebook, Vol. 2. (Illus.). 1981. 11.50 (ISBN 0-917704-11-8); pap. 6.50 (ISBN 0-917704-06-1); vol. 1 & 2 pap set avail. (ISBN 0-917704-09-6); vol. 1 & 2 cloth set avail. (ISBN 0-917704-13-4). Appropriate Techn Proj.

Darrow, Ken, ed. see Thorburn, Craig.

Darrow, Ken, et al. Appropriate Technology Sourcebook, Vol. II. (Illus.). 489p. 1981. 6.50 (ISBN 0-917704-06-1). Appropriate Techn Proj.

Darrow, Kenneth, ed. see Volunteers in Asia.

Darrow, Peter H. & Mestres, Ricardo A. Creative Financing in the 1980's. LC 83-62925. (Corporate Law & Practice Course Handbook Series: No. 432). 1983. write for info. PLI.

Darrow, Ralph C. House Journal Editing. LC 73-93505. x, 249p. 1974. pap. text ed. 5.95x (ISBN 0-8134-1628-0, 1628). Interstate.

Darrow, Robert A., jt. auth. see Benson, Lyman.

Darshana Shakti Ma, ed. see Svami Kripalvananda.

Darsie, M. L. Mental Capacity of American-Born Japanese Children. (Comparitive Psychology Monogr.: Vol. 3, No. 15). pap. 8.00 (ISBN 0-527-24850-9). Kraus Repr.

Darsie, Richard F. & Ward, Ronald A. The Identification & Geographical Distribution of Mosquitoes of North America, North of Mexico: Supplement Number One to Mosquito Systematics. (Illus.). 313p. 1981. 35.00 (ISBN 0-9606210-0-8); pap. 24.00 (ISBN 0-318-12861-6). Am Mosquito.

--Identification & Geographical Distribution of the Mosquitoes of North America North of Mexico. LC 81-50441. (Supplements to Mosquito Systematics Ser.). (Illus.). 315p. (Orig.). 1981. 24.00 (ISBN 0-9606210-0-8); pap. 30.00 (ISBN 0-9606210-1-6). Am Mosquito.

Darst, David M. The Complete Bond Book: A Guide to All Types of Fixed-Income Securities. (Illus.). 352p. (Orig.). 1975. 37.50 (ISBN 0-07-017390-7). McGraw.

--The Handbook of the Bond & Money Markets. LC 80-36816. (Illus.). 461p. 1981. 44.95 (ISBN 0-07-015401-5). McGraw.

Darst, H. W. Far Above Rubies. 128p. (Orig.). 1982. pap. 2.50 (ISBN 0-89114-110-3). Baptist Pub Hse.

Darst, Mrs. H. W. Missions in the Mountains. (Illus.). 116p. 1979. pap. 2.50 (ISBN 0-89114-085-9). Baptist Pub Hse.

Darst, Paul W. & Armstrong, George P. Outdoor Adventure Activities for School & Recreation Programs. LC 80-66363. (Orig.). 1980. pap. text ed. 14.95x (ISBN 0-8087-0489-3). Burgess.

Darst, Paul W., jt. auth. see Pangrazi, Robert P.

Darst, Paul W., et al. Systematic Observation Instrumentation for Physical Education. LC 82-83250. 352p. (Orig.). 1983. pap. 17.95 (ISBN 0-88011-094-5). Leisure Pr.

Darst, Sheila S., ed. see Kachelmeier, Glenda S.

Darst, Sheila S., ed. see Salter, Charles A. & De Lerma, Carlotta S.

Darst, Shelia S., ed. see Barrett, Anna P.

Darst, Shelia S., ed. see Evey, Ethel L.

Dart, Alan, jt. auth. see Cardy, Lynn.

Dart, Alan K. ESL Grammar Workbook 1A. 125p. 1984. pap. text ed. 5.95 (ISBN 0-13-283839-7). P-H.

--ESL Grammar Workbook 1B. 125p. 1984. pap. text ed. 5.95 (ISBN 0-13-283847-8). P-H.

--ESL Grammar Workbook 2A. 125p. 1984. pap. text ed. 5.95 (ISBN 0-13-283854-0). P-H.

--ESL Grammar Workbook 2B. 125p. 1984. pap. text ed. 5.95 (ISBN 0-13-283862-1). P-H.

Dart, Allan K. ESL Grammar Exercise Book, No. 1. (Illus.). 250p. 1985. pap. text ed. 10.95 (ISBN 0-13-283870-2). P-H.

--ESL Grammar Exercise Book, No. 1A. (Illus.). 128p. 1985. pap. text ed. 5.95 (ISBN 0-13-283888-5). P-H.

--ESL Grammar Exercise Book, No. 1B. (Illus.). 128p. 1985. pap. text ed. 5.95 (ISBN 0-13-283896-6). P-H.

--ESL Grammar Exercise Book, No. 2. (Illus.). 250p. 1985. pap. text ed. 12.95 (ISBN 0-13-283904-0). P-H.

--ESL Grammar Exercise Book, No. 2A. (Illus.). 128p. 1985. pap. text ed. 5.95 (ISBN 0-13-283912-1). P-H.

--ESL Grammar Exercise Book, No. 2B. (Illus.). 128p. 1985. pap. text ed. 5.95 (ISBN 0-13-283920-2). P-H.

--ESL Grammar Quiz Book for Intermediate to Advanced Students of English As a Second Language. 256p. 1982. pap. 12.95 (ISBN 0-13-283812-5). P-H.

Dart, Allen K. ESL Grammar Handbook for Intermediate to Advanced Students of English as a Second Language. 256p. 1982. pap. 12.50 (ISBN 0-13-283804-4). P-H.

--ESL Grammar Workbook 1: For Intermediate Speakers & Writers of English as a Second Language. 1978. pap. text ed. 12.95 (ISBN 0-13-283663-7). P-H.

--ESL Grammar Workbook 2: For Intermediate Speakers & Writers of English As a Second Language. 1978. pap. text ed. 12.95 (ISBN 0-13-283671-8). P-H.

Dart, C. J. & Smith, D. A. Woodwork for Winemakers. (Illus.). 143p. Date not set. pap. 5.95 (ISBN 0-900841-17-6, Pub. by Aztex Corp). Argus Bks.

Dart, Francis. Teaching Science as a Second Culture. Ives, Kenneth, ed. (Illus.). 60p. 1983. pap. 4.00 (ISBN 0-89670-009-7). Progresiv Pub.

Dart, John O. & Johnson, Daniel M. Oregon: Wet, High, & Dry. 365p. (Orig.). 1981. pap. 13.95 (ISBN 0-913244-53-8). Hapi Pr.

Dart, M. C. & Jenkins, S. H. Disposal of Sludge to Sea, Vol. 14, No. 3. pap. 40.00x (ISBN 0-08-029093-0). Pergamon.

Dart, P. J., jt. ed. see Ayanaba, A.

Dart, Peter. Pudovkin's Films & Film Theory. LC 74-986. (Dissertations on Film Ser.). 1974. 15.00 (ISBN 0-405-04874-2). Ayer Co Pubs.

Dart, R. K. & Stretton, R. J. Microbiological Aspects of Pollution Control. 2nd, rev. ed. (Fundamentals of Pollution Control & Environmental Sciences Ser.: Vol. 6). 266p. 1980. 57.50 (ISBN 0-444-41918-7). Elsevier.

Dart, Raymond A. Adventures with the Missing Link. 3rd ed. (Illus.). 255p. 6.95 (ISBN 0-936676-29-9). Better Baby.

Dart, S. Leonard & Tubbs F., Eldred. The Mini Module Manual. 1976. pap. text ed. 3.00 (ISBN 0-915242-17-6). Pygmalion Pr.

Dart, Thurston. Interpretation of Music. pap. 5.95xi (ISBN 0-06-131978-3, TB1978, Torch). Har-Row.

Dartez, Cecilia C. The Louisiana Plantation Coloring Book. (Illus.). 32p. (Orig.). 1985. pap. 1.75 (ISBN 0-88289-473-0). Pelican.

Dartford, Gerald P. The British Constitution. 1978. pap. text ed. 3.75x (ISBN 0-88334-107-7). Ind Sch Pr.

--The French Revolution. (gr. 9-12). 1972. pap. text ed. 4.75x (ISBN 0-88334-046-1). Ind Sch Pr.

Dartford, Mark, jt. ed. see Brown, Ashley.

Dartington, T., et al. Life Together. LC 81-11311. 148p. 1981. 8.95x (ISBN 0-422-77900-8, NO. 3573, Pub. by Tavistock England). Methuen Inc.

Dartmen-Arlaand, Flora. Story of Montesano. 40p. pap. 3.95 (ISBN 0-8466-0177-X, S177). Shorey.

Dartmouth College Library, Hanover, N. H. Dictionary Catalog of the Stefansson Collection on the Polar Regions, 8 Vols. 1967. Set. lib. bdg. 720.00 (ISBN 0-8161-0676-2, Hall Library). G K Hall.

Dartnall, H. J. see Autrum, H., et al.

Dartnell, G. E. & Goddard, E. H. A Glossary of Words Used in the County of Wiltshire. (English Dialect Society Publications Ser.: No. 69). pap. 25.00 (ISBN 0-317-16094-X). Kraus Repr.

Dartnell Institute of Business Research Staff, compiled by. Dartnell's Definitive Survey of Microcomputer Practices & Usage in the United States & Canada. 325p. 1984. three-ring binder 130.50 (ISBN 0-317-04225-4). Dartnell Corp.

D'Artois, Philippe, jt. auth. see Le Seneschal, Jean.

Darton, F. Harvey. Essays of the Year 1933-1934. 1973. Repr. of 1934 ed. 20.00 (ISBN 0-8274-1645-8). R West.

--From Surtees to Sassoon: Some English Contrasts 1838-1928. LC 77-6713. 1931. lib. bdg. 20.00 (ISBN 0-8414-3822-6). Folcroft.

--Vincent Crummles: His Theatre & His Times. LC 79-173157. Repr. of 1926 ed. 24.50 (ISBN 0-405-08431-5, Pub. by Blom). Ayer Co Pubs.
Darton, F. Harvey, jt. auth. see Sawyer, Charles J.
Darton, F. J. Arnold Bennett. LC 73-20384. (English Literature Ser., No. 33). 1974. lib. bdg. 39.95x (ISBN 0-8383-1769-3). Haskell.
--Children's Books in England. 3rd ed. Alderson, Brian, ed. LC 81-6161. (Illus.). 450p. 1982. 29.95 (ISBN 0-521-24020-4). Cambridge U Pr.
--J. M. Barrie. LC 73-21740. (English Literature Ser., No. 33). 1974. lib. bdg. 31.95x (ISBN 0-8383-1780-4). Haskell.
--The Marches of Wessex. 1922. 30.00 (ISBN 0-8482-3687-4). Norwood Edns.
Darton, Frederick J. Arnold Bennett. LC 70-131681. 1971. Repr. of 1913 ed. 19.00x (ISBN 0-403-00568-X). Scholarly.
--J. M. Barrie. 1929. lib. bdg. 12.50 (ISBN 0-8414-2438-1). Folcroft.
--J. M. Barrie. LC 74-131682. 1970. Repr. of 1929 ed. 11.00x (ISBN 0-403-00569-8). Scholarly.
Darton, Harvey. Arnold Bennett. 127p. 1980. Repr. lib. bdg. 17.50 (ISBN 0-89760-131-9). Telegraph Bks.
--Plates Illustrative of the Vocabulary for the Deaf & Dumb. 69.95 (ISBN 0-8490-0841-7). Gordon Pr.
Darton, Harvey F. Arnold Bennett. 127p. 1982. lib. bdg. 17.50 (ISBN 0-8495-1139-9). Arden Lib.
--From Surtees to Sassoon: Some English Contrasts 1938-1928. 222p. 1980. Repr. lib. bdg. 27.50 (ISBN 0-8492-4219-3). R West.
Darton, J. M. Famous Girls Who Have Become Illustrious Women: Forming Models for Imitation for the Young Women of England. facsimile ed. LC 79-38751. (Essay Index Reprint Ser). Repr. of 1864 ed. 21.00 (ISBN 0-8369-2644-7). Ayer Co Pubs.
Darton, Michael, ed. A Modern Concordance to the New Testament. LC 75-34831. 1977. 12.95 (ISBN 0-385-07901-X). Doubleday.
Darton, Nelson H. Catalogue & Index of Contributions to North American Geology: 1732-1891. Cohen, I. Bernard, ed. LC 79-7958. (Three Centuries of Science in America Ser.). 1980. Repr. of 1896 ed. lib. bdg. 86.00x (ISBN 0-405-12539-9). Ayer Co Pubs.
Dartsch, B., ed. Concrete According to German Standards: Production, Testing & Quality Control. 1977. 10.00 (ISBN 0-9960095-7-4, Pub. by Beton Bks W Germany). Heyden.
Darty, Peter. The Pocketbook of Porcelain & Pottery Marks. 1974. 12.50 (ISBN 0-685-53252-6). ARS Ceramica.
Darty, Trudy, jt. auth. see Potter, Sandra.
Darushenkov, O. Cuba, el Camino De la Revolucion. 330p. (Span.). 1980. 8.95 (ISBN 0-8285-1490-9, Pub. by Progress Pubs USSR). Imported Pubns.
D'Arusmont, Frances W. Life, Letters & Lectures: 1834-1844. LC 72-2598. (American Women Ser.). 1972. 20.00 (ISBN 0-405-04454-2). Ayer Co Pubs.
--Views of Society & Manners in America. Baker, Paul R., ed. LC 63-10878. pap. 79.30 (ISBN 0-317-10071-8, 2002996). Bks Demand UMI.
Daruvala, J. C., ed. Tensions of Economic Development in Southeast Asia. LC 73-19306. (Illus.). 163p. 1974. Repr. of 1962 ed. lib. bdg. 22.50x (ISBN 0-8371-7321-3, DAED). Greenwood.
Daruvar, Ives De see De Daruvar, Ives.
Daruwalla, K. N. Apparition in April. 8.00 (ISBN 0-89253-454-0); flexible cloth 4.80 (ISBN 0-89253-455-9). Ind-US Inc.
--Under Orion. (Writers Workshop Redbird Ser.). 93p. 1975. 8.00 (ISBN 0-88253-728-8); flexible bdg. 4.80 (ISBN 0-89253-597-0). Ind-US Inc.
Daruwalla, Keki N. Sword & Abyss: Short Stories. 1979. 7.95x (ISBN 0-7069-0680-2, Pub. by Vikas India). Advent NY.
Darvall, Frank O. Popular Disturbances & Public Order in Regency England. LC 68-58973. Repr. of 1934 ed. lib. bdg. 35.00x (ISBN 0-678-00458-7). Kelley.
Darvall, Lixi. How to Get What You Want in Nine Languages (incl. Hebrew) 160p. 1982. pap. 4.95 (ISBN 9-6524-7014-7, Carta Isreal). Hippocrene Bks.
Darvas, F. & Knoll, J., eds. Chemical Structure - Biological Activity Relationships, Quantitative Approaches: Proceedings of the Third Congress of the Hungarian Pharmacological Society, Budapest, 1979. LC 80-41281. (Advances in Pharmacological Research & Practice Ser.: Vol. III). 355p. 1981. 74.00 (ISBN 0-08-026388-7). Pergamon.
Darvas, Nicolas. Over the Counter Profits. 143p. 1985. 28.50 (ISBN 0-911156-44-5). Porter.
Darvas, Robert & Lukacs, Paul. Spotlight on Card Play: A New Approach to the Practical Analysis of Bridge Hands. (Master Bridge Ser.). (Illus.). 160p. 1982. pap. 8.50 (ISBN 0-575-03078-X, Pub. by Gollancz England). David & Charles.
Darveau, Mary, ed. see Casola, Matteo A.
Darveau, Mary, ed. see Winterflood, James.
Darveniza, M. Electrical Properties of Wood & Line Design. (Illus.). 197p. (Orig.). 1980. pap. text ed. 36.25x (ISBN 0-7022-1523-6). U of Queensland Pr.
Darvi, A. Pretty Babies: An Insider's Look at the World of the Hollywood Child Star. 288p. 1983. 14.95 (ISBN 0-07-015402-3). McGraw.
Darvil, Fred T., Jr. Hiking the North Cascades. LC 81-14451. (Sierra Club Totebook Ser.). (Illus.). 384p. (Orig.). 1982. pap. 9.95 (ISBN 0-87156-297-9). Sierra.
Darvill, Fred T. Mountaineering Medicine: A Wilderness Medical Guide. 11th, rev. ed. LC 85-62029. 60p. 1985. pap. 2.95 (ISBN 0-89997-055-9). Wilderness Pr.
Darvill, Fred T., Jr. Mountaineering Medicine: A Wilderness Medical Guide. 10th ed. Winnett, Thomas, ed. LC 82-62849. (Illus.). 60p. 1983. pap. 2.95 (ISBN 0-89997-021-4). Wilderness Pr.
--Stehekin: The Enchanted Valley. LC 80-16628. (Illus.). 128p. (Orig.). 1981. pap. 6.95 (ISBN 0-913140-42-2). Signpost Bk Pub.
Darwall, Stephen, ed. see Butler, Joseph.
Darwall, Stephen L. Impartial Reason. LC 82-22046. 288p. 1983. 24.95x (ISBN 0-8014-1560-8). Cornell U Pr.
--Impartial Reason. LC 82-22046. 261p. (Orig.). 1985. 24.95 (ISBN 0-8014-1560-8); pap. text ed. 9.95x (ISBN 0-8014-9348-X). Cornell U Pr.
Darwent, Brian, ed. see Saroyan, William.
Darwick, Richard. Case Against Hillman. 1980. pap. 2.25 (ISBN 0-8439-0818-1, Pub. by Nordon Pubns). Dorchester Pub Co.
Darwin, Andrew. Canals & Rivers of Britain. (Illus.). 1977. 13.95 (ISBN 0-8038-1213-2). Hastings.
Darwin, B. Dickens. LC 73-8958. (Studies in Dickens, No. 52). 1973. Repr. of 1933 ed. lib. bdg. 35.95x (ISBN 0-8383-1710-3). Haskell.
Darwin, Bernard. Dickens. 1933. lib. bdg. 12.50 (ISBN 0-8414-2439-X). Folcroft.
Darwin, Bernard A. Dickens Advertiser: A Collection of the Advertisements in the Original Parts of Novels by Charles Dickens. LC 72-152553. (Studies in Dickens, No. 52). 1971. Repr. of 1930 ed. lib. bdg. 33.95x (ISBN 0-8383-1234-9). Haskell.
Darwin, Charles. Autobiography & Selected Letters. Darwin, Francis, ed. 1892. pap. 5.95 (ISBN 0-486-20479-0). Dover.
--Autobiography & Selected Letters. Darwin, Francis, ed. 14.00 (ISBN 0-8446-1947-7). Peter Smith.
--Autobiography of Charles Darwin. Barlow, Nora, ed. (Illus.). 1969. pap. 6.95 (ISBN 0-393-00487-2, Norton Lib). Norton.
--Book of Darwin. Simpson, George G., intro. by. 224p. (Orig.). 1983. pap. 6.95 (ISBN 0-671-43126-9). WSP.
--The Collected Papers of Charles Darwin, Vols. I & II. Barrett, Paul H., ed. LC 76-606. (Illus.). 1977. lib. bdg. 40.00x set (ISBN 0-226-13657-4); pap. 12.50 (ISBN 0-226-13658-2, P886, Phoen). U of Chicago Pr.
--Darwin. Date not set. price not set (ISBN 0-670-25691-9). Viking.
--Darwin on Earthworms: The Formation of Vegetable Mould Through the Action of Worms. (Illus.). 160p. 1976. 7.95 (ISBN 0-916302-10-5); pap. 5.95 (ISBN 0-916302-06-7). Bookworm Pub.
--The Descent of Man & Selection in Relation to Sex. LC 80-8679. (Illus.). 935p. 1981. 45.00x (ISBN 0-691-08278-2); pap. 12.50x (ISBN 0-691-02369-7). Princeton U Pr.
--The Essential Darwin. Jastrow, Robert, ed. Korey, Kenneth A. 348p. 1984. 19.45i (ISBN 0-316-45826-0); pap. 10.45i (ISBN 0-316-45827-9). Little.
--The Expression of Emotions in Man & Animals. LC 82-62301. (Classics in Psychology & Psychiatry Ser.). 374p. 1979. pap. 20.00 (ISBN 0-86187-306-8). F Pinter Pubs.
--Expression of the Emotions in Man & Animals. LC 65-17286. (Illus.). 1965. pap. 9.00x (ISBN 0-226-13656-6, P526, Phoen). U of Chicago Pr.
--Fertilization of Orchids by Insects. (Orchid Ser.). 1980. Repr. of 1862 ed. text ed. 27.50 (ISBN 0-930576-20-9). E M Coleman Ent.
--The Formation of Vegetable Mould, Through the Action of Worms: With Observations on Their Habits. 10/1985 ed. (Illus.). 348p. pap. 11.95 (ISBN 0-226-13663-9). U of Chicago Pr.
--The Fossil Balanidae & Verrucidae. 1854. pap. 6.00 (ISBN 0-384-10850-4). Johnson Repr.
--The Fossil Lepadidae. 1851. pap. 14.00 (ISBN 0-384-10860-1). Johnson Repr.
--The Illustrated Origin of Species. (Illus.). 240p. 1979. 25.00 (ISBN 0-8090-5735-2); pap. 12.95 (ISBN 0-8090-1397-5). Hill & Wang.
--Journal of Researches into the Natural History & Geology of the Countries Visited During the Voyage of H. M. S. "Beagle" Round the World, under the Command of Capt. Fitz Roy, R. A. 1977. Repr. of 1892 ed. lib. bdg. 30.00 (ISBN 0-8482-0544-8). Norwood Edns.
--Metaphysics, Materialism, & the Evolution of the Mind: Early Writings of Charles Darwin. LC 80-15763. 1980. pap. 6.95x (ISBN 0-226-13659-0, P906, Phoen). U of Chicago Pr.
--A Monograph of the Sub-Class Cirripedia, 2 Vols. 1851-1853. Set. 88.00 (ISBN 0-384-10870-9). Johnson Repr.
--The Movements & Habits of Climbing Plants. 1977. Repr. of 1891 ed. lib. bdg. 40.00 (ISBN 0-8492-0621-9). R West.
--Natural Selection. Stauffer, R. C., ed. LC 72-95406. (Illus.). 1975. 110.00 (ISBN 0-521-20163-2). Cambridge U Pr.
--On the Origin of Species: A Facsimile of the First Edition. Mayr, Ernst, intro. by. LC 63-17196. 502p. 1975. pap. 8.95 (ISBN 0-674-63752-6). Harvard U Pr.
--Origin of Species. 1962. pap. 4.95 (ISBN 0-02-092120-9, Collier). Macmillan.
--Origin of Species. pap. 3.50 (ISBN 0-451-62102-6, ME2102, Ment). NAL.
--The Origin of Species. abr. ed. Appleman, Philip, ed. 1975. pap. text ed. 3.95x (ISBN 0-393-09219-4). Norton.
--The Origin of Species. Irvine, Charlotte & Irvine, William, eds. LC 56-7502. pap. 3.95 (ISBN 0-8044-6105-8). Ungar.
--The Origin of Species & the Descent of Man. LC 36-27228. 8.95 (ISBN 0-394-60398-2). Modern Lib.
--The Origin of the Species. (Rowman & Littlefield University Library). 488p. 1972. 15.00x (ISBN 0-87471-662-4); pap. 8.00x (ISBN 0-87471-663-2). Rowman.
--Origin of the Species. 1982. pap. 3.95 (ISBN 0-14-043205-1). Penguin.
--The Origins of Species. 1982. pap. 8.00 (ISBN 0-318-04039-5, DEL-05136, Evman). Biblio Dist.
--The Structure & Distribution of Coral Reefs. LC 84-79. (Illus.). 239p. 1984. pap. 7.95 (ISBN 0-8165-0844-5). U of Ariz Pr.
--The Substance of the Descent of Man. 1978. Repr. of 1926 ed. lib. bdg. 20.00 (ISBN 0-8492-0685-5). R West.
--The Various Contrivances by Which Orchids Are Fertilised by Insects. LC 83-18186. (Illus.). 275p. 1984. lib. bdg. 20.00x (ISBN 0-226-13661-2); pap. text ed. 9.95 (ISBN 0-226-13662-0). U of Chicago Pr.
--The Voyage of Charles Darwin. Ralling, Christopher, ed. LC 79-916. (Illus.). 1980. 12.50 (ISBN 0-8317-9212-4, Mayflower Bks). Smith Pubs.
--Voyage of the "Beagle". 1979. 10.95x (ISBN 0-460-00104-3, Evman); pap. 6.95x (ISBN 0-460-01104-9, Evman). Biblio Dist.
--Voyage of the Beagle. LC 62-2990. 1962. 6.95 (ISBN 0-385-02767-2, Anchor). Natural Hist.
--Voyage of the Beagle. LC 62-2990. Date not set. 6.95 (ISBN 0-385-02767-2). Doubleday.
Darwin, Charles & Keynes, Richard. Charles Darwin's Journal of a Voyage in HMS Beagle. ltd. ed. (Illus.). 700p. 1979. hand bound leather 460.00 (ISBN 0-904351-12-2). Genesis Pubns.
Darwin, Charles G. The New Conceptions of Matter. facsimile ed. (Select Bibliographies Reprint Ser). Repr. of 1931 ed. 20.00 (ISBN 0-8369-6610-4). Ayer Co Pubs.
--The Next Million Years. LC 73-5264. 210p. 1973. Repr. of 1953 ed. lib. bdg. 15.00x (ISBN 0-8371-6876-7, DANM). Greenwood.
Darwin, Charles R. The Descent of Man. 1902. 30.00 (ISBN 0-8274-2165-6). R West.
--The Descent of Man & His Selection in Relation to Sex. LC 72-3894. (Illus.). xvi, 688p. 1972. 42.50 (ISBN 0-404-08409-5). AMS Pr.
--The Different Forms of Flowers on Plants of the Same Species. LC 72-3900. (Illus.). viii, 352p. 1972. 42.50 (ISBN 0-404-08414-1). AMS Pr.
--The Effects of Cross & Self Fertilisation in the Vegetable Kingdom. 1889. 40.00 (ISBN 0-8274-2230-X). R West.
--The Effects of Cross & Self Fertilisation in the Vegetable Kingdom, Vol. 13. LC 72-3898. viii, 482p. 1972. 42.50 (ISBN 0-404-08413-3). AMS Pr.
--The Expression of Emotions in Man & Animals. 1873. 35.00 (ISBN 0-8274-2323-3). R West.
--Expression of the Emotions in Man & Animals. Repr. of 1897 ed. 42.50 (ISBN 0-404-08410-9). AMS Pr.
--Expression of the Emotions in Man & Animals. LC 73-90703. Repr. of 1955 ed. lib. bdg. 22.50x (ISBN 0-8371-2291-0, DAEM). Greenwood.
--The Formation of Vegetable Mould, Through the Action of Worms, with Observations on Their Habits. LC 72-3903. (Illus.). vii, 326p. 1972. 42.50 (ISBN 0-404-08416-8). AMS Pr.
--Foundations of the Origin of Species. Darwin, Francis, ed. LC 10-1422. 1909. 16.00 (ISBN 0-527-21610-0). Kraus Repr.
--Geological Obsevations on the Volcanic Islands & Parts of South America Visited during the Voyage of H.M.S. Beagle. LC 72-3889. (Illus.). xiii, 648p. 1972. 42.50 (ISBN 0-404-08403-6). AMS Pr.
--Insectivorous Plants. 2nd rev. ed. LC 70-151602. Repr. of 1893 ed. 27.50 (ISBN 0-404-01928-5). AMS Pr.
--Insectivorous Plants, Vol. 12. LC 72-3897. (Illus.). x, 462p. 1972. 42.50 (ISBN 0-404-08412-5). AMS Pr.
--Journal of Researches into the Natural History & Geology of the Countries Visited during the Voyage of the H.M.S. Beagle Round the World, under the Command of Capt. Fitz Roy R.N, 2 Vols. LC 72-3887. (Illus.). x, 519p. 1972. 42.50 (ISBN 0-404-08401-X). AMS Pr.
--Life & Letters of Charles Darwin, 3 Vols. Darwin, Francis, ed. (Sources of Science Ser: No. 102). 1969. Repr. of 1888 ed. Set. 110.00 (ISBN 0-384-10900-4). Johnson Repr.
--The Life & Letters of Charles Darwin, 2 Vols. Darwin, Francis, ed. LC 72-3904. (Illus.). 1972. Vol. I. (ISBN 0-404-08417-6). Vol. II (ISBN 0-404-08418-4). 85.00 set. AMS Pr.
--The Movements & Habits of Climbing Plants. LC 72-3896. (Illus.). viii, 208p. 42.50 (ISBN 0-404-08411-7). AMS Pr.
--The Origin of Species. 1914. 2 vols in 1 40.00 (ISBN 0-8274-3077-9). R West.
--The Origin of Species by Means of Natural Selection, 2 vols. LC 72-3891. (Illus.). Vol. I. (ISBN 0-404-08404-4). Vol. II (ISBN 0-404-08405-2). 85.00 set. AMS Pr.
--The Power of Movement in Plants. 2nd ed. LC 65-23402. 1966. Repr. of 1881 ed. lib. bdg. 55.00 (ISBN 0-306-70921-X). Da Capo.
--The Power of Movement in Plants. 1892. 40.00 (ISBN 0-8274-3193-7). R West.
--The Power of Movement in Plants. 3rd ed. LC 72-3901. (Illus.). x, 592p. 1972. 42.50 (ISBN 0-404-08415-X). AMS Pr.
--The Structure & Distribution of Coral Reefs. 3rd ed. LC 73-147085. (Illus.). xx, 344p. 1972. 42.50 (ISBN 0-404-08402-8). AMS Pr.
--The Variation of Animals & Plants Under Domestication, 2 Vols. LC 72-3893. (Illus.). 1972. Vol. I. (ISBN 0-404-08407-9). Vol. II (ISBN 0-404-08408-7). 85.00. AMS Pr.
--The Various Contrivances by Which Orchids are Fertilised by Insects. 2nd ed. LC 72-3892. (Illus.). xvi, 300p. 1972. write for info. (ISBN 0-404-08406-0). AMS Pr.
--Works, 18 Vols. LC 73-147085. Repr. of 1897 ed. Set. 765.00 (ISBN 0-404-08400-1); 42.50 ea. AMS Pr.
Darwin, Charles R. & Wallace, Alfred R. Evolution by Natural Selection. LC 58-14868. 1971. Repr. of 1958 ed. 32.00 (ISBN 0-384-10875-X, B132). Johnson Repr.
Darwin, Erasmus. The Letters of Erasmus Darwin. King-Hele, D. G., ed. (Illus.). 375p. 1981. 99.00 (ISBN 0-521-23706-8). Cambridge U Pr.
--Zoonomia, or the Laws of Organic Life, 2 Vols. LC 79-147964. Repr. of 1796 ed. Set. 95.00 (ISBN 0-404-08215-7). AMS Pr.
Darwin, Francis. Charles Darwin: His Life Told in An Autobiographical Chapter & in A Selected Series of His Published Letters. 348p. 1983. Repr. of 1902 ed. lib. bdg. 60.00 (ISBN 0-89987-176-3). Darby Bks.
--The Life & Letters of Charles Darwin, 2 vols. 1973. Repr. of 1893 ed. 75.00 (ISBN 0-8274-1406-4). R West.
--Rustic Sounds & Other Studies in Literature & Natural History. facs. ed. LC 69-17572. (Essay Index Reprint Ser). 1917. 17.00 (ISBN 0-8369-0069-3). Ayer Co Pubs.
--Springtime, & Other Essays. facs. ed. LC 67-23201. (Essay Index Reprint Ser). 1920. 17.00 (ISBN 0-8369-0364-1). Ayer Co Pubs.
Darwin, Francis, ed. The Life & Letters of Charles Darwin, 2 vols. 1981. Repr. of 1891 ed. lib. bdg. 125.00 set (ISBN 0-8495-1133-X). Arden Lib.
Darwin, Francis, ed. see Darwin, Charles.
Darwin, Francis, ed. see Darwin, Charles R.
Darwin, Francis D. The English Mediaeval Recluse. LC 73-4825. 1973. lib. bdg. 12.50 (ISBN 0-8414-1865-9). Folcroft.
Darwin, Gary. Darwin's Thumb Tip Miracles. Fenton, Robert & Fenton, Irene, eds. (Illus.). 129p. (Orig.). (gr. 8 up). 1981. 20.00 (ISBN 0-939024-00-4); text ed. 20.00 (ISBN 0-686-98459-5); pap. 13.95 (ISBN 0-939024-01-2). Rare Pub.
Darwin, George. Scientific Papers: 1907-16, 5 vols. LC 8-16429. 1976. Set. 300.00 (ISBN 0-527-21620-8). Kraus Repr.
Darwin, John. Britain, Egypt & the Middle East. LC 80-14718. 1981. 27.50 (ISBN 0-312-09736-0). St Martin.
Darwin, Leonard. The Need for Eugenic Reform (London, Nineteen Twenty-Six) Rosenberg, Charles, ed. LC 83-48532. (The History of Hereditarian Thought Ser.). 529p. Date not set. Repr. of 1926 ed. lib. bdg. 63.00 (ISBN 0-8240-5803-8). Garland Pub.
Darwish, Mahmoud. The Music of Human Flesh. Johnson-Davies, Denys, tr. from Arabic. (Modern Arab Writers Ser.). 96p. (Orig.). 1980. pap. 6.00x (ISBN 0-89410-203-6). Three Continents.
Darwish, Mahmud, et al. Victims of a Map. 168p. 1984. 22.00x (ISBN 0-86356-112-8, Pub. by Zed Pr England); pap. 7.95 (ISBN 0-86356-022-9, Pub. by Zed Pr England). Biblio Dist.
Dary, David. Comanche. (Public Education Ser.: No. 5). 19p. pap. 1.00 (ISBN 0-317-04771-X). U of KS Mus Nat Hist.
--Cowboy Culture: A Saga of Five Centuries. LC 80-2699. (Illus.). 416p. 1981. 18.50 (ISBN 0-394-42605-3). Knopf.
--True Tales of Old-Time Kansas. Orig. Title: True Tales of the Old-Time Plains. (Illus.). 336p. (Orig.). 1984. pap. 9.95 (ISBN 0-7006-0250-X). U Pr of KS.
Dary, David A. The Buffalo Book. 448p. 1983. pap. 3.95 (ISBN 0-380-00475-5, 62786-8, Discus). Avon.

--The Buffalo Book: The Full Saga of the American Animal. LC 73-13211. (Illus.). 374p. 1973. 20.00 (ISBN 0-8040-0653-9, 82-73575, SB); ltd. ed. o.p. 100.00 (ISBN 0-8040-0717-9, 82-73971). Ohio U Pr.

Dary, Davis. Cowboy Culture. 1982. pap. 7.95 (ISBN 0-380-60632-1, 60632-1). Avon.

Daryabadi, A. M. Holy Quaran Arabic-English. 22.50 (ISBN 0-686-83591-3). Kazi Pubns.

Daryabadi, A. Majid. Tafsir-ul-Quran, Vol. I-III. 49.50 (ISBN 0-317-14641-6). Kazi Pubns.

Daryanani, Gobind. Principles of Active Network Synthesis & Design. LC 76-20659. 495p. 1976. 45.50 (ISBN 0-471-19545-6). Wiley.

Daryanani, Sital. Building Systems Design with Programmable Calculators. 1980. 44.95 (ISBN 0-07-015415-5). McGraw.

Daryl, Philippe. Public Life in England. Frith, Henry, tr. 1978. Repr. lib. bdg. 25.00 (ISBN 0-8495-1038-4). Arden Lib.

Daryusl, A. A., et al. Persian Words in English. Commager, Steele, ed. Incl. The German Influence on the English Vocabulary; H.W. Fowler; The Dutch Influence on English Vocabulary; American Variations; Fine Writing; Names, Designations, & Appelations; Linguistic Self-Criticism; The Formation & Use of Compound Epithets in English Poetry; Northern Words in Modern English. (Society for Pure English Ser.: Vol. 5). 1979. lib. bdg. 46.00 (ISBN 0-8240-3669-7). Garland Pub.

Darzins, Egons. The Bacteriology of Tuberculosis. LC 57-8918. pap. 125.00 (ISBN 0-317-27940-8, 2055853). Bks Demand UMI.

Das. Microevolution. (Microevolution Ser.: No. 4). 104p. 1981. text ed. 12.50x (ISBN 0-391-02641-0, Pub. by Concept India). Humanities.

--Pesticide Analysis. 1981. 55.25 (ISBN 0-8247-1087-8). Dekker.

Das, A. C. Introduction to the Study of Society. 1972. 6.95 (ISBN 0-8426-0401-4). Orient Bk Dist.

--Rgvedic India, 2 vols. 1971. Repr. of 1971 ed. Set. 29.50 (ISBN 0-89684-306-8). Orient Bk Dist.

Das, A. C., jt. auth. see Halim, A.

Das, Arvind. Agrarian Unrest & Socio-Economic Change, 1900-1980. 1983. 28.00x (ISBN 0-8364-0967-1, Pub. by Manohar India). South Asia Bks.

Das, Arvind N. Agrarian Movements in India: Studies on 20th Century Bihar. (Library of Peasant Studies: No. 5). (Illus.). 200p. 1982. text ed. 29.50x (ISBN 0-7146-3216-3, F Cass Co). Biblio Dist.

Das, B. M. Fundamentals of Soil Dynamics. 400p. 1983. 41.50 (ISBN 0-444-00705-9). Elsevier.

Das, B. S. The Sikkim Saga. (Illus.). 1983. text ed. 18.95x (ISBN 0-7069-1971-8, Pub. by Vikas India). Advent NY.

Das, Binod S. Studies in the Economic History of Orissa from Ancient Times to 1833. 1978. 11.50x (ISBN 0-8364-0200-6). South Asia Bks.

Das, Braja. Advanced Soil Mechanics. (Illus.). 528p. 1982. text ed. 48.00 (ISBN 0-07-015416-3). McGraw.

Das, Braja M. Introduction to Soil Mechanics. 1st ed. LC 79-16729. pap. 68.50 (ISBN 0-317-27202-0, 2023864). Bks Demand UMI.

--Principles of Geotechnical Engineering. 1985. text ed. write for info. (ISBN 0-534-03765-8, 21R4400, Pub. by PWS Engineering). PWS Pubs.

--Soil Mechanics Laboratory Manual. LC 82-1451. 250p. 1982. pap. text ed. 13.95x (ISBN 0-910554-36-6). Engineering.

Das, Brajananda. Ophthalmology for General Practioners. 196p. 1984. text ed. 25.00x (ISBN 0-86590-306-9, Sterling Pubs India). Apt Bks.

Das, Deb K. The Eyes of Autumn: An Experiment in Poetry. 13p. 1975. 6.00 (ISBN 0-88253-706-7); flexible bdg. 4.00 (ISBN 0-86578-116-8). Ind-US Inc.

--The Fire Canto. 8.00 (ISBN 0-89253-487-7); flexible cloth 4.00 (ISBN 0-89253-488-5). Ind-US Inc.

--The Labyrinths: A Long Poem. (Bluebird Book). 26p. 1975. 8.00 (ISBN 0-88253-713-X); pap. text ed. 4.00 flexible bdg. (ISBN 0-89253-598-9). Ind-US Inc.

--The Night Before Us. 8.00 (ISBN 0-89253-489-3); flexible cloth 4.00 (ISBN 0-89253-490-7). Ind-US Inc.

--Through a Glass Darkly. (Writers Workshop Redbird Ser.). 53p. 1975. 8.00 (ISBN 0-89253-519-9); pap. 3.00 (ISBN 0-88253-723-7). Ind-US Inc.

Das, Deb K., tr. see Upanisads.

Das, Dilip K. Migration of Financial Resources to Developing Countries. 250p. 1985. 29.95 (ISBN 0-312-53217-2). St Martin.

Das, G. D. & Kreutzberg, G. W. Evaluation of Interstitial Nerve Cells in the Central Nervous System: A Correlative Study Using Acetylcholinesterase & Golgi Techniques. LC 64-20582. (Advances in Anatomy, Embryology & Cell Biology: Vol. 41, Pt. 1). (Illus.). 1969. pap. 17.70 (ISBN 0-387-04091-9). Springer-Verlag.

Das, G. D., jt. ed. see Wallace, R. B.

Das, G. K. & Beer, John, eds. E. M. Forster: A Human Exploration; Centenary Essays. LC 79-84339. 1979. 40.00x (ISBN 0-8147-1768-3). NYU Pr.

Das, H. C. Tantricism: A Study of the Yogini Cult. (Illus.). 88p. 1981. text ed. 22.00x (ISBN 0-391-02791-3, 41007, Pub. by Sterling India). Humanities.

Das, Hari H. Subhas Chandra Bose & the Indian National Movement. text ed. 37.50x (ISBN 0-86590-104-X, Pub. by Sterling Pubs India). Apt Bks.

Das, J., jt. auth. see Dutta Majumdar, J.

Das, J. P. Chitra Pothi: Illustrated Palm Leaf Manuscripts from Orissa. 160p. 1984. text ed. 30.50x (ISBN 0-391-03202-X, Pub. by Arnold Heinemann India). Humanities.

--Puri Paintings. 200p. 1982. text ed. 54.25x (ISBN 0-391-02577-5). Humanities.

--The Underdog-A Play. (Library of Modern Indian Writing). 48p. 1984. pap. text ed. 8.95x (ISBN 0-7069-2582-3, Pub. by Vikas India). Advent NY.

Das, J. P. & Baine, David. Mental Retardation for Special Educators. (Illus.). 332p. 1978. pap. 37.75x spiral (ISBN 0-398-03666-7). C C Thomas.

Das, J. P. & Mulcaby, R., eds. Theory & Research in Learning Disabilities. LC 82-112219. 296p. 1982. 37.50x (ISBN 0-306-41112-1, Plenum Pr). Plenum Pub.

Das, J. P., et al. Simultaneous & Successive Cognitive Processes. LC 78-20039. (Educational Psychology Ser.). 1979. 33.00 (ISBN 0-12-203150-4). Acad Pr.

Das, Jatin. Poems. (Redbird Bk.). 1976. 8.00 (ISBN 0-89253-537-7); flexible bdg. 4.00 (ISBN 0-89253-098-7). Ind-US Inc.

Das, Jibanananda. Banalata Sen. Lal, P., tr. from Bengali. 20p. 1975. pap. text ed. 4.00 (ISBN 0-88253-511-0). Ind-US Inc.

Das, K. G. Controlled-Release Technology: Bioengineering Aspects. LC 82-11052. 225p. 1983. 57.95 (ISBN 0-471-08680-0, Pub. by Wiley-Interscience). Wiley.

--Organic Mass Spectrometry. 1981. 25.00x (ISBN 0-686-72958-7, Pub. by Oxford & IBH India). State Mutual Bk.

Das, Kamala. The Descendants. (Writers Workshop Redbird Ser.). 35p. 1975. o.si. 8.00 (ISBN 0-88253-526-9); pap. text ed. 4.00 (ISBN 0-88253-525-0). Ind-US Inc.

Das, M. N. Partition & Independence of India. 344p. 1985. text ed. 23.00x (ISBN 0-391-02787-5). Humanities.

Das, M. N. & Giri, N. C. Design & Analysis of Experiments. LC 79-19286. 1981. 15.95x (ISBN 0-470-26861-1). Halsted Pr.

Das, M. S., ed. Trace Analysis & Technological Development. LC 83-12788. 407p. 1983. 42.95x (ISBN 0-470-27462-X). Halsted Pr.

Das, Man S. & Bardis, Panos D., eds. The Family in Asia. 1979. text ed. 35.00x (ISBN 0-04-301097-0). Allen Unwin.

Das, Man S. & Jesser, Clinton J., eds. The Family in Latin America. 1980. text ed. 40.00x (ISBN 0-7069-0800-7, Pub. by Vikas India). Advent NY.

Das, Man S., jt. ed. see Cavan, Ruth S.

Das, Man S., jt. ed. see Harry, Joseph.

Das, Man S., jt. ed. see Smith, T. Lynn.

Das, Manas M. Thomas Hardy-Poet of Tragic Vision: A Study of Hardy's Poetic Sensibility. 160p. 1983. text ed. 11.25x (ISBN 0-391-02805-7). Humanities.

Das, Manmohan. Peasant Agriculture in Assam: A Structural Analysis. xx, 290p. 1984. 50.00x (ISBN 0-86590-322-0, Pub. by Inter-India Pubns N Delhi). Apt Bks.

Das, Manoj. Books Forever. (Nehru Library for Children). (Illus.). (gr. 2-8). 1979. pap. 2.00 (ISBN 0-89744-175-3). Auromere.

--The Vengeance & Other Stories. 106p. 1980. 8.95 (ISBN 0-86578-191-5). Ind-US Inc.

Das, Nabagopal. The Indian Economy Under Planning. LC 72-907412. 140p. 1972. 7.50x (ISBN 0-89684-415-3). Orient Bk Dist.

Das, Nilima, ed. see Alfassa, Mira.

Das, O. P. The Magic Deer & Other Stories. (Vikas Library of Modern Indian Writing). 120p. 1983. text ed. 15.00x (ISBN 0-7069-2264-6, Pub. by Vikas India). Advent NY.

Das, P. C., jt. auth. see Sibinga, C. T.

Das, P. C., jt. ed. see Sibings, C. T.

Das, R. J. Joseph Conrad: A Study in Existential Vision. 132p. 1980. text ed. 10.50x (ISBN 0-391-01915-5). Humanities.

Das, R. K., jt. auth. see Sahu, D.

Das, R. R., jt. auth. see Misra, R.

Das, R. R., et al. Teaching of Home Science. 2nd ed. 146p. 1984. text ed. 13.95x (ISBN 0-86590-184-8, Pub. by Sterling India). Apt bks.

Das, Ram. Appropriate Technology. 1981. 11.95 (ISBN 0-533-04744-7). Vantage.

Das, Ranjan. Managing Diversification: The General Management Process. 1981. 14.00x (ISBN 0-8364-0710-5, Pub. by Macmillan India). South Asia Bks.

Das, S. C. Tibetan-English Dictionary. (Tibetan & Eng.). Repr. of 1970 ed. 45.00x (ISBN 0-87902-125-X). Orientalia.

--Tibetian Studies. Chattopadhyaya, Alaska, ed. 1985. 49.00x (ISBN 0-317-20274-X, Pub. by K P Bagchi & Co India). State Mutual Bk.

Das, S. C. & Kazi, I. D. Tibetan-English, English-Tibetan Dictionary, 2 vols. (Tibetan & Eng.). Set. 70.00 (ISBN 0-686-77964-9). Heinman.

Das, S. Chandra see Chandra Das, S.

Das, S. K. Cynewulf & the Cynewulf Canon. 59.95 (ISBN 0-87968-987-0). Gordon Pr.

Das, S. K. & Kear, B. H., eds. Rapidly Solidified Crystalline Alloys. avail. Metal Soc.

Das, S. R., et al. Introductory Physics: A Modern Approach. 121p. 1981. 29.00x (ISBN 0-86125-510-0, Pub. by Orient Longman India). State Mutual Bk.

Das, Sarat C. Tibetan-English Dictionary. rev ed. 1353p. 1985. Repr. of 1902 ed. text ed. 25.00x (ISBN 0-86590-722-6, Pub. by Gautau Pub Hse India). Apt Bks.

Das, Singh M. Contemporary Sociology in the United States. 329p. 1983. text ed. 35.00x (ISBN 0-7069-2104-6, Pub. by Vikas India). Advent NY.

Das, Sukla. Crime & Punishment in Ancient India, Circa AD 300 to AD 1100. 1977. 11.00x (ISBN 0-88386-980-2). South Asia Bks.

--Socio-Economic Life of Northern India. 1980. 22.50 (ISBN 0-8364-0609-5, Abhina India). South Asia Bks.

Das, Sunhit R., jt. auth. see Chopra, Kasturi L.

Das, T. K., jt. ed. see Flamholtz, Eric G.

Das, T. P. & Hahn, E. L. Nuclear Quadrupole Resonance Spectroscopy. (Solid State Physics: Suppl. 1). 1958. 56.00 (ISBN 0-12-607761-4). Acad Pr.

Das, Veena. Structure & Cognition: Aspects of Hindu Caste & Ritual. 2nd ed. 1982. 19.95x (ISBN 0-19-561395-3). Oxford U Pr.

Dasa, Mandalesvara, ed. see Dasa Goswami, Satsvarupa.

Dasa, Mandalesvara, ed. see Das Goswami, Satsvarupa.

Dasa, Mandalesvara, et al, eds. see Goswami, Satsvarupa D.

Dasa, Mathuresa, ed. see Das Goswami, Satsvarupa.

Dasa, Yogesvara & Dasi, Jyotirmayi-Devi. A Gift of Love: The Story of Sudama Brahmin. LC 82-8874. (Illus.). 32p. (gr. 5-8). 1982. PLB 7.00 (ISBN 0-89647-015-6). Bala Bks.

Dasa Goswaini, Satsvarupa. Living with the Scriptures, Vol. 1. Dattatreya dasa, ed. 120p. 1984. text ed. 5.00 (ISBN 0-911233-26-1). Gita Nagari.

Dasa Goswami, Satsvarupa. Handbook for Krishna Consciousness. 380p. 1983. 5.95 (ISBN 0-318-03098-5). Gita Nagari.

--He Lives Forever. Dasa, Mandalesvara, ed. 80p. 1980. 2.00 (ISBN 0-318-03099-3). Gita Nagari.

--In Praise of the Mahajanas & Other Poems. Dasi, Binala, ed. 100p. 1984. pap. text ed. 2.95 (ISBN 0-911233-20-2). Gita Nagari.

Dasa Goswami, Satvarupa. Prabhupada Nectar, Vol. 3. Bimala dasi, ed. 160p. 1985. pap. text ed. 2.00 (ISBN 0-911233-24-5). Gita Nagari.

Dasah, Bernard Z., jt. auth. see Kahl, Alfred L.

Da San Gimignano, Folgore. The Months of the Year. (Illus.). 1951. 5.00 (ISBN 0-87482-016-2). Wake-Brook.

DaSanto, J. A., ed. Mathematical Methods & Applications of Scattering Theory: Proceedings. (Lecture Notes in Physics Ser.: Vol. 130). 331p. 1980. pap. 26.00 (ISBN 0-387-10023-7). Springer-Verlag.

D'Asaro, Barbara. Be Young & Vital: The Nutrition-Exercise Plan. LC 78-24260. (Illus.). 191p. 1979. pap. 7.95 (ISBN 0-89490-022-6). Enslow Pubs.

Dasbach, Fernando L. Blight or Bloom. 198p. 1981. 12.50 (ISBN 0-686-28998-6). Regenbogen-Verlag.

--The Father Has Come. 113p. 1981. 10.00 (ISBN 0-686-28999-4). Regenbogen-Verlag.

Dascal, Marcelo. Pragmatics & the Philosophy of Mind. (Pragmatics & Beyond Ser.: VI: 1). 198p. 1983. pap. 22.00 (ISBN 90-272-2503-6). Benjamins North Am.

Dascalu, D. Electronic Processes in Unipolar Solid State Devices. 1977. 33.00 (ISBN 0-9961000-3-2, Pub. by Abacus England). Heyden.

--Transit Time Effects in Unipolar Solid-State Devices. 1977. 33.00 (ISBN 0-9961003-6-9, Pub. by Abacus England). Heyden.

Dasch. Neotropic Mesochorinae -(Hymenoptera, Ichneumonidae) (Memoirs Ser: No. 22). (Illus.). 509p. 1974. 40.00x (ISBN 0-686-17149-7). Am Entom Inst.

Dasch, Clement E. Ichneumon-Flies of America North of Mexico: Pt. 8. Subfamily. Cremastinae Memoir 29. (Illus.). 702p. 1979. 50.00x (ISBN 0-686-40424-6). Am Entom Inst.

--Ichneumonidae of America North of Mexico: Pt. 5 Subfamily Diplazontinae. (Memoirs Ser: No. 3). (Illus.). 1964. 25.00x (ISBN 0-686-00422-1). Am Entom Inst.

--Ichneumonidae of America North of Mexico: Pt. 6 Subfamily Mesochorinae. (Memoirs Ser: No. 16). (Illus.). 376p. 1971. 40.00x (ISBN 0-686-01269-0). Am Entom Inst.

Daschbach, Edwin. Interpreting Scripture: A Catholic Response to Fundamentalism. 144p. 1985. pap. 6.95 (ISBN 0-697-02110-6). Wm C Brown.

Dascher, Paul E. & Janell, Paul A. Accounting: A Book of Readings. LC 80-70470. 539p. 1983. pap. text ed. 13.95x (ISBN 0-931920-30-2). Dame Pubns.

Dascher, Paul E., jt. auth. see Copeland, Ronald M.

Dascher, Paul E., jt. auth. see Hindelang, Thomas J.

Daschler, John. Supervision in the Hospitality Industry. Harless, Marjorie, ed. 1983. 34.95 (ISBN 0-86612-016-5). Educ Inst Am Hotel.

Dasen, P. R., jt. auth. see Berry, J. W.

Dasen, Pierre. Piagetian Psychology. 1977. 33.95 (ISBN 0-89876-080-1). Gardner Pr.

Dasen, Pierre, ed. Piagetian Psychology: Cross-Cultural Contributions. LC 76-22199. 379p. 1977. 18.95x (ISBN 0-470-15186-2). Halsted Pr.

Dasenbrock, David. Battlestar BASIC for the TRS-80. LC 83-61060. 12.95 (ISBN 0-672-22006-7). Sams.

Dasenbrock, David H. User's Guide to Microcomputer Buzzwords. LC 83-60161. 110p. 1983. pap. text ed. 9.95 (ISBN 0-672-22049-0, 22049). Sams.

Dasenbrock, Reed W. The Literary Vorticism of Ezra Pound & Wyndham Lewis: Towards the Condition of Painting. LC 84-20179. 288p. 1985. text ed. 25.00x (ISBN 0-8018-2486-9). Johns Hopkins.

Dasent, Arthur I. Nell Gwyn Sixteen Fifty to Sixteen Eighty-Seven. LC 70-82824. 1924. 22.00 (ISBN 0-405-08432-3, Blom Pubns). Ayer Co Pubs.

--Speakers of the House of Commons from the Earliest Times to the Present Day. (Illus.). 1965. 29.50 (ISBN 0-8337-0773-6). B Franklin.

Dasent, G. W., tr. see De Paola, Tomie.

Dasent, G. W., tr. see Vigfussen, Gudbrand.

Dasent, George W. East o' the Sun & West o' the Moon. LC 70-97214. (Illus.). xv, 418p. (gr. 1 up). 1970. pap. 6.00 (ISBN 0-486-22521-6). Dover.

--East o' the Sun & West o' the Moon. (Norwegian Folk Tales). (Illus.). 15.50 (ISBN 0-8446-0573-5). Peter Smith.

--Popular Tales from the Norse. (Folklore & Society, House Ser). 1969. Repr. of 1888 ed. 29.00 (ISBN 0-384-10940-3). Johnson Repr.

--Popular Tales from the Norse: With an Introductory Essay on the Origin & Diffusion of Popular Tales. 3rd ed. LC 74-136733. clii, 443p. 1971. Repr. of 1888 ed. 43.00x (ISBN 0-8103-3796-7). Gale.

--The Story of Burnt Njal: From the Icelandic of the Njals Saga. 1979. Repr. lib. bdg. 12.50 (ISBN 0-8495-1100-3). Arden Lib.

Dasent, George W., tr. Story of Burnt Njal. 1971. 9.95x (ISBN 0-460-00558-8, Evman); pap. 3.50x (ISBN 0-460-01558-3, Evman). Biblio Dist.

Dasent, George W., tr. see Asbjornsen, Peter C.

Dasent, Sir George W., tr. see Rask, Rasmus K.

Dasent, W. E. Inorganic Energetics: An Introduction. LC 81-17958. (Cambridge Texts in Chemistry & Biochemistry Ser.). 200p. 1982. 22.95 (ISBN 0-521-24027-1); pap. 11.95 (ISBN 0-521-28406-6). Cambridge U Pr.

--Nonexistent Compounds: Compounds of Low Stability. LC 65-27436. pap. 47.80 (ISBN 0-317-08402-X, 2055035). Bks Demand UMI.

Dasgopta. Computer Architecture: A Synthesis. 1986. price not set (ISBN 0-471-82310-4). Wiley.

Das Goswami, Satsvarupa. Readings in Vedic Literature. 1985. 7.95 (ISBN 0-912776-88-9). Bhaktivedanta.

Das Goswami, Hridayananda. Srimad Bhagavatam. 12.95 (ISBN 0-89213-126-8). Bhaktivedanta.

--Srimad Bhagavatam. 12.95 (ISBN 0-89213-129-2). Bhaktivedanta.

--Srimad Bhagavatam. 12.95 (ISBN 0-89213-130-6). Bhaktivedanta.

Das Goswami, Satsvar upa. Reading Reform. Dattatreya dasa, ed. 120p. 1985. pap. text ed. 4.00 (ISBN 0-911233-28-8). Gita Nagari.

Das Goswami, Satsvarupa. Letters from Srila Prabhupada, Vol. 1. Mandalesvara dasa & Gaura Purnima dasa, eds. 274p. (Orig.). 1982. pap. text ed. 3.95 (ISBN 0-911233-03-2). Gita Nagari.

--Life with the Perfect Master. Dasa, Mathuresa, ed. 110p. 1983. pap. text ed. 3.50 (ISBN 0-911233-17-2). Gita Nagari.

--Lilamrta, Vol. 5. (Illus.). 297p. 12.95 (ISBN 0-89213-119-5). Bhaktivedanta.

--Lilmarta, Vol. 6. (Illus.). 12.95 (ISBN 0-89213-120-9). Bhaktivedanta.

--Living with the Scriptures, Vol. 2. Dattatreya dasa, ed. 120p. 1985. text ed. 5.00 (ISBN 0-911233-27-X). Gita Nagari.

--One Hundred & Eight Rosebushes: Preaching in Germany. Mandalesvara dasa & Bimala dasi, eds. (Prabupada-lila Ser.). 44p. (Orig.). 1982. pap. text ed. 2.00 (ISBN 0-911233-04-0). Gita-Nagari.

--Prabhupada. (Illus.). 387p. 1983. pap. 2.95 (ISBN 0-89213-127-6). Bhaktivedanta.

--Prabhupada: He Built a House in Which the Whole World Could Live. 7.95 (ISBN 0-89213-133-0). Bhaktivedanta.

--Prabhupada Nectar, Bk. 2. Dasi, Bimala, ed. 145p. pap. 4.99 (ISBN 0-911233-23-7). Gita Nagari.

--Prabhupada Nectar, Vol. 4. Bimala dasi, ed. 160p. 1985. pap. text ed. 2.00 (ISBN 0-911233-29-6). Gita Nagari.

--Remembering Srila Prabhupada. Dasa, Mandalesvara, ed. 1983. Bk. 1 & 2, 108p. pap. text ed. 3.95 (ISBN 0-911233-13-X); Bk. 3 & 4, 100p. pap. text ed. 4.95 (ISBN 0-911233-14-8); Set. (ISBN 0-911233-12-1); Bk. 5, 101p. pap. text ed. 3.95 (ISBN 0-911233-15-6); Bk. 6, 98p. pap. text ed. 3.95 (ISBN 0-911233-16-4). Gita Nagari.

--Srila Prbhupada in Latin America. Dasa, Mandalesvara & Dasi, Bimala, eds. (Prabhupada-lila). (Orig.). Vol. 7. pap. text ed. 2.00 (ISBN 0-911233-05-9). Gita-Nagari.

--Vaisnava Behavior: Twenty-Six Qualities of a Devotee. Dasa, Mandalesvara, ed. 201p. 1984. text ed. 5.50 (ISBN 0-911233-18-0). Gita Nagari.

Das Goswami, Satsvarupa see Goswami, Satsvarupa das.

Das Goswami, Satvarupa. Prabhupada Nectar, Vol. 5. Bimala dasi, ed. 160p. 1985. pap. text ed. 2.00 (ISBN 0-911233-31-8). Gita Nagari.
--The Worshipable Deity & Other Poems. Bimala dasi, ed. 140p. 1985. pap. text ed. 4.00 (ISBN 0-911233-30-X). Gita Nagari.
Das Gupta. Principles & Practice of Acute Cardiac Care. 1984. 59.95 (ISBN 0-8151-2279-9). Year Bk Med.
Dasgupta, A. K. Economic Theory & the Developing Countries. LC 74-83520. 250p. 1975. 22.50 (ISBN 0-312-23590-9). St Martin.
--Epochs of Economic Theory. 224p. 1985. 24.95x (ISBN 0-631-13786-6). Basil Blackwell.
--Phases of Capitalism & Economic Theory & Other Essays. 168p. 1983. 14.95x (ISBN 0-19-561565-4). Oxford U Pr.
Dasgupta, Ajit K. Agriculture & Economic Development in India. 1973. 9.00 (ISBN 0-686-20191-4). Intl Bk Dist.
--Economic Freedom, Technology & Planning for Growth. 1973. 9.00 (ISBN 0-686-20217-1). Intl Bk Dist.
Dasgupta, Ajit K., jt. auth. see Chaudhri, D. P.
Das Gupta, Ashin. Malabar in Asian Trade: 1740-1800. LC 66-44074. (Cambridge South Asian Studies). pap. 54.00 (ISBN 0-317-26009-X, 2024446). Bks Demand UMI.
Dasgupta, Biplab. The New Agrarian Technology & India. 1980. 17.50x (ISBN 0-8364-0635-4, Pub. by Macmillan India). South Asia Bks.
--Oil Industry in India. 257p. 1971. 34.00x (ISBN 0-7146-2583-3, F Cass Co). Biblio Dist.
--Selected Studies on the Dynamics, Patterns & Consequences of Migration: Migration & Development: Major Features of Migratory Movement in India, Vol. 3. (Reports & Papers in the Social Sciences: No. 52). (Illus.). 39p. 1983. pap. text ed. 5.00 (ISBN 92-3-102011-0, U1279, UNESCO). Unipub.
Das Gupta, Chidananda. The Cinema of Satyajit Ray. (Illus.). 88p. 1980. text ed. 32.50x (ISBN 0-7069-1035-4, Pub. by Vikas India). Advent NY.
Dasgupta, Gautam, ed. see Breuer, Lee.
Dasgupta, Gautam, jt. ed. see Marranca, Bonnie.
Das Gupta, Jyotirindra. Language Conflict & National Development: Group Politics & National Language Policy in India. LC 75-94992. (Center for South & Southeast Asia Studies, UC Berkeley). 1970. 34.00x (ISBN 0-520-01590-8). U of Cal Pr.
Dasgupta, K. K. Essentials of Marx's Capital. 431p. 1984. text ed. 37.50x (ISBN 0-86590-528-2, Pub. by Sterling Pubs India). Apt Bks.
Dasgupta, Mary A. The Circus of Love. 8.00 (ISBN 0-89253-463-X); flexible cloth 4.80 (ISBN 0-89253-464-8). Ind-US Inc.
--The Peacock Smiles. 8.00 (ISBN 0-89253-471-0); flexible cloth 4.00 (ISBN 0-89253-472-9). Ind-US Inc.
Dasgupta, Mary A., ed. Hers: English Verse by Indian Women. (Writers Workshop Redbirds Ser.). 106p. 1978. flexible bndg. 6.00 (ISBN 0-86578-040-4). Ind-US Inc.
Dasgupta, P. S. & Heal, G. M. Economic Theory & Exhaustible Resources. LC 79-51749. (Cambridge Economic Handbooks Ser.). 1980. 54.50 (ISBN 0-521-22991-X); pap. 19.95 (ISBN 0-521-29761-3). Cambridge U Pr.
Dasgupta, Partha. The Control of Resources. (Illus.). 240p. 1983. text ed. 18.50x (ISBN 0-674-16980-8). Harvard U Pr.
Dasgupta, S. Yoga As Philosophy & Religion. lib. bdg. 79.95 (ISBN 0-87968-104-7). Krishna Pr.
--Yoga As Philosophy & Religion. 1978. Repr. 9.95 (ISBN 0-8426-0488-X). Orient Bk Dist.
Dasgupta, S. K. Commercial & Industrial Law. 306p. 1984. 30.00x (ISBN 0-86590-186-4, Pub. by Sterling India). Apt Bks.
--Industrial Law. 274p. 1984. pap. 8.95x (ISBN 0-86590-185-6). Apt Bks.
Dasgupta, S. N. Hindu Mysticism. 1977. 12.95 (ISBN 0-8426-0929-6). Orient Bk Dist.
--A History of Indian Philosophy, 5 vols. 1975. Set. 56.00 (ISBN 0-8426-0963-6). Orient Bk Dist.
--Religion & Rational Outlook. 1974. Repr. 9.95 (ISBN 0-8426-0661-0). Orient Bk Dist.
--Yoga Philosophy in Relation to Other Systems of Indian Thought. 390p. Repr. 13.00 (ISBN 0-89581-406-4). Asian Human Pr.
Dasgupta, Samir. Bengali Poems on Calcutta. 1973. 15.00 (ISBN 0-88253-324-X); pap. text ed. 6.75 (ISBN 0-88253-795-4). Ind-US Inc.
--Paling Shadows. (Writers Workshop Redbird Ser.). 1975. 8.00 (ISBN 0-88253-606-0); pap. text ed. 4.80 (ISBN 0-88253-605-2). Ind-US Inc.
Dasgupta, Samir, ed. see Dey, Bishnu.
Dasgupta, Sipra. Class Relations & Technological Change in Indian Agriculture. 1981. 16.00x (ISBN 0-8364-0676-1, Pub. by Macmillan India). South Asia Bks.
Das Gupta, Sipra. The Home Book of Indian Cookery. 184p. 1980. pap. 6.95 (ISBN 0-571-11508-X). Faber & Faber.
Dasgupta, Somesh. Come, Solitude, Speak to Me. 8.00 (ISBN 0-89253-683-7); flexible cloth 4.80 (ISBN 0-89253-684-5). Ind-US Inc.
Dasgupta, Subhoranjan. Bodhisattva. 8.00 (ISBN 0-89253-465-6); flexible cloth 4.00 (ISBN 0-89253-466-4). Ind-US Inc.
--Nandini Night. (Writers Workshop Redbird Ser.). 1975. 8.00 (ISBN 0-88253-582-X); pap. text ed. 4.00 (ISBN 0-88253-581-1). Ind-US Inc.
--Pritish Nandy. (Indian Writers Ser.: Vol. XII). 1977. 8.50 (ISBN 0-89253-450-8). Ind-US Inc.
Dasgupta, Subrata. The Design & Description of Computer Architectures. LC 83-21826. 300p. 1984. 40.95x (ISBN 0-471-89616-0, Pub. by Wiley-Interscience). Wiley.
Das Gupta, Tapas K. Tumors of the Soft Tissue. (Illus.). 700p. 1983. 98.00 (ISBN 0-8385-9045-4). ACC.
Dasgupta, Uma. Rise of an Indian Public. 1978. 16.00x (ISBN 0-8364-0292-8). South Asia Bks.
Dash, B. & Kashyap, L. Diagnosis & Treatment of Diseases in Ayurveda. (Todarananda Ayurveda Saukhyam Ser.: No. 4). 160p. 1982. text ed. 35.00x (ISBN 0-391-02839-1, Pub. by Concept India). Humanities.
Dash, Bhagan & Kashyap, Lalitesh. Basic Principles of Ayurveda. 655p. 1980. 39.25x (ISBN 0-391-02208-3). Humanities.
Dash, Bhagwan & Kashyap, L. Diagnosis & Treatment of Diseases in Ayurveda. (Todarananda Ayurveda Saukhyam: Vol. 2). 640p. 1981. text ed. 35.00x (ISBN 0-391-02472-8, Pub. by Concept India). Humanities.
Dash, Bhagwan & Kashyap, Lalitesh. Basic Principles of Ayurveda. (Illus.). 628p. 1980. 44.95x (ISBN 0-940500-34-5). Asia Bk Corp.
Dash, Irene G. Wooing, Wedding, & Power: Women in Shakespeare's Plays. LC 81-4046. (Illus.). 256p. 1981. 26.00x (ISBN 0-231-05238-3); pap. 13.00 (ISBN 0-231-05239-1). Columbia U Pr.
Dash, J. G. Films on Solid Surfaces. 1975. 59.50 (ISBN 0-12-203350-7). Acad Pr.
Dash, J. G. & Ruvalds, J., eds. Phase Transitions in Surface Films. LC 79-28484. (NATO ASI Series B, Physical Sciences: Vol. 51). 379p. 1980. 59.50 (ISBN 0-306-40348-X, Plenum Pr). Plenum Pub.
Dash, J. Michael. Literature & Ideology in Haiti: 1915-1961. 1981. 28.50x (ISBN 0-389-20092-1). B&N Imports.
Dash, Michael, jt. auth. see Bailey, Joyce.
Dash, Norman. Yesterday's Los Angeles. LC 76-21249. (Historic Cities Ser.: No. 26). (Illus.). 208p. 1976. 12.95 (ISBN 0-912458-70-4). E A Seemann.
Dash, Samuel, et al. Eavesdroppers. LC 71-136498. (Civil Liberties in American History Ser). (Illus.). 1971. Repr. of 1959 ed. lib. bdg. 35.00 (ISBN 0-306-70074-3). Da Capo.
Dash, Stanley A., Jr. How to Save Money on Legal Fees. 1984. pap. 12.95 (ISBN 0-517-55178-0). Crown.
Dash, V. & Kashyap, L., eds. Materia Medica of Ayurveda. 1980. text ed. 40.50x (ISBN 0-391-01813-2). Humanities.
Dash, Vaidya B. Fundamentals of Ayurvedic Medicine. 2nd ed. 246p. 1980. text ed. 24.95 (ISBN 0-940500-05-1, Pub. by Bansal-India). Asia Bk Corp.
--Fundamentals of Ayurvedic Medicine. 3rd ed. 246p. 1982. 28.50 (ISBN 0-317-17433-9, Pub. by Cultural Integration). Auromere.
--Handbook of Ayurveda. 221p. (Orig.). 1983. 28.00 (ISBN 0-317-17437-1, Pub. by Cultural Integration). Auromere.
D'A. Shaw, Robert. Jobs & Agricultural Development. LC 79-145446. (Monographs: No. 3). 84p. 1970. 1.00 (ISBN 0-686-28692-8). Overseas Dev Council.
--Rethinking Economic Development. (Development Papers: No. 8). 58p. 1972. pap. 1.00 (ISBN 0-686-28680-4). Overseas Dev Council.
Dashefsky, Arnold, ed. Contemporary Jewry, Vol. 7. 160p. 1985. 19.95x (ISBN 0-87855-979-5). Transaction Bks.
--Contemporary Jewry, Vol. 8. 160p. 1986. 19.95 (ISBN 0-88738-097-2). Transaction Bks.
--Contemporary Jewry, Vol. 8. 160p. 1986. 19.95 (ISBN 0-88738-097-2). Transaction Bks.
Dasher, Thomas E. William Faulkner's Characters: An Index to the Published & Unpublished Fiction. LC 80-9033. 450p. 1981. lib. bdg. 73.00 (ISBN 0-8240-9305-4). Garland Pub.
Dashew, Linda, jt. auth. see Dashew, Steve.
Dashew, Steve. Blue Water Handbook: A Guide to Cruising Seamanship. (Illus.). 320p. 1984. 24.95 (ISBN 0-688-04195-7, Hearst Marine Bks). Morrow.
Dashew, Steve & Dashew, Linda. The Circumnavigators' Handbook. (Illus.). 1983. 35.50 (ISBN 0-393-03275-2). Norton.
Dashiell, Alfred, ed. see Canby, Henry S.
Dashti, Ali. In Search of Omar Khayyam. Elwell-Sutton, L. P., tr. from Persian. LC 77-168669. 276p. 1971. 26.00x (ISBN 0-231-03188-2). Columbia U Pr.
--Twenty Three Years: A Study of the Prophetic Career of Mohammad. Bagley, F. R., tr. from Persian. 224p. 1985. 17.50 (ISBN 0-04-297048-2). Allen Unwin.
Dasi, Bimala, ed. see Das Goswami, Satsvarupa.
Dasi, Bimali, ed. see Goswami, Satsvarupa das.
Dasi, Binala, ed. see Dasa Goswami, Satsvarupa.
Dasi, Jyotirmayi-Devi, jt. auth. see Dasa, Yogesvara.
Da Silva, A. Martins, et al, eds. Biorhythms & Epilepsy. 256p. 1985. text ed. 38.00 (ISBN 0-88167-124-X). Raven.
Da Silva, Andrew J. Do from the Octave of Man Number Four: The Awakening & Crisis, Vol. 1. Sajkovic, Olivera, ed. LC 85-71128. 128p. 1985. 12.00 (ISBN 0-9614941-0-7). Borderline NY.
Da Silva, Armando. Tai Yu Shan: Traditional Ecological Adoptation in a South Chinese Island. (Asian Folklore & Social Life Monograph: No. 32). 1972. 14.00 (ISBN 0-89986-032-X). Oriental Bk Store.
Da Silva, F. H. Lopes see Niedermeyer, Ernst & Lopes da Silva, F. H.
Da Silva, J. R., jt. ed. see Williams, R. J.
DaSilva, Leon. Mercenary-Green Hell. 1976. pap. 1.50 (ISBN 0-685-73458-7, LB388, Leisure Bks). Dorchester Pub Co.
Da Silva, Manuel A., ed. Thermochemistry & Its Applications to Chemical & Biochemical. 1984. lib. bdg. 97.00 (ISBN 0-318-00440-2, Pub. by Reidel Holland). Kluwer Academic.
DaSilva, R. Making Money in Filmmaking. 1986. cancelled (ISBN 0-442-21948-2). Van Nos Reinhold.
Da Silva, Rachel, jt. ed. see Wilson, Barbara.
DaSilva, Willard H. New York Matrimonial Practice: New York Practice Systems Library Selection. LC 79-91156. 87.50; Suppl. 1984. 37.00; Suppl. 1983. 32.00. Lawyers Co-Op.
Da Silva, Z. S. Usted y Yo: Primer Paso. 1975. 6.84 (ISBN 0-02-270100-1). Macmillan.
--Vuelo, Level 3. 1971. 8.96 (ISBN 0-02-270770-0). Macmillan.
DaSilva, Zenia S. A Concept Approach to Spanish. 3rd ed. 1975. text ed. 23.95 scp (ISBN 0-06-041531-2, HarpC); scp tape manual 10.30 (ISBN 0-06-041511-8); scp tapes 351.25 (ISBN 0-06-047476-9). Har-Row.
Da Silva, Zenia S. Margenes: Historia Intima del Pueblo Hispano. 2nd ed. (Illus.). 300p. 1972. pap. text ed. 14.00 scp (ISBN 0-06-041534-7, HarpC). Har-Row.
--On with Spanish: A Concept Approach. 3rd ed. 438p. 1982. text ed. 22.50 scp (ISBN 0-06-041525-8, HarpC); instr's manaul avail. (ISBN 0-06-361511-8); scp tapes 391.00 (ISBN 0-06-047443-2); scp tape manual 9.95 (ISBN 0-06-041526-6). Har-Row.
--Panorama: Lectures Primeras. (Illus.). 144p. 1973. pap. text ed. 10.95 scp (ISBN 0-06-041517-7, HarpC). Har-Row.
--Spanish: A Short Course. 2nd ed. (Illus.). 1980. text ed. 23.95 scp (ISBN 0-06-041524-X, HarpC); instructor's manual avail. (ISBN 0-06-361507-X); scp wkbk. & tape man 9.00 (ISBN 0-06-041518-5); scp tapes 391.00 (ISBN 0-06-047492-0). Har-Row.
--Spanish: A Short Course. 3rd ed. 374p. 1985. text ed. 25.50 scp (ISBN 0-06-041513-4, HarpC); tape manual avail. (ISBN 0-06-041514-2). Har-Row.
Dasilva, Zenia Sacks. Beginning Spanish: A Concept Approach. 5th ed. 536p. 1983. text ed. 23.95 scp (ISBN 0-06-041508-8, HarpC); scp wkbk. 11.50 (ISBN 0-06-041509-6); instr's. manual avail. (ISBN 0-06-361538-X); scp cassettes 350.00 (ISBN 0-06-047442-4); scp reel tapes 350.00 (ISBN 0-06-047446-7). Har-Row.
Da Silva Araquen, Endaldo, tr. see Braun, O.
Dasmann, R. F. Environmental Conservation. 5th ed. LC 83-21767. 486p. 1984. 24.95 (ISBN 0-471-89141-X). Wiley.
Dasmann, Raymond, jt. auth. see Yocom, Charles.
Dasmann, Raymond F. California's Changing Environment. Hundley, Norris & Schutz, John A., eds. LC 81-66064. (Golden State Ser.). (Illus.). 110p. 1981. pap. text ed. 6.95x (ISBN 0-87835-116-7). Boyd & Fraser.
--Destruction of California. 1966. pap. 2.95 (ISBN 0-02-072800-X, Collier). Macmillan.
--Wildlife Biology. 2nd ed. LC 80-19006. 212p. 1981. 27.00x (ISBN 0-471-08042-X). Wiley.
Dasmann, Raymond F. & Poore, Duncan. Ecological Guidelines for Balanced Land Use: Conservation & Development in High Mountains. (Illus.). 40p. 1979. pap. 10.00 (ISBN 2-88032-100-X, IUCN77, IUCN). Unipub.
Dasmann, Raymond F., et al. Ecological Principles for Economic Development. LC 72-8597. 252p. 1973. pap. 28.95 (ISBN 0-471-19606-1, Pub. by Wiley-Interscience). Wiley.
Dasmann, William. Deer Range: Improvement & Management. 2nd ed. LC 80-28280. (Illus.). 176p. 1981. lib. bdg. 15.95x (ISBN 0-89950-027-7). McFarland & Co.
Das Melwani, Murli see Melwani, Murli D.
Dasnoy, A. Paul Maas: Catalog Raisonne. (Illus.). 277p. (Fr.). 1975. 65.00 (ISBN 0-912728-97-3). Newbury Bks.
Daso, Satyendra Kimar see Das Satyendra Kimar.
Dass, Arvind. Agrarian Relations in India. 1980. 18.50x (ISBN 0-8364-0648-6, Pub. by Manohar India). South Asia Bks.
Dass, Baba H. Cat & Sparrow. LC 81-51915. (Illus.). 32p. (gr. k-3). 1982. 6.95 (ISBN 0-918100-06-2). Sri Rama.
--The Magic Gem: A Story Coloring Book. LC 76-10032. (Illus.). 32p. (Orig.). (ps-2). 1976. pap. 2.25 (ISBN 0-918100-07-0). Sri Rama.
Dass, Baba Hari. Sweeper to Saint: Stories of Holy India. Renu, Ma, ed. LC 80-52021. (Illus.). 208p. (Orig.). 1980. pap. 6.95 (ISBN 0-918100-03-8). Sri Rama.
Dass, Baba Hari, et al. Silence Speaks--from the Chalkboard of Baba Hari Dass. LC 76-53902. (Illus.). 224p. (Orig.). 1977. pap. 5.95 (ISBN 0-918100-01-1). SRI Rama.
Dass, Ram. Grist for the Mill. 1979. pap. 3.95 (ISBN 0-553-24228-8). Bantam.
--How Can I Help? Stories & Reflections on Service. Lippe, Toinette, ed. LC 84-48734. 1985. pap. 5.95 (ISBN 0-394-72947-1). Knopf.
--Journey of Awakening: A Mediator's Guidebook. 1978. pap. 3.95 (ISBN 0-553-22793-9). Bantam.
--Miracle of Love: Stories About Neem Karoli Baba. (Illus.). 1979. pap. 12.95 (ISBN 0-525-47611-3, 01257-380). Dutton.
--The Only Dance There Is. LC 73-14054. 295p. 1974. pap. 5.95 (ISBN 0-385-08413-7, Anch). Doubleday.
Dassanayake, M. D., ed. A Handbook to the Flora of Ceylon, Vol. IV. rev. ed. 545p. 1983. lib. bdg. 25.00 (ISBN 90-6191-067-6, Pub. by Balkema RSA). IPS.
Das Satyendra Kimar. Cynewulf & the Cynewulf Canon. LC 73-17006. 1942. lib. bdg. 27.50 (ISBN 0-8414-7701-9). Folcroft.
Dassesse, M., jt. auth. see Isaacs, S.
D'Assier, Adolphe. Posthumous Humanity. Olcott, H. S., ed. & tr. from French. LC 81-50204. (Secret Doctrine Reference Ser.). 384p. 1981. Repr. of 1887 ed. 16.00 (ISBN 0-913510-36-X). Wizards.
D'Assigny, Marius. The Art of Memory: A Treatise Useful for Such as Are to Speak in the Public. LC 83-46046. (Scientific Awakening in the Restoration Ser.: No. 1). 128p. 1985. Repr. of 1697 ed. 45.00 (ISBN 0-404-63301-3). AMS Pr.
D'Assigny, Marius, tr. see Gautruche, Pierre.
Dasso, jt. auth. see Ringl.
Dasso, C. H. Nuclear Physics. 782p. (Proceedings). 1982. 104.25 (ISBN 0-444-86401-6, I-88-82, North-Holland). Elsevier.
Dasso, J., jt. auth. see Ring, A., III.
Dasso, Jerome. Computerized Assessment Administration. LC 73-83136. 1974. 14.00 (ISBN 0-88329-001-4). Intl Assess.
Dasso, Jerome & Kuhn, Gerald W. Real Estate Finance. (Illus.). 464p. 1983. 29.95 (ISBN 0-13-762757-2). P-H.
Dasso, Jerome, jt. auth. see Ring, Alfred A.
Dasso, Jerome, et al. Fundamentals of Real Estate. (Illus.). 1977. ref. ed. 27.95 (ISBN 0-13-343426-5); student guide 12.95 (ISBN 0-13-343442-7). P-H.
Dassori, F. Davis & Rothman, David C. Estate Planning Considerations for Plan Participants: No. B368. (Tax & Estate Planning Considerations for Qualified Plans Ser.). 27p. 1980. pap. 6.00 (ISBN 0-317-31208-1). Am Law Inst.
Dassow, Ethel, jt. auth. see Jackson, W. H.
Dasta, Joseph F., jt. auth. see Majerus, Thomas C.
Dastrup, Boyd L. Crusade in Nuremberg: Military Occupation, 1945-1949. LC 85-927. (Contributions in Military History Ser.: No. 47). (Illus.). 160p. 1985. lib. bdg. 27.50 (ISBN 0-313-24847-8, DCN/). Greenwood.
--U. S. Army Command & General Staff Colllege: A Centennial History. (Illus.). 154p. 1982. 25.00x (ISBN 0-89745-033-7). Sunflower U Pr.
Dastur, J. F. Medicinal Plants of India & Pakistan. 3rd ed. 212p. 1985. text ed. 9.95x (ISBN 0-916638-30-8). Meyerbooks.
Daswani, C. J. Adverbials of Time & Location in English. 140p. 1977. pap. 4.95x (ISBN 0-86125-004-4, Pub by Orient Longman India). Apt Bks.
Data Communications Magazine Staff, ed. Interface Proceedings '84. 1984. softcover 40.00 (ISBN 0-317-04545-8). McGraw.
Data General Corporation, jt. auth. see Burstein, Harvey.
Data Notes Publishing Staff. Aluminum Recycling: Data Notes. LC 83-90732. 30p. 1983. pap. text ed. 4.95 (ISBN 0-911569-40-5, Pub. by Data Notes). Prosperity & Profits.
--Automobile Recycling: Data Notes. LC 83-90735. 30p. pap. text ed. 4.95 (ISBN 0-911569-50-2, Pub. by Data Notes). Prosperity & Profits.
--Candlemaking: Data Notes. (Bibliography Ser.). 25p. 1983. pap. text ed. 2.50 (ISBN 0-911569-63-4, Pub. by Data Notes). Prosperity & Profits.
--Clothing Recycling: Data Notes. 1983. pap. text ed. 9.95 (ISBN 0-911569-49-9, Pub. by Data Notes). Prosperity & Profits.
--College by Television. 26p. 1983. pap. text ed. 4.95 (ISBN 0-911569-24-3, Pub. by Data Notes). Prosperity & Profits.
--Colleges That Offer Credit for Life Experience: A Directory. 300p. 1983. text ed. 49.95 (ISBN 0-911569-07-3, Pub. by Data Notes). Prosperity & Profits.
--Diets: A Reading Bibliography. 16p. 1983. pap. 3.00 (ISBN 0-911569-67-7, Pub. by Data Notes). Prosperity & Profits.
--Directory of Flea Market Directories, Books, References. LC 83-90737. 200p. 1984. pap. text ed. 8.95 (ISBN 0-911569-57-X, Pub. by Data Notes). Prosperity & Profits.
--Directory of Women's Associations & Organizations Based in Iowa. Date not set. pap. text ed. cancelled (ISBN 0-911569-34-0, Pub. by Data Notes). Prosperity & Profits.

--Directory of Women's Associations & Organizations Based in Jersey. Date not set. pap. text ed. cancelled (Pub. by Data Notes). Prosperity & Profits.

--Directory of Women's Associations & Organizations Based in Massachusetts. Date not set. pap. text ed. cancelled (ISBN 0-911569-30-8, Pub. by Data Notes). Prosperity & Profits.

--Directory of Women's Associations & Organizations Based in Maryland. Date not set. pap. text ed. cancelled (ISBN 0-911569-36-7, Pub. by Data Notes). Prosperity & Profits.

--Directory of Women's Associations & Organizations Based in Minnesota. Date not set. pap. text ed. cancelled (Pub. by Data Notes). Prosperity & Profits.

--Directory of Women's Associations & Organizations Based in New York. Date not set. pap. text ed. cancelled (ISBN 0-911569-26-X, Pub. by Data Notes). Prosperity & Profits.

--Directory of Women's Associations & Organizations Based in Texas. Date not set. pap. text ed. cancelled (ISBN 0-911569-29-4, Pub. by Data Notes). Prosperity & Profits.

--Equipment Recycling: Data Notes. LC 83-90736. 30p. 1983. pap. text ed. 4.95 (ISBN 0-911569-48-0, Pub. by Data Notes). Prosperity & Profits.

--Furniture Recycling: Data Notes. 30p. 1983. pap. 4.95 (ISBN 0-911569-45-6, Pub. by Data Notes). Prosperity & Profits.

--Glass Recycling: Data Notes. LC 83-90730. 30p. 1983. pap. text ed. 4.95 (ISBN 0-911569-42-1, Pub. by Data Notes). Prosperity & Profits.

--How to Form a Corporation, Network, Cooperative, Barter Organization, Club, or Association: Data Notes. 50p. 1983. pap. text ed. 15.95 (ISBN 0-911569-56-1, Pub. by Data Notes). Prosperity & Profits.

--Kitchen Recycling: Data Notes. LC 83-90733. 35p. 1983. pap. text ed. 9.95 (ISBN 0-911569-51-0, Pub. by Data Notes). Prosperity & Profits.

--Metal Recycling: Data Notes. LC 83-90729. 30p. 1983. pap. text ed. 9.95 (ISBN 0-911569-44-8, Pub. by Data Notes). Prosperity & Profits.

--One Thousand & More Places to Look for Continuing Education. 200p. 1983. text ed. 49.95 (ISBN 0-911569-05-7, Pub. by Data Notes). Prosperity & Profits.

--Paper Recycling: Data Notes. LC 83-90731. 30p. 1983. pap. text ed. 9.95 (ISBN 0-911569-41-3, Pub. by Data Notes). Prosperity & Profits.

--Refunding Periodicals, Books, Clubs, Associations: A Directory. LC 83-90727. 200p. 1983. text ed. 8.95 (ISBN 0-911569-06-5, Pub. by Data Notes). Prosperity & Profits.

--Rubber Recycling: Data Notes. 30p. 1983. pap. text ed. 4.95 (ISBN 0-911569-43-X, Pub. by Data Notes). Prosperity & Profits.

--Self Storage & Mini Storage: Data Notes. 30p. 1983. pap. text ed. 9.95 (ISBN 0-911569-52-9, Pub. by Data Notes). Prosperity & Profits.

--Shelter Recycling: Data Notes. 30p. 1983. pap. text ed. 9.95 (ISBN 0-911569-46-4, Pub. by Data Notes). Prosperity & Profits.

--Telemarketing, Telephone Sales & Telephone Soliciting; Data Notes. LC 83-90724. 1983. 3.95 (ISBN 0-911569-04-9, Pub. by Data Notes). Prosperity & Profits.

--Telephone Repair & Operations: Bibliography References: Data Notes. LC 83-90725. 25p. 1983. pap. 2.95 (ISBN 0-911569-64-2, Pub. by Data Notes). Prosperity & Profits.

--Trade Show & Exhibition Calendars: Data Notes. LC 83-90725. 25p. 1985. pap. 3.95 (ISBN 0-911569-65-0, Pub by Data Notes). Prosperity & Profits.

--U. S. Directory of Places to Locate Recyclable Scrap. 60p. 1983. text ed. 19.95 (ISBN 0-911569-14-6, Pub. by Data Notes). Prosperity & Profits.

--Vegetarian Associations, Organizations, Periodicals, Cooking Schools & More: International Directory. 100p. 1983. pap. text ed. 19.95 (ISBN 0-911569-53-7, Pub. by Data Notes). Prosperity & Profits.

--Women's Associations & Organizations Based in England: A Directory. Date not set. pap. text ed. 9.95 (ISBN 0-911569-39-1, Pub. by Data Notes). Prosperity & Profits.

--Women's Associations & Organizations: Midwest Region Directory. Date not set. pap. text ed. 9.95 (ISBN 0-911569-27-8, Pub. by Data Notes). Prosperity & Profits.

--Women's Associations & Organizations: Mountain Region Directory. Date not set. pap. text ed. 9.95 (ISBN 0-911569-28-6, Pub. by Data Notes). Prosperity & Profits.

--Women's Associations & Organizations: Northeast Region Directory. Date not set. pap. text ed. 9.95 (ISBN 0-911569-32-4, Pub. by Data Notes). Prosperity & Profits.

--Women's Associations & Organizations: Pacific Coast, Hawaii & Alaska Directory. Date not set. pap. text ed. 9.95 (ISBN 0-911569-31-6, Pub. by Data Notes). Prosperity & Profits.

--Women's Associations & Organizations: Southwest Regional Directory. Date not set. pap. text ed. 9.95 (ISBN 0-911569-37-5, Pub. by Data Notes). Prosperity & Profits.

--Wood Recycling: Data Notes. LC 83-90734. 30p. 1983. pap. text ed. 4.95 (ISBN 0-911569-47-2, Pub. by Data Notes). Prosperity & Profits.

Data Notes Publishing Staff, compiled by. Creative Financing Data Notes. 65p. 10.95 (ISBN 0-911569-00-6, Pub. by Data Notes). Prosperity & Profits.

--Data Notes Bibliographical Reference Handbook. 250p. pap. text ed. 22.95 (ISBN 0-911569-01-4, Pub. by Data Notes). Prosperity & Profits.

--Generics Data Notes. LC 83-90730. 75p. 10.95 (ISBN 0-911569-02-2, Pub. by Data Notes). Prosperity & Profits.

Data Notes Research. Cooking School Alternatives: Mountain States Regional Directory. 58p. 1985. pap. text ed. 7.95 (ISBN 0-911569-35-9, Pub. by Data Notes). Prosperity & Profits.

--Cooking School Alternatives: Pacific Coast, Alaska & Hawaii Regional Directory. 28p. 1985. pap. text ed. 7.95 (ISBN 0-911569-38-3, Pub. by Data Notes). Prosperity & Profits.

--Cooking School Alternatives: Southern Regional Directory. 60p. 1985. pap. text ed. 7.95 (ISBN 0-911569-33-2, Pub. by Data Notes). Prosperity & Profits.

--Ginseng Poetry Pages: Data with Bibliography. 18p. 1985. pap. text ed. 2.75 (ISBN 0-911569-82-0, Pub. by Data Notes). Prosperity & Profits.

Data Notes Research Division Staff. Law Practice: Requirements by State. 25p. 1985. pap. text ed. 6.95 (ISBN 0-911569-79-0, Pub. by Data Notes). Prosperity & Profits.

Data Notes Research Project. Aloe Vera Poetry Pages: Data with Bibliography. 15p. 1985. pap. text ed. 2.75 (ISBN 0-911569-81-2, Pub. by Data Notes). Prosperity & Profits.

--Garlic Poetry Pages: Data with Bibliography. 12p. 1985. pap. text ed. 2.75 (ISBN 0-911569-84-7, Pub. by Data Notes). Prosperity & Profits.

--Ginger Poetry Pages: Data with Bibliography. 11p. 1985. pap. text ed. 2.75 (ISBN 0-911569-80-4, Pub. by Data Notes). Prosperity & Profits.

Data Notes Research Staff. Direct Sales, Commission Sales: Data Notes. LC 83-90738. (Bibliography Ser.). 60p. 1984. pap. 4.95 (ISBN 0-911569-61-8, Pub. by Data Notes). Prosperity & Profits.

--Home Businesses Data Notes. (Bibliography Ser.). 35p. 1984. pap. text ed. 7.95 (ISBN 0-911569-58-8, Pub. by Data Notes). Prosperity & Profits.

--Information & Referral Services: Data Notes. 60p. 1984. pap. text ed. 4.95 (ISBN 0-911569-59-6, Pub. by Data Notes). Prosperity & Profits.

--New Age Consciousness, Metaphysics & Parapsychology: Data Notes. 15p. 1984. pap. 3.50 (ISBN 0-911569-66-9, Pub. by Data Notes). Prosperity & Profits.

--Old Fashioned, Bygone, Yesteryear & Way Back When Products Catalogs: A Directory. LC 83-90728. 100p. 1984. pap. text ed. 3.95 (ISBN 0-911569-62-6, Pub. by Data Notes). Prosperity & Profits.

--Pennystock Publications Books, Etc. Data Notes. LC 83-90739. 25p. 1984. pap. text ed. 3.95 (ISBN 0-911569-60-X, Pub. by Data Notes). Prosperity & Profits.

Data Notes Research Staff, compiled by. References for Debtor's or Bill Payor's; Data Notes. 75p. 12.95 (ISBN 0-911569-03-0, Pub. by Data Notes). Prosperity & Profits.

Data Processing Management Association Staff & Washington Chapter Staff. CDP Examguide. (Computers & Information Processing Systems for Business Ser.). 126p. 1984. pap. 22.45 (ISBN 0-471-80444-4). Wiley.

Dataller, Roger. Drama & Life. 179p. 1982. Repr. of 1938 ed. lib. bdg. 25.00 (ISBN 0-89760-139-4). Telegraph Bks.

DataMyte Corporation. DataMyte Handbook: A Practical Guide to Computerized Data Acquisition for Statistical Quality Control. 432p. (Orig.). 1984. pap. 25.00 (ISBN 0-930345-00-2). DataMyte Corp.

--DataMyte Handbook: A Practical Guide to Computerized Data Acquisition for Statistical Process Control. 2nd ed. Houston, Jerry, ed. 530p. 1985. pap. 30.00 (ISBN 0-930345-01-0). DataMyte Corp.

Datan, Nancy, ed. Transitions of Aging. LC 80-528. 1980. 26.00 (ISBN 0-12-203580-1). Acad Pr.

Datan, Nancy & Reese, Hayne W., eds. Life-Span Developmental Psychology: Dialectical Perspectives on Experimental Research. 1977. 42.50 (ISBN 0-12-203560-7). Acad Pr.

Datan, Nancy, et al. A Time to Reap: The Middle Age of Women in Five Israeli Subcultures. LC 80-26776. 208p. 1981. text ed. 18.50x (ISBN 0-8018-2516-4). Johns Hopkins.

Datan, Nancy, et al, eds. Life-Span Developmental Psych. 304p. text ed. 36.00 (ISBN 0-89859-536-3). L Erlbaum Assocs.

Datapro-McGraw-Hill. Datapro-McGraw-Hill Guide to Apple Software. 2nd ed. 1985. 22.95 (ISBN 0-07-015406-6). McGraw.

--Datapro-McGraw-Hill Guide to CP-M Software. 2nd ed. 1985. 22.95 (ISBN 0-07-015408-2). McGraw.

--Datapro-McGraw-Hill Guide to IBM PC Software. 2nd ed. 1985. 22.95 (ISBN 0-07-015407-4). McGraw.

Datapro Research Corp. Microcomputer Literacy Program: All about Personal Computers. 89p. 1983. write for info. manual. McGraw.

Datapro Research Corporation. Datapro-McGraw Hill Guide to Apple Software. 267p. 1983. pap. 19.95 (ISBN 0-07-015403-1, Pub. by Datapro). McGraw.

--Datapro-McGraw-Hill Guide to Apple Software. 2nd ed. LC 84-20022. 350p. 1984. pap. 22.95 (ISBN 0-07-015406-6). Datapro Res.

--Datapro-McGraw Hill Guide to CP-M Software. 241p. 1984. pap. 19.95 (ISBN 0-07-015404-X, Pub. by Datapro). McGraw.

--Datapro-McGraw-Hill Guide to CP-M Software. 2nd ed. LC 84-20034. 386p. 1984. pap. 22.95 (ISBN 0-07-015408-2). Datapro Res.

--Datapro-McGraw-Hill Guide to IBM PC Software. 2nd ed. LC 84-20021. 390p. 1984. pap. 22.95 (ISBN 0-07-015407-4). Datapro Res.

--Who's Who in Microcomputing. 1983. pap. 39.95 (ISBN 0-07-015405-8, Pub. by Datapro). McGraw.

Datar, Kiran K. Malaysia: Quest for Politics or Consensus. 272p. 1983. text ed. 27.50x (ISBN 0-7069-1972-6, Pub. by Vikas India). Advent NY.

Date, C. J. Database: A User's Guide. (Illus.). 320p. 1983. pap. 12.95 (ISBN 0-201-11358-9). Addison-Wesley.

--Introduction to Database Systems, Vol. I. 3rd ed. LC 80-17603. (IBM Systems Programming Ser.). (Illus.). 704p. 1981. text ed. 32.95 (ISBN 0-201-14471-9). Addison-Wesley.

--Introduction to Database Systems, Vol. II. LC 82-3900. 480p. 1983. text ed. 29.95 (ISBN 0-201-14474-3). Addison-Wesley.

Date, V. H. Spiritual Treasures of St. Ramadasa. 1975. 13.50 (ISBN 0-8426-0805-2). Orient Bk Dist.

--Upanishads Retold. 1979. 11.50x (ISBN 0-8364-0492-0); text ed. 7.00x (ISBN 0-8364-0493-9). South Asia Bks.

Datenverarbeitung, Gruppe, jt. ed. see Bundestag, Deutscher.

Dater, Judy. Imogen Cunningham: A Portrait. LC 79-2375. (Illus.). 1979. 24.95 (ISBN 0-8212-0751-2, 417890). NYGS.

Datesh, John N. The Janus Murder. 1979. pap. 1.75 (ISBN 0-8439-0649-9, Leisure Bks). Dorchester Pub Co.

--The Nightmare Machine. 1979. pap. 1.75 (ISBN 0-505-51372-2, Pub. by Tower Bks). Dorchester Pub Co.

Datesman, Susan K., ed. Women, Crime, & Justice. Scarpitti, Frank R. (Illus., Orig.). 1980. pap. text ed. 8.95x (ISBN 0-19-502676-4). Oxford U Pr.

Datesman, Susan K., jt. ed. see Scarpitti, Frank R.

Dathorne, O. R. African Literature in the Twentieth Century. 1976. pap. 6.50x (ISBN 0-8166-0769-9). U of Minn Pr.

--The Black Mind: A History of African Literature. LC 74-76744. pap. 137.30 (ISBN 0-317-27935-1, 2055854). Bks Demand UMI.

--Dark Ancestor: The Literature of the Black Man in the Caribbean. LC 80-22581. xii, 292p. 1981. 27.50x (ISBN 0-8071-0757-3). La State U Pr.

Dathorne, O. R., ed. Caribbean Narrative. 1966. pap. text ed. 5.50x (ISBN 0-435-98221-4). Heinemann Ed.

--Caribbean Verse. 1967. pap. text ed. 4.50x (ISBN 0-435-98220-6). Heinemann Ed.

--Journal of Caribbean Studies: A Bi-Annual Journal, Vol. 1, Nos. 2 & 3, Vol. 2, Nos. 1, 2 & 3. 1250p. 1981. pap. 6.00 per issue (ISBN 0-686-88938-X, Pub. by Assoc Carib Stud). Three Continents.

Dathorne, Ronald. Dele's Child. LC 84-51445. 200p. 1985. 18.00 (ISBN 0-89410-421-7); pap. 8.00 (ISBN 0-89410-422-5). Three Continents.

Dati, Gregorio, jt. auth. see Pitti, Buonaccorso.

Da Tiepolo, Giovanni B. Drawings of Tiepolo. Millier, Arthur, ed. (Master Draughtsman Ser). (Illus., Orig.). treasure trove bdg. 9.95x (ISBN 0-87505-035-2); pap. 4.95 (ISBN 0-87505-188-X). Borden.

Datig, Fred A. Cartridges for Collectors, 3 Vols. Vol. I. 9.95 ea. (ISBN 0-87505-096-4). Vol. II (ISBN 0-87505-097-2). Vol. III (ISBN 0-87505-098-0). Borden.

--Luger Pistol. rev. ed. 14.95 (ISBN 0-87505-107-3). Borden.

Datin, Richard C. Elegance on C. Street: Virginia City's International Hotel. (Illus.). 48p. 1985. 3.95 (ISBN 0-913814-76-8). Nevada Pubns.

Datlow, Ellen, ed. The First Omni Book of Science Fiction. 1984. pap. 3.95 (ISBN 0-8217-1319-1). Zebra.

--Fourth Omni Book of Science Fiction. 1985. pap. 3.95 (ISBN 0-8217-1630-1). Zebra.

--The Second Omni Book of Science Fiction. 1984. pap. 3.95 (ISBN 0-8217-1320-5). Zebra.

--The Third Omni Book of Science Fiction. 1985. pap. 3.95 (ISBN 0-8217-1575-5). Zebra.

Datnow, Boris. Computerventures, 8 manuals. 347p. (Orig.). (gr. 3-9). 1984. Set. pap. text ed. 59.95 (ISBN 0-913956-16-3). EBSCO Ind.

--Computerventures Byte, No. 1. (Illus.). 42p. (Orig.). (gr. 3-9). 1984. pap. text ed. 8.95 (ISBN 0-913956-06-6). EBSCO Ind.

--Computerventures Byte, No. 2. (Illus.). 43p. (Orig.). (gr. 3-9). 1984. pap. text ed. 8.95 (ISBN 0-913956-07-4). EBSCO Ind.

--Computerventures Byte, No. 3. (Illus.). 64p. (Orig.). (gr. 3-9). 1984. pap. text ed. 9.95 (ISBN 0-913956-08-2). EBSCO Ind.

--Computerventures Byte, No. 4. (Illus.). 33p. (Orig.). (gr. 3-9). 1984. pap. text ed. 8.95 (ISBN 0-913956-09-0). EBSCO Ind.

--Computerventures Byte, No. 5. (Illus.). 65p. (Orig.). (gr. 3-9). 1984. pap. text ed. 9.95 (ISBN 0-913956-10-4). EBSCO Ind.

--Computerventures Byte, No. 6. (Illus.). 39p. (gr. 3-9). 1984. pap. text ed. 8.95 (ISBN 0-913956-11-2). EBSCO Ind.

--Computerventures Byte, No. 7. (Illus.). 35p. (Orig.). (gr. 3-9). 1984. pap. text ed. 7.95 (ISBN 0-913956-12-0). EBSCO Ind.

--Computerventures Byte, No. 8. (Illus.). 27p. (Orig.). (gr. 3-9). 1984. pap. text ed. 5.95 (ISBN 0-913956-13-9). EBSCO Ind.

Datnow, Claire L. Computerventures-1: Instructor's Guide & Reference Manual-A BASIC Computer Curriculum for Beginners. (Illus.). 123p. (Orig.). 1984. tchr's. ed. 20.00 (ISBN 0-913956-14-7). EBSCO Ind.

Datnow, Claire-Louise, et al. Downtown-An Outdoor Classroom. (Illus.). 54p. 1981. 10.00 (ISBN 0-943994-07-1). Birmingham Hist Soc.

Dato, Daniel P., ed. Georgetown University Round Table on Languages & Linguistics: Developmental Psycholinguistics, Theory & Applications. LC 58-31607. (Georgetown Univ. Round Table Ser.: 1975). 297p. (GURT 1975). 1975. pap. 6.95 (ISBN 0-87840-110-5). Georgetown U Pr.

Daton, Liz, jt. auth. see Christie, Anna.

Dator, James & Bezold, Clement. Judging the Future. LC 81-51228. 151p. 1981. pap. text ed. 11.00x (ISBN 0-8248-0770-7, Soc Sci Res Inst). UH Pr.

D'Atri, J. E. & Ziller, W. Naturally Reductive Metrics & Einstein Metrics on Compact Lie Groups. LC 79-7. (Memoirs Ser.: No. 215). 72p. 1982. pap. 13.00 (ISBN 0-8218-2215-2). Am Math.

Datskevich, V. The Green Island. 59p. 1980. 3.60 (ISBN 0-8285-2015-1, Pub. by Progress Pubs USSR). Imported Pubns.

Datt, S. C. & Srivastava, S. B. Foundation Course: Science & Society. 242p. 1985. pap. text ed. 10.95x (ISBN 0-7069-2669-2, Pub. by Vikas India). Advent NY.

Datta, A. State Municipal Fiscal Relations: A Comparative Study of Australia & India. LC 82-73258. (Centre for Research on Federal Financial Relations Research Monograph: No. 37). 70p. 1983. pap. text ed. 14.95 (ISBN 0-86784-140-0, 1617, Pub. by ANUP Australia). Australia N U P.

Datta, Amaresh. Captive Moments. (Redbird Bk.). 1976. 8.00 (ISBN 0-89253-528-8); flexible bdg. 4.00 (ISBN 0-89253-082-0). Ind-US Inc.

Datta, Ansu. Education & Society: A Sociology of African Education. LC 84-40338. 206p. 1985. 25.00 (ISBN 0-312-23720-0). St Martin.

Datta, Couri. Of Amaranths & Else. 1983. 5.95 (ISBN 0-533-05691-8). Vantage.

Datta, Dhirendra M. Philosophy of Mahatma Gandhi. 168p. 1953. pap. 8.50x (ISBN 0-299-01014-7). U of Wis Pr.

Datta, Gautam & Meerman, Jacob. Household Income or Household Income per Capita in Welfare Comparisons. (World Bank Staff Working Paper: No. 378). 32p. 1980. pap. 3.00 (ISBN 0-686-39730-4, WP-0378). World Bank.

Datta, K. K. Anti-British Plots & Movements Before 1857. 1970. 5.50x (ISBN 0-8426-0169-4). Verry.

Datta, Lois-Ellin, ed. Evaluation in Change. (Sage Research Progress Series in Evaluation: Vol. 12). 160p. 1981. 20.00 (ISBN 0-8039-1731-7); pap. 9.95 (ISBN 0-8039-1732-5). Sage.

Datta, Lois-Ellin & Perloff, Robert, eds. Improving Evaluations. LC 79-13627. (Sage Focus Editions: Vol. 12). (Illus.). 280p. 1979. 28.00 (ISBN 0-8039-1240-4); pap. 14.00 (ISBN 0-8039-1241-2). Sage.

Datta, Naomi, ed. Antibiotic Resistance in Bacteria. (Illus.). 111p. 1984. pap. text ed. 22.00 (ISBN 0-443-02947-4). Churchill.

Datta, S. K., ed. Earthquake Ground Motion & Its Effects On Structures. (AMD Ser.: Vol. 53). 197p. 1982. 40.00 (H00241). ASME.

Datta, Supriyo. Surface Acoustic Wave Devices. (Illus.). 208p. 1986. text ed. 42.95 (ISBN 0-13-877911-2). P-H.

Datta, Surajit K. De see De Datta, Surajit K.

Datta, V. N. Madan Lal Dhingra & the Revolutionary Movement. 1978. 9.50x (ISBN 0-8364-0206-5). South Asia Bks.

Datta, V. N. & Gleghorn, B. E., eds. A Nationalist Muslim & Indian Politics. LC 75-902114. 352p. 1974. 14.00 (ISBN 0-333-90023-5). South Asia Bks.

Datta-Chaudhuri, Mrinal, jt. auth. see Lefeber, Louis.

Dattagupta, S., jt. ed. see Agarwal, G. S.

Dattaray, Rajatbaran. A Critical Survey of the Life & Works of Ksemendra. 1974. 9.00 (ISBN 0-88386-574-2). South Asia Bks.

Datta-Ray, Sunanda K. Smash & Grab: Annexation of Sikkim. 300p. 1984. text ed. 32.50x (ISBN 0-7069-2509-2, Pub. by Vikas India). Advent NY.

Dattatreya. Avadhuta Gita of Dattatreya. Ashokananda, Swami, tr. from Sanskrit. 1978. pap. 3.95 (ISBN 0-87481-482-0). Vedanta Pr.

Dattatreya dasa, ed. see Dasa Goswaini, Satsvarupa.

Dattatreya dasa, ed. see Das Goswami, Satsvar upa.

Dattatreya dasa, ed. see Das Goswami, Satsvarupa.

D'Attilio, Anthony. Seashore Life Coloring Book. 48p. 1973. pap. 2.25 (ISBN 0-486-22930-0). Dover.

D'Attilio, Anthony, jt. auth. see Radwin, George E.

D'Attilio, Robert, tr. see Galleani, Luigi.

Datwyler, Scott, jt. auth. see Schimpf, Ann.

Datye, Deshav Vinayak & Vaidya, Ashok Amrut. Chemical Processing of Synthetic Fibers & Blends. LC 83-19809. 565p. 1984. 80.00x (ISBN 0-471-87654-2, Pub. by Wiley-Interscience). Wiley.

Datyner, Arved. Surfactants in Textile Processing. (Surfactant Science Ser.: No. 14). (Illus.). 232p. 1983. 49.50 (ISBN 0-8247-1812-7). Dekker.

Datz & Datz. Processing Words with Your IBM PC, PC XT or PC Compatible. 232p. 1984. 15.95 (ISBN 0-317-06579-3, 6359). Hayden.

Datz, Frederick L. Gamuts in Nuclear Medicine. 302p. 1983. 29.95 (ISBN 0-8385-3075-3). ACC.

Datz, I. Mortimer. Power Transmission & Automation for Ships & Submersibles. (Illus.). 190p. 45.00 (ISBN 0-85238-074-7, FN23, FNB). Unipub.

Datz, S., ed. Physics of Electronic & Atomic Collisions: Abstracts of Contributed Papers, 2 Vols. 1220p. 1981. Set. pap. 138.50 (ISBN 0-444-86322-2, North-Holland). Elsevier.

--Physics of Electronic & Atomic Collisions: Invited Papers of the International Conference on the Physics of Electronic & Atomic Collisions, XIIth, Gatlinburg, TN, July 15-21, 1981. 872p. 1982. 140.50 (ISBN 0-444-86323-0, North-Holland). Elsevier.

Datz, Sheldon, et al. Atomic Collisions in Solids, 2 vols. Incl. Vol. 1. 502p. 75.00x (ISBN 0-306-38211-3); Vol. 2. 477p. 75.00x (ISBN 0-306-38212-1). LC 74-26825. 1975. price 135.00 set (Plenum Pr). Plenum Pub.

Dau, G. J., jt. ed. see Nichols, R. W.

Dau, W. H., tr. see Walther, Carl F.

Daub, Edward E. Fire. LC 77-26664. (Read About Science). (Illus.). (gr. k-3). 1978. PLB 14.25 (ISBN 0-8393-0080-8). Raintree Pubs.

--Fire. LC 77-26664. (Read about Science Ser.). (Illus.). 48p. (gr. 2-5). 1983. pap. 9.27g (ISBN 0-8393-0294-0). Raintree Pubs.

Daub, Edward E., et al. Comprehending Technical Japanese. LC 74-5900. 440p. 1975. 32.50x (ISBN 0-299-06680-0). U of Wis Pr.

Daub, Guida H., jt. auth. see Seese, William S.

Daube, David. The Exodus Pattern in the Bible. LC 78-9920. 1979. Repr. of 1963 ed. lib. bdg. 24.75 (ISBN 0-313-21190-6, DAEX). Greenwood.

--Forms of Roman Legislation. LC 78-12308. 111p. 1979. Repr. of 1956 ed. lib. bdg. 24.75x (ISBN 0-313-21146-9, DAFR). Greenwood.

--The New Testament & Rabbinic Judaism. LC 73-2191. (The Jewish People; History, Religion, Literature Ser.). Repr. of 1956 ed. 38.50 (ISBN 0-405-05257-X). Ayer Co Pubs.

--Roman Law. 205p. 1969. 17.50x (ISBN 0-85224-051-1, Pub. by Edinburgh U Pr Scotland). Columbia U Pr.

Daube, Jasper R., et al. Medical Neurosciences: An Approach to Anatomy, Pathology, & Physiology by Systems & Levels. 1978. text ed. 34.50 (ISBN 0-316-17361-4, Little Med Div); pap. text ed. 24.95 (ISBN 0-316-17362-2). Little.

Dauben, Joseph W. The History of Mathematics from Antiquity to the Present: A Selective Bibliography. Multhauf, Robert & Wells, Ellen, eds. LC 81-43364. (Reference Library of the Humanities: Bibliographies of the History of Science & Technology Ser.). 508p. 1984. lib. bdg. 80.00 (ISBN 0-8240-9284-8). Garland Pub.

Dauben, Joseph W., ed. Mathematical Perspectives: Essays on Mathematics & Its Historical Development. LC 80-1781. 1981. 43.50 (ISBN 0-12-204050-3). Acad Pr.

Dauben, Joseph W. & Sexton, Virginia S., eds. History & Philosophy of Science: Selected Papers, Vol. 412. 1983. 33.00x (ISBN 0-89766-217-2); pap. 33.00x (ISBN 0-89766-218-0). NY Acad Sci.

Dauben, William G. Organic Reactions, Vol. 29. LC 42-20265. 457p. 1983. 49.50 (ISBN 0-471-87490-6, Pub. by Wiley-Interscience). Wiley.

--Organic Reactions, Vol. 30. (Organic Reactions Ser.). 592p. 1984. 54.50 (ISBN 0-471-89013-8, 2201, Pub. by Wiley-Interscience). Wiley.

--Organic Reactions, Vol. 32. LC 42-20265. (Organic Reactions Ser.: 2201). 533p. 1984. 54.95 (ISBN 0-471-88101-5, Pub. by Wiley-Interscience). Wiley.

Dauben, William G., ed. Organic Reactions, Vol. 21. LC 42-20265. (Organic Reactions Ser.). 428p. 1984. Repr. of 1974 ed. lib. bdg. 42.50 (ISBN 0-89874-777-5). Krieger.

--Organic Reactions, Vol. 22. LC 42-20265. 486p. 1984. Repr. of 1975 ed. 42.50 (ISBN 0-89874-795-3). Krieger.

--Organic Reactions, Vol. 23. LC 42-20265. 528p. 1984. Repr. of 1976 ed. 42.50 (ISBN 0-89874-796-1). Krieger.

--Organic Reactions, Vol. 24. LC 42-20265. 444p. 1984. Repr. of 1976 ed. 42.50 (ISBN 0-89874-797-X). Krieger.

--Organic Reactions, Vol. 25. LC 42-20265. 518p. 1984. Repr. of 1977 ed. 42.50 (ISBN 0-89874-798-8). Krieger.

--Organic Reactions, Vol. 26. LC 42-20265. (Organic Reactions Ser.). 496p. 1984. Repr. of 1979 ed. lib. bdg. 42.50 (ISBN 0-89874-778-3). Krieger.

--Organic Reactions, Vol. 31. LC 42-20265. (Organic Reactions Ser.: 2-201). 376p. 1984. 44.50 (ISBN 0-471-88671-8, Pub by Wiley Interscience). Wiley.

Dauben, William G., et al, eds. Organic Reactions, Vol. 22. LC 42-20265. 486p. 1984. Repr. of 1975 ed. 42.50 (ISBN 0-89874-795-3). Krieger.

Daubenmire, Rexford. Plant Geography: With Special Reference to North America. (Physiological Cology Ser.). 1978. 47.00 (ISBN 0-12-204150-X). Acad Pr.

--Plants & Environment: A Textbook of Plant Autecology. 3rd ed. LC 73-13826. 422p. 1974. 38.50 (ISBN 0-471-19636-3). Wiley.

Daubeny, Ulric. Orchestral Wind Instruments, Ancient & Modern. facs. ed. (Select Bibliographies Reprint Ser). 1920. 16.00 (ISBN 0-8369-5597-8). Ayer Co Pubs.

--Orchestral Wind Instruments Ancient & Modern. 1977. lib. bdg. 59.95 (ISBN 0-8490-2380-7). Gordon Pr.

Dauber, Kenneth. Rediscovering Hawthorne. LC 76-45893. Repr. of 1977 ed. 47.20 (ISBN 0-8357-9510-1, 2014030). Bks Demand UMI.

Dauber, Milton A. Revenue Act of 1964. 160p. 1964. pap. 2.64 (ISBN 0-317-30794-0, B316). Am Law Inst.

Dauber, Roslyn & Cain, Melinda, eds. Women & Technological Change in Developing Countries. LC 80-21653. (AAAS Selected Symposium Ser.: No. 53). 266p. 1980. pap. 28.50x (ISBN 0-89158-791-8). Westview.

Daubert, Darlene M., jt. auth. see Brownstein, Oscar L.

Daubert, James R. & Rothert, Eugene A., Jr. Horticultural Therapy at a Psychiatric Hospital. (Illus.). 120p. (Orig.). 1981. pap. 10.00 (ISBN 0-939914-03-4). Chi Horticult.

--Horticultural Therapy for the Mentally Handicapped. (Illus.). 118p. 1981. pap. 10.00 (ISBN 0-939914-04-2). Chi Horticult.

Daubert, James R., jt. auth. see Rothert, Eugene A.

Daubert, James R., jt. auth. see Rothert, Eugene A., Jr.

Daubert, T. E. Chemical Engineering Thermodynamics. (Chemical Engineering Ser.). 496p. 1985. 40.00 (ISBN 0-07-015413-9). McGraw.

Daubier, Jean. History of the Chinese Cultural Revolution. Seaver, Richard, tr. 1974. pap. 2.95 (ISBN 0-394-71843-7, V-843, Vin). Random.

D'Aubigne, Agrippa. Oeuvres. Weber, ed. (Bibliotheque de la Pleiade). 29.95 (ISBN 0-685-34179-8). French & Eur.

--Les Tragiques, 4 tomes. Garnier & Plattard, eds. (Soc. des Textes Francais Modernes). Set. 34.50 (ISBN 0-685-34180-1). French & Eur.

--Les Tragiques. McFarlane, I. D., ed. (Renaissance Library). 184p. (Fr.). 1970. 32.50 (ISBN 0-485-13803-4, Pub. by Athlone Pr Ltd); pap. 14.95 (ISBN 0-485-12803-9). Longwood Pub Group.

D'Aubigne, Merle. The Reformation in England, 2 vols. 1977. Vol. 1. 16.95 (ISBN 0-85151-059-0); Vol. 2. 16.95 (ISBN 0-85151-094-9); Set. 30.95 (ISBN 0-85151-214-3). Banner of Truth.

Daubitz, Paul. The Public Manager's Phone Book. 250p. 1985. text ed. 50.00 (ISBN 0-89006-151-3). Artech Hse.

Daubitz, Paul & Ross, Robert. The Public Manager's Phone Book. 142p. 1979. 35.00 (ISBN 0-686-98039-5). Telecom Lib.

Daudel, D., et al, eds. Structure & Dynamics of Molecular Systems. 1985. lib. bdg. 39.50 (ISBN 90-277-1977-2, Pub. by Reidel Holland). Kluwer Academic.

Daudel, P. Radioactive Tracers in Chemistry & Industry. 2nd ed. Eisner, U., tr. from Fr. 210p. 1960. 27.00x (ISBN 0-85264-101-X, Pub. by Griffin England). State Mutual Bk.

Daudel, R. Quantum Theory of Chemical Reactivity. LC 73-75762. 1973. lib. bdg. 31.50 (ISBN 90-277-0265-9, Pub. by Reidel Holland); pap. 24.00 (ISBN 90-277-0420-1). Kluwer Academic.

Daudel, R. & Pullman, A., eds. Quantum Theory of Chemical Reactions. 1982. lib. bdg. 32.50 (ISBN 90-277-1467-3, Pub. by Reidel Holland). Kluwer Academic.

Daudel, R., ed. see First International Congress of Quantum Chemistry, Menton, France, July 4-10, 1973.

Daudel, Raymond. Quantum Chemistry. LC 82-23688. 558p. 1983. 97.00x (ISBN 0-471-90135-0, Wiley-Interscience). Wiley.

--Quantum Theory of the Chemical Bond. LC 74-82700. Orig. Title: Theorie Quantique De la Liaison Chimique. 1974. lib. bdg. 26.00 (ISBN 90-277-0264-0, Pub. by Reidel Holland); pap. text ed. 14.00 (ISBN 90-277-0528-3, Pub. by Reidel Holland). Kluwer Academic.

Daudel, Raymond & Sandorfy, Camille. Semiempirical Wave-Mechanical Calculations Polyatomic Molecules: A Current Review. LC 74-140525. (Yale Series in the Sciences). (Illus.). pap. 36.80 (ISBN 0-317-13001-3, 2016797). Bks Demand UMI.

Daudel, Raymond, et al, eds. Quantum Theory of Chemical Reactions: Collision Theory, Reaction Path, Static Indices, Vol. 1. 1980. lib. bdg. 34.00 (ISBN 90-277-1047-3, Pub. by Reidel Holland). Kluwer Academic.

--Quantum Theory of Chemical Reactions: Solvent Effect, Reaction Mechanisms, Photochemical Processes, Vol. 11. 340p. 1980. PLB 42.00 (ISBN 90-277-1182-8, Pub. by Reidel Holland). Kluwer Academic.

Dauderis, Henry. Basic Accounting. 2nd Canadian ed. 1978. text ed. 17.95 (ISBN 0-03-928001-2, Pub. by HR&W Canada); Instructor's Manual & Transparencies with Purchase of Textbook avail. (ISBN 0-685-86066-3); student self study guide 4.95 (ISBN 0-03-928002-0). HR&W.

Daudet, Alphonse. L' Arlesienne. deluxe ed. 1100.00 (ISBN 0-685-34888-1). French & Eur.

--L' Arlesienne. 110p. 1965. 9.95 (ISBN 0-686-55584-8). French & Eur.

--La Belle-Nivernaise, & Other Stories. LC 77-130056. (Short Story Index Reprint Ser). 1895. 14.00 (ISBN 0-8369-3643-4). Ayer Co Pubs.

--La Chevre de Monsieur Seguin. (Illus.). 20p. 1972. 7.95 (ISBN 0-686-55585-6). French & Eur.

--Contes Choisis. (Illus.). 186p. 1977. 6.95 (ISBN 0-686-55586-4). French & Eur.

--Contes Du Lundi. 1962. pap. 3.95 (ISBN 0-685-11104-0, 1058). French & Eur.

--Les Contes du Lundi. 344p. 1969. 13.95 (ISBN 0-686-55587-2). French & Eur.

--La Doulou. 244p. 1931. 6.95 (ISBN 0-686-55588-0). French & Eur.

--L' Elixir du Reverend Pere Gaucher. (Illus.). 31p. 1977. 7.95 (ISBN 0-686-55589-9). French & Eur.

--L' Evangeliste. 294p. 1952. 3.95 (ISBN 0-686-55590-2). French & Eur.

--Fromont Jeune et Risler Aine. 306p. 1953. 6.95 (ISBN 0-686-55591-0). French & Eur.

--Letters from My Mill & Letters to an Absent One. facsimile ed. LC 72-37266. (Short Story Index Reprint Ser.). Repr. of 1900 ed. 18.00 (ISBN 0-8369-4077-6). Ayer Co Pubs.

--Letters from My Windmill. Davies, Frederick, tr. from Fr. Ardizzone, Edward, ed. (Classic Ser). 1978. pap. 4.95 (ISBN 0-14-044334-7). Penguin.

--Lettres De Mon Moulin. (Easy Readers, Ser. A). 48p. (Fr.). 1976. pap. text ed. 3.25 (ISBN 0-88436-225-6, 40266). EMC.

--Lettres De Mon Moulin. (Illus.). 1962. 15.50 (ISBN 0-685-11290-X, 848); pap. 3.95 (ISBN 0-685-11291-8, 848). French & Eur.

--Lettres de Mon Moulin. deluxe ed. 428.00 (ISBN 0-685-34889-X). French & Eur.

--Lettres de Mon Moulin. Pleasants, Jeanne V., ed. 1965. pap. text ed. 4.25 (ISBN 0-940630-05-2, T-7021). Playette Corp.

--Monday Tales. facsimile ed. LC 78-113654. (Short Story Index Reprint Ser.). 1900. 19.00 (ISBN 0-8369-3383-4). Ayer Co Pubs.

--Le Nabab. 250p. 1950. 6.95 (ISBN 0-686-55592-9). French & Eur.

--Numa Roumestan. 348p. 1950. 6.95 (ISBN 0-686-55593-7). French & Eur.

--Le Petit Chose. 420p. 1948. 8.95 (ISBN 0-686-55594-5). French & Eur.

--Les Rois En Exil. 1940. 7.95 (ISBN 0-686-55596-1). French & Eur.

--Sapho. 256p. 1950. 8.95 (ISBN 0-686-55597-X). French & Eur.

--Le Secret de Maitre Cornille. (Illus.). 32p. 1964. 7.95 (ISBN 0-686-55598-8). French & Eur.

--Soutien De Famille. 460p. 1898. 6.95 (ISBN 0-686-55599-6). French & Eur.

--Suffering: Eighteen Eighty-Seven to Eighteen Ninety-Five. 1934. 29.50x (ISBN 0-686-51319-3). Elliots Bks.

--Tartarin de Tarascon. (Coll. Prestige). 1965. 27.95 (ISBN 0-685-11580-1). French & Eur.

--Tartarin de Tarascon. (Class. Garnier). pap. 6.95 (ISBN 0-685-34887-3). French & Eur.

--Tartarin de Tarascon. (Illus.). 159p. 1977. 3.95 (ISBN 0-686-55600-3). French & Eur.

--Tartarin of Tarascon. Bd. with Tartarin on the Alps. 1954. 12.95x (ISBN 0-460-00423-9, Evman). Biblio Dist.

--Tartarin sur les Alpes. 3.95 (ISBN 0-686-55601-1). French & Eur.

--Le Tresor d'Arlatan. (Illus.). 160p. 1897. 11.95 (ISBN 0-686-55602-X). French & Eur.

--Vacances en Bretagne: Pirioc. Extraits. (Illus.). 60p. 1973. 6.95 (ISBN 0-686-55603-8). French & Eur.

Daudet, Alphonse, et al. Quinze Histoires de Provence. (Illus.). 220p. 1977. 8.95 (ISBN 0-686-55595-3). French & Eur.

Daudet, Leon. Alphonse Daudet. 1973. Repr. of 1898 ed. 17.50 (ISBN 0-8274-1414-5). R West.

Daudet, Lula C. & Roberts, Ruth C. Pinto Beans & a Silver Spoon. 144p. 1980. 9.95 (ISBN 0-8059-2724-7). Dorrance.

Daudet, Yves, jt. auth. see Debbasch, Charles.

Daudistel, Howard, et al. Criminal Justice: Situations & Decisions. LC 76-41970. 1979. text ed. 24.95 (ISBN 0-275-49890-5, HoltC) (ISBN 0-03-039426-0). HR&W.

Daudon, Rene. French in Review. 2nd ed. 433p. 1962. text ed. 18.95 (ISBN 0-15-528850-4, HC); tapes, 10 reels 125.00 (ISBN 0-15-528851-2, HC). HarBraceJ.

Dauenhauer, Bernard P. Silence: The Phenomenon & Its Ontological Significance. LC 80-7683. (Studies in Phenomenology & Existential Philosophy). 224p. 1980. 20.00x (ISBN 0-253-11021-1). Ind U Pr.

Dauenhauer, Bernard P., tr. see Le Senne, Rene.

Dauenhauer, Richard. Glacier Bay Concerto. (Alaskana Book Ser.: No. 38). 120p. (Orig.). 1980. 12.95 (ISBN 0-935094-02-4); pap. 4.95 (ISBN 0-935094-04-0). Alaska Pacific.

--Phrenologies. (Orig.). 1981. pap. 6.00 (ISBN 0-914476-90-4). Thorp Springs.

Dauenhauer, Richard & Binham, Philip, eds. Snow in May: An Anthology of Modern Finnish Writing 1945-1972. LC 74-4967. (Illus.). 389p. 1978. 29.50 (ISBN 0-8386-1583-X). Fairleigh Dickinson.

Dauer, Carl C., et al. Infectious Diseases. LC 68-15635. (Vital & Health Statistics Monographs, American Public Health Association). 1968. 17.50x (ISBN 0-674-45350-6). Harvard U Pr.

Dauer, Dorothea W. Schopenhauer As Transmitter of Buddhist Ideas. (European University Studies: Series 1, German Language & Literature: Vol. 15). 39p. 1969. 6.55 (ISBN 3-261-00014-7). P Lang Pubs.

Dauer, Manning J., ed. Florida's Politics & Government. 2nd ed. LC 80-20723. (Orig.). 1984. pap. 18.00x (ISBN 0-8130-0797-6). U Presses Fla.

Dauer, Manning, Jr. The Adams Federalists. LC 84-12995. xxiii, 381p. 1984. Repr. of 1953 ed. lib. bdg. 45.00x (ISBN 0-313-22663-6, DAAD). Greenwood.

Dauer, Rosamond. Bullfrog & Gertrude Go Camping. LC 78-13740. (Greenwillow Read-Alone Bks.). (Illus.). 40p. (gr. 1-3). 1980. 8.75 (ISBN 0-688-80207-9); PLB 8.88 (ISBN 0-688-84207-0). Greenwillow.

--Bullfrog Grows up. LC 75-19097. (Greenwillow Read-Alone Bks.). (Illus.). 56p. (gr. 1-4). 1976. PLB 8.88 (ISBN 0-688-84020-5). Greenwillow.

--The Three Hundred Pound Cat. (Illus.). 32p. 1983. pap. 2.25 (ISBN 0-380-62745-0, 62745-0, Camelot). Avon.

Dauer, Victor & Pangrazi, Robert. Dynamic Physical Education for Elementary School Children. 7th ed. LC 78-69796. 1983. text ed. 25.95x (ISBN 0-8087-4417-8). Burgess.

Dauer, Victor P. & Pangrazi, Robert P. Dynamic Physical Education for Elementary School Children. 8th, rev. ed. (Illus.). 608p. 1986. text ed. price not set (ISBN 0-8087-4444-5). Burgess.

Dauer, Victor P., jt. auth. see Pangrazi, Robert P.

Daufouy, P., jt. auth. see Van Der Straeton, S.

Daugaard, J. Symptoms & Signs in Occupational Diseases. 1979. 20.95 (ISBN 0-8151-2293-4). Year Bk Med.

D'Augelli, Anthony, et al. Helping Others. LC 80-17819. 170p. 1980. pap. text ed. 10.75 pub net (ISBN 0-8185-0401-3). Brooks-Cole.

Daugert, Stanley M. The Philosophy of Thorstein Veblen. vii, 134p. Repr. of 1950 ed. lib. bdg. 15.00x (ISBN 0-87991-651-6). Porcupine Pr.

Daugette, Marion. Hank's Hank. 32p. 1982. 5.95 (ISBN 0-89962-275-5). Todd & Honeywell.

Daughaday, W. H., ed. Endocrine Control of Growth. (Current Endocrinology Ser.: Vol. 1). 276p. 1981. 45.50 (ISBN 0-444-00434-3, Biomedical Pr). Elsevier.

Daughaday, William H., jt. auth. see Odell, William D.

Daugherty, Charles, jt. auth. see Maxson, Linda.

Daugherty, Charles M. Six Artists Paint a Landscape. LC 75-11511. (Illus.). 128p. 1983. pap. 14.95 (ISBN 0-89134-064-5). North Light Pub.

Daugherty, D. H., et al. A Bibliography of Periodical Literature in Musicology & Allied Fields, No. 1 & 2. LC 71-177974. 148p. 1971. Repr. of 1940 ed. lib. bdg. 35.00 (ISBN 0-306-70413-7). Da Capo.

Daugherty, Don G., jt. auth. see Talley, Harry E.

Daugherty, Harry M. The Inside Story of the Harding Tragedy. facsimile ed. (Select Bibliographies Reprint Ser). Repr. of 1932 ed. 25.50 (ISBN 0-8369-5833-0). Ayer Co Pubs.

--Inside Story of the Harding Tragedy. LC 75-27054. 348p. 1975. pap. 4.95 (ISBN 0-88279-118-4). Western Islands.

Daugherty, J. S. & Powell, R. E. Sheet-Metal Pattern Drafting & Shop Problems. rev. ed. 196p. 1975. pap. text ed. 16.88 (ISBN 0-02-665680-9). Bennett IL.

Daugherty, James. Andy & the Lion. LC 38-27390. (Illus.). 80p. (gr. 1-4). 1938. PLB 12.95 (ISBN 0-670-12433-8). Viking.

--The Landing of the Pilgrims. LC 80-21430. (Landmark Bks.). (Illus.). 160p. (gr. 5-9). 1981. pap. 3.95 (ISBN 0-394-84697-4). Random.

Daugherty, Lynn B. Why Me? Help for Victims of Child Sexual Abuse (Even If They Are Adults Now) LC 84-61863. 112p. (Orig.). 1985. pap. 7.95 (ISBN 0-941300-01-3). Mother Courage.

Daugherty, Richard D. Early Man in Washington. (Illus.). 66p. 1959. 0.50 (ISBN 0-686-34735-8). Geologic Pubns.

Daugherty, Richard D., jt. auth. see Kirk, Ruth.

Daugherty, Sarah B. The Literary Criticism of Henry James. LC 80-36753. xiv, 232p. 1981. 19.95x (ISBN 0-8214-0440-7, 82-83277); pap. 10.00x (ISBN 0-8214-0697-3, 82-84663). Ohio U Pr.

Daugherty, Tracy E. College Students Tell It Like It Is: What College Is Really Like. LC 83-51572. (Illus.). 192p. 1984. pap. 7.95 (ISBN 0-9613096-0-1). Sara Pubns.

Daugherty, William E. A Psychological Warfare Casebook. LC 58-2297. pap. 160.00 (ISBN 0-317-08179-9, 2003848). Bks Demand UMI.

Daughety, Andrew R., ed. Analytical Studies in Transport Economics. (Illus.). 329p. Date not set. price not set (ISBN 0-521-26810-9). Cambridge U Pr.

Daughters, Charles G. Wells of Discontent. Bruchey, Stuart & Carosso, Vincent P., eds. LC 78-18959. (Small Business Enterprise in America Ser.). (Illus.). 1979. Repr. of 1937 ed. lib. bdg. 27.50x (ISBN 0-405-11463-X). Ayer Co Pubs.

Daughters of Bilitis. The Ladder, 9 vols. LC 75-12330. (Homosexuality Ser.). 1975. Repr. 328.50x (ISBN 0-405-07371-2). Ayer Co Pubs.

Daughters of St. Paul. ABC's Dictionary. write for info. Dghtrs St Paul.

--Adventures of Peter & Paul. 120p. 1984. 10.00 (ISBN 0-8198-0726-5). Dghtrs St Paul.

--Alive in the Spirit. rev. ed. (Way, Truth & Life Ser.). (Illus.). (gr. 5). 1974. text ed. 2.75 (ISBN 0-8198-0282-4); tchr's manual 5.75 (ISBN 0-8198-0283-2); activity bk. 1.50 (ISBN 0-8198-0284-0); parents' guide 01.25 (ISBN 0-8198-0285-9). Dghtrs St Paul.

--All or Nothing. 1976. 2.00 (ISBN 0-8198-0382-0); pap. 0.95 (ISBN 0-8198-0383-9). Dghtrs St Paul.

--Always with Jesus. 1973. 3.95 (ISBN 0-8198-0265-4); pap. 2.95 (ISBN 0-8198-0714-1). Dghtrs St Paul.

--Basic Catechism Manual, Vol. I. (gr. 1-6). 1981. pap. 5.95 (ISBN 0-8198-1107-6). Dghtrs St Paul.

--Basic Catechism Manual, Vol. II. (gr. 7-12). 1981. pap. 5.95 (ISBN 0-8198-1106-8). Dghtrs St Paul.

--Boy with a Mission. 1967. 3.00 (ISBN 0-8198-0229-8). Dghtrs St Paul.

--A Brief Catholic Dictionary for Young People. 1977. pap. text ed. 1.00 (ISBN 0-8198-0389-8). Dghtrs St Paul.

--Brief Review for Confirmation. 1973. pap. 0.75 (ISBN 0-8198-0250-6). Dghtrs St Paul.

--Brief Summary of the Ten Commandments. 1976. pap. text ed. 1.75 (ISBN 0-8198-0386-3). Dghtrs St Paul.

--Came the Dawn. (Encounter Ser.). (Illus.). 102p. 1982. 3.00 (ISBN 0-8198-1402-4, EN0045); pap. 2.00 (ISBN 0-8198-1403-2). Dghtrs St Paul.

--Catherine of Siena. (Encounter Ser.). (gr. 3 up). 1975. 3.00 (ISBN 0-8198-0395-2). Dghtrs St Paul.

--Choose Your Tomorrow. 1975. pap. 1.95 (ISBN 0-8198-0488-6). Dghtrs St Paul.

--Christ Lives in Me. rev. ed. (Way, Truth & Life Ser.). (Illus.). (gr. 2). 1973. text ed. 2.00 (ISBN 0-8198-0308-1); tchr's manual 5.50 (ISBN 0-8198-0309-X); activity bk. 1.00 (ISBN 0-8198-0310-3); parent guide 1.25 (ISBN 0-8198-0311-1). Dghtrs St Paul.

--Christ of Vatican Two. (St. Paul Editions). (Illus.). 1968. 2.00 (ISBN 0-8198-0024-4); pap. 1.00 (ISBN 0-8198-0025-2). Dghtrs St Paul.

--Christ: Our Way to the Father. rev. ed. (Way, Truth & Life Ser.). (Illus.). (gr. 3). 1973. text ed. 2.00 (ISBN 0-8198-0300-6); tchrs. manual 5.50 (ISBN 0-8198-0301-4); activity bk. 1.00 (ISBN 0-8198-0302-2); parent guide 0.95 (ISBN 0-8198-0303-0). Dghtrs St Paul.

--Christ's Law of Love. rev. ed. (Way, Truth & Life Ser.). (Illus.). (gr. 4). 1973. text ed. 2.50 (ISBN 0-8198-0296-4); tchrs manual 5.50 (ISBN 0-8198-0297-2); activity bk. 1.50 (ISBN 0-8198-0298-0); parent guide 1.25 (ISBN 0-8198-0299-9). Dghtrs St Paul.

--Communicators for Christ. 1973. 5.00 (ISBN 0-8198-0249-2). Dghtrs St Paul.

--The Conscience Game. 1966. 3.00 (ISBN 0-8198-0231-X). Dghtrs St Paul.

--The Daughters of St. Paul: 50 Years of Service in the U.S.A. 1932-1982. (Illus.). 295p. 1982. 15.00 (ISBN 0-8198-1805-4, MS0133). Dghtrs St Paul.

--David. 0.75 (ISBN 0-8198-1800-3). Dghtrs St Paul.

--Documents on Renewal for Religious. LC 74-75621. 1974. pap. 3.50 (ISBN 0-8198-0319-7). Dghtrs St Paul.

--Drawing Near Him with Confidence. 1976. 3.95 (ISBN 0-8198-0403-7); pap. 2.95 (ISBN 0-8198-0404-5). Dghtrs St Paul.

--Faces of Courage. (Illus.). 1974. 5.00 (ISBN 0-8198-0292-1); pap. 4.00 (ISBN 0-8198-0293-X). Dghtrs St Paul.

--Faith We Live By. LC 68-59044. (Divine Master Ser., Vol. 3). (Illus.). 1969. 7.50 (ISBN 0-8198-0039-2); pap. 6.00 (ISBN 0-8198-0040-6); discussion & project manual 0.60 (ISBN 0-8198-0041-4). Dghtrs St Paul.

--Fifty-Seven Saints for Boys & Girls. (Illus.). (gr. 5-8). 1963. 7.50 (ISBN 0-8198-0044-9); pap. 6.50 (ISBN 0-8198-0045-7). Dghtrs St Paul.

--Flame in the Night. 1967. 3.00 (ISBN 0-8198-0234-4). Dghtrs St Paul.

--Gamble for God. (Encounter Bk.). (Illus.). 132p. (gr. 3-8). 1984. 3.00 (ISBN 0-8198-3033-X); pap. 2.00 (ISBN 0-8198-3034-8). Dghtrs St Paul.

--Gentle Revolutionary. (Encounter Ser.). (gr. 3 up). 1978. 3.00 (ISBN 0-8198-0358-8). Dghtrs St Paul.

--Giae Ly Can Ban. Tueng, Andrew, tr. Orig. Title: Basic Catachism. 202p. (Orig., Vietnamese.). 1983. pap. text ed. 2.00 (ISBN 0-8198-3035-6). Dghtrs St Paul.

--God Loves Me. (gr. 1-6). 1982. pap. 1.95 (ISBN 0-8198-3032-1); teacher's manual 3.95 (ISBN 0-8198-3031-3). Dghtrs St Paul.

--God or Nothing? 222p. 1985. 4.00 (ISBN 0-8198-3039-9); pap. 3.00 (ISBN 0-8198-3040-2). Dghtrs St Paul.

--God the Father Sent His Son. rev. ed. (Way, Truth & Life Ser.). (Illus.). (gr. 1). 1973. text ed. 2.00 (ISBN 0-8198-0286-7); tchrs. manual 5.50 (ISBN 0-8198-0287-5); activity bk. 1.00 (ISBN 0-8198-0288-3); parent guide 1.25 (ISBN 0-8198-0289-1). Dghtrs St Paul.

--God's People on the Move. LC 68-59042. (Divine Master Ser.). (gr. 10). pap. 2.50 (ISBN 0-8198-0348-0); rev. tchr's. manual 3.95 (ISBN 0-8198-0349-9). Dghtrs St Paul.

--God's Secret Agent. 1967. 3.00 (ISBN 0-8198-0236-0). Dghtrs St Paul.

--Heaven. 1977. 3.50 (ISBN 0-8198-0419-3); pap. 2.50 (ISBN 0-8198-0420-7). Dghtrs St Paul.

--Heroes from Every Walk of Life. 1981. 5.00 (ISBN 0-8198-3303-7); pap. 4.00 (ISBN 0-8198-3304-5). Dghtrs St Paul.

--His Saving Love. rev. ed. (Way, Truth & Life Ser.). (Illus.). (gr. 7). 1976. text ed. 2.75 (ISBN 0-8198-0340-5); tchrs. manual 6.95 (ISBN 0-8198-0341-3); activity bk. 1.60 (ISBN 0-8198-0342-1); parent guide 1.50 (ISBN 0-8198-0343-X). Dghtrs St Paul.

--I Learn About Jesus. 1973. 5.50 (ISBN 0-8198-0246-8); pap. 4.00 (ISBN 0-8198-0247-6). Dghtrs St Paul.

--I Learn About Jesus: Projects & Activities for Pre-Schoolers. 1973. pap. 1.00 (ISBN 0-8198-0245-X). Dghtrs St Paul.

--I Pray with Jesus. 1978. deluxe ed. 6.00 (ISBN 0-8198-0535-1); plastic bdg. 3.00 (ISBN 0-8198-0537-8). Dghtrs St Paul.

--Into the Woods & Other Favorite Verses. LC 73-89937. (Illus.). 1974. 5.50 (ISBN 0-8198-0281-6). Dghtrs St Paul.

--Introductions to the Books of the New Testament. 1977. pap. 1.00 (ISBN 0-8198-0421-5). Dghtrs St Paul.

--Joey. 1980. 3.00 (ISBN 0-8198-3907-8); pap. 2.00 (ISBN 0-8198-3908-6). Dghtrs St Paul.

--Karol from Poland. write for info. Dghtrs St Paul.

--Light in the Grotto. 1972. 3.00 (ISBN 0-8198-4409-8); pap. 2.00 (ISBN 0-8198-4410-1). Dghtrs St Paul.

--Live the Mass. rev. ed. (Way, Truth & Life Ser.). (Illus.). (gr. 6). text ed. 1.75 (ISBN 0-8198-0272-7); tchr's. manual 3.95 (ISBN 0-8198-0273-5); activity bk. 0.85 (ISBN 0-8198-0274-3); parent guide 0.69 (ISBN 0-8198-0275-1). Dghtrs St Paul.

--Live the Truth-Give the Truth. rev. ed. (Way, Truth & Life Ser.). (Illus.). (gr. 8). 1976. text ed. 2.75 (ISBN 0-8198-0304-9); tchr's. manual 6.95 (ISBN 0-8198-0305-7); activity bk. 1.60 (ISBN 0-8198-0306-5); parent guide 1.50 (ISBN 0-8198-0307-3). Dghtrs St Paul.

--Living & Growing Through the Eucharist. 1976. 7.00 (ISBN 0-8198-0432-0); pap. 6.00 (ISBN 0-8198-0433-9). Dghtrs St Paul.

--Mass Means of Communication. (Illus., Orig.). 5.00 (ISBN 0-8198-0096-1); pap. 4.00 (ISBN 0-8198-0097-X). Dghtrs St Paul.

--Master Plan Revealed. (Divine Master Ser.). (gr. 9). pap. 3.00 (ISBN 0-8198-0346-4); rev. project & discussion manual o.s.i. 3.95 (ISBN 0-8198-0347-2). Dghtrs St Paul.

--Media Impact & You. 1981. 2.95 (ISBN 0-8198-4702-X); pap. 1.95 (ISBN 0-686-73820-9). Dghtrs St Paul.

--Moments for Prayer. plastic bdg. 1.00 (ISBN 0-8198-0277-8); pap. 0.40 (ISBN 0-8198-0278-6). Dghtrs St Paul.

--More Than a Knight. (Encounter Ser.). (Illus.). 100p. 1982. 3.00 (ISBN 0-8198-4714-3, EN0204); pap. 2.00 (ISBN 0-8198-4715-1). Dghtrs St Paul.

--Mother Cabrini. 1977. 3.50 (ISBN 0-8198-0440-1); pap. 2.50 (ISBN 0-8198-0441-X). Dghtrs St Paul.

--Mother Seton. 1975. 3.95 (ISBN 0-8198-0487-8). Dghtrs St Paul.

--My Favorite Prayers & Reflections. 1973. plastic bdg. 5.00 (ISBN 0-8198-0276-X). Dghtrs St Paul.

--Obedience: The Greatest Freedom. 1966. 4.00 (ISBN 0-8198-0106-2). Dghtrs St Paul.

--Prayers for Young Adults. 1985. 4.00 (ISBN 0-8198-5822-6). Dghtrs St Paul.

--Preparing to Receive Jesus Christ. (Way, Truth & Life Ser.). 1978. 1.75 (ISBN 0-8198-0548-3); tchr's manual 3.50 (ISBN 0-8198-0549-1); activity book 1.00 (ISBN 0-8198-0550-5). Dghtrs St Paul.

--Really Living. LC 68-59042. (Divine Master Ser.). (gr. 11). pap. 3.00 (ISBN 0-8198-0350-2); rev. tchr's. manual 3.95 (ISBN 0-8198-0351-0). Dghtrs St Paul.

--Religion for the People of Today. LC 78-160576. (Illus.). 1971. pap. 1.25 (ISBN 0-8198-0345-6). Dghtrs St Paul.

--Religious Life in the Light of Vatican 2. (Orig.). 4.00 (ISBN 0-8198-0132-1). Dghtrs St Paul.

--St. Paul: A Good Friend of Jesus. 1980. 2.50 (ISBN 0-8198-6811-6); pap. 1.75 (ISBN 0-8198-6810-8). Dghtrs St Paul.

--St. Paul Mass Book for Children. (Illus.). 1973. 1.75 (ISBN 0-8198-0336-7); pap. 1.00 (ISBN 0-8198-0337-5). Dghtrs St Paul.

--St. Rita of Cascia: Saint of the Impossible. LC 73-91992. 1973. 3.95 (ISBN 0-8198-0335-9). Dghtrs St Paul.

--Saints for Young People for Every Day, Vol. 1, Jan.-june, Vol. 2, July-dec. (Illus.). (gr. 4-8). 6.00 ea. (ISBN 0-8198-0143-7); pap. 4.50 ea. (ISBN 0-8198-0144-5). Dghtrs St Paul.

--Seven Spiritual Works of Mercy. 1979. 1.75 (ISBN 0-8198-6805-1); pap. 1.00 (ISBN 0-8198-6806-X). Dghtrs St Paul.

--Sixteen Documents of Vatican Two. pap. 3.25 (ISBN 0-8198-0146-1). Dghtrs St Paul.

--Spiritual Life in the Bible. 1980. 5.95 (ISBN 0-686-76825-6); pap. 4.00 (ISBN 0-8198-6813-2). Dghtrs St Paul.

--The Teachings & Miracles of Jesus. 1981. 5.00 (ISBN 0-686-73821-7); pap. 4.00 (ISBN 0-8198-7302-0). Dghtrs St Paul.

--Teenagers Today. 1981. 4.00 (ISBN 0-8198-7303-9); pap. 3.00 (ISBN 0-8198-7304-7). Dghtrs St Paul.

--Thoughts of the Servant of God, Mother Thecla Merlo. LC 68-59045. 1974. flexible plastic 2.25 (ISBN 0-8198-0509-2). Dghtrs St Paul.

--When Jesus Was Born. (Illus.). 1973. plastic bdg. 2.00 (ISBN 0-8198-0326-X); pap. 1.25 (ISBN 0-8198-0327-8). Dghtrs St Paul.

--Where the Gospel Meets the World. 1977. 6.95 (ISBN 0-8198-0482-7); pap. 5.00 (ISBN 0-8198-0483-5). Dghtrs St Paul.

--Where's Grandma? write for info. Dghtrs St Paul.

--Wind & Shadows. (Encounter Ser.). (gr. 4-7). 3.00 (ISBN 0-8198-0174-7); pap. 2.00 (ISBN 0-8198-0175-5). Dghtrs St Paul.

--Woman of Faith. (Illus.). 1965. 3.00 (ISBN 0-8198-0179-8). Dghtrs St Paul.

--Women of the Bible. LC 71-145574. (Illus.). 5.95 (ISBN 0-8198-0322-7); pap. 4.95 (ISBN 0-8198-0323-5). Dghtrs St Paul.

--Women of the Gospel. LC 74-32122. 1975. 5.95 (ISBN 0-8198-0495-9); pap. 4.95 (ISBN 0-8198-0496-7). Dghtrs St Paul.

--Yes Is Forever. (Encounter Ser.). (Illus.). 109p. 1982. 3.00 (ISBN 0-8198-8700-5, EN0260); pap. 2.00 (ISBN 0-8198-8702-1). Dghtrs St Paul.

Daughters of St. Paul, ed. Bible Stories for Everyone. 1956. 6.00 (ISBN 0-8198-0008-2); pap. 5.00 (ISBN 0-8198-0009-0). Dghtrs St Paul.

--Catechism of Modern Man. 3rd rev. ed. 1971. 7.95 (ISBN 0-8198-0015-5); pap. 6.95 (ISBN 0-8198-0016-3). Dghtrs St Paul.

--Church's Amazing Story. rev. ed. LC 68-59043. (Divine Master Ser., Vol. 2). (gr. 10). 1969. 6.00 (ISBN 0-8198-0028-7); pap. 5.00 (ISBN 0-8198-0029-5); teacher's manual 2.75 (ISBN 0-8198-0030-9). Dghtrs St Paul.

--Dimensions of the Priesthood. new ed. 1973. 5.75 (ISBN 0-8198-0253-0); pap. 4.50 (ISBN 0-8198-0254-9). Dghtrs St Paul.

--Drawing Near Him with Confidence. (Chinese.). 1978. 3.95 (ISBN 0-8198-1801-1); pap. 2.95 (ISBN 0-8198-1802-X). Dghtrs St Paul.

--One Family Under God. (Divine Master Ser.). (Orig.). 1968. 3.00 (ISBN 0-8198-0109-7); pap. 2.00 (ISBN 0-8198-0110-0). Dghtrs St Paul.

Daughters of St. Paul, compiled by. Scriptural Meditations on the Rosary. 1981. 3.50 (ISBN 0-8198-6814-0). Dghtrs St Paul.

Daughters of St. Paul, compiled by see Pope John Paul, II.

Daughters Of St. Paul, ed. see Pope Paul VI.

Daughters of St. Paul, tr. Yes to Life. 1977. 6.95 (ISBN 0-8198-0485-1); pap. 5.95 (ISBN 0-8198-0486-X). Dghtrs St Paul.

Daughters Of St. Paul, tr. see Alberione, James.

Daughters of St. Paul, tr. see Alberione, James.

Daughters of St. Paul, tr. see Del Mazza, Valentino.

Daughters of St. Paul, tr. see Ricciardi, Antonio.

Daughters of St. Paul Editorial Staff. Looking Ahead to Marriage. (Divine Master Ser.). (Illus.). 1969. 5.25 (ISBN 0-8198-0259-X); pap. 4.25 (ISBN 0-8198-0260-3); discussion & projects manual 0.50 (ISBN 0-8198-0261-1). Dghtrs St Paul.

Daughters of St Paul. Basic Catechism. 1980. 3.00 (ISBN 0-8198-0622-6); pap. 2.00 (ISBN 0-8198-0623-4). Dghtrs St Paul.

--Blessed Kateri Takakwitha: Mohawk Maiden. 1980. 3.75 (ISBN 0-8198-1100-9); pap. 2.25 (ISBN 0-8198-1101-7). Dghtrs St Paul.

--Father Damien of Molokai. 1979. pap. 0.95 (ISBN 0-8198-0640-4). Dghtrs St Paul.

--Moments of Decision. 1976. 5.00 (ISBN 0-8198-0445-2); pap. 4.00 (ISBN 0-8198-0446-0). Dghtrs St Paul.

--Morality Today: The Bible in My Life. 1979. 3.25 (ISBN 0-8198-0620-X); pap. 2.25 (ISBN 0-8198-0621-8). Dghtrs St Paul.

--My Massbook. (gr. 3 up). 1978. plastic bdg. 2.00 (ISBN 0-8198-0361-8); pap. 1.25 (ISBN 0-8198-0362-6). Dghtrs St Paul.

--My Prayer Book. (gr. 3 up). 1978. plastic bdg. 2.00 (ISBN 0-8198-0359-6); pap. 1.25 (ISBN 0-8198-0360-X). Dghtrs St Paul.

--Saint Paul for Every Day of the Year. 1979. 6.00 (ISBN 0-686-63641-4); pap. 4.50 (ISBN 0-8198-0646-3). Dghtrs St Paul.

--Saints for Young People for Every Day of the Year, Vol. 2. (Illus.). (gr. 4 up). 6.00 (ISBN 0-8198-0647-1); pap. 4.50 (ISBN 0-8198-0648-X). Dghtrs St Paul.

--We Make a Promise. (gr. 3 up). 1978. plastic bdg. 1.75 (ISBN 0-8198-0373-1); pap. 1.00 (ISBN 0-8198-0374-X). Dghtrs St Paul.

--Your Right to Be Informed. LC 68-59042. (Divine Master Ser.: Vol. 1). 1969. 7.95 (ISBN 0-8198-0518-1); pap. 6.50 (ISBN 0-8198-0519-X); teacher manual 8.50 (ISBN 0-8198-0520-3). Dghtrs St Paul.

Daughters Of The American Revolution - Georgia. Historical Collections of the Joseph Habersham Chapter, Vol. 1. Peel, Mrs. William L., ed. LC 67-26474. 352p. 1967. Repr. of 1902 ed. 20.00 (ISBN 0-8063-0088-4). Genealog Pub.

--Historical Collections of the Joseph Habersham Chapter, Vol. 2. Peel, Mrs. William L., ed. LC 67-26474. 726p. 1968. Repr. of 1902 ed. 30.00 (ISBN 0-8063-0089-2). Genealog Pub.

--Historical Collections of the Joseph Habersham Chapter, Vol. 3. Peel, Mrs. William, ed. LC 67-26474. 293p. 1968. Repr. of 1910 ed. 18.50 (ISBN 0-8063-0090-6). Genealog Pub.

Daughtery, R. L. & Franzini, J. B. Fluid Mechanics with Engineering Applications. 8th ed. LC 84-10050. 640p. 1985. 40.95 (ISBN 0-07-015441-4). McGraw.

Daughton, Rosalee. Sara Becomes a Witch. 80p. 1982. 7.95 (ISBN 0-89962-283-6). Todd & Honeywell.

Daughtrey, Anne S., et al. Basic Business & Economic Education. 1982. text ed. 8.35 (ISBN 0-538-24130-6, X13). SW Pub.

Daughtrey, William H., Jr. & Gross, Malvern, Jr. Museum Accounting Handbook. (Illus.). 158p. pap. 12.00 (ISBN 0-317-32307-5); pap. 8.50 members (ISBN 0-317-32308-3). Am Assn Mus.

Daughtry, Dewitt C., ed. Thoracic Trauma. 1980. text ed. 38.50 (ISBN 0-316-17380-0). Little.

Daughtry, Duanne. What's Inside. LC 83-19565. (Borzoi Bks.). (Illus.). 32p. (ps-k). 1984. 7.95 (ISBN 0-394-86249-X); 8.99 (ISBN 0-394-96249-4). Knopf.

Daughtry, Jolyne, jt. auth. see McConnell, Sharon.

D'Augustine, Charles H. Multiple Methods of Teaching Mathematics in the Elementary School. 2nd ed. (Illus.). 416p. 1984. pap. text ed. 13.50 (ISBN 0-8191-4012-0). U Pr of Amer.

Daujat, Jean. The Faith Applied. 1963. 5.95 (ISBN 0-933932-22-7). Scepter Pubs.

Daul, Von C., et al. Landolt-Bornstein: Part A-Atoms, Inorganic Radicals & Radicals in Metal Complexes. LC 62-53136. (Numerical Data & Functional Relationships in Science & Technology Ser.). (Illus.). 1977. 161.70 (ISBN 0-387-08019-8). Springer-Verlag.

D'Aulaire, Edgar P., jt. auth. see D'Aulaire, Ingri.

D'Aulaire, Emily & D'Aulaire, Ola. Chimps & Baboons. Bourne, Russell & Rifkin, Natalie S., eds. LC 74-80051. (Ranger Rick's Best Friends Ser.). (Illus.). 32p. (gr. 1-6). 1974. 2.00 (ISBN 0-912186-14-3). Natl Wildlife.

D'Aulaire, Ingri & D'Aulaire, Edgar P. Abraham Lincoln. rev. ed. (gr. k-4). 1957. 12.95a (ISBN 0-385-07669-X); PLB (ISBN 0-385-07674-6). Doubleday.

--Animals Everywhere. (ps-1). 1954. PLB 7.95 (ISBN 0-385-07703-3). Doubleday.

--Benjamin Franklin. (Illus.). (gr. 1-4). 1950. 11.95 (ISBN 0-385-07219-8). Doubleday.

--Columbus. LC 55-9011. (gr. k-4). PLB 9.95 (ISBN 0-385-07262-7). Doubleday.

--D'Aulaires' Book of Greek Myths. LC 62-15877. (Illus.). 1962. 17.95a (ISBN 0-385-01583-6); PLB (ISBN 0-385-07108-6). Doubleday.

--D'Aulaires Book of Greek Myths. 1962. pap. 9.95 (ISBN 0-385-15787-8, Zephyr). Doubleday.

--D'Aulaires' Trolls. LC 76-158897. 64p. (gr. 1-5). 1972. 8.95a (ISBN 0-385-08255-X); PLB o.p. (ISBN 0-385-01275-6); pap. 2.95 (ISBN 0-385-13339-1, Zephyr). Doubleday.

--Don't Count Your Chicks. 48p. (ps-1). 1973. PLB 10.95 (ISBN 0-385-07609-6). Doubleday.

--George Washington. (Illus.). 64p. (gr. 1-4). 13.95 (ISBN 0-385-07306-2). Doubleday.

--Norse Gods & Giants. LC 67-19109. (Illus.). 160p. (gr. 3-7). 1967. write for info. (ISBN 0-385-04908-0); 14.95 (ISBN 0-385-07235-X). Doubleday.

--Pocahontas. (Illus.). 48p. (gr. 1-4). 1949. 9.95 (ISBN 0-385-07454-9). Doubleday.

D'Aulaire, Ola, jt. auth. see D'Aulaire, Emily.

D'Ault-Dumesnil, G. E. Dictionnaire Historique, Geographique et Biographique des Croisades. Migne, J. P., ed. (Nouvelle Encyclopedie Theologique Ser.: Vol. 18). 619p. (Fr.). Repr. of 1852 ed. lib. bdg. 79.00x (ISBN 0-89241-265-8). Caratzas.

Daum. Extrahepatic Biliary Atresia. (Gastroenterology Ser.). 336p. 1983. 45.00 (ISBN 0-8247-7017-X). Dekker.

Daum, E. & Schenk, W. A Dictionary of Russian Verbs. LC 76-17455. (Orig., Rus. & Eng.). 1983. 22.50x (ISBN 0-88254-420-9). Hippocrene Bks.

Daum, Edmund & Schenk, W. Deutsch-Russisches Woerterbuch. 15th ed. (Ger. & Rus.). 1976. 13.50 (ISBN 0-686-56602-5, M-7333, Pub. by Max Hueber). French & Eur.

--Russich-Deutsches Woerterbuch. 7th ed. (Rus. & Ger.). 1976. 17.50 (ISBN 3-19-006219-6, M-7606, Pub. by Max Hueber). French & Eur.

Daum, Peggy, ed. The Best Cook on the Block. (Illus.). 202p. 1979. pap. 4.95 (ISBN 0-686-34428-6). Milwaukee Journal.

Daum, Susan M. & Stellman, Jeanne M. Work Is Dangerous to Your Health: A Handbook of Health Hazards in the Workplace & What You Can Do about Them. pap. 5.95 (ISBN 0-394-71918-2, V-918, Vin). Random.

Daum, Susan M., jt. auth. see Stellman, Jeanne M.

Daum, V. & Schenk. Dictionary of Russian Verbs (Russian-English) 750p. (Rus. & Eng.). 1980. 75.00x (ISBN 0-569-08093-2, Pub. by Collet's). State Mutual Bk.

Daumal, Rene. Mount Analogue: A Novel of Symbolically Authentic Non-Euclidean Adventures in Mountain Climbing. Shattuck, Roger, tr. from Fr. 120p. 1974. pap. 4.95 (ISBN 0-14-003947-3). Penguin.

--A Night of Serious Drinking. Coward, David & Lovatt, E. A., trs. 121p. 1985. pap. 7.95 (ISBN 0-87773-335-X, 74217-6). Shambhala Pubns.

--Rasa, or Knowledge of the Self. Levi, Louise L., tr. from Fr. LC 81-22389. 128p. 1982. 12.95 (ISBN 0-8112-0824-9); pap. 5.95 (ISBN 0-8112-0825-7, NDP530). New Directions.

Daumantas, Juozas L. Fighters for Freedom. 1975. 9.95 (ISBN 0-87141-049-4). Manyland.

Daumard, Adeline, ed. Les Fortunes Francaises Au XIXe Siecle: Enquete Sur la Repartition & la Composition Des Capitaux Prives a Paris, Lyon, Lille, Bordeaux & Toulouse D'apres L'enregistrement Des Declarations De Succession. (Civilisation & Societes: No. 27). (Illus.). 1973. pap. 46.00x (ISBN 90-2797-288-5). Mouton.

Daumas, ed. Histoire Generale des Techniques, 3 tomes. Incl. Tome I. Les Origines de la Civilisation Technique. 66.80 (ISBN 0-685-35926-3); Tome II. Les Premieres Etapes du Machinsisme. 66.80 (ISBN 0-685-35927-1); Tome III. L' Expansion du Machinisme. 66.80 (ISBN 0-685-35928-X). French & Eur.

Daumas, Lisa, tr. see Keppe, Norberto R., et al.

Daumas, Maurice. Histoire de la Science. (Historique Ser.). write for info. French & Eur.

Daumas, Maurice, ed. The History of Technology & Invention, Vol. 3. (Illus.). 1978. 30.00 (ISBN 0-517-52037-0). Crown.

--History of Technology & Invention: Progress Through the Ages, 2 vols. Incl. Vol. 1. The Origins of Technological Civilization (ISBN 0-517-50727-7); Vol. 2. The First Stages of Mechanization (ISBN 0-517-50728-5). (Illus.). 1969. 30.00 ea. Crown.

--A History of Technology & Invention Progress Through the Ages, Vol. 1: The Origins of Technological Civilization to 1450. 520p. 1980. 60.00x (ISBN 0-7195-3730-4, Pub. by Murray Pubs England). State Mutual Bk.

--History of Technology & Invention Process Through the Ages, Vol. 2: The First Stages of Mechanization 1450-1725. 694p. 1980. 60.00x (ISBN 0-7195-3731-2, Pub. by Murray Pubs England). State Mutual Bk.

--A History of Technology & Invention Progress Through the Ages, Vol. 3: The Expansion of Mechanization 1725-1860. 700p. 1980. 60.00x (ISBN 0-7195-3732-0, Pub. by Murray Pubs England). State Mutual Bk.

Daume, Daphne, ed. Britannica Book of the Year, 1984. 1984. write for info. Ency Brit Inc.

Daumeister, W., ed. Electron Microscopy at Molecular Dimensions. (Proceedings in Life Sciences). (Illus.). 300p. 1980. 66.00 (ISBN 0-387-10131-4). Springer-Verlag.

Daumel, Gerd. Concrete in the Garden. 63p. 5.00 (ISBN 0-318-13142-0, CCP0603). Am Soc Conc Constr.

Daumier, Honore. Businessmen & Finance. Adhemar, Jean, notes by. LC 82-84245. (Illus.). 272p. 1983. 32.95 (ISBN 0-86710-054-0). Edns Vilo.

--Daumier & Music. (Music Reprint Ser.). 1983. lib. bdg. 25.00 (ISBN 0-306-76054-1). Da Capo.

--Daumier: One Hundred Twenty Great Lithographs. Ramus, Charles, ed. LC 77-83928. (Illus.). 1978. pap. 6.95 (ISBN 0-486-23512-2). Dover.

--Doctors & Medicine. LC 81-66415. 136p. 1981. 32.95 (ISBN 0-86710-001-X). Edns Vilo.

--Drawings of Daumier. Longstreet, Stephen, ed. (Master Draughtsman Ser). (Illus., Orig.). treasure trove bdg. 9.95x (ISBN 0-87505-003-4); pap. 4.95 (ISBN 0-87505-156-1). Borden.

--Lawyers & Justice. LC 81-66417. 136p. 1981. 32.95 (ISBN 0-86710-002-8). Edns Vilo.

--Lawyers & Law Courts. portfolio of loose prints ed. (Illus.). 12.50 (ISBN 0-87505-152-9). Borden.

--Liberated Women. LC 81-72091. (Illus.). 116p. 1982. 32.95 (ISBN 0-86710-020-6). Edns Vilo.

Daun, Lowell G., jt. auth. see Hooley, James R.

Daunce, Edward. A Briefe Discourse of the Spanish State, with a Dialogue Intituled Philobasilis. LC 72-6281. (English Experience Ser.: No. 73). 52p. 1968. Repr. of 1590 ed. 7.00 (ISBN 90-221-0073-1). Walter J Johnson.

Dauncey, Elizabeth, jt. auth. see Dowliing, Marion.

Dauncey, Helen. Is It Poisonous, 1980. 1980. pap. text ed. 2.95 (ISBN 0-933916-04-3). IMS Pr.

DauNe, Michele. Chicken Town. 160p. 1985. 10.00 (ISBN 0-682-40238-9). Exposition Pr FL.

Dauney, William. Ancient Scottish Melodies. LC 73-4533. (Maitland Club, Glasgow. Publications: No. 43). Repr. of 1838 ed. 22.00 (ISBN 0-404-53099-0). AMS Pr.

Dauns, John & Hofmann, Karl. Representation of Rings by Sections. LC 52-42839. (Memoirs: No. 83). 180p. 1983. pap. 10.00 (ISBN 0-8218-1283-1, MEMO-83). Am Math.

Daunt, Achilles. Our Sea Coast Heroes: Stories of the Wreck & Rescue, Origin, History & Principles of the Construction of the Lightboat. 1977. lib. bdg. 69.95 (ISBN 0-8490-2393-9). Gordon Pr.

Daunt, J. G., ed. see International Conference on Low Temperature Physics (9th: 1964: Columbus, Ohio).

Daunt, John G. Helium Three: Proceedings of the Second Symposium on Liquid & Solid Helium Three. 198p. 1960. 4.50 (ISBN 0-8142-0042-7). Ohio St U Pr.

Daunt, John G. & Lerner, E., eds. Monolayer & Submonolayer Helium Films. LC 73-12930. 160p. 1973. 35.00x (ISBN 0-306-30757-X, Plenum Pr). Plenum Pub.

Daunt, P. E. Comprehensive Values. (Organization in Schools Ser.). 1975. text ed. 16.50x (ISBN 0-435-80270-4). Heinemann Ed.

Daunt, W. J. A Life Spent for Ireland. 440p. 1972. Repr. of 1896 ed. 20.00x (ISBN 0-7165-0025-6, BBA 02157, Pub. by Irish Academic Pr Ireland). Biblio Dist.

Daunt-Mergens, Diana O., ed. Cave Research Foundation Personnel Manual. 3rd ed. (Illus.). 176p. 1981. pap. 5.00 (ISBN 0-939748-05-3). Cave Bks Mo.

Daunton, M. J. House & Home in the Victorian City. (Studies in Urban History). 1983. text ed. 65.00 (ISBN 0-7131-6384-4). E Arnold.

Daunton, Martin. Royal Mail: The History of the Post Office since 1840. (Illus.). 340p. 1985. 29.50 (ISBN 0-485-11280-9, Pub. by Athlone Pr Ltd). Longwood Pub Group.

Daunton, N. G., et al, eds. Mechanisms of Motion-Induced Vomiting. (Journal: Brain, Behavior & Evolution: Vol. 23, No. 1-2). (Illus.). 80p. 1983. pap. 22.25 (ISBN 3-8055-3790-5). S Karger.

Dauphin, Sue. Houston by Stages: A History of the Theatre in Houston. 1981. 14.95 (ISBN 0-89015-303-5). Eakin Pubns.

Dauphinais, Raymond, tr. see Moran, Hugh.

D'Aurevilly, Barbey. Oeuvres Romanesques Completes, 2 tomes. Petit, ed. (Bibliotheque de la Pleiade). Set. 67.45 (ISBN 0-685-34096-1). French & Eur.

D'Aurevilly, Jules B. The Diaboliques. 1925. 40.00 (ISBN 0-686-18159-X). Havertown Bks.

D'Auri, Laura, ed. see Sanadi, Lalita.

D'Auria, Antonio, jt. auth. see Baroni, Daniele.

D Auria, John M. & Gilchrist, Alan B. Chemistry & the Environment: Laboratory Experience. LC 72-82803. pap. 42.60 (ISBN 0-317-08680-4, 2013067). Bks Demand UMI.

D'Auria, Michael & Ryan, Herbert F. Legal Terms & Concepts in Criminal Justice. 2nd. ed. 168p. 1982. pap. 7.95 (ISBN 0-89529-153-3). Avery Pub.

Dausch, D. & Honegger, H. Timolol Ophthalmic Solution in the Treatment of Glaucoma. LC 78-72505. 1978. 3.00 (ISBN 0-911910-95-6). Merck-Sharp-Dohme.

Dause, Charles A., jt. auth. see Ziegelmueller, George W.

Dausey, Gary. The Youth Leader's Sourcebook. 320p. 1983. 14.95 (ISBN 0-310-29310-3). Zondervan.

Daussant, J. Seed Portions. LC 82-71240. 1983. 55.00 (ISBN 0-12-204380-4). Acad Pr.

Dausset, J., jt. ed. see Fougereau, M.

Dausset, Jean & Svejgaard, Arne. HLA & Disease. 332p. 1977. 39.95 (ISBN 0-686-86253-8). Krieger.

Dausset, Jean, jt. ed. see Rapaport, Felix T.

Daussett, J., jt. ed. see Fougereau, M.

Dauster, F. & Lyday, L. En un Acto: Diez Piezas Hispanoamericanas. 2nd ed. 1983. 11.95 (ISBN 0-8384-1229-7). Heinle & Heinle.

Dauster, Frank. Xavier Villaurrutia. (World Authors Ser.). 1971. lib. bdg. 15.95 (ISBN 0-686-82929-8). Irvington.

Dauten, Dale A. Quitting: Knowing When to Leave. 216p. 1980. 12.95 (ISBN 0-8027-0660-6). Walker & Co.

Dauten, Dale Alan, jt. auth. see Gentle, Jimmie.

D' Auteroche, Jean Chappe see Chappe d'Auteroche, Jean.

Dautov, Sh. A. & Aizenberg, L. A. Differential Forms Orthogonal to Holomorphic Functions or Forms, &Their Properties. (Translations of Mathematical Monographs: Vol. 56). 38.00 (ISBN 0-8218-4508-X). Am Math.

Dautrebande, L. Microaerosols: Physiology, Pharmacology, Therapeutics. 1962. 76.00 (ISBN 0-12-204350-2). Acad Pr.

Dauven, Jean. The Powers of Hypnosis. (Illus.). 254p. 1980. pap. 5.95 (ISBN 0-8128-1391-X). Stein & Day.

D'Auvergne, Edmund B. Pierre Loti. LC 72-103180. 1970. Repr. of 1926 ed. 21.00x (ISBN 0-8046-0817-2, Pub. by Kennikat). Assoc Faculty Pr.

D'Auvergne, Martial. Amant Rendu Cordelier a l'Observance d'Amours. (Societe Des Anciens Textes Francais Ser: Vol. 15). (Fr.). 1881. 25.00 (ISBN 0-686-76885-X); pap. 19.00 (ISBN 0-384-56560-3). Johnson Repr.

Dauvillier, A. Cosmic Dust. 15.00 (ISBN 0-685-28350-X). Philos Lib.

Dauvillier, Jean. Le Mariage En Droit Canonique Oriental. LC 80-2357. Repr. of 1936 ed. 35.00 (ISBN 0-404-18905-9). AMS Pr.

Dauw, Dean C. Creativity & Innovation in Organizations. 4th ed. 380p. 1980. pap. text ed. 15.95x (ISBN 0-917974-42-5). Waveland Pr.

--Feeling Better: Building Self-Esteem. (Illus.). 134p. (Orig.). 1985. pap. text ed. 6.95x (ISBN 0-88133-157-0). Waveland Pr.

--Increasing Your Self Esteem: How to Feel Better about Yourself. (Illus.). 128p. 1980. pap. text ed. 6.50x (ISBN 0-917974-43-3). Waveland Pr.

--New Educational Methods for Increasing Religious Effectiveness. pap. 0.65 (ISBN 0-8199-0389-2, L38532). Franciscan Herald.

--Sex Therapy Innovations. 63p. (Orig.). 1984. pap. 5.00x (ISBN 0-88133-086-8). Waveland Pr.

--Stranger in Your Bed: A Guide to Emotional Intimacy. LC 78-23444. 120p. 1979. 15.95 (ISBN 0-88229-472-5). Nelson-Hall.

--Up Your Career. 3rd ed. LC 79-57133. (Illus.). 256p. 1980. pap. text ed. 9.95x (ISBN 0-917974-40-9). Waveland Pr.

Dauwen, Norton. Henry James-Zabel. 14.95 (ISBN 0-670-40491-8). Viking.

Dauwer, Leo P. Boston's St. Patrick's Day Irish. 1984. 6.95 (ISBN 0-8158-0429-6). Chris Mass.

--I Remember Southie: A Boston Bicentennial Celebration. (Illus.). 157p. 1975. pap. 6.95 (ISBN 0-8158-0329-X). Chris Mass.

Dauxion-Lavaysse, Jean F. Statistical, Commercial & Political Description of Venezuela, Trinidad, Margarita, & Tobago. LC 70-97363. Repr. of 1820 ed. 21.50x (ISBN 0-8371-2445-X, DAV&, Pub. by Negro U Pr). Greenwood.

Dauzat, A., et al. Nouveau Dictionnaire Etymologique. (Fr., Fr). 27.50 (ISBN 2-03-020210-X, 3612). Larousse.

Dauzat, Albert. Dictionnaire des noms de famille et prenoms de France. (Fr). 23.50 (ISBN 2-03-020260-6, 3615). Larousse.

--Nouveau Dictionnaire Etymologique. 6th ed. 856p. (Fr.). 1971. 23.50 (ISBN 0-686-57269-6, F-135950). French & Eur.

Dauzat, Albert, et al. Dictionnaire Etymologique des Noms de Rivieres et de Montagnes en France. (Fr.). 1978. pap. 35.00 (ISBN 0-686-56974-1, M-6101). French & Eur.

Dauzat, Joann, jt. auth. see Dauzat, Sam V.

Dauzat, Sam V. & Dauzat, Joann. Reading: The Teacher & the Learner. LC 80-19435. 447p. 1981. 25.95 (ISBN 0-471-02668-9). Wiley.

Dauzet, Albert. Dictionnaire des Noms de Famille et Prenoms de France. (The International Library of Names Ser.). (Fr.). 1985. Repr. of 1880 ed. text ed. 39.50x (ISBN 0-8290-1233-8). Irvington.

Davajan, jt. auth. see Mishell.

Davajan, Val, jt. auth. see Mishell, Daniel R., Jr.

Daval, Jean-Luc. Oil Painting: From Van Eyck to Rothko. LC 85-42920. (Illus.). 140p. 1985. 35.00 (ISBN 0-8478-0628-6). Rizzoli Intl.

Davalos, Armando H. & Union of Writers & Artists of Cuba. Cultural Policy in Cuba: Partial Proceedings from the 3rd Congress of the Union of Writers & Artists of Cuba. Dochniak, Jim, ed. 48p. (Orig.). 1985. pap. 2.50 (ISBN 0-937724-04-1). Shadow Pr.

Davanagh, Brian M. BASIC for Beginners. 128p. 1978. 29.95 (ISBN 0-7157-1344-2, Pub. by H McDougall UK). State Mutual Bk.

Davaney, Sheila G., ed. Feminism & Process Thought: The Harvard Divinity School-Claremont Center for Process Studies Symposium Papers. LC 81-3942. (Symposium Ser.: Vol. 6). 144p. 1980. 19.95x (ISBN 0-88946-903-2). E Mellen.

Davanloo, H., ed. Short-Term Dynamic Therapy. LC 80-67986. 432p. 1980. 30.00 (ISBN 0-87668-418-5). Aronson.

Davanne, A. La Photographie, 2 vols. in 1. Bunnell, Peter C. & Sobieszek, Robert A., eds. LC 76-23052. (Sources of Modern Photography Ser.). (Illus., Fr.). 1979. lib. bdg. 37.00x (ISBN 0-405-09615-1). Ayer Co Pubs.

Davar, Dhun R., jt. auth. see Davar, Rustom S.

Davar, R. S. Personnel Management & Industrial Relations in India. 1976. 12.00 (ISBN 0-7069-0392-7). Intl Bk Dist.

Davar, Rustom S. & Davar, Dhun R. The Art of Damaging: A Sequel. (Illus.). 1979. 15.00x (ISBN 0-7069-0783-3, Pub. by Vikas India). Advent NY.

Davaras, Costis. Guide to Cretan Antiquities. LC 76-4600. (Illus.). 370p. 1976. 18.00 (ISBN 0-8155-5044-8, NP). Noyes.

Davau, Maurice & Lallemand, Maurice. Dictionnaire du Francais Vivant. 1360p. (Fr.). 1972. pap. 26.50 (ISBN 0-686-56975-X, M-6102). French & Eur.

Davauz, Jean-Baptiste, et al. The Symphonie Concertante. Brook, Barry S., et al, eds. (The Symphony Ser.). 568p. 1983. lib. bdg. 90.00 (ISBN 0-8240-3835-5). Garland Pub.

Dave, H. T. Life & Philosophy of Shree Swaminarayan. new ed. Shepard, Leslie, ed. (Illus.). 274p. 1974. 8.95 (ISBN 0-04-294082-6). Weiser.

Dave, Indu. The Basic Essentials of Counselling. 212p. 1984. pap. text ed. 5.95x (ISBN 0-86590-216-X, Pub. by Sterling Pubs India). Apt Bks.

Dave, J. The Human Predicament in Hardy's Novels. 224p. 1985. text ed. 29.50x (ISBN 0-391-03340-9). Humanities.

Dave, R. H. Lifelong Education & School Curriculum: Interim Findings of an Exploratory Study on School Curriculum, Structures & Teacher Education in the Perspective of Lifelong Education. (UIE Monographs: Unesco Institute for Education: No. 1). 90p. (Orig., 3rd Printing 1975). 1973. pap. 5.00 (ISBN 92-820-1004-X, U354, UNESCO). Unipub.

Dave, R. H. & Stiemerling, N. Lifelong Education & the School: Abstracts & Bibliography. (UIE Monographs: Unesco Institute for Education: No. 2). 154p. (Orig.). 1974. pap. 5.00 (ISBN 92-820-0005-2, U355, UNESCO). Unipub.

Dave, Ravindra H., jt. auth. see Skager, R.

Dave, Ravindra H., ed. Foundations of Life-Long Education, Vol. 1. 1977. pap. text ed. 19.25 (ISBN 0-08-021191-7). Pergamon.

Da Veiga, H. Beirao, ed. Fluid Dynamics: Lectures Given at the 3rd 1982 Session of the Centro Internazionale Matematico Estivo (C. I. M. E.) Held at Varenna, Italy, August 22-September 1, 1982. (Lecture Notes in Mathematics: Vol. 1047). vii, 193p. (Fr. & Eng.). 1984. pap. 12.00 (ISBN 0-387-12893-X). Springer-Verlag.

D'Avenant, Charles. Essay upon the Government of the English Plantations on the Continent of America, 1701. Wright, Louis B., ed. LC 76-141118. (Research Library of Colonial Americana). 1972. Repr. of 1945 ed. 18.00 (ISBN 0-405-03334-6). Ayer Co Pubs.

Davenant, Charles. The Political & Commercial Works Relating to the Trade & Revenue of England: 1771 Edition, 5 vols. 1981. write for info. (ISBN 0-08-027649-0, HE 074); microfiche 175.00 (ISBN 0-686-79355-2). Pergamon.

D'Avenant, David. What the Sophisticated Man of the World Ought to Know About Women. (Illus.). 1980. 51.45 (ISBN 0-89266-213-1). Am Classical Coll Pr.

D'Avenant, William. Love & Honour & the Siege of Rhodes. Tupper, James W., ed. 1909. 30.00 (ISBN 0-8274-2999-1). R West.

Davenant, William. Works of Sir William Davenant, 2 Vols. LC 67-31454. 1968. Set. 55.00 (ISBN 0-405-08433-1, Blom Pubns); 27.50 ea. Vol. 1 (ISBN 0-405-08434-X). Vol. 2 (ISBN 0-405-08435-8). Ayer Co Pubs.

D'Avenel, Georges. Fortune Privee a Travers Sept Siecles. LC 68-56732. (Research & Source Works Ser.: No. 212). (Fr). 1968. Repr. of 1895 ed. 26.50 (ISBN 0-8337-4062-8, 60). B Franklin.

--Histoire Economique De la Propriete Des Salaires, Des Denrees et De Tous les Prix on General Depuis L'An 1200 Jusqu'en L'An 1800, 7 vols. LC 68-56751. (Research & Source Works Ser.: No. 236). (Fr). 1969. Repr. of 1894 ed. 313.00 (ISBN 0-8337-4063-6, 61, 61). B Franklin.

D'Avennes, P. Arab Art: As Seen Through the Monuments of Cairo from the Seventh Century to the Eighteenth. Erythraspis, J. I., tr. 265p. 1983. text ed. 150.50x (ISBN 0-86356-000-8, Pub. by Al Saqi UK). Humanities.

D'Avennes, Prisse. L' Art Arabe D'apres les Monuments Du Kaire Depuis le 7th Siecle Jusqu'a la Fin Du 18th, 4 vols. 1974. Repr. of 1974 ed. Set. lib. bdg. 1263.00 (ISBN 9-0277-9005-1, Pub. by Reidel Holland). Kluwer Academic.

Davenport. Paediatric Anethesia. 3rd ed. (Illus.). 284p. 1982. text ed. 32.00 (ISBN 0-8391-1740-X). Univ Park.

Davenport, jt. auth. see O'Bryne.

Davenport, A. T., ed. see TMS-AIME Fall Meeting, Chicago, 1977.

Davenport, Adams W. Famous Books: Sketches in the Highways & Byeways of English Literature. 1979. Repr. lib. bdg. 30.00 (ISBN 0-8492-0098-9). R West.

Davenport, Albert M. Cleopatra: Her Intimate & Mysterious Life Fully Revealed. (Illus.). 143p. 1982. Repr. of 1893 ed. 77.45 (ISBN 0-89901-040-7). Found Class Reprints.

Davenport, Alfred. Camp & Field Life of the Fifth New York Infantry: Duryee Zouaves. 485p. 1984. Repr. of 1879 ed. 32.50 (ISBN 0-913419-05-2). Butternut Pr.

Davenport, Arnold, ed. The Poems of John Marston. 394p. 1961. 45.00x (ISBN 0-85323-292-X, Pub. by Liverpool Univ England). State Mutual Bk.

--The Poems of Joseph Hall, Bishop of Exeter & Norwich. 310p. 1969. 49.00x (ISBN 0-85323-282-2, Pub. by Liverpool Univ England). State Mutual Bk.

Davenport, Basil, ed. Portable Roman Reader. (Viking Portable Library: No. 56). 1977. pap. 7.95 (ISBN 0-14-015056-0). Penguin.

Davenport, Basil, et al. Science Fiction Novel: Imagination & Social Criticism. 3rd ed. LC 58-7492. 1969. 7.50 (ISBN 0-911682-02-3); pap. 4.00 (ISBN 0-911682-13-9). Advent.

Davenport, Beatrix C., ed. see Morris, Gouverneur.

Davenport, Benjamin R. Blood Will Tell. facsimile ed. LC 78-38645. (Black Heritage Library Collection). Repr. of 1902 ed. 21.75 (ISBN 0-8369-9003-X). Ayer Co Pubs.

--The Crime of Caste in Our Country: Bullets, 1861-Ballots 1892. text ed. 25.25 (ISBN 0-8369-9248-2, 9102). Ayer Co Pubs.

Davenport, Betty L. Textures & Patterns for the Rigid Heddle Loom. 1980. 6.50 (ISBN 0-932394-03-5). Dos Tejedoras.

Davenport, Byron. Handbook of Drilling Practices. LC 84-662. (Illus.). 192p. 1984. 32.95x (ISBN 0-87201-120-8). Gulf Pub.

Davenport, Charles, jt. auth. see O'Byrne, John C.

Davenport, Charles B. The Feebly Inhibited: Nomadism, or the Wandering Impulse, with Special Reference. Rosenberg, Charles, ed. LC 83-48533. (The History of Hereditarian Thought Ser.). 156p. 1985. Repr. of 1915 ed. lib. bdg. 25.00 (ISBN 0-8240-5804-6). Garland Pub.

--Heredity in Relation to Eugenics. LC 73-180571. (Medicine & Society in America Ser.). (Illus.). 320p. 1972. Repr. of 1911 ed. 22.00 (ISBN 0-405-03946-8). Ayer Co Pubs.

--Race Crossing in Jamaica. LC 77-106833. Repr. of 1929 ed. 31.00x (ISBN 0-8371-3455-2, DRC&). Greenwood.

Davenport, Cyril. The Book: Its History & Development. LC 79-164212. (Tower Bks.). (Illus.). viii, 258p. 1971. Repr. of 1930 ed. 37.00x (ISBN 0-8103-3944-7). Gale.

--The Book: Its History & Development. 1977. lib. bdg. 59.95 (ISBN 0-8490-1528-6). Gordon Pr.

--Byways Among English Books. 1973. Repr. of 1927 ed. 25.00 (ISBN 0-8274-1644-X). R West.

--Cameos. facsimile ed. 16p. pap. 2.95 (ISBN 0-8466-6005-9, U5). Shorey.

Davenport, Dana. The Dilettante Book of Chocolates: Lore & Recipes from America's Most Prestigious Chocolatier. LC 84-48153. (Illus.). 240p. (Orig.). 1985. pap. 10.95 (ISBN 0-06-091223-5, PL 1223, PL). Har-Row.

Davenport, Diana. One-Parent Families. 1979. 21.00 (Pub. by Batsford England). David & Charles.

--The Power Eaters. 320p. 1980. pap. 2.75 (ISBN 0-449-24287-0, Crest). Fawcett.

--Wild Spenders. 288p. 1984. 14.95 (ISBN 0-02-529810-0). Macmillan.

--Wild Spenders. 272p. 1985. pap. 3.95 (ISBN 0-380-69894-3). Avon.

Davenport, Don, jt. auth. see Wells, Robert W.

Davenport, Donald J. Street Art. (Illus.). 56p. 1982. pap. 15.00 trade manual saddle stitched (ISBN 0-9606640-0-9). D J Davenport.

Davenport, E. H., jt. auth. see Cooke, Sidney R.

Davenport, Eileen, ed. see Fleming, Harold L.

Davenport, Elizabeth O., jt. auth. see Davenport, George L.

Davenport, Elsie G. Your Handspinning. (Illus.). 1981. pap. 5.50 (ISBN 0-910458-01-4). Select Bks.

--Your Handweaving. (Illus.). 1981. pap. 5.50 (ISBN 0-910458-03-0). Select Bks.

--Your Yarn Dyeing. (Illus.). 1981. pap. 5.50 (ISBN 0-910458-02-2). Select Bks.

Davenport, F. G., jt. auth. see Andrews, C. M.

Davenport, F. M. Primitive Traits in Religious Revivals: A Study in Mental & Social Evolution. 1977. lib. bdg. 59.95 (ISBN 0-8490-2478-1). Gordon Pr.

Davenport, Frances G. A Classified List of Printed Original Materials for English Manorial & Agrarian History During the Middle Ages. (Radcliffe College Monographs: No. 6). 1964. Repr. of 1894 ed. 20.00 (ISBN 0-8337-0774-4). B Franklin.

--Economic Development of a Norfolk Manor, 1086-1565. (Illus.). 106p. 1967. Repr. 27.50x (ISBN 0-7146-1297-9, F Cass Co). Biblio Dist.

--Economic Development of a Norfolk Manor, 1085-1585. LC 67-16349. (Illus.). Repr. of 1906 ed. 25.00x (ISBN 0-678-05041-4). Kelley.

Davenport, Francis G. Ante-bellum Kentucky: A Social History, 1800-1860. LC 83-10871. xviii, 238p. 1983. Repr. of 1943 ed. lib. bdg. 29.75 (ISBN 0-313-24113-9, DAAN). Greenwood.

Davenport, Francis G., ed. European Treaties Bearing on the History of the United States & Its Dependencies to 1815, 4 vols. 18.00 ea.; Set. 72.00 (ISBN 0-8446-1148-4). Peter Smith.

Davenport, Frederick M. Primitive Traits in Religious Revivals. LC 72-163669. Repr. of 1905 ed. 15.00 (ISBN 0-404-01929-3). AMS Pr.

--Primitive Traits in Religious Revivals. LC 68-58053. Repr. of 1905 ed. 22.50x (ISBN 0-8371-0378-9, DAR&). Greenwood.

Davenport, George L. & Davenport, Elizabeth O. The Genealogies of the Families of Cohasset. LC 84-61011. (Illus.). 720p. 1984. Repr. of 1909 ed. 45.00 (ISBN 0-89725-051-6). NE History.

Davenport, Guy. Apples & Pears & Other Stories. LC 84-60685. (Illus.). 320p. 1984. 20.00 (ISBN 0-86547-159-2). N Point Pr.

--Archilochus, Sappho, Alkman: Three Lyric Poets of the Seventh Century B.C. (Cal Ser.: No. 698). 176p. 1984. pap. 7.95 (ISBN 0-520-05223-4). U of Cal Pr.

--Cities on Hills: A Study of I-XXX of Ezra Pound's Cantos. Litz, Walton, ed. LC 83-9272. (Studies in Modern Literature: No. 25). 294p. 1983. 39.95 (ISBN 0-8357-1455-1). UMI Res Pr.

--Da Vinci's Bicycle: Ten Stories by Guy Davenport. LC 78-22513. 1979. pap. 5.95 (ISBN 0-8018-2220-3). Johns Hopkins.

--Eclogues: Eight Stories by Guy Davenport. LC 80-29027. (Illus.). 256p. 1981. 20.00 (ISBN 0-86547-029-4); pap. 11.00 (ISBN 0-86547-030-8). N Point Pr.

--The Geography of the Imagination. LC 80-23870. 400p. 1981. pap. 15.00 (ISBN 0-86547-001-4). N Point Pr.

--Tatlin. LC 81-48197. (Poetry & Fiction Ser.). 272p. 1982. text ed. 7.95 (ISBN 0-8018-2800-7). Johns Hopkins.

Davenport, Guy, ed. see Agassiz, Louis.

Davenport, Guy, ed. & tr. see Herondas.

Davenport, Guy, tr. & intro. by. Archilochos, Sappho, Alkman: Three Lyric Poets of the Late Greek Bronze Age. LC 78-65467. 1980. 22.50x (ISBN 0-520-03823-1). U of Cal Pr.

Davenport, Guy, tr. see Heraclitus of Ephesus & Diogenes, the Cynic.

Davenport, H. The Higher Arithmetic. 5th ed. LC 81-21786. 180p. 1982. 27.95 (ISBN 0-521-24422-6); pap. 10.95 (ISBN 0-521-28678-6). Cambridge U Pr.

--The Higher Arithmetic: An Introduction to the Theory of Numbers. 172p. 1983. pap. 4.50 (ISBN 0-486-24452-0). Dover.

--Multiplicative Number Theory. (Graduate Texts in Mathematics Ser.: Vol. 74). 177p. 1980. 25.00 (ISBN 0-387-90533-2). Springer-Verlag.

Davenport, H. M, jt. auth. see Felidae, Thomas.

Davenport, Herbert J. Economics of Alfred Marshall. LC 65-19648. Repr. of 1935 ed. 37.50x (ISBN 0-678-00095-6). Kelley.

--Economics of Enterprise. LC 66-21668. Repr. of 1913 ed. 37.50x (ISBN 0-678-00424-2). Kelley.

--Outlines of Economic Theory. LC 67-29500. Repr. of 1896 ed. 35.00x (ISBN 0-678-00389-0). Kelley.

--Value & Distribution. LC 64-17406. Repr. of 1908 ed. 37.50x (ISBN 0-678-00036-0). Kelley.

Davenport, Horace W. ABC of Acid-Base Chemistry: The Elements of Physiological Blood-Gas Chemistry for Medical Students & Physicians. 6th rev. ed. LC 79-88230. 1974. 10.00x (ISBN 0-226-13705-8); pap. text ed. 5.95x (ISBN 0-226-13703-1). U of Chicago Pr.

--A Digest of Digestion. 2nd ed. (Illus.). 161p. 1978. pap. 14.95 (ISBN 0-8151-2326-4). Year Bk Med.

--An Eagle-Feather: The Short Life of Albert Moser, M.D., a Footnote to the Life of Walter B. Cannon. (Illus.). 1974. 2.50 (ISBN 0-686-05841-0). F A Countway.

--Physiology of the Digestive Tract. 5th ed. (Illus.). 1982. 28.50 (ISBN 0-8151-2330-2); pap. 23.50 (ISBN 0-8151-2329-9). Year Bk Med.

Davenport, J. H. On the Integration of Agebraic Function. (Lecture Notes in Computer Science: Vol. 102). 197p. 1981. pap. 14.00 (ISBN 0-387-10290-6). Springer-Verlag.

Davenport, J. S. German Talers Seventeen Hundred to Eighteen Hundred. 1979. 36.00 (ISBN 0-686-51598-6, Pub. by Spink & Son England). S J Durst.

Davenport, James A., jt. auth. see Boles, Harold W.

Davenport, Joe & Lawson, Todd. The Empire of Howard Hughes. LC 75-16010. 1975. pap. 2.95 (ISBN 0-914024-22-1). SF Arts & Letters.

Davenport, John. An Apologetical Reply to a Book Called: An Answer to the Unjust Complaint of W.B. (English Experience Ser.: No. 792). 1977. Repr. of 1636 ed. lib. bdg. 35.00 (ISBN 90-221-0792-2). Walter J Johnson.

--Environmental Stress & Behavioural Adaptation. 128p. 1984. text ed. 26.50x (ISBN 0-7099-0829-6, Pub. by Croom Helm England); pap. text ed. 14.50x (ISBN 0-7099-0854-7, Pub. by Croom Helm England). Sheridan.

--Graphics for the Dot-Matrix Printer. Date not set. price not set. S&S.

--A Just Complaint Against an Unjust Doer, Mr. J. Paget. LC 76-57376. (English Experience Ser.: No. 793). 1977. Repr. of 1634 ed. lib. bdg. 5.00 (ISBN 90-221-0793-0). Walter J Johnson.

--Letters of John Davenport, Puritan Divine. Calder, Isabel M., ed. 1937. 65.00x (ISBN 0-685-69794-0). Elliots Bks.

--U. S. Economy. LC 64-25754. 1965. pap. 1.25 (ISBN 0-911956-09-3). Constructive Action.

Davenport, John, jt. auth. see Thomas, Dylan.

Davenport, John C. Houston. Lubeck, Scott, ed. (Illus.). 254p. 1985. pap. 9.95 (ISBN 0-932012-80-9). Texas Month Pr.

--The Texas Monthly Guidebooks: Houston. 4th ed. 288p. 1985. pap. 9.95 (ISBN 0-932012-80-9). Texas Month Pr.

Davenport, John L., ed. see Mitchell, Roy.

Davenport, John W. Baseball Graphics. LC 79-52663. 1979. pap. 7.95 (ISBN 0-934794-00-6). First Impressions.

--Baseball's Pennant Races: A Graphic View. LC 81-67611. (Illus.). 1981. 19.95 (ISBN 0-934794-03-0); pap. 12.95 (ISBN 0-934794-02-2). First Impressions.

Davenport, Lynne. Home Transcribing: Could You? Should You? (Illus.). 150p. (Orig.). 1984. pap. 9.95 (ISBN 0-9613200-0-1). Dalyn Pr.

Davenport, Marcia. The Constant Image. 1982. pap. 2.95 (ISBN 0-380-60723-9, 60723-9). Avon.

--East Side, West Side. LC 78-74647. 1979. Repr. of 1947 ed. lib. bdg. 14.00x (ISBN 0-8376-0428-1). Bentley.

--East Side, West Side. 384p. 1982. pap. 2.95 (ISBN 0-380-58958-3, 58958-3). Avon.

--Mozart. 1979. pap. 4.95 (ISBN 0-380-45534-X, 60162-1). Avon.

--Mozart. (Illus.). 1956. lib. rep. ed. 20.00 (ISBN 0-684-14504-9, ScribT). Scribner.

--My Brother's Keeper. LC 78-74646. 1979. Repr. of 1954 ed. 14.00x (ISBN 0-8376-0429-X). Bentley.

--My Brother's Keeper. 512p. 1982. pap. 3.50 (ISBN 0-380-59865-5, 59865-5). Avon.

--Of Lena Geyer. 488p. 1982. pap. 3.50 (ISBN 0-380-57471-3, 57471-3). Avon.

--Too Strong for Fantasy. 1979. pap. 3.50 (ISBN 0-380-45195-6, 45195-6, Discus). Avon.

--The Valley of Decision. LC 78-74648. 1979. Repr. of 1942 ed. lib. bdg. 16.50x (ISBN 0-8376-0427-3). Bentley.

--The Valley of Decision. 768p. 1983. pap. 4.50 (ISBN 0-380-63891-6, 63891-6). Avon.

Davenport, Marge. Best of the Old Northwest. LC 80-83780. (Illus., Orig.). 1981. pap. 6.95 (ISBN 0-938274-00-7). Paddlewheel.

--Northwest Glory Days. (Illus.). 208p. (Orig.). 1983. pap. 6.95 (ISBN 0-938274-02-3). Paddlewheel.

--Wild Berry Magic: Pick the Berries. (Illus., Orig.). 1981. pap. 3.95 (ISBN 0-938274-01-5). Paddlewheel.

Davenport, Mariana B. The Stone - the Word. LC 73-86530. 84p. 1973. 4.00 (ISBN 0-8233-0193-1). Golden Quill.

Davenport, Marilyn. Double-Ups. (Illus.). 32p. (Orig.). (gr. k-6). 1979. pap. 3.50 (ISBN 0-8431-4037-2, 001-4). Troubador Pr.

Davenport, May. Two Plays. LC 75-55603. (gr. 5-12). 1977. 2.50x (ISBN 0-9603118-0-7). Davenport.

Davenport, May, ed. Courage: An Anthology of Short Stories, Articles & Poems. LC 79-26261. (Orig.). (gr. 6-9). 1979. pap. text ed. 6.00x (ISBN 0-9603118-3-1). Davenport.

--Involvement: An Anthology of Short Stories, Articles & Poems. LC 77-90390. (gr. 9-12). 1977. 4.50x (ISBN 0-9603118-1-5); wkbk 2.50x (ISBN 0-9603118-2-3). Davenport.

Davenport, May K. A Time to Fantasize. LC 80-69294. (Illus.). 130p. (Orig.). (gr. 5-12). 1980. pap. 5.00x (ISBN 0-9603118-7-4). Davenport.

--A Time to Fantasize. 130p. 1980. 4.50 (ISBN 0-9603118-7-4). MD Bks.

Davenport, Michael, et al, eds. Current Topics in English Historical Linguistics. (Odense University Studies in Enlgish: Vol. 4). 293p. 1983. pap. text ed. 24.50x (ISBN 87-7492-411-7). Humanities.

Davenport, Michael G. The Fully Illustrated Book of the Most Notorious French Females at the Beginning of the Century. (A Memoir Collection of Significant Historical Personalities Ser.). (Illus.). 113p. 1983. 98.75 (ISBN 0-86650-048-0). Gloucester Art.

Davenport, Neil. The United Kingdom Patent System: A Brief History. 136p. 1979. text ed. 18.50x (ISBN 0-85937-157-3). Sheridan.

Davenport, Odessa, jt. auth. see Porter, Mae R.

Davenport, Peter, jt. ed. see Thompson, Philip.

Davenport, R. Edward. Free to Share. LC 82-62743. 183p. (Orig.). 1983. pap. text ed. 6.95 (ISBN 0-87148-337-8). Pathway Pr.

--Person to Person Evangelism. new ed. LC 77-23716. 1978. pap. 2.95 (ISBN 0-87148-691-1). Pathway Pr.

Davenport, R. L., jt. auth. see Kutscher, Charles F.

Davenport, Reuben B. The Death-Blow to Spiritualism: Being the True Story of the Fox Sisters. LC 75-36836. (Occult Ser.). 1976. Repr. of 1888 ed. 19.00x (ISBN 0-405-07949-4). Ayer Co Pubs.

Davenport, Richard. Outline of Animal Development. LC 78-62548. (Life Sciences Ser.). (Illus.). 1979. text ed. 24.95 (ISBN 0-201-01814-4). Addison-Wesley.

Davenport, Rita. Degrazia & Mexican Cookery. LC 82-80299. (Illus.). 86p. 1982. 8.95 (ISBN 0-87358-307-8). Northland.

--Making Time, Making Money: A Step-By-Step Program to Set Your Goals & Achieve Success. 256p. 1982. 14.95 (ISBN 0-312-50801-8); pap. 6.95 (ISBN 0-312-50802-6). St Martin.

--Sourdough Cookery. LC 77-71168. (Illus.). 1977. pap. 7.95 (ISBN 0-89586-155-0). H P Bks.

Davenport, Robert. The City-Night Cap. Monie, Willis J. & Orgel, Stephen, eds. LC 78-66832. (Renaissance Drama Ser.). 1979. lib. bdg. 26.00 (ISBN 0-8240-9739-4). Garland Pub.

--King John & Matilda: A Critical Edition. Davis, Joyce O., ed. LC 79-54334. (Renaissance Drama Ser.). 200p. 1980. lib. bdg. 26.00 (ISBN 0-8240-4452-5). Garland Pub.

--Works of Robert Davenport. Bullen, A. H., ed. LC 68-24819. 27.50 (ISBN 0-405-08436-6, Pub. by Blom). Ayer Co Pubs.

Davenport, Roxanne W., ed. Model Cities Reports: A Bibliographic Guide to the Microfiche Collection. 98p. 1981. pap. text ed. 50.00 (ISBN 0-667-00589-7). Microfilming Corp.

--Rehabilitation & Handicapped Literature, Nineteen Seventy Nine Update: A Guide to the Microform Collection. 61p. 1981. 25.00 (ISBN 0-667-00636-2). Microfilming Corp.

--Rehabilitation & Handicapped Literature, 1980 Update: A Guide to the Microform Collection. 91p. 1981. pap. text ed. 25.00 (ISBN 0-667-00637-0). Microfilming Corp.

Davenport, Russell W. The Dignity of Man. LC 72-10694. 338p. 1973. Repr. of 1955 ed. lib. bdg. 20.00x (ISBN 0-8371-6614-4, DADI). Greenwood.

Davenport, Russell W., jt. auth. see Fortune Magazine.

Davenport, Stephen E. & Green, Philip P. Special Use & Conditional Use Districts: A Way to Impose More Specific Zoning Controls. LC 83-621940. 1980. pap. 3.50 (ISBN 0-318-01109-3). U of NC Inst Gov.

Davenport, T. C., ed. Rheology of Lubricants. (Illus.). 148p. 1973. 22.25 (ISBN 0-85334-473-6, Pub. by Elsevier Applied Sci England). Elsevier.

Davenport, T. R. South Africa: A Modern History. 1977. o. p. 35.00x (ISBN 0-8020-2261-8); pap. 10.95 (ISBN 0-8020-6312-8). U of Toronto Pr.

Davenport, Thomas, jt. auth. see Fundabunk, Lila.

Davenport, Thomas, jt. auth. see Fundaburk, Emma L.

Davenport, W. Probability & Random Processes: An Introduction for Applied Scientists & Engineers. 1970. 49.00 (ISBN 0-07-015440-6). McGraw.

Davenport, W. A. The Art of the Gawain-Poet. 233p. 1978. 36.50 (ISBN 0-485-11173-X, Pub. by Athlone Pr Ltd); pap. 12.95 (ISBN 0-485-12050-X). Longwood Pub Group.

--Fifteenth Century English Drama: The Early Moral Plays & their Literary Relations. LC 82-3665. 160p. 1982. text ed. 37.50x (ISBN 0-8476-7120-8). Rowman.

Davenport, W. H. The One Culture. LC 70-106054. 1971. 15.25 (ISBN 0-08-016322-X). Pergamon.

Davenport, Walter. Power & Glory, the Life of Boies Penrose. LC 77-100525. (BCL Ser. I). (Illus.). Repr. of 1931 ed. 11.50 (ISBN 0-404-01938-2). AMS Pr.

Davenport, Wilbur B. & Root, William L. An Introduction to the Theory of Random Signals & Noise. LC 57-10220. pap. 98.30 (ISBN 0-317-28211-5, 2055968). Bks Demand UMI.

Davenport, William, jt. auth. see Cox, J. Halley.

Davenport, William B. & Henson, Ray D. Secured Transactions II. 147p. 1966. pap. 2.64 (ISBN 0-317-32261-3, B387). Am Law Inst.

Davenport, William B. & Murray, Daniel R. Secured Transactions. LC 78-54289. write for info. Am Law Inst.

--Secured Transactions. 457p. 1978. 40.00 (ISBN 0-317-32259-1, B388). Am Law Inst.

Davenport-Hines, R. P. Dudley Docker: The Life & Times of a Trade Warrior. (Illus.). 280p. 1985. 44.50 (ISBN 0-521-26557-6). Cambridge U Pr.

Davenport-Hines, R. P., ed. Histoy, Markets & Bagmen. 220p. 1985. text ed. write for info. (ISBN 0-566-05066-8). Gower Pub Co.

Daventry, Paula. Sasakawa, the Warrior for Peace: Global Philanthropist. (Illus.). 143p. 1981. pap. 7.50 (ISBN 0-08-028126-5). Pergamon.

Daverman, Elizabeth, tr. see Du Perron, E.

Davern, Cedric I. Genetics. (Scientific American Reader Ser.). (Illus.). 331p. pap. text ed. 12.95 (ISBN 0-317-06257-3). W H Freeman.

Davern, Cedric I., intro. by. Genetics: Readings from Scientific American. LC 80-25208. (Illus.). 331p. 1981. pap. text ed. 12.95 (ISBN 0-7167-1201-6). W H Freeman.

Davern, W. A., jt. auth. see Lhuede, E. P.

Daves, Charles W., ed. The Uses & Misuses of Tests: Examining Current Issues in Educational & Psychological Testing. LC 84-47982. (Social & Behavioral Science Ser.). 1984. 20.95x (ISBN 0-87589-614-6). Jossey-Bass.

Daves, Francis M. Alapha Bet of Curious Animals. 64p. 1976. pap. 2.95 (ISBN 0-89783-026-1). Cherokee.

--Cherokee Woman. LC 72-81196. 448p. 1973. 14.95 (ISBN 0-87797-067-X). Cherokee.

--Rhyming Words for Insects, Animals & Birds. 78p. 1975. pap. 2.95 (ISBN 0-89783-027-X). Larlin Corp.

Daves, M. L. Cardiac Roentgenology. 1981. 89.50 (ISBN 0-8151-2323-X). Year Bk Med.

Daves, Michael. Young Readers Book of Christian Symbolism. (Illus.). (gr. 5 up). 1967. 11.95 (ISBN 0-687-46824-8). Abingdon.

Daveson, Mons. Land of Tomorrow. (Harlequin Romances Ser.). 192p. 1982. pap. 1.50 (ISBN 0-373-02461-4). Harlequin Bks.

--Mackenzie Country. (Harlequin Romances Ser.). 192p. 1983. pap. 1.75 (ISBN 0-373-02575-0). Harlequin Bks.

--My Lord Kasseem. (Harlequin Romances Ser.). 192p. 1983. pap. 1.75 (ISBN 0-686-37699-4). Harlequin Bks.

Davey, Alfred. Learning to Be Prejudiced: Growing up in Multi-Ethnic Britain. 224p. 1984. pap. text ed. 19.95 (ISBN 0-7131-6402-6). E Arnold.

Davey, Anthony. Discourse Production: A Computer Model of Some Aspects of a Speaker. 168p. 1979. 24.00x (ISBN 0-85224-339-1, Pub. by Edinburgh U Pr Scotland). Columbia U Pr.

Davey, B. J. Lawless & Immoral: Policing a Country Town, 1838-1857. LC 83-40185. 198p. 1984. 22.50 (ISBN 0-312-47561-6). St Martin.

Davey, Cyril. Horseman of the King (John Wesley) 1964. pap. 2.50 (ISBN 0-87508-605-5). Chr Lit.

--Monk Who Shook the World (Martin Luther) 1960. pap. 2.50 (ISBN 0-87508-614-4). Chr Lit.

--Never Say Die: Story of Gladys Aylward. 1964. pap. 2.50 (ISBN 0-87508-616-0). Chr Lit.

--On the Clouds to China (J. Hudson Taylor) 1964. pap. 2.50 (ISBN 0-87508-617-9). Chr Lit.

--Saint in the Slums (Kagawa of Japan) 1968. pap. 2.50 (ISBN 0-87508-620-9). Chr Lit.

Davey, Cyril J. March of Methodism. 1952. 5.00 (ISBN 0-8022-0345-0). Philos Lib.

Davey, D. Mackenzie & Harris, Marjorie. Judging People: A Guide to Orthodox & Unorthodox Methods of Assessment. (Illus.). 176p. 1982. 18.95 (ISBN 0-07-084581-6). McGraw.

Davey, Frank. Louis Dudek & Raymond Souster. LC 80-691215. (Studies in Canadian Literature). 208p. (Orig.). 1980. pap. 6.95x (ISBN 0-295-95831-6, Pub. by Douglas & McIntyre Canada). U of Wash Pr.

Davey, G. C. Animal Models of Human Behavior: Conceptual, Evolutionary & Neurobiological Perspectives. 371p. 1983. 52.95 (ISBN 0-471-90038-9). Wiley.

Davey, Gilbert. Fun with Hi-Fi. Cox, Jack, ed. (Learning with Fun). (Illus.). 64p. 1974. 13.50x (ISBN 0-7182-0083-7, SpS). Sportshelf.

--Fun with Short Wave Radio. rev. ed. Cox, Jack, ed. (Learning with Fun Ser.). (Illus.). 64p. text ed. 13.50x (ISBN 0-7182-1319-X, Sps). Sportshelf.

Davey, Graham. Animal Learning & Conditioning. (Illus.). 512p. 1981. pap. text ed. 21.00 (ISBN 0-8391-4149-1). Univ Park.

Davey, Graham, ed. Applications of Conditioning Theory. (Psychology in Progress Ser.). 1981. 25.00x (ISBN 0-416-73560-6, NO.3459); pap. 11.50x (ISBN 0-416-73570-3, 3458). Methuen Inc.

Davey, H. & Mercer, H. Real Estate Principles in California. 4th ed. 1981. 26.95 (ISBN 0-13-765685-8). P-H.

Davey, Harold W., et al. Contemporary Collective Bargaining. 4th ed. (Illus.). 448p. 1982. text ed. 28.95 (ISBN 0-13-169771-4). P-H.

Davey, Henry. History of English Music. 3rd ed. LC 69-15620. (Music Ser). 1969. Repr. of 1921 ed. lib. bdg. 42.50 (ISBN 0-306-71133-8). Da Capo.

Davey, Herbert. The Law Relating to the Mentally Defective. (Historical Foundations of Forensic Psychiatry & Psychology Ser.). 568p. 1980. Repr. of 1914 ed. lib. bdg. 55.00 (ISBN 0-306-76070-3). Da Capo.

Davey, Homer C. & Sharum, Albert. Financing Real Estate in California. 1976. text ed. 26.50 scp (ISBN 0-06-453607-6, HarpC); instr. manual avail. (ISBN 0-06-453620-3). Har-Row.

Davey, Homer C., jt. auth. see Driscoll, Donald C.

Davey, J. T. & Johnston, H. B. The African Migratory Locust (Locusta Migratoria Migratorioides) R & FO in Nigeria. 91p. 1956. 35.00x (ISBN 0-85135-009-7, Pub. by Centre Overseas Research). State Mutual Bk.

Davey, James E. Riches of Grace. pap. 0.95 (ISBN 0-87509-127-X). Chr Pubns.

Davey, Jocelyn. Murder in Paradise. 192p. 1982. 11.95 (ISBN 0-8027-5459-7). Walker & Co.

--Murder in Paradise. 240p. 1983. pap. 2.95 (ISBN 0-380-64659-5, 64659). Avon.

--Treasury Alarm. LC 80-52081. 229p. 1981. 10.95 (ISBN 0-8027-5431-7). Walker & Co.

Davey, John. Mining Coal. (Junior Reference Ser.). (Illus.). 64p. (gr. 6 up). 1976. 8.95 (ISBN 0-7136-1596-6). Dufour.

Davey, John, jt. auth. see Case, Doug.

Davey, Joseph. As Any Mountain of Its Snows. (American Fiction Ser.: Vol. 2). 96p. (Orig.). 1980. pap. 3.95 (ISBN 0-934040-15-X). Quality Ohio.

Davey, Judy. The Other Side of the Bedpan. (Illus.). 1979. 4.95 (ISBN 0-89962-006-X). Todd & Honeywell.

Davey, Keith. Australian Desert Life. 8.50x (ISBN 0-392-07552-0, SpS). Sportshelf.

Davey, Kenneth. Financing Regional Government: International Practices & Their Relevance to the Third World. LC 82-11132. (Public Administration in Developing Countries Ser.). 193p. 1983. 29.95x (ISBN 0-471-10356-X, Pub. by Wiley-Interscience). Wiley.

Davey, L. E. & Verstraeten, A. Indian Certificate Chemistry. 374p. 1981. 30.00x (ISBN 0-86125-663-8, Pub. by Orient Longman India). State Mutual Bk.

Davey, Neil K. Netsuke: A Comprehensive Study Based on the M.T. Hindson Collection. rev. ed. (Illus.). 576p. 1982. 120.00 (ISBN 0-85667-013-8, Pub. by Sotheby Pubns England). Biblio Dist.

--Netsuke: A Comprehensive Study Based on the M. T. Hindson Collection. rev. ed. (Illus.). 580p. 85.00 (ISBN 0-85667-116-9, Pub. by Sotheby Pubns England). Biblio Dist.

Davey, Nelson J. These Are the Times. 1983. 8.95 (ISBN 0-533-05555-5). Vantage.

Davey, Patrick J. Defenses Against Unnegotiated Cash Tender Offers. (Report Ser.: No. 726). 29p. 1977. pap. 15.00 (ISBN 0-8237-0160-3); pap. 5.00 member. Conference Bd.

--Dividend Reinvestment Programs. LC 76-43198. (Report Ser.: No. 699). (Illus.). 50p. 1976. pap. 15.00 (ISBN 0-8237-0133-6); pap. 5.00 member. Conference Bd.

--Financial Management of Company Pension Plans. (Report Ser: No. 611). 117p. (Orig.). 1973. pap. 17.50 (ISBN 0-8237-0022-4); pap. 3.50 member. Conference Bd.

--Leasing: Experiences & Expectations. (Report Ser.: No. 791). (Illus.). v, 58p. (Orig.). 1980. pap. 50.00 (ISBN 0-8237-0222-7); pap. 10.00 member. Conference Bd.

Davey, R., et al, eds. Electrical Inspection. (Engineering Craftsmen: No. G24). (Illus.). 1969. spiral bdg. 47.50x (ISBN 0-85083-066-4). Trans-Atlantic.

Davey, R. J., et al. Studies on Mesozoic & Caenozoic Dinoflagellate Cysts. (Illus.). 272p. 1983. pap. text ed. 90.00x (ISBN 0-565-00879-X, Pub. by Brit Mus Nat Hist England). Sabbot-Natural Hist Bks.

Davey, Rosemary. Under the Indian Turquois Sky. 1985. 9.95 (ISBN 0-87770-339-6). Ye Galleon.

Davey, Samuel. Darwin, Carlyle & Dickens. LC 77-116791. (English Literature Ser., No. 33). 1970. Repr. of 1876 ed. lib. bdg. 49.95x (ISBN 0-8383-1033-8). Haskell.

Davey, W. G. & Redman, W. C. Techniques in Fast Reactor Critical Experiments. LC 79-119375. 314p. 1970. 20.40 (ISBN 0-677-02680-3, 450006). Am Nuclear Soc.

Davey, William G., ed. Intercultural Theory & Practice: A Case Method Approach. (Illus.). 190p. (Orig.). 1981. text ed. 12.50 (ISBN 0-933934-08-4). Soc Intercult Ed Train & Res.

Davia, Diane W. Call Back the Dawn. 336p. 1985. pap. 3.25 (ISBN 0-380-89703-2). Avon.

Davia, N. C. & Thomas, D. An Assessment of the Model Six-V Oil Skimm ER Supplied by Engineering & General Equipment Ltd., 1980. 1981. 30.00x (ISBN 0-686-97036-5, Pub. by W Spring England). State Mutual Bk.

Davia, N. C., jt. auth. see Thomas, D. H.

Daviau, Donald & Johns, Jorun. Correspondence of Stefan Zweig with Raoul Auernheimer & Richard Beer-Hofmann. LC 83-70922. (Studies in German Literature, Linguistics, & Culture: Vol. 20). (Illus.). 300p. 1983. 28.00x (ISBN 0-938100-22-X). Camden Hse.

Daviau, Donald, tr. see Urbach, Reinhard.

Daviau, Donald G. Hermann Bahr. (World Author Ser.). 1985. lib. bdg. 22.95 (ISBN 0-8057-6592-1, Twayne). G K Hall.

Daviau, Donald G. & Buelow, George J. The "Ariadne Auf Naxos" of Hugo von Hofmannsthal & Richard Strauss. (Studies in the Germanic Languages & Literatures: No. 80). ix, 269p. 1975. 19.50x (ISBN 0-8078-8080-9). U of NC Pr.

Daviau, Donald G. & Fischer, Ludwig, eds. Exil: Wirkung und Wertung. LC 85-70743. 330p. 1985. text ed. 27.00x (ISBN 0-938100-36-X). Camden Hse.

--Das Exilerlebnis: Verhandlungen des vierten Symposium uber Deutsche und oesterreichische Exilliteratur. LC 81-70544. (Illus.). 516p. (Ger.). 1982. 37.00x (ISBN 0-938100-17-3). Camden Hse.

Daviau, Donald G., ed. see Schnitzler, Arthur & Auernheimer, Raoul.

David. Definitions & Divisions of Philosophy. Kendall, Bridget & Thomson, Robert W., trs. LC 83-3308. (Armenian Texts & Studies). 216p. 1983. 17.50 (ISBN 0-89130-616-1, 21 02 05); pap. 13.00. Scholars Pr GA.

--In Defense of the South. LC 76-20902. (Illus.). 99p. 1976. 14.00 (ISBN 0-9601044-1-0). Bon Mot Pubns.

David, A. R. A Guide to Religious Ritual at Abydos. 182p. 1981. pap. text ed. 40.50x (ISBN 0-85668-060-5, Pub. by Aris & Phillips England). Humanities.

David, A. R., ed. The Manchester Museum Mummy Project. 1979. 25.50 (ISBN 0-7190-1293-7, Pub. by Manchester Univ Pr-). Longwood Pub Group.

David, A. Rosalie. The Ancient Egyptians: Religious Beliefs & Practices. (Religious Beliefs & Practices Ser.). 250p. 1982. 26.00x (ISBN 0-7100-0877-5); pap. 10.00 (ISBN 0-7100-0878-3). Routledge & Kegan.

David, Al. Peaceful Revolution Handbook. 120p. (Orig.). 1982. pap. 3.50 (ISBN 0-9611682-0-X). Rel Psych.

David, Alfred. The Strumpet Muse: Art & Morals in Chaucer's Poetry. LC 76-11939. (Illus.). 288p. 1977. 22.50x (ISBN 0-253-35517-6). Ind U Pr.

David, Alfred & Meek, Mary E. The Twelve Dancing Princesses & Other Fairy Tales. LC 73-16517. (Midland Bks.: No. 173). (Illus.). 320p. (gr. 1-6). 1974. 20.00x (ISBN 0-253-36100-1); pap. 5.95x (ISBN 0-253-20173-X). Ind U Pr.

David, Alfred, jt. ed. see Pace, George B.

David, Andrew. Famous Criminal Trials. LC 79-17543. (On Trial Ser.). (Illus.). (gr. 5 up). 1979. PLB 7.95 (ISBN 0-8225-1427-3). Lerner Pubns.

--Famous Military Trials. LC 79-17537. (On Trial Ser.). (Illus.). (gr. 5 up). 1980. PLB 7.95 (ISBN 0-8225-1428-1). Lerner Pubns.

--Famous Political Trials. LC 79-16923. (On Trial Ser.). (Illus.). (gr. 5 up). 1980. PLB 7.95 (ISBN 0-8225-1429-X). Lerner Pubns.

--Famous Supreme Court Cases. LC 79-16579. (On Trial Ser.). (Illus.). (gr. 5 up). 1980. PLB 7.95 (ISBN 0-8225-1426-5). Lerner Pubns.

David, Andrew & Moran, Tom. River Thrill Sports. LC 82-24966. (Superwheels & Thrill Sports Bks.). (Illus.). 48p. (gr. 4up). 1983. PLB 8.95 (ISBN 0-8225-0506-1). Lerner Pubns.

David, Ann. How to Get Out of Debt & Stay Out of Debt. 160p. 1980. 5.95 (ISBN 0-346-12480-8). Cornerstone.

David, Anne. Get Out & Stay Out of Debt. 1981. 5.95 (ISBN 0-346-12480-8). Cornerstone.

David, Antony E. & David, Rosalie. Ancient Egypt. LC 84-50695. (History As Evidence Ser.). (Illus.). 37p. (gr. 4-7). 1984. PLB 9.90 (ISBN 0-531-03744-4). Watts.

David, Arie E. The Strategy of Treaty Termination: Lawful Breaches & Retaliations. LC 74-82748. 368p. 1975. 33.00x (ISBN 0-300-01718-9). Yale U Pr.

David, Arthur, tr. see Maimonides, Moses.

David, Bruce & Tartaglia, Gary. Successful Self Publishing on a Shoestring. (Illus.). 75p. (Orig.). wkbk. 6.95x (ISBN 0-9609734-5-1). Worthprinting.

David, Bruce, ed. see Tartaglia, Gary.

David, Bruce E. How to Get Everything you Want from Life: The Secret of Power. 62p. (Orig.). 1982. pap. 10.00x (ISBN 0-9609734-0-0). Worth Print.

--Principles for Profitable Advertising: A Handbook for Small Business. 2nd, rev. ed. LC 82-99849. 120p. 1983. 10.00x (ISBN 0-9609734-1-9); wkbk 9.95 (ISBN 0-317-13026-9); spiral bd. 8.95 (ISBN 0-317-13027-7). Worth Print.

--Shortcuts to Establishing AAA Credit: Even after Bankruptcy. Fintor, Craig, ed. (Illus.). 1984. 12.95 (ISBN 0-9609734-4-3); write for info wkbk. Worthprinting.

David C. Cook Editors. Ambush. LC 77-77277. (Illus.). (gr. 2-5). 1977. pap. 1.95 (ISBN 0-89191-076-X, 08748). Cook.

David, Carl. Collecting & Care of Fine Art. Michelman, Herbert, ed. 160p. 1981. Outlet 2.98 (ISBN 0-517-54287-0, Michelman Books). Crown.

David, Charles W. Robert Curthose, Duke of Normandy. LC 78-63356. (The Crusades & Military Orders: Second Ser.). (Illus.). 296p. Repr. of 1920 ed. 32.50 (ISBN 0-404-17007-2). AMS Pr.

David, Charles W., ed. see Du Pont De Nemours, Victor M.

David, Chella S., jt. auth. see Ferrone, Soldano.

David, Chella S., jt. ed. see Panayi, G. S.

David, D. J. & Staley, H. B. Analytical Chemistry of Polyurethanes. LC 78-12430. (High Polymer Ser.: Vol. 16, Pt. 3). 1979. Repr. of 1969 ed. lib. bdg. 39.50 (ISBN 0-88275-753-9). Krieger.

David, D. J., et al. The Craniosyntoses: Causes, Natural History, & Management. (Illus.). 340p. 1982. 99.50 (ISBN 0-387-11274-X). Springer-Verlag.

David, Deborah S. & Brannon, Robert. Forty-Nine Percent Majority: The Male Sex Role. LC 75-18152. 352p. 1976. pap. text ed. 12.95 (ISBN 0-394-34834-6, RanC). Random.

David, Deirdre. Fictions of Resolution in Three Victorian Novels. LC 80-16262. 304p. 1981. 31.00x (ISBN 0-231-04980-3). Columbia U Pr.

David, Ebenezer. Rhode Island Chaplain in the Revolution. Black, Jeannette D. & Roelker, W. Greene, eds. LC 73-159068. 1971. Repr. of 1949 ed. 19.50x (ISBN 0-8046-1662-0, Pub. by Kennikat). Assoc Faculty Pr.

David, Ed. The Intelligent Idiot's Guide to Getting the Most Out of Your Home Video Equipment. rev. ed. LC 82-13292. (Illus.). 224p. (Orig.). 1982. lib. bdg. 19.90 (ISBN 0-89471-178-4); pap. 9.95 (ISBN 0-89471-177-6). Running Pr.

David, Edward, ed. Inside Asquith's Cabinet: From the Diaries of Charles Hobhouse. LC 77-84941. (Illus.). 1978. 27.50x (ISBN 0-312-41868-X). St Martin.

David, Edward M. & Lee, Maurice D., III. Course Materials on Lifetime & Testamentary Estate Planning. 4th ed. 174p. 1982. pap. 25.00 (ISBN 0-686-40803-9, B409). Am Law Inst.

David, Elaine. A Teacher's Guide to Teaching BASIC in the Elementary Schools. 1982. 5.95 (ISBN 0-318-01731-8). E David Assoc.

David, Elizabeth. Elizabeth David Classics: Mediterranean Food, French Country Cooking, Summer Cooking. LC 80-7648. (Illus.). 672p. 1980. 15.95 (ISBN 0-394-49153-X). Knopf.

--English Bread & Yeast Cookery: American Edition. Hess, Karen, notes by. 1982. pap. 10.95 (ISBN 0-14-046539-1). Penguin.

--French Country Cooking. (Handbook Ser.). 1959. pap. 4.95 (ISBN 0-14-046043-8). Penguin.

--French Provincial Cooking. rev. ed. LC 80-8369. (Illus.). 520p. 1982. write for info (ISBN 0-06-014827-6, HarpT). Har-Row.

--French Provincial Cooking. (Handbook Ser.). 1964. pap. 6.95 (ISBN 0-14-046099-3). Penguin.

--Italian Food. (Handbook Ser.). 1964. pap. 5.95 (ISBN 0-14-046098-5). Penguin.

--Mediterranean Food. rev. ed. (Handbooks Ser). 1956. pap. 4.95 (ISBN 0-14-046027-6). Penguin.

--An Omelette & a Glass of Wine. 320p. 1985. 17.95 (ISBN 0-670-80769-9). Viking.

--Spices, Salts, & Aromatics in the English Kitchen. (Handbook Ser.). 280p. (Orig.). 1972. pap. 4.95 (ISBN 0-14-046163-9). Penguin.

--Summer Cooking. (Illus.). 1980. pap. 3.95 (ISBN 0-14-046100-0). Penguin.

David, Ella M., jt. auth. see Holmes, Thomas E.

David, Ephraim. Sparta Between Empire & Revolution: 404-243 B.C. rev. ed. Connor, W. R., ed. LC 80-2646. (Monographs in Classical Studies). 1981. lib. bdg. 30.00 (ISBN 0-405-14033-9). Ayer Co Pubs.

David, F. N. A First Course in Statistics. 2nd ed. (Griffin Monograph: No. 31). (Illus.). 1971. Repr. of 1953 ed. 10.75x (ISBN 0-02-843740-3). Hafner.

David, F. N. & Barton, D. E. Combinatorial Chance. 356p. 1962. text ed. 18.50x (ISBN 0-85264-057-9). Lubrecht & Cramer.

David, F. N., et al. Symmetric Function & Allied Tables. 278p. 1966. lib. bdg. 22.95x (ISBN 0-521-04788-9). Lubrecht & Cramer.

--Symmetric Function & Allied Tables. 278p. 1966. 27.00x (ISBN 0-85264-702-6, Pub. by Griffin England). State Mutual Bk.

David, Felicien. Melodies Orientales & Other Piano Works. (Music Reprint Ser.). 100p. 1985. Repr. lib. bdg. write for info (ISBN 0-306-76214-5). Da Capo.

David, Ferd, ed. see Corelli, A.

David, Florence N. Games, Gods & Gambling: The Origins & History of Probability & Statistical Ideas from the Earliest Times to the Newtonian Era. (Illus.). 1962. pap. 14.25x (ISBN 0-02-843710-1). Hafner.

David, G., jt. ed. see Teichroew, D.

David, Georges & Price, Wendel S., eds. Human Artificial Insemination & Semen Preservation. LC 80-19402. 656p. 1980. 69.50x (ISBN 0-306-40547-4, Plenum Pr). Plenum Pub.

David, Gwenda, tr. see Kracaver, Siegfried.

David, Gwenda, tr. see Silone, Ignazio.

David, Gwenda, tr. see Strasser, Otto.

David, H. The Computer Package STATCAT: Source Programs & User Manual. 800p. 1982. 102.25 (ISBN 0-444-86453-9, I-289-82, North Holland). Elsevier.

David, H. A. Method of Paired Comparisons. (Griffin's Statistical Monographs & Courses: Vol. 12). 1963. 9.75x (ISBN 0-02-843730-6). Hafner.

David, H. A. & Moeschberger, M. L. The Theory of Competing Risks. LC 78-58917. (Griffin's Statistical Monographs & Courses: No. 39). 1978. 16.25x (ISBN 0-02-843690-3). Macmillan.

David, H. A., ed. Contributions to Survey Sampling & Applied Statistics: Papers in Honor of H. O. Hartley. 1978. 72.00 (ISBN 0-12-204750-8). Acad Pr.

--Order Statistics. 2nd ed. LC 80-16928. (Probability & Mathematical Statistics Ser.). 360p. 1981. 50.95x (ISBN 0-471-02723-5, Pub. by Wiley-Interscience). Wiley.

David, Hans T. J. S. Bach's Musical Offering: History, Interpretation, & Analysis. LC 72-165391. 1972. pap. 4.50 (ISBN 0-486-22768-5). Dover.

--Music of the Moravians in America from the Archives of the Moravian Church at Bethlehem Pa, 2 vols. Incl. Vol. 1. Ten Sacred Songs. Dencke, J., et al.; Vol. 2. Six Quintets. Peter, John F. write to C. F. Peters Corp., NY for prices (ISBN 0-685-22862-2). NY Pub Lib.

David, Hans T., jt. auth. see Rau, Albert G.

David, Hans T. & Mendel, Arthur, eds. Bach Reader. rev. ed. (Illus.). 1966. pap. 12.95 (ISBN 0-393-00259-4, Norton Lib). Norton.

David, Hans T., ed. see Pachelbel, Carl T.

David, Henry. History of the Haymarket Affair. 2nd ed. LC 58-7136. 1958. Repr. of 1936 ed. 25.00x (ISBN 0-8462-0163-1). Russell.

David, Herbert A. & David, Herbert T., eds. Statistics: An Appraisal. 664p. 1984. text ed. 31.25x (ISBN 0-8138-1721-8). Iowa St U Pr.

David, Herbert T., jt. ed. see David, Herbert A.

David, I., jt. auth. see Sindell, Joseph M.

David, Irene, jt. auth. see David, Lester.

David, Irwin T. & Sturgeon, C. Eugene. How to Evaluate & Improve Internal Controls in Government Units. LC 81-83910. (Illus.). 111p. 1981. pap. 18.00 Nonmember (ISBN 0-686-84336-3); pap. 16.00 Member (ISBN 0-686-84337-1). Municipal.

David, Isabelle. Lebanese Cookery: An Easy Way. LC 77-539. (Illus.). 160p. 1982. 8.95 (ISBN 0-9607824-0-9). Laughing Sams Pr.

David, J., ed. see Reiter, Russel J.

David, Jack, jt. auth. see Lecker, Robert.

David, Jack, jt. ed. see Lecker, Robert.

David, Jacques. French in Africa: A Guide to the Teaching of French in a Foreign Language. (Source Books on Curricula & Methods). 230p. (Co-published with Evans Brothers Ltd., London). 1975. pap. 10.50 (ISBN 92-3-101038-7, U255, UNESCO). Unipub.

David, Janina. A Square of Sky & a Touch of Earth: A Wartime Childhood in Poland. 352p. 1981. pap. 5.95 (ISBN 0-14-004810-3). Penguin.

David, Janina, tr. see Ziemian, Joseph.

David, Jay. The Meeting Book: Never Be Lonely Again. 1979. pap. 2.95 (ISBN 0-346-12391-7). Cornerstone.

--The Scarsdale Murder. 1981. pap. 2.50 (ISBN 0-8439-0866-1, Pub. by Nordon Pubns). Dorchester Pub Co.

David, Joe. The Fire Within. LC 81-65447. 245p. 1981. 10.95x (ISBN 0-939360-00-4); pap. 4.95x (ISBN 0-939360-01-2). Bks for All Times.

David, John R., jt. ed. see Bloom, Barry R.

David, Jonathan, jt. auth. see Thurman, Judith.

David, Jules. American Political & Economic Penetration of Mexico, 1877-1920. Bruchey, Stuart & Bruchey, Eleanor, eds. LC 76-5001. (American Business Abroad Ser.). 1976. lib. bdg. 36.50x (ISBN 0-405-09269-5). Ayer Co Pubs.

David, Jules, ed. Perspectives in American Diplomacy. (Individual Publication Ser.). 1978. lib. bdg. 24.50x (ISBN 0-405-09162-1). Ayer Co Pubs.

David, Karen. Numerology Asks: Who Do You Think You Are Anyway? rev. ed. 167p. 1985. pap. 7.95 (ISBN 0-87500-009-6). RKM Pub Co.

David, Kenneth G. & Cowley, James C. Pastoral Care in Schools & Colleges: With Specific Reference to Health Education & to Drugs, Alcohol, & Smoking. 439p. 1982. 30.00x (ISBN 0-7131-0476-7, Pub. by Careers Con England). State Mutual Bk.

David, Leonard, jt. auth. see Borg, Nicholas.

David, Lester & David, Irene. Ike & Mamie. large print ed. LC 82-5869. (Illus.). 410p. 1982. Repr. of 1981 ed. 12.95 (ISBN 0-686-82639-6). Thorndike Pr.

David, Lester, jt. auth. see Sanford, Charlotte.

David, M. Geostatistical Ore Reserve Estimation. (Developments in Geomathematics: Vol. 2). 364p. 1977. 55.50 (ISBN 0-444-41532-7). Elsevier.

David M. World's Best Dirty Limericks. (Illus.). 192p. 1982. 8.95 (ISBN 0-8184-0324-1). Lyle Stuart.

David, M. & Lezine, I. Early Child Care in France. (International Monographs on Early Child Care). 164p. 1975. 27.95 (ISBN 0-677-05210-3). Gordon.

David, M. H. Environmental Quality & Social Behavior: Strategies for Research. 1973. pap. 7.75 (ISBN 0-309-02048-4). Natl Acad Pr.

David, Marjorie. The Primavera. (Orig.). 1981. pap. 2.50 (ISBN 0-671-83520-3). PB.

--Primavera. 208p. 1983. 14.50 (ISBN 0-671-45273-8, Poseidon). PB.

David, Martin & Smeeding, Timothy, eds. Horizontal Equity, Uncertainty & Economic Well-Being. LC 85-5879. 496p. 1985. 48.00 (ISBN 0-226-13726-0). U of Chicago Pr.

David, Martin A. The Dancer's Audition Book. LC 82-50546. (Illus.). 160p. 1982. 15.95 (ISBN 0-8069-7046-4); lib. bdg. 18.79 (ISBN 0-8069-7047-2); pap. 8.95 (ISBN 0-8069-7638-1). Sterling.

David, Martin H., jt. ed. see Joeres, Erhard F.

David, Mary E. Passages of Time: An Australian Woman 1890-1974. (Illus.). 1978. 14.95x (ISBN 0-7022-0951-1). U of Queensland Pr.

David, Megan. The American Bride. 224p. 1983. pap. 2.25 (ISBN 0-451-12481-2, Sig). NAL.

David, Michael, jt. ed. see Saunders, Peter E.

David, Miriam E. Reform, Reaction & Resources: The Three R's of Educational Planning. 244p. 1977. 20.00x (ISBN 0-85633-127-9, Pub. by NFER Nelson UK). Taylor & Francis.

--The State, the Family, & Education. (Radical Social Policy Ser.). 304p. (Orig.). 1980. pap. 17.50x (ISBN 0-7100-0601-2). Routledge & Kegan.

David, Nicholas, jt. auth. see Bricker, Harvey M.

David, Nicholas, jt. auth. see Daniels, Steve.

David, Nicholas & Bricker, Harvey, eds. Excavation of the Abri Pataud, les Eyzies (Dordogne) The Noaillian, Level 4. (American School of Prehistoric Research Bulletin: No. 37). (Illus.). 400p. 1985. pap. 35.00x (ISBN 0-87365-540-0). Peabody Harvard.

David, Nina. TV Season 1976-77. 336p. 1978. lib. bdg. 25.00x (ISBN 0-912700-22-X). Oryx Pr.

--TV Season 74-75. 200p. 1981. 25.00 (ISBN 0-912700-20-3, Oryx Pr). NY Zoetrope.

--TV Season 75-76. 225p. 1981. 11.95 (ISBN 0-912700-21-1, Oryx Pr). NY Zoetrope.

--TV Season 76-77. 275p. 1981. 11.95 (ISBN 0-912700-22-X, Oryx Pr). NY Zoetrope.

--TV Season 77-78. 300p. 1981. 11.95 (ISBN 0-912700-23-8, Oryx Pr). NY Zoetrope.

David, P., et al, eds. Dynamics of Nuclear Fission & Related Collective Phenomena, Bad Honnef, Germany 1981: Proceedings. (Lecture Notes in Physics: Vol. 158). 462p. 1982. pap. 26.00 (ISBN 0-387-11548-X). Springer-Verlag.

David, Paul, et al. Politics of National Party Conventions. rev. ed. Sproul, ed. 11.75 (ISBN 0-8446-1948-5). Peter Smith.

David, Paul A. Technical Choice Innovation & Economic Growth: Essays on American & British Experience in the Nineteenth Century. LC 74-76583. pap. 86.00 (ISBN 0-317-26014-6, 2024448). Bks Demand UMI.

David, Paul A. & Reder, Melvin W., eds. Nations & Households in Ecnomic Growth: Essays in Honor of Moses Abramovitz. 1973. 68.50 (ISBN 0-12-205050-9). Acad Pr.

David, Paul T. Barriers to Youth Employment, Vol. 1. facsimile ed. LC 74-1678. (Children & Youth Ser.). 124p. 1974. Repr. of 1942 ed. 14.00 (ISBN 0-405-05957-4). Ayer Co Pubs.

--Party Strength in the United States 1872-1970. LC 77-183897. xii, 310p. 1972. 20.00x (ISBN 0-8139-0396-3). U Pr of Va.

David, Paul T. & Ceasar, James W. Proportional Representation in Presidential Nominating Politics. LC 79-4387. xv, 298p. 1980. 17.95x (ISBN 0-8139-0787-X). U Pr of Va.

David, Paul T. & Pollock, Ross. Executives for Government: Central Issues of Federal Personnel Administration. LC 76-48706. 1977. Repr. of 1958 ed. lib. bdg. 17.00x (ISBN 0-8371-9335-4, DAEG). Greenwood.

David, Paul T. & Everson, David H., eds. The Presidential Election & Transition, 1980-1981. LC 82-19145. 304p. 1983. 24.95x (ISBN 0-8093-1109-7). S Ill U Pr.

David, Paul T., et al. The Politics of National Party Conventions. rev. ed. 394p. 1984. pap. text ed. 12.25 (ISBN 0-8191-4002-3). U Pr of Amer.

David, R. & De Vries, H. French Legal System. LC 58-9194. 1958. 10.50 (ISBN 0-379-00043-1). Oceana.

David, R., jt. ed. see Ticho, U.

David, R. W. Shakespeare in the Theatre. LC 77-82494. (Illus.). 278p. 1981. pap. 17.95 (ISBN 0-521-28490-2). Cambridge U Pr.

--Shakespeare in the Theatre. LC 77-82494. (Illus.). 1978. 34.50 (ISBN 0-521-21833-0). Cambridge U Pr.

David, Rene. Arbitration in International Trade. LC 84-5700. Date not set. price not set (ISBN 9-06-544164-6, Pub. by Kluwer Law Netherlands). Kluwer Academic.

--French Law: Its Structure, Sources, & Methodology. Kindred, Michael, tr. from Fr. LC 74-181563. xviii, 222p. 1972. 22.50x (ISBN 0-8071-0248-2). La State U Pr.

David, Rene & Brierly, John E. Major Legal Systems in the World Today: An Introduction to the Comparative Study of Law. 2nd ed. LC 78-67751. 1978. 30.00 (ISBN 0-02-907590-4); pap. text ed. 18.95 (ISBN 0-02-907610-2). Free Pr.

David, Richard. Hakluyt's Voyages. 672p. 1981. 27.50 (ISBN 0-395-31556-5). HM.

--Janus of Poets: An Essay on the Dramatic Value of Shakespeare's Poetry Both Good & Bad. facsimile ed. (Select Bibliographies Reprint Ser). 1935. 18.00 (ISBN 0-8369-5253-7). Ayer Co Pubs.

--Janus of Poets: Being an Essay on the Dramatic Value of Shakespeare's Poetry Both Good & Bad. LC 75-115397. Repr. of 1935 ed. 12.50 (ISBN 0-404-01939-0). AMS Pr.

--Shakespeare & the Players. LC 74-20519. 1961. lib. bdg. 10.00 (ISBN 0-8414-3787-4). Folcroft.

David, Richard W., ed. see Shakespeare, William.

David, Rosalie. Cult of the Sun: Myth & Magic in Ancient Egypt. (Illus.). 208p. 1980. 24.50 (ISBN 0-460-04284-X, BKA 03250, Pub. by J. M. Dent England). Biblio Dist.

--The Macclesfield Collection of Egyptian Antiquities. (Macclesfield Collection Ser.). (Illus.). 76p. 1980. text ed. 44.50x (ISBN 0-85668-129-6, Pub. by Aris & Phillips England). Humanities.

David, Rosalie, jt. auth. see David, Antony E.

David, Rosalie, ed. Mysteries of the Mummies. (Illus.). 1979. 14.95 (ISBN 0-684-16171-0, ScribT). Scribner.

David, Rosalie A. & Tapp, Edward, eds. Evidence Embalmed: Modern Medicine & the Mummies of Ancient Egypt. LC 84-2649. (Illus.). 175p. 1985. 19.50 (ISBN 0-7190-1079-9, Pub. by Manchester Univ Pr); pap. 9.00 (ISBN 0-7190-1082-9). Longwood Pub Group.

David, S. A., ed. Trends in Welding Research. 1982. 67.00 (ISBN 0-87170-150-2). ASM.

David, S. A., jt. ed. see Abbaschian, G. J.

David, S. A., ed. see Engineering Foundation Conference on Modeling of Casting & Welding Processes II, New Hampshire, July 31 - August 5, 1983.

David, Saul. The Industry: Life in the Hollywood Fast Lane. LC 80-5783. 278p. 1981. 13.95 (ISBN 0-8129-0971-2). Times Bks.

David, Sheri I. With Dignity: The Search for Medicare & Medicaid. LC 84-27941. (Contributions in Political Science Ser.: No. 12). 224p. 1985. lib. bdg. 27.95 (ISBN 0-313-24720-X, DWD/). Greenwood.

David, Stephen M. & Peterson, Paul E. Urban Politics & Public Policy: The City in Crisis. 2nd ed. LC 75-45450. 351p. (Orig.). 1976. pap. text ed. 9.95 (ISBN 0-275-64290-9, HoltC). HR&W.

David, Steven R. Defending Third World Regimes from Coups d'Etat. 100p. (Orig.). 1985. lib. bdg. 15.25 (ISBN 0-8191-4643-9); pap. text ed. 6.75 (ISBN 0-8191-4644-7). U Pr of Amer.

David, Suzy, ed. The Sephardic Kosher Kitchen. LC 84-8150. 228p. 1985. 14.95 (ISBN 0-8246-0303-6). Jonathan David.

David, Wilfred L. The IMF Policy Paradigm: The Macroeconomics of Stabilization, Structural Adjustment, & Development. LC 85-4408. 160p. 1985. 34.95 (ISBN 0-03-004408-1). Praeger.

David, Wilfred L., ed. Public Finance, Planning & Economic Development: Essays in Honor of Ursula Hicks. LC 73-77734. (Illus.). 349p. 1973. 37.50x (ISBN 0-8290-0201-4). Irvington.

David, William. The Harmonics of Sound, Color & Vibration. (Illus.). 160p. (Orig.). 1980. pap. 8.50 (ISBN 0-87516-411-0). De Vorss.

David, Zdenek V., jt. auth. see Kann, Robert A.

Davida, M., jt. auth. see Sullivan, M. Paulinus.

Davidar, E. R. & Joshi, Jagadish. The Runaway Elephant Calf. (Illus.). 24p. (Orig.). (gr. k-3). 1980. pap. 2.00 (ISBN 0-89744-216-4, Pub. by Children's Bk Trust India). Auromere.

David Ben Abraham. The Hebrew-Arabic Dictionary of the Bible, Known As Kitab Jami al-Alfaz (Agron, 2 vols. Skoss, Solomon L., ed. LC 78-63565. (Yale Oriental Ser. Researches: Nos. 20-21). (Hebrew & Arabic.). Repr. of 1945 ed. Set. 97.50 (ISBN 0-404-60290-8). AMS Pr.

Davidescu, D. & Davidescu, V. Evaluation of Fertility by Plant & Soil Analysis. 1982. 69.00 (ISBN 0-9961005-1-2, Pub. by Abacus England). Heyden.

Davidescu, V., jt. auth. see Davidescu, D.

Davidge, R. W. Mechanical Behaviour of Ceramics. LC 77-90206. (Solid State Science Ser.). (Illus.). 1979. 49.50 (ISBN 0-521-21915-9). Cambridge U Pr.

--Mechanical Behaviour of Ceramics. LC 77-90206. (Cambridge Solid State Science Ser.). (Illus.). 1980. pap. 12.95 (ISBN 0-521-29309-X). Cambridge U Pr.

Davidge, William F. & Hollman, Kenneth W. An Analysis of Mississippi Industrial Location Factors. 1978. 4.00 (ISBN 0-938004-02-6). U MS Bus Econ.

Davidheiser, Bolton. Evolution & Christian Faith. 1969. pap. 6.95 (ISBN 0-87552-251-3). Presby & Reformed.

Davidian, H. H. Rhododendron Species: The Lepidotes, Vol. I. LC 81-23232. (Illus.). 470p. 1982. cloth 59.95 (ISBN 0-917304-71-3). Timber.

David-Juba, Robert. Flights...Into Time. 2nd ed. LC 82-81680. (Illus.). 66p. 1982. pap. 7.95 (ISBN 0-686-82317-6, JNP-03). Joyful Noise.

Davidman, Joy. Letter to a Comrade. LC 75-144744. (Yale Ser. of Younger Poets: No. 37). Repr. of 1938 ed. 18.00 (ISBN 0-404-53837-1). AMS Pr.

--Smoke on the Mountain: An Interpretation of the Ten Commandments. LC 54-6099. 140p. 1970. pap. 5.95 (ISBN 0-664-24919-1). Westminster.

Davidman, Lyn, jt. auth. see Brewer, Joan S.

David-Neel, Alexandra. Buddhism. pap. 3.50 (ISBN 0-380-46185-4, 63594-1, Discus). Avon.

--Buddhism. LC 77-10308. 1978. 8.95 (ISBN 0-312-10680-7). St Martin.

--Magic & Mystery in Tibet. 1971. pap. 5.95 (ISBN 0-486-22682-4). Dover.

--The Power of Nothingness. large print ed. LC 82-10387. 217p. 1982. Repr. of 1982 ed. 10.95 (ISBN 0-89621-382-X). Thorndike Pr.

--Secret Oral Teachings in Tibetan Buddhist Sects. 1967. pap. 4.95 (ISBN 0-87286-012-4). City Lights.

--A Tibetan Tale of Love & Magic. L'Estrange, Vidar, tr. 224p. 1982. 30.00x (ISBN 0-85978-080-5, Pub. by Neville Spearman Ltd England). State Mutual Bk.

David-Neel, Alexandra & Yongden, Lama. The Superhuman Life of Gesar of Ling. Bolle, Kees W., ed. LC 77-79120. (Mythology Ser.). 1978. Repr. of 1934 ed. lib. bdg. 34.50x (ISBN 0-405-10532-0). Ayer Co Pubs.

--The Superhuman Life of Gesar of Ling. LC 81-12190. 271p. 1981. pap. 10.00 (ISBN 0-87773-753-3, Prajna). Great Eastern.

David-Novotney, Karen & Schwarz, Ted. Glamour & Fashion Photography. (Illus.). 192p. 1985. 24.95 (ISBN 0-240-51702-4). Focal Pr.

Davidoff. Handbook of the Spinal Cord, Vol. 1. 592p. 1983. 69.75 (ISBN 0-8247-1708-2). Dekker.

--Handbook of the Spinal Cord, Vols. 2 & 3. 864p. 1984. Set. 125.00 (ISBN 0-8247-7091-9). Dekker.

Davidoff, Doris S., jt. auth. see Davidoff, Philip G.

Davidoff, Frank & Rossi, John, eds. Digital Video One. (Illus.). 114p. 1982. pap. text ed. 25.00 (ISBN 0-940690-02-0). Soc Motion Pic & TV Engrs.

Davidoff, Henry, ed. Pocket Book of Quotations. 1983. pap. 3.95 (ISBN 0-671-47622-X). PB.

Davidoff, L. M., et al. Neuroradiology Workshop. Incl. Vol. 1. Scalp, Skull & Meninges. (Illus.). 264p. 1961. 98.00 (ISBN 0-8089-0112-5, 790991); Vol. 2. Intracranial Tumors Other Than Meningiomas. (Illus.). 410p. 1963. 121.00 (ISBN 0-8089-0113-3, 790992); Vol. 3. Non-Neoplastic Intracranial Lesions. (Illus.). 584p. 1968. 150.50 (ISBN 0-8089-0114-1, 7909-93). LC 60-16433. Grune.

Davidoff, Leonore & Hawthorn, Ruth. A Day in the Life of a Victorian Domestic Servant. (Victorian Day Ser.). 1976. pap. text ed. 5.95x (ISBN 0-04-942143-3). Allen Unwin.

Davidoff, Linda & Williams, Cynthia. Executive Orders: A New Strategy to Use Public Agencies to Increase Voter Registration. 5.00 (ISBN 0-318-04609-1). Conf Alt State & Local.

Davidoff, Linda L. Introduction to Psychology. 2nd ed. (Illus.). 1980. text ed. 32.95 (ISBN 0-07-015504-6). McGraw.

Davidoff, M., jt. auth. see Kaufmann, P.

Davidoff, Marsha, jt. auth. see Katz, Richard.

Davidoff, Martin. Satellite Experimenter's Handbook. LC 83-71699. 10.00 (ISBN 0-87259-004-6). Am Radio.

Davidoff, Philip G. & Davidoff, Doris S. Sales & Marketing for Travel & Tourism. (Illus.). 296p. 1983. pap. text ed. 18.00 (ISBN 0-935920-09-9). Natl Pub Black Hills.

Davidoff, Zino. The Connoisseur's Book of Cigar. (Illus.). 96p. 1984. 12.95 (ISBN 0-07-015460-0). McGraw.

Davidov, H. Botanical Dictionary: Russian-English-German-French-Latin. 335p. (Rus., Eng., Ger., Fr. & Lat.). 1981. Repr. of 1960 ed. lib. bdg. 28.00x (ISBN 3-87429-197-9). Lubrecht & Cramer.

Davidov, R. Palestine Question. 248p. 1985. pap. 4.95 (ISBN 0-8285-2998-1, Pub. by Progress Pubs USSR). Imported Pubns.

Davidovici, Sorin, ed. see Sydenham, Peter H.

Davidovitch, David. The Ketuba: Jewish Marriage Contracts Through the Ages. 2nd ed. (Illus.). 1974. 26.50 (ISBN 0-87203-054-7). Hermon.

--The Ketuba: Jewish Marriage Contracts Through the Ages. LC 82-1247. (Illus.). 120p. 1985. 29.95 (ISBN 0-915361-21-3, Dist. by Watts). Adama Pubs Inc.

Davidovits, Joseph. The Book of Stone: Alchemy & Pyramids, Vol. 1. 2nd ed. James, Andrew C. & James, Jacqueline, trs. from Fr. (Illus.). 252p. 1984. pap. text ed. 11.95 (ISBN 2-902933-09-6). Geopolymer Inst.

Davidovits, P. & McFadden, D. L., eds. Alkali Halide Vapors: Structure, Spectra, & Reaction Dynamics. LC 78-4812. 1979. 85.50 (ISBN 0-12-204250-6). Acad Pr.

Davidow, Jeffrey. A Peace in Southern Africa: The Lancaster House Conference on Rhodesia, 1979. (Special Studies on Africa). 128p. 1984. lib. bdg. 16.75x (ISBN 0-86531-703-8). Westview.

Davidow, Joel. Antitrust Guide for International Marketing & Distribution. LC 83-7805. (Corporate Practice Ser.). Date not set. price not set. BNA.

Davidow, M. Moscow Diary. 1980. 6.45 (ISBN 0-8285-1897-1, Pub. by Progress Pubs USSR). Imported Pubns.

--People's Theatre: From the Box Office to the Stage. 248p. 1977. 6.95 (ISBN 0-8285-0931-X, Pub. by Progress Pubs USSR). Imported Pubns.

--Third Soviet Generation. 221p. 1983. 6.95 (ISBN 0-8285-2685-0, Pub. by Progress Pubs USSR). Imported Pubns.

Davidow, Mike. Cities Without Crisis. LC 76-5415. 240p. 1976. 10.00 (ISBN 0-7178-0448-8). Intl Pubs Co.

--Cities Without Crisis. LC 76-5415. pap. 60.00 (ISBN 0-317-20522-6, 2022861). Bks Demand UMI.

--Life Without Landlords. 32p. 1973. pap. 0.40 (ISBN 0-87898-100-4). New Outlook.

Davidow-Goodman, Ann. Let's Draw Animals. (Illus.). (gr. 1-5). 1960. 2.95 (ISBN 0-448-02917-0, G&D); PLB 5.99 (ISBN 0-448-03326-7). Putnam Pub Group.

--Let's Draw Dinosaurs. LC 77-94034. (Step-by-Step Books Ser.). (Illus.). (gr. 1-6). 1978. pap. 2.95 (ISBN 0-448-14990-7, G&D). Putnam Pub Group.

Davidowicz, Lucy S. The Golden Tradition: Jewish Life & Thought in Eastern Europe. LC 84-5560. 512p. 1984. pap. 11.95 (ISBN 0-8052-0768-6). Schocken.

Davidowitz, Steve. Betting Thoroughbreds: A Professional's Guide for the Horseplayer. Rev. ed. (Illus.). 232p. 1983. pap. 7.95 (ISBN 0-525-48046-3, 0772-230). Dutton.

Davids, Anthony. Children in Conflict: A Casebook. LC 73-20108. 227p. 1974. pap. text ed. 17.95 (ISBN 0-471-19699-1). Wiley.

Davids, C. A., ed. see Robertson, George C.

Davids, C. Rhys. Gotama, the Man. LC 78-72409. Repr. of 1928 ed. 25.00 (ISBN 0-404-17273-3). AMS Pr.

--The Milinda Question; An Inquiry into Its Place in the History of Buddhism with a Theory As to Its Author. LC 78-72411. Repr. of 1930 ed. 22.50 (ISBN 0-404-17275-X). AMS Pr.

--Outlines of Buddhism; a Historical Sketch. LC 78-72412. Repr. of 1934 ed. 18.50 (ISBN 0-404-17276-8). AMS Pr.

--Wayfarer's Words, 3 vols. LC 78-72414. Repr. of 1942 ed. Set. 125.00 (ISBN 0-404-17600-3). AMS Pr.

--What Was the Original Gospel in 'Buddhism'? LC 78-72416. Repr. of 1938 ed. 17.00 (ISBN 0-404-17277-6). AMS Pr.

Davids, C. Rhys, ed. Khuddaka-Nikaya: The Minor Anthologies of the Pali Canon, 4 vols. Repr. of 1931 ed. 105.00 set (ISBN 0-404-17640-2). AMS Pr.

Davids, C. Rhys, intro. by. Stories of the Buddha. LC 78-72444. Repr. of 1929 ed. 30.00 (ISBN 0-404-17316-0). AMS Pr.

Davids, Carolina A. The Birth of Indian Psychology & Its Development in Buddhism. LC 78-72405. Repr. of 1936 ed. 37.50 (ISBN 0-404-17267-9). AMS Pr.

--Buddhism: A Study of the Buddhist Norm. LC 78-72408. Repr. of 1912 ed. 25.00 (ISBN 0-404-17269-5). AMS Pr.

--Buddhism: Its Birth & Dispersal. rev. ed. LC 78-72407. Repr. of 1934 ed. 25.00 (ISBN 0-404-17268-7). AMS Pr.

--A Manual of Buddhism for Advanced Students. LC 78-72410. Repr. of 1932 ed. 32.50 (ISBN 0-404-17274-1). AMS Pr.

Davids, Jules, ed. American Diplomatic & Public Papers, the United States & China: The Sino-Japanese War to the Russo-Japanese War, 14 vols. LC 81-9058. (Series 3). 4500p. 1982. Set. lib. bdg. 850.00 (ISBN 0-8420-2185-X). Scholarly Res Inc.

--American Diplomatic & Public Papers, the United States & China: The United States, China & the Imperial Rivalries, 1861-93, 18 vols. LC 79-12914. (Series 2). 1979. Set. lib. bdg. 1100.00 (ISBN 0-8420-2136-1). Scholarly Res Inc.

--The Inquiry Handbooks. LC 74-21632. (41 vols. in 20). 1975. Repr. of 1918 ed. 900.00 (ISBN 0-8420-1798-4). Scholarly Res Inc.

Davids, Kenneth & Duniec, M. L. Coffee: A Revised Guide to Buying, Brewing & Enjoying. rev. ed. LC 80-27222. (Illus.). 192p. 1981. pap. 7.95 (ISBN 0-89286-186-X). One Hund One Prods.

Davids, L. E. Instant Business Dictionary. (Career Institute Instant Reference Library). 1971. 4.95 (ISBN 0-531-02012-6). Watts.
Davids, L. Robert. This Date in Baseball History. rev. ed. (Illus.). 56p. (Orig.). 1982. pap. 2.50 (ISBN 0-910137-00-5). Soc Am Baseball Res.
Davids, L. Robert, ed. Baseball Historical Review. (Illus.). 112p. 1981. 4.00 (ISBN 0-910137-15-3). Soc Am Baseball Res.
--Baseball Research Journal, 1975. 2nd ed. (Illus.). 112p. 1983. pap. 3.00 (ISBN 0-910137-02-1). Soc Am Baseball Res.
--Baseball Research Journal, 1976. 2nd ed. (Illus.). 128p. 1983. pap. 4.00 (ISBN 0-910137-03-X). Soc Am Baseball Res.
--Baseball Research Journal, 1977. 2nd ed. (Illus.). 144p. 1983. pap. 4.00 (ISBN 0-910137-04-8). Soc Am Baseball Res.
--Baseball Research Journal, 1978. 2nd ed. (Illus.). 116p. 1983. pap. 4.00 (ISBN 0-910137-05-6). Soc Am Baseball Res.
--Baseball Research Journal, 1979. 2nd ed. (Illus.). 160p. 1983. pap. 5.00 (ISBN 0-910137-06-4). Soc Am Baseball Res.
--Baseball Research Journal, 1981. (Illus.). 188p. (Orig.). 1981. 5.00 (ISBN 0-910137-17-X). Soc Am Baseball Res.
--Baseball Research Journal, 1983. (Illus.). 188p. (Orig.). 1983. pap. 5.00 (ISBN 0-910137-08-0). Soc Am Baseball Res.
--Great Hitting Pitchers. (Illus.). 70p. 1979. pap. 2.50 (ISBN 0-910137-14-5). Soc Am Baseball Res.
--Minor League Baseball Stars. Rev. ed. (Illus.). 128p. 1984. 5.00 (ISBN 0-910137-12-9). Soc Am Baseball Res.
--Minor League Baseball Stars, Vol. II. (Illus.). 158p. 1985. pap. 5.00 (ISBN 0-910137-13-7). Soc Am Baseball Res.
Davids, Lewis E. Dictionary of Banking & Finance. (Quality Paperback Ser.: No. 336). 1979. pap. 7.95 (ISBN 0-8226-0336-5). Littlefield.
--Dictionary of Banking & Finance. 229p. 1980. Repr. of 1978 ed. 15.00x (ISBN 0-8476-6132-6). Rowman.
--Dictionary of Insurance. 5th ed. (Quality Paperback Ser: No. 62). (Orig.). 1977. pap. 6.95 (ISBN 0-8226-0062-5). Littlefield.
--Dictionary of Insurance. 6th, rev. ed. LC 83-16091. (Helix Bks.: No. 381). 338p. 1984. 21.95x (ISBN 0-8476-7340-5); pap. 7.95 (ISBN 0-8226-0381-0). Rowman & Allanheld.
--Instant Business Dictionary. LC 78-150232. 320p. 1970. 4.95 (ISBN 0-911744-07-X). Career Pub IL.
Davids, Lewis E., jt. auth. see Spero, Herbert.
Davids, Marilyn. A Love So Fresh. (Rapture Romance Ser.: No. 50). 192p. 1984. pap. 1.95 (ISBN 0-451-12635-1, Sig). NAL.
Davids, Peter. Commentary on James: New International Greek Testament Commentary. 226p. 1982. 15.95 (ISBN 0-8028-2388-2). Eerdmans.
Davids, Peter H. James: A Good News Commentary. LC 83-47720. (The Good News Commentary Ser.). 176p. (Orig.). 1983. pap. 7.64 (ISBN 0-06-061697-0, RD-499, HarpR). Har-Row.
Davids, Rhys. Buddhism: Its History & Literature. lib. bdg. 79.95 (ISBN 0-87968-510-7). Krishna Pr.
--Buddhist Birth Stories; or Jataka Tales: The Oldest Collection of Folklore Extant. Williams, Thomas, tr. Dorson, Richard M., ed. LC 77-70620. (International Folklore Ser.). 1977. Repr. of 1880 ed. lib. bdg. 36.50x (ISBN 0-405-10090-6). Ayer Co Pubs.
--Buddhist Suttas. lib. bdg. 79.95 (ISBN 0-87968-511-5). Krishna Pr.
--Poems of Cloister & Jungle, a Buddhist Anthology. 59.95 (ISBN 0-8490-0849-2). Gordon Pr.
--Sakya of Buddhist Origins. lib. bdg. 79.95 (ISBN 0-87968-512-3). Krishna Pr.
--Vinaya Texts, 3 vols. lib. bdg. 300.00 (ISBN 0-87968-513-1). Krishna Pr.
Davids, Rhys T., tr. see Fausboll, V.
Davids, Richard C. Lords of the Arctic: A Journey among the Polar Bears. (Illus.). 224p. 1982. 29.95 (ISBN 0-02-529630-2). Macmillan.
--Man Who Moved a Mountain. LC 75-99609. (Illus.). 270p. 1972. pap. 5.95 (ISBN 0-8006-1237-X, 1-1237). Fortress.
Davids, Robert L., ed. Insider's Baseball. (Illus.). 288p. 1983. 15.95 (ISBN 0-684-17905-9, ScribT). Scribner.
Davids, T. Rhys. Buddhism: Being a Sketch of the Life & Teachings of Guatama, the Buddha. LC 78-72417. Repr. of 1877 ed. 28.00 (ISBN 0-404-17278-4). AMS Pr.
Davids, T. W. Buddhist Suttas. (Sacred Bks. of the East: Vol. 11). 18.00 (ISBN 0-89581-520-6). Asian Human Pr.
--Jaina, Sutras. (Sacred Bks. of the East Ser.: Vol. 22, 45). both vols. 36.00 (ISBN 0-89581-525-7); 18.00 ea. Asian Human Pr.
--The Questions of King Milinda. (Sacred Books of the East: Vols. 35, 36). both vols. 36.00 (ISBN 0-89581-531-1); 18.00 ea. Asian Human Pr.
Davids, T. W. & Oldenberg, H. Vinaya Texts. (Sacred Bks. of the East: Vols. 13, 17, 20). 3 vols. 54.00 (ISBN 0-89581-522-2); 18.00 ea. Asian Human Pr.
Davids, Thomas W. Buddhist India. LC 78-38349. (Select Bibliographies Reprint Ser). Repr. of 1903 ed. 28.00 (ISBN 0-8369-6766-6). Ayer Co Pubs.
Davidse, J. Integration of Analogue Electronic Circuit. 1979. 55.00 (ISBN 0-12-204450-9). Acad Pr.
Davidsen, Leif. The Sardine Deception. Nunnally, Tiina & Murray, Steve, trs. from Danish. 192p. (Orig.). 1985. pap. 6.95 (ISBN 0-940242-15-X). Fjord Pr.
Davidsohn, A. & Milwidski, B. M. Synthetic Detergents. 6th ed. LC 77-13133. 265p. 1978. 37.95 (ISBN 0-470-99312-X). Halsted Pr.
Davidson. The People's Cause. (Longman Studies in African History). (Illus.). 224p. (Orig.). 1981. pap. text ed. 12.95x (ISBN 0-582-64681-2). Longman.
--Standard Stories from the Operas. 992p. 19.95 (ISBN 0-370-00259-8, Pub. by the Bodley Head). Merrimack Pub Cir.
Davidson, A. B. Biblical & Literary Essays. 1902. 20.00 (ISBN 0-8274-1933-3). R West.
Davidson, A. E. & Davidson, C. N., eds. The Art of Margaret Atwood: Essays in Criticism. 304p. 1981. 18.95 (ISBN 0-88784-080-9, Pub. by Hse Anansi Pr Canada). U of Toronto Pr.
Davidson, A. K. Zen Gardening. 1981. 29.00x (ISBN 0-09-146301-7, Pub. by Rider England). State Mutual Bk.
Davidson, A. N., et al, eds. Functional & Structural Proteins of the Nervous System. Mandel, Paul & Morgan, Ian. LC 72-91937. (Advances in Experimental Medicine & Biology Ser.: Vol. 32). 286p. 1972. 42.50x (ISBN 0-306-39032-9, Plenum Pr). Plenum Pub.
Davidson, Alan. Mediterranean Seafood. LC 81-13691. (Illus.). xii, 481p. 1981. 19.95 (ISBN 0-8071-0972-X); pap. 9.95 (ISBN 0-8071-0973-8). La State U Pr.
--North Atlantic Seafood. (Illus.). 1980. 15.95 (ISBN 0-670-51524-8). Viking.
--Seafood of South-East Asia. (Illus.). 366p. 1985. 15.95x (ISBN 0-8139-1073-0, Pub. by Prospect England). U Pr of Va.
Davidson, Alan & Davidson, Jane, trs. Dumas on Food. (Illus.). 328p. 1980. 24.95 (ISBN 0-7181-1842-1, Pub. by Michael Joseph). Merrimack Pub Cir.
Davidson, Alan, tr. see Dumas, Alexandre.
Davidson, Alastair. Antonio Gramsci: Towards an Intellectual Bibliography. (International Library of Social & Political Thought). 1977. text ed. 20.00x (ISBN 0-391-00671-1). Humanities.
--The Theory & Practice of Italian Communism. 302p. 14.95 (ISBN 0-85036-265-2). Kapitan Szabo.
Davidson, Alex. The Acoustic & Electric Guitar Repair Handbook. (Illus.). 240p. (Orig.). 1983. pap. 13.95 (ISBN 0-8306-1309-9, 1309). TAB Bks.
Davidson, Alexander, Jr., jt. auth. see Barrett, C. Waller.
Davidson, Alice J. Because I Love You. (Illus.). 128p. 1981. 12.95 (ISBN 0-8007-1281-1). Revell.
--Loving One Another. (Illus.). 128p. 1984. 12.95 (ISBN 0-8007-1388-5). Revell.
--Reflections of Love. (Illus.). 128p. 1982. 12.95 (ISBN 0-8007-1327-3). Revell.
--The Story of Baby Jesus. (Alice in Bibleland Ser.). (Illus.). 32p. (ps-3). 1985. 4.95 (ISBN 0-8378-5072-X). Gibson.
--The Story of Baby Moses. (Alice in Bibleland Ser.). (Illus.). 32p. (ps-3). 1985. 4.95 (ISBN 0-8378-5071-1). Gibson.
--The Story of Creation. (The Alice in Bibleland Storybooks). (Illus.). 32p. (gr. k-1). 1984. 4.95 (ISBN 0-8378-5066-5). Gibson.
--The Story of David & Goliath. (Alice in Bibleland Ser.). (Illus.). 32p. (ps-3). 1985. 4.95 (ISBN 0-8378-5070-3). Gibson.
--The Story of Jonah. (The Alice in Bibleland Storybooks). (Illus.). 32p. (gr. k-1). 1984. 4.95 (ISBN 0-8378-5068-1). Gibson.
--The Story of Noah. (The Alice in Bibleland Storybooks). (Illus.). 32p. (gr. k-1). 1984. 4.95 (ISBN 0-8378-5067-3). Gibson.
--The Story of the Loaves & Fishes. (Alice in Bibleland Ser.). (Illus.). 32p. (ps-3). 1985. 4.95 (ISBN 0-8378-5073-8). Gibson.
Davidson, Amanda. Teddy at the Seaside. (Illus.). 1984. 7.95 (ISBN 0-03-071026-X). HR&W.
--Teddy Cleans the House. (Illus.). 12p. (gr. k). 1985. 3.95 (ISBN 0-03-004999-7). HR&W.
--Teddy Goes Outside. (Illus.). 12p. (gr. k). 1985. 3.95 (ISBN 0-03-005004-9). HR&W.
--Teddy Goes Shopping. (Illus.). 12p. (gr. k). 1985. 3.95 (ISBN 0-03-005002-2). HR&W.
--Teddy's Birthday. LC 84-19298. (Illus.). (ps-2). 1985. 7.95 (ISBN 0-03-002887-6). HR&W.
--Teddy's Favorite Food. (Illus.). 12p. (gr. k). 1985. 3.95 (ISBN 0-03-005003-0). HR&W.
--Teddy's First Christmas. LC 82-82092. (Illus.). 24p. (ps-2). 1982. 7.95 (ISBN 0-03-062616-1). HR&W.
Davidson, Amy S., ed. see Van Vlierden, Carl & Stevens, Wendelle C.
Davidson, Andrea. Music in the Night. (Harlequin American Romance Ser.). 256p. 1983. pap. 2.25 (ISBN 0-373-16016-X). Harlequin Bks.
--Untamed Possession. (Harlequin American Romance Ser.). 256p. 1983. pap. 2.25 (ISBN 0-373-16021-6). Harlequin Bks.
Davidson, Angus, tr. see Berto, Giuseppe.
Davidson, Angus, tr. see Ginzburg, Natalia.
Davidson, Angus, tr. see Moravia, Alberto.
Davidson, Angus, tr. see Praz, Mario.
Davidson, Ann. How I Conquered Arthritis & Thanked the Lord. LC 85-90614. 102p. (Orig.). 1985. pap. 4.95 (ISBN 0-9614581-3-5). Amys.
Davidson, Anne A. WordBach Willie. (Illus.). 42p. (Orig.). (gr. k-2). 1984. pap. 5.95 (ISBN 0-9613763-0-9). Neuse Pr.
Davidson, Anne B. Once There Was: Poems. LC 76-42835. 80p. 1976. 5.00 (ISBN 0-8233-0255-5). Golden Quill.
Davidson, Arnold E. Conrad's Endings: A Study of the Five Major Novels. Litz, Walton, ed. LC 84-8508. (Studies in Modern Literature: No. 39). 134p. 1984. 24.95 (ISBN 0-8357-1587-6). UMI Res Pr.
--Jean Rhys. LC 84-28022. (Literature & Life Ser.). 160p. 1985. 13.95 (ISBN 0-8044-2143-9). Ungar.
--Mordecai Richler. LC 82-40282. (Literature & Life Ser.). 190p. 1983. 12.95 (ISBN 0-8044-2140-4). Ungar.
Davidson, Arthur. Eliot Enigma. LC 74-18248. 1959. lib. bdg. 10.00 (ISBN 0-8414-3736-X). Folcroft.
Davidson, Audrey. Substance & Manner: Studies in Music & the Other Arts. (Illus.). 1977. pap. 4.95 (ISBN 0-930276-00-0). Hiawatha Pr.
Davidson, Audrey & Fay, Judith. Phantasy in Childhood. LC 77-38129. 188p. 1972. Repr. of 1952 ed. lib. bdg. 18.75x (ISBN 0-8371-6327-7, DAPH). Greenwood.
Davidson, Audrey E. The Quasi-Dramatic St. John Passions from Scandinavia & Their Medieval Background. (Early Drama, Art & Music Monograph: No. 3). (Illus.). viii, 135p. 1981. pap. 8.95 (ISBN 0-918720-14-1). Medieval Inst.
Davidson, Audrey E. & Davidson, Clifford, eds. Sacra Profana: Studies in Sacred & Secular Music for Johannes Riedel. (Minnesota Monographs in Music: No. 1). (Illus.). vi, 292p. 1984. 35.00x (ISBN 0-9614757-0-6). Friends Minn Music.
Davidson, Avram. Clash of Star-Kings. 1983. pap. 2.50 (ISBN 0-441-11050-9, Pub. by Ace Science Fiction). Ace Bks.
--Masters of the Maze. 1976. pap. 1.25 (ISBN 0-532-12439-1). Woodhill.
--Or All the Seas with Oysters. 1976. pap. 1.25 (ISBN 0-671-80806-0). WSP.
--Peregrine: Secundus. (Orig.). 1981. pap. 2.25 (ISBN 0-425-04829-2). Berkley Pub.
--The Phoenix & the Mirror. 288p. 1983. pap. 2.50 (ISBN 0-441-66156-4). Ace Bks.
Davidson, Avram, ed. Magic for Sale. 224p. 1983. pap. 2.75 (ISBN 0-441-51535-5, Pub. by Ace Science Fiction). Ace Bks.
Davidson, B. R. European Farming in Australia: An Economic History of Australian Farming. 438p. 1981. 64.00 (ISBN 0-444-41993-4). Elsevier.
--Experimental Research & Farm Productions. 1969. pap. 8.00x (ISBN 0-85564-008-1, Pub. by U of W Austral Pr). Intl Spec Bk.
--The Northern Myth: Limits to Agricultural & Pastoral Development in Tropical Australia. (Illus.). 320p. 1972. o.p. 2nd ed. (ISBN 0-522-83577-5, Pub. by Melbourne U Pr); pap. 13.00x 3rd ed. (ISBN 0-522-84035-3, Pub. by Melbourne U Pr). Intl Spec Bk.
Davidson, Barbara K. There Was a Little Boy. 1968. 2.00 (ISBN 0-936426-03-9). Play Schs.
Davidson, Basil. Africa in History: Themes & Outlines. enl. & rev. ed. 320p. 1974. pap. 6.95 (ISBN 0-02-031260-1, Collier). Macmillan.
--The African Genius: An Introduction to Social & Cultural History. (Illus.). 1970. pap. 9.70i (ISBN 0-316-17432-7, Pub by Atlantic Monthly Pr). Little.
--The African Slave Trade. rev. enl. ed. 312p. 1981. 16.95 (ISBN 0-316-17439-4, Pub. by Atlantic Monthly Pr); pap. 8.70i (ISBN 0-316-17438-6). Little.
--Can Africa Survive? Arguments Against Growth Without Development. LC 74-6490. 1974. pap. 5.95 (ISBN 0-316-17434-3). Little.
--Ghana: An African Portrait. LC 75-13608. (Illus.). 160p. 1976. 30.00 (ISBN 0-912334-65-7); pap. 18.50 (ISBN 0-89381-009-6). Aperture.
--A History of West Africa, 1000-1800. Buah, F. A. & Ade Ajayi, J. F., eds. (The Growth of African Civilisation Ser.). (Illus.). 1978. pap. text ed. 10.95x (ISBN 0-582-60340-4). Longman.
--Let Freedom Come: Africa in Modern History. LC 78-5924. 1978. (Pub. by Atlantic Monthly Pr); pap. 9.70i (ISBN 0-316-17437-8, Pub. by Atlantic Monthly Pr). Little.
--The Lost Cities of Africa. rev. ed. (Illus.). 1970. pap. 7.25 (ISBN 0-316-17431-9, Pub. by Atlantic Monthly Pr). Little.
--Modern Africa. LC 82-14941. 256p. 1983. pap. 8.95x (ISBN 0-582-65525-0). Longman.
--No Fist is Big Enough to Hide the Sky: The Liberation of Guinea Bissau & Cape Verde. 208p. 1982. pap. 11.50x (ISBN 0-905762-93-2, Pub. by Zed Pr England). Biblio Dist.
--Scenes from the Anti-Nazi War. LC 81-81696. 288p. 1981. 16.00 (ISBN 0-85345-587-2); pap. 6.50 (ISBN 0-85345-588-0). Monthly Rev.
Davidson, Basil, et al, eds. Behind the War in Eritrea. 150p. 1981. pap. text ed. 8.95x (ISBN 0-85124-302-9). Barber Pr.
Davidson, Ben. The Skateboard Book. rev. ed. (Illus.). 1979. pap. 4.95 (ISBN 0-448-12484-X, G&D). Putnam Pub Group.
Davidson, Benjamin. Analytical Hebrew & Chaldee Lexicon. (Hebrew.). 24.95 (ISBN 0-310-20290-6, Pub. by Bagster). Zondervan.
Davidson, Bill, jt. auth. see Caesar, Sid.
Davidson, Bill R. To Keep & Bear Arms. 2nd ed. LC 75-93455. 275p. 1978. 14.95 (ISBN 0-87364-145-0). Paladin Pr.
Davidson, Billee, jt. auth. see Short, Pat.
Davidson, Billie, jt. auth. see Short, Pat.
Davidson, Bruce. Bruce Davidson Photographs. LC 78-73352. 168p. 30.00 (ISBN 0-671-40067-3); pap. text ed. 17.50 (ISBN 0-671-40068-1). Agrinde Pubns.
--Bruce Davidson Photographs. (An Agrinde Bk.). (Illus.). 1981. 30.00; pap. 17.50. Dodd.
--Subway. LC 82-47812. 100.00 (ISBN 0-394-52293-1). Knopf.
Davidson, C. J., et al, eds. The Drama of the Middle Ages: Comparative & Critical Essays. LC 81-68995. (Studies of the Middle Ages: No. 4). (Illus.). 400p. 1982. Repr. 32.50 (ISBN 0-404-61434-5). AMS Pr.
Davidson, C. N., jt. ed. see Davidson, A. E.
Davidson, C. T. Upon This Rock, 3 vols. 692p. 1973. Vol. 1. 11.95 (ISBN 0-934942-16-1); Vol. 2. 14.95 (ISBN 0-934942-17-X); Vol. 3. 13.95 (ISBN 0-934942-18-8). White Wing Pub.
Davidson, C. T., jt. auth. see Willing, Ora M.
Davidson, C. W. Transmission Lines For Communications. LC 78-4546. 218p. 1982. 21.95x (ISBN 0-470-27358-5). Halsted Pr.
--Wideband Voltage Amplifiers. 1974. pap. text ed. 18.95x (ISBN 0-7002-0235-8). Intl Ideas.
Davidson, Caroline. The Ham House Kitchen. (Illus.). 64p. (Orig.). 1985. pap. 6.95 (ISBN 0-317-30082-2, Pub. by Victoria & Albert Mus UK). Faber & Faber.
--A Woman's Work Is Never Done: A History of Housework in the British Isles 1650-1950. (Illus.). 256p. 1983. 19.95 (ISBN 0-7011-3901-3, Pub. by Chatto & Windus). Merrimack Pub Cir.
Davidson, Carson. Fast Talking Dolphin. (gr. 4-6). 1978. pap. 1.95 (ISBN 0-590-05367-1). Scholastic Inc.
Davidson, Cathy N. Critical Essays on Ambrose Bierce. (Critical Essays on American Literature Ser.). 1982. 30.00 (ISBN 0-8161-8393-7, Twayne). G K Hall.
--The Experimental Fictions of Ambrose Bierce: Structuring the Ineffable. LC 83-16844. x, 166p. 1984. 15.95x (ISBN 0-8032-1666-1). U of Nebr Pr.
Davidson, Cathy N. & Broner, E. M., eds. The Lost Tradition: Mothers & Daughters in Literature. LC 79-4832. 1980. 17.95 (ISBN 0-8044-2083-1); pap. 8.95 (ISBN 0-8044-6112-0). Ungar.
Davidson, Chandler. Biracial Politics: Conflict & Coalition in the Metropolitan South. LC 76-185951. xviii, 302p. 1972. 30.00x (ISBN 0-8071-0246-6). La State U Pr.
Davidson, Chandler, ed. Minority Vote Dilution. LC 84-10883. 298p. 1984. 24.95 (ISBN 0-88258-156-2). Howard U Pr.
Davidson, Charles. Studies in the English Mystery Plays. LC 68-752. (Studies in Drama, No. 39). 1969. Repr. of 1892 ed. lib. bdg. 39.95x (ISBN 0-8383-0536-9). Haskell.
Davidson, Charles T. & Davidson, Pearle V. These Tell of Miracles. 1978. pap. 3.95 (ISBN 0-934942-15-3). White Wing Pub.
Davidson, Christine V. & Abramowitz, Stephen I. Women as Patient. LC 80-80350. (Special Issue of Psychology of Woman Quarterly Ser.: Vol. 4, No. 3). 129p. 1980. pap. 9.95 (ISBN 0-89885-015-0). Human Sci Pr.
Davidson, Clarissa S. God's Man: The Story of Pastor Niemoeller. LC 78-21065. 1979. Repr. of 1959 ed. lib. bdg. 22.50x (ISBN 0-313-21065-9, DAGM). Greenwood.
Davidson, Cliff I., jt. auth. see Nriagu, Jerome O.
Davidson, Clifford. Drama & Art: An Introduction to the Use of Evidence from the Visual Arts for the Study of Early Drama. (Early Drama, Art, & Music Ser.). (Illus.). 1977. pap. 4.95x (ISBN 0-918720-00-1). Medieval Inst.
--From Creation to Doom: The York Cycle of Mystery Plays. LC 83-45273. (Studies in the Middle Ages: No. 5). (Illus.). 288p. 1984. 32.50 (ISBN 0-404-61435-3). AMS Pr.
--The Primrose Way: A Study of Shakespeare's Macbeth. LC 75-150380. (Comparative Literature Studies Ser). 105p. 1970. pap. 10.00 (ISBN 0-87423-006-3). Westburg.
--Star Poems & Other Poems. LC 76-27932. (Illus.). 1976. pap. 5.00 (ISBN 0-87423-021-7). Westburg.
Davidson, Clifford & O'Connor, David E. York Art: A Subject List of Extant & Lost Art Including Items Relevant to Early Drama. (Early Drama, Art, & Music Ser.). (Illus.). 1978. 14.95x (ISBN 0-918720-05-2); pap. 8.95x (ISBN 0-918720-04-4). Medieval Inst.
Davidson, Clifford, ed. Torquato Tasso's Aminta Englisht: The Henry Reynolds Translation of 1628. LC 72-78233. (North American Mentor Texts Ser: No. 1). (Illus.). 80p. 1972. pap. 10.00 (ISBN 0-87423-007-1). Westburg.
Davidson, Clifford & Gianakaris, C. J., eds. Drama in the Twentieth Century: Comparative & Critical Essays. LC 83-45289. (Illus.). 400p. 1984. 32.50 (ISBN 0-404-61581-3). AMS Pr.
Davidson, Clifford, jt. ed. see Davidson, Audrey E.

Davidson, Clifford, et al, eds. Drama in the Renaissance. LC 83-45277. (Studies in the Renaissance: No. 12). 1985. 32.50 (ISBN 0-404-62282-8). AMS Pr.

Davidson, D. & Harman, G., eds. Semantics of Natural Language. 2nd ed. LC 73-76427. (Synthese Library: No. 40). 769p. 1973. lib. bdg. 50.00 (ISBN 90-277-0304-3, Pub. by Reidel Holland); pap. 18.50 (ISBN 90-277-0310-8, Pub. by Reidel Holland). Kluwer Academic.

Davidson, D. & Hintikka, K. J., eds. Words & Objections: Essays on the Work of W. V. Quine. (Synthese Library: No. 21). 366p. 1975. lib. bdg. 42.00 (ISBN 90-277-0074-5, Pub. by Reidel Holland); pap. 21.00 (ISBN 90-277-0602-6). Kluwer Academic.

Davidson, D., ed. see TMS-AIME Fall Meeting, Philadelphia, Oct. 3-5, 1983.

Davidson, D. A., jt. ed. see Bridges, E. M.

Davidson, D. L. & Lenman, J. A. Neurological Therapeutics. 350p. 1981. text ed. 57.95x (ISBN 0-8464-1216-0). Beekman Pubs.

--Neurological Therapeutics. 250p. text ed. cancelled (ISBN 0-272-79616-6). Pitman Pub MA.

Davidson, Daniel S. Aboriginal Australian & Tasmanian Rock Carvings & Paintings. LC 36-32912. (American Philosophical Society, Philadelphia. Memoirs Ser.: Vol. 5). pap. 43.80 (ISBN 0-317-10424-1, 2000353). Bks Demand UMI.

--A Preliminary Consideration of Aboriginal Australian Decorative Art. LC 38-6677. (American Philosophical Society, Philadelphia. Memoirs Ser.: Vol. 9). pap. 40.80 (ISBN 0-317-10408-X, 2000358). Bks Demand UMI.

Davidson, Daniel V., et al. Business Law: Principles & Cases. LC 83-23863. 1024p. 1984. text ed. write for info. (ISBN 0-534-01456-9). Kent Pub Co.

Davidson, David & Blot, David. Write from the Start. 1983. pap. text ed. 7.95 (ISBN 0-88377-395-3). Newbury Hse.

Davidson, David, jt. auth. see Blot, David.

Davidson, David & Suresh, Subra, eds. Fatigue Crack Growth Threshold Concepts. LC 84-70400. (Illus.). 565p. 1984. 53.00 (ISBN 0-89520-475-4). Metal Soc.

Davidson, David L., jt. ed. see Zusman, Jack.

Davidson, David M. Current Approaches to the Teaching of Grammar in ESL. (Language in Education Ser.: No. 5). 23p. 1978. pap. 3.95x (ISBN 0-15-599056-X). Ctr Appl Ling.

Davidson, Diane, ed. see Shakespeare, William.

Davidson, Donald. The Attack on Leviathan: Regionalism & Nationalism in the United States. 12.75 (ISBN 0-8446-1149-2). Peter Smith.

--Essays on Actions & Events. 1980. 32.50x (ISBN 0-19-824529-7); pap. 9.95x (ISBN 0-19-824637-4). Oxford U Pr.

--Inquiries into Truth & Interpretation. 292p. 1984. 29.95x (ISBN 0-19-824617-X); pap. 10.95x (ISBN 0-19-875046-3). Oxford U Pr.

--Still Rebels, Still Yankees & Other Essays. 2nd ed. LC 70-168395. (Library of Southern Civilization). xx, 284p. 1957. 27.50x (ISBN 0-8071-0038-2). La State U Pr.

--Tennessee: Vol. 1: the Old River-Frontier to Secession. LC 78-15103. 1979. 16.95 (ISBN 0-87049-265-9). U of Tenn Pr.

Davidson, Donald & Suppes, Patrick. Decision Making: An Experimental Approach. LC 77-13439. 1977. Repr. of 1957 ed. lib. bdg. 19.75x (ISBN 0-8371-9854-2, DAVD). Greenwood.

Davidson, Donald, ed. British Poetry of the Eighteen Nineties. Repr. of 1937 ed. 59.00x (ISBN 0-403-08915-8). Somerset Pub.

Davidson, Donald, intro. by. The Fugitive-A Magazine of Verse: April 1922 to December 1925, 4 vols. in 1. authorized ed. 18.00 (ISBN 0-8446-1192-1). Peter Smith.

Davidson, Donald A. Soils & Land Use Planning. (Topics in Applied Geography Ser.). (Illus.). 128p. 1980. pap. text ed. 11.50x (ISBN 0-582-48985-7). Longman.

Davidson, Donald L. Nuclear War & the American Churches: Ethical Positions on Modern Warfare. 200p. 1983. pap. 21.50x (ISBN 0-86531-706-2). Westview.

Davidson, E. E., jt. auth. see Scheps, Clarence.

Davidson, E. H., ed. see Poe, Edgar Allan.

Davidson, Edward H. Jonathan Edwards: The Narrative of a Puritan Mind. LC 68-7254. pap. 43.80 (ISBN 0-317-07848-8, 2005489). Bks Demand UMI.

--Poe: A Critical Study. LC 57-12965. 1957. 20.00x (ISBN 0-674-67450-2, Belknap Pr). Harvard U Pr.

Davidson, Elizabeth H. Establishment of the English Church in Continental American Colonies. (Duke University. Trinity College Historical Society. Historical Papers: No. 20). Repr. of 1936 ed. 24.50 (ISBN 0-404-51770-6). AMS Pr.

Davidson, Elizabeth W., ed. Pathogenesis of Invertebrate Microbial Diseases. LC 81-65007. 576p. 1981. text ed. 42.50x (ISBN 0-86598-014-4). Allanheld.

Davidson, Ellen, jt. auth. see Schneidewind, Nancy.

Davidson, Eric H. Gene Activity in Early Development. 1977. 35.50 (ISBN 0-12-205160-2). Acad Pr.

Davidson, Eric H. & Firtel, Richard A. Molecular Biology of Development. (UCLA Symposium on Molecular & Cellular Biology, New Ser.: Vol. 19). 712p. 1984. 96.00 (ISBN 0-8451-2618-0). A R Liss.

Davidson, F., ed. see Emerson, R. W.

Davidson, Florence E., jt. auth. see Blackman, Margaret B.

Davidson, Francis. Davison's Poetical Rhapsody, 2 vols. Bullen, A. H., ed. 1978. Repr. of 1890 ed. lib. bdg. 75.00 set (ISBN 0-8495-0472-4). Arden Lib.

Davidson, Frank P. & Cox, John S. Macro: Reindustrializing America & the World. Guarnaschelli, Maria, ed. LC 83-62049. (Illus.). 294p. 1983. 17.95 (ISBN 0-688-02182-4). Morrow.

Davidson, Frank P., et al. Macroengineering & the Infra-Structure of Tomorrow. 1979. lib. bdg. 30.00x (ISBN 0-89158-294-0). Westview.

Davidson, Frank P., jt. ed. see Salkeld, Robert.

Davidson, Fraser P. The Judiciary & the Development of Employment Law. 240p. 1984. text ed. 32.95x (ISBN 0-566-00481-X). Gower Pub Co.

Davidson, G. Genetic Control of Insect Pests. 1974. 33.00 (ISBN 0-12-205750-3). Acad Pr.

Davidson, George. The ABC's of Air Travel. LC 84-71960. (Illus.). 90p. (Orig.). 1984. pap. 4.95 (ISBN 0-931921-00-7). ABC's Air.

--The Tracks & Landfalls of Bering & Chirikof on the Northwest Coast of America. 44p. 1973. (ISBN 0-87770-112-1). Ye Galleon.

Davidson, George I. The ABC's of Air Travel. LC 84-71960. (Illus.). 80p. (Orig.). 1984. pap. 4.95 (ISBN 0-317-19112-8). Atlas Pub.

Davidson, Georgie. Origami. LC 75-44992. (Larousse Craft Ser.). (Illus.). 1978. pap. 8.95 (ISBN 0-88332-027-4, 8036). Larousse.

Davidson, Gladys. Stories of the Ballets. LC 49-6942. 486p. 1979. 15.95 (ISBN 0-370-00320-9, Pub. by the Bodley Head). Merrimack Pub Cir.

Davidson, Glen, ed. The Hospice: Development & Administration. 2nd ed. LC 84-19211. (Death Education, Aging, & Health Care Ser.). (Illus.). 300p. 1985. 34.95 (ISBN 0-89116-370-0). Hemisphere Pub.

Davidson, Glen W. Living with Dying. LC 74-14186. 112p. (Orig.). 1975. pap. 5.50 (ISBN 0-8066-1468-4, 10-3980); study guide 00.30 (10-3981). Augsburg.

--Understanding Mourning: A Guide for Those Who Grieve. 112p. (Orig.). 1984. pap. 5.50 (ISBN 0-8066-2080-3, 10-6805). Augsburg.

Davidson, Glenn D. Tool Grinding & Sharpening Handbook. LC 84-24121. (Illus.). 128p. (Orig.). 1985. pap. 6.95 (ISBN 0-8069-7904-6). Sterling.

Davidson, Gordon, jt. auth. see McLaughlin, Corinne.

Davidson, Grace G. Early Records of Georgia (the Earliest Records of Wilkes County, Georgia, 2 vols. (Illus.). 1967. Repr. of 1933 ed. 37.50 (ISBN 0-89308-006-3). Southern Hist Pr.

--Historical Collections of the Georgia Chapters, Daughters of the American Revolution: Records of Richmond County, Georgia. Formerly St. Paul's Parish, Vol. 2. (Illus.). 1968. Repr. of 1927 ed. 20.00 (ISBN 0-89308-007-1). Southern Hist Pr.

Davidson, Graeme J. & Macdonald, Mary. Anyone Can Pray: A Guide to Methods of Christian Prayer. LC 82-62921. 208p. (Orig.). 1983. pap. 7.95 (ISBN 0-8091-2542-0). Paulist Pr.

Davidson, Gregory. Practical Pascal Programs. (Illus.). 205p. pap. 15.99 (ISBN 0-07-582633-X, BYTE Bks). McGraw.

Davidson, Gregory, jt. auth. see Poole, Lon.

Davidson, Gustav. All Things Are Holy. limited ed. LC 78-146980. (Living Poets' Library Ser.). (Illus.). pap. 2.50 (ISBN 0-686-01280-1). Dragons Teeth.

Davidson, Gustov. A Dictionary of Angels: Including the Fallen Angels. LC 66-19757. (Illus.). 1972. 22.95 (ISBN 0-02-906940-8); pap. 11.95 (ISBN 0-02-907050-3). Free Pr.

Davidson, H. Ellis. Gods & Myths of Northern Europe. (Orig.). 1965. pap. 4.95 (ISBN 0-14-020670-1, Pelican). Penguin.

Davidson, H. F., jt. auth. see Certon, M. J.

Davidson, H. R. The Viking Road to Byzantium. 341p. 1976. 21.50x (ISBN 0-87471-834-1). Rowman.

Davidson, H. R., ed. The Journey to the Other World. (Folklore Society Mistletoe Ser.). 149p. 1975. 13.50x (ISBN 0-87471-613-6). Rowman.

Davidson, H. W., et al. Manufactured Carbon. 1968. 18.00 (ISBN 0-08-012667-7); pap. 7.00 (ISBN 0-08-012666-9). Pergamon.

Davidson, Harold & Mechlenburg, Roy. Nursery Management: Administration & Culture. (Illus.). 464p. 1981. text ed. 29.95 (ISBN 0-13-627455-2). P-H.

Davidson, Harold G. Edward Borein: Cowboy Artist. LC 74-2063. limited ed. 100.00 (ISBN 0-385-02777-X). Doubleday.

--Jimmy Swinnerton: The Artist & His Work. (Illus.). 160p. 1985. 24.95 (ISBN 0-688-03710-0, Hearst Bks). Morrow.

Davidson, Harriet. T. S. Eliot & Hermeneutics: Absence & Interpretation in the Waste Land. LC 84-21757. 152p. 1985. text ed. 17.50x (ISBN 0-8071-1208-9). La State U Pr.

Davidson, Harry, ed. The Fully Illustrated Book of Nineteenth Century British Art with Rare & Original Engravings of the Period. (Illus.). 89p. 1981. 185.85 (ISBN 0-86650-018-9). Gloucester Art.

Davidson, Helen H., jt. auth. see Klopfer, Bruno.

Davidson, Henry M. Good Christian Men. facsimile ed. LC 70-142616. (Essay Index Reprint Ser). Repr. of 1940 ed. 19.00 (ISBN 0-8369-2390-1). Ayer Co Pubs.

Davidson, Herbert. Proofs for Eternity, Creation, & the Existence of God in Medieval Islamic & Jewish Philosophy. (Studies in Northeast Culture & Society: Vol. 7). 500p. 1985. price not set (ISBN 0-89003-180-0); pap. 62.00 (ISBN 0-89003-181-9). Undena Pubns.

Davidson, Herbert A. The Philosophy of Abraham Shalom: A Fifteenth-Century Exposition & Defense of Maimonides. LC 65-63470. (University of California Publications. Near Eastern Studies: Vol. 5). pap. 29.80 (ISBN 0-317-08847-5, 2014820). Bks Demand UMI.

Davidson, Herbert A., ed. see Averroes.

Davidson, Herbert A., ed. see Averrois.

Davidson, Hilda, ed. Saxo Grammaticus: The History of the Danes, Vol. 1-Englist Text. Fisher, Peter, tr. 297p. 1979. 36.50x (ISBN 0-8476-6221-7). Rowman.

Davidson, Hilda E. Patterns of Folklore. 133p. 1978. 11.50x (ISBN 0-8476-6092-3). Rowman.

--Saxo Grammaticus: History of the Danes, Vol. II. Fisher, Peter, tr. (Illus.). 209p. 1980. 35.00x (ISBN 0-8476-6938-6). Rowman.

Davidson, Hilda R. & Russell, W. M., eds. The Folklore of Ghosts. (Mistletoe Bks.: No. 15). 282p. 1981. text ed. 30.00x (ISBN 0-85991-079-2, Pub. by Boydell & Brewer). Biblio Dist.

Davidson, Homer K. Black Jack Davidson: Life of General John W. Davidson. 1974. 15.50 (ISBN 0-87062-109-2). A H Clark.

Davidson, Homer L. Beginner's Guide to TV Repair. 3rd ed. (Illus.). 272p. 1985. 18.95 (ISBN 0-8306-0897-4, 1897); pap. 12.95 (ISBN 0-8306-1897-X). TAB Bks.

--Practical Microwave Oven Repair. (Illus.). 364p. (Orig.). 1984. 19.95 (ISBN 0-8306-0667-X, 1667); pap. 13.95 (ISBN 0-8306-1667-5). TAB Bks.

--Thirty Three Photovoltaic Projects. (Illus.). 272p. (Orig.). 1982. 16.95 (ISBN 0-8306-2467-8, 1467); pap. 10.95 (ISBN 0-8306-1467-2). TAB Bks.

Davidson, Howard A., jt. auth. see Horowitz, Robert M.

Davidson, Hugh M. Audience, Words, & Art: Studies in Seventeenth-Century French Rhetoric. LC 65-18737. 213p. 1965. 5.00 (ISBN 0-8142-0043-5). Ohio St U Pr.

--Blaise Pascal. (World Authors Ser.: No. 701). 165p. 1983. lib. bdg. 16.95 (ISBN 0-8057-6548-4, Twayne). G K Hall.

--The Origins of Certainty: Means & Meanings in Pascal's "Pensees". LC 78-12768. 1979. lib. bdg. 16.00x (ISBN 0-226-13716-3). U of Chicago Pr.

Davidson, Hugh M., jt. auth. see Dube, Pierre H.

Davidson, Hugh M. & Dube, Pierre H., eds. A Concordance to Pascal's "Pensees". LC 75-16808. (Cornell Concordances Ser.). 1488p. 1975. 75.00x (ISBN 0-8014-0972-1). Cornell U Pr.

Davidson, I., jt. auth. see Ginzberg, L.

Davidson, I. see Ginzberg, L. & Davidson, I.

Davidson, I., et al, eds. Electronic Maintenance, Vol. 2. (Engineering Craftsmen: No. J24). (Illus.). 1970. spiral bdg. 43.50x (ISBN 0-89563-005-2). Trans-Atlantic.

Davidson, Ian D. Britain & the Making of Europe. LC 74-182185. 1972. text ed. 22.50 (ISBN 0-312-09800-6). St Martin.

Davidson, Ingledew C. The Ballads & Songs of Yorkshire. 1978. Repr. of 1860 ed. lib. bdg. 35.00 (ISBN 0-8495-2607-8). Arden Lib.

Davidson, Isobel. Real Stories from Baltimore County History. LC 70-9245. (Illus.). x, 296p. Repr. of 1917 ed. 35.00x (ISBN 0-8103-5033-5). Gale.

Davidson, Israel. Parody in Jewish Literature. LC 77-163670. (Columbia University. Oriental Studies: No. 2). Repr. of 1907 ed. 24.50 (ISBN 0-404-50492-2). AMS Pr.

--Thesaurus of Medieval Hebrew Poetry, 4 Vols. rev. ed. (Library of Jewish Classics). 1970. Set. 150.00x (ISBN 0-87068-003-X). Ktav.

Davidson, Israel, ed. see Solomon Ibn Gabirol.

Davidson, J. New Mathematics. (Teach Yourself Ser.). 1974. pap. 4.95 (ISBN 0-679-12326-1). McKay.

Davidson, J. A., intro. by. Resource Developments in the Eighties. (Chemeca Ser.). 338p. (Orig.). 1982. pap. text ed. 54.00x (ISBN 0-85825-169-8, Pub. by Inst Engineering Australia). Brookfield Pub Co.

Davidson, J. F., ed. Fluidization. Keairns, D. L. LC 77-82495. (Illus.). 1978. 69.50 (ISBN 0-521-21943-4). Cambridge U Pr.

Davidson, J. F., jt. ed. see Von Kaulla, K. N.

Davidson, J. L. Prophets of Deceit. 1960. 5.25 (ISBN 0-88027-016-0). Firm Foun Pub.

Davidson, J. M. Barron's Card Guide to Russian Grammar. 1964. pap. text ed. 1.75 (ISBN 0-8120-5072-X). Barron.

Davidson, J. M. C., ed. see Chekhov, Anton P.

Davidson, J. Morrison. Concerning Four Precursors of Henry George & the Single Tax & Also the Land Gospel According to Winstanley the Digger. LC 77-115317. 1971. Repr. of 1899 ed. 15.00x (ISBN 0-8046-1108-4, Pub. by Kennikat). Assoc Faculty Pr.

Davidson, J. N. & Cohn, W. E., eds. Progress in Nucleic Acid Research, Vol. 31. 1984. 58.00 (ISBN 0-12-540031-4). Acad Pr.

Davidson, J. N., jt. ed. see Chargaff, Erwin.

Davidson, J. N., et al, eds. Progress in Nucleic Acid Research & Molecular Biology: An International Series. Incl. Vol. 3. 1964. 71.50 (ISBN 0-12-540003-9); Vol. 4. 1965. 71.50 (ISBN 0-12-540004-7); Vol. 5. 1966. 71.50 (ISBN 0-12-540005-5); Vol. 6. 1967. 71.50 (ISBN 0-12-540006-3); Vol. 7. 1967. 71.50 (ISBN 0-12-540007-1); Vol. 8. 1968. 71.50 (ISBN 0-12-540008-X); Vol. 9. 1969. 71.50 (ISBN 0-12-540009-8); Vol. 10. 1970. 71.50 (ISBN 0-12-540010-1); Vol. 11. 1971. 75.00 (ISBN 0-12-540011-X); Vol. 12. 1972. 55.00 (ISBN 0-12-540012-8); Vol. 13. 1973. 65.00 (ISBN 0-12-540013-6); Vol. 20. 1977. 59.50 (ISBN 0-12-540020-9); Vol. 21. 1978. 50.00 (ISBN 0-12-540021-7); Vol. 22. 1979. 55.00 (ISBN 0-12-540022-5). Acad Pr.

Davidson, J. P. & Kern, Bernard D., eds. Fifth Symposium on the Structure of Low-Medium Mass Nuclei. LC 73-77254. (Illus.). 312p. 1973. 25.00x (ISBN 0-8131-1293-1). U Pr of Ky.

Davidson, J. R. Strachan see Strachan-Davidson, J. R.

Davidson, J. S. Grenada: A Study in Politics & the Limits of International Law. 200p. 1986. text ed. write for info. (ISBN 0-566-05052-8). Gower Pub Co.

Davidson, James. Effective Time Management: A Practical Workbook. LC 78-6126. 104p. 1978. pap. 9.95 (ISBN 0-87705-332-4). Human Sci Pr.

Davidson, James, jt. auth. see Sellmeyer, Ralph.

Davidson, James D. The Squeeze. 1981. pap. 2.95 (ISBN 0-671-42127-1). PB.

Davidson, James J. The Artistic Work of James L. Davidson: A Pictorial Look at an Artist. 1983. 6.95 (ISBN 0-533-05356-0). Vantage.

--The Vision of an Artist & Writer. 1981. 6.95 (ISBN 0-533-04806-0). Vantage.

Davidson, James J., ed. Creative Children of God. 1984. 6.95 (ISBN 0-533-05967-4). Vantage.

Davidson, James R. A Dictionary of Protestant Church Music. LC 74-30101. 349p. 1975. 21.00 (ISBN 0-8108-0788-2). Scarecrow.

Davidson, James W. The Island of Formosa: Past & Present. LC 77-86949. (Illus.). Repr. of 1903 ed. 55.00 (ISBN 0-404-16704-7). AMS Pr.

Davidson, James W. & Lytle, Mark H. After the Fact: The Art of Historical Detection. LC 81-13747. 1982. 22.95 (ISBN 0-394-52322-9). Knopf.

--After the Fact: The Art of Historical Detection, 2 vols. (Orig.). 1982. 1 vol. ed. 15.00 (ISBN 0-394-32965-1, RanC); Vol. 1. pap. text ed. 9.00 (ISBN 0-394-32129-4); Vol. 2. pap. text ed. 9.00 (ISBN 0-394-32890-6). Random.

--After the Fact: The Art of Historical Detection, 2 vols. 2nd ed. 1986. Vol. 1. pap. text ed. price not set (ISBN 0-394-35476-1); Vol. 2. pap. text ed. price not set (ISBN 0-394-35477-X); Combined binding. pap. text ed. price not set (ISBN 0-394-35475-3). Knopf.

Davidson, James W. & Rugge, John. The Complete Wilderness Paddler. 1976. 15.95 (ISBN 0-394-49347-8). Knopf.

--The Complete Wilderness Paddler. LC 82-40021. 288p. 1982. pap. 5.95 (ISBN 0-394-71153-X, Vin). Random.

Davidson, Jane, jt. tr. see Davidson, Alan.

Davidson, Jane, tr. see Dumas, Alexandre.

Davidson, Jean. Oswald's Game. (Illus.). 344p. 1986. pap. 7.95 (ISBN 0-393-30265-2). Norton.

Davidson, Jeffrey, jt. auth. see Watson, Thomas.

Davidson, Jeffrey L. Political Partnerships: Neighborhood Residents & Their Council Members. LC 79-13107. (City & Society Ser.: Vol. 5). (Illus.). 231p. 1979. 25.00 (ISBN 0-8039-1050-9); pap. 12.50 (ISBN 0-8039-1051-7). Sage.

Davidson, Jeffrey P., jt. auth. see Connor, Richard A., Jr.

Davidson, Jim. How to Plan Your Life. LC 79-19803. (Illus.). 126p. 1979. 5.95 (ISBN 0-88289-236-3). Pelican.

Davidson, Joan, jt. auth. see Wibberley, Gerald.

Davidson, Joan W., ed. see Wilson, Woodrow.

Davidson, Joel & Komp, R. J. The Solar Electric Home: A Photovoltaics How-To Handbook. LC 83-70647. (Illus.). 200p. 1983. pap. 11.95 (ISBN 0-937948-04-7). AATEC Pubns.

Davidson, John. Complete Poems, 2 vols. Set. 200.00 (ISBN 0-87968-917-X). Gordon Pr.

--A Full Account of the Wonderful Mission of Earl Lavender. Fletcher, Ian & Stokes, John, eds. LC 76-20049. (Decadent Consciousness Ser.: Vol. 7). 1977. Repr. of 1894 ed. lib. bdg. 46.00 (ISBN 0-8240-2756-6). Garland Pub.

--The Long Road North. 145p. (Orig.). 1981. pap. 5.95 (ISBN 0-932012-15-9). Texas Month Pr.

--The Man Forbid & Other Essays: Pre-Shakespearianism, Meredith. 1973. Repr. of 1910 ed. 20.00 (ISBN 0-8274-1646-6). R West.

Davidson, John & Casady, Cort. The Singing Entertainer: A Contemporary Study of the Art & Business of Being a Professional. 240p. 1982. pap. 14.95 (ISBN 0-88284-194-7). Alfred Pub.

Davidson, John & Lloyd, Richard, eds. Conservation & Agriculture. LC 77-697. 252p. 1978. 58.95x (ISBN 0-471-99502-9, Pub. by Wiley-Interscience). Wiley.

Davidson, John F. & Harrison, O. Fluidised Particles. LC 63-22979. (Illus.). pap. 46.30 (ISBN 0-317-10893-X, 2050790). Bks Demand UMI.

Davidson, John F., ed. Progress in Chemical Fibrinolysis & Thrombolysis, Vol. 5. (Illus.). 1981. text ed. 75.00 (ISBN 0-443-02328-X). Churchill.

Davidson, John F., et al, eds. Progress in Chemical Fibrinolysis & Thrombolysis, Vol. 3. LC 75-14335. 631p. 1978. 80.50 (ISBN 0-89004-137-7). Raven.

Davidson, John H. Agricultural Law, 2 vols. 10th ed. LC 81-1964. (Construction Law-Land Use Environmental Publications). 1035p. 1983. 140.00 (ISBN 0-07-015432-5, Shepards-McGraw). McGraw.

Davidson, John K. Clinical Diabetes Mellitus. (Illus.). 512p. 1985. text ed. 75.00 (ISBN 0-86577-122-7). Thieme-Stratton.

Davidson, John M. Eminent English Liberals in & Out of Parliament. facsimile ed. LC 70-37521. (Essay Index Reprint Ser). Repr. of 1880 ed. 18.00 (ISBN 0-8369-2542-4). Ayer Co Pubs.

Davidson, John P. Collective Models of the Nucleus. LC 68-18665. 1968. 57.50 (ISBN 0-12-205250-1). Acad Pr.

Davidson, Jon R. The Buying & Goodbying of Behaviorism's Way: Confessions & Perspectives of an Ex-Behaviorist. LC 76-52140. 1978. 8.95 (ISBN 0-87212-079-1). Libra.

Davidson, Josephine, jt. auth. see Reggio, Kathryn.

Davidson, Judith. Japan: Where East Meets West. (Discovering Our Heritage Ser.). (Illus.). 112p. (gr. 5 up). 1983. PLB 10.95 (ISBN 0-87518-230-5). Dillon.

Davidson, Julian M., jt. ed. see Davidson, Richard J.

Davidson, Kathryn & Glassman, Elizabeth. Transfixed by Light: Photographs from the Menil Foundation Clinic. LC 81-80810. (Menil Foundation Ser.). (Illus.). 1980. pap. write for info. (ISBN 0-939594-00-5). Menil Found.

Davidson, Kenneth M. Megamergers: Corporate America's Billion-Dollar Takeovers. 432p. 1985. 24.95 (ISBN 0-88730-058-8). Ballinger Pub.

Davidson, Khoren K. Odyssey of an Armenian of Zeitoun. LC 84-90122. 257p. 1985. 14.95 (ISBN 0-533-06202-0). Vantage.

Davidson, L. Using the Magic of Word Power to Multiply Real Estate Sales. 1973. 49.50 (ISBN 0-13-939694-2). P-H.

Davidson, L. A. The Shape of the Tree: New York, New York. 48p. 1982. pap. 3.00 (ISBN 0-941190-02-1). Wind Chimes.

Davidson, Laurie & Gordon, Laura K. The Sociology of Gender. 1979. pap. 18.50 (ISBN 0-395-30588-8). HM.

Davidson, Leola, jt. auth. see Hansen, Gerry.

Davidson, Les. High Income Shortcuts That Multiply Real Estate Sales & Commissions Fast. 1975. 49.50 (ISBN 0-13-387514-8). Exec Reports.

--Using the Magic of Word Power to Multiply Real Estate Sales. 1973. 49.50 (ISBN 0-13-939694-2). Exec Reports.

Davidson, Levette J. Guide to American Folklore. LC 74-97313. Repr. of 1951 ed. lib. bdg. 19.25 (ISBN 0-8371-2552-9, DAAF). Greenwood.

Davidson, Levette J. & Bostwick, Prudence. Literature of the Rocky Mountain West 1803-1903. LC 70-91039. 1970. Repr. of 1939 ed. 35.00x (ISBN 0-8046-0649-8, Pub. by Kennikat). Assoc Faculty Pr.

Davidson, Levette J., ed. Poems of the Old West. facs. ed. LC 68-58824. (Granger Index Reprint Ser). 1951. 16.00 (ISBN 0-8369-6012-2). Ayer Co Pubs.

Davidson, Lionel. The Chelsea Murders. (Crime Monthly Ser.). 1980. pap. 2.95 (ISBN 0-14-005136-8). Penguin.

--The Menorah Men. LC 82-47556. 288p. 1982. pap. 2.84i (ISBN 0-06-080592-7, P592, PL). Har-Row.

--The Night of Wenceslas. LC 82-47557. 224p. 1982. pap. 2.84i (ISBN 0-06-080595-1, P595, PL). Har-Row.

--The Rose of Tibet. LC 82-47558. 288p. 1982. pap. 2.84i (ISBN 0-06-080593-5, P593, PL). Har-Row.

Davidson, M. An Easy Outline of Astronomy. 1943. 15.00 (ISBN 0-686-17420-8). Ridgeway Bks.

--The Stars & the Mind: A Study of the Impact of Astronomical Development on Human Thought. 59.95 (ISBN 0-8490-1121-3). Gordon Pr.

Davidson, M. J. & Cooper, C. L. Women at Work: An International Survey. 300p. 1985. 34.95 (ISBN 0-471-90459-7). Wiley.

Davidson, Margaret. Five True Dog Stories. (gr. k-3). 1977. pap. 1.50 (ISBN 0-590-08793-2, Schol Pap). Scholastic Inc.

--Five True Horse Stories. (gr. 2-6). 1979. pap. 1.50 (ISBN 0-590-05737-5, Schol Pap). Scholastic Inc.

--The Golda Meir Story. rev. ed. LC 75-39297. 212p. (gr. 5 up). 1976. reinforced bdg. 13.95 (ISBN 0-684-16877-4, ScribJ). Scribner.

--Helen Keller. (Illus.). (gr. k-3). 1973. pap. 2.25 (ISBN 0-590-08899-8). Scholastic Inc.

--Helen Keller: Centennial Edition. new ed. 128p. (gr. 6-10). 1980. 6.95 (ISBN 0-8038-3015-7). Hastings.

--Helen Keller's Teacher. (gr. 4-6). 1972. pap. 2.25 (ISBN 0-590-02224-5). Scholastic Inc.

--I Have a Dream: The Story of Martin Luther King. (Illus.). 128p. (Orig.). (gr. 2-5). 1986. pap. 2.25 (ISBN 0-590-33312-7, Lucky Star). Scholastic Inc.

--Nine True Dolphin Stories. 72p. (gr. 2-6). 1975. 9.95g (ISBN 0-8038-5037-9). Hastings.

--Nine True Dolphin Stories. (Illus.). (gr. k-3). 1974. pap. 1.75 (ISBN 0-590-03058-2). Scholastic Inc.

--Wild Animal Families. new ed. 64p. (gr. 2-5). 1980. 7.95 (ISBN 0-8038-8098-7). Hastings.

Davidson, Margaret C., jt. ed. see Maunder, Elwood R.

Davidson, Marilyn & Cooper, Cary. Stress & the Woman Manager. LC 83-9666. 260p. 1983. 27.50 (ISBN 0-312-76610-6). St Martin.

Davidson, Marion & Blue, Martha. Making It Legal: A Law Primer for the Craftmaker, Visual Artist, & Writer. (Illus.). 1979. pap. 8.95 (ISBN 0-07-015431-7). McGraw.

Davidson, Mark. Uncommon Sense: The Life & Thought of Ludwig von Bertalanffy (1901-1972), Father of General Systems Theory. LC 82-16900. 256p. 1983. 15.95 (ISBN 0-87477-165-X). HM.

Davidson, Marshall & Stillinger, Elizabeth. The American Wing in the Metropolitan Museum of Art. Ralston, Susan, ed. (Illus.). 352p. 1985. 50.00 (ISBN 0-394-54847-7). Knopf.

Davidson, Marshall B. The American Wing: A Guide. Stillinger, Penny, ed. (Illus.). 176p. 1980. pap. 9.95 (ISBN 0-87099-238-4). Metro Mus Art.

--The Drawing of America: Eyewitnesses to History. LC 82-16465. (Illus.). 256p. 1983. 49.50 (ISBN 0-8109-0807-7). Abrams.

--New York: A Pictorial History. (Illus.). 360p. 1981. pap. 14.95 (ISBN 0-684-17287-9, ScribT). Scribner.

Davidson, Marshall B. & Stillinger, Elizabeth. The American Wing. (Illus.). 352p. 1985. 39.50 (ISBN 0-87099-309-7). Metro Mus Art.

Davidson, Martin J. & Gottlieb, Benjamin M., eds. Unconventional Methods in Exploration for Petroleum & Natural Gas, No. III. LC 83-8653. (Illus.). 282p. 1984. 50.00 (ISBN 0-87074-188-8). SMU Press.

Davidson, Mary F. The Dye Pot. 3rd rev. ed. 1981. pap. text ed. 3.00 (ISBN 0-686-10137-5). M F Davidson.

Davidson, Mary S. A Superstar Called Sweetpea. 144p. (YA) (gr. 6-9). 1982. pap. 1.95 (ISBN 0-440-97877-7, LFL). Dell.

--A Superstar Called Sweetpea. LC 80-11985. 144p. 1980. 11.50 (ISBN 0-670-68478-3). Viking.

Davidson, Max. The Wolf. 224p. 1984. 15.95 (ISBN 0-7043-2387-7, Pub. by Quartet Bks). Merrimack Pub Cir.

Davidson, Mayer B. Diabetes Mellitus: Diagnosis & Treatment. LC 81-84. 480p. 1981. Combined Ed. 25.00 set (ISBN 0-471-09543-5, Pub. by Wiley Med). Wiley.

Davidson, Michael. The Landing of Rochambeau. 80p. 1985. 15.00 (ISBN 0-930901-25-8); pap. 7.00 (ISBN 0-930901-26-6). Burning Deck.

Davidson, Michael, tr. see Mehnert, Klaus.

Davidson, Muriel. The Thursday Woman. 1982. pap. 2.95 (ISBN 0-425-04505-6). Berkley Pub.

Davidson, Neil. Neurotransmitter Amino Acids. 1976. 33.00 (ISBN 0-12-205950-6). Acad Pr.

Davidson, Nicole & UNITAR, eds. Paths to Peace: The UN Security & Its Presidency. LC 80-20166. (Pergamon Policy Studies on International Politics). 424p. 1981. 47.00 (ISBN 0-08-026322-4). Pergamon.

Davidson, Norman. Astronomy & the Imagination. (Illus.). 229p. 1985. 25.00 (ISBN 0-7102-0371-3). Routledge & Kegan.

--Crime & the Environment. 1981. 26.50x (ISBN 0-312-17198-6). St Martin.

Davidson, Norman, jt. ed. see Rich, Alexander.

Davidson, Orlando R., et al. The Deadeyes: The Story of the 96th Infantry Division. (Divisional Ser.: No. 20). (Illus.). 310p. 1981. Repr. of 1947 ed. 25.00 (ISBN 0-89839-051-6). Battery Pr.

Davidson, P. Everyday Math Made Easy. 272p. 1984. 8.95 (ISBN 0-07-049628-5). McGraw.

--Moonlighting: A Complete Guide to Over 200 Exciting Part-Time Jobs. 288p. 1983. 14.95 (ISBN 0-07-049601-3); pap. 7.95 (ISBN 0-07-049607-2). McGraw.

Davidson, P., et al. Wildwater West Virginia, Vol. 1. rev., exp. ed. Williams, Barbara E., ed. (Illus., Orig.). 1985. pap. 10.95 (ISBN 0-89732-021-2). Menasha Ridge.

--Wildwater West Virginia, Vol. 2. Williams, Barbara E., ed. (Illus., Orig.). 1985. pap. 10.95 (ISBN 0-89732-029-8). Menasha Ridge.

Davidson, Pamela & Norman, Jill. Russian Phrase Book. 1980. pap. 3.95 (ISBN 0-14-005079-5). Penguin.

Davidson, Park O. & Davidson, Sheena M., eds. Behavioral Medicine: Changing Health Lifestyles. LC 79-14944. 1979. 25.00 (ISBN 0-87630-200-2). Brunner Mazel.

Davidson, Paul. Are You Sure It's Arthritis? A Guide to Soft-Tissue Rheumatism. 224p. 1985. 15.95 (ISBN 0-02-529770-8). Macmillan.

--International Money & the Real World. LC 81-6777. 450p. 1981. 37.95x (ISBN 0-470-27256-2). Halsted Pr.

--Money & the Real World. 2nd ed. LC 77-16113. 428p. 1978. pap. text ed. 21.95x (ISBN 0-470-99217-4). Halsted Pr.

Davidson, Paul, jt. auth. see Burrell, Bob.

Davidson, Paul C., jt. auth. see Burrell, Robert G.

Davidson, Pearle V., jt. auth. see Davidson, Charles T.

Davidson, Percy E. Recapitulation Theory & Human Infancy. LC 70-176714. (Columbia University. Teachers College. Contributions to Education: No. 65). Repr. of 1914 ed. 22.50 (ISBN 0-404-55065-7). AMS Pr.

Davidson, Peter. Earn Money at Home. (McGraw-Hill Paperback Ser.). 1982. pap. 6.95 (ISBN 0-07-049606-4). McGraw.

Davidson, Philip. Propaganda & the American Revolution. (Illus.). 476p. 1973. pap. 3.45x (ISBN 0-393-00703-0). Norton.

Davidson, Philip G. Propaganda & the American Revolution, 1763-1789. xvi, 460p. 1941. 30.00 (ISBN 0-8078-0343-X). U of NC Pr.

Davidson, Phillip L. SWAT (Special Weapons & Tactics) (Illus.). 148p. 1979. photocopy ed. 16.75x (ISBN 0-398-03890-2). C C Thomas.

Davidson, R., jt. auth. see Clarke, Loyal.

Davidson, R. J. Methods in Nonlinear Plasma Theory. (Pure & Applied Physics Ser.). 1972. 63.00 (ISBN 0-12-205450-4). Acad Pr.

Davidson, R. L. Handbook of Water-Soluble Gums & Resins. 1980. 57.50 (ISBN 0-07-015471-6). McGraw.

Davidson, R. L., jt. auth. see Bland, William F.

Davidson, R. Theodore. Chicano Prisoners: The Key to San Quentin. (Illus.). 196p. 1983. pap. text ed. 7.95 (ISBN 0-88133-050-7). Waveland Pr.

Davidson, Ralph B. The Art of Making Concrete Pottery & Garden Furniture Easily Explained. (Illus.). 211p. 1984. 77.45 (ISBN 0-86650-124-X). Gloucester Art.

Davidson, Ralph H. & Lyon, William F. Insect Pests of Farm, Garden & Orchard. 7th ed. LC 78-31366. 596p. 1981. pap. text ed. 24.00 (ISBN 0-471-86314-9). Wiley.

Davidson, Ralph K. Price Discrimination in Selling Gas & Electricity. LC 78-64222. (Johns Hopkins University. Studies in the Social Sciences. Seventy-Second Ser. 1954: 1). 192p. 1982. Repr. of 1955 ed. 24.50 (ISBN 0-404-61325-X). AMS Pr.

--Price Discrimination in Selling Gas & Electricity. LC 75-35023. (The Johns Hopkins University Series in History & Political Science: No. 72, No. 1). 1976. Repr. of 1955 ed. lib. bdg. 18.25x (ISBN 0-8371-8575-0, DAPRD). Greenwood.

Davidson, Richard. The Gentleman from Hyde Park. 6p. (Orig.). 1982. pap. 0.75 (ISBN 0-934776-04-0). Bard Pr.

--Heirs of a Mongrel. LC 85-50841. 182p. 1985. pap. 7.00 (ISBN 0-913793-03-5). Teal Pr.

--Somatic Cell Genetics. 1984. 52.95 (ISBN 0-87933-120-8). Van Nos Reinhold.

Davidson, Richard J. & Davidson, Julian M., eds. Psychobiology of Consciousness. LC 79-316. 508p. 1980. 39.50x (ISBN 0-306-40138-X, Plenum Pr). Plenum Pub.

Davidson, Richard J. & Schwartz, Gary E., eds. Consciousness & Self-Regulation: Advances in Research & Theory, Vol. 3. 242p. 1983. 25.00x (ISBN 0-306-41214-4, Plenum Pr). Plenum Pub.

Davidson, Richard J., jt. ed. see Fox, Nathan A.

Davidson, Richard J., jt. ed. see Goleman, Daniel.

Davidson, Richard L. & De La Cruz, Felix F. Somatic Cell Hybridization. LC 74-75725. 312p. 1974. 45.50 (ISBN 0-911216-75-8). Raven.

Davidson, Richard M. Typology in Scripture: A Study of Hermeneutical Tupos Structures. (Andrews University Seminary Doctoral Dissertation Ser.: Vol. 2). 496p. (Orig.). 1981. pap. 10.95 (ISBN 0-943872-34-0). Andrews Univ Pr.

Davidson, Robert. The Bible in Religious Education. 72p. 1980. pap. 5.00x (ISBN 0-905312-10-4, Pub. by Scottish Academic Pr Scotland). Columbia U Pr.

--History of the Presbyterian Church in the State of Kentucky: Preliminary Sketch of the Churches in the Valley of Virginia. 371p. 1974. Repr. of 1847 ed. 8.95 (ISBN 0-87921-024-9). Attic Pr.

--Jeremiah, Vol. 1: Chapters 1 to 20. LC 83-14598. (Daily Study Bible - Old Testament Ser.). 176p. 1983. 12.95 (ISBN 0-664-21394-4); pap. 6.95 (ISBN 0-664-24476-9). Westminster.

--Modification of Pathological Behavior. 1979. 35.00 (ISBN 0-89876-078-X). Gardner Pr.

Davidson, Robert, jt. auth. see Black, Matthew.

Davidson, Robert, ed. Creative Ideas for Advent. 114p. (Orig.). 1980. pap. 9.95 (ISBN 0-940754-06-1). Ed Ministries.

--Genesis, Chapters Twelve to Fifty. LC 78-12892. (Cambridge Bible Commentary on the New English Bible, Old Testament Ser.). (Illus.). 1979. 39.50 (ISBN 0-521-22485-3); pap. 14.95x (ISBN 0-521-29520-3). Cambridge U Pr.

--Genesis, Chapters 1-11. LC 72-93675. (Cambridge Bible Commentary on the New English Bible, Old Testament Ser.). 200p. (Orig.). 1973. pap. 8.95x (ISBN 0-521-09760-6). Cambridge U Pr.

Davidson, Robert B., jt. auth. see Reitman, A.

Davidson, Robert F. Philosophies Men Live by. 2nd ed. LC 73-21684. 1974. text ed. 27.95 (ISBN 0-03-011851-4, HoltC). HR&W.

Davidson, Robert G. Gathering the Pieces. 88p. (Orig.). 1985. pap. 9.95 (ISBN 0-940754-30-4). Ed Ministries.

--What Do They Expect of Me? 80p. 1986. pap. 9.95 (ISBN 0-940754-32-0). Ed Ministries.

Davidson, Robert G., ed. Creative Ideas for Lent. 120p. (Orig.). 1985. pap. 9.95 (ISBN 0-940754-25-8). Ed Ministries.

Davidson, Robert L. & Sittig, Marshall, eds. Water-Soluble Resins. 2nd ed. LC 68-9136. 240p. 1968. 15.95 (ISBN 0-686-86267-8). Krieger.

Davidson, Robert L., ed. see Volk, William.

Davidson, Robert M. Coronary Heart Disease: Contemporary Patient Management. 1985. text ed. write for info. (ISBN 0-87488-874-3). Med Exam.

Davidson, Robert S., ed. Modification of Pathological Behavior: Experimental Analysis of Etiology & Behavior Therapy. LC 78-69. 588p. 1979. 27.95x (ISBN 0-470-99386-3). Halsted Pr.

Davidson, Robyn. Tracks. 1983. pap. 3.95 (ISBN 0-394-72167-5). Pantheon.

Davidson, Roger. Whitehall & the Labour Problem in Late Victorian & Edwardian Britain: A Study in Official Statistics & Social Control. LC 84-21424. 294p. 1985. 32.50 (ISBN 0-7099-0832-6, Pub. by Croom Helm Ltd). Longwood Pub Group.

Davidson, Roger, et al. Congress & Its Members. 2nd ed. LC 85-463. 477p. 1985. 19.95 (ISBN 0-87187-345-1); pap. 14.95 (ISBN 0-87187-325-7). Congr Quarterly.

Davidson, Roger H. The Politics of Comprehensive Manpower Legislation. LC 72-10874. (Policy Studies in Employment & Welfare: No. 15). pap. 32.00 (ISBN 0-317-19878-5, 2023092). Bks Demand UMI.

--The Role of the Congressman. LC 68-27986. 1969. 27.50x (ISBN 0-672-53587-4). Irvington.

Davidson, Roger H. & Levitan, Sar A. Antipoverty Housekeeping: The Administration of the Economic Opportunity Act. LC 68-65876. (Policy Papers in Human Resources & Industrial Relations Ser.: No. 9). (Orig.). 1968. pap. 2.50x (ISBN 0-87736-109-6). U of Mich Inst Labor.

Davidson, Roger H., jt. auth. see Patterson, Samuel C.

Davidson, Ronald C. & Marion, Jerry B. Mathematical Methods for Introductory Physics with Calculus. 2nd ed. LC 79-19656. 232p. 1980. pap. text ed. 18.95x (ISBN 0-7216-2919-9). SCP.

Davidson, Rosalie. Dinosaurs from A to Z. LC 83-7231. (Science Bks.). (Illus.). 56p. (gr. 3-6). 1983. PLB 11.95 (ISBN 0-516-00516-2). Childrens.

Davidson, S. & Weil, R. Handbook of Cost Accounting. 1978. 44.95 (ISBN 0-07-015452-X). McGraw.

Davidson, Sam R. Engineering Economics: Problems & Solutions. LC 83-11792. 224p. (Orig.). 1983. pap. text ed. 12.00 (ISBN 0-668-05862-5, 5862). Arco.

Davidson, Sara. Friends of the Opposite Sex. LC 83-45111. 288p. 1984. 15.95 (ISBN 0-385-13381-2). Doubleday.

--Friends of the Opposite Sex. 1985. pap. 3.95 (ISBN 0-317-18905-0). PB.

--Loose Change. 1985. pap. 4.50 (ISBN 0-671-50434-7). PB.

--Loose Change. 416p. 1984. pap. 4.95 (ISBN 0-671-50434-7). WSP.

--Real Property. 384p. 1981. pap. 2.95 (ISBN 0-671-41269-8). PB.

Davidson, Sarah A., jt. ed. see Blegen, Theodore C.

Davidson, Sharon V., jt. auth. see Bussman, John W.

Davidson, Sharon V., ed. Alcoholism & Health. LC 80-12354. 216p. 1980. text ed. 36.50 (ISBN 0-89443-292-3). Aspen Systems.

Davidson, Sheena M., jt. ed. see Davidson, Park O.

Davidson, Sidney & Schinder, James. Fundamentals of Accounting. 5th ed. LC 74-80399. 1975. text ed. 31.95x (ISBN 0-03-082803-1); instr's. manual 20.00 (ISBN 0-03-089652-5). Dryden Pr.

Davidson, Sidney, jt. auth. see Ventolo, William.

Davidson, Sidney, ed. see Ventolo, William L., Jr.

Davidson, Sidney, et al. Intermediate Accounting: Concepts, Methods & Uses. 4th ed. 1985. text ed. 40.95x (ISBN 0-03-058923-1); study guide 13.95x (ISBN 0-03-058926-6); instr's. manual 19.95 (ISBN 0-03-058924-X); test bank 100.00 (ISBN 0-03-058928-2). Dryden Pr.

--CPA Exam Booklet: Intermediate Accounting. 112p. 1984. pap. 10.95x (ISBN 0-03-071937-2). Dryden Pr.

Davidson, Sidney I., ed. Recent Advances in Ophthalmology, No. 6. LC 82-9495. (Illus.). 113p. 1983. pap. text ed. 24.00 (ISBN 0-443-01660-7). Churchill.

Davidson, Stanley, et al. Human Nutrition & Dietetics. 7th ed. (Illus.). 1979. text ed. 37.00 (ISBN 0-443-01765-4); pap. text ed. 49.50 (ISBN 0-443-01764-6). Churchill.

Davidson, Stephen M. Medicaid Decisions: Systematic Analysis of the Cost Problem. LC 80-10998. 1980. prof ref 29.95x (ISBN 0-88410-142-8). Ballinger Pub.

Davidson, Stephen M., et al. The Cost of Living Longer: National Health Insurance & the Elderly. LC 79-2756. 160p. 1980. 24.50 (ISBN 0-669-03242-5). Lexington Bks.

Davidson, Sue, ed. Justice for Young Women: Close-up on Critical Issues. LC 82-7848. 142p. (Orig.). 1982. pap. 5.50x (ISBN 0-9608696-0-3, AACR2). New Dir Young Women.
--The Second Mile: Contemporary Approaches in Counseling Young Women. 185p. (Orig.). 1983. pap. 7.50 (ISBN 0-9608696-2-X). New Dir Young Women.
Davidson, Sue, jt. ed. see Jensen, Joan M.
Davidson, Sue, jt. ed. see Rosen, Ruth.
Davidson, Sydney. The Plant Accounting Regulations of the Federal Power Commission: A Critical Analysis. Brief, Richard P., ed. LC 77-87296. (Development of Contemporary Accounting Thought Ser). 1978. Repr. of 1952 ed. lib. bdg. 20.00x (ISBN 0-405-10936-9). Ayer Co Pubs.
Davidson, Sydney, et al. Accounting: The Language of Business. 6th ed. LC 84-5974. 1984. pap. 8.95 (ISBN 0-913878-33-2). T Horton & Dghts.
Davidson, T. Rousseau & Education According to Nature. 59.95 (ISBN 0-8490-0976-6). Gordon Pr.
Davidson, Terence M. Manual of Otolaryngology: Head & Neck Surgery. 208p. 1984. 19.50 (ISBN 0-8089-1650-5, 7909-95). Grune.
Davidson, Theodore, ed. Polymers in Electronics. LC 83-25782. (ACS Symposium Ser.: No. 242). 605p. 1984. lib. bdg. 79.95x (ISBN 0-8412-0823-9). Am Chemical.
Davidson, Thomas. Aristotle & Ancient Educational Ideals. 1969. 22.50 (ISBN 0-8337-0777-9). B Franklin.
--Education of the Greek People, & Its Influence on Civilization. LC 74-136402. (BCL Ser. I). Repr. of 1894 ed. 18.50 (ISBN 0-404-01944-7). AMS Pr.
--The Education of the Greek People & Its Influence on Civilization. 1977. Repr. 29.00x (ISBN 0-403-07980-2). Scholarly.
--Education of the Wage-Earners: Contribution Toward Solution of Educational Problems of Democracy. Bakewell, Charles M., ed. LC 77-160419. (Research & Source Works Ser.: No. 722). 1971. Repr. of 1904 ed. lib. bdg. 20.50 (ISBN 0-8337-0778-7). B Franklin.
--The Fossil Brachiopoda, 2 Vols. 1850-1856. pap. 83.00 (ISBN 0-384-10960-8). Johnson Repr.
--History of Education. LC 74-121286. (BCL Ser. I). Repr. of 1900 ed. 12.50 (ISBN 0-404-01945-5). AMS Pr.
--History of Education. (Research & Source Ser.: No. 835). 1971. Repr. of 1969 ed. lib. bdg. 12.50 (ISBN 0-8337-0779-5). B Franklin.
--A History of Education. 1979. Repr. of 1900 ed. lib. bdg. 22.50 (ISBN 0-8492-4200-2). R West.
--Philosophy of Goethe's Faust. LC 68-24963. (Studies in German Literature, No. 13). 1969. Repr. of 1906 ed. lib. bdg. 39.95x (ISBN 0-8383-0933-X). Haskell.
--Rousseau & Education According to Nature. LC 70-136373. Repr. of 1898 ed. 17.50 (ISBN 0-404-01977-3). AMS Pr.
--Rousseau & Education According to Nature. LC 70-108469. 1970. Repr. of 1898 ed. 15.00x (ISBN 0-403-00427-6). Scholarly.
Davidson, Versa H. In His Presence. 160p. 1983. 8.95 (ISBN 0-89962-292-5). Todd & Honeywell.
--The Shadow of God. 320p. 1980. 7.95 (ISBN 0-89962-026-4). Todd & Honeywell.
Davidson, W. E. Catechism of Bible Doctrine. pap. 1.95 (ISBN 0-8054-9103-1). Broadman.
Davidson, W. S. Havens of Refuge: A History of Leprosy in Western Australia. 1979. 24.00x (ISBN 0-85564-141-X, Pub. by U of W Austral Pr); pap. 18.00x. Intl Spec Bk.
Davidson, W. S., jt. auth. see Fairweather, G. W.
Davidson, Wilburt C. Davidson's Complete Pediatrician. 9th ed. Arena, Jay M., ed. LC 78-98492. pap. 160.00 (ISBN 0-317-26674-8, 2055995). Bks Demand UMI.
Davidson, William. The Houseplant Survival Manual: How to Keep Your Houseplants. 192p. 1982. 17.95 (ISBN 0-8317-4589-4). Smith Pubs.
--An Illustrated Guide to Foliage House Plants. LC 83-83422. (Illustrated Gardening Guides Ser.). (Illus.). 160p. 1984. 9.95 (ISBN 0-668-06196-0, 6196-0). Arco.
--Wage & Salary Administration in a Changing Economy. 250p. 1984. manual 91.50 (ISBN 0-85013-145-6). Dartnell Corp.
Davidson, William, jt. auth. see Hochmuth, Milton.
Davidson, William, et al. Evaluation Strategies in Criminal Justice. (Pergamon General Psychology Ser.: No. 97). 206p. 1981. 33.00 (ISBN 0-08-024664-8). Pergamon.
Davidson, William F. An Early History of Free Will Baptists, Vol. 1. (Free Will Baptist History Ser.). 1974. 7.95 (ISBN 0-89265-037-0); pap. 4.95 (ISBN 0-89265-022-2). Randall Hse.
Davidson, William H. The Amazing Race: Winning the Technorivalry With Japan. LC 83-12353. 270p. 1984. 17.95 (ISBN 0-471-88711-0). Wiley.
--Experience Effects in International Investment & Technology Transfer. Dufey, Gunter, ed. LC 80-39884. (Research for Business Decisions Ser.: No. 34). 158p. 1981. 39.95 (ISBN 0-8357-1148-X). UMI Res Pr.
--Global Strategic Management. (Marketing Management Ser.). 348p. 1982. 34.95x (ISBN 0-471-09314-9, Pub. by Ronald Pr). Wiley.
Davidson, William L. Political Thought in England: The Utilitarians, from Bentham to J. S. Mill. LC 79-1624. 1981. Repr. of 1916 ed. 23.50 (ISBN 0-88355-929-3). Hyperion Conn.
--The Stoic Creed. Vlastos, Gregory, ed. LC 78-19341. (Morals & Law in Ancient Greece Ser.). 1979. Repr. of 1907 ed. lib. bdg. 23.00x (ISBN 0-405-11535-0). Ayer Co Pubs.
Davidson, William R. Wholesale Wine Trade in Ohio. 1954. pap. 1.50x (ISBN 0-87776-074-8, 74). Ohio St U Admin Sci.
Davidson, William R. & Sweeney, Daniel J. Retailing Management. 5th ed. LC 83-23378. 779p. 1984. text ed. 34.95 (ISBN 0-471-05717-7); write for info. (ISBN 0-471-87811-1). Wiley.
Davidson, William R., jt. auth. see Lowry, James R.
Davidson, William V. Historical Geography of the Bay Islands, Honduras: Anglo-Hispanic Conflict in the Western Caribbean. (Illus.). 1974. 16.95x (ISBN 0-87651-207-4); pap. 9.50x (ISBN 0-686-96890-5). Southern U Pr.
Davidson Pratt, J. & West, T. F. Services for the Chemical Industry. 1968. pap. 11.50 (ISBN 0-08-012664-2). Pergamon.
Davidson Pratt, J., jt. auth. see Hardie, D. W.
Davidzon, M. & Yurlov, V. Dushanbe: A Guide. 95p. 1983. 6.95 (ISBN 0-8285-2758-X, Pub. by Raduga Pubs USSR). Imported Pubns.
Davie, Cedric T. Musical Structure & Design. (Illus.). 1966. pap. 3.95 (ISBN 0-486-21629-2). Dover.
--Scotland's Music. 56p. 1981. 10.00x (ISBN 0-85158-136-6, Pub. by Blackwood & Sons England). State Mutual Bk.
Davie, Cedric T. & McVicar, George, eds. Oxford Scottish Song Book. 1969. pap. 4.60 (ISBN 0-19-330271-3); pap. 2.10x melody ed. (ISBN 0-19-330272-1). Oxford U Pr.
Davie, Charmian, et al. Child Development & Child Care: The Young Child at Home. 224p. 1984. 12.00x (ISBN 0-7005-0641-1, Pub. by NFER Nelson UK). Taylor & Francis.
--The Young Child at Home. 224p. 1984. 12.00 (ISBN 0-7005-0641-1). Taylor & Francis.
Davie, D. Selected Poems. 124p. 1985. pap. 7.50x (ISBN 0-85635-595-X). Carcanet.
Davie, Donald. Articulate Energy: An Inquiry into the Syntax of English Poetry. LC 77-158901. 1971. Repr. of 1955 ed. 29.00x (ISBN 0-403-01316-X). Scholarly.
--Collected Poems: 1970-1983. LC 83-50745. 176p. 1984. text ed. 14.95 (ISBN 0-268-00745-4, 85-07451). U of Notre Dame Pr.
--Dissentient Voice. LC 81-40455. 192p. 1982. text ed. 16.95 (ISBN 0-268-00852-3). U of Notre Dame Pr.
--Events & Wisdoms. LC 65-21077. (Wesleyan Poetry Program: Vol. 27). (Orig.). 1965. 15.00x (ISBN 0-8195-2027-6); pap. 6.95 (ISBN 0-8195-1027-0). Wesleyan U Pr.
--Ezra Pound. LC 81-21857. viii, 134p. 1982. pap. 4.95 (ISBN 0-226-13753-8, Phoen). U of Chicago Pr.
--Ezra Pound. new ed. LC 76-112. (Modern Masters Ser). 128p. 1976. 9.95 (ISBN 0-670-30392-5). Viking.
--A Gathered Church: The Literature of the English Dissenting Interest, 1700-1930. (The Clark Lectures 1976). 1978. 17.50x (ISBN 0-19-519999-5). Oxford U Pr.
--In the Stopping Train: And Other Poems. 1980. text ed. 11.95x (ISBN 0-19-520175-2). Oxford U Pr.
--New & Selected Poems. LC 61-14214. (Wesleyan Poetry Program: Vol. 12). (Orig.). 1961. 15.00x (ISBN 0-8195-2012-8); pap. 6.95 (ISBN 0-8195-1012-2). Wesleyan U Pr.
--These the Companions: Recollections. 1982. 27.95 (ISBN 0-521-24511-7). Cambridge U Pr.
--Thomas Hardy & British Poetry. LC 70-188291. 1972. 18.95x (ISBN 0-19-501572-X). Oxford U Pr.
--Three for Water Music. 64p. (Orig.). 1981. pap. text ed. 9.00x (ISBN 0-85635-363-9, Pub. by Carcanet New Pr England). Humanities.
--Trying to Explain. (Poets on Poetry Ser.). 1979. pap. 7.95 (ISBN 0-472-06310-3). U of Mich Pr.
Davie, Donald, ed. Augustan Lyric. (The Poetry Bookshelf Ser.). 1974. pap. text ed. 5.00x (ISBN 0-435-15701-9). Heinemann Ed.
--The New Oxford Book of Christian Verse. 1982. 27.50 (ISBN 0-19-213426-4). Oxford U Pr.
--Russian Literature & Modern English Fiction: A Collection of Critical Essays. LC 65-18337. (Patterns of Literary Criticism Ser.). pap. 62.50 (ISBN 0-317-09846-2, 2020052). Bks Demand UMI.
Davie, Donald, ed. & tr. see Pasternak, Boris.
Davie, Elspeth. Creating a Scene. 304p. 1984. 8.95 (ISBN 0-7145-0730-X). Riverrun NY.
--Providings. pap. 8.95 (ISBN 0-7145-0665-6). Riverrun NY.
--The Spark. 304p. 1984. pap. 6.95 (ISBN 0-7145-0537-4). Riverrun NY.
--The Traveller's Room. 160p. 1985. 15.95 (ISBN 0-241-11439-X, Pub. by Hamish Hamilton England). David & Charles.
Davie, Ian. Jesus Perusha. 160p. (Orig.). 1985. pap. 8.95 (ISBN 0-89281-069-6, Dist. by Inner Tradit). Lindisfarne Pr.
Davie, J. T. & Morrison, R. Recursive Descent Compiling. LC 81-6778. (Computers & Their Applications). 195p. 1981. pap. 29.95x (ISBN 0-470-27361-5). Halsted Pr.
Davie, John, ed. see Austen, Jane.
Davie, Judith F., jt. auth. see Wright, Keith C.
Davie, Maurice, ed. Refugees in America: Committee for the Study of Recent Immigration from Europe. LC 74-1513. (Illus.). 453p. 1974. Repr. of 1947 ed. lib. bdg. 25.00x (ISBN 0-8371-7390-6, DARA). Greenwood.
Davie, Maurice, ed. see Sumner, William G.
Davie, Maurice R. Constructive Immigration Policy. 1923. pap. 19.50x (ISBN 0-685-69809-2). Elliots Bks.
--Evolution of War. LC 68-15822. Repr. of 1929 ed. 29.50x (ISBN 0-8046-0099-6, Pub. by Kennikat). Assoc Faculty Pr.
--World Immigration. LC 82-48299. (The World Economy Ser.). 588p. 1983. lib. bdg. 72.00 (ISBN 0-8240-5354-0). Garland Pub.
Davie, Maurice R., ed. see Sumner, William G.
Davie, Michael, ed. The Diaries of Evelyn Waugh. 1977. 19.95 (ISBN 0-316-17450-5). Little.
Davie, Peter. Pastoral Care & the Parish. 102p. 1984. 24.95x (ISBN 0-631-13225-2); pap. 8.95x (ISBN 0-631-13226-0). Basil Blackwell.
Davie, Ronald & Butler, Neville R. From Birth to Seven: The Second Report of the National Child Development Survey. (Studies in Child Development). 150p. 1972. text ed. 34.50x (ISBN 0-391-00419-0); pap. text ed. 9.00x (ISBN 0-582-32493-9). Humanities.
Davies. Conduction System of the Heart. 1982. text ed. 119.95 (ISBN 0-407-00133-6). Butterworth.
--Inside the Chip. (Computer & Electronics Ser.). (gr. 6 up). 1984. 8.95 (ISBN 0-86020-730-7); PLB 12.95 (ISBN 0-88110-145-1); pap. 5.95 (ISBN 0-86020-729-3). EDC.
--Ohio Probate Practice, Nineteen Seventy-Four to Nineteen Eighty. 6th ed. 3000p. 1983. 180.00 (Pub by Addams & Hosford); latest suppl. incl. Anderson Pub Co.
Davies & Beatty. Literature of the Romantic Period, 1750-1850. 228p. 1982. 40.00x (ISBN 0-85323-353-5, Pub. by Liverpool Univ England). State Mutual Bk.
Davies, jt. auth. see Gatland.
Davies & Johnson, A. M., eds. Peter Skene Ogden's Snake Country Journal 1826-1827. (Hudson's Bay Record Society Publications Ser.: Vol. 23). pap. 52.00 (ISBN 0-317-15521-0). Kraus Repr.
Davies, A. Meaning of the Dead Sea Scrolls. pap. 1.95 (ISBN 0-451-62097-6, ME2097, Ment). NAL.
Davies, A., et al, eds. Interlanguage. 384p. 1985. 35.00s (ISBN 0-85224-499-1, Pub. by Edinburgh U Press, Scotland). Columbia U Pr.
Davies, A. C. The Science & Practice of Welding: Practice of Welding, Vol. 2. 8th ed. (Illus.). 350p. 1985. 49.50 (ISBN 0-521-26114-7); pap. 17.95 (ISBN 0-521-27840-6). Cambridge U Pr.
--The Science & Practice of Welding: Welding Science & Technology, Vol. 1. 8th ed. (Illus.). 320p. 1984. 39.50 (ISBN 0-521-26113-9); pap. 12.95 (ISBN 0-521-27839-2). Cambridge U Pr.
Davies, A. Emil. Investments Abroad. Wilkins, Mira, ed. LC 76-29984. (European Business Ser.). 1977. Repr. of 1927 ed. lib. bdg. 18.00x (ISBN 0-405-09749-2). Ayer Co Pubs.
Davies, A. F. Skills, Outlooks, Passions: A Psychoanalytic Contribution to the Study of Politics. 2nd ed. LC 78-54575. (Illus.). 456p. 1981. 64.50 (ISBN 0-521-22081-5); pap. 19.95 (ISBN 0-521-29349-9). Cambridge U Pr.
Davies, A. J. & Rudland, P. S. Medical & Biological Perspectives in Cancer Research. 1985. write for info. (ISBN 0-89573-423-0, Pub. by Ellis Horwood Ltd UK). VCH Pubs.
Davies, A. J. & Carter, R. L., eds. Contemporary Topics in Immunobiology, Vol. 2: Thymus Dependency. LC 78-165398. (Illus.). 384p. 1973. 39.50x (ISBN 0-306-37802-7, Plenum Pr). Plenum Pub.
Davies, A. Mervyn. Presbyterian Heritage. LC 65-10136. (Orig.). 1965. pap. 3.50 (ISBN 0-8042-0972-3). John Knox.
Davies, Adriana, ed. see Ormond, Richard & Rogers, Malcolm.
Davies, Alan, ed. Language & Learning in Early Childhood. 1977. Heinemann Ed.
--Language & Learning in Home & School. xi, 179p. (Orig.). 1982. pap. text ed. 19.50x (ISBN 0-435-10192-7). Heinemann Ed.
--Problems of Language & Learning. 1975. text ed. 17.50x (ISBN 0-435-10190-0). Heinemann Ed.
Davies, Alan J. The Finite Element Method: A First Approach. (Oxford Applied Mathematics & Computing Science Ser.). (Illus.). 1980. pap. 26.95x (ISBN 0-19-859631-6). Oxford U Pr.
Davies, Alan T., ed. Antisemitism & the Foundations of Christianity. LC 79-65620. 276p. 1979. pap. 7.95 (ISBN 0-8091-2219-7). Paulist Pr.
Davies, Alastair, ed. An Annotated Critical Bibliography of Modernism, No. 1. LC 82-13864. (Harvester-Barnes & Noble Annotated Critical Biblographies Ser.). 276p. 1982. text ed. 35.00x (ISBN 0-389-20303-3). B&N Imports.
Davies, Alfred T. John Calvin: Many Sided Genius. LC 83-45609. Date not set. Repr. of 1947 ed. 18.50 (ISBN 0-404-19827-9). AMS Pr.
Davies, Alice I. Allart van Everdingen. LC 77-94692. (Outstanding Dissertations in the Fine Arts Ser.). 1978. lib. bdg. 77.00 (ISBN 0-8240-3223-3). Garland Pub.
Davies, Alistair. Early Modernism, Nineteen Hundred to Nineteen Twenty-Five: H. G. Wells, Wyndham Lewis, D. H. Lawrence, T. S. Eliot & Virginia Woolf. LC 84-12460. 192p. 1985. 27.50x (ISBN 0-389-20519-2, 08081). B&N Imports.
Davies, Andrew. Conrad's War. 128p. (gr. 5 up). 1980. 7.95 (ISBN 0-517-54007-X). Crown.
--Conrad's War. 144p. (gr. 5 up). 1982. pap. 2.25 (ISBN 0-440-91452-3, LFL). Dell.
--Marmalade & Rufus. LC 83-1804. (Illus.). 96p. (gr. 3-7). 1983. 8.95 (ISBN 0-517-54632-9). Crown.
--Where Did the Forties Go? A Popular History. 135p. (Orig.). 1984. pap. 5.95 (ISBN 0-86104-758-3). Pluto Pr.
Davies, Andrew, jt. auth. see Widdicombe, John.
Davies, Ann. Inspirational Thoughts on the Tarot. 1983. 6.00 (ISBN 0-938002-05-8). Builders of Adytum.
--This Is Truth about the Self. 3rd ed. 1984. 2.25 (ISBN 0-938002-03-1). Builders of Adytum.
Davies, Anthony H. Practice of Marketing Research. (Illus.). 1973. pap. text ed. 21.00x (ISBN 0-434-90296-9). Intl Ideas.
--The Practice of Marketing Research. 264p. 1984. pap. 14.95 (ISBN 0-434-90293-4, Pub. by W Heinemann Ltd). David & Charles.
Davies, B. String of Amber: The Heritage of the Mennonites. (Illus.). 1973. 15.00 (ISBN 0-685-47308-2). Heinman.
Davies, B. J. Design Engineering. 1984. 82.75 (ISBN 0-444-86817-8, I-509-83). Elsevier.
Davies, B. J., ed. Design Engineering, 1984: Proceedings of the 7th Annual Conference, Birmingham, UK, 25-27, September 1984. 530p. 1985. 92.75 (ISBN 0-444-87624-3, North-Holland). Elsevier.
Davies, Barbara S. & Davies, J. Clarence, 3rd. The Politics of Pollution. 2nd ed. LC 74-20996. (Studies in Contemporary America). 256p. 1975. pap. 8.40scp (ISBN 0-02-327900-1). Macmillan.
Davies, Benedict, tr. see Birnbaum, Stanley.
Davies, Benjamin. Baker's Harmony of the Gospels. (Baker's Paperback Reference Library). 192p. 1983. pap. 6.95 (ISBN 0-8010-2928-7). Baker Bk.
Davies, Benjamin & Mitchell, Edward. Hebrew & Lexicon to the Old Testament. 800p. Date not set. 22.95 (ISBN 0-8254-2453-4). Kregel.
Davies, Bernita J. & Rooney, Francis J. Research in Illinois Law. LC 54-12404. (Research Publications in the Law Ser.). 68p. 1954. 7.50 (ISBN 0-379-11652-9). Oceana.
Davies, Bettilu D. Marty & the Scholarship. (The Marty Ser.). (Orig.). (gr. 7-9). 1984. pap. 3.95 (ISBN 0-8024-1902-X). Moody.
--Marty's Double Life. (Marty Ser.). (Orig.). 1983. pap. 3.95 (ISBN 0-8024-0272-0). Moody.
--Really, Marty! 128p. (gr. 6-10). 1981. pap. 2.95 (ISBN 0-8024-9299-1). Moody.
--Tall Trouble. LC 81-11326. (Marty Ser.). 160p. 1981. pap. 2.95 (ISBN 0-8024-8112-4). Moody.
Davies, Bleddyn. Universality, Selectivity & Effectiveness in Social Policy. LC 80-457434. (Studies in Social Policy & Welfare). 1978. text ed. 27.00x (ISBN 0-435-82266-7). Gower Pub Co.
--Variations in Children's Services among Urban Authorities. 159p. 1972. pap. text ed. 6.25x (ISBN 0-7135-1676-3, Pub. by Bedford England). Brookfield Pub Co.
Davies, Bleddyn P. Variations in Services for the Aged. 164p. 1971. pap. text ed. 6.25x (ISBN 0-7135-1621-6, Pub. by Bedford England). Brookfield Pub Co.
Davies, Brian. Introduction to Clinical Psychiatry. 3rd ed. 1981. pap. 11.00 (ISBN 0-522-84227-5, Pub. by Melbourne U Pr). Intl Spec Bk.
--An Introduction to the Philosophy of Religion. 1982. 17.95x (ISBN 0-19-219158-6); pap. 6.95x (ISBN 0-19-289145-6). Oxford U Pr.
--Seal Song. (Large Format Ser). (Illus.). 1979. pap. 7.95 (ISBN 0-14-004740-9). Penguin.
--Seal Song. (Illus.). 1978. 19.95 (ISBN 0-670-62668-6, Studio). Viking.
--Social Control & Education. 1976. pap. 7.50x (ISBN 0-416-55810-0, NO. 6369). Methuen Inc.
Davies, Brian, jt. ed. see Walsh, Michael.
Davies, Brian E., ed. Applied Soil Trace Elements. LC 79-40640. 482p. 1980. 79.95 (ISBN 0-471-27625-1, Pub. by Wiley-Interscience). Wiley.
Davies, Brian L. German Army Uniforms & Insignia, 1933-1945. LC 77-4302. (Illus.). 224p. 1983. pap. 12.95 (ISBN 0-668-05804-8, 5804). Arco.
Davies, Brian L. & Turner, Pierre. German Uniforms of the Third Reich, 1933-1945. LC 80-77. (Illus.). 1980. pap. 7.95 (ISBN 0-668-04940-5). Arco.
Davies, Bronwyn. Life in the Classroom & the Playground: The Accounts of Primary School Children. (Social Worlds of Childhood Ser.). 224p. 1983. 27.50x (ISBN 0-7100-9210-5). Routledge & Kegan.
Davies, Bruce & Thomas, Geoffrey, eds. Science & Sporting Performance: Management or Manipulation? (Illus.). 1982. 35.00x (ISBN 0-19-857594-7). Oxford U Pr.

Davies, C., et al. Organization for Program Management. LC 78-27660. 240p. 1980. 53.95 (ISBN 0-471-27571-9, Pub. by Wiley-Interscience). Wiley.

Davies, C. S. Peace, Print & Protestantism, Fourteen Fifty to Fifteen Fifty-Eight. 1976. 16.95x (ISBN 0-19-520118-3). Oxford U Pr.

--Peace, Print & Protestantism: 1450 to 1558. (Paladin History of England Ser.). 365p. 1983. pap. 7.95 (ISBN 0-586-08266-2, Pub. by Granada England). Academy Chi Pubs.

Davies, C. Stella & Levitt, John. What's in a Name? 112p. (Orig.). 1981. pap. 5.95 (ISBN 0-7100-0685-3). Routledge & Kegan.

Davies, Carole B. & Graves, Anne A., eds. Ngambika: Studies of Women in African Literature. LC 85-71385. 256p. 1985. 29.95 (ISBN 0-86543-017-9); pap. 9.95 (ISBN 0-86543-018-7). Africa Res.

Davies, Cecil W. Theatre for the People: The Story of the Volksbuhne. LC 77-73794. 191p. 1977. text ed. 12.50x (ISBN 0-292-78021-4). U of Tex Pr.

Davies, Celia. Brian Hatton. (Illus.). 1979. 20.00 (ISBN 0-900963-84-0, Pub. by Terence Dalton England). State Mutual Bk.

--Clean Clothes on Sunday. (Illus.). 1979. 20.00 (ISBN 0-900963-59-X, Pub. by Terence Dalton England). State Mutual Bk.

Davies, Celia, ed. Rewriting Nursing History. 226p. 1980. 28.50x (ISBN 0-389-20153-7). B&N Imports.

Davies, Charles. Time out in New Zealand. 1984. 8.95 (ISBN 0-533-05851-1). Vantage.

Davies, Charles M. Broad Church. Wolff, Robert L., ed. LC 75-1505. (Victorian Fiction Ser.). 1975. Repr. of 1875 ed. lib. bdg. 73.00 (ISBN 0-8240-1579-7). Garland Pub.

--Heterodox London or Phases of Free Thought in the Metropolis, 2 Vols. in 1. LC 69-17494. Repr. of 1874 ed. 50.00x (ISBN 0-678-00469-2). Kelley.

--Philip Paternoster: A Tractarian Love Story, 1858. Wolff, Robert L., ed. LC 75-477. (Victorian Fiction Ser.). 1975. lib. bdg. 66.00 (ISBN 0-8240-1555-X). Garland Pub.

--Unorthodox London or Phases of Religious Life in the Metropolis. LC 69-17495. Repr. of 1875 ed. 37.50x (ISBN 0-678-00470-6). Kelley.

--Verts; or, the Three Creeds, 1876. Wolff, Robert L., ed. LC 75-1506. (Victorian Fiction Ser.). 1975. lib. bdg. 66.00 (ISBN 0-8240-1580-0). Garland Pub.

Davies, Charles N., ed. Aerosol Science. 1967. 74.00 (ISBN 0-12-205650-7). Acad Pr.

Davies, Chris, et al, eds. Jesus: One of Us. 148p. 1981. pap. 3.95 (ISBN 0-87784-618-9). Inter Varsity.

Davies, Christie, jt. auth. see Brandon, Ruth.

Davies, Christie, jt. ed. see Dhavan, Rajeev.

Davies, Cornelia Oakes, jt. auth. see Clark, Charlotte.

Davies, D. Telecommunications: Developing Reading Skills in English. (Materials for Language Practice Ser.). (Illus.). 70p. 1985. pap. 3.95 (ISBN 0-08-031096-6, Pub. by PPL). Pergamon.

Davies, D. A. Waves, Atoms, & Solids. LC 77-2192. (Illus.). 320p. 1978. pap. text ed. 19.95x (ISBN 0-582-44174-9). Longman.

Davies, D. B., et al. Soil Management. 4th ed. (Illus.). 287p. 1982. 22.95 (ISBN 0-85236-118-1, Pub. by Farming Pr UK). Diamond Farm Bk.

Davies, D. E. Seasonal Breeding & Migrations of the Desert Locust (Schistocerca Gregaria Forskal) in North-Eastern Africa & the Middle East. 1952. 35.00x (ISBN 0-85135-010-0, Pub. by Centre Overseas Research). State Mutual Bk.

Davies, D. H., ed. Zambia in Maps. LC 73-653626. (Graphic Perspectives in Developing Countries Ser). 128p. 1972. text ed. 34.60x (ISBN 0-8419-0081-7, Africana). Holmes & Meier.

Davies, D. Hywel. The Welsh Nationalist Party, Nineteen Twenty-Five to Nineteen Forty-Five: A Call to Nationhood. 278p. 1983. text ed. 24.75x (ISBN 0-7083-0841-4, Pub. by Univ of Wales Pr England). Humanities.

Davies, D. I. & Parrott, M. J. Free Radicals in Organic Synthesis. (Reactivity & Structure: Vol. 7). 1978. 37.00 (ISBN 0-387-08723-0). Springer-Verlag.

Davies, D. M., ed. Textbook of Adverse Drug Reactions. (Illus.). 700p. 1985. 67.50 (ISBN 0-19-261479-7). Oxford U Pr.

Davies, D. R. Lead in Petrol. 51p. (Orig.). 1980. pap. text ed. 2.50 (ISBN 0-86740-041-2, 1012, Pub. by ANUP Australia). Australia N U P.

--Reinhold Niebuhr: Prophet from America. facs. ed. (Select Bibliographies Reprint Ser). 1945. 13.00 (ISBN 0-8369-5324-X). Ayer Co Pubs.

Davies, D. R. & Parasuraman, R. The Psychology of Vigilance. LC 81-67890. (Organizational & Occupational Psychology Ser.). 1982. 39.50 (ISBN 0-12-206180-2). Acad Pr.

Davies, D. R. & Schackleton, V. J. Psychology & Work. (Essential Psychology Ser.). 1975. pap. 4.50x (ISBN 0-416-82290-8, NO. 2728). Methuen Inc.

Davies, D. R., jt. auth. see Parasuraman, Raja.

Davies, D. R., jt. auth. see Tighe, J. R.

Davies, D. R., jt. ed. see Jones, D. G.

Davies, D. S., jt. auth. see Brown, S. S.

Davies, D. W. Dutch Influences on English Culture, 1558-1625. LC 64-18226. (Folger Guides to the Age of Shakespeare). 1964. pap. 3.95 (ISBN 0-918016-13-4). Folger Bks.

--Scott E. Haselton & His Abbey Garden Press. (Illus.). 26p. 1985. 25.00 (ISBN 0-87093-182-2). Dawsons.

Davies, D. W. & Barber, D. L. Communication Networks for Computers. LC 73-2775. (Computing Ser). 575p. 1973. 89.95x (ISBN 0-471-19874-9, Pub. by Wiley-Interscience). Wiley.

Davies, D. W. & Price, W. L. Security for Computer Networks: An Introduction to Data Security in Teleprocessing & Electronic Funds Transfer. (Computing Ser.). 300p. 1984. 34.95 (ISBN 0-471-90063-X). Wiley.

--Security in Teleprocessing & EPT Encryptian & Authentication in Computer Networks. LC 84-3662. (Computing Ser. 1-320). 300p. 1984. 34.95. Wiley.

Davies, D. W., ed. see Williams, Roger.

Davies, D. W., et al. Computer Networks & Their Protocols. LC 78-21973. (Wiley Series in Computing). 487p. 1979. 71.95 (ISBN 0-471-99750-1, Pub. by Wiley Interscience). Wiley.

Davies, Daniel R. & Hosler, Fred W. Challenge of School Board Membership. 1949. 2.50 (ISBN 0-910354-03-0). Chartwell.

Davies, David. The Case of Labourers in Husbandry Stated & Considered, 3 pts. Incl. Pt. 1. A View of Their Distressed Condition; Pt. 2. The Principal Causes of Their Growing Distress & Number, & of the Consequent Increase of the Poor Rate; Pt. 3. Means of Relief Proposed. LC 67-29501. 200p. Repr. of 1795 ed. 32.50x (ISBN 0-678-00863-9). Kelley.

--The Evergreen Tree. 1971. 3.75 (ISBN 0-910330-18-2). Grant Dahlstrom.

Davies, David, jt. auth. see Bussink, Willem.

Davies, David B., et al, eds. Structural Molecular Biology Methods & Applications. LC 81-23540. (NATO Advanced Study Institutes Series A, Life Sciences: Vol. 45). 540p. 1982. 65.00x (ISBN 0-306-40982-8, Plenum Pr). Plenum Pub.

Davies, David D. Financial Management: Art, Not Science. LC 85-7843. Date not set. price not set (ISBN 0-07-084771-1). McGraw.

Davies, David H., jt. auth. see Pincus, Alexis G.

Davies, David H., jt. ed. see Pincus, Alexis G.

Davies, David P. Handling the Big Jets. 3rd ed. (Illus.). 324p. 1973. 34.95 (ISBN 0-903083-01-9). Pan Am Nav.

Davies, David W. World of the Elseviers. LC 70-98751. 1971. Repr. of 1954 ed. lib. bdg. 18.75x (ISBN 0-8371-3084-0, DAWE). Greenwood.

Davies, David W. & Wrigley, Elizabeth S., eds. Concordance to the Essays of Francis Bacon. LC 73-8947. 392p. 1973. 85.00x (ISBN 0-8103-1004-X). Gale.

Davies, Derek A. Thailand. LC 72-100627. (This Beautiful World Ser.: Vol. 65). (Illus.). 138p. (Orig.). 1981. pap. 5.25 (ISBN 0-87011-116-7). Kodansha.

Davies, Derek A. C. Greek Islands. LC 73-158639. (This Beautiful World Ser.: Vol. 27). (Illus.). 130p. (Orig.). 1971. pap. 4.95 (ISBN 0-87011-154-X). Kodansha.

--Ireland. LC 72-77797. (This Beautiful World Ser.: Vol. 37). (Illus.). 118p. (Orig.). 1972. pap. 4.95 (ISBN 0-87011-180-9). Kodansha.

Davies, Diana. Songs of Love. 1976. pap. cancelled (ISBN 0-88238-979-3). Baraka Bk.

Davies, Don, ed. Communities & Their Schools. (Study of the Schooling in the United States Ser.). 352p. 1981. 21.95 (ISBN 0-07-015503-8). McGraw.

Davies, Don & Zerchykov, Ross, eds. Citizen Participation in Education: Annotated Bibliography. 2nd ed. 386p. 1978. pap. text ed. 15.00 (ISBN 0-917754-05-0). Inst Responsive.

Davies, Don, et al. Patterns of Citizen Participation in Educational Decisionmaking: Grassroots Perspectives; Diverse Forms of Participation. 961p. (Orig.). 1979. pap. 6.00 (ISBN 0-917754-08-5). Inst Responsive.

--Patterns of Citizen Participation in Educational Decision Making: Grassroots Perspectives, Diverse Forms of Participation, Vol. 2. 95p. 1979. 6.00 (ISBN 0-317-36770-6). Inst Responsive.

--Federal & State Impact on Citizen Participation in the Schools. 147p. 1978. 5.00 (ISBN 0-317-34488-9). Inst Responsive.

--Federal & State Impact on Citizen Participation in the Schools. 147p. (Orig.). 1978. pap. text ed. 5.00 (ISBN 0-917754-04-2). Inst Responsive.

Davies, Donald G. & Barnes, Charles D., eds. Regulation of Ventilation & Gas Exchange. (Research Topics in Physiology). 1978. 49.50 (ISBN 0-12-204650-1). Acad Pr.

Davies, Donald W. The Security of Data in Networks. (Tutorial Texts Ser.). 241p. 1981. 20.00 (ISBN 0-8186-0366-6, Q366). IEEE Comp Soc.

Davies, Dorothy K., compiled by. Race Relations in Rhodesia: A Survey for 1972-73. 458p. 1975. 23.75x (ISBN 0-87471-651-9). Rowman.

Davies, E. B., jt. auth. see London Mathematical Society Ser.

Davies, E. B., ed. Quantum Theory of Open Systems. 1976. 37.00 (ISBN 0-12-206150-0). Acad Pr.

Davies, E. L. & Grove, E. J. Dartmouth: The Royal Naval College, Seventy-Five Years in Pictures. (Illus.). 96p. 1980. 14.95 (ISBN 0-85997-462-6). McCartan Maritime.

Davies, E. T. Political Ideas of Richard Hooker. LC 75-159177. 1972. Repr. of 1946 ed. lib. bdg. 14.00x (ISBN 0-374-92073-7). Octagon.

Davies, Ebenezer. American Scenes & Christian Slavery. LC 70-123671. Repr. of 1849 ed. 21.00 (ISBN 0-404-00026-6). AMS Pr.

--American Scenes & Christian Slavery. (American Studies). 1969. Repr. of 1849 ed. 28.00 (ISBN 0-384-10985-3). Johnson Repr.

Davies, Ebenezer T. Episcopacy & the Royal Supremacy in the Church of England in the XVI Century. LC 78-13202. 1978. Repr. of 1950 ed. lib. bdg. 24.75x (ISBN 0-313-20626-0, DAER). Greenwood.

Davies, Edward. The Art of War & Englands Traynings. LC 68-54633. (English Experience Ser.: No. 37). 1968. Repr. of 1619 ed. 30.00 (ISBN 90-221-0037-5). Walter J Johnson.

--Celtic Researches, on the Origin, Traditions & Language, of the Ancient Britons. Feldman, Burton & Richardson, Robert D., eds. LC 78-60902. (Myth & Romanticism Ser.: Vol. 8). (Illus.). 1979. lib. bdg. 80.00 (ISBN 0-8240-3557-7). Garland Pub.

Davies, Edward, II. Anthracite Aristocracy: Leadership & Social Change in the Hard Coal Regions of Northeastern Pennsylvania, 1800-1930. LC 85-2947. 295p. 1985. 27.00 (ISBN 0-87580-107-2). N Ill U Pr.

Davies, Eirian. On the Semantics of Syntax: Mood & Condition in English. (Croom Helm Linguistic Ser.). 1979. text ed. 26.50x (ISBN 0-391-00936-2). Humanities.

Davies, Emily. Higher Education of Women. LC 77-37688. Repr. of 1866 ed. 21.50 (ISBN 0-404-56742-8). AMS Pr.

--Thoughts on Some Questions Relating to Women: 1860-1908. LC 73-14557. Repr. of 1910 ed. 24.50 (ISBN 0-404-56741-X). AMS Pr.

Davies, Eric, jt. ed. see Meints, Russel H.

Davies, Eryl. Ocean Frontiers. LC 79-14041. (How It Works Ser.). (gr. 4-6). 1980. 11.50 (ISBN 0-670-52026-8). Viking.

--Prophecy & Ethics: Isaiah & the Ethical Traditions of Israel. (Journal for the Study of the Old Testament, Supplement: No. 16). 1981. 20.75x (ISBN 0-905774-26-4, Pub. by JSOT Pr England). Eisenbrauns.

Davies, Evan. The Book of Dulwich. 1977. 40.00x (ISBN 0-86023-003-1). State Mutual Bk.

Davies, Evelyn & Town, Peter. The Man with No Name. (Heinemann Guided Readers Ser.). 1977. pap. 2.00x (ISBN 0-435-27050-8). Heinemann Ed.

Davies, Evelyn & Whitney, Norman. Reasons for Reading. (Reading Comprehension Course). (Orig.). 1980. pap. text ed. 5.50x (ISBN 0-435-28036-8); tchr's guide 6.50x (ISBN 0-435-28037-6). Heinemann Ed.

--Strategies for Reading. (Reading Comprehension Course Ser.). (Orig.). 1981. pap. text ed. 6.50x (ISBN 0-435-28940-3); tchrs. ed. 7.50x (ISBN 0-435-28941-1). Heinemann Ed.

Davies, F. L. & Law, B. A., eds. Advances in Microbiology & Biochemistry of Cheese & Fermented Milk. 268p. 1984. 42.00 (ISBN 0-85334-287-3, Pub. by Elsevier Applied Sci England). Elsevier.

Davies, Frances. Fortune's Darling. (Second Chance at Love Ser.: No. 296). 192p. 1985. pap. 2.25 (ISBN 0-425-08518-X). Berkley Pub.

--Love Thy Neighbor. (Second Chance at Love Ser.: No. 192). 192p. 1984. pap. 1.95 (ISBN 0-515-07808-5). Jove Pubns.

--Mysterious East. (Second Chance at Love Ser.: No. 239). 192p. 1985. pap. 1.95 (ISBN 0-425-07766-7). Berkley Pub.

Davies, Frederick. Snow in Venice. 208p. 1985. pap. 2.95 (ISBN 0-931773-44-X). Critics Choice Paper.

Davies, Frederick, tr. see Daudet, Alphonse.

Davies, Frederick, tr. see France, Anatole.

Davies, Frederick, tr. see Goldoni, Carlo.

Davies, Frederick, tr. see Labiche, Eugene M.

Davies, Frederick H., tr. see Goldoni, Carlo.

Davies, G., et al, eds. Perceiving & Remembering Faces. LC 81-66698. 1981. 49.50 (ISBN 0-12-206220-5). Acad Pr.

Davies, G. A., ed. Structural Impact & Crashworthiness, Vol. 1. 272p. 1984. 42.00 (ISBN 0-85334-288-1, I-258-84, Pub. by Elsevier Applied Sci England). Elsevier.

Davies, G. I. The Way of the Wilderness. LC 77-95442. (Society for Old Testament Monographs). (Illus.). 1979. 32.50 (ISBN 0-521-22057-2). Cambridge U Pr.

Davies, G. J. Purchasing International Freight Services. Gray, R., ed. 200p. 1985. text ed. 41.95x (ISBN 0-566-02497-7). Gower Pub Co.

Davies, G. J., jt. auth. see Padmanabham, K. A.

Davies, G. L. & Stephens, Nicholas. Ireland. (Illus.). 1978. 20.95x (ISBN 0-416-84640-8, NO.2841). Methuen Inc.

Davies, G. N. Cost & Benefit of Fluoride in the Prevention of Dental Caries. (Offset Pub.: No. 9). (Also avail. in French). 1974. pap. 8.00 (ISBN 92-4-170009-2). World Health.

Davies, G. Russ. Mapping the VIC. 386p. (Orig.). 1984. pap. 14.95 (ISBN 0-942386-24-8). Compute Pubns.

Davies, Garth W., jt. auth. see Bingham, John E.

Davies, Gary. International Logistics. 106p. 1981. 89.00x (ISBN 0-86176-072-7, Pub. by MCB Pubns). State Mutual Bk.

--Managing Export Distribution. (Illus.). 192p. 1985. pap. 17.50 (ISBN 0-434-90298-5, Pub. by W Heinemann Ltd). David & Charles.

Davies, Geoff. Practical Primary Drama. vii, 63p. 1983. pap. text ed. 4.50x (ISBN 0-435-18236-6). Heinemann Ed.

Davies, Geoff, ed. Nineteen Seventy-Nine Astronautics Convention: Proceedings, 2 pts. 314p. (Orig.). 1981. pap. text ed. 40.00 (ISBN 0-9596726-5-6, Pub. by Astronautical Soc W Australia). Univelt Inc.

Davies, Geoffrey, ed. Forensic Science. LC 75-9986. (ACS Symposium Ser.: No. 13). 1975. 23.95 (ISBN 0-8412-0280-X). Am Chemical.

Davies, Geoffrey M. Office Diagnosis & Management of Chronic Obstructive Pulmonary Disease. LC 81-8386. (Illus.). 135p. 1981. text ed. 8.95 (ISBN 0-8121-0823-X). Lea & Febiger.

Davies, Gladys K. Carl R. Krafft: An Artist's Life. (Illus.). 1982. 6.95 (ISBN 0-533-05123-1). Vantage.

Davies, Glyn A. Mathematical Methods in Engineering: Guidebook 5. (Handbook of Applicable Mathematics Ser.: Nos. 1-475). 458p. 1984. pap. 31.95 (ISBN 0-471-10331-4, Pub. by Wiley Interscience). Wiley.

--Virtual Work in Structural Analysis. LC 81-15926. 325p. 1982. 42.95x (ISBN 0-471-10112-5, Pub. by Wiley-Interscience). Wiley.

Davies, Godfrey. Early Stuarts, 1603-1660. 2nd ed. (Illus.). 1959. 32.00x (ISBN 0-19-821704-8). Oxford U Pr.

--Essays on the Later Stuarts. LC 74-20075. (Illus.). 133p. 1975. Repr. of 1958 ed. lib. bdg. 22.50x (ISBN 0-8371-7842-8, DAEL). Greenwood.

--Wellington & His Army. LC 74-8376. (Illus.). 154p. 1974. Repr. of 1954 ed. lib. bdg. 15.00x (ISBN 0-8371-7566-6, DAWA). Greenwood.

Davies, Godfrey, jt. ed. see Haller, William.

Davies, Graham I., ed. see Bartlett, John A.

Davies, Graham I., ed. see Moorey, Roger.

Davies, Granville, jt. auth. see Churchill, Bob.

Davies, Gynne H. Overcoming Food Allergies: How to Identify & Remove the Causes. (Illus.). 152p. 1985. pap. 8.95 (ISBN 0-906798-45-0, Pub. by Salem Hse Ltd). Merrimack Pub Cir.

Davies, H. & Whaton, M. Better BASIC. (Computers & Electronics Ser.). (Illus.). 48p. (gr. 6 up). 1983. 8.95 (ISBN 0-86020-734-X); lib. bdg. 12.95 (ISBN 0-88110-139-7); pap. 5.95 (ISBN 0-86020-733-1). EDC.

Davies, Helen, ed. Libraries in West Africa. 199p. 1982. lib. bdg. 23.00 (ISBN 3-598-10440-5). K G Saur.

Davies, Henry R. Conway & the Menai Ferries. (History & Law Ser.). 342p. 1942. text ed. 27.75x (ISBN 0-7083-0108-8, Pub. by Univ of Wales Pr England). Humanities.

Davies, Henry W. & Grace, Harvey. Music & Worship. LC 74-24067. Repr. of 1935 ed. 21.50 (ISBN 0-404-12894-7). AMS Pr.

Davies, Herbert A. Outline History of the World. new ed. Blount, C. H., ed. (Illus.). 1976. pap. 6.95x (ISBN 0-19-580350-7). Oxford U Pr.

Davies, Hilary, tr. see Hoeper, Claus-Juergen, et al.

Davies, Horton. The Ecumenical Century: 1900-1965. (Worship & Theology in England Ser.: Vol. 5). 1965. 37.50 (ISBN 0-691-07145-4). Princeton U Pr.

--The English Free Churches. 2nd. ed. LC 85-7684. vii, 208p. 1985. Repr. of 1963 ed. lib. bdg. 37.50x (ISBN 0-313-20838-7, DAEF). Greenwood.

--Great South African Christians. LC 70-104242. Repr. of 1951 ed. lib. bdg. 15.00x (ISBN 0-8371-3916-3, DAGC). Greenwood.

--Mirror of the Ministry in Modern Novels. facsimile ed. LC 70-111824. (Essay Index Reprint Ser.). 1959. 19.00 (ISBN 0-8369-1601-8). Ayer Co Pubs.

Davies, Horton & Davies, Marie-Helene. Holy Days & Holidays. LC 80-69875. 256p. 1982. 30.00 (ISBN 0-8387-5018-4). Bucknell U Pr.

Davies, Horton, ed. Studies of the Church in History: Essays Honoring Robert S. Paul on his Sixty-Fifth Birthday, Vol. X. (Pittsburgh Theological Monographs. New Series: No. 5). 276p. (Orig.). 1983. pap. 19.95 (ISBN 0-686-45571-1). Pickwick.

Davies, Horton M. Catching the Conscience. LC 84-71181. 169p. (Orig.). 1984. pap. 7.50 (ISBN 0-936384-21-2). Cowley Pubns.

Davies, Hugh & Yard, Sally. Francis Bacon. (Modern Masters Ser.). (Illus.). 128p. 1985. 29.95 (ISBN 0-89659-447-5); pap. 16.95 (ISBN 0-89659-448-3). Abbeville Pr.

Davies, Hugh. International Electronic Music Catalog. 1968. 35.00x (ISBN 0-262-04012-3). MIT Pr.

Davies, Hugh M. Francis Bacon: The Early & Middle Years, 1928-1958. LC 77-94731. (Outstanding Dissertations in the Fine Arts Ser.). 325p. 1982. lib. bdg. 37.00 (ISBN 0-8240-3224-1). Garland Pub.

Davies, Hugh S. Browning & the Modern Novel. LC 76-43278. 1976. Repr. of 1962 ed. lib. bdg. 6.00 (ISBN 0-8414-3793-9). Folcroft.

Davies, Hugh S; see Bloomfield, Paul.

Davies, Hugh S. & Watson, George, eds. The English Mind: Studies in the English Moralists Presented to Basil Wiley. LC 64-21539. pap. 77.50 (ISBN 0-317-08838-6, 2050742). BKs Demand UMI.

Davies, Hugh W. Catalog of Early German Books in the Library of C. Fairfax Murray, 2 Vols. 240.00x (ISBN 0-87556-067-9). Saifer.

Davies, Hunter. The Beatles. 2nd, rev. ed. 405p. 1985. pap. 8.95 (ISBN 0-07-015526-7). McGraw.

--Flossie Teacake-Again. (Illus.). 128p. (gr. 3-7). 1985. laminated boards 9.95 (ISBN 0-370-30554-X, Pub. by the Bodley Head). Merrimack Pub Cir.

--Flossie Teacake Strikes Back! (Illus.). 128p. (gr. 3-7). 1985. laminated boards 9.95 (ISBN 0-370-30622-8, Pub. by the Bodley Head). Merrimack Pub Cir.

--Flossie Teacakes's Fur Coat. (Illus.). 136p. (gr. 3-7). 1985. laminated boards 9.95 (ISBN 0-370-30933-2, Pub. by the Bodley Head). Merrimack Pub Cir.

--A Walk Round London's Parks. (Illus.). 256p. 1983. 21.00 (ISBN 0-241-11040-8, Pub. by Hamish Hamilton England). David & Charles.

--William Wordsworth: A Biography. LC 80-66004. (Illus.). 1980. 17.95 (ISBN 0-689-11087-1). Atheneum.

Davies, Hunter & Herrmann, Frank. Great Britain. (Illus.). 288p. 1983. 24.95 (ISBN 0-241-10755-5, Pub. by Hamish Hamilton England). David & Charles.

Davies, Hywel D. The Welsh Nationalist Party, 1925-1945: A Call to Nationhood. LC 83-11221. 300p. 1983. 27.50 (ISBN 0-312-86190-7). St Martin.

Davies, I. Aging in Animals. (Studies in Biology: No. 151). 64p. 1983. pap. text ed. 8.95 (ISBN 0-7131-2863-1). E Arnold.

Davies, I. & Sigee, D. C., eds. Cell Aging & Cell Death. (Illus.). 350p. 1985. 39.50 (ISBN 0-521-26172-4). Cambridge U Pr.

Davies, Ian, jt. auth. see Raistrick, Duncan.

Davies, Ioan. African Trade Unions. LC 76-44461. 1976. Repr. of 1966 ed. lib. bdg. 20.25x (ISBN 0-8371-9081-9, DAATU). Greenwood.

Davies, Ivor. It's a Triumph. (Illus.). 237p. 19.95 (ISBN 0-85429-182-2, F182). Haynes Pubns.

Davies, Ivor K. Competency Based Learning: Management, Technology, & Design. Orig. Title: The Management of Learning. 254p. 1973. text ed. 40.95 (ISBN 0-07-084420-8). McGraw.

--Instructional Technique. (Illus.). 352p. 1980. text ed. 16.95x (ISBN 0-07-015502-X). McGraw.

Davies, J. Kobon. (Descriptive Grammar Ser.). 264p. 1981. pap. 40.00 (ISBN 0-7099-0878-4, Pub. by Croom Helm Ltd). Longwood Pub Group.

Davies, J. & Hughes, S. Investment in the British Economy. (Studies in the British Economy). 1980. Heinemann Ed.

Davies, J., ed. Esenin: A Biography in Memoirs, Letters, & Documents. 286p. 1982. 30.00. Ardis Pubs.

Davies, J., et al. Guide to the Study of Soil Ecology. 1973. text ed. 12.40 (ISBN 0-13-370973-6); pap. text ed. 10.84 (ISBN 0-13-370965-5). P-H.

Davies, J. C. Mr. Fish & the Alabama Claims: A Chapter in Diplomatic History. LC 71-95065. (Select Bibliographies Reprint Ser.). 158p. 1972. Repr. of 1893 ed. lib. bdg. 16.00 (ISBN 0-8290-0485-8). Irvington.

--When Men Revolt & Why. LC 74-142361. 1971. 12.95 (ISBN 0-02-907310-3). Free Pr.

Davies, J. Clarence. Neighborhood Groups & Urban Renewal. LC 65-27764. (Metropolitan Politics Ser.). 235p. 1966. 29.00x (ISBN 0-231-02792-3). Columbia U Pr.

Davies, J. Clarence, et al. Training for Environmental Groups. LC 84-9443. 125p. (Orig.). 1984. pap. 11.95 (ISBN 0-89164-083-5). Conservation Foun.

Davies, J. Clarence, 3rd, jt. auth. see Davies, Barbara S.

Davies, J. Conway, ed. Captae Antiquae Rolls 11-20. (Pipe Roll Society, London: Ser. 2, vol. 33). Repr. of 1960 ed. 48.00 (ISBN 0-317-16518-6). Kraus Repr.

--Cartae Antiquae Rolls: 11-20. (Pipe Roll Society, London: No. 2, vol. 33). 48.00 (ISBN 0-317-16523-2). Kraus Repr.

Davies, J. G. The Early Christian Church. (Twin Brooks Ser.). 1980. pap. 9.95 (ISBN 0-8010-2906-6). Baker Bk.

--Temples, Churches & Mosques: A Guide to the Appreciation of Religious Architecture. LC 82-13130. (Illus.). 256p. 1982. 27.50 (ISBN 0-8298-0634-2). Pilgrim NY.

Davies, J. G. & Van Zyl, P. A Shaker Dance Service Reconstucted. 1984. pap. 3.00 (ISBN 0-941500-34-9). Sharing Co.

Davies, J. G., ed. The Westminster Dictionary of Worship. LC 78-25582. (Illus.). 400p. 1979. 18.95 (ISBN 0-664-21373-1). Westminster.

Davies, J. Glyn. Welsh Metrics. LC 78-72625. (Celtic Language & Literature: Goidelic & Brythonic). Repr. of 1911 ed. 14.50 (ISBN 0-404-17547-3). AMS Pr.

Davies, J. Griffith & Worts, F. R. England in the Middle Ages: Its Problems & Legacies. 298p. 1983. Repr. of 1928 ed. lib. bdg. 75.00 (ISBN 0-89987-178-X). Darby Bks.

Davies, J. H., ed. Letter to the Hebrews. (Cambridge Bible Commentary on the New English Bible, New Testament Ser.). 1967. 16.95 (ISBN 0-521-04222-4); pap. 8.95x (ISBN 0-521-09408-9). Cambridge U Pr.

Davies, J. K. Democracy & Classical Greece. (Fontana History of the Ancient World Ser.). 1978. text ed. 22.75x (ISBN 0-391-00766-1). Humanities.

--Democracy & Classical Greece. LC 83-45337. (Illus.). 292p. 1978. pap. 7.95x (ISBN 0-8047-1226-3). Stanford U Pr.

--Mormon Gold: The Story of the Mormon Argonauts. 440p. (Orig.). 1984. pap. 12.95 (ISBN 0-913420-20-4). Olympus Pub Co.

Davies, J. Kenneth & Ovard, Glen F. Economics & the American System. new ed. 1975. 12.48 (ISBN 0-397-40231-7); tchr's. manual 2.40 (ISBN 0-397-40232-5); tests 1.92 (ISBN 0-685-59114-X). Harper Row.

Davies, J. L. & Williams, M. A. Landform Evolution in Australia. new ed. (Illus.). 1978. text ed. 26.50 (ISBN 0-7081-1194-7, Pub. by ANUP Australia). Australia N U P.

Davies, J. M. Manual of Stressed Skin Diaphram Design. 441p. 1982. 82.50 (ISBN 0-471-87485-X). Wiley.

Davies, J. M., jt. auth. see Bryan, E. R.

Davies, J. Meredith. Community Health, Preventive Medicine & Social Services. 5th ed. (Illus.). 496p. 1983. pap. 14.95 (ISBN 0-7216-0937-6, Pub. by Bailliere-Tindall). Saunders.

Davies, J. S., ed. Amino Acids & Peptides. (Chemistry Sourcebooks Ser.). 800p. 69.95 (ISBN 0-412-26950-3, Pub. by Chapman & Hall). Methuen Inc.

Davies, J. T. Turbulence Phenomena: An Introduction to the Eddy Transfer of Momentum, Mass & Heat, Particularly at Interfaces. 1972. 75.00 (ISBN 0-12-206070-9). Acad Pr.

Davies, J. W. Mulching Effects on Plant Climate & Yield. (Technical Note Ser.: No. 136). xii, 118p. 1975. pap. 20.00 (ISBN 92-63-10388-7, W159, WMO). Unipub.

--Physiological Responses to Burning Injury. 1982. 71.00 (ISBN 0-12-206080-6). Acad Pr.

Davies, Jack. Legislative Law & Process. (Nutshell Ser.). 279p. 1975. pap. 7.95 (ISBN 0-317-00034-9). West Pub.

Davies, Jack & Lawry, Robert P. Institutions & Methods of the Law: Introductory Teaching Materials. LC 81-23956. (American Casebook Ser.). 542p. 1982. text ed. 17.95 (ISBN 0-314-64216-1). West Pub.

Davies, James. Hesiod & Theognis. 1923. 25.00 (ISBN 0-8274-3944-X). R West.

Davies, James A. John Forster: A Literary Life. LC 83-3792. (Illus.). 328p. 1983. text ed. 29.50x (ISBN 0-389-20391-2). B&N Imports.

Davies, James B. & MacDonald, Glenn M. Information in the Labour Market: Job-Worker Matching & Its Implications for Education in Ontario. (Ontario Economic Council Research Studies: No. 29). 200p. (Orig.). 1984. pap. 15.00 (ISBN 0-8020-3403-9). U of Toronto Pr.

Davies, James C. Baronial Opposition to Edward II: Its Character & Policy. 644p. 1967. Repr. of 1918 ed. 37.50x (ISBN 0-7146-1466-1, BHA-01466, F Cass Co). Biblio Dist.

--Human Nature in Politics: The Dynamics of Political Behavior. LC 77-13870. (Illus.). 1978. Repr. of 1963 ed. lib. bdg. 31.25x (ISBN 0-8371-9870-4, DAHN). Greenwood.

Davies, James P. Sing, with Understanding. 1966. 3.75 (ISBN 0-910452-02-4). Covenant.

Davies, Jane, jt. auth. see Andrian, Gustave W.

Davies, Jane B., intro. by see Howe, Katherine S. & Warren, David B.

Davies, Jane D. Le Compagnon Du Petit Prince: Cahier d'Exercises sur le Texte de Sainte-Exupery. 120p. 1975. pap. text ed. 6.95 (ISBN 0-15-550448-7, HC); instructor's man. avail. (ISBN 0-15-550449-5). HarBraceJ.

Davies, Jeffrey W., jt. auth. see Hall, Timothy C.

Davies, Jill. A Garden of Miracles: Herbal Drinks for Health, Pleasure & Beauty. 1985. 16.95 (ISBN 0-8253-0285-4); pap. 9.95 (ISBN 0-8253-0286-2). Beaufort Bks NY.

--Herbs & Herb Gardens. (Shire Album Ser.: No. 111). (Illus.). 32p. (Orig.). 1985. pap. 3.50 (ISBN 0-85263-656-3, Pub. by Shire Pubns England). Seven Hills Bks.

--The Living Herbalist: First Steps Towards Natural Healing. (Illus.). 128p. 1985. 10.95 (ISBN 0-241-11412-8, Pub. by Hamish Hamilton England). David & Charles.

Davies, John. Cardiff & the Marquesses of Bute. (Studies in Welsh History: No. 3). 347p. 1980. text ed. 32.00x (ISBN 0-7083-0761-2, Pub. by Univ of Wales Pr England). Humanities.

--Christians, Politics & Violent Revolution. LC 75-42517. pap. 56.00 (ISBN 0-317-26642-X, 2025118). Bks Demand UMI.

--Complete Works, 2 vols. Grosart, Alexander B., ed. (Chertsey Worthies' Library: No. 3). Repr. of 1878 ed. Set. 49.50 (ISBN 0-404-50293-8). Vol. 1 (ISBN 0-404-50381-0). Vol. 2 (ISBN 0-404-50382-9). AMS Pr.

--Orchestra: Or, a Poem of Dancing. LC 70-161962. 1947. Repr. 29.00x (ISBN 0-403-01333-X). Scholarly.

--Poems. Krueger, Robert, ed. (Oxford English Texts Ser). (Illus.). 1974. 59.00x (ISBN 0-19-812716-2). Oxford U Pr.

--Reg Butler. (Illus.). 88p. pap. 9.95 (ISBN 0-905005-99-6, Pub. by Salem Hse Ltd). Merrimack Pub Cir.

--The Scottish Forester. 69p. 1981. 10.00x (ISBN 0-85158-130-7, Pub. by Blackwood & Sons England). State Mutual Bk.

--A Tahitian & English Dictionary. LC 75-35188. (Eng. & Tahitian.). Repr. of 1851 ed. 31.50 (ISBN 0-404-14217-6). AMS Pr.

--The Visitor's Book. LC 85-71576. 68p. 1985. pap. 9.95 (ISBN 0-907476-41-4, Pub. by Poetry Wales Pr UK). Dufour.

--Wittes Pilgrimage, (by Poeticall Essaies) Through a World of Amorous Sonnets, Etc. LC 79-84099. (English Experience Ser.: No. 919). 172p. 1979. Repr. of 1605 ed. lib. bdg. 17.00 (ISBN 90-221-0919-4). Walter J Johnson.

--The Writing School-Master. LC 76-57376. (English Experience Ser.: No. 794). 1977. Repr. of 1636 ed. lib. bdg. 9.50 (ISBN 90-221-0794-9). Walter J Johnson.

Davies, John, ed. The Diaries of William Grierson. 288p. 1981. 40.00x (ISBN 0-85158-152-8, Pub. by Blackwood & Sons Scotland). State Mutual Bk.

--Everyman's Book of Nonsense. (Everyman's Library). 254p. 1981. 13.95 (ISBN 0-460-04479-6, Evman, Evman). Biblio Dist.

--Everyman's Book of Nonsense. (Everyman's Library). (Illus.). 254p. 1982. pap. text ed. 3.95x (ISBN 0-460-01277-0, Evman). Biblio Dist.

Davies, John, ed. see Douglas, David.

Davies, John, tr. see Scarron, Paul.

Davies, John, jt. auth. see Spenser, Edmund.

Davies, John A., jt. auth. see Field, Paul E.

Davies, John B. The Psychology of Music. LC 77-92339. (Illus.). 240p. 1978. 17.50x (ISBN 0-8047-0980-7); pap. 6.95 (ISBN 0-8047-1057-0, SP-158). Stanford U Pr.

Davies, John D. The Faith Abroad. (Faith & the Future Ser.). 163p. 1984. 24.95x (ISBN 0-631-13183-3); pap. 8.95x (ISBN 0-631-13221-X). Basil Blackwell.

--Phrenology: Fad & Science: A Nineteenth Century American Crusade. LC 70-122405. (Illus.). xiii, 203p. 1971. Repr. of 1955 ed. 18.50 (ISBN 0-208-00952-3, Archon). Shoe String.

Davies, John E., jt. auth. see Beck, J. Walter.

Davies, John G. Daily Life of Early Christians. LC 75-91757. Repr. of 1953 ed. lib. bdg. 15.00x (ISBN 0-8371-2413-1, DAEC). Greenwood.

--The Early Christian Church. LC 75-3989. (Illus.). 314p. 1976. Repr. of 1965 ed. lib. bdg. 24.00x (ISBN 0-8371-7696-4, DAECC). Greenwood.

Davies, John H., ed. Some Welsh Legends & Other Poems. LC 77-94572. 1979. Repr. of 1893 ed. lib. bdg. 35.00 (ISBN 0-89341-181-7). Longwood Pub Group.

Davies, John K. Wealth & the Power of Wealth in Classical Athens. rev. ed. Connor, W. R., ed. LC 80-2647. (Monographs in Classical Studies). 1981. lib. bdg. 22.00 (ISBN 0-88143-019-6). Ayer Co Pubs.

Davies, John L. Geographical Variation in Coastal Development. 2nd ed. LC 76-30821. (Geomorphology Texts Ser.: Vol. 4). (Illus.). 1980. pap. text ed. 18.95x (ISBN 0-582-49006-5). Longman.

Davies, John L. & Lockwood, Geoffrey. Universities: The Management Challenge. 288p. 1985. 22.00X (ISBN 0-7005-0609-8, Pub. by NFER Nelson UK). Taylor & Francis.

Davies, John L., ed. Working Men's College, 1854-1904. LC 75-144594. Repr. of 1904 ed. 21.50 (ISBN 0-404-01978-1). AMS Pr.

Davies, John P., Jr. Foreign & Other Affairs. 11.25 (ISBN 0-8446-0576-X). Peter Smith.

Davies, John S. Beginning to Compose. Incl. Bk. 1. Writing Melodies (ISBN 0-19-321063-0); Bk. 2. Writing in Two Parts (ISBN 0-19-321064-9). (gr. 4-6). 1976. pap. 4.25 ea. (ISBN 0-686-86546-4); tchr's bk. 5.25 (ISBN 0-19-321062-2). Oxford U Pr.

Davies, John S., ed. English Chronicle, of the Reigns of Richard Second, Henry Fourth, Henry Fifth, Henry Sixth, Written Before the Year 1471. LC 73-166036. (Camden Society, London. Publications. First Ser.: No. 64). Repr. of 1856 ed. 28.00 (ISBN 0-404-50164-8). AMS Pr.

Davies, John T. The Legend Makers. 1983. 12.95 (ISBN 0-686-34309-3). Bk Pools.

Davies, John T. & Rideal, Eric K. Interfacial Phenomena. 2nd ed. 1963. 77.00 (ISBN 0-12-206056-3). Acad Pr.

Davies, Jonathan, jt. auth. see Brenner, Vincent C.

Davies, Jonathan C. Folk-Lore of West & Mid-Wales. LC 74-3208. (Folklore Ser). 22.50 (ISBN 0-88305-160-5). Norwood Edns.

--Folklore of West & Mid Wales. 348p. 1980. Repr. of 1911 ed. lib. bdg. 38.50 (ISBN 0-8414-1874-8). Folcroft.

Davies, Joseph E. Fundamentals of Housing Study: A Determination of Factors Basic to an Understanding of American Housing Problems. LC 74-176715. (Columbia University. Teachers College. Contributions to Education: No. 759). Repr. of 1938 ed. 22.50 (ISBN 0-404-55759-7). AMS Pr.

Davies, Julian & Littlewood, Barbara S. Elementary Biochemistry: An Introduction to the Chemistry of Living Cells. (Biology Ser.). (Illus.). 1979. ref. 29.95 (ISBN 0-13-252809-6). P-H.

Davies, K. G. Documents of the American Revolution, 1770-1783, Vols. 8 & 9. Incl. Vol. 8. Transcript 1774. 296p (ISBN 0-7165-2093-1); Vol. 9. Transcript Jan.-June, 1775. 244p (ISBN 0-7165-2094-X). 1976. 50.00x ea. (Pub. by Irish Academic Pr Ireland). Biblio Dist.

--Documents of the American Revolution 1770-1783: Transcripts 1776, Vol. 12. (Colonial Office Ser.). 308p. 1976. 50.00x (ISBN 0-7165-2097-4, Pub. by Irish Academic Pr Ireland). Biblio Dist.

--The North Atlantic World in the Seventeenth Century. Shafer, Boyd C., ed. LC 74-78994. (Europe & the World in the Age of Expansion Ser: Vol. 4). (Illus.). 368p. 1974. 12.50x (ISBN 0-8166-0713-3); pap. 5.95 (ISBN 0-8166-0779-6). U of Minn Pr.

Davies, K. G., ed. Documents of the American Revolution, 1770-1783. Incl. Vol. 10. Calendar 1 July 1775-1776. 60.00x (ISBN 0-7165-2095-8); Vol. 11. Transcripts 1775 July-December. 246p. 50.00x (ISBN 0-7165-2096-6). (Colonial Office Ser.). 1976 (Pub. by Irish Academic Pr Ireland). Biblio Dist.

--Documents of the American Revolution, 1770-1783, Vols. 1-7. Incl. Vol. 1. Calendar 1770-1771. 528p. 1973. 60.00x (ISBN 0-7165-2086-9); Vol. 2. Transcript 1770. 340p. 1973. 50.00x (ISBN 0-7165-2087-7); Vol. 3. Transcript 1771. 308p. 1973. 50.00x (ISBN 0-7165-2088-5); Vol. 4. Calendar 1772-1773. 502p. 1973. 60.00x (ISBN 0-7165-2089-3); Vol. 5. Transcript 1772. 314p. 1974. 50.00x (ISBN 0-7165-2090-7); Vol. 6. Transcripts 1773. 298p. 1974. 50.00x (ISBN 0-7165-2091-5); Vol. 7. Calendar June,1774-1775. 440p. 1974. 60.00x (ISBN 0-7165-2092-3). 21 vol. set 850.00 (ISBN 0-7165-2085-0, Pub. by Irish Academic Pr Ireland). Biblio Dist.

--Documents of the American Revolution: Calendar 1777-1778, Vol. 13. (Colonial Office Ser.). 488p. 1976. 60.00x (ISBN 0-7165-2098-2, Pub. by Irish Academic Pr Ireland). Biblio Dist.

--Documents of the American Revolution 1770-1783: Calender 1781-1783 with Addenda 1770-1780, Vol. 19. (Colonial Office Ser.). 550p. 1978. 60.00x (ISBN 0-7165-2104-0, Pub by Irish Academic Pr Ireland). Biblio Dist.

--Documents of the American Revolution 1770-1783: Calendar 1779-1780, Vol. 16. (Colonial Office Ser.). 556p. 1977. 60.00x (ISBN 0-7165-2101-6, Pub. by Irish Academic Pr Ireland). Biblio Dist.

--Documents of the American Revolution, 1770-1783: Transcripts 1781, Vol. 20. (Colonial Office Ser.). 316p. 1980. 50.00x (ISBN 0-7165-2105-9, Pub. by Irish Academic Pr Ireland). Biblio Dist.

--Documents of the American Revolution 1770-1783: Transcripts 1777, Vol. 14. (Colonial Office Ser.). 306p. 1977. 50.00x (ISBN 0-7165-2099-0, Pub. by Irish Academic Pr Ireland). Biblio Dist.

--Documents of the American Revolution 1770-1783: Transcripts 1778, Vol. 15. (Colonial Office Ser.). 1977. 50.00x (ISBN 0-7165-2100-8, Pub. by Irish Academic Pr Ireland). Biblio Dist.

--Documents of the American Revolution 1770-1783: Transcripts 1779, Vol. 17. (Colonial Office Ser.). 296p. 1977. 50.00x (ISBN 0-7165-2102-4, Pub. by Irish Academic Pr Ireland). Biblio Dist.

--Documents of the American Revolution 1770-1783: Transcripts 1780, Vol. 18. (Colonial Office Ser.). 296p. 1978. 50.00x (ISBN 0-7165-2103-2, Pub. by Irish Academic Pr Ireland). Biblio Dist.

--Documents of the American Revolution 1770-1783, Vol. 21, Transcripts & Addenda: 1782-1783, Vol. 21. (Colonial Offices Ser.). 1980. 50.00x (ISBN 0-7165-2106-7, Pub. by Irish Academic Pr Ireland). Biblio Dist.

Davies, Karen. At Home in Manhattan: Modern Decorative Arts, 1925 to the Depression. (Illus.). 120p. (Orig.). 1983. pap. 12.50x (ISBN 0-89467-028-X). Yale Art Gallery.

Davies, Katherine. Enlightenment Comes in the Dark. 96p. 1983. 6.95 (ISBN 0-87516-521-4). De Vorss.

Davies, Kathryn. The Soviets at Geneva: The U. S. S. R. & the League of Nations, 1919-1939. LC 75-39051. (Russian Studies: Perspectives on the Revolution Ser). 315p. 1977. Repr. of 1934 ed. 25.00 (ISBN 0-88355-430-5). Hyperion Conn.

Davies, Keith A. Landowners in Colonial Peru. (Latin American Monograph Ser.: No. 61). (Illus.). 247p. 1985. text ed. 22.50x (ISBN 0-292-74639-3). U of Tex Pr.

Davies, Ken. Ken Davies: Artist at Work. (Illus.). 144p. 1978. 19.95 (ISBN 0-8230-2578-0). Watson-Guptill.

Davies, Kenneth G. The Royal African Company. 390p. 1975. Repr. of 1957 ed. lib. bdg. 23.00x (ISBN 0-374-92074-5). Octagon.

Davies, Kirk. Earth's Final Hours. 330p. (Orig.). 1982. pap. 9.95 (ISBN 0-9609174-0-3). Pacific Inst.

Davies, L., jt. auth. see Watts, C. T.

Davies, Laurence. Cesar Franck & His Circle. LC 77-4231. (Music Reprint Ser.). (Illus.). 1977. Repr. of 1970 ed. lib. bdg. 39.50 (ISBN 0-306-77410-0). Da Capo.

--Franck. (The Master Musicians Ser.). (Illus.). 160p. 1975. 13.50x (ISBN 0-460-03134-1, Pub. by J. M. Dent England). Biblio Dist.

--Ravel Orchestral Music. LC 70-536005. (BBC Music Guides Ser.). (Illus.). 64p. 1971. pap. 4.95 (ISBN 0-295-95108-7). U of Wash Pr.

Davies, Laurence, ed. see Conrad, Joseph.

Davies, Lawson. The Garden of Earthly Delights. 208p. 1985. 13.95 (ISBN 0-7181-2433-2, Pub. by Michael Joseph). Merrimack Pub Cir.
Davies, Lewis. A Key to the British Species of Simulidae (Diptera) in the Larval, Pupal & Adult Stages. 1968. 20.00x (ISBN 0-900386-12-6, Pub. by Freshwater Bio). State Mutual Bk.
Davies, Louise. Easy Cooking for One or Two. (Handbook Ser). 1981. pap. 6.95 (ISBN 0-14-046379-8). Penguin.
Davies, Lynn. Pupil Power: Deviance & Gender in School. 190p. 1984. 33.00x (ISBN 1-85000-007-7, Pub. by Falmer Pr); pap. 19.00x (ISBN 1-85000-006-9, Pub. by Falmer Pr). Taylor & Francis.
Davies, M. Functions of Biological Membranes. (Outline Studies in Biology). 1973. pap. 7.50 (ISBN 0-412-11350-3, NO. 6080, Pub. by Chapman & Hall). Methuen Inc.
Davies, M., ed. see Stewart-Tull, D. E.
Davies, M. Benedict, tr. see Boros, Ladislaus.
Davies, M. R. The Law of Burial, Cremation & Exhumation. 1974. 50.00x (ISBN 0-7219-0062-3, Pub. by Shaw & Sons). State Mutual Bk.
Davies, M. S., et al. A Directory of Clothing Research. 136p. 1968. 35.00x (ISBN 0-686-63762-3). State Mutual Bk.
Davies, Mansel, ed. Dielectric & Related Molecular Processes, Vols. 1-3. LC 72-83457. Vol. 1. 1966-71 literature 41.00 (ISBN 0-85186-505-4); Vol. 2. 1972-73 literature 43.00 (ISBN 0-85186-515-1); Vol. 3. 1974-76 literature 57.00 (ISBN 0-85186-525-9). Am Chemical.
Davies, Margaret G. Enforcement of English Apprenticeship: A Study in Applied Mercantilism, 1563-1642. LC 56-5174. (Economic Studies: No. 97). 1956. 20.00x (ISBN 0-674-25450-3). Harvard U Pr.
Davies, Margaret L., ed. Life As We Have Known It. 184p. 1975. pap. 5.95 (ISBN 0-393-00772-3, Norton Lib). Norton.
--Maternity: Letters from Working Women. 1979. pap. 3.95 (ISBN 0-393-00894-0, Norton Lib). Norton.
Davies, Margery. Woman's Place Is at the Typewriter: Office Work & Office Workers, 1870-1930. LC 82-13694. (Class & Culture Ser.). 264p. 1982. text ed. 27.95 (ISBN 0-87722-291-6). Temple U Pr.
Davies, Margery W. Woman's Place Is at the Typewriter: Office Work & Office Workers, 1870-1930. (Class & Culture Ser.). 256p. 1984. pap. 9.95 (ISBN 0-87722-368-8). Temple U Pr.
Davies, Marie-Helene. Laughter in a Genevan Gown: The Works of Frederick Buechner, 1970-1980. LC 83-14205. pap. 52.00 (ISBN 0-317-30136-5, 2025319). Bks Demand UMI.
--Reflections of Renaissance England: Life, Thought, & Religion Mirrored in Illustrated Pamphlets. (Pittsburgh Theological Monographs New Ser.: No. 18). 1985. pap. write for info. (ISBN 0-915138-68-9). Pickwick.
Davies, Marie-Helene, jt. auth. see Davies, Horton.
Davies, Marilyn A., jt. auth. see Foley, Theresa S.
Davies, Martin. The Essential Social Worker. (Community Care Practice Handbook Ser.). (Orig.). 1981. pap. text ed. 12.00x (ISBN 0-435-82268-3). Gower Pub Co.
--The Essential Social Worker: A Guide to Positive Practice. 2nd ed. 250p. 1985. text ed. write for info. (ISBN 0-566-00985-4). Gower Pub Co.
--Meaning, Quantification, Necessity. (International Library of Philosophy). 260p. 1981. 34.95x (ISBN 0-7100-0759-0). Routledge & Kegan.
Davies, Martin, ed. see Brown, Allan.
Davies, Martin, ed. see Cohen, Ruth & Rushton, Andree.
Davies, Martin, ed. see Crompton, Margaret.
Davies, Martin, ed. see Davis, Leonard.
Davies, Martin, ed. see Jones, R. & Kerslake, A.
Davies, Martin, ed. see Mortimer, Eunice.
Davies, Martin, ed. see Wendelken, Claire.
Davies, Martin, ed. see Wright, David.
Davies, Mary, jt. auth. see Doling, John.
Davies, Mary E., et al. So You Want to Be an Innkeeper. LC 85-13623. (Illus.). 240p. (Orig.). 1985. pap. 9.95 (ISBN 0-89286-252-1). One Hund One Prods.
Davies, Merton & Murray, Bruce C. The View from Space: Photographic Exploration of the Planets. LC 75-16887. 1971. pap. 11.00x (ISBN 0-231-08330-0). Columbia U Pr.
Davies, Michael. Archbishop Lefebvre & Religious Liberty. 17p. 1980. pap. 1.00 (ISBN 0-89555-143-8). TAN Bks Pubs.
--Communion Under Both Kinds- an Ecumenical Surrender. 1980. pap. 1.00 (ISBN 0-89555-141-1). TAN Bks Pubs.
--Open Lesson to a Bishop. 1980. pap. 1.00 (ISBN 0-89555-142-X). Tan Bks Pubs.
Davies, Michael & Riffenburgh, Ralph S. The Complete Medical Guide to Cataracts: Large Type. (Illus.). 144p. (Orig.). pap. write for info. cancelled (ISBN 0-941022-02-1). Appleton Davies.
Davies, Miranda, ed. Third World-Second Sex: Women's Struggles & National Liberation. (Illus.). 1983. 21.95x (ISBN 0-86232-017-8, Pub. by Zed Pr England); pap. 9.95x (ISBN 0-86232-029-1). Biblio Dist.
Davies, N. de G. see De G. Davies, N.
Davies, N. de Garis. A Corpus of Inscribed Egyptian Funerary Cones, Pt. I. (Illus.). 7p. 1957. text ed. 45.50x (ISBN 0-900416-12-2, Pub. by Aris & Philips England). Humanities.
Davies, Nicholas B., jt. auth. see Krebs, John R.
Davies, Nicholas B., jt. ed. see Krebs, John R.
Davies, Nigel. The Ancient Kingdoms of Mexico. 288p. 1984. pap. 5.95 (ISBN 0-14-022232-4, Pelican). Penguin.
--The Aztecs: A History. LC 80-12141. (Illus.). 384p. 1980. pap. 10.95 (ISBN 0-8061-1691-9). U of Okla Pr.
--Human Sacrifice: In History & Today. LC 80-21981. (Illus.). 320p. 1981. 14.95 (ISBN 0-688-03755-0). Morrow.
--The Toltec Heritage: From the Fall of Tula to the Rise of Tenochtitlan. LC 78-21384. (CAI Ser.: Vol. 153). (Illus.). 1980. 25.00 (ISBN 0-8061-1505-X). U of Okla Pr.
Davies, Nina. Scenes from Some Theban Tombs. (Private Tombs at Thebes Ser.: Vol. IV). 22p. 1963. text ed. 26.50x (ISBN 0-686-73619-2, Pub. by Aris & Philips England). Humanities.
Davies, Nina de Garis. Scenes from Some Theban Tombs. 58p. 1963. 45.00x (ISBN 0-900416-17-3, Pub. by Griffith Inst). State Mutual Bk.
Davies, Nina M. Tutankhamun's Painted Box. 22p. 1962. pap. 30.50x (ISBN 0-900416-22-X, Pub. by Aris & Philips England). Humanities.
Davies, Nina M. & Gardiner, A. H. Tut Ankhamun's Painted Box. 27p. 1962. 50.00x (ISBN 0-900416-22-X, Pub. by Griffith Inst). State Mutual Bk.
Davies, Noelle. Education for Life: A Danish Pioneer. 59.95 (ISBN 0-8490-0087-4). Gordon Pr.
Davies, Norman. God's Playground: A History of Poland, 2 vols. (Illus.). 1232p. 1982. 100.00x set (ISBN 0-231-04326-0). Columbia U Pr.
--God's Playground, A History of Poland: Vol. 1, The Origins to 1795. (Illus.). 560p. 1982. 50.00x (ISBN 0-231-05350-9). Columbia U Pr.
--God's Playground, A History of Poland: Vol. 2, 1795 to the Present. 672p. 1982. 50.00x (ISBN 0-231-05352-5). Columbia U Pr.
--Heart of Europe: A Short History of Poland. LC 83-22003. (Illus.). 1984. 35.00 (ISBN 0-19-873060-8). Oxford U Pr.
--Poland Past & Present: Select Bibliography of Works in English. (Illus.). 175p. 1976. lib. bdg. 26.00 (ISBN 0-89250-010-7). Orient Res Partners.
--The Tomb of Rekh-Mi-Re at Thebes: Metropolitan Museum of Art Egyptian Expedition Publications, 2 vols. in 1, Vol. 11. LC 75-168403. (Metropolitan Museum of Art Publications in Reprint). (Illus.). 374p. 1972. Repr. of 1943 ed. 47.50 (ISBN 0-405-02267-0). Ayer Co Pubs.
--White Eagle, Red Star: Polish Soviet War 1919-1920. (Illus.). 308p. 1985. pap. 9.95 (ISBN 0-901149-23-3, Pub. by Orbis Bks Ltd England). Hippocrene Bks.
Davies, Norman De Garis. The Tomb of Ken-Amun at Thebes: Metropolitan Museum of Art Egyptian Expedition Publications, 2 vols. in 1, Vol. 5. LC 78-168401. (Metropolitan Museum of Art Publications in Reprint). (Illus.). 208p. 1972. Repr. of 1930 ed. 39.00 (ISBN 0-405-02267-0). Ayer Co Pubs.
--The Tomb of Nefer-Hotep at Thebes: Metropolitan Museum of Art Egyptian Expedition Publications, 2 vols in 1, Vol. 9. LC 71-168402. (Metropolitan Museum of Art Publications in Reprint). (Illus.). 192p. 1972. Repr. of 1933 ed. 39.00 (ISBN 0-405-02236-0). Ayer Co Pubs.
Davies, Oliver. Roman Mines in Europe. Finley, Moses, ed. LC 79-4966. (Ancient Economic History Ser.). (Illus.). 1980. Repr. of 1935 ed. lib. bdg. 30.50x (ISBN 0-405-12354-X). Ayer Co Pubs.
Davies, Olwyn. Reber Two Thousand-Five. 1983. 10.00 (ISBN 0-533-05467-2). Vantage.
Davies, Owen, jt. auth. see Edelhart, Mike.
Davies, Owen, ed. The Omni Book of Computers & Robots. 413p. 1983. pap. 3.95 (ISBN 0-8217-1276-4). Zebra.
--The Omni Book of Medicine. pap. 3.95 (ISBN 0-8217-1364-7). Zebra.
--The Omni Book of Space. 1983. pap. 3.95 (ISBN 0-8217-1275-6). Zebra.
--The Omni Book of the Paranormal & the Mind. pap. 3.95 (ISBN 0-8217-1365-5). Zebra.
--Omni Complete Catalog of Hardware & Peripherals. 352p. 1984. 19.95 (ISBN 0-02-529830-5); pap. 12.95 (ISBN 0-02-008300-9). Macmillan.
--Omni Complete Catalog of Software & Accessories. 352p. 1984. 19.95 (ISBN 0-02-529820-8); pap. 12.95 (ISBN 0-02-008310-6). MacMillan.
Davies, Owen & Goldsmith, Peter, eds. Statistical Methods in Research & Production. (Illus.). 512p. 1984. text ed. 21.95 (ISBN 0-582-45087-X). Longman.
Davies, Owen L., ed. The Design & Analysis of Industrial Experiments. 2nd ed. LC 77-12563. pap. 160.00 (ISBN 0-317-27871-1, 2025259). Bks Demand UMI.
Davies, Owens & Edelhart, Mike. Omni Online Database Directory 1985. rev. ed. 384p. 1985. pap. 14.95 (ISBN 0-02-079920-9, Collier). Macmillan.
Davies, P. A. & Runcorn, S. K., eds. Mechanisms of Continental Drift & Plate Tectonics. 1981. 72.00 (ISBN 0-12-206160-8). Acad Pr.
Davies, P. A., ed. see Specialist Symposium on Geophysical Fluid Dynamics, European Geophysical Society, Fourth Meeting, Munich September, 1977.
Davies, P. C. The Accidental Universe. LC 81-21592. (Illus.). 160p. 1982. 22.95 (ISBN 0-521-24212-6); pap. 10.95 (ISBN 0-521-28692-1). Cambridge U Pr.
--The Forces of Nature. LC 78-72084. (Illus.). 1979. 44.50 (ISBN 0-521-22523-X). Cambridge U Pr.
--The Physics of Time Asymmetry. LC 74-81536. 1974. 38.50x (ISBN 0-520-02825-2); pap. 6.50x (ISBN 0-520-03247-0). U of Cal Pr.
--Quantum Mechanics. (Student Physics Ser.). 12800p. (Orig.). 1984. pap. text ed. 9.95x (ISBN 0-7100-9962-2). Routledge & Kegan.
--The Search for Gravity Waves. (Illus.). 160p. 1980. 15.95 (ISBN 0-521-23197-3). Cambridge U Pr.
--Space & Time in the Modern Universe. LC 76-27902. (Illus.). 1977. 37.50 (ISBN 0-521-21445-9); pap. 14.95 (ISBN 0-521-29151-8). Cambridge U Pr.
Davies, P. C., jt. auth. see Birrell, N. D.
Davies, P. C. W. The Forces of Nature. 2nd ed. (Illus.). 270p. Date not set. price not set (ISBN 0-521-30933-6); pap. price not set (ISBN 0-521-31392-9). Cambridge U Pr.
Davies, P. L. Biochemistry: Level Three. (Illus.). 224p. (Orig.). 1980. pap. text ed. 18.95x (ISBN 0-7121-0276-0). Trans-Atlantic.
Davies, P. M. Steps to Follow: A Guide to the Treatment of Adult Hemiplegia Based on the Concept of K. & B. Bobath. (Illus.). 335p. 1985. pap. 24.50 (ISBN 0-387-13436-0). Springer-Verlag.
Davies, P. M. & Coxon, A. P., eds. Key Texts in Multidimensional Scaling. LC 82-9320. xx, 352p. 1982. text ed. 20.00x (ISBN 0-435-82253-5). Heinemann Ed.
Davies, P. N. Sir Alfred Jones: Entrepreneur Par Excellence. LC 78-312287. 1978. 15.00x (ISBN 0-905118-17-0). Intl Pubns Serv.
Davies, P. O'Connor. Actions & Uses of Ophthalmic Drugs. 2nd ed. 1981. text ed. 69.95 (ISBN 0-407-93272-0). Butterworth.
Davies, Pamela & Gothefors, Leif. Bacterial Infections in the Fetus & Newborn Infant. (Major Problems in Clinical Pediatrics: Vol. 26). (Illus.). 350p. 1984. 30.00 (ISBN 0-7216-1185-0). Saunders.
Davies, Pamela A., et al. Medical Care of Newborn Babies. (Clinics in Developmental Medicine Ser.: Vols. 44 & 45). 363p. 1972. 32.00 (ISBN 0-433-32375-2, Pub. by Spastics Intl England). Lippincott.
Davies, Paul. The Edge of Infinity. 1983. pap. 7.95 (ISBN 0-671-46062-5, Touchstone Bks). S&S.
--God & the New Physics. 320p. 1983. 17.95 (ISBN 0-671-47688-2). S&S.
--God & the New Physics. 272p. 1984. pap. 7.95 (ISBN 0-671-52806-8, Touchstone Bks). S&S.
--Superforce: The Search for a Grand Unified Theory of Nature. LC 84-5473. 288p. 1984. 16.95 (ISBN 0-671-47685-8). S&S.
Davies, Paul & Freedland, Mark. Labour Law: Text & Materials. 2nd ed. (Law in Context Ser.). xiii, 964p. 1984. text ed. 45.00x (ISBN 0-297-78089-1, Pub. by Weidenfeld & Nicolson England). Rothman.
Davies, Paul, et al. Wild Orchids. 1982. 50.00x (ISBN 0-7011-2642-6, Pub. by Chatto Bodley Head England). State Mutual Bk.
--Wild Orchids of Britain & Europe. (Illus.). 256p. 1983. 17.95 (ISBN 0-7011-2642-6, Pub. by Chatto & Windus). Merrimack Pub Cir.
Davies, Penny. Growing up in the Medieval Times. (Growing Up Ser.). (gr. 7-12). 1980. 14.95 (ISBN 0-7134-0483-3, Pub. by Batsford England). David & Charles.
Davies, Peter. Roots: Family Histories of Familiar Words. (Illus.). 224p. 1981. 24.95 (ISBN 0-07-015449-X). McGraw.
--The Truth about Kent State. (Illus.). 241p. 1973. 10.00 (ISBN 0-374-27938-1). FS&G.
--The Truth about Kent State. 1973. pap. 3.50 (ISBN 0-374-51041-5, Noonday). FS&G.
Davies, Peter, ed. Trading in West Africa, 1840-1920. 209p. 1976. text ed. 20.00x (ISBN 0-8419-5504-2, Africana). Holmes & Meier.
Davies, Peter N. Henry Tyrer: A Liverpool Shipping Agent & His Enterprise 1879-1979. 159p. 1979. 25.00x (ISBN 0-85664-966-X, Pub. by Croom Helm Ltd). Longwood Pub Group.
Davies, Phil & Walsh, Dermot. Alcohol Problems & Alcohol Control in Europe. 320p. 1983. 28.50 (ISBN 0-89876-090-9). Gardner Pr.
Davies, Philip. Qumran. 1982. 35.00x (ISBN 0-7188-2458-X, Pub. by Lutterworth Pr England). State Mutual Bk.
Davies, Philip J. & Neve, Brian, eds. Cinema, Politics & Society in America. 1982. 25.00x (ISBN 0-312-13901-2). St Martin.
--Cinema, Politics & Society in America. 266p. 1985. pap. 12.95 (ISBN 0-312-13902-0). St Martin.
Davies, Philip R. The Damascus Covenant: An Interpretation of the "Damascus Document". (Journal for the Study of the Old Testament, Supplement Ser.: No. 25). 267p. 1983. text ed. 28.00x (ISBN 0-905774-50-7, Pub. by JSOT Pr England); pap. text ed. 18.50x (ISBN 0-905774-51-5, Pub. by JSOT Pr England). Eisenbrauns.
--Qumran. (Cities of the Biblical World Ser.). 1983. pap. 6.95 (ISBN 0-8028-1034-9). Eerdmans.
Davies, Phillips G., tr. see Thomas, R. D.
Davies, R. & Grant, M. D. Forgotten Railways, Chilterns & Cotswolds. (Illus.). 256p. 1984. 19.95 (ISBN 0-946537-07-0). David & Charles.
--London & Its Railways. (Illus.). 224p. (Orig.). 1983. 26.50 (ISBN 0-7153-8107-5). David & Charles.
--Railway History in Pictures: Chilterns & Cotswolds. 1977. 13.50 (ISBN 0-7153-7299-8). David & Charles.
Davies, R., ed. Developments in Food Microbiology, Vol. 1. (Illus.). 219p. 1982. 48.00 (ISBN 0-85334-999-1, Pub. by Elsevier Applied Sci England). Elsevier.
Davies, R., jt. ed. see Lovelock, D. W.
Davies, R., et al. Intermediate Moisture Foods. (Illus.). 306p. 1976. 48.00 (ISBN 0-85334-702-6, Pub. by Elsevier Applied Sci England). Elsevier.
Davies, R. D., ed. see I.A.U. Symposium, No. 46 Jodrell Bank, England, August 5-7, 1970.
Davies, R. E. Airlines of Latin America Since Nineteen-Nineteen. (Illus.). 704p. 1984. 47.50x (ISBN 0-87474-358-3, DALA). Smithsonian.
--Airlines of the United States Since 1914. LC 82-600203. (Illus.). 746p. 1983. Repr. of 1972 ed. text ed. 39.95x (ISBN 0-87474-356-7). Smithsonian.
--A History of the World's Airlines. LC 82-72843. (Airlines History Project Ser.). (Illus.). 608p. 1983. Repr. of 1967 ed. 57.50 (ISBN 0-404-19325-0). AMS Pr.
Davies, R. G. Computer Programming in Quantitative Biology. 1972. 77.50 (ISBN 0-12-206250-7). Acad Pr.
Davies, R. G., jt. auth. see Richards, O. W.
Davies, R. G. & Denton, J. H., eds. The English Parliament in the Middle Ages. LC 81-3423. (Middle Ages Ser.). 212p. 1981. 27.50x (ISBN 0-8122-7802-X). U of Pa Pr.
Davies, R. L. Retail & Commercial Planning. LC 83-51435. 384p. 1984. 35.00 (ISBN 0-312-67798-7). St Martin.
Davies, R. L. & Rogers, D. S. Store Location & Assessment Research. 380p. 1984. 34.95 (ISBN 0-471-90381-7, Pub. by Wiley-Interscience). Wiley.
Davies, R. Peter. Mixed Ability Grouping. 224p. 1982. 30.00x (ISBN 0-85117-075-7, Pub. by M Temple Smith). State Mutual Bk.
Davies, R. R., et al. Welsh Society & Nationhood: Historical Essays Presented to Glanmor Williams. (Illus.). 238p. 1984. text ed. 48.00x (ISBN 0-7083-0860-0, Pub. by Univ of Wales Pr). Humanities.
Davies, R. T., ed. Medieval English Lyrics. LC 72-8279. (Granger Index Reprint Ser). 1972. Repr. of 1964 ed. 21.00 (ISBN 0-8369-6386-5). Ayer Co Pubs.
--Medieval English Lyrics. 384p. 1966. pap. 8.95 (ISBN 0-571-06571-6). Faber & Faber.
Davies, R. T., ed. see Johnson, Samuel.
Davies, R. Trevor. Four Centuries of Witch-Belief. LC 74-180026. Repr. of 1947 ed. 27.50 (ISBN 0-405-08437-4). Ayer Co Pubs.
Davies, R. Trevor, tr. from Lat. & Fr. Documents Illustrating the History of Civilization in Medieval England: 1066-1500. 413p. 1982. Repr. of 1926 ed. lib. bdg. 50.00 (ISBN 0-8495-1140-2). Arden Lib.
Davies, R. W. The Socialist Offensive: The Collectivization of Soviet Agriculture, Nineteen Twenty-Nine to Nineteen Thirty. LC 79-15263. (Industrialization of Soviet Russia: Vol. 1). (Illus.). 512p. 1980. text ed. 37.50x (ISBN 0-674-81480-0). Harvard U Pr.
--The Soviet Collective Farm: 1929-1930. LC 79-15273. (Industrialization of Soviet Russia: Vol. 2). 256p. 1980. text ed. 18.50x (ISBN 0-674-82600-0). Harvard U Pr.
Davies, R. W., jt. auth. see Wheatcroft, S. G.
Davies, R. W., ed. Soviet Investment for Planned Industrialisation, 1929-1937, Policy & Practice: Selected Papers from the Second World Congress for Soviet & East European Studies. (Orig.). 1985. pap. 16.00 (ISBN 0-933884-32-X). Berkeley Slavic.
--The Soviet Union. (Illus.). 1978. pap. text ed. 8.95x (ISBN 0-04-947023-X). Allen Unwin.
Davies, Reginald T. The Golden Century of Spain, 1501-1621. LC 83-45426. Repr. of 1937 ed. 36.00 (ISBN 0-404-20073-7). AMS Pr.
--The Golden Century Spain, Fifteen Hundred One to Sixteen Twenty-One. LC 84-19806. (Illus.). xi, 327p. 1984. Repr. of 1937 ed. lib. bdg. 39.75x (ISBN 0-313-24678-5, DAGO). Greenwood.
Davies, Rhys. The Best of Rhys Davies. 8.50 (ISBN 0-7153-7756-6). David & Charles.
Davies, Richard. Chester's Triumph in Honor of Her Prince, As It Was Performed Upon St. George's Day, 1610. 1844. 14.00 (ISBN 0-384-10990-X). Johnson Repr.
Davies, Richard E. Handbook for Doctor of Ministry Projects: An Approach to Structured Observation Ministry. (Illus.). 238p. (Orig.). 1984. lib. bdg. 23.75 (ISBN 0-8191-3763-4); pap. text ed. 12.00 (ISBN 0-8191-3764-2). U Pr of Amer.
Davies, Robert. York Records of the Fifteenth Century. 304p. 1976. Repr. of 1843 ed. 20.00x (ISBN 0-8476-1290-2). Rowman.
Davies, Robert, ed. Life of Marmaduke Rawdon of York. (Camden Society, London. Publications, First Ser.: No. 85). Repr. of 1863 ed. 28.00 (ISBN 0-404-50185-0). AMS Pr.

--York Records of the Fifteenth Century. 304p. 1976. Repr. of 1843 ed. text ed. 21.50x (ISBN 0-904586-02-2, Pub. by Alan Sutton England). Humanities.

Davies, Robert, et al. The Struggle for South Africa: A Reference Guide to Movements, Organizations & Institutions, 2 vols. (Africa Ser.). 1984. Vol. 1, 278p. 29.50x (ISBN 0-86232-224-3, Pub. by Zed Pr England); pap. 10.75 (ISBN 0-86232-225-1, Pub. by Zed Pr England); Vol. 2, 206p. 29.50x (ISBN 0-86232-256-1); pap. 10.75 (ISBN 0-86232-257-X). Biblio Dist.

Davies, Robert A. Timber. (Poetry Chapbook Ser.). 1979. 4.50 (ISBN 0-932191-01-0). Mr Cogito Pr.

Davies, Robert A., jt. auth. see Gogol, John M.

Davies, Robert B. Peacefully Working to Conquer the World: Singer Sewing Machine in Foreign Markets, 1854-1920. Bruchey, Stuart & Bruchey, Eleanor, eds. LC 76-5000. (American Business Abroad Ser.). 1976. 36.00x (ISBN 0-405-09270-9). Ayer Co Pubs.

Davies, Robert H. Capital, State & White Labour in South Africa Nineteen Hundred - Nineteen Sixty: An Historical Materialist Analysis of Class Formation & Class Relations. LC 79-1517. (Humanities Studies in African Political Economy: No. 2). 1979. text ed. 40.50x (ISBN 0-391-01030-1). Humanities.

Davies, Robert W. The Development of the Soviet Budgetary System. LC 78-23596. 1979. Repr. of 1958 ed. lib. bdg. 32.50x (ISBN 0-313-21191-4, DADS). Greenwood.

Davies, Robertson. The Deptford Trilogy. (Penguin Fiction Ser.). 864p. 1985. pap. text ed. 8.95 (ISBN 0-14-006500-8). Penguin.

--Fifth Business. 1977. pap. 4.95 (ISBN 0-14-004387-X). Penguin.

--High Spirits. LC 83-47878. 208p. (Orig.). 1983. pap. 5.95 (ISBN 0-14-006505-9). Penguin.

--High Spirits. LC 83-47878. 208p. 1983. 14.95 (ISBN 0-670-37154-8, Dist. by Penguin). Viking.

--Leaven of Malice. 1980. pap. 4.95 (ISBN 0-14-005433-2). Penguin.

--The Manticore. 1977. pap. 4.95 (ISBN 0-14-004388-8). Penguin.

--The Mirror of Nature. (Alexander Lectures Ser.). 144p. 1983. pap. 6.50 (ISBN 0-8020-6536-8). U of Toronto Pr.

--A Mixture of Frailties. 384p. 1980. pap. 4.95 (ISBN 0-14-005432-4). Penguin.

--One Half of Robertson Davies. 1978. pap. 5.95 (ISBN 0-14-004967-3). Penguin.

--One Half of Robertson Davies. 1978. 12.95 (ISBN 0-670-52608-8). Viking.

--The Rebel Angels. LC 81-51907. 320p. 1982. 13.95 (ISBN 0-670-59063-0). Viking.

--The Rebel Angels. 1983. pap. 4.95 (ISBN 0-14-006271-8). Penguin.

--Tempest Tost. 1980. pap. 3.95 (ISBN 0-14-005431-6). Penguin.

--What's Bred in the Bone. 1985. price not set (ISBN 0-670-80916-0). Viking.

--World of Wonders. 1977. pap. 4.95 (ISBN 0-14-004389-6). Penguin.

--World of Wonders. LC 75-38778. 288p. 1976. 12.95 (ISBN 0-670-78812-0). Viking.

Davies, Robetson. The Personal Art: Reading to Good Purposes (Victorian Novel & Victorian Theatre, Victorian Shakespeare, Shakespeare Novels) 268p. 1983. Repr. of 1961 ed. lib. bdg. 40.00 (ISBN 0-89987-177-1). Darby Bks.

Davies, Ron, jt. auth. see Zerchykrov, Ross.

Davies, Rosaleen. I Can't Help Smiling. 70p. (Orig.). 1978. pap. 1.50 (ISBN 0-85640-148-X, Pub. by Blackstaff Pr). Longwood Pub Group.

Davies, Ross. Retail Planning in the European Community. 228p. 1979. text ed. 37.25x (ISBN 0-566-00308-2). Gower Pub Co.

Davies, Ross L. Marketing Geography with Special Reference to Retailing. 1977. pap. 14.95x (ISBN 0-416-70700-9, 6079). Methuen Inc.

Davies, Ross L. & Champion, Anthony G., eds. The Future for the City Centre. (Special Publications of the Institute of British Geographers Ser.: No. 14). 1983. 39.50 (ISBN 0-12-206240-X). Acad Pr.

Davies, Rowland. Journal of the Very Rev. Rowland Davies, from March 8, 1688-9, to September 29, 1690. Caulfield, Richard, ed. LC 71-163674. (Camden Society, London. Publications, First Ser.: No. 68). Repr. of 1857 ed. 28.00 (ISBN 0-404-50168-0). AMS Pr.

--Journal of the Very Rev. Rowland Davies, Ll.D. Dean of Ross from March 8, 1688-9 to September 29, 1690. 1857. 28.00 (ISBN 0-384-10995-0). Johnson Repr.

Davies, Rupert E. The Problems of Authority in the Continental Reformers: A Study of Luther, Zwingli, & Calvin. LC 78-5871. 1978. Repr. of 1946 ed. lib. bdg. 20.00x (ISBN 0-313-20487-X, DAPA). Greenwood.

--Problems of Authority in the Continental Reformers: A Study of Luther, Zwingli, & Calvin. LC 78-59015. 1979. Repr. of 1946 ed. 15.95 (ISBN 0-88355-689-8). Hyperion Conn.

Davies, Rupert E., ed. Approach to Christian Education. 1956. 5.00 (ISBN 0-8022-0352-3). Philos Lib.

Davies, Rupert E., jt. ed. see Flew, Robert N.

Davies, Russ. Mapping the IBM PC & PCjr. Compute Editors, ed. 352p. (Orig.). 1985. pap. 18.95 (ISBN 0-942386-92-2). Compute Pubns.

Davies, Ruth A. The School Library Media Program: Instructional Force for Excellence. 3rd ed. LC 79-20358. 580p. 1979. 18.50 (ISBN 0-8352-1244-0). Bowker.

Davies, Ruth A., jt. auth. see Clendening, Corinne P.

Davies, S. The Diffusion of Process Innovations. LC 78-15143. 1979. 42.50 (ISBN 0-521-22193-5). Cambridge U Pr.

Davies, S., ed. Renaissance Views of Man. 214p. 1978. pap. 5.95 (ISBN 0-7190-0726-7, Pub. by Manchester Univ Pr). Longwood Pub Group.

Davies, S. B., jt. ed. see Burrows, G. D.

Davies, S. G., ed. Organotransition Metal Chemistry: Applications to Organic Synthesis. (Organic Chemistry Ser.: Vol. 2). (Illus.). 428p. 1982. 85.00 (ISBN 0-08-026202-3). Pergamon.

Davies, S. J. In Spite of Dungeons. 160p. 1978. pap. text ed. 8.00x (ISBN 0-904387-11-9, Pub. by Alan Sutton England). Humanities.

Davies, S. J., jt. auth. see Busby, John R.

Davies, S. L. Peace, Print & Protestantism, Fourteen Fifty to Fifteen Eighty. 1976. 24.50x (ISBN 0-8464-0706-X). Beekman Pubs.

Davies, Samuel. Collected Poems. Davis, Richard B., ed. LC 68-17019. 1968. 40.00x (ISBN 0-8201-1011-6). Schol Facsimiles.

Davies, Saunders, tr. see Lauer, Hans E.

Davies, Stan G. James Joyce: A Portrait of the Artist. LC 75-11940. (Illus.). 336p. 1982. pap. 11.95 (ISBN 0-8128-6171-X). Stein & Day.

Davies, Stanley P. Social Control of the Mentally Deficient. LC 75-17215. (Social Problems & Social Policy Ser.). (Illus.). 1975. Repr. of 1930 ed. 32.00x (ISBN 0-405-07486-7). Ayer Co Pubs.

Davies, Stanley P. & Ecob, E. G. The Mentally Retarded in Society. 2nd ed. LC 58-59911. 248p. 1959. 27.50x (ISBN 0-231-02220-4). Columbia U Pr.

Davies, Stephen. The Diffusion of Process Innovations. LC 78-15143. pap. 51.80 (ISBN 0-317-28007-4, 2025580). Bks Demand UMI.

Davies, Stevan L. The Gospel of Thomas & Christian Wisdom. 160p. 1983. pap. 9.95 (ISBN 0-8164-2456-X, Pub. by Seabury). Winston Pr.

--The Revolt of the Widows: The Social World of the Apocryphal Acts. LC 80-11331. 150p. 1980. 12.95x (ISBN 0-8093-0958-0). S Ill U Pr.

Davies, Stevie. Emily Bronte: The Artist As Free Woman. 170p. 1984. 14.95 (ISBN 0-85635-459-7). Carcanet.

--Images of Kinship in "Pardise Lost". Milton's Politics & Christian Liberty. LC 82-17485. 256p. 1983. text ed. 21.00 (ISBN 0-8262-0392-2). U of Mo Pr.

--Renaissance Views of Man. (Literature in Context Ser.). 203p. 1979. text ed. 27.50x (ISBN 0-06-491621-9). B&N Imports.

Davies, Stevie, ed. The Bronte Sisters: Selected Poems. (The Fyfield Ser.). 120p. pap. 7.50 (ISBN 0-85635-131-8). Carcanet.

Davies, Sue, tr. see Schnitzler, Arthur.

Davies, T. Protection of Industrial Power Systems. 32.50 (ISBN 0-08-029322-0); pap. 15.00 (ISBN 0-08-029321-2). Pergamon.

Davies, T. & Lewis, O. A Supplementary English Glossary. 736p. 1983. lib. bdg. 200.00 (ISBN 0-8495-1143-7). Arden Lib.

Davies, T. L. Bible English: Chapters on Old & Disused Expressions. 1875. 25.00 (ISBN 0-8274-1932-5). R West.

--A Supplementary English Glossary. 1875. 25.00 (ISBN 0-8274-3557-6). R West.

Davies, T. Lewis. English Glossary: A Supplementary. 736p. 1980. Repr. of 1881 ed. lib. bdg. 125.00 (ISBN 0-8495-1119-4). Arden Lib.

Davies, Terry F. Autoimmune Endocrine Disease. LC 82-17318. 279p. 1983. 64.50 (ISBN 0-471-09778-0, Pub. by Wiley-Interscience). Wiley.

Davies, Thomas. Dramatic Miscellanies - on Several Plays of Shakespeare, 3 Vols. LC 75-163675. Repr. of 1784 ed. Set. 140.00 (ISBN 0-404-01990-0). AMS Pr.

--Memoirs of the Life of David Garrick, 2 vols. Jones, Stephen, ed. LC 73-82825. 1808. Set. 55.00 (ISBN 0-405-08438-2); 27.50 ea. Vol. 1 (ISBN 0-405-08439-0). Vol. 2 (ISBN 0-405-08440-4). Ayer Co Pubs.

Davies, Thomas D. Concise Tables for Sight Reduction. LC 84-45259. (Illus.). 64p. (Orig.). 1984. pap. text ed. 8.50 (ISBN 0-87033-325-9). Cornell Maritime.

--Sight Reduction Tables for Sun, Moon, & Planets: Assumed Altitude Method of Celestial Navigation. LC 81-9725. 247p. 1982. spiral text ed. 27.50x (ISBN 0-87033-276-7). Cornell Maritime.

--Star Sight Reduction Tables for Forty-Two Stars: Assumed Altitude Method of Celestial Navigation. LC 79-7464. 370p. 1980. spiral 28.50x (ISBN 0-87033-250-3). Cornell Maritime.

Davies, Thomas L. Supplementary English Glossary. LC 68-23468. 1968. Repr. of 1881 ed. 53.00x (ISBN 0-8103-3245-0). Gale.

Davies, Thomas M., Jr. Indian Integration in Peru: A Half Century of Experience, 1900-1948. LC 73-80965. (Illus.). xii, 204p. 1974. 16.95x (ISBN 0-8032-0834-0). U of Nebr Pr.

Davies, Thomas M., Jr., ed. see Guevara, Che.

Davies, Thomas M., Jr., jt. ed. see Loveman, Brian.

Davies, Thomas W. Magic, Divination & Demonology Among the Hebrews & Their Neighbors. 1898. 12.50x (ISBN 0-87068-051-X). Ktav.

Davies, Tom. The Electric Harvest. 256p. 1985. 15.95 (ISBN 0-450-06079-9, New Eng Lib). David & Charles.

Davies, Tom & Hodder, John. Stained Glass Hours: Modern Pilgrimage. (Illus.). 161p. 1985. 28.00 (ISBN 0-450-06053-5, New Eng Lib). David & Charles.

Davies, Tom, et al. Government & Local Labour Market Policy Implementation. LC 84-10235. 245p. 1984. text ed. 34.50x (ISBN 0-566-00750-9). Gower Pub Co.

Davies, Uri, jt. auth. see Lehn, Walter.

Davies, Valentine. Miracle on Thirty-Fourth Street. Repr. lib. bdg. 13.95 (ISBN 0-88411-934-3, Pub. by Aeonian Pr). Amereon Ltd.

--Miracle on Thirty-Fourth Street. LC 47-4221. 11.95 (ISBN 0-15-160239-5). HarBraceJ.

--Miracle on Thirty-Fourth Street. (Illus.). (gr. k up). 1984. 15.95 (ISBN 0-15-254526-3, HJ). HarBraceJ.

Davies, W. Brian, et al. Education Theory & Its Foundation Disciplines. 160p. (Orig.). 1984. pap. 10.95x (ISBN 0-7100-9763-8). Routledge & Kegan.

Davies, W. D. Christian Origins & Judaism. LC 73-2192. (The Jewish People; History, Religion, Literature Ser.). Repr. of 1962 ed. 22.00 (ISBN 0-405-05258-8). Ayer Co Pubs.

--The Gospel & the Land: Early Christianity & Jewish Territorial Doctrine. LC 72-82228. 1974. 32.50x (ISBN 0-520-02278-5). U of Cal Pr.

--Invitation to the New Testament. LC 65-17223. 1969. pap. 9.95 (ISBN 0-385-04767-3, Anch). Doubleday.

--Jewish & Pauline Studies. LC 82-48620. 432p. 1983. text ed. 29.95 (ISBN 0-8006-0694-9). Fortress.

--Paul & Rabbinic Judaism: Some Rabbinic Elements in Pauline Theology. LC 80-8049. 448p. 1980. pap. 14.95 (ISBN 0-8006-1438-0, 1-1438). Fortress.

--System Identification for Self-Adaptive Control. LC 70-128756. pap. 98.50 (ISBN 0-317-08013-X, 2022540). Bks Demand UMI.

--The Territorial Dimension of Judaism. LC 81-53. 160p. 1982. 15.95 (ISBN 0-520-04331-6). U of Cal Pr.

Davies, W. D., ed. Cambridge History of Judaism: Introduction, the Persian Period, Vol. 1. Finkelstein, Louis. LC 77-85704. 461p. 1984. 59.50 (ISBN 0-521-21880-2). Cambridge U Pr.

Davies, W. H. The Complete Poems of W. H. Davies. 1965. 26.50x (ISBN 0-8195-3055-7). Wesleyan U Pr.

--Later Days. 1985. pap. 4.95x (ISBN 0-19-281864-3). Oxford U Pr.

--Shorter Lyrics of the Twentieth Century 1900-1922. Repr. of 1922 ed. lib. bdg. 10.00 (ISBN 0-8414-2443-8). Folcroft.

--Young Emma. LC 80-70274. 158p. 1981. 9.95 (ISBN 0-8076-1009-7). Braziller.

Davies, W. J. German Army Handbook. LC 73-86000. (Illus.). 1977. pap. 6.95 (ISBN 0-668-04291-5). Arco.

--The Ravenglass & Eskdale Railway. LC 81-65680. (Illus.). 204p. 1981. 14.95 (ISBN 0-7153-8194-6). David & Charles.

--Ravenglass & Eskdale Railway. LC 68-23817. (Illus.). 1968. 14.95x (ISBN 0-678-05593-9). Kelley.

--The Romney, Hythe & Dymchurch Railway. (Railway History Ser). (Illus.). 184p. 1975. 14.95 (ISBN 0-7153-6827-3). David & Charles.

Davies, W. Pennar. E. Tegla Davies. (Writers of Wales Ser.). 100p. 1983. pap. text ed. 6.75x (ISBN 0-7083-0842-2, Pub. by Univ of Wales Pr England). Humanities.

Davies, W. V., jt. auth. see James, T. G.

Davies, W. X. Countdown WW II No. 3: Operation Choke Point. 240p. 1984. pap. 2.95 (ISBN 0-425-07135-9). Berkley Pub.

--Countdown WW III, No. 2: Operation Black Sea. 240p. 1984. pap. 2.95 (ISBN 0-425-07012-3). Berkley Pub.

Davies, W. X., jt. auth. see Strategic Operation Group.

Davies, W. X., jt. auth. see Strategic Operations Group.

Davies, Walford & Ley, Henry G., eds. Church Anthem Book: One Hundred Anthems. rev. ed. 1959. 16.00x (ISBN 0-19-353106-2). Oxford U Pr.

Davies, Walford, ed. & notes by see Wordsworth, William.

Davies, Wallace E. Patriotism on Parade: The Story of Veterans' & Hereditary Organizations in America, 1783-1900. LC 55-11951. (Historical Studies: No. 66). 1955. 25.00x (ISBN 0-674-65800-0). Harvard U Pr.

Davies, Wayne. Urban Social Structure: A Multi-Variate Structural Analysis of Cardiff & its Region. (Social Science Monography: No. 8). 183p. 1983. pap. text ed. 11.00x (ISBN 0-7083-0833-3, Pub. by Univ of Wales England). Humanities.

Davies, Wayne K. Factorial Ecology. LC 83-20617. 409p. 1984. text ed. 39.50x (ISBN 0-566-00599-9). Gower Pub Co.

Davies, Wendy. An Early Welsh Microcosm: Studies in the Llandaff Charters. (Royal Historical Society-Studies in History Ser.: Vol. 9). 208p. 1978. text ed. 28.00x (ISBN 0-901050-33-4, Pub. by Swiftbks England). Humanities.

--An Early Welsh Microcosm: Studies in the Llandaff Charters. 1982. 70.00X (ISBN 0-901050-33-4, 07549805, Pub. by Royal Hist Soc England). State Mutual Bk.

--Wales in the Early Middle Ages. (Studies in the Early History of Britain: Vol. 2). 300p. 1982. text ed. 40.50x (ISBN 0-7185-1163-8, Leicester). Humanities.

Davies, William. The Setting of the Sermon on the Mount. LC 64-630. pap. 140.80 (ISBN 0-317-26320-X, 2024449). Bks Demand UMI.

Davies, William, jt. auth. see Smetham, Sarah.

Davies, William D. Sermon on the Mount. (Orig.). 1966. pap. 9.95 (ISBN 0-521-09384-8, 384). Cambridge U Pr.

Davies, William H. Captive Lion & Other Poems. 1921. 24.50x (ISBN 0-685-89738-9). Elliots Bks.

Davies-Rodgers, Ellen. Education: Then, Now & Yon. 5.00 (ISBN 0-685-84988-0). Plantation.

--The Great Book: Calvary Protestant Episcopal Church. Memphis, Tennessee 1832-1972. 1973. 30.00 (ISBN 0-685-84989-9). Plantation.

--Heirs Through Hope: The Episcopal Diocese of West Tennessee. LC 83-50733. 1983. 30.00 (ISBN 0-317-05919-X). Plantation.

--The Holy Innocents: The Story of a Historic Church & Country Parish. (Illus.). 12.00 (ISBN 0-685-84990-2). Plantation.

--The Romance of the Episcopal Church in West Tennessee. 12.00 (ISBN 0-685-84991-0). Plantation.

Davies-Rogers, Ellen. Our Ancestors. LC 85-61051. 1985. write for info. Plantation.

--A Tree Is Lighted. LC 84-90673. (Illus.). 1984. 5.00 (ISBN 0-317-19588-3). Plantation.

Daviess, Maria T. Seven Times Seven. Baxter, Annette K., ed. LC 79-8786. (Signal Lives Ser.). (Illus.). 1980. Repr. of 1924 ed. lib. bdg. 34.50x (ISBN 0-405-12834-7). Ayer Co Pubs.

Davila, Angelamaria. Animal fiero y tierno. LC 81-68085. 68p. 1981. pap. 4.95 (ISBN 0-940238-50-0). Ediciones Huracan.

Davila, Maria D. Castro De see Castro De Davila, Maria D.

Davila, Mario L., tr. see Abreu-Gomez, Emilo.

Davila, Virgilio. Complete Works of Virgilio Davila. (Puerto Rico Ser.). 1979. lib. bdg. 75.00 (ISBN 0-8490-2900-7). Gordon Pr.

Davin, D. M. Closing Times. 1975. 17.50x (ISBN 0-19-212197-9). Oxford U Pr.

Davin, Delia. Woman-Work: Women & the Party in Revolutionary China. (Illus.). 1979. pap. 5.95 (ISBN 0-19-285080-6, GB 566, GB). Oxford U Pr.

Davin, L. E. Conditions de Croissance des Economies Regionales en Etat de Suremploi: Le Cas de Liege. Bd. with Le Destin Europeen de la Meuse. Delmer, A. (Economies et Societes Series L: No. 5). 1959. pap. 11.00 (ISBN 0-317-16155-5). Kraus Repr.

Davin, N. F. The Irishman in Canada. 718p. 1969. Repr. of 1877 ed. 30.00x (ISBN 0-7165-0060-4, Pub. by Irish Academic Pr Ireland). Biblio Dist.

Davinci, Ladislao, tr. from Italian. The Madrid Codices of Leonardo Da Vinci. LC 73-23091. 1974. 400.00 (ISBN 0-07-037194-6). McGraw.

Da Vinci, Leonardo. Codex Atlanticus. 12000.00 (ISBN 0-384-32302-2). Johnson Repr.

--Codex on the Flight of Birds. 295.00 (ISBN 0-384-32299-9). Johnson Repr.

--A Collection of Reproduction of the Original Drawings from the Rare, Personal Notebook by Leonardo Da Vinci. (Illus.). 99p. 1984. 117.45 (ISBN 0-86650-112-6). Gloucester Art.

--The Corpus of the Anatomical Studies in the Collection of Her Majesty Queen Elizabeth II at the Royal Library, Windsor Castle. facsimile ed. 1978. 8000.00. Johnson Repr.

--Drawings of Da Vinci. Belt, Elmer, ed. (Master Draughtsman Ser). (Illus.). (Orig.). treasure trove bdg. 9.95x (ISBN 0-87505-004-2); pap. 4.95 (ISBN 0-87505-157-X). Borden.

--Landscapes, Plants & Water Studies. 5500.00 (ISBN 0-384-32301-4). Johnson Repr.

--Leonardo da Vinci: Codex Trivulzianus. until October 1, 1984 thereafter 345.00 295.00 (ISBN 0-384-32296-4). Johnson Repr.

--Leonardo da Vinci Drawings. (Illus.). 1983. pap. 2.75 (ISBN 0-486-23951-9). Dover.

--Leonardo on the Human Body. O'Malley, Charles D. & Saunders, J. B., trs. (Fine Art Ser.). (Illus.). 506p. 1983. pap. 10.95 (ISBN 0-486-24483-0). Dover.

DaVinci, Leonardo. Leonardo On the Human Body. 1984. 18.50 (ISBN 0-8446-6111-2). Peter Smith.

Da Vinci, Leonardo. The Madrid Codices of Leonardo da Vinci. Reti, Ladislao, tr. from Ital. LC 73-23091. 1974. Deluxe First Edition English-language 1250.00 (ISBN 0-07-037207-1, Pub. by McGraw-Hill). Universal Book Co.

--The Notebooks of Leonardo Da Vinci, 2 vols. Richter, Jean-Paul, ed. (Illus.). Set. 36.00 (ISBN 0-8446-4535-4). Peter Smith.

--The Notebooks of Leonardo Da Vinci. Richter, Irma A., ed. (World's Classics Ser.). (Illus.). 1982. pap. 4.95 (ISBN 0-19-281538-5). Oxford U Pr.

--Transcriptions of the Codex Atlanticus, 12 vols. Set. 900.00 (ISBN 0-384-32303-0). Johnson Repr.

Da Vinci, Leonardo see Leonardo da Vinci.

Davin-Power, Maurice. Shadows in the Sun. (Irish Play Ser.). pap. 2.95x (ISBN 0-912262-64-8). Proscenium.

Davinson, D. E. The Periodicals Collection. 244p. 1978. 26.50x (ISBN 0-233-96918-7, 05776-2, Pub. by Gower Pub Co England). Lexington Bks.

Davinson, Donald. Academic & Legal Deposit Libraries. 2nd ed. (Examination Guide Ser). 100p. 1969. 14.50 (ISBN 0-208-00879-9, Archon). Shoe String.

--Bibliographic Control. 2nd ed. 164p. 1981. 12.00 (ISBN 0-85157-319-3, Pub. by Bingley England). Shoe String.

--Reference Service. 235p. 1980. text ed. 17.50 (ISBN 0-85157-291-X, Pub. by Bingley England). Shoe String.

Davio, M., et al. Digital Systems with Algorithm Implementation. 654p. 1983. 58.95 (ISBN 0-471-10413-2); pap. 34.95 (ISBN 0-471-10414-0). Wiley.

Davio, Marc, et al. Discrete & Switching Functions. 1978. text ed. 127.95x (ISBN 0-07-015509-7). McGraw.

Davis. Black Communities Social Security. 1977. pap. 10.50 (ISBN 0-8191-0282-2). U Pr of Amer.

--British Bus Fleets No. 10 Northern. pap. 4.00x (ISBN 0-392-08670-0, SpS). Sportshelf.

--Careers in a Medical Center. (Early Career Ser.). (Illus.). 32p. (gr. k-3). pap. 2.95 (ISBN 0-317-31312-6). Creative Ed.

--Cheerleading & Baton Twirling. rev. ed. (Illus.). 128p. (gr. 6 up). 1982. pap. 1.75 (ISBN 0-448-15686-5, Pub. by Tempo). Ace Bks.

--Cheese, Vols. 2 & 3. Vol. 2. 16.00 (ISBN 0-444-19952-7). Elsevier.

--Davis Dictionary of the Bible. 24.95 (ISBN 0-8054-1124-0). Broadman.

--Forms for Pleading under the Georgia Civil Practice Act: 1983 Edition. incl. latest supplement 49.95 (ISBN 0-686-90339-0); separate gum-strpped supplement, 1984 8.95; separate supplement, 1984 17.95. Harrison Co GA.

--Handbook on Georgia Practice. incl. latest supplement 47.95 (ISBN 0-686-90359-5); separate supplement, 1983 23.95 (ISBN 0-686-90360-9). Harrison Co GA.

--The Law & Medical Practice. 250p. 1985. 28.00 (ISBN 0-683-12104-9). Williams & Wilkins.

--Real Estate: Closings. (The Law in Georgia Ser.). incl. latest pocket part supplement 24.95 (ISBN 0-686-90562-8); separate pocket part supplement, 1983 10.95 (ISBN 0-686-90563-6). Harrison Co GA.

--Real Estate: Title Examinations. (The Law in Georgia Ser.). incl. latest pocket part supplement 24.95 (ISBN 0-686-90564-4); separate pocket part supplement, 1983 10.95 (ISBN 0-686-90565-2). Harrison Co GA.

--Scientific Foundations of Pediatrics. 2nd ed. (Illus.). 1116p. 1982. text ed. 150.00 (ISBN 0-8391-1747-7). Univ Park.

--Using the Biological Literature. (Books in Library & Information Science: Vol. 35). 272p. 1981. 45.00 (ISBN 0-8247-7209-1). Dekker.

Davis & Cornwell. Introduction to Environmental Engineering. 1985. text ed. write for info. (ISBN 0-534-04137-X, 21R4300, Pub. by PWS Engineering). PWS Pubs.

Davis & McKay. The Relaxation & Stress Reduction Workbook. 2nd ed. (Illus.). 208p. 1982. 22.50 (ISBN 0-934986-08-8); pap. 12.50 (ISBN 0-934986-04-5). New Harbinger.

Davis & Pokhrel, Durga. Planning Non-Formal Education for the Dakas of Nepal. 54p. 1984. 7.00 (ISBN 0-318-04172-3). Am-Nepal Ed.

Davis & Shulman. Georgia Practice & Procedure. 4th ed. incl. latest pocket part supplement 69.00 (ISBN 0-686-90363-3); separate pocket part supplement, 1983 (for use in 1985) 41.95 (ISBN 0-686-90364-1); separate pocket part suppl. 1984 (for use in 1985) 41.95. Harrison Co GA.

Davis, jt. auth. see Cutler.

Davis, jt. auth. see Hall.

Davis, jt. auth. see McCurley.

Davis, jt. auth. see Nelson.

Davis, jt. auth. see Nemoy, Elizabeth M.

Davis, jt. auth. see Pfaltzgraff.

Davis, jt. auth. see Templer.

Davis, jt. auth. see Tillman.

Davis, jt. ed. see Usdin, E.

Davis, tr. see Hennig, Willi.

Davis, jt. auth. see Pfaltzgraff.

Davis, et al, eds. Contemporary Issues in Biomedical Ethics. LC 78-71406. (Contemporary Issues in Biomedicine, Ethics, & Society Ser.). 300p. 1979. 29.50 (ISBN 0-89603-002-4). Humana.

Davis, A. Drug Treatment in Intestinal Helminthiasis. (Also avail. in French). 1973. 6.40 (ISBN 92-4-156036-3). World Health.

--Microwave Semiconductor Circuit Design. 1984. 47.50 (ISBN 0-442-27211-1). Van Nos Reinhold.

Davis, A. & Sims, D. Weathering of Polymers. (Illus.). 300p. 1983. 64.75 (ISBN 0-85334-226-1, I-266-83, Pub. by Elsevier Applied Sci England). Elsevier.

Davis, A., tr. see Graeff, H. & Kuhn, W.

Davis, A. C., jt. ed. see Scott, P. H.

Davis, A. C., III, jt. auth. see Shvyrkov, V.

Davis, A. Douglas. Classical Mechanics. Date not set. text ed. price not set (ISBN 0-12-206340-6). Acad Pr.

Davis, A. E. & Bolin, T. D. Symptom Analysis & Physical Diagnosis in Medicine. 1977. pap. text ed. 13.50 (ISBN 0-08-021244-1). Pergamon.

Davis, A. Jann. Please See My Need. (Illus.). 1981. pap. 5.95x (ISBN 0-9609184-0-X). Satellite Cont.

Davis, A. M. The Origin of the National Banking System. Bruchey, Stuart, ed. LC 80-1142. (The Rise of the Commercial Banking Ser.). 1981. Repr. of 1910 ed. lib. bdg. 24.00x (ISBN 0-405-13644-7). Ayer Co Pubs.

Davis, A. R. T'ao Yuan-ming: His Works & Their Meaning, 2 Vols. LC 82-22092. (Cambridge Studies in Chinese History, Literature & Institutions). 320p. 1984. Set. 125.00 (ISBN 0-521-25347-0). Cambridge U Pr.

Davis, A. R., ed. Modern Japanese Poetry. Kirkup, James, tr. from Japanese. (Asian & Pacific Writing Ser.). 1979. pap. 14.95x (ISBN 0-7022-1148-6). U of Queensland Pr.

Davis, A. R., jt. ed. see Kennedy, Eberhard C.

Davis, Abraham L., ed. The U. S. Supreme Court & the Uses of Social Science Data. LC 73-8983. 150p. 1975. pap. text ed. 5.95x (ISBN 0-8422-0338-9). Irvington.

Davis, Adelle. Eat Right to Keep Fit. 3.95x. Cancer Control Soc.

--Let's Cook It Right. 640p. 1970. pap. 4.50 (ISBN 0-451-12583-5, Sig). NAL.

--Let's Cook It Right. 1970. 6.95x (ISBN 0-15-150166-1); pap. 1.75x (ISBN 0-686-36360-4). Cancer Control Soc.

--Let's Eat Right to Keep Fit. 1970. pap. 3.95x (ISBN 0-451-07951-5). Cancer Control Soc.

--Let's Eat Right to Keep Fit. rev. ed. LC 75-134581. 1970. 8.95 (ISBN 0-15-150304-4). HarBraceJ.

--Let's Eat Right to Keep Fit. 1970. pap. 3.95 (ISBN 0-451-12736-6, AE2736, Sig). NAL.

--Let's Get Well. pap. 3.95x (ISBN 0-451-09147-7). Cancer Control Soc.

--Let's Get Well. LC 65-19054. 1972. pap. 3.50 (ISBN 0-451-09852-8). NAL.

--Let's Get Well. LC 65-19054. 1965. 16.95 (ISBN 0-15-150372-9). HarBraceJ.

--Let's Get Well. pap. 3.95 (ISBN 0-451-12726-9, AE2726, Sig). NAL.

--Let's Have Healthy Children. pap. 3.95x (ISBN 0-451-11128-1). Cancer Control Soc.

--Let's Have Healthy Children. rev. ed. Mendel, Marshall, rev. by. 1981. pap. 3.95 (ISBN 0-451-11024-2, AE1024, Sig). NAL.

--Let's Stay Healthy. 408p. 1983. pap. 4.95 (ISBN 0-451-11998-3, AE1998, Sig). NAL.

--You Can Get Well. 1975. pap. 2.95 (ISBN 0-87904-033-5). Lust.

Davis, Alan. Children in Clinics: A Sociological Analysis of Medical Work with Children. 300p. 1982. 27.00x (ISBN 0-422-77370-0, NO. 3715, Pub. by Tavistock). Methuen Inc.

--What Your Dreams Mean. 1969. pap. 3.50 (ISBN 0-553-24843-X). Bantam.

Davis, Alan, ed. Maps: The Eighties. 100p. cancelled (ISBN 0-943216-02-8). MoonsQuilt Pr.

Davis, Albert R. The Anatomy of Biomagnetism. 1982. 7.95 (ISBN 0-533-05046-4). Vantage.

Davis, Albert R. & Rawls, Walter C., Jr. The Magnetic Blueprint of Life. 1979. 10.95 (ISBN 0-682-49215-9). Exposition Pr FL.

--The Magnetic Effect. 1975. 8.50 (ISBN 0-682-48312-5). Exposition Pr FL.

--Magnetism & Its Effects on the Living System. LC 74-84423. (Illus.). 1974. 9.50 (ISBN 0-682-48087-8, University). Exposition Pr FL.

--The Rainbow in Your Hands. 1976. 6.95 (ISBN 0-682-48543-8). Exposition Pr FL.

Davis, Albert R., jt. auth. see Rawls, Walter, Jr.

Davis, Alexander. The Native Problem in South Africa. Bd. with Review of the Problem in West & West-Central Africa. Stewart, W. R. LC 76-78368. x, 242p. Repr. of 1903 ed. 19.75x (ISBN 0-8371-1340-7, DAN&). Greenwood.

Davis, Alexander J. Rural Residences. (Architecture & Decorative Art Ser.). 1980. Repr. of 1838 ed. 95.00 (ISBN 0-306-71165-6). Da Capo.

Davis, Alexandra & Davis, O. B. Exercises in Reading & Writing. LC 82-17719. (gr. 8-12). 1982. pap. 5.75x (ISBN 0-86709-031-6). Boynton Cook Pubs.

Davis, Alice V. Timothy Turtle. LC 40-32634. (Illus.). (gr. 1-4). 1972. pap. 3.95 (ISBN 0-15-690450-0, VoyB). HarBraceJ.

Davis, Allan F., ed. For Better or Worse: The American Influence in the World. LC 80-1048. (Contributions in American Studies: No. 51). (Illus.). xiv, 195p. 1981. lib. bdg. 29.95 (ISBN 0-313-22342-4, DBO/). Greenwood.

Davis, Allen. Jane Addams on Peace & Freedom, 1914-1935. LC 71-147761. (Library of War & Peace: Documentary Anthologies). 1976. lib. bdg. 46.00 (ISBN 0-8240-0501-5). Garland Pub.

Davis, Allen F. American Heroine: The Life & Legend of Jane Addams. LC 73-82664. (Illus.). 1973. pap. 9.95 (ISBN 0-19-501897-4, GB427, GB). Oxford U Pr.

--American Heroine: The Life & Legend of Jane Addams. 1983. 14.50 (ISBN 0-8446-6016-7). Peter Smith.

--Spearheads for Reform: The Social Settlements & the Progressive Movement, 1890 to 1914. 340p. 1985. 25.00 (ISBN 0-8135-1072-4); pap. 10.00 (ISBN 0-8135-1073-2). Rutgers U Pr.

Davis, Allen F. & Woodman, Harold D. Conflict & Consensus in Early American History. 5th ed. 1980. pap. text ed. 11.95 (ISBN 0-669-02489-9). Heath.

--Conflict & Consensus in Modern American History. 5th ed. 1980. pap. text ed. 11.95 (ISBN 0-669-02490-2). Heath.

Davis, Allen F., jt. auth. see Watts, J. F.

Davis, Allen F. & Haller, Mark H., eds. The Peoples of Philadelphia: A History of Ethnic Groups & Lower Class Life, 1790-1940. LC 72-95879. 311p. 1973. 27.95 (ISBN 0-87722-053-0); pap. 8.95 (ISBN 0-87722-035-2). Temple U Pr.

Davis, Allen F., ed. see Bremer, William W.

Davis, Allen F., ed. see Terrie, Philip G.

Davis, Allison. Leadership, Love & Aggression. LC 82-21342. 256p. 1983. 15.95 (ISBN 0-15-149348-0). HarBraceJ.

--Psychology of the Child in the Middle Class. LC 60-15158. (Horace Mann Lecture, 1960 Ser.). pap. 15.20 (ISBN 0-317-08019-9, 2017875). Bks Demand UMI.

Davis, Almer J. The Manchilde: An Imaginary Tale. Seller, Howard J., ed. LC 80-81274. 312p. 1981. 10.95 (ISBN 0-936800-00-3). Ironwood Calif.

Davis, Almond H. The Female Preacher: Memoir of Salome Lincoln, Afterwards the Wife of Elder Junia S. Mowry. LC 72-2599. (American Women Ser.: Images & Realities). (Illus.). 168p. 1972. Repr. of 1843 ed. 13.50 (ISBN 0-405-04489-5). Ayer Co Pubs.

Davis, Alva L. & McDavid, Raven I., Jr., eds. A Compilation of the Work Sheets of the Linguistic Atlas of the United States & Canada & Associated Projects. 2nd ed. LC 78-100481. (Midway Reprint Ser). 106p. 1974. pap. 5.75x (ISBN 0-226-13806-2). U of Chicago Pr.

Davis, Andrew M. Currency & Banking in the Province of the Massachusetts-Bay, 2 Vols. LC 68-55700. (Illus.). Repr. of 1900 ed. Set. 57.50x (ISBN 0-678-00637-7). Kelley.

--Journey of Moncacht-Ape. 1968. Repr. of 1883 ed. 5.50 (ISBN 0-87770-009-5). Ye Galleon.

Davis, Andrew M., ed. Colonial Currency Reprints Sixteen Niney-Two To Seventeen Fifty-One, 4 vols. (Prince Society Ser.: Nos. 32-35). Repr. of 1910 ed. 81.00 (ISBN 0-8337-0789-2). B Franklin.

--Colonial Currency Reprints 1682-1751, 4 Vols. LC 64-14707. Repr. of 1910 ed. 150.00x (ISBN 0-678-00041-7). Kelley.

Davis, Angela. If They Come in the Morning: Voices of Resistance. (Illus.). 256p. 1971. 9.95 (ISBN 0-89388-022-1). Okpaku Communications.

Davis, Angela Y. Women, Race & Class. 1981. 15.95 (ISBN 0-394-51039-9). Random.

--Women, Race & Class. LC 82-40414. 288p. 1983. pap. 5.95 (ISBN 0-394-71351-6, Vin). Random.

Davis, Ann, jt. ed. see Brook, Eve.

Davis, Ann E., et al. Schizophrenics in the New Custodial Community: Five Years after the Experiment. LC 74-11383. 242p. 1974. 12.00 (ISBN 0-8142-0215-2). Ohio St U Pr.

Davis, Ann S., ed. Guide to Reprints. LC 66-29279. 1025p. 1984. 85.00 (ISBN 0-918086-09-4). Guide to Reprints.

--Guide to Reprints: 1981 Edition, 2 vols. rev ed. LC 66-29279. 974p. 1981. 75.00 (ISBN 0-918086-07-8). Guide to Reprints.

--Guide to Reprints: 1983 Edition. 87.50 (ISBN 0-918086-09-4). Guide to Reprints.

--Guide to Reprints, 1985. LC 66-29279. 1985. 95.00 (ISBN 0-918086-11-6). Guide to Reprints.

Davis, Anne B., jt. auth. see Kalkman, Markian E.

Davis, Anne J. & Aroskar, Mila A. Ethical Dilemmas in Nursing Practice. 2nd ed. (Illus.). 352p. 1983. pap. 16.95 (ISBN 0-8385-2274-2). ACC.

Davis, Anne J. & Krueger, Janelle C., eds. Patients, Nurses, Ethics. LC 80-57573. 245p. 1980. pap. text ed. 9.95 (ISBN 0-937126-84-5). Am Journal Nurse.

Davis, Anne M. None to Comfort Me. LC 78-21963. 1978. 3.98 (ISBN 0-89587-005-3). Blair.

Davis, Anthony. Working in Journalism. 1982. 26.00x (ISBN 0-7134-3324-8, Pub. by Careers Con England). State Mutual Bk.

Davis, Anthony J., jt. auth. see Klinger, Donald E.

Davis, Anthony J., jt. auth. see Klingner, Donald E.

Davis, Archie K. Boy Colonel of the Confederacy: The Life & Times of Henry King Burgwyn, Jr. (Illus.). 580p. 1985. 29.95. U of NC Pr.

Davis, Arnold R. & Miller, Donald C. Science Games. 1974. pap. 3.95 (ISBN 0-8224-6303-2). Pitman Learning.

Davis, Arthur & Parker, Ben. Brutes & Savages. LC 78-55557. (Illus.). 1978. pap. 1.00 (ISBN 0-912760-73-7). Valkyrie Pub Hse.

Davis, Arthur K. Folk-Songs of Virginia. LC 79-163676. Repr. of 1949 ed. 26.50 (ISBN 0-404-01987-0). AMS Pr.

--Matthew Arnold's Letters: A Descriptive Checklist. LC 68-14092. pap. 90.90 (ISBN 0-317-10551-5, 2011424). Bks Demand UMI.

--Thorstein Veblen's Social Theory. Zuckerman, Harriet & Merton, Robert K., eds. LC 79-8989. (Dissertations on Sociology). 1980. lib. bdg. 42.00x (ISBN 0-405-12961-0). Ayer Co Pubs.

Davis, Arthur K., Jr. Traditional Ballads of Virginia. LC 78-79458. (Illus.). 634p. 1969. Repr. of 1929 ed. 13.95 (ISBN 0-8139-0269-X). U Pr of Va.

Davis, Arthur P. From the Dark Tower: Afro-American Writers, 1900 to 1960. LC 73-88969. 306p. 1974. 14.95 (ISBN 0-88258-004-3). Howard U Pr.

--From the Dark Tower: Afro-American Writers, 1900 to 1960. LC 73-88969. 1981. pap. 7.95 (ISBN 0-88258-058-2). Howard U Pr.

Davis, Audrey B. Circulation Physiology & Medical Chemistry in England, 1650-1680. (Illus.). 263p. 1973. 10.00x (ISBN 0-87291-059-8). Coronado Pr.

--Medicine & Its Technology: An Introduction to the History of Medical Instruments. LC 80-25202. (Contributions in Medical History Ser.: No. 7). (Illus.). 224p. 1981. lib. bdg. 45.00 (ISBN 0-313-22807-8, DMT/). Greenwood.

Davis, Audrey B. & Merzbach, Uta C. Early Auditory Studies: Activities in the Psychology Laboratories of American Universities. LC 75-619025. (Smithsonian Studies in History & Technology: No. 31). (Illus.). pap. 20.00 (ISBN 0-317-08276-0, 2004230). Bks Demand UMI.

Davis, B. Database in Perspective. 110p. 1980. pap. 26.25 (ISBN 0-471-89442-7). Wiley.

--The Selection of Database Software. LC 77-365114. (Illus.). 1977. 180.00x (ISBN 0-85012-173-6). Intl Pubns Serv.

--The Traditional English Pub. (Illus.). 192p. (Orig.). 1981. text ed. 26.25x (ISBN 0-85139-055-2, Pub. by Architectural Pr England). Humanities.

Davis, B., ed. see Yahya, Saad.

Davis, B. N. K. Insects on Nettles. (Cambridge Naturalists' Handbks.: No. 1). (Illus.). 68p. 1983. 16.95 (ISBN 0-521-23904-4). Cambridge U Pr.

Davis, B. P. The Economics of Automatic Testing: Electronics Components & Sub-Assemblies. 320p. 1982. 49.50 (ISBN 0-07-084584-0). McGraw.

Davis, Barbara. Edward S. Curtis: The Life & Times of a Shadowcatcher. (Illus.). 256p. 1985. 40.00 (ISBN 0-87701-346-2). Chronicle Bks.

Davis, Barbara, jt. auth. see Stuart, Richard B.

Davis, Barbara, ed. The Cruising World Best of People & Food Cookbook. LC 83-9523. (Illus.). 384p. 1983. 22.50 (ISBN 0-915160-56-0). Seven Seas.

Davis, Barbara, et al. The Evaluation of Composition Instruction. LC 80-68774. 230p. (Orig.). 1981. pap. 7.50x (ISBN 0-918528-11-9). Edgepress.

Davis, Barbara G. & Humphreys, Sheila. Evaluating Intervention Programs: Applications from Women's Programs in Math & Science. 256p. 1985. pap. text ed. 15.95x (ISBN 0-8077-2787-3). Tchrs Coll.

Davis, Barbara N. The Journey & Elders of the Tribe. (Orig.). 1984. pap. 6.00 (ISBN 0-9613450-0-4). Dovebks.

Davis, Barry. Understanding DC Power Supplies. (Illus.). 240p. 1983. 22.95 (ISBN 0-13-936831-0); pap. 12.95 (ISBN 0-13-936823-X). P-H.

Davis, Bart. Blind Prophet. LC 82-45241. 336p. 1983. 15.95 (ISBN 0-385-17980-4). Doubleday.

--Blind Prophet. 352p. 1985. pap. 3.50 (ISBN 0-553-24871-5). Bantam.

--A Conspiracy of Eagles. 400p. (Orig.). 1984. pap. 3.95 (ISBN 0-553-25142-2). Bantam.

Davis, Ben. Rapid Healing Foods. LC 79-22770. 1980. 18.95 (ISBN 0-13-753137-0, Parker). P-H.

--Rapid Healing Foods. 1982. pap. 4.95 (ISBN 0-13-753038-2, Reward). P-H.

--The Traditional English Pub: A Way of Drinking. (Illus.). 170p. 1981. 32.50x (ISBN 0-85139-055-2). Nichols Pub.

Davis, Benjamin F. Study of Shorthand Teaching: Comparison & Outcomes in the Learning of Effected by Differences in Teaching Methodology. LC 78-176716. (Columbia University. Teachers College. Contributions to Education: No. 693). Repr. of 1936 ed. 22.50 (ISBN 0-404-55693-0). AMS Pr.

Davis, Bernard. Food Commodities-Catering, Processing, Storing. 1978. pap. 16.50 (ISBN 0-434-90297-7, Pub. by W Heinemann Ltd). David & Charles.

Davis, Bernard & Davis, Elizabeth, eds. Poets of the Early Seventeenth Century. (Boutledge English Texts). 1967. pap. 5.95x (ISBN 0-7100-4512-3). Routledge & Kegan.

Davis, Bernard B. & Wood, W. Gibson, eds. Homeostatic Function & Aging. (Aging Ser.: Vol. 30). 1985. text ed. write for info. (ISBN 0-88167-139-8). Raven.

Davis, Bernard D. Microbiology. 3rd ed. (Illus.). 1274p. 1980. 49.00 (ISBN 0-06-140691-0, 14-06917, Harper Medical). Lippincott.

Davis, Bernard D. & Flaherty, Patricia, eds. Human Diversity: Its Causes & Social Significance. LC 76-7002. (American Academy of Arts and Sciences Ser.). 192p. 1976. prof ref 16.50x (ISBN 0-88410-047-2). Ballinger Pub.

Davis, Bertam H. A Proof of Eminence: The Life of Sir John Hawkins. LC 72-75389. pap. 116.50 (ISBN 0-317-09251-0, 2015814). Bks Demand UMI.

Davis, Bertha. How to Take a Test. (First Bks.). (Illus.). 72p. 1984. lib. bdg. 8.90 (ISBN 0-531-04824-1). Watts.

--How to Write a Composition. (First Bk.). (Illus.). 72p. (gr. 4-6). 1985. PLB 9.40 (ISBN 0-531-10042-1). Watts.

Davis, Bertha & Arnof, Dorothy. How to Fix What's Wrong with Our Schools: A Toolkit for Concerned Parents. LC 83-5102. 216p. 1983. 14.95 (ISBN 0-89919-193-2); pap. 6.95 (ISBN 0-89919-216-5). Ticknor & Fields.

Davis, Bertha & Whitfield, Susan. The Coal Question. LC 82-4716. (Impact Ser.). (Illus.). 96p. (gr. 7 up). 1982. PLB 9.90 (ISBN 0-531-04484-X). Watts.

Davis, Bertha, et al. The Postcards of Bucks County As Printed by the Arnold Bros. (Illus.). 80p. pap. 4.95 (ISBN 0-9610608-0-8). Wash Cross Card.

Davis, Bertram H. Johnson Before Boswell. LC 72-12309. 222p. 1973. Repr. of 1960 ed. lib. bdg. 24.75x (ISBN 0-8371-6691-8, DAJA). Greenwood.

--Thomas Percy. (English Authors Ser.). 13.50 (ISBN 0-8057-6804-1, Twayne). G K Hall.

Davis, Beth, jt. auth. see Lass, Bonnie.

Davis, Bette. What These Eyes Have Seen: Reminscences by... (Illus.). 256p. 1986. 16.95 (ISBN 0-525-24365-8). Dutton.

Davis, Bette, jt. auth. see Stine, Whitney.

Davis, Betty J. The Storytellers in Marguerite de Navarre's Heptameron. LC 77-93406. (French Forum Monographs: No. 9). 203p. (Orig.). 1978. pap. 9.50x (ISBN 0-917058-08-9). French Forum.

Davis, Beverly J. Chant of the Centuries. Rev. ed. (Illus.). 240p. 1984. text ed. 32.00 (ISBN 0-87443-064-X); tchr's manual 4.00 (ISBN 0-87443-065-8). Benson.

Davis, Bill & Tree, C. The Kennedy Library. (Illus.). 128p. 1980. pap. 9.95 (ISBN 0-916838-36-6). Schiffer.

Davis, Bill, jt. auth. see Davis, Deborah.

Davis, Bill C. Mass Appeal. 80p. 1981. pap. 2.50 (ISBN 0-380-77396-1, 77396-1, Bard). Avon.

Davis, Billie. Teaching to Meet Crisis Needs. LC 83-82815. 128p. (Orig.). 1984. pap. text ed. 2.95 (ISBN 0-88243-609-0, 02-0609). Gospel Pub.

Davis, Bob. Cock-A-Doodle-Dew. (Orig.). 1973. pap. 1.25 (ISBN 0-532-12165-1, 532-12165-125). Woodhill.

Davis, Bob, photos by. Faces of Japan. LC 78-55092. (Illus.). 108p. 1978. 15.50 (ISBN 0-87011-338-0). Kodansha.

Davis, Bob J. & American Trucking Assn. Annotated Bibliography of the Motor Carrier Industry. 77p. 1976. pap. text ed. 4.00 (ISBN 0-88711-053-3). Am Trucking Assns.

Davis, Bob J., ed. Information Sources in Transportation, Material Management, & Physical Distribution: An Annotated Bibliography & Guide. LC 75-23864. (Orig.). 1976. lib. bdg. 65.00 (ISBN 0-8371-8379-0, DBT/). Greenwood.

Davis, Bowman O., et al. Conceptual Human Physiology. 640p. 1985. text ed. 34.95 (ISBN 0-675-20252-3); study guide 9.95 (ISBN 0-675-20420-8); additional supplements avail. Merrill.

Davis, Boyd H. & O'Cain, Raymond, eds. First Person Singular: Papers from the Conference on an Oral Archive for the History of American Linguistics (Charlotte NC, March 9-10, 1979) (Studies in the History of Linguistics). 239p. 1980. 33.00x (ISBN 90-272-4502-9). Benjamins North Am.

Davis, Brian, ed. see National Computing Centre.

Davis, Brian L. Badges & Insignia of the Third Reich, 1933-1945. (Illus.). 160p. 1983. 17.95 (ISBN 0-7137-1130-2, Pub. by Blandford Pr England). Sterling.

--British Army Cloth Insignia: Nineteen Forty to the Present. (Illus.). 68p. 1985. 9.95 (ISBN 0-85368-709-9, Pub. by Arms & Armour). Sterling.

--British Army Uniforms & Insignia of WW II. (Illus.). 276p. 1984. 19.95 (ISBN 0-85368-609-2, Pub. by Arms & Armour Pr). Sterling.

--German Combat Uniforms of World War Two, Vol. 1. (Uniforms Illustrated Ser.: Vol. 5). (Illus.). 1984. pap. 7.95 (ISBN 0-85368-667-X, Arms & Armour Pr). Sterling.

Davis, Britton. The Truth about Geronimo. Quaife, M. M., ed. LC 75-37958. (Illus.). xxx, 263p. 1976. pap. 5.25 (ISBN 0-8032-5840-2, BB 622, Bison). U of Nebr Pr.

Davis, Bruce. The Drawings of Ciro Ferri. Freedberg, S. J., ed. (Outstanding Dissertations in Fine Arts Ser.). (Illus.). 430p. 1985. Repr. of 1982 ed. 55.00 (ISBN 0-8240-6854-8). Garland Pub.

--In Honor of Ebria Feinblatt: 1947-1985. (Bulletin Ser.: Vol. 28). (Illus.). 64p. (Orig.). 1984. pap. 5.00x (ISBN 0-87587-120-8). LA Co Art Mus.

--The Magical Child Within You. LC 76-55831. (Illus., Orig.). 1977. pap. 5.95 (ISBN 0-89087-422-0). Celestial Arts.

Davis, Bruce & Davis, Genny W. The Heart of the Healing. 280p. 1985. pap. 6.95 (ISBN 0-553-34222-3). Bantam.

Davis, Bruce & Wright, Genny. Hugs & Kisses. LC 77-5283. (Illus.). 96p. 1978. 4.95 (ISBN 0-89480-008-6, 155); pap. 3.50 (ISBN 0-89480-106-6, 307). Workman Pub.

Davis, Bruce, jt. auth. see Davis, Genny W.

Davis, Bruce, jt. auth. see Feinblatt, Ebria.

Davis, Bruce L., compiled by. Criminological Bibliographies: Uniform Citations to Bibliographies, Indexes, & Review Articles of the Literature of Crime Study in the United States. LC 78-59442. 1978. lib. bdg. 35.00 (ISBN 0-313-20545-0, DCR/). Greenwood.

Davis, Bryn D., ed. Research into Nurse Education. 208p. 1983. pap. 17.50 (ISBN 0-7099-0825-3, Pub. by Croom Helm Ltd). Longwood Pub Group.

Davis, Burke. Black Heroes of the American Revolution. LC 75-42218. (Illus.). 96p. (gr. 5 up). 1976. 9.95 (ISBN 0-15-208560-2, HJ). HarBraceJ.

--The Campaign That Won America: The Story of Yorktown. (Illus.). 319p. 1979. pap. 2.50 (Pub. by Eastern Natl Park). Eastern Acorn.

--George Washington & the American Revolution. 1975. 15.00 (ISBN 0-394-46388-9, BYR). Random.

--The Long Surrender. LC 83-42767. 316p. 1985. 19.45 (ISBN 0-394-52083-1). Random.

--Marine! The Life of Lt. Gen. Lewis B. Puller USMC. (Illus.). 1962. 17.45i (ISBN 0-316-17502-1). Little.

--Sherman's March. LC 79-5550. (Illus.). 1980. 17.50 (ISBN 0-394-50739-8). Random.

--The Southern Railway: Road of the Innovators. LC 84-15343. (Illus.). 390p. 1985. 19.95 (ISBN 0-8078-1636-1). U of NC Pr.

--The Summer Land. 224p. 1975. pap. 1.50 (ISBN 0-89176-374-0, 6374). Mockingbird Bks.

--To Appomattox. 444p. Repr. 3.95 (ISBN 0-915992-17-5). Eastern Acorn.

Davis, Burnie. How to Activate Miracles in Your Life & Ministry. 125p. 1982. pap. 3.95 (ISBN 0-89274-230-5, HH-230). Harrison Hse.

Davis, Burt. Chloride Pathways in the Wilsonville Alabama SRC-I Pilot Plant, Processing High Chlorine Coal. 28p. 1983. pap. text ed. 5.00 (ISBN 0-86607-017-6). Inst Mining & Minerals.

Davis, Burtron H. & Hettinger, William P., Jr., eds. Heterogeneous Catalysis: Selected American Histories. LC 83-8745. (ACS Symposium Ser.: No. 222). 536p. lib. bdg. 49.95x (ISBN 0-8412-0778-X). Am Chemical.

Davis, C., et al, eds. The Geometric Vein: The Coxeter Festschrift. (Illus.). 512p. 1981. 54.00 (ISBN 0-387-90587-1). Springer-Verlag.

Davis, C. Dean, jt. auth. see Davis, David M.

Davis, C. G., et al. Entity-Relationship Approach to Software Engineering. 1984. 59.00 (ISBN 0-444-86777-5, I-493-83). Elsevier.

Davis, C. N., et al. The Official Military Atlas of the Civil War: Atlas to Accompany the Official Records of the Union & Confederate Armies. 66.00 (ISBN 0-405-18842-0, 19368). Ayer Co Pubs.

Davis, C. R. Von Kleist: From Hussar to Panzer Marshal. LC 79-90615. (Illus.). 112p. 1979. pap. 9.95 (ISBN 0-935856-00-5). Lancer.

Davis, C. Thomas. Incorporation & Business Guide for Oregon. 2nd ed. 114p. 1984. pap. write for info. Self Counsel Pr.

Davis, Calvin D. United States & the Second Hague Peace Conference: American Diplomacy & International Organization, 1899-1914. LC 75-17353. x, 380p. 1976. 25.00 (ISBN 0-8223-0346-9). Duke.

Davis, Calvin O. Junior High School Education. 1926. 22.50 (ISBN 0-932062-49-0). Sharon Hill.

Davis, Calvin V. & Sorensen, K. E. Handbook of Applied Hydraulics. 3rd ed. (Illus.). 1968. 87.50 (ISBN 0-07-015538-0). McGraw.

Davis, Carl S. & Schmidt, Marlin R., eds. Differential Treatment of Drug & Alcohol Abusers. LC 76-54203. 1977. 9.95 (ISBN 0-88280-048-5). ETC Pubns.

Davis, Carlton G., jt. ed. see Coppedge, Robert O.

Davis, Carol B. Home Is North. LC 74-75634. 68p. 1974. 4.00 (ISBN 0-8233-0200-8). Golden Quill.

Davis, Carolina A., rev. by see Buddhaghosa.

Davis, Carolyn. Making Every Moment Count. (Illus.). 1980. 7.95 (ISBN 0-87707-225-6). CSA Pr.

Davis, Catherine M., jt. auth. see Davis, Emmett A.

Davis, Celia. Far to Go. (Illus.). 1979. 20.00 (ISBN 0-686-26045-7, Pub. by Terence Dalton England). State Mutual Bk.

Davis, Charles. American Sailing Ships: Their Plans & History. Date not set. 14.00 (ISBN 0-8446-6136-8). Peter Smith.

--Theology & Political Society. LC 80-40014. 180p. 1980. 27.95 (ISBN 0-521-22538-8). Cambridge U Pr.

--Twelve Essays. 1973. text ed. 4.50 (ISBN 0-88429-003-4). Collegiate Pub.

--Twelve Essays. 1975. text ed. 5.50 (ISBN 0-685-61974-5). Collegiate Pub.

--Why I Left the Roman Catholic Church. 1976. pap. 3.00 (ISBN 0-911826-11-4). Am Atheist.

Davis, Charles A., ed. Welding & Brazing of Carbon Steels, 2 bks. LC 76-44372. (Metalworking & Manufacturing Processes Ser.). (Illus.). Bk. 1-Arc Welding. pap. 43.00 (ISBN 0-317-09871-3, 2019480); Bk. 2-High-Deposition-Rate & Special-Application Welding. pap. 34.80 (ISBN 0-317-09872-1). Bks Demand UMI.

Davis, Charles A., ed. see American Society for Metals.

Davis, Charles B. Adventures & Letters of Richard Harding Davis. (American Newspapermen 1790-1933 Ser.). (Illus.). iii, 417p. 1974. Repr. of 1917 ed. 18.50x (ISBN 0-8464-0024-3). Beekman Pubs.

--Adventures & Letters of Richard Harding Davis. 1917. 18.00 (ISBN 0-8274-1818-3). R West.

--Borderland of Society. facs. ed. LC 79-140328. (Short Story Index Reprint Ser). 1898. Repr. 15.00 (ISBN 0-8369-3720-1). Ayer Co Pubs.

--Lodger Overhead, & Others. LC 71-121533. (Short Story Index Reprint Ser). (Illus.). 1909. 22.00 (ISBN 0-8369-3489-X). Ayer Co Pubs.

--Richard Harding Davis. (American Newspapermen Coll. Ser.). (Illus.). 1974. Repr. of 1917 ed. 20.00x (ISBN 0-8464-0024-3). Beekman Pubs.

--Stage Door. LC 74-122693. (Short Story Index Reprint Ser). 1908. 18.00 (ISBN 0-8369-3526-8). Ayer Co Pubs.

--Tales of the Town. facsimile ed. LC 78-167447. (Short Story Index Reprint Ser.). Repr. of 1911 ed. 21.50 (ISBN 0-8369-3973-5). Ayer Co Pubs.

Davis, Charles C. Marine & Fresh Water Plankton. (Illus.). 562p. 1955. 18.50x (ISBN 0-87013-016-1). Mich St U Pr.

Davis, Charles G. American Sailing Ships. (Antique Transporation Ser.). 240p. 1984. pap. 5.95 (ISBN 0-486-24658-2). Dover.

--Rigs of the Nine Principal Types of American Sailing Vessels. (Illus.). pap. 0.95 (ISBN 0-87577-028-2). Peabody Mus Salem.

--Shipping & Craft in Silhouette. LC 70-162509. (Tower Bks.). (Illus.). 221p. 1972. Repr. of 1929 ed. 40.00x (ISBN 0-8103-3945-5). Gale.

Davis, Charles H. Early Families of Wallingford, Connecticut. LC 78-71272. 363p. (With new index). 1979. Repr. of 1870 ed. 18.50 (ISBN 0-8063-0834-6). Genealog Pub.

Davis, Charles H. & Lundeen, Gerald W. Illustrative Computer Programming for Libraries: Selected Examples for Information Specialists. 2nd ed. LC 81-1128. (Contributions in Librarianship & Information Science Ser.: No. 39). (Illus.). 120p. 1981. lib. bdg. 17.50 (ISBN 0-313-22151-0, DAD/). Greenwood.

Davis, Charles H. & Rush, James E. Guide to Information Science. LC 78-75240. (Illus.). 1979. lib. bdg. 35.00 (ISBN 0-313-20982-0, DGI/). Greenwood.

--Guide to Information Science. LC 78-75240. xvii, 305p. 1980. pap. text ed. 9.95 (ISBN 0-313-22603-2, DGI:). Greenwood.

--Information Retrieval & Documentation in Chemistry. LC 72-791. (Contributions in Librarianship & Information Science: No. 8). 1974. lib. bdg. 25.00 (ISBN 0-8371-6364-1, DAI/). Greenwood.

Davis, Charles S. The Cotton Kingdom in Alabama. LC 73-16160. (Perspectives in American History Ser.: No. 3). (Illus.). 233p. 1974. Repr. of 1939 ed. lib. bdg. 19.50x (ISBN 0-87991-329-0). Porcupine Pr.

Davis, Charles T.. Black Is the Color of the Cosmos: Essays on Afro-American Literature. (Critical Studies on Black Life & Culture). lib. bdg. 61.00 (ISBN 0-8240-9315-1). Garland Pub.

--Dante's Italy & Other Essays. LC 83-3600. (Middle Ages Ser.). 352p. 1984. 35.00x (ISBN 0-8122-7883-6). U of Pa Pr.

--The Manufacture of Paper. LC 72-5042. (Technology & Society Ser.). (Illus.). 625p. 1972. Repr. of 1886 ed. 34.00 (ISBN 0-405-04694-4). Ayer Co Pubs.

Davis, Charles T., jt. auth. see Fabre, Michel.

Davis, Charles T. & Gates, Henry L., Jr., eds. The Slave's Narrative. (Illus.). 1984. 27.95x (ISBN 0-19-503276-4). Oxford U Pr.

Davis, Charles T., ed. see Goldstraw, Irma E.

Davis, Charlie. All Around Our Town. (Illus.). 1977. lib. bdg. 15.00 (ISBN 0-930000-04-8); pap. 6.95 (ISBN 0-930000-05-6). Mathom.

--That Band from Indiana. (Illus.). 1982. 15.00 (ISBN 0-930000-19-6); pap. 8.95 (ISBN 0-930000-20-X). Mathom.

Davis, Charlie, ed. see Membership of the Society.

Davis, Cheri. W. S. Merwin. (United States Authors Ser.). 1981. lib. bdg. 12.50 (ISBN 0-8057-7301-0, Twayne). G K Hall.

Davis, Christopher. A Peep into the Twentieth Century. 1985. 5.95 (ISBN 0-87795-711-8). Arbor Hse.

--Plains Indians. (Civilization Library Ser.). (Illus.). 32p. (gr. 4up). 1984. lib. bdg. 9.40 (ISBN 0-531-03479-8, Gloucester Pr). Watts.

Davis, Christopher M., jt. ed. see Stern, Robert M.

Davis, Clara. The Move of God: Azusa Street to Now. 80p. (Orig.). 1983. pap. 2.95 (ISBN 0-88144-016-7, CPS-016). Christian Pub.

Davis, Cos H., Jr. Building Bridges. LC 84-17476. 1985. pap. 3.95 (ISBN 0-8054-5659-7). Broadman.

--Children & the Christian Faith. LC 79-50339. 1979. pap. 4.95 (ISBN 0-8054-6221-X). Broadman.

--Ministering to Mobile Families. LC 80-71222. 1982. pap. 3.95 (ISBN 0-8054-3232-9). Broadman.

Davis, Craig, jt. auth. see Clark, Buddy.

Davis, Cullom, et al. Oral History: From Tape to Type. LC 77-4403. 156p. pap. 10.00x (ISBN 0-8389-0230-8). ALA.

Davis, Cullom, et al, eds. The Public & the Private Lincoln: Contemporary Perspectives. LC 79-9803. 192p. 1979. 18.95x (ISBN 0-8093-0921-1). S Ill U Pr.

Davis, Curtis C. Chronicler of the Cavaliers: A Biography of the Virginia Novelist, Dr. William A. Caruthers. 1953. 5.00 (ISBN 0-685-78316-2). Dietz.

--That Ambitious Mr Legare: The Life & Times of James M. Legare of South Carolina, Including a Collected Edition of His Verse. LC 76-86191. xx, 338p. 1971. 17.95x (ISBN 0-87249-166-8). U of SC Pr.

Davis, Cushman K. Law in Shakespeare. 2nd ed. LC 72-163677. Repr. of 1884 ed. 20.00 (ISBN 0-404-01988-9). AMS Pr.

--A Treatise on International Law Including American Diplomacy. xiii, 368p. 1982. Repr. of 1901 ed. lib. bdg. 30.00x (ISBN 0-8377-0441-3). Rothman.

Davis, D., jt. auth. see Stevens, R.

Davis, D. D., tr. see Pinel, Philippe.

Davis, D. Jack, ed. Behavioral Emphasis in Art Education. 202p. 1975. 12.50 (ISBN 0-937652-10-5). Natl Art Ed.

Davis, D. R. Food Container Corrosion. 350p. 1985. write for info. (ISBN 0-913655-35-X, Pub. By Ellis Horwood Ltd UK). VCH Pubs.

Davis, D. W. Elizabethans Errant. LC 67-16462. 1967. 9.50 (ISBN 0-8014-0098-8). Brown Bk.

Davis, D. Webster, jt. auth. see Jackson, Giles B.

Davis, Dale. How to Quickly & Accurately Master ECG-Interpretation. (Illus.). 350p. 1985. pap. text ed. 19.75 (ISBN 0-397-50665-1, Lippincott Medical). Lippincott.

Davis, Dales, jt. auth. see Thiessen, Frank.

Davis, Daniel S. Behind Barbed Wire: The Imprisonment of Japanese Americans During World War II. (Illus.). 224p. (gr. 7 up). 1982. 12.95 (ISBN 0-525-26320-9, 01258-370). Dutton.

Davis, Danny. Commodore 64 Machine Language for the Absolute Beginner. (Illus.). 194p. (Orig.). 1984. 14.95 (ISBN 0-86161-145-4). Melbourne Hse.

Davis, Daphne. Stars! LC 83-590. (Illus.). 280p. 1983. 29.95 (ISBN 0-941434-34-6). Stewart Tabori & Chang.

--Stars. 280p. 1984. pap. 14.95 (ISBN 0-671-53083-6, Fireside). S&S.

Davis, Dave D., ed. Perspectives on Gulf Coast Prehistory. LC 84-3686. (Ripley P. Bullen Monographs in Anthropology & History: No. 5). (Illus.). 1984. 24.50 (ISBN 0-8130-0756-9). U Presses Fla.

Davis, David. African Workers & Apartheid. 44p. 1978. pap. 1.35 (ISBN 0-904759-19-9). Intl Defense & Aid.

Davis, David B. Antebellum American Culture: An Interpretive Anthology. 1979. pap. text ed. 12.95 (ISBN 0-669-01476-1). Heath.

--Homicide in American Fiction, 1798-1860: A Study in Social Values. 364p. 1968. pap. 6.95x (ISBN 0-8014-9066-9, CP66). Cornell U Pr.

--The Problem of Slavery in the Age of Revolution, 1770-1823. LC 74-9214. 576p. 1975. 34.50x (ISBN 0-8014-0888-1); pap. 9.95x (ISBN 0-8014-9156-8). Cornell U Pr.

--The Slave Power Conspiracy & the Paranoid Style. LC 79-96257. (The Walter Lynwood Fleming Lectures in Southern History). 97p. 1982. text ed. 12.95x (ISBN 0-8071-0922-3); pap. text ed. 4.95x (ISBN 0-8071-1034-5). La State U Pr.

--The Slave Power Conspiracy & the Paranoid Style. LC 79-96257. pap. 20.80 (ISBN 0-317-28748-6, 2051639). Bks Demand UMI.

--Slavery & Human Progress. 1984. 25.00 (ISBN 0-19-503439-2). Oxford U Pr.

Davis, David B., ed. The Fear of Conspiracy: Images of Un-American Subversion from the Revolution to the Present. LC 70-12775. 396p. 1972. pap. 11.95x (ISBN 0-8014-9113-4, CP113). Cornell U Pr.

Davis, David C., et al, eds. Service Parts Management Reprints. LC 82-72118. 123p. 1982. pap. 10.50 (ISBN 0-935406-19-0). Am Prod & Inventory.

Davis, David E. Behavior as an Ecological Factor. LC 79-3006. (Benchmark Papers in Ecology Ser.: Vol. 2). 390p. 1974. 51.95 (ISBN 0-87933-132-1). Van Nos Reinhold.

Davis, David E., ed. CRC Handbook of Census Methods for Terrestrial Vertebrates. 424p. 1982. 125.00 (ISBN 0-8493-2970-1). CRC Pr.

Davis, David H. Energy Politics. 3rd ed. LC 81-51846. 323p. 1982. 16.95 (ISBN 0-312-25204-8); pap. text ed. 11.95 (ISBN 0-312-25205-6). St Martin.

Davis, David M. & Davis, C. Dean. Texas Health Law Reporter, Vol. 1, No. 1. 16p. 1984. looseleaf with binder 60.00 (ISBN 0-409-25043-0). Butterworth TX.

Davis, Dean, jt. auth. see Martin, Vaughn.

Davis, Dean, ed. see Sherman, Robert G.

Davis, Deane C. Justice in the Mountains: Stories & Tales by a Vermont Country Lawyer. LC 80-82866. (Illus.). 192p. 1980. 9.95 (ISBN 0-933050-05-4); pap. 6.95 (ISBN 0-933050-06-2). New Eng Pr VT.

--Nothin' But the Truth: More Yankee Yarns. LC 82-80343. (Illus.). 224p. 1982. 10.95 (ISBN 0-933050-10-0); pap. 6.95 (ISBN 0-933050-14-3). New Eng Pr VT.

Davis, Deborah & Davis, Bill. The Children of God: The Inside Story. LC 83-26025. 240p. (Orig.). 1984. 9.95 (ISBN 0-310-27840-6). Zondervan.

Davis, Deering, et al. Alexandria Houses: 1750-1830. (Illus.). 128p. 1982. 7.98 (ISBN 0-517-01730-X, Am Legacy Pr). Crown.

--Georgetown Houses of the Federal Period: 1780-1830. (Illus.). 128p. 1982. 7.98 (ISBN 0-517-01732-6). Crown.

Davis, Delbert D. The Giant Panda: A Morphological Study of Evolutionary Mechanisms. LC 64-8995. (Chicago Natural History Museum, Fieldiana; Zoology Memoirs Ser.: Vol. 3). pap. 84.80 (ISBN 0-317-29989-1, 2051831). Bks Demand UMI.

Davis, Dennis, jt. auth. see Kraus, Sidney.

Davis, Dennis K. & Baran, Stanley J. Mass Communication & Everyday Life: A Perspective on Theory & Effects. 240p. 1980. pap. text ed. write for info. (ISBN 0-534-00883-6). Wadsworth Pub.

Davis, Dennis M. & Clapp, Steve. The Third Wave & the Local Church. 175p. (Orig.). 1983. pap. 8.00 (ISBN 0-914527-54-1). C-Four Res.

Davis, Denny C., jt. auth. see Hall, Carl W.

Davis, Derek R. An Introduction to Psychopathology. 4th ed. (Illus.). 1984. pap. write for info. (ISBN 0-19-261488-6). Oxford U Pr.

Davis, Desmond. Theatre for Young People. LC 81-4388. 221p. 1981. 15.95 (ISBN 0-8253-0075-4). Beaufort Bks NY.

Davis, Devra, jt. ed. see Ng, Lorenz K.

Davis, Diane. Something Is Wrong at My House. LC 84-62129. (Illus.). 40p. (Orig.). (gr. 1-6). 1985. PLB 8.95 (ISBN 0-943990-11-4); pap. 3.00 (ISBN 0-943990-10-6). Parenting Pr.

Davis, Dick. Hold'em Poker Bible. LC 83-72831. 256p. 1983. 14.95 (ISBN 0-89227-104-3). Commonwealth Pr.

--In the Distance. 1975. pap. 4.95 (ISBN 0-685-78871-7, Pub. by Anvil Pr). Small Pr Dist.

--What the Mind Wants. 20p. 1984. pap. 4.00 (ISBN 0-941150-22-4). Barth.

--Wisdom & Wilderness: The Achievement of Yvor Winters. LC 82-4809. 256p. 1983. 22.50x (ISBN 0-8203-0631-2). U of Ga Pr.

Davis, Dick, jt. auth. see Reynolds, Angus.

Davis, Dick, ed. Thomas Traherne: Selected Writings. (The Fyfield Ser.). 94p. pap. 7.50 (ISBN 0-85635-231-4). Carcanet.

Davis, Dick, tr. see Farid ud-Din Attar.

Davis, Dick, tr. see Ginzburg, Natalia.

Davis, Dineh M. Wordperfect for the IBM PC. 1985. 17.95 (ISBN 0-03-071867-8). CBS Ed.

Davis, Don, jt. auth. see Badmaieff, Alexis.

Davis, Don D. Induced Task Competence & Effects on Problem Solving Behavior. (Illus.). 52p. (Orig.). 1980. pap. text ed. 3.00 (ISBN 0-907152-00-7). Prytaneum Pr.

--The Unique Animal. (Illus.). 336p. 1981. 25.00 (ISBN 0-907152-02-3); pap. 12.95 (ISBN 0-907152-01-5). Prytaneum Pr.

Davis, Donald. The Late Augustans. (The Poetry Bookshelf). 1958. pap. text ed. 5.00x (ISBN 0-435-15019-7). Heinemann Ed.

Davis, Donald D. I Had a Wonderful Time. (Illus.). 160p. Date not set. 16.95 (ISBN 0-89016-088-0); pap. 8.95 (ISBN 0-89016-087-2). Lightning Tree.

Davis, Donald G., Jr., jt. auth. see Harris, Michael H.

Davis, Donald G., Jr., ed. Libraries & Culture: Proceedings of Library History Seminar VI. (Illus.). 475p. 1981. text ed. 25.00x (ISBN 0-292-74632-6). U of Tex Pr.

Davis, Dorothy. History of Harrison County, West Virginia. Sloan, Elizabeth, ed. (Illus.). 1970. Repr. of 1972 ed. buckram 22.50 (ISBN 0-87012-088-3). McClain.

--John George Jackson. 1976. 18.50 (ISBN 0-87012-241-X). McClain.

Davis, Dorothy C. Reading Through the Newspaper. 1980. 4.95 (ISBN 0-88252-108-X). Paladin Hse.

Davis, Dorothy M. & McGeary, Bernice K. Cooking for Two. 91p. 1980. pap. 5.50 (ISBN 0-318-11770-3). Gov Printing Office.

Davis, Dorothy S. Lullaby of Murder. 224p. 1984. 12.95 (ISBN 0-684-18086-3, ScribT). Scribner.

--Scarlet Night. 208p. 1981. pap. 2.25 (ISBN 0-380-55129-2, 55129). Avon.

--Scarlet Night. 1980. 9.95 (ISBN 0-684-16492-2). Scribner.

--Tales for a Stormy Night: The Collected Crime Stories. 224p. 1984. 13.95 (ISBN 0-88150-030-5, Foul Play). Countryman.

Davis, Douglas. Artculture: Essays on the Post-Modern. LC 76-27504. (Icon Editions). (Illus.). 1978. (HarpT); pap. 5.95i (ISBN 0-06-430080-3, IN-80, HarpT). Har-Row.

--There's an Elephant in the Garage. LC 79-11378. (Illus.). (ps-5). 1979. 7.95 (ISBN 0-525-41050-3). Dutton.

Davis, Douglas, intro. by. Photography as Fine Art: The Gallery of World Photography, Vol. I. (Illus.). 224p. 1983. 42.50 (ISBN 0-525-24184-1, 04126-1240). Dutton.

Davis, Duane. Bang-Up Futures. 12p. 1983. pap. 1.00 (ISBN 0-686-46858-9). Samisdat.

Davis, Duane & Cosenza, Robert. Business Research for Decision-Making. LC 84-15412. 576p. 1985. text ed. write for info. (ISBN 0-534-04107-8). Kent Pub Co.

Davis, Dwight F., jt. auth. see Bramble, Donna L.

Davis, E. Challenging Colonialism: Bank Misr & Egyptian Industrialization, 1920-1941. 1982. 25.00 (ISBN 0-691-07640-5). Princeton U Pr.

--Yeats' Early Contacts with French Poetry. LC 74-6014. 1961. lib. bdg. 9.50 (ISBN 0-8414-3752-1). Folcroft.

Davis, E., ed. The Microcirculation in Diabetes. (Advances in Microcirculation: Vol. 8). (Illus.). 1979. 49.00 (ISBN 3-8055-2916-3). S Karger.

--Raynaud Update: Pathophysiology & Treatment. (Advances in Microcirculation: Vol. 12). (Illus.). vi, 162p. 1985. 58.75 (ISBN 3-8055-3992-4). S Karger.

Davis, E. A. La Placebo Play. 1980. 5.50 (ISBN 0-682-49646-4). Exposition Pr FL.

Davis, E. A., jt. auth. see Mott, Nevill.

Davis, E. Adams. Of the Night Wind's Telling: Legends from the Valley of Mexico. (Illus.). 270p. 1976. pap. 6.95 (ISBN 0-8061-1304-9). U of Okla Pr.

Davis, E. E. see De Heusch, Luc.

Davis, E. H. & Campbell-Allen, D. The Profession of a Civil Engineer: Studies in Honour of John Roderick. LC 79-670361. 1979. 29.00x (ISBN 0-424-00064-4, Pub. by Sydney U Pr). Intl Spec Bk.

Davis, E. H., jt. auth. see Poulos, H. G.

Davis, E. H., jt. auth. see Squier, Ephraim G.

Davis, E. K. The Poky Little Puppy at the Fair. (Little Golden Sniff-It Bks.). 16p. (ps-1). 1981. 3.50 (ISBN 0-307-13203-X, Golden Bks). Western Pub.

Davis, E. P. The Consumption Function in Macroeconomic Models: A Comparative Study. (Bank of England Technical Series of Discussion Papers: No. 1). pap. 20.00 (ISBN 0-317-27738-3, 2019470). Bks Demand UMI.

--A Recursive Model of Personal Sector Expenditure & Accumulation. (Bank of England. Technical Series. Discussion Papers: No. 6). pap. 25.00 (ISBN 0-317-20795-4, 2024789). Bks Demand UMI.

Davis, E. W. & Yeomans, K. A. Company Finance & the Capital Market. LC 74-16990. (Department of Applied Economics, Occasional Papers: No. 39). (Illus.). 200p. 1975. 32.50 (ISBN 0-521-20144-6); pap. 16.95 (ISBN 0-521-09792-4). Cambridge U Pr.

Davis, E. Z. Translations of German Poetry in American Magazines. 59.95 (ISBN 0-8490-1227-9). Gordon Pr.

Davis, Earl, jt. ed. see Miller, Ted L.

Davis, Earl C. Christ at the Door. 1985. pap. 5.95 (ISBN 0-8054-6249-X). Broadman.

--Forever, Amen. LC 81-67199. 1982. pap. 4.50 (ISBN 0-8054-1953-5). Broadman.

--Somebody Cares. LC 81-71255. 1983. 7.50 (ISBN 0-8054-5211-7). Broadman.

Davis, Earle. The Flint & the Flame: The Artistry of Charles Dickens. 333p. 1982. Repr. of 1964 ed. lib. bdg. 35.00 (ISBN 0-89760-142-4). Telegraph Bks.

Davis, Ed. Appalachian Day. 12p. 1985. 1.00 (ISBN 0-317-19194-2). Samisdat.

--Teachers As Curriculum Evaluators. (Classroom & Curriculum in Australia Ser.: No. 4). 180p. 1981. text ed. 22.50x (ISBN 0-86861-090-9). Allen Unwin.

Davis, Edith & McGinnis, Esther. Parent Education: A Survey of the Minnesota Program. LC 76-141544. (Univ. of Minnesota, the Institute of Child Welfare Monograph: No. 17). (Illus.). 153p. 1975. Repr. of 1939 ed. lib. bdg. 22.50x (ISBN 0-8371-5891-5, CWDP). Greenwood.

Davis, Edith, jt. auth. see Davis, Lionel.

Davis, Edith A. The Development of Linguistic Skills in Twins, Singletons with Siblings, & Only Children from Age Five to Ten Years. LC 72-141543. (Univ. of Minnesota Institute of Child Welfare Monographs: No. 14). (Illus.). 165p. 1975. Repr. of 1937 ed. lib. bdg. 17.50x (ISBN 0-8371-5890-7, CWDL). Greenwood.

Davis, Edith M., et al. Health Care for the Urban Poor: Directions for Policy. LC 82-8868. (Conservation of Human Resources Ser.: No. 21). 226p. 1983. text ed. 30.00x (ISBN 0-86598-088-8). Rowman & Allanheld.

Davis, Edith S. Whether White or Black, a Man. facsimile ed. LC 77-37590. (Black Heritage Library Collection). Repr. of 1898 ed. 17.25 (ISBN 0-8369-8966-X). Ayer Co Pubs.

Davis, Edward, jt. ed. see Norgren, Jill.

Davis, Edward D. A Half Century of Struggle for Freedom in Florida. LC 82-50932. 1982. write for info. (ISBN 0-9610068-0-3). Drake's Ptg & Pub.

Davis, Edward E. Bruno the Pretzel Man. LC 84-47630. (Illus.). 64p. (gr. 2-5). 1984. 11.06i (ISBN 0-06-021398-1); PLB 10.89g (ISBN 0-06-021399-X). HarpJ.

--Into the Dark: A Beginner's Guide to Developing & Printing Black & White Negatives. LC 78-11284. (Illus.). 224p. (gr. 5 up). 1979. 9.95 (ISBN 0-689-30676-8). Atheneum.

Davis, Edward G. Maryland & North Carolina in the Campaign of 1780-1781, with a Preliminary Notice of the Revolution, in Which the Troops of the Two States Won Distinction. LC 72-14418. (Maryland Historical Society. Fund-Publications: No. 33). Repr. of 1893 ed. 18.00 (ISBN 0-404-57633-8). AMS Pr.

Davis, Edward J., jt. auth. see Cooney, Thomas J.

Davis, Edward M. Staff One: Perspectives on Effective Police Management. (Illus.). 1978. ref. ed. o.p. 21.95 (ISBN 0-13-840256-6); pap. text ed. 15.95 (ISBN 0-13-840249-3). P-H.

Davis, Edward M. & Newcomb, William W., eds. Exhibicion de la Coleccion Peruana Danciger. Benavides, Magdalena, tr. from Span. (Illus.). 1960. pap. 3.00 (ISBN 0-87959-024-6). U of Tex H Ransom Ctr.

--A Preview of the Danciger Peruvian Collection. LC 60-63787. (Illus.). 1960. pap. 3.00 (ISBN 0-87959-023-8). U of Tex H Ransom Ctr.

Davis, Edward W. Pioneering with Taconite. LC 64-64494. (Illus.). 246p. 1964. 8.50 (ISBN 0-87351-023-2). Minn Hist.

Davis, Edward W., ed. Project Management: Techniques, Applications & Managerial Issues. 2nd ed. 1983. pap. text ed. 32.00 (ISBN 0-89806-043-5). Inst Indus Eng.

Davis, Edward Z. Translations of German Poetry in American Magazines, 1741-1810. LC 66-27663. 1966. Repr. of 1905 ed. 35.00x (ISBN 0-8103-3209-4). Gale.

Davis, Edwin A. Louisiana: A Narrative History. 3rd ed. 1971. 25.00 (ISBN 0-87511-504-7); text ed. 20.00 (ISBN 0-87511-021-5). Claitors.

--Story of Louisiana, 4 Vols. Vol. 1. 30.00x (ISBN 0-685-08213-X); Vol. 2. 30.00x (ISBN 0-685-08214-8); Vol. 3. 30.00x (ISBN 0-685-08215-6); Vol. 4. 35.00x (ISBN 0-685-08216-4); Set. 79.50x (ISBN 0-685-08217-2). Claitors.

Davis, Edwin A. & Hogan, William R. The Barber of Natchez. LC 54-10885. (Illus.). 278p. 1973. pap. text ed. 7.95x (ISBN 0-8071-0212-1). La State U Pr.

Davis, Edwin A. & Suarez, Raleigh A. Louisiana: The Pelican State. 5th ed. LC 84-21760. 400p. (Orig.). 1985. 19.95 (ISBN 0-8071-1144-9). La State U Pr.

Davis, Edwin A., ed. see Barrow, Bennet H.

Davis, Edwin W. Functional Pattern Technique for Classification of Jobs. LC 73-176712. (Columbia University. Teachers College. Contributions to Education Ser.: No. 844). Repr. of 1942 ed. 22.50 (ISBN 0-404-55844-5). AMS Pr.

Davis, Eleanor H. Abraham Fornander: A Biography. LC 78-31368. (Illus.). 336p. 1979. 13.95 (ISBN 0-8248-0459-7). UH Pr.

Davis, Eliza T. Frederick County, Virginia Marriages, 1771-1825. LC 41-8991. 129p. Repr. of 1941 ed. write for info. (ISBN 0-685-65065-0). Va Bk.

--Surry County Records, Surry County, Virginia, 1652-1684. LC 80-52582. 156p. 1980. Repr. of 1950 ed. 12.50 (ISBN 0-8063-0904-0). Genealog Pub.

--Wills & Administrations of Surry County, Virginia, 1671-1750. LC 80-67936. 184p. 1980. Repr. of 1955 ed. 15.00 (ISBN 0-8063-0899-0). Genealog Pub.

Davis, Elizabeth. A Guide to Midwifery: Heart & Hands. (Illus.). 224p. (Orig.). 1981. pap. 9.00 (ISBN 0-912528-22-2). John Muir.

Davis, Elizabeth, jt. ed. see Davis, Bernard.

Davis, Elizabeth A. Index to the New World Recorded Anthology of American Music. 224p. 1981. pap. text ed. 7.95x (ISBN 0-393-95172-3). Norton.

Davis, Elizabeth A., ed. Massachusetts General Hospital, Department of Nursing, Gynecological Standards of Care. 1984. pap. text ed. 25.00 (ISBN 0-8359-4250-3). Reston.

Davis, Ellen N. The Vapheio Cups & Aegean Gold & Silver Ware. LC 76-23609. (Outstanding Dissertations in the Fine Arts). (Illus.). 492p. 1977. Repr. of 1973 ed. lib. bdg. 76.00 (ISBN 0-8240-2681-0). Garland Pub.

Davis, Elmer. History of the New York Times, 1851-1921. LC 70-144968. (Illus.). 1971. Repr. of 1921 ed. 59.00x (ISBN 0-403-00937-5). Scholarly.

Davis, Elmer H. But We Were Born Free. LC 73-138585. 229p. Repr. of 1954 ed. lib. bdg. 15.00x (ISBN 0-8371-5784-6, DABF). Greenwood.

--By Elmer Davis. facs. ed. Davis, Robert L., ed. LC 77-117780. (Essay Index Reprint Ser.). 1964. 24.50 (ISBN 0-8369-1798-7). Ayer Co Pubs.

--History of the New York Times, 1851-1921. LC 72-95092. Repr. of 1921 ed. lib. bdg. 37.50x (ISBN 0-8371-2578-2, DAHT). Greenwood.

--Not to Mention the War. facsimile ed. LC 71-107692. (Essay Index Reprint Ser.). 1940. 21.50 (ISBN 0-8369-1602-6). Ayer Co Pubs.

Davis, Elsie S. Descendants of Jacob Young of Shelby County, Kentucky: Including President Harry S. Truman. LC 80-70981. (Illus.). 171p. (Orig.). 1980. pap. 11.00 (ISBN 0-9605618-0-3). E S Davis.

Davis, Elwin N., ed. see Mid-America Spectroscopy Symposium (15th; 1964; Chicago. IL).

Davis, Elwood C. Methods & Techniques Used in Surveying Health & Physical Education in City Schools: An Analysis & Evaluation. LC 70-176711. (Columbia University. Teachers College. Contributions to Education: No. 515). Repr. of 1932 ed. 22.50 (ISBN 0-404-55515-2). AMS Pr.

Davis, Elwood C., jt. auth. see Nance, Virginia L.

Davis, Emily. Ancient Americans: The Archaeological Story of Two Continents. 1931. 20.00 (ISBN 0-8482-3674-2). Norwood Edns.

Davis, Emma Lou, ed. The Ancient Californians: Rancholabrean Hunters of the Mojave Lakes Country. (Science Ser.: No. 29). (Illus.). 193p. 1978. 10.00 (ISBN 0-938644-09-2). Nat Hist Mus.

Davis, Emmett. Clues in the Desert. LC 83-8626. (Adventure Diaries). (Illus.). 32p. (gr. 3-6). 1983. PLB 14.65g (ISBN 0-940742-29-2). Raintree Pubs.

--Only in Dreams. LC 83-8627. (Imagination Bks.). (Illus.). 32p. (gr. k-3). 1983. PLB 14.65g (ISBN 0-940742-15-2). Raintree Pubs.

--Only in Dreams. LC 83-8627. (Imagination Clippers Ser.). (Illus.). 32p. (gr. k-3). 1984. PLB 27.97 (ISBN 0-8172-2282-0); cassette 14.00. Raintree Pubs.

--Press & Politics in British Western Punjab, 1836-1947. 1985. 22.00x (ISBN 0-8364-1261-3, Pub. by Academic India). South Asia Bks.

--See No Evil. LC 83-8609. (Adventure Diaries). (Illus.). 32p. (gr. 3-6). 1983. PLB 14.65g (ISBN 0-940742-14-4). Raintree Pubs.

Davis, Emmett A. & Davis, Catherine M. Mainstreaming Library Services for Disabled People. LC 80-12280. 208p. 1980. 15.00 (ISBN 0-8108-1305-X). Scarecrow.

Davis, Enid. A Comprehensive Guide to Children's Literature with a Jewish Theme. LC 80-54139. 190p. 1981. 18.95x (ISBN 0-8052-3760-7). Schocken.

--Liberty Cap. LC 77-17208. (Illus.). 225p. 1978. pap. 4.95 (ISBN 0-915864-15-0). Academy Chi Pubs.

Davis, Eric. Sangres. (Orig.). pap. cancelled (ISBN 0-932238-23-8, Pub. by Avant Bks). Slawson Comm.

Davis, Esther G. A Taste of Mexico: A Primer of Mexican Cooking. Rand, Elizabeth, ed. LC 76-43616. (Illus.). 1976. plastic comb bdg. 4.95 (ISBN 0-914488-11-2). Rand-Tofua.

Davis, Ethelyn C., et al, eds. Teaching Sociology: An Annotated Bibliography. 3rd ed. 168p. 1979. 4.00 (ISBN 0-317-33285-6). Am Sociological.

Davis, F. Hadland. Myths and Legends of Japan. 1978. Repr. of 1912 ed. lib. bdg. 45.00 (ISBN 0-8495-1008-2). Arden Lib.

--Myths & Legends of Japan. 1976. lib. bdg. 59.95 (ISBN 0-8490-2328-9). Gordon Pr.

Davis, F. Hadland, ed. Jami, Persian Mystic & Poet. 103p. 1981. pap. 3.25 (ISBN 0-88004-003-3). Sunwise Turn.

Davis, F. James. Minority-Dominant Relations: A Sociological Analysis. LC 77-90659. 1978. pap. text ed. 13.95x (ISBN 0-88295-209-9). Harlan Davidson.

--Understanding Minority Dominant Relations: Sociological Contributions. LC 77-90671. 1979. pap. text ed. 19.95x (ISBN 0-88295-210-2). Harlan Davidson.

Davis, Fei-Ling. Primitive Revolutionaries of China: A Study of Secret Societies in the Late Nineteenth Century. LC 76-45585. 261p. 1977. 14.00x (ISBN 0-8248-0522-4). UH Pr.

Davis, Ferdinand & Lybbert, Donald. Essentials of Counterpoint. 2nd ed. LC 77-81504. 1977. pap. 9.95x (ISBN 0-8061-1445-2). U of Okla Pr.

Davis, Ferdinand, tr. see Gedalge, Andre.

Davis, Flora. Inside Intuition: What We Know About Nonverbal Communication. 240p. 1975. pap. 2.50 (ISBN 0-451-11117-6, AE1117, Sig). NAL.

Davis, Flora, jt. auth. see Raphael, Dana.

Davis, Floyd J. & Foster, Henry H. Society & the Law: New Meaning for an Old Profession. LC 78-5643. vi, 488p. 1978. Repr. of 1962 ed. lib. bdg. 36.25x (ISBN 0-313-20445-4, DASL). Greenwood.

Davis, Forrest, jt. auth. see Hunter, Robert.

Davis, Frances A., jt. ed. see Parker, Robert P.

Davis, Frances P. A Fearful Innocence. LC 81-11793. (Illus.). 269p. 1981. 14.95 (ISBN 0-87338-260-9). Kent St U Pr.

Davis, Frances R. & Parker, Robert P., Jr., eds. Teaching for Literacy: Reflections on the Bullock Report. LC 78-16898. 1978. text ed. 12.95x (ISBN 0-87586-060-5); pap. text ed. 7.95x (ISBN 0-87586-061-3). Agathon.

Davis, Francis W. Horse Packing in Pictures. LC 75-946. 1975. 11.95 (ISBN 0-684-14259-7, ScribT). Scribner.

Davis, Frank. The Frank Davis Seafood Notebook. LC 82-24679. (Illus.). 256p. 1983. 14.95 (ISBN 0-88289-309-2). Pelican.

Davis, Frank & Williams, Alice D. One Hundred Years Ago. 1980. pap. 4.95 (ISBN 0-910286-79-5). Boxwood.

Davis, Frank G. The Economics of Black Community Development: An Analysis & Program for Autonomous Growth & Development. 1976. pap. text ed. 12.00 (ISBN 0-8191-0008-0). U Pr of Amer.

Davis, Frank M. I Am the American Negro. facsimile ed. LC 70-178471. (Black Heritage Library Collection). Repr. of 1937 ed. 10.00 (ISBN 0-8369-8920-1). Ayer Co Pubs.

Davis, Franklin M. Across the Rhine. Time-Life Books, ed. (World War II Ser.). (Illus.). 208p. 1980. 14.95 (ISBN 0-8094-2542-4). Time-Life.

Davis, Franklin T., jt. ed. see Wadsworth, Milton E.

Davis, Fred. Snooker. (Illus.). 1978. 10.95 (ISBN 0-7136-1740-3). Transatlantic.

--Yearning for Yesterday: A Sociology of Nostalgia. LC 78-19838. 1979. 12.95 (ISBN 0-02-906950-5). Free Pr.

Davis, Frederic E. & PC World Editors. Hardware for the IBM PC & XT. 256p. 1985. pap. 16.95 (ISBN 0-671-49278-0, Pub. by Computer Bks). S&S.

Davis, Frederic E., jt. auth. see Aldridge, Adele.

Davis, Frederick B., ed. Modern Educational Developments: Another Look. LC 66-27610. 1966. pap. 3.00x (ISBN 0-8134-0889-X, 889). Interstate.

Davis, Frederick G., jt. ed. see Robertson, Jack C.

Davis, G. A., jt. ed. see Beasley, Daniel S.

Davis, G. Albyn. A Survey of Adult Aphasia. (Illus.). 384p. 1983. 28.95 (ISBN 0-13-878207-5). P-H.

Davis, G. Albyn & Wilcox, M. Jeanne. Adult Aphasia Rehabilitation: Applied Pragmatics. (Illus.). 200p. 1985. 25.00 (ISBN 0-933014-07-4). College-Hill.

--Adult Aphasia Rehabilitation: Applied Pragmatics. (Illus.). 200p. 1985. pap. 19.50 (ISBN 0-88744-195-5). College-Hill.

Davis, G. B. & Olsen, M. H. Management Information Systems: Conceptual Foundations, Structure & Development. 2nd ed. (Management Info Ser.). 1985. 34.95 (ISBN 0-07-015828-2). McGraw.

Davis, G. B. & Olson, M. H. Elementary Structured COBOL: A Step by Step Approach. 3rd ed. 416p. 1985. 23.95 (ISBN 0-07-015788-X). McGraw.

Davis, G. Gervaise, et al. Software Protection: Practical & Legal Steps to Protect & Market Computer Programs. 400p. 1985. 42.95 (ISBN 0-442-21903-2). Van Nos Reinhold.

Davis, G. Gervaise, III. Software Protection: Practical & Legal Steps to Protect Computer Programs. 400p. 1985. 35.00 (ISBN 0-534-02703-2). Lifetime Learn.

Davis, G. P. What Shall the Public Schools Do for the Feeble Minded? (Harvard Studies in Education: Vol. 10, Pt. 1). 1927. pap. 19.00 (ISBN 0-384-11005-3). Johnson Repr.

Davis, G. T. Metlakahtla: Mission to Tsimshean Indians. facs. ed. (Shorey Indian Ser.). (Illus.). 128p. pap. 10.95 (ISBN 0-8466-0019-6, S19). Shorey.

Davis, Garold N. German Thought & Culture in England, 1700-1770. LC 78-62900. (University of North Carolina Studies in Comparative Literature Ser.: No. 47). Repr. of 1969 ed. 38.00 (ISBN 0-8357-9703-1, 2017229). Bks Demand UMI.

Davis, Garry. My Country Is the World. Honan, William, ed. LC 84-82393. (Illus.). 223p. 1984. pap. 4.95 (ISBN 0-931545-01-3). Juniper Ledge Pub.

--World Government, Ready or Not! LC 84-23362. (Illus.). 400p. 1984. pap. 14.95 (ISBN 0-931545-00-5). Juniper Ledge Pub.

Davis, Gary. What Now McBride? 99p. 1982. 7.95 (ISBN 0-934126-22-4). Randall Bk Co.

Davis, Gary & Scott, Joseph. Training Creative Thinking. LC 78-8376. 316p. 1978. Repr. of 1971 ed. lib. bdg. 18.50 (ISBN 0-88275-688-5). Krieger.

Davis, Gary A. Creativity Is Forever. 152p. 1983. pap. text ed. 9.95 (ISBN 0-8403-3080-4). Kendall-Hunt.

--Educational Psychology: Theory & Practice. 704p. (Orig.). 1983. pap. text ed. 23.95 (ISBN 0-394-34909-1, RanC); wkbk. 5.95 (ISBN 0-394-34911-3). Random.

Davis, Gary A. & Rimm, Sylvia. Education of the Gifted & Talented. (Illus.). 416p. 1985. text ed. 25.95 (ISBN 0-13-236597-9). P-H.

Davis, Gary A., ed. Imagination Express. new ed. 68p. (Orig.). (gr. 3-9). 1973. text ed. 5.95 (ISBN 0-914634-12-7). DOK Pubs.

Davis, Gene. Agriculture & Automotive Diesel Mechanics. (Illus.). 256p. 1983. 20.95 (ISBN 0-13-018838-7). P-H.

Davis, Gene, jt. auth. see Baldwin, Deirdra.

Davis, Genny W. & Davis, Bruce. Love & Money: Your Secret Source of Wealth. 96p. 1982. pap. 4.95 (ISBN 0-02-530010-5); pap. 59.40 12-copy prepack (ISBN 0-02-530020-2). Macmillan.

Davis, Genny W., jt. auth. see Davis, Bruce.

Davis, George. Coming Home. (Howard University Press Library of Contemporary Literature). 208p. 1984. pap. 6.95 (ISBN 0-88258-118-X). Howard U Pr.

--Man & the Adirondack Environment: A Primer. (Adirondack Museum Monographs). (Illus.). 1977. 2.50 (ISBN 0-686-74848-4). Adirondack Mus.

--The Posthumous Papers of the Pickwick Club. LC 72-3167. (Studies in Dickens, No. 52). 1972. Repr. of 1928 ed. lib. bdg. 29.95x (ISBN 0-8383-1533-X). Haskell.

Davis, George & Watson, Glegg. Black Life in Corporate America: Swimming in the Mainstream. LC 81-43064. (Illus.). 216p. 1982. 14.95 (ISBN 0-385-14701-5, Anchor Pr). Doubleday.

--Black Life in Corporate America: Swimming in the Mainstream. LC 81-43064. (Anchor Literary Library). 216p. 1985. pap. 7.95 (ISBN 0-385-14702-3). Doubleday.

Davis, George H. Structural Geology of Rocks & Regions. LC 83-17076. 492p. 1984. text ed. 37.45 (ISBN 0-471-09267-3). Wiley.

Davis, George H. & Velikanov. Hydrological Problems Arising from the Development of Energy: A Preliminary Report. (Technical Papers in Hydrology: No. 17). (Illus.). 32p. 1979. pap. 5.00 (ISBN 92-3-101685-7, U912, UNESCO). Unipub.

Davis, George K., jt. auth. see Harper, Alfred E.

Davis, George L. & Shannon, Samuel H. Institutions of American Government. LC 73-621. 145p. 1973. 20.00x (ISBN 0-8422-5087-5); pap. text ed. 4.75x (ISBN 0-8422-0295-1). Irvington.

Davis, George M. The Origin & Evolution of the Gastropod Family Pomatiopsidae, with Emphasis on the Mekong River Triculinae. (Monograph: No. 20). (Illus.). 120p. 1979. pap. 14.00 (ISBN 0-910006-28-8). Acad Nat Sci Phila.

Davis, George P., jt. auth. see Burnham, John H.

Davis, George R. The Local Network Handbook. (Illus.). 260p. 1982. pap. 29.95 (ISBN 0-07-015823-1). McGraw.

Davis, George T. A Navy Second to None: The Development of Modern American Naval Policy. LC 77-110826. (Illus.). xiii, 508p. Repr. of 1940 ed. lib. bdg. 24.75x (ISBN 0-8371-3226-6, DANS). Greenwood.

Davis, George W. Posthumous Papers of the Pickwick Club. LC 73-14971. 1928. lib. bdg. 10.00 (ISBN 0-8414-3681-9). Folcroft.

Davis, Georgia. Astrology & Love. 13th ed. 1977. pap. 1.50 (ISBN 0-685-11794-4, Argent Bks). Merit Pubns.

--Astrology Sex. 12th ed. 1977. pap. 1.25 (ISBN 0-685-11795-2, Argent Bks). Merit Pubns.

Davis, Gerald C., ed. Setting Free the Ministry of the People of God. 120p. (Orig.). 1984. pap. 1.75 (ISBN 0-88028-038-7). Forward Movement.

Davis, Gerald L. I Got the World in Me & I Can Sing It, You Know: A Study of the Performed African American Sermon. LC 85-2544. (Illus.). 272p. 1986. text ed. 24.95 (ISBN 0-8122-7987-5). U of Pa Pr.

Davis, Geraldine. Horary Astrology. rev. & enl. ed. (Illus.). 1970. 8.95 (ISBN 0-912504-35-8); pap. 5.95 (ISBN 0-912504-01-3). Sym & Sign.

Davis, Gibbs. Fishman & Charly. LC 82-23350. 160p. (gr. 5 up). 1983. PLB 8.95 (ISBN 0-395-33882-4). HM.

--Katy's First Haircut. LC 85-2435. (Illus.). (gr. k-3). 1985. 12.95 (ISBN 0-395-38942-9). HM.

--The Other Emily. LC 83-18913. (Illus.). 32p. (gr. k-3). 1984. PLB 10.95 (ISBN 0-395-35482-X, 5-84351). HM.

--Swann Song. LC 81-18066. 192p. (gr. 7 up). 1982. 9.95 (ISBN 0-02-726280-4). Bradbury Pr.

Davis, Glenn. Childhood & History in America. LC 76-27774. 281p. 1977. 18.95 (ISBN 0-914434-03-9); pap. 10.95 (ISBN 0-914434-04-7). Psychohistory Pr.

Davis, Glenn & Helfand, Gary. The Uncertain Balance: Federal Regulators in a Changing Political Economy. (Illus.). 208p. (Orig.). 1985. pap. text ed. 9.95x (ISBN 0-89529-185-1). Avery Pub.

Davis, Glenn B., jt. auth. see Bradford, Murray.

Davis, Glenn B., jt. auth. see Bradford, W. M.

Davis, Glenn B., jt. auth. see Bradford, W. Murray.

Davis, Gloria, ed. What Is Modern Indonesian Culture? LC 79-18979. (Papers in International Studies, Southeast Asia Ser.: No. 52). 1979. pap. 18.00x (ISBN 0-89680-075-X, 82-90538, Ohio U Ctr Intl). Ohio U Pr.

Davis, Gordon. Bloody Bush. (Sergeant Ser.: No. 3). 288p. (Orig.). 1980. pap. 2.25 (ISBN 0-89083-647-7). Zebra.

--Death Train. (The Sgt. Ser.: No. 1). 256p. (Orig.). 1980. pap. 2.25 (ISBN 0-89083-600-0). Zebra.

--The Goering Treasure. 288p. (Orig.). 1980. pap. 2.25 (ISBN 0-89083-692-2). Zebra.

Davis, Gordon B. Computers & Information Processing. (Illus.). 1977. text ed. 35.95 (ISBN 0-07-015564-X). McGraw.

--Introduction to Electronic Computers. 3rd ed. (Illus.). 1977. text ed. 41.95 (ISBN 0-07-015825-8). McGraw.

--Management Information Systems: Conceptual Foundations, Structure & Development. (Illus.). 480p. 1974. text ed. 35.95 (ISBN 0-07-015827-4). McGraw.

Davis, Gordon B. & Everest, Gordon. Readings in Management Information Systems. 1976. pap. 26.95 (ISBN 0-07-015835-5). McGraw.

Davis, Gordon B. & Hoffman, Thomas R. FORTRAN 77: A Structured Disciplined Style. 2nd ed. 416p. 1983. pap. text ed. 26.95 (ISBN 0-07-015903-3). McGraw.

Davis, Gordon B. & Parker, Clyde A. Writing the Doctoral Dissertation. LC 78-7598. 1979. pap. 5.95 (ISBN 0-8120-0997-5). Barron.

Davis, Gordon B., et al. Auditing & EDP. 1983. study guide vinyl 15.00 (ISBN 0-317-03800-1). Am Inst CPA.

Davis, Grace, jt. auth. see Miles, Austin.

Davis, Grania. The King & the Mangoes. (Jataka Tales for Children). (Illus.). 24p. (gr. 1-6). 1983. 4.95 (ISBN 0-913546-27-5). Dharma Pub.

--The Proud Peacock & the Mallard. (Jataka Tales for Children Ser.). (Illus.). 24p. (gr. 1-6). 1983. pap. 4.95 (ISBN 0-913546-70-4). Dharma Pub.

Davis, Grant, jt. ed. see Hutnik, Russell.

Davis, Grant M. Collective Ratemaking in the Motor Carrier Industry. (Illus.). 154p. 1980. pap. text ed. 7.95 (ISBN 0-8134-2138-1). Interstate.

Davis, Grant M. & Dillard, John E., Jr. Physical Logistics Management. LC 83-10300. (Illus.). 566p. 1983. lib. bdg. 35.75 (ISBN 0-8191-3342-6); pap. text ed. 22.00 (ISBN 0-8191-3343-4). U Pr of Amer.

Davis, Grant M. & Shephard, Eugene H. Motor Carrier Rate Structure: The Need for Basic Revision. LC 78-24194. 144p. 1979. 36.95 (ISBN 0-03-049136-3). Praeger.

Davis, Grant M., ed. Motor Carrier Economics, Regulation, & Operation. LC 81-40650. 452p. 1981. lib. bdg. 32.25 (ISBN 0-8191-1927-X); pap. text ed. 17.50 (ISBN 0-8191-1928-8). U Pr of Amer.

--Transportation Regulation: A Pragmatic Assessment. LC 76-1359. 1976. pap. text ed. 4.95x (ISBN 0-8134-1792-9, 1792). Interstate.

Davis, Granville D. The University Council on Education for Public Responsibility, 1961-1975. LC 75-2281. 130p. 1975. pap. 2.75 (ISBN 0-87060-068-0, OCP 43). Syracuse U Cont Ed.

Davis, Gregory H. Technology: Humanism or Nihilism: A Critical Analysis of the Philosophical Basis & Practice of Modern Technology. LC 81-40178. 304p. (Orig.). 1981. lib. bdg. 24.00 (ISBN 0-8191-1776-5); pap. text ed. 12.00 (ISBN 0-8191-1777-3). U Pr of Amer.

Davis, Gregson, tr. from Fr. Non-Vicious Circle: Twenty Poems of Aime Cesaire. LC 83-42791. (Illus.). 168p. 1984. 18.50x (ISBN 0-8047-1207-7). Stanford U Pr.

Davis, Guillermo H. Gramatica Elemental del Griego del Nuevo Testamento. McKibben, Jorge F., tr. 240p. 1980. Repr. of 1978 ed. 4.75 (ISBN 0-311-42008-7). Casa Bautista.

Davis, Gwen. Marriage. LC 81-66966. 288p. 1981. 12.95 (ISBN 0-87795-335-X). Arbor Hse.

--Marriage. 1983. pap. 3.50 (ISBN 0-8217-1122-9). Zebra.

--Romance. 1983. 14.50 (ISBN 0-87795-497-6). Arbor Hse.

--Romance. 288p. 1984. pap. 3.50 (ISBN 0-8217-1406-6). Zebra.

Davis, H. Beginning Gymnastics for College Women. (Illus.). pap. 4.50 wrappers (ISBN 0-8363-0011-4). Jenkins.

Davis, H., et al. The Testing of Engineering Materials. 4th ed. 480p. 1982. 44.00x (ISBN 0-07-015656-5). McGraw.

Davis, H. C. & Bridgeman, J. C. Three Minute Declamations for College Men. facs. ed. LC 68-58819. (Granger Index Reprint Ser). 1890. 18.00 (ISBN 0-8369-6013-0). Ayer Co Pubs.

Davis, H. Grady. Design for Preaching. LC 58-5749. (Orig.). 1958. 9.95 (ISBN 0-8006-0806-2, 1-806). Fortress.

Davis, H. L. Essays & Short Stories. 325p. (Orig.). 1985. pap. 10.95 (ISBN 0-89301-109-6). U Pr of Idaho.

--Honey in the Horn. 512p. 1962. pap. 4.95 (ISBN 0-380-01831-4, 68882, Bard). Avon.

--Honey in the Horn. LC 35-16787. 380p. 1975. 15.95 (ISBN 0-910220-76-X). Berg.

--The Selected Poems of H. L. Davis. 2nd ed. Burmaster, O., ed. LC 77-83226. (Ahsahta Press Modern & Contemporary Poets of the West). (Orig.). 1978. pap. 3.00 (ISBN 0-916272-07-9). Ahsahta Pr.

Davis, H. S. Culture & Diseases of Game Fishes. (Illus.). 1953. 34.00x (ISBN 0-520-00293-8). U of Cal Pr.

Davis, H. Ted, jt. ed. see Aris, Rutherford.

Davis, H. W., ed. Medieval England. new ed. Orig. Title: Bernard's Companion to English History. 1977. Repr. of 1924 ed. lib. bdg. 45.00 (ISBN 0-8495-1006-6). Arden Lib.

--Medieval England. 632p. 1984. Repr. of 1924 ed. lib. bdg. 100.00 (ISBN 0-8495-1145-3). Arden Lib.

Davis, H. W., ed. see Batiffol, Louis.

Davis, Hallowell & Silverman, Richard S. Hearing & Deafness. 4th ed. LC 77-22533. 1978. pap. 31.95 (ISBN 0-03-089980-X, HoltC). HR&W.

Davis, Hallowell, jt. auth. see Stevens, Stanley S.

Davis, Hallowell, jt. ed. see Owen, Jeffrey H.

Davis, Hannah & Kapantais, Gloria. Characteristics of Pharmacists: United States, 1978-79. Olmstead, Mary, ed. (Series 14: No. 28). 60p. 1983. pap. text ed. 1.75 (ISBN 0-8406-0279-0). Natl Ctr Health Stats.

Davis, Harold A. An International Community on the St. Croix. 1974. pap. 6.95 (ISBN 0-89101-029-7). U Maine Orono.

Davis, Harold B. & Gottlieb, Sybil, eds. Current Trends in Dynamic Personality Theory: Problems of Normal & Disturbed Development. LC 72-8722. 340p. 1972. text ed. 29.00x (ISBN 0-8422-5068-9). Irvington.

Davis, Harold E. The Fledgling Province: Social & Cultural Life in Colonial Georgia 1733-1776. LC 76-2570. (Institute of Early American History & Culture Ser.). (Illus.). xi, 306p. 1976. 25.00 (ISBN 0-8078-1267-6). U of NC Pr.

--Hinsdale of Hiram: The Life of Burke Aaron Hinsdale, Pioneer Educator 1837-1900. 1971. student ed. 5.50 (ISBN 0-87419-041-X); lib. bdg. 8.00 (ISBN 0-87419-028-2). U Pr of Wash.

--History & Power: The Social Relevance of History. LC 83-12385. 170p. 1983. lib. bdg. 22.50 (ISBN 0-8191-3412-0); pap. text ed. 11.00 (ISBN 0-8191-3413-9). U Pr of Amer.

--History of Latin America. LC 68-28843. (gr. 9-12). Repr. of 1968 ed. 120.00 (ISBN 0-8357-9906-9, 2012552). Bks Demand UMI.

--Latin American Leaders. LC 68-56189. Repr. of 1949 ed. 19.50 (ISBN 0-8154-0271-6). Cooper Sq.

--Latin American Thought: A Historical Introduction. LC 78-181564. 1974. pap. text ed. 9.95 (ISBN 0-02-907160-7). Free Pr.

--Latin American Thought: A Historical Introduction. LC 78-181564. 270p. 1972. 25.00x (ISBN 0-8071-0249-0). La State U Pr.

--Makers of Democracy in Latin America. LC 68-56190. Repr. of 1945 ed. 19.50 (ISBN 0-8154-0272-4). Cooper Sq.

--Revolutionaries, Traditionalists & Dictators in Latin America. LC 72-77988. 1973. lib. bdg. 20.00 (ISBN 0-8154-0420-4). Cooper Sq.

Davis, Harold E., ed. Government & Politics in Latin America. LC 58-5649. (Illus.). pap. 136.30 (ISBN 0-317-08734-7, 2012551). Bks Demand UMI.

Davis, Harold E., ed. see Inman, Samuel G.

Davis, Harold E., et al. Latin American Diplomatic History: An Introduction. LC 76-58901. vii, 302p. 1977. 27.50x (ISBN 0-8071-0260-1); pap. 7.95x (ISBN 0-8071-0286-5). La State U Pr.

Davis, Harold Eugene. Social Science Trends in Latin America Through Nineteen Fifty. 1950. 2.50 (ISBN 0-87419-010-X). U Pr of Wash.

Davis, Harold L. Beulah Land. LC 75-136062. 1971. Repr. of 1949 ed. lib. bdg. 19.75x (ISBN 0-8371-5212-7, DABL). Greenwood.

--Honey in the Horn. LC 83-45745. Repr. of 1935 ed. 34.50 (ISBN 0-404-20074-5). AMS Pr.

--Team Bells Woke Me, & Other Stories. LC 73-13321. 300p. 1974. Repr. of 1953 ed. lib. bdg. 19.75x (ISBN 0-8371-7125-3, DATB). Greenwood.

--Winds of Morning. LC 77-138586. 344p. 1972. Repr. of 1952 ed. lib. bdg. 24.75x (ISBN 0-8371-5785-4, DAWM). Greenwood.

Davis, Harold S., et al. Modern Approaches to School Organization. 1974. pap. text ed. 9.95x (ISBN 0-8422-0368-0). Irvington.

Davis, Harold T. Analysis of Economic Time Series. (Cowles Commission Monograph Ser., No. 6). 1941. 8.50 (ISBN 0-911536-18-3). Trinity U Pr.

--Introduction to Nonlinear Differential & Integral Equations. 1960. pap. 8.95 (ISBN 0-486-60971-5). Dover.

--Political Statistics. 364p. 1954. 7.00 (ISBN 0-911536-14-0). Trinity U Pr.

--Studies in Differential Equations. Scott, Walter, ed. LC 56-14277. (Northwestern University Series in Mathematical & Physical Sciences: No. 3). pap. 30.00 (ISBN 0-317-08636-7, 2006876). Bks Demand UMI.

--Summation of Series. 140p. 1962. 6.00 (ISBN 0-911536-19-1). Trinity U Pr.

Davis, Harold T. & Fisher, Vera. Tables of Mathematical Functions, Vol. 3. 1962. 8.75 (ISBN 0-911536-17-5). Trinity U Pr.

Davis, Harold T. & Holcomb, George L. Moliere Resumes. LC 71-168524. 241p. 1971. text ed. 6.00 (ISBN 0-911536-39-6). Trinity U Pr.

Davis, Harriet E., ed. Pioneers in World Order. facs. ed. LC 70-128232. (Essay Index Reprint Ser). 1944. 19.00 (ISBN 0-8369-1913-0). Ayer Co Pubs.

Davis, Harry C., ed. Commencement Parts: Valedictories, Salutatories, Orations, Essays, Class Poems, Ivy Orations, Toasts. facsimile ed. LC 74-152149. (Granger Index Reprint Ser.). Repr. of 1898 ed. 29.00 (ISBN 0-8369-6252-4). Ayer Co Pubs.

Davis, Harry F. & Snider, Arthur D. Introduction to Vector Analysis. 4th ed. LC 78-27618. 1979. text ed. 39.00 (ISBN 0-205-06598-8, EDP 566598). Allyn.

Davis, Harry L. & Silk, Alvin J., eds. Behavioral & Management Science in Marketing. LC 77-18878. pap. 69.50 (ISBN 0-317-10218-4, 2055606). Bks Demand UMI.

Davis, Harwell G. The Legend of Landsee. LC 76-40829. 1976. 6.95 (ISBN 0-87397-106-X). Strode.

Davis, Hassoldt. Land of the Eye: A Narrative of the Labors, Adventures, Alarums & Excursions of the Denis-Roosevelt Asiatic Expedition to Burma, China, India & the Lost Kingdom of Nepal. 1979. Repr. of 1940 ed. lib. bdg. 25.00 (ISBN 0-8492-0670-7). R West.

Davis, Hayne, ed. Among the World's Peacemakers: An Epitome of the Interparliamentary Union. LC 70-147454. (Library of War & Peace; Peace Leaders: Biographies & Memoirs). 1973. lib. bdg. 46.00 (ISBN 0-8240-0249-0). Garland Pub.

Davis, Hazel. Personnel Administration in Three Non-Teaching Services of the Public Schools. LC 76-178802. (Columbia University. Teachers College. Contributions to Education: No. 784). Repr. of 1939 ed. 22.50 (ISBN 0-404-55784-8). AMS Pr.

Davis, Hazel K., jt. ed. see Davis, James E.

Davis, Hazel R., jt. auth. see Davis, James E.

Davis, Helen C., ed. Constitutions, Electoral Laws, Treaties of States in the Near & Middle East. LC 79-99886. Repr. of 1953 ed. 27.50 (ISBN 0-404-01995-1). AMS Pr.

Davis, Helen E. Kindred: Davis-Stansbury Lines. 1977. 10.00 (ISBN 0-8059-2413-2). Dorrance.

--Tolstoy & Nietzsche. LC 72-119083. (Studies in Comparative Literature, No. 35). 1970. Repr. of 1929 ed. lib. bdg. 39.95x (ISBN 0-8383-1079-6). Haskell.

Davis, Helene. Nightblind. Kaplan, Peter, ed. 1976. 3.00x (ISBN 0-915176-17-3). Pourboire.

Davis, Henry. A Forgotten Heritage: The Story of the Early American Rifle. 1976. Repr. of 1941 ed. 9.95 (ISBN 0-88227-008-7). Gun Room.

Davis, Henry B. Electrical & Electronic Technologies: A Chronology of Events & Inventors to 1900. LC 81-9179. 221p. 1981. 16.00 (ISBN 0-8108-1464-1). Scarecrow.

--Electrical & Electronic Technologies: A Chronology of Events & Inventors from 1900 to 1940. LC 82-16739. 220p. 1983. 16.00 (ISBN 0-8108-1590-7). Scarecrow.

--Electrical & Electronic Technologies: A Chronology of Events & Inventors from 1940 to 1980. LC 84-13957. 321p. 1985. 25.00 (ISBN 0-8108-1726-8). Scarecrow.

Davis, Henry C. Both Sides Speak. 92p. 1976. pap. 7.50 (ISBN 0-934914-09-5). NACM.

Davis, Henry M. Use of State High School Examinations As an Instrument for Judging the Work of Teachers. LC 77-176713. (Columbia University. Teachers College. Contributions to Education: No. 611). Repr. of 1934 ed. 22.50 (ISBN 0-404-55611-6). AMS Pr.

Davis, Henry W. Charlemagne (Charles the Great) The Hero of Two Nations. (Select Bibliographies Reprint Ser.). 1972. Repr. of 1899 ed. 26.50 (ISBN 0-8369-9957-6). Ayer Co Pubs.

--The Political Thought of Heinrich Von Treitschke. LC 72-9084. 295p. 1973. Repr. of 1915 ed. lib. bdg. 16.25x (ISBN 0-8371-6568-7, DAPT). Greenwood.

Davis, Henry W. & Whitwell, R. J., eds. Regesta Regum Anglo-Normannorum, 1066 to 1135, 2 vols. LC 80-2220. Repr. of 1956 ed. Set. 150.00 (ISBN 0-404-18796-X); 75.00 ea. AMS Pr.

Davis, Herbert. Nineteenth-Century Studies. LC 72-194751. 1973. Repr. of 1940 ed. lib. bdg. 20.00 (ISBN 0-8414-2444-6). Folcroft.

Davis, Herbert, ed. see Congreve, William.

Davis, Herbert, ed. see Pope, Alexander.

Davis, Herbert, ed. see Swift, Jonathan.

Davis, Herbert J. The Satire of Jonathan Swift. LC 79-17603. 1979. Repr. of 1947 ed. lib. bdg. 27.50x (ISBN 0-313-22068-9, DAJS). Greenwood.

Davis, Herbert J., et al, eds. Nineteenth Century Studies. LC 69-10083. 1969. Repr. of 1940 ed. lib. bdg. 19.75x (ISBN 0-8371-0057-7, DANC). Greenwood.

Davis, Herm, jt. auth. see Kennedy, Joyce L.

Davis, Hester, jt. ed. see McGimsey, Charles R.

Davis, Hilarie. Super Think: A Guide for Asking Thought-Provoking Questions. Bachelis, Faren, ed. 88p. 1982. tchrs. ed. 8.50 (ISBN 0-931724-21-X). Dandy Lion.

Davis, Horace. American Constitutions: The Relations of the Three Departments As Adjusted by a Century. LC 78-63753. (Johns Hopkins University. Studies in the Social Sciences. Third Ser. 1885: 9-10). Repr. of 1885 ed. 11.50 (ISBN 0-404-61024-2). AMS Pr.

--American Constitutions: The Relations of the Three Departments As Adjusted by a Century. 1973. pap. 9.00 (ISBN 0-384-11006-1). Johnson Repr.

Davis, Horace A. The Judicial Veto. LC 78-146152. (American Constitutional & Legal History Ser). 1971. Repr. of 1914 ed. lib. bdg. 22.50 (ISBN 0-306-70093-X). Da Capo.

Davis, Horace B. Nationalism & Socialism: Marxist & Labor Theories of Nationalism to 1917. LC 67-19255. 258p. 1967. pap. 10.00 (ISBN 0-85345-293-8, PB-2938). Monthly Rev.

--Toward a Marxist Theory of Nationalism. LC 77-91740. 294p. 1980. pap. 7.50 (ISBN 0-85345-516-3); 17.50 (ISBN 0-85345-441-8). Monthly Rev.

Davis, Horace B., ed. & tr. see Luxemburg, Rosa.

Davis, Horace B., ed. see Luxemburg, Rosa.

Davis, Howard. Frank Parsons: Prophet, Innovator, Counselor. LC 69-11514. 176p. 1969. pap. 5.85x (ISBN 0-8093-0360-4). S Ill U Pr.

Davis, Howard & Scase, Richard. Western Capitalism & State Socialism: Comparative Perspectives. 220p. 1985. 24.95x (ISBN 0-631-14001-8); pap. 9.95x (ISBN 0-631-14002-6). Basil Blackwell.

Davis, Howard & Walton, Paul, eds. Language, Image, Media. LC 83-3124. (Illus.). 320p. 1984. 29.95x (ISBN 0-312-46747-8). St Martin.

Davis, Howard H. Beyond Class Images: Explorations in the Structure of Social Consciousness. (Social Analysis Ser.). 213p. 1979. 32.00 (ISBN 0-85664-801-9, Pub. by Croom Helm Ltd). Longwood Pub Group.

Davis, Hubert, ed. A January Fog Will Freeze a Hog & Other Weather Folklore. LC 76-54333. (Illus.). (gr. 1-4). 1977. reinforced lib. bdg. 6.95 (ISBN 0-517-52811-8). Crown.

Davis, Hubert J. Great Dismal Swamp: Its Science, History & Folklore. (Illus.). 1971. 8.50 (ISBN 0-930230-11-6). Johnson NC.

--Myths & Legends of the Great Dismal Swamp. (Illus.). 112p. 1981. 7.50 (ISBN 0-930230-42-6). Johnson NC.

--Pon My Honor Hit's the Truth: Tales from the South Western Virginia Mountains. (Illus.). 1973. 6.50 (ISBN 0-930230-19-1). Johnson NC.

Davis, Hurk. Blood on the Rhine. (Orig.). 1969. pap. 0.95 (ISBN 0-87067-171-5, BH171). Holloway.

Davis, I., ed. Disasters & the Small Dwelling. 220p. 1981. 33.00 (ISBN 0-08-024753-9). Pergamon.

Davis, Ian. Jesus Purusha. 144p. 1985. pap. 8.95 (ISBN 0-89281-069-6). Inner Tradit.

Davis, Ian A. Forty-Four Dynamic ZX-81 Games & Recreations. (Illus.). 1984. pap. 13.95 (ISBN 0-13-329144-8). P-H.

Davis, Inez S. Story of the Church. new ed. 1981. pap. 18.00 (ISBN 0-8309-0188-4). Herald Hse.

Davis, Inger P. Adolescents: Theoretical & Helping Perspectives. 1985. lib. bdg. 38.95 (ISBN 0-89838-165-7). Kluwer Nijhoff.

Davis, J. History of the Welsh Baptist: AD Sixty-Three to Seventeen Seventy. 1982. Repr. of 1835 ed. 15.00 (ISBN 0-686-91934-3). Church History.

--Land & Family in Pisticci. (London School of Economics Monographs on Social Anthropology: No. 48). (Illus.). 200p. 1973. 36.50 (ISBN 0-485-19548-8, Pub. by Athlone Pr Ltd). Longwood Pub Group.

Davis, J., jt. auth. see Stephenson, G. M.

Davis, J., ed. Choice & Change: Essays in Honor of Lucy Mair. (London School of Economics Monographs on Social Anthropology: No. 50). 259p. 1974. 38.50 (ISBN 0-485-19550-X, Pub. by Athlone Pr Ltd). Longwood Pub Group.

--Religious Organization & Religious Experience. (ASA Monograph). 1982. 30.00 (ISBN 0-12-206580-8). Acad Pr.

Davis, J. A., et al, eds. Parent-Baby Attachment in Premature Infants. LC 83-40171. (Illus.). 336p. 1983. 30.00 (ISBN 0-312-59657-X). St Martin.

Davis, J. Bancroft. Mister Fish & the Alabama Claims: A Chapter in Diplomatic History. facsimile ed. (Select Bibliographies Reprint Ser). 1893. 19.00 (ISBN 0-8369-5067-4). Ayer Co Pubs.

Davis, J. Boyce & Knight, E. Leslie. CVR Fitness: A Basic Guide for Cardio-Vascular-Respiratory Exercise. 2nd ed. (Illus.). 1983. pap. text ed. 11.95 (ISBN 0-8403-3019-7, 40301901). Kendall-Hunt.

Davis, J. C. Utopia & the Ideal Society: A Study of English Utopian Writing, 1516-1700. 410p. 1981. 59.50 (ISBN 0-521-23396-8). Cambridge U Pr.

--Utopia & the Ideal Society: A Study of English Utopian Writing 1516-1700. LC 80-40743. 434p. 1983. pap. 15.95 (ISBN 0-521-27551-2). Cambridge U Pr.

Davis, J. C., jt. auth. see Sheehan, H. L.

Davis, J. Cary. Recuardos de Guatemala. 1970. 4.95. S Ill U Pr.

--Recuerdos de Guatemala: A Spanish Reader. LC 71-93880. (Illus.). 256p. (Span.). 1970. 4.95 (ISBN 0-8093-0415-5). S Ill U Pr.

Davis, J. Cary, jt. auth. see Canfield, D. Lincoln.

Davis, J. D. Blue Gold: The Political Economy of Natural Gas. (World Industry Studies: No. 3). 300p. 1984. text ed. 29.50 (ISBN 0-04-338112-X). Allen Unwin.

--Davis Dictionary of the Bible. 5th rev. ed. 840p. 1972. Repr. 18.95 (ISBN 0-8007-0061-9). Revell.

Davis, J. D. & Merriman, D., eds. Observations on the Ecology & Biology of Western Cape Cod Bay, Massachusetts. (Lecture Notes on Coastal & Estuarine Studies: Vol. 11). x, 289p. 1984. pap. 22.00 (ISBN 0-387-96084-8). Springer-Verlag.

Davis, J. E., jt. auth. see Torrey, R. A.

Davis, J. F., tr. see Ma Chi-Yuan.

Davis, J. Kent, jt. auth. see Stein, Michael D.

Davis, J. M. Making America Work Again. LC 83-7706. 294p. 12.95 (ISBN 0-517-55117-9). Crown.

Davis, J. M., jt. ed. see Domino, E. F.

Davis, J. M., ed. see International Missionary Council - Department Of Social And Economic Research.

Davis, J. Madison, III. Blackletter: A Novella. pap. write for info. (ISBN 0-912288-22-1). Perivale Pr.

Davis, J. Mearle, ed. see International Missionary Council - Department of Social & Economic Research & Council.

Davis, J. Merle, ed. Modern Industry & the African. 2nd ed. 450p. 1967. Repr. of 1933 ed. 32.50x (ISBN 0-7146-1650-8, BHA-01650, F Cass Co). Biblio Dist.

Davis, J. P. How to Pass the Bar Examination. (Illus.). 200p. 1985. 17.50x (ISBN 0-914970-21-6); pap. text ed. 9.95x (ISBN 0-914970-19-4). Conch Mag.

Davis, J. Peter. Sonnets in the Colloquial. 1983. 6.95 (ISBN 0-533-05638-1). Vantage.

Davis, J. R. Instabilities in MOS Devices. (Electrocomponent Science Monographs). 192p. 1981. 34.75 (ISBN 0-677-05590-0). Gordon.

Davis, J. R., jt. auth. see Banet, B. A.

Davis, J. Ronnie. New Economics & the Old Economists. LC 71-126162. 1971. 7.95x (ISBN 0-8138-1165-1). Iowa St U Pr.

Davis, J. Ronnie & Hulett, Joe R. An Analysis of Market Failure: Externalities, Public Goods, & Mixed Goods. LC 77-12344. (University of Florida Social Sciences Monographs: No. 61). (Illus.). 1977. pap. 3.50 (ISBN 0-8130-0587-6). U Presses Fla.

Davis, J. Ronnie & Meyer, Charles W. Principles of Public Finance. (Illus.). 448p. 1983. 29.95 (ISBN 0-13-709881-2). P-H.

Davis, J. W. & Michel, D. J., eds. Topical Conference on Ferritic Alloys for Use in Nuclear Energy Technologies. LC 84-61008. (Illus.). 657p. 1984. 61.00 (ISBN 0-89520-458-4). Metal Soc.

Davis, J. W., ed. see TMS Nuclear Metallurgy Committee Conference, Snowbird, Utah, June 19-23, 1983.

Davis, J. W., ed. see TMS Nuclear Mettalurgy Committee Conference, Snowbird, Utah, June 19-23, 1983.

Davis, J. W., et al, eds. Philosophical Logic. (Synthese Library: No. 20). 277p. 1969. lib. bdg. 29.00 (ISBN 90-277-0075-3, Pub. by Reidel Holland). Kluwer Academic.

Davis, J. William & Wright, Ruth. Texas: Political Practice & Public Policy. 3rd ed. (Government Ser.). 1982. pap. 12.95 (ISBN 0-8403-2792-7). Kendall Hunt.

Davis, Jack & Loveless, E. E. The Administrator & Educational Facilities. LC 80-1445. 272p. 1981. lib. bdg. 23.00 (ISBN 0-8191-1391-3); pap. text ed. 12.75 (ISBN 0-8191-1392-1). U Pr of Amer.

Davis, Jack, jt. auth. see Hart, Stan.

Davis, Jack E. The Spanish of Argentina & Uruguay: An Annotated Bibliography for 1940-1978. (Janua Linguarum Series Maior: No. 105). 360p. 1982. text ed. 51.20 (ISBN 90-279-3339-1). Mouton.

Davis, Jack E., tr. see Leon-Portilla, Miguel.

Davis, Jackson. Africa Advancing: A Study of Rural Education & Agriculture in West Africa & Belgian Congo. LC 72-98717. (Illus.). Repr. of 1945 ed. 19.75x (ISBN 0-8371-2791-2, DAA&, Pub. by Negro U Pr). Greenwood.

--Management of Channel Catfish in Kansas. (Miscellaneous Publications: No. 21). 56p. 1959. pap. 3.00 (ISBN 0-686-79821-X). U of KS Mus Nat Hist.

Davis, Jacquelyn K. & Pfaltzgraff, Robert L., Jr. The Atlantic Alliance & U. S. Global Strategy. LC 83-18642. (Special Report Ser.). 44p. 1983. pap. 7.50 (ISBN 0-89549-051-X). Inst Foreign Policy Anal.

--Power Projection & the Long-Range Combat Aircraft: Missions, Capabilities & Alternative Designs. LC 81-82130. (Special Report Ser.). 37p. 1981. 6.50 (ISBN 0-89549-033-1). Inst Foreign Policy Anal.

Davis, Jacquelyn K., jt. auth. see Pfaltzgraff, Robert L., Jr.

Davis, Jacquelyn K., jt. auth. see Pfalzgraff, Robert L., Jr.

Davis, Jacquelyn K., et al. Salt II & U. S.-Soviet Strategic Forces. LC 79-2713. (Special Reports Ser.). 75p. 1979. 5.00 (ISBN 0-89549-016-1). Inst Foreign Policy Anal.

Davis, James. Our Communities & Others: Study Book. Hawke, Sharryl D. & Combs, Eunice A., eds. (Illus.). 57p. (gr. 3). 1983. pap. 4.50 (ISBN 0-943068-74-6). Graphic Learning.

Davis, James, jt. ed. see Brandstatter, Hermann.

Davis, James A. Do People Like Me Have Any Control Over Politics? A Study of the Locus of Political Control As Perceived by Mexican-American Adolescents of South Texas. LC 80-65614. 140p. 1981. perfect bdg. 11.50 (ISBN 0-86548-029-X). R & E Pubs.

--Education for Positive Mental Health: A Review of Existing Research & Recommendations for Future Studies. LC 64-15607. (Monographs in Social Research: No. 5). 1965. 7.95x (ISBN 0-202-09009-4). NORC.

--Elementary Survey Analysis. (Methods of Social Science Ser). (Illus.). 1971. pap. text ed. 17.95 (ISBN 0-13-260547-3). P-H.

--Fifty-First Virginia Infantry. (The Virginia Regimental Histories Ser.). (Illus.). 1985. 16.45 (ISBN 0-930919-13-0). H E Howard.

--General Social Survey, 1972. 1973. codebk. write for info. (ISBN 0-89138-060-4). ICPSR.

--General Social Survey, 1973. 1974. codebk. write for info. (ISBN 0-89138-073-6). ICPSR.

--General Social Survey, 1974. LC 75-36289. 1975. codebk. write for info. (ISBN 0-89138-119-8). ICPSR.

--Great Aspirations: The Graduate School Plans of America's College Seniors. LC 64-15603. (NORC Monographs in Social Research Ser.: No. 1). 1964. 11.95x (ISBN 0-202-09004-3). NORC.

--Studies in Social Change Since 1948, Vol. 1: Methodological. (Report Ser: No. 127-A). 1976. 4.50x (ISBN 0-932132-19-7). NORC.

--Studies in Social Change Since 1948, Vol. 2: Substantive. (Report Ser: No. 127-B). 1976. 7.00x (ISBN 0-932132-20-0). NORC.

--Undergraduate Career Decisions: Correlates of Occupational Choice. LC 64-15604. (NORC Monographs in Social Research Ser.: No. 2). (Illus.). 1965. 9.95x (ISBN 0-202-09007-8). NORC.

--An Unfair Advantage: The Mental Part of Sports & Business. LC 84-50120. (Illus.). 215p. (Orig.). 1984. 19.95 (ISBN 0-915377-00-4); pap. 13.95 (ISBN 0-915377-01-2). Trad Pub.

--Wisdom & Spirit: An Investigation of 1 Corinthians 1.18-3.20 Against the Background of Jewish Sapiential. (Traditions in the Greco-Roman Period Ser.). 270p. (Orig.). 1984. lib. bdg. 24.50 (ISBN 0-8191-4210-7); pap. text ed. 13.50 (ISBN 0-8191-4211-5). U Pr of Amer.

Davis, James A. & Gebhard, Ruth. Great Books & Small Groups. LC 77-24390. 1977. Repr. of 1961 ed. lib. bdg. 18.50x (ISBN 0-8371-9742-2, DAGB). Greenwood.

Davis, James A. & Smith, Tom W. General Social Surveys, 1972-1982: Cumulative Codebook. 1982. 10.00 (ISBN 0-932132-27-8). NORC.

--General Social Surveys, 1972-1985: Cumulative Codebook. (National Data Program for The Social Science Ser.: No. 6). 450p. 1985. pap. text ed. 12.50x (ISBN 0-932132-32-4). NORC.

Davis, James A., jt. auth. see Davis, Richard H.

Davis, James A., ed. see Goodman, Leo A.

Davis, James A., et al. Americans View the Military: Public Opinion in 1982. (Report Ser.: No. 131). 1983. 8.00 (ISBN 0-932132-29-4). NORC.

Davis, James B. La Quete de Paul Gadenne: Une Morale pour Notre Epoque. 96p. (Fr.). 1979. 9.95 (ISBN 0-917786-18-1). Summa Pubns.

Davis, James C. The Decline of the Venetian Nobility As a Ruling Class. LC 78-64238. (Johns Hopkins University. Studies in the Social Sciences. Eightieth Ser. 1962: 2). Repr. of 1962 ed. 17.50 (ISBN 0-404-61343-8). AMS Pr.

--A Venetian Family & Its Fortune, 1500-1900: The Dona & the Conservation of Their Wealth. LC 74-26309. (Memoirs Ser.: Vol. 106). (Illus.). 1975. 6.50 (ISBN 0-87169-106-X). Am Philos.

Davis, James E. Chicago: Copy Master File. new ed. Hawke, Sharryl D., et al, eds. 225p. 1986. pap. 65.00 (ISBN 0-87746-010-8). Graphic Learning.

--Chicago: Study Book. Hawke, Sharryl D., et al, eds. 80p. 1986. pap. 4.90 study book (ISBN 0-87746-011-6). Graphic Learning.

--Chicago: Teachers Guide. Hawke, Sharryl D., et al, eds. 153p. 1986. pap. 15.00 (ISBN 0-87746-009-4). Graphic Learning.

--Our Communities: And Other Study Book Ser. Hawke, Sharryl D. & Combs, Eunice A., eds. (Illus.). 1983. pap. 360.00 ser. of 105 (ISBN 0-943068-98-3). Graphic Learning.

--Our Communities & Others: Manual. Hawke, Sharryl D. & Combs, Eunice A., eds. (Illus.). 323p. (gr. 3). 1983. duplication masters 69.00 (ISBN 0-943068-52-5). Graphic Learning.

Davis, James E. & Davis, Hazel R. Women's Studies. 108p. 1981. 5.50 (ISBN 0-8141-5811-0). NCTE.

Davis, James E., jt. auth. see Helburn, Suzanne W.

Davis, James E., ed. Dealing with Censorship. LC 79-4053. 228p. 1979. pap. text ed. 10.00 (ISBN 0-8141-1062-2, 10622); pap. text ed. 7.75 members. NCTE.

--Fiction for Adolescents: Theory & Practice. 97p. 1977. 6.50 (ISBN 0-8141-1669-8); members 5.00 (ISBN 0-317-35270-9). NCTE.

--Planning a Social Studies Program: Activities, Guidelines, & Resources. 2nd ed. LC 83-681. 284p. 1983. pap. 17.00 (ISBN 0-89994-266-0). Soc Sci Ed.

--Teaching Shakespeare. 74p. (Reprinted from Spring 1976 Focus of the Southeastern Ohio Council of Teachers of English). 4.50 (ISBN 0-317-35336-5, 52325); members 3.75 (ISBN 0-317-35337-3). NCTE.

Davis, James E. & Davis, Hazel K., eds. Licking County Writing Project. 127p. 1982. 6.00 (ISBN 0-8141-2811-4). NCTE.

Davis, James F. Almanzar. facsimile ed. LC 70-144153. (Short Story Index Reprint Ser.). (Illus.). Repr. of 1918 ed. 17.00 (ISBN 0-8369-3768-6). Ayer Co Pubs.

--A Survey of the Spherical Space Form Problem. (Mathematical Reports Ser.: vol.2, pt. 2). 72p. 1985. pap. text ed. 19.00 (ISBN 3-7186-0250-4). Harwood Academic.

Davis, James H. Group Performance. Kiesler, Charles A., ed. (Psychology-Topics in Social Psychology). 115p. 1969. pap. text ed. 11.95 (ISBN 0-394-34806-0, RanC). Random.

Davis, James H., jt. auth. see Stephenson, G. M.

Davis, James H., Jr. Fenelon. (World Authors Ser.). 1979. lib. bdg. 15.95 (ISBN 0-8057-6384-8, Twayne). G K Hall.

Davis, James M. Mules, Donkeys & Burros. 1983. 5.95 (ISBN 0-8062-2178-X). Carlton.

--Raids: A Guide to Planning, Coordinating, & Executing Searches & Arrests. 138p. 1982. 23.50x (ISBN 0-398-04649-2). C C Thomas.

Davis, James O. & Laragh, John H., eds. Hypertension: Mechanisms, Diagnosis & Management. (Illus.). 288p. 1977. text ed. 18.95 (ISBN 0-913800-07-4). HP Pub Co.

Davis, James P. How to Make it through Law School: A Guide for Minority & Disadvantaged Students. 150p. 1982. 15.00x (ISBN 0-914970-23-2); pap. 7.50 (ISBN 0-914970-24-0). Conch Mag.

Davis, James R. Help Me, I'm Hurt: The Child Abuse Handbook. 168p. 1982. 9.95 (ISBN 0-8403-2747-1); pap. text ed. 9.95. Kendall-Hunt.

--The Sentencing Dispositions of New York City Lower Court Criminal Judges. LC 82-45016. (Illus.). 230p. (Orig.). 1982. lib. bdg. 25.00 (ISBN 0-8191-2566-0); pap. text ed. 12.50 (ISBN 0-8191-2567-9). U Pr of Amer.

--Street Gangs: Youth, Biker, & Prison Groups. 160p. 1982. pap. text ed. 7.95 anc casebound (ISBN 0-8403-2750-1). Kendall-Hunt.

Davis, James R. & Cushing, Barry E. Accounting Information Systems: A Book of Readings. LC 78-74681. pap. 17.95 (ISBN 0-201-01099-2). Addison-Wesley.

Davis, James W. National Conventions in an Age of Party Reform. LC 82-9382. (Contributions in Political Science Ser.: No. 91). 384p. 1983. lib. bdg. 35.00 (ISBN 0-313-23048-X, DNC/). Greenwood.

--National Conventions: Nominations Under the Big Top. rev. ed. Dillon, Mary E., ed. LC 77-189866. (Politics of Government Ser.). 124p. (Orig.). 1973. pap. 3.95 (ISBN 0-8120-0443-4). Barron.

--Presidential Primaries: Road to the White House. LC 79-54062. (Contributions in Political Science Ser.: No. 41). 1980. lib. bdg. 29.95 (ISBN 0-313-22057-3, DPP/). Greenwood.

Davis, James W., Jr. & Dolbeare, Kenneth M. Little Groups of Neighbors: The Selective Service System. LC 80-25861. xv, 276p. 1981. Repr. of 1968 ed. lib. bdg. 42.50x (ISBN 0-313-22777-2, DALN). Greenwood.

Davis, Jane. The Dynamics of Prostar. 300p. 1985. pap. 19.95 (ISBN 0-87094-669-2). Dow Jones-Irwin.

--Why Does the Tiger Have Stripes? LC 77-29165. (Illus.). (ps-4). 1978. PLB 6.95 (ISBN 0-89565-018-5). Childs World.

Davis, Janice. Cook & Color with Recipe Rabbit. (Illus.). (gr. 4-9). 1978. pap. 2.50 (ISBN 0-931318-01-7). Walnut AZ.

--Cowboy Jeans & Chili Beans. (Scratch-Sniff Color Ser.). (gr. 4-9). 1980. pap. 2.95 (ISBN 0-931318-04-1). Walnut AZ.

--The Merry Christmas Mice. (Scratch-Sniff-Color Ser.). (Illus.). (gr. 4-9). 1978. pap. 2.95 (ISBN 0-931318-02-5). Walnut AZ.

--A Tale of the Butterscotch Bears. (Scratch-Sniff-Color Ser.). (Illus.). (gr. 4-9). 1980. pap. 2.95 (ISBN 0-931318-05-X). Walnut AZ.

Davis, Jean. Straw Plait. (Shire Album Ser.: No. 78). (Illus.). 32p. (Orig.). 1981. pap. 2.95 (ISBN 0-85263-580-X, Pub. by Shire Pubns England). Seven Hills Bks.

Davis, Jean, jt. auth. see Kahn, Sandra S.

Davis, Jed H. & Evans, Mary J. Theatre, Children & Youth. 1982. text ed. 22.50 (ISBN 0-87602-016-3); pap. 19.00 (ISBN 0-87602-017-1). Anchorage.

Davis, Jed H., ed. Theatre Education: Mandate for Tomorrow. 60p. 1985. pap. 6.00 (ISBN 0-87602-023-6). Anchorage.

Davis, Jeff C., Jr. Advanced Physical Chemistry: Molecules, Structure, & Spectra. (Illus.). 632p. 1965. 39.95x (ISBN 0-471-06719-9, Pub. by Wiley-Interscience). Wiley.

Davis, Jefferson. Jefferson Davis, Constitutionalist: His Letters, Papers & Speeches, 10 Vols. Rowland, Dunbar, ed. LC 71-163682. Repr. of 1923 ed. Set. 425.00 (ISBN 0-404-02000-3); 42.50 ea. AMS Pr.

--Papers of Jefferson Davis: Vol. 2, June 1841-July 1846. McIntosh, James T., ed. LC 76-152704. (Illus.). xlii, 806p. 1975. 40.00x (ISBN 0-8071-0082-X). La State U Pr.

--Papers of Jefferson Davis: Vol. 3, July 1846 - Dec. 1848. McIntosh, James T., ed. LC 76-152704. (Illus.). xxxiv, 598p. 1981. 37.50x (ISBN 0-8071-0786-7). La State U Pr.

--Papers of Jefferson Davis: 1808-1840, Vol. 1. Monroe, Haskell M., Jr. & McIntosh, James T., eds. LC 76-152704. (Illus.). xcii, 594p. 1971. 37.50x (ISBN 0-8071-0943-6). La State U Pr.

--The Papers of Jefferson Davis, 1849-1852, Vol. IV. Crist, Linda L., ed. LC 76-152704. (Illus.). 511p. 1985. text ed. 37.50x (ISBN 0-8071-1037-X). La State U Pr.

--Rise & Fall of the Confederate Government. abr. ed. 16.75 (ISBN 0-8446-0074-1). Peter Smith.

Davis, Jefferson & Stephens, Alexander. Robert E. Lee. Simpson, Harold B., ed. 1983. 10.00 (ISBN 0-912172-28-2). Hill Jr Coll.

Davis, Jefferson, ed. see Confederate States of America - Constitutional Convention.

Davis, Jennie. In God's Great Way. LC 82-7446. (Illus.). 32p. (gr. 1-2). 1982. lib. bdg. 4.95 (ISBN 0-89693-201-X). Dandelion Hse.

--Julie's New Home: A Story about Being a Friend. (Making Choices Ser.). (Illus.). 30p. (gr. k-3). 1983. 9.65 (ISBN 0-516-06384-7). Childrens.

--Praise Him, Praise Him! (ps-3). 1982. pap. text ed. 4.95 (ISBN 0-89693-208-7, Sonflower Bks). SP Pubns.

--Praise Him! Praise Him! LC 82-7238. (Illus.). 32p. (ps-k). 1982. lib. bdg. 4.95 (ISBN 0-89693-208-7). Dandelion Hse.

Davis, Jennie, jt. auth. see Buerger, Jane.

Davis, Jerome. Capitalism & Its Culture. 1979. Repr. of 1935 ed. lib. bdg. 30.00 (ISBN 0-8492-0696-0). R West.

--Russian Immigrant. LC 69-18770. (American Immigration Collection Ser., No. 1). 1969. Repr. of 1922 ed. 9.00 (ISBN 0-405-00518-0). Ayer Co Pubs.

Davis, Jerome, ed. New Russia: Between the First & Second Five-Year Plans. facs. ed. LC 68-22909. (Essay Index Reprint Ser). 1933. 17.00 (ISBN 0-8369-0365-X). Ayer Co Pubs.

Davis, Jerome D. High-Cost Oil & Gas Resources. (Illus.). 266p. 1981. 40.00 (ISBN 0-85664-588-5, Pub. by Croom Held Ltd). Longwood Pub Group.

Davis, Jerry C. Rehabbing for Profit. (Illus.). 224p. 1981. 31.50 (ISBN 0-07-015695-6). McGraw.

Davis, Jerry S. & Van Dusen, William D. Guide to the Literature of Student Financial Aid. 166p. 1978. pap. 7.00 (ISBN 0-87447-053-6, 238620). College Bd.

Davis, Jessica H., ed. see Weigle, Marta.

Davis, Jessica M. Farce. (The Critical Idiom Ser.). 1978. 5.50 (ISBN 0-416-81580-4, NO. 2159). Methuen Inc.

Davis, Jim. Garfield A to Z Zoo. LC 83-17697. (Garfield Mini-Storybooks). (Illus.). 24p. (ps-5). 1984. pap. 1.25 (ISBN 0-394-86483-2, BYR). Random.

--Garfield at Large. 1984. pap. 5.95 (ISBN 0-345-32007-7). Ballantine.

--Garfield Book of the Seasons. LC 83-17814. (Garfield Mini-Storybooks). (Illus.). 24p. (gr. k-5). 1984. pap. 1.25 (ISBN 0-394-86482-4). Random.

--Garfield Counts to Ten. LC 83-60602. (Shape Bks.). (Illus.). 24p. (ps). 1983. bds. 2.95 comb-bound (ISBN 0-394-86123-X). Random.

--Garfield Eats His Heart Out. (Illus.). 128p. (Orig.). 1984. pap. 5.95 (ISBN 0-345-32018-2). Ballantine.

--Garfield Gains Weight. 128p. (Orig.). 1984. pap. 5.95 (ISBN 0-345-32008-5). Ballantine.

--Garfield Goes to a Picnic. LC 82-60879. (Sniffy Bks.). (Illus.). 24p. (ps-1). 1983. pap. 3.95 (ISBN 0-394-85634-1). Random.

--Garfield Goes to the Farm. (Deluxe Coloring Bks.). 64p. (ps-3). 1985. pap. 2.95 (ISBN 0-394-87614-8, BYR). Random.

--Garfield Goes Underground. LC 83-60600. (Garfield Mini-Storybks.). (Illus.). 32p. (gr. k-5). 1983. pap. 1.25 (ISBN 0-394-86121-3). Random.

--Garfield: His Nine Lives. (Illus.). 128p. (Orig.). 1984. pap. 8.95 (ISBN 0-345-32061-1); 17.45 (ISBN 0-345-32074-3). Ballantine.

--Garfield in Space. LC 83-6061. (Garfield Mini-Storybks.). (Illus.). 32p. (gr. k-5). 1983. pap. 1.25 (ISBN 0-394-86122-1). Random.

--Garfield Loses His Feet. 128p. 1984. pap. 5.95 (ISBN 0-345-31805-6). Ballantine.

--Garfield Makes It Big. 1985. pap. 5.95 (ISBN 0-345-31928-1). Ballantine.

--Garfield Mix & Match Storybook. (Garfield Ser.). (Illus.). 1982. spiral plastic 3.95 (ISBN 0-394-85444-6). Random.

--Garfield on the Town. pap. 4.95 (ISBN 0-345-31542-1). Ballantine.

--Garfield Rolls On. (Orig.). 1985. pap. 5.95 (ISBN 0-345-32634-2). Ballantine.

--Garfield Sits Around the House. 128p. 1984. pap. 5.95 (ISBN 0-345-32011-5). Ballantine.

--Garfield Takes the Cake. (Orig.). 1984. pap. 5.95 (ISBN 0-345-32009-3). Ballantine.

--Garfield the Knight in Shining Armor. (Garfield Ser.). (Illus.). 32p. (ps). 1982. pap. 1.25 (ISBN 0-394-85446-2). Random.

--Garfield: The Knight in Shining Armor. (Illus.). 32p. 1984. Repr. of 1983 ed. 8.98 (ISBN 0-87660-013-5). I J E Bk Pub.

--Garfield Tips the Scales. 128p. 1984. pap. 4.95 (ISBN 0-345-31271-6). Ballantine.

--The Garfield Treasury. (Orig.). 1984. pap. 8.95 (ISBN 0-345-32106-5). Ballantine.

--Garfield Water Fun. (Bathtime Books). (Illus.). 10p. (gr. 1-4). 1985. vinyl 2.95 (ISBN 0-394-87360-2, BYR). Random.

--Garfield Weighs in. (Orig.). 1984. pap. 5.95 (ISBN 0-345-32010-7). Ballantine.

--Here Comes Garfield. 1984. pap. 5.95 (ISBN 0-345-32012-3). Ballantine.

--My Little Pony Through the Seasons. (Deluxe Coloring Bks.). (Illus.). 64p. (ps-3). 1985. pap. 2.95 (ISBN 0-394-87387-4, BYR). Random.

--The Second Garfield Treasury. 120p. 1983. pap. 7.95 (ISBN 0-345-31225-2). Ballantine.

--The Third Garfield Treasury. 1985. pap. 8.95 (ISBN 0-345-32635-0). Ballantine.

Davis, Jim, jt. auth. see Byron, H. J.

Davis, Jim R. Garfield Bigger Than Life: His Third Book. 122p. 1984. pap. 5.95 (ISBN 0-345-32007-7). Ballantine.

Davis, Jimmie, Jr. Revenge of the Great Magician. 1984. 6.00 (ISBN 0-8062-2331-6). Carlton.

Davis, Jinnie Y. & Richardson, John V. Calligraphy: A Source Book. LC 81-19360. 224p. 1982. lib. bdg. 35.00 (ISBN 0-87287-277-7). Libs Unl.

Davis, Joan & Mason, Celestine. Intensive Care of the Respiratory. 1986. cancelled (ISBN 0-442-22006-5). Van Nos Reinhold.

Davis, Joan E. & Mason, Celestine B. Neurologic Critical Care. 1979. 18.95 (ISBN 0-442-22004-9). Van Nos Reinhold.

Davis, Joe. Hawaiian Song Album. 2.95x. Wehman.

Davis, Joe L. James Branch Cabell. (Twayne's United States Authors Ser). 1962. pap. 5.95x (ISBN 0-8084-0167-X, T21, Twayne). New Coll U Pr.

--Sons of Ben: Jonsonian Comedy in Caroline England. LC 67-11271. 253p. 1967. 10.95x (ISBN 0-8143-1302-7). Wayne St U Pr.

Davis, Joe T. Legendary Texans. 1982. 9.95 (ISBN 0-89015-336-1). Eakin Pubns.

--Legendary Texans, Vol. II. (Illus.). 1985. 10.95 (ISBN 0-89015-473-2). Eakin Pubns.

Davis, Joel. Endorphins: New Waves in Brain Chemistry. LC 83-24017. (Illus.). 264p. 1984. 16.95 (ISBN 0-385-27856-X, Dial). Doubleday.

Davis, Johanna. Machine Knitting: To Suit Your Mood. (Illus.). 96p. 1983. 17.95 (ISBN 0-7207-1298-X, Pub. by Michael Joseph). Merrimack Pub Cir.

--Machine Knitting: To Suit Your Mood. (Illus.). 96p. 1984. pap. 10.95 (ISBN 0-7207-1470-2). Merrimack Pub Cir.

Davis, John. Energy, to Use or Abuse. 192p. 1980. softcover 10.00x (ISBN 0-905381-00-9, Pub. by Gresham England). State Mutual Bk.

--The Evasive Peace. LC 79-142227. 1970. pap. 6.00 (ISBN 0-911026-01-0). New World Press NY.

--The First Settlers of Virginia: An Historical Novel. 2nd ed. LC 78-64070. Repr. of 1805 ed. 37.50 (ISBN 0-404-17059-5). AMS Pr.

--Gifts You Wouldn't Give Your Mother. (Illus.). 64p. 1985. pap. 5.95 (ISBN 0-312-32716-1). St Martin.

--Heresy & Reformation in the Southeast of England, 1520-1559. (Royal Historical Society, Studies in History: No. 34). 178p. 1983. text ed. 29.00x (ISBN 0-391-02874-X, Pub. by Swiftbks England). Humanities.

--Nebraska Map Studies Program: Activity Manual. 1st ed. Yockstick, M. L., ed. (Illus.). (gr. 4). 1980. Duplication Master 49.00 (ISBN 0-943068-54-1); 5.00 (ISBN 0-943068-53-3). Graphic Learning.

--Program Organization in Western Australia's District High Schools. Simpson, Patricia M., ed. (Research Ser.: No. 1). (Illus.). xix, 162p. (Orig.). 1983. pap. 21.00x (ISBN 0-909751-74-9, Pub. by U of W Austral Pr). Intl Spec Bk.

--The Seaman Speculum, or Complete School-Master. Edson, Merritt A., Jr., intro. by. (Illus.). viii, 164p. 1985. pap. 45.00 (ISBN 0-9603456-1-2). Nautical Res.

--Strike a Giant Bell. 1980. 3.00 (ISBN 0-8198-6815-9); pap. 2.00 (ISBN 0-8198-6816-7). Dghtrs St Paul.

--Voyages & Works of John Davis the Navigator. Markham, Albert H., ed. & intro. by. LC 71-134714. (Hakluyt Society, First Ser.: No. 59). (Illus.). 1970. Repr. of 1880 ed. lib. bdg. 32.00 (ISBN 0-8337-2241-7). B Franklin.

Davis, John & Baldridge, Alan. The Bird Year: A Book for Birders with Special Reference to the Monterey Bay Area. 1980. pap. 5.95 (ISBN 0-910286-62-0). Boxwood.

Davis, John, jt. auth. see Hall, Robert.

Davis, John A. Merchants, Monopolists, & Contractors: A Study of Economic Activity & Society in Bourbon Naples 1815-1860. Bruchey, Stuart, ed. LC 80-2802. (Dissertations in European Economic History II). (Illus.). 1981. lib. bdg. 35.50x (ISBN 0-405-13986-1). Ayer Co Pubs.

--Regional Organization of the Social Security Administration. LC 68-59254. (Columbia University Studies in the Social Sciences: No. 571). Repr. of 1950 ed. 24.50 (ISBN 0-404-51571-1). AMS Pr.

Davis, John A., ed. Gramsci & Italy's Passive Revolution. LC 79-53440. (Illus.). 278p. 1979. text ed. 27.50x (ISBN 0-06-491609-X). B&N Imports.

Davis, John A., jt. ed. see Kitzinger, Sheila.

Davis, John C. The Furrows of Freedom. LC 61-11032. pap. 3.25 (ISBN 0-912806-14-1). Long Hse.

--Statistics & Data Analysis in Geology. LC 72-6792. (Illus.). 550p. 1973. 48.50 (ISBN 0-471-19895-1). Wiley.

Davis, John D. Davis Dictionary of the Bible. 1954. 24.95 (ISBN 0-8010-2805-1). Baker Bk.

--Davis Dictionary of the Bible. 896p. 1981. 45.00x (ISBN 0-7208-0240-7, Pub. by Pickering & Inglis Scotland). State Mutual Bk.

--English Silver at Williamsburg. LC 75-4814. (Williamsburg Decorative Arts Ser.). (Illus.). viii, 254p. (Orig.). 1976. pap. 11.00x (ISBN 0-87935-028-8). U Pr of Va.

--Genesis & Semitic Tradition. (Twin Brooks Ser.). 1980. pap. 4.95 (ISBN 0-8010-2902-3). Baker Bk.

--The Interview as Arena: Strategies in Standardized Interviews & Psychotherapy. LC 73-107647. 1971. 15.00x (ISBN 0-8047-0729-4). Stanford U Pr.

Davis, John E. An Introduction to Tool Marks, Firearms & the Striagraph. 302p. 1958. photocopy ed. 25.50x (ISBN 0-398-00402-1). C C Thomas.

Davis, John F. An Audience with Jesus. 134p. 1982. 4.00 (ISBN 0-8198-0721-4, SP0008); pap. 3.00 (ISBN 0-8198-0722-2). Dghtrs St Paul.

--China, During the War & since the Peace, 2 vols. LC 72-79816. (China Library Ser.). (Illus.). 1972. Repr. of 1852 ed. Set. lib. bdg. 42.00 (ISBN 0-8420-1369-5). Scholarly Res Inc.

--Chinese Novels. LC 76-43332. 1976. Repr. of 1822 ed. 45.00x (ISBN 0-8201-1278-X). Schol Facsimiles.

Davis, John G. Seize the Wind. LC 84-40627. 372p. 1985. 15.95 (ISBN 0-8128-3006-7). Stein & Day.

Davis, John H. The Kennedys: Dynasty & Disaster Eighteen Forty-Eight to Nineteen Eighty-Four. 944p. 1985. pap. 5.95 (ISBN 0-07-015862-2). McGraw.

--The Kennedys: Dynasty & Disaster, 1848-1983. LC 83-19566. (Illus.). 784p. 1984. 24.95 (ISBN 0-07-015860-6). McGraw.

Davis, John H., ed. Summary of the Colloquium on Public Law 94-210. (Lincoln Institute Monograph: No. 77-3). 1977. pap. text ed. 1.00 (ISBN 0-686-20039-X). Lincoln Inst Land.

Davis, John H., Jr. The Peat Deposits of Florida, Their Occurrence, Development, & Uses. (Illus.). 250p. 1946. 1.00 (ISBN 0-318-17292-5, B 30). FL Bureau Geology.

Davis, John J. Abortion & the Christian. 128p. 1984. pap. 4.95 (ISBN 0-87552-221-1). Presby & Reformed.

--Biblical Numerology. (Orig.). 1968. pap. 4.50 (ISBN 0-8010-2813-2). Baker Bk.

--Biblical Numerology. pap. 4.95 (ISBN 0-88469-063-6). BMH Bks.

--The Birth of a Kingdom: Studies in I & II Samuel & I Kings I-II. pap. 4.95 (ISBN 0-88469-053-9). BMH Bks.

--Conquest & Crisis: Studies in Joshua, Judges & Ruth. (Illus.). pap. 5.95 (ISBN 0-88469-052-0). BMH Bks.

--Foundations of Evangelical Theology: A Contextualized Approach. 232p. 1984. pap. 9.95 (ISBN 0-8010-2937-6). Baker Bk.

--Hebrew Language Chart. pap. 1.75 (ISBN 0-8010-2865-5). Baker Bk.

--Moses & Gods of Egypt. (Old Testament Studies). pap. 7.95 (ISBN 0-8010-2814-0). Baker Bk.

--Moses & the Gods of Egypt: Studies in Exodus. (Illus.). pap. 7.95 (ISBN 0-88469-068-7). BMH Bks.

--Paradise to Prison: Studies in Genesis. LC 74-30753. (Old Testament Studies). 384p. 1975. 14.95 (ISBN 0-8010-2838-8). Baker Bk.

--Paradise to Prison: Studies in Genesis. 14.95 (ISBN 0-88469-050-4). BMH Bks.

--Perfect Shepherd. (Illus., Orig.). 1980. pap. 4.50 (ISBN 0-8010-2905-8). Baker Bk.

--Perfect Shepherd. pap. 5.50 (ISBN 0-88469-110-1). BMH Bks.

--Theology Primer. LC 81-67093. 128p. (Orig.). 1981. pap. 5.95 (ISBN 0-8010-2912-0). Baker Bk.

--Your Wealth in God's World. 144p. 1984. pap. 4.95 (ISBN 0-87552-219-X). Presby & Reformed.

Davis, John J. & Whitcomb, John C. A History of Israel. (Old Testament Studies). 1980. 17.95 (ISBN 0-8010-2888-4). Baker Bk.

--History of Israel. 15.95 (ISBN 0-88469-061-X). BMH Bks.

Davis, John J., ed. The Necessity of Systematic Theology. 144p. 1980. pap. 7.95 (ISBN 0-8010-2903-1). Baker Bk.

Davis, John L. The Danish Texans. 1st ed. LC 79-63226. (Illus.). 122p. 1979. pap. text ed. 6.95 (ISBN 0-933164-57-2). U of Tex Inst Tex Culture.

--Danish Texans. 2nd ed. (Illus.). 168p. 1983. pap. 9.95 (ISBN 0-86701-010-X). U of Tex Inst Tex Culture.

--Houston: A Historical Portrait. (Illus.). 183p. 1983. 25.00 (ISBN 0-88426-062-3). Encino Pr.

--San Antonio: A Historical Portrait. (Illus.). 1978. 20.00 (ISBN 0-88426-055-0). Encino Pr.

--Treasure, People, Ships & Dreams. (Illus.). 75p. 1977. pap. 5.95 (ISBN 0-933164-20-3). U of Tex Inst Tex Culture.

Davis, John M. & Greenblatt, David, eds. Psychopharmacology Update: New & Neglected Areas. (Seminars in Psychiatry Ser.). 208p. 1979. 26.50 (ISBN 0-8089-1156-2, 790996). Grune.

Davis, John M. & Maas, James W., eds. The Affective Disorders. LC 83-3731. (Illus.). text ed. 27.50x, 448P. 1983 ed. (ISBN 0-88048-002-5, 48-002-5); pap. text ed. 19.95X, 448P. 1985 ed. (ISBN 0-88048-214-1, 48-214-1). Am Psychiatric.

Davis, John M., et al. An Atlas of Pedodontics. 2nd ed. (Illus.). 425p. 1980. 37.50 (ISBN 0-7216-2977-6). Saunders.

Davis, John M., jt. ed. see Blasewitz, A. G.

Davis, John P. Corporations: Study of the Origin & Development of Great Business Combinations & of Their Relation to the Authority of the State, 2 Vols. LC 74-164479. (Research & Source Works Ser.: No. 813). 1971. Repr. of 1905 ed. lib. bdg. 48.00 (ISBN 0-8337-0788-4). B Franklin.

--The Union Pacific Railway. LC 73-2501. (Big Business; Economic Power in a Free Society Ser.). Repr. of 1894 ed. 20.00 (ISBN 0-405-05082-8). Ayer Co Pubs.

Davis, John W., ed. Value & Valuation: Axiological Studies in Honor of Robert S. Hartman. LC 72-146661. 1972. 24.95x (ISBN 0-87049-130-X). U of Tenn Pr.

Davis, John W. & Anderson, Roy C., eds. Parasitic Diseases of Wild Mammals. facsimile ed. LC 72-103854. (Illus.). 1971. pap. 25.65x (ISBN 0-8138-2455-9). Iowa St U Pr.

Davis, John W., jt. ed. see Hoff, Gerald L.

Davis, John W., et al, eds. Infectious & Parasitic Diseases of Wild Birds. LC 71-88003. pap. 88.50 (ISBN 0-317-30472-0, 2024823). Bks Demand UMI.

--Infectious Diseases of Wild Mammals. 2nd ed. 446p. 1981. text ed. 36.95x (ISBN 0-8138-0445-0). Iowa St U Pr.

Davis, Joseph C. & Walker, Claxton. Buying Your House: A Complete Guide to Inspection & Evaluation. LC 75-5477. (Illus.). 252p. 1975. 12.95 (ISBN 0-87523-184-5). Emerson.

--Wage the Energy War at Home. LC 78-51121. (Illus.). 1978. 10.95 (ISBN 0-87523-191-8). Emerson.

Davis, Joseph K., et al. Literature. 1977. text ed. 17.90x (ISBN 0-673-15009-7). Scott F.

Davis, Joseph L. Sectionalism in American Politics, 1774-1787. LC 76-11310. 252p. 1977. 29.50x (ISBN 0-299-07020-4). U of Wis Pr.

Davis, Joseph S. Wheat & the AAA. LC 76-172868. (FDR & the Era of the New Deal Ser.). 468p. 1973. Repr. of 1935 ed. 59.50 (ISBN 0-306-70375-0). Da Capo.

Davis, Joy E., jt. auth. see Edwards, Lawrence.

Davis, Joy M. A Woman's Song. LC 83-70376. (Orig.). 1984. pap. 5.95 (ISBN 0-8054-5243-5). Broadman.

Davis, Joyce E. Chrysalis. Bennett, Heather, ed. LC 80-84927. 170p. 1981. 6.95 (ISBN 0-913420-91-3). Olympus Pub Co.

--Moonlight & Murder. (Orig.). 1981. pap. 1.95 (ISBN 0-8439-8036-2, Tiara Bks). Dorchester Pub Co.

Davis, Joyce O., ed. see Davenport, Robert.

Davis, Judith. Making Love: A Woman's Guide. 144p. 1984. pap. 3.50 (ISBN 0-451-13732-9, Sig). NAL.

--Queen: An Illustrated Biography. (Illus.). 96p. (Orig.). 1981. pap. 8.95 (ISBN 0-906071-91-7). Proteus Pub NY.

--Richard Gere: An Unauthorized Biography. 1983. pap. 2.95 (ISBN 0-451-12682-3, Sig). NAL.

Davis, Judith, jt. auth. see Toral, Judith.

Davis, Judy & Spellman, Shirley. Cardiac Rehabilitation for the Patient & Family. (Illus.). 176p. 1980. pap. text ed. 14.95 (ISBN 0-8359-0678-7). Reston.

Davis, Judy & Spillman, Shirley. Intermedics: Cardiac Rehabilitation for Patient & Family. 1981. pap. 4.80 (ISBN 0-8359-3131-5). Reston.

Davis, Judy G., jt. auth. see Davis, William R.

Davis, Julia F; see O'Neal, William B.

Davis, Julia M. & Hardick, Edward J. Rehabilitative Audiology for Children & Adults. LC 81-7427. 509p. 1981. 35.00 (ISBN 0-471-03560-2). Wiley.

Davis, Julian C. Rorschach Location Charts. 1958. spiral bdg. 18.00 (ISBN 0-8089-0594-5, 790998). Grune.

Davis, Julian C. & Foreyt, John P. Mental Examiner's Source Book. (Illus.). 248p. 1975. 29.50x (ISBN 0-398-03410-9). C C Thomas.

Davis, Julie. The Allure Book: How to Be the Woman Men Want & Women Want to Be. (Illus.). 192p. 1984. pap. 7.95 (ISBN 0-553-34074-3). Bantam.

--The Gathering Passion. 1978. pap. 1.95 (ISBN 0-8439-0527-1, Leisure Bks). Dorchester Pub Co.

--Three Hundred Sixty-Five Diet Tips. 208p. 1985. pap. 3.50 (ISBN 0-345-31848-X). Ballantine.

Davis, Julie & Weiss, Herman. How to Get Married: A Proven Plan for Finding the Right Mate. 64p. (Orig.). 1983. pap. 2.95 (ISBN 0-345-31102-7). Ballantine.

Davis, Julie, jt. auth. see Sartin, Janet.

Davis, Julie, jt. auth. see Wolf, Michael D.

Davis, Juliet, jt. auth. see Cox, Deborah.

Davis, K. & Newstrom, J. Human Behavior at Work. 7th ed. (Management Ser.). 544p. 1985. 29.95 (ISBN 0-07-015566-6); 9.95 (ISBN 0-07-015569-0). McGraw.

--Organizational Behavior: Readings & Exercises. 7th ed. (Management Ser.). 448p. 1985. 17.95 (ISBN 0-07-015508-9). McGraw.

Davis, K., jt. auth. see Werther, W. B.

Davis, K. E., jt. ed. see Gergen, K. J.

Davis, K. R. Marketing Management. 5th ed. 841p. 1985. 34.95 (ISBN 0-471-89532-6). Wiley.

Davis, K. Roscoe & McKeown, Patrick G. Quantitative Models for Management. 2nd ed. LC 83-24813. 784p. 1984. text ed. write for info. (ISBN 0-534-03122-6). Kent Pub Co.

Davis, K. Roscoe, jt. auth. see Leitch, Robert A.

Davis, Karen. National Health Insurance: Benefits, Costs, & Consequences. (Studies in Social Economics). 182p. 1975. 22.95 (ISBN 0-8157-1760-1); pap. 8.95 (ISBN 0-8157-1759-8). Brookings.

Davis, Karen & Rowland, E. Diane. Medicare Policy: New Directions for Health & Long-Term Care. LC 85-45048. 160p. 1985. text ed. 19.50x (ISBN 0-8018-2874-0). Johns Hopkins.

Davis, Karen & Schoen, Cathy. Health & the War on Poverty: A Ten-Year Appraisal. (Studies in Social Economics). 1978. 22.95 (ISBN 0-8157-1758-X); pap. 8.95 (ISBN 0-8157-1757-1). Brookings.

Davis, Katharine B. Factors in the Sex Life of Twenty-Two Hundred Women. LC 70-169379. (Family in America Ser.). 456p. 1972. Repr. of 1929 ed. 30.00 (ISBN 0-405-03856-9). Ayer Co Pubs.

Davis, Katherine, et al. The Little Drummer Boy. LC 68-25714. (Illus.). 32p. 1982. 4.95 (ISBN 0-02-749530-2). Macmillan.

Davis, Kathryn. At the Wind's Edge. (The Dakotas Ser.). 384p. (Orig.). 1983. pap. 3.25 (ISBN 0-523-43009-4). Pinnacle Bks.

--The Endless Sky. (The Dakotas Ser.: Bk. 2). 464p. (Orig.). 1984. pap. 3.50 (ISBN 0-523-41737-3). Pinnacle Bks.

--Memories & Ashes. 368p. 1985. pap. 3.95 (ISBN 0-515-08325-9). Jove Pubns.

Davis, Katie. Sentence Combing & Paragraph Construction. 244p. 1983. pap. text ed. write for info. (ISBN 0-02-327880-3). Macmillan.

Davis, Katie B. Federico Garcia Lorca & Sean O'Casey: Powerful Voices in the Wilderness. (Salzburg Studies in English Literature: Poetic Drama & Poetic Theory: No. 43). 1978. text ed. 25.50x (ISBN 0-391-01357-2). Humanities.

Davis, Katrina. Toothpick Building Illustrated. (Illus.). 48p. (Orig.). 1980. pap. 3.95 (ISBN 0-937242-04-7). Scandia Pubs.

Davis, Kay. Fugue & Fresco: Structures in Pound's Cantos. LC 84-61103. (Ezra Pound Scholarship Ser.). (Illus.). 125p. 1984. 18.00 (ISBN 0-915032-07-4); pap. 12.95 (ISBN 0-915032-08-2). Natl Poet Foun.

Davis, Keagle & Perry, William E. Auditing Computer Applications: A Basic Systematic Approach. 601p. 1982. 55.00x (ISBN 0-471-05482-8, Pub. by Ronald Pr). Wiley.

Davis, Keith. Human Behavior at Work. 6th ed. (Management Ser.). (Illus.). 576p. 1981. text ed. 31.95x (ISBN 0-07-015516-X). McGraw.

Davis, Keith & Newstrom, John. Organizational Behavior: Readings & Exercises. 6th ed. (Management Ser.). (Illus.). 468p. 1981. text ed. 17.95 (ISBN 0-07-015500-3). McGraw.

Davis, Keith, ed. Advances in Descriptive Psychology, Vol. 1. 400p. 1981. 45.50 (ISBN 0-89232-179-2). Jai Pr.

Davis, Keith, ed. see Miles, Raymond E.

Davis, Keith, et al. Business & Society: Concepts & Policy Issues. 4th ed. (Management Ser.). (Illus.). 672p. 1980. text ed. 31.95x (ISBN 0-07-015532-1). McGraw.

Davis, Keith E. & Mitchell, Thomas O., eds. Advances in Descriptive Psychology, Vol. 4. 1985. 52.50 (ISBN 0-89232-358-2). Jai Pr.

Davis, Keith F. Desire Charnay: Expeditionary Photographer. LC 81-52052. (Illus.). 192p. 1981. 29.95 (ISBN 0-8263-0592-X). U of NM Pr.

Davis, Ken. Better Business Writing: A Process Approach. 320p. 1983. 16.50 (ISBN 0-675-20015-6). Additional supplements may be obtained from publisher. Merrill.

Davis, Ken & Hollowell, John, eds. Inventing & Playing Games in the English Classroom: A Handbook for Teachers. LC 77-22925. 160p. (Orig.). 1977. pap. 7.50 (ISBN 0-8141-2372-4). NCTE.

Davis, Kenn. Dead to Rights. 224p. 1981. pap. 2.25 (ISBN 0-380-78295-2, 78295). Avon.

--Words Can Kill. (Orig.). 1984. pap. 2.50 (ISBN 0-317-05464-3, Crest). Fawcett.

Davis, Kenneth. FDR: The New York Years, 1928-1933. price not set. Random.

Davis, Kenneth & Henvey, Thom. Restoring & Reupholstering Furniture. Stoner, Carol, ed. (Illus.). 176p. 1982. 21.95 (ISBN 0-87857-429-8, 14-123-0). Rodale Pr Inc.

Davis, Kenneth & Webster, Frederick E. Sales Force Management. LC 68-20549. pap. 160.00 (ISBN 0-317-28587-4, 2055189). Bks Demand UMI.

Davis, Kenneth C. Discretionary Justice: A Preliminary Inquiry. LC 80-16898. xii, 233p. 1980. Repr. of 1969 ed. lib. bdg. 24.75x (ISBN 0-313-22503-6, DADC). Greenwood.

--Discretionary Justice: A Preliminary Inquiry. LC 69-12591. 245p. 1971. pap. 5.95x (ISBN 0-252-00153-2). U of Ill Pr.

--Two-Bit Culture: The Paperbacking of America. LC 83-22767. 430p. 1984. 18.95 (ISBN 0-395-34398-4); pap. 9.95 (ISBN 0-395-35535-4). HM.

Davis, Kenneth C., ed. Discretionary Justice in Europe & America. LC 75-38842. 224p. 1976. 17.50 (ISBN 0-252-00579-1). U of Ill Pr.

Davis, Kenneth L. & Berger, Philip A., eds. Brain Acetylcholine & Neuropsychiatric Disease. LC 79-862. 614p. 1979. 59.50x (ISBN 0-306-40157-6, Plenum Pr). Plenum Pub.

Davis, Kenneth P. Land Use. 1976. text ed. 40.95 (ISBN 0-07-015534-8). McGraw.

Davis, Kenneth P., jt. auth. see Brown, A. A.

Davis, Kenneth R. Anabaptism & Asceticism. LC 73-19593. 384p. 1974. 15.95x (ISBN 0-8361-1195-8). Herald Pr.

--Marketing Management. 4th ed. LC 80-19924. (Marketing Ser.). 778p. 1981. 36.45x (ISBN 0-471-05948-X). Wiley.

Davis, Kenneth R. & Webster, Frederick E., Jr., eds. Readings in Sales Force Management. LC 68-20550. (Illus.). pap. 118.80 (ISBN 0-317-10053-X, 2012394). Bks Demand UMI.

Davis, Kenneth S. Kansas: A Bicentennial History. (States & the Nation Ser). (Illus.). 1976. 14.95 (ISBN 0-393-05593-0, Co-Pub by AASLH). Norton.

--Kansas: A History. (States & the Nation Ser.). (Illus.). 1984. pap. 7.95 (ISBN 0-393-30179-6). Norton.

Davis, Kenneth S., ed. Paradox of Poverty in America. (Reference Shelf Ser.: Vol. 41, No. 2). 1969. 8.00 (ISBN 0-8242-0107-8). Wilson.

Davis, Kingsley. A Structural Analysis of Kinship: Prolegomena to the Sociology of Kinship. Zuckerman, Harriet & Merton, Robert K., eds. LC 79-8990. (Dissertations on Sociology Ser.). 1980. lib. bdg. 38.00x (ISBN 0-405-12962-9). Ayer Co Pubs.

Davis, Kingsley, ed. Demography Series, 20 vols. 1976. Set. 643.50x (ISBN 0-405-07980-X). Ayer Co Pubs.

Davis, Kingsley & Styles, Frederick G., eds. California's Twenty Million. LC 76-4573. (Population Monograph Ser.: No. 10). 1976. Repr. of 1972 ed. lib. bdg. 37.50x (ISBN 0-8371-8832-6, DACM). Greenwood.

Davis, Kortright. Cross & Crown in Barbados: Caribbean Political Religion in the Late 19th Century. (European University Studies: No. 23, Vol. 212). 195p. 1983. 24.20 (ISBN 3-8204-7781-0). P Lang Pubs.

--Mission for Caribbean Change. (IC-Studies in the Intercultural History of Christianity: Vol. 28). 300p. 1982. pap. 32.10 (ISBN 3-8204-5732-1). P Lang Pubs.

Davis, L. J. Bad Money. 224p. 1982. 12.95 (ISBN 0-312-06524-8). St Martin.

--Bad Money. 1983. pap. 3.50 (ISBN 0-451-62245-6, Ment). NAL.

--Christina Onassis: A Modern Greek Tragedy. LC 82-82786. (Illus.). 352p. 1983. 13.95 (ISBN 0-88015-008-4). Empire Bks.

--Walking Small. LC 74-75686. 224p. 1974. 6.95 (ISBN 0-8076-0748-7). Braziller.

Davis, L. M., jt. auth. see Winn, Charles S.

Davis, L. V. Dallas Blue. 240p. (Orig.). 1982. pap. 2.50 (ISBN 0-505-51785-X, Pub. by Tower Bks). Dorchester Pub Co.

Davis, L. Wilson. Go Find! Training Your Dog to Track. LC 72-88977. (Illus.). 160p. 1984. 12.95 (ISBN 0-87605-550-1). Howell Bk.

Davis, Lance & North, Douglass C. Institutional Change & American Economic Growth. LC 70-155584. pap. 72.80 (ISBN 0-317-26011-1, 2024447). Bks Demand UMI.

Davis, Lance E., jt. auth. see Payne, Peter L.

Davis, Lanny J. A User's Guide to Computer Contracting: Forms, Techniques, Strategies. LC 84-9667. 1984. 75.00 (ISBN 0-15-004368-6, Law & Business). HarBraceJ.

Davis, Lanny J. & Allen, Don A. A User's Guide to Computer Contracting: Forms, Techniques & Strategies. 620p. 1984. Supplements avail. 75.00 (ISBN 0-317-29411-3, #H43686). HarBraceJ.

Davis, Lanny J. & Ortner, Charles B. Negotiating Computer Contracts. LC 84-198741. (Illus.). write for info. Amer Bar Assn.

Davis, Larry. Air War over Korea. (Aircraft Special Ser.). (Illus.). 96p. 1982. 8.95 (ISBN 0-89747-137-7, 6035). Squad Sig Pubns.

--B-17 in Action. (In Action Ser.: No. 1063). (Illus.). 58p. 1984. pap. 4.95 (ISBN 0-89747-152-0). Squad Sig Pubns.

--F-4 Phantom II in Action. Campbell, Jerry, ed. (Aircraft in Action Ser.). (Illus.). 58p. 1984. pap. 4.95 (ISBN 0-89747-154-7). Squad Sig Pubns.

--F-84 Thunderjet. (Aircraft in Action Ser.: No. 1061). (Illus.). 50p. 1983. saddlestitch 4.95 (ISBN 0-89747-147-4). Squad Sig Pubns.

--F-86 in Color. (Fighting Colors Ser.). (Illus.). 1984. pap. 5.95 (ISBN 0-89747-110-5, 6502). Squad Sig Pubns.

--F-86 Sabre in Action. (Aircraft in Action Ser.). (Illus.). 1984. pap. 4.95 (ISBN 0-89747-032-X, 1033). Squad Sig Pubns.

--Mig Alley. 80p. 1985. pap. 7.95 (ISBN 0-89747-081-8, 6020). Squad Sig Pubns.

--P-47 Thunderbolt in Action. 50p. 1985. pap. 4.95 (ISBN 0-89747-161-X, 1067). Squad Sig Pubns.

--P-50 Mustang in Color. (Fighting Colors Ser.). (Illus.). 32p. 1984. pap. 5.95 (ISBN 0-89747-135-0, 6505). Squad Sig Pubns.

--P-80 Shooting Star in Action. (Aircraft in Action Ser.). (Illus.). 1984. pap. 4.95 (ISBN 0-89747-099-0, 1040). Squad Sig Pubns.

Davis, Larry, jt. auth. see Bard, Ray.

Davis, Larry E., ed. Ethnicity in Social Group Work Practice. LC 84-6628. (Social Work with Groups Ser.: Vol. 7, No. 3). 134p. 1984. text ed. 19.95 (ISBN 0-86656-323-7, B323). Haworth Pr.

Davis, Larry N. Planning, Conducting, & Evaluating Workshops. LC 74-82809. 310p. 1975. text ed. 17.95 (ISBN 0-89384-002-5); pap. 12.95 (ISBN 0-89384-001-7). Learning Concepts.

Davis, Lawrence. Theory of Action. (Foundations of Philosophy Ser.). 1979. ref. 17.95 (ISBN 0-13-913152-3); pap. text ed. 13.95 (ISBN 0-13-913145-0). P-H.

Davis, Lawrence B. Immigrants, Baptists & the Protestant Mind in America. LC 72-81264. pap. 60.00 (ISBN 0-8357-9682-5, 2019040). Bks Demand UMI.

Davis, Lawrence M. English Dialectology: An Introduction. LC 81-23164. (Illus.). 164p. 1983. text ed. 19.75 (ISBN 0-8173-0113-5); pap. text ed. 9.95 (ISBN 0-8173-0114-3). U of Ala Pr.

Davis, Lawrence M; see Bryant, Margaret M.

Davis, Lawrence M., et al. Studies in Linguistics in Honor of Raven I. McDavid Jr. LC 77-156749. 461p. 1972. 26.75 (ISBN 0-8173-0010-4); limited edition 35.75 (ISBN 0-8173-0005-8). U of Ala Pr.

Davis, Lee E. In Charge. LC 84-4969. 1984. pap. 4.95 (ISBN 0-8054-6404-2). Broadman.

Davis, Lee N. The Corporate Alchemists: Profit Takers & Problem Makers in the Chemical Industry. LC 83-25014. 320p. 1984. 15.95 (ISBN 0-688-02187-5). Morrow.

--Frozen Fire: Where Will It Happen Next? LC 78-74808. 1979. pap. 6.95 (ISBN 0-913890-30-8). Brick Hse Pub.

Davis, Lennard J. Factual Fictions: The Origins of the English Novel. LC 82-12815. 272p. 1983. 26.00x (ISBN 0-231-05420-3); pap. 14.50x (ISBN 0-231-05421-1). Columbia U Pr.

Davis, Lenwood & Hill, George H. Religious Broadcasting, Nineteen Twenty to Nineteen Eighty-Three: A Selectively Annotated Bibliography. (Reference Library of Social Science). 1984. lib. bdg. 40.00 (ISBN 0-8240-9015-2). Garland Pub.

Davis, Lenwood G. The Black Aged in the United States: An Annotated Bibliography. LC 80-1193. xviii, 200p. 1980. lib. bdg. 29.95 (ISBN 0-313-22560-5, DAB/). Greenwood.

--Black Colleges in the United States. (Dasein Literary Society Ser.). 350p. (Orig.). lib. bdg. 39.50 (ISBN 0-915833-26-3); pap. 13.95 (ISBN 0-915833-29-8). Drama Jazz Hse Inc.

--The Black Family in the United States: A Selected Bibliography of Annotated Books, Articles, & Dissertations on Black Families in America. LC 77-89109. 1978. lib. bdg. 29.95 (ISBN 0-8371-9851-8, DBF/). Greenwood.

--Black-Jewish Relations in the United States, 1752-1984: A Selected Bibliography. LC 84-4685. (Bibliographies & Indexes in Afro-American & African Studies: No. 1). xv, 130p. 1984. lib. bdg. 29.95 (ISBN 0-313-23329-2, DBB/). Greenwood.

--Black Women in the Cities, Eighteen Seventy-Two to Nineteen Seventy-Five: A Bibliography of Published Works on the Life & Achievements of Black Women in Cities in the U. S, Nos. 751-752. 2nd ed. 1975. 7.50 (ISBN 0-686-20343-7). CPL Biblios.

--Blacks in the American West: A Working Bibliography, No. 984. 2nd ed. 1976. 5.00 (ISBN 0-686-20388-7). CPL Biblios.

--Blacks in the State of Ohio, 1800-1976: A Preliminary Survey, Nos. 1208-1209. 1977. 8.50 (ISBN 0-686-19690-2). CPL Biblios.

--I Have a Dream: The Life & Times of Martin Luther King, Jr. LC 70-154202. 303p. 1973. Repr. of 1969 ed. lib. bdg. 19.75x (ISBN 0-8371-5977-6, DHD&). Greenwood.

--A Paul Robeson Research Guide: A Selected Annotated Bibliography. LC 82-11680. xxv, 879p. 1982. lib. bdg. 49.95 (ISBN 0-313-22864-7, DPR/). Greenwood.

--Sickle Cell Anemia: A Preliminary Survey, Nos. 1042-1043. 2nd ed. 1976. 9.50 (ISBN 0-686-20397-6). CPL Biblios.

Davis, Lenwood G. & Hill, George. Blacks in the American Armed Forces, 1776-1983: A Bibliography. LC 84-15697. (Bibliographies & Indexes in Afro-American & African Studies: No. 3). xv, 198p. 1985. lib. bdg. 35.00 (ISBN 0-313-24092-2, DAV/). Greenwood.

Davis, Lenwood G. & Sims, Janet L. Black Artists in the United States: An Annotated Bibliography of Books, Articles, & Dissertations on Black Artists, Seventeen Seventy-Nine to Nineteen Seventy-Nine. LC 79-8576. 160p. 1980. lib. bdg. 35.00 (ISBN 0-313-22082-4, DBA/). Greenwood.

Davis, Lenwood G., ed. The Black Family in Urban Areas in the U. S., 1965-1974: A Bibliography of Published Works on the Black Family in Urban Areas in the U. S, Nos. 808-809. 2nd ed. 1975. 8.50 (ISBN 0-686-20354-2). CPL Biblios.

Davis, Lenwood G., compiled by. Joe Louis: A Bibliography of Articles, Books, Pamphlets, Records, & Archival Materials. LC 83-1732. xxiii, 232p. 1983. lib. bdg. 29.95 (ISBN 0-313-23327-6, DAJ/). Greenwood.

--The Ku Klux Klan: A Bibliography. LC 82-21136. xv, 643p. 1984. lib. bdg. 49.95 (ISBN 0-313-22949-X, DKK/). Greenwood.

Davis, Lenwood G., ed. The Woman in American Society: A Selected Bibliography, Nos. 787-788. 2nd ed. 1975. 10.00 (ISBN 0-686-20355-0). CPL Biblios.

Davis, Lenwood G. & Daniels, Belinda S., eds. Black Athletes in the United States: A Bibliography of Books, Articles, Autobiographies & Biographies on Black Professional Athletes in the United States, 1880 to 1981. LC 81-6334. 288p. 1981. lib. bdg. 29.95 (ISBN 0-313-22976-7, DBL/). Greenwood.

Davis, Lenwood G. & Moore, Marsha L., eds. Malcolm X: A Selected Bibliography. LC 83-18329. xiii, 146p. 1984. lib. bdg. 29.95 (ISBN 0-313-23061-7, DAM/). Greenwood.

Davis, Lenwood G. & Sims, Janet L., eds. Marcus Garvey: An Annotated Bibliography. LC 80-653. xvi, 200p. 1980. lib. bdg. 29.95 (ISBN 0-313-22131-6, DMG/). Greenwood.

Davis, Lenwood G., compiled by. Blacks in the Cities, Nineteen Hundred to Nineteen Seventy Four: A Bibliography, Nos. 787-788. 2nd ed. 1975. 8.00 (ISBN 0-686-20353-4). CPL Biblios.

--Ecology of Blacks in the Inner City: An Exploratory Bibliography, Nos. 785-786. 1975. 8.00 (ISBN 0-686-20352-6). CPL Biblios.

Davis, Leo G. Challenging Lexicograpers Re Spelling Reform. 1983. 6.95 (ISBN 0-8062-2181-X). Carlton.

Davis, Leonard. Residential Care: A Community Resource. (Community Care Practice Handbook Ser.). viii, 118p. (Orig.). 1982. pap. text ed. 8.50x (ISBN 0-435-82264-0). Gower Pub Co.

--Sex & the Social Worker. Davies, Martin, ed. (Community Care Practice Handbook Ser.). 120p. (Orig.). 1983. pap. text ed. 8.50x (ISBN 0-435-82263-2). Gower Pub Co.

Davis, Leslie. Budget Decorating with Flair When Selling Your Home. (Illus.). 48p. (Orig.). 1984. pap. 3.95 (ISBN 0-9614214-0-1). Davis & Co.

--The Splintered Moon. (Velvet Glove Ser.: No. 19). 224p. 1985. pap. 2.25 (ISBN 0-380-89785-7). Avon.

--A Touch of Scandal. (Velvet Glove Ser.: No. 16). 192p. 1985. pap. 2.25 (ISBN 0-380-89667-2). Avon.

Davis, Levi, jt. auth. see Scott, Stanley.

Davis, Lionel & Davis, Edith. Keyboard Instruments. LC 62-18818. (Musical Books for Young People Ser). (gr. 5-11). 1963. PLB 4.95 (ISBN 0-8225-0057-4). Lerner Pubns.

Davis, Lisa E. & Taran, Isabel C., eds. The Analysis of Hispanic Texts: Current Trends in Methodology. LC 76-45294. (Second York College Colloquium). 1976. lib. bdg. 22.00x (ISBN 0-916950-03-4); pap. 14.00x (ISBN 0-916950-17-4). Biling Rev-Pr.

Davis, Lloyd & Irwin, Robert. Contemporary American Poetry: A Checklist. LC 75-19028. 183p. 1975. 16.50 (ISBN 0-8108-0832-3). Scarecrow.

Davis, Lloyd E., ed. Handbook of Small Animal Therapeutics. (Illus.). 718p. 1985. text ed. 55.00 (ISBN 0-443-08294-4). Churchill.

Davis, Lola A. Towards a New World Religion. 256p. 1983. pap. 16.00 (ISBN 0-942494-77-6). Coleman Pub.

Davis, Lorraine, ed. see Calasibetta, Charlotte M.

Davis, Louis E. & Cherns, Albert B., eds. Quality of Working Life: Cases & Commentary, Vol. 2. LC 74-24370. 1975. 22.95 (ISBN 0-02-907330-8); pap. text ed. 14.95 (ISBN 0-02-907340-5). Free Pr.

--The Quality of Working Life: Problems, Prospects & the State of the Art, Vol.1. LC 74-24369. 1975. pap. text ed. 16.95 (ISBN 0-02-907380-4). Free Pr.

Davis, Louise. Nashville Tales. LC 81-13778. (Frontier Tales of Tennessee Ser.: No. 3). 214p. 1981. 7.95 (ISBN 0-88289-294-0). Pelican.

Davis, Louise L. Frontier Tales of Tennessee. LC 76-18122. 190p. 1983. pap. 7.95 (ISBN 0-88289-422-6). Pelican.

--More Tales of Tennessee. 192p. 1983. pap. 7.95 (ISBN 0-88289-423-4). Pelican.

Davis, Lowery. The Unpardonable Sin. 10p. pap. text ed. 1.00x (ISBN 0-8134-1455-5, 1455). Interstate.

Davis, Lydia. Sketches for a Life of Wassilly. 32p. 1981. pap. 3.50 (ISBN 0-930794-45-1). Station Hill Pr.

--Story & Other Stories. Date not set. pap. 5.00 (ISBN 0-317-28696-X). Figures.

Davis, Lydia, tr. see Blanchot, Maurice.

Davis, Lydia, tr. see Chesneaux, Jean, et al.

Davis, Lydia, tr. see Chesneaux, Jean.

Davis, Lydia, tr. see Detrez, Conrad.

Davis, Lydia, tr. see Friedlander, Saul & Hussein, Mahmoud.

Davis, Lydia, tr. see Giroud, Francoise.

Davis, Lydia, tr. see Sartre, Jean-Paul.

Davis, Lynn. The Lynn Davis Guide to Personal Ads: How to Meet People; Safely, Selectively, Successfully. Meehan, Trudy, ed. LC 83-60285. (Illus.). 128p. (Orig.). 1983. pap. 4.95 (ISBN 0-9610742-0-5, Dist. by Golden-Lee Book Distributors, Inc.). Purcell Prods.

--Na Pa'i Ki'i: The Photographers in the Hawaiian Islands, 1845-1900. LC 80-70100. (Special Publication Ser.: No. 69). (Illus.). 48p. 1980. pap. 5.50 (ISBN 0-910240-29-9). Bishop Mus.

Davis, Lynn E., jt. auth. see Brown, Harold.

Davis, Lynn L., ed. see Dillon, Richard.

Davis, M. Multiaxial Actions on Manifolds. LC 78-3765. (Lecture Notes in Mathematics: Vol. 643). 1978. pap. 14.00 (ISBN 0-387-08667-6). Springer-Verlag.

--Visual Design in Dress. 1980. 26.95 (ISBN 0-13-942409-1). P-H.

Davis, M., ed. The Undecidable: Basic Papers on Undecidable Propositions, Unsolvable Problems & Computable Functions. LC 65-3996. 440p. 1965. 36.50 (ISBN 0-911216-01-4). Raven.

Davis, M., et al. Drug Reactions & the Liver. (Illus.). 400p. text ed. cancelled (ISBN 0-272-79620-4). Pitman Pub MA.

Davis, M., et al, eds. Drug Reactions & the Liver. 300p. 1981. text ed. 62.00x (ISBN 0-8464-1220-9). Beekman Pubs.

Davis, M. Edward & Meilach, Dona. Doctor Discusses Menopause & Estrogens. (Illus.). 1980. pap. 2.99 (ISBN 0-910304-26-2). Budlong.

Davis, M. H. Eagles. 384p. 1982. pap. 2.95 (ISBN 0-449-24557-8, Crest). Fawcett.

--Linear Estimation & Stochastic Control. LC 77-23389. 1977. pap. text ed. 16.95x (ISBN 0-412-15130-8). Halsted Pr.

--Linear Estimation & Stochastic Control. 1977. (Pub. by Chapman & Hall); pap. 16.95x (ISBN 0-412-15130-8, NO. 6563). Methuen Inc.

--Stochastic Control & Nonlinear Filtering. (Tata Institute Lectures on Mathematics Ser.). iv, 109p. 1984. pap. 7.10 (ISBN 0-387-13343-7). Springer-Verlag.

Davis, M. I. IBM Series One Design Decisions: Architecture. (Illus.). 48p. (Orig.). 1979. pap. text ed. 5.20 (ISBN 0-933186-01-0, G360-0060). IBM Armonk.

Davis, M. M. Kit Carson: A View of His Life & Times. LC 83-51112. (Illus.). 96p. (Orig.). 1984. pap. 5.95 (ISBN 0-9611028-1-0). Salt Warrior Pr.

Davis, M. M; see Bernard, William S.

Davis, Mac. Great Sports Humor. (Illus.). 128p. (gr. 3-7). 1982. pap. 4.95 (ISBN 0-448-12327-4, G&D). Putnam Pub Group.

--Strange & Incredible Sports Happenings. Powers, Richard, ed. (Illus.). 128p. (gr. 3-7). 1982. pap. 4.95 (ISBN 0-448-12326-6, G&D). Putnam Pub Group.

Davis, Madeleine & Wallbridge, David. Boundary & Space: An Introduction to the Work of D. W. Winnicott. LC 81-10034. 212p. 1981. 22.50 (ISBN 0-87630-251-7). Brunner-Mazel.

Davis, Madeleine, ed. see Winnicott, D. W.

Davis, Maggie. Diamonds & Pearls. 352p. 1985. pap. 3.95 (ISBN 0-425-07705-5). Berkley Pub.

Davis, Maggie S. The Best Way to Ripton. LC 82-2940. (Illus.). 32p. (ps-3). 1982. Reinforced bdg. 8.95 (ISBN 0-8234-0459-5). Holiday.

--Choices of a Growing Woman. LC 81-1083. 1982. 7.95 (ISBN 0-87491-418-3); pap. 4.95. Acropolis.

--Grandma's Secret Letter. LC 80-23331. (Illus.). 32p. (ps-3). 1982. reinforced bdg. 12.95 (ISBN 0-8234-0382-3). Holiday.

--Rickety Witch. LC 84-498. (Illus.). 32p. (ps-3). 1984. reinforced bdg. 9.95 (ISBN 0-8234-0521-4). Holiday.

Davis, Malcolm, jt. auth. see Plath, Carl.

Davis, Marbury, et al. Our Jobs, Our Health: A Woman's Guide to Occupational Safety & Health. 90p. pap. 6.00 (ISBN 0-317-17655-2). Mass Coalition.

Davis, Marcella Z. Living with Multiple Sclerosis: A Social Psychological Analysis. 80p. 1973. 9.50x (ISBN 0-398-02850-8). C C Thomas.

Davis, Margaret D. Piero Della Francesca's Mathematical Treatises. (Illus.). 165p. 1983. pap. 17.50 (ISBN 0-8390-0320-X). Abner Schram Ltd.

Davis, Margaret R. Families in a Working World: The Impact of Organizations on the Domestic Life. Steinmetz, Suzanne K., ed. LC 82-446. (Praeger Studies on Changing Issues in the Family). 256p. 1982. 31.95 (ISBN 0-03-059774-9). Praeger.

Davis, Margaret T. A Baby Might Be Crying. (The Breadmaker Trilogy Ser.). 224p. 1983. 13.95 (ISBN 0-8052-8152-5, Pub. by Allison & Busby England). Schocken.

--The Breadmakers. (The Breadmakers Trilogy Ser.). 224p. 1983. 13.95 (ISBN 0-8052-8151-7, Pub. by Allison & Busby England). Schocken.

--A Sort of Peace. (The Breadmakers Trilogy Ser.). 224p. 1983. 13.95 (ISBN 0-8052-8153-3, Pub. by Allison & Busby England). Schocken.

Davis, Margo, jt. ed. see Wilson, Page.

Davis, Maria H., jt. auth. see Freeman, Marie E.

Davis, Marianna W. Transformational Grammar & Written Sentences. (Janua Linguarum Ser. Didactica: No. 2). 1973. pap. text ed. 10.40x (ISBN 90-2792-384-1). Mouton.

Davis, Marilyn. The Little Fly. (Illus.). (ps-2). 1977. pap. 3.00 (ISBN 0-682-48739-2). Exposition Pr FL.

Davis, Mark E. Numerical Methods & Modeling for Chemical Engineers. LC 83-21590. 258p. 1984. 28.95 (ISBN 0-471-88761-7, Pub. by Wiley); solutions (Nonsaleable) 10.00 (ISBN 0-471-88252-6). Wiley.

Davis, Mark H. & Vinter, Richard. Stochastic Modelling & Control. (Monographs on Statistics & Applied Probability). 350p. 1985. 39.95x (ISBN 0-317-17595-5, 6874, Pub. by Chapman & Hall England). Methuen Inc.

Davis, Martha. Methods of Perceiving Patterns of Small Group Behavior. LC 78-322618. (Illus.). iv, 75p. (Orig.). 1977. pap. text ed. 5.95x (ISBN 0-932582-11-7). Dance Notation.

--Towards Understanding the Intrinsic in Body Movement. new ed. LC 74-7857. (Body Movement Perspectives in Research Ser). (Illus.). 192p. 1975. 31.00x (ISBN 0-405-06200-1). Ayer Co Pubs.

--Understanding Body Movement: An Annotated Bibliography. LC 73-37652. 1676p. 1971. 21.00 (ISBN 0-405-00286-6). Ayer Co Pubs.

--Understanding Body Movement: An Annotated Bibliography. LC 82-1096. 200p. 1982. 20.00x (ISBN 0-253-36163-X). Ind U Pr.

Davis, Martha & Skupien, Janet. Body Movement & Nonverbal Communication: An Annotated Bibliography, 1971-1981. LC 81-7881. 320p. 1982. 29.50x (ISBN 0-253-34101-9). Ind U Pr.

Davis, Martha, jt. auth. see McKay, Matthew.

Davis, Martha, ed. Anthropological Perspectives of Movement: An Original Anthology. LC 74-9162. (Body Movement Perspectives in Research). (Illus.). 203p. 1975. Repr. text ed. 25.50x (ISBN 0-405-06201-X). Ayer Co Pubs.

--Body Movement: Perspectives in Research, 10 vols. (Illus.). 1975. Set. 84.00x (ISBN 0-405-06197-8). Ayer Co Pubs.

--Interaction Rhythms: Periodicity in Communicative Behavior. LC 81-2936. 336p. 1982. 34.95 (ISBN 0-89885-003-7). Human Sci Pr.

--Psychoanalytic Perspectives of Movement: An Original Anthology. LC 74-9161. (Body Movement Perspectives in Research Ser). 164p. 1975. Repr. 30.00x (ISBN 0-405-06199-4). Ayer Co Pubs.

--Recognition of Facial Expression: An Original Anthology. LC 74-9160. (Body Movement Perspectives in Research Ser). 252p. 1975. Repr. 32.00x (ISBN 0-405-06198-6). Ayer Co Pubs.

Davis, Martha, jt. auth. see McKay, Matthew.

Davis, Martin. Computability & Unsolvability. (Mathematics Ser.). 288p. 1983. pap. 6.50 (ISBN 0-486-61471-9). Dover.

--A First Course in Functional Analysis. (Notes on Mathematics & Its Applications Ser.). 122p. (Orig.). 1966. pap. 26.95 (ISBN 0-677-01155-5). Gordon.

--Lectures on Modern Mathematics. (Notes on Mathematics & Its Applications Ser.). 196p. 1967. 57.75 (ISBN 0-677-00200-9). Gordon.

Davis, Marvin. Rank & Rivalry: The Politics of Inequality in Rural West Bengal. LC 82-9747. (Cambridge Studies in Cultural Systems). (Illus.). 280p. 1983. 42.50 (ISBN 0-521-24657-1); pap. 15.95 (ISBN 0-521-28880-0). Cambridge U Pr.

Davis, Mary. August Norieri. 1970. pap. 1.00 (ISBN 0-911116-39-7). Pelican.

--Careers in a Bank. LC 72-7645. (Early Career Bks.). (Illus.). 36p. (gr. 3-5). 1973. PLB 5.95 (ISBN 0-8225-0308-5). Lerner Pubns.

--Careers in a Medical Center. LC 72-7657. (Early Career Bks). (Illus.). 36p. (gr. 2-5). 1973. 5.95 (ISBN 0-8225-0310-7). Lerner Pubns.

--Careers in Baseball. LC 72-7646. (Early Career Bks.). (Illus.). 36p. (gr. 2-5). 1973. PLB 5.95 (ISBN 0-8225-0313-1). Lerner Pubns.

--Careers in Printing. LC 72-5416. (Early Career Bks.). (Illus.). 36p. (gr. 2-5). 1973. PLB 5.95 (ISBN 0-8225-0306-9). Lerner Pubns.

--Careers with a Telephone Company. LC 72-5412. (Early Career Bks.). (Illus.). 36p. (gr. 2-5). 1973. PLB 5.95 (ISBN 0-8225-0302-6). Lerner Pubns.

--Shetland Sheep Dogs. 135p. 7.95 (ISBN 0-317-11558-8). Diamond Farm Bk.

Davis, Mary B. James Elroy Flecker: A Critical Study. (Salzburg Studies in English Literature: Poetic Drama & Poetic Theory: No. 33). 1977. text ed. 25.50x (ISBN 0-391-01358-0). Humanities.

Davis, Mary E. Elephant's Track & Other Stories. facsimile ed. LC 78-94714. (Short Story Index Reprint Ser.). 1896. 19.00 (ISBN 0-8369-3093-2). Ayer Co Pubs.

Davis, Mary K. & Giammattei, Helen. More Needlepoint from America's Great Quilt Designs. LC 77-5305. (Illus.). 208p. 1978. 12.50 (ISBN 0-89480-005-1, 152). Workman Pub.

--Needlepoint from America's Great Quilt Designs. LC 75-8815. (Illus.). 172p. 1974. 10.95 (ISBN 0-911104-42-9, 055). Workman Pub.

Davis, Mary L. Polly & the President. LC 67-15697. (General Juvenile Bks). (Illus.). (gr. k-5). 1967. PLB 3.95g (ISBN 0-8225-0264-X). Lerner Pubns.

--Women Who Changed History: Five Famous Queens of Europe. LC 74-11899. (Real World Ser.). (Illus.). 104p. (gr. 5 up). 1975. PLB 6.95 (ISBN 0-8225-0638-6). Lerner Pubns.

Davis, Mary L. & Pack, Greta. Mexican Jewelry. (Illus.). 278p. 1982. pap. 10.95 (ISBN 0-292-75073-0). U of Tex Pr.

Davis, Mary O. Metanoia: A Transformational Journey. LC 84-71551. 154p. 1984. pap. 7.95 (ISBN 0-87516-544-3). De Vorss.

Davis, Matthew L. Memoirs of Aaron Burr, with Miscellaneous Selections from His Correspondence, 2 Vols. facsimile ed. (Select Bibliographies Reprint Ser). 1836. Set. 50.00 (ISBN 0-8369-5213-8). Ayer Co Pubs.

Davis, Matthew L., ed. Memoirs of Aaron Burr, 2 Vols. LC 73-152836. (Era of the American Revolution Ser). 1971. Repr. of 1836 ed. Set. lib. bdg. 85.00 (ISBN 0-306-70139-1). Da Capo.

Davis, Maxine. Through the Stratosphere. LC 46-4775. 1946. 2.75 (ISBN 0-911090-06-1). Pacific Bk Supply.

Davis, Mel. The Aplhanauts. 182p. 1985. 7.25 (ISBN 0-89697-246-1). Intl Univ Pr.

--High Uinta Trails. (Illus.). 132p. 1974. pap. 3.50 (ISBN 0-915272-02-4). Wasatch Pubs.

Davis, Mel, jt. auth. see Bottcher, Betty.

Davis, Mel, ed. see Mitchell, Finis.

Davis, Mel, ed. see Petzoldt, Paul.

Davis, Melinda D. Winslow Homer: An Annotated Bibliography of Periodical Literature. LC 75-29243. 138p. 1975. 16.00 (ISBN 0-8108-0876-5). Scarecrow.

Davis, Melodie M. For the Next Nine Months: Meditations for Expectant Mothers. 256p. 1983. pap. 3.95 (ISBN 0-310-45542-1). Zondervan.

--On Troublesome Creek. LC 83-18541. 112p. (Orig.). 1983. pap. 5.95 (ISBN 0-8361-3347-1). Herald Pr.

Davis, Merrell R. Melville's Mardi: A Chartless Voyage. (Yale Studies in English Ser.: No. 119). xv, 240p. 1967. Repr. of 1952 ed. 18.50 (ISBN 0-208-00069-0, Archon). Shoe String.

Davis, Michael. William Blake: A New Kind of Man. LC 77-71059. (Illus.). 1977. 27.50x (ISBN 0-520-03443-0); pap. 6.95 (ISBN 0-520-03456-2). U of Cal Pr.

Davis, Michael, jt. auth. see Miller, Arthur R.

Davis, Michael, ed. In A Wiltshire Village: Scenes from Rural Victorian Life, Selected from the Writings of Alfred Williams. 192p. 1981. pap. text ed. 10.00x (ISBN 0-904387-62-3, 61185, Pub. by Alan Sutton England). Humanities.

Davis, Michael, ed. see Ellsworth Community College.

Davis, Michael, ed. see Ellsworth COmmunity College.

Davis, Michael, ed. see Ellsworth Community College.

Davis, Michael H. Business Law in Egypt. 350p. 1983. 53.00 (ISBN 90-654-4086-0, Pub. by Kluwer Law Netherlands). Kluwer Academic.

Davis, Michael M. Paying Your Sickness Bills. LC 77-180572. (Medicine & Society in America Ser). 292p. 1972. Repr. of 1931 ed. 19.00 (ISBN 0-405-03947-6). Ayer Co Pubs.

Davis, Michael M., Jr. Psychological Interpretations of Society. LC 71-76682. (Columbia University. Studies in the Social Sciences: No. 87). Repr. of 1909 ed. 20.00 (ISBN 0-404-51087-6). AMS Pr.

Davis, Michael M., Jr. & Warner, Andrew R. Dispensaries, Their Management & Development: A Book for Administrators, Public Health Workers. Rosenkrantz, Barbara G., ed. LC 76-25658. (Public Health in America Ser.). (Illus.). 1977. Repr. of 1918 ed. PLB 33.00 (ISBN 0-405-09813-8). Ayer Co Pubs.

Davis, Michele S. A Dramatist & His Characters: Jose Cid Perez. LC 83-60447. (Senda de Estudios y Ensayos). (Illus.). 184p. (Orig.). 1983. pap. 13.95 (ISBN 0-918454-33-6). Senda Nueva.

Davis, Mick. Prevent Burglary: An Aggressive Approach to Total Home Security. (Illus.). 1985. 18.95 (ISBN 0-13-699265-X, Busn); pap. 7.95 (ISBN 0-13-699257-9). P-H.

Davis, Mike. From Populism to Reaganism: Politics & Economy in the History of the U. S. Working Class. 288p. (Orig.). 1985. 25.00 (ISBN 0-8052-7269-0, Pub. by Verso England); pap. 8.95 (ISBN 0-8052-7270-4, Pub. by Verso England). Schocken.

Davis, Mike, et al, eds. The Year Left: An American Socialist Yearbook. 300p. (Orig.). 1985. 25.00 (ISBN 0-8052-7266-6, Pub. by Verso England); pap. 8.95 (ISBN 0-8052-7267-4, Pub. by Verso England). Schocken.

Davis, Mildred. Scorpion. 1979. pap. 1.95 (ISBN 0-671-82113-X). PB.

Davis, Milt. You Can Live Life As It Was Meant to Be: Leader's Guide. LC 80-50541. (Study & Grow Electives). 64p. 1985. pap. 3.95 (ISBN 0-8307-1015-9, 6101999). Regal.

Davis, Mitchell P. Talk Show Guest Directory. 104p. 1985. pap. 25.00 (ISBN 0-934333-00-9). Broadcast Inter.

Davis, Morris. Interpreters for Nigeria: The Third World & International Public Relations. LC 77-2345. 208p. 1977. 17.50x (ISBN 0-252-00552-X). U of Ill Pr.

Davis, Morton. Mathematically Speaking. 484p. 1980. text ed. 20.95 (ISBN 0-15-555190-6, HC); instr's manual avail. (ISBN 0-15-555191-4). HarBraceJ.

Davis, Morton & Whitener, John C. The Role of Vision in the Multidisciplinary Approach to Children with Learning Disabilities: Proceedings from Learning Disabilities Institute II. 326p. 1982. pap. 24.50x spiral (ISBN 0-398-04665-4). C C Thomas.

Davis, Morton D. Game Theory: A Nontechnical Introduction. Rev. ed. LC 83-70771. 250p. 1983. 20.00x (ISBN 0-465-02627-3); pap. 9.95 (ISBN 0-465-02628-1, TB-5105). Basic.

Davis, Moshe. America & the Holy Land Series, 72 vols. (Illus.). 1977. Repr. lib. bdg. 2212.50 (ISBN 0-405-10220-8). Ayer Co Pubs.

--The Emergence of Conservative Judaism: The Historical School in 19th Century America. LC 77-22180. (The Jacob R. Schiff Library of Jewish Contributions to American Democracy: No. 15). (Illus.). 1977. Repr. of 1965 ed. lib. bdg. 36.25x (ISBN 0-8371-9792-9, DAECJ). Greenwood.

--From Dependence to Mutuality: The American Jewish Community & World Jewry. (Texts & Studies). (Hebrew.). 1970. 10.00 (ISBN 0-911934-07-3). Am Jewish Hist Soc.

--Mordecai M. Kaplan Jubilee Volume, 2 Vols. 1953. Set. 50.00x (ISBN 0-685-13740-6, Pub. by Jewish Theol Seminary). Ktav.

Davis, Moshe, ed. Call to America to Build Zion: An Original Anthology. LC 77-70723. (America & the Holy Land Ser.). 1977. lib. bdg. 20.00x (ISBN 0-405-10306-9). Ayer Co Pubs.

--Christian Protagonists for Jewish Restoration: An Orginal Anthology. LC 77-70678. (America & the Holy Land Ser.). 1977. lib. bdg. 20.00x (ISBN 0-405-10221-6). Ayer Co Pubs.

--Holy Land Missions & Missionaries: An Original Anthology. LC 77-70703. (America & the Holy Land Ser.). (Illus.). 1977. lib. bdg. 20.00x (ISBN 0-405-10259-3). Ayer Co Pubs.

--Israel: Its Role in Civilization. LC 77-70673. (America & the Holy Land Ser.). 1977. Repr. of 1956 ed. lib. bdg. 31.00 (ISBN 0-405-10241-0). Ayer Co Pubs.

--Pioneer Settlement in the Twenties: An Original Anthology. LC 77-70699. (America & the Holy Land Ser.). 1977. lib. bdg. 20.00x (ISBN 0-405-10250-X). Ayer Co Pubs.

--With Eyes Toward Zion: Scholars Coloquium on America-Holy Land Studies. LC 77-2493. (America & the Holy Land Ser.). (Illus.). 1977. lib. bdg. 24.50x (ISBN 0-405-10312-3). Ayer Co Pubs.

--World Jewry & the State of Israel. LC 77-72730. (Indivual Publications Ser.). 1977. lib. bdg. 14.00x (ISBN 0-405-10305-0). Ayer Co Pubs.

--The Yom Kippur War: Israel & the Jewish People. LC 74-10466. 381p. 1974. 11.00 (ISBN 0-405-06192-7). Ayer Co Pubs.

--Zionism in Transition. LC 80-67905. 1980. lib. bdg. 24.00x (ISBN 0-405-13825-3). Ayer Co Pubs.

--Zionism in Transition. 1980. pap. 8.00 (ISBN 0-930832-61-2). Herzl Pr.

Davis, Moshe, ed. see Adler, Cyrus & Margalith, Aaron M.

Davis, Moshe, ed. see Alvan, Bond.

Davis, Moshe, ed. see Babcock, Maltbie D.

Davis, Moshe, ed. see Badt-Strauss, Bertha.

Davis, Moshe, ed. see Barclay, James T.

Davis, Moshe, ed. see Bartlett, Samuel C.

Davis, Moshe, ed. see Bliss, Frederick J.

Davis, Moshe, ed. see Bloomgarden, Yehoash.

Davis, Moshe, ed. see Browne, John R.

Davis, Moshe, jt. ed. see Burnet, David S.

Davis, Moshe, ed. see Cox, Samuel S.

Davis, Moshe, ed. see Cresson, Warder.

Davis, Moshe, ed. see Crossman, Richard.

Davis, Moshe, ed. see De Hass, Frank S.

Davis, Moshe, ed. see Field, Frank M.

Davis, Moshe, ed. see Fosdick, Harry E.
Davis, Moshe, ed. see Fulton, John.
Davis, Moshe, ed. see Gilmore, Albert F.
Davis, Moshe, ed. see Gordon, Benjamin L.
Davis, Moshe, ed. see Holmes, John H.
Davis, Moshe, ed. see Hoofien, Sigfried.
Davis, Moshe, ed. see Intercollegiate Zionist Association of America.
Davis, Moshe, ed. see Isaacs, Samuel H.
Davis, Moshe, ed. see Isreal, John & Lundt, Henry.
Davis, Moshe, ed. see Johnson, Sarah B.
Davis, Moshe, ed. see Kallen, Horace M.
Davis, Moshe, ed. see Krimsky, Joseph.
Davis, Moshe, ed. see Kyle, Melvin G.
Davis, Moshe, ed. see Lipsky, Louis.
Davis, Moshe, ed. see Lynch, William F.
Davis, Moshe, ed. see Macalister, Robert A.
Davis, Moshe, ed. see McCrackan, William D.
Davis, Moshe, ed. see Merrill, Selah.
Davis, Moshe, ed. see Miller, Ellen C.
Davis, Moshe, ed. see Minor, Clorinda.
Davis, Moshe, ed. see Morris, Robert.
Davis, Moshe, ed. see Morton, Daniel O.
Davis, Moshe, ed. see Odenheimer, William H.
Davis, Moshe, ed. see Olin, Stephen.
Davis, Moshe, ed. see Palmer, Edward H.
Davis, Moshe, ed. see Paton, Lewis B.
Davis, Moshe, ed. see Prime, William C.
Davis, Moshe, ed. see Rifkind, Simon H., et al.
Davis, Moshe, ed. see Rix, Herbert.
Davis, Moshe, ed. see Robinson, Edward.
Davis, Moshe, ed. see Salo, Baron W. & Baron, Jennette M.
Davis, Moshe, ed. see Schaff, Philip.
Davis, Moshe, ed. see Smith, Ethan.
Davis, Moshe, ed. see Smith, George A., et al.
Davis, Moshe, ed. see Sneersohn, Haym Z.
Davis, Moshe, ed. see Szold, Henrietta.
Davis, Moshe, ed. see Talmage, Thomas.
Davis, Moshe, ed. see Taylor, Baynard.
Davis, Moshe, ed. see Thompson, George, et al.
Davis, Moshe, ed. see Van Dyke, Henry.
Davis, Moshe, ed. see Vester, Bertha H.
Davis, Moshe, ed. see Wallace, Edwin S.
Davis, Moshe, ed. see Ware, William.
Davis, Moshe, ed. see Worsley, Israel.
Davis, Murray S. Intimate Relations. LC 73-1859. (Illus.). 1973. 14.95 (ISBN 0-02-907020-1); pap. 6.95 (ISBN 0-02-907200-X). Free Pr.
--Smut: Erotic Reality-Obscene Ideology. LC 82-16061. 328p. 1983. 22.50 (ISBN 0-226-13791-0). U of Chicago Pr.
--Smut: Erotic Reality-Obscene Ideology. LC 82-16061. xxviii, 314p. 1985. pap. 10.95 (ISBN 0-226-13792-9). U of Chicago Pr.
Davis, Myer D. Shetaroth, Hebrew Deeds of English Jews Before 1290. 410p. 1888. text ed. 74.52x (ISBN 0-576-80111-9, Pub. by Gregg Intl Pubs England). Gregg Intl.
Davis, Myron W. & Van Woerkom, Carol. A Safe Change of Pace for the Beginning Jogger. (Illus.). 64p. 1981. 4.95 (ISBN 0-8403-2576-2). Kendall-Hunt.
Davis, N. Edward & Maisel, Edward. Have Your Baby, Keep Your Figure. rev. ed. LC 63-13231. (Illus.). 1979. pap. 4.95 (ISBN 0-8128-6039-X). Stein & Day.
Davis, Nanciellen. Ethnicity & Ethnic Group Persistance in an Acadian Village in Maritime Canada. LC 83-45352. (Immigrant Communities & Ethnic Minorities in the United States & Canada Ser.). (Illus.). 256p. 1985. 38.50 (ISBN 0-404-19405-2). AMS Pr.
Davis, Nancy. Vocabulary Improvement. 3rd ed. 1978. pap. text ed. 19.95x (ISBN 0-07-015543-7). McGraw.
Davis, Nanette J. From Crime to Choice: The Transformation of Abortion in America. LC 85-8018. (Contributions in Women's Studies Ser.: No. 60). (Illus.). 1985. lib. bdg. 35.00 (ISBN 0-313-24929-6, DCC/). Greenwood.
Davis, Nanette J. & Anderson, Bo. Social Control: The Production of Deviance in the Modern State. LC 83-136. 364p. 1983. text ed. 19.95x (ISBN 0-8290-0727-X). Irvington.
Davis, Nanette J. & Keith, Jone M. Women & Deviance: Issues in Social Conflict & Change, an Annotated Bibliography. LC 82-49164. (Applied Social Science Bibliographies Ser.: Vol. 1). 300p. 1984. text ed. 35.00 (ISBN 0-8240-9165-5). Garland Pub.
Davis, Natalie Z. The Return of Martin Guerre. 176p. 1984. pap. 5.95 (ISBN 0-674-76691-1). Harvard U Pr.
--Society & Culture in Early Modern France: Eight Essays by Natalie Zemon Davis. LC 74-82777. (Illus.). 1975. 27.50x (ISBN 0-8047-0868-1); pap. 10.95 (ISBN 0-8047-0972-6, SP-142). Stanford U Pr.
Davis, Natalie Zemon. The Return of Martin Guerre. (Illus.). 176p. 1983. 15.00 (ISBN 0-674-76690-3). Harvard U Pr.
Davis, Nathan. Writings in Jazz. 3rd ed. 185p. 1985. pap. text ed. 12.95 (ISBN 0-89787-804-3). Gorsuch Scarisbrick.
Davis, Nathaniel. The Last Two Years of Salvador Allende. LC 84-23774. (Illus.). 480p. 1985. 24.95 (ISBN 0-8014-1791-0). Cornell U Pr.
Davis, Nathaniel, ed. Graduate Research in Afro-American Studies: A Bibliography of Doctoral Dissertations & Master's Theses Completed at the University of California, Los Angeles, 1942-1980. (CAAS Special Publications). (Illus.). 46p. (Orig.). 1981. pap. 1.95 (ISBN 0-934934-12-6). Ctr Afro-Am Stud.
Davis, Neil M. Medical Abbreviations: Twenty-Three Hundred Conveniences at the Expense of Communications & Safety. 2nd ed. 63p. 1985. pap. 3.25 (ISBN 0-931431-02-6). Davis Assocs.
Davis, Neil M. & Cohen, Michael R. Medication Errors: Causes & Prevention. (Illus.). 288p. 1981. text ed. 15.95x (ISBN 0-89313-051-6). G F Stickley.
Davis, Nigel. The Rampant God: Eros Throughout the World. LC 84-60201. 291p. 1984. 17.95 (ISBN 0-688-03094-7). Morrow.
Davis, Nigel, jt. auth. see Meinhardt, Peter.
Davis, Norma A. Trade Winds Cookery. 1956. spiral bdg. 5.00 (ISBN 0-685-09015-9). Dietz.
Davis, Norman. Journeys to the Past. 1980. 9.95 (ISBN 0-910286-83-3); pap. 6.95 (ISBN 0-910286-78-7). Boxwood.
Davis, Norman, ed. The Paston Letters. (The World's Classics Ser.). (Illus.). 1983. pap. 6.95 (ISBN 0-19-281615-2, GB). Oxford U Pr.
--Paston Letters & Papers of the Fifteenth Century, Pt. 2. (Illus.). 1976. 98.00x (ISBN 0-19-812555-0). Oxford U Pr.
Davis, Norman, ed. see Sweet, Henry.
Davis, Norman, et al. A Chaucer Glossary. 1979. 29.95x (ISBN 0-19-811168-1); pap. 10.95x (ISBN 0-19-811171-1). Oxford U Pr.
Davis, Norman M. The Complete Book of United States Coin Collecting. rev. ed. 341p. 1976. 15.95 (ISBN 0-02-529880-1). Macmillan.
Davis, O. B. Introduction to Biblical Literature. 1976. pap. text ed. 9.25x (ISBN 0-8104-5834-9). Boynton Cook Pubs.
--Introduction to the Novel. rev., 2nd ed. (gr. 10 up). 1976. pap. text ed. 8.00x (ISBN 0-8104-6030-0). Boynton Cook Pubs.
Davis, O. B., jt. auth. see Davis, Alexandra.
Davis, O. K. Gramblings Gridiron Glory. (Illus.). 110p. 1983. pap. 7.95 (ISBN 0-9610262-0-0). O K Davis.
Davis, O. L., ed. Perspectives on Curriculum Development: 1776-1976. LC 76-39962. 1976. 9.50 (ISBN 0-87120-078-3, 610-76078). Assn Supervision.
Davis, O. L., Jr. Schools of the Past: A Treasury of Photographs. LC 76-12175. (Fastback Ser.: No.80). 50p. (Orig.). 1976. pap. 0.75 (ISBN 0-87367-080-9). Phi Delta Kappa.
Davis, O. L., Jr., jt. ed. see English, Fenwick W.
Davis, O. L., Jr., jt. ed. see Mehlinger, Howard.
Davis, Olive. Stockton: Sunrise Port on the San Joaquin. (Illus.). 152p. 1984. 22.95 (ISBN 0-89781-093-7). Windsor Pubns Inc.
Davis, Oscar, Jr. Save Your Marriage. 1982. 4.95 (ISBN 0-8062-2000-7). Carlton.
Davis, Ossie. Escape to Freedom: A Play About Young Frederick Douglass. LC 77-25346. 128p. (gr. 7 up). 1978. 11.50 (ISBN 0-670-29775-5). Viking.
--Langston: A Play. LC 82-70314. 144p. (gr. 7 up). 1982. 11.95 (ISBN 0-385-28543-4). Delacorte.
Davis, Oswald H. George Gissing, a Study in Literary Leanings. LC 74-3007. 1966. lib. bdg. 15.00 (ISBN 0-8414-3729-7). Folcroft.
--The Master. 206p. 1980. Repr. of 1966 ed. lib. bdg. 25.00 (ISBN 0-8482-0641-X). Norwood Edns.
--The Master: A Study of Arnold Bennett. 1979. Repr. of 1966 ed. lib. bdg. 22.50 (ISBN 0-8414-1899-3). Folcroft.
Davis, Owen. Voice. 1973. signed 4.00 (ISBN 0-685-78956-X, Pub. by Grosseteste); sewn in wrappers 1.00 (ISBN 0-685-78957-8). Small Pr Dist.
Davis, P., ed. Single Cell Protein. 1975. 47.00 (ISBN 0-12-206550-6). Acad Pr.
Davis, P., et al. Wemyss Ware: A Decorative Scottish Pottery. (Illus.). 120p. 1985. 55.00x (ISBN 0-7073-0354-0, Pub. by Scottish Academic Pr Scotland). Columbia U Pr.
Davis, P. H. & Cullen, J. The Identification of Flowering Plant Families. LC 78-8125. (Illus.). 1979. 29.95 (ISBN 0-521-22111-0); pap. 8.95x (ISBN 0-521-29359-6). Cambridge U Pr.
Davis, P. H. & Heywood, V. H. Principles of Angiosperm Taxonomy. 578p. 1973. Repr. of 1963 ed. 32.50 (ISBN 0-88275-129-8). Krieger.
Davis, P. H., jt. auth. see Stearn, W. T.
Davis, P. H., ed. The Flora of Turkey, 6 vols. 60.00x ea., vols. 1-4 (Pub. by Edinburgh U Pr Scotland). Vol. 1, 1965 (ISBN 0-85224-159-3). Vol. 2, 1965 (ISBN 0-85224-000-7). Vol. 3, 1970 (ISBN 0-85224-154-2). Vol. 4, 1973 (ISBN 0-85224-208-5). Vol. 5, 1975. 100.00x (ISBN 0-85224-280-8, Pub. by Edinburgh U Pr Scotland); Vol. 6, 1979. 125.00x (ISBN 0-85224-336-7, Pub. by Edinburgh U Pr Scotland); Vol. 7. 125.00 (ISBN 0-85224-396-0). Columbia U Pr.
Davis, P. J. The Lore of Large Numbers. LC 61-13842. (New Mathematical Library: No. 6). 165p. 1975. pap. 10.00 (ISBN 0-88385-606-9). Math Assn.
--The Schwarz Function & Its Applications. 241p. 1974. 19.00 (ISBN 0-88385-017-6, CAM-17); members 14.00 (ISBN 0-317-37232-7). Math Assn.
Davis, P. Michael & Whiteside, Frederick W. A Practical Guide to Preparing a Fiduciary Income Tax Return. 7th ed. 1978. pap. 11.50 1983 supplement (ISBN 0-88450-059-4, 1706-B). Lawyers & Judges.
Davis, P. Michael, jt. auth. see Crumbley, D. Larry.
Davis, P. R., ed. Performance Under Sub-Optimal Condition. 1971. pap. text ed. 21.00x (ISBN 0-85066-044-0). Intl Ideas.
--Performance Under Sub-Optimal Conditions. 104p. 1971. pap. 22.00x (ISBN 0-85066-044-0). Taylor & Francis.
Davis, P. W. History of the National Woman's Rights Movement for Twenty Years, with the Proceedings of the Decade Meeting, 1870. Repr. of 1871 ed. 16.00 (ISBN 0-527-22000-0). Kraus Repr.
Davis, P. W. & Solomon, E. P. The World of Biology. 2nd ed. 1979. text ed. 34.95 (ISBN 0-07-015552-6). McGraw.
Davis, P. W., ed. see Linguistic Association of Canada & the U.S.
Davis, P. William, jt. auth. see Solomon, Eldra P.
Davis, Pat. The Badminton Coach: A Manual for Coaches, Teachers & Players. 3rd, rev. ed. (Illus.). 160p. (gr. 9 up). text ed. 23.50x (ISBN 0-7182-1243-6, SpS). Sportshelf.
--Badminton: The Complete Practical Guide. (Illus.). 192p. 1982. 21.50 (ISBN 0-7153-8163-6). David & Charles.
--The Guinness Book of Badminton. (Illus.). 166p. 1984. 14.95 (ISBN 0-85112-271-X, Pub. by Guinness Superlatives England). Sterling.
Davis, Patricia. End of the Line: Alexander J. Cassatt & Pennsylvania Railroad. LC 78-977. 1978. 20.00 (ISBN 0-88202-181-8). Watson Pub Intl.
Davis, Patricia A. Suicidal Adolescents. 108p. 1983. 18.50x (ISBN 0-398-04866-5). C C Thomas.
--Two Hundred One Russian Verbs Fully Conjugated in All the Tenses. LC 67-26140. 1970. text ed. 9.95 o.p (ISBN 0-8120-6050-4); pap. text ed. 6.95 (ISBN 0-8120-0271-7). Barron.
Davis, Patricia A. & Oprendek, Donald V. Making Progress in Russian. LC 71-170354. 518p. (Rus). 1973. 27.50x (ISBN 0-471-00682-3). Wiley.
Davis, Patricia M. see Jakway, Martha & De Davis, Patricia M.
Davis, Patricia M. see Larson, Mildred L.
Davis, Patricia M., jt. ed. see Larson, Mildred L.
Davis, Patricia T. A Family Tapestry: Five Generations of the Curwens of Walnut Hill & Their Various Relatives. LC 72-14325. (Illus.). 224p. 1972. lib. bdg. 10.00 (ISBN 0-915010-15-1). Sutter House.
--Together They Built a Mountain. LC 74-14727. (Illus.). 196p. 1974. 6.95 (ISBN 0-915010-00-3). Sutter House.
Davis, Paul. A Bright Defiance. (Illus.). 48p. 1983. pap. 4.75 (ISBN 0-935284-34-6). Patrice Pr.
--Faces. LC 85-70861. (Illus.). 160p. (ps). 1985. 24.95 (ISBN 0-914919-04-0). Friendly Pr NY.
--Something Else Than Birds: Poems of the Warfare & the Joy of Being Alive. LC 81-11262. (Illus.). 148p. 1981. 9.95 (ISBN 0-935284-22-2). Patrice Pr.
Davis, Paxton. Three Days. LC 79-22676. (Illus.). 132p. (gr. 7 up). 1980. 8.95 (ISBN 0-689-30764-0). Atheneum.
Davis, Peggy. New Icons. 16p. 1980. pap. 2.00 (ISBN 0-913198-15-3, Lucky Heart Books). Salt Lick.
Davis, Penny A., jt. auth. see McCurley, Robert L., Jr.
Davis, Percival, jt. auth. see Friar, Wayne.
Davis, Peter. Flora of Turkey, Vol. 9. 256p. 1986. 125.00x (ISBN 0-85224-516-5, Pub. by Edinburgh U Pr Scotland). Columbia U Pr.
--Hometown. 1983. pap. 6.95 (ISBN 0-671-47059-0, Touchstone Bks). S&S.
--The Social Context of Dentistry. 176p. 1980. 27.50 (ISBN 0-7099-0152-6). Croom Helm.
Davis, Phil. Beyond the Zone System. (Illus.). 192p. 1982. 19.95 (ISBN 0-930764-23-4); wkbk 8.95 (ISBN 0-930764-28-5); pap. 14.95 (ISBN 0-930764-37-4). Curtin & London.
--The Dancer's Death. 176p. 1981. pap. 2.25 (ISBN 0-380-76612-4, 76612-4). Avon.
--Photography. 4th ed. 462p. 1982. pap. text ed. write for info. (ISBN 0-697-03219-1); instructor's manual avail. (ISBN 0-697-03220-5). Wm C Brown.
--Photography. 4th ed. 366p. 1982. pap. 18.95 (ISBN 0-697-09957-1). Wm C Brown.
--The University (Pictorial) LC 67-30753. 1967. 14.95 (ISBN 0-472-27900-9). U of Mich Pr.
Davis, Philip. The Field of Social Service. 436p. 1974. Repr. of 1902 ed. lib. bdg. 45.00 (ISBN 0-87821-277-9). Milford Hse.
--Immigration & Americanization. 1920. 17.50 (ISBN 0-686-17695-2). Quality Lib.
--Memory & Writing: From Wadsworth to Lawrence. LC 83-12242. (Liverpool English Texts & Studies: No. 21). 564p. 1983. 31.50x (ISBN 0-389-20342-4, 07186). B&N Imports.
Davis, Philip E., ed. Moral Duty & Legal Responsibility: A Philosophical-Legal Casebook. 2nd ed. (Orig.). Date not set. price not set (ISBN 0-8290-0681-8). Irvington.
Davis, Philip J. Circulant Matrices. LC 79-10551. (Pure & Applied Mathematics Ser.). 250p. 1979. 39.95 (ISBN 0-471-05771-1, Pub. by Wiley-Interscience). Wiley.
--Interpolation & Approximation. LC 75-2568. (Illus.). 416p. 1975. pap. text ed. 7.00 (ISBN 0-486-62495-1). Dover.
--The Mathematics of Matrices. LC 84-5647. 368p. 1984. Repr. of 1965 ed. lib. bdg. 26.50 (ISBN 0-89874-756-2). Krieger.
--Schwarz Function & Its Applications. LC 74-77258. (Carus Monograph: No. 17). 241p. 1973. 16.50 (ISBN 0-88385-017-6). Math Assn.
Davis, Philip J. & Chinn, William G. Three Point One Four One Six & All That. 1985. pap. 11.95 (ISBN 0-8176-3304-9). Birkhauser.
Davis, Philip J. & Hersh, Reuben. The Mathematical Experience. 460p. 1981. 27.95x (ISBN 0-8176-3018-X). Birkhauser.
Davis, Philip J. & Rabinowitz, Philip. Methods of Numerical Integration. 2nd ed. LC 83-13522. (Computer Science & Mathematics Monograph). 1984. 52.00 (ISBN 0-12-206360-0). Acad Pr.
Davis, Philip W., ed. see Bennett, Michael, et al.
Davis, Phillip J. The Thread: A Mathematical Yarn. 196p. 1983. 12.95 (ISBN 0-8176-3097-X). Birkhauser.
Davis, Phyllis & Hershelman, N. L. Medical Shorthand. 2nd ed. LC 80-29003. 323p. 1981. pap. 18.95x (ISBN 0-471-06024-0). Wiley.
Davis, Phyllis E. Medical Terminology: A Programmed Text. 1976. incl. cassette 76.00 (ISBN 0-471-80202-6). Wiley.
Davis, Polly. English Structure in Focus. 1977. pap. text ed. 12.95 (ISBN 0-88377-077-6); answer key 3.95 (ISBN 0-88377-100-4); tchrs. manual 3.95 (ISBN 0-88377-095-4). Newbury Hse.
Davis, Polly Ann. Alben W. Barkley: Senate Majority Leader & Vice President. Freidel, Frank, ed. LC 78-62380. (Modern American History Ser.: Vol. 6). 1979. lib. bdg. 36.00 (ISBN 0-8240-3630-1). Garland Pub.
Davis, Porter. Unusual Sex Practices. 1968. pap. 1.00 (ISBN 0-87497-143-8). Assoc Bk.
Davis Publications, jt. auth. see Queen, Ellery.
Davis, R. & Wells, C. H. J. Spectral Problems in Organic Chemistry. (Illus.). 200p. 1984. pap. text ed. 10.95 (ISBN 0-412-00561-1, 9019, Pub. by Chapman & Hall England). Methuen Inc.
Davis, R., et al, eds. Advanced Bacterial Genetics. LC 80-25695. 254p. (Orig.). 1980. lab manual 38.00x (ISBN 0-87969-130-1). Cold Spring Harbor.
Davis, R. A., Jr., ed. Coastal Sedimentary Environments. 2nd, rev. ed. (Illus.). xvii, 716p. 1985. 39.80 (ISBN 0-387-96097-X). Springer-Verlag.
Davis, R. A., Jr., jt. ed. see Greenwood, B.
Davis, R. C., jt. ed. see Cutler, W. G.
Davis, R. D. & Hucker, G., eds. Environmental Effects of Organic & Inorganic Contaminants in Sewage Sludge. 1983. lib. bdg. 36.95 (ISBN 90-277-1586-6, Pub. by Reidel Holland). Kluwer Academic.
Davis, R. F., et al, eds. Processing of Crystalline Ceramics. LC 78-18441. (Materials Science Research Ser.: Vol. 11). 696p. 1978. 95.00 (ISBN 0-306-40035-9, Plenum Pr). Plenum Pub.
Davis, R. G. The San Francisco Mime Troupe: The First Ten Years. LC 74-19943. (Illus.). 220p. 1975. 14.00 (ISBN 0-87867-058-0); pap. 5.95 (ISBN 0-87867-059-9). Ramparts.
Davis, R. H. & Wallace-Hadrill, J. M., eds. The Writing of History in the Middle Ages: Essays Presented to Richard William Southern. (Illus.). 1981. 57.00x (ISBN 0-19-822556-3). Oxford U Pr.
Davis, R. H. C. A History of Medieval Europe: From Constantine to St. Louis. (Illus.). 1971. pap. text ed. 14.95 (ISBN 0-582-48208-9). Longman.
Davis, R. Harvard. General Practice for Students of Medicine. (Monographs for Students of Medicine Ser.). 1975. 19.00 (ISBN 0-12-328850-9). Acad Pr.
Davis, R. Hunt, Jr. Bantu Education & the Education of Africans in South Africa. LC 72-85206. (Papers in International Studies: Africa Ser.: No. 14). (Illus.). 1972. pap. 4.50x (ISBN 0-89680-047-4, 82-91650, Ohio U Ctr Intl). Ohio U Pr.
Davis, R. M. Power Diode & Thyristor Circuits, No. 7. (IEE Monograph Series). 279p. 1979. 20.00 (ISBN 0-901223-90-5, Pub. by Peregrinus London). Inst Elect Eng.
--The Woods: The Human Self & the Realism of Jesus. 79p. 1971. pap. 4.00 (ISBN 0-9600434-0-3, 03). Camda.
Davis, Ralph. English Overseas Trade Fifteen Hundred to Seventeen Hundred. (Studies in Economic & Social History). 1973. pap. 4.00x (ISBN 0-333-14419-8). Humanities.
--The Industrial Revolution & British Overseas Trade. (Illus.). 1978. text ed. 21.00x (ISBN 0-391-00925-7, Leicester); pap. text ed. 10.75x (ISBN 0-391-00927-3). Humanities.
--The Rise of the Atlantic Economies. Wilson, Charles, ed. (World Economic History Ser.). 340p. 1973. pap. 11.95 (ISBN 0-8014-9143-6, CP143). Cornell U Pr.
Davis, Ralph, ed. Leadership & Institutional Renewal. LC 84-82370. (Higher Education Ser.: No. 49). (Orig.). 1985. pap. text ed. 9.95x (ISBN 0-87589-747-9). Jossey-Bass.
Davis, Ralph C. Fundamentals of Top Management. Chandler, Alfred D., ed. LC 79-7539. (History of Management Thought & Practice Ser.). 1980. Repr. of 1951 ed. lib. bdg. 68.50x (ISBN 0-405-12324-8). Ayer Co Pubs.

--Principles of Business Organization & Operation. 4th ed. LC 72-9522. (Management History Ser.: No. 16). (Illus.). 150p. 1973. Repr. of 1937 ed. 20.00 (ISBN 0-87960-019-5). Hive Pub.

Davis, Ralph C., jt. auth. see Baker, Alton W.

Davis, Randall & Lenat, Douglas. Knowledge-Based Systems in Artificial Intelligence: Two Case Studies. (Artificial Intelligence Ser.). (Illus.). 416p. 1982. text ed. 51.95 (ISBN 0-07-015557-7). McGraw.

Davis, Ray J. Arizona Workers' Compensation. 406p. 1980. 34.35 (ISBN 0-910039-02-X). Az Law Inst.

--Ecology & Conservation of Natural Resources. 1978. lib. bdg. 7.70 (ISBN 0-931054-02-8). Clark Pub.

Davis, Raymond E. & Kelly, J. W. Elementary Plane Surveying. 4th ed. (Illus.). 1967. text ed. 45.00 (ISBN 0-07-015771-5). McGraw.

Davis, Raymond E., et al. Surveying Theory & Practice. 6th ed. (Illus.). 1120p. 1981. text ed. 46.00 (ISBN 0-07-015790-1). McGraw.

--Principles of Chemistry. LC 83-19271. 884p. 1984. text ed. 38.95x (ISBN 0-03-060458-3). SCP.

Davis, Raymond G., jt. auth. see Harder, Marvin A.

Davis, Reba B. & Balderson, John L. Word Processing Supervision. 320p. 1984. text ed. 26.35 scp (ISBN 0-672-98448-2); scp instr's. guide 7.33 (ISBN 0-672-98449-0). Bobbs.

Davis, Rebecca, tr. see Seike, Kiyosi.

Davis, Rebecca H. Life in the Iron Mills & Other Stories. 242p. 1985. pap. 7.95 (ISBN 0-935312-39-0). Feminist Pr.

--Margaret Howth. LC 77-104437. Repr. of 1862 ed. lib. bdg. 19.50 (ISBN 0-8398-0353-2). Irvington.

--Silhouettes of American Life. 1972. Repr. of 1892 ed. lib. bdg. 22.50 (ISBN 0-8422-8033-2). Irvington.

--Waiting for the Verdict. LC 68-57520. Repr. of 1867 ed. lib. bdg. 27.50 (ISBN 0-8398-0354-0). Irvington.

Davis, Rebecca M., ed. see Niwano, Nikkyo.

Davis, Reed E. The Art & Skill of Real Estate Selling: Fifty-Eight Years in the Business. LC 80-51433. 118p. 1981. 7.95 (ISBN 0-533-04691-2). Vantage.

Davis, Reed E. & Davis, Steve. From Aviation Section Signal Corps to United States Air Force. 1984. 11.95 (ISBN 0-533-05756-6). Vantage.

Davis, Rich, jt. auth. see Stein, Shifra.

Davis, Richard. The English Rothschilds. LC 83-10517. 1984. 17.95 (ISBN 0-8078-1575-6). U of NC Pr.

--The Human Queen: Learn How to Be a Queen. 1984. 4.95 (ISBN 0-8062-2097-X). Carlton.

Davis, Richard & Stone, Jeff. Treasures of the Aquarians: The Sixties Rediscovered. (Nonfiction Ser.). 96p. (Orig.). 1985. pap. 6.95 (ISBN 0-14-008036-8). Penguin.

Davis, Richard A. Principles of Oceanography. 2nd ed. LC 76-10436. (Illus.). 1977. text ed. 27.95 (ISBN 0-201-01464-5). Addison-Wesley.

Davis, Richard A., compiled by. Neurosurgical Contributions of Loyal Davis: Selected Papers & Retrospective Commentaries. LC 72-93113. (Illus.). Repr. of 1973 ed. 66.20 (ISBN 0-8357-9551-9, 2016658). Bks Demand UMI.

Davis, Richard A., Jr. Depositional Systems: A Genetic Approach to Sedimentary Geology. (Illus.). 560p. 1983. 37.95 (ISBN 0-13-198960-X, Busn). P-H.

Davis, Richard B. A Colonial Southern Bookshelf: Reading in the Eighteenth Century. LC 78-3832. (Mercer University Lamar Memorial Lecture Ser.: No. 21). 152p. 1979. 13.50x (ISBN 0-8203-0450-6). U of Ga Pr.

--Intellectual Life in Jefferson's Virginia, 1790-1830. LC 64-13548. pap. 130.80 (ISBN 0-317-28043-0, 2025559). Bks Demand UMI.

--Intellectual Life in the Colonial South, 1585-1763, 3 vols. LC 77-1370. (Illus.). 1978. Set. slipcased 85.00x (ISBN 0-87049-210-1). U of Tenn Pr.

--Literature & Society in Early Virginia, 1608-1840. LC 72-89896. (Southern Literary Studies). xxiv, 332p. 1973. 30.00x (ISBN 0-8071-0215-6). La State U Pr.

Davis, Richard B., jt. auth. see Steiner, Charles V., Jr.

Davis, Richard B., compiled by. American Literature Through Bryant. LC 76-79172. (Goldentree Bibliographies in Language & Literature Ser.). 160p. (Orig.). 1969. pap. 6.95x (ISBN 0-88295-510-1). Harlan Davidson.

Davis, Richard B., ed. see Davies, Samuel.

Davis, Richard B., ed. see Fitzhugh, William.

Davis, Richard B., ed. see Foster, Augustus J.

Davis, Richard C., compiled by. Inventory of the Records of the California State Council of Lumber & Sawmill Workers, AFL-CIO. 1976. pap. 1.00 (ISBN 0-89030-027-5). Forest Hist Soc.

--Inventory of the Records of the National Forest Products Association. (Guides to Forest & Conservation History of North America, No. 3). 1976. pap. 1.00 (ISBN 0-89030-031-3). Forest Hist Soc.

Davis, Richard C. & Miller, Linda A., eds. Guide to the Cataloged Collections in the Manuscript Department of the William R. Perkins Library, Duke University. LC 79-28688. 1005p. 1980. lib. bdg. 30.50 (ISBN 0-87436-299-7). ABC-Clio.

Davis, Richard C., ed. see Forest History Society.

Davis, Richard H. About Paris. LC 70-96879. Repr. of 1895 ed. lib. bdg. 14.00 (ISBN 0-8398-0355-9). Irvington.

--Aging: Prospects & Issues. rev. ed. 9.95 (ISBN 0-669-05729-0). Hollander Co.

--At a New Mining Camp: Creede of Colorado, 1892. Jones, William R., ed. (Illus.). 32p. 1977. pap. 1.00 (ISBN 0-89646-018-5). Outbooks.

--Bar Sinister. LC 77-90081. Repr. of 1903 ed. 8.00 (ISBN 0-404-01996-X). AMS Pr.

--Bar Sinister. LC 69-13877. Repr. of 1903 ed. lib. bdg. 18.75 (ISBN 0-8371-1965-0, DABS). Greenwood.

--Bar Sinister. 1903. 6.00x (ISBN 0-403-00017-3). Scholarly.

--Cinderella, & Other Stories. facs. ed. LC 70-90579. (Short Story Index Reprint Ser). 1896. 17.00 (ISBN 0-8369-3062-2). Ayer Co Pubs.

--Cuban & Puerto Rican Campaigns. facsimile ed. (Select Bibliographies Reprint Ser). (Illus.). 1898. 29.00 (ISBN 0-8369-5278-2). Ayer Co Pubs.

--Dealing with Death. 1973. pap. 5.00 (ISBN 0-88474-025-0, 05753-3). Lexington Bks.

--Dealing with Death. (Andrus Gerontology Ser.). 4.95 (ISBN 0-686-94884-X). Hollander Co.

--Episodes in Van Bibber's Life. facsimile ed. LC 75-101795. (Short Story Index Reprint Ser.). 1899. 13.00 (ISBN 0-8369-3183-1). Ayer Co Pubs.

--The Exiles & Other Stories. 1972. 28.00 (ISBN 0-8422-8034-0). Irvington.

--Gallegher & Other Stories. (Illus.). Repr. of 1891 ed. 12.50 (ISBN 0-404-01997-8). AMS Pr.

--Gallegher & Other Stories. 1972. Repr. of 1894 ed. 9.50 (ISBN 0-8422-8035-9). Irvington.

--Gallegher & Other Stories. LC 71-131684. (Illus.). 1970. Repr. of 1904 ed. 10.00x (ISBN 0-403-00571-X). Scholarly.

--Lion & the Unicorn. facsimile ed. LC 71-94715. (Short Story Index Reprint Ser.). 1899. 17.00 (ISBN 0-8369-3094-0). Ayer Co Pubs.

--Ranson's Folly. facsimile ed. LC 79-152938. (Short Story Index Reprint Ser.). (Illus.). Repr. of 1902 ed. 20.00 (ISBN 0-8369-3797-X). Ayer Co Pubs.

--Ranson's Folly & Other Stories. (Classics Ser). (gr. 9 up). 1968. pap. 1.95 (ISBN 0-8049-0192-9, CL-192). Airmont.

--Real Soldiers of Fortune. (Illus.). 240p. 1981. Repr. of 1906 ed. 12.95 (ISBN 0-87364-239-2). Paladin Pr.

--Rulers of the Mediterranean. facsimile ed. LC 76-38788. (Essay Index Reprint Ser). Repr. of 1893 ed. 21.00 (ISBN 0-8369-2645-5). Ayer Co Pubs.

--Soldiers of Fortune. 300p. Repr. lib. bdg. 16.95x (ISBN 0-89966-284-6). Buccaneer Bks.

--Soldiers of Fortune. LC 74-96880. (Illus.). Repr. of 1897 ed. lib. bdg. 11.00 (ISBN 0-8398-0356-7). Irvington.

--Soldiers of Fortune. LC 73-129186. (Illus.). 1971. Repr. of 1897 ed. 39.00 (ISBN 0-403-00479-9). Scholarly.

--Stories for Boys. facsimile ed. LC 73-150472. (Short Story Index Reprint Ser.). Repr. of 1891 ed. 18.00 (ISBN 0-8369-3812-7). Ayer Co Pubs.

--Television & the Aging Audience. LC 80-68093. (Illus.). 107p. (Orig.). 1980. 12.00x (ISBN 0-88474-096-X, 05731-2); pap. 8.00x (05732-0). Lexington Bks.

--Van Bibber & Others, Vol. 1. LC 72-5865. (Short Story Index Reprint Ser.). Repr. of 1892 ed. 21.00 (ISBN 0-8369-4208-6). Ayer Co Pubs.

--Year from a Reporter's Notebook. LC 70-125691. (American Journalists Ser). (Illus.). 1970. Repr. of 1898 ed. 23.00 (ISBN 0-405-01668-9). Ayer Co Pubs.

--Young Winston Churchill: A Biography Written in 1906. 7.00 (ISBN 0-8363-0110-2). Jenkins.

Davis, Richard H. & Davis, James A. The Television Image of America's Elderly. LC 83-47933. 288p. 1985. 27.50x (ISBN 0-669-06764-4). Lexington Bks.

Davis, Richard H., ed. Aging: Prospects & Issues. 3rd rev. ed. LC 80-53413. 427p. 1981. pap. 15.00x (ISBN 0-88474-097-8, 05729-0). Lexington Bks.

--Non-Profit Homes for the Aging: Planning, Development & Programming. 94p. 1973. pap. 3.00 (ISBN 0-88474-002-1). U of S Cal Pr.

--Religion & Aging: The Behavioral & Social Sciences Look at Religion & Aging. 84p. 1967. pap. 3.00 (ISBN 0-88474-009-9). U of S Cal Pr.

Davis, Richard H., jt. ed. see Unterman, Israel.

Davis, Richard H., et al. The Great Streets of the World. Repr. of 1892 ed. 45.00 (ISBN 0-686-19889-1). Ridgeway Bks.

Davis, Richard L. & Robertson, David M. Textbook of Neuropathology. 976p. 1985. 129.95 (ISBN 0-683-02343-8). Williams & Wilkins.

Davis, Richard M. Thesis Projects in Science & Engineering. LC 78-65255. (Illus.). 1979. pap. text ed. 8.95 (ISBN 0-312-79963-2). St Martin.

Davis, Richard W. Political Change & Continuity: A Buckinghamshire Study. (Library of Politics & Society). 262p. 1972. 19.50 (ISBN 0-208-01307-5, Archon). Shoe String.

Davis, Rita. Simple Yet Stunning Quilts. (Illus.). 80p. 1981. pap. 8.95 (ISBN 0-942152-07-7). R C Pubns OR.

Davis, Robert. Gerald Griffin. (English Authors Ser.). 1980. lib. bdg. 15.95 (ISBN 0-8057-6799-1, Twayne). G K Hall.

--Learning Mathematics: The Cognitive Science Approach to Mathematics Education. LC 84-2853. 300p. 1984. text ed. 34.50 (ISBN 0-89391-245-X). Ablex Pub.

--Padre Porko. (Illus.). 297p. (gr. 4-6). 1948. 6.95 (ISBN 0-8234-0085-9). Holiday.

--Selling Special Market Software. 224p. 1984. pap. 16.95. Wiley.

Davis, Robert, jt. auth. see Dahl, Richard C.

Davis, Robert, jt. auth. see Denny, Ray.

Davis, Robert, jt. ed. see Hsu, Jeng.

Davis, Robert A. Engineers, Pump Operators, Drivers Handbook, Vol. 1. 1968. pap. 9.00x (ISBN 0-89368-308-6). Davis Pub Co.

--Engineers, Pump Operators, Drivers Handbook, Vol. 2. 1972. pap. 9.00x (ISBN 0-89368-309-4). Davis Pub Co.

--Fire Lieutenant's-Captain's Handbook, Vol. 1. 1966. pap. 9.00x (ISBN 0-89368-305-1). Davis Pub Co.

--Fire Lieutenant's-Captain's Handbook, Vol. 2. 1972. pap. 7.75x (ISBN 0-89368-306-X). Davis Pub Co.

--Police Sergeant's Handbook, Vol. 1. 1968. pap. 9.00x (ISBN 0-89368-016-8). Davis Pub Co.

Davis, Robert C. Final Mutiny: Reinhard Goering, His Life & Art. LC 83-49394. (Stanford German Studies: Vol. 21). 316p. (Orig.). 1985. text ed. 26.66 (ISBN 0-8204-0098-X). P Lang Pubs.

Davis, Robert C., ed. The Fictional Father: Lacanian Readings of the Text. LC 80-26222. 224p. 1981. lib. bdg. 16.00x (ISBN 0-87023-111-1). U of Mass Pr.

--The Grapes of Wrath: A Collection of Critical Essays. 157p. 1982. 10.95 (ISBN 0-13-363358-6); pap. 4.95 (ISBN 0-13-363341-1). P-H.

--Lacan & Narration: The Psychoanalytic Difference in Narrative Theory. LC 84-47946. 1984. pap. text ed. 10.95x (ISBN 0-8018-2414-1). Johns Hopkins.

Davis, Robert C. & Schleifer, Ronald, eds. Rhetoric & Form: Deconstruction at Yale. LC 84-40692. 232p. 1985. 16.95x (ISBN 0-8061-1895-4). U of Okla Pr.

Davis, Robert D., jt. auth. see Moon, Robert A.

Davis, Robert E. The Imagical World of Bossons. (Illus.). 238p. 1982. write for info. (ISBN 0-9614255-0-4). R E Davis.

--Response to Innovation: A Study of Popular Argument about New Mass Media. Loweth, Garth S., ed. LC 75-21430. (Dissertations on Film Ser.). 1976. lib. bdg. 46.50x (ISBN 0-405-07533-2). Ayer Co Pubs.

Davis, Robert E., Jr. Selling Your Software. (General Trade Books). 224p. 1985. pap. 16.95 (ISBN 0-471-80737-0). Wiley.

Davis, Robert F., et al, eds. Emergent Process Methods for High-Technology Ceramics. (Materials Science Research Ser.: Vol. 17). 809p. 1984. 95.00x (ISBN 0-306-41677-8, Plenum Pr). Plenum Pub.

Davis, Robert G. C. P. Snow. LC 65-16381. (Columbia Essays on Modern Writers Ser.: No. 8). 48p. (Orig.). 1965. pap. 2.50 (ISBN 0-231-02669-2, MW8). Columbia U Pr.

--John Dos Passos. (Pamphlets on American Writers Ser: No. 20). (Orig.). 1962. pap. 1.25x (ISBN 0-8166-0277-8, MPAW20). U of Minn Pr.

--Ten Modern Masters. 3rd ed. 583p. 1972. pap. text ed. 14.95 (ISBN 0-15-590281-4, HC); instr's. manual avail. (ISBN 0-15-590282-2). HarBraceJ.

Davis, Robert G. & Issacs, Larry. Elementary Physical Education: Growing Through Movement. (Illus.). 396p. (Orig.). 1983. 19.95x (ISBN 0-89459-193-2). Hunter Textbks.

Davis, Robert H. & Maurice, Arthur B. The Caliph of Bagdad. 1931. Repr. 30.00 (ISBN 0-8482-3662-9). Norwood Edns.

Davis, Robert H., et al. Learning System Design. (Illus.). 320p. 1974. text ed. 36.95 (ISBN 0-07-074334-7). McGraw.

Davis, Robert K., et al. The Range of Choice in Water Management: A Study of Dissolved Oxygen in the Potomac Estuary. LC 68-27737. (Illus.). pap. 53.50 (ISBN 0-317-10648-1, 2019821). Bks Demand UMI.

Davis, Robert L., ed. see Davis, Elmer H.

Davis, Robert M. A Catalogue of the Evelyn Waugh Collection at the Humanities Research Center: The University of Texas at Austin. LC 80-50840. 376p. 1981. 25.00x (ISBN 0-87875-194-7). Whitston Pub.

--Evelyn Waugh, Aprentice. 275p. 1985. 34.95 (ISBN 0-937664-65-0). Pilgrim Bks OK.

--Evelyn Waugh, Writer: The Making of a Man of Letters. 342p. 1980. 26.95x (ISBN 0-937664-00-6). Pilgrim Bks OK.

Davis, Robert M., ed. Steinbeck: A Collection of Critical Essays. 1972. 12.95 (ISBN 0-13-846659-9, Spec). P-H.

Davis, Robert M., et al, eds. A Bibliography of Evelyn Waugh. 500p. 1985. 28.50 (ISBN 0-87875-313-3). Whitston Pub.

Davis, Robert P. Control Tower. 288p. 1981. pap. 2.95 (ISBN 0-449-24470-9, Crest). Fawcett.

--The Divorce. 368p. 1982. pap. 3.25 (ISBN 0-441-14999-5). Ace Bks.

--The Divorce. 1980. 12.95 (ISBN 0-688-03725-9). Morrow.

Davis, Robert P., jt. auth. see Schmidt, J. William.

Davis, Robert P., jt. auth. see Stobart, John.

Davis, Robert R., Jr. Lexicon of Historical & Political Terms. Reed, R., ed. LC 81-83626. (Illus.). 125p. 1982. pap. 7.95 (ISBN 0-88247-612-2). R & E Pubs.

Davis, Robert S., et al. Atlas of Endoscopic Urology. 250p. Date not set. price not set (ISBN 0-7216-2989-X). Saunders.

Davis, Robert S., Jr. The American Revolution in the Georgia Backcountry: An Anthology. 250p. 1985. write for info. (ISBN 0-89308-350-X, GA 45). Southern Hist Pr.

--The Georgia Black Book: Morbid, Macabre, & Disgusting Records of Genealogical Value. (Illus.). 456p. 1982. 35.00 (ISBN 0-89308-291-0, GA 63). Southern Hist Pr.

--Georgia Citizens & Soldiers of the American Revolution. 350p. 1979. 30.00 (ISBN 0-89308-169-8); pap. 23.50 (ISBN 0-89308-411-5). Southern Hist Pr.

--Research in Georgia: With a Special Emphasis Upon the Georgia Department of Archives & History. (Illus.). 268p. 1981. write for info. o. s. i. (ISBN 0-89308-199-X); 20.00 (ISBN 0-686-96889-1). Southern Hist Pr.

--The Wilkes County Papers, Seventeen Seventy-Three to Eighteen Thirty-Three. 338p. 1979. 35.00 (ISBN 0-89308-170-1); pap. 28.50 softcover (ISBN 0-89308-410-7). Southern Hist Pr.

Davis, Robert S., Jr. & Lucas, Silas E., Jr. The Families of Burke County, Georgia, 1755 to 1855: A Census. (Illus.). 816p. 1981. 40.00 (ISBN 0-89308-211-2). Southern Hist Pr.

Davis, Robert S., Jr., jt. auth. see Dorsey, James E.

Davis, Robert S., Jr., jt. ed. see Lucas, Silas E., Jr.

Davis, Robert T., et al. Marketing Management Casebook. 4th ed. 1984. 30.95 (ISBN 0-256-03017-0). Irwin.

Davis, Rodney. Real Estate. LC 79-155. (Career Competencies in Marketing). (Illus.). (gr. 11-12). 1979. pap. text ed. 8.68 (ISBN 0-07-015672-7). McGraw.

Davis, Roger. Case Studies in Pharmacy Practice. 204p. 1979. text ed. 23.00 (ISBN 0-910769-00-1). Am Coll Apothecaries.

Davis, Roger & Northcutt, Glenn, eds. Fish Neurobiology, Vol. II: Higher Brain Areas & Functions. (Illus.). 328p. 1983. text ed. 45.00x (ISBN 0-472-10019-X). U of Mich Pr.

Davis, Roger, jt. ed. see Northcutt, Glenn.

Davis, Roger E. The Organists' Manual: Technical Studies & Selected Compositions for the Organ. 1985. pap. text ed. 19.95x (ISBN 0-393-95461-7). Norton.

Davis, Roger L., jt. auth. see Huffman, D. C., Jr.

Davis, Roger T. & Leathers, Charles W. Behavior & Pathology of Aging in Rhesus Monkeys. LC 85-5255. (MP Ser.: Vol. 8). 326p. 1985. write for info. (ISBN 0-8451-3407-8). A R Liss.

Davis, Ron. Women & Horses. (Illus., Orig.). 1981. pap. 3.00x (ISBN 0-914140-11-6). Carpenter Pr.

Davis, Ron, jt. auth. see Linville, Jack, Jr.

Davis, Ron, et al. You Can Teach Adults Successfully. (Training Successful Teachers Ser.). 48p. (Orig.). 1984. pap. 2.50 (ISBN 0-87239-808-0, 3208). Standard Pub.

Davis, Ron L. A Forgiving God in an Unforgiving World. 1984. pap. 5.95 (ISBN 0-89081-431-7). Harvest Hse.

--Gold in the Making. LC 83-21931. 160p. 1984. pap. 4.95 (ISBN 0-8407-5869-3). Nelson.

Davis, Ronald F. & Starleaf, Karen. Microkey. (Illus.). 43p. (Orig.). 1982. pap. 11.95 (ISBN 0-915961-50-4). Awareness Marketing.

Davis, Ronald J. Augustus Thomas. (United States Authors Ser.: No. 478). 1984. lib. bdg. 18.50 (ISBN 0-8057-7419-X, Twayne). G K Hall.

Davis, Ronald L. Good & Faithful Labor: From Slavery to Sharecropping in the Natchez District, 1860-1890. LC 81-13367. (Contributions in American History Ser.: No. 100). (Illus.). xv, 225p. 1982. lib. bdg. 27.50 (ISBN 0-313-23134-6, DFL/). Greenwood.

--A History of Music in American Life, Vol. 1: The Formative Years, 1620-1865. LC 79-25359. 320p. 1982. lib. bdg. 22.50 o.p (ISBN 0-89874-002-9); pap. 12.50 (ISBN 0-89874-622-1). Krieger.

--A History of Music in American Life, Vol. 2: The Gilded Years, 1865-1920. LC 79-25359. 286p. 1980. lib. bdg. 20.50 (ISBN 0-89874-003-7); pap. 11.50 (ISBN 0-89874-623-X). Krieger.

--A History of Music in American Life, Vol. 3: The Modern Era, 1920 to the Present. LC 79-25359. 462p. 1981. lib. bdg. 36.50 (ISBN 0-89874-004-5); pap. 19.50 (ISBN 0-89874-624-8). Krieger.

--Opera in Chicago. (Illus.). 393p. 1985. Repr. of 1966 ed. 29.50 (ISBN 0-8290-0225-1). Irvington.

--Twentieth Century Cultural Life in Texas. (Texas History Ser.). (Illus.). 50p. 1981. pap. text ed. 1.95x (ISBN 0-89641-072-2). American Pr.

Davis, Ronald L., jt. auth. see Hussian, Richard A.

Davis, Ronald L., ed. A History of Music in American Life. LC 79-25359. 69.50 (ISBN 0-89874-080-0); pap. 39.50 set (ISBN 0-89874-625-6). Krieger.

--Social & Cultural Life in the 1920's. LC 72-171520. (American Problem Ser.). 133p. 1972. pap. 5.95 (ISBN 0-03-084159-3, Pub. by HR&W). Krieger.

Davis, Ronald W. Ethnological Studies on the Kru Coast. (Liberian Studies Monographs: No. 5). 1976. 8.50 (ISBN 0-916712-04-4). Liberian Studies.

Davis, Ross & Bloedel, James, eds. Cerebellar Stimulation for Spasticity & Seizures. LC 84-4254. 360p. 1984. 105.00 (ISBN 0-8493-6067-6). CRC Pr.

Davis, Roy E. Conscious Immortality. 150p. 1978. pap. 2.95 (ISBN 0-87707-216-7). CSA Pr.

--Freedom Is New. 189p. 1980. pap. 3.95 (ISBN 0-87707-221-3). CSA Pr.

--How to Use the Technique of Creative Imagination. LC 74-75315. pap. 2.50 (ISBN 0-87707-016-4). CSA Pr.

--Light on the Spiritual Path. 138p. 1984. pap. 3.95 (ISBN 0-317-20861-6). CSA Pr.

--Miracle Man of Japan: The Life & Work of Masaharu Taniguchi, One of the Most Influential Spiritual Leaders of Our Time. (Illus., Orig.). pap. 3.00 (ISBN 0-87707-048-2). CSA Pr.

--My Personal Fulfillment Plan Workbook. 32p. 1984. pap. 3.95 (ISBN 0-317-20868-3). CSA Pr.

--Open Your Life to Infinite Good. 128p. 1983. 4.95 (ISBN 0-317-20865-9). CSA Pr.

--Philosophy & Practice of Yoga. 192p. 1983. pap. 4.95 (ISBN 0-317-20862-4). CSA Pr.

--Potential Is Within You. 172p. 1982. 7.95 (ISBN 0-317-20867-5). CSA Pr.

--Science of Kriya Yoga. 192p. 1984. 7.95 (ISBN 0-317-20860-8). CSA Pr.

--This Is Reality. 160p. 1983. pap. 3.95 (ISBN 0-317-20863-2). CSA Pr.

--Who is the True Guru. 192p. 1981. pap. 4.95 (ISBN 0-317-20864-0). CSA Pr.

Davis, Ruby, ed. see Clark, Barbara R.

Davis, Rupert Hart see Sassoon, Seigfried.

Davis, Rupert Hart see Sassoon, Siegfried.

Davis, Russell G., jt. auth. see McGinn, Noel F.

Davis, S. Hong Kong in Its Geographical Setting. LC 70-179188. (Illus.). Repr. of 1949 ed. 20.00 (ISBN 0-404-54818-0). AMS Pr.

Davis, S., et al, eds. see Olivier, Charles B.

Davis, S. H. Victims of the Miracle. (Illus.). 1977. 37.50 (ISBN 0-521-21738-5); pap. 9.95 (ISBN 0-521-29246-8). Cambridge U Pr.

Davis, S. H., ed. Frontiers in Fluid Mechanics. Lumley, J. L. (Illus.). 340p. 1985. 34.00 (ISBN 0-387-15361-6). Springer-Verlag.

Davis, S. K. Bible Crossword Puzzle Book. (Quiz & Puzzle Bks). (gr. k-3). 1969. pap. 2.95 (ISBN 0-8010-2812-4). Baker Bk.

Davis, S. M. The Life & Times of Sir Philip Sidney. 1973. Repr. of 1858 ed. 40.00 (ISBN 0-8274-0060-8). R West.

Davis, S. Rufus. The Federal Principle: A Journey Through Time in Quest of Meaning. LC 75-32673. 1978. 30.00x (ISBN 0-520-03146-6). U of Cal Pr.

Davis, S. S., et al, eds. Microspheres & Drug Therapy: Pharmaceutical, Immunological & Medical Aspects. 448p. 1985. 105.75 (ISBN 0-444-80577-X). Elsevier.

Davis, Sam. The Form of Housing. 320p. 1981. pap. 16.95 (ISBN 0-442-27218-9). Van Nos Reinhold.

Davis, Sammy, Jr. Hollywood in a Suitcase. 256p. 1981. pap. 2.95 (ISBN 0-425-05091-2). Berkley Pub.

Davis, Samuel M. Rights of Juvenile: The Juvenile Justice System. 2nd ed. LC 80-12465. 1980. 65.00 (ISBN 0-87632-104-X); student edition 22.50. Boardman.

--Rights of Juveniles. 2nd ed. (The Juvenile Justice System Ser.). 1983. write for info. Boardman.

Davis, Samuel P. History of Nevada, 2 vols. (Illus.). 1272p. 1984. Set. 75.00 (ISBN 0-913814-58-X). Nevada Pubns.

Davis, Sandra T. Intellectual Change & Political Development in Early Modern Japan: Ono Azusa, a Case Study. LC 76-14762. 328p. 1979. 28.50 (ISBN 0-8386-1953-3). Fairleigh Dickinson.

Davis, Sara D. & Beidler, Philip D., eds. The Mythologizing of Mark Twain. LC 83-9166. (The Alabama Symposium on English & American Literature). (Illus.). 208p. 1984. 20.00 (ISBN 0-8173-0199-2); pap. 9.95 (ISBN 0-8173-0201-8). U of Ala pr.

Davis, Scott, ed. American Athletics Annual: 1983 Edition. 1983. 10.00 (ISBN 0-686-46900-3). Athletics Cong.

--American Athletics Annual: 1984 Edition. 1984. 12.00 (ISBN 0-317-11295-3). Athletics Cong.

Davis, Scott, jt. ed. see Sloss, Leon.

Davis, Scott M., jt. auth. see Soleri, Paolo.

Davis, Sharon. Marvin Gaye. (Illus.). 128p. 1984. 18.95 (ISBN 0-86276-194-8); pap. 10.95 (ISBN 0-86276-193-X). Proteus Pub NY.

Davis, Sheila. The Craft of Lyric Writing. LC 84-22080. 350p. 1985. 16.95 (ISBN 0-89879-149-9). Writers Digest.

Davis, Shelby C. Reservoirs of Men: A History of the Black Troops of French West Africa. LC 79-107505. Repr. of 1934 ed. 19.75x (ISBN 0-8371-3776-4, DRE&). Greenwood.

Davis, Shelton H. & Hodson, Julie. Witnesses to Political Violence in Guatemala: The Suppression of a Rural Development Movement. Simon, Laurence R., ed. (Impact Audit Ser.: No. 2). (Illus.). 54p. (Orig.). 1984. pap. 5.00 (ISBN 0-910281-00-9). Oxfam Am.

Davis, Shelton H., jt. auth. see Narby, Jeremy.

Davis, Shelton H. & Mathews, Robert O., eds. America in the Nineteen Eighties: Issues for Anthropologists. LC 81-67481. (Working Paper Ser.: No. 2). (Orig.). 1981. pap. 4.00 (ISBN 0-932978-05-3). Anthropology Res.

Davis, Shelton H., jt. ed. see Wright, Robin M.

Davis, Shirley M., jt. auth. see Swain, Philip H.

Davis, Sidney A. The Saddler. (Illus.). 64p. (Orig.). 1980. pap. 6.50 (ISBN 0-85263-527-3, Pub. by Shire Pubns England). Seven Hills Bks.

Davis, Skye. Trailside Shelters. LC 77-21610. (Packit Ser.). 224p. 1977. pap. 5.95 (ISBN 0-8117-2268-6). Stackpole.

Davis, Sonia H. The Private Life of H. P. Lovecraft. Joshi, S. T., frwd. by. 38p. (Orig.). 1985. pap. 3.95 (ISBN 0-318-04718-7). Necronomicon.

Davis, Stanley, et al. Geology: Our Physical Environment. 1975. text ed. 36.95 (ISBN 0-07-015680-8). McGraw.

Davis, Stanley M. Managing Corporate Culture. LC 84-11142. 144p. 16.95 (ISBN 0-88410-997-6). Ballinger Pub.

Davis, Stanley M., ed. Managing & Organizing Multinational Corporations. LC 77-1760. 1979. text ed. 65.00 (ISBN 0-08-021267-0); pap. text ed. 15.50 (ISBN 0-08-021266-2). Pergamon.

Davis, Stanley M., et al. Matrix. LC 77-81192. (An Organization Development Ser.). 1977. pap. text ed. 10.95 (ISBN 0-201-01115-8). Addison-Wesley.

Davis, Stanley N. & De Wiest, Roger J. M. Hydrogeology. 463p. 1966. 40.50 (ISBN 0-471-19900-1). Wiley.

Davis, Stephen. Bob Marley. LC 82-40398. (Illus.). 288p. 1985. pap. 9.95 (ISBN 0-385-17956-1, Dolp). Doubleday.

--Faith, Skepticism & Evidence. 233p. 1978. 20.00 (ISBN 0-8387-2039-0). Bucknell U Pr.

--Hammer of the Gods: The Led Zeppelin Saga. LC 84-24776. (Illus.). 352p. 1985. 15.95 (ISBN 0-688-04507-3). Morrow.

Davis, Stephen & Simon, Peter. Reggae Bloodlines. LC 76-42428. (Illus.). 1977. pap. 10.95 (ISBN 0-385-12330-2, Anch). Doubleday.

--Reggae International. LC 82-61223. 1983. pap. 14.95 (ISBN 0-394-71313-3). Knopf.

Davis, Stephen, jt. ed. see Trubowitz, Sidney.

Davis, Stephen C. California Gold Rush Merchant: The Journal of Stephen Chapin Davis. Richards, Benjamin B., ed. LC 73-21490. (Illus.). 124p. 1974. Repr. of 1956 ed. lib. bdg. 15.00x (ISBN 0-8371-6408-7, DAGR). Greenwood.

Davis, Stephen T. Logic & the Nature of God. 200p. 1984. 9.95 (ISBN 0-8028-3321-7). Eerdmans.

Davis, Stephen T., ed. Encountering Evil: Live Options in Theodicy. LC 80-84647. 1981. pap. 8.95 (ISBN 0-8042-0517-5). John Knox.

Davis, Steve. Programming Animation & Graphics for the TI 99-4A. Brown, Rachel, ed. (Computer Literacy Ser.). 1983. 9.95 (ISBN 0-88049-070-5, 7263). Milton Bradley Co.

--Programs for the TI Home Computer. LC 82-90783. 128p. (Orig.). (gr. 5 up). 1983. pap. 14.95 (ISBN 0-911061-00-2). S Davis Pub.

--Programs for the TI Home Computer. 1984. pap. 14.95 (ISBN 0-13-729534-0). P-H.

Davis, Steve, jt. auth. see Davis, Reed E.

Davis, Steve, ed. see Molesworth, Ralph.

Davis, Steve, et al. The Electric Mailbox: A User's Guide to Electronic Mail Services. LC 84-91756. 260p. 1985. pap. 19.95 (ISBN 0-911061-14-2). S Davis Pub.

Davis, Steven, ed. Causal Theories of Mind: Action, Knowledge, Memory, Perception & Reference. LC 83-15082. (Foundations of Communications Ser.). x, 421p. 1983. 71.20x (ISBN 3-11-007730-2). De Gruyter.

Davis, Steven & Mithun, Marianne, eds. Linguistics, Philosophy & Montague Grammar. 354p. 1979. text ed. 23.50x (ISBN 0-292-74625-3). U of Tex Pr.

Davis, Steven A. How to Stay Healthy in an Unhealthy World. LC 82-12581. 288p. 1983. 12.50 (ISBN 0-688-01574-3). Morrow.

Davis, Steven I. The Euro-Bank: Its Origins, Management & Outlook. 2nd ed. LC 80-13337. 154p. 1980. 32.95x (ISBN 0-470-26955-3). Halsted Pr.

--The Management of International Banks. (International Banking Ser.). 227p. 1984. 29.50x (ISBN 0-8448-1456-3). Crane Russak Co.

Davis, Susan. I Choose to Belong. (My Church Teaches Ser.). 1979. pap. 1.65 (ISBN 0-8127-0237-9). Review & Herald.

--Password to Heaven. (My Church Teaches Ser.). 32p. (gr. k-3). 1980. pap. 2.50 (ISBN 0-8127-0298-0). Review & Herald.

--A Way to Remember. Davis, Tom, ed. 32p. (ps up). 1980. pap. 2.95 (ISBN 0-8280-0023-9). Review & Herald.

--When God Lived in a Tent. (My Church Teaches Ser.). (Illus.). (ps-1). 1978. 1.95 (ISBN 0-8127-0181-X). Review & Herald.

--Will the Real Me Please Stand Up. (Redwood Ser.). 79p. Date not set. pap. 4.50 (ISBN 0-8163-0479-3). Pacific Pr Pub Assn.

Davis, Susan G. Parades & Power: Street Theatre in Nineteenth Century Philadelphia. (Illus.). 288p. 1986. 32.95 (ISBN 0-87722-394-7). Temple U Pr.

Davis, Susan S. Patience & Power: The Lives of Morrocan Village Women. 200p. 1982. (ISBN 0-87073-503-9); pap. 9.95 (ISBN 0-87073-504-7). Schenkman Bks Inc.

Davis, Suzannah. No Bed of Roses. 1984. 13.95 (ISBN 0-8027-0827-7). Walker & Co.

Davis, Sydney. Know to Mystery. LC 77-74868. 1978. 5.00 (ISBN 0-87212-078-3). Libra.

Davis, Sydney G. & Tregear, Mary. Man Kok Tsui: Archaeological Site 30, Lantau Island, Hong Kong. pap. 20.00 (ISBN 0-317-11286-4, 2017697). Bks Demand UMI.

Davis, T. Neil. Alaska Science Nuggets. LC 82-80679. (Illus.). 233p. (Orig.). 1982. pap. 15.95 (ISBN 0-915360-02-0). Geophysical Inst.

--Energy-Alaska. LC 83-51414. (Illus.). 400p. 1984. 19.95 (ISBN 0-912006-07-2). U of Alaska Pr.

Davis, T. Patrick. New Methods of Rectification: Lincoln. 154p. avail. (ISBN 0-86690-254-6). Am Fed Astrologers.

Davis, T. W. Rhys. On the Ancient Coins & Measures of Ceylon. (Illus.). 1975. pap. 8.00 (ISBN 0-916710-24-6). Obol Intl.

Davis, T. Wesley. Secular Humanism: Humanist Psychology in Public Education. 1984. 6.95 (ISBN 0-8062-2332-4). Carlton.

Davis, Ted see Penn, Gerald M.

Davis, Ted J., ed. see Agricultural Sector Symposium, 3rd.

Davis, Ted S. Constant Processes. (Illus.). 1978. 29.50 (ISBN 0-685-19863-4). Constant Soc.

Davis, Tenney L., tr. see Bacon, Roger.

Davis, Tenny L. Chemistry of Powder & Explosives. 500p. 1972. Repr. of 1943 ed. 14.00 (ISBN 0-913022-00-4). Angriff Pr.

Davis, Terence. The Gothick Taste. LC 75-10733. (Illus.). 168p. 45.00 (ISBN 0-8386-1746-8). Fairleigh Dickinson.

Davis, Terry. Mysterious Ways. 1984. 15.95 (ISBN 0-670-50224-3). Viking.

--Vision Quest. (Windstone Ser.). 204p. 1985. 2.95 (ISBN 0-553-24527-9); pap. 2.50 (ISBN 0-553-14815-X). Bantam.

--Vision Quest. 1979. 8.95 (ISBN 0-670-74722-X). Viking.

Davis, Thadious, jt. ed. see Harris, Trudier.

Davis, Thadious, jt. ed. see Harris, Trudior.

Davis, Thadious M. Faulkner's "Negro". Art & the Southern Context. LC 82-7327. 266p. 1982. 25.00x (ISBN 0-8071-1047-7); pap. 10.95x (ISBN 0-8071-1064-7). La State U Pr.

Davis, Theresa. Fragrance Sense. 1985. pap. 6.95 (ISBN 0-449-90107-6, Columbine). Fawcett.

Davis, Thomas. Experimentation with Microprocessor Applications. (Orig.). 1980. pap. text ed. 17.95 (ISBN 0-8359-1812-2). Reston.

--National & Historical Ballads, Songs, & Poems. (Folklore Ser.). 1869. 20.00 (ISBN 0-8482-3690-4). Norwood Edns.

--Thomas Davis, Selections from His Prose & Poetry. LC 75-28810. (Illus.). 392p. Repr. of 1914 ed. 39.00 (ISBN 0-404-13803-9). AMS Pr.

Davis, Thomas A. Horse Owners & Breeders Tax Manual. 928p. 90.00 (ISBN 0-318-12777-6). Am Horse Coun.

Davis, Thomas A., ed. see Habenicht, Donna & Bell, Anne.

Davis, Thomas B. Defense of the Ruffians: A Dialogue with Conscience. 14p. 1977. pap. 2.50 (ISBN 0-88053-007-3, M-13). Macoy Pub.

Davis, Thomas D. Philosophy: An Introduction Through Original Fiction & Discussion. LC 78-12329. 1978. pap. text ed. 10.00x (ISBN 0-394-32048-4). Random.

Davis, Thomas G. Saved & Certain. (Orig.). 1955. pap. 3.95 (ISBN 0-8054-1611-0). Broadman.

Davis, Thomas J. A Rumor of Revolt: The "Great Negro Plot" in Colonial New York. LC 82-48427. 336p. 1985. 19.95 (ISBN 0-02-907740-0). Free Pr.

Davis, Thomas M. & Davis, Virginia L., eds. Edward Taylor vs. Solomon Stoddard: The Nature of the Lord's Supper. (American Literary Manuscripts Ser.). 1981. lib. bdg. 31.50 (ISBN 0-8057-9653-3, Twayne). G K Hall.

--Edward Taylor's "Church Records" & Related Sermons. (American Literary Manuscripts Ser.). 1981. lib. bdg. 36.50 (ISBN 0-8057-9650-9, Twayne). G K Hall.

--Edward Taylor's Minor Poetry. (American Literary Manuscripts Ser.). 1981. lib. bdg. 36.50 (ISBN 0-8057-9654-1, Twayne). G K Hall.

--The Unpublished Writings of Edward Taylor, 3 vols. (American Literary Manuscripts Ser.). 1981. Set. lib. bdg. 93.95 (ISBN 0-8057-9655-X, Twayne). G K Hall.

Davis, Thomas O. Prose Writings. text ed. 14.75 (ISBN 0-8369-8153-7, 8293). Ayer Co Pubs.

Davis, Thomas W. The Corps Roots the Loudest: A History of VMI Athletics. LC 85-13446. (Illus.). 400p. 1986. 20.00x (ISBN 0-8139-1069-2). U Pr of Va.

Davis, Thomas W., ed. Committees for Repeal of the Test & Corporation Acts: Minutes, 1786-90, 1827-8. 1978. 50.00x (ISBN 0-686-96607-4, Pub by London Rec Soc England). State Mutual Bk.

Davis, Thomas W., et al. Computer-Aided Analysis of Electrical Networks. LC 72-80234. (Illus.). pap. 111.50 (ISBN 0-317-09130-1, 2015044). Bks Demand UMI.

Davis, Thomas X., tr. see William of St. Thierry.

Davis, Thulani. Playing the Changes. viii, 64p. 1985. 16.00 (ISBN 0-8195-5139-2); pap. 8.95 (ISBN 0-8195-6139-8). Wesleyan U Pr.

Davis, Timothy C. In Search of Perlas Grandes. LC 84-72655. (Orig.). 1985. pap. 5.95 (ISBN 0-89636-152-7). Accent Bks.

Davis, Tom & Ross, Marilyn. Be Tough or Be Gone. (Illus.). 1984. pap. 6.95 (ISBN 0-914269-09-7). N Trails.

Davis, Tom, ed. see Davis, Susan.

Davis, Tom, ed. see Down, Goldie.

Davis, Tom, ed. see Hannum, Harold E.

Davis, Tracy, ed. Information America: Sources of Print & Nonprint Materials Available from Organizations, Industry, Government Agencies & Specialized Publishers, Master Volume. 815p. 1985. lib. bdg. 110.00 (ISBN 0-918212-79-0). Neal-Schuman.

Davis, Uri. Israel: Utopia Incorporated. 182p. 1977. 10.00x (ISBN 0-905762-12-6, Pub. by Zed Pr England). Biblio Dist.

Davis, Varina. Jefferson Davis: Ex-President of the Confederate States of America, a Memoir by His Wife, 2 vols. facsimile ed. (Select Bibliographies Reprint Ser). Repr. of 1890 ed. Set. 95.00 (ISBN 0-8369-6611-2). Ayer Co Pubs.

Davis, Vincent. The Politics of Innovation: Patterns in Navy Cases. (Monograph Series in World Affairs: Vol. 4, 1966-67 Ser., Bk. 3). 54p. (Orig.). 1967. 3.95 (ISBN 0-87940-013-7). Monograph Series.

Davis, Vincent, ed. The Post Imperial Presidency. LC 79-67064. 202p. 1980. 33.95 (ISBN 0-03-055741-0). Praeger.

--The Post-Imperial Presidency. LC 79-67064. 190p. 1980. pap. text ed. 7.95x (ISBN 0-87855-747-4). Transaction Bks.

Davis, Vincent, ed. see Bucknell, Howard, III.

Davis, Vincent, ed. see Conant, Melvin A.

Davis, Vincent, ed. see Gray, Colin S.

Davis, Virginia L., jt. ed. see Davis, Thomas M.

Davis, W. First Blood. LC 82-17014. (Civil War Ser.). 1983. lib. bdg. 19.94 (ISBN 0-8094-4701-0, Pub. by Time-Life). Silver.

--Hints to Philanthropists. 176p. 1971. Repr. of 1821 ed. 20.00x (ISBN 0-7165-1564-4, Pub. by Irish Academic Pr Ireland). Biblio Dist.

Davis, W., jt. auth. see Harrap, K. R.

Davis, W., et al, eds. The Control of Tumour Growth & Its Biological Bases. (Developments in Oncology Ser.). 1983. lib. bdg. 77.00 (ISBN 0-89838-603-9, Pub. by Martinus Nijhoff Netherlands). Kluwer Academic.

Davis, W. A. Another Generation. (Orig.). 1985. text ed. 5.25 (ISBN 0-87148-019-0); pap. 4.25 (ISBN 0-87148-020-4); instr's. guide 7.95 (ISBN 0-87148-021-2). Pathway Pr.

Davis, W. Eugene. The Celebrated Case of Esther Waters: The Collaboration of George Moore & Barrett H. Clark on "Esther Waters: A Play". 168p. (Orig.). 1985. lib. bdg. 22.75 (ISBN 0-8191-4221-2); pap. text ed. 11.25 (ISBN 0-8191-4222-0). U Pr of Amer.

Davis, W. Eugene & Gerber, Helmut E., eds. Thomas Hardy: An Annotated Bibliography of Writings about Him, Vol. II. LC 72-7514. (The Annotated Secondary Bibliography Series on English Literature in Transition, 1880-1920). 735p. 1983. 35.00 (ISBN 0-87580-091-2). N Ill U Pr.

Davis, W. Eugene, jt. ed. see Gerber, Helmut E.

Davis, W. Grayburn, jt. auth. see McCormick, John.

Davis, W. Hardy. Aiming for the Jugular in New Orleans. LC 75-16561. 1976. 14.95 (ISBN 0-87949-035-7). Ashley Bks.

Davis, W. Hersey. Greek Papyri of the First Century. 84p. 1980. 6.00 (ISBN 0-89005-332-4). Ares.

Davis, W. Hersey, jt. auth. see Robertson, A. T.

Davis, W. J. The British Trades Union Congress: History & Recollections. LC 83-48477. (The World of Labour - English Workers 1850-1890 Ser.). 158p. 1984. lib. bdg. 25.00 (ISBN 0-8240-5705-8). Garland Pub.

--The Federal Reserve System: Legal or Illegal? 1982. lib. bdg. 59.95 (ISBN 0-87700-357-2). Revisionist Pr.

--Nineteenth Century Token Coinage. 1979. Repr. of 1906 ed. 35.00 (ISBN 0-915262-28-2). S J Durst.

--Racial Chaos & Criminal Anarchy: The Prelude to Black Revolution. 1982. lib. bdg. 59.95 (ISBN 0-87700-412-9). Revisionist Pr.

Davis, W. J. & Waters, A. W. Tickets & Passes of Great Britain & Ireland. 1977. 40.00 (ISBN 0-685-51520-6, Pub by Spink & Son England). S J Durst.

Davis, W. Jackson. The Seventh Year: Industrial Civilization in Transition. (Illus.). 1979. 19.95 (ISBN 0-393-05693-7); pap. text ed. 7.95x (ISBN 0-393-09027-2). Norton.

Davis, W. M. The Coral Reef Problem. LC 75-45469. 612p. 1976. Repr. of 1928 ed. 39.50 (ISBN 0-88275-383-5). Krieger.

--Studies in Revelation. 1976. pap. 2.75 (ISBN 0-88027-044-6). Firm Foun Pub.

--The Way to Get What You Want. 1941. pap. 3.50 (ISBN 0-88027-022-5). Firm Foun Pub.

Davis, W. M., jt. auth. see Showalter, G. H.

Davis, W. N. California Indians Five: Sagebrush Corner - Opening of California's Northeast. (American Indian Ethnohistory Ser: California & Basin - Plateau Indians). (Illus.). lib. bdg. 51.00 (ISBN 0-8240-0775-1). Garland Pub.

Davis, W. R. Classical Fields, Particles & the Theory of Relativity. 418p. 1970. 79.75 (ISBN 0-677-02570-X). Gordon.
Davis, W. S. Computers & Business Information Processing & BASIC: Getting Started. 1981. package 22.95 (ISBN 0-201-13299-0). Addison-Wesley.
--Computers & Business Information Processing & FORTRAN: Getting Started. 1981. package 22.95 (ISBN 0-201-13298-2). Addison-Wesley.
--Information Processing Systems: An Introduction to Modern Computer-Based Information Systems. 2nd ed. 1981. 26.95 (ISBN 0-201-03183-3); student wkbk. 7.95 (ISBN 0-201-03185-X); transparencies 18.00 (ISBN 0-201-03577-4); instr's manual 2.95 (ISBN 0-201-03184-1). Addison-Wesley.
--Information Processing Systems & BASIC: Getting Started. 1981. 22.95 (ISBN 0-201-13297-4). Addison-Wesley.
--Information Processing Systems & FORTRAN: Getting Started. 1981. 22.95 (ISBN 0-201-13296-6). Addison-Wesley.
Davis, W. T., ed. Bradford's History of Plymouth Plantation 1606-1646. (Original Narratives Ser.). 436p. 1959. Repr. of 1908 ed. 21.50x (ISBN 0-686-63939-1). B&N Imports.
Davis, W. W. El Gringo: New Mexico & Her People. LC 82-2735. (Illus.). 432p. 1982. 29.50x (ISBN 0-8032-1665-3); pap. 7.95 (ISBN 0-8032-6558-1, BB 800, Bison). U of Nebr Pr.
Davis, Wade. The Serpent & the Rainbow. 1986. price not set. S&S.
--Ted & Dottie in a Day of Fun. (Illus.). (gr. 1-2). 1967. text ed. 6.84 (ISBN 0-87443-032-1). Benson.
Davis, Wally. Crime Crushers. 92p. (Orig.). 1984. pap. 4.95 (ISBN 0-916063-08-9). Fragments West.
Davis, Walter A. The Act of Interpretation: A Critique of Literary Reason. LC 77-13803. 1978. 16.00x (ISBN 0-226-13795-3). U of Chicago Pr.
Davis, Walter R. Idea & Act in Elizabethan Fiction. LC 68-56307. 1969. 32.00 (ISBN 0-691-06162-9). Princeton U Pr.
Davis, Walter R., ed. see Campion, Thomas.
Davis, Warren B. & Cromie, Richard M. The Future Is Now. 110p. (Orig.). 1984. pap. 4.95 (ISBN 0-914733-03-6). Desert Min.
Davis, Warren J. Japan, the Air Menace of the Pacific. LC 73-111751. (American Imperialism: Viewpoints of United States Foreign Policy, 1898-1941). 1970. Repr. of 1928 ed. 13.00 (ISBN 0-405-02010-4). Ayer Co Pubs.
Davis, Wayne A. An Introduction to Logic. (Illus.). 600p. 1986. text ed. 26.95 (ISBN 0-13-486259-7). P-H.
Davis, Wayne H., jt. auth. see Barbour, Roger W.
Davis, Wendy M. Aids to Make You Able: Self-Help Devices for Disabled Persons. LC 81-4085. (Illus.). 155p. 1981. spiralbound 8.95 (ISBN 0-8253-0066-5). Beaufort Bks NY.
Davis, Wilbur W., jt. auth. see Blake, Maurice C.
Davis, Willard O. Evolution & Revelation. 6.95 (ISBN 0-88027-097-7). Firm Foun Pub.
Davis, William. Bench & Bar of the Commonwealth of Massachusetts, 2 vols. (American Constitutional & Legal History Ser). 1299p. 1974. Repr. of 1895 ed. Set. lib. bdg. 145.00 (ISBN 0-306-70612-1). Da Capo.
--The Corporate Infighter's Handbook: Winning the Office War. (Illus.). 144p. 1985. pap. 10.95 (ISBN 0-283-99133-X, Pub. by Sidgwick & Jackson). Merrimack Pub Cir.
--Fantasy: A Practical Guide to Escapism. (Illus.). 222p. 1984. 16.95 (ISBN 0-283-98949-1, Pub. by Sidgwick & Jackson). Merrimack Pub Cir.
--History of the Judiciary of Massachusetts. LC 74-8535. (American Constitutional & Legal History Ser). xxiv, 446p. 1974. Repr. of 1900 ed. lib. bdg. 55.00 (ISBN 0-306-70613-X). Da Capo.
--The Rich. 232p. 1983. 16.95 (ISBN 0-531-09893-1). Watts.
--The Special Educator: Strategies for Succeeding in Today's Schools. LC 83-9513. 202p. (Orig.). 1983. pap. text ed. 16.00 (ISBN 0-936104-32-5, 0083). Pro Ed.
Davis, William, jt. auth. see Nichols, John Treadwell.
Davis, William, jt. auth. see Schultes, Richard.
Davis, William, ed. Best Business Hotels: A World Guide for the Discerning Traveller. 1985. 75.00 (ISBN 0-912289-54-6). St James Pr.
Davis, William, ed. see Nitsch, Susan L.
Davis, William A. Maydays & Mermaids. 152p. 1983. 10.00 (ISBN 0-89540-133-9, SB-133). Sun Pub.
Davis, William C. Battle at Bull Run: A History of the First Major Campaign of the Civil War. LC 76-42322. (Illus.). xiv, 298p. 1981. pap. text ed. 8.95 (ISBN 0-8071-0867-7). La State U Pr.
--The Battle of New Market. LC 82-18705. (Illus.). 249p. 1983. pap. 7.95 (ISBN 0-8071-1078-7). La State U Pr.
--Breckinridge: Statesman, Soldier & Symbol. LC 73-77658. (Southern Biography Ser.). (Illus.). xxii, 688p. 1974. 40.00x (ISBN 0-8071-0068-4). La State U Pr.
--Brother Against Brother. LC 82-17014. (Civil War Ser.). 1983. lib. bdg. 19.94 (ISBN 0-8094-4701-0, Pub. by Time-Life). Silver.
--Brother Against Brother. (Illus.). 176p. 1984. 14.95 (ISBN 0-8094-4700-2). Time Life.
--Civil War Parks: The Story Behind the Scenery. LC 83-83006. (Story Behind the Scenery Ser.). (Illus.). 64p. (Orig.). 1984. pap. 8.95 (ISBN 0-916122-96-4). KC Pubns.
--The Deep Waters of the Proud. LC 81-43307. (Imperiled Union 1861-1865 Ser.: Vol. 1). (Illus.). 320p. 1982. 19.95 (ISBN 0-385-14894-1). Doubleday.
--Duel Between the First Ironclads. LC 75-11071. (Illus.). xii, 220p. 1981. pap. 7.95 (ISBN 0-8071-0868-5). La State U Pr.
--Gettysburg: The Story Behind the Scenery. LC 83-80606. (Illus.). 48p. 1983. 8.95 (ISBN 0-916122-90-5); pap. 3.75 (ISBN 0-916122-89-1). KC Pubns.
--The Orphan Brigade: The Kentucky Confederates Who Couldn't Go Home. LC 82-18700. (Illus.). 318p. 1983. pap. 8.95 (ISBN 0-8071-1077-9). La State U Pr.
--Stand in the Day of Battle. LC 82-45521. (Imperiled Union 1861-1865 Ser.: Vol. 2). (Illus.). 336p. 1983. 19.95 (ISBN 0-385-14895-X). Doubleday.
Davis, William C., jt. auth. see Angle, Paul.
Davis, William C., jt. auth. see Fickett, Wildon.
Davis, William C., jt. auth. see Mother Earth News Staff.
Davis, William C., ed. see National Historical Society.
Davis, William D., ed. Jerome Witkin: Paintings & Drawings, a Decade of Work. (Illus.). 48p. 1983. pap. 7.50 (ISBN 0-911209-27-1). Penn St Art.
Davis, William E. The Special Educator: Meeting the Challenge for Professional Growth. LC 84-16886. 288p. (Orig.). 1985. pap. text ed. 17.00 (ISBN 0-936104-39-2, 0084). Pro Ed.
Davis, William F. Educator's Resource Guide to Special Education: Terms-Laws-Tests-Organizations. 350p. 1980. text ed. 29.95 (ISBN 0-205-06876-6, 246876). Allyn.
--Every Cloud Has One. 1985. 7.95 (ISBN 0-8062-2477-0). Carlton.
Davis, William G. Social Relations in a Philippine Market: Self-Interest & Subjectivity. LC 71-145783. 1973. 35.00x (ISBN 0-520-01904-0). U of Cal Pr.
Davis, William H. Beginner's Grammar of the Greek New Testament. 1923. 12.49x (ISBN 0-06-061710-1, HarpR). Har-Row.
--English Essayists: A Reader's Handbook. LC 72-5356. 1972. Repr. of 1916 ed. lib. bdg. 15.00 (ISBN 0-8414-0045-8). Folcroft.
--Philosophy of Religion. LC 75-92048. (Way of Life Ser: No. 114). (Orig.). 1969. pap. 3.95 (ISBN 0-89112-114-5). Bibl Res Pr.
--Science & Christian Faith. LC 68-21524. (Way of Life Ser: No. 104). 1968. pap. 3.95 (ISBN 0-89112-104-8). Bibl Res Pr.
--Seventy-Five Years in California. rev. & enl. ed. Small, Harold A., ed. LC 66-11279. (Illus.). 1967. 27.50 (ISBN 0-910760-08-X). Brick Row.
Davis, William H. see Golf Digest Editors.
Davis, William H. see Golf Digest Magazine Editors.
Davis, William J. & Waters, Arthur W. Tickets & Passes of Great Britain & Ireland, Struck or Engraved on Metal, Ivory, Etc. LC 73-16244. 1969. Repr. of 1904 ed. 35.50 (ISBN 0-8337-0794-9). B Franklin.
Davis, William K., et al. Laboratory Exercises for General Botany. 4th ed. (Illus.). 94p. 1981. pap. text ed. 5.95x (ISBN 0-89641-067-6). American Pr.
--Laboratory Exercises for General Zoology. 3rd ed. (Illus.). 131p. 1980. pap. text ed. 5.95x (ISBN 0-89641-030-7). American Pr.
Davis, William M. Coral Reef Problem. Repr. of 1928 ed. 37.50 (ISBN 0-404-01998-6). AMS Pr.
--Nimrod of the Sea. LC 72-78905. (Illus.). 416p. 1972. 8.95 (ISBN 0-8158-0283-8). Chris Mass.
Davis, William R. Development & Present Status of Negro Education in East Texas. LC 75-178798. (Columbia University. Teachers College. Contributions to Education: No. 626). Repr. of 1934 ed. 22.50 (ISBN 0-404-55626-4). AMS Pr.
Davis, William R. & Davis, Judy G. Roger's Rules of Public Relations. (Illus.). 100p. (Orig.). 1984. pap. 8.95 (ISBN 0-915113-01-5). Bizarre Butterfly.
Davis, William S. BASIC: Getting Started. 69p. 1981. pap. text ed. 7.95 (ISBN 0-201-03258-9). Addison-Wesley.
--Computer & Business Information Processing. 2nd ed. LC 82-6864. (Illus.). 448p. 1983. pap. text ed. 19.95 (ISBN 0-201-11118-7); instr's manual 2.95 (ISBN 0-201-11119-5); wkbk 6.95 (ISBN 0-201-11121-7); write for info. trans. masters. Addison-Wesley.
--Computers & Business Information Processing. LC 80-10946. 448p. 1981. pap. text ed. 17.95 (ISBN 0-201-03161-2); 7.95 (ISBN 0-201-03713-0). Addison-Wesley.
--Day in Old Athens. LC 60-16707. (Illus.). (gr. 7 up). 12.00x (ISBN 0-8196-0111-X). Biblo.
--Day in Old Rome. LC 61-24993. (Illus.). (gr. 7 up). 12.00x (ISBN 0-8196-0106-3). Biblo.
--FORTRAN-Getting Started. 1980. pap. text ed. 7.95 (ISBN 0-201-03104-3). Addison-Wesley.
--A Friend of Caesar: A Tale of the Fall of the Roman Republic (Time, 50-47 B. C.) 1977. Repr. of 1922 ed. lib. bdg. 22.50 (ISBN 0-8482-0542-1). Norwood Edns.
--The NECEN Voyage. LC 84-24392. 1985. 9.95 (ISBN 0-201-11979-X). Addison-Wesley.
--Operating Systems. 2nd ed. (Illus.). 448p. 1983. text ed. 29.95 (ISBN 0-201-11116-0); instrs' manual 2.95 (ISBN 0-201-11117-9). Addison-Wesley.
--Readings in Ancient History: Greece & the East. 1912. 20.00 (ISBN 0-686-20107-8). Quality Lib.
--Systems Analysis & Design a Structured Approach. 432p. 1983. pap. text ed. 24.95 (ISBN 0-201-10271-4); instr's manual 2.95 (ISBN 0-201-10272-2). Addison-Wesley.
--Tools & Techniques for Structured Systems Analysis & Design. LC 83-4629. 208p. 1983. pap. 15.95 (ISBN 0-201-10274-9). Addison-Wesley.
Davis, William S. & Fisher, Richard H. COBOL: An Introduction to Structured Logic & Modular Program Design. 1979. pap. 22.95 (ISBN 0-201-01431-9); instrs'. manual 2.95 (ISBN 0-201-01432-7). Addison-Wesley.
Davis, William S. & McCormack, Allison. Information Age. LC 78-55817. 1979. text ed. 23.95 (ISBN 0-201-01101-8); manual 2.95 (ISBN 0-201-01102-6). Addison-Wesley.
Davis, William S., et al, eds. Anasazi Subsistence & Settlement on White Mesa, San Juan County, Utah. (Illus.). 644p. (Orig.). 1985. lib. bdg. 36.50 (ISBN 0-8191-4800-8); pap. text ed. 24.75 (ISBN 0-8191-4801-6). U Pr of Amer.
Davis, William V. One Way to Reconstruct the Scene. LC 79-22810. (Yale Ser. of Younger Poets: No. 75). 1980. 13.95x (ISBN 0-300-02481-9); pap. 5.95x (ISBN 0-300-02503-3). Yale U Pr.
Davis, William W. Fries Rebellion, 1798-1799. LC 78-90171. (Mass Violence in America). Repr. of 1899 ed. 10.50 (ISBN 0-405-01305-1). Ayer Co Pubs.
--El Gringo. LC 72-9438. (The Far Western Frontier Ser.). (Illus.). 436p. 1973. Repr. of 1857 ed. 24.00 (ISBN 0-405-04968-4). Ayer Co Pubs.
Davis, Winborn E., jt. auth. see Knight, Paul E.
Davis, Winifred, ed. see Dubin, Fraida & Olshtain, Elite.
Davis, Winston. Dojo: Magic & Exorcism in Modern Japan. LC 79-64219. (Illus.). xx, 324p. 1980. 27.50x (ISBN 0-8047-1053-8); pap. 9.95 (ISBN 0-8047-1131-3, SP-7). Stanford U Pr.
Davis-Debeuneure, Linda, jt. auth. see Makris, Barbara L.
Davis-Friedmann, Deborah. Long Lives: Chinese Elderly & the Communist Revolution. (Harvard East Asian Ser.: No. 100). (Illus.). 160p. 1983. text ed. 20.00x (ISBN 0-674-53860-9). Harvard U Pr.
Davis-Gardner, Angela. Felice. LC 81-40234. 430p. 1982. 13.50 (ISBN 0-394-52009-2). Random.
Davis-Goff, Annabel. Night Moves. 288p. 1983. pap. 3.50 (ISBN 0-441-57487-4). Ace Bks.
Davis-Hawke, Sharryl, ed. see Van de Water, H. Keith, et al.
Davison, A. & Gordon, Peter. Games & Simulations in Action. (Woburn Educational Ser.). 200p. 1982. 18.50x (ISBN 0-7130-0150-X, Pub. by Woburn Pr England); pap. 9.95x (ISBN 0-7130-4002-5). Biblio Dist.
Davison, A., ed. Physical & Inorganic Chemistry. (Topics in Current Chemistry Ser.: Vol. 111). (Illus.). 194p. 1983. 39.50 (ISBN 0-387-12065-3). Springer-Verlag.
Davison, A., et al, eds. New Concepts Two. (Topics in Current Chemistry: Vol. 42). (Illus.). iv, 158p. 1973. 35.00 (ISBN 0-387-06399-4). Springer-Verlag.
--Three-Membered Rings. LC 51-5497. (Topics in Current Chemistry: Vol. 40). (Illus.). iv, 149p. 1973. 33.00 (ISBN 0-387-06265-3). Springer-Verlag.
Davison, A. M., ed. see European Dialysis & Transplant Association Staff.
Davison, A. N., ed. Biochemical Correlates of Brain Structure & Function. 1977. 65.00 (ISBN 0-12-206650-2). Acad Pr.
Davison, A. N. & Cuzner, M. L., eds. The Suppression of Experimental Allergic Encephalomyelitis & Multiple Sclerosis. LC 79-41796. 1980. 55.00 (ISBN 0-12-206660-X). Acad Pr.
Davison, A. N. & Thompson, R. H., eds. The Molecular Basis of Neuropathology. LC 81-86190. (Illus.). 693p. 1981. monograph 120.00 (ISBN 0-89640-068-9). Igaku-Shoin.
Davison, A. N., jt. ed. see Paoletti, R.
Davison, Alex M. A Synopsis of Renal Diseases. (Illus.). 192p. 1981. pap. text ed. 17.50 (ISBN 0-7236-0569-6). PSG Pub Co.
Davison, Alex M. & Guillou, Pierre J., eds. Proceedings of the European Dialysis & Transplant Association-European Renal Association, No. 21. 1200p. 1985. 82.50 (ISBN 0-272-79804-5, Pitman Med UK). Urban & S.
Davison, Archibald. Bach & Handel. (Music Reprint Ser.). 77p. 1985. Repr. of 1951 ed. 18.50 (ISBN 0-306-76258-7). Da Capo.
--Protestant Church Music in America. 59.95 (ISBN 0-8490-0905-7). Gordon Pr.
Davison, Archibald T. Bach & Handel, the Consummation of the Baroque in Music. LC 51-10950. pap. 21.00 (ISBN 0-317-10116-1, 2006011). Bks Demand UMI.
--Choral Conducting. LC 40-27315. 1940. 7.95x (ISBN 0-674-12800-1). Harvard U Pr.
Davison, Archibald T. & Apel, Willi, eds. Historical Anthology of Music, 2 vols. Incl. Vol. 1. Oriental, Medieval, & Renaissance Music. rev. ed. (Illus.). 258p. 1949 (ISBN 0-674-39300-7); Vol. 2. Baroque, Rococo, & Pre-Classical Music. (Illus.). 303p. 1950 (ISBN 0-674-39301-5). LC 49-4339. 20.00 ea. Harvard U Pr.
Davison, Brian. Explore a Castle. (Illus.). 128p. (gr. 4-6). 1983. 11.00 (ISBN 0-241-10763-6, Pub. by Hamish Hamilton England). David & Charles.
Davison, Charles. The Founders of Seismology. Albritton, Claude C., Jr., ed. LC 77-6518. (History of Geology Ser.). 1978. Repr. of 1927 ed. lib. bdg. 18.00 (ISBN 0-405-10441-3). Ayer Co Pubs.
Davison, D. J. The Environmental Factor: An Approach for Managers. LC 77-20123. 183p. 1978. 42.95x (ISBN 0-470-99351-0). Halsted Pr.
Davison, Dennis. Dryden. (Literature in Perspective Ser.). (Illus.). 151p. 1968. 6.00x (ISBN 0-87471-244-0). Rowman.
Davison, Dennis, ed. The Penguin Book of Eighteenth-Century English Verse. (Poetry Ser.). 320p. 1973. pap. 5.95 (ISBN 0-14-042169-6). Penguin.
Davison, Edward. Some Modern Poets & Other Critical Essays. 255p. 1980. Repr. lib. bdg. 35.00 (ISBN 0-89987-157-7). Century Bookbindery.
--Some Modern Poets & Other Critical Essays. 255p. 1980. Repr. of 1928 ed. lib. bdg. 35.00 (ISBN 0-89760-149-1). Telegraph Bks.
Davison, Edward L. Some Modern Poets, & Other Critical Essays. facs. ed. LC 68-16926. (Essay Index Reprint Ser). 1968. Repr. of 1928 ed. 18.00 (ISBN 0-8369-0366-8). Ayer Co Pubs.
--Some Modern Poets & Other Critical Essays. 1928. Repr. 15.50 (ISBN 0-8274-3459-6). R West.
Davison, Ellen S. Forerunners of Saint Francis & Other Studies. Richards, Gertrude R., ed. LC 77-85270. Repr. of 1927 ed. 34.50 (ISBN 0-404-16120-0). AMS Pr.
Davison, Frank, tr. see Alain-Fournier.
Davison, G. C. & Neale, J. Abnormal Psychology: An Experimental Clinical Approach. 4th ed. 1985. price not set (ISBN 0-471-88876-1). Wiley.
Davison, G. C. & Neale, J. M. Abnormal Psychology: An Experimental Clinical Approach. 3rd ed. 823p. 1982. 32.95 (ISBN 0-471-06159-X); pap. 12.95 (ISBN 0-471-07735-6). Wiley.
Davison, G. C., jt. auth. see Goldfried, M. R.
Davison, Graeme. The Rise & Fall of Marvellous Melbourne. 1979. 15.00x (ISBN 0-522-84191-0, Pub. by Melbourne U Pr). Intl Spec Bk.
Davison, J. F. Programming for Digital Computers. (Illus.). 186p. 1962. 42.95 (ISBN 0-677-00210-6). Gordon.
Davison, James F., ed. Cases & Readings on Administrative Law. LC 72-108388. 777p. Repr. of 1952 ed. lib. bdg. 36.75x (ISBN 0-8371-3811-6, DAAL). Greenwood.
Davison, Jane, jt. auth. see Vila, Bob.
Davison, Jaquie. Cancer Winner. 7.95 (ISBN 0-686-29905-1). Cancer Control Soc.
--I Am a Housewife. LC 72-91284. (Illus.). iv, 108p. (Orig.). 1972. pap. 1.95 (ISBN 0-685-30126-5). Guild Bks.
Davison, Jean. The Golden Torrent. LC 77-7012. 1978. 10.95 (ISBN 0-385-12856-8). Doubleday.
--Oswald's Game. LC 83-8351. (Illus.). 288p. 1983. 17.95 (ISBN 0-393-01764-8). Norton.
Davison, June & Schaub, Ardella. Piano Progress, Bk. I. Podolsky, Leo, ed. 1967. 2.00 (ISBN 0-913650-43-9). Columbia Pictures.
--Piano Progress, Bk. II. Podolsky, Leo, ed. 1967. 2.00 (ISBN 0-913650-44-7). Columbia Pictures.
--Piano Progress, Bk. III. Podolsky, Leo, ed. 1968. 2.00 (ISBN 0-913650-45-5). Columbia Pictures.
--Piano Progress for the Partially Sighted, Bk. IA. Podolsky, Leo, ed. 1972. 4.00 (ISBN 0-913650-13-7). Columbia Pictures.
--Piano Progress for the Partially Sighted, Bk. IB. Podolsky, Leo, ed. 1972. 4.00 (ISBN 0-913650-14-5). Columbia Pictures.
--Piano Progress for the Partially Sighted, Bk. 2A. Podolsky, Leo, ed. 1967. 4.00 (ISBN 0-913650-15-3). Columbia Pictures.
--Piano Progress for the Partially Sighted, Bk. 2B. Podolsky, Leo, ed. 1967. 4.00 (ISBN 0-913650-16-1). Columbia Pictures.
--Piano Progress for the Partially Sighted, Bk. 3A. Podolsky, Leo, ed. 1974. 6.00 (ISBN 0-913650-17-X). Columbia Pictures.
--Piano Progress for the Partially Sighted, Bk. 3B. Podolsky, Leo, ed. 1974. 6.00 (ISBN 0-913650-18-8). Columbia Pictures.
--Piano Progress-Primary Book. Podolsky, Leo, ed. 1968. 2.00 (ISBN 0-913650-42-0). Columbia Pictures.
--The Piano Way to Music Piano Speller. Podolsky, Leo, ed. 1957. 2.50 (ISBN 0-913650-46-3). Columbia Pictures.
--The Piano Way to Music Reader, Bk. I. Podolsky, Leo, ed. 1957. 2.50 (ISBN 0-913650-47-1). Columbia Pictures.
--The Piano Way to Music Reader, Bk. II. Podolsky, Leo, ed. 1957. 2.50 (ISBN 0-913650-48-X). Columbia Pictures.
--The Piano Way to Music Reader, Bk. III. Podolsky, Leo, ed. 1957. 2.50 (ISBN 0-913650-49-8). Columbia Pictures.

Davison, Kenneth E. The Presidency of Rutherford B. Hayes. LC 79-176289. (Contributions in American Studies: No. 3). 1972. lib. bdg. 29.95 (ISBN 0-8371-6275-0, DPH/). Greenwood.

Davison, Kenneth E., jt. auth. see Burke, James L.

Davison, Kenneth E., ed. American Presidency: A Guide to Information Sources. LC 73-17552. (The American Studies Information Guide Series, Gale Information Guide Library: Vol. 11). 200p. 1983. 60.00x (ISBN 0-8103-1261-1). Gale.

Davison, L., jt. ed. see Aifantis, E. C.

Davison, Marguerite P. A Handweavers Pattern Book. rev ed. (Illus.). 1951. 18.00 (ISBN 0-9603172-0-1). M P Davison.

--A Handweavers Source Book. (Illus.). 1953. pap. text ed. 10.95 (ISBN 0-9603172-1-X). M P Davison.

Davison, Mark L. Multidimensional Scaling. LC 82-17403. (Probability & Mathematical Statistics: Applied Probability & Statistic Section Ser.). 242p. 1983. 29.95 (ISBN 0-471-86417-X, Pub. by Wiley-Interscience). Wiley.

Davison, Marshall B. A History of Art: From Twenty-Five Thousand B.C. to the Present. LC 83-16110. (The Random House Library of Knowledge). (Illus.). 112p. (gr. 5 up). 1984. pap. 8.95 (ISBN 0-394-85181-1, BYR); PLB 9.99 (ISBN 0-394-95181-6). Random.

Davison, Ned. Eduardo Barrios. LC 70-120478. (World Authors Ser.). 1970. lib. bdg. 15.95 (ISBN 0-8057-2112-6). Irvington.

Davison, Nigel, ed. see De La Rue, Pierre.

Davison, P. H., ed. see Shakespeare, William.

Davison, Peter. Barn Fever & Other Poems. LC 80-69364. 64p. 1981. 10.00 (ISBN 0-689-11126-6); pap. 5.95 (ISBN 0-689-11163-0). Atheneum.

--The Breaking of the Day & Other Poems. LC 75-21578. (Yale Ser. of Younger Poets: No. 60). Repr. of 1964 ed. 18.00 (ISBN 0-404-53860-6). AMS Pr.

--Contemporary Drama & the Popular Dramatic Tradition in England. LC 79-55526. 206p. 1983. text ed. 28.50x (ISBN 0-389-20232-0). B&N Imports.

--Dark Houses. LC 77-177946. 1971. pap. 4.00 (ISBN 0-912604-07-7). Halty Ferguson.

--Hamlet. (Text & Performance). 80p. 1983. pap. text ed. 5.45x (ISBN 0-333-33994-0, Pub. by MacMillan, England). Humanities.

--Popular Appeal in English Drama to Eighteen Fifty. LC 79-55528. 234p. 1982. text ed. 28.50x (ISBN 0-389-20231-2). B&N Imports.

--Praying Wrong: New & Selected Poems, 1957-1984. LC 84-45061. 192p. 1984. 18.95 (ISBN 0-689-11499-0); pap. 9.95 (ISBN 0-689-11500-8). Atheneum.

--Pretending to Be Asleep. LC 70-103824. (Orig.). 1970. pap. 2.95 (ISBN 0-689-10309-3). Atheneum.

--A Voice in the Mountain. LC 77-76552. 1977. pap. 4.95 (ISBN 0-689-10812-5). Atheneum.

--Walking the Boundaries. LC 73-93708. 128p. 1974. 6.95 (ISBN 0-689-10608-4). Atheneum.

Davison, Peter, ed. Critics & Apologists of the English Theatre: A Selection of Seventeenth Century Pamphlets in Facsimile. 106p. 1972. 30.00 (ISBN 0-384-11008-8). Johnson Repr.

--Theatrum Redivivum, 17 vols. Repr. 535.00 (ISBN 0-384-59985-0). Johnson Repr.

Davison, Peter, ed. see Blount, Roy, Jr.

Davison, Peter, ed. see Jacobson, Dan.

Davison, Peter, ed. see Jonnes, Jill.

Davison, Peter, ed. see Kunitz, Stanley.

Davison, Peter, ed. see Mowat, Farley.

Davison, Peter, ed. see Orwell, George.

Davison, Peter, et al, eds. Uses of Literacy: Media. LC 77-90618. (Literary Taste, Culture & Mass Communication Ser.: Vol. 9). 1978. lib. bdg. 44.00x (ISBN 0-85964-044-2). Chadwyck-Healey.

--Art & Changing Civilisation. LC 77-90612. (Literary Taste, Culture & Mass Communication Ser.: Vol. 4). 1978. lib. bdg. 42.00x (ISBN 0-85964-039-6). Chadwyck-Healey.

--Art & Social Life. LC 77-90611. (Literary Taste, Culture & Mass Communication Ser.: Vol. 3). 1978. lib. bdg. 40.00x (ISBN 0-85964-039-6). Chadwyck-Healey.

--Authorship. LC 77-90619. (Literary Taste, Culture & Mass Communication: Vol. 10). 1978. lib. bdg. 47.00x (ISBN 0-85964-045-0). Chadwyck-Healey.

--Bookselling, Reviewing & Reading. LC 77-90621. (Literary Taste, Culture & Mass Communication: Vol. 12). 1978. lib. bdg. 47.00x (ISBN 0-85964-047-7). Chadwyck-Healey.

--Content & Taste: Religion & Myth. LC 77-90615. (Literary Taste, Culture & Mass Communication: Vol. 7). 1978. lib. bdg. 47.00x (ISBN 0-85964-042-6). Chadwyck-Healey.

--The Cultural Debate: Part I. LC 77-90622. (Literary Taste, Culture & Mass Communication: Vol. 13). 1978. lib. bdg. 40.00x (ISBN 0-85964-048-5). Chadwyck-Healey.

--The Cultural Debate: Part II Indexes. LC 77-90623. (Literary Taste, Culture & Mass Communication Ser.: Vol. 14). 1978. lib. bdg. 42.00x (ISBN 0-85964-049-3). Chadwyck-Healey.

--Culture & Mass Culture. LC 77-90608. (Literary Taste, Culture & Mass Communication Ser.: Vol. 1). 1978. lib. bdg. 47.00x (ISBN 0-85964-036-1). Chadwyck-Healey.

--Literature & Society. LC 77-90613. (Literary Taste, Culture & Mass Communication Ser.: Vol. 5). 1978. lib. bdg. 40.00x (ISBN 0-85964-040-X). Chadwyck-Healey.

--Mass Media & Mass Communication. LC 77-90610. (Literary Taste, Culture & Mass Communication: Vol. 2). 1978. 49.00x (ISBN 0-85964-037-X). Chadwyck-Healey.

--The Sociology of Literature. LC 77-90614. (Literary Taste, Culture & Mass Communication Ser.: Vol. 6). 1978. lib. bdg. 49.00x (ISBN 0-85964-041-8). Chadwyck-Healey.

--Theater & Song. LC 77-90616. (Literary Taste, Culture & Mass Communication Ser.: Vol. 8). 1978. lib. bdg. 42.00x (ISBN 0-85964-043-4). Chadwyck-Healey.

--The Writer & Politics. LC 77-90620. (Literary Taste, Culture & Mass Communication Se.: Vol. 11). 1978. 42.00x (ISBN 0-85964-046-9). Chadwyck-Healey.

Davison, Peter H. & Brown, Arthur, eds. The Fair Maid of the Exchange. LC 82-45716. (Malone Society Reprint Ser.: No. 116). Repr. of 1962 ed. 40.00 (ISBN 0-404-63117-7). AMS Pr.

Davison, Philip. Twist & Shout. 92p. 1983. 10.95 (ISBN 0-86322-022-3, Pub. by Brandon Bks); pap. 4.95 (ISBN 0-86322-047-9). Longwood Pub Group.

Davison, Richard A. Charles G. Norris. (United States Authors Ser.: No. 445). 1983. lib. bdg. 18.95 (ISBN 0-8057-7404-1, Twayne). G K Hall.

Davison, Robert E., ed. Illinois Handbook of Criminal Law Decisions. 1983. pap. 20.00 (ISBN 0-318-02521-3). Illinois Bar.

Davison, Roderic H. Reform in the Ottoman Empire, 1856-1876. LC 73-148618. 1973. Repr. of 1963 ed. text ed. 17.50x (ISBN 0-87752-135-2). Gordian.

--Reform in the Ottoman Empire, 1856-1876. LC 63-12669. pap. 123.30 (ISBN 0-317-09287-1, 2000890). Bks Demand UMI.

Davison, Ronald. Synastry: Understanding Human Relationships Through Astrology. 335p. 10.95 (ISBN 0-943358-05-1). Aurora Press.

Davison, Ronald C. The Unemployed. Leventhal, F. M., ed. (English Workers & the Coming of the Welfare State, 1918-1945). 292p. 1985. lib. bdg. 35.00 (ISBN 0-8240-7610-9). Garland Pub.

Davison, S. G., ed. Progress in Surface Science, Vols. 1-7. Incl. Vol. 1, 4 pts. Vol. 1, 1971 Complete. 81.00 (ISBN 0-08-016878-7); Pts 1-4. pap. 15.50 ea.; Pt. 1. pap. (ISBN 0-08-016549-4); Pt. 2, 1971. pap. (ISBN 0-08-016629-6); Pt. 3, 1972. pap. (ISBN 0-08-016815-9); Pt. 4. 1972. pap. (ISBN 0-08-016792-6); Vol. 2, 4 pts. 1972. Vol. 2, Complete. 81.00 (ISBN 0-08-017135-4); Pts. 1-4. pap. 15.50 ea.; Pt. 1. pap. (ISBN 0-08-016934-1); Pt. 2. pap. (ISBN 0-08-016879-5); Pt. 3. pap. (ISBN 0-08-016944-9); Pt. 4. pap. (ISBN 0-08-016952-X); Vol. 3, 4 pts. Vol. 3, Complete. 81.00 (ISBN 0-08-017150-8); Pts. 1-4. pap. 15.50 ea.; Pt. 1. pap. (ISBN 0-08-016981-3); Pt. 2, 1972. pap. (ISBN 0-08-017045-5); Pt. 3, 1972. pap. (ISBN 0-08-017046-3); Pt. 4, 1973. pap. (ISBN 0-08-017127-3); Vol. 4, 3 pts. 1974. Vol. 4, Complete. 81.00 (ISBN 0-08-017778-6); Pts. 1-3. pap. 15.50 ea.; Pt. 1-1973. pap. Pt. 2. pap. (ISBN 0-08-017790-5); Pt. 3. pap. (ISBN 0-08-017798-0); Vol. 5, 4 pts. 1974. Vol. 5, Complete. 81.00 (ISBN 0-08-017791-3); Pts. 1-4. pap. 15.50 ea.; Pt. 1-1974. pap. (ISBN 0-08-017904-5); Pt. 2-1974. pap. (ISBN 0-08-017792-1); Pt. 3-1974. pap. (ISBN 0-08-018051-5); Pt. 4-1975. pap. (ISBN 0-08-018150-3); Vol. 6, 3 pts. 1975. Pt. 1. pap. 8.00 (ISBN 0-08-018223-2); Pt. 2. pap. 22.00 (ISBN 0-08-018974-1); Pt. 3. pap. 12.50 (ISBN 0-08-018975-X); Vol. 6-7 Complete-1978. 77.00 (ISBN 0-08-019460-5); Vol. 7, 3 pts. 1976. Pt. 1. pap. 10.00 (ISBN 0-08-018977-6); Pt. 2. pap. 12.00 (ISBN 0-08-018978-4); Pt. 3. pap. 11.00 (ISBN 0-08-018979-2); Vol. 9 Complete. 273p. 1980. 81.00 (ISBN 0-08-026052-7). pap. write for info. Pergamon.

--Progress in Surface Science, Vol. 10, No. 1. (Illus.). 164p. 1981. pap. 28.00 (ISBN 0-08-027154-5). Pergamon.

--Progress in Surface Science, Vol. 11. LC 77-141188. 378p. 1983. 106.00 (ISBN 0-08-030875-9, 17). Pergamon.

--Progress in Surface Science, Vol. 12. 436p. 1983. 110.00 (ISBN 0-08-030876-7). Pergamon.

--Progress in Surface Science, Vol. 13. LC 77-141188. 355p. 1985. 110.00 (ISBN 0-08-030886-4). Pergamon.

--Progress in Surface Science, Vol. 14. LC 77-141188. 423p. 1985. 110.00 (ISBN 0-08-030887-2). Pergamon.

Davison, Stanley S. Leadership of the Reclamation Movement, 1875-1902. Bruchey, Stuart, ed. LC 78-53545. (Development of Public Land Law in the U. S. Ser.). (Illus.). 1979. lib. bdg. 21.00x (ISBN 0-405-11365-X). Ayer Co Pubs.

Davison, T. The Cross & the Sabre. pap. 8.95 (ISBN 0-937816-33-7). Tech Data.

Davison, W. Phillips. The Berlin Blockade: A Study in Cold War Politics. Zuckerman, Harriet & Merton, Robert K., eds. LC 79-8992. (Dissertations on Sociology Ser.). (Illus.). 1980. Repr. of 1958 ed. lib. bdg. 40.00x (ISBN 0-405-12963-7). Ayer Co Pubs.

Davison, W. Phillips & Gordenker, Leon, eds. Resolving Nationality Conflicts: The Role of Public Opinion Research. LC 80-15128. 256p. 1980. 38.95 (ISBN 0-03-056229-5). Praeger.

Davison, W. Phillips, et al. News from Abroad & the Foreign Policy Public. LC 80-68024. (Headline Ser.: No. 250). (Illus.). 64p. (Orig.). 1980. pap. 3.00 (ISBN 0-87124-063-7). Foreign Policy.

Davison, William T. Mystics & Poets. LC 77-924. 1977. lib. bdg. 25.00 (ISBN 0-8414-3680-0). Folcroft.

--Mystics & Poets. 167p. 1980. Repr. of 1936 ed. lib. bdg. 25.00 (ISBN 0-8482-0639-8). Norwood Edns.

Davison, Z. C; see Reed, C. E.

Davis Philip, A. G., ed. Finding Charts: Contributions of Van Vleck Obs, Vol. 2. 1985. pap. 15.00 (ISBN 0-9607902-6-8). Davis Pr.

Davis Philip, A. G. & Latham, D. W., eds. Stellar Radial Velocities. 1985. 42.00 (ISBN 0-933485-01-8); pap. 32.00 (ISBN 0-933485-00-X). Davis Pr.

Davisson, A., ed. Kentucky Harmony: A Collection of Psalms, Tunes, Hymns & Anthems. 1976. 8.50 (ISBN 0-8066-1546-X, 11-9249). Augsburg.

Davisson, Bud. The World of Sport Aviation. LC 82-1054. (Illus.). 242p. 1982. 24.00 (ISBN 0-87851-151-2). Hearst Bks.

Davisson, Charles, tr. see Unger, Georg.

Davisson, Charles N. & Wilhelm, Ross. Economic Effects of the Wage-Price Guideposts. (Michigan Business Papers: No. 45). 1967. pap. 1.50 (ISBN 0-87712-094-3). U Mich Busn Div Res.

Davisson, Darrell D., jt. auth. see Fredericksen, Burton B.

Davisson, Emmett D. Art & Mysteries in Tombs, Mummies & Catacombs. (Illus.). 1980. deluxe ed. 97.45 deluxe binding (ISBN 0-930582-63-2). Gloucester Art.

Davisson, Lee D., jt. auth. see Gray, Robert M.

Davisson, Lee D. & Gray, Robert M., eds. Data Compression. LC 76-3629. (Benchmark Papers in Electrical Engineering: Vol. 14). 400p. 1976. 65.00 (ISBN 0-12-786326-5). Acad Pr.

Davisson, Lee D., jt. ed. see Gray, Robert M.

Davisson, Lisa, tr. see Unger, Georg.

Davisson, William I. Information Processing. LC 76-109528. 276p. 1970. pap. 12.50x (ISBN 0-306-50010-8, Plenum Pr). Plenum Pub.

Davisson, William I. & Bonello, Frank J. Computer-Assisted Instruction in Economics. LC 76-642. 208p. 1976. text ed. 22.95 (ISBN 0-268-00715-2). U of Notre Dame Pr.

Davisson, William I. & Harper, James E. European Economic History: The Ancient World. LC 75-172518. (Illus.). 1972. 34.50x (ISBN 0-89197-153-X); pap. text ed. 12.95x (ISBN 0-89197-154-8). Irvington.

Davisson, William I. & Uhran, John J., Jr. NDTRAN: A Primer for a Systems Dynamics Interpreter. (Illus.). pap. text ed. write for info. (ISBN 0-89651-504-4). Icarus.

Davitt, Michael. Boer Fight for Freedom. LC 72-5540. (Black Heritage Library Collections). 1972. Repr. of 1902 ed. 60.00 (ISBN 0-8369-9137-0). Ayer Co Pubs.

--The Boer Fight for Freedom. 59.95 (ISBN 0-87968-764-9). Gordon Pr.

--Within the Pale: The True Story of Anti-Semitic Persecutions in Russia. facsimile ed. LC 74-27976. (Modern Jewish Experience Ser.). 1975. Repr. of 1903 ed. 25.50x (ISBN 0-405-06705-4). Ayer Co Pubs.

Davitt, Thomas E. The Basic Values in Law: A Study of the Ethics-Legal Implications of Psychology & Anthropology. LC 68-24357. 1968. pap. 12.95 (ISBN 0-87462-451-7). Marquette.

--The Elements of Law. LC 59-10419. 1959. pap. 12.95 (ISBN 0-87462-475-4). Marquette.

--Ethics in the Situation. LC 72-121300. 1978. pap. 9.95 (ISBN 0-87462-450-9). Marquette.

Davitz, J. R. Language of Emotion. (Personality & Psychopathology: Vol. 6). 1969. 41.50 (ISBN 0-12-206450-X). Acad Pr.

Davitz, Joel & Davitz, Lois. Making It: Forty & Beyond, Surviving the Mid-Life Crisis. 1979. pap. 6.95 (ISBN 0-03-051561-0). Winston Pr.

Davitz, Joel, jt. auth. see Davitz, Lois.

Davitz, Joel R. & Davitz, Lois J. A Guide for Evaluating Research Plans in Psychology & Education. LC 67-25063. pap. 20.00 (ISBN 0-317-10282-6, 2005465). Bks Demand UMI.

Davitz, Joel R. & Davitz, Lois L. Evaluating Research Plans in the Behavioral Sciences: A Guide. LC 77-20296. 1977. pap. 4.50x (ISBN 0-8077-2544-7). Tchrs Coll.

--Inferences of Patients' Pain & Psychological Distress: Studies of Nursing Behaviors. (Illus.). 1981. text ed. 25.00 (ISBN 0-8261-3360-6). Springer Pub.

Davitz, Joel R., jt. auth. see Davitz, Lois J.

Davitz, Joel R., jt. auth. see Davitz, Lois L.

Davitz, Joel R., et al. The Communication of Emotional Meaning. LC 75-31360. 1976. Repr. of 1964 ed. lib. bdg. 24.75x (ISBN 0-8371-8527-0, DACE). Greenwood.

--Terminology & Concepts in Mental Retardation. LC 62-61261. (Orig.). 1964. pap. text ed. 5.50x (ISBN 0-8077-1233-7). Tchrs Coll.

Davitz, Lois & Davitz, Joel. How to Live (Almost) Happily with a Teenager. 240p. 1983. pap. 3.95 (ISBN 0-451-13727-2, Sig). NAL.

Davitz, Lois, jt. auth. see Davitz, Joel.

Davitz, Lois J. & Davitz, Joel R. Nurses' Responces to Patient's Suffering. (Orig.). 1980. pap. text ed. 14.95 (ISBN 0-8261-2921-8). Springer Pub.

Davitz, Lois J., jt. auth. see Davitz, Joel R.

Davitz, Lois L. Baby Hunger: Every Woman's Longing for a Baby. 144p. (Orig.). 1984. pap. 6.95 (ISBN 0-86683-810-4, 8402). Winston Pr.

Davitz, Lois L. & Davitz, Joel R. How to Live (Almost) Happily with a Teenager. 230p. (Orig.). 1982. pap. 8.95 (ISBN 0-86683-624-1, AY8208). Winston Pr.

Davitz, Lois L., jt. auth. see Davitz, Joel R.

Davmier, Honore, illus. Actors, Actresses, & the Theatre. (Illus.). 15 prints in portfolio 12.50 (ISBN 0-87505-216-9). Borden.

Davock, Marcia. Cruising Guide to Tahiti & the French Society Islands. Wilensky, Julius M., ed. LC 85-50922. (Illus.). 272p. (Orig.). 1985. pap. 29.95 (ISBN 0-918752-04-3). Wescott Cove.

D'Avray, D. L. The Preaching of the Friars: Sermons Diffused from Paris Before Thirteen Hundred. 320p. 1984. 45.00 (ISBN 0-19-822772-8). Oxford U Pr.

Davril, Robert. Le Drame De John Ford. 550p. 1979. Repr. of 1954 ed. lib. bdg. 100.00 (ISBN 0-8495-1051-1). Arden Lib.

Davrout, L., tr. see Wieger, L.

Davson. The Eye. 1974. Vol. 5. 84.00 (ISBN 0-12-206755-X); Vol. 6. 78.00 (ISBN 0-12-206756-8). Acad Pr.

Davson, H. Physiology of the Eye. 4th ed. 1980. 85.00 (ISBN 0-12-206745-2). Acad Pr.

Davson, H., jt. ed. see Bito, L.

Davson, Hugh. The Eye: Vegetative Physiology & Biochemistry, 2 vols. 3rd ed. 1984. Vol. 1A. 80.00 (ISBN 0-12-206901-3); Vol. 1B. 70.00 (ISBN 0-12-206921-8). Acad Pr.

--The Eye: Visual Optics & Optical Space Sense. 2nd ed. Date not set. Vol. 4. price not set (ISBN 0-12-206754-1). Acad Pr.

Davson, Hugh & Segal, M. B. Introduction to Physiology, Vols. 1-3. Incl. Vol. I. Basic Mechanisms. 576p. 1975. 29.50 (ISBN 0-8089-0896-0, 791001); Vol. II. Basic Mechanisms. 494p. 1975; Vol. III. Control Mechanisms. 656p. 1976. 29.50 (ISBN 0-686-57753-1, 791003). Grune.

--Introduction to Physiology: Vol. IV, Mechanisms of Motor Control. 620p. 1978. 29.50 (ISBN 0-8089-0899-5, 791004). Grune.

--Introduction to Physiology, Vol. V: Control of Reproduction. 610p. 1980. 54.50 (ISBN 0-8089-0900-2, 791005). Grune.

Davson, Hugh, jt. auth. see Zadunaisky, Jose.

Davson, Hugh, ed. Eye. 2nd ed. Vol. 1. 1969. 89.50 (ISBN 0-12-206751-7); Vol. 2A 1976. 90.00 (ISBN 0-12-206752-5); Vol. 2B 1977. 90.00 (ISBN 0-12-206762-2); Vol. 3. 1970. 64.50 (ISBN 0-12-206753-3). Acad Pr.

Davson, Hugh, jt. ed. see Zadunaisky, Jose A.

Davy, A. J., jt. ed. see Jefferies, R. L.

Davy, B. & Graham, M., eds. Disease of Fish Cultured for Food in Southeast Asia: Report of a Workshop Held in Cisarua, Bogor, Indonesia, 28 Nov.-1-Dec. 1978. 32p. 1979. pap. 5.00 (ISBN 0-88936-226-2, IDRC139, IDRC). Unipub.

Davy, C. see Steiner, Rudolf.

Davy, C., tr. see Steiner, Rudolf.

Davy, Charles. Words in the Mind: Exploring Some Effects of Poetry, English & French. 178p. 1983. Repr. of 1965 ed. lib. bdg. 30.00 (ISBN 0-89987-179-8). Darby Bks.

Davy, Charles, ed. Footnotes to the Film. LC 75-124004. (Literature of Cinema, Ser. 1). Repr. of 1938 ed. 17.00 (ISBN 0-405-01610-7). Ayer Co Pubs.

Davy, Charles, tr. see Steiner, Rudolf.

Davy, Don. Anatomy & Life Drawing. LC 77-91042. 1978. pap. 4.95 (ISBN 0-8008-0196-2, Pentalic). Taplinger.

--Drawing Animals & Birds. LC 77-91048. 1978. pap. 4.95 (ISBN 0-8008-2268-4, Pentalic). Taplinger.

--Drawing Boats & Water. LC 80-50085. (Illus.). 96p. 1980. pap. 4.95 (ISBN 0-8008-2269-2, Pentalic). Taplinger.

--Drawing Buildings. LC 81-50606. (Illus.). 66p. 1981. pap. 4.95 (ISBN 0-8008-2267-6, Pentalic). Taplinger.

Davy, E. G. A Survey of Meteorological & Hydrological Data Available in Six Sahelian Countries of West Africa. vi, 120p. (Orig., Eng. & Fr.). 1974. pap. 15.00 (ISBN 92-63-10379-8, W#149, WMO). Unipub.

Davy, E. J. & Mattei, F. An Evaluation of Climate & Water Resources for Development of Agriculture in the Sudano-Sahelian Zone of West Africa. (Special Environmental Reports: No. 9). (Illus.). 289p. (Eng. & Fr., Prepared in Co-operation with the United Nations Environment Programme). 1976. pap. 40.00 (ISBN 92-63-10459-X, W255, WMO). Unipub.

Davy, Elizabeth & Davy, Karen. TOEFL Reading Comprehension & Vocabulary Workbook. 1st ed. LC 83-3717. 256p. (Orig.). 1983. pap. 7.95 (ISBN 0-668-05594-4, 5594). Arco.

Davy, F. B. & Chouinard, A., eds. Induced Fish Breeding in Southeast Asia: Report of a Workshop Held in Singapore, 25-28 Nov. 1980. 48p. 1981. pap. 7.50 (ISBN 0-88936-306-4, IDRC178, IDRC). Unipub.

Davy, F. Brian & Graham, Michael, eds. Bivalve Culture in Asia & the Pacific: Proceeding of a Workshop Held in Singapore, 16-19 Feb. 1982. 90p. 1983. pap. 8.00 (ISBN 0-88936-343-9, IDRC200, IDRC). Unipub.

Davy, G., jt. auth. see Moret, A.

Davy, Georges. La Foi Juree. LC 74-25746. (European Sociology Ser.). 390p. 1975. Repr. 29.00x (ISBN 0-405-06501-9). Ayer Co Pubs.

--L' Homme, le Fait Social & le Fait Politique. (Textes De Sciences Sociales: No. 9). (Illus.). 1973. pap. 11.20x (ISBN 90-2797-171-4). Mouton.

Davy, Humphry. Salmonia. (Illus.). 273p. 1970. boxed 10.75 (ISBN 0-88395-004-9). Freshet Pr.

Davy, Humphry B. The Collected Works of Sir Humphry Davy, 9 Vols. Davy, John, ed. 1972. Repr. Set. 260.00 (ISBN 0-384-11010-X). Johnson Repr.

Davy, John. West Indies Before & since Emancipation Compromising the Windward & Leeward Islands' Military Command. 1971. Repr. of 1854 ed. 45.00x (ISBN 0-7146-1935-3, F Cass Co). Biblio Dist.

Davy, John, ed. Work Arising from the Life of Rudolf Steiner. 232p. 1975. 12.95 (ISBN 0-85440-293-4, Pub. by Steinerbooks); pap. 5.50 (ISBN 0-85440-294-2). Anthroposophic.

Davy, John, ed. see Davy, Humphry B.

Davy, Karen, jt. auth. see Davy, Elizabeth.

Davy, Kate. Richard Foreman & the Ontological-Hysteric Theatre. Beckerman, Bernard, ed. LC 81-10380. (Theater & Dramatic Studies: No. 2). 266p. 1981. 44.95 (ISBN 0-8357-1220-6). UMI Res Pr.

Davy, Kate, ed. Richard Foreman: Plays & Manifestos. LC 75-27117. (Drama Review Ser.). 229p. 1976. 35.00x (ISBN 0-8147-2560-0); pap. 20.00 (ISBN 0-8147-2561-9). NYU Pr.

Davy, Kitty L. Love Alone Prevails: A Story of Life with Meher Baba. LC 81-85849. (Illus.). 727p. 1981. 25.00 (ISBN 0-913078-43-3). Sheriar Pr.

Davy McKee Corp. Fuel Alcohol: Report & Analysis of Plant Conversion Potential to Fuel Alcohol Production. 125p. 1981. pap. 29.50x (ISBN 0-89934-095-4, B016). Solar Energy Info.

Davy, Norman. British Scientific Literature in the 17th Century. LC 71-105777. 1970. Repr. of 1953 ed. 21.00x (ISBN 0-8046-0947-0, Pub. by Kennikat). Assoc Faculty Pr.

Davy, R. & Mazzucchelli, R. H., eds. Geochemical Exploration in Arid & Deeply Weathered Environments: Proceedings of the Regional Meeting of the Australian Branch of the Association of Exploration Geochemists Held in Perth, Western Australia, May 1983. 376p. 1984. Repr. 81.50 (ISBN 0-444-42412-1). Elsevier.

Davy, Yvonne. Africa's Diamonds. Tyson-Flyn, Juanita, ed. (Daybreak Ser.). 96p. 1983. pap. 4.95 (ISBN 0-8163-0512-9). Pacific Pr Pub Assn.

--Trail of Peril. Wheeler, Gerald, ed. LC 83-17835. (A Banner Bk.). (Illus.). 94p. (Orig.). 1984. pap. 5.95 (ISBN 0-8280-0223-1). Review & Herald.

Davydoff, Alexander. Russian Sketches: Memoirs. Davydoff-Dax, Olga, tr. LC 84-22586. (Illus.). 303p. 1984. pap. 15.00 (ISBN 0-938920-56-1). Hermitage.

Davydoff-Dax, Olga, tr. see Davydoff, Alexander.

Davydov, A. S. Biology & Quantum Mechanics. Oliver, D., tr. LC 81-15833. (International Series on Natural Philosophy: Vol. 109). (Illus.). 250p. 1981. 50.00 (ISBN 0-08-026392-5). Pergamon.

--Quantum Mechanics, Vol. 1. 2nd ed. Ter Haar, D., tr. 760p. 1976. 25.00 (ISBN 0-08-020437-6); text ed. 76.00 (ISBN 0-08-020438-4). Pergamon.

--Solutions in Molecular Systems. 1985. lib. bdg. 54.00 (ISBN 90-277-1854-7, Pub. by Reidel Netherlands). Kluwer Academic.

--Theory of Molecular Excitations. LC 72-75767. 313p. 1971. 45.00x (ISBN 0-306-30440-6, Plenum Pr). Plenum Pub.

Davydov, Gavriil. Two Voyages to Russian America, 1802-1807. Pierce, Richard A., ed. Bearne, Colin, tr. (Alaska History Ser.: No. 10). (Illus.). 1977. 16.50x (ISBN 0-919642-75-6). Limestone Pr.

Davydov, V. I. Germanium. 422p. 1966. 106.50 (ISBN 0-677-20610-0). Gordon.

Davydov, Yu. Myth, Philosophy, Avant-Gardism. Beraha, Laura & Miller, Alex, trs. 296p. 1983. 9.95 (ISBN 0-8285-2618-4, Pub. by Progress Pubs USSR). Imported Pubns.

Davydychev, L. Hands Up! Public Enemy No. 1. 1980. 6.45 (ISBN 0-8285-1914-5, Pub. by Progress Pubs USSR). Imported Pubns.

Davye, Arnold, et al. Lagonga: A History of the Marque. 1979. 32.00 (ISBN 0-7153-7695-0). David & Charles.

Davys, Mary. The Reform'd Coquet. Bd. with Familiar Letters Betwixt a Gentleman & a Lady; The Mercenary Lover: or the Unfortunate Heiresses. Haywood, Eliza. LC 72-170558. (Foundations of the Novel Ser.: Vol. 42). lib. bdg. 61.00 (ISBN 0-8240-0554-6). Garland Pub.

Daw, Ednah. How I Grow African Violets. (Illus.). 108p. (Orig.). 1983. pap. 7.95 (ISBN 0-85091-164-8, Pub. by Lothian). Intl Spec Bk.

Daw, George. Gun Patents 1864. 1982. 15.00x (ISBN 0-87556-251-5). Saifer.

Daw, Prasanta, ed. The Two Great Indian Artists. 1978. 8.00x (ISBN 0-8364-0277-4). South Asia Bks.

Daw, Stephen. Music of Johann Sebastian Bach: The Choral Works. LC 78-68624. (Illus.). 240p. 1981. 24.50 (ISBN 0-8386-1682-8). Fairleigh Dickinson.

Dawa-Samdup, Kazi, tr. from Tibetan. Shrichakrasambhara Tantra: A Buddhist Tantra. 255p. 1984. Repr. of 1919 ed. lib. bdg. 22.50x (ISBN 0-88181-000-2). Canon Pubns.

Dawber, P. G., jt. auth. see Elliot, J. P.

Dawber, Rodney, jt. auth. see Rook, Arthur.

Dawber, Thomas R. The Framingham Study: The Epidemiology of Atherosclerotic Disease. LC 80-11189. (Commonwealth Fund Ser.). 1980. text ed. 20.00x (ISBN 0-674-31730-0). Harvard U Pr.

Dawdy, Doris O. Annotated Bibliography of American Indian Paintings. LC 66-27358. 1968. soft cover 2.50 (ISBN 0-934490-05-8). Mus Am Ind.

--Artists of the American West: A Biographical Dictionary, Vol. II. LC 72-91919. xiv, 345p. 1981. 24.00x (ISBN 0-8040-0352-1, 82-75059, Pub by Swallow). Ohio U Pr.

--Artists of the American West: A Biographical Dictionary of Artists Born Before 1900, Vol. 3. xvi, 568p. 1985. text ed. 35.00x (ISBN 0-8040-0851-5, Swallow). Ohio U Pr.

--Artists of the American West: A Biographical Dictionary, Vol. I. LC 72-91919. 275p. 1974. 24.00x (ISBN 0-8040-0607-5, 82-73294, SB). Ohio U Pr.

Dawe, Charles W., et al. One to One: Resources for Conference-Centered Writing. 2nd ed. 1984. write for info. tchr's ed. (ISBN 0-316-17726-1); student ed. 12.95 (ISBN 0-316-17725-3). Little.

Dawe, Clyde J., ed. The Chromosome: Structural & Functional Aspects. (In Vitro Journal Back Volumes: Vol. 1). 107p. 1965. 15.00 (ISBN 0-317-36060-4). Tissue Culture Assn.

Dawe, Clyde J., et al, eds. Phyletic Approaches to Cancer. 410p. 49.50x (ISBN 0-89955-404-0, Pub. by Japan Sci Soc Japan). Intl Spec Bk.

Dawe, D. J. Matrix & Finite Element Analysis of Structures. (Illus.). 1984. 49.00x (ISBN 0-19-856211-X). Oxford U Pr.

Dawe, Donald G. Jesus: The Death & Resurrection of God. 252p. pap. 15.95 (ISBN 0-317-20332-0). John Knox.

Dawe, Donald G. & Carman, John B., eds. Christian Faith in a Religiously Plural World. LC 78-50927. 200p. (Orig.). 1978. pap. 7.95 (ISBN 0-88344-083-0). Orbis Bks.

Dawe, Gerald, ed. The Younger Irish Poets. 184p. (Orig.). 1982. pap. 10.95 (ISBN 0-317-07230-7, Pub. by Blackstaff Pr). Longwood Pub Group.

Dawe, Gerald & Longley, Edna, eds. Across a Roaring Hill: The Protestant Imagination in Modern Ireland. 156p. 1985. 16.50 (ISBN 0-85640-334-2, Pub. by Blackstaff Pr). Longwood Pub Group.

Dawe, Jessamon. Writing Business & Economic Papers, Theses & Dissertations. (Quality Paperback: No. 96). (Orig.). 1975. pap. 5.95 (ISBN 0-8226-0096-X). Littlefield.

Dawe, Jessamon, jt. auth. see Lord, William J.

Dawe, R. A. & Wilson, D. C., eds. Developments in Petroleum Engineering, No. 1. 288p. 1985. 54.00 (ISBN 0-85334-358-6, Pub. by Elsevier Applied Sci England). Elsevier.

Dawe, R. D., ed. see Sophocles.

Daweewarn, D. Brahamism in Southeast Asia. 322p. 1982. text ed. 40.50x (ISBN 0-391-02581-3, Pub. by Sterling India). Humanities.

Da-Wei, Kwo. Chinese Brushwork: Its History, Aesthetics, & Techniques. LC 81-65013. (Illus.). 220p. 1981. 37.50 (ISBN 0-8390-0267-X, Allanheld Schram). Abner Schram Ltd.

Dawes, Anna, jt. auth. see Dawes, Trevern.

Dawes, B. & Lumsden, W. H., eds. Advances in Parasitology, Vol. 16. (Serial Publication Ser.). 1978. 70.00 (ISBN 0-12-031716-8). Acad Pr.

Dawes, Benjamin. Trematoda. 1946. 87.50 (ISBN 0-521-07219-0). Cambridge U Pr.

Dawes, Benjamin, ed. Advances in Parasitology. Incl. Vol. 1. 1963; Vol. 4. 1967. 70.00 (ISBN 0-12-031704-4); Vol. 5. 1968. 55.00 (ISBN 0-12-031705-2); Vol. 6. 1969. 75.00 (ISBN 0-12-031706-0); Vol. 7. 1969. 75.00 (ISBN 0-12-031707-9); Vol. 8. 1970. 60.00 (ISBN 0-12-031708-7); Vol. 9. 1971. 55.00 (ISBN 0-12-031709-5); Vol. 10. 1972. 70.00 (ISBN 0-12-031710-9); Vol. 11. 1974. 98.00 (ISBN 0-12-031711-7); Vol. 12. 1974. 85.00 (ISBN 0-12-031712-5); Vol. 13. 1975. 70.00 (ISBN 0-12-031713-3); Vol. 14. 1976. 80.00 (ISBN 0-12-031714-1); Vol. 15. 1977. 70.00 (ISBN 0-12-031715-X). Acad Pr.

Dawes, Charles G. The Banking System of the United States & Its Relation to the Money & Business of the Country. Bruchey, Stuart, ed. LC 80-1143. (The Rise of Commercial Banking Ser.). 1981. Repr. of 1894 ed. lib. bdg. 12.00x (ISBN 0-405-13645-5). Ayer Co Pubs.

Dawes, Clinton J. Marine Algae of the West Coast of Florida. LC 73-22107. (Illus.). 272p. 1974. 15.00x (ISBN 0-87024-258-X). U of Miami Pr.

--Marine Botany. LC 1-7527. 628p. 1981. 53.50 (ISBN 0-471-07844-1, Pub. by Wiley-Interscience). Wiley.

Dawes, E. A. Microbial Energetics. (Tertiary Level Biology Ser.). (Illus.). 192p. 1985. text ed. 39.95 (ISBN 0-412-01041-0, 9432, Pub by Chapman & Hall); pap. text ed. 19.95 (ISBN 0-412-01051-8, 9433, Pub. by Chapman & Hall). Methuen Inc.

--Microbial Energetics. (Illus.). 192p. 1985. 39.95 (ISBN 0-412-01041-0, 9444); pap. 19.95 (ISBN 0-412-01051-8, 9445). Methuen Inc.

--Quantitative Problems in Biochemistry. 6th ed. (Illus.). 340p. 1980. text ed. 32.00x (ISBN 0-582-44402-0). Longman.

Dawes, Edwin A. A Vonetta: Mistress of Mystery. (Illus.). 1983. pap. 5.00x (ISBN 0-916638-28-6). Meyerbooks.

Dawes, Elizabeth & Baynes, Norman H., trs. from Greek. Three Byzantine Saints. 275p. 1977. pap. 7.95 (ISBN 0-913836-44-3). St Vladimirs.

Dawes, Elizabeth A., tr. see Comnena, Anna.

Dawes, Frank. Debussy Piano Music. LC 71-105438. (BBC Music Guides Ser.). (Illus.). 64p. 1971. pap. 4.95 (ISBN 0-295-95107-9, BBC14). U of Wash Pr.

--Not in Front of the Servants: A True Portrait of English Upstairs-Downstairs Life. LC 73-16961. 1974. 8.95 (ISBN 0-8008-5605-8). Taplinger.

Dawes, Hugh N. Public Finance & Economic Development: Spotlight on Jamaica. LC 81-40176. (Illus.). 162p. (Orig.). 1982. lib. bdg. 24.00 (ISBN 0-8191-2091-X); pap. text ed. 11.25 (ISBN 0-8191-2092-8). U Pr of Amer.

Dawes, I. W. & Sutherland, I. W. Microbial Physiology. (Illus.). 192p. 1976. pap. text ed. 15.60x (ISBN 0-632-00278-6). Blackwell Pubns.

Dawes, J. N. & Robson, L. L. Citizen to Soldier: Australia Before the Great War: Recollections of Members of the First A.I.F. 1977. 19.00x (ISBN 0-522-84124-4, Pub. by Melbourne U Pr). Intl Spec Bk.

Dawes, Jean D. & Magilton, J. R. Cemetery of St. Helen-on-the-Walls: Aldwark, York. (Archaeology of York Ser: Vol. 12). 132p. 1980. pap. text ed. 24.50x (ISBN 0-900312-88-2, Pub. by Coun Brit Archaeology). Humanities.

Dawes, John. Design & Planning of Swimming Pools. LC 79-40059. 276p. 1979. 53.95 (ISBN 0-8436-0169-8). Van Nos Reinhold.

--The Freshwater Aquarium Questions & Answers. 128p. 1984. 29.00x (ISBN 0-947728-00-7, Pub. by R Royce UK). State Mutual Bk.

Dawes, Kathleen A., ed. see Dawes, Walter A.

Dawes, Mike. The Flytier's Manual. 160p. 1985. pap. 13.95 (ISBN 0-88317-130-9). Stoeger Pub Co.

Dawes, Robin, ed. see Brother Lawrence.

Dawes, Rosemary N., jt. auth. see Champagne, Anthony.

Dawes, Rufus R. Sixth Wisconsin Infantry. 1984. 30.00 (ISBN 0-89029-079-2). Pr of Morningside.

Dawes, Trevern & Dawes, Anna. Highlights of New Zealand. (Illus.). 120p. (Orig.). 1984. pap. 14.95 (ISBN 0-7233-0676-1, Pub. by Salem Hse Ltd). Merrimack Pub Cir.

Dawes, Walter A. Bold Challenge. (Illus.). 103p. (Orig.). 1980. pap. 5.95 (ISBN 0-938792-14-8). New Capernaum.

--Christianity Four Thousand Years Before Jesus. Dawes, Kathleen A., ed. (Illus.). 63p. (Orig.). 1982. pap. 4.95 (ISBN 0-938792-17-2). New Capernaum.

--The Ghost of Old Capernaum. (Illus.). 358p. (Orig.). 1980. pap. text ed. 24.95 (ISBN 0-938792-00-8). New Capernaum.

--The Hidden Gospel. Dawes, Kathleen A., ed. (Orig.). 1985. pap. 8.95 (ISBN 0-938792-21-0). New Capernaum.

--Impact: The Religion of the Twenty-First Century. (Illus.). 79p. (Orig.). 1980. pap. text ed. 8.95 (ISBN 0-938792-05-9). New Capernaum.

Dawes, William M. The Circle & the Conic Curves. 4.95 (ISBN 0-8283-1620-1). Branden Pub Co.

--The Hyperbola & the Parabola. LC 72-86314. 75p. 1973. text ed. 9.75 (ISBN 0-8283-1485-3). Branden Pub Co.

Dawidoff, Robert. The Education of John Randolph. 1979. 19.95x (ISBN 0-393-01242-5). Norton.

--The Education of John Randolph. 352p. Date not set. pap. 6.95 (ISBN 0-393-95287-8). Norton.

Dawidowicz, L. S., et al, eds. For Max Weinreich on His Seventieth Birthday: Studies in Jewish Language, Literature & Society. 1964. 66.00x (ISBN 0-686-22430-2). Mouton.

Dawidowicz, Lucy. Holocaust Reader. LC 75-33740. pap. 9.95x (ISBN 0-87441-236-6). Behrman.

--The Jewish Presence: Essays on Identity & History. LC 78-6236. 1978. pap. 3.95 (ISBN 0-15-646221-4, Harv). HarBraceJ.

Dawidowicz, Lucy S. Holocaust & the Historians. LC 80-29175. (Illus.). 200p. 1983. pap. 16.50x (ISBN 0-674-40566-8); pap. text ed. 5.95 (ISBN 0-674-40567-6). Harvard U Pr.

--On Equal Terms: Jews in America, 1881-1981. 200p. 1982. 12.95 (ISBN 0-03-061658-1). HR&W.

--On Equal Terms: Jews in America 1881-1981. 1984. pap. 6.95 (ISBN 0-03-071058-8). HR&W.

--The War Against the Jews: 1933-1945. 640p. 1976. pap. 4.95 (ISBN 0-553-23477-3). Bantam.

Dawidowicz, Lucy S. & Goldstein, Leon J. Politics in a Pluralist Democracy. LC 74-9630. 100p. 1974. Repr. of 1963 ed. lib. bdg. 22.50x (ISBN 0-8371-7599-2, DAPD). Greenwood.

Dawidziak, Mark. The Barter Theatre Story. LC 82-22667. 1982. 8.50 (ISBN 0-913239-03-8). Appalach Consortium.

Dawis, Rene V. & Lofquist, Lloyd. A Psychological Theory of Work Adjustment: An Individual-Differences Model & Its Applications. LC 83-23381. (Illus.). 192p. 1984. 25.00x (ISBN 0-8166-1316-8). U of Minn Pr.

Dawisha, Adeed, ed. Islam in Foreign Policy. LC 83-7458. 250p. 1984. 27.95 (ISBN 0-521-25815-4). Cambridge U Pr.

--Islam in Foreign Policy. 202p. 1985. pap. 11.95 (ISBN 0-521-27740-X). Cambridge U Pr.

Dawisha, Adeed & Dawisha, Karen, eds. The Soviet Union in the Middle East: Perspectives & Policies. 168p. 1982. text ed. 17.50x (ISBN 0-8419-0796-X); pap. text ed. 9.50x (ISBN 0-8419-0797-8). Holmes & Meier.

Dawisha, Adeed I. Syria & the Lebanese Crisis. LC 80-85. 200p. 1980. 27.50 (ISBN 0-312-78203-9). St Martin.

Dawisha, Karen. The Kremlin & the Prague Spring. LC 83-21351. (International Crises Behavior Ser.: Vol. 4). 256p. 1984. text ed. 34.50 (ISBN 0-520-04971-3). U of Cal Pr.

--Soviet Foreign Policy Towards Egypt. LC 78-10539. 276p. 1979. 27.50x (ISBN 0-312-74837-X). St Martin.

Dawisha, Karen & Hanson, Philip, eds. Soviet-East European Dilemmas. LC 80-28573. 226p. 1981. text ed. 27.50x (ISBN 0-8419-0697-1); pap. text ed. 11.50x (ISBN 0-8419-0698-X). Holmes & Meier.

Dawisha, Karen, jt. ed. see Dawisha, Adeed.

Dawkins. Landlord & Tenant: Lease Forms & Clauses, 2 vols. (The Law in Georgia Ser.). Sold as set only. incl. latest pocket part supplement 24.95 ea. (ISBN 0-686-90403-6); separate pocket part supplements,1981 11.45 (ISBN 0-686-90404-4). Harrison Co GA.

Dawkins, ed. Immunogenetics in Rheumatology. (International Congress Ser.: No. 602). 390p. 1983. 91.50 (ISBN 0-444-90293-7, Excerpta Medica). Elsevier.

Dawkins, Cecil. Charleyhorse. 1985. 15.95 (ISBN 0-670-80631-5). Viking.

--The Live Goat. LC 75-138781. 1971. 15.00 (ISBN 0-06-010998-X). Ultramarine Pub.

Dawkins, H. C. & Field, D. R. A Long-Term Surveillance System for British Woodland Vegetation. 1978. 40.00x (ISBN 0-85074-038-X, Pub. by For Lib Comm England). State Mutual Bk.

Dawkins, J. V., ed. Developments in Polymer Characterization, 4 vols. (Illus.). Vol. 1, 1978. 44.50 (ISBN 0-85334-789-1, Pub. by Elsevier Applied Sci England); Vol. 2, 1980. 53.75 (ISBN 0-85334-909-6); Vol. 3, 1982. 61.00 (ISBN 0-85334-119-2); Vol. 4, 1983. 61.00 (ISBN 0-85334-180-X). Elsevier.

Dawkins, Lee. The Beast of Revelation: Thirteen the Number of Man Six Threescore & Six? or Six Threescore to the Power & Six?...Nine? 68p. 1982. 5.00 (ISBN 0-682-49887-4). Exposition Pr FL.

--The Mystery Babylon - Revelation 17-5: Is It America? 103p. 1983. 7.00 (ISBN 0-682-49965-X). Exposition Pr FL.

Dawkins, Louisa. Natives & Strangers. 416p. 1985. 17.95 (ISBN 0-395-36553-8). HM.

Dawkins, Marian S. Animal Suffering: The Science of Animal Welfare. 1980. 24.00 (ISBN 0-412-22580-8, NO.6407, Pub. by Chapman & Hall England); pap. 11.95 (ISBN 0-412-22590-5, NO.6406). Methuen Inc.

Dawkins, Marvin P. Alcohol & the Black Community: Exploratory Studies of Selected Issues. LC 79-93301. 130p. 1980. 10.95 (ISBN 0-86548-006-0). R & E Pubs.

Dawkins, Peter J., jt. auth. see Bosworth, Derek L.

Dawkins, R. M. The Nature of the Cypriot Chronicle of Leontios Makhairas. 32p. pap. 4.00 (ISBN 0-89005-334-0). Ares.

Dawkins, R. M., ed. see Machairas, Leontios.

Dawkins, Richard. The Extended Phenotype: The Gene As the Unit of Selection. LC 81-9889. 320p. 1982. text ed. 26.95 (ISBN 0-7167-1358-6). W H Freeman.

--The Extended Phenotype: The Gene As the Unit of Selection. 1983. pap. 7.95 (ISBN 0-19-857609-9, GB 760). Oxford U Pr.

--The Selfish Gene. LC 76-29168. 1976. pap. 6.95 (ISBN 0-19-520000-4, GB500, GB). Oxford U Pr.

Dawkins, Richard, ed. Oxford Surveys in Evolutionary Biology 1984, Vol. 1. (Illus.). 227p. 1985. 35.00 (ISBN 0-19-854158-9). Oxford U Pr.

Dawkins, Richard M. Forty-Five Stories from the Dodekanese. Dorson, Richard M., ed. LC 80-742. (Folklore of the World Ser.). 1980. Repr. of 1950 ed. lib. bdg. 90.50x (ISBN 0-405-13308-1). Ayer Co Pubs.

--Modern Greek in Asia Minor. LC 78-67703. (The Folktale). Repr. of 1916 ed. 49.50 (ISBN 0-404-16077-8). AMS Pr.

Dawkins, Richard M., ed. & tr. Modern Greek Folktales. LC 74-9217. 491p. 1974. Repr. of 1953 ed. lib. bdg. 28.00x (ISBN 0-8371-7630-1, DAGF). Greenwood.

Dawkins, Richard M., ed. & tr. from Gr. More Greek Folktales. LC 74-9218. 178p. 1974. Repr. of 1955 ed. lib. bdg. 15.00x (ISBN 0-8371-7631-X, DAMGF). Greenwood.

Dawley, Alan. Class & Community: The Industrial Revolution in Lynn. LC 75-29049. (Harvard Studies in Urban History Ser.). (Illus.). 1979. 22.50x (ISBN 0-674-13390-0); pap. 7.95x (ISBN 0-674-13395-1). Harvard U Pr.

Dawley, Alan & Buhle, Paul, eds. Working for Democracy: American Workers from the Revolution to the Present. LC 85-5845. (Illus.). 144p. 1985. 12.95x (ISBN 0-252-01220-8); pap. 4.95x (ISBN 0-252-01221-6). U of Ill Pr.

Dawley, Donald L. What Auditors Should Know about Data Processing. Farmer, Richard N., ed. LC 83-17879. (Research for Business Decisions Ser.: No. 63). 250p. 1983. 39.95 (ISBN 0-8357-1483-7). UMI Res Pr.

Dawley, Gloria & Sorger, James. What to Do until the Doctor Calls Back. Guindon, Kathleen M., ed. (Illus.). 96p. (Orig.). 1982. 10.95 (ISBN 0-942696-01-8); pap. 5.95 (ISBN 0-942696-00-X). Transmediacom.

Dawley, Gloria, jt. auth. see Dawley, Joseph.

Dawley, Joseph & Dawley, Gloria. The Painter's Problem Book: Twenty Problem Subjects & How to Paint Them. (Illus.). 152p. 1973. 22.50 (ISBN 0-8230-3515-8). Watson-Guptill.

Dawley, Powel M. Our Christian Heritage: Revised & Expanded. 4th ed. LC 78-62062. 1978. pap. 5.50 (ISBN 0-8192-1243-1); leader's guide 2.50x (ISBN 0-8192-4086-9). Morehouse.

Dawlwy, Harold H., Jr. Friendship: How to Make & Keep Friends. (Illus.). 176p. 1980. (Spec); pap. 4.95 (ISBN 0-13-330852-9). P-H.

Dawn. Roots & Wings. 18p. 1967. pap. 2.00 (ISBN 0-932264-03-4). Trask Hse Bks.

Dawn, C. Ernest. From Ottomanism to Arabism: Essays on the Origins of Arab Nationlism. LC 72-88953. pap. 56.00 (ISBN 0-317-11133-7, 2020255). Bks Demand UMI.

Dawn, Marva J. I'm Lonely Lord-How Long? The Psalms for Today. LC 83-47721. 176p. 1984. 12.45 (ISBN 0-06-067201-3, HarpR). Har-Row.

Dawood, M. Y. Oxytocin, Vol. 2. Horrobin, D. F., ed. (Annual Research Reviews Ser.). 181p. 1984. 28.00x (ISBN 0-88831-112-5). Eden Pr.

Dawood, M. Yusoff. Dysmenorrhea. (Illus.). 478p. 1981. lib. bdg. 28.50 (ISBN 0-683-02364-0). Williams & Wilkins.

Dawood, M. Yusoff, et al, eds. Premenstrual Syndrome & Dysmenorrhea. LC 84-7571. (Illus.). 247p. 1984. text ed. 29.50 (ISBN 0-8067-0411-X). Urban & S.

Dawood, N. J. The Penguin Tales from Thousand & One Nights. (Fiction Ser.). (Illus.). 272p. 1985. pap. 6.95 (ISBN 0-14-009023-1). Penguin.

Dawood, N. J., ed. see Khaldun, Ibn.

Dawood, N. J., tr. Koran. (Classics Ser.). 1956. pap. 3.95 (ISBN 0-14-044052-6). Penguin.

--Tales from the Thousand & One Nights. (Classics Ser.). (Orig.). 1973. pap. 3.95 (ISBN 0-14-044289-8). Penguin.

Daws, Gavan. Holy Man: Father Damien of Molokai. 328p. 1984. pap. 8.95 (ISBN 0-8248-0920-3). UH Pr.

--Shoal of Time: A History of the Hawaiian Islands. LC 73-92053. 507p. 1974. pap. 7.95 (ISBN 0-8248-0324-8). UH Pr.

Daws, Gavan & Bushnell, O. A. Illustrated Atlas of Hawaii. LC 70-152566. (Illus.). 1970. pap. 5.95 (ISBN 0-89610-034-0). Island Herit.

Daws, Ron. Running Your Best: The Committed Runner's Guide to Training & Racing. (Illus.). 1985. pap. 8.95 (ISBN 0-8289-0559-2). Greene.

Dawson & Drover. Early English Clocks. (Illus.). 550p. 1982. 119.50 (ISBN 0-902028-59-6). Antique Collect.

Dawson, ed. The Small Computer in Medicine. 1984. 25.00 (ISBN 0-9901003-5-9, Pub. by Abacus England). Heyden.

Dawson, et al. Modern Russian, Vol. I. 480p. 1980. plus 24 audio-cassettes 195.00x (ISBN 0-88432-044-8, B101). J Norton Pubs.

--Modern Russian II. 479p. 1980. plus 24 audio cassettes 195.00x (ISBN 0-88432-056-1, B125). J Norton Pubs.

Dawson, A. C. & Dawson, L. M. Dicho y Hecho: Beginning Spanish, A Simplified Approach. 2nd ed. 439p. 1985. 23.95 (ISBN 0-471-87901-0). Wiley.

--Workbook of Written Exercises to Accompany Dicho Y Hecho: Beginning Spanish. 214p. 1985. pap. 9.95 (ISBN 0-471-81082-7). Wiley.

Dawson, A. J. Finn the Wolfhound. LC 63-7894. (gr. 7-9). 1966. pap. 0.75 (ISBN 0-15-630998-X, VoyB). HarBraceJ.

Dawson, A. M., et al, eds. Recent Advances in Medicine, No. 19. (Recent Advances in Medicine Ser.). (Illus.). 341p. 1981. pap. text ed. 28.00 (ISBN 0-443-02946-6). Churchill.

Dawson, Adele. Health, Happiness & the Pursuit of Herbs. LC 79-21182. (Illus.). 1980. pap. 9.95 (ISBN 0-8289-0363-8). Greene.

Dawson, Adele G. James Franklin Gilman: Nineteenth Century Painter. LC 75-20929. 168p. 1975. 15.00 (ISBN 0-914016-20-2). Phoenix Pub.

Dawson, Aileen. Bernard Moore. (Illus.). 116p. 1982. 37.50 (ISBN 0-903685-12-4, 1250019, Pub. by R Dennis Pubns UK). Seven Hills Bks.

--Masterpieces of Wedgwood in the British Museum. LC 84-48053. (Illus.). 160p. 1984. 27.50x (ISBN 0-253-33688-0); pap. 17.50x (ISBN 0-253-28610-7). Ind U Pr.

Dawson, Aileen & Dennis, Richard. Bernard Moore: Master Potter. (Orig.). pap. 2.95 (ISBN 0-317-02541-4, Pub. by Victoria & Albert Mus UK). Faber & Faber.

Dawson, Alastair G., jt. auth. see Smith, David E.

Dawson, Albert C. & Dawson, Laila M. Dicho y Hecho: Beginning Spanish: A Simplified Approach. LC 80-19506. 456p. 1981. 25.45x (ISBN 0-471-06476-9). wkbk. 13.45x (ISBN 0-471-06103-4); tapes 1.00 (ISBN 0-471-06475-0). Wiley.

Dawson, Amy. Bobbin Lacemaking for Beginners. (Illus.). 88p. 1984. pap. 5.95 (ISBN 0-7137-1496-4, Pub. by Blandford Pr England). Sterling.

Dawson, Andrew, ed. Planning in Eastern Europe. 320p. 1986. 35.00 (ISBN 0-312-61412-8). St Martin.

Dawson, Andrew H. The Land Problem in the Developed Economy. LC 83-24360. 280p. 1984. 27.50x (ISBN 0-389-20456-0, 08017). B&N Imports.

Dawson, Anthony B. Indirections: Shakespeare & the Art of Illusion. LC 78-6016. 1978. 25.00x (ISBN 0-8020-5413-7). U of Toronto Pr.

Dawson, Arthur & Simon, Ronald. The Practical Management of Asthma. 288p. 1983. text ed. 39.50 (ISBN 0-8089-1595-9, 791008). Grune.

Dawson, Barbara. The Technique of Metal Thread Embroidery. (Illus.). 216p. 1982. pap. 9.75 (ISBN 0-7134-3919-X). Branford.

Dawson, Barbara & Feibelman, Barbara. Sexuality Education: A Family Life Education Curriculum for Parents & Young Adolescents. LC 84-61333. 82p. (Orig.). (gr. 4-8). 1984. pap. 7.95 (ISBN 0-934586-14-4). Plan Parent.

Dawson, Bonnie. Women's Films in Print: An Annotated Guide to Eight Hundred Films Made by Women. LC 74-80642. 1975. pap. 10.00x (ISBN 0-912932-02-3). Booklegger Pr.

Dawson, C. E. Indo-Pacific Pipefishes: Red Sea to the Americas. LC 84-48414. (Illus.). 230p. 1985. 48.00x (ISBN 0-917235-00-2). Gulf Coast Lab.

Dawson, Carl. Victorian Noon: English Literature in 1850. LC 78-13939. 1979. text ed. 27.50x (ISBN 0-8018-2110-X). Johns Hopkins.

Dawson, Carl, ed. Matthew Arnold, the Poetry. (The Critical Heritage Ser). 480p. 1973. 38.50x (ISBN 0-7100-7565-0). Routledge & Kegan.

Dawson, Carl & Pfordresher, John, eds. Matthew Arnold: Prose Writings. (The Critical Heritage Ser.). 1979. 34.00x (ISBN 0-7100-0244-0). Routledge & Kegan.

Dawson, Carley, tr. see Poulet, Georges.

Dawson, Chandler, jt. auth. see Schachter, Julius.

Dawson, Chester S. American History As Interpreted in Literature. 1980. lib. bdg. 69.95 (ISBN 0-87700-295-9). Revisionist Pr.

Dawson, Chris, jt. auth. see Armstrong, Pat.

Dawson, Christopher. Christianity & the New Age. 1985. 10.95 (ISBN 0-918477-02-6); pap. 7.95 (ISBN 0-918477-01-8). Sophia Inst Pr.

--Christianity in East & West. Mulloy, John J., ed. 224p. 1981. pap. text ed. 5.95 (ISBN 0-89385-015-2). Sugden.

--Dynamics of World History. Mulloy, John J., ed. 509p. 1978. pap. 9.95 (ISBN 0-89385-003-9). Sugden.

--The Judgement of the Nations. 1977. Repr. lib. bdg. 25.00 (ISBN 0-8482-0546-4). Norwood Edns.

--Medieval Essays. 271p. 1984. Repr. of 1953 ed. lib. bdg. 45.00 (ISBN 0-89760-176-9). Telegraph Bks.

--Mission to Asia. (Medieval Academy Reprints for Teaching Ser.). 228p. 1981. pap. 6.95 (ISBN 0-8020-6436-1). U of Toronto Pr.

--Religion & the Modern State. 1977. Repr. lib. bdg. 20.00 (ISBN 0-8482-0547-2). Norwood Edns.

--Tackle Sailing This Way. (Illus.). (gr. 9 up). pap. 8.95x (ISBN 0-392-04859-0, SpS). Sportshelf.

Dawson, Christopher H. Beyond Politics. facsimile ed. LC 74-111825. (Essay Index Reprint Ser.). 1939. 14.00 (ISBN 0-8369-1603-4). Ayer Co Pubs.

--Enquiries into Religion & Culture. facs. ed. LC 68-29200. (Essay Index Reprint Ser.). 1933. 24.50 (ISBN 0-8369-0367-6). Ayer Co Pubs.

--Medieval Essays. facs. ed. LC 68-58785. (Essay Index Reprint Ser). 1954. 18.00 (ISBN 0-8369-0070-7). Ayer Co Pubs.

--Progress & Religion, an Historical Enquiry. LC 79-104266. Repr. of 1929 ed. lib. bdg. 27.50x (ISBN 0-8371-3917-1, DAPR). Greenwood.

--Religion & Culture. LC 77-27183. (Gifford Lectures Ser.: 1947). 232p. Repr. of 1948 ed. 27.50 (ISBN 0-404-60498-6). AMS Pr.

--Religion & the Rise of Western Culture. LC 77-27181. (Gifford Lectures: 1948-49). Repr. of 1950 ed. 21.50 (ISBN 0-404-60499-4). AMS Pr.

--The Spirit of the Oxford Movement. LC 75-30020. Repr. of 1934 ed. 16.50 (ISBN 0-404-14025-4). AMS Pr.

Dawson, Christopher H., ed. The Mongol Mission. LC 78-63334. (The Crusades & Military Orders: Second Ser.). Repr. of 1955 ed. 26.50 (ISBN 0-404-17008-0). AMS Pr.

Dawson, Clayton L., et al. Modern Russian, 2 pts. Incl. Part 1 (ISBN 0-87840-169-5). with 24 cassettes in an album 120.00 set (ISBN 0-87840-182-2). LC 77-5837. 1977. Repr. of 1964 ed. 14.95 ea. (ISBN 0-87840-170-9). Georgetown U Pr.

Dawson, Clint. Hourly Selling: Your Fast Track to Sales Success. 12.95 (ISBN 0-13-395013-1); pap. 6.95 (ISBN 0-13-395005-0). P-H.

Dawson, Coningsby W., jt. auth. see Dawson, William J.

Dawson, Dan T. & Mellott, M. Numbers for You & Me. (gr. k-1). pap. text ed. 5.68 (ISBN 0-13-625392-X); teachers' manual o.p. 1.95 (ISBN 0-685-04689-3, 62654-9). P-H.

Dawson, Daniel. The Mexican Adventure. facsimile ed. (Select Bibliographies Reprint Ser). Repr. of 1935 ed. 26.50 (ISBN 0-8369-6682-1). Ayer Co Pubs.

--The Mexican Adventure. 1976. lib. bdg. 59.95 (ISBN 0-8490-2232-0). Gordon Pr.

Dawson, David. Trapped! LC 82-23015. 256p. 1983. pap. 3.95 (ISBN 0-8307-0871-5, 5018002). Regal.

Dawson, David, et al. Schizophrenia in Focus: Guidelines for Treatment & Rehabilitation. 176p. 1983. 24.95 (ISBN 0-89885-096-7). Human Sci Pr.

Dawson, David M., et al. Entrapment Neuropathies. 307p. 1983. text ed. 37.50 (ISBN 0-316-17742-3). Little.

Dawson, E. R., tr. see Akheizer, N. I.

Dawson, E. R., tr. see Akheizer, N. I. & Glazman, I. M.

Dawson, E. R., tr. see Naimark, M. A.

Dawson, E. Y. Marine Red Algae of Pacific Mexico: Ceramiales, Dasyaceae, Rhodomelaceae, Part 8. (Illus.). 1963. pap. 8.00 (ISBN 3-7682-0209-7). Lubrecht & Cramer.

Dawson, E. Yale. Cacti of California. (California Natural History Guides: No. 18). (Illus.). 1966. pap. 3.95 (ISBN 0-520-00299-7). U of Cal Pr.

--Seashore Plants of Northern California. (California Natural History Guides: No. 20). 1966. pap. 3.25 (ISBN 0-520-00301-2). U of Cal Pr.

--Seashore Plants of Southern California. (California Natural History Guides: No. 19). 1966. pap. 2.95 (ISBN 0-520-00300-4). U of Cal Pr.

Dawson, E. Yale & Foster, Michael S. Seashore Plants of California. LC 81-19690. (California Natural History Guides Ser.: No. 47). (Illus.). 226p. 1983. 15.95 (ISBN 0-520-04138-0); pap. 7.95 (ISBN 0-520-04139-9). U of Cal Pr.

Dawson, E. Yale, jt. auth. see Abbott, Isabella A.

Dawson, Edwin C. James Hannington First Bishop of Eastern Equatorial Africa. LC 69-19355. (Illus.). Repr. of 1887 ed. 21.75x (ISBN 0-8371-0985-X, DAH&, Pub. by Negro U Pr). Greenwood.

Dawson, Ein. The San Diego Bargain Book. (Illus.). 168p. 1984. pap. 6.95 (ISBN 0-9607696-4-1). Carol Mendel.

Dawson, Fielding. Delayed: Not Postponed. Owen, Maureen, ed. LC 77-21162. (Illus.). 1978. pap. 2.00 (ISBN 0-916382-17-6). Telephone Bks.

--Krazy Kat & Seventy-Six More, Collected Stories: 1950-1976. 378p. 1982. 17.50 (ISBN 0-87685-564-8); signed ed. 25.00 (ISBN 0-87685-565-6); pap. 12.50 (ISBN 0-87685-563-X). Black Sparrow.

--Penny Lane. 160p. (Orig.). 1977. pap. 4.50 (ISBN 0-87685-314-9). Black Sparrow.

--Three Penny Lane. 150p. (Orig.). 1981. signed ed. 20.00 (ISBN 0-87685-447-1); pap. 5.00 (ISBN 0-87685-446-3). Black Sparrow.

--Tiger Lillies: An American Childhood. LC 84-4170. 224p. 1984. 16.75 (ISBN 0-8223-0593-3). Duke.

--Two Penny Lane. 160p. (Orig.). 1977. pap. 4.50 (ISBN 0-87685-316-5). Black Sparrow.

--Virginia Dare, Stories 1976-1981. 178p. (Orig.). 1985. 14.00 (ISBN 0-87685-618-0); pap. 8.50 (ISBN 0-87685-617-2); signed ed. 25.00 (ISBN 0-87685-619-9). Black Sparrow.

Dawson, Frances E., tr. see Steiner, Rudolf.

Dawson, Francis W. Reminiscences of Confederate Service, 1861-1865. Wiley, Bell I., ed. LC 79-26720. (Library of Southern Civilization). xii, 220p. 1980. 20.00x (ISBN 0-8071-0689-5). La State U Pr.

Dawson, Frank G. Nuclear Power: Development & Management of a Techology. LC 75-40880. (Illus.). 332p. 1976. 30.00x (ISBN 0-295-95445-0). U of Wash Pr.

Dawson, Frank G. & Head, Ivan L. International Law, National Tribunals, & Rights of Aliens, Vol. 10. (Procedural Aspects of International Law Ser.). 1971. 20.00x (ISBN 0-8156-2152-3). U Pr of Va.

Dawson, Gaynor W. Harzardous Waste Management. 1985. 60.00 (ISBN 0-471-82268-X). Wiley.

Dawson, Geoffrey. A Book of Broadsheets. 1975. Repr. of 1928 ed. 35.00 (ISBN 0-8274-4080-4). R West.

--A Second Book of Broadsheets. 1975. Repr. of 1929 ed. 35.00 (ISBN 0-8274-4081-2). R West.

Dawson, Geoffrey, ed. A Second Book of Broadsheets. 301p. 1980. Repr. lib. bdg. 40.00 (ISBN 0-89987-152-6). Darby Bks.

Dawson, George. Biographical Lectures (Milton, John Bunyan, Daniel Defoe, Swift, Johnson, Goldsmith, Chaucer, Cowper, Pope & Byron, Lamb, Wordsworth, Coleridge, Carlyle, Thackeray) St Clair, George, ed. 1973. lib. bdg. 20.00 (ISBN 0-8414-2445-4). Folcroft.

--The Haidas. facsimile ed. (Shorey Indian Ser.). 10p. pap. 0.95 (ISBN 0-8466-0096-X, S96). Shorey.

Dawson, George C., jt. auth. see Gordon, Sanford D.

Dawson, George G. Healing: Pagan & Christian. LC 75-23704. Repr. of 1935 ed. 26.50 (ISBN 0-404-13256-1). AMS Pr.

Dawson, George G., jt. auth. see Gordon, Sanford D.

Dawson, George M. Notes & Observations on the Kwakiool People of the Northern Part of Vancouver Island & Adjacent Coasts, Made During the Summer of 1885: With a Vocabulary of About Seven Hundred Words. 37p. 1977. pap. 3.50 (ISBN 0-87770-118-0). Ye Galleon.

Dawson, Giles. The Life of William Shakespeare. LC 79-65979. (Folger Guides to the Age of Shakespeare). 1979. pap. 3.95 (ISBN 0-918016-06-1). Folger Bks.

Dawson, Giles, ed. July & Julian. LC 82-45705. (Malone Society Reprint Ser.: No.103). Repr. of 1955 ed. 40.00 (ISBN 0-404-63102-9). AMS Pr.

Dawson, Glen. Hungarians in the United States. 13p. 1972. imitation vellum 15.00 (ISBN 0-317-11651-7). Dawsons.

Dawson, Glen, jt. auth. see Helen, Mary.

Dawson, Grace. No Little Plans: Fairfax County's PLUS Program for Managing Growth. 168p. 1977. pap. 7.95x (ISBN 0-87766-185-5, 17100). Urban Inst.

Dawson, H. B. New York City During the American Revolution. 59.95 (ISBN 0-8490-0727-5). Gordon Pr.

Dawson, Henry B. Sons of Liberty in New York. LC 71-90172. (Mass Violence in America Ser). Repr. of 1859 ed. 11.00 (ISBN 0-405-01306-X). Ayer Co Pubs.

Dawson, I. M. An Atlas of Gastrointestinal Pathology. (Current Histopathology Ser.: Vol. 6). (Illus.). 150p. 1983. text ed. 59.50 (ISBN 0-397-50454-3, 65-72671, Lippincott Medical). Lippincott.

Dawson, J. B. Kimberlites & Their Xenoliths. (Minerals & Rocks: Vol. 15). (Illus.). 252p. 1980. 53.00 (ISBN 0-387-10208-6). Springer-Verlag.

--Understanding the TI PC: A Programming Digest. 108p. (Orig.). 1985. pap. 9.95 (ISBN 0-9615084-0-X). Prosoft AZ.

Dawson, J. Frank. Place Names in Colorado. 1976. pap. 1.75x (ISBN 0-87315-067-8). Golden Bell.

Dawson, J. G., tr. see D'Entreves, A. P.

Dawson, J. G., tr. see Thomas Aquinas.

Dawson, J. L. & Blowers, G. H., eds. Perspectives in Asian Cross-Cultural Psychology: Selected Papers of the First Asian Regional Conference of the IACCP, March 19-23, 1979. 1981. pap. 11.25 (ISBN 90-265-0359-8, Pub. by Swets & Zeitlinger Netherlands). Hogrefe Intl.

Dawson, J. William. Modern Ideas of Evolution. 1977. pap. 8.95 (ISBN 0-88202-167-2, Sci Hist). Watson Pub Intl.

Dawson, Jack, ed. see Logan, Thaddeus.

Dawson, James. Australia Aborigines. (AIAS New Ser.: No. 26). 103p. 1981. text ed. 23.75x (ISBN 0-391-02220-2, Pub. by Australian Inst Australia). Humanities.

Dawson, James, jt. auth. see Perry, Susan.

Dawson, Jan. Films of Hellmuth Costard. 1979. pap. 3.50 (ISBN 0-918432-24-3). NY Zoetrope.

Dawson, Jan & Wenders, Wim. Wim Wenders. (Illus., Orig.). 1977. pap. 5.00 (ISBN 0-918432-04-9). NY Zoetrope.

Dawson, Jan C. The Unusable Past: America's Puritan Tradition, 1830-1930. LC 83-27091. (Studies in the Humanities). 150p. 1984. 16.50 (ISBN 0-89130-721-4, 00 01 04); pap. 10.95 (ISBN 0-89130-722-2). Scholars Pr GA.

Dawson, Jim. Whitetail Hunting. LC 82-5661. (Illus.). 192p. 14.95 (ISBN 0-8117-1872-7). Stackpole.

Dawson, John. Seventeenth Virginia Cavalry: Or Wildcat Cavalry. 1982. 15.00 (ISBN 0-89029-310-4). Pr of Morningside.

Dawson, John & Phillips, Melanie. Doctors' Dilemmas: Medical Ethics & Contemporary Science. 224p. (Orig.). 1985. 17.95 (ISBN 0-416-01111-X, 9341); pap. 9.50 (ISBN 0-416-01121-7, 9342). Methuen Inc.

Dawson, John, jt. auth. see Kirby, David.

Dawson, John & Lord, Dennis, eds. Shopping Centre Development: Policies & Prospects. 280p. 1985. 37.50 (ISBN 0-89397-225-8). Nichols Pub.

Dawson, John A. Commercial Distribution in Europe. LC 81-2123. 1982. 27.50 (ISBN 0-312-15264-7). St Martin.

--Retail Geography. 248p. 1980. 39.95x (ISBN 0-470-27014-4, Pub. by Hlasted Pr). Wiley.

--Shopping Center Development. LC 82-12674. (Topics in Applied Geography). (Illus.). 160p. 1983. pap. text ed. 11.95 (ISBN 0-582-30068-1). Longman.

Dawson, John A., ed. The Marketing Environment. LC 78-31680. 1979. 35.00x (ISBN 0-312-51530-8). St Martin.

Dawson, John C. High Plains Yesterday: From XIT Days through Drought & Depression. (Illus.). 248p. 1985. 14.95 (ISBN 0-89015-516-X). Eakin Pubns.

--Lakanal the Regicide. facs. ed. (Select Bibliographies Reprint Ser.). 1948. 19.00 (ISBN 0-8369-5520-X). Ayer Co Pubs.

--Toulouse in the Renaissance: The Floral Games, University & Student Life: Etienne Dolet. (Columbia University. Studies in Romance Philology & Literature: No. 33). Repr. of 1923 ed. 18.50 (ISBN 0-404-50633-X). AMS Pr.

Dawson, John P. Gifts & Promises: Continental & American Law Compared. LC 79-23034. (Storrs Lectures on Jurisprudence, Yale Law School, 1978). 1980. pap. text ed. 24.00x (ISBN 0-300-02446-0). Yale U Pr.

--The Oracles of the Law. xix, 520p. 1978. Repr. of 1968 ed. lib. bdg. 49.50x (ISBN 0-313-20260-5, DAOL). Greenwood.

Dawson, John W. The Cancer Patient. LC 78-52192. (Religion & Medicine Ser.). 1978. pap. 5.50 (ISBN 0-8066-1662-8, 10-0960). Augsburg.

Dawson, Joseph C. Seeking Shelter: How to Find & Finance an Energy-Efficient Home. LC 83-61369. (Illus.). 256p. 1983. 17.95 (ISBN 0-688-00902-6). Morrow.

--Seeking Shelter: How to Find & Finance an Energy-Efficient Home. (Illus.). 256p. 1983. pap. 12.95 (ISBN 0-688-00903-4, Quill NY). Morrow.

Dawson, Joseph G., III. Army Generals & Reconstruction: Louisiana, 1862-1877. LC 81-11735. (Illus.). xvi, 294p. 1982. text ed. 27.50x (ISBN 0-8071-0896-0). La State U Pr.

Dawson, Joseph M. America's Way in Church, State & Society. LC 79-15522. 1980. Repr. of 1953 ed. lib. bdg. 22.50x (ISBN 0-313-22006-9, DAAW). Greenwood.

--Baptists & the American Republic. Gaustad, Edwin S., ed. LC 79-52584. (The Baptist Tradition Ser.). 1980. Repr. of 1956 ed. lib. bdg. 21.00x (ISBN 0-405-12451-1). Ayer Co Pubs.

--A Thousand Months to Remember: An Autobiography. 306p. 1964. 4.95 (ISBN 0-918954-03-7). Baylor Univ Pr.

Dawson, L. M., jt. auth. see Dawson, A. C.

Dawson, L. R., jt. ed. see Gibson, J. M.

Dawson, Laila M., jt. auth. see Dawson, Albert C.

Dawson, Lawrence, ed. see Licht, Hans.

Dawson, Lawrence H., ed. see Licht, Hans.

Dawson, Loleta & Huntting, Marion. European War Fiction in English Personal Narratives. LC 76-27527. 1976. Repr. of 1921 ed. lib. bdg. 15.00 (ISBN 0-89341-054-3). Longwood Pub Group.

Dawson, Louis W. Colorado High Routes: Aspen-Vail-Crested Butte Ski Tours, Including the Tenth Mountain Trail. (Illus.). 240p. (Orig.). 1985. pap. 9.95 (ISBN 0-89886-099-7). Mountaineers.

Dawson, M. The Ethics of Socrates: A Compilation. 59.95 (ISBN 0-8490-0133-1). Gordon Pr.

Dawson, M. M. The Ethics of Socrates. LC 74-30274. (Studies in Philosophy, No. 40). 1974. lib. bdg. 59.95x (ISBN 0-8383-2042-2). Haskell.

Dawson, Margaret, tr. see Steiner, Rudolf.

Dawson, Martha E. & Markun, Patricia M., eds. Children & Intercultural Education. LC 72-97348. 72p. 1974. pap. 3.50x (ISBN 0-87173-004-9). ACEI.

Dawson, Mary M. A Complete Guide to Crochet Stitches. (Illus.). 128p. 1973. pap. 4.50 (ISBN 0-517-50019-1). Crown.

Dawson, Michael E., jt. auth. see Grings, William W.

Dawson, Miles M. Ethical Religion of Zoroaster. LC 73-90100. (BCL Ser. I). Repr. of 1931 ed. 22.50 (ISBN 0-404-01999-4). AMS Pr.

Dawson, Miles M., ed. Wisdom of Confucius. pap. 2.50 (ISBN 0-8283-1462-4, 18, IPL). Branden Pub Co.

Dawson, Nadine. Light of Truth Beaming on the Human Race. 1980. 9.00 (ISBN 0-682-49576-X). Exposition Pr FL.

Dawson, Nelson L. Louis D. Brandeis, Felix Frankfurter & the New Deal. vii, 272p. 1980. 19.50 (ISBN 0-208-01817-4, Archon). Shoe String.

Dawson, Nelson L., jt. ed. see Harrison, Lowell H.

Dawson, Nicholas. California in Forty-One, Texas in Fifty-One. (Illus.). 9.50 (ISBN 0-8363-0017-3). Jenkins.

Dawson, Owen L. Studies of Relief & Rehabilitation in China. LC 78-74350. (Modern Chinese Economy Ser.). 126p. 1980. lib. bdg. 20.00 (ISBN 0-8240-4285-9). Garland Pub.

Dawson, P. M. The Unacknowledged Legislator: Shelley & Politics. 1980. 52.00x (ISBN 0-19-812095-8). Oxford U Pr.

Dawson, P. R. & Wilkinson, A. The Effectiveness of Fluxes in Secondary Brass Remelting, 1977. 1981. 40.00x (ISBN 0-686-97074-8, Pub. by W Spring England). State Mutual Bk.

Dawson, P. R., jt. auth. see Murray, Peter S.

Dawson, P. R., jt. auth. see Rao, S.

Dawson, P. R., jt. auth. see Wilkinson, A.

Dawson, P. S., ed. Microbial Growth. LC 74-26644. (Benchmark Papers in Microbiology Ser: Vol. 8). 400p. 1975. 68.00 (ISBN 0-12-786330-3). Acad Pr.

Dawson, Peter E. Evaluation, Diagnosis, & Treatment of Occlusal Problems. LC 74-12409. 407p. 1974. 64.95 (ISBN 0-8016-1216-0). Mosby.

Dawson, Peter P. & Gallegos, Frederick. Case Study II: MEDCO, Inc. (Illus.). 89p. 1973. pap. text ed. 9.95 (ISBN 0-574-17920-8, 13-0920); instr's guide avail. (ISBN 0-574-17921-6, 13-0921). SRA.

Dawson, Peter S. & King, Charles E. Population Biology: Retrospect & Prospect. 240p. 1983. 29.50 (ISBN 0-231-05252-9). Columbia U Pr.

Dawson, Philip. Provincial Magistrates & Revolutionary Politics in France, 1789-1795. LC 74-182816. (Historical Monographs Ser: No. 66). (Illus.). 416p. 1972. 27.50x (ISBN 0-674-71960-3). Harvard U Pr.

Dawson, R., jt. ed. see Duursma, E. K.

Dawson, R. M., et al. Data for Biochemical Research. 500p. 1985. 45.00x (ISBN 0-19-855358-7). Oxford U Pr.

Dawson, Ralph E., III & Dawson, Shirley. Cherokee-English Interliner, First Epistle of John of the New Testament. 25p. (Eng. & Cherokee.). 1982. spiral bdg. 2.50 (ISBN 0-940392-11-9). Indian U Pr OK.

Dawson, Raymond. Confucius. (Past Masters Ser.). 1982. pap. 3.95 (ISBN 0-19-287536-1). Oxford U Pr.

--A New Introduction to Classical Chinese. 1984. 32.00x (ISBN 0-19-815461-5); pap. 17.95x (ISBN 0-19-815460-7). Oxford U Pr.

Dawson, Raymond H. The Decision to Aid Russia, 1941. LC 73-16798. 315p. 1974. Repr. of 1959 ed. lib. bdg. 35.00x (ISBN 0-8371-7231-4, DAAR). Greenwood.

Dawson, Richard D. Cop-a-Form Charts & Graphs. (Office Copier Library Ser.). 64p. 1983. pap. text ed. 8.95 (ISBN 0-914567-04-7). Cop-A-Form.

--Cop-a-Form Columnar & Data Grid Sheets. (Office Copier Library Ser.). 64p. (Orig.). 1983. pap. text ed. 8.95 (ISBN 0-914567-03-9). Cop-A-Form.

--Cop-a-Form General Office Forms. (Office Copier Library Ser.). 64p. (Orig.). 1983. pap. 8.95 (ISBN 0-914567-01-2). Cop-A-Form.

--Cop-a-Form States & U. S. Maps. (Office Copier Library Ser.). 64p. (Orig.). 1983. pap. text ed. 8.95 (ISBN 0-914567-02-0). Cop-A-Form.

Dawson, Richard E., et al. Political Socialization. 2nd ed. (Series in Comparative Politics). 226p. 1977. pap. text ed. 12.95 (ISBN 0-316-17741-5). Little.

Dawson, Robert L., ed. International Directory of Eighteenth-Century Studies. 404p. 1981. 45.00x (ISBN 0-7294-0258-4, Pub. by Voltaire Found). State Mutual Bk.

Dawson, Robert M. Democratic Government in Canada. 4th ed. Ward, Norman, rev. by. LC 71-163808. 1971. pap. 7.50 (ISBN 0-8020-6128-1). U of Toronto Pr.

Dawson, Robert M., ed. Development of Dominion Status, 1900-1936. 466p. 1965. Repr. of 1937 ed. 30.00x (ISBN 0-7146-1467-X, BHA-01467, F Cass Co). Biblio Dist.

Dawson, Robert O. Sentencing: The Decision As to Type, Length, & Conditions of Sentence. 428p. 1969. pap. 7.95 (ISBN 0-316-17739-3). Little.

--Sentencing: The Decision as to Type, Length, & Conditions of Sentence. xxxii, 428p. 1969. pap. 6.00 (ISBN 0-686-90533-4). Am Bar Foun.

--Standards Relating to Adjudication. LC 77-1755. (IJA-ABA Juvenile Justice Standards Project Ser.). 112p. 1980. prof ref 22.50 (ISBN 0-88410-236-X); pap. 12.50 (ISBN 0-88410-809-0). Ballinger Pub.

Dawson, Robert O. & Dix, George E. Texas Criminal Procedure. LC 83-73210. (Cases & Materials Ser.). (Illus.). 1984. write for info. Bender.

Dawson, Roger. You Can Get Anything You Want: But You Have to Do More Than Ask. 1985. 15.95 (ISBN 0-910019-34-7). Invest Tax Pubn.

Dawson, Rosemary B., jt. auth. see Hardgrove, Carol B.

Dawson, S. W. Drama & the Dramatic. (Critical Idiom Ser.). 1970. pap. 5.50 (ISBN 0-416-17280-6, NO.2160). Methuen Inc.

Dawson, Samuel A. Freedom of the Press: A Study of the Legal Doctrine of 'Qualified Privilege' 120p. 1982. Repr. of 1924 ed. lib. bdg. 22.50x (ISBN 0-8377-0516-9). Rothman.

Dawson, Samuel E. A Study: With Critical & Explanatory Notes of Alfred Tennyson's Poem "the Princess". LC 72-13042. 1973. lib. bdg. 10.00 (ISBN 0-8414-1040-2). Folcroft.

Dawson, Sarah M. A Confederate Girl's Diary. Robertson, James I., Jr., ed. LC 70-170604. (Civil War Centennial Ser). 473p. 1972. Repr. of 1960 ed. lib. bdg. 26.00x (ISBN 0-8371-6250-5, DACG). Greenwood.

Dawson, Shirley, jt. auth. see Dawson, Ralph E., III.

Dawson, Steve, ed. see Blaisdell, Frank.

Dawson, T. J. Monotremes & Marsupials. (Studies in Biology: No. 150). 80p. 1983. pap. text ed. 8.95 (ISBN 0-7131-2853-4). E Arnold.

Dawson, T. L. Chapter Four - Carpet & Yarn Printing. 75.00x (ISBN 0-686-98203-7, Pub. by Soc Dyers & Colour); pap. 50.00x (ISBN 0-686-98204-5). State Mutual Bk.

Dawson, T. R. Five Classics of Fairy Chess. (Illus.). 9.00 (ISBN 0-8446-4727-6). Peter Smith.

Dawson, Thomas. The Good Huswifes Jewell & the Second Part of the Good Huswifes Jewel. LC 77-6868. (English Experience Ser.: No. 865). 1977. Repr. of 1596 ed. lib. bdg. 14.00 (ISBN 90-221-0865-1). Walter J Johnson.

Dawson, Thomas & Skiff, F. J. Ute War: A History of the White River Massacre. 1980. pap. 6.95 (ISBN 0-933472-04-8). Johnson Bks.

Dawson, Thomas C. South American Republics, 2 Vols. Repr. of 1903 ed. Set. 45.00 (ISBN 0-404-02011-9). AMS Pr.

Dawson, Thomas H. Offshore Structural Engineering. (Illus.). 352p. 1983. text ed. 41.95 (ISBN 0-13-633206-4). P-H.

--Theory & Practice of Solid Mechanics. LC 76-26010. (Illus.). 281p. 1976. 45.00x (ISBN 0-306-30931-9, Plenum Pr). Plenum Pub.

Dawson, Townes L. & Mounce, Earl W. Business Law: Text & Cases. 4th ed. 1979. text ed. 29.95 (ISBN 0-669-01690-X); instr's. maual 1.95 (ISBN 0-669-01691-8). Heath.

Dawson, V. H. Date Production & Protection: Special Reference to North Africa & the Near East. (Plant Production & Protection Papers: No. 35). 313p. 1982. pap. 22.50 (ISBN 92-5-101121-4, F2313, FAO). Unipub.

Dawson, Virginia D. The Lamp. (Illus.). 48p. 1981. 25.00 (ISBN 0-88014-030-5). Mosaic Pr OH.

Dawson, W. H. Matthew Arnold & His Relation to the Thought of Our Time. LC 74-12203. 1904. lib. bdg. 25.00 (ISBN 0-8414-3774-2). Folcroft.

Dawson, W. J. The Makers of Modern Prose: A Popular Handbook to the Greater Prose Writers of the Century. 1977. Repr. of 1899 ed. lib. bdg. 20.00 (ISBN 0-8414-3659-2). Folcroft.

--The Man Jesus Christ. 1977. lib. bdg. 59.95 (ISBN 0-8490-2199-5). Gordon Pr.

--Quest & Vision: Essays in Life & Literature (Shelley, Meredith, Wordsworth, Longfellow, Eliot) LC 76-15282. 1973. lib. bdg. 25.00 (ISBN 0-8414-3720-3). Folcroft.

--Wordsworth & His Message in Quest & Vision. 1892. Repr. 15.00 (ISBN 0-8274-3749-8). R West.

Dawson, W. R. Bride of Pegasus: Studies in Magic, Mythology & Folklore. lib. bdg. 79.95 (ISBN 0-87968-514-X). Krishna Pr.

Dawson, W. W. & Enoch, J. M., eds. Foundations of Sensory Science. (Illus.). 615p. 1984. 108.00 (ISBN 0-387-12967-7). Springer Verlag.

Dawson, Warren R. The Beginnings: Egypt & Assyria. LC 75-23650. (Clio Medica: No. 1). Repr. of 1930 ed. 9.50 (ISBN 0-404-58901-4). AMS Pr.

Dawson, Warren R., ed. The Banks Letters: A Calendar of the Manuscript Correspondence of Sir Joseph Banks Preserved in the British Museum, the British Museum (Natural History) & Other Collections in Great Britain. 965p. 1958. 94.00x (ISBN 0-565-00085-3, Pub. by Brit Mus Nat Hist England). Sabbot-Natural Hist Bks.

Dawson, Warren R., tr. see Capart, Jean.

Dawson, William F. Christmas, Its Origin & Associations, Together with Its Historical Events & Festive Celebrations During Nineteen Centuries. LC 68-54857. 1968. Repr. of 1902 ed. 58.00x (ISBN 0-8103-3351-1). Gale.

Dawson, William H. Bismarck & State Socialism: An Exposition of the Social & Economic Legislation of Germany Since 1804. LC 79-106366. 1970. Repr. of 1890 ed. 8.00x (ISBN 0-403-00192-7). Scholarly.

--German Empire, Eighteen Sixty-Seven to Nineteen Fourteen, 2 Vols. 992p. 1966. Repr. of 1919 ed. Set. 40.00 (ISBN 0-208-00025-9, Archon). Shoe String.

--German Life in Town & Country. 1977. Repr. 35.00 (ISBN 0-403-08061-4). Scholarly.

--The German Workman: A Study in National Efficiency. LC 77-87732. Repr. of 1906 ed. 25.50 (ISBN 0-404-16505-2). AMS Pr.

--Germany under the Treaty. (Select Bibliographies Reprint Ser.). 1972. Repr. of 1933 ed. 20.25 (ISBN 0-8369-9958-4). Ayer Co Pubs.

--Matthew Arnold & His Relation to the Thought of Our Time. 450p. 1980. Repr. of 1904 ed. lib. bdg. 35.00 (ISBN 0-89987-154-2). Darby Bks.

--Municipal Life & Government in Germany. LC 84-48286. (The Rise of Urban Britain Ser.). 507p. 1985. lib. bdg. 60.00 (ISBN 0-8240-6288-4). Garland Pub.

--Social Insurance in Germany, Eighteen Eighty-Three to Nineteen Eleven. LC 78-32002. (Illus.). xi, 283p. Repr. of 1912 ed. lib. bdg. 24.75x (ISBN 0-8371-5446-4, DASI). Greenwood.

Dawson, William J. Makers of English Fiction. 3rd facs. ed. LC 74-142617. (Essay Index Reprint Ser). 1905. 18.00 (ISBN 0-8369-2043-0). Ayer Co Pubs.

--The Makers of English Fiction. 1973. lib. bdg. 20.00 (ISBN 0-8414-2446-2). Folcroft.

--The Makers of English Prose. 308p. 1982. Repr. of 1906 ed. lib. bdg. 35.00 (ISBN 0-89760-141-6). Telegraph Bks.

--Quest & Vision. 286p. 1980. Repr. of 1892 ed. lib. bdg. 30.00 (ISBN 0-8495-1058-9). Arden Lib.

Dawson, William J. & Dawson, Coningsby W. The Great English Letter-Writers, 2 vols. 1978. Repr. of 1909 ed. lib. bdg. 50.00 (ISBN 0-8495-1029-5). Arden Lib.

--The Great English Letter-Writers, 2 vols. 1980. Set. lib. bdg. 50.00 (ISBN 0-8492-4218-5). R West.

Dawson, William L. Instrumentation in the Speech Clinic. LC 73-86410. (Illus.). 56p. 1973. pap. text ed. 1.50x (ISBN 0-8134-6549-4, 6549). Interstate.

Dawson, William M., jt. auth. see Mokwa, Michael P.

Dawtrey, John. Falstaff Saga. LC 71-103181. 1970. Repr. of 1927 ed. 21.00 (ISBN 0-8046-0818-0, Pub. by Kennikat). Assoc Faculty Pr.

Dawydoff, W. Technical Dictionary of High Polymers: English, French, German, Russian. 1969. 145.00 (ISBN 0-08-013112-3). Pergamon.

Dax, Peter, tr. see Berrondo, Marie.

Daxl, Rainer, jt. auth. see Swenzey, Sean.

Day. High Density Lipoproteins. 728p. 1981. 95.00 (ISBN 0-8247-1220-X). Dekker.

--If You Fight-Fight Fair. (Out Ser.). 1984. 0.99 (ISBN 0-8163-0597-8). Pacific Pr Pub Assn.

--Sales Management Simulation. 1985. pap. write for info. (ISBN 0-471-82361-9). Wiley.

Day, jt. auth. see Philipp.

Day, A., jt. auth. see Kuykendall, R.

Day, A. C. Compatible FORTRAN. LC 77-95444. (Illus.). 1979. 22.95 (ISBN 0-521-22027-0). Cambridge U Pr.

--FORTRAN Techniques. LC 72-78891. (Illus.). 104p. 1972. 22.95 (ISBN 0-521-08549-7); pap. 10.95 (ISBN 0-521-09719-3). Cambridge U Pr.

Day, A. Colin. Text Processing. (Computer Science Text Ser.: No. 20). 150p. 1984. 29.95 (ISBN 0-521-24432-3); pap. 12.95 (ISBN 0-521-28683-2). Cambridge U Pr.

Day, A. Grove. Books about Hawaii: Fifty Basic Authors. LC 77-7997. 138p. 1977. text ed. 9.95x (ISBN 0-8248-0561-5). UH Pr.

--History Makers of Hawaii: A Biographical Dictionary. LC 84-60784. 192p. casebound 16.95 (ISBN 0-935180-09-5); pap. 12.95 (ISBN 0-317-12361-0). Mutual Pub HI.

--James A. Michener. 2nd ed. (United States Authors Ser.). 1977. lib. bdg. 12.50 (ISBN 0-8057-7184-0, Twayne). G K Hall.

--Kamehameha, First King of Hawaii. Hazama, Dorothy, ed. (Hawaii's Cultural Heritage Ser.: Vol. 5). (Illus.). 64p. (gr. 4 up). 1974. pap. 3.50x (ISBN 0-911776-25-7). Hogarth.

--Modern Australian Prose, Nineteen Hundred One to Nineteen Seventy-Five: A Guide to Information Sources, Vol. 32. Day, A. Grove, ed. LC 74-11536. (American Literature, English Literature & World Literatures in English Information Guide Ser.). 425p. 1980. 60.00x (ISBN 0-8103-1243-3). Gale.

--The Sky Clears: Poetry of the American Indians. LC 65-38538. xiv, 204p. 1964. pap. 3.95 (ISBN 0-8032-5047-9, BB 142, Bison). U of Nebr Pr.

Day, A. Grove, jt. auth. see Leib, Amos P.

Day, A. Grove, jt. auth. see Michener, James A.

Day, A. Grove & Stroven, Carl, eds. Best South Sea Stories. LC 64-12430. 320p. 1985. pap. 2.95 (ISBN 0-935180-12-5). Mutual Pub Hi.

--A Hawaiian Reader. LC 59-14048. 392p. Repr. of 1959 ed. 2.95 (ISBN 0-935180-07-9). Mutual Pub HI.

--Spell of Hawaii. LC 69-11908. 346p. 1985. pap. 2.95 (ISBN 0-935180-08-7). Mutual Pub Hi.

Day, A. Grove, ed. see Becke, Louis.

Day, A. Grove, ed. see London, Jack.

Day, A. Grove, ed. & intro. by see Stevenson, Robert L.

Day, A. Grove, ed. see Twain, Mark.

Day, Adrian. International Investment Opportunities: How & Where to Invest Overseas Successfully. New ed. LC 83-9345. 400p. 1983. 17.95 (ISBN 0-688-02078-X). Morrow.

--Investing Without Borders. 1981. 17.95 (ISBN 0-932496-10-5). Alexandria Hse.

Day, Adrienne. In Search of a Song, Vol. 4. Fisher, Barbara & Spiegel, Richard, eds. (Illus.). 27p. (Orig.). 1983. pap. 2.00 (ISBN 0-934830-29-0). Ten Penny.

Day, Alan. History: A Reference Handbook. 354p. 1977. 25.00 (ISBN 0-208-01536-1, Linnet). Shoe String.

Day, Alan E. Discovery & Exploration: The Old World. 295p. 1980. 32.50 (ISBN 0-85157-256-1, Pub. by Bingley England). Shoe String.

--J. B. Priestley: An Annotated Bibliography. LC 78-68251. (Garland Reference Library of the Humanities). 350p. 1980. lib. bdg. 48.00 (ISBN 0-8240-9798-X). Garland Pub.

--Search for the Northwest Passage. LC 83-48202. 600p. 1985. lib. bdg. 78.00 (ISBN 0-8240-9288-0). Garland Pub.

Day, Alan E., ed. Archaeology: A Reference Handbook. 319p. 1978. 22.50 (ISBN 0-208-01672-4, Linnet). Shoe String.

Day, Alan J. & East, Roger. Government Economic Agencies of the World: An International Directory of Governmental Organizations Concerned with Economic Development & Planning. LC 84-26861. (A Keesing's Reference Publication Ser.). 1985. 78.00x (ISBN 0-8103-2104-1). Gale.

Day, Alan J., ed. Border & Territorial Disputes. (Illus.). 450p. 1982. 78.00x (ISBN 0-8103-2030-4, Pub. by Longman). Gale.

Day, Alan J. & Degenhardt, Henry W., eds. Political Parties of the World. LC 80-83467. 432p. 1980. 90.00x (ISBN 0-582-90252-5). Gale.

Day, Albert E. An Autobiography of Prayer. 1979. pap. 3.95x (ISBN 0-8358-0384-8). Upper Room.

--Discipline & Discovery. rev. ed. 1977. pap. 3.50x (ISBN 0-8358-0354-6). Upper Room.

Day, Albert E. & Wagner, James K. Letters on the Healing Ministry. 144p. 1986. pap. 6.95 incl. study guide (ISBN 0-317-30215-9, Dist. by Abingdon). Upper Room.

Day, Alexandra. Good Dog, Carl. LC 85-70419. (Illus.). 36p. (Orig.). (ps up). 1985. 11.95 (ISBN 0-88138-062-8, Star & Elephant Bks.); pap. 7.95 (ISBN 0-88138-052-0). Green Tiger Pr.

Day, Angel. Daphnis & Chloe. 1890. Repr. 30.00 (ISBN 0-8274-2143-5). R West.

Day, Angell. English Secretary. LC 67-10122. 1967. Repr. of 1599 ed. 45.00 (ISBN 0-8201-1012-4). Schol Facsimiles.

Day, Arnold. Patient with a Psychiatric Disorder. 1983. pap. text ed. 4.50 (ISBN 0-06-318274-2). Har-Row.

Day, Arthur G. Coronado's Quest: The Discovery of the Southwestern States. LC 81-13443. xvi, 419p. 1982. Repr. of 1964 ed. lib. bdg. 35.00x (ISBN 0-313-23207-5, DACO). Greenwood.

Day, Arthur G., ed. The Sky Clears: Poetry of the American Indians. LC 83-1576. xiii, 204p. 1983. Repr. of 1951 ed. lib. bdg. 27.50x (ISBN 0-313-23883-9, DASK). Greenwood.

Day, B. F. Building Acoustics. (Illus.). 120p. 1969. 13.00 (ISBN 0-444-20047-9, Pub. by Elsevier Applied Sci England). Elsevier.

Day, Barbara. Early Childhood Education: Creative Learning Activities. 2nd ed. 320p. 1983. text ed. write for info. (ISBN 0-02-327940-0). Macmillan.

--Open Learning in Early Childhood. 2nd ed. (Illus.). 224p. 1975. pap. text ed. write for info. (ISBN 0-02-327950-8, 32795). Macmillan.

Day, Barbara B. Thinking & Doing: Youth and a New International Economic Order. (Illus.). 96p. 1980. pap. 7.50 (ISBN 92-3-101841-8, U1075, UNESCO). Unipub.

Day, Barbara D. & Drake, Kay N. Early Children Education: Curriculum Organization & Classroom Management. LC 83-70920. 165p. (Orig.). 1983. pap. text ed. 7.50 (ISBN 0-87120-118-6). Assn Supervision.

Day, Beth. Glacier Pilot. LC 57-6781. (Illus.). 1976. pap. 4.95 (ISBN 0-89174-009-0). Comstock Edns.

Day, Beth, jt. auth. see Schiff, Jacqui L.

Day, Bradford M., ed. The Checklist of Fantastic Literature in Paperbound Books. LC 74-15961. (Science Fiction Ser). 128p. 1975. Repr. 12.00x (ISBN 0-405-06326-1). Ayer Co Pubs.

--The Supplemental Checklist of Fantastic Literature. LC 74-15962. (Science Fiction Ser). 160p. 1975. Repr. 11.00x (ISBN 0-405-06327-X). Ayer Co Pubs.

Day, Bradford M., et al, eds. Bibliography of Adventure: Mundy, Burroughs, Rohmer, Haggard. rev. ed. LC 77-84282. (Lost Race & Adult Fantasy Ser.). 1978. lib. bdg. 17.00x (ISBN 0-405-11019-7). Ayer Co Pubs.

Day, C., tr. see Steiner, Rudolf.

Day, C. J., jt. auth. see Shaw, W. C.

Day, C. Nixon. Hodio. LC 84-9074. (Illus.). 208p. (Orig.). 1984. pap. 9.95 (ISBN 0-934802-13-0). ICS Bks.

Day, C. R. The Music & Musical Instruments of Southern India & the Decan. (Illus.). 182p. 1983. text ed. 32.50x (ISBN 0-86590-133-3). Apt Bks.

Day, Carol, ed. see Junior League of Portland, Inc.

Day, Carol O. & Day, Edmund. The New Immigrants. (Impact Ser.). 128p. (gr. 7 up). 1985. lib. bdg. 10.90 (ISBN 0-531-04929-9). Watts.

Day, Caroline. Study of Some Negro-White Families in the U. S. LC 76-106857. (Illus.). Repr. of 1932 ed. 27.00x (ISBN 0-8371-3479-X, DNF&, Pub. by Negro U Pr). Greenwood.

Day, Charles E., ed. Atherosclerosis Drug Discovery. LC 76-5395. (Advances in Experimental Medicine & Biology: Vol. 67). 477p. 1976. 49.50x (ISBN 0-306-39067-1, Plenum Pr). Plenum Pub.

Day, Charles E. & Levy, Robert S., eds. Low Density Lipoproteins. LC 76-25840. (Illus.). 465p. 1976. 52.50x (ISBN 0-306-30934-3, Plenum Pr). Plenum Pub.

Day, Chris, jt. auth. see Rees, Mervy.

Day, Christine R., ed. see Williams, Tennessee.

Day, Christopher. The Jacaltec Language. (Language Science Monographs: No. 12). 136p. 1973. pap. text ed. 12.00x (ISBN 0-686-27751-1). Mouton.

--The Jacaltec Language. (Language Science Monographs: Vol. 12). viii, 136p. (Orig.). 1973. pap. text ed. 8.50x (ISBN 0-87750-176-9). Res Ctr Lang Semiotic.

Day, Christopher & Norman, John L., eds. Issues in Educational Drama. (Curriculum Books For Teachers Monograph). 197p. 1984. 27.00x (ISBN 0-905273-66-4, Pub. by Falmer Pr); pap. 14.00x (ISBN 0-905273-65-6). Taylor & Francis.

Day, Clarence. The Best of Clarence Day. 22.95 (ISBN 0-88411-528-3, Pub. by Aeonian Pr). Amereon Ltd.

--In the Green Mountain Country. 1934. 29.50x (ISBN 0-686-50044-X). Elliots Bks.

--Life with Father. (YA) 1957. 10.95 (ISBN 0-394-43319-X). Knopf.

--Life With Father. 1981. Repr. lib. bdg. 16.95x (ISBN 0-89966-430-X). Buccaneer Bks.

--Life with Father. (General Ser.). 1984. lib. bdg. 13.95 (ISBN 0-8161-3755-2, Large Print Bks). G K Hall.

--Life with Father. 18.95 (ISBN 0-88411-527-5, Pub. by Aeonian Pr). Amereon Ltd.

--Scenes from the Mesozoic & Other Drawings. 1935. 29.50x (ISBN 0-686-51306-1). Elliots Bks.

Day, Clarence A. Ezekiel Holmes, Father of Maine Agriculture. 1968. pap. 4.95 (ISBN 0-89101-016-5). U Maine Orono.

--Farming in Maine. 1963. pap. 4.95 (ISBN 0-89101-009-2). U Maine Orono.

Day, Clarence B. The Philosophers of China. 1978. pap. 5.95 (ISBN 0-8065-0622-9). Citadel Pr.

Day, Clive. A History of Commerce. LC 82-48300. (The World Economy Ser.). 676p. 1982. lib. bdg. 72.00 (ISBN 0-8240-5355-9). Garland Pub.

Day, Colin. A London FORTRAN Course. rev. ed. (Illus.). 86p. 1975. pap. 14.95 (ISBN 0-485-12018-6, Pub. by Athlone Pr Ltd). Longwood Pub Group.

Day, Cyrus L. Art of Knotting & Splicing. 3rd rev. ed. LC 55-10028. (Illus.). 225p. 1970. 18.95 (ISBN 0-87021-083-1). Naval Inst Pr.

--The Art of Knotting & Splicing. 3rd ed. (Illus.). 225p. 1970. 18.95 (ISBN 0-87021-083-1); bulk rates avail. Naval Inst Pr.

--Knot & Splices. 1983. pap. 3.50 (ISBN 0-8286-0094-5). J De Graff.

Day, Cyrus L. & Murrie, Eleanore B. English Song-Books. LC 75-8964. Repr. of 1936 ed. lib. bdg. 10.00 (ISBN 0-8414-3809-9). Folcroft.

Day, Cyrus L., ed. see D'Urfey, Thomas.

Day, D., jt. auth. see Hull, T.

Day, D. A., jt. ed. see Douce, R.

Day, D. E. Relaxation Processes in Glasses: Special Journal Issue. 1974. Repr. 57.50 (ISBN 0-444-10613-8, North-Holland). Elsevier.

Day, Dabney, et al. Learning to Remember: Procedures for Teaching Recall. 1978. 18.50 (ISBN 0-87879-194-9). Acad Therapy.

Day, Dan. Ever Been Irritated? (Uplook Ser.). 31p. 1972. pap. 0.79 (ISBN 0-8163-0070-4, 05630-9). Pacific Pr Pub Assn.

--Hurting. (Uplook Ser.). 1978. pap. 0.79 (ISBN 0-8163-0088-7, 08889-8). Pacific Pr Pub Assn.

--I've Got This Problem with Sex... (Uplook Ser.). 32p. (YA) 1973. pap. 0.79 (ISBN 0-8163-0012-7, 09790-7). Pacific Pr Pub Assn.

--Why I'm an Adventist. LC 73-91871. (Stories That Win). 1974. pap. 0.95 (ISBN 0-8163-0274-X, 23665-3). Pacific Pr Pub Assn.

Day, Dave. Electric Flight. (Illus.). 96p. (Orig.). 1984. pap. 9.95 (ISBN 0-85242-822-7, Pub by ARGUS). Aztex.

--Electric Flight. (Illus.). 95p. 1983. pap. 10.95 (ISBN 0-85242-822-7, Pub. by Argus Bks. Ltd. (England)). Motorbooks Intl.

Day, David. The Doomsday Book of Animals: A Natural History of Vanished Species. LC 81-43018. (Illus.). 288p. 1981. 40.00 (ISBN 0-670-27987-0, Studio); pap. 14.95 (ISBN 0-670-27988-9). Viking.

Day, David, jt. auth. see Jackson, Albert.

Day, David, et al. Castles. 192p. (Orig.). 1984. 24.95 (ISBN 0-553-05066-4). Bantam.

Day, David E. Early Childhood Education: A Human Ecological Approach. 1983. text ed. 17.35x (ISBN 0-673-16029-7). Scott F.

Day, Dawn. The Adoption of Black Children. LC 77-18585. (Illus.). 1979. 20.00 (ISBN 0-669-02107-5). Lexington Bks.

Day, Donald. The Autobiography of Will Rogers. 20.95 (ISBN 0-89190-330-5, Pub. by Am Repr). Amereon Ltd.

--Onward Christian Soldiers. 210p. (Orig.). 1982. pap. 7.00 (ISBN 0-939482-03-7). Noontide.

Day, Donald & Trohan, Walter. Onward Christian Soldiers Nineteen Twenty to Nineteen Forty-two: Propaganda, Censorship, & One Man's Struggle to Herald the Truth. 1982. lib. bdg. 69.95 (ISBN 0-87700-450-1). Revisionist Pr.

Day, Donald, ed. Autobiography of Will Rogers. 1980. pap. 1.95 (ISBN 0-380-00213-2, 34397). Avon.

Day, Donald, jt. ed. see Boatright, Mody C.

Day, Donald, ed. see Houston, Samuel.

Day, Donald, ed. see Rogers, Will.

Day, Donald B. Index to the Science Fiction Magazines, 1926-1950. rev. ed. 1982. lib. bdg. 50.00 (ISBN 0-8161-8591-3, Hall Reference). G K Hall.

Day, Donald D. This I Believe. 224p. 1972. pap. 1.95 (ISBN 0-9600500-1-9). Three D Pubs.

Day, Dorothy. By Little & By Little: The Selected Writings of Dorothy Day. Ellsberg, Robert, ed. LC 82-48887. 1983. 17.95 (ISBN 0-394-52499-3); pap. 9.95 (ISBN 0-394-71432-6). Knopf.

--Loaves & Fishes: The Story of the Catholic Worker Movement. LC 82-48433. (Illus.). 240p. 1983. pap. 7.64i (ISBN 0-06-061771-3, RD/434, HarpR). Har-Row.

--The Long Loneliness: An Autobiography. LC 81-4727. (Illus.). 1981. pap. 7.64i (ISBN 0-06-061751-9, RD363, HarpR). Har-Row.

--Therese. 1979. 7.95 (ISBN 0-87243-090-1). Templegate.

Day, Douglas. Malcolm Lowry: A Biography. (Galaxy Bks.). (Illus.). 1973. pap. 9.95 (ISBN 0-19-503523-2, GB777). Oxford U Pr.

Day, Douglas, ed. see Faulkner, William.

Day, Edmund, jt. auth. see Day, Carol O.

Day, Edmund E. Education for Freedom & Responsibility: Selected Essays. facsimile ed. Konvitz, Milton R., ed. LC 78-142618. (Essay Index Reprint Ser). Repr. of 1952 ed. 18.00 (ISBN 0-8369-2391-X). Ayer Co Pubs.

Day, Edmund E. & Thomas, Woodlief. The Growth of Manufacturers, 1899-1923. LC 75-22811. (America in Two Centuries Ser). 1976. Repr. of 1928 ed. 17.00x (ISBN 0-405-07682-7). Ayer Co Pubs.

Day, Edward. The Catholic Church Story. rev ed. LC 78-73834. (Illus.). 192p. (Orig.). 1975. pap. 3.95 (ISBN 0-89243-105-9, 65300). Liguori Pubns.

Day, Emily F. The Princess of Manoa. (Illus.). 1977. pap. 1.00 (ISBN 0-912180-16-1). Petroglyph.

Day, Faye & Geistfeld, Annette. Books Too Good to Miss. (Illus.). 53p. 1984. pap. 7.50 (ISBN 0-912773-04-9). One Hund Twenty Creat.

--Productive Thinking Activities. 56p. (Orig.). 1985. pap. 6.00 (ISBN 0-912773-11-1). One Hund Twenty Creat.

--Tales Too Good To Miss. (Illus.). 44p. 1983. pap. 7.50 (ISBN 0-912773-03-0). One Hund Twenty Creat.

Day, Frank. Sir William Empson: An Annotated Bibliography. Cain, William E., ed. LC 82-49130. (Modern Critics & Critical Schools Ser.: vol. 8). 180p. 1984. lib. bdg. 64.00 (ISBN 0-8240-9207-4). Garland Pub.

Day, Frank P. Rockbound. LC 73-81763. (Literature of Canada, Poetry & Prose in Reprint). pap. 81.00 (ISBN 0-317-26917-8, 2023609). Bks Demand UMI.

Day, Fraser, jt. auth. see Carriere, Dean.

Day, G. S. Buyer Attitudes and Brand Choice Behavior. LC 74-81374. 1970. 12.95 (ISBN 0-02-907210-7). Free Pr.

Day, G. S., jt. auth. see Aaker, D. A.

Day, Gene. Future Day. (Illus.). 1979. 5.95x (ISBN 0-918348-03-X). NBM.

Day, George & McCormick, Herb. Out There: The Intimate Story of the Longest, Loneliest Sailboat Race. LC 84-5293. (Illus.). 240p. 1984. 17.95 (ISBN 0-915160-59-5). Seven Seas.

Day, George E. A Practical Treatise on the Domestic Management & Most Important Diseases of Advanced Life. Kastenbaum, Robert, ed. LC 78-22198. (Aging & Old Age Ser.). 1979. Repr. of 1849 ed. lib. bdg. 17.00x (ISBN 0-405-11815-5). Ayer Co Pubs.

Day, George F. The Uses of History in the Novels of Vardis Fisher. (Vardis Fisher Ser). 1974. lib. bdg. 69.95 (ISBN 0-87700-225-8). Revisionist Pr.

Day, George S. Analysis for Strategic Market Decisions. (Illus.). 270p. 1985. pap. text ed. 7.95 (ISBN 0-314-85227-1). West Pub.

--Strategic Business Planning: The Pursuit of Competitive Advantage. (Strategic Marketing Ser.). (Illus.). 200p. 1984. pap. text ed. 16.95 (ISBN 0-314-77884-5). West Pub.

Day, George S., jt. auth. see Aaker, David A.

Day, George S., jt. ed. see Aaker, David A.

Day, Gina. Tell No Tales. 176p. 1984. pap. 2.95 (ISBN 0-8128-8020-X). Stein & Day.

Day, Glenn R., jt. auth. see Likes, Robert C.

Day, Graham & Caldwell, Lesley, eds. Diversity & Decomposition in the Labour Market. 224p. 1982. text ed. 36.50x (ISBN 0-566-00556-5). Gower Pub Co.

Day, Grove D. Captain Cook. O'Connell, Patrick, ed. (Hawaii Cultural Heritage Ser.: Vol. 7). (Illus.). (gr. 4 up). 1977. pap. 3.50x (ISBN 0-911776-31-1). Hogarth.

Day, Gwynn M. The Joy Beyond. 1979. 3.95 (ISBN 0-8010-2893-0). Baker Bk.

Day, H. Benefit & Cost Analysis of Hydrological Forecasts: A State-of-the-Art-Report. (Operational Hydrology Reports: No. 3). (Illus.). 26p. 1973. pap. 12.00 (ISBN 0-685-39011-X, W259, WMO). Unipub.

Day, H. J., et al, eds. Thrombosis: Animal & Clinical Models. LC 78-7219. (Advances in Experimental Medicine & Biology Ser.: Vol. 102). 346p. 1978. 49.50x (ISBN 0-306-40009-X, Plenum Pr). Plenum Pub.

Day, Harvey. Encyclopaedia of Natural Health & Healing. LC 78-24666. (Illus.). 1979. 7.95 (ISBN 0-912800-62-3). Woodbridge Pr.

--Yoga Illustrated Dictionary. (Illus.). 1970. 9.95 (ISBN 0-87523-177-2). Emerson.

Day, Holliday D. The Shape of Space, George Sugarman. Allen, Jane A., ed. (Illus.). 144p. (Orig.). 1981. pap. 20.00 (ISBN 0-936364-06-8). Joslyn Art.

Day, Holman. Aunt Shaw's Pet Jug. (Illus., Orig.). 1983. pap. 1.95 (ISBN 0-89621-079-0). Thorndike Pr.

--Hoskin's Cow. 1983. pap. 1.95 (ISBN 0-89621-080-4). Thorndike Pr.

Day, Horace & Grob, Gerald N., eds. The Opium Habit, with Suggestions as to the Remedy. LC 80-1224. (Addiction in America Ser.). 1981. Repr. of 1868 ed. lib. bdg. 29.00x (ISBN 0-405-13580-7). Ayer Co Pubs.

Day, Howard D. Guide for Adult School Crossing Guards. (Illus.). 34p. 1971. Set Of 10. spiral 24.50x (ISBN 0-398-02171-6). C C Thomas.

Day, Hughes W. Beside Still Waters. 418p. 1979. 9.95 (ISBN 0-8341-0599-3). Beacon Hill.

Day, Hy I., ed. Advances in Intrinsic Motivation & Aesthetics. LC 81-2766. 515p. 1981. 49.50x (ISBN 0-306-40606-3, Plenum Pr). Plenum Pub.

Day, Isobel, jt. auth. see Bewley, Beulah R.

Day, J. D., jt. ed. see Pryor, J. B.

Day, J. Edward. My Appointed Round: 929 Days As Postmaster General. 1965. 6.50 (ISBN 0-87012-149-9). McClain.

Day, J. Laurence. Press Coverage of the Falklands Conflict. LC 83-198373. (UFSI Reports Ser.: No. 47). U Field Staff Intl.

Day, J. S. & Krisch, A. D., eds. History of ZGS the Argonne, 1979. LC 80-67694. (AIP Conference Proceedings: No. 60). 453p. 1980. lib. bdg. 23.75 (ISBN 0-88318-159-2). Am Inst Physics.

Day, J. Wentworth. The Modern Shooter. 1976. Repr. 15.00x (ISBN 0-85409-954-9, CRR). Charles River Bks.

Day, James. Literary Background to Bach's Cantatas. (Student's Music Library-Historical & Critical Studies Ser). (Illus.). 1961. 10.95 (ISBN 0-234-77522-X). Dufour.

--Vaughan Williams. rev. ed. (Master Musicans Ser.: No. M112). (Illus.). 1975. pap. 7.95 (ISBN 0-8226-0722-0). Littlefield.

--Vaughan Williams. (The Master Musicians Ser.). (Illus.). 238p. 1975. 13.50x (ISBN 0-460-03162-7, Pub. by J. M. Dent England). Biblio Dist.

Day, James, jt. auth. see Le Huray, Peter.

Day, James A. Perspectives in Kinanthropometry. 1985. text ed. write for info. (ISBN 0-87322-008-0, BDAY0008). Human Kinetics.

Day, James F. Migrant Education. LC 75-7967. 96p. 1975. 6.00 (ISBN 0-8022-2169-6). Philos Lib.

Day, James M. Captain Clint: Peoples Texas Ranger. 1980. 17.50 (ISBN 0-87244-055-9). Texian.

Day, James M, jt. ed. see Laufer, William S.

Day, James M., ed. see Parker, Morris B.

Day, Janis K. A Working Approach to Human Relations in Organizations. LC 79-24589. 1980. pap. text ed. 16.50 pub net (ISBN 0-8185-0347-5). Brooks-Cole.

Day, Jeremiah. An Examination of President Edwards' Inquiry on the Freedom of the Will. LC 75-3125. Repr. of 1841 ed. 28.00 (ISBN 0-404-59125-6). AMS Pr.

--An Inquiry Respecting the Self-Determining Power of the Will: Or, Contingent Volition. LC 75-950. Repr. of 1838 ed. 18.00 (ISBN 0-404-59001-2). AMS Pr.

Day, Jerry, jt. auth. see Peck, Dave.

Day, Jo Anne C. Art Nouveau Cut & Use Stencils. (Illus.). 64p. 1977. pap. 3.95 (ISBN 0-486-23443-6). Dover.

--Early American Cut & Use Stencils. LC 75-17179. (Illus.). 64p. (Orig.). 1975. pap. 3.95 (ISBN 0-486-20231-3). Dover.

--Pennsylvania Dutch Cut & Use Stencils. LC 75-17180. (Illus.). 64p. (Orig.). 1975. pap. 3.95 (ISBN 0-486-20574-6). Dover.

Day, Jo Anne C., ed. Decorative Silhouettes of the Twenties for Designers & Craftsmen. LC 73-89255. (Pictorial Archive Ser.). (Illus.). 160p. (Orig.). 1975. pap. 4.50 (ISBN 0-486-23152-6). Dover.

Day, JoAnne C. Decorative Silhouettes of the Twenties for Designers & Craftsmen. (Illus.). 10.25 (ISBN 0-8446-5178-8). Peter Smith.

--Early American Stencils: 54 Cut-&-Use Stencils. 14.75 (ISBN 0-8446-5179-6). Peter Smith.

--Pennsylvania Dutch Stencils: Forty-Three Cut-&-Use Stencils. 11.25 (ISBN 0-8446-5180-X). Peter Smith.

Day, Jocelyn. Island Fires. 192p. 1983. pap. 1.95 (ISBN 0-515-07238-9). Jove Pubns.

--The Marrying Kind. (Second Chance at Love Ser.: No. 128). 1983. pap. 1.95 (ISBN 0-515-07216-8). Jove Pubns.

--Sometimes a Lady. (Second Chance at Love Ser.: No. 196). 192p. 1984. pap. 1.95 (ISBN 0-515-07812-3). Jove Pubns.

--The Steele Heart. (Second Chance at Love Ser.: No. 52). 1982. pap. 1.75 (ISBN 0-317-06891-1, 06148-4). Jove Pubns.

--Tarnished Rainbow, No. 82. 1984. pap. 1.75 (ISBN 0-515-06693-1). Jove Pubns.

Day, John. An Economic History of Athens under Roman Domination. LC 72-7887. (Greek History Ser). Repr. of 1942 ed. 23.50 (ISBN 0-405-04781-9). Ayer Co Pubs.

--God's Conflict with the Dragon & the Sea in the Old Testament: Echoes of a Canaanite Myth. (University of Cambridge Oriental Publications Ser.: No. 35). 208p. 1985. 49.50 (ISBN 0-521-25600-3). Cambridge U Pr.

--Law Tricks. LC 82-45693. (Malone Society Reprint Ser.: No. 91). Repr. of 1949 ed. 40.00 (ISBN 0-404-63090-1). AMS Pr.

--Works of John Day. Bullen, A. H., ed. 25.00x (ISBN 0-87556-044-X). Saifer.

Day, John & Chettle, Henry. Blind Beggar of Bednal Green. (Tudor Facsimile Texts. Old English Plays: No. 143). Repr. of 1914 ed. 49.50 (ISBN 0-404-53443-0). AMS Pr.

Day, John, tr. see Ladurie, Emmanuel L.

Day, John A., jt. auth. see Schaefer, Vincent J.

Day, John C. Managing the Lower Rio Grande: An Experience in International River Development. LC 70-129457. (Research Papers Ser.: No. 125). 1970. pap. 10.00 (ISBN 0-89065-032-2, 125). U Chicago Dept Geog.

Day, John F. Bloody Ground. LC 79-57571. (Illus.). 352p. 1981. 28.00 (ISBN 0-8131-1454-3); pap. 9.00 (ISBN 0-8131-0148-4). U Pr of Ky.

Day, John W., Jr., jt. ed. see Hall, Charles A.

Day, Joseph. The Glory of Athens. 213p. 1980. 20.00 (ISBN 0-89005-346-4). Ares.

Day, K. R. & Day, K. R. Alvis: The Story of the Red Triangle. (Illus.). cloth hardback 18.95 (ISBN 0-85614-063-5, F394). Haynes Pubns.

Day, Kenneth, intro. by. William Caxton & Charles Knight. (Illus.). 240p. pap. 8.95 (ISBN 0-913720-06-2, Sandstone). Beil.

Day, Kenneth F. Eden Phillpotts on Dartmoor. (Illus.). 248p. 1981. 17.50 (ISBN 0-7153-8118-0). David & Charles.

Day, Kent C. & Dibble, David S. Archeological Survey of the Flaming Gorge Reservoir Area, Wyoming-Utah. (Upper Colorado Ser.: No. 9). Repr. of 1963 ed. 22.50 (ISBN 0-404-60665-2). AMS Pr.

Day, Kent C., jt. ed. see Moseley, Michael E.

Day, L. B. Bengal Peasant Life. 383p. 1984. Repr. of 1923 ed. text ed. 35.50x (ISBN 0-391-03333-6, Pub. by Cosmo India). Humanities.

Day, Lal B. Bengal Peasant Life. new ed. LC 76-44747. Repr. of 1920 ed. 34.50 (ISBN 0-404-15946-X). AMS Pr.

--Folk-Tales of Bengal. LC 78-67727. (The Folktale). Repr. of 1883 ed. 25.00 (ISBN 0-404-16138-3). AMS Pr.

Day, Langston. The Life & Art of W. Heath Robinson. (Illus.). 1977. Repr. of 1947 ed. 25.00x (ISBN 0-7158-1180-0). Charles River Bks.

--New Worlds Beyond the Atom. 1963. Devin.

Day, Lawrence, jt. auth. see Hodgson, Julian.

Day, LeGrand E. A New Dimension of Freedom. 1977. 4.95 (ISBN 0-87881-064-1). Mojave Bks.

Day, LeRoy J. Dynamic Christian Fellowship. rev. ed. (Orig.). pap. 2.95 (ISBN 0-8170-0226-X). Judson.

Day, Lewis C. The Mind in Chains: Socialism & the Cultural Revolution. LC 72-7243. 1972. Repr. of 1937 ed. lib. bdg. 29.50 (ISBN 0-8414-0279-5). Folcroft.

--Notable Images of Virtue: Emily Bronte, George Meredith, W. B. Yeats. LC 74-3179. 1973. lib. bdg. 10.00 (ISBN 0-8414-5724-7). Folcroft.

--We're Not Going to Do Nothing. 1978. lib. bdg. 10.00 (ISBN 0-8495-1017-1). Arden Lib.

--We're Not Going to Do Nothing. LC 74-4379. 1973. lib. bdg. 10.00 (ISBN 0-8414-3741-6). Folcroft.

Day, Lewis F. Alphabets Old & New. 59.95 (ISBN 0-87968-591-3). Gordon Pr.

--Alphabets Old & New for the Use of Craftsmen. 3rd ed. LC 68-23148. 1968. Repr. of 1910 ed. 30.00x (ISBN 0-8103-3301-5). Gale.

--Nature & Ornament: Nature the Raw Material of Design. LC 74-137355. (Illus.). 1971. Repr. of 1930 ed. 34.00x (ISBN 0-8103-3328-7). Gale.

--Nature in Ornament. LC 70-159852. (Illus.). 1971. Repr. of 1898 ed. 40.00x (ISBN 0-8103-3207-8). Gale.

--Ornament & Its Application. LC 71-136735. (Illus.). 1971. Repr. of 1904 ed. 40.00x (ISBN 0-8103-3324-4). Gale.

--Pattern Design. LC 78-21373. (Illus.). 1979. 14.95 (ISBN 0-8008-6268-6, Pentalic); pap. 9.95 (ISBN 0-8008-6270-8, Pentalic). Taplinger.

--Penmanship of the Sixteenth, Seventeenth, & Eighteenth Centuries. LC 78-58919. (Illus.). 1979. pap. 7.95 (ISBN 0-8008-6277-5, Pentalic). Taplinger.

Day, Lewis F. & Buckle, Mary. Art in Needlework: A Book about Embroidery. LC 74-159927. Repr. of 1900 ed. 34.00x (ISBN 0-8103-3062-8). Gale.

Day, Lillian. Paganini of Genoa. LC 77-181135. 318p. 1929. Repr. 39.00 (ISBN 0-403-01536-7). Scholarly.

Day, Lincoln. Analyzing Population Trends: Differential Fertility in a Pluralistic Society. LC 83-40176. 272p. 1984. 27.95 (ISBN 0-312-03281-1). St Martin.

Day, Lucille. Self-Portrait with Hand Microscope. 52p. 1982. pap. 4.95 (ISBN 0-917658-18-3). BPW & P.

Day, M., jt. auth. see Tivers, J.

Day, M. H. Fossil History of Man. rev. ed. Head, J. J., ed. (Carolina Biological Readers Ser.). (Illus.). 16p. (gr. 10 up). 1984. pap. 1.60 (ISBN 0-317-27340-X). Carolina Biological.

Day, M. H., ed. Human Evolution. (Symposia of the Society for the Study of Human Biology Ser.: Vol. II). 162p. 1973. 19.00x (ISBN 0-85066-061-0). Taylor & Francis.

--Vertebrate Locomotion. (Symposia of the Zoological Society of London Ser.: No. 48). 1981. 89.50 (ISBN 0-12-613348-4). Acad Pr.

Day, M. J. Plasmids. (Studies in Biology: No. 142). 64p. 1982. pap. text ed. 8.95 (ISBN 0-7131-2846-1). E Arnold.

Day, M. M. Normed Linear Spaces. 3rd ed. (Ergebnisse der Mathematik und Ihrer Grenzgebiete: Vol. 21). viii, 211p. 1973. 33.00 (ISBN 0-387-06148-7). Springer-Verlag.

Day, Malcolm M. Thomas Traherne. (English Authors Ser.). 1982. lib. bdg. 16.95 (ISBN 0-8057-6742-8, Twayne). G K Hall.

Day, Marie F. Kingdom Come: Fact or Fantasy. 1983. 7.95 (ISBN 0-533-05309-9). Vantage.

Day, Mark. Yuletide Lost. 1981. 4.25 (ISBN 0-89536-484-0). CSS of Ohio.

Day, Martin S. The Many Meanings of Myth. 574p. 1984. lib. bdg. 25.75 (ISBN 0-8191-3821-5); pap. text ed. 20.75 (ISBN 0-8191-3822-3). U Pr of Amer.

Day, Mary S. Scheubel As an Algebraist. LC 78-176708. (Columbia University. Teachers College. Contributions to Education: No. 219). Repr. of 1926 ed. 22.50 (ISBN 0-404-55219-6). AMS Pr.

Day, Mary W., ed. The Socio-Cultural Dimensions of Mental Health. LC 83-91012. 168p. 1985. 13.95 (ISBN 0-533-06004-4). Vantage.

Day, Michael. Autonomic Pharmacology. (Illus.). 1979. pap. text ed. 16.25 (ISBN 0-443-01790-5). Churchill.

Day, Michael, jt. auth. see Tivers, Jacqueline.

Day, Michael H. Guide to Fossil Man. 3rd rev. ed. LC 77-10517. 1978. Repr. of 1965 ed. lib. bdg. 24.00x (ISBN 0-226-13888-7). U of Chicago Pr.

Day, Mildred L. The Rise of Gawain, Nephew of Arthur: De Ortu Waluuanii Nepotis Arturi. Wilhem, James J. & Nelson, Lowry, eds. LC 83-48237. (Library of Medieval Literature). 150p. 1984. lib. bdg. 30.00 (ISBN 0-8240-9423-9). Garland Pub.

Day, Millard F. Basic Bible Doctrine. 1953. pap. 2.95 (ISBN 0-8024-0239-9). Moody.

Day, N. E., jt. auth. see Breslow, N. E.

Day, N. E. & Boice, J. C., Jr., eds. Second Cancer in Relation to Radiation Treatment for Cervical Cancer: Results of a Cancer Registry Collaboration. (Illus.). 1984. 30.00x (ISBN 0-19-723052-0). Oxford U Pr.

Day, N. K. & Good, R. A., eds. Biological Amplification Systems in Immunology. LC 76-56828. (Comprehensive Immunology Ser.: Vol. 2). (Illus.). 340p. 1977. 42.50x (ISBN 0-306-33102-0, Plenum Pr). Plenum Pub.

Day, N. R. David's Faithfulness. 85p. (Orig.). 1979. pap. 6.95 (ISBN 0-940754-02-9). Ed Ministries.

--Your Faith Is Growing! 51p. (Orig.). 1981. pap. 5.45 (ISBN 0-940754-10-X). Ed Ministries.

Day, N. Raymond. From Palm Sunday to Easter. 45p. (Orig.). 1979. pap. 5.45 (ISBN 0-940754-01-0). Ed Ministries.

Day, Nancy R. Help Yourself to Health. 80p. 1980. 2.95 (ISBN 0-317-35467-1). New Readers.

Day, Nicolas, jt. auth. see Simpson, Ken.

Day, P., ed. Electronic Structure & Magnetism of Inorganic Compounds, Vols. 1-6. Incl. Vol. 1. 1970-71 Literature. 1972. 32.00 (ISBN 0-85186-251-9); Vol. 2. 1971-72 Literature. 1973. 37.00 (ISBN 0-85186-261-6); Vol. 3. 1972-73 Literature. 1974. 43.00 (ISBN 0-85186-271-3); Vol. 4. 1973-74 Literature. 1976. 45.00 (ISBN 0-85186-281-0); Vol. 5. 1974-75 Literature. 1977. 54.00 (ISBN 0-85186-291-8); Vol. 6. 1979. 70.00 (ISBN 0-85186-610-7, Pub. by Royal Soc Chem London). LC 72-78529. Am Chemical.

Day, P., ed. see NATO Advanced Study Institute, Inorganic Laboratory, St. John's College, Oxford, September 8-18, 1974.

Day, Paul W. Matthew Arnold & the Philosophy of Vico. 1964. 10.00 (ISBN 0-8274-2691-7). R West.

Day, Peter, ed. Emission & Scattering Techniques: Studies of Inorganic Molecules, Solids, & Surfaces. 400p. 1981. 48.00 (ISBN 90-277-1317-0, Pub. by Reidel Holland). Kluwer Academic.

Day, Peter R. Genetics of Host-Parasite Interaction. LC 73-17054. (Illus.). 238p. 1974. text ed. 25.95 (ISBN 0-7167-0844-2). W H Freeman.

Day, Peter R., ed. The Genetic Basis of Epidemics in Agriculture, Vol. 287. (Annals of the New York Academy of Sciences). 400p. 1977. 37.00x (ISBN 0-89072-033-9). NY Acad Sci.

Day, Philip R., Jr. In Search of Community College Partnerships. (Keeping America Working Ser.: No. 2). (Illus.). 58p. (Orig.). 1985. pap. 9.00 (ISBN 0-87117-148-1). Am Assn Comm Jr Coll.

Day, Phyllis J., et al. Social Working: Exercises in Generalist Practice. (Illus.). 288p. 1984. pap. 15.95 (ISBN 0-13-819516-1). P-H.

Day, R. A. & Underwood, Arthur L. Quantitative Analysis. 5th ed. (Illus.). 704p. 1986. text ed. 38.95 (ISBN 0-13-746728-1). P-H.

Day, R. A., Jr. & Underwood, Arthur L. Quantitative Analysis. 4th ed. (Illus.). 1980. text ed. 37.95 (ISBN 0-13-746545-9); pap. 9.95 solutions manual (ISBN 0-13-746560-2); lab manual 14.95 (ISBN 0-13-746552-1). P-H.

Day, R. H. & Cigno, A. Modelling Economic Change: The Recursive Programming Approach. (Contributions to Economic Analysis Ser.: Vol. 117). 448p. 1978. 70.25 (ISBN 0-444-85056-2, North Holland). Elsevier.

Day, Ralph E. Our Church of God Faith for Children. 1961. pap. 1.25 (ISBN 0-87148-652-0). Pathway Pr.

--Our Church of God Faith: For Young People & Adults. 1959. pap. 1.95 (ISBN 0-87148-651-2). Pathway Pr.

Day, Ralph L., tr. see Ness, Thomas E.

Day, Rhonda, ed. see Garcia, Joseph G.

Day, Richard. Automotive Engine Tuning. 1981. pap. text ed. 16.95 (ISBN 0-8359-0270-6). Reston.

Day, Richard B., ed. Crisis & the "Crash" Soviet Studies of the West (1917-1939) 320p. 1981. 22.50 (ISBN 0-8052-7097-3, Pub. by NLB England). Schocken.

Day, Richard B., ed. & tr. see Bukharin, Nikolai I.

Day, Richard C. When in Florence. LC 85-10171. 216p. 1986. 14.95 (ISBN 0-385-23157-1). Doubleday.

Day, Richard E. Beacon Lights of Grace: Twelve Biographical Vignettes. facs. ed. LC 71-148210. (Biography Index Reprint Ser.). 1947. 17.00 (ISBN 0-8369-8057-3). Ayer Co Pubs.

Day, Richard E., jt. auth. see Pound, Arthur.

Day, Richard H., jt. auth. see Kamrany, Nake M.

Day, Richard H., ed. Economic Analysis & Agricultural Policy. 368p. 1982. text ed. 35.00x (ISBN 0-8138-0532-5). Iowa St U Pr.

Day, Richard H. & Robinson, Stephen M., eds. Mathematical Topics in Economic Theory & Computation. LC 72-96283. v, 149p. 1972. text ed. 12.50 (ISBN 0-89871-045-6). Soc Indus-Appl Math.

Day, Richard H., ed. see Symposium, University of Wisconsin, Madison, October, 1974.

Day, Richard R., ed. Issues in English Creoles: Papers from the 1975 Hawaii Conference. (Varieties of English Around the World, General Ser.: No. 2). iii, 188p. (Orig.). 1980. pap. 19.00x (ISBN 3-87276-245-1, Pub. by J Groos W Germany). Benjamins North Am.

Day, Robert. The Last Cattle Drive. LC 83-16887. 224p. 1983. Repr. of 1977 ed. 12.95 (ISBN 0-7006-0243-7). U Pr of KS.

Day, Robert A. How to Write & Publish a Scientific Paper. 2nd ed. (Professional Writing Ser.). (Illus.). 181p. 1983. 17.95 (ISBN 0-89495-021-5); pap. text ed. 11.95 (ISBN 0-89495-022-3). ISI Pr.

Day, Rosemary. The Witch & the Owl. (Illus.). 28p. 1981. 11.00x (ISBN 0-460-06886-5, BKA 03659, Pub. by J. M. Dent England). Biblio Dist.

Day, Ross. The International Monetary Chaos & the Advancing Necessary Revolution in the World Financial Order. (Illus.). 1977. 65.00x (ISBN 0-918968-00-3). Inst Econ Finan.

Day, Ross H. & Stanley, Gordon V. Studies in Perception. 1977. 14.50x (ISBN 0-85564-121-5, Pub. by U of W Austral Pr). Intl Spec Bk.

Day, S. The Writer's Workbook. 2nd ed. 240p. 1984. 9.95 (ISBN 0-07-016154-2). McGraw.

Day, S., jt. auth. see McMahon, E.

Day, S. R. & Good, R. A., eds. Membranes & Viruses in Immunopathology: Proceedings. 1973. 65.00 (ISBN 0-12-207250-2). Acad Pr.

Day, Samuel P. Down South; Or an Englishman's Experience at the Seat of the American War, 2 Vols. LC 79-164480. (Research & Source Works Ser.: No. 349). 1971. Repr. of 1862 ed. Set. lib. bdg. 43.00 (ISBN 0-8337-0797-3). B Franklin.

Day, Satis B. & Day, Stacey B. A Hindu Interpretation of the Hand & Its Portents As Practiced by the Palmists of India. LC 73-85296. 5.50 (ISBN 0-912922-25-7). U of Minn Bell.

Day, Sherman. Historical Collections of the State of Pennsylvania. LC 69-18290. (Keystone State Historical Publications Ser.: No. 1). (Illus.). 1969. Repr. of 1843 ed. 48.50x (ISBN 0-87198-501-2). Friedman.

--Historical Collections of the State of Pennsylvania. LC 69-18290. (Keystone State Historical Publications Ser.). (Illus.). 1843. Repr. 48.50x (ISBN 0-8046-8501-0, Pub. by Kennikat). Assoc Faculty Pr.

Day, Stacey. Tuluak & Amaulik. LC 73-93517. (Illus.). 176p. 1973. 6.50 (ISBN 0-912922-07-9). U of Minn Bell Mus.

Day, Stacey, ed. A Companion to the Life Sciences, Vol. 1. 1979. 28.95 (ISBN 0-442-22010-3). Van Nos Reinhold.

Day, Stacey B. Biologos & Biopsychosocial Synthesis: The SAMA Foundation Lectures, Calabar, West Africa, 1982. LC 84-82409. 130p. 1985. 35.00X (ISBN 0-934314-75-6). INTL Found Biosocial Dev.

--The Biopsychosocial Imperative: Understanding the Biologos & General Systems Theory Approach to Biocommunications As the Psychospiritual Anatomy of Good Health. LC 81-84483. 60p. 1981. 25.00 (ISBN 0-934314-06-3). Intl Found Biosocial Dev.

--Creative Health & Health Enhancement: Individual Initiative & Responsibility for Self Health & Wellness. LC 81-81300. (Monograph on Health Communications & Biopsychosocial Health). (Illus.). 1982. lib. bdg. 150.00x (ISBN 0-934314-07-1, SBD/HES82SKI). Intl Found Biosocial Dev.

--Death & Attitudes Towards Death. LC 72-76821. Orig. Title: Proceedings A Symposium of the Bell Museum, Univ. of Minn. Med. School. 94p. (Orig.). 1984. Repr. of 1972 ed. 10.00 (ISBN 0-934314-76-4). Intl Found Biosocial Dev.

--Health Communications. LC 79-87888. (Illus.). 356p. (Orig.). 1979. pap. 26.50 (ISBN 0-934314-00-4). Intl Found Biosocial Dev.

--The Idle Thoughts of a Surgical Fellow: Being An Account of Experimental Surgical Studies 1956-1966. LC 68-31066. (Illus.). 344p. 1984. 25.00x (ISBN 0-934314-99-3). Intl Found Biosocial Dev.

--The Way of a Physician: The Biologos, Biopsychosocial Way, Survival & the Parasympathetic Towards an Ethic & a Way of Life. LC 81-80988. (Monograph Series on Health Communications & Biopsychosocial Health). Orig. Title: Le Medicine Reprend Lui-Meme. 80p. 1982. write for info. (ISBN 0-934314-04-7, SBD/BIO/81SKI); lib. bdg. 25.00 (ISBN 0-686-87149-9). Intl Found Biosocial Dev.

Day, Stacey B., jt. auth. see Day, Satis B.

Day, Stacey B., ed. Ethics in Medicine in a Changing Society. LC 73-85309. (Bell Symposia Ser.). (Orig.). 1973. pap. 2.50 (ISBN 0-912922-04-4). U of Minn Bell.

--Image of Science & Society. (Biosciences Communications: Vol. 3, No. 1). 1977. 8.25 (ISBN 3-8055-2690-3). S Karger.

--Intergrated Medicine. (Companion to the Life Sciences Ser.: Vol. 2). 625p. 1981. 37.95 (ISBN 0-442-25163-7). Van Nos Reinhold.

--Life Stress. (Companion to the Life Sciences Ser.: Vol. III). 416p. 1982. 36.95 (ISBN 0-442-26294-9). Van Nos Reinhold.

--Some Systems of Biological Communication. (Biosciences Communications: Vol. 3, No. 5-6). (Illus.). 1977. 24.25 (ISBN 3-8055-2817-5). S Karger.

--Trauma: Clinical & Biological Aspects. LC 74-30105. 389p. 1975. 45.00x (ISBN 0-306-30834-7, Plenum Pr). Plenum Pub.

--What Is a Scientist? Memorial Issue for Professor Oscar Bodansky. (Biosciences Communications: Vol. 4, No. 5). 1978. pap. 8.25 (ISBN 3-8055-2967-8). S Karger.

Day, Stacey B. & Brandejs, Jan F., eds. Computers for Medical Office & Patient Management. 224p. 1982. 21.95 (ISBN 0-442-21316-6). Van Nos Reinhold.

Day, Stacey B., et al. Biopsychosocial Health. LC 80-85218. 225p. 1980. pap. 15.00 (ISBN 0-934314-02-0). Intl Found Biosocial Dev.

--Readings in Oncology. LC 80-80708. (Foundation Publication Ser.). (Illus.). 227p. (Orig.). 1980. pap. 15.00x (ISBN 0-934314-01-2). Intl Found Biosocial Dev.

Day, Stacey B., et al, eds. Cancer Invasion & Metastasis: Biologic Mechanisms & Therapy. LC 77-83695. (Progress in Cancer Research & Therapy Ser: Vol. 5). 540p. 1977. 63.00 (ISBN 0-89004-184-9). Raven.

--Miscellaneous Papers of the Bell Museum of Pathobiology. LC 73-91360. (Orig.). 1973. pap. 2.50 (ISBN 0-912922-05-2). U of Minn Bell.

Day, Susan & McMahan, Elizabeth. The Writer's Resource: Readings for Composition. 416p. 1983. pap. text ed. 14.95 (ISBN 0-07-016152-6). McGraw.

Day, Susan, jt. auth. see McMahan, Elizabeth.

Day, T. J., jt. auth. see Jackson, Roscoe G., II.

Day, Terence P. The Conception of Punishment in Early Indian Literature. (Editions Ser.: No. 2). 332p. 1982. pap. text ed. 11.00x (ISBN 0-919812-15-5, Pub. by Wilfrid Laurier U Pr). Humanities.

Day, Theodore E., et al. Taxes, Financial Policy & Small Business. LC 85-40016. 192p. 1985. 24.00x (ISBN 0-669-10393-4). Lexington Bks.

Day, Thomas I. Dietrich Bonhoeffer on Christian Community & Common Sense. LC 83-25900. (Toronto Studies in Theology: Vol. 11). 248p. 1983. 49.95x (ISBN 0-88946-752-8). E Mellen.

Day, U. N. The Government of the Sultanate. LC 72-901571. 219p. 1972. 7.50x (ISBN 0-89684-398-X). Orient Bk Dist.

Day, Virgil. The Equal Employment Compliance Manual. LC 77-14116. 1977. 230.00 (ISBN 0-317-20374-6). Callaghan.

Day, W. & Atkin, R. K., eds. Wheat Growth & Modeling. (NATO ASI Series A, Life Sciences: Vol. 86). 420p. 1985. 65.00x (ISBN 0-306-41933-5, Plenum Pr). Plenum Pub.

Day, W. A. The Thermodynamics of Simple Materials with Fading Memory. LC 77-183992. (Springer Tracts in Natural Philosophy: Vol. 22). (Illus.). 152p. 1972. 23.00 (ISBN 0-387-05704-8). Springer-Verlag.

Day, William. Genesis on Planet Earth: The Search for Life's Beginning. 2nd ed. LC 83-21900. 320p. 1984. 36.00x (ISBN 0-300-02954-3); pap. 12.95x (ISBN 0-300-03202-1, Y-494). Yale U Pr.

Day, William H. Maximizing Small Business Profits: With Precision Management. LC 78-9407. 1979. 13.95 (ISBN 0-13-566257-5, Spec); pap. 6.95 (ISBN 0-13-566240-0, Spec). P-H.

Day, William P. In the Circles of Fear & Desire: A Study of Gothic Fantasy. LC 84-28004. 1985. lib. bdg. 17.50 (ISBN 0-226-13890-9); pap. text ed. price not set (ISBN 0-226-13891-7). U of Chicago Pr.

Daya, Sr. The Guru & the Disciple. 1976. pap. 2.95 (ISBN 0-911564-26-8). Vedanta Ctr.

Dayal, A. K., jt. auth. see Dayal, I.

Dayal, Baghubir & Barrow, A. E. An Outline of Indian History & Culture, Vol. 1. 300p. 1984. pap. text ed. 8.95 (ISBN 0-86131-449-2, Pub. by Orient Longman Ltd India). Apt Bks.

Dayal, Har. The Bodhisattva Doctrine in Buddhist Sanskrit Literature. 1975. Repr. 22.50 (ISBN 0-89684-180-4). Orient Bk Dist.

--The Bodhisattva Doctrine in Buddhist Sanskrit Literature. 416p. 1978. pap. 7.95 (ISBN 0-87728-425-3). Weiser.

Dayal, I. & Dayal, A. K. Organization for Management in Developing Countries. (Management in Developing Societies Ser.: No. 1). 274p. 1983. text ed. 13.50x (ISBN 0-391-03076-0, Pub. by Concept India). Humanities.

Dayal, Ishwar. District Administration, India. LC 76-904844. 1976. 9.50 (ISBN 0-333-90143-6). South Asia Bks.

Dayal, John & Bose, Ajoy. The Shah Commission Begins: India Under Emergency. 1978. 13.50x (ISBN 0-8364-0179-4). South Asia Bks.

Dayal, R. An Integrated System of World Models. (North-Holland Systems & Control Ser.: Vol. 2). 398p. 1981. 59.75 (ISBN 0-444-86272-2, North-Holland). Elsevier.

Dayal, R., jt. auth. see Khanne, K. C.

Dayal, Raghubir & Barrow, A. E. An Outline of Indian History & Culture, Vol. 2. 2nd, rev. ed. 350p. 1983. pap. text ed. 8.95x (ISBN 0-86131-450-6, Pub. by Orient Longman Ltd India). Apt Bks.

Dayal, Raghubir, jt. auth. see Khanna, K. C.

Dayal, T. H. Ancient Culture of India. (Illus.). 261p. 1981. text ed. 37.00x (ISBN 0-391-02657-7). Humanities.

Dayal, Vijay S. Clinical Otolaryngology. (Illus.). 304p. 1981. 28.75i (ISBN 0-397-50499-3, Lippincott Medical). Lippincott.

--Clinical Otolaryngology. (Illus.). 355p. 1981. Set. text ed. 29.50 (ISBN 0-397-50499-3, 65-06430, Lippincott Medical). Lippincott.

Dayan, Joan, tr. see Depestre, Rene.

Dayan, Moshe. Breakthrough: A Personal Account of the Egypt-Israel Peace Negotiations. 1981. 15.00 (ISBN 0-394-51225-1). Knopf.

--Diary of the Sinai Campaign. LC 78-27859. (Illus.). 1979. Repr. of 1966 ed. lib. bdg. 24.75x (ISBN 0-313-20928-6, DADO). Greenwood.

Dayan, Rodney S. & Practising Law Institute. Mortgage-Backed Securities: Mortgage Pass-Throughs, CMOs, & Builder Bonds. LC 84-61683. (Real Estate Law & Practice Course Handbook Ser. No.250). (Illus.). Date not set. price not set. PLI.

Dayan, Yael. My Father, His Daughter. 320p. 1985. 17.95 (ISBN 0-374-21695-9). FS&G.

Dayanand. Autobiography of Dayanand Saraswati. Yadav, K. C., ed. LC 76-900170. 1976. Repr. 6.00x (ISBN 0-88386-740-0). South Asia Bks.

Dayananda, James Y., ed. Eden Phillpotts (Eighteen Sixty-Two to Nineteen Sixty) Selected Letters. LC 83-26125. (Illus.). 334p. 1984. lib. bdg. 25.75 (ISBN 0-8191-3827-4); pap. text ed. 15.50 (ISBN 0-8191-3828-2). U Pr of Amer.

Dayananda, M. A., ed. Diffusion in Solids: Recent Developments. LC 85-8897. 295p. 1985. avail. (ISBN 0-89520-493-2). Metal Soc.

Dayani, Elizabeth, jt. auth. see Riccardi, Betty.

Dayasena, P. J., ed. Microprocessor Applications in Manufacturing Industry: Bibliography. 1981. 36.00 (ISBN 0-85296-227-4). Inst Elect Eng.

Dayasena, P. J. & Deighton, S., eds. Microprocessor Applications in Electrical Engineering, 1977-1978: Bibliography. 1980. 38.00 (ISBN 0-85296-453-6). Inst Elect Eng.

Daydi-Tolson, Santiago. The Post-Civil War Spanish Social Poets. (World Authors Ser.). 1983. lib. bdg. 20.95 (ISBN 0-8057-6533-6, Twayne). G K Hall.

--Voces y Ecos en la Poesia de Jose Angel Valente. LC 83-51783. 200p. 1984. pap. 25.00 (ISBN 0-89295-034-X). Society Sp & Sp Am.

Daydi-Tolson, Santiago, ed. Five Poets of Aztlan. LC 83-71140. 224p. 1985. 18.95x (ISBN 0-916950-41-7); pap. 11.00x (ISBN 0-916950-42-5). Biling Rev-Pr.

--Vicente Aleixandre: A Critical Appraisal. LC 81-65036. (Studies in Literary Analysis). 336p. 1981. lib. bdg. 22.00x (ISBN 0-916950-21-2); pap. text ed. 14.00x (ISBN 0-916950-20-4). Biling Rev-Pr.

Dayee, Frances S. Private Zone. 32p. (Orig.). 1984. pap. text ed. 2.95 (ISBN 0-446-38053-9). Warner Bks.

--Private Zone: A Book Teaching Children Sexual Assault Prevention Tools. Meyer, Linda D., ed. (Illus.). 30p. (Orig.). (ps-3). 1982. PLB 8.00 (ISBN 0-9603516-5-5). C Franklin Pr.

Dayer, Roberta A. Bankers & Diplomats in China Nineteen Seventeen to Nineteen Twenty-Five: The Anglo-American Relationship. 324p. 1981. 30.00x (ISBN 0-7146-3118-3, F Cass Co). Biblio Dist.

Dayhoff, M. O., ed. Atlas of Protein Sequence & Structure, Vol. 5, Suppl. No. 2. LC 65-29342. 1976. 15.00 (ISBN 0-912466-05-7). Natl Biomedical.

--Atlas of Protein Sequence & Structure, Vol. 5, Suppl. No. 1. LC 65-29342. 1973. pap. 5.00 (ISBN 0-912466-04-9). Natl Biomedical.

--Atlas of Protein Sequence & Structure, Vol. 5, Suppl. No. 3. LC 65-29342. 1979. pap. 25.00 (ISBN 0-912466-07-3). Natl Biomedical.

Dayhoff, M. O., et al. Protein Segment Dictionary 78. LC 76-28614. 1978. pap. 99.00 (ISBN 0-912466-08-1). Natl Biomedical.

Dayhoff, Margaret O., et al. Nucleic Acid Sequence Database, Vol 1. LC 81-84122. (Illus.). xiv, 214p. (Orig.). 1981. text ed. 35.00 (ISBN 0-912466-09-X); pap. text ed. 25.00 (ISBN 0-686-79304-8). Natl Biomedical.

Day-Lewis, Cecil. Collected Poems. LC 78-14113. 1980. Repr. of 1954 ed. 25.00 (ISBN 0-88355-785-1). Hyperion Conn.

--The Colloquial Element in English Poetry. 1978. Repr. of 1947 ed. lib. bdg. 10.00 (ISBN 0-8495-1014-7). Arden Lib.

--The Colloquial Element in English Poetry. LC 73-559. 1973. lib. bdg. 9.50 (ISBN 0-8414-1478-5). Folcroft.

Day Lewis, Cecil. Hope for Poetry. LC 74-5140. 1939. lib. bdg. 10.00 (ISBN 0-8414-5722-0). Folcroft.

Day-Lewis, Cecil. A Hope for Poetry. LC 76-7980. 1976. Repr. of 1939 ed. lib. bdg. 18.75x (ISBN 0-8371-8847-4, LEHFP). Greenwood.

--The Poetic Image. LC 83-45427. Repr. of 1947 ed. 22.00 (ISBN 0-404-20075-3). AMS Pr.

--Revolution in Writing. LC 74-14996. 1974. Repr. of 1935 ed. lib. bdg. 15.00 (ISBN 0-8414-3797-1). Folcroft.

Day-Lewis, Cecil, ed. English Lyric Poems Fifteen Hundred to Nineteen Hundred. LC 61-7707. (Goldentree Bks. in English Literature). (Orig.). 1961. pap. text ed. 12.95x (ISBN 0-89197-146-7). Irvington.

Day-Lewis, Cecil & Lehman, John, eds. The Chatto Book of Modern Poetry: Nineteen Fifteen to Nineteen Fifty-Five. LC 77-25967. 1978. Repr. of 1956 ed. lib. bdg. 27.50x (ISBN 0-313-20099-8, DLCB). Greenwood.

Day-Lewis, Cecil & Lehmann, John, eds. The Chatto Book of Modern Poetry, Nineteen Fifteen to Nineteen Fifty-Five. Repr. of 1956 ed. 29.00 (ISBN 0-403-03067-6). Somerset Pub.

Day-Lewis, J. & Coningsby, W. A New Anthology of Modern Verse 1920-1940. 1945. lib. bdg. 10.00 (ISBN 0-8414-2448-9). Folcroft.

Day-Lewis, Tamasin, ed. The Englishwoman's Kitchen. (Illus.). 144p. 1983. 22.95 (ISBN 0-7011-2652-3, Pub. by Chatto & Windus). Merrimack Pub Cir.

Dayley, Jon P. Tzutujil Grammar. LC 84-28118. (Publications in Linguisitics: Vol. 107). 1985. 22.00x (ISBN 0-317-27127-X). U of Cal Pr.

Daynard, J., tr. see Gazdanov, Gaito.

Daynes, Byron W. & Tatalovich, Raymond. Contemporary Readings in American Government. (Orig.). 1980. pap. text ed. 11.95 (ISBN 0-669-01163-0). Heath.

Daynes, Byron W., jt. auth. see Tatalovich, Raymond.

Daynes, R. & Butler, B. The Videodisk Book: A Guide & Directory, 1984. 478p. 1984. 75.00 (ISBN 0-471-80342-1). Wiley.

Dayney, Randy & Cohen, Joel H. Winning Roller Skating: Figure & Freestyle. LC 76-6260. (Winning Ser.). (Illus.). 1977. pap. 5.95 (ISBN 0-8092-8153-8). Contemp Bks.

Dayrell, Elphinstone. Folk Stories from Southern Nigeria, West Africa. LC 77-76488. Repr. of 1910 ed. 17.50x (ISBN 0-8371-1125-0, DAS&, Pub. by Negro U Pr). Greenwood.

--Why the Sun & the Moon Live in the Sky. (Illus.). (gr. k-3). 1977. PLB 7.95 (ISBN 0-395-06741-3); pap. 1.95 (ISBN 0-395-25381-0, Sandpiper). HM.

Dayringer, Richard. God Cares for You. LC 83-70210. (Orig.). 1984. pap. 5.95 (ISBN 0-8054-5232-X). Broadman.

Dayringer, Richard, ed. Pastor & Patient. LC 80-70247. 240p. 1981. 25.00 (ISBN 0-87668-437-1). Aronson.

Days, G. D., ed. McCarthy Era-Beginning of the End: The Audio Cassette. LC 80-740530. cassette 9.00 (ISBN 0-918628-08-3). Congeros Pubns.

--Threshold of the McCarthy Era: The Audio Cassette. LC 80-740529. cassette 11.00 (ISBN 0-918628-07-5). Congeros Pubns.

Days, Mary L., ed. see Conard, Rebecca & Nelson, Christopher H.

Dayton, Brandt. The Swami & Sam: A Yoga Book. LC 77-150884. (Illus.). 95p. (Orig.). 1976. pap. 0.95 (ISBN 0-89389-014-6). Himalayan Pubs.

Dayton, Brandt, ed. Practical Vedanta: Selected Works of Swami Rama Tirtha. LC 78-10567. 341p. 1978. 8.95 (ISBN 0-89389-038-3). Himalayan Pubs.

Dayton, C. M. Design of Educational Experiments. 1970. text ed. 42.95 (ISBN 0-07-016174-7). McGraw.

Dayton, Daonald W., ed. see McPherson, Aimee S.

Dayton, David. The Lost Body of Childhood. LC 79-16222. (Illus., Orig.). 1979. pap. 4.50 (ISBN 0-914278-25-8). Copper Beech.

Dayton, Delbert H., jt. ed. see Cooper, Max D.

Dayton, Delbert H., jt. ed. see Ogra, P. L.

Dayton, Donald W. Discovering an Evangelical Heritage. LC 75-36750. (Illus.). 160p. 1976. pap. 6.68i (ISBN 0-06-061780-2, RD 142, HarpR). Har-Row.

Dayton, Donald W., ed. Account of the Union Meeting for the Promotion of Scriptual Holiness: Held at Oxford, August 29, to September 7, 1874. (The Higher Christian Life Ser.). 388p. 1985. 50.00 (ISBN 0-8240-6401-1). Garland Pub.

--The Devotional Writings of Robert Pearsall Smith & Hannah Whitall Smith. (The Higher Christian Life Ser.). 477p. 1985. lib. bdg. 60.00 (ISBN 0-8240-6444-5). Garland Pub.

--The Higher Christian Life. (The Higher Christian Life Ser.). 204p. 1985. 25.00 (ISBN 0-8240-6400-3). Garland Pub.

--Holiness Tracts Defending the Ministry of Women. (The Higher Christian Life Ser.). 304p. 1985. 40.00 (ISBN 0-8240-6411-9). Garland Pub.

--Late Nineteenth Century Revivalist Teachings of the Holy Spirit. (The Higher Christian Life Ser.). 320p. 1985. 40.00 (ISBN 0-8240-6412-7). Garland Pub.

--The Sermons of Charles F. Parham. (The Higher Christian Life Ser.). 261p. 1985. lib. bdg. 35.00 (ISBN 0-8240-6413-5). Garland Pub.

--Seven "Jesus Only" Tracts. (The Higher Christian Life Ser.). 379p. 1985. lib. bdg. 45.00 (ISBN 0-8240-6414-3). Garland Pub.

--Three Early Pentecostal Tracts. (The Higher Christian Life Ser.). 441p. 1985. 55.00 (ISBN 0-8240-6415-1). Garland Pub.

--The Work of T. B. Barratt. (The Higher Christian Life Ser.). 435p. 1985. 55.00 (ISBN 0-8240-6404-6). Garland Pub.

Dayton, Donald W. & Robeck, Cecil M., eds. Witness to Pentecost: The Life of Frank Bartleman. (The Higher Christian Life Ser.). 439p. 1985. 55.00 (ISBN 0-8240-6405-4). Garland Pub.

Dayton, Donald W., ed. see Boardman, W. E.

Dayton, Donald W., ed. see Brooks, John P.

Dayton, Donald W., jt. ed. see Bryant, M. Darrol.

Dayton, Donald W., ed. see Carter, Russell K.

Dayton, Donald W., ed. see Daniels, W. H.

Dayton, Donald W., ed. see Fairchild, James H.

Dayton, Donald W., ed. see Figgis, John B.

Dayton, Donald W., ed. see Fleisch, Paul.

Dayton, Donald W., ed. see Girvin, E. A.

Dayton, Donald W., ed. see Gordon, Earnest B.

Dayton, Donald W., ed. see Hills, A. M.

Dayton, Donald W., ed. see Horner, Ralph C.

Dayton, Donald W., ed. see LaBerge, Agnes N.

Dayton, Donald W., ed. see Lee, Luther.

Dayton, Donald W., ed. see McDonald, William & Searless, John E.

Dayton, Donald W., ed. see McLean, A. & Easton, J. W.

Dayton, Donald W., ed. see Mahan, Asa.

Dayton, Donald W., ed. see Montgomery, Carrie J.

Dayton, Donald W., ed. see Palmer, Phoebe.

Dayton, Donald W., jt. ed. see Palmer, Phoebe.

Dayton, Donald W., ed. see Palmer, Phoebe.

Dayton, Donald W., ed. see Palmer, Phoebe & Wheatley, Richard.

Dayton, Donald W., ed. see Pardington, G. P.

Dayton, Dorothy. The Epic of Alexandra. LC 79-22391. (Illus.). 1979. 4.98 (ISBN 0-89587-015-0). Blair.

Dayton, E. & Wilson, S., eds. The Future of World Evangelization: Unreached People '84. 720p. 1984. pap. 12.00 (ISBN 0-912552-42-5). MARC.

--The Refugees Among Us: Unreached People '83. 523p. 1982. pap. 9.00 (ISBN 0-912552-38-7). MARC.

Dayton, Ed. Faith That Goes Further: Facing the Contradictions of Life. LC 84-14693. 1984. pap. 5.95 (ISBN 0-88070-062-9). Multnomah.

Dayton, Ed & Wilson, Samuel. The Future of World Evangelization: The Lausanne Movement. 1984. 5.50 (ISBN 0-912552-42-5). MARC.

Dayton, Edward & Fraser, David. Planning Strategies for World Evangelization. LC 79-27014. (Orig.). 1980. pap. 15.95 (ISBN 0-8028-1832-3). Eerdmans.

Dayton, Edward & Wagner, C. Peter. Unreached Peoples '80. LC 79-57522. 1980. pap. 8.95 (ISBN 0-89191-837-X). Cook.

Dayton, Edward, jt. auth. see Wagner, C. Peter.

Dayton, Edward R. God's Purpose & Man's Plans. 64p. 1982. pap. 4.50 (ISBN 0-912552-11-5). MARC.

--That Everyone May Hear Workbook. 54p. 1983. pap. 4.00 (ISBN 0-317-03977-6). MARC.

--Tools for Time Management: Time-Saving Tools for Managing your Life. 224p. 1983. pap. 6.95 (ISBN 0-310-23221-X). Zondervan.

--What Ever Happened to Commitment? 224p. 1983. pap. 6.95 (ISBN 0-310-23161-2). Zondervan.

Dayton, Edward R. & Engstrom, Ted W. Strategy for Leadership. 240p. 1979. 13.95 (ISBN 0-8007-0994-2). Revell.

--Strategy for Living: How to Make the Best Use of Your Time & Abilities. LC 76-3935. (Orig.). 1976. pap. 6.95 (ISBN 0-8307-0424-8, 5403405); wkbk. 4.95 (ISBN 0-8307-0476-0, 5202000). Regal.

Dayton, Edward R., ed. That Everyone May Hear. 3rd ed. 91p. 1983. pap. 3.50 (ISBN 0-912552-41-7). MARC.

Dayton, Eldorous L. Chantefable: The Story of the Roman Poet Catullus & His Love for Lesbia in Prose & English Verse. 120p. 1982. 16.95 (ISBN 0-943602-00-9). Gardnor Hse.

--Give 'Em Hell Harry: An Informal Biography of the Terrible Tempered Mr. T. LC 56-9833. pap. 64.00 (ISBN 0-317-28243-3, 2022707). Bks Demand UMI.

Dayton, Howard. Your Money: Frustration or Freedom? 1979. pap. 4.95 (ISBN 0-8423-8725-0). Tyndale.

Dayton, Laura. I'd Rather Be Me. LC 78-72137. (Illus.). (gr. k-3). Date not set. price not set (ISBN 0-89799-115-X); pap. price not set (ISBN 0-89799-062-5). Dandelion Pr.

--LeRoy's Birthday Circus. LC 81-2205. (Illus.). 32p. (ps-3). 1982. 6.75 (ISBN 0-525-66744-X). Dandelion Pr.

--Mommies & Daddies Work. LC 78-73532. (Illus.). (ps-2). Date not set. price not set (ISBN 0-89799-158-3); pap. price not set (ISBN 0-89799-076-5). Dandelion Pr.

Dayton, Laura, jt. auth. see Dunlap, Carla.

Dayton, Laura, retold by. More Aesop's Fables. LC 78-73537. (Illus.). (gr. 2-5). Date not set. price not set (ISBN 0-89799-149-4); pap. price not set (ISBN 0-89799-067-6). Dandelion Pr.

Dayton, Lily. Caught in the Middle. (Candlelight Ecstasy Supreme Ser.: No. 63). (Orig.). 1985. pap. 2.50 (ISBN 0-440-11129-3). Dell.

Dayton, Linnea. Kidding Around with the Macintosh. 224p. (Orig.). (gr. 2 up). 1985. pap. 9.95 (ISBN 0-915391-11-2, Pub. by Microtrend). Slawson Comm.

Dayton, Neil A. New Facts on Mental Disorders. Grob, Gerald N., ed. LC 78-22558. (Historical Issues in Mental Health Ser.). (Illus.). 1979. Repr. of 1940 ed. lib. bdg. 34.50x (ISBN 0-405-11912-7). Ayer Co Pubs.

Dayton, O. William. Athletic Training & Conditioning. rev. ed. pap. 98.80 (ISBN 0-317-29301-X, 2055670). Bks Demand UMI.

Dayton Philharmonic Women's Association. Mud Pies & Silver Spoons: A Cookbook. Quinlivan, Lorraine, ed. (Illus.). 368p. 1985. 11.95x (ISBN 0-9614169-0-4). Dayton Phil.

Dayton, Rick. Macintosh Microsoft BASIC. price not set. P-H.

--Understanding the Macintosh. 1984. pap. text ed. 18.95 (ISBN 0-8359-8054-5). Reston.

Dayton, Seymour, et al. Controlled Clinical Trial of a Diet High in Unsaturated Fat in Preventing Complications of Atherosclerosis. (Monograph: Vol. 25). (Illus., Orig.). 1969. pap. text ed. 4.00 (ISBN 0-87493-005-7, 73-017A). Am Heart.

Dayus, Kathleen. Her People. (Illus.). 194p. 1983. pap. 7.95 (ISBN 0-86068-275-7, Pub. by Virago Pr). Merrimack Pub Cir.

Dazai, Osamu. No Longer Human. Keene, Donald, tr. from Jap. & intro. by. LC 58-9509. 192p. 1973. pap. 5.95 (ISBN 0-8112-0481-2, NDP357). New Directions.

--Return to Tsugaru: Travels of a Purple Tramp. LC 84-48694. 216p. 1985. 16.95 (ISBN 0-87011-686-X). Kodansha.

--The Setting Sun. rev. ed. Keene, Donald, tr. from Japanese. LC 56-13350. (Illus.). 1968. pap. 4.95 (ISBN 0-8112-0032-9, NDP258). New Directions.

Daze. Practical Guide to Neonatal Nursing. (Illus.). 288p. 1984. pap. text ed. 24.00 (ISBN 0-8391-1875-9, 19453). Univ Park.

Daze, Ann M. & Scanlon, John W. Code Pink: A Practical System for Neonatal-Perinatal Resuscitation. (Illus.). 168p. 1981. pap. text ed. 20.00 (ISBN 0-8391-1670-5). Univ Park.

Dazeley, G. H. Organic Chemistry. LC 69-10061. 1969. text ed. 19.95x (ISBN 0-521-07171-2). Cambridge U Pr.

D'Azevedo, Warren L. The Artist Archetype in Gola Culture. 1970. 3.50 (ISBN 0-686-11766-2). Liberian Studies.

--Straight with the Medicine: Narratives of Washoe Followers of the Tipi Way. (Illus.). 64p. (Orig.). 1985. pap. 5.95 (ISBN 0-930588-19-3). Heyday Bks.

Dazhina, I. M., et al, eds. see Kollantai, Alexandra.

D'Azzo, John & Houpis, Constantine. Linear Control System Analysis & Design. 2nd ed. (Electrical Engineering Ser.). (Illus.). 864p. 1981. text ed. 45.00 (ISBN 0-07-016183-6). McGraw.

D'Azzo, John J. & Houpis, Constantine. Feedback Control System Analysis & Synthesis. 2nd ed. (Electronic & Electrical Engineering Ser.). 1966. text ed. 45.00 (ISBN 0-07-016175-5). McGraw.

D'Bulow, Henri. Prescription for Success: How to Become Successful. Hartmann, Hans W., ed. LC 81-52564. 128p. (Orig.). 1982. 12.95 (ISBN 0-940656-01-9); pap. 9.95 (ISBN 0-940656-00-0). Ultima Corp.

D'Campo, G. Basic Technical Drawing. (Illus.). 376p. 1977. pap. 15.95x (ISBN 0-86125-432-5, Pub by Orient Longman India). Apt Bks.

D'Costa, David, jt. auth. see Tarlov, Edward.

D'Cruz, E. India: The Quest for Nationhood. 1967. 6.25 (ISBN 0-89684-558-3). Orient Bk Dist.

D'Cruz, Fleck. Canada Can Compete: Strategic Management of the Canadian Industrial Portfolio. 1985. pap. text ed. 18.00x (ISBN 0-88645-020-9, Pub. by Inst Res Pub Canada). Brookfield Pub Co.

D'Cruz, Fvan C. All about High Blood Pressure. 224p. 1979. 30.00x (ISBN 0-86125-006-0, Pub. by Orient Longman India). State Mutual Bk.

D'Cruz, Ivan. Echocardiographic Diagnosis. 1983. write for info. (ISBN 0-02-326120-X). MacMillan.

D-Din-Ahmed, Shemsu see Ahmed, Shemsu-D-Din.

DDR Central Statistical Board. Statistical Pocket Book of the German Democratic Republic, 1982. 27th ed. LC 63-47828. (Illus.). 160p. 1982. 7.50x (ISBN 0-8002-3128-7). Intl Pubns Serv.

De, Amalendu. Islam in Modern India. 1984. 21.00x (ISBN 0-8364-1128-5, Pub. by UK Paul). South Asia Bks.

De, Francois R. European Security & France. Nice, Richard, tr. from Fr. LC 84-8780. 162p. 1984. 19.95x (ISBN 0-252-01176-7). U of Ill Pr.

De, Ira. The Hunt & Other Poems. 8.00 (ISBN 0-89253-467-2); flexible cloth 4.00 (ISBN 0-89253-468-0). Ind-US Inc.

De, La Mare Peter see De La Mare, Peter.

De La Rive Box. Illustrated Lamborghini Buyer's Guide. (Buyer's Guide Ser). (Illus.). 160p. 1983. pap. 13.95 (ISBN 0-87938-173-6). Motorbooks Intl.

De, La Ronciere see De La Ronciere & Delort.

De, Nitish, et al. Managing & Developing New Forms of Work Organization. (Management Development Ser.: No. 16). (Illus.). 158p. (Orig.). 1980. pap. 11.40 (ISBN 92-2-102145-9). Intl Labour Office.

De, Nitish R. Alternative Designs of Human Organizations. 1985. 25.00 (ISBN 0-8039-9480-X). Sage.

De, P. Waard-Dekking see De Jonge, Mrs. P.

De, Riet Vernon Van see Van De Riet, Vernon, et al.

De, S. C. Public Speeches in Ancient & Medieval India. 1977. 9.00x (ISBN 0-686-22669-0). Intl Bk Dist.

De, S. K. Bengal's Contribution to Sanskrit Literature & Studies in Bengal Vaisnavism. 150p. 1974. Repr. 4.00 (ISBN 0-88065-047-8, Pub. by Messers Today Tomorrows Printers & Publishers India). Scholarly Pubns.

--History of Sanskrit Poetics. LC 76-911225. 1976. Repr. of 1960 ed. 18.50x (ISBN 0-88386-853-9). South Asia Bks.
--Some Problems of Sanskrit Poetics. 1981. 12.00x (ISBN 0-8364-0733-4, Pub. by Mukhopadhyay). South Asia Bks.
--Treatment of Love in Sanskrit Literature. 87p. 1983. Repr. of 1929 ed. text ed. 16.25x (ISBN 0-391-03321-2, Pub. by Cosmo India). Humanities.
De, Schaps H. see Schutz, Albert & Schaps, Hilda W.
Dea, Kay & Sixth NASW Professional Symposium, 1979, eds. Perspectives for the Future: Social Work Practice in the 80s. LC 80-83988. 192p. (Orig.). 1980. pap. text ed. 12.95x (ISBN 0-87101-089-5). Natl Assn Soc Wkrs.
De Abajian, James T., ed. Blacks in Selected Newspapers, Censuses & Other Sources, an Index to Names & Subjects. 1977. lib. bdg. 335.00 (ISBN 0-8161-0056-X, Hall Library). G K Hall.
De Aberle, S. B. The Pueblo Indians of New Mexico: Their Land, Economy & Civil Organization. LC 49-2640. (American Anthropological Association Memoirs). Repr. of 1948 ed. 11.00 (ISBN 0-527-00569-X). Kraus Repr.
De Acha, Eduardo. Marxismo y Derecho. LC 84-72917. (Coleccion Cuba y sus Jueces Ser.). 158p. (Orig.). 1985. pap. 9.95 (ISBN 0-89729-364-9). Ediciones.
--Una Nota de Derecho Penal. LC 82-71757. 184p. (Orig., Span.). 1982. 12.95 (ISBN 0-89729-314-2). Ediciones.
--Pesimismo. LC 83-82918. 112p. (Orig., Span.). 1984. pap. 5.00 (ISBN 0-89729-340-1). Ediciones.
Deacon, Alan. In Search of the Scrounger. 110p. 1976. pap. text ed. 7.50x (ISBN 0-7135-1992-4, Pub. by Bedford England). Brookfield Pub Co.
Deacon, G., jt. ed. see Charnock, H.
Deacon, G. E. R. & Deacon, Margaret B., eds. Modern Concepts of Oceanography. LC 81-6239. (Benchmark Papers in Geology Ser.: Vol. 61). 386p. 1982. 48.95 (ISBN 0-87933-390-1). Van Nos Reinhold.
Deacon, Gene E. Kid Tested Menus with Kitchen & Lunchroom Techniques for Day Care Centers. LC 81-90547. (Illus.). 120p. (Orig.). 1981. pap. 10.00 (ISBN 0-941790-01-0). Gold Crest.
--Secrets to Day School Success. (Illus.). 242p. (Orig.). 1979. pap. 14.95 (ISBN 0-941790-00-2). Gold Crest.
Deacon, George. The Antarctic Circumpolar Ocean. (Studies in Polar Research). (Illus.). 170p. 1985. 24.95 (ISBN 0-521-25410-8). Cambridge U Pr.
--John Clare & the Folk Tradition. 288p. 1982. 55.00x (ISBN 0-86300-008-8, Pub. by Sinclair Browne Arch England). State Mutual Bk.
Deacon, J. W. Introduction to Modern Mycology. 2nd ed. (Illus.). 272p. 1984. pap. 15.95x (ISBN 0-632-01156-4). Blackwell Pubns.
Deacon, James E. Fish Populations, Following a Drought, in the Neosho & Marais Des Cygnes Rivers of Kansas. (Museum Ser.: Vol. 13, No. 9). 69p. 1961. pap. 3.75 (ISBN 0-686-79822-8). U of KS Mus Nat Hist.
Deacon, James E. & Metcalf, Artie L. Fishes of the Wakarusa River in Kansas. (Museum Ser.: Vol. 13, No. 6). 14p. 1961. 1.25 (ISBN 0-317-04824-4). U of KS Mus Nat Hist.
Deacon, Joe. Winding Down a Psychiatric Private Practice. LC 85-7341. (Private Practice Monograph). 112p. 1985. pap. text ed. 15.00x (ISBN 0-88048-103-X, 48-103-X). Am Psychiatric.
Deacon, John. Tobacco Tortured, or the Filthie Fume of Tobacco Refined. LC 68-54634. (English Experience Ser.: No. 42). 194p. 1968. Repr. of 1616 ed. 21.00 (ISBN 90-221-0042-1). Walter J Johnson.
Deacon, John & Walker, John. Dialogicall Discourses of Spirits & Devils, Declaring Their Proper Essence. LC 76-57377. (English Experience Ser.: No. 795). 1977. Repr. of 1601 ed. lib. bdg. 37.00 (ISBN 90-221-0795-7). Walter J Johnson.
Deacon, Margaret B. Oceanography: Concepts & History. LC 76-27682. (Benchmark Papers in Geology Ser.: Vol. 35). 1978. 44.50 (ISBN 0-87933-202-6). Van Nos Reinhold.
Deacon, Margaret B., jt. ed. see Deacon, G. E. R.
Deacon, Renee M. Bernard Shaw As Artist-Philosopher: An Exposition of Shavianism. LC 74-990. 1973. Repr. of 1910 ed. lib. bdg. 10.00 (ISBN 0-8414-3717-3). Folcroft.
Deacon, Richard. The Chinese Secret Service. LC 74-5817. (Illus.). 544p. 1974. 14.95 (ISBN 0-8008-1478-9). Taplinger.
--Escape! 192p. 1980. 42.00x (ISBN 0-563-17772-1, Pub. by BBC Pubns). State Mutual Bk.
--A History of the British Secret Service. 6.95 (ISBN 0-586-05116-3). Academy Chi Pubs.
--The Israeli Secret Service. 2nd ed ed. LC 78-5685. (Illus.). 326p. 1985. pap. 3.95 (ISBN 0-8008-4268-5). Taplinger.
--Kempei Tai: A History of the Japanese Secret Service. LC 82-20564. (Illus.). 306p. 14.95 (ISBN 0-8253-0131-9). Beaufort Bks NY.
--Kempei Tai: A History of the Japanese Secret Service. 320p. 1985. pap. 3.95 (ISBN 0-425-07458-7). Berkley Pub.
--Microwave Cookery. 1978. pap. 3.95 (ISBN 0-553-24021-8). Bantam.
--Napoleon's Book of Fate. Orig. Title: The Book of Fate: Its Origins & Uses. 1977. 10.00 (ISBN 0-8065-0564-8); pap. 4.95 (ISBN 0-8065-0577-X). Citadel Pr.
--Richard Deacon's Microwave Cookery. LC 73-93782. (Illus.). 160p. 1977. pap. 7.95 (ISBN 0-912656-73-5). H P Bks.
--William Caxton: The First English Editor, Printer, Merchant & Translator. (Illus.). 198p. 1976. 18.50x (ISBN 0-8476-6030-3). Rowman.
Deacon, Richard & West, Nigel. Spy! 192p. 1980. 30.00x (ISBN 0-563-17729-2, Pub. by BBC Pubns). State Mutual Bk.
Deacon, Robert T. & Johnson, Bruce M. Forestlands: Public & Private. LC 84-22699. (Illus.). 360p. 1985. pap. 12.95 (ISBN 0-88410-392-7). PIPPR.
Deacon, Ruth E. & Firebaugh, Francille M. Family Resource Management: Principles & Applications. 369p. 1980. text ed. 29.95x (ISBN 0-205-06994-0, 4569946, Pub. by Longwood Div); tchr's. manual (ISBN 0-205-07000-0, 457000); instrs' manual (ISBN 0-205-07000-0). Allyn.
De Acosta, Joseph. The Natural & Moral History of the Indies, 2 Vols. Markham, Clements R., ed. LC 75-134715. (Hakluyt Society Ser.: No. 60-61). 1970. Set. lib. bdg. 60.50 (ISBN 0-8337-0798-1). B Franklin.
De Acosta, Mercedes. Here Lies the Heart. LC 75-13709. (Homosexuality). 1975. Repr. of 1960 ed. 18.00x (ISBN 0-405-07360-7). Ayer Co Pubs.
Deady, Matthew P. Pharisee Among Philistines: The Diary of Judge Matthew P. Deady, 1871-1892, 2 vols. Clark, Malcolm, Jr., intro. by. LC 74-75363. (Illus.). 702p. 1975. 27.95 (ISBN 0-87595-046-9); deluxe ed. 30.00 (ISBN 0-686-96825-5); pap. 21.95 (ISBN 0-87595-080-9). Oreg Hist Soc.
Deag, John. Social Behavior of Animals. (Studies in Biology: No. 118). 96p. 1980. pap. text ed. 8.95 (ISBN 0-7131-2770-8). E Arnold.
Deagan, Kathleen, ed. Spanish St. Augustine: The Archaeology of a Colonial Creole Community (Monographs) (Studies in Historical Archaeology). 1983. 39.50 (ISBN 0-12-207880-2). Acad Pr.
Deagan, Kathleen A. Archaeology at the National Greek Orthodox Shrine, St. Augustine, Florida: Microchange in 18th Century Spanish Colonial Material Culture. LC 76-31. (Illus.). 1976. 7.50 (ISBN 0-8130-0555-8). U Presses Fla.
Deaglio, Mario. Private Enterprise & Public Emulation. (Institute of Economic Affairs, Research Monographs: No. 5). pap. 2.50 technical (ISBN 0-255-69593-4). Transatlantic.
Deagon, Ann. Carbon Fourteen. LC 74-79483. 72p. 1974. 7.50x (ISBN 0-87023-170-7); pap. 4.00 (ISBN 0-87023-171-5). U of Mass Pr.
--The Diver's Tomb. 192p. 1984. 13.95 (ISBN 0-312-21378-6, Pub. by Marek). St Martin.
--Habitats. LC 82-84084. 1982. 12.00 (ISBN 0-940580-24-1); pap. 6.00 (ISBN 0-940580-25-X). Green River.
--The Pentekontaetia: The Great Fifty Years. (Orig.). 1985. special ed. 25.00 (ISBN 0-317-17613-7); pap. 6.00 (ISBN 0-931956-21-8). Water Mark.
--Poetics South. LC 74-21265. 54p. 1974. 7.95 (ISBN 0-910244-83-9). Blair.
--There Is No Balm in Birmingham. LC 75-41623. (Third Godine Poetry Chapbook Ser.). 1978. 5.00 (ISBN 0-87923-177-7). Godine.
De Aguiar, Ricardo W., tr. see Furtado, Celso.
De Ajuriaguerra, J. Handbook of Child Psychiatry & Psychology. Lorion, Raymond P., tr. LC 80-80094. 678p. 1980. text ed. 34.50x (ISBN 0-89352-031-4). Masson Pub.
Deak, Edit. Rope Drawings by Patrick Ireland: An Exhibition. (Illus.). 32p. 1977. pap. 3.00x (ISBN 0-934418-04-7). La Jolla Mus Contemp Art.
Deak, Etienne & Deak, Simone. Dictionnaire des Americanismes. 6th ed. 928p. (Fr.). 1974. 25.00 (ISBN 0-686-56976-8, M-6103). French & Eur.
Deak, Francis, jt. auth. see Shotwell, James T.
Deak, Francis & Jessup, Philip, eds. A Collection of Neutrality Laws, Regulations & Treaties of Various Countries, 2 vols. LC 70-138607. 1970. Repr. of 1939 ed. lib. bdg. 53.00x (ISBN 0-8371-5715-3, DENL). Greenwood.
Deak, Gloria-Gilda. American Views: Prospects & Vistas. LC 76-40041. (Illus.). 134p. 1976. 25.00 (ISBN 0-87104-263-0). NY Pub Lib.
Deak, Istvan. Everyman in Europe: Essays in Social History, Vol. 1. 224p. 1981. pap. text ed. 17.95 (ISBN 0-13-293621-6). P-H.
--The Lawful Revolution: Louis Kossuth & the Hungarians, 1848-1849. LC 78-22063. Orig. Title: Reluctant Rebels. (Illus.). 416p. 1979. 29.00x (ISBN 0-231-04602-2). Columbia U Pr.
Deak, Simone, jt. auth. see Deak, Etienne.
De'ak, Stephen. David Popper: Violoncello Virtuoso & Composer. (Illus.). 320p. 1980. 17.95 (ISBN 0-87666-621-7, Z-32). Paganiniana Pubns.
Deakin, Alfred. Crisis in Victorian Politics, 1879-1881. 1957. 8.00x (ISBN 0-522-83582-1, Pub. by Melbourne U Pr). Intl Spec Bk.
--Federated Australia. LaNauze, T. A., ed. 1968. 20.00x (ISBN 0-522-83842-1, Pub. by Melbourne U Pr Australia). Intl Spec Bk.
Deakin, B. M. & Pratten, C. F. Effects of the Temporary Employment Subsidy. LC 81-10239. (Department of Applied Economics Occasional Paper Ser.: No. 53). (Illus.). 256p. 1982. 34.50 (ISBN 0-521-24358-0). Cambridge U Pr.
Deakin, Edward B. & Maher, Michael W. Cost Accounting. 1984. 33.95x (ISBN 0-256-02789-7); study guide 11.95x (ISBN 0-256-02790-0). Irwin.
Deakin, James. Lobbyists. 1966. 9.00 (ISBN 0-8183-0180-5). Pub Aff Pr.
--Straight Stuff: The Reporters, the Government & the Truth. LC 83-19521. 386p. 1984. 17.95 (ISBN 0-688-02204-9). Morrow.
Deakin, James, jt. auth. see Cormier, Frank.
Deakin, Joan. Scuba Diving. (Illus.). 160p. 1981. 11.95 (ISBN 0-7153-7952-6). David & Charles.
Deakin, Mary H. The Early Life of George Eliot. 188p. 1980. Repr. of 1913 ed. lib. bdg. 30.00 (ISBN 0-8495-1121-6). Arden Lib.
--The Early Life of George Eliot. 1973. Repr. of 1913 ed. 30.00 (ISBN 0-8492-0681-2). R West.
Deakin, Michael, jt. auth. see Frost, David.
Deakin, Motley F. Rebecca West. (English Authors Ser.). 1980. 13.50 (ISBN 0-8057-6788-6, Twayne). G K Hall.
Deakin, Nicholas & Ungerson, Clare. Leaving London: Planned Mobility & the Inner City. LC 78-307623. 1977. text ed. 40.00x (ISBN 0-435-85930-7). Gower Pub Co.
Deakin, Rose. Database Primer: An Easy-to-Understand Guide to Database Management Systems. (Plume Computer Bks.). (Illus.). 128p. 1984. pap. 9.95 (ISBN 0-452-25492-2, Plume). NAL.
--Understanding Microcomputers: An Introduction to the New Personal Computers for Home & Office. 1983. pap. 3.50 (ISBN 0-451-12427-8, Sig). NAL.
Deakin, Rose & Willmot, Phyllis. Participation in Local Social Services: An Explanatory Study - Discussion Paper. 1979. 22.00x (ISBN 0-317-05800-2, Pub. by Natl Inst Social Work). State Mutual Bk.
Deakin, T. Testament of a Roach-Eating Saint. 64p. 1973. text ed. 8.00x (ISBN 0-900821-18-3, Pub. by C Woolf UK). Humanities.
Deakins, Roger L., tr. see Heywood, Ellis.
Deal, jt. auth. see Barth.
Deal, Alice B., jt. ed. see Mihalyka, Jean M.
Deal, Babs. Friendships, Secrets & Lies. 1979. pap. 2.25 (ISBN 0-449-24253-6, Crest). Fawcett.
Deal, Jacquelyn see Meltzer, Lawrence.
Deal, S. A Season of Letters. write for info. (ISBN 0-943216-01-X). MoonsQuilt Pr.
Deal, Samuel J., et al. Experimental Microbiology for the Health Sciences. 4th ed. 1976. spiral bdg. 14.95x (ISBN 0-8087-0436-2). Burgess.
Deal, Shirley H. The Cruising Cook. LC 77-78074. 288p. 1977. polyvinyl 3-ring notebook 15.95 (ISBN 0-930006-00-3). S Deal Assoc.
Deal, Susan S. The Dark Is a Door. Burmaster, O., ed. (Ahsahta Press Modern & Contemporary Poetry of the West Ser.). 50p. (Orig.). 1984. pap. 3.00 (ISBN 0-916272-25-7). Ahsahta Pr.
--No Moving Parts. 2nd ed. Burmaster, O., ed. LC 80-67909. (Ahsahta Press Modern & Contemporary Poets of the West Ser.). 60p. 1980. pap. 3.00 (ISBN 0-916272-15-X). Ahsahta Pr.
Deal, Terrence & Nolan, Robert, eds. Alternative Schools: Ideologies, Realities, Guidelines. LC 78-18505. (Illus.). 336p. 1978. 25.95x (ISBN 0-88229-383-4); pap. 13.95x (ISBN 0-88229-613-2). Nelson-Hall.
Deal, Terrence, jt. ed. see Baldridge, J. Victor.
Deal, Terrence E. & Kennedy, Allan A. Corporate Cultures: The Rites & Rituals of Corporate Life. 1984. pap. 8.95 (ISBN 0-201-10287-0). Addison-Wesley.
Deal, Terrence E., jt. auth. see Bolman, Lee G.
Deal, William. God's Answer for the Unequally Yoked. LC 80-67387. 96p. 1980. pap. 2.95 (ISBN 0-89107-182-2). Good News.
Deal, William S. After Death, What? 1977. 1.75 (ISBN 0-686-19329-6). Crusade Pubs.
--Battling with the Devil & Depression. 1975. pap. 1.95 (ISBN 0-686-11024-2). Crusade Pubs.
--Christian's Daily Manna. 0.95 (ISBN 0-686-13721-3). Crusade Pubs.
--Daily Christian Living. LC 62-22195. 1962. pap. 0.95 (ISBN 0-686-05840-2). Crusade Pubs.
--Faith, Facts & Feelings. 3rd ed. 1978. pap. 0.95 (ISBN 0-686-05527-6). Crusade Pubs.
--The Furnace of Affliction. 6th ed. 1978. 1.50 (ISBN 0-686-05833-X). Crusade Pubs.
--Happiness & Harmony in Marriage. pap. 2.95 (ISBN 0-686-13723-X). Crusade Pubs.
--Heart Talks on the Deeper Life. 1960. 1.50 (ISBN 0-686-05838-0). Crusade Pubs.
--How May I Know I Am Saved? 1973. pap. 0.60, 3 for 1.50, 5 for 2.50, 10 for 5.00 (ISBN 0-686-05834-8). Crusade Pubs.
--The March of Holiness Through the Centuries. 1978. pap. 2.50 (ISBN 0-686-05528-4). Crusade Pubs.
--New Light on the Shepherd Psalm. 1982. 3.95. Crusade Pubs.
--The Other Shepherd. 1982. 1.95 (ISBN 0-686-38053-3). Crusade Pubs.
--Picking a Partner. 2.95 (ISBN 0-686-13716-7). Crusade Pubs.
--Pictorial Introduction to the Bible. (Baker's Paperback Reference Library). 440p. 1982. pap. 12.95 (ISBN 0-8010-2926-0). Baker Bk.
--Pictorial Introduction to the Bible. large print 12.95 (ISBN 0-686-13725-6); pap. 7.95. Crusade Pubs.
--A Pictorial Introduction to the Bible. LC 67-20517. 438p. 1982. pap. 12.95 (ISBN 0-89081-363-9). Harvest Hse.
--Problems of the Spirit-Filled Life. 2.95 (ISBN 0-686-13724-8). Crusade Pubs.
--The Tinker of Bedford: A Historical Fiction on the Life & Times of John Bunyan. 1977. pap. 3.50 (ISBN 0-686-19330-X). Crusade Pubs.
--What Every Young Christian Should Know. 1982. 1.95. Crusade Pubs.
--Workmen of God. 1975. pap. 0.95 (ISBN 0-686-11025-0). Crusade Pubs.
Deal, Zack J., III. Serf & State Peasant Agriculture: Kharkov Province, 1842-1861. Bruchey, Stuart, ed. LC 80-2803. (Dissertations in European Economic History II). (Illus.). 1981. lib. bdg. 43.00x (ISBN 0-405-13987-X). Ayer Co Pubs.
De Alba, Joaquin. Violence in America: De Tocqueville's America Revisited. LC 70-75126. 1969. pap. 3.95 (ISBN 0-87491-120-6). Acropolis.
De Albertis, Gustave G. The Dollar & the Approaching Collapse of the United States & of the World Economies. (Illus.). 131p. 1984. 137.45x (ISBN 0-86722-071-6). Inst Econ Pol.
De Alcantara, Cynthia H. Anthropological Perspectives on Rural Mexico. (International Library of Anthropology). 245p. 1984. 32.95x (ISBN 0-7100-9923-1). Routledge & Kegan.
De Alcedo, Antonio. Geographical & Historical Dictionary of America & the West Indies, 5 Vols. Thompson, George A., tr. LC 70-146788. (Research & Source Works Ser: No. 627). 1971. Repr. of 1812 ed. Set. lib. bdg. 220.00 (ISBN 0-8337-3525-X). B Franklin.
De Alcega, Juan. A Tailor's Pattern Book: From Spain in the Year 1589. 279p. limited ed 35.00x (ISBN 0-318-01133-6). Robin & Russ.
Deale, Edgar. Catalogue of Contemporary Irish Composers. 2nd ed. 80p. 1973. lib. bdg. 8.50 (ISBN 0-85342-464-0, Pub. by Mercier Pr Ireland). Irish Bk Ctr.
De Alencar, Jose M. see Alencar, Jose M. de.
De Alessi, Louis. Some Economic Aspects of Government Ownership & Regulation: Essays From Economia Pubblica. LC 82-84249. (LEC Occasional Paper). 40p. 1983. pap. 3.00 (ISBN 0-916770-12-5). Law & Econ U Miami.
Dealey, J. Q. Growth of American State Constitutions. LC 75-124891. (American Constitutional & Legal History Ser). 308p. 1972. Repr. of 1915 ed. lib. bdg. 39.50 (ISBN 0-306-71985-1). Da Capo.
Dealey, James Q. Sociology: Its Development & Applications. 1920. 25.00 (ISBN 0-8482-7751-1). Norwood Edns.
--Sociology: Its Simpler Teachings & Applications. 1978. Repr. of 1909 ed. lib. bdg. 25.00 (ISBN 0-8492-0684-7). R West.
Dealey, Ted. Diaper Days of Dallas. LC 75-11544. (Illus.). 192p. 1975. Repr. of 1966 ed. 12.50 (ISBN 0-87074-140-3). SMU Press.
De Almeida, Hermione. Byron & Joyce Through Homer: Don Juan & Ulysses. 256p. 1981. 25.00x (ISBN 0-231-05092-5). Columbia U Pr.
De Alonso, Irma T. see Dutta, Manoranjan & Alonso, Irma T.
De Alteriis, Anthony, tr. see Mejetta, M. & Spada, S.
Dealtry, William. The Laborer: A Remedy for His Wrongs. LC 76-89729. (American Labor, from Conspiracy to Collective Bargaining Ser). 420p. 1969. Repr. of 1869 ed. 23.50 (ISBN 0-405-02116-X). Ayer Co Pubs.
De Alvarado, Pedro. An Account of the Conquest of Guatemala in 1524. Mackie, Sedley J., ed. (Cortes Society Ser.). 1924. 18.00 (ISBN 0-527-19723-8). Kraus Repr.
--An Account of the Conquest of Guatemala in 1524. Mackie, Sedley J., ed. LC 77-88568. 1977. Repr. of 1924 ed. lib. bdg. 15.00 (ISBN 0-89341-275-9). Longwood Pub Group.
De Alvarez, Josefina R. Dictionary of Puerto Rican Literature, 2 vols. (Puerto Rico Ser.). 1979. Set. lib. bdg. 250.00 (ISBN 0-8490-2906-6). Gordon Pr.
DeAlvarez, Leo P., ed. see Berns, Laurence, et al.
De Alvarez, Leo P., tr. see Machiavelli, Niccolo.
De Alvarez, Russell R., ed. The Kidney in Pregnancy. LC 76-13184. (Wiley Clinical Obstetrics & Gynecology Ser.). Repr. of 1976 ed. 62.30 (ISBN 0-8357-9919-0, 2015190). Bks Demand UMI.
--Textbook of Gynecology. LC 76-10816. pap. 140.50 (ISBN 0-317-28609-9, 2055418). Bks Demand UMI.
Dealy, John M. Rheometers for Molten Plastics: A Practical Guide to Testing & Property Measurement. 300p. 1981. 39.50 (ISBN 0-442-21874-5). Van Nos Reinhold.
Dealy, Ross. The Politics of An Erasmian Lawyer: Vasco de Quiroga. (Humana Civilitas Ser.: Vol.3). 34p. 1976. pap. 4.90x (ISBN 0-89003-015-4). Undena Pubns.
Deam, C. C. Flora of Indiana. 1981. Repr. of 1940 ed. 32.50 (ISBN 3-7682-0696-3). Lubrecht & Cramer.
--Flora of Indiana. (Reprints of U. S. Floras Ser.: Vol. 6). (Illus.). 1236p. 1984. lib. bdg. 35.00 (ISBN 3-7682-0696-3). Lubrecht & Cramer.
Deamer, David. Being Human. 1981. text ed. 32.95 (ISBN 0-03-022076-9, CBS C); instr's manual 19.95 (ISBN 0-03-045036-5). SCP.

Deamer, David W., ed. Light Transducing Membranes: Structure, Function & Evolution. 1978. 44.00 (ISBN 0-12-207650-8). Acad Pr.

Deamer, Elizabeth T. Olga's Prelude to Wine for the Thirsty Beginner. Schpitfeir, Olga, ed. (Illus.). 96p. (Orig.). 1985. pap. 7.95 (ISBN 0-9607330-1-9). Schpitfeir.

De Amicis, E. Spain & the Spaniards, 2 vols. 1976. lib. bdg. 250.00 (ISBN 0-8490-2639-3). Gordon Pr.

De Amicis, Edmondo. Holland & Its People. Tilton, Caroline, tr. from It. LC 72-3433. (Essay Index Reprint Ser.). Repr. of 1880 ed. 36.50 (ISBN 0-8369-2887-3). Ayer Co Pubs.

--Morocco: Its People & Places, 2 vols. 1976. lib. bdg. 250.00 (ISBN 0-8490-2282-7). Gordon Pr.

--Studies of Paris. LC 72-3348. (Essay Index Reprint Ser.). Repr. of 1879 ed. 19.00 (ISBN 0-8369-2888-1). Ayer Co Pubs.

Deamicis, Edmondo. Studies of Paris: (Victor Hugo, Emile Zola) 276p. 1981. Repr. of 1882 ed. lib. bdg. 35.00 (ISBN 0-8495-1062-7). Arden Lib.

Dean. Careers with an Airline. (Early Career Ser.). (Illus.). 32p. (gr. k-3). pap. 2.95 (ISBN 0-317-31307-X). Creative Ed.

Dean & Acuff. The S.D.N. Theory of Music. pap. 1.95 (ISBN 0-88027-058-6). Firm Foun Pub.

Dean, jt. auth. see Haddad, A.

Dean, A. C., et al, eds. Continuous Culture: Applications & New Fields. (Continuous Culture Ser.). 364p. 1976. 62.95 (ISBN 0-470-98984-X). Halsted Pr.

--Continuous Culture: Biotechnology, Environmental & Medical Applications, No. 8. 322p. 1984. 84.95x (ISBN 0-470-20042-1). Halsted Pr.

Dean, A. E., ed. see Didactic Systems, Inc.

Dean, A. E., ed. see National Bureau of Standards.

Dean, A. E., ed. see NFPA.

Dean, A. E., ed. see Purington, Robert & Patterson, Wade.

Dean, A. E., ed. see Urban Institute, NFPA.

Dean, Alan H., jt. auth. see McDonald, Jack R.

Dean, Alexander & Carra, Lawrence. Fundamental of Play Directing. 4th ed. LC 79-26236. 417p. 1980. text ed. 25.95 (ISBN 0-03-021551-X, HoltC). HR&W.

Dean, Alfred, ed. Depression in Multidisciplinary Perspective. 275p. 1985. 27.50 (ISBN 0-87630-370-X). Brunner-Mazel.

Dean, Amy, ed. see Bugbee, Percy.

Dean, Amy E. & Tower, Keith. Fire Protection Guide on Hazardous Materials. 7th ed. LC 78-59832. 1978. pap. 12.50 (ISBN 0-87765-130-2, SPP-1D). Natl Fire Prot.

Dean, Amy E., ed. Flash Point Index of Trade Liquids. 9th ed. LC 78-54003. 1978. pap. text ed. 5.50 (ISBN 0-87765-127-2, SPP-51). Natl Fire Prot.

--State Fire Marshals Conference Report. LC 77-87129. 1977. pap. text ed. 7.50 (ISBN 0-87765-110-8). Natl Fire Prot.

Dean, Amy E., ed. see Best, Richard L.

Dean, Amy E., ed. see Dixon, Robert G., Jr.

Dean, Amy E., ed. see NFPA Technical Reference Library.

Dean, Amy E., ed. see NFPA & U.S. Department of Transportation.

Dean, Anabel. Bats the Night Fliers. LC 73-11975. (General Juvenile Bks). (Illus.). 32p. (gr. 7 up). 1974. PLB 5.95 (ISBN 0-8225-0291-7). Lerner Pubns.

--Fire! How Do They Fight It? LC 77-17635. (Illus.). 1978. text ed. 9.95 (ISBN 0-664-32626-9). Westminster.

--Going Underground: All about Caves & Caving. LC 83-23232. (Doing & Learning Bks). (Illus.). 144p. (gr. 5 up). 1984. PLB 10.95 (ISBN 0-87518-255-0). Dillon.

--Plants That Eat Insects: A Look at Carnivorous Plants. LC 75-38480. (Science Books for Young People). (Illus.). (gr. 5-12). 1977. PLB 5.95 (ISBN 0-8225-0299-2). Lerner Pubns.

--Strange Partners: The Story of Symbiosis. LC 75-38479. (Science Books for Young People). (Illus.). (gr. 5-12). 1976. PLB 5.95 (ISBN 0-8225-1100-2). Lerner Pubns.

--Up, Up, & Away! The Story of Ballooning. LC 79-23427. (Illus.). 192p. 1980. Westminster.

--Wind Sports. LC 82-13460. (Illus.). 170p. (gr. 5-9). 12.95 (ISBN 0-664-32696-X). Westminster.

Dean, Andrew. Wages & Earnings. (Reviews of United Kingdom Statistical Sources Ser.: Vol. XIII). 1980. 53.00 (ISBN 0-08-024060-7). Pergamon.

Dean, Ann, jt. auth. see Schechter, Alan N.

Dean, Audrey Vincente. Wooden Spoon Puppets. LC 75-28202. (Illus.). 1976. 10.95 (ISBN 0-8238-0204-3). Plays.

Dean, B. Introduction to Strong Interactions. 394p. 1976. 74.25 (ISBN 0-677-02750-8). Gordon.

Dean, B. & Goldhar, J., eds. Management of Research & Innovation. (TIMS Studies in the Management Sciences: Vol. 15). 300p. 1981. 32.50 (ISBN 0-444-86009-6, North-Holland). Elsevier.

Dean, Barbara. Wellspring: A Story from the Deep Country. LC 79-2606. (Illus.). 208p. 1979. pap. 6.00 (ISBN 0-933280-01-7). Island CA.

Dean, Bashford. A Bibliography of Fishes, 3 vols. 1973. Set. 112.00 (ISBN 3-87429-036-0). Lubrecht & Cramer.

Dean, Beryl. Embroidery in Religion & Ceremonial. (Illus.). 288p. 1982. 37.50 (ISBN 0-7134-3325-6). Branford.

Dean, Bessie. Aprendamos el Plan de Dios. Balderas, Eduardo, tr. from Eng. LC 80-82256. (Books for LDS Children Ser.). Orig. Title: Let's Learn God's Plan. (Illus.). 64p. (Orig., Span.). (gr. k-3). 1980. pap. text ed. 3.95 (ISBN 0-88290-135-4). Horizon Utah.

--God Hears My Prayers. (Children's Inspirational Coloring Bk.). (Illus.). (ps-3). 1978. pap. 1.25 (ISBN 0-88290-110-9). Horizon Utah.

--God Loves Me. (Children's Inspirational Coloring Bk.). (Illus.). (ps-3). 1979. pap. 1.25 (ISBN 0-88290-108-7). Horizon Utah.

--I'm Happy When I'm Good. (Children's Inspirational Coloring Bk.). (Illus.). (ps-3). 1979. pap. 1.25 (ISBN 0-88290-109-5). Horizon Utah.

--It's Fun to Read the Bible. (Children's Inspirational Coloring Bk.). (Illus.). (ps-3). 1979. pap. 1.25 (ISBN 0-88290-112-5). Horizon Utah.

--Lessons Jesus Taught. (Children's Inspirational Coloring Books). (Illus.). 72p. (Orig.). (gr. k-5). 1980. pap. 2.50 (ISBN 0-88290-146-X). Horizon Utah.

--Let's Choose the Right. LC 76-29302. (Books for LDS Children Ser.). (Illus.). (ps-3). 1976. pap. 3.95 (ISBN 0-88290-072-2). Horizon Utah.

--Let's Go to Church. LC 76-3995. (Books for Lds Children Ser.). (Illus.). 64p. (ps-3). 1976. pap. 3.95 (ISBN 0-88290-062-5). Horizon Utah.

--Let's Learn About Jesus: A Child's Coloring Book of the Life of Christ. (Children's Inspirational Coloring Bk.). (Illus.). (ps-6). 1979. pap. 2.50 (ISBN 0-88290-131-1). Horizon Utah.

--Let's Learn God's Plan. LC 78-52114. (Illus.). 1978. pap. 3.95 (ISBN 0-88290-092-7). Horizon Utah.

--Let's Learn of God's Love. LC 79-89367. (Books for LDS Children). (Illus.). (ps-3). 1979. pap. 3.95 (ISBN 0-88290-124-9). Horizon Utah.

--Let's Learn the First Principles. LC 78-70366. (Books for LDS Children). (Illus.). (ps-3). 1978. pap. 3.95 (ISBN 0-88290-104-4). Horizon Utah.

--Let's Love One Another. LC 77-74492. (Books for Lds Children Ser.). (Illus.). (ps-3). 1978. pap. 3.95 (ISBN 0-88290-077-3). Horizon Utah.

--Living the Golden Rule. (Children's Inspirational Coloring Bk.). (Illus.). (ps-3). 1979. pap. 1.25 (ISBN 0-88290-113-3). Horizon Utah.

--Paul, God's Special Missionary. (Story Books to Color.). 72p. (Orig.). (gr. k-5). 1980. pap. 2.50 (ISBN 0-88290-152-4). Horizon Utah.

--Paul's Letters. (Story Books to Color). (Illus.). 72p. (Orig.). (gr. k-5). 1981. pap. 2.50 (ISBN 0-88290-170-2). Horizon Utah.

--Stories Jesus Told: A Child's Coloring Book of the Parables of Jesus. (Children's Inspirational Coloring Bk.). (Illus.). (ps-6). 1979. pap. 2.50 (ISBN 0-88290-132-X). Horizon Utah.

--Sunday's Are Special. (Children's Inspirational Coloring Bk.). (Illus.). (ps-3). 1979. pap. 1.25 (ISBN 0-88290-111-7). Horizon Utah.

Dean, Beth. Folkloric in Australia. (Illus.). 90p. 1981. text ed. 9.95 (ISBN 0-85807-017-0, 3010, Pub. by Pacific Pubns Australia). Australia N U P.

Dean, Blanche, et al. Wildflowers of Alabama & Adjoining States. LC 73-10585. (Illus.). 230p. 1973. pap. 14.75 1983 (ISBN 0-8173-0147-X). U of Ala Pr.

Dean, Blanche E. Birds. (Southern Regional Nature Ser). (Illus.). pap. 5.00 (ISBN 0-87651-018-7). Southern U Pr.

--Ferns. (Southern Regional Nature Ser.). (Illus.). 1969. pap. 12.00 (ISBN 0-87651-019-5). Southern U Pr.

--Happy Trails. (Southern Regional Nature Ser.). (Illus.). 1969. pap. 5.00 (ISBN 0-87651-020-9). Southern U Pr.

Dean, Britten. China & Great Britain: The Diplomacy of Commercial Relations, 1860-1864. LC 73-75059. (East Asian Monographs Ser: No. 50). 1973. pap. 11.00x (ISBN 0-674-11725-5). Harvard U Pr.

Dean, Burton V., ed. Operations Research in Research & Development. LC 77-18041. 302p. 1978. Repr. of 1963 ed. lib. bdg. 18.50 (ISBN 0-88275-647-8). Krieger.

Dean, C. G. Red Ring Disease of Coconut. 70p. 1979. 49.00x (ISBN 0-85198-455-X, Pub. by CAB Bks England). State Mutual Bk.

Dean, Carol. One Last Kiss. 1982. pap. 2.95 (ISBN 0-8217-1112-1). Zebra.

Dean, Charles W. & De Bruyn Kops, Mary. The Crime & the Consequences of Rape. 152p. 1982. 17.50x (ISBN 0-398-04552-6). C C Thomas.

Dean, Chris & Whitlock, Quentin. The Handbook of Computer-Based Training. 250p. 1982. 26.50 (ISBN 0-89397-132-4). Nichols Pub.

Dean, Claire, jt. auth. see Dean, Jay.

Dean, Coleen L., jt. auth. see Schmid, George H.

Dean, D. H., et al, eds. Gene Structure & Expression. LC 80-17606. (Ohio State University Biosciences Colloquia: No. 6). (Illus.). 369p. 1980. 22.50x (ISBN 0-8142-0321-3). Ohio St U Pr.

Dean, D. L. Discrete Field Analysis of Structural Systems. (International Centre for Mechanical Sciences Ser.: No. 203). 1977. 23.00 (ISBN 0-387-81377-2). Springer-Verlag.

Dean, Dave. Now Is Your Time to Win. Vries, Vickie De, ed. 128p. 1985. pap. 2.50 (ISBN 0-8423-4727-5). Tyndale.

Dean, Dave & Hefley, Marti. Now Is Your Time to Win. 1983. 8.95 (ISBN 0-8423-4724-0). Tyndale.

Dean, David. Architecture of the 1930's. (Illus.). 160p. 1983. pap. 15.00 (ISBN 0-8478-0484-4). Rizzoli Intl.

--English Shopfronts from Contemporary Source Books, 1792-1840. (Illus.). 1970. 20.00 (ISBN 0-85458-270-3). Transatlantic.

Dean, David, jt. auth. see Stegmaier, Harry, Jr.

Dean, David M. Defender of the Race: James Theodore Holly, Black Nationalist Bishop. 150p. 1979. 16.95x (ISBN 0-931186-02-1). Lambeth Pr.

Dean, Dudley. The Man from Riondo. 160p. 1981. pap. 1.75 (ISBN 0-449-14231-0, GM). Fawcett.

Dean, Edith, jt. auth. see Andersen, Georg.

Dean, Edwin. Education & Economic Productivity. 240p. 1984. professional reference 29.95 (ISBN 0-88410-943-7). Ballinger Pub.

Dean, Elizabeth P. Jodie: One Little Ewe Lamb. 96p. 1984. pap. 4.95 (ISBN 0-8010-2938-4). Baker Bk.

Dean, Frank. The Complete Book of Trick & Fancy Riding. LC 60-13312. (Illus.). 1975. boxed 14.95 (ISBN 0-87004-240-8). Caxton.

--Cowboy Fun. LC 79-91384. (Illus.). 160p. 1980. 10.95 (ISBN 0-8069-4608-3); PLB 13.29 (ISBN 0-8069-4609-1). Sterling.

Dean, G. C. Science & Technology for Development: Technology Policy & Industrialization in the People's Republic of China. 108p. 1979. pap. 11.50 (ISBN 0-88936-210-6, IDRC130, IDRC). Unipub.

Dean, G. D., jt. auth. see Read, Bryan E.

Dean, G. W. & Wells, M. C. The Case for Continuously Contemporary Accounting. LC 83-49438. (Accounting History & the Development of a Profession Ser.). 440p. 1984. lib. bdg. 40.00 (ISBN 0-8240-6305-8). Garland Pub.

--Current Cost Accounting: Identifying the Issues, A Book of Readings, Vol. 1. (Illus.). 214p. (Orig.). 1979. pap. text ed. 13.95x (ISBN 0-909203-81-4). Dame Pubns.

Dean, G. W. & Wells, M. C., eds. Forerunners of Realizable Values Accounting in Financial Reporting. LC 82-82486. (Accountancy in Transition Ser.). 342p. 1985. lib. bdg. 50.00 (ISBN 0-8240-5334-6). Garland Pub.

Dean, Genevieve C. Science & Technology in the Development of Modern China: An Annotated Bibliography. LC 74-76296. 279p. 1974. 32.00x (ISBN 0-7201-0376-2). Mansell.

Dean, Gloria. The Dean Mountain Story. 1982. pap. 4.00 (ISBN 0-317-06955-1). Potomac Appalach.

Dean, Gregory D., jt. auth. see Read, Brian E.

Dean, H. Manufacturing: Industry & Careers. 1975. pap. text ed. 8.84 (ISBN 0-13-555839-5). P-H.

Dean, H. & Dean, M. Counselling in a Troubled Society. 160p. 1981. 30.00x (ISBN 0-686-81145-3, Pub. by Quatermaine England). State Mutual Bk.

Dean, H. E. Judicial Review & Democracy. 11.50 (ISBN 0-8446-1956-6). Peter Smith.

Dean, Hank L. Biology of Plants: Laboratory Exercises. 5th ed. 288p. 1982. write for info. wire coil bdg (ISBN 0-697-04708-3). Wm C Brown.

Dean, Ian. Industrial Narrow Gauge Railways. (Shire Album Ser.: No. 145). (Orig.). 1985. pap. 3.50 (ISBN 0-85263-752-7, Pub. by Shire Pubns England). Seven Hills Bks.

Dean, Inga. Memory & Desire. 1985. 16.95 (ISBN 0-670-80439-8). Viking.

Dean, J. Planning Library Education Programmes. 144p. 1972. 17.00x (ISBN 0-233-95760-X, 05778-9, Pub. by Gower Pub Co England). Lexington Bks.

Dean, J. & Padarathsingh, M. The Biological Relevance of Immune Suppression Induced by Therapeutic & Environmental Chemicals. 346p. 1981. 37.50 (ISBN 0-442-24429-0). Van Nos Reinhold.

Dean, J. Michael. Cardiac Arrest Simulation Program. 1984. software for Apple II 225.00 (ISBN 0-89443-859-X). Aspen Systems.

Dean, J. Michael & Booth, Frank V. Microcomputer in Critical Care: A Practical Approach. 368p. 1985. 32.50 (ISBN 0-683-02401-9). Williams & Wilkins.

Dean, Jack H., et al, eds. Immunotoxicology & Pharmacology. (Target Organ Toxicology Ser.). 520p. 1985. text ed. 98.00 (ISBN 0-89004-838-X). Raven.

Dean, James, compiled by. Health Administration, Vol. 14. LC 81-69298. (Business Administration Reading Lists & Courses Outlines). 317p. 1981. pap. text ed. 15.00 (ISBN 0-88024-026-1). Eno River Pr.

--Industrial Relations. LC 81-69293. (Business Administration Reading Lists & Course Outlines: Vol. 5). 163p. 1981. pap. text ed. 13.00 (ISBN 0-88024-017-2). Eno River Pr.

--International Banking & Finance, Vol. 3. LC 81-69291. (Business Administration Reading Lists & Course Outlines Ser.). 145p. (Orig.). 1981. pap. text ed. 12.00 (ISBN 0-88024-015-6). Eno River Pr.

--International Business, Vol. 4. LC 81-69292. (Business Administration Reading Lists & Course Outlines Ser.). 130p. (Orig.). 1981. pap. text ed. 11.00 (ISBN 0-88024-016-4). Eno River Pr.

--Marketing I, Vol. 8. LC 81-69326. (Business Administration reading Lists & Course Outlines Ser.). 192p. 1981. pap. text ed. 14.00 (ISBN 0-88024-020-2). Eno River Pr.

--Marketing II, Vol. 9. LC 81-69324. (Business Administration Reading Lists & Course Outlines). 221p. 1981. pap. text ed. 14.00 (ISBN 0-88024-021-0). Eno River Pr.

Dean, James & Schwindt, Richard, eds. Accounting II, Vol. 7. LC 81-69295. (Business Administration Reading Lists & Course Outlines Ser.). 194p. (Orig.). 1981. pap. text ed. 12.00 (ISBN 0-88024-019-9). Eno River Pr.

--Business, Goverment & Society, Vol. 13. LC 81-69297. (Business Administration Reading Lists & Course Outlines Ser.). 134p. (Orig.). 1981. pap. text ed. 10.00 (ISBN 0-88024-025-3). Eno River Pr.

--Business Policy & Strategy, Vol. 12. LC 81-69296. (Business Administration Reading Lists & Course Outlines Ser.). 153p. (Orig.). 1981. pap. text ed. 10.00 (ISBN 0-88024-024-5). Eno River Pr.

Dean, James M., ed. see Chaucer, Geoffrey.

Dean, James S. Robert Greene: A Reference Guide. (Reference Guides to Literature Ser.). 1984. lib. bdg. 55.00 (ISBN 0-8161-7854-2, Hall Reference). G K Hall.

Dean, James S., Jr., jt. auth. see Benfield, Warren A.

Dean, James W. & Schwindt, Richard, eds. Finance I, Vol. 1. LC 81-69326. (Business Administration Reading Lists & Course Outlines Ser.). 131p. (Orig.). 1981. pap. text ed. 12.00 (ISBN 0-88024-013-X). Eno River Pr.

Dean, Jay & Dean, Claire. How Damage is Done in The Name of Christ! LC 82-90134. 102p. (Orig.). 1982. pap. 3.95 (ISBN 0-943416-00-0). Plus Seven Bks.

Dean, Jeanne A. Employment, Work & Health Sciences: Subject Analysis Index With Research Bibliography. LC 85-47848. 150p. 1985. 29.95 (ISBN 0-88164-368-8); pap. 21.95 (ISBN 0-88164-369-6). ABBE Pubs Assn.

Dean, Jeff. Architectural Photography: Techniques for Architects, Preservationists, Historians, Photographers, & Urban Planners. LC 81-12830. (Illus.). 144p. 1982. 20.95 (ISBN 0-910050-54-6). AASLH Pr.

Dean, Jeffrey S. Chronological Analysis of Tsegi Phase Sites in Northeastern Arizona. LC 69-16330. (Papers of the Laboratory of Tree-Ring Research Ser.: No. 3). 207p. 1969. pap. 12.50x (ISBN 0-8165-0195-5). U of Ariz Pr.

Dean, Jennifer B. Careers in a Department Store. LC 72-5411. (Early Career Bks.). (Illus.). 36p. (gr. 2-5). 1973. PLB 5.95 (ISBN 0-8225-0301-8). Lerner Pubns.

--Careers with an Airline. LC 72-5413. (Early Career Bks.). (Illus.). 36p. (gr. 2-5). 1973. PLB 5.95 (ISBN 0-8225-0303-4). Lerner Pubns.

Dean, Joan. Managing the Secondary School. 240p. 1985. 24.50 (ISBN 0-89397-222-3). Nichols Pub.

--Organising Learning in the Primary School Classroom. (Teaching 5-13 Ser.). 232p. 1983. 29.00 (ISBN 0-7099-0822-9, Pub. by Croom Helm Ltd); pap. 11.50 (ISBN 0-7099-0823-7). Longwood Pub Group.

Dean, Joan F. Tom Stoppard: Comedy As a Moral Matrix. LC 80-26400. (A Literary Frontier Edition). 128p. 1981. text ed. 8.00x (ISBN 0-8262-0332-9). U of Mo Pr.

Dean, Joe, jt. auth. see Hall, Joe B.

Dean, Joel. Capital Budgeting: Top Management Policy on Plant, Equipment, & Product Development. LC 51-11344. (Illus.). 174p. 1951. 30.00x (ISBN 0-231-01847-9). Columbia U Pr.

Dean, John. Blind Ambition. (gr. 11-12). 1979. pap. 2.75 (ISBN 0-671-82343-4). PB.

--Games Make Spelling Fun: Activities for Better Spelling. rev. ed. 1973. pap. 4.50 (ISBN 0-8224-3255-2). Pitman Learning.

--Restless Wanderers: Shakespeare & the Pattern of Romance. (Orig.). 1979. text ed. 25.50x (ISBN 0-391-01708-X). Humanities.

Dean, John, jt. auth. see Henke, James T.

Dean, John A. & Rains, Theodore C., eds. Flame Emission & Atomic Absorption Spectrometry, 2 vols. Incl. Vol. 1. Theory. pap. 114.00 (ISBN 0-317-10435-7); Vol. 2. Components & Techniques. pap. 96.00 (ISBN 0-317-10436-5). LC 76-78830. pap. (2055080). Bks Demand UMI.

--Flame Emission & Atomic Absorption Spectrometry: Components & Techniques, Vol. 2. LC 76-78830. pap. 94.50 (ISBN 0-317-28665-X, 2055081). Bks Demand UMI.

Dean, John F. Writing Well. 1985. pap. 6.95 (ISBN 0-8224-7530-8). Pitman Learning.

Dean, John P. & Rosen, Alex. Manual of Intergroup Relations. LC 56-5141. 1963. pap. 4.50x (ISBN 0-226-13933-6, Phoen). U of Chicago Pr.

Dean, John P., et al. A Manual of Intergroup Relations. LC 56-5141. pap. 55.00 (ISBN 0-317-07766-X, 2022504). Bks Demand UMI.

Dean, John W., ed. Captain John Mason Fifteen Eighty-Six to Sixteen Thirty-Five. LC 3-24569. (Prince Society Pubns.: No. 17). 1966. Repr. of 1887 ed. 32.00 (ISBN 0-8337-0810-4). B Franklin.

Dean, John W., III. Lost Honor. LC 82-61776. 1982. 15.95 (ISBN 0-936906-15-4). Stratford Pr.

Deane, Seamus. Celtic Revivals: Essays in Modern Irish Literature, Eighteen Eighty to Nineteen Eighty. LC 85-5233. 208p. 1985. 29.95 (ISBN 0-571-13500-5). Faber & Faber.
--Gradual Wars. 64p. 1975. Repr. of 1972 ed. 8.00x (ISBN 0-7165-2153-9, Pub. by Irish Academic Pr Ireland). Biblio Dist.
--Rumours. LC 78-301258. 1977. pap. text ed. 7.00x (ISBN 0-85105-320-3, Dolmen Pr). Humanities.
Deane, Sidney M., tr. see Anselm, St.
Deane, Silas. The Deane Papers: Collections of the New-York Historical Society, 1886-90, 5 vols. LC 1-13394. 25.00 set (ISBN 0-685-73896-5). U Pr of Va.
Deane, Sonia. Doctors in Love. DeRoin, Gene, ed. (Aston Hall Presents Ser.). (Orig.). 1979. pap. 1.50 (ISBN 0-89936-005-X). Aston Hall.
Deane, Tony & Shaw, Tony. The Folklore of Cornwall. (Folklore of the British Isles Ser.). 217p. 1975. 16.50x (ISBN 0-87471-695-0). Rowman.
Deane, W. J. & Kirt, T. Studies in the First Book of Samuel. 509p. 1983. lib. bdg. 19.00 Smythe Sewn (ISBN 0-86524-150-3, 0902). Klock & Klock.
Deane, Wallace. Fijian Society: Or, The Sociology & Psychology of the Fijians. LC 75-32813. Repr. of 1921 ed. 24.50 (ISBN 0-404-14117-X). AMS Pr.
Deane-Drummond, Anthony. Riot Control. LC 75-7555. 158p. 1975. 14.00x (ISBN 0-8448-0711-7). Crane-Russak Co.
Deanesly, Margaret. History of the Medieval Church, Five Ninety to Fifteen Hundred. 9th ed. 1969. pap. 12.50x (ISBN 0-416-18100-7, NO. 2163). Methuen Inc.
--The Incendium Amoris of Richard Rolle of Hampole. LC 74-9872. 1915. 45.00 (ISBN 0-8414-3760-2). Folcroft.
--The Lollard Bible & Other Medieval Biblical Versions. LC 77-84722. Repr. of 1920 ed. 37.50 (ISBN 0-404-16125-1). AMS Pr.
--The Pre-Conquest Church in England. 2nd ed. (Ecclesiastical History of England Ser.). 376p. 1963. text ed. 30.00x (ISBN 0-06-491638-3). B&N Imports.
De Angeli, Marguerite. Book of Nursery & Mother Goose Rhymes. (Illus.). (gr. k-5). 1954. 16.95 (ISBN 0-385-07232-5). Doubleday.
--Copper-Toed Boots. (gr. k-4). 1938. 5.95 (ISBN 0-385-07264-3). Doubleday.
--The Door in the Wall. (Illus.). 124p. (gr. 4-6). 1984. pap. 2.25 (ISBN 0-590-33853-6, Apple Paperbacks). Scholastic Inc.
DeAngeli, Marguerite. The Door in the Wall: Story of Medieval London. LC 64-7025. (Illus.). 111p. (gr. 3-6). 10.95a (ISBN 0-385-07283-X); PLB (ISBN 0-385-05743-1). Doubleday.
De Angeli, Marguerite. Fiddlestrings. LC 73-82243. 128p. (gr. 4-7). 1974. PLB 4.95 (ISBN 0-385-08437-4). Doubleday.
--Friendship & Other Poems. LC 79-6857. (Illus.). 48p. 1981. 6.95a (ISBN 0-385-15854-8). Doubleday.
DeAngeli, Marguerite. Henner's Lydia. 76p. (gr. 2-5). 1936. 9.95 (ISBN 0-385-07318-6). Doubleday.
De Angeli, Marguerite. The Lion in the Box. LC 74-33676. 80p. (gr. 3-7). 1975. 6.95 (ISBN 0-385-03317-6). Doubleday.
--Marguerite De Angeli's Book of Nursery & Mother Goose Rhymes. (Illus.). (gr. k-5). 1979. pap. 6.95 (ISBN 0-385-15291-4, Zephyr). Doubleday.
DeAngeli, Marguerite. Marguerite DeAngeli's Book of Nursery & Mother Goose Rhymes. (Illus.). 192p. (ps-3). 1953. pap. 6.95 (ISBN 0-385-15291-4, Zephyr). Doubleday.
DeAngelis, Catherine. Pediatric Primary Care. 3rd ed. 1984. 29.95 (ISBN 0-316-17783-0). Little.
De Angelis, George & Francis, Edward P. The Ford Model "A"-As Henry Built It. 3rd ed. (Illus.). 244p. 1983. 17.95 (ISBN 0-911383-02-6). Motor Cities.
DeAngelis, George, jt. auth. see Francis, Edward P.
De Angelis, Jacqueline, jt. ed. see Rodriguez, Aleida.
De Angelis, Michele & Lentz, Thomas. Architecture in Islamic Painting. Walsh, Peter L., ed. (Illus.). 32p. (Orig.). 1982. pap. 7.50 (ISBN 0-916724-51-4). Fogg Art.
DeAngelis, Richard A. Blue-Collar Workers & Politics: A French Paradox. (Illus.). 286p. 1982. 28.00 (ISBN 0-7099-0815-6, Pub. by Croom Helm Ltd). Longwood Pub Group.
DeAngelis, Robert. Radiologic Science Workbook. 256p. 1982. 17.95 (ISBN 0-03-060619-5). Praeger.
DeAngelis, William. Acting Out the Gospels. LC 81-84919. 96p. 1982. pap. 9.95 (ISBN 0-89622-136-9). Twenty-Third.
--School Year Liturgies. (Illus.). 64p. (Orig.). 1985. pap. 9.95 (ISBN 0-89622-218-7). Twenty-Third.
De Angelis Bothwell, Sr. Mary. God Is Good. LC 73-5752. (Christ Our Life Ser.). (Illus.). 138p. (gr. 1). 1979. pap. text ed. 3.80 (ISBN 0-8294-0290-X); tchrs' ed 9.95 (ISBN 0-8294-0291-8). Loyola.
DeAngelo, Linda E. The Auditor-Client Contractual Relationship: An Economic Analysis. Dufey, Gunter, ed. LC 81-12923. (Research for Business Decisions Ser.: No. 43). 140p. 1981. 34.95 (ISBN 0-8357-1241-9). UMI Res Pr.
De Angioy, Rosella. Exotic Pasta: Seventy New Recipes for Very Different Pasta Dishes. LC 85-11606. (Illus.). 96p. 1985. 12.95 (ISBN 0-906053-84-6). Faber & Faber.
De Angulo, Gui, ed. see Angulo, Jaime de.
De Angulo, Jaime. How the World Was Made: Old Time Stories, Vol. 2. Callahan, Bob, ed. LC 73-78143. (Jaime De Angulo Library). (Illus.). 1976. 10.00 (ISBN 0-913666-13-0). Turtle Isl Foun.
--Jaime De Angulo Reader. Callahan, Bob, ed. LC 78-59741. (New World Writing Ser.). (Illus.). 1979. pap. 8.95 (ISBN 0-913666-30-0). Turtle Isl Foun.
--Shabegok: Old Time Stories, Vol. 1. Callahan, Bob, ed. LC 73-78142. (Jaime De Angulo Library: Vol. 1). (Illus.). 1976. 10.00 (ISBN 0-913666-12-2). Turtle Isl Foun.
De Angulo, Jaime see Angulo, Jaime de.
Deanin, Rudolph D. & Crugnola, Aldo M., eds. Toughness & Brittleness of Plastics. LC 76-41267. (Advances in Chemistry Ser.: No. 154). 1976. 49.95 (ISBN 0-8412-0221-4). Am Chemical.
Deans, Alan, ed. Australian Mining, Minerals & Oil. 610p. 1984. 110.00x (ISBN 0-317-04431-1, NO. 5060). Methuen Inc.
Deans, Alexander S. The Bee Keepers Encyclopedia. LC 75-23248. (Illus.). 1979. Repr. of 1949 ed. 65.00x (ISBN 0-8103-4176-X). Gale.
Deans, James. Tales from the Totem of the Hidery. (Folklore Ser). 15.00 (ISBN 0-8482-7752-X). Norwood Edns.
Deans, Laurie, jt. auth. see Roberts, Garbut.
Deans, Marjorie. Meeting at the Sphinx: Gabriel Pascal's Production of Bernard Shaw's Caesar & Cleopatra. Repr. 20.00 (ISBN 0-8274-2700-X). R West.
Deans, Nora L. Aquatic Life in the John G. Shedd Aquarium: A Guide to Exhibit Animals. (Illus.). 272p. (Orig.). 1983. pap. 6.95 guidebook (ISBN 0-9611074-0-5). Shedd Aquarium.
Deans, Stanley R. The Radon Transform & Some of Its Applications. LC 83-1125. 289p. 1983. 37.95x (ISBN 0-471-89804-X, Pub. by Wiley-Interscience). Wiley.
De Anton, Haberkamp G., jt. ed. see Haensch, G.
De Antonio, Emile & Tuchman, Mitch. Painters Painting. LC 83-21526. (Illus.). 192p. 1984. 19.95 (ISBN 0-89659-418-1). Abbeville Pr.
De Anza, Frank. Corporate State & the Inevitable New Structure in the Economic & Political Order. 1978. 67.50x (ISBN 0-930008-03-0). Inst Econ Pol.
Dear, Ian. Fastnet: The Story of a Great Ocean Race. (Illus.). 192p. 1981. 25.00 (ISBN 0-7134-0997-5, Pub. by Batsford England). David & Charles.
Dear, James. American Covert Action. 54p. 1976. pap. 3.00 (ISBN 0-318-00191-8). LBJ Sch Pub Aff.
Dear, Michael, jt. auth. see Clark, Gordon L.
Dear, Michael J. & Scott, Allen J. Urbanization & Urban Planning in Capitalist Societies. 1981. 33.00 (ISBN 0-416-74640-3, NO. 2869); pap. 18.00x (ISBN 0-416-74650-0, NO. 6382). Methuen Inc.
Dear, Michael J. & Taylor, S. Martin. Not on Our Street: Community Attitudes to Mental Health Care. 200p. 1982. 19.95 (ISBN 0-85086-096-2, NO. 8010, Pub. by Pion England). Methuen Inc.
Dear, William. Dungeon Master: The Disappearance of James Dallas Egbert, III. 1984. 16.95 (ISBN 0-395-35536-2). HM.
--The Dungeon Master: The Disappearance of James Dallas Egbert III. 352p. 1985. pap. 3.95 (ISBN 0-345-32695-4). Ballantine.
De Aragon, Maximo. The Pearl. LC 80-83435. (Illus.). 50p. (Orig.). (gr. 7-12). 1984. pap. 2.95 (ISBN 0-932906-08-7). Pan-Am Publishing Co.
De Aragon, Ray J. City of Candy & Streets of Ice Cream. LC 79-52960. (Miss Miffit Story Time Bks.). (Illus., Orig.). (gr. 1-6). 1979. text ed. 5.95 (ISBN 0-932906-05-2); pap. 2.50 (ISBN 0-932906-04-4). Pan-Am Publishing Co.
--The Great Lovers. (Non-Fiction Ser.). (Illus.). 104p. (Orig.). 1984. pap. 5.95 (ISBN 0-932906-10-9). Pan-Am Publishing Co.
--Padre Martinez & Bishop Lamy. 3rd ed. LC 78-70565. (History Ser.). (Illus.). 1978. pap. 7.95 (ISBN 0-932906-00-1). Pan-Am Publishing Co.
De Aragon, Ray J. see Aragon, Ray J. De.
De Aragon, Ray J. see Aragon, Ray J. de.
De Aragon, Ray J., tr. see Sanchez, Pedro.
De Araoz, J., et al. Principles & Practices of Cholera Control. (Public Health Papers Ser: No. 40). 139p. (Avail. in Eng., Fr., Rus. & Span.). 1970. pap. 3.60 (ISBN 92-4-130040-X, 298). World Health.
De Araujo, Virginia, ed. see Andrade, Carlos D.
Dearborn, Benjamin. The Columbian Grammar. 59.95 (ISBN 0-87968-909-9). Gordon Pr.
Dearborn, David C., frwd. by see Wyman, Thomas B.
Dearborn, Elwyn. The Down East Printmaker: Carroll Thayer Berry. (Illus.). 1983. limited ed. 60.00 (ISBN 0-89272-169-3); trade ed. 29.95 (ISBN 0-89272-164-2). Down East.
Dearborn, George van N. see Quantz, J. Q.
Dearborn, George Van Ness. The Psychology of Clothing. Bd. with Some Imaginal Factors Influencing Verbal Expression. Shaw, E. E. Repr. of 1918 ed; The Learning Curve Equation. Thurstone, L. L. Repr. of 1919 ed; The Effect of Alcohol on the Intelligent Behavior of the White Rat & Its Progeny. Arlitt, A. H. Repr. of 1919 ed; The Form of the Learning Curves for Memory. Kjerstad, C. L. Repr. of 1919 ed; An Introspective Analysis of the Process of Comparing. Fernberger, S. W. Repr. of 1919 ed. (Psychological Monographs, General & Applied: Vol. 26). pap. 36.00 (ISBN 0-317-15622-5). Kraus Repr.
Dearborn, Georgia, illus. Sweet Wild World: Selections from Thoreau's Journals. (Illus.). 142p. (Orig.). 1982. 12.95 (ISBN 0-89182-059-0); pap. 6.95 (ISBN 0-89182-060-4). Charles River Bks.
Dearborn, Henry. Revolutionary War Journals, 1775-1783. facsimile ed. Brown, Lloyd A. & Peckham, Howard H., eds. LC 74-102233. (Select Bibliographies Reprint Ser). 1939. 29.00 (ISBN 0-8369-5118-2). Ayer Co Pubs.
Dearborn, Mona L. Anson Dickinson: The Celebrated Miniature Painter 1779-1852. LC 83-70635. 224p. 1983. pap. text ed. 7.95 (ISBN 0-940748-86-X). Conn Hist Soc.
Dearborn, Ned. Trapping on the Farm. 38p. pap. 3.95 (ISBN 0-8466-6028-8, U28). Shorey.
Dearborn, Ned H. Oswego Movement in American Education. LC 71-176709. (Columbia University. Teachers College. Contributions to Education: No. 183). Repr. of 1925 ed. 22.50 (ISBN 0-404-55183-1). AMS Pr.
--Oswego Movement in American Education. LC 74-89171. (American Education: Its Men, Institutions & Ideas, Ser. 1). 1969. Repr. of 1925 ed. 16.00 (ISBN 0-405-01409-0). Ayer Co Pubs.
Dearborn, Walter F., et al. Data on the Growth of Public School Children. (SRCD Ser.: Vol. 3, No. 1). 1938. 12.00 (ISBN 0-527-01501-6). Kraus Repr.
Dearden, C. W. The Stage of Aristophanes. (University of London Classical Studies: Vol. VII). (Illus.). 203p. 1976. 46.50 (ISBN 0-485-13707-0, Pub. by Athlone Pr Ltd). Longwood Pub Group.
Dearden, Garry, jt. ed. see Parlett, Malcolm.
Dearden, Harold. Devilish but True: The Doctor Looks at Spiritualism. (Illus.). 288p. 1975. Repr. of 1936 ed. 14.95x (ISBN 0-8464-0324-2). Beekman Pubs.
--Devilish but True: The Doctor Looks at Spiritualism. (Illus.). 288p. (Orig.). 1975. Repr. of 1936 ed. 14.50x (ISBN 0-87471-683-7). Rowman.
Dearden, J. C., ed. Quantitative Approaches to Drug Design: Proceedings of the Fourth European Symposium on Chemical Structure Biological Activity: Bath, U.K., Sept. 6-9, 1982. (Pharmacochemistry Library: Vol. 6). 296p. 1983. 64.00 (ISBN 0-444-42200-5). Elsevier.
Dearden, J. S. John Ruskin. (Clarendon Biography Ser.). (Illus.). pap. 3.50 (ISBN 0-912728-75-2). Newbury Bks.
Dearden, Jeannette & Stig-Nielsen, Karin. Spoken Danish. bk. I, units 1-12, 1976 341p. 10.00x (ISBN 0-87950-044-1); bk. II, units 13-30, 1980 567 p. 15.00x (ISBN 0-87950-045-X); bk. I & cassettes 65.00x (ISBN 0-87950-051-4); cassettes, 6 dual track 60.00x (ISBN 0-87950-050-6). Spoken Lang Serv.
Dearden, John. Cost Accounting & Financial Control Systems. LC 73-184160. 1973. text ed. 38.95 (ISBN 0-201-01507-2). Addison-Wesley.
--Essentials of Cost Accounting. (Orig.). 1969. pap. text ed. 19.50 (ISBN 0-201-01484-X); instr's. guide o.p. 0.50. Addison-Wesley.
Dearden, John & Shank, John. Financial Accounting & Reporting: A Contemporary Emphasis. (Illus.). 544p. 1975. ref. ed. 34.95 (ISBN 0-13-314757-6). P-H.
Dearden, Paul F. The Rhode Island Campaign of 1778: Inauspicious Dawn of Alliance. LC 78-68920. (Illus.). 169p. 1980. 6.95 (ISBN 0-917012-17-8). RI Pubns Soc.
Dearden, R. F. Philosophy of Primary Education: An Introduction. LC 68-21589. (Students' Library of Education). 1968. pap. text ed. 8.00x (ISBN 0-7100-6648-1). Humanities.
--Problems in Primary Education. (Students Library of Education Ser.). 1976. 18.95x (ISBN 0-7100-8363-7); pap. 8.95x (ISBN 0-7100-8364-5). Routledge & Kegan.
--Theory & Practice in Education. 192p. 1984. 19.95x (ISBN 0-7100-9910-X). Routledge & Kegan.
Dearden, R. F., et al. Educational & the Development of Reason, 3 pts. Incl. Pt. 1. Critique of Current Educational Aims. pap. 9.95x (ISBN 0-7100-8084-0); Pt. 2. Reason. pap. 9.95x (ISBN 0-7100-8101-4); Pt. 3. Education & Reason. pap. 9.95x (ISBN 0-7100-8102-2). 1975. pap. Routledge & Kegan.
Dearden, Seton. The Arabian Knight: A Study of Sir Richard Burton. 1936. 25.00 (ISBN 0-8274-1875-2). R West.
--Burton of Arabia. LC 77-18851. 1936. 30.00 (ISBN 0-8414-3796-3). Folcroft.
--A Nest of Corsairs: The Fighting Karamanlis of Tripoli. (Illus.). 1977. 22.00 (ISBN 0-7195-3279-5). Transatlantic.
Dearden, Warren. A Free Country. 1979. pap. 3.00 (ISBN 0-913028-68-1). North Atlantic.
DeArdo, A. J. & Ratz, G. A. Thermomechanical Processing of Microalloyed Austenite: Proceedings. Pittsburgh, 1981. (Illus.). 680p. 45.00 (ISBN 0-89520-398-7); members 30.00 (ISBN 0-317-36286-0); student members 15.00 (ISBN 0-317-36287-9). ASM.
Deardorff, Anna, ed. see Folk-Williams, John A., et al.
DeAre, Diana R., jt. auth. see Huff, David L.
Dearen, Patrick. The Illegal Man. 1981. pap. 2.25 (ISBN 0-8439-0872-6, Leisure Bks). Dorchester Pub Co.
--Starflight to Faroul. (Orig.). 1980. pap. 1.95 (ISBN 0-505-51600-4, Pub. by Tower Bks). Dorchester Pub Co.
De Arenas, Bibi Armas see Armas de Arenas, Bibi.
Dearhammer, William G. Unbundling Credit Department Costs. LC 84-16618. (Illus.). 76p. (Orig.). 1984. pap. text ed. 27.00 (ISBN 0-936742-19-4). Robt Morris Assocs.
Dearholt, Donald & McSpadden, William. Electromagnetic Wave Propagation. (Illus.). 480p. 1973. text ed. 58.00 (ISBN 0-07-016205-0). McGraw.
Dearing, Brian E., jt. auth. see Hartwig, Frederick.
Dearing, C. L. American Highway Policy: Urban Dimension. LC 77-74939. (American Federalism Ser.). (Illus.). 1978. Repr. of 1941 ed. lib. bdg. 26.50x (ISBN 0-405-10486-3). Ayer Co Pubs.
Dearing, Charles L. & Owen, Wilfred. National Transportation Policy. LC 79-28670. (Illus.). xiv, 459p. 1980. Repr. of 1949 ed. lib. bdg. 37.50x (ISBN 0-313-22301-7, DENT). Greenwood.
Dearing, Charles L., et al. ABC of the NRA. (Brookings Institution Reprint Ser). Repr. of 1934 ed. lib. bdg. 25.00x (ISBN 0-697-00154-7). Irvington.
Dearing, Frank. About God & You. LC 82-14054. 1982. pap. 4.95 (ISBN 0-88270-545-8). Bridge Pub.
Dearing, James. Making Money Making Music. LC 82-7617. 305p. 1982. pap. 12.95 (ISBN 0-89879-101-4). Writers Digest.
Dearing, John, ed. Calculator Tips & Routines: Especially for the HP-41C 41CV. LC 81-90355. 136p. 1981. 15.00 (ISBN 0-942358-00-7). Corvallis Software.
Dearing, Mary R. Veterans in Politics. LC 74-9625. (Illus.). 523p. 1974. Repr. of 1952 ed. lib. bdg. 29.50x (ISBN 0-8371-7605-0, DEVP). Greenwood.
Dearing, Trevor. God & Healing of the Mind. 1983. pap. 4.95 (ISBN 0-88270-549-0). Bridge Pub.
--Supernatural Healing Today. LC 78-71527. 1979. pap. 4.95 (ISBN 0-88270-324-2, Pub. by Logos). Bridge Pub.
--Wesleyan & Tractarian Worship. LC 66-72190. 1966. text ed. 15.00x (ISBN 0-8401-0531-2). A R Allenson.
Dearing, Vinton A. A Manual of Textual Analysis. LC 82-20947. ix, 108p. 1983. Repr. of 1959 ed. lib. bdg. 32.50x (ISBN 0-313-23734-4, DEMA). Greenwood.
Dearing, Vinton A. see Dryden, John.
Dearing, Vinton A., ed. see Gay, John.
Dearle, N. B. Dictionary of Official War-Time Organizations. (Economic & Social History of the World British Ser.). 1928. 75.00x (ISBN 0-317-27446-5). Elliots Bks.
Dearle, Norman B. Economic Chronicle of the Great War For Great Britain & Ireland: 1914-1919. (Economic & Social History of the World War Ser.). 1929. 75.00x (ISBN 0-686-83531-X). Elliots Bks.
Dearling, Robert. The Music of Mozart: The Symphonies. LC 78-68625. (Illus.). 232p. 1982. 26.50 (ISBN 0-8386-2335-2). Fairleigh Dickerson.
Dearling, Robert, jt. auth. see Blokker, Roy.
Dearling, Robert, et al. Guinness Book of Music Facts & Feats. (Illus.). 288p. 1983. 19.95 (ISBN 0-85112-212-4, Pub. by Guinness Superlatives). Sterling.
--Music Facts & Feats. rev. ed. (Illus.). 288p. 1981. 19.95 (ISBN 0-85112-212-4, Pub. by Guinness Superlatives England). Sterling.
Dearlove, J. E. Accomodating the Chaos: Samuel Beckett's Nonrelational Art. LC 81-12465. 172p. 1981. 18.75 (ISBN 0-8223-0462-7). Duke.
Dearlove, John. The Politics of Policy in Local Government. LC 73-77179. (Illus.). 300p. 1973. 34.50 (ISBN 0-521-20244-2). Cambridge U Pr.
--The Reorganization of British Local Government. LC 78-18092. 1979. 44.50 (ISBN 0-521-22341-5); pap. 13.95 (ISBN 0-521-29456-8). Cambridge U Pr.
Dearlove, John & Saunders, Peter. Introduction to British Politics: Analysing a Capitalist Democracy. 416p. 1985. 45.00x (ISBN 0-7456-0010-7); pap. 14.95x (ISBN 0-7456-0011-5). Basil Blackwell.
De Armas, F. A. The Invisible Mistress: Aspects of Feminism & Fantasy in the Golden Age. (Biblioteca Siglo De Oro Ser.). 1976. pap. 10.00 (ISBN 84-399-5958-3). Biblio Siglo.
De Armas, Frederick, et al, eds. Critical Perspectives on Calderon de la Barca. LC 80-53823. 150p. (Orig.). 1981. pap. 25.00 (ISBN 0-89295-004-8). Society Sp & Sp-Am.
DeArmas, Frederick A. The Four Interpolated Stories in the "Roman Comique". Their Sources & Unifying Function. (Studies in the Romance Languages & Literatures: No. 100). 144p. 1971. pap. 8.50x (ISBN 0-8078-9100-2). U of NC Pr.
De Armas, Jose R. & Steele, Charles W. Cuban Consciousness in Literature: 1923-1974. LC 78-53265. (Coleccion Antologias). 1978. pap. 12.00 (ISBN 0-89729-166-2). Ediciones.
DeArment, Robert K. Bat Masterson: The Man & the Legend. LC 78-21383. (Illus.). 1979. 19.95 (ISBN 0-8061-1522-X). U of Okla Pr.
--Knights of the Green Cloth: The Saga of the Frontier Gamblers. LC 81-16196. (Illus.). 432p. 1982. 19.95 (ISBN 0-8061-1726-5). U of Okla Pr.

Dearmer, Percy. Songs of Praise. Vaughan Williams, Ralph & Shaw, Martin, eds. Incl. Music Ed. rev. & enl. ed. 1932. 19.95x (ISBN 0-19-231207-3). Oxford U Pr.
--A Subject Index of Hymns in the English Hymnal & Songs of Praise. 59.95 (ISBN 0-8490-1159-0). Gordon Pr.
Dearmer, Percy, et al. The Oxford Book of Carols. 1928. pap. 12.00x (ISBN 0-19-353315-4). Oxford U Pr.
Dearmer, Percy, et al, eds. Oxford Book of Carols. 1964. Repr. of 1928 ed. 18.00x (ISBN 0-19-353314-6); words & melody 6.95x (ISBN 0-19-313118-8). Oxford U Pr.
--Oxford Book of Carols for Schools. (gr. 1-6). 1956. piano ed. 6.75x (ISBN 0-19-330830-4); melody ed. 2.50x (ISBN 0-19-330831-2). Oxford U Pr.
De Armond, Dale. Berry Woman's Children. LC 84-29760. (Illus.). 40p. (gr. 1 up). 1985. 10.25 (ISBN 0-688-05814-0); lib. bdg. 10.88 (ISBN 0-688-05815-9). Greenwillow.
--Dale De Armond: A First Book Collection of Her Prints. LC 79-18388. (Illus., Orig.). 1979. pap. 14.95 (ISBN 0-88240-131-9). Alaska Northwest.
--Juneau: A Book of Woodcuts. LC 73-82791. (Illus.). 56p. 1973. pap. 12.95 slipcased (ISBN 0-88240-021-5). Alaska Northwest.
--Raven: A Collection of Woodcuts. LC 75-23002. (Illus.). 132p. (Orig.). 1975. slip-cased 100.00 (ISBN 0-88240-040-1). Alaska Northwest.
DeArmond, Robert N. Alaska: 1867-1959. (Alaska Historical Commission Studies in History: No. 18). (Illus.). 20p. (Orig.). 1981. pap. 3.00 (ISBN 0-943712-02-5). Alaska Hist.
De Armond, Robert N., ed. see Pierce, W. H.
De Armond, Robert N. see Atwood, Evangeline.
DeArmond, Stephen J., et al. Structure of the Human Brain: A Photographic Atlas. 2nd ed. (Illus.). 1976. pap. text ed. 17.95x (ISBN 0-19-502073-1). Oxford U Pr.
De Armond Marchant, Alexander N. Boundaries of the Latin American Republics: An Annotated List of Documents, 1493-1943. (Latin America Ser.). 1979. lib. bdg. 59.95 (ISBN 0-8490-2876-0). Gordon Pr.
Dearnaley, E. J. & War, P. B., eds. Aircrew Stress in Wartime Operations. 1979. 39.00 (ISBN 0-12-207750-4). Acad Pr.
Dearness, John L. & Angus, Robert B., Jr. Applied Avionics. 3rd ed. (Illus.). 523p. 1982. text ed. 39.00 (ISBN 0-942354-01-X); tchrs' guide 10.00 (ISBN 0-942354-02-8). Bowens Pub Div.
Dearnley, M. Margiad Evans. (Writers of Wales Ser.). 108p. 1982. pap. text ed. 6.75x (ISBN 0-7083-0820-1, Pub. by Univ of Wales Pr England). Humanities.
De Arrillano, E. Ramirez & Sundararaman, D. Topics in Several Complex Variables. (Research Notes in Mathematics Ser.: No. 112). 300p. 1985. pap. text ed. 18.95 (ISBN 0-273-08656-1). Pitman Pub MA.
Dearstyne, Howard, tr. see Malevich, Kasimir.
DeArteaga, William. Past Life Visions: A Christian Exploration. 256p. 1983. pap. 9.95 (ISBN 0-8164-2414-4, Pub. by Seabury). Winston Pr.
Dearth, FLorean. Construction & Utilization of Visual Aids in Dental Health Education. LC 74-18988. (Illus.). 132p. 1974. 14.00 (ISBN 0-913590-26-6). Slack Inc.
Deary, Terry. Calamity Kate. LC 82-1326. (The Good Time Library). (Illus.). 112p. (gr. 2-6). 1982. lib. bdg. 8.95g (ISBN 0-87614-195-5). Carolrhoda Bks.
--The Custard Kid. LC 81-21693. (The Good Time Library). (Illus.). 96p. (gr. 2-6). 1982. PLB 8.95g (ISBN 0-87614-188-2). Carolrhoda Bks.
--The Lambton Worm. LC 82-1327. (The Good Time Library). (Illus.). 88p. (gr. 3-7). 1982. lib. bdg. 8.95g (ISBN 0-87614-196-3). Carolrhoda Bks.
Deas, Walter. Australian Fishes in Color. (Illus.). 1973. 6.00 (ISBN 0-912728-47-7). Newbury Bks.
Deasey, Denison. Education under Six. LC 77-21081. 1978. 27.50x (ISBN 0-312-23748-0). St Martin.
Deasey-Spinetta, Patricia M., jt. auth. see Spinetta, John J.
Deasington, R. X.25 Explained: Protocols for Packet Switching Networks. (Computer Communications Ser.). 1985. 21.95 (ISBN 0-470-20183-5). Halsted Pr.
Deasington, R. J. A Practical Guide to Computer Communications & Networking. LC 84-4617. (Computers & Their Applications Ser.: 1-403). 126p. 1984. pap. text ed. 24.95x (ISBN 0-470-20078-2). Halsted Pr.
Deason, Dee & Deason, Velma. World Outreach Intercessory Prayer Warriors. 1983. pap. 2.50 (ISBN 0-910709-40-8). PTL Repro.
Deason, Hilary J., compiled by. AAAS Science Book List for Children. 3rd ed. LC 75-169601. 268p. (gr. 4-12). 1972. casebd. 8.95 (ISBN 0-87168-202-8). AAAS.
Deason, Velma, jt. auth. see Deason, Dee.
De Aspurz-Iriarte, Lazaro. The Franciscan Calling. Kelly, Sr. Marie, tr. 300p. 1975. 6.95 (ISBN 0-8199-0538-0). Franciscan Herald.
De Assis, Joaquim M. Machado see Machado de Assis, Joaquim M.
De Assis, Machado. Dom Casmurro. 1980. pap. 2.95 (ISBN 0-380-49668-2, 49668-2, Bard). Avon.
--Epitaph of a Small Winner. 1977. pap. 3.50 (ISBN 0-380-01712-1, 59659-8, Bard). Avon.
--Helena. Caldwell, Helen, tr. from Portugese. LC 83-17966. 197p. 1984. 14.95 (ISBN 0-520-04812-1). U of Cal Pr.
--Philosopher or Dog? 288p. 1982. pap. 3.95 (ISBN 0-380-58982-6, 58982-6, Bard). Avon.
Deassis, Machado J. & Neto, C. Brazilian Tales. Goldberg, Isaac, tr. 1977. lib. bdg. 59.95 (ISBN 0-8490-1551-0). Gordon Pr.
D'Easum, Dick. Dowager of Discipline: The Life of Dean of Women Permeal French. LC 81-51334. (GEM Books: Historical). (Illus.). 150p. (Orig.). 1981. pap. 11.95 (ISBN 0-89301-080-4). U Pr of Idaho.
--Sawtooth Tales. LC 76-24379. (Illus.). 1977. pap. 7.95 (ISBN 0-87004-259-9). Caxton.
Deasy, C. M. & Lasswell, Thomas. Designing Places for People. (Illus.). 160p. 1985. 27.50 (ISBN 0-8230-7152-9, Whitney Lib). Watson-Guptill.
Deasy, Mary. The Hour of Spring. LC 76-6334. (Irish Americans Ser). 1976. Repr. of 1948 ed. 30.00 (ISBN 0-405-09330-6). Ayer Co Pubs.
Deasy, Richard M., ed. see Staples, William R.
De'Ath, E., jt. auth. see Pugh, G.
Deatherage. Steamboating on the Missouri River in the Sixties. 1984. pap. 2.00 (ISBN 0-87770-043-5). Ye Galleon.
Deatherage, F. E. Food for Life. LC 75-15502. (Illus.). 434p. 1975. 24.50x (ISBN 0-306-30816-9, Plenum Pr). Plenum Pub.
Deathridge, John & Dahlhaus, Carl. The New Grove Wagner. Sadie, Stanley, ed. (The New Grove Composer Biography Ser.). (Illus.). 1984. 17.95 (ISBN 0-393-01688-9); pap. 7.95 (ISBN 0-393-30092-7). Norton.
Deaton, Agnus & Muellbauer, John. Economics & Consumer Behavior. LC 79-17090. 1980. 54.50 (ISBN 0-521-22850-6); pap. 22.95 (ISBN 0-521-29676-5). Cambridge U Pr.
Deaton, Angus. Essays in the Theory & Measurement of Consumer Behavior. 300p. 1981. 52.50 (ISBN 0-521-22565-5). Cambridge U Pr.
Deaton, Donald B., ed. Glossary of Printing Terms. 58p. 1973. 27.00 (ISBN 0-318-12163-8); members 16.00 (ISBN 0-318-12164-6). AATCC.
Deaton, William. Statistical Analysis for Microcomputers. (Illus.). 96p. 1984. incl. disk 49.95 (ISBN 0-88056-217-X). Dilithium Pr.
Deats, Paul, Jr., jt. auth. see Stotts, Herbert E.
Deats, Paul, Jr., ed. Toward a Discipline of Social Ethics: Essays in Honor of Walter George Muelder. LC 70-189020. 1972. 5.00 (ISBN 0-87270-018-6). Boston U Sch of Theology.
De Aureliani, Vittorio. Why Even Competent Businessmen Fail when Managing Their Own Businesses: The Negatives You Ought to Know. (Illus.). 102p. 1984. 77.85x (ISBN 0-86654-103-9). Inst Econ Finan.
Deaux, John. The Saints Joke Book. (Illus.). 48p. (Orig.). 1981. pap. 2.95 (ISBN 0-937552-08-9). Quail Ridge.
Deaux, Kay. The Behavior of Women & Men. LC 75-23856. 1976. pap. text ed. 9.00 pub net (ISBN 0-8185-0177-4). Brooks-Cole.
Deaux, Kay & Ullman, Joseph C. Women of Steel: Female Blue-Collar Workers in the Basic Steel Industry. 208p. 1983. 24.95 (ISBN 0-03-062008-2). Praeger.
Deaux, Kay & Wrightsman, Lawrence C. Social Psychology in the Eighties. 4th ed. LC 83-7379. (Psychology Ser.). 700p. 1983. text ed. 22.00 pub net (ISBN 0-534-02926-4). Brooks-Cole.
Deaver, B. & Ruvalds, John, eds. Advances in Superconductivity. (NATO ASI Series B, Physics: Vol. 100). 538p. 1983. 75.00x (ISBN 0-306-41388-4, Plenum Pr). Plenum Pub.
Deaver, B. S., Jr., et al, eds. Future Trends in Superconductive Electronics. LC 78-66638. (AIP Conference Proceedings: No. 44). (Illus.). 1979. lib. bdg. 22.00 (ISBN 0-88318-143-6). Am Inst Physics.
Deaver, Jeff. The Complete Law School Companion. LC 84-2290. 189p. 1984. pap. 8.95 (ISBN 0-471-80445-2). Wiley.
Deaver, Korra, compiled by. Rock Crystal: The Magic Stone. LC 85-50463. 64p. (Orig.). 1985. pap. 3.95 (ISBN 0-87728-577-2). Weiser.
Deaver, Robert. Opera Plots Made Easy. 70p. (Orig.). 1985. pap. 4.95 (ISBN 0-932665-00-4). Deaver Corp.
Deaville, Alfred S. The Colonial Postal System & Postage Stamps of Vancouver Island & British Columbia Eighteen Forty-Nine to Eighteen Seventy-One. LC 79-67392. 224p. 1980. Repr. of 1928 ed. lib. bdg. 35.00x (ISBN 0-88000-111-9). Quarterman.
Deavours, Cipher & Kruh, Louis. Machine Cryptography & Modern Cryptanalysis. 1985. text ed. 56.00 (ISBN 0-89006-161-0). Artech Hse.
De Ayala, Ramon P. Belarmino & Apolonio. Baumgarten, Murray & Berns, Gabriel, trs. from Span. 1983. pap. 5.95 (ISBN 0-520-04958-6, CAL 626). U of Cal Pr.
De Ayala, Ramon Perez see Perez de Ayala, Ramon.
De Azara, Don Felix. Apuntamientos para la Historia Natural de los Quadrupedos del Paraguay y Rio de la Plata, 2 vols. in one. Sterling, Keir B., ed. LC 77-81077. (Biologists & Their World Ser.). (Span.). 1978. Repr. of 1802 ed. lib. bdg. 52.00x (ISBN 0-405-10645-9). Ayer Co Pubs.
De Azavedo, Carlos. Churches of Portugal. LC 85-50365. (Illus.). 206p. 1985. 38.50 (ISBN 0-935748-66-0). Scala Books.
De Azcarate, P. League of Nations & National Minorities: An Experiment. (Studies in the Administration of International Law & Organization). Repr. of 1945 ed. 21.00 (ISBN 0-527-00883-4). Kraus Repr.
De Azcarate, Pablo. Mission in Palestine, Nineteen Forty-Eight to Nineteen Fifty-Two. LC 66-30659. 1966. 6.75 (ISBN 0-916808-07-6). Mid East Inst.
Deb, Arabinda. India & Bhutan: A Study in Frontier Political Relations, 1772-1865. LC 76-905259. 1976. 7.50x (ISBN 0-88386-913-6). South Asia Bks.
Deb, B. M. The Force Concept in Chemistry. 480p. 1981. 37.50 (ISBN 0-442-26106-3). Van Nos Reinhold.
Deb, D. Flora of Tripura State, Vegetation: Ophioglossaceae-Staphyleaceae, Vol. 1. (International Bio Science Ser.: Vol. 9). (Illus.). 484p. 1981. 50.00 (ISBN 0-88065-231-4, Pub. by Messers Today & Tomorrow Printers & Publishers). Scholarly Pubns.
De Baca, Carlos. Vicente Silva: The Terror of Las Vegas. (Wild & Woolly West Ser: No. 35). (Illus.). 1978. 8.00 (ISBN 0-910584-50-8); pap. 2.00 (ISBN 0-910584-93-1). Filter.
De Baca Gilbert, Fabiola C. The Good Life: New Mexico Traditions & Food. (Illus.). 104p. 1982. pap. 5.95 (ISBN 0-89013-137-6). Museum NM Pr.
De Bacan, Alvaro. Relation of the Expongnable Attempt & Conquest of the Ylande of Tercera. LC 76-57352. (English Experience Ser.: No. 772). 1977. Repr. of 1584 ed. lib. bdg. 6.00 (ISBN 90-221-0772-8). Walter J Johnson.
DeBach, P. Biological Control by Natural Enemies. LC 73-90812. (Illus.). 325p. 1974. 49.50 (ISBN 0-521-20380-5); pap. 14.95 (ISBN 0-521-09835-1). Cambridge U Pr.
Debahy, Moses. Dictionary Hebrew Verbs. (Hebrew & Arabic.). 1974. 15.00x (ISBN 0-86685-123-2). Intl Bk Ctr.
De Baillie, Katrine. How to Cook Forsoothly. (Illus.). 170p. (Orig.). 1979. plastic ring 5.50 (ISBN 0-943228-02-6). Raymonds Quiet Pr.
--Medieval Costume. (Illus.). 180p. (Orig.). 1980. pap. 5.25 (ISBN 0-943228-01-8). Raymonds Quiet Pr.
De Bairacli-Levy, Juliette. Common Herbs for Natural Health. LC 73-91335. (Illus.). 198p. 1974. pap. 3.95 (ISBN 0-8052-0436-9). Schocken.
--The Complete Herbal Book for the Dog. LC 72-3339. 1973. 8.95 (ISBN 0-668-02649-9); pap. 5.95 (ISBN 0-668-04181-1). Arco.
De Bairacli Levy, Juliette. Traveler's Joy. LC 78-61327. 1979. 8.95 (ISBN 0-87983-182-0); pap. 4.95 (ISBN 0-87983-183-9). Keats.
DeBakey, Lois. The Scientific Journal: Editorial Policies & Practices--Guidelines for Editors, Reviewers & Authors. LC 76-6046. 129p. 1976. text ed. 13.95 (ISBN 0-8016-1223-3). Mosby.
DeBakey, Michael E. & Gotto, Anthony M., Jr. Factors Influencing the Course of Myocardial Ischemia. (Argenteuil Symposia Ser.: Vol. 7). 1983. 84.75 (ISBN 0-444-80472-2, I-382-83). Elsevier.
Debakey, Michael E., jt. auth. see Beebe, Gilbert W.
DeBakey, Michael E., ed. Advances in Cardiac Valves: Clinical Perspectives. (Illus.). 274p. 1983. 35.00 (ISBN 0-914316-40-0). Yorke Med.
DeBakey, Michael E., et al. The Living Heart Diet: Professional Edition. 425p. 1984. text ed. 29.95 (ISBN 0-89004-672-7). Raven.
De Bakker, H. Major Soils & Soil Regions in the Netherlands. (Illus.). 1979. lib. bdg. 53.00 (ISBN 9-06193-590-3, Pub. by Junk Pubs Netherlands). Kluwer Academic.
--Major Soils & Soil Regions in the Netherlands. 192p. 105.00x (ISBN 0-686-45853-2, Pub. by CAB Bks England). State Mutual Bk.
De Bakker, J. W. & Van Vliet, J., eds. Algorithmic Languages: Proceedings of the IFIP TC-2 International Symposium, October 1981. 432p. 1982. 45.00 (ISBN 0-444-86285-4, North-Holland). Elsevier.
De Bakker, M. Mathematical Theory of Program Correctness. 1980. 44.95 (ISBN 0-13-562132-1). P-H.
DeBallester, Archimandrite P. The Subconscious Orthodoxy of the Spanish Race. Orthodox Christian Educational Society, ed. 8p. (Orig.). 1978. pap. 0.30x (ISBN 0-938366-46-7). Orthodox Chr.
De Balzac, Honore. Beatrix. (Coll. Prestige). 1962. 27.95 (ISBN 0-685-11037-0). French & Eur.
--Beatrix. Regard, ed. (Class. Garnier). pap. 9.95 (ISBN 0-685-34069-4). French & Eur.
--Beatrix: Le Livre de Poche Classique. pap. 9.95 (ISBN 0-685-34070-8). French & Eur.
--Le Cabinet des Antiques. Castex, ed. (Coll. Prestige). 1958. 27.95 (ISBN 0-685-34071-6); pap. 9.95 (ISBN 0-686-66833-2). French & Eur.
--Les Chouans. (Le Livre de Poche Classique). pap. 3.95 (ISBN 0-685-34075-9). French & Eur.
--Les Chouans. Regard, ed. (Class Garnier). pap. 9.95 (ISBN 0-685-34073-2). French & Eur.
--Les Chouans. Regard, ed. (Coll. Prestige). 27.95 (ISBN 0-685-34074-0). French & Eur.
--Chouans. (Penguin Classics Ser.). 1972. pap. 5.95 (ISBN 0-14-044260-X). Penguin.
--Colonel Chabert. 1964. pap. 3.95 (ISBN 0-685-11095-8, 1140). French & Eur.
--Conjugal Life. 1958. 3.75 (ISBN 0-685-06549-9). Assoc Bk.
--Correspondances a l'exception Ides Lettres de Mme. Hanska, 5 Vols. Pierrot, ed. 1961-67. pap. 18.95 ea; Tome 1, (1809-Mai 1832. (ISBN 0-685-11112-1); Tome 2, (juin 1832-1835. (ISBN 0-685-11113-X); Tome 3, (1836-1837) (ISBN 0-685-11114-8); Tome 4,(1840-Avril 1845) (ISBN 0-685-11115-6); Tome 5, (mai 1845-1850) (ISBN 0-685-11116-4). French & Eur.
--Cousin Bette. Crawford, Marion A., tr. (Classics Ser.). (Orig.). 1965. pap. 4.95 (ISBN 0-14-044160-3). Penguin.
--Le Cousin Pons. 1962. pap. 4.95 (ISBN 0-685-11119-9, 989). French & Eur.
--Le Cousin Pons. Allem, ed. (Class. Garnier). pap. 15.95 (ISBN 0-685-34076-7). French & Eur.
--Le Cousin Pons. Allem, ed. (Coll. Prestige). 27.95 (ISBN 0-685-34077-5). French & Eur.
--Cousine Bette. 1955. pap. 4.95 (ISBN 0-685-11120-2, 952). French & Eur.
--La Cousine Bette. Allem, ed. (Class. Garnier). pap. 10.95 (ISBN 0-685-34078-3). French & Eur.
--La Cousine Bette. Allem, ed. (Coll. Prestige). 27.95 (ISBN 0-685-34079-1). French & Eur.
--Le Cure de Tours, La Grenadiere, L'Illustre Gaudissart. Berard, ed. (Coll GF). pap. 4.95 (ISBN 0-685-34081-3). French & Eur.
--Le Cure De Tours, Pierette. Allem, ed. 1965. pap. 7.95 (ISBN 0-685-11124-5). French & Eur.
--Le Cure de Tours, Pierette. Allem, ed. (Coll. Prestige). 27.95 (ISBN 0-685-34080-5). French & Eur.
--Cure De Village. 1965. pap. 4.95 (ISBN 0-685-11125-3, 1563). French & Eur.
--La Duchesse de Langeais. Bd. with Fille aux Yeux d'Or. 1958. pap. 4.95 (ISBN 0-685-23885-7, 356). French & Eur.
--Eugenie Grandet. (Literature Ser). (gr. 10-12). 1970. pap. text ed. 4.83 (ISBN 0-87720-746-1). AMSCO Sch.
--Eugenie Grandet. 1965. pap. 3.95 (ISBN 0-685-11176-8, 1414). French & Eur.
--Eugenie Grandet. Castex, ed. (Class. Garnier). pap. 9.95 (ISBN 0-685-34082-1). French & Eur.
--Eugenie Grandet. Castex, ed. (Coll. Prestige). 27.95 (ISBN 0-685-34083-X). French & Eur.
--Eugenie Grandet, 2 Vols. (Nouveaux Classiques Larousse). (Illus., Fr.). pap. 2.95 ea. Larousse.
--Eugenie Grandet. Crawford, M. A., tr. (Classic Ser.). 1955. pap. 3.95 (ISBN 0-14-044050-X). Penguin.
--Femme De Trente Ans. (Coll. GF). 1962. pap. 3.95 (ISBN 0-685-11182-2, 2201). French & Eur.
--La Femme de Trente Ans. Allem, ed. (Class. Garnier). pap. 9.95 (ISBN 0-685-34084-8). French & Eur.
--La Femme de Trente Ans. Allem, ed. (Coll. Prestige). 27.95 (ISBN 0-685-34085-6). French & Eur.
--Harlot High & Low. Heppenstall, Rayner, tr. (Ping Classic Ser.). 1970. pap. 4.95 (ISBN 0-14-044232-4). Penguin.
--Illusions Perdues. Adam, ed. (Class. Garnier). pap. 14.95 (ISBN 0-685-34086-4). French & Eur.
--Illusions Perdues. Adam, ed. (Coll. Prestige). 27.95 (ISBN 0-685-34087-2). French & Eur.
--Les Illusions perdues, 2 pts. (Documentation thematique). (Fr.). pap. 2.95 ea. Pt. 1 (368). Pt. 2 (369). Larousse.
--Lys Dans la Vallee. 1965. pap. 4.50 (ISBN 0-685-11298-5, 1461). French & Eur.
--Le Lys dans la Vallee. (Coll. Prestige). 27.95 (ISBN 0-685-34088-0). French & Eur.
--La Maison du Chat-qui-pelote. Castex, ed. Incl. Vendetta; Le Bal de Sceaux. (Classiques Garnier Ser.). pap. 6.95 (ISBN 0-685-23883-0). French & Eur.
--Medecin De Campagne. (Classiques Garnier). 1965. pap. 13.95 (ISBN 0-685-11354-X). French & Eur.
--Le Medecin de Campagne. Allem, ed. (Coll. Prestige). 27.95 (ISBN 0-685-34089-9). French & Eur.
--Le Medecin de Campagne. Citron, ed. (Coll. GF). pap. 4.95 (ISBN 0-685-34090-2). French & Eur.
--Oeuvres Completes, 24 tomes. (Avec notes et appendices publ. sons la signature de la societe des etudes balzaciennes). Set. 1250.00 (ISBN 0-685-34067-8). French & Eur.
--Oeuvres Completes Illustrees, 25 tomes. Ducourneau, ed. Set. 950.00 (ISBN 0-685-34068-6). French & Eur.
--Peau de Chagrin. (Coll. GF). 1960. pap. 3.95 (ISBN 0-685-11483-X, 1701). French & Eur.
--La Peau de Chagrin. Allem, ed. (Class. Garnier). pap. 9.95 (ISBN 0-685-34091-0). French & Eur.
--Pere Goriot. (Classics Ser). (gr. 10 up). pap. 1.50 (ISBN 0-8049-0084-1, CL-84). Airmont.
--Pere Goriot. 1960. pap. 3.95 (ISBN 0-685-11486-4, 757). French & Eur.
--Le Pere Goriot. Castex, ed. (Class. Garnier). pap. 9.95 (ISBN 0-685-34092-9). French & Eur.
--Le Pere Goriot. Castex, ed. (Coll. Prestige). 27.95 (ISBN 0-685-34093-7). French & Eur.
--Pere Goriot, 2 Vols. (Documentation thematique). (Fr). pap. 2.95 ea. Larousse.

--Pere Goriot. Reed, Henry, tr. (Orig.). 1962. pap. 2.95 (ISBN 0-451-51976-0, CE1812, Sig Classics). NAL.
--Pere Goriot. 14.95 (ISBN 0-88411-598-4, Pub. by Aeonian Pr). Amereon Ltd.
--Physiology of Marriage. (Black & Gold Lib). 1943. 6.95 (ISBN 0-87140-983-6, Co-Pub with Tudor). Liveright.
--Rabouilleuse. 1960. pap. 4.50 (ISBN 0-685-11520-8, 543). French & Eur.
--La Recherche de l'Absolu. Bd. with Messe de l'Athee. pap. 4.50 (ISBN 0-685-23884-9, 2163). French & Eur.
--Seraphita. LC 83-83172. (Spiritual Fiction Publications: Vol. 6). 224p. 1985. cloth 14.00 (ISBN 0-8334-0005-3, Spiritual Fiction). Garber Comm.
--Splendeurs et Miseres des Courtisanes. (Coll. GF). pap. 4.50 (ISBN 0-685-34094-5). French & Eur.
--Ursule Mirouet. pap. 4.50 (ISBN 0-685-23960-8, 2449). French & Eur.
De Balzac, Honore see Balzac, Honore De.
De Balzac, Honore see Balzac, Honore de.
De Balzac, Honore see Balzac, Honore De.
De Balzac, Honore see Peyrazat, Jean E.
DeBand, Roy E., jt. auth. see Bess, C. W.
De Bandt, Jacques, et al. European Studies in Development. LC 79-26811. 1980. 35.00x (ISBN 0-312-27086-0). St Martin.
DeBanks, Henward M. & Ginalski, William. The Franchise Option: Expanding Your Business Through Franchising. LC 80-65946. (Illus.). 187p. 1980. 34.50 (ISBN 0-936898-00-3). Franchise Group.
DeBarbadillo, John J. & Snape, Edwin, eds. Sulfide Inclusions in Steel: An International Symposium, 7-8 November, 1974, Port Chester, New York Proceedings. LC 75-19315. (Materials-Metalworking Technology Ser.: No. 6). (Illus.). pap. 127.00 (ISBN 0-317-09688-5, 2051903). Bks Demand UMI.
Debarbat, S. & Guinot, B. La Methode Des Hauteurs Egales En Astronomie. (Cours et Documents De Mathematiques et De Physique Ser.). 150p. (Fr.). 1970. 45.25 (ISBN 0-677-50250-8). Gordon.
DeBardeleben, Martha G. Fear's Answer: A Case History in Nouthetic Counseling. 1981. pap. 3.75 (ISBN 0-87552-236-X). Presby & Reformed.
De Bargh, David J. Christ in My Life. 1977. 4.50 (ISBN 0-8198-0396-0); pap. text ed. 3.50 (ISBN 0-8198-0397-9). Dghtrs St Paul.
DeBarra, G. Measure Theory & Integration. LC 81-13510. (Mathematics & Its Applications Ser.). 260p. 1981. 69.95x (ISBN 0-470-27232-5). Halsted Pr.
De Barranco, Clara, tr. see Dinkmeyer, Don & McKay, Gary.
De Barrios, Miguel. La Poesia Religiosa de Miguel De Barrios. Scholberg, Kenneth R., ed. 369p. (Orig., Sp.). 1962. pap. 5.00 (ISBN 0-8142-0108-3). Ohio St U Pr.
De Barrios, Virginia B. A Guide to Tequila, Mezcal & Pulque. 65p. 1971. pap. 3.50 (ISBN 0-912434-12-0). Ocelot Pr.
De Barry, Brett, jt. auth. see Nee, Victor G.
De Barry Barnett, Edward. Explosives. 1980. lib. bdg. 150.00 (ISBN 0-8490-3154-0). Gordon Pr.
De Bartha, Georges, jt. auth. see Duncan, Alastair.
De Barthe, Joe. Life & Adventures of Frank Grouard. Stewart, Edgar I., ed. LC 58-11651. (Illus.). Repr. of 1958 ed. 74.50 (ISBN 0-8357-9731-7, 2016209). Bks Demand UMI.
De Bartolo, Dick. The Return of a Mad Look at Old Movies. pap. 1.25 (ISBN 0-451-06835-1, Y6835, Sig). NAL.
De Bartolo, Dick & Clarke, Bob. Mad Vertising. (Orig.). 1972. pap. 1.25 (ISBN 0-451-06739-8, Y6739, Sig). NAL.
DeBartolo, Dick & Edwing, Don. Mad Murders the Movies. 192p. 1985. pap. 2.50 (ISBN 0-446-30886-2). Warner Bks.
Debartolo, Dick & North, Harry. The Mad Book of Sex & Violence & Home Cooking. 192p. (Orig.). 1983. pap. 1.95 (ISBN 0-446-30033-0). Warner Bks.
De Bartolo, Dick & North, Henry. Mad Guide to Fraud & Deception. (Illus.). 192p. (Orig.). 1981. pap. 1.95 (ISBN 0-446-30465-4). Warner Bks.
DeBartolo, Dick & Torres, Angelo. A Mad Look at TV. (Illus.). 192p. (Orig.). (YA) 1974. pap. 1.75 (ISBN 0-446-94436-X). Warner Bks.
DeBartolo, Dick & Woodbridge, George. A Mad Guide to Leisure Time. (Illus.). 192p. (Orig.). 1983. pap. 1.95 (ISBN 0-446-30466-2). Warner Bks.
DeBartolo, Joseph A. In Further Pursuit of Trivial Pursuit: Baby Boomers Edition. (Illus.). 450p. 1985. pap. 13.95 (ISBN 0-930281-01-2). Sarsaparilla.
--In Further Pursuit of Trivial Pursuit. (Illus.). 444p. (Orig.). 1984. pap. 13.95 (ISBN 0-930281-00-4). Sarsaparilla.
--The Original Chicago Trivia Book. (Illus.). 250p. 1985. pap. 8.95 (ISBN 0-930281-03-9). Sarsaparilla.
De Bary, Anton. Comparative Morphology & Biology of the Fungi, Mycetozoa, & Bacteria. Balfour, I. B., ed. Garnsey, E. H., tr. Repr. of 1887 ed. 50.00 (ISBN 0-384-11145-9). Johnson Repr.
DeBary, Brett, tr. Three Works by Nakano Shigeharu. (East Asia Papers: No. 21). 166p. 1979. 7.00 (ISBN 0-318-04626-1). Cornell China-Japan Pgm.
DeBary, Theodore & Haboush, Jahyun K., eds. The Rise of Neo-Confucianism in Korea. 512p. 1985. 45.00x (ISBN 0-231-06052-1). Columbia U pr.
De Bary, W. T., ed. Sources of Indian Tradition, 2 vols. LC 58-4146. (Introductions to the Oriental Classics & Records of Civilization: Sources & Studies Ser.). Vol. 1, 585 Pgs. 13.00x (ISBN 0-231-08600-8); Vol. 2, 384 Pgs. 11.00x (ISBN 0-231-08601-6). Columbia U Pr.
De Bary, W. Theodore, ed. The Unfolding of Neo-Confucianism. LC 74-10929. (Neo-Confucian Series & Studies in Oriental Culture: No. 10). 593p. 1975. 36.00x (ISBN 0-231-03828-3); pap. 17.50x (ISBN 0-231-03829-1). Columbia U Pr.
De Bary, W. Theodore & Bloom, Irene, eds. Principle & Practicality: Essays in Neo-Confucianism & Practical Learning. LC 78-11530. (Neo-Confucian Series & Studies in Oriental Culture). 1979. 36.00x (ISBN 0-231-04612-X); pap. 18.00x (ISBN 0-231-04613-8). Columbia U Pr.
DeBary, W. Theodore, jt. ed. see Chan, Hok-Lam.
De Bary, W. Theodore, ed. see Conference on Oriental Classics in General Education (1958: Columbia University) Staff.
De Bary, William T. Guide to Oriental Classics. 2nd ed. Embree, T., ed. LC 63-20463. (Companions to Asian Studies). 1974. 20.00x (ISBN 0-231-03891-7); pap. 10.50 (ISBN 0-231-03892-5). Columbia U Pr.
--The Liberal Tradition in China. (Neo-Confucian Studies). 130p. 1983. 20.00x (ISBN 0-231-05666-4). Columbia U Pr.
--Neo-Confucian Orthodoxy & the Learning of the Mind-&-Heart. LC 81-3809. 288p. 1981. 28.50x (ISBN 0-231-05228-6). Columbia U Pr.
De Bary, William T., ed. The Buddhist Tradition: In India, China & Japan. 448p. 1972. pap. 5.95 (ISBN 0-394-71696-5, V702, Vin). Random.
--Self & Society in Ming Thought. LC 78-101229. (Neo-Confucian Series & Studies in Oriental Culture). 550p. 1970. 34.00x (ISBN 0-231-03271-4); pap. 17.00x (ISBN 0-231-08313-0). Columbia U Pr.
--Sources of Chinese Tradition, 2 Vols. LC 60-9911. (Records of Civilization, Sources & Studies & Introduction to Oriental Classics Ser.). 1960. 1 vol. ed. o.p 30.00x (ISBN 0-231-02255-7); Vol. 1, 578 P. pap. 14.00x (ISBN 0-231-08602-4); Vol. 2, 322 P. pap. 12.00x (ISBN 0-231-08603-2). Columbia U Pr.
De Bary, William T. & Embree, Ainslie T., eds. Approaches to Asian Civilizations. LC 63-20226. (Companions to Asian Studies). 290p. 1964. 26.00x (ISBN 0-231-02648-X). Columbia U Pr.
De Bary, William T., tr. see Saikaku, Ihara.
De Basily, Lascelle. Memoirs of a Lost World. LC 75-29793. 308p. 1975. 9.95x (ISBN 0-8179-4151-7). Hoover Inst Pr.
De Basily, Nicolas. Memoirs. LC 70-175450. (Publications Ser.: No. 125). 201p. 1973. 8.95x (ISBN 0-8179-6251-4). Hoover Inst Pr.
De Basily, Nicolas see Basily, Nicolas de.
De Bastyai, Lorant. All My Life with Hunting Birds. 265p. 1982. 33.00x (ISBN 0-85435-454-9, Pub. by Neville Spearman Ltd England). State Mutual Bk.
De Bat, Alfred, ed. Advertising Photography in Chicago, 1985. (Illus.). 150p. 1985. pap. 25.00 (ISBN 0-917001-01-X). R Silver.
Debate, Alfred, ed. The Professional Photographer. (Illus.). 80p. (J). subscr. incl. membership 22.10ann., monthly (ISBN 0-318-16209-1). Prof Photog.
Debate Study Group & Tharchin, Sermey G., eds. Logic & Debate Tradition of India, Tibet & Mongolia: History, Reader & Sources. 281p. (Orig.). 1979. pap. 9.50 (ISBN 0-918753-00-7, Pub by Rashi Gempil Ling). Mahayana.
De Bauw, F. & Dewit, B. China Trade Law. 478p. 1983. Published in Eng. & Fr. 68.00 (ISBN 90-654-4113-1, Pub. by Kluwer Law Netherlands). Kluwer Academic.
Debavpatnaik, P., jt. auth. see Olander, William.
De Baye, J. The Industrial Arts of the Anglo-Saxons. 1980. Repr. of 1893 ed. lib. bdg. 40.00 (ISBN 0-89341-380-1). Longwood Pub Group.
De Baz, Petros. The Story of Medicine. LC 74-84858. (Illus.). 100p. 1975. 6.00 (ISBN 0-8022-2154-8). Philos Lib.
Debbasch, Charles & Daudet, Yves. Lexique des Termes Politiques. 280p. (Fr.). 1978. pap. 14.95 (ISBN 0-686-57285-8, M-4652). French & Eur.
DeBear, Constance, jt. auth. see Burger, Isabel.
De Bear, Nicol, jt. auth. see Jones, Thora B.
Debease, Gloria, jt. auth. see Forbes, Adrienne.
De Beau Chesne, John & Baildon, John. A Booke Containing Divers Sortes of Hands, As Well As the English & French Secretarie. LC 77-6875. (English Experience Ser.: No. 867). 1977. Repr. of 1602 ed. lib. bdg. 10.50 (ISBN 90-221-0867-8). Walter J Johnson.
De Beauclair, Inez. Studies on Botel Tobago & Yap. (Asian Folklore & Social Life Monograph: No. 19). (Eng. & Ger.). 1971. 19.00 (ISBN 0-89986-021-4). Oriental Bk Store.
Debeaufort, jt. auth. see De Beaufort-Wijnholds, J. A.
De Beaufort, Raphael L., ed. & tr. see Sand, George.
De Beaufort, Simon. Yellow Earth, Green Jade: Constants in Chinese Political Mores. LC 78-56502. (Studies in International Affairs: No. 41). (gr. 10 up). 1979. text ed. 8.95x (ISBN 0-87674-044-1); pap. text ed. 3.95x (ISBN 0-87674-043-3). U Pr of Amer.
--Yellow Earth, Green Jade: Constants in Chinese Political Mores. (Harvard Studies in International Affairs: No. 41). 90p. 1984. pap. text ed. 7.25 (ISBN 0-8191-4059-7). U Pr of Amer.
De Beaufort-Wijnholds, J. A. & Debeaufort. The Need for International Reserves & Credit Facilities. (Publications of the Netherlands Institute of Bankers & Stock Brokers Ser: No. 31). 1977. pap. 23.00 (ISBN 90-207-0713-2, Pub. by Martinus Nijhoff Netherlands). Kluwer Academic.
De Beaugrande, R. & Dressler, W. Introduction to Text Linguistics. LC 80-40581. (Longman Linguistics Library). (Illus.). 288p. 1981. text ed. 19.95x (ISBN 0-582-55486-1); pap. text ed. 12.95x (ISBN 0-582-55485-3). Longman.
De Beaugrande, Robert. Text, Discourse, & Process: Toward a Multidisciplinary Science of Texts. (Advances in Discourse Processes Ser.: Vol. 4). 1980. text ed. 39.50x (ISBN 0-89391-033-3). Ablex Pub.
De Beaugrande, Robert see Beaugrande, Robert de.
De Beaugrande, Robert, tr. see Schmidt, Siegfried J.
De Beaujoyeulx, Balthazar. Le Balet Comique. Facsimile ed. McGowan, Margaret M., intro. by. LC 81-18827. (Medieval & Renaissance Texts & Studies: Vol. 6). 224p. (Fr.). 1982. 16.00 (ISBN 0-86698-012-1). Medieval & Renaissance NY.
De Beaumachais, P. Caron. Complete Figaro Plays. Wells, John, tr. from Fr. 500p. Date not set. 35.00 (ISBN 0-7145-3700-4). Riverrun NY.
De Beaumanoir, jt. auth. see Philippe De Remi.
De Beaumarchais, Pierre. The Barber of Seville. Luciani, Vincent, tr. from Fr. Bd. with The Marriage of Figaro. (World Classics in Tr.). (Eng.). 1965. pap. 5.95 (ISBN 0-8120-0029-3). Barron.
--The Barber of Seville & The Marriage of Figaro. Wood, John, tr. (Classics Ser.). 224p. 1964. pap. 3.95 (ISBN 0-14-044133-6). Penguin.
--Barbier de Seville. (Documentation thematique). (Illus., Fr.). pap. 2.95 (ISBN 0-685-13807-0, 22). Larousse.
--Le Mariage de Figaro, 2 Vols. (Documentation thematique). (Illus.). Set. pap. 2.95 ea. Larousse.
De Beaumarchais, Pierre A. Le Mariage de Figaro. (Fr.). 1965. pap. 5.90 (ISBN 0-685-23344-8). French & Eur.
--Theatre Complet, Parades, Lettres Relatives a son Theatre. Allem & Courant, eds. (Bibl de la Pleiade). 1954. 22.50 (ISBN 0-685-11590-9). French & Eur.
De Beaumont, E & Allinson, A. The Sword & Womankind: The Influence of the Sword Upon Moral & Social Status of Women. 1977. lib. bdg. 59.95 (ISBN 0-8490-2722-5). Gordon Pr.
De Beaumont, Gustave & De Tocqueville, Alexis. On the Penitentiary System in the United States & Its Application in France. LC 79-431. (Arcturus Books, Paperbacks). 264p. 1979. pap. 9.95x (ISBN 0-8093-0913-0). S Ill U Pr.
De Beaumont, Gustave & De Toqueville, Alexis. On the Penitentiary System in the United States & Its Applications in France. unabr. ed. (Criminology, Law Enforcement, & Social Problems Ser.). (Illus.). Date not set. 14.00 (ISBN 0-87585-204-1). Patterson Smith.
De Beaumont, Gustave, jt. auth. see De Tocqueville, Alexis.
De Beaumont, Gustave A. Marie, or Slavery in the United States: A Novel of Jacksonian America. 1958. 20.00x (ISBN 0-8047-0545-3). Stanford U Pr.
De Beaumont, Madame L. Beauty & the Beast. LC 76-57884. (Illus.). (gr. k-3). 1978. 9.95 (ISBN 0-02-726400-9). Bradbury Pr.
De Beaumont de la Bonniere, G. & De Tocqueville, Alexis. On the Penitentiary System in the United States, & Its Application to France; with an Appendix on Penal Colonies; Also Statistical Notes. LC 68-58029. Repr. of 1833 ed. lib. bdg. 35.00x (ISBN 0-678-00670-9). Kelley.
De Beauregard, Oliver Costa see Costa De Beauregard, Oliver.
De Beausobre, Isaac see Beausobre, Isaac de.
De Beauvais, Vincent. De Eruditione Filiorum Nobilium. Steiner, Arpad, ed. (Mediaeval Academy of America Ser). (Lat). Repr. of 1938 ed. 18.00 (ISBN 0-527-01699-3). Kraus Repr.
De Beauvais-Nangis, Nicolas D. Memoires du Marquis de Beauvais-Nangis et Journal du Proces du Marquis de la Boulaye. 1862. 43.00 (ISBN 0-384-03695-3); pap. 37.00 (ISBN 0-685-13509-8). Johnson Repr.
De Beauvoir, Simone. Adieux: A Farewell to Sartre. O'Brian, Patrick, tr. LC 83-19327. 453p. 1984. 19.45 (ISBN 0-394-53035-7). Pantheon.
--Adieux: A Farewell to Satre. O'Brian, Patrick, tr. 1985. pap. 8.95 (ISBN 0-394-72898-X). Pantheon.
--L' Amerique au Jour le Jour: Voyages. 9.95 (ISBN 0-685-37185-9). French & Eur.
--Belles Images. (Coll. Soleil). 1966. 10.95 (ISBN 0-685-11041-9); pap. 3.95 (ISBN 0-686-66414-0). French & Eur.
--The Blood of Others. Senhouse, Roger & Moyse, Yvonne, trs. (Modern Writers Ser.). 1984. pap. 7.95 (ISBN 0-394-72411-9). Pantheon.
--Les Bouches Inutiles. pap. 3.95 (ISBN 0-685-37186-7). French & Eur.
--Brigitte Bardot & the Lolita Syndrome. LC 78-169346. (Arno Press Cinema Program). (Illus.). 100p. 1972. Repr. of 1960 ed. 20.00 (ISBN 0-405-03912-3). Ayer Co Pubs.
--Deuxieme Sexe, 2 tomes. (Coll. Idees). 1949. Set. pap. 9.00 (ISBN 0-685-11134-2). French & Eur.
--Ethics of Ambiguity. 1962. pap. 4.95 (ISBN 0-8065-0160-X, 107). Citadel Pr.
--Faut-Il Bruler Sade? (Coll. Idees). pap. 3.95 (ISBN 0-685-37187-5). French & Eur.
--La Femme Rompue. (Coll. Soleil). 10.50 (ISBN 0-685-37188-3); pap. 3.95 (ISBN 0-686-66851-0). French & Eur.
--Force De L'age. 1960. 15.95 (ISBN 0-685-11196-2); pap. 3.95 (ISBN 0-686-66420-5). French & Eur.
--Force Des Choses. (Coll. Soleil). 1963. 18.50 (ISBN 0-685-11197-0); pap. 9.90 (ISBN 0-686-66421-3). French & Eur.
--Invitee: Roman. (Coll. Soleil). 1943. 15.50 (ISBN 0-685-11256-X); pap. 4.50 (ISBN 0-685-37189-1). French & Eur.
--The Mandarins. LC 79-65852. 610p. 1979. pap. 8.95 (ISBN 0-89526-898-1). Regnery-Gateway.
--Mandarins: Roman. (Coll. Blanche). 1961. 13.95 (ISBN 0-685-11340-X). French & Eur.
--Memoires d'une Jeune Fille Rangee. 1958. 8.50 (ISBN 0-685-11359-0). French & Eur.
--Memoirs of a Dutiful Daughter. 1974. pap. 7.64i (ISBN 0-06-090351-1, CN351, CN). Har-Row.
--Mort Tres Douce. (Coll. Soleil). 1964. 10.50 (ISBN 0-685-11609-3). French & Eur.
--Pour une Morale de l'Ambiguite, Pyrrhus et Cineas. (Coll. Idees). pap. 4.50 (ISBN 0-685-37190-5). French & Eur.
--Sang Des Autres. 1945. 6.50 (ISBN 0-685-11555-0). French & Eur.
--Second Sex. Parshley, H. M., tr. 1953. 25.00 (ISBN 0-394-44415-9). Knopf.
--Second Sex. LC 74-4241. 1974. pap. 5.95 (ISBN 0-394-71227-7, V-227, Vin). Random.
--Tous Les Hommes Sont Mortels: Roman. (Coll. Soleil). 1946. 14.50 (ISBN 0-685-11602-6). French & Eur.
--Tout Compte Fait. (Coll. Soleil). 29.75 (ISBN 0-685-37192-1). French & Eur.
--La Vieillesse. (Coll. Soleil). 22.75 (ISBN 0-685-37193-X). French & Eur.
--When Things of the Spirit Come First. O'Brian, Patrick, tr. (Modern Writers Ser.). 1984. pap. 6.95 (ISBN 0-394-72235-3). Pantheon.
--When Things of the Spirit Come First: Five Early Tales. O'Brian, Patrick, tr. 256p. 1982. 13.45 (ISBN 0-394-52216-8). Pantheon.
--Who Shall Die? Francis, Claude & Gontier, Fernande, trs. from Fr. LC 83-63137. Orig. Title: Les Bouches Inutiles. 66p. (Orig.). 1983. pap. 6.95 (ISBN 0-915535-00-9). River Pr.
De Beck, Billy. Barney Google: An Original Compilation. First Collection of the Complete First Year of the Daily Strip, 1919-1920. Blackbeard, Bill, ed. LC 76-53038. (Classis American Comic Series). 1977. 15.95 (ISBN 0-88355-631-6); pap. 6.95 (ISBN 0-88355-630-8). Hyperion Conn.
De Becker, Eric V. Survey of Some Japanese Tax Laws. (Studies in Japanese Law & Government). 182p. 1979. Repr. of 1931 ed. 18.50 (ISBN 0-89093-218-2). U Pubns Amer.
De Becker, Joseph E. Elements of Japanese Law: Studies in Japanese Law & Government. 1979. Repr. of 1916 ed. 34.00 (ISBN 0-89093-210-7). U Pubns Amer.
--Principles & Practice of the Civil Code of Japan: A Complete Theoretical & Practical Exposition of the Motifs of the Japanese Civil Code, 2 vols. (Studies in Japanese Law & Government). 852p. 1979. Repr. of 1921 ed. Set. 60.00 (ISBN 0-89093-216-6). U Pubns Amer.
De Becker, Joseph E., tr. from Japanese. Annotated Civil Code of Japan, 4 vols. (Studies in Japanese Law & Government). 1200p. 1979. 95.00 (ISBN 0-89093-215-8). U Pubns Amer.
DeBedts, Ralph F. Recent American History, Vol. VI: 1933 Through World War II. LC 73-84298. pap. 87.50 (ISBN 0-317-28000-7, 2055805). Bks Demand UMI.
Debee, Rajlukshmee. The Owl & Other Poems. Debee, Rajlukshmee, tr. from Bengali. (Writers Workshop Redbird Ser.). 1975. 12.00 (ISBN 0-88253-604-4); pap. text ed. 4.80 (ISBN 0-88253-603-6). Ind-US Inc.
De Beer, Carel, jt. auth. see Jackson, Melvin.
DeBeer, E. S., jt. auth. see Locke, John.
De Beer, E. S., ed. see Locke, John.
DeBeer, E. S., ed. see Locke, John.
De Beer, E. S., ed. see Locke, John.
De Beer, G. R. Sir Hans Sloane & the British Museum. LC 74-26258. (History, Philosophy & Sociology of Science Ser.). (Illus.). 1975. Repr. of 1953 ed. 22.00x (ISBN 0-405-06586-8). Ayer Co Pubs.
De Beer, G. R., ed. see Goodrich, Edwin S.

DeBeer, Gavin. Adaptation. rev ed. Head, J. J., ed. LC 77-88028. (Carolina Biology Readers Ser.). (Illus.). 16p. (gr. 10 up). 1978. pap. 1.60 (ISBN 0-89278-222-6, 45-9622). Carolina Biological.

De Beer, Gavin. Archaeopteryx Lithographica: A Study Based on the British Museum Specimen. (Illus.). 68p. 1966. Repr. of 1954 ed. 22.50x (ISBN 0-565-00224-4, Pub. by Brit Mus Nat Hist England). Sabbot-Natural Hist Bks.

DeBeer, Gavin. Autobiographies: Charles Darwin & Thomas Henry Huxley. (Illus.). 1983. pap. 5.95 (ISBN 0-19-285131-4). Oxford U Pr.

De Beer, Gavin. Charles Darwin: Evolution by Natural Selection. LC 74-1779. (British Men of Science Ser.). 1976. Repr. of 1964 ed. lib. bdg. 27.50x (ISBN 0-8371-7378-7, DECD). Greenwood.

--Early Travellers in the Alps. (Illus.). 1967. 5.95 (ISBN 0-8079-0041-9); pap. 2.95 (ISBN 0-8079-0042-7). October.

De Beer, Gavin R. The Development of the Vertebrate Skull. (Illus.). xxiv, 730p. 1985. pap. text ed. 22.50x (ISBN 0-226-13960-3); 45.00x (ISBN 0-226-13958-1). U of Chicago Pr.

De Beer, Gavin R., ed. see Locke, John.

De Beer, Peter H., jt. auth. see Leonard, Robert J.

De Begona, Mauricio. Cristo Yanqui. LC 82-84263. 777p. (Orig., Span.). 1984. pap. 19.00 (ISBN 0-89729-323-1). Ediciones.

De Bekker, L. J. The Plot Against Mexico. 1976. lib. bdg. 59.95 (ISBN 0-8490-0844-1). Gordon Pr.

Debel, Niels H. The Veto Power of the Governor of Illinois. (Illinois Studies in the Social Sciences: Vol. 6). 1917. 12.00 (ISBN 0-384-11165-3). Johnson Repr.

Debelak, Marianne, et al. Creating Innovative Classroom Materials for Teaching Young Children. 321p. 1981. pap. text ed. 20.95 spiral bdg. (ISBN 0-15-515786-8, HC). HarBraceJ.

De Bellaigue, Geoffrey. Furniture, Clocks, Gilt Bronzes, 2 vols. (The Waddesdon Catalogues Ser.). (Illus.). 904p. text ed. 100.00 (ISBN 0-7078-0010-2, Pub. by P Wilson Pubs). Sotheby Pubns.

--The Louis XVI Service: The Sevres Porcelain in the Collection of Her Majesty the Queen, Vol. 1. (Illus.). 224p. Date not set. price not set (ISBN 0-521-26637-8). Cambridge U Pr.

De Bellay, Jaochim. Regrets: Choix de poemes. (Documentation thematique). (Illus., Fr.). 1975. pap. 2.95 (ISBN 0-685-64173-2). Larousse.

De Bellefonds, Y. Linant see Linant De Bellefonds, Y.

DeBelleroche, J. Presynaptic Receptors: Mechanisms & Functions. 223p. 1982. 74.95 (ISBN 0-470-27345-3). Halsted Pr.

De Belleroche, J. & Dockray, G. J., eds. Cholecystokinin (CCK) in the Nervous System. 132p. 1984. text ed. 33.80x (ISBN 0-89573-369-2). VCH Pubs.

De Bellis, Jack, ed. Sidney Lanier, Henry Timrod & Paul Hamilton Hayne: A Reference Guide. 1978. lib. bdg. 26.00 (ISBN 0-8161-7967-0, Hall Reference). G K Hall.

DeBellis, Robert, et al, eds. Medical Care of the Dying Patient. 30.00 (ISBN 0-405-13947-0). Ayer Co Pubs.

--The House Staff & Thanatology. 15.00 (ISBN 0-405-14211-0). Ayer Co Pubs.

De Belot, Raymond. The Struggle of the Mediterranean, 1939-1945. Field, James A., Jr., tr. LC 51-12459. pap. 76.50 (ISBN 0-317-26671-3, 2055993). Bks Demand UMI.

DeBenedetti, Charles. The Peace Reform in American History. LC 79-2173. 274p. 1980. 18.50x (ISBN 0-253-13095-6). Ind U Pr.

--The Peace Reform in American History. LC 79-2173. 264p. (Orig.). 1984. pap. 8.95x (ISBN 0-253-20320-1, 320, MB). Ind U Pr.

De Benedetti, Edoardo. Visualizations in the Realm of Historical Predictions in the Light of the Kondratieff Theory. (Illus.). 131p. 1983. 97.45x (ISBN 0-86722-041-4). Inst Econ Pol.

DeBenedetti, Leo V. A Glossary of Latin Philosophical Terms Translated into English with Explanatory Elucidations. 89p. 1984. pap. 23.75 (ISBN 0-89266-492-4). Am Classical Coll Pr.

DeBenedetti, Leonardo. The Racial Inequality of the Human Race & the Leadership Rights of the Historical Elite. (Illus.). 117p. 1981. 63.85 (ISBN 0-89266-316-2). Am Classical Coll Pr.

DeBenedetti, Rodolfe. How to Conduct an Investigation of Your Unconscious Self for the Discovery of the Mystery You Carry within Yourself. (Illus.). 165p. 1986. 87.45 (ISBN 0-89920-126-1). Am Inst Psych.

De Benedict, Spinoza see Spinoza, Benedict de.

De Benedictis, Daniel J. Complete Real Estate Advisor. 1977. pap. 4.95 (ISBN 0-346-12212-0). Cornerstone.

--The Complete Real Estate Advisor. rev. ed. 1983. pap. 3.95 (ISBN 0-671-49855-X). PB.

--The Complete Real Estate Advisor. Rev. ed. 1983. pap. 6.95 (ISBN 0-346-12578-2). Cornerstone.

DeBenedictis, Matthew M. The Social Thought of Saint Bonaventure: A Study in Social Philosophy. LC 73-138108. 276p. 1946. Repr. lib. bdg. 19.75x (ISBN 0-8371-5684-X, DESB). Greenwood.

De Benedittis, Suzanne M. Teaching Faith & Morals. 200p. (Orig.). 1981. pap. 8.95 (ISBN 0-86683-621-7). Winston Pr.

Debenham, Michael J. Microprocessors: An Introduction to the Principles & Applications. 1979. 25.00 (ISBN 0-08-024206-5); pap. 9.50 (ISBN 0-08-024207-3). Pergamon.

De Benitez, Ana M. Cocina Prehispanica. bilingual ed. (Illus., Eng., Span.). 1977. pap. 7.95x (ISBN 0-685-79831-3). Adlers Foreign Bks.

--Prehispanic Cookbook (Cocina Prehispanica) 1960. pap. 12.50 (ISBN 0-911268-24-3). Heinman.

Debenjak, D. Modern Dictionary Slovene-German-Slovene. 608p. (Slovene & Ger.). 1981. leatherette 14.95 (ISBN 0-686-97402-6, M-9702). French & Eur.

De Berard, F. B. Famous Tales of Barbarians & Savages. LC 72-5688. (Black Heritage Library Collections). 1972. Repr. of 1899 ed. 20.00 (ISBN 0-8369-9138-9). Ayer Co Pubs.

De Berceo, Gonzalo. Milagros De Nuestra Senora. Devoto, Daniel, ed. 3.50 (ISBN 0-685-11394-9). French & Eur.

De Bercy, Drouin. L' Europe et L'Amerique Comparees, 2 vols. (Illus.). 884p. 1968. Repr. of 1818 ed. Set. 45.00 (ISBN 0-8398-0369-9). Parnassus Imprints.

De Berdt, Dennys. Letters of Dennys De Berdt, 1757-70. facsimile ed. (Select Bibliographies Reprint Ser). Repr. of 1911 ed. 17.00 (ISBN 0-8369-5931-0). Ayer Co Pubs.

De Berg, Jean. The Image. 2nd ed. Southgate, Patsy, tr. LC 75-32905. (Illus.). 1966. pap. 1.95 (ISBN 0-394-17400-3, B307, BC). Grove.

De Bernard, B., et al, eds. Calcium-Binding Proteins, 1983. (Developments in Biochemistry Ser.: Vol. 25). 472p. 1983. 94.00 (ISBN 0-444-80537-0, I-450-83, Biomedical Pr). Elsevier.

De Bernardi, J. Mario. The Catalog Showroom Formula. LC 73-92730. 224p. 1974. 12.95 (ISBN 0-86730-515-0). Lebhar Friedman.

DeBernardis, Amo. Use of Instructional Materials. LC 60-11477. (Illus., Orig.). 1960. pap. text ed. 3.95x (ISBN 0-89197-461-X). Irvington.

De Bernardis, Frank & O'Connor, Fank. The Only Smart Book on Meetings. 1985. 15.95 (ISBN 0-931933-12-9). Richardson & Steirman.

De Bersaques, J., ed. Symposium sur les tumeurs cutanees des enfants. Gent. November 1978. (Journal: Dermatologica: Vol. 161, Suppl. 1, 1980). (Illus.). iv, 160p. 1981. pap. 7.75 (ISBN 3-8055-2238-X). S Karger.

De Bertier de Sauvigny, G. & Pinkney, David H. History of France. rev. & enl. ed. Friguglietti, James, tr. LC 82-20978. (Illus.). 446p. 1983. text ed. 29.95 (ISBN 0-88273-426-1); pap. 19.95 (ISBN 0-88273-425-3). Forum Pr Il.

De Bertier De Sauvigny, Guillaume. Bourbon Restoration. Case, Lynn M., tr. LC 67-17175. Repr. of 1966 ed. 128.50 (ISBN 0-8357-9746-5, 2051109). Bks Demand UMI.

Debertin, David L. Agricultural Production Economics. 623p. 1986. price not set (ISBN 0-02-328060-3). Macmillan.

Debertin, K. & Mann, W. B. Gamma & X-Ray Spectrometry Techniques & Applications. 25.00 (ISBN 0-08-029159-7). Pergamon.

De Bertrand, Anthoine see Expert, Henry.

De Berville, M. The Story of the Chevalier Boyard. Walford, Edith, ed. 1978. Repr. of 1880 ed. lib. bdg. 20.00 (ISBN 0-8492-3047-0). R West.

Debes, John L., jt. auth. see Fransecky, Roger B.

De Betancourt, Ethel Rios. Marmol, Bronce y Barro. LC 81-10286. (Illus.). 686p. Date not set. 20.00 (ISBN 0-8477-0874-8). U of PR Pr.

Debets, G. F. Physical Anthropology of Afghanistan. LC 72-116739. (Russian Translation Ser.: Vol. 5, No. 1). 1970. pap. 7.50x (ISBN 0-87365-763-2). Peabody Harvard.

DeBetz, Barbara. A Primer of Clinical Hypnosis. (Illus.). 256p. 1985. 24.50 (ISBN 0-88416-486-1). PSG Pub Co.

DeBetz, Barbara & Baker, Samm S. Erotic Focus: The New Way to Enhance Your Sexual Pleasure. LC 84-20765. 1985. 14.95 (ISBN 0-453-00484-9). NAL.

Debevec, et al, eds. United States Documents in the Propaganda Fide Archives, Vol. 9. 1982. 40.00 (ISBN 0-88382-210-5). AAFH.

--United States Documents in the Propaganda Fide Archiives, Vol. 8. 1980. 40.00 (ISBN 0-88382-208-3). AAFH.

Debever, Robert, ed. Elie Cartan & Albert Einstein: Letters on Absolute Parallelism. LC 78-73832. 1979. 32.00 (ISBN 0-691-08229-4). Princeton U Pr.

Debevoise, Neilson C. Political History of Parthia. LC 38-10721. (Illus.). 1968. Repr. of 1938 ed. lib. bdg. 19.00x (ISBN 0-8371-0374-6, DEPA). Greenwood.

De Bevoise, Wynn. The Contribution of Education to Economic Productivity: Schooling in a Technological Society. LC 83-81508. xiv, 50p. (Orig.). 1983. pap. 5.95 (ISBN 0-86552-085-2). U of Oreg ERIC.

De Beys, C. see Beys, C. De & Protzman, M. I.

De Beze, Theodore. Abraham Sacrifiant. (French Renaissance Classics, House Ser). (Fr). 1969. Repr. of 1550 ed. 15.00 (ISBN 0-384-04090-X). Johnson Repr.

--A Discourse Conteyning the Life & Death of John Calvin. LC 77-38153. (English Experience Ser.: No. 433). 80p. 1972. Repr. of 1564 ed. 11.50 (ISBN 90-221-0433-8). Walter J Johnson.

De Bhaldraithe, Tomas, tr. see O'Sullivan, Humphrey.

De Bhardraithe, T. English-Irish Dictionary. (Eng. & Irish.). 1959. 12.50x (ISBN 0-686-00860-X). Colton Bk.

DeBiase, Louis A. How to Break into Politics on a Shoestring. 61p. (Orig.). (gr. 9-12). 1981. pap. 4.95 (ISBN 0-686-31571-5). Louvin Pub.

De Bibar, Geronimo. Cronica y Relacion Copiosa y Verdadera De los Reynos De Chile, Vol. 2. Leonard, Irving & Cruz, Guillermo F., eds. (Illus.). 1966. pap. 30.00 (ISBN 0-911028-09-9). Newberry.

Debicki, Andrew & Pupo-Walker, Enrique. Estudios Hispanoamericanos in Honor of J. J. Arrom. (Studies in the Romance Languages & Literatures: No. 158). 291p. 1974. pap. 16.00x (ISBN 0-8078-9158-4). U of NC Pr.

Debicki, Andrew P. Damaso Alonso. LC 74-75876. (World Authors Ser.). 1970. lib. bdg. 15.95. Irvington.

--Poetry of Discovery: The Spanish Generation of 1956-1971. LC 82-40171. 248p. 1982. 22.00x (ISBN 0-8131-1461-6). U Pr of Ky.

De Biedma, Luis H., ed. see Relacam, Verdadeira.

De Billon, Francois. Le Fort Inexpugnable De L'honneur Du Sexe Femenin. Repr. of 1555 ed. 55.00 (ISBN 0-384-04270-8). Johnson Repr.

De Biran, Pierre Maine see Maine De Biran, Pierre.

De Biro, Elizabeth. Hungarian Cooking. 15.00 (ISBN 0-87557-098-4, 098-4). Saphrograph.

De Birriel, Marta C. see Birriel, Marta C. & Williams, J. Clifton.

Debischop, Eric. Tahiti Nui. Young, Edward, tr. (Illus.). 1959. 12.00 (ISBN 0-8392-1109-0). Astor-Honor.

De Blacam, Mark. The Control of Private Rented Dwellings. 200p. 1985. 20.00x (ISBN 0-9508725-2-0, Pub. by Irish Academic Pr Ireland). Biblio Dist.

DeBlase, Anthony F. & Martin, Robert E. A Manual of Mammalogy: With Keys to Families of the World. 2nd ed. 448p. 1980. write for info. wire coil (ISBN 0-697-04591-9). Wm C Brown.

De Blase, Betty E. Survivor of a Tarnished Ministry. 176p. (Orig.). 1983. pap. text ed. 5.95 (ISBN 0-913621-00-5). Truth CA.

DeBlasio, Charles. My Three-Year Career. 1983. 6.95 (ISBN 0-8062-1914-9). Carlton.

De Blasis, Celese. The Tiger's Woman. 1982. pap. 3.95 (ISBN 0-440-11820-4). Dell.

De Blasis, Celeste. The Proud Breed. 892p. 1981. pap. 2.95 (ISBN 0-449-23905-5, Crest). Fawcett.

--Swan's Chance. LC 85-5999. 560p. 1985. pap. 17.95 (ISBN 0-553-05092-3). Bantam.

--Wild Swan. LC 83-46001. 592p. 1984. 16.95 (ISBN 0-553-05059-1). Bantam.

--Wild Swan. 1985. pap. 3.95 (ISBN 0-317-19737-1). Bantam.

DeBlassie, Paul, III. Inner Calm: A Christian Answer to Modern Stress. LC 84-52377. 128p. 1985. pap. 3.95 (ISBN 0-89243-229-2). Liguori Pubns.

DeBlassie, Richard. Counseling with Adolescents: A Christian Perspective. 100p. 1983. pap. 4.95 (ISBN 0-911519-04-1). Richelieu Court.

De Blassie, Richard R. & Anderson, John. Helping the Troubled. 179p. 1981. pap. 3.95 (ISBN 0-8189-1163-8). Alba.

DeBlassie, Richard R., ed. Measuring & Evaluating Pupil Progress. LC 74-8974. 210p. 1974. 29.00x (ISBN 0-8422-5184-7); pap. text ed. 7.25x (ISBN 0-8422-0434-2). Irvington.

De Blazac, Honore see Balzac, Honore de.

Deble, Isabell. The School Education of Girls: An International Comparative Study on School Wastage Among Girls & Boys at the First & Second Levels of Education. (Illus.). 180p. 1980. pap. 10.50 (ISBN 92-3-101782-9, U1058, UNESCO). Unipub.

De Blecourt, J. J., ed. Patient Compliance. (Illus.). 58p. (Orig.). 1980. pap. 13.50 (ISBN 3-456-80917-4, Pub. by Hans Huber Switzerland). J K Burgess.

De Bles, Arthur. How to Distinguish the Saints in Art by Their Costumes, Symbols & Attributes. LC 68-18018. 1975. Repr. of 1925 ed. 70.00x (ISBN 0-8103-4125-5). Gale.

De Bles, Arthur see De Bles, Arthur.

Debliek, Ruth & Quinn, Virginia. Psych Path- A Handbook of Instruction to Accompany Psychology: Its Principles & Meanings. 336p. 1982. pap. text ed. 15.95 (ISBN 0-8403-2734-X). Kendall-Hunt.

De Blij, H. J. Earth: A Topical Geography. 2nd ed. LC 79-18051. 472p. 1980. 33.95 (ISBN 0-471-05169-1). Wiley.

DeBlij, H. J. Human Geography: Culture, Society & Space. 2nd ed. 656p. 1982. 36.00 (ISBN 0-471-08557-X). Wiley.

De Blij, Harm J. Africa South. LC 62-14295. Repr. of 1962 ed. 77.80 (ISBN 0-8357-9445-8, 2014770). Bks Demand UMI.

--Dar es Salaam: A Study in Urban Geography. LC 63-18014. pap. 25.30 (ISBN 0-317-27599-2, 2014769). Bks Demand UMI.

--Geography: Regions & Concepts. 4th ed. LC 80-17961. 587p. 1985. text ed. 30.95 (ISBN 0-471-88596-7). study guide 5.95 (ISBN 0-471-81083-5). Wiley.

--Mombasa: An African City. LC 68-17731. pap. 45.50 (ISBN 0-317-27588-7, 2014854). Bks Demand UMI.

--Wine Regions of the Southern Hemisphere. LC 84-17949. (Illus.). 269p. 1985. 32.95x (ISBN 0-8476-7390-1). Rowman & Allanheld.

De Blij, Harm J. & Martin, Esmond B. African Perspectives. 1981. 19.95x (ISBN 0-416-31790-1, NO.3023). Methuen Inc.

Deblij, Harm J., jt. auth. see Glassner, Martin I.

DeBlij, Harm Jan. Wine: A Geographic Appreciation. LC 82-20648. (Illus.). 254p. 1983. text ed. 18.95 (ISBN 0-86598-091-8). Rowman & Allanheld.

De Bloch, Jean see Bloch, Jean De.

Deblock, Nick J. Elsevier's Dictionary of Public Health. LC 76-676387. 196p. (Eng., Fr., Span., Ital., Dutch & Ger.). 1976. 47.00 (ISBN 0-444-41395-2). Elsevier.

DeBlois, Peter, jt. auth. see Grassi, Rosanna.

De Blois, Pierre. Hystore Job: Adaptation en Vers Francaise du Compenonm in Job de Pierre de Blois. Bates, Robert C., ed. 1937. 14.50x (ISBN 0-686-83574-3). Elliots Bks.

DeBloois, Michael L., ed. Videodisc-Microcomputer Courseware Design. LC 81-22161. 192p. 1982. 26.95 (ISBN 0-87778-183-4). Educ Tech Pubns.

De Blumenthal, Vera. Folk Tales from the Russian. LC 78-74512. (Children's Literature Reprint Ser.). (Illus.). (gr. 4-5). 1979. Repr. of 1903 ed. 16.75x (ISBN 0-8486-0216-1). Core Collection.

Debnam, Betty. The Mini Page Kids' Cookbook. LC 78-59687. 1978. spiral bd. 5.95 (ISBN 0-8362-4202-5). Andrews McMeel Parker.

Debnam, Betty & Avery, Lois. The Mini Page & Your Newspaper Activity Book. 128p. (gr. k-6). 1980. pap. 5.95 (ISBN 0-8362-4209-2). Andrews McMeel Parker.

Debnam, Geoffrey. The Analysis of Power: Core Elements & Structure. LC 83-4556. 150p. 1984. 19.95 (ISBN 0-312-03284-6). St Martin.

Debnath, L. Advances in Nonlinear Waves, Vol. 2. (Research Notes in Mathematics Ser.: No. 111). 350p. 1985. pap. text ed. 25.95 (ISBN 0-273-08648-0). Pitman Pub MA.

Debnath, L., ed. Advances in Nonlinear Waves, Vol. 1. (Research Notes Ser.: No. 95). 350p. 1984. pap. text ed. 25.95 (ISBN 0-273-08609-X). Pitman Pub MA.

Debnath, Lokenath, ed. Nonlinear Waves. LC 83-15102. 350p. 1983. 42.50 (ISBN 0-521-25468-X). Cambridge U Pr.

Debner, Claudia & Leone, Bruno, eds. Chemical Dependency. (Opposing Viewpoints Bks.). (Illus.). 150p. (Orig.). 1985. lib. bdg. 11.95 (ISBN 0-89908-376-5); pap. 6.95 (ISBN 0-89908-351-X). Greenhaven.

Debney, L. M., jt. ed. see Singleton, W. T.

Debo, Angie. And Still the Waters Run: The Betrayal of the Five Civilized Tribes. LC 84-7282. (Illus.). 448p. (Orig.). pap. 12.95 (ISBN 0-8061-1903-9). U of Okla Pr.

--Geronimo: The Man, His Time, His Place. LC 76-13858. (The Civilization of the American Indian Ser: No.142). (Illus.). 500p. 1976. 24.95 (ISBN 0-8061-1333-2); pap. 12.95 (ISBN 0-8061-1828-8). U of Okla Pr.

--History of the Indians of the United States. LC 73-108802. (Civilization of the American Indian Ser.: Vol. 106). (Orig.). 1970. 21.95 (ISBN 0-8061-0911-4). U of Okla Pr.

--A History of the Indians of the United States. LC 73-108802. (The Civilizations of the American Indian Ser.: Vol. 106). (Illus.). 464p. 1984. pap. 12.95 (ISBN 0-8061-1888-1). U of Okla Pr.

--Oklahoma: Foot-Loose & Fancy Free. LC 81-17865. (Illus.). xi, 258p. 1982. Repr. of 1949 ed. lib. bdg. 27.50x (ISBN 0-313-23085-4, DEOK). Greenwood.

--Prairie City: The Story of an American Community. LC 85-71340. (Illus.). 272p. 1985. 14.95 (ISBN 0-933031-00-9); pap. 9.95 (ISBN 0-933031-01-7). Coun Oak Bks.

--Rise & Fall of the Choctaw Republic. 2nd ed. LC 69-7973. (Civilization of the American Indian Ser.: No. 6). (Illus.). 1934. pap. 9.95 (ISBN 0-8061-1247-6). U of Okla Pr.

--The Road to Disappearance: A History of the Creek Indians. (CAI Ser.). (Orig.). 1979. pap. 12.95 (ISBN 0-8061-1532-7). U of Okla Pr.

Debo, Angie, ed. see Cushman, Horatio B.

Debo, Darrell. Burnet County History, 2 vols. 1980. 60.00 (ISBN 0-89015-229-2). Eakin Pubns.

Debo, Harvey V. & Diamant, Leo. Construction Superintendent's Job Guide. LC 79-17979. (Series on Practical Construction Guides). 166p. 1980. 34.95 (ISBN 0-471-20457-9, Pub. by Wiley-Interscience). Wiley.

Debo, Richard K. Revolution & Survival: The Foreign Policy of Soviet Russia 1917-18. 475p. 1979. 60.00x (ISBN 0-85323-144-3, Pub. by Liverpool Univ England). State Mutual Bk.

--Revolution & Survival: The Foreign Policy of Soviet Russia, 1917-1918. LC 78-9671. 1979. 32.50x (ISBN 0-8020-5411-0). U of Toronto Pr.

De Board, Robert. Counseling People at Work. 137p. 1983. text ed. 31.00x (ISBN 0-566-02376-8). Gower Pub UK.

--Counselling People at Work. 152p. 1983. text ed. 31.00x (ISBN 0-566-02376-8). Gower Pub Co.

--The Psychoanalysis of Organizations: A Psychoanalytic Approach to Behaviour in Groups & Organizations. 158p. 1978. 18.00x (ISBN 0-422-76520-1, NO. 2730, Pub. by Tavistock England); pap. 10.50x (ISBN 0-422-76530-9, NO. 2731). Methuen Inc.

De Bock, G., jt. ed. see Vokaer, R.

De Bock, Harold, jt. ed. see Wilhoit, G. Cleveland.

De Bodinat, Henri. Influence in the Multinational Corporation: The Case of Manufacturing. Bruchey, Stuart, ed. LC 80-567. (Multinational Corporations Ser.). 1980. lib. bdg. 33.50x (ISBN 0-405-13364-2). Ayer Co Pubs.

De Bodin De Saint-Laurent, Jean. Idees Monetaires et Commerciales De Jean Bodin. 1969. Repr. of 1907 ed. 20.50 (ISBN 0-8337-0314-5). B Franklin.

Deboeck, Guido & Kinsey, Bill. Managing Information for Rural Development: Lessons from Eastern Africa. (Working Paper: No. 379). vii, 70p. 1980. 5.00 (ISBN 0-686-36070-2, WP-0379); pap. 3.00 (ISBN 0-686-39645-6). World Bank.

Deboeck, Guido & Ng, Ronald. Monitoring Rural Development in East Asia. (Working Paper: No. 439). 91p. 1980. 5.00 (ISBN 0-686-36072-9, WP-0439). World Bank.

De Boer, C., jt. auth. see Chretien de Troyes.

DeBoer, C. H., jt. auth. see Harrison, R. G.

De Boer, E. & Viergever, M. A., eds. Mechanics of Hearing. 1983. lib. bdg. 36.00 (ISBN 90-247-2878-9, Pub. by Martinus Nijhoff Netherlands). Kluwer Academic.

De Boer, Frederick, jt. auth. see Bandem, I. M.

DeBoer, J. B. & Fischer, D. Interior Lighting. (Philips Technical Library). (Illus.). 1978. text ed. 69.50x (ISBN 0-333-25670-0). Scholium Intl.

DeBoer, J. B., jt. auth. see Van Bommel, W. J.

De Boer, Jan & Baillie, Thomas W., eds. Disasters: Medical Organization. (Illus.). 112p. 1980. 19.75 (ISBN 0-08-025491-8). Pergamon.

De Boer, Janet. Dyeing for Fibres & Fabrics. (Illus.). 81p. (Orig.). 1984. pap. write for info. R L Shep.

DeBoer, John C. Let's Plan: A Guide to the Planning Process for Voluntary Organizations. LC 72-124329. (Illus., Orig.). 1970. pap. 3.95 (ISBN 0-8298-0177-4). Pilgrim NY.

De Boer, John J. Teaching Secondary English. LC 76-100155. Repr. of 1951 ed. lib. bdg. 18.00x (ISBN 0-8371-3426-9, DETS). Greenwood.

De Boer, Leobert E., ed. Workshop on the Conservation of the Orangutan. LC 82-7722. (Illus.). 353p. 1982. 76.00 (ISBN 90-6193-702-7, Pub. by Junk Pubs Netherlands). Kluwer Academic.

Deboer, Majorie. The Whitbourne Legacy. 1985. pap. 2.50 (ISBN 0-451-13658-6, Sig). NAL.

DeBoer, Marjorie. Crown of Desire. 704p. (Orig.). 1983. pap. 3.95 (ISBN 0-8439-1166-2, Leisure Bks). Dorchester Pub Co.

--The Unwelcome Suitor. 1984. pap. 2.50 (ISBN 0-451-13108-8, Sig). NAL.

De Boer, P., jt. ed. see Searle, A. G.

DeBoer, Paul, jt. auth. see Kavet, Herbert I.

De Boer, Paul M. Price Effects in Input-Output Relations: A Theoretical & Empirical Study for the Netherlands 1949-1967. (Lecture Notes in Economics & Mathematical Systems: Vol. 201). (Illus.). 140p. 1982. 13.00 (ISBN 0-387-11550-1). Springer-Verlag.

DeBoer, Piet, jt. auth. see Hoppenfeld, Stanley.

De Boer, S. P. & Driessen, E. J. Biographical Dictionary of Soviet Dissidents. 1982. lib. bdg. 165.00 (ISBN 90-247-2538-0, Pub. by Martinus Nijhoff Netherlands). Kluwer Academic.

De Boer, Theo. Foundations of Critical Psychology. Plantinga, Theodore, tr. 196p. 1982. text ed. 17.00x (ISBN 0-8207-0158-0). Duquesne.

De Boisdeffre, Pierre, jt. auth. see Alberes, Rene M.

De Boissiere, Ralph. Rum & Coca-Cola. 352p. 1984. 16.95 (ISBN 0-8052-8195-9, Pub. by Allison & Busby England). Schocken.

De Boissmont, Alexander-Jacques-Francois Brierre see Brierre De Boismont, Alexandre-Jacques-Francois.

De Bokx, ed. Viruses of Potatoes & Seed-Potato Production. 232p. 1971. 17.50 (ISBN 90-220-0358-2, PDC100, PUDOC). Unipub.

De Bolt, Alice, ed. Journal of Holistic Health, Vol. IX. Shapiro, Shelby. LC 78-59776. (Illus.). 144p. 1984. pap. 12.00 (ISBN 0-939410-13-3). Mandala Holistic.

DeBolt, Alice & Shapiro, Shalby, eds. The Journal of Holistic Health, Vol. VIII. 1983. write for info. (ISBN 0-939410-12-5). Mandala Holistic.

DeBolt, Alice & Shapiro, Shelby, eds. Journal of Holistic Health, Vol. VII. (Illus.). 120p. 1982. pap. 12.00 (ISBN 0-939410-10-9). Mandala Holistic.

De Bolt, Joseph W., ed. The Happening Worlds of John Brunner: Critical Explorations in Science Fiction. (National University Publications Literary Criticism Ser.). 1975. 19.50x (ISBN 0-8046-9124-X, Pub. by Kennikat). Assoc Faculty Pr.

DeBolt, Margaret W. Georgia Sampler Cookbook. Browder, Robyn, ed. LC 82-19841. (Regional Cookbook Ser.). (Illus.). 300p. (Orig.). 1983. pap. 8.95 (ISBN 0-89865-283-9). Donning Co.

--Savannah Spectres. Friedman, Robert, ed. LC 82-23455. (Illus., Orig.). 1985. pap. 7.95 (ISBN 0-89865-201-4). Donning Co.

DeBolt, Margaret W. & Law, Emma. Savannah Sampler Cookbook. LC 78-1078. (Illus.). 298p. 1978. pap. 8.95 (ISBN 0-915442-49-3). Donning Co.

De Bona, Maurice, Jr. God Rejected: A Summary of Atheistic Thought. LC 75-46088. 1976. 4.95 (ISBN 0-916698-00-9); pap. 2.95 (ISBN 0-916698-01-7). Desserco Pub.

De Bone, Edward & De Saint-Arnold, Michael. The Learn-to-Think Coursebook. 245p. 1982. 25.00 (ISBN 0-88496-199-0). E De Bono.

De Bonfils Templer, Margherita see Templer, Margherita D.

Deboni, Franco. Authentic Art Deco Jewelry Designs. 1983. 13.50 (ISBN 0-8446-6001-9). Peter Smith.

Deboni, Franco, ed. Authentic Art Deco Jewelry Designs: 700 Illustrations. (Antiques Ser.). (Illus.). 96p. (Orig.). 1983. pap. 5.00 (ISBN 0-486-24346-X). Dover.

De Bono, E. Lateral Thinking. pap. 6.95 (ISBN 0-06-090325-2, CN325, CN). Har-Row.

DeBono, Edward. Future Positive. 234p. 1980. 20.00 (ISBN 0-85117-171-0). Transatlantic.

De Bono, Edward. New Think. 224p. 1971. pap. 4.50 (ISBN 0-380-01426-2, Discus). Avon.

--Tactics: The Art & Science of Success. 192p. 1984. 17.45i (ISBN 0-316-17790-3). Little.

--Teaching Thinking. 1977. 18.00 (ISBN 0-85117-085-4). Transatlantic.

--Wordpower. 1977. pap. 4.95i (ISBN 0-06-090568-9, CN 568, CN). Har-Row.

Debons, Anthony, et al. Information Science: An Introduction. (Professional Librarian Ser.). 150p. 1985. 36.50 (ISBN 0-86729-153-2); pap. 27.50 (ISBN 0-86729-152-4). Knowledge Indus.

--Information Science: An Introduction. 150p. 1985. 36.50 (ISBN 0-86729-153-2); pap. 27.50 (ISBN 0-86729-152-4). Knowledge Indus.

Deboo, Gordon J. & Burrous, Clifford N. Integrated Circuits & Semiconductor Devices: Theory & Application. 2nd ed. (Illus.). 1977. text ed. 34.25 (ISBN 0-07-016246-8). McGraw.

DeBoodt, M. & Gabriels, D., eds. Assessment of Erosion. LC 80-41170. 563p. 1980. 94.95x (ISBN 0-471-27899-8, Pub. by Wiley-Interscience). Wiley.

De Boor, C. A Practical Guide to Splines. (Applied Mathematical Sciences Ser.: Vol. 27). (Illus.). 1978. pap. 22.00 (ISBN 0-387-90356-9). Springer-Verlag.

De Boor, C., jt. auth. see Conte, S. D.

De Boor, Carl, ed. Mathematical Aspects of Finite Elements in Partial Differential Equations. 1974. 23.00 (ISBN 0-12-208350-4). Acad Pr.

De Boor, Carl & Golub, Gene H., eds. Recent Advances in Numerical Analysis. (Mathematics Research Center Symposia Ser.). 1978. 32.50 (ISBN 0-12-208360-1). Acad Pr.

De Boor, Carl G., ed. see Nicephorus.

De Boor, W. & Grossarth-Maticek, R., eds. Radikalismus Untersuchungen Zur Persoenlichkeitsentwicklung Westdeutscher Studenten in den Jahren-1973. (Schriftenreihe des Instituts fuer Konfliktforschung: No. 5). (Illus.). 1979. 5.75 (ISBN 3-8055-3035-8). S Karger.

De Boor, W. & Kohlmann, G., eds. Obsessionsdelikte. (Schriftenreihe des Instituts fuer Konfliktforschung: No. 6). 1980. pap. 7.75 (ISBN 3-8055-3015-3). S Karger.

De Boos, A. G. Chemical Testing & Analysis. 51p. 1974. 70.00x (ISBN 0-686-63753-4). State Mutual Bk.

De Booy, Theodoor N. Virgin Islands, Our New Possessions & the British Islands. LC 72-109318. (Illus.). Repr. of 1918 ed. 25.00x (ISBN 0-8371-3584-2, BVI&). Greenwood.

Debor, Jane & Isabel, Linda. Banner Designs for Celebrating Christians. 1984. pap. 5.95 (ISBN 0-570-03930-4, 12-2865). Concordia.

De Borchgrave, Arnaud & Moss, Robert. The Spike. 1981. pap. 3.95 (ISBN 0-380-54270-6, 68387-3). Avon.

De Borchgrave, Arnaud, jt. auth. see Moss, Robert.

Debord, Guy. Negacion y Consumo En la Cultura. 3.00 (ISBN 0-931106-07-9). TVRT.

--Society of the Spectacle. 1983. 2.00x (ISBN 0-934868-07-7). Black & Red.

De Borhegy, Stephen F. & Body, E. Santuario de Chimayo. (Illus.). 32p. 1982. pap. 2.75 (ISBN 0-317-17600-5). Ancient City Pr.

De Borms, C. T., jt. auth. see Bailly, H. C.

De Born, Bertran. Poesies Completes De Bertran de Born. Repr. of 1888 ed. 25.00 (ISBN 0-384-04081-0). Johnson Repr.

DeBortali-Tregerthan, Gail, jt. auth. see Watson, David L.

De Bosis, Lauro. Icaro. 1933. 22.50 (ISBN 0-932062-50-4). Sharon Hill.

De Bosschere, Jean see Bosschere, Jean de & Morris, M. C.

DeBosset, C. P. Proceedings in Parga & the Ionian Islands. (Illus.). 1976. 15.00 (ISBN 0-916710-27-0). Obol Intl.

De Bourbourg, Charles E. Brasseru see Brasseur De Bourbourg, Charles E.

De Bourgoing, Jean, ed. see Franz Joseph, I.

De Bourrienne, Louis A. Memoirs of Napoleon Bonaparte, 4 vols. Phipps, R. W., ed. 1765p. Date not set. Repr. of 1891 ed. Set. lib. bdg. 350.00 (ISBN 0-89760-219-6). Telegraph Bks.

De Bourrienne, Louis F. Memoirs of Napoleon, 3 vols. Repr. Set. 50.00 (ISBN 0-8482-3688-2). Norwood Edns.

De Bovis, Edmond. Tahitian Society: Before the Arrival of the Europeans. 2nd ed. (Monograph Ser.: No. 1). pap. 6.95 (ISBN 0-939154-04-8). Inst Polynesian.

De Bow, J. B. Industrial Resources of the Southern & Western States, 3 Vols. LC 65-26362. Repr. of 1852 ed. Set. 125.00x (ISBN 0-678-00143-X). Kelley.

Debow, J. B. Statistical View of the United States. (Demographic Monographs). 408p. 1970. 60.25 (ISBN 0-677-02200-X). Gordon.

De Boyer Argens, Jean Baptiste see Baptiste De Boyer Argens, Jean.

De Boysson-Bardies, Benedicte see Boysson-Bardies, Benedicte De.

De Bra, Lemuel. Ways That Are Wary. facsimile ed. LC 79-101796. (Short Story Index Reprint Ser.). 1925. 18.00 (ISBN 0-8369-3184-X). Ayer Co Pubs.

Debra, Opstal Van see Van Opstal, Debra.

De Brabander, Guido L. Regional Specialization, Employment & Economic Growth in Belgium from 1846 to 1970. Bruchey, Stuart, ed. LC 80-2797. (Dissertations in European Economic History II). (Illus.). 1981. lib. bdg. 27.50x (ISBN 0-405-13981-0). Ayer Co Pubs.

De Brabander, M., et al, eds. Cell Movement & Neoplasia: Proceedings of the Annual Meeting of the Cell Tissue & Organ Culture Study Group, Held at the Janssen Research Foundation, Beerse, Belgium, May 1979. (Illus.). 174p. 1980. 42.00 (ISBN 0-08-025534-5). Pergamon.

De Braganca, Aquino. African Liberation Reader: Documents of the National Liberation Movements: Vol III The Strategy of Liberation. Wallerstein, Immanuel, ed. 244p. 1982. 26.95x (ISBN 0-86232-069-0, Pub. by Zed Pr England); pap. 10.50x (ISBN 0-86232-120-4, Pub. by Zed Pr England). Biblio Dist.

--African Liberation Reader: Documents of the National Liberation Movements: Vol. II The National Liberation Movements. Wallerstein, Immanuel, ed. 244p. 1982. 26.95x (ISBN 0-86232-068-2, Pub. by Zed Pr England); pap. 10.50x (ISBN 0-86232-119-0, Pub. by Zed Pr England). Biblio Dist.

De Brahm, William G. The Atlantic Pilot. De Vorsey, Louis, ed. LC 73-18036. (Floridiana Facsimile & Reprint Ser.). (Illus.). 112p. 1974. Repr. of 1772 ed. 6.50 (ISBN 0-8130-0366-0). U Presses Fla.

De Brand, Roy E. Children's Sermons for Special Occasions. LC 82-72228. (Orig.). 1983. pap. 3.95 (ISBN 0-8054-4927-2). Broadman.

--The Cross & Beyond. LC 83-70374. 1984. pap. 4.95 (ISBN 0-8054-2250-1). Broadman.

De Branganca, Aquino. African Liberation Reader: Documents of the National Liberation Movements: Vol. I The Anatomy of Colonialism. Wallerstein, Immanuel, ed. 244p. 1982. 26.95x (ISBN 0-86232-067-4, Pub. by Zed Pr England); pap. 10.50x (ISBN 0-86232-118-2, Pub. by Zed Pr England). Biblio Dist.

De Brantome, Abbe. The Brass Ring. 1971. pap. 1.95 (ISBN 0-87140-258-0). Liveright.

De Brantome, Pierre B. Lives of Fair & Gallant Ladies. (Black & Gold Lib). (Illus.). 1933. 7.95 (ISBN 0-87140-973-9, Co-Pub with Tudor). Liveright.

De Brasunas, Anton & Stansbury, E. E., eds. Symposium on Corrosion Fundamentals: A Series of Lectures Presented at the University of Tennessee Corrosion Conference at Knoxville on March 1-3, 1955. LC 56-13073. pap. 65.30 (ISBN 0-317-10658-9, 2022212). Bks Demand UMI.

De Brath, Stanley, tr. see Geley, Gustave.

De Brath, Stanley, tr. see Richet, Charles.

De Bray, Lys. Cottage Garden Year. (Illus.). 160p. 1983. 19.95x (ISBN 0-460-04513-X, Pub. by J M Dent England). Biblio Dist.

--The Manual of Old-Fashioned Flowers. (Illus.). 1985. 15.95 (ISBN 0-902280-91-0). Interbook.

--The Wild Garden. (Illus.). 1978. 19.95 (ISBN 0-8317-9430-5, Mayflower Bks). Smith Pubs.

De Bray, Reginald G. Guide to the East Slavonic Languages: Guide to the Slavonic Languages, Part 3. 3rd rev. ed. 254p. 1980. 25.95 (ISBN 0-89357-062-1). Slavica.

--Guide to the South Slavonic Languages: Guide to the Slavonic Languages, Part 1. 3rd rev. ed. 399p. 1980. 26.95 (ISBN 0-89357-060-5). Slavica.

DeBray, Reginald G. Guide to the West Slavonic Languages: Guide to the Slavonic Languages, Part 2. 3rd rev. ed. 483p. 80. 29.95 (ISBN 0-89357-061-3). Slavica.

Debray, Regis. Critique of Political Reason. 384p. 1983. 27.50 (ISBN 0-8052-7141-4, Pub. by NLB England); pap. 11.50 (ISBN 0-8052-7142-2). Schocken.

--Revolution in the Revolution? Armed Struggle & Political Struggle in Latin America. Ortiz, Bobbye, tr. from Fr., Span. LC 80-19409. 126p. 1980. Repr. of 1967 ed. lib. bdg. 24.75x (ISBN 0-313-22669-5, DERE). Greenwood.

--Teachers, Writers, Celebrities: The Intellectuals of Modern France. 251p. 1981. text ed. 19.95 (ISBN 0-8052-7086-8, Pub. by NLB England); pap. 9.95 (ISBN 0-8052-7101-5). Schocken.

DeBray, X. B. A Sketch of the History of DeBray's 26th Regiment of Texas Cavalry. (Illus.). pap. 7.50x (ISBN 0-686-05286-2). Globe Pubs Texas.

Debre, R., et al. Poliomyelitis. (Monograph Ser: No. 26). (Illus.). 408p. 1955. 10.80 (ISBN 92-4-140026-9). World Health.

De Breau Armand De, Quatrefages see Quatrefages de Breau, Armand de.

Debreczeni, L. A., jt. ed. see Hutas, I.

Debreczeny, Paul. The Other Pushkin: A Study of Alexander Pushkin's Prose Fiction. LC 81-85449. 392p. 1983. 32.50x (ISBN 0-8047-1143-7). Stanford U Pr.

--Temptations of the Past. LC 82-3051. 110p. 1982. pap. 6.50 (ISBN 0-938920-17-0). Hermitage.

Debreczeny, Paul, ed. American Contributions to the Ninth International Congress of Slavists, Kiev 1983, Vol. 2: Literature, Poetics, History. 400p. (Orig., Eng. & Slavic.). 1983. pap. 19.95 (ISBN 0-89357-113-X). Slavica.

Debreczeny, Paul & Zeldin, Jesse, eds. Literature & National Identity: Nineteenth-Century Russian Critical Essays. LC 77-109598. xxvi, 188p. 1970. 16.95x (ISBN 0-8032-0748-4). U of Nebr Pr.

Debreczeny, Paul, tr. see Pushkin, Alexander.

De Breffny, Brian. In the Steps of St. Patrick. (Illus.). 1982. 9.98 (ISBN 0-500-24110-4). Thames Hudson.

--Irish Family Names: Arms, Origins & Locations. (Illus.). 190p. 1982. 19.95 (ISBN 0-393-01612-9). Norton.

--Irish Family Names: Arms, Origins, & Locations. 50.00x (ISBN 0-7171-1225-X). State Mutual Bk.

--Land of Ireland. LC 79-11461. (Illus.). 1979. 19.95 (ISBN 0-8109-8066-5). Abrams.

--My First Naked Lady. 192p. 1982. 14.95 (ISBN 0-241-10614-1, Pub. by Hamish Hamilton England). David & Charles.

De Breffny, Brian & Ffolliott, Rosemary. The Houses of Ireland. LC 80-51981. (Illus.). 240p. 1985. pap. 11.95 (ISBN 0-500-27351-0). Thames Hudson.

--The Houses of Ireland: Domestic Architecture from the Medieval Castle to the Edwardian Villa. (Illus.). 240p. 1981. 12.98 (ISBN 0-500-24091-4). Thames Hudson.

De Breffny, Brian & Mott, George. The Churches & Abbeys of Ireland. (Illus.). 1976. 14.95 (ISBN 0-393-04441-6). Norton.

De Breffny, Brian, ed. Ireland: A Cultural Encyclopedia. LC 83-1533. (Illus.). 256p. 1984. 24.95 (ISBN 0-87196-260-8). Facts on File.

--The Irish World. LC 77-6659. (Illus.). 1977. 45.00 (ISBN 0-8109-1120-5). Abrams.

DeBremaecker, J. Geophysics: The Earth's Interior. 352p. 1985. 29.95 (ISBN 0-471-87815-4). Wiley.

De Bremont Anna, Contesse. Oscar Wilde & His Mother. LC 72-2155. (English Biography Ser., No. 31). 1972. Repr. of 1911 ed. lib. bdg. 59.95x (ISBN 0-8383-1457-0). Haskell.

DeBrentani-Laroche. Readings in Canadian Marketing. 1983. pap. 10.95 (ISBN 0-8403-3143-6). Kendall-Hunt.

Debrer, M. Riga: A Guide. 156p. 1982. 6.95 (ISBN 0-8285-2586-2, Pub. by Progress Pubs USSR). Imported Pubns.

De Bretteville, Sheila L., jt. auth. see Nodal, Al.

Debretts, Peerage, jt. auth. see Ashe, Geoffrey.

Debreu, Gerard. Mathematical Economics: Twenty Papers of Gerard Debreu. LC 82-12875. (Econometric Society Monographs in Pure Theory). 320p. 1983. 34.50 (ISBN 0-521-23736-X). Cambridge U Pr.

--Theory of Value: An Axiomatic Analysis of Economic Equilibrium. (Cowles Foundation Mongraph: No. 17). 128p. 1972. pap. 4.95x (ISBN 0-300-01559-3, Y-251). Yale U Pr.

DeBrigard, Raul & Helmer, Olaf. Some Potential Societal Developments: 1970-2000. 140p. 1970. 10.50 (ISBN 0-318-14422-0, R7). Inst Future.

De Brincat, Matthew see Brincat, Matthew De.

De Brissiere, P. Caribbean Cookery. (Chinese & Eng.). pap. 3.95 (ISBN 0-87557-100-X, 100-X). Saphrograph.

De Brisson, Pierre R., jt. auth. see Saugnier.

DeBrizzi, John A. Ideology & the Rise of Labor Theory in America. LC 82-12024. (Contributions in Labor History Ser.: No. 14). 224p. 1983. lib. bdg. 29.95 (ISBN 0-313-23614-3, DID/). Greenwood.

De Broglie, Louis. Revolution in Physics: A Non-Mathematical Survey of Quanta. Niemeyer, Ralph W., tr. LC 76-95113. Repr. of 1953 ed. lib. bdg. 18.75x (ISBN 0-8371-2582-0, BRRP). Greenwood.

De Broglie, Marie-Blanche & Zukas, Harriet. The Cuisine of Normandy: French Regional Cooking with Princess Marie-Blanche de Broglie. LC 84-9020. 1984. 18.95 (ISBN 0-395-36552-X). HM.

De Broucker, Jose. Dom Helder Camara: The Violence of a Peacemaker. Briffault, Herma, tr. from Fr. LC 78-135536. (Illus.). 154p. 1970. 6.95x (ISBN 0-88344-099-7). Orbis Bks.

De Brouker, Jose, ed. see Camara, Dom H.

Debrovner, Charles M., ed. Premenstrual Tension: A Multidisciplinary Approach. LC 81-6659. 112p. 1982. 19.95x (ISBN 0-89885-019-3). Human Sci Pr.

Deb Roy, H. L. A Tribe in Transition. 222p. 1981. text ed. 19.00x (ISBN 0-391-02911-8). Humanities.

DeBruicker, F. Stewart, et al. Cases in Consumer Behavior. 2nd ed. (Illus.). 336p. 1986. pap. text ed. 19.95 (ISBN 0-13-118332-X). P-H.

De Bruicker, S., jt. auth. see Ward, S.

DeBruicker, Stewart, jt. auth. see Reibstein, David J.

De Bruijn, N. G. Asymptotic Methods in Analysis. viii, 200p. 1982. pap. 4.50 (ISBN 0-486-64221-6). Dover.

De Bruin, A. Biochemical Toxicology of Environmental Agents. 154p. 1976. 253.25 (ISBN 0-444-41455-X, Biomedical Pr). Elsevier.

DeBruin, Jerome E. Hey Teach: Are You a Teacher? (Illus.). 1977. pap. 8.95 (ISBN 0-9602200-0-3). JED.

DeBruin, Jerry. Cardboard Carpentry. (gr. 3-8). 1979. 8.95 (ISBN 0-916456-39-0). JED.

--Creative, Hands-on Science Experiences. (gr. k-9). 1980. 12.95 (ISBN 0-916456-87-0, GA 165). Good Apple.

--Young Scientists Explore Animals, Bk. 2. (gr. 4-7). 1982. 3.95 (ISBN 0-86653-073-8, GA 406). Good Apple.

--Young Scientists Explore Inner & Outer Space. (Superific Science Ser.). (Illus.). 32p. (gr. 4-7). 1983. wkbk. 3.95 (ISBN 0-86653-152-1, GA 457). Good Apple.

--Young Scientists Explore the Five Senses. (Superific Science Ser.). (Illus.). 32p. (gr. 4-7). 1983. wkbk. 3.95 (ISBN 0-86653-114-9, GA 455). Good Apple.

--Young Scientists Explore the Moon, Bk. 3. (gr. 4-7). 1982. 3.95 (ISBN 0-86653-074-6, GA 407). Good Apple.

--Young Scientists Explore the Weather. (Superific Science Ser.). (Illus.). 32p. (gr. 4-7). 1983. wkbk. 3.95 (ISBN 0-86653-129-7, GA 456). Good Apple.

--Young Scientists Explore the World Around Them, Bk. 1. (gr. 4-7). 1982. 3.95 (ISBN 0-86653-072-X, GA 405). Good Apple.

DeBruin, Jerry & Sherperak, Rita. Touching & Teaching Metrics. (gr. k-8). 1977. 11.95 (ISBN 0-916456-08-0). JED.

DeBruin, Jerry, et al. Touching & Teaching Metric: Dulpicating Masters for the Primary Grades. (gr. k-3). 1978. 8.95 (ISBN 0-916456-26-9). JED.

--Touching & Teaching Metics: Duplicating Masters for the Intermediate Grades. 244p. (gr. k-8). 1978. 8.95 (ISBN 0-916456-27-7). Good Apple.

De Bruin, M. G. & Van Rossum, H., eds. Pade Approximation & Its Applications, Amsterdam 1980: Proceedings. (Lecture Notes in Mathematics Ser.: Vol. 888). 383p. 1981. pap. 22.00 (ISBN 0-387-11154-9). Springer-Verlag.

Debruin, Richard. One-Hundred Topographic Maps. 128p. (Orig.). 1970. pap. text ed. 6.95 (ISBN 0-8331-1704-1). Hubbard Sci.

De Brun, Padraig & Herbert, Marie. Catalogue of Irish Manuscripts in Cambridge Libraries. 260p. Date not set. price not set (ISBN 0-521-30261-7). Cambridge U Pr.

De Brunhoff, Jean. Babar & Father Christmas. (Illus.). (ps). 1949. 5.95 (ISBN 0-394-80578-X, BYR); PLB 6.99 (ISBN 0-394-90578-4). Random.

--Babar & His Children. Haas, Merle, tr. (Illus.). (ps). 1954. 5.95 (ISBN 0-394-80577-1, BYR); PLB 6.99 (ISBN 0-394-90577-6). Random.

--Babar & Zephir. Haas, Merle, tr. (Illus.). (ps). 1942. 6.95 (ISBN 0-394-80579-8, BYR); PLB 5.99 (ISBN 0-394-90579-2). Random.

--Babar the King. (Illus.). (ps). 1937. 5.95 (ISBN 0-394-80580-1, BYR); PLB 5.99 (ISBN 0-394-90580-6). Random.

--Meet Babar & His Family. (Illus.). (ps-1). 1973. pap. 1.95 (ISBN 0-394-82682-5, BYR). Random.

--The Story of Babar. (Illus.). (ps). 1937. 5.95 (ISBN 0-394-80575-5, BYR); PLB 5.99 (ISBN 0-394-90575-X). Random.

--The Story of Babar. (Illus.). 48p. 1984. Oversized Facsimile ed. 12.95 (ISBN 0-394-86823-4, BYR). Random.

--Travels of Babar. (Illus.). (ps). 1937. 6.95 (ISBN 0-394-80576-3, BYR); PLB 6.99 (ISBN 0-394-90576-8). Random.

--The Travels of Babar. LC 85-2236. (Illus.). 48p. (ps up). 1985. Repr. of 1934 ed. 14.95 (ISBN 0-394-87453-6, BYR). Random.

--Voyage De Babar. (Illus., Fr & Span.). bds. 6.50 (ISBN 0-685-11626-3). French & Eur.

De Brunhoff, Jean & De Brunhoff, Laurent. Babar's Anniversary Album. LC 81-5182. (Illus.). 144p. (ps-3). 1981. 15.95 (ISBN 0-394-84813-6). Random.

De Brunhoff, L. La Fete De Celesteville. (gr. 4-6). 6.50 (ISBN 0-685-33969-6). French & Eur.

De Brunhoff, Laurent. Babar a la Mer. (Fr.). (gr. 2-3). 2.50 (ISBN 0-685-11023-0). French & Eur.

--Babar a New York. (Illus.). (gr. 4-6). bds. 6.50 (ISBN 0-685-11024-9). French & Eur.

--Babar & the Ghost. LC 80-5753. (Illus.). 32p. 1981. PLB 6.99 (ISBN 0-394-94660-X); pap. 4.95 boards (ISBN 0-394-84660-5). Random.

--Babar & the Professor. new ed. (Illus.). (gr. k-2). 1966. (BYR); PLB 6.99 (ISBN 0-394-90590-3). Random.

--Babar Artiste Peintre. (Fr.). (gr. 2-3). 2.50 (ISBN 0-685-28424-7). French & Eur.

--Babar Chez le Docteur. (Fr.). (gr. 2-3). 2.50 (ISBN 0-685-28425-5). French & Eur.

--Babar En Ballon. (Fr.). (gr. 2-3). 2.50 (ISBN 0-685-28422-0). French & Eur.

--Babar En Promenade. (Fr.). (gr. 2-3). 2.50 (ISBN 0-685-11026-5). French & Eur.

--Babar et ce coquin d'Arthur. (Illus., Fr.). (gr. 4-6). bds. 7.95 (ISBN 0-685-11027-3). French & Eur.

--Babar et le Prof. Grifaton. (Fr.). (gr. 2-4). 7.95 (ISBN 0-685-28434-4). French & Eur.

--Babar et ses Enfants. (Fr.). (gr. 2-3). 2.50 (ISBN 0-685-28436-0). French & Eur.

--Babar Fait Du Ski. (Fr.). (gr. 2-3). 2.50 (ISBN 0-685-11029-X). French & Eur.

--Babar Jardinier. (Fr.). (gr. 2-3). 2.50 (ISBN 0-685-11030-3). French & Eur.

--Babar Learns to Cook. LC 78-11769. (Picturebacks Ser.). (Illus.). (ps-1). 1979. PLB 4.99 (ISBN 0-394-94108-X, BYR); pap. 1.95 (ISBN 0-394-84108-5). Random.

--Babar Loses His Crown. LC 67-21918. (gr. k-3). 1967. PLB 6.99 (ISBN 0-394-90045-6). Beginner.

--Babar Visits Another Planet. (Illus.). (ps-2). 1972. (BYR); PLB 5.99 (ISBN 0-394-92429-0). Random.

--Babar's ABC. LC 83-2987. (Illus.). 36p. (gr. k-1). 1985. PLB 6.99 (ISBN 0-394-95920-5); pap. 6.95 (ISBN 0-394-85920-0). Random.

--Babar's Birthday Surprise. (ps-2). 1970. (BYR). Random.

--Babar's Book of Color. LC 84-42737. (Illus.). 36p. (ps-2). 1984. 6.95 (ISBN 0-394-86896-X, BYR); PLB 7.99 (ISBN 0-394-96896-4). Random.

--Babar's Bookmobile. LC 73-22775. (Illus.). 24p. (ps-2). 1974. 5.95 (ISBN 0-394-82660-4, BYR). Random.

--Babar's Coloring Book. (Illus.). 64p. (ps-3). pap. 2.95 (ISBN 0-394-86812-9, BYR). Random.

--Babar's Fair. Haas, Merle, tr. (Illus.). (ps). 1961. (BYR); PLB 7.99 (ISBN 0-394-90584-9). Random.

--Babar's French Lessons. (Illus.). (ps). 1963. 7.95 (ISBN 0-394-80587-9, BYR). Random.

--Babar's Mystery. LC 78-55912. (Illus.). (gr. 1-3). 1978. 4.95 (ISBN 0-394-93920-4, BYR); PLB 6.99. Random.

--Babar's Trunk, 4 bks. Incl. Babar at the Seashore; Babar the Gardener; Babar Goes Skiing; Babar on a Picnic. (Illus.). (ps-2). 1969. Set. slipcased 6.95 (ISBN 0-394-80585-2). Random.

--Chateau Du Roi Babar. (Fr.). (gr. 3-8). 7.95 (ISBN 0-685-11078-8). French & Eur.

--Couronnement De Babar. (Fr.). (gr. 2-3). 2.50 (ISBN 0-685-28420-4). French & Eur.

--Enfance De Babar. (Fr.). (gr. 2-3). 2.50 (ISBN 0-685-28421-2). French & Eur.

--Histoire De Babar. (Fr.). (gr. 2-4). 7.95 (ISBN 0-685-28435-2). French & Eur.

--Je Parle Allemand Avec Babar. (Illus., Fr.). (gr. 4-6). 7.95 (ISBN 0-685-11271-3). French & Eur.

--Je Parle Anglais Avec Babar. (Illus., Fr.). (gr. 4-6). 7.95 (ISBN 0-685-11272-1). French & Eur.

--Je Parle Espagnol Avec Babar. (Illus., Fr.). (gr. 4-6). 7.95 (ISBN 0-685-11273-X). French & Eur.

--Je Parle Italien Avec Babar. (Fr.). (gr. 4-6). 7.95 (ISBN 0-685-11274-8). French & Eur.

--Meet Babar & His Family. (Pictureback Book & Cassette Library Ser.). (Illus.). 32p. (ps-1). 1985. pap. 4.95 incl. cassette (ISBN 0-394-87653-9). Random.

--The One Pig with Horns. Howard, Richard, tr. from Fr. LC 78-4917. (Illus.). (gr. k-3). 1979. PLB 5.99 (ISBN 0-394-93673-6). Pantheon.

--Roi Babar. (Fr.). (gr. 4-6). 1975. 7.95 (ISBN 0-685-11533-X). French & Eur.

--Vive le Roi Babar. (Fr.). (gr. 2-3). 2.50 (ISBN 0-685-28423-9). French & Eur.

De Brunhoff, Laurent, jt. auth. see De Brunhoff, Jean.

DeBrunner. Orthopedic Diagnosis. 1982. 20.95 (ISBN 0-8151-2371-X). Year Bk Med.

De Brunoff, Laurent. Babar Saves the Day. LC 76-11684. (Picturebacks Ser.). (Illus.). (gr. 3-6). 1976. pap. 1.95 (ISBN 0-394-83341-4, BYR). Random.

De Brux, J., et al, eds. The Endometrium: Hormonal Impacts. LC 81-8529. 176p. 1981. 35.00x (ISBN 0-306-40749-3, Plenum Pr). Plenum Pub.

De Bruyn, Chris, et al, eds. Purine Metabolism in Man IVA: Clinical & Therapeutic Aspects. (Advances in Experimental Medicine & Biology Ser.: Vol. 165A). 544p. 1983. 75.00x (ISBN 0-306-41363-9, Plenum Pr). Plenum Pub.

De Bruyn, Chris H., et al, eds. Purine Metabolism in Man IVB: Biochemical, Immunological, & Cancer Research. (Advances in Experimental Medicine & Biology Ser.: Vol. 165B). 509p. 1983. 69.50x (ISBN 0-306-41364-7, Plenum Pr). Plenum Pub.

DeBruyn, Monica. Lauren's Secret Ring. Fay, Ann, ed. LC 79-27261. (Concept Bk.: Level 1). (Illus.). (gr. 1-3). 1980. PLB 10.75 (ISBN 0-8075-4391-8). A Whitman.

DeBruyn, Robert L. Before You Can Discipline. LC 83-62446. 172p. (Orig.). 1984. pap. text ed. 17.95 (ISBN 0-914607-03-0). Master Tchr.

--Causing Others to Want Your Leadership. LC 76-29223. 184p. 1976. 12.95 (ISBN 0-914607-06-5). Master Tchr.

--Understanding & Relating to Parents... Professionally. LC 84-62205. 66p. (Orig.). 1985. pap. price not set (ISBN 0-914607-21-9). Master Tchr.

--Welcome to Teaching... & Our Schools. LC 84-60402. 60p. (Orig.). 1985. price not set (ISBN 0-914607-05-7). Master Tchr.

DeBruyn, Robert L. & Benjamin, James M. Mastering Meetings. LC 83-62444. 107p. (Orig.). 1984. pap. 5.95 (ISBN 0-914607-02-2). Master Tchr.

DeBruyn, Robert L. & Larson, Jack L. You Can Handle Them All. LC 83-62445. 320p. (Orig.). 1984. text ed. 24.95 (ISBN 0-914607-04-9). Master Tchr.

De Bruyne, K. I., et al. Semimicro Chemistry. rev. ed. (gr. 9-12). 1966. pap. text ed. 10.92 (ISBN 0-03-052860-7, Holte); tchrs' manual o.p. 1.12 (ISBN 0-03-052865-8). HR&W.

De Bruyn Kops, Mary, jt. auth. see Dean, Charles W.

De Bruz, J. & Gautrey, J. P., eds. Clinical Pathology of the Endocrine Ovary. 300p. 1984. lib. bdg. 45.00 (ISBN 0-85200-854-6, Pub. by MTP Pr England). Kluwer Academic.

DeBruzzi, D. J., jt. auth. see Healy, J. J.

Debry, G., ed. Nutrition, Food & Drug Interactions in Man. (World Review of Nutrition & Dietetics: Vol. 43). (Illus.). x, 210p. 1984. 70.75 (ISBN 3-8055-3800-6). S Karger.

Debry, R. K. Communicating with Display Terminals. 256p. 1985. 36.95 (ISBN 0-07-016185-2). McGraw.

De Bryant, Ramona L. Poemas y Cuentos. LC 84-52378. (Senda Poetica Ser.). 120p. (Orig., Span.). 1985. pap. 6.95 (ISBN 0-918454-44-1). Senda Nueva.

Debs, Eugene V. Eugene V. Debs Speaks. Tussey, Jean, ed. LC 72-108720. (Illus.). 1970. pap. 7.95 (ISBN 0-87348-132-1). Path Pr NY.

--His Life, Writings & Speeches. 59.95 (ISBN 0-8490-0303-2). Gordon Pr.

--John Swinton: Radical Editor & Leader. 59.95 (ISBN 0-8490-0458-6). Gordon Pr.

--Walls & Bars. LC 74-172574. (Criminology, Law Enforcement, & Social Problems Ser.: No. 161). (With intro & index added). 1973. Repr. of 1927 ed. 8.00x (ISBN 0-87585-161-4). Patterson Smith.

--Walls & Bars. 3rd ed. 286p. 1983. Repr. of 1927 ed. lib. bdg. 19.95 (ISBN 0-88286-010-0). C H Kerr.

Debs, Theodore. Sidelights: Incidents in the Life of Eugene V. Debs. (Illus.). 32p. 1980. lib. bdg. 12.95 (ISBN 0-88286-090-9); pap. 2.00 (ISBN 0-88286-091-7). C H Kerr.

De Buck, A. Egyptian Reading Book I: Exercises & Middle Egyptian Texts. 1977. 20.00 (ISBN 0-89005-213-1). Ares.

De Bude, Guy see Doi Chrysostomus.

De Buen-de Arguero, Nuria, tr. see Saccomanno, Geno.

Debuigne, Gerard. Dictionnaire des Plantes Qui Guerissent. 250p. (Fr.). 1972. pap. 6.95 (ISBN 0-686-56860-5, M-6638). French & Eur.

--Dictionnaire Vins. (Illus., Fr.). pap. 8.50 (ISBN 0-03-075459-3, 3742). Larousse.

--Larousse Des Plantes Qui Guerissent. 256p. (Fr.). 1974. 42.50 (ISBN 0-686-56977-6, M-6104). French & Eur.

--Larousse des plantes qui guerissent. new ed. (Illus.). 254p. (Fr.). 1974. 38.95x (ISBN 2-03-019013-6). Larousse.

--Larousse des vins. (Illus.). 271p. (Fr.). 1970. 47.50x (ISBN 2-03-019010-1). Larousse.

DeBurgh, David. The Maturing Salesian. 1977. pap. 3.95 (ISBN 0-89944-028-2). Don Bosco Multimedia.

DeBurgh, David, tr. see Wirth, Morand.

DeBurgh, W. G. From Morality to Religion. LC 70-102568. 1970. Repr. of 1938 ed. 29.50x (ISBN 0-8046-0728-1, Pub. by Kennikat). Assoc Faculty Pr.

De Burgos, Julia. Cancion de la Verdad Sencilla. LC 82-71883. (Vortice Ser.). (Illus.). 64p. (Orig., Span.). 1982. pap. 4.95 (ISBN 0-940238-66-7). Ediciones Huracan.

--Poema en Veinte Surcos. LC 83-82116. (Illus.). 72p. (Orig.). 1983. pap. 4.95 (ISBN 0-940238-23-3). Ediciones Huracan.

De Bury, Blaz. Moliere & the French Classical Drama. 1973. Repr. of 1846 ed. 25.00 (ISBN 0-8274-1508-7). R West.

De Bury, Richard. Love of Books: The Philobiblon of Richard De Bury. Gollancz, I., ed. Thomas, E. C., tr. LC 66-23971. (Medieval Library). Repr. of 1926 ed. 17.50 (ISBN 0-8154-0042-X). Cooper Sq.

De Bury, Yetta B. French Literature of To-Day. 1973. Repr. of 1898 ed. 20.00 (ISBN 0-8274-1405-6). R West.

De Bury, Yetta Blaze see Blaze De Bury, Yetta.

Debus, A. English Paracelsians. 1965. 10.75 (ISBN 0-444-99961-2). Elsevier.

Debus, A. G. Man & Nature in the Renaissance. LC 77-91085. (Cambridge History of Science Ser.). (Illus.). 1978. 29.95 (ISBN 0-521-21972-8); pap. 10.95 (ISBN 0-521-29328-6). Cambridge U Pr.

Debus, Allen G., ed. A Symposium Held at UCLA in Honor of C. D. O'Malley. (Illus.). 1974. 39.50x (ISBN 0-520-02226-2). U of Cal Pr.

Debuskey, Matthew. The Chronically Ill Child & His Family. 224p. 1970. 16.75x (ISBN 0-398-00410-2). C C Thomas.

Debussy, Claude. Debussy, Prelude to the Afternoon of a Faun. Austin, William W., ed. (Critical Score Ser). 1970. pap. 8.95x (ISBN 0-393-09939-3). Norton.

--Pelleas et Melisande in Full Score. (Music Scores to Play & Study). 410p. 1985. pap. 14.95 (ISBN 0-486-24825-9). Dover.

--Piano Music Eighteen Eighty-Eight to Nineteen Hundred Five. 175p. 1972. pap. 5.95 (ISBN 0-486-22771-5). Dover.

--The Poetic Debussy: A Collection of His Song Texts & Selected Letters. Cobb, Margaret G., ed. Miller, Richard, tr. LC 81-19010. (Illus.). 318p. 1982. 22.95x (ISBN 0-930350-28-6). NE U Pr.

--Songs, Eighteen Eighty to Nineteen Hundred & Four. Benson, Rita, ed. (Orig.). 1981. pap. 6.95 (ISBN 0-486-24131-9). Dover.

Debussy, Claude & Nicholas, John, eds. Pelleas & Melisande, No. 9. Mac Donald, Hugh, tr. from Fr. (English National Opera Guide: Libretto, Articles: No. 9). 128p. 1982. pap. 4.95 (ISBN 0-7145-3906-6). Riverrun NY.

Debussy, Claude see Rameau, Jean Philippe.

Debussy, Claude, et al. Three Classics in the Aesthetic of Music. pap. 3.95 (ISBN 0-486-20320-4). Dover.

DeButts, Mary C., ed. Growing Up in the Eighteen Fifties: The Journal of Agnes Lee. LC 84-10452. (Illus.). 171p. 1984. 11.95x (ISBN 0-8078-1622-1). U of NC Pr.

D'Eca, Raul & Greenfield, Eric V. Portuguese Grammar. 1979. pap. 5.50i (ISBN 0-06-460185-4, CO 185, COS). B&N NY.

D'Eca, Raul, jt. ed. see Hanke, Lewis.

De Cadenet, J. J., jt. auth. see Castro, Rene.

De Calba, Marti J., jt. auth. see Martorell, Joanot.

De Callieres. On the Manner of Negotiating with Princes. Whyte, A. F., tr. from Fr. LC 82-21800. 160p. 1983. pap. text ed. 9.75 (ISBN 0-8191-2923-2). U Pr of Amer.

Decalo, Samuel. Coups & Army Rule in Africa: Studies in Military Style. LC 75-18169. (Illus.). 352p. 1976. pap. 8.95x (ISBN 0-300-01995-5). Yale U Pr.

--Historical Dictionary of Chad. LC 77-23585. (African Historical Dictionaries Ser.: No. 13). 437p. 1977. 27.50 (ISBN 0-8108-1046-8). Scarecrow.

--Historical Dictionary of Dahomey. LC 75-42168. (African Historical Dictionaries Ser.: No. 7). 231p. 1976. 20.00 (ISBN 0-8108-0833-1). Scarecrow.

--Historical Dictionary of Niger. LC 79-15704. (African Historical Dictionaries Ser.: No. 20). 376p. 1979. 27.50 (ISBN 0-8108-1229-0). Scarecrow.

--Historical Dictionary of Togo. LC 76-14926. (African Historical Dictionaries Ser.: No. 9). 261p. 1976. 20.00 (ISBN 0-8108-0942-7). Scarecrow.

De Camara, Idalia F. Dictados Para Transcripcion. pap. 6.00 (ISBN 0-8477-2607-X). U of PR Pr.

De Cameens, Luis Vaz. Lusiads. Atkinson, William C., tr. (Classics Ser.). 1975. pap. 3.95 (ISBN 0-14-044026-7). Penguin.

De Cameron, Luis. Impressionism, Expressionism & the Influence of War on Art. (Illus.). 133p. 1983. 117.45 (ISBN 0-86650-071-5). Gloucester Art.

De Camoens, Luis. The Lusiad; or the Discovery of India. Feldman, Burton & Richardson, Robert, eds. LC 78-60914. (Myth & Romanticism Ser.: Vol. 6). 1980. lib. bdg. 80.00 (ISBN 0-8240-3555-0). Garland Pub.

De Camoes, L. Os Lusiadas. Ford, Jeremiah D., ed. (Harvard Studies in Romance Languages Ser.). 1946. 37.00 (ISBN 0-527-01120-7). Kraus Repr.

De Camoes, Luiz. The Lusiads. 75.00 (ISBN 0-87968-318-X). Gordon Pr.

De Camp, Catherine C., jt. auth. see De Camp, L. Sprague.

De Camp, Catherine C., ed. Creatures of the Cosmos. LC 77-22748. (Illus.). 152p. (gr. 5-9). 1977. 7.95 (ISBN 0-664-32621-8). Westminster.

DeCamp, Harry S. One Man's Healing from Cancer. 160p. 1983. 8.95 (ISBN 0-8007-1354-0). Revell.

DeCamp, Howard. Conan of Cimmeriria, No. 2. 189p. 1985. pap. 2.75 (ISBN 0-441-11455-5). Ace Bks.

De Camp, J. E. see Franz, Shepherd I.

DeCamp, L. Sprague. The Ancient Engineers. 1980. pap. 2.95 (ISBN 0-345-29347-9). Ballantine.

De Camp, L. Sprague. The Bronze God of Rhodes. Stine, Hank, ed. LC 82-23470. (Illus.). 338p. (Orig.). 1983. cancelled (ISBN 0-89865-286-3). Donning Co.

--Citadels of Mystery. 1973. pap. 1.25 (ISBN 0-345-23215-1). Ballantine.

--The Fallible Fiend. 160p. 1981. pap. 1.95 (ISBN 0-345-29367-3, Del Rey). Ballantine.

--The Fringe of the Unknown. LC 83-60205. 205p. 1983. 17.95 (ISBN 0-87975-204-1); pap. 9.95 (ISBN 0-87975-217-3). Prometheus Bks.

--The Hand of Zei. (Illus.). 200p. 1981. 20.50 (ISBN 0-913896-20-9). Owlswick Pr.

DeCamp, L. Sprague. The Hostage of Zir. LC 77-10137. 1982. pap. 2.50 (ISBN 0-441-34296-5, Dist. by Putnam). Ace Bks.

De Camp, L. Sprague. The Hostage of Zir. 224p. 1982. pap. 2.50 (ISBN 0-441-34296-5, Pub. by Ace Science Fiction). Ace Bks.

--Literary Swordsmen & Sorcerers: The Makers of Heroic Fantasy. (Illus.). 1976. 10.00 (ISBN 0-87054-076-9). Arkham.

--Lost Continents: The Atlantis Theme in History, Science & Literature. (Illus.). 1970. pap. 5.50 (ISBN 0-486-22668-9). Dover.

--Lost Continents: The Atlantis Theme in History, Science, & Literature. 16.00 (ISBN 0-8446-0535-2). Peter Smith.

--The Prisoner of Zhamanak. 1983. pap. 2.50 (ISBN 0-441-67937-4, Pub. by Ace Science Fiction). Ace Bks.

--The Purple Pterodactyls. Baen, Jim, ed. 1980. pap. 2.25 (ISBN 0-441-69190-0). Ace Bks.

--The Purple Pterodactyls: The Adventures of W. Wilson Newbury, Ensorcelled Financier. (W. Wilson Newbury Ser.). 1979. 15.00 (ISBN 0-932096-02-6). Phantasia Pr.

--The Ragged Edge of Science. LC 79-92640. (Illus.). 254p. 1980. 16.00 (ISBN 0-913896-06-3). Owlswick Pr.

--Rogue Queen. (Illus.). 176p. pap. text ed. 7.95 (ISBN 0-312-94396-2). Bluejay Bks.

--The Unbeheaded King. 1983. 9.95 (ISBN 0-345-30773-9, Del Rey). Ballantine.

De Camp, L. Sprague & Carter, Lin. Conan of Aquilonia. (Conan Ser.: No. 11). 1983. pap. 2.50 (ISBN 0-441-11612-4, Ace Science Fiction). Ace Bks.

DeCamp, L. Sprague & Carter, Lin. Conan the Barbarian. 1982. pap. 2.50 (ISBN 0-553-22544-8). Bantam.

De Camp, L. Sprague & De Camp, Catherine C. The Bones of Zora. 272p. 1984. pap. 2.75 (ISBN 0-441-07012-4). Ace Bks.

--Footprints on Sand. (Illus.). 1981. 12.00 (ISBN 0-911682-25-2). Advent.

--Science Fiction Handbook, Revised: How to Write & Sell Imaginative Stories. 1977. pap. 3.95 (ISBN 0-07-016198-4). McGraw.

--Spirits, Stars, & Spells: The Profits & Perils of Magic. LC 65-25470. (Illus.). 348p. 1980. 17.00 (ISBN 0-913896-17-9). Owlswick Pr.

De Camp, L. Sprague & Pratt, Fletcher. The Compleat Enchanter. 416p. (Orig.). 1976. pap. 2.95 (ISBN 0-345-31435-2). Ballantine.

--The Compleat Enchanter: The Magical Misadventures of Harold Shea. 432p. (Orig.). 1980. pap. 2.50 (ISBN 0-345-28929-3, Del Rey Bks.). Ballantine.

--Land of Unreason. (Illus.). 224p. 1985. pap. 7.95 (ISBN 0-312-94278-8). Bluejay Bks.

De Camp, L. Sprague see De Camp, L. Sprague.

De Camp, L. Sprague, jt. auth. see Howard, Robert E.

De Camp, L. Sprague see Sprague de Camp, L.

De Camp, L. Sprague, ed. see Howard, Robert E.

De Camp, L. Sprague, et al. Dark Valley Destiny: The Life of Robert E. Howard. LC 83-15635. (Illus.). 416p. 1983. 16.95 (ISBN 0-312-94074-2); ltd., signed, collector's ed. 40.00 (ISBN 0-312-94075-0). Bluejay Bks.

DeCamp, Lane, et al, trs. see Kindsfather, William, et al.

De Camp, Sprague L. The Queen of Zamba. (Krishna Ser.). 224p. 1983. pap. 2.50 (ISBN 0-441-69658-9). Ace Bks.

De Camp, Sprague L. & Carter, Lin. Conan of the Isles. (Conan Ser.: No. 12). 1983. pap. 2.75 (ISBN 0-441-11620-5, Pub. by Ace Science Fiction). Ace Bks.

De Camp, Sprague L. & Howard, Robert E. Conan, the Usurper. (Conan Ser.: No. 8). 192p. 1983. pap. 2.50 (ISBN 0-441-11602-7, Pub. by Ace Science Fiction). Ace Bks.

DeCampoli, Giuseppe. The Statics of Structural Components: Understanding the Basics of Structural Design. LC 82-20122. 296p. 1983. 29.95 (ISBN 0-471-87169-9, Pub. by Wiley-Interscience). Wiley.

De Campoli, Giuseppe. Strength of Structural Materials: Understanding Basic Structural Design. LC 84-3569. 461p. 1984. text ed. 34.95 (ISBN 0-471-89082-0, Pub. by Wiley-Interscience). Wiley.

De Campos, Deoclecio Redig. Michelangelo: The Last Judgment. 1979. 100.00 (ISBN 0-385-12299-3). Doubleday.

De Cande, R. La Musique. 550p. (Fr.). 42.50 (ISBN 0-686-56978-4, M-6105). French & Eur.

De Candolle, A. P. Collection de Memoires pour servir a l'Histoire du Regne Vegetal et plus specialement pour servir de complement a quelques parties du Prodromus Regni Vegetabilis. (Illus.). 1972. 87.50 (ISBN 3-7682-0728-5). Lubrecht & Cramer.

De Candolle, Alphonse. Histiore Des Sciences et Des Savants Depuis Deux Siecles. Cohen, I. Bernard, ed. LC 80-2116. (Development of Science Ser.). (Illus.). 1981. lib. bdg. 50.00x (ISBN 0-405-13836-9). Ayer Co Pubs.

De Candolle, Augustin P. & Sprengel, Kurt. Elements of the Philosophy of Plants: Containing the Principles of Scientific Botany. Sterling, Keir B., ed. LC 77-81123. (Biologists & Their World Ser.). (Illus.). 1978. Repr. of 1821 ed. lib. bdg. 40.00x (ISBN 0-405-10719-6). Ayer Co Pubs.

Decanio, Stephen J. Agriculture in the Postbellum South: The Economics of Production & Supply. 1975. 35.00x (ISBN 0-262-04047-6). MIT Pr.

De Capriles, Miguel A. Modern Financial Accounting: 1001-1088. 166p. 1962. pap. 5.00x (ISBN 0-8377-0505-3). Rothman.

DeCaprio, A. Clear & Simple Guide to Business Spelling. (Clear & Simple Guides Ser.). 128p. (Orig.). 1981. pap. 5.95 (ISBN 0-671-42222-7). Monarch Pr.

DeCaprio, Annie. A Modern Approach to Business English. LC 73-90044. 1974. pap. text ed. 15.67 scp (ISBN 0-672-96102-4). Bobbs.

--A Modern Approach to Business Spelling. 2nd ed. LC 78-3421. 1979. pap. text ed. 15.67 scp (ISBN 0-672-97206-9); scp tchr's manual 7.33 (ISBN 0-672-97207-7). Bobbs.

De Capua, A. G. German Baroque Poetry: Interpretive Readings. LC 73-152521. Repr. of 1973 ed. 55.30 (ISBN 0-8357-9595-0, 2010105). Bks Demand UMI.

DeCarava, Roy. Roy DeCarava: Photographs. Alinder, James, ed. LC 81-68286. (Illus.). 192p. 1982. 40.00 (ISBN 0-933286-26-0); Deluxe ed. 750.00 (ISBN 0-933286-29-5). Friends Photography.

De Carcaradec, Maria. Mural Ceramics in Turkey. Conlon, James, tr. from Fr. (Illus.). 150p. (Orig.). 1981. pap. 12.50. Heinman.

De Cardona, Mariana R. Essays on the Generation of the Thirties. (Puerto Rico Ser.). 1979. lib. bdg. 59.95. Gordon Pr.

De Cardonda, Nicolas. Geographic & Hydrographic Descriptions... of the Kingdom of California (1632) Mathes, Michael, ed. & tr. (Baja California Travels Ser.: No. 35). (Illus.). 111p. 1974. 18.00 (ISBN 0-87093-235-7). Dawsons.

Decareau, Robert V. Microwaves in the Food Processing Industry. (Food Science & Technology Ser.). Date not set. 37.50 (ISBN 0-12-208430-6). Acad Pr.

Decareau, Robert V., jt. auth. see Goldblith, Samuel A.

Decarie, Therese G. Intelligence & Affectivity in Early Childhood: An Experimental Study of Jean Piaget's Object Concept & Object Relations. LC 65-28439. 230p. (Orig.). 1966. text ed. 22.50 (ISBN 0-8236-2720-9). Intl Univs Pr.

Decarie, Therese G., et al. The Infant's Reaction to Strangers. Diamanti, Joyce, tr. from Fr. LC 73-8080. (Illus.). 238p. (Orig.). 1973. text ed. 22.50 (ISBN 0-8236-2650-4). Intl Univs Pr.

DeCarle, Don. Practical Clock Repairing. 18.95x (ISBN 0-685-22074-5). Wehman.

--Practical Watch Repairing. 18.95x (ISBN 0-685-22078-8). Wehman.

De Carli, Franco. The World of Fish. Richardson, Jean, tr. LC 79-1436. (Abbeville Press Encyclopedia of Natural Science). (Illus.). 1979. 13.95 (ISBN 0-89659-035-6); pap. 7.95 (ISBN 0-89659-029-1). Abbeville Pr.

DeCarlo, Joseph P. Fundamentals of Flow Measurement: An Independent Learning Module of the Instrument Society of America. LC 83-12686. 288p. 1984. text ed. 39.95x (ISBN 0-87664-627-5). Instru Soc.

DeCarlo, Tessa, tr. see Luxemburg, Rosa.

De Carmoy, Guy. Energy for Europe. 1977. pap. 5.25 (ISBN 0-8447-3243-5). Am Enterprise.

--Foreign Policies of France, Nineteen Forty-Four to Nineteen Sixty-Eight. Halperin, Elaine P., tr. LC 71-85446. 1970. 16.50x (ISBN 0-226-13991-3). U of Chicago Pr.

De Caro, Francis A., compiled by. Women & Folklore: A Bibliographic Survey. LC 83-12837. xiv, 170p. 1983. lib. bdg. 29.95 (ISBN 0-313-23821-9, DWF/). Greenwood.

Decarpentry. Academic Equitation. Bartle, Nicole, tr. from Fr. (Illus.). pap. 7.95 (ISBN 0-85131-036-2, NC51, Dist. by Miller). J A Allen.

--Academic Equitation. 280p. 1981. 40.00x (ISBN 0-85131-036-2, Pub. by Allen & Co.). State Mutual Bk.

De Carvajal, M. Tragedia Josephina. Gillet, S. E., ed. (Elliott Monographs in the Romance Languages & Literature Ser). Repr. of 1932 ed. 25.00 (ISBN 0-527-02631-X). Kraus Repr.

De Carvalho, Maria C. Karl R. Poppers Philosophie der Wissenschaftlichen und der Vorwissenschaft-Lichen Erfahrung. (European University Studies Ser.: No. 20, Vol. 95). 203p. (Ger.). 1982. 24.75 (ISBN 3-8204-7206-1). P Lang Pubs.

De Carvalho, Sergio. The Origins of Human Lymphomas. 2nd ed. (Illus.). 120p. 1985. pap. write for info. (ISBN 0-930376-40-4). Chem-Orbital.

Decary, Francine & Rock, Gail A., eds. Platelet Serology. (Current Studies in Hematology & Blood Transfusion: No. 52). (Illus.). x, 150p. 1986. 41.75 (ISBN 3-8055-4208-9). S Karger.

De Casas, Celso A. Pelon Drops Out. LC 79-84473. (Illus.). 1979. pap. 6.00 (ISBN 0-89229-006-4). Tonatiuh-Quinto Sol Intl.

De Caso, Jacques, tr. see Rodin, Auguste.

De Casseres, Benjamin. Don Marquis. 59.95 (ISBN 0-8490-0055-6). Gordon Pr.

--Fantasie Impromptu. 59.95 (ISBN 0-8490-0156-0). Gordon Pr.

--Forty Immortals. 59.95 (ISBN 0-8490-0184-6). Gordon Pr.

--James Gibbons Huneker. LC 77-17168. 1977. lib. bdg. 15.00 (ISBN 0-8414-1895-0). Folcroft.

--James Gibbons Huneker. 59.95 (ISBN 0-8490-0433-0). Gordon Pr.

--James Gibbons Huneker. 62p. 1980. Repr. of 1925 ed. lib. bdg. 15.00 (ISBN 0-8492-4215-0). R West.

--Mencken & Shaw: The Anatomy of America's Voltaire & England's Other John Bull. 1930. Repr. 25.00 (ISBN 0-8274-2727-1). R West.

--Works, 3 vols. 300.00 (ISBN 0-87968-467-4). Gordon Pr.

De Castells, Matilde O. & Lionetti, Harold E. La Lengue Espanola: Grammatica y Cultura. 3rd ed. 539p. (Span.). 1983. text ed. 21.95 (ISBN 0-02-320110-X, Pub by. Scribner). Macmillan.

De Castille, Vernon. Man's Self-Discovery in the Order of the Universe. 1979. 57.50 (ISBN 0-89266-147-X). Am Classical Coll Pr.

De Castillejo, Irene Claremont see Claremont De Castillejo, Irene.

De Castres, Elizabeth. A Collector's Guide to Tea Silver 1670-1900. 1977. 25.00 (ISBN 0-685-87551-2). State Mutual Bk.

De Castries, Duc. The Lives of the Kings & Queens of France. LC 79-2205. (Illus.). 1979. 20.00 (ISBN 0-394-50734-7). Knopf.

De Castro, Adolph see Castro, Adolph de.

De Castro, Fernando J. & Jaeger, Robert W. Clinical Toxicology Manual. LC 77-78898. 1978. pap. 9.50 (ISBN 0-87125-039-X). Cath Health.

De Castro, J. Paul, ed. see Fielding, Henry.

DeCastro, Josue. The Geopolitics of Hunger. rev. & enl. ed. LC 52-5012. 524p. 1977. 18.50 (ISBN 0-85345-357-8); pap. 7.50 (ISBN 0-85345-456-6). Monthly Rev.

De Castro, Josue. Of Men & Crabs. LC 79-139980. 1979. 7.95 (ISBN 0-8149-0667-2). Vanguard.

DeCastro, Norma S. Mental Health Nursing. 192p. 1984. pap. text ed. 14.95 (ISBN 0-8403-3269-6). Kendall-Hunt.

De Castroverde, Waldo. El Circulo de la Muerte. LC 84-80921. (Coleccion Caniqui Ser.). 153p. (Orig., Span.). 1984. pap. 8.95 (ISBN 0-89729-349-5). Ediciones.

De Castro Y Bellius, Guillem. Premiere Partie Des Mocedades Del Cid De Don Guillen De Castro. Repr. of 1890 ed. 28.00 (ISBN 0-384-07870-2). Johnson Repr.

De Castro Y Rossi, Adolfo see Castro Y Rossi, Aldolfo De.

De Catanzaro, C. J. Symeon, the New Theologian: The Discourses. LC 80-82414. (Classics of Western Spirituality Ser.). 416p. 1980. 11.95 (ISBN 0-8091-0292-7); pap. 9.95 (ISBN 0-8091-2230-8). Paulist Pr.

Decatanzaro, Carmino J., tr. see Cabasilas, Nicholas.

De Catanzaro, Denys. Suicide & Self-Damaging Behavior: A Sociobiological Perspective. LC 81-12872. (Personality & Psychopathology Ser.). 1981. 33.50 (ISBN 0-12-163880-4). Acad Pr.

DeCato, Clifford M. & Wicks, Robert J. Case Studies of the Clinical Interpretation of the Bender Gestalt Test: Illustrations of the Interpretive Process for Graduate Training & Continuing Professional Education. (Illus.). 152p. 1976. photocopy ed. 17.75x (ISBN 0-398-03554-7). C C Thomas.

Decato, Clifford M., jt. auth. see Bell, Albert A.

Decato, Clifford M., et al. Rorschach Scoring: A Workbook for the Perceptanalytic System. LC 84-9566. 224p. 1984. spiral bound 25.00 (ISBN 0-87630-364-5). Brunner-Mazel.

Decatur Junior Service League Inc. Cotton Country Cooking. 407p. Repr. of 1972 ed. 9.00 (ISBN 0-9614406-0-0). Decatur Jr Serv.

Decatur, Stephen. The Private Affairs of George Washington. LC 77-86596. (American Scene Ser.). 1969. Repr. of 1933 ed. 45.00 (ISBN 0-306-71416-7). Da Capo.

Decaudin, jt. auth. see Kihm.

Decaudin, ed. see Apollinaire, Guillaume.

De Cauhe, Joana Raspall see Raspall de Cauhe, Joana, et al.

De Caussade, Jean-Pierre. Abandonment to Divine Providence. LC 74-2827. 120p. 1975. pap. 2.95 (ISBN 0-385-02544-0, Im). Doubleday.

--The Sacrament of the Present Moment: Self Abandonment to the Divine Providence. Muggeridge, Kitty, tr. from Fr. LC 81-48206. 128p. 1982. 8.61i (ISBN 0-06-061809-4, HarpR). Har-Row.

De Caux, Len. The Living Spirit of the Wobblies. LC 76-1865. 180p. 1978. 7.50 (ISBN 0-7178-0431-3); pap. 2.95 (ISBN 0-7178-0432-1). Intl Pubs Co.

Decavalles, Adonis. Ransoms to Time: Selected Poems. Friar, Kimon, tr. from Gr. LC 82-49314. 144p. 1984. 18.50 (ISBN 0-8386-3180-0). Fairleigh Dickinson.

Decavalles, Adonis, et al, eds. Voice of Cyprus. 1966. 8.50 (ISBN 0-8079-0132-6). October.

Decavelles, Andonis. Pandelis Prevelakis & the Value of a Heritage. Woodhead, Jean H., tr. from Gr. Stavrou, Theofanis G., ed. Bd. with Rethymno as a Style of Life. Prevelakis, Pandelis. (Modern Greek History & Culture Ser.). 1981. 10.00 (ISBN 0-935476-08-3). Nostos Bks.

De Cayeux, Andre. Three Billion Years of Life. Clemow, Joyce E., tr. LC 68-31779. (Illus.). 1970. pap. 2.45 (ISBN 0-8128-1349-9). Stein & Day.

DeCecco, John P. & Richards, Arlene. Growing Pains: Uses of School Conflict. 8.95 (ISBN 0-87945-029-0). Fed Legal Pubn.

De Cecco, John P., ed. Bashers, Baiters, Bigots. LC 84-19121. 208p. 1985. pap. text ed. 7.95 (ISBN 0-918393-02-7). Harrington Pk.

DeCecco, John P., ed. Bisexual & Homosexual Identities: Critical Clinical Issues. LC 84-4569. (Research on Homosexuality Ser.: No. 9). 106p. 1984. text ed. 19.95 (ISBN 0-86656-300-8, B300). Haworth Pr.

De Cecco, John P., ed. Gay Personality & Sexual Labeling. LC 84-22578. 120p. 1985. pap. text ed. 6.95 (ISBN 0-918393-01-9). Harrington Pk.

--Homophobia: An Overview. LC 84-8959. (Journal of Homosexuality Ser.: Vol. 10, No. 1-2). 208p. 1984. text ed. 24.95 (ISBN 0-86656-356-3, B356). Haworth Pr.

--Origins of Sexuality & Homosexuality. Shively, Michael. LC 84-22563. 184p. 1985. pap. text ed. 7.95 (ISBN 0-918393-00-0). Harrington Pk.

DeCecco, John P. & Shively, Michael G., eds. Bisexual & Homosexual Identities: Critical Theoretical Issues. LC 83-26371. (Research on Homosexuality Ser.: Vol. 9, Nos. 2/3). 174p. 1984. text ed. 22.95 (ISBN 0-86656-271-0, B271). Haworth Pr.

De Cecco, Marcello. The International Gold Standard. LC 83-42534. 275p. 1983. 27.50 (ISBN 0-312-42203-2). St Martin.

De Cecco, Marcello, ed. International Economic Adjustment: Small Countries & the European Economic System. LC 82-23164. 275p. 1983. 37.50x (ISBN 0-312-42050-1). St Martin.

De Celeyran, Mary Tapie see Beaute, Georges & Tapie de Celeyran, Mary.

De Cervantes, Miguel. Don Quijote. (Span). 7.50x (ISBN 0-686-00858-8). Colton Bk.

--Don Quixote. (Classics Ser). (gr. 11 up). 1967. pap. 2.75 (ISBN 0-8049-0153-8, CL-153). Airmont.

--Don Quixote. unabr. ed. Starkie, Walter, tr. (Orig.). 1957. pap. 4.95 (ISBN 0-451-51821-7, CE1821, Sig Classics). NAL.

--Don Quixote. Jones, Joseph R. & Douglas, Kenneth, eds. (Critical Editions Ser.). 1981. 29.95 (ISBN 0-393-04514-5); pap. text ed. 9.95x (ISBN 0-393-09018-3). Norton.

--Don Quixote. (Now Age Illustrated V Ser.). (Illus.). 64p. (gr. 4-12). 1979. text ed. 5.00 (ISBN 0-88301-399-1); pap. text ed. 1.95 (ISBN 0-88301-387-8); student activity bk 1.25 (ISBN 0-88301-411-4). Pendulum Pr.

--Don Quixote. Cohen, John M., tr. (Classics Ser.). (Orig.). (YA) (gr. 9 up). 1951. pap. 5.95 (ISBN 0-14-044010-0). Penguin.

--Don Quixote. (Classics for Kids). 32p. (gr. 8 up). 1985. pap. 3.60 (ISBN 0-382-06957-9). Silver.

--Don Quixote. Smollett, Tobias, tr. from Span. 986p. 1986. 19.95 (ISBN 0-374-14232-7); pap. 9.95 (ISBN 0-374-51943-9). FS&G.

--Obras Completas. (Span). 34.95x (ISBN 0-685-20243-7). Schoenhof.

--Six Exemplary Novels. De Onis, Harriet, ed. Incl. Dialogue of the Dogs; Gypsy Maid; Illustrious Kitchen Maid; Jealous Hidalgo; Master Glass; Rinconete & Cortadillo. LC 61-8942. (Illus.). (gr. 9 up). 1961. pap. text ed. 5.95 (ISBN 0-8120-0159-1). Barron.

De Cervantes, Miguel see Cervantes, Miguel de.

De Cervantes, Miguel, ed. Fesstival De Flor y Canto. (Span.). 1976. pap. text ed. 4.95 (ISBN 0-88474-031-5). U of S Cal Pr.

De Cervantes, Miquel see Cervantes, Miquel De.

De Cervantes Saavedra, Miguil see Cervantes Saavedra, Miguil de.

De Cervera, Alejo. The Statute of Limitations in American Conflicts of Law. LC 65-23494. 5.00 (ISBN 0-8477-3001-8). U of PR Pr.

--The Statute of Limitations in American Conflicts of Law. 197p. 1966. 12.50 (ISBN 0-317-30244-2). Oceana.

--Statutes of Limitations in American Conflicts of Law. LC 65-23494. 189p. 1966. 12.50 (ISBN 0-379-00259-0). Oceana.

De Chamblain De Marivaux, Pierre C. Le Paysan Parvenu: Or, the Fortunate Peasant. LC 78-60836. (Novel 1720-1805 Ser.: Vol. 2). 1979. lib. bdg. 37.00 (ISBN 0-8240-3651-4). Garland Pub.

De Chambrun, Adolphe. The Executive Power in the United States: A Study of Constitutional Law. LC 74-75460. 303p. 1974. Repr. of 1874 ed. 35.00x (ISBN 0-912004-13-4). W W Gaunt.

De Chambrun, Clara L. The Making of Nicholas Longworth: Annals of an American Family. facsimile ed. (Select Bibliographies Reprint Ser.). Repr. of 1933 ed. 26.50 (ISBN 0-8369-5882-9). Ayer Co Pubs.

De Chambrun, Clara Longworth see Longworth de Chambrun, Clara.

De Chambrun, Rene. Pierre Laval: Traitor or Patriot? Stein, Elly, tr. (Illus.). 256p. 1984. 15.95 (ISBN 0-684-18095-2, ScribT). Scribner.

De Champigny, Victor. Legends & Romance of the Great Castles of the Renaissance. (The Library of Historical Culture Ser.). (Illus.). 176p. 1982. 57.45 (ISBN 0-89266-345-6). Am Classical Coll Pr.

DeChancie, John. Red Limit Freeway. 256p. pap. 2.75 (ISBN 0-441-71122-7, Pub. by Ace Science Fiction). Ace Bks.

--Starriger. 272p. 1983. pap. 2.75 (ISBN 0-441-78304-X, Pub. by Ace Science Fiction). Ace Bks.

--Starrigger. 272p. 1984. pap. 2.75 (ISBN 0-441-78304-X). Ace Bks.

Dechanet, J. M. Yoga in Ten Lessons. 1980. pap. 2.95 (ISBN 0-346-12428-X). Cornerstone.

Dechanet, Jean M. William of St. Thierry: The Man & His Work. Strachen, Richard, tr. from Fr. LC 73-152485. (Cistercian Studies: No. 10). 192p. 1972. 10.95 (ISBN 0-87907-810-3). Cistercian Pubns.

Dechant, Emarld V. Psychology in Teaching Reading. 2nd ed. 1977. text ed. 30.95 (ISBN 0-13-736686-8). P-H.

Dechant, Emerald. Diagnosis & Remediation of Reading Disability. (Illus.). 512p. 1981. text ed. 28.95 (ISBN 0-13-208454-6). P-H.

--Teacher's Directory of Reading Skill Aids & Materials. LC 81-406. 274p. 1981. 19.95 (ISBN 0-13-888255-X, Parker). P-H.

Dechant, Emerald V. Improving the Teaching of Reading. 3rd ed. (Illus.). 512p. 1982. reference 29.95 (ISBN 0-13-453423-9). P-H.

De Chant, John M. Devilbirds: The Story of the United States Marine Corps Aviation in World War II. LC 79-16257. Repr. of 1947 ed. 16.95 (ISBN 0-89201-050-9). Zenger Pub.

De Chantelou, Paul F. Diary of the Cavaliere Bernini's Visit to France. Blunt, Anthony, ed. Corbett, Margery, tr. (Illus.). 376p. 1985. text ed. 47.00x (ISBN 0-691-04028-1). Princeton U Pr.

--Journal Du Voyage En France Du Cavalier Bernin: (Giovanni Lorenzo Bernini, 1598-1680) LC 72-86907. (Illus.). 300p. 1973. Repr. of 1930 ed. lib. bdg. 22.50 (ISBN 0-8337-0531-8). B Franklin.

De Chantigny, J. A., ed. Hilaire Belloc's Prefaces: Written for Fellow Authors. LC 76-178120. 347p. 1971. 10.00 (ISBN 0-8294-0209-8). Loyola.

De Chardin, Pierre T. see Teilhard de Chardin, Pierre.

De Chardin, Pierre Teilhard see Teilhard De Chardin, Pierre.

De Chardin, Teilhard. Building the Earth. 7.95 (ISBN 0-87193-078-1). Dimension Bks.

--Le Groupe Zoologique Humain, Structure et Directions Evolutives. (Coll. les Savants et le Monde Ser.). pap. 6.95 (ISBN 0-685-36591-3). French & Eur.

De Charlevoix, F. X. History & General Description of New France. 6 Vols. Shea, John G., tr. (The American West Ser.). (Illus.). 1962. 59.95 (ISBN 0-8294-0011-7). Loyola.

De Charms, Desiree & Breed, Paul. Songs in Collections: An Index. 1966. 38.00 (ISBN 0-911772-53-7); pap. 11.00 (ISBN 0-911772-54-5). Info Coord.

DeCharms, Richard. Enhancing Motivation: Change in the Classroom. enl. ed. 300p. 1985. text ed. 27.50x (ISBN 0-8290-1248-6); pap. text ed. 14.95x (ISBN 0-8290-1249-4). Irvington.

De Charriere, Isabella A. Four Tales by Zelide. facs. ed. LC 75-140327. (Short Story Index Reprint Ser.). 1926. 18.00 (ISBN 0-8369-3719-8). Ayer Co Pubs.

De Chary, Pauline, tr. see Von Klarwill, Victor.

De Chasca, Edmund S. John Gould Fletcher & Imagism. LC 77-10795. 1978. 19.00x (ISBN 0-8262-0229-2). U of Mo Pr.

De Chastellux, Francois J. Travels in North-America, in the Years 1780-1782, 2 Vols. LC 67-29046. (Eyewitness Accounts of the American Revolution Ser., No. 1). 1968. Repr. of 1787 ed. Set. 24.00 (ISBN 0-405-01109-1); Vol. 1. 14.00 (ISBN 0-405-01135-0); Vol. 2. 11.50 (ISBN 0-405-01127-X). Ayer Co Pubs.

De Chateaubriand, Francois R. Rene. (Documentation thematique). (Illus., Fr.). pap. 2.95 (ISBN 0-685-14065-2, 42). Larousse.

De Chateaubriand, Francois-Rene. Memoires d'Outre-Tombe, 2 vols. (Documentation thematique). (Fr). pap. 2.95 ea. Larousse.

De Chateaubriand, Francois-Rene see Chateaubriand, Francois-Rene de.

De Chateaubriand, Rene. Atala. Letessier, ed. Bd. with Rene; Les Aventures du Dernier Abencerage. (Class. Garnier). pap. 6.95 (ISBN 0-685-34882-2). French & Eur.

--Atala, Rene. Reboul, ed. (Coll GF). 1958. pap. 2.95 (ISBN 0-685-11016-8, 3209). French & Eur.

--Memoires D'Outre-Tombe, 2 tomes. Levaillant & Moulnier, eds. (Bibl. de la Pleiade). 1947-50. Set. leather bdg. 67.45 (ISBN 0-685-11358-2). French & Eur.

--Oeuvres Romanesques et Voyages, Tome I. Regard, ed. Incl. Atala; Rene; Les Natchez; Le Voyage en Amerique; La Vie de Rance. (Bibliotheque De la Pleiade). 27.50 (ISBN 0-685-34883-0). French & Eur.

--Oeuvres Romanesques et Voyages, Tome II. Regard, ed. Incl. Les Martyrs; Le Dernier Abencerage; Itineraire de Paris a Jerusalem; Voyage en Italie. (Bibliotheque De la Pleiade). 29.95 (ISBN 0-685-34884-9). French & Eur.

De Chateaubriand, Viscount. The Emotional & Supernatural Substance in the Realm of Poetry. 159p. 1984. 89.15 (ISBN 0-89901-224-8). Found Class Reprints.

--The Genius of Christianity, 2 vols. White, Charles I., tr. 245p. 1985. 117.35 (ISBN 0-89901-223-X). Found Class Reprints.

De Chavigny, Camille, ed. The Napoleon's Book of Dreams & Fate. (Illus.). 155p. 1984. 88.95 (ISBN 0-89920-115-6). Am Inst Psych.

De Chazal, Malcolm. Sens-Plastique. 2nd, rev. ed. Weiss, Irving, ed. LC 79-25078. 163p. (Orig.). 1980. pap. 8.00 (ISBN 0-915342-29-4). SUN.

Dechema. Eighth International Congress on Catalysis, 6 vols. 1984. text ed. 384.00x (ISBN 0-89573-371-4). VCH Pubs.

Dechema, ed. Third European Congress on Biotechnology, 3 vols. 2014p. 1984. Set. pap. 275.30x (ISBN 0-89573-414-1). VCH Pubs.

DECHEMA, Deutsche Gesellschaft Fuer Chemisches Apparatewesen E. V., ed. Biotechnology: Proceedings of the First European Congress on Biotechnology. (Dechema Monographs: Vol. 82). 304p. 1979. pap. 37.50x (ISBN 3-527-10765-7). VCH Pubs.

--Characterization of Immobilized Biocatalysts. (DECHEMA Monographs: Vol. 84). 400p. (Orig.). 1980. pap. 46.00x (ISBN 3-527-10767-3). VCH Pubs.

Dechend, Hertha Von see De Santillana, Giorgio & Von Dechend, Hertha.

De Chene, Brent. The Historical Phonology of Vowel Length. Hankamer, Jorge, ed. (Outstanding Dissertations in Linguistics Ser.). 313p. 1985. 35.00 (ISBN 0-8240-5423-7). Garland Pub.

De Chenier, Louis. Present State of the Empire of Morocco, 2 Vols. in 1. 1788. 52.00 (ISBN 0-384-08620-9). Johnson Repr.

De Cherisey, Christine. My Village in Nepal: Tsiza & the Caravans. LC 85-2193. (Illus.). 48p. (gr. 4 up). PLB 12.95 (ISBN 0-382-09007-1). Silver.

DeCherney. High Risk Pregnancy & Perinatology. Date not set. write for info. (ISBN 0-444-00865-9). Elsevier.

DeCherney, Alan. Patient Management Problems: Obstetrics & Gynecology. LC 79-24563. 128p. (Orig.). 1980. pap. 11.95 (ISBN 0-668-04364-4). ACC.

DeCherney, Alan H., ed. Ectopic Pregnancy. 1985. text ed. 29.00 (ISBN 0-8391-2005-2, 20159). Univ Park.

Dechert, Hans & Raupach, Manfred, eds. Temporal Variables in Speech: Studies in Honor of Frieda Goldman-Eisler. (Janua Linguarum, Series Maior: No. 86). 1979. text ed. 36.00x (ISBN 90-279-7946-4). Mouton.

Dechert, Hans W. & Raupach, Manfred. Temporal Variables in Speech: Studies in Honour of Frieda Golman-Eisler. (Janua Linguarum Ser.: Maior 86). 370p. 1980. 36.00 (ISBN 90-279-7946-4). Mouton.

Dechert, Hans W. & Raupach, Manfred, eds. Towards a Cross-Linguistic Assessment of Speech Production. (Kassler Arbeiten zur Sprache und Literatur: Vol. 7). 129p. 1980. pap. 13.70 (ISBN 3-8204-6003-9). P Lang Pubs.

Dechert, Hans W., et al. Transfer & Interference in Language: A Selected Bibliography. (Library & Information Sources in Linguistics Ser.: 14). 1985. 52.00x (ISBN 90-272-3735-2). Benjamins North Am.

Dechert, Hans W., et al, eds. Second Language Productions. (Tuebinger Beitraege zur Linguistik: 240). 297p. (Orig.). 1984. pap. 31.00x (ISBN 3-87808-257-6, Pub. by G N Verlag Germany). Benjamins North AM.

De Chiara, Edith, jt. auth. see Uhlin, Donald H.

DeChiara, J. & Koppelman, L. E. Time-Saver Standard for Site Planning. (Illus.). 849p. 1984. 75.00 (ISBN 0-07-016266-2). McGraw.

DeChiara, J., ed. Time-Saver Standards for Residential Development. (Illus.). 910p. 1984. 75.00 (ISBN 0-07-016217-4). McGraw.

De Chiara, Joseph. Handbook of Architectural Details for Commercial Buildings. 512p. 1980. 55.00 (ISBN 0-07-016215-8). McGraw.

--Site Planning Standards. LC 77-9440. (Illus.). 1977. 49.50 (ISBN 0-07-016216-6). McGraw.

De Chiara, Joseph & Callender, John. Time-Saver Standards for Building Types. 2nd ed. 1088p. 1980. 75.00 (ISBN 0-07-016265-4). McGraw.

DeChiara, Joseph & Koppelman, Lee. Urban Planning & Design Criteria. 3rd ed. 702p. 1982. 69.50 (ISBN 0-442-21946-6). Van Nos Reinhold.

De Chiara, Joy. The Fairfield County Bargain Hunter's Notebook. 52p. 1980. 4.25 (ISBN 0-9613971-0-1). Bargain Hunt Ntebks.

De Chico, Catherine. Mobius. LC 85-50092. 94p. 1985. 6.95 (ISBN 0-938232-63-0); pap. 4.95 (ISBN 0-317-18274-9). Winston-Derek.

De Chirico, Giorgio. Memoirs of Giorgio De Chirico. Crosland, Margaret, tr. LC 74-102694. (Illus.). 1971. 13.95x (ISBN 0-87024-125-7). U of Miami Pr.

DECHMA, Deutsche Gesellschaft Fuer Chemisches Apparatewesen E. V., ed. Microbiology Applied to Biotechnology: Proceedings XIIth International Congress of Microbiology. (DECHEMA Monographs: Vol. 83). 230p. (Orig.). 1979. pap. text ed. 25.80x (ISBN 3-527-10766-5). VCH Pubs.

DeChow, Georgeen H. Curriculum Design for Associate Degree Nursing Programs: Factors in Program Direction. 26p. 1980. 4.95 (ISBN 0-88737-182-5, 23-1833). Natl League Nurse.

DeChow, Georgeen H. & Rines, Alice R. Preparing the Associate Degree Graduate. 71p. 1977. 6.95 (ISBN 0-88737-212-0, 23-1661). Natl League Nurse.

DeChristoforo, R. J. Woodworking Techniques: Joints & Their Applications. (Illus.). 1979. ref.ed. 23.95 (ISBN 0-8359-8785-X). Reston.

De Chungara, Domitila B. & Viezzer, Moema. Let Me Speak! Testimony of Domitila, a Woman of the Bolivian Mines. Ortiz, Victoria, tr. LC 77-91757. 235p. 1979. 12.50 (ISBN 0-85345-445-0); pap. 7.00 (ISBN 0-85345-485-X). Monthly Rev.

Deci, Edward L. Intrinsic Motivation. LC 75-17613. (Perspectives in Social Psychology Ser.). (Illus.). 335p. 1975. 22.50x (ISBN 0-306-34401-7, Plenum Pr). Plenum Pub.

--The Psychology of Self-Determination. LC 80-8373. 1980. 24.00 (ISBN 0-669-04045-2); pap. 11.00x (ISBN 0-669-09813-2). Lexington Bks.

Deci, Edward L., jt. auth. see Gilmer, B. V.

Deci, Edward L., jt. ed. see Vroom, Victor H.

DeCicco, Paul R. Life Safety Considerations in Atrium Buildings. 1982. 4.35 (ISBN 0-686-37667-6, TR 82-3). Society Fire Protect.

De Cieza De Leon, Pedro. Travels of Pedro De Cieza De Leon 1532-50. Markham, Clements R., tr. 1964. Repr. of 1864 ed. 60.50 (ISBN 0-8337-2235-2). B Franklin.

Decius, J. C. & Hexter, R. M. Molecular Vibrations in Crystals. 1977. 59.95 (ISBN 0-07-016227-1). McGraw.

De Civrieux, Marc. Watunna: An Orinoco Creation Cycle. Guss, David, ed. LC 80-82440. (Illus.). 216p. 1980. 20.00 (ISBN 0-86547-002-2); pap. 12.50 (ISBN 0-86547-003-0). N Point Pr.

Deck, Allan. Francisco Javier Alagre: A Study in Mexican Literary Criticism, Vol. 13. 112p. 1976. 18.00. Jesuit Hist.

Deck, E., jt. ed. see Folta, J.

Deck, John N. Nature, Contemplation, & the One: A Study in the Philosophy of Plotinus. LC 67-98055. pap. 36.30 (ISBN 0-317-08774-6, 2014184). Bks Demand UMI.

Deck, Mary C. A Book about Kitties. (Illus., Orig.). (gr. 2). 1978. pap. 2.50 (ISBN 0-8431-0457-0). Price Stern.

Deckard, Barbara S. The Women's Movement: Political, Socioeconomic, & Psychological Issues. 3rd ed. 500p. 1983. pap. text ed. 15.50 scp (ISBN 0-06-041615-7, HarpC). Har-Row.

Deckel, jt. auth. see Presley.

Decker & Du Plessis. Synopsis of Surgical Anatomy. 12th ed. 1986. price not set. PSG Pub Co.

Decker, Barbara, jt. auth. see Decker, Robert.

Decker, Carol W. Me & You & Other Things. 1980. 6.95 (ISBN 0-87881-083-8). Mojave Bks.

Decker, Celia A. & Decker, John R. Planning & Administering Early Childhood Programs. 3rd ed. 1984. pap. 22.50 (ISBN 0-675-20116-0). Merrill.

Decker, Clarence R. The Victorian Conscience. LC 77-8021. 1977. Repr. of 1952 ed. lib. bdg. 24.75x (ISBN 0-8371-9684-1, DEVC). Greenwood.

Decker, Clarence R., jt. ed. see Angoff, Charles.

Decker, David L. Social Gerontology: An Introduction to the Dynamics of Aging. 304p. 1980. text ed. 18.95 (ISBN 0-316-17918-3). Little.

Decker, David L. & Shichor, David. Urban Structure & Victimization. LC 79-1865. 128p. 1982. 17.50 (ISBN 0-669-02951-3). Lexington Bks.

Decker, David R. The Political, Economic, & Labor Climate in Argentina. Northrup, Herbert R., frwd. by. LC 83-81084. (Multinational Industrial Relations Ser.: No. 4f). 131p. (Orig.). 1983. pap. 20.00 (ISBN 0-89546-041-6). Indus Res Unit-Wharton.

Decker, David R. & Duran, Ignacio. The Political, Economic, & Labor Climate in Colombia. LC 82-82996. (Multinational Industrial Relations Ser.: No. 4e). 1982. pap. 18.00 (ISBN 0-89546-025-4). Indus Res Unit-Wharton.

Decker, DeLynn. The Power Of Patriotism. LC 81-50387. (Power Tales Ser.). pap. write for info. (ISBN 0-911712-84-4). Promised Land.

Decker, Donald M. Luis Durand. LC 79-120022. (World Authors Ser.). 1971. lib. bdg. 15.95 (ISBN 0-8057-2276-9). Irvington.

Decker, Donald M. & Decker, Mary L. Reflections on Elegance: Pasadena's Huntington Hotel since 1906. LC 84-180900. (Illus.). 68p. (Orig.). 1984. pap. 5.95 (ISBN 0-918329-01-9). Royal Lit.

Decker, Dorothy. Stripe Presents the ABC's. (Stripe Adventure Ser.). (Illus.). 64p. (gr. k-3). 1984. PLB 10.95 (ISBN 0-87518-266-6, Gemstone Bks). Dillon.

--Stripe Visits New York. (Stripe Adventure Ser.). (Illus.). 48p. (gr. k-3). 1985. PLB 9.95 (ISBN 0-87518-267-4, Gemstone Bks). Dillon.

Decker, Douglas, jt. auth. see Mackie, Dustin.

Decker, Ed & Hunt, Dave. The God Makers. LC 83-82319. 192p. 1984. pap. 6.95 (ISBN 0-89081-402-3). Harvest Hse.

Decker, Eugene, jt. ed. see Teague, Richard D.

Decker, Fred W. Science Travel Guide: The Guide to Technological Expositions, Museums, Landmarks, & Science Originals. 1971. pap. 1.95X (ISBN 0-88246-017-X). Oreg St U Bkstrs.

--Weather Map Study. rev ed. 1981. pap. 1.25x (ISBN 0-931778-02-6). Weather Wkbk.

--The Weather Workbook. rev ed. 1981. pap. 8.00x (ISBN 0-931778-03-4). Weather Wkbk.

Decker, Hannah. Freud in Germany: Revolution & Reaction in Science, 1893-1907. LC 77-20062. (Psychological Issues Ser.: Monograph 41). 360p. (Orig.). 1977. text ed. 28.50 (ISBN 0-8236-2023-9); pap. text ed. 22.50 (ISBN 0-8236-2022-0). Intl Univs Pr.

Decker, Harold A. & Herford, Julius, eds. Choral Conducting: A Symposium. LC 72-94347. (Illus.). 320p. 1973. 28.95 (ISBN 0-13-133355-0). P-H.

Decker, J., tr. see Taminiaux, J.

Decker, Jack. TRS-80 ROM Routines Documented. 126p. 1983. pap. text ed. 19.95 (ISBN 0-915363-01-1). Alter Source.

Decker, Jake. Deadly Snow. (The Force: No. 1). 256p. (Orig.). 1984. pap. 2.50 (ISBN 0-523-42079-X). Pinnacle Bks.

--Death's Little Sister. (The Force Ser.: No. 2). 224p. (Orig.). 1984. pap. 2.50 (ISBN 0-523-42127-3). Pinnacle Bks.

Decker, Jane. Death Comes Home. (The Force Ser.: No. 4). (Orig.). 1985. pap. 2.95 (ISBN 0-523-42424-8). Pinnacle Bks.

Decker, Jay B. All about Junk: How to Cash in on Other Peoples Junk & Make a Fortune. LC 84-60970. 63p. (Orig.). 1984. pap. text ed. 4.95 (ISBN 0-88247-741-2). R & E Pubs.

Decker, John A. Labor Problems in the Pacific Mandates. LC 75-30053. (Institute of Pacific Relations). Repr. of 1940 ed. 24.50 (ISBN 0-404-59517-0). AMS Pr.

Decker, John F. Prostitution: Regulation & Control. (New York University Criminal Law Education & Research Center Publication Ser.: Vol. 13). xxvi, 572p. 1979. 65.00x (ISBN 0-8377-0507-X). Rothman.

--Prostitution: Regulation & Control. (New York University Criminal Law Education & Research Center Publication Ser.). 65.00 (ISBN 0-317-31423-8). Rothman.

Decker, John R., jt. auth. see Decker, Celia A.

Decker, Larry, ed. Volunteer Coordinator's Guide. 6th ed. 61p. 1969. pap. 4.00 (ISBN 0-943272-07-6, 07-6). Inst Recreation Res.

Decker, Larry E. Foundation of Community Education. LC 72-83687. 69p. 1980. Repr. 3.95 (ISBN 0-930388-06-2). Comm Collaborators.

--People Helping People. (Community Education How to Ser.). 24p. 1977. pap. 1.25 (ISBN 0-87812-152-8). Pendell Pub.

Decker, Larry E., jt. auth. see Decker, Virginia A.

Decker, Larry E., jt. ed. see Schoeny, Donna H.

Decker, Leslie E. Railroads, Lands & Politics: The Taxation of the Railroad Land Grants, 1864-1897. LC 64-11940. (Illus.). 447p. 1964. 35.00x (ISBN 0-87057-084-6). U Pr of New Eng.

Decker, Malcolm. Brink of Revolution: New York in Crisis, 1765-1776. (Illus.). 1964. 10.00 (ISBN 0-87266-005-2). Argosy.

--Ten Days of Infamy. LC 68-20204. (Illus.). 1968. Repr. of 1968 ed. 17.00 (ISBN 0-405-00053-7). Ayer Co Pubs.

Decker, Malcolm, ed. Eyewitness Accounts of the American Revolution, Ser. 1, 34 bks. (Illus.). 1968. Repr. Set. 1947.50 (ISBN 0-405-01100-8). Ayer Co Pubs.

--Eyewitness Accounts of the American Revolution, Ser. 2, 42 bks. (Illus.). 1969. Repr. Set. 702.00 (ISBN 0-405-01101-6). Ayer Co Pubs.

--Eyewitness Accounts of the American Revolution, Ser. 3, 35 bks. (Illus.). 1971. Repr. Set. 526.00 (ISBN 0-405-01187-3). Ayer Co Pubs.

Decker, Margaret S. Lark & Sky. 112p. 1972. pap. 3.00 (ISBN 0-913976-04-0). Discovery Bks.

--Mr. Billiwicket's Burro. (Illus.). 51p. (gr. k-5). 1980. cancelled (ISBN 0-913976-08-3). Discovery Bks.

--Mr. Billiwicket's Burro: Ten Stories. (Illus.). (gr. 1-3). 1980. 5.00 (ISBN 0-682-49565-4). Exposition Pr FL.

Decker, Marjorie A. The Christian Mother Goose Baby Album in Rhyme. (Illus.). 30p. 1982. lib. bdg. 12.95 (ISBN 0-933724-12-8). Decker Pr Inc.

--Christian Mother Goose: Benjamin Bumblebee's Little Color-Grams. (Little Color-Grams Ser.). (Illus.). 96p. (gr. k-4). 1981. Decker Pr Inc.

--Christian Mother Goose Book. LC 78-78337. (Mother Goose Trilogy Ser.: Vol. I). (Illus.). 112p. (gr. k-4). 1978. 11.95 (ISBN 0-933724-00-4). Decker Pr Inc.

--Christian Mother Goose: Brother Rabbit's Little Color-Grams. (Illus.). 96p. (gr. k-4). 1981. Decker Pr Inc.

--Christian Mother Goose: Charlie Cricket's Little Color-Grams. (Little Color-Grams Ser.). (Illus.). 96p. (gr. k-4). 1981. Decker Pr Inc.

--Christian Mother Goose: Color-Me Keepsakes. (Color-Me Ser.). (Illus.). 64p. (gr. k-4). 1981. pap. 1.95 (ISBN 0-933724-05-5). Decker Pr Inc.

--Christian Mother Goose: Color-Me Praises. (Color-Me Ser). (Illus.). 64p. 1981. pap. 1.95 (ISBN 0-933724-03-9). Decker Pr Inc.

--Christian Mother Goose: Color-Me Rhymes No. 1. (Color-Me Ser.). (Illus.). 64p. (gr. k-4). 1981. pap. 1.95 (ISBN 0-933724-02-0). Decker Pr Inc.

--Christian Mother Goose: Color-Me Rhymes, No. 2. (Color-Me Ser.). (Illus.). 64p. (gr. k-4). 1981. pap. 1.95 (ISBN 0-933724-04-7). Decker Pr Inc.

--Christian Mother Goose: Grandpa Mole's Little Color-Grams. (Little Color-Grams Ser.). (Illus.). 96p. (gr. k-4). 1981. Decker Pr Inc.

--The Christian Mother Goose Treasury. LC 80-69167. (Christian Mother Goose Trilogy: Vol. II). (Illus.). 112p. (gr. k-4). 1980. PLB 11.95 (ISBN 0-933724-01-2). Decker Pr Inc.

--The Christian Mother Goose Trilogy, 3 Vols. (Illus.). 336p. (ps-4). 1983. PLB 35.50 (ISBN 0-933724-14-4). Decker Pr Inc.

--Life in Christian Mother Goose Land. LC 83-70989. (Christian Mother Goose Trilogy: Vol. III). (Illus.). 112p. (gr. k-4). 1983. PLB 11.95 (ISBN 0-933724-13-6). Decker Pr Inc.

Decker, Mary L., jt. auth. see Decker, Donald M.

Decker, Mathew. An Essay on the Causes of the Decline of the Foreign Trade, Consequently of the Value of Lands of Britain, & on the Means to Restore Both. (History of English Economic Thought Ser). 1970. Repr. of 1744 ed. 19.00 (ISBN 0-384-11170-X). Johnson Repr.

Decker, Matthew. Essay on the Causes of the Decline of the Foreign Trade. 4th ed. LC 67-29502. Repr. of 1751 ed. 27.50x (ISBN 0-678-00864-7). Kelley.

Decker, Nan. The Caption Workbook. (Caption Kit Ser.). (Illus.). 27p. (gr. 5-8). 1984. pap. text ed. 3.50x (ISBN 0-913072-61-3). Natl Assn Deaf.

Decker, Natasha. Seventy-Six Ways to Save Our Nation. 1977. 2.95 (ISBN 0-89036-063-4). Hawkes Pub Inc.

Decker, Peter, ed. see Barker, John.

Decker, Peter, ed. see Carroll, Charles.

Decker, Peter, ed. see De Rosenthal, Gustavus.

Decker, Peter, ed. see Drayton, John.

Decker, Peter, ed. see Feltman, William.

Decker, Peter, ed. see Graydon, Alexander.

Decker, Peter, ed. see Laurens, John.

Decker, Peter, ed. see Lee, Henry.

Decker, Peter, jt. ed. see Moore, Frank.

Decker, Peter, ed. see Morris, Margaret.

Decker, Peter, ed. see Roberts, Lemuel.

Decker, Peter, ed. see Robin, Abbe.

Decker, Peter, ed. see Smith, Joshua H.

Decker, Peter, ed. see Smith, William.

Decker, Peter, ed. see Stedman, Charles.

Decker, Peter, ed. see Thacher, James.

Decker, Peter R. Fortunes & Failures: White-Collar Mobility in 19th-Century San Francisco. LC 77-12557. (Studies in Urban History). 1978. 22.50x (ISBN 0-674-31118-3). Harvard U Pr.

Decker, Phillip J. & Nathan, Barry R. Behavior Modeling Training: Principles & Applications. LC 84-18155. 256p. 1985. 28.95x (ISBN 0-03-069883-9); pap. 15.95x (ISBN 0-03-001404-2). Praeger.

Decker, Randall E. Patterns of Exposition 8. 1982. pap. text ed. 11.95 (ISBN 0-316-17924-8); tchrs' manual avail. (ISBN 0-316-17925-6). Little.

Decker, Randall E. & Schwegler, Robert A. Decker's Patterns of Exposition. 1984. 11.95 (ISBN 0-316-17926-4) (ISBN 0-316-17927-2). Little.

Decker, Raymond F., compiled by see American Society for Metals Staff.

Decker, Robert & Decker, Barbara. Volcanoes. LC 80-20126. (Geology Ser.). (Illus.). 244p. 1981. pap. text ed. 11.95 (ISBN 0-7167-1242-3). W H Freeman.

Decker, Robert & Marquez, Esther T. The Proud Mexicans. (Illus.). 250p. (gr. 7-12). 1976. pap. 5.95 (ISBN 0-88345-254-5, 18450). Regents Pub.

Decker, Robert O. The Whaling City: A History of New London. LC 74-30794. (Illus.). 413p. 1976. 15.00 (ISBN 0-87106-053-1). New London County.

--Whaling Industry of New London. LC 72-87999. (Illus.). 202p. 1973. casebound 15.00 (ISBN 0-87387-056-5); softbound o.p. 10.00 (ISBN 0-87387-055-7). Shumway.

Decker, Scott H. Criminalization, Victimization & Structural Correlates of Twenty Six American Cities. LC 79-65265. 130p. 1980. 11.95 (ISBN 0-86548-007-9). R & E Pubs.

Decker, Scott H., jt. auth. see Academy of Criminal Justice Sciences Staff.

Decker, Virginia A. & Decker, Larry E. The Funding Process: Grantsmanship & Proposal Development. LC 77-92892. 120p. 1978. pap. text ed. 6.95 (ISBN 0-930388-02-X). Comm Collaborators.

Decker, William. The Holdouts. 1981. pap. 1.95 (ISBN 0-671-42081-X). PB.

--To Be a Man. 1981. pap. 1.95 (ISBN 0-671-42082-8). PB.

Deckert, Frank. Big Bend: Three Steps to the Sky. Pearson, John R., ed. (Illus.). 40p. (Orig.). 1981. pap. 3.95 (ISBN 0-912001-03-8). Big Bend.

Deckert, Frank J., ed. see Rudig, Doug.

Deckinger, Larry, jt. auth. see Singer, Jules.

Deckshot, K., ed. see Garrett, Charles L.

Deckter, Jack Van see Van Deckter, Jack.

De Clarac, Pierre, ed. Dictionnaire Universel Des Lettres. 23.00 (ISBN 0-685-11144-X). French & Eur.

De Claremont, Lewis. Ancient Book of Formulas. 3.95. Wehman.

--Ancients Book of Magic. 3.95x. Wehman.

--Seven Keys to Power. 3.95x (ISBN 0-685-22105-9). Wehman.

Declareuil, Joseph. Rome, the Law-Giver. Parker, Edward A., tr. LC 73-98752. xvi, 400p. Repr. of 1927 ed. lib. bdg. 20.75x (ISBN 0-8371-2796-3, DERL). Greenwood.

De Clark, Catalina, tr. see Dana, H. E. & Mantey, J. R.

De Cleir, Piaras V. Polymers in Injection Molding. LC 85-51316. 170p. 1985. 44.00 (ISBN 0-938648-25-X). T-C Pubns CA.

De Clemente, Elizabeth M., jt. auth. see Van Ness, Bethann.

De Clements, Barthe. How Do You Lose Those Ninth Grade Blues? LC 83-5750. 144p. (gr. 3-7). 1983. 11.50 (ISBN 0-670-38122-5, Viking Kestrel). Viking.

DeClements, Barthe. How Do You Lose Those Ninth Grade Blues? 144p. (gr. 7 up). 1984. pap. 2.25 (ISBN 0-590-33195-7, Point). Scholastic Inc.

--Nothing's Fair in Fifth Grade. LC 80-54195. 144p. (gr. 3-7). 1981. 10.95 (ISBN 0-670-51741-0). Viking.

--Nothing's Fair in Fifth Grade. 144p. (gr. 4-6). 1982. pap. 2.25 (ISBN 0-590-33947-8, Apple Paperbacks). Scholastic Inc.

--Seventeen & In-Between. 180p. (gr. 7-9). 1984. 11.95 (ISBN 0-670-63615-0, Viking Kestrel). Viking.

--Seventeen & In-Between. 144p. (Orig.). (gr. 7 up). 1985. pap. 2.25 (ISBN 0-590-33559-6, Point). Scholastic Inc.

Declerck, A. C. Interaction Epilepsy Sleep Antiepileptics: A Clinical Neurophysiological Study. 200p. 1983. pap. text ed. 12.25 (ISBN 90-265-0459-4, Pub. by Swets & Zeitlinger Netherlands). Hogrefe Intl.

DeClerck, Fred & Vanhoutte, Paul M., eds. Five-Hydroxytryptamine in Peripheral Reactions. 242p. 1982. text ed. 48.50 (ISBN 0-89004-772-3). Raven.

De Clercq, E. & Walker, R. T., eds. Targets for the Design of Antiviral Agents. (NATO ASI Series A, Life Sciences: Vol. 73). 390p. 57.50x (ISBN 0-306-41618-2, Plenum Pr). Plenum Pub.

De Clercq, Guido, jt. auth. see Steenbergen, Jacques.

De Clercq, H., et al, eds. Concept & Practice of Therapeutic Teams. LC 83-1958. (Progress in Clinical Pharmacy Ser.). 272p. 1984. 37.50 (ISBN 0-521-25595-3). Cambridge U Pr.

DeClermont, Andre R. & Wheeler, John. Standard Catalog of British Colonial & Commonwealth Coins. Bruce, Colin R., II, ed. LC 85-50753. (Illus.). 704p. 1986. 29.50 (ISBN 0-87341-076-9). Krause Pubns.

De Clerq, C., jt. auth. see Johl, S. S.

Decleve. Heidegger und Kant. (Phaenomenologica Ser: No. 40). 1970. lib. bdg. 45.00 (ISBN 90-247-5016-4, Pub. by Martinus Nijhoff Netherlands). Kluwer Academic.

DeCleyre, V., jt. auth. see Lum, Dyer D.

De Cleyre, Voltairine. The First Mayday: The Haymarket Speeches 1895-1910. (Illus.). 53p. (Orig.). 1982. pap. 2.50 (ISBN 0-904564-35-5). Left Bank.

--Selected Works of Voltairine De Cleyre. Berkman, Alexander & Havel, H., eds. (Great Women Ser.). 484p. 1972. Repr. of 1914 ed. lib. bdg. 75.00 (ISBN 0-87700-191-X). Revisionist Pr.

DeCleyre, Voltairine. Written in Red: Selected Poems. Rosemont, Franklin, ed. (Poets of Revolt Ser.: No. 2). 56p. 1985. lib. bdg. 14.95 (ISBN 0-88286-146-8); pap. 3.95 (ISBN 0-88286-121-2). C H Kerr.

DeCleyre, Voltarine. The First Mayday: Haymarket Speeches of Voltarine de Cleyre. 1984. lib. bdg. 79.95 (ISBN 0-87700-630-X). Revisionist Pr.

DeClouet, Fredric. Cooking with St. Clair. Jones, Will, ed. LC 78-74175. 1978. pap. write for info. (ISBN 0-9602228-0-4). Dectur Corp.

DeClue, Charlotte. Without Warning. 24p. (Orig.). 1985. pap. 3.50 (ISBN 0-936574-08-9). Strawberry Pr NY.

Decock, Jean, tr. see Laude, Jean.

Decock, Jean-Pierre. Mirage. (Illus.). 72p. (Orig.). 1985. pap. 5.95 (ISBN 0-85368-705-6, Pub. by Arms & Armour). Sterling.

De Cogolin, Joseph B. Chabert see Chabert De Cogolin, Joseph B.

Decoin, Didier. Laurence. 1976. pap. 1.50 (ISBN 0-532-15218-2). Woodhill.

De Coinci, Gautier. Tumbler of Our Lady & Other Miracles. Kemp-Welch, A., tr. (Medieval Library). (Illus.). Repr. of 1926 ed. 17.50 (ISBN 0-8154-0076-4). Cooper Sq.

De Coligny-Saligny, Jean. Memoires. 1841. 28.00 (ISBN 0-384-09546-1); pap. 22.00 (ISBN 0-384-09545-3). Johnson Repr.

De Combray, Richard. Armani. (Illus.). 224p. 150.00 (ISBN 0-8478-5418-3). Rizzoli Intl.

De Comeau, Alexander. Monk's Magic. Reginald, R. & Melville, Douglas, eds. LC 77-84213. (Lost Race & Adult Fantasy Ser.). 1978. Repr. of 1931 ed. lib. bdg. 22.00x (ISBN 0-405-10968-7). Ayer Co Pubs.

De Commynes, Philippe. Memoirs of Philippe De Commynes, Vol. 1, Bks 1-5 & Vol. 2, Bks. 6-8. Kinser, Samuel, ed. Cazeaux, Isabelle, tr. from Fr. LC 68-9363. (Illus.). xvi, 368p. 1969. Vol. 1. 19.95x (ISBN 0-87249-130-7); Vol. 2. 19.95x (ISBN 0-87249-224-9); Set. 39.95x (ISBN 0-87249-199-4). U of SC Pr.

DeConde, Alexander. American Diplomatic History in Transformation. LC 76-47093. (AHA Pamphlets: No. 702). 1976. pap. text ed. 1.50 (ISBN 0-87229-022-0). Am Hist Assn.

--The American Secretary of State. LC 75-27680. 182p. 1976. Repr. of 1962 ed. lib. bdg. 22.50x (ISBN 0-8371-8453-3, DEAS). Greenwood.

De Conde, Alexander. Entangling Alliance. LC 73-16799. 536p. 1974. Repr. of 1958 ed. lib. bdg. 33.00x (ISBN 0-8371-7232-2, DEEA). Greenwood.

--A History of American Foreign Policy, Vol. II: Global Power, 1900 to Present. 3rd ed. LC 78-143911. 448p. 1979. pap. text ed. 15.95x (ISBN 0-02-327980-X, Pub. by Scribner). Macmillan.

--A History of American Foreign Policy, Vol. I: Grow to World Power, 1700-1914. 3rd ed. LC 78-143911. 416p. 1978. pap. text ed. 15.95 (ISBN 0-02-327970-2, Pub. by Scribner). Macmillan.

DeConde, Alexander. This Affair of Louisiana. LC 76-12468. xii, 325p. 1979. pap. 8.95x (ISBN 0-8071-0497-3). La State U Pr.

DeConde, Alexander, ed. Encyclopedia of American Foreign Policy, 3 vols. LC 78-5453. 1978. Set. 200.00 (ISBN 0-684-15503-6, ScribR). Scribner.

De Conde, Alexander, ed. Isolation & Security: Ideas & Interests in 20th Century American Foreign Policy. LC 57-13022. Repr. of 1957 ed. 41.50 (ISBN 0-8357-9108-4, 2017897). Bks Demand UMI.

DeConde, Alexander, ed. see Bailey, Thomas A.

De Condillac, Etienne Bonnot. The Philosophical Works of Etienne Bonnot de Condillac. Philip, Franklin & Lane, Harlan, trs. from Fr. 448p. 1982. text ed. 39.95x (ISBN 0-89859-181-3). L Erlbaum Assocs.

Deconinck, F., jt. auth. see Bossuyt, A.

Deconinck, F., ed. Information Processing in Medical Imaging. LC 84-1121. 1984. lib. bdg. 84.00 (ISBN 0-89838-677-2, Pub. by Martinus Nijhoff Netherlands). Kluwer Academic.

Deconinck, F., jt. ed. see Jonckheer, M. H.

De Constant, D'Estaurnelles. America & Her Problems. Paul, H. B., ed. LC 73-13127. (Foreign Travelers in America, 1810-1935 Ser.). 570p. 1974. Repr. 38.50x (ISBN 0-405-05449-1). Ayer Co Pubs.

De Coppens, Peter R. Ideal Man in Classical Sociology: The Views of Comte, Durkheim, Pareto, & Weber. LC 75-27174. 272p. 1976. 19.95x (ISBN 0-271-01206-4). Pa St U Pr.

--The Nature & Use of Ritual. 1977. pap. text ed. 9.50 (ISBN 0-8191-0341-1). U Pr of Amer.

--Spiritual Perspective II: The Spiritual Dimension & Implications of Love, Sex, & Marriage. LC 80-6302. 175p. (Orig.). 1981. pap. text ed. 10.50 (ISBN 0-8191-1512-6). U Pr of Amer.

De Coppet, Laura see Coppet, Laura de & Jones, Alan.

De Cordemoy, Geraud see Cordemoy, Geraud de.

De Cordoba, Pedro. Christian Doctrine for the Instruction & Information of the Indians. Stoudemire, Sterling A., tr. LC 79-121681. 1970. 7.95x (ISBN 0-87024-159-1). U of Miami Pr.

De Cordova, Lorenzo. Echoes of the Flute. (Illus.). 64p. 1972. lib. bdg. 11.95 (ISBN 0-941270-03-3); pap. 3.50 (ISBN 0-941270-02-5). Ancient City Pr.

De Cornulier, Benoit. Meaning Detachment. (Pragmatics & Beyond Ser.). vi, 124p. 1980. pap. 16.00 (ISBN 90-272-2502-8, 7). Benjamins North Am.

De Corrales, Jeanne Frankel. Nine Days to Istanbul. (Poineer Paperback Ser.). (Orig.). 1981. pap. 2.50 (ISBN 0-933770-07-3). Kalimat.

De Corso, S. M., jt. ed. see Clark, J. S.

De Cortivron, Isabelle, jt. auth. see Resnick, Margery.

De Cosnac, Daniel. Memoires, 2 vols. 1852. Set. 86.00 (ISBN 0-384-09890-8); Set. pap. 74.00 (ISBN 0-685-13504-7). Johnson Repr.

DeCosse, Barbara, ed. see Papy, Frank.

DeCosse, Jerome, jt. ed. see Condon, Robert E.

DeCosse, Jerome J., ed. Gastrointestinal Cancer I. Sherlock, Paul. 544p. 1981. 75.00 (ISBN 90-247-2461-9, Pub. by Martinus Nijhoff Netherlands). Kluwer Academic.

--Large Bowel Cancer: Clinical Surgery International, Vol. 1. (Illus.). 225p. 1981. text ed. 29.00 (ISBN 0-443-02126-0). Churchill.

DeCosse, Jerome J. & Sherlock, Paul, eds. Clinical Management of Gastrointestinal Cancer. (Cancer Treatment & Research Ser.). 386p. 1984. text ed. 72.50 (ISBN 0-89838-601-2, Pub. by Martinus Nijhoff Netherlands). Kluwer Academic.

De Cosse, Jerome J., jt. ed. see Condon, Robert E.

De Costa, Gomes B. German Language Attainment: A Sample Survey of Universities & Colleges in the U. K. (Wissenschaftliche Bibliothek: No. 14). 101p. (Orig.). 1975. pap. 15.00x (ISBN 3-87276-152-8, Pub by J Groos W Verlag Germany). Benjamins North Am.

DeCosta, Miriam, ed. Blacks in Hispanic Literature: A Collection of Critical Essays. (Literary Criticism Ser). 1976. 15.00x (ISBN 0-8046-9140-1, Pub. by Kennikat). Assoc Faculty Pr.

DeCosta, Rene. The Poetry of Pablo Neruda. LC 78-18008. 1979. 15.00x (ISBN 0-674-67980-6). Harvard U Pr.

De Costa, Rene. The Poetry of Pablo Neruda. 256p. 1982. pap. text ed. 5.95x (ISBN 0-674-67981-4). Harvard U Pr.

--Vincente Huidobro: The Careers of a Poet. (Illus.). 1984. 39.95x (ISBN 0-19-815789-4). Oxford U Pr.

De Coster, Charles T. Flemish Legends. Taylor, Harold, tr. LC 78-74513. (Children's Literature Reprint Ser.). (Illus.). (gr. 7 up). 1979. Repr. of 1920 ed. 18.75x (ISBN 0-8486-0217-X). Core Collection.

Decoster, D. T., et al. Accounting for Managerial Decision Making. 2nd ed. LC 77-15785. (Wiley Series Accounting & Information Systems). 438p. 1978. pap. text ed. 28.45 (ISBN 0-471-02204-7). Wiley.

Decoster, David & Mable, Phylis. Student Development & Education in College Residence Halls. (ACPA Student Personnel Monograph: No. 18). 278p. 1974. pap. 7.00; pap. 5.50 members (ISBN 0-911547-71-1, 72159W34). Am Assn Coun Dev.

DeCoster, David & Mabel, Phyllis, eds. Understanding Today's Students. LC 80-84303. (Student Services Ser.: No. 16). 1981. pap. text ed. 8.95x (ISBN 0-87589-864-5). Jossey-Bass.

DeCoster, David A., jt. ed. see Brown, Robert D.

Decoster, Don T. & Schafer, Eldon L. Management Accounting: A Decision Emphasis. 3rd ed. Incl. Study Guide to Accompany Management Accounting. 197p. 1982. pap. 15.45 (ISBN 0-471-89010-3). 720p. 1982. pap. 35.45 (ISBN 0-471-09811-6). Wiley.

De Coster, Jean. Dictionary for Automotive Engineering: English-French-German. 298p. 1982. lib. bdg. 28.00 (ISBN 3-598-10430-8). K G Saur.

DeCoster, Miles. Economics: Money. 1984. 9.95 (ISBN 0-932526-08-X). Nexus Pr.

Decoteau, A. E. Exhibiting Birds. (Illus.). 192p. 1983. 19.95 (ISBN 0-87666-830-9, H-1036). TFH Pubns.

--The Handbook of Amazon Parrots. (Illus.). 221p. 1980. 14.95 (ISBN 0-87666-892-9, H-1025). TFH Pubns.

--Handbook of Cockatoos. (Illus.). 159p. 1981. 19.95 (ISBN 0-87666-826-0, H-1030). TFH Pubns.

--The Handbook of Macaws. (Illus.). 128p. 1982. 19.95 (ISBN 0-87666-844-9, H-1044). TFH Pubns.

DeCoto, Jean. Heart's Awakening. (Superromances Ser.). 384p. 1982. pap. 2.50 (ISBN 0-373-70029-6, Pub. by Worldwide). Harlequin Bks.

De Coulanges, Fustel. The Ancient City. 59.95 (ISBN 0-87968-624-3). Gordon Pr.

--Ancient City. 15.25 (ISBN 0-8446-1960-4). Peter Smith.

De Coulanges, Numa D. The Ancient City: A Classic Study of the Religious & Civil Institutions of Ancient Greece & Rome. LC 79-3703. 1980. pap. 7.95x (ISBN 0-8018-2304-8). Johns Hopkins.

De Coulon, F., jt. ed. see Kunt, M.

De Courcy, G. see Revesz, Geza.

De Courcy, G. I., tr. see Misch, Ludwig.

De Courcy, G. I. C., tr. see Ringbom, Nils-Eric.

DeCoursey, Michael, jt. auth. see Lang, Hans J.

De Coursey, R. The Human Organism. 5th ed. 1980. text ed. 36.95 (ISBN 0-07-016275-1). McGraw.

DeCoursey, Russell M. Laboratory Manual of Human Anatomy & Physiology. 2nd ed. (Illus.). 256p. 1974. pap. text ed. 18.95 (ISBN 0-07-016239-5). McGraw.

DeCoursey, Virginia. Ever This Night. 288p. (Orig.). 1983. pap. 3.95 (ISBN 0-440-12236-8). Dell.

De Courtivron, Isabelle. Violette Leduc. (World Author Ser.). 1985. lib. bdg. 22.95 (ISBN 0-8057-6607-3, Twayne). G K Hall.

De Courtivron, Isabelle see Courtivron, Isabelle de & Resnick, Margery.

De Courtivron, Isabelle, jt. ed. see Marks, Elaine.

De Coussemaker, Edmond. L'Art harmonique aux XIIe et XIIIe Siecles. (Illus.). 550p. (Fr.). 1964. Repr. of 1865 ed. 55.00x (ISBN 0-8450-2501-5). Broude.

De Coussemaker, Edmond, ed. Drames liturgiques du moyen age, texte et musique. (Illus.). 370p. (Fr., Lat.). 1964. Repr. of 1860 ed. 57.50x (ISBN 0-8450-1004-2). Broude.

De Coussemaker, Edmond, ed. see De la Halle, Adam.

De Covarrubias Horozco, Sebastian. Tesoro de la Lengua Castellana, O Espanola. (Span., Microphoto Reprod). 1927. 7.50 (ISBN 0-87535-020-8). Hispanic Soc.

DeCoy, Robert H. Big Black Fire. (Orig.). 1969. pap. 0.95 (ISBN 0-87067-166-9, BH166). Holloway.

--Cold Black Preach. 224p. 1983. pap. 2.25 (ISBN 0-87067-220-7, BH220). Holloway.

--Nigger Bible. (Orig.). 1967. pap. 2.95 (ISBN 0-87067-804-3, BH804). Holloway.

De Craemer, Willy. The Jamaa & the Church: A Bantu Catholic Movement in Zaire. (Oxford Studies in African Affairs). 1977. 49.50x (ISBN 0-19-822708-6). Oxford U Pr.

De Craemer, Willy & Fox, Renee C. The Emerging Physician: A Sociological Approach to the Development of a Congolese Medical Profession. LC 67-26615. (Studies Ser.: No. 19). 1968. pap. 4.50 (ISBN 0-8179-3192-9). Hoover Inst Pr.

DeCraon, Pierre, jt. auth. see Amauri, Maurice.

De Crauzat, E. Steinlen: The Graphic Work. (Illus.). 248p. (Fr.). 1983. Repr. of 1913 ed. 95.00 (ISBN 0-915346-71-0). A Wofsy Fine Arts.

De Crebillon, M. The Opportunities of a Night. Sutton, Eric, tr. LC 70-174388. Repr. of 1925 ed. 20.00 (ISBN 0-405-08401-3). Ayer Co Pubs.

De Crespo, Patria C., jt. auth. see Falcon, Luis N.

De Crevecoeur, J. Hector. Letters from an American Farmer. 1982. pap. 5.95x (ISBN 0-460-01640-7, Evman). Biblio Dist.

--Letters from an American Farmer. Repr. of 1782 ed. 11.25 (ISBN 0-8446-1139-5). Peter Smith.

De Crevecoeur, J. Hector St. John see St. John de Crevecoeur, J. Hector.

De Crevecoeur, St. John. Sketches of Eighteenth Century America. Boudin, H. L., et al, eds. LC 72-83505. Repr. of 1925 ed. 26.50 (ISBN 0-405-08406-4). Ayer Co Pubs.

DeCristoforo, R. J. Concrete & Masonry: Techniques & Design. (Illus.). 384p. 1975. 23.95 (ISBN 0-87909-149-5). Reston.

De Cristoforo, R. J. De Cristoforo's Complete Book of Power Tools: Stationary & Portable Tools. LC 72-90933. (A Popular Science Bk.). (Illus.). 448p. 1973. 16.95i (ISBN 0-06-010999-8, HarpT). Har-Row.

--De Cristoforo's House Building Illustrated. LC 77-6659. (Popular Science Bk.). (Illus.). 1978. 19.18i (ISBN 0-06-010987-4, HarpT). Har-Row.

DeCristoforo, R. J. Handyman's Guide to Concrete & Masonry. (Illus.). 1978. pap. 10.95 (ISBN 0-8359-2752-0). Reston.

--Power Tool Woodworking for Everyone. rev. ed. LC 83-22995. (Illus.). 360p. 1983. 31.95 (ISBN 0-8359-5567-2). Shopsmith.

De Croix, Rick C. The Reel Life of Chaplin's Little Fellow. 1986. pap. price not set. Jayell Ent.

Decroocq, Daniel. Catalytic Cracking of Heavy Petroleum Fractions. LC 84-71685. (Illus.). 136p. 1984. 42.95x (ISBN 0-87201-143-7). Gulf Pub.

Decroos, Jean F. The Long Journey: Social Integration & Ethnicity Maintenance among Urban Basques in the San Francisco Bay Region. LC 83-8808. 144p. 1983. 14.00x (ISBN 0-8046-9319-6). Assoc Faculty Pr.

DeCrow, Karen, jt. auth. see Seidenberg, Robert.

DeCrow, Roger. New Learning for Older Americans. 1975. 5.75 (ISBN 0-88379-011-4). A A A C E.

De Crow, Roger. Older Americans: New Uses of Mature Ability. 1978. 3.00 (ISBN 0-87117-073-6). Am Assn Comm Jr Coll.

DeCrow, Roger, ed. Adult Education Dissertation Abstracts 1963-1967. League, Nehume. 1970. 8.50 (ISBN 0-88379-001-7). A A A C E.

Decsy, Gy & Hodge, C. T., eds. Global Linguistic Connections. 154p. 1983. 26.00 (ISBN 0-931922-12-7). Eurolingua.

Decsy, Gyula. Yurak Chrestomathy. LC 65-63391. (Uralic & Altaic Ser: Vol. 50). (Orig., Yurak). 1966. pap. text ed. 4.50x (ISBN 0-87750-004-5). Res Ctr Lang Semiotic.

Decsy, Gyula, ed. Sprachherkunftsforschung, Vol. I: Einleitung & Phonogenese. (Bibliotheca Nostratica: Vol 2). 87p. 1977. 22.00 (ISBN 3-447-01861-5). Eurolingua.

--Sprachherkunftsforschung, Vol. II: Semogenese-Palaosemiotik. (Bibliotheca Nostratica: Vol. 2). 78p. 1981. 22.00 (ISBN 0-931922-06-2). Eurolingua.

--Ural-Altaische Jahrbucher, Vol. 56. 186p. 1984. 48.00 (ISBN 0-931922-17-8). Eurolingua.

Decsy, Gyula & Bodrogligeti, A. J., eds. Ural-Altaische Jahrbucher: 1977, Vol. 49. 177p. 1977. 48.00 (ISBN 3-447-01806-2). Eurolingua.

--Ural-Altaische Jahrbucher: 1978, Vol. 50. 207p. 1978. 48.00 (ISBN 3-447-01891-7). Eurolingua.

--Ural-Altaische Jahrbucher: 1981, Vol. 53. 172p. 1981. 48.00 (ISBN 0-931922-08-9). Eurolingua.

--Ural-Altaische Jahrbucher: 1982, Vol. 54. 172p. 1982. 48.00 (ISBN 0-931922-09-7). Eurolingua.

Decsy, Gyula & Brodrogligeti, A. J., eds. Ural-Altaische Jahrbucher: 1979, Vol. 51. 183p. 1979. 48.00 (ISBN 0-931922-00-3). Eurolingua.

--Ural-Altaische Jahrbucher: 1980, Vol. 52. 191p. 1980. 48.00 (ISBN 0-931922-05-4). Eurolingua.

Decsy, Gyula & Dimov-Bogoev, Christo, eds. Eurasia Nostratica: Festschrift fuer Karl Heinrich Menges, 2 vols. in 1. (Bibliotheca Nostratica Ser.: Vol. 1). 473p. 1977. 86.00 (ISBN 3-447-01834-8). Eurolingua.

Decsy, Gyula, intro. by. First Votyak Grammar. LC 67-63038. (Uralic & Altaic Ser.: Vol. 81). Orig. Title: Socinenija Prinadle-Zascija K Grammatike Votskago Jazyka. (Rus.). 1967. pap. text ed. 7.50x (ISBN 0-87750-031-2). Res Ctr Lang Semiotic.

Decsy, Janos. Prime Minister Gyula Andrassy's Influence on Habsburg Foreign Policy. (East European Monographs: No. 52). 177p. 1979. 20.00x (ISBN 0-914710-44-3). East Eur Quarterly.

De Cuenca, Pilar, tr. see McNaught, Harry.

De Curet, Miriam De Anda see Curet de De Anda, Miriam.

DeCusa, Nicolas. Idiota de Mente. Miller, Clyde L., tr. LC 77-812. (Bilingual Editions of Classics in Philosophy & Science: Ser. 3). 1980. 20.00 (ISBN 0-913870-65-X). Abaris Bks.

De Cusa, Nicolas. Unity & Reform: Selected Writings of Nicholas De Cusa. Dolan, John P., ed. 1962. 22.95x (ISBN 0-268-00287-8). U of Notre Dame Pr.

De Custine, Marquis. Zaprisky O Rossik: The Notes About Russia. 2nd ed. Kustanovich, K., ed. 160p. (Orig., Russian.). pap. 15.00 (ISBN 0-940294-07-9). Silver Age Pub.

De Czege, A. Wass. Eliza & the House that Jack Built. LC 82-71386. 1982. 15.00 (ISBN 0-87934-027-4). Danubian.

De Czege, A. Wass, compiled by. The History of Astor on the St. Johns. LC 82-70902. 1982. pap. 4.00 (ISBN 0-87934-026-6). Danubian.

De Czege, Albert W., et al. Transylvanian Hungarian Folk Art. (Illus.). 80p. 1983. 16.00 (ISBN 0-87934-029-0). Danubian.

DED Vibrations Conference 1975, Washington, D. C. Vibration Testing--Instrumentation & Data Analysis: Presented at ASME/DED Vibrations Conference, Washington, D. C. Magrab, Edward B. & Shinaishin, Osman A., eds. LC 75-8349. (American Society of Mechanical Engineers Series - Applied Mechanics Division: Vol. 12). (Illus.). pap. 37.00 (ISBN 0-317-09976-0, 2015395). Bks Demand UMI.

De Dan, Kiley see Kiley, Dan De.

De Danois, Vivian. Abortion & the Moral Degeneration of the American Medical Profession. (A Science of Man Library Bk). 92p. 1975. 51.50 (ISBN 0-913314-56-0). Am Classical Coll Pr.

--Abortion, The Claims of the Body & the Deceit of "Choice". (Illus.). 1978. deluxe ed. 67.50 (ISBN 0-930582-10-1). Gloucester Art.

--God & Abortion. (A Science of Man Library Bk). 1979. 51.50 (ISBN 0-89266-160-7). Am Classical Coll Pr.

De Daruvar, Ives. The Tragic Fate of Hungary: A Country Carved up Alive at Trianon. (Illus., Eng.). casebound 10.00 (ISBN 0-912404-03-5). Alpha Pubns.

De Datta, Surajit K. Principles & Practices of Rice Production. LC 80-28941. 618p. 1981. 49.95x (ISBN 0-471-08074-8, Pub. by Wiley-Interscience). Wiley.

De Davila, E. Paradise in Mexico: Cuernavaca. 1976. lib. bdg. 59.95 (ISBN 0-8490-2408-0). Gordon Pr.

De Davila, Maria D. Castro see Castro De Davila, Maria D.

De Davis, Patricia M., jt. auth. see Jakway, Martha.

Dede, Vivian. Mr. Dumb Jokes. 1982. pap. 1.95 (ISBN 0-570-08407-5, 39-1082). Concordia.

DeDecker, Mary. Flora of the Northern Mojave Desert, California. LC 84-12151. (Special Publication Ser.: No. 7). (Illus.). 184p. (Orig.). 1984. pap. 8.95x (ISBN 0-943460-09-3). Calif Native.

--Mines of the Eastern Sierra. (Illus.). 1966. wrappers 2.95 (ISBN 0-910856-15-X). La Siesta.

De Deckker, P. T., ed. see Pritchard, George.

De Deguileville, Guillaume see Deguileville, Guillaume de.

De Deguilleville, Guillaume. The Pilgrimage of the Life of Man, Pts. 1-3. Furnivall, F. J. & Locock, K. B., eds. (EETS, ES Ser.: Nos. 77, 83, & 92). Repr. of 1904 ed. 90.00 (ISBN 0-527-00279-8). Kraus Repr.

De Deguilleville, Guillaume see Deguilleville, Guillaume de.

De Deiros, Norma H. C. Dramatizaciones Infantiles Para Dias Especiales. 96p. 1983. pap. 2.50 (ISBN 0-311-07606-8). Casa Bautista.

Dedek, John. Contemporary Sexual Morality. LC 79-152319. 1972. pap. 5.95 (ISBN 0-8362-0513-8). Andrews McMeel Parker.

Dedekind, R., jt. auth. see Lejeune-Dirichlet, P. G.

Dedekind, Richard. Essays on the Theory of Numbers. Beman, Wooster W., tr. 1901. pap. 3.50 (ISBN 0-486-21010-3). Dover.

De Del Rio, Amelia A. see Del Rio, Amelia A.

De Del Rio, Amelia Agostini. Leon Felipe: El Hombre y el Poeta. (Span.). 1980. pap. 7.80 (ISBN 84-499-4047-8). Edit Mensaje.

Dedera, Don. Artistry in Clay: Contemporary Pottery of the Southwest. LC 84-62423. (Illus.). 94p. (Orig.). 1985. pap. 9.95 (ISBN 0-87358-371-X). Northland.

--Navajo Rugs: How to Find, Evaluate, Buy & Care for Them. LC 74-31617. (Illus.). 128p. 1975. pap. 8.95 (ISBN 0-87358-138-5). Northland.

Dederer, John M. Making Bricks Without Straw: Nathaniel Greene's Southern Campaign & Mao Tse-Tung's Mobile War. (Illus.). 98p. 1983. pap. text ed. 7.50x (ISBN 0-89745-049-3). Sunflower U Pr.

Dederichs, P. H. & Zeller, R. Point Defect in Metals II: Dynamical Properties & Diffusion Controlled Reactions. (Springer Tracts in Modern Physics: Vol. 87). 1980. 45.00 (ISBN 0-387-09623-X). Springer-Verlag.

Dederichs, P. H., et al. Metals: Phonon States of Elements. Electron States & Fermi Surfaces of Alloys. Hellwege, K. H. & Olsen, J. L., eds. (Landolt-Boernstein Ser.: Vol. 13, Group III). (Illus.). 500p. 1981. 348.10 (ISBN 0-387-09774-0). Springer-Verlag.

Dedeyan, Charles. Dante En Angleterre. Repr. of 1966 ed. 30.00 (ISBN 0-8274-1589-3). R West.

--Dante En Angleterre Moyen Age: Renaissance. 223p. 1984. Repr. of 1961 ed. lib. bdg. 50.00 (ISBN 0-89760-177-7). Telegraph Bks.

Dedeyan, Charles, jt. auth. see Montaigne, Michel de.

Dedichen, L. Fransk-Norsk Ordbok. 373p. (Fr.). 1979. 29.95 (ISBN 82-573-0068-3, M-9457). French & Eur.

De Diego, Fernando. La Ingenia Hidalgo Don Quijote De la Mancha, De Cervantes. (Illus.). 1977. 35.00x (ISBN 84-400-3582-9). Esperanto League North Am.

De Diego, Jose. Complete Works of Jose De Diego, 2 vols. (Puerto Rico Ser.). 1979. Set. lib. bdg. 250.00 (ISBN 0-8490-2893-0). Gordon Pr.

De Dienes, Andre. Exotic Nudes. (Illus.). 4.95 (ISBN 0-910550-04-2). Elysium.

--Glory of De Dienes Women. (Illus.). 7.95 (ISBN 0-910550-05-0). Elysium.

--Sun-Warmed Nudes. (Illus.). 10.00 (ISBN 0-910550-15-8, Dist. by Lyle Stuart). Elysium.

De Dietrich, Suzanne. God's Unfolding Purpose: A Guide to the Study of the Bible. Brown, Robert M., tr. LC 60-6169. 1960. Westminster.

--The Witnessing Community: The Biblical Record of God's Purpose. LC 58-5020. 180p. 1978. pap. 3.95 (ISBN 0-664-24199-9). Westminster.

Dedieu, Joseph. Montesquieu et la Tradition Politique Anglaise En France: Les Sources Anglaises de "l'Espirit des Lois". 1969. Repr. of 1909 ed. 26.50 (ISBN 0-8337-0804-X). B Franklin.

Dedijer, Vladimir. Tito. LC 72-4269. (World Affairs Ser.: National & International Viewpoints). 450p. 1972. Repr. of 1953 ed. 32.00 (ISBN 0-405-04565-4). Ayer Co Pubs.

De Dillmont, Th. The Complete Encyclopedia of Needlework. LC 78-72286. (Illus.). 787p. 1972. lib. bdg. 19.80 (ISBN 0-914294-36-9); pap. 7.95 (ISBN 0-914294-00-8). Running Pr.

De Dillmont, Therese. The Complete DMC Encyclopedia of Needlework. (Illus.). 700p. Date not set. pap. 9.95 (ISBN 0-685-20554-1). Toggitt.

Dedini. A Much Much Better World. (Illus.). 128p. 1985. pap. 6.95 (ISBN 0-914845-50-0). Microsoft.

De Djunkovskoy, E., jt. auth. see Lacroix.

Dedmon, Emmett. Fabulous Chicago. rev. ed. LC 81-66024. (Illus.). 480p. 1983. pap. 9.95 (ISBN 0-689-70639-1, 288). Atheneum.

Dedmond, Francis B. Sylvester Judd. (United States Authors Ser.). 1980. lib. bdg. 14.50 (ISBN 0-8057-7305-3, Twayne). G K Hall.

Dedner, Burghard. Carl Sternheim. (World Authors Ser.). 1982. lib. bdg. 19.95 (ISBN 0-8057-6518-2, Twayne). G K Hall.

Dedo, Douglas D., ed. Aesthetic Facial Surgery, Vol. 3. 304p. 1984. 79.00 (ISBN 0-8089-1616-5, 7910-12). Grune.

Dedo, Herbert H. & Shipp, Thomas. Spastic Dysphonia: A Surgical & Voice Therapy Treatment Program. LC 80-65193. (Illus.). 94p. 1980. pap. text ed. 13.00 (ISBN 0-933014-58-9). College-Hill.

De Dombal, E. T., jt. ed. see IFIP TC Four Working Conference.

De Dombal, F. T. Diagnosis of Acute Abdominal Pain. (Illus.). 192p. 1981. pap. text ed. 13.75 (ISBN 0-443-01901-0). Churchill.

De Dombal, F. T., jt. ed. see Rozen, P.

DeDomenico Reichert, Katherine. Pasta with a Flair. (Illus.). 160p. 1984. 14.95 (ISBN 0-87518-283-6). Dillon.

Dedova, V., jt. auth. see Volkov, M.

Dedron, P. & Itard, J. Mathematics & Mathematicians, No. 1. 326p. 1978. pap. 10.00x (ISBN 0-335-00246-3, Pub. by Open Univ Pr). Taylor & Francis.

--Mathematics & Mathematicians, No. 2. 222p. 1978. pap. 10.00x (ISBN 0-335-00247-1, Pub. by Open Univ Pr). Taylor & Francis.

Deduck, Patricia A. Realism, Reality & the Fictional Theory of Alain Robbe-Grillet & Anais Nin. LC 82-13549. 118p. 1982. lib. bdg. 21.75 (ISBN 0-8191-2719-1); pap. text ed. 9.50 (ISBN 0-8191-2720-5). U Pr of Amer.

De Duve, Christian. A Guided Tour of the Living Cell, Vols. I & II. (Illus.). 423p. Set. 55.95 (ISBN 0-7167-5002-3). W H Freeman.

--A Guided Tour of the Living Cell, Vols. I & II. (Scientific American Library). (Illus.). 463p. 1984. Set. 55.95. Vol. I (ISBN 0-7167-5002-3). Vol. II (ISBN 0-7167-5006-6). pap. 33.95 student ed. (ISBN 0-7167-6002-9). Sci Am Bks.

--A Guided Tour of the Living Cell. LC 84-29818. (Illus.). 433p. 1985. pap. 33.95 (ISBN 0-7167-6002-9). W H Freeman.

De Dwyer. Chicano Voices. Adams, ed. (Multi-Ethnic Literature Ser.). (gr. 9-12). 1975. pap. text ed. 7.24 (ISBN 0-395-20579-4). HM.

Dee, Anne P. The Cloth Dollmaker's Source Book: A Guide to the Best in Mail Order for Cloth Doll & Soft Toy Making. LC 85-13460. (Illus.). 256p. (Orig.). 1985. pap. 12.95 (ISBN 0-932620-52-3). Betterway Pubns.

Dee, D. J. Nurse Jackie's Prize. 1984. 8.95 (ISBN 0-8034-8446-1, Avalon). Bouregy.

--Nurse Mickey's Crisis. (YA) 1983. 8.95 (ISBN 0-317-17580-7, Avalon). Bouregy.

Dee, Elaine E. Nineteenth-Century American Landscape Drawings in the Collection of the Cooper-Hewitt Museum: The Smithsonian Institution's National Museum of Design. Akre, Nancy, et al, eds. LC 82-72122. (The Cooper-Hewitt Museum Collection Handbook Ser.). (Illus.). 36p. (Orig.). 1982. pap. 3.95x (ISBN 0-910503-17-6). Cooper-Hewitt.

Dee, Elaine E. & Michie, Thomas. Japanese Woodblock Prints in the Collection of Cooper-Hewitt Museum: The Smithsonian Institution's National Museum of Design. LC 79-51624. (The Cooper-Hewitt Museum Collection Handbook Ser.). (Illus.). 36p. (Orig.). 1979. pap. 3.95x (ISBN 0-910503-06-0). Cooper-Hewitt.

Dee, Elaine E., jt. auth. see Zocchi, Giusseppe.

Dee, John. Enochian Evocation. James, Geoffrey, ed. LC 83-80338. (Illus.). c, 250p. 1983. 40.00 (ISBN 0-935214-06-2). Heptangle.

--General & Rare Memorials Pertaining to Perfecte Arte of Navigation. LC 68-54635. (English Experience Ser.: No. 62). 82p. 1968. Repr. of 1577 ed. 28.00 (ISBN 90-221-0062-6). Walter J Johnson.

--Letter containing a most Brief Discourse Apologetical. 011 FRJohn Dee. LC 83. LC 72-5972. (English Experience Ser.: No. 502). 1973. Repr. of 1599 ed. 6.00 (ISBN 90-221-0502-4). Walter J Johnson.

--Private Diary of Dr. John Dee & the Catalogue of His Library of Manuscripts. Halliwell, James O., ed. (Camden Society, London. Publications, First Ser.: No. 19). Repr. of 1842 ed. 19.00 (ISBN 0-404-50119-2). AMS Pr.

--Private Diary of Dr. John Dee & the Catalogue of His Library of Manuscripts. 1842. 19.00 (ISBN 0-384-11180-7). Johnson Repr.

--Stagger Lee. 192p. 1974. pap. 1.50 (ISBN 0-532-15121-6). Woodhill.

Dee, M. M. Adventures of Dusty. (Illus.). 48p. (gr. k-4). 1984. 9.95 (ISBN 0-937460-39-7). Hendrick-Long.

--The Adventures of L. A. (Illus.). 48p. (gr. k-4). 1983. 9.95 (ISBN 0-937460-37-0). Hendrick-Long.

Dee, Margaret. Face the Music, Bk. I. 1955. 1.75 (ISBN 0-913650-36-6). Columbia Pictures.

--Face the Music, Bk. II. 1955. 1.75 (ISBN 0-913650-37-4). Columbia Pictures.

--Get Acquainted Book, Bk. I. 1953. 1.75 (ISBN 0-913650-32-3). Columbia Pictures.

--On We Go, Bk. II. 1953. 1.75 (ISBN 0-913650-33-1). Columbia Pictures.

--Tips for Pianists. 1956. 1.25 (ISBN 0-913650-39-0). Columbia Pictures.

--Touch Technique Fpr Every Pianist. 1955. 1.50 (ISBN 0-913650-40-4). Columbia Pictures.

Dee, Miss. Health, Astrology & Spirituality. 160p. 1984. 11.00 (ISBN 0-86690-247-3, 2366-01). Am Fed Astrologers.

--The Yod, Your Special Life Purpose. 72p. 1983. 7.95 (ISBN 0-86690-234-1, 2287-01). Am Fed Astrologers.

Dee, Nerys. Fortune-Telling by Playing Cards: A New Guide to the Ancient Art of Cartomancy. 160p. 1982. pap. 7.95 (ISBN 0-85030-266-8). Newcastle Pub.

--Your Dreams & What They Mean. 160p. 1984. pap. 9.95 (ISBN 0-85030-353-2). Newcastle Pub.

Dee, Ron. Boundaries. LC 77-94074. 1979. 12.95 (ISBN 0-87949-125-6). Ashley Bks.

Dee, Ruby, ed. Glowchild & Other Poems. LC 72-77858. 112p. (gr. 7 up). 1972. 5.95 (ISBN 0-89388-040-X). Okpaku Communications.

Dee, Wilma. Hoosier Cooking: Yesteryear & Today. LC 83-80929. (Illus.). 120p. 1983. spiral bdg 5.95 (ISBN 0-932970-37-0). Fayova Pubns.

Deeb, K. Abu, ed. Al-Jurja-Ni's Theory of Poetic Imagery. (Approaches to Arabic Literature: No. 1). 341p. 1979. text ed. 42.50x (ISBN 0-85668-117-2, Pub. by Aris & Phillips England). Humanities.

Deeb, Marius. The Lebanese Civil War. LC 79-19833. (Praeger Special Studies). 176p. 1980. 34.95 (ISBN 0-03-039701-4). Praeger.

Deeb, Marius K. & Deeb, Mary J. Libya Since the Revolution: Aspects of Social & Political Development. LC 81-19985. 172p. 1982. 27.95 (ISBN 0-03-058308-X). Praeger.

Deeb, Mary J., jt. auth. see Deeb, Marius K.

Deeb, Norman A. Cloud Nine: A Seminar on Educational Philosophy. LC 75-377. (Illus.). 128p. 1975. 7.50 (ISBN 0-8022-2165-3). Philos Lib.

Deecke, L., jt. ed. see Kornhuber, H. H.

Deedat, A. Is Bible God's Word? 1981. 2.75 (ISBN 0-686-97857-9). Kazi Pubns.

--Quran, the Ultimate Miracle. pap. 2.95 (ISBN 0-686-63913-8). Kazi Pubns.

--Was Jesus Crucified? pap. 1.50 (ISBN 0-686-63916-2). Kazi Pubns.

--What the Bible Says about Muhammad? 1.75 (ISBN 0-686-63917-0). Kazi Pubns.

Deeds, Daphne & Bell, David. Collecting: The Phoenix Art Museum, 1957-1984. LC 84-62598. 44p. 1984. pap. 7.50x (ISBN 0-910407-13-4). Phoenix Art.

Deeds, Daphne A., jt. auth. see Bell, David.

Deedy, John. Your Aging Parents. 192p. (Orig.). 1984. pap. 7.95 (ISBN 0-88347-160-4). Thomas More.

Deegan. Kareem Abdul-Jabbar. (Sports Superstars Ser.). (Illus.). 32p. (gr. 3-9). 7.95 (ISBN 0-317-31213-8). Creative Ed.

--The Who. (Rock 'n Pop Stars Ser.). (Illus.). 32p. (gr. 4-12). PLB 7.95 (ISBN 0-317-31150-6). Creative Ed.

Deegan, Arthur. Management Succession Planning. Date not set. 19.95 (ISBN 0-471-82527-1). Wiley.

Deegan, Arthur X., II & O'Donovan, Thomas R. Management by Objectives for Hospitals. 2nd ed. LC 82-3929. 338p. 1982. 34.00 (ISBN 0-89443-658-9). Aspen Systems.

Deegan, Arthur X., 2nd. Coaching: A Management Skill for Improving Individual Performance. LC 79-619. 1979. pap. text ed. 11.95 (ISBN 0-201-01266-9). Addison-Wesley.

Deegan, Dorothy Y. Stereotype of the Single Woman in American Novels. 1969. lib. bdg. 22.00x (ISBN 0-374-92090-7). Octagon.

Deegan, James F. An Econometric Model of the Gulf Coast Oil & Gas Exploration Industry. Bruchey, Stuart, ed. LC 78-22672. (Energy in the American Economy Ser.). (Illus.). 1979. lib. bdg. 16.00x (ISBN 0-405-11975-5). Ayer Co Pubs.
Deegan, Jim E. The Moments in Between. LC 84-90444. 64p. 1984. 6.50 (ISBN 0-8233-0396-9). Golden Quill.
Deegan, John. The Masks of Command. 1985. write for info. (ISBN 0-670-45988-7). Viking.
Deegan, Mary J. Jane Addams & the Men of the Chicago School, 1892-1918. 385p. (Orig.). 1985. 34.95 (ISBN 0-88738-077-8). Transaction Bks.
Deegan, Mary Jo & Brooks, Nancy A. Women & Disability: The Double Handicap. 180p. 1984. cloth 24.95. Transaction Bks.
Deegan, Paul. Animals of East Africa. LC 72-140641. (World's People Ser.). (Illus.). (gr. 5-12). 1971. PLB 7.95 (ISBN 0-87191-050-0). Creative Ed.
--Catfish Hunter. (Sports Superstars Ser.). (Illus.). (gr. 3-9). 1979. pap. 3.95 (ISBN 0-89812-159-0). Creative Ed.
--O. J. Simpson. LC 73-17056. (Creative Superstars Ser.). 1974. pap. 3.95 (ISBN 0-89812-166-3). Creative Ed.
Deegan, Paul & Larson, Bruce. Hospital: Life in a Medical Center. LC 76-156064. (gr. 5-9). 1970. PLB 7.95 (ISBN 0-87191-052-7). Creative Ed.
Deegan, Paul, ed. see Coffey, Richard A.
Deegan, Paul J. Almost a Champion. LC 74-14517. (Dan Murphy Sports Ser). 40p. (gr. 3-6). 1975. PLB 7.95 (ISBN 0-87191-402-6). Creative Ed.
--The Basic Strokes. LC 75-41383. (Sports Instruction Ser.). (Illus.). (gr. 3-9). 1976. PLB 8.95 (ISBN 0-87191-502-2); pap. 3.95 (ISBN 0-686-67434-0). Creative Ed.
--Bunting & Baserunning. LC 75-15817. (Creative Education Sports Instructional Bk. Ser.). (Illus.). 32p. (gr. 3-9). 1975. PLB 8.95 (ISBN 0-87191-431-X). Creative Ed.
--Catching the Football. LC 74-34572. (Creative Education Sports Instructional Bk.). (Illus.). 32p. (gr. 3-9). 1975. pap. 3.95 (ISBN 0-89812-133-7). Creative Ed.
--Checking & Defensive Play. LC 76-13849. (Sports Instruction Ser.). (Illus.). (gr. 3-9). 1976. PLB 8.95 (ISBN 0-87191-525-1); pap. 3.95 (ISBN 0-686-67439-1). Creative Ed.
--Close but Not Quite. LC 74-16334. (Dan Murphy Sports Ser.). 40p. (gr. 3-6). 1975. PLB 7.95 (ISBN 0-87191-405-0); pap. 3.95 (ISBN 0-89812-152-3). Creative Ed.
--Dan Moves up. LC 74-17069. (Dan Murphy Sports Ser.). 40p. (gr. 3-6). 1975. PLB 7.95 (ISBN 0-87191-406-9); pap. 3.95 (ISBN 0-89812-153-1). Creative Ed.
--Hitting the Baseball. LC 75-12750. (Creative Education Sports Instructional Bk.). (Illus.). 32p. (gr. 3-6). 1975. PLB 8.95 (ISBN 0-87191-430-1); pap. 3.95 (ISBN 0-89812-136-1). Creative Ed.
--Important Decision. LC 74-14514. (Dan Murphy Sports Ser.). (Illus.). 40p. (gr. 3-6). 1975. PLB 7.95 (ISBN 0-87191-401-8); pap. 3.95 (ISBN 0-89812-154-X). Creative Ed.
--The Jump Shot & the Layup. LC 75-11680. (Creative Education Sports Instructional Bk.). (Illus.). 32p. (gr. 3-6). 1975. PLB 8.95 (ISBN 0-87191-432-8); pap. 3.95 (ISBN 0-89812-139-6). Creative Ed.
--Passing the Football. LC 75-1479. (Creative Education Sports Instructional Bks.). (Illus.). 32p. (gr. 3-6). 1975. pap. 3.95 (ISBN 0-89812-132-9). Creative Ed.
--Pitching the Baseball. (Creative Education Sports Instructional Bks.). (Illus.). 32p. (gr. 3-6). 1975. PLB 8.95 (ISBN 0-87191-429-8); pap. 3.95 (ISBN 0-89812-135-3). Creative Ed.
--Placekicking & Punting. LC 75-2026. (Creative Education Sports Instructional Bks.). (Illus.). 32p. (gr. 3-6). 1975. pap. 3.95 (ISBN 0-89812-134-5). Creative Ed.
--Scoring: The Shots. LC 76-12423. (Sports Instruction Ser.). (Illus.). (gr. 3-9). 1976. PLB 8.95 (ISBN 0-87191-526-X); pap. 3.95 (ISBN 0-686-67438-3). Creative Ed.
--Serving & Returning. LC 75-31813. (Sports Instruction Ser.). (Illus.). (gr. 3-9). 1976. PLB 8.95 (ISBN 0-87191-495-6); pap. 3.95 (ISBN 0-686-67433-2). Creative Ed.
--The Set Shot. LC 75-11913. (Creative Education Sports Instructional Bks.). (Illus.). 32p. (gr. 3-6). 1975. PLB 8.95 (ISBN 0-87191-433-6); pap. 3.95 (ISBN 0-89812-138-8). Creative Ed.
--Shooting in a Game. LC 75-11776. (Creative Education Sports Instructional Bks.). (Illus.). 32p. (gr. 3-6). 1975. PLB 8.95 (ISBN 0-87191-434-4); pap. 3.95 (ISBN 0-89812-140-X). Creative Ed.
--Skates & Skating. LC 76-5812. (Sports Instruction Ser.). (Illus.). (gr. 3-9). 1976. PLB 8.95 (ISBN 0-87191-514-6); pap. 3.95 (ISBN 0-686-67436-7). Creative Ed.
--Stickhandling & Passing. LC 76-8444. (Sports Instruction Ser.). (Illus.). (gr. 3-9). 1976. PLB 8.95 (ISBN 0-87191-520-0); pap. 3.95 (ISBN 0-686-67437-5). Creative Ed.
--Team Manager. LC 74-14515. (Dan Murphy Sports Ser.). (Illus.). 40p. (gr. 3-6). 1974. PLB 7.95 (ISBN 0-87191-403-4); pap. 3.95 (ISBN 0-89812-155-8). Creative Ed.
--Tournaments. LC 74-149436. (Dan Murphy Sports Ser.). 40p. (gr. 3-6). 1975. PLB 7.95 (ISBN 0-87191-404-2); pap. 3.95 (ISBN 0-89812-156-6). Creative Ed.
--Volleying & Lobs. LC 75-35614. (Sports Instruction Ser.). (Illus.). (gr. 3-9). 1976. PLB 8.95 (ISBN 0-87191-496-4); pap. 3.95 (ISBN 0-686-67435-9). Creative Ed.
Deegan, William L. The Management of Student Affairs Programs in Community Colleges: Revamping Processes & Structures. (Horizon Issues Monograph Ser.). 52p. 1982. pap. 5.00 (ISBN 0-87117-126-0). Am Assn Comm Jr Coll.
--Managing Student Programs: Methods, Models, Muddles. (Illus.). 240p. 1981. 14.95 (ISBN 0-88280-083-3). ETC Pubns.
Deegan, William L. & Gollattscheck, James F., eds. Ensuring Effective Governance. LC 84-82366. (Community College Ser.: No. 49). (Orig.). 1985. pap. text ed. 9.95x (ISBN 0-87589-739-8). Jossey-Bass.
Deehr, C. S. & Holtet, J. A., eds. Exploration of the Polar Upper Atmosphere. 1981. 58.00 (ISBN 90-277-1225-5, Pub. by Reidel Holland). Kluwer Academic.
De El, Amelia Agustini see De Del Rio, Amelia Agostini.
Deel, Evelyn K. The Virgin Wife. LC 83-258166. 1985. 15.95 (ISBN 0-87949-246-5). Ashley Bks.
Deelder, C. L. Synopsis of Biological Data on the Eel: Anguilla anguilla (Linnaeus, 1758) (Fisheries Synopsis Ser.: No. 80, Rev. 1). 73p. 1985. pap. 7.50 (ISBN 92-5-102166-X, F2724, FAO). Unipub.
Deeley, Lilla. Favorite Hungarian Recipes. 88p. 1972. pap. 2.75 (ISBN 0-486-22846-0). Dover.
--Favorite Hungarian Recipes. (Illus.). 12.00 (ISBN 0-8446-4537-0). Peter Smith.
Deeley, P. D., et al. Ferroalloys & Alloying Additives Handbook. LC 81-51501. 127p. 1981. 25.00 (ISBN 0-9606196-0-7). Shieldalloy.
Deeley, T. J., ed. The Planning of Radiotherapy Departments. 1980. 50.00x (ISBN 0-686-69955-6, Pub. by Brit Inst Radiology). State Mutual Bk.
--Topical Reviews in Radiotherapy & Oncology, Vol. 1. (Topical Reviews Ser.). (Illus.). 288p. 1980. text ed. 34.00 (ISBN 0-7236-0538-6). PSG Pub Co.
Deeley, T. J., et al. Guide to Oncological Nursing. 1974. 7.50 (ISBN 0-443-01089-7). Churchill.
Deeley, Thomas J., ed. Topical Reviews in Radiotherapy & Oncology, Vol. 2. (Illus.). 264p. 1982. text ed. 39.50 (ISBN 0-7236-0616-1). PSG Pub Co.
Deelman, H. T., et al. see Tilanus, C. B.
Deely, John. Introducing Semiotic: Its History & Doctrine. LC 82-47782. (Advances in Semiotics Ser.; Midland Bks.: Bk. 287). 264p. (Orig.). 1982. 22.50x (ISBN 0-253-33080-7); pap. 8.95 (ISBN 0-253-20287-6). Ind U Pr.
--Tractatus de Signis. LC 82-17658. 1985. 65.00x (ISBN 0-520-04252-2). U of Cal Pr.
Deely, John, ed. see Bouissac, Paul.
Deely, John, ed. see Calahan, John C.
Deem, Bill, jt. auth. see Muchow, Kenneth.
Deem, Bill, et al. Digital Computer Circuits & Concepts. 3rd ed. (Illus.). 1980. text ed. 31.95 (ISBN 0-8359-1299-X); free instrs'. manual (ISBN 0-8359-1300-7). Reston.
Deem, Bill R. Electronics Math. 2nd ed. (Illus.). 624p. 1986. text ed. 32.95 (ISBN 0-13-252321-3). P-H.
Deem, Rosemary. Women & Schooling. (Education Bks). 1980. pap. 8.95 (ISBN 0-7100-8958-9). Routledge & Kegan.
Deem, Rosemary, ed. Co-Education Reconsidered. (Gender & Education Ser.). 128p. 1984. pap. 13.00x (ISBN 0-335-10417-7, Pub. by Open Univ Pr). Taylor & Francis.
--Schooling for Women's Work. 160p. (Orig.). 1980. pap. 18.00x (ISBN 0-7100-0576-8). Routledge & Kegan.
Deem, William R. Electronics Math. (Illus.). 576p. 1981. text ed. 31.95 (ISBN 0-13-252304-3). P-H.
Deemer, Bill. Diana. (Orig.). 1966. pap. 1.00 (ISBN 0-940556-01-4). Coyote.
--This Is Just to Say. bilingual ed. Hyner, Stefan, tr. from Eng. (Orig., Ger.). 1981. pap. 4.00 (ISBN 0-940556-03-0). Coyote.
Deemer, W. L. An Experimental Comparison of Two Shorthand Systems. (Harvard Studies in Education: Vol. 28). 1942. pap. 24.00 (ISBN 0-384-11190-4). Johnson Repr.
Deeming, Bill, jt. auth. see Deeming, Sue.
Deeming, Sue & Deeming, Bill. Canning. (Illus.). 192p. 1983. pap. 7.95 (ISBN 0-89586-185-2). H P Bks.
--Soups & Sandwiches. (Illus.). 160p. 1983. pap. 6.95 (ISBN 0-89586-216-6). H P Bks.
Deeming, Terry, jt. auth. see Bowers, Richard.
Deems, Betty. Easy-to-Make Felt Ornaments for Christmas & Other Occasions. LC 76-18405. (Dover Needlework Ser). (Illus.). 32p. (Orig.). 1976. pap. 3.50 (ISBN 0-486-23389-8). Dover.
Deems, Edward M., ed. Holy-Days & Holidays: A Treasury of Historical Material, Sermons in Full & in Brief, Suggestive Thoughts & Poetry, Relating to Holy Days & Holidays. LC 68-17940. 1968. Repr. of 1902 ed. 65.00x (ISBN 0-8103-3352-X). Gale.
Deems, Eugene F., Jr. & Pursley, Duane. North American Furbearers: A Contemporary Reference. (Illus.). 217p. 1983. text ed. 14.00 (ISBN 0-932108-08-3). IAFWA.
Deen. Managerial Economics. 1951. 28.95 (ISBN 0-13-549972-0); pap. 9.95 ref. ed. op (ISBN 0-13-549980-1). P-H.
Deen, Edith. All of the Women of the Bible. LC 55-8621. 1955. 18.22 (ISBN 0-06-061810-8, HarpR). Har-Row.
Deen, Jeannie M., ed. see Harper, Annie E.
Deen, Leonard W. Conversing in Paradise: Poetic Genius and Identity-as-Community in Blake's Los. LC 82-20307. 288p. 1983. text ed. 23.00 (ISBN 0-8262-0396-5). U of Mo Pr.
Deen, Rosemary, jt. auth. see Ponsot, Marie.
Deen, S. M. & Hammersley, P., eds. Data Bases International Conference, University of Aberdeen, July 1980: Proceedings. (British Computer Society Workshop Ser.). 300p. 1980. 76.95 (ISBN 0-471-25658-7, Wiley Heyden). Wiley.
--Databases. LC 81-13191. 250p. 1981. 44.95x (ISBN 0-470-27295-3). Halsted Pr.
--Icod-Two Second International Conference, 1983. (The PCS Workshop Ser.). 376p. 1983. 49.95x (ISBN 0-471-90309-4, Pub. by Wiley-Interscience). Wiley.
Deen, S. M. & Hemmersley, P., eds. Databases: Second British National Conference on Database Held at Bristol July 1982. 240p. 1984. text ed. write for info. (ISBN 0-471-90365-5, Pub. by Wiley Heyden). Wiley.
Deener, D. R., jt. auth. see Howard, L. V.
Deener, David R. De Lege Pactorum: Essays in Honor of R. R. Wilson. LC 70-101129. pap. 72.00 (ISBN 0-8357-9101-7, 2017898). Bks Demand UMI.
Deeney, Daniel. Peasant Lore from Gaelic Ireland. LC 77-26163. 1978. Repr. of 1900 ed. lib. bdg. 15.00 (ISBN 0-8414-1866-7). Folcroft.
--Peasant Lore from Gaelic Ireland. 1978. 14.50 (ISBN 0-685-86826-5). Porter.
Deeney, John J., ed. Chinese-Western Comparative Literature Theory & Strategy. 220p. 1981. 22.50x (ISBN 0-295-95810-3, Pub. by Chinese Univ Hong Kong). U of Wash Pr.
Deeny, A. A., jt. auth. see Roe, F. J.
Deeny, Kevin J., jt. auth. see Junkins, David R.
De Eon, Luis P. Lyrics of Luis De Leon. Bell, Aubrey F., tr. from Span. LC 76-48433. (Library of World Literature Ser.). 1978. Repr. of 1928 ed. 14.00 (ISBN 0-88355-562-X). Hyperion Conn.
Deep, Sam & Sussman, Lyle. COMEX: Communication Experience in Human Relations. 1984. text ed. 12.60 (ISBN 0-538-07070-6, G07). SW Pub.
Deepak, A., jt. ed. see Hobbs, Peter V.
Deepak, A., jt. ed. see Ruhnke, Lothar H.
Deepak, Adarsh, ed. Atmospheric Aerosols: Their Formation, Optical Properties, & Effects. LC 81-51934. (Illus.). 1982. 47.50 (ISBN 0-937194-01-8). A Deepak Pub.
--Inversion Methods in Atmospheric Remote Sounding. 1977. 57.50 (ISBN 0-12-208450-0). Acad Pr.
--Remote Sensing of Atmospheres & Oceans. LC 80-18881. 1980. 55.00 (ISBN 0-12-208460-8). Acad Pr.
Deepak, Adarsh & Rao, K. R., eds. Applications of Remote Sensing for Rice Production. (Illus.). 1985. 49.00 (ISBN 0-937194-03-4). A Deepak Pub.
Deepak, Adarsh, jt. ed. see Gerber, Hermann E.
Deepak, Adarsh, jt. ed. see Singh, Jag J.
Deepak, Lal. The Poverty of "Development Economics". (Hobart Paperbacks: No. 16). 1983. pap. 10.95 technical (ISBN 0-255-36163-7, Pub. by Inst Econ Affairs). Transatlantic.
Deeping, Warwick. Fox Farm. 1976. lib. bdg. 17.75x (ISBN 0-89968-021-6). Lightyear.
--Kitty. 1976. lib. bdg. 16.75x (ISBN 0-89968-020-8). Lightyear.
--The Red Saint. 1976. lib. bdg. 16.75x (ISBN 0-89968-024-0). Lightyear.
Deer, Josef. The Dynastic Porphyry Tombs of the Norman Period in Sicily. LC 60-3574. (Dumbarton Oaks Studies: Vol. 5). (Illus.). 188p. 1959. 20.00x (ISBN 0-88402-005-3). Dumbarton Oaks.
Deer, Richard E. The Lawyer's Basic Corporate Practice Manual. 2nd ed. 282p. 1978. looseleaf bound 35.00 (ISBN 0-317-32234-6, B154). Am Law Inst.
Deer, Richard E., jt. auth. see American Law Institute-American Bar Association Committee on Continuing Professional Education.
Deer, Richard E., jt. auth. see Pantzer, Kurt F.
Deer, Richard E., ed. The Lawyer's Basic Corporate Practice Manual: No. B154. 2nd ed. 282p. 1978. loose-leaf 35.00 (ISBN 0-317-30823-8). Am Law Inst.
Deer, W. A., et al. Rock Forming Minerals: Disilicates & Ring Silicates, Vol. 1B. 608p. 1985. 125.00 (ISBN 0-470-26634-1). Halsted Pr.
--Rock Forming Minerals: Orthosilicates, Vol. 1A. 2nd ed. 919p. 1982. 149.95x (ISBN 0-470-26633-3). Halsted Pr.
--Rock Forming Minerals, Vol. 5. 372p. 1962. 39.95x (ISBN 0-471-20524-9). Halsted Pr.
--Rock Forming Minerals, Vol. 1. 333p. 1962. 34.95x (ISBN 0-471-20518-4). Halsted Pr.
--Rock Forming Minerals, Vol. 4. 435p. 1963. 39.95x (ISBN 0-471-20523-0). Halsted Pr.
Deer, William A., et al. Introduction to Rock Forming Minerals. 528p. 1966. pap. 29.95x (ISBN 0-470-20516-4). Halsted Pr.
Deere & Company. Electrical Systems: Compact Equipment. (Fundamentals of Service Compact Equipment Ser.). (Illus.). 1982. pap. text ed. 10.00 (ISBN 0-86691-028-X); wkbk. 4.60 (ISBN 0-86691-031-X). Deere & Co.
--Engines (Consumer Products) (Illus.). 100p. (Orig.). 1982. pap. text ed. 11.05 (ISBN 0-86691-004-2); wkbk. 4.60 (ISBN 0-86691-035-2). Deere & Co.
--Hydraulics: Compact Equipment. (Fundamentals of Service Compact Equipment Ser.). (Illus.). 124p. 1983. pap. text ed. 8.80 (ISBN 0-86691-029-8); wkbk. 3.80 (ISBN 0-86691-032-8). Deere & Co.
--Power Trains: Compact Equipment. (Funadamentals of Service Compact Equipment Ser.). (Illus.). 104p. 1983. pap. text ed. 8.80 (ISBN 0-86691-030-1); wkbk. 3.80 (ISBN 0-86691-033-6). Deere & Co.
Deere, Carmen & Leal, Magdalena Leon de. Women in Andean Agriculture: Peasant Production & Rural Wage Employment in Colombia & Peru. International Labour Office, ed. (Women, Work & Development Ser.: No. 4). xii, 172p. (Orig.). 1983. pap. 11.40 (ISBN 92-2-103106-3, ILO 205). Intl Labour Office.
Deere, Carmen Diana & Leon de Leal, Magdalena. Women in Andean Agriculture: Peasant Production & Rural Wage Employment in Colombia & Peru. (Women, Work & Development Ser.: No. 4). 172p. 1983. pap. 11.40 (ISBN 92-2-103106-3, ILO205, ILO). Unipub.
Deere, Derek H., ed. Corrosion in Marine Environment International Sourcebook I: Ship Painting & Corrosion. LC 76-15600. 259p. 1977. 74.95x (ISBN 0-470-15203-6). Halsted Pr.
Deere, Don U., jt. ed. see Dunnicliff, John.
Deerfield, William, jt. auth. see Porter, Darrell.
Deerforth, Daniel. Knock Wood! Superstition Through the Ages. LC 79-164220. 200p. 1974. Repr. of 1928 ed. 43.00x (ISBN 0-8103-3964-1). Gale.
Deering, Christopher, jt. auth. see Smith, Steven.
Deering, Paul L., jt. auth. see Balshone, Bruce L.
Deering, Warren H., et al. California Administrative Mandamus. LC 66-64355. xxiv, 463p. 1966. 50.00 (ISBN 0-88124-003-6). Cal Cont Ed Bar.
Deering, William M., jt. auth. see Lubar, Joel F.
Deery, Ruth. Scholar Dollars. (gr. 3-6). 1982. 5.95 (ISBN 0-86653-057-6, GA 415). Good Apple.
Dees, Anne, ed. see Zeyen, Dorothy D.
Dees, Jerome S. Sir Thomas Elyot & Roger Ascham: A Reference Guide. 1981. 29.50 (ISBN 0-8161-8353-8, Hall Reference). G K Hall.
Dees, Jesse W. Jim Crow. LC 70-138004. (Illus.). Repr. of 1951 ed. cancelled (ISBN 0-8371-5651-3, DJC&, Pub. by Negro U Pr). Greenwood.
Dees, Marvelle, ed. Heirs Together. (Illus.). 242p. 1970. 8.95 (ISBN 0-912315-30-X). Word Aflame.
De Escalante, Bernardino see Escalante, Bernardino de.
De Escudero, Jose A; see Carroll, H. Bailey & Haggard, J. Villasana.
Deese, David & Nye, Joseph, eds. Energy & Security. LC 80-19922. 512p. 1980. prof ref 14.95 (ISBN 0-88410-640-3). Ballinger Pub.
Deese, David A., jt. ed. see Williams, Frederick C.
Deese, Helen, jt. auth. see Axelrod, Steven G.
Deese, J., jt. auth. see Szalay, L. B.
Deese, James. American Freedom & the Social Sciences. 232p. 1985. 25.00x (ISBN 0-231-05914-0). Columbia U Pr.
--Thought into Speech: The Psychology of a Language. (Century Psychology Ser.). (Illus.). 160p. 1984. text ed. 24.95 (ISBN 0-13-919944-6). P-H.
Deese, James, jt. auth. see Szalay, Lorand B.
Deese, James E. The Structure of Associations in Language & Thought. LC 65-26181. pap. 58.00 (ISBN 0-317-10518-3, 2003839). Bks Demand UMI.
Deeter, Allen C. Heirs of a Promise. new ed. 48p. 1972. pap. 1.95 (ISBN 0-87178-359-2). Brethren.
Deetjen, P., et al. Physiology of the Kidney & of Water Balance. LC 72-85949. (Illus.). 145p. 1975. pap. 18.00 (ISBN 0-387-90048-9). Springer-Verlag.
--Wasser und Elektrolythaushalt: Physiologie und Pathophysiologie. (Handbuch der Infusionstherapie und Klinischen Ernaehrung: Band 1). viii, 160p. 1984. 33.75 (ISBN 3-8055-3745-X). S Karger.
Deetz, Charles H. & Adams, Oscar S. Elements of Map Projection with Applications to Map & Chart Construction. 5th ed. LC 77-89015. Repr. of 1945 ed. lib. bdg. 32.25x (ISBN 0-8371-2268-6, DEMP). Greenwood.
Deetz, James. In Small Things Forgotten: The Archaeology of Early American Life. LC 76-50760. (Illus.). 1977. pap. 4.95 (ISBN 0-385-08031-X, Anch). Doubleday.
Deetz, Stanley, ed. Phenomenology in Rhetoric & Communication. LC 81-43514. (Current Continental Research Ser.: No. 3). (Illus.). 246p. (Orig.). 1982. lib. bdg. 26.00 (ISBN 0-8191-2087-1); pap. text ed. 12.75 (ISBN 0-8191-2088-X). U Pr of Amer.
De Eudaly, Maria S. Capacitando a Maestros De Ninos. 1982. pap. 1.30 (ISBN 0-311-11035-5). Casa Bautista.
Deevey, E. S., ed. Growth by Intussusception: Ecological Essays in Honor of G. Evelyn Hutchinson. (Conn. Academy of Arts & Sciences Transactions, Vol. 44). (Illus.). 441p. 1973. pap. 37.50 (ISBN 0-208-01293-1). Shoe String.

Deevey, Edward S., Jr. Limnologic Studies in Middle America with a Chapter on Aztec Limnology. (Connecticut Academy of Arts & Sciences Transactions Ser.: Vol. 39). 1957. 15.00 (ISBN 0-317-03799-4). Shoe String.

De Fabry, Anne & Hilgar, Marie-France. Etudes Autour d'Alcools. LC 85-61599. 209p. (Fr.). 1985. 18.95 (ISBN 0-317-31672-9). Summa Pubns.

DeFalco, Joseph. The Hero in Hemingway's Short Stories. 1977. Repr. of 1963 ed. lib. bdg. 30.00 (ISBN 0-8495-1000-7). Arden Lib.

--The Hero in Hemingway's Short Stories. LC 78-16871. Repr. of 1963 ed. lib. bdg. 30.00 (ISBN 0-8414-1884-5). Folcroft.

DeFalco, Joseph, ed. see Cranch, Christopher P.

De Falla, Manuel. On Music & Musicians. 136p. 1979. 14.95 (ISBN 0-7145-2600-2, Dist by Scribner); pap. 7.95 (ISBN 0-7145-2735-1). M Boyars.

De Fallois. Simenon. pap. 11.50 (ISBN 0-685-36579-4). French & Eur.

Defant, F. see Wiin-Nielsen, A.

DeFanti, Charles L., Jr. The Wages of Expectation: A Biography of Edward Dahlberg. LC 77-94390. (Gotham Library). 1978. 35.00x (ISBN 0-8147-1763-2). NYU Pr.

DeFantini, Beatriz C., tr. see Moran, Patrick R.

Defaux, Gerard. Le Curieux, le glorieux et la sagesse du monde dans la premiere moitie du XVIe siecle: L'exemple de Panurge. LC 81-71430. (French Forum Monographs: No. 34). 196p. (Orig.). 1982. pap. 15.00x (ISBN 0-917058-33-X). French Forum.

--Moliere, ou les Metamorphoses du Comique: De la Comedie Morale Au Triomphe De la Folie. LC 79-53401. (French Forum Monographs: No. 18). 370p. (Fr.). 1980. pap. 17.50x (ISBN 0-917058-17-8). French Forum.

Defaux, Gerard, ed. see Yale French Studies.

De Favia, Gussie. Around Moma's Kitchen: Authenic Portuguese Recipes. LC 83-50000. 1976. 6.95 (ISBN 0-915176-23-8). Job Shop.

Defay, Raymond & Prigogine, I. Surface Tension & Adsorption with the Collaboration of A. Bellemans. LC 61-71787. pap. 116.00 (ISBN 0-317-08947-1, 2003639). Bks Demand UMI.

De Faye, Eugene. Origen & His Work. LC 78-16959. 1926. 22.50 (ISBN 0-8414-3684-3). Folcroft.

De Faye, Eugene see Faye, Eugene De.

De Federico De Onis, Ensayo. Disciplina y Rebeldia. 51p. 1915. 0.75 (ISBN 0-318-14255-4). Hispanic Inst.

De Federico De Onis, Ensayos, et al. Antonia Merce - la Argentina. 50p. 0.80 (ISBN 0-318-14238-4). Hispanic Inst.

Defeis, Elizabeth, jt. auth. see Halberstam, Malvina.

De Feldy, L. Elizabeth. Common Sense Etiquette: For Business Women, Wives, Mistresses. (Illus.). 119p. 1983. lib. bdg. 18.00x (ISBN 0-935402-15-2). Intl Comm Serv.

DeFelice, Eugene A., jt. ed. see Kostis, John B.

De Felice, Frank, ed. A Primer on Business Finance. LC 73-20489. 1974. 34.75x (ISBN 0-8422-5132-4); pap. text ed. 12.50x (ISBN 0-686-77022-6). Irvington.

DeFelice, James. Filmguide to Odd Man Out. LC 74-6519. (Indiana University Press Filmguide Ser.: No. 9). pap. 23.80 (ISBN 0-8357-9209-9, 2017616). Bks Demand UMI.

DeFelice, Louis J. Introduction to Membrane Noise. LC 80-16163. 516p. 1981. 49.50x (ISBN 0-306-40513-X, Plenum Pr). Plenum Pub.

De Felice, Louise, jt. auth. see Gray, Juanita.

DeFelice, Louise, jt. auth. see Tovey, Luanne.

De Felice, Renzo. Fascism: An Informal Introduction to Its Theory & Practice. An Interview with Michael A. Ledeen. LC 76-13006. (Issues in Contemporary Civilization). pap. 32.00 (ISBN 0-317-20613-3, 2024155). Bks Demand UMI.

--Interpretations of Facism. Everett, Brenda H., tr. 1977. 16.50x (ISBN 0-674-45962-8). Harvard U Pr.

--Jews in an Arab Land: Libya, 1835-1970. Roumani, Judith, tr. 436p. 1985. 22.50x (ISBN 0-292-74016-6). U of Tex Pr.

De Felitta, Frank. The Entity. 480p. 1979. pap. 3.95 (ISBN 0-446-30136-1). Warner Bks.

--For Love of Audrey Rose. 464p. (Orig.). 1982. pap. 3.95 (ISBN 0-446-30206-6). Warner Bks.

--Golgotha Falls. 1985. pap. 3.95 (ISBN 0-671-50776-1). PB.

--Golgotha Falls: A Novel. 1984. 15.95 (ISBN 0-671-50775-3). S&S.

--Oktoberfest. 208p. 1980. pap. 2.50 (ISBN 0-380-53546-7, 53546-7). Avon.

--Sea Trial. 288p. 1980. pap. 2.95 (ISBN 0-380-81414-5, 81414-5). Avon.

Defeller, F. X. & Perennes, F. Dictionnaire de Biographie Chretienne, 3 vols. Migne, J. P., ed. (Nouvelle Encyclopedie Theologique Ser.: Vols. 1-3). 2352p. (Fr.). Repr. of 1851 ed. lib. bdg. 298.00x (ISBN 0-89241-254-2). Caratzas.

De Fenelon, Marquis. Adventures of Telemachus. Wight, O. W., ed. Hawkesworth, tr. 1977. Repr. of 1882 ed. lib. bdg. 50.00 (ISBN 0-8495-1610-2). Arden Lib.

De Fenin, Pierre. Memoires. 1837. 34.00 (ISBN 0-384-15455-7); pap. 28.00 (ISBN 0-384-15460-3). Johnson Repr.

De Fenoyl, Pierre. Photography Album Number One. (An Agrinde Bk.). (Illus.). 1981. 50.00. Dodd.

De Fenoyl, Pierre, ed. Photography Album, No. 1. LC 79-20063. (Illus.). 232p. (Fr. & Eng.). 50.00 (ISBN 0-9601068-3-9). Agrinde Pubns.

Defensive Tips, Inc. Staff & Penkivich, Robert R. Drinking & Driving Is No Accident: The Inside Story. (Defensive Tips Ser.: Vol. 1). 200p. 1985. pap. 14.95 (ISBN 0-933531-07-9). Defensive Tips.

De Fer, Hugo. The Art & Science of Stimulating the Force & Daring of Your Inventiveness Faculties. (Illus.). 1976. 57.50 (ISBN 0-89266-034-1). Am Classical Coll Pr.

--Jewish Ethics & Catholic Doctrine. LC 78-167699. (Illus.). 32p. 1972. 49.25 (ISBN 0-913314-08-0). Am Classical Coll Pr.

--The Metaphysics of Inventiveness. (Illus.). 200p. 1976. 44.15 (ISBN 0-913314-72-2). Am Classical Coll Pr.

De Ferdinandy, Magdalena, et al, trs. see Ferdinandy, Miguel De.

De Ferdinandy, Miguel. El Emperador Carlos V. 4.35 (ISBN 0-8477-0826-8); pap. 3.75 (ISBN 0-8477-0827-6). U of PR Pr.

--En Torno al Pensar Historico, 2 bks. Set. pap. 3.35 (ISBN 0-8477-0828-4). U of PR Pr.

DeFerranti, David. Paying for Health Services in Developing Countries: An Overview. (Staff Working Paper: No. 721). 132p. 8.00 (ISBN 0-318-11947-1, WP 0721). World Bank.

Deferrari, R. J., tr. see Hugh Of St. Victor.

Deferrari, Roy J. Memoirs of the Catholic University of America 1918-1960. 5.00 (ISBN 0-8198-0103-8). Dghtrs St Paul.

--Some Problems of Catholic Higher Education in the United States. (Orig.). 1963. 3.00 (ISBN 0-8198-0149-6). Dghtrs St Paul.

Deferrari, Roy J., ed. Essays on Catholic Education in the U. S. (Essay Index Reprint Ser.). 566p. Repr. of 1942 ed. lib. bdg. 12.00 (ISBN 0-8290-0814-4). Irvington.

--Essays on Catholic Education in the United States. LC 71-90629. (Essay Index Reprint Ser.). 1942. 33.00 (ISBN 0-8369-1347-7). Ayer Co Pubs.

Defert, Thierry, jt. auth. see Lepape, Claude.

DeFeudis, F. & DeFeudis, P. Elements of the Behavioral Code. 1978. 66.00 (ISBN 0-12-208760-7). Acad Pr.

De Feudis, F. V. Central Cholinergic Systems & Behavior. 1975. 47.00 (ISBN 0-12-208750-X). Acad Pr.

DeFeudis, F. V., jt. ed. see Mandel, Paul.

DeFeudis, Francis V., jt. ed. see Mandel, Paul.

DeFeudis, P., jt. auth. see DeFeudis, F.

De Feyter, C. A. Industrial Policy & Shipbuilding: Changing Economic Structures in the Low Countries, 1600-1980. 200p. (Orig.). 1982. pap. 19.00x (ISBN 90-6194-323-X). Benjamins North Am.

--Industrial Policy & Shipbuilding: Changing Economic Structures in the Low Countries, 1600-1980. 353p. 1982. pap. text ed. 19.00x (ISBN 90-6194-323-X, Pub. by HES Pub Holland). Humanities.

Deffand, Madame du. Letters to & from Madame Du Deffand & Julie De Lespinasse. limited ed. Smith, W. H., ed. 1938. 39.50x (ISBN 0-685-69810-6). Elliots Bks.

Deffenbacher, Kenneth A., jt. auth. see Brown, Evan L.

Deffeyes, jt. auth. see Judson, S.

Deffner, Don. Bound to Be Free. LC 80-81841. 1980. pap. 7.95 (ISBN 0-933350-38-4). Morse Pr.

Deffner, Donald. I Hear Two Voices, God! LC 12-2817. 1983. pap. 4.95 (ISBN 0-570-03882-0). Concordia.

--Please Talk to Me, God! (Continued Applied Christianity). 1983. pap. 4.95 (ISBN 0-570-03899-5, 12-2981). Concordia.

--Voices & Choices. 1984. pap. 4.95 (ISBN 0-570-03939-8, 12-2874). Concordia.

--You Promised Me God. LC 12-2792. (Illus.). 1981. pap. 4.95 (ISBN 0-570-03827-8). Concordia.

Deffner, Donald, jt. auth. see Andersen, Richard.

Deffner, Donald L. Come Closer to Me, God! 1982. pap. 4.95 (ISBN 0-570-03851-0, 12-2806). Concordia.

Deffner, Wenonah S. Scripture Word Search. (Quiz & Puzzle Bks.). 1980. pap. 2.45 (ISBN 0-8010-2897-3). Baker Bk.

Deffontaines, Pierre, jt. auth. see Journaux, Andre.

Deficit, George, jt. auth. see Deficit, Ron.

Deficit, Ron & Deficit, George. Everything Must Go! 128p. 1985. 3.95 (ISBN 0-918222-74-5). Apple Wood.

De Fiebre, Henry. Grandpa, Book 1. LC 82-62527. 64p. 1982. pap. 5.95 (ISBN 0-89821-046-1). Reiman Assocs.

De Fiebre, Henry, ed. Grandpa, Book II. LC 82-62527. 64p. 1984. pap. 5.95 (ISBN 0-89821-062-3). Reiman Assocs.

De Figueiredo, D. G., ed. Differential Equations, Sao Paulo, Brazil, 1981: Proceedings. (Lecture Notes in Mathematics: Vol. 957). 301p. 1982. pap. 18.00 (ISBN 0-387-11951-5). Springer-Verlag.

De Figueiredo, M. P. & Splittstoesser, D. F. Food Microbiology: Public Health & Spoilage Aspects. (Illus.). 1976. lib. bdg. 50.00 (ISBN 0-87055-209-0). AVI.

DeFigueiredo, R. J., jt. ed. see Jain, K. C.

De Figuerdo, Antonio, jt. auth. see Norman, Jill.

De Figueroa, Martin Fernandez see Fernandez De Figueroa, Martin.

De Filippi, Joseph, jt. auth. see Contant, Clement.

De Filippi, Joseph see Lacroix, Paul.

De Filippis, Michele. The Literary Riddle in Italy in the Eighteenth Century. LC 68-63064. 208p. 1983. Repr. of 1967 ed. lib. bdg. 19.95x (ISBN 0-89370-763-5). Borgo Pr.

De Filippo, Eduardo. Filumena. Waterhouse, Keith & Hall, Willis, trs. 1978. pap. text ed. 6.00x (ISBN 0-435-23202-9). Heinemann Ed.

--Saturday, Sunday, Monday. Waterhouse, Keith & Hall, Willis, trs. 1974. pap. text ed. 5.50x (ISBN 0-435-23201-0). Heinemann Ed.

DeFilipps, Robert A., jt. auth. see Ayensu, Edward S.

DeFillippo, J. NHE Life Skills Workbook I. 1981. pap. 5.95 (ISBN 0-201-05048-X, World Language Div). Addison-Wesley.

--NHE Lifeskills Workbook II. 1982. pap. 5.95 (ISBN 0-201-05049-8). Addison-Wesley.

De Finis, Francesco, jt. auth. see Pantaleo, Mario.

De Fiore, Gaspare. Composing & Shading Your Drawings: The Drawing Course, Vol. 2. (Illus.). 192p. 1985. 24.95 (ISBN 0-8230-0878-9). Watson-Guptill.

De Fiori, Vittorio E. Mussolini, the Man of Destiny. Pei, Mario A., tr. from Italian. LC 78-63673. (Illus.). 288p. 1982. Repr. of 1928 ed. 28.00 (ISBN 0-404-16933-3). AMS Pr.

DeFleur, Lois B., jt. auth. see Winfield, Betty H.

DeFleur, Melvin & Ball-Rokeach, Sandra J. Theories of Mass Communication. 4th ed. LC 81-8215. (Illus.). 288p. 1981. text ed. 22.50x (ISBN 0-582-28278-0); pap. text ed. 16.45x (ISBN 0-582-28277-2). Longman.

DeFleur, Melvin & Lowery, Shearon. Milestones in Mass Communication Research. LC 82-14043. (Illus.). 448p. 1983. pap. text ed. 14.95x (ISBN 0-582-28353-1). Longman.

DeFleur, Melvin, et al. Sociology. 2nd ed. LC 76-12523. 1977. pap. text ed. 15.95 (ISBN 0-394-33300-4, RanC). Random.

DeFleur, Melvin L. Social Problems in American Society. LC 82-81108. 640p. 1982. text ed. 27.95 (ISBN 0-395-32567-6); instr's. manual 2.00 (ISBN 0-395-32568-4); study guide 8.50 (ISBN 0-395-32569-2); test bank 2.00 (ISBN 0-395-33955-3). HM.

DeFleur, Melvin L. & D'Antonio, William. Sociology: Human Society. 4th ed. 475p. 1984. text ed. 25.00 (ISBN 0-394-33742-5, RanC). Random.

DeFleur, Melvin L. & Dennis, Everette E. Understanding Mass Communication. LC 80-82762. (Illus.). 528p. 1981. pap. text ed. 18.50 (ISBN 0-395-29722-2); instr's manual 1.00 (ISBN 0-395-29723-0). HM.

--Understanding Mass Communication. 2nd ed. LC 84-81983. 608p. 1985. pap. text ed. 17.95 (ISBN 0-395-35929-5); instr's. manual with test items 2.00 (ISBN 0-395-36398-5). HM.

De Fleury, C. Rohault. La Sainte Vierge: Etudes Archeologiques et Iconographiques, 2 vols. (Illus., Fr.). Repr. of 1878 ed. Set. 325.00x (ISBN 0-89241-154-6). Caratzas.

Defliese, Philip L., jt. ed. see Chippindale, Warren.

Defliese, Philip L., et al. Montgomery's Auditing: College Edition. 10th ed. LC 84-5289. 1179p. 1984. text ed. 36.95 (ISBN 0-471-07756-9); cancelled (ISBN 0-471-81177-7); cancelled (ISBN 0-471-81178-5). Wiley.

De Flumiani, Carlo M. The Cylinder Theory in Dynamic Exhibitional Charts Depicting the Traumatic Extremes of the Stock Market: The Excesses of the National Economy & the Dangerous Extravagances of History from Which New Nations Are Born & Old Nations Die. 1977. 67.85 (ISBN 0-89266-064-3). Am Classical Coll Pr.

--The Eternal Principles of Managerial Excellence for the Benefit of Businessmen: Corporate Executives, Junior Clerks, Housewives, Students, Politicians, Statesmen & Anyone Genuinely Interested in Improving His Station in Life. (Illus.). 1977. 59.75 (ISBN 0-89266-061-9). Am Classical Coll Pr.

Defoe. Robinson Crusoe. (Children's Classic Ser.). (gr. 3-6). 1981. 6.95 (ISBN 0-86020-554-1, Usborne-Hayes); pap. 2.95 (ISBN 0-86020-553-3). EDC.

Defoe, Daniel. Account of the Conduct & Proceedings of the Pirate Gow: The Original of Sir Walter Scott's Captain Cleveland. LC 77-122230. (Research & Source Works Ser.: No. 517). 1970. Repr. of 1896 ed. lib. bdg. 18.50 (ISBN 0-8337-0805-8). B Franklin.

--Best of Defoe's Review. facs. ed. Payne, William L., ed. LC 73-128233. (Essay Index Reprint Ser). 1951. 21.50 (ISBN 0-8369-1873-8). Ayer Co Pubs.

--Colonel Jack: The History & Remarkable Life of the Truly Honorable Colonel Jacque, Commonly Called Colonel Jack. Monk, Samuel H., ed. (Oxford English Novels Ser). 1965. pap. 4.95x (ISBN 0-19-281076-6, OPB). Oxford U Pr.

--Complete English Gentleman. Bulbring, Karl K., ed. LC 74-2440. 1890. lib. bdg. 35.00 (ISBN 0-8414-3733-5). Folcroft.

--Complete English Tradesman, 2 vols in 1. 1970. Repr. of 1726 ed. text ed. 36.50 (ISBN 0-8337-0808-2). B Franklin.

--Conjugal Lewdness, or Matrimonial Whoredom. LC 67-10178. 1967. Repr. of 1727 ed. 50.00x (ISBN 0-8201-1013-2). Schol Facsimiles.

--The Consolidator or Memoirs of Sundry Transactions from the World in the Moon. LC 75-170513. (Foundations of the Novel Ser.: Vol. 9). lib. bdg. 61.00 (ISBN 0-8240-0521-X). Garland Pub.

--Daniel Defoe: His Life & Recently Discovered Writing Extending from 1716-1729, 3 Vols. Lee, William, ed. LC 78-82017. (Research & Source Works Ser.: No. 369). (Illus.). 1969. Repr. of 1869 ed. lib. bdg. 77.00 (ISBN 0-8337-2047-3). B Franklin.

--Daniel Defoe's Tour Through Great Britain, 2 vols. 1968. Repr. of 1927 ed. 65.00x (ISBN 0-7146-1298-7, F Cass Co). Biblio Dist.

--Defoe's Review, 9 Vols. Bd. in 22 Pts. facsimile ed. 1704-1713. Repr. of 1938 ed. Set. 900.00 (ISBN 0-404-19513-X). AMS Pr.

--Due Preparations for the Plague, As Well for Soul As Body. LC 74-13434. (Illus.). Repr. of 1895 ed. 32.50 (ISBN 0-404-07925-3). AMS Pr.

--The Earlier Life & Chief Earlier Works of Daniel Defoe. Morley, Henry, ed. 1968. Repr. of 1889 ed. 30.50 (ISBN 0-8337-0809-0). B Franklin.

--The Farther Adventures of Robinson Crusoe, Being the Second & Last Part of His Life. LC 74-13446. (Illus.). Repr. of 1895 ed. 32.50 (ISBN 0-404-07912-1). AMS Pr.

--The Fortunate Mistress, 2 vols. LC 74-13447. (Illus.). Repr. of 1895 ed. 32.50 ea.; Vol. 1. (ISBN 0-404-07922-9); Vol. 2. (ISBN 0-404-07923-7). AMS Pr.

--The Fortunes & Misfortunes of Moll Flanders. Starr, G. A., ed. (World's Classics Ser.). 1981. pap. 2.95 (ISBN 0-19-281570-9). Oxford U Pr.

--The Fortunes & Misfortunes of the Famous Moll Flanders, 2 vols. LC 74-13449. (Illus.). Repr. of 1895 ed. 32.50 ea.; Vol. 1. (ISBN 0-404-07917-2); Vol. 2. (ISBN 0-404-07918-0). AMS Pr.

--The Four Years Voyages of Captain George Roberts. LC 79-170566. (Foundations of the Novel Ser.: Vol. 47). 1973. lib. bdg. 61.00 (ISBN 0-8240-0559-7). Garland Pub.

--Giving Alms, No Charity & Employing the Poor: A Grievance to the Nation. (History of English Economic Thought Ser). 1970. Repr. of 1704 ed. 16.00 (ISBN 0-384-11193-9). Johnson Repr.

--The History & Remarkable Life of the Truly Honourable Colonel Jacque, 2 vols. (Illus.). Repr. of 1895 ed. 32.50 ea.; Vol. 1. (ISBN 0-404-07920-2); Vol. 2. (ISBN 0-404-07921-0). AMS Pr.

--The History of the Life & Adventures of Mr. Duncan Campbell. LC 74-13463. (Illus.). Repr. of 1895 ed. 32.50 (ISBN 0-404-07914-8). AMS Pr.

--Journal of Plague Year. Burgess, Anthony, ed. (English Library). 1966. pap. 2.95 (ISBN 0-14-043015-6). Penguin.

--A Journal of the Plague Year. LC 74-13469. (Illus.). Repr. of 1895 ed. 32.50 (ISBN 0-404-07919-9). AMS Pr.

--A Journal of the Plague Year. 1977. 11.95x (ISBN 0-460-00289-9, Evman); (Evman). Biblio Dist.

--A Journal of the Plague Year. 240p. 1984. pap. 4.95 (ISBN 0-452-00689-9, Mer). NAL.

--The King of Pirates, Being an Account of the Famous Enterprises of Captain Avery. LC 74-13451. (Illus.). Repr. of 1895 ed. 32.50 (ISBN 0-404-07926-1). AMS Pr.

--The Life, Adventures, & Piracies of the Famous Captain Singleton. LC 74-13433. (Illus.). Repr. of 1895 ed. 32.50 (ISBN 0-404-07916-4). AMS Pr.

--The Life, Adventures, & Piracies of the Famous Captain Singleton... Being Set on Shore in the Island of Madagascar. LC 70-170544. (Foundations of the Novel Ser.: Vol. 33). 1972. lib. bdg. 61.00 (ISBN 0-8240-0545-7). Garland Pub.

--The Life & Strange & Surprising Adventures of Robinson Crusoe, of York, Mariner. LC 74-13442. (Illus.). Repr. of 1895 ed. 32.50 (ISBN 0-404-07911-3). AMS Pr.

--The Life & Strange Surprising Adventures of Robinson Crusoe. Crowley, J. Donald, ed. (World's Classics Ser.). 1981. pap. 2.95 (ISBN 0-19-281555-5). Oxford U Pr.

--The Manufacturer, Vols. 1-86. Bd. with The British Merchant; The Weaver. LC 78-11810. 1979. Repr. of 1720 ed. 60.00x (ISBN 0-8201-1324-7). Schol Facsimiles.

--The Meditations of Daniel Defoe. LC 77-23230. 1977. Repr. of 1946 ed. lib. bdg. 10.00 (ISBN 0-8414-4949-X). Folcroft.

--Memoirs of a Cavalier. LC 74-13443. (Illus.). Repr. of 1895 ed. 32.50 (ISBN 0-404-07915-6). AMS Pr.

--Memoirs of a Cavalier. LC 74-170545. (Novel in England, 1700-1775 Ser). 1972. lib. bdg. 61.00 (ISBN 0-8240-0546-5). Garland Pub.

--Memoirs of an English Officer & Other Stories. 1981. 20.00x (ISBN 0-575-00421-5, Pub. by Gollancz England). State Mutual Bk.

--Moll Flanders. (Classics Ser). (gr. 11 up). 1969. pap. 1.95 (ISBN 0-8049-0200-3, CL-200). Airmont.

--Moll Flanders. 1977. pap. 2.50x (ISBN 0-460-01837-X, DEL-04243, Evman). Biblio Dist.

--Moll Flanders. Sutherland, James, ed. LC 59-16265. (YA) (gr. 9 up). 1959. pap. 5.50 (ISBN 0-395-05129-0, 3-47665, RivEd). HM.

--Moll Flanders. (YA) 1950. pap. 3.95 (ISBN 0-394-30908-1, T8, Mod LibC). Modern Lib.
--Moll Flanders. (Orig.). 1962. pap. 2.75 (ISBN 0-451-51845-4, CE1845, Sig Classics). NAL.
--Moll Flanders. Kelly, Edward, ed. (Critical Editions Ser.). 500p. 1973. pap. text ed. 8.95x (ISBN 0-393-09412-X). Norton.
--Moll Flanders. (English Library). 1978. pap. 2.95 (ISBN 0-14-043107-1). Penguin.
--Moll Flanders. (Illus.). (gr. 9 up). pap. 0.60 (ISBN 0-671-46120-6). WSP.
--Moll Flanders. 451p. 1983. Repr. lib. bdg. 18.95x (ISBN 0-89966-313-3). Buccaneer Bks.
--Moll Flanders. (Modern Library College Editions). 1950. pap. text ed. 3.95 (ISBN 0-394-30908-1, RanC). Random.
--A New Voyage Round the World, by a Course Never Sailed Before. LC 74-13444. (Illus.). Repr. of 1895 ed. 32.50 (ISBN 0-404-07924-5). AMS Pr.
--Novels & Miscellaneous Works of Daniel Defoe, 20 Vols. Scott, Walter, ed. LC 79-154120. Repr. of 1841 ed. Set. 630.00 (ISBN 0-404-09300-0); 31.50 ea. AMS Pr.
--The Novels & Selected Writings of Daniel Defoe: Shakespeare Head Edition, 14 vols. 300p. 1974. Repr. of 1923 ed. Set. 250.00x (ISBN 0-87471-521-0). Rowman.
--The Pirate Gow. 88p. 1981. 25.00x (ISBN 0-903065-22-3, Pub. by Wright Pub Scotland). State Mutual Bk.
--Plan of the English Commerce, 3 Pts. 2nd ed. LC 67-20365. Repr. of 1730 ed. 45.00x (ISBN 0-678-00316-5). Kelley.
--Robinson Crusoe. (Classics Ser). (gr. 6 up). 1964. pap. 2.95 (ISBN 0-8049-0022-1, CL-22). Airmont.
--Robinson Crusoe. (Literature Ser.). (gr. 7-12). 1970. pap. text ed. 5.00 (ISBN 0-87720-736-4). AMSCO Sch.
--Robinson Crusoe. (Bantam Classics Ser.). 288p. (gr. 7-12). 1981. pap. text ed. 1.95 (ISBN 0-553-21105-6). Bantam.
--Robinson Crusoe. 1977. 12.95x (ISBN 0-460-00059-4, Evman); pap. 2.50x (ISBN 0-460-01059-X, Evman). Biblio Dist.
--Robinson Crusoe. (Span.). 9.95 (ISBN 84-241-5636-6). E Torres & Sons.
--Robinson Crusoe. (Illus.). (gr. 4-6). 1952-63. il. jr. lib. o.p. 5.95 (ISBN 0-448-05821-9, G&D); Companion Lib. Ed. o.p. 2.95 (ISBN 0-448-05467-1); deluxe ed. 10.95 (ISBN 0-448-06021-3); PLB 3.79 (ISBN 0-448-03260-0). Putnam Pub Group.
--Robinson Crusoe. (RL 6). pap. 1.95 (ISBN 0-451-51606-0, CJ1606, Sig Classics). NAL.
--Robinson Crusoe. Shinagel, Michael, ed. (Critical Editions Ser.). 399p. 1975. pap. text ed. 5.95x (ISBN 0-393-09231-3). Norton.
--Robinson Crusoe. Fago, John N., ed. (Now Age Illustrated IV Ser.). (Illus.). (gr. 4-12). 1978. text ed. 5.00 (ISBN 0-88301-332-0); pap. text ed. 1.95 (ISBN 0-88301-320-7); activity bk. 1.25 (ISBN 0-88301-344-4). Pendulum Pr.
--Robinson Crusoe. Ross, Angus, ed. (English Library Ser.). (YA) (gr. 9 up). 1966. pap. 2.95 (ISBN 0-14-043007-5). Penguin.
--Robinson Crusoe. abr. ed. Lasson, Robert, ed. LC 67-25784. (Pacemaker Classics Ser.). (Illus., Orig., Abridged adapted to grade 2 reading level). (gr. 2,RL 2.8). 1967. pap. text ed. 4.92 (ISBN 0-8224-9225-3); tchrs' manual free. Pitman Learning.
--Robinson Crusoe. (Regents Illustrated Classics Ser.). 62p. (gr. 7-12). 1982. pap. text ed. 2.75 (ISBN 0-88345-469-6, 20418). Regents Pub.
--Robinson Crusoe. (Bambi Classics Ser.). (Illus.). 384p. (Orig.). 1981. pap. 3.95 (ISBN 0-89531-067-8, 0221-48). Sharon Pubns.
--Robinson Crusoe. 1982. Repr. lib. bdg. 17.95x (ISBN 0-89966-403-2). Buccaneer Bks.
--Robinson Crusoe. (Illus.). 368p. 1983. 18.95 (ISBN 0-684-17946-6); Deluxe, numbered, boxed ed. 75.00 (ISBN 0-684-17947-4). Scribner.
--Robinson Crusoe. LC 84-50438. (Classics for Kids Ser.). 1984. 5.96 (ISBN 0-382-06815-7). Silver.
--Robinson Crusoe. (Classics for Kids Ser.). 32p. (gr. 2 up). 1985. pap. 3.60 (ISBN 0-382-06958-7). Silver.
--Robinson Crusoe. 19.95 (ISBN 0-88411-594-1, Pub. by Aeonian Pr). Amereon Ltd.
--Robinson Crusoe. LC 84-52575. (Classics for Kids Ser.). (Illus.). 32p. (Span.). (gr. 3 up). 1985. pap. 3.60 (ISBN 0-382-09024-1). Silver.
--Robinson Crusoe & Other Writings. Sutherland, James, ed. LC 77-77300. (Gotham Library). 416p. 1977. pap. 12.50x (ISBN 0-8147-7785-6). NYU Pr.
--Robinson Crusoe & the Farther Adventures of Robinson Crusoe. 320p. 1968. pap. 2.95 (ISBN 0-671-47227-5). WSP.
--Romances & Narratives, 16 Vols. Aitken, George, ed. (Illus.). Repr. of 1895 ed. Set. 520.00 (ISBN 0-404-07910-5); 32.50 ea. AMS Pr.
--Romans: Moll Flanders, Mme. Veal, Memoires d'un Canalier, Vie Du Capitaine Singleton, Etc, Vol. 2. 1760p. 42.95 (ISBN 0-686-56494-4). French & Eur.
--Romans: Robinson Crusoe, Journal de l'Annee de la Peste, Jean Gow, Jean Sheppard, Etc, Vol. 1. 1376p. 41.50 (ISBN 0-686-56493-6). French & Eur.
--Roxana. Blewett, David, ed. 1982. pap. 4.95 (ISBN 0-14-043149-7). Penguin.
--Roxana. Jack, Jane, ed. (World's Classics Ser.). 1981. pap. 3.95 (ISBN 0-19-281563-6). Oxford U Pr.
--Roxana: The Fortunate Mistress. 1979. pap. 2.25 (ISBN 0-451-51190-5, CE1190, Sig Classics). NAL.
--Serious Reflections During the Life & Surprising Adventures of Robinson Crusoe, with His Vision of the Angelic World. LC 74-13445. (Illus.). Repr. of 1895 ed. 32.50 (ISBN 0-404-07913-X). AMS Pr.
--Tour Thro' London About the Year 1725. Beeton, Mayson M. & Chancellor, E. Beresford, eds. LC 68-56542. (Illus.). Repr. of 1929 ed. 30.00 (ISBN 0-405-08441-2, Blom Pubns). Ayer Co Pubs.
--A Tour Through the Whole Island of Great Britain. 1974. Repr. of 1962 ed. 12.95x (ISBN 0-460-10820-4, Evman). Biblio Dist.
--Tour Through the Whole Island of Great Britain. 1978. pap. 5.95 (ISBN 0-14-043066-0). Penguin.
--The Versatile Defoe: An Anthology of Uncollected Writings by Daniel Defoe. Curtis, Laura A., ed. (Illus.). 469p. 1979. 26.50x (ISBN 0-8476-6149-0). Rowman.
Defoe, Daniel & Knill, Harry. Pirates. Knill, Harry, ed. (Illus.). 64p. 1975. pap. 3.50 (ISBN 0-88388-027-X). Bellerophon Bks.
Defoe, Daniel see Swan, D. K.
Defoe, Louis V., ed. see Belasco, David.
Defoe, M., jt. ed. see George, B.
DeFoe, Mark. Bringing Home Breakfast, BW/4. new ed. Fleming, Harold, ed. (Black Willow Chapbook Ser.). (Illus.). 20p. (Orig.). 1982. pap. 3.00 (ISBN 0-910047-02-2). Black Willow.
Defoe, Mark, et al, eds. Laurel Review: A Literary Periodical. pap. text ed. 4.00 (ISBN 0-686-32950-3). W VA Wesleyan.
DeFoe, Martha, jt. ed. see George, B.
Defoggi, Ernest. Unlocking the Mystery of How the Mind Creates Time: An Engineer's Analysis. (Illus.). 1979. 8.95 (ISBN 0-9602372-1-6). E Defoggi.
DeFonblanque, Edward B. Political & Military Episodes in the Latter Half of the Eighteenth Century Derived from the Life & Correspondence of the Right Hon. John Burgoyne. LC 72-8667. (American Revolutionary Ser.). Repr. of 1879 ed. lib. bdg. 36.00x (ISBN 0-8398-0378-8). Irvington.
DeFontaine, F. G., ed. see Dickens, Charles.
De Fontbrune, Jean-Charles. Nostradamus 2: Into the Twenty-First Century. 1984. pap. 9.95 (ISBN 0-03-003678-X, Owl Bks). HR&W.
De Fontenay, Elisabeth. Diderot: Reason & Resonance. Mehlman, Jeffrey, tr. from Fr. LC 82-9649. 274p. 1982. 14.95 (ISBN 0-8076-1035-6). Braziller.
De Fontenelle, Maurice. The Early History of French Painting. (Illus.). 121p. 1981. 49.85 (ISBN 0-930582-93-4). Gloucester Art.
De Fontenelle Bernard Le, Bovier see Le Bovier De Fontenelle, Bernard.
De Fontgalland, Bernard. World Railway Systems. Hoskins, V., tr. 220p. 1984. 29.95 (ISBN 0-521-24541-9). Cambridge U Pr.
Deford, Frank. Alex: The Life of a Child. LC 83-47863. 224p. 1983. 13.95 (ISBN 0-670-11195-3). Viking.
--Alex: The Life of a Child. 1984. pap. 2.95 (ISBN 0-451-13198-3, Sig). NAL.
--Everybody's All-American. LC 81-65287. 324p. 1981. 13.95 (ISBN 0-670-30035-7). Viking.
--Lite Reading: The Lite Beer from Miller Commericial Scrapbook. (Illus.). 112p. 1984. pap. 6.95 (ISBN 0-14-006813-9). Penguin.
De Ford, Miriam A. They Were San Franciscans. facs. ed. LC 70-117781. (Essay Index Reprint Ser). 1941. 22.00 (ISBN 0-8369-1914-9). Ayer Co Pubs.
De Ford, Miriam A. & Jackson, Joan S., eds. Who Was When? 3rd ed. LC 76-2404. 184p. 1976. 38.00 (ISBN 0-8242-0532-4). Wilson.
DeFord, Sara & Lott, Clarinda H. Forms of Verse: British & American. LC 77-94257. (Illus.). 393p. (Orig.). 1971. 12.50 (ISBN 0-89197-169-6). Irvington.
--Forms of Verse, British & American. LC 77-94257. 393p. Repr. 15.00 (ISBN 0-390-26000-2, Pub. by Appleton-Century Crofts). New Poets.
De Ford, Sara, et al, eds. The Pearl. De Ford, Sara, et al, trs. LC 67-13376. (Crofts Classics Ser.). 1967. pap. text ed. 3.75x (ISBN 0-88295-003-7). Harlan Davidson.
De Ford, Tamara. Like It Is: From Voices of Today's Youth. Faville, Mary & Otero, Ray, eds. (Illus.). 205p. 1981. pap. text ed. 8.95 (ISBN 0-931908-06-X, Multi-Cultural). Sag Scriptory.
--We Are the Children. (Illus.). 1977. pap. text ed. 2.95 (ISBN 0-931908-00-0). Sag Scriptory.
--We Are the Children with Feelings We Don't Understand: Are We O. K.? Sanchez, Ray A., ed. (Illus.). 1978. pap. text ed. 7.95 (ISBN 0-931908-01-9, Multi-Cultural). Sag Scriptory.
De Forest, Elizabeth K. The Gardens & Grounds at Mount Vernon: How George Washington Planned & Planted Them. (Illus.). 116p. 1982. cloth 17.95x (ISBN 0-8139-0989-9, Pub. by Mt Vernon Ladies); pap. 8.95x (ISBN 0-8139-0988-0). U Pr of Va.
De Forest, Grant E. God in the American Schools: Religious Education in a Pluralistic Society. (Illus.). 1979. 49.50 (ISBN 0-89266-181-X). Am Classical Coll Pr.
De Forest, Izette. The Leaven of Love: A Development of the Psychoanalytic Theory & Technique of Sandor Ferenczi. LC 65-14585. pap. 56.00 (ISBN 0-317-10287-7, 2010213). Bks Demand UMI.
De Forest, J. W. Oriental Acquaintance: Letters from Syria. 1978. Repr. of 1856 ed. lib. bdg. 50.00 (ISBN 0-8495-1028-7). Arden Lib.
De Forest, John W. The Bloody Chasm. facsimile ed. LC 72-38011. (Black Heritage Library Collection). Repr. of 1881 ed. 17.50 (ISBN 0-8369-8979-1). Ayer Co Pubs.
--Collected Works, 17 vols. Incl. History of the Indians of Connecticut. 1851. Repr. 49.00x (ISBN 0-403-00426-8); Oriental Acquaintance. 1856. Repr. 39.00x (ISBN 0-403-04562-2); European Acquaintance. 1858. Repr. 39.00 (ISBN 0-403-04563-0); Seacliff. 1859. Repr. 39.00 (ISBN 0-403-04564-9). Somerset Pub; Miss Ravenel's Conversion from Secession to Loyalty. 1867. Repr. 29.00x (ISBN 0-403-03090-0); Overland. 1871. Repr. 18.00 (ISBN 0-403-04565-7); Kate Beaumont. 1872. Repr. 16.00x (ISBN 0-403-04566-5); The Wetherel Affair. 1873. Repr. 18.00 (ISBN 0-403-04567-3); Honest John Vane. 1875. Repr. 16.00x (ISBN 0-403-04568-1); Playing the Mischief. 1875. Repr. 16.00x (ISBN 0-403-04569-X); Justine's Lovers. 1878. Repr. 18.00 (ISBN 0-403-04570-3); Irene, the Missionary. 1879. Repr. 31.00 (ISBN 0-403-04571-1); The Bloody Chasm. 1881. Repr. 23.00 (ISBN 0-403-04572-X); A Lover's Revolt. 1898. Repr. 34.00 (ISBN 0-403-04573-8); The Deforests of Avesnes. 1900. Repr. 25.00 (ISBN 0-403-04574-6); The Downing Legends. 1901. Repr. 18.00 (ISBN 0-403-04575-4); Poems: Medley & Palestina. 1902. Repr. 18.00 (ISBN 0-403-04576-2). Set. 395.00 (ISBN 0-403-03455-8). Somerset Pub.
DeForest, John W. The Downing Legends-Stories in Rhyme. Incl. The Witch of Shiloh; The Last of the Wampanoags; The Gentle Earl; The Enchanted Voyage. 1901. 16.50x (ISBN 0-685-91097-0). Elliots Bks.
De Forest, John W. Honest John Vane. Rubin, Joseph J., ed. (Monument Edition Ser.). 22.50x (ISBN 0-271-00318-9). Pa St U Pr.
--Kate Beaumont. Rubin, Joseph J., ed. (Monument Edition Ser.). 22.50x (ISBN 0-271-00319-7). Pa St U Pr.
--Playing the Mischief. Rubin, Joseph J., ed. (Monument Edition Ser.). 22.50x (ISBN 0-271-00320-0). Pa St U Pr.
DeForest, John W. Poems: Medley & Palestina. 1902. 16.50x (ISBN 0-685-89770-2). Elliots Bks.
De Forest, John W. Union Officer in the Reconstruction. Potter, David M. & Croushore, James H., eds. LC 68-12523. xxx, 211p. 1968. Repr. of 1948 ed. 17.00 (ISBN 0-208-00097-6, Archon). Shoe String.
--Volunteer's Adventures: A Union Captain's Record of the Civil War. Croushore, James H., ed. (Illus.). xviii, 237p. 1970. Repr. of 1946 ed. 17.50 (ISBN 0-208-00951-5, Archon). Shoe String.
--Witching Times. Appel, Alfred, Jr., ed. (Masterworks of Literature Ser.). 1967. 10.95x (ISBN 0-8084-0332-X); pap. 7.95x (ISBN 0-8084-0333-8). New Coll U Pr.
DeForest, P. R. & Gaenssien, R. E. Forensic Science: An Introduction to Criminalistics. (McGraw-Hill Ser. in Criminology & Criminal Justice). (Illus.). 480p. 1983. 25.95 (ISBN 0-07-016267-0). McGraw.
DeForest, Robert W. & Veiller, Lawrence, eds. Tenement House Problem: Including the Report of the New York State Tenement House Commission of 1900, 2 Vols. in 1. LC 75-112537. (Rise of Urban America). (Illus.). 1970. Repr. of 1903 ed. 59.50 (ISBN 0-405-02446-0). Ayer Co Pubs.
DeForest, W. S. Photoresist: Materials & Processes. 1975. 46.50 (ISBN 0-07-016230-1). McGraw.
De Foret, Nancy C. Charon's Daughter. (Illus.). 1977. 12.50 (ISBN 0-87140-628-4); pap. 5.95 (ISBN 0-87140-116-9). Liveright.
De Fornaro, Carlo. Carranza & Mexico. 1976. lib. bdg. 59.95 (ISBN 0-87968-814-9). Gordon Pr.
DeForrest, Roland. The Wildon Affair. 256p. 1983. pap. 2.75 (ISBN 0-446-30207-4). Warner Bks.
De Forto, Rocco Z. Philosophy in Medicine, Science & Health: Subject Analysis Index with Reference Bibliography. LC 84-47864. 150p. 1985. 29.95 (ISBN 0-88164-402-1); pap. 21.95 (ISBN 0-88164-403-X). ABBE Pubs Assn.
DeFossard, Esta. Reading in Focus: Learning to Get the Message. 2nd ed. (gr. 9-12). 1985. pap. text ed. 8.95 wkbk. (ISBN 0-538-05660-6, E66). SW Pub.
De Fossard, Esta see Rinsky, Lee A. & Fossard, Esta de.
De Foucauld, Charles. Come, Let Us Sing a Song Unknown. 2.95 (ISBN 0-87193-080-3). Dimension Bks.
Defourneaux, Marcelin. Daily Life in Spain in the Golden Age. Branch, Newton, tr. (Illus.). 1971. 20.00x (ISBN 0-8047-1036-8); pap. 7.95 (ISBN 0-8047-1029-5, SP-153). Stanford U Pr.
De Fournival, Richard. Master Richard's "Bestiary of Love" & "Response". Beer, Jeanette, tr. Date not set. price not set. U of Cal Pr.
DeFoyer, Crispin. Christmas Games for Adults & Children. (Oleander Games & Pastimes Ser.: Vol. 7). (Illus.). 64p. 1982. 9.95 (ISBN 0-906672-08-2); pap. 4.95 (ISBN 0-906672-09-0). Oleander Pr.
De Fraga Frangipane, E., jt. auth. see Pearson, E. A.
Defrain, John, jt. auth. see LeMasters, E. E.
DeFrain, John D., et al. Coping with Sudden Infant Death. 128p. 1982. 18.00 (ISBN 0-669-05453-4); pap. 9.95 (ISBN 0-669-05583-2). Lexington Bks.
De France, Galeriede. Alechinsky a la Ligne. 1977. pap. 29.95 (ISBN 0-8120-0956-8). Barron.
Defrance, Henry. The Elements of Dowsing. (Illus.). 83p. 1979. pap. 6.50 (ISBN 0-7135-0246-0). Transatlantic.
De France, J. F., jt. ed. see Chronister, R. B.
DeFrance, J. J. Communications Electronics Circuits. 2nd ed. LC 71-187116. 1972. text ed. 37.95 (ISBN 0-03-083139-3, HoltC). HR&W.
--General Electronic Circuits. 2nd ed. LC 75-25718. 1976. text ed. 28.95 (ISBN 0-03-015481-2, HoltC). HR&W.
DeFrance, Jon F., ed. The Septal Nuclei. LC 76-43348. (Advances in Behavioral Biology Ser.: Vol. 20). 550p. 1976. 65.00x (ISBN 0-306-37920-1, Plenum Pr). Plenum Pub.
DeFrance, Joseph J. Electrical Fundamentals. 2nd ed. (Illus.). 672p. 1983. text ed. 37.95 (ISBN 0-13-247262-7). P-H.
De France, Marie. Medieval Fables. Beer, Jeanette, tr. (Illus.). 72p. 1983. 14.95 (ISBN 0-396-08169-X). Dodd.
De Francesco, Grete see Francesco, Grete de.
De Francia, Peter. Fernand Leger. LC 83-42878. (Illus.). 288p. 1983. 36.00x (ISBN 0-300-03067-3). Yale U Pr.
--Fernand Leger. 280p. 35.00 (ISBN 0-317-18843-7). Yale U Pr.
De Francia, Rubio J., jt. ed. see Peral, I.
De Francis, J. Colonialism & Language Policy in Vietnam. 1977. 19.00x (ISBN 90-279-7643-0). Mouton.
De Francis, J., compiled by. A Chinese-English Glossary of the Mathematical Sciences. 286p. (Chinese & Eng.). 1964. 42.20 (ISBN 0-8218-0018-3, UMI-2004670); pap. 37.20 members (ISBN 0-317-32956-1). Am Math.
DeFrancis, John. Advanced Chinese. (Illus.). 1967. text ed. 49.00x (ISBN 0-300-00406-0); pap. text ed. 19.95x (ISBN 0-300-00056-1). Yale U Pr.
--Advanced Chinese Reader. LC 68-8364. (Illus.). 1969. pap. text ed. 19.95x (ISBN 0-300-01083-4). Yale U Pr.
--Annotated Quotations from Chairman Mao. LC 74-20080. (Linguistic Ser). 336p. 1975. text ed. 31.00x (ISBN 0-300-01749-9). Yale U Pr.
--Beginning Chinese. 2nd, rev ed. LC 76-5099. (Yale Linguistic Ser.). 1976. text ed. 47.00x (ISBN 0-300-02054-6); pap. text ed. 12.95x (ISBN 0-300-02058-9). Yale U Pr.
--Beginning Chinese Reader, 2 pts. 2nd ed. LC 76-5103. 1977. Pt. I. text ed. 47.00x (ISBN 0-300-02056-2); Pt. II. 47.00x (ISBN 0-300-02057-0); Pts. I & II. pap. 15.95x vol. I (ISBN 0-300-02060-0); pap. 15.95x vol. 2 (ISBN 0-300-02061-9). Yale U Pr.
--Character Text for Advanced Chinese. (Illus.). 1966. pap. text ed. 21.95x (ISBN 0-300-00063-4). Yale U Pr.
--Character Text for Beginning Chinese. 2nd ed. LC 76-5105. 1976. text ed. 47.00x (ISBN 0-300-02055-4); pap. 13.95x (ISBN 0-300-02059-7). Yale U Pr.
--Character Text for Intermediate Chinese. (Illus.). 1965. pap. text ed. 18.95x (ISBN 0-300-00062-6). Yale U Pr.
--The Chinese Language: Fact & Fantasy. LC 84-8546. 342p. 1984. text ed. 20.00x (ISBN 0-8248-0866-5). UH Pr.
--Intermediate Chinese. 1964. pap. text ed. 18.95x (ISBN 0-300-00064-2). Yale U Pr.
De Francis, John. Nationalism & Language Reform in China. LC 74-187315. xii, 306p. 1972. Repr. of 1950 ed. lib. bdg. 24.00x (ISBN 0-374-92095-8). Octagon.
DeFrancis, John. Things Japanese in Hawaii. (Illus.). 224p. 1973. pap. 9.50 (ISBN 0-8248-0233-0). UH Pr.
DeFrancis, John, ed. Supplementary Readers for Intermediate Chinese Reader, 5 vols. Incl. Vol. 1. The White Haired Girl. Chi-Yu Ho (ISBN 0-88710-116-X); Vol. 2. Red Detachment of Women. Chi-Yu Ho (ISBN 0-88710-117-8); Vol. 3. Episodes from Dream of the Red Chamber. Li, Louise H (ISBN 0-88710-118-6); Vol. 4. Sun Yat-sen. Yung Teng Chia-Yee; Vol. 5. Wu Sung Kills a Tiger. Yung Teng Chia-Yee. 1976. 3.00 ea. (ISBN 0-88710-120-8). Far Eastern Pubns.
DeFrancis, John, ed. see Lindell, Kristina.
DeFrancis, John, ed. see Yee, Dennis K.
DeFrancis, John, ed. see Yung, Teng C.
De Francis, John, tr. see Ma, Ho-t'ien.
DeFrancis, John, et al. Intermediate Chinese Reader, 2 Pts. Pt. 1. pap. 19.95x (ISBN 0-300-00065-0); Pt. 2. pap. text ed. 19.95x (ISBN 0-300-00066-9). Yale U Pr.
DeFrancis, John, jt. auth. see Liang, James C.
De Francis, John F. Chinese-English Glossary of the Mathematical Sciences. LC 64-16997. pap. 71.50 (ISBN 0-317-08625-1, 2004670). Bks Demand UMI.

De Francisco, Cesar P., ed. see World Congress of Psychiatry, 6th, Honolulu, Hawaii, August-September 1977.

De Franco, Ellen B. Learning Activities for Preschool Children. LC 74-29661. 128p. 1975. pap. 6.95 (ISBN 0-913420-50-6). Olympus Pub Co.

DeFranco, Ellen B. TV On-Off: Better Family Use of Television. 1980. pap. 9.95 (ISBN 0-673-16453-5). Scott F.

DeFrees, Madeline. Magpie on the Gallows. 96p. 1982. 12.00 (ISBN 0-914742-66-3); pap. 6.00 (ISBN 0-914742-65-5). Copper Canyon.

--When Sky Lets Go. LC 76-55838. (Braziller Series of Poetry). 1978. 6.95 (ISBN 0-8076-0844-0); pap. 3.95 (ISBN 0-8076-0845-9). Braziller.

De Freine, Sean. The Great Silence. abr. ed. 128p. 1978. pap. 4.95 (ISBN 0-85342-516-7, Pub. by Mercier Pr Ireland). Irish Bks Media.

De Freitas, A. Falcao see World Congress on Ballistocardiography & Cardiovascular Dynamics, 2nd, Oporto, 1969.

De Freitas, M. H., jt. auth. see Blyth, F. G.

Defreitas, M. H., jt. auth. see Blyth, F. G.

DeFreitas', Stan. Stan DeFreitas Complete Guide to Florida Gardening. (Illus.). 384p. 1984. 19.95 (ISBN 0-87833-341-X). Taylor Pub.

Defremery, C. & Sanguinetti, B. R. The Travels of Ibn Buttuta, 1325-1354, Vol. 3. Gibb, H. A. R., ed. 232p. 1971. 30.00x (ISBN 0-686-79461-3, Pub. by Hakluyt Soc England). State Mutual Bk.

Defremery, C., tr. see Gibb, H. A.

Defremery, G., tr. see Batoutah, Ibn.

Defries, Amelia D. Pioneers of Science. facs. ed. LC 74-117782. (Essay Index Reprint Ser). 1928. 17.00 (ISBN 0-8369-1646-8). Ayer Co Pubs.

Defries, Esther P. Browning Primer. LC 70-103182. 1970. Repr. of 1892 ed. 19.50x (ISBN 0-8046-0819-9, Pub. by Kennikat). Assoc Faculty Pr.

--A Browning Primer. 1979. Repr. of 1892 ed. lib. bdg. 15.00 (ISBN 0-8492-0694-4). R West.

--A Browning Primer: Being a Companion to the Pocket-Volume of Selections from the Poetical Works of Robet Browning. 1978. Repr. of 1893 ed. lib. bdg. 12.50 (ISBN 0-8495-1010-4). Arden Lib.

DeFries, J. C., jt. auth. see McClearn, G. E.

De Fries, Lewis. The Sunday Express Book of European Holidays. (Illus.). 202p. 1985. pap. 7.95 (ISBN 0-86072-076-4, Pub. by Quartet Bks). Merrimack Pub Cir.

DeFries, Zira, et al, eds. Sexuality: New Perspectives. LC 84-28991. (Contributions in Psychology Ser.: No. 6). (Illus.). 448p. 1985. lib. bdg. 45.00 (ISBN 0-313-24207-0, DFS/). Greenwood.

DeFriese, Gordon H. & Barker, Ben D., eds. Assessing Dental Manpower Requirements: Alternative Approaches for State & Local Planning. LC 82-11383. 184p. 1982. prof ref 25.00 (ISBN 0-88410-746-9). Ballinger Pub.

De Froe, A. Laurence Sterne & His Novels Studied in the Light of Modern Psychology. LC 72-193729. lib. bdg. 35.00 (ISBN 0-8414-2451-9). Folcroft.

De Froment, Diana. Art at Auction Nineteen Seventy-Eight to Nineteen Seventy-Nine: Two Hundred & Forty-Fifth Season. (Illus.). 496p. 1979. 45.00 (ISBN 0-85667-063-4, Pub. by Sotheby Pubns England). Biblio Dist.

De Froment, Diana & Lewis, Lynn, eds. Art at Auction: The Year at Sotheby Parke Bernet - 1977-78. (Illus.). 496p. 1978. 45.00x (ISBN 0-85667-049-9, Pub. by Sotheby Pubns England). Biblio Dist.

Defromont, Hubert J. Les Constructions Perfectives Du Verbe Anglais Contemporain: Etude Comparee De L'aspect Transcendant Dans les Systemes Verbaux Anglais & Francais. (Janua Linguarum, Series Practica: No. 185). 1973. pap. 20.80 (ISBN 0-686-21259-2). Mouton.

De Frost, Elizabeth K. The Gardens & Grounds at Mount Vernon: How George Washington Planned & Planted Them. (Illus.). 116p. 15.00 (ISBN 0-318-01685-0); pap. 6.00 (ISBN 0-318-01686-9). Mt Vernon Ladies.

Deftos, L. J. Medullary Thyroid Carcinoma. (Beitraege zur Onkologie. Contributions to Oncology: Vol. 17). (Illus.). x, 114p. 1983. pap. 35.50 (ISBN 3-8055-3703-4). S Karger.

De Funiak, William Q. & Vaughn, Michael J. Principles of Community Property. 2nd ed. LC 72-101099. pap. 143.80 (ISBN 0-317-28651-X, 2055347). Bks Demand UMI.

De Fusco, Renato. Le Corbusier, Designer--Furniture, 1929. LC 77-81368. 1977. 19.95 (ISBN 0-8120-5148-3). Barron.

De Gaeger, Charles. The Linz File: The Plunder of Europe's Art. 240p. 1981. 29.50x (ISBN 0-906671-30-2, Pub. by Webb & Bower). State Mutual Bk.

Degaeta, Paul F. They Only Played Cards. 160p. 1982. 7.95 (ISBN 0-89962-262-3). Todd & Honeywell.

De Gaetano, Giovanni & Garattini, Silvio, eds. Platelets: A Multidisciplinary Approach. LC 78-66352. (Monographs of the Mario Negri Institute for Pharmacological Research). 501p. 1978. 62.50 (ISBN 0-89004-252-7). Raven.

DeGaetano, Jean. Speech Improvement Duplicating Masters, 2 vols. 1973. Set 1. text ed. 10.95x (ISBN 0-8134-1124-6). Set 3. text ed. 10.95x (ISBN 0-8134-1537-3). Interstate.

DeGaetano, Jean G. Articulation-Language Development: Games from B to Z. 1985. text ed. write for info. (ISBN 0-8134-2495-X, 2495). Interstate.

De Galan, L. Analytical Spectrometry. (Illus.). 1981. text ed. 37.50 (ISBN 0-9960017-1-9, Pub. by A Hilger England). Heyden.

De Galba, Marti J., jt. auth. see Martorell, Joanot.

De Galiana Mingot, Tomas see Mingot, Tomas De Galiana.

De Galinanes, Maria T. B. see Universidad de Puerto Rico, Centro de Investigaciones Sociales.

DeGalindez, Jesus see Ireland, Gordon & Galindez, Jesus de.

De Galindez, Suarez J. The Era of Trujillo: Dominican Dictator. LC 72-79292. pap. 81.50 (ISBN 0-317-28617-X, 2055403). Bks Demand UMI.

De Galvez, Bernardo. Diario. 52p. 1966. pap. 5.00 (ISBN 0-686-70401-0). South Pass Pr.

--Instructions for Governing the Interior Provinces of New Spain, 1786. Worcester, Donald E., ed. LC 67-24723. (Quivira Society Publications, Vol. 12). 1967. Repr. of 1951 ed. 17.00 (ISBN 0-405-00086-3). Ayer Co Pubs.

De Galway, Alberic. Assess Your Chess Fast. 1978. (Pub. by Batsford England); pap. 12.95 (ISBN 0-7134-1056-6). David & Charles.

De Gamboa, Pedro S. History of the Incas. Markham, Clements, ed. Bd. with Execution of the Inca Tupac Amaru, 1571. De Ocampo, Baltaser. 1610; Supplement: A Narrative of the Vice-Regal Embassy to Vilcabamba, 1571, & of the Execution of the Inca Tupac Amaru, December, 1571. De Oviedo, Gabriel. 1573. (Hakluyt Society Works Ser.: No. 2, Vol. 22). (Illus.). Repr. of 1907 ed. 42.00 (ISBN 0-317-15714-0). Kraus Repr.

De Gamboa, Pedro Sarmiento see Sarmiento De Gamboa, Pedro.

De Gamez, Tana. Alicia Alonso: At Home & Abroad. 1970. 10.00 (ISBN 0-8065-0218-5). Citadel Pr.

Deganawidah. Ranger's Guide to Useful Plants of Eastern Wilds. (Illus.). 1964. 3.95 (ISBN 0-8158-0086-X). Chris Mass.

De Gandavo P. De, Magalhaes see De Magalhaes De Gandavo, P.

Deganello, G. Transition Metal Complexes of Cyclic Polyolefins. (Organometallic Chemistry Ser.). 1979. 99.50 (ISBN 0-12-207950-7). Acad Pr.

De Gange, Susan see Verniero, Joan.

DeGange, Susan & Verniero, Joan, eds. Food & Beverage Market Research Report. 117p. (Orig.). 1984. pap. text ed. 95.00 (ISBN 0-931634-39-3). FIND-SVP.

DeGange, Susan, jt. ed. see Verniero, Joan.

Degani, Meir H. Astronomy Made Simple. rev. ed. LC 76-2836. (Made Simple Ser.). 224p. 1976. pap. 4.95 (ISBN 0-385-08854-X). Doubleday.

Degano, Jack. A Call to Ministry: Reflections on Lay Volunteer Ministries. 72p. 1981. 4.00 (ISBN 0-318-14585-5). Intl Liaison.

Degano, P. & Sandewall, E., eds. Integrated Interactive Computing Systems. 374p. 1983. 51.00 (ISBN 0-444-86595-0, I-176-83, North Holland). Elsevier.

De Garay, Alfonso L., et al, eds. Genetic & Anthropological Studies of Olympic Athletes. 1974. 45.00 (ISBN 0-12-208650-3). Acad Pr.

De Garcia, Carmen I. Raffucci see Raffucci de Garcia, Carmen I.

De Garcia Diaz, Eva S. see Diaz, Eva S.

De Garis, James. The Lemonade River. 1982. 5.95 (ISBN 0-533-05093-6). Vantage.

DeGaris, Roger, tr. see Bulychev, Kirill.

DeGaris, Roger, tr. see Gakov, Vladimir.

DeGaris, Roger, tr. see Strugatsky, Arkady & Strugatsky, Boris.

De Garmo, Charles. Herbart & Herbartism. Brickman, William W., ed. LC 79-12853. (Educational Ser.). Repr. of 1895 ed. 25.00. Folcroft.

--Herbart & the Herbartians. 1979. Repr. of 1896 ed. lib. bdg. 30.00 (ISBN 0-8414-1894-2). Folcroft.

DeGarmo, E. Paul & Kohser, Ronald A. Materials & Processes in Manufacturing. 6th ed. (Illus.). 1024p. 1984. text ed. write for info. (ISBN 0-02-328620-2). Macmillan.

DeGarmo, E. Paul & Sullivan, William. Engineering Economy. 7th ed. (Illus.). 600p. 1984. text ed. write for info. (ISBN 0-02-328600-8). Macmillan.

DeGarsault, F. A. The Art of the Tennis-Racket-Maker & of Tennis. Leftwich, Catherine W., tr. LC 77-93557. (Illus.). 1977. Repr. 25.00x (ISBN 0-685-87124-X). Racquet Sports.

Degas, Hilaire. Drawings of Degas. Longstreet, Stephen, ed. (Master Draughtsman Ser). (Illus., Orig.). treasure trove bdg. 9.95x (ISBN 0-87505-005-0); pap. 4.95 (ISBN 0-87505-158-8). Borden.

Degas, Hilaire G. Drawings. (Illus.). 1974. pap. 5.95 (ISBN 0-486-21233-5). Dover.

--My Friend Degas. Curtiss, Mina, ed. LC 64-22375. (Illus.). pap. 34.50 (ISBN 0-317-10028-9, 2005236). Bks Demand UMI.

De Gasparin, Agenor. Uprising of a Great People: The United States in 1861 to Which Is Added a Word of Peace Between England & the United States. facsimile ed. Booth, Mary L., tr. LC 75-95066. (Select Bibliographies Reprint Ser). 1861. 27.50 (ISBN 0-8369-5068-2). Ayer Co Pubs.

De Gaspe Philippe, J. Aubert see Aubert De Gaspe, Philippe J.

Degasperis, A., jt. auth. see Calogero, F.

De Gast, Robert. The Lighthouses of the Chesapeake. LC 73-8216. pap. 46.00 (ISBN 0-317-29786-4, 2017030). Bks Demand UMI.

--Western Wind, Eastern Shore: A Sailing Cruise around the Eastern Shore of Maryland, Delaware & Virginia. LC 75-10924. (Illus.). 192p. 1975. 14.95 (ISBN 0-8018-1767-6). Johns Hopkins.

De Gasztold, Carmen B. Creature's Choir. (Illus., Fr.). (gr. 3-8). 14.95 (ISBN 0-685-11121-0). French & Eur.

--Prayers from the Ark. (Fr.). (gr. 3-8). 14.95 (ISBN 0-685-11511-9). French & Eur.

--Prayers from the Ark & the Creatures' Choir. Godden, Rumer, tr. (Poets Ser.). 1976. pap. 4.95 (ISBN 0-14-042200-5). Penguin.

De Gaulle, Charles. The Army of the Future. LC 74-5925. 1976. Repr. of 1941 ed. lib. bdg. 22.50x (ISBN 0-8371-7525-9, GAAF). Greenwood.

--The Complete War Memoirs of Charles de Gaulle: 1940-1946. Howard, Richard, tr. from Fr. (Quality Paperbacks Ser.). 1048p. 1984. pap. 14.95 (ISBN 0-306-80227-9). Da Capo.

--La Discorde Chez l'Ennemi. 1973. 3.95 (ISBN 0-686-55604-6). French & Eur.

--Discours et Messages, 5 tomes. Incl. Tome I. Pendant la Guerre (Juin 1940-Janv. 1946; Tome II. Dans L'attente (Fev. 46-Avr. 58; Tome III. Vers le Renouveau (Mai 58-Juill. 62; Tome IV. Pour l'Effort (Aout 62-Dec. 65; Tome V. Vers le Terme (Jano. 66-Avril 69. 24.50 ea. French & Eur.

--The Edge of the Sword. LC 75-26731. 128p. 1975. Repr. of 1960 ed. lib. bdg. 22.50x (ISBN 0-8371-8366-9, GAES). Greenwood.

--Le Fil De L'epee. 1961. 14.95 (ISBN 0-685-11184-9). French & Eur.

--La France et Son Armee. 14.95 (ISBN 0-685-34131-3). French & Eur.

--Memoires de Guerre, 3 tomes. Incl. Tome I. L' Appel (1940-1942; Tome II. L' Unite (1942-1944; Tome III. Le Salut (1944-1946. (Fr.). 1954-61. 27.50 ea. French & Eur.

--Memoires d'Espoir, 2 tomes. Incl. Tome I. Le Renouveau 1958-1962; Tome II. L' Effort (1962. 11.95 ea. French & Eur.

De Gaultier, Jules. Bovarysm. Spring, Geraldm., tr. LC 72-109168. 1970. 8.75 (ISBN 0-8022-2314-1). Philos Lib.

--From Kant to Nietzsche. facs. ed. LC 70-134080. (Essay Index Reprint Ser.). 1961. 19.00 (ISBN 0-8369-2157-7). Ayer Co Pubs.

--From Kant to Nietzsche. LC 60-13643. 1961. 4.75 (ISBN 0-8022-1625-0). Philos Lib.

De Gaury, Gerald. Rulers of Mecca. LC 78-63458. (Pilgrimages Ser.). (Illus.). 1982. Repr. of 1954 ed. 34.50 (ISBN 0-404-16517-6). AMS Pr.

De Gaury, Gerald & Winstone, H. V. The Spirit of the East. 17.50 (ISBN 0-7043-2230-7, Pub. by Quartet England). Charles River Bks.

DeGaury, Gerald & Winstone, H. V., eds. Spirit of the East. 240p. (Orig.). 1984. pap. 9.95 (ISBN 0-7043-3447-X, Pub. by Quartet Bks). Merrimack Pub Cir.

De Gautel, Beatrice see Carillon, Annie & Goutel, Beatrice de.

De Gaviria, Maria C., ed. see National Library of Peru.

De Gayangos, Don Pascual. Catalogue of the Manuscripts in the Spanish Language in the British Museum, 4 vols. 2821p. 1981. 275.00x set (ISBN 0-686-72038-5, Pub. by Brit Lib England). State Mutual Bk.

De Gayangos, P., tr. see Al-Maqqari, Ahmed.

De Gayangos, Pascual, tr. see Cortes, Hernando.

De G. Davies, N. The Rock Tombs of El Amarna, Pt. VI. 1975. 99.00x (ISBN 0-85698-050-1, Pub. by Egypt Exploration). State Mutual Bk.

Degeest, Achille. Saint Joseph Commentary on the Sunday Readings, 3 vols. 3.95 ea. Year A (341/04). Year B (342/04). Year C (343/04). Catholic Bk Pub.

De Geigel, Alma S. see Handschuh, Jeanne & Simounet de Geigel, Alma.

De Geijer, W., tr. see Ducros, Louis.

De Gelder, Beatrice, ed. Knowledge & Representation. (International Library of Psychology). 190p. 1982. 31.95x (ISBN 0-7100-0922-4). Routledge & Kegan.

Degelius, Gunnar. The Lichen Flora of the Island of Vega in Nordland, Northern Norway. (Acta Regiae Societatis Scientiarum et Litterarum Gothoburgensis, Botanica Ser.: No. 2). 127p. 1982. pap. text ed. 17.50x (ISBN 91-85252-30-1, Pub. by Acta Universitatis Sweden). Humanities.

Degen, Bruce. Aunt Possum & the Pumpkin Man. LC 76-58685. (Illus.). (ps-1). 1977. PLB 9.89 (ISBN 0-06-021413-9). HarpJ.

--Jamberry. LC 82-47708. (Illus.). 32p. (ps-1). 1983. 7.64i (ISBN 0-06-021416-3); PLB 9.89g (ISBN 0-06-021417-1). HarpJ.

--Jamberry. LC 82-47708. (Trophy Picture Bk.). (Illus.). 32p. (ps-1). 1985. pap. 2.84i (ISBN 0-06-443068-5, Trophy). HarpJ.

--The Little Witch & the Riddle. LC 78-19475. (I Can Read Bk.). (Illus.). 64p. (gr. k-3). 1980. PLB 9.89 (ISBN 0-06-021415-5). HarpJ.

Degen, Clara, jt. ed. see Stearns, Betty.

Degen, H. & Cox, Raymond P., eds. Gas Enzymology. 1985. lib. bdg. 44.00 (ISBN 90-277-1900-4, Pub. by Reidel Holland). Kluwer Academic.

Degen, Marie L. The History of the Woman's Peace Party. LC 78-64176. (Johns Hopkins University. Studies in the Social Sciences. Fifty-Seventh Ser. 1939: 3). Repr. of 1939 ed. 24.00 (ISBN 0-404-61285-7). AMS Pr.

--The History of the Woman's Peace Party. LC 72-81980. (John Hopkins Studies in Hist. & Pol. Sci. Ser.: No. 57, No. 3). 268p. 1974. Repr. of 1939 ed. lib. bdg. 21.00 (ISBN 0-8337-5275-8). B Franklin.

--History of the Women's Peace Party. LC 76-147442. (Library of War & Peace; Histories of the Organized Peace Movement). 1972. lib. bdg. 46.00 (ISBN 0-8240-0232-6). Garland Pub.

Degen, Paula, jt. auth. see Wescott, Lynanne.

Degen, R. & Neidermeyer, E., eds. Epilepsy, Sleep & Sleep Deprivation. 380p. 1985. 85.25 (ISBN 0-444-80521-4, I-163-84). Elsevier.

Degenhard, William. The Regulators. 598p. 1981. pap. 11.95 (ISBN 0-933256-23-X). Second Chance.

--The Regulators. LC 80-54849. 598p. 1981. Repr. of 1943 ed. 22.50 (ISBN 0-933256-22-1). Second Chance.

Degenhardt, Alan J., jt. ed. see Degenhardt, Henry W.

Degenhardt, Henry W. Treaties & Alliances of the World. 3rd ed. 409p. 1981. 85.00x (ISBN 0-8103-1602-1, Pub. by Longman). Gale.

Degenhardt, Henry W. & Degenhardt, Alan J., eds. Political Dissent: An International Guide to Dissident, Extra-Parliamentary, Guerrila & Illegal Political Movements. 600p. 1983. 90.00x (ISBN 0-8103-2050-9, Pub. by Longman). Gale.

Degenhardt, Henry W., jt. ed. see Day, Alan J.

Degenhardt, M. A. Education & the Value of Knowledge. (Introductory Series in Philosophy of Education). 128p. 1982. pap. text ed. 7.50x (ISBN 0-04-370116-7). Allen Unwin.

Degenhardt, Richard. Belleek. (Illus.). 210p. 1982. 25.00 (ISBN 0-942620-03-8). Portfolio Pr.

Degenhart, Bernhard & Schmitt, Annegrit. Jacopo Bellini: The Louvre Album of Drawings. Mecklenburg, Frank, tr. from Ger. LC 84-12355. (Illus.). 204p. 1984. 80.00 (ISBN 0-8076-1097-6). Braziller.

Degenhart, Karen. The Birth of Poet. 1983. pap. 3.95 (ISBN 0-916337-00-6). New Vision.

--Dark Night Where Angels Tread. (Illus.). 76p. (Orig.). 1979. pap. text ed. 3.95x (ISBN 0-916337-01-4). New Vision.

Degenhart, Laura, jt. auth. see Dahl, Patricia.

Degenkolb, Oris H. Concrete Box Girder Bridges. (Monograph No. 10). 1977. 29.25 (ISBN 0-685-85763-8) (ISBN 0-685-85764-6). ACI.

--Concrete Box Girder Bridges. (American Concrete Institute Monograph Ser: No. 10). (Illus.). 106p. 1977. text ed. 14.50x (ISBN 0-8138-1815-X). Iowa St U Pr.

De Gennaro, Angelo A. Philosophy of Benedetto Croce, an Introduction. LC 69-10084. Repr. of 1961 ed. lib. bdg. 15.00x (ISBN 0-8371-0058-5, DEBC). Greenwood.

DeGennaro, Angelo A., tr. see Croce, Benedetto.

De Gennes, J. L., et al, eds. Latent Dyslipoproteinemias & Atherosclerosis. 334p. 1984. text ed. 51.50 (ISBN 0-89004-306-X). Raven.

De Gennes, Pierre-Gilles. Scaling Concepts in Polymer Physics. LC 78-21314. 319p. 1979. 59.50x (ISBN 0-8014-1203-X). Cornell U Pr.

Degens, E. T., et al. Inorganic Biochemistry. LC 76-2616. (Topics in Current Chemistry: Vol. 64). 1976. 40.00 (ISBN 0-387-07636-0). Springer-Verlag.

Degens, T. Friends. 160p. (gr. 7 up). 1981. 9.95 (ISBN 0-670-33051-5). Viking.

--The Game on Thatcher Island. LC 77-24166. 160p. (gr. 7 up). 1977. 7.95 (ISBN 0-670-33393-X). Viking.

--Transport Seven-Forty One-R. 176p. (gr. 7 up). 1974. 11.50 (ISBN 0-670-72429-7). Viking.

--The Visit. LC 82-2600. 168p. (gr. 7 up). 1982. 10.95 (ISBN 0-670-74712-2). Viking.

Degenshein, Joan & Stern, Naomi M. Successful Cosmetic Selling. rev. ed. LC 71-144088. (Chain Store Age Bks.). (Illus.). 1978. pap. 14.95 (ISBN 0-86730-403-0). Lebhar Friedman.

De George, Frances V., jt. auth. see Osborne, Richard H.

DeGeorge, James, jt. auth. see Olson, Gary.

DeGeorge, R. T. Classical & Contemporary Metaphysics: A Source Book. 332p. 1962. 18.50 (ISBN 0-03-011310-5). Krieger.

De George, R. T. & Scanlan, J. P., eds. Marxism & Religion in Eastern Europe. LC 75-33051. (Sovietica Ser: No. 36). 180p. 1976. lib. bdg. 39.50 (ISBN 90-277-0636-0, Pub. by Reidel Holland). Kluwer Academic.

De George, Richard T. Business Ethics. 1982. text ed. write for info. (ISBN 0-02-328000-X). Macmillan.

--Business Ethics. 2nd ed. 714p. 1986. pap. price not set (ISBN 0-02-328010-7). Macmillan.

--The Nature & Limits of Authority. LC 85-8128. 320p. 1985. 27.50x (ISBN 0-7006-0269-0); pap. text ed. 12.95x (ISBN 0-7006-0270-4). U Pr of KS.

--Patterns of Soviet Thought: The Origins & Development of Dialectical & Historical Materialism. LC 66-17026. (Ann Arbor Paperbacks Ser.: No. AA-160). pap. 77.00 (ISBN 0-317-09962-0, 2051056). Bks Demand UMI.

DeGeorge, Richard T. The Philosopher's Guide to Sources, Research Tools, Professional Life, and Related Fields. LC 79-91437. 220p. 1980. 22.50x (ISBN 0-7006-0200-3). U Pr of KS.

De George, Richard T., ed. Semiotic Themes. (University of Kansas Humanistic Studies: No. 53). (Illus.). 284p. 1981. pap. 12.00 (ISBN 0-686-28731-2). U of KS Pubns.

DeGeorge, Richard T. & Pichler, Joseph A., eds. Ethics, Free Enterprise, & Public Policy: Original Essays on Moral Issues in Business. 1978. pap. text ed. 9.95x (ISBN 0-19-502425-7). Oxford U Pr.

Degerbol, Magnus. Zoology I: Mammals. LC 74-20244. (Thule Expedition, 5th, 1921-24: Vol. 2, Pts. 4-5). (Illus.). 1976. Repr. of 1935 ed. 57.50 (ISBN 0-404-58309-1). AMS Pr.

De Gerez, Toni see Gerez, Toni de.

Degering, Etta. Gallaudet: Friend of the Deaf. LC 79-83923. xiv, 178p. (gr. 7 up). 1982. pap. 5.95 (ISBN 0-913580-84-8). Gallaudet Coll.

Degering, Etta B. Once Upon a Bible Time. Van Dolson, Bobbie J., ed. LC 76-14118. (Illus.). (gr. k-3). 1976. 7.95 (ISBN 0-8280-0052-2). Review & Herald.

Degering, F., ed. Organic Chemistry. 6th ed. 1965. pap. 5.50x (ISBN 0-06-460006-8, CO 7000, COS). B&N NY.

Degering, Hermann. Lettering: Modes of Writing in Western Europe. 1978. pap. 8.95 (ISBN 0-8008-4727-X, Pentalic). Taplinger.

Degering, Klaus. Defoes Gesellschaftsknzeption. (Bochum Studies in English: No. 5). (Illus.). 512p. (Orig., Ger.). 1977. pap. 28.00x (ISBN 90-6032-079-4). Benjamins North Am.

Degeste, Beatrix Chanson. The Romance of the Chevelere Assigne. Aldenham, Lord, ed. (EETS, ES Ser.: No. 6). pap. 12.00 (ISBN 0-527-00221-6). Kraus Repr.

De Geus, Leonard F. Job Seeker's Guide: Getting Yours & Making It in the 80's, Your Way, 2 Vols. (Orig.). 1984. 25.00 set (ISBN 0-916541-00-2); Vol. 1, Merchandising Your Job Talents, 67 pgs. pap. text ed. 15.00 (ISBN 0-916541-01-0); Vol. 2, The Perfect InFlation Hedge: Your Own Business!, 59 pgs. pap. text ed. 15.00 (ISBN 0-916541-02-9). Woods Creek Pr.

De Geus, Leonard F., ed. see Bibb, Benjamin O.

Degge, Rogena M., jt. auth. see McFee, June K.

Degh, Linda. People in the Tobacco Belt: Four Lives. Dorson, Richard M., ed. LC 80-792. (Folklore of the World Ser.). (Illus.). 1980. Repr. of 1975 ed. lib. bdg. 28.50x (ISBN 0-405-13331-6). Ayer Co Pubs.

Degh, Linda, ed. Folktales of Hungary. Halasz, Judit, tr. LC 64-19846. (Folktales of the World Ser). 1965. 14.00x (ISBN 0-226-14023-7); pap. 6.95x (ISBN 0-226-14024-5, FW6). U of Chicago Pr.

--Indiana Folklore: A Reader. LC 79-2970. (Midland Bks.: No. 239). (Illus.). 320p. 1980. 20.00x (ISBN 0-253-10986-8); pap. 7.95x (ISBN 0-253-20239-6). Ind U Pr.

--Studies in East European Folk Narrative. (AFS Biblographic & Special Ser.: No. 30). 696p. 1978. 25.00x (ISBN 0-292-77544-X). U of Tex Pr.

Deghan, Bijan & Webster, Grady L. Morphology & Infrageneric Relationships of the Genus "Jatropha" (Euphorbiaceae) LC 77-83116. (Publications in Botany Ser.: Vol. 74). 1979. 17.50x (ISBN 0-520-09585-5). U of Cal Pr.

De Ghelderode, Michel see Ghelderode, Michel De.

Deghy, Guy. Cafe Royal: Ninety Years of Bohemia. LC 79-8061. Repr. of 1955 ed. 25.00 (ISBN 0-404-18372-7). AMS Pr.

DeGiacomo, F. P. Chiropractic Analysis Through Palpation. McDonnell, James, ed. (Illus.). 192p. 1980. 15.00 (ISBN 0-938470-00-0). NY Chiro Coll.

DeGidio, Sandra. R. C. I. A: The Rites Revisited. 144p. (Orig.). 1984. pap. 7.95 (ISBN 0-86683-837-6, 8436). Winston Pr.

De Gidio, Sandra. Re-Treat Your Family to Lent. 50p. (Orig.). 1983. pap. text ed. 1.95 (ISBN 0-86716-022-5). St Anthony Mess Pr.

De Giorgio, A., ed. see IFAC Symposium, Bari, Italy, May 1979.

Degiorgio, V. & Corti, M., eds. Physics of Amphiphiles: Micelles, Vesicles & Microemulsions: Proceedings of the International School of Physics, Enrico Fermi Course XC, Varenna, Italy, 19-29 July, 1983. 900p. 1985. 148.25 (ISBN 0-444-86940-9, North-Holland). Elsevier.

Degiorgio, V., et al, eds. Light Scattering in Liquids & Macromolecular Solutions. LC 80-20472. 305p. 1980. 49.50x (ISBN 0-306-40558-X, Plenum Pr). Plenum Pub.

De Girardin, Emile, jt. auth. see Blanqui, Jerome A.

DeGivry, Grillot. Witchcraft, Magic & Alchemy. lib. bdg. 95.00 (ISBN 0-87968-515-8). Krishna Pr.

De Givry, Grillot see Givry, Grillot De.

Degler, Carl. The Other South: Southern Dissenters in the Nineteenth Century. LC 82-14429. 392p. 1982. text ed. 24.95X (ISBN 0-930350-33-2); pap. text ed. 9.95x (ISBN 0-930350-34-0). NE U Pr.

Degler, Carl, ed. see Gilman, Charlotte P.

Degler, Carl N. Affluence & Anxiety: America since Nineteen Forty-Five. 2nd ed. 210p. 1975. pap. 10.80 (ISBN 0-673-07956-2). Scott F.

--The Age of the Economic Revolution: 1876-1900. 2nd ed. 1977. pap. 10.80 (ISBN 0-673-07967-8). Scott F.

--At Odds: Women & the Family in America, from the Revolution to the Present. 1980. 29.95x (ISBN 0-19-502657-8). Oxford U Pr.

--At Odds: Women & the Family in America from the Revolution to the Present. 1980. pap. 11.95 (ISBN 0-19-502934-8, GB 645, GB). Oxford U Pr.

--Out of Our Past: The Forces That Shaped Modern America. 3rd. ed. LC 83-48021. 1984. pap. 9.95xi (ISBN 0-06-131985-6, TB1985, Torch). Har-Row.

--Place Over Time: The Continuity of Southern Distinctiveness. LC 77-586. (Walter Lynwood Fleming Lectures in Southern History Ser.). 1977. 12.95x (ISBN 0-8071-0299-7); pap. 5.95x. La State U Pr.

Degler, Carl N., ed. The New Deal. LC 73-78319. (New York Times Bks.). 239p. Date not set. pap. text ed. 8.95x (ISBN 0-317-30664-2). Wiener Pub Inc.

Degler, Carl N., ed. see Gilman, Charlotte P.

Degler, Carl N., ed. see Potter, David M.

Degler, Carl N., et al. The Democratic Experience, 3 vols. 5th ed. 1981. pap. 20.60x (ISBN 0-673-15450-5); Vol. 1. pap. text ed. 14.10x (ISBN 0-673-15451-3); Vol. 2. pap. text ed. 14.10x (ISBN 0-673-15452-1). Scott F.

Degler, Lois. Man & God. LC 74-28943. (Illus.). 1975. pap. 3.00 (ISBN 0-930422-04-X). Dennis-Landman.

Degli Antelminelli, F. Castracane see Castracane Degli Antelminelli, F.

Degnan, Colleen. Building Competency in Two-Three Word Verbs. (Illus.). 128p. 1986. pap. text ed. 10.95 (ISBN 0-13-086018-2). P-H.

De Gobineau, A. de see Gobineau, A. de.

De Gobineau, Arthur. Inequality of the Races. 1966. pap. 5.00 (ISBN 0-911038-02-7). Noontide.

--The Pleiads. Scanlan, J. F., tr. from Fr. 359p. 1981. Repr. of 1928 ed. lib. bdg. 30.00 (ISBN 0-89984-234-8). Century Bookbindery.

Degoff, R. A. Construction Management: Basic Principles for Architects, Engineers & Owners. (Construction Management & Engineering Ser.). 384p. 1985. 44.95 (ISBN 0-471-81459-8). Wiley.

DeGoff, Robert A. & Friedman, Howard A. Construction Management: Basic Principles for Facility Planners & Design Professionals. (Construction Management & Engineering Ser.: No. 1-102). 375p. 1984. 44.95x (ISBN 0-317-11515-4, Pub. by Wiley-Interscience). Wiley.

DeGolia. Object Lessons Using Common Things. 1954. 2.95 (ISBN 0-88207-026-6). Victor Bks.

De Golia, Jack. Everglades: The Story Behind the Scenery. LC 78-71200. (Illus.). 1978. 8.95 (ISBN 0-916122-56-5); pap. 3.75 (ISBN 0-916122-55-7). KC Pubns.

DeGolyer, Everett, Jr. The Track Going Back: A Century of Transcontinental Railroading. pap. 14.95 (ISBN 0-317-31519-6, Dist. by Univ. of Texas Pr.). Amon Carter.

De Golyer, Everett L., Jr. The Track Going Back: A Century of Transcontinental Railroading 1869-1969. LC 74-88245. (Illus.). 207p. 1979. pap. 14.95 (ISBN 0-88360-007-2). Amon Carter.

De Goma, F. S., jt. auth. see Marole, L. T.

De Gomez, Madeleine Angelique Poisson see Poisson De Gomez, Madeleine Angelique.

De Goncourt, Edmond & De Goncourt, Jules. French Eighteenth Century Painters. (Illus.). 1981. 12.95x (ISBN 0-8014-9218-1, Pub. by Phaidon England). Cornell U Pr.

--Germinie Lacerteux. Tancock, Leonard, tr. (Classics Ser.). 160p. 1985. pap. 5.95 (ISBN 0-14-044438-6). Penguin.

De Goncourt, Edmond L. see Goncourt, Edmond L. & Goncourt, Jules A. De.

De Goncourt, Jules, jt. auth. see De Goncourt, Edmond.

De Goncourt, Jules A. see Goncourt, Edmond L. & Goncourt, Jules A. De.

De Gongora, Luis see Gongora, Luis De.

De Gongora, Luis see Gongora, Luis de.

De Gongoray Argote, Luis. Obras Poeticas. Foulche-Delbosc, Raymond, ed. (Sp). 1970. Repr. of 1921 ed. 12.00 (ISBN 0-87535-008-9). Hispanic Soc.

De Gonzales, Ela R. Yanette Sings. (Illus.). 32p. (gr. 1-6). 1984. 5.95 (ISBN 0-89962-455-3). Todd & Honeywell.

DeGonzalez, Fe Acosta & DeMatos, Isabel Freire. Matematicas Modernas En el Nivel Elemental: Guia Metodologica. (Illus.). 6.25 (ISBN 0-8477-2700-9); pap. 5.00 (ISBN 0-8477-2701-7). U of PR Pr.

De Gonzalez, Fe Acosta see Acosta de Gonzalez, Fe.

De Gonzalez, Nelly, jt. ed. see Diaz, Jorge.

De Gorbea, Josefina Q., et al. Reglas Para Ordenar Alfabeticamente. (Span.). 1977. text ed. 2.00 (ISBN 0-538-22971-3, V971). SW Pub.

--Sistemas de Archivar y Control de Documentos. (Span.). 1977. text ed. 7.35 (ISBN 0-538-22970-5, V97). SW Pub.

De Gorog, Ralph. Dictionnaire inverse de l'ancien francais. LC 81-18874. (Medieval & Renaissance Texts & Studies: Vol. 4). 272p. (Fr.). 1981. 25.00 (ISBN 0-86698-010-5). Medieval & Renaissance NY.

--Lexique Francais Moderne - Ancien Francais. LC 72-91996. 488p. (Fr.). 1973. 28.00x (ISBN 0-8203-0312-7). U of Ga Pr.

De Goscinny. Le Devin. (Coll. Asterix). (gr. 7-9). 7.95 (ISBN 0-685-33972-6). French & Eur.

--La Serpe d'Or. (Coll. Asterix). (gr. 7-9). 7.95 (ISBN 0-685-33971-8). French & Eur.

De Goscinny, Rene. Asterix & Caesar's Gift. (Asterix Ser.). 1977. 7.95x (ISBN 0-340-21588-7); pap. 4.95x. Intl Learn Syst.

--Asterix & Cleopatra. (Asterix Ser.). (Illus.). 1976. 7.95x (ISBN 0-340-04239-7); pap. 4.95x (ISBN 0-686-31734-3). Intl Learn Syst.

--Asterix & the Big Fight. (Asterix Ser.). (Illus.). 1976. 7.95x (ISBN 0-340-04238-9); pap. 4.95x (ISBN 2-2050-6906-3). Intl Learn Syst.

--Asterix & the Cauldron. (Asterix Ser.). (Illus.). 1976. 7.95x (ISBN 0-340-20212-2); pap. 4.95x (ISBN 2-2050-6912-8). Intl Learn Syst.

--Asterix & the Chieftain's Shield. (Asterix Ser.). 1977. 7.95x (ISBN 0-340-21394-9); pap. 4.95x. Intl Learn Syst.

--Asterix & the Goths. (Asterix Ser.). (Illus.). 1976. 7.95x (ISBN 0-340-18491-4); pap. 4.95x (ISBN 0-686-31735-1). Intl Learn Syst.

--Asterix & the Great Crossing. (Asterix Ser.). (Illus.). 1976. 7.95x (ISBN 0-340-20211-4); pap. 4.95x (ISBN 0-686-31736-X). Intl Learn Syst.

--Asterix & the Laurel Wreath. (Asterix Ser.). (Illus.). 1976. 7.95x (ISBN 0-340-19107-4); pap. 4.95x (ISBN 0-686-31737-8). Intl Learn Syst.

--Asterix & the Roman Agent. (Asterix Ser.). (Illus.). 1976. 7.95x (ISBN 0-340-16540-5); pap. 4.95x (ISBN 2-205-06914-4). Intl Learn Syst.

--Asterix apud Gothos. (Asterix Ser.). (Illus., Latin.). 1976. 7.95x (ISBN 0-686-19936-7). Intl Learn Syst.

--Asterix at the Olympic Games. (Asterix Ser.). (Illus.). 1976. 7.95x (ISBN 0-340-15591-4); pap. 4.95x (ISBN 0-686-31739-4). Intl Learn Syst.

--Asterix auf Korsika. (Asterix Ser.). (Illus., Ger.). 1976. 7.95x (ISBN 0-686-19937-5). Intl Learn Syst.

--Asterix aux Jeux Olympiques. (Fr.). (gr. 7-9). 7.95 (ISBN 0-685-23424-X). French & Eur.

--Asterix chez les Bretons. (Fr.). (gr. 7-9). 7.95 (ISBN 0-685-23430-4). French & Eur.

--Asterix Chez les Helvetes. (Illus., Fr.). (gr. 7-9). 7.95 (ISBN 0-685-28427-1). French & Eur.

--Asterix e gli Allori di Cesare. (Asterix Ser.). (Ital.). 1976. 4.95x (ISBN 0-686-10694-6). Intl Learn Syst.

--Asterix e il Paiolo. (Asterix Ser.). (Illus., Ital.). 1976. 4.95x (ISBN 0-686-19938-3). Intl Learn Syst.

--Asterix e il Regalo Di Cesare. (Asterix Ser.). (Ital.). 1976. 4.95x (ISBN 0-686-10693-8). Intl Learn Syst.

--Asterix en Corcega. (Asterix Ser.). (Illus., Span.). 1976. 5.95x (ISBN 84-7419-083-5). Intl Learn Syst.

--Asterix en Hispanie. (Illus., Fr.). (gr. 7-9). 7.95 (ISBN 0-685-28428-X). French & Eur.

--Asterix en los Juegos Olimpicos. (Asterix Ser.). (Illus., Span.). 1976. 5.95x (ISBN 84-7419-045-2). Intl Learn Syst.

--Asterix et Cleopatre. (Fr.). (gr. 7-9). 7.95 (ISBN 0-685-23434-7). French & Eur.

--Asterix et le Chaudron. (Illus., Fr.). (gr. 7-9). 7.95 (ISBN 0-685-28429-8). French & Eur.

--Asterix et les Goths. (Fr.). (gr. 7-9). 7.95 (ISBN 0-685-23426-6). French & Eur.

--Asterix et les Normands. (Fr.). (gr. 7-9). 7.95 (ISBN 0-685-23431-2). French & Eur.

--Asterix Gallus. (Asterix Ser.). (Illus., Lat.). 1976. 7.95x (ISBN 0-686-19940-5). Intl Learn Syst.

--Asterix Gladiador. (Asterix Ser.). (Illus., Span.). 1976. 5.95x (ISBN 0-686-28601-4). Intl Learn Syst.

--Asterix Gladiateur. (Fr.). (gr. 7-9). 7.95 (ISBN 0-685-23427-4). French & Eur.

--Asterix Gladiator. (Asterix Ser.). (Illus., Lat.). 1976. 7.95x (ISBN 0-686-19941-3). Intl Learn Syst.

--Asterix in Britain. (Asterix Ser.). (Illus.). 1976. 7.95x (ISBN 2-205-06907-1); pap. 4.95x (ISBN 2-205-06907-1). Intl Learn Syst.

--Asterix in Spain. (Asterix Ser.). (Illus.). 1976. 7.95x (ISBN 0-340-14934-5); pap. 4.95x (ISBN 0-686-31741-6). Intl Learn Syst.

--Asterix in Switzerland. (Asterix Ser.). (Illus.). 1976. 7.95x (ISBN 0-340-17062-X); pap. 4.95x (ISBN 0-686-34392-1). Intl Learn Syst.

--Asterix la Zizanie. (Illus., Fr.). (gr. 7-9). 7.95 (ISBN 0-685-28426-3). French & Eur.

--Asterix le Gaulois. (Fr.). (gr. 7-9). 7.95 (ISBN 0-685-23425-8). French & Eur.

--Asterix Legionnaire. (Fr.). (gr. 7-9). 7.95 (ISBN 0-685-23432-0). French & Eur.

--Asterix the Gladiator. (Asterix Ser.). (Illus.). 1976. 7.95x (ISBN 0-340-10479-1); pap. 4.95x (ISBN 2-205-06903-9). Intl Learn Syst.

--Asterix the Legionary. (Asterix Ser.). (Illus.). 1976. 7.95x (ISBN 0-340-10392-2); pap. 4.95x (ISBN 0-686-31743-2). Intl Learn Syst.

--Asterix und Kleopatra. (Asterix Ser.). (Ger.). 1977. 7.95x (ISBN 0-686-10695-4). Intl Learn Syst.

--Le Bouclier Arverne. (Fr.). (gr. 7-9). 7.95 (ISBN 0-685-23433-9). French & Eur.

--Le Combat des Chefs. (Fr.). (gr. 7-9). 7.95 (ISBN 0-685-23429-0). French & Eur.

--The Golden Sickle. (Asterix Ser.). (Illus.). 1976. 7.95x (ISBN 2-205-06901-2); pap. 3.95x (ISBN 0-686-31744-0). Intl Learn Syst.

De Goscinny., Rene. La Gran Travesia. (Asterix Ser.). (Illus., Span.). 1976. 5.95x (ISBN 84-02-04451-4). Intl Learn Syst.

De Goscinny, Rene. Die Lorbeeren Des Casars. (Asterix Ser.). (Illus., Ger.). 1976. 5.95x (ISBN 0-686-19973-1). Intl Learn Syst.

--The Mansion of the Gods. (Asterix Ser.). (Illus.). 1976. 7.95x (ISBN 0-340-17719-5); pap. 4.95x (ISBN 2-2050-6916-0). Intl Learn Syst.

--El Regalo Del Cesar. (Asterix Ser.). (Illus., Span.). 1976. 5.95x (ISBN 0-686-34393-X). Intl Learn Syst.

--Der Seher. (Asterix Ser.). (Illus., Ger.). 1976. 5.95x (ISBN 0-686-19948-0). Intl Learn Syst.

--The Soothsayer. (Asterix Ser.). (Illus.). 1976. 5.95x (ISBN 0-340-19525-8). Intl Learn Syst.

--Die Trabantenstadt. (Asterix Ser.). (Illus., Ger.). 1976. 7.95x (ISBN 0-686-19994-4). Intl Learn Syst.

De Goscinny, Rene & Uderzo, M. Domaine des Dieux. (Illus., Fr.). (gr. 7-9). 7.95 (ISBN 0-685-28430-1). French & Eur.

De Gourmont, Remy. Book of Masks. facs. ed. Lewis, J., tr. LC 67-26745. (Essay Index Reprint Ser.). 1921. 15.00 (ISBN 0-8369-0490-7). Ayer Co Pubs.

--Natural Philosophy of Love. Pound, Ezra, tr. (Black & Gold Lib). (Illus.). 1944. 6.95 (ISBN 0-87140-951-8, Co-Pub with Tudor). Liveright.

--Philosophic Nights in Paris. facsimile ed. Goldberg, I., tr. LC 68-8465. (Essay Index Reprint Ser). 1920. 17.00 (ISBN 0-8369-1293-4). Ayer Co Pubs.

De Gourmont, Remy see Gourmont, Remy de.

DeGourville, Frank. Universal School of Street Fighting. (Illus.). 1984. pap. 7.95 (ISBN 0-931981-03-4). Am Martial Arts Pub.

De Gouy, et al. The Ultimate Sandwich Book: With Over 700 Delicious Sandwich Creations. LC 82-537. (Illus.). 160p. (Orig.). 1982. lib. bdg. 12.90 (ISBN 0-89471-163-6); pap. 5.95 (ISBN 0-89471-164-4). Running Pr.

De Gouy, Louis P. The Bread Tray: Nearly 600 Recipes for Homemade Breads, Rolls, Muffins, & Biscuits. LC 73-88329. vii, 463p. 1974. pap. 5.95 (ISBN 0-486-23000-7). Dover.

--The Bread Tray: 600 Recipes for Homemade Breads, Rolls, Muffins, & Biscuits. 11.25 (ISBN 0-8446-5024-2). Peter Smith.

--Creative Hamburger Cookery. LC 73-88330. 128p. 1974. pap. 3.95 (ISBN 0-486-23001-5). Dover.

--Creative Hamburger Cookery: One Hundred Two Unusual Recipes for Caseroles, Meat Loaves & Hamburgers. 11.25 (ISBN 0-8446-5025-0). Peter Smith.

--Ice Cream & Ice Cream Desserts: 470 Recipes. 14.25 (ISBN 0-8446-5026-9). Peter Smith.

--Ice Cream & Ice Cream Desserts: 470 Tested Recipes for Ice Creams, Coupes, Bombes, Frappes, Ices, Mousses, Parfaits, Sherberts, Etc. LC 73-88333. 281p. 1974. pap. 4.95 (ISBN 0-486-22999-8). Dover.

--The Pie Book: 419 Recipes. LC 73-88331. 384p. 1974. pap. 5.95 (ISBN 0-486-22997-1). Dover.

--The Pie Book: 419 Recipes. 12.00 (ISBN 0-8446-5027-7). Peter Smith.

--The Soup Book. LC 73-88332. 428p. 1974. pap. 5.95 (ISBN 0-486-22998-X). Dover.

--The Soup Book: 770 Recipes. 12.75 (ISBN 0-8446-5028-5). Peter Smith.

DeGowin, Elmer L. & DeGowin, Richard L. Bedside Diagnostic Examination. 4th ed. (Illus.). 952p. 1981. write for info. (ISBN 0-02-328030-1). Macmillan.

DeGowin, Richard L., jt. auth. see DeGowin, Elmer L.

De Graaf, A. M., jt. ed. see Hooper, H. O.

DeGraaf, Donald E. Macrophysics. 2nd ed. LC 80-70717. (Illus.). 618p. 1981. pap. text ed. 17.00x (ISBN 0-930402-07-3). Crystal MI.

--Microphysics. 3rd ed. LC 83-71906. (Illus.). 660p. 1983. pap. text ed. 15.00x (ISBN 0-930402-12-X). Crystal MI.

--The Physical Universe. 4th ed. LC 81-65520. (Illus.). 495p. 1983. 13.75x (ISBN 0-930402-11-1). Crystal MI.

De Graaf, Frank. Marine Tropical Aquarium Guide. (Illus.). 282p. (YA) 1982. 14.95 (ISBN 0-87666-805-8, PL-2017). TFH Pubns.

De Graaf, H. J. Early Printing in Indonesia. Clair, Colin, ed. LC 75-78401. (Spread of Printing Ser). (Illus., Orig.). 1969. pap. 9.75 (ISBN 0-8390-0020-0). Abner Schram Ltd.

De Graaf, Janny, jt. auth. see Schmid, Alex.

De Graaf, Kaspar & Garrett, Malcolm. Culture Club: When Cameras Go Crazy. (Illus.). 96p. 1983. pap. 7.95 (ISBN 0-312-17879-4). St Martin.

De Graaf, Kasper & Garrett, Malcolm. Duran Duran: Their Story. (Illus.). 32p. 1984. pap. 3.95 (ISBN 0-86276-171-9). Proteus Pub NY.

DeGraaf, Richard M. & Rudis, Deborah D. Amphibians & Reptiles of New England: Habitats & Natural History. LC 83-5125. (Illus.). 96p. 1983. 14.00x (ISBN 0-87023-399-8); pap. 6.95 (ISBN 0-87023-400-5). U of Mass Pr.

DeGraaf, Richard M. & Witman, Gretchin M. Trees, Shrubs, & Vines for Attracting Birds: A Manual for the Northeast. LC 78-19698. (Illus.). 160p. 1981. pap. 11.50 (ISBN 0-87023-202-9). U of Mass Pr.

De Graaf, T. J. Cosmic Mutons & Neutrinos. write for info. Pergamon.

De Graaff, John H. Van see Van De Graaff, John H., et al.

DeGraeve, Frank P. & Flinn, Frank K., eds. Paradigms & Parameters in Christianity. (Orig.). Date not set. text ed. price not set (ISBN 0-913757-16-0, Pub. by New Era Bks.); pap. text ed. price not set (ISBN 0-913757-17-9). Paragon Hse.

DeGraff, Amy. The Tower & the Well: A Psychological Interpretation of the Fairy Tales of Madame D'Aulnoy. 136p. (Eng. & Fr.). 1984. pap. 12.00 (ISBN 0-917786-03-3). Summa Pubns.

De Graft, J. C. Beneath the Jazz & Brass. (African Writers Ser.). 1975. pap. text ed. 6.00x (ISBN 0-435-90166-4). Heinemann Ed.

De Graft, Joe. Muntu. (African Writers Ser.: No. 264). 104p. (Orig.). 1984. pap. text ed. 4.00x (ISBN 0-435-90264-4). Heinemann Ed.

De Grahl, Wolfgang. The Parrot Family: Parakeets-Budgerigars-Cockatiels-Lovebirds-Lories-Macaws. LC 83-17940. (Illus.). 176p. 1985. 12.95 (ISBN 0-668-06039-5); pap. 7.95 (ISBN 0-668-06043-3). Arco.

De Grainville, Jean B. The Last Man: Or, Omegarus & Syderia, a Romance in Futurity, 2 vols. in 1. LC 77-84246. (Lost Race & Adult Fantasy Ser.). 1978. Repr. of 1806 ed. lib. bdg. 35.50x (ISBN 0-405-10992-X). Ayer Co Pubs.

De Grana, Lydia Diaz. El Supervisor Universitario de la Practica Docente. pap. 3.75 (ISBN 0-8477-2707-6). U of PR Pr.

De Grand, Alexander J. Italian Fascism: Its Origins & Development. LC 81-23132. (Illus.). xiv, 174p. 1982. 16.50x (ISBN 0-8032-1652-1); pap. 7.95 (ISBN 0-8032-6553-0, BB 727, Bison). U of Nebr Pr.

--The Italian Nationalist Association & the Rise of Fascism in Italy. LC 77-24633. xii, 238p. 1978. 19.95x (ISBN 0-8032-0949-5). U of Nebr Pr.

De Grandmaison, C. Dictionnaires Heraldique. Migne, J. P., ed. (Nouvelle Encyclopedie Theologique Ser.: Vol. 13). 688p. (Fr.). Repr. of 1852 ed. lib. bdg. 90.00x (ISBN 0-89241-262-3). Caratzas.

De Grandpre. Histoire de la Litterature Francaise du Quebec, 4 tomes. Set. 144.50 (ISBN 0-685-35932-8). French & Eur.

De Grandsaigne, J. African Short Stories: An Anthology. LC 85-1930. 208p. 1985. 27.50 (ISBN 0-312-01029-X). St Martin.

De Grange, McQuilkin. Nature & Elements of Sociology. 1953. 65.00x (ISBN 0-686-83631-6). Elliots Bks.

Degras, Jane. Calendar of Soviet Documents on Foreign Policy, 1917-1941. LC 79-4912. 1981. Repr. of 1948 ed. 23.00 (ISBN 0-88355-962-5). Hyperion Conn.

Degras, Jane, ed. Communist International: Documents. Incl. Vol. 1: 1919-22. 464p. 47.50x (ISBN 0-7146-1554-4); Vol. 2: 1923-1928. 584p. 47.50x (ISBN 0-7146-1555-2); Vol. 3: 1929-1943. 494p. 47.50x (ISBN 0-7146-1556-0). 1971 (F Cass Co). Biblio Dist.

--Soviet Documents on Foreign Policy: Vol. I-1917-1924, Vol. II-1925-1932, Vol. III-1933-1941. 1978. Repr. of 1953 ed. lib. bdg. 115.00x set (ISBN 0-374-92096-6). Octagon.

--Soviet Planning: Essays in Honour of Naum Jasny. LC 81-19072. (Illus.). xi, 225p. 1982. Repr. of 1964 ed. lib. bdg. 25.00x (ISBN 0-313-23203-2, DESP). Greenwood.

Degras, Jane, tr. see Monnerot, Jules.

DeGrasse, Robert W., Jr. & Council on Economic Priorities. Military Expansion, Economic Decline: The Impact of Military Spending on U. S. Economic Performance. rev. ed. LC 83-12680. 260p. 1983. 25.00 (ISBN 0-87332-258-4); pap. 11.95 (ISBN 0-87332-260-6). M E Sharpe.

De Grauwe, Paul. Macro-Economic Theory for the Open Economy. 336p. 1983. text ed. 38.50x (ISBN 0-566-00622-7). Gower Pub Co.

DeGrauwe, Paul & Peeters, Theo, eds. Exchange Rates in Multi-Country Econometric Models. LC 83-13922. 298p. 1984. 35.00 (ISBN 0-312-27402-5). St Martin.

De Grauwe, Paul, et al. Exchange Rates, Money & Output: The European Experience. LC 84-11692. 350p. 1985. 32.50 (ISBN 0-312-27403-3). St Martin.

DeGrave, Philip. Unholy Moses. LC 84-28676. (Crime Club Ser.). 192p. 1985. 12.95 (ISBN 0-385-19741-1). Doubleday.

De Gravelles, Virginia W., intro. by see Cushman, Margery.

DeGravelles, William D. & Kelley, John H. Injuries Following Rear-End Automobile Collisions. (Illus.). 256p. 1969. 23.75x (ISBN 0-398-00414-5). C C Thomas.

De Gravemont, Ulysses B. The Historical & Political Forces Which Are Subterraneously & Inflexibly Leading the World to a Final & Maximal Military Climax. (Illus.). 166p. 1985. 179.85 (ISBN 0-317-18524-1). Inst Econ Pol.

DeGraw, Imelda G. The Denver Art Museum: Quilts & Coverlets. LC 74-7687. (Illus.). 1974. pap. 6.50 (ISBN 0-914738-02-X). Denver Art Mus.

DeGraw, Linda & Wallin, Barbara J. Children's Favorite Parties. 96p. (Orig.). 1985. pap. 9.95 (ISBN 0-934318-49-2). Falcon Pr MT.

DeGraw, Ronald. Red Arrow: The First Hundred Years. Sebree, Mac, ed. (Interubans Special Ser.: 96). (Illus.). 160p. 1985. 31.95 (ISBN 0-916374-67-X). Interurban.

DeGrazia. Supporting Art & Culture. pap. 11.95 (ISBN 0-317-07058-4). Lieber-Atherton.

De Grazia, Alfred. Chaos & Creation: An Introduction to Quantavolution in Human & Natural History. (Quantavolution Ser.). (Illus.). xiii, 336p. 1981. 22.00x (ISBN 0-940268-00-0). Metron Pubns.

--The Disastrous Love Affair of Moon & Mars. (Quantavolution Ser.). 278p. (Orig.). 1984. pap. 17.00X (ISBN 0-940268-09-4). Metron Pubns.

--Divine Succession: A Science of Gods Old & New. (Quantavolution Ser.). 204p. 1983. pap. 14.00x (ISBN 0-940268-05-1). Metron Pubns.

--Eight Bads - Eight Goods: The American Contradictions. 8.25 (ISBN 0-8446-5818-9). Peter Smith.

--Lately Tortured Earth: Exoterrestrial Forces & Quantavolutions in the Earth Sciences. (Quantavolution Ser.). 516p. 1983. 28.00x (ISBN 0-940268-06-X). Metron Pubns.

--Public & Republic. LC 84-22449. xiv, 271p. 1985. Repr. lib. bdg. 35.00x (ISBN 0-313-24679-3, DEPR). Greenwood.

De Grazia, Alfred see Grazia, Alfred De.

De Grazia, Alfred see Grazia, Alfred de.

De Grazia, Alfred see Grazia, Alfred de & Milton, Earl R.

De Grazia, Alfred, jt. auth. see Schlesinger, Arthur M., Jr.

De Grazia, Alfred, tr. see Michels, Roberto.

De Grazia, Anne-Marie. Le Pigeon d'Argile: The Clay Pigeon. 104p. 1984. pap. 14.00x (ISBN 0-940268-99-X). Metron Pubns.

DeGrazia, Diane. Correggio & His Legacy: Sixteenth Century Emilian Drawings. LC 83-24943. (Illus.). 1984. pap. 24.95 (ISBN 0-89468-072-2). Natl Gallery Art.

De Grazia, Edward & Newman, Roger K. Banned Films: Movies, Censors & the First Amendment. 532p. 1982. 29.95 (ISBN 0-8352-1509-1); pap. 19.95 (ISBN 0-8352-1511-3). Bowker.

DeGrazia, Emilio. Enemy Country. Date not set. pap. 7.50 (ISBN 0-317-28738-9). New Rivers Pr.

DeGrazia, Emilio, et al. Likely Stories: A Collection of Untraditional Fiction. McPherson, Bruce R., ed. LC 82-129270. 224p. 1981. 14.50 (ISBN 0-914232-42-8); pap. 7.95 (ISBN 0-914232-41-X). McPherson & Co.

Degrazia, Joseph. Math Is Fun. (Illus.). 11.95 (ISBN 0-89490-111-7). Enslow Pubs.

--Mind Bogglers. 159p. 1984. pap. 5.95 (ISBN 0-13-583246-2). P-H.

De Grazia, Raffaele. Clandestine Employment: The Situation in the Industrialised Market Economy Countries. International Labour Organisation Staff, ed. vii, 118p. 1984. pap. 10.00 (ISBN 92-2-103833-5). Intl Labour Office.

De Grazia, Sebastian. Of Time, Work & Leisure. LC 73-12379. 572p. 1973. lib. bdg. write for info. (ISBN 0-527-22100-7); pap. 20.00 (ISBN 0-527-22101-5). Kraus Repr.

--The Political Community: A Study of Anomie. LC 77-90967. (Midway Reprint). 1978. pap. text ed. 10.00x (ISBN 0-226-14071-7). U of Chicago Pr.

De Grazia, Victoria. The Culture of Consent: Mass Organization of Leisure in Fascist Italy. LC 80-24361. (Illus.). 304p. 1981. 39.50 (ISBN 0-521-23705-X). Cambridge U Pr.

DeGrazia, Victoria, tr. see Hobsbawm, Eric.

De Graziani, Vincenzo G. The Franco-German Coalition & the Emergence of a New International Superpower: Its Effects Upon the Future Course of History. (Illus.). 1979. deluxe ed. 75.75x (ISBN 0-930008-31-6). Inst Econ Pol.

DeGre, Gerard. The Social Compulsions of Ideas: Toward a Sociological Analysis of Knowledge. Levitt, Cyril, ed. 264p. 1984. 39.95 (ISBN 0-88738-003-4). Transaction Bks.

--Society & Ideology: An Inquiry into the Sociology of Knowledge. Coser, Lewis A. & Powell, Walter W., eds. LC 79-6991. (Perennial Works in Sociology Ser.). 1979. Repr. of 1943 ed. lib. bdg. 15.00x (ISBN 0-405-12091-5). Ayer Co Pubs.

Degre, S. G., ed. Myocardial Revascularization in Acute Conditions. (Bibliotheca Cardiologica Ser.: No. 39). (Illus.). vi, 178p. 1985. 49.00 (ISBN 3-8055-4142-2). S Karger.

De Greaf, Donald E. Microphysics. (Illus.). 640p. 1985. pap. text ed. 17.50x (ISBN 0-930402-13-8). Crystal MI.

Degreef, E. & Van Buggenhaut, J. Trends in Mathematical Psychology. (Advances in Psychology Ser.: Vol. 20). 1984. 61.75 (ISBN 0-444-87512-3, I-241-84). Elsevier.

DeGreen, Keith P. Creating a Success Environment. LC 79-64210. (Illus.). 1979. 12.95 (ISBN 0-934174-02-4). Summit Ent.

DeGreene, K. B. The Adaptive Organization: Anticipation & Management of Crisis. LC 81-13112. 394p. 1982. 38.95x (ISBN 0-471-08296-1, Pub. by Wiley-Interscience). Wiley.

De Gregoire, Abbe Henri. Oeuvres, 14 Vols. 1977. Set. lib. bdg. 695.00 (ISBN 3-262-00007-8). Kraus Intl.

DeGregori, Thomas R. A Theory of Technology: Continuity & Change in Human Development. 176p. (Orig.). 1985. pap. text ed. 13.50x (ISBN 0-8138-1778-1). Iowa St U Pr.

DeGregorio, George. Joe DiMaggio: An Informal Biography. LC 80-6159. 272p. 1981. 14.95 (ISBN 0-8128-2777-5); pap. 10.95 (ISBN 0-8128-6178-7). Stein & Day.

DeGregorio, William A. The Complete Book of U. S. Presidents. LC 83-23201. (Illus.). 691p. 1984. 22.50 (ISBN 0-934878-36-6). Dembner Bks.

De Gregory, Augustus. What Everyone Should Know about Death. (Library of the Phenomena of the Mind). (Illus.). 147p. 1982. 47.85 (ISBN 0-89266-344-8). Am Classical Coll Pr.

Degrell, I. Atlas of the Diseases of the Mammary Gland: Atlas der Brustdruesenerkrankungen. (Illus.). 186p. 1976. 59.75 (ISBN 3-8055-2219-3). S Karger.

Degrelle, Leon. Epic: The Story of the Waffen SS. (Illus.). 69p. (Orig.). 1983. pap. 4.00 (ISBN 0-939484-12-9). Inst Hist Rev.

--Epic: The Story of the Waffen SS. 1983. lib. bdg. 79.95 (ISBN 0-87700-465-X). Revisionist Pr.

--Letter to the Pope on His Visit to Auschwitz. 1982. lib. bdg. 59.95 (ISBN 0-87700-346-7). Revisionist Pr.

Degremont Company. Water Treatment Handbook. 5th ed. LC 79-87503. 1186p. 1979. 89.95x (ISBN 0-470-26749-6). Halsted Pr.

Degremont Company Editors. Water Treatment Handbook. LC 72-96505. (Illus.). 1116p. 1973. 40.00 (ISBN 0-686-02503-2). Taylor-Carlisle.

Degrijse, Omer. Going Forth: Missionary Consciousness in Third World Catholic Churches. LC 83-19337. 112p. (Orig.). 1984. pap. 6.95 (ISBN 0-88344-427-5). Orbis Bks.

De Grivart, tr. see Crawford, Williame & Kerstrat, Francoise.

De Groat, Diane, illus. Robert Louis Stevenson's a Child's Garden of Verses to Color. (Color-&-Keep Bks.). (Illus.). 64p. (ps-3). 1985. pap. 2.95 (ISBN 0-394-87275-4, BYR). Random.

DeGroat, Florence. Animal Stories. 88p. (gr. 2-6). 1983. pap. 2.50 (ISBN 0-87516-509-5). De Vorss.

--A Fairy's Workday. 65p. (gr. 1-6). 1983. pap. 1.95 (ISBN 0-87516-508-7). De Vorss.

--Resurrection. LC 81-67782. (Universal Man Ser.: Vol. 2). (Illus.). 168p. (Orig.). 1981. pap. text ed. 6.50 (ISBN 0-87516-456-0). De Vorss.

--Tales from Galilee. 96p. (Orig.). (gr. 4 up). 1982. pap. 4.50 (ISBN 0-87516-485-4). De Vorss.

--This Drama Called Life: An Introduction to Advanced Christianity. (Illus.). 49p. 1984. pap. 6.95 (ISBN 0-942494-89-X). Coleman Pub.

--Universal Man. LC 80-69413. 117p. 1981. pap. 6.50 (ISBN 0-87516-428-5). De Vorss.

De Groer, Leon. Decorative Arts in Europe Seventeen Ninety to Eighteen Fifty. LC 85-42864. (Illus.). 360p. 1985. 75.00 (ISBN 0-8478-0621-9). Rizzoli Intl.

DeGrolier, Eric. The Organization of Information Systems for Government & Public Administration. (Documentation, Libraries & Archives: Studies & Research: No. 8). (Illus.). 163p. 1979. pap. 10.00 (ISBN 92-3-101595-8, U919, UNESCO). Unipub.

De Grolier, Eric, ed. Glossogenetics: The Origin & Evolution of Language. LC 83-232. (Models of Scientific Thought: Vol. VI). (Illus.). 557p. 1983. 38.50 (ISBN 3-7186-0158-3). Harwood Academic.

DeGrood, D. Dialectics & Revolution, Vol. 3. (Philosophical Currents Ser.: No. 28). 270p. 1983. pap. text ed. 28.25x (ISBN 90-6032-210-X, Pub. by Gruner Holland). Humanities.

Degrood, David. Dialectics & Revolution. (Philosophical Currents Ser.: No. 25). 1980. pap. text ed. 28.00x (ISBN 9-0603-2154-5). Humanities.

--Dialectics & Revolution, Vol. 4. (Philosophical Currents Ser.: Vol. 31). 296p. 1984. pap. text ed. 28.25x (ISBN 90-6032-243-6, Pub. by B R Gruner Netherlands). Humanities.

--Haeckel's Theory of the Unity of Nature. (Praxis Ser.: Vol.8). 100p. 1982. pap. text ed. 14.50x (ISBN 90-6032-216-9). Humanities.

DeGrood, David H. Consciousness & Social Life. (Philosophical Currents Ser.: Vol. 15). 112p. (Orig.). 1976. pap. 14.00x (ISBN 90-6032-067-0, Pub. by B R Gruener Netherlands). Benjamins North Am.

--Dialectics & Revolution, Vol. 1. (Philosophical Currents Ser.: No. 21). 1978. pap. text ed. 23.50x (ISBN 90-6032-097-2). Humanities.

--Dialectics & Revolution, Vol. 2. (Philosophical Currents Ser.; No. 25). (Orig.). 1978. pap. text ed. 29.00x (ISBN 90-6032-154-5). Humanities.

--Philosophies of Essence: An Examination of the Category of Essence. 2nd ed. (Praxis Ser.: No. 1). 1976. pap. text ed. 17.75x (ISBN 90-6032-076-X). Humanities.

--Radical Currents in Contemporary Philosophy. LC 73-110806. 286p. 1971. 15.00 (ISBN 0-87527-029-8). Fireside Bks.

DeGroot, jt. auth. see Turk.

De Groot, Adriaan. Methodology: Foundations of Inference & Research in the Behavioral Sciences. (Psychological Studies: No. 6). 1969. text ed. 30.00x (ISBN 90-2796-250-2). Mouton.

De Groot, Adriaan D. Methodologie: Grondslagen Van Onderzoek En Denken in De Gedragswetenschappen. 1975. 27.75x (ISBN 90-2797-721-6). Mouton.

--Standpunt: Over Onderwijs, Democratie En Wetenschap. 1971. 11.60x (ISBN 90-2796-917-5). Mouton.

--Thought & Choice in Chess. 2nd ed. (Psychological Studies: No. 4). 1978. text ed. 33.60x (ISBN 0-686-27037-1). Mouton.

De Groot, Adriaan D. & Van Naerssen, R. F. Studietoetsen: Construeren, Afnemen, Analyseren, Vol. 1. 1973. 8.80x (ISBN 90-2797-217-6). Mouton.

--Studietoetsen: Construeren, Afnemen, Analyseren, Vol. 2. (Illus.). 1975. 8.00x (ISBN 90-2797-831-X). Mouton.

Degroot, Bob, jt. auth. see Turk, Phillip.

De Groot, C. Hofstede. Beschreibendes und Kritisches Verzeichnis der Werke der Hervorragendsten Hollandischen Maler des XVIIJh. (A Catalogue Raisonne of the Works of the Most Eminent Dutch Painters of the Seventeenth Century). 1976. lib. bdg. 100.00x (ISBN 0-85964-024-8). Chadwyck-Healey.

--A Catalogue Raisonne of the Works of the Most Eminent Dutch Painters of the Seventeenth Century, 2 vols. Hawke, E. G., ed. 6128p. 1976. Repr. of 1927 ed. Set. 200.00x (ISBN 0-85964-023-X). Chadwyck-Healey.

De Groot, David, jt. auth. see Dalenburg, Cornelia.

De Groot, E. C., jt. auth. see Mouwen, J. M.

De Groot, Irene. Landscape Etchings by the Dutch Masters of the Seventeenth Century. 1980. 35.00 (ISBN 0-670-41770-X, Studio). Viking.

--Sailing Ships in Dutch Prints. LC 82-80141. (Illus.). 32p. 1982. pap. 7.75 (ISBN 0-88397-040-6, Pub. by Intl Exhibit Foun). C E Tuttle.

De Groot, Irene & Vorstman, Robert. Sailing Ships. 280p. 1981. 75.00x (ISBN 0-86092-052-6, Pub. by Fraser Bks). State Mutual Bk.

De Groot, Irene, jt. auth. see Niemeijer, J. W.

De Groot, J. Correlative Neuroanatomy of Computed Tomography & Magnetic Resonance Imaging. LC 83-22175. (Illus.). 248p. 1984. text ed. 45.00 (ISBN 0-8121-0917-1). Lea & Febiger.

De Groot, J. J. Le Cope du Mahayana en Chine: Amsterdam, 1892. LC 78-74288. (Oriental Religions Ser.: Vol. 15). 281p. 1980. lib. bdg. 40.00 (ISBN 0-8240-3917-3). Garland Pub.

DeGroot, J. J. The Religious System of China, 6 vols. 1982. Repr. of 1892 ed. 130.00 (ISBN 0-89986-346-9). Oriental Bk Store.

De Groot, J. J. Sectarianism & Religious Persecution in China: A Page in the History of Religions, 2 vols. 872p. 1972. Repr. of 1903 ed. 55.00x (ISBN 0-7165-2034-6, Pub. by Irish Academic Pr Ireland). Biblio Dist.

De Groot, John H. Shakespeares-'The Old Faith.' facs. ed. LC 68-57315. (Essay Index Reprint Ser.). 1946. 18.00 (ISBN 0-8369-0368-4). Ayer Co Pubs.

De Groot, Klaas. Bioceramics of Calcium Phosphate. 152p. 1983. 52.00 (ISBN 0-8493-6456-6). CRC Pr.

DeGroot, Leslie J., ed. Endocrinology, 3 vols. LC 78-24043. 1979. Vol. 1, 592pps. 70.50 (ISBN 0-8089-1114-7, 791017); Vol.2, 800pps. 93.50 (ISBN 0-8089-1168-6, 791018); Vol. 3, 880pps. 99.00 (ISBN 0-8089-1169-4, 791019). Grune.

DeGroot, Leslie J., et al. The Thyroid & Its Diseases. 5th ed. LC 83-27411. 907p. 1984. 65.00 (ISBN 0-471-88688-2, Pub. by Wiley Med). Wiley.

Degroot, Leslie J., et al, eds. Radiation Associated Thyroid Carcinoma. LC 77-79894. 560p. 1977. 56.00 (ISBN 0-8089-1044-2, 791015). Grune.

DeGroot, M. H. Optimal Statistical Decisions. 1970. text ed. 47.95 (ISBN 0-07-016242-5). McGraw.

DeGroot, Morris H., jt. auth. see Carnegie-Mellon University.

DeGroot, Morris H., jt. auth. see Cyert, Richard M.

De Groot, Roy A. The Auberge of the Flowering Hearth. 512p. 1984. pap. 4.95 (ISBN 0-345-32006-9). Ballantine.

--Cooking with the Cuisinart Food Processor. LC 76-46586. 1977. 14.95 (ISBN 0-07-016273-5). McGraw.

DeGroot, S. R. & Mazur, P. Non-Equilibrium Thermodynamics. 544p. 1984. pap. 10.95 (ISBN 0-486-64741-2). Dover.

De Groot, S. R., et al. Relativistic Kinetic Theory: Principles & Applications. 418p. 1980. 78.75 (ISBN 0-444-85453-3, North-Holland). Elsevier.

DeGroot, W., ed. Stormwater Detention Facilities. LC 82-73613. 439p. 1982. pap. 31.00x (ISBN 0-87262-348-3). Am Soc Civil Eng.

DeGroot, Wm. L. Tennis & You. (Illus.). 1984. pap. text ed. 6.95x (ISBN 0-89582-124-9). Morton Pub.

DeGroote, Betty. Judo Vignettes: 1882 to 1985. Lubbert, Hal & DeGroote, H. W., eds. (Illus.). 120p. 1985. pap. 25.00 (ISBN 0-933099-26-6). Kodokan IA Pub.

DeGroote, H. W., ed. see DeGroote, Betty.

DeGroote, Harry W., ed. see Lubbert, Hal.

De Grouchy, Jean & Turleau, Catherine. Clinical Atlas of Human Chromosomes. 2nd ed. LC 83-16839. 487p. 1984. 65.00 (ISBN 0-471-89205-X, Pub. by Wiley Med). Wiley.

DeGrove, John M. Land, Growth, & Politics. LC 83-63441. (Illus.). 435p. 1984. 33.95 (ISBN 0-918286-31-X). Planners Pr.

DeGruchy, John W. Bonhoeffer & South Africa: Theology in Dialogue. 128p. (Orig.). 1984. pap. 9.95 (ISBN 0-8028-0042-4). Eerdmans.
--The Church Struggle in South Africa. LC 78-26761. 1978. pap. 7.95 (ISBN 0-8028-1786-6). Eerdmans.
De Gruchy, John W. & Villa-Vicencio, Charles. Resistance & Hope: South African Essays in Honor of Beyers Naude. 224p. (Orig.). 1985. pap. 11.95 (ISBN 0-8028-0098-X). Eerdmans.
De Gruchy, John W. & Villa-Vicencio, Charles, eds. Apartheid Is a Heresy. 208p. (Orig.). 1983. pap. 5.95 (ISBN 0-8028-1972-9). Eerdmans.
De Grucy, Clare, jt. auth. see Martin, Lillien J.
De Gruijter, D. N., jt. ed. see Crombag, H. G.
De Gruijter, J. J. Numerical Classification of Soils & Its Application in Survey. (Agricultural Research Reports: No. 855). (Illus.). 1978. pap. 22.00 (ISBN 90-220-0608-5, PDC59, PUDOC). Unipub.
De Grummond, Jane L. Renato Beluche: Smuggler, Privateer, & Patriot, 1780 to 1860. LC 82-14969. (Illus.). 328p. 1983. text ed. 27.50x (ISBN 0-8071-1054-X). La State U Pr.
De Grummond, Lena & Delaune, Lynn. Jeb Stuart. LC 62-16298. (Illus.). 160p. (gr. 4-6). 1979. pap. 4.95 (ISBN 0-88289-247-9). Pelican.
De Grummond, Nancy T. see Grummond, Nancy T. de.
De Grunwald, C. Metternich. Todd, D., tr. 1977. lib. bdg. 59.95 (ISBN 0-8490-2231-2). Gordon Pr.
De Gubernatis, Angelo. La Mythologie Des Plantes: Ou les Legendes Du Regne Vegetal. Bolle, Kees W., ed. LC 77-79128. (Mythology Ser.). 1978. Repr. of 1882 ed. lib. bdg. 52.00x (ISBN 0-405-10539-8). Ayer Co Pubs.
--Zoological Mythology or the Legends of Amimals, 2 vols. in 1. Bolle, Kees W., ed. LC 77-79129. (Mythology Ser.). 1978. Repr. of 1872 ed. lib. bdg. 68.50x (ISBN 0-405-10540-1). Ayer Co Pubs.
De Gubernatis, Angelo see Gubernatis, Angelo De.
De Guevara, Antonio see Guevara, Antonio de.
De Guibert, Joseph. The Jesuits: Their Spiritual Doctrine & Practice. Young, W. J., tr. LC 64-21430. 717p. 1964. pap. 8.00 (ISBN 0-912422-09-2). Inst Jesuit.
Deguileville, Guillaume de. The Pylgremage of the Sowle. Lydgate, J., tr. LC 74-28845. (English Experience Ser.: No. 726). 1975. Repr. of 1483 ed. 24.00 (ISBN 90-221-0740-X). Walter J Johnson.
Deguilleville, Guillaume de. The Booke of the Pylgremage of the Sowle. Cust, Katherine I., ed. Caxton, William, tr. from Fr. LC 78-180445. (Illus.). Repr. of 1859 ed. 21.50 (ISBN 0-404-56612-X). AMS Pr.
Deguilleville, Guillaume De see De Deguilleville, Guillaume.
DeGuilmo, Joseph M. Electricity-Electronics: Principles & Applications. LC 79-54909. (Electronics Technology Ser.). (Illus.). 706p. (Orig.). 1982. pap. 26.80 (ISBN 0-8273-1686-0); instr's. guide 5.25 (ISBN 0-8273-1687-9). Delmar.
Deguine, Jean-Claude. Emperor Penguin. LC 74-5224. (Illus.). 40p. 1974. 7.50 (ISBN 0-8289-0236-4). Greene.
De Guise, Giorgio. The Ignorant Man's Guide to the Mysteries of Metaphysics. (Illus.). 111p. 1984. 37.85x (ISBN 0-89266-465-7). Am Classical Coll Pr.
De Gutierrez, Edna L., tr. see Ton, Mary E.
De Gutierrez, Edna L., tr. see Wood, Fred M.
De Gutierrez, Frances A., tr. see Olson, Joan & Olson, Gene.
Deguy, Michel. Given Giving: Selected Poems. Eshleman, Clayton, tr. LC 84-40332. 144p. 1985. 19.95 (ISBN 0-520-04728-1). U of Cal Pr.
De Guzman, Domingo see Domingo De Guzman, Saint.
De Guzman, Miguel & Miguel. Real Variable Methods in Fourier Analysis. (Mathematical Studies Ser.: Vol. 46). 392p. 1981. 61.75 (ISBN 0-444-86124-6, North-Holland). Elsevier.
DeGuzman, Videa P. Syntactic Derivation of Tagalog Verbs. LC 78-11029. (Oceanic Linguistic Special Publication: No. 16). 1978. pap. text ed. 15.00x (ISBN 0-8248-0627-1). UH Pr.
DeHaan, Dan. The God You Can Know. (Moody Press Electives Ser.). 1985. pap. text ed. 3.95 (ISBN 0-8024-0697-1); leader's guide 2.50 (ISBN 0-8024-0698-X). Moody.
--Steve Bartkowski: Intercepted: A Game Plan for Spiritual Growth. (Illus.). 160p. 1981. pap. 5.95 (ISBN 0-8007-5075-6, Power Bks). Revell.
DeHaan, Daniel F. The God You Can Know. LC 81-16948. 180p. 1982. pap. 5.95 (ISBN 0-8024-3008-2). Moody.
DeHaan, Dennis J., ed. Windows on the Word. 1984. pap. 4.95 (ISBN 0-8010-2946-5). Baker Bk.
De Haan, F. F. & Van De Ven, A. E. Le Mot Juste. (Illus.). 1977. pap. text ed. 4.50x (ISBN 0-582-33112-9). Longman.
De Haan, Ger. Conditions on Rules. 248p. 1981. 25.00x (ISBN 90-70176-35-1); pap. 15.60x (ISBN 90-70176-08-4). Foris Pubns.
De Haan, J. P. Rigging Equipment & Outfit of Seagoing Ships, Pt. 1. 464p. 1957. 200.00x (ISBN 0-85950-070-5, Pub. by Stam Pr England). State Mutual Bk.
--Rigging Equipment & Outfit of Seagoing Ships, Pt. 2. 692p. 1961. 250.00x (ISBN 0-85950-075-6, Pub. by Stam Pr England). State Mutual Bk.
DeHaan, John D. Kirk's Fire Investigation. 2nd ed. LC 82-16078. 352p. 1983. text ed. 29.95 (ISBN 0-471-09279-7). Wiley.
De Haan, M. J., jt. ed. see Gumbert, J. P.
DeHaan, Martin R. Broken Things: Why We Suffer. 144p. 1982. pap. 4.95 (ISBN 0-310-23277-5). Zondervan.
--The Chemistry of the Blood. 160p. 1983. pap. 4.95 (ISBN 0-310-23291-0). Zondervan.
De Haan, Martin R. Daniel the Prophet. 1947. 11.95 (ISBN 0-310-23320-8). Zondervan.
DeHaan, Martin R. Daniel the Prophet. 340p. 1983. pap. 8.95 (ISBN 0-310-23321-6). Zondervan.
De Haan, Martin R. Days of Noah. 5.95 (ISBN 0-310-23331-3). Zondervan.
DeHaan, Martin R. Five Hundred Eight Answers to Bible Questions. 1979. pap. 5.95 (ISBN 0-310-23341-0). Zondervan.
De Haan, Martin R. Hebrews. pap. 6.95 (ISBN 0-310-23371-2). Zondervan.
DeHaan, Martin R. The Jew & Palestine in Prophecy. 1978. pap. 5.95 (ISBN 0-310-23381-X). Zondervan.
De Haan, Martin R. Law or Grace. 1965. pap. 6.95 (ISBN 0-310-23401-8). Zondervan.
DeHaan, Martin R. Pentecost & After. 1978. pap. 5.95 (ISBN 0-310-23421-2). Zondervan.
--Portraits of Christ in Genesis. 1978. pap. 5.95 (ISBN 0-310-23431-X). Zondervan.
--Religion o Cristo? Orig. Title: Religion or Christ. 64p. (Span.). 1970. pap. 1.50 (ISBN 0-8254-1153-X). Kregel.
De Haan, Martin R. Revelation. 1956. 12.95 (ISBN 0-310-23440-9). Zondervan.
DeHaan, Martin R. Second Coming of Jesus. 1978. pap. 6.95 (ISBN 0-310-23461-1). Zondervan.
De Haan, Martin R. Signs of the Times. 1951. 5.95 (ISBN 0-310-23471-9). Zondervan.
--Simon Peter. 1954. 6.95 (ISBN 0-310-23481-6). Zondervan.
--Studies in First Corinthians. 1978. pap. 6.95 (ISBN 0-310-23311-9). Zondervan.
DeHaan, Martin R. The Tabernacle. 1979. pap. 6.95 (ISBN 0-310-23491-3). Zondervan.
DeHaan, Martin R. & Bosch, H. G. Bread for Each Day. large print ed. 1979. Kivar 10.95 (ISBN 0-310-23267-8); 12.95 (ISBN 0-310-23260-0). Zondervan.
--Our Daily Bread. 384p. 1983. pap. 9.95 (ISBN 0-310-25827-8). Zondervan.
DeHaan, R. F. Return Unto Me. pap. 2.00 (ISBN 0-686-14199-7). Rose Pub MI.
DeHaan, Richard W. Como Ser Feliz. Orig. Title: How to Be Happy. 64p. (Span.). 1978. pap. 1.95. Kregel.
--Pray: God Is Listening. 80p. (Orig.). 1980. pap. 2.50 (ISBN 0-310-23542-1). Zondervan.
--The Secret of a Happy Home. (Direction Bks.). 88p. 1982. pap. 2.95 (ISBN 0-8010-2916-3). Baker Bk.
De Haan, Richard W. & Bosch, Henry G., eds. Our Daily Bread Favorites. 384p. 1971. 10.95 (ISBN 0-310-23590-1). Zondervan.
De Haan, Rosemarie. Reflections on Marriage. (Illus.). 48p. 1972. pap. 1.95 (ISBN 0-917814-04-5). Astroart Ent.
De Haan, Vici. Bicycling the Colorado Rockies. LC 82-423. (Illus.). 120p. (Orig.). 1982. pap. 6.95 (ISBN 0-87108-615-8). Pruett.
DeHaan, Vici. Bike Rides of the Colorado Front Range. 1981. pap. 7.50 (ISBN 0-87108-574-7). Pruett.
--The Runner's Guide to Boulder County. LC 81-71143. (Illus.). 200p. 1982. pap. 7.95 (ISBN 0-941388-01-8). Am Trend Pub.
DeHaan, Warren V. The Optometrist's & Ophthalmologist's Guide to Pilot's Vision. LC 81-69431. 200p. 1982. 33.00 (ISBN 0-941388-00-X). Am Trend Pub.
De Haas, C. E. Nature & the Country in English Poetry of the First Half of the Eighteenth Century. LC 74-3086. 1928. lib. bdg. 25.00 (ISBN 0-8414-3735-1). Folcroft.
De Haas, Elsa. Antiquities of Bail: Origin & Historical Development in Criminal Cases to the Year 1275. LC 72-163693. Repr. of 1940 ed. 17.50 (ISBN 0-404-02067-4). AMS Pr.
DeHaas, Frank. Bolt Action Rifles. Rev. ed. LC 73-16310000005. 448p. 1984. pap. 14.95 (ISBN 0-910676-69-0). DBI.
De Haas, Frank see Haas, Frank de.
De Haas, Michel, jt. ed. see Goldscheider, Robert.
Dehaine, M., jt. auth. see Camille, Cl.
De Halacsy, E. Conspectus Florae Graecae & Supplementum Prim, 4 vols. in 3. 1969. Set. 210.00 (ISBN 3-7682-7192-7). Lubrecht & Cramer.
De Haller, R. Aspergillosis & Farmer's Lung in Man & Animal. Suter, F., ed. 329p. 1974. 90.00 (ISBN 3-456-00364-1, Pub. by Holdan Bk Ltd UK). State Mutual Bk.
DeHaller, Rodolphe, jt. ed. see Junod, Alain F.
De'Ham, Claude, illus. Playtime. (Moments Ser.). 20p. (Orig.). 1975. pap. 2.00 (ISBN 0-85953-038-8, Pub. by Child's Play England). Playspaces.
De Hamel, Christopher. Glossed Books of the Bible & the Origins of the Paris Book Trade. (Illus.). 129p. 1985. 75.00 (ISBN 0-85991-145-4, Pub. by Boydell & Brewer). Longwood Pub Group.
Dehan, Vici. Hiking Trails of the Boulder Mountain Area. (Illus.). 1984. pap. 7.50 (ISBN 0-87108-678-6). Pruett.
Deharbe, Joseph. A Full Catechism of the Catholic Religion. 1979. lib. bdg. 59.95 (ISBN 0-8490-2924-4). Gordon Pr.
De Hart, Allen. Hiking the Old Dominion: The Trails of Virginia. LC 83-19586. (Sierra Club Totebk.). (Illus.). 480p. (Orig.). 1984. pap. 10.95 (ISBN 0-87156-812-8). Sierra.
DeHart, Allen. North Carolina Hiking Trails. (Illus.). 346p. (Orig.). 1982. pap. 12.95 (ISBN 0-910146-37-3). Appalach Mtn.
De Hart, Allen. South Carolina Hiking Trails. LC 83-49035. (Illus.). 288p. 1984. pap. 8.95 (ISBN 0-88742-009-5). East Woods.
DeHart, Don. All about Bears. 96p. 1971. pap. 2.95 (ISBN 0-933472-41-2). Johnson Bks.
De Hart, Don. Oh, for the Life of a Guide. (Illus.). 1968. pap. 2.95 (ISBN 0-933472-42-0). Johnson Bks.
DeHart, Florence E. The Librarian's Psychological Commitments: Human Relations in Librarianship. LC 79-7059. (Contributions in Librarianship & Information Science: No. 27). 1979. lib. bdg. 27.50 (ISBN 0-313-21329-1, DLC/). Greenwood.
DeHart, Jess. Hallmarks of a Heritage: A Literary Outline of Unique Southern Cultures. LC 83-83113. (Illus.). 200p. 1984. 10.95 (ISBN 0-913861-00-6). Hamlet Hse.
De Hart, Jess. Plantations of Louisiana. LC 82-325. (Illus.). 160p. 1982. spiral bound 9.95 (ISBN 0-88289-338-6). Pelican.
DeHart, Roy L., ed. Fundamentals of Aerospace Medicine. LC 84-19359. (Illus.). 985p. 1985. text ed. write for info. (ISBN 0-8121-0880-9). Lea & Febiger.
DeHart, Steven. The Meininger Theater: 1776-1926. Beckerman, Bernard, ed. LC 81-11453. (Theater & Dramatic Studies: No. 4). 250p. 1981. 39.95 (ISBN 0-8357-1227-3). UMI Res Pr.
Dehart, William C. Observations on Military Law & the Constitution & the Practice of Courts Marital. Mersky, Roy M. & Jacobstein, J. Myron, eds. (Classics in Legal History Reprint Ser.: Vol. 18). 433p. 1973. Repr. of 1859 ed. lib. bdg. 35.00 (ISBN 0-89941-017-0). W S Hein.
De Hartmann, Olga, jt. auth. see De Hartmann, Thomas.
De Hartmann, Thomas. Our Life with Mister Gurdjieff. LC 64-22661. (Illus.). 1964. 17.50 (ISBN 0-8154-0058-6). Cooper Sq.
De Hartmann, Thomas & De Hartmann, Olga. Our Life with Mr. Gurdjieff. rev. ed. LC 83-47722. 160p. 1983. pap. 7.64 (ISBN 0-06-061865-5, RD 469, HarpR). Har-Row.
De Hartog, Jan. The Commodore. LC 84-48591. 376p. 1985. 16.30 (ISBN 0-06-039041-7, C&M Bessie Bk). Har-Row.
--The Inspector. 14.95 (ISBN 0-88411-069-9, Pub. by Aeonian Pr). Amereon Ltd.
--The Lamb's War. LC 78-20201. 500p. 1980. 13.41i (ISBN 0-06-010995-5, HarpT). Har-Row.
--The Lamb's War. 512p. 1983. pap. 3.95 (ISBN 0-449-20019-1, Crest). Fawcett.
--The Spiral Road. 22.95 (ISBN 0-88411-071-0, Pub. by Aeonian Pr). Amereon Ltd.
--Star of Peace. 1985. pap. 3.95 (ISBN 0-451-13473-7, Sig). NAL.
--The Trail of the Serpent. LC 80-8228. (Cornelia & Michael Bessie Bks.). 208p. 1983. 13.41i (ISBN 0-06-039018-2, HarpT). Har-Row.
--The Trail of the Serpent. LC 83-22018. 224p. 1984. pap. 6.95 (ISBN 0-452-25513-9, Plume). NAL.
De Hartog, Jan see Hartog, Jan de.
De Harven, Emile. Caminos Peligrosos. LC 75-38833. (Illus.). 140p. 1976. pap. 5.95 (ISBN 0-88436-259-0, 70253). EMC.
--Chemins Dangereux. LC 75-38836. (Illus.). 140p. 1976. pap. 5.95 (ISBN 0-88436-260-4, 40256). EMC.
--Gefahrliche Wege. LC 75-29089. (Illus.). 140p. 1976. pap. 5.95 (ISBN 0-88436-256-6, 45252). EMC.
--Suivez la Piste. LC 77-10091. 1972. pap. 5.75 (ISBN 0-912022-30-2, 40257). EMC.
De Hass, Frank S. Buried Cities Recovered: Explorations in Bible Lands. Davis, Moshe, ed. LC 77-70774. (America & the Holy Land). (Illus.). 1977. lib. bdg. 40.00x (ISBN 0-405-10242-9). Ayer Co Pubs.
De Hass, Wills. History of the Early Settlement & Indian Wars of Western Virginia. 1980. Repr. of 1851 ed. 15.00 (ISBN 0-87012-002-6). McClain.
DeHaven, Charlotte, jt. auth. see DeHaven, Kent C.
DeHaven, Edna P. Teaching & Learning the Language Arts. 2nd ed. 1983. text ed. 26.95 (ISBN 0-316-17935-3); avail. tchr's. manual (ISBN 0-316-17936-1). Little.
DeHaven, Kent C. & DeHaven, Charlotte. What's on Tap. (Illus., Orig.). 1982. pap. 4.95 (ISBN 0-910879-00-1). Trends & Custom.
DeHaven, Martha L., jt. auth. see Walker, Jacilyn G.
De Haven, Tom. Funny Papers. 384p. 1985. 15.95 (ISBN 0-670-33251-8). Viking.
--Jersey Luck. LC 80-7602. 208p. 1980. 9.95i (ISBN 0-06-011087-2, HarpT). Har-Row.
De Havenon, Andre, ed. A Touch of Paris: A Selective Guide to Paris in Plain English. (Illus.). 255p. (Orig.). 1980. pap. 7.95 (ISBN 0-933982-14-3). Bradt Ent.
De Havilland, Geoffrey. Sky Fever. 261p. 1981. 30.00 (ISBN 0-906393-02-7, Pub. by Airlife England). State Mutual Bk.
DeHay, Jerry M., jt. auth. see Mondy, R. Wayne.
De Heathcote, Niels, jt. auth. see McKie, Douglas.
De Heer, Joseph. Phenomenological Thermodynamics with Applications to Chemistry. (Illus.). 496p. 1986. text ed. 44.95 (ISBN 0-13-662172-4). P-H.
De Heere, R. F. Scheltema & Bakker, A. R. Buoyance & Stability of Ships. 222p. 1970. 80.00x (ISBN 0-85950-081-0, Pub. by Stam Pr England). State Mutual Bk.
Dehejia, Harsha V. The Allergy Book: A Family Guide. (Illus.). 184p. 1982. pap. 6.95 (ISBN 0-8092-5772-6). Contemp Bks.
Dehejia, Vidya. Early Buddhist Rock Temples. LC 75-158835. (Studies in Ancient Art & Archaeology Ser.). (Illus.). 193p. 1972. 37.50x (ISBN 0-8014-0651-X). Cornell U Pr.
--Early Stone Temples of Orissa. LC 78-54434. 217p. 1979. 29.95 (ISBN 0-89089-092-7). Carolina Acad Pr.
--Living & Dying: An Inquiry into the Enigma of Death & After-Life. 1979. 8.95x (ISBN 0-7069-0815-5, Pub. by Vikas India). Advent NY.
De Hemingford, Walter. Chronicon Domini Walteri de Hemingburgh, Vulgo Heminford Nuncupati, 2 vols. Repr. of 1850 ed. Set. 86.00 (ISBN 0-317-16153-9). Kraus Repr.
De Heredia, Jose M. The Trophies: Sonnets. Sewall, Frank, tr. 1977. lib. bdg. 59.95 (ISBN 0-8490-2769-1). Gordon Pr.
--The Trophies, with Other Sonnets. O'Hara, John M. & Hervey, John, trs. from Fr. LC 76-48425. (Library of World Literature Ser.). 1978. Repr. of 1929 ed. 19.50 (ISBN 0-88355-546-8). Hyperion Conn.
De Heredia, Jose M. see Heredia, Jose M. De.
De Heredia, Jose-Maria. Les Trophees. Ince, W. N., ed. (French Poets Ser.). 178p. (Fr.). 1979. 32.50 (ISBN 0-485-14709-2, Pub. by Athlone Pr Ltd); pap. 14.95 (ISBN 0-485-12709-1). Longwood Pub Group.
De Hernandez Carrera, Armida O., ed. El Vuela del Triunfador. (Span.). Date not set. pap. 3.95 (ISBN 0-87148-306-8). Pathway Pr.
De Herrera Y Tordesillas, Antonio see Herrera Y Tordesillas, Antonio De.
Dehesa, J. S., et al, eds. Interacting Bosons in Nuclei, Granada, Spain 1981: Proceedings. (Lecture Notes in Physics: Vol. 161). 209p. 1982. pap. 15.00 (ISBN 0-387-11572-2). Springer-Verlag.
--Mathematical & Computational Methods in Nuclear Physics. (Lecture Notes in Physics Ser.: Vol. 209). vi, 276p. 1984. pap. 16.50 (ISBN 0-387-13392-5). Springer-Verlag.
De Heusch, Luc. The Cinema & Social Sciences: A Survey of Ethnographic & Sociological Films. Bd. with International Directory of Sample Survey Centres (Outside the U. S. A.) International Committee for Social Sciences Documentation. 1960; The Social Science Activities of Some Eastern European Academies of Science. 1964; Attitude Change; a Review & Bibliography of Selected Research. Davis, E. E. 1965; International Repertory of Sociological Research Centres (Outside the U. S. A.) 1965; International Organizations in the Social Sciences. rev. ed. (UNESCO SSCH RP Ser.: Nos. 16 & 21). 1962. pap. 49.00 (ISBN 0-317-16491-0). Kraus Repr.
--Sacrifice in Africa. O'Brien, Linda & Morton, Alice, trs. LC 84-4887. (African Systems of Thought Ser.). 320p. 1985. 22.50x (ISBN 0-253-35038-7). Ind U Pr.
--Why Marry Her? Society & Symbolic Structures. Lloyd, Janet, tr. (Cambridge Studies in Social Anthropology: No. 33). (Illus.). 240p. 1981. 49.50 (ISBN 0-521-22460-8). Cambridge U Pr.
De Hita, Arcipreste see Arcipreste de Hita.
Dehlinger, P. Marine Gravity. (Oceanography Ser.: Vol. 22). 322p. 1978. 83.00 (ISBN 0-444-41680-3). Elsevier.
Dehlvi, A. M. A. The Finality of Prophethood. pap. 1.25 (ISBN 0-686-18424-6). Kazi Pubns.
Dehmel, Richard. Poems. 59.95 (ISBN 0-8490-0846-8). Gordon Pr.
--Richard Dehmel's Gesammelte Werke, 10 Vols. in 3. LC 76-163694. (BCL Ser. I). Repr. of 1913 ed. Set. 110.00 (ISBN 0-404-02070-4). AMS Pr.
Dehmlow, Eckehard & Dehmlow, Sigrid. Phase Transfer Catalysis. 2nd ed. Ebel, Hans F., ed. (Monographs in Modern Chemistry: Vol. 11). (Illus.). xi, 386p. 1983. 69.00x (ISBN 0-89573-035-9). VCH Pubs.
Dehmlow, Sigrid, jt. auth. see Dehmlow, Eckehard.
Dehn, Thomas & Sandrick, Karen. How Doctors Can Use DRG Data. (Orig.). 1983. pap. 4.00 (ISBN 0-916499-01-4). Care Comm Inc.
Dehn, Virginia, ed. Adolf Dehn Drawings. LC 71-134016. (Illus.). 208p. 1971. 22.00x (ISBN 0-8262-0100-8). U of Mo Pr.
Dehnbostel, Nancy L. & Hartman, Mary E. P.E.P.P.E.R. Dinosaurs Procedural Educational Plan for Primary Enrichment Resource Activities. (Illus.). 72p. (Orig.). 1981. pap. text ed. 5.95 (ISBN 0-914634-95-X). DOK Pubs.

--Space. (The P.E.P.P.E.R. Ser.). (Illus.). 44p. (gr. 1-6). 1982. 5.95 (ISBN 0-88047-010-0, 8205). DOK Pubs.

--Superheroes. (The P.E.P.P.E.R. Ser.). (Illus.). 48p. (gr. 1-6). 1983. pap. 5.95 Tchr Enrichment Bk (ISBN 0-88047-026-7, 8306). DOK Pubs.

Dehner, Louis P., jt. ed. see Humphrey, G. Bennett.

DeHoghton, C. Company: Law, Structure & Reform. LC 76-124642. (Studies of the Modern Corporation). 1970. 10.00 (ISBN 0-02-907240-9). Free Pr.

DeHoghton, Charles. The Company: Law, Structure & Reform in Eleven Countries. (Political & Economic Planning Ser.). 1970. text ed. 35.00x (ISBN 0-04-347001-7). Allen Unwin.

De Hojeda, Diego see Hojeda, Diego de.

De Hollanda, Francisco see Hollanda, Francisco De.

Dehoney, Wayne. An Evangelical's Guidebook to the Holy Land. LC 73-85698. pap. 8.95 (ISBN 0-8054-5701-1). Broadman.

De Honnecourt, Villard. The Sketchbook of Villard de Honnecourt. Bowie, Theodore, ed. LC 82-15540. (Illus.). 144p. 1982. lib. bdg. 35.00x (ISBN 0-313-23747-6, VISK). Greenwood.

De Hoog, F. R., jt. ed. see Anderson, R. S.

De Hoog, Ruth H. Contracting Out for Human Services: Economic, Political & Organizational Perspectives. LC 83-24292. (SUNY Series in Urban Public Policy). 180p. 1984. 29.50x (ISBN 0-87395-893-4); pap. text ed. 12.95x (ISBN 0-87395-894-2). State U NY Pr.

De Hooge, Romein. Famous Etchings: Les Indes Orientales. 104p. 1981. 99.50x (ISBN 0-686-79052-9, Pub. by BV Uitgerij W Van Hoeue). State Mutual Bk.

De Horst, Adrian Van see Van De Horst, Adrian.

De Hostos, Adolfo, ed. Bibliography & Index of the Work of Eugenio Maria De Hostos. (Puerto Rico Ser.). 1979. lib. bdg. 99.75 (ISBN 0-8490-2873-6). Gordon Pr.

De Hostos, Eugenio C. see Hostos, Eugenio C. De.

De Hostos, Eugenio M. Complete Works of Eugenio Maria De Hostos, 20 vols. (Puerto Rico Ser.). 1979. Set. lib. bdg. 50.00 ea. (ISBN 0-8490-2891-4). Gordon Pr.

De Hostos, Eugenio M. see Hostos, Eugenio M. De.

De Hoveden, Roger see Hoveden, Roger de.

DeHoyos, Genieve. Stewardship, the Divine Order. LC 81-82055. 200p. 1982. 6.95 (ISBN 0-88290-191-5, 1065). Horizon Utah.

De Hoyos, Ladislas. Klaus Barbie: The Untold Story. Courtin, Nicholas, tr. (Illus.). 336p. 1985. 17.95 (ISBN 0-07-016297-2). McGraw.

DeHoyos, R., tr. see Crowther, Duane S.

Deh Ta Hsiung. The Home Book of Chinese Cookery. (Illus.). 200p. 1978. pap. 3.95 (ISBN 0-571-11283-8). Faber & Faber.

Dehuai, Peng. Memoirs of a Chinese Marshal. Grimes, Sara, ed. Longpu, Zheng, tr. from Chinese. (Illus.). 523p. (Orig.). 1984. pap. 7.95 (ISBN 0-8351-1052-4). China Bks.

De Hucck Doherty, Catherine see Doherty, Catherine de Hucck.

De Hueck Doherty, Catherine. Soul of my Soul: Reflections from a Life of Prayer. 128p. (Orig.). 1985. pap. 4.95 (ISBN 0-87793-298-0). Ave Maria.

De Hunter, Elena Mellado see Mellado De Hunter, Elena.

De Huszar, George B. Fundamentals of Voluntary Health Care. LC 61-9382. 1962. 6.00 (ISBN 0-87004-070-7). Caxton.

De Huszar, George B., ed. Persistent International Issues. LC 79-142645. (Essay Index Reprint Ser.). Repr. of 1947 ed. 20.00 (ISBN 0-8369-2772-9). Ayer Co Pubs.

DeHuszar, William I. Mortgage Loan Administration. (Illus.). 480p. 1972. text ed. 38.95 (ISBN 0-07-016257-3). McGraw.

De Huszar Allen, Marguerite. The Faust Legend: Popular Formula & Modern Novel. (Germanic Studies in America: Vol. 53). 178p. 1985. text ed. 16.50 (ISBN 0-8204-0210-9). P Lang Pubs.

De Ibarbourou, Juan. Elegia. (Illus.). 3.75 (ISBN 0-8477-3206-1). U of PR Pr.

Deibel, Franz. Dorothea Schlegel Als Schriftstellerin Im Zusammenhang Mit der Romantischen Schule. (Ger). 18.00 (ISBN 0-384-11196-3); pap. 13.00 (ISBN 0-685-02239-0). Johnson Repr.

Deibert, Alvin N. B. J. & the Language of the Woodland. LC 82-24422. (Illus.). 48p. (Orig.). (gr. 2-6). 1983. pap. 4.95 (ISBN 0-87743-701-7, 353-019, Pub. by Bellwood Pr). Baha'i.

Deibler, Ellis. Semantic Relationships of Gahuku Verbs. (SIL Linguistic & Related Fields Ser.: No. 48). 159p. 1974. pap. 8.00x (ISBN 0-88312-058-5); microfiche 2.25x (ISBN 0-88312-458-0). Summer Inst Ling.

Deich, A., jt. auth. see Rylsky, M.

Deich, Ruth F. & Hodges, Patricia M. Language Without Speech. 256p. 1977. 20.00x (ISBN 0-285-64847-0, Pub. by Souvenir Pr). State Mutual Bk.

Deicher, H. & Schulz, L. C., eds. Arthritis: Models & Mechanisms. (Illus.). 309p. 1981. pap. 36.00 (ISBN 0-387-10781-9). Springer-Verlag.

Deichert, Jerome. Nebraska Population Projections, 1985-2020. (Nebraska Economic & Business Report Ser.: No. 32). 1982. 17.50 (ISBN 0-318-02059-9). Bur Busn Res U Nebr.

Deichert, Jerome A. Economic Impact of the University of Nebraska-Lincoln on the Lincoln Area Economy. 1979p. write for info. Bur Busn Res U Nebr.

Deichert, Jerome A. & Ralston, Anne S. In-migration of Young Adults in Nebraska: Characteristics, Motivations, & Implications. (Nebraska Economic & Business Report: No. 26). 1979. 5.00 (ISBN 0-686-26980-2). Bur Busn Res U Nebr.

Deichert, Jerome A., jt. auth. see Love, Douglas O.

Deichert, Jerome A., jt. auth. see Pursell, Donald E.

Deichert, Jerome A., et al. Migration Patterns of Young Adults in Nebraska. (Nebraska Economic & Business Report: No. 25). 1978. 5.00 (ISBN 0-686-28413-5). Bur Busn Res U Nebr.

Deichgraeber, Karl. Die Epidemien und das Corpus Hippocraticum: Voruntersuchung zu einer Geschichte der koischen Aerzteschule. 187p. 1971. Repr. 33.60x (ISBN 3-11-003635-5). De Gruyter.

Deichman, E. S., et al. Working with the Elderly Manual & Guide: Manual & Guide. rev. ed. 100p. 1985. pap. 12.95 (ISBN 0-932910-53-X). Potentials Development.

Deichmann, Paul. German Air Force Operations in Support of the Army. LC 68-22550. (German Air Force in World War 2 Series). (Illus.). 1968. Repr. of 1962 ed. 17.00 (ISBN 0-405-00040-5). Ayer Co Pubs.

Deichmann, W. B., ed. Toxicology & Occupational Medicine. (Developments in Toxicology & Environmental Science Ser.: Vol. 4). 480p. 1979. 86.00 (ISBN 0-444-00288-X, Biomedical Pr). Elsevier.

Deichmann, W. J. Bladder Cancer. LC 67-23390. 296p. 1967. 12.50 (ISBN 0-87527-005-0). Green.

Deichmann, William B. Safe Farming & Gardening. 1972. pap. 3.00 (ISBN 0-89970-077-2, OP-389). AMA.

D'Eichthal, Gustave. A French Sociologist Looks at Britain: Gustave d'Eichthal & British Society in 1828. Ratcliffe, Barrie M., ed. Chaloner, W. H., tr. LC 77-1899. 192p. 1977. 13.75x (ISBN 0-87471-963-1). Rowman.

Deif, A. S. Advanced Matrix Theory for Scientists & Engineers. 256p. 1982. 39.95x (ISBN 0-470-27316-X). Halsted Pr.

Deigendesch, Paul, ed. see Moore, Lolita D.

Deighan, Maurice. County Court Practice & Procedure. 1980. 40.00x (ISBN 0-686-97089-6, Pub. by Fourmat England). State Mutual Bk.

Deighton, L. C. Encyclopedia of Education, 10 vols. 1971. Set. 199.00 (ISBN 0-02-895300-2). Macmillan.

Deighton, Lee. Fight for the Valley. 160p. 1981. pap. 1.75 (ISBN 0-345-29076-3). Ballantine.

--Tomahawk. 156p. 1981. pap. 1.75 (ISBN 0-345-29431-9). Ballantine.

--You'll Never Hang Me. 160p. 1981. pap. 1.75 (ISBN 0-345-29119-0). Ballantine.

Deighton, Lee C. Vocabulary Development in the Classroom. LC 59-8372. pap. 15.00 (ISBN 0-8357-9611-6, 2015778). Bks Demand UMI.

Deighton, Len. Berlin Game. LC 83-48104. 289p. 1984. 15.95 (ISBN 0-394-53407-7). Knopf.

--Berlin Game. (General Ser.). 1984. lib. bdg. 16.95 (ISBN 0-8161-3685-8, Large Print Bks). G K Hall.

--The Berlin Game. 320p. 1986. pap. 4.50 (ISBN 0-345-31498-0). Ballantine.

--The Billion Dollar Brain. 256p. 1984. pap. 3.50 (ISBN 0-425-07372-6). Berkley Pub.

--Blitzkrieg. 1982. pap. 9.95 (ISBN 0-345-29426-2). Ballantine.

--Blitzkrieg: From the Rise of Hitler to the Fall of Dunkirk. LC 79-3482. (Illus.). 1980. pap. 9.95 (ISBN 0-345-29426-2). Knopf.

--Bomber. 1971. pap. 3.95 (ISBN 0-451-13689-6, Sig). NAL.

--Catch a Falling Spy. 1981. pap. 2.75 (ISBN 0-671-44259-7). PB.

--Catch a Falling Spy. 288p. 1985. pap. 3.50 (ISBN 0-345-31568-5). Ballantine.

--An Expensive Place to Die. 1984. pap. 3.50 (ISBN 0-425-07373-4). Berkley Pub.

--Fighter. 1982. pap. 9.95 (ISBN 0-345-29821-7). Ballantine.

--Fighter: The True Story of the Battle of Britain. LC 77-20356. (Illus.). 1978. 16.95 (ISBN 0-394-42757-2). Knopf.

--Funeral in Berlin. 272p. 1984. pap. 3.50 (ISBN 0-425-07402-1). Berkley Pub.

--Goodbye, Mickey Mouse. LC 82-47813. 355p. 1982. 14.95 (ISBN 0-394-51259-6). Knopf.

--Goodbye, Mickey Mouse. (General Ser.). 1983. lib. bdg. 19.95 (ISBN 0-8161-3544-4, Large Print Bks). G K Hall.

--Goodbye, Mickey Mouse. 384p. 1983. pap. 3.95 (ISBN 0-345-31146-9). Ballantine.

--Horse under Water. 1984. pap. 3.50 (ISBN 0-425-07403-X). Berkley Pub.

--Ipcress File. 1976. pap. 2.75 (ISBN 0-345-30453-5). Ballantine.

--London Match. 1985. 16.95 (ISBN 0-317-20674-5). Knopf.

--Mexico Set. Gottlieb, Robert, ed. LC 84-48500. 384p. 1985. 16.95 (ISBN 0-394-53525-1). Knopf.

--Mexico Set. 408p. 1986. pap. 4.50 (ISBN 0-345-31499-9). Ballantine.

--Spy Story. 1983. pap. 3.50 (ISBN 0-671-47164-3, 80058). PB.

--Spy Story. 272p. 1985. pap. 3.95 (ISBN 0-345-31569-3). Ballantine.

--SS-GB. 1984. pap. 3.95 (ISBN 0-345-31809-9). Ballantine.

--SS-GB. 1980. pap. 2.95 (ISBN 0-345-29317-7). Ballantine.

--SS-GB. 1979. 10.95 (ISBN 0-394-50409-7). Knopf.

--XPD. 1983. pap. 3.95 (ISBN 0-345-31337-2). Ballantine.

--XPD. LC 80-7629. 384p. 1981. 12.95 (ISBN 0-394-51258-8). Knopf.

--Yesterday's Spy. 224p. 1976. pap. 2.95 (ISBN 0-446-30882-X). Warner Bks.

Deighton, Len, ed. see Goodenough, Simon.

Deighton, S., ed. Computers in Developing Countries: A Bibliography. 1981. 44.00 (ISBN 0-85296-228-2). Inst Elect Eng.

--Microprocessor Applications in Home & Office, 1977-1978: Bibliography. 1979. 23.00 (ISBN 0-85296-449-8). Inst Elect Eng.

--Microprocessor Applications in Science & Medicine, 1977-1978: Bibliography. 1979. 28.00 (ISBN 0-85296-448-X). Inst Elect Eng.

--The New Criminals: A Bibliography of Computer Related Crime. 2nd ed. 1979. 23.00 (ISBN 0-85296-456-0). Inst Elect Eng.

Deighton, S. & Mayne, K. D., eds. Microprocessor Applications in Engineering, 1977-1978: Bibliography. 1979. 23.00 (ISBN 0-85296-454-4). Inst Elect Eng.

Deighton, S., jt. ed. see Dayasena, P. J.

Deighton, Suzan, et al, eds. Computers & Information Processing World Index. 626p. 1984. lib. bdg. 85.00 (ISBN 0-89774-116-1, Co-Pub. with Gower Pub. Co). Oryx Pr.

Deignan, Margaret C., jt. auth. see Tolor, Alexander.

Deignan, Paul T., jt. auth. see McCarthy, Martha M.

Deihl, David. Quill. 1980. pap. 1.75 (ISBN 0-505-51472-9, Pub. by Tower Bks). Dorchester Pub Co.

Deike, Robert J., et al. Minnesota Real Estate Law Digest. 1983. looseleaf 85.00 (ISBN 0-917126-94-7). Butterworth MN.

Deikman, Arthur J. The Observing Self: Mysticism & Psychotherapy. LC 81-70486. 208p. 1983. pap. 7.95 (ISBN 0-8070-2951-3, BP 652). Beacon Pr.

Deily, R. L., ed. IISS Commentary Special Reports I: Steel Plants USA 1960-1980. 150p. 1979. 50.00 (ISBN 0-317-34774-8). Iron & Steel.

--Steel Industry in Brief: Japan. 156p. 1977. pap. 75.00 (ISBN 0-317-34776-4). Iron & Steel.

Deily, R. L. & Pietrucla, W. E., eds. Steel Industry in Brief: Databook USA. 144p. 1977. pap. 75.00 (ISBN 0-317-34775-6). Iron & Steel.

De Imaz, Jose L. Los Que Mandan (Those Who Rule) Astiz, Carlos A., tr. from Span. LC 69-12100. 1970. 34.50x (ISBN 0-87395-044-5); pap. 10.95x (ISBN 0-87395-073-9). State U NY Pr.

Deimel, Diana. Vision Victory. 4.00x (ISBN 0-686-29907-8). Cancer Control Soc.

--Vision Victory. 196p. 3.00 (ISBN 0-318-15692-X). Natl Health Fed.

Deimer, Petra. Parrots. (Pet Care Ser.). 80p. 1983. pap. 3.95 (ISBN 0-8120-2630-6). Barron.

Deimling, K. Nonlinear Functional Analysis. (Illus.). xiv, 450p. 1985. 39.00 (ISBN 0-387-13928-1). Springer-Verlag.

--Ordinary Differential Equations in Banach Spaces. (Lecture Notes in Mathematics: Vol. 596). 1977. 13.00 (ISBN 0-387-08260-3). Springer-Verlag.

Deimling, Paula, ed. Writer's Market '86. 1056p. 1985. 19.95 (ISBN 0-89879-198-7, 2709). Writers Digest.

Deindorfer, Robert G., ed. America's One Hundred One Most High Falutin', Big Talkin' Knee Slappin', Golly Whoppers & Tall Tales: The Best of the Burlington Liars' Club. LC 80-51618. (Illus.). 128p. (Orig.). 1980. pap. 3.95 (ISBN 0-89480-136-8, 244). Workman Pub.

Deindorfer, Scott. Dear Scott. LC 77-5304. (Illus.). 1978. 3.95 (ISBN 0-89480-007-8, 153). Workman Pub.

Deiner, Penny L. Resources for Teaching Young Children with Special Needs. LC 82-84254. 564p. 1983. pap. text ed. 21.95 (ISBN 0-15-576627-9, HC). HarBraceJ.

Deiner, Royce. How to Finance a Growing Business. 414p. 1974. 14.95x (ISBN 0-8464-1108-3). Beekman Pubs.

Deines, Elaine. Staffing for DRGs: A Unit-Specific Approach for Nurse Managers. LC 83-81646. (Help Series of Management Guides). 130p. 1983. pap. 15.95 (ISBN 0-933036-20-5). Ganong W L Co.

--Staffing for DRGs-Part II: Nursing Care Strategies for DRG-Specific Staffing. LC 83-81646. (HELP Series of Management Guides). 128p. 1985. pap. 15.95 (ISBN 0-933036-21-3). Ganong W L Co.

Deinhard, Hanna. Meaning & Expression: Toward a Sociology of Art. LC 83-18526. (Illus.). 120p. 1983. Repr. of 1970 ed. lib. bdg. 25.00x (ISBN 0-313-24252-6, DEMX). Greenwood.

Deinhardt, Carol L. Personality Assessment & Psychological Interpretation. (Illus.). 256p. 1983. 24.75x (ISBN 0-398-04752-9). C C Thomas.

Deinhardt, Friedrich & Deinhardt, J., eds. Viral Hepatitis: Laboratory & Clinical Science. (Liver: Normal Function & Disease Ser.: Vol. 3). 608p. 1983. 89.75 (ISBN 0-8247-1801-1). Dekker.

Deinhardt, J., jt. ed. see Deinhardt, Friedrich.

Deinhart, Ligita & Pinsel, E. Melvin. Power Lunching. (A Turnbull & Willoughby Bk.). 228p. 6.95 (ISBN 0-943084-21-0). Contemp Bks.

Deinzer, Harvey T. Development of Accounting Thought. LC 83-49107. (Accounting History & the Development of a Profession Ser.). 192p. 1984. lib. bdg. 25.00 (ISBN 0-8240-6321-X). Garland Pub.

De Iongh, Daniel Crena see Crena De Iongh, Daniel.

Deirmendjian, D. Electromagnetic Scattering on Spherical Polydispersions. LC 68-28759. pap. 78.00 (ISBN 0-317-08591-3, 2007761). Bks Demand UMI.

Deiros, P. A. Que Paso con Estos Pecados? 144p. 1979. pap. 2.50 (ISBN 0-311-42063-X). Casa Bautista.

Deiros, Pablo. El Cristiano y los Problemas Eticos. 112p. 1982. pap. 3.50 (ISBN 0-311-46064-X). Casa Bautista.

Deiros, Pablo, compiled by. Figuras De Plata. 200p. 1978. pap. 3.95 (ISBN 0-311-42053-2, Edit Mundo). Casa Bautista.

Deiros, Pablo A., tr. see Duval, Evelyn M.

Deis, Paul. Inventory & Production Management in the 1980's. (Illus.). 384p. 1983. 25.95 (ISBN 0-13-502559-1). P-H.

D'Eisenberg, Reis. The Classical Riding School. (Illus.). 1979. 9.95 (ISBN 0-670-22509-6, The Vendome Pr.). Viking.

Deisler, Paul F., Jr. Reducing the Carcinogenic Risks in Industry. (Occupation Safety & Health Ser.). 288p. 1984. 55.00 (ISBN 0-8247-7250-4). Dekker.

Deiss, Joseph J. Herculaneum: Italy's Buried Treasure. LC 84-48097. (Illus.). 224p. 1985. pap. 12.45i (ISBN 0-06-091205-7, CN). Har-Row.

--Herculaneum: Italy's Buried Treasure. LC 84-48097. (Illus.). 224p. 1985. 22.07 (ISBN 0-06-015376-8, HarpT). Har-Row.

Deiss, Lucien. Springtime of the Liturgy: Liturgical Texts of the First Four Centuries. rev. ed. O'Connell, Matthew J., tr. from Fr. LC 79-15603. 307p. 1979. pap. 10.00 (ISBN 0-8146-1023-4). Liturgical Pr.

Deissman, Adolf. Light from the Ancient East. (Twin Brooks Ser). 1978. pap. 10.95 (ISBN 0-8010-2886-8). Baker Bk.

Deissman, Adolph. Paul: A Study in Social & Religious History. Wilson, William W., tr. 1958. 12.75 (ISBN 0-8446-1965-5). Peter Smith.

Deist, Wilhelm. The Wehrmacht & German Rearmament. 164p. 1981. 30.00x (ISBN 0-8020-2423-8). U of Toronto Pr.

Deist, Wilhelm, ed. The German Military in the Age of Total War. LC 84-734779. 352p. 1985. 36.75 (ISBN 0-907582-14-1, Pub. by Berg Pubs). Longwood Pub Group.

Deitchman, Seymour J. The Best-Laid Schemes: A Tale of Social Research & Bureaucracy. LC 75-31736. 1976. text ed. 20.00x (ISBN 0-262-04049-2). MIT Pr.

--Military Power & the Advance of Technology: General Purpose Military Forces in the 1980's & Beyond. Rev. ed. LC 83-50434. (Special Studies in Military Affairs). 278p. 1983. lib. bdg. 29.50x (ISBN 0-86531-573-6); pap. 13.50x (ISBN 0-86531-574-4). Westview.

Deitel, Barbara, jt. auth. see Deitel, Harvey M.

Deitel, Harvey, jt. auth. see Lorin, Harold.

Deitel, Harvey M. Introduction to Computer Programming with the BASIC Language. LC 77-2960. (Illus.). 1977. pap. 21.95 ref. ed. (ISBN 0-13-480137-7). P-H.

--An Introduction to Operating Systems. Rev. ed. LC 83-7153. 704p. 1983. text ed. 36.95 (ISBN 0-201-14501-4). Addison-Wesley.

--VAX-11 BASIC: A Structural Approach. (Illus.). 256p. 1985. pap. text ed. 18.95 (ISBN 0-13-940966-1). P-H.

Deitel, Harvey M. & Deitel, Barbara. Introduction to Computers & Data Processing. 1985. text ed. 22.50i (ISBN 0-12-209020-9); study guide avail. (ISBN 0-12-209021-7); 10.00i (ISBN 0-12-209023-3); slide package avail. (ISBN 0-12-209024-1); transparencies avail. (ISBN 0-12-209022-5). Acad Pr.

Deitel, Mervyn. Nutrition in Clinical Surgery. 2nd ed. 350p. 1985. 65.00 (ISBN 0-683-24507-4, 2450-7). Williams & Wilkins.

Deiter, Ronald H. The Story of Metro: Politics & Transport in Washington. Sebree, Mac, ed. (Interurbans Special Ser.: 101). 120p. 1985. pap. 14.95 (ISBN 0-916374-70-X). Interurban.

Deitering. Action, Gestures, & Bodily Attitudes. (Illus.). 96p. 1980. 9.95 (ISBN 0-318-16436-1). Sacred Dance Guild.

Deitering, Carolyn. Actions, Gestures & Bodily Attitudes. LC 80-51058. 1980. pap. 10.95 (ISBN 0-89390-021-4). Resource Pubns.

--The Liturgy As Dance & the Liturgical Dancer. (Illus.). 144p. 1984. pap. 8.95 (ISBN 0-8245-0654-5). Crossroad NY.

Deitrich, Jeff. Reluctant Resister. (Illus.). 1983. 17.00 (ISBN 0-87775-156-0); pap. 7.00 (ISBN 0-87775-157-9). Unicorn Pr.

Deitrick, Bernard E. A Basic Book List for Church Libraries. 2nd rev ed. LC 77-4093. 1983. pap. 3.00x (ISBN 0-915324-10-5); pap. 2.40 members. CSLA.

--Know Your Neighbor's Faith. LC 83-7259. (Orig.). 1983. pap. 3.00x (ISBN 0-915324-19-9); pap. 2.40 members. CSLA.

Deitsch, Clarence R., jt. auth. see Dilts, David A.

Deitsch, Cyrel, jt. ed. see Blau, Esther.

Deitsch, Marian, ed. Directory of U. S. & Canadian Marketing Surveys & Services: Supplements Through 1983. 4th ed. 1981. loose-leaf 145.00 (ISBN 0-917148-75-4). Kline.

--Kline Guide to Packaging. Rich, Susan. (Illus.). 324p. 1980. pap. 70.00. Kline.

Deitsch, Marian & Rauch, James, eds. Kline Guide to Energy. LC 81-81264. (Illus.). 525p. 1981. pap. 85.00 (ISBN 0-917148-20-7). Kline.

Deitsch, Marian, jt. ed. see Kollonitsch, Valerie.

Deitschmann, Craig, et al. Poetry Peddlers: Two from Music City Country. 128p. (Orig.). 1984. pap. 6.95 (ISBN 0-939298-46-5, 465). J M Prods.

Deitz, Granville. Mountain Memories. (Illus.). 124p. 1980. pap. 5.00 (ISBN 0-934750-30-0). Jalamap.

Deitz, Samuel M. & Hummel, John H. Discipline in the Schools: A Guide to Reducing Misbehavior. LC 78-18269. (Illus.). 280p. 1978. pap. 19.95 (ISBN 0-87778-128-1). Educ Tech Pubns.

Deitzer, Bernard A. & Shilliff, Karl A. Contemporary Management Incidents. LC 76-44998. (Management Ser.). Repr. of 1977 ed. 52.00 (ISBN 0-8357-9140-8, 2016551). Bks Demand UMI.

De Jaager, Gerald. The Best Management Resources: Developing Management Skills: A Self-Directed Approach, Bk. 2. LC 84-51544. 373p. 1985. 80.00 (ISBN 0-916001-01-6). Seiler Doar.

--The Management Skills Inventory: Developing Management Skills: A Self-Directed Approach. LC 84-51543. (Bk 1). 78p. (Orig.). 1985. pap. 20.00 (ISBN 0-916001-00-8). Seiler Doar.

De Jaeger, Charles. The Linz File: Hitler's Plunder of Europe's Art. 1982. 12.95 (ISBN 0-03-061463-5). HR&W.

--Paul Is a Maltese Boy. LC 68-13444. (Children Everywhere Ser.: No. 6). (Illus.). (gr. 2-4). 1968. PLB 5.95 (ISBN 0-8038-5699-7). Hastings.

DeJaeger, Robert, jt. ed. see Mathe, Georges.

De Jaegher, Paul, ed. An Anthology of Christian Mysticism. 1977. 7.95 (ISBN 0-87243-073-1). Templegate.

De Jaegher, Raymond. Enemy Within. 1968. pap. 1.95 (ISBN 0-912080-21-3). Guild Bks.

De Jager, C., ed. The Brightest Stars. (Geophysics & Astrophysics Monographs: No. 19). 472p. 1981. PLB 73.50 (ISBN 90-277-1109-7, Pub. by Reidel Holland); pap. 31.50 (ISBN 90-277-1109-7). Kluwer Academic.

--Highlights of Astronomy, Vol. 2. LC 71-159657. 793p. 1971. 79.00 (ISBN 90-277-0189-X, Pub. by Reidel Holland). Kluwer Academic.

--Transactions of the International Astronomical Union: Reports on Astronomy, Vol. 14a. LC 30-10103. 566p. 1970. lib. bdg. 50.00 (ISBN 90-277-0154-7, Pub. by Reidel Holland). Kluwer Academic.

--Transactions of the International Astronomical Union: Reports on Astronomy, Vol. 15a. LC 73-81827. 762p. 1973. lib. bdg. 105.00 (ISBN 90-277-0340-X, Pub. by Reidel Holland). Kluwer Academic.

De Jager, C. & Nieuwenhuijzen, H., eds. Image Processing Techniques in Astronomy. LC 75-23032. (Astrophysics & Space Science Library: No. 54). xi, 418p. 1975. lib. bdg. 53.00 (ISBN 90-277-0650-6, Pub. by Reidel Holland). Kluwer Academic.

De Jager, C., ed. see Biderberg Conference, Arnhem, Holland, April 17-21, 1967.

De Jager, C., ed. see General Assembly 14th,Brighton,1970.

De Jager, C., ed. see Symposium, University of Utrecht, 1963.

De Jager, E. M., jt. ed. see Eckhaus, W.

De Janvry, Alain. The Agrarian Question & Reformism in Latin America. LC 81-4147. (Illus.). 352p. 1981. text ed. 28.50x (ISBN 0-8018-2531-8); pap. text ed. 9.95x (ISBN 0-8018-2532-6). Johns Hopkins.

DeJardin, Charie. Computer Gardening Made Simple. (Illus.). 32p. 1984. pap. 2.95 (ISBN 0-915765-20-9). Natl Pr Inc.

DeJarnette, Harriette. Follow the North Star. 384p. (Orig.). 1982. pap. 3.25 (ISBN 0-8439-1073-9, Leisure Bks). Dorchester Pub Co.

De Jarnette, Harriette. Follow the North Star. 384p. 1985. pap. 3.75 (ISBN 0-8439-2221-4, Leisure Bks). Dorchester Pub Co.

DeJarnette, Harriette. The Passion Stone. 1980. pap. 2.75 (ISBN 0-8439-0840-8, Pub. by Nordon Pubns). Dorchester Pub Co.

--The Passion Stone. 384p. 1984. pap. 3.50 (ISBN 0-8439-2095-5). Dorchester Pub Co.

De Jasay, Anthony. The State. 256p. 1985. 24.95x (ISBN 0-631-14025-5). Basil Blackwell.

DeJay, Ralph. Guitar-Plus. (Illus.). 1979. pap. 4.00 (ISBN 0-682-49408-9). Exposition Pr FL.

DeJean, Joan. Libertine Strategies: Freedom & the Novel in Seventeenth Century France. LC 81-38431. (Illus.). 235p. 1981. 17.50x (ISBN 0-8142-0325-6). Ohio St U Pr.

--Literary Fortifications: Rousseau, Laclos, Sade. LC 84-42593. (Illus.). 336p. 1984. text ed. 36.50 (ISBN 0-691-06611-6). Princeton U Pr.

DeJean, Joan E. Scarron's Roman Comique: A Comedy of the Novel-A Novel of Comedy, French Language & Literature, Vol. 46. (European University Studies: Ser. 13). 110p. 1977. pap. 19.60 (ISBN 3-261-02943-9). P Lang Pubs.

DeJ Ellis, Maria see Ellis, Maria deJ.

Dejerine, Joseph J. & Gauckler, E. Psychoneuroses & Their Treatment by Psychotherapy. Jelliffe, Smith E., tr. LC 75-16697. (Classics in Psychiatry Ser.). 1976. Repr. of 1913 ed. 31.00x (ISBN 0-405-07425-5). Ayer Co Pubs.

De Jersey, Katherine & Taves, Isabella. Destiny Times Six: An Astrologer's Case Book. LC 70-122815. 312p. 1970. 5.95 (ISBN 0-87131-004-X). M Evans.

DeJesu, Gil. Developing Confidence & Self-Expression: A Do-It-Yourself Manual of Instruction. Dickinson, Janice, ed. 150p. (Orig.). 1986. pap. 7.50 (ISBN 0-918935-02-4). Magnoart Pubns.

--How to Attract Your Love-Life-Partner: A Do-It-Yourself Manual of Instruction. Dickinson, Janice, ed. 200p. (Orig.). 1984. pap. 9.50 (ISBN 0-918935-99-7). Magnoart Pubns.

DeJesu, Gil, jt. auth. see Edgerly, Webster.

De Jesus, Carolina M. Child of the Dark: The Diary of Carolina Maria De Jesus. (Illus.). 1964. pap. 2.50 (ISBN 0-451-62294-4, ME2294, Ment). NAL.

De Jesus, Ed C., ed. The Tobacco Monopoly in the Philippines: Bureaucratic Enterprise & Social Change, 1766-1880. (Illus.). 244p. 1981. 25.00x (ISBN 0-686-30372-5, Pub. by Ateneo de Manila U Pr Philippines); pap. 17.00x (ISBN 0-686-30373-3). Cellar.

De Jesus, Ed. C., jt. ed. see McCoy, Alfred W.

De Jesus, Gonzalo. Fray Jose De Guadalupe Mojica: Mid Guia y Mi Estrella. (Illus.). 100p. 1976. 2.00 (ISBN 0-8199-0570-4). Franciscan Herald.

De Jesus Toro, Rafael see Toro, Rafael J.

De Jeu, W. H. Physical Properties of Liquid Crystalline Materials. 140p. 1980. 45.25 (ISBN 0-677-04040-7). Gordon.

De Jim, Strange. Visioning. LC 79-66208. (Illus.). 112p. (Orig.). 1979. pap. 5.95 (ISBN 0-9605308-0-0). Ash-Kar Pr.

Dejnozka, Edward L. Educational Administration Glossary. LC 83-5719. xii, 247p. 1983. lib. bdg. 39.95 (ISBN 0-313-23301-2, DEA/). Greenwood.

Dejnozka, Edward L. & Kapel, David E., eds. The American Educators' Encyclopedia. LC 81-6664. (Illus.). xvii, 597p. 1982. lib. bdg. 75.00 (ISBN 0-313-20954-5, DDE/). Greenwood.

DeJohn, Marie, illus. Christmas Words: See & Say Fun for the Very Young. LC 83-63316. (Illus.). 12p. (ps). 1984. bds. 1.95 (ISBN 0-394-86746-7, BYR). Random.

DeJoia, Alex & Stenton, Adrian. Terms in Systemic Linguistics. LC 80-5089. 1980. 20.00 (ISBN 0-312-79180-1). St Martin.

De Joinville, Jean. Histoire De Saint Louis. De Wailly, N., ed. 1868. 38.00 (ISBN 0-384-27721-7); pap. 32.00 (ISBN 0-384-27720-9). Johnson Repr.

De Joinville, Jean, jt. auth. see De Villehardouin, Geoffrey.

De Joly, Robert. Memoires of a Speleologist: The Adventurous Life of a Famous French Cave Explorer. Kurz, Peter, tr. LC 73-31836. (Illus.). 185p. (Orig.). 1975. 10.50 (ISBN 0-914264-08-7); pap. 5.95 (ISBN 0-914264-09-5). Cave Bks MO.

De Jonah, Brian see Chatzidakis, Manolis.

DeJong. The Dutch Reformed Church in the American Colonies. LC 78-17216. 1978. pap. 8.95 (ISBN 0-8028-1741-6). Eerdmans.

De Jong. Yearbook of Neurology & Neurosurgery, 1985. 1985. 44.95 (ISBN 0-8151-2407-4). Year Bk Med.

DeJong, Alexander D. Help & Hope for the Alcoholic. 128p. 1982. pap. 4.95 (ISBN 0-8423-1408-3). Tyndale.

De Jong, Ben, tr. see Jackins, Harvey.

DeJong, Benjamin. God's Promise for Today. 1974. Repr. 3.25 (ISBN 0-89081-212-8). Harvest Hse.

De Jong, Benjamin R. Uncle Ben's Instant Clip Quotes. 128p. 1985. pap. 5.95 (ISBN 0-8010-2954-6). Baker Bk.

--Uncle Ben's Quotebook. 1976. 11.95 (ISBN 0-8010-2851-5). Baker Bk.

DeJong, Benjamin R. Uncle Ben's Quotebook. 1976. pap. 8.95 (ISBN 0-89081-023-0). Harvest Hse.

De Jong, Constance. At Night. 80p. 1985. 12.95 (ISBN 0-934378-49-5); pap. 5.95 (ISBN 0-934378-50-9). Tanam Pr.

--I.T.I.L.O.E. 24p. (Orig.). 1983. pap. 3.00 (ISBN 0-917061-15-2). Top Stories.

DeJong, Constance & Glass, Philip. Satyagraha: M. K. Gandhi in South Africa, 1893-1914. (Illus.). 80p. (Orig.). 1983. 12.95 (ISBN 0-934378-43-6); pap. 5.95 (ISBN 0-934378-44-4). Tanam Pr.

DeJong, Dola. The Field. Perkins, Maxwell, ed. Van Duyn, A. V., tr. from Dutch. LC 79-84437. 1979. 15.95 (ISBN 0-933256-02-7); pap. 7.95 (ISBN 0-933256-05-1). Second Chance.

--The Field. Van Duym, A. V., tr. LC 79-84437. 215p. 1983. pap. 5.95 (ISBN 0-933256-39-6). Second Chance.

De Jong, Dola see Jong, Dola De.

De Jong, E. J., jt. auth. see Jancic, S. J.

De Jong, E. J. & Jancic, S. J., eds. Industrial Crystallization, '78. 588p. 1979. 106.50 (ISBN 0-686-63101-3, North Holland). Elsevier.

De Jong, E. W., jt. auth. see Westbroek, P.

De Jong, Frits J., et al, eds. Quadrilingual Economics Dictionary. 1981. lib. bdg. 48.00 (ISBN 90-247-2243-8, Pub. by Martinus Nijhoff Netherlands). Kluwer Academic.

DeJong, Gerben. Three Models of Independent Living in the Netherlands, No. 27. (International Exchange of Experts & Information in Rehabilitation Ser.). Date not set. pap. price not set (ISBN 0-939986-40-X). World Rehab Fund.

De Jong, Gordon F. Appalachian Fertility Decline. LC 68-12966. (Illus.). 154p. 1968. pap. 7.00x (ISBN 0-8131-1160-9). U Pr of Ky.

De Jong, Gordon F. & Gardner, Robert W., eds. Migration Decision Making: Multidisciplinary Approaches to Microlevel Studies in Developed & Developing Countries. (Illus.). 408p. 1981. 41.00 (ISBN 0-08-026305-4). Pergamon.

DeJong, H. W., jt. ed. see Jacquemin, A. P.

De Jong, Henry W., ed. The Structure of European Industry. 1981. 49.50 (ISBN 90-247-2416-3, Pub. by Martinus Nijhoff Netherlands). Kluwer Academic.

De Jong, J. W., ed. Mi la Ras Pa'i Rnam Thar: Texte Tibetian De la Vie De Milarepa. (Indo-Iranian Monographs: No. 4). 1959. 22.00x (ISBN 90-2790-052-3). Mouton.

--Tibetan Studies. 384p. 1984. write for info. (ISBN 0-89581-042-5). Asian Human Pr.

De Jong, James. Into His Presence: Perspectives on Reformed Worship. Date not set. pap. 7.25 (ISBN 0-933140-99-1). Bd of Pubns CRC.

De Jong, Marvin. Programming & Interfacing the Sixty-Five Two, with Experiments. LC 79-67130. 416p. 1980. pap. 17.95 (ISBN 0-672-21651-5, 21651). Sams.

De Jong, Marvin L. Apple II Assembly Language. LC 82-50015. 336p. 1982. pap. 15.95 (ISBN 0-672-21894-1, 21894). Sams.

DeJong, Marvin L. Assembly Language Programming with the Commodore 64. (Illus.). 320p. 1984. pap. 19.95 (ISBN 0-89303-319-7); bk. & diskette 39.95 (ISBN 0-89303-311-1); diskette 20.00 (ISBN 0-89303-327-8). Brady Comm.

DeJong, Meindert. Along Came a Dog. LC 57-9265. (Illus.). (gr. 3-6). 1958. PLB 11.89 (ISBN 0-06-021421-X). HarpJ.

--Along Came a Dog. LC 57-9265. (Illus.). 192p. (gr. 4-7). 1980. pap. 1.95 (ISBN 0-06-440114-6, Trophy). HarpJ.

--Big Goose & the Little White Duck. LC 63-15322. (Illus.). (gr. 1-5). 1963. PLB 13.89 (ISBN 0-06-021431-7). HarpJ.

--Cat That Walked a Week. LC 43-16877. (Illus.). (gr. 1-5). 1943. HarpJ.

--Good Luck Duck. LC 50-6809. (Illus.). (gr. 3-7). 1959. HarpJ.

--A Horse Came Running. LC 71-110. (Illus.). 160p. (gr. 5-7). 1970. 9.95 (ISBN 0-02-726540-4). Macmillan.

--House of Sixty Fathers. LC 56-8148. (Illus.). (gr. 5 up). 1956. PLB 11.89 (ISBN 0-06-021481-3). HarpJ.

--Hurry Home, Candy. LC 53-8536. (Illus.). (gr. 4-6). 1953. PLB 12.89 (ISBN 0-06-021486-4). HarpJ.

--Hurry Home, Candy. (Illus.). (gr. 4-6). 1953. pap. 2.95 (ISBN 0-06-440025-5, Trophy). HarpJ.

--Journey from Peppermint Street. (Illus.). (gr. 5 up). 1974. pap. 3.95 (ISBN 0-06-440011-5, Trophy). HarpJ.

--Shadrach. LC 53-5250. (Illus.). (gr. 1-5). 1953. PLB 11.89 (ISBN 0-06-021546-1). HarpJ.

--Shadrach. LC 53-5250. (Illus.). 192p. (gr. 3-6). 1980. pap. 1.95 (ISBN 0-06-440115-4, Trophy). HarpJ.

--Wheel on the School. LC 54-8945. (Illus.). (gr. 3-6). 1954. 13.41i (ISBN 0-06-021585-2); PLB 13.89 (ISBN 0-06-021586-0). HarpJ.

--Wheel on the School. LC 54-8945. (Illus.). (gr. 3-6). 1954. pap. 2.95 (ISBN 0-06-440021-2, Trophy). HarpJ.

De Jong, Norman. Christian Approaches to Learning Theory: A Symposium; Major Papers Delivered at the First Annual Conference at Trinity Christian College, November 11-12, 1983. 234p. 1985. 22.50 (ISBN 0-8191-4319-7, Pub. by Trinity Christ Coll). U Pr of Amer.

--Christian Approaches to Learning Theory: A Symposium; Major Papers Delivered at the First Annual Conference at Trinity Christian College, November 11-12, 1983. 234p. (Orig.). 1985. pap. 12.00 (ISBN 0-8191-4320-0, Pub. by Trinity Christ Coll). U Pr of Amer.

--Christianity & Democracy. 1978. pap. 4.95 (ISBN 0-934532-08-7). Presby & Reformed.

DeJong, Norman. Education in the Truth. 1969. pap. 7.95 (ISBN 0-87552-252-1). Presby & Reformed.

DeJong, Paul S., et al. Engineering Graphics: Communication, Analysis, & Creative Design. 5th ed. 1982. pap. text ed. 22.95 (ISBN 0-8403-2725-0). Kendall-Hunt.

De Jong, Ralph. The Life of Mary Magdalene in the Paintings of the Great Masters, 2 vols. (Illus.). 1979. deluxe ed. 117.45 (ISBN 0-930582-30-6). Gloucester Art.

De Jong, Rudolph H. Local Anesthetics. 2nd ed. (Illus.). 364p. 1977. 45.75x (ISBN 0-398-03611-X). C C Thomas.

Dejong, Russell N. A History of American Neurology. 170p. 1982. text ed. 26.00 (ISBN 0-89004-680-8). Raven.

--Year Book of Neurology & Neurosurgery, 1984. 1984. 44.95 (ISBN 0-8151-2408-2). Year Bk Med.

DeJong, Russell N., ed. Year Book of Neurology & Neurosurgery, 1982. 1982. 44.95 (ISBN 0-8151-2423-6). Year Bk Med.

--Year Book of Neurology & Neurosurgery, 1981. 1981. 44.95 (ISBN 0-8151-2421-X). Year Bk Med.

--Year Book of Neurology & Neurosurgery, 1983. 1983. 44.95 (ISBN 0-8151-2424-4). Year Bk Med.

De Jong, T. & Maeder, A., eds. Star Formation. (Symposium of the International Astronomical Union: No. 75). 1977. lib. bdg. 39.50 (ISBN 90-277-0796-0, Pub. by Reidel Holland); pap. 24.00 (ISBN 90-277-0797-9). Kluwer Academic.

De Jong, Tine H. Amse see Amse-De Jong, Tine H.

De Jong, W., ed. Experimental & Genetic Models of Hypertension. (Handbook of Hypertension Ser.: Vol. 4). 556p. 1984. 118.75 (ISBN 0-444-90336-4, I-224-84). Elsevier.

De Jong, W. A., jt. ed. see Van den Berg, P. J.

De Jonge, Alex. The Weimar Chronicle: Prelude to Hitler. 1979. pap. 5.95 (ISBN 0-452-00515-9, F515, Mer). NAL.

De Jonge, Alfred R. Gottfried Kinkel As Political & Social Thinker. LC 70-163695. (Columbia University. Germanic Studies, Old Ser.: No. 30). Repr. of 1926 ed. 21.00 (ISBN 0-404-50430-2). AMS Pr.

DeJonge, Eric. Victorian Period Furniture: 1840-1860. (Illus.). 72p. (Orig.). 1982. pap. 4.95 (ISBN 0-940166-02-X). Old Main Bks.

De Jonge, H. J., jt. ed. see Augustijn.

De Jonge, Joanne. Bats & Bugs & Snakes & Slugs. (Voyager Ser.). 64p. (Orig.). 1981. pap. 2.50 (ISBN 0-8010-2914-7). Baker Bk.

De Jonge, Joanne E. All Nature Sings. (My Father's World Ser.). (Illus.). 144p. (gr. 5-12). 1985. pap. write for info. (ISBN 0-930265-12-2, 85-7724). Bd of Pubns CRC.

DeJonge, Joanne E. A Beautiful Gift. 64p. 1985. pap. 4.95 (ISBN 0-8010-2950-3). Baker Bk.

De Jonge, Joanne E. My Listening Ears. LC 85-7372. (My Father's World Ser.). (Illus.). 144p. (gr. 5-12). 1985. pap. write for info. (ISBN 0-930265-09-2). Bd of Pubns CRC.

--Of Skies & Seas. LC 85-7391. (My Father's World Ser.). (Illus.). 144p. (gr. 5-12). 1985. pap. write for info. (ISBN 0-930265-11-4). Bd of Pubns CRC.

--The Rustling Grass. LC 85-7762. (My Father's World Ser.). (Illus.). 144p. 1985. pap. write for info. (ISBN 0-930265-10-6). Bd of Pubns CRC.

DeJonge, Joanne E. Skin & Bones. 105p. 1985. pap. 7.95 (ISBN 0-8010-2953-8). Baker Bk.

De Jonge, M. The Testaments of the Twelve Patriarchs: A Study of Their Text, Composition & Origin. (Van Gorcum's Theologische Bibliotheek: No. 25). 1975. pap. text ed. 27.00x (ISBN 90-232-1339-4). Humanities.

De Jonge, Marinus. Jesus: Stranger from Heaven & Son of God. Steely, John E., ed. LC 77-9984. (Soceity of Biblical Literature. Sources for Biblical Studies: No. 11). Repr. of 1977 ed. 61.50 (ISBN 0-8357-9575-6, 2017532). Bks Demand UMI.

--Outside the Old Testament. (Camridge Commentaries on the Writings of the Jewish & Christian World 200 B.C. to 200 A.D. Ser.). 264p. Date not set. price not set (ISBN 0-521-24249-5); pap. price not set (ISBN 0-521-28554-2). Cambridge U Pr.

De Jonge, P. Philological & Historical: Commentary on Ammianus Marcellinus XVII. (Ammianus Marcellinus Ser.). xi, 404p. 1977. 36.00x (ISBN 90-6088-052-8, Pub. by Boumas Boekhuis Netherlands). Benjamins North AM.

--Philological & Historical: Commentary on Ammianus Marcellinus XVIII. (Ammianus Marcellinus Ser.). xii, 308p. 1980. 29.00x (ISBN 90-6088-065-X, Pub. by Boumas Boekhuis Netherlands). Benjamins North AM.

--Philological & Historical Commentary on Ammianus Marcellinus XVI. (Ammianus Marcellinus Ser.). xii, 304p. 1972. 35.00x (ISBN 90-6088-035-8, Pub. by Boumas Boekhuis Netherlands). Benjamins North AM.

De Jonge, Mrs. P. Philological & Historical: Commentary on Ammianus Marcellinus XIX. De Waard-Dekking, P., tr. from Dutch. (Ammianus Marcellinus Ser.). ix, 279p. 1982. 27.00x (ISBN 90-6088-072-2, Pub. by Boumas Boekhuis Netherlands). Benjamins North AM.

De Jongh, Brian. Companion Guide to Mainland Greece. (Illus.). 456p. 1983. 16.95 (ISBN 0-13-154567-1); pap. 8.95 (ISBN 0-13-154559-0). P-H.

De Jongh, D. M., tr. see Beth, E. W.

De Jongh, L. J. & Miedema, A. R. Experiments on Simple Magnetic Magnetic Model Systems. 270p. 1974. pap. 19.00x (ISBN 0-85066-085-8). Taylor & Francis.

DeJonghe, Marty & Earhart, Caroline. Power Up! Kids' Guide to the Apple IIe-IIc. (Illus.). 180p. (gr. 3-6). 1984. pap. 14.95 (ISBN 0-89588-212-4). SYBEX.

--Power Up! Kids' Guide to the Commodore 64. LC 84-50363. (Illus.). 192p. (gr. 3-6). 1984. pap. 14.95 (ISBN 0-89588-188-8). SYBEX.

De Jongh-Kearl, Susan, tr. see Beth, E. W.

De Jongh Osborne, Lilly. Four Keys to El Salvador. LC 83-1506. (Illus.). x, 221p. 1983. Repr. of 1956 ed. lib. bdg. 29.75x (ISBN 0-313-22968-6, OSFK). Greenwood.
De Joode, Ton & Stolk, Anthonie. The Backyard Bestiary. LC 82-47803. (Illus.). 1982. 25.00 (ISBN 0-394-52824-7). Knopf.
De Jorio, Andrea. La Mimca Degli Antichi Investigata nel Gestire Napoletano. (Classics of Antrhropology Ser.). 80.00 (ISBN 0-8240-9646-0). Garland Pub.
De Josselin De Jong, P. E., ed. Structural Anthropology in the Netherlands. (Translation Ser.: No. 17). (Illus.). 1977. pap. 31.00 (ISBN 90-247-1944-5, Pub. by Martinus Nijhoff Netherlands). Kluwer Academic.
De Jourlet, Marie. Legacy of Windhaven. (The Windhaven Saga). 1978. pap. 3.50 (ISBN 0-523-41784-5). Pinnacle Bks.
--Return to Windhaven. 320p. 1985. pap. 3.95 (ISBN 0-523-42594-5). Pinnacle Bks.
--Storm Over Windhaven. 1977. pap. 3.50 (ISBN 0-523-41967-8). Pinnacle Bks.
--Trials of Windhaven. (Orig.). 1982. pap. 3.50 (ISBN 0-523-42013-7). Pinnacle Bks.
--Windhaven Plantation. (Orig.). 1982. pap. 3.50 (ISBN 0-523-42006-4). Pinnacle Bks.
--Windhaven's Bounty. 512p. (Orig.). 1981. pap. 3.50 (ISBN 0-523-41110-3). Pinnacle Bks.
--Windhaven's Crisis. 448p. (Orig.). 1981. pap. 3.50 (ISBN 0-523-41748-9). Pinnacle Bks.
--Windhaven's Destiny. (Windhaven's Saga Ser.: No. 12). 448p. (Orig.). 1983. pap. 3.75 (ISBN 0-523-41888-4). Pinnacle Bks.
--Windhaven's Fury. 320p. (Orig.). 1985. pap. 3.95 (ISBN 0-523-42595-3). Pinnacle Bks.
--Windhaven's Glory. 448p. (Orig.). 1985. pap. 3.95 (ISBN 0-523-41890-6). Pinnacle Bks.
--Windhaven's Hope. 448p. (Orig.). 1983. pap. 3.95 (ISBN 0-523-41889-2). Pinnacle Bks.
--Windhaven's Peril. (Windhaven Ser.). 1982. pap. 3.50 (ISBN 0-523-41968-6). Pinnacle Bks.
--Windhaven's Triumph. 448p. (Orig.). 1982. pap. 3.50 (ISBN 0-523-41111-1). Pinnacle Bks.
Dejours, Pierre, ed. Principles of Comparative Respiratory Physiology. 2nd ed. LC 74-25821. 251p. 1981. 32.50 (ISBN 0-444-80279-7, North-Holland). Elsevier.
De Jouvenel, Bertrand. Sovereignty: An Inquiry into the Political Good. Huntington, J. F., tr. LC 57-9548. 1957. 20.00x (ISBN 0-226-14161-6). U of Chicago Pr.
De Jouvenel, Bertrand see Jouvenel, Bertrand de.
Dejovine, F. Anthony. Young Hero in American Fiction: A Motif for Teaching Literature. LC 79-130792. (Orig.). 1971. pap. text ed. 9.95x (ISBN 0-89197-476-8). Irvington.
Deju, Raul, et al. The Environment & Its Resources. 340p. 1972. 56.75 (ISBN 0-677-14120-3). Gordon.
Deju, Raul A. Regional Hydrology Fundamentals. (Illus.). 222p. 1971. 57.75 (ISBN 0-677-03860-7). Gordon.
De Julio, Mary A. Quilts from Montgomery County, New York. (Illus.). 24p. (Orig.). 1981. pap. 3.00 (ISBN 0-9608694-0-9). Montgomery Hist.
DeJulio, Maryann, tr. see Hocquard, Emmanuel.
De Jussieu-Pontcarral, Pierre. Encyclopedie de l'electricite, 2 vols. (Illus.). 1970. 82.50x ea. Larousse.
Dejussieu-Pontcarral, Pierre. Encyclopedie De l'Electricite, 1: Production et Distribution. 1700p. (Fr.). 1969. 89.50 (ISBN 0-686-57135-5, M-6190). French & Eur.
--Encyclopedie de l'Electricite, 2: Application. 1024p. (Fr.). 1970. 89.50 (ISBN 0-686-56979-2, M-6106). French & Eur.
De Juvigny, F. Leonard, jt. auth. see Fair, D. E.
De Juvigny, F. Leonard, jt. auth. see Wadsworth, J. E.
De Kadt, E., et al, eds. see Conference on Blood Viscosity in Heart Disease, Thromboembo-Lism & Cancer, Sydney Australia, May, 1978.
De Kadt, Ellen, tr. see Medvedev, Zhores A. & Medvedev, Roy A.
De Kadt, Emanuel, ed. Tourism-Passport to Development? Perspectives on the Social & Cultural Effects of Tourism in Developing Countries: Perspectives on the Social & Cultural Effects of Tourism in Developing Countries. (World Bank Research Publication Ser.). 1979. 24.95x (ISBN 0-19-520149-3); pap. 9.95x (ISBN 0-19-520150-7). Oxford U Pr.
De Kadt, Emmanuel J. British Defence Policy & Nuclear War. 144p. 1964. 24.00x (ISBN 0-7146-1558-7, F Cass Co). Biblio Dist.
De Kait, Ellen see Medvedev, Roy A.
Dekar, Paul R. & Ban, Joseph D., eds. In the Great Tradition. 240p. 1982. 25.00 (ISBN 0-8170-0972-8). Judson.
DeKay. World's Greatest Left-Handers. pap. 5.95 (ISBN 0-87131-449-5, 0578-170). Dutton.
DeKay, Charles. Barye: Life & Works of Antoine Louis Barye. LC 73-163696. (BCL Ser. I). (Illus.). Repr. of 1889 ed. 49.50 (ISBN 0-404-02068-2). AMS Pr.
De Kay, Charles, tr. see Von Embden, Ludwig.
DeKay, James E. Anniversary Address on the Progress of the Natural Sciences of the United States. LC 76-125737. (American Environmental Studies). 1970. Repr. of 1826 ed. 11.50 (ISBN 0-405-02662-5). Ayer Co Pubs.
De Kay, James T. A Billion Dollars. LC 77-24416. (Illus.). 64p. 1977. pap. 1.95 (ISBN 0-87131-238-7). M Evans.
--Left-Handed Book. LC 66-23271. (Illus.). 64p. 1966. pap. 3.50 (ISBN 0-87131-156-9). M Evans.
--Meet Christopher Columbus. LC 68-23104. (Step-up Books Ser.). (Illus.). (gr. 2-6). 1968. (BYR); PLB 5.99 (ISBN 0-394-90071-5). Random.
--Meet Martin Luther King Jr. LC 78-79789. (Step-up Books Ser.). (gr. 3-6). 1969. 4.95 (ISBN 0-394-80055-9, BYR); PLB 5.99 (ISBN 0-394-90055-3). Random.
--The Natural Superiority of the Left-Hander. LC 79-15824. (Illus.). 128p. 1979. pap. 3.95 (ISBN 0-87131-307-3). M Evans.
De Kay, James T. & Huffaker, Sandy. The World's Greatest Left-Handers. LC 85-1474. (Illus.). 128p. 1984. pap. 5.95 (ISBN 0-87131-449-5). M Evans.
De Kay, Ormond, tr. see Larteguy, Jean.
De Kay, Ormonde. Late Bloomers. 288p. 1985. 16.95 (ISBN 0-917657-47-0). D I Fine.
--Snorkes & the Waterwitch. LC 83-4458. (Illus.). 32p. (ps-3). 1983. pap. 1.95 (ISBN 0-394-86086-1). Random.
DeKay, Ormonde, ed. N'Heures Souris Rames: The Coucy Castle Manuscript. 64p. (Fr.). 1985. pap. 5.95 (ISBN 0-312-57246-8). St Martin.
Deke, Castleman, ed. see Dalton, Bill.
Dekeijzer, A., jt. auth. see Kaplan, Frederic M.
DeKeijzer, Arne J., jt. auth. see Kaplan, Fredric.
De Keijzer, Arne J. see Posner, Arlene & Keijzer, Arne J. De.
De Kemeseye, Johannes. Roll of the Household Expenses of Richard De Swinfield, Bishop of Hereford, 1289-1290, 2 Vols. 1854-1855. 65.00 (ISBN 0-384-29130-9). Johnson Repr.
De Kemeseye, Johannes see Kemeseye, Johannes de.
Deken, Joseph. Computer Images: State of the Art. (Illus.). 200p. 1983. pap. 16.95 (ISBN 0-941434-40-0). Stewart Tabori & Chang.
--The Electronic Cottage: Everyday Living with Your Personal Computer in the 1980's. LC 81-14016. (Illus.). 320p. 1981. 15.95 (ISBN 0-688-00664-7). Morrow.
De Kerbrech, Richard P., jt. auth. see Williams, David L.
De Kerchove, Nicole Nealey-van see Van De Kerchove, Nicole N.
De Kerchove, Rene. International Maritime Dictionary. 2nd ed. 1983. 40.00 (ISBN 0-442-02062-7). Van Nos Reinhold.
De Kernion, Jean B., jt. auth. see Skinner, Donald G.
De Kerpely, Theresa. Of Love & Wars. LC 83-40584. 500p. 1984. 19.95 (ISBN 0-8128-2967-0). Stein & Day.
De Kerpley, Theresa. Arabesque. 312p. 1985. pap. 3.50 (ISBN 0-8128-8111-7). Stein & Day.
De Kerval, Alastor see Kerval, Alastor de.
De Kervasdove, Jean, et al, eds. The End of an Illusion: The Future of Health Policy in Western Industrialized Nations. LC 83-18030. (Comparative Studies of Health Systems & Medical Care). (Illus.). 300p. 1985. 28.50x (ISBN 0-520-04726-5). U of Cal Pr.
De Ketchiva, Paul. Confessions of a Croupier. 1978. lib. bdg. 59.95 (ISBN 0-8490-1663-0). Gordon Pr.
De Keyser, Euginie. La Sculpture Contemporaine en Belgique. (Illus.). 259p. (Fr.). 30.00 (ISBN 0-912729-22-8). Newbury Bks.
Dekeyser, W., et al, eds. Electron Emission Spectroscopy. LC 73-83559. 1973. lib. bdg. 79.00 (ISBN 90-277-0366-3, Pub. by Reidel Holland). Kluwer Academic.
DeKieffer, Donald. How to Lobby Congress: A Guide for the Citizen Lobbyist. LC 81-4621. 228p. 1982. pap. 8.95 (ISBN 0-396-07969-5). Dodd.
De Kieffer, Donald, jt. auth. see De Villiers, Les.
DeKieffer, Donald E. Doing Business with Romania. (Illus.). 180p. (Orig.). 1985. pap. 8.50 (ISBN 0-916673-02-2). Business Bks CT.
DeKiewiet, C. W. History of South Africa, Social & Economic. 1941. pap. 15.95x (ISBN 0-19-821638-6). Oxford U Pr.
De Kiewiet, Cornelis W. Imperial Factor in South Africa. 341p. 1965. Repr. of 1937 ed. 30.00x (ISBN 0-7146-1651-6, BHA-01651, F Cass Co). Biblio Dist.
De Kiewiet, Cornelius W. The Anatomy of South African Misery. LC 83-5635. (The Whidden Lectures Ser., 1956). viii, 88p. 1983. Repr. of 1956 ed. lib. bdg. 25.00x (ISBN 0-313-23960-6, DEAN). Greenwood.
De Kimpe, C. R., tr. see Duchaufour, Philippe.
Dekin, Albert A., Jr. Arctic Archaeology: An Annotated Bibliography & History. LC 75-5120. (Reference Library of Natural Science: No. 1). (Illus.). 200p. 1975. lib. bdg. 37.00 (ISBN 0-8240-1084-1). Garland Pub.
Dekin, Timothy. Carnival. 20p. (Orig.). 1984. pap. 4.00 (ISBN 0-941150-31-3). Barth.
Dekker, Casimir. The Unknown Art of Becoming a Spiritual Lover. (Illus.). 97p. 1984. 57.75 (ISBN 0-89920-074-5). Am Inst Psych.
Dekker, E., ed. see International Congress on Alcoholism & Drug Dependence, Amsterdam, September, 4-9, 1972.
Dekker, Eduard D. see Multatuli, pseud.
Dekker, George. Coleridge & the Literature of Sensibility. (Critical Studies). 270p. 1978. text ed. 27.50x (ISBN 0-686-83548-4). B&N Imports.
Dekker, George, ed. Donald Davie: The Responsibilities of Literature. LC 83-61320. 220p. 1984. 12.95 (ISBN 0-915032-38-4). Natl Poet Foun.
Dekker, George & McWilliams, John P., eds. Fenimore Cooper: The Critical Heritage. (The Critical Heritage Ser). 318p. 1985. 29.95x (ISBN 0-7100-7635-5); pap. 15.00 (ISBN 0-7102-0514-7). Routledge & Kegan.
Dekker, J. & Georgopoulos, S. G., eds. Fungicide Resistance in Crop Protection. 273p. 1982. pap. 31.50 (ISBN 90-220-0797-9, PDC245, Pudoc). Unipub.
Dekker, J., ed. see Symposium in Pure Mathematics, New York, 1961.
Dekker, James C., tr. see Hanks, Thomas D.
Dekker, John. Torches of Joy. LC 84-72007. 192p. (Orig.). 1985. pap. 5.95 (ISBN 0-89107-339-6). Good News.
Dekker, John, jt. auth. see Briggs, Asa.
Dekker, Julian. How to Master the Forces of Your Imagination for the Pursuit of Your Scientific Objectives. (Illus.). 1978. deluxe ed. 47.50 (ISBN 0-930582-07-1). Gloucester Art.
Dekker, K. & Verwer, J. G. Stability of Runge-Kutta Methods for Stiff Nonlinear Differential Equations. (CWI Monographs: No. 2). 308p. 1984. 35.25 (ISBN 0-444-87634-0, North-Holland). Elsevier.
Dekker, L. & Savastano, G., eds. Simulation of Systems, 1979. 1170p. 1980. 138.50 (ISBN 0-444-86123-8, North-Holland). Elsevier.
Dekker, Thomas. The Belman of London Bringing to Light the Most Notorious Villanies That Are Now Practised in the Kingdome. LC 73-6117. (English Experience Ser.: No. 584). 68p. 1973. Repr. of 1608 ed. 7.00 (ISBN 90-221-0584-9). Walter J Johnson.
--Dramatic Works of Thomas Dekker, 4 vols. Bowers, Fredson, ed. 1953-61. Vol. 1. 75.00 (ISBN 0-521-04808-7); Vol. 2. 77.50 (ISBN 0-521-04809-5); Vol. 3. 75.00 (ISBN 0-521-04810-9); Vol. 4. 75.00 (ISBN 0-521-04811-7). Cambridge U Pr.
--Gull's Hornbook. McKerrow, R. M., ed. LC 74-136374. Repr. of 1904 ed. 14.00 (ISBN 0-404-02069-0). AMS Pr.
--The Gull's Hornbook. McKerrow, R. B., ed. 1905. lib. bdg. 15.00 (ISBN 0-8414-2452-7). Folcroft.
--The Gull's Hornbook. Mc Kerrow, R. B., ed. 120p. 1983. Repr. of 1907 ed. lib. bdg. 45.00 (ISBN 0-89987-172-0). Darby Bks.
--Lanthorne & Candle-Light, or the Bell-Mans Second Nights Walke. LC 73-6118. (English Experience Ser.: No. 585). 86p. 1973. Repr. of 1608 ed. 9.50 (ISBN 90-221-0585-7). Walter J Johnson.
--Noble Soldier. LC 74-133655. (Tudor Facsimile Texts. Old English Plays: No. 140). Repr. of 1913 ed. 49.50 (ISBN 0-404-53440-6). AMS Pr.
--The Plague Pamphlets of Thomas Dekker. 1978. Repr. of 1925 ed. lib. bdg. 30.00 (ISBN 0-8492-0680-4). R West.
--The Plague Pamphlets of Thomas Dekker. LC 73-161963. 268p. 1925. Repr. 39.00x (ISBN 0-403-01319-4). Scholarly.
--Shoemaker's Holiday. Lawlis, Merritt, ed. LC 78-14915. (gr. 10up). 1979. pap. text ed. 3.50 (ISBN 0-8120-0314-4). Barron.
--The Shoemakers Holiday. Smallwood, R. L., et al, eds. LC 79-87579. (Revels Plays Ser.). 244p. 1979. text ed. 20.00x (ISBN 0-8018-2293-9). Johns Hopkins.
--The Shoemaker's Holiday. Palmer, D. J., ed. (New Mermaid Ser.). 1976. pap. 4.95x (ISBN 0-393-90005-3). Norton.
--Thomas Dekker: The Wonderful Year, the Gull's Horn-Book, Penny Wise, Pound Foolish, English Villainies Discovered by Lantern & Candlelight & Selected Writing. Pendry, Eric D., ed. LC 68-88991. (Stratford-Upon-Avon Library). (Illus.). 1968. 25.00x (ISBN 0-674-88486-8). Harvard U Pr.
--The Welsh Embassador. LC 82-45779. (Malone Society Reprint Ser.: No. 48). Repr. of 1920 ed. 40.00 (ISBN 0-404-63048-0). AMS Pr.
Dekker, Thomas & Webster, John. Northward Ho. LC 75-133655. (Tudor Facsimile Texts. Old English Plays: No. 119). Repr. of 1914 ed. 49.50 (ISBN 0-404-53419-8). AMS Pr.
--Sir Thomas Wyatt. LC 75-133655. (Tudor Facsimile Texts. Old English Plays: No. 122). Repr. of 1914 ed. 49.50 (ISBN 0-404-53422-8). AMS Pr.
--Westward Ho. LC 79-133656. (Tudor Facsimile Texts. Old English Plays: No. 123). Repr. of 1914 ed. 49.50 (ISBN 0-404-53423-6). AMS Pr.
Dekker, Thomas see Bald, Robert C.
Dekker, Thomas see Jonson, Ben.
Dekker, Thomas see Maas, H.
Dekker, Thomas, jt. auth. see Middleton, Thomas.
Dekker, Thomas, ed. see Middleton, Thomas.
Dekker, Thomas, et al. The Witch of Edmonton. (Methuen Student Editions). (Illus.). 128p. 1983. pap. 3.95 (ISBN 0-413-53260-7, NO. 3969). Methuen Inc.
Dekkers, N. W. The Cornea in Measles. (Monographs in Ophthalmology: No. 3). 121p. 1982. 29.00 (ISBN 90-6193-803-1, Pub. by Junk Pubs Netherlands). Kluwer Academic.
Dekko, Dottie. The Fast Lane Diet: The Forteen-Day Weight Loss Program for Everyone on the Fast Track to Success. 224p. 1985. 14.95 (ISBN 0-07-016298-0). McGraw.
De Kleen, Tyra. Mudras: The Ritual Hand-Poses of the Buddha Priests & the Shiva Priests of Bali. 1970. 5.00 (ISBN 0-8216-0119-9). Univ Bks.
DeKlerk, Peter & DeRidder, Richard R., eds. Perspectives on the Christian Reformed Church. 1983. 14.95 (ISBN 0-8010-2934-1). Baker Bk.
De Klerk, R. The Puritans in Africa. 2nd ed. 39.00x (ISBN 0-901720-71-2, Pub. by R Collings UK). State Mutual Bk.
De Klerk, W. The Thirstland. Rex Collings Ltd., ed. 39.00x (ISBN 0-86036-045-8, Pub. by R Collings UK). State Mutual Bk.
Dekmejian, R. Hrair. Egypt under Nasir: A Study in Political Dynamics. LC 70-152520. (Illus.). Repr. of 1971 ed. 96.50 (ISBN 0-8357-9593-4, 2010956). Bks Demand UMI.
--Islam in Revolution: Fundamentalism in the Arab World. (Contemporary Issues in the Middle East Ser.). 224p. 1985. text ed. 26.00x (ISBN 0-8156-2329-1); pap. text ed. 12.95x (ISBN 0-8156-2330-5). Syracuse U Pr.
--Patterns of Political Leadership: Egypt, Israel, Lebanon. LC 74-20940. (Illus.). xi, 356p. 1975. 44.50x (ISBN 0-87395-291-X). State U NY Pr.
De Knight, Freda. Ebony Cookbook: A Date with a Dish. 1962. 9.95 (ISBN 0-87485-003-7). Johnson Chi.
Dekock, John B. Extending Family Practice Medical Services to 24 Hours in Rural Areas: Studies of a Demonstration Model. (Illus.). 1975. pap. 3.95 (ISBN 0-916552-05-5). Acoma Bks.
De Kock, M. A. Dynamic Bronchoscopy. 1977. 71.00 (ISBN 0-387-08109-7). Springer-Verlag.
DeKock, M. H. Central Banking. 4th ed. LC 74-78896. 318p. 1974. 27.50 (ISBN 0-312-12740-5). St Martin.
DeKock, Roger L. & Gray, Harry B. Chemical Structure & Bonding. 1980. 36.95 (ISBN 0-8053-2310-4). Benjamin-Cummings.
DeKock, Victor. Those in Bondage. LC 76-122865. 1971. Repr. of 1950 ed. 21.00x (ISBN 0-8046-1368-0, Pub by Kennikat). Assoc Faculty Pr.
De Kohen, Clara I., tr. see Selsam, Millicent.
De Kok, Winifred. You & Your Child. 1955. 5.00 (ISBN 0-685-78050-3). Philos Lib.
DeKok, Winifred, tr. see Marais, Eugene N.
De Koninck & Ivic. Topics in Arithmetical Functions. (Mathematics Studies Ser.: Vol. 43). 262p. 1980. 47.00 (ISBN 0-444-86049-5, North Holland). Elsevier.
De Koninck, Rodolphe, jt. auth. see Gibbons, David.
De Koning, A. J. & Jenner, F. A., eds. Phenomenology & Psychiatry. 288p. 1982. 43.50 (ISBN 0-8089-1432-4, 791022). Grune.
DeKornfeld, T. J. Pharmacology for Respiratory Therapy. 1978. 12.95 (ISBN 0-8151-2425-2). Year Bk Med.
DeKornfeld, Thomas J. Anesthesiology: Continuing Education Review. 2nd ed. 1983. pap. text ed. 26.00 (ISBN 0-87488-353-9). Med Exam.
DeKornfeld, Thomas J. & Finch, Jay S. Respiratory Care Case Studies, Vol. 1. 3rd ed. (Illus.). 1982. 22.00 (ISBN 0-87488-019-X). Med Exam.
DeKornfeld, Thomas J., jt. auth. see Israel, Jacob S.
Dekornfeld, Thomas J., ed. Selected Papers in Respiratory Therapy. 2nd ed. 1979. pap. 24.00 (ISBN 0-87488-525-6). Med Exam.
DeKornfeld, Thomas J. & Detmar, Michael W., eds. Anesthesiology. 6th ed. LC 61-66847. (Medical Examination Review Bk.: No. 12). 1980. pap. 24.50 (ISBN 0-87488-112-9). Med Exam.
Dekornfeld, Thomas J., et al. Respiratory Therapy Examination Review Book, Vol. 2. 2nd ed. 1974. spiral bdg. 13.25 (ISBN 0-87488-344-X). Med Exam.
De Koros, Alexander Csoma see Csoma de Koros, Alexander.
De Kort, Kees, illus. What the Bible Tells Us: Third Series, 4 bks. Incl. A Baby Called John. 28p (ISBN 0-8066-1770-5, 10-0538); Jesus & a Little Girl. 28p (ISBN 0-8066-1771-3, 10-3479); The Son Who Left Home. 28p (ISBN 0-8066-1773-X, 10-5852); Jesus Goes Away. 28p (ISBN 0-8066-1774-8, 10-3510). (gr. 1-4). 1980. pap. 1.75 ea. Augsburg.
DeKosky, Robert K. Knowledge & Cosmos: Development & Decline of the Medieval Perspective. LC 79-66226. 1979. text ed. 23.50 (ISBN 0-8191-0814-6); pap. text ed. 15.00 (ISBN 0-8191-0815-4). U Pr of Amer.
DeKoster, Lester. Work: The Meaning of Your Life. 95p. (Orig.). 1982. pap. 3.95 (ISBN 0-934874-04-2). Chr Lib Pr.
DeKoster, Lester, jt. auth. see Berghoef, Gerard.
DeKoven, Marianne. A Different Language: Gertrude Stein's Experimental Writing. LC 82-70558. (Illus.). 208p. 1983. 22.50x (ISBN 0-299-09210-0). U of Wis Pr.
De Koven, Reginald. Songs of Childhood. 59.95 (ISBN 0-8490-1084-5). Gordon Pr.
Dekovic, Gene. This Blessed Land. LC 80-84495. (Illus.). 112p. 1982. 12.95 (ISBN 0-937088-00-5). Illum Pr.
Dekovic, Gene, ed. see Emerson, Ralph Waldo.

De Kreter, D. M., et al, eds. The Pituitary & Testis: Clinical & Experimental Studies. (Monographs on Endocrinology: Vol. 25). (Illus.). 200p. 1983. 52.00 (ISBN 0-387-11874-8). Springer-Verlag.

Dekretser, David, jt. ed. see Burger, Henry.

De Krey, Gary S. A Fractured Society: The Politics of London in the First Age of Party, 1688-1715. (Illus.). 420p. 1985. 34.50 (ISBN 0-19-820067-6). Oxford U Pr.

De Kruif, Paul. Hunger Fighters. LC 67-32084. (gr. 7-12). 1967. pap. 0.95 (ISBN 0-15-642430-4, Harv). HarBraceJ.

--Microbe Hunters. LC 67-34588. 1966. pap. 5.95 (ISBN 0-15-659413-7, Harv). HarBraceJ.

De Kruyter, Arthur H. Journey into Joy. 192p. 1984. 9.95. Revell.

DeKruyter, Arthur H. Love Makes Life. 1981. pap. 4.95 (ISBN 0-8423-3849-7). Tyndale.

DeKryger, et al. Auto Mechanics: Theory & Servicing. 1986. text ed. 17.50 (IE09). SW Pub.

DeKryger, William J., jt. auth. see Peterson, John C.

DeKryger, William J., et al. Auto Mechanics: Theory & Service. Sprague & Sturzenberger, eds. (Automotive Ser.). (Illus.). 800p. 1985. text ed. 23.48x (ISBN 0-538-33090-2); write for info. (ISBN 0-538-33091-0); instr's. manual avail. (ISBN 0-538-33092-9). SW Pub.

De Kunffy, Charles. Creative Horsemanship: Training Suggestions for Dressage. (Illus.). 224p. 1984. 19.95 (ISBN 0-668-05965-6, 5965). Arco.

de la, Walter Mare see De La Mare, Walter.

Delaat, Adrian N. Microbiology for the Allied Health Professions. 3rd ed. LC 83-24833. (Illus.). 1984. 24.50 (ISBN 0-8121-0910-4). Lea & Febiger.

De Laat, P. J. M. Model for Unsaturated Flow Above a Shallow Water-Table, Applied to a Regional Subsurface Flow Problem. (Agricultural Research Reports: No. 895). 133p. 1980. pap. 11.00 (ISBN 90-220-0725-1, PDC244, PUDOC). Unipub.

De Labac, jt. auth. see Teilhard De Chardin, Pierre.

De la Barca, Calderon see Bentley, Eric.

De la Barca, Pedro C. Celos Aun Del Aire Matan. Stroud, Matthew D., tr. LC 80-54543. (Illus.). 219p. (Sp. & Eng.). 1981. 15.00 (ISBN 0-911536-90-6); pap. 10.00 (ISBN 0-939980-01-0). Trinity U Pr.

--Three Comedies by Pedro Calderon de la Barca. Muir, Kenneth & MacKenzie, Ann L., trs. LC 85-5369. 256p. 1985. 25.00 (ISBN 0-8131-1546-9); pap. 9.00 (ISBN 0-8131-0166-2). U Pr of Ky.

De La Bathie, H. Perrier. Flora of Madagascar: Orchids. Humbert, H., ed. Beckman, Steven D., tr. from French. LC 82-90881. (Illus.). 542p. 1982. 65.00x (ISBN 0-9609434-0-4). S D Beckman.

De La Bedoyere, Michael. The Life of Baron Von Hugel. 366p. 1982. Repr. of 1951 ed. lib. bdg. 45.00 (ISBN 0-89760-089-4). Telegraph Bks.

De La Bere, R. John Heywood: Entertainer. LC 72-188001. 1937. lib. bdg. 20.00 (ISBN 0-8414-2454-3). Folcroft.

De La Bierre, Gustave H. The History of Hallucinations in the Growth of Mankind. (Illus.). 141p. 1984. 95.75 (ISBN 0-89266-471-1). Am Classical Coll Pr.

De La Billardiere, J. J. Sertum Austro-Caledonicum. (Illus.). 1968. Repr. of 1825 ed. 56.00 (ISBN 3-7682-0541-X). Lubrecht & Cramer.

De La Boetie, Etienne. Politics of Obedience. 1984. lib. bdg. 79.95 (ISBN 0-87700-648-2). Revisionist Pr.

de la Bonniere, G. De Beaumont see De Beaumont de la Bonniere, G. & De Tocqueville, Alexis.

De LaBrosse, Olivier see Henry, Antonir Marie & LaBrosse, Olivier De.

De La Bruyere, Jean. Caracteres. 1962. pap. 6.50 (ISBN 0-685-11061-3); pap. 4.50 pocket ed. (ISBN 0-685-11062-1). French & Eur.

--Caracteres, 2 Vols. (Documentation thematique). (Illus., Fr.). pap. 2.95 ea. Larousse.

--Les Caracteres de Theophrastre, traduits du grec avec Les Caracteres, ou Les Moeurs de ce siecle. Garagon, ed. (Class. Garnier). pap. 14.95 (ISBN 0-685-34227-1). French & Eur.

--Les Caracteres de Theophrastre, traduits du grec avec Les Caracters, ou Les Moeurs de ce siecle. Garpon, ed. (Coll. Prestige). 27.95 (ISBN 0-685-34228-X). French & Eur.

--Oeuvres Completes. Benda, ed. (Bibl. de la Pleiade). 1935. 35.95 (ISBN 0-685-11445-7). French & Eur.

De La Casa, Enrique C. La Novela Antioquena. 100p. 2.00 (ISBN 0-318-14294-5). Hispanic Inst.

Delacato, Carl H. The Diagnosis & Treatment of Speech & Reading Problems. (Illus.). 200p. 1963. 17.75x (ISBN 0-398-00418-8). C C Thomas.

--The Elementary School of the Future: A Guide for Parents. 108p. 1969. 11.50x (ISBN 0-398-00419-6). C C Thomas.

--Neurological Organization & Reading. 200p. 1973. spiral 17.75x (ISBN 0-398-00420-X). C C Thomas.

--The Treatment & Prevention of Reading Problems: The Neuropsychological Approach. 136p. 1971. 15.50x (ISBN 0-398-00421-8). C C Thomas.

--The Ultimate Stranger: The Autistic Child. rev. ed. 240p. 1984. pap. 9.00 (ISBN 0-87879-446-8, 446-8, Arena Press). Acad Therapy.

De la Ceppede, Jean. Theorems. Bosley, Keith, tr. from Fr. 132p. 1983. text ed. 19.50x (ISBN 0-85635-450-3, Pub. by Carcanet Pr England). Humanities.

De Lacey & O'Leary, trs. from Coptic. Fragmentary Coptic Hymns from the Wadi N Natrum: Part One Translation. 1973. pap. 4.00 (ISBN 0-686-08835-2). British Am Bks.

Delach, Mary K. Happy Mama & Her Auto-Fly. LC 76-8721. (Illus.). (gr. k-4). 1976. 5.95 (ISBN 0-914598-29-5). Padre Prods.

De La Chavignerie, Emile B. & Auvray, Louis. Dictionnaire General, 5 vols. Rosenblum, Robert, ed. LC 78-68412. (Dictionnaire General Ser.). 2000p. 1979. Repr. of 1885 ed. lib. bdg. 500.00 (ISBN 0-8240-3539-9). Garland Pub.

De la Cierva, Patronato J. Diccionario Ruso-Espanol de la Ciencia y la Tecnica. 2nd ed. 700p. (Span.). 1972. 50.00 (ISBN 84-237-0407-6, S-50249). French & Eur.

De Laclos, Choderlos. Dangerous Acquaintances. Aldington, Richard, tr. from Fr. (Open University Set Text Ser.). (Orig.). 1979. pap. 7.95 (ISBN 0-7100-8858-2). Routledge & Kegan.

De Laclos, Choderlos see Laclos, Choderlos de.

De Laclos, P. Choderlos see Choderlos De Laclos, P.

De La Colombiere, Claude, jt. auth. see Saint-Jure, Jean B.

Delacorta, pseud. Diva. Bair, Lowell, tr. from Fr. 1983. 9.95 (ISBN 0-671-47056-6). Summit Bks.

--Diva. 192p. 1984. pap. 2.75 (ISBN 0-345-31265-1). Ballantine.

--Lola. 176p. 1985. pap. 2.95 (ISBN 0-345-31268-6). Ballantine.

--Lola: A Novel. 1985. 9.95 (ISBN 0-671-47752-8). Summit Bks.

--Luna. Reiter, Victoria, tr. (Gorodish-Alba Ser.). 128p. 1984. 9.95 (ISBN 0-671-49379-5). Summit Bks.

--Luna. 176p. 1985. pap. 2.95 (ISBN 0-345-31266-X). Ballantine.

--Vida. Reiter, Victoria, tr. from Fr. 1985. 12.95 (ISBN 0-671-60424-4). Summit Bks.

Delacorte, Peter. Levantine. LC 84-14744. 1985. 15.95 (ISBN 0-393-01881-4). Norton.

Delacorte, Peter & Witte, Michael C. The Book of Terns. (Large Format Ser). (Illus.). 1978. pap. 4.95 (ISBN 0-14-004905-3). Penguin.

Delacorte, Toni, et al. How to Get Free Press: The Step-By-Step Guide to Successful Media Coverage for Your Business, Organization, or Political Campaign. 240p. 1984. pap. 6.95 (ISBN 0-380-68189-7, 68189-7). Avon.

De La Costa, Horacio. Five Plays. ii, 148p. (Orig.). 1982. pap. 8.25 (ISBN 971-10-0025-3, Pub. by New Day Philippines); pap. text ed. 8.25 (ISBN 971-10-0026-1). Cellar.

De La Costa, Horacio, jt. auth. see Delaney, John P.

Delacoste, Frederique & Newman, Felice, eds. Fight Back: Feminist Resistance to Male Violence. LC 81-68220. (Illus.). 400p. (Orig.). 1981. pap. 13.95 (ISBN 0-939416-01-8). Cleis Pr.

Delacote, G., ed. Physics Teaching in Schools. 404p. 1978. pap. 49.00x (ISBN 0-85066-136-6). Taylor & Francis.

Delacour, ed. see Labiche, Eugene.

Delacour, Jean. Dictionnaire des Mots d'Esprit. 352p. (Fr.). 1976. pap. 15.95 (ISBN 0-686-56849-4, M-6627). French & Eur.

--Pheasant Breeding & Care. (Illus.). 1978. 14.95 (ISBN 0-87666-434-6, AP-6450). TFH Pubns.

--The Pheasants of the World. 2nd ed. 432p. 1983. 55.00 (ISBN 0-904558-37-1). Triplegate.

--Wild Pigeons & Doves. rev. ed. (Illus.). 189p. 1980. 14.95 (ISBN 0-87666-968-2, AP-6810). TFH Pubns.

De La Court, Pieter. The True Interest & Political Maxims of the Republic of Holland. LC 78-38278. (The Evolution of Capitalism Ser.). 520p. 1972. Repr. of 1746 ed. 34.50 (ISBN 0-405-04117-9). Ayer Co Pubs.

De la Coze, Minerva. A Little Fairy Tale for Little People. 23p. 1983. 5.95 (ISBN 0-533-05618-7). Vantage.

Delacre, Georges. El Tiempo En Perspectiva. pap. 5.00 (ISBN 0-8477-0505-6). U of PR Pr.

Delacre, Georges, ed. see Wells, Henry.

Delacre, Lulu. Lullabies. (Mother Goose Board Bks.). (ps-5). 1984. 2.95 (ISBN 0-671-49686-7, Little Simon). S&S.

Delacretaz, J., et al. Color Atlas of Medical Mycology. 187p. 1976. 300.00 (ISBN 3-456-80230-7, Pub. by Holdan Bk Ltd UK). State Mutual Bk.

Delacretaz, J. E. Color Atlas of Medical Mycology. (Illus.). 1977. 85.00 (ISBN 0-8151-2422-8). Year Bk Med.

Delacroix, Charles P. The Scientific Analysis of Great Paintings. (Illus.). 168p. 1985. 93.65 (ISBN 0-86650-163-0). Gloucester Art.

Delacroix, Eugene. The Journal of Eugene Delacroix. Wellington, Herbert, ed. Norton, Lucy, tr. (Landmarks in Art History Ser.). (Illus.). 517p. 1980. pap. 14.95 (ISBN 0-8014-9196-7). Cornell U Pr.

Delacroix, Ferdinand V. Drawings of Delacroix. Price, Vincent, ed. (Master Draughtsman Ser). (Illus., Orig.). treasure trove bdg. 9.95x (ISBN 0-87505-006-9); pap. 4.95 (ISBN 0-87505-159-6). Borden.

De La Croix, Horst. Military Considerations in City Planning: Fortifications. LC 72-143398. (Planning & Cities Ser). (Illus.). 1971. 7.95 (ISBN 0-8076-0585-9); pap. 3.95 (ISBN 0-8076-0584-0). Braziller.

De la Croix, Horst & Tansey, Richard G. Gardener's Art Through the Ages, 2 vols. 7th ed. 922p. 1980. Set. text ed. 28.95 (ISBN 0-15-503758-7, HC); Vol. I - Ancient, Medieval, & Non-European Art. pap. text ed. 19.95 (ISBN 0-15-503759-5); Vol. II - Renaissance & Modern Art. pap. text ed. 19.95 (ISBN 0-15-503760-9); study guide 9.95 (ISBN 0-15-503761-7). HarBraceJ.

De la Croix, Robert. A History of Piracy. 1978. pap. 1.95 (ISBN 0-532-19210-9). Woodhill.

Delacruz, Chester, jt. auth. see Sewell, George E.

De La Cruz, F. & LaVeck, G. D., eds. Human Sexuality & the Mentally Retarded. LC 72-92057. 1973. 22.50 (ISBN 0-87630-063-8). Brunner-Mazel.

De la Cruz, Felix see Lubs, Herbert & Cruz, Felix de la.

De La Cruz, Felix F., jt. auth. see Davidson, Richard L.

De la Cruz, Felix F., ed. Trisomy Twenty-One (Down Syndrome) (NICHD-Mental Retardation Research Center Ser.). (Illus.). 318p. 1980. 22.00 (ISBN 0-8391-1588-1). Pro-Ed.

De la Cruz, Sov J. El Sueno. Campion, John, tr. LC 83-4719. pap. 5.00 (ISBN 0-914476-93-9). Thorp Springs.

De la Cruz Aymes, Maria & Buckley, Francis J. Fe y Cultura: Manual de Direccion. 64p. (Orig.). 1986. pap. 5.95 (ISBN 0-8091-2748-2). Paulist Pr.

De la Cruz Aymes, Maria, et al. Growing with God. (God with Us Program). 112p. (Orig.). 1983. pap. text ed. 3.69 (ISBN 0-8215-1121-1); tchr's ed. 10.86 (ISBN 0-8215-1131-9); wkbk. 1.65 (ISBN 0-8215-1151-3); compact ed 3.18 (ISBN 0-8215-1101-7). Sadlier.

--Growing with Jesus. 144p. (Orig.). 1983. pap. text ed. 3.69 (ISBN 0-8215-1122-X); 10.86 (ISBN 0-8215-1132-7); wkbk. 1.65 (ISBN 0-8215-1152-1); compact ed. 3.18 (ISBN 0-8215-1102-5). Sadlier.

De La Cuesta, Felip Arroyo see Arroyo De La Cuesta, Felipe.

De Lacy, E. A., ed. see Philodemus.

De Lacy, Ph. H., ed. see Philodemus.

DeLadurantey, Joseph C. & Sullivan, Daniel R. Criminal Investigation Standards. (Illus.). 1979. text ed. 22.80 scp (ISBN 0-06-041609-2, HarpC); inst. manual avail. (ISBN 0-06-361610-6). Har-Row.

De Laet, Siegfried J. Portorium: Etude Sur L'organisation Douaniere Chez les Romains, Surtout a L'epoque Du Haut-Empire. LC 75-7312. (Roman History Ser.). (Fr.). 1975. Repr. 38.50x (ISBN 0-405-07194-9). Ayer Co Pubs.

De La Falaise, Maxime. Food in Vogue. LC 79-8920. (Illus.). 336p. 1980. 15.95 (ISBN 0-385-09220-2). Doubleday.

De La Falonaise, Clarence J. A Collection of Reproductions in Full Colours of the Masterpieces of the French Impressionists. (Illus.). 113p. 1984. 137.45 (ISBN 0-86650-094-4). Gloucester Art.

De Lafayette, Madame. The Princesse de Cleves. Mitfod, Nancy, tr. from Fr. (Classics Ser.). 1978. pap. 4.95 (ISBN 0-14-044337-1). Penguin.

De Lafayette, Marie see Lafayette, Marie.

De La Fayette, Marie M. Princesse de Cleves. (Coll. Folio). 1958. 4.50 (ISBN 0-685-11514-3). French & Eur.

De La Fayette, Marie-Madeleine. La Princesse de Cleves. (Documentation Thematique Ser.). (Illus., Fr.). pap. 2.95 (ISBN 0-685-14059-8, 143). Larousse.

Delafield, E. Love Prescription. (Stories That Win Ser.). 64p. 1980. pap. 0.95 (ISBN 0-8163-0410-6). Pacific Pr Pub Assn.

Delafield, E. M. The Brontes: Their Lives Recorded by Their Contemporaries. 1980. Repr. of 1935 ed. 27.50x (ISBN 0-930466-18-7). Meckler Pub.

--Diary of a Provincial Lady. (Illus.). 388p. 1982. pap. 7.95 (ISBN 0-89733-053-6). Academy Chi Pubs.

--I Visited the Soviets: The Provincial Lady in Russia. (Provincial Lady Ser.: No. 4). 1985. pap. 8.95 (ISBN 0-89733-156-7). Academy Chi Pubs.

--The Provincial Lady in America. 245p. 1984. pap. 8.95 (ISBN 0-89733-110-9). Academy Chi Pubs.

--Provincial Lady in London. 302p. 1983. pap. 8.95 (ISBN 0-89733-085-4). Academy Chi Pubs.

--The Provincial Lady in Russia. 343p. pap. 8.95 (ISBN 0-89733-156-7). Academy Chi Pubs.

De Lafontaine, Henry C. The King's Musick: A Transcript of Records Relative to Music & Musicians. LC 70-169648. 522p. 1973. Repr. of 1909 ed. lib. bdg. 49.50 (ISBN 0-306-70269-X). Da Capo.

De La Fontaine, Jean. Contes, 3 tomes. Set. deluxe ed. 950.00 (ISBN 0-685-34230-1). French & Eur.

--Fables, 2 tomes. Incl. Tome I, Livre I-VI; Tome II, Livres VII-XII. (Fr.). 1962. Set. pap. 9.90 (ISBN 0-685-36015-6). French & Eur.

--Fables Choisies, 2 Vols. (Documentation thematique). (Illus., Fr.). pap. 2.95 (ISBN 0-685-13914-X). Larousse.

--Oeuvres Completes, 2 tomes. Incl. Tome I. Fables, Contes et Nouvelles. Gross & Schiffrin, eds. 35.95 (ISBN 0-685-35866-6); Tome II. Oeuvres diverses. Clarac, ed. 39.95 (ISBN 0-685-35867-4). (Bibl. de la Pleiade). 1933. French & Eur.

De La Fontaine, Jean & Calder, Alexander. Selected Fables. Clark, Eunice, tr. (Illus.). 86p. pap. 3.50 (ISBN 0-486-21878-3). Dover.

De la Fontaine, Jean see Fontaine, Jean de la.

De La Fontainerie, Francois, tr. see La Fontainerie.

De Lafora, Nicholas. Frontiers of New Spain. Kinnaird, Lawrence, ed. LC 67-24724. (Quivira Society Publications, Vol. 13). 1967. Repr. of 1958 ed. 17.00 (ISBN 0-405-00087-1). Ayer Co Pubs.

De La Fronde, Eugene. An Introduction to Psychology. (The Library of Scientific Psychology). (Illus.). 1979. 47.15 (ISBN 0-89266-178-X). Am Classical Coll Pr.

De La Fuente, Julio, jt. auth. see Malinowski, Bronislaw.

De La Fuente, Julio, ed. see Malinowski, Bronislaw.

De La Fuente, Mario. I Like You Gringo-But. 1974. pap. 2.50 (ISBN 0-914778-08-0). Phoenix Bks.

De La Fuente, Patricia, ed. Chicano. (Illus.). 64p. 1982. 4.00 (ISBN 0-938884-02-6). RiverSedge Pr.

De La Fuente, Tomas. Abraham y Jose el patriarca: personas importantes de la Biblia. (Illus.). 76p. (Span.). 1982. pap. 2.50 (ISBN 0-940048-03-5). Austin Bilingual Lang Ed.

--La Hermosa Historia de Jesus: Ordenada, Simplificada y Brevemente Explicada. 1983. pap. 4.95 (ISBN 0-311-04658-4). Casa Bautista.

De La Fuente, Tomas, tr. see Cowan, Marvin W.

De La Fuente, Tomas R. Jesus Nos Habla Por Medio De Sus Parabolas. 160p. 1978. 2.95 (ISBN 0-311-04344-5). Casa Bautista.

De La Fuye, Allotte. Jules Vernes: Sa Vie, son Oeuvre. 8.95 (ISBN 0-685-37140-9). French & Eur.

De la Garza, Rodolfo. The Mexican-American Experience: An Interdisciplinary Anthology. (Illus.). 432p. 1985. text ed. 25.00x (ISBN 0-292-75088-9); pap. 14.95x (ISBN 0-292-75083-8). U of Tex Pr.

DeLage, Ida. ABC Christmas. LC 77-14604. (Once Upon an ABC Ser.). (Illus.). (gr. k-4). 1978. PLB 7.47 (ISBN 0-8116-4355-7). Garrard.

--ABC Easter Bunny. LC 78-14829. (Once Upon an ABC Ser.). (Illus.). (gr. k-4). 1979. PLB 7.47 (ISBN 0-8116-4356-5). Garrard.

--ABC Fire Dogs. LC 77-591. (Once Upon an ABC Ser.). (Illus.). (gr. k-4). 1977. PLB 7.47 (ISBN 0-8116-4351-4). Garrard.

--ABC Halloween Witch. LC 77-5469. (Once Upon an ABC Ser.). (Illus.). (gr. k-4). 1977. lib. bdg. 7.47 (ISBN 0-8116-4353-0). Garrard.

--ABC Pigs Go to Market. LC 77-23317. (Once Upon an ABC Ser.). (Illus.). (gr. k-4). 1977. lib. bdg. 7.47 (ISBN 0-8116-4350-6). Garrard.

--ABC Pirate Adventure. LC 77-3171. (Once Upon an ABC Ser.). (Illus.). (gr. k-4). 1977. PLB 7.47 (ISBN 0-8116-4352-2). Garrard.

--ABC Santa Claus. LC 77-5629. (Once Upon an ABC Ser.). (Illus.). (gr. k-4). 1978. PLB 7.47 (ISBN 0-8116-4354-9). Garrard.

--ABC Triplets at the Zoo. LC 79-13265. (Once Upon an ABC Ser.). (Illus.). 32p. (gr. k-4). 1980. PLB 7.47 (ISBN 0-8116-4357-3). Garrard.

--Am I a Bunny? LC 77-11639. (Ida De Lage Bks.). (Illus.). (gr. k-2). 1978. lib. bdg. 7.47 (ISBN 0-8116-6072-9). Garrard.

--A Bunny Ride. LC 74-14818. (Ida DeLage Bks.). (Illus.). 32p. (gr. k-2). 1975. PLB 7.47 (ISBN 0-8116-6065-6). Garrard.

--Bunny School. LC 76-17625. (Ida DeLage Bks.). (Illus.). 32p. (gr. k-2). 1976. PLB 6.69 (ISBN 0-8116-6071-0). Garrard.

--Farmer & the Witch. LC 66-12674. (Old Witch Bks.). (Illus.). (gr. k-4). 1966. PLB 7.47 (ISBN 0-8116-4050-7). Garrard.

--Frannie's Flower. LC 79-11724. (Ida DeLage Bks.). (Illus.). (gr. k-2). 1979. PLB 7.47 (ISBN 0-8116-6076-1). Garrard.

--Good Morning, Lady. LC 73-22084. (Ida DeLage Bks.). (Illus.). 32p. (gr. k-2). 1974. PLB 7.47 (ISBN 0-8116-6051-6). Garrard.

--Hello, Come in. LC 71-156079. (Venture Ser.). (Illus.). 40p. (gr. 1). 1971. PLB 7.47 (ISBN 0-8116-6708-1). Garrard.

--Old Witch & Her Magic Basket. LC 78-58520. (Old Witch Ser.). (Illus.). (gr. k-4). 1978. PLB 7.47 (ISBN 0-8116-4063-9). Garrard.

--The Old Witch & the Crows. LC 81-13227. (Old Witch Bks.). (Illus.). 48p. (gr. k-4). 1983. PLB 7.47 (ISBN 0-8116-4067-1). Garrard.

--The Old Witch & the Dragon. LC 78-11283. (Old Witch Ser.). (Illus.). (gr. k-4). 1979. lib. bdg. 7.47 (ISBN 0-8116-4064-7). Garrard.

--The Old Witch & the Ghost Parade. LC 77-18185. (Old Witch Ser.). (Illus.). (gr. k-4). 1978. PLB 7.47 (ISBN 0-8116-4062-0). Garrard.

--Old Witch & the Snores. LC 75-95748. (Old Witch Bks.). (Illus.). (gr. k-4). 1970. PLB 7.47 (ISBN 0-8116-4056-6). Garrard.

--Old Witch & the Wizard. LC 73-16039. (Old Witch Bks.). (Illus.). 48p. (gr. k-4). 1974. PLB 7.47 (ISBN 0-8116-4060-4). Garrard.

--The Old Witch Finds a New House. LC 79-11732. (Old Witch Bks.). (Illus.). (gr. k-4). 1979. PLB 7.47 (ISBN 0-8116-4065-5). Garrard.

--The Old Witch Gets a Surprise. LC 80-24223. (Old Witch Bks.). (Illus.). 48p. (gr. k-4). 1981. lib. bdg. 7.47 (ISBN 0-8116-4066-3). Garrard.

--Old Witch Goes to the Ball. LC 69-15830. (Old Witch Bks.). (Illus.). (gr. k-4). 1969. PLB 7.47 (ISBN 0-8116-4055-8). Garrard.

--The Old Witch's Party. LC 75-45232. (Old Witch Bks.). (Illus.). 48p. (gr. k-4). 1976. PLB 7.47 (ISBN 0-8116-4061-2). Garrard.

--Pilgrim Children Come to Plymouth. LC 80-29180. (Illus.). 48p. (gr. 1-5). 1981. lib. bdg. 7.47 (ISBN 0-8116-6084-2). Garrard.

--The Pilgrim Children on the Mayflower. LC 79-21812. (Ida DeLage Bks.). (Illus.). 48p. (gr. 1-5). 1980. PLB 7.47 (ISBN 0-8116-4315-8). Garrard.

--Pink Pink. LC 72-11015. (Venture Ser.). (Illus.). 40p. (gr. 1). 1973. PLB 7.47 (ISBN 0-8116-6725-1). Garrard.

--The Squirrel's Tree Party. LC 78-58523. (Ida DeLage Bks.). (Illus.). (gr. k-2). 1978. PLB 7.47 (ISBN 0-8116-6073-7). Garrard.

--Weeny Witch. LC 68-10173. (Old Witch Bks.). (Illus.). (gr. k-4). 1968. PLB 7.47 (ISBN 0-8116-4052-3). Garrard.

--What Does a Witch Need? LC 76-143305. (Old Witch Bks.). (Illus.). (gr. k-4). 1971. PLB 7.47 (ISBN 0-8116-4058-2). Garrard.

--Witchy Broom. LC 69-10373. (Old Witch Bks.). (Illus.). (gr. k-4). 1969. PLB 7.47 (ISBN 0-8116-4054-X). Garrard.

Delagi, Edward F. & Perotto, Aldo. Anatomic Guide for Electromyographer: The Limbs. 2nd ed. (Illus.). 224p. 1982. 21.75x (ISBN 0-398-03951-8). C C Thomas.

De Lagny, Germain. Knout & the Russians: Or, the Muscovite Empire, the Czar, & His People. LC 74-115528. (Russia Observed, Series I). 1970. Repr. of 1854 ed. 19.00 (ISBN 0-405-03020-7). Ayer Co Pubs.

Delagran, Louise, ed. Economy Motel Guide. LC 82-23953. 416p. 1984. pap. 6.95 (ISBN 0-88166-015-9). Meadowbrook.

--Free Stuff for Kids. 7th, rev. ed. LC 81-2416. (Illus.). 120p. (gr. 2-8). 1983. pap. 2.95 (ISBN 0-88166-010-8). Meadowbrook.

--Free Stuff for Kids. 8th, rev. ed. (Illus.). 113p. (gr. 1-8). 1984. pap. 2.95 (ISBN 0-88166-060-4). Meadowbrook.

Delagran, Louise, ed. see Braganti, Nancy & Devine, Elizabeth.

Delagran, Louise, ed. see Lansky, Bruce.

Delagran, Louise, ed. see Masters, M.

Delagran, Louise, ed. see Meadowbrook Reference Group.

Delagran, Louise, et al, eds. see Masters, M.

De La Grange, Henry-Louis. Mahler. LC 72-76147. (Illus.). 1008p. 1973. 17.50 (ISBN 0-385-00524-5). Doubleday.

Del Aguila, F., et al, eds. Supersymmetry, Supergravity & Related Topics: Proceedings of the XVth GIFT International Seminar on Theoretical Physics, Sant Feliu de Guixols, Girona, Spain, June 4-9, 1984. 550p. 1984. 60.00x (ISBN 9971-966-79-4, Pub. by World Sci Singapore); pap. 28.00x (ISBN 9971-966-80-8, Pub. by World Sci Singapore). Taylor & Francis.

Del Aguila, Juan see Aguila, Juan del.

De Laguna, Asela R., ed. Images & Identities: The Puerto Rican in Two World Contexts. 275p. 1985. 24.95 (ISBN 0-88738-060-3); pap. 14.95 (ISBN 0-88738-617-2). Transaction Bks.

De Laguna, Asela Rodriguez-Seda see Rodriguez-Seda de Laguna, Asela.

De Laguna, Frederica. The Archaeology of Cook Inlet, Alaska. LC 74-5832. Repr. of 1934 ed. 57.50 (ISBN 0-404-11637-X). AMS Pr.

--The Prehistory of Northern North America As Seen from the Yukon. LC 76-43687. (Society for American Archaeology Memoirs.: No. 3). Repr. of 1947 ed. 54.50 (ISBN 0-404-15520-0). AMS Pr.

--The Story of a Tlingit Community: Problem in the Relationship Between Archaeological, Ethnological & Historical Methods. Repr. of 1960 ed. 39.00x (ISBN 0-403-03698-4). Scholarly.

De Laguna, Frederica, jt. auth. see Birket-Smith, Kaj.

De Laguna, Frederica, ed. Selected Papers from the "American Anthropologist" 1888-1920. 930p. 1976. text ed. 15.00 (ISBN 0-913167-04-5); pap. 10.00 (ISBN 0-318-04015-8). Am Anthro Assn.

De Laguna, Theodore see Laguna, Theodore De.

De la Halle, A. The Chansons of Adam De la Halle. Marshall, J. H., ed. (Medieval French Texts). 148p. (Fr.). 1971. pap. text ed. 6.95 (ISBN 0-7190-0461-6, Pub. by Manchester Univ Pr). Longwood Pub Group.

De la Halle, Adam. Oeuvres completes du trouvere Adam de la Halle Poesies et musique. De Coussemaker, Edmond, ed. (Illus.). 516p. (Fr.). 1964. Repr. of 1872 ed. 60.00x (ISBN 0-8450-1003-4). Broude.

De la Harpe, Jean-Baptiste. The Historical Journal of the Establishment of the French in Louisiana. Conrad, Glenn R., ed. Koenig, Virginia & Cain, Joan, trs. (USL History Ser.: No. 3). 150p. 1985. 12.95 (ISBN 0-940984-24-5). U of SW LA Ctr LA Studies.

De la Harpe, P. Classical Banach-Lie Algebras & Banach-Lie Groups of Operators in Hilbert Space. LC 72-88729. (Lecture Notes in Mathematics: Vol. 285). 160p. 1972. pap. 9.00 (ISBN 0-387-05984-9). Springer-Verlag.

Delahay, Paul. Double Layer & Electrode Kinetics. LC 65-16404. pap. 83.30 (ISBN 0-317-09078-X, 2009033). Bks Demand UMI.

--New Instrumental Methods in Electrochemistry: Theory, Instrumentation, & Applications to Analytical & Physical Chemistry. LC 80-16170. 456p. 1980. Repr. of 1954 ed. 29.50 (ISBN 0-89874-222-6). Krieger.

Delahay, Paul & Tobias, Charles W. Advances in Electrochemistry & Electrochemical Engineering, Vol. 8. LC 61-15021. 406p. 1971. 36.50 (ISBN 0-471-87526-0). Krieger.

Delahaye, Brian L., jt. auth. see Smith, Barry J.

Delahaye, Ernest. Documents relatifs a Paul Verlaine: Lettres, dessins, pages inedites recueillis et decrits. LC 77-10258. Repr. of 1919 ed. 20.00 (ISBN 0-404-16313-0). AMS Pr.

De La Haye, John, et al. Governments of the United States & California. 5th ed. 432p. 1982. pap. text ed. write for info. (ISBN 0-697-07710-1). Wm C Brown.

Delahaye, Michael. On the Third Day: A Novel of Suspense. 320p. 1984. 15.95 (ISBN 0-02-530560-3). MacMillan.

De La Haye, Yves, ed. see Marx, Karl & Engels, Friedrich.

Delahoyde, Melinda. Fighting for Life. 96p. (Orig.). 1984. pap. 3.95 (ISBN 0-89283-138-3). Servant.

DeLahunta, Alexander. Veterinary Neuroanatomy & Clinical Neurology. 2nd ed. LC 76-4246. (Illus.). 1983. text ed. 36.95 (ISBN 0-7216-3029-4). Saunders.

De Lahunta, Alexander, jt. auth. see Evans, Howard E.

De Lahunta, Alexander, jt. auth. see Noden, Drew M.

Delahunty, R. J. Spinoza. (Arguments of the Philosophers Ser.). 352p. 1985. 49.95x (ISBN 0-7102-0375-6). Routledge & Kegan.

De la Iglesia, F. A. see Feuer, G. & Iglesia, F. A. de la.

De la Iglesia, Maria E. The International Catalogue of Catalogues: The Complete Guide to World-Wide Shopping by Mail. rev. ed. LC 81-48041. (Illus.). 224p. (Orig.). 1982. 21.11i (ISBN 0-06-014985-X, HarpT); pap. 10.53i (ISBN 0-06-090942-0, CN 942, HarpT). Har-Row.

Delaigue, Joelle, jt. auth. see Schneider, Jost.

Delaisement, ed. see De Maupassant, Guy.

Delaisi, Francis. Political Myths & Economic Realities. LC 70-137938. (Economic Thought, History & Challenge Ser). 1971. Repr. of 1927 ed. 37.50x (ISBN 0-8046-1442-3, Pub. by Kennikat). Assoc Faculty Pr.

Delaisse, L. M. A Century of Dutch Manuscript Illumination. (California Studies in the History of Art: No. VI). (Illus.). 1968. 80.00x (ISBN 0-520-00315-2). U of Cal Pr.

Delaisse, L. M., et al. Illuminated Manuscripts. (The Waddesdon Catalogues Ser.). (Illus.). 608p. 1985. text ed. 75.00 (ISBN 0-7078-0070-6, Pub. by P Wilson Pubs). Sotheby Pubns.

De Lajarte, Theodore, ed. see Campra, Andre.

De Lajarte, Theodore, ed. see Lully, Jean-Baptiste.

De Lajarte, Theodore, ed. see Rameau, Jean-Philippe.

De Lalande, Joseph. Astronomie, 3 Vols. 1965. Repr. of 1792 ed. Set. 145.00 (ISBN 0-384-31065-6). Johnson Repr.

De Lalande, Michel-Richard & Destouches, Andre-Cardinal. Les Elements. D'Indy, Vincent, ed. (Chefs-d'oeuvre classiques de l'opera francais Ser.: Vol. 14). (Illus.). 344p. (Fr.). 1972. pap. 27.50x (ISBN 0-8450-1114-6). Broude.

De La Lavoissier, Gaston. Europe, Italy & the Rebuilding of the Holy Roman Empire. (Illus.). 131p. 1984. 97.85x (ISBN 0-86722-059-7). Inst Econ Pol.

De La Luz, Antonio. La Empresa y la Funcion de Personal. 7.50 (ISBN 0-8477-2620-7); pap. 6.25 (ISBN 0-8477-2609-6). U of PR Pr.

De La Luz, Antonio, et al. Contabilidad Practica Del Siglo XX. (Span.). 1974. text ed. 9.40 (ISBN 0-538-02800-9, B80). SW Pub.

De Lamadrid, Jesus G., jt. auth. see Argabright, Loren.

Delamaide, Darrell. Debt Shock: The Full Story of the World Credit Crisis. LC 83-45009. 288p. 1984. 15.95 (ISBN 0-385-18899-4). Doubleday.

--Debt Shock: The Full Story of the World Credit Crisis. LC 83-45009. 288p. 1985. pap. text ed. 9.95 (ISBN 0-385-18900-1, Anchor). Doubleday.

De La Malle, Adolphe Dureau see Dureau De La Malle, Adolphe.

Delamar, Gloria T. Children's Counting-Out Rhymes, Fingerplays, Jump Rope & Bounce-Ball Chants & Other Rhythms: A Comprehensive English-Language Reference. LC 82-24904. 224p. 1983. lib. bdg. 19.95x (ISBN 0-89950-064-1). McFarland & Co.

De Lamar, Marie & Rothstein, Elisabeth. The Reconstructed 1790 Census of Georgia Substitutes for Georgia's Lost 1790 Census. LC 84-73075. 235p. 1985. Repr. of 1976 ed. 20.00 (ISBN 0-8063-1111-8). Genealog Pub.

--Records of Washington County, Georgia. LC 84-73076. 184p. 1985. Repr. of 1975 ed. 18.50 (ISBN 0-8063-1110-X). Genealog Pub.

De la Mare, F. R. see Mare, R. F. De la.

Delamare, J. & Delamare, Th. Dictionnaire Francais-Anglais et Anglais-Francais des Termes Techniques de Medecine. 714p. (Eng. & Fr.). 1970. 39.95 (ISBN 0-686-56980-6, M-6107). French & Eur.

Delamare, Jean, jt. auth. see Garnier, Marcel.

De la Mare, P. B. & Bolton, R. Electrophilic Additions to Unsaturated Systems. 2nd ed. (Studies in Organic Chemistry: Vol. 9). 378p. 1982. 95.75 (ISBN 0-444-42030-4). Elsevier.

De La Mare, Peter. Electrophilic Halogenation: Reaction Pathways Involving Attack by Electrophilic Halogens on Unsaturated Compounds. LC 75-13451. (Cambridge Chemistry Texts Ser.). pap. 60.80 (ISBN 0-317-20854-3, 2024444). Bks Demand UMI.

Delamare, Th., jt. auth. see Delamare, J.

De La Mare, W. Lewis Carroll. LC 72-2127. (English Literature Ser., No. 33). 1972. Repr. of 1932 ed. lib. bdg. 75.00x (ISBN 0-8383-1489-9). Haskell.

--Rupert Brooke & the Intellectual Imagination. LC 72-3166. (English Literature Ser., No. 33). 1972. Repr. of 1919 ed. lib. bdg. 29.95x (ISBN 0-8383-1515-1). Haskell.

De la Mare, Walter. Behold, This Dreamer! 720p. (Orig.). 1984. pap. 12.95 (ISBN 0-571-13298-7). Faber & Faber.

--Best Stories of Walter de la Mare. 400p. (Orig.). 1983. pap. 7.95 (ISBN 0-571-13076-3). Faber & Faber.

--Checklist. Cecil, D., ed. 1956. lib. bdg. 10.00 (ISBN 0-8414-2457-8). Folcroft.

--Collected Poems. LC 79-670359. 480p. 1979. 19.95 (ISBN 0-571-11381-8); pap. 9.95 (ISBN 0-571-11382-6). Faber & Faber.

--De La Mare, Walter. Hadfield, John, ed. (Pocket Poet Ser.). 1962. pap. 2.00 (ISBN 0-8023-9044-7). Dufour.

--Early One Morning. 1977. Repr. of 1935 ed. lib. bdg. 49.00x (ISBN 0-374-92098-2). Octagon.

--Eight Tales. 1971. 5.00 (ISBN 0-87054-055-6). Arkham.

--Eighteen-Eighties: Essays. LC 73-158497. 1971. Repr. of 1930 ed. 39.00x (ISBN 0-403-01295-3). Scholarly.

--Lewis Carroll. LC 73-13510. 1932. lib. bdg. 10.00 (ISBN 0-8414-3662-2). Folcroft.

--Lewis Carroll. 1978. 18.50 (ISBN 0-685-87740-X). Porter.

--Memoirs of a Midget. (Twentieth-Century Classics Ser.). 1982. pap. 6.95 (ISBN 0-19-281344-7). Oxford U Pr.

--Molly Whuppie. LC 82-83099. (Illus.). 32p. (gr. 1 up). 1983. 10.95 (ISBN 0-374-35000-0). FS&G.

--Peacock Pie. 1958. 7.95 (ISBN 0-571-04683-5); pap. 3.50 (ISBN 0-571-05609-1). Faber & Faber.

--Peacock Pie. (Fanfares Ser.). 122p. (gr. 4 up). 1980. pap. 3.25 (ISBN 0-571-18014-0). Faber & Faber.

--Poetry in Prose. LC 76-25537. 1935. lib. bdg. 8.50 (ISBN 0-8414-3738-6). Folcroft.

--Poetry in Prose. 1978. 18.50 (ISBN 0-685-87741-8). Porter.

--The Return. Reginald, R. & Menville, Douglas, eds. LC 75-46266. (Supernatural & Occult Fiction Ser.). 1976. Repr. of 1910 ed. lib. bdg. 23.50x (ISBN 0-405-08124-3). Ayer Co Pubs.

--Selected Poems. 208p. 1973. pap. 5.95 (ISBN 0-571-10401-0). Faber & Faber.

--Songs of Childhood. 106p. (gr. 3 up). pap. 3.50 (ISBN 0-486-21972-0). Dover.

--Songs of Childhood. 13.50 (ISBN 0-8446-1966-3). Peter Smith.

--Stories from the Bible. (Illus.). 418p. (gr. 3). 1985. pap. 6.95 (ISBN 0-571-11086-X). Faber & Faber.

--Tales Told Again. (Faber Fanfares Ser.). (Illus.). 208p. (Orig.). (gr. 4-7). 1980. pap. 3.25 (ISBN 0-571-18013-2). Faber & Faber.

De La Mare, Walter see Fellows of the Royal Society of Literature of the UK.

De la Mare, Walter see Ramal, Walter, pseud.

De La Mare, Walter J. Memoirs of a Midget. LC 83-45428. Repr. of 1941 ed. 38.00 (ISBN 0-404-20076-1). AMS Pr.

--Pleasures & Speculations. facsimile ed. LC 76-90630. (Essay Index Reprint Ser). 1940. 19.50 (ISBN 0-8369-1255-1). Ayer Co Pubs.

--Private View: Essays on Literature. LC 78-14114. 1979. Repr. of 1953 ed. 24.20 (ISBN 0-88355-786-X). Hyperion Conn.

--Wind Blows Over. facsimile ed. LC 71-113655. (Short Story Index Reprint Ser.). 1936. 20.00 (ISBN 0-8369-3384-2). Ayer Co Pubs.

Delamarre. Dictionnaire Francais-Anglais et Anglais-Francais des Termes Techniques De Medecine. (Fr. & Eng.). 49.95 (ISBN 0-685-36680-4). French & Eur.

De La Marre, jt. auth. see Cazes.

De La Mars, Claude H. The Life & Art of Jean-Louis-Ernest Meissonier. (The Great Art Masters of History Ser.). (Illus.). 119p. 1984. 47.55 (ISBN 0-86650-119-3). Gloucester Art.

De Lamartine, A. Poemes Choisis. Barbier, J. L., ed. (Modern French Text Ser.). (Fr.). 1921. pap. text ed. 7.95 (ISBN 0-7190-0147-1, Pub. by Manchester Univ Pr). Longwood Pub Group.

De Lamartine, Alphonse. Jocelyn. (Coll. GF). 1960. pap. 3.95 (ISBN 0-685-11277-2). French & Eur.

--Meditations. Bd. with Nouvelles Meditations. pap. 3.95 (ISBN 0-685-23882-2). French & Eur.

--Meditations. Letessier, ed. (Class. Garnier). pap. 18.50 (ISBN 0-685-34926-8). French & Eur.

--Meditations. Letessier, ed. (Coll. Prestige). 27.50 (ISBN 0-685-34927-6). French & Eur.

--Meditations Poetiques. (Documentation Thematique Ser.). (Illus., Fr.). pap. 2.95 (ISBN 0-685-13988-3, 151). Larousse.

--Oeuvres Poetiques Completes. Guyard, ed. (Bibl. de la Pleiade). 1963. 45.00 (ISBN 0-685-11460-0). French & Eur.

De Lamartine, Alphonse see Lamartine, Alphonse de.

Delamater, Jerome. Dance in the Hollywood Musical. Kirkpatrick, Diane, ed. LC 81-7513. (Studies in Cinema: No. 4). 324p. 1981. 44.95 (ISBN 0-8357-1198-6). UMI Res Pr.

DeLamater, John & MacCorquodale, Patricia. Premarital Sexuality: Attitudes, Relationships, Behavior. LC 78-65019. 314p. 1979. 32.50x (ISBN 0-299-07840-X). U of Wis Pr.

Delamater, John, jt. auth. see Fidell, Linda S.

De la Maza, L. M. & Peterson, E. M., eds. Medical Virology. 408p. 1982. 75.00 (ISBN 0-444-00709-1, Biomedical Pr). Elsevier.

De La Maza, Luis M. & Peterson, Ellena, eds. Medical Virology IV. 460p. 1985. text ed. 20.00 (ISBN 0-89859-765-X). L Erlbaum Assocs.

De La Maza, M. & Patterson, E. M., eds. Medical Virology III: Proceedings of the 1983 International Symposium on Medical Virology, Oct. 19-21, 1983, Anaheim, Ca. 400p. 1984. 65.00 (ISBN 0-444-00829-2). Elsevier.

Delambre, Jean B. Histoire De l'Astronomie Ancienne, 2 Vols. facsimile ed. 1817. Set. 105.00 (ISBN 0-384-11203-X). Johnson Repr.

--Histoire de L'astronomie du Moyen Age. 1965. Repr. of 1819 ed. 55.00 (ISBN 0-384-11265-X). Johnson Repr.

--Histoire De L'astronomie Moderne, 2 Vols. (Sources of Science, House Ser.: No. 25). (Fr). 1969. Repr. of 1821 ed. Set. 140.00 (ISBN 0-384-11300-1). Johnson Repr.

Delamere, Catherine, jt. auth. see Calhoun, George M.

Dela Mirandola, Giovanni Pico. Oracion Acerca De la Dignidad Del Hombre. pap. 1.50 (ISBN 0-8477-0712-1). U of PR Pr.

Delamont, Sara. Interaction in the Classroom. 2nd ed. (Contemporary Sociology of the School Ser.). 128p. 1983. pap. 7.95 (ISBN 0-416-35880-2, NO. 3956). Methuen Inc.

--Readings on Interaction in the Classroom. (Contemporary Sociology of the School Ser.). 368p. 1984. pap. text ed. 12.95 (ISBN 0-416-35220-0, 3971). Methuen Inc.

--Sex Roles & the School. 128p. 1980. 17.50x (ISBN 0-416-71310-6, NO. 3436); pap. 7.50x (ISBN 0-416-71320-3, NO. 3437). Methuen Inc.

--Sociology of Women: An Introduction. 256p. (Orig.). 1980. text ed. 21.50x (ISBN 0-04-301119-5). Allen Unwin.

Delamont, Sara & Duffin, Lorna, eds. The Nineteenth Century Woman: Her Cultural & Physical World. LC 77-28236. 213p. 1978. text ed. 27.50x (ISBN 0-06-491660-X). B&N Imports.

Delamont, Sara, jt. ed. see Chanan, Gabriel.

Delamore, I. W., jt. auth. see Israels, M. G.

De La Mothe, Francois De Salignac see Fenelon & De Salignac De La Mothe, Francois.

De la Motte, Guillaume see Motte, Guillaume de la.

Delamotte, Philip H. The Practice of Photography. 2nd ed. LC 72-9193. (The Literature of Photography Ser.). Repr. of 1855 ed. 15.00 (ISBN 0-405-04903-X). Ayer Co Pubs.

DeLamotte, Roy C. The Alien Christ. LC 80-5902. 276p. 1980. lib. bdg. 24.00 (ISBN 0-8191-1304-2); pap. text ed. 12.50 (ISBN 0-8191-1305-0). U Pr of Amer.

--Jalaluddin Rumi: Songbird of Sufism. LC 80-5884. 187p. 1980. lib. bdg. 21.75 (ISBN 0-8191-1286-0); pap. text ed. 10.25 (ISBN 0-8191-1287-9). U Pr of Amer.

Delamotte, Yves. Grievance Procedure in an American Enterprise. (Fr.). 1966. 3.00 (ISBN 0-89215-051-3). U Cal LA Indus Rel.

Delamotte, Yves & Takezawa, S. Quality of Working Life in International Perspective. International Labour Office, ed. ix, 89p. (Orig.). 1984. pap. 8.55 (ISBN 92-2-103402-X). Intl Labour Office.

Delana, Alice & Reick, Cynthia, eds. On Common Ground: A Selection of Hartford Writers. 156p. 1975. pap. 5.95 (ISBN 0-317-35970-3). Stowe-Day.

Delana, Alice & Reik, Cynthia, eds. On Common Ground: A Selection of Hartford Writers. (Illus.). 1975. pap. 5.95 (ISBN 0-917482-03-4). Stowe-Day.

De Laney, Edward F., ed. see Jones, Thomas.

Delancey, Mark & Delancey, Virginia. A Bibliography of Cameroon. LC 75-1165. (African Bibliography Ser.: Vol. 4). 675p. 1975. text ed. 45.00x (ISBN 0-8419-0167-8, Africana). Holmes & Meier.

DeLancey, Mark W. African International Relations: An Annotated Bibliography. 366p. 1980. 29.50x (ISBN 0-89158-680-6). Westview.

DeLancey, Mark W. & Normand, Elizabeth L. Nigeria: A Bibliography of Politics, Government, Administration, & Internal Relations. LC 84-123087. (The Archival & Bibliographical Ser.). Date not set. price not set (ISBN 0-918456-36-3). Crossroads MA.

DeLancey, Mark W., ed. Aspects of International Relations in Africa. (African Humanities Ser.). 253p. (Orig.). 1980. pap. 9.00 (ISBN 0-941934-28-4). Indiana Africa.

Delancey, Virginia, jt. auth. see Delancey, Mark.

DeLancy, Elaine. Quiltcraft: New Dimensions from Past Traditions. 160p. 1985. 12.95 (ISBN 0-8329-0391-4). New Century.

Delancy, Patrick R., jt. auth. see Gleim, Irvin N.

Delancy, Patrick R., et al. GAAP: Interpretation & Application. 550p. 1985. pap. 24.95 (ISBN 0-471-86144-8). Wiley.

DeLand, Antoinette. Fielding's Far East. (Illus.). 582p. (Orig.). 1984. pap. 14.95 FPT (ISBN 0-688-01577-8, Pub. by Fielding). Morrow.

--Fielding's Worldwide Cruises. 2nd rev. ed. (Illus.). 400p. 1984. pap. 12.95 (ISBN 0-688-03947-2). Fielding Travel Bks.

--Fielding's Worldwide Guide to Cruises. rev. ed. LC 82-62320. (Illus.). 416p. 1982. pap. 12.95 (ISBN 0-688-01648-0). Morrow.

Deland, Charles E. The Aborigines of South Dakota. LC 76-43688. (South Dakota Historical Collections: 3). 1977. Repr. of 1906 ed. 30.00 (ISBN 0-404-15521-9). AMS Pr.

Deland, E. C., jt. auth. see Lance, G. N.

De Land, E. C., ed. Information Technology in Health Science Education. LC 78-7201. 624p. 1978. 85.00x (ISBN 0-306-31113-5, Plenum Pr). Plenum Pub.

Deland, Frank H. Cerebral Radionuclide Angiography. LC 72-292. pap. 79.80 (ISBN 0-317-07793-7, 2016660). Bks Demand UMI.

Deland, Frank H., et al. Atlas of Nuclear Medicine, Vol. 1, Brain. LC 74-81820. pap. 57.30 (ISBN 0-317-07792-9, 2016659). Bks Demand UMI.

Deland, Isidore. The United States, Europe, Israel & the Approaching Collapse of the World Order. (Illus.). 1978. deluxe ed. 69.50x (ISBN 0-930008-00-6). Inst Econ Pol.

Deland, Margaret. The Awakening of Helena Richie. LC 78-96881. (Illus.). Repr. of 1906 ed. lib. bdg. 19.00 (ISBN 0-8398-0358-3). Irvington.

--Florida Days. LC 83-137206. (Illus.). 200p. 1983. pap. 7.95 (ISBN 0-910923-01-9). Pineapple Pr.

--Floriday Day. (Illus.). 1978. Repr. of 1889 ed. lib. bdg. 35.00 (ISBN 0-8492-0690-1). R West.

--John Ward, Preacher. LC 67-29263. (Americans in Fiction Ser.). lib. bdg. 14.00 (ISBN 0-8398-0359-1); pap. text ed. 7.95x (ISBN 0-8290-0134-4). Irvington.

Deland, Margaret W. Doctor Lavendar's People. LC 70-90102. (BCL Ser. II). (Illus.). 1969. Repr. of 1903 ed. 14.00 (ISBN 0-404-02074-7). AMS Pr.

--Doctor Lavendar's People. LC 75-113656. (Short Story Index Reprint Ser.). 1903. 19.00 (ISBN 0-8369-3385-0). Ayer Co Pubs.

--Doctor Lavendar's People. 1972. Repr. of 1903 ed. 13.00 (ISBN 0-8422-8036-7). Irvington.

--Doctor Lavendar's People. LC 77-129345. (Illus.). 1971. Repr. of 1903 ed. 12.00x (ISBN 0-403-00478-0). Scholarly.

--Mister Tommy Dove & Other Stories. facsimile ed. LC 75-94716. (Short Story Index Reprint Ser.). 1893. 18.00 (ISBN 0-8369-3095-9). Ayer Co Pubs.

--Old Chester Days. LC 79-113657. (Short Story Index Reprint Ser.). 1937. 21.00 (ISBN 0-8369-3386-9). Ayer Co Pubs.

--Old Chester Tales. LC 70-97884. (BCL Ser. I). Repr. of 1898 ed. 18.50 (ISBN 0-404-02075-5). AMS Pr.

--Old Chester Tales. 1972. Repr. of 1898 ed. lib. bdg. 18.00 (ISBN 0-8422-8037-5). Irvington.

--Wisdom of Fools. LC 72-98567. (Short Story Index Reprint Ser.). 1897. 17.00 (ISBN 0-8369-3141-6). Ayer Co Pubs.

De Land, T. A. & Smith, Davis, eds. Northern Alabama, Historical & Biographical. LC 75-45365. (Illus.). 776p. 1976. Repr. of 1888 ed. 50.00 (ISBN 0-87152-224-1). Reprint.

De Landa, D. Relacion De las Cosas De Yucatan. Tozzer, A., tr. (Harvard University Peabody Museum of Archaeology & Ethnology Papers). Repr. of 1941 ed. 66.00 (ISBN 0-527-01245-9). Kraus Repr.

De Landa, Diego. Landa's Relacion de las Cosas de Yucatan. Tozzer, Alfred M., ed. LC 83-45906. Repr. of 1941 ed. 48.00 (ISBN 0-404-20150-4). AMS Pr.

De Landscheere, G. Empirical Research in Education. (Educational Sciences Ser.). 113p. 1982. pap. text ed. 11.50 (ISBN 92-3-102023-4, U1268, UNESCO). Unipub.

De Landsheere, Gilbert. Dictionnaire de l'Evaluation et de la Recherche en Education. 352p. (Fr.). 1979. 62.50 (ISBN 0-686-56981-4, M-6108). French & Eur.

Delaney & Laney. The Osmonds. 32p. (gr. 4-6). 1975. pap. 3.95 (ISBN 0-89812-113-2). Creative Ed.

Delaney, A. Monster Tracks? LC 79-2671. (Illus.). 32p. (ps-1). 1981. 9.57i (ISBN 0-06-021588-7); PLB 9.89g (ISBN 0-06-021589-5). HarpJ.

Delaney, Anita J., ed. Black Task Force Report. LC 78-24566. (Project on Ethnicity Ser.). 37p. 1979. pap. 4.00 (ISBN 0-87304-171-2). Family Serv.

Delaney, Anita J., jt. ed. see Mizio, Emelicia.

Delaney, Betty. The Magic of Spellbinder. LC 84-91754. 200p. 1985. pap. 19.95 (ISBN 0-911061-12-6). S Davis Pub.

Delaney, C. F. Electronics for the Physicist with Applications. LC 79-42737. 306p. 1980. 53.95x (ISBN 0-470-26902-2); pap. 28.95x (ISBN 0-470-26903-0). Halsted Pr.

Delaney, C. F., ed. Rationality & Religious Belief. LC 79-63359. (Studies in the Philosophy of Religion: No. 1). 1979. text ed. 12.95x (ISBN 0-268-01602-X, 85-16023); pap. text ed. 5.95x (ISBN 0-268-01603-8, 85-16031). U of Notre Dame Pr.

Delaney, C. F., et al. The Synoptic Vision: Essays on the Philosophy of Wilfrid Sellars. LC 76-22406. 1977. text ed. 17.95x (ISBN 0-268-01596-1). U of Notre Dame Pr.

Delaney, Caldwell. Confederate Mobile: A Pictorial History. LC 70-172006. (Illus.). 1971. 25.00 (ISBN 0-940882-12-4). Haunted Bk Shop.

--Deep South. (Illus.). 1981. Repr. of 1942 ed. 15.00 (ISBN 0-940882-00-0). Haunted Bk Shop.

--A Mobile Sextet. (Illus.). 187p. 1981. 15.00 (ISBN 0-940882-15-9). Haunted Bk Shop.

--The Phoenix Volunteer Fire Company of Mobile, 1838-1888. (Illus., Orig.). 1967. pap. 2.00 (ISBN 0-914334-00-X). Museum Mobile.

--Remember Mobile. (Illus.). 242p. 1980. Repr. of 1948 ed. 15.00 (ISBN 0-940882-13-2). Haunted Bk Shop.

--The Story of Mobile. rev. ed. (Illus.). 352p. 1981. Repr. of 1953 ed. 15.00 (ISBN 0-940882-14-0). Haunted Bk Shop.

Delaney, Caldwell, ed. Raphael Semmes, Rear Admiral, Confederate States Navy, Brigadier General, Confederate States Army. (Illus.). 1978. 25.00 (ISBN 0-914334-05-0); pap. 10.00 (ISBN 0-914334-06-9). Museum Mobile.

Delaney, Caldwell, ed. see Craighead, Erwin.

Delaney, Cornelius F. Mind & Nature: A Study in the Naturalistic Philosophies of Cohen, Woodbridge & Sellars. LC 70-75150. 1969. 19.95 (ISBN 0-268-00313-0). U of Notre Dame Pr.

Delaney, E. J. & Feehan, J. M. Comic History of Ireland. 125p. 1951. pap. 4.50 (ISBN 0-85342-058-0, Co-dist. by Irish Bks Media). Irish Bk Ctr.

Delaney, Edmund. The Connecticut River: New England's Historic Waterway. LC 83-80635. (Illus.). 182p. 1983. pap. 9.95 (ISBN 0-87106-980-6). Globe Pequot.

Delaney, Edmund T., et al. Greenwich Village: A Photographic Guide. LC 74-78593. (Illus.). 128p. (Orig.). 1976. pap. 5.95 (ISBN 0-486-23114-3). Dover.

Delaney, F. M., jt. ed. see Rast, N.

Delaney, Frank. Betjeman Country. (Illus.). 233p. 1984. 18.95 (ISBN 0-340-34151-3, Pub. by Hodder & Stoughton UK). David & Charles.

Delaney, Frank & Lewinski, Jorge. James Joyce's Odyssey: A Guide to the Dublin of Ulysses. LC 81-83276. (Illus.). 224p. 1982. 19.95 (ISBN 0-03-060457-5). HR&W.

Delaney, Gayle. Living Your Dreams. LC 78-20590. 240p. 1981. pap. 7.68 (ISBN 0-06-250201-8, CN 4018, HarpR). Har-Row.

Delaney, H. M. & Jason, R. Abdominal Trauma: Surgical & Radiologic Diagnosis. (Illus.). 224p. 1981. 49.00 (ISBN 0-387-90502-2). Springer-Verlag.

Delaney, J. B., jt. ed. see Najarian, J. S.

Delaney, J. P., jt. auth. see Najarian, J. S.

Delaney, Jack. Palm Springs a la Carte. LC 77-21834. (Illus.). 1978. pap. 3.95 (ISBN 0-88280-055-8). ETC Pubns.

Delaney, Jack J. Media Program in the Elementary & Middle School: Its Organization & Administration. (Illus.). 222p. 1976. 17.50 (ISBN 0-208-01344-X, Linnet). Shoe String.

--Steinbeck: A Biography. (Illus.). Date not set. price not set (ISBN 0-8022-2476-8). Philos Lib.

Delaney, John. How to Brief a Case: An Introduction to Legal Reasoning. LC 83-72289. 133p. (Orig.). 1983. 9.95 (ISBN 0-9608514-1-0). J Delaney Pubns.

--How to Do Your Best on Law School Exams. LC 82-90278. 156p. 1982. 10.95 (ISBN 0-9608514-0-2). J Delaney Pubns.

Delaney, John J. Dictionary of American Catholic Biography. LC 83-25524. 624p. 1984. 24.95 (ISBN 0-385-17878-6). Doubleday.

--Dictionary of Saints. LC 79-7783. (Illus.). 648p. 1980. 24.95 (ISBN 0-385-13594-7). Doubleday.

--A Dictionary of Saints. 648p. 1982. 45.00x (ISBN 0-7182-2170-2, Pub. by Windmill Pr). State Mutual Bk.

--Pocket Dictionary of Saints. LC 82-45479. 528p. 1983. pap. 6.95 (ISBN 0-385-18274-0, Im). Doubleday.

--Saints Are Now: Eight Portraits of Modern Sanctity. LC 82-45866. 224p. 1983. pap. 4.50 (ISBN 0-385-17356-3, Im). Doubleday.

Delaney, John J., ed. Saints for All Seasons. LC 77-81438. 1978. pap. 3.95 (ISBN 0-385-12909-2, Im). Doubleday.

--Woman Clothed with the Sun. LC 60-5922. 1961. pap. 4.50 (ISBN 0-385-08019-0, Im). Doubleday.

Delaney, John J., tr. The Practice of the Presence of God. LC 77-70896. 1977. pap. 2.95 (ISBN 0-385-12861-4, Im). Doubleday.

Delaney, John P. & De La Costa, Horacio. Just for Fun & Other Stories. 1971. wrps. 4.50x (ISBN 0-686-09492-1). Cellar.

Delaney, John P. & Varco, Richard L., eds. Controversies in Surgery, Two. (Illus.). 464p. 1983. 49.95 (ISBN 0-7216-3038-3). Saunders.

Delaney, John P., jt. ed. see Najarian, John S.

Delaney, John P., jt. ed. see Varco, Richard L.

Delaney, Joseph H. & Stiegler, Marc. Valentina: Soul in Sapphire. 320p. 1984. pap. 3.50 (ISBN 0-671-55916-8, Pub. by Baen Bks). PB.

Delaney, Laurence. Blood Red Wine. (Orig.). 1981. pap. 2.95 (ISBN 0-440-10714-8). Dell.

--Sea Ranch. (Orig.). 1984. pap. 3.50 (ISBN 0-440-17674-3). Dell.

Delaney, M. C. Henry's Special Delivery. (Illus.). 144p. (gr. 3-6). 1984. 9.95 (ISBN 0-525-44081-X, 0966-290). Dutton.

--The Marigold Monster. LC 82-14739. (Illus.). 32p. (ps-3). 1983. 9.95 (ISBN 0-525-44023-2, 0966-290). Dutton.

Delaney, Mary M. Of Irish Ways. (BN 4000 Ser.). pap. 6.50 (ISBN 0-06-464035-3, BN 4035, BN). B&N NY.

--Of Irish Ways. (BN 4035 Ser.). 368p. 1979. pap. 6.50i. Har-Row.

Delaney, Matilda S. Whitman Massacre. facs. ed. 46p. pap. 3.95 (ISBN 0-8466-0130-3, S130). Shorey.

Delaney, Michael, jt. auth. see Hakala, Donald.

Delaney, Ned. Terrible Things Could Happen. LC 82-10051. (Illus.). 32p. (gr. k-3). 1983. 10.25 (ISBN 0-688-01282-5); PLB 10.88 (ISBN 0-688-01284-1). Lothrop.

--Two Strikes, Four Eyes. (Illus.). (gr. k-3). 1976. PLB 11.95 reinforced bdg. (ISBN 0-395-24744-6). HM.

Delaney, Patrick R. & Adler, James R. GAAP: A Transaction Approach. 500p. 1984. text ed. write for info. (ISBN 0-471-86144-8). Wiley.

Delaney, Patrick R. & Gleim, Irvin N. CPA Examination Review 1984 Edition: Auditing, Vol. 2. 552p. 1984. pap. 21.95x (ISBN 0-471-88222-4). Wiley.

--CPA Examination Review 1984 Edition: Theory & Practice, Vol. 1. 1368p. 1984. pap. 31.95x (ISBN 0-471-88221-6). Wiley.

--CPA Examination Review 1984 Edition: Vol. 3 - Business Law. 588p. 1984. pap. 21.95x (ISBN 0-471-88219-4). Wiley.

--CPA Examination Review: 1985 Edition, 3 pts. Incl. Theory & Practice. 1423p. Part I. pap. 31.95 (ISBN 0-471-81900-X); Auditing. 589p. Part II. pap. 21.95 (ISBN 0-471-81899-2); Business Law. 563p. Part III. pap. 21.95 (ISBN 0-471-81901-8). Set. pap. 75.85 (ISBN 0-471-81898-4). Wiley.

--CPA Examination Solutions: May, 1983. (1645). 189p. 1983. pap. text ed. 15.95 (ISBN 0-471-89825-2). Wiley.

Delaney, Patrick R., jt. auth. see Gleim, Irvin N.

DeLaney, Rex. Grow Younger after Forty: A Scientific Approach to the Problem of Aging. (Illus.). 182p. (Orig.). 1974. pap. 5.00 (ISBN 0-89955-420-2, Pub. by R Delaney). Intl Spec Bk.

--Self Attainment Through Transitional Sleep: How to Improve Your Mind & Body. Orig. Title: Health Through Transitional Sleep. (Illus.). 150p. (Orig.). 1961. pap. 5.00 (ISBN 0-89955-419-9, Pub. by R. Delaney). Intl Spec Bk.

Delaney, Robert F. The Literature of Communism in America: A Selected Reference Guide. LC 62-6923. pap. 111.80 (ISBN 0-317-10348-2, 2005378). Bks Demand UMI.

Delaney, Ronald. Hounds & Terriers. (Illus.). 112p. 1984. 9.95 (ISBN 0-7137-1371-2, Pub. by Blandfrod Pr England). Sterling.

Delaney, Shelagh. The Lion in Love. 104p. 1961. pap. 6.95 (ISBN 0-413-38330-X, NO. 2999). Methuen Inc.

--A Taste of Honey. (Orig.). 1959. pap. 3.95 (ISBN 0-394-17480-1, E159, Ever). Grove.

Delaney, Sue. The Lord, the Lion & Mutn. pap. 0.95 (ISBN 0-89985-995-X). Christ Nations.

--Mutu Finds the Way to Heaven. pap. 0.95 (ISBN 0-89985-996-8). Christ Nations.

Delaney, W. How to Run a Growing Company. 1983. pap. 6.95 (ISBN 0-8144-7590-6). AMACOM.

--The Thirty Most Common Problems in Management & How to Solve Them. 1982. pap. 14.95 (ISBN 0-8144-5536-0). AMACOM.

Delaney, W., Jr. Physicians' Guide to Oculosystemic Diseases: Ophthalmoscopic Physical Diagnosis. 1982. 49.50 (ISBN 0-87489-250-3). Med Economics.

Delaney, William A. Manager's Tricks of the Trade: How to Solve 30 Common Management Problems. LC 83-69735. 192p. 1983. pap. 6.95 (ISBN 0-8144-7603-1). AMACOM.

--Micromanagement: How to Solve the Problems of Growing Companies. 176p. 1981. 14.95 (ISBN 0-8144-5642-1). AMACOM.

--Micromanagement: How to Solve the Problems of Growing Companies. LC 80-69691. pap. 43.50 (ISBN 0-317-20787-3, 2023914). Bks Demand UMI.

--So You Want To Start a Business! 216p. 1984. 16.95 (ISBN 0-13-823915-0, Busn); pap. 9.95 (ISBN 0-13-823907-X). P-H.

--The Thirty Most Common Problems in Management & How to Solve Them. LC 81-69375. pap. 48.00 (ISBN 0-317-19939-0, 2023569). Bks Demand UMI.

--Why Small Businesses Fail: Don't Make the Same Mistake Once. 204p. 1984. 16.95 (ISBN 0-13-959016-1, Busn); pap. 9.95 (ISBN 0-13-959008-0). P-H.

DeLange, Deon. More Techniques of Beading Earrings II. Smith, Monte, ed. (Illus.). 94p. 1985. pap. 8.95 (ISBN 0-943604-12-5). Eagles View.

Delange, F. Endemic Goitre & Thyroid Function in Central Africa. Falkner, F., et al, eds. (Monographs in Pediatrics: Vol. 2). (Illus.). xvi, 160p. 1974. 34.50 (ISBN 3-8055-1687-8). S Karger.

Delange, F. & Iteke, G. B. Nutritional Factors Involved in the Goitrogenic Action of Cassava. 100p. 1982. pap. 9.00 (ISBN 0-88936-315-3, IDRC184, IDRC). Unipub.

Delange, F., et al, eds. Pediatric Thyroidology. (Pediatric & Adolescent Endocrinology: Vol. 14). (Illus.). x, 412p. 1985. 117.25 (ISBN 3-8055-3968-1). S Karger.

De Lange, Mauarice F., tr. see Danielou, Cardinal Jean.

De Lange, N. R. Origen & the Jews. LC 75-36293. (Oriental Publications Ser.: No. 25). 160p. 1977. 39.50 (ISBN 0-521-20542-5). Cambridge U Pr.

DeLange, Nicholas, tr. see Oz, Amos.

De Lange, Nicholas, tr. see Oz, Amos.

De Lange, P. J. Samuel Butler: Critic & Philosopher. LC 68-716. (English Biography Ser., No. 31). 1969. Repr. of 1925 ed. lib. bdg. 49.95x (ISBN 0-8383-0537-7). Haskell.

DeLange, Samuel A., jt. auth. see DeVlieger, Marinus.

Delanghe, Jules A. The Philosophy of Jesus: Real Love. LC 72-96805. 1973. 4.95 (ISBN 0-8059-1821-3). Dorrance.

Delanghe, R., jt. auth. see Brackt, F.

Delanglez, Jean. The French Jesuits in Lower Louisiana (1700-1763) LC 73-3576. (Catholic University of America. Studies in American Church History: No. 21). Repr. of 1935 ed. 46.00 (ISBN 0-404-57771-7). AMS Pr.

--A Jean Delanglez, S. J., Anthology: Observations on Mississippi Valley & Trans-Mississippi Indians. Wedel, Mildred M., ed. LC 83-47637. (The North American Indian Ser.). 399p. 1985. lib. bdg. 50.00 (ISBN 0-8240-5890-9). Garland Pub.

Delanglez, Jean, ed. see Garraghan, Gilbert J.

De Langre, Jacques. Do-In Primer. (Illus.). 128p. (Orig.). 1985. cancelled (ISBN 0-916508-26-9); pap. cancelled (ISBN 0-916508-27-7). Happiness Pr.

--Do-In Two: Art of Rejuvenation. 1985. pap. cancelled. Happiness Pr.

--First Book of Do-In. 1983. pap. 4.00 (ISBN 0-916508-01-3). Happiness Pr.

--Food Consciousness for Spiritual Development. LC 80-84993. (Illus., Orig.). 1980. pap. 6.00 (ISBN 0-916508-05-6). Happiness Pr.

--Food for Spiritual Development. 1984. pap. cancelled (ISBN 0-916508-05-6). Happiness Pr.

--Seasalt & Your Life. LC 80-84990. (Illus.). 128p. (Orig.). 1984. 10.00 (ISBN 0-916508-08-0). Happiness Pr.

--Seasalt's Hidden Power: The Scientific Proof Finding & Identifying & Usage Manual. 1984. pap. 3.00 (ISBN 0-916508-35-8). Happiness Pr.

De Langre, Jacques & De Langre, Yvette. Brown Rice Cookbook: Traditional World-Wide Western Recipes. (Illus.). 32p. (Orig.). 1984. pap. 4.00 (ISBN 0-916508-21-8). Happiness Pr.

--The Magic Spectacles: Instant Unique Principle Comprehension, Art Edition. (Illus.). 1984. pap. 8.00 (ISBN 0-916508-04-8). Happiness Pr.

De langre, Jacques & Kervan, L. Natural Leavened Bread, Its Biology & Alchemy: The Layperson's Guide to Bread Quality Search, Evaluation & Revaloration. 1984. pap. 10.00 (ISBN 0-916508-36-6). Happiness Pr.

De Langre, Jacques, jt. auth. see Aihara, Herman.

De Langre, Jacques, jt. auth. see Ohsawa, Georges.

De Langre, Jacques, ed. see De Langre, Yvette.

De Langre, Jacques, ed. see Kervan, L. C.

De langre, Jacques, et al. Do-In Primer: Regenerative Universal Necessity. 1985. pap. 20.00 (ISBN 0-916508-46-3). Happiness Pr.

--Survival First Aid: Outlasting Cataclysms & Nuclear Attacks. 1985. pap. cancelled (ISBN 0-916508-13-7). Happiness Pr.

De Langre, Yvette. Cooking Good Food with Grains & Vegetables. De Langre, Jacques, ed. LC 80-84991. (Illus.). 128p. (Orig.). 1984. spiral bdg. 12.00 (ISBN 0-916508-11-0); pap. 9.00 (ISBN 0-916508-12-9). Happiness Pr.

De Langre, Yvette, jt. auth. see De Langre, Jacques.

Delank, Claudia. Die Struktur des Zylklus "Four Quartets" Von T. S. Eliot. (European University Studies: No. 14, Vol. 104). 327p. (Ger.). 1982. 37.35 (ISBN 3-8204-5810-7). P Lang Pubs.

Delannay. Characterization of Heterogeous Catalysts. (Chemical Industries Ser.). 392p. 1984. 65.00 (ISBN 0-8247-7100-1). Dekker.

Delannoy, ed. see Cocteau, Jean.

DeLano, Agnes. Reflective Writing. 1979. Repr. of 1937 ed. lib. bdg. 25.00 (ISBN 0-8492-4202-9). R West.

Delano, Alonzo. Life on the Plains & Among the Diggings, Being Scenes & Adventures of an Overland Journey to California. LC 72-9440. (The Far Western Frontier Ser.). (Illus.). 396p. 1973. Repr. of 1854 ed. 24.50 (ISBN 0-405-04970-6). Ayer Co Pubs.

Delano, Amasa. A Narrative of Voyages and Travels in the Northern & Southern Hemispheres. (Illus.). 598p. 1970. Repr. of 1817 ed. 35.00 (ISBN 0-8398-0360-5). Parnassus Imprints.

Delano, Anne. Field Hockey. (Physical Education Activities Ser.). 80p. 1967. pap. text ed. write for info. (ISBN 0-697-07010-7); tchrs.' manual o.p. avail. (ISBN 0-697-07217-7). Wm C Brown.

Delatush, Edith. The Cape Cod Affair. (Ecstasy Ser.: No. 395). (Orig.). 1986. pap. 2.25 (ISBN 0-440-11004-1). Dell.

--Hand in Hand. (Candlelight Ecstasy Ser.: No. 371). (Orig.). 1985. pap. 2.25 (ISBN 0-440-13417-X). Dell.

--When Midnight Comes. (Candlelight Ecstasy Ser.: No. 333). 192p. (Orig.). 1985. pap. 2.25 (ISBN 0-440-19433-4). Dell.

De Laubenfels, David J. Mapping the World's Vegetation: Regionalization of Formations & Flora. (Geographical Ser.: No. 4). (Illus.). 304p. 1975. text ed. 27.95x (ISBN 0-8156-2172-8). Syracuse U Pr.

De Lauer, Marjel. The Traders. 384p. (Orig.). 1981. pap. 2.75 (ISBN 0-440-18586-6). Dell.

DeLauer, Marjel. Where Rivers Run Gold. 288p. (Orig.). 1984. pap. 3.50 (ISBN 0-440-19511-X). Dell.

DeLauer, Marjel Jean. The Mystery of the Phantom Billionaire. Young, Billie, ed. LC 72-83301. 1972. 12.95 (ISBN 0-87949-005-5). Ashley Bks.

Delaughter, Thomas J. Malachi: Messenger of Divine Love. LC 75-40410. 160p. (Orig.). 1976. 6.00 (ISBN 0-914520-08-3); pap. text ed. 5.00 (ISBN 0-914520-07-5). Insight Pr.

Delaume, George R. Law & Practice of Transnational Contracts. 1984. looseleaf 100.00 (ISBN 0-317-30260-4). Oceana.

Delaume, Georges. Transnational Contracts: Applicable Law & Settlement of Disputes, 6 bndrs, Vol. 1. LC 74-30028. 1976. Set. looseleaf suppl. to 1979 600.00 (ISBN 0-379-10200-5). Oceana.

Delaume, Georges R. American-French Private International Law. 2nd ed. LC 61-13055. (Bilateral Studies in Private International Law: No. 2). 221p. 1961. 15.00 (ISBN 0-379-11402-X). Oceana.

--Transnational Contract: Law & Practice. 1983. looseleaf 125.00 (ISBN 0-317-01155-3). Oceana.

Delaunay, Charles. Django Reinhardt. James, Michael, tr. from Fr. (Quality Paperbacks Ser.). (Illus.). 247p. 1982. pap. 7.95 (ISBN 0-306-80171-X). Da Capo.

--Django Reinhardt (Jazz) (Roots of Jazz Ser.). 247p. 1981. 25.00 (ISBN 0-306-76057-6). Da Capo.

--New Hot Discography. 1948. 24.95 (ISBN 0-910468-04-4). Criterion Mus.

Delaunay, Sonia. Sonia Delaunay: Art into Fashion. Date not set. cancelled. Braziller.

--Sonia Delaunay's Alphabet. LC 72-172414. (Illus.). (ps-3). 1972. 10.10i (ISBN 0-690-75258-X). Crowell Jr Bks.

Delaune, Lynn, jt. auth. see De Grummond, Lena.

Delauney, Robert & Delauney, Sonia. The New Art of Color: The Writings of Robert & Sonia Delauney. Cohen, Arthur A., ed. (Documents of 20th Century Art Ser.). 1978. 19.95 (ISBN 0-670-50636-2). Viking.

Delauney, Sonia, jt. auth. see Delauney, Robert.

Delauney, W. E. & Land, W. A. Principles & Practice of Dermatology. 1984. text ed. 45.00 (ISBN 0-409-49331-7). Butterworth.

Delaunois, A. L., ed. Biostatistics in Pharmacology. new ed. LC 78-40220. (International Encyclopedia of Pharmacology & Therapeutics: Section 7, Vol. 3). (Illus.). 1979. text ed. 89.00 (ISBN 0-08-021514-9). Pergamon.

--Biostatistics in Pharmacology, Vol. 1-2. 1128p. 1973. Set. text ed. 150.00 (ISBN 0-08-016556-7). Pergamon.

DeLaura, David, ed. see Newman, John H.

DeLaura, David J., ed. Victorian Prose: A Guide to Research. LC 73-80586. (Reviews of Research). xvi, 560p. 1973. 25.00x (ISBN 0-87352-250-8, Z41); pap. 14.50x (ISBN 0-87352-251-6, Z42). Modern Lang.

DeLaurence, L. W. Silent Friend. 8.95 (ISBN 0-685-22110-5). Wehman.

DeLaurence, Lauron W. Master Key. 14.50x (ISBN 0-685-22037-0). Wehman.

De Laurentis, Anthony C. You are Never Too Old to Live: For People from 35 to 100 Who are Eager for New Challenges in Life. (Illus.). 117p. 1983. 49.75 (ISBN 0-89266-394-4). Am Classical Coll Pr.

DeLaurentis, Rocky. Laughing & Griping with the 97th Seabees. Fitting, Frances, ed. 192p. (Orig.). 1983. pap. 4.95 (ISBN 0-912495-01-4). San Diego Pub Co.

De Laurentis, Teresa & Heath, Stephen, eds. The Cinematic Apparatus. 213p. pap. 11.95 (ISBN 0-312-13908-X). St Martin.

De Lauretis, Teresa see Lauretis, Teresa de.

DeLauretis, Teresa & Heath, Stephen, eds. The Cinematic Apparatus. 1980. 25.00 (ISBN 0-312-13907-1). St Martin.

De Lauretis, Teresa see Lauretis, Teresa de, et al.

DeLaurier, Nancy, ed. Slide Buyers Guide. 4th ed. LC 80-84877. (Visual Resources Association Guides). 128p. 1980. 9.00 (ISBN 0-938852-07-8). Visual Resources Assn.

De Laussat, Pierre C. Memoirs of My Life. Bush, Robert D., ed. LC 77-12113. xxiii, 137p. 1977. text ed. 17.50x (ISBN 0-8071-0365-9). La State U Pr.

DeLauter, Roger. Eighteenth Virginia Cavalry. (The Virginia Regimental Histories Ser.). (Illus.). 1985. 16.45 (ISBN 0-930919-18-1). H E Howard.

De Lautreamont, Comte, pseud. Les Chants de Maldoror. Wernham, Guy, tr. LC 66-12289. 1947. pap. 9.95 (ISBN 0-8112-0082-5, NDP207). New Directions.

--Oeuvres Completes. Bd. with Oeuvres Completes. Nouveau, Germain. Walzer, ed. (Bibliotheque de la Pleiade). 39.95 (ISBN 0-685-34928-4). French & Eur.

De la Valdene, Guy. Making Game: An Essay on Woodcock. (Illus.). 204p. 1985. 20.00 (ISBN 0-317-30090-3). Willow Creek.

De La Vallieres, William. The Theory, Application & Practice of the Point & Figure Method of Stock Market Chart Analysis. (The New Stock Market Library). (Illus.). 1978. 197.50 (ISBN 0-89266-126-7). Am Classical Coll Pr.

Delavan, Elizabeth. Lake Country Views. 1985. 12.95 (ISBN 0-533-06547-X). Vantage.

De La Vega, Garcilasco. Incas. 448p. 1964. pap. 3.50 (ISBN 0-380-01269-3, 45542-0, Discus). Avon.

De la Vega, Garcilaso see Garcilaso de la Vega.

De La Vega, John. Mexican Real Estate: Law & Practices Affecting Private U. S. Ownership. LC 75-27888. 78p. 1976. pap. 3.95 (ISBN 0-8165-0534-9). U of Ariz Pr.

De La Vega, Marguerite. Some Factors Affecting Leadership of Mexican-Americans in a High School. LC 74-76562. 1974. Repr. of 1951 ed. soft bdg. 9.95 (ISBN 0-88247-290-9). R & E Pubs.

De La Vega, Sara L. & Parr, Carmen S. Avanzando: Gramatica Espanola y Lectura. LC 77-18537. 133p. 1978. pap. 21.00 (ISBN 0-471-02731-6); wkbk. A 14.00 (ISBN 0-471-02732-4); wkbk. B 14.00 (ISBN 0-471-02733-2). Wiley.

De Laveleye, Emile. Primitive Property. Marriott, G. R., tr. from Fr. xlvii, 356p. 1985. Repr. of 1878 ed. lib. bdg. 35.00x (ISBN 0-8377-0817-6). Rothman.

Delavignette, Robert. Freedom & Authority in French West Africa. 152p. 1968. Repr. of 1950 ed. 30.00x (ISBN 0-7146-1652-4, BHA-01652, F Cass Co). Biblio Dist.

Delaville Le Roulx, Joseph. La France en Orient au XIVe Siecle, 2 vols. LC 78-63335. (The Crusades & Military Orders: Second Ser.). Repr. of 1886 ed. Set. 37.50 (ISBN 0-404-17020-X). AMS Pr.

Delaware Technical & Community College, English Department. Writing Skills for Technical Students. 400p. 1982. pap. text ed. 15.95 (ISBN 0-13-970665-8). P-H.

Delaware University Staff. Delaware Notes. text ed. 12.25 (ISBN 0-8369-8120-0, 8260). Ayer Co Pubs.

Delbanco, Andrew. William Ellery Channing: An Essay on the Liberal Spirit in America. LC 80-19304. 256p. 1981. text ed. 15.00x (ISBN 0-674-95335-5). Harvard U Pr.

Delbanco, Dawn Ho. Art from Ritual: Ancient Chinese Bronze Vessels from the Arthur M. Sackler Collection. (Illus.). 208p. Date not set. pap. 20.00 (ISBN 0-916724-54-9). Fogg Art.

Delbanco, Nicholas. About My Table: And Other Stories. LC 83-61367. 160p. 1983. 11.95 (ISBN 0-688-02157-3). Morrow.

--The Beaux Arts Trio. LC 84-1125. (Illus.). 256p. 1985. 15.95 (ISBN 0-688-04001-2). Morrow.

--Group Portrait: Conrad, Crane, Ford, Wells, & James. LC 81-16787. (Illus.). 192p. 1982. 11.50 (ISBN 0-688-01017-2). Morrow.

--Group Portrait: Joseph Conrad, Stephen Crane, Ford Madox Ford, Henry James, H. G. Wells. LC 84-60484. 224p. 1984. pap. 5.95 (ISBN 0-688-02143-3, Quill NY). Morrow.

--Possession. LC 76-27834. 1977. 8.95 (ISBN 0-688-03146-3). Morrow.

--Sherbrookes. LC 78-11141. 1978. 8.95 (ISBN 0-688-03406-3). Morrow.

--Sherbrookes. LC 81-21020. (The Sherbrookes Trilogy). 250p. 1982. pap. 7.25 (ISBN 0-688-00979-4, Quill NY). Morrow.

--Stillness. LC 80-14395. 224p. 1980. 9.95 (ISBN 0-688-03708-9). Morrow.

--Stillness. (The Sherbrookes Trilogy). 1982. pap. 7.25 (ISBN 0-688-00978-6, Quill NY). Morrow.

Delbanco, Nicholas, jt. ed. see Heimert, Alan.

Delbanco, Nocholas. Possession. LC 81-20994. (The Sherbrookes Trilogy). 216p. 1982. pap. 7.25 (ISBN 0-688-00980-8, Quill NY). Morrow.

Del Barco, Miguel. Ethnology & Linguistics of Baja California. Tiscareno, Froylan, tr. (Baja California Travels Ser.: No. 44). 112p. 1981. 30.00 (ISBN 0-87093-244-6). Dawsons.

Del Barco, Miguel & Tiscareno, Froylan, trs. The Natural History of Baja California. (Baja California Travel Ser.: No. 43). (Illus.). 298p. 1980. 50.00 (ISBN 0-87093-243-8). Dawson's.

Delbecq, Andre & Filley, Alan. Program & Project Management in a Matrix Organization: A Case Study. (Wisconsin Business Monographs: No. 9). (Orig.). 1974. pap. 5.00 (ISBN 0-86603-001-8). Bur Busn Wis.

DelBene, Ron & Montgomery, Herb. Alone with God: A Place for Your Time Together. 120p. (Orig.). 1984. pap. 4.95 (ISBN 0-86683-856-2, 8434). Winston Pr.

--Breath of Life: Discovering Your Breath Prayer. 108p. (Orig.). 1981. pap. 3.95 (ISBN 0-86683-639-X). Winston Pr.

--Hunger of the Heart. 96p. (Orig.). 1983. pap. 4.95 (ISBN 0-86683-801-5). Winston Pr.

Del Bigio, G. & Gottschalk, C. M. INIS: Descriptive Cataloguing Rules. Ruckenbacker, E., ed. (INIS Reference Ser.: No. 1, Rev. 6). 90p. 1985. pap. 7.50 (ISBN 92-0-178085-0, IN1R6, IAEA). Unipub.

Delblanc, Sven. The Castrati. Williams, C. W., tr. from Swedish. LC 79-88924. 151p. 1979. 7.95 (ISBN 0-89720-020-9). Karoma.

--Speranza. Austin, Paul B., tr. from Swedish. LC 83-47872. 176p. 1983. 14.95 (ISBN 0-670-66245-3). Viking.

Del Bo, Dino. Italian Catholics in Crisis. Bricca, John, tr. 1957. 4.95 (ISBN 0-87462-404-5). Marquette.

Del Boca, Angelo. Ethiopian War: Nineteen Thirty-Five to Nineteen Forty-One. Cummins, P. D., tr. LC 71-79562. 1969. 24.00x (ISBN 0-226-14217-5). U of Chicago Pr.

Del Boca, Frances K., jt. ed. see Ashmore, Richard D.

Del Bonta, Robert J. & Berkson, Carmel. In Praise of Hoysala Art. LC 80-901926. (Illus.). 106p. 1979. 22.50x (ISBN 0-8002-2440-X). Intl Pubns Serv.

Del Borgo, S. Classical Faces & Figures from the 16th to the 19th Century Fully Illustrated & Described. (Science of Man Library Bks.). (Illus.). 115p. 1981. 77.85 (ISBN 0-89901-028-8). Found Class Reprints.

DelBourgo, David. Fairfax & Other Poems. 80p. (Orig.). 1985. pap. 5.00 (ISBN 0-930844-14-9). Quest Pub.

Delbridge, A., ed. The Macquarie Dictionary. (Illus.). 2000p. Date not set. 45.00x (ISBN 0-87196-959-9). Facts On File.

Delbridge, Pauline N., jt. auth. see Boyle, Elisabeth L.

Delbruck, Hans. History of the Art of War Within the Framework of Political History: The Middle Ages. Renfroe, Walter J., Jr., tr. from Ger. LC 72-792. (Contributions in Military History Ser.: No. 26). 711p. 1982. lib. bdg. 65.00 (ISBN 0-8371-8164-X, DED/). Greenwood.

--History of the Art of War Within the Framework of Political History, Vol. II: The Germans. Renfroe, Walter J., Jr., tr. from Ger. LC 72-792. (Contributions in Military History Ser.: No. 20). (Illus.). 552p. 1980. lib. bdg. 55.00 (ISBN 0-8371-8163-1, DEC/). Greenwood.

--History of the Art of War Within the Framework of Political History, Vol. I: Antiquity. Renfroe, Walter J., Jr., tr. from Ger. LC 72-792. (Contributions in Military History Ser.: No. 9). (Illus.). 604p. 1975. lib. bdg. 55.00 (ISBN 0-8371-6365-X, DEB/). Greenwood.

--History of the Art of War Within the Framework of Political History: The Modern Era. Renfroe, Walter J., Jr., tr. LC 72-792. (Contributions in Military History Ser.: No. 39). xi, 487p. (Ger.). 1985. lib. bdg. 75.00 (ISBN 0-8371-8165-8, DEE/). Greenwood.

Delbruck, Max. Mind from Matter: An Essay on Evolutionary Epistemology. Stent, Gunther, ed. (Illus.). 300p. 1985. 30.00 (ISBN 0-86542-306-7). Blackwell Sci.

--Mind from Matter: An Essay on Evolutionary Epistemology. Stent, Gunther & Presti, David, eds. (Illus.). 316p. 1985. pap. 14.95 (ISBN 0-86542-311-3). Blackwell Pubns.

Delbrueck, Berthold, jt. auth. see Brugmann, Karl.

Delbrueck, Richard. Die Consulardiptychen und verwandte Denkmaeler. (Studien Zur Spaetantiken Kunstgeschichte: Vol. 2). (Illus.). 296p. Repr. of 1929 ed. write for info. (ISBN 3-11-005704-2). De Gruyter.

--Spaetantike Kaiserportraits. (Studien zur spaetantiken Kunstgeschichte, Vol. 8). (Illus.). xx, 252p. 1978. Repr. of 1933 ed. 170.00x (ISBN 3-11-005700-X). De Gruyter.

Del Bueno, Dorothy. A Financial Guide for Nurses: Investing in Yourself & Others. (Illus.). 240p. 1982. text ed. 14.95 (ISBN 0-86542-007-6). Blackwell Sci.

Del Bueno, Dorothy J. Case Studies in Pharmacology. LC 75-30281. 1976. pap. text ed. 7.95 (ISBN 0-316-17984-1). Little.

Del Buono, Barbara, jt. auth. see Del Buono, John.

Del Buono, John & Del Buono, Barbara. When Two Become One: The Miracle in Marriage. 1976. 10.00 (ISBN 0-9605698-0-4); soft cover 6.40 (ISBN 0-9605698-1-2). Ellingsworth Pr.

Del Carmen, Vicente F. Rizal: An Encyclopedic Collection, Vol. 2. (Illus.). 205p. 1983. 15.75 (ISBN 971-10-0060-1, Pub. by New Day Philippines); pap. 10.75 (ISBN 971-10-0061-X). Cellar.

Del Caro, Adrian. Dionysian Aesthetics: The Role of Destruction in Creation as Reflected in the Life & Works of Friedrich Nietzsche. (European University Studies: Series 20, Philosophy: Vol. 69). 157p. 1980. 20.65 (ISBN 3-8204-6819-6). P Lang Pubs.

Del Carril, Bonifacio, tr. see Saint-Exupery, Antione De.

Del Castillo, Adelaida, jt. ed. see Mora, Magdalena.

Del Castillo, Bernal Diaz see Diaz Del Castillo, Bernal.

Del Castillo, Hernando. Cancionero General. facsim. ed. 1904. 23.00 (ISBN 0-527-15300-1). Kraus Repr.

Del Castillo, Richard G. La Familia: Chicano Families in the Urban Southwest, 1848 to the Present. LC 84-40356. 224p. 1984. text ed. 18.95 (ISBN 0-268-01272-5, 85-12725); pap. text ed. 7.95 (ISBN 0-268-01273-3, 85-12733). U of Notre Dame Pr.

Del Cecchetti, Giovanni see Leopardi, Giacomo.

Del Cervo, Diane M., ed. Witchcraft in Europe & America: Guide to the Microfilm Collection. 111p. 1983. 50.00 (ISBN 0-89235-074-1). Res Pubns Conn.

Del Cervo, Diane M., ed. see Research Publications.

Del Chiaro, Mario A. Classical Art: Sculpture. LC 84-23651. (Illus.). 112p. (Orig.). 1984. pap. 18.00 (ISBN 0-89951-055-8). Santa Barb Mus Art.

--Etruscan Red-Figured Vase-Painting at Caere. LC 73-85785. 1975. 65.00x (ISBN 0-520-02578-4). U of Cal Pr.

--The Genucillia Group: A Class of Etruscan Red-Figured Plates. LC 57-9900. (University of California Publications in Classical Archaeology: Vol. 3, No. 4). pap. 35.00 (ISBN 0-317-29118-1, 2021332). Bks Demand UMI.

Del Conde, Teresa, jt. auth. see Mexican Ministry Art Staff.

Del Corso, Dante, jt. ed. see Conte, Gianni.

Delcorta. Nana. Reiter, Victoria, tr. from Fr. (Gorodish-Alba Ser.: No. 2). 128p. 1984. 9.95 (ISBN 0-671-49210-1). Summit Bks.

Delcroix, Maurice & Hallyn, Fernand, eds. Thanatos Clasique. (Etudes Litteraires Francaise Ser.: No. 20). 165p. (Orig., Fr.). 1982. pap. 23.00x (ISBN 3-87808-899-X). Benjamins North Am.

Del Dario, Rafaela Contreras see Dario, Rafaela Contreras de.

Delden, E. Standard Fabrication Practices for Cane Sugar Mills. (Sugar Ser.: Vol. 1). 254p. 1981. 59.75 (ISBN 0-444-41958-6). Elsevier.

D'Elden, Karl H. Van see Van D'Elden, Karl H.

Del Deo, Josephine C., jt. auth. see Tod, Osma G.

Delderfeld, R. F. To Serve Them All My Days. 688p. 1984. pap. text ed. 4.95 (ISBN 0-671-45927-9). WSP.

Delderfield, Eric R. Eric Delderfield's Book of True Animal Stories. LC 76-126288. (Illus.). (gr. 4-6). 4.95 (ISBN 0-8008-2510-1). Taplinger.

--Kings & Queens of England. LC 81-48535. 172p. 14.95 (ISBN 0-8128-2863-1); pap. 7.95 (ISBN 0-8128-6161-2). Stein & Day.

--Kings & Queens of England. 11.95 (ISBN 0-89190-587-1, Pub. by Am Repr). Amereon Ltd.

--West Country Historic Houses & Their Families, Vol. 2: Dorset, Wiltshire & N. Somerset. 11.95 (ISBN 0-7153-4910-4). David & Charles.

Delderfield, R. F. Imperial Sunset. LC 79-31696. (Illus.). 320p. 1980. pap. 9.95 (ISBN 0-8128-6056-X). Stein & Day.

--Napoleon's Marshals. LC 66-16287. (Illus.). 1980. pap. 8.95 (ISBN 0-8128-6055-1). Stein & Day.

--To Serve Them All My Days. 688p. 1982. pap. 4.95 (ISBN 0-671-45927-9). PB.

Del Duca, Louis & Del Duca, Patrick. Commercial, Business & Trade Laws: Italy. 1983. loose-leaf 125.00 (ISBN 0-379-22002-4). Oceana.

Del Duca, Patrick, jt. auth. see Del Duca, Louis.

De Le, Vergne. Orleans Digest of Laws (with Moreau Lislet Notes) 1972. 25.00. Claitors.

Deleage, Andre. La Capitation Du Bas-Empire. LC 75-7313. (Roman History Ser.). (Illus., Fr.). 1975. Repr. 23.50x (ISBN 0-405-07195-7). Ayer Co Pubs.

de Leal, Magdalena Leon see Deere, Carmen & Leal, Magdalena Leon de.

Delear, Frank J. Airplanes & Helicopters of the U. S. Navy. (Illus.). 144p. (gr. 5 up). 1982. PLB 10.95 (ISBN 0-396-08031-6). Dodd.

--Famous First Flights Across the Atlantic. LC 79-12808. (Illus.). (gr. 7). 1979. 8.95 (ISBN 0-396-07704-8). Dodd.

--Helicopters & Airplanes of the U.S. Army. LC 77-6495. (Illus.). (gr. 5 up). 1977. 7.95 (ISBN 0-396-07476-6). Dodd.

Deledda, Grazia. After the Divorce. Ashe, Susan, tr. 1985. pap. 8.95 (ISBN 0-7043-3485-2, Pub. by Quartet Bks). Merrimack Pub Cir.

--L'Edera. (Easy Reader, C. Ser.). 96p. (Ital.). 1981. pap. text ed. 4.25 (ISBN 0-88436-884-X, 55257). EMC.

--The Mother. new ed. Steegman, Mary G., tr. from Ital. LC 82-13995. 252p. 1982. 16.00 (ISBN 0-89783-022-9). Larlin Corp.

--The Mother. LC 23-16660. 239p. 1974. lib. bdg. 15.95 (ISBN 0-910220-57-3). Berg.

DeLee. Safeguarding Motherhood. 7th ed. LC 65-1126. (Illus.). 188p. 1976. pap. text ed. 5.50 (ISBN 0-397-50365-2, 65-01126, Lippincott Medical). Lippincott.

De Lee, James, et al. Developing Teaching Competencies. LC 79-9910. 72p. 1979. pap. 4.95 (ISBN 0-88289-215-0). Pelican.

De Leener, M. F., jt. auth. see Resibois, P.

De Leenheer, A. P. & Roncucci, R. R., eds. Quantitative Mass Spectrometry in Life Sciences, Vol. II. 502p. 1979. 89.50 (ISBN 0-444-41760-5). Elsevier.

DeLeenheer, A. P., ed. see International Symposium on Quantitative Mass Spectrometry in Life Sciences, 1st, State University of Ghent Belgium June 16-18 1976.

DeLeeuw, Adele. The Boy with Wings. LC 74-15860. 1971. 8.95 (ISBN 0-87874-001-5, Nautilus). Galloway.
--Casey Jones Drives an Ice Cream Train. LC 74-152792. (American Folktales Ser.). (Illus.). (gr. 2-5). 1971. PLB 7.47 (ISBN 0-8116-4029-9). Garrard.
--John Henry, Steel-Drivin' Man. LC 66-20136. (American Folktales Ser.). (Illus.). (gr. 2-5). 1966. PLB 7.47 (ISBN 0-8116-4004-3). Garrard.
--Paul Bunyan & His Blue Ox. LC 68-10710. (American Folktales Ser.). (Illus.). (gr. 2-5). 1968. PLB 7.47 (ISBN 0-8116-4007-8). Garrard.
--Paul Bunyan Finds a Wife. LC 69-11771. (American Folktales Ser.). (Illus.). (gr. 2-5). 1969. PLB 7.47 (ISBN 0-8116-4013-2). Garrard.
De Leeuw, Adele. Remembered with Love: Letters to My Sister. LC 81-86639. (Illus.). 160p. 1982. 10.95 (ISBN 0-912650-03-6). Brookdale Pr.
DeLeeuw, Adele. Who Can Kill the Lion. LC 66-20137. (Fantasy Ser.). (Illus.). 48p. (gr. k-4). 1966. PLB 7.47 (ISBN 0-8116-4051-5). Garrard.
Deleeuw, Dianne & Lehrman, Steve. Figure Skating. LC 77-76798. 1978. 8.95 (ISBN 0-689-10820-6). Atheneum.
De Leeuw, J. H. see Von Mises, Richard & Von Karman, Theodore.
De Leeuw, P. W. & Guinee, P. A., eds. Laboratory Diagnosis in Neonatal Calf & Pig Diarrhea: Current Topics in Veterinary Medicine & Animal Science, No. 13. 210p. 1981. 32.00 (ISBN 90-247-2527-5, Pub. by Martinus Nijhoff Netherlands). Kluwer Academic.
De Leeuw, S., jt. auth. see Southworth, R.
De Leevw, Adolph L. Rambling Through Science. LC 72-315. (Essay Index Reprint Ser.). Repr. of 1932 ed. 21.00 (ISBN 0-8369-2788-5). Ayer Co Pubs.
DeLegall, Walter & Johnston, Percy. Computer Dictionary. (Desein Literary Society Ser.). 400p. 1984. lib. bdg. 32.95 (ISBN 0-915833-18-2); pap. text ed. 17.50 (ISBN 0-915833-20-4). Drama Jazz Hse Inc.
Delehanty, Randolph. California: A Guide Book. (Illus.). 1984. pap. 12.95 (ISBN 0-15-615300-9, Harv). HarBraceJ.
--San Francisco: Walks & Tours in the Golden Gate City. (Illus.). 340p. 1980. pap. 11.95 (ISBN 0-385-27106-9, Dial). Doubleday.
Delehanty, Suzanne. Paul Thek-Processions. LC 77-92423. 1977. pap. 12.00 (ISBN 0-88454-023-5). U of Pa Contemp Art.
Delehanty, Suzanne & Ashton, Dore. Eight Abstract Painters. (Illus.). 1978. pap. 5.00 (ISBN 0-88454-024-3). U of Pa Contemp Art.
Delehanty, Suzanne & Pincus-Witten, Robert. Improbable Furniture. (Illus.). 48p. 1977. pap. 10.00 (ISBN 0-88454-022-7). U of Pa Contemp Art.
Delehaye, Hippolyte. Les Legendes Grecques Des Saints Militaires. LC 75-7314. (Roman History Ser.). (Fr.). 1975. Repr. 21.00x (ISBN 0-405-07196-5). Ayer Co Pubs.
--The Legends of the Saints. LC 77-26797. 1907. 30.00 (ISBN 0-8414-3657-6). Folcroft.
--Les Origines du Culte des martyrs. 2nd, rev. ed. LC 78-63459. (The Crusades & Military Orders: Second Ser.). Repr. of 1933 ed. 40.00 (ISBN 0-404-16518-4). AMS Pr.
Delehaye, Hippolyte & Halkin, Francois. Synaxaires Byzantins, Menolugues, Typica. 322p. 1977. 60.00x (ISBN 0-86078-010-4, Pub. by Variorum). State Mutual Bk.
De Leiris, Alain. The Drawings of Edouard Manet. LC 68-13017. (Studies in the History of Art: No. 10). 1969. 90.00x (ISBN 0-520-01547-9). U of Cal Pr.
De Leiris, Lucia. Shells of the World Coloring Book. (Coloring Bks.). (Illus.). 45p. (Orig.). (gr. 2 up). 1982. pap. 2.50 (ISBN 0-486-24368-0). Dover.
Delellis. Diagnostic Immunohistochemistry. LC 81-4949. (Masson Monographs in Diagnostic Pathology: Vol. 2). (Illus.). 360p. 1981. 69.50x (ISBN 0-89352-126-4). Masson Pub.
DeLellis, Ronald A., ed. Advances in Immunohistochemistry. (Monographs in Diagnostic Pathology: Vol. 7). (Illus.). 384p. 1984. 69.50 (ISBN 0-89352-215-5). Masson Pub.
De Le Mahotiers, Stuart see Mahotiers, Stuart De Le.
Delen. Histoire De la Gravure Dans les Anciens Pays-Bas et Dans les Provinces Belges, Jusgn'a la Fin du Des Origines Siezieme Siecle, 3 vols. in one. LC 73-127252. (Graphic Art Ser.). 1971. Repr. of 1931 ed. lib. bdg. 175.00 (ISBN 0-306-71114-1). Da Capo.
De Leomos, Antonio A. see Briquet de Leomos, Antonio A.
De Leon, Arnoldo. San Angelenos: Mexican Americans in San Angelo, Texas. (Illus.). 176p. (Orig.). 1985. pap. 12.95 (ISBN 0-938036-05-X). Mulberry Ave Bks.
--The Tejano Community, 1836-1900. LC 81-52053. (Illus.). 288p. 1982. 19.95x (ISBN 0-8263-0586-5). U of NM Pr.
--They Called Them Greasers: Anglo Attitudes toward Mexicans in Texas, 1821-1900. 167p. 1983. 19.95 (ISBN 0-292-70363-5); pap. 8.95 (ISBN 0-292-78054-0). U of Tex Pr.
De Leon, Daniel. Abolition of Poverty. 8th ed. 1969. pap. text ed. 0.50 (ISBN 0-935534-00-8). NY Labor News.
--As to Politics. 128p. 1966. pap. 0.60 (ISBN 0-935534-03-2). NY Labor News.
--The Ballot & the Class Struggle. 8th ed. 1971. pap. text ed. 0.50 (ISBN 0-935534-04-0). NY Labor News.
--The Burning Question of Trades Unionism. 1977. pap. 0.50 (ISBN 0-935534-32-6). NY Labor News.
--Capitalism Means War! 3rd ed. 1970. pap. 0.50 (ISBN 0-935534-33-4). NY Labor News.
--Industrial Unionism: Selected Editorials. 4th ed. 80p. 1944. 0.50 (ISBN 0-935534-16-4). NY Labor News.
--Marxian Science & the Colleges. 3rd ed. 96p. 1944. 2.00 (ISBN 0-935534-19-9); pap. 0.75 (ISBN 0-935534-20-2). NY Labor News.
--Reform or Revolution. 1977. pap. 0.50 (ISBN 0-935534-37-7). NY Labor News.
--Socialism vs. Anarchism. 1970. pap. 0.50 (ISBN 0-935534-39-3). NY Labor News.
--A Socialist in Congress: His Conduct & Responsibilities. 5th ed. 1962. pap. 0.50 (ISBN 0-935534-41-5). NY Labor News.
--Socialist Landmarks. 2nd ed. 1977. pap. 1.50 (ISBN 0-935534-29-6). NY Labor News.
--Socialist Reconstruction of Society. 20th ed. 1977. pap. 0.50 (ISBN 0-935534-42-3). NY Labor News.
--The Vatican in Politics. 4th ed. 1962. pap. text ed. 0.50 (ISBN 0-935534-31-8). NY Labor News.
--What Means This Strike? 10th ed. 1972. pap. 0.50 (ISBN 0-935534-44-X). NY Labor News.
DeLeon, David. The American As Anarchist: Reflections on Indigenous Radicalism. LC 78-58290. 1979. 24.50x (ISBN 0-8018-2126-6). Johns Hopkins.
De Leon, Fidel. Espanol: Material Para el Hispano. 1978. pap. text ed. 12.95 (ISBN 0-88408-098-6). Sterling Swift.
De Leon, Fray L. The Unknown Light: The Poems of Fray Luis de Leon. Barnstone, Willis, tr. LC 79-15030. 1979. 39.50x (ISBN 0-87395-394-0); pap. 12.95x (ISBN 0-87395-419-X). State U NY Pr.
De Leon, George, ed. Phoenix House: Studies in a Therapeutic Community (1968-1973) 214p. 1974. text ed. 29.75x (ISBN 0-8422-7238-0). Irvington.
De Leon, George Falewski see Symposium on Muscular Dystrophy, Jerusalem 1976.
De Leon, Luis P. Lyrics of Wis De Leon. 1976. lib. bdg. 59.95 (ISBN 0-8490-2191-X). Gordon Pr.
De Leon, M. & Rodrigues, P. R. Generalized Classical Mechanics & Field Theory: A Geometrical Approach of Lagrangian & Hamiltonian Formalisms Involving Higher Order Derivatives. (Mathematics Studies: Vol. 112). 290p. 1985. 44.50 (ISBN 0-444-87753-3, North Holland). Elsevier.
De Leon, Pedro de Cieza see Cieza de Leon, Pedro D.
DeLeon, Peter. Development & Diffusion of the Nuclear Power Reactor: A Comparative Analysis. LC 79-12988. 352p. 1979. prof ref 30.00 (ISBN 0-88410-682-9). Ballinger Pub.
DeLeon, Peter, jt. auth. see Brewer, Garry D.
De Leon, Thomas C. Belles, Beaux & Brains of the Sixties. LC 74-3937. (Women in America Ser). (Illus.). 476p. 1974. Repr. of 1909 ed. 36.50x (ISBN 0-405-06084-X). Ayer Co Pubs.
DeLeon, Thomas C. Four Years in Rebel Capitals. LC 83-9280. (Collectors Library of the Civil War). (gr. 7 up). 1983. Kivar binding 26.60 (ISBN 0-8094-4462-3, Pub. by Time-Life). Silver.
De Leon, Virgil. The Failure of Modern Art As an Aesthetic Instrument for the Emotional & Moral Uplifting of Mankind. (Illus.). 1978. deluxe bdg. 57.50 (ISBN 0-930582-00-4). Gloucester Art.
De Leon-Cieza, Pedro. The Incas of Pedro De Cieza De Leon. Von Hagen, Victor W., ed. (Civilization of the American Indian Ser.: No. 53). 1976. 29.50 (ISBN 0-8061-0433-3). U of Okla Pr.
De Leon Felipe, Poesias. Versos y Oraciones De Caminante. (Libro II). 104p. 1.10 (ISBN 0-318-14316-X). Hispanic Inst.
De Lepervanche, Marie M. Indians in White Australia: An Account of Race, Class & Indian Immigration to Eastern Australia. (Studies in Society: No. 22). 196p. 1984. text ed. 28.50x (ISBN 0-86861-295-2). Allen Unwin.
De Lepervanche, Marie M., jt. ed. see Bottomley, Gill.
Delepiere, Octave. A Sketch of the History of Flemish Literature from the Twelfth Century Down to the Present Time. LC 72-3215. (Studies in European Literature, No. 56). 1972. Repr. of 1860 ed. lib. bdg. 49.95x (ISBN 0-8383-1521-6). Haskell.
Delepine, D., jt. auth. see Hotyat, Fernand.
De Lerin, O. S. D., tr. see Hudson, R. Lofton.
De Lerin, Olivia, tr. see Crane, J. D.
De Lerin, Olivia S. Enviame a Mi: Aventuras de los esposos Davis, fundadores de la C. B. P. 64p. 1980. pap. 1.75 (ISBN 0-311-01062-8). Casa Bautista.
De Lerin, Olivia S. D., tr. see Bisagno, Juan.
De Lerma, Carlotta S., jt. auth. see Salter, Charles A.
De Lerma, Dominique-Rene. Bibliography of Black Music: Afro-American Idioms, Vol. 2. LC 80-24681. (Encyclopedia of Black Music Ser.). 240p. 1981. lib. bdg. 35.00 (ISBN 0-313-23144-3, DBI/02). Greenwood.
--Bibliography of Black Music: Reference Materials, Vol. 1. LC 80-24681. (Encyclopedia of Black Music Ser.). xv, 124p. 1981. lib. bdg. 29.95 (ISBN 0-313-21340-2, DBI/01). Greenwood.
--Charles Edward Ives Eighteen Seventy-Four to Nineteen Fifty-Four: A Bibliography of His Music. LC 72-99083. Repr. of 1970 ed. 56.00 (ISBN 0-8357-9359-1, 2015385). Bks Demand UMI.
--Igor Fedorovitch Stravinsky, 1882-1971: A Practical Guide to Publications of His Music. LC 74-79152. 150p. 1974. 13.50x (ISBN 0-87338-158-0). Kent St U Pr.
De Lerma, Dominique-Rene, et al. Reflections on Afro-American Music. LC 72-619703. 271p. 1973. 14.00x (ISBN 0-87338-135-1). Kent St U Pr.
De Lerma, Dominque-Rene see Lerma, Dominque-Rene De.
Delery, Linda, ed. Four World's Fair 1984: The Official Guidebook. 160p. 1984. 10.95 (ISBN 0-317-12232-0). Picayune Pr.
--Nineteen Eighty-Four World's Fair: The Official Guidebook. (Illus.). 160p. 1984. pap. 6.25. Picayune Pr.
--Official World's Fair Preview & Vacation Planner. (Illus.). 112p. 1983. pap. 3.75. Picayune Pr.
Delery, Simone De La Soucher see Delery, Simone De La Souchere.
Delery, Simone De La Souchere. Napoleon's Soldiers in America. LC 74-186543. (Illus.). 224p. 1972. 15.00 (ISBN 0-911116-58-3). Pelican.
Delesio, Michael L. Love Beyond Reason. 1982. 7.95 (ISBN 0-533-05392-7). Vantage.
De Lesseps, Ferdinand M. The Suez Canal: Letters & Documents Descriptive of Its Rise & Progress in 1854-56. LC 74-83185. (Islam & Mideast Ser.). 1976. Repr. of 1876 ed. 29.00 (ISBN 0-8420-1748-8). Scholarly Res Inc.
De Lesseps, Jean. Travels in Kamtschatka, During the Years 1787 & 1788. LC 72-115557. (Russia Observed, Series I). 1970. Repr. of 1790 ed. 32.00 (ISBN 0-405-03043-6). Ayer Co Pubs.
Delessert, Etienne. The Endless Party. Tabberner, Jeffrey, tr. from Fr. Orig. Title: San Fin la Fete. (Illus.). (ps-3). 1981. 11.95 (ISBN 0-19-279753-0). Oxford U Pr.
Delessert, Etienne, ed. see Gallaz, Chrsitophe.
De L'est, Paul. The Ancient Curse. 280p. 1984. 16.95 (ISBN 0-9614372-0-0); pap. 9.95 (ISBN 0-9614372-1-9). Stamberger Pub.
De l'Estocart, Paschal see Expert, Henry.
Delestre-Poirson, Charles-Gaspard, jt. auth. see Scribe, Eugene.
Deletant, Andrea & Deletant, Dennis. Romania. (World Bibliographical Ser.: No. 59). 280p. 1985. 40.00 (ISBN 1-85109-002-9, Pub. by ABC-Clio Pr England). ABC-Clio.
Deletant, Dennis. Colloquial Romanian. (Routledge Colloquial Ser.). (Orig.). 1983. pap. 13.95 (ISBN 0-7100-0834-1). Routledge & Kegan.
Deletant, Dennis, jt. auth. see Deletant, Andrea.
De Leu, Barbara, jt. auth. see Walters, Julie.
De Leusse, Claude. For Love of Anne. 1976. pap. 1.25 (ISBN 0-532-12332-8). Woodhill.
Deleuze, Gilles. Kant's Critical Philosophy. Tomlinson, Hugh & Habberjam, Barbara, trs. from Fr. LC 84-7548. 110p. 1985. 22.50x (ISBN 0-8166-1341-9). U of Minn Pr.
--Nietzsche & Philosophy. Tomlinson, Hugh, tr. from Fr. (European Perspectives Ser.). 221p. 1985. pap. 10.00x (ISBN 0-231-05669-9). Columbia U Pr.
Deleuze, Gilles & Guattari, Felix. Anti-Oedipus. (Richard Seaver Bk). 1977. 16.95 (ISBN 0-670-12941-0). Viking.
--Anti-Oedipus: Capitalism & Schizophrenia. Hurley, Robert, et al, trs. from Fr. 424p. 1983. pap. 14.95 (ISBN 0-8166-1225-0). U of Minn Pr.
Deleuze, Gilles & Tomlinson, Hugh. Nietzsche & Philosophy. LC 82-17676. (European Perspectives Ser.). 275p. 1983. 28.00x (ISBN 0-231-05668-0). Columbia U Pr.
Deleuze, Jean P. Practical Instruction in Animal Magnetism. Hartshorn, Thomas, tr. from Fr. (Hypnosis & Altered States of Consciousness Ser.). 1982. Repr. of 1843 ed. lib. bdg. 45.00 (ISBN 0-306-76074-6). Da Capo.
De Leval, M., jt. ed. see Stark, J.
Delevoryas, Theodore. Plant Diversification. 2nd ed. LC 76-30858. 144p. 1977. pap. text ed. 17.95x (ISBN 0-03-080133-8, HoltC). HR&W.
Delevoy, R. L. Jean Brusselmans: Catalog Raisonne. (Illus.). 443p. (Fr.). 1975. 65.00 (ISBN 0-912728-98-1). Newbury Bks.
Delevoy, Robert L. & Skira-Rizzoli. Symbolists & Symbolism. (Illus.). 230p. 1982. pap. 17.50 (ISBN 0-8478-0430-5). Rizzoli Intl.
De Ley, Herbert. The Movement of Thought: An Essay on Intellect in Seventeenth-Century France. LC 84-16128. 176p. 1985. 19.95x (ISBN 0-252-01165-1). U of Ill Pr.
De Ley, Herbert, ed. Saint-Simon Memorialist. LC 75-4491. 153p. 1975. pap. 9.95 (ISBN 0-252-00556-2). U of Ill Pr.
Delf, George. Jomo Kenyatta: Towards Truth About "the Light of Kenya". LC 75-17469. 215p. 1975. Repr. of 1961 ed. lib. bdg. 22.50x (ISBN 0-8371-8307-3, DEJK). Greenwood.
Delfeld, Paula. The Indian Priest: Philip B. Gordon, 1885-1948. 1977. 5.95 (ISBN 0-8199-0650-6). Franciscan Herald.
Delffs, Sofie, tr. see Scheffel, Josef V.
Delfinado, Mercedes. Culicine Mosquitoes of the Philippines. (Memoirs Ser: No. 7). (Illus.). 252p. 1966. 20.00x (ISBN 0-686-00417-5). Am Entom Inst.
Delfinado, Mercedes D. & Hardy, D. Elmo. A Catalog of the Diptera of the Oriental Region, Vol. 3. LC 74-174544. 1977. text ed. 40.00x (ISBN 0-8248-0346-9). UH Pr.
--Catalog of the Diptera of the Oriental Region, Vol. 1: Suborder Nematocera. LC 74-174544. 350p. 1973. text ed. 30.00x (ISBN 0-8248-0205-5). UH Pr.
--A Catalog of the Diptera of the Oriental Region, Vol. 2: Suborder Brachycera, Suborder Cyclorrhapha Through Division Aschiza. LC 74-174544. 480p. 1975. text ed. 30.00x (ISBN 0-8248-0274-8). UH Pr.
Delfinado, Mercedes D., jt. auth. see Hardy, D. Elmo.
Delfiner, Henry. The Vienna Broadcasts to Slovakia, 1938-1939: A Case Study in Subversion. (East European Monographs: No. 7). 142p. 1974. 20.00x (ISBN 0-914710-00-1). East Eur Quarterly.
Delfosse, Claude M., jt. ed. see Oren, Tuncer I.
Del Fosse, E. S. Proceedings of the Fifth International Symposium on Biological Control of Weeds. 647p. 1981. pap. 90.00x (ISBN 0-643-02837-4, Pub. by CAB Bks England). State Mutual Bk.
Del Fosse, E. S., ed. Biological Control of Weeds. 648p. 1982. 60.00x (ISBN 0-643-02837-4, Pub. by CSIRO Australia). State Mutual Bk.
--Biological Control of Weeds, Fifth International Symposium. (Illus.). 649p. 1982. pap. 35.00 (ISBN 0-643-02837-4, Pub. by CSIRO). Intl Spec Bk.
Delfs, Robert. Good Food of Szechwan: Down to Earth Chinese Cooking. LC 74-77960. (Illus.). 124p. 1974. 12.50 (ISBN 0-87011-231-7). Kodansha.
Delft, A. Van see Van Delft, A. & Nijkamp, P.
Delgado. The Best Short Plays: 1985. (Best Short Plays Ser.). 276p. 1985. 14.95 (ISBN 0-8019-7541-7). Chilton.
Delgado, Abelardo. Letters to Louise. LC 82-50707. 1982. pap. 5.00 (ISBN 0-89229-008-0). Tonatiuh-Quinto Sol Intl.
Delgado, Christopher L., jt. ed. see Zartman, William I.
Delgado, Conchita, tr. see Cummins, D. Duane.
Delgado, Enrique, jt. ed. see Cline, William R.
Delgado, Gabriel. A Love Story. 64p. (Orig.). pap. 1.25 (ISBN 0-89228-046-8). Impact Bks MO.
Delgado, Gary. Organizing the Movement: The Roots & Growth of ACORN. (Labor & Social Change Ser.). 256p. 1986. 24.95 (ISBN 0-87722-393-9). Temple U Pr.
Delgado, George. El Hotel Durascamas y Otras Historietas. (No. 1). (Illus.). 120p. (Spa. & Eng.). 1985. pap. 4.25 (ISBN 0-940038-02-1). Andante Pub.
Delgado, Gibert L., ed. The Hispanic Deaf: Issues & Challenges for Bilingual Special Education. LC 84-8130. x, 224p. 1984. 14.95 (ISBN 0-913580-88-0). Gallaudet Coll.
Delgado, Gregorio & Smith, Julian P. Management of Complications in Gynecologic Oncology. LC 81-16135. 287p. 1982. 45.00 (ISBN 0-471-05993-5, Pub. by Wiley Med). Wiley.
Delgado, Guillermo, jt. tr. see Hillman, Grady L.
Delgado, James P. Alcatraz: The Story Behind the Scenery. LC 85-80214. (Illus.). 48p. (Orig.). 1984. pap. text ed. 3.75 (ISBN 0-88714-001-7). KC Pubns.
Delgado, Jeanne H., ed. Advice to Farm Women. (Wisconsin Stories Ser.). 27p. pap. 1.25 (ISBN 0-686-76158-8). State Hist Soc Wis.
Delgado, Jose M. Physical Control of the Mind: Toward a Psychocivilized Society. Anshen, Ruth N., ed. (Illus.). 280p. 1971. 22.50x (ISBN 0-8290-0574-9). Irvington.
--Physical Control of the Mind: Toward a Psychcivilized Society. Anshen, Ruth N., ed. pap. 2.95 (ISBN 0-8290-1765-8). Irvington.
Delgado, Osiris. Historical Synopsis of the Plastic Arts in Puerto Rico. (Puerto Rico Ser.). 1979. lib. bdg. 59.95 (ISBN 0-8490-2933-3). Gordon Pr.
Delgado, Ramon. The Best Short Plays 1983. LC 83-8006. (Best Short Plays Ser.). 264p. 1983. 13.95 (ISBN 0-8019-7296-5). Chilton.
--The Best Short Plays 1984. LC 83-8006. 252p. 1984. 13.95 (ISBN 0-8019-7411-9). Chilton.
--A Little Holy Water. (Illus.). 59p. 1983. pap. 2.75x (ISBN 0-88680-110-9). I E Clark.
Delgado, Ramon, ed. The Best Short Plays Nineteen Eighty-Two. 1982. 12.95 (ISBN 0-8019-7144-6). Chilton.
Delgado-Escueta, Antonio V., et al, eds. Status Epilepticus: Mechanisms of Brain Damage & Treatment. (Advances in Neurology Ser.: Vol. 34). (Illus.). 580p. 1983. 93.50 (ISBN 0-89004-623-9). Raven.
Delgado-Martins, Maria R. Aspects de l'Accent en Portugais. (Hamburger Phonetische Beitraege Ser.: No.39). 206p. (Orig.). 1982. pap. text ed. 17.00x (ISBN 3-87118-532-9, Pub. by Helmut Buske Verlag Hamburg). Benjamins North Am.
Delgass, William, et al. Spectroscopy in Heterogeneous Catalysis. LC 78-27885. 1979. 49.50 (ISBN 0-12-210150-2). Acad Pr.
Delgatto, John, et al, eds. see Griffin, Sid.

Delgaty, Alfa & Sanchez, Agustin R. Diccionario Tzotzil de San Andres con Variaciones Dialectales. (Vocabularios Indigenas: No. 22). (Illus.). 481p. (Orig., Tzotzil & Span.). 1978. pap. 10.00 (ISBN 0-88312-674-5); microfiche (5) 5.72x (ISBN 0-88312-372-X). Summer Inst Ling.

Del Giudice, Paula J. Microwave Game & Fish Cookbook: Quick, Convenient Recipes for Concocting the Tastiest, Juiciest, Most Succulent Wild Meat & Fish Meals You've Ever Eaten. Schnell, Judith, ed. (Illus.). 160p. 1985. pap. 12.95 (ISBN 0-8117-2191-4). Stackpole.

Del Greco, A. A. Giacomo Leopardi in Hispanic Literature. 1952. 12.50x (ISBN 0-913298-63-8). S F Vanni.

Del Guercio, Louis R. Multilingual Manual for Medical History-Taking. 1972. spiral bdg. 8.95 (ISBN 0-316-18025-4). Little.

Delhaye, J. M. & Cognet, G., eds. Measuring Techniques in Gas-Liquid Two-Phase Flows: Symposium, Nancy, France, July 5-8, 1984. (International Union of Theoretical & Applied Mechanics (IUTAM)). 760p. 1984. 59.00 (ISBN 0-387-12736-4). Springer-Verlag.

Delhaye, J. M., et al. Thermohydraulics of Two-Phase Systems for Industrial Design & Nuclear Engineering. LC 80-14312. (Hemisphere Series in Thermal & Fluids Engineering). (Illus.). 544p. 1980. text ed. 59.95 (ISBN 0-07-016268-9). McGraw.

Delhaye, Jean. Art Deco Posters & Graphics. (Illus.). 96p. 1984. pap. 9.95 (ISBN 0-312-05202-2). St Martin.

Del Hierro, Audrey & Campbell, Jane. Loved into Life. 176p. 1985. pap. 5.95 (ISBN 0-310-60881-3, Pub. by Chosen Bks). Zondervan.

D'Elia, Anthony A., Jr. By Choice: The Right School for Your Child! LC 84-91015. 70p. (Orig.). 1984. pap. 6.00 (ISBN 0-9613749-1-8). Personal Assocs.

D'Elia, Anthony N. The Adirondack Rebellion. (Illus.). 1979. text ed. 10.00 (ISBN 0-686-25749-9). Onchiota Bks.

D'Elia, Donald. The Spirits of Seventy-Six: A Catholic Inquiry. 182p. (Orig.). pap. 6.95 (ISBN 0-931888-10-7). Christendom Pubns.

D'Elia, Joseph A., jt. auth. see Bedworth, Albert E.

De Liano, Ignacio G. Dali. LC 83-61925. (Illus.). 128p. 1984. pap. 14.95 (ISBN 0-8478-0522-0). Rizzoli Intl.

Delibes, Miguel. The Hedge. Lopez-Morillas, Frances M., tr. from Span. LC 83-7567. (Twentieth Century Continental Fiction Ser.). 160p. 1983. 20.00 (ISBN 0-231-05460-2). Columbia U Pr.

Delicado, Francisco. Portrait of Lozana: The Exuberant Andalusian Woman. Damiani, Bruno M., tr. 33.00 (ISBN 0-916379-15-9). Scripta.

Delicostopoulos, A. J. Greek Idioms. (Illus.). 1977. pap. 15.00 (ISBN 0-686-77966-5). Heinman.

--Greek (Modern) for Foreigners. (Illus.). 1977. pap. 20.00 (ISBN 0-686-77965-7). Heinman.

De Liefde, John. Six Months among the Charities of Europe. 910p. 1974. Repr. of 1865 ed. lib. bdg. 65.00 (ISBN 0-87821-278-7). Milford Hse.

Deliere, J. & Lafayette, R. Connaitre La France. 1983. 13.95 (ISBN 0-8384-1163-0). Heinle & Heinle.

Deligiorgis, Stavros. Narrative Intellection in the "Decameron". LC 74-26802. 249p. 1975. text ed. 20.00 (ISBN 0-87745-049-8). U of Iowa Pr.

De Ligne. Oeuvres Choisies du Prince de Ligne: Nouvelle Anthologie Critique. Guy, Basil, ed. (Stanford French & Italian Studies: No. 13). xlvi, 282p. (Fr.). 1978. pap. 25.00 (ISBN 0-915838-28-1). Anma Libri.

Deligne, P., et al. Hodge Cycles, Motives, & Shimura Varieties. (Lecture Notes in Mathematics: Vol. 900). 414p. 1981. pap. 24.00 (ISBN 0-387-11174-3). Springer-Verlag.

De Liguori, Alphonse. How to Converse Continually & Familiarly with God. Aubin, tr. 2.95 (ISBN 0-8198-0062-7). Dghtrs St Paul.

Delilah Communications, Ltd., ed. The Compleat Beatles Nineteen Sixty-Two to Nineteen Seventy. Abridged ed. (Illus.). 192p. (Orig.). 1984. pap. 9.95 (ISBN 0-88715-008-X). Delilah Comm.

--The Delilah Rock & Roll Handbook. (Illus.). 128p. (Orig.). 1984. pap. 4.95 (ISBN 0-88715-002-0). Delilah Comm.

--More Rear Views. (Illus.). 96p. (Orig.). 1984. pap. 8.95 (ISBN 0-88715-006-3). Delilah Comm.

Delilah Communications Ltd. Staff, ed. Bowiepix. (Illus.). 32p. 1983. pap. 4.95 (ISBN 0-933328-85-0). Delilah Bks.

Delilah Communications Staff. The Compleat Beatles. abr. ed. (Illus.). 176p. 1985. pap. 9.95 (ISBN 0-8092-5149-3). Contemp Bks.

Delilez, Jean-Pierre. La Planification Dans les Pays D'economie Capitaliste. (Confluence Ser.: No. 14). 1968. pap. 14.00x (ISBN 90-2796-011-9). Mouton.

Delille, Edward. Some French Writers. facsimile ed. LC 78-37526. (Essay Index Reprint Ser). Repr. of 1893 ed. 18.00 (ISBN 0-8369-2543-2). Ayer Co Pubs.

DeLillo, Don. End Zone. 208p. 1983. pap. 3.95 (ISBN 0-671-49302-7). WSP.

--Great Jones Street. LC 83-6928. 272p. pap. 5.95 (ISBN 0-394-71718-X, Vin). Random.

--The Names. LC 82-48012. 1982. 13.95 (ISBN 0-394-52814-X). Knopf.

--The Names. LC 83-5763. 352p. 1983. pap. 5.95 (ISBN 0-394-71564-0, Vin). Random.

--Players. 1984. pap. 5.95 (ISBN 0-394-72382-1, Vin). Random.

--Ratner's Star. LC 80-10927. 448p. 1980. pap. 7.95 (ISBN 0-394-74495-0, Vin). Random.

--Running Dog. LC 77-26674. 1978. 8.95 (ISBN 0-394-50143-8). Knopf.

--Running Dog. LC 79-2159. 1979. pap. 6.95 (ISBN 0-394-74121-8, Vin). Random.

--White Noise. LC 84-40375. 352p. 1985. 16.95 (ISBN 0-670-80373-1, E Sifton Bks). Viking.

DeLillo, Nicholas J., jt. auth. see Mallozzi, John S.

Delillo, Nicholas T. Advanced Calculus with Applications. 1982. text ed. 31.95x (ISBN 0-02-328220-7). Macmillan.

De Lima, Agnes. Our Enemy the Child. LC 78-89172. (American Education: Its Men, Institutions & Ideas, Ser. 1). 1969. Repr. of 1926 ed. 21.00 (ISBN 0-405-01410-4). Ayer Co Pubs.

DeLima, Clara R. Tomorrow Will Always Come. 1965. 9.95 (ISBN 0-8392-1141-4). Astor-Honor.

De Lima, Jorge. Brazilian Psalm. Wager, Willis, tr. 1977. lib. bdg. 59.95 (ISBN 0-8490-1549-9). Gordon Pr.

De Lima, Suzanne, jt. auth. see Hemingway, Mary M.

Deliman, Tracy & Smolowe, John. Holistic Medicine. 1982. text ed. 18.95 (ISBN 0-8359-2844-6); pap. 12.95 (ISBN 0-8359-2843-8). Reston.

De Limce, Alison, jt. auth. see Silk, Gerald.

De Lincy, M. Le-Roux see Philippe De Remi.

De Lincy Antoine Le, Roux see Leroux De Lincy, Antoine J.

Delinde, C. A. Skiing. 7.50x (ISBN 0-392-09172-0, SpS). Sportshelf.

Delinsky, Barbara. Finger Prints. 1984. pap. 3.95 (ISBN 0-318-01774-1, Pub. by Worldwide). Harlequin Bks.

De Lint, Charles. The Harp of the Grey Rose. Reynolds, Kay, ed. LC 84-13806. (The Adventures of Cerwin Songweaver Ser.). (Illus.). 240p. 1985. pap. 7.95 (ISBN 0-89865-374-6). Donning Co.

--Moonheart. 496p. 1984. pap. 2.95 (ISBN 0-441-53719-7). Ace Bks.

--Mulengro: A Romany Tale. 368p. 1985. pap. 3.50 (ISBN 0-441-54484-3) (ISBN 0-317-31758-X). Ace Bks.

--The Riddle of the Wren. 320p. 1984. pap. 2.75 (ISBN 0-441-72229-6). Ace Bks.

DeLint, George J. The United Nations. pap. text ed. 2.50 (ISBN 90-271-1151-0, Pub. by Martinus Nijhoff Netherlands). Kluwer Academic.

De Lint, J. G. Rembrandt. Repr. 20.00 (ISBN 0-8482-3695-5). Norwood Edns.

DeLio, Thomas. Circumscribing the Open Universe: Essays on John Cage, Morton Feldman, Christian Wolff, Robert Ashley, Alvin Lucier. 120p. (Orig.). 1984. lib. bdg. 18.75 (ISBN 0-8191-3747-2); pap. text ed. 8.25 (ISBN 0-8191-3748-0). U Pr of Amer.

DeLio, Thomas, ed. Contiguous Lines: Issues & Ideas in the Music of the '60's & '70's. LC 84-19549. 232p. (Orig.). 1985. lib. bdg. 23.50 (ISBN 0-8191-4329-4); pap. text ed. 10.75 (ISBN 0-8191-4330-8). U Pr of Amer.

De Lion, Gwoffrey, et al. Chronicles of the Crusades. Giles, John A. & Johnes, Thomas, trs. LC 73-84862. (Bohn's Antiquarian Library Ser.). Repr. of 1848 ed. 27.50 (ISBN 0-404-50014-5). AMS Pr.

De Lippe, Aschwin. Indian Medieval Sculpture: About 550-1250 A.D. (Illus.). 412p. 1978. 93.75 (ISBN 0-444-85086-4, North-Holland). Elsevier.

DeLisa, Joel A. & Mackenzie, Keith. Manual of Nerve Conduction Velocity Techniques. 158p. 1982. pap. text ed. 20.50 (ISBN 0-89004-656-5). Raven.

Delisi, C. Antigen Antibody Interactions. (Lecture Notes in Biomathematics: Vol. 8). 1976. pap. 13.00 (ISBN 0-387-07697-2). Springer-Verlag.

DeLisi, C. & Blumenthal, R., eds. Physical Chemical Aspects of Cell Surface Events in Cellular Regulation. (Developments in Cell Biology Ser.: Vol. 4). 394p. 1979. 79.25 (ISBN 0-444-00311-8, Biomedical Pr). Elsevier.

Delisi, C., jt. ed. see Eisenfeld, J.

Delisi, Charles & Hiernaux, Jacques R., eds. Regulation of Immune Response Dynamics, Vols. I, II. 184p. 1982. Vol. I, 176pp. 55.00 (ISBN 0-8493-6632-1); Vol. II, 184pp. 55.00 (ISBN 0-8493-6633-X). CRC Pr.

De Lisle, C. Business Interest Calculations: A Practical Guide. (Waterlow's Practitioner's Library). 228p. 1985. pap. 21.50 (ISBN 0-08-039231-8). Pergamon.

Delisle, Fanny. A Study of Shelley's "a Defence of Poetry". A Textual & Critical Evaluation, 2 vols. (Salzburg Studies in English Literature,Romantic Reassessment: Nos.27-28). 633p. 1974. Set. pap. text ed. 50.75x (ISBN 0-391-01359-9). Humanities.

Delisle, Francoise, tr. see Scheikevitch, Marie.

Delisle, James, et al. The Muffs Peer Identification Instrument for Grades 2-5. 1984. wkbk. 15.00 (ISBN 0-89824-124-3). Trillium Pr.

Delisle, James R. Gifted Children Speak Out. LC 83-42916. 192p. 1984. 14.95 (ISBN 0-8027-0752-1). Walker & Co.

Delisle, Leopold V. Le Cabinet Des Manuscripts De la Bibliotheque Imperiale, 4 vols. LC 78-125018. 1974. lib. bdg. 206.00 (ISBN 0-8337-0819-8, 0-8337-0819). B Franklin.

--Etudes sur la Condition de la Classe Agricole et l'Etat de l'Agriculture en Normandie au Moyen Age. 1965. Repr. of 1906 ed. 45.00 (ISBN 0-8337-0820-1). B Franklin.

Delisle, Leopold V., ed. Rouleaux Des Morts Du IXe Au XVe Siecle. 1866. 43.00 (ISBN 0-384-11361-3); pap. 37.00 (ISBN 0-384-11360-5). Johnson Repr.

De L'Isle-Adam, Villers. Eve of the Future Eden. Rose, Marilyn G., tr. from French. 260p. 1981. 15.00x (ISBN 0-87291-150-0). Coronado Pr.

De Liso, Oscar see Liso, Oscar De.

DeLisser, H. G. Jane's Career. (Caribbean Writers Ser.). 1972. pap. text ed. 6.50x (ISBN 0-435-98540-X). Heinemann Ed.

De Lisser, Herbert G. Jane's Career. LC 78-162467. (Colonial Novel Ser). 207p. 1971. text ed. 27.50x (ISBN 0-8419-0078-7, Africana). Holmes & Meier.

De Lisser, R. Lionel. Picturesque Catskills, Greene County. (Illus.). 1983. pap. 7.50 (ISBN 0-685-12167-4). Hope Farm.

De Lisser, Richard. Picturesque Ulster. 1984. Repr. 9.95 (ISBN 0-317-14701-3). Hope Farm.

Delitala, Giuseppe, et al, eds. Opioid Modulation of Endocrine Function. (Frontiers in Neuroscience Ser.). 296p. 1984. text ed. 54.50 (ISBN 0-88167-024-3). Raven.

Delitzsch, F., jt. auth. see Gloag, P. J.

Delitzsch, Franz. Commentary on the Epistle to the Hebrews, 2 vols. 1978. Set. 31.50 (ISBN 0-86524-110-4, 5801). Klock & Klock.

--A New Commentary on Genesis, 2 vols. 1978. Set. 30.50 (ISBN 0-86524-131-7, 0101). Klock & Klock.

Delitzsch, Franz, jt. auth. see Keil, Carl F.

Delius, F. Delius: A Life in Letters, Eighteen Sixty-Two to Nineteen Hundred & Eight. Carley, Lionel, ed. 500p. 1982. 95.00x (ISBN 0-85967-656-0, Pub. by Scolar England). State Mutual Bk.

Delius, Jean, jt. auth. see DiPasquale, Dominic.

Delius, Peter. The Land Belongs to Us: The Pedi Polity, the Boers, & the British in Nineteenth-Century Transvaal. LC 83-17938. (Perspectives on Southern Africa Ser.: Vol. 35). (Illus.). 278p. 1984. lib. bdg. 28.50x (ISBN 0-520-05148-3). U of Cal Pr.

Deliusin, Lev. The Cultural Revolution in China. 1976. lib. bdg. 59.95 (ISBN 0-8490-1693-2). Gordon Pr.

Delivanis, Demetre J. & Cleveland, William C. Greek Monetary Developments, 1939-1948: A Case Study of the Consequences of World War II for the Monetary System of a Small Nation. LC 49-47294. (Indiana Univrsity, Indiana University Publications, Social Science Ser.: No. 6). pap. 49.00 (ISBN 0-317-28583-1, 2055206). Bks Demand UMI.

Deliz, Monserrate. Hymn of Puerto Rico: Critical Studies of "La Borinquena". (Puerto Rico Ser.). 1979. lib. bdg. 59.95 (ISBN 0-8490-2942-2). Gordon Pr.

--Songs & Folklore of Puerto Rico. (Puerto Rico Ser.). 1979. lib. bdg. 59.95 (ISBN 0-8490-3007-2). Gordon Pr.

Deliz, Wenceslao S., jt. ed. see Ramirez, Rafael L.

Delk, Marcus, jt. auth. see Schein, Jerome.

Dell, Carl W., Jr. Treating the School Age Stutterer: A Guide for Clinicians. LC 79-67284. 110p. (Orig.). pap. 1.50 (ISBN 0-933388-11-X). Speech Found Am.

Dell, Catherine. In Spain. (Span.). Date not set. pap. 6.95 (ISBN 0-8219-0149-4, 70282). EMC.

Dell, Catherine, jt. auth. see Paton, John.

Dell, Cecily. A Primer for Movement Description Using Effort Shape & Supplementary Concepts. 2nd rev. ed. LC 78-111086. (Illus.). 1970. pap. text ed. 9.50x (ISBN 0-932582-03-6). Dance Notation.

Dell, Cecily & Crow, Aileen. Space Harmony: Basic Terms. rev. ed 1977 ed. (Illus.). 24p. 1984. pap. text ed. 3.00 (ISBN 0-932582-12-5). Dance Notation.

Dell, Christopher. Lincoln & the War Democrats: The Grand Erosion of Conservative Tradition. LC 73-21227. 455p. 1975. 35.00 (ISBN 0-8386-1466-3). Fairleigh Dickinson.

Dell, David J., et al. Guide to Hindu Religion. 1981. lib. bdg. 47.00 (ISBN 0-8161-7903-4, Hall Reference). G K Hall.

Dell, Edmund, ed. see Hill, Christopher.

Dell, Edmund, jt. ed. see Hill, John E.

Dell, Ethel. The Knave of Diamonds. (Barbara Cartland's Library of Love: Vol. 3). 280p. 1979. 12.95x (ISBN 0-7156-1379-0, Pub. by Duckworth England). Biblio Dist.

Dell, Ethel M. The Bars of Iron. (Barbara Cartland's Library of Love: Vol. 9). 278p. 1979. 12.95x (ISBN 0-7156-1384-7, BPA-03480, Pub. by Duckworth England). Biblio Dist.

--The Bars of Iron. 1975. lib. bdg. 21.50x (ISBN 0-89966-066-5). Buccaneer Bks.

--Charles Rex. (Barbara Cartland's Library of Love: Vol. 18). 216p. 1980. 12.95x (ISBN 0-7156-1478-9, BPA-03489, Pub. by Duckworth England). Biblio Dist.

--Greatheart. (Barbara Cartland's Library of Love: Vol. 15). 247p. 1980. 12.95x (ISBN 0-7156-1475-4, Pub. by Duckworth England). Biblio Dist.

--House of Happiness: And Other Stories. LC 72-5866. (Short Story Index Reprint Ser.). Repr. of 1927 ed. 20.00 (ISBN 0-8369-4209-4). Ayer Co Pubs.

--The Hundredth Chance. (Barbara Cartland's Library of Love: Vol. 5). 306p. 1979. 12.95x (ISBN 0-7156-1381-2, Pub. by Duckworth England). Biblio Dist.

--The Knave of Diamonds. 1975. lib. bdg. 21.50x (ISBN 0-89966-069-X). Buccaneer Bks.

--The Passer-by: And Other Stories. LC 72-5867. (Short Story Index Reprint Ser). Repr. of 1925 ed. 20.00 (ISBN 0-8369-4210-8). Ayer Co Pubs.

--The Reason Why. 402p. Repr. of 1925 ed. lib. bdg. 20.95x (ISBN 0-88411-293-4, Pub. by Aeonian Pr). Amereon Ltd.

--Rosa Mundi, & Other Stories. LC 79-121535. (Short Story Index Reprint Ser.). 1921. 22.00 (ISBN 0-8369-3491-1). Ayer Co Pubs.

--Swindler & Other Stories. facs. ed. LC 72-140329. (Short Story Index Reprint Ser). 1914. 21.00 (ISBN 0-8369-3721-X). Ayer Co Pubs.

--The Way of an Eagle. 398p. Repr. of 1925 ed. lib. bdg. 20.95x (ISBN 0-88411-294-2, Pub. by Aeonian Pr). Amereon Ltd.

--The Way of an Eagle. (Barbara Cartland's Library of Love: Vol. 7). 193p. 1979. 12.95x (ISBN 0-7156-1383-9, Pub. by Duckworth England). Biblio Dist.

Dell, F. Generative Phonology. LC 79-14139. (Illus.). 1980. 47.50 (ISBN 0-521-22484-5); pap. 12.95x (ISBN 0-521-29519-X). Cambridge U Pr.

Dell, Floyd. Diana Stair. LC 74-26100. Repr. of 1932 ed. 39.50 (ISBN 0-404-58419-5). AMS Pr.

--King Arthur's Socks & Other Village Plays. LC 77-70353. (One-Act Plays in Reprint Ser.). 1977. Repr. of 1922 ed. 16.50x (ISBN 0-8486-2014-3). Core Collection.

--Love in Greenwich Village. LC 73-128730. (Short Story Index Reprint Ser.). 1926. 18.00 (ISBN 0-8369-3621-3). Ayer Co Pubs.

--Love in the Machine Age: A Psychological Study of the Transition from Patriarchal Society. LC 73-4608. 428p. 1973. Repr. of 1930 ed. lib. bdg. 26.00x (ISBN 0-374-92104-0). Octagon.

--Upton Sinclair: A Study in Social Protest. LC 73-133826. Repr. of 1927 ed. 24.50 (ISBN 0-404-02076-3). AMS Pr.

--Women As World Builders: Studies in Modern Feminism. LC 75-21810. (Pioneers of the Woman's Movement: an International Perspective Ser.). 104p. 1976. Repr. of 1913 ed. 13.00 (ISBN 0-88355-258-2). Hyperion-Conn.

Dell, Penelope. Nettie & Sissie: A Biography of Ethel M. Dell & Her Sister Ella. (Illus.). 1978. 16.95 (ISBN 0-241-89663-0, Pub. by Hamish Hamilton England). David & Charles.

Dell Puzzle Publications, jt. ed. see Moore, Rosalind.

Dell Puzzle Publications Editors. The Dell Big Book of Crosswords & Pencil Puzzles, No. 3. Moore, Rosalind, ed. 400p. (Orig.). 1983. pap. 7.95 (ISBN 0-440-51882-2, Dell Trade Pbks). Dell.

Dell, Ralph B., jt. auth. see Winters, Robert W.

Dell, Robert W. & Dell, Yvonne. Foster Parenting: Is It for You. 1984. 7.95 (ISBN 0-533-05857-0). Vantage.

Dell, Sidney. The Inter-American Development Bank: A Study in Development Financing. LC 70-185778. (Special Studies in International Economics & Development). 1972. 29.75x (ISBN 0-275-28606-1). Irvington.

--On Being Grandmotherly: The Evolution of IMF Conditionality. LC 81-6888. (Essays in International Finance Ser.: No. 144). 1981. pap. text ed. 2.50x (ISBN 0-88165-051-X). Princeton U Int Finan Econ.

Dell, Sidney & Lawrence, Roger. The Balance of Payments Adjustment Process in Developing Countries. LC 79-22818. (Pergamon Policy Studies Ser.). 120p. 1980. 21.00 (ISBN 0-08-025577-9). Pergamon.

Dell, Susanne. Murder into Manslaughter: The Diminished Responsibility Defense in Practice. (Maudsley Monographs). (Illus.). 1984. 26.95x (ISBN 0-19-712151-9). Oxford U Pr.

--Silent in Court. 64p. 1971. pap. text ed. 5.00 (ISBN 0-7135-1576-7, Pub. by Bedford England). Brookfield Pub Co.

Dell, Yvonne, jt. auth. see Dell, Robert W.

Della Bitta, Albert J., jt. auth. see Loudon, David.

Della Buono, Carmen J. Rare Early Essays on Nathaniel Hawthorne. 200p. 1979. lib. bdg. 27.00 (ISBN 0-8482-0635-5). Norwood Edns.

Della Casa, Giovanni. Galateo: A Treatise of the Manners & Behaviours. Peterson, Robert, tr. LC 73-26476. (English Experience Ser.: No. 120). 122p. 1969. Repr. of 1576 ed. 16.00 (ISBN 90-221-0120-7). Walter J Johnson.

Della Cava, Ralph. Miracle at Joaseiro. LC 76-127364. (Institute for Latin American Studies). (Illus.). 324p. 1970. 28.00x (ISBN 0-231-03293-5). Columbia U Pr.

Dellacherie, C. & Meyer, P. A. Probabilities & Potential. (North Holland Mathematical Studies: No. 29). 190p. 1979. 42.75 (ISBN 0-7204-0701-X, North-Holland). Elsevier.

Della Corte, Andrea see Corte, Andrea Della.

Dellacorte, Betty. Shelter from the Storm. 306p. 1985. pap. 9.95 (ISBN 0-933843-00-3). Villa Pr AZ.

Della-Dora, Delmo & Blanchard, Lois J., eds. Moving Toward Self-Directed Learning. LC 79-64506. 1979. pap. text ed. 4.75 (ISBN 0-87120-094-5, 611-79166). Assn Supervision.

Della-Dora, Delmo, ed. see Banks, James A., et al.

Della Fazia, Alba, ed. see Anouilh, Jean.

Dellamere, Wanda. Call of the Heart. (Superromances Ser.). 384p. 1982. pap. 2.50 (ISBN 0-373-70024-5, Pub. by Worldwide). Harlequin Bks.

Della Mirandola, Giovanni Pico see Pico Della Mirandola, Giovanni.

Della Mirandola, Giovanni Pico see Pico della Mirandola, Giovanni.

Della Mirandola, Giovanni Pico see Pico Della Mirandola, Giovanni.

DellaNeva, JoAnn. Song & Counter-Song: Sceve's Delie & Petrarch's Rime. LC 83-81597. (French Forum Monographs: 49). 128p. 1983. pap. 10.00x (ISBN 0-917058-49-6). French Forum.

De Llano, Rodriguez. Falta una Pagina Que Trate de Eso. 61p. (Span.). 1978. 7.50 (ISBN 0-317-11653-3). Dawsons.

Dell'Antonio, G., et al, eds. Mathematical Problems in Theoretical Physics: International Conference, Held in Rome, June 6-15, 1977. (Lecture Notes in Physics: Vol. 80). 1979. pap. 27.00 (ISBN 0-387-08853-9). Springer-Verlag.

Della Porta, G., ed. see International Pigment Cell Conference - 6th.

Della Porta, Giambattista. I Due Fratelli Rivali: The Two Rival Brothers. Clubb, Louise G., tr. from Italian. LC 78-64458. 350p. 1980. 28.50x (ISBN 0-520-03786-3). U of Cal Pr.

Dellaquila, William. The Metaphysics of History at the End of the Twentieth Century. (Illus.). 1977. 69.45 (ISBN 0-89266-028-7). Am Classical Coll Pr.

Dellar, Fred & Wootton, Richard. The Country Music Book of Lists. LC 84-40110. (Illus.). 176p. 1984. pap. 9.95 (ISBN 0-8129-6339-3). Times Bks.

Della Torre, K. W. Von see Von Dalla Torre, K. W. & Harms, H.

Della Torree, Edward, et al. The Electromagnetic Field. LC 79-23788. 1980. Repr. of 1979 ed. text ed. 44.50 (ISBN 0-89874-100-9). Krieger.

Della Valle, George. The New, Fully Illustrated Book in Vibrant Colors of the Most Dramatic Flowers in the Universe. (Illus.). 107p. 1982. 69.75 (ISBN 0-89266-322-7). Am Classical Coll Pr.

Della Valle, Pietro. The Travels of Pietro Della Valle to India, 2 Vols. Grey, Edward, ed. Hovers, G., tr. (Illus.). 58.00 (ISBN 0-8337-0822-8). B Franklin.

Della Volpe, Galvano. Critique of Taste. 1978. 18.50 (ISBN 0-8052-7001-9, Pub by NLB). Schocken.

--Rousseau & Marx & Other Writings. Fraser, John, tr. from Ital. 1979. text ed. 18.75x (ISBN 0-391-01211-8). Humanities.

Delle Colonne, G. Guido de Columnis: Historia Destructionis Troiae. Griffin, Nathanial E., ed. (Med Acad Amer Pubns). 1936. 21.00 (ISBN 0-527-01696-9). Kraus Repr.

Dellenbach, Carolyn M., jt. auth. see Clasper, James W.

Dellenbarger, Lynn E., Jr. Common Stock Valuation in Industrial Mergers. LC 66-30593. (Illus.). 1966. 6.95 (ISBN 0-8130-0057-2). U Presses Fla.

Dellenbaugh, F. S. The North Americans of Yesterday. 1977. lib. bdg. 69.95 (ISBN 0-8490-2351-3). Gordon Pr.

Dellenbaugh, Frederick S. A Canyon Voyage: The Narrative of the Second Powell Expedition Down the Colorado River from Wyoming, & the Explorations, in the Years 1871 & 1872. LC 84-8648. (Illus.). 277p. 1984. pap. 9.95 (ISBN 0-8165-0880-1). U of Ariz Pr.

--The North-Americans of Yesterday: A Comparative Study of North-American Indian Life, Customs, & Products, on the Theory of the Ethnic Unity of Race. LC 74-7950. (Illus.). Repr. of 1906 ed. 44.50 (ISBN 0-404-11837-2). AMS Pr.

Dellenbrant, Jan-Ake. Soviet Regional Policy: A Quantitative Inquiry into the Social & Political Development of the Soviet Republics. 208p. 1980. pap. text ed. 30.50x (ISBN 0-391-01797-7). Humanities.

Dellepiane, Angela B., jt. auth. see Szmuk, Szilvia E.

Deller, Anthony W. Patent Claims, 3 vols. 2nd ed. LC 76-112643. 1971. 199.50 (ISBN 0-686-14534-8); Suppl. 1984. 44.00; Suppl. 1983. 34.00. Lawyers Co-Op.

Deller, Karlheinz & Watanabe, Kazuke. STT 366: Deutungsbersuch 1982 & other articles. (Assur Ser.: Vol. 3, Issue 4). 40p. (Ger.). 1983. pap. 6.00x (ISBN 0-89003-004-9). Undena Pubns.

Delles, Roger. Assessment of Effectiveness Measures for Local Government Recreation Agencies in Oregon. 99p. 1974. pap. 4.00 (ISBN 0-943272-09-2). Inst Recreation Res.

De Llevada, Nilda C. De Mi Alma A Mi Pueblo: Prosa Y Poesia. Yanez, Roberto, ed. LC 83-80993. (Illus., Orig.). 1983. pap. 5.00 (ISBN 0-88696-000-2). Editorial D O.

Dellheim, Charles. The Face of the Past: The Preservation of the Medieval Inheritance in Victorian England. LC 82-4486. (Illus.). 225p. 1983. 32.50 (ISBN 0-521-23645-2). Cambridge U Pr.

Delli Carpini, Michael X. Stability & Change in American Politics: The Coming of Age of the Generation of the 1960's. 304p. 1986. text ed. 35.00x (ISBN 0-8147-1780-2). NYU Pr.

Delligan, William. Time nor Tide. 352p. 1983. 16.95 (ISBN 0-525-24104-3, 01646-490). Dutton.

--Time nor Tide. 400p. 1984. pap. 3.50 (ISBN 0-523-42148-6). Pinnacle Bks.

Dellinger, Ann M. Legal Guide for North Carolina School Board Members. 70p. 1978. 2.50 (ISBN 0-686-39471-2). U of NC Inst Gov.

Dellinger, Annetta. A Birthday Party for Jesus. (Little Happy Day Bks.). (Illus.). 24p. (gr. 5-7). 1985. pap. 0.49 (ISBN 0-87239-939-7, 2195). Standard Pub.

--Color, Color, Everywhere. (Little Happy Day Bks.). (Illus.). 24p. (ps-2). 1985. 0.49 (ISBN 0-87239-937-0, 2193). Standard Pub.

--Happy Talk. 1982. pap. 5.95 (ISBN 0-570-03859-6, 12-2953). Concordia.

--More Happy Talk. 1984. pap. 5.95 (ISBN 0-570-03929-0, 12-2864). Concordia.

--You Are Special to Jesus. 1984. pap. 4.95 (ISBN 0-570-04089-2, 56-1457). Concordia.

Dellinger, Annetta E. Angels Are My Friends. 32p. (gr. 5-9). 1985. 5.95 (ISBN 0-570-04120-1, 56-1531). Concordia.

--Good Manners for God's Children. 1984. pap. 3.95 (ISBN 0-570-04093-0, 56-1461). Concordia.

--Hugging. LC 84-21505. (What Is It? A Value Ser.). (Illus.). 32p. (gr. k-3). lib. bdg. 7.45 (ISBN 0-89565-301-X). Childs World.

--I Talk to God. LC 84-50287. (Little Happy Day Bks.). (Illus.). 24p. (Orig.). (ps-1). 1984. pap. 0.45 (ISBN 0-87239-802-1, 2162). Standard Pub.

--My First Easter Book. LC 84-21512. (My First Bks.). (Illus.). 32p. 1985. lib. bdg. 10.35 (ISBN 0-516-02904-5); pap. 2.95 (ISBN 0-516-42904-3). Childrens.

--My Good Manners Book. LC 84-50285. (Little Happy Day Bks.). (Illus.). 24p. (Orig.). (ps-1). 1984. pap. 0.45 (ISBN 0-87239-803-X, 2163). Standard Pub.

Dellinger, Bill & Freeman, Bill. The Competitive Runner's Training Book. (Illus.). 144p. 1985. 13.95 (ISBN 0-02-530570-0, Collier); pap. 6.95 (ISBN 0-02-023840-1). Macmillan.

Dellinger, David, jt. ed. see Albert, Michael.

DelliQuadri, Lyn & Breckenridge, Kati. The New Mother Care: Helping Yourself Through the Emotional & Physical Transitions of Motherhood. LC 77-88008. 228p. 1984. pap. 6.95 (ISBN 0-87477-315-6). J P Tarcher.

Delliquadri, Lyn, ed. Drawings: Eighty-First Exhibition by Artists of Chicago & Vicinity. 32p. (Orig.). 1985. pap. 6.95 (ISBN 0-86559-071-0). Art Inst Chi.

DelliQuadri, Lyn, ed. see Allen, Harold & Frumkin, Deborah S.

DelliQuadri, Lyn, ed. see Kuh, Katharine & Adrian, Denis.

Dellis, A. N., tr. see Lominadze, D. G.

Dell'Isola, A. J. V. E. in Construction Industry. 181p. 1973. 46.00 (ISBN 0-318-16557-0, A1005); members 41,50 (ISBN 0-318-16558-9). Soc Am Value E.

Dell'Isola, Alphonse & Kirk, Stephen J. Life Cycle Cost Data. (Illus.). 160p. 1982. 36.95 (ISBN 0-07-016282-4). McGraw.

--Life Cycle Costing for Design Professionals. (Illus.). 288p. 1981. 39.95 (ISBN 0-07-016280-8). McGraw.

Dell'Isola, Alphonse J. Value Engineering in the Construction Industry. 3rd ed. 376p. 1983. 38.50 (ISBN 0-442-26202-7). Van Nos Reinhold.

Dell'Isola, Frank. Thomas Merton: A Bibliography. rev. ed. LC 74-79148. (Serif Ser.: No. 31). 200p. 1975. 12.00x (ISBN 0-87338-156-4). Kent St U Pr.

Del Litto, ed. see Stendhal.

Del Litto, Victor, ed. see Stendhal.

Dellman, H. D., et al, eds. Comparative Endocrinology of Prolactin. LC 77-1871. (Advances in Experimental Medicine & Biology: Vol. 80). 229p. 1977. 35.00x (ISBN 0-306-39080-9, Plenum Pr). Plenum Pub.

Dellmann, Horst-Dieter & Brown, Esther M., eds. Textbook of Veterinary Histology. 2nd ed. LC 81-8439. (Illus.). 460p. 1981. text ed. 37.50 (ISBN 0-8121-0792-6). Lea & Febiger.

Dello Buono, Carmen J. Rare Early Essays on William Shakespeare: First Series. 202p. 1980. lib. bdg. 27.00 (ISBN 0-8482-0648-7). Norwood Edns.

Dello Buono, Carmen J. Rare Early Essays on Charles Dickens. 207p. 1980. lib. bdg. 27.50 (ISBN 0-8482-0647-9). Norwood Edns.

--Rare Early Essays on Charles Dickens. (Rare Early Essay Ser). 1978. lib. bdg. 27.50 (ISBN 0-8482-0632-0). Norwood Edns.

--Rare Early Essays on Edgar Allan Poe. 211p. 1981. lib. bdg. 27.50 (ISBN 0-8482-3676-9). Norwood Edns.

--Rare Early Essays on Geoffrey Chaucer. 219p. 1981. lib. bdg. 27.50 (ISBN 0-8482-3677-7). Norwood Edns.

--Rare Early Essays on George Eliot. 202p. 1980. lib. bdg. 27.00 (ISBN 0-8482-3661-0). Norwood Edns.

--Rare Early Essays on George Eliot. 211p. 1980. lib. bdg. 25.00 (ISBN 0-8482-3660-2). R West.

--Rare Early Essays on John Keats. 208p. 1980. lib. bdg. 27.00 (ISBN 0-8482-3675-0). Norwood Edns.

--Rare Early Essays on John Milton. 204p. 1981. lib. bdg. 27.00 (ISBN 0-8482-3682-3). Norwood Edns.

--Rare Early Essays on Lord Byron. 203p. 1981. lib. bdg. 27.00 (ISBN 0-8482-3654-8). Norwood Edns.

--Rare Early Essays on Percy Bysshe Shelley. 220p. 1981. lib. bdg. 27.50 (ISBN 0-8482-3653-X). Norwood Edns.

--Rare Early Essays on Ralph Waldo Emerson. 206p. 1980. Repr. lib. bdg. 27.50 (ISBN 0-8414-3875-7). Norwood Edns.

--Rare Early Essays on Ralph Waldo Emerson. 1979. lib. bdg. 27.50 (ISBN 0-8482-0633-9). Norwood Edns.

--Rare Early Essays on Samuel Johnson. 208p. 1981. lib. bdg. 27.50 (ISBN 0-8482-3657-2). Norwood Edns.

--Rare Early Essays on Samuel Taylor Coleridge. 205p. 1981. lib. bdg. 25.00 (ISBN 0-8482-3678-5). Norwood Edns.

--Rare Early Essays on Sidney & Spenser. 215p. 1981. lib. bdg. 27.50 (ISBN 0-8482-3679-3). Norwood Edns.

--Rare Early Essays on the Age of Johnson. 208p. 1981. lib. bdg. 27.50 (ISBN 0-8482-3655-6). Norwood Edns.

--Rare Early Essays on the Brontes. 218p. 1980. lib. bdg. 27.00 (ISBN 0-8482-0646-0). Norwood Edns.

--Rare Early Essays on Walt Whitman. 202p. 1980. lib. bdg. 27.50 (ISBN 0-8482-3699-8). Norwood Edns.

--Rare Early Essays on William Shakespeare: Second Series. 205p. 1980. lib. bdg. 27.00 (ISBN 0-8482-3650-5). Norwood Edns.

--Rare Early Essays on William Shakespeare: Third Series. 206p. 1980. lib. bdg. 27.50 (ISBN 0-8482-3651-3). Norwood Edns.

Dello Buono, Carmen J., ed. Rare Early Essays on Milton & Bunyan. 214p. 1981. lib. bdg. 27.50 (ISBN 0-8482-3683-1). Norwood Edns.

--Rare Early Essays on William Wordsworth. (First Ser.). 210p. 1981. lib. bdg. 27.50 (ISBN 0-8482-3680-7). Norwood Edns.

--Rare Essays on William Wordsworth. (Second Ser.). 214p. 1981. lib. bdg. 27.50 (ISBN 0-8482-3681-5). Norwood Edns.

Delloff, Linda M., ed. see Sittler, Joseph A.

Dellor, Ralph, jt. auth. see Ibbotson, Doug.

Dell Orto, Arthur, jt. ed. see Marinelli, Robert.

Dell'Orto, Luisa F. Ancient Rome: Life & Art. (Illus.). 96p. (Orig.). 1982. pap. 12.50 (ISBN 0-935748-46-6). Scala Books.

Dellosa, Janet & Carson, Patti. Addition Facts: Sums to Ten. (Let's Learn Ser.). (Illus.). 32p. (gr. 1-2). 1984. pap. 1.79 (ISBN 0-88724-076-3, CD-7019). Carson-Dellos.

--Birthday Fun Book. (Stick-Out-Your-Neck Ser.). (Illus.). 32p. (ps-2). 1982. pap. 1.25 (ISBN 0-88724-034-8, CD-8005). Carson-Dellos.

--The Color Words. (Let's Learn Ser.). (Illus.). 32p. (ps-1). 1983. pap. 1.79 (ISBN 0-88724-001-1, CD-7002). Carson-Dellos.

--Easter Fun Book. (Stick-Out-Your-Neck Ser.). (Illus.). 32p. (ps-1). 1982. pap. 1.25 (ISBN 0-88724-050-X, CD-8004). Carson-Dellos.

--Fall Preschool & Kindergarten Practice. (Stick-Out-Your-Neck Ser.). (Illus.). 32p. (ps-k). 1983. pap. 1.79 (ISBN 0-88724-046-1, CD-8022). CArson-Dellos.

--Farm Fun Book. (Stick-Out-Your-Neck Ser.). (Illus.). 32p. (ps-2). 1984. pap. 1.25 (ISBN 0-88724-020-8, CD-8035). Carson-Dellos.

--Holiday Story Starters. (Stick-Out-Your-Neck Ser.). (Illus.). 64p. (gr. 2 up). 1984. pap. 5.95 (ISBN 0-88724-114-X, CD-0026). Carson-Dellos.

--Let's Learn Counting One to Ten. (Let's Learn Ser.). (Illus.). 32p. (ps-k). 1984. pap. 1.79 (ISBN 0-88724-091-7, CD-7030). Carson-Dellos.

--The Letters A-Z. (Let's Learn Ser.). (Illus.). 32p. (ps-1). 1984. pap. 1.79 (ISBN 0-88724-093-3, CD-7032). Carson-Dellos.

--Matching: Similarities & Differences. (Let's Learn Ser.). (Illus.). 32p. (ps-1). 1983. pap. 1.79 (ISBN 0-88724-010-0, CD-7011). Carson-Dellos.

--Reproducible Blank Holiday Patterns. (Stick-Out-Your-Neck Ser.). (Illus.). 32p. (gr. k-6). 1984. pap. 1.98 (ISBN 0-88724-032-1, CD-0913). Carson-Dellos.

--Sporty Blank Reproducible Worksheets. (Stick-Out-Your-Neck Ser.). (Illus.). 32p. (gr. 1 up). 1984. pap. 6.95 (ISBN 0-88724-031-3, CD-0919). Carson-Dellos.

--Thanksgiving Fun Book. (Stick-Out-Your-Neck Ser.). (Illus.). 32p. (ps-2). 1981. pap. 1.25 (ISBN 0-88724-052-6, CD-8007). Carson-Dellos.

--Thanksgiving Preschool & Kindergarten Practice. (Stick-Out-Your-Neck Ser.). (Illus.). 32p. (ps-k). 1983. pap. 1.79 (ISBN 0-88724-048-8, CD-8024). Carson-Dellos.

--Winter Fun Book. (Stick-Out-Your-Neck Ser.). (Illus.). 32p. (ps-2). 1984. pap. 1.25 (ISBN 0-88724-060-7, CD-8048). Carson-Dellos.

--Year Round Holiday Fun Book. (Stick-Out-Your-Neck Ser.). (Illus.). 32p. (ps-2). 1984. pap. 1.25 (ISBN 0-88724-058-5, CD-8043). Carson-Dellos.

Dellosa, Janet, jt. auth. see Carson, Patti.

Dellosa, JAnet, jt. auth. see Carson, Patti.

Dellosa, Janet, jt. auth. see Carson, Patti.

DEllosa, Janet, jt. auth. see Carson, Patti.

Dellosa, Janet, jt. auth. see Carson, Patti.

Dellosa, Janet, et al. All about Me. (Let's Learn Ser.). (Illus.). 32p. (ps-1). 1983. pap. 1.79 (ISBN 0-88724-009-7, CD-7010). Carson-Dellos.

--Colors & Counting Zero Through Nine. (Stick-Out-Your-Neck Ser.). (Illus.). 32p. (ps-1). 1984. pap. 1.98 (ISBN 0-88724-158-1, CD-0922). Carson-Dellos.

--Consonants & Counting Zero Through Twenty. (Stick-Out-Your-Neck Ser.). (Illus.). 32p. (ps-2). 1984. pap. 1.98 (ISBN 0-88724-161-1, CD-0921). Carson-Dellos.

--Positions: under, on, Beside, in, Behind. (Let's Learn Ser.). (Illus.). 32p. (ps-1). 1983. pap. 1.79 (ISBN 0-88724-007-0, CD-7008). Carson-Dellos.

Dell'Osso, Bernardino. Of Human Values. 1985. 12.95 (ISBN 0-533-06264-0). Vantage.

Dellow, E. L. A First Course in Proof Correcting. 1979. 40.00x (ISBN 0-85298-411-1, Pub. by Mechanical Eng Pubns). State Mutual Bk.

Dellow, P. Beads. 30p. 1985. 5.95 (ISBN 0-533-06327-2). Vantage.

Dellums, Ronald V. Defense Sense: The Search for a Rational Military Policy. 376p. 1983. 29.95 (ISBN 0-88410-942-9); pap. 9.95 (ISBN 0-88410-957-7). Ballinger Pub.

Dellums, Ronald V., et al. Nuclear California: An Investigative Report. Kaplan, David E., ed. LC 82-1213. (Illus.). 144p. (Orig.). 1982. pap. 5.95 (ISBN 0-9607166-0-2). Greenpeace-Ctr Invest Re.

Delly, John G., ed. Teaching Microscopy, Vol. 52. LC 76-39606. (Illus.). 1977. 18.00 (ISBN 0-904962-05-9). Microscope Pubns.

Delmage, Lewis, tr. see Ignatius, Saint.

Delman, Abner J., jt. auth. see Stein, Emanuel.

Delman, Abner J., et al. Dynamic Cardiac Auscultation & Phonocardiography: A Graphic Guide. LC 77-16990. pap. 160.00 (ISBN 0-317-07790-2, 2016661). Bks Demand UMI.

Delman, David. Murder in the Family. LC 84-18693. (Crime Club Ser.). 192p. 1985. 11.95 (ISBN 0-385-19806-X). Doubleday.

Del Mar, Alexander. Barbara Villiers. 59.95 (ISBN 0-87968-705-3). Gordon Pr.

--Collected Works. 500.00 (ISBN 0-87968-887-4). Gordon Pr.

--A History of Monetary Crimes. 59.95 (ISBN 0-8490-0337-7). Gordon Pr.

--History of Monetary Systems. Fasc. ed. LC 83-61903. 444p. 1983. 25.00 (ISBN 0-915032-26-0); pap. 15.95 (ISBN 0-915032-27-9). Natl Poet Foun.

--History of Money in America. 59.95 (ISBN 0-8490-0338-5). Gordon Pr.

--The History of Money in America from the Earliest Times to the Establishment of the Constitution. LC 68-58459. (Research & Source Ser.: No. 323). 1969. Repr. of 1899 ed. 20.50 (ISBN 0-8337-0827-9). B Franklin.

--History of Money in Ancient Countries from Earliest Times to the Present. 1969. Repr. of 1885 ed. 24.00 (ISBN 0-8337-0826-0). B Franklin.

--History of the Precious Metals. 2nd rev ed. LC 68-18230. Repr. of 1902 ed. 37.50x (ISBN 0-678-00475-7). Kelley.

--A History of the Precious Metals from Earliest Times to the Present. 2nd ed. LC 68-58460. (Research & Source Ser.: No. 324). 1969. Repr. of 1902 ed. 23.50 (ISBN 0-8337-0828-7). B Franklin.

--Money & Civilization. pap. 5.00 (ISBN 0-913022-20-9). Angriff Pr.

--Money & Civilization. 1969. 29.00 (ISBN 0-8337-0829-5). B Franklin.

--Roman & Moslem Moneys. 59.95 (ISBN 0-8490-0968-5). Gordon Pr.

--Science of Money. 2nd ed. LC 68-5846. (Research & Source Ser.: No. 322). 1969. Repr. of 1896 ed. 20.50 (ISBN 0-8337-0830-9). B Franklin.

--The Science of Money. 59.95 (ISBN 0-8490-1002-0). Gordon Pr.

--The Worship of Augustus Caesar. Repr. of 1899 ed. 10.00 (ISBN 0-913022-19-5). Angriff Pr.

DelMar, D. Operations & Industrial Management: Designing for Productivity. (Management Ser.). 672p. 1985. 32.95 (ISBN 0-07-016287-5). McGraw.

Del Mar, Donald. Classics in Scientific Management. Collons, Roger D., ed. LC 75-20471. 457p. 1976. 26.75 (ISBN 0-8173-8701-3). U of Ala Pr.

Delmar, Ken. Winning Moves: The Body Language of Selling. 304p. 1985. 17.50 (ISBN 0-446-51301-6). Warner Bks.

Del Mar, Marcia. A Cuban Story. LC 79-17551. 1979. 3.98 (ISBN 0-89587-011-8). Blair.

Del Mar, Norman. Anatomy of the Orchestra. LC 81-11559. 512p. 1982. 42.50x (ISBN 0-520-04500-9). U of Cal Pr.

--Anatomy of the Orchestra. (Cal Ser.: No. 675). (Illus.). 528p. 1984. pap. 14.95 (ISBN 0-520-05062-2). U of Cal Pr.

--Confusion & Error in the Orchestral Repertoire. 256p. 1981. 35.00x (ISBN 0-903873-37-0, Pub. by Eulenburg England). State Mutual Bk.

--Mahler's Sixth Symphony: A Study. (Eulenburg Music Bks.). (Illus.). 153p. 1982. pap. 22.50 (ISBN 0-903873-29-X). Da Capo.

--Orchestral Variations: Confusion & Error in the Orchestral Repertoire. (Eulenburg Music Ser.). (Illus.). 240p. 1982. pap. text ed. 22.50 (ISBN 0-903873-37-0). Da Capo.

Delmar, Rosalind, tr. see Aleramo, Sibilla.

Delmar-Morgan, Edward. Normandy Harbors & Pilotage. 1979. 29.95x (ISBN 0-8464-0073-1). Beekman Pubs.
--North Sea Harbors & Pilotage. 1979. 37.00x (ISBN 0-8464-0070-7). Beekman Pubs.
Delmas, B, jt. auth. see D'Olier, J.
Delmas, J., ed. see IFAC-IFORS Symposium, Toulouse, France, Mar. 1979.
Delmas-Harrap. Dictionnaire des Affaires Francais-Anglais, Anglais-Francais. (Fr. & Eng.). 65.50 (ISBN 0-685-36681-2). French & Eur.
Del Mastro, M. L. The Stairway of Perfection. LC 78-60288. 1979. pap. 4.95 (ISBN 0-385-14059-2, Im). Doubleday.
Del Mastro, M. L., tr. Revelations of Divine Love: Juliana of Norwich. LC 76-52004. 1977. pap. 3.95 (ISBN 0-385-12297-7, Im). Doubleday.
Del Mastro, M. L., jt. tr. see Meisel, Anthony C.
Del Mastro, M. L., tr. see Rolle, Richard.
Del Mazza, Valentino. Good News for the Liturgical Community: Cycle B. 1980. 5.95 (ISBN 0-8198-3004-6); pap. 4.95 (ISBN 0-8198-3005-4). Dghtrs St Paul.
--Good News for the Liturgical Community: Cycle C. rev. ed. 1981. 5.95 (ISBN 0-8198-0573-4); pap. 4.95 (ISBN 0-8198-3003-8). Dghtrs St Paul.
--Our Lady among Us. 1978. 4.00 (ISBN 0-8198-0363-4); pap. 3.00 (ISBN 0-8198-0364-2). Dghtrs St Paul.
--Secrets for Finding Happiness in Marriage. Daughters of St. Paul, tr. 84p. 1983. 3.00 (ISBN 0-317-13552-X); pap. 2.00 (ISBN 0-8198-6856-6). Dghtrs St Paul.
Delmenico, J., jt. auth. see Farnworth, A. J.
Delmer, A; see Davin, L. E.
De L. Milosz, O. V. Fourteen Poems by O. V. de L. Milosz. Rexroth, Kenneth, tr. 68p. (Fr.). 1984. pap. 6.95 (ISBN 0-914742-71-X). Copper Canyon.
Delmon, B. & Froment, G., eds. Catalyst Deactivation: Proceedings. (Studies in Surface Science & Catalysis: Vol. 6). 602p. 1980. 117.00 (ISBN 0-444-41920-9). Elsevier.
Delmon, B. & Jannes, G., eds. Catalysis: Heterogeneous & Homogeneous: Proceedings of the International Symposium, Brussels, 1974. 550p. 1975. 113.00 (ISBN 0-444-41346-4). Elsevier.
Delmon, B., et al, eds. Preparation of Catalyts: Scientific Basis for the Preparation of Heterogeneous Catalysis. (Studies in Surface Science & Catalyses: Vol. 1). 706p. (Proceedings). 1976. 127.75 (ISBN 0-444-41428-2). Elsevier.
Delmon, B., jt. ed. see Bonnelle, J. P.
Delmon, B., et al, eds. see International Symposium, Louvain, Sept., 1978.
Delmont, J., ed. Milk Intolerances & Rejection. (Illus.). x, 170p. 1983. pap. 59.75 (ISBN 3-8055-3546-5). S Karger.
Delmont, J., ed. see Gastroenterological Symposium, 3rd.
Delmont, J., ed. see Symposium on Hepato-Gastroenterology of the University Hospital Center of Nice, 1st, August 1972.
Delmonte, Diana. Dynamics in the Arts. 1974. 3.95 (ISBN 0-8315-0144-8). Speller.
Delmonte, J. Age Dating. 1986. cancelled (ISBN 0-442-22087-1). Van Nos Reinhold.
Delmonte, John. Technology of Carbon & Graphite Fiber Composites. 464p. 1981. 36.50 (ISBN 0-442-22072-3). Van Nos Reinhold.
--Technology of Carbon & Graphite Fiber Composites. (Illus.). 464p. 1981. 36.50 (ISBN 0-686-48237-9, 0213). T-C Pubns CA.
Delmore, Alton. Truth is Stranger than Publicity. Wolfe, Charles K., ed. 188p. 1977. pap. 5.95 (ISBN 0-915608-05-7). Country Music Found.
Delmore, Diana. Anthea. 1985. pap. 2.50 (ISBN 0-446-32833-2). Warner Bks.
--Dorinda. 208p. 1985. pap. 2.50 (ISBN 0-446-32805-7). Warner Bks.
--Leonie. LC 83-14791. 192p. 1984. 12.95 (ISBN 0-8027-0755-6). Walker & Co.
--Leonie. 208p. 1985. pap. 2.50 (ISBN 0-446-32835-9). Warner Bks.
Delmotte, P. H., jt. ed. see Gonsette, R. E.
Del Negro, John T. & Levenson, Harvey S. Depreciation & the Investment Tax Credit: With Tax Planning. LC 83-70021. (Illus.). 1983. Looseleaf. looseleaf 140.00 (ISBN 0-317-12894-9). Bender.
DeLo, James S. & Green, William A. Multicultural Transactions: A Workbook Focusing on Communication Between Groups. LC 80-69328. 125p. 1981. perfect bdg. 11.50 (ISBN 0-86548-030-3). R & E Pubs.
DeLoach, et al, eds. Red Blood Cells As Carriers for Drugs. (Bibliotheca Haematologica: No. 51). (Illus.). viii, 162p. 1985. 44.25 (ISBN 3-8055-3940-1). S Karger.
De Loach, Allen. Literary Assays: Portraits of Writers. 1984. 4.00 (ISBN 0-934834-44-X). White Pine.
De Loach, Allen, ed. see Mottram, Eric.
DeLoach, Charlene. A Metamorphosis: Adjustment to Severe Physical Disability. (Special Education Ser.). 320p. 1981. text ed. 26.95x (ISBN 0-07-016281-6). McGraw.
DeLoach, Charlene P. & Wilkins, Ronnie D. Independent Living: Services for the Disabled & Elderly. LC 82-21949. (Illus.). 288p. 1983. 20.00 (ISBN 0-8391-1794-9). Pro Ed.
DeLoach, Christopher. Using Your Guitar. 1980. pap. 2.95 (ISBN 0-8256-2378-2, Amsco Music). Music Sales.
DeLoach, Clarence, Jr., ed. The Faith Once Delivered. (Illus.). 170p. 1974. 6.95 (ISBN 0-88428-033-0). Parchment Pr.
DeLoach, Jane E. General Surgical Nursing. (Nursing Outline Ser.). 1979. pap. 13.25 (ISBN 0-87488-393-8). Med Exam.
DeLoach, Jim C. Digital Systems: Principles & Applications. 3rd ed. (Illus.). 176p. 1985. lab manual 14.95 (ISBN 0-13-212473-4). P-H.
DeLoach, Marva L., jt. ed. see Josey, E. J.
Deloache, Michel, jt. auth. see St. John's Episcopal Church.
Delobeau, F. The Environment of the Earth. LC 71-170338. (Astrophysics & Space Science Library: No. 28). 113p. 1972. 21.00 (ISBN 90-277-0208-X, Pub. by Reidel Holland). Kluwer Academic.
Delobel, C. & Adiba, M. Relational Database Systems. Hollett, M. L., tr. 470p. 1985. 65.00 (ISBN 0-444-87718-5, North-Holland). Elsevier.
Delobel, C. & Litwin, W., eds. Distributed Data Bases. 368p. 1980. 68.00 (ISBN 0-444-85471-1, North-Holland). Elsevier.
Deloche, Maximin. La Crise Economique Au Seizeime Siecle et la Crise Actuelle. LC 71-132525. (Research & Source Works Ser.: No. 623). 1971. Repr. of 1922 ed. lib. bdg. 16.50 (ISBN 0-8337-0831-7). B Franklin.
Delocorta. Nana. 192p. 1984. pap. 2.75 (ISBN 0-345-31267-8). Ballantine.
De Lodzia, George, jt. auth. see Wasmuth, William J.
Deloe, Jesse B. Sweeter Than Honey. pap. 4.95 (ISBN 0-88469-105-5). BMH Bks.
Deloffre, ed. see Prevost, Abbe.
Deloger, James E., jt. auth. see Gagnor, Raymond A.
Delogne, P. Leaky Feeders & Subsurface Radio Communications. (IEE Electromagnetic Waves Ser.: No. 14). 304p. 1982. 76.00 (ISBN 0-906048-77-X, EW014, Pub. by Peregrinus England). Inst Elect Eng.
Delogu, Orlando E. United Nations List of National Parks & Equivalent Reserves, 1980. (Environmental Policy & Law Papers: No. 7). 162p. 1980. pap. 8.00 (ISBN 2-88032-406-8, IUCN80, IUCN). Unipub.
Delogu, Orlands & Soell, Hermann. Fiscal Measures for Environmental Protection: Two Divergent Views. (Environmental Policy & Law Papers: NO. 11). (Illus.). 77p. 1976. pap. 10.00 (ISBN 2-88032-081-X, IUCN63, IUCN). Unipub.
De Loi, Raimon. Trails of the Troubadours. 1973. Repr. of 1926 ed. 30.00 (ISBN 0-8274-1394-7). R West.
Deloitte, Haskins & Sells. Summary Reporting of Financial Information, 2 vols, Vols. 1 & 2. Vol. 1, 1983. 8.00 (ISBN 0-317-06337-5); Vol. 2, 1984. 8.00 (ISBN 0-317-06338-3). Finan Exec.
Deloitte, Haskins, & Sells. Taxation in Europe. 60.00x (ISBN 0-686-44520-1, Pub. by Oyez Longman Pub England). State Mutual Bk.
Deloitte, Haskins & Sells & High Technology Industry Group. Tax Aspects of High Technology Operations. 500p. 1984. text ed. 65.00x (ISBN 0-471-88874-5, Pub. by Ronald Pr). Wiley.
De Lollis, Nicholas J. Adhesives: Adherends, Adhesion. LC 79-1371. 352p. 1980. lib. bdg. 29.50 (ISBN 0-88275-981-7). Krieger.
De Lolme, J. L. & Machelon, Jean-Pierre. The Constitution of England & les Idees Politiques De J.L. De Lolme: 1741-1806, 2 vols. in one. Mayer, J. P., ed. LC 78-67366. (European Political Thought Ser.). (Eng. & Fr.). 1979. Repr. of 1807 ed. lib. bdg. 50.50x (ISBN 0-405-11714-0). Ayer Co Pubs.
De Lolme, Jean L. The Rise & Progress of the English Constitution, 2 vols. Berkowitz, David S. & Thorne, Samuel E., eds. LC 77-86589. (Classics of English Legal History in the Modern Era Ser.: Vol. 82). 1334p. 1979. lib. bdg. 121.00 (ISBN 0-8240-3069-9). Garland Pub.
Delomenie, Dominique, jt. auth. see Maurice, Marc.
Delon, Floyd G., jt. auth. see Beckham, Joseph.
Delon, Floyd G., jt. auth. see Garber, Lee O.
Delon, P. J. International Health Regulations - a Practical Guide. (Also avail. in French). 1975. pap. 2.00 (ISBN 92-4-158002-X). World Health.
Delone, B. N. & Faddeev, D. K. Theory of Irrationalities of the Third Degree. LC 63-21548. (Translations of Mathematical Monographs: Vol. 10). 509p. 1978. pap. 49.00 (ISBN 0-8218-1560-1, MMONO-10). Am Math.
Delone, N. B. & Krainov, V. P. Atoms in Strong Light Fields. (Springer Series in Chemical Physics: Vol. 28). (Illus.). 350p. 1985. 49.00 (ISBN 0-387-12412-8). Springer-Verlag.
DeLone, Peter. Literature & Materials for Sightseeing. 352p. (Orig.). 1980. pap. text ed. 21.95 (ISBN 0-03-044626-0, HoltC). HR&W.
DeLone, Richard & Carnegie Council. Small Futures: Children, Inequality, & the Limits of Liberal Reform. LC 77-92536. 1979. 12.95 (ISBN 0-15-183128-9). HarBraceJ.
Delone, Richard, et al. Aspects of Twentieth Century Music. (Illus.). 541p. 1974. 29.95 (ISBN 0-13-049346-5). P-H.
De Lone, Richard P., jt. auth. see Thomson, William.
Deloney, Thomas. The Novels of Thomas Deloney. Lawlis, Merritt E., ed. LC 77-18010. (Illus.). 1978. Repr. of 1961 ed. lib. bdg. 37.50x (ISBN 0-313-20105-6, DENO). Greenwood.
Delong. History of American Buildings: California, 4 vols. Incl. New York, 8 vols; Texas, 2 vols. 1979. lib. bdg. 109.00 ea. Garland Pub.
--Medical Acronyms & Abbreviations. 276p. 1985. 10.95 (ISBN 0-87489-392-5). Med Economics.
DeLong, Charles E. The Murder of Julia Bulette: Virginia City, Nevada, 1867--with the Life & Confession of John Millian, Convicted Murderer. Jones, William R., ed. 16p. 1978. pap. 1.00 (ISBN 0-89646-044-4). Outbooks.
De Long, David G. The Architecture of Bruce Goff Buildings & Projects, 1916-1974, 2 vols. LC 76-23610. (Outstanding Dissertations in the Fine Arts - 2nd Series - American). (Illus.). 943p. 1976. Repr. Set. lib. bdg. 146.00 (ISBN 0-8240-2682-9). Garland Pub.
DeLong, David G., ed. New York, 8 vols. Incl. Vol. 1. lib. bdg. 100.00 (ISBN 0-8240-3186-5); Vol. 2. lib. bdg. 100.00 (ISBN 0-8240-3187-3); Vol. 3. lib. bdg. 100.00 (ISBN 0-8240-3188-1); Vol. 4. lib. bdg. 100.00 (ISBN 0-8240-3189-X); Vol. 5. lib. bdg. 100.00 (ISBN 0-8240-3190-3); Vol. 6. lib. bdg. 100.00 (ISBN 0-8240-3191-1); Vol. 7. lib. bdg. 100.00 (ISBN 0-8240-3192-X); Vol. 8. lib. bdg. 100.00 (ISBN 0-8240-3193-8). (Historic American Buildings). 1979. lib. bdg. 600.00 set (ISBN 0-686-70456-8). Garland Pub.
DeLong, Deanna. How to Dry Foods. LC 79-88010. (Illus.). 1979. pap. 7.95 (ISBN 0-89586-024-4). H P Bks.
Delong, Dwight M. & Freytag, Paul H. Four Genera of World Gyponinae: Gypona, Gyponana, Rugosana, & Reticana. 1964. 4.00 (ISBN 0-86727-050-0). Ohio Bio Survey.
Delong, Fred. Delong's Guide to Bicycles & Bicycling. LC 74-4133. (Illus.). 1978. pap. 12.95 (ISBN 0-8019-6686-8). Chilton.
Delong, Fred J. Aim for a Job in Drafting. LC 68-10505. (Aim High Vocational Guidance Ser.). (gr. 7 up). 1976. PLB 8.97 (ISBN 0-8239-0365-6). Rosen Group.
DeLong, Fredrick C. Laughing All the Way to the Bank: The Earning Money Formula. (Exploring Careers Ser.). 1982. lib. bdg. 8.97 (ISBN 0-8239-0547-0). Rosen Group.
DeLong, George W. Her Long Black Hair: Poetic Thoughts & Love Stories. LC 81-90306. (Illus.). 128p. (Orig.). 1981. pap. 5.00 (ISBN 0-9603414-1-2). DeLong & Assocs.
--Waterfront Living: How to Buy Real Estate on the Water. LC 79-57321. (Illus., Orig.). pap. 10.00 (ISBN 0-9603414-0-4). DeLong & Assoc.
DeLong, Howard. Profile of Mathematical Logic. (Intermediate Mathematics Geometry Topology Ser). 1970. text ed. 22.95 (ISBN 0-201-01499-8). Addison-Wesley.
DeLong, Kathy. Descendants of Benjamin & Dorcas Ames of Connecticut: 1786-1979. (Illus.). 205p. 1980. 10.95 (ISBN 0-87881-097-8). Mojave Bks.
DeLong, Lea. Nature's Forms--Nature's Forces: The Work of Alexandre Hogue. LC 84-60404. (Illus.). 216p. (Orig.). 1984. pap. 25.00 (ISBN 0-86659-005-6). SW Art Assn.
DeLong, Lea R. Nature's Forms, Nature's Forces: The Art of Alexandre Hogue. LC 84-60404. (Illus.). 221p. 1984. pap. 19.95 (ISBN 0-8061-1917-9). U of Okla Pr.
De Long, Patrick D. Art in the Humanities. 2nd ed. 1970. pap. text ed. 14.95 (ISBN 0-13-046979-3). P-H.
DeLong, Sylvia. Charting Presidential Elections. 160p. 14.00 (ISBN 0-86690-030-6, 2456-011). Am Fed Astrologers.
--Guideposts to Mystical & Mundane Interpretations. 152p. 8.50 (ISBN 0-86690-066-7, 1061-01). Am Fed Astrologers.
DeLong, Thomas A. The DeLongs of New York & Brooklyn: A Huguenot Family Portrait. LC 75-189091. (Illus.). 203p. 1972. 9.95 (ISBN 0-912980-01-X). Sasco.
--Mighty Music Box: The Golden Age of Musical Radio. LC 77-94433. (Illus.). 335p. 1980. 14.95 (ISBN 0-86533-000-X). Sasco.
--Pops: Paul Whiteman, King of Jazz. LC 83-19291. (Illus.). 352p. 1983. 17.95 (ISBN 0-8329-0264-0). New Century.
De Longchamps, Joanne. The Hungry Lions. LC 74-19783. 60p. 1975. Repr. of 1963 ed. lib. bdg. 18.75x (ISBN 0-8371-7806-1, DEHL). Greenwood.
--The Schoolhouse Poems. 1976. pap. 2.50 (ISBN 0-915596-14-8). West Coast.
--Warm Bloods, Cold Bloods. (Illus.). 44p. (Orig.). 1982. pap. text ed. 10.00 (ISBN 0-915596-25-3). West Coast.
--Wishing Animal: Poems. LC 72-115829. 1970. 7.95 (ISBN 0-8265-1157-0). Vanderbilt U Pr.
DeLonge, Deon. Techniques of Beading Earrings. Smith, Monte, ed. 76p. (Orig.). 1984. pap. 7.95 (ISBN 0-943604-03-6). Eagles View.
De Longueville, Thomas see Longueville, Thomas de.
De Looff, James L. Commuter Airlines: A Study of the History & Operational Requirements. 1979. 10.00 (ISBN 0-682-49315-5, University). Exposition Pr FL.
De Loor, G. P., ed. Radar Remote Sensing. (Remote Sensing Reviews Ser.: Vol. 1, No. 1). 185p. 1984. 47.50 (ISBN 3-7186-0132-X). Harwood Academic.
De Loore, C. W., jt. ed. see Conti, Peter S.
De Lopez, Awilda P. & Ortiz, Ernesto R. En la Calle Estabas: La Vida En una Institucion De Menores. 2nd ed. 3.75 (ISBN 0-8477-2415-8); pap. 3.40 (ISBN 0-8477-2416-6). U of PR Pr.
Delopez, Awilda Palau. Esbozo de la Historia Legal de las Instituciones y Tribunales de Menores en Puerto Rico. 3.75 (ISBN 0-8477-2417-4). U of PR Pr.
Delora, Joann S., et al. Understanding Human Sexuality. LC 79-89744. (Illus.). 1980. pap. text ed. 20.95 (ISBN 0-395-28255-1); instr's. manual 1.00 (ISBN 0-395-28256-X). HM.
--Understanding Sexual Interaction. 2nd ed. (Illus.). 672p. 1981. text ed. 25.50 (ISBN 0-395-29724-9); instr's manual 1.00 (ISBN 0-395-29725-7). HM.
DeLorean, Cristina F. & Cohen, Sherry S. Cristina Ferrare's Style: How to Have It in Every Part of Your Life. 1984. 16.95 (ISBN 0-671-46849-9). S&S.
DeLorean, Donna. Passions of the Heart. 1985. 10.95 (ISBN 0-533-06642-5). Vantage.
DeLorean, John. De Lorean. 304p. 1985. 17.95 (ISBN 0-310-37940-7, Pub. by Zondervan Bks). Zondervan.
DeLorean, John & Schwartz, Ted. DeLorean. 1985. price not set. Zondervan.
De Lorely, Augustus. The Civilization of the Computer & the Brutalization of American Culture. (Illus.). 119p. 1983. 77.85x (ISBN 0-86654-088-1). Inst Econ Finan.
De Lorenzo, David L., ed. see Gallaudet, Edward M.
DeLorenzo, Lorisa M., jt. auth. see DeLorenzo, Robert J.
DeLorenzo, Robert J. & DeLorenzo, Lorisa M. Total Child Care: From Birth to Age Five. LC 78-55847. (Illus.). 1129p. 1982. 29.95 (ISBN 0-385-12593-3). Doubleday.
De Lorenzo, Ronald. Problem Solving in General Chemistry. 496p. 1981. pap. text ed. 12.95 (ISBN 0-669-02924-6). Heath.
Deloria, D. J., jt. auth. see Weikart, D. P.
Deloria, Ella. Dakota Texts. LC 73-3550. (American Ethnological Society. Publications: No. 14). Repr. of 1932 ed. 34.50 (ISBN 0-404-58164-1). AMS Pr.
Deloria, Ella, jt. auth. see Boas, Franz.
Deloria, S., jt. auth. see Weikart, D. P.
Deloria, Vine, Jr. Behind the Trail of Broken Treaties: An Indian Declaration of Independence. 3296p. 1985. pap. 9.95 (ISBN 0-292-70754-1). U of Tex Pr.
--Custer Died for Your Sins. (YA) 1970. pap. 3.50 (ISBN 0-380-00250-7, 64477-0). Avon.
--God Is Red. 1983. pap. 3.95 (ISBN 0-440-33044-0, LE). Dell.
--The Indian Affair. (Orig.). 1974. pap. 2.50 (ISBN 0-377-00022-1). Friend Pr.
--The Metaphysics of Modern Existence. LC 76-8708. (Native American Publishing Program Ser.). 1978. 8.95i (ISBN 0-06-450250-3, HarpR). Har-Row.
--A Sender of Words: Essays in Memory of John G. Neihardt. LC 84-9054. 196p. 1984. 15.95 (ISBN 0-935704-22-1). Howe Brothers.
Deloria, Vine, Jr. & Lytle, Clifford M. American Indians, American Justice. 278p. 1983. text ed. 19.95x (ISBN 0-292-73833-1); pap. 9.95 (ISBN 0-292-73834-X). U of Tex Pr.
--The Nations Within: The Past & Future of American Indian Sovereignity. LC 84-42663. 336p. 1984. pap. 11.95 (ISBN 0-394-72566-2). Pantheon.
Deloria, Vine, Jr., ed. American Indian Policy in the Twentieth Century. LC 85-1057. 272p. 1985. 16.95 (ISBN 0-8061-1897-0). U of Okla Pr.
Deloria, Vine, Jr., jt. ed. see Cadwalader, Sandra L.
Delorit, Richard, et al. Crop Production. 4th ed. 1973. text ed. 31.52 (ISBN 0-13-194761-3). P-H.
DeLorm, R. T. & Kersten, L. CALCOMP Programming for Digital Plotters. 234p. 1976. pap. 11.95x (ISBN 0-8032-6550-6). U of Nebr Pr.
DeLorme & Ekelund. Macroeconomics. 1983. 27.95 (ISBN 0-256-02685-8). Business Pubns.
Delorme, David, jt. auth. see Vanderweide, Harry.
DeLorme, David, jt. auth. see Vanderweide, Harry.
DeLorme, David, ed. The Maine Atlas & Gazetteer. rev. ed. (Atlas & Gazetteer Ser.). (Illus.). 96p. 1984. pap. 9.95 (ISBN 0-89933-035-5). DeLorme Pub.
--The New Hampshire Atlas & Gazetteer. rev. ed. (Atlas & Gazetteer Ser.). (Illus.). 88p. 1983. pap. 9.95 (ISBN 0-89933-004-5). DeLorme Pub.
--The Vermont Atlas & Gazetteer. rev. ed. (Atlas & Gazetteer Ser.). (Illus.). 88p. (Orig.). 1983. pap. 9.95 (ISBN 0-89933-005-3). DeLorme Pub.
DeLorme Publishing Company Staff. Bicycling: A Cyclist's Guide to Maine's Scenic Beauty. (Maine Geographic Ser.). (Illus.). 48p. (Orig.). 1983. pap. 2.95 (ISBN 0-89933-066-5). DeLorme Pub.
--Wildlife Signatures: A Guide to the Identification of Tracks & Scat. Abridged ed. (Maine Geographic Ser.). (Illus.). 48p. 1983. pap. 2.95 (ISBN 0-89933-064-9). DeLorme Pub.
Delorme, Robert L. Latin America: A Social Science Bibliography, 1979-1983. 225p. 1984. lib. bdg. 45.00 (ISBN 0-87436-394-2). ABC-Clio.

--Latin America: Social Science Information Sources, 1967-1979. LC 80-327. 262p. 1981. lib. bdg. 32.75 (ISBN 0-87436-292-X). ABC-Clio.

De Lorrabeiti, Michael. The Borribles Go for Broke. 288p. 1984. pap. 2.50 (ISBN 0-441-07024-8, Pub. by Ace Science Fiction). Ace Bks.

De Lorre, C. & Willis, A., eds. Wolf-Rayet Stars: Observations, Physics, Evolution. 1982. 69.50 (ISBN 90-277-1469-X, Pub. by Reidel Holland); pap. 34.50 (ISBN 90-277-1470-3). Kluwer Academic.

De Lorris, Guillaume. Roman de la Rose. Nichols, Stephen G., Jr., ed. LC 67-25114. (Medieval French Literature Ser). (Orig., Fr.,.). 1967. pap. text ed. 6.95x (ISBN 0-89197-496-2). Irvington.

De Lorris, Guillaume & De Meun, Jean. Roman De La Rose, 5 Vols. Langlois, E., ed. 1914-24. Set. 190.00 (ISBN 0-384-51882-6); Set. pap. 160.00 (ISBN 0-384-51883-4). Johnson Repr.

--Romance of the Rose. Robbins, Harry W., tr. 1962. pap. 10.50 (ISBN 0-525-47090-5, 01019-310). Dutton.

--The Romance of the Rose. Dahlberg, Charles, tr. from Fr. LC 83-40017. Orig. Title: Roman de la Rose. (Illus.). 468p. 1983. pap. 16.00x (ISBN 0-87451-267-0). U Pr of New Eng.

De Lorris, Guillaume see Lorris, Guillaume De & Meur, Jean De.

Delort, jt. auth. see De La Ronciere.

De los Reyes, M. Philomene. The Biblical Theme in Modern Drama. 189p. 1979. text ed. 14.00x (ISBN 0-8248-0633-6, Pub. by U of Philippines Pr); pap. text ed. 8.50x (ISBN 0-8248-0644-1, Pub. by U of Philippines Pr). UH Pr.

De Lott, O. I., jt. auth. see Wysong, E. M.

De Loubriel, Estela C. The Formation of the Puerto Rican People: Catalonians, Balearic Islanders & Valencianos. (Puerto Rico Ser.). 1979. lib. bdg. 59.95 (ISBN 0-8490-2920-1). Gordon Pr.

De Lourdes Cabrera, Yvette. Decima in Puerto Rico: Historical Survey & Analysis of the Ten Line Stanza Composition As an Expression of the Puerto Rican Spirit. (Puerto Rico Ser.). 1979. lib. bdg. 59.95 (ISBN 0-8490-2905-8). Gordon Pr.

De Loyola, Ignatius see St. Ignatius.

De Loyola Brandao, Ignacio. Zero. Watson, Ellen, tr. 272p. 1983. pap. 4.50 (ISBN 0-380-84533-4, 84533, Bard). Avon.

DeLozier, James E. & Gagnon, Raymond O. National Ambulatory Medical Care Survey 1973 Summary, U. S. May 1973 - April 1974. Stevenson, Taloria, ed. LC 75-35700. (Series 13: No. 21). 73p. 1976. pap. text ed. 1.75 (ISBN 0-8406-0057-7). Natl Ctr Health Stats.

DeLozier, M. Wayne. The Marketing Communications Process. (Illus.). 1976. text ed. 33.95 (ISBN 0-07-016302-2). McGraw.

DeLozier, M. Wayne & Woodside, Arch G. Marketing Management: Strategies & Cases. (Marketing & Management Ser.). 1978. text ed. 28.95 (ISBN 0-675-08417-2). Merrill.

DeLozier, M. Wayne, jt. auth. see Lewison, Dale.

DeLozier, M. Wayne, et al. Experiential Learning Exercises in Marketing. 1977. pap. text ed. 16.55x (ISBN 0-673-16085-8). Scott F.

DeLozier, Wayne. Consumer Behavior Dynamics: A Casebook. (Business Ser.). 1977. text ed. 15.95 (ISBN 0-675-08504-7). Additional supplements may be obtained from publisher. Merrill.

Delp, Edward J., jt. ed. see Buda, Andrew J.

Delp, Frank. Aircraft Governors. (Aviation Technician Training Course Ser.). 50p. (Orig.). 1982. pap. text ed. 4.95 (ISBN 0-89100-156-5, EA-AGV). Aviation Maintenance.

--Aircraft Propellers & Controls. (Aviation Technician Training Course Ser.). (Illus.). 156p. 1979. pap. text ed. 6.95 (ISBN 0-89100-097-6, EA-APC). Aviation Maintenance.

--Commercial Pilot Question Book Including Answers, Explanations, & References. rev. ed. (Pilot Training Ser.). 475p. 1985. pap. text ed. 12.95 (ISBN 0-89100-261-8, EA-FAA-T-8080-2C). Aviation Maintenance.

--Flight Instructor Question Book Including Answers, Explanations, & References. rev. ed. (Pilot Training Ser.). 300p. 1985. pap. text ed. 10.95 (ISBN 0-89100-263-4, EA-FAA-T-8080-3C). Aviation Maintenance.

Delp, Jeanne L. & Martinson, Ruth A. A Handbook for Parents of Gifted & Talented (Also Helpful for Educators) 102p. 5.75 (ISBN 0-318-02117-X); excerpt (13 pg.) 1.10 (ISBN 0-318-02118-8). NSLTIGT.

--A Handbook for Parents of Gifted & Talented (Also Helpful for Educators) 102p. 5.25 (ISBN 0-318-16007-2, 6); excerpt 0.95 (ISBN 0-318-16008-0). NSLTIGT.

Delp, Mahlon H. & Manning, Robert T. Major's Physical Diagnosis: An Introduction to the Clinical Process. 9th ed. (Illus.). 650p. 1981. text ed. 22.50 (ISBN 0-7216-3002-2). Saunders.

Delp, Paul S. The Gentle Way. LC 76-51006. 1977. 8.50 (ISBN 0-8022-2198-X). Philos Lib.

--The Life of Mind. LC 82-61238. (Illus.). 125p. (Orig., PB). 1983. pap. 10.00 (ISBN 0-935356-05-3). Mills Pub Co.

Delp, Peter. Systems Tools for Project Planning. LC 77-7588. 1976. pap. text ed. 15.00 (ISBN 0-89249-021-7). Intl Development.

Delp, Robert. Digital Electronics Through Experimentation. 2nd ed. (Illus.). 98p. (Orig.). 1984. pap. text ed. 6.00x (ISBN 0-911908-11-0). Tech Ed Pr.

Delpar, Helen. The Discoverers: An Encyclopedia of Explorers & Exploration. LC 79-9259. (Illus.). 1979. 49.95 (ISBN 0-07-016264-6). McGraw.

--Red Against Blue: The Liberal Party & Colombian Politics, 1863-1899. LC 79-19081. (Illus.). 320p. 1981. text ed. 23.50 (ISBN 0-8173-0030-9). U of Ala Pr.

Del Pazzo, Bob, ed. Radio Contacts, 1984. 149.00 (ISBN 0-935224-19-X). Larimi Comm.

--Television Contacts, 1984. 144.00 (ISBN 0-935224-20-3). Larimi Comm.

--TV News, 1984. 99.00 (ISBN 0-935224-21-1). Larimi Comm.

Delpech, Henri M. La Tactique au XIII siecle, 2 vols. LC 78-63493. Repr. of 1886 ed. Set. 110.00 (ISBN 0-404-17140-0). AMS Pr.

Delpel, Jean J. Visages de la France. (Illus.). 1983. 29.95 (ISBN 2-03-523103-5, 3808). Larousse.

Delpel, Jean-Jacques. Landmarks of France. Orig. Title: Visages de la France. (Illus.). 160p. (English.). 1983. 29.95 (ISBN 2-03-523104-3, 8083). Larousse.

Delph, Edward W. The Silent Community: Public Homosexual Encounters. LC 78-629. (Sociological Observations Ser.: No. 3). pap. 46.50 (ISBN 0-317-08749-5, 2021886). Bks Demand UMI.

Delph, John & Delph, Shirley. Factory Decoys of Mason, Stevens, Dodge & Peterson. LC 80-52025. (Illus.). 168p. 35.00 (ISBN 0-916838-33-1). Schiffer.

Delph, John, jt. auth. see Delph, Shirley.

Delph, Shirley & Delph, John. New England Decoys. LC 81-51445. (Illus.). 159p. 1981. 35.00 (ISBN 0-916838-54-4). Schiffer.

Delph, Shirley, jt. auth. see Delph, John.

Delphian School Faculty. Learning Book. (Basics of Education Ser.: No. 2). (Illus.). 140p. 1983. pap. 10.00 (ISBN 0-89739-004-0). Heron Bks.

Delphos, William A. Washington's Best Kept Secrets: A U. S. Government Guide to International Business. LC 83-16671. 270p. 1983. 50.00x (ISBN 0-471-87944-4). Wiley.

Delphy, Christine. Close to Home: A Materialist Analysis of Women's Oppression. Leonard, Diana, ed. & tr. from Fr. LC 84-40285. 240p. 1984. lib. bdg. 18.00x (ISBN 0-87023-453-6); pap. 8.95 (ISBN 0-87023-454-4). U of Mass Pr.

Del Polito, Carolyn M. & Barresi, Josephine G., eds. Alliances in Health & Education: Serving Youngsters with Special Needs. 236p. 1982. pap. 27.95 (ISBN 0-317-12905-8). Ramsco Pub.

Delporte, pseud. Romeo & Smurfette & Twelve Other Smurfy Stories. LC 82-60258. (Smurf Adventures Ser.). (Illus.). 48p. (gr. 4-7). 1983. 2.95 (ISBN 0-394-85618-X). Random.

Del Portillo, Alvaro see Portillo, Alvaro del.

Del Porto, Heriberto. La Decadencia de la Familia Aristocrativa y Su Reflejo en la Novela Espanola Moderna. LC 81-69539. (Coleccion Polymita Ser.). 150p. (Orig., Span.). 1984. pap. 12.95 (ISBN 0-89729-302-9). Ediciones.

Del Pozo, Cal. The Back Book: The Complete Health & Exercise Program to Cure Your Aching Back. (Illus.). 1983. pap. 6.95 (ISBN 0-87795-515-8, Pub. by Priam); 10-copy prepack 69.50 (ISBN 0-87795-567-0). Arbor Hse.

--Twenty Days to a Trimmer Torso. 64p. (Orig.). pap. 3.50 (ISBN 0-346-12588-X). Cornerstone.

Del Prado, Oscar Nunez see Nunez Del Prado, Oscar & Whyte, William F.

Del Punta, Francesco, ed. Guillelmi de Ockham: Opera Philosophica, Vol. 3. 1979. 29.00 (ISBN 0-686-27931-X). Franciscan Inst.

Del Rae, Dolores. How to Get a Nightclub Gig: A Singer's Guide. 150p. (Orig.). 1985. pap. 9.95 (ISBN 0-930867-04-1). S O S Pubs.

Del Ray, Lester, ed. see Coblentz, Stanton A.

Del Ray, Lester, ed. see Cummings, Ray.

Del Ray, Lester, ed. see Fletcher, George U.

Del Ray, Lester, ed. see Fort, Charles.

Del Ray, Lester, ed. see Jones, Neil R.

Del Ray, Lester, ed. see Kuttner, Henry.

Del Ray, Lester, ed. see Lafferty, R. A.

Del Ray, Lester, ed. see Piper, H. Beam.

Del Ray, Lester, ed. see Pohl, Frederick & Kornbluth, C. M.

Del Ray, Lester, ed. see Smith, Cordwainer.

Del Ray, Lester, ed. see Stasheff, Christopher.

Del Ray, Lester, ed. see Taine, John.

Del Re, G., et al. Electronic States of Molecules & Atom Clusters. (Lecture Notes in Chemistry: Vol. 13). (Illus.). 180p. 1980. pap. 21.00 (ISBN 0-387-09738-4). Springer-Verlag.

Del Regato, Juan A. & Spjut, Harlan J. Ackerman & Del Ragato's Cancer: Diagnosis, Treatment, & Prognosis. 5th ed. LC 76-26170. (Illus.). 1014p. 1977. pap. 84.95 (ISBN 0-8016-1250-0). Mosby.

Del Rey, Judy L., ed. Stellar Science Fiction Stories, No. 7. 224p. (Orig.). 1981. pap. 2.50 (ISBN 0-345-29473-4, Del Rey). Ballantine.

Del Rey, Judy L., ed. see Heinlein, Robert A.

Del Rey, Judy-Lynn, ed. Stellar Science Fiction Stories, No. 6. 192p. (Orig.). 1981. pap. 2.25 (ISBN 0-345-28969-2, Del Rey). Ballantine.

Del Rey, Lester. Attack from Atlantis. 176p. 1982. pap. 1.95 (ISBN 0-345-30501-9, Del Rey). Ballantine.

--The Best of Lester Del Rey. (A Del Rey Bk.). 384p. 1986. pap. 3.95 (ISBN 0-345-32933-3). Ballantine.

--The Eleventh Commandment. 192p. 1981. pap. 2.50 (ISBN 0-345-29641-9, Del Rey). Ballantine.

--The Fantastic Art of Boris Vallejo. 1981. 12.95 (ISBN 0-345-27521-7, Del Rey). Ballantine.

--Moon of Mutiny. 192p. 1982. pap. 1.95 (ISBN 0-345-30606-6, Del Rey). Ballantine.

--The Mysterious Planet. 1982. pap. 1.95 (ISBN 0-345-30418-7, Del Rey). Ballantine.

--Outpost of Jupiter. 1982. pap. 1.95 (ISBN 0-345-30505-1, Del Rey). Ballantine.

--Police Your Planet. 1981. pap. 2.25 (ISBN 0-345-29858-6, Del Rey). Ballantine.

--Rocket Jockey. 1982. pap. 1.95 (ISBN 0-345-30655-4, Del Rey). Ballantine.

--Science Fiction: Nineteen Twenty-Six to Nineteen Seventy-Six. (Library of Science Fiction). 1975. lib. bdg. 29.00 (ISBN 0-8240-1446-4). Garland Pub.

Del Rey, Lester, ed. The Best of C. L. Moore. LC 77-5293. 1977. Repr. of 1976 ed. 9.95 (ISBN 0-8008-0722-7). Taplinger.

Del Rey, Lester, ed. see Bester, Alfred.

Del Rey, Lester, ed. see Capek, Karel.

Del Rey, Lester, ed. see Coblentz, Stanton A.

Del Rey, Lester, ed. see Farmer, Philip J.

Del Rey, Lester, ed. see Fort, Charles.

Del Rey, Lester, ed. see Gail, Otto W.

Del Rey, Lester, ed. see Hubbard, L. Ron.

Del Rey, Lester, ed. see Kuttner, Henry.

Del Rey, Lester, ed. see LeGuin, Ursula K.

Del Rey, Lester, ed. see Pangborn, Edgar.

Del Rey, Lester, ed. see Piper, H. Beam.

Del Rey, Lester, ed. see Smith, Edward E.

Del Rey, Lester, ed. see Smith, Edward E. & Garby, Lee H.

Del Rey, Lester, ed. see Smith, George O.

Del Rey, Lester, ed. see Stapledon, Olaf.

Del Rey, Lester, ed. see Van Vogt, A. E.

Del Rey, Lester, ed. see Zelazny, Roger.

Del Rio, Amelia A. Del Yunque a los Pirineos. (Span.). 1982. pap. 8.00 (ISBN 84-499-5836-9). Edit Mensaje.

--Puertorriquenos en Nueva York. (Span.). 1970. pap. 5.50 (ISBN 0-317-02313-6). Edit Mensaje.

Del Rio, Amelia A., jt. auth. see Del Rio, Angel.

Del Rio, Amelia A., ed. Flores del Romancero, II. LC 73-93965. 202p. (Span.). 1983. pap. 5.50 (ISBN 0-8477-3502-8). U of PR Pr.

Del Rio, Angel. Torquemada En la Hoguera, De Benito Perez Galdos. xlviii, 131p. (Sp.). bulk 0.80 (ISBN 0-318-14310-0). Hispanic Inst.

Del Rio, Angel & Bernadete, M. J. El Concepto contemporaneo de Espana: Antologia De Ensayos. 737p. 5.25 (ISBN 0-318-14250-3). Hispanic Inst.

Del Rio, Angel & Del Rio, Amelia A. Antologia General de La Literatura Espanola. (Span.). 1982. 19.95 (ISBN 0-86515-001-X). Edit Mensaje.

Del Rio, Angel, ed. Responsible Freedom in the Americas. Repr. of 1955 ed. lib. bdg. 27.75x (ISBN 0-8371-0199-9, RIFA). Greenwood.

Del Rio, Carmen D. see Rio, Carmen D.

Del Rio, Eduardo, ed. see RIUS.

Delrio, Giovanni & Brachet, J., eds. Steroids & Their Mechanism of Action in Non Mammalian Vertebrates. 239p. 1980. text ed. 35.50 (ISBN 0-89004-487-2). Raven.

Del Rio, Ignacio. A Guide to the Archivo Franciscano of the National Library of Mexico. (Miscellaneous Ser.). 1975. 20.00 (ISBN 0-88382-257-1). AAFH.

Del Rosario, Pilar Barbosa see Barbosa del Rosario, Pilar.

Del Rosario Marquez, Nieves. Raices y Alas (Poesias Para Ninos y Jovenes) LC 81-65415. (Coleccion Espejo De Paciencia). (Illus., Orig.). 1981. pap. 5.00 (ISBN 0-89729-289-8). Ediciones.

--Una Isla, la Mas Bella. LC 81-65414. (Coleccion Espejo De Paciencia Ser.). 62p. (Orig.). 1981. pap. 4.50 (ISBN 0-89729-288-X). Ediciones.

Del Russo, Luihi. International Protection of Human Rights. 1970. 14.00 (ISBN 0-685-41584-8). Lerner Law.

De L. Ryals, Clyde see Ryals, Clyde de L.

Delsarte, F. Delsarte: System of Oratory. 14.95x (ISBN 0-685-21930-5). Wehman.

Del Sesto, Steven L. Science, Politics, & Controversy: Civilian Nuclear Power in the United States 1946-1974. (Special Studies in Sci., Tech., & Pub. Policy). 260p. 1981. 29.50x (ISBN 0-89158-566-4); pap. text ed. 13.50x (ISBN 0-86531-255-9). Westview.

Delsol, Paula. Chinese Astrology. 1983. pap. 3.50 (ISBN 0-446-30831-5). Warner Bks.

Delson, Donn. The Dictionary of Marketing & Related Terms in the Motion Picture Industry. LC 79-67865. (Entertainment Communication Ser.: Vol. 1). 70p. (Orig.). 1979. pap. text ed. 7.95 (ISBN 0-9603574-0-8). Bradson.

Delson, Donn & Hurst, Walter E. Delson's Dictionary of Radio & Record Industry Terms. Posner, Neil, ed. LC 80-24486. (Entertainment Communication Ser.: Vol. 2). 112p. (Orig.). 1981. pap. 9.95 (ISBN 0-9603574-2-4). Bradson.

Delson, Donn & Michalove, Ed. Delson's Dictionary of Cable, Video & Satellite Terms. Posner, Neil, ed. LC 82-17767. (Entertainment Communications Ser.: Vol. 3). (Orig.). 1982. pap. 6.95 (ISBN 0-9603574-3-2, A-4). Bradson.

Delson, Eric. Ancestors. cancelled. A R Liss.

--Ancestors: The Hard Evidence. 378p. 1985. 49.50 (ISBN 0-8451-0249-4). A R Liss.

Delson, Eric, jt. auth. see Szalay, Frederick S.

Delson, J. K., jt. auth. see Slonim, M. A.

Delson, Paula. Chinese Astrology. (Illus.). 248p. 1982. Repr. 11.95 (ISBN 0-88254-700-3). Hippocrene Bks.

Delson, Roberta M. New Towns for Colonial Brazil: Spatial & Social Planning the 18th Century. LC 79-9347. (Dellplain Latin American Studies Ser.: No. 2). pap. 57.00 (ISBN 0-317-28278-6, 2022596). Bks Demand UMI.

--Readings in Caribbean History & Economics: An Introduction to the Region. (Caribbean Studies). 360p. 1981. 69.50 (ISBN 0-677-05280-4). Gordon.

Delteil, Loys, ed. Le Peintre-Graveur Illustre, 32 vols, Vols. 1-16. Incl. Vol. 1. J. F. Millet, Th. Rousseau, Jules Dupre, J. Barthold Jongkind. 20.00 (ISBN 0-306-78501-3); Vol. 2. Charles Meryon. 35.00 (ISBN 0-306-78502-1); Vol. 3. J. A. D. Ingres & Eugene Delacroix. 60.00 (ISBN 0-306-78503-X); Vol. 4. Anders Zorn. 45.00 (ISBN 0-306-78504-8); Vol. 5. C. Corot. 35.00 (ISBN 0-306-78505-6); Vol. 6. Rude, Barye, Carpeaux, Rodin. 20.00 (ISBN 0-306-78506-4); Vol. 7. Paul Huet. 27.50 (ISBN 0-306-78507-2); Vol. 8. Eugene Carriere. 25.00 (ISBN 0-306-78508-0); Vol. 9. Edgar Degas. 35.00 (ISBN 0-306-78509-9); Vols. 10 & 11. Toulouse-Lautrec. Set. 140.00 (ISBN 0-685-24299-4); Vol. 10. 70.00 ea. (ISBN 0-306-78510-2). Vol. 11 (ISBN 0-306-78511-0); Vol. 12. Gustave Leheutre. 32.50 (ISBN 0-306-78512-9); Vol. 13. Charles-Francois Daubigny. 40.00 (ISBN 0-306-78513-7); Francisco Goya. Vol. 14. 79.50 (ISBN 0-306-78514-5); Vol. 15. o. p. 70.00 (ISBN 0-306-78515-3); Vol. 16. Jean-Francois Raffaeli. 35.00 (ISBN 0-306-78516-1). LC 68-27720. (Graphic Art Ser). 1969. Da Capo.

--Le Peintre-Graveur Illustre, 32 vols, Vols. 17-32. Incl. Vol. 17. Camille Pissaro, Alfred Sisley, Auguste Renoir. 75.00 (ISBN 0-306-78517-X); Vol. 18. Theodore Gericault. 35.00 (ISBN 0-306-78518-8); Vol. 19. Henri Leys, Henri de Braekeleer, James Ensor. 59.50 (ISBN 0-306-78519-6); Vols. 20-29. Honore Daumier. Set. 595.00 (ISBN 0-306-78520-X); Vol. 30. Albert Besnard. 49.50 (ISBN 0-306-78530-7); Vol. 31. Jean Frelaut. lib. bdg. 55.00 (ISBN 0-306-78531-5); Vol. 32. Appendix. Wechsler, Herman J. 30.00 (ISBN 0-306-78532-3). LC 68-27720. (Graphic Art Ser). Da Capo.

Delton, Jina. Two Blocks Down. 1982. pap. 1.50 (ISBN 0-451-11477-9, AW1477, Sig Vista). NAL.

Delton, Judy. Angel in Charge. (Illus.). 160p. (gr. 2-5). 1985. 11.95 (ISBN 0-395-37488-X). HM.

--Back Yard Angel. (Illus.). 112p. (gr. 2-5). 1983. 8.95 (ISBN 0-395-33883-2). HM.

--Back Yard Angel. (Star Challenge Ser.). (Illus.). 112p. (gr. 3 up). 1984. pap. 2.25 (ISBN 0-440-40445-2, YB). Dell.

--Bear & Duck on the Run. Tucker, Kathleen, ed. LC 83-25987. (Just for Fun Bks.). (Illus.). 32p. (ps-3). 1984. PLB 10.25 (ISBN 0-8075-0594-3). A Whitman.

--A Birthday Bike for Brimhall. LC 83-21025. (Carolrhoda On My Own Bks.). (Illus.). 56p. (gr. k-4). 1985. PLB 8.95 (ISBN 0-87614-256-0). Carolrhoda Bks.

--Brimhall Turns Detective. LC 82-9582. (Carolrhoda On My Own Bks). (Illus.). 48p. (gr. k-3). 1983. PLB 8.95g (ISBN 0-87614-203-X). Carolrhoda Bks.

--Duck Goes Fishing. Fay, Ann, ed. LC 83-17116. (Just for Fun Bks.). (Illus.). 32p. (ps-3). 1983. PLB 10.25 (ISBN 0-8075-1722-4). A Whitman.

--The Elephant in Duck's Garden. (Illus.). 32p. (gr. k-3). 1985. 10.25 (ISBN 0-8075-1959-6). A Whitman.

--The Goose Who Wrote a Book. LC 81-15475. (Carolrhoda on My Own Bks.). (Illus.). 40p. (gr. k-3). 1982. PLB 8.95g (ISBN 0-87614-179-3). Carolrhoda Bks.

--Groundhog's Day at the Doctor. LC 80-20327. (Illus.). 48p. (ps-3). 1981. 5.95 (ISBN 0-8193-1041-7); PLB 5.95 (ISBN 0-8193-1042-5). Parents.

--I Never Win! LC 80-27618. (A Carolrhoda on My Own Bk). (Illus.). 32p. (gr. k-3). 1981. PLB 8.95g (ISBN 0-87614-139-4). Carolrhoda Bks.

--I'll Never Love Anything Ever Again: Concept Bks. Fay, Ann, ed. (Illus.). 32p. (ps-3). 1985. PLB 10.25 (ISBN 0-8075-3521-4). A Whitman.

--I'm Telling You Now. LC 82-17714. (Illus.). 32p. (ps-k). 1983. 9.95 (ISBN 0-525-44037-2, 0966-290). Dutton.

--I'm Telling You Now. Durell, Ann, ed. LC 82-17714. (Unicorn Paperbacks Ser.). (Illus.). 32p. (ps-k). 1985. pap. 3.95 (ISBN 0-525-44221-9). Dutton.

--It Happened on Thursday. Pacini, Kathy, ed. LC 77-19086. (Concept Bks.). (Illus.). (gr. 1-3). 1978. PLB 10.25 (ISBN 0-8075-3669-5). A Whitman.

--Kitty in High School. LC 84-523. 128p. (gr. 2-5). 1984. 10.95 (ISBN 0-395-35334-3, 5-84405). HM.

--Kitty in High School. (YA) 1984. 10.95 (ISBN 0-317-07658-2). HM.

--Kitty in the Middle. 136p. (gr. k-6). 1980. pap. 1.50 (ISBN 0-440-44437-3, YB). Dell.

--Kitty in the Middle. (Illus.). (gr. 2-5). 1979. 6.95 (ISBN 0-395-28004-4). HM.

--Kitty in the Summer. 160p. (gr. 3-7). 1982. pap. 2.50 (ISBN 0-440-44495-0, YB). Dell.

--Kitty in the Summer. (Illus.). (gr. 2-5). 1980. 8.95 (ISBN 0-395-29456-8). HM.

--Lee Henry's Best Friend. Fay, Ann, ed. LC 79-16902. (Concept Bk.: Level I). (Illus.). (gr. k-3). 1980. PLB 10.25 (ISBN 0-8075-4417-5). A Whitman.

--My Mom Hates Me in January. LC 77-5749. (Concept Books). (Illus.). (gr. 1-3). 1977. PLB 10.25 (ISBN 0-8075-5356-5). A Whitman.

--My Mother Lost Her Job Today. Fay, Ann, ed. LC 80-19067. (Concept Bks.). (Illus.). 32p. (gr. k-3). 1980. PLB 10.25 (ISBN 0-8075-5359-X). A Whitman.

--Near Occasion of Sin. LC 84-4597. 160p. (gr. 7 up). 1984. 12.95 (ISBN 0-15-256738-0, HJ). HarBraceJ.

--The New Girl at School. LC 79-11409. (Illus.). (gr. k-3). 1979. 9.95 (ISBN 0-525-35780-7, 0966-290). Dutton.

--On a Picnic. LC 78-1240. (Illus.). 64p. (gr. k-3). 1979. PLB 6.95a (ISBN 0-385-12945-9). Doubleday.

--Only Jody. (Illus.). (gr. 2-5). 1982. 7.95 (ISBN 0-395-32080-1). HM.

--Only Jody. (Illus.). 112p. (gr. 2-6). pap. 2.25 (ISBN 0-440-46678-4, YB). Dell.

--A Pet for Duck & Bear. Fay, Ann, ed. LC 82-1932. (Illus.). 32p. (gr. k-3). 1982. PLB 10.25 (ISBN 0-8075-6522-9). A Whitman.

--Rabbit's New Rug. LC 79-16639. (Illus.). 40p. (ps-3). 1980. 5.95 (ISBN 0-8193-1009-3); PLB 5.95 (ISBN 0-8193-1010-7). Parents.

--The Twenty-Nine Most Common Writing Mistakes & How to Avoid Them. LC 84-27117. (Writer's Basic Bookshelf Ser.). 73p. 1985. 9.95 (ISBN 0-89879-172-3). Writers Digest.

--Walk on a Snowy Night. LC 81-48660. (Illus.). 32p. (gr. k-3). 1982. PLB 11.89. HarpJ.

Delton, Judy & Knox-Wagner, Elaine. The Best Mom in the World. Pacini, Kathy, ed. LC 78-27238. (Concept Bk.: Level I). (Illus.). (gr. k-2). 1979. PLB 10.25 (ISBN 0-8075-0665-6). A Whitman.

Delton, Julie. My Uncle Nikos. LC 81-43317. (Illus.). 32p. (gr. 1-4). 1983. 10.53i (ISBN 0-690-04164-0); PLB 10.89g (ISBN 0-690-04165-9). Crowell Jr Bks.

Del Toro, Josefina. A Bibliography of the Collective Biography of Spanish America. 1976. lib. bdg. 59.95 (ISBN 0-87968-741-X). Gordon Pr.

Del Toro, V. Electromechanical Devices for Energy Conversion & Control Systems. 1968. ref. ed. 39.95 (ISBN 0-13-250068-X). P-H.

Del Toro, Vincent. Electric Machines & Power Systems. (Illus.). 720p. 1985. text ed. 41.95 (ISBN 0-13-248709-8). P-H.

--Electrical Engineering Fundamentals. (Illus.). 832p. 1972. ref. ed. 36.95 (ISBN 0-13-247056-X). P-H.

--Electrical Engineering Fundamentals. 2nd ed. (Illus.). 896p. 1986. text ed. 39.95 (ISBN 0-13-247131-0). P-H.

Del Tredici, Peter. A Giant among the Dwarfs: The Mystery of Sargent's Weeping Hemlock. (Illus.). 109p. 1983. 15.00x (ISBN 0-913728-34-9). Theophrastus.

Del Tredici, Robert. The People of Three Mile Island. LC 80-13558. (Illus.). 128p. (Orig.). 1980. pap. 7.95 (ISBN 0-87156-237-5). Sierra.

Delu, Christian. French Provincial Cuisine. rev. ed. LC 81-14861. (Illus.). 200p. 1981. 17.95 (ISBN 0-8120-5436-9). Barron.

De Lubac, Henri. A Brief Catechesis on Nature & Grace. Arnandez, Richard, tr. from Fr. LC 83-82108. 308p. (Orig.). 1984. pap. 10.95 (ISBN 0-89870-035-3). Ignatius Pr.

De Lubac, Henry. The Un-Marxian Socialist: A Study of Proudhon. 1978. Repr. of 1948 ed. lib. bdg. 20.50x (ISBN 0-374-95138-1). Octagon.

De Lubicz, Isha S. The Opening of the Way. Gleadow, Rupert, tr. LC 81-782. 256p. 1981. pap. 8.95 (ISBN 0-89281-015-7). Inner Tradit.

De Lubicz, Isha Schwaller see Schwaller de Lubicz, Isha.

De Lubicz, R. A. Schwaller see Schwaller de Lubicz, R. A.

De Lubicz Milosz, Oscar V. The Noble Traveller: The Life & Selected Writings of Oscar V. de Lubicz Milosz. Gascoyne, David, et al, trs. from Fr. LC 84-25029. (Illus.). 504p. (Orig.). 1985. 24.95 (ISBN 0-89281-066-1, Dist. by Inner Tradit); pap. 14.95 (ISBN 0-89281-064-5). Lindisfarne Pr.

Deluc, Yves & Ruck, Heribert. Prisunic. LC 82-12756. (Illus.). 48p. (Fr.). (gr. 7-12). 1982. pap. text ed. 2.35 (ISBN 0-88436-905-6, 40287); pap. text ed. 12.00 cassette. EMC.

De Luca, Anthony. Freud & Future Religious Experience. LC 75-3782. 290p. 1976. 12.50 (ISBN 0-8022-2173-4). Philos Lib.

De Luca, Anthony J. Freud & Future Religious Experience. (Quality Paperback Ser.: No. 330). 263p. 1977. pap. 4.95 (ISBN 0-8226-0330-6). Littlefield.

Deluca, Anthony R. Great Power Rivalry at the Turkish Straits: The Montreux Conference & Convention of 1936. (East European Monographs: No. 77). 216p. 1981. 20.00x (ISBN 0-914710-71-0). East Eur Quarterly.

--Personality, Power, & Politics: The Historical Significance of Napoleon, Bismark, Lenin, & Hitler. 144p. 1983. 17.25 (ISBN 0-87073-616-7); pap. 9.95 (ISBN 0-87073-617-5). Schenkman Bks Inc.

DeLuca, Arnold A. The Idea Machine. LC 75-24150. (Illus.). 252p. 1975. 29.50 (ISBN 0-317-17224-7). Dynamo Inc.

DeLuca, Arold A. Special Sections & Promotions. (Illus.). 48p. 1981. pap. 5.00 (ISBN 0-317-17222-0). Dynamo Inc.

DeLuca, Carlo J., jt. auth. see Basmajian, John V.

DeLuca, Charles J. & DeLuca, Diana M. Pacific Marine Life: A Survey of Pacific Ocean Invertebrates. LC 76-12228. 1976. pap. 2.75 (ISBN 0-8048-1212-8). C E Tuttle.

DeLuca, Diana M., jt. auth. see DeLuca, Charles J.

DeLuca, Donald R., jt. auth. see Burch, William R., Jr.

De Luca, Gioia see Boehringer, Erich.

De Luca, Gioia, jt. auth. see Ziegenaus, Oskar.

DeLuca, H. F. Vitamin D: Metabolism & Function. (Monographs on Endocrinology: Vol. 13). (Illus.). 1979. 20.00 (ISBN 0-387-09182-3). Springer-Verlag.

DeLuca, H. F., ed. Handbook of Lipid Research, Vol. 2: The Fat-Soluble Vitamins. LC 78-2009. (Illus.). 299p. 1978. 35.00x (ISBN 0-306-33582-4, Plenum Pr). Plenum Pub.

DeLuca, H. F. & Anast, C. S., eds. Pediatric Diseases Related to Calcium. 450p. 1980. 56.00 (ISBN 0-444-00361-4, Biomedical Pr). Elsevier.

DeLuca, H. F. & Suttie, J. W., eds. Fat-Soluble Vitamins. 550p. 1970. 50.00x (ISBN 0-299-05600-7). U of Wis Pr.

De Luca, Hector F. & Frost, H. M., eds. Osteoporosis. (Recent Advances in Pathogenesis & Treatment Ser.). (Illus.). 528p. 1981. text ed. 53.00 (ISBN 0-8391-1630-6). Univ Park.

DeLuca, Helen. Mountains to Climb. (Illus.). 128p. (Orig.). 1983. pap. 6.95 (ISBN 0-918342-18-X). Cambric.

DeLuca, J. Practical Problems in Mathematics for Printers. LC 76-3942. 1976. pap. 6.00 (ISBN 0-8273-1280-6); instructor's guide 1.75 (ISBN 0-8273-1286-5). Delmar.

DeLuca, Kathleen D. & Salerno, Sandra C. Helping Professionals Connect with Families with Handicapped Children. 448p. 1984. 39.50x (ISBN 0-398-04868-1). C C Thomas.

De Luca, Luigi M., ed. see New York Academy of Sciences, March 10-12, 1980.

Deluca, Marlene & McElroy, William, eds. Bioluminescience & Chemiluminescence: Basic Chemistry & Analytical Applications. 1981. 59.50 (ISBN 0-12-208820-4). Acad Pr.

Deluca, Michael, jt. auth. see Michaelides, Stephen.

Deluca, Sam. Football Made Easy. 320p. 1983. pap. 6.95 (ISBN 0-8246-0296-X). Jonathan David.

De Luca, Sam. Junior Football Playbook. LC 73-80413. (Illus.). 128p. (gr. 4-8). 1973. 5.95 (ISBN 0-8246-0150-5). Jonathan David.

De Luca, Stuart M. Television's Transformation. LC 80-15254. 1980. 14.95 (ISBN 0-498-02474-1). A S Barnes.

Deluca, Stuart M., jt. auth. see Stone, Alfred R.

DeLuca, Stuart M., jt. auth. see Stone, Alfred R.

De Luca, V. A. Thomas De Quincey: The Prose of Vision. 184p. 1980. 17.50x (ISBN 0-8020-5480-3). U of Toronto Pr.

DeLuca, Virginia & Wolfson, Randy. Couples with Children. LC 81-3268. 190p. 1981. 12.95 (ISBN 0-934878-07-2). Dembner Bks.

Deluca, Virginia, jt. auth. see Wolfson, Randy M.

DeLucca, John. Reason & Experience: Dialogues in Modern Philosophy. LC 72-91229. 448p. 1973. text ed. 10.95x (ISBN 0-87735-517-7). Freeman Cooper.

DeLucca, R. C. Check List of the Birds of the Maltese Islands. rev. ed. 1969. wrappers 25.00x (ISBN 0-317-07053-3, Pub. by EW Classey UK). State Mutual Bk.

De'Lucchi, Lorna, ed. & tr. An Anthology of Italian Poems: 13th-19th Century. 359p. 1981. Repr. of 1922 ed. lib. bdg. 40.00 (ISBN 0-89987-031-7). Darby Bks.

De Lucchi, Lorna see Lucchi, Lorna De.

Delucchi, Vittorio L., ed. Studies in Biological Control. LC 75-16867. (International Biological Programme Ser.: No. 9). pap. 80.00 (ISBN 0-317-29377-X, 2024479). Bks Demand UMI.

De Luce, J. & Wilder, H. T., eds. Language in Primates: Perspectives & Implications. (Springer Series in Language & Communication: Vol. 11). (Illus.). xi, 198p. 1983. 28.00 (ISBN 0-387-90798-X); pap. 17.00 (ISBN 0-387-90799-8). Springer-Verlag.

Deluce, Robert. Complete Method of Prediction. LC 76-51421. (Illus.). 200p. 1978. pap. text ed. 8.75 (ISBN 0-88231-027-5). Asi Pubs, Inc.

--Horary Astrology. 4th ed. (Illus.). 1978. pap. 8.95 (ISBN 0-88231-035-6). ASI Pubs Inc.

DeLucia, Alan A. Compact Atlas of Idaho. (Illus.). 117p. (Orig.). 1983. pap. 20.95x (ISBN 0-940982-02-1). Ctr Bus Devel & Res.

DeLucia, Alan A., et al. Mineral Atlas: Pacific Northwest. LC 80-52312. 38p. (Orig.). 1980. pap. 9.95 (ISBN 0-89301-072-3). U Pr of Idaho.

DeLucia, Russell J. & Jacoby, Henry D. Energy Planning for Developing Countries: A Study of Bangladesh. LC 81-20726. (Johns Hopkins Studies in Development). 320p. 1982. text ed. 28.50x (ISBN 0-8018-2769-8). Johns Hopkins.

Delumeau, Jean. Catholicism Between Luther & Voltaire: A New View of the Counter-Reformation. Moiser, Jeremy, tr. LC 77-4005. 314p. 1977. 21.50 (ISBN 0-664-21341-3). Westminster.

Delupis, Ingrid. Finance & Protection of Investments in Developing Countries. 183p. 1973. 21.95 (ISBN 0-7161-0173-4, Pub. by Wiley). Krieger.

--International Law & the Independent State. LC 73-94048. 236p. 1974. 32.50x (ISBN 0-8448-0317-0). Crane-Russak Co.

DeLury, George E., ed. World Encyclopedia of Political Systems & Parties, 2 vols. Incl. Vol. 1. Afghanistan-Mozambique (ISBN 0-87196-781-2); Vol. 2. Nepal-Zimbabwe & Smaller Countries & Microstates (ISBN 0-87196-780-4). LC 83-1541. 1296p. 1983. Set. 120.00 (ISBN 0-317-01064-6). Facts on File.

Delury, George G., ed. The World Encyclopedia of Political Systems & Parties, 2 Vols. (Illus.). 1200p. 1983. 120.00x (ISBN 0-87196-574-7). Facts on File.

Deluscar, Horace. Was Poet William Shakespeare a Cuckoo Imposter, 2 vols. (Vol. 1 61pp; Vol. 2 57pp.). 1981. Repr. of 1913 ed. Set. lib. bdg. 100.00 (ISBN 0-89987-160-7). Darby Bks.

De Luxan, Diego P. Expedition into New Mexico Made by Antonio De Espejo 1582-1583. Hammond, George P., ed. LC 67-24713. (Quivira Society Publications, Vol. 1). 1967. Repr. of 1929 ed. 17.00 (ISBN 0-405-00088-X). Ayer Co Pubs.

Deluz, Adriane. Organisation Sociale & Tradition Orale: Les Guro De Cote-D'ivoire. (Cahiers De L'homme, Nouvelle Serie: No. 9). (Illus.). 1971. pap. 14.00x (ISBN 90-2796-770-9). Mouton.

Del Valle-Inclan, Ramon. The Pleasant Memoirs of the Marquis De Bradomin (Four Sonatas) Broun, May H. & Walsh, Thomas, trs. 1978. Repr. of 1924 ed. lib. bdg. 30.00 (ISBN 0-8482-0618-5). Norwood Edns.

Del Vasto, Lanza. Definitions of Nonviolence. Sidgwick, Jean, tr. from Fr. 27p. (Orig.). 1972. pap. 1.00 (ISBN 0-934676-06-2). Greenlf Bks.

Del Vecchio, Anthony & Del Vecchio, Mary. Preparing for the Sacrament of Marriage. LC 80-67721. (Illus.). 144p. (Orig.). 1980. pap. 3.95 (ISBN 0-87793-208-5). Ave Maria.

Del Vecchio, Giorgio. Formal Bases of Law. Lisle, John, tr. LC 68-54757. (Modern Legal Philosophy Ser.: Vol. 10). Repr. of 1914 ed. 35.00x (ISBN 0-678-04521-6). Kelley.

--Man & Nature: Selected Essays. Newman, Ralph A., ed. Campbell, A. H., tr. LC 72-75156. 1969. 13.95x (ISBN 0-268-00316-5). U of Notre Dame Pr.

Del Vecchio, John M. The Thirteenth Valley. 688p. 1983. pap. 4.50 (ISBN 0-553-25041-8). Bantam.

Del Vecchio, Mary, jt. auth. see Del Vecchio, Anthony.

Del Vecchio, Robert J. Physiological Aspects of Flight. LC 77-82675. 1977. pap. 10.00 (ISBN 0-917428-05-6). Dowling.

Delvert, Jean. Le Paysan Combodgien. (Le Monde D'outre-Mer Passe & Present, Etudes: No. 10). 1961. pap. 41.60x (ISBN 90-2796-167-0). Mouton.

Delves, L. M. & Freeman, T. L. Analysis of Global Expansion Methods: Weakly Asymtotically Diagonal Systems. LC 80-42084. (Computational Mathematics & Application Ser.). 1981. 55.00 (ISBN 0-12-208880-8). Acad Pr.

Delves, L. M. & Mohamed, J. L. Computational Methods for Integral Equations. 350p. Date not set. price not set (ISBN 0-521-26629-7). Cambridge U Pr.

Delves, L. M., jt. auth. see Hennell, M. A.

Delves, L. M. & Walsh, J., eds. Numerical Solution of Integral Equations. (Illus.). 1974. 39.95x (ISBN 0-19-853342-X). Oxford U Pr.

Delves, Tony. Issues in Teaching English. (The Second Century in Australian Education Ser.: Vol. 7). 1972. pap. 8.50x (ISBN 0-522-84028-0, Pub. by Melbourne U Pr Australia). Intl Spec Bk.

Delvin, J. P. Pulmonary & Antiallergic Drugs. LC 84-11905. (Chemistry & Pharmacology of Drugs Ser. (1-406)). 400p. 1985. text ed. 75.00x (ISBN 0-471-87395-0, Pub. by Wiley-Interscience). Wiley.

Delving, Michael. The Devil Finds Work. 1977. pap. 1.50 (ISBN 0-8439-0487-9, Leisure Bks). Dorchester Pub Co.

Delvolve, Jean. Religion, Critique et Philisophique Positive Chez Pierre Bayle. (Research & Source Works Ser.: No. 836). 1971. Repr. of 1906 ed. lib. bdg. 29.50 (ISBN 0-8337-4073-3, 74-166962). B Franklin.

Delvolve, Jean-Louis & Von Breitenstein, Detlev. Arbitration in France: The French Law of National & International Arbitration. 176p. 1983. Trilingual Ed. (Fr., Ger., & Eng.) 38.00 (ISBN 90-654-4098-4, Pub. by Kluwer Law Netherlands). Kluwer Academic.

Delwiche, C. C. Denitrification, Nitrification, & Atmospheric Nitrous Oxide. LC 80-22698. 286p. 1981. 53.50x (ISBN 0-471-04896-8, Pub. by Wiley-Interscience). Wiley.

Delworth, Ursula, et al. Student Services: A Handbook for the Profession. LC 80-8008. (Higher Education Ser.). 1980. text ed. 27.95x (ISBN 0-87589-476-3). Jossey-Bass.

--Student Paraprofessionals: A Working Model for Higher Education. (ACPA Student Personnel Monograph: No. 17). 80p. 1974. pap. 5.00 (ISBN 0-911547-73-8, 72158W34); pap. 3.75 (ISBN 0-686-34306-9). Am Assn Coun Dev.

Delworth, Ursula, et al, eds. Crisis Center Hotline: A Guidebook to Beginning & Operating. 160p. 1972. 15.75x (ISBN 0-398-02561-4). C C Thomas.

Delyannis, A. A., jt. auth. see Max Planck Society for the Advancement of Science, Gemelin Institute for Inorganic Chemistry.

Delyannis, A. E. & Delyannis, E. E. Seawater & Desalting, Vol. 1. 180p. 1980. 39.00 (ISBN 0-387-10206-X). Springer-Verlag.

Delyannis, E. E., jt. auth. see Delyannis, A. E.

De Lynn, Eileen. Secrets of How to Have the Latest Pant Styles: Style Pants or Restyle Pants & Save Money. Boyce, D. E., ed. (Illus.). 128p. 1982. 18.95 (ISBN 0-941110-01-X); pap. 14.95 (ISBN 0-941110-00-1). Seagulls Artistic.

DeLyre, Wolf & Johnson, Orlen. Essentials of Dental Radiography for Dental Assistants & Hygienists. 3rd ed. (Illus.). 464p. 1985. text ed. 25.95 (ISBN 0-13-285693-X). P-H.

DeLys, Claudia. Giant Book of Superstitions. 1979. pap. 5.95 (ISBN 0-8065-0721-7). Citadel Pr.

De Lys, Claudia. Treasury of Parenthood & Its Folklore. 5.00 (ISBN 0-8315-0016-6). Speller.

De Lys, Claudia & Rhudy, Frances. Centuries of Cats. LC 78-120176. 1971. pap. 5.95 (ISBN 0-685-53687-4). Silvermine.

DeLys, Edith. Jean De Reszke Teaches Singing to Edith De Lys: A True Copy of the Lesson Notebooks of Edith De Lys, Includes 41 Lessons, 23 Vocal Exercises, 230 Notations. (Illus.). 83p. (Orig.). 1979. lesson bk. 15.00 (ISBN 0-686-28440-2). L Volan.

DeLyser, Femmy. Jane Fonda's Workout Book for Pregnancy, Birth & Recovery. 1982. 19.95 (ISBN 0-671-43219-2). S&S.

Delza, Sophia. T'ai Chi Ch'uan. rev. ed. 192p. 1972. pap. 3.95 (ISBN 0-346-12329-1). Cornerstone.

--T'ai Chi Ch'uan: Body & Mind in Harmony (Integration of Meaning & Method) Neville, Robert C., ed. 250p. 1985. lib. bdg. 34.50 (ISBN 0-88706-029-3); pap. text ed. 10.95 (ISBN 0-88706-030-7). State U NY Pr.

Delzanne, Eugene S. How to Evaluate Properly a Work of Art. (Illus.). 117p. 1980. 48.75 (ISBN 0-930582-79-9). Gloucester Art.

Delzell, Charles F. Italy in the Twentieth Century. LC 80-71044. (AHA Pamphlets, 428). 80p. (Orig.). (gr. 9-12). 1981. pap. text ed. 3.50 (ISBN 0-87229-024-7). Am Hist Assn.

--Mussolini's Enemies: The Italian Anti-Fascist Resistance. LC 61-7406. pap. 160.00 (ISBN 0-317-09495-5, 2000562). Bks Demand UMI.

Delzell, Charles F., ed. The Unification of Italy, 1859-1861, Cavour, Mazzini, or Garibaldi? LC 76-15352. (European Problem Studies Ser.). 126p. 1976. pap. text ed. 5.95 (ISBN 0-88275-658-3). Krieger.

Dem, Tidiane. Masseni: A Novel. Frenaye, Frances, tr. from Fr. LC 82-36. (The Pegasus Prize for Literature Ser.). 174p. 1982. 14.95 (ISBN 0-8071-1011-6). La State U Pr.

De Maar, Harko G. Elizabethan & Modern Romanticism in the Eighteenth Century. 1924. lib. bdg. 22.50 (ISBN 0-8414-3755-6). Folcroft.

--A History of Modern English Romanticism. LC 74-3327. 1974. lib. bdg. 22.00 (ISBN 0-8414-3725-4). Folcroft.

--History of Modern English Romanticism. LC 72-141657. (Studies in Poetry, No. 38). 1969. Repr. of 1924 ed. lib. bdg. 39.95x (ISBN 0-8383-0538-5). Haskell.

De Maar, Harko Gerrit. A History of Modern English Romanticism. 246p. 1980. Repr. of 1924 ed. lib. bdg. 30.00 (ISBN 0-8492-4217-7). R West.

De Mably, Gabriel B. see Mably, Gabriel B. de.

De Mably, Gabriel Bonnot. Remarks Concerning the Government & the Laws of the United States of America, in Four Letters, Addressed to Mr. Adams, from the French, of the Abbe De Mably. LC 72-6273. Repr. of 1785 ed. 23.50 (ISBN 0-8337-2160-7). B Franklin.

Demac, Donna A. Keeping America Uninformed: Government Secrecy in the 1980's. LC 84-1013. 192p. 1984. pap. 8.95 (ISBN 0-8298-0721-7). Pilgrim NY.

De Macario, Everly, jt. ed. see Macario, Alberto J.

Demachy, C. Puyo, jt. auth. see Demacy, Robert.

Demacy, Robert & Demachy, C. Puyo. Les Procedes d'art en Photographie. Sobieszek, Robert A. & Bunnell, Peter C., eds. LC 76-24673. (Sources of Modern Photography Ser.). (Illus., Fr.). 1979. Repr. of 1906 ed. lib. bdg. 17.00x (ISBN 0-405-09649-6). Ayer Co Pubs.

De Madariaga, Isabel. Russia in the Age of Catherine the Great. LC 80-21993. 710p. 1982. 52.00x (ISBN 0-300-02515-7, Y-419); pap. 16.95x (ISBN 0-300-02843-1). Yale U Pr.

De Madariaga, Salvador. Americans. facs. ed. LC 68-29229. (Essay Index Reprint Ser.). 1968. Repr. of 1930 ed. 13.75 (ISBN 0-8369-0661-6). Ayer Co Pubs.
--Don Quixote: Introductory Essays in Psychology. 159p. Repr. of 1935 ed. lib. bdg. 30.00 (ISBN 0-8492-6841-9). R West.
--Englishmen, Frenchmen, Spaniards. 256p. 1981. Repr. of 1928 ed. lib. bdg. 30.00 (ISBN 0-89984-309-3). Century Bookbindery.
--Essays with a Purpose. 192p. Repr. of 1954 ed. lib. bdg. 35.00 (ISBN 0-8492-6839-7). R West.
--Genius of Spain, & Other Essays on Spanish Contemporary Literature. facs. ed. LC 68-22927. (Essay Index Reprint Ser). 1923. 14.75 (ISBN 0-8369-0662-4). Ayer Co Pubs.
De Madariaga, Salvador see Madariaga, Salvador De.
De Madariaga, Salvador De see Madariaga, Salvador De.
De Madariaga, Salvadore. Bolivar. LC 79-16763. (Illus.). 1979. Repr. of 1952 ed. lib. bdg. 42.50x (ISBN 0-313-22029-8, MABO). Greenwood.
De Madariaga, Salvadore see Madariaga, Salvadore De.
De Madariage, S. Anarchy or Hierarchy. Repr. of 1937 ed. 17.00 (ISBN 0-527-60100-4). Kraus Repr.
De Madlener, Judith Cooper see Cooper Madlener, Judith.
De Maeyer, E. & Schellekens, H., eds. The Biology of the Interferon System 1983: Proceedings of the Second International TNO Meeting on the Biology of the Interferon System, Held in Rotterdam, the Netherlands, 18-22 April, 1983. 564p. 1983. 95.75 (ISBN 0-444-80531-1, I-335-83, Biomedical Pr). Elsevier.
De Magalhaes, Pero. The Histories of Brazil, 2 vols. in 1. Stetson, John B., Jr., tr. LC 77-88576. 1977. Repr. of 1922 ed. lib. bdg. 40.00 (ISBN 0-89341-282-1). Longwood Pub Group.
De Magalhaes De Gandavo, P. Histories of Brazil, 2 Vols. in 1. (Cortes Scoiety Ser.). Repr. of 1922 ed. 32.00 (ISBN 0-527-19725-4). Kraus Repr.
De Magrina, Emilio. Atlas of Therapeutic Proctology. 185p. 1984. 85.00 (ISBN 0-7216-3036-7). Saunders.
De Mailles, Jacques see Mailles, Jacques de.
De Mailly Nesle, Solange. Astrology: History, Symbols, & Signs. (Illus.). 197p. (Orig.). 1985. pap. 14.95 (ISBN 0-89281-105-6). Inner Tradit.
Demain, A. L. & Solomon, N. A., eds. Antibiotics Containing the Beta-Lactam Structure II. (Handbook of Experimental Pharmacology Ser.: Vol. 67, II). (Illus.). 500p. 1983. 127.00 (ISBN 0-387-12131-5). Springer-Verlag.
Demain, Arnold L. & Solomon, Nadine A. Biology of Industrial Microorganisms. (Biotech Ser.). 1985. text ed. 41.95 (ISBN 0-8053-2451-8). Benjamin-Cummings.
Demaine, Jack. Contemporary Theories in the Sociology of Education. 192p. 1983. pap. text ed. 13.00x (ISBN 0-333-23449-9, Pub. by Macmillan England). Humanities.
De Maio, Gerald, jt. auth. see Kushner, Harvey W.
DeMaio, Joe, jt. auth. see Curtin, Dennis.
De Mairet, Jean see Mairet, Jean De & Lancaster, H. C.
De Maison, J., et al see Hellwege, K. H. & Hellwege, A. M.
De Maisse, Andre H. De Maisse. LC 76-15982. 1976. Repr. of 1931 ed. lib. bdg. 20.00 (ISBN 0-8414-4822-1). Folcroft.
De Maisse, Monsieur. De Maisse Journal. 1931. 20.00 (ISBN 0-8482-3663-7). Norwood Edns.
De Maistre, Joseph M. see Maistre, Joseph M. De.
Demaitre, Edmund. Eyewitness: A Journalist Covers the Twentieth Century. LC 81-2311. (Illus.). 450p. 1981. 17.50 (ISBN 0-8044-1218-9). Ungar.
De Malave, Florita Z. Charles W. Moore, North American Architect. (Architecture Ser.: Bibliography A 1344). 1985. pap. 2.00 (ISBN 0-89028-314-1). Vance Biblios.
De Malave, Florita Z. Louis see Louis de Malave, Florita Z.
De Malherbe, M. C., jt. auth. see De Malherbe, R.
De Malherbe, R. & De Malherbe, M. C. Risk Analysis in Some Production & Refining Systems in the Petroleum Industry. 1981. 41.00 (ISBN 0-9961073-3-9, Pub. by VDI W Germany). Heyden.
--Risk Analysis in Transportation Systems. 1981. 41.00 (ISBN 0-9961073-4-7, Pub. by VDI W Germany). Heyden.
De Mallac, Guy. Boris Pasternak: His Life & Art. LC 81-2616. (Illus.). 464p. 1981. 26.95 (ISBN 0-8061-1660-9). U of Okla Pr.
DeMallie, Raymond, ed. The Sixth Grandfather: Black Elk's Teachings Given to John G. Neihardt. LC 83-14452. (Illus.). xxx, 462p. 1985. pap. 9.95 (ISBN 0-8032-6564-6, BB 945, Bison). U of Nebr Pr.
DeMallie, Raymond J., ed. The Sixth Grandfather: Black Elk's Teachings Given to John G. Neihardt. LC 83-14452. xxx, 462p. 1984. 19.95x (ISBN 0-8032-1664-5); pap. 9.95 (ISBN 0-8032-6564-6, BB 945, Bison). U of Nebr Pr.
DeMallie, Raymond J., ed. see Walker, James R.
De Malpas Grey Egerton, Philip, ed. see Grey De Wilton, Arthur G.
De Malynes, Gerard. Center of the Circle of Commerce. LC 66-21687. Repr. of 1623 ed. 22.50x (ISBN 0-678-00296-7). Kelley.
--Maintenance of Free Trade. LC 73-115927. Repr. of 1622 ed. lib. bdg. 22.50x (ISBN 0-678-00644-X). Kelley.
De Malynes, Gerard see Malynes, Gerard De.
De Malynes, Gerrard. Englands View, in the Unmasking of Two Paradoxes: With a Replication unto the Answer of Maister John Bodine. LC 79-38254. (The Evolution of Capitalism Ser.). 208p. 1972. Repr. of 1603 ed. 16.00 (ISBN 0-405-04126-8). Ayer Co Pubs.
De Man. Allegories of Reading. LC 79-64075. 1979. pap. 8.95x (ISBN 0-300-02845-8). Yale U Pr.
Deman, Barry A. Van see Van Deman, Barry A. & McDonald, Ed.
De Man, Henri. Joy in Work. Stein, Leon, ed. LC 77-70513. (Work Ser.). 1977. Repr. of 1929 ed. lib. bdg. 20.00 (ISBN 0-405-10182-1). Ayer Co Pubs.
De Man, Henry. The Psychology of Marxian Socialism. Paul, Eden & Paul, Cedar, trs. 518p. 1984. pap. 19.95 (ISBN 0-87855-992-2). Transaction Bks.
Deman, Henry. The Psychology of Socialism. LC 73-14152. (Perspectives in Social Inquiry Ser.). 514p. 1974. Repr. 30.00x (ISBN 0-405-05498-X). Ayer Co Pubs.
DeMan, J. M. Principles of Food Chemistry. Rev. ed. (Illus.). 1980. pap. 27.50 (ISBN 0-87055-287-2). AVI.
De Man, Paul. Blindness & Insight: Essays in the Rhetoric of Contemporary Criticism. 2nd, rev. ed. (Theory & History of Literature Ser.: Vol. 7). 288p. 1983. 29.50x (ISBN 0-8166-1134-3); pap. 12.95 (ISBN 0-8166-1135-1). U of Minn Pr.
DeMan, Paul. The Rhetoric of Romanticism. LC 84-3213. 300p. 1984. 24.00x (ISBN 0-231-05526-9). Columbia U Pr.
De Man, Paul, ed. see Flaubert, Gustave.
Demana, Franklin D., et al. Transition to College Mathematics. (Illus.). 592p. 1984. 26.95 (ISBN 0-201-11153-5); teacher's guide 3.95 (ISBN 0-201-11154-3). Addison-Wesley.
Demand, Carlo. Airplanes of the Second World War Coloring Book. 48p. 1981. pap. 2.50 (ISBN 0-486-24107-6). Dover.
--Airplanes of World War I Coloring Book. 48p. 1979. pap. 2.25 (ISBN 0-486-23807-5). Dover.
--Classic Racing Cars of the World Coloring Book. (Illus.). 48p. (Orig.). (gr. 3 up). 1982. pap. 2.50 (ISBN 0-486-24294-3). Dover.
Demand, Nancy H. Thebes in the Fifth Century. (States & Cities of Ancient Greece Ser.). 208p. 1983. 21.95x (ISBN 0-7100-9288-1). Routledge & Kegan.
De Mandeville, Bernard. A Treatise of the Hypochondriack & Hysterick Passions. LC 75-16717. (Classics in Psychiatry Ser.). 1976. Repr. of 1711 ed. 23.50x (ISBN 0-405-07445-X). Ayer Co Pubs.
De Mandiargues, Andre P. Blaze of Embers. FitzLyon, April, tr. from Fr. 1980. 10.95 (ISBN 0-7145-0131-X). Riverrun NY.
De Mandiargues, Andre P., ed. Henri Cartier-Bresson Photo Portraits. (Illus.). 1985. 50.00 (ISBN 0-500-54109-4). Thames Hudson.
Demange, Sandrine. Le Coeur Dans le Nuages. (Collection Colombine Ser.). 192p. 1983. pap. 1.95 (ISBN 0-373-48073-3). Harlequin Bks.
Demangeon, Albert. Sources de la Geographie de la France au Archives Nationales. 1969. Repr. of 1905 ed. 18.50 (ISBN 0-8337-0832-5). B Franklin.
De Manhar, Nurho. The Zohar: Bereshith. 3rd ed. (Secret Doctrine Reference Ser.). 432p. 1985. 20.00 (ISBN 0-913510-53-X). Wizards.
Demao, Kong & Lan, Ke. In the Mansion of Confucius' Descendants. Roberts, Rosemary, tr. from Chinese. (China Spotlight Ser.). (Illus.). 292p. (Orig.). 1984. pap. 6.95 (ISBN 0-8351-1395-7). China Bks.
De Mar, Alex. The Middle Ages Revisited: The Roman Government, Religion & Their Relations to Britain. 371p. 1983. Repr. of 1900 ed. lib. bdg. 100.00 (ISBN 0-89760-146-7). Telegraph Bks.
DeMar, Clarence. Marathon. LC 81-83460. (Illus.). 156p. 1981. Repr. of 1937 ed. 9.95 (ISBN 0-933050-09-7). New Eng Pr VT.
Demarais Studio Press, Inc. Erotic Photography, an Exhibition. LC 81-70902. (Illus.). 102p. (Orig.). 1981. pap. 12.95 (ISBN 0-9607462-1-8). Demarais Studio.
Demaray, Donald. How Are You Praying. 176p. (Orig.). 1985. pap. 5.95 (ISBN 0-310-23841-2, Pub. by F. Asbury Pr). Zondervan.
--Near Hurting People: The Pastoral Ministry of Robert Moffat Fine. (Illus.). 1978. pap. 3.50 (ISBN 0-89367-024-3). Light & Life.
Demaray, Donald E. Basic Beliefs. 1958. pap. 3.95 (ISBN 0-8010-2827-2). Baker Bk.
--Introduction to Homiletics. 140p. 1978. pap. 4.95 (ISBN 0-8010-2892-2). Baker Bk.
--Watch Out for Burnout: Its Signs, Prevention, & Cure. 112p. (Orig.). 1983. pap. 4.95 (ISBN 0-8010-2930-9). Baker Bk.
Demaray, Donald E. & Brother Lawrence, eds. The Practice of the Presence of God. (Devotional Classics Ser). 64p. 1975. pap. 2.45 (ISBN 0-8010-2844-2). Baker Bk.
Demaray, John G. The Invention of Dante's 'Commedia' LC 73-86888. (Illus.). 208p. 1974. 24.50x (ISBN 0-300-01664-6). Yale U Pr.
--Milton & the Masque Tradition: The Early Poems, Arcades & Comus. LC 68-14254. (Illus.). 1968. 15.00x (ISBN 0-674-57550-4). Harvard U Pr.
--Milton's Theatrical Epic: The Invention & Design of Paradise Lost. LC 79-23139. (Illus.). 1980. text ed. 16.50x (ISBN 0-674-57615-2). Harvard U Pr.
Demaray, Kathleen. Instruye al Nino. Orig. Title: Train up a Child. (Illus.). 24p. (Span.). 1982. Spiral Wire Bound 5.95 (ISBN 0-89367-085-5). Light & Life.
--Train up a Child. 24p. spiral 5.95 (ISBN 0-89367-059-6). Light & Life.
DeMarce, Virginia E. Mercenary Troops from Anhalt-Zerbst, Germany, During the American Revolution, 2 Pt. (German-American Genealogical Research Monograph Ser.: No. 19). (Orig.). 1984. pap. 12.00 ea. (ISBN 0-915162-21-0). Westland Pubns.
De Marchi, Attilio. Il Culto Privato di Roma Antica, 2 vols. in 1. facsimile ed. LC 75-10641. (Ancient Religion & Mythology Ser.). (Illus., It.). 1976. Repr. 40.00x (ISBN 0-405-07011-X). Ayer Co Pubs.
DeMarco, Carl. Pharmacy & the Law. 2nd ed. LC 84-2991. 464p. 1984. 39.50 (ISBN 0-89443-591-4). Aspen Systems.
DeMarco, Donald. Abortion, in Perspective. 1982. pap. 5.95 (ISBN 0-910728-07-0). Hayes.
--The Anesthetic Society. 182p. (Orig.). 1982. pap. 6.95 (ISBN 0-931888-09-3). Christendom Pubns.
DeMarco, Gordon. October Heat. 2nd ed. 250p. 1985. pap. 5.95 (ISBN 0-917583-01-9). Don't Call Frisco.
De Marco, Guy. Ships in Bottles. LC 84-52714. (Illus.). 64p. 1985. pap. 6.95 (ISBN 0-88740-033-7). Schiffer.
DeMarco, Guy. Third from the Sun. 265p. 1981. 10.00 (ISBN 0-682-49670-7, Banner). Exposition Pr FL.
De Marco, Joseph P. The Social Thought of W. E. B. Du Bois. LC 83-6547. 203p. (Orig.). 1983. lib. bdg. 23.50 (ISBN 0-8191-3235-7); pap. text ed. 12.25 (ISBN 0-8191-3236-5). U Pr of Amer.
De Marco, Roland R. Italianization of African Natives: Government Native Education in the Italian Colonies, 1890-1937. LC 76-176710. (Columbia University. Teachers College. Contributions to Education: No. 880). Repr. of 1943 ed. 22.50 (ISBN 0-404-55880-1). AMS Pr.
DeMarco, Thomas J. Basic Dental Sciences Review. LC 73-88021. (Medical Review Ser.). 1975. pap. 12.95 (ISBN 0-668-03396-7). ACC.
--Clinical Dental Sciences Review. LC 74-17914. (Arco Review Ser.). 1974. pap. 12.95 (ISBN 0-668-03383-5). ACC.
DeMarco, Tom. Concise Notes on Software Engineering. LC 79-66408. (Illus.). 104p. (Orig.). 1979. pap. 9.50 (ISBN 0-917072-16-2). Yourdon.
--Controlling Software Projects: Management Measurement & Estimation. (Illus.). 296p. 1982. pap. 28.50 (ISBN 0-917072-32-4). Yourdon.
--Structured Analysis & System Specification. LC 78-51285. (Illus.). 368p. (Orig.). 1979. pap. 27.50 (ISBN 0-917072-07-3). Yourdon.
DeMarco, William. Going Prepaid: A Strategic Planning Decision. 1985. write for info. (ISBN 0-933948-87-5). Ctr Res Ambulatory.
De Marco, William M. Ethnics & Enclaves: Boston's Italian North End. Berkhofer, Robert, ed. LC 81-16508. (Studies in American History & Culture: No. 31). 176p. 1981. 39.95 (ISBN 0-8357-1251-6). UMI Res Pr.
De Mare, Eric. The Victorian Woodblock Illustrators. 200p. 1981. 100.00x (ISBN 0-900406-58-5, Pub. by Fraser Bks). State Mutual Bk.
--The Victorian Woodblock Illustrators. (Illus.). 200p. 1982. 55.00 (ISBN 0-913720-32-1). Beil.
--Wren's London. 128p. 1977. 12.95 (ISBN 0-7181-1586-4, Pub. by Michael Joseph). Merrimack Pub Cir.
De Mare, G. R. Mercury Photosensitization. Date not set. price not set. Elsevier.
DeMare, George. Communicating at the Top: What You Need to Know About Communicating to Run an Organization. LC 78-31951. 270p. 1979. 23.50 (ISBN 0-471-05681-2, Pub. by Wiley-Interscience). Wiley.
DeMare, George, jt. auth. see Steil, Lyman K.
Demaree, Albert L. The American Agricultural Press: 1819-1860. LC 73-16296. (Perspectives in American History Ser.: No. 4). (Illus.). 430p. Repr. of 1941 ed. lib. bdg. 35.00x (ISBN 0-87991-331-2). Porcupine Pr.
DeMaree & McKinnon Fegan. Idaho Supplement to "Fundamentals of Real Estate" & "Real Estate Principles & Practice". 8th ed. 1981. pap. 5.95 (ISBN 0-13-765917-2). P-H.
Demaree, Doris C. Bible Stories for Children. Incl. Exciting Adventures (ISBN 0-87162-235-1, D1445); Followers of God (ISBN 0-87162-236-X, D1446); Helping Others (ISBN 0-87162-237-8, D1447); Bible Boys & Girls. 1970 (ISBN 0-87162-002-2, D1443); Bible Heroes (ISBN 0-87162-004-9, D1444); Living for Jesus (ISBN 0-87162-238-6, D1448). (Illus.). (gr. k-4). 1974. pap. 1.50 ea. Warner Pr.
Demaree, Kristyna P., ed. Continuity & Change in Latin America. (Proceedings of the Pacific Coast Council on Latin American Studies: Vol. 9). (Illus.). 130p. (Orig.). 1982. pap. 12.00 (ISBN 0-916304-54-X). SDSU Press.
Demaree, Richard S., jt. auth. see Marquardt, William C.
Demarest, Arthur A. Viracocha: The Nature & Antiquity of the Andean High God. Condon, Lorna, ed. LC 81-80344. (Peabody Museum Monograph: No. 6). (Illus.). 102p. (Orig.). 1981. pap. text ed. 8.00x (ISBN 0-87365-906-6). Peabody Harvard.
Demarest, Arthur A., jt. auth. see Conrad, Geoffrey W.
Demarest, Arthur J. Resettlement. 166p. 1970. 6.50x (ISBN 0-911038-75-2, New Voices). Noontide.
Demarest, Bruce, jt. ed. see Lewis, Gordon R.
Demarest, Bruce A. General Revelation: Historical Views & Contemporary Issues. 320p. 1982. 12.95 (ISBN 0-310-44550-7). Zondervan.
--Who Is Jesus? 132p. 1983. pap. 4.50 (ISBN 0-88207-103-3). SP Pubns.
--Who Is Jesus. Chen, Ruth T., tr. (Basic Doctrine Ser.: Bk. 1). 1985. pap. write for info. (ISBN 0-941598-26-8). Living Spring Pubns.
Demarest, Chris L. Benedict Finds a Home. LC 81-15586. (Illus.). 32p. (ps-1). 1982. 11.75 (ISBN 0-688-00154-8); PLB 11.88 (ISBN 0-688-00586-1). Lothrop.
--Clemens' Kingdom. LC 82-12731. (Illus.). 32p. (gr. k-3). 1983. 11.75 (ISBN 0-688-01655-3); PLB 11.88 (ISBN 0-688-01657-X). Lothrop.
Demarest, David P., Jr., ed. From These Hills, from These Valleys: Selected Fiction about Western Pennsylvania. LC 75-15088. 1976. 12.95 (ISBN 0-8229-1123-X). U of Pittsburgh Pr.
Demarest, Judith H., jt. auth. see Roper, Gary C.
Demarest, Kathy K., ed. see Miller, William J., Jr.
Demarest, R. J., jt. auth. see Noback, C. R.
Demarest, Robert, jt. auth. see Noback, Charles.
Demarest, Robert J., jt. auth. see Fink, B. Raymond.
Demarest, Robert J., jt. auth. see Kratzer, Guy L.
Demarest, Rosemary. Accounting Information Sources. LC 70-120908. (Management Information Guide Ser.: No. 18). 1970. 60.00x (ISBN 0-8103-0818-5). Gale.
Demarest, Victoria B. God, Woman & Ministry. (Illus.). 1978. 6.95 (ISBN 0-912760-61-3). Valkyrie Pub Hse.
--A Violin, a Lily & You. LC 76-42917. 1976. pap. 1.95 (ISBN 0-912760-28-1). Valkyrie Pub Hse.
Demaret, H., jt. ed. see Denolin, H.
Demaret, Paul. Patents, Territorial Restrictions, & EEC Law: A Legal & Economic Analysis. (IIC Studies: Vol. 2). 147p. 1978. pap. 26.50x (ISBN 0-89573-016-2). VCH Pubs.
De Margerie, Bertrand. Christ for the World. Carroll, Malachy, tr. from Fr. write for info (ISBN 0-8199-0460-0); pap. 3.95 (ISBN 0-8199-0485-6). Franciscan Herald.
--The Christian Trinity in History. Fortman, E. J., tr. from Fr. LC 81-8735. 1982. cloth 29.95 (ISBN 0-932506-14-3). St Bedes Pubns.
--Human Knowledge of Christ. 1980. 2.95 (ISBN 0-8198-3301-0); pap. 1.50 (ISBN 0-8198-3302-9). Dghtrs St Paul.
--Remarried Divorcees & Eucharistic Communion. 1980. pap. 1.95 (ISBN 0-8198-6401-3). Dghtrs St Paul.
--A Theological Retreat. 280p. 1977. 8.95 (ISBN 0-8199-0584-4). Franciscan Herald.
DeMaria. How Management Wins Union Organizing Campaigns. 1980. pap. 19.95 (ISBN 0-917386-32-9). Exec Ent Inc.
De Maria, jt. auth. see Hughes.
DeMaria, A. see Levine, Albert K.
DeMaria, Anthony N. Two-Dimensional Echocardiography. LC 81-50609. (Illus.). 1985. text ed. write for info. (ISBN 0-914316-25-7). Yorke Med.
De Maria, Gary. The Closet. LC 80-11677. (Illus., Orig.). 1980. pap. 5.95 (ISBN 0-89407-020-7). Strawberry Hill.
DeMaria, Richard. Communal Love at Oneida: A Perfectionist Vision of Authority, Property & Sexual Order. 2nd. ed. LC 78-60958. (Texts & Studies in Religion: Vol. 2). 248p. 1983. 49.95x (ISBN 0-88946-988-1). E Mellen.
De Maria, Robert. Brothers. 352p. 1984. pap. 3.95 (ISBN 0-345-31936-2). Ballantine.
DeMaria, Robert. The Language of Grammar. LC 63-15677. 1973. 10.00 (ISBN 0-88427-008-4); pap. text ed. 5.95 (ISBN 0-88427-009-2). North River.
De Maria, Robert. Stone of Destiny. 384p. 1985. pap. 3.95 (ISBN 0-345-28625-1). Ballantine.
DeMarinis, Rick. Cinder. 212p. 1978. 7.95 (ISBN 0-374-12364-0). FS&G.
Demaris, Ovid. Captive City: Chicago in Chains. 1969. 6.95 (ISBN 0-8184-0018-8). Lyle Stuart.
--The Last Mafioso. 560p. 1981. pap. 3.95 (ISBN 0-553-20230-8). Bantam.
--The Vegas Legacy. 528p. 1983. 15.95 (ISBN 0-385-29215-5). Delacorte.
--The Vegas Legacy. 1984. pap. 3.95 (ISBN 0-440-19288-9). Dell.
De Marivaux, Pierre. Fausses Confidences. (Documentation thematique). (Fr). pap. 2.95 (ISBN 0-685-13917-4, 171). Larousse.
--Jeu de l'Amour et du Hasard. (Documentation thematique). (Fr). pap. 2.95 (ISBN 0-685-13955-7, 169). Larousse.
--Seven Comedies by Marivaux. Mandel, Oscar & Mandel, Adrienne, eds. LC 68-16386. 1968. 29.00x (ISBN 0-686-60850-X). Irvington.

De Marivaux, Pierre C. Romans, Recits, Contes et Nouvelles. Arland, ed. (Bibliotheque de la Pleiade). 24.95 (ISBN 0-685-34042-2). French & Eur.
--Up from the Country; Infidelities; the Game of Love & Chance. 384p. 1980. pap. 5.95 (ISBN 0-14-044303-7). Penguin.

De Marivaux, Pierre C. De Chamblain see De Chamblain De Marivaux, Pierre C.

De Marly, Diana. Costume on the Stage: 1600-1940. LC 82-8799. (Illus.). 168p. 1982. text ed. 27.50x (ISBN 0-389-20317-3). B&N Imports.

DeMarly, Diana. Fashion for Men: An Illustrated History. (Illus.). 168p. 1985. 42.50x (ISBN 0-8419-1013-8). Holmes & Meier.

De Marly, Diana. The History of Haute Couture Eighteen Fifty to Nineteen Fifty. LC 79-22987. (Illus.). 216p. 1980. 44.50x (ISBN 0-8419-0586-X). Holmes & Meier.

De Marmon, P., tr. see Bergeret, L. F.

De Marne, Henri. Entering the Remodeling Field: A Manual for Small-Volume Builders. 96p. 1977. pap. 12.00 (ISBN 0-86718-050-1); pap. 9.00 members. Natl Assn Home.

Demarolle, P. Villon: Un Testament ambique. new ed. (Collection themes et textes). (Orig., Fr.). 1973. pap. 6.75 (ISBN 2-03-035019-2, 2648). Larousse.

Demarquez, Suzanne. Manuel de Falla. (Music Reprint Ser.). viii, 253p. 1983. Repr. of 1968 ed. lib. bdg. 27.50 (ISBN 0-306-76204-8). Da Capo.

De Marr, jt. auth. see Bakerman.

DeMarr, Mary Jean & Bakerman, Jane S. The Adolescent in the American Novel 1961-1982. 400p. 1985. 25.00 (ISBN 0-8044-3067-5). Ungar.

DeMarre & Kantrowitz. Applied Biomedical Electronics for Technicians. (Biomedical Engineering & Instrumentation Ser.: Vol. 7). 1979. 34.75 (ISBN 0-8247-6759-4). Dekker.

DeMarre, Dean & Michaels, David. Bioelectronic Measurements. (Illus.). 304p. 1983. 29.95 (ISBN 0-13-076398-5). P-H.

Demars & Chaney, eds. Geotechnical Properties, Behavior, & Performance of Calcareous Soils - STP 777. 414p. 1982. 39.00 (ISBN 0-8031-0787-0, 04-777000-38). ASTM.

De Marsily, G., et al, eds. Predictive Geology with Emphasis on Nuclear-Waste Disposal: Proceedings of Papers Presented at Sessions Sponsored by the International Association for Mathematical Geology at the 26th International Geological Congress in Paris, July 1980. (Computers & Geology Ser.: Vol. 4). (Illus.). 222p. 1981. 39.00 (ISBN 0-08-026246-5). Pergamon.

De Martin, Elena L., jt. auth. see Marshall, William H.

De Martinez, Maria C. Childrens Games & Songs in Puerto Rico. (Puerto Rico Ser.). 1979. lib. bdg. 59.95 (ISBN 0-8490-2883-3). Gordon Pr.
--Popular Poetry in Puerto Rico: Origins & Themes. (Puerto Rico Ser.). 1979. lib. bdg. 69.95 (ISBN 0-8490-2986-4). Gordon Pr.

De Martinez, Violeta S., tr. see Stowell, Gordon.

De Martini, Francesco, jt. ed. see Burstein, Elias.

De Martini, Joseph. Expedition Diamonds. 1983. 7.70 (ISBN 0-8062-1963-7). Carlton.

DeMartini, Rodney J. Be with Me Lord: Prayers for the Sick. LC 82-71881. 96p. (Orig.). 1982. pap. 2.95 (ISBN 0-87793-256-5). Ave Maria.

De Martinis, Carlo, ed. see Portonovo Conferences on Endocrine Pharmacology, Compartmental Models & Control Systems, 1st & 2nd.

DeMartinis, Rick. Cinder. 1980. pap. 1.95 (ISBN 0-380-48298-3, 48298). Avon.

De Martino, James E. Simple Estate Planning & Will Writing: A Home Study Course. (Home Study Ser.). 41p. 1982. 24.00 (ISBN 0-939926-15-6); audio tape avail. (ISBN 0-939926-14-8). Fruition Pubns.

DeMartino, Manfred, ed. Human Autoerotic Practices. LC 78-8766. 378p. 1979. 34.95 (ISBN 0-87705-373-1); pap. 14.95 (ISBN 0-87705-403-7). Human Sci Pr.

DeMartino, Manfred F. Dreams & Personality Dynamics. 396p. 1959. 36.50x (ISBN 0-398-00427-7). C C Thomas.

DeMas, Don Sinibaldo. L'Ideographie. 193p. 1983. Repr. of 1863 ed. lib. bdg. 200.00 (ISBN 0-89984-948-2). Century Bookbindery.

Demas, J. N., ed. Excited State Lifetime Measurements: Monograph. LC 82-16253. 288p. 1983. 47.50 (ISBN 0-12-208920-0). Acad Pr.

Demas, Kathleen J. From Behind the Veil. 121p. (Orig.). 1983. pap. 4.95 (ISBN 0-87743-186-8, 332-108). Baha'i.

DeMas, Sinibaldo Don see DeMas, Don Sinibaldo.

De Mas-Latrie, Louis. Traites de Paix et de Commerce et Documents Divers Concernant les Relations des Chretiens avec les Arabes de l'Afrique Septentrionale Au Moyen Age, 2 Vols. 1964. Repr. of 1886 ed. 73.00 (ISBN 0-8337-2278-6). B Franklin.

DeMasters, Carol. Christmas & Holiday Cooking. (Illus.). 80p. (Orig.). 1985. pap. 4.95 (ISBN 0-8249-3051-7). Ideals.
--Dining In: Milwaukee. (Dining In Ser.). 210p. (Orig.). 1981. pap. 8.95 (ISBN 0-89716-099-1). Peanut Butter.
--Wok Cookbook. (Illus.). 1983. pap. 3.50 (ISBN 0-8249-3017-7). Ideals.

DeMatos, Isabel Freire, jt. auth. see DeGonzalez, Fe Acosta.

Dematteis, Phillip. Max Stirner Versus Karl Marx: Individuality & the Social Organism. 1975. lib. bdg. 69.95 (ISBN 0-87700-239-8). Revisionist Pr.

De Mattos, A. T., tr. see Maeterlinck, Maurice.

De Mattos, A. Teiseira, tr. see Grenard, F.

De Mattos, Alexander, tr. see De Tocqueville, Alexis.

De Mattos, Alexander, tr. see Leblanc, Maurice.

De Mattos, Alexander T., tr. see Couperus, L.

De Mattos, Alexander T., tr. see Leblanc, Maurice.

DeMattos, Jack. Masterson & Roosevelt. LC 84-17591. (The Early West Ser.). (Illus.). 151p. 1984. 12.95 (ISBN 0-932702-31-7). Creative Texas.

DeMattos, Jack, ed. see Masterson, William B.

De Maulde, L. & LaClaviere, R. The Women of the Renaissance: A Study of Feminism. 1976. lib. bdg. 69.95 (ISBN 0-8490-2835-3). Gordon Pr.

De Maulde, R. The Women of the Renaissance: A Study of Feminism. LC 78-15352. 1978. Repr. of 1905 ed. lib. bdg. 57.50 (ISBN 0-8414-3665-7). Folcroft.

De Mauni, Roger. Franco-Prussian War. Clarke, David S., ed. (Military Memoirs Ser.). 151p. 1970. 16.50 (ISBN 0-208-01081-5, Archon). Shoe String.

De Mauny, Erik, tr. see Moreux, Serge.

De Mauny, Erik, tr. see Nemirovsky, Irene.

De Maupassant, see Maupassant.

De Maupassant, Guy. Bel Ami. Delaisement, ed. (Coll. Class. Garnier). 1960. pap. 3.95 (ISBN 0-685-11039-7). French & Eur.
--Bel Ami. Delaisement, ed. (Coll. Prestige). 27.95 (ISBN 0-685-34940-3). French & Eur.
--Best Short Stories of Guy De Maupassant. (Classics Ser). (gr. 9 up). pap. 1.50 (ISBN 0-8049-0161-9, CL-161). Airmont.
--Boule de Suif. 1961. pap. 3.95 (ISBN 0-685-11052-4, 650). French & Eur.
--Boule de Suif et Autres Contes Normands. Bancquart, ed. (Coll. Prestige). 27.95 (ISBN 0-685-34941-1). French & Eur.
--The Complete Novels of Guy De Maupassant. 756p. 1980. Repr. of 1928 ed. lib. bdg. 35.00 (ISBN 0-89987-564-5). Darby Bks.
--Contes et Nouvelles, 2 tomes. 1956. Set. 97.95 (ISBN 0-685-11105-9). French & Eur.
--Contes et nouvelles, 2 vols. (Documentation thematique). (Fr). pap. 2.95 ea. Larousse.
--Fort Comme la Mort. 1963. pap. 3.95 (ISBN 0-685-11198-9, 1084). French & Eur.
--Horla. 1962. pap. 3.95 (ISBN 0-685-11237-3, 840). French & Eur.
--A Life. Laurie, Marjorie, tr. from Fr. LC 76-48440. (Library of World Literature Ser.). 1978. Repr. of 1930 ed. 16.50 (ISBN 0-88355-576-X). Hyperion Conn.
--Mademoiselle Fifi. 1960. pap. 3.95 (ISBN 0-685-11303-5, 583). French & Eur.
--Mademoiselle Fifi & Other Stories. Galsworthy, Ada, tr. Incl. Old Mother Savage; Piece of String; Sale; Two Friends; Duel; Umbrella; At Sea. (Illus.). pap. 3.00 (ISBN 0-8283-1446-2, IPL). Branden Pub Co.
--Maison Tellier. 1961. pap. 3.95 (ISBN 0-685-11333-7, 760). French & Eur.
--Misti. pap. 3.95 (ISBN 0-685-23907-1, 2156). French & Eur.
--Oeuvres Completes, 16 tomes. Pia, ed. Set. deluxe ed. 2450.00 (ISBN 0-685-34942-X). French & Eur.
--Peter Ibbetson. (Illus.). 418p. 1980. Repr. lib. bdg. 25.00 (ISBN 0-89984-152-X). Century Bookbindery.
--Pierre & Jean. LC 76-48441. (Library of World Literature Ser.). 1978. Repr. of 1923 ed. lib. bdg. 19.50 (ISBN 0-88355-578-6). Hyperion Conn.
--Pierre et Jean. 1962. pap. 3.95 (ISBN 0-685-11493-7). French & Eur.
--Quinze Contes. Green, F. C., ed. (Fr). 1943. text ed. 8.95 (ISBN 0-521-05693-4). Cambridge U Pr.
--Romans. 1959. 42.50 (ISBN 0-685-11534-8). French & Eur.
--Selected Short Stories. Colet, Roger, tr. (Classics Ser). 1971. pap. 3.95 (ISBN 0-14-044243-X). Penguin.
--Short Stories. Laurie, Marjorie, tr. 1979. 12.95x (ISBN 0-460-00907-9, Evman); pap. 4.50x (ISBN 0-460-01907-4, Evman). Biblio Dist.
--Short Stories of De Maupassant. Repr. of 1941 ed. 35.00 (ISBN 0-89987-097-X). Darby Bks.
--Two Friends. Redpath, Ann, ed. (Classic Short Stories Ser.). (Illus.). 32p. (gr. 8 up). 1985. PLB 8.95 (ISBN 0-88682-003-0). Creative Ed.
--Une Vie. 1959. pap. 4.50 (ISBN 0-685-11610-7, 478). French & Eur.
--Works, 17 vols. 1975. Repr. of 1903 ed. deluxe ed. 375.00 (ISBN 0-8274-4056-1). R West.

De Maupassant, Guy see Maupassant, Guy D.

De Maupassant, Guy see Maupassant, Guy De.

De Maupassant, Guy see Peyrazat, Jean E.

De Maupertuis, Pierre-Louis M. Earthly Venus. Boas, Simone B., tr. 1966. 13.00 (ISBN 0-384-35930-2). Johnson Repr.

De Mauro, T. Ludwig Wittgenstein: His Place in the Development of Semantics. (Foundations of Language Supplementary Ser.: No. 3). 62p. 1967. lib. bdg. 13.00 (ISBN 90-277-0029-X, Pub. by Reidel Holland). Kluwer Academic.

De Maury, Eric, jt. ed. see Selwyn, Victor.

Demaus, A. B. Motoring in the Twenties & Thirties. 1979. 18.95 (ISBN 0-7134-1538-X, Pub. by Batsford England). David & Charles.

De Mause, Alan. Guitar Power. LC 75-16979. (Illus., Orig.). 1976. pap. 6.95 (ISBN 0-8256-2816-4, Amsco Music). Music Sales.

DeMause, Lloyd. Foundations of Psychohistory. LC 81-90307. (Illus.). 350p. 1982. 32.95 (ISBN 0-940508-00-1); pap. 12.95 (ISBN 0-940508-01-X). Creative Roots.
--Reagan's America. LC 82-73581. 200p. 1984. 21.95 (ISBN 0-940508-02-8). Creative Roots.

DeMause, Lloyd, ed. The History of Childhood. 460p. 1974. 28.00 (ISBN 0-914434-00-4). Psychohistory Pr.
--The New Psychohistory. LC 75-14687. (Illus.). 300p. 1975. 18.95 (ISBN 0-914434-01-2). Psychohistory Pr.

De Mause, Lloyd, et al. A Bibliography of Psychohistory. LC 75-5140. (Reference Library of Social Science: No. 6). 200p. 1975. lib. bdg. 22.00 (ISBN 0-8240-9999-0). Garland Pub.

De Mausse, Alan. How to Play Musical Guitar. 1978. pap. 4.95 (ISBN 0-8256-2360-X, Amsco Music). Music Sales.

DeMaw, Doug. Practical RF Design Manual. (Illus.). 288p. 1982. 29.95 (ISBN 0-13-693754-3). P-H.

DeMaw, M. Ferromagnetic-Core Design & Application Handbook. 1980. 28.95 (ISBN 0-13-314088-1). P-H.

De May, Bonnie C., jt. auth. see Choate, Sharr.

DeMay, John A. Discovery: How to Win Your Case Without Trial. 199p. 1982. 34.95 (ISBN 0-13-215640-7, Busn). P-H.

De Mayo, Paul, ed. Rearrangements in Ground & Excited States, Vol. 1. LC 79-51675. (Organic Chemistry Ser.). 1980. 84.00 (ISBN 0-12-481301-1). Acad Pr.
--Rearrangements in Ground & Excited States, Vol. 2. LC 79-51675. (Organic Chemistry Ser.). 1980. 77.00 (ISBN 0-12-481302-X). Acad Pr.

De Mayo, Welington, jt. auth. see Palis, Jacob, Jr.

De Mazan, J. Les Doctrines Economiques De Colbert. LC 72-85104. Repr. of 1900 ed. 19.50 (ISBN 0-8337-2309-X). B Franklin.

De Mazariegos, Lazaro, jt. auth. see Marjil de Jesus, Antonio.

Demazure, M. & Gabriel, P. Introduction to Algebraic Geometry & Algebraic Groups. (Mathematics Studies: Vol. 39). 358p. 1980. 44.75 (ISBN 0-444-85443-6, North-Holland). Elsevier.

Demb, A. Computer Systems for Human Systems. LC 77-30730. (Illus.). 186p. 1979. 48.00 (ISBN 0-08-023029-6). Pergamon.

Dembeck, Adeline A. Guidebook to Man-Made Textile Fibers & Textured Yarns of the World: Film-To-Yarn Non-Wovens. 3rd ed. LC 68-28677. 1969. leatherette 11.00 (ISBN 0-911546-01-4). United Piece.

Dember, William & Warm, Joel. Psychology of Perception. 2nd ed. LC 78-16099. 1979. text ed. 29.95 (ISBN 0-03-006426-0, HoltC); instr's. manual 25.00 (ISBN 0-03-048431-6). HR&W.

Dember, William N., et al. General Psychology. 2nd ed. 352p. 1984. text ed. 26.95x (ISBN 0-89859-265-8); instr's. manual 10.95x (ISBN 0-89859-315-8); study guide 10.95x (ISBN 0-89859-314-X). L Erlbaum Assocs.

Dembitz, Lewis N. Jewish Services in Synagogue & Home. facs. ed. LC 74-27977. (Modern Jewish Experience Ser.). 1975. Repr. of 1898 ed. 40.00x (ISBN 0-405-06706-2). Ayer Co Pubs.

Dembo, David, et al, eds. Global School Education at the Grass Roots: Profiles of School-Based Programs. 160p. 1984. looseleaf bdg. 20.00 (ISBN 0-936876-18-2). Learn Res Intl Stud.

Dembo, Jonathan. Unions & Politics in Washington State, 1885-1935. Burke, Robert E. & Freidel, Frank, eds. (Modern American History Ser.). 83.00 (ISBN 0-8240-5654-X). Garland Pub.

Dembo, L. S., ed. Criticism: Speculative & Analytical Essays. 160p. 1968. pap. 7.95x (ISBN 0-299-04974-4). U of Wis Pr.
--Interviews with Contemporary Writers: Second Series. LC 82-51092. 384p. 1983. 25.00x (ISBN 0-299-09330-1); pap. 10.95x (ISBN 0-299-09334-4). U of Wis Pr.

Dembo, L. S. & Pondrom, Cyrena N., eds. Contemporary Writer: Interviews with Sixteen Novelists & Poets. LC 71-176410. 318p. 1972. 22.50x (ISBN 0-299-06141-8); pap. 11.75x (ISBN 0-299-06144-2). U of Wis Pr.

Dembo, L. S. & Pratt, Annis, eds. Doris Lessing: Critical Essays. LC 74-5909. pap. 46.00 (ISBN 0-8357-9774-0, 2010188). Bks Demand UMI.

Dembo, L. S., jt. ed. see Krieger, Murray.

Dembo, Myron. Teaching for Learning. 2nd ed. 1981. pap. text ed. 17.35x (ISBN 0-673-16450-0). Scott F.

Dembo, R. S., jt. ed. see Avriel, M.

Dembofsky, Thomas J., ed. see Dorf, Richard C.

Dembofsky, Thomas J., ed. see Ferri, Robert & Silverberg, Barry.

Dembofsky, Thomas J., ed. see Trafalgar House Publishing Inc.

Dembovsky, V. Plasma Metallurgy: The Principles. (Materials Science Monographs: No. 23). 280p. 1985. 109.25 (ISBN 0-444-99603-6). Elsevier.

Dembowski, Frederick L., ed. Administrative Uses for Microcomputers: Hardware, Vol. 2. 101p. 1983. 15.95 (ISBN 0-910170-28-2). Assn Sch Busn.
--Administrative Uses for Microcomputers: Software, Vol. 1. 143p. 1983. 15.95 (ISBN 0-910170-27-4). Assn Sch Busn.
--Administrative Uses for Microcomputers: Word Processing & Office Management, Vol. 3. 151p. 1983. 15.95 (ISBN 0-910170-29-0). Assn Sch Busn.

Dembowski, Peter F. Jean Froissart & His Meliador: Context, Craft & Sense. LC 82-84728. (The Edward C. Armstrong Monographs on Medieval Literature: No. 2). 196p. 1983. pap. 15.00x (ISBN 0-917058-44-5). French Forum.

Dembrinski, P., ed. Mathematical Foundation of Computer Science: Proceedings. (Lecture Notes in Computer Science Ser.: Vol. 88). 723p. 1980. pap. 42.00 (ISBN 0-387-10027-X). Springer-Verlag.

Dembroski, T. M. & Schmidt, T. H., eds. Biobehavioral Bases of Coronary Heart Disease. (Karger Biobehavioral Medicine Series: Vol. 2). (Illus.). xviii, 482p. 1983. 67.75 (ISBN 3-8055-3629-1). S Karger.

Dembroski, T. M., et al, eds. Coronary Prone Behavior. LC 78-9947. (Illus.). 1978. 23.00 (ISBN 0-387-08876-8). Springer-Verlag.

Dembrowski, Harry E. The Union of Lublin: Polish Federalism in the Golden Age. (East European Monographs: No. 116). 380p. 1982. 35.00x (ISBN 0-88033-009-0). East Eur Quarterly.

Demby, William. Beetlecreek. 223p. 1972. Repr. of 1950 ed. 7.50x (ISBN 0-911860-12-6). Chatham Bkseller.

Demchak, Barry, jt. auth. see Willner, Eliakim.

Demcy, Arthur I. How to Cope with United States Customs. LC 76-16154. (Legal Almanac Ser.: No. 77). 123p. 1976. lib. bdg. 5.95 (ISBN 0-379-11103-9). Oceana.

Deme. Semiconductor Detectors for Nuclear Radiation Management. 1971. 33.75 (ISBN 0-9960017-4-3, Pub. by A Hilger England). Heyden.

Deme, Laszlo, jt. auth. see Deme, Lazlo.

Deme, Lazlo & Deme, Laszlo. The Radical Left in the Hungarian Revolution of 1848. (East European Monographs: No. 19). 162p. 1976. 20.00x (ISBN 0-914710-12-5). East Eur Quarterly.

De Medici, Lorenzo, jt. auth. see Gionanni, Cosimo.

De Medici, Lorenzo see Medici, Lorenzo de.

De'Medici Society Editors. The Masterpieces by George Frederick Watts in Full Colours. (Illus.). 118p. 1984. 93.85 (ISBN 0-86650-110-X). Gloucester Art.

De Medrano, Lopez. Involutions on Manifolds. LC 74-139952. (Ergebnisse der Mathematik und Ihrer Grenzgebiete: Vol. 59). (Illus.). 1971. 28.00 (ISBN 0-387-05092-2). Springer-Verlag.

DeMeer, Van see Van DeMeer.

DeMeester, Tom R. & Skinner, David B., eds. Esophageal Disorders: Pathophysiology & Therapy. (American College of Chest Physicians Ser.). (Illus.). 688p. 1985. text ed. 98.50 (ISBN 0-89004-447-3). Raven.

De Meillon, Botha, jt. auth. see Freeman, Paul.

DeMeis, Leopold. The Sarcoplasmic Reticulum: Transport & Energy Transduction. LC 81-2325. 182p. 1981. 52.50 (ISBN 0-471-05025-3). Krieger.

De Mejo, Oscar. The Forty-Niner. LC 84-48340. (Illus.). 48p. (gr. k-3). 1985. 11.06i (ISBN 0-06-021577-1); PLB 11.89g (ISBN 0-06-021578-X). HarpJ.
--My America. LC 82-22794. (Contemporary Artists Ser.). (Illus.). 120p. 1983. 40.00 (ISBN 0-8109-1804-8). Abrams.
--There's a Hand in the Sky. LC 83-2320. (Illus.). 64p. (gr. 4 up). 1983. 11.95 (ISBN 0-394-85667-8, Pant Bks Young); PLB 11.99 (ISBN 0-394-95667-2). Pantheon.

Demel, John T. & Miller, Michael J. Introduction to Computer Graphics. 425p. 1984. write for info. solutions manual. Wadsworth Pub.

DeMello, Anthony. Sadhana: A Way to God. LC 84-6735. 144p. (Christian Exercises in Eastern Form.). 1984. pap. 4.95 (ISBN 0-385-19614-8, Im). Doubleday.

De Mello, Anthony. Sadhana: A Way to God, Christian Exercises in Eastern Form. LC 78-70521. (Study Aids on Jesuit Topics: No. 9). 146p. 1978. 6.00 (ISBN 0-912422-38-6); pap. 4.95 (ISBN 0-912422-46-7). Inst Jesuit.

DeMello, Anthony. Song of the Bird. LC 84-10105. (Illus.). 192p. 1984. pap. 5.95 (ISBN 0-385-19615-6, Im). Doubleday.
--Wellsprings: A Book of Spiritual Exercises. LC 84-13655. 216p. 1985. 12.95 (ISBN 0-385-19616-4). Doubleday.

De Mello, George. Espanol Contemporaneo. 1974. text ed. 20.50 scp (ISBN 0-06-041613-0, HarpC). Har-Row.

De Mello, Walmor C., ed. Electrical Phenomena in the Heart. (Clinical Engineering Ser). 1972. 70.00 (ISBN 0-12-208950-2). Acad Pr.

DeMello, Walmor C., ed. Intercellular Communication. LC 76-46379. 268p. 1977. 32.50x (ISBN 0-306-30958-0, Plenum Pr). Plenum Pub.

De Melo, Dias. Dark Stones. Gavea-Brown Publications, ed. McNab, Gregory, tr. from Portugese. LC 83-80781. Orig. Title: Pedras Negras. 200p. (Orig.). 1984. pap. 4.50 (ISBN 0-943722-05-5). Gavea-Brown.

De Melo, Jaime, jt. auth. see Dervis, Kemal.

DeMena, Henry F. How to Increase Parish Income. 144p. 1982. pap. 12.95 (ISBN 0-89622-160-1). Twenty-Third.

De Mena, Juan. Coplas de los Siete Pecados Mortales: Second & Third Continuations. Rivera, Gladys, ed. 25.50 (ISBN 0-916379-16-7). Scripta.

De Mendelssohn, Peter. Japan's Political Warfare. LC 72-4674. (International Propaganda & Communications Ser.). 192p. 1972. Repr. of 1944 ed. 15.00 (ISBN 0-405-04758-4). Ayer Co Pubs.

De Mendieta, Emmanuel A. Mount Athos: The Garden of the Panaghia. Incl. Pt. 1. A History of the Monastic Confederation of Athos; Pt. 2. The Present Legal Position of Mount Athos; Pt. 3. The Life of the Monks of Athos. 360p. 1972. 35.50x (ISBN 0-8002-0853-6). Intl Pubns Serv.

De Menezes, Carlos A. Flora do Archipelago da Madeira. (Floras of the World Ser.: Vol. 4). 282p. (Port.). 1984. pap. text ed. 50.40 (ISBN 3-87429-214-2). Lubrecht & Cramer.

De Menezes, Ruth. You Can Type for Doctors at Home! 72p. 1981. pap. 8.95 (ISBN 0-941358-00-3). Claremont CA.

De Menil, Alexander N. Literature of the Louisiana Territory. LC 72-172193. (Research & Source Works Ser.: No. 855). 1971. Repr. of 1904 ed. lib. bdg. 23.50 (ISBN 0-8337-2364-2). B Franklin.

De Menil, Dominique, intro. by. Constant Companions: An Exhibition of Mythological Animals, Demons, & Monsters. (Illus.). 1964. pap. 6.00 (ISBN 0-914412-19-1). Inst for the Arts.

De Menil, Dominique, ed. Jim Love up to Now. LC 80-82000. (Illus.). 1980. pap. 8.00 (ISBN 0-914412-16-7). Inst for the Arts.

--Secret Affinities: Words & Images by Rene Magritte. LC 76-45518. 1976. 2.00 (ISBN 0-914412-12-4). Inst for the Arts.

De Menil, Dominique, intro. by. Through the Porthole: Exhibition Catalog. (Publication of the Rice University Institute for the Arts). (Illus.). 1965. pap. 2.50 (ISBN 0-913456-89-6). Interbk Inc.

--Unromantic Agony: An Exhibition. (Illus.). 1965. pap. 2.50 (ISBN 0-914412-26-4). Inst for the Arts.

De Menil, Dominique see Lemagny, J. C.

De Menil, G. Stabilization Policy in France & the Federal Republic of Germany. Westphal, U., ed. (Contributions to the Economic Analysis Ser.: Vol. 153). 384p. 1985. 70.50 (ISBN 0-444-87529-8, North-Holland). Elsevier.

De Menil, George. Economic Summitry. 88p. 1983. pap. 8.95 (ISBN 0-87609-004-8). Coun Foreign.

De Menil, Lois P. Who Speaks for Europe: The Case of De Gaulle. LC 77-77137. 1978. 19.95x (ISBN 0-312-87025-6). St Martin.

Dement, William C. Some Must Watch While Some Must Sleep: Exploring the World of Sleep. (Illus.). 160p. 1978. pap. text ed. 5.95x (ISBN 0-393-09001-9). Norton.

Dement, William C., jt. auth. see Miles, Laughton E.

Dement, William C., jt. ed. see Guilleminault, Christian.

DeMente, Boye. Bachelor's Japan. LC 67-11428. (Orig.). 1967. pap. 5.95 (ISBN 0-8048-0052-9). C E Tuttle.

De Mente, Boye. Businessman's Language Guide to Japan. 1982. pap. 3.00 (ISBN 0-914778-16-1). Phoenix Bks.

--Eros' Revenge: The Brave New World of American Sex. LC 78-78307. 1979. pap. 6.95 (ISBN 0-914778-21-8). Phoenix Bks.

--Exotic Japan: The Traveler's Wonderland. LC 72-71128. (Illus.). 160p. 1976. pap. 4.95 (ISBN 0-914778-12-9). Phoenix Bks.

--Face-Reading for Fun & Profit. LC 68-19163. (Illus.). 1979. pap. 2.95 (ISBN 0-914778-18-8). Phoenix Bks.

--Guide to Arizona's Indian Reservations. 1985. pap. 4.95 (ISBN 0-914778-14-5). Phoenix Bks.

--How to Do Business in Japan: A Guide for International Businessmen. 1983. 9.95 (ISBN 0-914778-15-3). Phoenix Bks.

--How to Order Chinese Food. LC 82-80460. 64p. 1982. pap. 4.95 (ISBN 0-914778-43-9). Phoenix Bks.

--Japanese Language Guide: For Travelers & the Travel Industry. 164p. Date not set. pap. 4.95 (ISBN 0-914778-42-0). Phoenix Bks.

--Japanese Manners & Ethics in Business. LC 75-3916. 1980. pap. 9.95 (ISBN 0-914778-00-5). Phoenix Bks.

DeMente, Boye. The Japanese Way of Doing Business: A Practical Guide to Motivations, Techniques & Goals of Japanese Business. 156p. 1982. 11.95 (ISBN 0-13-509174-8); pap. 5.95 (ISBN 0-13-509166-7). P-H.

De Mente, Boye. Kicking the Smoking Habit. 1978. pap. 2.00 (ISBN 0-914778-10-2). Phoenix Bks.

--P'S & Cues for Travellers in Japan. (Illus.). 102p. (Orig.). 1974. pap. 5.50 (ISBN 4-07-971838-1, Pub. by Shufunomoto Co Ltd Japan). C E Tuttle.

--Reading Your Way Around Japan. (Illus.). 1979. pap. 4.95 (ISBN 0-914778-20-X). Phoenix Bks.

--Retiring in Arizona: Senior Citizen's Shangri-la. 1980. pap. 6.95 (ISBN 0-914778-07-2). Phoenix Bks.

--Secrets of Graceful Living. LC 78-71128. 1980. pap. 4.95 (ISBN 0-914778-22-6). Phoenix Bks.

--Shopping Your Way Around Japan. (Illus.). 166p. 1983. pap. 6.25 (ISBN 4-89788-016-5, Pub. by Lotus Pr Japan). C E Tuttle.

--Tourist & the Real Japan: How to Avoid Pitfalls & Get the Most Out of Your Trip. LC 67-15318. (Orig.). 1966. pap. 4.95 (ISBN 0-8048-0593-8). C E Tuttle.

--The Whole Japan Book. LC 83-61461. (Illus.). 352p. 1983. pap. 14.95 (ISBN 0-914778-52-8). Phoenix Bks.

--Women of the Orient. 2nd ed. LC 84-42989. 1985. pap. 4.95 (ISBN 0-914778-57-9). Phoenix Bks.

De Mente, Boye see Mente, Boye de.

DeMente, Boye, ed. Images of Japan: A Photographic Souvenir. (Illus.). 190p. 1982. pap. 7.95 (ISBN 4-89788-013-0, Pub. by Lotus Pr Japan). C E Tuttle.

DeMente, Boye, ed. see Buckley, Mort.

De Mente, Boye, ed. see Fournier, Mark E.

De Mente, Boye, ed. see Longo, Peter.

De Mente, Boye, ed. see Nash, Grace C.

De Mente, Boye, ed. see Stuart, Karlton.

Dementyev, I. U. S. A., Imperialists & Anti-Imperialists. 351p. 1979. 7.45 (ISBN 0-8285-1598-0, Pub. by Progress Pubs USSR). Imported Pubns.

Demeny, Paul, jt. auth. see Coale, Ansley J.

Demeny, Paul & Mauldin, W. Parker, eds. Population Growth & Labor Absorption in the Developing World: 1960-2000. 1985. write for info. Population Coun.

DeMeo, J. N. & DeMeo, John F. California Deposition & Discovery Practice: Release 18. 1983. Updates avail. 300.00 (#250); looseleaf 1983 115.00; looseleaf 1984 135.00. Bender.

DeMeo, John F., jt. auth. see DeMeo, J. N.

De Meo, Victoria, jt. auth. see Dutton, Beth.

DeMeo, Victoria, jt. auth. see Dutton, Beth.

Demerac, M., ed. Advances in Genetics: Serial Publication, Vol. 23. 1985. 42.00 (ISBN 0-12-017623-8). Acad Pr.

Demerast, Kathy K., ed. see Miller, William J., Jr.

Demerath, N. J., et al. Dynamics of Idealism: White Activists in a Black Movement. LC 75-148656. (Jossey-Bass cience Ser.). Repr. of 1971 ed. 63.00 (ISBN 0-8357-9317-6, 2013918). Bks Demand UMI.

Demerath, N. J., et al, eds. Social Policy & Sociology. (Studies in Quantitative Relations Ser.). 1975. 49.50 (ISBN 0-12-209450-6). Acad Pr.

Demerath, N. J., 3rd & Marwell, Gerald. Sociology: Perspectives & Applications. 618p. 1976. text ed. 21.95 scp (ISBN 0-06-041617-3, HarpC). Har-Row.

Demerath, Nicholas J., jt. ed. see Vance, Rupert B.

De Mercado, Maria A., tr. see Twitchell, Paul.

Demerec, M. Advances in Genetics, Vol. 22. (Serial Publication). 1984. 40.00 (ISBN 0-12-017622-X). Acad Pr.

Demerec, M., ed. Advances in Genetics. Incl. Vol. 1. 1947 (ISBN 0-12-017601-7); Vol. 2. 1948 (ISBN 0-12-017602-5); Vol. 3. 1950 (ISBN 0-12-017603-3); Vol. 4. 1951 (ISBN 0-12-017604-1); Vol. 5. 1953 (ISBN 0-12-017605-X); Vol. 6. 1954 (ISBN 0-12-017606-8); Vol. 7. 1955 (ISBN 0-12-017607-6); Vol. 8. 1956 (ISBN 0-12-017608-4); Vol. 9. 1958 (ISBN 0-12-017609-2); Vol. 10. Caspari, E. W. & Thoday, J. M., eds. 1961 (ISBN 0-12-017610-6); Vol. 11. 1963 (ISBN 0-12-017611-4); Vol. 12. 1964 (ISBN 0-12-017612-2); Vol. 13. 1965 (ISBN 0-12-017613-0); Vol. 14. Caspari, E. W., ed. 1968 (ISBN 0-12-017614-9); Vol. 15. Caspari, E. W., ed. 1970 (ISBN 0-12-017615-7); Vol. 16. Caspari, E. W., ed. 1971 (ISBN 0-12-017616-5); Vol. 17. The Genetics of Tribolium & Related Species. 1973. 75.00 (ISBN 0-12-017617-3); Vol. 18. 1976. 75.00 (ISBN 0-12-017618-1); Vol. 19. 1977. 75.00 (ISBN 0-12-017619-X); Suppl. 1. The Genetics of Tribolium & Related Species. Sokoloff, Alexander. 1966. 55.00 (ISBN 0-12-017661-0). Vols. 1-16. 75.00 ea. Acad Pr.

--Advances in Genetics, Vol. 20. 1979. 70.00 (ISBN 0-12-017620-3). Acad Pr.

--Advances in Genetics, Vol. 21. LC 47-30313. (Serial Publication Ser.). 384p. 1982. 50.00 (ISBN 0-12-017621-1). Acad Pr.

Demeritt, Dwight B., Jr. Maine-Made Guns & Their Makers. LC 73-91769. (Maine Heritage Ser.: No. 2). (Illus.). 1973. 22.00 (ISBN 0-913764-04-3). Maine St Mus.

Demers, Aline, jt. auth. see Chaplin, James P.

Demers, Jan. What Do You Do with A..... (Predictable Readings Bks.). (Illus.). 24p. (gr. k-4). 1985. 7.95 (ISBN 0-87406-034-6, Dist. by Sterling). Willowisp Pr.

Demers, Laurence & Shaw, Leslie, eds. Evaluation of Liver Function: A Multifaceted Approach to Clinical Diagnosis. LC 78-13314. (Illus.). 222p. 1978. text ed. 22.50 (ISBN 0-8067-0400-4). Urban & S.

Demers, Patricia, ed. A Garland from the Golden Age: Children's Literature from 1850-1900. (Illus.). 1984. pap. 14.95x (ISBN 0-19-540414-9). Oxford U Pr.

Demers, R. A. & Moyles, R. G., eds. From Instruction to Delight: An Anthology of Children's Literature to 1850. (Illus.). 1982. pap. text ed. 11.95x (ISBN 0-19-540384-3). Oxford U Pr.

Demers, W. A., ed. see Green, Kerry & Leocha, Charles.

Demers, W A., ed. see Green, Kerry & Leocha, Charles A.

Demers, W. A., ed. see Kitfield, James & Walker, William.

Demers, W. A., ed. see Leocha, Charles.

De Mertens, Charles. An Account of the Plague Which Raged at Moscow, 1771. 1977. Repr. of 1799 ed. 19.00 (ISBN 0-89250-007-7). Orient Res Partners.

Demery. Macroeconomics. LC 83-710. (Illus.). 1984. pap. text ed. 14.95 (ISBN 0-582-29570-X). Longman.

Demes, B. Biomechanics of the Primate Skull Base. (Advances in Anatomy, Embryology & Cell Biology Ser.: Vol. 94). (Illus.). 70p. 1985. pap. 22.00 (ISBN 0-387-15290-3). Springer-Verlag.

De Mesquita, Bruce B., et al. Forecasting Political Events: The Future of Hong Kong. LC 85-8166. (Illus.). 277p. 1985. 22.00x (ISBN 0-300-03519-5). Yale U Pr.

De Messieres, Nicole. Reina the Galgo. 160p. (gr. 7 up). 1981. 9.95 (ISBN 0-525-66749-0). Lodestar Bks.

Demeter, ed. IED Courthouse Directory. 1985. 15.00 (ISBN 0-89419-355-4). Inst Energy.

Demeter, George. Demeter's Manual of Parliamentary Law & Procedure: The Blue Book Edition. 1969. 10.45 (ISBN 0-316-18030-0, Pub by Atlantic Monthly Pr). Little.

Demeter, Richard L. Primer, Presses, & Composing Sticks: Women Printers of the Colonial Period. 1979. 7.50 (ISBN 0-682-49195-0, University). Exposition Pr FL.

Demetillo, Ricardo. Barter in Panay. 134p. (Orig.). pap. 9.00x (ISBN 971-10-0168-3, Pub. by New Day Philippines). Cellar.

Demetillo, Ricaredo. Lazarus, Troubadour. 1974. wrps. 2.75x (ISBN 0-686-18693-1). Cellar.

Demetracopoulou, E., jt. ed. see Arnakis, G. G.

Demetracopulou, E., jt. ed. see Arnakis, G. G.

Demetrakopoulos, Stephanie. Listening to Our Bodies: The Rebirth of Feminine Wisdom. LC 81-70489. 256p. 1983. 13.50x (ISBN 0-8070-6704-0); pap. 7.95 (ISBN 0-8070-6705-9, BP 667). Beacon Pr.

Demetriades, Chrysses. Cyprus in International Tax Planning 1980: A Practical Guide for Foreign Firms & Individuals. 464p. 72.00 (ISBN 0-686-41011-4). Kluwer Academic.

Demetrio, Francisco R. Christianity in Context. 134p. 1981. pap. 5.50x (ISBN 0-686-32576-1, Pub. by New Day Phillipines). Cellar.

Demetrios, George. When Greek Meets Greek. LC 76-116949. (Short Story Index Reprint Ser). (Illus.). 1947. 18.00 (ISBN 0-8369-3452-0). Ayer Co Pubs.

Demetrius. Demetrius on Style. Connor, W. R., ed. LC 78-18597. (Greek Texts & Commentaries Ser.). (Gr. & Eng.). 1979. Repr. of 1902 ed. lib. bdg. 25.50x (ISBN 0-405-11438-9). Ayer Co Pubs.

Demetrius see Aristotle.

Demetropoulos, Andrew & Wolff, Kenneth. Elementary Algebra. 448p. 1984. text ed. write for info. (ISBN 0-02-328580-X). Macmillan.

Demetropoulos, Andrew & Wolff, Kenneth C. Elementary Algebra. 176p. 1984. write for info. supplement (ISBN 0-02-328650-4). Macmillan.

Demetropoulos, Andrew & Wolff, Kenneth. Intermediate Algebra. 560p. 1985. text ed. price not set (ISBN 0-02-328530-3); write for info. solutions manual (ISBN 0-02-328640-7). Macmillan.

Demetrulias, Diana & Deutsch, Alleen. New Audiences for Teacher Education. LC 82-60797. (Fastback Ser.: No. 178). 50p. 1982. pap. 0.75 (ISBN 0-87367-178-3). Phi Delta Kappa.

Demetz, Hana. The House on Prague Street. (General Ser.). 1980. lib. bdg. 12.95 (ISBN 0-8161-3143-0, Large Print Bks). G K Hall.

Demetz, Peter. Postwar German Literature: A Critical Introduction. LC 73-114169. 264p. 1970. text ed. 27.50x (ISBN 0-8290-0198-0). Irvington.

Demetz, Peter, ed. see Fontane, Theodor.

De Meude-Monpas, Jean J. see Meude-Monpas, Jean J. de.

De Meulenaere, Herman & MacKay, P. Mendes II. Hall, E. S. & Bothmer, B., eds. (Illus.). 243p. 1976. text ed. 70.50x (ISBN 0-85668-001-X, Pub. by Aris & Phillips England). Humanities.

De Meun, Jean, jt. auth. see De Lorris, Guillaume.

De Meur, Jean see Lorris, Guillaume De & Meur, Jean De.

De Mey, M. The Cognitive Paradigm. 1982. 43.50 (ISBN 90-277-1382-0, Pub. by Reidel Holland). Kluwer Academic.

De Mey, Marc. The Cognitive Paradigm. (Orig.). 1984. pap. text ed. 19.50 (ISBN 90-277-1600-5, Pub. by Reidel Holland). Kluwer Academic.

De Meyer, John. Benjamin Franklin Calls on the President. 1939. 10.00 (ISBN 0-8274-1924-4). R West.

De Meyer, R. Metabolic Adaptation to Extrauterine Life. 370p. 1982. 58.00 (ISBN 90-247-2484-8, Pub. by Martinus Nijhoff Netherlands). Kluwer Academic.

De Meynard, Barbier C., tr. see Khurdadbeh.

De Meza, Barbara S. Business Letter Handbook: Spanish-English, English-Spanish. (gr. 12 up). 1984. pap. text ed. 5.45 (ISBN 0-88345-520-X, 17765). Regents Pub.

De Meza, David & Osborne, Michael. Problems in Price Theory. LC 80-16597. (Illus.). xiv, 302p. 1980. pap. 12.00x (ISBN 0-226-14294-9). U of Chicago Pr.

De Mezieres, Philippe. Figurative Representation of the Presentation of the Virgin Mary in the Temple. Haller, Robert S., ed. & tr. LC 71-125315. xliv, 97p. 1971. 11.95x (ISBN 0-8032-0780-8). U of Nebr Pr.

Demi. The Adventures of Marco Polo. LC 81-13228. (Illus.). 32p. (gr. 1-4). 1982. 6.95 (ISBN 0-03-061263-2). HR&W.

--Cinderella on Wheels. LC 82-2996. (Illus.). 12p. (gr. 1-4). 1983. 9.95 (ISBN 0-03-059473-1). HR&W.

--Demi's Find the Animal ABC. (Illus.). 48p. (ps up). 1985. 7.95 (ISBN 0-448-18970-4, G&D). Putnam Pub Group.

--Follow the Line. LC 81-4072. (Illus.). 48p. 1981. 4.95 (ISBN 0-03-059112-0). HR&W.

--Hide & Seek with Wilma Worm. LC 82-63207. (Follow-Me Bks.). (Illus.). 26p. (ps). 1983. 3.50 (ISBN 0-394-86020-9). Random.

--Watch Harry Grow! LC 84-60109. (Follow-Me Bks.). (Illus.). 26p. (ps-1). 1984. bds. 3.50 (ISBN 0-394-86857-9, Pub. by BYR). Random.

--Where Is It? LC 78-22634. (Illus.). (gr. 1-3). 1980. PLB 9.95 (ISBN 0-385-14847-X). Doubleday.

--Where Is Willie Worm? LC 80-53680. (Follow-Me Bks.). (Illus.). 24p. (ps-1). 1981. 3.95 (ISBN 0-394-84759-8). Random.

Demianski, M. Relativistic Astrophysics. (International Studies of Natural Philosophy: Vol. 110). (Illus.). 300p. 1985. 45.00 (ISBN 0-08-025042-4). Pergamon.

Demianski, M., ed. Physics of the Expanding Universe. (Lecture Notes in Physics: Vol. 109). 1979. pap. 17.00 (ISBN 0-387-09562-4). Springer-Verlag.

Demiashkevich, Michael. The National Mind: English, French, German. 1979. Repr. of 1938 ed. lib. bdg. 45.00 (ISBN 0-8495-1104-6). Arden Lib.

DeMichele, Michael D. The Italian Experience in America: A Pictorial History. LC 81-71921. (Illus.). 144p. 15.00 (ISBN 0-9607870-0-3); lib. bdg. write for info. U Scranton Ethnic.

De Michele, Vincenzo. Diccionario: Atlas De Mineralogia. 2nd ed. 216p. (Span.). 1978. 11.50 (ISBN 84-307-8288-5, S-50260). French & Eur.

Demidoff, Lorna B. How to Raise & Train a Siberian Husky. (Orig.). pap. 2.95 (ISBN 0-87666-391-9, DS-1118). TFH Pubns.

Demidoff, Lorna B., jt. auth. see Jennings, Michael.

Demidovich, B., ed. Problems in Mathematical Analysis. (Russian Monographs). 496p. 1969. 106.50 (ISBN 0-677-20840-5). Gordon.

Demidovich, B. P. & Maron, I. A. Computational Mathematics. 668p. 1981. 10.80 (ISBN 0-8285-0704-X, Pub. by Mir Pubs USSR). Imported Pubns.

Demidovich, B. P., jt. auth. see Efimov, A. V.

Demidovich, B. P., jt. auth. see Kudryavtsev, V. A.

Demidovich, Boris, ed. Problems in Mathematical Analysis. MIR Publishers, tr. from Rus. 496p. 1975. text ed. 18.00x (ISBN 0-8464-0761-2). Beekman Pubs.

Demikhov, Vladimir P. Experimental Transplantation of Vital Organs. Haigh, Basil, tr. from Russian. LC 61-17721. (Illus.). pap. 75.00 (ISBN 0-317-07940-9, 2020648). Bks Demand UMI.

De Milan, Luis. El Maestro. Jacobs, Charles, ed. LC 70-78939. (Illus.). 328p. 1970. 32.50x (ISBN 0-271-00091-0). Pa St U Pr.

DeMile, James W. Power Punch: Bruce Lee's 1 & 3 Power Punch. 7th ed. (Illus.). 1984. pap. 3.95 (ISBN 0-918642-02-7). Tao of Wing.

--Tao of E Wing Chun Do, 2 pts, Vol. 1, pt. 1. 4th ed. (Illus.). 1983. 6.95 ea. (ISBN 0-918642-01-9); Pt. 1. Pt. 2. Tao of Wing.

--Tao of Wing Chun Do, Vol. 2. 3rd ed. (Illus.). 1982. 6.95 (ISBN 0-918642-03-5). Tao of Wing.

D'Emilio, John. Sexual Politics, Sexual Communities: The Making of a Homosexual Minority in the United States, 1940-1970. LC 82-16000. 262p. 1983. 20.00x (ISBN 0-226-14265-5). U of Chicago Pr.

--Sexual Politics, Sexual Communities: The Making of a Homosexual Minority in the United States, 1940-1970. LC 82-16000. 268p. 1984. pap. 7.95 (ISBN 0-226-14266-3). U of Chicago Pr.

D'Emilio, John, ed. Civil Rights Struggle: Leaders in Profile. 1979. lib. bdg. 22.50 (ISBN 0-87196-460-0). Facts on File.

D'Emilio, Sandra & Baird, Joseph A., Jr. Joseph A. Fleck: An Early Taos Painter. LC 85-2980. (Illus.). 64p. 1985. pap. 6.95 (ISBN 0-89013-152-X). Museum NM Pr.

De Mille, A. B. Literature in the Century. 548p. 1983. Repr. of 1902 ed. lib. bdg. 50.00 (ISBN 0-89984-813-3). Century Bookbindery.

DeMille, A. B., ed. American Poetry. LC 77-94805. (Granger Poetry Library). (Illus.). 1978. Repr. of 1923 ed. 38.50x (ISBN 0-89609-082-5). Granger Bk.

De Mille, Agnes. And Promenade Home. (Series in Dance). 1980. Repr. of 1956 ed. lib. bdg. 25.00 (ISBN 0-306-79614-7). Da Capo.

--Dance to the Piper. (Series in Dance). (Illus.). 342p. 1980. Repr. of 1951 ed. lib. bdg. 27.50 (ISBN 0-306-79613-9); Set. 45.00 (ISBN 0-306-79615-5). Da Capo.

--Dance to the Piper & Promenade Home: A Two-Part Autobiography. (Quality Paperbacks Ser.). (Illus.). xii, 643p. 1982. pap. 10.95 (ISBN 0-306-80161-2). Da Capo.

De Mille, Andrew. Fund Raising Consultancy & Public Relations. 1981. 90.00 (ISBN 0-86176-089-1, Pub. by MCB Pubns). State Mutual Bk.

De Mille, Anna G. Henry George, Citizen of the World. Shoemaker, Don C., ed. LC 79-138218. (Illus.). 276p. 1972. Repr. of 1950 ed. lib. bdg. 22.75x (ISBN 0-8371-5575-4, DEHG). Greenwood.

DeMille, Cecil B. The Autobiography of Cecil B. DeMille. Hayne, Donald, ed. LC 82-49241. (Cinema Classics Ser.). 475p. 1984. lib. bdg. 55.00 (ISBN 0-8240-5757-0). Garland Pub.

De Mille, James. A Strange Manuscript Found in a Copper Cylinder. LC 74-15964. (Science Fiction Ser). (Illus.). 291p. 1975. Repr. 21.00x (ISBN 0-405-06285-0). Ayer Co Pubs.

DeMille, Jancie F. Kendra's Surprise: A Child's First Visit to Zion. 1981. pap. 1.00 (ISBN 0-686-46196-7). Zion.

DeMille, Janice. From Spring to Spring: Growing up in Zion National Park. 32p. 1.50 (ISBN 0-915630-16-8). Schocken.

DeMille, Janice F. Bushy's Secret Spot: A Child's Introduction to the Zion Nature School. (Illus.). 32p. 1981. pap. 1.00 (ISBN 0-915630-15-X). Zion.

DeMille, Nelson. Cathedral. 1982. pap. 3.95 (ISBN 0-440-11620-1). Dell.

De Mille, Nelson. The Talbot Odyssey. 432p. 1984. 16.95 (ISBN 0-385-29322-4). Delacorte.

DeMille, Nelson. The Talbot Odyssey. 1985. pap. 3.95 (ISBN 0-440-18488-6). Dell.

--Word of Honor. 448p. 1985. 17.50 (ISBN 0-446-51280-X). Warner Bks.

De Mille, Richard. Put Your Mother on the Ceiling: Children's Imagination Games. 192p. 1981. 9.95 (ISBN 0-915520-39-7). Santa Barb Pr.

De Mille, Richard, ed. The Don Juan Papers: Further Castaneda Controversies. (Illus.). 520p. 19.95 (ISBN 0-915520-25-7); pap. 10.95 (ISBN 0-915520-24-9). Santa Barb Pr.

Demille, Robert. Put Your Mother on the Ceiling. 1976. pap. 4.95 (ISBN 0-14-004379-9). Penguin.

Demillo, Richard A., et al, eds. Foundations of Secure Computation. 1978. 49.50 (ISBN 0-12-210350-5). Acad Pr.

Deming, Barbara. Prison Notes of an Anti-War Activist. 1966. lib. bdg. 19.95 (ISBN 0-88286-107-7). C H Kerr.

--Prisons That Could Not Hold. (Illus.). 288p. (Orig.). 1985. pap. 7.95 (ISBN 0-933216-15-7). Spinsters Ink.

--Two Essays: On Anger & New Men, New Women. 32p. 1982. pap. 2.45 (ISBN 0-86571-024-4). New Soc Pubs.

--We Have Always Lived in the Castle. 224p. 1984. pap. 4.95 (ISBN 0-14-007107-5). Penguin.

Deming, Basil S. Evaluating Job-Related Training Programs. 144p. 1983. 22.00 (ISBN 0-13-292292-4). P-H.

Deming, Brian. Jackson: An Illustrated History. (Illus.). 148p. 1984. 19.95 (ISBN 0-89781-113-5). Windsor Pubns Inc.

Deming, Clarence. Yale Yesterday. 254p. 1980. Repr. lib. bdg. 30.00 (ISBN 0-89987-150-X). Darby Bks.

--Yale Yesterdays. 254p. 1984. Repr. of 1915 ed. lib. bdg. 50.00 (ISBN 0-8492-4224-X). R West.

Deming, Doris R. Touch of Infinity. 1984. 6.75 (ISBN 0-8062-2224-7). Carlton.

Deming, Dorothy. The Practical Nurse. Reverby, Susan, ed. LC 83-49138. (The History of American Nursing Ser.). 370p. 1984. Repr. of 1947 ed. lib. bdg. 45.00 (ISBN 0-8240-6509-3). Garland Pub.

Deming, H. G. Water: The Fountain of Opportunity. Gillam, W. S. & McCoy, W. S., eds. (Illus.). 1975. 25.00x (ISBN 0-19-501841-9). Oxford U Pr.

Deming, Mary & Haddard, Joyce. Follow the Sun: International Cookbook for Young People. LC 82-61563. (Illus.). 96p. (gr. 4-12). 1982. pap. 6.50 (ISBN 0-9609188-0-9). Sun Scope.

Deming, Philander. Adirondack Stories. 1972. Repr. of 1880 ed. 18.50 (ISBN 0-8422-8038-3). Irvington.

--Story of a Pathfinder. LC 77-128731. (Short Story Index Reprint Ser). 1907. 17.00 (ISBN 0-8369-3622-1). Ayer Co Pubs.

--Tompkins & Other Folks: Stories of the Hudson & the Adirondacks. 1972. Repr. of 1885 ed. lib. bdg. 22.50 (ISBN 0-8422-8039-1). Irvington.

Deming, Richard. Metric Power: Why & How We Are Going Metric. LC 74-5039. 192p. (gr. 5 up). 1974. 8.95 (ISBN 0-525-66380-0). Lodestar Bks.

--The Paralegal: A New Career. LC 79-27172. 1979. 7.95 (ISBN 0-525-66655-9). Lodestar Bks.

Deming, Robert H. Ceremony & Art: Robert Herrick's Poetry. (De Proprietatibus Litterarum Ser. Practica: No. 64). 1974. pap. text ed. 19.20x (ISBN 90-2792-621-2). Mouton.

Deming, Robert H., ed. A Bibliography of James Joyce Studies. Rev., 2nd ed. (Reference Publications Ser.). 1977. lib. bdg. 41.50 (ISBN 0-8161-7969-7, Hall Reference). G K Hall.

Deming, Romine R. Divergent Corrections. 1977. soft bdg. 10.95 (ISBN 0-88247-417-0). R & E Pubs.

Deming, W. E. Quality, Productivity, & Competitive Position. LC 82-61320. (Illus.). 373p. (Orig.). 1982. pap. text ed. 45.00 (ISBN 0-911379-00-2). Ctr Adv Eng Stud.

Deming, W. Edwards. Out of the Crisis. (Illus.). 500p. 1985. 49.00 (ISBN 0-911379-01-0); text ed. 49.00 (ISBN 0-317-19993-5). Ctr Adv Eng Stud.

Deming, William E. Sample Design in Business Research. LC 60-6451. (Probability & Mathematical Statistics Ser.). 517p. 1960. 58.50x (ISBN 0-471-20724-1, Pub. by Wiley-Interscience). Wiley.

--Some Theory of Sampling. 602p. 1984. pap. 14.95 (ISBN 0-486-64684-X). Dover.

--Statistical Adjustment of Data. 261p. 1984. pap. 6.95 (ISBN 0-486-64685-8). Dover.

Demir, Soliman. Arab Development Funds in the Middle East. LC 79-503. (Pergamon Policy Studies). 1979. 33.00 (ISBN 0-08-022489-X). Pergamon.

--The Kuwait Fund & the Political Economy of Arab Regional Development. LC 75-45305. (Special Studies). (Illus.). 160p. 1976. text ed. 39.95 (ISBN 0-275-22980-7). Praeger.

De Miranda, Francisco see Miranda, Francisco de.

De Miranda, Francisco see Miranda, Francisco De.

Demirchian, K. S. Soviet Armenia. Ludwick, Percy, tr. 98p. 1984. 5.95 (ISBN 0-8285-2839-X, Pub. by Progress Pubns USSR). Imported Pubns.

DeMirjian, Arto, Jr. & Nelson, Eve, eds. Front Page History of the World Wars: As Reported by the New York Times. LC 76-7428. (Illus.). 1976. 7.98x (ISBN 0-405-06674-0). Ayer Co Pubs.

DeMirjian, Arto, Jr., jt. ed. see Keylin, Arleen.

Demis, D. Joseph, et al, eds. see Loose Leaf Reference Services.

Demisch, Edwin, jt. auth. see Schodorf, Konrad.

Demise, Phil. What I Don't Know for Sure. (Burning Deck Poetry Ser.). 1978. pap. 10.00 signed ed (ISBN 0-930900-55-3). Burning Deck.

Demitsas, Margarites. Sylloge Inscriptionum Graecarum et Latinarum Macedoniae, 2 vols. 1046p. 1980. 125.00 (ISBN 0-89005-324-3). Ares.

Demko, George, ed. Regional Development: Problems & Policies in Eastern & Western Europe. LC 84-40039. 283p. 1984. 27.95 (ISBN 0-312-66905-4). St Martin.

Demko, George J. Russian Colonization of Kazakhstan, 1896-1916. (Uralic & Altaic Ser.: No. 99). (Orig.). 1969. pap. text ed. 11.00x (ISBN 0-87750-082-7). Res Ctr Lang Semiotic.

Demko, George J. & Fuchs, Roland J., eds. Geographical Perspectives in the Soviet Union: A Selection of Readings. Demko, George J. & Fuchs, Roland J., trs. LC 74-9853. (Illus.). 756p. 1974. 30.00x (ISBN 0-8142-0196-2). Ohio St U Pr.

--Geographical Studies on the Soviet Union: Essays in Honor of Chauncy D. Harris. LC 84-2498. (Research Papers: No. 211). 294p. 1984. pap. 10.00 (ISBN 0-89065-116-7). U Chicago Dept Geog.

Demko, George J., ed. see Anuchin, V. A.

Demko, George J., tr. see Demko, George J. & Fuchs, Roland J.

Demling, L. & Ottenjanm, R., eds. Gastrointestinal Motility: International Symposium, July 1969. 1971. 20.00 (ISBN 0-12-209050-0). Acad Pr.

Demling, L., jt. ed. see Lutz, H.

Demling, L., et al. Atlas of Enteroscopy. Soergel, K. H. & Pease, H., trs. from Ger. LC 75-11709. (Illus.). 270p. 1975. 140.00 (ISBN 0-387-07292-6). Springer-Verlag.

--Endoscopy & Biopsy of the Esophagus & Stomach. 2nd ed. (Illus.). 226p. 1982. text ed. 65.00 (ISBN 0-7216-3023-5). Saunders.

Demmon, E. L. Opportunities in Forestry Careers. rev. ed. LC 74-25903. (Illus.). 1975. text ed. 6.60 (ISBN 0-8442-6442-3); pap. text ed. 4.95 (ISBN 0-8442-6441-5). Natl Textbk.

Demmon, Elwood L., jt. auth. see Eldredge, Inman F.

Demnitz. Read English, Bk. 3. (Speak English Ser.). (Illus.). 80p. (Orig.). 1981. pap. text ed. 4.95 (ISBN 0-88499-677-8). Inst Mod Lang.

Demo, J. J. Structure, Constitution, & General Characteristics of Wrought Ferritic Stainless Steels - STP 619. 72p. 1976. 7.50 (ISBN 0-8031-0793-5, 04-619000-02). ASTM.

De Moges. Recollections of Baron Gros's Embassy to China & Japan in 1857-1858. LC 72-79818. (China Library Ser.). (Illus.). 1972. Repr. of 1860 ed. lib. bdg. 32.00 (ISBN 0-8420-1366-0). Scholarly Res Inc.

De Moges, Marquis. Recollections of Baron Gros's Embassy to China & Japan in 1857 to 1858. 376p. 1972. Repr. of 1860 ed. 35.00x (ISBN 0-7165-2039-7, Pub. by Irish Academic Pr). Biblio Dist.

De Moivre, A. Doctrine of Chances or, a Method of Calculating the Probabilities of Events in Play. 257p. 1967. Repr. of 1738 ed. 45.00x (ISBN 0-7146-1058-5, BHA-01058, F Cass Co). Biblio Dist.

DeMoivre, Abraham. The Doctrine of Chances: A Method of Calculating the Probabilities of Events in Play, Including Treatise on Annuities. 3rd ed. 1967. lib. bdg. 40.00x (ISBN 0-697-00052-4); pap. 7.50x (ISBN 0-89197-736-8). Irvington.

De Moivre, Abraham. Doctrine of Chances, or A Method of Calculating the Probabilities of Events in Play: Including a Treatise on the Annuities of Lives. 3rd ed. LC 66-23756. 380p. 1967. 15.95 (ISBN 0-8284-0200-0). Chelsea Pub.

Demokan, M. S. Mode-Locking in Solid-State & Semiconductor Lasers. LC 82-8610. 227p. 1982. 44.95x (ISBN 0-471-10498-1, Pub. by Res Stud Pr). Wiley.

Demolen, Richard, ed. Richard Mulcaster's Positions. LC 77-168389. (Classics in Education Ser.). 1970. text ed. 11.50 (ISBN 0-8077-1238-8); pap. 5.95x (ISBN 0-8077-1235-3). Tchrs Coll.

DeMolen, Richard L., ed. Erasmus. LC 73-89992. (Documents of Modern History Ser.). 208p. 1974. 18.95 (ISBN 0-312-25795-3). St Martin.

--Erasmus of Rotterdam: A Quincentennial Symposium. LC 76-125264. 151p. 1971. text ed. 29.00x (ISBN 0-8290-0170-0). Irvington.

--Essays on the Works of Erasmus. LC 78-3481. 1978. 25.00x (ISBN 0-300-02177-1). Yale U Pr.

--Leaders of the Reformation. LC 83-51423. 360p. 1984. 39.50 (ISBN 0-941664-05-8). Susquehanna U.

De Molina. Antona Garcia. Wilson, M., ed. (Spanish Texts). 136p. (Span.). 1957. pap. text ed. 5.95 (ISBN 0-7190-0208-7). Manchester.

De Molina, N. see Molina, N. de.

De Molina, Sara Pais, tr. see Haas, Harold I.

De Molina, Tirso. La Venganza de Tamar. Peterson, A. K., ed. LC 69-10572. pap. 39.50 (ISBN 0-317-20843-8, 202442). Bks Demand UMI.

De Molina, Tirso see Bentley, Eric.

De Molina, Tirso see Molina, Tirso De.

De Molinari, Gustavo see Molinari, Gustavo De.

Demolins, Edmond. Anglo-Saxon Superiority. (Select Bibliographies Reprint Ser.). 1972. Repr. of 1898 ed. 22.00 (ISBN 0-8369-6875-1). Ayer Co Pubs.

De Moll, Lane & Coe, Gigi, eds. Stepping Stones: Appropriate Technology & Beyond. LC 78-54392. (Illus., Orig.). 1978. 14.50x (ISBN 0-8052-3694-5). Schocken.

De Monclos, Jean-Marie P. Etienne-Louis Boullee: Theoretician of Revolutionary Architecture. LC 72-92833. (Illus.). 128p. 1974. 6.95 (ISBN 0-8076-0672-3); pap. 3.95 (ISBN 0-8076-0671-5). Braziller.

De Moncrif, Augustin-Paradis. The Adventures of Zeloide & Amanzarifdine. 1929. 25.00 (ISBN 0-932062-48-2). Sharon Hill.

De Moncrif, Francois A. see Moncrif, Francois A. De.

De Moncrif, Paradis. The Adventures of Zeloide. Moncrieff, C. Scott, tr. LC 75-172542. Repr. of 1929 ed. 22.00 (ISBN 0-405-08794-2). Ayer Co Pubs.

DeMond, C. W. Price, Waterhouse & Company in America: A History of a Public Accounting Firm. Brief, Richard P., ed. LC 80-1485. (Dimensions of a Accounting Firm). 1981. Repr. of 1951 ed. lib. bdg. 40.00x (ISBN 0-405-13515-7). Ayer Co Pubs.

DeMond, Robert O. The Loyalists in North Carolina During the Revolution. LC 78-65828. 286p. 1979. Repr. of 1940 ed. 15.00 (ISBN 0-8063-0839-7). Genealog Pub.

De Mondeville, Henri. Chirurgie De Maitre Henri De Mondeville, 2 Vols. Bos, A., ed. 1965. Set. 77.00 (ISBN 0-384-05155-3); Set. pap. 65.00 (ISBN 0-384-05156-1). Johnson Repr.

De Mondonville, Jean-Joseph C. Jubilate: Motet for Five Chorus, etc. Borroff, Edith, ed. (Music Reprint Ser., 1977). (Illus.). 1977. Repr. of 1961 ed. text ed. 5.75 (ISBN 0-306-77411-9). Da Capo.

Demone, Harold & Harshbarger, Dwight, eds. A Handbook of Human Service Organizations. LC 73-12280. 600p. 1974. text ed. 44.95 (ISBN 0-87705-120-8). Human Sci Pr.

Demoney, Jerry & Meyer, Susan E. Pasteups & Mechanicals: A Step-by-Step Guide to Preparing Art for Reproduction. (Illus.). 176p. 1982. 22.50 (ISBN 0-8230-3924-2). Watson-Guptill.

De Monfort, St. Louis. The Secret of the Rosary. Barbour, Mary, tr. from Fr. 1976. pap. 1.00 (ISBN 0-89555-056-3). TAN Bks Pubs.

De Monforti, Vittorio D. The Nature & Power of the Holy Ghost: Discoveries Into One of the Major & Most Mysterious Forces in the Universe. (Illus.). 107p. 1984. 77.95x (ISBN 0-89266-439-8). Am Classical Coll Pr.

De Monfreid, Henry. Hashish. (Travel Library). 224p. 1985. pap. 5.95 (ISBN 0-317-19406-2). Penguin.

Demong, Phyllis. Celebearties & Other Bears. 128p. 1982. pap. 3.95 (ISBN 0-380-57034-3, 57034-3). Avon.

--It's a Pig World Out There. 1981. pap. 4.95 (ISBN 0-380-53082-1, 53082-1). Avon.

--Rare & Undone Saints. LC 80-16731. (Illus.). 96p. 1981. 4.95 (ISBN 0-8397-7071-5). Eriksson.

--Rare & Undone Saints. 96p. 1983. pap. 3.95 (ISBN 0-380-63081-8, 63081-8). Avon.

Demongeot, J., et al. Dynamical Systems & Cellular Automata. 1985. 39.50 (ISBN 0-12-209060-8). Acad Pr.

Demonstration Project Asian Americans. Filipinos: Forgotten Asian Americans Seventeen Sixty-Three to Nineteen Sixty-Three. 256p. 1983. pap. text ed. 11.95 (ISBN 0-8403-2897-4). Kendall-Hunt.

De Monstrelet, Enguerrand. Chronique D'Enguerrand De Monstrelet, 6 Vols. Douet D'Arcq, L., ed. 1857-62. Set. 255.00 (ISBN 0-384-39781-6); Set. pap. 220.00 (ISBN 0-384-39780-8). Johnson Repr.

De Monstrelet, Enquerrand see Monstrelet, Enguerrand De.

DeMont, Billie C. & DeMont, Roger A. Accountability: An Action Model for the Public Schools. (Illus.). 1975. 9.95 (ISBN 0-88280-023-X). ETC Pubns.

DeMont, Roger, et al. Busing, Taxes & Desegregation. 74p. 1973. pap. text ed. 1.50x (ISBN 0-8134-1554-3, 1554). Interstate.

DeMont, Roger A., jt. auth. see DeMont, Billie C.

De Montaigne, Michel. Essais, 2 tomes. Rat, ed. (Classiques Garnier). 1962. Set. pap. 19.90 (ISBN 0-685-11169-5). French & Eur.

--Essais. Francon, Marcel, ed. (Fr). 1969. pap. text ed. 5.95x (ISBN 0-685-20237-2). Schoenhof.

--Essais. Chapman, J. Carol & Mouret, Francois J. L., eds. (Renaissance Library). 202p. (Fr.). 1978. 18.95 (ISBN 0-485-13810-7, Pub. by Athlone Pr Ltd). Longwood Pub Group.

--Essays, III. Florio, John, tr. 1976. 14.95x (ISBN 0-460-00442-5, Evman). Biblio Dist.

--Essays, Pt. 1. Florio, John, tr. 1976. 14.95x (ISBN 0-460-00440-9, Evman). Biblio Dist.

--Montaigne's Essays & Selected Writings. Frame, Donald M., ed. (Orig., Fr. & Eng.). 1969. pap. 12.95 (ISBN 0-312-54635-1). St Martin.

De Montaigne, Michel see Montaigne, Michel D.

De Montaigne, Michel see Montaigne, Michel De.

De Montaigne, Michel see Montaigne, Michel de.

De Montaigne, Michel E. The Complete Essays of Montaigne. Frame, Donald M., tr. 1958. 35.00 (ISBN 0-8047-0485-6); pap. 15.95 (ISBN 0-8047-0486-4, SP1). Stanford U Pr.

--The Complete Works of Montaigne: Essays, Travel Journal, Letters. Frame, Donald M., tr. 1957. 42.50 (ISBN 0-8047-0484-8). Stanford U Pr.

--Essais, 3 Vols. (Documentation thematique). (Illus., Fr.). pap. 2.95 ea. Larousse.

--Essays, II. Florio, John, tr. 1976. 14.95x (ISBN 0-460-00441-7, Evman). Biblio Dist.

De Montalembert, M. R. & Clement, J. Fuelwood Supplies in the Developing Countries. (Forestry Papers: No. 42). 134p. (Eng., Fr. & Span.). 1983. pap. text ed. 9.75 (ISBN 92-5-101252-0, F2429, FAO). Unipub.

De Montault, X. Barbier. Traite d'Iconographie Chretienne. (Illus.). 972p. (Fr.). Repr. of 1890 ed. lib. bdg. 200.00x (ISBN 0-89241-137-6). Caratzas.

De Montbrial, Thierry. Energy: The Countdown: A Report to the Club of Rome. LC 78-41103. (Illus.). 1979. 48.00 (ISBN 0-08-024225-1); pap. 15.50 (ISBN 0-08-024224-3). Pergamon.

De Montchrestien, Antoine. Aman: A Critical Edition. Repr. of 1939 ed. 30.00 (ISBN 0-8492-9951-9). R West.

--Two Tragedies: Hector & la Reine d'Escosse. Smith, C. N., ed. (Renaissance Library). 152p. (Fr.). 1972. 36.50 (ISBN 0-485-13805-0, Pub. by Athlone Pr Ltd); pap. 16.95 (ISBN 0-485-12805-5). Longwood Pub Group.

De Monte, Alpha. In Return For... 240p. 1983. 11.00 (ISBN 0-682-49934-X, Banner). Exposition Pr FL.

DeMonte, Claudia, jt. auth. see Bachrach, Judy.

De Monte, John, ed. A Collection & Portfolio of Golf Humor. 18p. (Orig.). 1984. pap. 3.00 (ISBN 0-9605176-2-6). Raycol Prods.

De Monte, Philippe. The Complete Works of Philippe de Monte, Vols. 1-29. Van den Borren, Charles & Van Nuffel, Julius, eds. Incl. Vol. 1. Missa "Inclina cor meum" (ISBN 0-8450-1501-X); Vol. 2. Motettum "O bone Jesu," tripartitum. Van Doorslaer, George & Nuffel, Julius Van, eds. (ISBN 0-8450-1502-8); Vol. 3. Missa Sine nomine, 2a (ISBN 0-8450-1503-6); Vol. 4. Missa "O altitudo divitiarum" (ISBN 0-8450-1504-4); Vol. 5. Missa "Ultimi miei sospiri" (ISBN 0-8450-1505-2); Vol. 6. Madrigalium Spiritualium cum sex vocibus: Liber Primus. Van Doorslaer, George, ed (ISBN 0-8450-1506-0); Vol. 7. Missa sine nomine (ISBN 0-8450-1507-9); Vol. 8. Missa "Ancor che col partire" (ISBN 0-8450-1508-7); Vol. 9. Missa "Reviens Vers moi" (ISBN 0-8450-1509-5); Vol. 10. Missa "Nasce la pena mia" (ISBN 0-8450-1510-9); Vol. 11. Missa Sine nomine, Ia (ISBN 0-8450-1511-7); Vol. 12. Canticum Magnificat (ISBN 0-8450-1512-5); Vol. 13. Missa de "Requiem" (ISBN 0-8450-1513-3); Vol. 14. Missa "la dolce vista" (ISBN 0-8450-1514-1); Vol. 15. Collectio decem Motettorum 5-6-7 et 8 vocum (ISBN 0-8450-1515-X); Vol. 16. Missa quaternis vocibus (ISBN 0-8450-1516-8); Vol. 17. Liber Septimus Motettorum cum quinque vocibus (ISBN 0-8450-1517-6); Vol. 18. Missa Sex vocum (ISBN 0-8450-1518-4); Vol. 19. Liber quartus Madrigalium quatuor vocum (ISBN 0-8450-1519-2); Vol. 20. Collectio Decem Carminum Gallicorum, Alias Chansons Francaises 4-5 Vocum (ISBN 0-8450-1520-6); Vol. 21. Missa super "Cara la vita mia" (ISBN 0-8450-1521-4); Vol. 22. Liber quartus Motettorum quinque vocum (ISBN 0-8450-1522-2); Vol. 23. Missa "Quando lieta sperai" (ISBN 0-8450-1523-0); Vol. 24. Missa "Cum sit omnipotens rector Olympi" (ISBN 0-8450-1524-9); Vol. 25. Cantiones (ISBN 0-8450-1525-7); Vol. 26. Missa "Aspice Domine" (ISBN 0-8450-1526-5); Vol. 27. Missa "Quomodo dilexi" (ISBN 0-8450-1527-3); Vol. 28. Missa "Sine nomine" (ISBN 0-8450-1528-1); Vol. 29. Missa "Sine nomine" (ISBN 0-8450-1529-X). 2808p. (Repr. of 1927-39 ed.). 1966. Set. pap. 525.00x (ISBN 0-8450-1500-1); pap. 22.50x ea. Broude.

De Montespan, Madame. The Intimate Memoirs of Madame de Montespan, 2 vols. (Illus.). 308p. 1984. Repr. of 1907 ed. Set. 165.00 (ISBN 0-89901-174-8). Found Class Reprints.

De Montesquieu, C. see Montesquieu, C. de.

De Montesquieu, Charles. Esprit des lois, 2 Vols. (Fr). pap. 2.95 ea. Larousse.

--Lettres Persanes. (Documentation Thematique Ser.). (Fr). pap. 2.95 (ISBN 0-685-13969-7, 218). Larousse.

De Montesquieu, Charles-Louis. De l'Esprit des Lois, 2 tomes. (Coll. Prestige). Set. 55.95 (ISBN 0-685-34045-7). French & Eur.

--Lettres Persanes. (Selection Litteraire Bordas). pap. 3.95 (ISBN 0-685-34048-1). French & Eur.

--Lettres Persanes. Verniere, ed. (Classiques Garnier). pap. 14.95 (ISBN 0-685-34046-5). French & Eur.

--Lettres Persanes. Verniere, ed. (Coll. Prestige). 27.95 (ISBN 0-685-34047-3). French & Eur.

--Oeuvres Completes, 2 tomes. Caillois, ed. (Bibliotheque de la Pleiade). Set. 79.50 (ISBN 0-685-34044-9). French & Eur.

De Montfaucon, Abbe N., ed. Le Comte de Gabalis. (Illus.). 182p. 1984. 16.95 (ISBN 0-932785-10-7); pap. 10.95 (ISBN 0-932785-09-3). Philos Pub.

De Montfort, Louis. True Devotion. LC 63-12679. 1973. 3.50 (ISBN 0-8198-0517-3); pap. 2.50. Dghtrs St Paul.

De Montfort, St. Louis. Love of Eternal Wisdom. 4.95 (ISBN 0-910984-51-4); pap. 2.95 (ISBN 0-910984-05-0). Montfort Pubns.

De Montfort, St. Louis Marie. True Devotion to the Blessed Virgin. 4.95 (ISBN 0-910984-49-2); pap. 3.95 (ISBN 0-910984-50-6). Montfort Pubns.

De Montgolfier, Bernard see Montgolfier, Bernard de.

De Montherlant, Henri. Le Bestiaire Celeste. deluxe ed. 787.50 (ISBN 0-685-36992-7). French & Eur.

--Bestiaires. (Coll. Soleil). 1957. 13.95 (ISBN 0-685-11046-X). French & Eur.

--Bestiaires. (Documentation thematique). (Illus., Fr.). pap. 2.95 (ISBN 0-685-13809-7, 220). Larousse.

--Carnets, 4 tomes. Incl. Tome I. (1935-1939) pap. 10.95 (ISBN 0-685-35868-2); Tome II. (1942-1943) pap. 8.50 (ISBN 0-685-35869-0); Tome III. (1932-1934) pap. 10.50 (ISBN 0-685-35870-4); Tome IV. (1930-1932) 10.50 (ISBN 0-685-35871-2). 1956-68. pap. French & Eur.

--Les Celibataires. 1958. 7.95 (ISBN 0-685-11070-2). French & Eur.

--Le Chaos et la Nuit. (Coll. Soleil). 1963. 13.25 (ISBN 0-685-11075-3). French & Eur.

--Essais. 1963. lea. 38.50 (ISBN 0-685-01985-3). French & Eur.

--Fils De Personne. Bd. with Un Incompris. (Coll. Soleil). 1944. 13.25 (ISBN 0-685-35872-0). French & Eur.

--Guerre Civile. (Coll. Soleil). 1965. 13.25 (ISBN 0-685-11226-8). French & Eur.

--Theatre, 5 tomes. Set. 525.00 (ISBN 0-685-11587-9). French & Eur.

De Montherlant, Henry. Aux Fontaines de Desir. La Petite Infante de Castille. pap. 7.50 (ISBN 0-685-36971-4). French & Eur.

--Cardinal d'Epagne. (Coll. Soleil). 1960. 11.50 (ISBN 0-685-11063-X); pap. 3.95 (ISBN 0-686-66416-7). French & Eur.

--Celles qu'on Prend dans ses Bras. pap. 4.95 (ISBN 0-685-36974-9). French & Eur.

--Chant de Mimos, Pasiphae. (Coll. Las Peintres du Livre). (Illus.). deluxe ed. 27.50 (ISBN 0-685-36993-5). French & Eur.

--Le Chaos et la Nuit. (Illus.). deluxe ed. 787.50 (ISBN 0-685-36994-3). French & Eur.

--Demain il fera Jour. pap. 4.50 (ISBN 0-685-36975-7). French & Eur.

--Discours de Reception a l'Academie Francaise. pap. 6.50 (ISBN 0-685-36976-5). French & Eur.

--Don Juan. pap. 3.95 (ISBN 0-685-36977-3). French & Eur.

--Don Juan. (Illus.). deluxe ed. 481.25 (ISBN 0-685-36995-1). French & Eur.

--Encore un Instant de Bonheur. pap. 3.95 (ISBN 0-685-36978-1). French & Eur.

--L' Etoile du Soir. (Illus.). deluxe ed. 36.75 (ISBN 0-685-36996-X). French & Eur.

--L' Exil et Malatesta. (L'Avant-Scene). pap. 6.95 (ISBN 0-685-36979-X). French & Eur.

--The Fire That Consumes. Cox, Vivian, tr. from Fr. LC 80-51842. Orig. Title: La Ville Dont le Prince Est un Enfant. 92p. 1980. 30.00 (ISBN 0-9604392-1-8). G F Ritchie.

--Les Garcons. (Coll. Soleil). 19.25 (ISBN 0-685-36980-3). French & Eur.

--The Girls. 639p. 1985. pap. 11.95 (ISBN 0-88184-115-3). Carroll & Graf.

--Histoire d'amour de la Rose de Sable. 7.95 (ISBN 0-685-36981-1). French & Eur.

--L' Infini est du Cote de Malatesta. pap. 3.95 (ISBN 0-685-36982-X). French & Eur.

--Les Jeunes Filles, 4 tomes. Incl. Tome I. Les/Jeunes Filles. 7.95 (ISBN 0-685-35873-9); Tome 2. Pitie pour les Femmes. 4.50 (ISBN 0-685-35874-7); Tome 3. Le Demon du Bien. 4.95 (ISBN 0-685-35875-5); Tome 4. Les Lepreuses. 3.95 (ISBN 0-685-35876-3). French & Eur.

--Maitre De Santiago. (Coll. Soleil). 1962. 13.25 (ISBN 0-685-11334-5). French & Eur.

--Malatesta. (Coll. Soleil). 1965. 13.25 (ISBN 0-685-11336-1). French & Eur.

--La Maree du Soir: Carnets, 1968-1971. (Coll. Soleil). 17.50 (ISBN 0-685-36983-8); pap. 9.95 (ISBN 0-686-55525-2). French & Eur.

--Mariette Lydis. (Illus.). deluxe ed. 65.75 (ISBN 0-685-36997-8). French & Eur.

--Mors et Vita, Service Inutile. pap. 6.50 (ISBN 0-685-36984-6). French & Eur.

--Oeuvre Romanesque, 8 vols. Set. 612.50 (ISBN 0-685-11433-3). French & Eur.

--Les Olympiques. (Coll. Soleil). 13.25 (ISBN 0-685-23905-5). French & Eur.

--La Petite Infante de Castille. (Illus.). deluxe ed. 215.00 (ISBN 0-685-36998-6). French & Eur.

--Port-Royal. (Coll. Soleil). (Fr.). 1960. 13.25 (ISBN 0-685-11501-1). French & Eur.

--Reine Morte. 1957. 11.95 (ISBN 0-685-11525-9). French & Eur.

--Romans et Oeuvres De Fiction Non Theatrales. (Bibl de la Pleiade). 1960. 42.95 (ISBN 0-685-11538-0). French & Eur.

--La Rose de Sable. (Coll. Soleil). 20.95 (ISBN 0-685-36985-4). French & Eur.

--Service Inutile. 3.95 (ISBN 0-685-36986-2). French & Eur.

--Le Songe. pap. 4.95 (ISBN 0-685-36987-0). French & Eur.

--Sur les Femmes. 14.95 (ISBN 0-685-36988-9). French & Eur.

--Textes sous une Occupation (1940-1944) pap. 6.95 (ISBN 0-685-36989-7). French & Eur.

--Theatre. (Bibl. de Pleiade). 1965. 39.95 (ISBN 0-685-11588-7). French & Eur.

--La Tragedie Sans Masque: Notes de Theatre. 16.50 (ISBN 0-685-36990-0). French & Eur.

--Le Treizieme Cesar. (Coll. Soleil). 13.95 (ISBN 0-685-36991-9). French & Eur.

--Va Jouer avec Cette Poussiere: Carnets (1958-1964) 1966. 11.50 (ISBN 0-685-11612-3). French & Eur.

--Ville Dont le Prince Est un Enfant. 1963. pap. 13.50 (ISBN 0-685-11620-4). French & Eur.

--Voyageur Solitaire Est Un Diable. 1961. pap. 10.95 (ISBN 0-685-11627-1). French & Eur.

--Un Voyageur Solitaire est un Diable. (Illus.). deluxe ed. 341.25 (ISBN 0-685-36999-4). French & Eur.

De Montherlant, Henry see Montherlant, Henry de.

De Montmorency, J. E. Thomas A'Kempis: His Age & Book. LC 73-103183. 1970. Repr. of 1906 ed. 28.00x (ISBN 0-8046-0820-2, Pub by Kennikat). Assoc Faculty Pr.

De Montmort, R. Essay D'analyse Sur les Jeux De Hazard. LC 79-1226. (Illus.). 463p. (Fr) 1980. Repr. of 1714 ed. text ed. 35.00 (ISBN 0-8284-0307-4). Chelsea Pub.

De Montreville, Doris & Crawford, Elizabeth D., eds. Fourth Book of Junior Authors & Illustrators. LC 78-115. 370p. 1978. 22.00 (ISBN 0-8242-0568-5). Wilson.

De Montreville, Doris & Hill, Donna, eds. Third Book of Junior Authors. LC 75-149381. (Illus.). 1972. 18.00 (ISBN 0-8242-0408-5). Wilson.

De Montrond, M. Dictionnaire des Abbayes et Monasteres ou Histoire Des Establissements Religieux. Migne, J. P., ed. (Troisieme et Derniere Encyclopedie Theologique Ser.: Vol. 16). 614p. (Fr.). Repr. of 1856 ed. lib. bdg. 81.00x (ISBN 0-89241-299-2). Caratzas.

De Montule, E. Travels in America, 1816-1817. Seeber, E. D., tr. Repr. of 1950 ed. 16.00 (ISBN 0-527-64550-8). Kraus Repr.

De Monvel, L. Boutet, et al, eds. Mathematics et Physique. (Progress in Mathematics: Vol. 37). 456p. 1983. text ed. 37.95 (ISBN 0-8176-3154-2). Birkhauser.

De Monvel, Roger B. Cervantes & the Magicians. LC 72-3201. (Studies in Spanish Literature, No. 36). 1972. Repr. of 1934 ed. lib. bdg. 39.95x (ISBN 0-8383-1531-3). Haskell.

Demopoulas, William & Marras, Ausonio. Language Learning & Concept Acquisition. Phlyshyn, Zenon, ed. (Theoretical Issues in Cognitive Science Ser.: Vol. 1). 288p. 1985. text ed. 32.50 (ISBN 0-89391-316-2). Ablex Pub.

De Moraes, Borba & Berrien, William. Manual Bibliografico De Estudos Brasileiros. 1976. lib. bdg. 59.95 (ISBN 0-8490-2203-7). Gordon Pr.

De Moraes, Ruben B. Bibliographia Brasiliana, 2 vols. rev. ed. LC 82-620036. (Reference Ser.: Vol. 10). (Illus.). 1114p. 1983. Set. lib. bdg. 150.00x (ISBN 0-87903-109-3). UCLA Lat Am Ctr.

De Moraes, Vinicius. The Joy of Rio. Gullar, Ferreira, tr. LC 80-51190. Orig. Title: Rio. (Illus.). 160p. (Port.). 1980. 19.95 (ISBN 0-86565-005-5). Vendome.

De Morais, A., ed. see Ferreira, J. Albino.

De Morais, Armando. Dicionario De Ingles-Portugues. 1966. 16.00x (ISBN 0-686-19950-2). Intl Learn Syst.

De Morais, O., ed. see Ferreira, J. Albino.

De Morales, Leonard C. Luis Gonzalez Obregon: 1865-1938: Chronicler of Mexico City. 164p. 3.00 (ISBN 0-318-14285-6). Hispanic Inst.

DeMorant, George S. Chinese Acupunture, Vol. 1. Zmiewski, Paul, ed. Grinnell, Lawrence, et al, trs. from Fr. 500p. 1986. 25.00 (ISBN 0-912111-11-9). Paradigm Pubns.

DeMorant, Soulie G. Chinese Acupunture, Vol. 2. Zmiewski, Paul, ed. Grinnell, Lawrence, et al, trs. 500p. 1986. 25.00 (ISBN 0-912111-12-7). Paradigm Pubns.

Demorest, Jean-Jacques, tr. see Moraze, Charles.

De Morga, A. History of the Philippine Islands, from Their Discovery by Magellan in 1521 to the Beginning of the Seventeenth Century, with Descriptions of Japan, China & Adjacent Countries, 2 Vols. in 1. Repr. of 1907 ed. 27.00 (ISBN 0-527-65000-5). Kraus Repr.

De Morga, Antonio. Philippine Islands: Moluccas, Siam, Cambodia, Japan & China at the Close of the Sixteenth Century. Stanley, Henry J., tr. 1964. 32.00 (ISBN 0-8337-2460-6). B Franklin.

De Morgan, Augustus. Budget of Paradoxes, 2 Vols. facsimile ed. Smith, David E., ed. (Select Bibliographies Reprint Ser.). 1915. Set. 55.00 (ISBN 0-8369-5119-0). Ayer Co Pubs.

--Elementary Illustrations of the Differential & Integral Calculus. 152p. 16.95 (ISBN 0-87548-158-2). Open Court.

--The Encyclopedia of Eccentrics. Smith, David E., ed. 416p. 1974. pap. 12.95 (ISBN 0-87548-194-9). Open Court.

--An Essay on Probabilities. LC 80-2119. (Development of Science Ser.). (Illus.). lib. bdg. 30.00x (ISBN 0-405-13885-7). Ayer Co Pubs.

--On the Study & Difficulties of Mathematics. 2nd ed. 295p. 19.95 (ISBN 0-87548-187-6). Open Court.

De Morgan, Augustus, jt. auth. see Smith, David E.

DeMorgan, J. Manuel De Numismatique Orientale. 1985. 30.00 (ISBN 0-317-17360-X); pap. 20.00 (ISBN 0-89005-405-3). Ares.

--Manuel de Numismatique Orientale de l'Antiquite et du Moyen Age. (Illus., Fr.). 1979. 30.00 (ISBN 0-916710-44-0); pap. 20.00 (ISBN 0-916710-45-9). Obol Intl.

De Morgan, Jacques. Prehistoric Man: A General Outline of Prehistory. 1924. 20.00 (ISBN 0-8482-3693-9). Norwood Edns.

--Prehistoric Man: A General Outline of Prehistory. 1977. Repr. of 1924 ed. lib. bdg. 40.00 (ISBN 0-8492-0609-X). R West.

De Morgue, Jacques Le Moyne. Portraits of Plants by Jacques le Moyne de Morgues. (Illus.). 64p. 1984. pap. 13.95 (ISBN 0-905209-52-4, Pub. by Victoria & Albert Mus UK). Faber & Faber.

De Mori, Renato. Computer Models of Speech Using Fuzzy Algorithms. (Advanced Applications in Pattern Recognition Ser.). 508p. 1983. 59.50x (ISBN 0-306-41381-7, Plenum Pr). Plenum Pub.

DeMori, Renato, jt. ed. see Suen, Ching Y.

De Morinni, J., tr. see Foch, Ferdinand.

De Mornay, Charlotte A. Memoires, 2 vols. 1869. Set. 67.00 (ISBN 0-384-40148-1); Set. pap. 55.00 (ISBN 0-384-40149-X). Johnson Repr.

Demoro, Harre. The Key Route: Book One. Walker, Jim, ed. (Interurbans Special Ser.: 95). (Illus.). 168p. 1985. 31.95 (ISBN 0-317-14470-7). Interurban.

Demoro, Harre, jt. auth. see Wurm, Ted.

Demoro, Harre W. Electric Railway Pioneer: Commuting on the Northwestern Pacific 1903-1941. LC 81-20193. (Special Ser.: No. 84). (Illus.). 136p. 1983. 24.95 (ISBN 0-916374-55-6). Interurban.

--Southern Pacific Bay Area Steam. LC 78-72990. (Illus.). 144p. 1979. 25.00 (ISBN 0-89685-037-4). Chatham Pub CA.

De Morsang, Marguerite. Of Men of Women: Poems. 4.95 (ISBN 0-686-74606-6). Crambruck.

Demory, Richard, jt. auth. see Megill, Donald D.

Demos, George D., jt. auth. see Bennett, James C.

Demos, George D., jt. auth. see Gowan, John C.

Demos, George D., jt. ed. see Gallagher, Philip J.

Demos, Jean, tr. see Tsatsos, Ioanna.

Demos, Jean, tr. see Tsatsos, Jeanne.

Demos, John. Little Commonwealth: Family Life in Plymouth Colony. (Illus.). 1970. pap. 5.95 (ISBN 0-19-501355-7, 344, GB). Oxford U Pr.

Demos, John, ed. Remarkable Providences. LC 74-160130. (American Culture Ser). 1972. 8.95 (ISBN 0-8076-0617-0); pap. 4.95 (ISBN 0-8076-0616-2). Braziller.

Demos, John & Boocock, Sarane, eds. Turning Points: Historical & Sociological Essays on the Family. 1978. lib. bdg. 22.00x (ISBN 0-685-87016-2, 14284-1); pap. 10.95x (ISBN 0-685-87017-0, 14286-8). U of Chicago Pr.

Demos, John P. Entertaining Satan: Witchcraft & the Culture of Early New England. LC 81-22463. 1982. 29.95x (ISBN 0-19-503131-8). Oxford U Pr.

--Entertaining Satan: Witchcraft & the Culture of Early New England. (Illus.). 1982. pap. 9.95 (ISBN 0-19-503378-7, GB742, GB). Oxford U Pr.

Demos, Peter G., Jr. Casino Supervision: A Basic Guide. LC 83-72779. (Illus.). 160p. (Orig.). 1983. pap. 24.95x (ISBN 0-913421-00-6). CSI Pr.

Demos, Terrence C. Bone Radiologic Case Studies. LC 82-62398. 256p. 1983. 24.50 (ISBN 0-943432-02-2). Slack Inc.

DeMoss, Arthur, ed. The Family Album: 1978 Edition. DeMoss, Nancy. (Illus.). 1977. 9.95 (ISBN 0-87981-086-6). Holman.

DeMoss, Arthur, jt. ed. see DeMoss, Nancy.

DeMoss, Marguerite. The Scarlet Storm. 272p. (Orig.). 1981. pap. 2.50 (ISBN 0-8439-0971-4, Leisure Bks). Dorchester Pub Co.

DeMoss, Nancy see DeMoss, Arthur.

DeMoss, Nancy & DeMoss, Arthur, eds. The Family Album. LC 66-21900. 1982. Repr. of 1979 ed. 10.95 (ISBN 0-8054-5117-X). Broadman.

DeMoss, Ted & Tamasy, Robert. The Gospel & the Briefcase. 128p. 1984. pap. 5.95 (ISBN 0-8423-1152-1). Tyndale.

DeMoss, Virginia. Runner's World Vitamin Book. 204p. 1982. spiral bdg. 11.95 (ISBN 0-89037-146-6). Anderson World.

--Runner's World Vitamin Book. (Instructional Bk.: No. 9). (Illus.). 204p. 1983. pap. 9.95 (ISBN 0-89037-271-3). Anderson World.

De Moss, William F. Influence of Aristotle's Politics & Ethics on Spenser. LC 72-123758. Repr. of 1920 ed. 11.50 (ISBN 0-404-02077-1). AMS Pr.

Demostenes, Rojas R. ABC Del Archivo. (Span.). 1982. text ed. 7.45 (ISBN 0-538-22980-2, V98). SW Pub.

Demosthenes. Against Meidias. Warmington, E. H., ed. Bd. with Against Androtion; Against Aristocrates; Against Timocrates; Against Aristogeiton 1 & 2, 21-26. (Loeb Classical Library: No. 299). (Gr. & Eng.). 12.50x (ISBN 0-674-99330-6). Harvard U Pr.

--All the Orations of Demosthenes. 2nd cor. ed. Leland, Thomas, tr. LC 76-161787. Repr. 37.50 (ISBN 0-404-54113-5). AMS Pr.

--De Corona. Warmington, E. H., ed. Bd. with De Falsa Legatione, 18 & 19. (Loeb Classical Library: No. 155). (Gr. & Eng.). 12.50x (ISBN 0-674-99171-0). Harvard U Pr.

--Demosthenes Against Androtion & Against Timocrates. 2nd ed. Vlastos, Gregory, ed. LC 78-14602. (Morals & Law in Ancient Greece Ser.). (Gr. & Eng.). 1979. Repr. of 1893 ed. lib. bdg. 23.00x (ISBN 0-405-11581-4). Ayer Co Pubs.

--Demosthenes on the Crown. Vlastos, Gregory, ed. LC 78-19354. (Morals & Law in Ancient Greece Ser.). (Eng. & Greek.). 1979. Repr. of 1901 ed. lib. bdg. 27.00x (ISBN 0-405-11547-4). Ayer Co Pubs.

--Demosthenes, Volumina 8 et 9: Scholia Graeca ex Codicibus Aucta et Emendata, ex Recensione Gulielmi Dindorfiu, 2 vols. LC 72-7888. (Greek History Ser.). (Gr. & Latin.). Repr. of 1851 ed. Set. 54.00 (ISBN 0-405-04782-7); Vol. 8. 30.50 (ISBN 0-405-04783-5); Vol. 9. 27.50 (ISBN 0-405-04784-3). Ayer Co Pubs.

--The First Philippic & the Olynthiacs of Demosthenes. Connor, W. R., ed. LC 78-18599. (Greek Texts & Commentaries Ser.). (Illus., Gr. & Eng.). 1979. Repr. of 1897 ed. lib. bdg. 25.50x (ISBN 0-405-11440-0). Ayer Co Pubs.

--Funeral Speech. Warmington, E. H., ed. Bd. with Erotic Essay; Exordia; Letters; General Index. (Loeb Classical Library: No. 374). (Gr. & Eng.). 12.50x (ISBN 0-674-99412-4). Harvard U Pr.

--Olynthiacs 1-3. Warmington, E. H., ed. Bd. with Philippic 1; On the Peace; Philippic 2; On Halonnesus; On the Chersonese; Philippics 3 & 4; Answer to Philip's Letter; On Organization; On the Navy-Boards; For the Liberty of the Rhodians; For the People of Megalopolis; On the Treaty with Alexander; Against Leptines, 1-7 & 20. (Loeb Classical Library: No. 238). (Gr. & Eng.). 12.50x (ISBN 0-674-99263-6). Harvard U Pr.

--On the Peace: Second Philippic on Chersonesus & Third Philippic. Connor, W. R., ed. LC 78-18602. (Greek Text Commentaries Ser.). 1979. Repr. of 1900 ed. lib. bdg. 25.50x (ISBN 0-405-11443-5). Ayer Co Pubs.

--Orationes, 3 vols. Incl. Vol. 1. Nos. 1-19. Butcher, S. H., ed. 1903. 24.00x (ISBN 0-19-814518-7); Vol. 3. Nos. 41-60. Butcher, S. H., ed. 1931.. 22.50x (ISBN 0-19-814521-7); Vol. 2, Pt. 2. Nos. 27-40. Rennie, W., ed. 1921. (Oxford Classical Texts Ser.). Oxford U Pr.

--Orationes, 3 Vols. Dindorf, F. & Blass, F., eds. 1822p. 1985. 45.00 (ISBN 0-89005-414-2). Ares.

--Orations of Demosthenes, 2 vols. Kennedy, C. R., ed. 1977. Set. lib. bdg. 250.00 (ISBN 0-8490-2378-5). Gordon Pr.

--Private Orations, 3 Vols. (Loeb Classical Library: No. 318, 346, 351). 12.50x ea. Nos. 27-40 (ISBN 0-674-99351-9). Nos. 41-49 (ISBN 0-674-99381-0). Nos. 50-58 (ISBN 0-674-99386-1). Harvard U Pr.

--Public Orations. 1967. Repr. of 1954 ed. 7.95x (ISBN 0-460-00546-4, Evman). Biblio Dist.

--Select Private Orations of Demosthenes, 2 vols. in 1, Pts. I & II. Connor, W. R., ed. LC 78-18601. (Greek Texts & Commentaries Ser.). (Illus.). 1979. Repr. of 1898 ed. lib. bdg. 48.50 (ISBN 0-405-11442-7). Ayer Co Pubs.

--Selected Private Speeches. Carey, C. & Reid, R. A., eds. (Cambridge Greek & Latin Classics Ser.). 250p. Date not set. price not set (ISBN 0-521-23960-5); pap. price not set (ISBN 0-521-28373-6). Cambridge U Pr.

--The Speech of Demosthenes Against the Law of Leptines. Sandys, John E., ed. LC 78-18605. (Greek Texts Commentaries Ser.). (Illus.). 1979. Repr. of 1890 ed. lib. bdg. 14.00x (ISBN 0-405-11445-1). Ayer Co Pubs.

--The Three Orations in Favour of the Olynthians with Fower Orations Against King Philip. Wilson, Thomas, tr. LC 68-54637. (English Experience Ser.: No. 54). 200p. 1968. Repr. of 1570 ed. 21.00 (ISBN 90-221-0054-5). Walter J Johnson.

DeMott, Barbara. Dogon Masks: A Structural Study of Form & Meaning. Seidel, Linda, ed. LC 81-16308. (Studies in the Fine Arts: Iconography: No. 4). 220p. 1982. 39.95 (ISBN 0-8357-1274-5). UMI Res Pr.

DeMott, Harold. Beacon Small-Group Bible Studies, Daniel: Daring to Live by Faith. Wolf, Earl C., ed. 96p. (Orig.). 1985. pap. 2.50 (ISBN 0-8341-0962-X). Beacon Hill.

DeMott, Robert. Steinbeck's Reading: A Catalogue of Books Owned & Borrowed. LC 80-8516. 1983. lib. bdg. 52.00 (ISBN 0-8240-9468-9). Garland Pub.

Demott, Robert J. & Marovitz, Sanford E., eds. Artful Thunder - Versions of the Romantic Tradition in American Literature - in Honor of Howard P. Vincent. LC 74-21886. (Illus.). 328p. 1975. 19.00x (ISBN 0-87338-172-6). Kent St U Pr.

De Motte Green, Catherine. The Dynamic Balance Sheet: A German Theory of Accounting. Brief, Richard P., ed. LC 80-1497. (Dimensions of Accounting Theory & Practice Ser.). 1981. lib. bdg. 39.00x (ISBN 0-405-13491-6). Ayer Co Pubs.

Demou, Doris B. A Part of Myself I Give to You: A Collection of Poems. 40p. 1976. softcover 4.00 (ISBN 0-9604794-0-6). M Demou & Assocs.

De Moubray, George A. Matriarchy in the Malay Peninsula & Neighbouring Countries. LC 77-87025. 304p. Repr. of 1931 ed. 34.50 (ISBN 0-404-16810-8). AMS Pr.

De Moulin, Daniel see Moulin, Daniel de.

Demoulin, Hubert. Epimenide de Crete. Vlastos, Gregory, ed. LC 78-19344. (Morals & Law in Ancient Greece Ser.). (Fr. & Gr.). 1979. Repr. of 1901 ed. lib. bdg. 12.00x (ISBN 0-405-11539-3). Ayer Co Pubs.

De Mourgues, Odette. Metaphysical Baroque & Precieux Poetry. LC 73-1144. 1953. lib. bdg. 30.00 (ISBN 0-8414-1850-0). Folcroft.

--Two French Moralists. LC 77-82506. (Major European Authors Ser.). 1978. 39.50 (ISBN 0-521-21823-3). Cambridge U Pr.

DeMouy, Jane K. Katherine Anne Porter's Women: The Eye of Her Fiction. 238p. 1983. text ed. 22.50x (ISBN 0-292-79018-X). U of Tex Pr.

Demouzon. A Rotten Deal. (Orig.). Date not set. 8.95 (ISBN 0-85690-089-3). Peebles Pr.

DeMoya, Armando & DeMoya, Dorothy. Sex & Health: A Practical Encyclopedia of Sexual Medicine. LC 80-5799. 304p. 1982. 19.95 (ISBN 0-8128-2794-5). Stein & Day.

DeMoya, Armando, et al. Sex & Health: A Practical Guide to Sexual Medicine. LC 80-5799. (Illus.). 369p. 1984. pap. 12.95 (ISBN 0-8128-6220-1). Stein & Day.

DeMoya, Dorothy, jt. auth. see DeMoya, Armando.

DeMoya, Dorothy, et al. RN's Sex Q & A: Candid Advice for You & Your Patients. 1983. pap. 15.95 (ISBN 0-87489-360-7). Med Economics.

Dempewolff, Richard, ed. Lost Cities & Forgotten Tribes. 1976. pap. 1.95 (ISBN 0-671-80809-5). WSP.

Dempewolff, Richard F., jt. auth. see Feinberg, Mortimer R.

Dempf, Alois. Christliche Staatsphilosophie in Spanien. Mayer, J. P., ed. LC 78-67344. (European Political Thought Ser.). (Ger.). 1979. Repr. of 1937 ed. lib. bdg. 12.00x (ISBN 0-405-11691-8). Ayer Co Pubs.

Dempsey, Al. The Italian Connection: Pulsar No. 2. 192p. 1982. 20.00x (ISBN 0-7278-0652-1, Pub. by Severn Hse). State Mutual Bk.

--The Red Falcons. 240p. 1982. 20.00x (ISBN 0-7278-0531-2, Pub. by Severn Hse). State Mutual Bk.

--The Stendal Raid. (Orig.). 1985. pap. 3.95 (ISBN 0-931773-17-2). Critics Choice Paper.

Dempsey, Al, jt. auth. see Moore, Robin.

Dempsey, B., jt. auth. see Perrin, D. D.

Dempsey, B., jt. ed. see Serjeant, E. P.

Dempsey, Charles. Annibale Carracci & the Beginnings of Baroque Style. 1977. 22.00 (ISBN 0-686-92334-0). J J Augustin.

Dempsey, D. Love...& the Days of. LC 75-24149. 1975. 4.95 (ISBN 0-9601968-1-1). Papa's Pr.

Dempsey, David & Zimbardo, Philip G. Psychology & You. 1978. text ed. 22.75x (ISBN 0-673-15086-0). Scott F.

Dempsey, David, et al. Death, the Press & the Public: Presentations to, for & by the Media & Other Professionals. 15.50 (ISBN 0-405-14023-1). Ayer Co Pubs.

Dempsey, David K. The Way We Die: An Investigation of Death & Dying in America Today. LC 76-51356. (McGraw-Hill Paperback Ser.). 1977. pap. 5.95 (ISBN 0-07-016340-5). McGraw.

Dempsey, Hugh & Harper, J. Russell. History in Their Blood: The Indian Portraits of Nicholas De Grandmaison. LC 82-6103. (Illus.). 128p. 1982. 35.00 (ISBN 0-933920-32-6). Hudson Hills.

Dempsey, Hugh A. Big Bear: The End of Freedom. LC 84-13105. (Illus.). 227p. 1985. 22.95 (ISBN 0-8032-1668-8). U of Nebr Pr.

--Charcoal's World. LC 79-14920. (Illus.). x, 178p. 1979. 15.95x (ISBN 0-8032-1651-3); pap. 3.95 (ISBN 0-8032-6552-2, BB 717, Bison). U of Nebr Pr.

--Red Crow, Warrior Chief. LC 80-51872. (Illus.). viii, 247p. 1980. 18.95x (ISBN 0-8032-1657-2). U of Nebr Pr.

Dempsey, J. Travis. Autobiography of Black Politics. (Illus.). 580p. 1985. price not set (ISBN 0-941484-05-X). Urban Res Inst.

Dempsey, Jack. Championship Fighting: Explosive Punching & Aggressive Defense. Cuddy, Jack, ed. (Illus.). 205p. Date not set. pap. 8.95 (ISBN 0-913111-00-7). Centerline.

Dempsey, James M. Fiber Crops. LC 74-4259. 1975. 18.50 (ISBN 0-8130-0449-7). U Presses Fla.

Dempsey, Janet. Washington's Last Cantonment: High Time for a Peace. (Illus.). 250p. 1986. 25.95 (ISBN 0-912526-39-4). Lib Res.

Dempsey, Jerome A. & Reed, Charles E., eds. Muscular Exercise & the Lung. (Illus.). 416p. 1977. 50.00x (ISBN 0-299-07220-7). U of Wis Pr.

Dempsey, John A. Basic Digital Electronics with MSI Applications. LC 75-9009. 320p. 1976. text ed. 29.95 (ISBN 0-201-01478-5). Addison-Wesley.

--Experimentation with Digital Electronics. 1976. 13.95 (ISBN 0-201-01479-3). Addison-Wesley.

Dempsey, John J. The Family & Public Policy: The Issue of the 1980s. LC 81-1740. (Illus.). 180p. 1981. text ed. 18.95 (ISBN 0-933716-15-X, 15X). P H Brookes.

Dempsey, Michael & Barrett, Norman. Atlas of the Arab World. (Culture Atlas Ser.). (Illus.). 128p. 1983. 16.95x (ISBN 0-87196-138-5). Facts on File.

Dempsey, Michael W., ed. Illustrated Fact Book of Science. LC 82-16412. (Illus.). 236p. 1983. 9.95 (ISBN 0-668-05729-7, 5729). Arco.

Dempsey, Mike, ed. Pipe Dreams: Early Advertising Art from the Imperial Tobacco Company. (Illus.). 96p. 1983. pap. 11.95 (ISBN 0-907516-12-2, Pub by Michael Joseph). Merrimack Pub Cir.

Dempsey, P. E., jt. ed. see Sluzalis, L. I.

Dempsey, Paul. How to Repair Briggs & Stratton Engines. 2nd ed. (Illus.). 192p. 1984. 15.95 (ISBN 0-8306-0687-4, 1687); pap. 8.95 (ISBN 0-8306-1687-X). TAB Bks.

--How to Repair Briggs & Stratton Engines. 2nd ed. 196p. 1985. pap. 8.95 (ISBN 0-8306-1687-X). Wallace-Homestead.

--How to Repair Diesel Engines. LC 75-20847. (Illus.). 308p. 1975. o.p 15.95 (ISBN 0-8306-5817-3); pap. 10.95 (ISBN 0-8306-4817-8, 817). TAB Bks.

--How to Repair Small Gasoline Engines. 2nd ed. LC 76-45056. 1976. pap. 9.95 (ISBN 0-8306-5917-X, 917). TAB Bks.

Dempsey, Raymond J., ed. see D'Amico, Ferninando & Valentini, Gabriele.

Dempsey, Richard A. & Traverso, Henry P. Scheduling the Secondary School. 96p. (Orig.). 1983. pap. 8.00. Natl Assn Principals.

Dempsey, S. J., jt. auth. see Topping, Victor.

Dempsey, Sandy. Women in Love. (Herland Ser.: No. 7). 52p. (Orig.). 1985. pap. 5.00 (ISBN 0-934996-30-X). Am Stud Pr.

Dempsey, Sheryll. Nursing Crosswords & Other Word Games. LC 73-17491. (Illus.). 100p. 1974. 5.95 (ISBN 0-8463-0600-X). Trainex Pr.

Dempsey, T. Delphic Oracle: Its Early History, Influence & Fall. LC 69-13234. Repr. of 1918 ed. 15.00 (ISBN 0-405-08442-0). Ayer Co Pubs.

Dempsey, Tom. The TRS-80 Beginner's Guide to Games & Graphics. 1984. 16.95 (ISBN 0-317-06048-1); pap. 16.95 (ISBN 0-936200-10-3). Blue Cat.

Dempster, Chris & Tomkins, Dave. Fire Power. 500p. 1980. 13.95 (ISBN 0-312-29115-9). St Martin.

Dempster, Derek, jt. auth. see Wood, Derek.

Dempster, Germaine. Dramatic Irony in Chaucer. 1959. text ed. 13.00x (ISBN 0-391-00492-1). Humanities.

Dempster, J. P. The Population Dynamics of the Moroccan Locust (Dociostaurus Maroccanus Thunb) in Cyprus. 1957. 35.00x (ISBN 0-85135-011-9, Pub. by Centre Overseas Research). State Mutual Bk.

Dempster, L. T. & Jepson, W. L. Flora of California: Vol. 4, Pt. 2, Rubiaceae. (Illus.). 47p. 1979. pap. 3.00x (ISBN 0-935628-08-8). Jepson Herbarium.

Dempster, Lauramay T. The Genus Galium (Rubiaceae) in Mexico & Central America. (Publications in Botany Ser.: No. 73). 1978. pap. 14.00x (ISBN 0-520-09578-2). U of Cal Pr.

Dempster, M. A., jt. auth. see Adby, P. R.

Dempster, M. A., ed. Stochastic Programming. LC 77-92826. (Institute of Mathematics & Its Applications Conference Ser.). 1980. 95.00 (ISBN 0-12-208250-8). Acad Pr.

Dempster, M. A. & Lenstra, J. K., eds. Deterministic & Stochastic Scheduling. 1982. 48.00 (ISBN 90-277-1397-9, Pub. by Reidel Holland). Kluwer Academic.

Dempster, Nigel. H. R. H. the Princess Margaret: A Life Unfulfilled. (Illus.). 208p. (Orig.). 1983. pap. 4.95 (ISBN 0-7043-3413-5, Pub. by Quartet Bks). Merrimack Pub Cir.

Dempster, Stuart. The Modern Trombone: A Definition of Its Idioms. LC 76-14309. (The New Instrumentation Ser.: Vol. III). 1979. 27.50x (ISBN 0-520-03252-7). U of Cal Pr.

Dempster, Thomas. Thomae Dempsteri Historia Ecclesiastica Gentis Scotorum: Sive, De Scriptoribus Scotis, 2 Vols. Irving, David, ed. LC 72-163685. (Bannatyne Club, Edinburgh. Publications: No. 21). Repr. of 1829 ed. Set. 75.00 (ISBN 0-404-52725-6). AMS Pr.

Dempster, W. J. Patrick Matthew & Natural Selection. 1984. 39.00 (ISBN 0-86228-065-6, Pub. by P Harris Scotland). State Mutual Bk.

Dempster-Ogden, Linda & De Renne, Charlotte. Chronic Obstructive Pulmonary Disease: Program Guidelines for Health Professionals. (Illus.). 1984. text ed. 21.50 (ISBN 0-943596-04-1, RAMSCO 00700). Ramsco Pub.

Dempsy, Paul. How to Convert Your Car, Van or Pickup to Diesel. (Illus.). 1978. pap. 7.95 (ISBN 0-8306-7968-5, 968). TAB Bks.

Demsetz, H. Economic, Legal & Political Dimensions of Competition. (Lectures in Economics Ser.: Vol. 4). 126p. 1982. 27.75 (ISBN 0-444-86442-3, North-Holland). Elsevier.

Demske, Dick. Carpentry & Woodworking. Roundtable Press, ed. LC 83-15094. (Illus.). 160p. (Orig.). 1983. 17.95 (ISBN 0-932944-63-9); pap. 6.95 (ISBN 0-932944-62-0). Creative Homeowner.

--Electrical Installations & Repairs. Wolf, Donald D. & Wolf, Margot L., eds. LC 76-8372. (Adventures in Home Repair Ser.). (Illus.). 1977. pap. 3.95 (ISBN 0-8326-2211-7, 7701). Delair.

--Exterior Home Repairs. Wolf, Donald D. & Wolf, Margot L., eds. LC 76-52268. (Adventures in Home Repair Ser.). (Illus.). 1979. pap. 3.95 (ISBN 0-8326-2216-8, 7704). Delair.

--Home Comfort. Wolf, Donald D. & Wolf, Margot L., eds. LC 76-52269. (Adventures in Home Repair Ser.). (Illus.). 1979. pap. 3.95 (ISBN 0-8326-2217-6, 7703). Delair.

--Home Repair Book. Wolf, Margot L. & Wolf, Donald D., eds. LC 78-13807. (Illus.). 1979. 19.95 (ISBN 0-8326-2238-9, 7720); deluxe ed. 19.95 (ISBN 0-8326-2239-7, 7721). Delair.

--Home Repairs Made Easy. Wolf, Donald D., ed. LC 79-84283. (Illus.). 1979. pap. 9.95 (ISBN 0-8326-2240-0, 7725). Delair.

--Interior Home Repairs. Wolf, Donald D. & Wolf, Margot L., eds. LC 76-52267. (Adventures in Home Repair Ser.). (Illus.). 1979. pap. 3.95 (ISBN 0-8326-2215-X, 7705). Delair.

--Painting, Paneling, & Wallpapering. Wolf, Donald D. & Wolf, Margot L., eds. LC 76-8373. (Adventures in Home Repair Ser.). (Illus.). 1977. pap. 3.95 (ISBN 0-8326-2212-5, 7702). Delair.

--Plumbing. Wolf, Donald D. & Wolf, Margot L., eds. LC 76-8370. (Adventures in Home Repair Ser.). (Illus.). 1976. pap. 3.95 (ISBN 0-8326-2210-9, 7700). Delair.

Demske, James A., tr. see Rahner, Karl.

Demske, James M. Being, Man, & Death: A Key to Heidegger. LC 70-94065. pap. 46.00 (ISBN 0-8357-9783-X, 2011252). Bks Demand UMI.

Demske, R. J. Instant Home Repair. LC 72-91408. (Illus.). 320p. 1973. 4.95 (ISBN 0-911744-13-4). Career Pub IL.

Demski. Instant Home Repair Guide. (Career Institute Instant Reference Library). 1973. 4.95 (ISBN 0-531-02086-X). Watts.

Demski, Joel S. Information Analysis. 2nd ed. LC 80-15971. (A-W Paperback Series in Accounting). 200p. 1980. pap. text ed. 10.50 (ISBN 0-201-01231-6). Addison-Wesley.

Demski, Joel S. & Feltham, Gerald A. Cost Determination: A Conceptual Approach. (Illus.). 272p. 1976. text ed. 16.75x (ISBN 0-8138-0360-8). Iowa St U Pr.

Demtroeder, W. Laser Spectroscopy: Basic Concepts & Instrumentation. (Springer Series in Chemical Physics: Vol. 5). (Illus.). 694p. 1981. 39.00 (ISBN 0-387-10343-0). Springer-Verlag.

De Mundo, Sara. Index to Spanish American Collective Biography: The River Plate Countries, Vol. 4. (Reference Publications in Area Studies). 1985. lib. bdg. 85.00 (ISBN 0-8161-8650-2). G K Hall.

De Mundo Lo, Sara. Index to Spanish American Collective Biography: Vol. 2-Mexico. 1982. lib. bdg. 68.00 (ISBN 0-8161-8529-8, Hall Reference). G K Hall.

--Index to the Spanish American Collective Biography: The Andean Countries, Vol. 1. 1981. lib. bdg. 62.50 (ISBN 0-8161-8181-0, Hall Reference). G K Hall.

--Julio Cortazar: His Works & His Critics. 280p. 1985. pap. 32.50 (ISBN 0-932759-00-9). Albatross.

De Mundo Lo, Sara see Lo, Sara de Mundo.

De Mundo Lo, Sara & Garner, Jane, eds. Basic Documents of the Seminar on the Acquisition of Latin American Library Materials, 2 pts. (Orig.). 1985. pap. 5.00 (ISBN 0-917617-05-3). SALALM.

Demura, F. Sai: Karate Weapon of Self-Defense. 7.50x (ISBN 0-685-63776-X). Wehman.

--Shito-Ryu Karate. 8.95x (ISBN 0-685-38450-0). Wehman.

Demura, Fumio. Advanced Nunchaku. 1976. 6.95x (ISBN 0-685-88116-4). Wehman.

--Bo: Karate Weapon of Self Defense. Johnson, Gil & Adachi, Geraldine, eds. LC 76-13757. (Ser. 124). (Illus.). 1976. pap. text ed. 7.50 (ISBN 0-89750-019-9). Ohara Pubns.

--Kama: Karate Weapon of Self-Defense. Lee, Mike, ed. LC 84-61149. (Series 436). (Orig.). 1984. pap. 7.95 (ISBN 0-89750-101-2). Ohara Pubns.

--Nunchaku. 6.95x (ISBN 0-685-38448-9). Wehman.

--Nunchaku Karate Weapon of Self-Defense. LC 78-183341. (Ser. 111). (Illus.). 1971. pap. text ed. 6.95 (ISBN 0-89750-006-7). Ohara Pubns.

--Sai Karate Weapon of Self-Defense. LC 74-83597. (Ser. 115). (Illus.). 1974. pap. text ed. 7.50 (ISBN 0-89750-010-5). Ohara Pubns.

--Shito-Ryu Karate. LC 74-169720. (Ser. 110). (Illus.). 1971. pap. text ed. 8.95 (ISBN 0-89750-005-9). Ohara Pubns.

--Tonfa: Karate Weapon of Self-Defense. Lee, Gregory, ed. LC 82-81557. (Series 417). (Illus.). 144p. (Orig.). 1982. pap. 7.95 (ISBN 0-89750-080-6). Ohara Pubns.

Demura, Fumio & Allee, John G. Bo, Karate Weapon of Self Defense. 6.95x (ISBN 0-685-70670-2). Wehman.

Demura, Fumio & Ivan, Dan. Advanced Nunchaku. Johnson, Gilbert & Adachi, Geraldine, eds. LC 76-40816. (Ser. 126). (Illus.). 1976. pap. text ed. 6.95 (ISBN 0-89750-021-0). Ohara Pubns.

--Street Survival: A Pratical Guide to Self Defense. LC 79-1946. (Illus.). 1979. pap. 11.50 (ISBN 0-87040-440-7). Japan Pubns USA.

De Muralt, Andre. The Idea of Phenomenology: Husserlian Exemplarism. Breckon, Garry L., tr. from Fr. LC 73-94433. (Studies in Phenomenology & Existential Philosophy). 1974. text ed. 26.95 (ISBN 0-8101-0448-2). Northwestern U Pr.

Demus, D. & Richter, L. Textures of Liquid Crystals. (Illus.). 228p. 1978. 108.90x (ISBN 0-89573-015-4). VCH Pubs.

Demus, Otto. Byzantine Mosaic Decoration: Aspects of Monumental Art in Byzantium. (Illus.). 162p. 1976. 25.00 (ISBN 0-89241-018-3). Caratzas.

--The Mosaics of San Marco in Venice: Part I: Eleventh & Twelfth Centuries; Part II: The Thirteenth Century, 4 vols. LC 82-2787. (Illus.). 1984. Slip-cased set. 350.00x (ISBN 0-226-14289-2); fiche 500.00 (ISBN 0-226-68975-1). U of Chicago Pr.

De Musset, Alfred. Les Caprices de Marianne. (Documentation thematique). (Fr). pap. 2.95 (ISBN 0-685-13814-3, 222). Larousse.

--Chandelier: Un Caprice. (Documentation thematique). 2.95 (ISBN 0-685-36195-0, 260). Larousse.

--Confession D'un Enfant Du Siecle. Allem, ed. (Coll. Class. Garnier). 1962. pap. 10.95 (ISBN 0-685-11099-0). French & Eur.

--La Confession d'un Enfant du Siecle. Allem, ed. (Coll. Prestige). 27.95 (ISBN 0-685-34951-9). French & Eur.

--Contes d'Espagne et d'Italie. Rees, Margaret, ed. (French Poets Ser.). 181p. (Fr.). 1973. 32.50 (ISBN 0-485-14703-3, Pub. by Athlone Pr Ltd); pap. 14.95 (ISBN 0-485-12703-2). Longwood Pub Group.

--Fantasio: Il ne faut jurer de rien. (Documentation thematique). (Fr). pap. 2.95 (ISBN 0-685-13915-8, 223). Larousse.

--Il Ne Faut Jurer De Rien. 1965. pap. 2.95 (ISBN 0-685-11242-X). French & Eur.

--Lorenzaccio. (Illus.). 1964. pap. 2.95 (ISBN 0-685-11297-7). French & Eur.

--Lorenzaccio. (Documentation Thematique). (Fr). pap. 2.95 (ISBN 0-685-13973-5, 224). Larousse.

--Oeuvres Completes, 3 tomes. Allem, ed. Incl. Tome I. Poesies Completes. 33.95 (ISBN 0-685-34948-9); Tome II. Theatre Complete. 42.95 (ISBN 0-685-34949-7); Tome III. Oeuvres Completes en Prose. 37.50 (ISBN 0-685-34950-0). (Bibliotheque de la Pleiade). French & Eur.

--Oeuvres Completes, 12 tomes. Set. deluxe ed. 850.00 (ISBN 0-685-34952-7); Set. deluxe ed. 1487.50 (ISBN 0-685-34953-5). French & Eur.

--On ne badine pas avec l'amour. (Documentation thematique). (Fr). pap. 2.95 (ISBN 0-685-14014-8, 225). Larousse.

--Poesies. (Documentation thematique). (Fr). pap. 2.95 (ISBN 0-685-14019-9, 226). Larousse.

Demuth, Jack & Demuth, Patricia. City Horse. (Illus.). (gr. 3-5). 1979. 7.95 (ISBN 0-396-07650-5). Dodd.

--Hannon: Police Horse. (Illus.). 96p. (gr. 3-6). 1983. pap. 1.95 (ISBN 0-590-31701-6). Scholastic Inc.

DeMuth, James. Small Town Chicago: The Comic Perspective of Finley Peter Dunne, George Ade, & Ring Lardner. (National University Publications, Interdisciplinary Urban Ser.). 1980. 12.50x (ISBN 0-8046-9252-1, Pub. by Kennikat). Assoc Faculty Pr.

Demuth, Katherine & Sekhesa, Tholoana. Basic SeSotho: An Oral Approach. (African Language Texts Ser.). (Orig.). 1978. pap. text ed. 5.00 (ISBN 0-941934-24-1). Indiana Africa.

Demuth, Norman. Albert Roussel: A Study. LC 78-66890. (Encore Music Editions Ser.). (Illus.). 1979. Repr. of 1947 ed. 16.00 (ISBN 0-88355-736-3). Hyperion Conn.

--An Anthology of Musical Criticism. LC 72-138219. 397p. 1972. Repr. of 1947 ed. lib. bdg. 26.75x (ISBN 0-8371-5576-2, DEMC). Greenwood.

--French Opera: Its Development to the Revolution. (Music Reprint, 1978 Ser.). (Illus.). 1978. Repr. of 1963 ed. lib. bdg. 35.00 (ISBN 0-306-77576-X). Da Capo.

--Musical Trends in the Twentieth Century. LC 73-6258. (Illus.). 359p. 1975. Repr. of 1952 ed. lib. bdg. 30.75x (ISBN 0-8371-6896-1, DEMT). Greenwood.

--Ravel. LC 78-59016. (Encore Music Editions Ser.). (Illus.). 1979. Repr. of 1947 ed. 22.45 (ISBN 0-88355-690-1). Hyperion Conn.

--Vincent D'Indy, 1851-1931. LC 73-6259. (Illus.). 117p. 1974. Repr. of 1951 ed. lib. bdg. 15.00x (ISBN 0-8371-6895-3, DEVD). Greenwood.

Demuth, Patricia. Joel: Growing up on Farm Man. (Illus.). 96p. (gr. 4-7). 1982. PLB 12.95 (ISBN 0-396-07997-0). Dodd.

Demuth, Patricia, jt. auth. see Demuth, Jack.

Demuynck, M., et al, eds. Biogas Plants in Europe: A Practical Handbook. (Solar Energy in the European Community Ser.: No. E, Vol. 6). 1984. lib. bdg. 53.00 (Pub. by Reidel Holland). Kluwer Academic.

Demyanov, V. & Malozemov, V. N. Introduction to Minimax. Louvish, D., tr. from Rus. LC 74-8156. 307p. 1974. 44.95x (ISBN 0-470-20850-3). Halsted Pr.

DeMyer, William. Technique of the Neurologic Examination. 3rd, rev. ed. (Illus.). 1980. text ed. 37.00 (ISBN 0-07-016352-9). McGraw.

DeMyer, William, ed. see Pre Test Service, Inc.

Demykina, G. Lost Girl & the Scallywags. 96p. 1982. 4.95 (ISBN 0-8285-2527-7, Pub. by Progress Pubs USSR). Imported Pubns.

Den, Douglas Uyl see Uyl, Douglas D.

Den, Van Hoek see Van den Hoek, C.

Denaerde, Stefan & Stevens, Wendelle C. UFO... Contact from Planet Iarga. Lodge, Jim, tr. from Dutch. (UFO Fact Bks.). Orig. Title: Buitenaardse Beschaving. (Illus.). 368p. 1982. lib. bdg. 15.95 (ISBN 0-9608558-1-5). UFO Photo.

Denaes, Raymond. General Guide to Paris Street Atlas. 1980. pap. 10.95 (ISBN 0-933982-04-6, Pub by Editions L'indispensable). Bradt Ent.

Denan, Corinne. Dragon & Monster Tales. new ed. LC 79-66329. (Illus.). 48p. (gr. 3-6). 1980. PLB 7.59 (ISBN 0-89375-326-2); pap. 1.95 (ISBN 0-89375-325-4). Troll Assocs.

--Giant Tales. new ed. LC 79-66330. (Illus.). 48p. (gr. 3-6). 1980. lib. bdg. 7.59 (ISBN 0-89375-328-9); pap. 1.95 (ISBN 0-89375-327-0). Troll Assocs.

--Goblin Tales. new ed. LC 79-66326. (Illus.). 48p. (gr. 3-6). 1980. lib. bdg. 7.59 (ISBN 0-89375-320-3); pap. 1.95 (ISBN 0-89375-319-X). Troll Assocs.

--Hair-Raising Tales. LC 79-66334. (Illus.). 48p. (gr. 5-7). 1980. PLB 7.59 (ISBN 0-89375-334-3); pap. 1.95 (ISBN 0-89375-333-5). Troll Assocs.

--Haunted House Tales. LC 79-66335. (Illus.). 48p. (gr. 5-7). 1980. PLB 7.59 (ISBN 0-89375-336-X); pap. text ed. 1.95 (ISBN 0-89375-335-1); cassette avail. Troll Assocs.

--Once upon a Time Tales. LC 79-66337. (Illus.). 48p. (gr. 2-6). 1980. lib. bdg. 7.59 (ISBN 0-89375-340-8); pap. 1.95 (ISBN 0-89375-339-4). Troll Assocs.

--Strange & Eerie Tales. new ed. LC 79-66336. (Illus.). 48p. (gr. 4-6). 1980. lib. bdg. 7.59 (ISBN 0-89375-338-6); pap. 1.95 (ISBN 0-89375-337-8). Troll Assocs.

--Tales of Magic & Spells. (Illus.). 48p. (gr. 3-6). 1980. PLB 7.59 (ISBN 0-89375-318-1); pap. text ed. 1.95 (ISBN 0-89375-317-3); cassette avail. Troll Assocs.

--Tales of the Ugly Ogres. LC 79-66333. (Illus.). 48p. (gr. 3-6). 1980. PLB 7.59 (ISBN 0-89375-332-7); pap. text ed. 1.95 (ISBN 0-89375-331-9). Troll Assocs.

--Troll Tales. new ed. LC 79-66327. (Illus.). 48p. (gr. 3-6). 1980. lib. bdg. 7.59 (ISBN 0-89375-322-X); pap. 1.95 (ISBN 0-89375-321-1); cassette avail. Troll Assocs.

--Witch Tales. new ed. LC 79-66328. (Illus.). 48p. (gr. 3-6). 1980. lib. bdg. 7.59 (ISBN 0-89375-324-6); pap. 1.95 (ISBN 0-89375-323-8). Troll Assocs.

--Wizard Tales. new ed. LC 79-66331. (Illus.). 48p. (gr. 3-6). 1980. lib. bdg. 7.59 (ISBN 0-89375-330-0); pap. 1.95 (ISBN 0-89375-329-7). Troll Assocs.

Denan, Jay. Burnout: Funny Car Races. LC 79-64700. (Illus.). 32p. (gr. 4-9). 1980. PLB 9.79 (ISBN 0-89375-256-8); pap. 2.50 (ISBN 0-89375-257-6). Troll Assocs.

--The Glory Ride, Road Racing. LC 79-52179. (Illus.). 32p. (gr. 4-9). 1980. PLB 9.79 (ISBN 0-89375-254-1); pap. 2.50 (ISBN 0-89375-255-X). Troll Assocs.

--Hot on Wheels: The Rally Scene. LC 79-64701. (Illus.). 32p. (gr. 4-9). 1980. PLB 9.79 (ISBN 0-89375-258-4); pap. 2.50 (ISBN 0-89375-259-2). Troll Assocs.

--Start Your Engines: Racing the Championship Trail. LC 79-64702. (Illus.). 32p. (gr. 4-9). 1980. PLB 9.79 (ISBN 0-89375-260-6); pap. 2.50 (ISBN 0-89375-261-4). Troll Assocs.

De Nanteuil, Luc. David. (Library of Great Painters). (Illus.). 168p. 1985. 40.00 (ISBN 0-8109-0833-6). Abrams.

Denardo, Eric V. Dynamic Programming: Models & Applications. (Illus.). 240p. 1982. 34.95 (ISBN 0-13-221507-1). P-H.

DeNardo, G. & Doebner, H., eds. Differential Geometric Methods in Theoretical Physics: Proceedings of June 30-July 3, 1981 Conference, Trieste, Italy. vi, 294p. 1983. 33.00x (ISBN 9971-950-58-8, Pub. by World Sci Singapore). Taylor & Francis.

Denardo, G., et al, eds. Group Theoretical Methods in Physics: Proceedings of the XIIth International Colloquium, Held at the International Centre for Theoretical Physics, Trieste, Italy, Sept. 5-11, 1983. (Lecture Notes in Physics Ser.: Vol. 201). xxvii, 518p. 1984. pap. 23.00 (ISBN 0-387-13335-6). Springer-Verlag.

DeNardo, James. Power in Numbers: The Political Strategy of Protest & Rebellion. LC 84-42880. (Illus.). 240p. 1985. text ed. 25.00x (ISBN 0-691-07682-0). Princeton U Pr.

Denault, Gerard F., tr. see Houzeau, Jean-Charles.

DeNault, Phyllis M., jt. auth. see Jacobs, Erwin M.

De Navacelle, Thierry. Sublime Marlene. Smith, Carey L., tr. from Fr. LC 84-50458. (Illus.). 160p. 1984. 14.95 (ISBN 0-312-77468-0). St Martin.

De Navarre, Marguerite. The Heptameron. Chilton, Paul A., tr. (Classics Ser.). 544p. 1984. pap. 7.95 (ISBN 0-14-044355-X). Penguin.

--Oeuvres Choisies, 2 vols. Clive, H. P., ed. Incl. Vol. 1. Poemes; Vol. 2. Theatre et Nouvelles (ISBN 0-89197-323-0). LC 68-12125. (Medieval French Literature Ser). (Fr.). 1968. pap. text ed. 4.95x ea. Irvington.

--Tales from the 'Heptameron' Clive, H. P., ed. (Renaissance Library). 184p. (Fr.). 1970. pap. 18.95 (ISBN 0-485-12801-2, Pub. by Athlone Pr Ltd). Longwood Pub Group.

De Navarrete, Martin F. Biblioteca Maritima Espanola, 2 vols. LC 68-58225. (Bibliography & Reference Ser.: No. 244). (Span). 1969. Repr. of 1851 ed. 98.00 (ISBN 0-8337-1115-6). B Franklin.

De Navarro, J. M. The Finds from the Site of La Tene: Scabbards & the Swords Found in Them. 498p. 1979. 55.00x (ISBN 0-19-725909-X). State Mutual Bk.

Denavit-Saubie, M., jt. ed. see Bianchi, A. L.

Denber, H. C., jt. auth. see Rinkle, Max.

Denber, Herman, ed. Schizophrenia: Theory, Diagnoses & Treatment. 1978. 55.00 (ISBN 0-8247-6711-X). Dekker.

Denber, Herman C., ed. Psychopharmacological Treatment: Theory & Practice. (Modern Pharmacology-Toxicology Ser: Vol. 2). 320p. 1975. 55.00 (ISBN 0-8247-6229-0). Dekker.

Den Berg, J. H. Van see Van Den Berg, J. H.

Den Berg, Jan H. Van see Van Den Berg, Jan H.

Den Berg, Leo Van see Klaasen, Leo & Burns, Leland.

Den Berghe, Van see Van Den Berghe.

Denbigh, J. S., jt. auth. see Denbigh, K. G.

Denbigh, K. G. An Inventive Universe. LC 75-13561. 220p. 1975. 8.95 (ISBN 0-8076-0802-5). Braziller.

Denbigh, K. G. & Denbigh, J. S. Entropy in Relation to Incomplete Knowledge. 164p. 1985. 34.50 (ISBN 0-521-25677-1). Cambridge U Pr.

Denbigh, K. G. & Turner, J. C. Chemical Reactor Theory: An Introduction. 3rd ed. LC 83-7557. 250p. 1984. 42.50 (ISBN 0-521-25645-3); pap. 15.95 (ISBN 0-521-27630-6). Cambridge U Pr.

Denbigh, Kenneth G. The Principles of Chemical Equilibrium. 4th ed. (Illus.). 506p. 1981. 67.50 (ISBN 0-521-23682-7); pap. 21.95 (ISBN 0-521-28150-4). Cambridge U Pr.

--Three Concepts of Time. 160p. 1981. pap. 22.00 (ISBN 0-387-10757-6). Springer-Verlag.

Denbigh, Kenneth G. & Turner, J. C. Chemical Reactor Theory: An Introduction. LC 76-123661. pap. 59.00 (ISBN 0-317-10504-3, 2013219). Bks Demand UMI.

Den Bleyker, Merle, jt. auth. see Hendricks, William C.

Denbo, Bruce F., ed. see Wharton, Mary E. & Bowen, Edward L.

DenBoer, Gordon. The Documentary History of the First Federal Elections, 1788-1790, Vol. II. LC 74-5903. 800p. 1984. text ed. 50.00x (ISBN 0-299-09510-X). U of Wis Pr.

Den Boer, James. Lost in Blue Canyon. (Orig.). 1979. pap. 5.00 (ISBN 0-87922-108-9). Christopher's Bks.

Den Boer, James, jt. auth. see Olson, Charles.

Denborough, M. A., ed. Australia & Nuclear War. LC 84-148159. 224p. 1985. 34.50 (ISBN 0-949614-05-X, Pub by Croom Helm Ltd); pap. 15.50 (ISBN 0-949614-09-2, Pub. by Croom Helm Ltd). Longwood Pub Group.

Den Borren, Charles Van see Van Den Borren, Charles.

Denbow, William. Chandler. 1977. pap. 1.50 (ISBN 0-505-51169-X, Pub. by Tower Bks). Dorchester Pub Co.

Den Bulcke, D. Van & Halsberghe, E. Employment Decision-Making in Multinational Enterprises: Survey Results from Belgium. International Labour Office Staff, ed. (Working Papers: No. 32). (Illus.). v, 102p. 1984. pap. 8.55 (ISBN 92-2-103832-7). Intl Labour Office.

Denburg, Joseph K. Van see Van Denburg, Joseph K.

Denburgh, John Van see Van Denburgh, John.

Denby, Charles. Indignant Heart: A Black Worker's Journal. LC 78-65368. 300p. 1978. 15.00 (ISBN 0-89608-093-5); pap. 7.50 (ISBN 0-89608-092-7). South End Pr.

Denby, Cumore B. Mystical Lady. 80p. 1981. 7.50 (ISBN 0-87881-095-1). Mojave Bks.

Denby, Edwin. Collected Poems. LC 75-23024. 1975. 17.95 (ISBN 0-916190-00-5); pap. 8.95 (ISBN 0-916190-01-3). Full Court NY.

--Mrs. W's Last Sandwich. 1972. 6.95. Horizon.

Denby, Ron. American Lives. LC 85-4280. 304p. (Orig.). 1985. pap. 7.95 (ISBN 0-915175-13-4). Knights Pr.

Denby-Wrightson, Kathryn, jt. auth. see Fry, Joan.

D'Encarnacao, Patricia, jt. auth. see D'Encarnacao, Paul.

D'Encarnacao, Paul & D'Encarnacao, Patricia. How to Love Yourself Unconditionally. LC 82-99980. (Illus.). 96p. 1983. pap. 12.95 with cassette (ISBN 0-9610048-0-0). Metamorphosis Pr.

D'Encausse, Helene C. Confiscated Power. LC 82-47521. (A Cornelia & Michael Bessie Bk.). 415p. 1982. 19.18i (ISBN 0-06-039009-3, HarpT). Har-Row.

--Decline of an Empire: The Soviet Socialist Republic in Revolt. LC 80-8402. (Illus.). 304p. 1981. pap. 6.95xi (ISBN 0-06-131988-0, TB 1988, Torch). Har-Row.

--A History of the Soviet Union Nineteen Seventeen to Nineteen Fifty-Three: Volume 1: Lenin - Revolution & Power. Ionescu, Valence, tr. from Fr. 288p. (Orig.). 1982. pap. text ed. 11.95 (ISBN 0-582-29559-9). Longman.

--A History of the Soviet Union 1917-1953: Vol. 2, Stalin-Order Through Terror. Ionescu, Valence, tr. from Fr. LC 81-8132. 288p. (Orig.). 1982. pap. text ed. 11.95x (ISBN 0-582-29560-2). Longman.

Dence, Joseph B. Mathematical Techniques in Chemistry. LC 75-16337. 442p. 1975. text ed. 43.00 (ISBN 0-471-20319-X, Pub. by Wiley-Interscience). Wiley.

--Steroids & Peptides: Selected Chemical Aspects for Biology, Biochemistry & Medicine. LC 79-21236. 418p. 1980. 74.95 (ISBN 0-471-04700-7, Pub. by Wiley-Interscience). Wiley.

Dence, Thomas P. The FORTRAN Cookbook. 2nd ed. LC 84-8695. (Illus.). 240p. 1984. 18.95 (ISBN 0-8306-0737-4); pap. 11.95 (ISBN 0-8306-1737-X, 1737). TAB Bks.

--Solving Math Problems in BASIC. (Illus.). 392p. 1983. 19.95 (ISBN 0-8306-0264-X, 1564); pap. 15.50 (ISBN 0-8306-0164-3). TAB Bks.

Dencher, Ted. Why I Left Jehovah's Witnesses. 1966. pap. 5.95 (ISBN 0-87508-160-6). Chr Lit.

Denck, H., ed. see Paquet, K. J., et al.

Dencke, J., et al see David, Hans T.

Dencker, Sven-Jonas. Hospital Based Community Support Services Recovering Chronic Schizophrenics, No. 2. (International Exchange of Information in Rehabilitation Ser.). 83p. 1980. write for info. (ISBN 0-939986-03-5). World Rehab Fund.

Dendel, Esther W. African Fabric Crafts: Sources of African Design & Technique. LC 72-6627. (Illus.). 160p. 1974. 10.95 (ISBN 0-8008-0150-4). Taplinger.

--Designing from Nature: A Source Book for Artists & Craftsmen. LC 77-92756. 1978. 10.95 (ISBN 0-8008-2173-4); pap. 5.95 (ISBN 0-8008-2174-2). Taplinger.

Dendinger, Lloyd N., ed. E. E. Cummings: The Critical Reception. (American Critical Tradition Ser.: No. 8). (Illus.). 1979. lib. bdg. 21.50x (ISBN 0-89102-124-8). B Franklin.

Dendle, Brian J. Galdos: The Mature Thought. LC 80-51013. (Studies in Romance Languages: No. 23). 216p. 1980. 20.00x (ISBN 0-8131-1407-1). U Pr of Ky.

Dendle, Brian J., ed. see Galdos, Benito P.

Den Dooren, L. E., jt. auth. see Van Iterson, G.

DenDooven, Gweneth R., jt. auth. see Borglum, Lincoln.

Dendrinos, Dimitrios S. Urban Revolution: Studies in the Mathematical Ecology of Cities. (Illus.). 1985. 27.95 (ISBN 0-19-823249-7). Oxford U Pr.

Dendurent, H. O., ed. Thomas De Quincey: A Reference Guide. 1978. lib. bdg. 22.00 (ISBN 0-8161-7840-2, Hall Reference). G K Hall.

Dendy, Arthur, ed. Problems of Modern Science: A Series of Lectures Delivered at King's College (University of London) LC 72-314. (Essay Index Reprint Ser.). Repr. of 1922 ed. 18.00 (ISBN 0-8369-2789-3). Ayer Co Pubs.

Dendy, P., ed. Human Tumour in Short Term Culture: Techniques & Clinical Applications. 1976. 60.00 (ISBN 0-12-209850-1). Acad Pr.

Dendy, Philip P., ed. Technical Advances in Biomedical Physics. 1984. lib. bdg. 57.00 (ISBN 90-247-2934-3, Pub. by Martinus Nijhoff Netherlands). Kluwer Academic.

Dendy, Philip P. & Hill, Bridget T., eds. Human Tumour Drug Sensitivity Testing in Vitro: Techniques & Clinical Applications. 1984. 60.00 (ISBN 0-12-209860-9). Acad Pr.

Dendy, Walter C. The Philosophy of Mystery. LC 74-2364. 1845. lib. bdg. 35.00 (ISBN 0-8414-3723-8). Folcroft.

Deneau, Daniel P. Byron's Narrative Poems of Eighteen Thirteen. (Salzburgstudies in English Literature, Romantic Reassessment Ser.: No. 55). 106p. 1975. pap. text ed. 25.50x (ISBN 0-391-01360-2). Humanities.

De Nebesky-Wojkowitz, Rene see Nebesky-Wojkowitz, Rene De.

Denecke, H., jt. ed. see Heberer, G.

Denecke, H. J. & Meyer, R. Corrective & Reconstructive Rhinoplasty. Oxtoby, L., tr. (Plastic Surgery of Head & Neck: Vol. 1). (Illus.). 1967. 289.10 (ISBN 0-387-03757-8). Springer-Verlag.

DeNeef, A. L. Spenser & the Motives of Metaphor. LC 82-14837. 205p. 1983. 31.75 (ISBN 0-8223-0487-2). Duke.

De Neef, J. & De Nottolander, G., eds. Coagulation Disorders in Obstetrics. (International Congress Ser.: No. 123). 1966. 13.00 (ISBN 90-219-0070-X, Excerpta Medica). Elsevier.

De Neef, Leigh. This Poetick Liturgie: Robert Herrick's Ceremonial Mode. LC 74-75910. 200p. 1974. 14.75 (ISBN 0-8223-0323-X). Duke.

Deneen, Lawrence J. & Hessellund, Thorvald A. Vocational Rehabilitation of the Injured Worker. 192p. 1981. 24.95 (ISBN 0-931290-62-7). Alchemy Bks.

Denef, Lawrence W., tr. see Lapide, Pinchas & Stuhlmacher, Peter.

Denef, Lawrence W., tr. see Loewenich, Walther.

Denekamp, Juliana. Cell Kinetics & Cancer Therapy. (Illus.). 176p. 1982. 24.75x (ISBN 0-398-04580-1). C C Thomas.

Deneke, Frederick J., jt. auth. see Grey, Gene W.

De Nemours, Pierre-Samuel Du Pont. Oeuvres Politiques Et Economiques, 10 Vols. 1979. lib. bdg. 550.00 (ISBN 3-262-01205-X). Kraus Intl.

De Nemours Victor M. Du, Pont see Du Pont De Nemours, Victor M.

Denenberg, Herbert. Getting Your Money's Worth. 1974. pap. 8.50 (ISBN 0-8183-0133-3). Pub Aff Pr.

Denenberg, Herbert S., jt. auth. see Kimball, Spencer L.

Denenberg, Herbert S., et al. Risk & Insurance. 2nd ed. 1974. 32.95 (ISBN 0-13-781294-9). P-H.

Denenberg, Richard, jt. auth. see Denenberg, Tia.

Denenberg, Tia & Denenberg, Richard. Alcohol & Drugs: Issues in the Workplace. 216p. 1983. 32.00 (ISBN 0-87179-410-1). BNA.

Denenberg, Victor H., ed. Education of the Infant & Young Child. LC 77-137617. 1970. 28.50 (ISBN 0-12-209150-7). Acad Pr.

De Nerval, Gerard. Aurelia. Bd. with La Pandora; Les Chimeres. (Le Livre de Poche Classique Ser.). pap. 4.50 (ISBN 0-685-34958-6). French & Eur.

--The Chimeras. Jay, Peter, tr. (French Poetry Ser.). (Illus.). 96p. 1985. 17.50 (ISBN 0-933806-34-5). Black Swan CT.

--Les Chimeres. Rinsler, Norma, ed. (French Poets Ser.). 144p. (Fr.). 1973. 32.50 (ISBN 0-485-14702-5, Pub. by Athlone Pr Ltd); pap. 14.95 (ISBN 0-485-12702-4, Pub. by Athlone Pr Ltd). Longwood Pub Group.

--Les Filles Du Feu. Bd. with Les Chimeres. (Coll. GF). 1961. pap. 3.95 (ISBN 0-685-36017-2, 6904). French & Eur.

--Journey to the Orient. Glass, Norman, tr. 216p. 1985. pap. 6.95 (ISBN 0-918825-09-1). Moyer Bell Ltd.

--Oeuvres, 2 vols. Beguin & Richer, eds. (Bibl. de la Pleiade). 1952-56. Set. 91.95 (ISBN 0-685-11437-6). French & Eur.

--Oeuvres, Tome I. Lemaitre, ed. Incl. Petits Chateaux de Boheme; Les Illumines; Les Nuits d'Octobre; Promenades et Souvenirs; Les Filles du Feu; Les Chimeres; La Pandora; Aurelia. (Class. Garnier). pap. 12.95 (ISBN 0-685-34955-1). French & Eur.

--Oeuvres, Tome I. Lemaitre, ed. Incl. Petits Chateaux de Boheme; Les Illumines; Les Nuits d'Octobre; Promenades et Souvenirs; Les Filles du Feu; Les Chimeres; La Pandora; Aurelia. (Coll. Selecta). 12.95 (ISBN 0-685-34956-X). French & Eur.

--Oeuvres. Lemaitre, ed. Incl. Voyage En Orient. (Coll. Prestige). 21.95 (ISBN 0-685-34957-8). French & Eur.

De Nerval, Gerard see Nerval, Gerard de.

Denes, Agnes. Isometric Systems in Isotropic Space, Map Projections from the Study of Distortions, 1973-1979. LC 79-66223. (Illus.). 100p. 1979. 75.00x (ISBN 0-89822-007-6). Visual Studies.

Denes, Gabor. The Story of the Imperial: The Life & Times of Torquay's Great Hotel. LC 81-68502. (Illus.). 160p. 1982. 21.50 (ISBN 0-7153-8051-6). David & Charles.

Denes, Peter B. & Pinson, Elliot N. The Speech Chain: The Physics & Biology of Spoken Language. LC 74-180069. 192p. 1973. pap. 4.50 (ISBN 0-385-04238-8, Anch). Doubleday.

Denes, Tibor. Fak, Tavak, Tengerek. LC 66-29554. (Hungarian). 1967. pap. 5.00 (ISBN 0-911050-29-9). Occidental.

De Nettancourt, D., jt. ed. see Magnien, E.

De Neufville, Judith I., ed. The Land Use Policy Debate in the United States. (Environment, Development, & Public Policy - Environmental Policy & Planning Ser.). 284p. 1981. text ed. 29.50x (ISBN 0-306-40718-3, Plenum Pr). Plenum Pub.

DeNeufville, R. & Stafford, J. Systems Analysis for Engineers & Managers. 48.00 (ISBN 0-07-016370-7). McGraw.

De Neuvillate, Alfonso. Reindorf. (Illus.). 236p. 1984. 75.00; deluxe ed. 300.00 (ISBN 0-933516-66-5). Alpine Bk Co.

Denevan, William M., ed. The Native Population of the Americas in 1492. LC 75-32071. 376p. 1976. 29.50x (ISBN 0-299-07050-6). U of Wis Pr.

DeNeve, Rose, jt. auth. see Holmes, Nigel.

DeNevers, Noel. Fluid Mechanics. LC 78-91144. (Engineering Ser). 1970. text ed. 31.95 (ISBN 0-201-01497-1). Addison-Wesley.

DeNevi, Don. Tragic Train "the City of San Francisco" Development & Historic Wreck of a Streamliner. LC 77-3499. (Illus.). 1977. 19.95 (ISBN 0-87564-525-9). Superior Pub.

--Western Pacific. LC 78-11258. (Illus.). 1978. 15.95 (ISBN 0-87564-530-5). Superior Pub.

DeNevi, Don & Moholy, Noel. Junipero Serra: The Illustrated Story of the Franciscan Founder of California's Missions. LC 84-47718. (Illus.). 256p. 1985. 12.45i (ISBN 0-06-061876-0, HarpR). Har-Row.

DeNevi, Don & Moulin, Thomas. Gabriel Moulin's Peninsula. Bonnett, Wayne, ed. (Illus.). 184p. 1985. 45.00 (ISBN 0-915269-01-5). Windgate Pr.

DeNevi, Don, jt. auth. see Saul, Eric.

Denevi, Marco. Ceremonia Secreta y Otros Cuentos. Yates, Donald A., ed. (Sp). 1965. pap. text ed. 2.50x (ISBN 0-685-14844-0). Macmillan.

--Rosaura a las Diez. Yates, Donald A., ed. (Illus.). 219p. (Span.). 1964. pap. text ed. 9.95 (ISBN 0-02-328440-4, Pub. by Scribner). Macmillan.

Denfeld, Duane. A Guide to World War II Museums, Relics & Sites in Europe. 222p. 1979. pap. 25.00x (ISBN 0-89126-079-X). MA-AH Pub.

Denffer, Ahmad von see Von Denffer, Ahmad.

Deng, Francis. Security Problems: An African Predicament. LC 81-71701. (Hans Wolff Memorial Lecture Ser.). 1982. pap. text ed. 5.00 (ISBN 0-941934-35-7). Indiana Africa.

Deng, Francis, jt. ed. see Collins, Robert.

Deng, Francis M. Africans of Two Worlds: The Dinka in Afro-Arab Sudan. LC 77-76305. 1978. 27.50x (ISBN 0-300-02149-6). Yale U Pr.

--Dinka Folktales: African Stories from the Sudan. LC 73-82901. (Illus.). 200p. 1974. text ed. 32.50x (ISBN 0-8419-0138-4, Africana). Holmes & Meier.

--The Dinka of the Sudan. (Illus.). 174p. 1984. pap. text ed. 7.95x (ISBN 0-88133-082-5). Waveland Pr.

Deng, Ming-Dao. The Wandering Taoist. LC 82-48925. (Illus.). 224p. 1983. 14.37i (ISBN 0-06-250225-5, HarpR). Har-Row.

Dengel, R. Dance & Be Charming. (Ballroom Dance Ser.). 1985. lib. bdg. 74.50 (ISBN 0-87700-765-9). Revisionist Pr.

Dengerink, Don, jt. auth. see Green, Lee.

Dengerink, H. A. & Cross, H. J., eds. Training Professionals for Rural Mental Health. LC 81-16288. viii, 135p. 1982. 11.95x (ISBN 0-8032-1660-2). U of Nebr Pr.

Dengerink, H. A., jt. ed. see Carr, J. E.

Dengevin, K. The Idea of Justice in Christian Perspective. 1978. pap. 2.95 (ISBN 0-88906-102-5). Radix Bks.

Dengler. Fanny Crosby, Writer of Eight Thousand Songs. 3.95 (ISBN 0-318-18159-2). WCTU.

Dengler, Dieter. Escape from Laos. LC 78-32056. 224p. 1979. 12.95 (ISBN 0-89141-076-7). Presidio Pr.

--Escape from Laos. 1982. pap. 2.95 (ISBN 0-8217-1113-X). Zebra.

Dengler, J. C. Let's Start Investing: Millions for Millions. 160p. 1984. 9.95 (ISBN 0-8059-2931-2). Dorrance.

Dengler, Mariana. A Pebble in Newcomb's Pond. (gr. 6 up). 1980. pap. 1.95 (ISBN 0-448-17131-7, Pub. by Tempo). Ace Bks.

Dengler, Marianna. A Certain Kind of Courage. (gr. 6 up). 1983. pap. 1.95 (ISBN 0-448-13574-4, Pub by Tempo). Ace Bks.

Dengler, Marianne. Vicki. 135p. (gr. 7 up). 1980. pap. 1.95 (ISBN 0-590-31324-X). Scholastic Inc.

Dengler, Sandy. Arizona Longhorn Adventure. LC 18-60. (Pioneer Family Adventure Ser.). 128p. (gr. 5-8). 1980. pap. 2.95 (ISBN 0-8024-0299-2). Moody.

--The Chain Five Mystery. (The Daniel Tremain Adventures Ser.). 128p. (Orig.). 1984. pap. 2.95 (ISBN 0-8024-1901-1). Moody.

--Fanny Crosby: Writer of Eight Thousand Songs. (Orig.). 1985. pap. 3.95 (ISBN 0-8024-2529-1). Moody.

--The Horse Who Loved Picnics. LC 80-10691. (Pioneer Family Adventure Ser.). 128p. (gr. 4-8). 1980. pap. 2.95 (ISBN 0-8024-3589-0). Moody.

--Mystery at McGeehan Ranch. LC 81-18694. (Pioneeer Family Adv. Ser.). 128p. 1982. pap. 2.95 (ISBN 0-8024-2972-6). Moody.

--Socorro Island Treasure. LC 82-22864. (Daniel Tremain Adventures Ser.). 128p. (gr. 5-8). 1983. pap. 3.95 (ISBN 0-8024-7813-1). Moody.

--Song of the Nereids. 192p. 1984. pap. 1.95 (ISBN 0-310-46472-2, Serenade-Saga). Zondervan.

--Summer of the Wild Pig. (Pioneer Family Adventure Ser.). (gr. 6-8). 1979. pap. 2.95 (ISBN 0-8024-8429-8). Moody.

--Summer Snow. 192p. 1984. pap. 1.95 (ISBN 0-310-46432-3, Serenade-Saga). Zondervan.

--Three in One Pioneer Family Adventure Series. 1985. pap. 3.95 (ISBN 0-8024-6365-7). Moody.

Dengrove, Edward. Hypnosis & Behavior Therapy. (Illus.). 428p. 1976. 36.75x (ISBN 0-398-03336-6). C C Thomas.

Den Haag, Ernest Van see Van Den Haag, Ernest.

Denham, Alice. The Ghost & Mrs. Muir. 132p. Repr. of 1968 ed. lib. bdg. 13.95 (ISBN 0-88411-826-6, Pub. by Aeonian Pr). Amereon Ltd.

Denham, Diana. Gypsies in Social Space. LC 80-51689. 120p. 1981. perfect bound 10.00 (ISBN 0-918660-14-9). Ragusan Pr.

Denham, Foxy & Whitehead, Pinky. Building It: Muscle Building & Steroids. (Illus.). 300p. (Orig.). 1985. 28.95x (ISBN 0-911238-87-5); pap. 15.95x (ISBN 0-911238-80-8). B of A.

Denham, H. M. The Ionian Islands to Rhodes: A Sea-Guide. (Illus.). 1976. 19.95 (ISBN 0-393-03195-0). Norton.

--Southern Turkey, the Levant & Cyprus: A Sea-Guide to the Coasts & Islands. (Illus.). 1976. 19.95 (ISBN 0-393-03198-5). Norton.

--The Tyrrhenian: A Sea-Guide to Its Coasts & Islands. (Illus.). 1976. 19.95 (ISBN 0-393-03196-9). Norton.

Denham, H. W. Road Transport Records. 12.50x (ISBN 0-392-04425-0, SpS). Sportshelf.

Denham, Hardy R., Jr. After You've Said I Do. 96p. (Orig.). 1983. pap. 6.95 (ISBN 0-939298-18-X). J M Prods.

--Marriage Renewal Sourcebook. 96p. (Orig.). 1983. pap. 6.95 (ISBN 0-939298-24-4, 244). J M Prods.

Denham, Henry. Inside the Nazi Ring: A Naval Attache in Germany. (Illus.). 224p. 1985. 24.50 (ISBN 0-8419-1024-3). Holmes & Meier.

Denham, John. Poetical Works of Sir John Denham. 2nd ed. Banks, Theodore H., ed. xviii, 326p. 1969. 25.00 (ISBN 0-208-00155-7, Archon). Shoe String.

Denham, John W. & Pickard, C. Glenn. Clinical Roles in Rural Health Centers. LC 78-27733. (Rural Health Center Ser.). (Illus.). 80p. 1979. prof ref 15.00x (ISBN 0-88410-537-7); pap. 9.95x (ISBN 0-88410-543-1). Ballinger Pub.

Denham, Ken. Guinea Pigs & Chinchillas. (Illus.). 93p. 1977. pap. 3.95 (ISBN 0-7028-1075-4). Avian Pubns.

Denham, Ken, ed. see Christie, Irene.

Denham, M. J., ed. Care of the Long-Stay Elderly Patient. (Illus.). 236p. 1983. text ed. 29.50x (ISBN 0-7099-0809-1); pap. 14.50x (ISBN 0-7099-0820-2). Sheridan.

--Care of the Long-Stay Elderly Patient. (Illus.). 240p. 1983. text ed. 32.50x (ISBN 0-7099-0809-1, Pub. by Croom Helm England); pap. text ed. 18.50x (ISBN 0-7099-0820-2). Sheridan.

Denham, Michael A. The Denham Tracts, Vol. I-II: A Collection of Folk-Lore. Hardy, James, ed. (Folk-Lore Society, London, Monography: Vols. 29 & 35). pap. 66.00. Kraus Repr.

Denham, Robert. Northrop Frye: A Supplementary Bibliography. 67p. (Orig.). 1979. pap. 5.00 (ISBN 0-931182-02-6). Iron Mtn Pr.

Denham, Robert D. Northrop Frye: An Enumerative Bibliography. LC 73-20345. (Author Bibliographies Ser.: No. 14). 149p. 1974. 16.50 (ISBN 0-8108-0693-2). Scarecrow.

--Northrop Frye & Critical Method. 1978. text ed. 23.75x (ISBN 0-271-00546-7). Pa St U Pr.

Denham, Robert D., intro. by see Frye, Northrop.

Denham, Robert D., ed. see Frye, Northrop.

Den Hamer, H. E. Interordering: A New Method of Component Orientation. (Studies in Mechanical Engineering: Vol. 2). 160p. 1981. 51.00 (ISBN 0-444-41933-0). Elsevier.

Denhard, J. G. & Grider, John D. Complete Guide to Fiduciary Accounting. LC 80-28061. 218p. 1981. 39.95 (ISBN 0-13-160572-0, Busn). P-H.

Denhardt, Bob. The Quarter Horse. LC 82-45893. (Illus.). 256p. 1983. Repr. of 1941 ed. 14.95 (ISBN 0-89096-144-1). Tex A&M Univ Pr.

Denhardt, David T. Replication of DNA. Head, John J., ed. LC 83-71256. (Carolina Biology Readers Ser.). 16p. (gr. 10 up). 1983. pap. 1.60 (ISBN 0-89278-320-6, 45-9720). Carolina Biological.

Denhardt, J., Jr. Complete Guide to Estate Accounting & Taxes. 2nd ed. 1978. 39.95 (ISBN 0-13-160242-X). P-H.

Denhardt, Robert B. In the Shadow of Organization. LC 80-23775. (Studies in Government & Public Policy). 168p. 1981. 17.95x (ISBN 0-7006-0210-0). U Pr of KS.

--Theories of Public Organization. LC 83-7996. (Public Administration Ser.). 275p. 1983. text ed. 10.00 pub net (ISBN 0-534-02736-9). Brooks-Cole.

Denhardt, Robert M. Foundation Dams of the American Quarter Horse. 240p. 1982. 22.95 (ISBN 0-8061-1820-2). U of Okla Pr.

--Foundation Sires of the American Quarter Horse. LC 75-40956. 1976. 19.95 (ISBN 0-8061-1337-5). U of Okla Pr.

--The Horse of the Americas. LC 74-5955. 1975. pap. 10.95 (ISBN 0-8061-1724-9). U of Okla Pr.

--The King Ranch Quarter Horses: And Something of the Ranch & the Men That Bred Them. LC 73-123340. (Illus.). 1978. Repr. of 1970 ed. 26.95 (ISBN 0-8061-0924-6). U of Okla Pr.

--Quarter Horses: A Story of Two Centuries. (Illus.). 1967. 16.95 (ISBN 0-8061-0753-7). U of Okla Pr.

--The Quarter Running Horse: America's Oldest Breed. LC 78-21381. 1979. 27.95 (ISBN 0-8061-1500-9). U of Okla Pr.

Den Hartog, Adel P. & Van Staveren, Wija A. Manual for Social Surveys on Food Habits & Consumption in Developing Countries. 114p. 1984. pap. text ed. 7.50 (ISBN 90-220-0838-X, PDC265, Pudoc). Unipub.

Den Hartog, Jacob P. Mechanics. 1948. pap. 7.50 (ISBN 0-486-60754-2). Dover.

--Strength of Materials. 1949. pap. 6.00 (ISBN 0-486-60755-0). Dover.

Den Hartog, Jacob P., ed. see Prandtl, Ludwig & Tietjens, O. G.

Den Hartog Jager, W. A. see Jager, W. A. den Hartog.

Den Hartog Jager, W. A., et al, eds. Neurology. (International Congress Ser.: Nos. 427 & 434). 1978. 137.50 (ISBN 0-444-90017-9); pap. 53.00 (ISBN 0-444-90004-7). Elsevier.

Den Hengel, John W. Van. The Home of Meaning: The Hermeneutics of the Subject of Paul Ricoeur. LC 82-40204. 356p. (Orig.). 1982. lib. bdg. 29.75 (ISBN 0-8191-2602-0); pap. text ed. 15.50 (ISBN 0-8191-2603-9). U Pr of Amer.

Den Hengst, D. The Prefaces in the Historia Augusta. 188p. 1981. pap. text ed. 23.50x (ISBN 90-6032-224-X, Pub. by Gruner Amsterdam). Humanities.

Den Hoek, C. van see Van den Hoek, C.

Denhoff & Feldman. Developmental Disabilities. (Pediatric Habilitation Ser.: Vol. 2). 328p. 1981. 29.50 (ISBN 0-8247-1565-9). Dekker.

Denhoff, Eric. Cerebral Palsy the Preschool Years: Diagnosis, Treatment & Planning. 144p. 1968. 15.75x (ISBN 0-398-00432-3). C C Thomas.

Denhoff, Eric & Feldman, Steven A. Developmental Disabilities: Management Through Diet & Medication. (Pediatric Habilitation Ser.: Vol. 2). (Illus.). 280p. 1981. 29.50 (ISBN 0-8247-1565-9). Dekker.

Denholm, Richard. Basic Math with Applications. 1982. pap. text ed. 20.60x (ISBN 0-673-15233-2). Scott F.

Denholm-Young, N. Collected Papers. 317p. 1969. text ed. 27.75x (ISBN 0-900768-21-5, Pub. by Univ of Wales Pr England). Humanities.

Denholm-Young, Noel. Seignorial Administration in England. 196p. 1963. 26.00x (ISBN 0-7146-1468-8, F Cass Co). Biblio Dist.

Denholm-Young, Sally. Supersecretary: You Office Survival Guide. 160p. 25.00x (ISBN 0-907070-00-0, Pub. by Settle & Bendall UK); pap. 20.00x (ISBN 0-907070-01-9). State Mutual Bk.

Denholtz, Elaine. Having It Both Ways: Married Women with Lovers. LC 81-40336. 324p. 1981. 12.95 (ISBN 0-8128-2819-4). Stein & Day.

Deni, Richard L. Programming Microcomputers for Psychology Experiments. 180p. 1985. pap. text ed. write for info. (ISBN 0-534-05442-0). Wadsworth Pub.

DeNicola, Alejandro F. & Blaquier, Jorge A. Physiopathology of Hypophysial Disturbances & Diseases of Reproduction. LC 82-15219. (Progress in Clinical & Biological Research Ser.: Vol. 87). 352p. 1982. 36.00 (ISBN 0-8451-0087-4). A R Liss.

De Nicola, P., et al. Nail Diseases in Internal Medicine. (Illus.). 128p. 1974. 14.75x (ISBN 0-398-03178-9). C C Thomas.

Denicola, Robert C., jt. auth. see Brown, Ralph S.

De Nicolas, Antonio T. Avatara: The Humanization of Philosophy Through the Bhagavad Gita. LC 76-152. 1976. 12.50 (ISBN 0-89254-001-X); pap. 8.50 (ISBN 0-89254-002-8). Nicolas-Hays.

--Meditations Through the Rg Veda: Four-Dimensional Man. LC 76-39692. 1976. 12.95 (ISBN 0-89254-004-4). Nicolas-Hays.

De Nicolas, Antonio T. & Moutsopolous, Evanghlos, eds. God: Experience or Origin. (God Ser.). (Orig.). 1985. text ed. 12.95 (ISBN 0-913757-24-1, Pub. by New Era Bks); pap. text ed. price not set (ISBN 0-913757-25-X, Pub. by New Era Bks). Paragon Hse.

De Nicolas, Antonio T., ed. see Lincoln, Victoria.

De Nicolay, Nicolas see Nicolay, Nicolas de.

Denie, jt. auth. see Manion, Jim.

Denieffe, Joseph. A Personal Narrative of the Irish Revolutionary Brotherhood. (Illus.). 324p. 1969. Repr. of 1906 ed. 20.00x (ISBN 0-7165-0044-2, BBA 03073, Pub. by Irish Academic Pr). Biblio Dist.

Denies, Mark, jt. auth. see Meyers, Thomas.

Denig, Edwin T. Five Indian Tribes of the Upper Missouri: Sioux, Arickaras, Assiniboines, Crees & Crows. Ewers, John C., ed. LC 61-9005. (Civilization of the American Indian Ser.: No. 59). (Illus.). 1961. 16.95 (ISBN 0-8061-0493-7); pap. 7.95 (ISBN 0-8061-1308-1). U of Okla Pr.

--Indian Tribes of Upper Missouri. facs. ed. (Shorey Indian Ser.). 292p. Repr. of 1930 ed. 15.95 (ISBN 0-8466-0152-4, S152). Shorey.

--Of the Crow Nation. Ewers, John C., ed. LC 76-43690. (BAE. Bulletin: 151). Repr. of 1953 ed. 14.50 (ISBN 0-404-15532-4). AMS Pr.

Deniker, Joseph. The Races of Man: Outline of Anthropology & Ethnography. facsimile ed. (Select Bibliographies Reprint Ser). Repr. of 1900 ed. 45.00 (ISBN 0-8369-5932-9). Ayer Co Pubs.

Denikin, Anton. The White Army. 1973. lib. bdg. 59.95 (ISBN 0-8490-1290-2). Gordon Pr.

Denikin, Anton I. The Russian Turmoil, Memoirs: Military, Social & Political. LC 73-2306. (Russian Studies: Perspectives on the Revolution Ser.). (Illus.). 344p. 1973. Repr. of 1922 ed. 29.85 (ISBN 0-88355-100-4). Hyperion Conn.

--The White Army. Zvegintzov, Catherine, tr. from Rus. LC 73-2307. (Russian Studies: Perspectives on the Revolution Ser.). (Illus.). 367p. 1973. Repr. of 1930 ed. 25.00 (ISBN 0-88355-101-2). Hyperion Conn.

Denilson, E., ed. see Csoma, Sandor K.

Denim, B. C. Different Is Not The Same As Wrong. 1982. pap. 1.95 (ISBN 0-570-08408-3, 39-1083). Concordia.

Dening, Greg. Islands & Beaches: Discourse on a Silent Land, Marquesas, 1774-1880. (Illus.). 367p. 1980. text ed. 27.50x (ISBN 0-8248-0721-9). UH Pr.

Dening, Walter. Japan in Days of Yore. 422p. 1982. 39.00x (Pub. by E-W Pubns England). State Mutual Bk.

--Life of Toyotomi Hideyoshi. 3rd ed. LC 79-136391. (BCL Ser. II). Repr. of 1930 ed. 18.50 (ISBN 0-404-02078-X). AMS Pr.

Denis, Christopher. The Films of Shirley Maclaine. (Illus.). 256p. 1982. pap. 8.95 (ISBN 0-8065-0795-0). Citadel Pr.

--The Films of Shirley Maclaine. (Illus.). 1980. 14.95 (ISBN 0-8065-0693-8). Citadel Pr.

Denis, Claude St. Kashi-No-Bo. pap. 1.50 (ISBN 0-686-00694-1). Assoc Bk.

Denis, Ernest. La Boheme Depius la Montagne-Blanche, 2 vols. 1981. Repr. Set. lib. bdg. 59.00x (ISBN 0-686-71907-7). Scholarly.

--Boheme Depuis la Montagne - Blanche, 2 Vols. LC 70-144973. (Fr). 1971. Repr. of 1903 ed. Set. 59.00 (ISBN 0-403-00941-3). Scholarly.

--Fin de l'Independance Boheme, 2 vols. LC 76-151601. (BCL Ser. I). Repr. of 1890 ed. Set. 85.00 (ISBN 0-404-02087-9). AMS Pr.

--Huss et les guerres hussites. LC 77-8424. Repr. of 1930 ed. 34.00 (ISBN 0-404-16126-X). AMS Pr.

Denis, Ferdinand. Monde Enchante: Cosmographie et Histoire Naturelle Fantastiques Du Moyen Age. 1965. Repr. of 1845 ed. 23.50 (ISBN 0-8337-0833-3). B Franklin.

Denis, Gabriel. Reign of Jesus Thru Mary. 5.50 (ISBN 0-910984-03-4). Montfort Pubns.

Denis, George, tr. see Tertz, Abram & Sinyavsky, Andrei.

Denis, Jean. Traite de L'Accord de L'Espinette. 2nd ed. LC 68-16229. (Music Ser.). 1969. Repr. of 1650 ed. 19.50 (ISBN 0-306-70950-3). Da Capo.

Denis, Jean-Jerome. Le Tresor. LC 82-10317. (Illus.). 32p. (Fr.). (gr. 7-12). 1982. pap. text ed. 1.95 (ISBN 0-88436-910-2, 40284); cassette 12.00. EMC.

Denis, John. Alistair MacLean's Hostage Tower. 192p. 1983. pap. 2.50 (ISBN 0-449-20086-8, Crest). Fawcett.

Denis, Keith. Canoe Trails Through Quetico. (Illus.). 1960. pap. 7.50 (ISBN 0-8020-3046-7). U of Toronto Pr.

Denis, L., et al, eds. Clinical Bladder Cancer. LC 81-15855. 214p. 1982. text ed. 29.50 (ISBN 0-306-40835-X, Plenum Pr). Plenum Pub.

Denis, Louis, et al, eds. Controlled Clinical Trials in Urologic Oncology. (European Organization for Research on Treatment of Cancer (EORTC) Monograph: Vol. 13). 350p. 1984. text ed. 59.50 (ISBN 0-89004-152-0). Raven.

Denis, Michael J. Connecticut. (New England Towns & Counties Ser.). 45p. 1984. pap. 5.00 (ISBN 0-318-04594-X). Danbury Hse Bks.

--Genealogical Researching in Eastern Canada: An Address Guide. (Genealogical Researching Address Guides Ser.). 39p. (Orig.). 1981. pap. 4.00 (ISBN 0-318-12046-1). Danbury Hse Bks.

--Genealogical Researching in Eastern Canada. 39p. 1981. pap. 4.00 (ISBN 0-318-04592-3). Danbury Hse Bks.

--Genealogical Researching in New England: An Address Guide. (Genealogical Researching Address Guides Ser.). 71p. 1982. pap. 7.50 (ISBN 0-318-12047-X). Danbury Hse Bks.

--Genealogical Researching in New England. 71p. 1982. pap. 7.50 (ISBN 0-318-02995-2). Danbury Hse Bks.

--Genealogical Researching in Ontario: An Address Guide. (Genealogical Researching Address Guides Ser.). 11p. (Orig.). 1984. pap. 2.00 (ISBN 0-318-12048-8). Danbury Hse Bks.

--Machias, Maine, Families, 1767-1827. 21p. 1984. pap. 2.50 (ISBN 0-318-04602-4). Danbury Hse Bks.

--Machias, Maine, Marriages, 1767-1827. 20p. 1984. pap. 2.50 (ISBN 0-318-04604-0). Danbury Hse Bks.

--Maine. (New England Towns & Counties Ser.). 73p. 1981. pap. 7.50 (ISBN 0-318-04595-8). Danbury Hse Bks.

--Maine Towns & Counties. (New England Towns & Counties Ser.). 73p. (Orig.). 1981. pap. 7.50 (ISBN 0-318-12049-6). Danbury Hse Bks.

--Massachusetts. (New England Towns & Counties Ser.). 46p. 1984. pap. 5.00 (ISBN 0-318-04596-6). Danbury Hse Bks.

--Massachusetts Towns & Counties. (New England Towns & Counties Ser.). 46p. 1984. pap. 5.00 (ISBN 0-318-12050-X). Danbury Hse Bks.

--New Hampshire. (New England Towns & Counties Ser.). 27p. 1982. pap. 3.00 (ISBN 0-318-04597-4). Danbury Hse Bks.

--New Hampshire Towns & Counties. (New England Towns & Counties Ser.). 27p. (Orig.). 1982. pap. 3.00 (ISBN 0-318-12051-8). Danbury Hse Bks.

--Rhode Island. (New England Towns & Counties Ser.). 1983. pap. 2.00 (ISBN 0-318-04598-2). Danbury Hse Bks.

--Rhode Island Towns & Counties. (New England Towns & Counties Ser.). 8p. (Orig.). 1983. pap. 2.00 (ISBN 0-318-12052-6). Danbury Hse Bks.

--Scarboro, Maine, Marriages of the Second Congregational Church. 21p. 1983. pap. 2.50 (ISBN 0-318-04600-8). Danbury Hse Bks.

--Vermont. (New England Towns & Counties Ser.). 35p. 1983. pap. 2.50 (ISBN 0-318-04599-0). Danbury Hse Bks.

--Vermont Towns & Counties. (New England Towns & Counties Ser.). 35p. (Orig.). 1983. pap. 3.50 (ISBN 0-318-12053-4). Danbury Hse Bks.

--York, Maine, Marriages, 1697-1760. 25p. 1985. pap. 3.00 (ISBN 0-318-04605-9). Danbury Hse Bks.

Denis, Michael J., ed. Connecticut Towns & Counties. (New England Towns & Counties Ser.). 45p. (Orig.). 1985. pap. 5.00 (ISBN 0-318-12045-3). Danbury Hse Bks.

Denis, Paul. Opportunities in Dance. (VGM Career Bks.). (Illus.). 160p. 1983. 7.95 (ISBN 0-8442-6657-4, 6657-4, Passport Bks.); pap. 5.95 (ISBN 0-8442-6658-2, 6658-2). Natl Textbk.

Denis, Peter, jt. ed. see Preston, Adrian.

Denis, Philippe. Notebook of Shadows: Selected Poems, 1974-1980. Irwin, Mark, tr. from Fr. LC 82-82907. (Contemporary European Poetry Ser.). Orig. Title: Cahier d'ombres. 68p. (Orig.). 1982. pap. 5.00 (ISBN 0-910321-00-0). Globe Pr.

Denis, Pierre. The Argentine Republic, Its Development & the Progress. McCabe, Joseph, tr. LC 75-41073. Repr. of 1922 ed. 26.50 (ISBN 0-404-14530-2). AMS Pr.

--Brazil. 1977. lib. bdg. 59.95 (ISBN 0-8490-1541-3). Gordon Pr.

Denis, R. G. Gambling Times Guide to Thoroughbred Racing. (Illus., Orig.). 1984. pap. text ed. 5.95 (ISBN 0-89746-005-7). Gambling Times.

Denis, Serge & Maraval, Marcel. Dictionnaire Espagnol-Francais. 1774p. (Fr. & Eng.). 1968. pap. 26.50 (ISBN 0-686-56983-0, M-6110). French & Eur.

Denis, Serge, et al. Le Dictionnaire Espagnol-Francais et Francais-Espagnol. new ed. 904p. (Span. & Fr.). 1976. 36.95 (ISBN 0-686-56984-9, M-6111). French & Eur.

Denisen, Ervin L. Principles of Horticulture. 2nd ed. (Illus.). 1979. text ed. 24.95 (ISBN 0-02-328380-7); write for info (ISBN 0-685-96773-5). Macmillan.

Denisoff, R. Serge. Great Day Coming: Folk Music & the American Left. LC 74-155498. (Music in American Life Ser). (Illus.). Repr. of 1971 ed. 58.00 (ISBN 0-8357-9680-9, 2019042). Bks Demand UMI.

--Sing a Song of Social Significance. rev ed. LC 78-186631. 1983. 19.95 (ISBN 0-87972-036-0); pap. 6.95 (ISBN 0-87972-272-X). Bowling Green Univ.

--Solid Gold: The Popular Record Industry. LC 74-20194. (Cultural & Society Ser). (Illus.). 504p. 1981. pap. 14.95 (ISBN 0-87855-586-2). Transaction Bks.

--Tarnished Gold: The Record Industry Revisited. 350p. 1985. pap. 16.95 (ISBN 0-88738-618-0); cloth 29.95 (ISBN 0-88738-068-9). Transaction Bks.

--Waylon: A Biography. LC 82-24786. (Illus.). 392p. 1983. 16.95 (ISBN 0-87049-387-6). U of Tenn Pr.

--Waylon: A Biography. (Illus.). 375p. 1984. pap. 10.95 (ISBN 0-312-85848-5). St Martin.

Denisoff, R. Serge & Wahrman, Ralph. An Introduction to Sociology. 3rd ed. 640p. 1983. pap. text ed. write for info. (ISBN 0-02-328430-7). Macmillan.

Denisoff, R. Serge, et al. Theories & Paradigms in Contemporary Sociology. LC 73-90894. 451p. 1974. pap. text ed. 13.50 (ISBN 0-87581-169-8). Peacock Pubs.

Denison, Cara D., et al, eds. European Drawings, Thirteen Seventy-Five to Eighteen Twenty-Five. (Illus.). 1981. 75.00x (ISBN 0-19-520258-9). Oxford U Pr.

Denison, David O. & Forman, Arthur S. Archaeological Investigations in South Halawa Valley, Ewa District, Island of Oahu-Phase II. (Departmental Report: No. 71-9). 64p. 1971. pap. 3.00 (ISBN 0-910240-77-9). Bishop Mus.

Denison, Early, ed. see Symposium of Fluid Mechanics in the Petroleum Industry (1975: Houston, TX).

Denison, Edward. Letters & Other Writings. Leighton, Baldwyn, ed. 303p. 1974. Repr. of 1875 ed. lib. bdg. 30.00 (ISBN 0-87821-276-0). Milford Hse.

Denison, Edward F. Accounting for Slower Economic Growth: The United States in the 1970s. LC 79-20341. 212p. 1979. 29.95 (ISBN 0-8157-1802-0); pap. 10.95 (ISBN 0-8157-1801-2). Brookings.

--Accounting for United States Economic Growth: 1929-1969. LC 74-278. 355p. 1974. 29.95 (ISBN 0-8157-1804-7); pap. 11.95 (ISBN 0-8157-1803-9). Brookings.

--Why Growth Rates Differ: Postwar Experience in Nine Western Countries. 1967. 22.95 (ISBN 0-8157-1806-3); pap. 8.95 (ISBN 0-8157-1805-5). Brookings.

Denison, Edward F. & Chung, William K. How Japan's Economy Grew So Fast: The Sources of Postwar Expansion. LC 76-10836. pap. 71.30 (ISBN 0-317-30402-X, 2024963). Bks Demand UMI.

Denison, Herbert. A Treatise on Photogravure. Lyons, Nathan, ed. LC 73-22263. (Visual Studies Reprint Ser.). 1974. pap. 6.50 (ISBN 0-87992-004-1). Light Impressions.

--A Treatise on Photogravure. Lyons, Nathan, ed. (Reprint & Research Ser.). (Illus.). 142p. 1974. 11.95 (ISBN 0-87992-005-X); pap. 6.50 (ISBN 0-87992-004-1). Visual Studies.

Denison, J. H. The Enlargement of Personality: Behavior Patterns & Their Formation. 1930. 30.00 (ISBN 0-8495-6271-6). Arden Lib.

Denison, John H., Jr., jt. auth. see Ruppert, Karl.

Denison, Mary A. Out of Prison. facsimile ed. LC 74-164558. (American Fiction Reprint Ser). Repr. of 1864 ed. 26.50 (ISBN 0-8369-7034-9). Ayer Co Pubs.

Denison, Oliver. Images of Mystic Seaport. (Illus., Orig.). 1979. pap. 3.95 (ISBN 0-933614-01-2). Peregrine Pr.

Denison, Raymond A., jt. ed. see Martin, Michael J.

Denison, Robert. Acanthodii. Kuhn, O. & Schultze, H. P., eds. (Handbook of Paleoichthyology: Vol. 5). (Illus.). 62p. 1979. text ed. 41.30x (ISBN 3-437-30291-4). Lubrecht & Cramer.

--Placodermi. Kuhn, O. & Schultz, H. P., eds. (Handbook of Paleoichthyology: Vol. 2). (Illus.). 128p. 1978. text ed. 55.05x (ISBN 3-437-30265-5). Lubrecht & Cramer.

Denison, T. S. Friday Afternoon Dialogues. facs. ed. LC 79-139763. (Granger Index Reprint Ser). 1879. 17.00 (ISBN 0-8369-6217-6). Ayer Co Pubs.

--A Mexican-Aryan Comparative Vocabulary. (Span.). 1976. lib. bdg. 59.95 (ISBN 0-8490-0613-9). Gordon Pr.

Denison, Thomas S. An Iron Crown: A Tale of the Great Republic. LC 74-22779. Repr. of 1885 ed. 34.50 (ISBN 0-404-58420-9). AMS Pr.

Denisov, E. T. Liquid-Phase Reaction Rate Constants. LC 73-79419. 795p. 1974. 110.00x (ISBN 0-306-65160-2, IFI Plenum). Plenum Pub.

Denisov, E. T., et al. Liquid-Phase Oxidation of Oxygen-Containing Compounds. (Studies in Soviet Science-Physical Sciences Ser.). (Illus.). 369p. 1978. 59.50x (ISBN 0-306-10936-0, Consultants). Plenum Pub.

Denisov, P. N. Principles of Constructing Linguistic Models. LC 72-88205. (Janua Linguarum, Ser. Minor: No. 91). 173p. (Orig.). 1973. pap. text ed. 20.00x (ISBN 90-2792-376-0). Mouton.

Denisov, P. N., ed. see Lenin, V. I.

Denis-Papin, Maurice. Dictionnaire Analogique et de Synonymes Pour la Resolution des Problemes des Mots Croises. 6th ed. (Fr.). 1970. pap. 6.95 (ISBN 0-686-56786-2, M-6582, Pub. by Albin Michel). French & Eur.

--Dictionnaire Des Mots Croises. 384p. (Fr.). 1978. pap. 11.95 (ISBN 0-686-56883-4, F-137060). French & Eur.

Denissov, A. I., ed. see Voronine, V. V., et al.

Deniston, Lynn O., et al, eds. Community Health Agency Evaluation. 24p. 1976. 4.95 (ISBN 0-88737-235-X, 21-1643). Natl League Nurse.

Deniston, Richard, ed. see Bloch, Iwan.

Denisyuk, Yu. N. Fun with Maths & Physics. 355p. 1984. 9.95 (ISBN 0-8285-2894-2, Pub by Mir Pubs USSR). Imported Pubns.

--Fundamentals of Holography. 136p. 1985. pap. 3.95 (ISBN 0-8285-2876-4, Pub by Mir Pubs USSR). Imported Pubns.

Denitch, Bogdan. A New Foreign & Defense Policy for the United States. 180p. Date not set. 14.95x (ISBN 0-86598-141-8). Rowman & Allanheld.

Denitch, Bogdan, ed. Democratic Socialism: The Mass Left in Advanced Industrial Societies. LC 81-65021. 192p. 1981. text ed. 31.95x (ISBN 0-86598-015-2). Allanheld.

--Legitimation of Regimes: International Frameworks for Analysis. LC 78-63117. (Sage Studies in International Sociology: Vol. 17). (Illus.). 305p. 1979. 28.00 (ISBN 0-8039-9898-8); pap. 14.00 (ISBN 0-8039-9899-6). Sage.

Denitch, Bogdan D. The Legitimation of a Revolution: The Yugoslav Case. LC 75-18170. 272p. 1976. 27.50x (ISBN 0-300-01906-8). Yale U Pr.

Denitto, Dennis. Film: Form & Feeling. 576p. 1985. pap. text ed. 20.50 scp (ISBN 0-06-041629-7, HarpC). Har-Row.

Denizeau, Claude. Dictionnaire des Parlers Arabes de Syrie, Liban et Palestine. 581p. (Fr. & Arabic.). 1961. pap. 49.95 (ISBN 0-686-57090-1, M-6112). French & Eur.

Denk, Roland. The Complete Sailing Guide. (Illus.). 142p. 1983. 12.95 (ISBN 0-7158-0829-X, Pub. by EP Publishing England). Sterling.

--The Complete Sailing Handbook. (Illus.). 352p. 1980. 29.95 (ISBN 0-8317-1600-2, Mayflower Bks). Smith Pubs.

--Sailing. (EP Sports Ser.). (Illus.). 1973. 6.95 (ISBN 0-7158-0581-9). Charles River Bks.

Denker, Arnold S. My Best Games of Chess 1929-75. Orig. Title: If You Must Play Chess. 190p. 1981. pap. 5.95 (ISBN 0-486-24035-5). Dover.

Denker, Bert & Denker, Ellen. The Rocking Chair Book. (Illus.). 1979. pap. 7.95 (ISBN 0-8317-7418-5, Mayflower Bks). Smith Pubs.

--The Warner Collector's Guide to American Pottery & Porcelain. (Illus.). 256p. (Orig.). 1982. pap. 9.95 (ISBN 0-446-97631-8). Warner Bks.

Denker, Bert, jt. auth. see Denker, Ellen.

Denker, Ellen & Denker, Bert. The Main Street Pocket Guide to North American Pottery & Porcelain. rev. ed. (Illus.). 256p. 1985. pap. 7.95 (ISBN 0-915590-79-4). Main Street.

Denker, Ellen, jt. auth. see Denker, Bert.

Denker, Ellen P. The Chinese Influence in America. (Illus.). 96p. 1985. pap. price not set (ISBN 0-87577-153-X). Peabody Mus Salem.

Denker, Henry. The Director. 1971. pap. 1.95 (ISBN 0-380-00669-3, 29355). Avon.

--Error of Judgment. 1984. pap. 3.95 (ISBN 0-671-81959-3). PB.

--The Healers. LC 82-20374. 352p. 1983. 14.95 (ISBN 0-688-01585-9). Morrow.

--The Healers. 464p. 1984. pap. 3.95 (ISBN 0-380-67405-X, 67405). Avon.

--Kincaid. LC 84-60199. 320p. 1984. 15.95 (ISBN 0-688-02365-7). Morrow.

--Outrage. LC 81-22551. 320p. 1982. 13.95 (ISBN 0-688-01113-6). Morrow.

--Outrage. 320p. 1983. pap. 3.50 (ISBN 0-380-62802-3, 62802). Avon.

--Robert, My Son. LC 85-7244. 352p. 1985. 16.95 (ISBN 0-688-05957-0). Morrow.

Denker, Joel, jt. auth. see Bhaerman, Steve.

Denker, Joel S. Unions & Universities: The Rise of the New Labor Leader. LC 80-67093. 198p. 1981. text ed. 23.95x (ISBN 0-916672-58-1). Allanheld.

Denker, M. & Jacobs, K., eds. Ergodic Theory: Proceedings, Oberwolfach, Germany, 11-17 June 1978. (Lecture Notes in Mathematics: Vol. 729). 1979. pap. 17.00 (ISBN 0-387-09517-9). Springer-Verlag.

Denker, Manfred. Theory in Nonparametric: Asymptotic Distribution. Fischer, Gerd, ed. 210p. 1985. pap. 13.00 (ISBN 3-528-08905-9, 99040031X, Pub. by Vieweg & Sohn Germany). Heyden.

Denkinger, Emma M. Immortal Sidney. 1931. Repr. 35.00 (ISBN 0-8274-2558-9). R West.

Denkinger, Marc, ed. see Olivier, Juste.

Denkstein, Vladimir, et al, eds. Prague. LC 78-58354. (Great Centers of Art Ser.). (Illus.). 1979. 35.00 (ISBN 0-8390-0225-4, Allanheld & Schram). Abner Schram Ltd.

Denktash, Rauf. The Cyprus Triangle. 224p. 1982. text ed. 17.95x (ISBN 0-04-327066-2). Allen Unwin.

Denlinger, A. Martha. Real People. rev. ed. LC 74-16966. 96p. 1981. pap. 3.50. Herald Pr.

Denlinger, Donald M., jt. auth. see Warner, James A.

Denlinger, Ken & Attner, Paul. Redskin Country: An Inside Look at Washington Redskins' Football. LC 83-80699. (Illus.). 192p. 1983. 12.95 (ISBN 0-88011-191-7). Leisure Pr.

Denlinger, Martha. Real People. rev. ed. LC 74-16966. (Illus.). 96p. 1975. pap. 3.50 (ISBN 0-8361-1960-6). Herald Pr.

Denlinger, Milo G. Complete Boxer. 3rd ed. LC 69-19392. (Complete Breed Book Ser.). (Illus.). 304p. 1982. 15.95 (ISBN 0-87605-060-7). Howell Bk.

Denlinger, Milo G., et al. New Complete Great Dane. 3rd ed. LC 62-20219. (Complete Breed Book Ser.). (Illus.). 352p. 1983. 14.95 (ISBN 0-87605-161-1). Howell Bk.

Denlinger, Sutherland & Gary, Charles B. War in the Pacific: A Study of Navies, Peoples, & Battle Problems. LC 77-111752. (American Imperialism: Viewpoints of United States Foreign Policy, 1898-1941). 1970. Repr. of 1936 ed. 20.00 (ISBN 0-405-02011-2). Ayer Co Pubs.

Denlinger, William, et al. Complete Chihuahua. 4th ed. LC 63-21874. (Complete Breed Book Ser.). (Illus.). 256p. 1983. 15.95 (ISBN 0-87605-100-X). Howell Bk.

Denman, Clarence P. The Secession Movement in Alabama. facsimile ed. LC 79-170695. (Black Heritage Library Collection). Repr. of 1933 ed. 16.25 (ISBN 0-8369-8885-X). Ayer Co Pubs.

Denman, D. R. The King's Vista. 368p. 1973. 50.00x (ISBN 0-900394-14-5, Pub. by Geographical Pubns). State Mutual Bk.

--The Place of Property. 150p. 1978. 45.00x (ISBN 0-900394-20-X, Pub. by Geographical Pubns). State Mutual Bk.

Denman, Eugene D., jt. auth. see Adams, Roy N.

Denman, G. L., ed. see AIP Conference.

Denman, R. P., jt. auth. see Dunlop, Jocelyn.

Denman, Scott, jt. auth. see Bossong, Ken.

Denmark, F. L., jt. auth. see Sherman, J. A.

Denmark, Florence, ed. Who Discriminates Against Women? LC 74-78560. (Sage Contemporary Social Science Issues Ser.: No. 15). (Illus.). pap. 36.00 (ISBN 0-317-08953-6, 2021887). Bks Demand UMI.

Denmark, Florence L., jt. auth. see Unger, Rhoda K.

Denmark, Florence L., ed. Psychology: The Leading Edge. (Annals of the New York Academy of Sciences Ser.: Vol. 340). 114p. 1980. 22.00x; pap. 22.00x (ISBN 0-89766-078-1). NY Acad Sci.

Denmark, Florence L., jt. ed. see Salzinger, Kurt.

Denmark, Florence L., et al, eds. Women: A PDI Reference Work, Vol. 1. LC 75-5161. 626p. 1977. 39.95x (ISBN 0-88437-001-1). Psych Dimensions.

Denn, M. Process Fluid Mechanics. 1980. 39.95 (ISBN 0-13-723163-6). P-H.

Denn, Morton. Process Modelling. 304p. 1985. text ed. price not set (ISBN 0-273-08704-5). Pitman Pub MA.

Denn, Morton M., jt. auth. see Russell, T. Fraser.

Denne, Constance A., ed. see Cooper, James F.

Denne, Robert. Property Taxation in the U. S. An Annotated Bibliography, Pt. I, Alabama-Maine. Incl. Property Taxation in the U.S.; An Annotated Bibliography: Pt. II Maryland - North Carolina. Denne, Robert. (Bibliographic Ser.: No. 3B). 82p. 1978. 14.50 (ISBN 0-88329-023-5); Property Taxation in the U.S.; An Annotated Bibliography: Pt. III, North Dakota - Wyoming & All States. (Bibliographic Ser.: No. 3C). 99p. 1978. 16.00 (ISBN 0-88329-022-7). (Bibliographic Ser.: No.3A). 80p. 1978. 14.00 (ISBN 0-88329-024-3). Intl Assess.

Denne, Robert C. Assessment Sales Ratio Studies. (Bibliographic Ser.). 57p. 1977. 12.00 (ISBN 0-88329-047-2). Intl Assess.

--Computer-Assisted Apprasial & Assessment Systems. (Bibliographic Ser.: No.2). 88p. 1977. 15.00 (ISBN 0-88329-046-4). Intl Assess.

Denne, W. Magnetic Compass Deviation & Correction. 3rd ed. 165p. 1979. 17.50x (ISBN 0-85174-332-3). Sheridan.

Dennehy, Henry E. see Sheehan, Patrick A.

Dennehy, Raymond. Reason & Dignity. LC 81-40364. 152p. 1982. lib. bdg. 22.50 (ISBN 0-8191-1898-2); pap. text ed. 9.75 (ISBN 0-8191-1899-0). U Pr of Amer.

Dennehy, Raymond, ed. see Muggeridge, Malcolm, et al.

Dennell, R. European Economic Prehistory: A New Approach. 1983. 27.00 (ISBN 0-12-209180-9). Acad Pr.

Dennen, William H. & Moore, Bruce R. Geology & Engineering. 448p. 1986. text ed. price not set (ISBN 0-697-00128-8). Wm C Brown.

Dennenberg, Herb. Herb Denenberg's Smart Shopper's Guide. LC 80-66978. 208p. 1980. pap. 6.95 (ISBN 0-8019-7003-2). Chilton.

Denneny, Michael. Decent Passions: A Book of Real Love Stories. 224p. (Orig.). 1984. pap. 6.95 (ISBN 0-932870-39-2). Alyson Pubns.

Denneny, Michael, ed. The Christopher Street Reader. Ortleb, Charles, et al. LC 84-1847. 432p. 1984. pap. 7.95 (ISBN 0-399-50812-0, Wideview). Putnam Pub Group.

Denner, Patricia. Language Through Play. LC 72-84851. (Illus.). (ps-1). 1969. pap. 8.95 (ISBN 0-405-00118-5). Ayer Co Pubs.

Dennerline, Jerry. The Chia-Ting Loyalists: Confucian Leadership & Social Change in Seventeenth-Century China. LC 80-21417. (Historical Publications Miscellany Ser.: No. 126). (Illus.). 416p. 1981. text ed. 47.00 (ISBN 0-300-02548-3). Yale U Pr.

Dennerstein, L. & De Senarclens, M. The Young Woman: Psychosomatic Aspects of Obstetrics & Gynaecology. (International Congress Ser.: Vol. 618). 1983. 93.75 (ISBN 0-444-90316-X). Elsevier.

Dennerstein, L., jt. auth. see Burrows, G.

Dennerstein, L. & Burrows, G. D., eds. Handbook of Psychosomatic Obstetrics & Gynaecology. 516p. 1983. 153.25 (ISBN 0-444-80444-7, Biomedical Pr). Elsevier.

Dennerstein, Lorraine, et al. Gynaecology, Sex & Psyche. LC 79-670113. 1978. pap. 18.00x (ISBN 0-522-84148-1, Pub. by Melbourne U Pr Australia). Intl Spec Bk.

--Hysterectomy: A Book to Help You Deal with the Physical & Emotional Aspects. (Illus.). 1982. 11.95x (ISBN 0-19-554371-8); pap. 6.95x (ISBN 0-19-554366-1). Oxford U Pr.

Dennery, Etienne. Asia's Teeming Millions. LC 70-115201. 1971. Repr. of 1931 ed. 22.50x (ISBN 0-8046-1094-0, Pub by Kennikat). Assoc Faculty Pr.

Dennes, William R. Some Dilemmas of Naturalism. facs. ed. (Select Bibliographies Reprint Ser). 1960. 14.50 (ISBN 0-8369-5551-X). Ayer Co Pubs.

Dennett, D. C. Content & Consciousness. (International Library of Philosophy & Scientific Method). 1969. text ed. 16.75x (ISBN 0-391-01015-8). Humanities.

Dennett, Daniel C. Brainstorms: Philosophical Essays on Mind & Psychology. LC 78-13723. (Bradford Bks.). 353p. 1980. text ed. 30.00x (ISBN 0-262-04064-6); pap. 10.95 (ISBN 0-262-54037-1). MIT Pr.

--Elbow Room: The Varieties of Free Will Worth Wanting. 256p. 1984. 19.95x (ISBN 0-262-04077-8); pap. 10.00 (ISBN 0-262-54042-8). MIT Pr.

Dennett, Daniel C., jt. auth. see Hofstadter, Douglas R.

Dennett, Daniel C., jt. ed. see Hofstadter, Douglas R.

Dennett, E. The Step I Have Taken. Daniel, R. P., ed. 53p. pap. 3.50 (ISBN 0-88172-140-9). Believers Bkshelf.

Dennett, Jane & James, Edward. Europe Against Poverty. 256p. 1982. text ed. 26.75x (ISBN 0-7199-1074-9, Pub. by Bedford England). Brookfield Pub Co.

Dennett, M. F. Fire Investigation: A Practical Guide for Fire Students & Officers, Insurance Investigators, Loss Adjustors, & Police Officers. (Illus.). 80p. 1980. 20.00 (ISBN 0-08-024741-5); pap. 9.75 (ISBN 0-08-024742-3). Pergamon.

Dennett, M. W. Birth Control Laws. LC 70-119053. (Civil Liberties in American History Ser). 1970. 35.00 (ISBN 0-306-71942-8). Da Capo.

Dennett, Richard E. At the Back of the Black Man's Mind, or Notes on the Kingly Office in West Africa. (Illus.). 288p. 1968. Repr. of 1906 ed. 29.50x (ISBN 0-7146-1653-2, F Cass Co). Biblio Dist.

--Nigerian Studies, or the Religious & Political Systems of the Yoruba. new ed. (Illus.). 236p. 1968. 28.50x (ISBN 0-7146-1654-0, F Cass Co). Biblio Dist.

--Notes on the Folklore of the Fjort. LC 78-67705. (The Folktale). Repr. of 1898 ed. 19.00 (ISBN 0-404-16078-6). AMS Pr.

Dennett, Tyler. Americans in Eastern Asia. LC 79-703. 1979. Repr. of 1922 ed. lib. bdg. 46.00x (ISBN 0-374-92115-6). Octagon.

--Roosevelt & the Russo-Japanese War. 1958. 11.75 (ISBN 0-8446-1150-6). Peter Smith.

Denney, Frank C. Trigonometry. 1976. text ed. 23.50 scp (ISBN 0-06-382560-0, HarpC). Har-Row.

Denney, George & Barker, Wayne G. Solving Cryptograms in Spanish. 164p. (Orig.). 1985. pap. text ed. 9.80 (ISBN 0-89412-058-1). Aegean Park Pr.

Denney, James. The Death of Christ. LC 81-81100. (The Shephard Illustrated Classics Ser.). (Illus.). 372p. 1981. pap. 6.95 (ISBN 0-87983-258-4). Keats.

Denney, M. Ray, jt. auth. see Evans, Sharon.

Denney, Michael, ed. see Mordden, Ethan.

Denney, Myron K. A Matter of Choice: An Essential Guide to Every Aspect of Abortion. 192p. (Orig.). 1983. pap. 9.95 (ISBN 0-671-46372-1, Fireside). S&S.

Denney, R. C. Dictionary of Spectroscopy. 2nd ed. 208p. 1982. 39.95x (ISBN 0-471-87478-7, Pub. by Wiley-Interscience). Wiley.

Denney, Reuel. Connecticut River & Other Poems. LC 79-144745. (Yale Ser. of Younger Poets: No. 38). Repr. of 1939 ed. 18.00 (ISBN 0-404-53838-X). AMS Pr.

--Conrad Aiken. (Pamphlets on American Writers Ser: No. 38). (Orig.). 1964. pap. 1.25x (ISBN 0-8166-0330-8, MPAW38). U of Minn Pr.

--In Praise of Adam. LC 61-18887. (Phoenix Poets Ser). 1961. pap. 1.50 (ISBN 0-226-14301-5, PP3, Phoen). U of Chicago Pr.

Denney, Robert W. How to Market Legal Services. LC 84-5255. 288p. 1984. 29.95 (ISBN 0-442-21980-6). Van Nos Reinhold.

--Marketing Accounting Services. 256p. 1983. 24.95 (ISBN 0-442-22003-0). Van Nos Reinhold.

Denney, Ronald C. Dictionary of Chromatography. 2nd ed. 229p. 1982. 50.95 (ISBN 0-471-87477-9, Pub. by Wiley-Interscience). Wiley.

Dennie, Joseph. The Lay Preacher. LC 43-9749. 1979. Repr. of 1796 ed. lib. bdg. 35.00x (ISBN 0-8201-1204-6). Schol Facsimiles.

Denning & Phillips. Llewellyn's Practical Guide to Astral Projection. 6th ed. LC 79-88141. (Illus.). 1984. pap. 7.95 (ISBN 0-87542-181-4). Llewellyn Pubns.

--Triumph of Light. LC 75-2428. (Magical Philosophy Ser.: Vol. 4). (Illus.). 251p. 1978. 10.00 (ISBN 0-87542-179-2). Llewellyn Pubns.

Denning, Adam. C at a Glance. (Illus.). 180p. 1985. pap. 19.95 (ISBN 0-317-19449-6, 9564, Pub. by Chapman & Hall England). Methuen Inc.

Denning, Charles H., Jr. First Aid for Horses. (Orig.). pap. 3.00 (ISBN 0-87980-189-1). Wilshire.

Denning, Dennis. We Are One in the Lord: Developing Caring Groups in the Church. LC 81-14958. 96p. (Orig.). 1982. pap. 5.50 (ISBN 0-687-44281-8). Abingdon.

Denning, Dorothy E. Cryptography & Data Security. LC 81-15012. (Computer Science Ser.). (Illus.). 500p. 1982. text ed. 36.95 (ISBN 0-201-10150-5). Addison-Wesley.

Denning, Mark. Beyond the Prize. (Private Library Collection). 1985. mini-bound 6.95 (ISBN 0-938422-17-0). SOS Pubns CA.

--Die Fast, Die Happy. (Private Library Collection). 1985. mini-bound 6.95 (ISBN 0-938422-14-6). SOS Pubns CA.

--Din of Inequity. 160p. 1984. 11.95 (ISBN 0-312-21087-6). St Martin.

--The Golden Lure. (Orig.). 1981. pap. 1.75 (ISBN 0-505-51664-0, Pub. by Tower Bks). Dorchester Pub Co.

--Shades of Gray. (Private Library Collection). 1985. mini-bound 6.95 (ISBN 0-938422-20-0). SOS Pubns CA.

--The Swiss Abduction. 1981. pap. 1.95 (ISBN 0-8439-0858-0, Leisure Bks). Dorchester Pub Co.

Denning, Melita. The Inner World of Fitness. Weschcke, Carl L., ed. (Practical Guide Ser.). 240p. (Orig.). 1985. pap. 7.95 (ISBN 0-87542-165-2, L-165). Llewellyn Pubns.

Denning, Melita & Phillips, Osborne. The Llewellyn Inner Guide to Magickal States of Consciousness: Working the Paths of the Tree of Life. Weschcke, Carl L., ed. LC 83-82527. (Inner Guide Ser.). (Illus.). 416p. 1985. pap. 12.95 (ISBN 0-87542-194-6, L-194). Llewellyn Pubns.

--The Llewellyn Inner Guide to Planetary Magic: Spheres of Power & Attainment. Weschcke, Carl L., ed. LC 82-83316. (Inner Guides Ser.). (Illus.). 400p. (Orig.). 1985. pap. 12.95 (ISBN 0-87542-193-8, L-193). Llewellyn Pubns.

--The Llewellyn Practical Guide to Creative Visualization: The Dynamic Way to Success, Love, Plenty & Spiritual Power. 2nd ed. Weschcke, Carl L., ed. LC 83-80168. (Practical Guide Ser.). (Illus.). 250p. 1985. pap. 7.95 (L-183). Llewellyn Pubns.

--Llewellyn Practical Guide to the Development of Psychic Powers. 5th ed. LC 83-80170. 1984. 7.95 (ISBN 0-87542-191-1). Llewellyn Pubns.

--The Llewellyn Practical Guide to the Evocation of the Gods. Weschcke, Carl L., ed. LC 83-80161. (Practical Guide Ser.). (Illus.). 240p. 1986. pap. 7.95 (ISBN 0-87542-187-3, L-187). Llewellyn Pubns.

--Llewellyn Practical Guide to the Magic of Sex. 2nd ed. Weschcke, Carl L., intro. by. LC 83-80171. 336p. 1985. 6.95 (ISBN 0-87542-192-X, L-192). Llewellyn Pubns.

--The Llewellyn Practical Guide to the Magick of the Tarot. Weschcke, Carl L., ed. LC 82-83428. (Practical Magick Ser.). (Illus.). 252p. (Orig.). 1983. pap. 6.95 (ISBN 0-87542-198-9). Llewellyn Pubns.

--Mysteria Magica. 2nd, rev. & expanded ed. Weschcke, Carl L., ed. LC 83-80176. (Magical Philosophy Ser.). (Illus.). 540p. 1985. pap. 15.00 (ISBN 0-87542-196-2, L-196). Llewellyn Pubns.

--The Sword & the Serpent: The Structure & Psychology of Magick. Weschcke, Carl L., ed. (Magical Philosophy). (Illus.). 500p. 1985. pap. 15.00 (ISBN 0-87542-197-0, L-197). Llewellyn Pubns.

Denning, Melits & Phillips, Osborne. Voudoun Fire: The Living Reality of the Mystical Religions. LC 79-3375. (Mystery Religions Series: No. 1). (Illus.). 172p. (Orig.). 1979. pap. 9.95 (ISBN 0-87542-699-9). Llewellyn Pubns.

Denning, Peter J., jt. auth. see Coffman, Edward G., Jr.

Denning, Peter J., et al. Machines, Languages & Computation. (Automatic Computation Ser.). (Illus.). 1978. ref. ed. 34.95 (ISBN 0-13-542258-2). P-H.

Denninger, Richard. Anatomy of the Pure & of the Impure Love. (Intimate Life of Man Library Bk.). (Illus.). 1979. 51.75 (ISBN 0-89266-177-1); spiral bdg. 37.95 (ISBN 0-685-67718-4). Am Classical Coll Pr.

Dennis, A. J., jt. ed. see Cooke, M.

Dennis, Alfred L. Adventures in American Diplomacy, Eighteen Ninety-Six to Nineteen Hundred & Six. (Political Science Ser). 1969. Repr. of 1928 ed. 45.00 (ISBN 0-384-11385-0). Johnson Repr.

--The Anglo-Japanese Alliance. 1923. pap. 8.00 (ISBN 0-384-11395-8). Johnson Repr.

Dennis, Alfred P. The Romance of World Trade. 1977. lib. bdg. 59.95 (ISBN 0-8490-2538-9). Gordon Pr.

Dennis, Anthony J., jt. auth. see Cooke, Marcus.

Dennis, Anthony J., jt. ed. see Bjorseth, Alf.

Dennis, Anthony J., jt. ed. see Cooke, Marcus.

Dennis, Barbara D. & Stern, James L. Arbitration Promise & Performance. (National Academy of Arbitrators: 36th Annual Meeting, 1983). 300p. 1984. text ed. 30.00 (ISBN 0-87179-437-3). BNA.

Dennis, Barbara D., ed. see National Academy of Arbitrators-24th Annual Meeting.

Dennis, Barbara D., ed. see National Academy of Arbitrators-25th Annual Meeting.

Dennis, Barbara D., ed. see National Academy of Arbitrators-26th Meeting.

Dennis, Barbara D., ed. see National Academy of Arbitrators-27th Annual Meeting.

Dennis, Barbara D., ed. see National Academy of Arbitrators-28th Annual Meeting.

Dennis, Barbara D., ed. see National Academy of Arbitrators-29th Annual Meeting.

Dennis, Barbara D., ed. see National Academy of Arbitrators-30th Annual Meeting.

Dennis, Barbara D., ed. see National Academy of Arbitrators-32nd Annual Meeting.

Dennis, Barbara D., jt. ed. see Stern, James L.

Dennis, Ben & Case, Betsy. Houseboat: Reflections of North America's Floating Homes...History, Architecture, & Lifestyles. new ed. 1977. 14.95 (ISBN 0-918484-00-6); pap. 9.95 (ISBN 0-918484-01-4). Smugglers.

Dennis, Benjamin D. The Gbandes: A People of the Liberian Hinterland. LC 72-88580. 1973. 27.95x (ISBN 0-911012-50-8). Nelson-Hall.

Dennis, Brian. Experimental Music in Schools: Towards a New World of Sound. 1970. pap. 4.75 (ISBN 0-19-323195-6); materials 1-20 3.25 (ISBN 0-19-323196-4). Oxford U Pr.

Dennis, Carl. Climbing Down. LC 75-38779. 80p. 1976. 6.95 (ISBN 0-8076-0814-9); pap. 3.95 (ISBN 0-8076-0815-7). Braziller.

--A House of My Own. Howard, Richard, ed. LC 74-77524. (Braziller Series of Poetry). 80p. 1974. 6.95 (ISBN 0-8076-0753-3); pap. 3.95 (ISBN 0-8076-0754-1). Braziller.

--The Near World. LC 84-27296. 80p. (Orig.). 1985. 12.95 (ISBN 0-688-04824-2). Morrow.

--The Near World. LC 84-26379. 77p. 1985. pap. 5.95 (ISBN 0-688-04825-0, Quill). Morrow.

--Signs & Wonders. LC 79-3210. (Princeton Series of Contemporary Poets). 69p. 1979. 15.00x (ISBN 0-691-06407-5); pap. 5.95 (ISBN 0-691-01360-8). Princeton U Pr.

Dennis, Charles H. Eugene Field's Creative Years. 1924. 25.00 (ISBN 0-8274-2318-7). R West.

--Eugene Field's Creative Years. LC 72-144971. 339p. 1924. Repr. 24.00x (ISBN 0-403-00939-1). Scholarly.

Dennis, Clifford E. King Joker, a King in Search of a Civilization. 1970. 6.00 (ISBN 0-686-00964-9). Willoughby.

Dennis, Clifford J. Laboratory Manual for Introductory Entomology. 3rd ed. 112p. 1974. write for info. wire coil (ISBN 0-697-04702-4). Wm C Brown.

Dennis, Colin, ed. Post-Harvest Pathology of Fruits & Vegatables. (Food Science & Technology Ser.). 1983. 46.00 (ISBN 0-12-210680-6). Acad Pr.

Dennis, David M., jt. auth. see Adler, Kraig.

Dennis, Deborah E., jt. ed. see Zikmund, Joseph.

Dennis, Denise & Willmarth, Susan. Black History for Beginners. (Illus.). 176p. 1984. 14.95 (ISBN 0-86316-069-7); pap. 6.95 (ISBN 0-86316-068-9). Writers & Readers.

Dennis, Doug, ed. Reading: Meeting Childrens Special Needs. iv, 201p. (Orig.). 1984. pap. text ed. 12.50x (ISBN 0-435-10200-1). Heinemann Ed.

Dennis, E. S., jt. ed. see Hohn, B.

Dennis, Earle S. & Smith, Jane E. Marriage Bonds of Bedford County, Virginia, 1755-1800. LC 75-4010. 99p. 1981. pap. 6.00 (ISBN 0-8063-0669-6). Genealog Pub.

Dennis, Edward A. see Colowick, Sidney P. & Kaplan, Nathan O.

Dennis, Ervin A. Applied Photography. LC 84-23047. 512p. 1985. text ed. 18.60 (ISBN 0-8273-2292-5); instr's. guide 4.80 (ISBN 0-8273-2294-1); student manual 6.80 (ISBN 0-8273-2293-3). Delmar.

--Lithographic Technology. LC 79-16756. 1980. scp 28.99 (ISBN 0-672-97164-X); scp tchr's manual 7.33 (ISBN 0-672-97165-8); scp student manual 11.49 (ISBN 0-672-97166-6). Bobbs.

Dennis, Ervin A. & Jenkins, John D. Comprehensive Graphic Arts. 2nd ed. (Illus.). 576p. 1983. text ed. 32.60 scp (ISBN 0-672-97681-1); scp instr's guide 7.33 (ISBN 0-672-97682-X); scp wkbk 8.40 (ISBN 0-672-98447-4). Bobbs.

Dennis, Eve. Everyman's Nature Reserve: Ideas for Action. (Illus.). 256p. 1973. 7.50 (ISBN 0-7153-5918-5). David & Charles.

Dennis, Everette, et al. Enduring Issues in Mass Communication. (Mass Communication Ser.). (Illus.). 1978. pap. text ed. 18.95 (ISBN 0-8299-0173-6). West Pub.

Dennis, Everette, jt. auth. see Hage, George.

Dennis, Everette E. & Merrill, John C. Media & Contemporary Society. (Illus.). 288p. 1983. pap. text ed. write for info. (ISBN 0-02-328510-9). Macmillan.

Dennis, Everette E., jt. auth. see DeFleur, Melvin L.

Dennis, Everette E., et al, eds. Justice Hugo Black & the First Amendment. 1978. text ed. 12.50x (ISBN 0-8138-1905-9). Iowa St U Pr.

Dennis, Frank A., ed. The Journal of Mississippi History: Index to Volumes I-XX. text ed. 40.00 (ISBN 0-318-03036-5). Mississippi De.

--Southern Miscellany: Essays in Honor of Glover Moore. LC 80-20373. 202p. 1981. 6.95 (ISBN 0-87805-129-5). U Pr of Miss.

Dennis, G. E. International Financial Flows: A Statistical Handbook. LC 83-25557. 376p. 1984. 24.00x (ISBN 0-669-07788-7). Lexington Bks.

Dennis, George. Cities & Cemeteries of Etruria. LC 84-8431. (Illus.). 416p. 1985. 47.50x (ISBN 0-691-03575-X); pap. 14.50x (ISBN 0-691-00214-2). Princeton U Pr.

Dennis, George T. Byzantium & the Franks, Tirteen Fifty to Fourteen Twenty. 320p. 1982. 75.00x (ISBN 0-86078-097-X, Pub. by Variorum England). State Mutual Bk.

Dennis, George T., ed. & tr. The Letters of Manuel II Palaeologus. LC 77-14898. (Dumbarton Oaks Texts: Vol. 4). 315p. 1977. 35.00x (ISBN 0-88402-068-1). Dumbarton Oaks.

Dennis, George T., ed. & tr. see Emperor Maurice.

Dennis, Harry. Water & Power: The Peripheral Canal & Its Alternatives. LC 81-68547. 128p. (Orig.). 1981. pap. 4.95 (ISBN 0-913890-49-9). Brick Hse Pub.

Dennis, Helen, ed. Retirement Preparation: What Retirement Specialists Need to Know. LC 83-48130. 224p. 1984. 25.00 (ISBN 0-669-06949-3); pap. 14.00x (ISBN 0-669-08338-0). Lexington Bks.

Dennis, Henry C. The American Indian, 1492-1976: A Chronology & Fact Book. 2nd ed. LC 76-46440. (Ethnic Chronology Ser.). 177p. 1977. 8.50 (ISBN 0-379-00526-3). Oceana.

Dennis, Ivanette, ed. see Richardson Woman's Club.

Dennis, J. G. & Murawski, H. International Tectonic Lexicon: A Prodrome. (International Union of Geological Sciences Ser.). 153p. 1979. pap. text ed. 24.00x (ISBN 3-510-65092-1). Lubrecht & Cramer.

Dennis, J. G., ed. Orogeny. LC 81-6436. (Benchmark Papers in Geology: Vol. 62). 380p. 1982. 47.95 (ISBN 0-87933-394-4). Van Nos Reinhold.

Dennis, J. Richard. Fractions Are Parts of Things. LC 73-127603. (Illus.). 40p. (gr. 2-5). 1971 (ISBN 0-690-31520-1). PLB 11.89 (ISBN 0-690-31521-X); pap. 1.45 (ISBN 0-690-31522-8, TYC-J). Crowell Jr Bks.

Dennis, J. Richard & Kansky, Robert. Instructional Computing: An Action Guide for Educators. 1984. pap. 15.50x (ISBN 0-673-16606-6). Scott F.

Dennis, Jack, jt. auth. see Easton, David.

Dennis, James M. Karl Bitter: Architectural Sculptor, 1867-1915. (Illus.). 316p. 1967. 27.50x (ISBN 0-299-04450-5). U of Wis Pr.

Dennis, Jessie M., jt. auth. see Wilkinson, Charles K.

Dennis, Joe. Spreading Truth. 64p. 1979. pap. text ed. 1.95 (ISBN 0-89114-086-7); tchrs. ed. 1.95 (ISBN 0-89114-087-5). Baptist Pub Hse.

Dennis, John. The Age of Pope. facsimile ed. (Select Bibliographies Reprint Ser). Repr. of 1894 ed. 18.00 (ISBN 0-8369-5765-2). Ayer Co Pubs.

--The Age of Pope: Seventeen Hundred to Seventeen Forty-Four. 1978. Repr. of 1924 ed. lib. bdg. 25.00 (ISBN 0-8495-1023-6). Arden Lib.

--The Critical Works of John Dennis. Hooker, Edward N., ed. LC 39-5971. Vol. 1: 1692-1711. pap. 137.30 (ISBN 0-317-28816-4, 2020537); Vol. 2: 1711-1729. pap. 160.00 (ISBN 0-317-28817-2). Bks Demand UMI.

--Dr. Johnson. LC 72-10146. 1972. Repr. of 1905 ed. lib. bdg. 10.00 (ISBN 0-8414-0662-6). Folcroft.

--The Impartial Critick. Bd. with Miscellaneous Letters & Essays. Gildon, Charles. LC 72-170436. (The English Stage Ser.: Vol. 21). 1973. lib. bdg. 61.00 (ISBN 0-8240-0604-6). Garland Pub.

--O, Promised Land. 160p. 1982. pap. text ed. 8.95 (ISBN 0-88377-237-X). Newbury Hse.

--The Plays of John Dennis. Backscheider, Paula R., ed. LC 78-66657. (Eighteenth-Century English Drama Ser.: Vol. 14). 1980. lib. bdg. 73.00 (ISBN 0-8240-3588-7). Garland Pub.

--Studies in English Literature: Pope, Defoe, Matthew Prior, Steele, the Wartons, Southey, the English Sonnet. 1973. Repr. of 1883 ed. 35.00 (ISBN 0-8274-1642-3). R West.

Dennis, John, jt. auth. see Griffin, Suzanne M.

Dennis, John see Law, William.

Dennis, John, ed. Robert Southey. 447p. 1980. Repr. of 1894 ed. lib. bdg. 30.00 (ISBN 0-89984-155-4). Century Bookbindery.

Dennis, John E. & Schnabel, Robert B. Numerical Methods for Unconstrained Optimization & Nonlinear Equations. (Illus.). 272p. 1983. text ed. 35.95 (ISBN 0-13-627216-9). P-H.

Dennis, John G. Structural Geology. 532p. 1972. 38.95 (ISBN 0-471-06746-6). Wiley.

Dennis, John M., et al. English Through Drama: An Introduction to Language-Learning Activities Developed by Mark Rittenberg and Penelope Kreitzer. (Illus.). 54p. 1980. pap. 7.95x (ISBN 0-88084-001-3). Alemany Pr.

Dennis, John V. Beyond the Bird Feeder: The Habits & Behavior of Feeding Station Birds When They Are Not at Your Feeder. LC 81-47491. (Illus.). 224p. 1981. 14.95 (ISBN 0-394-50890-4). Knopf.

--A Complete Guide to Bird Feeding. 1975. 16.95 (ISBN 0-394-47937-8). Knopf.

--The Wildlife Gardener. LC 84-48653. 1985. 17.95 (ISBN 0-394-53582-0). Knopf.

Dennis, K. C. Blood Red! LC 81-51252. 156p. 1983. 8.95 (ISBN 0-533-05049-9). Vantage.

Dennis, Lane T., ed. The Letters of Francis A. Schaeffer. LC 85-70473. 250p. (Orig.). 1985. 14.95 (ISBN 0-89107-361-2, Crossway Bks). Good News.

Dennis, LaRae. Know Your Poison. 1972. pap. text ed. 3.95x (ISBN 0-88246-026-9). Oreg St U Bkstrs.

Dennis, Larry, jt. auth. see Graham, David.

Dennis, Larry, jt. auth. see Kostis, Peter.

Dennis, Larry, jt. auth. see Lohren, Carl.

Dennis, Larry, ed. see Toski, Bob & Flick, Jim.

Dennis, Laurie B., jt. auth. see Dennis, Terry L.

Dennis, Lawrence. Coming American Fascism. LC 73-180397. Repr. of 1936 ed. 29.50 (ISBN 0-404-56118-7). AMS Pr.

--The Dynamics of War & Revolution. 296p. 1980. pap. 10.00 (ISBN 0-911038-91-4). Inst Hist Rev.

--The Dynamics of War & Revolutions. 69.95 (ISBN 0-87700-151-0). Revisionist Pr.

--Operational Thinking for Survival. LC 73-85338. 1969. 5.95 (ISBN 0-87926-003-3). R Myles.

--A Trial on Trial. 1978. lib. bdg. 75.00 (ISBN 0-87700-292-4). Revisionist Pr.

Dennis, Lawrence & Martin, James J. The Dynamics of War & Revolution. 2nd ed. 259p. 1941. pap. 10.00 (ISBN 0-911038-91-4, Inst Hist Rev). Noontide.

Dennis, Lawrence & St. George, Maximillian. A Trial on Trial. 502p. 1984. pap. 11.00 (ISBN 0-939484-20-X). Inst Hist Rev.

Dennis, Lawrence E. & Jacobs, Renata M., eds. The Arts in Higher Education. LC 68-57442. (Jossey-Bass Series in Higher Education). pap. 44.00 (ISBN 0-317-10531-0, 2013941). Bks Demand UMI.

Dennis, Lawrence J. & Eaton, William E., eds. George S. Counts: Educator for a New Age. LC 79-28182. 167p. 1980. 14.95x (ISBN 0-8093-0954-8). S Ill U Pr.

Dennis, Leah H., et al. Word Lists from the South: Tobacco Words. (Publications of the American Dialect Society Ser.: No. 2). 72p. 1944. pap. 4.95 (ISBN 0-8173-0602-1). U of Ala Pr.

Dennis, Lee. Warman's Antique American Games: 1840-1940. LC 85-50969. (Warman's Price Key Ser.). (Illus.). 224p. (Orig.). 1985. pap. 14.95 (ISBN 0-911594-08-6). Warman.

Dennis, Lisl. Shooting Portraits on Location. (Illus.). 144p. 1985. 24.95 (ISBN 0-8174-5875-1, Amphoto); pap. 16.95 (ISBN 0-8174-5876-X). Watson-Guptill.

Dennis, Lorraine B. Psychology of Human Behavior for Nurses. 3rd ed. LC 67-10729. (Illus.). 1967. 14.95 (ISBN 0-7216-3011-1). Saunders.

Dennis, Lorraine B. & Hassol, Joan. Introduction to Human Development & Health Issues. (Illus.). 320p. 1983. pap. 15.95 (ISBN 0-7216-3030-8). Saunders.

Dennis, Margaret W., jt. ed. see Dennis, Wayne.

Dennis, Marshall. Mortgage Lending Fundamentals & Practices. 2nd ed. 1983. text ed. 24.95 (ISBN 0-8359-4653-3); avail. (ISBN 0-8359-4654-1). Reston.

--Residential Mortgage Lending. 1985. text ed. 25.95 (ISBN 0-8359-6654-2); instr's. manual avail. (ISBN 0-8359-6662-3). Reston.

Dennis, Martha, jt. ed. see Colowick, Sidney.

Dennis, Martha G. see Colowick, Sidney P. & Kaplan, Nathan O.

Dennis, Mary Cable. The Tail of the Comet. 1937. 30.00 (ISBN 0-8274-3564-9). R West.

Dennis, Maureen, jt. ed. see Boller, Francois.

Dennis, Muriel, ed. Chosen Children. 150p. 1987. 6.95 (ISBN 0-89107-154-7). Good News.

Dennis, Nigel. Cards of Identity. 304p. 1984. pap. 4.95 (ISBN 0-14-006608-X). Penguin.

--An Essay on Malta. LC 73-83041. (Illus.). 64p. 1974. 8.95 (ISBN 0-8149-0732-6). Vanguard.

Dennis, Nigel F. Dramatic Essays. LC 77-28431. 1978. Repr. of 1962 ed. lib. bdg. 22.50x (ISBN 0-313-20244-3, DEDR). Greenwood.

Dennis, P. O., et al, eds. Food Control in Action. (Illus.). 280p. 1981. 42.75 (ISBN 0-85334-894-4, Pub. by Elsevier Applied Sci England). Elsevier.

Dennis, Patrick. Auntie Mame. LC 54-11512. 224p. 1954. 11.95 (ISBN 0-8149-0085-2). Vanguard.

Dennis, Phil & Minter, Greg. Games Commodores Play. (Games Computers Play Ser.). 250p. (Orig.). 1984. pap. 14.95 (ISBN 0-88190-121-0, BO121). Datamost.

Dennis, Philip. Gibraltar. (Islands Ser.). (Illus.). 144p. 1985. 22.00 (ISBN 0-317-30187-X). David & Charles.

Dennis, R. Fungus Flora of Venezuela & Adjacent Countries. 1970. 45.85 (ISBN 3-7682-0692-0). Lubrecht & Cramer.

Dennis, R. K. Algebraic K-Theory: Proccedings, Oberwolfach, FRG 1980, Vol. 1. (Lecture Notes in Mathematics Ser.: Vol. 966). 407p. 1982. pap. 22.00 (ISBN 0-387-11965-5). Springer-Verlag.

Dennis, R. K., ed. Algebraic K-Theory: Proceedings, Oberwolfach, FRG, 1980, Vol. II. (Lecture Notes in Mathematics: Vol. 967). 409p. 1982. pap. 22.00 (ISBN 0-387-11966-3). Springer-Verlag.

Dennis, R. L. The British Butterflies: Their Origin & Establishment. 60.00x (ISBN 0-317-07035-5, Pub. by EW Classey UK). State Mutual Bk.

Dennis, R. W. British Ascomycetes. 3rd rev. & enl. ed. (Illus.). 1981. 70.00 (ISBN 3-7682-0552-5). Lubrecht & Cramer.

Dennis, R. W., jt. auth. see Wakefield, E. M.

Dennis, R. W., et al. New Check List of British Agarics & Boleti. 1974. Repr. of 1960 ed. 14.00 (ISBN 3-7682-0935-0). Lubrecht & Cramer.

Dennis, Richard. English Industrial Cities of the Nineteenth Century: A Social Geography. (Studies in Historical Geography: No. 4). (Illus.). 336p. 1984. 49.50 (ISBN 0-521-24922-8). Cambridge U Pr.

Dennis, Richard, jt. auth. see Dawson, Aileen.

Dennis, Richard, ed. Handbook on Aerosols. ERDA Technical Information Center. LC 75-33965. 148p. 1976. pap. 11.75 (ISBN 0-87079-024-2, TID-26608); microfiche 4.50 (ISBN 0-87079-237-7, TID-26608). DOE.

Dennis, Richard J., jt. auth. see Clout, Hugh D.

Dennis, Robert L., jt. auth. see Doyle, Jean M.

Dennis, Ronald A., ed. see Jones, William C.

Dennis, Rosemary. Path of the Lonely Ones. LC 79-89516. (Illus.). 1979. 3.50 (ISBN 0-918482-02-X). Ageless Bks.

Dennis, Rutledge M., jt. auth. see Moeser, John V.

Dennis, Stephen N., ed. see National Trust for Historic Preservation.

Dennis, Terry L. Apple Pascal: A Problem-Solving Approach. (Illus.). 400p. 1985. pap. text ed. 16.95 (ISBN 0-314-85228-X). West Pub.

Dennis, Terry L. & Dennis, Laurie B. Microcomputer Models for Management Science: Text & Software. (Illus.). 350p. 1985. pap. text ed. write for info. (ISBN 0-314-93171-6). West Pub.

Dennis, Virginia, jt. auth. see Gillenwater, Susan.

Dennis, W. H. Foundations of Iron & Steel Metallurgy. (Illus.). 246p. 1967. 15.00 (ISBN 0-444-20006-1, Pub. by Elsevier Applied Sci England). Elsevier.

Dennis, W. M., ed. see ASTM Committee D-19 on Water.

Dennis, Wayne. The Hopi Child. LC 75-169380. (Family in America Ser). (Illus.). 232p. 1972. Repr. of 1940 ed. 16.00 (ISBN 0-405-03857-7). Ayer Co Pubs.

Dennis, Wayne & Skinner, B. F. Current Trends in Psychology. 225p. 1982. Repr. of 1947 ed. lib. bdg. 45.00 (ISBN 0-8495-1141-0). Arden Lib.

Dennis, Wayne, ed. Readings in General Psychology. facsimile ed. LC 71-167334. (Essay Index Reprint Ser). Repr. of 1949 ed. 31.00 (ISBN 0-8369-2493-2). Ayer Co Pubs.

Dennis, Wayne & Dennis, Margaret W., eds. The Intellectually Gifted: An Overview. LC 76-41850. (Illus.). 352p. 1976. 56.00 (ISBN 0-8089-0962-2, 791025). Grune.

Dennis, Wesley. Flip. (ps-1). 1977. pap. 2.95 (ISBN 0-14-050203-3, Puffin). Penguin.

--Flip. LC 41-2939. (Illus.). 58p. (ps-1). 1941. 11.50 (ISBN 0-670-31876-0). Viking.

--Flip & the Morning. LC 51-13521. (Illus.). (ps-1). 1977. pap. 3.95 (ISBN 0-14-050204-1, Puffin). Penguin.

Dennis, William E. On the Way to Jericho. 1983. 4.50 (ISBN 0-89536-959-1). CSS of Ohio.

Dennis, William J. Documentary History of the Tacna-Arica Dispute. LC 75-130329. (Latin-American History & Culture Ser). 1971. Repr. of 1927 ed. 22.50cx (ISBN 0-8046-1391-5, Pub. by Kennikat). Assoc Faculty Pr.

--Tacna & Arica: An Account of the Chile-Peru Boundary Dispute & of the Arbitrations by the United States. (Illus.). xviii, 332p. 1967. Repr. of 1931 ed. 20.00 (ISBN 0-208-00466-1, Archon). Shoe String.

--Tacna & Arica: An Account of the Chile-Peru Boundary Dispute & of the Arbitration by the United States. 1931. 18.50x (ISBN 0-686-83802-5). Elliots Bks.

Dennison, Darwin. The Dine System: For Better Nutrition & Health. 128p. 1981. pap. text ed. 9.95 (ISBN 0-8403-2371-9). Kendall-Hunt.

--The Dine System: The Nutritional Plan for Better Health. LC 82-8254. (Mosby Medical Library). (Illus.). 196p. 1982. pap. 8.95 (ISBN 0-452-25367-5, 1258-6). Mosby.

Dennison, Darwin, et al. Alcohol & Behavior: An Activated Education Approach, No. 1. LC 79-25741. 1980. pap. text ed. 12.95 (ISBN 0-8016-1252-7). Mosby.

Dennison, Edward F. Sources of Economic Growth in the U. S. & the Alternatives Before Us. 279p. 1962. pap. 6.00 (ISBN 0-87186-213-1). Comm Econ Dev.

Dennison, George. Lives of Children. LC 74-85566. 320p. 1970. pap. 4.95 (ISBN 0-394-70863-6, V638, Vin). Random.

--Luisa Domic. LC 85-42734. 192p. 1985. 14.37 (ISBN 0-06-015480-2, HarpT). Har-Row.

--Shawno. LC 84-1434. 96p. 1984. 10.95 (ISBN 0-8052-3917-0). Schocken.

--Shawno: Large Print Books. 1985. lib. bdg. 11.95 (ISBN 0-8161-3876-1). G K Hall.

Dennison, George M. The Dorr War: Republicanism on Trial, 1831-1861. LC 75-3543. 264p. 1976. 24.00x (ISBN 0-8131-1330-X). U Pr of Ky.

Dennison, Henry S. Organization Engineering. LC 73-169665. (Management History Ser.: No. 4). 214p. 1972. Repr. of 1931 ed. 22.50 (ISBN 0-87960-001-2). Hive Pub.

Dennison, James T., Jr. The Market Day of the Soul: The Puritan Doctrine of the Sabbath in England, 1532-1700. LC 83-6990. (Illus.). 188p. (Orig.). 1983. lib. bdg. 22.50 (ISBN 0-8191-3204-7); pap. text ed. 11.00 (ISBN 0-8191-3205-5). U Pr of Amer.

Dennison, John M. Analysis of Geologic Structures. (Illus.). 1968. text ed. 14.95x (ISBN 0-393-09801-X, NortonC). Norton.

Dennison, Lisa. New Horizons in American Art: 1985 Exxon National Exhibition. (Illus.). 144p. (Orig.). 1985. pap. write for info. (ISBN 0-89207-050-1). S R Guggenheim.

Dennison, Lisa, jt. auth. see Waldman, Diane.

Dennison, Mark A. Preparing for the Greatest Two Years of Your Life. pap. 3.95 (ISBN 0-89036-128-2). Hawkes Pub Inc.

Dennison, Milo. Blackstone's Magic Adventure: The Case of the Gentleman Ghost, No. 2. pap. 1.95 (ISBN 0-8125-6253-4). Tor Bks.

--Blackstone's Magic Adventure: The Case of the Mummy's Tomb, No. 1. pap. 1.95 (ISBN 0-8125-6251-8). Tor Bks.

--Blackstone's Magic Adventure: The Case of the Phantom Treasure, No. 3. pap. 1.95 (ISBN 0-8125-6255-0). Tor Bks.

--The Case of the Gentleman Ghost. (Blackstone's Magic Adventures Ser.). 128p. (Orig.). 1985. pap. 1.95 (ISBN 0-8125-6253-4, Dist. by Pinnacle Bks, Warner Pub Services & St. Martin). Tor Bks.

--The Case of the Mummy's Tomb. (Blackstone's Magic Adventures Ser.). 128p. (Orig.). 1985. pap. 1.95 (ISBN 0-8125-6251-8, Dist. by Pinnacle Bks, Warner Pub Services & St. Martin). Tor Bks.

--The Case of the Phantom Treasure. (Blackstone's Magic Adventures Ser.). 128p. (Orig.). 1985. pap. 1.95 (ISBN 0-8125-6255-0, Dist. by Pinnacle Bks, Warner Pub Services & St. Martin). Tor Bks.

Dennison, Sally. Alternative Literary Publishing: Five Modern Histories. LC 84-8700. (Illus.). 224p. (Orig.). 1984. 12.95 (ISBN 0-87745-126-5); pap. 9.95 (ISBN 0-87745-127-3). U of Iowa Pr.

Dennison, Sam. Scandalize My Name: Black Imagery in American Popular Music, Vol. 13. (Critical Studies on Black Life & Culture). 1981. lib. bdg. 73.00 (ISBN 0-8240-9309-7). Garland Pub.

Dennison, W. F. Educational Finance & Resources. 288p. 1984. 26.50 (ISBN 0-7099-0842-3, Pub. by Croom Helm Ltd). Longwood Pub Group.

Dennison, Walter. Studies in East Christian & Roman Art. (Humanistic Ser.: Vol. 12). Repr. of 1918 ed. 37.00 (ISBN 0-384-38812-4). Johnson Repr.

Denniston, Carter, jt. auth. see Crow, James F.

Denniston, Denie, jt. auth. see Cohen, Stanley B.

Denniston, Denise, jt. auth. see Goldhaber, Nat.

Denniston, George. Orca Breaching. 2nd. ed. (Illus.). 48p. 1985. pap. 3.95 (ISBN 0-933457-05-7). Random Motion.

Denniston, J. D. Greek Literary Criticism. 224p. 1981. Repr. of 1924 ed. lib. bdg. 35.00 (ISBN 0-89984-157-0). Century Bookbindery.

Denniston, J. D., ed. see Aeschylus.

Denniston, J. D., ed. see Euripides.

Denniston, John D. Greek Literary Criticism. (Library of Greek Thought: No. 1). Repr. of 1924 ed. 18.50 (ISBN 0-404-07801-X). AMS Pr.

--Greek Literary Criticism. LC 74-103222. (Classics Ser.). 1971. Repr. of 1924 ed. 21.00x (ISBN 0-8046-1198-X, Pub. by Kennikat). Assoc Faculty Pr.

--Greek Particles. 2nd ed. 1954. 52.00x (ISBN 0-19-814307-9). Oxford U Pr.

--Greek Prose Style. LC 78-31880. 1979. Repr. of 1952 ed. lib. bdg. 27.50x (ISBN 0-313-20960-X, DEGP). Greenwood.

Denniston, K. J. & Enquist, L. W., eds. Recombinant DNA. LC 80-14100. (Benchmark Papers in Microbiology Ser.: Vol. 15). 391p. 1981. 56.95 (ISBN 0-87933-378-2). Van Nos Reinhold.

Denniston, Lyle W. The Reporter & the Law: Techniques of Covering the Courts. 1980. 17.50 (ISBN 0-8038-6341-1); pap. text ed. 9.95x (ISBN 0-8038-6343-8). Hastings.

Dennistoun, James, ed. Cartularium Comitatus De Levanax Ab Initio Seculi Decimi Tertii Usque Ad Annum 1398. LC 72-1044. (Maitland Club, Glasgow. Publications: No. 24). Repr. of 1833 ed. 16.50 (ISBN 0-404-52969-0). AMS Pr.

--Coltness Collections. LC 72-1031. (Maitland Club, Glasgow. Publications: No. 58). Repr. of 1842 ed. 45.00 (ISBN 0-404-53047-8). AMS Pr.

Dennistoun, James, ed. see Cochrane, Andrew.

Dennis Willows, A. O., ed. The Mollusca, Vol. 8: Neurobiology & Behavior, Pt. 1. Date not set. price not set (ISBN 0-12-751408-2). Acad Pr.

Dennler, Louise. Food Preparation: Study Course. 2nd ed. (Illus.). 176p. 1985. pap. text ed. 14.95x (ISBN 0-8138-0805-7). Iowa St U Pr.

Denno, Deborah W. & Schwarz, Ruth M. Biological, Psychological, & Environmental Factors in Delinquency & Mental Disorder: An Interdisciplinary Bibliography. LC 85-5620. (Bibliographies & Indexes in Sociology Ser.: No. 4). xii, 222p. 1985. lib. bdg. 37.50 (ISBN 0-313-24939-3, DBP/). Greenwood.

Denno, R. F. & Dingle, H., eds. Insect Life History Patterns: Habitat & Geographic Variation. (Proceedings in Life Sciences Ser.). (Illus.). 225p. 1981. 36.00 (ISBN 0-387-90591-X). Springer-Verlag.

Denno, Robert F. & McClure, Mark S. Variable Plants & Herbivores in Natural & Managed Systems. 1983. 64.00 (ISBN 0-12-209160-4). Acad Pr.

Dennon, Jack. CP-M Revealed. 1983. pap. 15.95 (ISBN 0-8104-5204-9, 5204). Hayden.

Dennon, Jerry. The Salmon Cookbook. LC 77-25088. (Illus.). 120p. 1978. pap. 5.95 (ISBN 0-914718-30-4). Pacific Search.

Dennon, Lester E., ed. see Russell, Bertrand.

Denny, jt. auth. see White.

Denny, Arthur A. Pioneer Days on Puget Sound. (Shorey Historical Ser.). 84p. pap. 4.95 (ISBN 0-8466-0195-8, S195). Shorey.

--Pioneer Days on Puget Sound. rev. ed. 1980. 14.95 (ISBN 0-87770-226-8). Ye Galleon.

Denny, Brewster C. Seeing American Foreign Policy Whole. LC 84-16390. 210p. 1985. 19.95x (ISBN 0-252-01181-3). U of Ill Pr.

Denny, Don. The Annunciation from the Right: From Early Christian Times to the Sixteenth Century. LC 76-23611. (Outstanding Dissertations in the Fine Arts - 2nd Ser. - Fifteenth Century). (Illus.). 1978. Repr. of 1965 ed. lib. bdg. 55.00 (ISBN 0-8240-2683-7). Garland Pub.

Denny, Ebenezer. Military Journal of Major Ebenezer Denny, An Officer in the Revolutionary & Indian Wars. LC 70-140860. (Eyewitness Accounts of the American Revolution Ser., No. 3). 1970. Repr. of 1859 ed. 23.50 (ISBN 0-405-01214-4). Ayer Co Pubs.

Denny, Emily I. Blazing the Way. (Illus.). 504p. 1984. Repr. of 1909 ed. 24.95 (ISBN 0-939806-05-3). Hist Soc Seattle.

Denny, Frederick M. An Introduction to Islam. 368p. 1985. text ed. write for info. (ISBN 0-02-328520-6). Macmillan.

Denny, Frederick M. & Taylor, Rodney L. The Holy Book in Comparative Perspective. LC 85-8473. (Comparative Religion Ser.). 1985. 19.95 (ISBN 0-87249-453-5). U of SC Pr.

Denny, George. The Dread Fishwish. (Illus.). 1974. 8.95 (ISBN 0-88395-024-3). Freshet Pr.

Denny, Harold N. Dollars for Bullets: The Story of American Rule in Nicaragua. LC 79-25688. (Illus.). 411p. 1980. Repr. of 1929 ed. lib. bdg. 42.50x (ISBN 0-313-22269-X, DEDB). Greenwood.

Denny, Hugh W. Grounding for the Control of EMI. Price, Edward R., ed. LC 82-63066. 1983. text ed. 42.00 (ISBN 0-932263-17-8). White Consult.

Denny, J. O., jt. auth. see Armstrong, Leroy.

Denny, James. Death of Christ. 1982. lib. bdg. 12.50 (ISBN 0-86524-090-6, 9507). Klock & Klock.

--Jesus & the Gospel. 1977. lib. bdg. 59.95 (ISBN 0-8490-2095-6). Gordon Pr.

Denny, Jon S. Careers in Cable TV. LC 82-48660. 288p. 1984. pap. 7.64i (ISBN 0-06-463588-0, HarpT). Har-Row.

Denny, Ludwell. America Conquers Britain. 1981. lib. bdg. 75.00 (ISBN 0-686-71625-6). Revisionist Pr.

--We Fight for Oil. 1979. lib. bdg. 59.95 (ISBN 0-8490-3014-5). Gordon Pr.

--We Fight for Oil. LC 75-6468. (History & Politics of Oil Ser.). 297p. 1976. Repr. of 1928 ed. 19.75 (ISBN 0-88355-287-6). Hyperion Conn.

Denny, M. Ray. Comparative Psychology: An Evolutionary Analysis of Animal Behavior. LC 79-21123. 496p. 1980. pap. 38.00x (ISBN 0-471-70930-1). Wiley.

Denny, Norman & Filmer-Sankey, Josephine. The Bayeux Tapestry: The Norman Conquest 1066. 86p. 1984. 15.00 (ISBN 0-00-195058-4, Pub. by Salem Hse Ltd). Merrimack Pub Cir.

Denny, Norman, jt. auth. see Tournier, Michel.

Denny, Norman, tr. see Hugo, Victor.

Denny, Norman, tr. see Renoir, Jean.

Denny, Patrick, ed. The Ecology & Management of African Wetland Vegetation. (Geobotany Ser.). 1985. lib. bdg. 78.50 (ISBN 90-6193-509-1, Pub. by Junk Pubs Netherlands). Kluwer-Academic.

Denny, Randal. The Habit of Happiness. 1976. 2.50 (ISBN 0-8341-0399-0). Beacon Hill.

Denny, Randal E. Wind in the Rigging. 120p. 1985. pap. 4.50 (ISBN 0-8341-0937-9). Beacon Hill.

Denny, Ray & Davis, Robert. Understanding Behavior: Foundations & Applications. 1981. 18.95 (ISBN 0-88252-113-6). Paladin Hse.

Denny, Stephen, et al see Bates, Martin & Dudley-Evans, Tony.

Denny, Walter A. Stories from the Old Ones: As Told to Walter A. Denny. (Illus., Orig.). (gr. 4 up). 1979. pap. 4.95 (ISBN 0-686-27639-6). Rising Wolf.

Denny, Walter B. Oriental Rugs. Gilchrist, Brenda, ed. LC 78-62734. (Smithsonian Illustrated Library of Antiques). (Illus.). 127p. (Orig.). 1979. 9.95 (ISBN 0-910503-24-9). Cooper-Hewitt Museum.

Denny-Brown. The Cerebral Control of Movement. 222p. 1982. 50.00x (ISBN 0-85323-001-3, Pub. by Liverpool Univ England). State Mutual Bk.

Denny-Brown, D., ed. see Sherrington, Charles.

Denny-Brown, Derek, et al. Handbook of Neurological Examination & Case Recording. 3rd ed. LC 81-13315. 1982. text ed. 6.95x spiral bdg. (ISBN 0-674-37101-1). Harvard U Pr.

Dennys, Joyce. Henrietta's War: News from the Home Front. (Illus.). 160p. 1985. 12.95 (ISBN 0-233-97829-1, Pub. by A Deutsch England). David & Charles.

Dennys, N. B. The Folk-Lore of China: And Its Affinities with That of the Aryan & Semitic Races. LC 72-84000. Repr. of 1876 ed. 20.00 (ISBN 0-405-08443-9, Blom Pubns). Ayer Co Pubs.

Dennys, Nicholas B. The Folk-Lore of China, & Its Affinities with That of the Aryan & Semitic Races. LC 79-89262. (Illus.). iv, 163p. 1972. Repr. of 1876 ed. 43.00x (ISBN 0-8103-3932-3). Gale.

Dennys, Rodney. Heraldry & the Heralds. 288p. 1981. 50.00x (ISBN 0-224-01643-1, Pub. by Cape England). State Mutual Bk.

--Heraldry & the Heralds. (Illus.). 288p. 1982. 24.95 (ISBN 0-224-01643-1, Pub. by Jonathan Cape). Merrimack Pub Cir.

Deno, Stanley, jt. ed. see Merkin, Phylis.

Denoeu, Francois. Sommets Litteraires Francais. rev. ed. 1967. text ed. 22.95 (ISBN 0-669-04826-7). Heath.

Denoeu, Francois & Hall, R. A., Jr. Spoken French. LC 74-152740. (Spoken Language Ser.). 230p. 1973. pap. 10.00x Units 1-12 (ISBN 0-87950-080-8); 6 dual track cassettes 60.00x (ISBN 0-87950-085-9); bk. & cassettes 65.00x (ISBN 0-87950-086-7). Spoken Lang Serv.

Denoeu, Francois & Sices, David. Two Thousand & One French & English Idioms: Idiotismes Francais et Anglais 2001. 1982. pap. text ed. 8.95 (ISBN 0-8120-0435-3). Barron.

De Nogales, Rafael. Looting of Nicaragua. LC 70-111726. (American Imperialism: Viewpoints of United States Foreign Policy, 1898-1941). 1970. Repr. of 1928 ed. 21.00 (ISBN 0-405-02041-4). Ayer Co Pubs.

--The Looting of Nicaragua. 1976. lib. bdg. 59.95 (ISBN 0-8490-0555-8). Gordon Pr.

De Nogent, Guibert. The Autobiography of Guibert, Abbot of Nogent-Sous-Coucy. Bland, C. C., tr. from Lat. LC 79-11248. 1980. Repr. of 1926 ed. lib. bdg. 24.75x (ISBN 0-313-21460-3, GUAU). Greenwood.

De Nolhac, Pierre. Petrarch & the Ancient World. LC 74-6226. 1907. lib. bdg. 25.00 (ISBN 0-8414-3756-4). Folcroft.

Denolin, H., ed. Psychological Problems Before & after Myocardial Infarction. (Advances in Cardiology: Vol. 29). viii, 156p. 1982. 41.75 (ISBN 3-8055-3424-8). S Karger.

Denolin, H. & Demaret, H., eds. Neural Control of the Cardiovascular System & Orthostatic Regulation: Proceedings Basel 1975. (Cardiology: Vol. 61, Suppl. 1). (Illus.). 250p. 1976. 30.00 (ISBN 3-8055-2260-6). S Karger.

Denolin, H., ed. see International Congress on Cardiac Rehabilitation, Hamburg, 1st, September 1977.

Denomme, Robert T. The French Parnassian Poets. LC 72-185260. (Crosscurrents-Modern Critiques Ser.). 160p. 1972. 6.95x (ISBN 0-8093-0575-5). S Ill U Pr.

--Nineteenth-Century French Romantic Poets. LC 69-11504. (Crosscurrents-Modern Critiques Ser.). 188p. 1969. 7.95x (ISBN 0-8093-0343-4). S Ill U Pr.

Denomy, A. J. The Heresy of Courtly Love. 11.25 (ISBN 0-8446-1151-4). Peter Smith.

Denomy, Alexander J., ed. see Agnes, Saint.

Denomy, Alexander J., ed. see Oresme, Nicole.

Denon, Vivant. Travels in Upper & Lower Egypt, 3 vols. in 1. LC 73-6275. (The Middle East Ser.). Repr. of 1803 ed. 86.00 (ISBN 0-405-05331-2). Ayer Co Pubs.

Denoon, David B., ed. The New International Economic Order: A U. S. Response. LC 79-1997. (A UNA-USA Bk.). 1979. 35.00x (ISBN 0-8147-1769-1); pap. 18.50x (ISBN 0-8147-1770-5). NYU Pr.

Denoon, Donald. Settler Capitalism: The Dynamics of Dependent Development in the Southern Hemisphere. (Illus.). 1983. 49.50x (ISBN 0-19-828291-5). Oxford U Pr.

Denoon, Donald & Nyeko, Balaam. Southern Africa since 1800. 2nd ed. 256p. 1984. pap. text ed. 14.95 (ISBN 0-582-72707-3). Longman.

De Noriega, L. A. & Leach, F. Broadcasting in Mexico. (Case Studies on Broadcasting Systems). (Orig.). 1979. pap. 17.95x (ISBN 0-7100-0416-8). Routledge & Kegan.

DeNoter, R. & Vuillermoz, P. Dictionnaire des Synonymes. 284p. (Fr.). 1969. 43.95 (ISBN 0-686-57091-X, M-6113). French & Eur.

De Nottolander, G., jt. ed. see De Neef, J.

Den Ouden, C., ed. Thermal Storage of Solar Energy. 378p. 1982. 39.50 (ISBN 90-247-2492-9, Pub. by Martinus Nijhoff Netherlands). Kluwer Academic.

Den Ouden, C., jt. ed. see Steemers, T. C.

De-Nour, A. Kaplan, jt. auth. see Czaczkes, J. W.

Denova, Charles C. Establishing a Training Function: A Guide for Management. LC 72-122813. 160p. 1971. 23.95 (ISBN 0-87778-005-6). Educ Tech Pubns.

De Noyelles, Diana A. & Smith, Joan D. Women in California: A Guide to Organizations & Resources. LC 76-4327. (California Information Guides Ser.). 1977. pap. 16.75x (ISBN 0-912102-26-8). Cal Inst Public.

Dens, Jean-Pierre. L' Honnete Homme et la Critique du Gout: Esthetique et Societe au XVIIe Siecle. LC 81-68005. (French Forum Monographs: No. 28). 157p. (Orig.). 1981. pap. 9.50x (ISBN 0-917058-27-5). French Forum.

Denscombe, Martin, ed. The Social Organization of Classroom Control. 1980. 30.00x (ISBN 0-686-64956-7, Pub. by Nafferton England). State Mutual Bk.

Denscombe, Martyn. Classroom Control: A Sociological Perspective. 240p. 1985. text ed. 25.00x (ISBN 0-04-371094-8). Allen Unwin.

Densford, Katherine & Everett, Millard. Ethics for Modern Nurses. Reverby, Susan, ed. LC 83-49137. (The History of American Nursing Ser.). 260p. 1984. Repr. of 1946 ed. lib. bdg. 30.00 (ISBN 0-8240-6510-7). Garland Pub.

Densham, A. B., tr. see Zhbankov, Rostislav G.

Densley, Barbara. The ABC's of Home Food Dehydration. LC 75-23565. 112p. (Orig.). 1975. pap. 5.95 (ISBN 0-88290-051-X). Horizon Utah.

--New Concepts in Dehydrated Food Cookery: Hundreds of New Ideas & Tested Recipes for Enjoying Home Dehydrated Foods. LC 79-89357. 1979. pap. 7.95 (ISBN 0-88290-126-5). Horizon Utah.

Denslow, Van B. Modern Thinkers: Principally Upon Social Science; What They Think & Why. facsimile ed. LC 72-38744. (Essay Index Reprint Ser). Repr. of 1880 ed. 25.50 (ISBN 0-8369-2646-3). Ayer Co Pubs.

Denslow, William R. Ten Thousand Famous Freemasons, 4 vols. 1979. Repr. Set. slip cover 29.95 (ISBN 0-88053-072-3). Macoy Pub.

Densmore, D., tr. see Tchernia, P.

Densmore, Frances. American Indians & Their Music. (American Studies). 1926. 18.00 (ISBN 0-384-11405-9). Johnson Repr.

--Cheyenne & Arapaho Music. 111p. 1964. Repr. of 1936 ed. 5.00 (ISBN 0-916561-12-7). Southwest Mus.

--Chippewa Customs. (Landmarks in Anthropology Ser). 1970. Repr. of 1929 ed. 24.00 (ISBN 0-384-11410-5). Johnson Repr.

--Chippewa Customs. LC 79-15400. (Borealis Books Ser.). (Illus.). 204p. 1979. pap. 7.95 (ISBN 0-87351-142-5). Minn Hist.

--Chippewa Customs. Repr. of 1929 ed. 29.00x (ISBN 0-403-03556-2). Scholarly.

--Chippewa Music, 2 vols. LC 77-164513. (Illus.). 1972. Repr. of 1913 ed. Set. lib. bdg. 49.50 (ISBN 0-306-70459-5). Da Capo.

--Chippewa Music. (2 vols. in one). Repr. 15.00 (ISBN 0-87018-067-3). Ross.

--Choctaw Music. LC 72-1883. (Music Ser.). (Illus.). 110p. 1972. Repr. of 1943 ed. lib. bdg. 19.50 (ISBN 0-306-70511-7). Da Capo.

--Dakota & Ojibwe People in Minnesota. LC 77-72282. (Illus.). 55p. (gr. 7-9). 1977. pap. 3.50 (ISBN 0-87351-111-5). Minn Hist.

--Handbook of the Collection of Musical Instruments in the United States National Museum. LC 79-155231. (Music Ser). 1971. Repr. of 1927 ed. lib. bdg. 29.50 (ISBN 0-306-70167-7). Da Capo.

--How Indians Use Wild Plants for Food, Medicine & Crafts. (Illus.). 162p. 1974. pap. 3.95 (ISBN 0-486-23019-8). Dover.

--How Indians Use Wild Plants for Food, Medicine & Crafts. Orig. Title: Use of Plants by the Chippewa Indians. (Illus.). 14.25 (ISBN 0-8446-5029-3). Peter Smith.

--Mandan & Hidatsa Music. LC 72-1886. (Music Ser.). (Illus.). 236p. 1972. Repr. of 1923 ed. lib. bdg. 25.00 (ISBN 0-306-70514-1). Da Capo.

--Menominee Music. LC 72-1882. (Music Ser.). (Illus.). 286p. 1972. Repr. of 1932 ed. lib. bdg. 27.50 (ISBN 0-306-70510-9). Da Capo.

--Music of Acoma, Isleta, Cochiti, & Zuni Pueblos. LC 72-1877. (Music Ser.). (Illus.). 142p. 1972. Repr. of 1957 ed. lib. bdg. 19.50 (ISBN 0-306-70505-2). Da Capo.

--Music of Santo Domingo Pueblo, New Mexico. 186p. 1938. 5.00 (ISBN 0-916561-53-4). Southwest Mus.

--Music of the Indians of British Columbia. LC 72-1879. (Music Ser.). (Illus.). 118p. 1972. Repr. of 1943 ed. lib. bdg. 19.50 (ISBN 0-306-70507-9). Da Capo.

--The Music of the North American Indian, 14 vols. in 13. (Music Ser.). 1972. Set. 295.00 (ISBN 0-306-70517-6). Da Capo.

--Nootka & Quileute Music. LC 72-1885. (Music Ser.). (Illus.). 416p. 1972. Repr. of 1939 ed. lib. bdg. 39.50 (ISBN 0-306-70513-3). Da Capo.

--Northern Ute Music. LC 72-1887. (Music Ser.). (Illus.). 236p. 1972. Repr. of 1922 ed. lib. bdg. 25.00 (ISBN 0-306-70515-X). Da Capo.

--Papago Music. LC 72-1881. (Music Ser.). (Illus.). 276p. 1972. Repr. of 1929 ed. lib. bdg. 25.00 (ISBN 0-306-70509-5). Da Capo.

--Pawnee Music. LC 72-1880. (Music Ser.). 160p. 1972. Repr. of 1929 ed. lib. bdg. 19.50 (ISBN 0-306-70508-7). Da Capo.

--Seminole Music. LC 72-1878. (Music Ser.). (Illus.). 276p. 1972. Repr. of 1956 ed. lib. bdg. 25.00 (ISBN 0-306-70506-0). Da Capo.

--Study of Indian Music. facs. ed. 32p. pap. 3.95 (ISBN 0-8466-0113-3, S113). Shorey.

--Teton Sioux Music. LC 72-1889. (Music Ser.). (Illus.). 722p. 1972. Repr. of 1918 ed. lib. bdg. 49.50 (ISBN 0-306-70516-8). Da Capo.

--Yuman & Yaqui Music. LC 72-1884. (Music Ser.). (Illus.). 272p. 1972. Repr. of 1932 ed. lib. bdg. 25.00 (ISBN 0-306-70512-5). Da Capo.

Densmore, Francis. Chippewa Music. Repr. of 1911 ed. 29.00x (ISBN 0-403-03557-0). Scholarly.

Densmore, Raymond E. The Coal Miner of Appalachia. 1977. 3.75 (ISBN 0-87012-258-4). McClain.

Denson, Alan. A Bibliography of the Writings of A. E. (Collected Edition of the Writings of G. W. Russell Ser.: No. IX). Date not set. text ed. price not set (ISBN 0-391-01089-1). Humanities.

--Letters from A. E. (Collected Edition of the Writings of G. W. Russell VII). 1980. text ed. write for info. (ISBN 0-391-01139-1). Humanities.

Denson, Alan, ed. The Poetry of A. E. (Collected Edition of the Writings of G.W. Russell Ser. V). 1980. text ed. write for info. (ISBN 0-391-01144-8). Humanities.

Denson, Wil. Aladdin McFaddin. 24p. (Piano-Vocal Score, Music by Michael Cunningham). 1978. pap. 6.00 (ISBN 0-88680-005-6). I E Clark.

Denson, Wil & Cunningham, Michael. Aladdin McFaddin. (Illus.). 44p. 1977. pap. 2.50 (ISBN 0-88680-004-8); royalty 35.00 (ISBN 0-317-03621-1). I E Clark.

Den Steinen, Karl Von see Von Der Steinen, Karl.

Dent, A., tr. see Andrist, Friedrich.

Dent, Alan. Animals & Monsters. LC 72-13625. (World of Shakespeare Ser: Vol. 1). 160p. 1973. 5.50 (ISBN 0-8008-0274-8). Taplinger.

--Mrs. Patrick Campbell. LC 72-9046. (Illus.). 333p. 1973. Repr. of 1961 ed. lib. bdg. 22.50x (ISBN 0-8371-6560-1, DECA). Greenwood.

--Preludes & Studies. LC 75-105778. 1970. Repr. of 1942 ed. 21.00x (ISBN 0-8046-0948-9, Pub. by Kennikat). Assoc Faculty Pr.

--The World of Shakespeare. LC 78-20691. 1979. pap. 7.95 (ISBN 0-8008-8597-X). Taplinger.

Dent, Alan, ed. see Shaw, George B.

Dent, Anthony. Cleveland Bay Horses. (Illus.). 1978. 4.95 (ISBN 0-85131-283-7, NL51, Dist. by Miller). J A Allen.

Dent, Anthony, ed. International Modern Plays. Incl. Life of the Insects. Capek, Karel; Mask & the Face. Chiarelli, Luigi; Infernal Machine. Cocteau, Jean; Hannele. Hauptmann, Gerhart; Miss Julie. Strindberg, August. 1973. pap. 2.50x (ISBN 0-460-01989-9, Evman). Biblio Dist.

Dent, Anthony, tr. see Geurts, Reiner.

Dent, Arthur. The First Book of Adam the Computer. (Illus.). 208p. (Orig.). 1984. 14.95 (ISBN 0-8306-0720-X, 1720); pap. 9.95 (ISBN 0-8306-1720-5). TAB Bks.

--The First Book of the IBM PCjr. (Illus.). 208p. 1984. 14.95 (ISBN 0-8306-0760-9); pap. 9.95 (ISBN 0-8306-1760-4, 1760). TAB Bks.

--The Plaine Mans Path-Way to Heaven. LC 74-80173. (English Experience Ser.: No. 652). 430p. 1974. Repr. of 1601 ed. 29.00 (ISBN 90-221-0652-7). Walter J Johnson.

Dent, Borden D. Principles of Thematic Design. (Geography Ser.). (Illus.). 400p. 1984. 30.95 (ISBN 0-201-11334-1). Addison-Wesley.

Dent, C. M. Protestant Reformers in Elizabethan England. (Oxford Theological Monographs). 272p. 1985. 37.50x (ISBN 0-19-826723-1). Oxford U Pr.

Dent, Colin. Construction Cost Appraisal: DCF Techniques in the Construction Industry. LC 75-322708. pap. 45.50 (ISBN 0-317-27869-X, 2025266). Bks Demand UMI.

--Construction Measurement: Elementary Substructures & Superstructures. 364p. 1980. pap. 18.50x (ISBN 0-246-11256-5, Pub. by Granada England). Sheridan.

Dent, David, jt. auth. see Young, Anthony.

Dent, E. J., tr. see Berlioz, Hector.

Dent, E. J., tr. see Pushkin, Alexander.

Dent, Edward. Ferruccio Busoni. (Eulenburg Music Books). (Illus.). 390p. 1982. pap. text ed. 15.00 (ISBN 0-903873-02-8). Da Capo.

--The Rise of Romantic Opera. Dean, Winton, ed. LC 76-14029. (Illus.). 1976. 42.50 (ISBN 0-521-21337-1). Cambridge U Pr.

Dent, Edward, tr. see Mozart, Wolfgang & Nicholas, John.

Dent, Edward J. Alessandro Scarlatti: His Life & Works. LC 76-181140. 252p. 1960. Repr. 49.00x (ISBN 0-403-01541-3). Scholarly.

--Foundations of English Opera. 2nd ed. LC 65-18501. (Music Ser). 1965. Repr. of 1928 ed. lib. bdg. 29.50 (ISBN 0-306-70905-8). Da Capo.

--Mozart's Operas: A Critical Study. 2nd ed. LC 83-45429. Repr. of 1947 ed. 32.50 (ISBN 0-404-20077-X). AMS Pr.

--Opera. rev. ed. LC 78-14482. (Illus.). 1978. Repr. of 1968 ed. lib. bdg. 27.50x (ISBN 0-313-20563-9, DEOP). Greenwood.

--The Rise of Romantic Opera. Dean, Winton, ed. LC 78-62111. 1979. pap. 12.95 (ISBN 0-521-29659-5). Cambridge U Pr.

--A Theatre for Everybody: The Story of the Old Vic & Sadler's Wells. LC 78-59017. (Illus.). 1979. Repr. of 1945 ed. 23.50 (ISBN 0-88355-691-X). Hyperion Conn.

Dent, Edward J., tr. see Ponte, Lorenzo Da.

Dent, George, jt. auth. see Sims, Albert E.

Dent, H. C. Education in England & Wales. (Illus.). 171p. 1977. 18.00 (ISBN 0-208-01742-9, Linnet). Shoe String.

--Education in Transition. LC 73-8255. 244p. 1974. Repr. of 1948 ed. lib. bdg. 22.50x (ISBN 0-8371-6976-3, DEET). Greenwood.

Dent, Huntley. The Feast of Santa Fe: Cooking of the American Southwest. 333p. 1985. 16.95 (ISBN 0-671-47686-6). S&S.

Dent, J. B. & Blackie, M. J. Systems Simulation in Agriculture. (Illus.). 180p. 1979. 31.50 (ISBN 0-85334-827-8, Pub. by Elsevier Applied Sci England). Elsevier.

Dent, J. B., jt. ed. see Blackie, M. J.

Dent, James. James Dent Strikes Again. (Illus.). 200p. 1984. 5.95 (ISBN 0-934750-43-2). Jalamap.

--James Dent Strikes Again. 1984. 5.95 (ISBN 0-934750-43-2). McClain.

Dent, John C. The Story of the Upper Canadian Rebellion: Largely Derived from Original Sources & Documents Upper Canadian Rebellion. 52.00 (ISBN 0-8369-7157-4, 7989). Ayer Co Pubs.

Dent, Joseph B., et al. Fundamentals of Engineering Graphics, SI. 3rd ed. 504p. 1983. pap. text ed. write for info. (ISBN 0-02-328490-0). Macmillan.

Dent, Julian. Crisis in Finance: Crown, Financiers & Society in Seventeenth-Century France. LC 73-80084. 288p. 1973. 27.50 (ISBN 0-312-17360-1). St Martin.

Dent, Martin. Nigeria: The Politics of Military Rule. 200p. 1985. text ed. 30.00x (ISBN 0-7146-3138-8, BHA-03138, F Cass Co). Biblio Dist.

Dent, N. J. The Moral Psychology of the Virtues. LC 83-26208. (Cambridge Studies in Philosophy). 240p. 1984. 34.50 (ISBN 0-521-25726-3). Cambridge U Pr.

Dent, Nicholas. How to Sail. LC 78-78116. 1979. 11.95 (ISBN 0-312-39613-9). St Martin.

--How to Sail: A Practical Course in Boat Handling. (Illus.). 128p. pap. 9.95 (ISBN 0-312-39625-2). St Martin.

Dent, R. W. Proverbial Language in English Drama Exclusive of Shakespeare, 1495-1616: An Index. LC 83-17922. 600p. 1984. text ed. 49.95x (ISBN 0-520-05169-6). U of Cal Pr.

--Shakespeare's Proverbial Language: An Index. 378p. 1981. 35.00x (ISBN 0-520-03894-0). U of Cal Pr.

Dent, Roxanne. Bitter Harvest. 528p. (Orig.). 1984. pap. 3.95 (ISBN 0-446-80994-2). Warner Bks.

--Island of Fear. 1973. pap. 0.75 (ISBN 0-380-01305-3, 15032). Avon.

Dent, Thomas L., ed. Pancreatic Disease: Diagnosis & Therapy. LC 81-81493. (Illus.). 576p. 1981. 69.50 (ISBN 0-8089-1376-X, 791028). Grune.

Dent, Tom. Blue Lights & River Songs. LC 81-82659. 75p. 1982. pap. 4.50x perfect bd. (ISBN 0-916418-31-6). Lotus.

Dent, W. Practical Cataloguing. 1966. 6.00 (ISBN 0-8022-0382-5). Philos Lib.

Den Tak Richard, Van see Van Den Tak, Richard.

Dentan, Robert C. First Reader in Biblical Theology: The Design of the Scriptures. 1965. pap. 5.95 (ISBN 0-8164-2022-X, SP20, Pub. by Seabury). Winston Pr.

--First, Second Kings & First, Second Chronicles. LC 59-10454. (Layman's Bible Commentary Ser., Vol. 7). 1964. pap. 4.95 (ISBN 0-8042-3067-6). John Knox.

--Holy Scriptures: A Survey. (Orig.). 1949. pap. 5.95 (ISBN 0-8164-2031-9, SP1, Pub. by Seabury). Winston Pr.

Dentan, Robert K. The Semai: A Nonviolent People of Malaya. LC 78-16352. 1979. pap. text ed. 9.50 (ISBN 0-03-045376-3, HoltC). HR&W.

Dente, Leonard A. Veblen's Theory of Social Change. Bruchey, Stuart, ed. LC 76-39826. (Nineteen Seventy-Seven Disseratations Ser.). (Illus.). 1977. lib. bdg. 29.00x (ISBN 0-405-09906-1). Ayer Co Pubs.

Denti, Elisabetta. Vanished Dreams of a Poet: Poems from a Foreign Land. 56p. (Orig.). 1985. pap. write for info. (ISBN 0-9614723-0-8). Elisabetta Denti.

Denti, Renzo. Dizionario Tecnico Italiano-Inglese, Inglese-Italiano. 10th rev. ed. 1811p. (Eng. & Ital.). 1981. 78.00x (ISBN 88-203-1052-X). S F Vanni.

Dentinger, Don. Helga & the Christmas Star. (Reading Readiness Ser.). (Illus.). 32p. (ps-2). 1981. pap. text ed. 2.95 (ISBN 0-941802-03-5, CL-4). Creat Learning.

--If Animals Could Talk. (Reading Readiness Ser.). (Illus.). 32p. (Orig.). (ps-2). pap. 2.95 (ISBN 0-941802-02-7, CL-3). Creat Learning.

--Judy's Raggedy Ann. (Reading Readiness Ser.). 32p. (Orig.). (ps-2). 1981. pap. text ed. 2.95 (ISBN 0-941802-01-9, CL-2). Creat Learning.

--Read with Me. (Reading Readiness Ser.). (Illus.). 32p. (ps). 1981. pap. 2.95 (ISBN 0-941802-00-0, CL-1). Creat Learning.

Dentinger, Jane. First Hit of the Season. LC 83-20700. (Crime Club Ser.). 192p. 1984. 11.95 (ISBN 0-385-19409-9). Doubleday.

--First Hit of the Season. 1985. pap. 3.50 (ISBN 0-440-12535-9). Dell.

De Oliveira Marques, A. H. Daily Life in Portugal in the Late Middle Ages. Wyatt, S. S., tr. (Illus.). 372p. 1971. 21.50x (ISBN 0-299-05580-9). U of Wis Pr.

De Oliveira Martins, J. P. History of Iberian Civilization. Bell, Aubrey F., tr. LC 71-81778. 292p. 1969. Repr. of 1929 ed. 23.50 (ISBN 0-8154-0300-3). Cooper Sq.

De Oliveira Setubal, Paulo see Setubal, Paulo de Oliveira.

De Olivera Marques, Antonia H. History of Portugal. Incl. Vol. 1. From Lusitania to Empire. (Illus.). 507p. 34.00x (ISBN 0-231-03159-9); Vol. 2. From Empire to Corporate State. 2nd rev. ed. 310p. 30.00x (ISBN 0-231-04162-4). LC 77-184748. 1972. pap. 20.00x (ISBN 0-686-66878-2) (ISBN 0-231-08353-X). Columbia U Pr.

De Olivieri, Evelyn R., tr. see Blazier, Kenneth D.

De Olivieri, Matilde Vilarino see Vilarino De Olivieri, Matilde.

Deonanan, Carlton R., jt. auth. see Deonanan, Venus E.

Deonanan, Venus E. & Deonanan, Carlton R. Teaching Spanish in the Secondary School in Trinidad, West Indies: A Curriculum Perspective. 373p. 1980. pap. text ed. 15.75 LC 79-6199. (ISBN 0-8191-1005-1). U Pr of Amer.

Deonarain, M. A BASIC Course in Computer Programming. 1984. 8.95 (ISBN 0-8062-2317-0). Carlton.

De Onis, Federico. Espana en America. 2nd ed. 7.50 (ISBN 0-8477-3140-5). U of PR Pr.

De Onis, Federico & De Torre, Emilio. Canciones Espanolas. (Seleccion III y IV). 75p. (Sp.). 2.00 (ISBN 0-318-14244-9). Hispanic Inst.

De Onis, Federico see Schindler, Kurt.

De Onis, Federico see Seminario De Estudios Hispanicos & Onis, Federico de.

De Onis, Harriet see Alegria, Ciro.

De Onis, Harriet, ed. see De Cervantes, Miguel.

De Onis, Harriet, tr. from Span. Life of Lazarillo De Tormes. (gr. 11 up). 1959. pap. text ed. 3.95 (ISBN 0-8120-0128-1). Barron.

De Onis, Harriet, tr. see Alegria, Ciro.

De Onis, Harriet, tr. see Freyre, Gilberto.

De Onis, Harriet, tr. see Guzman, Martin L.

De Onis, Harriet, tr. see Perez Galdos, Benito.

De Onis, Harriet, tr. see Reyes, Alfonso.

De Onis, Harriet, tr. see Valdes, Armando P.

De Onis, Jone. The United States as Seen by Spanish American Writers: 1776-1890. 226p. 4.00 (ISBN 0-318-14313-5). Hispanic Inst.

De Onis, Jose. Melville y el Mundo Hispanico. (UPREX, E. Literarios: No. 38). pap. 1.85 (ISBN 0-8477-0038-0). U of PR Pr.

--The United States As Seen by Spanish American Writers (1776-1890) LC 74-26684. (Cultural Relations Between the U. S. & the Hispanic World Ser.: Vol. 1). 236p. 1975. Repr. of 1952 ed. 10.00x (ISBN 0-87752-184-0). Gordian.

De Ortiz, Sutti R. Uncertainties in Peasant Farming: A Colombian Case. (London School of Economics Monographs on Social Anthropology: No. 46). (Illus.). 294p. 1973. 38.50 (ISBN 0-485-19546-1, Pub. by Athlone Pr Ltd). Longwood Pub Group.

De Osma, Guillermo. Mariano Fortuny: His Life & Work. LC 80-51134. (Illus.). 224p. 1985. pap. 25.00 (ISBN 0-8478-0641-3). Rizzoli Intl.

De Otero, Blas. Esto No Es un Libro. 2.50 (ISBN 0-8477-3210-X); pap. 1.85 (ISBN 0-8477-3211-8). U of PR Pr.

De Oviedo, Gabriel see De Gamboa, Pedro S.

De Oviedo, Gonzalo F. see Oviedo, Gonzalo F. de.

De Pace, M. The dBASE III: A Practical Guide. (Illus.). 160p. (Orig.). 1985. pap. 19.95 (ISBN 0-00-383076-4, Pub. by Collins England). Sheridan.

De Pace, M. see Pace, M. de.

De Pacheco, Blanca Silvestrini see Silvestrini De Pacheco, Blanca.

De Padua, Fernando. New Frontiers of Electrocardiology: Proceedings. Macfarlane, Peter W., ed. 538p. 1981. 103.95 (ISBN 0-471-10041-2, Pub. by Res. Stud Pr). Wiley.

De Pagter, Henk & Van Raan, Richard. The Valuation of Goods for Customs Purposes. 92p. 1982. 22.00 (ISBN 90-654-4023-2, Pub. by Kluwer Law Netherlands). Kluwer Academic.

De Palacios, Alicia Puyana see Puyana De Palacios, Alicia.

De Palchi, Alfredo. Alfredo De Palchi: Sessions with My Analyst. Salomon, I. L., tr. from It. 1971. 5.95 (ISBN 0-8079-0167-9); pap. 2.95 (ISBN 0-8079-0168-7). October.

De Palerne, Guillaume. The Romance of William of Palerne. Skeat, W. W., ed. (EETS, ES Ser.: No. 1). Repr. of 1867 ed. 35.00 (ISBN 0-527-00211-9). Kraus Repr.

De Palerne, Guillaume & Sims, Norman T. William of Palerne. LC 75-37599. 1975. lib. bdg. 40.00 (ISBN 0-8414-7549-0). Folcroft.

DePalma, Anthony F. Surgery of the Shoulder. 3rd ed. (Illus.). 768p. 1983. text ed. 82.50 (ISBN 0-397-50492-6, 65-06349, Lippincott Medical). Lippincott.

DePalma, Anthony F. & Rothman, Richard H. The Intervertebral Disc. LC 73-97546. pap. 94.80 (ISBN 0-317-29995-6, 2051844). Bks Demand UMI.

DePalma, David J. & Foley, Jeanne M. Moral Development: Current Theory & Research. LC 75-14211. 206p. 1975. text ed. 24.95x (ISBN 0-89859-116-3). L Erlbaum Assocs.

De Palma, Vito. Be Not Conformed... LC 78-54418. 1979. 10.00 (ISBN 0-9601672-0-X). Cross Bks.

DePaola, Dominick P., et al, eds. Preventive Dentistry. LC 77-94885. (Illus.). 308p. 1979. 31.00 (ISBN 0-88416-162-5). PSG Pub Co.

De Paola, Helena, jt. auth. see Mueller, Carol S.

De Paola, T. Andy: That's My Name. (ps-2). 1973. 9.95x (ISBN 0-13-036731-1, Pub. by Treehouse); pap. 3.95 (ISBN 0-13-036749-4). P-H.

--Charlie Needs a Cloak. 1974. 10.95x (ISBN 0-13-128355-3). P-H.

DePaola, T., jt. auth. see Jennings, M.

De Paola, Tomie. Big Anthony & the Magic Ring. LC 78-23631. (Illus.). 32p. (ps-3). 1979. 12.95 (ISBN 0-15-207124-5, HJ). HarBraceJ.

--Big Anthony & the Magic Ring. LC 78-23631. (Illus.). (gr. k-3). 1979. pap. 3.95 (ISBN 0-15-611907-2, VoyB). HarBraceJ.

--Bill & Pete. LC 78-5330. (Illus.). (gr. k-2). 1978. 9.95 (ISBN 0-399-20646-9, Putnam); pap. 5.95 (ISBN 0-399-20650-7, Putnam). Putnam Pub Group.

--The Cat on the Dovrefell: A Christmas Tale. Dasent, G. W., tr. LC 78-26340. (Illus.). 32p. (gr. k-3). 1979. (Putnam); pap. 3.95 (ISBN 0-399-20685-X, Putnam). Putnam Pub Group.

--Charlie Needs a Cloak. (Illus.). 32p. (ps-2). 1982. pap. 3.95 (ISBN 0-13-128280-8, Pub. by Treehouse). P-H.

--The Cloud Book. LC 74-34493. (Illus.). 32p. (gr. k-3). 1975. reinforced bdg. 11.95 (ISBN 0-8234-0259-2). Holiday.

DePaola, Tomie. The Cloud Book. LC 74-34493. (Illus.). 32p. (gr. k-3). 1984. pap. 5.95 (ISBN 0-8234-0531-1). Holiday.

De Paola, Tomie. The Clown of God. LC 78-3845. (Illus.). (gr. k up). 1978. 10.95 (ISBN 0-15-219175-5, HJ). HarBraceJ.

--The Clown of God. LC 78-3845. (Illus.). (ps-3). 1978. pap. 6.95 (ISBN 0-15-618192-4, VoyB). HarBraceJ.

--The Comic Adventures of Old Mother Hubbard & Her Dog. LC 80-19270. (Illus.). 32p. (ps-3). 1981. 11.95 (ISBN 0-15-219541-6, HJ). HarBraceJ.

--The Comic Adventures of Old Mother Hubbard & Her Dog. LC 80-19270. (Illus.). 32p. (ps-3). 1981. pap. 5.95 (ISBN 0-15-219542-4, VoyB). HarBraceJ.

DePaola, Tomie. Country Farm. (Magic Windows Ser.). (Illus.). 9p. 1984. pap. 4.95 (ISBN 0-399-21056-3, Philomel). Putnam Pub Group.

De Paola, Tomie. The Family Christmas Tree Book. LC 80-12081. (Illus.). 32p. (ps-3). 1980. reinforced bdg. 11.95 (ISBN 0-8234-0416-1). Holiday.

DePaola, Tomie. The Family Christmas Tree Book. LC 80-12081. (Illus.). 32p. (gr. k-3). 1984. pap. 5.95 (ISBN 0-8234-0535-4). Holiday.

De Paola, Tomie. Fin M'Coul. (Illus.). 32p. (gr. k-3). 1981. reinforced bdg. 12.95 (ISBN 0-8234-0384-X); pap. 5.95 (ISBN 0-8234-0385-8). Holiday.

--Francis: The Poor Man of Assisi. LC 81-6984. (Illus.). 48p. (gr. 2-5). 1982. reinforced 14.95 (ISBN 0-8234-0435-8). Holiday.

--The Friendly Beasts: An Old English Christmas Carol. (Illus.). 32p. 1981. 10.95 (ISBN 0-399-20739-2); pap. 4.95 (ISBN 0-399-20777-5). Putnam Pub Group.

--Giorgio's Village. (Illus.). (gr. 1 up). 1982. 11.95 (ISBN 0-399-20854-2, Putnam). Putnam Pub Group.

--Helga's Dowry. LC 76-54953. (Illus.). 32p. (ps-3). 1977. 12.95 (ISBN 0-15-233701-6, HJ). HarBraceJ.

--Helga's Dowry. LC 76-54953. (Illus.). 32p. (ps-3). 1977. pap. 6.95 (ISBN 0-15-640010-3, VoyB). HarBraceJ.

--The Hunter & the Animals: A Wordless Picture Book. LC 81-2875. (Illus.). 32p. (ps-3). 1981. reinforced bdg. 11.95 (ISBN 0-8234-0397-1); pap. 5.95 (ISBN 0-8234-0428-5). Holiday.

--The Kids' Cat Book. LC 79-2090. (Illus.). 32p. (gr. k-3). 1979. reinforced bdg. 11.95 (ISBN 0-8234-0365-3). Holiday.

DePaola, Tomie. The Kids' Cat Book. LC 79-2090. 32p. (gr. k-3). 1984. pap. 5.95 (ISBN 0-8234-0534-6). Holiday.

De Paola, Tomie. The Knight & the Dragon. (Illus.). 32p. (gr. k-2). 1980. 10.95 (ISBN 0-399-20707-4, Peppercorn); pap. 4.95 (ISBN 0-399-20708-2). Putnam Pub Group.

--The Lady of Guadalupe. LC 79-19610. (Illus.). 48p. (gr. k-3). 1980. reinforced bdg. 13.95 (ISBN 0-8234-0373-4); pap. 4.95 (ISBN 0-8234-0403-X). Holiday.

--The Legend of Old Befana. LC 80-12293. (Illus.). 32p. (gr. k-3). 1980. pap. 3.95 (ISBN 0-15-243817-3, VoyB). HarBraceJ.

DePaola, Tomie. Marianna May & Nursey. LC 82-9364. (Illus.). 32p. (ps-3). 1983. reinforced bdg. 12.95 (ISBN 0-8234-0473-0). Holiday.

De Paola, Tomie. Michael Bird-Boy. (Illus.). (ps-2). 1975. (Pub. by Treehouse); pap. 5.95; 3.95 (ISBN 0-13-580811-1). P-H.

--Mother Goose Story Streamers. (Illus.). 28p. (ps-3). 1984. 4.95 (ISBN 0-399-21004-0, Putnam). Putnam Pub Group.

DePaola, Tomie. The Mysterious Giant of Barletta. LC 83-18445. (Illus.). 32p. (ps-3). 1984. 12.95 (ISBN 0-15-256347-4, HJ). HarBraceJ.

--Nana Upstairs & Nana Downstairs. (Illus.). (gr. 1-3). 1978. pap. 3.95 (ISBN 0-14-050290-4, Puffin). Penguin.

De Paola, Tomie. Nana Upstairs & Nana Downstairs. new ed. (Illus.). 32p. (ps-3). 1973. PLB 7.99 (ISBN 0-399-60787-0). Putnam Pub Group.

DePaola, Tomie. Noah & the Ark. (Illus.). 40p. (Orig.). (ps-4). 1983. pap. 5.95 (ISBN 0-86683-699-3, AY8268). Winston Pr.

--Noah & the Ark. (Illus.). 32p. (ps-2). 1983. 12.95 (ISBN 0-86683-819-8, AY8451). Winston Pr.

De Paola, Tomie. Now One Foot, Now the Other. (Illus.). 48p. (gr. 3-7). 1981. 9.95 (ISBN 0-399-20774-0, Putnam); pap. 4.95 (ISBN 0-399-20775-9). Putnam Pub Group.

--Nuestra Senora de Guadalupe. Belpre, Pura, tr. LC 79-19609. (Illus.). 48p. (Span.). (gr. 1-3). 1980. reinforced bdg. 10.95 (ISBN 0-8234-0374-2); pap. 4.95 (ISBN 0-8234-0404-8). Holiday.

--Oliver Button Is a Sissy. LC 78-12624. (Illus.). 48p. (ps-3). 1979. 9.95 (ISBN 0-15-257852-8, HJ). HarBraceJ.

--Oliver Button Is a Sissy. LC 78-12624. (Illus.). (gr. k-3). 1979. pap. 3.95 (ISBN 0-15-668140-4, VoyB). HarBraceJ.

--Pancakes for Breakfast. LC 77-15523. (Illus.). (ps-2). 1978. 9.95 (ISBN 0-15-259455-8, HJ). HarBraceJ.

DePaola, Tomie. Pancakes for Breakfast. LC 77-15523. (Illus.). 32p. (ps-3). 1978. pap. 4.95 (ISBN 0-15-670768-3, VoyB). HarBraceJ.

De Paola, Tomie. The Popcorn Book. LC 77-21456. (Illus.). 32p. (gr. k-3). 1978. reinforced bdg. 11.95 (ISBN 0-8234-0314-9). Holiday.

--The Popcorn Book. (gr. k-3). 1979. pap. 1.95 (ISBN 0-590-03142-2). Scholastic Inc.

DePaola, Tomie. The Popcorn Book. LC 77-21456. (Illus.). 32p. (gr. k-3). 1984. pap. 5.95 (ISBN 0-8234-0533-8). Holiday.

De Paola, Tomie. The Prince of the Dolomites. LC 79-18524. (Illus.). (gr. k-3). 1980. 8.95 (ISBN 0-15-263528-9, HJ). HarBraceJ.

--The Prince of the Dolomites. LC 79-18524. (Illus.). 48p. (ps-3). 1980. pap. 4.50 (ISBN 0-15-674432-5, VoyB). HarBraceJ.

--The Quicksand Book. LC 76-28762. (Illus.). 32p. (ps-3). 1977. reinforcd bdg. 11.95 (ISBN 0-8234-0291-6). Holiday.

DePaola, Tomie. The Quicksand Book. LC 76-28762. (gr. k-3). 1984. pap. 5.95 (ISBN 0-8234-0532-X). Holiday.

--Sing, Pierrot, Sing: A Picture Book in Mime. LC 83-8403. (Illus.). 32p. (ps-3). 1983. 12.95 (ISBN 0-15-274988-8, HJ). HarBraceJ.

De Paola, Tomie. Songs of the Fog Maiden. LC 78-12822. (Illus.). 32p. (ps-3). 1979. reinforced bdg. 8.95 (ISBN 0-8234-0341-6). Holiday.

DePaola, Tomie. The Story of the Three Wise Kings. LC 83-4609. (Illus.). (ps-5). 1983. 11.95 (ISBN 0-399-20998-0, Putnam); pap. 4.95 (ISBN 0-399-20999-9). Putnam Pub Group.

De Paola, Tomie. Strega Nona. LC 75-11565. (Illus.). (ps-3). 1975. 10.95x (ISBN 0-13-851600-6, Pub. by Treehouse); pap. 4.95 (ISBN 0-13-851592-1). P-H.

--Strega Nona's Magic Lessons. LC 80-28260. (Illus.). (ps-3). 1982. 12.95 (ISBN 0-15-281785-9, HJ). HarBraceJ.

DePaola, Tomie. Strega Nona's Magic Lessons. LC 80-28260. (Illus.). 32p. (ps-3). 1984. pap. 6.95 (ISBN 0-15-281786-7, VoyB). HarBraceJ.

De Paola, Tomie. Things to Make & Do for Valentine's Day. (gr. k-4). 1985. pap. 1.50 (ISBN 0-590-11821-8). Scholastic Inc.

--Things to Make & Do for Valentine's Day. (Things to Make & Do Ser.). (Illus.). 48p. (gr. k-3). 1976. PLB 8.90 (ISBN 0-531-01187-9). Watts.

--Watch Out for the Chicken Feet in Your Soup. LC 74-8201. (Illus.). (ps-3). 1974. PLB 9.95 (ISBN 0-13-945782-8, Pub. by Treehouse); pap. 3.95 (ISBN 0-13-945766-6). P-H.

--When Everyone Was Fast Asleep. (Picture Puffin Ser.). (Illus.). (gr. k-2). 1979. pap. 3.95 (ISBN 0-14-050310-2, Puffin). Penguin.

De Paola, Tomie see Keller, Charles & Baker, Richard.

De Paola, Tomie see Paola, Tomie de.

DePaola, Tomie, retold by. & illus. The Legend of the Bluebonnet: An Old Tale of Texas. LC 82-12391. (Illus.). (ps-3). 1983. 10.95 (ISBN 0-399-20937-9, Putnam); pap. 4.95 (ISBN 0-399-20938-7). Putnam Pub Group.

DePaola, Tomie, illus. David & Goliath. (Bible Story Cutout Bks.). (Illus., Orig.). (gr. k-6). 1984. 32 pages 12.95, (ISBN 0-86683-820-1, 8452); pap. 5.95, 40 pages (ISBN 0-86683-700-0, 8469). Winston Pr.

De Paola, Tomie, illus. & retold by. Fin M'Coul: The Giant of Knockmany Hill. LC 80-2254. (Illus.). 32p. (ps-3). 1981. reinforced bdg. 12.95 (ISBN 0-8234-0384-X); pap. 5.95 (ISBN 0-8234-0385-8). Holiday.

DePaola, Tomie, illus. Queen Esther. (Bible Story Cutout Bks.). (Illus., Orig.). (gr. k-6). 1984. 32p 12.95, (ISBN 0-86683-822-8, 8454); pap. 4.95, 40p (ISBN 0-86683-702-7, 8271). Winston Pr.

--Tomie dePaola's Mother Goose. (Illus.). 128p. 1985. 17.95 (ISBN 0-399-21258-2, Putnam). Putnam Pub Group.

De Paor, Liam, jt. auth. see De Paor, Maire.

De Paor, Maire. Early Irish Art. (Aspects of Ireland Ser.: Vol. 3). (Illus.). 57p. 1979. pap. 5.95 (ISBN 0-906404-03-7, Pub. by Dept Foreign Ireland). Irish Bks Media.

De Paor, Maire & De Paor, Liam. Early Christian Ireland. (Illus.). 1978. pap. 8.95 (ISBN 0-500-27110-0). Thames Hudson.

Depardon, Raymond & Taback, Carol, illus. Aperture, No. 89. (Illus.). 80p. 1983. pap. 12.50 (ISBN 0-89381-112-2). Aperture.

Deparment of Agriculture. Living on a Few Acres. (Illus.). 1979. pap. 4.95 (ISBN 0-452-25215-6, Z5215, Plume). NAL.

Departamento De Ciencias Fisicas. Ciencias Fisicas. 9th ed. 5.00 (ISBN 0-8477-2308-9). U of PR Pr.

Departamento De Espanol, Facultad De Estudios Generales, UPR. Manual De Nociones y Ejercicios Gramaticales: Unidad De Composicion y Otras Destrezas Linguisticas. enl. rev. ed. LC 76-4501. 136p. (Span.). 1976. pap. text ed. 2.15 (ISBN 0-8477-3164-2). U of PR Pr.

Department for the Aging, City of New York. Older Women in the City. Kastenbaum, Robert, ed. LC 78-73649. (Aging & Old Age Ser.). 1979. lib. bdg. 17.00x (ISBN 0-405-11839-2). Ayer Co Pubs.

Department of Aviation Education. Federal Aviation Regulations. 3rd. ed. LC 80-67616. 1982. pap. 3.95 (ISBN 0-912682-32-9). Aero Products.

--Flight Training Manual. LC 80-70568. 1981. pap. 9.95 (ISBN 0-912682-28-0). Aero Products.

--Instrument Rating: Complete Programmed Course. LC 67-8700. 412p. 1969. pap. 4.95 (ISBN 0-685-62815-9). Aero Products.

--Manual of Flight: Private & Commercial Pilot. 332p. 1973. pap. 14.95 (ISBN 0-685-62814-0). Aero Products.

Department of Commerce, ed. Inventory of Research Units in Pennsylvania. 464p. (Orig.). 1983. pap. 10.25 (ISBN 0-8182-0016-2). Commonweal PA.

Department of Cultural Affairs, City of New York. The New York Fine Artists Source Book. 160p. 1983. pap. 6.95 (ISBN 0-201-06023-X). Addison-Wesley.

--The New York Writer's Source Book. 160p. 1983. pap. 6.68 (ISBN 0-201-06024-8). Addison-Wesley.

Department of Energy. Photovoltaic Energy Systems: Program Summary. 220p. 1980. pap. 34.95x (ISBN 0-89934-070-9, P-040). Solar Energy Info.

--Solar Energy: A Status Report. pap. 6.95 (ISBN 0-930978-43-9, V-022). Solar Energy Info.

--Solar Heating & Cooling: Commercial Buildings Demonstration Project Summaries. 1978. pap. 14.95x (ISBN 0-930978-35-8, H-021). Solar Energy Info.

--Solar Heating & Cooling: Research & Development Project Summaries. pap. 14.95x (ISBN 0-930978-36-6, H-009). Solar Energy Info.

--Solar Thermal Power Systems: Program Summary. 270p. 1979. pap. 29.95x (ISBN 0-89934-127-6, T-041). Solar Energy Info.

Department of Foreign Affairs. Facts about Ireland. 2nd ed. (Illus.). 258p. 1981. 14.95 (ISBN 0-906404-10-X, Pub. by Dept Foreign Ireland). Irish Bks Media.

Department of Foreign Affairs Staff, ed. Facts about Ireland. 6th, rev. ed. (Illus.). 255p. 1985. pap. 8.95 (ISBN 0-906404-21-5, Pub. by Dept Foreign Ireland). Irish Bks Media.

Department of Geography, University of Hawaii, compiled by. Atlas of Hawaii. LC 72-91236. (Illus.). 232p. 1973. 19.95 (ISBN 0-8248-0259-4). UH Pr.

Department of Geography, University of Hawaii. Atlas of Hawaii. 2nd ed. LC 82-675462. (Illus.). 238p. 1983. pap. 29.95 deluxe softcover (ISBN 0-8248-0837-1). UH Pr.

Department of International Economic & Social Affairs. Population Bulletin of the United Nations, No. 16-1984. 89p. 1985. pap. 11.00 (UN84/13/6 5071, UN). Unipub.

Department of Oriental History Staff, University of London. Handbook of Oriental History. Philips, C. H., ed. (RHS Guides & Handbooks Ser.: No. 6). 265p. 1963. Repr. of 1951 ed. 7.50 (ISBN 0-901050-16-4, Pub. by Boydell & Brewer). Longwood Pub Group.

Department of Paintings in the Rijkmuseum. All the Paintings in the Rijk-Museum, Amsterdam. Schwartz, Gary, tr. from Dutch. (Illus.). 800p. 1976. 100.00 (ISBN 0-8390-0161-4). Abner Schram Ltd.

Department of Paintings Museum of Fine Arts. Summary Catalogue of European Paintings. (Illus.). 368p. 1985. write for info. (ISBN 0-87846-230-9). Mus Fine Arts Boston.

Department of Romantic Languages of the University of California Members. Literary & Philological Studies. 1978. Repr. of 1919 ed. lib. bdg. 50.00 (ISBN 0-8414-0060-1). Folcroft.

Department of State, jt. ed. see Office of Strategic Studies.

Department of Statistics, Wellington, N.Z. New Zealand Official Yearbook 1980. 85th ed. LC 7-21753. (Illus.). 1027p. 1980. 17.50x (ISBN 0-8002-2885-5). Intl Pubns Serv.

Department of the Air Force. Air Force Manual - AFM 64-5: Search & Rescue-Survival. (Illus.). 1969. soft cover 6.95 (ISBN 0-930294-15-7). World Wide OR.
--Survival! Air Force Manual 64-5. (Illus.). 144p. 1979. pap. 8.00 (ISBN 0-87364-167-1). Paladin Pr.
Department of the Army. First Aid for Soldiers: An Army Field Manual. 1982. lib. bdg. 75.00 (ISBN 0-87700-402-1). Revisionist Pr.
--Guerilla Warfare. 1982. lib. bdg. 75.00 (ISBN 0-87700-400-5). Revisionist Pr.
--Ranger Training & Operations. 1982. lib. bdg. 75.00 (ISBN 0-87700-376-9). Revisionist Pr.
Department of the Interior, U. S. Geologicaal Survey, Monograph & Osborn, Henry F. The Titanotheres of Ancient Wyoming, Dakota, & Nebraska. Gould, Stephen J., ed. LC 79-83341. (The History of Paleontology Ser.: 55 2vols.). (Illus.). 1980. Repr. of 1929 ed. Set. lib. bdg. 224.00x (ISBN 0-405-12729-4); lib. bdg. 112.00xa. Vol. 1 (ISBN 0-405-12730-8). Vol. 2 (ISBN 0-405-12731-6). Ayer Co Pubs.
Department of Transportation. Private Pilot Practical Test Standards: S. E. Land. 114p. (Orig.). pap. text ed. 4.95 (ISBN 0-941272-25-7). Astro Pubs.
Department or the Army, ed. Hand-to-Hand Combat. 1982. lib. bdg. 69.95 (ISBN 0-87700-405-6). Revisionist Pr.
De Pascale, Marc. Book of Spells. LC 70-163218. (Illus.). 1978. pap. 4.95 (ISBN 0-8008-0934-3). Taplinger.
DePasquale, Michael, Jr. Learn the Martial Arts in Eight Weeks. (Orig.). 1983. pap. 8.95 (ISBN 0-671-47469-3, Wallaby). S&S.
--Martial Arts for Young Athletes. Schwartz, Betty, ed. 128p. (Orig.). (gr. 3 up). 1984. pap. 7.95 (ISBN 0-671-50733-8). Wanderer Bks.
De Pasquale, Michael, Jr. Woman's Guide to Self Defense. 1980. pap. 3.95 (ISBN 0-346-12455-7). Cornerstone.
DePasquale, Nicholas P. & Bruno, Michael S. Cardiology Case Studies. 2nd ed. LC 79-91847. 1980. pap. 21.50. Med Exam.
DePasquale, Nicholas P., jt. auth. see Burch, George E.
DePasquale, Nicholas P. & Bruno, Michael S., eds. Cardiology Case Studies. 1973. spiral bdg. 21.50 (ISBN 0-87488-001-7). Med Exam.
De Patterson, Paulina G. Te Damos Gracias, Dios. (Illus.). 28p. 1981. pap. 0.60 (ISBN 0-311-38508-7). Casa Bautista.
Depaul & Mount St. Vincent Center. Administrative Manual of Policies & Procedures for Long Term Care Facilities. LC 75-21141. (Orig.). 1976. pap. 10.00 (ISBN 0-87125-028-4). Cath Health.
DePaul, Don. Caterfly. LC 76-39691. (Illus.). 1977. pap. 4.25 (ISBN 0-8356-0490-X, Quest). Theos Pub Hse.
De Paul, Vincent. Correspondence, Conferences, Documents, Vol. 1. Law, Helen M., et al, trs. from Fr. & Lat. Kilar, Jacqueline, ed. LC 83-63559. 675p. 1985. 28.00 (ISBN 0-317-27157-1). New City.
De Paula, F. Clive. Management Accounting in Practice. 4th ed. 1972. 15.95x (ISBN 0-8464-0587-3); pap. 11.50x (ISBN 0-686-77031-5). Beekman Pubs.
--Techniques of Business Control. 1973. pap. 8.95 (ISBN 0-8464-0911-9). Beekman Pubs.
De Paula, F. R. see Paula, F. R.
De Paula, Frederic & Zeff, Stephen A. Developments in Accounting: With a Profile of the Author. Brief, Richard P., ed. LC 77-87268. (Development of Contemporary Accounting Thought Ser). 1978. Repr. of 1948 ed. lib. bdg. 24.50x (ISBN 0-405-10897-4). Ayer Co Pubs.
DePaula, H. & Mueller, C. Marketing Today's Fashion. 1980. 24.95 (ISBN 0-13-558155-9). P-H.
De Pauley, William C. Candle of the Lord. facsimile ed. LC 75-107693. (Essay Index Reprint Ser). 1937. 16.00 (ISBN 0-8369-1496-1). Ayer Co Pubs.
--The Candle of the Lord: Studies in the Cambridge Platonists. (Church Historical Society, London, New Ser.: No. 28). pap. 23.00 (ISBN 0-317-15604-7). Kraus Repr.
De Paulo, Tomie. The First Christmas. (A Festive Pop-Up Bk.). (Illus.). 6p. 1984. 12.95 (ISBN 0-399-21070-9, Putnam). Putnam Pub Group.
De Pauw, Corneille. Recherches Philosophiques Sur les Americans, 3 vols. 1078p. 1968. Repr. of 1770 ed. Set. 40.00 (ISBN 0-8398-1555-7). Parnassus Imprints.
De Pauw, John W. Soviet-American Trade Negotiations. LC 78-25883. (Praeger Special Studies). 200p. 1979. 39.95 (ISBN 0-03-048446-4). Praeger.
DePauw, John W. U. S.-Chinese Trade Negotiations. LC 80-27254. 252p. 1981. 39.95 (ISBN 0-03-056688-6). Praeger.
Depauw, Karen, jt. auth. see Seaman, Janet.
DePauw, Karen P., ed. National Association for Physical Education in Higher Education Annual Conference: Proceedings, Vol. IV. LC 81-646183. 1983. pap. text ed. 15.00x (ISBN 0-931250-64-1, NPR0004). Human Kinetics.
De Pauw, Linda G. Founding Mothers: Women of America in the Revolutionary Era. (Illus.). 228p. (gr. 7 up). 1975. 13.95 (ISBN 0-395-21896-9). HM.
--Seafaring Women. (gr. 7 up). 1982. 10.95 (ISBN 0-395-32434-3). HM.
De Pauw, Linda Grant, ed. Documentary History of the First Federal Congress of the United States of America, March 4, 1789-March 3,1791. Incl. Vol. 1. Senate Legislative Journal. 800p. 1972. 35.00x (ISBN 0-8018-1280-1); Vol. 2. Senate Executive Journal & Related Documents. 592p. 1974. 32.50x (ISBN 0-8018-1572-X); Vol. 3. House of Representatives Journal. 466p. 1977. 35.00x (ISBN 0-8018-1819-2). (DH). Johns Hopkins.
De Paz, A. Campos, jt. auth. see Cortes-Prieto, J.
De Pedrolo, Manuel. Final Trajectory: Seven Science Fiction Stories. Forcadas, Albert M. & Quinn, Shelley, trs. Date not set. 7.95 (ISBN 0-8062-2409-6). Carlton.
De Peguilhan, Aimeric see Aimeric De Peguilhan.
Depel, Jim. The Baseball Handbook for Coaches & Players. LC 75-19308. (Illus.). 96p. 1976. (ScribT); pap. 9.95 (ISBN 0-684-14265-1, ScribT). Scribner.
Deperet, Charles. The Transformations of the Animal World: Being the Authorized Translation of "Les Transformations Du Monde Animal. Gould, Stephen J., ed. LC 79-8330. (The History of Paleontology Ser.). 1980. Repr. of 1909 ed. lib. bdg. 32.50x (ISBN 0-405-12711-1). Ayer Co Pubs.
Depestre, Rene. A Rainbow for the Christian West. Dayan, Joan, tr. LC 76-45047. 272p. 1977. 15.00x (ISBN 0-87023-229-0). U of Mass Pr.
--Vegetations of Splendor. Hirschman, Jack, tr. from Fr. 25p. (Orig.). 1981. pap. 1.00 (ISBN 0-917702-10-7). Vanguard Bks.
De Peters, Amalia B., jt. auth. see Lombardi, Ronald P.
Depew, Arthur M. Game Book. (Game & Party Books). 1977. pap. 6.95 (ISBN 0-8010-2877-9). Baker Bk.
Depew, Chauncey M. My Memories of Eighty Years: Mark Twain. 1924. 25.00 (ISBN 0-8274-2781-6). R West.
Depew, Chauncey M., ed. Seventeen Ninety-Five to Eighteen Ninety-Five: One Hundred Years of American Commerce, 2 Vols. LC 68-28623. (Illus.). 1968. Repr. of 1895 ed. Set. lib. bdg. 49.50x (ISBN 0-8371-0377-0, DEAC). Greenwood.
Depew, David J., ed. The Greeks & the Good Life. 280p. lib. bdg. 25.00 (ISBN 0-937622-00-1); pap. text ed. 7.95 (ISBN 0-937622-01-X). CSU Fullerton.
Depew, David J. & Weber, Bruce H., eds. Evolution at a Crossroads: The New Biology & the New Philosophy of Science. 288p. 1985. text ed. 25.00x (ISBN 0-262-04079-4). MIT Pr.
Depew, Wally. Nine Essays on Concrete Poems. (Illus.). 68p. (Orig.). 1974. pap. 3.00 (ISBN 0-914974-00-9). Holmgangers.
Depeyrot, Michel, jt. auth. see Faurre, Pierre.
De Pina, Araujo A. Portuguese-English, English-Portuguese Technical Dictionary, 2 vols. (Port. & Eng.). Set. 130.00 (ISBN 0-685-79115-7). Heinman.
D'Epinay, Christian L. Haven of the Masses: A Study of the Pentecostal Movement in Chile. Sandle, Marjorie, tr. (World Studies of Churches in Mission). 1969. pap. 4.95 (ISBN 0-377-82931-5, Pub. by Lutterworth England). Friend Pr.
De Pinero, Europa Gonzales, ed. Schools in Transition. LC 72-96731. 1973. pap. text ed. 2.95x (ISBN 0-8134-1551-9, 1551). Interstate.
De Pinero, Gonzales, ed. Accountability & Change in Education. LC 72-80336. 72p. 1972. pap. text ed. 2.50x (ISBN 0-8134-1473-3, 1473). Interstate.
De Pinto, Vivian. English Biography in the Seventeenth Century. 1951. Repr. 11.50 (ISBN 0-8274-2250-4). R West.
D'Epiro, Peter. A Touch of Rhetoric: Ezra Pound's Malatesta Cantos. Litz, Walton, ed. LC 83-5729. (Studies in Modern Literature: No. 2). 172p. 1983. 34.95 (ISBN 0-8357-1404-7). UMI Res Pr.
De Pisan, C. see Pisan, C. de.
De Pisan, Christine. Book of the Duke of True Lovers. Kemp-Welch, Alice, et al, trs. LC 66-23313. (Illus.). Repr. of 1926 ed. 18.50 (ISBN 0-8154-0177-9). Cooper Sq.
--Oeuvres Poetiques, 3 Vols. Roy, M., ed. 1965. 109.00 (ISBN 0-384-46593-5); pap. 91.00 (ISBN 0-384-46594-3). Johnson Repr.
--The Treasure of the City of Ladies: Or the Book of Three Virtues. Lawson, Sarah, tr. (Classics Ser.). 192p. 1985. pap. 4.95 (ISBN 0-14-044453-X). Penguin.
De Pisan, Christine see Pisan, Christine.
De Pizan, Christine. The Book of the City of Ladies. Richards, E. J., tr. from Fr. (Illus.). 336p. 1982. 17.95 (ISBN 0-89255-061-9). Persea Bks.
--A Medieval Woman's Mirror of Honor: The Treasury of the City of Ladies. Cosmen, Madeleine P., ed. Willard, Charity C., tr. from Old French. & intro. by. (Illus.). 265p. 1985. pap. 12.95 (ISBN 0-916491-22-6). Persea Bks.
De Planhol, Xavier see Planhol, Xavier De.
De Plata, Edith M. Mexican Vegetarian Cooking: Exotic & Spicy Recipes Using Wholefood Ingredients. 128p. (Orig.). 1984. pap. 6.95 (ISBN 0-7225-0789-5). Thorsons Pubs.
De Platt, Lyman. Una Guia genealogico-historica de Latinoamerica. (Illus., Span.). 1978. pap. 6.95 (ISBN 0-916552-14-4). Acoma Bks.
DePlatt, Lyman, ed. Genealogical Historical Guide to Latin America. LC 78-75146. (Genealogy & Local History Ser.: Vol. 4). 1978. 60.00x (ISBN 0-8103-1389-8). Gale.
De Plou, Dafne C., tr. see Drakeford, John W.
De Plou, Dafne C., tr. see Harty, Robert & Harty, Annelle.
DePoe, Charles E., et al. Laboratory Manual for General Botany. (Illus.). 176p. 1983. 10.95x (ISBN 0-88136-010-4). Jostens.
De Poerck, R. A., jt. auth. see Krug, C. A.
De Poix, Carol. Jo, Flo & Yolanda. (Illus.). 35p. (Orig.). (ps-1). 1973. pap. 3.00 (ISBN 0-914996-04-5). Lollipop Power.
DePol, Dennis R. & Cheremisinoff, Paul N. Emergency Response to Hazardous Materials Incidents. LC 84-51633. 121p. 1984. pap. 19.00 (ISBN 0-87762-371-6). Technomic.
De Poleo, Patty W., jt. auth. see Ferrer, Jami.
De Polnay, Peter. Garibaldi: The Legend & the Man. LC 75-22641. (Illus.). 234p. 1976. Repr. of 1960 ed. lib. bdg. 17.50x (ISBN 0-8371-8361-8, DEGA). Greenwood.
De Pomaine, Edouard. Cooking in Ten Minutes. LC 84-28774. 144p. 1985. pap. 5.95 (ISBN 0-571-13599-4). Faber & Faber.
De Pomiane, Edouard. The Jews of Poland: Recollections & Recipes. Bacon, Josephine, tr. from Fr. (Jewish Cookery Classics Ser.). (Illus.). 256p. 1985. 9.95 (ISBN 0-910231-02-8); pap. 9.95. Pholiota.
De Pompei, Roberta, jt. auth. see Blosser, Jean.
DePonceau, Arthur. Kill the Envious Moon. 1985. 12.50 (ISBN 0-682-40213-3). Exposition Pr FL.
De Poncins, Gontran. Kabloona. 339p. 1985. pap. 9.95 (ISBN 0-88184-171-4). Carroll & Graf.
De Poncins, Leon. Freemasonry & the Vatican. 1982. lib. bdg. 69.95 (ISBN 0-87700-351-3). Revisionist Pr.
--Judaism & the Vatican. 1982. lib. bdg. 65.00 (ISBN 0-87700-381-5). Revisionist Pr.
--State Secrets: How the Jews Operate Behind Our "Democratic Governments". 1982. lib. bdg. 69.95 (ISBN 0-87700-420-X). Revisionist Pr.
DePoncins, Leon V. Freemasonry & the Vatican. 59.95 (ISBN 0-8490-0196-X). Gordon Pr.
--Judaism & the Vatican. 59.95 (ISBN 0-8490-0466-7). Gordon Pr.
--Secret Powers Behind the Revolution. 59.95 (ISBN 0-8490-1013-6). Gordon Pr.
De Pons, Beatriz. Crecer Contigo. 80p. 1978. pap. 2.25 (ISBN 0-311-40037-X). Casa Bautista.
De Pons, Francois R. see Pons, Francois R. de.
De Ponsard, Pierre see Ronsard, Pierre de.
De Pont, J. J., jt. ed. see Bonting, S. L.
DePont, J. J., jt. ed. see Watts, A.
De Pontgibaud, Chevalier. A French Volunteer of the War of Independence. Douglas, Robert B., ed. & tr. LC 73-76558. (Eyewitness Accounts of the American Revolution Ser. 2). 220p. 1969. Repr. of 1898 ed. 13.50 (ISBN 0-405-01171-7). Ayer Co Pubs.
De Poor, Betty M., tr. Dios, Tu y Tu Familia. (Dios, Tu y la Vida). Orig. Title: Deus, Voce E Sua Familia. 1981. Repr. of 1978 ed. 0.95 (ISBN 0-311-46202-2). Casa Bautista.
DePorte, A. W. The Atlantic Alliance at Thirty-Five. LC 84-81644. (Headline Ser.: No. 268). (Illus.). 64p. (Orig.). (gr. 11-12). 1984. pap. 3.00 (ISBN 0-87124-091-2). Foreign Policy.
--Europe & the Superpower Balance. LC 79-92257. (Headline Ser.: No. 247). (Illus.). 80p. (gr. 11-12). 1979. pap. 3.00 (ISBN 0-87124-058-0). Foreign Policy.
DePorte, Anton W. The Atlantic Alliance. (Headline Ser.: 268). 1984. 3.00 (ISBN 0-87124-091-2). Foreign Policy.
--DeGaulle's Foreign Policy: 1944-1946. LC 67-29624. 1968. 20.00x (ISBN 0-674-19550-7). Harvard U Pr.
--Europe Between the Super Powers: The Enduring Balance. LC 78-8123. 1979. 33.00x (ISBN 0-300-02229-8); pap. 8.95x (ISBN 0-300-02595-5). Yale U Pr.
De Porte, Michael V. Nightmares & Hobbyhorses: Swift, Sterne, & Augustan Ideas of Madness. LC 73-78048. (Illus.). 164p. 1974. 12.50 (ISBN 0-87328-061-X). Huntington Lib.
De Pougy, Liane. My Blue Notebooks. Athill, Diana, tr. from Fr. LC 79-1659. (Illus.). 1979. 15.00i (ISBN 0-06-011083-X, HarpT). Har-Row.
De Pourtales, Guy. Richard Wagner: The Story of an Artist. May, Lewis, tr. from Fr. LC 76-138173. (Illus.). 1972. Repr. of 1932 ed. lib. bdg. 25.25x (ISBN 0-8371-5630-0, PORW). Greenwood.
Depp, Roberta J., jt. ed. see Wynar, Bohdan S.
Deppe, Gunter. Chemotherapy of Gynecologic Cancer. LC 83-26779. 404p. 1984. 58.00 (ISBN 0-8451-0232-X). A R Liss.
Deppe, Theodore R. Management Strategies in Financing Parks & Recreation. LC 82-21840. 166p. 1983. text ed. 22.45 (ISBN 0-471-09966-X). Wiley.
Deppert, Joahim. India & the West. 33.00 (ISBN 0-89410-536-1, Pub. by UBSPD India). Three Continents.
Deppert, Jochim. India & the West. 1984. 42.50x (ISBN 0-8364-1152-8, Pub. by Manohar India). South Asia Bks.
Depping, George B. Histoire du Commerce entre la Levant et l'Europe, depuis les Croisades Jusqu'a la Foundation des Colonies d'Amerique. LC 77-115814. (Research & Source Works Ser.: No. 425). (Fr). 1970. Repr. of 1830 ed. Set. text ed. 49.50 (ISBN 0-8337-0836-8). B Franklin.
DePratter, Chester B., ed. The Late Prehistoric Southeast: A Sourcebook. LC 83-47624. (The North American Indian Ser.). 548p. 1985. lib. bdg. 65.00 (ISBN 0-8240-5881-X). Garland Pub.
De Preaumont, Charles. La Medecine a portee de la main. (Collection que faire?). (Illus.). 1978. pap. 7.95x (ISBN 2-03-001201-7). Larousse.
DePree, Gladis. Festival! 208p. 1985. 12.95 (ISBN 0-310-44110-2, Pub. by J Markham Bks). Zondervan.
DePree, Gladis & DePree, Gordon. A Time to Grow. 112p. (Orig.). 1981. pap. 3.95 (ISBN 0-310-23681-9). Zondervan.
DePree, Gladis, jt. auth. see DePree, Gordon.
DePree, Gordon & DePree, Gladis. Faces of God. LC 80-14384. 128p. 1980. pap. 5.95 (ISBN 0-664-24350-9). Westminster.
DePree, Gordon, jt. auth. see DePree, Gladis.
Depres, Josquin. Sammlung Ausgewaehlter Kompositionen zu 4, 5 und 6 Stimmen. Eitner, Robert & Schlecht, Raymund, eds. (Publikation aelterer praktischer und theoretischer Musikwerke Ser.: Vol. VI). (Illus., Ger., Lat.). 1967. Repr. of 1877 ed. write for info. (ISBN 0-8450-1706-3). Broude.
De Pressense, Domitille. Emily. Cutler, Ebbitt, tr. from Fr. LC 77-79545. (The Emily Ser.). (Illus.). (ps-1). 1977. 3.95 (ISBN 0-88776-077-5). Tundra Bks.
--Emily & Arthur. Cutler, Ebbitt, tr. from French. LC 77-79546. (The Emily Ser.). (Illus.). (ps-1). 1977. 3.95 (ISBN 0-88776-078-3). Tundra Bks.
De Pressense, E. Jesus Christ: His Times, Life & Work. 1978. Repr. of 1898 ed. lib. bdg. 50.00 (ISBN 0-8495-1032-5). Arden Lib.
De Prez, Caroline S. & De Prez, Richard J. Resume & Job Hunting Guide for Present & Future Veterans: How to Make Your Military Training Count in Civilian Job Markets. 192p. 1984. pap. 7.95 (ISBN 0-668-06129-4, 6129-4). Arco.
Deprez, K. Sociolinguistics in the Low Countries. LC 84-24240. (Studies in the Science of Language Series: No. 5). 359p. (Orig.). 1983. pap. 44.00x (ISBN 90-272-2321-1). Benjamins North Am.
De Prez, Richard J., jt. auth. see De Prez, Caroline S.
Depriest, Launder. Reliability in the Acquisitions Process. (Statistics Lecture Notes). 296p. 1983. 35.00 (ISBN 0-8247-1792-9). Dekker.
De Priester, W., jt. ed. see Brederoo, P.
De Prieto, Aura M. Las Tecnicas de la Investigacion. (Span.). 1979. text ed. 6.95 (ISBN 0-538-22220-4, V22). SW Pub.
DePrist, jt. auth. see Wegman.
De Proft, Melanie & Culinary Arts Institute Staff, eds. The American Family Cookbook. rev. ed. LC 71-158818. (Illus.). 848p. 1980. 14.95 (ISBN 0-8326-0536-0, 1105-N). Delair.
Dept. of Aviation Education. Commercial Pilot: Complete Programmed Course. 3rd ed. LC 67-8618. (Illus.). 412p. 1969. 4.95 (ISBN 0-912682-01-9). Aero Products.
Dept. of Defense-Defense Supply Agency. Defense in-Plant Quality Assurance Program. 1976. 14.95x (ISBN 0-912702-08-7). Global Eng.
Dept. of Foreign Affairs Staff. Facts About Ireland. (Illus.). 258p. pap. 8.95 (ISBN 0-317-31813-6, Pub by Dept Foreign Ireland). Irish Bks Media.
Dept. of Indian & Northern Affairs at Quebec, tr. see Harper, Linda.
Dept. of Public Information, jt. auth. see United Nations.
Depta, Victor. The Creek. LC 72-85541. 64p. 1973. 7.95 (ISBN 0-8214-0121-1, 82-81230). Ohio U Pr.
--The House. 1978. pap. 2.50 (ISBN 0-685-90002-9). New Rivers Pr.
Depue, Richard A., ed. The Psychobiology of the Depressive Disorders: Implications for the Effects of Stress. LC 79-51676. (Personality & Psychopathology Ser.). 1979. 45.00 (ISBN 0-12-211650-X). Acad Pr.
De Purucker, G. Clothed with the Sun: The Mystery-Tale of Jesus the Avatara. rev. ed. Small, Emmett & Todd, Helen, eds. Orig. Title: The Story of Jesus. 56p. 1972. pap. 1.00 (ISBN 0-913004-06-5). Point Loma Pub.
--Dialogues of G. de Purucker, 3 vols. Conger, Arthur L., ed. LC 79-65630. 1948. Set. 25.00 (ISBN 0-911500-59-6). Theos U Pr.
--The Esoteric Tradition, 2 vols. 2nd ed. LC 73-81738. 1973. Set. 20.00 (ISBN 0-911500-65-0); Set. pap. 14.00 (ISBN 0-911500-66-9). Theos U Pr.
--Fountain-Source of Occultism. Knoche, Grace F., ed. LC 72-92155. 1974. 15.00 (ISBN 0-911500-70-7); pap. 9.00 (ISBN 0-911500-71-5). Theos U Pr.
--The Four Sacred Seasons. LC 79-63565. 1979. 5.00 (ISBN 0-911500-83-9); pap. 2.75 (ISBN 0-911500-84-7). Theos U Pr.
--Fundamentals of the Esoteric Philosophy. 2nd, rev. ed. Knoche, Grace F., ed. LC 78-74258. 1979. 14.00 (ISBN 0-911500-63-4); pap. 8.00 (ISBN 0-911500-64-2). Theos U Pr.
--Golden Precepts. LC 76-49638. 1977. pap. 2.50 (ISBN 0-8356-0491-8, Quest). Theos Pub Hse.

--Golden Precepts: A Guide to Enlightened Living. rev. 3rd ed. Todd, Helen & Small, W. Emmett, eds. 170p. 1971. pap. 2.50 (ISBN 0-913004-02-2, 913004-02). Point Loma Pub.
--Golden Precepts of Esotericism. 3rd, rev. ed. LC 78-74257. 1979. 5.00 (ISBN 0-911500-85-5); pap. 3.00 (ISBN 0-911500-86-3). Theos U Pr.
--Mahatmas & Genuine Occultism. rev. ed. Small, Emmett & Todd, Helen, eds. Orig. Title: The Masters & the Path of Occultism. 100p. 1972. pap. 1.50 (ISBN 0-913004-07-3). Point Loma Pub.
--Man in Evolution. 2nd rev. ed. Knoche, Grace F., ed. LC 76-45503. 1977. pap. 6.00 (ISBN 0-911500-55-3). Theos U Pr.
--Occult Glossary. LC 53-37086. (A Compendium of Oriental & Theosophical Terms). 1972. 7.50 (ISBN 0-911500-50-2); pap. 4.00 (ISBN 0-911500-51-0). Theos U Pr.
--Studies in Occult Philosophy. LC 73-81739. 1973. 14.00 (ISBN 0-911500-52-9); pap. 8.00 (ISBN 0-911500-53-7). Theos U Pr.
--Wind of the Spirit. abr. ed. Small, W. Emmett & Todd, Helen, eds. 282p. 1971. pap. 3.25 (ISBN 0-913004-00-6). Point Loma Pub.
--Wind of the Spirit. 2nd, rev. ed. LC 84-50118. 328p. 1984. 10.00 (ISBN 0-911500-67-7); pap. 5.00 (ISBN 0-911500-68-5). Theos U Pr.
--Word Wisdom in the Esoteric Tradition. (Study Ser.: No. 2). 1980. 5.95 (ISBN 0-913004-35-9, 913004-35). Point Loma Pub.
De Purucker, G. & Tingley, Katherine. H. P. Blavatsky: The Mystery. rev. ed. Small, W. Emmett & Todd, Helen, eds. (Illus.). 256p. 1974. pap. 5.25 (ISBN 0-913004-14-6). Point Loma Pub.
De Purucker, G. De see De Purucker, G.
De Pury, Simon, ed. see Cocks, Anna S. & Truman, Charles.
Deputy, Erby C. Predicting First Grade Reading Achievement: A Study in Reading Readiness. LC 77-176705. (Columbia University. Teachers College. Contributions to Education: No. 426). Repr. of 1930 ed. 22.50 (ISBN 0-404-55426-1). AMS Pr.
De Puy, Blanche, tr. see Marias, Julian.
Depuy, Charles H., jt. ed. see Shapiro, Robert H.
De Puy, Henry C. A Steady Progress: From Creation to Christ. (Illus.). 1982. 12.95 (ISBN 0-533-05250-5). Vantage.
De Puy, Henry F. A Bibliography of the English Colonial Treaties with the American Indians. LC 78-164820. Repr. of 1917 ed. 11.50 (ISBN 0-404-07123-6). AMS Pr.
--A Bibliography of the English Colonial Treaties with the American Indians. LC 78-108471. 1917. Repr. 10.00x (ISBN 0-403-00425-X). Scholarly.
De Puy, Henry W. Ethan Allen - the Green Mountain Heroes of '76, with a Sketch of the Early History of Vermont. facsimile ed. (Select Bibliographies Reprint Ser). 1853. 26.50 (ISBN 0-8369-5022-4). Ayer Co Pubs.
DePuy, Norman. Help in Understanding Theology. 1980. pap. 3.95 (ISBN 0-8170-0847-0). Judson.
Dequasie, Andrew. Thirsty. 1983. 11.95 (ISBN 0-8027-4017-0). Walker & Co.
De Quehen, Hugh, ed. see Butler, Samuel.
De Queiroz, Rachel see Queiroz, Rachel de.
Dequeker, J. Atlas of Radiology of Rheumatic Disorders. (Illus.). 184p. 1982. 50.00 (ISBN 0-8385-0453-1). ACC.
Dequeker, J. V. & Johnston, C. C., Jr., eds. Non-Invasive Bone Measurements: Methodological Problems Proceedings. 266p. 1982. pap. 33.00 (ISBN 0-904147-47-9). IRL Pr.
De Queljoe, David. Marginal Man in a Colonial Society: Abdoel Moeis' Salah Asuahan. LC 74-620028. (Papers in International Studies: Southeast Asia Ser.: No. 32). 1974. pap. 4.00x (ISBN 0-89680-019-9, 82-90330, Ohio U Ctr Intl). Ohio U Pr.
De Queljoe, David H. Marginal Man in a Colonial Society: Abdoel Moeis' Salah Asuhan. LC 74-620028. (Papers in International Studies: Southeast Asia Ser.: No. 32). pap. 20.00 (ISBN 0-317-10085-8, 2007451). Bks Demand UMI.
De Quental, Anthero. Sonnets & Poems. Morley, S. Griswold, tr. from Portuguese. LC 77-137073. 133p. Repr. of 1922 ed. lib. bdg. 18.75x (ISBN 0-8371-5536-3, GUSP). Greenwood.
--Sonnets & Poems of Anthero De Quental. 59.95 (ISBN 0-8490-1088-8). Gordon Pr.
De Quesada, Gonzalo. War in Cuba, Being a Full Account of Her Great Struggle for Freedoms. LC 79-111731. (American Imperialism: Viewpoints of United States Foreign Policy, 1898-1941). 1970. Repr. of 1896 ed. 37.50 (ISBN 0-405-02047-3). Ayer Co Pubs.
De Quevedo y Villegas, Francisco G. see Quevedo y Villegas, Francisco G. de.
De Queyroz, Fernao see Queyroz, Fernao De.
DeQuille, Dan. History of the Big Bonanza. 488p. 1983. pap. (ISBN 0-913814-66-0). Nevada Pubns.
De Quille, Dan, pseud. A History of the Comstock Silver Lode & Mines, Nevada & the Great Basin Region, Lake Tahoe & the High Sierras. LC 72-9439. (The Far Western Frontier Ser.). 162p. 1973. Repr. of 1889 ed. 17.00 (ISBN 0-405-04969-2). Ayer Co Pubs.
Dequin, Henry C. Librarians Serving Disabled Children & Young People. 303p. 1983. lib. bdg. 22.50 (ISBN 0-87287-364-1). Libs Unl.

De Quincey, Thomas. Biographies of Shakespeare, Pope, Goethe, & Schiller. LC 75-164822. (Illus.). Repr. of 1862 ed. 24.50 (ISBN 0-404-02079-8). AMS Pr.
--Collected Writings, 14 vols. Masson, David, ed. LC 68-58566. Repr. of 1890 ed. Set. 315.00 (ISBN 0-404-02100-X); 22.50 ea. AMS Pr.
--The Collected Writings, 14 Vols. new & enl. ed. Masson, David, ed. (English Literary Reference Ser). 1969. Repr. of 1889 ed. Set. 540.00 (ISBN 0-384-11325-7); 40.00 ea. Johnson Repr.
--Confessions of an English Opium-Eater & Other Writings. Lindop, Grevel, ed. (The World's Classics Ser.). 304p. 1985. pap. 3.95 (ISBN 0-19-281675-6). Oxford U Pr.
--English Mail-Coach & Other Essays. 1970. Repr. of 1912 ed. 7.95x (ISBN 0-460-00609-6, Evman). Biblio Dist.
--Klosterheim. LC 82-8517. 192p. (Orig.). 1982. pap. 5.95 (ISBN 0-912800-98-4). Woodbridge Pr.
--Political Economy & Politics, Being Volume Nine of His Collected Writings. Masson, David, ed. LC 66-21670. Repr. of 1897 ed. 37.50x (ISBN 0-678-00680-6). Kelley.
--Selected Essays on Rhetoric. Burwick, Frederick, ed. LC 67-21038. (Landmarks in Rhetoric & Public Address Ser.). 329p. 1967. 11.95x (ISBN 0-8093-0262-4). S Ill U Pr.
--Uncollected Writings, 2 vols. Hogg, James, ed. 716p. Repr. of 1890 ed. Set. 54.00x (ISBN 3-4870-4887-6). Adlers Foreign Bks.
De Quincey, Thomas & Musgrove, S. Niels Klim: Being an Incomplete Translation. 62p. 1984. Repr. of 1953 ed. lib. bdg. 15.00 (ISBN 0-89987-421-5). Darby Books.
DeQuincey, Thomas & Ward, Aileen. Confessions of an English Opium Eater. 336p. 1985. pap. 4.95 (ISBN 0-88184-130-7). Carroll & Graf.
De Quincey, Thomas see De Quincy, Thomas.
De Quincey, Thomas, tr. see Holberg, Ludvig.
De Quincy, Leon P. The Village Poet. 40p. 1984. pap. 5.95 (ISBN 0-915885-01-8). Intl Lit Pub Inc.
De Quincy, Thomas. Confessions of an English Opium-Eater. 1978. Repr. of 1907 ed. 12.95x (ISBN 0-460-00223-6, Evman). Biblio Dist.
--Confessions of an English Opium Eater. Hayter, Alethea, ed. (English Library). 1971. pap. 3.95 (ISBN 0-14-043061-X, EL61). Penguin.
--Reminiscences of the English Lake Poets. LC 83-45741. Repr. of 1929 ed. 31.50 (ISBN 0-404-20078-8). AMS Pr.
Dequine, M., jt. auth. see Padover, C. E.
De Quiros, Beltran. La Otra Cara de la Moneda. LC 83-82388. (Coleccion Caniqui). 62p. (Orig., Span.). 1984. pap. 5.95 (ISBN 0-89729-342-8). Ediciones.
Der Ling. Golden Phoenix. LC 70-101799. (Short Story Index Reprint Ser.). 1932. 18.00 (ISBN 0-8369-3187-4). Ayer Co Pubs.
Der, Mehden, Fred R. Von see Von Der Mehden, Fred R., pseud.
Der, R. T. Van Paardt see Hijmans, B. L., Jr. & Van der Paardt, R. T.
der, Tak Herman G. Van see Tak, Herman G. van der.
Der, Van Werff see Van Der Werff, A. & Huls, H.
Derache, R., ed. see Commission of the European Communities.
De Rachewiltz, Igor. Index to the Secret History of the Mongols. LC 70-183993. (Uralic & Altaic Ser: Vol. 121). 347p. (Orig.). 1972. pap. text ed. 18.00x (ISBN 0-87750-166-1). Res Ctr Lang Semiotic.
De Rachewiltz, Mary. Ezra Pound, Father & Teacher: Discretions. LC 73-143717. (Illus.). 336p. 1975. pap. 4.75 (ISBN 0-8112-0589-4, NDP405). New Directions.
De Rachwiltz, I. & Wang, M. Index to Biographical Material in Chin & Yuan Literary Works - Third Series. LC 78-52594. (Faculty of Asian Studies Oriental Monograph: No. 26). 341p. 1980. pap. text ed. 13.50 (ISBN 0-7081-0179-8, 0556). Australia N U P.
De Rais, Gilles. Laughter for the Devil: The Trials of Gilles de Rais, Companion-in-Arms of Joan of Arc (1440) Hyatte, Reginald, tr. LC 83-20801. 1984. 22.50 (ISBN 0-8386-3190-8). Fairleigh Dickinson.
Derakhshani, Mani, tr. see Beaute, Georges & Tapie de Celeyran, Mary.
D'Eramo, Nello. Neurological Symptoms in Blood Diseases. Iliffe, John, tr. LC 72-1871. pap. 74.30 (ISBN 0-317-26197-5, 2052069). Bks Demand UMI.
De Ransijat, Chevalier Bosredon see Bosredon de Ransijat, Chevalier.
De Ranter, C. J., jt. auth. see Horn, A. S.
D'Erasmo, Martha, jt. auth. see Burger, Sarah G.
DeRasor, Roberto. Alcohol Distillers Manual. 205p. 1980. pap. 12.95 (ISBN 0-686-92650-1). Rutan Pub.
Derato, F. C. Automotive Ignition Systems: Diagnosis & Repair. LC 81-8285. 320p. 1982. 20.50x (ISBN 0-07-016501-7). McGraw.
Derato, Frank C. & Curtis, Lory V. Automotive Diagnosis & Tuneup. 3rd ed. LC 83-893. (Illus.). 432p. 1983. text ed. 22.85 (ISBN 0-07-032603-7). McGraw.
Der Bagdasarian, Nicholas. The Austro-German Rapprochement, 1870-1879: From the Battle of Sedan to the Dual Alliance. LC 74-199. 334p. 1976. 28.50 (ISBN 0-8386-1527-9). Fairleigh Dickinson.

Der Bedrosian, Robert & Der Bedrosian, Zabel, eds. A Picture Book of Armenian Miniatures. (Illus.). 63p. (Orig.). 1968. pap. 2.50 (ISBN 0-318-15084-0). Natl Assn Arm.
Der Bedrosian, Zabel, jt. ed. see Der Bedrosian, Robert.
Der Beets, Richard Van see Bowen, James K. & Van Der Beets, Richard.
Derber, Charles. The Pursuit of Attention: Power & Individualism in Everyday Life. 1983. pap. 5.95 (ISBN 0-19-503368-X, GB750, GB). Oxford U Pr.
Derber, Milton. The American Idea of Industrial Democracy, 1865-1965. LC 70-100376. pap. 142.30 (ISBN 0-317-28794-X, 2020216). Bks Demand UMI.
Derber, Milton & Young, Edwin, eds. Labor & the New Deal. LC 70-169656. (Fdr & the Era of the New Deal Ser.). 394p. 1972. Repr. of 1957 ed. lib. bdg. 39.50 (ISBN 0-306-70364-5). Da Capo.
Derbers, Milton & Stein, Leon, eds. The Aged & Society. LC 79-8665. (Growing Old Ser.). (Illus.). 1980. Repr. of 1950 ed. lib. bdg. 22.00 (ISBN 0-405-12783-9). Ayer Co Pubs.
Derbigny, Irving A. General Education in the Negro College. LC 72-97448. Repr. of 1947 ed. 19.75x (ISBN 0-8371-2694-0, DEN&, Pub. by Negro U Pr). Greenwood.
Der Borcht, Pieter Van see Bochius, Johannes & Van Der Borcht, Pieter.
Derby, George H. Phoenixiana: Or, Sketches & Burlesques. LC 72-174198. Repr. of 1856 ed. 28.00 (ISBN 0-404-05045-X). AMS Pr.
--The Squibob Papers. LC 76-174199. (Illus.). Repr. of 1865 ed. 28.00 (ISBN 0-404-05046-8). AMS Pr.
Derby, Harry L. The Hand Cannons of Imperial Japan. Reidy, John & Welge, Albert, eds. LC 82-90099. (Illus.). 304p. 1981. 37.95 (ISBN 0-940424-00-2). Derby Pub.
Derby, Hasket, ed. see LeForestier, Francois.
Derby, Mark. Element of Risk. 1977. 20.00 (ISBN 0-685-80015-6). State Mutual Bk.
Derby, William L. The Tall Ships Pass: The Story of the Last Years of Deepwater Square-Rigged Sail. LC 72-121378. pap. 125.30 (ISBN 0-317-08228-0, 2001853). Bks Demand UMI.
Derbyshire, A. Leslie. Mastering Management. LC 80-83028. 300p. 1981. 16.95 (ISBN 0-88290-159-1, 2046). Horizon Utah.
Derbyshire, D. C. Hixkaryana. (Descriptive Grammars Ser.). 208p. 1979. pap. 40.00 (ISBN 0-7099-0877-6, Pub. by Croom Held Ltd). Longwood Pub Group.
Derbyshire, Desmond. Textos Hixkaryana. 206p. 1965. pap. 2.75x (ISBN 0-88312-649-4); microfiche 3.00 (ISBN 0-88312-499-8). Summer Inst Ling.
Derbyshire, Desmond C. Hitkaryana & Linguistic Typology. LC 85-50398. (Summer Institute of Linguists Publications in Linguistics Ser.: No. 76). 250p. (Orig.). 1985. pap. 20.00 (ISBN 0-88312-082-8); (3) 3.80microfiche (ISBN 0-88312-988-4). Summer Inst Ling.
Derbyshire, Edward, ed. Geomorphology & Climate. LC 75-4523. Repr. of 1976 ed. 99.80 (ISBN 0-8357-9899-2, 2016026). Bks Demand UMI.
Derbyshire, Jane. The Flower Arranger's Year. (Illus.). 160p. 1984. 18.95 (ISBN 0-00-411655-0, Pub. By Salem Hse Ltd). Merrimack Pub Cir.
Derbyshire, Robert C. Medical Licensure & Discipline in the United States. LC 78-17712. xiv, 183p. 1978. Repr. of 1969 ed. lib. bdg. 18.50x (ISBN 0-313-20528-0, DEML). Greenwood.
Derche. Etudes de Textes Francais, 6 tomes. Set. 47.90 (ISBN 0-685-36706-1). French & Eur.
D'Ercole, Joseph A., jt. auth. see Ontjes, David A.
Dercourt, J. & Paquet, J. Geology: Principles & Methods. LC 85-70437. (Illus.). 350p. 1985. text ed. 34.95x (ISBN 0-87201-319-7). Gulf Pub.
Derden, John K., jt. auth. see Dorsey, James E.
Der Donck, Adriaen Van see Van Der Donck, Adriaen.
DeReamer, Russell. Modern Safety & Health Technology. LC 79-17487. 615p. 1980. 49.95x (ISBN 0-471-05729-0, Pub. by Wiley-Interscience). Wiley.
De Reamer, Russell. Modern Safety Practices. LC 58-12708. 372p. 1958. 18.50 (ISBN 0-471-20361-0, Pub. by Wiley). Krieger.
De Reaumur, Rene A. F. The Natural History of Ants from an Unpublished Manuscript in the Archives of the Academy of Sciences of Paris. Egerton, Frank N., 3rd, ed. Wheeler, Morton, tr. LC 77-74211. (History of Ecology Ser.). 1978. Repr. of 1926 ed. lib. bdg. 23.50x (ISBN 0-405-10382-4). Ayer Co Pubs.
De Rebecque, Constant & Benjamin, Henri. Dupolytheisme Romain: Considere dans ses rapports avec la philosophie grecque et la religion chertienne. Bolle, Kees W., ed. LC 77-79118. (Mythology Ser.). (Fr.). 1978. Repr. of 1833 ed. lib. bdg. 59.50 (ISBN 0-405-10530-4). Ayer Co Pubs.
DeRebello, D. M. Formal Schooling & Personal Efficacy. 1979. 14.50 (ISBN 0-89684-510-9). Orient Bk Dist.
De Recondo, A. M., ed. New Approaches in Eukaryotic DNA Replication. 374p. 1983. 47.50x (ISBN 0-306-41182-2, Plenum Pr). Plenum Pub.

Derecskey, Susan. The Hungarian Cookbook: The Pleasures of Hungarian Food & Wine. LC 72-79654. (Illus.). 480p. 1972. 15.34i (ISBN 0-06-011004-X, HarpT). Har-Row.
De Reed, Alicia C., tr. see Hoover, John P.
De Reede, Rien see Reede, Rien de.
De Reeder, P. L., ed. Environmental Programmes of Intergovernmental Organizations. 1978. loose-leaf bdg. 39.50 (ISBN 90-0148-002-0, Pub. by Martinus Nijhoff Netherlands). Kluwer Academic.
De Reedy, Ginette D., tr. see Wallace, Lew.
De Regniers, B Schenk see Schenk de Regniers, Beatrice.
De Regniers, Beatrice. Jack & the Beanstalk. LC 85-7946. (Illus.). 48p. (gr. 2). 1985. 12.95 (ISBN 0-689-31174-5, McElderry Bk). Atheneum.
De Regniers, Beatrice S. A Bunch of Poems & Verses. LC 76-28324. (Illus.). 40p. (gr. 1-5). 1976. 7.95 (ISBN 0-395-28881-9, Clarion). HM.
--How Joe the Bear & Sam the Mouse Got Together. (Illus.). 48p. (Orig.). (ps-3). 1983. pap. 2.25 (ISBN 0-590-32831-X). Scholastic Inc.
--It Does Not Say Meow. LC 72-75704. (Illus.). 40p. (ps-3). 1972. 10.95 (ISBN 0-395-28822-3, Clarion); pap. 3.95 (ISBN 0-89919-043-X). HM.
--Laura's Story. LC 78-12623. (Illus.). (ps-1). 1979. 9.95 (ISBN 0-689-30677-6). Atheneum.
--Little Sister & the Month Brothers. LC 75-4594. (Illus.). 48p. (ps-3). 1976. 8.95 (ISBN 0-8164-3147-7, Clarion). HM.
--Little Sister & the Month Brothers. LC 75-4594. (Illus.). 48p. (ps-3). 1984. PLB 8.95 (Clarion); pap. 4.95 (ISBN 0-89919-316-1). HM.
--May I Bring a Friend? LC 64-19562. (Illus.). (ps-2). 1964. PLB 11.95 (ISBN 0-689-20615-1). Atheneum.
--May I Bring a Friend? (Illus.). (ps-2). 1974. pap. 4.95 (ISBN 0-689-70405-4, A-32, Aladdin). Atheneum.
--Picture Book Theater: The Mysterious Stranger & the Magic Spell. (Illus.). 40p. (ps-3). 1982. 11.50 (ISBN 0-89919-061-8, Clarion). HM.
--Red Riding Hood. LC 79-175561. (Illus.). 48p. (ps-3). 1972. pap. 1.95 (ISBN 0-689-70435-6). Atheneum.
--So Many Cats. (Illus.). (ps-3). 1985. 13.95 (ISBN 0-317-30692-8, Clarion). HM.
--So Many Cats! LC 85-3739. 32p. (ps-3). 1985. 12.95 (ISBN 0-89919-322-6). Ticknor & Fields.
--This Big Cat & Other Cats I've Known. LC 84-21498. (Illus.). 32p. 1985. 9.95 (ISBN 0-517-55538-7). Crown.
--Waiting for Mama. LC 83-14982. (Illus.). 32p. (ps-2). 1984. PLB 9.95 (ISBN 0-89919-222-X, Clarion). HM.
De Regniers, Beatrice S. & Haas, Irene. Little House of Your Own. LC 55-5236. (Illus.). (gr. k-3). 1955. 6.95 (ISBN 0-15-245787-9, HJ). HarBraceJ.
De Regniers, Beatrice S. see Schenk De Regniers, Beatrice.
de Regniers, Beatrice Schenk see Regniers, Beatrice Schenk de.
Deregowski, J. B. Distortion in Art: The Eye & the Mind. (International Library of Psychology). (Illus.). 256p. 1984. 50.00x (ISBN 0-7100-9516-3). Routledge & Kegan.
--Illusions, Patterns & Pictures. (AP Ser. in Cognition & Perception). 1981. 45.00 (ISBN 0-12-210750-0). Acad Pr.
Deregowski, J. B. & Dzjurawiec, S. Expiscations in Cross-Cultural Psychology. 462p. 1983. pap. text ed. 22.75 (ISBN 90-265-0450-0, Pub. by Swets & Zeitlinger Netherlands). Hogrefe Intl.
De Reichel, Alicia D., jt. auth. see Reichel-Dolmatoff, Gerardo.
Derek, Kelly. A Layman's Introduction to Robotics. (Illus.). 220p. 1985. 27.95 (ISBN 0-317-28908-X). Petrocelli.
Derek, Sean C. Cast of Characters. (Illus.). 336p. (Orig.). 1982. pap. 3.50 (ISBN 0-8439-1126-3, Leisure Bks). Dorchester Pub Co.
Derek, Sean C., ed. see Evans, Linda.
De Remusat, Charles. L' Angleterre au XVIIIE siecle, 2 vols. in one. Mayer, J. P., ed. LC 78-67378. (L' Angleterre au XVIIIe siecle). (Fr.). 1979. Repr. of 1865 ed. lib. bdg. 71.50x (ISBN 0-405-11728-0). Ayer Co Pubs.
De Remusat, Charles F. see Remusat, Charles F. de.
Deren, Coke van see Coke, Van Deren.
Deren, Maya. Divine Horseman: The Living Gods of Haiti. LC 83-16228. (Illus.). 350p. 1984. 20.00 (ISBN 0-914232-64-9, Documentext); pap. 10.00 (ISBN 0-914232-63-0). McPherson & Co.
De Reneville. Aventure De L'Absolu. (Phaenomenologica Ser.: No. 48). 1972. lib. bdg. 39.50 (ISBN 90-247-1319-6, Pub. by Martinus Nijhoff Netherlands). Kluwer Academic.
Dereniak, E. L. & Crowe, D. G. Optical Radiation Detectors. LC 84-7356. (Pure & Applied Optics Ser. (1-349)). 300p. 1984. text ed. 42.50x (ISBN 0-471-89797-3, Pub. by Wiley-Interscience). Wiley.
De Renne, Charlotte, jt. auth. see Dempster-Ogden, Linda.
Derenne, Eudore. Les Proces D'impiete Intentes Aux Philosophes a Athenes Au Vme & Au Ivme Siecles. facsimile ed. LC 75-13260. (History of Ideas in Ancient Greece Ser.). (Fr.). 1976. Repr. of 1930 ed. 17.00x (ISBN 0-405-07302-X). Ayer Co Pubs.

De Renty, Ivan. The Businessman's Everyday English to Spanish Dictionary: El Mundo De Negocios. (Eng. & Span.). 1978. pap. 9.95 (ISBN 84-7143-118-1, 8138). Larousse.

De Renzi, E. Disorders of Space Exploration & Cognition. 265p. 1982. 47.95 (ISBN 0-471-28024-0). Wiley.

De Renzo, D. J., ed. Biodegradation Techniques for Industrial Organic Wastes. LC 80-12834. (Pollution Technology Review Ser. 65; Chemical Technology Review Ser. 158). (Illus.). 358p. 1980. 28.00 (ISBN 0-8155-0800-X). Noyes.

--Cogeneration Technology & Economics for the Process Industries. LC 82-22279. (Energy Technology Review: No. 81). (Illus.). 395p. 1983. 42.00 (ISBN 0-8155-0932-4). Noyes.

--European Technology for Obtaining Energy from Solid Waste. LC 78-61896. (Energy Technology Review No. 34: Pollution Technology Review No. 54). (Illus.). 281p. 1978. 39.00 (ISBN 0-8155-0730-5). Noyes.

--Industrial Energy Conservation Technologies & Research Opportunities. LC 83-3944. (Energy Tech. Rev. 82). (Illus.). 704p. (Orig.). 1983. 64.00 (ISBN 0-8155-0941-3). Noyes.

--Nitrogen Control & Phosphorus Removal in Sewage Treatment. LC 78-59820. (Pollution Technology Review Ser.: No. 44). 1978. 32.00 (ISBN 0-8155-0711-9). Noyes.

--Pollution Control Technology for Industrial Wastewater. LC 81-38394. (Pollution Technology Review 80). (Illus.). 712p. 1981. 48.00 (ISBN 0-8155-0855-7). Noyes.

--Wind Power: Recent Developments. LC 79-14069. (Energy Technology Review Ser.: No. 46). (Illus.). 347p. 1979. 36.00 (ISBN 0-8155-0759-3). Noyes.

De Resende, Garcia. Cancioneiro, Geral: Cum Predilegio. 1516. 40.00 (ISBN 0-527-74700-9). Kraus Repr.

Dereshinsky, Ralph M. & Berkowitz, Alan D. The NLRB & Secondary Boycotts. rev. ed. LC 81-52616. (Labor Relations & Public Policy Ser.: No. 4). 349p. 1981. pap. 22.00 (ISBN 0-89546-027-0). Indus Res Unit-Wharton.

Dereske, Jo. Glom Gloom. LC 85-7451. 240p. (gr. 4-6). 1985. 13.95 (ISBN 0-689-31131-1). Atheneum.

De Retz, Cardinal. Memoires, La Conjuration du Comte de Fiesque et Pamphlets. 1256p. 37.50 (ISBN 0-686-56554-1). French & Eur.

Derevitzky. Fiddleheads & Mustard Blossoms. (Illus.). 1979. pap. 4.95 (ISBN 0-89272-074-3). Down East.

--Lobster Pots & Sea Rocket Sandwiches. (Illus.). 1979. pap. 5.95 (ISBN 0-89272-075-1). Down East.

Derevitzky, Catherine. Tansy Cakes with Honey. (Illus.). 1980. pap. 4.95 (ISBN 0-89272-097-2, 310). Down East.

De Reyna, Rudy. Creative Painting from Photographs. (Illus.). 160p. 1975. 22.50 (ISBN 0-8230-1092-9). Watson-Guptill.

--How to Draw What You See. (Illus.). 176p. 1972. 14.50 (ISBN 0-8230-1460-6). Watson-Guptill.

--Magic Realist Watercolor Painting. (Illus.). 144p. 1978. 22.50 (ISBN 0-8230-2957-3). Watson-Guptill.

--Realist Techniques in Water Media. (Illus.). 80p. 1984. pap. 6.95 (ISBN 0-8230-4511-0). Watson-Guptill.

De Reyna, Rudy, jt. auth. see Blake, Wendon.

Derfler, Frank. TRS-80 Data Communications. (Illus.). 159p. 1982. 18.95 (ISBN 0-13-931238-2); pap. 12.95 (ISBN 0-13-931220-X). P-H.

Derfler, Frank J., Jr. & InfoWorld Editors. InfoWorld's Essential Guide to the IBM PC. (InfoWorld's Essential Guides Ser.). 250p. (Orig.). 1984. pap. 16.95 (ISBN 0-06-669002-1). Har Row.

Derfler, Frank, Jr. Microcomputer Data Communications Systems. 129p. 1982. 17.95 (ISBN 0-13-580720-4); pap. 18.95 (ISBN 0-13-580712-3). P-H.

Derfler, Frank, Jr. & Stallings, Frank. A Manager's Guide to Local Networks. (Illus.). 154p. 1983. 21.95 (ISBN 0-13-549766-3); pap. 14.95 (ISBN 0-13-549758-2). P-H.

Derfler, Leslie. President & Parliament: A Short History of the French Presidency. LC 82-16133. x, 286p. 1983. 20.00 (ISBN 0-8130-0733-X). U Presses Fla.

--The Third French Republic, Eighteen-Seventy to Nineteen-Forty. LC 82-177. (Anvil Ser.). 192p. 1982. pap. text ed. 6.95 (ISBN 0-89874-480-6). Krieger.

Derfler, Leslie, ed. Alexandre Millerand: The Socialist Years. (Issues in Contemporary Politics, Historical & Theoretical Perspectives Ser.: No. 4). 1977. text ed. 20.00x (ISBN 0-686-22642-9). Mouton.

Derfner, Mary F. & Wolf, Arthur D. Court Awarded Attorney Fees, 3 vols. 1983. Updates avail. looseleaf 240.00 (ISBN 0-317-09750-4, 168); looseleaf 1984 50.00. Bender.

Der Foenander, Orwell. Shop Stewards & Shop Committees. 1965. 14.00x (ISBN 0-522-83600-3, Pub. by Melbourne U Pr). Intl Spec Bk.

Dergarabedian, Paul, ed. see Gov. Rockefeller Symposium Winrock, Arkansas, Oct. 1970.

De Rham, G. Differentiable Manifolds. Smith, F. R., tr. from Fr. (Grundlehren der mathematischen Wissenschaften. A Series of Comprehensive Studies in Mathematics: Vol. 266). (Illus.). 180p. 1984. 28.50 (ISBN 0-387-13463-8). Springer-Verlag.

Derham, W., ed. see Hooke, Robert.

Derham, William. Physico-Theology: A Demonstration of the Being & Attributes of God, from His Works of Creation. Egerton, Frank N., 3rd, ed. LC 77-74212. (History of Ecology Ser.). 1978. Repr. of 1716 ed. lib. bdg. 37.50 (ISBN 0-405-10383-2). Ayer Co Pubs.

Derham, William, ed. see Ray, John.

Der Horst, Pieter W. van see Van der Horst, Pieter W.

Der-Houssikian, Haig, ed. see Conference on African Linguistics, Seventh.

Der Hovanessian, Diana. How to Choose Your Past. LC 78-67675. 1978. 6.95 (ISBN 0-933706-00-6); pap. 3.95 (ISBN 0-933706-01-4). Ararat Pr.

Der Hovanessian, Diana & Margossian, Marzbed, trs. from Armenian. Sacred Wrath: The Selected Poems of Vahan Tekeyan. LC 81-20559. 176p. 1982. 12.50 (ISBN 0-935102-08-6); pap. 7.50 (ISBN 0-935102-09-4). Ashod Pr.

Der Hovanessian, Diana, tr. see Kouchag, Nahabed.

Der Hovanessian, Diana, tr. see Manoogian, Torkom.

Deri, M. Ferroelectric Ceramics. 106p. 1969. 37.25 (ISBN 0-677-61450-0). Gordon.

Deri, Susan K. Symbolization & Creativity. LC 83-26482. xii, 364p. 1984. text ed. 40.00 (ISBN 0-8236-6292-6). Intl Univs Pr.

Deriabin, Peter. The Secret World, No. 21. (Espionage-Intelligence Library). 416p. 1982. pap. 3.50 (ISBN 0-345-30416-0). Ballantine.

--The Watchdogs of Terror. (Foreign Intelligence Bk.). 469p. 1984. 24.00x (ISBN 0-89093-674-9). U Pubns Amer.

Deriada, Leoncio P. The Road to Mawab & Other Stories. 160p. (Orig.). 1984. pap. 8.75x (ISBN 971-10-0084-9, Pub. by New Day Philippines). Cellar.

De Ribier, Gabriel. Repertoire Des Traites De Paix, de Commerce, D'alliance, Etc., Conventions et Autres Actes Conclus Entre Toutes les Puissances Du Globe, Depuis 1867 Jusqua Nos Jours, 2 vols. in 1. Repr. of 1899 ed. 52.00 (ISBN 0-527-75160-X). Kraus Repr.

De Ricci, S. & Wilson, W. J. Census of Medieval & Renaissance Manuscripts in the United States & Canada, 2 vols. Incl. Supplement. Bond, W. H. & Faye, C. U. 1962. 51.00 (ISBN 0-685-23298-0). Repr. of 1940 ed. Set. 171.00 (ISBN 0-527-75200-2). Kraus Repr.

De Ricci, Seymour. Bibliography of Shelley's Letters Published & Unpublished. LC 68-56595. (Bibliography & Reference Ser.: No. 112). 1969. Repr. of 1927 ed. 22.50 (ISBN 0-8337-2979-9). B Franklin.

--Book Collector's Guide. 1970. Repr. of 1921 ed. 35.50 (ISBN 0-8337-2980-2). B Franklin.

--English Collectors of Books & Manuscripts 1530-1930 & Their Mark of Ownership. 1969. Repr. of 1930 ed. 22.50 (ISBN 0-8337-2982-9). B Franklin.

Derick & Baker. FORTH Encyclopedia. 2nd ed. 25.00 (ISBN 0-318-01344-4). Mountain View Pr.

--FORTH Encyclopedia: Pocket Guide. 7.00 (ISBN 0-318-01345-2). Mountain View Pr.

Derick, Mitch & Baker, Linda. Pocket Guide to FORTH. (Micro Computer Ser.). pap. 6.95 (ISBN 0-201-10103-3). Addison-Wesley.

De Rico, Ul. The Rainbow Goblins. (Illus.). 1978. 24.95 (ISBN 0-500-95005-9). Thames Hudson.

--The Rainbow Goblins. (Illus.). 36p. 1979. pap. 13.85 (ISBN 0-446-38204-3). Warner Bks.

--The Ring of the Nibelung. (Illus.). 204p. 1980. 24.98 (ISBN 0-500-23324-1). Thames Hudson.

DeRidder, Margaret D. New Career Opportunities in Health & Human Services. LC 83-15585. (Illus.). 178p. 1984. pap. 8.95 (ISBN 0-668-06103-0). Arco.

De Ridder, Richard R., jt. auth. see Brink, William P.

DeRidder, Richard R., jt. auth. see Brink, William P.

DeRidder, Richard R., jt. ed. see DeKlerk, Peter.

De Ridder-Barzin, Louise. Le Pessimisme De Thomas Hardy. LC 76-16485. 1976. Repr. of 1932 ed. lib. bdg. 25.00 (ISBN 0-8414-3776-9). Folcroft.

De Riencourt, Amaury. The Eye of Shiva: Eastern Mysticism & Science. LC 80-22032. 221p. 1981. 8.95 (ISBN 0-688-00036-3); pap. 4.95 (ISBN 0-688-00038-X). Morrow.

Derig, Betty & Sharp, Flo. The Idaho Rambler: For Gadabouts & Stay-at-Homes. rev. ed. LC 82-80104. 266p. (Orig.). 1982. pap. 7.95 (ISBN 0-686-38094-0). Rambler Pr.

DeRighi, R. The Story of the Penny Black. 8.95. StanGib.

Derigs, U., jt. auth. see Burkhard, R. E.

De Rijk, L. M. Logica Modernorum: On the 12th Century Theories of Fallacy, Vol. 1. (Philosophical Texts & Studies: No. 6). 1979. text ed. 65.25x (ISBN 90-232-0440-9). Humanities.

De Rijk, Lambertus M. Logica Modernorum, Vol. 2. (Philosophical Texts & Studies: Vol. 16). 1967. text ed. 107.00x. Humanities.

De Rinaldis, Aldo. Neapolitan Painting of the Seicento. LC 75-11055. 1976. Repr. of 1929 ed. lib. bdg. 45.00 (ISBN 0-87817-177-0). Hacker.

Dering, Edward. M. Derings Workes: More at Large Than Ever Hath Heer-to-Fore Been Printed, 3 pts. LC 74-38171. (English Experience Ser.: No. 448). 692p. 1972. Repr. of 1597 ed. 95.00 (ISBN 90-221-0448-6). Walter J Johnson.

--Parliamentary Diary of Sir Edward Dering, 1670-73. Henning, Basil D., ed. (Yale Historical Pubs. Miscellany Ser.: No. XVI). 1940. 59.50x (ISBN 0-685-69825-4). Elliots Bks.

Dering, Edward H. Sherborne; or, the House at the Four Ways, 1875. Wolff, Robert L., ed. LC 75-457. (Victorian Fiction Ser.). 1976. lib. bdg. 73.00 (ISBN 0-8240-1536-3). Garland Pub.

De Rios, Marlene D. Hallucinogens: Cross-Cultural Perspectives. LC 84-7244. 224p. 1984. 22.50x (ISBN 0-8263-0737-X). U of NM Pr.

DeRis, Margaret, tr. see Steiner, Rudolf.

De Rishanger, William see Rishanger, William de.

DeRisi, William J. & Butz, George. Writing Behavioral Contracts: A Case Simulation Practice Manual. (Illus.). 94p. (Orig.). 1975. pap. text ed. 8.95 (ISBN 0-87822-123-9, 1239). Res Press.

De River, J. Paul. Crime & the Sexual Psychopath. (Illus.). 384p. 1958. 27.50x (ISBN 0-398-00436-6). C C Thomas.

--The Sexual Criminal: A Psychoanalytical Study. 2nd ed. (Illus.). 400p. 1956. photocopy ed. 39.50x (ISBN 0-398-00437-4). C C Thomas.

De Rivera, Joseph. A Structural Theory of the Emotions. LC 76-53916. (Psychological Issues Monograph: No. 40). 178p. 1977. text ed. 20.00 (ISBN 0-8236-6171-7); pap. text ed. 17.50 (ISBN 0-8236-6170-9). Intl Univs Pr.

De Rivera, Joseph, ed. Conceptual Encounters: A Method for the Exploration of Human Experience. LC 80-6068. 382p. 1981. lib. bdg. 28.25 (ISBN 0-8191-1961-X); pap. text ed. 15.50 (ISBN 0-8191-1962-8). U Pr of Amer.

De Rivera, Robert V. Euromart, Eurodollars, Stateless Currencies & the Coming Eruption of a Major Economic & Political Crisis. (Illus.). 1979. deluxe ed. 67.50x (ISBN 0-930008-24-3). Inst Econ Pol.

De Rivero, Oswaldo. New Economic Order & International Development Law. LC 79-41222. 132p. 1980. 22.00 (ISBN 0-08-024706-7). Pergamon.

Derk, Francis H. Names of Christ: A Pocket Guide. LC 75-44928. 176p. 1976. pap. 3.50 (ISBN 0-87123-390-8, 200390). Bethany Hse.

Der Kaloustian, V. M. & Kurban, A. K. Genetic Diseases of the Skin. LC 78-25740. (Illus.). 1979. 120.00 (ISBN 0-387-09151-3). Springer-Verlag.

Derkatsch, Inessa. Transparent Watercolor: Painting Methods & Materials. (Illus.). 1980. text ed. 25.95 (ISBN 0-13-930321-9, Spec); pap. text ed. 12.95 (ISBN 0-13-930313-8, Spec). P-H.

Derkinderen, F. & Crum, R. L. Readings in Strategy for Corporate Investment. 224p. (Orig.). 1981. pap. text ed. 19.95 (ISBN 0-273-01635-0). Pitman Pub MA.

Derkinderen, Frans G. & Crum, Roy L. Project Set Strategies. (Nijenrode Studies in Business: Vol. 4). 1979. lib. bdg. 20.75 (ISBN 0-89838-014-6, Pub. by Martinus Nijhoff Netherlands). Kluwer Academic.

--Risk, Capital Costs & Project Financing Decisions. (Nijenrode Studies in Business: Vol. 6). 288p. 1980. lib. bdg. 22.00 (ISBN 0-89838-046-4, Pub. by Martinus Nijhoff Netherlands). Kluwer Academic.

Derkinderen, Frans G., jt. ed. see Crum, Roy L.

Der Kroef, Justus M. Van see Van Der Kroef, Justus M.

Derksen, Sandy & Nash, Connie. The Other Side of Sorrow. LC 81-52281. 128p. (Orig.). 1982. pap. 5.95 (ISBN 0-8066-1913-9, 10-4840). Augsburg.

Der Kulk, W. Van see Schouten, Jan A. & Van Der Kulk, W.

Der Leeden, Fritz van see Van der Leeden, Frits.

Der Leeuw, J. J. Van see Van Der Leeuw, J. J.

Derlega, Valerian & Janda, Louis H. Personal Adjustment: Selected Readings. 1979. pap. text ed. 11.90x (ISBN 0-673-15288-X). Scott F.

Derlega, Valerian & Grzelak, Janusz, eds. Cooperation & Helping Behavior: Theories & Research. LC 81-19130. 1981. 47.50 (ISBN 0-12-210820-5). Acad Pr.

Derlega, Valerian J. Communication, Intimacy & Close Relationships. 1984. 36.00 (ISBN 0-12-210840-X). Acad Pr.

Derlega, Valerian J. & Janda, Louis. Personal Adjustment: The Psychology of Everyday Life. 2nd ed. 1981. text ed. 26.05x (ISBN 0-673-15470-X). Scott F.

Derlega, Valerian J. & Janda, Louis H. Personal Adjustment: The Psychology of Everyday Life. 3rd ed. 1986. text ed. 22.95x (ISBN 0-673-18197-9). Scott F.

Derleth, August. A Boy's Way. 109p. 1947. 4.95 (ISBN 0-88361-045-0). Stanton & Lee.

--The Chronicles of Solar Pons. 1973. 7.95 (ISBN 0-87054-005-X, Mycroft & Moran). Arkham.

--Collected Poems, Nineteen Thirty-Seven to Nineteen Sixty-Seven. 302p. 1967. 9.95 (ISBN 0-88361-048-5). Stanton & Lee.

--Dwellers in Darkness. 1976. 7.95 (ISBN 0-87054-074-2). Arkham.

--Harrigan's File. LC 75-2522. 1975. 7.95 (ISBN 0-87054-070-X). Arkham.

--A House Above Cuzco. LC 75-76502. 67p. 1969. 10.00 (ISBN 0-88361-053-1). Stanton & Lee.

--Return to Walden West. LC 75-125927. (SAC Prairie Saga Ser.). 233p. 1970. 8.95 (ISBN 0-88361-064-7). Stanton & Lee.

--Sac Prairie People. LC 75-125927. (SAC Prairie Saga Ser.). 322p. 1948. 6.95 (ISBN 0-88361-065-5). Stanton & Lee.

--The Shadow in the Glass. LC 62-8520. (Wisconsin Saga Ser.). 471p. 1963. 8.95 (ISBN 0-88361-066-3). Stanton & Lee.

--The Solar Pons Omnibus, 2 Vols. LC 76-17995. (Illus.). 1982. 39.95 set (ISBN 0-87054-006-8, Mycroft & Moran). Arkham.

--Some Notes on H. P. Lovecraft. 50p. (Orig.). 1982. pap. 3.95 (ISBN 0-318-04720-9). Necronomicon.

--Some Notes on H.P. Lovecraft. LC 73-16283. 1959. lib. bdg. 9.50 (ISBN 0-8414-3701-7). Folcroft.

--Someone in the Dark. 335p. 1980. Repr. of 1941 ed. lib. bdg. 15.50x (ISBN 0-89968-213-8). Lightyear.

--Three Literary Men: A Memoir of Sinclair Lewis, Sherwood Anderson & Edgar Lee Masters. LC 78-11518. Repr. of 1963 ed. lib. bdg. 12.50 (ISBN 0-8414-3686-X). Folcroft.

--The Three Straw Men. LC 72-76504. (A Steve & Sim Mystery Ser.). 143p. 1970. 5.95 (ISBN 0-88361-071-X). Stanton & Lee.

--Village Daybook. (SAC Prairie Saga Ser.). 306p. 1947. 7.95 (ISBN 0-88361-072-8). Stanton & Lee.

--Walden West. LC 61-14127. (SAC Prairie Saga Ser.). 262p. 1961. 8.95 (ISBN 0-88361-073-6). Stanton & Lee.

--West of Morning. LC 60-16459. 64p. 1960. 4.95 (ISBN 0-88361-075-2). Stanton & Lee.

--The Wind Leans West. LC 70-76506. (The Wisconsin Saga Ser.). 323p. 1969. 8.95 (ISBN 0-88361-077-9). Stanton & Lee.

--A Wisconsin Harvest. 338p. 1966. 8.95 (ISBN 0-88361-080-9). Stanton & Lee.

--Wisconsin in Their Bones. LC 61-6918. (SAC Prairie Saga Ser.). 265p. 1961. 7.95 (ISBN 0-88361-081-7). Stanton & Lee.

--The Wisconsin: River of a Thousand Isles. LC 85-40367. 368p. 1985. pap. 12.95 (ISBN 0-299-10374-9). U of Wis Pr.

Derleth, August, jt. auth. see Lovecraft, H. P.

Derleth, August, ed. Dark of the Moon. LC 73-80374. (Granger Index Reprint Ser.). 1947. 22.00 (ISBN 0-8369-6056-4). Ayer Co Pubs.

--Fire & Sleet & Candlelight. LC 72-11987. (Granger Index Reprint Ser.). 1973. Repr. of 1961 ed. 18.00 (ISBN 0-8369-6402-0). Ayer Co Pubs.

--New Poetry Out of Wisconsin. 307p. 1969. 8.95 (ISBN 0-88361-058-2). Stanton & Lee.

Derleth, August, ed. see Lovecraft, H. P., et al.

Derleth, August, ed. see Lovecraft, H. P.

Derleth, August, ed. see Lovecraft, Howard P.

Derleth, August, et al. Only Place We Live. Lefebvre, Mark E., ed. LC 76-13755. (Illus.). 186p. 1976. 12.95 (ISBN 0-88361-040-X). Stanton & Lee.

Derleth, August W. Some Notes on H. P. Lovecraft. 50p. 1980. Repr. of 1959 ed. lib. bdg. 10.00 (ISBN 0-8495-1059-7). Arden Lib.

--Three Literary Men. 56p. 1980. Repr. of 1963 ed. lib. bdg. 15.00 (ISBN 0-8482-0645-2). Norwood Edns.

--Writing Fiction. LC 72-141413. 1971. Repr. of 1946 ed. lib. bdg. 18.75x (ISBN 0-8371-4694-1, DEWF). Greenwood.

Derlith, James, ed. see Konizeski, Dick.

Derloshon, Gerald B. & Potter, James E. The Success Merchants: A Guide to the Major Influences & People in the Human Potential Movement. 203p. 1982. 12.95 (ISBN 0-13-863415-7); pap. 5.95 (ISBN 0-13-863407-6). P-H.

Derloshon, Jerry, jt. auth. see McCaffrey, Mike.

Derman, Cyrus. Finite State Markovian Decision Processes. (Mathematics in Science & Engineering Ser.: Vol. 67). 1970. 49.50 (ISBN 0-12-209250-3). Acad Pr.

Derman, Martha. The Friendstone. 160p. (gr. 4-7). 1981. 8.95 (ISBN 0-8037-2472-1). Dial Bks Young.

Derman, Sylvia, ed. see Tarthang Tulku.

Derman, William. Serfs, Peasants, & Socialists: A Former Serf Village in the Republic of Guinea. LC 78-117148. 1973. 32.00x (ISBN 0-520-01728-5). U of Cal Pr.

Derman, William & Whiteford, Scott, eds. Social Impact Analysis & Development Planning in the Third World. (Social Impact Assessment Ser.). 250p. 1985. pap. text ed. 18.50x (ISBN 0-86531-786-0). Westview.

Der Manuelian, Lucy & Eiland, Murray L., Jr. Weavers, Merchants, & Kings: The Inscribed Rugs of Armenia. (Illus.). 211p. (Orig.). 1984. 38.00 (ISBN 0-912804-18-1); pap. 19.95 (ISBN 0-912804-17-3). Kimbell Art.

Der Marel, R. Van see Van der Marel, R. & Beutelspacher, H.

Der Meer, Ron Van see Van Der Meer, Ron.

Der Mehden, Fred R. Von see Von der Mehden, Fred R.

Der Meid, Louise B. Van see Van Der Meid, Louise B.

Dermek, Aurel. Fungorum Rariorum Icones Coloratae, Pt. 4. (Illus.). 20p. 1985. pap. 14.00x (ISBN 0-318-11897-1). Lubrecht & Cramer.

--Fungorum Rariorum Icones Coloratae: Boletes II, Pars XIII. (Illus.). 15p. 1984. pap. text ed. 14.00x (ISBN 3-7682-0419-7). Lubrecht & Cramer.
--Mushrooms & Other Fungi. (Illus.). 224p. 1985. 8.95 (ISBN 0-668-06304-1). Arco.
Dermenghem, Emile. Muhammad & the Islamic Tradition. Watt, Jean M., tr. from Fr. LC 81-47412. (Spiritual Masters Ser.). (Illus.). 192p. 1981. 16.95 (ISBN 0-87951-130-3). Overlook Pr.
--Muhammad & the Islamic Tradition. Watt, Jean M., tr. LC 81-47412. 192p. pap. 6.95 (ISBN 0-87951-170-2). Overlook Pr.
Dermer, Irwin. Witch's Hat. (Illus.). 1980. 8.95 (ISBN 0-233-97800-3). Andre Deutsch.
Dermer, Joseph. How to Write Successful Foundation Proposals. pap. 11.50 (ISBN 0-686-24207-6). Public Serv Materials.
--The New How to Raise Funds from Foundations. pap. 11.50 (ISBN 0-686-24206-8). Public Serv Materials.
--New Ways to Succeed with Foundations: A Guide for the Reagan Years. pap. 19.50 (ISBN 0-686-37107-0). Public Serv Materials.
Dermer, Joseph, ed. America's Most Successful Fund Raising Letters. 19.95 (ISBN 0-686-24210-6). Public Serv Materials.
--A Treasury of Successful Appeal Letters. 1985. pap. 49.50 (ISBN 0-914977-07-5). Public Serv Materials.
--Where America's Large Foundations Make Their Grants: 1983-1984 Edition. 1983. pap. 44.50 (ISBN 0-686-37909-8). Public Serv Materials.
--Where America's Large Foundations Make Their Grants: 1980-81 Edition. pap. 7.00 (ISBN 0-686-24208-4). Public Serv Materials.
Dermer, Joseph & Wertheimer, Stephen, eds. The Complete Guide to Corporate Fund Raising. pap. 16.75 (ISBN 0-686-37106-2). Public Serv Materials.
--The Complete Guide to Corporate Fund Raising. 112p. 1982. pap. 17.75 (ISBN 0-318-17143-0, C85). Natl Ctr Cit Involv.
Dermer, O. C. & Ham, G. E. Ethylenimine & Other Aziridines: Chemistry - Applications. 1969. 95.50 (ISBN 0-12-209650-9). Acad Pr.
Dermer, Otis C., jt. auth. see Waller, George R.
Der Merwe, Alwyn Van see Van Der Merwe, Alwyn.
Der Merwe, Henrik van see Van Der Merwe, Henrik.
Der Meulen, Jan van see Van der Meulen, Jan & Price, Nancy W.
Dermine, J. Pricing Policies of Financial Intermediaries. (Studies in Contemporary Economics: Vol. 5). 174p. 1984. pap. 14.50 (ISBN 0-387-13080-2). Springer Verlag.
D'Ermo, Dominique. The Chef's Dessert Cookbook. LC 75-13679. 1976. pap. 8.95 (ISBN 0-689-70571-9, 239). Atheneum.
--Dominique's Famous Fish, Game & Meat Recipes. 1981. pap. 8.95 (ISBN 0-87491-080-3). Acropolis.
Dermody, Eugene M., jt. auth. see Reifert, Gail.
Dermott, S. F. The Origin of the Solar System. LC 77-7547. 668p. 1978. 144.95 (ISBN 0-471-99529-0, Pub. by Wiley-Interscience); pap. 61.95 (ISBN 0-471-27585-9, Pub. by Wiley-Interscience). Wiley.
Dermott, Vern. Planet Finders. 1977. pap. 1.25 (ISBN 0-532-12499-5). Woodhill.
Dermout, Maria. The Ten Thousand Things. Beekman, E. M., ed. Koning, Hans, tr. from Dutch. LC 82-21867. (Library of the Indies). 320p. 1983. Repr. of 1958 ed. lib. bdg. 19.00x (ISBN 0-87023-384-X). U of Mass Pr.
--The Ten Thousand Things. 1984. pap. 7.95 (ISBN 0-394-72443-7, Vin). Random.
Dern, John P. Genealogical Contribution Reprinted from the Albany Protocol: Wilhelm Christoph Berkenmeyer's Chronicle of Lutheran Affairs in New York Colony, 1731-1750. 1981. pap. 3.75 (ISBN 0-686-97286-4). Hope Farm.
Dern, John P., jt. auth. see Hitselberger, Mary F.
Dernay, Eugene. Longitudes & Latitudes in the U.S. 128p. 1945. 6.00 (ISBN 0-86690-067-5, 1062-01). Am Fed Astrologers.
--Longitudes & Latitudes Throughout the World. 148p. 1948. 6.00 (ISBN 0-86690-068-3, 1063-01). Am Fed Astrologers.
Dernbach, John C. & Singleton, Richard V., II. A Practical Guide to Legal Writing & Legal Method. xviii, 246p. 1981. pap. text ed. 12.50x (ISBN 0-8377-0513-4). Rothman.
Dernberger, Robert, jt. auth. see Eckstein, Alexander.
Dernberger, Robert, ed. China's Development Experience in Comparative Perspective: A Social Science Research Council Study. LC 80-418. (East Asian Ser.: No. 93). 358p. 1980. text ed. 30.00x (ISBN 0-674-11890-1). Harvard U Pr.
Dernberger, Robert F. Economic Consequences & Future Implications of Population Growth in China. LC 81-15119. (Papers of the East-West Population Institute Ser.: No. 76). v, 32p. (Orig.). 1981. pap. text ed. 1.00 (ISBN 0-86638-015-9). E W Center HI.
Dernberger, Robert F. & Hartwell, Robert M. Coterminal Characteristics of Political Units & Economic Regions in China. xi, 199p. 1983. pap. 10.00 (ISBN 0-89264-054-5). U of Mich Ctr Chinese.
Dernburg, T. Macroeconomics. 7th ed. 480p. 1985. 29.95 (ISBN 0-07-016536-X). McGraw.
Derner, Otis C., jt. auth. see Eubanks, I. Dwaine.
Der Nersessian, Sirarpie see Nersessian, Sirarpie Der.
Dernocoeur, Kate. Streetsense: Communications, Safety, & Control. (Illus.). 256p. 1984. pap. text ed. 14.95 (ISBN 0-89303-867-9). Brady Comm.
Dernoncourt, Wayne L., jt. auth. see Robinson, James W.
De Robeck, Nesta. Praise the Lord. 1967. 4.50 (ISBN 0-8199-0086-9, L38643). Franciscan Herald.
De Robeck, Nesta see Robeck, Nesta D.
DeRobertis, E. Synaptic Receptors: Isoloation & Molecular Biology. (Modern Pharmacology-Toxicology Ser.: Vol. 4). 408p. 1975. 69.75 (ISBN 0-8247-6237-1). Dekker.
De Robertis, E. & Schacht, J., eds. Neurochemistry of Cholinergic Factors. 1974. 15.00 (ISBN 0-7204-7502-3, North Holland). Elsevier.
DeRobertis, E. D. & DeRobertis, E. M., Jr. Cell & Molecular Biology. 7th ed. 1980. text ed. 40.95x (ISBN 0-03-056749-1, CBS C). SCP.
--Essentials of Cell & Molecular Biology. 1981. text ed. 36.95x (ISBN 0-03-057713-6, CBS C); study guide 10.95 (ISBN 0-03-059736-6); instr's manual 9.95 (ISBN 0-03-059734-X). SCP.
DeRobertis, E. M., Jr., jt. auth. see DeRobertis, E. D.
DeRobertis, Eduardo & Schacht, Jochen, eds. Neurochemistry of Cholinergic Receptors. LC 73-91105. 156p. 1974. 26.50 (ISBN 0-911216-66-9). Raven.
De Robertis, Francesco M. & Norr, Dieter. Lavoroe Lavoratori Nel Mondo Romano & Zur Sozialen und Rechtlichen Bewertung der Freien Arbeit in Rom. Francesco M. Finley, Moses, ed. LC 79-4967. (Ancient Economic History Ser.). (Ger. & It.). 1980. Repr. of 1965 ed. lib. bdg. 39.00x (ISBN 0-405-12355-8). Ayer Co Pubs.
De Robespierre, Maximilien M. Oeuvres de Maximilien Robespierre, 3 Vols. LC 77-131412. (Research & Source Works: No. 565). (Fr). 1970. Repr. of 1840 ed. Set. 88.50 (ISBN 0-8337-3028-2). B Franklin.
De Robigne, Bennett M. Trial of D. M. Bennett: Upon the Charge of Depositing Prohibited Matter in the Mail. LC 72-8110. (Civil Liberties in American History Ser). 202p. 1973. Repr. of 1879 ed. lib. bdg. 27.50 (ISBN 0-306-70525-7). Da Capo.
De Rocaberti, Hughes B. see Rocaberti, Hugues B. de.
De Rocco, Jovan. I Was Once a Tree. (Illus.). 1979. 6.00 (ISBN 0-682-49424-0). Exposition Pr FL.
DeRocco, Jovan. Legend of the Truant Tree. (Illus.). 112p. 1982. 6.50 (ISBN 0-682-49804-1). Exposition Pr FL.
De Rochambeau, Jean B. Memoirs of the Marshall Count De Rochambeau. LC 74-140880. (Eyewitness Accounts of the American Revolution Ser., No. 3). 1970. Repr. of 1838 ed. 11.50 (ISBN 0-405-01212-8). Ayer Co Pubs.
Deroche, Andre & Huldebrand, Nicholas. The Principles of Autobody Repairing & Repainting. 3rd ed. (Illus.). 672p. 1981. text ed. 29.95 (ISBN 0-13-705665-6). P-H.
DeRoche, Edward F. An Administrator's Guide for Evaluating Programs & Personnel. 274p. 1981. 29.95x (ISBN 0-205-07252-6, 237252, Pub. by Longwood Div). Allyn.
De Roche, Edward F. How School Administrators Solve Problems. LC 84-16021. 316p. 1984. 24.95 (ISBN 0-13-431271-6, Busn). P-H.
DeRoche, Edward F. & Infantino, Robert L. Real World Reading Activities for Teachers & Students. 138p. 1983. spiral bdg. 13.75x (ISBN 0-398-04827-4). C C Thomas.
DeRoche, Frederick W. & McDougall, Mary A. Now It's Your Move: A Guide for the Outplaced Employee. (Illus.). 224p. 1984. 17.95 (ISBN 0-13-625434-9); pap. 8.95 (ISBN 0-13-625426-8). P-H.
Deroche, G. Informations Touristiques: Le Monde. (Illus., Fr.). pap. 3.50x (ISBN 0-88332-245-5, 3941). Larousse.
De Roche, Halina. The Weekend. 1983. 7.95 (ISBN 0-8062-2143-7). Carlton.
De Roche, Joseph. The Heath Introduction to Poetry. 2nd ed. 464p. 1983. pap. text ed. 6.95 (ISBN 0-669-06446-7). Heath.
De Rochefoucauld, La Duc see Rochefoucauld, La Duc De.
De Rochemont, Richard, jt. auth. see Root, Waverley.
De Rocher, F., jt. auth. see Hagiwara, M. P.
DeRocher, Francoise & DeRocher, Gregory. Options: Apercus de la France. LC 79-27245. 140p. 1980. pap. text ed. 15.00x (ISBN 0-471-04260-9). Wiley.
DeRocher, Gregory, jt. auth. see DeRocher, Francoise.
De Rocher, Gregory see Rocher, Gregory De.
De Rocher, Gregory D. see Joubert, Laurent.
De Rochon, Alexis M. A Voyage to Madagascar & the East Indies. Repr. of 1792 ed. 42.00 (ISBN 0-384-51590-8). Johnson Repr.
De Rockville, Alphonse, ed. The Fibonacci Method of Trading in Stocks & Commodities, 2 vols. (Illus.). 1979. deluxe ed. 147.50x (ISBN 0-918968-39-9). Inst Econ Finan.
De Rodriguez, Berta Cabanillas see Cabanillas De Rodriguez, Berta.
De Rodriguez, Carmela V. Poemas en Prosa. 2.50 (ISBN 84-399-8110-4). Edit Mensaje.
Derogy, Jacques & Carmel, Hesi. Untold History of Israel. LC 78-74552. Orig. Title: L' Histoire Secrete d'Israel. (Illus.). 396p. (Orig.). 1980. pap. 7.95 (ISBN 0-394-17651-0, E756, Ever). Grove.
De Rohan, Pierre, ed. Federal Theatre Plays: 3 Plays. LC 72-2386. (Illus.). 1973. lib. bdg. 25.00 (ISBN 0-306-70494-3). Da Capo.
De Rohan, Rodema & Raymond, eds. The Pleasure Book. 2nd ed. (Illus.). 190p. (Orig.). 1982. pap. 5.00 (ISBN 0-943228-00-X). Raymonds Quiet Pr.
DeRoin, Gene, ed. see Bromige, Iris.
DeRoin, Gene, ed. see Cowen, Frances.
DeRoin, Gene, ed. see Deane, Sonia.
DeRoin, Gene, ed. see Faid, Mary.
DeRoin, Gene, ed. see Gordon, Yvonne.
DeRoin, Gene, ed. see Gorman, Beth.
DeRoin, Gene, ed. see Hill, Lorna.
DeRoin, Gene, ed. see Holt, Helen.
DeRoin, Gene, ed. see McMaster, Mary.
DeRoin, Gene, ed. see Manley-Tucker, Audrie.
DeRoin, Gene, ed. see Marsh, Jean.
DeRoin, Gene, ed. see Morgan, Arlene.
DeRoin, Gene, ed. see Munro, Mary.
DeRoin, Gene, ed. see Newman, Mona.
DeRoin, Gene, ed. see Saunders, Anne.
DeRoin, Gene, ed. see Stewart, Isobel.
DeRoin, Gene, ed. see Tucker, Audrie M.
DeRoin, Gene, ed. see Vernon, Marjorie.
DeRoin, Gene, ed. see Warby, Marjorie.
DeRoin, Gene, ed. see Weigh, Iris.
De Rojas, Fernando. Celestina. (Illus.). 1970. Repr. of 1909 ed. 7.50 (ISBN 0-87535-001-1). Hispanic Soc.
De Rojas, Fernando see Rojas, Fernando de.
De Rola, Klossowski. Alchemy: The Secret of Art. (Art & the Cosmos Ser.). (Illus.). 128p. 1973. pap. 4.95 (ISBN 0-380-01012-7, 16907). Avon.
De Rola, Stanislas Klossowski see Klossowski de Rola, Stanislas.
Derolez, Albert. Library of Raphael De Marctellis. 335p. 1980. text ed. 84.25x (ISBN 90-6439-191-2). Humanities.
De Rome, Peter. The Erotic World of Peter de Rome. 192p. (Orig.). 1984. pap. 7.50 (ISBN 0-907040-46-2, Pub. by GMP England). Alyson Pubns.
De Romilly, Jacqueline. The Rise & Fall of States According to Greek Authors. LC 75-31056. 1977. 12.50x (ISBN 0-472-08762-2). U of Mich Pr.
DeRomilly, Jacqueline. A Short History of Greek Literature. Doherty, Lillian, tr. from French. LC 84-16457. (Illus.). 296p. 1985. lib. bdg. 27.00x (ISBN 0-226-14311-2); pap. 9.95 (ISBN 0-226-14312-0). U of Chicago Pr.
De Romilly, Jacqueline. Thucydides & Athenian Imperialism. Vlastos, Gregory, ed. Thody, Philip, tr. from Eng. & Greek. LC 78-19381. (Morals & Law in Ancient Greece Ser.). 1979. Repr. of 1963 ed. lib. bdg. 30.50x (ISBN 0-405-11570-9). Ayer Co Pubs.
De Ronsard, P. Odes, Hymns & Other Poems, Vol. II. Castor, G. & Cave, T., eds. (Medieval French Texts). 304p. (Fr.). 1977. pap. 9.95 (ISBN 0-7190-0673-2, Pub. by Manchester Univ Pr). Longwood Pub Group.
--Poems of Love, Vol. 1. Castor, G. & Cave, T., eds. (Medieval French Texts Ser.). 162p. (Fr.). 1975. pap. text ed. 6.95 (ISBN 0-7190-0609-0, Pub. by Manchester Univ Pr). Longwood Pub Group.
De Ronsard, Pierre. Amours. 1963. 16.95 (ISBN 0-685-10995-X); pap. 4.50 pocket ed. (ISBN 0-685-10996-8, 1242). French & Eur.
--Oeuvres, 8 tomes. Silver, ed. Incl. Tomes I Et II. Oeuvres. Set. 47.25 (ISBN 0-685-34194-1); Tome III. Les Odes. 33.25 (ISBN 0-685-34195-X); Tome IV. Les Quatres Premiers Livres de la Franciade - Le Bocage Royal. 33.25 (ISBN 0-685-34196-8); Tome V. Les Eglogues et les Mascarades - Les Elegies. 52.50 (ISBN 0-685-34197-6); Tome VI. Les Hymnes. 43.75 (ISBN 0-685-34198-4); Tome VII. Les Poemes - Discours des Miseres de Ce Temps. 38.50 (ISBN 0-685-34199-2); Tome VIII. Les Epitaphes de Divers Sujets - Index des Tomes I a VIII. 45.50 (ISBN 0-685-34200-X). French & Eur.
--Oeuvres Completes, 2 vols. Cohen, ed. (Bibl. de la Pleiade). 1938. Set. 77.45 (ISBN 0-685-11446-5). French & Eur.
--Selected Poems. Scollen, Christine M., ed. 184p. (Fr.). 1974. 14.95 (ISBN 0-485-13807-7, Pub. by Athlone Pr Ltd). Longwood Pub Group.
--Songs & Sonnets of Pierre De Ronsard. Page, Curtis H., tr. from Fr. LC 76-48455. (Library of World Literature Ser.). 1978. Repr. of 1924 ed. 15.00 (ISBN 0-88355-604-9). Hyperion Conn.
--Sonnets Pour Helene. Wolfe, Humbert, tr. from Fr. LC 76-48456. (Library of World Literature Ser.). 1978. Repr. of 1934 ed. lib. bdg. 21.00 (ISBN 0-88355-606-5). Hyperion Conn.
--Sonnets Pour Helene. Wolfe, Humbert, tr. 291p. 1982. lib. bdg. 45.00 (ISBN 0-89984-527-4). Century Bookbindery.
De Ronsard, Pierre, et al. La Fleur des musiciens de P. de Ronsard. Expert, Henry, ed. (Illus.). 116p. (Fr.). 1965. pap. 25.00x (ISBN 0-8450-1245-2). Broude.
De Roo, P. History of America Before Columbus According to Documents & Approved Authors: American Aborigenes & European Immigrants, 2 vols. (Caribbean Ser.). 1979. Set. lib. bdg. 250.00 (ISBN 0-8490-2934-1). Gordon Pr.
DeRoo, Sally. Exploring Our Environment: A Resource Guide-Manual: Animals. (Exploring Our Environment Ser.). (Illus.). 207p. (gr. 3-6). 1979. tchr's. ed. 6.50 (ISBN 0-89039-144-0). Ann Arbor FL.
--Exploring Our Environment: A Resource Guide-Manual-Plants. (Illus.). 168p. 1977. instr.'s manual 6.00 (ISBN 0-89039-208-0). Ann Arbor Fl.
--Exploring Our Environment: Animals Student Materials One. (Exploring Our Environment Ser.). (Illus.). 22p. (gr. 3-6). 1979. wkbk. 1.00 (ISBN 0-89039-146-7). Ann Arbor Fl.
--Exploring Our Environment: Animals Student Materials Two. (Exploring Our Environment Ser.). (Illus.). 32p. (gr. 3-6). 1979. wkbk. 1.00 (ISBN 0-89039-148-3). Ann Arbor FL.
--Exploring Our Environment: Plants-Student Materials 1. (Illus.). 32p. (gr. 3-6). 1977. wkbk 1.00 (ISBN 0-89039-229-3). Ann Arbor FL.
--Exploring Our Environment: Plants-Student Materials 2. 32p. (gr. 3-6). 1977. wkbk 1.00 (ISBN 0-89039-231-5). Ann Arbor FL.
De Roos, Robert W. The Thirsty Land: The Story of the Central Valley Project. LC 48-10963. pap. 30.00 (ISBN 0-317-27233-0, 2025083). Bks Demand UMI.
De Roos, Willy. North-West Passage. LC 80-82413. (Illus.). 1981. 4.95 (ISBN 0-87742-087-4). Intl Marine.
De Roover, Raymond. Business, Banking, & Economic Thought in Late Medieval & Early Modern Europe. Kirshner, Julius, ed. LC 73-87307. 392p. 1976. 20.00x (ISBN 0-226-72545-6); pap. text ed. 6.00x (ISBN 0-226-72546-4). U of Chicago Pr.
--Money, Banking & Credit in Mediaeval Bruges. 1983. Repr. of 1948 ed. 25.00 (ISBN 0-910956-25-1). Medieval Acad.
--San Bernardino of Siena & Sant Antonino of Florence. (Kress Library Publications: No. 19). (Illus.). 1967. pap. 8.95x (ISBN 0-678-09913-8, Baker Lib). Kelley.
De Roover, Raymond A. Rise & Decline of the Medici Bank: 1397-1494. LC 63-11417. (Studies in Business History: No. 21). (Illus.). 1963. 27.50x (ISBN 0-674-77145-1). Harvard U Pr.
De Rooy, F. P. Documentary Credits. 1984. lib. bdg. 50.00 (ISBN 90-6544-075-5, Pub. by Kluwer Law Netherlands). Kluwer Academic.
--Documentary Credits 1983. 250p. 40.00 (ISBN 0-686-41012-2). Kluwer Academic.
DeRopp, Robert S. Warrior's Way: The Challenging Life Games. 1984. 18.25 (ISBN 0-8446-6174-0). Peter Smith.
De Roque, Carmen I. Modulos de Contabilidad Introductoria. (Span.). 1979. text ed. 8.55 wkbk. (ISBN 0-538-22010-4, V01). SW Pub.
DeRosa, Paul & Stern, Gary H. In the Name of Money: A Professional's Guide to the Federal Reserve, Interest Rates & Money. (Illus.). 192p. 1980. 24.95 (ISBN 0-07-016521-1). McGraw.
De Rosa, Peter. Prayers for Pagans & Hypocrites. LC 78-27802. (Illus.). 1979. 6.95 (ISBN 0-688-03449-7). Morrow.
De Rosario. Vocabulario Puertorriqueno. (Span.). 1966. 10.95 (ISBN 0-87751-010-5, Pub by Troutman Press). E Torres & Sons.
De Rosario, Vega. El Hombre Que Vion de la Lluvia. (Romance Real Ser.). 192p. (Span.). 1981. pap. 1.50 (ISBN 0-88025-008-9). Roca Pub.
--Los Malditos Amores. (Romance Real Ser.). 192p. (Span.). 1981. pap. 1.50 (ISBN 0-88025-006-2). Roca Pub.
Derose, A. J., jt. auth. see Cowper, C. J.
DeRose, Peter & McGuire, S. W. A Concordance to the Works of Jane Austen, 3 Vols. LC 82-48281. 1647p. 1982. lib. bdg. 303.00 (ISBN 0-8240-9245-7). Garland Pub.
De Rose, Peter L. Jane Austen & Samuel Johnson. LC 78-7813. 133p. 1980. lib. bdg. 23.25 (ISBN 0-8191-1073-6); pap. text ed. 9.25 (ISBN 0-8191-1074-4). U Pr of Amer.
DeRosemond, Peggy. A Royal Romance Paper Dolls. (gr. 8-12). 1984. pap. 4.00 (ISBN 0-914510-14-2). Evergreen.
De Rosenthal, Gustavus. Journal of a Volunteer Expedition to Sandusky: From May 24 to June 13, 1782. Decker, Peter, ed. LC 77-77111. (Eyewitness Accounts of the American Revolution Ser., No. 2). 1969. Repr. of 1894 ed. 13.00 (ISBN 0-405-01177-6). Ayer Co Pubs.
DeRosier, Arthur H., Jr. Removal of the Choctaw Indians. LC 70-111044. (Illus.). 1970. 14.95 (ISBN 0-87049-113-X); pap. text ed. 6.95 (ISBN 0-87049-329-9). U of Tenn Pr.
De Rosier, John. Chuck Foreman. (Sports Superstars Ser.). (Illus.). (gr. 3-9). 1976. pap. 3.95 (ISBN 0-89812-168-X). Creative Ed.
DeRosis, Helen. Women & Anxiety. 1981. pap. 8.95 (ISBN 0-385-29121-3, Delta). Dell.
De Rosis, Helen A. Working with Patients: Introductory Guidelines for Psychotherapists. LC 77-896. 1977. 10.50x (ISBN 0-87586-057-5). Agathon.
De Rosis, Helen A. & Pellegrino, Victoria Y. The Book of Hope: How Women Can Overcome Depression. 1977. pap. 4.50 (ISBN 0-553-24064-1). Bantam.

De Rosnay, Joel. The Macroscope: A New World Scientific System. Edwards, Robert I., tr. LC 76-5122. (Illus.). 1979. 15.95i (ISBN 0-06-011029-5, HarpT). Har-Row.

De Rosnay, Joel see Rosnay, Joel de.

De Rosny, Eric. Healers in the Night. Barr, Robert R., tr. from Fr. LC 85-5659. 304p. (Orig.). 1985. pap. 13.95 (ISBN 0-88344-199-3). Orbis Bks.

DeRossi, Claude & Hopper, David. Software Interfacing: A User & Supplier Guide. (Illus.). 208p. 1984. 29.95 (ISBN 0-13-822353-X). P-H.

De Rossi, Claude J. Learning BASIC Fast. rev. ed. LC 74-3355. (Illus.). 1979. pap. text ed. 17.95 (ISBN 0-8359-3977-4). Reston.

Derossi, Flavia. The Technocratic Illusion: A Study of Managerial Power in Italy. LoBello, Susan, tr. from Italian. LC 81-14341. 284p. 1982. 30.00 (ISBN 0-87332-185-5). M E Sharpe.

De Rossi, Rita H., jt. ed. see Rossi, Roberto A.

Der Osten, Hans H. Von see Von der Osten, Hans H. & Schmidt, Erich F.

De Rostyne, Catherine van see Van de Rostyne, Catherine & Schnell, Marilyn.

De Rothschild, Guy. The Whims of Fortune: The Memoirs of Guy de Rothschild. LC 84-42630. 325p. 1985. 19.45 (ISBN 0-394-54054-9). Random.

DeRothschild, J. A., jt. auth. see Williams, M.

De Rothschild, James A., jt. auth. see Williams, Mary.

De Rothschild, James E. Catalogue des Livres Composant la Bibliotheque de Feu M. le Baron Rothschild, 5 Vols. Picot, Emile, ed. Repr. of 1884 ed. 215.00 (ISBN 0-8337-3070-3). B Franklin.

De Rothschild, P see De Rothschild, Phillipine.

De Rothschild, Philippe & Littlewood, Joan. Baron Philippe: The Very Candid Autobiography of Baron Philippe de Rothschild. 1984. 16.95 (ISBN 0-517-55557-3). Crown.

De Rothschild, Phillipine. Mouton Rothschild: Paintings for the Labels 1945-1981. (Illus.). 144p. 1983. pap. 14.50i (ISBN 0-8212-1557-4, 585963); 39.00 (ISBN 0-8212-1555-8, 585955). NYGS.

De Rothschild, Salomon. A Casual View of America: The Home Letters of Salomon De Rothschild, 1859-1861. Diamond, Sigmund, tr. 1961. 12.50x (ISBN 0-8047-0053-2). Stanford U Pr.

De Rothwell, Helene F. see Rothwell, Helene De F.

Derouane, E. G. & Lucas, A. A., eds. Electronic Structure & Reactivity of Metal Surfaces. LC 76-10692. (NATO ASI Series B, Physics: Vol. 16). 633p. 1976. 89.50x (ISBN 0-306-35716-X, Plenum Pr). Plenum Pub.

De Rouck, A., jt. ed. see Francois, J.

De Rouffignac, Ann E. Lucas. The Contemporary Peasantry in Mexico: A Class Analysis. LC 85-6317. 224p. 1985. 30.95 (ISBN 0-03-071868-6). Praeger.

DeRouge, J. & Feaurdent, F. The Coins of the Nomes & Prefecture of Roman Egypt. (Illus., Fr.). 1979. 20.00 (ISBN 0-916710-41-6); pap. 10.00 (ISBN 0-685-95531-1). Obol Intl.

DeRouge, J. & Feuardent, F. Monnaies Des Nomes D'Egypte. 1985. 20.00 (ISBN 0-89005-396-0); pap. 10.00 (ISBN 0-89005-395-2). Ares.

De Rougement, Denis. Love in the Western World. Belgion, Montgomery, tr. from Fr. 400p. (Eng.). 1983. 35.00x (ISBN 0-691-06515-2); pap. 9.95x (ISBN 0-691-01393-4). Princeton U Pr.

De Rougemont, D. Future Within Us. (Systems Science & World Order Library). 254p. 1983. 50.00 (ISBN 0-08-027395-5); pap. 16.00 (ISBN 0-08-027394-7). Pergamon.

De Rougemont, Denis. Dramatic Personages. Howard, Richard, tr. LC 72-153246. (Essay & General Literature Index Reprint Ser). 1971. Repr. of 1964 ed. 21.00x (ISBN 0-8046-1499-7, Pub. by Kennikat). Assoc Faculty Pr.

--Man's Western Quest: The Principles of Civilization. Belgion, Montgomery, tr. LC 73-3757. 197p. 1973. Repr. of 1957 ed. lib. bdg. 15.00x (ISBN 0-8371-6850-3, ROWQ). Greenwood.

De Rougemont, Denis, ed. The State of the Union of Europe: Report of the CADMOS Group to the European People. 1979. pap. 10.50 (ISBN 0-08-024476-9). Pergamon.

De Roussan, Jacques. Beyond the Sun: Au Dela Du Soleil. LC 76-179432. (Astronomy for Children Ser.). (Illus.). (gr. k-4). 1977. 2.95 (ISBN 0-88776-031-7). Tundra Bks.

--If I Came from Mars: Si J'etais Martien. LC 76-58700. (Astronomy for Children Ser.). (Illus.). (gr. k-4). 1977. 2.95 (ISBN 0-88776-032-5). Tundra Bks.

De Roussy De Sales, Raoul, ed. see Hitler, Adolph.

De Routisie, Albert see Routisie, Albert de.

De Rouver, Camillus A. The Anti-European Policy of the Washington Myopic Foreign Office Bureaucrats. (Illus.). 103p. 1984. 99.95x (ISBN 0-86722-059-7). Inst Econ Pol.

Derow, Ellan O., jt. auth. see Carley, Michael J.

Derow, Peter, jt. auth. see Bagnall, Roger.

De Roy Moore, Tui. Galapagos: Islands Lost in Time. LC 80-5360. (Illus.). 144p. 1980. 30.00 (ISBN 0-670-33361-1, Studio); pap. 14.95 (ISBN 0-670-33362-X). Viking.

Derozio, Henry. Henry Derozio: Poems. Lal, P., ed. 67p. 1975. 14.00 (ISBN 0-88253-716-4); pap. 6.75 (ISBN 0-88253-848-9). Ind-US Inc.

Der Plas, Leendert Van see Van Der Plas, Leendert.

Derr, C. Brooklyn, ed. Work, Family & the Career: New Frontiers in Theory & Research. LC 80-13598. 380p. 1980. 37.95 (ISBN 0-03-056717-3). Praeger.

Derr, Don A. & Small, Leslie, eds. Property Rights in Transition. 243p. 1977. text ed. 29.50x (ISBN 0-8422-5252-5); pap. text ed. 8.95x (ISBN 0-8422-0554-3). Irvington.

Derr, Jill M. Sarah M. Kimball. 20p. pap. 1.95 (ISBN 0-941214-05-2). Signature Bks.

Derr, Thomas S. Barriers to Ecumenism: The Holy See & the World Council on Social Questions. LC 82-18761. 112p. (Orig.). 1983. pap. 7.95 (ISBN 0-88344-031-8). Orbis Bks.

Derre, Jean Rene, jt. auth. see Constant, Benjamin.

Derrett, D. R. Ship Stability for Master & Mates. 3rd rev. ed. 1972. 30.00 (ISBN 0-540-01403-6). Heinman.

--Ship Stability for Masters & Mates. 4th ed. (Illus.). 420p. 1984. text ed. 24.50x (ISBN 0-540-07388-1, Pub. by Stanford Maritime). Sheridan.

Derrett, J. Duncan. The Death of a Marriage Law: Epitaph for the Rishis. LC 77-93389. 228p. 1978. 18.95 (ISBN 0-89089-056-0). Carolina Acad Pr.

Derrett, J. Duncan, tr. see Lingat, Robert.

Derrey, Francois. The Earth Is Alive: Origins of the Earth & the Solar System. Roy, Gregor, tr. from Fr. 1968. 14.95x (ISBN 0-8464-0346-3). Beekman Pubs.

Derrick. The Dental Annual 1986. 1986. price not set (ISBN 0-7236-0838-5). PSG Pub Co.

--Field Ionization & Field Desorption Mass Spectrometry. 1978. write for info. (ISBN 0-685-84731-4). Elsevier.

Derrick, Beckett. Stephensons' Britain. (Illus.). 240p. 1984. 21.00 (ISBN 0-7153-8269-1). David & Charles.

Derrick, Christopher. C. S. Lewis & the Church of Rome. LC 80-83049. 225p. (Orig.). 1981. pap. 8.95 (ISBN 0-89870-009-4). Ignatius Pr.

--Church Authority & Intellectual Freedom. LC 81-80209. 113p. (Orig.). 1981. pap. 7.95 (ISBN 0-89870-011-6). Ignatius Pr.

--The Delicate Creation. 144p. 1972. 9.95 (ISBN 0-8159-5304-6). Devin.

--Escape from Scepticism: Liberal Education As If Truth Mattered. 1977. pap. text ed. 3.95 (ISBN 0-89385-002-0). Sugden.

--Joy Without a Cause: Selected Essays of Christopher Derrick. 254p. 1979. pap. 5.95 (ISBN 0-89385-004-7). Sugden.

--The Rule of Peace. LC 80-20804. 1980. 4.95 (ISBN 0-932506-01-1). St Bedes Pubns.

--Sex & Sacredness: A Catholic Homage to Venus. LC 82-80302. 219p. (Orig.). 1982. pap. 9.95 (ISBN 0-89870-018-3). Ignatius Pr.

--That Strange Divine Sea: Reflections on Being a Catholic. LC 83-80190. 189p. (Orig.). 1983. pap. 8.95 (ISBN 0-89870-029-9). Ignatius Pr.

--Too Many People? A Problem in Values. 120p. (Orig.). 1985. pap. 6.95 (ISBN 0-89870-071-X). Ignatius Pr.

Derrick, David. Boat Maintenance. (Illus.). 128p. 1984. 18.95 (ISBN 0-7153-8412-0). David & Charles.

--Navigation for Offshore & Ocean Sailors. LC 81-67008. (Illus.). 160p. 1981. 19.95 (ISBN 0-7153-8086-9). David & Charles.

Derrick, Deborah. Bibliography of Youth: Youth Work & Provision for Youth. 1976. 35.00x (ISBN 0-902095-26-9, Pub. by Natl Youth Bur England). State Mutual Bk.

Derrick, John & Oppenheim, Phillip. A Handbook of New Office Technology. 320p. 1982. 110.00x (ISBN 0-7126-0020-5, Pub. by Century Pub Co). State Mutual Bk.

Derrick, June. The Child's Acquisition of Language. 64p. 1977. 6.00x (ISBN 0-85633-110-4, Pub. by NFER Nelson UK). Taylor & Francis.

--Language Needs of Minority Group Children. 68p. 1977. 6.00x (ISBN 0-85633-118-X, Pub. by NFER Nelson UK). Taylor & francis.

Derrick, Lionel. Assassination Factor. (Penetrator Ser.: No. 40). 192p. (Orig.). 1981. pap. 1.75 (ISBN 0-523-41114-6). Pinnacle Bks.

--City of the Dead. (Penetrator Ser.: No. 53). 208p. (Orig.). 1984. pap. 2.50 (ISBN 0-523-41958-9). Pinnacle Bks.

--Cruise into Chaos. (Penetrator Ser.: No. 39). 192p. (Orig.). 1980. pap. 1.75 (ISBN 0-523-40924-9). Pinnacle Bks.

--Deep Cover Blast-off. (Penetrator Ser.: No. 44). 208p. (Orig.). 1981. pap. 1.95 (ISBN 0-523-41407-2). Pinnacle Bks.

--Jungle Blitz. (The Penetrator Ser.: No. 48). 192p. (Orig.). 1982. pap. 2.25 (ISBN 0-523-41680-6). Pinnacle Bks.

--Penetrator: Hell's Hostages, No. 41. 192p. (Orig.). 1981. pap. 1.75 (ISBN 0-523-41116-2). Pinnacle Bks.

--Penetrator, No. 46: Terrorist Torment. 192p. 1982. pap. 1.95 (ISBN 0-523-41553-2). Pinnacle Bks.

--Penetrator, No. 47: Orphan Army. 208p. (Orig.). 1982. pap. 2.25 (ISBN 0-523-41554-0). Pinnacle Bks.

--Quaking Terror. (Penetrator Ser.: No. 45). 208p. (Orig.). 1982. pap. 1.95 (ISBN 0-523-41398-X). Pinnacle Bks.

--Rampage in Rio. (Penetrator Ser.: No. 43). 208p. (Orig.). 1981. pap. 1.95 (ISBN 0-523-41157-X). Pinnacle Bks.

--Satan's Swarm. (The Penetrator Ser.: No. 49). 192p. (Orig.). 1983. pap. 2.25 (ISBN 0-523-41681-4). Pinnacle Bks.

Derrick, Michael. The Portugal of Salazar. (Select Bibliographies Reprint Ser). 1972. Repr. of 1938 ed. 12.50 (ISBN 0-8369-9959-2). Ayer Co Pubs.

Derrick, Paul. Men over Industry. 1980. lib. bdg. 59.95 (ISBN 0-8490-3079-X). Gordon Pr.

Derrick, Sara M. & Bachman, Kelly L. Hospitalized Children Play & Play Activities. (Illus.). 106p. (Orig.). 1983. pap. write for info. (ISBN 0-89279-049-0). S M Derrick.

Derrick, William R. Complex Analysis & Applications. 2nd ed. LC 83-6865. (Mathematics Ser.). 256p. 1984. text ed. write for info. (ISBN 0-534-02853-5). Wadsworth Pub.

Derrick, William R. & Grossman, Stanley I. Elementary Differential Equations with Applications. 2nd ed. (Mathematics Ser.). (Illus.). 576p. 1981. text ed. 31.95 (ISBN 0-201-03162-0); answer bk. 2.00 (ISBN 0-201-03166-3). Addison-Wesley.

--Elementary Differential Equations with Applications: A Short Course. 2nd ed. (Mathematics Ser.). (Illus.). 384p. 1981. text ed. 27.95 (ISBN 0-201-03164-7). Addison-Wesley.

Derricke, John. The Image of Irelande, with a Discoverie of Woodkarne. (Illus.). 242p. 1985. ltd. ed. 100.00 (ISBN 0-85640-296-6, Pub. by Blackstaff Pr). Longwood Pub Group.

Derricott, R. & Chissick, Seymour S. Rebuild. LC 81-21942. (Properties of Materials Safety & Environmental Factors). 286p. 1982. 48.95x (ISBN 0-471-10173-7, Pub. by Wiley-Interscience). Wiley.

Derricott, R., jt. auth. see Blyth, W. A.

Derricott, R., jt. auth. see Chissick, S. S.

Derricott, Ray, ed. Curriculum Continuity: Primary to Secondary. 192p. 1985. 13.00 (ISBN 0-7005-0671-3). Taylor & Francis.

Derricott, Robert & Chissick, Seymour. Energy Conservation & Thermal Insulation: Properties of Materials. LC 80-41587. (Safety & Environmental Factors Ser.). 785p. 1981. 100.00x (ISBN 0-471-27930-7, Pub. by Wiley-Interscience). Wiley.

Derricotte, Toi. The Empress of the Death House. LC 77-91700. 51p. 1978. perfect bdg. 3.50x (ISBN 0-916418-12-X). Lotus.

--Natural Birth. LC 83-2071. (Feminist Ser.). 62p. (Orig.). 1983. 13.95 (ISBN 0-89594-102-3); pap. 5.95 (ISBN 0-89594-101-5). Crossing Pr.

Derricourt, Nick, jt. ed. see Craig, Gary.

Derricourt, Robin. Man on the Kafue: The Archaeology & History of the Itezhitezhi Area of Zambia. LC 84-6293. (Illus.). 272p. 1985. text ed. 35.00x (ISBN 0-936508-10-8). Barber Pr.

Derrida, Jacques. The Archaeology of the Frivolous: Reading Condillac. Leavey, John P., Jr., tr. from Fr. (Duquesne Studies - Philosophical Ser.: Vol. 37). 130p. 1981. text ed. 11.45x (ISBN 0-391-01636-9). Duquesne.

--Dissemination. Johnson, Barbara, tr. LC 81-3359. 400p. 1981. 26.00x (ISBN 0-226-14327-9). U of Chicago Pr.

--Dissemination. Johnson, Barbara, tr. LC 81-3359. xxiv, 366p. 1983. pap. 11.95x (ISBN 0-226-14334-1). U of Chicago Pr.

--Edmund Husserl's The Origin of Geometry: An Introduction. Leavey, John P., tr. from Fr. LC 77-13723. 1977. 12.95 (ISBN 0-89254-006-0). Nicolas-Hays.

--Margins of Philosophy. Bass, Alan, tr. from Fr. LC 82-11137. 1983. lib. bdg. 22.50x (ISBN 0-226-14325-2); pap. 10.95 (ISBN 0-226-14326-0). U of Chicago Pr.

--Of Grammatology. Spivak, Gayatri C., tr. LC 76-17226. (Illus.). 446p. 1977. 30.00x (ISBN 0-8018-1841-9); pap. 8.95 (ISBN 0-8018-1879-6). Johns Hopkins.

--Positions. Bass, Alan, tr. from Fr. LC 80-17620. 1981. 11.95x (ISBN 0-226-14332-5); pap. 5.00x (ISBN 0-226-14331-7). U of Chicago Pr.

--Signeponge-Signsponge. Rand, Richard, tr. from Fr. 1984. 21.00x (ISBN 0-231-05446-7). Columbia U Pr.

--Signeponge: Siigneponge. Rand, Richard, tr. 160p. 1985. pap. text ed. 12.00x (ISBN 0-231-05447-5). Columbia U Pr.

--Speech & Phenomena: And Other Essays on Husserl's Theory of Signs. Allison, David B., tr. from Ger. LC 72-80565. (Studies in Phenomenology & Existential Philosophy). 1973. text ed. 18.95 (ISBN 0-8101-0397-4); pap. text ed. 7.95 (ISBN 0-8101-0590-X). Northwestern U Pr.

--Spurs: Nietzsche's Styles. Harlow, Barbara, tr. from Fr. LC 79-31. vi, 166p. 1981. pap. 6.95x (ISBN 0-226-14333-3). U of Chicago Pr.

--Writing & Difference. Bass, Alan, tr. from Fr. LC 77-25933. 1978. lib. bdg. 25.00x (ISBN 0-226-14328-7). U of Chicago Pr.

--Writing & Difference. Bass, Alan, tr. from Fr. LC 77-25933. 1980. pap. 11.00x (ISBN 0-226-14329-5, P865, Phoen). U of Chicago Pr.

Derriere, Pierre. Up Yours! 1976. pap. 0.95 (ISBN 0-8439-0325-2, Leisure Bks). Dorchester Pub Co.

Derrig, Leslie A. & Westdyk, Roxanne H. Mommy in the Sky. LC 83-73248. (Working Mommy Ser.: Vol. 2). (Illus.). 32p. (Orig.). (gr. k-5). 1983. pap. 6.95 (ISBN 0-915479-68-0). Cottage Pub Co.

Derry, Charles M., jt. ed. see Ra'anan, Uri.

Derry Historical Research Committee. From Turnpike to Interstate: The 150 Years of Derry, N. H. LC 77-20952. (Illus.). 1977. 12.00 (ISBN 0-914016-47-4). Phoenix Pub.

Derry, John & Derry, Reg. Spectral Universe. 1983. 7.95 (ISBN 0-533-05502-4). Vantage.

Derry, Joseph T. Story of the Confederate States; or, History of the War for Southern Independence Embracing the Early Settlement of the Country, Trouble with the Indians, the French, Revolutionary & Mexican Wars. 19.50 (ISBN 0-405-12295-0). Ayer Co Pubs.

Derry, Reg, jt. auth. see Derry, John.

Derry, T. Oslo. (Tanum of Norway Tokens Ser). pap. 7.00x (ISBN 0-89918-484-7, N484). Vanous.

Derry, T. K. A History of Modern Norway, 1814-1972. (Illus.). 1973. 42.00x (ISBN 0-19-822503-2). Oxford U Pr.

--A History of Scandinavia: Norway, Sweden, Denmark, Finland, & Iceland. LC 78-14284. 1979. pap. 13.95 (ISBN 0-8166-0936-5). U of Minn Pr.

--A History of Scandinavia: Norway, Sweden, Denmark, Finland, & Iceland. 1979. 25.00x (ISBN 0-8166-0835-0). U of Minn Pr.

Derry, Thomas K. A Short History of Norway. LC 79-10688. (Illus.). 1979. Repr. of 1968 ed. lib. bdg. 24.75x (ISBN 0-313-21467-0, DESH). Greenwood.

Derry, Thomas K. & Williams, Trevor I. Short History of Technology from the Earliest Times to A. D. 1900. (Illus.). 1961. o. p. 29.95x (ISBN 0-19-500142-7); pap. 13.95x (ISBN 0-19-881231-0, OPB). Oxford U Pr.

Derry, Warren, ed. see Burney, Fanny.

Derry Youth & Community Workshop Ltd. of Northern Ireland. Port of Derry Ship List. 108p. 1984. perfect bdg. 13.95 (ISBN 0-318-03874-9). Closson Pr.

Dersal, William R. Van see Van Dersal, William R.

Dersal, William R. van see Van Dersal, William R.

Dersch, James E. Band-Aids. 3rd ed. Bash, Richard M., ed. (Illus.). 162p. 1981. wire bound 9.95 (ISBN 0-938408-06-2, 1811-BA). Bash Educ Serv.

Dersh, Rhoda. The School Budget: It's Your Money-It's Your Business. LC 79-90677. 1979. pap. 4.95 (ISBN 0-934460-10-8). NCCE.

Dershem, Larry D. Library of Congress Classification Class K Subclass KF Law of the United States Cumulative Schedule. (AALL Publications Ser.: No. 20). 1984. loose-leaf 75.00x (ISBN 0-8377-0118-X). Rothman.

--Library of Congress Classification Class K: Subclass K Law (General) Cumulative Schedule & Index. (AALL Publications Ser.: No. 24). 1985. loose-leaf 60.00x (ISBN 0-8377-0122-8). Rothman.

Dershem, Larry D., ed. Library of Congress Classification Class K, Subclass KF Law of the United States Cumulative Index. (AALL Publication Ser.: No. 18). vii, 326p. 1982. loose-leaf 35.00x (ISBN 0-8377-0115-5). Rothman.

Dershowitz. Evolution of Programs. (Progress in Computer Science Ser.: Vol. 5). 1983. 24.95 (ISBN 3-7643-3156-9); pap. 16.95 (ISBN 0-8176-3171-2). Birkhauser.

Dershowitz, Alan M. The Best Defense. 1982. 16.95 (ISBN 0-394-50736-3). Random.

--The Best Defense. LC 82-40426. (Illus.). 464p. 1985. pap. 6.95 (ISBN 0-394-71380-X, Vin). Random.

Der Smissen, Betty van see Van der Smissen, Betty.

Der Smissen, Betty Van see Van Der Smissen, Betty.

Derssenbrock, El, et al, trs. see Wright, Michael.

Der Starre, H. van see Van der Starre, H.

Derstine, Gerald. Destined to Mature. 144p. (Orig.). 1984. pap. 3.50 (ISBN 0-88368-147-1). Whitaker Hse.

Derstine, Gerald & Layman, Joanne. Following the Fire. LC 79-91216. 1980. 4.95 (ISBN 0-88270-486-9, Pub. by Logos). Bridge Pub.

Der Tak, Herman G. van see Squire, Lyn & Van der Tak, Herman G.

Derthick, Martha. Between State & Nation: Regional Organizations of the United States. LC 74-727. 1974. 22.95 (ISBN 0-8157-1812-8); pap. 8.95 (ISBN 0-8157-1811-X). Brookings.

--Influence of Federal Grants: Public Assistance in Massachusetts. LC 73-95919. (Joint Center for Urban Studies Publications Ser). 1970. 17.50x (ISBN 0-674-45425-1). Harvard U Pr.

--New Towns in-Town: Why a Federal Program Failed. LC 73-187564. 102p. 1972. pap. 6.95x (ISBN 0-87766-022-0, 70006). Urban Inst.

--Policymaking for Social Security. LC 78-24811. 1979. 29.95 (ISBN 0-8157-1816-0); pap. 11.95 (ISBN 0-8157-1815-2). Brookings.

--Uncontrollable Spending for Social Services Grants. 80p. 1975. pap. 8.95 (ISBN 0-8157-1813-6). Brookings.

Derthick, Martha A. National Guard in Politics. LC 65-11588. (Political Studies Ser). 1965. 15.00x (ISBN 0-674-60200-5). Harvard U Pr.

Dertinger, Charles J. Reflections. 1983. write for info. (ISBN 0-8062-2043-0). Carlton.

Dertouzos, Michael. Threshold Logic: A Synthesis Approach. (Press Research Monographs: No. 32). 1965. 27.50x (ISBN 0-262-04009-3). MIT Pr.

Dertouzos, Michael L. & Moses, Joel, eds. The Computer Age: A Twenty-Year View. 1979. pap. text ed. 10.95 (ISBN 0-262-54036-3). MIT Pr.

Dertouzos, Michael L., et al. Systems, Networks & Computation: Basic Concepts. LC 79-4556. 528p. 1979. Repr. of 1972 ed. lib. bdg. 29.50 (ISBN 0-88275-916-7). Krieger.

Dertschland, Bundesrepublik, tr. see Arbeitsgemeinschaft Ausseruniversitarer Historischer Forschungseinrichtungen.

Derucher & Heins. Bridges & Pier Protective Systems & Devices. (Civil Engineering Ser.: Vol. 1). 1979. 49.75 (ISBN 0-8247-6895-7). Dekker.

Derucher, K., jt. auth. see Heins, C. P., Jr.

Derucher, Kenneth & Heins, Conrad. Materials for Civil & Highway Engineers. (Illus.). 416p. 1981. text ed. 37.95 (ISBN 0-13-560490-7). P-H.

De Ruggiero, Guido. The History of European Liberalism. Collingwood, R. C., tr. 1977. lib. bdg. 59.95 (ISBN 0-8490-1975-3). Gordon Pr.

--History of European Liberalism. Collingwood, R. C., tr. 19.00 (ISBN 0-8446-1970-1). Peter Smith.

Derugin, Vladimir, ed. see Chrysostomos, Archimandrite & Ambrosios, Hieromonk.

Deruguine, Tania, tr. see Dyadkin, Iosif G.

DeRuiter, Gerald L., jt. auth. see Allen, Pat.

DeRuiter, James, jt. auth. see Gearheart, Bill R.

DeRuiter, James A. & Wansart, William L. Psychology of Learning Disabilities: Application & Educational Practice. LC 82-4108. 245p. 1982. 30.00 (ISBN 0-89443-687-2). Aspen Systems.

De Rulhiere, Claude. History or Anecdotes of the Revolution in Russia, in the Year 1762. LC 72-115581. (Russia Observed, Series I). 1970. Repr. of 1797 ed. 14.00 (ISBN 0-405-03060-6). Ayer Co Pubs.

Derus, David. A Passion for the Hidden City. (Illus.). 52p. (Orig.). 1977. pap. text ed. 5.00 (ISBN 0-942908-04-X). Pancake Pr.

DeRusso, P. M., et al. State Variables for Engineers. LC 65-21443. 608p. 1965. 57.50 (ISBN 0-471-20380-7). Wiley.

De Ruth, Jan. Painting Portraits, Nudes & Clothed Figures. (Illus.). 144p. 1981. 22.50 (ISBN 0-8230-3728-2). Watson-Guptill.

Dervaes, Claudine. The Travel Agent Training Workbook, 6 pts. (Illus.). 694p. 1985. Pt. 1. 30.00; Pts. 2-6. 25.00 ea. (ISBN 0-318-03041-1); Set. 125.00. Solitaire Pub.

--The Travel Agent's Dictionary. 1985. 15.95. Solitaire Pub.

Derveer, Paul D. Van see Van Derveer, Paul D. & Haas, Leonard E.

Dervenn. Brittany. LC 82-70578. (Illus.). 120p. 1982. 22.50 (ISBN 0-86710-019-2). Edns Vilo.

Derveur, Paul W. Van see Lian & Van Der Veur, Paul W.

Dervin, A. Daniel. Bernard Shaw: A Psychological Study. LC 73-8301. 350p. 1975. 24.50 (ISBN 0-8387-1418-8). Bucknell U Pr.

Dervin, Brenda. Progress in Communication Sciences, Vol. 3. Voigt, Melvin J., ed. (Communication & Information Sciences Ser.). 350p. 1982. text ed. 39.50 (ISBN 0-89391-081-3). Ablex Pub.

Dervin, Brenda & Voigt, Melvin J. Progress in Communication Sciences, Vol. 6. (Progress in Communication Sciences Ser.). 332p. 1985. text ed. 39.50 (ISBN 0-89391-306-5). Ablex Pub.

Dervin, Brenda & Voigt, Melvin J., eds. Progress in Communication Sciences, Vol. 4. (Communication & Information Science Ser.). 304p. 1983. text ed. 35.00 (ISBN 0-89391-102-X). Ablex Pub.

Dervin, Brenda, jt. ed. see Voigt, Melvin.

Dervin, Brenda, jt. ed. see Voigt, Melvin J.

Dervin, Daniel. A "Strange Sapience": The Creative Imagination of D. H. Lawrence. LC 84-2681. (Illus.). 256p. 1984. lib. bdg. 23.50x (ISBN 0-87023-455-2). U of Mass Pr.

--Through a Freudian Lens Deeply: A Psychoanalysis of Cinema. (Advances in Psychoanalysis Ser.: Vol. 5). 176p. text ed. write for info. (ISBN 0-88163-018-7). Analytic Pr.

Dervis, Kemal & De Melo, Jaime. A General Equilibrium Analysis of Foreign Exchange of Foreign Exchange Shortages in a Developing Economy. (Working Paper: No. 443). 32p. 1982. pap. 3.00 (ISBN 0-686-39743-6, WP-0443). World Bank.

Dervis, Kemal, et al. General Euquilibrium Models for Development Policy. LC 81-12307. 1982. 44.50 (ISBN 0-521-24490-0); pap. 19.95 (ISBN 0-521-27030-8). Cambridge U Pr.

Dervis, Kermal, et al. Policy Analysis of Shadow Pricing, Foreign Borrowing, & Resource Extraction in Egypt. 186p. 5.00 (ISBN 0-318-02817-4, WP0622). World Bank.

Dervish, H. B. M. Journeys with a Sufi Master. Griffiths, A. L., ed. Tiryaqi, A. W. T., tr. 1982. 15.95 (ISBN 0-900860-95-2, Pub. by Octagon Pr England). Ins Study Human.

Dervitsiotis, Kostas. Operations Management. (Industrial Engineering & Management Science). (Illus.). 784p. 1980. text ed. 42.00x (ISBN 0-07-016537-8). McGraw.

Der Vlugt, Ebel Van see Van Der Vlugt, Ebed.

Der Waerden, B. L. Van see Van Der Waerden, B. L.

Der Wal, H. J. Van see International Congress on Alcoholism & Drug Dependence, Amsterdam, September, 4-9, 1972.

Der Wal, John Van see Croom, George E., Jr. & Van Der Wal, John.

Der Wee, Hermann Van see Van der Wee, Hermann & Vinogradov, Vladimir A.

Derwich, Jenny B. & Latos, Mary. Dictionary Guide to United States Pottery & Procelain: Nineteenth & Twentieth Century. LC 83-82232. (Illus.). 276p. 1984. pap. 30.00x (ISBN 0-317-02738-7). Jenstan.

Derwing, Bruce L. & Priestly, Tom M. Reading Rules for Russian: A Systematic Approach to Russian Spelling & Pronunciation with Notes on Dialectal & Stylistic Variation. (Illus.). vi, 247p. (Orig.). 1980. pap. 11.95 (ISBN 0-89357-066-4). Slavica.

Derwing, Bruce L., jt. auth. see Schutz, Noel W., Jr.

Dery, David. Computers in Welfare: The MIS-Match. LC 81-224. (Managing Information Ser.: Vol. 3). (Illus.). 264p. 1981. 25.00 (ISBN 0-8039-1610-8). Sage.

--Problem Definition in Policy Analysis. (Studies in Government & Public Policy). (Illus.). 160p 1984. 19.95x (ISBN 0-7006-0261-5). U Pr of KS.

Dery, Tiber. The Portuguese Princess. 1981. pap. 4.95 (ISBN 0-7145-0486-6). Riverrun NY.

Deryagin, B. V., ed. Research in Surface Forces, Vols. 1 & 3. LC 62-15549. Vol. 1, 1963, 190p. 32.50x (ISBN 0-306-18201-7, Consultants); Vol. 3, 1971 448p. 55.00 (ISBN 0-306-18203-3). Plenum Pub.

--Research in Surface Forces: Surface Forces in Thin Films & Disperse Systems, Vol. 4. LC 64-20561. (Illus.). 341p. 1975. 55.00 (ISBN 0-306-18204-1, Consultants). Plenum Pub.

Deryagin, B. V., et al. Adhesion of Solids. LC 78-1843. (Studies in Soviet Science--Physical Sciences Ser.). (Illus.). 473p. 1978. 72.50x (ISBN 0-306-10941-7, Consultants). Plenum Pub.

Derz, Friedrich W., ed. ChemBUYdirect: International Chemical Buyers Directory, 3 vols. 1974-76. Set. 259.00x (ISBN 3-11-004688-1). De Gruyter.

Derzhavina, M. Central V. I. Lenin Museum. 111p. 1979. 4.95 (ISBN 0-8285-1790-8, Pub by Progress Pubs USSR). Imported Pubns.

--Volgograd: A Short Guide. 173p. 1979. 8.45 (ISBN 0-8285-1653-7, Pub. by Progress Pubs USSR). Imported Pubns.

Der Zouwen, J. Van see Geyer, R. F. & Zouwen, J. van der.

Desa, A. Principles of Electronic Instrumentation. LC 80-28240. 280p. 1981. pap. 34.95x (ISBN 0-470-27135-3). Halsted Pr.

De Sa, A. Principles of Electronic Instrumentation. 280p. 1981. 50.00x (ISBN 0-7131-2799-6, Pub. by E Arnold England). State Mutual Bk.

Desa, Joe V., jt. auth. see Claussen, Claus F.

De Sabata, Victor, tr. see Bertolini, Alberto M.

De Sabato Swinton, Elizabeth. The Graphic Art of Onchi Koshiro (Eighteen Ninety-One to Nineteen Fifty-Five) Innovation & Tradition. Freedberg, S. J., ed. (Outstanding Dissertations in Fine Arts Ser.). (Illus.). 510p. 1985. Repr. of 1980 ed. 60.00 (ISBN 0-8240-6868-8). Garland Pub.

De Sabbata, V., ed. The Origin & Evolution of Galaxies: Proceedings of the Course of the International School of Cosmology & Gravitation, 7th, Erice, Trapani, Scicily, May 11-23, 1981. 222p. 1982. 44.00x (ISBN 9971-950-05-7, 99600810H, Pub. by World Sci Singapore). Taylor & Francis.

De Sabbata, V. & Schmutzer, E., eds. Unified Field Theories of More Than Four Dimensions Including Exact Solutions: Proceedings of the 8th Course of the International School Cosmology & Gravitation Erice, Trapani, Siciliy, May 20-June 1, 1982. viii, 458p. 1983. 53.00x (ISBN 9971-950-50-2, Pub. by World Sci Singapore). Taylor & Francis.

De Sabbata, V. & Weber, J., eds. Topics in Theoretical & Experimental Gravitation Physics. LC 77-14029. (NATO ASI Series B, Physics: Vol. 27). 354p. 1977. 52.50x (ISBN 0-306-35727-5, Plenum Pr). Plenum Pub.

De Sabbath, Venzo, jt. ed. see Bergmann, Peter G.

De Sackerville, Wellington. Beautiful Women in Art & Poetry. (Illus.). 1979. deluxe ed. 42.15 (ISBN 0-930582-39-X). Gloucester Art.

De Sade. Oeuvres Completes, 30 tomes. Set. 250.00 (ISBN 0-685-34060-0). French & Eur.

De Sade, Marquis Adelaide of Brunswick. x1954 ed. Ryland, Hobart, tr. LC 72-11856. 168p. 1973. 16.50 (ISBN 0-8108-0574-X). Scarecrow.

Desade, Marquis see Sade, Marquis De.

Desaguliers, J. T., tr. see Mariotte, Edme.

Desai, A. R. Rural Sociology in India. 5th ed. 1985. Repr. of 1978 ed. 30.00x (ISBN 0-8364-1284-2, Pub. by Popular Prakashan). South Asia Bks.

--Urban Family & Family Planning in India. 224p. 1980. Repr. 22.95x (ISBN 0-940500-70-1). Asia Bk Corp.

Desai, Amrit. Happiness Is Now. LC 82-80489. 72p. (Orig.). 1982. pap. 4.50 (ISBN 0-940258-03-X). Kripalu Pubns.

Desai, Anita. Clear Light of Day. LC 80-7603. 224p. 1980. 12.45i (ISBN 0-06-010984-X, HarpT). Har-Row.

--Clear Light of Day. 190p. 1982. pap. 4.95 (ISBN 0-14-005860-5). Penguin.

--Cry the Peacock. (Orient Paperbacks Ser.). 218p. 1983. pap. 4.50 (ISBN 0-86578-083-8). Ind-US Inc.

--Fire on the Mountain. LC 77-3788. 1977. 12.45i (ISBN 0-06-011066-X, HarpT). Har-Row.

--Fire on the Mountain. 152p. 1983. pap. 3.95 (ISBN 0-14-005347-6). Penguin.

--Games at Twilight. 144p. 1983. pap. 3.95 (ISBN 0-14-005348-4). Penguin.

--In Custody. LC 84-48154. 204p. 1985. 16.95 (ISBN 0-06-039038-7, C&M Bessie Bk). Har-Row.

--Voices in the City. 2nd ed. 257p. 1982. pap. 5.95 (ISBN 0-88253-250-2). Ind-US Inc.

--Where Shall We Go This Summer? 2nd ed. 157p. 1982. pap. 4.50 (ISBN 0-86578-125-7). Ind-US Inc.

Desai, B. B., jt. auth. see Salunkhe, D. K.

Desai, Barney & Marney, Cardiff. The Killing of the Imam: South African Tyranny Defied. 9.95 (ISBN 0-7043-2183-1, Pub. by Quartet England); pap. 3.95 (ISBN 0-7043-3212-4, Pub. by Quartet England). Charles River Bks.

Desai, C. S. Elementary Finite Element Method. (Civil Engineering & Engineering Mechanics Ser.). (Illus.). 1979. ref. ed. 36.95 (ISBN 0-13-256636-2). P-H.

Desai, C. S. & Abel, John F. Introducing to the Finite Element Method: A Numerical Method for Engineering Analysis. (Illus.). 1972. 27.95 (ISBN 0-442-22083-9). Van Nos Reinhold.

Desai, C. S. & Siriwardane, H. J. Constitution Laws for Engineering Materials with Emphasis on Geologic Materials. (Illus.). 464p. 1984. 40.95 (ISBN 0-13-167940-6). P-H.

Desai, C. S. & Gallagher, R. H., eds. Mechanics of Engineering Materials. (Numerical Methods in Engineering Ser.). 691p. 1984. 45.00 (ISBN 0-471-90276-4). Wiley.

Desai, C. S., ed. see Symposium, Chicago, Illinois, August, 3-6, 1981.

Desai, Chintamani N. Shakespearean Comedy. LC 79-144595. Repr. of 1952 ed. 19.50 (ISBN 0-404-02099-2). AMS Pr.

Desai, Dolat. Recent Concept of Social Studies. 1962. 3.50x (ISBN 0-8426-1235-1). Verry.

Desai, Gunvant M., jt. ed. see Mellor, John W.

Desai, I. P. The Craft of Sociology & Other Essays. 158p. 1981. text ed. 13.50x (ISBN 0-391-02710-7). Humanities.

Desai, J. D., ed. see Gandhi, M. K.

Desai, Kalpana. Treasures of the Heras Institute. LC 76-905157. (Illus.). 1976. 20.00x (ISBN 0-88386-923-3). South Asia Bks.

Desai, Mahadev. Day to Day with Mahatma Gandhi: Secretary's Diary 1917-1927 & 1932, 10 Vols. Parikh, N. D. & Dalal, C. B., eds. Nilkanth, H. G. & Desai, V. G., trs. 3800p. 1984. Set. text ed. 190.00 (ISBN 0-934676-64-X). Greenlf Bks.

--A Righteous Struggle. 105p. 1983. pap. 1.25 (ISBN 0-934676-34-8). Greenlf Bks.

--The Story of Bardoli Satyagraha. 257p. 1983. pap. 3.25 (ISBN 0-934676-46-1). Greenlf Bks.

Desai, Mahadev, tr. see Gandhi, M. K.

Desai, Meghnad. Marxian Economics. (Quality Paperback Ser.: No. 348). 265p. (Orig.). 1979. pap. 8.95 (ISBN 0-8226-0348-9). Littlefield.

--Marxian Economics. 265p. 1979. 27.50x (ISBN 0-8476-6204-7). Rowman.

--Testing Monetarism. LC 81-21360. 1982. 27.50 (ISBN 0-312-79356-1). St Martin.

--Testing Monetarism. 250p. 1981. pap. 13.50 (ISBN 0-86187-225-8). F Pinter Pubs.

Desai, Meghnad, ed. Agrarian Power & Productivity in South Asia. LC 84-16333. 1985. 25.00x (ISBN 0-520-05369-9). U of Cal Pr.

Desai, Meghnad, jt. ed. see Kumar, Dharma.

Desai, Morarji. The Story of My Life, 3 vols. LC 78-40613. 1979. text ed. 44.00 (ISBN 0-08-023566-2). Pergamon.

Desai, Narayan. Bliss to Be Young with Gandhi. (Childhood Memoirs Ser.: Vol. I). (Orig.). 1984. pap. write for info. cancelled (ISBN 0-940460-01-7). Peace & Gladness.

--Childhood Memoirs, 2 Vols. (Orig.). 1984. pap. write for info. (ISBN 0-940460-03-3). Peace & Gladness.

--Handbook for Satyagrahis: A Manual for Volunteers of Total Revolution. 1982. pap. 3.95 perfect bdg. (ISBN 0-86571-002-3). New Soc Pubs.

--Towards a Nonviolent Revolution. 176p. 9.75 (ISBN 0-686-96939-1). Greenlf Bks.

Desai, P. The Bokaro Steel Plant. 1972. pap. 15.00 (ISBN 0-444-10388-0, North-Holland). Elsevier.

Desai, P., jt. auth. see Bose, A.

Desai, P. B. Planning in India. 1980. text ed. 17.95x (ISBN 0-7069-0832-5, Pub. by Vikas India). Advent NY.

Desai, P. D. Shivambu Cure: Guide to Treatment. 3rd ed. 116p. pap. 9.95 (ISBN 0-88697-000-8). Life Science.

Desai, Padma, ed. Marxism, Central Planning & the Soviet Economy: Economic Essays in Honor of Alexander Erlich. (Illus.). 352p. 1983. 37.50x. MIT Pr.

Desai, Pramod D., jt. auth. see Hultgren, Ralph.

Desai, R. W., ed. Johnson on Shakespeare. 1979. text ed. 13.50x (ISBN 0-86131-120-5). Humanities.

Desai, Rupin W. Sir John Falstaff Knight. LC 75-5210. (Comparative Literature Studies Ser). 133p. pap. 10.00 (ISBN 0-87423-013-6). Westburg.

Desai, S. K. Santha Rama Rau. (Indian Writers Ser.: Vol. Xiii). 1977. 8.50 (ISBN 0-89253-451-6). Ind-US Inc.

Desai, Santilal M., ed. see Patel, R. M.

Desai, Santosh N. Hinduism in Thai Life. 163p. 1980. 23.95x (ISBN 0-940500-66-3, Pub by Popular Prakashan India). Asia Bk Corp.

Desai, Sudha V. Social Life in Maharashtra Under the Peshwas. 220p. 1980. 29.95 (ISBN 0-940500-72-8). Asia Bk Corp.

Desai, T. The East India Company. 282p. 1984. text ed. 30.50x (ISBN 0-391-03218-6, Pub. by Kanak Pubns India). Humanities.

Desai, V. G., tr. see Desai, Mahadev.

Desai, V. G., tr. see Gandhi, M. K.

Desai, V. V., jt. auth. see Sharma, D. P.

Desai, Yogi A. Love Is an Awakening. Sarasohn, Lisa, ed. (Illus.). 40p. (Orig.). 1984. pap. 2.00 (ISBN 0-940258-14-5). Kripalu Pubns.

--The Wisdom of the Body. Sarasohn, Lisa, ed. (Illus.). 40p. (Orig.). 1984. pap. 2.00 (ISBN 0-940258-13-7). Kripalu Pubns.

--Working Miracles of Love: A Collection of Teachings. LC 85-50126. (Illus.). 184p. 1985. pap. text ed. 5.95 (ISBN 0-940258-15-3). Kripalu Pubns.

De Sainliens, Claude. The Elizabethan Home. LC 74-9894. 1930. 15.00 (ISBN 0-8414-3209-0). Folcroft.

De St. Cyr, Hugues. Poesies De Uc De Saint-Circ. Repr. of 1913 ed. 25.00 (ISBN 0-384-24870-5). Johnson Repr.

De St. Georges, Georges G. The Gentleman's Dictionary. LC 77-103247. 240p. 1983. Repr. of 1970 ed. lib. bdg. 39.95x (ISBN 0-89370-782-1). Borgo Pr.

De St. Jeor, Owanna. Bad Timing. LC 83-40425. 192p. 1984. 12.95 (ISBN 0-8027-0774-2). Walker & Co.

De Saint Arnaud, Michael H. NewSell. LC 84-18546. 215p. 1984. 50.00 (ISBN 0-932648-56-8). Boardroom.

De Saint-Arnold, Michael, jt. auth. see De Bone, Edward.

De Saint-Denys, Hervey. Dreams & How to Guide Them. Schatzman, Morton, ed. 174p. 1982. text ed. 13.50x (ISBN 0-7156-1584-X, Pub. by Duckworth England). Biblio Dist.

De Sainte-Beuve, Charles-Agustin. Oeuvres, 2 tomes, Tome II. Incl. Portraits Litteraires (Fin; Portraits de Femmes. (Bibl. de Pleiade). 1950. 24.95 (ISBN 0-685-36019-9). French & Eur.

De Sainte-Beuve, Charles-Augustin. Oeuvres, 2 tomes, Tome I. Incl. Premiers Lundis; Portraits Litteraires. (Bibl. de la Pleiade). 1950. 22.50 (ISBN 0-685-36018-0). French & Eur.

--Port-Royal, 3 tomes. 1953-1955. Set. 79.95 (ISBN 0-685-11502-X). French & Eur.

De Sainte Colombe, Paul. Grapho-Therapeutics: Pen & Pencil Therapy. 1966. pap. 8.95 (ISBN 0-87516-297-5). De Vorss.

De Saint-Evremond, Charles see Saint-Evremond, Charles De.

De Saint-Evremond, Charles S. The Letters of Saint Evremond. Hayward, John, ed. LC 72-83506. (Illus.). 436p. 1930. 27.50 (ISBN 0-405-08908-2). Ayer Co Pubs.

De Saint-Exupery, Antoine. Carnets. pap. 12.50 (ISBN 0-685-37086-0). French & Eur.

--Citadelle. 1965. 13.95 (ISBN 0-685-23936-5). French & Eur.

--Courrier Sud. (Coll. Soleil). 1956. 12.95 (ISBN 0-685-11118-0). French & Eur.

--Lettres a Sa Mere. pap. 4.95 (ISBN 0-685-37088-7). French & Eur.

--Lettres a un Otage. 76p. 1970. pap. 4.95 (ISBN 0-685-37087-9). French & Eur.

--Lettres de Jeunesse (1923-1931) pap. 4.95 (ISBN 0-685-37089-5). French & Eur.

De Saint Exupery, Antoine. The Little Prince. 10.95 (ISBN 0-89190-331-3, Pub. by Am Repr). Amereon Ltd.

De Saint-Exupery, Antoine. Oeuvres. (Bibl. de la Pleiade). 1953. 33.95 (ISBN 0-685-11436-8). French & Eur.

--Pages Choisies. pap. 8.50 (ISBN 0-685-37085-2). French & Eur.

--Petit Prince. (Illus., Fr.). 1946. pap. 1.50 (ISBN 0-685-11488-0). French & Eur.

--Petit Prince. (Fr.). (gr. 3-8). 10.95 (ISBN 0-685-28443-3). French & Eur.

--Petit Prince. (Illus., Fr.). pap. 1.95 (ISBN 0-685-20246-1). Schoenhof.

--Pilote De Guerre. (Coll. Soleil). (Illus., Fr.). 1953. 13.95 (ISBN 0-685-11494-5). French & Eur.

--Regulus vel Pueri soli Sapiunt: The Little Prince. Haury, Augusto, tr. from Fr. (Illus.). 96p. (Latin.). 1985. pap. 3.95 (ISBN 0-15-676300-1, Harv). HarBraceJ.

--Un Sens a la Vie. pap. 10.50 (ISBN 0-685-37090-9). French & Eur.

--Terre des Hommes. (Coll. Soleil). 1954. 13.50 (ISBN 0-685-11584-4). French & Eur.

--Terre des Hommes. (Documentation thematique). (Illus., Fr.). pap. 2.95 (ISBN 0-685-14081-4, 305). Larousse.

--Vol De Nuit. (Coll. Soleil). 1953. 13.50 (ISBN 0-685-11624-7). French & Eur.

De Saint-Exupery, Antoine see Saint-Exupery, Antoine De.

De Saint-Exupery, Antoine see Saint-Exupery, Antoine de.

De Saint-Exupery, Antoine see Saint-Exupery, Antoine De.

De Saint-Exupery, Antoine see Saint-Exupery, Antoine de.

De Saint-Foix, G., jt. auth. see De Wyzewa, T.

De Saint-Georges, Chevalier. Masters of the Violin. Banat, Gabriel, ed. 75.00 (ISBN 0-384-03183-8). Johnson Repr.

De Saint-Germain, C. Practical Astrology. LC 80-19738. 257p. 1980. Repr. of 1973 ed. lib. bdg. 15.90x (ISBN 0-89370-618-3). Borgo Pr.

--The Practice of Palmistry. 410p. 1973. pap. 6.95 (ISBN 0-87877-019-4, P-19). Newcastle Pub.

--The Practice of Palmistry for Professional Purposes. LC 80-23774. 416p. 1980. Repr. of 1973 ed. lib. bdg. 16.95x (ISBN 0-89370-619-1). Borgo Pr.

De Saint Phalle, Thibaut. Trade, Inflation, & the Dollar. (Illus.). 1981. 35.00x (ISBN 0-19-502970-4). Oxford U Pr.

--U. S. Productivity & Competitiveness in International Trade, Vol. II. LC 80-68434. (Significant Issues Ser.: No. 12). 134p. 1980. 5.95 (ISBN 0-89206-028-X). CSI Studies.

De St. Phalle, Thibaut, jt. ed. see Stirling, Catherine.

De Saint-Pierre, Bernardin see Peyrazat, Jean E.

De Saint-Pierre, Jacques H. Bernardin see Bernardin De Saint-Pierre, Jacques H.

De Saint Pierre, Michel. The New Priests. 209p. 1966. pap. 1.95 (ISBN 0-912414-18-9). Lumen Christi.

De Saint-Simon, Claude-Henri. Oeuvres Completes, 7 tomes. Set. write for info. (ISBN 0-685-34971-3). French & Eur.

De Saint-Val, Alix. Le Mage des Monts Noirs. (Collection Colombine Ser.). 192p. 1983. pap. 1.95 (ISBN 0-373-48085-7). Harlequin Bks.

De Saint-Victor, Niepce. Recherches Photographiques. Bunnell, Peter C. & Sobieszek, Robert A., eds. LC 76-23058. (Sources of Modern Photography Ser.). (Fr.). 1979. Repr. of 1855 ed. lib. bdg. 17.00x (ISBN 0-405-09622-4). Ayer Co Pubs.

Desaive, Jean-Paul, et al. Medecins, Climat & Epidemies a la Fin Du XVIIIe Siecle. (Civilisations & Societes: No. 29). (Illus.). 1972. pap. 21.60x (ISBN 90-2797-013-0). Mouton.

De Salazar, Francisco Cervantes see Cervantes De Salazar, Francisco.

De Sales, Francis. The Sermons of St. Francis de Sales on Prayer. Fiorelli, Lewis, ed. Visitation Nuns, tr. LC 84-52310. 51p. 1985. pap. 3.00 (ISBN 0-89555-258-2). Tan Bks Pubs.

De Sales, Saint Francoise. Treatise on the Love of God. Mackey, Henry B., tr. LC 71-156190. xiiv, 555p. Repr. of 1942 ed. lib. bdg. 31.50x (ISBN 0-8371-6139-8, FRLG). Greenwood.

De Sales, R. de Roussy see Roussy de Sales, R. de.

De Sales, Raoul De Roussy see Hitler, Adolph.

De Salignac De La Mothe, Francois, jt. auth. see Fenelon.

De Salignac de la Mothe-Fenelon, Francoise. Along the Royal Way. Helms, Hal M., ed. LC 83-61406. 152p. (Orig.). 1984. pap. 4.95 (ISBN 0-941478-20-3). Paraclete Pr.

De Salles, Frances. Doctor's Diet Cookbook. 5th ed. 1977. pap. 2.95 (ISBN 0-89596-213-6, Success). Merit Pubns.

--Weight Losers Diet Cookbook. 9th ed. 1974. pap. 1.25 (ISBN 0-89596-232-2, Basic Hlth). Merit Pubns.

De Saltinbene, Virginius. Thoughts in Contemplation of the Feminine Nude in the Realm of Art. (Illus.). 117p. 1984. 125.85x (ISBN 0-89266-441-X). Am Classical Coll Pr.

De Salvatierra, Juan M. Selected Letters about California. Burrus, Ernest J., tr. (Baja California Travel Ser.: No. 25). 280p. 1971. 30.00 (ISBN 0-87093-225-X). Dawsons.

De Salvio, Alfonso. Dante & Heresy. LC 73-2721. (Select Bibliographies Reprint Ser). 1973. Repr. of 1936 ed. 14.00 (ISBN 0-8369-7158-2). Ayer Co Pubs.

De Salvio, Alfonso, tr. see Galilei, Galileo.

DeSalvo, Jim. Poem: One Half off. LC 77-83888. 1977. saddlestitched 2.00 (ISBN 0-930460-66-9). Armchair Pr.

DeSalvo, John A., ed. see Adams, Frank O.

De Salvo, Louise. Virginia Woolf's "First Voyage". A Novel in the Making. 202p. 1980. 23.50x (ISBN 0-8476-6199-7). Rowman.

DeSalvo, Louise & Leaska, Mitchell A., eds. The Letters of Vita Sackville-West to Virginia Woolf. LC 84-60758. (Illus.). 400p. 1984. 17.95 (ISBN 0-688-03963-4). Morrow.

DeSalvo, Louise A., ed. see Woolf, Virginia.

Desan, W. The Marxism of Jean-Paul Sartre. 11.50 (ISBN 0-8446-1971-X). Peter Smith.

De Sanchez Hidalgo, Lydia see Sanchez Hidalgo, Efrain & Sanchez Hidalgo, Lydia.

De Sanctis, E., jt. ed. see Atti, C. Ciofi.

DeSanctis, Paul, jt. auth. see Atkinson, William.

De Sane, John W. Analogies & Black History: A Programmed Approach. 176p. 1983. write for info (ISBN 0-939296-03-9). Bond Pub Co.

De San Pedro, Diego see San Pedro, Diego de.

De Santa Ana, Julio. Towards a Church of the Poor. LC 80-25667. 210p. (Orig.). 1981. pap. 8.95 (ISBN 0-88344-502-6). Orbis Bks.

De Santa Ana, Julio, ed. Separation Without Hope? LC 80-12831. 198p. (Orig.). 1980. pap. 8.95 (ISBN 0-88344-456-9). Orbis Bks.

De Santes, Zerlina. Martin De Porres. write for info. Dghtrs St Paul.

De Santi, Roger. Trends & Issues of Diagnostic & Remedial Readings. LC 81-43680. 202p. (Orig.). 1982. lib. bdg. 26.00 (ISBN 0-8191-2219-X); pap. text ed. 12.25 (ISBN 0-8191-2220-3). U Pr of Amer.

De Santi, Roger J., ed. Teacher's Needs & Concerns Regarding Reading Instruction: Findings, Strategies, & Applications. LC 83-10219. 166p. (Orig.). 1983. lib. bdg. 22.50 (ISBN 0-8191-3365-5); pap. text ed. 11.00 (ISBN 0-8191-3366-3). U Pr of Amer.

De Santiago, Carmen R. El Desarrollo Constitucional De Puerto Rico: Documentos y Casos. 2nd ed. pap. 3.00 (ISBN 0-8477-2221-X). U of PR Pr.

De Santillana, George see Santillana, George De.

De Santillana, Giorgio. Reflections on Men & Ideas. 1968. pap. 8.95x (ISBN 0-262-54012-6). MIT Pr.

De Santillana, Giorgio & Von Dechend, Hertha. Hamlet's Mill. LC 69-13267. 505p. 1977. pap. 9.95 (ISBN 0-87923-215-3). Godine.

--Hamlet's Mill: An Essay on Myth & the Frame of Time. LC 69-13267. (Illus.). 1969. 15.00 (ISBN 0-87645-008-7, Pub. by Gambit). Harvard Common Pr.

De Santis, Daniel V., jt. auth. see Levin, Edward.

De Santis, Hugh. The Diplomacy of Silence: The American Foreign Service, the Soviet Union, & the Cold War 1933 to 1947. LC 80-16676. 1980. 23.00x (ISBN 0-226-14337-6). U of Chicago Pr.

--The Diplomacy of Silence: The American Foreign Service, the Soviet Union, & the Cold War, 1933-1947. LC 83-4935. 270p. 1983. pap. 9.95x (ISBN 0-226-14338-4). U of Chicago Pr.

DeSantis, Josephine. Grubby: The Absent Minded Gopher. (Illus.). 64p. (ps-6). 1981. 5.95 (ISBN 0-89962-226-7). Todd & Honeywell.

DeSantis, Kenny. A Doctor's Tools. (Illus.). 48p. (ps-1). 1985. PLB 9.95 (ISBN 0-396-08516-4); pap. 3.95 (ISBN 0-396-08739-6). Dodd.

De Santis, Marie. California Currents: An Exploration of the Ocean's Pleasures, Mysteries & Dilemmas. (Illus.). 248p. 1985. 15.95 (ISBN 0-89141-191-7). Presidio Pr.

DeSantis, Marie. Neptune's Apprentice: Adventures of a Pacific Fisherwoman. (Illus.). 248p. 1984. 15.95 (ISBN 0-89141-200-X). Presidio Pr.

De Santis, Vincent, compiled by. Gilded Age, Eighteen Seventy-Seven to Eighteen Ninety-Six. LC 72-96558. (Goldentree Bibliographies in American History Ser.). 168p. (Orig.). 1973. pap. 6.95x (ISBN 0-88295-536-5). Harlan Davidson.

De Santis, Vincent P. Republicans Face the Southern Question: The New Departure Years, 1877-1897. LC 78-64231. (Johns Hopkins University. Studies in the Social Sciences. Seventy-Seventh Ser. 1959: 1). Repr. of 1959 ed. 13.00 (ISBN 0-404-61336-5). AMS Pr.

DeSantis, Vincent P. Republicans Face the Southern Question: The New Departure Years, 1877-1897. LC 69-13880. Repr. of 1959 ed. lib. bdg. 15.00x (ISBN 0-8371-1059-9, DERS). Greenwood.

--The Shaping of Modern America: Eighteen Seventy-Seven to Nineteen Sixteen. 1973. pap. text ed. 13.95x (ISBN 0-88273-110-6). Forum Pr IL.

De Santis, Zerlina. Castle Days & Gallant Knights. (ps-3). 1.75 (ISBN 0-8198-0194-1); pap. 1.00 (ISBN 0-8198-0195-X). Dghtrs St Paul.

--A Child's Story of Ancient Days. (Illus.). (ps-3). 1.75 (ISBN 0-8198-1410-5). Dghtrs St Paul.

--A Child's Story of Early Explorers. 1981. pap. 1.00 (ISBN 0-8198-1411-3). Dghtrs St Paul.

--A Child's Story of Saints, Past & Present. 1979. 1.75 (ISBN 0-8198-0567-X); pap. 1.00 (ISBN 0-8198-0568-8). Dghtrs St Paul.

--A Child's Story of the Baby Who Changed the World. (Illus.). (ps-3). 1.75 (ISBN 0-8198-0191-7). Dghtrs St Paul.

--Journeys with Mary. (Encounter Ser.). 155p. (gr. 4 up). 1982. 3.00 (ISBN 0-8198-3900-0, EN0165); pap. 2.00 (ISBN 0-8198-3910-8). Dghtrs St Paul.

DeSanto, et al. Statistics Through Problem Solving. 2nd ed. Avenoso, Frank & Cheifetz, Philip, eds. LC 73-77244. (gr. 9-12). 1978. pap. text ed. 16.50X (ISBN 0-916060-04-7). Math Alternatives.

De Santo, Charles. Dear Tim. LC 81-23744. 200p. (Orig.). 1982. pap. 7.95 (ISBN 0-8361-1991-6). Herald Pr.

De Santo, Charles P. Love & Sex Are Not Enough. LC 76-45731. 168p. 1977. pap. 3.95 (ISBN 0-8361-1809-X); Student Activity Bk. (48 p.) 1.25 (ISBN 0-8361-1865-0). Herald Pr.

DeSanto, J. A., ed. Ocean Acoustics. (Topics in Current Physics: Vol. 8). (Illus.). 1979. 46.00 (ISBN 0-387-09148-3). Springer-Verlag.

De Santo, R. S. Concepts of Applied Ecology. (Heidelberg Science Library). 1978. pap. 19.50 (ISBN 0-387-90301-1). Springer-Verlag.

De Santos Otero, Aurelio see Santos Otero, Aurelio De.

De Sapio, Rodolfo. Calculus for the Life Sciences. LC 77-21312. (Illus.). 740p. 1978. text ed. 29.95x (ISBN 0-7167-0371-8). W H Freeman.

Desarigny, Rudi. How to Make & Design Stuffed Toys. 16.50 (ISBN 0-8446-5668-2). Peter Smith.

DeSario, Jack & Langton, Stuart, eds. Symposium on Citizen Participation & Public Policy. (Orig.). 1984. pap. 8.00 (ISBN 0-918592-65-8). Policy Studies.

De Sarlo, Carmine R. TV Commercial Film Editing: Professional Motion Picture Pre-& Post-Production Including Animation, Rotoscoping, & Video Tape. LC 84-43231. 250p. 1985. pap. 29.95 (ISBN 0-89950-174-5). McFarland & Co.

Desarnis, Anna M., et al. Appleton's Review of Nursing for the New State Board Examination. 2nd ed. 464p. 1985. pap. write for info. (ISBN 0-8385-0207-5). ACC.

Desatnick, Robert L. The Business of Human Resource Management: A Guide for the Results Oriented Executive. LC 83-10241. 249p. 1983. 26.95x (ISBN 0-471-89172-X). Wiley.

Desatnick, Robert L. & Bennett, Margo L. Human Resource Management in the Multinational Company. LC 77-15803. 350p. 1978. 25.00x (ISBN 0-89397-031-X). Nichols Pub.

De Satnick, Shelly. Bridge for Everyone: A Step by Step Text & Workbook. 144p. 1982. pap. 9.95 (ISBN 0-380-81083-2, 89504-8). Avon.

--Everyone's Introduction to Bridge Conventions. 144p. (Orig.). 1984. pap. 6.95 (ISBN 0-380-89318-5). Avon.

DeSaulniers, Lawrence B. The Response in American Catholic Periodicals to the Crises of the Great Depression, 1930-1935. LC 83-23603. 198p. (Orig.). 1984. lib. bdg. 22.25 (ISBN 0-8191-3786-3); pap. text ed. 11.50 (ISBN 0-8191-3787-1). U Pr of Amer.

De Saunders, J. B. see O'Malley, Charles D. & Saunders, J. B. de.

De Saunders, J. B. see Saunders, J. B. de & O'Malley, C. D.

De Sausmarez, Maurice. Basic Design. 96p. 1982. 30.00x (ISBN 0-906969-22-0, Pub. by Benn Pubns). State Mutual Bk.

De Saussure, Ferdinand. Course in General Linguistics. Baskin, Wade, tr. 1966. pap. 6.95 (ISBN 0-07-016524-6). McGraw.

--Grundfragen der allgemeinen Sprachwissenschaft. 2nd ed. Bally, Charles & Sechehaye, Riedlinger, eds. Lommel, Herman, tr. xvi, 294p. (Ger.). 1983. pap. 10.40x (ISBN 3-11-000158-6). De Gruyter.

DeSautel, Madeline, tr. see Mattina, Anthony.

Desautels, Edouard J. Assembly Language Programming for PDP-11 & LSI-11 Computers: An Introduction to Computer Organization. 574p. 1982. pap. 23.95 (ISBN 0-697-08164-8); solutions manual avail. (ISBN 0-697-08165-6). Wm C Brown.

--Lotus 1-2-3 for the IBM Personal Computer & XT. (Microcomputer Power Ser.). 288p. 1984. pap. 16.95 (ISBN 0-697-09997-0); incl. disk 29.95 (ISBN 0-697-00337-X). Wm C Brown.

--Lotus 1-2-3 for the TI Professional Computer. 272p. 1984. 17.95 (ISBN 0-697-00377-9); incl. diskette o.p. 29.95 (ISBN 0-317-05722-7). Wm C Brown.

--SuperCalc for the Apple II Plus & IIe. (Microcomputer Power Ser.). 160p. 1983. 16.95 (ISBN 0-697-09920-2); incl. disk 32.95 (ISBN 0-697-09940-7). Wm C Brown.

--Symphony for the IBM Personal Computer & Compatible Computers. (Micropower Ser.). 200p. 1985. pap. 17.95 (ISBN 0-697-00600-X). Wm C Brown.

--VisiCalc for the Apple II Plus & IIe Computers. (Microcomputer Power Ser.). 164p. 1982. plastic comb 16.95 (ISBN 0-697-00345-0); deluxe ed. bk. & Diskette 27.95 (ISBN 0-697-00329-9). Wm C Brown.

--VisiCalc for the IBM Personal Computer. (Microcomputer Power Ser.). 156p. 1982. plastic comb 16.95 (ISBN 0-697-00344-2); deluxe ed. bk. & diskette 27.95 (ISBN 0-697-00327-2). Wm C Brown.

--VisiCalc for the TRS-80 Model III & IV Computers. (Micropower Ser.). 152p. 1982. plastic comb 16.95 (ISBN 0-697-00343-4); deluxe ed. bk. & diskette 27.95 (ISBN 0-697-00328-0). WM C Brown.

Desautels, Edouard J. & Laric, Michael V. SuperCalc for the IBM Personal Computer: Microcomputer Power Ser. 160p. 1983. plastic comb. 17.95 (ISBN 0-697-09930-X); incl. disk 29.95 (ISBN 0-697-00138-5). Wm C Brown.

Desautels, Joseph. Manuel des cures pour le bon Gouvernement Temporel Des Paroisses et des Fabriques dans le Bas-Canada. 1864. 24.00 (ISBN 0-384-11480-6). Johnson Repr.

--Manuel Des Cures Pour le Bon Gouvernement Temporel Des Paroisses et Des Fabriques Dans le Bas-Canada. (Canadiana Avant 1867: No. 10). 1968. 20.00x (ISBN 90-2796-335-5). Mouton.

Desautels, Paul E. The Gem Collection. new ed. LC 79-16475. (The Treasures in the Smithsonian Ser.: No. 1). (Illus.). 77p. 1980. 12.50 (ISBN 0-87474-360-5); pap. 8.95 (ISBN 0-87474-361-3). Smithsonian.

--Rocks & Minerals. LC 73-91134. (Collector's Series: No. 1). (Illus.). 160p. 1982. 3.95 (ISBN 0-448-04088-3, G&D). Putnam Pub Group.

de Sauvigny, G. de Bertier see De Bertier de Sauvigny, G. & Pinkney, David H.

De Sauvigny Guillaume De, Bertier see De Bertier De Sauvigny, Guillaume.

Desbarats, Peter. Gabrielle & Selena. LC 73-14661. (Illus.). 32p. (gr. k-3). 1974. pap. 0.95 (ISBN 0-15-634080-1, AVB87, VoyB). HarBraceJ.

Desbazielle, G., jt. auth. see Kaufman, A.

Desbiens, Jean P. For Pity's Sake. LC 65-28218. (French Canadian Renaissance Ser.). pap. 33.50 (ISBN 0-317-28413-4, 202292). Bks Demand UMI.

--The Impertinences of Brother Anonymous. LC 62-14443. (French Canadian Renaissance Ser.: Vol. 2). pap. 31.50 (ISBN 0-317-28410-X, 2022291). Bks Demand UMI.

Desboulmiers, Jean A. Histoire du theatre de l'Opera comique, 2 vols. 2nd ed. LC 76-43914. (Music & Theatre in France in the 17th & 18th Centuries Ser.). Repr. of 1770 ed. 97.50 (ISBN 0-404-60160-X). AMS Pr.

Desbrandes, R., jt. auth. see Ketchian, S.

Desbrandes, Robert. Encyclopedia of Well Logging. LC 85-70854. (Illus.). 450p. 1985. 79.95x (ISBN 0-87201-249-2). Gulf Pub.

Descarries, Laurent, et al. Monoamine Innervation of Cerebral Cortex. LC 84-10015. (Neurology & Neurobiology Ser.: Vol. 10). 376p. 1984. 68.00 (ISBN 0-8451-2711-X). A R Liss.

Des Cars, Guy. Amour de Ma Vie. 352p. 1956. 14.95 (ISBN 0-686-55605-4). French & Eur.

--Amour de Ma Vie. 320p. 1973. pap. 3.95 (ISBN 0-686-55606-2). French & Eur.

--L' Amour s'en va-t-en Guerre. 256p. 1953. 14.95 (ISBN 0-686-55607-0). French & Eur.

--L' Amour s'en va-t-en Guerre. 1978. pap. 3.95 (ISBN 0-686-55608-9). French & Eur.

--Le Boulevard des Illusions. 254p. 1966. 8.95 (ISBN 0-686-55609-7). French & Eur.

--La Brute. 304p. 1951. 10.95 (ISBN 0-686-55610-0). French & Eur.

--La Brute. 448p. 1960. pap. 3.95 (ISBN 0-686-55611-9). French & Eur.

--La Cathedrale De Haine. 280p. 1969. 9.95 (ISBN 0-686-55612-7). French & Eur.

--La Cathedrale De Haine. 320p. 1969. pap. 3.95 (ISBN 0-686-55613-5). French & Eur.

--Une Certaine Dame. 392p. 1971. 17.95 (ISBN 0-686-55614-3). French & Eur.

--Une Certaine Dame. 1978. pap. 4.95 (ISBN 0-686-55615-1). French & Eur.

--Cette Etrange Tendresse. 336p. 1960. 9.95 (ISBN 0-686-55616-X). French & Eur.

--Cette Etrange Tendresse. 320p. 1968. pap. 3.95 (ISBN 0-686-55617-8). French & Eur.

--Le Chateau De la Juive. 384p. 1958. 11.95 (ISBN 0-686-55618-6). French & Eur.

--Le Chateau de la Juive. 384p. 1966. pap. 4.50 (ISBN 0-686-55619-4). French & Eur.

--Le Chateau Du Clown. 349p. 1977. 16.95 (ISBN 0-686-55620-8). French & Eur.

--La Corruptrice. 272p. 1952. 11.95 (ISBN 0-686-55621-6). French & Eur.

--La Corruptrice. 384p. 1965. pap. 3.95 (ISBN 0-686-55622-4). French & Eur.

--La Dame Du Cirque. 256p. 1962. 9.95 (ISBN 0-686-55623-2). French & Eur.

--La Dame Du Cirque. 320p. 1968. pap. 3.95 (ISBN 0-686-55624-0). French & Eur.

--De Cape et de Plume. 520p. 1965. 15.95 (ISBN 0-686-55625-9). French & Eur.

--La Demoiselle d'Opera. 1953. 9.95 (ISBN 0-686-55626-7); pap. 3.95 (ISBN 0-686-55627-5). French & Eur.

--Le Donneur. 288p. 1973. 16.95 (ISBN 0-686-55628-3); pap. 3.95 (ISBN 0-686-55629-1). French & Eur.

--L' Entremetteuse. 384p. 1970. 11.95 (ISBN 0-686-55630-5); pap. 4.95 (ISBN 0-686-55631-3). French & Eur.

--L' Envouteuse. 416p. 1975. 22.50 (ISBN 0-686-55632-1). French & Eur.

--Un Faussaire. 9.95 (ISBN 0-686-55633-X); pap. 4.95 (ISBN 0-686-55634-8). French & Eur.

--Les Filles De Joie. 320p. 1967. 3.95 (ISBN 0-686-55635-6). French & Eur.

--Le Grand Monde. 624p. 1961. 17.95 (ISBN 0-686-55636-4). French & Eur.

--Le Grand Monde, Vol. 1: L'Alliee. 320p. 1972. 3.95 (ISBN 0-686-55637-2). French & Eur.

--Le Grand Monde, Vol. 2: La Trahison. 320p. 1972. 3.95 (ISBN 0-686-55638-0). French & Eur.

--L' Habitude d'Amour. 320p. 1966. 12.95 (ISBN 0-686-55639-9); pap. 3.95 (ISBN 0-686-55640-2). French & Eur.

--J'ose. 304p. 1974. 11.95 (ISBN 0-686-55645-3). French & Eur.

--La Justiciere. 1978. 15.95 (ISBN 0-686-55646-1). French & Eur.

--Louis II de Baviere du le Roi Foucroye: Documents hors Texte. 318p. 1975. 19.95 (ISBN 0-686-55647-X). French & Eur.

--Louis II de Baviere du le Roi Foucroye. 3.95 (ISBN 0-686-55666-6). French & Eur.

--Le Mage et les Signes De la Main. 240p. 1976. 10.95 (ISBN 0-686-55650-X). French & Eur.

--Le Mage: La Boule De Cristal, Vol. 1. 190p. 1974. 6.95 (ISBN 0-686-55648-8). French & Eur.

--La Maudite. 284p. 1970. 11.95 (ISBN 0-686-55651-8); pap. 3.95 (ISBN 0-686-55652-6). French & Eur.

--L' Officier Sans Nom. 200p. 1965. 7.95 (ISBN 0-686-55653-4); pap. 3.95 (ISBN 0-686-55654-2). French & Eur.

--La Revoltee. 314p. 1968. 15.95 (ISBN 0-686-55655-0); pap. 4.50 (ISBN 0-686-55656-9). French & Eur.

--Sang d'Afrique. 408p. 1963. 14.95 (ISBN 0-686-55657-7). French & Eur.

--Sang d'Afrique: L'Africain, Vol. 1. 1971. 3.95 (ISBN 0-686-55658-5). French & Eur.
--Sang d'Afrique: L'Amoureuse, Vol. 2. 1971. 3.95 (ISBN 0-686-55659-3). French & Eur.
--Les Sept Femmes. 384p. 1970. 3.95 (ISBN 0-686-55660-7). French & Eur.
--Toni, Roi du Cirque. (Illus.). 24p. 1977. 12.95 (ISBN 0-686-55661-5). French & Eur.
--La Tricheuse. 288p. 1957. 14.95 (ISBN 0-686-55662-3); pap. 3.95 (ISBN 0-686-55663-1). French & Eur.
--La Vie Secrete De Dorothee Gindt. 1973. 14.95 (ISBN 0-686-55664-X). French & Eur.
--La Vipere. 362p. 1969. 16.95 (ISBN 0-686-55665-8). French & Eur.
Des Cars, Guys. L' Impure. 344p. 1946. 16.95 (ISBN 0-686-55641-0); pap. 3.95 (ISBN 0-686-55642-9). French & Eur.
Descartes, et al. The Philosophical Writings. Cottingham, John & Murdoch, Dugald, trs. 456p. 1985. Vol. 1. 44.50 (ISBN 0-521-24594-X); Vol. 2. pap. 12.95 (ISBN 0-521-28807-X); 44.50 (ISBN 0-521-24595-8); pap. 12.95 (ISBN 0-521-28808-8). Cambridge U Pr.
Descartes, Rene. Descartes le Monde. Mahoney, Michael, tr. LC 77-86236. 1978. 20.00 (ISBN 0-913870-35-8). Abaris Bks.
--Discours De la Methode. (Illus.). 1965. pap. 4.50 (ISBN 0-685-11145-8). French & Eur.
--Discours de la methode. (Documentation thematique). (Illus., Fr.). pap. 2.95 (ISBN 0-685-13889-5, 80). Larousse.
--Discours de la Methode: Avec: Extraits de la Dioptrique, des Meteores, du Mond, de Homme, de Lettres et de la Vie de Descartes par Baillet. 254p. 1966. 4.50 (ISBN 0-686-55669-0). French & Eur.
--Discourse on Method. 2nd ed. Lafleur, Laurence J., tr. LC 60-13395. (Orig.). 1956. pap. 3.56 scp (ISBN 0-672-60180-X, LLA19). Bobbs.
--Discourse on Method. Cress, Donald A., tr. from Fr. Bd. with Meditations on First Philosophy. LC 80-10809. 120p. 1980. lib. bdg. 15.00 (ISBN 0-915144-85-9); pap. text ed. 4.25 (ISBN 0-915144-84-0). Hackett Pub.
--Discourse on Method. Cress, Donald A., ed. & tr. LC 79-28579. 64p. 1980. pap. text ed. 2.45 (ISBN 0-915144-83-2). Hackett Pub.
--Discourse on Method. Veitch, John, tr. from Fr. 93p. 1962. 12.00 (ISBN 0-87548-008-X); pap. 3.95 (ISBN 0-87548-009-8). Open Court.
--Discourse on Method & Meditations. Lafleur, Laurence J., tr. LC 60-13395. 1960. pap. 5.44 scp (ISBN 0-672-60278-4, LLA 89). Bobbs.
--Discourse on Method & Other Writings. Wollaston, tr. (Classics Ser.). (Orig.). 1968. pap. 3.95 (ISBN 0-14-044206-5). Penguin.
--Discourse on Method: Meditations on a First Philosophy, & Principles of Philosophy. 1975. 12.95x (ISBN 0-460-00570-7, Evman); pap. 3.50x (ISBN 0-460-01570-2, Evman). Biblio Dist.
--La Geometrie. (Illus.). 96p. 5.95 (ISBN 0-686-55671-2). French & Eur.
--La Geometrie. Smith, David E. & Latham, Marcia L., trs. from Fr. & Lat. (Illus.). xiii, 259p. 1952. 7.95 (ISBN 0-87548-168-X). Open Court.
--Geometry. (Eng. & Fr.). 1925. pap. 4.50 (ISBN 0-486-60068-8). Dover.
--Lettres. 2nd ed. 248p. 1964. 12.95 (ISBN 0-686-55672-0). French & Eur.
--Lettres a Regius et Remarques sur l'Explication de l'Esprit Humain. 216p. 1959. 15.00 (ISBN 0-686-55673-9). French & Eur.
--Meditations Metaphysiques. 7th ed. 320p. 1974. 12.95 (ISBN 0-686-55675-5). French & Eur.
--Meditations Methaphysiques. (Documentation Thematique Ser.). pap. 2.95 (ISBN 0-685-13987-5, 82). Larousse.
--Meditations of Descartes. Veitch, John, tr. from Fr. & Lat. xxxii, 290p. 1966. 4.95 (ISBN 0-87548-042-X). Open Court.
--Meditations on First Philosophy. 2nd ed. Lafleur, Laurence J., tr. 1960. pap. 4.24 scp (ISBN 0-672-60191-5, LLA29). Bobbs.
--Meditations on First Philosophy. Cress, Donald A., tr. from Lat. LC 78-78213. 76p. 1979. pap. text ed. 1.95 (ISBN 0-915144-57-3). Hackett Pub.
--Meditations on First Philosophy. Rubin, Ronald, tr. from Latin. 50p. (Orig.). 1984. pap. text ed. 3.50 (ISBN 0-941736-10-5). Arete Pr.
--Oeuvres, 11 tomes. Adam & Tannery, eds. Incl. Tome I. Correspondance (Avril 1622-Fevrier 1638) 36.95 (ISBN 0-685-34212-3); Tome II. Correspondance (Mars 1638 - Decembre 1639) 32.95 (ISBN 0-685-34213-1); Tome III. Correspondance (Janvier 1640-Juin 1643) 37.95 (ISBN 0-685-34214-X); Tome IV. Correspondance (Juillet 1643-Avril 1647) 37.95 (ISBN 0-685-34215-8); Tome V. Correspondance (Mai 1647 - Fevrier 1650) 36.95 (ISBN 0-685-34216-6); Tome VI. Discours de la Methode et Essais. 32.95 (ISBN 0-685-34217-4); Tome VII. Meditationes de Prima Philosophia. 27.95 (ISBN 0-685-34218-2); Tome VIII, Pt. 1. Principia Philosophiae. 15.95 (ISBN 0-685-34219-0); Tome VIII, Pt. 2. Epistola ad Voetium, Lettre Apologetique, Notas in Programma. 20.95 (ISBN 0-685-34220-4); Tome IX, Pt. 1. Meditations. 12.95 (ISBN 0-685-34221-2); Tome IX, Pt. 2. Principes. 14.95 (ISBN 0-685-34222-0); Tome X. Physico-Mathematica, Compendium Musicae, Regulea ad Directionem Ingenii, Recherche de la Verite, Supplement a la Correspondance. 37.95 (ISBN 0-685-34223-9); Tome XI. Le Monde, Description du Corps Humain, Passions de l'Ame, Anatomica, Varia. 37.95 (ISBN 0-685-34224-7). French & Eur.
--Oeuvres et Lettres: Avec: Discours de la Methode. 1424p. 1937. 42.95 (ISBN 0-686-55676-3). French & Eur.
--Oeuvres Philosophiques, 3 vols. Alquie, Ferdinand, ed. Incl. Vol. 1. 1618-1637. 1963. 18.50 (ISBN 0-686-57384-6); Vol. 2. 1638-1642. 1975. 22.50 (ISBN 0-686-57385-4); Vol. 3. 1643-1650. 1973. 37.50 (ISBN 0-686-57386-2). French & Eur.
--Les Passions de l'Ame. 1970. 3.95 (ISBN 0-686-55677-1). French & Eur.
--Philosophical Essays: Discourse on Method; Meditations; Rules for the Direction of the Mind. Lafleur, Laurence J., tr. LC 63-16951. (Orig.). 1964. pap. 7.87 scp (ISBN 0-672-60292-X, LLA99). Bobbs.
--Philosophical Letters. Kenny, Anthony, ed. & tr. LC 81-3431. 287p. 1981. pap. 10.95x (ISBN 0-8166-1060-6). U of Minn Pr.
--Philosophical Works, 2 Vols. Haldane, E. S. & Ross, G. R., eds. 1967. Vol. 1. 54.50 (ISBN 0-521-06943-2); Vol. 2. 54.50 (ISBN 0-521-06944-0); Vol. 1. pap. 13.95 (ISBN 0-521-09416-X); Vol. 2. pap. 13.95 (ISBN 0-521-09417-8). Cambridge U Pr.
--Philosophical Writings. Anscombe, Elizabeth & Geach, Peter T., eds. Anscombe, Elizabeth & Geach, Peter T., trs. LC 79-171798. 1971. pap. 7.20 scp (ISBN 0-672-61274-7, LLA198). Bobbs.
--Principes de la Philosophie, Vol. 1. 3rd ed. 158p. 1970. 9.95 (ISBN 0-686-55678-X). French & Eur.
--Principles of Philosophy. Miller, Reese P. & Miller, Valentine R., trs. 1983. lib. bdg. 59.00 (ISBN 0-686-37924-1, Pub by Reidel Holland). Kluwer Academic.
--Principles of Philosophy. Miller, Valentine R. & Miller, Resse P., trs. (Orig.). 1984. pap. text ed. 19.50 (ISBN 90-277-1754-0, Pub. by Reidel Holland). Kluwer Academic.
--Regles pour la Direction de l'Esprit. 152p. 1966. 9.95 (ISBN 0-686-55679-8). French & Eur.
--Regles Utiles et Claires Pour la Direction De L'Esprit et la Recherche De la Verite. (Archives Internationales D'Histoire Des Idees: No. 88). 1977. lib. bdg. 60.50 (ISBN 90-247-1907-0, Pub. by Martinus Nijhoff Netherlands). Kluwer Academic.
--Treatise of Man. Hall, Thomas S., tr. & commentary by. LC 76-173412. (Monographs in the History of Science Ser). (Illus., Fr. & Eng.). 1972. 15.00x (ISBN 0-674-90710-8). Harvard U Pr.
Descartes, Rene & Adam, Charles. Entretiens Avec Burman: Manuscrit de Gottingen. 2nd ed. 160p. 1975. 13.50 (ISBN 0-686-55670-4). French & Eur.
Descartes, Rene & Lewis, G. Meditationes, de Prima Philosophia: Meditations Metaphysiques. 178p. (Fr. & Lat.). 1967. 13.00 (ISBN 0-686-55674-7). French & Eur.
Descartes, Rene & Robinet, Andre. Cogito 75: Meditations Metaphysiques. 156p. 1976. 19.95 (ISBN 0-686-55667-4). French & Eur.
Descartes, Rene & Ross, G. R. The Philosophical Works of Descartes, Vol. 1. Haldane, Elizabeth S., ed. pap. 115.00 (ISBN 0-317-20587-0, 2024470). Bks Demand UMI.
Descartes, Rene, et al. The Rationalists: Five Basic Works on Rationalism. Incl. Discourse on Method. Descartes, Rene; Meditations. Descartes, Rene; Ethics. Spinoza, Benedict; Monadology. Liebniz, Gottfried W; Discourse on Metaphysics. Liebniz, Gottfried W. 1960. pap. 6.95 (ISBN 0-385-09540-6, Anch). Doubleday.
Descartes, S. L. Credit Institutions for Local Authorities in Latin America. LC 73-75403. 81p. 1973. pap. 1.50 (ISBN 0-913480-16-9). Inter Am U Pr.
Descartes, Sol L. Puerto Rico: Trasfondo de su Economia. LC 73-84204. 50p. (Sp.). 1973. pap. 1.95 (ISBN 0-913480-14-2). Inter Am U Pr.
Desch, H. E. Structural Surveying. 269p. 1970. 33.95 (ISBN 0-85264-167-2, Pub. by Griffin England). State Mutual Bk.
--Timber: Its Structure, Properties & Utilization. 6th ed. 416p. (Orig.). 1980. pap. text ed. 24.95x (ISBN 0-917304-62-4). Timber.
Desch, Samuel, tr. see Landa, L. N.
DesChamps, D. J. Why Pascal? 125p. 1984. pap. cancelled (ISBN 0-88056-302-8). Dilithium Pr.
Deschamps, Eustache. Oeuvres Completes, 11 Vols. 1878-1903. Set. 365.00 (ISBN 0-384-11491-1); pap. 28.00 ea.; Set. pap. 300.00 (ISBN 0-384-11490-3). Johnson Repr.
Deschamps, Fanny. The King's Garden. Frenaye, Frances & Wolf, Patricia, trs. LC 84-3804. 768p. 1985. 18.95 (ISBN 0-517-55085-7, Harmony). Crown.
Deschamps, Marion. French Home Cooking. 192p. 1986. pap. 3.50 (ISBN 0-345-32893-0). Ballantine.
Deschamps, Pierre. Dictionnaire de Geographie Ancienne et Moderne. 2nd ed. 1008p. (Fr.). 1965. 85.00 (ISBN 0-686-56814-1, M-6592). French & Eur.
Descharnes, Robert. Dali. LC 74-4257. (Library of Great Painters Ser.). (Illus.). 176p. 1976. 40.00 (ISBN 0-8109-0222-2). Abrams.
--Dali. (Master of Art Ser.). (Illus.). 128p. 1985. 19.95 (ISBN 0-8109-0830-1). Abrams.
--Dali: The Work, the Man. Morse, Eleanor R., tr. from Fr. (Illus.). 456p. 1984. 145.00 (ISBN 0-8109-0825-5). Abrams.
De Schauensee, Max. The Collector's Verdi & Puccini. LC 77-28264. (Keystone Books in Music Ser.: No. KB 46). 1978. Repr. of 1962 ed. lib. bdg. 16.00x (ISBN 0-313-20241-9, SCCV). Greenwood.
De Schauensee, Raadolphe M. & Phelps, William H., Jr. A Guide to the Birds of Venezuela. LC 76-45903. (Illus.). 1977. 70.00x (ISBN 0-691-08188-3); pap. 27.50 (ISBN 0-691-08205-7). Princeton U Pr.
De Schauensee, Rodolphe M. The Birds of China. Brown, Eleanor D., ed. LC 83-10314. (Illus.). 602p. 1984. 45.00 (ISBN 0-87474-362-1); pap. 29.95 (ISBN 0-87474-363-X). Smithsonian.
Deschenes, Jules, jt. auth. see Shetreet, Shimon.
De Schepper, Luc. Acupucture for the Practitioner. LC 85-90075. (Medical Sciences, General Medicine Ser.). (Illus.). 220p. (Orig.). 1985. 39.95 (ISBN 0-9614734-0-1). LDS Pubns.
DeScherer, Mildred, ed. Directory of Natural Science Centers 1984. (Illus.). 1985. pap. 15.00 spiral bd. (ISBN 0-317-20046-1). Natural Sci Youth.
DeSchill, Stefan. Introduction to Psychoanalytic Group Therapy. 6th, rev. ed. text ed. write for info. Am Mental Health Found.
DeSchill, Stefan & LaHullier, Denise. The Practice of Mental Health Groups: Increased Effectiveness in Psychoanalysis Translated into an Intensive, Low-Cost Treatment Method. write for info. Am Mental Health Found.
De Schill, Stefan, ed. The Challenge for Group Psychotherapy: Present & Future. LC 73-19952. 366p. (Orig.). 1974. text ed. 35.00 (ISBN 0-8236-0710-0). Intl Univs Pr.
Deschin, Celia. The Teenager in a Drugged Society. LC 72-190581. (Personal Guidance, Social Adjustment Ser). (gr. 7 up). 1972. PLB 8.97 (ISBN 0-8239-0226-9). Rosen Group.
Deschner, Donald. The Films of Cary Grant. LC 73-84151. (Illus.). 288p. 1983. pap. 9.95 (ISBN 0-8065-0376-9). Citadel Pr.
--The Films of Spencer Tracy. 1972. 8.95 (ISBN 0-8065-0017-4, C341); pap. 7.95 (ISBN 0-8065-0272-X). Citadel Pr.
--Films of W. C. Fields. (Illus.). 12.00 (ISBN 0-8065-0374-2); pap. 7.95 (ISBN 0-8065-0143-X). Citadel Pr.
Deschner, Gunther. Reinhard Heydrich: A Biography. Bance, Sandra & Woods, Brenda, trs. LC 80-6263. (Illus.). 340p. 1981. 18.95 (ISBN 0-8128-2809-7). Stein & Day.
Deschner, Jeanne P. The Hitting Habit: Anger Control for Battering Couples. LC 83-48413. 18.95 (ISBN 0-02-907780-X). Free Pr.
Deschner, John. Wesley's Christology: An Interpretation. 244p. 12.95 (ISBN 0-317-28507-6). SMU Press.
Deschner, Whit. Does the Wet Suit You? The Confessions of a Kayak Bum. LC 80-70510. (Illus.). 96p. 1981. pap. 6.45 (ISBN 0-9605388-0-1). Tern Pr.
De Schonen, Scania. La Memoire: Connaissance Active du Passe. LC 73-86214. (Connaissance et Language Ser: No. 3). 335p. (Fr.). 1975. pap. text ed. 28.40x (ISBN 90-2797-606-6). Mouton.
De Schutter, J., ed. see International Workshop on Appropriate Tech., Delft Univ. of Technology, Sept. 4-7, 1979.
De Schutter, R. Le Financement Interne au Congo Belge. (Economies et Societes Series F: No. 6). 1957. pap. 11.00 (ISBN 0-317-16833-9). Kraus Repr.
De Schweinitz, Edmund. Life & Times of David Zeisberger the Western Pioneer & Apostle of the Indians. LC 70-146391. (First American Frontier Ser). 1971. Repr. of 1870 ed. 39.00 (ISBN 0-405-02844-X). Ayer Co Pubs.
De Schweinitz, Edmund A. The Life & Times of David Zeisberger, the Western Pioneer & Apostle of the Indians. 1971. Repr. of 1870 ed. 50.00 (ISBN 0-384-11515-2). Johnson Repr.
De Schweinitz, K. see Schweintz, K. de, Jr.
Des Cilleuls, Alfred. Histoire et Regime De la Grande Industrie En France Au 17e et 18e Siecles. LC 70-126407. (Research & Source Works: No. 5). 1970. Repr. of 1898 ed. lib. bdg. 25.00 (ISBN 0-8337-0575-X). B Franklin.
Desclot, Bernardo. Chronicle of the Reign of King Pedro III of Aragon, 2 vols. Critchlow, F. L., tr. from Catalan. LC 79-8360. Repr. of 1928 ed. Set. 75.00 (ISBN 0-404-18340-9). AMS Pr.
Descloux, J. & Marti, J. T., eds. Numerical Analysis. (International Series of Numerical Mathematics: No. 37). 248p. 1977. pap. 37.95x (ISBN 0-8176-0939-3). Birkhauser.
Des Cognets, Louis, Jr. English Duplicates of Lost Virginia Records. LC 80-85117. 380p. 1981. Repr. of 1958 ed. 17.50 (ISBN 0-8063-0929-6). Genealog Pub.
Descola, Jean. Conquistadors. Barnes, Malcolm, tr. LC 72-122060. Repr. of 1957 ed. lib. bdg. 35.00x (ISBN 0-678-03151-7). Kelley.
Descombes, Vincent. Modern French Philosophy. Scott-Fox, L. & Harding, J. M., trs. 240p. 1981. 39.50 (ISBN 0-521-22837-9); pap. 13.95 (ISBN 0-521-29672-2). Cambridge U Pr.
Descotes, Maurice. Histoire de la Critique Dramatique en France. (Etudes Litteraires Francaise Ser.: No. 14). 407p. (Orig., Fr.). 1980. pap. 36.00x (ISBN 3-87808-893-0). Benjamins North Am.
D'Escoto, Miguel, tr. see Frei, Eduardo.
D'Escouchy, Mathieu. Chronique De Mathieu D'Escouchy, 3 Vols. 1863-1864. Set. 128.00 (ISBN 0-384-14650-3); Set. pap. 110.00 (ISBN 0-384-14651-1). Johnson Repr.
Descovich, G. C., jt. ed. see Lenzi, S.
Descovisch, G., ed. Soy Protein in the Preventin of Artherosclerosis. (Illus.). 150p. 1982. text ed. 29.00 (ISBN 0-85200-450-8, Pub. by MTP Pr England). Kluwer Academic.
Descovisch, G. & Lenzi, S., eds. Artherosclerosis: Clinical Evaluations & Therapy. (Illus.). 500p. 1982. text ed. 75.00 (ISBN 0-85200-449-4, Pub. By MTP Pr England). Kluwer Academic.
Desdunes, Rodolphe L. Our People & Our History. McCants, Sr. Dorothea O., tr. from Fr. LC 72-79329. xxviii, 154p. 1973. 14.95x (ISBN 0-8071-0223-7). La State U Pr.
De Segur, Comtesse. The Angel Inn. Aiken, Joan, tr. from Fr. LC 78-12784. (Illus.). 240p. (gr. 3 up). 1978. 11.95 (ISBN 0-916144-28-3); pap. 6.95 (ISBN 0-916144-29-1). Stemmer Hse.
De Segur, Louis. Memoirs & Recollections of Count Louis Philippe De Segur. LC 73-115584. (Russia Observed, Series I). 1970. Repr. of 1827 ed. 60.50 (ISBN 0-405-03061-4). Ayer Co Pubs.
De Segura, Juan see Segura, Juan de.
De Selincourt, ed. see Wordsworth, Dorothy.
De Selincourt, Aubrey. On Reading Poetry. LC 76-40218. 1952. lib. bdg. 8.50 (ISBN 0-8414-3700-9). Folcroft.
--Six Great Englishmen. LC 73-12820. 1953. lib. bdg. 25.00 (ISBN 0-8414-3658-4). Folcroft.
--Six Great Englishmen. 221p. 1980. lib. bdg. 25.00 (ISBN 0-8482-3652-1). Norwood Edns.
--Six Great Playwrights. LC 74-17310. 1974. Repr. of 1960 ed. lib. bdg. 27.00 (ISBN 0-8414-3805-6). Folcroft.
--Six Great Poets. LC 73-6998. 1956. lib. bdg. 27.50 (ISBN 0-8414-1868-3). Folcroft.
--Six Great Poets: Chaucer, Pope, Wordsworth, Shelley, Tennyson, the Brownings. Repr. of 1956 ed. 26.00x (ISBN 0-403-04283-6). Somerset Pub.
--Six Great Thinkers. LC 77-1363. 1977. lib. bdg. 20.00 (ISBN 0-8414-3816-1). Folcroft.
--Streams of Ocean. 1923. Repr. 15.00 (ISBN 0-8274-3527-4). R West.
--World of Herodotus. LC 81-83969. 400p. 1982. pap. 12.00 (ISBN 0-86547-070-7). N Point Pr.
De Selincourt, Aubrey, tr. see Arrian.
De Selincourt, Aubrey, tr. see Herodotus.
De Selincourt, Aubrey, tr. see Livy.
De Selincourt, Aubrey, tr. see Livy, Titus.
De Selincourt, Basil. English Secret, & Other Essays. facs. ed. LC 68-16927. (Essay Index Reprint Ser.). 1923. 15.00 (ISBN 0-8369-0369-2). Ayer Co Pubs.
--Towards Peace, & Other Essays, Critical or Constructive. facs. ed. LC 67-30205. (Essay Index Reprint Ser). 1932. 14.00 (ISBN 0-8369-0370-6). Ayer Co Pubs.
--Walt Whitman: A Critical Study. LC 64-66391. (Illus.). 1965. Repr. of 1914 ed. 8.00x (ISBN 0-8462-0609-9). Russell.
--William Blake. LC 72-162018. (Illus.). 1972. Repr. of 1909 ed. 28.50x (ISBN 0-8154-0389-5). Cooper Sq.
--William Blake. LC 70-173850. (Studies in Blake, No. 3). (Illus.). 1971. Repr. of 1909 ed. lib. bdg. 59.95x (ISBN 0-8383-1357-4). Haskell.
De Selincourt, E., ed. Journals of Dorothy Wordsworth, 2 Vols. (Illus.). 1970. Repr. of 1959 ed. Set. 45.00 (ISBN 0-208-00985-X, Archon). Shoe String.
De Selincourt, Ernest. The Early Letters of William & Dorothy Wordsworth: 1787 to 1805. 578p. 1983. Repr. of 1935 ed. lib. bdg. 150.00 (ISBN 0-89984-164-3). Century Bookbindery.
--Early Wordsworth. LC 73-1142. 1936. lib. bdg. 9.00 (ISBN 0-8414-1853-5). Folcroft.
--English Poets & the National Ideal. LC 73-7775. 1915. lib. bdg. 15.00 (ISBN 0-8414-1879-9). Folcroft.

--English Poets & the National Ideal. 119p. 1980. Repr. of 1916 ed. text ed. 20.00 (ISBN 0-8492-4226-6). R West.

--Notes in Correction of the Text of Wordsworth's Prelude. LC 74-16288. 1925. lib. bdg. 7.50 (ISBN 0-8414-3785-8). Folcroft.

--Oxford Lectures on Poetry. facs. ed. LC 67-23202. (Essay Index Reprint Ser). 1934. 17.00 (ISBN 0-8369-0371-4). Ayer Co Pubs.

--Oxford Lectures on Poetry. LC 73-13004. 1934. lib. bdg. 30.00 (ISBN 0-8414-3652-5). Folcroft.

De Selincourt, Ernest, ed. see Spenser, Edmund.

De Selincourt, Ernest, ed. see Wordsworth, William.

De Selincourt, Ernest, ed. see Wordsworth, William & Wordsworth, Dorothy.

De Selincourt, Hugh. Nine Tales. facsimile ed. LC 79-103506. (Short Story Index Reprint Ser.). 1918. 19.00 (ISBN 0-8369-3248-X). Ayer Co Pubs.

--Studies from Life. 1978. Repr. of 1934 ed. lib. bdg. 20.00 (ISBN 0-8492-0671-5). R West.

De Sena, Jorge. Sobre Esta Praia: Eight Meditations on the Coast of the Pacific. Griffin, Jonathan, tr. LC 79-114869. (Inklings Ser.: No. 1). (Port. & Eng.). 1979. pap. 3.00 (ISBN 0-930012-31-3). Mudborn.

De Senarclens, M., jt. auth. see Dennerstein, L.

De Sennevoy, Jean Dupotet see Dupotet de Sennevoy, Jean.

De Sephibus, G. Indication Dilution in Cardiology. 81p. 1980. 40.00 (ISBN 3-456-80968-9, Pub. by Holdan Bk Ltd UK). State Mutual Bk.

Deser, S., jt. ed. see Chretien, M.

Deser, S., jt. ed. see Levy, M.

Deser, Stanley, et al, eds. Lectures on Elementary Particles & Quantum Field Theory, 2 vols. 1971. Vol. 1. pap. 11.50x (ISBN 0-262-54013-4). MIT Pr.

Deseret Book Company, ed. Faith. LC 83-72343. 119p. 1983. 7.95 (ISBN 0-87747-980-1). Deseret Bk.

De Serio, Louis F. & Greenwell, Glen H., Jr. A Last Look. LC 79-67536. (Illus.). 1979. 20.00 (ISBN 0-9603568-0-0). De Serio.

De Sermisy, Claudin see Janequin, Clement, et al.

DeSerpa. Microeconomic Theory. 1985. 32.87 (ISBN 0-205-08339-0, 098339). Allyn.

De Serpa, Allan. The Mexican Contract. LC 84-223722. 148p. 1981. pap. 5.95 (ISBN 0-939460-15-7). M Hardy.

Deserrano, Irma G. Manual Para la Preparacion De Informes y Tesis. LC 76-11003. 1984. pap. 5.00 (ISBN 0-8477-2312-7). U of PR Pr.

De Serrano, Irma G. The Puerto Rico Teachers' Association & It's Relationship to Teacher Personnel Administration. 6.25 (ISBN 0-8477-2202-3); pap. 5.00 (ISBN 0-8477-2203-1). U of PR Pr.

--La Seleccion De Personal En el Servicio Publico De Puerto Rico. 5.60 (ISBN 0-8477-2204-X); pap. 4.35 (ISBN 0-8477-2205-8). U of PR Pr.

De Serrano, Irma Garcia see Garcia de Serrano, Irma.

De Serres, F. J. & Pero, Ronald W., eds. Individual Susceptibility to Genotoxic Agents in the Human Population. LC 84-11467. (Environmental Science Research Ser.: Vol. 30). 528p. 1984. 69.50x (ISBN 0-306-41679-4, Plenum Pr). Plenum Pub.

De Serres, F. J., et al, eds. Evaluation of Short Term Tests for Carcinogens. (Progress in Mutation Research Ser.: Vol. 1). 828p. 1981. 159.00 (ISBN 0-444-00570-6, Biomedical Pr). Elsevier.

De Serres, Frederic J., ed. Chemical Mutagens: Principles & Methods for Their Detection, Vol. 9. 320p. 1984. 42.50x (ISBN 0-306-41696-4, Plenum Pr). Plenum Pub.

De Serres, Frederick, jt. ed. see Ansari, Aftab A.

De Serres, Frederick J., ed. Chemical Mutagens: Principles & Methods for their Detection, Vol. 8. 370p. 1983. 45.00x (ISBN 0-306-41336-1, Plenum Pr). Plenum Pub.

--Genetic Consequences of Nucleotide Pool Imbalance. (Basic Life Sciences Ser.: Vol. 31). 504p. 1985. 69.50x (ISBN 0-306-41902-5, Plenum Pr). Plenum Pub.

De Serres, Frederick J. & Hollaender, A., eds. Chemical Mutagens: Principles & Methods for Their Detection, Vol. 6. LC 79-640909. (Illus.). 505p. 1980. 55.00x (ISBN 0-306-40364-1, Plenum Pr). Plenum Pub.

De Serres, Frederick J. & Hollaender, Alexander, eds. Chemical Mutagens: Principles & Methods for Their Detection, Vol. 7. LC 79-640909. 523p. 1982. 55.00x (ISBN 0-306-40771-X, Plenum Pr). Plenum Pub.

De Serres, Frederick J. & Shelby, Michael D., eds. Comparative Chemical Mutagenesis. LC 81-17887. (Environmental Science Research Ser.: Vol. 24). 1125p. 1981. text ed. 115.00 (ISBN 0-306-40930-5, Plenum Pr). Plenum Pub.

De Serres, Frederick J., jt. ed. see Hollaender, Alexander.

De Serres, Frederick J., et al, eds. Utilization of Mammalian Specific Locus Studies in Hazard Evaluation & Estimation of Genetic Risk. (Environmental Science Research Ser.). 325p. 1983. 45.00x (ISBN 0-306-41380-9, Plenum Pr). Plenum Pub.

De Serres, Olivier see Serres, Oliver de.

Desert First Works, Inc, ed. see Hallgren, Stephanie.

Desert, Gabriel. Une Societe Rurale Au XIX Siecle: Les Paysans Du Calvados, Eighteen Fifteen to Eighteen Ninty-Five. Bruchey, Stuart, ed. LC 77-77166. (Dissertations in European Economic History Ser.). (Illus., Fr.). 1977. lib. bdg. 70.50x (ISBN 0-405-10780-3). Ayer Co Pubs.

DeServille, Paul. Tubbo: The Great Peter's Run. 1982. 39.50x (ISBN 0-19-554304-1). Oxford U Pr.

De Sevigne. Madame de Sevigne: Selected Letters. Tancock, L. W., ed. 1982. pap. 5.95 (ISBN 0-14-044405-X). Penguin.

De Sevigne, Marie. Correspondance, 3 tomes. Duchene, ed. Incl. Tome I. (1644-1675) 41.50 (ISBN 0-685-34028-7); Tome II. (1676-1684) 45.95 (ISBN 0-685-34029-5); Tome III. (1684-1696) 53.95 (ISBN 0-685-34030-9). (Bibliotheque de la Pleiade). French & Eur.

--Lettres Choisies. (Documentation Thematique). (Illus., Fr.). pap. 2.95 (ISBN 0-685-13968-9, 314). Larousse.

De Seze, S. & Ryckewaert, A. Traite Maladies des Os et des Articulations Mise a Jour 1985. (Collection Medico-Chirurgicale). (Illus.). 168p. (Fr.). 1985. 36.00 (ISBN 0-318-04694-6). S M P F Inc.

Desfeuilles, Arthur. Lexique de la Langue de Moliere avec une, Vol. 1-2. (Fr.). 1900. Set. 64.00 (ISBN 0-8337-4744-4). B Franklin.

--Notice Bibliographique De Moliere. Despois, Eugene & Mesnard, Paul, eds. LC 70-126412. (Bibliography & Reference Ser.: No. 343). (Fr). 1970. Repr. of 1893 ed. lib. bdg. 23.50 (ISBN 0-8337-0839-2). B Franklin.

Des Fontaines, Una. Wedgwood Fairyland Lustre. LC 75-34505. 1976. 60.00 (ISBN 0-85667-022-7). Born-Hawes Pub.

Desforges, Charles, jt. auth. see Bennett, Neville.

Desforges, Charles, jt. auth. see Brown, Geoffrey.

Des Forges, Roger V. Hsi-Liang & the Chinese National Revolution. LC 73-77147. (Historical Publications, Miscellany Ser.: No. 99). (Illus.). Repr. of 1973 ed. 56.30 (ISBN 0-8357-9255-2, 2011092). Bks Demand UMI.

Desfosses, Helen, ed. Soviet Population Policy: Conflicts & Constraints. (Pergamon Policy Studies). 150p. 1981. 27.00 (ISBN 0-08-025976-6). Pergamon.

Desgodetz, Antoine. The Ancient Buildings of Rome. (Printed Sources of Western Art Ser.). (Illus.). 324p. (Fr.). 1981. pap. 75.00 slipcase (ISBN 0-915346-49-4). A Wofsy Fine Arts.

Des Grange, Jane. Long Island's Religious History. 5.95 (ISBN 0-911660-17-8). Yankee Peddler.

Desgranges, ed. see Pascal, Blaise.

De Shalit, Amos & Feshbach, Herman. Theoretical Nuclear Physics, Vol. 1: Nuclear Structure. LC 73-17165. 979p. 1974. 80.50x (ISBN 0-471-20385-8). Wiley.

Deshapande, V. D. Dr. Hedgewar. Sehadri, H. V., ed. 1983. 7.50x (ISBN 0-686-43920-1, Pub. by Sahitya Sindhi India). South Asia Bks.

Desharnais, A. A Review of Surgical Nursing. 1978. text ed. 15.95 (ISBN 0-07-016560-2). McGraw.

Desharnais, A., et al. Appleton's Practice Test in Nursing for the New State Board Examination. LC 81-71119. 60p. (Orig.). 1982. pap. text ed. 12.95x (ISBN 0-8385-0200-8, Appleton-Century Crofts). ACC.

Desharnais, Anna M., et al. Appleton's Review of Nursing for the New State Board Examination. 333p. 1982. pap. 16.95 (ISBN 0-8385-0201-6). ACC.

De Shazer, Steve. Keys to Solution in Brief Therapy. 1985. 18.50 (ISBN 0-393-70004-6). Norton.

--Patterns of Brief Family Therapy. LC 81-7239. (Family Therapy Ser.). 1982. 19.50 (ISBN 0-89862-038-4, 2038). Guilford Pr.

DeShazo, Peter. Urban Workers & Labor Unions in Chile, 1902-1927. LC 82-70557. (Illus.). 384p. 1983. 30.00x (ISBN 0-299-09220-8). U of Wis Pr.

Desh Bandhu & Chauhan, Eklavya. Current Trends in Indian Environment. 240p. 1977. 10.00 (ISBN 0-88065-080-X, Pub. by Messers Today & Tomorrows Printers & Publishers India). Scholarly Pubns.

Deshen, Schlomo, jt. auth. see Shokeid, Moshe.

Deshen, Shlomo & Zenner, Walter P. Jewish Societies in the Middle East: Community, Culture & Authority. LC 80-6285. (Illus.). 328p. (Orig.). 1982. lib. bdg. 29.00 (ISBN 0-8191-2578-4); pap. text ed. 14.25 (ISBN 0-8191-2579-2). U Pr of Amer.

Deshen, Shlomo, jt. auth. see Shokeid, Moshe.

Deshen, Solomon. Ethnic Boundaries & Cultural Paradigms: The Case of Southern Tunisian Immigrants in Israel. 35p. 1976. softcover 2.00 (ISBN 0-686-74366-0). ADELANTRE.

Deshimaru, Taisen. Questions to a Zen Master. Amphoux, Nancy, tr. 160p. 1985. pap. 8.95 (ISBN 0-525-48141-9, 0869-260). Dutton.

--The Zen Way to the Martial Arts: A Japanese Master Reveals the Secrets of the Samurai. Amphoux, Nancy, tr. (Illus.). 128p. 1983. pap. 5.95 (ISBN 0-525-93267-4, 0578-170). Dutton.

Deshler, Betty, intro. by. School Social Work & the Law. LC 80-83075. 192p. (Orig.). pap. text ed. 8.95 (ISBN 0-87101-088-7). Natl Assn Soc Wkrs.

Deshler, Donald, jt. auth. see Alley, Gordon.

Deshler, George O. Western States Fly-in Campground Directory. 2nd ed. (Illus.). 1978. pap. 5.95 (ISBN 0-911721-32-0). Aviation.

Deshman, Robert. Anglo-Saxon & Anglo-Scandinavian Art: An Annotated Bibliography. (Reference Publications in Art History Ser.). 1984. lib. bdg. 45.00 (ISBN 0-8161-8344-9, Hall Reference). G K Hall.

Deshmukh, C. D. Reflections on Finance, Education & Society. 1972. 9.95 (ISBN 0-8426-0416-2). Orient Bk Dist.

Deshmukh, C. D., ed. see Baba, Meher.

Deshmukh, D. G. Thoreau & Indian Thought: A Study of the Impact of Indian Thought on the Life of Henry David Thoreau. LC 80-2505. Repr. of 1974 ed. 19.50 (ISBN 0-404-19053-7). AMS Pr.

Deshmukh, V. M., jt. auth. see Tamoskar, B. G.

DeShong, Andrew. The Theatrical Designs of George Grosz. Foster, Stephen, ed. LC 82-1939. (Studies in the Fine Arts: The Avant-Garde Ser.: No. 22). 196p. 1982. 39.95 (ISBN 0-8357-1298-2). UMI Res Pr.

DeShong, Barbara R. The Special Educator: Stress & Survival. LC 81-1743. 230p. 1981. text ed. 29.95 (ISBN 0-89443-358-X). Aspen Systems.

Deshpande, C. D., et al. Impact of a Metropolitan City on the Surrounding Region. (Illus.). 167p. 1980. pap. text ed. 9.00x (ISBN 0-391-02206-7). Humanities.

Deshpande, D. L. Basic Tools. 64p. 1981. 20.00x (ISBN 0-86125-499-6, Pub. by Orient Longman India). State Mutual Bk.

Deshpande, D. L., ed. Basic Drawing. 68p. 1981. 20.00x (ISBN 0-86125-690-5, Pub. by Orient Longman India). State Mutual Bk.

Deshpande, Gauri. An Anthology of Indo-English Poetry. 162p. 1975. pap. text ed. 2.50 (ISBN 0-88253-455-6). Ind-US Inc.

--Between Births. 1975. 8.00 (ISBN 0-88253-508-0); pap. text ed. 4.00 (ISBN 0-88253-507-2). Ind-US Inc.

--Lost Love. 8.00 (ISBN 0-89253-685-3). Ind-US Inc.

Deshpande, K. S. University Library System in India. 1985. text ed. 25.00x (ISBN 0-86590-697-1, Pub. by Sterling Pubs India). Apt Bks.

Deshpande, Madhav. Critical Studies in Indian Grammarians I, Theory of Homogeneity (Savarnya) LC 75-36896. (The Michigan Papers in South & Southeast Asian Languages & Linguistics: No. 2). xiv, 221p. (Orig.). 1975. pap. 8.00x (ISBN 0-89148-052-8). Ctr S&SE Asian.

--Evolution of Syntactic Theory in Sanskrit Grammar: Syntax of the Sanskrit Infinitive Ser. (Linguista Extranea: Studia: No. 10). 164p. 1980. 10.50 (ISBN 0-89720-029-2); pap. 7.50 (ISBN 0-89720-030-6). Karoma.

Deshpande, Madhav & Hook, Peter, eds. Aryan & Non-Aryan in India. 315p. 1979. 21.00 (ISBN 0-89720-011-X); pap. 15.50 (ISBN 0-89720-012-8). Karoma.

Deshpande, Madhav M. Sociolinguistic Attitudes in India: An Historical Reconstruction. (Linguistica Extranea Ser.: Studia 5). 178p. 1979. lib. bdg. 10.50 (ISBN 0-89720-007-1); pap. 7.50 (ISBN 0-89720-008-X). Karoma.

Deshpande, Madhav M. & Hook, Peter E., eds. Aryan & Non-Aryan in India. LC 78-60016. (Michigan Papers on South & Southeast Asia: No. 14). xii, 315p. 1979. 21.00x (ISBN 0-89720-011-X); pap. 15.50x (ISBN 0-89148-014-5). Ctr S&SE Asian.

Deshpande, P. G. A Modern English-Gujarati Dictionary. (Eng. & Gujarati.). 1982. 29.95 (ISBN 0-19-561140-3). Oxford U Pr.

Deshpande, Pradeep B. Distillation Dynamics & Control. 420p. 1985. text ed. 49.95x (ISBN 0-87664-810-3). Instru Soc.

Deshpande, Pradeep B. & Ash, Raymond H. Elements of Computer Process Control with Advanced Control Applications. LC 80-82117. 424p. 1981. text ed. 47.95x (ISBN 0-87664-449-3). Instru Soc.

Deshpande, Pradeep B. & Ash, Raymond H., eds. Elements of Computer Process Control with Advanced Control Applications. (Illus.). 400p. 1983. 47.95 (ISBN 0-13-264093-7). P-H.

Deshpande, S. Roots & Shadows. 216p. 1983. pap. 4.95x (ISBN 0-86131-287-2, Pub. by Orient Longman India). Apt Bks.

Deshpande, S. R. Yadava Sculpture. (Illus.). 107p. 1985. text ed. 75.00x (ISBN 0-86590-715-3, Pub. by B R Pub Corp India). Apt Bks.

Deshpande, Shashi. Come Up & Be Dead: A Novel. 266p. 1983. text ed. 15.00x (ISBN 0-7069-2129-1, Pub. by Vikas India). Advent NY.

--The Dark Holds No Terrors. (Vikas Library of Modern Indian Writing: No. 3). 208p. 1980. text ed. 15.95x (ISBN 0-7069-1071-0, Pub. by Vikas India). Advent NY.

Deshpande, V. S. Women & the New Law. 1985. pap. text ed. 9.50 (ISBN 0-8364-1368-7, Pub. by Punjabi U India). South Asia Bks.

Deshpande, Vasant D. Towards Social Integration. 1978. 12.00x (ISBN 0-8364-0236-7). South Asia Bks.

Desia, A. R. India's Path of Development: A Marxist Approach. 1985. 22.00x (ISBN 0-8364-1332-6, Pub. by Popular Prakashan). South Asia Bks.

DeSiano, Frank. Searching for Sense: The Logic of Catholic Belief. LC 75-23155. 196p. 1975. pap. 2.45 (ISBN 0-8091-1886-6). Paulist Pr.

De Sica, Vittorio. Bicycle Thieves (The Bicycle Thief) (Lorrimer Classic Screenplay Ser.). (Illus.). pap. 8.95 (ISBN 0-8044-6113-9). Ungar.

Desiderato, O. Readings in General Psychology. 1969. pap. text ed. 12.95x (ISBN 0-8422-0047-9). Irvington.

Desiderato, O., ed. Introduction to Psychology: Selected Readings. 1970. pap. text ed. 8.95x (ISBN 0-8422-0096-7). Irvington.

Desiderio, D. M. Analysis of Neuropeptides by Liquid Chromatography & Mass Spectrometry. (Techniques & Instrumentation in Analytical Chemistry Ser.: No. 6). 236p. 1984. 61.00 (ISBN 0-444-42418-0). Elsevier.

Desiderio, Robert J., ed. see Shepard's & McGraw-Hill.

Design Collective Incorporated Columbus, Ohio, tr. see Planned Parenthood Federation of America, Inc.

Design Concept Associates. Homes in the Earth. (Illus.). 112p. 1980. pap. 7.95 (ISBN 0-87701-212-1). Chronicle Bks.

Design Council, ed. Equipment for Parks & Amenity Areas. 1979. pap. 25.00x (ISBN 0-85072-083-4, Pub. by Design Council England). Intl Spec Bk.

--Street Furniture. 192p. 1979. pap. 32.50x (ISBN 0-85072-082-6, Pub. by Design Council England). Intl Spec Bk.

Design Engineering Conference. New Design Standards for Flexible Couplings: Design Engineering Conference, Chicago, May 10, 1966. pap. 20.00 (ISBN 0-317-11086-1, 2011324). Bks Demand UMI.

Design Engineering Technical Conference Staff. Passenger Vibration in Transportation Vehicles: Presented at the Design Engineering Technical Conferenc, Chicago, Illinois, September 26-28, 1977. Berman, Alex & Hannibal, Alan J., eds. LC 77-82212. (AMD Ser.: Vol. 24). pap. 34.00 (ISBN 0-317-27775-8, 2015393). Bks Demand UMI.

Design Schools. Your Future in Art. (Illus.). 32p. (gr. 10-12). 1981. pap. text ed. 1.25 (ISBN 0-9607016-0-5). Design Schools.

--Your Future in Fashion. (Illus.). 32p. (gr. 10-12). 1983. pap. text ed. 1.25 (ISBN 0-9607016-1-3). Design Schools.

Designers Guild. Soft Furnishings. (Illus.). 1980. pap. 14.95 (ISBN 0-374-51614-6). FS&G.

Desikachar, T. K. Religiousness in Yoga: Lectures on Theory & Practice. Skelton, Mary L. & Carter, J. R., eds. LC 79-9643. (Illus.). 314p. 1980. text ed. 24.25 (ISBN 0-8191-0966-5); pap. text ed. 11.50 (ISBN 0-8191-0967-3). U Pr of Amer.

Desiles, Clara. Japan Today. (Illus.). 1979. bds. 14.95 (ISBN 2-85258-110-8, Pub. by J. A. Editions France). Hippocrene Bks.

De Silk, Eve. Rhythms of Life. 1984. 5.95 (ISBN 0-533-05988-7). Vantage.

De Silva, Clarence W. Dynamic Testing & Seismic Qualification Practice. LC 80-8879. 416p. 1982. 48.50x (ISBN 0-669-04393-1). Lexington Bks.

De Silva, Clarence W. & Wormley, David N. Automated Guideway Transit Analysis & Design. LC 80-8927. 304p. 1983. 40.00 (ISBN 0-669-04407-5). Lexington Bks.

De Silva, Colin. The Winds of Sinhala. LC 80-2954. (Illus.). 528p. 1982. 17.95 (ISBN 0-385-15952-8). Doubleday.

De Silva, D. M. Pemato Jayati Soko (Love Is the Bringer of Sorrow) De Silva, D. M., tr. from Singhalese. (Salzburg Studies in English Literature: Poetic Drama & Poetic Theory: No. 25). 55p. 1976. pap. text ed. 25.50x (ISBN 0-391-01524-9). Humanities.

De Silva, Derek see Sternlicht, Sanford & Silva, Derek De.

De Silva, Judith C., ed. Malaysia Official Year Book 1977. 17th ed. LC 62-41053. (Illus.). 576p. (Orig.). 1979. pap. 15.00x (ISBN 0-8002-2453-1). Intl Pubns Serv.

De Silva, K. M. A History of Sri Lanka. 550p. 1981. 45.00x (ISBN 0-520-04320-0). U of Cal Pr.

--Sri Lanka: A Survey. LC 77-73917. 1977. text ed. 25.00x (ISBN 0-8248-0568-2). UH Pr.

De Silva, Lynn A. The Problem of the Self in Buddhism & Christianity. LC 76-19860. (Library of Philosophy & Religion Ser). 1979. Repr. of 1975 ed. text ed. 24.50x (ISBN 0-06-491667-7). B&N Imports.

De Silva, M. A. & Siriwardenc, Reggie. Communication Policies in Sri Lanka: A Study Carried Out by a Committee Appointed by the Secretary to the Ministry of Education, Sri Lanka. (Communication Policy Studies). 59p. 1977. pap. 5.00 (ISBN 92-3-101416-1, U86, UNESCO). Unipub.

De Silva, M. W. Sinhalese & Other Island Languages in South Asia. (ARS Linguistica: 3). 75p. (Orig.). 1979. pap. 14.00x (ISBN 3-87808-353-X). Benjamins North Am.

De Silva, Padmasiri. An Introduction to Buddhist Psychology. (Library of Philosophy & Religion Ser.). 134p. 1979. text ed. 28.50x (ISBN 0-06-491666-9). B&N Imports.

De Silva, Robin & DuPont, Robert L. Treating the Marijuana-Dependent Person. LC 82-198647. 59p. 1981. pap. 2.95 (ISBN 0-942348-04-4). Am Council Drug Ed.

De Silva, S. B. The Political Economy of Underdevelopment. (International Library of Sociology). 640p. 1982. 50.00x (ISBN 0-7100-0469-9). Routledge & Kegan.

DeSilva, S. B. The Political Economy of Underdevelopment. (International Library of Sociology). 645p. 1984. pap. 23.95x (ISBN 0-7102-0273-3). Routledge & Kegan.

DeSimone, Diane, jt. auth. see Durden-Smith, Jo.

De Simone, Diane see Durden-Smith, Jo & Simone, Diane de.

De Simone, Donald. A Kiss on Each Cheek. 448p. (Orig.). 1981. pap. 2.95 (ISBN 0-523-40469-7). Pinnacle Bks.

--Railroaded to Resurrection. 204p. 1982. 13.95. ETC Pubns.

De Simoni, Felix. Mary Magdalene & the Theory of Sin, 2 vols. LC 72-84832. (Illus.). 35p. 1972. 97.45 (ISBN 0-913314-04-8). Am Classical Coll Pr.

Desimoni, Giovanni, et al, eds. Natural Products Synthesis through Pericyclic Reactions. LC 83-12303. (ACS Monographs: No. 180). 443p. 1983. lib. bdg. 89.95 (ISBN 0-8412-0757-7). Am Chemical.

De Sismondi, J. C. see Sismondi, J. C. De.

De Sismondi, Jean C. Simonde see Simonde De Sismondi, Jean C.

De Sivry, L. Dictionnaire Geographique, Historique, Descriptif, Archeologique des Pelegrinages, 2 vols. Migne, J. P., ed. (Encyclopedie Theologique Ser.: Vols. 43-44). 1328p. (Fr.). Repr. of 1851 ed. lib. bdg. 169.00x (ISBN 0-89241-248-8). Caratzas.

Des Jardins & McCall. Contemporary Issues in Business Ethics. 1984. write for info. (ISBN 0-534-03693-7). Wadsworth Pub.

Desjardins, A. U., tr. see Forestier, J., et al.

Des Jardins, Paul R., et al. Apple II & II Plus Microcomputer, BASIC & 6502. rev. ed. (Nanos Reference Cards Ser.). 16p. 1982. 4.95 (ISBN 0-915069-10-5). Nanos Sys.

--The Apple II & II Plus Microcomputer, BASIC. rev. ed. (Nanos Reference Cards Ser.). (Illus.). 14p. 1982. 3.95 (ISBN 0-915069-11-3). Nanos Sys.

--The Apple IIe. (Nanos Reference Cards Ser.). (Illus.). 16p. (Orig.). 1983. 4.95 (ISBN 0-915069-22-9). Nanos Sys.

--The Sixty-Five Hundred Two Microprocessor. (Nanos Reference Cards Ser.). 16p. (Orig.). 1983. pap. 4.95 (ISBN 0-915069-16-4). Nanos Sys.

Desk Top Seminar Staff. Handling Problem Employees: How to Take Corrective Action. (Professional Development Program Ser.). 172p. 1980. 90.00 (ISBN 0-471-88937-7). Wiley.

--How to Improve Listening Skills. (Professional Development Program Ser.). 192p. 1983. Trainer's Guide. 145.00 (ISBN 0-471-88933-4); 90.00 (ISBN 0-471-88934-2). Wiley.

--How to Improve Writing Skills. (Professional Development Program Ser.). 208p. 1983. Trainer's Guide. 145.00 (ISBN 0-471-88931-8); 90.00 (ISBN 0-471-88932-6). Wiley.

--Selecting the Right Supervisor. (Professional Development Program Ser.). 176p. 1981. 90.00 (ISBN 0-471-88880-X). Wiley.

--Selecting the Right Supervisor: Trainer's Edition. (Professional Development Program Ser.). 176p. 1981. 145.00 (ISBN 0-471-88940-7). Wiley.

Desk Top Seminars Staff. Handling Problem Employees: How to Take Corrective Action, Trainer's Edtion. (Professional Development Program Ser.). 192p. 1980. 125.00 (ISBN 0-471-88936-9). Wiley.

Deskins, Donald R., Jr. Minority Recruitment Data: An Analysis of Baccalaureate Degree Production in the United States. LC 83-19159. 819p. 1983. 55.00x (ISBN 0-86598-145-0). Rowman & Allanheld.

Deskins, W. E., jt. auth. see Bray, Henry G.

Des Landes Hessen, Bibliotheken, jt. ed. see Universitatsbibliothek Frankfurt am Main in Zusammenarbeit mit den Wissenschaftlichen.

Deslandres, Maurice C. Histoire Constitutionnelle de la France de 1789 a 1970, 3 vols. LC 78-67346. (European Political Thought Ser.). (Fr.). 1979. Repr. of 1937 ed. Set. lib. bdg. 145.50 (ISBN 0-405-11692-6). Ayer Co Pubs.

--Histoire Constitutionnelle de la France de 1789 a 1870, Vol. 1. 48.50 (ISBN 0-405-11842-2). Ayer Co Pubs.

--Histoire Constitutionnelle de la France de 1789 a 1870, Vol. 2. 48.50 (ISBN 0-405-11843-0). Ayer Co Pubs.

Des Lauriers, Austin M. The Experience of Reality in Childhood Schizophrenia. LC 62-15155. (Monograph Ser. on Schizophrenia: No. 6). 215p. (Orig.). 1962. text ed. 22.50 (ISBN 0-8236-1800-5). Intl Univs Pr.

Des Lauriers, Brian. Wealth for Women. Keane, Joyce, ed. LC 79-91054. 126p. (Orig.). 1980. pap. text ed. 9.90 (ISBN 0-686-27291-9). Progress Pr WA.

Desloge, Edward A. Classical Mechanics, Vol. 1. LC 81-11407. 519p. 1982. 48.50x (ISBN 0-471-09144-8, Pub. by Wiley-Interscience). Wiley.

--Classical Mechanics, Vol. 2. LC 81-11402. 492p. 1982. 56.95x (ISBN 0-471-09145-6, Pub. by Wiley-Interscience). Wiley.

Deslongchamps, P. Stereoelectronic Effects in Organic Chemistry. (Organic Chemistry Ser.: Vol. 1). (Illus.). 390p. 1983. 55.00 (ISBN 0-08-026184-1); pap. 27.50 (ISBN 0-08-029248-8). Pergamon.

Des Lozieres, Baudry & Narcisse, Louis. Voyage a la Louisiane, et Sur le Continent De L'amerique Septentrionale Fait Dans les Annees Seventeen Ninety-Four to Seventeen Ninety-Eight. (Illus.). 382p. 1968. Repr. of 1802 ed. 25.00 (ISBN 0-8398-0156-4). Parnassus Imprints.

Desmaison, Rene. Total Alpinism. Taylor, Jane, tr. from French. 200p. 1982. 27.95x (ISBN 0-8464-1278-0). Beekman Pubs.

Desmaisons. Psychiatry in Russia & Spain: An Original Anthology. LC 75-16729. (Classics in Psychiatry Ser.). (Fr. & Ger.). 1976. 24.50x (ISBN 0-405-07452-2). Ayer Co Pubs.

Desmarais, ed. see Mertin, Roger.

Desmarais, Charles, ed. Michael Bishop. LC 79-10942. (Illus.). 1979. pap. 4.95 (ISBN 0-932026-03-6). Columbia College Chi.

Des Marais, Philip. How to Get Government Grants. pap. 15.50 (ISBN 0-686-24214-9). Public Serv Materials.

Desmarchelier, J. M., et al. Residue Reviews, Vol. 63. LC 62-18595. 1976. 29.50 (ISBN 0-387-90164-7). Springer-Verlag.

Desmarets, Peter, jt. auth. see Neuner, Gerd.

Desmars, J. Un Precurseur D'Adam Smith en France: J. J. L. Graslin (1727-1790) LC 77-159696. 257p. (Fr.). 1973. Repr. of 1900 ed. 20.50 (ISBN 0-8337-0840-6). B Franklin.

Des Mas-Latrie, L. Dictionnaire de Statistique Religieuse. Migne, J. P., ed. (Nouvelle Encyclopedie Theologique Ser.: Vol. 9). 538p. (Fr.). Repr. of 1851 ed. lib. bdg. 69.00x (ISBN 0-89241-259-3). Caratzas.

Desmedt, J. E., ed. Attention, Voluntary Contraction & Event-Related Cerebral Potentials. (Progress in Clinical Neurophysiology: Vol. 1). 1977. 41.95 (ISBN 3-8055-2438-2). S Karger.

--Auditory Evoked Potentials in Man: Psychopharmacology Correlates of EPS. (Progress in Clinical Neurophysiology: Vol. 2). 1977. 41.75 (ISBN 3-8055-2626-1). S Karger.

--Cerebral Motor Control in Man: Cerebral Event-Related Potentials. (Progress in Clinical Neurophysiology: Vol. 4). (Illus.). 1977. 50.25 (ISBN 3-8055-2712-8). S Karger.

--Cognitive Components in Cerebral Event Related Potentials & Selective Attention. (Progress in Clinical Neurophysiology: Vol. 6). (Illus.). 1979. 50.25 (ISBN 3-8055-2760-8). S Karger.

--Computer-Aided Electromyography. (Progress in Clinical Neurophysiology Series: Vol. 10). (Illus.). x, 334p. 1983. 70.25 (ISBN 3-8055-3748-4). S Karger.

--Language & Hemispheric Specialization in Man: Cerebral Event-Related Potentials. (Progress in Clinical Neurophysiology: Vol. 3). (Illus.). 1977. 41.75 (ISBN 3-8055-2629-6). S Karger.

--Motor Unit Types, Recruitment & Plasticity in Health & Disease. (Progress in Clinical Neurophysiology: Vol. 9). (Illus.). x, 418p. 1981. 63.00 (ISBN 3-8055-1929-X). S Karger.

--New Developments in Electromyography & Clinical Neurophysiology. Incl. Vol. 1. New Concepts of the Motor Unit, Neuromuscular Disorders, Electromyographic Kinesiology. (Illus.). x, 700p. 102.25 (ISBN 3-8055-1451-4); Vol. 2. Pathological Conduction in Nerve Fibers, Electromyography of Sphincter Muscles, Automatic Analysis of Electrogram with Computers. (Illus.). x, 500p. 76.75 (ISBN 3-8055-1452-2); Vol. 3. Human Reflexes, Pathophysiology of Motor Systems, Methodology of Human Reflexes. (Illus.). x, 850p. 123.50 (ISBN 3-8055-1453-0). 1973. Set. 255.50 (ISBN 3-8055-1409-3). S Karger.

--Physiological Tremor, Pathological Tremor & Clonus. (Progress in Clinical Neurophysiology: Vol. 5). (Illus.). 1977. 41.75 (ISBN 3-8055-2713-6). S Karger.

--Spinal & Supraspinal Mechanisms of Voluntary Motor Control & Locomotion. (Progress in Clinical Neurophysiology: Vol. 8). (Illus.). x, 374p. 1980. 58.75 (ISBN 3-8055-0022-X). S Karger.

Desmedt, J. E., ed. see Quantitative Methods of Investigations in the Clinics of Neuromuscular Diseases International Symposium, Giessen, April 1974.

Desmedt, John E., ed. Clinical Uses of Cerebral, Brainstem & Spinal Somatosensory Evoked Potentials. (Progress in Clinical Neurophysiology: Vol. 7). (Illus.). 1979. 58.75 (ISBN 3-8055-2936-8). S Karger.

--Motor Control Mechanisms in Health & Disease: Advances in Neurology, Vol. 39. (Illus.). 1224p. 1983. 163.00 (ISBN 0-89004-723-5). Raven.

--Visual Evoked Potentials in Man: New Developments. (Illus.). 1977. text ed. 87.50x (ISBN 0-19-857393-6). Oxford U Pr.

DeSmet, P. J. New Indian Sketches. 175p. pap. 9.95 (ISBN 0-8466-4049-X, I49). Shorey.

De Smet, Peter J. Western Missions & Missionaries. 562p. 1972. Repr. of 1863 ed. 37.50x (ISBN 0-87471-318-8). Rowman.

De Smet, Pierre J. Life, Letters & Travels of Father Pierre Jean de Smet, 4 vols. LC 75-83418. (Religion in America Ser. I). 1969. Repr. of 1905 ed. 88.00 set (ISBN 0-405-00237-8); Vols. 1-2. 22.00 ea. Vol. 1 (ISBN 0-405-00238-6). Vol. 2 (ISBN 0-405-00239-4). Vols. 3-4. 22.00 ea. Vol. 3 (ISBN 0-405-00240-8). Vol. 4 (ISBN 0-405-00241-6). Ayer Co Pubs.

--Oregon Missions & Travels Over the Rocky Mountains in Eighteen Forty Six. 1979. 14.95 (ISBN 0-87770-132-6). Ye Galleon.

De Smet, Pierre-Jean. New Indian Sketches. 1985. 12.50 (ISBN 0-87770-336-1). Ye Galleon.

--Origin, Progress & Prospects of the Catholic Mission to the Rocky Mountains. 1971. pap. 1.00 (ISBN 0-87770-044-3). Ye Galleon.

De Smet, Robin. Published Music for the Viola Dagamba & Other Viols. LC 75-151302. (Detroit Studies in Music Bibliography Ser.: No. 18). 1971. pap. 2.00 (ISBN 0-911772-40-5). Info Coord.

De Smit, Bart N. From Person into Patient: A Mental Health Study. (Orig.). 1963. pap. text ed. 6.00x (ISBN 0-686-22432-9). Mouton.

De Smit, Jacob, jt. auth. see Kramer, Nicolas.

De Smith, Josie. El Hogar Que Dios Me Dio. 80p. 1981. pap. 2.10 (ISBN 0-311-46082-8). Casa Bautista.

De Smith, Josie see Smith, Josie De.

Desmond, Adrian. Archetypes & Ancestors: Palaeontology in Victorian London 1850-1875. LC 83-18104. 1984. lib. bdg. 22.50x (ISBN 0-226-14343-0). U of Chicago Pr.

--The Hot-Blooded Dinosaurs: A Revolution in Paleontology. (Illus.). 336p. 1976. 12.95 (ISBN 0-385-27063-1, Dial). Doubleday.

Desmond, Astra. Schumann Songs. LC 74-39503. (BBC Music Guides Ser.). (Illus.). 64p. (Orig.). 1972. pap. 4.95 (ISBN 0-295-95200-8). U of Wash Pr.

Desmond, Cecelia. Blessed James Salomoni. 1970. 2.00 (ISBN 0-8198-0000-7); pap. 1.00 (ISBN 0-8198-0001-5). Dghtrs St Paul.

Desmond, Charles. Wooden Ship-Building. 2nd ed. 232p. pap. 14.95 (ISBN 0-911572-37-6). Vestal.

Desmond, David P., jt. auth. see Maddux, James F.

Desmond, Glenn M. How to Value Professional Practices. 1980. 18.50 (ISBN 0-930458-03-6). Valuation.

Desmond, Glenn M. & Kelley, Richard E. Business Valuation Handbook. rev ed. LC 80-51554. 1980. 42.50 (ISBN 0-930458-02-8). Valuation.

Desmond, Humphrey. A. P. A. Movement: A Sketch. LC 69-18772. (American Immigration Collection Ser., No. 1). 1969. Repr. of 1912 ed. 10.00 (ISBN 0-405-00519-9). Ayer Co Pubs.

Desmond, J. Big John. MacLennan, Kathy, ed. LC 81-50391. 147p. 1981. pap. 5.95x perfect bound (ISBN 0-934044-04-X). Roush Bks.

--Deerskin Map. Date not set. price not set. Roush Bks.

--Here, There & Everywhere. 1984. perfect bound 5.95 (ISBN 0-934044-05-8). Roush Bks.

--Kansas Boy. MacLennan, Kathy, ed. LC 79-67031. 140p. (gr. 4-12). 1979. pap. 4.95x perfect bound (ISBN 0-934044-02-3). Roush Bks.

--A Voice Called. MacLennan, Kathy, ed. LC 79-63975. 107p. (gr. 4-12). 1979. pap. 4.95x perfect bound (ISBN 0-934044-01-5). Roush Bks.

Desmond, John. Louisiana's Antebellum Architecture. 1970. 5.95 (ISBN 0-87511-023-1). Claitors.

Desmond, John F., ed. A Still Moment: Essays on the Art of Eudora Welty. LC 78-3719. 1978. 16.00 (ISBN 0-8108-1129-4). Scarecrow.

Desmond, Kevin. Motorboating Facts & Feats. (Illus.). 256p. 1980. 19.95 (ISBN 0-900424-86-9, Pub by Guinness Superlatives England). Sterling.

--Richard Shuttleworth. (Illus.). 192p. 1982. 19.95 (ISBN 0-86720-629-2). Jane's Pub Inc.

Desmond, Margaret G. Modifying the Work Environment for the Physically Disabled: An Accessibility Checklist for Employers. LC 80-83500. (Illus.). 128p. 1981. 8.95 (ISBN 0-686-38822-4). Human Res Ctr.

Desmond, Ray. Bibliography of British Gardens. (Illus.). 224p. 1985. 30.00x (ISBN 0-906795-15-X). U Pr of Va.

--Dictionary of British & Irish Botanists & Horticulturists: Including Plant Collectors & Botanical Artists. 3rd ed. 747p. 1977. 99.50x (ISBN 0-8476-1392-5). Rowman.

Desmond, Ray, jt. auth. see Barr, Pat.

Desmond, Ray, jt. auth. see Satow, Michael.

Desmond, Ray, ed. Dictionary of British & Irish Botanists & Horticulturists. 3rd ed. 764p. 1977. cancelled (ISBN 0-85066-089-0). Taylor & Francis.

Desmond, Robert M., jt. auth. see Karlekar, Bhalchandra V.

Desmond, Robert W. Crisis & Conflict: World News Reporting Between Two Wars, 1920 to 1940, Vol. III. LC 82-8584. (World News Reporting Ser.). 544p. 1982. text ed. 38.00x (ISBN 0-87745-111-7). U of Iowa Pr.

--The Information Process: World News Reporting to the Twentieth Century. LC 77-9491. (World News Reporting Ser.: Vol. 1). 445p. 1978. text ed. 30.00x (ISBN 0-87745-070-6). U of Iowa Pr.

--The Press & World Affairs. LC 72-4665. (International Propaganda & Communications Ser.). (Illus.). 449p. 1972. Repr. of 1937 ed. 25.00 (ISBN 0-405-04746-0). Ayer Co Pubs.

--Tides of War: World News Reporting 1931-1945. LC 84-2504. (World News Reporting Ser.: Vol. IV). 608p. 1984. text ed. 30.00x (ISBN 0-87745-125-7). U of Iowa Pr.

--Windows on the World: World News Reporting Nineteen Hundred to Nineteen Twenty. LC 80-19397. (World News Reporting Ser.: Vol. 2). 626p. 1981. text ed. 45.00x (ISBN 0-87745-104-4). U of Iowa Pr.

Desmond, S. The Soul of Denmark. 1977. lib. bdg. 59.95 (ISBN 0-8490-2632-6). Gordon Pr.

Desmont, Mark, jt. ed. see Blaukopf, Kurt.

Desmore, Mary J., jt. auth. see Emanuelson, Kathy L.

Desmoulins, Camille. Oeuvres, 2 Vols in 1. LC 72-164282. Repr. of 1838 ed. 42.50 (ISBN 0-404-07124-4). AMS Pr.

--Oeuvres, 10 Vols. 1980. lib. bdg. 595.00 (ISBN 3-601-00189-6). Kraus Intl.

Desmyter, J., ed. see International Symposium on Basic Progress in Blood Transfusion, 6th, Brussels, Feb., 1972.

Desne, R., jt. auth. see Diderot, Denis.

Desnick, R. J., jt. ed. see Bishop, D. F.

Desnick, Robert J., ed. Enzyme Therapy in Genetic Diseases: Part 2. LC 79-48026. (Alan R. Liss Ser.: Vol. 16, No. 1). 1980. 77.00 (ISBN 0-686-29474-2). March of Dimes.

--Enzyme Therapy in Genetic Diseases: Proceedings, No. 2. 2nd ed. LC 79-48026. (Birth Defects: Original Article Ser.: Vol. XVI, No. 1). 568p. 1980. 77.00 (ISBN 0-8451-1035-7). A R Liss.

Desnick, Robert J. & Gatt, Shimon, eds. Gaucher Disease: A Century of Delineation & Research. LC 82-4611. (Progress in Clinical & Biological Research Ser.: Vol. 95). 764p. 1982. 76.00 (ISBN 0-8451-0095-5). A R Liss.

Desnick, Robert J. & Patterson, Donald F., eds. Animal Models of Inherited Metabolic Diseases. LC 82-8961. (Progress in Clinical & Biological Research Ser.: Vol. 94). 544p. 1982. 54.00 (ISBN 0-8451-0094-7). A R Liss.

Desnick, Shirley G. Geriatric Contentment: A Guide to Its Achievement in Your Home. 76p. 1971. 9.75x (ISBN 0-398-00440-4). C C Thomas.

Desnoes & Edmundo. Literatures in Transition: The Many Voices of the Caribbean Area. Minc, Rose S., ed. LC 82-84104. 180p. (Eng. & Span.). 1983. pap. 12.95 (ISBN 0-935318-10-0). Edins Hispamerica.

Desnoes, Edmundo & Luis, William. Los Dispositivos en la Flor: Cuba: Literatura desde la Revolucion. 557p. (Span.). 1981. 12.00 (ISBN 0-910061-03-3, 1104). Ediciones Norte.

Desnoes, Edmundo, ed. Los Dispositivos en la flor (Cuba: literatura desde la revolucion) 557p. (Span.). 1981. pap. 12.00 (ISBN 0-910061-03-3, 1104). Ediciones Norte.

De Snoo, H. S., jt. auth. see Coddington, E. A.

Desnos, Robert. Calixto: Avec: Contree. 64p. 1962. 3.95 (ISBN 0-686-55991-6). French & Eur.

--Chantefables. Annen, Sharon, tr. from Fr. LC 84-61257. (Illus.). 60p. (gr. 1-6). 1986. 10.95 (ISBN 0-9613938-0-7). Penstemon Pr.

--Chantefables et Chantefleurs. (Illus.). 7.95 (ISBN 0-686-55992-4). French & Eur.

--Cinema. 216p. 1966. 8.95 (ISBN 0-686-55993-2). French & Eur.

--Corps et Biens. 192p. 1968. 3.95 (ISBN 0-686-55994-0). French & Eur.

--Domaine Public. 424p. 1953. 11.95 (ISBN 0-686-55996-7). French & Eur.

--Fortunes. 192p. 1969. 3.95 (ISBN 0-686-55997-5). French & Eur.

--La Liberte ou l'Amour. 168p. 1962. 14.95 (ISBN 0-686-55998-3). French & Eur.

--Recits, Nouvelles et Poemes. 1975. 14.95 (ISBN 0-686-55999-1). French & Eur.

--Le Vin Est Tire. 208p. 1943. 3.95 (ISBN 0-686-56000-0). French & Eur.

Desnos, Robert & Dumas, Marie-Claire. Destinee Arbitraire. 88p. 1975. 4.95 (ISBN 0-686-55995-9). French & Eur.

Desnuelle, P., et al, eds. Structure-Function Relationships of Proteolytic Enzymes: Proceedings. 1970. 49.00 (ISBN 0-12-211850-2). Acad Pr.

Desoer, C. A. & Kuh, E. S. Basic Circuit Theory. LC 68-9551. 1969. text ed. 45.00 (ISBN 0-07-016575-0). McGraw.

Desoer, C. A. & Vidyasagar, M. Feedback Systems: Input-Output Properties. (Electrical Science Ser.). 1975. 75.00 (ISBN 0-12-212050-7). Acad Pr.

Desoer, C. A., jt. auth. see Callier, F. M.

Desoer, C. A., jt. auth. see Zadeh, L. A.

De Sola. The Spirit Moves: Dance & Prayer. 169p. 1977. 9.95 (ISBN 0-318-16446-9). Sacred Dance Guild.

De Sola, Carla. Learning Through Dance. LC 73-90083. 254p. 1974. pap. 7.95 (ISBN 0-8091-1807-6). Paulist Pr.

--The Spirit Moves: A Handbook of Dance & Prayer. LC 77-89743. (Illus.). 1977. pap. 9.95 (ISBN 0-918208-04-1). Liturgical Conf.

DeSola, R. Abbreviations Dictionary. 6th ed. 966p. 1981. 41.50 (ISBN 0-444-00380-0). Elsevier.

De Sola, Ralph. Abbreviations Dictionary. 7th ed. 1985. 45.00 (ISBN 0-444-00807-1). Elsevier.

--Crime Dictionary. 240p. 1982. 22.50 (ISBN 0-87196-443-0). Facts on File.

De Sola, Ralph, tr. Beethoven by Berlioz. LC 74-84541. 1975. pap. 2.95 (ISBN 0-8008-0711-1, Crescendo). Taplinger.

De Sola, Vivian, ed. see Skelton, John.

De Solac Pinto, Vivian. Seventeenth-Century Biographies. 31p. 1980. Repr. of 1955 ed. lib. bdg. 10.00 (ISBN 0-8492-2189-7). R West.
De Solac Pinto, Vivian see De Solac Pinto, Vivian.
De Sola-Morales, Ignasi. Gaudi. LC 83-62001. (Illus.). 128p. 1984. 14.95 (ISBN 0-8478-0525-5). Rizzoli Intl.
De Sola Pinto, V. see Pinto, V. de Sola.
De Sola Pinto, V., ed. see Sedley, Charles.
De Sola Pinto, Vivan see Pinto, Vivan De Sola.
De Sola Pinto, Vivian. D. H. Lawrence Prophet of the Midlands: A Lecture. LC 75-17879. Repr. of 1951 ed. lib. bdg. 9.50 (ISBN 0-8414-3677-0). Folcroft.
--John Skelton: A Selection from His Poems. 1979. Repr. of 1950 ed. lib. bdg. 20.00 (ISBN 0-8495-1041-4). Arden Lib.
De Sola Pinto, Vivian see Pinto, Vivian De Sola.
De Sola Pinto, Vivian see Pinto, Vivian De Sola & Rodway, Allan E.
De Sola Pinto, Vivian, ed. John Skelton: A Selection from His Poems. 1977. Repr. of 1950 ed. lib. bdg. 20.00 (ISBN 0-8482-2503-1). Norwood Edns.
--Poetry of the Restoration Sixteen Fifty-Three to Seventeen Hundred. (The Poetry Bookshelf). 1966. pap. text ed. 5.00x (ISBN 0-435-15047-2). Heinemann Ed.
De Sola Pinto, Vivian, ed. see Lawrence, D. H.
De Sola Pool, I., et al. Communication Flows: A Census in the United States & Japan. (Information, Research & Resource Reports Ser.: Vol. 3). 250p. 1984. 29.00 (ISBN 0-444-87521-2, I-192-84, North Holland). Elsevier.
De Sola Pool, Ithiel. Forecasting the Telephone. LC 82-22637. (Communications & Information Sciences Ser.). 192p. 1983. text ed. 27.50 (ISBN 0-89391-048-1). Ablex Pub.
De Sola Pool, Ithiel see Pool, Ithiel de Sola.
De Sola Pool, Ithiel, ed. The Prestige Press: A Comparative Study of Political Symbols. 1970. pap. 6.95x (ISBN 0-262-66022-9). MIT Pr.
--The Social Impact of the Telephone. 512p. 1977. pap. 10.95x (ISBN 0-262-66048-2). MIT Pr.
--Talking Back: Citizen Feedback & Cable Technology. 320p. 1973. 30.00x (ISBN 0-262-16056-0). MIT Pr.
De Sola Pool, Ithiel, et al. Candidates, Issues & Strategies: A Computer Simulation of the 1960 & 1964 Presidential Elections. 2nd rev. ed. 1965. pap. 5.95x (ISBN 0-262-66003-2). MIT Pr.
De Sola Sola de Pool, Ithiel see Pool, Ithiel de Sola.
DeSole, Daniel D. Wasted Lives: A Clinician's Indictment of Traditional Psychiatry. (Traditional Healing Ser.). 300p. Date not set. 25.00 (ISBN 0-932426-13-1). Trado-Medic.
DeSole, Gloria, jt. ed. see Hoffmann, Leonore.
De Sole, S. Entwicklung der Drelipore von Coprinus Radiatus (Bolt.) Fr. (Bibliotheca Mycologica 88). (Illus.). 148p. 1982. pap. 17.50 (ISBN 3-7682-1343-9). Lubrecht & Cramer.
De Soleinne, Martineau. Bibliotheque Dramatique De M. De Soleinne, 9 vols. in 8. LC 72-7273. Repr. of 1914 ed. 275.00 (ISBN 0-8337-3312-5). B Franklin.
De Solenni, Gino. Lope De Vega's El Brasil restituido. 306p. (Eng. & Span.). text ed. 2.60 (ISBN 0-318-14282-1). Hispanic Inst.
De Solms, Marie T., pseud. The Condition of Woman in the United States: A Traveller's Notes. Alger, Abby L., tr. LC 72-2590. (American Women Ser: Images & Realities). (Illus.). 292p. 1972. Repr. of 1895 ed. 19.00 (ISBN 0-405-04447-X). Ayer Co Pubs.
De Sommevoire, Alexis & Da Parigi, Tomaso. Tesoro Della Linqua Greca-Volgare Ed Italiana, Cioe Ricchissimo Dizzionario Greco-Volgare et Italiano, 2 vols. (Gr. & Ital.). Repr. of 1709 ed. lib. bdg. 175.00x (ISBN 0-89241-338-7). Pt. 1, Italian-Greek, viii, 513 Pages. Pt. 2, Greek-Italian, xxviii, 461 Pages. Caratzas.
Desonay. Ronsard Poete de l'Amour, 3 tomes. Incl. Tome I. Cassandre. 21.50 (ISBN 0-685-34201-8); Tome II. De Marie a Genevre. 21.50 (ISBN 0-685-34202-6); Tome III. Du Poete de la Cour au Chantre d'Helene. 23.95 (ISBN 0-685-34203-4). (Academie Royale de Belgique). French & Eur.
De Sormo, Maitland C. Heydays of the Adirondacks. LC 74-84746. (Illus.). 1975. 20.00 (ISBN 0-9601158-2-X); pap. 15.00 (ISBN 0-9601158-3-8). Adirondack Yes.
--Joe Call: The Lewis Giant. LC 81-3334. (Illus.). 1981. 12.50 (ISBN 0-9601158-7-0). Adirondack Yes.
--John Bird Burnham: Klondiker, Adirondacker & Eminent Conservationist. LC 78-50570. (Illus.). 1978. 12.50 (ISBN 0-9601158-5-4). Adirondack Yes.
DeSormo, Maitland C. Noah John Rondeau: Adirondack Hermit. (Illus.). 244p. Repr. of 1969 ed. 11.95 (ISBN 0-932052-37-1). North Country.
De Sormo, Maitland C. Seneca Ray Stoddard, Versatile Camera Artist. LC 72-905866. (Illus.). 1972. 20.00 (ISBN 0-9601158-1-1). Adirondack Yes.
--Summers on the Saranacs. LC 80-81853. (Illus.). 1980. 30.00 (ISBN 0-9601158-6-2). Adirondack Yes.
De Sormo, Maitland C., ed. see Stoddard, Seneca R.
De Sosa, Michael. Taking the Quantum Leap: Using the Sinclair QL Computer. 1985. price not set (ISBN 0-07-016578-5). McGraw.
Desotelle, Joanne R., ed. Who's Who Among American Law Students. 4th. ed. LC 81-645742. 364p. 1984. 35.00 (ISBN 0-317-19181-0). Summa Pub Bur.
--Who's Who Among American Law Students, 1983. LC 81-645742. 160p. 1982. 30.00 (ISBN 0-943960-00-2). Summa Pub Bur.
--Who's Who Among American Law Students, 1984. 3rd ed. LC 81-645742. 321p. 1983. 35.00 (ISBN 0-943960-00-2). Summa Pub Bur.
De Soto, Brown. Hawaii Recalls. LC 82-83322. (Illus.). 130p. (Orig.). 1982. pap. 12.95 (ISBN 0-9607938-2-8). Editions Ltd.
DeSoto, Carole. For Fun & Funds: Creative Fund-Raising Ideas for Your Organization. LC 83-8307. 208p. 1984. 15.95 (ISBN 0-13-324897-6, Busn); pap. 6.95 (ISBN 0-13-324889-5). P-H.
DeSoto, Clinton. Two Hundred Meters & Down, 1936. 1985. 4.00 (ISBN 0-87259-012-7). Am Radio.
DeSourdis, Ron, jt. auth. see Henry, Marilyn.
Desourteaux, Robert. Idees De William Thompson. (Research & Source Works Ser.: No. 640). 1971. Repr. of 1912 ed. lib. bdg. 19.50 (ISBN 0-8337-0842-2). B Franklin.
De Sousa, Maria. Lymphocyte Circulation: Experimental & Clinical Aspects. LC 80-40848. 259p. 1981. 69.95x (ISBN 0-471-27854-8, Pub. by Wiley-Interscience). Wiley.
De Sousa, Maria S., et al. The Effects of Hormones on Immunity, Vol. 2. LC 72-13691. (Illus.). 220p. 1973. text ed. 30.00x (ISBN 0-8422-7098-1). Irvington.
De Souto, Martha S. Group Travel Operations Manual. LC 83-61024. (The Travel Management Library). 1984. 22.95 (ISBN 0-916032-20-5). Merton Hse.
Desoutter, Denny. The Boat-Owner's Practical Dictionary. (Practical Handbooks for the Yachtsman Ser.). (Illus.). 1978. 14.95 (ISBN 0-370-30041-6). Transatlantic.
De Souza, Alfred, jt. auth. see Singh, Andre M.
De Souza, Alfred, ed. Children in India: Critical Issues in Human Development. 1980. 17.50x (ISBN 0-8364-0601-X, Pub. by Manohar India). South Asia Bks.
DeSouza, Alfred, ed. The Indian City. 2nd ed. 1983. 16.00x (ISBN 0-8364-0998-1, Pub. by Manohar India). South Asia Bks.
De Souza, Alfred, ed. The Indian City: Poverty, Ecology & Urban Development. 1979. 14.50x (ISBN 0-8364-0196-4). South Asia Bks.
DeSouza, Alfred, ed. Urban Growth & Urban Planning: Political Context & People's Priorities. 1984. pap. 6.00 (ISBN 0-8364-1242-7, Pub. by Indian Soc Inst). South Asia Bks.
De Souza, Alfred, ed. Women in Contemporary India. LC 76-900940. 1976. 18.50 (ISBN 0-88386-720-6). South Asia Bks.
Desouza, Alfred, ed. Women in Contemporary India & South Asia. rev. 2nd ed. 1981. 22.00x (ISBN 0-8364-0738-5, Pub. by Manohar India). South Asia Bks.
DeSouza, Amaury, jt. auth. see McDonough, Peter.
DeSouza, Anthony & Foust, Brady. World Space-Economy. 1979. text ed. 26.95 (ISBN 0-675-08292-7). Merrill.
DeSouza, Anthony, ed. The Politics of Change & Leadership Development: New Leaders in India & Africa. 1978. 15.00x (ISBN 0-8364-0192-1). South Asia Bks.
De Souza, Anthony, jt. ed. see Vogeler, Ingolf.
DeSouza, Glenn R. Energy Policy & Forecasting: Economic, Financial, & Technological Dimensions. LC 79-9671. (Arthur D. Little Bk.). 240p. 1981. 29.50x (ISBN 0-669-03614-5). Lexington Bks.
De Souza, Luis A. & Ribeiro, Lucia. Youth Participation in the Development Process: A Case Study in Panama. (International Bureau of Education Ser.: No. 18). 1976. pap. 5.00 (ISBN 92-3-101308-4, U735, UNESCO). Unipub.
De Souza, Maria. Living English for Portuguese-Speaking People. 15.95, with 4 LP records conversation manual & dictionary (ISBN 0-517-50820-6). Crown.
De Souza, Teotonio. Medieval Goa. 309p. 1981. text ed. 21.75x (ISBN 0-391-02352-7, Pub. by Concept India). Humanities.
Desowitz, Robert S. New Guinea Tapeworms & Jewish Grandmothers: Tales of Ecology, Parasites, & Progress. 1981. 12.95 (ISBN 0-393-01474-6). Norton.
--New Guinea Tapeworms & Jewish Grandmothers: Tales of Parasites & Peoples. 224p. 1983. pap. 3.95 (ISBN 0-380-64006-6, 64006-6, Discus). Avon.
D'Espagnat, B. In Search of Reality. Ehlers, A., tr. (Illus.). 210p. 1983. pap. 18.00 (ISBN 0-387-11399-1). Springer-Verlag.
D'Espagnat, B., ed. Foundations of Quantum Mechanics. (Italian Physical Society Ser.: Course 49). 1972. 86.00 (ISBN 0-12-368849-3). Acad Pr.
Despain, Goldie B. Tiny Ant Who Scared a Horned Toad. (Illus.). (ps-3). 1970. 4.25 (ISBN 0-8313-0029-9); PLB 6.19. Lantern.
De Spain, June. Little Cyanide Cookbook: B-17 Recipes. 5.95 (ISBN 0-912986-00-X). Cancer Control Soc.
--The Little Cyanide Cookbook: Delicious Recipes Rich in Vitamin B17. 192p. 1976. pap. text ed. 5.95 (ISBN 0-912986-00-X). Am Media.
Despain, R. O. The Malt-Ease Flagon: Your Complete Guide to Homebrewing. LC 78-24695. 1978. 8.95 (ISBN 0-913668-88-5); pap. 4.95 (ISBN 0-913668-87-7). Ten Speed Pr.
DeSpain, Richard. More Than a Memory: Little Rock's Historic Quapaw Quarter. LC 81-52796. (Illus.). 72p. 1981. pap. 9.95 (ISBN 0-914546-37-6). Rose Pub.
Despalatovic, Elinor M. Ljudevit Gaj & the Illyrian Movement. (East European Monographs: No. 12). 271p. 1976. 22.50x (ISBN 0-914710-05-2). East Eur Quarterly.
Despalatovic, Marijan, tr. see Gulyga, Arsenij.
Despard, Annabelle, tr. see Skirbekk, Sigurd.
DeSparks, C. Tractor Operating Book & Directory. 144p. 4.75. (ISBN 0-318-14908-7, G114). Midwest Old Settlers.
Desparmet, J. Contes populaires sur les ogres, recueillis a Bilda, 2 vols. LC 78-20144. (Collection de contes et de chansons populaires: Vols. 35-36). Repr. of 1910 ed. Set. 43.00 (ISBN 0-404-60385-8). AMS Pr.
Des Pas Feuquieres, Antoine. Memoirs Historical & Military: Containing a Distinct View of All the Considerable States of Europe. LC 68-54790. 1735-1736. Repr. lib. bdg. 42.50x (ISBN 0-8371-2662-2, FEMH). Greenwood.
De Spelder, Bruce E. Ratios of Staff to Line Personnel. 81p. 1962. pap. 2.00x (ISBN 0-87776-106-X, R-106). Ohio St U Admin Sci.
DeSpelder, Lynne & Strickland, Albert. Family Life Education: Resources for the Elementary Classroom. 339p. 1982. 24.95 (ISBN 0-941816-06-0). Network Pubns.
DeSpelder, Lynne A. & Prettyman, Nathalie. A Guidebook for Teaching Family Living. 281p. 1980. pap. 31.95x (ISBN 0-205-06977-0, 236977, Pub. by Longwood Div). Allyn.
DeSpelder, Lynne A. & Strickland, Albert L. The Last Dance: Encountering Death & Dying. LC 82-62054. 491p. 1983. text ed. 21.95 (ISBN 0-87484-535-1). Mayfield Pub.
Des Periers, Bonaventure. Bonaventure Des Periers's Novel Pastimes & Merry Tales. La Charite, Raymond C., ed. & tr. LC 70-190532. (Studies in Romance Languages: No. 6). 264p. 1972. 24.00x (ISBN 0-8131-1279-6). U Pr of Ky.
De Spindler, Irene, ed. see Congress on Occupational Therapy, 5th International, Zurich, 1970.
De Spinoza, Benedict. Ethics. Eliot, George, tr. from Lat. (Salzburg Romantic Reassessment Ser.: No. 102). 259p. 1981. pap. text ed. 25.50x (ISBN 0-391-02369-1, Pub. by Salzburg Austria). Humanities.
--Tractatus De Intellectus Emendatione. facs. ed. LC 78-94284. (Select Bibliographies Reprint Ser). 1899. 17.00 (ISBN 0-8369-5057-7). Ayer Co Pubs.
De Spinoza, Benedictus. Ethics. Boyle, Andrew, tr. Incl. On the Correction of the Understanding. 1977. Repr. of 1959 ed. 12.95x (ISBN 0-460-00481-6, Evman). Biblio Dist.
--The Principles of Descartes' Philosophy. Britan, Halbert H., tr. from Lat. LC 74-3096. 1978. pap. 6.75 (ISBN 0-87548-053-5). Open Court.
Despointes, Ann H., tr. see Grunchec, Philippe.
Despois, Eugene, ed. see Desfeuilles, Arthur.
De Sponde, Jean. Sonnets on Love & Death. Nugent, Robert, tr. LC 78-12395. 1979. Repr. of 1962 ed. lib. bdg. 22.50x (ISBN 0-313-21126-4, SPSL). Greenwood.
Despontin, M., et al. Macro-Economic Planning with Conflicting Goals: Proceedings of a Workshop Held at the Vrije Universiteit of Brussels, Beligum, December 10, 1982. (Lecture Notes in Economics & Mathematical Systems Ser.: Vol. 230). vi, 297p. 1984. pap. 20.00 (ISBN 0-387-13367-4). Springer-Verlag.
Despot, Maggi, tr. see Matura, Thaddee.
D'Espouy, Hector. Fragments from Greek & Roman Architecture: The Classical American Edition of Hector D'Espouy's Plates. Blatteau, John & Sears, Christiane, eds. (Illus.). 1981. pap. 9.95 (ISBN 0-393-00052-4). Norton.
Despres, David, jt. ed. see Adair, John.
DesPres, Terrence. The Survivor. 1983. pap. 3.95 (ISBN 0-671-46687-9). WSP.
Des Pres, Terrence. The Survivor: An Anatomy of Life in the Death Camps. 1976. 18.95x (ISBN 0-19-501952-0). Oxford U Pr.
--The Survivor: An Anatomy of Life in the Death Camps. (Illus.). 1976. pap. 7.95 (ISBN 0-19-502703-5, GB 596, GB). Oxford U Pr.
Desramaut, Francis. Don Bosco & the Spiritual Life. Luna, Roger M., tr. from Fr. LC 79-52674. (Orig.). 1979. pap. text ed. 10.95 (ISBN 0-89944-022-3). Don Bosco Multimedia.
Desroche, Henri. The American Shakers: From Neo-Christianity to Presocialism. Savacool, John K., ed. LC 78-123537. 368p. 1971. 20.00x (ISBN 0-87023-063-8). U of Mass Pr.
--Jacob & the Angel: An Essay in Sociologies of Religion. Savacool, John K., ed. & tr. from Fr. LC 72-77575. 196p. 1973. 15.00x (ISBN 0-87023-109-X). U of Mass Pr.
Desroche, Henri & Rambaud, Placide, eds. Villages En Developpement: Contribution a une Sociologie Villageois. (Recherches Cooperatives: No. 4). (Illus.). 1972. pap. 14.00x (ISBN 0-686-21260-6). Mouton.
Desroche, Henri, et al. Dieux D'hommes: Dictionnaire Des Messianismes & Millenarismes De L'ere Chretienne. 1969. 30.40x (ISBN 90-2796-415-7). Mouton.
Desroches-Noblecourt, Christiane. Tutankhamen. LC 63-15145. 1976. pap. 8.95 (ISBN 0-8212-0695-8, 857017). NYGS.
Desrosier, John N., jt. auth. see Desrosier, Norman W.
Desrosier, Norman W. & Desrosier, John N. Technology of Food Preservation. 4th ed. (Illus.). 1977. pap. 25.50 (ISBN 0-87055-286-4). AVI.
Desrosier, Norman W. & Tressler, Donald K. Fundamentals of Food Freezing. (Illus.). 1977. pap. text ed. 26.50 (ISBN 0-87055-290-2). AVI.
Desrosier, Norman W., jt. auth. see Sivetz, Michael.
Desrosier, Norman W., ed. Elements of Food Technology. (Illus.). 1977. pap. 29.50 (ISBN 0-87055-284-8). AVI.
Desrosiers, G. & Boulay, J. Vocabulaire des Assurances Sociales. 21p. (Fr.). 1971. pap. 3.95 (ISBN 0-7754-2274-6, M-9231). French & Eur.
Dessaigne, Jacques, jt. auth. see Carrere, Jean.
Dessain, C. S. The Spirituality of John Henry Newman. 160p. 1980. pap. 4.95 (ISBN 0-03-057843-4). Winston Pr.
Dessain, Charles S. John Henry Newman. 2nd ed. 1971. 15.00x (ISBN 0-8047-0778-2). Stanford U Pr.
Dessain, Charles S., ed. see Newman, John H.
Dessain, Stephen, ed. see Newman, John H.
Dessaint, Alain Y. Minorities of Southwest China: An Introduction to the Yi (Lolo) & Related Peoples & an Annotated Bibliography. LC 80-80017. (Bibliographies Ser.). 381p. 1980. 25.00 (ISBN 0-87536-250-8). HRAFP.
Dessaix, Paul. Montchretien et L'economie Politique Nationale. LC 79-146139. (Research & Source Works Ser.: No. 624). 1971. Repr. of 1901 ed. lib. bdg. 12.00 (ISBN 0-8337-0843-0). B Franklin.
Dessaix, Robert. Turgenev: The Quest for Faith. LC 80-66036. 222p. (Orig.). 1980. pap. text ed. 6.50 (ISBN 0-908160-55-0, 0591, Pub. by Faculty Arts Australia). Australia N U P.
Dessaix, Robert, tr. from Rus. The Mysterious Tales of Ivan Turgenev. LC 79-53661. (Orig.). (gr. 11-12). 1980. pap. text ed. 7.50 (ISBN 0-7081-1204-8, 0376, Pub. by ANUP Australia). Australia N U P.
Dessaix, Robert, tr. see Dostoyevsky, Fyodor.
Dessart, Donald J. & Suydam, Marilyn N. Classroom Ideas from Research on Secondary School Mathematics. LC 83-8279. (Illus.). 128p. 1983. pap. 6.00 (ISBN 0-87353-207-4). NCTM.
Dessart, George. Television in the Real World. 1978. pap. text ed. 10.95x (ISBN 0-8038-7172-4). Hastings.
Dessau, H. Inscriptiones Latinae Selectae, 5 vols. 1985. Set. 165.00 (ISBN 0-89005-274-3); Set. pap. 125.00 (ISBN 0-317-17356-1). Ares.
Dessau, Hermann. Geschichte der Romischen Kaiserzeit, 2 vols. LC 75-7316. (Roman History Ser.). 1975. Repr. Set. 106.00 (ISBN 0-405-07197-3); 53.00x ea. Vol. 1 (ISBN 0-405-07198-1). Vol. 2 (ISBN 0-405-07199-X). Ayer Co Pubs.
Dessau, J. Role of Multilateral Food Aid Programs. (World Food Programme Studies: No. 5). (Orig.). 1965. pap. 4.50 (ISBN 0-685-09405-7, F415, FAO). Unipub.
Dessauer, Herbert C. & Hafner, Mark S., eds. Collections of Frozen Tissues: Value, Management, Field & Laboratory Procedures, & Directory of Existing Collections. (Illus.). 74p. (Orig.). 1984. pap. 7.50 (ISBN 0-942924-10-X). Assn Syst Coll.
Dessauer, John. Book Publishing: What It Is, What It Does. 2nd ed. 248p. 1981. 29.95 (ISBN 0-8352-1325-0); pap. 15.95 (ISBN 0-8352-1326-9). Bowker.
Dessaulles, Louis A. Six Lectures Sur l'Annexion Du Canada Aux Etats-Unis. 1851. 15.00 (ISBN 0-384-11514-4). Johnson Repr.
--Six Lectures Sur L'Annexion Du Canada Aux Etats-Unis. (Canadiana Avant 1867: No. 11). 1968. 14.00 (ISBN 90-2796-336-3). Mouton.
Dessaur, C. I. Foundations of Theory-Formation in Criminology: A Methodological Analysis. (Methods & Models in the Social Sciences Ser: No. 2). 152p. 1971. text ed. 12.00x (ISBN 0-686-22484-1). Mouton.
--Science Between Culture & Counter Culture. 128p. 1975. pap. text ed. 12.75x (ISBN 90-255-9813-7). Humanities.
Desseaux, Jacques. Twenty Centuries of Ecumenism. 1984. pap. 4.95 (ISBN 0-8091-2617-6). Paulist Pr.
Dessel, Sabine Van see Van Dessel, Sabine.
Dessem, Ralph. Celebrating Advent in the Sanctuary. 1983. 2.00 (ISBN 0-89536-635-5). CSS of Ohio.
Dessem, Ralph, jt. auth. see Crouch, Tim.
Dessem, Ralph & Klempnauer, D. Gary, eds. Power of the Light. 1978. pap. 5.50 (ISBN 0-89536-330-5). CSS of Ohio.
Dessem, Ralph E. Participate! Family Night Programs. (Orig.). 1977. pap. 4.95 (ISBN 0-89536-280-5). CSS of Ohio.
--The Service of Lights. 1970. pap. 2.50 (ISBN 0-89536-220-1). CSS of Ohio.
--Shadows Around the Cross. 1973. 2.75 (ISBN 0-89536-211-2). CSS of Ohio.
--Were You There the Day the Sun Refused to Shine. 1973. 2.50 (ISBN 0-89536-260-0, 2317). CSS of Ohio.

Dessem, Ralph E. & Grossmann, Mary Lou. Twentieth Century Worship Services, Vol. 2. 1982. 10.00 (ISBN 0-89536-575-8). CSS of Ohio.
Dessem, Ralph E. & Runk, Wesley T. Making Confirmation Meaningful. 1971. pap. 2.50 (ISBN 0-89536-149-3). CSS of Ohio.
Dessem, Ralph E., ed. A Season to Return. 119p. 1976. pap. 5.25 (ISBN 0-89536-205-8). CSS of Ohio.
Dessem, Ralph E., compiled by. Twentieth Century Worship Services & Bulletins. 55p. (Orig.). 1975. pap. 8.25 (ISBN 0-89536-239-2). CSS of Ohio.
Dessemontet, F., jt. auth. see Ansay, T.
Dessemontet, F., jt. ed. see Ansay, T.
Dessemontet, Francois. The Legal Protection of Know-How in the United States of America. 2nd rev. ed. Clarke, H. W., tr. from Fr. (Studies in Researches of the Institute of Comparative Law, Faculty of Law of the University of Lausanne). 487p. 1976. pap. 30.00x (ISBN 0-8377-0504-5). Rothman.
Dessen, Alan C. Elizabethan Stage Conventions & Modern Interpreters. LC 83-23970. 224p. 1984. 29.95 (ISBN 0-521-25912-6). Cambridge U Pr.
--Jonson's Moral Comedy. LC 76-126900. pap. 50.60 (ISBN 0-8357-9461-X, 2014778). Bks Demand UMI.
Dessen, Alan C., ed. Renaissance Drama New Series XII. LC 67-29872. 225p. 1981. 24.95 (ISBN 0-8101-0547-0). Northwestern U Pr.
Dessen, Alan C., jt. ed. see Schoenbaum, S.
Dessent, Michael H. Baseball Becky. (gr. 4-8). 1982. 8.95 (ISBN 0-916392-80-5); pap. 5.95 (ISBN 0-916392-97-X). Oak Tree Pubns.
--California Corporation Manual, 3 vols. 2nd ed. LC 74-26211. write for info. Lawyers Co-Op.
Dessent, Tony, ed. What Is Important about Portage? 196p. 1984. 16.00x (ISBN 0-7005-0646-2, Pub. by NFER Nelson UK). Taylor & Francis.
Desser, David. The Samurai Films of Akira Kurosawa. Kirkpatrick, Diane, ed. LC 83-15563. (Studies in Cinema: No. 23). 172p. 1983. 39.95 (ISBN 0-8357-1495-0). UMI Res Pr.
Desser, S. S., jt. ed. see Mettrick, D. F.
Dessler, Alexander J., ed. Physics of the Jovian Magnetosphere. (Cambridge Planetary Science 3). (Illus.). 400p. 1983. 32.50 (ISBN 0-521-24558-3). Cambridge U Pr.
Dessler, E. E. Strive for the Truth: The World of Rav Dessler. Carmell, Aryeh, tr. from Hebrew. 1978. 7.95 (ISBN 0-87306-139-X); pap. 4.95 (ISBN 0-87306-177-2). Feldheim.
Dessler, G. Organization Theory: Integrating Structure & Behavior. 1980. 28.95 (ISBN 0-13-641886-4). P-H.
Dessler, Gary. Applied Human Relations. 1983. text ed. 24.95 (ISBN 0-8359-0180-7); instr's. manual free. Reston.
--Human Behavior: Improving Productivity at Work. (Illus.). 480p. 1980. text ed. 25.95 (ISBN 0-8359-2994-9); instrs' manual avail. (ISBN 0-8359-2995-7). Reston.
--Improving Productivity at Work: Motivating Today's Employees. 1983. text ed. 19.95 (ISBN 0-8359-3050-5). Reston.
--Management Fundamentals. 4th ed. LC 84-22263. 1985. text ed. 28.95 (ISBN 0-8359-4161-2); instr's manual avail. (ISBN 0-8359-4162-0); study guide 11.95 (ISBN 0-8359-4163-9). Reston.
--Organization & Management. 1982. text ed. 28.95 (ISBN 0-8359-5311-4); instrs'. manual avail. (ISBN 0-8359-5312-2). Reston.
--Organization & Management: A Contingency Approach. ref. ed. (Illus.). 1976. 22.95. P-H.
--Organization Theory: Integrating Structure & Behavior. 2nd ed. (Illus.). 448p. 1986. text ed. 28.95 (ISBN 0-13-641903-8). P-H.
--Personnel Management. 3rd ed. 1984. text ed. 27.95 (ISBN 0-8359-5507-9). Reston.
Dessler, N. W. Suggested Curriculum for the Day School. 7.00 (ISBN 0-914131-63-X, C01). Torah Umesorah.
Dessner, Lawrence J. The Homely Web of Truth: A Study of Charlotte Bronte's Novels. (De Proprietatibus Litterarum, Ser Practica: No 108). 126p. (Orig.). 1975. pap. text ed. 11.20x (ISBN 0-686-22597-X). Mouton.
--How to Write a Poem. LC 78-65447. 1979. 25.00x (ISBN 0-8147-1766-7); pap. 12.50x (ISBN 0-8147-1767-5). NYU Pr.
Dessoir, Max. Aesthetics & Theory of Art. Emery, Stephen A., tr. LC 68-22680. 454p. 1970. text ed. 14.95x (ISBN 0-8143-1383-3). Wayne St U Pr.
Dessouki, Ali E. Hillal. Islamic Resurgence in the Arab World. LC 81-12135. 286p. 1982. 37.95 (ISBN 0-03-059673-4). Praeger.
Dessouki, Ali E. Hillal, jt. ed. see Cudsi, Alex.
Dessy, Jeanne & Norton, Lee. Assessing Learning Time at the Co-op Training Station. 58p. 1985. 6.25 (ISBN 0-318-17849-4, SN 50). Natl Ctr Res Voc Ed.
De Stael. Ten Years Exile. 434p. 1969. 25.00x (ISBN 0-87556-075-X). Saifer.
De Stael, Madame. Correspondance Generale, 3 tomes. Jasinski, ed. Incl. Tome I, Pt. 1. Lettres de Jeunesse de 1777 a Aout 1788. 20.75 (ISBN 0-685-35000-2); Tome I, Pt. 2. 1788-1791. 20.75 (ISBN 0-685-35001-0); Tome II, Pt. 1. Lettres Inedites a Louis de Norbonne. 26.95 (ISBN 0-685-35002-9); Tome II, Pt. 2. Lettres Diverses de 1792 a Mai 1794. 27.95 (ISBN 0-685-35003-7); Tome III, Pt. 1. Lettres de Mezery et de Coppet (16 Mai 1794-16 Mai 1795) 27.95 (ISBN 0-685-35004-5); Tome III, Pt. 2. Lettres d'une Nouvelle Republicaine. 36.75 (ISBN 0-685-35005-3). French & Eur.
De Staercke, Andre, ed. NATO's Anxious Birth: The Way to the 1980's. LC 84-40609. (Illus.). 220p. 1985. 27.50 (ISBN 0-312-11469-9). St Martin.
D'Estaing, Giscard. Peace & East-West Relations. (The Singapore Lecture Ser.). (Orig.). 1984. pap. text ed. 9.50 (ISBN 9971-902-64-8, Pub. by Inst Southeast Asian Stud). Gower Pub Co.
Destang, Francoise, jt. auth. see Paschos, Jacqueline.
D'Este, Carlo. Decision in Normandy. (Illus.). 555p. 1983. 22.50 (ISBN 0-525-24218-X, 02184-660). Dutton.
DeStefano, Anthony. Dachau Treasure. 1977. pap. 1.50 (ISBN 0-532-15294-8). Woodhill.
--The Hard Edge. 1978. pap. 1.50 (ISBN 0-532-15329-4). Woodhill.
--A Minute to Pray, a Second to Die - Mondo. (No. 3). 1977. pap. 1.50 (ISBN 0-532-15272-7). Woodhill.
--The Sorceress. 1977. pap. 1.50 (ISBN 0-532-15285-9). Woodhill.
DeStefano, Johanna S. Language, the Learner & the School. LC 77-13511. 221p. 1978. pap. text ed. 19.95 (ISBN 0-471-02378-7). Wiley.
DeStefano, Patricia. Interlude of Widowhood. (Greeting Book Line Ser.). 48p. (Orig.). 1983. pap. 1.50 (ISBN 0-89622-200-4). Twenty-Third.
Destenay, Anne, tr. see Chesneaux, Jean, et al.
De Stevens, George. Diuretics. (Medicinal Chemistry Ser.: Vol. 1). 1963. 42.00 (ISBN 0-12-212156-2). Acad Pr.
De Stevens, George, ed. Analgetics. (Medicinal Chemistry Ser.: Vol. 5). 1965. 76.00 (ISBN 0-12-212150-3). Acad Pr.
Desti, Mary. The Untold Story: The Life of Isadora Duncan 1921-1927. (Ser. in Dance). (Illus.). 281p. 1981. Repr. of 1929 ed. lib. bdg. 29.50 (ISBN 0-306-76044-4). Da Capo.
Destin, E. J., jt. ed. see Cantraine, G.
Destine, J., jt. ed. see Cantraine, G.
Destler, Chester M. Joshua Coit: American Federalist, 1758-1798. LC 62-10571. (Illus.). 1962. 17.50x (ISBN 0-8195-3023-9). Wesleyan U Pr.
Destler, Chester M. see Weaver, Glenn.
Destler, I. M. Making Foreign Economic Policy. LC 79-5119. 256p. 1980. 22.95 (ISBN 0-8157-1822-5); pap. 8.95 (ISBN 0-8157-1821-7). Brookings.
--Presidents, Bureaucrats, & Foreign Policy: The Politics of Organizational Reform. LC 77-166368. 362p. 1972. pap. 13.95x (ISBN 0-691-02169-4). Princeton U Pr.
Destler, I. M. & Sato, Hideo, eds. Coping with U. S. Japanese Economic Conflicts. LC 81-47897. (Illus.). 320p. 1982. 28.50x (ISBN 0-669-05144-6). Lexington Bks.
Destler, I. M., et al. Managing an Alliance: The Politics of U. S.-Japanese Relations. 224p. 1976. 22.95 (ISBN 0-8157-1820-9); pap. 8.95 (ISBN 0-8157-1819-5). Brookings.
--The Textile Wrangle: Conflict in Japanese-American Relations, 1969-1971. LC 78-14429. 1979. 37.50x (ISBN 0-8014-1120-3). Cornell U Pr.
--Our Own Worst Enemy: The Unmaking of American Foreign Policy. 294p. 1984. 17.95 (ISBN 0-671-44278-3). S&S.
Destouches, Andre C. ISSE: Pastovale Heroique. Fajon, Robert, ed. Heroique, Pastoval. (French Opera in the 17th & 18th Centuries Ser.: No.1, Vol.XIV). (Illus.). 1984. lib. bdg. 95.00 (ISBN 0-918728-30-4). Pendragon NY.
Destouches, Andre-Cardinal. Isse. Salomon, Hector, ed. (Chefs-d'oeuvre classiques de l'opera francais Ser: Vol. 10). (Illus.). 282p. (Fr.). 1972. pap. 27.50x (ISBN 0-8450-1110-3). Broude.
Destouches, Andre Cardinal. Omphale. Salomon, Hector, ed. (Chefs-d'oeuvre classiques de l'opera francais ser.: Vol. 11). (Illus.). 346p. (Fr.). 1972. pap. 27.50x (ISBN 0-8450-1111-1). Broude.
Destouches, Andre-Cardinal, jt. auth. see De Lalande, Michel-Richard.
Destouches, J. L., ed. see E.W. Beth Memorial Colloquium, Paris, 1964.
Destouches, J. L., ed. see Logic & Foundations of Science, Institute Henri Poincare, Paris, May 1964.
D'Estree, Sabine, tr. see Reage, Pauline.
De Stroumillo, Elizabeth. Traveller's Guide to Greece. 1978. pap. 5.95 (ISBN 0-8038-2665-6). Hastings.
Destutt De Tracy, A. Treatise on Political Economy. LC 67-23018. Repr. of 1817 ed. 37.50x (ISBN 0-678-00656-3). Kelley.
Destutt De Tracy, Antoine L. Commentary & Review of Montesquieu's Spirit of Laws. 1967. Repr. of 1811 ed. 22.50 (ISBN 0-8337-0845-7). B Franklin.
De Sua, William J. Dante into English: A Study of the Translation of the Divine Comedy in Britain & America. Repr. of 1964 ed. 18.00 (ISBN 0-384-11523-3). Johnson Repr.
De Sua, William J., ed. see Friederich, Werner P. & Arndt, Walter W.
De Summers, Jessica. Gozo Al Grecer. 48p. 1981. pap. 1.10 (ISBN 0-311-38550-8, Edit Mundo). Casa Bautista.
De Surcy, Bernard B., ed. see De Wert, Giaches.
De Surgy, Paul. Mystery of Salvation. Sheed, Rosemary, tr. 1966. pap. 2.25x (ISBN 0-268-00185-5). U of Notre Dame Pr.
De Suria, Tomas. Tomas De Suria & His Voyage with Malaspina, 1791. 91p. 1980. 10.95 (ISBN 0-87770-239-X). Ye Galleon.
Desvignes-Parent. Marivaux et l'Angleterre: Essai sur une Creation Dramatique Originale. 52.50 (ISBN 0-685-34043-0). French & Eur.
DesVoigne, Merritt J. Being Small Wasn't Bad at All. LC 82-90097. (Orig.). 1982. pap. 4.95 (ISBN 0-686-84843-8). Littleman.
Desy, Jeanne, jt. auth. see Franchak, Stephen J.
De Sylva, Donald P. The Alfred C. Glassell, Jr. - University of Miami Argosy Expedition to Ecuador: Part 1: Introduction & Narrative. LC 72-125657. (Studies in Tropical Oceanography Ser: No. 11). 1972. 6.95x (ISBN 0-87024-171-0). U Miami Marine.
--Systematics & Life History of the Great Barracuda, Sphyraena Barracuda (Walbaum) (Studies in Tropical Oceanography Ser: No. 1). 1970. 7.95x (ISBN 0-87024-082-X). U Miami Marine.
De Sylva, Geoffrey F. John Ruskin's "Modern Painters I & II". A Phenomenological Analysis. Kuspit, Donald, ed. LC 81-13009. (Studies in the Fine Arts: Art Theory: No. 5). 296p. 1981. 39.95 (ISBN 0-8357-1233-8). UMI Res Pr.
De Syrmia, Edmond. At the Head of Nations: The Rise of the Papal & Princely House of Odescalchi. LC 76-44029. (Illus.). 116p. 1978. 10.00 (ISBN 0-914226-05-3). Cyclopedia.
Deszo, L. & Hajdu, P., eds. Theoretical Problems of Typology & the Northern Eurasian Languages. 184p. 1970. 28.00x (ISBN 90-6032-062-X). Benjamins North Am.
Deszo, Laszlo. Studies in Syntactic Typology & Contrastive Grammar. (Janua Linguarum Series Maior: No. 89). 207p. 1982. text ed. 42.00 (ISBN 90-279-3108-9). Mouton.
Deszoe, Laslo. Studies on Syntactic Topology & Contrastive Grammar. (Janua Linguarum, Series Practica). 1979. pap. text ed. 33.60x (ISBN 90-279-3108-9). Mouton.
Detacuden, Nam U. The Simplest Explanation of God Ever Explained. 230p. 1983. 13.50 (ISBN 0-682-49951-X). Exposition Pr FL.
DeTalavera, Frances & Custis, John P. Sumptuous Dining in Gaslight San Francisco (1875-1915) LC 83-45372. (Illus.). 240p. 1985. 17.95 (ISBN 0-385-19252-5). Doubleday.
Detaller, Roger see Eaglestone, Arthur A., pseud.
De Talleyrand-Perigord, Charles M. see Talleyrand-Perigord, Charles M. de.
De T. Alvim, Paulo, ed. Ecophysiology of Tropical Crops. 1977. 62.50 (ISBN 0-12-055650-2). Acad Pr.
DeTar, Delos F., ed. Molecular Mechanics: A Symposium. LC 77-14614. 1978. pap. text ed. 36.00 (ISBN 0-08-022070-3). Pergamon.
De Tarde, Alfred. Idee Du Juste Prix: Essai De Psychologie Economique. 1971. Repr. of 1907 ed. lib. bdg. 23.50 (ISBN 0-8337-3471-7). B Franklin.
De Tarr, Francis. The French Radical Party: From Herriot to Mendes-France. LC 80-18231. (Illus.). xx, 264p. 1980. Repr. of 1961 ed. lib. bdg. 27.50x (ISBN 0-313-22608-3, DEFR). Greenwood.
De Tassy, Joseph H. Garcin see Garcin De Tassy, Joseph H.
De Tavera, Joaquin P. see Craig, Austin.
Detection Club. The Floating Admiral. 320p. 1984. pap. 2.95 (ISBN 0-441-24098-4, Pub. by Charter Bks). Ace Bks.
Detection Club, ed. Verdict of Thirteen. 256p. 1980. pap. 2.25 (ISBN 0-345-28901-3). Ballantine.
Detel, Wofgang. Scientia Rerum Nature Occultarum Methodologische Studien Zur Physik Pierre Gassendis. (Quellen und Studien Zur Philosophie: Vol. 14). 1978. 39.60x (ISBN 3-11-007320-X). De Gruyter.
De Tella, G., jt. ed. see Kindleberger, Charles P.
Detels, P., ed. see Thomas, Deborah & Clauser, Suzanne S.
Detels, Pamela & Harris, Janet. Canoeing: Trips in Connecticut. (Illus.). 1977. pap. 3.95 (ISBN 0-931964-03-2). Birch Run Pub.
--Inside the Breakwater: A Guide to Coastal Conn. 1979. pap. 6.95 (ISBN 0-931964-02-4). Birch Run Pub.
De Teran, Lisa St. Aubin see St. Aubin de Teran, Lisa.
Deterding, David, tr. see Bo Yang.
Deterding, Henri. An International Oilman, as Told to Stanley Naylor. Wilkins, Mira, ed. LC 76-29771. (European Business Ser.). 1977. Repr. of 1934 ed. lib. bdg. 14.00x (ISBN 0-405-09784-0). Ayer Co Pubs.
Deterding, Paul E. Echoes of Pauline Concepts in the Speech at Antioch. (Concordia Student Journal Monograph Ser.: No. 1). (Illus.). 50p. (Orig.). 1980. pap. 2.50 (ISBN 0-911770-51-8). Concordia Student.
Detering, Alberta M. Of Times & People from Ohio, Vol. I: Distant Cousins. 200p. 1985. 15.00 (ISBN 0-682-40248-6). Exposition Pr FL.
Detering, Klaus. Automatische Erzeugung Englischer Satze. (Janua Linguarum, Series Practica: No. 170). (Illus.). 1970. 18.40x (ISBN 90-2792-501-1). Mouton.
Determann, H. Gel Chromatography: Gel Filtration, Gel Permeation, Molecular Sieves-a Laboratory Handbook. Gross, E. & Harkin, J. M., trs. LC 68-59064. (Illus.). 1968. 26.00 (ISBN 0-387-04450-7). Springer-Verlag.
De Terra, Helmut, et al. Tepexpan Man. Linton, Ralph, ed. (Illus.). 1949. 19.00 (ISBN 0-384-11525-X). Johnson Repr.
Detert, Richard A., jt. auth. see Curtis, Jack D.
Detert, Richard A., jt. auth. see Curtis, John D.
De Tevis, Rose, et al, eds. El Oro y el Futuro del Pueblo. (Illus.). 155p. 1979. pap. 5.00 (ISBN 0-918358-11-6). Pajarito Pubns.
De Thabrew. Popular Tropical Aquarium Plants. 1981. 30.00x (ISBN 0-686-98215-0, Pub. by Thornhill Pr England). State Mutual Bk.
De The, G., et al, eds. Oncogenesis & Herpesviruses II: Proceedings of a Symposium. Held in Nuremberg, Germany, Oct. 14-16, 1974, 2 pts. Incl. Pt. 1. Biochemistry of Viral Replication & in Vitro Transformation. 40.00 (ISBN 0-686-16808-9); Pt. 2. Epidemiology, Host Response & Control. 32.00 (ISBN 0-686-16809-7). (IARC Scientific Pub.: No. 11). 1975. World Health.
Detheridge, Joseph, compiled by. Chronology of Music Composers, 2 vols. LC 77-166270. (Illus.). 311p. 1972. Repr. of 1936 ed. Set. 59.00 (ISBN 0-403-01390-9). Scholarly.
Dethier. Newberry: The Life & Times of a Maine Clam. LC 81-66267. (Illus.). (gr. 4-6). 1981. pap. 6.95 (ISBN 0-89272-085-9). Down East.
Dethier, Jean. Down to Earth. (Illus.). 192p. 1983. 21.95 (ISBN 0-87196-691-3). Facts on File.
Dethier, V. G. The Ant Heap. LC 79-52701. (Illus.). 151p. 1979. 7.95 (ISBN 0-87850-034-0). Darwin Pr.
--The Hungry Fly: A Physiological Study of the Behavior Associated with Feeding. (Commonwealth Fund Ser.). (Illus.). 512p. 1976. text ed. 35.00x (ISBN 0-674-42710-6). Harvard U Pr.
--Man's Plague? Insects & Agriculture. LC 75-15216. (Illus.). 237p. (Orig.). 1976. 9.95 (ISBN 0-87850-026-X). Darwin Pr.
Dethier, Vincent G. The Ecology of a Summer House. LC 83-18007. (Illus.). 144p. 1984. lib. bdg. 15.00x (ISBN 0-87023-421-8); pap. 7.95 (ISBN 0-87023-422-6). U of Mass Pr.
--Fairweather Duck. LC 77-101628. 1970. 4.95 (ISBN 0-8027-0102-7). Walker & Co.
--To Know a Fly. LC 62-21838. (Illus.). 1963. pap. 7.95x (ISBN 0-8162-2240-1). Holden-Day.
--The World of the Tent-Makers: A Natural History of the Eastern Tent Caterpillar. LC 80-11361. (Illus.). 160p. 1980. lib. bdg. 13.50x (ISBN 0-87023-300-9); pap. 7.95 (ISBN 0-87023-301-7). U of Mass Pr.
Dethier, Vincent G. & Stellar, Eliot. Animal Behavior. 3rd ed. LC 78-110092. 1970. pap. 17.95 ref ed. (ISBN 0-13-037440-7). P-H.
Dethlefsen, Merle & Canfield, James D. Transition from Military to Civilian Life: How to Plan a Bright Future Now for You & Your Family. LC 84-10536. (Illus.). 256p. (Orig.). 1984. pap. 14.95 (ISBN 0-8117-2190-6). Stackpole.
Dethlefsen, Thorwald. Voices from Other Lives: Reincarnation As a Source of Healing. LC 76-30454. 252p. 1977. 7.95 (ISBN 0-87131-233-6). M Evans.
Dethlefson, Ronald, ed. Edison Blue Amberol Recordings: 1912-1914. (American Popular Series Live Recordings). (Illus.). 1980. 32.95 (ISBN 0-937612-00-6). A P M Pr.
--Edison Blue Amberol Recordings: 1915-1929. (Illus.). 512p. 1981. 49.50 (ISBN 0-686-78147-3). A P M Pr.
Dethloff, Henry, ed. see Auernheimer, Leonardo.
Dethloff, Henry, ed. see Maurice, S. Charles & Smithson, Charles W.
Dethloff, Henry, ed. see Pejovich, Steve.
Dethloff, Henry, ed. see Saving, Thomas R.
Dethloff, Henry C. A Centennial History of Texas A&M University: 1876-1976, 2 vols. LC 75-18687. (Centennial Series of the Association of Former Students: No. 1). 744p. 1975. boxed set 25.00 (ISBN 0-89096-007-0). Tex A&M Univ Pr.
--A Pictorial History of Texas A&M University: 1876-1976. LC 75-19559. (Centennial Ser. of the Association of Former Students: No. 2). (Illus.). 232p. 1975. 15.00 (ISBN 0-89096-006-2). Tex A&M Univ Pr.
Dethloff, Henry C. & Bryant, Keith L., Jr. Entrepreneurship: A U. S. Perspective. Pejovich, Steve, ed. (Series on Public Issues: No. 5). 22p. (Orig.). 1983. pap. 2.00 (ISBN 0-86599-014-X). Ctr Educ Res.

Dethloff, Henry C. & May, Irvin M., Jr. Southwestern Agriculture: Pre-Columbian to Modern. LC 81-48381. (Illus.). 320p. 1982. 23.75x (ISBN 0-89096-121-2). Tex A&M Univ Pr.

Dethloff, Henry C., jt. auth. see Bryant, Keith L., Jr.

Dethloff, Henry C., jt. auth. see Caddy, Douglas.

De Thomasis, Louis. My Father's Business: Creating a New Future for the People of God. 168p. (Orig.). 1984. pap. 6.95 (ISBN 0-87061-107-0). Chr Classics.

Detienne, Marcel. Dionysos Slain. Muellner, M. & Muellner, L., trs. LC 78-20518. 144p. 1979. 14.00x (ISBN 0-8018-2210-6). Johns Hopkins.

De Tio, Lola R. Complete Works of Lola Rodriguez De Tio, 3 vols. (Puerto Rico Ser.). 1979. Set. lib. bdg. 300.00 (ISBN 0-8490-2894-9). Gordon Pr.

Detjen, David W. The Germans in Missouri, Nineteen Hundred to Nineteen Eighteen: Prohibition, Neutrality & Assimilation. LC 84-2226. 256p. 1984. 23.00 (ISBN 0-8262-0446-5). U of Mo Pr.

Detjen, David W., jt. auth. see Schurtman, William.

Detjen, Gustav, Jr., ed. F. D. Roosevelt Handbook. (Philatelic Handbook). (Illus.). 107p. 1983. pap. text ed. 16.00 (ISBN 0-9612272-0-6). F D Roosevelt Phil Soc.

Detlaf, A., jt. auth. see Yavorsky, B.

Detlaf, A. A., jt. auth. see Yavorski, B. M.

Detlefsen, Ellen G., ed. see Association of Mental Health Librarians.

Detlof, Belva. Welfare Wonderland. 1968. pap. 1.00 (ISBN 0-911956-04-2). Constructive Action.

Detloff, Virginia. Index to Spring: An Annual of Archetypal Psychology & Jungian Thought, 1941-1979. LC 83-60224. 59p. 1983. pap. 6.00 (ISBN 0-88214-018-3). Spring Pubns.

Detlovs, V. K., et al. Nine Papers on Logic & Quantum Electrodynamics. American Mathematical Society, tr. LC 51-5559. (Translations Ser.: No. 2, Vol. 23). 1963. 27.00 (ISBN 0-8218-1723-X, TRANS 2-23). Am Math.

Detmar, Bernhard. Live Wisely, Live Well. 1955. 2.00 (ISBN 0-685-06574-X). Assoc Bk.

Detmar, Michael W., jt. ed. see DeKornfeld, Thomas J.

Detmer, Josephine & Pancoast, Patricia. Portland. Dibner, Martin, ed. LC 72-172820. (Illus.). 1973. collector's 25.00 (ISBN 0-9600612-0-7). Greater Portland.

Detmer, Richard C. & Smullen, Clinton W. Algebra Drill & Practice. 2nd ed. (A Software Microcomputer Program Ser.). 1982. user's guide 9.50scp (ISBN 0-06-041636-X, HarpC); complete package 125.00scp (ISBN 0-06-041635-1). Har-Row.

Detmold, M. J. The Unity of Law & Morality: A Refutation of Legal Positivism. (International Library of Philosophy). 288p. 1984. 25.00x (ISBN 0-7102-0030-7). Routledge & Kegan.

De Tocqueville, Alexis. Correspondence & Conversations of Alexis de Tocqueville with Nassau W. Senior, 2 vols in 1. 2nd ed. Simpson, M. C., ed. LC 68-30544. Repr. of 1872 ed. 39.50x (ISBN 0-678-00444-7). Kelley.

--De la Democratie en Amerique, 2 vols. Gain, ed. Set. 11.00 (ISBN 0-685-37121-2). French & Eur.

--Democracy in America, 2 vols. Bradley, Phillips, ed. (The American Past Ser.). 1944. Set. 30.00 (ISBN 0-394-42186-8). Knopf.

--Democracy in America. abr. ed. Heffner, Richard D., ed. pap. 3.95 (ISBN 0-451-62320-7, ME2320, Ment). NAL.

--Democracy in America. Hacker, Andrew, ed. Reeve, Henry, tr. 1971. pap. 1.50 (ISBN 0-671-48795-7). WSP.

DeTocqueville, Alexis. Democracy in America. Bender, Thomas, et al, eds. Reeve, Henry & Bowen, Francis, trs. LC 80-24544. (Modern Library College Edition). 603p. 1981. pap. text ed. 6.00 (ISBN 0-394-32675-X, RanC). Random.

De Tocqueville, Alexis. The European Revolution & Correspondence with Gobineau. Lukacs, John, ed. & tr. 12.75 (ISBN 0-8446-1152-2). Peter Smith.

--Journeys to England & Ireland. Mayer, J. P., ed. LC 78-67392. (European Political Thought Ser.). 1979. Repr. of 1958 ed. lib. bdg. 17.00x (ISBN 0-405-11745-0). Ayer Co Pubs.

--Old Regime & the French Revolution. Gilbert, Stuart, tr. 11.25 (ISBN 0-8446-1973-6). Peter Smith.

--The Recollections of Alexis De Tocqueville. Mayer, J. P., ed. De Mattos, Alexander, tr. LC 78-13685. 1979. Repr. of 1949 ed. lib. bdg. 20.50x (ISBN 0-313-21052-7, TRRE). Greenwood.

--Selected Letters on Politics & Society. Boesche, Roger, ed. Toupin, James, tr. from Fr. LC 84-2524. 288p. 1985. 24.95 (ISBN 0-520-05047-9). U of Cal Pr.

De Tocqueville, Alexis & De Beaumont, Gustave. Tocqueville & Beaumont on Social Reform. Drescher, Seymour, ed. & tr. LC 68-13576. 1968. lib. bdg. 17.50x (ISBN 0-88307-075-8). Gannon.

De Tocqueville, Alexis, jt. auth. see De Beaumont, Gustave.

De Tocqueville, Alexis, jt. auth. see De Beaumont de la Bonniere, G.

De Tocqueville, Alexis see Tocqueville, Alexis de.

De Tocqueville, Alexis see Tocqueville, Alexis De.

De Tocqueville, Alexis see Tocqueville, Alexis de.

De Tocqueville, Alexis, ed. see France Chambre des Deputes, 1814-1848 Staff.

De Tocqueville, Alexis C. Etudes Economiques, Politiques et Litteraires. LC 76-132539. (Fr). 1970. Repr. of 1865 ed. lib. bdg. 31.50 (ISBN 0-8337-3540-3). B Franklin.

--Journey to America. rev. ed. Mayer, J. P., ed. Lawrence, George, tr. from Fr. LC 80-22556. xvi, 424p. 1981. Repr. of 1971 ed. lib. bdg. 35.00x (ISBN 0-313-22712-8, TOJA). Greenwood.

De Tocqueville, Charles A. De la Democratie en Amerique. new ed. (Nouveaux Classiques Larousse). (Illus., Fr.). 1976. pap. 2.95 (ISBN 0-685-66281-0, 326). Larousse.

De Toledano, Ralph. The Municipal Doomsday Machine. LC 75-19174. 180p. 1976. pap. 1.95 (ISBN 0-916054-31-4, Dist. by Kampmann). Green Hill.

--Poems: You & I. LC 77-17944. 72p. 1978. 5.95 (ISBN 0-88289-173-1). Pelican.

De Tolnay, Charles. History & Technique of Old Master Drawings: A Handbook. LC 70-158334. (Illus.). 1972. Repr. of 1943 ed. 60.00 (ISBN 0-87817-107-X). Hacker.

De Tolnay, Charles Q. Michelangelo, 6 vols. Incl. Vol. 1. The Youth of Michelangelo. 1969. 85.00x (ISBN 0-691-03858-9); Vol. 2. The Sistine Ceiling. 1969. 85.00x (ISBN 0-691-03856-2); Vol. 3. The Medeci Chapel. 1970. 87.00 (ISBN 0-691-03854-6); Vol. 4. The Tomb of Julius Two. 1970. 87.00x (ISBN 0-691-03857-0); Vol. 5. The Final Period. 1970. 85.00x (ISBN 0-691-03855-4); Vol. 6. Michelangelo, Architect. 40.00x (ISBN 0-691-03853-8); Michelangelo: Sculpter-Painter-Architect. (One vol. condensation). 50.00 (ISBN 0-691-03876-7); pap. 19.50 (ISBN 0-691-00337-8). Princeton U Pr.

Detomasi, Don D. & Gartrell, J. W. Resources Communities: A Decade of Disruption. 210p. 1984. pap. 22.50x (ISBN 0-8133-0114-9). Westview.

De Toqueville, Alexis, jt. auth. see De Beaumont, Gustave.

De Toqueville, Alexis C. Democracy in America, 2 Vols. Vol. 1. 25.95 (ISBN 0-89190-262-7, Pub. by Am Repr); Vol. 2. 25.95 (ISBN 0-89190-263-5); Set of 2 Vols. 43.95 (ISBN 0-89190-572-3). Amereon Ltd.

De Toqueville, Alexis Comte see De Toqueville, Alexis C.

Detorie, Rick. Illustrated Tacky Trivia. 80p. 1985. 4.95 (ISBN 0-399-51182-2). Putnam Pub Group.

--Miss Lil. 96p. 1983. pap. 3.95 (ISBN 0-671-47005-1, Wallaby); pap. 43.45 12-copy counter display (ISBN 0-671-93150-4). S&S.

--No Good Lawyers. (Orig.). 1984. pap. 3.95 (ISBN 0-671-50907-1, Wallaby). PB.

Detorie, Rick & Coffee, Candis. Illustrated Sexual Trivia. (Illus.). 1984. pap. 3.50 (ISBN 0-943588-01-4). Baron-Scott Enterp.

De Tornyay, Rheba & Thompson, Martha A. Strategies for Teaching Nursing. 2nd ed. 274p. 1982. pap. 16.00 (ISBN 0-471-04523-3). Wiley.

De Toro, M. & Gisbert. Dictionnaire Bilingue Larousse, Francais-Espagnol, Espanol-Frances. (Apollo). (Fr. & Span.). 10.95 (ISBN 0-685-13857-7, 3774). Larousse.

De Toro Gisbert, M. Dictionnaire Bilingue: Francais-Espagnol, Espagnol-Francais. 546p. (Fr. & Span.). 1968. pap. text ed. 7.95 (ISBN 0-686-97445-X, S-36345). French & Eur.

De Torre, Emilio, jt. auth. see De Onis, Federico.

De Torre, Jacinto, tr. see Benteen, John.

De Torres, J., tr. see Chase, Glen.

De Torres, Jacinto, tr. see Benteen, John.

De Torres, Jacinto, tr. see Callie, M. K.

De Torres, Jacinto, tr. see Chase, Glen.

De Torres, Juan. Metropolitan America: The Development of Its Major Markets. LC 76-20381. (Report Ser.: No. 692). (Illus.). 101p. 1976. pap. 15.00 (ISBN 0-8237-0126-3); pap. 5.00 member. Conference Bd.

De Tott, Baron. Memoirs of Baron de Tott, 2 vols. in 1. LC 73-6303. (The Middle East Ser.). Repr. of 1785 ed. 46.50 (ISBN 0-405-05363-0). Ayer Co Pubs.

De Tourtoulon, Pierre. Philosophy in the Development of Law. Cohen, Morris R., ed. Read, M. M., tr. 1977. lib. bdg. 59.95 (ISBN 0-8490-2428-5). Gordon Pr.

--Philosophy in the Development of Law. Reed, Martha, tr. LC 68-54759. (Modern Legal Philosophy Ser.: Vol. 13). Repr. of 1922 ed. 37.50x (ISBN 0-678-04523-2). Kelley.

De Tourville, Abbe. Letters of Direction. LC 84-60628. 110p. 1984. pap. 3.95 (ISBN 0-8192-1346-2). Morehouse.

De Tousard, Louis see Tousard, Louis De.

De Tovar, M. Bara, jt. auth. see Peyrollaz, M.

De Tracy, A. Destutt see Destutt De Tracy, A.

De Tracy, Antoine L. Destutt see Destutt De Tracy, Antoine L.

Detre, L., ed. Non-Periodic Phenomena in Variable Stars. 490p. 1969. lib. bdg. 58.00 (ISBN 90-277-0115-6, Pub. by Reidel Hilland). Kluwer Academic.

Detrekoei, jt. auth. see Juo.

DeTreville, Stan, jt. auth. see DeTreville, Susan.

DeTreville, Susan & DeTreville, Stan. Butterflies & Moths. (Illus.). 32p. (Orig.). 1981. pap. 3.95 (ISBN 0-8431-1731-1). Troubador Pr.

De Trevino, Elizabeth B. Beyond the Gates of Hercules. LC 75-149227. 256p. 1971. 4.95 (ISBN 0-374-30673-7). FS&G.

De Trevino, Elizabeth B. see Trevino, Elizabeth B. De.

De Trevino, Elizabeth Borton see Trevino, Elizabeth Borton De.

Detrez, Conrad. A Weed for Burning. Davis, Lydia, tr. LC 83-22844. 272p. 1984. 13.95 (ISBN 0-15-195596-4). HarbraceJ.

Detrich, Richard L. & Steele, Nicola. How to Recover from Grief. 128p. 1983. pap. 7.95 (ISBN 0-8170-0989-2). Judson.

Detrick, Mia. Sushi. LC 81-12224. (Illus.). 112p. (Orig.). 1981. pap. 8.95 (ISBN 0-87701-238-5). Chronicle Bks.

Detrick, R. Blaine. I Met Jesus When He Ministered. 56p. 1976. pap. 3.50 (ISBN 0-89536-102-7). CSS of Ohio.

--I Met Jesus When He Was Born: Dramatic Monologues for Advent. 1976. pap. 3.50 (ISBN 0-89536-110-8). CSS of Ohio.

Detrie, Philippe. Techniques in Abdominal Surgery. Pryer, Richard R., tr. from Fr. LC 73-593870. pap. 31.80 (ISBN 0-317-26196-7, 2052070). Bks Demand UMI.

Detro, Gene. The Honey Dwarf. 1974. 5.95 (ISBN 0-913218-23-5); pap. 2.50 (ISBN 0-913218-24-3). Dustbooks.

--The Mary Caper. LC 81-51876. (Sunburst Originals Ser.: No. 10). (Illus.). 130p. (Orig.). 1982. pap. 4.65 (ISBN 0-934648-09-3). Sunburst Pr.

--Mary Militant. (Orig.). 1979. pap. 3.00 (ISBN 0-914974-24-6). Holmgangers.

--Moon Horns-Razor Door. LC 81-6493. 72p. 1981. pap. 3.95 (ISBN 0-914974-31-9). Holmgangers.

--When All the Wild Summer. (Kestrel Ser.: No. 7). 28p. 1983. pap. 3.00 (ISBN 0-914974-39-4). Holmgangers.

Detro, Gene, ed. see Stock, Susan.

De Trobriand, Philippe R. Military Life in Dakota: The Journal of Philippe Regis de Trobriand. Kane, Lucille M., ed. LC 81-14740. (Illus.). xxviii, 419p. 1982. 29.95x (ISBN 0-8032-1661-0); pap. 9.95 (ISBN 0-8032-6557-3, BB 788, Bison). U of Nebr Pr.

Detroit Historical Society. Cadillac & the Founding of Detroit: Commemorating the 275th Anniversary of the Founding of the City of Detroit. LC 76-25500. (Illus.). 116p. 1976. pap. 4.95 (ISBN 0-8143-1571-2). Wayne St U Pr.

Detroit Institute of Art. Detroit Collects Prints & Drawings. LC 76-168631. 52p. 1972. 5.00 (ISBN 0-8143-1486-4). Wayne St U Pr.

Detroit Institute Of Arts. The City Within. (Illus.). 36p. 1969. pap. 1.95 (ISBN 0-8143-1447-3). Wayne St U Pr.

--The Graphic Art of Rolf Nesch. LC 74-8117. (Illus.). 84p. 1969. pap. 5.00 (ISBN 0-8143-1446-5). Wayne St U Pr.

--The Legend of John Brown: Twenty-Two Gouaches by Jacob Lawrence. (Illus.). 62p. 1979. 6.00x (ISBN 0-8143-1633-6, Pub. by Detroit Inst Arts). Wayne St U Pr.

--Robert Hudson Tannahill Bequest to the Detroit Institute of Arts: A Catalogue Issued on the Occasion of the Exhibition. LC 71-122774. (Illus.). 209p. 1970. 14.95 (ISBN 0-8143-1445-7). Wayne St U Pr.

Detroit Institute of Arts, Grand Palais, Paris, jt. auth. see Philadelphia Museum of Art.

Detroit Marine Historical Society. Great Lakes Ships We Remember. rev. ed. Van der Linden, Peter J., ed. (Illus.). 415p. 1984. 24.75 (ISBN 0-912514-24-8). Freshwater.

--Great Lakes Ships We Remember II. Van der Linden, Peter J., ed. (Illus.). 400p. 1984. 34.75 (ISBN 0-912514-25-6). Freshwater.

Detroit Michigan News Staff. The Magic Season: The 1984 Detroit Tigers. 112p. 1984. pap. 5.95 (ISBN 0-89730-152-8). News Bks Intl.

Detroit Public Library. Automotive History Collection of the Detroit Public Library: A Simplified Guide to Its Holdings, 2 Vols. 1966. Set. 200.00 (ISBN 0-8161-0718-1, Hall Library). G K Hall.

--Catalog of the E. Azalia Hackley Memorial Collection of Negro Music, Dance & Drama. 1979. lib. bdg. 105.00 (ISBN 0-8161-0299-6, Hall Library). G K Hall.

De Troyes, Chrestien. Yvain (Le Chevalier au Lion) Reid, T. B., intro. by. (French Texts Ser.). 288p. (Orig., Fr.). 1984. pap. text ed. 7.95 (ISBN 0-7190-0134-X, Pub. by Manchester Univ Pr.). Longwood Pub Group.

De Troyes, Chretien. Lancelot: The Knight of the Cart. Rogers, Deborah W., tr. from Medieval Fr. (Records of Civilization: Sources & Studies: XCVII). 192p. 1984. 25.00x (ISBN 0-231-05862-4); pap. 12.00x (ISBN 0-231-05863-2). Columbia U Pr.

--Perceval: Or, The Story of the Grail. 1986. pap. text ed. 10.00 (ISBN 0-8203-0812-9). U of Ga Pr.

--Perceval: The Story of the Grail. Bryant, Nigel, tr. LC 82-3696. (Arthurian Studies: No. V). 318p. 1982. text ed. 47.50x (ISBN 0-8476-7201-8). Rowman.

--Yvain; or, the Knight with the Lion. Cline, Ruth H., tr. from Fr. LC 73-85026. 222p. 1975. pap. 6.95x. U of Ga Pr.

--Yvain Ou le Chevalier Au Lion. Nelson, Jan, et al, eds. LC 68-22800. (Medieval French Literature Ser). (Orig., Fr). 1968. pap. 6.95 (ISBN 0-89197-477-6). Irvington.

De Troyes, Chretien see Chretien De Troyes.

De Trueba, Don T. The Romance of History: Spain. 1979. Repr. lib. bdg. 30.00 (ISBN 0-8495-1049-X). Arden Lib.

De Tryon, Charles F. see Montalembert, Charles, pseud.

Detsch, Richard. Georg Trakl's Poetry: Toward a Union of Opposites. LC 82-42780. (Studies in German Literature). 160p. 1983. 22.50x (ISBN 0-271-00343-X). Pa St U Pr.

Detsicas, Alec. Collectanea Historica. 320p. 1981. text ed. 42.50x (ISBN 0-906746-02-7, Pub. by Alan Sutton England). Humanities.

Dett, Robert N., ed. Religious Folk Songs of the Negro. LC 72-1595. Repr. of 1927 ed. 21.50 (ISBN 0-404-09920-3). AMS Pr.

Dettelbach, Cynthia G. In the Driver's Seat: The Automobile in American Literature & Popular Culture. LC 75-35342. (Contributions in American Studies: No. 25). (Illus.). 160p. 1976. lib. bdg. 27.50 (ISBN 0-8371-8593-9, DDS/). Greenwood.

Detterman, Douglas. Current Topics in Human Intelligence, Vol. 1. (Current Topics in Human Intelligence Ser.). 344p. 1985. text ed. 39.50 (ISBN 0-89391-173-9). Ablex Pub.

Detterman, Douglas K. & Sternberg, Robert J., eds. How & How Much Can Intelligence Be Increased. LC 82-1787. 256p. 1982. 0.32.50 (ISBN 0-89391-117-8). Ablex Pub.

Detterman, Douglas K., jt. ed. see Sternberg, Robert J.

Dettlinger, Chet & Prugh, Jeff. The List. LC 84-158611. (Illus.). 516p. 1983. text ed. 14.95 (ISBN 0-942894-04-9). Strode Comm.

Dettman, B., jt. auth. see Bedford, Michael.

Dettman, John W. Applied Complex Variables. (Mathematics Ser.). 481p. 1984. pap. 10.00 (ISBN 0-486-64670-X). Dover.

Dettner, H. Fachwoerterbuch Fuer der Metalloberflaechenveredelung. 391p. (Ger. & Eng., Dictionary of Metal Refining). 1969. 20.95 (ISBN 3-87749-011-5, M-7397, Pub. by G. Siemens). French & Eur.

Dettre, Judith. One, Two, Three, Read! LC 79-52661. 1980. pap. 7.50 (ISBN 0-8224-5788-1). Pitman Learning.

Dettweiler, Hans, jt. ed. see Gnirss, Christa.

Detty, Elizabeth W., jt. auth. see Bryson, Joseph E.

De Turnebe, Odet. Satisfaction All Around: Les Contens. Beecher, Donald, tr. (Carleton Renaissance Plays Ser.). 102p. 1979. pap. text ed. 6.25x (ISBN 0-7709-0063-1, Pub. by Wilfred Laurier U Pr Canada). Humanities.

De Turo, Doreen M. The American Bench: Judges of the Nation. 3rd ed. LC 78-640695. 2500p. 1985. 170.00 (ISBN 0-931398-10-X). R B Forster.

Detweiler, Clinton. Ventriloquism in a Nutshell. (Illus.). 1974. pap. 4.00 (ISBN 0-686-20905-2, 065). Maher Ventril Studio.

Detweiler, Richard C. Mennonite Statements on Peace. 80p. (Orig.). 1968. pap. 1.50 (ISBN 0-8361-1581-3). Herald Pr.

--Mennonite Statements on Peace. 80p. 1968. pap. 1.50 (ISBN 0-8361-1581-3). Herald Hse.

Detweiler, Robert. Art, Literature, Religion: Life on the Borders. LC 82-3319. (AAR Thermatic Studies). 208p. 1983. 22.50 (ISBN 0-89130-578-5, 01 24 92). Scholars Pr GA.

--Four Spiritual Crises in Mid-Century American Fiction. facs. ed. LC 78-121461. (Essay Index Reprint Ser). 1964. 12.00 (ISBN 0-8369-1799-5). Ayer Co Pubs.

--Four Spiritual Crises in Mid-Century American Fiction. LC 64-63316. (University of Florida Humanities Monographs: No. 14). 1963. pap. 3.50 (ISBN 0-8130-0058-0). U Presses Fla.

--John Updike. (United States Authors Ser.). lib. bdg. 13.50 (ISBN 0-8057-0752-2, Twayne). G K Hall.

--John Updike. rev. ed. (United States Authors Ser.: No. 481). 208p. 1984. lib. bdg. 13.95 (ISBN 0-8057-7422-X, Twayne); pap. 5.95 (ISBN 0-8057-7429-7). G K Hall.

Detweiler, Robert & Kornweibel, Theodore. Slave & Citizen: A Critical Annotated Bibliography on Slavery & Race Relations in the Americas. 300p. 1983. pap. 6.00 (ISBN 0-686-84758-X). SDSU Press.

Detweiler, Robert, ed. Semeia Twenty-Three: Derrida & Biblical Studies. (Semeia Ser.). pap. 9.95 (ISBN 0-686-96296-6, 06 20 23). Scholars Pr GA.

Detweiler, Robert & Meeter, Glenn, eds. Faith & Fiction: The Modern Short Story. LC 78-32082. pap. 86.80 (ISBN 0-317-19817-3, 2023210). Bks Demand UMI.

Detweiler, Robert & Ruiz, Ramon, eds. Liberation in the Americas: Comparative Aspects of the Independence Movements in Mexico & the United States. 1978. 14.00 (ISBN 0-916304-41-8). SDSU Press.

--Liberation in the Americas: Comparative Aspects of the Independence Period in Mexico & the United States. LC 77-83491. 1978. 5.00x (ISBN 0-916304-30-2). SDSU Press.

Detweiler, Robert, ed. see Starr, Raymond.

Detweiler, Susan G. George Washington's Chinaware. LC 81-14993. (Illus.). 240p. 1982. 40.00 (ISBN 0-8109-1779-3). Abrams.

Detwiler, Donald S. Germany: A Short History. LC 76-4563. 288p. 1976. pap. 10.95x (ISBN 0-8093-0768-5). S Ill U Pr.

Detwiler, Donald S., jt. auth. see Mendelsohn, John.

Detwiler, Donald S., ed. World War Two German Military Studies, 10 pts. in 23 vols. Incl. Pt. 1. Introduction & Guide (ISBN 0-8240-4300-6); Pt. 2. The Extinct Series (European Theatre Interrogations, 2 pts. Pt. A (ISBN 0-8240-4301-4). Pt. B (ISBN 0-8240-4302-2); Pt. 3. Command Structure, 3 pts. Pt. A (ISBN 0-8240-4303-0). Pt. B (ISBN 0-8240-4304-9). Pt. C (ISBN 0-8240-4305-7); Pt. 4. The OKW (Oberkommando der Wehrmacht) War Diary Series, 5 pts. Pt. A (ISBN 0-8240-4306-5). Pt. B (ISBN 0-8240-4307-3). Pt. C (ISBN 0-8240-4308-1). Pt. D (ISBN 0-8240-4309-X). Pt. E (ISBN 0-8240-4310-3); Pt. 5. The Western Theatre (ISBN 0-8240-4311-1); Pt. 6. The Mediterranean Theatre, 2 pts. Pt. A (ISBN 0-8240-4312-X). Pt. B (ISBN 0-8240-4313-8); Pt. 7. The Eastern Theatre, 5 pts. Pt. A (ISBN 0-8240-4314-6). Pt. B (ISBN 0-8240-4315-4). Pt. C (ISBN 0-8240-4316-2). Pt. D (ISBN 0-8240-4317-0). Pt. E (ISBN 0-8240-4318-9); Pt. 8. Diplomacy, Strategy & Military Theory, 2 pts. Pt. A (ISBN 0-8240-4319-7). Pt. B (ISBN 0-8240-4320-0); Pt. 9. German Military Government (ISBN 0-8240-4321-9); Pt. 10. Special Topics, 2 pts. Pt. A (ISBN 0-8240-4322-7). Pt. B (ISBN 0-8240-4323-5). 1979. lib. bdg. 73.00 ea., vol. Garland Pub.

Detwiler, Donald S. & Burdick, Charles B., eds. Defense of the Homeland & the End of the War: Japanese Military Studies 1937-1949. (War in Asia & the Pacific Ser., 1937 to 1949: Vol. 12). 1980. lib. bdg. 74.00 (ISBN 0-8240-3296-9). Garland Pub.

--Introduction & Guide: Japanese & Chinese Studies & Documents, Vol. 1. (War in Asia & the Pacific Ser., 1937 to 1949). 460p. 1980. lib. bdg. 74.00 (ISBN 0-8240-3285-3). Garland Pub.

--Japan & the Soviet Union, Pt. 1. (War in Asia & the Pacific Ser., 1937 to 1949: Vol. 10). 670p. 1980. lib. bdg. 74.00 (ISBN 0-8240-3294-2). Garland Pub.

--Japan & the Soviet Union, Pt. 2. (War in Asia & the Pacific Ser., 1937 to 1949: Vol. 11). 610p. 1980. lib. bdg. 74.00 (ISBN 0-8240-3295-0). Garland Pub.

--Japanese Military Studies Nineteen Thirty-Seven to Nineteen Forty-Nine, Naval Armament Program & Naval Operations: Japanese & Chinese Studies & Documents, Vol. 4. (War in Asia & the Pacific Ser., 1937 to 1949). 550p. 1980. Part I. lib. bdg. 74.00 (ISBN 0-8240-3288-8); lib. bdg. 650.00 set of 15 vols. (ISBN 0-686-60107-6). Garland Pub.

--Japanese Military Studies Nineteen Thirty-Seven to Nineteen Forty-Nine, Naval Armament Program & Naval Operations: Japanese & Chinese Studies & Documents, Vol. 5. (War in Asia & the Pacific Ser., 1937 to 1949). 520p. 1980. Part II. lib. bdg. 74.00 (ISBN 0-8240-3289-6); lib. bdg. 845.00 set 15 vols. Garland Pub.

--Japanese Military Studies: The Southern Area: Japanese & Chinese Studies & Documents, Vol. 7. (War in Asia & the Pacific Ser., 1937 to 1949). 420p. 1980. Part II. lib. bdg. 75.00 (ISBN 0-8240-3291-8). Garland Pub.

--Japanese Military Studies 1937-1949: Command, Administration, & Special Operations; Japanese & Chinese Studies & Documents. (War in Asia & the Pacific Ser., 1937 to 1949: Vol. 3). 660p. 1980. lib. bdg. 75.00 (ISBN 0-8240-3287-X). Garland Pub.

--Japanese Military Studies 1937-1949: China, Manchuria, & Korea, Pt. 1. (War in Asia & the Pacific Ser., 1937 to 1949: Vol. 8). 630p. 1980. lib. bdg. 75.00 (ISBN 0-8240-3292-6). Garland Pub.

--Japanese Military Studies 1937-1949: China, Manchuria, & Korea, Pt. 2. (War in Asia & the Pacific Ser., 1937 to 1949: Vol. 9). 650p. 1980. lib. bdg. 75.00 (ISBN 0-8240-3293-4). Garland Pub.

--Japanese Military Studies, 1937-1949: Political Background of the War: Japanese & Chinese Studies & Documents, Vol. 2. (War in Asia & the Pacific Ser., 1937 to 1949). 500p. 1980. lib. bdg. 75.00 (ISBN 0-8240-3286-1). Garland Pub.

--Japanese Military Studies, 1937-1949: The Southern Area: Japanese & Chinese Studies & Documents, Vol. 6. (War in Asia & the Pacific Ser., 1937 to 1949). 530p. 1980. Part I. lib. bdg. 75.00 (ISBN 0-8240-3290-X). Garland Pub.

--Japanese Military Studies, 1937-1949: The Sino-Japanese & the Chinese Civil Wars, Pt. 1. (War in Asia & the Pacific Ser., 1937 to 1949: Vol. 13). 460p. 1980. lib. bdg. 75.00 (ISBN 0-8240-3297-7). Garland Pub.

--Japanese Military Studies, 1937-1949: The Sino-Japanese & the Chinese Civil Wars, Pt. 2. (War in Asia & the Pacific Ser., 1937 to 1949: Vol. 14). 610p. 1980. lib. bdg. 75.00 (ISBN 0-8240-3298-5). Garland Pub.

--Japanese Military Studies, 1939-1949: The Sino-Japanese & the Chinese Civil Wars, Pt. 3. (War in Asia & the Pacific Ser., 1937 to 1949: Vol. 15). 570p. 1980. lib. bdg. 75.00 (ISBN 0-8240-3299-3). Garland Pub.

Detwiler-Zapp, Diane & Dixon, William C. Lay Caregiving. LC 81-66519. (Creative Pastoral Care & Counseling Ser.). 1982. pap. 4.50 (ISBN 0-8006-0567-5, 1-567). Fortress.

De Tyard, Pontus, tr. see Perry, T. Anthony.

Detz, Joan. How to Write & Give a Speech: A Practical Guide for Executives, PR People, Managers, Fund-Raisers, Politicians, Educators, & Anyone Who Has to Make Every Word Count. 144p. 1984. 14.95 (ISBN 0-312-39627-9); pap. 5.95 (ISBN 0-312-39628-7). St Martin.

Deuber, Carl G. Vegetative Propagation of Conifers. 1940. pap. 39.50x (ISBN 0-686-51323-1). Elliots Bks.

Deubert, L. W. & Jenkins, C. B. Tooth-Coloured Filling Materials in Clinical Practice. 2nd ed. (Dental Practitioner Handbook Ser.: No. 16). (Illus.). 156p. 1982. pap. text ed. 18.50 (ISBN 0-7236-0628-5). PSG Pub Co.

Deuchar, Elizabeth M. Xenopus: The South African Clawed Frog. LC 73-18927. pap. 64.00 (ISBN 0-317-28860-1, 2020972). Bks Demand UMI.

Deuchar, Margaret. British Sign Language. (Language, Education & Society Ser.). (Illus.). 300p. (Orig.). 1984. 29.95x (ISBN 0-7100-9643-7). Routledge & Kegan.

Deuchler, Martina. Confucian Gentlemen & Barbarian Envoys: The Opening of Korea, 1875-1885. LC 76-57228. (Royal Asiatic Society Ser.). 324p. 1978. 27.50x (ISBN 0-295-95552-X). U of Wash Pr.

Deudney, Daniel. Rivers of Energy: The Hydropower Potential. LC 81-51798. (Worldwatch Papers). 1981. pap. 2.00 (ISBN 0-916468-43-7). Worldwatch Inst.

--Whole Earth Security: A Geopolitics of Peace. (Worldwatch Institute Papers: No. 55). 93p. 1983. pap. text ed. 2.95 (ISBN 0-916468-54-2, WW55, WW). Unipub.

--Whole-Earth Security: Geopolitics of Peace. LC 83-50619. (Worldwatch Papers Ser.). 1983. 2.00 (ISBN 0-916468-54-2). Worldwatch Inst.

Deudney, Daniel & Flavin, Christopher. Renewable Energy: The Power to Choose. 1983. Norton.

--Renewable Energy: The Power to Choose. 448p. 1984. 22.95 (ISBN 0-393-01999-3); pap. 8.95 (ISBN 0-393-30201-6). Norton.

Deudon, Eric H. Nietzsche En France: L'antichristianisme et la Critique, 1891-1915. LC 81-43820. 176p. (Orig.). 1982. lib. bdg. 26.00 (ISBN 0-8191-2339-0); pap. text ed. 11.75 (ISBN 0-8191-2340-4). U Pr of Amer.

Deudon, Eric H., ed. The Nightcharmer & Other Tales of Claude Seignolle. LC 83-45104. (Illus.). 112p. 1983. 9.95 (ISBN 0-89096-169-7). Tex A&M Univ Pr.

Deuel, Harry. Chester's Paradise. LC 70-2567. (Orig.). 1976. pap. 3.00 (ISBN 0-912860-00-6). Total Graphics.

Deuel, R. Z., jt. auth. see Hammel, E. A.

Deuel, Thorne. American Indian Ways of Life. facsimile ed. (Story of Illinois Ser.: No. 9). (Illus.). 80p. 1976. pap. 1.00 (ISBN 0-89792-018-X). Ill St Museum.

--The Human Factor in the Behavior of Peoples. (Scientific Papers Ser.: Vol. XIII). (Illus.). 204p. 1971. pap. 5.75 (ISBN 0-89792-047-3). Ill St Museum.

--Man's Venture in Culture. (Story of Illinois Ser.: No. 6). (Illus.). 40p. 1955. pap. 1.00 (ISBN 0-89792-008-2). Ill St Museum.

--Power Adaptations & Changing Cultures. (Scientific Papers Ser.: Vol. XV). (Illus.). 114p. 1976. pap. 4.00 (ISBN 0-89792-063-5). Ill St Museum.

Deuel, Thorne, jt. auth. see Cole, Fay-Cooper.

Deuel, William K. Kitchen Management for Institutions: Economies in Purchasing, Portioning & Preparation. 1975. 12.95 (ISBN 0-8104-9462-0). Hayden.

Deuflhard, Peter & Hairer, Ernst. Workshop on Numerical Treatment of Inverse Problems in Differential & Integral Equations. (Progress in Scientific Computing: Vol. 2). 372p. 1983. 27.50x (ISBN 0-8176-3125-9). Birkhauser.

D'Eugenio, Diane B. & Moersch, Martha S., eds. Developmental Programming for Infants & Young Children, 2 vols, Vols. 4 & 5. LC 80-50630. 100p. 1981. text ed. 12.50x (ISBN 0-472-08150-0). Vol. 4 Preschool Assessment & Application. Vol. 5 Preschool Developmental Profile. U of Mich Pr.

Deuink, James W. The Ministry of the Christian School Guidance Counselor. (Illus.). 175p. (Orig.). 1984. pap. 6.60 (ISBN 0-89084-273-6). Bob Jones Univ Pr.

Deuink, James W. & Herbster, Carl D. Effective Christian School Management. (Illus.). 255p. (Orig.). 1982. pap. 8.95 (ISBN 0-89084-190-X). Bob Jones Univ Pr.

Deuink, James W., ed. Some Light on Christian Education. (Illus.). 195p. (Orig.). 1984. pap. 4.95 (ISBN 0-89084-262-0). Bob Jones Univ Pr.

De Ullmann, Stephan. Epic of the Finnish Nation. 1977. lib. bdg. 59.95 (ISBN 0-8490-1780-7). Gordon Pr.

De Ulloa, Antonio. Voyage to South America. Leonard, Irving A., ed. LC 74-32438. (Illus.). 256p. 1975. pap. 6.50x (ISBN 0-87918-020-X). ASU Lat Am St.

De Ulloa, Antonio, jt. auth. see Juan, Jorge J.

De Ulloa, Don Antonio, jt. auth. see Juan, George.

De Ulloa, Leonor A., jt. auth. see Ulloa, Justo.

Deulofeu, et al. The Best from the Bottle. 1982. 12.95 (ISBN 0-399-50702-7, Periger). Putnam Pub Group.

Deumlich, Fritz. Surveying Instruments. 336p. 1981. text ed. 44.95x (ISBN 3-11-007765-5). De Gruyter.

De Unamuno, Miguel. Abel Sanchez & Other Stories. Kerrigan, Anthony, tr. pap. 3.95 (ISBN 0-89526-923-6). Regnery-Gateway.

DeUnamuno, Miguel. Cancionero-Diario Poetico. 486p. 5.00 (ISBN 0-318-14243-0). Hispanic Inst.

De Unamuno, Miguel. Peace in War: A Novel: Selected Works of Miguel de Unamuno, Vol. 1. Kerrigan, Anthony & Lacy, Allen, trs. from Span. LC 82-61390. (Bollingen Ser.: No. LXXXV-1). 300p. 1983. 35.00x (ISBN 0-691-09926-X). Princeton U Pr.

--Three Exemplary Novels & a Prologue. 228p. 1982. Repr. of 1930 ed. lib. bdg. 50.00 (ISBN 0-8495-5412-8). Arden Lib.

--Tragic Sense of Life. 14.00 (ISBN 0-8446-3100-0). Peter Smith.

De Unamuno, Miguel see Unamuno, Miguel de.

De Unamuno, Miguel see Unamuno, Miguel De.

De Unamuno y Jugo, Miguel see Unamuno y Jugo, Miguel De.

Deupree, Robert G. The Wholesale Marketing of Fruits & Vegetables in Baltimore. LC 78-64175. (Johns Hopkins University. Studies in the Social Sciences. Fifty-Seventh Ser. 1939: 2). 128p. 1982. Repr. of 1939 ed. 24.50 (ISBN 0-404-61284-9). AMS Pr.

Deur, Lynne. Doers & Dreamers: Social Reformers of the 19th Century. LC 79-128808. (Pull Ahead Bks). (gr. 5-11). 1972. PLB 5.95 (ISBN 0-8225-0462-6). Lerner Pubns.

--Indian Chiefs. LC 75-128807. (Pull Ahead Bks). (Illus.). (gr. 6-11). 1972. PLB 5.95 (ISBN 0-8225-0461-8). Lerner Pubns.

--Political Cartoonists. LC 72-128809. (Pull Ahead Bks). (Illus.). (gr. 5-11). 1972. PLB 5.95 (ISBN 0-8225-0463-4). Lerner Pubns.

Deuring, M. Lectures on the Theory of Algebraic Functions of One Variable. LC 72-97679. (Lecture Notes in Mathematics: Vol. 314). 151p. 1973. pap. 12.00 (ISBN 0-387-06152-5). Springer-Verlag.

Deursen, A. Van see Van Deursen, A.

Deusen, Glyndon G. Van see Perkins, Dexter.

Deusen, Glyndon G. Van see Van Deusen, Glyndon G.

Deusen, John G. Van see Van Deusen, John G.

Deusen, M. van see Van Deusen, M.

Deusen Edmund, Van see Van Deusen, Edmund.

Deuss, Jean, ed. Banking & Finance Collections. LC 83-26466. (Special Collections Ser.: Vol. 2, No. 3). 164p. 1984. text ed. 29.95 (ISBN 0-86656-252-4, B252). Haworth Pr.

Deussen, P., ed. Theoretical Computer Science Fifth Conference. (Lecture Notes in Computer Science Ser.: Vol. 104). 261p. 1981. pap. 19.00 (ISBN 0-387-10576-X). Springer-Verlag.

Deussen, Paul. Philosophy of the Upanishads. Geden, A. S., tr. (Orig.). 1966. pap. 8.50 (ISBN 0-486-21616-0). Dover.

--Philosophy of the Upanishads. Geden, A. S., tr. 11.25 (ISBN 0-8446-1974-4). Peter Smith.

Deutch, Howard E. High Profits Without Risk. (Illus.). 1977. 18.95 (ISBN 0-917244-01-X). Jefren Pub.

Deutch, John M. Prospects for Synthetic Fuels in the United States. 1982. 2.50x (ISBN 0-317-06611-0). Colo Assoc.

Deutch, Richard. Dime. 1970. 4.50 (ISBN 0-912284-09-9); signed ltd ed 10.00 (ISBN 0-685-02576-4); pap. 2.50 (ISBN 0-685-02577-2). New Rivers Pr.

Deutcsh, Arthur V. Starett. LC 78-57329. 1978. 8.95 (ISBN 0-87795-199-3). Arbor Hse.

Deutelbaum, Marshall, ed. Image on the Art & Evolution of Film: Photographs & Articles from the Magazine of the International Museum of Photography. LC 78-94843. (Illus.). 1979. pap. 8.95 (ISBN 0-486-23777-X). Dover.

Deutermann, P. T. OPS Officer's Manual. LC 79-89179. (Illus.). 216p. 1980. 14.95x (ISBN 0-87021-505-1). Naval Inst Pr.

--Ops Officer's Manual. (Illus.). 184p. 1980. 14.95 (ISBN 0-87021-505-1); bulk rates avail. Naval Inst Pr.

Deutman, A. F. & Cruysberg, J. R., eds. Neurogenetics & Neuro-Ophthalmology. (Documenta Ophthalmologica Proceedings Ser.: No. 17). 1978. lib. bdg. 87.00 (ISBN 90-6193-159-2, Pub. by Junk Pubs Netherlands). Kluwer Academic.

Deutrich, Mabel E. & Purdy, Virginia C., eds. Clio Was a Woman: Studies in the History of American Women. LC 79-15336. (National Archives Conference Ser.: Vol. 16). (Illus.). 1980. 19.95 (ISBN 0-88258-077-9). Howard U Pr.

Deutsch, jt. ed. see Hardgrave.

Deutsch, Albert. The Mentally Ill in America: A History of Their Care & Treatment from Colonial Times. 2nd ed. LC 49-7527. 535p. 1949. 42.50x (ISBN 0-231-01656-5). Columbia U Pr.

--Our Rejected Children. LC 74-1680. (Children & Youth Ser.: Vol. 29). 316p. 1974. Repr. of 1950 ed. 23.00x (ISBN 0-405-05958-2). Ayer Co Pubs.

--The Shame of the States. LC 73-2394. (Mental Illness & Social Policy; the American Experience Ser.). Repr. of 1948 ed. 17.00 (ISBN 0-405-05202-2). Ayer Co Pubs.

Deutsch, Albert, jt. auth. see Schneider, David M.

Deutsch, Albert, ed. Encyclopedia of Mental Health. LC 63-7150. 1970. Repr. of 1963 ed. 60.00 (ISBN 0-8108-0357-7). Scarecrow.

Deutsch, Alfred H. Still Full of Sap, Still Green. LC 79-21558. 130p. 1979. pap. 2.50 (ISBN 0-8146-1051-X). Liturgical Pr.

Deutsch, Alleen, jt. auth. see Demetrulias, Diana.

Deutsch, Armin J. & Klemperer, Wolfgang B., eds. Space Age Astronomy: An International Symposium. 1962. 92.50 (ISBN 0-12-213550-4). Acad Pr.

Deutsch, Arnold. The Human Resources Revolution: Communicate or Litigate. (Illus.). 1979. 21.50 (ISBN 0-07-016593-9). McGraw.

Deutsch, Arnold R. The Complete Job Book. 228p. (Orig.). 1980. pap. 6.95 (ISBN 0-346-12481-6). Cornerstone.

--How to Hold Your Job: Gaining Skills & Becoming Promotable in Difficult Times. 184p. 1984. 15.95 (ISBN 0-13-410621-0); pap. 7.95 (ISBN 0-13-410613-X). P-H.

Deutsch, Babette. Poetry Handbook: A Dictionary of Terms. 4th ed. 224p. 1982. pap. 5.72i (ISBN 0-06-463548-1, EH 548, EH). B&N NY.

--Poetry Handbook: A Dictionary of Terms. 4th ed. (Funk & W Bk.). 1982. pap. 5.72i (ISBN 0-06-463548-1, EH-548). T Y Crowell.

--Poetry Handbook: Dictionary of Terms. 4th ed. (Funk & W Bk.). 224p. 1974. 10.95i (ISBN 0-308-10088-3). Har-Row.

--Poetry in Our Time. LC 73-191121. 457p. 1975. Repr. of 1963 ed. lib. bdg. 32.50x (ISBN 0-8371-7309-4, DEPT). Greenwood.

Deutsch, Babette see Youtz, Phillip N.

Deutsch, Babette & Yarmolinsky, Avrahm, eds. Contemporary German Poetry. facs. ed. LC 77-76934. (Granger Index Reprint Ser). 1923. 17.00 (ISBN 0-8369-6010-6). Ayer Co Pubs.

--Modern Russian Poetry: An Anthology. LC 22-1307. 1968. Repr. of 1921 ed. 20.00 (ISBN 0-527-22200-3). Kraus Repr.

Deutsch, Babette, tr. see Babel, Isaac.

Deutsch, Babette, tr. & intro. by see Rilke, Rainer M.

Deutsch, Charles. Broken Bottles, Broken Dreams: Understanding & Helping the Children of Alcoholics. LC 81-5729. 232p. 1982. pap. text ed. 14.95x (ISBN 0-8077-2663-X). Tchrs Coll.

Deutsch, D. & Deutsch, J. A., eds. Short-Term Memory. 1975. 49.00 (ISBN 0-12-213350-1). Acad Pr.

Deutsch, David J., ed. see Chemical Engineering Magazine.

Deutsch, Dennis S. Protect Yourself: The Guide to Understanding & Negotiating Contracts for Business Computers & Software. LC 83-6524. 248p. 1983. 21.95 (ISBN 0-471-89217-3). Wiley.

Deutsch, Diana, ed. The Psychology of Music. LC 82-1646. (AO Series in Cognition & Perception). 1982. 54.50 (ISBN 0-12-213560-1). Acad Pr.

Deutsch, E., jt. ed. see Kleinberger, G.

Deutsch, Edward, et al, eds. Technetium in Chemistry & Nuclear Medicine. 246p. 1983. text ed. 50.50 (ISBN 8-885-03750-X). Raven.

Deutsch, Eliot. Advaita Vedanta: A Philosophical Reconstruction. LC 69-19282. 1969. pap. text ed. 5.95x (ISBN 0-8248-0271-3, Eastwest Ctr). UH Pr.

--The Bhagavad Gita. LC 81-40512. 206p. 1981. pap. text ed. 10.00 (ISBN 0-8191-1900-8). U Pr of Amer.

--Humanity & Divinity: An Essay in Comparative Metaphysics. LC 76-128081. 1970. 14.00x (ISBN 0-87022-190-6). UH Pr.

--On Truth: An Ontological Theory. LC 79-12754. 1979. text ed. 14.00x (ISBN 0-8248-0615-8). UH Pr.

--Personhood, Creativity & Freedom. LC 82-4891. 167p. 1982. text ed. 20.00x (ISBN 0-8248-0800-2). UH Pr.

--Studies in Comparative Aesthetics. LC 74-34028. (Society for Asian & Comparative Philosophy Monographs: No. 2). (Illus.). 112p. (Orig.). 1975. pap. text ed. 4.95x (ISBN 0-8248-0365-5). UH Pr.

Deutsch, Eliot & Van Buitenen, J. A. A Source Book of Advaita Vedeanta. LC 75-148944. pap. 65.60 (ISBN 0-317-12996-1, 2017216). Bks Demand UMI.

Deutsch, F., jt. ed. see Brosowski, F.

Deutsch, Felix & Murphy, William F. The Clinical Interview, 2 vols. Incl. Vol. 1. Diagnosis: A Method of Teaching Associative Exploration. 613p. text ed. 40.00 (ISBN 0-8236-0920-0); Vol. 2. Therapy: A Method of Teaching Sector Psychotherapy. 355p. text ed. 30.00x (ISBN 0-8236-0940-5). LC 54-12140. 1967. Intl Univs Pr.

Deutsch, Felix, ed. On the Mysterious Leap from the Mind to the Body: A Workshop Study on the Theory of Conversion. LC 59-8411. 1959. pap. 10.95 (ISBN 0-8236-8174-2, 023800). Intl Univs Pr.

Deutsch, Francine. Child Services: On Behalf of Children. LC 82-14570. (Psychology Ser.). 350p. 1982. pap. text ed. 13.50 pub net (ISBN 0-534-01221-3). Brooks-Cole.

Deutsch, Francine, jt. auth. see Hultsch, David F.

Deutsch, Georg, jt. auth. see Springer, Sally P.

Deutsch, Harold C. Conspiracy Against Hitler in the Twilight War. LC 68-22365. 1970. 15.00x (ISBN 0-8166-0473-8); pap. 3.45 (ISBN 0-8166-0550-5). U of Minn Pr.

--Memoires & Lettres de Marguerite de Valois. Gessard, M. F., ed. 43.00 (ISBN 0-384-35398-3); pap. 37.00 (ISBN 0-384-35388-6). Johnson Repr.
--The Revealing Intimate Memoirs of Marguerite De Valois. (Illus.). 1978. Repr. of 1831 ed. deluxe ed. 39.75 (ISBN 0-930582-11-X). Gloucester Art.
De Valois, Ninette. Come Dance with Me: A Memoir. (Ser. in Dance). (Illus.). 1980. Repr. of 1957 ed. lib. bdg. 22.50 (ISBN 0-306-79616-3). Da Capo.
--Come Dance With Me: A Memoir, 1898-1956. (Illus.). xvi, 234p. 1981. pap. 8.95 (ISBN 0-903102-02-1, Pub. by Dance Bks. England). Princeton Bk Co.
De Valuy, A. & Borel, B. The French Riviera: A Picture Guide. 1976. lib. bdg. 59.95 (ISBN 0-8490-1865-X). Gordon Pr.
Devamata, Sr. Days in an Indian Monastery. 3rd ed. 1975. pap. 5.50 (ISBN 0-911564-20-9). Vedanta Ctr.
--The Open Portal. 1929. 2.50 (ISBN 0-911564-35-7). Vedanta Ctr.
Devambez, Pierre. Diccionario de la Civilizacion Griega. 482p. (Span.). 1972. 37.50 (ISBN 84-233-0645-3, S-50367). French & Eur.
--Histoire de l'Art: Le Monde non Chretien, Vol. 1. (Historique Ser.). 2236p. 48.95 (ISBN 0-686-56450-2). French & Eur.
DeVan, William, jt. ed. see Maxwell, Carolyn.
Devander, Charles W. Van see Van Devander, Charles W.
De Vane, Lenchen Coleman. The Adventures of Tony, David & Marc: Reading from A-Z. 1976. 6.95 (ISBN 0-682-48435-0); tchr's. manual 4.00 (ISBN 0-682-48677-9). Exposition Pr FL.
DeVane, M. P., ed. see Tennyson, Alfred.
Devane, Richard S. The Failure of Individualism: A Documented Essay. LC 75-28664. (Illus.). 1976. Repr. lib. bdg. 21.75x (ISBN 0-8371-8484-3, DEFI). Greenwood.
DeVane, William C. American University in the Twentieth Century. LC 57-7496. (Davis Washington Mitchell Lectures). x, 72p. 1957. 10.95x (ISBN 0-8071-0432-9). La State U Pr.
De Vane, William C. Higher Education in Twentieth-Century America. LC 65-13839. (Library of Congress Series in American Civilization). 1965. 15.00x (ISBN 0-674-39150-0). Harvard U Pr.
De Vane, William C. & Knickerbocker, Kenneth L., eds. New Letters of Robert Browing. 413p. 1985. Repr. of 1951 ed. lib. bdg. 45.00 (ISBN 0-8492-2837-9). R West.
DeVane, William C., ed. see Browning, Robert.
DeVane, William C., ed. see Tennyson, Alfred.
Devanesen, Chandran D. S. The Making of the Mahatma. 1969. 23.50x (ISBN 0-8046-8808-7, Pub. by Kennikat). Assoc Faculty PR.
Devaney, Bob, et al. Devaney. (Illus.). 265p. 1981. 10.95 (ISBN 0-934904-14-6); pap. 7.95 (ISBN 0-934904-13-8). J & L Lee.
Devaney, D. M. & Eldredge, L. G., eds. Reef & Shore Fauna of Hawaii: Protozoa Through Ctenophora. LC 77-89747. (Special Publication Ser: No. 64 (1)). (Illus.). 290p. 1977. pap. 15.00 (ISBN 0-910240-22-1). Bishop Mus.
Devaney, Dennis M. & Kelly, Marion. Kaneohe: A History of Change. rev. ed. (Illus.). 300p. 1982. pap. 12.95 (ISBN 0-935848-14-2). Bess Pr.
Devaney, James. Poetry of Our Time. 1973. Repr. of 1952 ed. 15.00 (ISBN 0-8274-1619-9). R West.
Devaney, John. Blood & Guts: The True Story of General George S. Patton, U. S. A. LC 82-60636. (Illus.). 96p. (gr. 4-6). 1982. lib. bdg. 9.79 (ISBN 0-671-44273-2). Messner.
--The Bobby Orr Story. (Pro Hockey Library: No. 6). (Illus.). (gr. 5 up). 1973. (BYR); PLB 3.69 (ISBN 0-394-92612-9). Random.
--Great Upsets of Stanley Cup Hockey. LC 75-33969. (Sports Library). (Illus.). 96p. (gr. 3-6). 1976. PLB 7.98 (ISBN 0-8116-6678-6). Garrard.
--Secrets of the Super Athletes: Tips for Fans & Players-Soccer. (Illus., Orig.). (gr. 7 up). 1982. pap. 1.95 (ISBN 0-440-98399-1, LFL). Dell.
--Star Pass Receivers of the NFL. (NFL Punt, Pass & Kick Library: No. 17). (Illus.). (gr. 5 up). 1972. (BYR); PLB 3.69 (ISBN 0-394-92439-8). Random.
--Superstars of Sports: Today & Yesterday. 1979. pap. 2.25 (ISBN 0-532-22149-4). Woodhill.
--Where Are They Today? Great Sports Stars of Yesteryear. LC 84-17475. (Illus.). 288p. 1985. 16.95 (ISBN 0-517-55344-9); pap. 9.95 (ISBN 0-517-55345-7). Crown.
Devaney, John, jt. auth. see Lorimer, Lawrence T.
Devaney, Kathleen, ed. Building a Teachers' Center. 1979. pap. 9.75x (ISBN 0-8077-2566-8, Pub. by Teach Ctr Exchange). Tchrs Coll.
Devanna, Mary A. Male-Female Careers - the First Decade: A Study of MBA's. 1984. pap. 17.50 (ISBN 0-317-11513-8). Columbia U Res.
Devanna, Mary A., et al. Human Resource Management: Issues for the 1980's. 1983. pap. 15.00 (ISBN 0-317-11512-X). Columbia U Res.
Devanney, J. W., et al. Parable Beach: A Primer in Coastal Zone Management. 1976. text ed. 15.00x (ISBN 0-262-04052-2). MIT Pr.
Devant, David, jt. auth. see Maskelyne, Nevil.
Devanter, Linda Van see Van Devanter, Linda & Morgan, Christopher.
Devanter, Lynda Van see Van Devanter, Lynda & Morgan, Christopher.
DeVany, A. S. Master Optical Techniques. LC 80-24442. (Pure & Applied Optics Ser.). 600p. 1981. 67.50x (ISBN 0-471-07720-8, Pub. by Wiley-Interscience). Wiley.
De Vany, Arthur S., et al. A Property System Approach to the Electromagnetic Spectrum: A Legal-Economic-Engineering Study. (Cato Paper Ser.: No. 10). 87p. 1980. pap. 4.00x (ISBN 0-932790-11-9). Cato Inst.
Devaquet, A., et al. Triplet States One. (Topics in Current Chemistry Ser.: Vol. 54). (Illus.). iv, 164p. 1975. 42.00 (ISBN 0-387-07107-5). Springer-Verlag.
Devarahi, pseud. The Complete Guide to Synthesizers. (Illus.). 272p. 1982. pap. 21.95 (ISBN 0-13-160630-1). P-H.
Devaraj, T. L. Speaking of Ayurvedic Remedies for Common Diseases: Simple Remedies Based on Herbal Medicines. (Health & Cure Ser.). 1985. text ed. 17.95x (ISBN 0-317-19697-9, Pub. by Sterling Pubs India). Apt Bks.
Devaraja, N. K. An Introduction to Sankara's Theory of Knowledge. 2nd, rev. ed. 1972. 5.95 (ISBN 0-89684-227-4). Orient Bk Dist.
--The Mind & Spirit of India. 1967. 5.95 (ISBN 0-89684-281-9). Orient Bk Dist.
Devaraja, N. K., ed. Indian Philosophy Today. LC 75-908522. 1975. 13.50 (ISBN 0-333-90085-5). South Asia Bks.
Devarenne, M. Butterflies: A Colour Field Guide. (Illus.). 183p. 1984. 12.95 (ISBN 0-7153-8488-0). Hippocrene Bks.
De Vargas Y Ponce, Jose. A Voyage of Discovery to the Strait of Magellan. LC 77-88580. 1977. Repr. of 1820 ed. lib. bdg. 12.50 (ISBN 0-89341-286-4). Longwood Pub Group.
De Varigny, Charles see Varigny, Charles de.
Devaris, Dionisios P., jt. ed. see Wain, Harold J.
De Varthema, Ludovico, jt. auth. see Hammond, Lincoln D.
Devas, Dominic. Treatise on Prayer & Meditation. Repr. of 1926 ed. lib. bdg. 25.00 (ISBN 0-8495-1026-0). Arden Lib.
Devas, M., ed. Geriatric Orthopaedics. 1977. 39.50 (ISBN 0-12-213750-7). Acad Pr.
Devas, Nicolette. Two Flamboyant Fathers. (Illus.). 288p. 1985. pap. 9.95 (ISBN 0-241-11404-7, Pub. by Hamish Hamilton England). David & Charles.
DeVasure, John, jt. auth. see Champlin, Connie.
De Vattel, Emmerich. The Law of Nations. LC 75-31104. 664p. Repr. of 1863 ed. 57.50 (ISBN 0-404-13519-6). AMS Pr.
De Vaucouleurs, Antoinette, jt. auth. see De Vaucouleurs, Gerald H.
De Vaucouleurs, Antoinette, jt. auth. see De Vaucouleurs, Gerard.
De Vaucouleurs, Antoinette, jt. auth. see Longo, Guiseppe.
De Vaucouleurs, Gerald H. & De Vaucouleurs, Antoinette. Second Reference Catalogue of Bright Galaxies. LC 75-44009. (Texas University Monographs in Astronomy: No. 2). pap. 101.00 (ISBN 0-317-08632-4, 2021153). Bks Demand UMI.
De Vaucouleurs, Gerard & De Vaucouleurs, Antoinette. Reference Catalogue of Bright Galaxies. 276p. 1964. 30.00x (ISBN 0-292-73348-8). U of Tex Pr.
De Vaul, Diane. Iowa Legacy. (WEP Poetry Ser.: No. 3). (Orig.). 1979. pap. 1.50 (ISBN 0-917976-07-X). White Ewe.
DeVaul, R. A., ed. see Gildenberg, P. L.
DeVault, Christine, jt. auth. see Strong, Bryan.
DeVault, Don. Quantum Mechanical Tunnelling in Biological Systems. 2nd ed. LC 83-15445. (Illus.). 200p. 1984. 44.50 (ISBN 0-521-24904-X). Cambridge U Pr.
DeVault, Don C., jt. ed. see Chance, Britton.
Devault, Joseph J. Josue. (Bible Ser.). pap. 1.00 (ISBN 0-8091-5075-1). Paulist Pr.
DeVault, M. Vere, jt. auth. see Cooper, James M.
DeVault, Mary & Goldner, Paul. The Texas Instruments Software Digest. cancelled 12.95 (ISBN 0-89303-855-5). Brady Comm.
De Vaux, R. & Milik, J. T. Discoveries in the Judaean Desert: Qumran Grotte 4-11, Vol. 6. (Illus.). 1977. text ed. 52.00x (ISBN 0-19-826317-1). Oxford U Pr.
DeVaux, Roland. Ancient Israel, 2 Vols. 1965. Vol. 1, Social Institutions. pap. 6.95 (ISBN 0-07-016599-8, SP); Vol. 2, Religious Institutions. pap. 6.95 (ISBN 0-07-016600-5). McGraw.
De Vaux, Roland. The Early History of Israel. LC 78-1883. 914p. 1978. Westminster.
Devavrata Basu Ray, tr. see Vishwashrayananda, Swami.
De Vazquez, Margot Arce see Pales Matos, Luis.
De V. Booysen, P. & Tainton, N. M., eds. Ecological Effects of Fire in South African Ecosystems. (Ecological Studies: Analysis & Synthesis: Vol. 48). (Illus.). 440p. 1984. 33.50 (ISBN 0-387-13501-4). Springer-Verlag.
De V. Brunkow, Robert see Brunkow, Robert de V.
DeVeau, Frederic J. & Getty, Norris M. Selections from Ovid's Metamorphoses. (gr. 10-12). 1969. text ed. 10.95 (ISBN 0-88334-010-0). Ind Sch Pr.
DeVeaugh-Geiss, Joseph. Tardive Dyskinesia & Related Involuntary Movement Disorders. (Illus.). 224p. 1982. text ed. 37.00 (ISBN 0-7236-7006-4). PSG Pub Co.
DeVeaux, Alexis. Don't Explain (A Song of Billie Holiday) LC 78-19471. (Illus.). 160p. (gr. 7 up). 1980. PLB 10.89 (ISBN 0-06-021630-1). HarpJ.
Devecmon, William C. In Re Shakespeare's Legal Acquirements. LC 79-170139. Repr. of 1899 ed. 16.00 (ISBN 0-404-54212-3). AMS Pr.
De Veen, J. J. The Rural Access Roads Programme: Apropriate Technology in Kenya. International Labour Office, Geneva, ed. (Illus.). 175p. (Orig.). 1984. pap. 11.40 (ISBN 92-2-102204-8). Intl Labour Office.
De Veer, A. A., jt. ed. see Tjallingii, S. P.
DeVeer, Donald Van see Regan, Tom & Van DeVeer, Donald.
De Veer, Gerrit. Three Voyages of William Barents to the Arctic Regions, 1594, 1595, & 1596. 2nd ed. Beynen, K., ed. 1964. 32.00 (ISBN 0-8337-3622-1). B Franklin.
De Veer, Gerrit see Veer, Gerrit de.
DeVega, Felix L. La Dorotea. (Biblioteca De Cultura Basica Ser.). pap. 3.50 (ISBN 0-8477-0709-1). U of PR Pr.
De Vega, Lope. La Dorotea. Trueblood, Alan & Honig, Edwin, trs. from Span. 352p. 1985. text ed. 29.50x (ISBN 0-674-50590-5). Harvard U Pr.
--La Francesilla. McGrady, Donald, ed. 236p. 1981. pap. 19.00 (ISBN 84-499-4456-2). Biblio Siglo.
--Fuente Ovejuna. Colford, William E., tr. from Span. LC 68-26715. (Juxtalingual verse). 1969. pap. text ed. 9.00 (ISBN 0-8120-6020-2). Barron.
De Vega, Lope see Bentley, Eric.
De Vega, Lope see Lope de Vega.
De Vega, Lope see Vega, Lope De.
De Vega Carpio, L. F. El Sembrar en Buena Tierra. Fichter, William L., ed. (MLA GS Ser.). Repr. of 1944 ed. 13.00 (ISBN 0-527-92980-8). Kraus Repr.
De Vegh, Elizabeth. The Coral Boatmen. Reynolds, Julie & Darlington, Sandy, eds. LC 81-70080. (Illus.). 176p. (Orig.). 1982. pap. 3.95 (ISBN 0-9604152-3-8). Arrowhead Pr.
--In Transit. Reynolds, Julie & Darlington, Sandy, eds. LC 81-70082. (Illus.). 262p. 1982. pap. 4.50 (ISBN 0-9604152-4-6). Arrowhead Pr.
--Lime Valley. Darlington, Sandy, ed. LC 85-70445. 358p. (Orig.). 1985. pap. 7.50 (ISBN 0-9604152-8-9). Arrowhead Pr.
DeVegh, Elizabeth. Love: A Fearful Success. Darlington, Sandy, ed. 192p. (Orig.). 1983. pap. 3.95 (ISBN 0-9604152-7-0). Arrowhead Pr.
Devegh, Imre. The Pound Sterling. Wilkins, Mira, ed. LC 78-3908. (International Finance Ser.). 1978. Repr. of 1939 ed. lib. bdg. 14.00x (ISBN 0-405-11213-0). Ayer Co Pubs.
DeVelasco, Joe & Klug, Ron. Philippians: Living Joyfully. (Young Fisherman Bible Studyguide Ser.). (Illus.). 64p. (gr. 7-12). 1983. tchr's ed. 4.95 (ISBN 0-87788-682-2); saddle-stitched student's ed. 2.95 (ISBN 0-87788-681-4). Shaw Pubs.
DeVelasco, Joe, illus. The Illustrated Gospels. (Illus.). 1982. misc. format 18.95 (ISBN 0-89191-568-0). Cook.
De Velde, J. H. van see Van de Velde, J. H., et al.
De Velde, Roger G. van see Van de Velde, Roger G.
De Velde, T. H. Van see Van De Velde, T. A.
Develin, L. Patrick, ed. Political Persuasion in Presidential Campaigns. 275p. (Orig.). 1986. 29.95 (ISBN 0-88738-078-6). Transaction Bks.
Devellard, Jean-Paul, jt. auth. see Dolce, Donald.
De Vellis, Jean, jt. ed. see Perez-Polo, J. Regino.
Development Academy of the Philippines. Rootcrops, Your Cookmate. (Illus.). 115p. 1981. pap. 5.00x (ISBN 0-686-32454-4, Pub. by New Day Philippines). Cellar.
Development Planning & Research Associates, Inc., for U. S. Dept. of Agri., Manhattan, Kansas. Wind Energy Applications in Agriculture. 204p. 1982. pap. 29.50x (ISBN 0-89934-172-1, W064). Solar Energy Info.
De Ven, Andrew H. Van see Van De Ven, Andrew H.
Devendra, Canagasaby & Fuller, M. F. Pig Production in the Tropics. (Oxford Tropical Handbooks Ser.). (Illus.). 1979. text ed. 32.50x (ISBN 0-19-859474-7). Oxford U Pr.
Devendra Gani. Davva-Samgaha (Dravya-Samgaha) Goshal, Sarat C., ed. & intro. by. LC 73-3835. Repr. of 1917 ed. 27.50 (ISBN 0-404-57701-6). AMS Pr.
--Gommatsara Jiva-Kanda (the Soul) Jaini, Rai B., ed. & intro. by. LC 73-3839. Repr. of 1927 ed. 48.00 (ISBN 0-404-57705-9). AMS Pr.
--Gommatsara Karma-Kanda, Pts. 1 & 2. Jaini, Rai B. & Ji, Brachmachari S., eds. LC 73-3840. Repr. of 1927 ed. Set. 72.50 (ISBN 0-404-57712-1). AMS Pr.
Deventer, C. N. Van see Van Deventer, C. N.
Deventer, Marylon Van see Friends of the Earth Staff.
De Ventos, Xavier R. Heresies of Modern Art. Bernstein, Jerome, tr. from Span. LC 79-19613. 1980. 29.00x (ISBN 0-231-04458-5). Columbia U Pr.
Deveny, Mary A. Recommended Reference Books in Paperback. 317p. 1981. lib. bdg. 25.00 (ISBN 0-87287-269-6); pap. 19.50 (ISBN 0-87287-279-3). Libs Unl.
Devenyi, T. & Gergely, J. Amino Acid Peptides & Proteins. 1974. 56.00 (ISBN 0-444-41127-5). Elsevier.
DeVenzio, Dick. Hitting Your Targets. 96p. (Orig.). 1983. pap. 4.95 (ISBN 0-686-36862-2). Fool Court.
--Stuff! Good Players Should Know. (Illus.). 320p. 1983. 13.95 (ISBN 0-910305-00-5). Fool Court.
Dever, Alan. Community Health Analysis: A Holistic Approach. LC 79-26291. 409p. 1980. text ed. 36.50 (ISBN 0-89443-161-7). Aspen Systems.
Dever, G. E. Epidemiology in Health Services Management. 350p. 1984. 34.95 (ISBN 0-89443-850-6). Aspen Systems.
Dever, G. R., jt. ed. see Ettensohn, F. R.
Dever, Joe & Chalk, Gary. Fire on the Water. (Lone Wolf Ser.: Bk. 2). (Illus.). 192p. (gr. 7 up). 1985. 2.25 (ISBN 0-399-21218-3). Putnam Pub Group.
--Flight from the Dark. (Lone Wolf Ser.: Bk. 1). 192p. (gr. 7 up). 1985. 2.25 (ISBN 0-399-21217-5). Putnam Pub Group.
Dever, Joseph. Cushing of Boston: A Candid Portrait. 15.00 (ISBN 0-8283-1382-2). Branden Pub Co.
Dever, William G. Gezer One: Preliminary Report of the 1964-1966 Seasons. 1971. 35.00x (ISBN 0-87820-300-1, Pub. by Hebrew Union). Ktav.
--Gezer Two. 1974. 35.00x (ISBN 0-685-56198-4). Ktav.
Dever, William G. & Darrel, Lance H. A Manual of Field Excavation. 1979. 12.50x (ISBN 0-87820-303-6). Ktav.
De Vera, Jose M. Educational Television in Japan. LC 68-16432. 1968. 6.00 (ISBN 0-8048-0162-2). C E Tuttle.
Deverall, B. J. Defence Mechanisms of Plants. LC 76-12917. (Monographs in Experimental Biology Ser.: No. 19). (Illus.). 1977. 27.95 (ISBN 0-521-21335-5). Cambridge U Pr.
Deverall, B. J., jt. ed. see Helgeson, John P.
Deverall, Brian. Fungal Parasitism. 2nd ed. (Studies in Biology: No. 17). 72p. 1981. pap. text ed. 8.95 (ISBN 0-7131-2832-1). E Arnold.
Deverall, Brian J., jt. auth. see Bailey, John A.
Deverall, Joseph M., jt. ed. see Daly, Joseph M.
Deveraux, Jude. The Black Lyon. 1980. pap. 3.50 (ISBN 0-380-75911-X, 88930-7). Avon.
--Counterfeit Lady. (Orig.). 1985. pap. 3.95 (ISBN 0-671-43560-4). PB.
--The Enchanted Land. 1978. pap. 3.50 (ISBN 0-380-40063-4, 60112-5). Avon.
--Highland Velvet. (The Montgomery Annals: No. 2). (Orig.). 1982. pap. 2.95 (ISBN 0-671-45034-4). PB.
--Highland Velvet. (General Ser.). 1985. lib. bdg. 16.95 (ISBN 0-8161-3794-3, Large Print Bks). G K Hall.
--Highland Velvet. 1985. pap. 3.50 (ISBN 0-671-60073-7). PB.
--Sweetbriar. (Gregg Hardcovers Ser.). 1985. lib. bdg. 12.95 (ISBN 0-8398-2874-8, Gregg). G K Hall.
--Sweetbriar. 1985. pap. 3.95 (ISBN 0-671-60074-5). PB.
--Twin of Fire. 1985. pap. 3.95 (ISBN 0-671-50050-3). PB.
--Twin of Ice. 1985. pap. 3.95 (ISBN 0-671-50049-X). PB.
--Velvet Angel. (Orig.). 1983. pap. 3.50 (ISBN 0-671-45406-4, Little Simon). PB.
--Velvet Angel. (Large Print Books). 1985. lib. bdg. 13.95 (ISBN 0-8161-3793-5). G K Hall.
--Velvet Angel. 1985. pap. 3.95 (ISBN 0-317-19326-0). PB.
--Velvet Angel. 320p. 1985. Repr. of 1983 ed. deluxe ed. 35.00 (ISBN 0-88733-012-6, Brandywine Bks). Underwood Miller.
--The Velvet Promise. (Richard Gallen Bks.). 416p. 1981. pap. 3.50 (ISBN 0-671-49272-1). PB.
--The Velvet Promise. 1984. lib. bdg. 17.95 (ISBN 0-8161-3783-8, Large Print Bks). G K Hall.
--Velvet Promise. 1985. pap. 3.95 (ISBN 0-671-54756-9). PB.
--Velvet Song. (General Ser.). 1984. lib. bdg. 13.95 (ISBN 0-8161-3633-5, Large Print). G K Hall.
Deverdun, A. The True Mexico: Tenochtitlan. 1976. lib. bdg. 59.95 (ISBN 0-8490-2773-X). Gordon Pr.
De Vere, Aubrey. English Misrule & Irish Misdeeds. LC 77-102597. (Irish Culture & History Ser.). 1970. Repr. of 1848 ed. 24.00x (ISBN 0-8046-0775-3, Pub. by Kennikat). Assoc Faculty Pr.
--Essays, Chiefly Literary & Ethical. 1889. 14.00 (ISBN 0-8274-2291-1). R West.
--Irish Odes & Other Poems. 59.95 (ISBN 0-8490-0426-8). Gordon Pr.
--Recollections of Aubrey De Vere. 1897. Repr. 35.00 (ISBN 0-8274-3255-0). R West.
DeVere, Charles. Lasers. LC 84-80510. (Inside Story Ser.). (Illus.). 40p. (gr. 4 up). 1984. PLB 9.90 (ISBN 0-531-04869-1). Watts.
De Vere, Maximilian Schele see Schele De Vere, Maximilian.
Devereaux, Captain C. Venus in India: Love Adventures in Hindustan. 352p. 1983. pap. 3.95 (ISBN 0-446-30789-0). Warner Bks.
Devereaux, Charles. Venus in India. (Orig.). 1967. pap. 1.95 (ISBN 0-87067-611-3, BH611). Holloway.
Devereaux, Frederick L., Jr., ed. The Cavalry Manual of Horse Management. rev. ed. (Illus.). 236p. 1985. Repr. of 1979 ed. 17.95 (ISBN 0-8159-5227-9). Devin.
Devereaux, Jude. Casa Grande. 304p. 1982. pap. 3.95 (ISBN 0-380-80192-2, 80556-1). Avon.
--Lost Lady. Date not set. pap. 3.95 (ISBN 0-317-19271-X). PB.

--Sweetbriar. (Tapestry Romance Ser.). (Orig.). 1983. pap. 2.50 (ISBN 0-671-45035-2). PB.

--Velvet Song. (Montgomery Annals Ser.: No. 3). (Orig.). 1983. pap. 2.95 (ISBN 0-671-45404-8). PB.

Devereaux, Linda E. The Texas Navy: Freedom Fighters for the Republic of Texas. Ericson, Joe, ed. LC 83-81716. (Illus.). 1983. pap. 14.50 (ISBN 0-911317-21-X). Ericson Bks.

Deverell, C. Business Administration & Management. 4th ed. 1980. pap. 17.95 (ISBN 0-85258-188-2). Van Nos Reinhold.

--Communication: A Book for Students. 1978. pap. 14.95 (ISBN 0-85258-169-6). Van Nos Reinhold.

--Management Studies: Questions & Answers. 2nd ed. 1979. pap. 15.95 (ISBN 0-85258-177-7). Van Nos Reinhold.

--Office Administration. 1980. pap. 16.95 (ISBN 0-85258-187-4). Van Nos Reinhold.

Deverell, David, ed. see Deverell, Dore.

Deverell, Dore. How I Healed My Cancer Holistically. 4.95 (ISBN 0-686-29909-4). Cancer Control Soc.

--How I Healed My Cancer Holistically (& Discovered the Cancer Coverup) Deverell, David, ed. 172p. (Orig.). 1978. 4.95 (ISBN 0-686-30100-5). Psychenutrition.

Deverell, Gweneth. Follow the Sun...to Tahiti, to Western Samoa, to Fiji, to Melanesia, to Micronesia. (gr. 1-3). 1982. 3.95 (ISBN 0-377-00120-1). Friend Pr.

Deverell, William. High Crimes. LC 81-21409. 498p. 1982. 15.95 (ISBN 0-312-37221-3). St Martin.

--High-Crimes. 304p. 1984. pap. 3.50 (ISBN 0-553-24432-9). Bantam.

Devereux, E. J. Renaissance English Translations of Erasmus: A Bibliography to 1700. (Erasmus Ser.). 256p. 1983. 35.00x (ISBN 0-8020-2411-4). U of Toronto Pr.

Devereux, Edward C., Jr. Gambling & the Social Structure: A Sociological Study of Lotteries & Horse Racing in Contemporary America, 2 vols. Zuckerman, Harriet & Merton, Robert K., eds. LC 79-8993. (Dissertations on Sociology). 1980. Set. lib. bdg. 103.00 (ISBN 0-405-12964-5). Ayer Co Pubs.

Devereux, Frederick L., Jr. Famous American Horses. LC 75-13347. (Illus.). 128p. 1975. 24.95 (ISBN 0-8159-5512-X). Devin.

--Practical Navigation for the Yachtsman. (Illus.). 316p. 1972. 19.95 (ISBN 0-393-03171-3). Norton.

Devereux, G. A Book of Edwardian Etiquette. (Illus.). 1983. 8.95 (ISBN 0-04-942181-6). Allen Unwin.

Devereux, George. Basic Problems of Enthnopsychiatry. Gulati, Basia M., tr. from Fr. LC 79-11104. 1980. Repr. of 1970 ed. lib. bdg. 31.00x (ISBN 0-226-14355-4). U of Chicago Pr.

--Dreams in Greek Tragedy: An Ethno-Psycho-Analytic Study. LC 74-27288. 400p. 1976. 42.00x (ISBN 0-520-02921-6). U of Cal Pr.

--Ethnopsychoanalysis: Psychoanalysis & Anthropology As Complementary Frames of Reference. LC 74-16708. 1978. 41.00 (ISBN 0-520-02864-3). U of Cal Pr.

--From Anxiety to Method in the Behavioral Sciences. (New Babylon Studies in the Social Sciences: No. 3). 1967. text ed. 22.40x (ISBN 90-2796-025-9). Mouton.

--Mohave Ethnopsychiatry & Suicide: The Psychiatric Knowledge & the Psychic Disturbances of an Indian Tribe. Repr. of 1961 ed. 59.00x (ISBN 0-403-03650-X). Scholarly.

--A Study of Abortion in Primitive Societies. rev. ed. LC 75-10572. 390p. 1976. text ed. 35.00 (ISBN 0-8236-6245-4); pap. text ed. 10.95 (ISBN 0-8236-8311-7, 26245). Intl Univs Pr.

Devereux, George, ed. Psychoanalysis &.the Occult. 432p. 1970. text ed. 35.00 (ISBN 0-8236-5180-0); pap. text ed. 9.95 (ISBN 0-8236-8240-4, 25180). Intl Univs Pr.

Devereux, Hugo B. The Small State As the Major Troublemaker in History & the Need to Eliminate Its Existence for the Peace of the World. (Illus.). 1979. deluxe ed. 69.75x (ISBN 0-930008-34-0). Inst Econ Pol.

Devereux, James, ed. see Williams, Shirley & Zalaquett, Jose.

Devereux, Kathleen. Understanding Learning Difficulties. 144p. 1982. 32.00x (ISBN 0-335-10049-X, Pub. by Open Univ Pr); pap. 13.00x (ISBN 0-335-10053-8). Taylor & Francis.

Devereux, Owen F. Topics in Metallurgical Thermodynamics. LC 83-1115. 494p. 1983. 43.50x (ISBN 0-471-86963-5, Pub. by Wiley-Interscience). Wiley.

Devereux, Robert. The First Ottoman Constitutional Period: A Study of the Midhat Constitution & Parliament. LC 78-64239. (Johns Hopkins University. Studies in the Social Sciences. Eighty-First Ser. 1963: 1). Repr. of 1963 ed. 26.00 (ISBN 0-404-61344-6). AMS Pr.

Devereux, Robert & Wingfield, Anthony. True Copie of a Discourse Written by a Gentleman, Employed in the Late Voyage of Spaine & Portingale. LC 78-38172. (English Experience Ser.: No. 449). 1972. Repr. of 1589 ed. 9.50 (ISBN 90-221-0449-4). Walter J Johnson.

Devereux, Stephen E., jt. auth. see McGregor, Rob R.

Devereux, Weeks J. Handbook for Collecting Delinquent Property Taxes. 2nd ed. LC 84-16959. 40p. 1984. pap. 6.50 (ISBN 0-89854-102-6). U of GA Inst Govt.

DeVere-White, Ralph. Aspects of Male Infertility. (I.P.U. Ser.). (Illus.). 296p. 1982. lib. bdg. 40.25 (ISBN 0-683-02451-5). Williams & Wilkins.

De Vere White, Terence. Johnnie Cross. 160p. 1984. 12.95 (ISBN 0-312-44463-X). St Martin.

De Vergie, Adrienne & Kell, Mary K. Location Guide to the Manuscripts of Supreme Court Justices. rev. ed. (Tarlton Legal Bibliography Ser.: No. 24). 146p. 1981. 15.00 (ISBN 0-935630-07-4). U of Tex Tarlton Law Lib.

Devergnas, Meery, et al, trs. see Ratushinskaya, Irina.

DeVernisy, G., jt. auth. see Delattre, J.

DeVerona, Donna & Tarshis, Barry. Donna DeVerona's Hydro-Aerobics: Swim Your Way to Total Fitness. 192p. 1984. 17.95 (ISBN 0-02-531250-2). MacMillan.

De Verre, Felix M. The Fibonacci Theory of Commodity Futures Trading. (Illus.). 111p. 1980. deluxe ed. 71.35x text (ISBN 0-918968-70-4). Inst Econ Finan.

Devers, Delaney. A Heart Victorious. (To Have & To Hold Ser.: No. 40). 192p. 1984. pap. 1.95 (ISBN 0-515-07842-5). Jove Pubns.

--Lucky's Woman. (Second Chance at Love Ser.: No. 284). 192p. 1985. pap. 2.25 (ISBN 0-425-08465-5). Berkley Pub.

De Verteuil, Maurice. Maurice's Tropical Fruits Cookbook. pap. 3.95 (ISBN 0-8200-0806-0). Great Outdoors.

De Vesme, Alexandre, jt. auth. see Massar, Phyllis D.

De Vet, Therese see Shaw, Peter & Vet, Therese de.

De Veubeke, B. F., et al, eds. see CISM (International Center for Mechanical Sciences).

De Veubeke, B. M. A Course in Elasticity. (Applied Mathematical Sciences Ser.: Vol. 29). (Illus.). 1979. 22.95 (ISBN 0-387-90428-X). Springer-Verlag.

Devey, J. A Comparative Estimate of Modern English Poets. 1973. Repr. of 1873 ed. 65.00 (ISBN 0-8274-1618-0). R West.

De Vezins, Elie. Hounds for a Pack. Woolner, Lionel R., tr. (Illus.). 7.00 (ISBN 0-85131-210-1, Dist. by Sporting Book Center). J A Allen.

Devi, Gayatri. One Life's Pilgrimage. 1977. pap. 6.95 (ISBN 0-911564-27-6). Vedanta Ctr.

Devi, Gayatri & Rau, Santha R. Princess Remembers. LC 85-7442. (Illus.). 320p. 1985. pap. 11.95 (ISBN 0-385-19937-6, Anchor). Doubleday.

Devi, Indira & Roy, Dilip K. Pilgrims of the Stars. 2nd ed. (Illus.). 406p. 1985. pap. 14.95 (ISBN 0-931454-10-7). Timeless Bks.

Devi, Indra. Yoga for Americans. 1971. pap. 2.25 (ISBN 0-451-09869-2, E9869, Sig). NAL.

Devi, Maitreyi. It Does Not Die. (Translated from Bengali). flexible cloth 11.00 (ISBN 0-89253-645-4). Ind-US Inc.

--Rabindranath: The Man Behind His Poetry. (Illus.). 1978. 8.00 (ISBN 0-86578-122-2); pap. 4.00 (ISBN 0-86578-123-0). Ind-US Inc.

Devi, P. K., jt. ed. see Menon, M. K.

Devi, Ragini. Dances of India. LC 79-7751. (Dance Ser.). 1980. Repr. of 1962 ed. lib. bdg. 16.00x (ISBN 0-8369-9282-2). Ayer Co Pubs.

Devi, Ratan. Thirty Indian Songs from the Panjab & Kashmir. Coomaraswamy, Ananda K., ed. LC 77-94573. 1979. Repr. of 1913 ed. lib. bdg. 17.50 (ISBN 0-89341-406-9). Longwood Pub Group.

Devi, Savitri. Son of the Sun: The Life & Philosophy of Akhnaton, King of Egypt. 4th ed. LC 80-54808. (Illus.). 323p. 1981. Repr. of 1946 ed. 12.50 (ISBN 0-912057-17-3, G-534). AMORC.

Devi, Shakuntala. Mathematical Merry-Go-Round. 150p. 1978. 14.95x (ISBN 0-306-31031-7, Plenum Pr). Plenum Pub.

Devi, Shree. The Purple-Braided People. 8.00 (ISBN 0-89253-652-7); flexible cloth 4.80 (ISBN 0-89253-653-5). Ind-US Inc.

--Shades of Green. (Writers Workshop Redbird Ser). 1975. 8.00 (ISBN 0-88253-632-X); pap. text ed. 4.00 (ISBN 0-88253-631-1). Ind-US Inc.

Devi, Shyamasree & Lal, P. Tagore's Last Poems. Rev. ed. 29p. (Bengali.). 1980. 8.00 (ISBN 0-86578-120-6); pap. 4.00 (ISBN 0-86578-121-4). Ind-US Inc.

Devi, Shyamasree, tr. see Roy, Tarapada.

De Vic, Claude see Vic, Claude de.

De Vicente-Gella, Pilar. The Man with White Slacks. 1985. 6.95 (ISBN 0-533-06395-7). Vantage.

Devide, Charles, ed. see Steinitz, William.

De Vido, Alfredo. Designing Your Client's House: The Architect's Guide for Meeting Design Goals & Budgets. (Illus.). 208p. 1983. 27.50 (ISBN 0-8230-7142-1, Whitney Lib). Watson-Guptill.

--Innovative Approaches to Architectural Design & Construction. (Illus.). 216p. 1984. 32.50 (ISBN 0-8230-7291-6). Watson-Guptill.

Devieux, Violet S. The One Stringed Harp. 1980. 6.50 (ISBN 0-8233-0311-X). Golden Quill.

De Vighne, Harry C. The Time of My Life. (Illus.). 64p. 1984. pap. 6.95 (ISBN 0-88240-261-7). Alaska Northwest.

--The Time of My Life. (Illus.). 64p. 1984. 6.95 (ISBN 0-88240-260-9). Alaska Northwest.

De Vigny, A. Oeuvres Completes: Cinq-Mars, Servitude et Grandeur Militaires, Etc, Vol. 2. 1404p. 39.95 (ISBN 0-686-56465-0). French & Eur.

--Oeuvres Completes: Oeuvres en vers, Theatre en vers, La Defense Obstinee de la Poesie et des Poetes, Etc, Vol. 1. 1032p. 39.95 (ISBN 0-686-56464-2). French & Eur.

De Vigny, Alfred. Chatterton. Germain, ed. Bd. with Quitte pour la Peur. (Coll GF). 1964. pap. 2.95 (ISBN 0-685-36020-2). French & Eur.

--Chatterton. (Documentation Thematique). (Fr). pap. 2.95 (ISBN 0-685-13826-7, 270). Larousse.

--Cinq-Mars. (Coll. Livre Club). 6.50 (ISBN 0-685-23961-6). French & Eur.

--Les Destinees. Saulnier, ed. (Textes Litter Franc Ser.). pap. 6.95 (ISBN 0-685-37141-7). French & Eur.

--Destinees. (Documentation thematique Ser.). (Illus., Fr.). pap. 2.95 (ISBN 0-685-13849-6, 338). Larousse.

--Servitude Et Grandeur Militaires. Germain, ed. 1965. pap. 6.95 (ISBN 0-685-11560-7). French & Eur.

--Stello. Germain, ed. Bd. with Les Consultations du Docteur Noir; Daphne. (Class. Garnier). pap. 12.95 (ISBN 0-685-37142-5). French & Eur.

--Stello: A Session with Doctor Noir. Massey, Irving, tr. LC 68-48328. pap. 54.00 (ISBN 0-317-20719-9, 2023828). Bks Demand UMI.

De Vigo, Johannes see Vigo, Johannes de.

Devijver, Pierre A., jt. auth. see Ronse, Christian.

Devik, O., ed. Harvesting Polluted Waters: Waste Heat & Nutrient-Loaded Effluents in the Aquaculture. LC 75-40281. (Environmental Science Research Ser.: Vol. 8). (Illus.). 335p. 1976. 42.50x (ISBN 0-306-36308-9, Plenum Pr). Plenum Pub.

De Vila, Maria Arsuaga see Arsuaga De Vila, Maria.

Devilbiss, M. C. Women in the Armed Forces. LC 84-48010. 100p. 1985. lib. bdg. 15.00 (ISBN 0-8240-8911-1). Garland Pub.

De Villa, Alvaro, tr. see Benteen, John.

De Villa-Dei, Alexander. Das Doctrinale des Alexander de Villa-Dei: Mit Einleitung, Verzeichniss der Handschriften & Drucke. Reichling, Dietrich, ed. LC 74-14859. 1975. Repr. of 1893 ed. 26.50 (ISBN 0-8337-2920-9). B Franklin.

De Villafranca, George W. Driving Force: Muscle. LC 72-189425. (Katharine Asher Engel Lecture for 1971). (Illus.). 1972. pap. 1.50 (ISBN 0-87391-010-9). Smith Coll.

De Villamil, Richard. Newton, the Man. 112p. 1972. Repr. of 1931 ed. 28.00 (ISBN 0-685-27503-5). Johnson Repr.

DeVille, Jard. The Psychology of Leadership: Managing Resources & Relationships. LC 83-20495. 179p. 1984. 14.95 (ISBN 0-910580-74-X). Farnswth Pub.

--Psychology of Leadership: Managing Resources & Relationships. 1985. pap. 3.95 (ISBN 0-451-62389-4, Ment). NAL.

Deville, Lawrence. American Foreign Policy & American Business: The Two Worlds in Conflict, 2 vols. (Illus., Orig.). 1979. Set. 155.85 (ISBN 0-89266-143-7). Am Classical Coll Pr.

--American Foreign Policy & American Business: The Two Worlds in Conflict, 2 vols. (Illus.). 257p. 1983. 137.45 (ISBN 0-89266-419-3). Am Classical Coll Pr.

Deville, Lawrrence. The Conflict Between the Foreign Policy of the United States & the Economic Interests of the Large Corporations. (Illus.). 163p. 1983. 88.45x (ISBN 0-86722-043-0). Inst Econ Pol.

De Ville, Paul. The Concertina & How to Play It. (Illus.). 79p. 1905. pap. 4.50 (ISBN 0-8258-0159-1, 0-3311). Fischer Inc NY.

DeVille, Paul. Universal Method for Saxophone. 320p. 1907. pap. 15.00 (ISBN 0-8258-0146-X, 0532). Fischer Inc NY.

DeVille, Winston. Acadian Church Records, 1679-1757. 1974. 10.00 (ISBN 0-686-20850-1). Polyanthos.

De Ville, Winston. Colonial Louisiana Marriage Contracts: Pointe Coupee, Vol 3. Bd. with Vol. 4. Avoyelles. 10.00x. Claitors.

DeVille, Winston. First Settlers of Pointe Coupee: 1737-1750. 1975. 10.00 (ISBN 0-686-20866-8). Polyanthos.

De Ville, Winston. Louisiana Recruits: 1752-1758. 12.50 (ISBN 0-686-20880-3). Polyanthos.

--New Orleans French, 1720-1733: A Collection of Marriage Records Relating to the First Colonists of the Louisiana Province. LC 75-150967. 113p. 1973. 12.50 (ISBN 0-8063-0480-4). Genealog Pub.

De Villehardouin, Geoffrey & De Joinville, Jean. Chronicles of the Crusades. Shaw, Margaret R., tr. (Classics Ser.). (Orig.). 1963. pap. 5.95 (ISBN 0-14-044124-7). Penguin.

De Villehardouin, Geoffroi. De la Conqueste De Constantinoble. Paris, Paulin, ed. 1965. 39.00 (ISBN 0-685-92799-7); pap. 33.00 (ISBN 0-384-64581-X). Johnson Repr.

De Villehardouin, Geoffroi & Joinville. Memoirs of the Crusades. LC 83-1515. (Everyman's Library: History: No. 333). xli, 340p. 1983. Repr. of 1908 ed. lib. bdg. 45.00x (ISBN 0-313-23856-1, VIME). Greenwood.

De Villehardouin, Geoffroy. Conqueste de Constantinople. White, Julian E., Jr., ed. LC 68-16196. (Medieval French Literature Ser). (Orig., Fr.). 1968. pap. text ed. 4.95x (ISBN 0-89197-102-5). Irvington.

De Ville Leyda, Seraphia see Leyda, Seraphia De Ville.

Devillers, Philippe. Histoire De Viet-Nam De Dix-Neuf Cents Quarante & Dix-Neuf Cents Cinquante-Deux. LC 73-179189. (Illus.). Repr. of 1952 ed. 32.50 (ISBN 0-404-54819-9). AMS Pr.

DeVillez, Randy. Step by Step: College Writing. 3rd ed. 1980. pap. text ed. 12.95 (ISBN 0-8403-3306-4, 40330601). Kendall-Hunt.

De Villiers, J. A., jt. auth. see Harris, C. A.

DeVilliers, Jill, jt. auth. see DeVilliers, Peter.

De Villiers, Jill G. & De Villiers, Peter A. Language Acquisition. 1978. 15.00x (ISBN 0-674-50931-5). Harvard U Pr.

De Villiers, Les & De Kieffer, Donald. Doing Business with the U. S. A. (Illus.). 304p. 1984. pap. 12.95 (ISBN 0-916673-00-6). Business Bks CT.

De Villiers, Les see Villiers, Les de, et al.

DeVilliers, Peter & DeVilliers, Jill. Early Language. LC 78-9862. (Developing Child Ser.). (Illus.). 1979. text ed. 7.95x (ISBN 0-674-22140-0); pap. 3.95 (ISBN 0-674-22141-9). Harvard U Pr.

De Villiers, Peter A., jt. auth. see De Villiers, Jill G.

De Villiers, Victor. The Point & Figure Method of Anticipating Stock Price Movements. 1973. pap. 15.00 (ISBN 0-685-42039-6). Windsor.

De Villiers du Terrage, Marc. The Last Years of French Louisiana. Brasseaux, Carl A. & Conrad, Glenn R., eds. Phillips, Hosea, tr. LC 82-73751. 525p. 20.00x (ISBN 0-940984-05-9). U of SW LA Ctr LA Studies.

De Villiers-Sidani, Maria E., et al. Lexique de Prevention des Accidents. 137p. (Eng. & Fr.). 1980. pap. 4.95 (ISBN 0-686-97398-4, M-9225). French & Eur.

Devin-Adair Staff. Dogmatic Canons & Decrees of the Council of Trent, Vatican Council I, Plus the Decree on the Immaculate Conception & the Syllabus of Errors. LC 79-112469. (Eng.). 1977. pap. 5.00 (ISBN 0-89555-018-0). TAN Bks Pubs.

Devin, Flanna. Alien Encounter. 1981. pap. 1.95 (ISBN 0-8439-0898-X, Leisure Bks). Dorchester Pub Co.

Devin, Robert. A History of the Grassy Creek Baptist Church. Repr. 15.00 (ISBN 0-686-12337-9); vinyl back 8.00 (ISBN 0-686-12338-7). Church History.

Devinat, Paul. International Labour Office Studies & Reports. Chandler, Alfred D., ed. LC 79-7540. (Scientific Management in Europe: Economic Conditions No. 17, History of Management Thought & Practice Ser.: Economic Conditions, No. 17). 1980. Repr. of 1927 ed. lib. bdg. 25.50x (ISBN 0-405-12325-6). Ayer Co Pubs.

De Vincent, George, jt. auth. see Stern, Philip.

De Vinck, Catherine. A Garland of Straw. LC 81-65684. 96p. (Orig.). 1981. pap. 5.75 sewn bdg. (ISBN 0-911726-41-1). Alleluia Pr.

--A Liturgy. 28p. 1973. pap. 1.50 (ISBN 0-911726-36-5). Alleluia Pr.

--A Passion Play. LC 75-26326. 68p. 1975. 6.75 (ISBN 0-911726-16-0); pap. 4.75 (ISBN 0-911726-18-7). Alleluia Pr.

--Readings: John at Patmos & A Book of Hours. LC 78-55341. 68p. 1978. 5.75 (ISBN 0-911726-32-2); pap. 3.75 (ISBN 0-911726-33-0). Alleluia Pr.

De Vinck, Jose. Revelations of Women Mystics: From Middle Ages to Modern Times. LC 84-24485. 180p. (Orig.). 1985. pap. 5.95 (ISBN 0-8189-0478-X). Alba.

--The Virtue of Sex. LC 66-15236. 256p. 1966. 12.75 (ISBN 0-911726-14-4). Alleluia Pr.

--The Words of Jesus, with Key Readings from New & Old Testaments. 320p. 1977. deluxe ed. 30.00 boxed, slipcover, hand-made full morocco (ISBN 0-911726-26-8). Alleluia Pr.

--The Yes Book. 1976. pap. 3.75 (ISBN 0-685-77499-6). Franciscan Herald.

--The Yes Book: An Answer to Life (a Manual of Christian Existentialism) LC 77-190621. 200p. 1972. 8.75 (ISBN 0-911726-12-8); pap. 6.75 (ISBN 0-911726-11-X). Alleluia Pr.

De Vinck, Jose, jt. auth. see Raya, Joseph.

De Vinck, Jose, tr. see Bonaventure, St.

De Vinck, Jose M., ed. see Kucharek, Casimir.

De Vinck, Jose M., ed. see Raya, Joseph.

Devine, Andrew M. & Stephens, Laurence D. Language & Metre: Resolution, Porson's Bridge, & Their Prosodic Basis. LC 84-1395. (APA American Classical Studies). 1984. pap. 11.25 (ISBN 0-89130-735-4, 40 04 12). Scholars Pr GA.

--Two Studies in Latin Phonology. (Studia Linguistica et Philologica: No. 3). 1978. pap. 25.00 (ISBN 0-915838-42-7). Anma Libri.

DeVine, Bob. Uncle Bob Talks with My Central Nervous System. (Designed by God Ser.). 48p. (gr. 4-7). 1985. pap. 4.95 (ISBN 0-89191-945-7, 59451, Chariot Bks). Cook.

--Uncle Bob Talks with My Circulatory System. (Designed by God Ser.). 48p. (gr. 4-7). 1985. pap. 4.95 (ISBN 0-89191-943-0, 59436, Chariot Bks). Cook.

--Uncle Bob Talks with My Digestive System. (Designed by God Ser.). 48p. (gr. 4-7). 1985. pap. 4.95 (ISBN 0-89191-944-9, 59444, Chariot Bks). Cook.

--Uncle Bob Talks with My Respiratory System. (Designed by God Ser.). 48p. (gr. 4-7). 1985. pap. 4.95 (ISBN 0-89191-941-4, 59410, Chariot Bks). Cook.

Devine, Carl T. Inventory Valuation & Periodic Income. Brief, Richard P., ed. LC 80-1486. (Dimensions of Accounting Theory & Practice Ser.). 1981. Repr. of 1942 ed. lib. bdg. 22.00x (ISBN 0-405-13516-5). Ayer Co Pubs.

Devine, Charles, jt. auth. see Guerriero, Graham.

Devine, Charles J., Jr. & Stecker, John F. Urology in Practice. 1978. text ed. 52.50 (ISBN 0-316-18155-2, Little Med Div). Little.

Devine, D. F. & Kaufmann, J. E. Elementary Mathematics for Teachers. 740p. 1983. 32.50 (ISBN 0-471-86254-1). Wiley.

Devine, D. M. My Brother's Killer. LC 81-47093. 256p. 1981. pap. 2.40i (ISBN 0-06-080558-7, P 558, PL). Har-Row.

Devine, Dominic. This Is Your Death. 224p. 1982. 10.95 (ISBN 0-312-80052-5). St Martin.

Devine, Donald F. & Kaufmann, Jerome E. Elementary Mathematics. LC 76-24805. 525p. 1977. text ed. 31.95x (ISBN 0-471-20970-8); tchr's. manual 8.00 (ISBN 0-471-02394-9). Wiley.

Devine, Donald J. Does Freedom Work: Liberty & Justice in America. LC 77-15914. (Illus.). 1978. (Dist. by Kampmann); pap. 5.95 (ISBN 0-916054-56-X). Green Hill.

--Reagan Electionomics: How Reagan Ambushed the Pollsters, 1976-1984. 105p. 1984. 14.95 (ISBN 0-89803-130-3, Dist. by Kampmann). Green Hill.

Devine, Edward & Staudinger, Lennette. Biological Investigations: Lab Exercises for Introductory Biology. 3rd ed. 128p. 1983. pap. text ed. 8.95 (ISBN 0-8403-3060-X). Kendall-Hunt.

Devine, Edward T. Misery & Its Causes. LC 70-137161. (Poverty U.S.A. Historical Record Ser). 1971. Repr. of 1909 ed. 18.00 (ISBN 0-405-03100-9). Ayer Co Pubs.

--Principles of Relief. LC 74-137162. (Poverty U.S.A. Historical Record Ser). 1971. Repr. of 1904 ed. 25.00 (ISBN 0-405-03132-7). Ayer Co Pubs.

--The Spirit of Social Work. LC 75-17216. (Social Problems & Social Policy Ser.). 1976. Repr. of 1911 ed. 19.00x (ISBN 0-405-07487-5). Ayer Co Pubs.

Devine, Elizabeth, jt. auth. see Braganti, Nancy.

Devine, Elizabeth, ed. The Annual Obituary 1983. 1984. 55.00 (ISBN 0-912289-07-4). St James Pr.

--Annual Obituary 1984. 1985. 55.00 (ISBN 0-912289-53-8). St James Pr.

Devine, Elizabeth, et al, eds. Thinkers of the Twentieth Century: A Biographical, Bibliographical & Critical Dictionary. 643p. 1984. 75.00 (ISBN 0-8103-1516-5). Real Est Futures.

Devine, Frank J. El Salvador: Embassy Under Attack. 1981. 10.00 (ISBN 0-533-05000-6). Vantage.

Devine, George. Liturgical Renewal. LC 73-12923. 199p. (Orig.). 1973. pap. 3.95 (ISBN 0-8189-0281-7). Alba.

--Transformation in Christ. LC 70-39884. 125p. 1972. pap. 3.95 (ISBN 0-8189-0240-X). Alba.

Devine, George, ed. That They May Live: Theological Reflections on the Quality of Life. 314p. 1984. pap. text ed. 10.50 (ISBN 0-8191-3852-5, College Theo Soc). U Pr of Amer.

--A World More Human: A Church More Christian. 204p. 1984. pap. text ed. 9.25 (ISBN 0-8191-3851-7, College Theo Soc). U Pr of Amer.

Devine, George F., jt. ed. see Starr, William J.

Devine, J. T., jt. auth. see Ahlstrom, Trudy H.

Devine, Laurie. Nile. LC 82-16960. 476p. 1983. 16.95 (ISBN 0-671-45170-7). S&S.

--Nile. 544p. 1984. pap. 3.95 (ISBN 0-440-16419-2). Dell.

--Saudi. 520p. 1985. 17.95 (ISBN 0-671-47453-7). S&S.

Devine, Maria T., jt. auth. see Napolitano, Annamaria.

Devine, Marjorie M. & Pimentel, Marcia H. Dimensions of Food. 2nd ed. (Illus.). 1985. text ed. 19.50 (ISBN 0-87055-470-0). AVI.

Devine, Mary. Brujeria: A Study of Mexican American Folk-Magic. Weschcke, Carl L., ed. LC 82-83427. (Illus.). 266p. (Orig.). 1982. pap. 7.95 (ISBN 0-87542-775-8). Llewellyn Pubns.

Devine, Michael D., jt. auth. see Ballard, Steven C.

Devine, Michael D., et al. Energy from the West: A Technology Assessment of Western Energy Resource Development. LC 80-5936. (Illus.). 350p. 1981. 32.50 (ISBN 0-8061-1750-8); pap. 17.95 (ISBN 0-8061-1751-6). U of Okla Pr.

Devine, Michael J. John W. Foster: Politics & Diplomacy in the Imperial Era, 1873-1917. LC 80-17387. (Illus.). x, 187p. 1981. 18.00x (ISBN 0-8214-0437-7, 82-83244). Ohio U Pr.

Devine, P. J., et al. An Introduction to Industrial Economics. 4th ed. (Illus.). 500p. 1985. pap. text ed. 18.95x (ISBN 0-04-338124-3). Allen Unwin.

Devine, Peter, ed. see Gafney, Leo & Beers, John C.

Devine, Philip E. The Ethics of Homicide. LC 78-58055. 304p. 1978. 24.50x (ISBN 0-8014-1173-4). Cornell U Pr.

Devine, Robert, ed. see New York State Bar Association.

Devine, T. M. Farm Servants & Labour in Lowland Scotland, 1780-1914. 280p. 1984. text ed. 31.00x (ISBN 0-85976-105-3, Pub. by John Donald Scotland). Humanities.

--The Tobacco Lords: A Study of the Tobacco Merchants of Glasgow & Their Trading Activities. 222p. 1982. 37.00x (ISBN 0-85976-010-3, Pub. by Donald Pubs Scotland). State Mutual Bk.

Devine, T. M. & Dickson, D., eds. Ireland & Scotland, 1600-1850. 283p. 1983. text ed. 34.25x (ISBN 0-85976-089-8, Pub. by John Donald England). Humanities.

Devine, Thomas G. Listening Skills Schoolwide: Activities & Programs. 61p. (Orig.). 1982. pap. 6.50 (ISBN 0-8141-2956-0). NCTE.

--Teaching Study Skills: A Guide for Teachers. 334p. 1981. 29.95x (ISBN 0-205-07269-0, 237269, Pub. by Longwood Div). Allyn.

Devinne, Paul. Day of Prosperity: A Vision of the Century to Come. LC 73-154439. (Utopian Literature Ser). 1971. Repr. of 1902 ed. 21.00 (ISBN 0-405-03522-5). Ayer Co Pubs.

DeVinne, Theodore L. Invention of Printing. LC 68-17971. 1969. Repr. of 1876 ed. 48.00x (ISBN 0-8103-3302-3). Gale.

De Vinne, Theodore L. Manual of Printing Office Practice. (Bibliographical Reprint Ser.). 52p. 1978. 25.00 (ISBN 0-685-27169-2). Battery Pk.

--Manual of Printing Office Practice. Lew, Irving, ed. (Bibliographical Reprint Ser.). 1980. Repr. of 1926 ed. text ed. 25.00 ltd. ed. (ISBN 0-89782-003-7). Battery Pk.

--The Printers' Price List, a Manual for the Use of Clerks & Book-Keepers in Job Printing Offices. Bidwell, John, ed. LC 78-74396. (Nineteenth-Century Book Arts & Printing History Ser.: Vol. 10). 1980. lib. bdg. 46.00 (ISBN 0-8240-3884-3). Garland Pub.

--Treatise on Title Pages. LC 68-25308. (Reference Ser., No. 44). 1972. Repr. of 1904 ed. lib. bdg. 59.95x (ISBN 0-8383-0935-6). Haskell.

Devino, Gary T. Agribusiness Finance. 166p. 1981. pap. 13.00 (ISBN 0-8134-2191-8); pap. text ed. 9.75. Interstate.

Devino, W. Stanley, et al. A Study of Textile Mill Closings in Selected New England Communities. 1966. pap. 6.95 (ISBN 0-89101-014-9). U Maine Orono.

Devins, D. W. Energy: Its Physical Impact on the Environment. 572p. 1982. 40.50 (ISBN 0-471-09122-7). Wiley.

Devins, D. W., ed. see Workshop-Seminar on Momentum Wave Function Determination in Atomic, Molecular & Nuclear Systems, Indiana Univ., Bloomington, May 31-June 4, 1976.

De Viri, Anne. Indrani & I. LC 65-21134. (Orig.). 1966. 4.95 (ISBN 0-87376-004-2). Red Dust.

De Visan, Tancrede see Visan, Tancrede De.

De Visme Williamson, Rene see Williamson, Rene De Visme.

De Visscher, Charles. Theory & Reality in Public International Law. rev. ed. Corbett, P. E., tr. LC 67-21020. (Center of International Studies Ser). 1968. 48.50 (ISBN 0-691-09210-9). Princeton U Pr.

De Visscher, Michel, ed. The Thyroid Gland. (Comprehensive Endocrinology Ser.). 552p. 1980. 77.00 (ISBN 0-89004-342-6, 396). Raven.

Devisse, Jean & Courtes, Jean Marie. The Image of the Black in Western Art, Vol. II: From the Demonic Threat to the Incarnation of Sainthood. Bugner, Ladislas, ed. (Illus.). 288p. 1983. 70.00 (ISBN 0-939594-02-1). Menil Found.

Devisse, Jean & Mollat, Michel. The Image of the Black in Western Art, Vol. II: From the Pharaohs to the Fall of the Roman Empire, Pt. 2: Africans in the Christian Ordinance of the World (F ourteenth to the Sixteenth Century) Bugner, Ladislas, ed. (Illus.). 336p. 1983. 80.00 (ISBN 0-939594-03-X). Menil Found.

De Visser, Louis A., jt. auth. see Hosford, Ray.

De Visser, Marinus W. The Arhats in China & Japan. LC 78-70136. Repr. of 1923 ed. 27.50 (ISBN 0-404-17406-X). AMS Pr.

DeVita, et al. Important Advances in Oncology, 1985. LC 65-8469. 1984. 47.50 (ISBN 0-397-50680-5, Lippincott Medical). Lippincott.

DeVita, Joseph, jt. auth. see Goldstein, William.

DeVita, Vincent, et al. Aids: Etiology, Diagnosis, Treatment, & Prevention. (Illus.). 384p. 1985. text ed. 38.00 (ISBN 0-397-50697-X, Lippincott Medical). Lippincott.

--Cancer: Principles & Practice of Oncology. 2nd ed. (Illus.). 2336p. 1985. text ed. 125.00 (ISBN 0-397-50632-5, Lippincott Medical); Two vol. set. text ed. 157.50 (ISBN 0-397-50727-5). Lippincott.

DeVita, Vincent T., Jr. & Hellman, Samuel. Cancer: Principles & Practice of Oncology. (Illus.). 1926p. 1982. text ed. 125.00x (ISBN 0-397-50440-3, 65-05838, Lippincott Medical). Lippincott.

De Vitis, A. A. Roman Holiday: The Catholic Novels of Evelyn Waugh. LC 71-153314. (BCL Ser. I). Repr. of 1956 ed. 14.50 (ISBN 0-404-02119-0). AMS Pr.

De Vitis, A. A. & Kalson, Albert E. J. B. Priestley. (English Authors Ser.). 1980. lib. bdg. 13.50 (ISBN 0-8057-6774-6, Twayne). G K Hall.

DeVitis, Joseph L., jt. auth. see Rich, John M.

De Vito, Albert. Albert De Vito Piano Course, Bk. 1. 1968. pap. 2.95 (ISBN 0-934286-52-3). Kenyon.

--Chord Approach to Pop Organ Playing, Bk. 1. (Illus.). 1965. pap. 3.95 (ISBN 0-934286-49-3). Kenyon.

--Chord Approach to Pop Organ Playing, Bk. 2. (Illus.). 1965. pap. 3.95 (ISBN 0-934286-50-7). Kenyon.

--Chord Approach to Pop Piano Playing, Bk. 1. (Illus.). 1962. pap. 3.95 (ISBN 0-934286-29-9). Kenyon.

--Chord Approach to Pop Piano Playing, Bk. 2. (Illus.). 1962. pap. 3.95 (ISBN 0-934286-30-2). Kenyon.

--Chord Approach to Pop Piano Playing, Bk. 3. (Illus.). 1963. pap. 3.95 (ISBN 0-934286-31-0). Kenyon.

--Chord Approach to Pop Piano Playing, Bk. 4. (Illus.). 1963. pap. 3.95 (ISBN 0-934286-32-9). Kenyon.

DeVito, Albert. Chord Charts. (Illus.). 1980. 3.95 (ISBN 0-934286-00-0). Kenyon.

--Chord Dictionary. LC 75-40685. (Illus.). 1980. 4.95 (ISBN 0-934286-01-9). Kenyon.

--Chord Encyclopedia. LC 75-43441. (Illus.). 1980. 6.95 (ISBN 0-934286-02-7). Kenyon.

De Vito, Albert. Chord Pianist: Classical Favorites for Piano, Bk. B. (Illus.). 1966. pap. 3.95 (ISBN 0-934286-34-5). Kenyon.

--Chord Pianist: Standard Favorites for Piano, Bk. A. (Illus.). 1966. pap. 3.95 (ISBN 0-934286-33-7). Kenyon.

DeVito, Albert. Chord Progressions Made Easy for Organ. (Illus.). pap. 3.25 (ISBN 0-934286-27-2). Kenyon.

De Vito, Albert. Christmas Songs for Piano. 1968. pap. 2.95 (ISBN 0-934286-53-1). Kenyon.

--Contrasts for Two Pianos. 1977. pap. 3.95 (ISBN 0-934286-58-2). Kenyon.

DeVito, Albert. Dance Suite for Piano. (Orig.). 1977. pap. 3.25 (ISBN 0-934286-56-6) (ISBN 0-317-14731-5). Kenyon.

De Vito, Albert. Fake It for All Keyboard Instruments. LC 75-40687. (Illus.). 1976. 5.00 (ISBN 0-934286-05-1). Kenyon.

DeVito, Albert. Instrumental Chord Guide. pap. 3.95 (ISBN 0-934286-17-5). Kenyon.

De Vito, Albert. Melodic Organ Pedal Studies. 1969. pap. 3.25 (ISBN 0-934286-42-6). Kenyon.

--Modern Organ Course for All Organs, Bk. 1. 1964. pap. 3.95 (ISBN 0-934286-36-1). Kenyon.

--Modern Organ Course for All Organs, Bk. 2. 1964. pap. 3.95 (ISBN 0-934286-37-X). Kenyon.

--Modern Organ Course, for All Organs: Primer. 1964. pap. 3.95 (ISBN 0-934286-35-3). Kenyon.

DeVito, Albert. Piano Sonata No. I. (Orig.). 1979. pap. 5.00 (ISBN 0-934286-12-4). Kenyon.

De Vito, Albert. Playing the Chord Organ & Learning to Read Music. (Illus.). 1974. 4.95 (ISBN 0-934286-08-6). Kenyon.

DeVito, Albert. Pocket Dictionary of Chords. pap. 1.50 (ISBN 0-934286-18-3). Kenyon.

De Vito, Albert. Pocket Dictionary of Music Terms. LC 65-8450. 1965. 1.95 (ISBN 0-934286-09-4). Kenyon.

--Popular Organ Classics. 1964. pap. 3.25 (ISBN 0-934286-43-4). Kenyon.

--Popular Piano Classics. 1964. pap. 3.25 (ISBN 0-934286-51-5). Kenyon.

--Progressive Organ Solos, Bk. 1. 1964. pap. 3.95 (ISBN 0-934286-38-8). Kenyon.

--Progressive Organ Solos, Bk. 2. 1964. pap. 3.95 (ISBN 0-934286-39-6). Kenyon.

--Progressive Organ Solos, Bk. 3. 1965. pap. 3.95 (ISBN 0-934286-40-X). Kenyon.

--Progressive Organ Solos, Bk. 4. 1965. pap. 3.25 (ISBN 0-934286-41-8). Kenyon.

DeVito, Albert. Seven Novelettes for Piano. pap. 3.95 (ISBN 0-934286-15-9). Kenyon.

--Sonatina for Piano. (Illus.). 1985. write for info. (ISBN 0-934286-65-5). Kenyon.

--Toys for Piano. (Orig.). 1961. pap. 3.25 (ISBN 0-934286-54-X). Kenyon.

De Vito, Albert, ed. see Piano Teachers Congress Members.

De Vito, Albert K., ed. see Byman, Isabelle Y.

De Vito, Alfred. Creative Wellsprings for Science Teaching. LC 84-70142. (Illus.). 260p. (Orig.). (gr. 3-8). 1984. pap. 14.95 (ISBN 0-942034-02-3). Creat Ventures IN.

--Teaching with Eggs. (Illus.). 70p. (Orig.). (gr. 3-8). 1982. pap. 6.95 (ISBN 0-686-32839-6). Creat Ventures IN.

--Teaching with Quotes. (Illus.). 162p. (Orig.). 1983. pap. 10.95 (ISBN 0-942034-01-5). Creat Ventures IN.

Devito, Alfred & Krockover, Gerald. Activities Handbook for Energy Education. (Illus.). 192p. 1981. pap. 12.95 (ISBN 0-673-16464-0). Scott F.

DeVito, Alfred & Krockover, Gerald H. Creative Sciencing: A Practical Approach. 2nd ed. (Illus.). 262p. 1980. text ed. 17.95 (ISBN 0-316-18159-5); tchr's manual avail. (ISBN 0-316-18162-5). Little.

--Creative Sciencing: Ideas & Activities for Teachers & Children. 2nd ed. (Illus.). 388p. 1980. pap. text ed. 14.95 (ISBN 0-316-18161-7). Little.

DeVito, Carl L. Functional Analysis. (Pure & Applied Mathematics Ser.). 1978. 23.50 (ISBN 0-12-213250-5). Acad Pr.

DeVito, Joseph. The Elements of Public Speaking. 2nd ed. LC 83-16630. 358p. 1984. scp 16.95 (ISBN 0-06-041649-1, HarpC); write for info. inst. manual (ISBN 0-06-361629-7). Har-Row.

--The Psychology of Speech & Language: An Introduction to Psycholinguistics. LC 81-40762. (Illus.). 320p. 1981. pap. text ed. 12.75 (ISBN 0-8191-1820-6). U Pr of Amer.

DeVito, Joseph A. Communication: Concepts & Processes. 3rd ed. (Illus.). 320p. 1981. pap. text ed. 18.95 (ISBN 0-13-153411-4). P-H.

--Communicology: An Introduction to the Study of Human Communication. 2nd ed. 608p. 1982. text ed. 20.50 scp (ISBN 0-06-041652-1, HarpC); instr. manual avail. (ISBN 0-06-361632-7). Har-Row.

--Human Communication: The Basic Course. 3rd ed. 528p. 1985. pap. text ed. 18.50 scp (ISBN 0-06-041648-3, HarpC). Har-Row.

--The Interpersonal Communication Book. 3rd ed. 470p. 1983. pap. text ed. 15.50 scp (ISBN 0-06-041651-3, HarpC); instr's. manual avail. (ISBN 0-06-361631-9). Har-Row.

DeVito, Michael. The Church's Faith, Bk. I. pap. 3.95 (ISBN 0-941850-06-4). Sunday Pubns.

De Vito, Michael C. Connecticut's Old Timbered Crossings. (Illus.). 1964. 8.00x (ISBN 0-910506-01-9). De Vito.

DeVito, Michael C. Diary of a Trolley Road. (Illus.). 1975. 8.00x (ISBN 0-910506-16-7). De Vito.

--East Windsor, Through the Years. (Illus.). 1968. 10.75x (ISBN 0-910506-05-1). De Vito.

--East-Windsor, Through the Years. Borrup, Roger, ed. 1968. 8.00 (ISBN 0-910506-05-1). E Windsor.

De Vito, Michael J. The New York Review, 1905-1908. LC 77-75637. (Monograph Ser.: No. 34). (Illus.). 1977. 13.95x (ISBN 0-930060-14-8). US Cath Hist.

De Vito, Robert A. & Tapley, Richard P., eds. A View into a Modern, State-Operated Mental Health Facility: The Madden Zone Center. 152p. 1975. 34.50x (ISBN 0-398-03207-6). C C Thomas.

Devitt, Edward J. & Blackmar, Charles B. Federal Jury Practice & Instructions: Civil & Criminal. 3rd ed. write for info. West Pub.

DeVitt, Joan Q., jt. auth. see Benson, Evelyn P.

Devitt, Michael. Designation. LC 80-26471. 304p. 1981. 31.00x (ISBN 0-231-05126-3). Columbia U Pr.

--Realism & Truth. LC 84-42588. 256p. 1984. text ed. 25.00x (ISBN 0-691-07290-6). Princeton U Pr.

Devivre, Joe, jt. auth. see Devivre, O.

Devivre, O. & Devivre, Joe. Perfection Perception. (Illus.). 128p. 1981. pap. 5.00 (ISBN 0-933280-08-4). Island CA.

De Vlad Georgescu. Istoria Romanilor dela Origini Pin in Zilele Noastre, Vol. IV. 394p. (Romanian.). 1984. 25.00 (ISBN 0-912131-00-4). Am Romanian.

Devletian, J. H. & Wood, W. E. Factors Affecting Porosity in Aluminum Welds: A Review. 1983. bulletin no. 290 12.00 (ISBN 0-318-01895-0). Welding Res Coun.

DeVlieger, Marinus & DeLange, Samuel A. Brain Edema. LC 80-22983. 190p. 1981. 42.95 (ISBN 0-471-04477-6). Krieger.

De Vlieger, Marinus, ed. Handbook of Clinical Ultrasound. LC 78-14458. (Illus.). pap. 120.00 (ISBN 0-317-07798-8, 2051330). Bks Demand UMI.

Devlin, Albert J. Conversations with Tennessee Williams. (Literary Conversations Ser.). 1986. 17.95 (ISBN 0-87805-262-3); pap. 9.95 (ISBN 0-87805-263-1). U Pr of Miss.

Devlin, Albert J., ed. Eudora Welty's Chronicle: A Story of Mississippi Life. LC 82-19996. 240p. 1983. text ed. 20.00x (ISBN 0-87805-176-7). U Pr of Miss.

Devlin, Christopher. Hamlet's Divinity & Other Essays. facs. ed. (Essay Index Reprint Ser). 1963. 15.00 (ISBN 0-8369-1915-7). Ayer Co Pubs.

Devlin, D. D. The Author of Waverley. LC 71-146129. 142p. 1971. 16.50 (ISBN 0-8387-7925-5). Bucknell U Pr.

--De Quincey, Wordsworth & the Art of Prose. LC 82-20443. 132p. 1983. 22.50 (ISBN 0-312-19397-1). St Martin.

--Wordsworth & the Poetry of Epitaphs. 143p. 1980. 28.50x (ISBN 0-389-20040-9). B&N Imports.

Devlin, D. D., ed. Walter Scott. (Modern Judgement Ser.). 1970. 2.50 (ISBN 0-87695-094-2). Aurora Pubs.

Devlin, Denis, tr. see Perse, St. John.

Devlin, Georgia F., jt. auth. see Rome, Carol C.

Devlin, Gerard M. Paratrooper! The Saga of Parachute & Glider Combat Troops-1914 to 1945. LC 77-23674. (Illus.). 1979. 27.50 (ISBN 0-312-59654-5). St Martin.

--Silent Wings: The Saga of the U. S. Army & Marine Combat Glider Pilots During World War II. (Illus.). 560p. 1985. 27.95 (ISBN 0-312-72460-8). St Martin.

Devlin, Harry, jt. auth. see Devlin, Wende.

Devlin, J. Frank, et al. Sports Illustrated Badminton. rev. ed. LC 72-10556. 1973. pap. 2.95i (ISBN 0-397-00968-2, LP80). Har-Row.

Devlin, James E. Erskine Caldwell. (United States Authors Ser.: No. 469). 189p. 1984. lib. bdg. 15.95 (ISBN 0-8057-7410-6, Twayne). G K Hall.

Devlin, John F. The Bath Party: A History from Its Origins to 1966. LC 75-41903. (Publications Ser.: No. 156). 372p. 1976. 12.95 (ISBN 0-8179-6561-0). Hoover Inst Pr.

--Syria: Modern State in an Ancient Land. LC 82-15909. 135p. 1982. lib. bdg. 22.50x (ISBN 0-86531-185-4); pap. text ed. 11.95x (ISBN 0-8133-0021-5). Westview.

Devlin, Joseph. A Dictionary of Synonyms & Antonyms. 384p. 1982. pap. 2.95 (ISBN 0-446-31310-6). Warner Bks.

Devlin, K. Fundamentals of Contemporary Set Theory. (Universitext Ser.). 1979. pap. 15.00 (ISBN 0-387-90441-7). Springer-Verlag.

Devlin, K. J. The Axiom of Constructibility: A Guide for the Mathematician. LC 77-17119. (Lecture Notes in Mathematics Ser.: Vol. 617). 1977. pap. 14.00 (ISBN 0-387-08520-3). Springer-Verlag.

--Constructibility. (Perspectives in Mathematical Logic Ser.). (Illus.). 425p. 1984. 58.00 (ISBN 0-387-13258-9). Springer-Verlag.

--Sets, Functions & Logic. 90p. 1981. (Pub. by Chapman & Hall England); pap. 7.95x (ISBN 0-412-22670-7, NO. 2048). Methuen Inc.

Devlin, K. J. & Johnsbraten, H. The Souslin Problem. (Lecture Notes in Mathematics Ser.: Vol. 405). vii, 132p. 1974. pap. 13.00 (ISBN 0-387-06860-0). Springer-Verlag.

Devlin, Laura K. Looking Inward: Studies in James Joyce, E.M. Forster, & the Twentieth Century Novel. 1980. lib. bdg. 59.95 (ISBN 0-87700-269-X). Revisionist Pr.

Devlin, Mark. Stubborn Child. LC 84-45053. 288p. 1985. 15.95 (ISBN 0-689-11476-1). Atheneum.

Devlin, Paddy. Yes We Have No Bananas: Outdoor Relief in Belfast, 1920-1939. 192p. (Orig.). 1981. pap. 4.50 (ISBN 0-85640-246-X, Pub. by Blackstaff Pr). Longwood Pub Group.

Devlin, Patrick. Criminal Prosecution in England. 1958. 34.50x (ISBN 0-685-69811-4). Elliots Bks.

--Easing the Passing: The Trial of Dr. John Bodkin Adams. (Illus.). 240p. 1985. 15.95 (ISBN 0-370-30627-9, Pub. by the Boadley Head). Merrimack Pub Cir.

--Enforcement of Morals. 1965. pap. 6.95 (ISBN 0-19-500305-5, GB). Oxford U Pr.

--The Judge. 1979. 24.95x (ISBN 0-19-215949-6). Oxford U Pr.

--The Judge. xiv, 208p. 6.95x (ISBN 0-226-14356-2, Phoen). U of Chicago Pr.

--Too Proud to Fight: Woodrow Wilson's Neutrality. (Illus.). 1975. 32.50x (ISBN 0-19-215807-4). Oxford U Pr.

Devlin, Polly. Vogue Book of Fashion Photography: The First Sixty Years. LC 83-63560. (Illus.). 240p. 1984. pap. 14.95 (ISBN 0-688-03900-6, Quill NY). Morrow.

Devlin, Robert & Witham, Francis. Plant Physiology. 4th ed. 500p. 1983. text ed. write for info. (ISBN 0-87150-765-X, Pub. by Willard Grant Pr). PWS Pubs.

Devlin, Thomas M. Textbook of Biochemistry, Vol. 2. 400p. (Japanese.). 1984. write for info. (ISBN 0-471-88695-5). Wiley.

--Textbook of Biochemistry: With Clinical Correlations. LC 81-13063. 1265p. 1982. 39.95x (ISBN 0-471-05039-3, Pub. by Wiley Med). Wiley.

Devlin, Tim & Warnock, Mary. What Must We Teach. 160p. 1982. 32.00x (ISBN 0-85117-136-2, Pub. by M Temple Smith). State Mutual Bk.

Devlin, Wende & Devlin, Harry. Hang on Hester! LC 79-19400. (A Fun-to-Read-Bk.). (Illus.). (gr. 1-3). 1980. 10.00 (ISBN 0-688-41935-6); PLB 10.88 (ISBN 0-688-51935-0). Lothrop.

Devlin, William. We Crown Them All: An Illustrated History of Danbury. (Illus.). 144p. 1984. 22.95 (ISBN 0-89781-092-9). Windsor Pubns Inc.

De Vocht, C., jt. ed. see Hengeveld, H.

De Vocht, H. Comments on the Text of Ben Jonson's "Every Man Out of His Humour". (Materials for the Study of the Old English Drama Series 2: Vol. 14). pap. 21.00 (ISBN 0-317-15145-2). Kraus Repr.

--Everyman: A Comparative Study of Texts & Sources. (Material for the Study of the Old English Drama Ser.: No. 2, Vol. 20). pap. 21.00 (ISBN 0-317-15506-7). Kraus Repr.

--Studies on the Texts of Ben Jonson's "Poetaster" & "Seianus". (Materials for the Study of the English Drama Series 2: Vol. 27). pap. 11.00 (ISBN 0-317-15517-2). Kraus Repr.

De Vocht, H., ed. A Knack to Know an Honest Man. LC 82-45755. (Malone Society Reprint Ser.: No. 112). Repr. of 1916 ed. 40.00 (ISBN 0-404-63022-7). AMS Pr.

De Vocht, H., ed. see Baylie, Simon.

De Vocht, H., ed. see Heywood, Jasper.

De Vocht, H., ed. see Jonson, Ben.

De Vocht, H., ed. see Middleton, Thomas.

Devoe, Charles D. Maine Workers' Compensation Act: Practice & Procedure Second Supplement. 400p. 1985. pap. 20.00 (ISBN 0-89442-051-8). Tower Pub Co.

De Voe, James R., ed. Validation of the Measurement Process. LC 77-15555. (ACS Symposium Ser.: No. 63). 1977. 29.95 (ISBN 0-8412-0396-2). Am Chemical.

Devoe, Lilly. For Love of a Stranger. 352p. (Orig.). 1983. pap. 3.75 (ISBN 0-523-42081-1). Pinnacle Bks.

Devoe, Lily. Made in Heaven. 288p. (Orig.). 1985. pap. 3.50 (ISBN 0-523-43338-7). Pinnacle Bks.

DeVoe, Shirley S. The Art of the Tinsmith: English & American. LC 81-85999. 222p. 1982. 27.50 (ISBN 0-916838-59-5). Schiffer.

--English Papier Mache of the Georgian & Victorian Periods. LC 76-105502. (Illus.). 1971. 25.00x (ISBN 0-8195-4017-X). Wesleyan U Pr.

De Voe, Thomas F. The Market Assistant. LC 72-174033. (Illus.). 455p. 1975. Repr. of 1867 ed. 65.00x (ISBN 0-8103-4117-4). Gale.

--Market Book, Containing a Historical Account of the Public Markets in the Cities of New York, Boston, Philadelphia & Brooklyn Etc. 1969. Repr. of 1862 ed. 29.00 (ISBN 0-8337-0847-3). B Franklin.

--Market Book Containing a Historical Account of the Public Markets in the Cities of New York, Boston, Philadelphia & Brooklyn: Vol. 1: A History of the Public Markets in the City of New York. LC 72-121319. Repr. of 1862 ed. lib. bdg. 45.00x (ISBN 0-678-00685-7). Kelley.

De Vogel, C. J. Greek Philosophy, 3 Vols. 1960-1964. Vol. 1. text ed. 30.25x (ISBN 90-04-02356-9); Vol. 2. text ed. 30.25x (ISBN 90-04-02357-7); Vol. 3. text ed. 42.75x (ISBN 90-040374-3-8). Humanities.

--Philosophia: Studies in Greek Philosophy, Pt. 1. (Philosophical Texts & Studies: No. 19). 1970. text ed. 37.50x (ISBN 90-232-0733-5). Humanities.

De Vogue, Adalbert. The Rule of Saint Benedict: A Doctrinal & Spiritual Commentary. Hasbrouck, John B., tr. from Fr. (Cistercian Studies: No. 54). 1983. pap. 25.95 (ISBN 0-87907-854-5). Cistercian Pubns.

De Vogue, E. M. The Russian Novelists. LC 74-28331. (Studies in Russian Literature & Life, No. 100). 1974. lib. bdg. 49.95x (ISBN 0-8383-1949-1). Haskell.

Devol, George H. Forty Years a Gambler on the Mississippi. 1892. 14.00 (ISBN 0-384-11595-0). Johnson Repr.

Devol, Kenneth S., ed. Mass Media & the Supreme Court. rev. 3rd ed. (Communication Arts Bks.). 1982. pap. text ed. 22.50x (ISBN 0-8038-4741-6). Hastings.

De Volpi, A., et al. Born Secret: The H-Bomb, the "Progressive" Case & National Security. (Illus.). 320p. 1981. 19.25 (ISBN 0-08-025995-2). Pergamon.

De Volpi, Alexander. Proliferation, Plutonium & Policy: Institutional & Technological Impediments to Nuclear Weapons Propogation. (Pergamon Policy Studies). (Illus.). 1979. 46.00 (ISBN 0-08-023872-6). Pergamon.

De Voltaire, Francois. Candide. Torrey, Norman L., ed. LC 47-15086. (Crofts Classics Ser.). 1946. pap. text ed. 3.75x (ISBN 0-88295-100-9). Harlan Davidson.

De Voltaire, Francois M. Candide. Bd. with Zadig. (Classics Ser). pap. 1.50 (ISBN 0-8049-0117-1, CL-117). Airmont.

--Candide. (Documentation thematique). (Illus., Fr.). pap. 2.95 (ISBN 0-685-13813-5, 344). Larousse.

--Candide. Adams, Robert M., ed. (Critical Edition Ser). 1966. pap. 3.95x (ISBN 0-393-09649-1). Norton.

--Candide. Brumfitt, J. H., ed. 1968. pap. 10.95x (ISBN 0-19-832372-7). Oxford U Pr.

--Candide. Butt, John, tr. (Classics Ser.). (Orig.). 1950. pap. 2.25 (ISBN 0-14-044004-6). Penguin.

--Candide ou l'Optimisme. 1957. pap. 7.95 (ISBN 0-685-11059-1). French & Eur.

--Candide, Zadig & Selected Stories. Frame, Donald, tr. pap. 2.25 (ISBN 0-451-51980-9, Sig Classics). NAL.

--Correspondance, 4 tomes. Besterman, ed. Incl. Tome I. (1704-1738) deluxe ed. 52.50 (ISBN 0-685-36021-0); Tome II. (1739-1748) 52.50 (ISBN 0-685-36022-9); Tome III. 1749-1753. 43.95 (ISBN 0-685-36023-7); Tome IV. 1754-1757. 52.50 (ISBN 0-686-57664-0). (Bibl. de la Pleiade). French & Eur.

--Melanges. Van Den Heuval, ed. (Bibl. de la Pleiade). 1961. 44.95 (ISBN 0-685-11356-6). French & Eur.

--Oeuvres Historiques. Pomeau, ed. (Bibl. de la Pleiade). 1958. 41.50 (ISBN 0-685-11456-2). French & Eur.

--Oeuvres Philosophiques. (Documentation Thematique Ser.). (Fr). pap. 2.95 (ISBN 0-685-14012-1, 351). Larousse.

--Romans, 2 tomes. 1961. pap. 9.90 (ISBN 0-685-23962-4, 657). French & Eur.

--Romans et Contes. Groos, ed. (Bibl. de la Pleiade). 1933. 49.95 (ISBN 0-685-11535-6). French & Eur.

--Zadig: Le Monde comme il va. (Documentation thematique). 2.95 (ISBN 0-685-36197-7, 349). Larousse.

--Zaire. (Documentation thematique). (Fr). pap. 2.95 (ISBN 0-685-14100-4, 355). Larousse.

De Voltaire, Francois-Marie A. Oeuvres Completes, 18 tomes. Set. 275.00 (ISBN 0-685-34062-7). French & Eur.

--Romans et Contes. pap. 4.95 (ISBN 0-685-34063-5). French & Eur.

--Zadig. (Classiques de la civilisation francaise). pap. 3.95 (ISBN 0-685-34065-1). French & Eur.

--Zadig, Micromegas et Autres Contes. Grimal, ed. (Bibliotheque de Cluny). pap. 5.50 (ISBN 0-685-34064-3). French & Eur.

De Voltaire, M. Essays & Criticisms: Containing Letters on the Christian Religion, The Philosophy of History, The Ignorant Philosopher, & the Chinese Catechism. 120p. 1983. Repr. of 1982 ed. lib. bdg. 65.00 (ISBN 0-89987-878-4). Darby Bks.

Devoluy, Pierre & Borel, Pierre. The French Riviera. 1981. Repr. 10.00 (ISBN 0-8495-1011-2). Arden Lib.

Devon, Anne. Defiant Mistress. (Second Chance at Love Ser.: No. 105). 1983. pap. 1.75 (ISBN 0-515-06869-1). Jove Pubns.

Devon, D. G. Precious Objects. 272p. (Orig.). 1984. pap. 2.95 (ISBN 0-345-29850-0). Ballantine.

--Temple Kent. 288p. 1982. pap. 2.75 (ISBN 0-345-29848-9). Ballantine.

Devon, James. The Criminal & the Community. LC 83-49234. (Crime & Punishment in England, 1850-1922 Ser.). 348p. 1984. lib. bdg. 40.00 (ISBN 0-8240-6225-6). Garland Pub.

Devon, Marian. Miss Armstead Wears Black Gloves. 224p. (Orig.). 1985. pap. 2.50 (ISBN 0-449-20792-7, Crest). Fawcett.

Devon, Richard F. The First Few Bytes. 96p. (gr. 10-12). 1984. pap. text ed. 5.95 (ISBN 0-8403-3250-5). Kendall-Hunt.

Devon, T. K. & Scott, A. I. Handbook of Naturally Occurring Compounds, 2 vols. Incl. Vol. 1. Acetogenins, Shikimates & Carbohydrates. 1975. 76.50 (ISBN 0-12-213601-2); Vol. 2. Terpenes. 1972. 77.00 (ISBN 0-12-213602-0). Acad Pr.

DeVoney, Chris. IBM's Personal Computer. 2nd ed. 318p. (Orig.). 1983. pap. 17.95 (ISBN 0-88022-026-0, 14). Que Corp.

--Introducing the Apple IIc: Applications & Programming. LC 84-61397. 250p. (Orig.). 1984. pap. 12.95 (ISBN 0-88022-093-7, 152). Que Corp.

De Voney, Chris. MS-DOS User's Guide. 330p. 1984. pap. 16.95 (ISBN 0-88022-061-9, 20). Que Corp.

--PC-DOS User's Guide. 354p. 1984. pap. 16.95 (ISBN 0-88022-040-6, 30). Que Corp.

DeVoney, Chris, jt. auth. see Cobb, Douglas.

Devons, Ely. Essays in Economics. LC 79-17089. (Illus.). 203p. 1980. Repr. of 1961 ed. lib. bdg. 24.75x (ISBN 0-313-21296-1, DEEE). Greenwood.

Devons, S. High-Energy Physics & Nuclear Structure. LC 72-112272. 859p. 1970. 65.00x (ISBN 0-306-30473-2, Plenum Pr). Plenum Pub.

Devons, Samuel, ed. Biology & the Physical Sciences. LC 78-80272. 379p. 1969. 36.50x (ISBN 0-231-03134-3). Columbia U Pr.

Devonshire, R. L., tr. see Faguet, Emile.

De Voogd, Peter. Henry Fielding & William Hogarth: The Correspondence of the Arts. 195p. 1981. pap. text ed. 23.50x (ISBN 90-6203-543-4, Pub. by Rodopi Holland). Humanities.

De Voogt, H. J., jt. ed. see Schroeders, F. H.

De Voogt, H. J., et al. Urinary Cytology: Phase-Contrast Microscopy & Analysis of Stained Smears. (Illus.). 1977. 64.00 (ISBN 0-387-08042-2). Springer-Verlag.

De Voort, Alice M. Van see Van De Voort, Alice M.

De Vooys, Sijna. Psychological Element in the English Sociological Novel of the 19th Century. LC 68-2022. (Studies in Fiction, No. 34). 1969. Repr. of 1927 ed. lib. bdg. 49.95x (ISBN 0-8383-0539-3). Haskell.

Devor, Barbara. Aunt Maude & le Faisan d'Or. 1981. 6.00 (ISBN 0-682-49563-8). Exposition Pr FL.

De Voragine, Jacobus. Golden Legend. LC 72-88826. (Art Histories Collection Ser). Repr. of 1941 ed. 40.00 (ISBN 0-405-02227-1). Ayer Co Pubs.

Devorah-Leah. Lost in the Zoo. 30p. (ps-1). 1983. 7.95 (ISBN 0-910818-56-8); pap. 5.95 (ISBN 0-910818-57-6). Judaica Pr.

De Vore, Blanche B. In the Lair of the Fox. (Illus.). 1985. write for info. (ISBN 0-318-01384-3); pap. write for info. (ISBN 0-318-01385-1). CLCB Pr.

DeVore, Irven, jt. ed. see Lee, Richard B.

Devore, Jay. Probability & Statistics for Engineering & the Physical Sciences. LC 81-21744. (Statistics Ser.). (Illus.). 700p. 1982. pap. text ed. 28.50 pub net (ISBN 0-8185-0514-1). Brooks-Cole.

De Vore, M. Susan. Individualized Learning Program for the Profoundly Retarded. (Illus.). 256p. 1978. spiral vinyl 18.50x (ISBN 0-398-03728-0). C C Thomas.

De Vore, Nicholas. Encyclopedia of Astrology. (Quality Paperback Ser.: No. 323). 1977. pap. 5.95 (ISBN 0-8226-0323-3). Littlefield.

--Encyclopedia of Astrology. 435p. 1976. Repr. of 1947 ed. 12.50x (ISBN 0-87471-858-9). Rowman.

DeVore, Paul, ed. see Pytlik, Edward C., et al.

DeVore, Paul W. Technology: An Introduction. LC 79-53782. (Technology Ser.). (Illus.). 397p. 1980. text ed. 18.95 (ISBN 0-87192-115-4, 000-5). Davis Mass.

De Vore, R. A. The Approximation of Continuous Functions by Positive Linear Operators. LC 72-91891. (Lecture Notes in Mathematics: Vol. 293). viii, 289p. 1972. pap. 13.00 (ISBN 0-387-06038-3). Springer-Verlag.

DeVore, R. A. & Scherer, K., eds. Quantitative Approximation. LC 80-17554. 1980. 35.00 (ISBN 0-12-213650-0). Acad Pr.

DeVore, R. William & Graves, Donald H. Nineteen Eighty-Five Symposium on Surface Mining, Hydrology, Sedimentology & Reclamation: Proceedings. LC 83-60966. (Illus.). 600p. (Orig.). 1985. text ed. 45.00 (ISBN 0-89779-064-2, UKY BU139). OES Pubns.

DeVore, R. William & Huffsey, R. Nineteen Eighty-Five International Symposium on Urban Hydrology, Hydraulic & Infrastructures & Water Quality Control: Proceedings. (Illus.). 335p. (Orig.). 1985. pap. 33.50 (ISBN 0-89779-063-4, UKY BU138). OES Pubns.

De Vore, R. William, ed. Carnahan Conference on Crime Countermeasures: Proceedings 1979. Jackson, J. S. LC 79-64890. (Illus.). 182p. (Orig.). 1979. pap. 22.50 (ISBN 0-89779-018-9, UKY BU117). OES Pubns.

De Vore, R. William & Carpenter, Stanley B., eds. Symposium on Surface Mining Hydrology, Sedimentology, & Reclamation. LC 79-91553. (Illus.). 353p. (Orig.). 1979. pap. 33.50 (ISBN 0-89779-024-3, UKY BU119). OES Pubns.

DeVore, R. William & Graves, Donald H., eds. Nineteen Eighty-Four Symposium on Surface Mining, Hydrology, Sedimentology & Reclamation: Proceedings. LC 83-60966. (Illus.). 492p. (Orig.). 1984. pap. 45.00 (ISBN 0-89779-062-6, UKY BU136). OES Pubns.

--Proceedings, Symposium on Surface Mining, Hydrology, Sedimentology, & Reclamation, 1982. LC 82-51182. (Illus.). 728p. (Orig.). 1982. pap. 45.00 (ISBN 0-89779-054-5, UKY BU129). OES Pubns.

De Vore, R. William & Graves, Donald H., eds. Proceedings, 1980 Symposium on Surface Mining, Hydrology, Sedimentology, & Reclamation. LC 80-84399. (Illus.). 480p. 1980. 45.00 (ISBN 0-89779-044-8, UKY BU123). OES Pubns.

--Proceedings, 1981 Symposium on Surface Mining, Hydrology, Sedimentology & Reclamation. LC 81-84944. (Illus.). 558p. (Orig.). 1981. 45.00 (ISBN 0-89779-050-2, UKY BU126). OES Pubns.

--Proceedings, 1983 Symposium on Surface Mining, Hydrology, Sedimentology & Reclamation. LC 83-60966. (Illus.). 554p. (Orig.). 1983. pap. 45.00 (ISBN 0-89779-058-8, UKY BU 133). OES Pubns.

De Vore, R. William & Haan, Charles T., eds. International Symposium on Urban Storm Water Management: Proceedings 1978. 348p. 1978. pap. text ed. 33.50 (ISBN 0-89779-002-2, UKY BU116). OES Pubns.

De Vore, R. William & Huffsey, R., eds. Nineteen Eighty-Four International Symposium on Urban Hydrology, Hydrolics & Sediment Control: Proceedings. LC 83-60965. (Illus.). 284p. (Orig.). 1984. pap. 33.50 (ISBN 0-89779-060-X, UKY BU135). OES Pubns.

De Vore, R. William & Huffsey, R. R., eds. International Symposium on Urban Storm Runoff: Proceedings 1979. LC 79-66289. (Illus.). 365p. (Orig.). 1979. pap. 33.50 (ISBN 0-89779-020-0, UKY BU118). OES Pubns.

De Vore, R. William & Jackson, J. S., eds. Carnahan Conference on Crime Countermeasures: Proceedings, 1980. LC 79-644630. (Illus.). 160p. (Orig.). 1980. pap. 22.50 (ISBN 0-89779-030-8, UKY BU120). OES Pubns.

--Carnahan Conference on Security Technology: Proceedings, 1982. (Illus.). 194p. (Orig.). 1982. pap. 22.58 (ISBN 0-89779-052-9, UKY BU127). OES Pubns.

DeVore, R. William & Jackson, J. S., eds. Carnahan Conference on Security Technology, 1985: Proceedings. (Illus.). 181p. 1985. pap. 22.50 (ISBN 0-89779-061-8, UKY BU137). OES Pubns.

De Vore, R. William & Jackson, J. S., eds. Conference on Crime Countermeasures & Security, 1983: Proceedings. (Illus.). 117p. 1983. pap. 22.50 (ISBN 0-89779-055-3, UKY BU 130). OES Pubns.

--Proceedings, 1981 Carnahan Conference on Crime Countermeasures. LC 79-644630. (Illus.). 199p. (Orig.). 1981. pap. 22.50 (ISBN 0-89779-046-4, UKY BU124). OES Pubns.

DeVore, R. William & Jackson, J. S., eds. Proceedings, 1984 Carnahan Conference on Security Technology. 218p. 1984. pap. 22.50 (ISBN 0-89779-059-6, UKY BU134). OES Pubns.

De Vore, R. William & Jackson, J. S., eds. Security Through Science & Engineering: Proceedings, Third International Conference. LC 80-83300. (Illus.). 313p. 1980. pap. 33.50 (ISBN 0-89779-042-1, UKYBU122). OES Pubns.

De Vore, R. William & Jackson, John S., eds. Carnahan Conference on Crime Countermeasures, 1978: Proceedings. 175p. 1978. pap. text ed. 22.50 (ISBN 0-89779-000-6). OES Pubns.

De Vore, R. William & Wood, Don J., eds. Proceedings 1981 International Symposium on Urban Hydrology, Hydraulics & Sediment Control. LC 81-82243. (Illus.). 473p. (Orig.). 1981. pap. 33.50 (ISBN 0-89779-047-2, UKY BU125). OES Pubns.

De Vore, R. William, ed. see International Carnahan Conference.

De Vore, R. William, ed. see International Symposium, 1983.

DeVore, Ralph E., jt. auth. see Mallery, Mary S.

DeVore, Ronald A. & Sharpley, Robert C. Maximal Functions Measuring Smoothness. LC 83-21494. (Memoirs Ser.: No. 293). 116p. 1984. pap. 11.00 (ISBN 0-8218-2293-4). Am Math.

DeVore, Russell B. Practical Problems in Mathematics for Heating & Cooling Technicians. LC 79-57141. (Practical Problems in Mathematics Ser.). 192p. 1981. pap. text ed. 7.80 (ISBN 0-8273-1682-8); instr's. guide 4.20 (ISBN 0-8273-1683-6). Delmar.

DeVore, Wynetta & Schlesinger, Elfriede. Ethnic-Sensitive Social Work Practice. LC 80-27538. (Illus.). 285p. 1981. pap. text ed. 14.95 (ISBN 0-8016-1268-3). Mosby.
DeVorkin, David H. The History of Modern Astronomy & Astrophysics. LC 81-43349. 462p. 1985. lib. bdg. 79.00 (ISBN 0-8240-9283-X). Garland Pub.
De Vorsey, Louis. The Georgia-South Carolina Boundary: A Problem in Historical Geography. LC 81-10441. (Illus.). 192p. 1982. 20.00x (ISBN 0-8203-0591-X). U of Ga Pr.
DeVorsey, Louis & Parker, John, eds. In the Wake of Columbus: Islands & Controversy. (Illus.). 272p. 1985. 25.00 (ISBN 0-8143-1786-3). Wayne St U Pr.
De Vorsey, Louis, ed. see De Brahm, William G.
Devos, Anthony. The Pollution Reader: Based on the National Conference on "Pollution & Our Environment". Pearson, Norman, et al, eds. LC 68-31597. (Harvest House Environment Ser.). (Illus.). pap. 66.00 (ISBN 0-317-09460-2, 2022293). Bks Demand UMI.
DeVos, Antoon. Deer Farming. (Animal Production & Health Papers: No. 27). 60p. 1982. pap. 7.50 (ISBN 92-5-101137-0, F2362, FAO). Unipub.
Devos, Burnell H., Jr., jt. ed. see Connor, Joseph E.
De Vos, George & Romanucci-Ross, Lola. Ethnic Identity: Cultural Continuities & Change. xvi, 396p. 1983. pap. text ed. 14.00x (ISBN 0-226-14364-3). U of Chicago Pr.
DeVos, George, jt. auth. see Lee, Changsoo.
DeVos, George, ed. Institutions for Change in Japanese Society. LC 84-80606. (Research Papers & Policy Studies: No. 9). 236p. 1984. pap. 15.00x (ISBN 0-912966-69-6). IEAS.
DeVos, George A. Socialization for Achievement: Essays on the Cultural Psychology of the Japanese. LC 78-132420. 613p. 1973. pap. 13.50x (ISBN 0-520-02893-7). U of Cal Pr.
De Vos, George A., jt. auth. see Wagatsuma, Hiroshi.
De Vos, P. A., jt. auth. see Eales, P. G.
De Vos, Raymond. History of the Monies Medals & Tokens of Monaco. 1978. 0.00 (ISBN 0-685-51123-5); lib. bdg. 80.00x (ISBN 0-685-51124-3). S J Durst.
Devos, Richard & Conn, Charles P. Believe! 1983. pap. 2.95 (ISBN 0-671-45829-9). PB.
DeVos, Richard M. & Conn, Charles P. Believe! 128p. 1975. pap. 2.95 (ISBN 0-8007-8267-4, Spire). Revell.
--Believe. 160p. 1985. pap. 2.95 (ISBN 0-425-07456-0). Berkley Pub.
De Vos, Susan. The Old-Age Economic Security Value of Children in the Philippines & Taiwan. LC 84-6081. (Papers of the East-West Population Institute: No. 60-G). viii, 72p. 1984. pap. text ed. 3.00 (ISBN 0-86638-056-6). E W Center HI.
Devos, Ton. U. S. Multinationals & Worker Participation in Management: The American Experience in the European Community. LC 80-23597. xv, 229p. 1981. lib. bdg. 35.00 (ISBN 0-89930-004-9, DUM/, Quorum). Greenwood.
DeVos-Miller, Kathryn, jt. auth. see Rising, Trudy L.
DeVoss, James T., jt. auth. see Schoen, Robert H.
DeVoss, Lishka. How to Be a Waitress (or Waiter) Everything You Need to Know to Get the Right Job, Make Good Money, & Stay Sane. (Illus.). 128p. 1985. pap. 5.95 (ISBN 0-312-39537-X). St Martin.
De Voto, Bernard. Across the Wide Missouri. (Illus.). 1964. pap. 10.95 (ISBN 0-395-08374-5, 25, SenEd). HM.
DeVoto, Bernard. Across the Wide Missouri. (Illus.). 608p. 1981. 8.98 (ISBN 0-517-10266-8, Am Legacy Pr). Crown.
--The Course of Empire. LC 83-6626. (Illus.). xxii, 647p. 1983. pap. 12.95 (ISBN 0-8032-6559-X, BB 851, Bison). U of Nebr Pr.
De Voto, Bernard. Journals of Lewis & Clark. 1953. 22.50 (ISBN 0-395-07607-2). HM.
DeVoto, Bernard. Literary Fallacy. LC 69-16484. (Essay & General Literature Index Reprint Ser). 1969. Repr. of 1944 ed. 21.00x (ISBN 0-8046-0519-X, Pub. by Kennikat). Assoc Faculty Pr.
De Voto, Bernard. Mark Twain's America: A Study in the Correction of Ideas. 355p. (Orig.). 1985. pap. 9.95 (ISBN 0-89301-108-8). U Pr of Idaho.
Devoto, Bernard. The Portable Mark Twain. (Orig.). 1983. 18.75 (ISBN 0-670-73341-5). Viking.
De Voto, Bernard. The Year of Decision: 1864. 26.95 (ISBN 0-88411-292-6, Pub. by Aeonian Pr). Amereon Ltd.
De Voto, Bernard, ed. see Lewis, Meriwether & Clark, William.
De Voto, Bernard, ed. see Twain, Mark.
Devoto, Bernard, ed. see Twain, Mark.
De Voto, Bernard, ed. see Twain, Mark.
De-Voto, Bernard A. Across the Wide Missouri. LC 83-45742. (Illus.). Repr. of 1947 ed. 94.50 (ISBN 0-404-20079-6). AMS Pr.
De Voto, Bernard A. Easy Chair. facsimile ed. LC 78-167333. (Essay Index Reprint Ser). Repr. of 1955 ed. 20.00 (ISBN 0-8369-2433-9). Ayer Co Pubs.
--Forays & Rebuttals. LC 78-111826. (Essay Index Reprint Ser.). 1936. 27.50 (ISBN 0-8369-1604-2). Ayer Co Pubs.
--Hour. LC 76-106664. Repr. of 1951 ed. lib. bdg. 18.75x (ISBN 0-8371-3422-6, DEHO). Greenwood.
--Mark Twain's America. LC 78-4109. (Illus.). xix, 351p. 1978. Repr. of 1967 ed. lib. bdg. 35.00x (ISBN 0-313-20368-7, DEVMT). Greenwood.
--Minority Report. facs. ed. LC 71-142619. (Essay Index Reprint Ser). 1940. 21.00 (ISBN 0-8369-2105-4). Ayer Co Pubs.
Devoto, Daniel, ed. see De Berceo, Gonzalo.
Devoto, G. & Oli, G. C., eds. Dizionario della Lingua Italiano. 2712p. (Ital.). write for info. (M-9196). French & Eur.
Devoto, Giacomo. The Languages of Italy. Katainen, V. Louise, tr. LC 78-3391. (The History & Structure of Languages Ser.). 1978. lib. bdg. 30.00x (ISBN 0-226-14368-6). U of Chicago Pr.
--Linguistics & Literary Criticism. Edgerton, M. F., Jr., tr. 1963. 6.00x (ISBN 0-913298-08-5). S F Vanni.
De Voto, Mark, ed. see Piston, Walter.
De Voursney, Robert B. J. & Marshall, J. Paxton, eds. The Virginia Assembly on Land Use Policies: Issues for the Commonwealth. 119p. 1982. pap. 3.00 (ISBN 0-318-04163-4). U Va Inst Gov.
Devoy, J. Recollections of an Irish Rebel. 508p. 1979. Repr. of 1929 ed. 25.00x (ISBN 0-7165-0045-0, BBA 02226, Pub. by Irish Academic Pr Ireland). Biblio Dist.
DeVoy, Robert & Wise, Harold. The Capital Budget. Barker, Michael, ed. LC 79-67387. (Studies in State Development Policy: Vol. 9). 73p. 1979. pap. 9.95 (ISBN 0-934842-08-6). Coun State Plan.
DeVoy, Robert S., jt. auth. see Costonis, John J.
Devraux, Jude. Counterfeit Lady. (Large Print Books (General Ser.)). 1985. lib. bdg. 17.95 (ISBN 0-8161-3826-5). G K Hall.
Devreeese, J. T. & Van Doren, V., eds. Linear & Nonlinear Electron Transport in Solids. LC 76-15234. (NATO ASI Ser. B, Physics: Vol. 17). 634p. 1976. 89.50x (ISBN 0-306-35717-8, Plenum Pr). Plenum Pub.
Devrees, J. T. & Peeters, F., eds. Polarons & Excitons in Polar Semiconductors & Ionic Crystals. (NATO ASI Series B, Physics). 490p. 1984. 72.50x (ISBN 0-306-41498-8, Plenum Pr). Plenum Pub.
Devreese, J. T., ed. Polarons in Ionic Crystals & Polar Semiconductors: Proceedings of the 1971 Antwerp Advanced Study Institute. 1976. 76.75 (ISBN 0-444-10409-7, North-Holland). Elsevier.
--Theoretical Aspects & the New Developments in Magneto-Optics. LC 80-18871. (NATO ASI Series B, Physics: Vol. 60). 635p. 1981. 89.50x (ISBN 0-306-40555-5, Plenum Pr). Plenum Pub.
Devreese, J. T. & Van Doren, V. E., eds. Ab Initio Calculation of Phonon Spectra. 312p. 1983. 42.50x (ISBN 0-306-41119-9, Plenum Pr). Plenum Pub.
Devreese, J. T., jt. ed. see Papadoupoulos, G.
Devreese, J. T., et al, eds. Elementary Excitations in Solids, Molecules, & Atoms, 2 pts. Incl. Pt. A. 375p. 59.50x (ISBN 0-306-35791-7); Pt. B. 385p. 59.50x (ISBN 0-306-35792-5). LC 74-1247. (NATO ASI Series B, Physics: Vols. 2A & 2B). 1974 (Plenum Pr). Plenum Pub.
--Recent Developments in Condensed Matter Physics, Vol. 2: Metals, Disordered Systems, Surfaces & Interfaces. LC 80-28067. 496p. 1981. 75.00 (ISBN 0-306-40647-0, Plenum Pr). Plenum Pub.
--Recent Developments in Condensed Matter Physics, Vol. 3: Impurities, Excitons, Polarons, & Polaritons. LC 80-28067. 436p. 1981. 65.00 (ISBN 0-306-40648-9, Plenum Pr). Plenum Pub.
--Recent Developments in Condensed Matter Physics, Vol. 4: Low-Dimensional Systems, Phase Changes, & Experimental Techniques. LC 80-28067. 464p. 1981. 69.50 (ISBN 0-306-40649-7, Plenum Pr). Plenum Pub.
--Highly Conducting One Dimensional Solids. LC 78-11396. (Physics of Solids & Liquids Ser.). (Illus.). 435p. 1979. 65.00x (ISBN 0-306-40099-5, Plenum Pr). Plenum Pub.
--Recent Developments in Condensed Matter Physics, Vol. 1: Invited Papers. LC 80-28067. 874p. 1981. 95.00x (ISBN 0-306-40646-2, Plenum Pr). Plenum Pub.
Devreese, Josef T. & Van Camp, Piet, eds. Electronic Structure, Dynamics & Quantum Structural Properties of Condensed Matter: Proceedings of an Antwerp Advanced Study Institute Held in Priorij Cordsendank, Belgium, July 1-27, 1984. (NATO ASI Series B, Physics: Vol. 1211). 604p. 1985. 89.50x (ISBN 0-306-41912-2, Plenum Pr). Plenum Pub.
Devreese, Jozef T. & Brosens, Fons, eds. Electron Correlations in Solids, Molecules, & Atoms. (NATO ASI Series B, Physics: Vol. 81). 448p. 1983. 55.00x (ISBN 0-306-41027-3, Plenum Pr). Plenum Pub.
DeVriend, H. J., ed. The Old English Herbarium & Medicina de Quadrupedibus. (Early English Text Society, Original Ser.: No. 286). 1984. 57.00x (ISBN 0-19-722288-9). Oxford U Pr.
Devrient, Eduard. My Recollections of Felix Mendelssohn-Bartholdy & His Letters to Me. Macfarren, Natalia, tr. LC 72-163799. 307p. 1972. Repr. of 1869 ed. 35.00x (ISBN 0-8443-0002-0). Vienna Hse.
Devrient, Edward. My Recollections of Felix Mendelssohn-Bartholdy & His Letters to Me. Macfarren, Natalia, tr. LC 72-163799. 307p. Date not set. Repr. of 1869 ed. 65.00. Vienna Hse.
De Vries, A. Dictionary of Symbols & Imagery. 2nd. rev. ed. 516p. 1976. 66.00 (ISBN 0-444-10607-3, North-Holland). Elsevier.
Devries, A. & Kochva, E., eds. Toxins of Animal & Plant Origin, 3 vols. LC 71-130967. (Illus.). 1142p. 1973. Set. 212.50 (ISBN 0-677-14710-4); Vol. 1-1971,512. 106.50 (ISBN 0-677-12430-9); Vol. 2-1972,338. 72.75x (ISBN 0-677-12440-6); Vol. 3-1973,292. 68.25x (ISBN 0-677-12450-3). Gordon.
De Vries, Barend A. Transition Toward More Rapid & Labor-Intensive Industrial Development: The Case of the Philippines. (Working Paper: No. 424). 32p. 1980. pap. 3.00 (ISBN 0-686-39755-X, WP-0424). World Bank.
DeVries, Betty. Bible Activity Balloon. (Pelican Activity Ser.). pap. 0.89 (ISBN 0-8010-2891-4). Baker Bk.
--Bible Activity Capsule. (Pelican Activity Ser.). pap. 0.89 (ISBN 0-8010-2896-5). Baker Bk.
--Bible Treasures Activity Book. (Pelican Activity Ser.). pap. 0.89 (ISBN 0-8010-2895-7). Baker Bk.
--One Hundred One Bible Activity Sheets. 144p. 1983. pap. 5.95 (ISBN 0-8010-2931-7). Baker Bk.
De Vries, Carolyn. Grand & Ancient Forest: The Story of Andrew P. Hill & Big Basin Redwood State Park. LC 78-50221. (Illus.). 1978. 10.00 (ISBN 0-913548-51-0, Valley Calif); pap. 3.95 (ISBN 0-913548-55-3, Valley Calif). Western Tanager.
DeVries, David L. & Slavin, Robert E. Teams-Games-Tournament: A Final Report on the Research. (Technical Report Ser.: No. 7). 50p. 1978. pap. 12.00 (ISBN 0-912879-06-8). Ctr Creat Leader.
DeVries, David L., jt. auth. see Celluci, Anthony J.
DeVries, David L., jt. auth. see McCall, Morgan W., Jr.
DeVries, David L., et al. Teams-Games-Tournament: The Team Learning Approach. Langdon, Danny G., ed. LC 79-26378. (Instructional Design Library). 104p. 1980. 19.95 (ISBN 0-87778-157-5). Educ Tech Pubns.
--Performance Appraisal on the Line. LC 81-10328. 160p. 1981. 29.95 (ISBN 0-471-09254-1, Pub. by Wiley-Interscience). Wiley.
De Vries, David P. see Vries, David P. De.
DeVries, Duane. Dickens's Apprentice Years: The Making of a Novelist. LC 75-31403. 195p. 1976. text ed. 19.50x (ISBN 0-06-491672-3). B&N Imports.
DeVries, Duane, ed. see Brattin, Joel J. & Hornback, Bert G.
DeVries, Duane, ed. see Fennell, Francis L.
DeVries, Duane, ed. see Glancy, Ruth F.
DeVries, Duane, ed. see Manning, Sylvia.
De Vries, G., jt. auth. see Norrie, D. H.
De Vries, G. A. Contribution to the Knowledge of the Genus Cladosporium Linx Ex Fries: Thesis. (Illus.). 1967. 16.00 (ISBN 3-7682-0458-8). Lubrecht & Cramer.
De Vries, G. J., et al, eds. Sex Differences in the Brain, Relation Between Structure & Function: Proceedings of the 13th International Summer School of Brain Research, Held at the Royal Netherlands Academy of Arts & Sciences, Amsterdam, The Netherlands, 22-26 August 1983. (Progress in Brain Research Ser.: Vol. 61). 514p. 1984. 129.75 (ISBN 0-444-80532-X). Elsevier.
De Vries, Gerard, jt. auth. see Norrie, Douglas.
DeVries, Gerard, jt. ed. see Norrie, Douglas H.
De Vries, H. Mutation Theory, 2 Vols. in 1. Farmer, J. B. & Darbishire, trs. 1909-1910. 58.00 (ISBN 0-527-93470-4). Kraus Repr.
De Vries, H., jt. auth. see David, R.
De Vries, H., jt. auth. see Van Bekkum, O.
De Vries, H. P. & Rodriguez-Novas, J. The Law of the Americas. LC 65-27792. 352p. 1965. 20.00 (ISBN 0-379-00268-X). Oceana.
DeVries, Henri. Incarnate Son of God. pap. 2.75 (ISBN 0-87509-095-8). Chr Pubns.
De Vries, Henry P., jt. auth. see Parker School of Foreign & Comparitive Law, Columbia University.
Devries, Herbert. Health Science. LC 78-27588. (Illus.). 1979. 20.60x (ISBN 0-673-16334-2). Scott F.
DeVries, Herbert A. Physiology of Exercise for Physical Education & Athletics. 3rd ed. 592p. 1980. text ed. write for info. (ISBN 0-697-07169-3). Wm C Brown.
DeVries, Herbert A. & Hales, Dianne. Fitness after Fifty: An Exercise Prescription for Lifelong Health. 192p. 1982. 12.95 (ISBN 0-684-17485-5, ScribT); pap. 5.95 (ISBN 0-684-17922-9). Scribner.
DeVries, Hugo. Intracellular Pangenesis. Gager, C. S, tr. from Ger. 1910. 19.95 (ISBN 0-87548-209-0). Open Court.
De Vries, J. Economy of Europe in an Age of Crisis: 1600-1750. LC 75-30438. (Illus.). 240p. 1976. 37.50 (ISBN 0-521-21123-9); pap. 10.95 (ISBN 0-521-29050-3). Cambridge U Pr.
DeVries, J. Hendrick, tr. see Kuyper, Abraham.
De Vries, J. J. Inleiding Tot De Hydrologie Van Nederland. (Chemie En Technick Ser.: No. 2). (Illus.). 78p. (Ger.). 1976. pap. text ed. 6.50x (ISBN 90-6203-149-8). Humanities.
De Vries, J. L., jt. auth. see Jenkins, R.
DeVries, James. The Kingdom of Christ. LC 84-90313. 155p. (Orig.). 1984. pap. 3.00 (ISBN 0-9613181-0-4). Kingdom Bks.
DeVries, James E. Race & Kinship in a Midwestern Town: The Black Experience in Monroe Michigan, 1900-1915. LC 83-6508. (Blacks in the New World Ser.). 206p. 1984. 17.50x (ISBN 0-252-01084-1). U of Ill Pr.
De Vries, James E. You Can Live with a Heartache: Hope for Long-Term Heartaches. (Christian Counseling Aids Ser.). 1977. pap. 0.95 (ISBN 0-8010-2876-0). Baker Bk.
De Vries, Jan. Barges & Capitalism: Passenger Transportation in the Dutch Economy (1632-1839) 368p. 1981. pap. 19.00x (ISBN 90-6194-432-5, Pub. by Hes Pubs Netherlands). Benjamins North Am.
--The Dutch Rural Economy in the Golden Age: 1500-1700. LC 73-86889. (Economic History Ser). (Illus.). 326p. 1974. 33.00x (ISBN 0-300-01608-5). Yale U Pr.
--European Urbanization: Fifteen Hundred to Eighteen Hundred. (Illus.). 432p. 1984. text ed. 28.50x (ISBN 0-674-27015-0). Harvard U Pr.
--Heroic Song & Heroic Legend. Bolle, Kees W., ed. LC 77-79157. (Mythology Ser.). 1978. Repr. of 1963 ed. lib. bdg. 18.00x (ISBN 0-405-10566-5). Ayer Co Pubs.
--Perspectives in the History of Religions. Bolle, Kees W., tr. & intro. by. LC 76-20154. (Cal Ser.: No. 352). 1977. pap. 3.65 (ISBN 0-520-03300-0). U of Cal Pr.
De Vries, Jan Vredeman see Vredeman De Vries, Jan.
DeVries, Janet M. Learning the Pacific Way: A Guide for All Ages. (Orig.). 1982. pap. 3.95 (ISBN 0-377-00119-8). Friend Pr.
De Vries, Jetty, jt. auth. see Verleum, Jan.
DeVries, John, jt. auth. see Charlton, Andrew.
De Vries, John A. Eaglerock: The History of the Alexander Aircraft Company. Feitz, Leland, ed. (Illus.). 120p. 1984. 24.95 (ISBN 0-937080-17-9); pap. 19.95 (ISBN 0-937080-18-7). Century One.
Devries, John A. Taube, Dove of War. LC 77-91439. (World War I Aircraft Ser.). (Illus.). 84p. 1978. pap. 7.95 (ISBN 0-911852-82-4). Hist Aviation.
Devries, John H., tr. see Kuyper, Abraham.
DeVries, Keith, ed. see Dyson, R. H., et al.
De Vries, L. Woerterbuch der Reinen und Angewandten Physik, Vol. 1. (Ger. & Eng., Dictionary of Physics & Applied Physics). 1964. 38.00 (ISBN 3-486-30942-0, M-6954). French & Eur.
--Woerterbuch der Reinen und Angewandten Physik, Vol. 2. (Eng. & Ger., Dictionary of Physics & Applied Physics). 1964. 38.00 (ISBN 0-686-56615-7, M-6962). French & Eur.
De Vries, L. & Clason, W. E. Dictionary of Pure & Applied Physics: German-English. 367p. 46.75 (ISBN 0-444-40168-7). Elsevier.
De Vries, L. P. Nature of Poetic License. LC 77-749. 1930. lib. bdg. 10.00 (ISBN 0-8414-3800-5). Folcroft.
De Vries, Lini. Up from the Cellar. 1978. 9.95 (ISBN 0-917266-17-X). Vanilla.
De Vries, Lini M. Please God Take Care of the Mule. 127p. 1975. pap. 3.00 (ISBN 0-912434-19-8). Ocelot Pr.
DeVries, Louis. German-English Technical & Engineering Dictionary. 2nd ed. (Ger. & Eng.). 1966. 67.95 (ISBN 0-07-016631-5). McGraw.
DeVries, Louis & Hochman, Stanley. French-English Science & Technology Dictionary. 4th ed. (Fr. & Eng.). 1976. 39.95 (ISBN 0-07-016629-3). McGraw.
DeVries, Louis & Jacolev, Leon. German-English Science Dictionary. 4th ed. (Ger. & Eng.). 1978. 37.95 (ISBN 0-07-016602-1). McGraw.
DeVries, Louis & Kolb, Helga. Dictionary of Chemistry & Chemical Engineering, 2 vols. 2nd ed. Incl. Vol. 1. German-English. 1978. 150.00x; Vol. 2. English-German. LC 77-138815. 150.00x (ISBN 0-89573-025-1). (Ger. & Eng.). 1979. VCH Pubs.
De Vries, Louis P. The Nature of Poetic Literature. 1978. Repr. of 1930 ed. lib. bdg. 25.00 (ISBN 0-8482-0626-6). Norwood Edns.
De Vries, Manfred F. Organizational Paradoxes. 1980. 15.95 (ISBN 0-422-77270-4, NO. 2970, Pub. by Tavistock England). Methuen Inc.
De Vries, Manfred F. Kets see Zaleznik, Abraham & Kets de Vries, Manfred F.
De Vries, Margaret G. The International Monetary Fund, 1966-1971: The System Under Stress, 2 vols. Incl. Vol. 1. Narrative. xxii, 699p. 11.00 (ISBN 0-939934-09-4); Vol. 2. Documents. viii, 339p. 6.00 (ISBN 0-939934-10-8). 1976. Set. 15.00 (ISBN 0-939934-11-6). Intl Monetary.
--International Monetary Fund, 1972-1978: Cooperation on Trial, 3 vols. 1985. Vol. 1-Narrative & Analysis, 600 p. 25.00 (ISBN 0-939934-40-X); Vol. 2-Narrative & Analysis (Concluded), 600 p. 25.00 (ISBN 0-939934-41-8); Vol. 3-Documents, 600 p. 25.00 (ISBN 0-939934-42-6); Set. 60.00 (ISBN 0-939934-43-4). Intl Monetary.
DeVries, Marten & Berg, Robert L. The Use & Abuse of Medicine. LC 82-7563. 316p. 1982. 42.95 (ISBN 0-03-061702-2). Praeger.
De Vries, Mary. New Century Vest-Pocket Secretary's Handbook. LC 82-81063. 352p. 1980. pap. 2.95 (ISBN 0-8329-1342-1). New Century.

DeVries, Mary A. Complete Secretary's Handbook. 5th ed. 300p. 1982. 19.95 (ISBN 0-13-163410-0). P-H.
--The Prentice-Hall Complete Secretarial Letter Book. (Illus.). 1978. 17.50 (ISBN 0-13-695494-4, Busn); pap. 7.95 (ISBN 0-13-696682-9). P-H.
--Private Secretary's Encyclopedic Dictionary. 3rd ed. LC 83-11004. 556p. 1983. 19.95 (ISBN 0-13-711093-6, Busn). P-H.
De Vries, Mary A. Secretary's Almanac & Fact Book. 420p. 1985. 19.95 (ISBN 0-13-798307-7, Busn). P-H.
DeVries, Mary A. Secretary's Standard Reference Manual & Guide. (Illus.). 1977. 19.95 (ISBN 0-13-797712-3, Parker); pap. 5.95 (ISBN 0-13-797704-2). P-H.
DeVries, Mary A. see Prentice-Hall Editorial Staff.
De Vries, Peter. Blood of the Lamb. 1962. 10.95 (ISBN 0-316-18173-0). Little.
DeVries, Peter. Blood of the Lamb. 1982. pap. 5.95 (ISBN 0-14-006297-1). Penguin.
De Vries, Peter. Consenting Adults, or, the Duchess Will Be Furious. 244p. 1980. 10.95 (ISBN 0-316-18184-6). Little.
DeVries, Peter. Consenting Adults, or the Duchess Will Be Furious. 1981. pap. 4.95 (ISBN 0-14-005833-8). Penguin.
De Vries, Peter. Forever Panting. 288p. 1982. pap. 4.95 (ISBN 0-14-006188-6). Penguin.
--The Glory of the Hummingbird. 1974. 6.95 (ISBN 0-316-18199-4). Little.
--I Hear America Swinging. 1976. 7.95 (ISBN 0-316-18200-1). Little.
--Into Your Tent I'll Creep. LC 70-161422. 1971. 6.95 (ISBN 0-316-18198-6). Little.
DeVries, Peter. Madder Music. 1982. pap. 4.95 (ISBN 0-14-006133-9). Penguin.
--The Prick of Noon. 240p. 1985. 14.95 (ISBN 0-316-18205-2). Little.
De Vries, Peter. Sauce for the Goose. 1982. pap. 3.95 (ISBN 0-14-006281-5). Penguin.
--Slouching Towards Kalamazoo. 228p. 1983. 13.45i (ISBN 0-316-18172-2). Little.
--Slouching Towards Kalamazoo. 256p. 1984. pap. 4.95 (ISBN 0-14-007070-2). Penguin.
Devries, Peter. The Tunnel of Love. 1982. pap. 5.95 (ISBN 0-14-002200-7). Penguin.
DeVries, Pieter A. & Shapiro, Stephen R. Complications of Pediatric Surgery. LC 81-19678. 581p. 1982. 62.00 (ISBN 0-471-04887-9, Pub. by Wiley Med). Wiley.
De Vries, R. R., jt. ed. see Van Rood, J. J.
DeVries, Raymond G. Regulating Birth: Midwives, Medicine, & the Law. LC 84-16196. (Health, Society & Policy Ser.). 24.95 (ISBN 0-87722-379-3). Temple U Pr.
--Regulating Birth: Midwives, Medicine & the Law. 1985. 29.95. Temple U Pr.
DeVries, Rheta, jt. auth. see Kamii, Constance.
DeVries, Robert A., frwd. by see Commission on Education for Health Administration.
De Vries, Simon J. The Achievements of Biblical Religion: A Prolegomenon to Old Testament Theology. LC 83-3614. 558p. (Orig.). 1983. lib. bdg. 36.75 (ISBN 0-8191-3140-7); pap. text ed. 22.00 (ISBN 0-8191-3141-5). U Pr of Amer.
De Vries, Tineke Bartels see Bartels-De Vries, Tineke & Van Zon, Egbert.
De Vries, Tom. On the Meaning & Future of the European Monetary System. LC 80-20510. (Essays in International Finance Ser.: No. 138). 1980. pap. text ed. 2.50x (ISBN 0-88165-045-5). Princeton U Int Finan Econ.
De Vries, Vickie see Dean, Dave.
DeVries, W. R., ed. Computer Applications in Manufacturing Systems. (PED: Vol. 2). 101p. 1980. 18.00 (ISBN 0-317-06810-5, G00194). ASME.
--Computer Applications in Manufacturing Systems. 101p. 1980. 18.00 (ISBN 0-317-33464-6, G00194); members 9.00 (ISBN 0-317-33465-4). ASME.
De Vries, W. R. & Dornfield, D. A., eds. Inspection & Quality Control in Manufacturing Systems. (PED Ser.: Vol. 6). 1982. 24.00 (H00249). ASME.
De Vries, Walter, jt. auth. see Bass, Jack.
De Vries Vries, Manfred F. Kets see Kets De Vries, Manfred F.
Devroey, C., jt. ed. see Vanbreuseghemn, R.
Devroye, Luc & Gyorfi, Laszlo. Nonparametric Density Estimation: The L1 View. (Wiley Series in Probability & Mathematical Statistics - Probability & Mathematical Statistics Section). 368p. 1985. text ed. 37.95x (ISBN 0-471-81646-9, Pub. by Wiley-Interscience). Wiley.
Devsis Study Team. DEVSIS: The Preliminary Design of an International Information System for the Development Sciences. 247p. (Eng., Fr. & Span.). 1976. pap. 13.00 (ISBN 0-88936-084-7, IDRC65, IDRC). Unipub.
Devyer, F. T. Arbitration: Its Differences & Drawbacks. 1964. pap. 3.00x (ISBN 0-85564-034-0, Pub. by U of W Austral Pr). Intl Spec Bk.
De Vylder, F., et al, eds. Premium Calculation in Insurance. 1984. lib. bdg. 76.00 (ISBN 90-277-1732-X, Pub. by Reidel Holland). Kluwer Academic.
De Vylder, Stephan. Agriculture in Chains: A Case Study in Contradictions & Constraints. 192p. 1981. 25.00x (ISBN 0-86232-041-0, Pub. by Zed Pr England). Biblio Dist.
De Vyver, Frank T., jt. ed. see McKinney, John C.
Dew, Anthony. Making Rocking Horses. LC 84-2694. (Illus.). 128p. (Orig.). 1985. pap. 9.95 (ISBN 0-8069-7916-X). Sterling.
Dew, Desmond. Let's Try It This Way. 1983. 13.95 (ISBN 0-533-05383-8). Vantage.
Dew, Donald & Jensen, Paul J. Phonetic Processing: The Dynamics of Speech. 1977. text ed. 19.95 (ISBN 0-675-08594-2). Merrill.
Dew, Edward. Politics in the Altiplano: The Dynamics of Change in Rural Peru. (Latin American Monographs: No. 15). 234p. 1969. 12.50x (ISBN 0-292-78405-8). U of Tex Pr.
Dew, James F., jt. auth. see Wilhite, J. Portert.
Dew, Joan, jt. auth. see Pearl, Minnie.
Dew, John F. Dragonara: Poems. LC 76-58183. 78p. 1977. 5.00 (ISBN 0-8233-0259-8). Golden Quill.
Dew, P. M. & James, K. R. Introduction to Numerical Computation in Pascal. 304p. 1983. pap. 19.00 (ISBN 0-387-91216-9). Springer-Verlag.
Dew, Philip L. The Trial. Tice, Richard, ed. LC 84-12711. 250p. 1984. 8.95 (ISBN 0-87747-874-0). Deseret Bk.
Dew, Robb F. Dale Loves Sophie to Death. 217p. 1981. 11.95 (ISBN 0-374-13450-2). FS&G.
--Dale Loves Sophie to Death. (Contemporary American Fiction Ser.). 1982. pap. 4.95 (ISBN 0-14-006183-5). Penguin.
--The Time of Her Life. LC 84-4665. 240p. 1984. 12.95 (ISBN 0-688-03918-9). Morrow.
--The Time of Her Life. (General Ser.). 1985. lib. bdg. 14.95 (ISBN 0-8161-3816-8, Large Print Bks). G K Hall.
--The Time of Her Life. 224p. 1985. pap. 3.50 (ISBN 0-345-32542-7). Ballantine.
Dew, Thomas R. Lectures on the Restrictive System. LC 68-55701. Repr. of 1829 ed. 25.00x (ISBN 0-678-00441-2). Kelley.
--Review of the Debate on the Abolition of Slavery in the Virginia Legislature of 1831 & 1832. LC 75-110027. Repr. of 1832 ed. 15.00x (ISBN 0-8371-4114-1, DRB&). Greenwood.
Dew, Walton N. A Dyshe of Norfolk Dumplings. LC 77-11404. 1978. Repr. of 1898 ed. lib. bdg. 10.00 (ISBN 0-8414-3655-X). Folcroft.
De Waal, Esther. God under My Roof. 40p. (Orig.). 1985. pap. 1.50 (ISBN 0-941478-42-4). Paraclete Pr.
--Seeking God: The Way of St. Benedict. 160p. 1984. pap. 4.95 (ISBN 0-8146-1388-8). Liturgical Pr.
De Waal, Frans. Chimpanzee Politics: Power & Sex among Apes. Milnes, Janet, tr. from Dutch. LC 82-48115. (Illus.). 224p. 1983. 15.86i (ISBN 0-06-015113-7, HarpT). Har-Row.
--Chimpanzee Politics: Power & Sex among Apes. LC 82-48115. 224p. 1984. pap. 8.61i (ISBN 0-06-091125-5, CN 1125, CN). Har-Row.
De Waal, Hugo, tr. see Faber, Heije.
De Waal, M. Medicinal Herbs in the Bible. Meijlink, Jane, tr. from Dutch. 96p. 1984. pap. 5.95 (ISBN 0-87728-527-6). Weiser.
De Waal, Ronald B. International Sherlock Holmes: A Companion Volume to the World Bibliography of Sherlock Holmes & Dr. Watson. 621p. 1980. 57.50 (ISBN 0-208-01777-1, Archon). Shoe String.
De Waal Malefijt, Anne X. see Malefijt, Anne M.
De Waard, J. & Nida, E. A. Translator's Handbook on the Book of Ruth. (Helps for Translators Ser.). 111p. Repr. of 1973 ed. soft cover 2.90x (ISBN 0-8267-0107-8, 08518, Pub. by United Bible). Am Bible.
De Waard, J. & Smalley, W. A. Translator's Handbook on the Book of Amos. LC 80-490970. (Helps for Translators Ser.). 274p. Repr. of 1979 ed. soft cover 3.55x (ISBN 0-8267-0128-0, 08577, Pub. by United Bible). Am Bible.
De Waard, Jan, jt. auth. see Borg, Albert J.
De Waard, Romke. From Music Boxes to Street Organs. LC 67-27808. (Illus.). 1967. 12.95 (ISBN 0-911572-04-X). Vestal.
De Waard-Dekking, P., tr. see De Jonge, Mrs. P.
De Waarsenburg, Hans Van see Van De Waarsenburg, Hans & Barkan, Stanley H.
De Wachter, Maurice A., jt. auth. see Roy, David J.
De Waelhens. La Philosophie et les Experiences Naturelles. (Phaenomenologica Ser.: No. 9). 1961. lib. bdg. 24.00 (ISBN 90-247-0243-7, Pub. by Martinus Nijhoff Netherlands). Kluwer Academic.
De Wailly, N., ed. see De Joinville, Jean.
Dewald, J. The Formation of a Provincial Nobility: The Magistrates of the Parliament of Rouen, 1490-1610. LC 79-83986. 1980. 40.00 (ISBN 0-691-05283-2). Princeton U Pr.
Dewald, Paul A. Learning Process in Psychoanalysis Supervision. Date not set. price not set (BN#02965). Intl Univs Pr.
--Psychotherapy. 2nd ed. LC 72-145664. 1971. text ed. 16.95x (ISBN 0-465-06766-2). Basic.
Dewaldt, Franz, ed. Native Uprisings in Southwest Africa. 1976. 27.95x (ISBN 0-89712-019-1). Documentary Pubns.
DeWall, Robb, ed. Storyteller-Korczak. (Illus.). 60p. 1.90 (ISBN 0-318-17136-8). Crazy Horse.
De Walle, R. T. van see Van de Walle, R. T.
De Walsh, Faust C. Grillparzer As a Poet of Nature. LC 73-164827. (Columbia University. Germanic Studies, Old Ser.: No. 12). Repr. of 1910 ed. 11.50 (ISBN 0-404-50412-4). AMS Pr.
De Walt, B. R. Modernization in a Mexican Ejido. LC 78-3412. (Latin American Studies: No. 33). (Illus.). 1979. 44.50 (ISBN 0-521-22064-5). Cambridge U Pr.
DeWalt, Billie R. & Pelto, Pertti J., eds. Micro & Macro Levels of Analysis in Anthropology: Issues in Theory & Research. (WVSS Ser.). 210p. 1985. pap. text ed. 20.00x (ISBN 0-8133-0251-X). Westview.
DeWalt, Kathleen M. Nutritional Strategies & Agricultural Change in a Mexican Community. Kottak, Conrad, ed. LC 83-18303. (Studies in Cultural Anthropology: No. 6). 232p. 1983. 39.95 (ISBN 0-8357-1516-7). UMI Res Pr.
De Walterskirchen, Katalin. Vlaminck's Graphic Work. (Illus.). 280p. (Fr.). 1974. 95.00x (ISBN 0-915346-90-7). A Wofsy Fine Arts.
Dewan, John. Modern Open-Hole Log-Interpretation. LC 83-4228. 360p. 1983. 54.95 (ISBN 0-87814-233-9, P-4302). Pennwell Bks.
Dewan, John G., et al. The Organic Psychoses: A Guide to Diagnosis. (Illus.). pap. 46.00 (ISBN 0-317-07844-5, 2014186). Bks Demand UMI.
Dewan, M. L. Agriculture & Rural Development in India: A Case Study on the Dignity of Labour. 240p. 1982. text ed. 16.75x (ISBN 0-391-02722-0, Pub. by Concept). Humanities.
Dewan, Paras. Family Law: Law of Marriage & Divorce in India. 1983. text ed. 40.00x (ISBN 0-86590-156-2, Pub. by Sterling India). Apt Bks.
Dewan, Shashi & Straughen, Alan. Power Semiconductor Circuits. LC 75-8911. 523p. 1975. 45.50 (ISBN 0-471-21180-X, Pub. by Wiley-Interscience). Wiley.
Dewan, Wilfred F. Catholic Belief & Practice in an Ecumenical Age. (Orig.). 1966. pap. 1.95 (ISBN 0-8091-1510-7, Deus). Paulist Pr.
DeWane, Michael L., ed. see Kauffman, Draper, Jr.
Dewane, Michael L., ed. see Kauffman, Draper, Jr.
Dewar, Angela, jt. auth. see Banbury, Gisela.
Dewar, Darrell. Fundamental Math Workbooks & Answer Key. (Illus.). (gr. 7-12). 1972. wkbk. pt. 1 7.95 (ISBN 0-88499-043-5). wkbk. pt. 2 7.95 (ISBN 0-88499-044-3). Inst Mod Lang.
Dewar, David & Ellis, George. Low Income Housing Policy in South Africa: With Particular Reference to the Western Cape. (Illus.). 244p. 1979. pap. 15.00x (ISBN 0-8476-3285-7). Rowman.
Dewar, David, et al. Housing: A Comparative Evaluation of Urbanism in Cape Town. (Illus.). 207p. 1976. 24.00x (ISBN 0-8476-2399-8). Rowman.
Dewar, Deborah. Breast Cancer: A Woman's Handbook. LC 83-70328. 178p. (Orig.). 1983. pap. 8.95 (ISBN 0-89708-114-5). And Bks.
Dewar, Diana. All for Christ: Some Twentieth Century Martyrs. 1980. 18.95x (ISBN 0-19-213115-X); pap. 8.95x (ISBN 0-19-283024-4). Oxford U Pr.
--The Saint of Auschwitz: The Story of Maximilian Kolbe. LC 82-48926. (Illus.). 160p. (Orig.). 1983. pap. 5.72i (ISBN 0-06-061901-5, RD/460, HarpR). Har-Row.
Dewar, Donald. The Quality Circle Guide to Participation Management. 414p. 1982. 19.95 (ISBN 0-13-744987-9); pap. 9.95 (ISBN 0-13-744979-8). P-H.
Dewar, Donald L. El Circulo de Calidad Esto es Lo Que Tiene Que Saber Acerca de El. (Illus.). 29p. (Span.). 1982. pap. 0.75 (ISBN 0-937670-15-4). Quality Circle.
--Circulo de Calidad Manual del Lider y Guia de Instrucciones. (Illus.). 248p. (Span.). 1981. pap. 16.00 (ISBN 0-937670-09-X). Quality Circle.
--Circulo de Calidad Manual del Miembro. (Illus.). 246p. (Orig., Span.). 1981. pap. 11.00 (ISBN 0-937670-08-1). Quality Circle.
--Circulos de Calidad Respuestas para 100 Preguntas Pregunadas con Frecuencia. (Illus.). 48p. (Span.). 1982. pap. 4.25 (ISBN 0-937670-11-1). Quality Circle.
--Control Charts No. 1: Leader Manual & Instructional Guide. (Advance Quality Circle Ser.). (Illus.). 43p. (Orig.). 1982. pap. 12.00 (ISBN 0-937670-20-0). Quality Circle.
--Control Charts No. 1: Member Manual. (Advance Quality Circle Ser.). (Illus.). 43p. (Orig.). 1982. pap. 7.00 (ISBN 0-937670-25-1). Quality Circle.
--Control Charts No. 2: Leader Manual & Instructional Guide. (Advance Quality Circle Ser.). (Illus.). 43p. 1982. pap. 12.00 (ISBN 0-937670-21-9). Quality Circle.
--Control Charts No. 2: Member Manual. (Advance Quality Circle Ser.). (Illus.). 58p. 1982. pap. 7.00 (ISBN 0-937670-26-X). Quality Circle.
--Histograms: Leader Manual & Instructional Guide. (Advance Quality Circle Ser.). (Illus.). 50p. (Orig.). 1982. pap. 12.00 (ISBN 0-937670-19-7). Quality Circle.
--Histograms: Member Manual. (Advance Quality Circle Ser.). (Illus.). 50p. 1982. pap. 7.00 (ISBN 0-937670-24-3). Quality Circle.
--El Manual del Circulo de Calidad para el Facilitator. (Illus.). 496p. (Span.). 1982. pap. 60.00 (ISBN 0-937670-10-3). Quality Circle.
--The Quality Circle Handbook. (Quality Circle Leader Manual & Instructional Guide, Quality Circle Member Manual Ser.). 640p. 1980. pap. 60.00 (ISBN 0-937670-03-0). Quality Circle.
--Quality Circle Handbook for Financial Institutions. 3rd ed. (Illus.). 496p. 1982. pap. 60.00 (ISBN 0-937670-14-6). Quality Circle.
--Quality Circle Handbook for Health Care Facilities. 2nd ed. (Illus.). 496p. (Orig.). 1982. pap. 60.00 (ISBN 0-937670-07-3). Quality Circle.
--Quality Circle Leader Manual & Instructional Guide. (Quality Circle Member Manual: Quality Circle Handbook Ser.). 248p. 1980. pap. 16.00 (ISBN 0-937670-02-2). Quality Circle.
--Quality Circle Leader Manual & Instructional Guide for Financial Institutions. 3rd ed. (Illus.). 235p. (Orig.). 1982. 16.00 (ISBN 0-937670-12-X). Quality Circle.
--Quality Circle Member Manual. (Quality Circle Handbook & Quality Circle Leader Manual & Instructional Guide Ser.). (Illus.). 268p. (Orig.). 1980. pap. 11.00 (ISBN 0-937670-01-4). Quality Circle.
--Quality Circle Member Manual for Financial Institutions. 3rd ed. (Illus.). 268p. 1982. pap. 11.00 (ISBN 0-937670-13-8). Quality Circle.
--Quality Circle Member Manual for Health Care Facilities. 2nd ed. (Illus.). 268p. (Orig.). 1982. pap. 11.00 (ISBN 0-937670-05-7). Quality Circle.
--The Quality Circle: What You Should Know about It. (Illus.). 29p. 1980. pap. 0.75 (ISBN 0-937670-04-9). Quality Circle.
--The Quality Circle: What You Should Know about It - Financial Institutions. 3rd ed. (Illus.). 29p. 1982. pap. 0.75 (ISBN 0-937670-17-0). Quality Circle.
--The Quality Circle: What You Should Know about It - Health Care Facilities. 2nd ed. (Illus.). 29p. (Orig.). 1982. pap. 0.75 (ISBN 0-937670-16-2). Quality Circle.
--Quality Circles: Answers to One Hundred Frequently Asked Questions. rev. ed. (Illus.). 1980. pap. 4.25 (ISBN 0-937670-00-6). Quality Circle.
--Quality Circles Guidebook: How to Install Quality Circles in Your Organization. 81p. (Orig.). 1982. pap. 30.00 (ISBN 0-937670-28-6). Quality Circle.
--Scatter Diagrams: Leader Manual & Instructional Guide. (Advance Quality Circle Ser.). (Illus.). 58p. 1982. pap. 12.00 (ISBN 0-937670-22-7). Quality Circle.
--Scatter Diagrams: Member Manual. (Advance Quality Circle Ser.). (Illus.). 58p. 1982. pap. 7.00 (ISBN 0-937670-27-8). Quality Circle.
--Stratification: Leader Manual & Instructional Guide. (Advance Quality Circle Ser.). (Illus.). 42p. (Orig.). 1982. pap. 12.00 (ISBN 0-937670-18-9). Quality Circle.
--Stratification: Member Manual. (Advance Quality Circle Ser.). (Illus.). 42p. (Orig.). 1982. pap. 7.00 (ISBN 0-937670-23-5). Quality Circle.
Dewar, Evelyn. Perfumes of Arabia. 1984. pap. 2.95 (ISBN 0-8027-3088-4). Walker & Co.
Dewar, Hugo. Assassins at Large: Being a Fully Documented & Hitherto Unpublished Account of the Executions Outside Russia Ordered by the GPU. LC 79-2898. 203p. 1980. Repr. of 1952 ed. 22.00 (ISBN 0-8305-0069-3). Hyperion Conn.
Dewar, Jacqueline M., jt. auth. see Zill, Dennis G.
Dewar, Jeffrey D. Quality Circles at Work & Spreading in Utility Systems of Today. (Illus.). 64p. 1984. pap. 3.25 (ISBN 0-937670-31-6). Quality Circle.
Dewar, M. J., et al, eds. Organic Chemistry. (Topics in Current Chemistry: Vol. 105). (Illus.). 180p. 1982. 40.00 (ISBN 0-387-11636-2). Springer-Verlag.
--Radicals in Biochemistry. (Topics in Current Chemistry Ser.: Vol. 108). (Illus.). 140p. 1983. 24.00 (ISBN 0-387-11864-0). Springer-Verlag.
--Synthetic & Structural Problems. (Topics in Current Chemistry Ser.: Vol. 106). (Illus.). 170p. 1982. 41.00 (ISBN 0-387-11766-0). Springer-Verlag.
--Wittig Chemistry: Dedicated to Professor Dr. G. Wittig. (Topics in Current Chemistry Ser.: Vol. 109). (Illus.). 220p. 1983. 43.50 (ISBN 0-387-11907-8). Springer-Verlag.
Dewar, Margaret. Industry in Trouble: The Federal Government & the New England Fisheries. LC 82-10748. 244p. 1983. text ed. 34.95 (ISBN 0-87722-284-3). Temple U Pr.
--Labour Policy in U. S. S. R. 1917-1928. 1979. Repr. of 1956 ed. lib. bdg. 20.50x (ISBN 0-374-92148-2). Octagon.
Dewar, Margaret E., ed. Industry Vitalization: Toward a National Industrial Policy. (Illus.). 230p. 1982. 28.00 (ISBN 0-08-028829-4). Pergamon.
Dewar, Mary, ed. see Smith, Thomas.
Dewar, Michael. Brush Fire Wars: Minor Campaigns of the British Army Since 1945. LC 84-40337. 203p. 1984. 22.50 (ISBN 0-312-10674-2). St Martin.
Dewar, Michael J. & Dougherty, Ralph C. The PMO Theory of Organic Chemistry. LC 74-12196. (Illus.). 576p. 1975. 69.50 (ISBN 0-306-30779-0, Plenum Pr); pap. 17.50 (ISBN 0-306-20010-4). Plenum Pub.
De Wardener, H. E. The Kidney: An Outline of Normal & Abnormal Structure & Function. 4th ed. LC 73-175548. (Illus.). 440p. 1973. text ed. 27.50x (ISBN 0-443-01027-7). Churchill.
De Warren, Shaun. The Harris Visits the Garden of Everything. (Illus.). 32p. (ps-3). 1985. 12.95 (ISBN 0-913299-21-9, Pub. by Angelfood Bks). Stillpoint.

Dewart, Joanne. The Theology of Grace of Theodore of Mopsuestia. LC 65-18319. (Studies in Christian Antiquity: Vol. 16). 160p. 1971. 12.95x (ISBN 0-8132-0523-9). Cath U Pr.

Dewart, Leslie. Foundations of Belief. LC 69-17777. 1970. pap. 4.95 (ISBN 0-8164-2549-3). Winston Pr.

De Warville, Jean P. Brissot see Brissot De Warville, Jean P.

De Water, F. F. Van see Van De Water, F. F.

De Water, Frederick F. Van see Van De Water, Frederick F.

De Waters, Lillian. All Things Are Yours. (Practical Demonstration Ser.). pap. 0.95 (ISBN 0-686-05719-8). L De Waters.

--Atomic Age. (Atomic Ser). pap. 0.95 (ISBN 0-686-05723-6). L De Waters.

--The Christ Within. 5.95 (ISBN 0-686-05717-1). L De Waters.

--The Finished Kingdom. 5.95 (ISBN 0-686-05716-3). L De Waters.

--God & Oneself. pap. 3.00 (ISBN 0-686-05705-8). L De Waters.

--God Is All. pap. 0.95 (ISBN 0-686-05711-2). L De Waters.

--The Great Answer. 5.95 (ISBN 0-686-05715-5). L De Waters.

--Greater Works. pap. 1.25 (ISBN 0-686-05713-9). L De Waters.

--How to Have Abundance. pap. 0.95 (ISBN 0-686-05710-4). L De Waters.

--How to Have Dominion. pap. 0.95 (ISBN 0-686-05709-0). L De Waters.

--How to Have Health. pap. 0.95 (ISBN 0-686-05708-2). L De Waters.

--I Am Self. (The I Am That I Am Ser.). pap. 1.25 (ISBN 0-686-05726-0). L De Waters.

--The Kingdom Within. pap. 0.95 (ISBN 0-686-05712-0). L De Waters.

--Light. (Atomic Ser). pap. 0.95 (ISBN 0-686-05724-4). L De Waters.

DeWaters, Lillian. Light of the Eternal. 5.95 (ISBN 0-686-17824-6). L De Waters.

De Waters, Lillian. Loving Your Problem. (Practical Demonstration Ser). pap. 0.95 (ISBN 0-686-05721-X). L De Waters.

--Narrow Way. (Atomic Ser). pap. 0.95 (ISBN 0-686-05722-8). L De Waters.

--Practice of Reality. pap. 4.00 (ISBN 0-686-05706-6). L De Waters.

--Realities Supernal. (The I Am That I Am Ser). pap. 1.25 (ISBN 0-686-05727-9). L De Waters.

--The Seamless Robe. 5.95 (ISBN 0-686-17826-2). L De Waters.

--Self Revealing Light. (The I Am That I Am Ser). pap. 1.25 (ISBN 0-686-05725-2). L De Waters.

--The Time Is at Hand. (Practical Demonstration Ser). pap. 0.95 (ISBN 0-686-05720-1). L De Waters.

--True Identification. pap. 4.00 (ISBN 0-686-05707-4). L De Waters.

--Voice of Revelation. 5.95 (ISBN 0-686-05714-7). L De Waters.

DeWaters, Lillian. Who Am I. 5.95 (ISBN 0-686-17825-4). L De Waters.

De Waters, Lillian. The Word Made Flesh. (Practical Demonstration Ser.). pap. 0.95 (ISBN 0-686-05718-X). L De Waters.

De Waurin, Jehan. A Collection of the Chronicles & Ancient Histories of Great Britain, Now Called England, Albina-1431, 3 vols. Hardy, William & Hardy, Edward L., eds. (Rolls Ser.: No. 40). Repr. of 1891 ed. Set. 132.00 (ISBN 0-317-16687-5). Kraus Repr.

--Recueil des Croniques et Anchiennes Istories de la Grant: Bretaigne, a Present Nomme Engleterre par...Siegneur du Forestel; Albina-1471, 5 vols. Hardy, William & Hardy, Edward L., eds. (Rolls Ser.: No. 39). Repr. of 1891 ed. Set. 252.00. Kraus Repr.

De Wavrin, Jehan. Anchiennes Cronicques D'Engleterre, 3 Vols. 1858-1863. 100.00 (ISBN 0-384-66112-2); pap. 83.00 (ISBN 0-384-66113-0). Johnson Repr.

De Wayne, M. L., ed. Water, Human Values & the Eighties. 100p. 1981. pap. 15.25 (ISBN 0-08-028098-6). Pergamon.

Dewdney, A. K. The Planiverse: Computer Contact with a Two-Dimensional World. 1984. 16.50 (ISBN 0-671-46362-4, Poseidon); pap. 9.50 (ISBN 0-671-46363-2). PB.

Dewdney, Christopher. Spring Trances in the Control Emerald Night. 1978. Repr. perfect bound in wrappers 5.00 (ISBN 0-685-04174-3); signed ed. 7.50 (ISBN 0-686-66326-8). Figures.

Dewdney, J. C., ed. The U. S. S. R. in Maps. LC 52-1242. 128p. 1982. 32.50 (ISBN 0-8419-0760-9). Holmes & Meier.

Dewdney, J. C., jt. auth. see Symons, Leslie.

Dewdney, John C. A Geography of the Soviet Union. 3rd ed. LC 78-40992. (Pergamon Oxford Geography Ser.). (Illus.). 1979. text ed. 34.00 (ISBN 0-08-023739-8); pap. text ed. 13.25 (ISBN 0-08-023738-X). Pergamon.

Dewdney, P. E., jt. ed. see Roger, R. S.

Dewdney, Selwyn. Sacred Scrolls of the Southern Ojibway. LC 73-90150. 1974. 27.50x (ISBN 0-8020-3321-0). U of Toronto Pr.

Dewdwney, J. C., jt. auth. see Symons, L.

Dewe, J. A. History of Economics: Or, Economics As a Factor in the Making of History. 1977. lib. bdg. 59.95 (ISBN 0-8490-1973-7). Gordon Pr.

Dewe, Michael, jt. ed. see Fuhlrott, Rolf.

De Weck, A., jt. ed. see Schoenfeld, H.

De Weck, A. L., ed. Differentiated Lymphocyte Functions. (Progress in Allergy: Vol. 28). (Illus.). x, 286p. 1981. 61.75 (ISBN 3-8055-1834-X). S Karger.

--HLA & Allergy. (Monographs in Allergy: Vol. 11). (Illus.). 1977. 20.50 (ISBN 3-8055-2639-3). S Karger.

De Weck, A. L. & Rundgaard, H., eds. Allergic Reactions to Drugs. (Handbook of Experimental Pharmacology Ser.: Vol. 63). (Illus.). 775p. 1983. 150.00 (ISBN 0-387-12399-7). Springer-Verlag.

De Weck, Alain L., et al, eds. Biochemical Characterization of Lymphokines: Proceedings of the Second International Lymphokine Workshop. LC 80-289. 1980. 58.50 (ISBN 0-12-213950-X). Acad Pr.

DeWeerd, H. A., ed. see Marshall, George C.

Deweerd, Harvey A. Great Soldiers of the Two World Wars. facs. ed. LC 69-18926. (Essay Index Reprint Ser). 1941. 23.75 (ISBN 0-8369-1032-X). Ayer Co Pubs.

Deweerdt, Jacques. Vocabulaire Fondamental de Technologie. 272p. (Fr.). 1974. pap. 19.95 (ISBN 0-686-57280-7, M-4654). French & Eur.

DeWees, Aletha, tr. see Orizet, Jean.

Dewees, Christopher M. The Printer's Catch: An Artist's Guide to Pacific Coast Edible Marine Life. LC 83-51816. (Illus.). 128p. 1984. 26.95 (ISBN 0-930118-10-3). Sea Chall.

Dewees, D. N., et al. Economic Analysis of Environmental Policies. LC 75-38798. (Ontario Economic Council Research Studies). 1975. pap. 8.50 (ISBN 0-8020-3335-0). U of Toronto Pr.

Dewees, Donald N. Economics & Public Policy: The Automobile Pollution Case. 208p. 1974. 32.50x (ISBN 0-262-04043-3). MIT Pr.

Dewees, Eleanor. Those Four & Plenty More. Van Dolson, Bobbie J., ed. (gr. 2-5). 1981. pap. 4.95 (ISBN 0-8280-0092-1). Review & Herald.

Dewees, Francis P. Molly Maguires, the Origin, Growth, & Character of the Organization. 1877. 22.50 (ISBN 0-8337-0848-1). B Franklin.

Dewees, Jacob. Great Future of America & Africa. facs. ed. LC 75-154075. (Black Heritage Library Collection Ser). 1854. 15.25 (ISBN 0-8369-8786-1). Ayer Co Pubs.

--Great Future of America & Africa. LC 72-92425. 1854. 12.00x (ISBN 0-403-00158-7). Scholarly.

Deweese, Charles W. The Emerging Role of Deacons. LC 79-50337. 1980. pap. 3.75 (ISBN 0-8054-3512-3). Broadman.

Deweese, Charles W., ed. Resource Kit for Your Church's History. 1984. 11.95 (ISBN 0-939804-12-3). Hist Comm S Baptist.

Deweese, Charles W., ed. see Brown, Pat.

Deweese, Charles W., ed. see Sumners, Bill.

DeWeese, David F. & Saunders, William H. Textbook of Otolaryngology. 6th ed. LC 81-14162. (Illus.). 495p. 1982. text ed. 35.95 (ISBN 0-8016-1273-X). Mosby.

DeWeese, Gene. Adventures of a Two-Minute Werewolf. LC 82-45285. (Illus.). 132p. (gr. 5-8). 1983. 9.95a (ISBN 0-385-17453-5). Doubleday.

--The Adventures of a Two-Minute Werewolf. 128p. (gr. 5-9). 1984. pap. 2.25 (ISBN 0-399-21082-2). Putnam Pub Group.

--Black Suits from Outer Space. 160p. (gr. 5-8). 1985. 10.95 (ISBN 0-399-21261-2, Putnam). Putnam Pub Group.

--Computers in Entertainment & the Arts. (A Computer Applications Bk.). 96p. (gr. 7 up). 1984. 9.90 (ISBN 0-531-04843-8). Watts.

--A Different Darkness. LC 82-81381. 304p. 1982. pap. 2.95 (ISBN 0-86721-201-2). Jove Pubns.

--Nightmares from Space. (Triumph Books Ser.). (Illus.). 96p. (gr. 7up). 1981. lib. bdg. 8.90 (ISBN 0-531-04338-X). Watts.

--Something Answered. 288p. (Orig.). 1983. pap. 3.25 (ISBN 0-440-08067-3, Emerald). Dell.

De Weese, Gene, jt. auth. see Rogowski, Gini.

DeWeese, June L. & Humphreys, Jo A. Comparable Worth: An Annotated Bibliography. (CompuBibs Ser.: No. 12). 81p. 1985. pap. 15.00x (ISBN 0-914791-11-7). Vantage Info.

DeWeid. Hormones & the Brain. (Illus.). 352p. 1981. text ed. 42.50 (ISBN 0-8391-1645-4). Univ Park.

DeWelt, Don. Acts Made Actual. rev. ed. LC 59-20263. (The Bible Study Textbook Ser.). (Illus.). 1975. 13.80 (ISBN 0-89900-036-3). College Pr Pub.

--The Church in the Bible. (The Bible Study Textbook Ser.). (Illus.). 1958. 13.80 (ISBN 0-89900-049-5). College Pr Pub.

--If You Want to Preach. 2nd ed. LC 56-13226. 1964. pap. 3.95 (ISBN 0-89900-111-4). College Pr Pub.

--Leviticus. LC 75-328945. (The Bible Study Textbook Ser.). (Illus.). 1975. 14.30 (ISBN 0-89900-007-X). College Pr Pub.

--Nine Lessons on the Holy Spirit. 187p. 1978. 3.95 (ISBN 0-89900-116-5). College Pr Pub.

--The Power of the Holy Spirit, Vol. III. 3rd ed. 1972. pap. 3.95 (ISBN 0-89900-125-4). College Pr Pub.

--Power of the Holy Spirit, Vol. IV. 2nd ed. (Orig.). 1976. pap. 5.95 (ISBN 0-89900-126-2). College Pr Pub.

--Power of the Holy Spirit, Vol. II. 5th ed. (Orig.). 1971. pap. 3.95 (ISBN 0-89900-124-6). College Pr Pub.

--Power of the Holy Spirit, Vol. I. 8th ed. (Orig.). 1963. pap. 2.95 (ISBN 0-89900-123-8). College Pr Pub.

--Romans Realized. LC 72-1068. (The Bible Study Textbook Ser.). (Illus.). 1959. 12.20 (ISBN 0-89900-037-1). College Pr Pub.

--Ten Timely Truths. 1949. pap. 2.00 (ISBN 0-89900-135-1). College Pr Pub.

DeWelt, Don & Baird, John. What the Bible Says about Fasting. LC 79-57087. (What the Bible Says Ser.). 1984. 13.50 (ISBN 0-89900-077-0). College Pr Pub.

DeWelt, Don, jt. auth. see Kidwell, R. J.

DeWelt, Don, ed. see Rotherham, Joseph B.

De Wert, Giaches. Three Motets. De Surcy, Bernard B., ed. LC 68-8191. (Penn State Music Series, No. 19). 64p. pap. 5.00x (ISBN 0-271-09119-3). Pa St U Pr.

DeWerth, D. W. Energy Consumption of Contemporary Nineteen Seventy-Three Gas Range Burners & Pilots Under Typical Cooking Loads. 53p. 1974. pap. 5.00 (ISBN 0-318-12607-9, M50155). Am Gas Assn.

--A Study of Infra-Red Energy Generated by Radiant Gas Burners. 61p. 1962. 2.00 (ISBN 0-318-12707-5, U71141). Am Gas Assn.

Dewes, Simon. Marian: The Life of George Eliot. LC 74-28384. (English Literature Ser., No. 33). 1974. lib. bdg. 52.95x (ISBN 0-8383-1745-6). Haskell.

--Marion: The Life of George Eliot. LC 72-187523. 1939. lib. bdg. 15.00. Folcroft.

--Mrs. Delany. 25.00 (ISBN 0-8274-2770-0). R West.

D'Ewes, Simonds. Journal of Sir Simonds D'Ewes from the First Recess of the Long Parliament to the Withdrawal of King Charles from London. Coates, Willson H., ed. LC 71-122400. 1970. Repr. of 1942 ed. 32.50 (ISBN 0-208-00948-5, Archon). Shoe String.

--Journal of Sir Simonds D'Ewes From the First Recess of the Long Parliament to the Withdrawal of King Charles From London. Coates, Willson H., ed. 1942. 30.00x (ISBN 0-686-83599-9). Elliots Bks.

D'Ewes, Simonds, compiled by. A Compleat Journal of the Votes, Speeches & Debates Both of the House of Lords & House of Commons Throughout the Whole Reign of Queen Elizabeth, of Glorious Memory. LC 74-75952. 1974. Repr. of 1693 ed. 60.00 (ISBN 0-8420-1739-9). Scholarly Res Inc.

De Wesselow, M. R. Donkeys: Their Care & Management. 1969. 12.50x (ISBN 0-87556-076-8). Saifer.

De Wet, J. M. J., jt. auth. see Zeven, A. C.

Dewett, Don, jt. auth. see Van Buren, James.

Dewett, K. K. Modern Economic Theory: Micro & Macroanalysis. 1976. 5.50 (ISBN 0-89684-524-9). Orient Bk Dist.

Dewey, Ariane. Dorin & the Dragon. LC 81-6850. (Illus.). 32p. (gr. k-3). 1982. 11.75 (ISBN 0-688-00910-7); PLB 11.88 (ISBN 0-688-00911-5). Greenwillow.

--Febold Feboldson. LC 83-14222. (Illus.). 48p. (gr. 1-3). 1984. 10.25 (ISBN 0-688-02533-1); PLB 9.55 (ISBN 0-688-02534-X). Greenwillow.

--Laffite, the Pirate. LC 84-18727. (Illus.). 48p. (gr. 1-4). 1985. 11.75 (ISBN 0-688-04229-5); lib. bdg. 11.88 (ISBN 0-688-04230-9). Greenwillow.

--The Thunder God's Son. LC 80-16325. (Illus.). 32p. (gr. k-4). 1981. 11.75 (ISBN 0-688-80295-8); PLB 11.88 (ISBN 0-688-84295-X). Greenwillow.

Dewey, Ariane, jt. auth. see Aruego, Jose.

Dewey, Ariane, ed. & illus. Pecos Bill. LC 82-9229. (Illus.). 56p. (gr. k-3). 1983. 10.25 (ISBN 0-688-01410-0); PLB 10.88 (ISBN 0-688-01412-7). Greenwillow.

Dewey, Arthur J., jt. tr. see Cameron, Ron.

Dewey, Barbara. As You Believe. LC 85-7370. 208p. 1985. 18.95 (ISBN 0-933123-01-9). Bartholomew Bks.

--The Creating Cosmos. LC 85-70369. 128p. 1985. 16.95 (ISBN 0-933123-00-0). Bartholomew Bks.

--The Theory of Laminated Spacetime. LC 85-70368. (Illus.). 120p. 1985. 16.95 (ISBN 0-933123-02-7). Bartholomew Bks.

Dewey, Clive, ed. see Darling, Malcolm L.

Dewey, Clive J., jt. ed. see Chaudhuri, K. N.

Dewey, Davis & Shugrue, Martin. Banking & Credit. Bruchey, Stuart, ed. LC 80-1144. (The Rise of Commercial Banking Ser.). (Illus.). 1981. Repr. of 1922 ed. lib. bdg. 45.00x (ISBN 0-405-13646-3). Ayer Co Pubs.

Dewey, Davis R. Financial History of the United States. 12th ed. LC 67-30857. Repr. of 1934 ed. 37.50x (ISBN 0-678-00463-3). Kelley.

Dewey, Davis R. & Chaddock, Robert E. State Banking Before the Civil War & the Safety Fund Banking System in New York, 1829-1866. Repr. of 1910 ed. 27.00 (ISBN 0-384-11598-5). Johnson Repr.

Dewey, Davis R., ed. see Walker, Francis A.

Dewey, Donald. Modern Capital Theory. LC 65-22157. (Illus.). 238p. 1965. 26.00x (ISBN 0-231-02831-8). Columbia U Pr.

--Monopoly in Economics & Law. LC 76-5436. (Illus.). 328p. 1976. Repr. of 1959 ed. lib. bdg. 21.75x (ISBN 0-8371-8811-3, DEME). Greenwood.

--Theory of Imperfect Competition: A Radical Reconstruction. LC 73-79190. (Studies in Economics). (Illus.). 205p. 1969. 25.00x (ISBN 0-231-03164-5). Columbia U Pr.

Dewey, Ethel L., ed. see Dewey, Richard.

Dewey, Evelyn. Behavior Development in Infants: A Survey of the Literature on Prenatal & Postnatal Activity 1920-1932. LC 72-343. (Body Movement Ser.: Perspectives in Research). 334p. 1972. Repr. of 1935 ed. 22.00 (ISBN 0-405-03142-4). Ayer Co Pubs.

Dewey, George. Autobiography. LC 74-108813. (BCL Ser. I). (Illus.). Repr. of 1913 ed. 17.50 (ISBN 0-404-02121-2). AMS Pr.

Dewey, Godfrey. Relative Frequency of English Speech Sounds. rev. ed. (Studies in Education: No. 4). 1950. 14.00x (ISBN 0-674-75450-6). Harvard U Pr.

--Relative Frequency of English Speech Sounds. pap. 19.00 (ISBN 0-384-11599-3). Johnson Repr.

Dewey, H. W. & Kleimola, A. M., trs. Zakon Sudnyj Ljudem: Court Law for the People. (Michigan Slavic Materials: No. 14). 1977. pap. 5.00 (ISBN 0-930042-07-7). Mich Slavic Pubns.

Dewey, Horace W., ed. Muscovite Judicial Texts, 1488-1556. (Michigan Slavic Materials: No. 7). 1966. pap. 10.00 (ISBN 0-930042-02-6). Mich Slavic Pubns.

Dewey, J. F., et al, eds. Tectonics: A Selection of Papers. 150p. 23.00 (ISBN 0-08-028742-5). Pergamon.

Dewey, James F., jt. auth. see Dewey, William T.

Dewey, Joanna. Markan Public Debate: Literary Technique, Concentric Structure & Theology in Mark 2: 1-3: 6. LC 79-17443. (Society of Biblical Literature Ser.: No. 48). 14.95 (ISBN 0-89130-337-5, 06-01-48); pap. 9.95 (ISBN 0-89130-338-3). Scholars Pr GA.

Dewey, John. Child & the Curriculum & the School & Society. 2nd ed. LC 56-13578. (Illus.). 1956. pap. 5.95 (ISBN 0-226-14392-9, P3, Phoen). U of Chicago Pr.

--Child & the Curriculum & The School & the Society. LC 56-13578. 1956. 12.00x (ISBN 0-226-14394-5). U of Chicago Pr.

--Common Faith. (Terry Lectures Ser.). 1934. pap. 3.95x (ISBN 0-300-00069-3, Y18). Yale U Pr.

--Democracy & Education: An Introduction to the Philosophy of Education. 434p. 1982. Repr. of 1932 ed. lib. bdg. 30.00 (ISBN 0-89987-165-8). Darby Bks.

--Democracy & Education: An Introduction to the Philosophy of Education. 1966. pap. 10.95x (ISBN 0-02-907370-7). Free Pr.

--Dictionary of Education. Winn, Ralph B., ed. LC 72-139129. 150p. 1972. Repr. of 1959 ed. lib. bdg. 16.75 (ISBN 0-8371-5745-5, DEDE). Greenwood.

--The Early Works of John Dewey, 1882-1898, 5 vols. MLA-CEAA textual ed. Boydston, Jo Ann, ed. Incl. Vol. 1 (1882-1888): Collected Essays & Leibniz's New Essays Concerning the Human Understanding. Hahn, Lewis E., intro. by. LC 67-13938. 493p. 1969. 17.50x (ISBN 0-8093-0349-3); pap. 7.95 (ISBN 0-8093-0722-7); Vol. 2 (1887): Psychology. Schneider, Herbert W., intro. by. LC 67-13938. 420p. 1967. 19.95x (ISBN 0-8093-0282-9); pap. 6.95 (ISBN 0-8093-0723-5); Vol. 3 (1889-1892): Collected Essays & Outline of a Critical Theory of Ethics. Eames, S. Morris, intro. by. LC 67-13938. 495p. 1969. 17.50x (ISBN 0-8093-0402-3); pap. 7.95 (ISBN 0-8093-0724-3); Vol. 4 (1893-1894): Collected Essays & the Study of Ethics. Leys, Wayne A., intro. by. LC 67-13938. 463p. 1971. 17.50x (ISBN 0-8093-0496-1); pap. 7.95 (ISBN 0-8093-0725-1); Vol. 5 (1895-1898): Collected Essays. McKenzie, William R., intro. by. LC 67-13938. 670p. 1972. 18.95x (ISBN 0-8093-0540-2); pap. 8.95 (ISBN 0-8093-0726-X). LC 67-13938. pap. S Ill U Pr.

--Education Today. Ratner, Joseph, ed. LC 74-95118. Repr. of 1940 ed. lib. bdg. 65.00x (ISBN 0-8371-2550-2, DEED). Greenwood.

--Educational Situation. LC 71-89173. (American Education: Its Men, Institutions & Ideas, Ser. 1). 1969. Repr. of 1902 ed. 11.00 (ISBN 0-405-01411-2). Ayer Co Pubs.

--Essays in Honor of John Dewey on the Occasion of His Seventieth Birthday. 1970. lib. bdg. 26.50x (ISBN 0-374-92153-9). Octagon.

--Experience & Education. 1963. pap. 3.95 (ISBN 0-02-013660-9, Collier). Macmillan.

--Experience & Education. 1983. 12.75 (ISBN 0-8446-5961-4). Peter Smith.

--Experience & Education. 91p. 1938. 2.50 (ISBN 0-318-17241-0). Assn Exper Ed.

--Experience & Nature. 1929. pap. 6.95 (ISBN 0-486-20471-5). Dover.

--Experience & Nature. rev. ed. (Paul Carus Lectures Ser.). 380p. 1925. 29.95x (ISBN 0-87548-096-9); pap. 6.95 (ISBN 0-87548-097-7). Open Court.

--Experience & Nature. 14.50 (ISBN 0-8446-1975-2). Peter Smith.

--German Philosophy & Politics. facs. ed. (Select Bibliographies Reprint Ser.). 1915. 12.50 (ISBN 0-8369-5552-8). Ayer Co Pubs.

--Habits, Impulses & Intelligence in the Conduct of Human Nature, 2 vols. (Illus.). 341p. 1984. 205.75 (ISBN 0-89920-118-0). Am Inst Psych.

--How We Think: A Restatement of the Relation of Reflective Thinking to the Educative Process. 1933. text ed. 16.95 (ISBN 0-669-20024-7). Heath.

--Human Nature & Conduct. 1935. 5.95 (ISBN 0-394-60439-3). Modern Lib.

--The Influence of Darwin on Philosophy & Other Essays. 11.50 (ISBN 0-8446-1153-0). Peter Smith.

--Interest & Effort in Education. LC 74-18471. (Arcturus Books Paperbacks). 120p. 1975. pap. 6.95 (ISBN 0-8093-0716-2). S Ill U Pr.

--John Dewey: His Contribution to the American Tradition. Edman, Irwin, ed. LC 68-21327. 1968. Repr. of 1955 ed. lib. bdg. 18.75x (ISBN 0-8371-0404-1, EDCT). Greenwood.

--John Dewey on Education. Archambault, Reginald D., ed. & intro. by. LC 64-18939. xxx, 440p. 1974. pap. 11.00x (ISBN 0-226-14390-2, P598, Phoen). U of Chicago Pr.

--The Later Works of John Dewey, Nineteen Twenty-Five to Nineteen Fifty-Three: Volume 1, Nineteen Twenty-Five. Boydston, Jo Ann, et al, eds. LC 80-27285. 462p. 1981. 22.50x (ISBN 0-8093-0986-6). S Ill U Pr.

--The Later Works of John Dewey, Nineteen Twenty-Five to Nineteen Fifty-Three: Vol. 4, - 1929. 330p. 1984. 25.00 (ISBN 0-317-18490-3). S Ill U Pr.

--The Later Works of John Dewey, Nineteen Twenty-Three to Nineteen Twenty-Five: Vol. 5, 1929-1930. 480p. 1984. 30.00 (ISBN 0-8093-1162-3); pap. write for info. (ISBN 0-8093-1163-1). S Ill U Pr.

--Lectures in China, 1919-1920. Clopton, Robert W. & Ou, Tsuin-chen, trs. from Chinese. 343p. 1973. 18.00x (ISBN 0-8248-0212-8, Eastwest Ctr). UH Pr.

--Leibniz's New Essays Concerning the Human Understanding: A Critical Exposition. 1977. lib. bdg. 59.95 (ISBN 0-8490-2148-0). Gordon Pr.

--The Living Thoughts of Thomas Jefferson. 170p. 1982. Repr. of 1941 ed. lib. bdg. 20.00 (ISBN 0-89984-160-0). Century Bookbindery.

--The Living Thoughts of Thomas Jefferson. 170p. 1982. Repr. of 1941 ed. lib. bdg. 20.00 (ISBN 0-8495-1136-4). Arden Lib.

--The Living Thoughts of Thomas Jefferson. Mendel, Alfred O., ed. 173p. 1983. Repr. of 1940 ed. PLB 20.00 (ISBN 0-89760-148-3). Telegraph Bks.

--Logic: Theory of Inquiry. 1982. Repr. of 1938 ed. 44.50x (ISBN 0-89197-831-3). Irvington.

--The Middle Works of John Dewey, 1899-1924, 15 vols. MLA-CEAA textual ed. Boydston, Jo Ann, ed. Incl. Vol. 1 (1899-1901): Collected Articles & "The School & Society" & "The Educational Situation". Burnett, Joe R., intro. by. LC 76-7231. 480p. 1976. 19.95x (ISBN 0-8093-0753-7); pap. 8.95x 385pp. (ISBN 0-8093-1135-6); Vol. 2-Essays on Logical Theory, 1902-1903. Hook, Sidney, intro. by. LC 76-7231. Vol. 1p. 1976. 19.95x (ISBN 0-8093-0754-5); pap. 8.95x 397pp. (ISBN 0-8093-1136-4); Vol. 3-Essays on the New Empiricism, 1903-1906. Baysinger, Patricia R., ed. LC 76-7231. 495p. 1977. 19.95x (ISBN 0-8093-0775-8); pap. 8.95x 347pp. (ISBN 0-8093-1137-2); Vol. 4-Essays on Pragmatism & Truth, 1907-1909. Hahn, Lewis E. LC 76-7231. 471p. 1977. 19.95x (ISBN 0-8093-0776-6); pap. 8.95x 418pp. (ISBN 0-8093-1138-0); Vol. 5-Essays on Ethics, 1908. Stevenson, Charles L., intro. by. LC 76-7231. 652p. 1978. 24.95x (ISBN 0-8093-0834-7); pap. 9.95x 584pp. (ISBN 0-8093-1139-9); Nineteen Ten to Nineteen Eleven, Vol. 6. Thayer, H. S., intro. by. LC 76-7231. 597p. 1979. 24.95x (ISBN 0-8093-0835-5); Nineteen Twelve to Nineteen Fourteen, Vol. 7. Ross, Ralph, intro. by. LC 76-7231. 575p. 1979. 24.95x (ISBN 0-8093-0881-9); Nineteen Fifteen, Vol. 8. Hook, Sidney, intro. by. LC 76-7231. 582p. 1979. 24.95x (ISBN 0-8093-0882-7); Nineteen Sixteen, Vol. 9. Hook, Sidney, intro. by. LC 76-7231. 426p. 1980. 19.95x (ISBN 0-8093-0933-5); Vol. 10, 1916-1917. Hahn, Lewis E., intro. by. LC 76-7231. 575p. 1980. 24.95x (ISBN 0-8093-0934-3); Vol. 11, 1918-1919. Handin, Oscar & Handin, Lilian, eds. 491p. 1982. 25.00x (ISBN 0-8093-1003-1); Vol. 12, 1920. Ross, Ralph, intro. by. 346p. 1982. 22.50x (ISBN 0-8093-1004-X); Vol. 13, 1921-1922. Ross, Ralph, intro. by. LC 76-7231. 560p. 1983. 30.00x (ISBN 0-8093-1083-X); Vol. 14, 1922. Murphey, Murray G., intro. by. LC 76-7231. 352p. 1983. 22.50x (ISBN 0-8093-1084-8); Vol. 15, 1923-1924. Cohen, Carl, intro. by. LC 76-7231. 480p. 1983. 25.00x (ISBN 0-8093-1085-6). LC 76-7231. pap. S Ill U Pr.

--Moral Principles in Education. LC 74-18472. (Arcturus Books Paperbacks). 80p. 1975. pap. 3.45 (ISBN 0-8093-0715-4). S Ill U Pr.

--Outlines of a Critical Theory of Ethics. LC 71-92299. Repr. of 1957 ed. lib. bdg. 15.00x (ISBN 0-8371-2707-6, DETE). Greenwood.

--Philosophy of Education. (Quality Paperback: No. 126). 312p. 1971. pap. 4.95 (ISBN 0-8226-0126-5). Littlefield.

--Problems of Men. LC 68-19266. 1968. Repr. of 1946 ed. lib. bdg. 29.75x (ISBN 0-8371-0382-7, DEPM). Greenwood.

--Public & Its Problems. LC 76-178242. 236p. 1954. pap. 5.95x (ISBN 0-8040-0254-1, 82-71751, Pub. by Swallow). Ohio U Pr.

--The Public & Its Problems: An Essay in Political Inquiry. 224p. Repr. of 1946 ed. lib. bdg. 30.00 (ISBN 0-89760-179-3). Telegraph Bks.

--Reconstruction in Philosophy. 1957. pap. 9.95x (ISBN 0-8070-1585-7, BP48). Beacon Pr.

--The School & Society. LC 79-26919. (Arcturus Paperbacks). 124p. 1980. pap. 5.95 (ISBN 0-8093-0967-X). S Ill U Pr.

--Studies in Logical Theory. LC 75-3128. Repr. of 1903 ed. 27.50 (ISBN 0-404-59129-9). AMS Pr.

--The Study of Ethics: A Syllabus. 1976. lib. bdg. 59.95 (ISBN 0-8490-2710-1). Gordon Pr.

--Theory of the Moral Life. LC 60-9060. 1980. pap. text ed. 9.95x (ISBN 0-8290-0263-4). Irvington.

--Theory of Valuation. (Foundations of the Unity of Science Ser: Vol. 2, No. 4). 1939. pap. 4.00x (ISBN 0-226-57594-2). U of Chicago Pr.

--The Thinking Mechanisms of the Human Intellect & How to Develop Them Successfully. (An Intimate Life of Man Library Book). (Illus.). 143p. 1982. 77.85 (ISBN 0-89920-047-8). Am Inst Psych.

--Types of Thinking: Including a Survey of Greek Philosophy. Meyer, Samuel, ed. LC 83-13245. 251p. 1984. 15.95 (ISBN 0-8022-2404-0). Philos Lib.

--Way Out of Educational Confusion. LC 72-104267. Repr. of 1931 ed. lib. bdg. 15.00x (ISBN 0-8371-3918-X, DEEC). Greenwood.

--Wit & Wisdom of John Dewey. Johnson, A. H., ed. LC 69-13883. Repr. of 1949 ed. lib. bdg. 45.00x (ISBN 0-8371-0380-0, DEWW). Greenwood.

Dewey, John & Bentley, Arthur F. Knowing & the Known. LC 75-31432. 334p. 1976. Repr. of 1949 ed. lib. bdg. 25.00x (ISBN 0-8371-8498-3, DEKK). Greenwood.

Dewey, John & Kallen, Horace M. The Bertrand Russell Case. LC 78-37289. (Civil Liberties in American History Ser). 228p. 1972. Repr. of 1941 ed. lib. bdg. 29.00 (ISBN 0-306-70426-9). Da Capo.

Dewey, John, et al. Am I Getting an Education? LC 75-3114. (Philosophy of America Ser.). Repr. of 1929 ed. 15.00 (ISBN 0-404-59110-8). AMS Pr.

--Creative Intelligence: Essays in the Pragmatic Attitude. LC 78-120247. 1970. Repr. lib. bdg. 26.00x (ISBN 0-374-92151-2). Octagon.

--Art & Education: A Collection of Essays. 316p. 1982. Repr. of 1929 ed. lib. bdg. 40.00 (ISBN 0-8495-0229-2). Arden Lib.

--Not Guilty. new ed. LC 72-87928. 439p. 1973. Repr. of 1938 ed. 27.00 (ISBN 0-913460-00-1, Dist. by Path Pr NY). Monad Pr.

Dewey, Melvil. A Classification & Subject Index for Cataloguing & Arranging the Books & Pamphlets of a Library. lib. bdg. 59.95 (ISBN 0-8490-1637-1). Gordon Pr.

--Classification Decimale de Dewey et Index, 2 vols. Incl. Vol. 1. Tables Generales. 32.00x (ISBN 0-910608-14-8); Vol. 2. Index. 32.00x (ISBN 0-910608-15-6). 1974. Set. 64.00x (ISBN 0-910608-31-8). Forest Pr.

--Dewey Decimal Classification & Relative Index. 10th & abridged ed. LC 70-164427. 1971. 18.00x (ISBN 0-910608-13-X). Forest Pr.

--Dewey Decimal Classification & Relative Index, 3 vols. 18th ed. Incl. Vol. 1. Introduction & Tables. 20.00x (ISBN 0-910608-10-5); Vol. 2. Schedules. 20.00x; Vol. 3. Index. 20.00x (ISBN 0-910608-11-3). LC 78-140002. (Illus.). 2692p. 1971. Set. 60.00x (ISBN 0-685-26876-4). Forest Pr.

--Dewey Decimal Classification & Relative Index. 11th abridged ed. LC 78-12514. 1979. 29.00x (ISBN 0-910608-22-9). Forest Pr.

--Dewey Decimal Classification & Relative Index, 3 vols. 19th ed. LC 77-27967. 1979. Set. 105.00x (ISBN 0-910608-23-7); Vol 1, Introduction & Tables. 37.00x (ISBN 0-910608-19-9); Vol. 2, Schedules. 37.00x (ISBN 0-910608-20-2); Vol. 3, Index. 37.00x (ISBN 0-910608-21-0). Forest Pr.

--Dewey Decimal Classification for British Schools: Introduction. 3rd ed. 1977. 5.50x (ISBN 0-910608-18-0). Forest Pr.

--Dewey Decimal Classification: Proposed Revision of 780 Music. Sweeney, Russell, et al, eds. LC 80-16730. 1980. pap. text ed. 6.00x (ISBN 0-910608-25-3). Forest Pr.

--Sistema de Clasificacion Decimal, con adaptaciones para los paises de habla espanola, basado en la 18a edicion con adiciones de la 19a edicion, 3 vols. Aguayo, Jorge, tr. LC 80-24527. (Span.). 1980. Set. 81.00x (ISBN 0-910608-26-1); Vol. 1, Introduccion, Tablas Auxiliares. 28.00x (ISBN 0-910608-27-X); Vol. 2, Esquemas. 28.00x (ISBN 0-910608-28-8); Vol. 3, Indice. 28.00x (ISBN 0-910608-29-6). Forest Pr.

--Two Hundred (Religion) Class. LC 79-55849. 1980. Repr. saddlewire pap. 4.75 (ISBN 0-8054-3107-1). Broadman.

Dewey, Nikki. Orphan Foal Care. LC 81-69794. (Illus.). 64p. 1985. 8.00x (ISBN 0-940074-02-8). Family Tree Pony Farm.

--Sneak Peeks: A Hot Shots. LC 81-69907. (Illus.). 64p. 1984. cancelled (ISBN 0-940074-03-6). Family Tree Pony Farm.

--Stable Management. rev. ed. LC 81-69795. (Illus.). 64p. 1982. 8.00x (ISBN 0-940074-01-X). Family Tree Pony Farm.

Dewey, Orville. Moral Views of Commerce, Society & Politics. LC 68-27851. Repr. of 1838 ed. 35.00x (ISBN 0-678-00527-3). Kelley.

Dewey, Patrick R. Public Access Microcomputers: A Handbook for Librarians. LC 83-26776. (Professional Librarian Ser.). 151p. 1984. professional 34.50 (ISBN 0-86729-086-2, 230-BW); pap. 27.50 professional (ISBN 0-86729-085-4). Knowledge Indus.

Dewey, Richard. Recollections of Richard Dewey: Pioneer in American Psychiatry. Dewey, Ethel L., ed. LC 73-2395. (Mental Illness & Social Policy; the American Experience Ser.). Repr. of 1936 ed. 20.00 (ISBN 0-405-05203-0). Ayer Co Pubs.

Dewey, Robert E. & Gould, James A. Freedom: Its History, Nature & Varieties. 1970. pap. text ed. write for info. (ISBN 0-02-329500-7, 32950). Macmillan.

Dewey, Robert E. & Hurlbutt, Robert H. Introduction to Ethics. 1977. write for info. (ISBN 0-02-329480-9, 32948). Macmillan.

Dewey, Thomas B. The Brave Bad Girls. 248p. 1986. pap. 3.50 (ISBN 0-88184-176-5). Carroll & Graf.

--Deadline. 224p. 1984. pap. 3.50 (ISBN 0-88184-068-8). Carroll & Graf.

--The Mean Streets. 256p. 1985. pap. 3.50 (ISBN 0-88184-175-7). Carroll & Graf.

--A Sad Song Singing. Barzun, J. & Taylor, W. h., eds. LC 81-47377. (Crime Fiction 1950-1975 Ser.). 159p. 1982. lib. bdg. 18.00 (ISBN 0-8240-4980-2). Garland Pub.

--A Sad Song Singing. 192p. 1984. pap. 3.50 (ISBN 0-88184-067-X). Carroll & Graf.

Dewey, Veronica, tr. see Gorky, Maxim.

Dewey, W. A. Practical Homeopathic Therapeutics. 1979. 25.00x (ISBN 0-686-78828-1, Pub. by Bks India England). State Mutual Bk.

Dewey, William T. Marriages in Montpelier, Vermont. 1984. pap. 5.50 (ISBN 0-912606-17-7). Hunterdon Hse.

Dewey, William T. & Dewey, James F. Marriage Records of Barre & of Berlin, Washington County, Vermont. 64p. 1984. pap. 6.50 (ISBN 0-317-06489-4). Hunterdon Hse.

Dewey, Willis, jt. auth. see Boericke, William.

De Weydenthal, Jan B., et al. Poland Nineteen Eighty to Nineteen Eighty-Two: The Making of the Revolution. LC 82-48527. 368p. 1983. 28.00 (ISBN 0-669-06214-6). Lexington Bks.

De Wheat, Gaye, jt. auth. see Wheat, Ed.

Dewhirst, D., ed. see Houzeau, J. C. & Lancaster, A.

Dewhirst, John. A Child's Guide to the Apple Micro. (Illus.). 96p. Date not set. pap. price not set (ISBN 0-521-31300-7). Cambridge U Pr.

--A Child's Guide to the Commodore 64. (Illus.). 96p. 1985. pap. 7.95 (ISBN 0-521-31538-7). Cambridge U Pr.

Dewhirst, Martin & Farrell, Robert, eds. The Soviet Censorship. LC 73-9844. 177p. 1973. 17.50 (ISBN 0-8108-0674-6). Scarecrow.

Dew-Hughes, D., jt. auth. see Wyatt, Oliver H.

Dewhurst. Practical Pediatric & Adolescent Gynecology. (Reproductive Medicine Ser.: Vol. 1). 288p. 1980. 45.00 (ISBN 0-8247-6978-3). Dekker.

Dewhurst, C. J., jt. auth. see Chamberlain, Geoffrey.

Dewhurst, C. Kurt, et al. Artists in Aprons: Folk Art by American Women. (Illus.). 1979. pap. 9.95 (ISBN 0-525-47503-6). Dutton.

--Religious Folk Art in America: Reflections of Faith. (Illus.). 163p. 1983. 29.95 (ISBN 0-525-93300-X, 02908-870); pap. 16.95 (ISBN 0-525-48071-4, 01646-490). Dutton.

Dewhurst, D. J. An Introduction to Biomedical Instrumentation. 2nd ed. 288p. 1975. text ed. 59.00 (ISBN 0-08-018755-2); pap. text ed. 31.00 (ISBN 0-08-018884-2). Pergamon.

Dewhurst, Eileen. House That Jack Built. LC 84-6054. (Crime Club Ser.). 192p. 1984. 11.95 (ISBN 0-385-19578-8). Doubleday.

Dewhurst, J. Frederic, jt. auth. see Bossard, James H.

Dewhurst, J. Frederic, jt. auth. see Stewart, Paul W.

Dewhurst, John. Integrated Obstetrics & Gynaecology for Postgraduates. 3rd ed. (Illus.). 880p. 1982. text ed. 108.50 (ISBN 0-632-00684-6, B 1276-4). Mosby.

Dewhurst, John, jt. auth. see Chamberlain, Geoffrey.

Dewhurst, Kenneth. Dr. Thomas Sydenham (1624-1689) His Life & Original Writings. LC 66-19348. (Wellcome Institute of the History of Medicine). 1966. 32.50x (ISBN 0-520-00320-9). U of Cal Pr.

--John Locke, Physician & Philosopher. LC 83-48567. (The Philosophy of John Locke Ser.). 343p. 1985. lib. bdg. 40.00 (ISBN 0-8240-5602-7). Garland Pub.

Dewhurst, Kenneth & Reeves, Nigel. Friedrich Schiller-Medicine, Psychology, & Literature: With the First English Edition of His Complete Medical & Psychological Writings. LC 76-14308. 1978. 45.00x (ISBN 0-520-03250-0). U of Cal Pr.

Dewhurst, Robin. Approaching Retirement. 117p. (Orig.). 1976. pap. 5.75 (ISBN 0-85941-048-X). Woodhead-Faulkner.

Dewhurst, W. G. & Baker, G. B., eds. Pharmacotherapy of Affective Disorders: Theory & Practice. 500p. 1985. 45.00x (ISBN 0-8147-1777-2). NYU Pr.

De Wied, D., et al, eds. Neuropeptides & Behavior, Vol. 1. (International Encyclopedia of Pharmacology & Therapeutics Ser.). (Illus.). 480p. 1985. 95.00 (ISBN 0-08-032006-6, Pub by PPL). Pergamon.

De Wied, D., jt. ed. see Endroczi, E.

De Wiest, R., tr. see Polubarinova-Kochina, P.

De Wiest, Roger J. Night Flight to Brussels. LC 80-84739. 176p. 1981. 15.00 (ISBN 0-8022-2384-2). Philos Lib.

De Wiest, Roger J. M., jt. auth. see Davis, Stanley N.

De Wilamowitz-Moellendorf, Udalricus see Aeschylus.

De Wilde, Eliane, et al. Flemish Old Master Drawings: From the Royal Museums of Fine Arts of Belgium, Brussels. Morini, Raymond, tr. (Illus.). 114p. (Orig.). pap. 1.00 (ISBN 0-939802-09-0). High Mus Art.

De Wilde, John C., et al. Experiences with Agricultural Development in Tropical Africa. Incl. Vol. 1. The Synthesis. 22.50x (ISBN 0-8018-0163-X). LC 66-28504. (World Bank Ser). (Illus.). 264p. 1967. Johns Hopkins.

DeWilde, Marc. Closed Graph Theorems & Webbed Spaces. (Research Notes in Mathematics: No. 19). 158p. (Orig.). 1978. pap. text ed. 21.50 (ISBN 0-273-08403-8). Pitman Pub MA.

De Wilde, P., jt. auth. see Boite, R.

Dewilde, P. & May, C. A., eds. Links for the Future-Science, Systems & Services for Communication: Proceedings of the International Conference on Communications-ICC, 1984, Amsterdam, the Netherlands, 14-17, 1984, 2 pts. 1550p. 1984. Set. 160.00 (ISBN 0-444-87524-7, I-266-84, North Holland). Elsevier.

Dewilde, P., jt. ed. see Butheel, A.

De Wildemann, E. see Wildemann, E. De.

De Willard Smith, Percy. Deck Machinery. LC 73-12704. (Illus.). 135p. 1973. pap. 7.00x (ISBN 0-87033-185-X). Cornell Maritime.

De Wilton, Arthur G. Grey see Grey De Wilton, Arthur G.

DeWindt, Gaye. Mystical Poems. 1985. 8.00 (ISBN 0-682-40209-5). Exposition Pr FL.

De Windt, Gaye see Windt, Gaye de.

Dewindt, Hal, jt. auth. see Smith, Bubba.

DeWindt, Harry. The New Siberia. LC 76-27538. (Illus.). 1976. Repr. of 1896 ed. lib. bdg. 35.00 (ISBN 0-89341-044-6). Longwood Pub Group.

Dewine, Sue, jt. auth. see Phelps, Lynn.

DeWine, Sue, jt. auth. see Tortoriello, Thomas R.

Dewing, Alisa B. The Rapid Transit, Fast Food, No-Deposit, No-Return Reader. LC 83-632218. 116p. pap. 6.00 (ISBN 0-935834-28-1). Rainbow Books.

Dewing, Rolland. Wounded Knee: The Meaning & Significance of the Second Incident. 417p. 1984. text ed. 39.50x (ISBN 0-8290-1455-1); pap. text ed. 19.95x (ISBN 0-8290-1456-X). Irvington.

DeWinkle, Carl, jt. auth. see Marier, Donald.

De Winter, F., ed. Sun: Mankind's Future Source of Energy, 3 vols. 1979. text ed. 380.00 (ISBN 0-08-022725-2). Pergamon.

De Winter, Francis. Determination of the Relative Cost Effectiveness of Different Absorption Coatings in the Flat Plate Collector. (Illus.). 48p. 1978. pap. 9.95x (ISBN 0-930978-08-0, H-012). Solar Energy Info.

--How to Design & Build a Solar Swimming Pool Heater: With Sample Calculations, 2 vols. (Illus.). 1978. pap. 9.65x set (ISBN 0-930978-07-2, H-003). Solar Energy Info.

--Solar Energy & the Flat Plate Collector: An Annotated Bibliography. 31p. 1978. pap. 11.50x (ISBN 0-930978-09-9, H-004). Solar Energy Info.

De Winter, Francis, jt. auth. see Bereny, Justin A.

De Winter, Francis, ed. see Bereny, Justin A.

De Winter, Francis, jt. ed. see Clark, E. F.

De Winter, Francis, jt. ed. see Clark, Elizabeth F.

De Winter, Jan. How to Avoid Cancer. (Illus.). 96p. (Orig.). 1985. pap. 3.95 (ISBN 0-7137-1593-6, Pub. by Javelin England). Sterling.

De Winter, Patrick M. see Winter, Patrick M. de.

De Winton, Dorothy see Winton, Dorothy de.

Dewire, Robert, jt. auth. see Russo, Monica.

Dewis, M., et al. Product Liability. 220p. 1980. 24.95 (ISBN 0-434-90311-6, Pub. by W Heinemann Ltd). David & Charles.

Dewis, Malcolm, ed. Tolley's Health & Safety at Work Handbook. 1982. 95.00x (ISBN 0-85459-029-3, Pub. by Tolley Pub England). State Mutual Bk.

De Wispelaere, C., ed. Air Pollution Modeling & Its Application, Part I. LC 81-12020. (NATO Challenges of Modern Society Ser.: Vol. 1). 762p. 1981. 95.00x (ISBN 0-306-40820-1, Plenum Pr). Plenum Pub.

--Air Pollution Modeling & Its Application, III. (NATO Challenges in Modern Society Ser.: Vol. 5). 750p. 1983. 95.00x (ISBN 0-306-41491-0, Plenum Pr). Plenum Pub.

--Air Pollution Modeling & Its Applications, No. IV. (NATO Challenges for Modern Society Ser.: Vol. 7). 806p. 1985. 110.00x (ISBN 0-306-41908-4, Plenum Pr). Plenum Pub.

--Air Pollution Modeling & Its Application, Part II. (NATO-Challenges of Modern Society Ser.: Vol. 3). 886p. 1983. 110.00 (ISBN 0-306-41115-6, Plenum Pr). Plenum Pub.

De Wit, Augusta. Island India. 1923. 39.50x (ISBN 0-686-51407-6). Elliots Bks.

Dewit, B., jt. auth. see De Bauw, F.
De Wit, C. T. Simulation of Assimilation, Respiration & Transpiration of Crops. 148p. 1978. pap. 11.50 (ISBN 90-220-0601-8, PDC141, PUDOC). Unipub.
De Wit, C. T. & Goudriaan, J. Simulation of Ecological Processes. 2nd ed. 1978. pap. 10.00 (ISBN 90-220-0652-2, PDC144, PUDOC). Unipub.
DeWit, C. T. & Houdriaan, J. Simulation of Ecological Processes. 2nd ed. LC 78-5408. (Simulation Monographs). 174p. 1978. pap. 32.95x (ISBN 0-470-26357-1). Halsted Pr.
DeWit, C. T., et al. Simulation of Assimilation, Respiration & Transpiration of Crops. LC 78-11384. 140p. 1978. pap. 26.95x (ISBN 0-470-26494-2). Halsted Pr.
De Wit, Dorothy. Children's Faces Looking up: Program Building for the Storyteller. LC 78-10702. 156p. 1979. 15.00x (ISBN 0-8389-0272-3). ALA.
--The Talking Stone. LC 79-13798. 192p. (gr. 5 up). 1979. 13.00 (ISBN 0-688-80204-4); PLB 12.88 (ISBN 0-688-84204-6). Greenwillow.
De Wit, J. & Benton, A. L. Perspectives in Child Study: Integration of Theory & Practice. 190p. 1982. pap. text ed. 16.75 (ISBN 90-265-0399-7, Pub. by Swets & Zeitlinger Netherlands). Hogrefe Intl.
De Wit, Jan, jt. auth. see Hartup, Willfard W.
De Wit, Jan & Hartup, Willard W., eds. Deteminants & Origins of Aggressive Behavior. (New Babylon Studies in the Social Sciences: No. 22). 623p. 1974. text ed. 66.00 (ISBN 90-2797-671-6). Mouton.
De Wit, Joost & Barkan, Stanley H., eds. Fifty Dutch & Flemish Novelists. LC 79-87646. (Illus., Orig.). 1979. 25.00x (ISBN 0-89304-031-2, CCC118); pap. 15.00x (ISBN 0-89304-032-0). Cross Cult.
De Wit, Toke. Epiphytic Lichens & Air Pollution in the Netherlands. 1974. 21.00 (ISBN 3-7682-1059-6). Lubrecht & Cramer.
De Wit, Wim. The Amsterdam School: Dutch Expressionist Architecture 1915-1930. LC 83-72390. (Illus.). 172p. 1984. 25.00 (ISBN 0-262-04074-3). MIT Pr.
DeWitt, jt. ed. see DeWitt, C.
De Witt, Anton A. The Epicurean Pursuit of Pleasure. (The Essential Library of the Great Philosophers). (Illus.). 121p. 1982. 88.85 (ISBN 0-89901-071-7). Found Class Reprints.
DeWitt, Augusta. Java: Fact & Problems. (Illus.). 332p. 1985. 16.95x (ISBN 0-19-582609-4). Oxford U Pr.
De Witt, B. & Stora, R., eds. Les Houches, Course XL: Relativity, Groups & Topology II. (Les Houches: Vol. 40). 1985. 133.50 (ISBN 0-444-86858-5). Elsevier.
Dewitt, B. S. & Graham, N., eds. The Many Worlds of Interpretation of Quantum Mechanics: A Fundamental Exposition. (Princeton Series in Physics). 250p. 1973. 32.00 (ISBN 0-691-08126-3); pap. text ed. 13.50 (ISBN 0-691-08131-X). Princeton U Pr.
DeWitt, Bryce S. Dynamical Theory of Groups & Fields. (Documents on Modern Physics Ser.). 258p. 1965. pap. 69.50 (ISBN 0-677-00985-2). Gordon.
De Witt, Bryce S. Supermanifolds. (Monographs on Mathematical Physics). 350p. 1984. 59.50 (ISBN 0-521-25850-2). Cambridge U Pr.
DeWitt, C. & Matricon, J. Les Houches Lectures: 1969 Physical Problems in Biological Systems. 450p. 1970. 85.75 (ISBN 0-677-14020-7). Gordon.
DeWitt, C. & Stora, R. Les Houches Lectures: 1970, Statistical Mechanics & Quantum Field Theory. 568p. 1971. 150.25 (ISBN 0-677-13330-8). Gordon.
DeWitt, C. & DeWitt, eds. Les Houches Lectures: 1972, Black Holes. 564p. 1973. 120.75 (ISBN 0-677-15610-3). Gordon.
DeWitt, C. & Gillet, V., eds. Les Houches Lectures: 1968, Nuclear Physics. 814p. 1969. 153.95 (ISBN 0-677-13380-4). Gordon.
DeWitt, C. & Itzykson, C., eds. Les Houches Lectures: 1971, Particle Physics. LC 78-184148. (Illus.). 554p. 1973. 132.95 (ISBN 0-677-12560-7). Gordon.
DeWitt, C. & Peyraud, J., eds. Les Houches Lectures: 1972, Plasma Physics. 556p. 1975. 120.25 (ISBN 0-677-15740-1). Gordon.
DeWitt, C., et al, eds. Les Houches Lectures: 1966, High Energy Astrophyspics, 3 vols. Incl. Vol. 1. Radiosources & their Interpretations. 264p. 69.50 (ISBN 0-677-11130-4); Vol. 2. Elementary Processes & Acceleration Mechanisms. 344p. 93.75 (ISBN 0-677-11140-1); Vol. 3. General Relativity & High Density Astrophysics. 462p. 113.50 (ISBN 0-677-11150-9). LC 74-80848. 1070p. 1967-68. Set. 244.95 (ISBN 0-677-11160-6). Gordon.
DeWitt, Dave & Gerlach, Nancy. Fiery Cuisines: A Hot & Spicy Food Lover's Cookbook. 240p. pap. 7.95 (ISBN 0-8092-5148-5). Contemp Bks.
--Fiery Cuisines: A Hot & Spicy Food Lover's Cookbook. 240p. 1985. pap. 7.95 (ISBN 0-8092-5148-5). Contemp Bks.
--The Fiery Cuisines: The World's Most Delicious Hot Dishes. 224p. 1984. 13.95 (ISBN 0-312-29211-2). St Martin.
Dewitt, David. Answering the Tough Ones. 160p. 1980. pap. 5.95 (ISBN 0-8024-8971-0). Moody.
--Beyond the Basics. 1983. pap. 5.95 (ISBN 0-8024-0178-3). Moody.
Dewitt, David, jt. auth. see Incropera, Frank.
Dewitt, David, jt. ed. see Gross-Stein, Janice.
Dewitt, David M. Assassination of Abraham Lincoln & Its Expiation. facs. ed. (Select Bibliographies Reprint Ser). 1909. 17.00 (ISBN 0-8369-5574-9). Ayer Co Pubs.
--Judicial Murder of Mary E. Surratt. LC 71-108472. 1970. Repr. of 1895 ed. 49.00x (ISBN 0-403-00423-3). Scholarly.
Dewitt, David P., jt. auth. see Incropera, Frank P.
DeWitt, David P., ed. see Incropera, Frank P.
De Witt, Emmanuel see Witt, Emmanuel de.
DeWitt, Gill. First Navy Flight Nurse on a Pacific Battlefield. 1983. pap. 1.25 (ISBN 0-318-03066-7). Adm Nimitz Foun.
DeWitt Historical Society of Tompkins County. Images of Rural Life: Photographs of Verne Morton. (York State Bks.). (Illus.). 256p. 1984. 32.95 (ISBN 0-8156-0186-7); pap. 16.95 (ISBN 0-8156-0187-5). Syracuse U Pr.
De Witt, Howard. Violence in the Fields: California Filipino Farm Labor Unionization During the Great Depression. LC 79-65249. 125p. 1980. 10.95 (ISBN 0-86548-008-7). R & E Pubs.
DeWitt, Howard, jt. auth. see Cotten, Lee.
De Witt, Howard A. Anti-Filipino Movements in California: A History, Bibliography & Study Guide. LC 75-36567. 1976. perfect bdg. softcover 10.95 (ISBN 0-88247-377-8). R & E Pubs.
DeWitt, Howard A. The Beatles: Untold Tales. (Illus.). 284p. 1985. pap. text ed. 12.95 (ISBN 0-938840-03-7). Horizon Bks Ca.
--California Civilization: An Interpretation. LC 79-88729. 1979. pap. text ed. 18.50 (ISBN 0-8403-2088-4). Kendall-Hunt.
De Witt, Howard A. Chuck Berry: Rock'N'Roll Music. 2nd ed. (Rock & Roll Reference Ser.: No. 12). individual 16.50; institutions 24.50. Pierian.
DeWitt, Howard A. Images of Ethnic & Radical Violence in California Politics, 1917-1930. LC 74-31770. 1975. soft bdg. 12.95 (ISBN 0-88247-336-0). R & E Pubs.
--Readings in California Civilization: Interpretative Issues. LC 80-83492. 240p. 1981. pap. text ed. 13.95 (ISBN 0-8403-2311-5). Kendall-Hunt.
--Van Morrison: The Mystic's Music. (Illus.). 114p. (Orig.). 1983. pap. 10.95 (ISBN 0-938840-02-9). Horizon Bks CA.
DeWitt, Howard A. & Kirshner, Alan M. In the Course of Human Events: American Government. 296p. 1982. pap. text ed. 17.50 (ISBN 0-8403-2844-3). Kendall-Hunt.
De Witt, Ilse, tr. see Hadamovsky, Eugen.
DeWitt, J. Richard, tr. see Ridderbos, Herman N.
DeWitt, Jamie. Jamie's Turn. LC 84-13973. (Adventure Diaries Ser.). (Illus.). 32p. (gr. 3-6). 1984. PLB 14.65 (ISBN 0-940742-37-3). Raintree Pubs.
DeWitt, Jim. Breath Etchings. Skeens, Gary S., ed. (Illus.). 28p. (Orig.). 1984. pap. 2.50x (ISBN 0-934040-12-5). Quality Ohio.
--Cloud Reflections in My Soup. LC 83-90475. (Poetry for Schools Ser.). (Illus.). 64p. (Orig.). (gr. 3-12). 1984. pap. text ed. 5.95 (ISBN 0-915199-01-7). Pen Dec.
--Collecting Shrill Shadows. (Illus.). 52p. (Orig.). 1984. pap. cancelled (ISBN 0-915199-02-5). Pen Dec.
--Fingernail Souffle. (Poetry for Schools Ser.). (Illus.). 52p. (Orig.). (gr. 3-12). 1984. pap. cancelled (ISBN 0-915199-03-3). Pen Dec.
--Glints From the Sphinx's Right Eye. (Illus.). 64p. (Orig.). 1980. pap. 3.95 (ISBN 0-915199-99-8). Pen-Dec.
--Jammy Donuts a Season After. LC 83-90481. (Poetry for Schools Ser.). (Illus.). 64p. (Orig.). (gr. 4-12). 1984. pap. text ed. 5.95 (ISBN 0-915199-04-1). Pen-Dec.
--Means Something Else: Figures of Speech Writing Book, No. 1 & 2. (Figurative Language Ser.). 72p. (YA) (gr. 6-12). 1984. No. 1. pap. 3.00 ea. wkbk. (ISBN 0-915199-50-5); No. 2. pap. (ISBN 0-915199-51-3). Pen-Dec.
--The Open Heart Kiss Touch. (Poetry for Schools Ser.). (Illus.). 52p. (gr. 6-12). 1984. pap. cancelled (ISBN 0-915199-08-4). Pen Dec.
--Quiet-Time Thoughts. LC 83-90474. (Poetry for Schools Ser.). (Illus.). 64p. (Orig.). (gr. 3-10). 1984. pap. text ed. 5.95 (ISBN 0-915199-00-9). Pen Dec.
--Sex: Hot, Love: Warm. (Illus.). 64p. (Orig.). 1978. pap. 3.95 (ISBN 0-915199-97-1). Pen-Dec.
--Sharpshooting at Kinkajous. (Poetry for Schools Ser.). (Illus.). 52p. (gr. 3-12). 1984. pap. cancelled (ISBN 0-915199-06-8). Pen Dec.
--Skirt Tag: You're It. (Illus.). 52p. (Orig.). 1984. pap. cancelled (ISBN 0-915199-05-X). Pen Dec.
--Sprinting into Sun. (Illus.). 64p. (Orig.). 1979. pap. 3.95 (ISBN 0-915199-98-X). Pen-Dec.
--Starlooping into Comfort. (Poetry for Schools Ser.). (Illus.). 52p. (Orig.). (gr. 3-12). 1984. pap. cancelled (ISBN 0-915199-07-6). Pen Dec.
--Wallowing in Trivia Grits. (Illus.). 52p. (Orig.). 1984. pap. cancelled (ISBN 0-915199-09-2). Pen Dec.
Dewitt, Jim see Cassius, pseud.
DeWitt, Jim see Cassius, pseud.
Dewitt, John R. Amazing Love. 160p. (Orig.). 1981. pap. text ed. 4.45 (ISBN 0-85151-328-X). Banner of Truth.
--What Is the Reformed Faith? (Orig.). 1981. pap. text ed. 1.45 (ISBN 0-85151-326-3). Banner of Truth.
DeWitt, Lucille & Pittman, Alva. Mini Painting. (Illus., Orig.). 1974. pap. 8.95 (ISBN 0-917119-04-5, 451008). Priscillas Pubns.
DeWitt, Marguerite E., et al. Practical Methods in Choral Speaking. 1973. text ed. 2.50 (ISBN 0-686-09411-5). Expression.
DeWitt, Mary, ed. see Van Zant, Peter, et al.
Dewitt, Norman J., et al. College Latin. 1954. text ed. 19.60x (ISBN 0-673-05105-6). Scott F.
De Witt, Norman W. Epicurus & His Philosophy. LC 72-11234. 388p. 1973. Repr. of 1954 ed. lib. bdg. 65.00x (ISBN 0-8371-6639-X, DEEP). Greenwood.
DeWitt, R. Peter, Jr. The Inter-American Development Bank & Political Influence: With Special Reference to Costa Rica. LC 77-2929. (Special Studies). 222p. 1977. text ed. 39.95 (ISBN 0-275-24460-1). Praeger.
DeWitt, Robert H. Arise, Thy Light Is Come. (Orig.). 1957. pap. 1.75 (ISBN 0-8054-9703-X). Broadman.
Dewitt, Schulte. Zub the Tooth Fairy. 1982. 9.95 (ISBN 0-913730-06-8). Robinson Pr.
DeWitt, Stephen. Apple LOGO Activities. 1984. pap. text ed. 16.95x (ISBN 0-8359-0088-6). Reston.
DeWitt, Steve. Atari LOGO Activities. 1984. pap. 12.95 (ISBN 0-8359-0115-7). Reston.
--The Golden Kingdom. LC 83-81903. (Illus.). 299p. 1984. pap. text ed. 3.95 (ISBN 0-88155-026-4). IWP Pub.
Dewitt, Steve, tr. see Twitchell, Paul.
DeWitt, Steve, et al, trs. see Twitchell, Paul.
De Witt, Thomas E., tr. see Steinert, Marlis G.
De Witt, William H. Art & Graphics on the Apple II-IIe. (Professional Software Ser.). 1984. No. 1-598. incl. disk 39.90 (ISBN 0-471-80253-0, Wiley Professional Software); disk 24.95 (ISBN 0-471-80252-2). Wiley.
DeWitt, William H. Art & Graphics on the Apple II Plus. (Recreational Computing Ser.). 128p. 1984. pap. text ed. 14.95 (ISBN 0-471-88728-5, Pub. by Wiley Pr); software disk (Apple II) 24.95; book & disk set 39.90. Wiley.
De Witte, J. Atlas of the Ancient Coins Struck by the Emperors of the Gallic Empire. (Illus.). 1976. 10.00 (ISBN 0-89005-118-6). Ares.
DeWitt Jones, Edgar see Jones, Edgar DeWitt.
DeWitt-Morette, Cecile, ed. see I.A.U. Symposium No. 64, Warsaw, Poland, 5-8 September 1973.
Dewitz-Colpin, F. von see Seiger, H. F. & Von Dewitz-Colpin, F.
Dewjee, Audrey, ed. see Seacole, Mary.
De Wohl, Louis. Founded on a Rock: A History of the Catholic Church. LC 81-6557. 248p. 1981. Repr. lib. bdg. 23.50x (ISBN 0-313-23168-0, DEF0). Greenwood.
DeWolf, Gordon. Flora Exotica. LC 72-190443. (Illus.). 1978. pap. 7.95 (ISBN 0-87923-257-9); ltd. edition o.p. 35.00; 17.50. Godine.
DeWolf, L. Harold. Eternal Life: Why We Believe. LC 79-21670. 112p. 1980. pap. 6.95 (ISBN 0-664-24288-X). Westminster.
De Wolf, Paul P. The Noun-Class Systems of Proto-Benue-Congo. 1971. pap. text ed. 30.00 (ISBN 0-686-22527-9). Mouton.
DeWolf, Rose. How to Raise Your Man. 192p. 1984. pap. 3.50 (ISBN 0-446-32357-8). Warner Bks.
--How to Raise Your Man: The Problems of a New Style Woman in Love with an Old Style Man. 192p. 1983. 11.95 (ISBN 0-531-09808-7). Watts.
Dewolf, William F. A Competency-Based Instructional Module in Art Criticism: Task Analysis & Assessment Procedures. 47p. 1977. pap. text ed. 8.00 (ISBN 0-8191-0250-4). U Pr of Amer.
De Wolfe, Elsie. After All: From Colonial Times to the 20th Century. LC 74-3938. (Women in America Ser). (Illus.). 310p. 1974. Repr. of 1935 ed. 25.50x (ISBN 0-405-06085-8). Ayer Co Pubs.
--The House in Good Taste. fascimile ed. LC 75-1839. (Leisure Class in America Ser.). (Illus.). 1975. Repr. of 1913 ed. 25.00x (ISBN 0-405-06908-1). Ayer Co Pubs.
DeWolfe, Howe M. Bristol, Rhode Island: A Town Biography. 1930. 49.50x (ISBN 0-317-27417-1). Elliots Bks.
DeWolfe, Joyce & Herman, Sharon. Behavioral Objectives for Learning Disabilities (BOLD) 240p. (Orig.). 1982. text ed. 32.50 (ISBN 0-87562-071-X). Spec Child.
DeWolfe, R. H. Carboxylic Ortho Acid Derivatives: Preparation & Synthetic Applications. (Organic Chemistry Ser, Vol. 14). 1970. 90.00 (ISBN 0-12-214550-X). Acad Pr.
De Wolfe Howe, M. A., ed. see Child, Francis J. & Lowell, James R.
De Wolfe Howe, M. A., ed. see Fields, Mrs. Jame T.
De Wolff, Charles, et al. Conflicts & Contradiction: Work Psychologists in Europe. (Organizational & Occupational Psychology Ser.). 1981. 33.00 (ISBN 0-12-214650-6). Acad Pr.
DeWolff, Frederick A., et al, eds. Therapeutic Relevance of Drug Assays. (Boehaave Series for Postgraduate Medical Education: No. 14). 1979. lib. bdg. 35.00 (ISBN 90-6021-443-9, Pub. by Leiden Univ Holland). Kluwer Academic.
De Woronin, U. G. Zambezi Trails. (Illus.). Date not set. 12.00 (ISBN 0-930422-17-1). Dennis-Landman.
DeWoskin, Kenneth J. A Song for One or Two: Music & the Concept of Art in Early China. LC 81-19519. (Michigan Monographs in Chinese Studies: No. 42). (Illus.). 216p. (Orig.). 1982. pap. 7.00 (ISBN 0-89264-042-1). U of Mich Ctr Chinese.
DeWoskin, Kenneth J., tr. from Chinese. Doctors, Diviners, & Magicians of Ancient China. (Translations from the Oriental Classics Ser.). 224p. 1983. 24.00x (ISBN 0-231-05597-8); pap. 13.00x (ISBN 0-686-46049-9). Columbia U Pr.
Dews, Bobby. Georgia-Florida League Nineteen Thirty-Five to Nineteen Fifty-Eight: The Melody Lingers on. (Illus.). 1979. 6.00x (ISBN 0-940184-05-2). R P Dews.
Dews, D., jt. ed. see Fildes, R.
Dews, Jule N. Decision Structure of Organization. LC 78-53774. (Illus.). 120p. 1978. pap. 15.00 (ISBN 0-937300-00-4). Stoneridge Inst.
Dews, Margie P., ed. see Dews, Robert P.
Dews, P. B., ed. Caffeine: Perspectives from Recent Research. (Illus.). 260p. 1984. 29.00 (ISBN 0-387-13532-4). Springer-Verlag.
Dews, Peter. A Critique of French Philosophical Modernism. 224p. 1985. 25.00 (ISBN 0-8052-7231-3, Pub. by NLB England); pap. 7.95 (ISBN 0-8052-7232-1, Pub. by NLB England). Schocken.
Dews, Peter, jt. ed. see Thompson, Travis.
Dews, Peter B., ed. Festschrift for B. F. Skinner. LC 76-133193. (Century Psychology Ser). (Orig.). 1977. Repr. of 1970 ed. 37.00x (ISBN 0-89197-497-0). Irvington.
Dews, Peter B., jt. ed. see Thompson, Travis.
Dews, Peter B., et al. Marijuana: Biochemical, Physiological, & Pathological Effects. (Illus.). 220p. 1973. text ed. 32.50x (ISBN 0-8422-7094-9). Irvington.
Dews, Robert P. Early Joel. 2nd ed. 194p. 1982. 6.00x (ISBN 0-940184-03-6). R P Dews.
--Gentle Connecticut Georgian, Vol. I. Hogue, Mabel W. & Dews, Margie P., eds. (Rebel Bks.). (Illus.). 200p. 1981. 9.95x (ISBN 0-940184-07-9). R P Dews.
--Georgia-Florida League, Nineteen Thirty-Five to Nineteen Fifty-Eight: Extra Innings. (Illus.). 200p. 1985. pap. 6.00 (ISBN 0-940184-08-7). R P Dews.
--Mobile East. 228p. 1972. 5.00x (ISBN 0-940184-01-X). R P Dews.
Dewsbury, D. Mammalian Sexual Behavior. 1981. 52.50 (ISBN 0-87933-396-0). Van Nos Reinhold.
Dewsbury, Donald. A Comparative Psycholgy in the Twentieth Century. 1984. 34.95 (ISBN 0-87933-108-9). Van Nos Reinhold.
Dewsbury, Donald, ed. Foundations in Comparative Psychology. (Benchmark Papers in Behavior). 384p. 45.00 (ISBN 0-442-21753-6). Van Nos Reinhold.
--Leaders in the Study of Animal Behavior. LC 83-46153. (Illus.). 512p. 1985. 59.50 (ISBN 0-317-18333-8). Bucknell U Pr.
Dewsbury, Donald A. Comparative Animal Behavior. (Illus.). 1978. text ed. 38.95 (ISBN 0-07-016673-0). McGraw.
Dewsnap, James W., jt. auth. see Blackmon, Beverly S.
Dewsnap, Terence. Monarch Notes on Wolfe's Look Homeward Angel, of Time & the River & Other Writings. (Orig.). pap. 3.25 (ISBN 0-671-00702-5). Monarch Pr.
Dews-Skinner, P B. Festschrift for B. F. Skinner: 1970. 413p. 1970. 89.00 (ISBN 0-317-14269-0, Pub. by Holdan Bk Ltd UK). State Mutual Bk.
De Wulf, Lucienne. Faces of Venus: Prostitution Through the Ages. LC 79-55796. 225p. Date not set. 14.95 (ISBN 0-916728-31-5). Bks in Focus.
DeWulf, Lucienne & Fourestier, Marie-Francoise. Adventures with Liqueurs. LC 78-74589. (Illus.). 1979. text ed. 14.95 (ISBN 0-916728-14-5). Bks in Focus.
De Wulf, Maurice M. Philosophy & Civilization in the Middle Ages. Repr. of 1922 ed. lib. bdg. 15.00x (ISBN 0-8371-2521-9, WUMA). Greenwood.
De Wyzewa, T. & De Saint-Foix, G. W. A. Mozart: Sa Vie Musicale & Son Oeuvre, 2 vols. (Music Reprint Ser.). 2274p. 1980. Repr. of 1936 ed. Set. lib. bdg. 110.00 (ISBN 0-306-79561-2). Da Capo.
Dex, Shirley. The Sexual Division of Work: Conceptual Revolutions in the Social Sciences. 230p. 1985. 27.50 (ISBN 0-312-71349-5). St Martin.
Dexel, Thomas. Gebrauchsgerattypen, Band I: Ton und Holz. (Illus.). 274p. (Ger.). 1985. 90.00 (ISBN 3-7814-0107-3, Pub. by Klinkhardt & Biermann WG). Seven Hills Bks.
--Gebrauchsgerattypen, Band II: Das Metallgerat. (Illus.). 440p. (Ger.). 1985. 90.00 (ISBN 3-7814-0157-X, Pub. by Klinkhardt & Biermann WG). Seven Hills Bks.
--Gebrauchsglas. (Illus.). 248p. (Ger.). 1984. 80.00 (ISBN 3-7814-0208-8, Pub. by Klinkhardt & Biermann WG). Seven Hills Bks.
Dexeus, Santiago, Jr., et al. Colposcopy. Austin, Karl L., tr. from Span. LC 74-177752. (Major Problems in Obstetrics & Gynecology: Vol. 10). (Illus.). 1977. text ed. 28.00 (ISBN 0-7216-3050-2). Saunders.

Dexler, Paul. Vans. LC 77-6181. (Superwheels & Thrill Sports Bks.). (Illus.). (gr. 3-9). 1977. PLB 8.95 (ISBN 0-8225-0415-4). Lerner Pubns.

Dexler, Paul R. Yesterday's Cars. LC 79-1462. (Superwheels & Thrill Sports Bks.). (Illus.). (gr. 4 up). 1979. PLB 8.95 (ISBN 0-8225-0420-0). Lerner Pubns.

Dexter, A. L., jt. auth. see Burton, D. P.

Dexter, Arthur. Heinrich Heine's Life Told in His Own Words. Karpeles, Gustav, ed. 1893. Repr. 15.00 (ISBN 0-8274-3845-1). R West.

Dexter, Beverly L. Special Education & the Classroom Teacher: Concepts, Perspectives & Strategies. (Illus.). 272p. 1977. 33.50x (ISBN 0-398-03607-1). C C Thomas.

Dexter, Byron. The Years of Opportunity: The League of Nations, 1920-1926. 1967. 12.95 (ISBN 0-670-79376-0). Viking.

Dexter, Catherine. Gertie's Green Thumb. LC 82-21664. (Illus.). 128p. (gr. 4-7). 1983. 8.95 (ISBN 0-02-730200-8). Macmillan.

--The Oracle Doll. (YA) (gr. 10 up). 1985. 9.95 (ISBN 0-02-709810-9). Four Winds Pr.

--The Oracle Doll. LC 85-42803. 168p. (gr. 5-9). 1985. PLB 9.95 (ISBN 0-02-709810-9, Four Winds Pr). Macmillan.

Dexter, Colin. The Riddle of the Third Mile. 224p. 1984. 16.95 (ISBN 0-312-68228-X). St Martin.

--Service of All the Dead. (Murder Ink Ser.: No. 43). 1982. pap. 2.50 (ISBN 0-440-18026-0). Dell.

Dexter, D. Gilbert. Life & Works of Henry Wadsworth Longfellow. 59.95 (ISBN 0-8490-0524-8). Gordon Pr.

Dexter, D. J., jt. auth. see Wright, A. P.

Dexter, Dave, Jr. Jazz Cavalcade. LC 77-8035. (Roots of Jazz Ser.). (Illus.). 1977. Repr. of 1946 ed. lib. bdg. 25.00 (ISBN 0-306-77431-3). Da Capo.

Dexter, David S., ed. see American Institute of Certified Public Accountants.

Dexter, Edwin G. see Quantz, J. Q.

Dexter, Elizabeth W. Career Women of America. LC 77-153179. Repr. of 1950 ed. 25.00x (ISBN 0-678-03568-7). Kelley.

--Colonial Women of Affairs. 2nd, rev. ed. LC 71-153180. Repr. of 1931 ed. 25.0000347843x (ISBN 0-678-03569-5). Kelley.

Dexter, Franklin B. Biographical Sketches of the Graduates of Yale College, with Annals of the College History, Seventeen Hundred One to Eighteen Fifteen, 6 vols. (Two vols. are unbound). 1912. Set. 600.00x (ISBN 0-686-51346-0); vol. 100.00 ea. Elliots Bks.

--Sketch of the History of Yale University. 1887. 39.50x (ISBN 0-685-89783-4). Elliots Bks.

Dexter, Franklin B., ed. Documentary History of Yale University. LC 75-89174. (American Education: Its Men, Institutions & Ideas, Ser. 1). 1969. Repr. of 1916 ed. 17.00 (ISBN 0-405-01412-0). Ayer Co Pubs.

Dexter, Gerry L. International Broadcast Station Address Book. Ferrell, Jeanne C., ed. 128p. (Orig.). 1985. pap. 8.95 (ISBN 0-914542-15-X). Gilfer.

--QSL Address Book. 4th ed. 128p. (Orig.). 1984. pap. 6.95 (ISBN 0-914542-12-5). Gilfer.

--Shortwave Clandestine Confidential. (Illus.). 86p. (Orig.). 1984. pap. 8.95 (ISBN 0-916661-02-4, 203). Universal Elect.

--Shortwave Listening Today: Modern Guide to Shortwave Listening. (Illus.). 160p. (Orig.). 1984. pap. 9.95 (ISBN 0-317-13513-9). Universal Elect.

Dexter, Graham & Wash, Michael. Psychiatric Nursing Skills: A Patient-Centered Approach. 320p. (Orig.). 1985. pap. 12.95 (ISBN 0-7099-3617-6, Pub. by Croom Helm Ltd). Longwood Pub Group.

Dexter, Harriet. The Nuremberg Stove. (Illus.). 40p. 1981. pap. 2.50 (ISBN 0-88680-142-7); royalty 25.00 (ISBN 0-317-03607-6). I E Clark.

Dexter, Harry & Tobin, Raymond, eds. Pocket Encyclopedia of Music. 5.00 (ISBN 0-8022-0390-6). Philos Lib.

Dexter, Henry M. Congregationalism of the Last Three Hundred Years As Seen in Its Literature, 2 Vols. LC 65-58213. (Research & Source Ser.: No. 519). 1970. Repr. of 1880 ed. Set. lib. bdg. 53.00 (ISBN 0-8337-0851-1). B Franklin.

Dexter, Henry M. & Dexter, Morton. The England & Holland of the Pilgrims. LC 77-90433. (Illus.). 673p. 1978. Repr. of 1906 ed. 28.50 (ISBN 0-8063-0794-3). Genealog Pub.

Dexter, John, jt. auth. see Friedman, Martin.

Dexter, Kerry. Bazaars, Fairs & Festivals: A How-to Book. 1978. pap. 4.95 (ISBN 0-8192-1238-5). Morehouse.

--The Display Book. (Illus.). 1977. pap. 5.95 (ISBN 0-8192-1226-1). Morehouse.

Dexter, Lewis A. Representation Versus Direct Democracy in Fighting About Taxes. 124p. 1982. 14.95 (ISBN 0-87073-425-3); pap. 7.95 (ISBN 0-87073-426-1). Schenkman Bks Inc.

Dexter, Lewis A. & White, David M., eds. People, Society & Mass Communications. LC 64-11222. 1964. text ed. 17.95 (ISBN 0-02-907400-2). Free Pr.

Dexter, Lincoln A., ed. The Gosnold Discoveries in the North Part of Virginia, 1602. LC 82-90361. (Illus.). 1982. pap. text ed. 4.00x (ISBN 0-9601210-8-0). L A Dexter.

--Maps of Early Massachusetts. LC 79-51535. (Illus.). 1979. pap. text ed. 7.50x (ISBN 0-9601210-6-4). L A Dexter.

--Maps of Early Massachusetts. Rev. ed. LC 84-70419. (Illus.). 1984. pap. 7.50x (ISBN 0-9601210-4-8). L A Dexter.

Dexter, Lincoln A., ed. see Apes, William.

Dexter, Margaret & Harbert, Wally. The Home Help Service. 232p. 1983. 23.00x (ISBN 0-422-78680-2, NO. 4055); pap. 10.95x (ISBN 0-422-78690-X, NO. 4056). Methuen Inc.

Dexter, Morton, jt. auth. see Dexter, Henry M.

Dexter, Pete. God's Pocket. 312p. 1984. 14.95 (ISBN 0-394-53057-8). Random.

--God's Pocket. 288p. 1985. pap. 3.95 (ISBN 0-446-32811-1). Warner Bks.

Dexter, R. F., tr. see Loyer, Francois.

Dexter, Susan. The Ring of Allaire. 224p. 1985. pap. 2.75 (ISBN 0-345-31121-3, Del Rey). Ballantine.

--The Sword of Calandra. 352p. 1985. pap. 2.95 (ISBN 0-345-29717-2, Del Rey). Ballantine.

Dexter, W. Days in Dickensland. LC 72-3610. (Studies in Dickens, No. 52). (Illus.). 1972. Repr. of 1933 ed. lib. bdg. 49.95x (ISBN 0-8383-1559-3). Haskell.

--Mr. Pickwick's Pilgrimages. 59.95 (ISBN 0-8490-0645-7). Gordon Pr.

--The Origin of Pickwick. 59.95 (ISBN 0-8490-0775-5). Gordon Pr.

--Some Rogues & Vagabonds of Dickens. 59.95 (ISBN 0-8490-1080-2). Gordon Pr.

Dexter, W., ed. see Dickens, Charles.

Dexter, W. A. Field Guide to Astronomy Without a Telescope. (Earth Science Curriculum Project Pamphlet Ser.). (gr. 11-12). 1971. pap. text ed. 4.08 (ISBN 0-395-02623-7). HM.

Dexter, Walter. Dickens: The Story of the Life of the World's Favourite Author. LC 77-17827. 1977. Repr. of 1937 ed. lib. bdg. 12.50 (ISBN 0-8414-3653-3). Folcroft.

--Kent of Dickens. LC 72-2105. (Studies in Dickens, No. 52). 1972. Repr. of 1924 ed. lib. bdg. 49.95x (ISBN 0-8383-1482-1). Haskell.

--Love Romance of Charles Dickens. LC 74-18404. 1974. Repr. of 1936 ed. lib. bdg. 15.00 (ISBN 0-8414-3807-2). Folcroft.

--Mr. Pickwick's Pilgrimages. LC 72-3637. (Studies in Dickens, No. 52). 1972. Repr. of 1926 ed. lib. bdg. 49.95x (ISBN 0-8383-1587-9). Haskell.

--The Origin of Pickwick. LC 74-11255. 1936. 15.00 (ISBN 0-8414-3768-8). Folcroft.

--The Unpublished Letters of Charles Dickens to Mark Lennon. LC 73-16260. 1927. lib. bdg. 25.00 (ISBN 0-8414-3707-6). Folcroft.

Dexter, Walter, ed. see Dickens, Charles.

Dexter, Warren W. Ogam Consaine & Tifinag Alphabets-Ancient Uses. LC 84-70953. (Illus.). 72p. (Orig.). 1984. pap. text ed. 8.50 (ISBN 0-914960-44-X). Academy Bks.

Dey, Bishnu. Selected Poems. Dasgupta, Samir, ed. (Writers Workshop Saffronbird Ser). 1975. 12.00 (ISBN 0-88253-626-5); pap. text ed. 4.80 (ISBN 0-88253-625-7). Ind-US Inc.

Dey, Charmaine. The Magic Candle. 64p. 1982. pap. 3.50 (ISBN 0-942272-00-5). Original Pubns.

Dey, Denny, jt. auth. see Grim, Gary.

Dey, Frederic V. Magic Story. pap. 1.00 (ISBN 0-87516-020-4). De Vorss.

Dey, Frederick V. The Magic Story of Success. LC 78-50945. 1976. 6.00 (ISBN 0-912472-20-0). Miller Bks.

Dey, Ian, jt. auth. see Wood, Stephen.

Dey, J. N., tr. see Jnanatmananda, Swami.

Dey, J. N., tr. see Saradeshananda.

Dey, Lala K. The Intermediary World & Patterns of Perfection in Philo & Hebrews. LC 75-22457. (Society of Biblical Literature Dissertation Ser.: No.25). pap. 62.80 (ISBN 0-317-12981-3, 2017524). Bks Demand UMI.

Dey, Lilian, jt. auth. see Patankar, Pandit.

Dey, Mukul K. Methods of Experimental Psychology. LC 79-66485. 1979. pap. text ed. 10.25 (ISBN 0-8191-0818-9). U Pr of Amer.

Dey, Nano Lal see Lal Dey, Nando.

Dey, P. M. & Dixon, R. A. Biochemistry of Storage Carbohydrates in Green Plants. 1985. 79.00 (ISBN 0-12-214680-8). Acad Pr.

Dey, S. K. Destination Man: Towards a New World. 160p. 1982. text ed. 18.95x (ISBN 0-7069-1791-X, Pub. by Vikas India). Advent NY.

--Destination Man: Towards a New World. 1982. 40.00x (ISBN 0-686-94084-9, Pub. by Garlandfold England). State Mutual Bk.

Dey, Sitanath. Indian Life in the Sukla-Yajurveda. 1985. 17.50x (ISBN 0-8364-1347-4, Pub. by KL Mukhopadhyay). South Asia Bks.

Deydier, Christian. Chinese Bronzes. (Illus.). 252p. 60.00 (ISBN 0-8478-0323-6). Apollo.

Deyermond, A. D. The Petrarchan Sources of "la Celestina". LC 72-12554. 164p. 1975. Repr. of 1961 ed. lib. bdg. 18.75x (ISBN 0-8371-6724-8, DEPS). Greenwood.

Deyl, Z., ed. Separation Methods. (New Comprehensive Biochemistry Ser.: No. 18). 534p. 1984. 75.00 (ISBN 0-444-80527-3). Elsevier.

Deyl, Z. & Crambach, A., eds. Electrophoresis: A Survey of Techniques & Applications, Pt. B. (Journal of Chromatography Library: Vol. 18). 462p. 1982. 95.75 (ISBN 0-444-42114-9). Elsevier.

Deyl, Z., et al. Electrophoresis: A Survey of Techniques & Applications, Pt. A. Everaerts, F. M., ed. (Journal of Chromatography Library: Vol. 18). 1980. 91.50 (ISBN 0-444-41721-4). Elsevier.

Deyl, Z., et al, eds. Liquid Column Chromatography: A Survey of Modern Techniques & Applications. (Journal of Chromatography Library: Vol. 3). 1176p. 1975. 149.00 (ISBN 0-444-41156-9). Elsevier.

Deyl, Zdenek. Connective Tissue Research: Chemistry, Biology, & Physiology. Adam, Milan, ed. LC 81-954. (Progress in Clinical & Biological Research Ser.: Vol. 54). 262p. 1981. 28.00 (ISBN 0-8451-0054-8). A R Liss.

Deyo, Fredric C. Dependent Development & Industrial Order: An Asian Case Study. LC 80-22873. 154p. 1981. 32.95x (ISBN 0-03-047386-1). Praeger.

Deyo, Louise, ed. see Deyo, Stan.

Deyo, Stan. The Cosmic Conspiracy. Deyo, Louise & Deyo, Stan, eds. 200p. (Orig.). 1978. pap. 11.00 (ISBN 0-908477-00-7). Emissary Pubns.

Deyo, Stan, ed. see Deyo, Stan.

Deyoe, George P. Certain Trends in Curriculum Practices & Policies in State Normal Schools & Teachers Colleges. LC 70-176705. (Columbia University. Teachers College. Contributions to Education: No. 606). Repr. of 1934 ed. 22.50 (ISBN 0-404-55606-X). AMS Pr.

DeYonker, John F. & Tobin, Thomas E. Your Marriage. rev. ed. LC 68-57211. 1976. pap. 1.95 (ISBN 0-89243-059-1, 38850). Liguori Pubns.

De Young, Barbara, jt. auth. see Chen, Ching-Chih.

De Young, Barbara, jt. auth. see Chen, Ching-Chin.

Deyoung, Carol & Glittenberg, Jody. Out of Uniform & into Trouble Again. LC 82-62400. 120p. 1983. 16.00 (ISBN 0-913590-98-3). Slack Inc.

DeYoung, Donald B., jt. auth. see Whitcomb, John C.

De Young, Garry. Abraham Lincoln, Apostle of Freedom. 22p. pap. 1.00 (ISBN 0-317-03370-0). De Young Pr.

--Abraham Lincoln: Apostle of Freedom. 22p. (Orig.). 1983. pap. 2.50 (ISBN 0-936128-04-6). De Young Pr.

--Garry's Scrap Book. (Illus.). 150p. 1984. 25.00 (ISBN 0-936128-08-9); pap. 15.00 (ISBN 0-936128-07-0). De Young Pr.

--The Meaning of Christianity. 96p. 1982. text ed. 9.95x (ISBN 0-936128-02-X); pap. 7.95x (ISBN 0-686-81750-8); tchrs' ed. 7.95. De Young Pr.

--Quest for Justice: Systemic Discrimination in America. 83p. (Orig.). 1984. 9.00 (ISBN 0-936128-05-4); pap. 6.00 (ISBN 0-936128-06-2). De Young Pr.

De Young, Gary. Money Making Gardening. 7.50 (ISBN 0-936128-03-8). De Young Pr.

--Pocket Gopher & Other Poems from the Gopher State. (Illus.). 31p. pap. 1.50 (ISBN 0-936128-00-3). De Young Pr.

DeYoung, Gordon. Dial-a-Word from the Bible. (Quiz & Puzzle Bks). 1977. pap. 0.95 (ISBN 0-8010-2862-0). Baker Bk.

DeYoung, Harry A., jt. auth. see Hale, Leon.

DeYoung, John H., Jr. & Tilton, John E. Public Policy & the Diffusion of Technology. LC 78-50067. (Penn State Studies: No. 43). (Illus.). 1978. pap. text ed. 5.50x (ISBN 0-271-00547-5). Pa St U Pr.

DeYoung, Lillian. Dynamics of Nursing. 4th ed. LC 80-29477. (Illus.). 235p. 1981. pap. text ed. 17.95 (ISBN 0-8016-1283-7). Mosby.

DeYoung, Mary. Call to Reason: An Introduction to Atheism. 3rd ed. 1979. pap. 2.50 (ISBN 0-936128-01-1). De Young Pr.

De Young, Mary. The Sexual Victimization of Children. LC 82-17197. 190p. 1982. lib. bdg. 19.95 (ISBN 0-89950-063-3). McFarland & Co.

DeYoung, Sandra. The Neurologic Patient: A Nursing Perspective. (Illus.). 256p. 1983. 22.95 (ISBN 0-13-611475-X). P-H.

Deyries, Bernard & Lemery, Denys. The Story of Music in Cartoon. LC 82-1817. (Illus.). 1983. 12.95 (ISBN 0-668-05592-8). Arco.

Deyries, Bernard, et al. The Story of Music in Cartoon. LC 82-1817. (Illus.). 144p. 1982. 12.95 (ISBN 0-668-05592-8, 5592). Arco.

Deza, M. & Rosenberg, I. G., eds. Combinatorics 79, 2 pts. (Annals of Discrete Mathematics: Vols. 8 & 9). 1981. Set. (ISBN 0-444-86112-2); Pt. 1. 74.50 (ISBN 0-444-86110-6); Pt. 2. 74.50 (ISBN 0-444-86111-4). Elsevier.

Dezani-Ciancaglini, M. & Montanari, U., eds. International Symposium on Programming, Turin 1982: Proceedings. (Lecture Notes in Computer Science Ser.: Vol. 137). 406p. 1982. pap. 24.00 (ISBN 0-387-11494-7). Springer-Verlag.

De Zarate Salmeron, Geronimo. Relaciones. LC 66-27660. 122p. 1982. lib. bdg. 29.95x (ISBN 0-89370-728-7). Borgo Pr.

Dezart, Louis. Drawing for Publication. (Illus.). 128p. 1980. pap. 15.50 (ISBN 0-85139-184-2). Nichols Pub.

--Drawing for Publication: A Manual for Technical Illustrators. 128p. 1981. 30.00x (ISBN 0-85139-185-0, Pub. by Architectural England). State Mutual Bk.

De Zavala, Ann M., tr. see Cuadra, Pablo A.

DeZayas, Alfred M. Nemesis at Potsdam. rev. ed. (Illus.). 1979. pap. 10.95x (ISBN 0-7100-0410-9). Routledge & Kegan.

De Zeeluw, Gerard, jt. ed. see Jungermann, Helmut.

DeZeeuw, Anne M. & Foltz, Roger E. Sight Singing & Related Skills. rev. ed. 1975. pap. text ed. 9.95 (ISBN 0-88408-018-8). Sterling Swift.

--Sight Singing: Melodic Structures in Functional Tonality. 1978. pap. text ed. 7.95 (ISBN 0-88408-103-6). Sterling Swift.

Dezelsky, Thomas L., jt. auth. see Toohey, Jack V.

De Zendegui, Guillermo. Marti's Circle. Johnson, Scott, tr. from Span. 1980. lib. bdg. 59.95 (ISBN 0-8490-3061-7). Gordon Pr.

Dezettel, Louis M. & Philbin, Tom. Masons & Builders Library, 2 vols. 2nd ed. LC 83-22352. (Illus.). 1984. 12.95 ea. Vol. 1 (ISBN 0-672-23402-5). Vol. 2 (ISBN 0-672-23403-3). Set. 24.90 (ISBN 0-672-23401-7). Audel.

De Zirkoff, Boris. The Dream That Never Dies: Boris de Zirkoff Speaks Out on Theosophy. Small, W. Emmett, ed. (Illus.). 242p. 1983. pap. 11.50 lexitone (ISBN 0-913004-45-6). Point Loma Pub.

De Zirkoff, Boris, ed. H. P. Blavatsky: Collected Writings, Vol. XIV. LC 84-50694. (Illus.). 750p. 1985. text ed. 16.50 (ISBN 0-8356-0234-6, Quest). Theos Pub Hse.

De Zirkoff, Boris, ed. see Blavatsky, H. P.

De Zirkoff, Boris, ed. see Blavatsky, Helena P.

De Zoete, Beryl. The Other Mind, a Study of Dance in South India. Repr. 39.00 (ISBN 0-403-08185-8). Scholarly.

DeZoete, Beryl, tr. see Schmitz, Ettore.

De Zorzoli, Alicia, tr. see Conway, Jim & Conway, Sally.

Dezseran, Louis J. The Student Actor's Handbook: Theatre Games & Exercises. LC 75-270. (Illus.). 214p. 1975. pap. 11.95 (ISBN 0-87484-324-3). Mayfield Pub.

De Zulueta, Francis see Gaius.

DeZulueta, Julian, jt. auth. see Bruce-Chwatt, L. J.

DeZulueta, Tana. We Live in Italy. (Living Here Ser.). (gr. 6-8). PLB 9.90 (ISBN 0-531-04690-7). Watts.

De Zuluetta, Pedro. Trial of Pedro De Zuluetta. LC 76-82326. lxxiv, 410p. Repr. of 1844 ed. 25.00x (ISBN 0-8371-1659-7, ZUP&, Pub. by Negro U Pr). Greenwood.

De Zurara, Gomes E. Chronicle of the Discovery & Conquest of Guinea, 2 Vols. (Hakluy Society Ser.: Nos. 95 & 100). (Illus.). 1963. Repr. Set. 57.50 (ISBN 0-8337-0209-2). B Franklin.

DH - TE Research Studies. Peter Fleming: A Gentleman's Journey on Unbeaten Paths. LC 75-14403. 1975. pap. 3.50 (ISBN 0-686-11969-X). Bks Intl DH-TE.

--Politics of the Sea. LC 75-14401. 1975. pap. 3.50 (ISBN 0-686-11970-3). Bks Intl DH-TE.

--The Vatican & the Third World: Diplomacy & the Future. LC 75-14400. 1975. pap. 3.50 (ISBN 0-686-11971-1). Bks Intl DH-TE.

--Yukio Mishima: Japan's Prodigal Son. LC 75-14402. 1975. pap. 3.50 (ISBN 0-686-11972-X). Bks Intl DH-TE.

DH 01 TE Research Studies. Pacific Future of Canada. LC 75-14399. 1975. pap. 3.50 (ISBN 0-686-11968-1). Bks Intl DH-TE.

D'Haem, Jim, ed. see Walkowiak, J.

D'Haen, Theo. Text to Reader: A Communicative Approach to Fowles, Barth, Cortazar & Boon. (Utrecht Publications in Comparative Literature: 16). 162p. 1983. 33.00x (ISBN 90-272-2191-X); pap. 22.00x (ISBN 90-272-2201-0). Benjamins North Am.

D'Hainaut, L. Educational Systems Regulation: A Methodological Guide. (Educational Studies & Documents: No. 33). 60p. 1980. pap. 5.00 (ISBN 92-3-101606-7, U1066, UNESCO). Unipub.

Dhake, Arvind M. Television Engineering. (Illus.). 1980. 27.50 (ISBN 0-07-096389-4). McGraw.

Dhaleine, L. N. Hawthorne, sa vie et son oeuvre. LC 77-164828. (BCL Ser. I). Repr. of 1905 ed. 24.50 (ISBN 0-404-02122-0). AMS Pr.

Dhalla, M. N. Zoroastrian Civilization from the Earlist Times to the Downfall of the Last Zoroastrian Empire, 651 A. D. 1976. lib. bdg. 59.95 (ISBN 0-8490-2857-4). Gordon Pr.

--Zoroastrian Theology. lib. bdg. 79.95 (ISBN 0-87968-516-6). Krishna Pr.

Dhalla, Maneckji N. History of Zoroastrianism. LC 74-21256. Repr. of 1938 ed. 40.00 (ISBN 0-404-12806-8). AMS Pr.

--Our Perfecting World: Zarathushtra's Way of Life. LC 74-21257. Repr. of 1930 ed. 27.50 (ISBN 0-404-12807-6). AMS Pr.

--Zoroastrian Civilization: From the Earliest Times to the Downfall of the Last Zoroastrian Empire, 651 A.D. LC 74-21258. Repr. of 1922 ed. 30.00 (ISBN 0-404-12808-4). AMS Pr.

--Zoroastrian Theology from the Earliest Times to the Present Day. LC 70-131038. Repr. of 1914 ed. 30.00 (ISBN 0-404-02123-9). AMS Pr.

Dhalla, Maneckji N., ed. The Nyaishes, or Zoroastrian Litanies. LC 70-164829. (Columbia University. Indo-Iranian Ser.: No. 6). Repr. of 1908 ed. 22.00 (ISBN 0-404-50476-0). AMS Pr.

Dhalla, N. S., ed. Methods in Studying Cardiac Membranes, Vol. II. 344p. 1984. 98.00 (ISBN 0-8493-5996-1). CRC Pr.

Dhalla, Naranjan S. & Hearse, D. J., eds. Advances in Myocardiology, Vol. 6. 655p. 1985. 79.50x (ISBN 0-306-41759-6, Plenum Pr). Plenum Pub.

D'Ham, Claude. Sport. (Moment Ser.). 20p. (Orig.). 1975. pap. 2.00 (ISBN 0-85953-035-3, Pub. by Child's Play England). Playspaces.

D'Ham, Claude, illus. On the Farm. (Moments Ser.). (Illus., Orig.). 1975. pap. 2.00 (ISBN 0-85953-036-1, Pub. by Child's Play England). Playspaces.

--The Weather. (Moments Ser.). (Illus., Orig.). 1975. pap. 2.00 (ISBN 0-85953-037-X, Pub. by Child's Play England). Playspaces.

Dhames, Dudley. On Your Feet. 10.00x (ISBN 0-392-06109-0, SpS). Sportshelf.

Dhamija, Jasleen. Living Tradition of Iran's Crafts. (Illus.). 1979. 30.00x (ISBN 0-7069-0728-0, Pub. by Vikas India). Advent NY.

Dhamija, Jasleen, ed. Crafts of Gujarat. (Living Traditions of India Ser.). (Illus.). 192p. 1985. 27.50 (ISBN 0-295-96248-8). U of Wash Pr.

Dhamma-Kitti. A Manual of Buddhist Historical Traditions - Saddhamma - Sangaha. Law, Bimala C., tr. LC 78-72418. Repr. of 1941 ed. 21.50 (ISBN 0-404-17279-2). AMS Pr.

Dhammapada. The Buddha's Path of Virtue. 2nd ed. Woodward, F. L., tr. LC 78-72419. Repr. of 1929 ed. 21.50 (ISBN 0-404-17283-0). AMS Pr.

--Texts from the Buddhist Canon. Beal, Samuel, tr. from Chin. LC 78-72420. Repr. of 1878 ed. 22.50 (ISBN 0-404-17284-9). AMS Pr.

Dhammapadatthakatha. Buddhist Legends, 3 vols. Burlingame, Eugene W., tr. from Pali. LC 78-72421. Repr. of 1929 ed. Set. 105.00 (ISBN 0-404-17610-0). AMS Pr.

--The Commentary on the Dhammapada, 5 vols. in 4. Norman, H. C., ed. LC 78-72423. Repr. of 1915 ed. Set. 155.00 (ISBN 0-404-17620-8). AMS Pr.

Dhanagare, D. N. Peasant Movements in India, Nineteen Twenty to Nineteen Fifty. 1982. 28.00 (ISBN 0-19-561390-2). Oxford U Pr.

Dhanamjaya. Dasarupa: A Treatise on Hindu Dramaturgy. Haas, George C., tr. LC 75-164830. (Columbia University. Indo-Iranian Ser.: No. 7). Repr. of 1912 ed. 19.50 (ISBN 0-404-50477-9). AMS Pr.

Dhanapala, Jayantha. China & the Third World. 136p. 1984. text ed. 15.95x (ISBN 0-7069-2517-3, Pub. by Vikas India). Advent NY.

D'Hancarville. The Private Lives of the Twelve Caesars. Niemoeller, A. F., tr. 54p. 1983. Repr. of 1949 ed. 7.50x (ISBN 0-914937-03-0). Ind Pubns.

D'Hancarville, Pierre. Recherches sur l'Origine, l'Esprit et la Progres des Arts de Arts de la Grece. Feldman, Burton & Richardson, Robert D., eds. LC 78-60885. (Myth & Romanticism Ser.). 1984. lib. bdg. 240.00 (ISBN 0-8240-3561-5). Garland Pub.

Dhanda, Leila. Bonsai Culture. 141p. 1980. 40.00x (ISBN 0-686-84448-3, Pub. by Oxford & I B H India). State Mutual Bk.

Dhanda, R. P. & Kalevar, V. A Textbook of Clinical Ophthalmology, Vol. 1. 800p. 1985. pap. text ed. 35.00x (ISBN 0-7069-2705-2, Pub. by Vikas India). Advent NY.

Dhande, S. G., jt. auth. see Chakraborty, J.

Dhanens, Elisabeth. Van Eyck: The Ghent Altarpiece. (Art in Context Ser.). (Illus.). 1973. 16.95 (ISBN 0-670-74273-2). Viking.

D'Hangest, Germain. Walter Pater L'Homme et L'Oeuvre, 2 vols. 404p. 1983. Repr. of 1961 ed. Set. lib. bdg. 200.00 (ISBN 0-89987-399-5). Darby Bks.

Dhanji, Farid. El Salvador: Demographic Issues & Prospects. ii, 69p. 1979. pap. 20.00 (ISBN 0-686-36106-7, RC-7910). World Bank.

Dhar, D. N. The Chemistry of Chalcones & Related Compounds. LC 80-39560. 285p. 1981. 55.50 (ISBN 0-471-08007-1, Pub. by Wiley-Interscience). Wiley.

Dhar, Niranjan. Vedanta & the Bengal Renaissance: Progress or Reaction. LC 76-52210. 1977. 11.00x (ISBN 0-88386-837-7). South Asia Bks.

Dhar, R. N. Computer Aided Power System Operation & Analysis. (Illus.). 320p. 1983. 32.50 (ISBN 0-07-451580-2). McGraw.

Dhar, Sanat K., ed. Metal Ions in Biological Systems: Studies of Some Biomedical & Environmental Problems. (Advances in Experimental Medicine & Biology Ser.: Vol. 40). 318p. 1973. 45.00x (ISBN 0-306-39040-X, Plenum Pr). Plenum Pub.

Dhar, Sheila. Children's History of India. 7th rev. ed. (Illus.). 178p. (gr. 5-7). pap. text ed. 1.50x (ISBN 0-88253-919-1). Ind-US Inc.

Dhar, Somnath. Historical Tales of Kashmir. 10.00 (ISBN 0-89410-520-5, Pub. by UBSPD India). Three Continents.

Dhar, Trilok N. The Politics of Manpower Planning: Graduate Unemployment & the Planning of Higher Education in India. LC 75-905987. 1974. 13.00x (ISBN 0-88386-475-4). South Asia Bks.

Dhar, U. & Kachroo, P. Alpine Flora of Kashmir Himalaya. 350p. 1982. 92.00x (ISBN 0-686-45791-9, Pub. by United Bk Traders India). State Mutual Bk.

Dharamdasani, M. D., ed. Political Participation & Change in South Asia: In the Context of Nepal. 1985. 22.00x (ISBN 0-8364-1363-6, Pub. by Shalimar). South Asia Bks.

Dharma Publishing Staff, ed. & tr. see Buddha Sakyamuni.

Dharma Realm Buddhist University Faculty. Human Roots: Buddhist Stories for Young Readers, Vol. 2. (Illus.). 140p. (Orig.). (gr. 4-5). 1984. pap. 6.00 (ISBN 0-88139-017-8). Buddhist Text.

Dharmalingam, T., jt. auth. see Ramachandran, L.

Dharmaraj, Leela. Slum Silouette. 8.00 (ISBN 0-89253-551-2); flexible cloth 4.00 (ISBN 0-89253-552-0). Ind-US Inc.

Dharmaratna, M., compiled by see Gunasekera, Henry M.

D'Harnoncourt, Anne & Celant, Germano. Futurism & the International Avant-Garde. LC 80-83095. (Illus.). 144p. (Orig.). 1980. pap. 10.95 (ISBN 0-87633-037-5). Phila Mus Art.

D'Harnoncourt, Rene, jt. auth. see Bennett, Wendell C.

D'Harnoncourt, Rene, jt. auth. see Douglas, Frederic H.

Dhasmana, M. M. The Ramos of Arunachal. 1980. text ed. 17.75x (ISBN 0-391-01827-2). Humanities.

Dhatt, Gouri & Touzot, Gilbert. The Finite Element Method Displayed. LC 82-24843. 509p. 1984. 39.95x (ISBN 0-471-90110-5, Pub. by Wiley-Interscience). Wiley.

Dhaubhadel, Harsha N. Planning & Management of Special Education in Nepal. 60p. 1983. pap. 10.00 (ISBN 0-318-03447-6). Am-Nepal Ed.

Dhavalikar, M. K. Masterpieces of Indian Terracottas. (Illus.). 64p. 1981. text ed. 30.00x (ISBN 0-86590-034-5, Pub. by Taraporevala India). Apt Bks.

--Masterpieces of Rashtrakuta Art: The Kailas. (Illus.). 1983. text ed. 45.00x (ISBN 0-86590-233-X, Pub. by Taraporevala India). Apt Bks.

Dhavamony, M. & Geffre, C., eds. Buddhism & Christianity. (Concilium Ser.: Vol. 116). pap. 6.95 (ISBN 0-8245-0277-9). Crossroad NY.

Dhavamony, Mariasusai, ed. Evangelization, Dialogue & Development. (Documenta Missionalia Ser.: No. 5). 1972. pap. 10.00 (ISBN 0-8294-0323-X, Pub. by Gregorian U Pr). Loyola.

Dhavamony, Mariasusai, et al. Revelation in Christianity & Other Religions. (Studia Missionalia: Vol. 20). (Eng., Fr., & Ital.). 1971. pap. 10.00 (ISBN 0-8294-0324-8, Pub. by Gregorian U Pr). Loyola.

Dhavan, Rajeev & Davies, Christie, eds. Censorship & Obscenity. 187p. 1978. 18.50x (ISBN 0-8476-6054-0). Rowman.

Dhawan, B. N., ed. see Satellite Symposium International Congress of Pharmacology, Lucknow, India 8th, July 1981.

Dhawan, Y. P. Beyond the Guru. 227p. 1980. pap. 4.25 (ISBN 0-86578-060-9). Ind-US Inc.

Dheilly, Joseph. Dictionnaire Biblique. 1284p. (Fr.). 1964. 22.50 (ISBN 0-686-57092-8, M-6114). French & Eur.

D'hert, Ignace. Wittgenstein's Relevance for Theology. (European University Studies: Ser. 23, Vol. 44). 237p. 1978. pap. 27.15 (ISBN 3-261-03092-5). P Lang Pubs.

Dhiegh, Khigh, ed. The Golden Oracle: The Ancient Chinese Way to Prosperity. LC 82-18471. (Illus.). 176p. 1983. 15.95 (ISBN 0-668-05661-4); pap. 8.95 (ISBN 0-668-05913-3). Arco.

Dhiegh, Lnigh. I Ching: Taoist Book of Days for 1982. 224p. 1981. pap. 9.95 (ISBN 0-345-29833-0). Ballantine.

Dhillion, B. Reliability Engineering in Systems Design & Operation. 336p. 1982. 39.95 (ISBN 0-442-27213-8). Van Nos Reinhold.

Dhillon. Quality Control, Reliability, & Engineering Design. (Industrial Engineering Ser.). 392p. 1985. 49.50 (ISBN 0-8247-7278-4). Dekker.

Dhillon, B. S. & Singh, Chanan. Engineering Reliability: New Techniques & Applications. LC 80-18734. (Systems Engineering & Analysis Ser.). 339p. 1981. 45.95x (ISBN 0-471-05014-8, Pub. by Wiley-Interscience). Wiley.

Dhillon, Balbir S. Power System Reliability, Safety & Management. LC 82-72852. (Illus.). 350p. 1983. 45.00 (ISBN 0-250-40548-2). Butterworth.

Dhillon, Balbir S. & Reiche, Hans. Reliability & Maintainability Management. (Illus.). 288p. 1985. 36.95 (ISBN 0-442-27637-0). Van Nos Reinhold.

Dhillon, Balhir. Systems Reliability, Maintainability & Management. (Illus.). 376p. 1983. text ed. 29.95 (ISBN 0-89433-195-7). Petrocelli.

Dhillon, Glenda S. & Jackson, John J. Dhillon-Jackson Teaching Observation Inventory for Physical Education. 143p. 1983. pap. text ed. 7.20 (ISBN 0-87563-227-0). Stipes.

Dhillon, Gurdial S., jt. auth. see Singh, Kartar.

Dhillon, Sukhraj S. Health, Happiness & Longevity Eastern & Western Approach. (Illus.). 224p. (Orig.). 1983. pap. 13.95 (ISBN 0-87040-527-6). Japan Pubns USA.

Dhindsa, jt. auth. see McCann.

Dhindsa, D. S. & Schumacher, F. B., eds. Immunological Aspects of Infertility & Fertility Regulation. (Developments in Immunology Ser.: Vol. 9). 266p. 1980. 61.75 (ISBN 0-444-00405-X, Biomedical Pr). Elsevier.

Dhingra, Ashok K. & Pipes, Byron R., eds. New Composite Materials & Technology. LC 82-18467. (AICHE Symposium: Vol. 78). 1982. pap. 22.00 (ISBN 0-8169-0234-8, S-217); pap. 12.00 members (ISBN 0-686-47549-6). Am Inst Chem Eng.

Dhir, K. K. Ferns of the Northwestern Himalayas. (Bibliotheca Pteridologica 1). (Illus.). 1979. pap. text ed. 14.00x (ISBN 3-7682-1222-X). Lubrecht & Cramer.

Dhir, K. K. & Sood, A. Fern Flora of Mussoorie Hills. (Bibliotheca Pteridologica 2). (Illus.). 1981. pap. text ed. 14.00x (ISBN 3-7682-1232-7). Lubrecht & Cramer.

Dhir, R. K. & Munday, J. G. Advances in Concrete Slab Technology: Materials Design, Construction & Finishing. 1980. 140.00 (ISBN 0-08-023256-6). Pergamon.

Dhiravamsa. The Dynamic Way of Meditation. 160p. 1983. pap. 8.95 (ISBN 0-85500-163-1). Newcastle Pub.

--The Dynamic Way of Meditation: The Release & Cure of Pain & Suffering Through Vipassana Meditative Techniques. 160p. 1983. pap. 7.95 (ISBN 0-85500-163-1, Pub. by Turnstone Pr England). Sterling.

--A New Approach to Buddhism. LC 74-81623. 1974. pap. 3.95 (ISBN 0-913922-08-0). Dawn Horse Pr.

--The Way of Non-Attachment: The Practice of Insight Meditation. 160p. 1984. pap. 9.95 (ISBN 0-85500-210-7). Newcastle Pub.

Dhokalia, R. P. The Codification of Public International Law. LC 66-11927. 367p. 1970. 22.50 (ISBN 0-379-00264-7). Oceana.

D'Holbach, Paul H. Christianity Unveiled. 69.95 (ISBN 0-87968-068-7). Gordon Pr.

--Ecce Home Leucippe. 69.95 (ISBN 0-87968-077-6). Gordon Pr.

--A Letter from Thrasybus to Leucippe. 59.95 (ISBN 0-8490-0508-6). Gordon Pr.

--Letters to Eugenia. 59.95 (ISBN 0-8490-0514-0). Gordon Pr.

--Nature & Her Laws. 59.95 (ISBN 0-8490-0714-3). Gordon Pr.

D'Holbach, Paul H. & Meslier, Jean. Superstition in All Ages. 69.95 (ISBN 0-87968-108-X). Gordon Pr.

D'Holbach, Paul T. & Diderot, eds. The System of Nature Or, Laws of the Moral & Physical World, 2 vols. in 1. Robinson, H. D., tr. LC 79-143669. (Research & Source Works Ser.: No. 618). 1971. Repr. of 1836 ed. lib. bdg. 29.50 (ISBN 0-8337-0753-1). B Franklin.

Dhondt, Jan. Etudes Sur la Naissance Des Principautes Territoriales En France, IXe-IXe Siecle. LC 80-2033. Repr. of 1948 ed. 42.00 (ISBN 0-404-18560-6). AMS Pr.

Dhondy, Farrukh. Poona Company. 160p. (gr. 6-8). 1985. 11.95 (ISBN 0-575-03555-2, Pub. by Gollancz England). David & Charles.

Dhondy, Rarrukh. Romance, Romance & the Bride. 90p. (Orig.). 1985. pap. 8.95 (ISBN 0-571-13548-X). Faber & Faber.

Dhonte, Pierre. Clockwork Debt: Trade & the External Debt of Developing Countries. LC 79-1753. 144p. 1979. 22.50x (ISBN 0-669-02925-4). Lexington Bks.

Dhopeshwarkar, Govind A. Nutrition & Brain Development. LC 83-8139. (Illus.). 196p. 1983. 29.50 (ISBN 0-306-41060-5). Plenum Pub.

Dhorme, Edouard. A Commentary on the Book of Job. 906p. 1984. 24.95 (ISBN 0-8407-5421-3). Nelson.

Dhrymes, P. J. Distributed Lags: Problems of Estimation & Formulation. Rev. ed. (Advanced Textbooks in Economics: Vol. 14). 470p. 1981. 34.50 (ISBN 0-444-86013-4, North-Holland). Elsevier.

--Econometrics: Statistical Foundations & Applications. rev. ed. LC 74-10898. xvi, 592p. (Springer study ed.). 1974. pap. 32.00 (ISBN 0-387-90095-0). Springer Verlag.

--Mathematics for Econometrics. 2nd ed. 150p. 1984. pap. 19.80 (ISBN 0-387-90988-5). Springer-Verlag.

D'Hulst, R. A. Jacob Jordaens. LC 82-70747. (Illus.). 1982. 95.00x (ISBN 0-8014-1519-5). Cornell U Pr.

Dhundiraja, tr. Mudrarakshasa of Visakhadatta. 6th ed. 1976. pap. 6.50 (ISBN 0-8426-0906-7). Orient Bk Dist.

Dhurander, K. P. An Atlas of Assets & Liabilities of Rural Indian Households. 308p. 1985. text ed. 75.00x (ISBN 0-7069-2530-0, Pub by Vikas India). Advent NY.

Diab, Lutfy N., jt. auth. see Prothro, Edwin T.

Diab, Zuhair, ed. International Documents on Palestine, 1968. 510p. 1971. 25.00 (ISBN 0-88728-011-0). Inst Palestine.

Diabelli, Anton, et al. The Diabelli Variations: Variations on a Theme by Fifty Composers & Virtuosos. pap. 25.00 (ISBN 0-912028-09-2). Music Treasure.

Diabetes & Exercise Symposium, Sept., 1980, Olympia, Greece. Diabetes & Exercise Current Problems in Clinical Biochemistry: Proceedings, Vol. 2. Berger, Michael & Christacopoulos, Paris, eds. (Illus.). 200p. 1982. text ed. 29.50 (ISBN 3-456-81158-6, Pub. by Hans Huber Switzerland). J K Burgess.

Diabetes Education Center, Nassau Hospital, et al. Diabetes: The Comprehensive Self-Management Handbook. large print ed. LC 82-45392. (Illus.). 408p. 1984. 19.95 (ISBN 0-385-18292-9). Doubleday.

Diachenko, Gregory. Dukhovnija Posjevi. (Illus.). 475p. 1977. 20.00 (ISBN 0-317-30414-3); pap. 15.00 (ISBN 0-317-30415-1). Holy Trinity.

Diack, Hunter. Language for Teaching. 1967. 5.95 (ISBN 0-8022-0392-2). Philos Lib.

--Reading & the Psychology of Perception. LC 77-138220. (Illus.). 155p. 1972. Repr. of 1960 ed. lib. bdg. 18.75x (ISBN 0-8371-5577-0, DIRP). Greenwood.

Diacon, Diane. Residential Housing & Nuclear Attack. LC 84-17639. 146p. 1984. 23.50 (ISBN 0-7099-0868-7, Pub. by Croom Helm Ltd). Longwood Pub Group.

Diacono, Mario. Vito Acconci: Dal Testo-Azione Al Corpo Come Testo. LC 75-22995. (Illus.). 245p. (Ital.). 1975. 9.95 (ISBN 0-915570-03-3). Oolp Pr.

Diagram Group. The Brain: A User's Manual. 528p. 1983. pap. 4.95 (ISBN 0-425-06053-5). Berkley Pub.

--Comparisons. (Illus.). 240p. 1980. 15.00 (ISBN 0-312-15484-4). St Martin.

--Comparisons. (Illus.). 240p. 1982. pap. 9.95 (ISBN 0-312-15485-2). St Martin.

--The Complete Book of Exercises. 1986. cancelled (ISBN 0-442-21970-9). Van Nos Reinhold.

--Crossword Puzzles: How to Make Your Own. 160p. 1982. pap. 6.95 (ISBN 0-312-17689-9). St Martin.

--Enjoying Combat Sports. (Illus.). 159p. pap. 4.95 (ISBN 0-88317-099-X). Stoeger Pub Co.

--Enjoying Gymnastics. (Illus.). 159p. pap. 4.95 (ISBN 0-88317-096-5). Stoeger Pub Co.

--Enjoying Racquet Sports. (Illus.). 160p. pap. 4.95 (ISBN 0-88317-100-7). Stoeger Pub Co.

--Enjoying Skating. (Illus.). 160p. pap. 3.95 (ISBN 0-88317-101-5). Stoeger Pub Co.

--Enjoying Swimming & Diving. (Illus.). 160p. pap. 3.95 (ISBN 0-88317-102-3). Stoeger Pub Co.

--Enjoying Track & Field Sports. (Illus.). 160p. pap. 3.95 (ISBN 0-88317-104-X). Stoeger Pub Co.

--A Field Guide to Dinosaurs: The First Complete Guide to Every Dinosaur Now Known. (Illus.). 256p. 1983. pap. 8.95 (ISBN 0-380-83519-3, 83519-3). Avon.

--A Field Guide to Prehistoric Life. Date not set. price not set. Facts on File.

--Handtools of Arts & Crafts. (Illus.). 320p. 1981. 19.95 (ISBN 0-312-35860-1). St Martin.

--The Healthy Body: A Maintenance Manual. 1981. pap. 8.95 (ISBN 0-452-25352-7, Z5352, Plume). NAL.

--The Healthy Body: A Maintenance Manual. LC 81-82816. (Mosby Medical Library). (Illus.). 191p. 1982. pap. 8.95 (ISBN 0-452-25352-7, 1293-4). Mosby.

--How to Hold a Crocodile & Hundreds of Other Practical Tips, Fascinating Facts, Quizzes, Games & Pastimes. 1981. pap. 7.95 (ISBN 0-345-29577-3). Ballantine.

--The Human Body: A Comprehensive, Illustrated Guide to the Body & Its Functions. 544p. 1980. 24.95 (ISBN 0-87196-309-4). Facts on File.

--The Human Body on File. (Illus.). 300p. 1983. 145.00x (ISBN 0-87196-706-5). Facts on File.

--Logic Puzzles. 96p. 1983. pap. 1.75 (ISBN 0-345-30478-0). Ballantine.

--Man's Body. 1977. pap. 4.95 (ISBN 0-553-25348-4). Bantam.

--Maze Puzzles. 96p. (Orig.). 1983. pap. 1.75 (ISBN 0-345-30477-2). Ballantine.

--Musical Instruments of the World: An Illustrated Encyclopedia. (Illus.). 320p. 1978. 29.95 (ISBN 0-87196-320-5). Facts on File.

--Number Puzzles, No. 3. 96p. (Orig.). 1983. pap. 1.75 (ISBN 0-345-30479-9). Ballantine.

--The Parent's Emergency Guide: An Action Handbook for Childhood Illness & Accidents. 128p. 1984. pap. 6.95 (ISBN 0-87196-821-5). Facts on File.

--Picture Puzzles. 96p. (Orig.). 1983. pap. 1.75 (ISBN 0-345-30476-4). Ballantine.

--Predicting Your Future. 128p. 1983. pap. 5.95 (ISBN 0-345-30716-X). Ballantine.

--The Rule Book: The Authoritative Up-To-Date Illustrated Guide to the Regulations, History, & Object of All Major Sports. (Illus.). 432p. 1983. 9.95 (ISBN 0-312-69576-4). St Martin.

--The Scribner Guide to Orchestral Instruments. LC 83-179512. (Illus.). 119p. 1983. 9.95 (ISBN 0-684-17951-2, ScribT). Scribner.

--Sex: A User's Manual. 352p. 1983. pap. 4.50 (ISBN 0-425-07056-5). Berkley Pub.

--Sex: A User's Manual. (Illus.). 196p. 1981. pap. 9.95 (ISBN 0-399-50517-2, Perigee). Putnam Pub Group.

--The Sports Fan's Ultimate Book of Sports Comparisons: A Visual, Statistical & Factual Reference on Comparative Abilities, Records, Rules & Equipment. LC 81-21517. (Illus.). 192p. 1982. 14.95 (ISBN 0-312-75334-9). St Martin.

--The Sports Fan's Ultimate Book of Sports Comparisons: A Visual, Statistical & Factual Reference on Comparative Abilities, Records, Rules & Equipment. (Illus.). 192p. 1983. pap. 9.95 (ISBN 0-312-75335-7). St Martin.

--Weapons. (Illus.). 320p. 1980. 27.50 (ISBN 0-312-85946-5). St Martin.

--Woman's Body: An Owner's Manual. 1978. pap. 4.50 (ISBN 0-553-25486-3). Bantam.

Diakite, Madubuko. Film, Culture, & the Black Filmmaker. Jowett, Garth S., ed. LC 79-6679. (Issertations on Film, 1980 Ser.). 1980. lib. bdg. 21.00x (ISBN 0-405-12907-6). Ayer Co Pubs.

Diakonoff, I. M. Comparative Historical Vocabulary of Languages. (Bibliotheca Afroasiatica Ser.: Vol. 2-1). 42p. (Orig.). 1985. pap. text ed. 6.50x (ISBN 0-89003-161-4, BAA 2-1). Undena Pubns.

Diakonoff, Igor M. Prehistory of the Armenian People. LC 83-15429. write for info. (ISBN 0-88206-039-2). Caravan Bks.

Diakonov, I. M. & Neroznak, V. P. Phrygian. LC 85-453. 1985. write for info. (ISBN 0-88206-042-2). Caravan Bks.

Dial, Adolph & Eliades, David K. The Only Land I Know: A History of the Lumbee Indians. LC 74-80435. (Illus.). 240p. (Orig.). 1974. 9.75 (ISBN 0-913436-28-3); pap. 6.00 (ISBN 0-913436-29-1). Indian Hist Pr.

Dial, Hertha & Richter, Catherine. Little Blue Heaven. 1972. 4.50 (ISBN 0-87516-111-1). De Vorss.

Dial, James. The Harlot of Jericho. LC 74-33071. 177p. 1974. 6.95 (ISBN 0-89227-009-8). Commonwealth Pr.

Dial, James L. I Saw God. LC 75-37224. 63p. 1976. pap. 1.95 (ISBN 0-89227-000-4). Commonwealth Pr.

Dial, Joan. Echoes of War. LC 84-12715. 352p. 1984. 15.95 (ISBN 0-312-22546-6). St Martin.

Dial, Scott. New Clues to Steamboat Springs Lost Treasure. 1975. pap. 2.00 (ISBN 0-933472-28-5). Johnson Bks.

--A Place to Raise Hell-Cheyenne Saloons. 1977. pap. 2.00 (ISBN 0-933472-52-8). Johnson Bks.

Dial, Scott D. Silver Insights. (Illus.). 105p. (Orig.). 1982. pap. 25.00 (ISBN 0-912497-00-9). Silver D Invest Inc.

Diallo, A., jt. auth. see Chamberlain, R.

Diallo, Nafissatou. The Princess of Tiali. Woollcombe, Ann & Scherer, Barbara, trs. from Fr. LC 83-50541. (Illus.). 150p. 1985. 15.00 (ISBN 0-89410-411-X); pap. 7.00 (ISBN 0-89410-412-8). Three Continents.

Diaman, N. A. Ed Dean Is Queer. 2nd ed. LC 78-57153. (Illus.). 175p. 1981. pap. 7.95 (ISBN 0-931906-02-4). Persona Pr.

--The Fourth Wall. LC 79-92284. (Illus.). 128p. (Orig.). 1980. pap. 4.95 (ISBN 0-931906-01-6). Persona Pr.

--Reunion. LC 83-4051. 164p. (Orig.). 1983. pap. 8.95 (ISBN 0-931906-04-0). Persona Pr.

--Second Crossing. LC 82-7564. 240p. (Orig.). 1982. pap. 9.95 (ISBN 0-931906-03-2). Persona Pr.

Diamant, Alfred. Austrian Catholics & the First Republic: Democracy, Capitalism, & the Social Order, 1918-1934. LC 60-5745. pap. 84.30 (ISBN 0-317-09404-1, 2015226). Bks Demand UMI.

--Austrian Catholics & the Social Question, 1918-1933. LC 59-62692. (University of Florida Social Sciences Monographs: No. 2). 1959. pap. 3.50 (ISBN 0-8130-0059-9). U Presses Fla.

Diamant, B., et al, eds. see Collegium Internationale Allergologicum Symposium, 10th, Copenhagen, 1974.

Diamant, E., et al, eds. Surveys of Research in Transportation Technology: Presented at the Winter Annual Meeting of the ASME, November 11-15, 1973. LC 73-90322. (American Society of Mechanical Engineers, Applied Mechanics Division. AMD: Vol. 5). (Illus.). pap. 45.50 (ISBN 0-317-10236-2, 2016808). Bks Demand UMI.

Diamant, Leo, jt. auth. see Debo, Harvey V.

Diamant, Lincoln. Bernard Romans: Forgotten Patriot of the American Revolution, Military Engineer & Cartographer of West Point & the Hudson Valley. LC 85-5421. (Illus.). 160p. 1985. 15.95 (ISBN 0-916346-56-0). Harbor Hill Bks.

Diamant, Lincoln, ed. The Broadcast Communications Dictionary. 2nd, rev., enl. ed. 1978. 10.95 (ISBN 0-8038-0788-0). Hastings.

--Broadcast Communications Dictionary. 3rd, rev. ed. 1985. 15.95 (ISBN 0-8038-0807-0). Hastings.

Diamant, R. M. Energy Conservation Equipment. 156p. 1984. 29.50 (ISBN 0-89397-190-1). Nichols Pub.

--Total Energy. 1970. 22.00 (ISBN 0-08-006918-5). Pergamon.

Diamant, R. M. & Kut, David. District Heating & Cooling for Energy Conservation. LC 81-4110. 464p. 1981. 63.95x (ISBN 0-470-27182-5). Halsted Pr.

Diamant, Rolf, et al. A Citizen's Guide to River Conservation. LC 84-7799. (Illus.). 113p. (Orig.). 1984. pap. 7.95 (ISBN 0-89164-082-7). Conservation Foun.

Diamanti, J., tr. see Lebovici, Serge & Widlocher, K.

Diamanti, Joyce, tr. see Chauvin, Remy.

Diamanti, Joyce, tr. see Decarie, Therese G., et al.

Diamanti, Joyce, tr. see Droz, R. & Rahmy, M.

Diamanti, Joyce, tr. see Grunberger, Bela.

Diamond, Ann & Goodman, Frances B. Taste of the Bayou: Creole & Cajun Recipes. 156p. 1984. 5.95 (ISBN 0-89896-082-7). Larksdale.

Diamond, Arlyn & Edwards, Lee, eds. The Authority of Experience: Essays in Feminist Criticism. LC 76-8755. 320p. 1977. 17.50x (ISBN 0-87023-220-7). U of Mass Pr.

Diamond, Arthur S. The Evolution of Law & Order. LC 72-9372. 342p. 1973. Repr. of 1951 ed. lib. bdg. 21.00x (ISBN 0-8371-6580-6, DIEL). Greenwood.

--History & Origin of Language. 1965. pap. 1.95 (ISBN 0-8065-0127-8, 207). Citadel Pr.

Diamond, B, et al. West Africa Fertilizer Study: Regional Overview, Vol. I. (Technical Bulletin Ser.: T-3). 79p. (Orig.). 1977. pap. 4.00 (ISBN 0-88090-039-3). Intl Fertilizer.

Diamond, Bernard. Odyssey of Revenge. 204p. 1983. pap. 10.95 (ISBN 0-914366-21-1). Columbia Pub.

--Odyssey of Revenge. 204p. 1983. 10.95. Vanguard.

--Odyssey of Revenge. LC 83-15191. 208p. 1983. pap. 10.95 (ISBN 0-914366-21-1). Columbia Pub.

Diamond, Betty. The Traveling Kitchen: A Guide to Healthy, Independent Easting While Traveling. 1983. pap. 4.95 (ISBN 0-911238-88-3). B of A.

Diamond, Carlin J. Don't Label It...Love It! A Personal Journey to Peace of Mind. Amari-Amir, Lisa, ed. (Peace of Mind, Living It & Loving It Ser.). (Illus.). 100p. (Orig.). 1985. pap. 8.95 (ISBN 0-911761-46-2). Fifth Wave Pr.

Diamond, Charles & Frew, Ivor. The Facial Nerve. (Illus.). 1979. text ed. 49.50x (ISBN 0-19-261128-3). Oxford U Pr.

Diamond, Cora & Teichman, Jenny, eds. Intention & Intentionality: Essays in Honour of G. E. M. Anscombe. LC 79-2478. (Illus.). 265p. 1980. 39.50x (ISBN 0-8014-1275-7). Cornell U Pr.

Diamond, D. R. & McLoughlin, J. B. Progress in Planning, Vol. 13, (complete) (Illus.). 174p. 1981. 62.00 (ISBN 0-08-028398-5). Pergamon.

Diamond, D. R. & Spence, N. A. Regional Policy Evalution: Methodological Review & the Scottish Example. 170p. 1984. text ed. 33.50x (ISBN 0-566-00644-8). Gower Pub Co.

Diamond, D. R., ed. Progress in Planning, Vol. 20. (Illus.). 260p. 1984. 60.00 (ISBN 0-08-031490-2). Pergamon.

Diamond, D. R. & McLoughlin, J. B., eds. Progress in Planning, Vol. 7. (Illus.). 1979. 55.00 (ISBN 0-08-020333-7). Pergamon.

--Progress in Planning, Vol. 9. 300p. 1979. 55.00 (ISBN 0-08-025221-4). Pergamon.

--Progress in Planning, Vol. 10. (Illus.). 247p. 1980. 55.00 (ISBN 0-08-025788-7). Pergamon.

--Progress in Planning, Vol. 11. (Illus.). 280p. 1980. 55.00 (ISBN 0-08-025802-6). Pergamon.

--Progress in Planning, Vol. 12. 224p. 1980. 55.00 (ISBN 0-08-026100-0). Pergamon.

--Progress in Planning, Vol. 17. 268p. 1982. 62.00 (ISBN 0-08-029701-3). Pergamon.

--Progress in Planning, Vol. 18. (Illus.). 384p. 1983. 60.00 (ISBN 0-08-030415-X). Pergamon.

--Progress in Planning, Vol. 19. (Illus.). 280p. 1983. text ed. 60.00 (ISBN 0-08-031035-4). Pergamon.

--Progress in Planning, Vol. 21. (Illus.). 230p. 1985. 60.00 (ISBN 0-08-032325-1). Pergamon.

--Progress in Planning: Recent Researh in Urban & Regional Planning, 3 pts, Vol. 10. Incl. Pt. 1. Internal Migration & the Australian Urban System. McKay, J. & Whitelaw, J. S. pap. 10.00 (ISBN 0-08-023704-5); Pt. 2. Employment Decentralisation: Policy Instruments for Large Cities in Less Developed Countries. Townroe, P. M. pap. 10.00 (ISBN 0-08-023705-3); Pt. 3. The Geography of Industrial Reorganisation. Massey, Doreen & Meegan, Richard A. pap. 10.00 (ISBN 0-08-023706-1). (Illus.). 1979. write for info. Pergamon.

Diamond, Dan. True Gesture: Dream Poems. (Illus.). 31p. 1985. pap. 5.00 (ISBN 0-942292-00-6). Warthog Pr.

Diamond, Dan & McGoey, Peter. Hockey, the Illustrated History: An Official Publication of the National Hockey League. (Illus.). 256p. 1985. 19.95 (ISBN 0-385-23329-9). Doubleday.

Diamond, Denise. Living with Flowers: A Guide to Bringing Flowers into Your Daily Life. LC 81-18879. (Illus.). 288p. 1982. 19.95 (ISBN 0-688-00990-5). Morrow.

--Living with the Flowers: A Guide to Bringing Flowers into Your Daily Life. LC 81-18552. (Illus.). 288p. (Orig.). 1982. pap. 11.95 (ISBN 0-688-00991-3, Quill NY). Morrow.

Diamond, Donna, illus. & adapted by. Swan Lake. LC 79-11179. (Illus.). 32p. (gr. 2-6). 1980. reinforced bdg. 9.95 (ISBN 0-8234-0356-4). Holiday.

Diamond, Dorothy. Facts about Ulcers. pap. 1.00x (ISBN 0-392-11245-0, SpS). Sportshelf.

Diamond, Dorothy B., jt. auth. see Diamond, Walter H.

Diamond, Douglas & Tolley, George, eds. The Economics of Urban Amenities. (Studies in Urban Economics Ser.). 1982. 31.50 (ISBN 0-12-214840-1). Acad Pr.

Diamond, Edwin. Good News, Bad News. 1978. 22.50x (ISBN 0-262-04057-3); pap. 6.95x (ISBN 0-262-54035-5). MIT Pr.

--Sign off: The Last Days of Television. 288p. 1982. 27.50x (ISBN 0-262-04069-7); pap. 7.95 (ISBN 0-262-54039-8). MIT Pr.

--The Tin Kazoo: Television, Politics, & the News. LC 75-17905. 316p. 1975. pap. 5.95x (ISBN 0-262-54032-0). MIT Pr.

Diamond, Edwin & Bates, Stephen. The Spot: The Rise of Political Advertising on Television. (Illus.). 220p. 1984. 20.00 (ISBN 0-262-04075-1). MIT Pr.

Diamond, Edwin, et al. Telecommunications in Crisis: The First Amendment, Technology, & Deregulation. 1983. pap. 6.00 (ISBN 0-932790-39-9). Cato Inst.

Diamond, Eugene & Diamond, Rosemary. The Positive Values of Chastity. 1983. 7.50 (ISBN 0-8199-0829-0). Franciscan Herald.

Diamond, Eugene, jt. auth. see Horan, Denis.

Diamond, Frank B. Increase Your Profits in the Stock Market. 1967. pap. 1.95 (ISBN 0-346-12231-7). Cornerstone.

Diamond, Graham. Captain Sinbad. 250p. 1980. pap. 2.25 (ISBN 0-449-14341-4, GM). Fawcett.

--Cinnabar. 304p. 1985. pap. 2.95 (ISBN 0-449-12463-0, GM). Fawcett.

--Marrakesh. 288p. 1981. pap. 2.50 (ISBN 0-449-14443-7, GM). Fawcett.

--The Thief of Kalimar. 1979. pap. 2.95 (ISBN 0-449-14214-0, GM). Fawcett.

Diamond, H. G., jt. auth. see Pollard, Harry.

Diamond, H. G., ed. see Symposium in Pure Mathematics, St. Louis, 1972.

Diamond, Harold J. Music Criticism: An Annotated Guide to the Literature. LC 79-22279. 326p. 1979. 21.00 (ISBN 0-8108-1268-1). Scarecrow.

Diamond, Harriet & Dutwin, Phyllis. Grammar in Plain English. rev. ed. LC 75-2487. (gr. 9-12). 1977. pap. text ed. 7.95 (ISBN 0-8120-0545-7). Barron.

Diamond, Harriet & Dutwin, Physsil. The Science Test. rev. ed. (GED Ser.). 202p. 1985. pap. 6.85 (ISBN 0-8092-5586-3). Contemp Bks.

Diamond, Harriet, jt. auth. see Dutwin, Phillis.

Diamond, Harvey & Diamond, Marilyn. Fit for Life. 256p. 1985. 16.50 (ISBN 0-446-51322-9). Warner Bks.

Diamond, Hugh W. Face of Madness. Gilman, Sander L., ed. 1977. pap. 5.95 (ISBN 0-8065-0604-0). Citadel Pr.

Diamond, Irene. Astrology in the Holy Bible. new ed. (Illus.). 92p. (Orig.). 1982. pap. text ed. 10.00x (ISBN 0-941762-09-2). Psychic Forum.

--Families, Politics, & Public Policy: A Feminist Dialogue on Women & the State. LC 82-20357. 432p. 1983. 15.95 (ISBN 0-582-28268-3). Longman.

--Sex Roles in the State House. LC 76-49708. 1977. 9.95x (ISBN 0-300-02115-1). Yale U Pr.

Diamond, Irvin F. & Walker, Mike, eds. Tax Planning Tips from the Tax Adviser: 1984. 442p. 1982. pap. 19.50 (ISBN 0-686-70250-6). Am Inst CPA.

Diamond, J. & Pintel, G. Introduction to Contemporary Business. 1975. 25.75 (ISBN 0-13-487991-0); study guide o.p. 8.95 (ISBN 0-13-488015-3). P-H.

Diamond, Jacqueline. The Forgetful Lady. LC 83-40421. 153p. 1984. 12.95 (ISBN 0-8027-0760-2). Walker & Co.

--The Forgetful Lady. 192p. 1986. pap. 2.50 (ISBN 0-446-32795-6). Warner Bks.

--Lady in Disguise. 1982. 11.95 (ISBN 0-8027-0715-7). Walker & Co.

--A Lady of Letters. 192p. 1983. 12.95 (ISBN 0-8027-0741-6). Walker & Co.

--Song for a Lady. 192p. 1983. 11.95 (ISBN 0-8027-0724-6). Walker & Co.

Diamond, James S. Barukh Kurzweil & Modern Hebrew Literature. LC 82-16770. (Brown Judaic Studies). 232p. 1983. pap. 18.00 (ISBN 0-89130-595-5, 14 00 39). Scholars Pr GA.

Diamond, Jared M. Avifauna of the Eastern Highlands of New Guinea. (Illus.). 438p. 1972. 15.00 (ISBN 0-686-35800-7). Nuttall Ornith.

Diamond, Jared M., jt. ed. see Cody, Martin L.

Diamond, Jay & Pintel, Gerald. Applied Business Arithmetic. (Illus.). 336p. 1985. pap. text ed. 19.95 (ISBN 0-13-040155-2). P-H.

--Principles of Marketing. (Illus.). 1980. 23.95 (ISBN 0-13-701417-1); study guide 10.95 (ISBN 0-13-701425-2). P-H.

--Principles of Marketing. 3rd ed. (Illus.). 544p. 1986. text ed. 26.95 (ISBN 0-13-701392-2). P-H.

--Principles of Selling. (Illus.). 384p. 1985. text ed. 23.95 (ISBN 0-13-709957-6). P-H.

--Retail Buying. 2nd ed. (Illus.). 336p. 1985. text ed. 24.95 (ISBN 0-13-778713-8). P-H.

--Successful Selling. (Illus.). 384p. 1980. text ed. 18.95 (ISBN 0-8359-7246-1). Reston.

Diamond, Jay, jt. auth. see Pintel, Gerald.

Diamond, Jed. Inside Out: Becoming My Own Man. LC 83-90225. (Orig.). 1983. pap. 10.00 (ISBN 0-911761-35-7). Fifth Wave Pr.

Diamond, John. Behavioral Kinesiology. 1981. 18.95x (ISBN 0-686-76727-6). B Of A.

--Behavioral Kinesiology for the Dentist: An Introductory Overview. (BK Ser.). 40p. 1979. pap. 9.95x (ISBN 0-317-02751-4). B of A.

--BK--Behavioral Kinesiology: The New Science for Positive Health Through Muscle Testing. LC 78-2127. (Illus.). 1979. 8.95i (ISBN 0-06-010986-6, HarpT). Har-Row.

--The Collected Papers of John Diamond, M.D, 2 vols. 1983. pap. 19.95 ea. Vol. 1, 88p. (ISBN 0-911238-75-1). Vol. 2, 170p (ISBN 0-911238-76-X). B of A.

--Holistic Therapy: Lectures on a Spiritual Basis of Holistic Therapy. 67p. 1983. pap. 19.95x (ISBN 0-911238-79-4). B of A.

--Life Energy. (Illus.). 288p. 1985. 16.95 (ISBN 0-396-08489-3). Dodd.

--Life Energy in Music: Notes on Music & Sound, 2 Vols. 140p. 1983. Vol. I. pap. 19.95 (ISBN 0-915628-20-1); Vol. II. pap. 19.95 (ISBN 0-915628-21-X). Zeppelin.

--Re-Mothering Experience: How to Totally Love. Orig. Title: How to Totally Love. 90p. 1983. pap. 15.95x (ISBN 0-915628-13-9). Zeppelin.

--Some Contributions of Behavioral Kineseology to Art. (Behavioral Kinesiology Ser.). 73p. 1983. pap. 29.95 (ISBN 0-915628-14-7). Zeppelin.

--Speech, Language & the Power of Breath in Behavioral Kinesiology. (Behavioral Kinesiology Ser.). 85p. 1983. pap. 47.50 (ISBN 0-911238-77-8). B of A.

--Your Body Doesn't Lie. 208p. 1980. pap. 3.50 (ISBN 0-446-30859-5). Warner Bks.

--Your Body Doesn't Lie. 1979. 3.50x (ISBN 0-318-03768-8). Cancer Control Soc.

Diamond, Joseph & Kurucza, Robert M. Second Annual Financial Services Institute Handbook, 2 vols. (Corporate Law & Practice Course Handbook: No. 437-438). (Illus.). 1984. Set. 35.00 (ISBN 0-317-15184-3). PLI.

Diamond, Joseph, jt. auth. see Barnard, Kevin F.

Diamond, Lucy. Jesus by the Sea of Galilee. (Ladybird Ser). (Illus.). 1958. bds. 2.25 (ISBN 0-87508-840-6). Chr Lit.

--Jesus Calls His Disciples. (Ladybird Ser). (Illus.). 1959. bds. 2.25 (ISBN 0-87508-842-2). Chr Lit.

--Moses, Prince & Shepherd. (Ladybird Ser). (Illus.). 1954. bds. 2.25 (ISBN 0-87508-850-3). Chr Lit.

--Naaman & the Little Maid. (Ladybird Ser). (Illus.). 1959. bds. 2.25 (ISBN 0-87508-852-X). Chr Lit.

--Story of Daniel. (Ladybird Ser). (Illus.). 1958. bds. 2.25 (ISBN 0-87508-866-X). Chr Lit.

--Story of Joseph. (Ladybird Ser). (Illus.). 1954. bds. 2.25 (ISBN 0-87508-868-6). Chr Lit.

--Two Stories Jesus Told. (Ladybird Ser). (Illus.). 1959. bds. 2.25 (ISBN 0-87508-870-8). Chr Lit.

Diamond, Malcolm L. Martin Buber: Jewish Existentialist. 1968. lib. bdg. 17.50x (ISBN 0-88307-077-4). Gannon.

Diamond, Marian C. & Korenbrot, Carol C., eds. Hormonal Contraceptives, Estrogens & Human Welfare. 1978. 20.00 (ISBN 0-12-214750-2). Acad Pr.

Diamond, Marie J. Flaubert: The Problem of Aesthetic Discontinuity. 1975. 13.95x (ISBN 0-8046-9075-8, Pub. by Kennikat). Assoc Faculty Pr.

Diamond, Marilyn, jt. auth. see Diamond, Harvey.

Diamond, Martin. The Electoral College & the American Idea of Democracy. LC 77-81901. 1977. pap. 2.25 (ISBN 0-8447-3262-1). Am Enterprise.

--The Founding of the Democratic Republic. LC 80-84210. 190p. 1981. pap. text ed. 8.95 (ISBN 0-87581-271-6). Peacock Pubs.

--The Revolution of Sober Expectations. (Bicentnnial Lecture Ser.). 17p. 1974. pap. 1.00 (ISBN 0-8447-1301-5). Am Enterprise.

Diamond, Max & Ward, Jeremy H. Joust a Minute. (Illus.). 200p. 1982. 12.75 (ISBN 0-904573-65-6); pap. 6.75 (ISBN 0-904573-70-2). Caliban Bks.

Diamond, Michael A., jt. auth. see Arnold, Jerry L.

Diamond, Michael J. & Gowing, Peter G. Islam & Muslims: Some Basic Information. 100p. 1981. pap. 3.75x (ISBN 0-686-30367-9, Pub. by New Day Publishers Philippines). Cellar.

Diamond, Milton & Karlen, Arno. Sexual Decisions. (Illus.). 536p. 1980. text ed. 26.95 (ISBN 0-316-18388-1); instructor's manual free (ISBN 0-316-18390-3). Little.

Diamond, Milton, jt. auth. see Steinhoff, Patricia G.

Diamond, Milton, et al, eds. see Beach, Frank A.

Diamond, Neil, compiled by. The Neil Diamond Songbook. (Illus.). 400p. 1982. 29.95 (ISBN 0-933328-46-X). Delilah Bks.

Diamond, Norma. K'un Shen: A Taiwan Village. Spindler, George & Spindler, Louise, eds. (Case Studies in Cultural Anthropology). 128p. 1982. pap. text ed. 6.95x (ISBN 0-8290-0280-4). Irvington.

Diamond, Peter. A Search Equilibrium Approach to the Micro Foundations of Macro Economics. (Illus.). 40p. 1984. 10.00x (ISBN 0-262-04076-X). MIT Pr.

Diamond, Peter & Rothschild, Michael, eds. Uncertainty in Economics: Readings & Exercises. (Economic Theory Econometrics & Mathematical Economic Ser.). 1978. 25.00 (ISBN 0-12-214850-9). Acad Pr.

Diamond, Petra. Confidentially Yours. (To Have & to Hold Ser.: No. 31). 192p. 1984. pap. 1.95 (ISBN 0-515-07833-6). Jove Pubns.

Diamond, R. B., et al. Etude sur Les Engrais en Afrique de L'Ouest: Volume 1 - Apercu Regional. (Technical Bulletins Ser.: TF-3). (Illus.). 84p. (Orig., Fr.). 1977. pap. 4.00 (ISBN 0-88090-038-5). Intl Fertilizer.

--Etude sur les Engrais en Afrique de L'Ouest Vol. 2: Senegal. (Technical Bulletins Ser.: TF-4). (Illus.). 70p. (Orig., Fr.). 1977. pap. 4.00 (ISBN 0-88090-032-6). Intl Fertilizer.

--Etude sur les Engrais en Afrique de L'Quest Vol. 3: Mali. (Technical Bulletin Ser.: TF-5). (Illus.). 73p. (Orig., Fr.). 1976. pap. 4.00 (ISBN 0-88090-033-4). Intl Fertilizer.

--Etude sur les Engrais en Afrique de L'Ouest Vol. 4: Haute Volta. (Technical Bulletin Ser.: TF-6). (Illus.). 65p. (Orig., Fr.). 1977. pap. 4.00 (ISBN 0-88090-034-2). Intl Fertilizer.

--Etude sur les Engrais en Afrique de L'Ouest Vol. 5: Niger. (Technical Bulletin Ser.: TF-7). (Illus.). 51p. (Orig., Fr.). 1978. pap. 4.00 (ISBN 0-88090-035-0). Intl Fertilizer.

--Etude sur les Engrais en Afrique de L'Ouest Vol. 6: Tchad. (Technical Bulletin Ser.: TF-8). (Illus.). 63p. (Orig., Fr.). 1977. pap. 4.00 (ISBN 0-88090-036-9). Intl Fertilizer.

--Etude sur les Engrais en Afrique de L'Ouest Vol. 7: Mauritanie. (Technical Bulletin Ser.: TF-9). (Illus.). 42p. (Orig., Fr.). 1978. pap. 4.00 (ISBN 0-88090-037-7). Intl Fertilizer.

--West Africa Fertilizer Study: Mali, Vol. III. (Technical Bulletin T-5). (Illus.). 64p. (Orig.). 1976. pap. 4.00 (ISBN 0-88090-004-0). Intl Fertilizer.

--West Africa Fertilizer Study: Mauritania, Vol. VII. (Technical Bulletin T-9). (Illus.). 39p. (Orig.). 1978. pap. 4.00 (ISBN 0-88090-008-3). Intl Fertilizer.

--West Africa Fertilizer Study: Niger, Vol. V. (Technical Bulletin - T-7). (Illus.). 47p. (Orig.). 1978. pap. 4.00 (ISBN 0-88090-006-7). Intl Fertilizer.

--West Africa Fertilizer Study: Senegal, Vol. II. (Technical Bulletin, T-4). (Illus.). 64p. (Orig.). pap. 4.00 (ISBN 0-88090-003-2). Intl Fertilizer.

--West Africa Fertilizer Study: Upper Volta, Vol. IV. (Technical Bulletin - T-6). (Illus.). 60p. (Orig.). 1977. pap. 4.00 (ISBN 0-88090-005-9). Intl Fertilizer.

--West Africa Fertilizer Study: Chad, Vol. VI. (Technical Bulletin - T-8). (Illus.). 55p. (Orig.). 1977. pap. 4.00 (ISBN 0-88090-007-5). Intl Fertilizer.

Diamond, R. B., jt. auth. see Zalla, T.

Diamond, Ray B., jt. auth. see Martinez, Adolfo.

Diamond, Robert E. Old English: Grammar & Reader. LC 79-79477. (Waynebooks Ser: No. 38). 304p. 1970. text ed. 15.00x (ISBN 0-8143-1390-6); pap. text ed. 6.95x (ISBN 0-8143-1510-0). Wayne St U Pr.

Diamond, Robert M., et al. Instructional Development for Individualized Learning in Higher Education. LC 74-18398. 208p. 1975. pap. 24.95 (ISBN 0-87778-077-3). Educ Tech Pubns.

Diamond, Rosemary, jt. auth. see Diamond, Eugene.

Diamond, Seymour & Dalessio, Donald J. The Practicing Physician's Approach to Headache. 3rd ed. (Illus.). 166p. 1982. lib. bdg. 31.00 (ISBN 0-683-02503-1). Williams & Wilkins.

Diamond, Seymour & Diamond-Falk, Judi. Advice from the Diamond Headache Clinic. LC 82-8973. ix, 194p. 1982. 22.50 (ISBN 0-8236-0119-6). Intl Univs Pr.

--Advice From the Diamond Headache Clinic. 194p. 18.95 (ISBN 0-318-01577-3). Sphinx Pr.

Diamond, Seymour & Epstein, Mary F. Coping with Your Headaches. (Illus.). 96p. pap. 2.50 (ISBN 0-8326-2260-5, 7465). Delair.

Diamond, Seymour & Friedman, Arnold P. Headache. (Contemporary Patient Management Ser.). 1983. text ed. 20.00 (ISBN 0-87488-892-1). Med Exam.

Diamond, Seymour, et al, eds. Vasoactive Substances Relevant to Migraine. (Illus.). 112p. 1975. 14.75x (ISBN 0-398-03348-X). C C Thomas.

Diamond, Sheldon. Fundamental Concepts of Modern Physics. (gr. 11-12). 1970. pap. text ed. 8.42 (ISBN 0-87720-178-1). AMSCO Sch.

Diamond, Sheldon R., jt. auth. see Ahner, Walter L.

Diamond, Sidney A. Trademark Problems & How to Avoid Them. 2nd ed. LC 80-70205. 1981. 22.95 (ISBN 0-87251-059-X). Crain Bks.

Diamond, Sigmund. In Quest. LC 79-26717. (Illus.). 1980. 24.00x (ISBN 0-231-04842-4). Columbia U Pr.

--The Reputation of the American Businessman. 16.50 (ISBN 0-8446-0581-6). Peter Smith.

Diamond, Sigmund, ed. The Nation Transformed: The Creation of an Industrial Society. LC 63-17876. (American Epochs Ser). 1963. 10.00 (ISBN 0-8076-0247-7); pap. 4.95 (ISBN 0-8076-0395-3). Braziller.

Diamond, Sigmund, tr. see De Rothschild, Salomon.

Diamond, Stanley. In Search of the Primitive. LC 72-82195. 387p. 1981. pap. 9.95 (ISBN 0-87855-582-X). Transaction Bks.

--Totems. 96p. 1981. pap. 6.50 (ISBN 0-940170-02-7). Open Bk Pubns.

--Totems. 96p. (Orig.). 1983. pap. 6.50 (ISBN 0-317-17093-7). Station Hill Pr.

Diamond, Stanley, ed. Culture in History: Essays in Honor of Paul Radin. 1980. Repr. of 1960 ed. lib. bdg. 80.50x (ISBN 0-374-92155-5). Octagon.

--Theory & Practice: Essays Presented to Gene Weltfish. (Studies in Anthropology). 1979. text ed. 33.60 (ISBN 90-279-7958-8). Mouton.

--Toward a Marxist Anthropology: Problems & Perspectives. (World Anthropology Ser.). 1979. text ed. 36.00x (ISBN 90-279-7780-1). Mouton.

Diamond, Stephen C. Leveraged Buyouts. LC 84-73255. 1985. 35.00 (ISBN 0-87094-579-3). Dow Jones-Irwin.

Diamond, Susan A. Helping Children of Divorce: A Handbook for Parents & Teachers. LC 84-22191. 124p. 1985. 11.95 (ISBN 0-8052-3974-X). Schocken.

Diamond, Susan Z. Preparing Administrative Manuals. 160p. 1981. 24.95 (ISBN 0-8144-5631-6). AMACOM.

--Records Management. 192p. 1983. 21.95 (ISBN 0-8144-5729-0). Am Mgmt Assns.

Diamond, Susan Z., jt. ed. see Kristy, James E.

Diamond, Walter H. & Diamond, Dorothy B. International Tax Treaties of All Nations: Supplement & Cumulative Index. LC 73-33646. 1983. looseleaf 35.00 (ISBN 0-379-00745-2). Oceana.

--International Tax Treaties of All Nations. LC 75-33646. (Series A, 12 Vols. & Series B, & 18 Vols.). 1978. text ed. 50.00 ea. (ISBN 0-379-00725-8). Oceana.

Diamond, Walter H. & McCann, William J. Organizing & Operating a Foreign Sales Corporation. 1985. looseleaf 100.00 (ISBN 0-379-20194-1). Oceana.

Diamond, William. Development Banks. (World Bank Ser.). 128p. 1957. pap. 5.00x (ISBN 0-8018-0708-5). Johns Hopkins.

--The Economic Thought of Woodrow Wilson. LC 78-64192. (Johns Hopkins University. Studies in the Social Sciences. Sixty-First Ser. 1943). 216p. 1982. Repr. of 1943 ed. 24.50 (ISBN 0-404-61299-7). AMS Pr.

Diamond, William, ed. Development Finance Companies: Aspects of Policy & Operation. LC 68-27738. pap. 32.00 (ISBN 0-317-07755-4, 2021734). Bks Demand UMI.

Diamond, William & Raghavan, V. S., eds. Aspects of Development Bank Management. LC 81-48174. 1982. 29.95x (ISBN 0-8018-2571-7); pap. 12.95x (ISBN 0-8018-2572-5). Johns Hopkins.

Diamond, William J. Bulls, Bears & Massacres: A Proven System for Investing in the Stock Market. (Finance Ser.). (Illus.). 164p. 1982. 21.00 (ISBN 0-534-97945-9). Lifetime Learn.

--Practical Experiment Designs for Engineers & Scientists. 348p. 1981. text ed. 33.50x (ISBN 0-534-97992-0). Lifetime Learn.

--Practical Experiment Designs for Engineers & Scientists. 348p. 1981. 33.50 (ISBN 0-534-97992-0). Van Nos Reinhold.

Diamond, William M. Distribution Channels for Industrial Goods. 1963. 4.50x (ISBN 0-87776-114-0, R114). Ohio St U Admin Sci.

Diamond-Falk, Judi, jt. auth. see Diamond, Seymour.

Diamondis, Peter J. Underwater Photography Now. LC 83-136151. (Illus.). 154p. 1983. 14.95 (ISBN 0-9612110-0-8). P J Diamondis.

Diamonstein, Barbaralee. American Architecture Now II. LC 85-42870. (Illus.). 300p. 1985. pap. 25.00 (ISBN 0-8478-0612-X). Rizzoli Intl.

--Fashion: The Inside Story. LC 85-42865. (Illus.). 200p. 1985. pap. 19.95 (ISBN 0-8478-0610-3). Rizzoli Intl.

--Handmade in America: Conversations with Fourteen Craftmasters. LC 82-13941. (Illus.). 224p. 1983. 49.50 (ISBN 0-8109-1083-7). Abrams.

Diamonstein, Barbaralee, jt. auth. see Arnason, H. H.

Diamonstein, Barbaralee, ed. Collaboration: Artists & Architects. (Illus.). 176p. 1981. 32.50 (ISBN 0-8230-7126-X, Whitney Lib); pap. 16.95 (ISBN 0-8230-7123-5). Watson-Guptill.

Diamonstein, Barbarlee, et al. Louise Nevelson: Celebration-Deluxe. Pace Gallery Publications, ed. (Illus.). 64p. 1980. boxed 75.00 (ISBN 0-938608-31-2). Pace Gallery Pubns.

Diamont, Anita. The New Jewish Wedding. LC 84-24102. (Illus.). 1985. 16.95 (ISBN 0-671-49527-5). Summit Bks.

Diamonti, Joyce, tr. see Sow, I.

Diamos, Kerson D. The First Letters in Love: Stories of Nogales, Sonora, & the Guaymas, Sonora, Mexico Areas. 152p. (Orig., Eng. Span.). 1986. pap. 15.00 (ISBN 0-9614985-3-6). El Siglo Pubs.

--How to Speak Spanish, Pronto. 120p. (Orig.). 1985. pap. 15.00 (ISBN 0-9614985-2-8). El Siglo Pubs.

--Ojos del Griego (Greek's Springs) Ranch. 184p. (Orig.). 1985. pap. 7.95 (ISBN 0-9614985-0-1). El Siglo Pubs.

--Remembrance of Tucson's Past: Century Ago & More, & Less in Tucson Arizona. 150p. (Orig.). 1985. pap. 14.00 (ISBN 0-9614985-1-X). El Siglo Pubs.

Dian, Twila. A Color & Story Album for Horse Lovers. (Illus.). 32p. (Orig.). (gr. 3-8). 1982. pap. 3.95 (ISBN 0-8431-1740-0). Troubador Pr.

Diana. Zodiac Coloring Book. 1977. pap. 2.50 (ISBN 0-914350-24-2). Vulcan Bks.

Diana, Lewis. The Prostitute & Her Clients: Your Pleasure Is Her Business. 246p. 1985. 24.75x (ISBN 0-398-05042-2). C C Thomas.

Dianin, Sergei A. Borodin. Lord, Robert, tr. from Rus. (Illus.). xi, 356p. 1980. Repr. of 1963 ed. lib. bdg. 32.50x (ISBN 0-313-22529-X, DIBO). Greenwood.

Dianioux, A. J., jt. ed. see Dupuy, J.

Dianming, Wang, jt. auth. see Kong, Wu.

Di Antonio, Angelo. Spreadsheet Applications in Managerial Accounting. 1985. pap. text ed. 18.95 (ISBN 0-8359-6962-2). Reston.

Dianzani, M. U. & Gentilini, P., eds. Chronic Liver Disease. (Frontiers of Gastrointestinal Research Ser.: Vol. 9). (Illus.). viii, 250p. 1986. 69.00 (ISBN 3-8055-4205-4). S Karger.

Dianzani, M. U., jt. ed. see Gentilini, P.

Diara, Agadem L. Islam & Pan-Africanism. LC 72-91318. (Illus.). 120p. 1973. pap. 3.75 (ISBN 0-913358-04-5). Shabazz Pr.

Diara, Schavi M. Zora Neale Hurston & Jessie Redmond Fauset: Glistening Reflections from a Bygone Day. 64p. 1984. 5.50 (ISBN 0-682-40136-6). Exposition Pr FL.

Diarmid, Hugh Mac see Mac Diarmid, Hugh.

Dias, C. J. & Luckham, R., eds. Studies of Law in Social Change & Development: Lawyers in the Third World-Comparative & Developmental Perspectives. 25.00 (ISBN 0-686-35898-8); pap. 12.00 (ISBN 0-686-37202-6). Intl Ctr Law.

Dias, C. J., et al, eds. Lawyers in the Third World: Comparative & Developmental Perspectives. (Studies of Law in Social Change & Development: No. 3). (Illus.). 400p. 1983. text ed. 54.50x (ISBN 0-8419-9750-0, Africana). Holmes & Meier.

--Lawyers in the Third World: Comparative & Developmental Perspectives. 400p. 1981. 47.50 (ISBN 0-317-07367-2). Transnatl Pubs.

Dias, Luciano S., jt. auth. see Schafer, Michael F.

Dias, R. W. & Markesinis, B. S. Tort Law. (Illus.). 1984. 37.50 (ISBN 0-19-876150-3); pap. 24.95 (ISBN 0-19-876151-1). Oxford U Pr.

Dias, Susan. The Official NBC Olympic Activity Book for Kids. (gr. 2-5). 1980. pap. cancelled (ISBN 0-671-95641-8). Wanderer Bks.

Dias-Blve, Anthony. American Wine. LC 84-28631. (Illus.). 1985. 30.00 (ISBN 0-385-19191-X, Dial). Doubleday.

Diat, Louis. French Country Cooking for Americans. 1978. pap. 5.95 (ISBN 0-486-23665-X). Dover.

--French Country Cooking for Americans. 12.00 (ISBN 0-8446-5679-8). Peter Smith.

--Gourmet's Basic French Cookbook. Gourmet Magazine, ed. (Illus.). 1961. 27.50 (ISBN 0-394-54033-6). Gourmet Bks.

--Sauces, French & Famous. 1978. pap. 2.95 (ISBN 0-486-23663-3). Dover.

--Sauces: French & Famous. 12.50 (ISBN 0-8446-5677-1). Peter Smith.

Diaz. Derecho Mercantil. 300p. (Span.). 1983. pap. text ed. write for info. (ISBN 0-06-310500-4, Pub. by HarLA Mexico). Har-Row.

Diaz, Abby M., jt. auth. see Smith, Elizabeth Oakes.

Diaz, Abby M. see Smith, Elizabeth Oakes & Diaz, Abby M.

Diaz, Albert. The Airport Book: The Passenger's Guide to Major Airports in the United States & Canada. (Illus.). 1979. pap. 2.95 (ISBN 0-935866-00-0). Airport Bk Pr.

Diaz, Albert, ed. Microforms & Library Catalogs: A Reader. (Meckler Publishing's Series in Library Micrographics Management: No. 3). 1978. 20.95x (ISBN 0-913672-16-5). Microform Rev.

Diaz, Albert J. Microforms in Libraries: A Reader. (Meckler Publishing's Series in Library Micrographics Management: No. 1). (Illus.). 440p. 1975. pap. 9.95 (ISBN 0-913672-03-3). Microform Rev.

Diaz, Alfredo, tr. see Lima, Tiaga.

Diaz, Andres C. & Iorillo, Nino R. Conversacion y Controversia: Topicos de Siempre. LC 72-1757. (Illus.). 272p. 1973. text ed. 19.95 (ISBN 0-13-171934-3). P-H.

Diaz, Arcadio. Conversacion con Jose Luis Gonzalez. (Norte Ser.). 160p. 1977. pap. 3.50 (ISBN 0-940238-11-X). Ediciones Huracan.

Diaz, Arenas A., jt. ed. see McMahon, T. A.

Diaz, Eva S. Manual de Referencia Para la Oficina. (Span.). 1977. text ed. 4.80 (ISBN 0-538-22250-6, V25). SW Pub.

Diaz, J. & Ramos, I., eds. Formalization of Programming Concepts: Proceedings. (Lecture Notes in Computer Sciences Ser.: Vol. 107). 478p. 1981. pap. 26.50 (ISBN 0-387-10699-5). Springer-Verlag.

Diaz, J. B., ed. Alexander Weinstein Selecta. 629p. 1978. text ed. 53.95 (ISBN 0-273-08411-9). Pitman Pub MA.

Diaz, J. G. & Pai, S. I., eds. Fluid Dynamics & Applied Mathematics. (Illus.). 218p. 1962. 57.75 (ISBN 0-677-10110-4). Gordon.

Diaz, J I. Nonlinear Partial Differential Equations & Free Boundaries Vol. 1: Elliptic Equations. (Research Notes in Mathematics Ser.: No. 106). 250p. 1985. pap. text ed. write for info. (ISBN 0-273-08572-7). Pitman Pub MA.

Diaz, Janet. Ana Maria Matute. LC 70-125268. (World Authors Ser.). 1982. Repr. of 1971 ed. lib. bdg. 15.95 (ISBN 0-8290-1101-3). Irvington.

--Miguel Delibes. (World Authors Ser.). 1971. lib. bdg. 15.95 (ISBN 0-8290-0119-0). Irvington.

--Miguel Delibes. (World Authors Ser.). lib. bdg. 16.95 (ISBN 0-8057-2264-5, Twayne). G K Hall.

Diaz, Janet W. The Major Themes of Existentialism in the Works of Jose Ortega y Gasset. (Studies in the Romance Languages & Literatures: No. 94). 200p. 1970. pap. 11.00x (ISBN 0-8078-9094-4). U of NC Pr.

Diaz, Joaquin & Viana, Luis D. Romances Tradicionales de Castilla y Leon. (Spanish Ser: No. 7). 162p. 1981. 12.50x (ISBN 0-942260-22-8). Hispanic Seminary.

Diaz, John T., tr. see Benteen, John.

Diaz, Jorge & De Gonzalez, Nelly, eds. La Biblia lo Dice. (Illus.). 120p. (Span.). 1984. spiral bdg. 3.95 (ISBN 0-311-11453-9). Casa Bautista.

Diaz, Jorge E. Guia De Estudios Sobre Doctrina Cristiana. (Guias De Estudio). 88p. pap. 4.50 (ISBN 0-311-43500-9). Casa Bautista.

Diaz, Jorge E., jt. auth. see Crane, James D.

Diaz, Jorge E., tr. see Charley, Julian.

Diaz, Jorge E., tr. see Coleman, Lucien E., Jr.

Diaz, Jose Luis Martinez see Thomas, I. D., et al.

Diaz, Luis F. & Savage, George M. Resource Recovery from Municipal Solid Wastes, 2 vols. Incl. Vol. I. Primary Processing. 176p. 55.00 (ISBN 0-8493-5613-X); Vol. II. Final Processing. 192p (ISBN 0-8493-5614-8). 1982. 55.00 ea. CRC Pr.

Diaz, Manuel G. Neoclassicals in Puerto Rico. (Puerto Rico Ser.). 1979. lib. bdg. 59.95 (ISBN 0-8490-2975-9). Gordon Pr.

Diaz, May N. Tonala: Conservatism, Responsibility & Authority in a Mexican Town. LC 66-14566. 1966. 23.00x (ISBN 0-520-00321-7). U of Cal Pr.

Diaz, Modesto, jt. auth. see Aguera, Helen.

Diaz, Myriam, tr. see Charley, Julian.

Diaz, Olimpia, tr. see Balado, Jose L.

Diaz, Olimpia, tr. see McPhee, John.

Diaz, Olimpia, tr. see Norquist, Marilyn.

Diaz, Olimpia, tr. see Ruhnke, Robert.

Diaz, Olimpia, tr. see Tickle, John.

Diaz, Olimpia, Sr., tr. see Gonzalez-Balado, Jose.

Diaz, Olimpia, Sr., tr. see Tickle, John.

Diaz Alejandro, Carlos F. Essays on the Economic History of the Argentine Republic. new ed. LC 70-118727. (Economic Growth Center Pubns.). (Illus.). 1970. 50.00x (ISBN 0-300-01193-8). Yale U Pr.

Diaz Alejandro, Carlos F., jt. auth. see Bacha, Edmar L.

Diaz-Briquets, Sergio. The Health Revolution in Cuba. (Institute of Latin American Studies Special Publication Ser.). 245p. 1983. text ed. 19.95x (ISBN 0-292-75071-4). U of Tex Pr.

--International Migration Within Latin America & the Caribbean: An Overview Paper. LC 81-69418. 121p. 1982. pap. 9.95x (ISBN 0-913256-58-7). Ctr Migration.

Diaz-Cobo, Oscar. Bare Kills. (Illus.). 160p. 1982. pap. 10.00 (ISBN 0-87364-253-8). Paladin Pr.

--Unarmed Against the Knife. (Illus.). 88p. 1981. pap. 8.00 (ISBN 0-87364-243-0). Paladin Pr.

Diaz De Gamez. The Unconquered Knight: A Chronicle of the Deeds of Don Pero Nino. Evans, Joan, tr. LC 78-63494. Repr. of 1928 ed. 27.50 (ISBN 0-404-17143-5). AMS Pr.

Diaz De Grana, Lydia. Los Objetivos Educacionales: Criterios Basicos para la Evaluacion del Aprendizaje. LC 76-8191. 92p. (Orig., Span.). 1976. pap. 3.75 (ISBN 0-8477-2721-1). U of PR Pr.

Diaz Del Castillo, Bernal. Conquest of New Spain. Cohen, John M., tr. (Classics Ser.). (Orig.). (YA) (gr. 9 up). 1963. pap. 4.95 (ISBN 0-14-044123-9). Penguin.

--Discovery & Conquest of Mexico. 478p. 1956. pap. 10.95 (ISBN 0-374-50384-2). FS&G.

Diaz-Diocaretz, Myriam. The Transforming Power of Language: The Poetry of Adrienne Rich. v, 75p. (Orig.). 1984. pap. 10.00x (ISBN 90-6194-394-9, Pub. by Hes Pubs Netherlands). Benjamins North AM.

Diaz-Guerrero, R. Psychology of the Mexican: Culture & Personality. LC 74-23309. (Texas Pan American Ser.). 193p. 1975. 16.95x (ISBN 0-292-77512-1); pap. 7.95x (ISBN 0-292-76430-8). U of Tex Pr.

Diaz-Guerrero, R., jt. auth. see Spielberger, C. D.

Diaz-Guerrero, R. & Holtzman, W. H., eds. Personality Development in Two Cultures. (Human Development: Vol. 22, No. 5). (Illus.). 1979. pap. 11.50 (ISBN 3-8055-0120-X). S Karger.

Diaz-Guerrero, Rogelio, ed. see Figueroa, Richard A. & Ruiz, Nadeen T.

Diaz-Guerrero, Rogelio, jt. ed. see Spielberger, Charles D.

Diaz Plaja, Fernando. La Sociedad Espanola: Desde 1500 Hasta Nuestros Dias. 5.00 (ISBN 0-8477-3116-2); pap. 3.75 (ISBN 0-8477-3117-0). U of PR Pr.

Diaz-Plaja, Guillermo. A History of Spanish Literature. Harter, Hugh A., tr. from Span. LC 70-124524. 1971. 27.00x (ISBN 0-8147-1750-0). NYU Pr.

Diaz Quinones, Arcadio. El Almuerzo en la Hierba. LC 81-68088. (La Nave Y El Puerto Ser.). 174p. (Span.). 1982. pap. 5.95 (ISBN 0-940238-42-X). Ediciones Huracan.

Diaz-Retg, E. Diccionario de Dificultades de la Lengua Espanola. 344p. (Span.). 1963. 18.95 (ISBN 0-686-92537-8, S-37576). French & Eur.

Diaz-Rivera, Maria. Refranes Usados en Puerto Rico. LC 82-21680. (Coleccion Uprex, 64: Serie Lengua y Folklore). viii, 144p. (Orig., Span.). 1984. pap. 3.00 (ISBN 0-8477-0064-X). U of PR Pr.

Diaz-Rivera, Tulio. Hacia Donde Vamos?: Radiografia del Presente Cubano. LC 84-73320. (Coleccion Cuba y sus Jueces). 144p. (Orig., Span.). 1985. pap. 5.00 (ISBN 0-89729-367-3). Ediciones.

Diaz-Royo, Antonio. Loas-Loas. (De Orilla a Orilla Ser.). (Illus.). 16p. 1978. pap. 3.00 (ISBN 0-940238-03-9). Ediciones Huracan.

Diaz Valcarcel, Emilio. Schemes in the Month of March. Sebastiani, Nancy A., tr. from Span. LC 76-45296. Orig. Title: Figuraciones en el mes de marzo. 1979. lib. bdg. 18.00x (ISBN 0-916950-06-9); pap. text ed. 11.00x (ISBN 0-916950-05-0). Biling Rev-Pr.

Diaz-Valcarcel, Emilio. La Vision del Mundo en la Novela: Tiempo de silencio, de Luis Martin-Santos. 98p. (Orig., Spanish.). 1982. pap. 5.00 (ISBN 0-8477-3506-0). U of PR Pr.

Diaz Viana, Luis see Diaz, Joaquin & Viana, Luis D.

Diaz Zayas, Carmen E. & Benitez de Avila, Crucita. Practicas de Oficina. (Span.). 1978. text ed. 5.55 (ISBN 0-538-22890-3, V89). SW Pub.

Dib, Albert. Forms & Agreements for Architects, Engineers & Contractors, 3 vols. LC 75-37971. 1977. 235.00 (ISBN 0-87632-215-1). Boardman.

Dib, Mohammad. Omneros. Lettieri, Carol & Vangelisti, Paul, trs. 1978. pap. 3.00 sewn in wrappers (ISBN 0-88031-050-2). Invisible-Red Hill.

Dib, Mohammed. Who Remembers the Sea. Tremaine, Louis, tr. from Fr. LC 85-50529. 122p. 1985. 18.00 (ISBN 0-89410-444-6); pap. 8.00 (ISBN 0-89410-445-4). Three Continents.

Di Bartolo, B., ed. Luminescence of Inorganic Solids. LC 78-16681. 720p. 1978. 110.00x (ISBN 0-306-40034-0, Plenum Pr). Plenum Pub.

DiBartolo, Baldassare. Optical Interactions in Solids. LC 67-31206. 260p. 1968. 32.50 (ISBN 0-471-21276-8). Krieger.

Di Bartolo, Baldassare & Powell, Richard C. Phonons & Resonances in Solids. LC 75-35691. (Illus.). pap. 133.30 (ISBN 0-317-09219-7, 2012430). Bks Demand UMI.

Di Bartolo, Baldassare, ed. Collective Excitations in Solids. (NATO ASI Series B, Physics: Vol. 88). 711p. 1983. 95.00x (ISBN 0-306-41186-5, Plenum Press). Plenum Pub.

--Energy Transfer Processes in Condensed Matter, Vol. 114. (NATO ASI Ser.: Series B, Physics). 724p. 1985. 105.00x (ISBN 0-306-41826-6, Plenum Pr). Plenum Pub.

--Optical Properties of Ions in Solids. LC 75-1190. (NATO ASI Series B, Physics: Vol. 8). 490p. 1975. 75.00x (ISBN 0-306-35708-9, Plenum Pr). Plenum Pub.

--Radiationless Processes. LC 80-21961. (NATO ASI Series B, Physical Sciences: Vol. 62). 565p. 1981. 85.00 (ISBN 0-306-40577-6, Plenum Pr). Plenum Pub.

--Spectroscopy of the Excited State. LC 75-38526. (NATO ASI Series B, Physics: Vol. 12). 416p. 1976. 62.50x (ISBN 0-306-35712-7, Plenum Pr). Plenum Pub.

DiBattista, Maria. Virginia Woolf's Major Novels: The Fables of Anon. LC 79-18422. 1980. 27.00x (ISBN 0-300-02402-9). Yale U Pr.

DiBattista, William J., jt. ed. see Kaldor, George.

Dibb, Paul. The Soviet Union: The Incomplete Superpower. LC 85-8552. 300p. 1986. 35.00x (ISBN 0-252-01260-7). U of Ill Pr.

Dibb, Paul, ed. Australia's External Relations in the 1980s: The Interaction of Economic, Political & Strategic Factors. LC 83-40165. 224p. 1983. 25.00 (ISBN 0-312-06120-X). St Martin.

Dibben, A. A. The Cowdray Archives, Pt. 11. 234p. 1964. 25.00x (ISBN 0-686-75538-3, Pub. by W Sussex Rec off). State Mutual Bk.

Dibben, Martin J. Chemosystematics of the Lichen Genus Pertusaria in North America North of Mexico. 200p. 1980. 22.50 (ISBN 0-89326-036-3). Milwaukee Pub Mus.

Dibbert, Michael T. & Wichern, Frank B. Growth Groups. 160p. (Orig.). 1985. pap. 5.95 (ISBN 0-310-23121-3, Pub. by Minister Res Lib). Zondervan.

Dibble, Charles E. Codex en Cruz, 2 vols. 148p. 1981. 45.00x (ISBN 0-87480-124-9). U of Utah Pr.

Dibble, Charles E., jt. auth. see Anderson, Arthur J.

Dibble, Charles E., tr. see Leon-Portilla, Miguel.

Dibble, Charles E., tr. see Sahagun, Bernardino de.

Dibble, David S. & Kent, C. Day. A Preliminary Survey of the Fontenelle Reservoir, Wyoming. (Upper Colorado Ser: No. 7). Repr. of 1962 ed. 18.00 (ISBN 0-685-91138-1). AMS Pr.

Dibble, David S., jt. auth. see Day, Kent C.

Dibble, Ernest F. Young Prophet Niebuhr: Reinhold Niebuhr's Early Search for Social Justice. 1978. pap. text ed. 14.00 (ISBN 0-8191-0377-2). U Pr of Amer.

Dibble, J. Birney. Pan. 256p. 1985. pap. 2.95 (ISBN 0-8439-2238-9, Leisure Bks). Dorchester Pub Co.

Dibble, Jerry A. The Pythia's Drunken Song. (International Archives of the History of Ideas, Series Minor: No. 19). 1978. pap. 9.00 (ISBN 90-247-2011-7, Pub. by Martinus Nijhoff Netherlands). Kluwer Academic.

Dibble, L. Grace. Return Tickets to Southern Europe. 1981. 25.00x (ISBN 0-7223-1423-X, Pub. by Stockwell). State Mutual Bk.

Dibble, Peter, jt. auth. see Puckett, Dale.

Dibble, Roy F. Albion W. Tourgee, Chronicler of the Reconstruction. LC 68-16287. 1968. Repr. of 1921 ed. 21.50x (ISBN 0-8046-0109-7, Pub. by Kennikat). Assoc Faculty Pr.

Dibble, Vernon K. The Legacy of Albion Small. LC 74-16686. (Heritage of Sociology Ser). x, 256p. 1975. 20.00x (ISBN 0-226-14520-4). U of Chicago Pr.

Dibbs, Owen & Pereira, Patricia. Promoting Sales: A Systematic Approach to Benefit Selling; an ILO Programmed Book. 1976. 8.55 (ISBN 92-2-101393-6). Intl Labour Office.

Dibbs, Owen & Periera, Patricia. Promoting Sales: A Systematic Approach to Benefit Selling. ix, 248p. (An ILO Programmed Book). 1976. pap. 8.55 (ISBN 92-2-101393-6, ILO30, ILO). Unipub.

Dibden, Arthur J., ed. Academic Deanship in American Colleges & Universities. LC 67-22024. 283p. 1968. 8.95x (ISBN 0-8093-0302-7). S Ill U Pr.

Dibdin, Charles. The Professional Life of Mr. Dibdin, Written by Himself, 4 vols. in 2. LC 80-2272. Repr. of 1803 ed. Set. 150.00 (ISBN 0-404-18835-4). Vol. 1 (ISBN 0-404-18836-2). Vol. 2 (ISBN 0-404-18837-0). AMS Pr.

Dibdin, Thomas F. Bibliographical, Antiquarian, & Picturesque Tour in France & Germany, 3 Vols. 2nd ed. LC 76-111768. Repr. of 1829 ed. Set. 80.00 (ISBN 0-404-02130-1). AMS Pr.

Dibdin, Thomas J. Reminiscences of Thomas Dibdin, 2 Vols. LC 70-111769. Repr. of 1827 ed. Set. 67.50 (ISBN 0-404-02124-7). AMS Pr.

Dibelius, Martin. Fresh Approach to the New Testament & Early Christian Literature. LC 78-32096. 1979. Repr. of 1936 ed. lib. bdg. 24.75x (ISBN 0-8371-4219-9, DINT). Greenwood.

--From Tradition to Gospel. Wooff, Bertram L., tr. 328p. 1971. 27.50 (ISBN 0-227-67752-8). Attic Pr.

--James. Koester, Helmut, ed. Willims, Michael A., tr. LC 74-80428. (Hermeneia: a Critical & Historical Commentary on the Bible). 252p. 1975. 24.95 (ISBN 0-8006-6006-4, 20-6006). Fortress.

Dibelius, Martin & Conzelmann, Hans. The Pastoral Epistles. Koester, Helmut, ed. Buttolph, Philip & Yarbro, Adela, trs. from Ger. LC 71-157549. (Hermeneia: a Critical & Historical Commentary on the Bible). 1972. 19.95 (ISBN 0-8006-6002-1, 20-6002). Fortress.

Dibella, Geoffrey A., et al. Handbook of Partial Hospitalization. LC 81-12231. 450p. 1982. 32.50 (ISBN 0-87630-270-3). Brunner-Mazel.

Dibello, C., jt. ed. see Offord, R. E.

DiBello, P., jt. auth. see Amery, H.

DiBenedetto, A. T. The Structure & Properties of Materials. LC 67-11602. pap. 138.50 (ISBN 0-317-11001-2, 2004413). Bks Demand UMI.

DiBerardino, Marie, jt. ed. see Danielli, James F.

DiBernard, Barbara. Alchemy & Finnegans Wake. LC 79-22809. 1980. 49.50x (ISBN 0-87395-388-6); pap. 14.95x (ISBN 0-87395-429-7). State U NY Pr.

Dibert, Ken. Photography: Three Generations. LC 76-15520. 9.95 (ISBN 0-912216-11-5). Angel Pr.

DiBiaggio, John A., jt. auth. see Cooper, Thomas M.

Di'Bil b. 'Ali. Di'bil b. 'Ali: The Life and Writings of an Early 'Abbasid Poet. Zolondek, Leon, ed. & tr. LC 61-6553. 196p. 1961. 18.00x (ISBN 0-8131-1061-0). U Pr of Ky.

Dible, Donald. Business Startup Basics. 1981. text ed. 17.95 (ISBN 0-8359-0598-5); pap. text ed. 12.95 (ISBN 0-8359-0597-7). Reston.

--How to Plan & Finance a Growing Business. 1981. pap. 12.95 (ISBN 0-8359-2966-3). Reston.

--Small Businesss Success Secrets. 1981. pap. 10.00 (ISBN 0-8359-7010-8). Reston.

--Up Your Own Organization. rev. ed. 1985. text ed. 24.95 (ISBN 0-8359-8087-1); pap. 17.95 (ISBN 0-8359-8086-3). Reston.

--Up Your Own Organization! A Handbook on How to Start & Finance a New Business. 1981. pap. 12.00 (ISBN 0-8359-8088-X); text ed. 18.00 case O.P. Reston.

--What Everyone Should Know about Patents, Trademarks, & Copyright. LC 78-6780. 1981. text ed. 14.95 (ISBN 0-8359-8641-1); pap. 12.95 (ISBN 0-8359-8640-3). Reston.

Dible, Donald M., ed. Build a Better You-Starting Now, Vol. 1. LC 79-63064. 272p. 1979. 12.95 (ISBN 0-88205-200-4). Showcase Fairfield.

--Build a Better You-Starting Now, Vol. 2. LC 79-63064. 256p. 1980. 12.95 (ISBN 0-88205-201-2). Showcase Fairfield.

--Build a Better You-Starting Now, Vol. 3. LC 79-63064. 256p. 1980. 12.95 (ISBN 0-88205-202-0). Showcase Fairfield.

--Build a Better You-Starting Now, Vol. 4. LC 79-63064. 256p. 1980. 12.95 (ISBN 0-88205-203-9). Showcase Fairfield.

--Build a Better You-Starting Now, Vol. 5. LC 79-63064. 256p. 1980. 12.95 (ISBN 0-88205-204-7). Showcase Fairfield.

--Build a Better You-Starting Now, Vol. 6. LC 79-63064. 256p. 1980. 12.95 (ISBN 0-88205-205-5). Showcase Fairfield.

--Build a Better You-Starting Now, Vol. 7. LC 79-63064. 256p. 1980. 12.95 (ISBN 0-88205-206-3). Showcase Fairfield.

--Build a Better You-Starting Now, Vol. 8. LC 79-63064. 256p. 1981. 12.95 (ISBN 0-88205-207-1). Showcase Fairfield.

--Build a Better You-Starting Now, Vol. 9. LC 79-63064. 256p. 1982. 12.95 (ISBN 0-88205-208-X). Showcase Fairfield.

--Build a Better You-Starting Now, Vol. 10. LC 79-63064. 256p. 1982. 12.95 (ISBN 0-88205-209-8). Showcase Fairfield.

--Build a Better You-Starting Now, Vol. 11. LC 79-63064. 256p. 1983. 12.95 (ISBN 0-88205-210-1). Showcase Fairfield.

--Build a Better You-Starting Now, Vol. 12. LC 79-63043. 256p. 1983. 12.95 (ISBN 0-88205-211-X). Showcase Fairfield.

Dible, Henry. Pathology of Limb Ischaema. LC 67-27239. (Illus.). 110p. 1967. 9.00 (ISBN 0-87527-030-1). Green.

Diblos, Pablo E., et al. Atlas of Nuclear Medicine, Vol. 4, Bone. LC 74-81820. pap. 52.30 (ISBN 0-317-07791-0, 2016659). Bks Demand UMI.

Dibner, A. S., jt. auth. see Dibner, S. S.

Dibner, Bern. Heralds of Science. 1969. pap. 7.95x (ISBN 0-262-54004-5). MIT Pr.

--Heralds of Science. rev. ed. LC 80-25340. (Illus.). 96p. 1981. 14.95 (ISBN 0-88202-191-5); pap. 8.95 (ISBN 0-88202-192-3). Watson Pub Intl.

Dibner, D. R. & Dibner-Dunlap, A. Building Additions Design. 256p. 1985. 39.95 (ISBN 0-07-016761-3). McGraw.

Dibner, Martin. The Devil's Paintbrush. LC 82-45460. 360p. 1983. 16.95 (ISBN 0-385-15666-9). Doubleday.

Dibner, Martin, ed. see Detmer, Josephine & Pancoast, Patricia.

Dibner, S. S. & Dibner, A. S. Integration or Segregation for the Physically Handicapped Child? 228p. 1973. 25.75x (ISBN 0-398-02817-6). C C Thomas.

Dibner-Dunlap, A., jt. auth. see Dibner, D. R.

Dibona, Joseph, ed. One Teacher, One School: The Adam Reports on Indigenous Education in 19th Century India. 1983. 27.50x (ISBN 0-8364-1075-0, Pub. by Biblia Impex). South Asia Bks.

Di Brandi, Herman A. Introduction to Christian Doctrine. 128p. (Orig.). (gr. 11-12). 1976. pap. 4.95 (ISBN 0-8192-1194-X). Morehouse.

Di Brino, Nicholas. The History of the Morris Park Racecourse & the Morris Family. (Illus.). 48p. 1977. pap. 3.95 (ISBN 0-686-38455-5). Bronx County.

DiCaprio, Nicholas S. Adjustment: Fulfilling Human Potentials. (Illus.). 1980. text ed. 24.95 (ISBN 0-13-004101-7). P-H.

--Personality Theories Guides to Human Nature. 2nd ed. LC 82-15745. 564p. 1983. text ed. 32.95 (ISBN 0-03-059094-9). HR&W.

DiCapua, Rinaldo. Vologeso Re De Parti. Brown, Howard M., ed. LC 76-20970. (Italian Opera, 1640-1770 Ser.: Vol. 38). (Libretto by G. E. Luccarelli). 1978. lib. bdg. 77.00 (ISBN 0-8240-2641-1). Garland Pub.

DiCara, Leo V., ed. Limbic & Autonomic Nervous Systems Research. LC 74-17327. (Illus.). 441p. 1975. 35.00x (ISBN 0-306-30786-3, Plenum Pr). Plenum Pub.

DiCarlo, Joseph. Following Christ. (Faith & Life Ser.). (Illus.). 142p. (Orig.). (gr. 6). 1985. pap. 4.95 (ISBN 0-89870-065-5). Ignatius Pr.

DiCarlo, Louis M., et al. Speech After Laryngectomy. (Special Education & Rehabilitation Monograph: No. 1). (Illus.). 1956. 8.95x (ISBN 0-8156-2016-0). Syracuse U Pr.

Dicaro, Deborah. Patents. Spigai, Frances, ed. LC 82-72565. (Database Search Aids Ser.: Vol. 6). 174p. (Orig.). 1983. pap. 25.00 (ISBN 0-939920-08-5). Database Serv.

Dicaro, Deborah, ed. see Snow, Bonnie.

Di Carpegna, N. Firearms in the Princes Odescalchi Collection in Rome. (Illus.). 201p. (Eng.). 1976. Repr. of 1969 ed. 20.00 (ISBN 0-686-14971-8). Arma Pr.

Di Castri, F., et al, eds. Mediterranean-Type Shrublands: Ecosystems of the World Ser. (Vol. 11). 644p. 1981. 127.75 (ISBN 0-444-41858-X). Elsevier.

Dice, Kathy. From the Heart. (Orig.). 1984. pap. 1.95 (ISBN 0-931085-00-4). Parsons Pr.

Dice, Lee R. Man's Nature & Nature's Man: The Ecology of Human Communities. LC 72-9607. 329p. 1973. Repr. of 1955 ed. lib. bdg. 20.75x (ISBN 0-8371-6594-6, DIMN). Greenwood.

Di Certo, Joseph. The Wall People: In Search of a Home. LC 84-21535. (Illus.). 168p. (gr. 3 up). 1985. 11.95 (ISBN 0-689-31090-0). Atheneum.

DiCerto, Joseph J. Looking into TV. LC 82-42874. (Illus.). 96p. (gr. 4-6). 1983. PLB 8.79 (ISBN 0-671-45948-1). Messner.

Di Cesare, Mario. The Altar & the City: A Reading of Virgil's Aeneid. LC 74-3436. 278p. 1974. 26.00x (ISBN 0-231-03830-5); pap. 13.00x (ISBN 0-231-03831-3). Columbia U Pr.

DiCesare, Mario, ed. George Herbert & the Seventeenth Century Religious Poets. (Norton Critical Editions). 401p. 1978. pap. text ed. 8.95x (ISBN 0-393-09254-2). Norton.

Di Cesare, Mario A., jt. auth. see Mignani, Rigo.

Di Cesare, Mario A. & Fogel, Ephim, eds. A Concordance to the Poems of Ben Jonson. LC 78-59630. (Concordances Ser). 904p. 1978. 62.50x (ISBN 0-8014-1217-X). Cornell U Pr.

Di Cesare, Mario A. & Mignani, Rigo, eds. A Concordance to the Complete Writings of George Herbert. LC 76-56642. (Cornell Concordances Ser.). 1344p. 1977. 67.50x (ISBN 0-8014-1106-8). Cornell U Pr.

Di Cesare, Mario A., tr. see Ruiz, Juan.

Dicey, A. V. England's Case Against Home Rule. 324p. 1984. Repr. of 1886 ed. 42.00x (ISBN 0-85546-183-7, Pub. by Richmond Pub England). State Mutual Bk.

Dicey, Albert V. Introduction to the Study of the Law of the Constitution. LC 81-82778. 586p. 1982. 15.00 (ISBN 0-86597-002-5, Liberty Clas); pap. 7.00 (ISBN 0-86597-003-3). Liberty Fund.

--Lectures on the Relation Between Law & Public Opinion in England, During the Nineteenth Century. 2nd ed. LC 75-41074. Repr. of 1914 ed. 42.50 (ISBN 0-404-14532-9). AMS Pr.

--Lectures on the Relation Between Law & Public Opinion in England, During the Nineteenth Century. LC 81-2391. (Social Science Classics Ser.). 506p. 1981. pap. 19.95 write for info. (ISBN 0-87855-869-1). Transaction Bk.

--The Privy Council. LC 79-1625. 1981. Repr. of 1887 ed. 17.60 (ISBN 0-88355-930-7). Hyperion Conn.

--Thoughts on the Union Between England & Scotland. LC 77-114510. 1971. Repr. of 1920 ed. lib. bdg. 19.00x (ISBN 0-8371-4785-9, DIUE). Greenwood.

Dicey, E. M., tr. see Boutmy, Emile.

Dicey, Edward. Six Months in the Federal States. text ed. 27.25 (ISBN 0-8369-9221-0, 9075). Ayer Co Pubs.

Dicharry, Warren F. Greek Without Grief: An Outline Guide to New Testament Greek. rev ed. 1985. 8.95. Vincentian.

Dichele, Ernest M., et al. Massachusetts Corporate Tax Manual. LC 82-73441. xvii, 249p. Date not set. price not set. Mass Bar Assn.

Dichgans, J., ed. see International Congress on Physiological Sciences, 25th, Munich, 1971.

Dichgans, J., et al, eds. Cerebellar Functions. (Proceedings in Life Sciences Ser.). (Illus.). 350p. 1985. 48.50 (ISBN 0-387-13728-9). Springer-Verlag.

Di Chiara, G. & Gessa, G. L., eds. GABA & the Basal Ganglia. (Advances in Biochemical Psychopharmacology Ser.: Vol. 30). 252p. 1981. text ed. 41.00 (ISBN 0-89004-752-9). Raven.

--Glutamate As a Neurotransmitter. (Advances in Biochemical Psychopharmacology Ser.: Vol. 27). 464p. 1981. text ed. 71.00 (ISBN 0-89004-420-1). Raven.

DiChiara, James, jt. auth. see Conroy, Kathleen.

DiChiara, Robert. Hard-Boiled: Three Tough Cases for the Private Eye with Smarts. LC 84-48324. 176p. 1985. pap. 7.95 (ISBN 0-87923-554-3). Godine.

Di Chiro, Giovanni. Atlas of Detailed Normal Pneumoencephalographic Anatomy. 2nd ed. (Illus.). 360p. 1971. photocopy ed. 52.50x (ISBN 0-398-00447-1). C C Thomas.

Di Chiro, Giovanni, et al. Atlas of Pathologic Pneumoencephalographic Anatomy. (Illus.). 594p. 1967. photocopy ed. 115.00x (ISBN 0-398-00448-X). C C Thomas.

Dichter, Ernest. Packaging: The Sixth Sense. LC 73-76439. 160p. 1975. 22.50 (ISBN 0-8436-1103-0). Van Nos Reinhold.

--The Strategy of Desire. Assael, Henry & Craig, C. Samuel, eds. LC 84-46034. (The History of Advertising Ser.). 314p. 1985. lib. bdg. 35.00 (ISBN 0-8240-6728-2). Garland Pub.

--Total Self-Knowledge. LC 75-37981. 280p. 1976. pap. 4.95 (ISBN 0-8128-1919-5). Stein & Day.

Dichter, H. Handbook of American Sheet Music, 2 Pts. (Illus.). pap. 12.50 ea. (ISBN 0-87556-077-6). Saifer.

Dichter, Harry & Shapiro, Elliot. Early American Sheet Music 1768-1889. LC 77-70454. (Illus.). 1977. pap. 7.95 (ISBN 0-486-23364-2). Dover.

--Handbook of Early American Sheet Music: 1768-1889. (Illus.). 17.25 (ISBN 0-8446-5570-8). Peter Smith.

Dichtl, et al. Air-Cooled Aluminium Cylinder Heads. 1983. 30.00 (ISBN 0-9911000-2-6, Pub. by Aluminium W Germany). Heyden.

Dichtl, Rudolph J., jt. auth. see Jackson, John P.

DiCicco, Philip P., jt. auth. see Krutza, William J.

Dicicco, Philip P., jt. auth. see Krutza, William J.

DiCicco, Philip P., jt. auth. see Krutza, William J.

Dicicco, Philip P.; jt. auth. see Krutza, William J.

Dick, A. Emmy Noether: 1882-1935. (Supplement Ser.: No. 13). 72p. (Ger.). 1970. pap. 13.95x (ISBN 0-8176-0519-3). Birkhauser.

Dick, Alexandra, tr. see Lagerkvist, Par.

Dick, Aliki L. Padeia Through Laughter: Jonson's Aristophanic Appeal to Human Intelligence. LC 73-84787. (Studies in English Literature: No. 76). xi, 141p. (Orig.). 1974. pap. text ed. 17.60x (ISBN 90-2792-714-6). Mouton.

Dick, Auguste. Emmy Noether (1882-1935) 192p. 1980. pap. 14.95x (ISBN 0-8176-3019-8). Birkhauser.

Dick, B., jt. auth. see Dunphy, D. C.

Dick, Bernard F. The Anatomy of Film. LC 76-28140. 1978. pap. text ed. 12.95 (ISBN 0-312-03395-8). St Martin.

--Billy Wilder. (Filmmakers Ser.). 1980. lib. bdg. 13.50 (ISBN 0-8057-9274-0, Twayne). G K Hall.

--The Hellenism of Mary Renault. LC 71-188696. (Cross Currents-Modern Critiques Ser.). 156p. 1972. 6.95 (ISBN 0-8093-0576-3). S Ill U Pr.

--Hellman in Hollywood. LC 81-72044. (Illus.). 220p. 1982. 22.50 (ISBN 0-8386-3140-1). Fairleigh Dickinson.

--Joseph L. Mankiewicz. (Film Ser.). 172p. 1983. lib. bdg. 19.95 (ISBN 0-8057-9291-0, Twayne). G K Hall.

--The Star Spangled Screen: The American World War II Film. LC 85-9205. 304p. 1985. 26.00 (ISBN 0-8131-1531-0). U Pr of Ky.

Dick, Bernard F., ed. Dark Victory. LC 81-50822. (Wisconsin-Warner Bros. Screenplay Ser.). (Illus.). 216p. (Orig.). 1981. 17.50x (ISBN 0-299-08760-3); pap. 6.95 (ISBN 0-299-08764-6). U of Wis Pr.

Dick, Bruce M., jt. auth. see Illingworth, Charles.

Dick, Carson W., jt. auth. see Buchanan, Watson W.

Dick, Dancing. My Mind is an Ocean. LC 85-11333. 100p. 1985. Repr. of 1973 ed. lib. bdg. 19.95x (ISBN 0-89370-881-X). Borgo Pr.

Dick, David. All Modern Slavery Indefensible: Intended for All Places Where Slavery Does Exist. LC 72-6533. (Black Heritage Library Collection Ser.). 1972. Repr. of 1836 ed. 21.00 (ISBN 0-8369-9165-6). Ayer Co Pubs.

Dick, Donald, intro. by see Hawker, Margot, et al.

Dick, E., et al. GUIDE: Gathering up Information for Developmental Education for the TMR. 1979. spiral bound 18.95 (ISBN 0-87804-358-6). Mafex.

Dick, E. A., jt. auth. see Snell, W. H.

Dick, Ernst S., jt. ed. see Jankowsky, Kurt.

Dick, Esther A., jt. auth. see Snell, Walter.

Dick, Everett. Conquering the Great American Desert: Nebraska. LC 74-17591. (Nebraska State Historical Publications Ser.: Vol. 27). 456p. 1975. 10.95 (ISBN 0-686-18150-6). Nebraska Hist.

--The Lure of the Land: A Social History of the Public Lands from the Articles of Confederation to the New Deal. LC 66-13015. (Illus.). xiv, 413p. 1970. 28.95x (ISBN 0-8032-0725-5). U of Nebr Pr.

--The Sod-House Frontier, 1854-1890: A Social History of the Northern Plains from the Creation of Kansas & Nebraska to the Admission of the Dakotas. LC 78-24204. (Illus.). xxii, 612p. 1979. pap. 12.95 (ISBN 0-8032-6551-4, BB 700, Bison). U of Nebr Pr.

--Tales of the Frontier: From Lewis & Clark to the Last Roundup. LC 62-14664. (Illus.). x, 390p. 1963. 27.50x (ISBN 0-8032-0038-2); pap. 7.50 (ISBN 0-8032-5744-9, BB 539, Bison). U of Nebr Pr.

--Vanguards of the Frontier: A Social History of the Northern Plains & Rocky Mountains from the Fur Traders to the Sod Busters. LC 41-6157. (Illus.). xvii, 574p. 1965. pap. 9.95 (ISBN 0-8032-5048-7, BB 189, Bison). U of Nebr Pr.

Dick, George. Immunisation. (Illus.). 1978. text ed. 12.50x (ISBN 0-906141-10-9, Pub. by Update Pubns England). Kluwer Academic.

--Immunisation. 160p. 1978. 40.00x (ISBN 0-906141-10-9, Pub. by MTP Pr); pap. 25.00x (ISBN 0-906141-03-6). State Mutual Bk.

--Immunological Aspects of Infectious Diseases. (Illus.). 536p. 1979. text ed. 32.00 (ISBN 0-8391-1373-0). Univ Park.

Dick, Gerry, ed. Paradise Plus: A Selection of Stories from Air Niugini's in-Flight Magazine. LC 79-89558. (Illus.). 144p. 1980. 12.95 (ISBN 0-85807-044-8, 3028, Pub. by Pacific Pubns Australia). Australia N U P.

Dick, Ginger, jt. auth. see Smith, Richard D.

Dick, Harold G. & Robinson, Douglas H. The Golden Age of the Great Passenger Airships, Graf Zeppelin & Hindenburg. LC 84-600298. (Illus.). 200p. 1985. 24.95 (ISBN 0-87474-364-8, DIGA). Smithsonian.

Dick, James C. Violence & Oppression. LC 78-2235. 224p. 1979. 17.00x (ISBN 0-8203-0446-8). U of Ga Pr.

Dick, James C., ed. see Burns, Robert.

Dick, John H. Other Edens: The Sketchbook of an Artist Naturalist. LC 79-67270. (Illus.). 1979. 19.95 (ISBN 0-8159-6412-9). Devin.

Dick, Kay. Ivy & Stevie. (Illus.). 96p. (Orig.). 1983. pap. 5.95 (ISBN 0-8052-8136-3, Pub. by Allison & Busby England). Schocken.

--The Shelf. 109p. 1984. 12.95 (ISBN 0-241-11179-X, Pub. by Hamish Hamilton England). David & Charles.

Dick, Lenox. The Art & Science of Fly Fishing. 1977. pap. 3.95 (ISBN 0-8065-0587-7). Citadel Pr.

Dick, Lois H. Amy Carmichael: Let the Little Children Come. (Orig.). 1984. pap. 3.95 (ISBN 0-8024-0433-2). Moody.

--Devil on the Deck. 192p. (Orig.). 1984. pap. 9.95 (ISBN 0-8007-1201-3). Revell.

Dick, Manfred, ed. see Wentzlaff-Eggebert, Friedrich-Wilhelm.

Dick, Oliver L., ed. see Aubrey, John.

Dick, Pastor. Heavenly Groundwork. 196p. (Orig.). 1985. 3.95 (ISBN 0-934109-00-1). Banquet Hse.

Dick, Philip K. Blade Runner. 1982. pap. 2.75 (ISBN 0-345-30129-3, Del Rey). Ballantine.

--Clans of the Alphane Moon. 1979. lib. bdg. 13.50 (ISBN 0-8398-2598-6, Gregg). G K Hall.

--Clans of the Alphane Moon. 268p. 1984. pap. 6.95 (ISBN 0-312-94051-3). Bluejay Bks.

--The Cosmic Puppets. 192p. 1983. pap. 2.50 (ISBN 0-425-06276-7). Berkley Pub.

--Dr. Bloodmoney. (Orig.). 1980. pap. 2.25 (ISBN 0-440-11489-6). Dell.

--Dr. Bloodmoney. 304p. 1984. pap. 7.95 (ISBN 0-312-94105-6). Bluejay Bks.

--Dr. Futurity. 160p. 1984. pap. 2.50 (ISBN 0-425-07106-5). Berkley Pub.

--Eye in the Sky. 1979. lib. bdg. 15.95 (ISBN 0-8398-2481-5, Gregg). G K Hall.

--Flow My Tears, The Policeman Said. 1981. pap. 2.50 (ISBN 0-87997-969-0, UE1969). DAW Bks.

--The Game-Players of Titan. 1979. lib. bdg. 14.50 (ISBN 0-8398-2482-3, Gregg). G K Hall.

--I Hope I Shall Arrive Soon. LC 84-28660. (Science Fiction Ser.). 192p. 1985. 12.95 (ISBN 0-385-19567-2). Doubleday.

--In Milton Lumky Territory. 224p. 1984. 30.00 (ISBN 0-911499-09-1, Pub. by Dragon Pr.). Ultramarine Pub.

--The Man in the High Castle. 1984. pap. 2.75 (ISBN 0-425-07660-1). Berkley Pub.

--The Man in the High Castle. 1979. lib. bdg. 10.50 (ISBN 0-8398-2476-9, Gregg). G K Hall.

--The Man Whose Teeth Were All Exactly Alike. LC 83-91458. 240p. 19.50x (ISBN 0-9612970-0-X). Ziesing Mark.

--The Man Whose Teeth Were All Exactly Alike. LC 85-51149. 268p. 1985. pap. 9.95 (ISBN 0-317-19712-6). Ziesing Mark.

--Martian Time-Slip. 4th ed. 224p. 1981. pap. 2.25 (ISBN 0-345-29560-9). Ballantine.

--The Maze of Death. 1983. pap. 2.50 (ISBN 0-87997-830-9). DAW Bks.

--Now Wait for Last Year. (Science Fiction Ser.). 1981. pap. 2.50 (ISBN 0-87997-654-3, UE1654). DAW Bks.

--The Penultimate Truth. LC 83-25867. 208p. 1984. pap. 5.95 (ISBN 0-312-94356-3). Bluejay Bks.

--Puttering Around in a Small Land. 225p. 1985. 15.95 (ISBN 0-89733-149-4). Academy Chi Pubs.

--Radio Free Albemuth. 1985. 14.95 (ISBN 0-87795-762-2). Arbor Hse.

--A Scanner Darkly. 224p. 1984. pap. 2.50 (ISBN 0-87997-923-2). DAW Bks.

--The Three Stigmata of Palmer Eldritch. 1979. lib. bdg. 15.95 (ISBN 0-8398-2479-3, Gregg). G K Hall.

--The Three Stigmata of Palmer Eldritch. 192p. 1982. pap. 2.50 (ISBN 0-87997-810-4). Daw Bks.

--Time Out of Joint. 1979. lib. bdg. 15.95 (ISBN 0-8398-2480-7, Gregg). G K Hall.

--Time Out of Joint. LC 84-14585. 264p. 1984. Repr. 6.95 (ISBN 0-312-94427-6). Bluejay Bks.

--The Transmigration of Timothy Archer. 1983. pap. 2.95 (ISBN 0-671-46751-4, Timescape). PB.

--The Transmigration of Timothy Archer. LC 81-232182. 255p. 1982. 15.00 (ISBN 0-671-44066-7). Ultramarine Pub.

--UBIK. 176p. 1983. pap. 2.50 (ISBN 0-87997-859-7). DAW Bks.

--UBIK: The Screenplay. Thornhill, Ira M., ed. (Illus.). 160p. 1985. 23.00 (ISBN 0-911169-06-7); text ed. write for info. (ISBN 0-911169-07-5). Corroboree Pr.

--The Unteleported Man. 208p. (Orig.). 1983. pap. 2.75 (ISBN 0-425-06252-X). Berkley Pub.

--Vulcan's Hammer. 1979. lib. bdg. 12.50 (ISBN 0-8398-2484-X, Gregg). G K Hall.

--The World Jones Made. 1979. PLB 13.50 (ISBN 0-8398-2483-1, Gregg). G K Hall.

--The Zap Gun. 1979. lib. bdg. 13.50 (ISBN 0-8398-2494-7, Gregg). G K Hall.

--The Zap Gun. 256p. 1985. pap. 7.95 (ISBN 0-312-94488-8). Bluejay Bks.

Dick, Philip K. & Zelazny, Roger. Deus Irae. 192p. pap. 2.95 (ISBN 0-87997-887-2). Daw Bks.

--Deus Irae. LC 74-24580. 182p. 1976. 15.00 (ISBN 0-385-04527-1). Ultramarine Pub.

Dick, Richard J., jt. auth. see Hinkel, Daniel F.

Dick, Robert. The Other Flute: A Performance Manual of Contemporary Techniques with 33.3 RPM Mono Record. (Illus.). 1975. text ed. 28.50 (ISBN 0-19-322125-X). Oxford U Pr.

Dick, Robert C. Black Protest: Issues & Tactics. LC 72-794. 320p. 1974. lib. bdg. 29.95 (ISBN 0-8371-6366-8, DNA/). Greenwood.

Dick, Steven J. Plurality of Worlds: The Extraterrestrial Life Debate from Democritus to Kant. LC 81-10165. (Illus.). 246p. 1982. 39.50 (ISBN 0-521-24308-4); pap. 12.95 (ISBN 0-521-31985-4). Cambridge U Pr.

Dick, Stewart. Arts & Crafts of Old Japan. LC 77-94574. 1979. Repr. of 1905 ed. lib. bdg. 20.00 (ISBN 0-89341-237-6). Longwood Pub Group.

Dick, Susan, ed. see Woolf, Virginia.

Dick, Trevor J. Economic History of Canada: A Guide to Information Sources. LC 73-17571. (Economics Information Guide Ser.: Vol. 9). 1978. 60.00x (ISBN 0-8103-1292-1). Gale.

--An Economic Theory of Technological Change: The Case of Patents & United States Railroads, 1871-1950. LC 77-14769. (Dissertations in American History Ser.). 1978. 17.00 (ISBN 0-405-11031-6). Ayer Co Pubs.

Dick, W. Byron & His Poetry. LC 76-52949. (Studies in Byron, No. 5). 1977. lib. bdg. 42.95x (ISBN 0-8383-2142-9). Haskell.

Dick, W. C. Immunological Aspects of Rheumotology. 262p. 1981. 47.50 (ISBN 0-444-19474-6, Biomedical Pr). Elsevier.

Dick, W. Carson. An Introduction to Clinical Rheumatology. (Illus.). 200p. 1972. pap. 6.25 (ISBN 0-443-00762-4). Churchill.

Dick, Walter & Carey, Lou. The Systematic Design of Instruction. 2nd ed. 1985. pap. text ed. 16.95 (ISBN 0-673-18070-0). Scott F.

Dick, William. Byron & His Poetry. LC 73-120968. (Poetry & Life Ser.). Repr. of 1913 ed. 7.25 (ISBN 0-404-52508-3). AMS Pr.

--Byron & His Poetry. LC 74-16132. 1974. Repr. of 1913 ed. lib. bdg. 17.50 (ISBN 0-8414-3783-1). Folcroft.

Dick, William B. Dick's One Hundred Amusements. LC 67-16293. (Illus.). 184p. 1967. pap. 7.50 (ISBN 0-89366-051-5). Ultramarine Pub.

Dick, William B., compiled by. Dick's Festival Reciter: Containing Appropriate Pieces & Programs, Original & Selected for Washington's Birthday, Memorial Day... LC 78-39484. (Granger Index Reprint Ser.). Repr. of 1892 ed. 14.00 (ISBN 0-8369-6340-7). Ayer Co Pubs.

Dick, William M. Labor & Socialism in America: The Gompers Era. LC 71-189555. (National University Publications). 1972. 19.50x (ISBN 0-8046-9005-7, Pub. by Kennikat). Assoc Faculty Pr.

Dickason, A. Sheet Metal Drawing & Pattern Development. (Illus.). 364p. 1983. pap. text ed. 30.50x (ISBN 0-273-41163-2, SpS). Sportshelf.

Dickason, C. Fred. Angels, Elect & Evil. 256p. 1975. pap. 6.95 (ISBN 0-8024-0222-4). Moody.

Dickason, David H. Daring Young Men: The Story of the American Pre-Raphaelites. LC 69-13235. (Illus.). 1953. 20.00 (ISBN 0-405-08444-7, Blom Pubns). Ayer Co Pubs.

Dickason, Jean & Schult, Martha. Maternal & Infant Care. 2nd ed. (Illus.). 1979. text ed. 32.00 (ISBN 0-07-016796-6). McGraw.

Dickason, Jean, et al. Maternal & Infant Drugs & Nursing Intervention. (Illus.). 1978. pap. text ed. 18.95 (ISBN 0-07-016788-5). McGraw.

Dicke, Karen & Goeldner, C. R. Bibliography of Tourism & Travel Research Studies, Reports, & Articles, 9 vols. 1980. Set. 60.00 (ISBN 0-89478-052-2). U CO Busn Res Div.

--Colorado Ski Industry Characteristics & Financial Analysis. 1981. 25.00 (ISBN 0-686-69386-8). U CO Busn Res Div.

Dicke, Karen, jt. auth. see Goeldner, C. R.

Dicke, Robert H. Gravitation & the Universe. LC 78-107344. (Memoirs Ser.: Vol. 78). (Illus.). 1970. 5.00 (ISBN 0-87169-078-0). Am Philos.

--Theoretical Significance of Experimental Relativity. (Documents on Modern Physics Ser.). 168p. 1965. 45.25 (ISBN 0-677-00220-3). Gordon.

Dicke, Robert H. & Wittke, J. P. Introduction to Quantum Mechanics. 1960. 30.95 (ISBN 0-201-01510-2). Addison-Wesley.

Dicke, Robert, Jr., jt. auth. see Martin, Lance.

Dickel, Karl, ed. see Rowe, Alan J. & Mason, Richard O.

Dicken, Charles. American Notes. 248p. 1985. Repr. of 1842 ed. 14.95 (ISBN 0-312-02888-1). St Martin.

Dicken, Emily F., jt. auth. see Dicken, Samuel N.

Dicken, Peter & Lloyd, Peter. Modern Western Society. 1981. text ed. 31.50 (ISBN 0-06-318030-8, IntlDept); pap. text ed. 17.95 (ISBN 0-06-318048-0). Har-Row.

--Modern Western Society: A Geographical Perspective on Work, Home, & Well-Being. 396p. 1982. pap. text ed. 17.50 scp (ISBN 0-06-318048-0, HarpC). Har-Row.

Dicken, Peter, jt. auth. see Lloyd, Peter.

Dicken, Peter, jt. auth. see Lloyd, Peter E.

Dicken, Samuel N. Pioneer Trails of the Oregon Coast. 2nd ed. LC 70-176249. (Illus.). 78p. 1978. pap. 4.95 (ISBN 0-87595-030-2). Oreg Hist Soc.

Dicken, Samuel N. & Dicken, Emily F. Making of Oregon: A Study in Historical Geography. LC 79-89087. (Two Centuries of Oregon Geography Ser.: Vol. 1). (Illus.). 222p. pap. 12.95 (ISBN 0-87595-081-7). Oreg Hist Soc.

--Oregon Divided: A Regional Geography. LC 80-84480. (Two Centuries of Oregon Geography Ser.: Vol. 2). (Illus.). 192p. (gr. 10-12). 1982. 17.95 (ISBN 0-87595-082-5); pap. 10.95 (ISBN 0-87595-064-7). Oreg Hist Soc.

Dickens, A. G. The Counter-Reformation. (Library of World Civilization). (Illus.). 1979. pap. 7.95x (ISBN 0-393-95086-7). Norton.

--Lollards & Protestants in the Diocese of York. (No. 10). 280p. 1983. 27.00 (ISBN 0-907628-05-2); pap. 12.00 (ISBN 0-907628-06-0). Hambledon Press.

--Reformation & Society in Sixteenth Century Europe. (History of European Civilization Library). (Illus., Orig.). 1966. pap. text ed. 11.95 (ISBN 0-15-576455-1, HC). HarBraceJ.

Dickens, A. G. & Lit, D. Reformation Studies. 624p. 1983. 40.00 (ISBN 0-907628-04-4). Hambledon Press.

Dickens, A. G. & Tonkin, John M. The Reformation in Historical Thought. 456p. 1985. text ed. 33.50x (ISBN 0-674-75311-9). Harvard U Pr.

Dickens, Albert, jt. ed. see Andrews, Earl.

Dickens, Arthur G. English Reformation. LC 64-22987. (Fabric of British History Ser). 1968. pap. 8.95 (ISBN 0-8052-0177-7). Schocken.

Dickens, Arthur G. & Carr, Dorothy. Reformation in England to the Accession of Elizabeth 1. (Documents of Modern History Ser). (Orig.). 1968. pap. 11.95 (ISBN 0-312-66815-5). St Martin.

Dickens, Betty. Voice on the Southwind. Holley, Barbara, ed. (Orig.). 1982. pap. 3.50 (ISBN 0-933494-15-7). Earthwise Pubs.

Dickens, Cedric. Drinking with Dickens. (Illus.). 127p. 1983. 9.95 (ISBN 0-88254-879-4, 095071848). Hippocrene Bks.

Dickens, Charles. Adventures of Oliver Twist. (World's Classics Ser: No. 8). 12.95 (ISBN 0-19-250008-2). Oxford U Pr.

--American Notes. 11.25 (ISBN 0-8446-1154-9). Peter Smith.

--American Notes: A Journey. LC 85-10213. 264p. 1985. pap. 8.95 (ISBN 0-88064-023-5). Fromm Intl Pub.

--The Bagman's Story. (Classic Short Stories Ser.). 48p. 1983. PLB 8.95 (ISBN 0-87191-922-2). Creative Ed.

--Barnaby Rudge. 1966. 14.95x (ISBN 0-460-00076-4, Evman). Biblio Dist.

--Barnaby Rudge. Spence, G. W., ed. (English Library). 1974. pap. 5.95 (ISBN 0-14-043090-3). Penguin.

--Bleak House. (Heinemann Guided Readers Ser.: Upper Level). 1976. pap. text ed. 2.50x (ISBN 0-435-27032-X). Heinemann Ed.

--Bleak House. Zabel, M. D., ed. LC 56-58296. (YA) (gr. 9 up). 1956. pap. 6.50 (ISBN 0-395-05104-5, RivEd). HM.

--Bleak House. 1964. pap. 4.95 (ISBN 0-451-51739-3, CE1739, Sig Classics). NAL.

--Bleak House. (Critical Edition Ser.). (Illus.). pap. 9.95x 1977 (ISBN 0-393-09332-8). Norton.

--Bleak House. (English Library Ser). 976p. 1971. pap. 4.95 (ISBN 0-14-043063-6). Penguin.

--Bleak House. (Bantam Classics Ser.). (YA) (gr. 10-12). 1983. pap. 4.95 (ISBN 0-553-21193-5). Bantam.

--Bleak House. Date not set. pap. 10.95 (ISBN 0-394-60520-9). Modern Lib.

--The Bookman: Charles Dickens Number. 1914. 25.00 (ISBN 0-8274-1960-0). R West.

--Character Portraits from Dickens. Welsh, Charles, ed. LC 72-3628. (Studies in Dickens, No. 52). 1972. Repr. of 1908 ed. lib. bdg. 51.95x (ISBN 0-8383-1552-6). Haskell.

--Charles Dickens As Editor. Lehmann, R., ed. LC 73-38842. (Studies in Dickens, No. 52). 403p. 1972. Repr. of 1912 ed. lib. bdg. 59.95x (ISBN 0-8383-1393-0). Haskell.

--Charles Dickens As Editor. Lehmann, R. C., ed. LC 12-35530. Repr. of 1912 ed. 20.00 (ISBN 0-527-22500-2). Kraus Repr.

--Charles Dickens As Editor: Letters Written by Him to William Henry Wills As Sub-Editor. Lehmann, R. C., ed. 1912. 35.00 (ISBN 0-8274-2036-6). R West.

--Charles Dickens' Book of Memoranda. 1st ed. Kaplan, Fred, ed. LC 81-18872. (Harcourt Brace Jovanovich Fund Ser.: No. 2). (Illus.). 118p. 1982. 20.00 (ISBN 0-87104-279-7). NY Pub Lib.

--Charles Dickens: The Writer & His Work. facsimile ed. Floyd, M. & Floyd, P., eds. LC 74-920. (Biography Index Reprint Ser.). 1948. 12.50 (ISBN 0-8369-8196-0). Ayer Co Pubs.

--Child's History of England. (gr. 4-6). 1978. Repr. of 1907 ed. 9.95x (ISBN 0-460-00291-0, Evman). Biblio Dist.

--The Christmas Books. Stater, Michael, ed. (English Library Ser.). 1971. Vol. 1. pap. 3.95 (ISBN 0-14-043068-7); Vol. 2. pap. 3.95 (ISBN 0-14-043069-5). Penguin.

--Christmas Carol. (gr. 7 up). pap. 1.50 (ISBN 0-8049-0026-4, CL-26). Airmont.

--A Christmas Carol. 191p. 1981. Repr. PLB 13.95x (ISBN 0-89966-344-3). Buccaneer Bks.

--A Christmas Carol. (Children's Theatre Playscript Ser.). 1961. pap. 2.25x (ISBN 0-88020-070-7). Coach Hse.

--A Christmas Carol. 150p. 1980. Repr. PLB 13.95x (ISBN 0-89967-017-2). Harmony Raine.

--A Christmas Carol. Fagan, Tom, ed. (Now Age Illustrated IV Ser.). (Illus.). (gr. 4-12). 1978. text ed. 5.00 (ISBN 0-88301-325-8); pap. text ed. 1.95 (ISBN 0-88301-313-4); activity bk. 1.25 (ISBN 0-88301-337-1). Pendulum Pr.

--A Christmas Carol. 64p. (gr. 6 up). 4.95 (ISBN 0-88088-125-9). Peter Pauper.

--A Christmas Carol. LC 82-23321. (Illus.). 128p. (gr. 4-6). 1983. reinforced bdg. 14.95 (ISBN 0-8234-0486-2). Holiday.

--A Christmas Carol. (Illus.). 128p. 1983. 12.95 (ISBN 0-8037-0032-6, 01258-370). Dial Bks Young.

--A Christmas Carol. (Illus.). 128p. 1983. 11.95 (ISBN 0-671-45599-0, Little Simon). S&S.

--A Christmas Carol. LC 83-883. 128p. (gr. k-3). 1983. lib. bdg. 11.97 (ISBN 0-671-47646-7). Messner.

--A Christmas Carol. (Christmas Stories Ser.). 32p. 1983. PLB 8.95 (ISBN 0-87191-955-9). Creative Ed.

--A Christmas Carol. 240p. 1984. pap. 2.95 (ISBN 0-671-47369-7). WSP.

--A Christmas Carol. (Puffin Classics Ser.). 176p. (gr. 7). 1984. pap. 2.25 (ISBN 0-14-035027-6, Puffin). Penguin.

--A Christmas Carol. 1985. pap. 3.95 (ISBN 0-14-007120-2). Penguin.

--A Christmas Carol. Kennedy, Pam, ed. (Illus.). 32p. (gr. k-6). 1985. pap. 2.95 (ISBN 0-317-17954-3). Ideals.

--A Christmas Carol. (Fairy Tales & Fabels Ser.). (Illus.). 4.98 (ISBN 0-517-23159-X). Outlet Bk Co.

--A Christmas Carol. (Illus.). 80p. 1985. 14.95 (ISBN 0-317-31429-7). Barron.

--A Christmas Carol & Other Christmas Stories. 1984. pap. 2.75 (ISBN 0-451-51869-1, Sig Classics). NAL.

--A Christmas Carol: And The Chimes. 1978. 12.95x (ISBN 0-460-00239-2, Evman); pap. 2.50x (ISBN 0-460-01239-8, Evman). Biblio Dist.

--A Christmas Carol: Retold by A. Sweaney. (Oxford Progressive English Readers Ser.). (gr. k-6). 1975. pap. text ed. 3.50x (ISBN 0-19-580724-3). Oxford U Pr.
--A Christmas Carol: The Original Manuscript. 1971. pap. 5.95 (ISBN 0-486-20980-6). Dover.
--A Christmas Carol: The Original Manuscript. 15.75 (ISBN 0-8446-0078-4). Peter Smith.
--A Christmas Carol: The Public Reading Version. Collins, Philip, ed. (Illus.). 232p. 1971. 20.00 (ISBN 0-87104-228-2). NY Pub Lib.
--Christmas Stories. 512p. 1982. pap. 4.95x (ISBN 0-460-01414-5, Evman). Biblio Dist.
--Comic World of Dickens. 11.25 (ISBN 0-8446-1979-5). Peter Smith.
--The Complete Ghost Stories of Charles Dickens. Haining, Peter, ed. LC 82-13481. (Illus.). 342p. 1983. 15.95 (ISBN 0-531-09885-0). Watts.
--David Copperfield. (Classics Ser). (gr. 9 up). pap. 2.95 (ISBN 0-8049-0065-5, CL-65). Airmont.
--David Copperfield. (Bantam Classics Ser.). 832p. (Orig.). 1981. pap. text ed. 3.50 (ISBN 0-553-21189-7). Bantam.
--David Copperfield. 1975. Repr. of 1907 ed. 10.95x (ISBN 0-460-00242-2, Evman). Biblio Dist.
--David Copperfield. abr. ed. Fuller, Edmund, ed. 416p. 1958. pap. 2.50 (ISBN 0-440-31675-8, LE). Dell.
--David Copperfield. (Great Il. Classics). (Illus.). 1979. 8.95 (ISBN 0-396-07745-5). Dodd.
--David Copperfield. Ford, G. H., ed. LC 58-14706. (gr. 7 up). 1958. pap. 6.50 (ISBN 0-395-05122-3, RivEd). HM.
--David Copperfield. (RL 7). 1962. pap. 3.50 (ISBN 0-451-51907-8, Sig Classics). NAL.
--David Copperfield. Burgis, Nina, ed. (The Clarendon Dickens Ser.). (Illus.). 1981. 110.00x (ISBN 0-19-812492-9). Oxford U Pr.
--David Copperfield. (YA) (gr. 9-12). 1981. pap. 4.95 (ISBN 0-671-45106-5). PB.
--David Copperfield. Blount, Trevor, ed. (English Library Ser.). (Orig.). (YA) (gr. 9 up). 1966. pap. 3.95 (ISBN 0-14-043008-3). Penguin.
--David Copperfield. (Illus.). 795p. 1981. 55.00 (ISBN 0-913720-20-8); leather bound 95.00 (ISBN 0-913720-19-4). Beil.
--David Copperfield. 864p. pap. 4.95 (ISBN 0-671-45106-5). WSP.
--David Copperfield. 1982. Repr. lib. bdg. 21.95x (ISBN 0-89966-370-2). Buccaneer Bks.
--David Copperfield. Buckley, Jerome H., ed. (Norton Critical Edition Ser.). pap. write for info. (ISBN 0-393-95249-5). Norton.
--David Copperfield. (Great Illustrated Classics Ser.). (Illus.). 892p. 1984. 14.95 (ISBN 0-396-08256-4). Dodd.
--David Copperfield. Burgis, Nina, ed. (The World's Classics-Paperback Ser.). (Illus.). 1983. pap. 4.95 (ISBN 0-19-281609-8). Oxford U Pr.
--David Copperfield. (Madhuban Abridged Classics Ser.). 118p. 1983. pap. 3.95x (ISBN 0-7069-2468-1, Pub. by Vikas India). Advent NY.
--David Copperfield & de Grandes Esperances. 1564p. 41.50 (ISBN 0-686-56495-2). French & Eur.
--Dickens' London. 1923. 9.75 (ISBN 0-8274-2178-8). R West.
--Dickens to His Oldest Friend: Letters to Thomas Beard. Dexter, W., ed. LC 72-6506. (Studies in Dickens, No. 52). 315p. 1972. Repr. of 1932 ed. lib. bdg. 52.95x (ISBN 0-8383-1620-4). Haskell.
--Dickens V. Barrabas. LC 72-3173. (Studies in Dickens, No. 52). 1972. Repr. of 1930 ed. lib. bdg. 29.95x (ISBN 0-8383-1523-2). Haskell.
--Dickens vs Barabbas. LC 78-26151. 1930. lib. bdg. 20.00 (ISBN 0-8414-4172-3). Folcroft.
--Dombey & Son. pap. 3.95 (ISBN 0-451-51595-1, CE1595, Sig Classics). NAL.
--Dombey & Son. (English Library Ser.). 992p. 1970. pap. 5.95 (ISBN 0-14-043048-2). Penguin.
--Dombey & Son. Horsman, Alan, ed. (World's Classics Ser.). (Illus.). 1982. pap. 5.95 (ISBN 0-19-281565-2). Oxford U Pr.
--Dombey & Sons. 1964. pap. 4.95 (ISBN 0-452-00755-0, Mer). NAL.
--Dombey et Fils & Temps Difficils. 1376p. 42.95 (ISBN 0-686-56496-0). French & Eur.
--Don't Crowd. 59.95 (ISBN 0-8490-0058-0). Gordon Pr.
--The Earliest Letters of Charles Dickens: Written to His Friend Henry Kolle. LC 76-58366. 1977. Repr. of 1910 ed. lib. bdg. 20.00 (ISBN 0-8414-7555-5). Folcroft.
--Edwin Drood & Master Humphrey's Clock. 1970. Repr. of 1915 ed. 9.95x (ISBN 0-460-00725-4, Evman). Biblio Dist.
--The England of Dickens. 1925. 30.00 (ISBN 0-8274-2247-4). R West.
--Fireside Dickens. DeFontaine, F. G., ed. LC 77-148773. (Illus.). Repr. of 1883 ed. 30.00 (ISBN 0-404-08746-9). AMS Pr.
--George Silverman's Explanation. Stone, Harry, ed. (Illus.). 80p. 1985. 85.00 (ISBN 0-937048-36-4). CSUN.
--Great Expectations. (Classics Ser). (gr. 9 up). pap. 2.95 (ISBN 0-8049-0068-X, CL-68). Airmont.
--Great Expectations. (Literature Ser.). (gr. 9-12). 1970. pap. text ed. 5.58 (ISBN 0-87720-725-9). AMSCO Sch.
--Great Expectations. (Bantam Classics Ser.). 454p. (gr. 9-12). 1981. pap. 2.50 (ISBN 0-553-21113-7). Bantam.
--Great Expectations. 1979. pap. 2.25x (ISBN 0-460-01234-7, Evman). Biblio Dist.
--Great Expectations. Crompton, Louis, ed. LC 62-21261. 1964. pap. 9.08 scp (ISBN 0-672-60967-3, LL2). Bobbs.
--Great Expectations. 2nd ed. LC 72-177918. (Rinehart Editions). 1972. pap. text ed. 12.95 (ISBN 0-03-077900-6, HoltC). HR&W.
--Great Expectations. (YA) (RL 9). pap. 2.50 (ISBN 0-451-51932-9, CE1871, Sig Classics). NAL.
--Great Expectations. (Enriched Classics Edition). (Illus.). 1982. pap. 3.50 (ISBN 0-671-46200-8). PB.
--Great Expectations. (Now Age Illustrated V Ser.). (Illus.). 64p. (gr. 4-12). 1979. text ed. 5.00 (ISBN 0-88301-400-9); pap. text ed. 1.95 (ISBN 0-88301-388-6); student activity bk. 1.25 (ISBN 0-88301-412-2). Pendulum Pr.
--Great Expectations. Calder, Angus, ed. (English Lib.). (Orig.). (YA) (gr. 9 up). 1965. pap. 2.95 (ISBN 0-14-043003-2). Penguin.
--Great Expectations. Shefter, Harry, ed. (Enriched Classics Edition Ser.). 528p. pap. 2.95 (ISBN 0-671-42071-2). WSP.
--Great Expectations. LC 84-62236. (Illus.). 432p. 1985. 12.95 (ISBN 0-89577-205-1). RD Assn.
--Great Expectations. (Illus.). 640p. 1985. 14.95 (ISBN 0-396-08687-X). Dodd.
--Great Expectations with Reader's Guide. (gr. 10-12). 1975. pap. text ed. 8.58 (ISBN 0-87720-800-X); tchrs ed. 5.35 (ISBN 0-87720-900-6). AMSCO Sch.
--Hard Times. (Bantam Classics Ser.). 301p. (gr. 9-12). 1981. pap. 1.95 (ISBN 0-553-21016-5). Bantam.
--Hard Times. 1974. 9.95x (ISBN 0-460-01292-4, Evman); pap. 3.95x (ISBN 0-460-11292-9, Evman). Biblio Dist.
--Hard Times. Clay, N. L., ed. (The Guide Novel Ser.). pap. text ed. 4.50x (ISBN 0-435-16236-5). Heinemann Ed.
--Hard Times. pap. 1.95 (ISBN 0-451-51335-5, CJ1335, Sig Classics). NAL.
--Hard Times. Ford, George H. & Monod, Sylvere, eds. (Critical Editions). (Annotated). 1966. pap. text ed. 6.95x (ISBN 0-393-09639-4, NortonC). Norton.
--Hard Times. Craig, David, ed. (English Library Ser.). 1969. pap. 2.25 (ISBN 0-14-043042-3). Penguin.
--Hard Times. Krishnan, S. V., ed. (Sangam Abridged Texts Ser.). xii, 107p. (Orig.). 1983. pap. text ed. 4.95x (ISBN 0-86131-176-0, Pub. by Orient Longman Ltd India). Apt Bks.
--Hard Times. (Book Notes Ser.). 1985. pap. 2.50 (ISBN 0-8120-3518-6). Barron.
--Hard Times for These Times. Watt, William W., ed. LC 58-7847. (Rinehart Editions). 1958. pap. text ed. 8.95 (ISBN 0-03-009875-0, HoltC). HR&W.
--The Illustrated Life & Adventures of Nicholas Nickleby. (Illus.). 464p. 1982. 19.95 (ISBN 0-02-531350-9). Macmillan.
--Illustrations from Dickens. (Illus.). 1974. 4.95 (ISBN 0-87482-042-1). Wake-Brook.
--The Letters of Charles Dickens: The Pilgrim Edition, Vol. 4, 1844 to 1846. Tillotson, Kathleen & Burgis, Nina, eds. (Illus.). 1977. text ed. 59.00x (ISBN 0-19-812475-9). Oxford U Pr.
--The Letters of Charles Dickens: The Pilgrim Edition, Vol. 3, 1842-1843. House, Madeline, et al, eds. 1974. 64.00x (ISBN 0-19-812474-0). Oxford U Pr.
--Letters of Charles Dickens to Wilkie Collins. LC 73-20382. (Studies in Dickens, No. 52). 1974. lib. bdg. 49.95x (ISBN 0-8383-1823-1). Haskell.
--Letters of Charles Dickens Vol. 2: 1840-1841. House, Madeline & Storey, Graham, eds. 1969. 69.00x (ISBN 0-19-811478-8). Oxford U Pr.
--The Letters of Charles Dickens: Vol. 5, 1847-1949. Storey, Graham & Fielding, Kenneth J., eds. (Illus.). 1981. 115.00x (ISBN 0-19-812514-3). Oxford U Pr.
--The Letters of Charles Dickens: 1820-1839, Vol. 1. House, Madeline & Story, Graham, eds. 1982. Repr. of 1965 ed. text ed. 94.00x (ISBN 0-19-811447-8). Oxford U Pr.
--Letters to Wilkie Collins. Repr. of 1892 ed. 15.00 (ISBN 0-527-22510-X). Kraus Repr.
--Life & Adventures of Nicholas Nickleby. TV tie-in ed. Slater, Michael, ed. 1982. pap. 4.95 (ISBN 0-14-006454-0). Penguin.
--The Life & Adventures of Nicholas Nickleby. LC 82-21971. (Illus.). 1344p. 1983. 40.00 (ISBN 0-8122-7873-9); pap. 19.95 2 vol. set (ISBN 0-8122-1135-9). U of Pa Pr.
--The Life & Adventures of Nicholas Nickleby. 1982. pap. 4.50 (ISBN 0-451-51633-8, CE1633, Sig Classics). NAL.
--The Life & Adventures of Nicholas Nickleby. (Illus.). 720p. 1983. 5.98 (ISBN 0-517-40800-7, Avenel). Outlet Bk Co.
--The Life of Our Lord. LC 80-22131. (Illus.). 128p. 1981. Repr. of 1934 ed. 9.95 (ISBN 0-664-21382-0). Westminster.
--Little Dorrit. 1980. pap. 3.50 (ISBN 0-451-51294-4, CE1294, Sig Classics). NAL.
--Little Dorrit. Sucksmith, Harvey P., ed. (The Claredon Dickens Ser.). (Illus.). 1979. 82.00x (ISBN 0-19-812513-5). Oxford U Pr.
--Little Dorrit. Holloway, John, ed. (English Library Ser.). 1968. pap. 5.95 (ISBN 0-14-043025-3). Penguin.
--Little Dorrit. Sucksmith, Harvey P., ed. (World's Classics Ser.). (Illus.). 1982. pap. 6.95 (ISBN 0-19-281592-X). Oxford U Pr.
--The Love Romance of Charles Dickens, Told in His Letters to Maria Beadnell. LC 36-30973. Repr. of 1936 ed. 11.00 (ISBN 0-527-22520-7). Kraus Repr.
--Le Magasin d'Antiquites & Barnabe Rudge. 1480p. 39.95 (ISBN 0-686-56498-7). French & Eur.
--The Magic Fishbone. (Children's Theatre Playscript Ser.). 1961. pap. 2.25x (ISBN 0-88020-039-1). Coach Hse.
--Magic Fishbone. LC 53-10806. (Illus.). (gr. 3 up). 1953. 8.95 (ISBN 0-8149-0296-0). Vanguard.
--La Maison d'Apre-Vent & Recits Pour Noel et Autres. write for info. French & Eur.
--Martin Chuzzlewit. Furbank, P. N., ed. (English Library). 1968. pap. 6.95 (ISBN 0-14-043031-8). Penguin.
--Martin Chuzzlewit. Cardwell, Margaret, ed. (The Clarendon Dickens Ser.). (Illus.). 1982. 95.00x (ISBN 0-19-812488-0). Oxford U Pr.
--Martin Chuzzlewit. Monod, Sylvere & Rawson, Claude, eds. (Unwin Critical Library). 192p. 1985. text ed. 25.00x (ISBN 0-04-800028-0). Allen Unwin.
--Martin Chuzzlewitt. Cardwell, Margaret, ed. (World Classics Ser.). 1984. pap. 6.95 (ISBN 0-19-281676-4). Oxford U Pr.
--Mickey's Christmas Carol. Disney Studio Staff, ed. LC 84-9491. (Illus.). (gr. k up). 1984. pap. 5.95 (ISBN 0-517-55525-5). Crown.
--Miscellaneous Papers: A Collection of His Journalistic Writings, 2 vols. Repr. of 1908 ed. 130.00 (ISBN 0-527-22605-X). Kraus Repr.
--Mr. & Mrs. Charles Dickens: His Letters to Her. Dexter, Walter, ed. LC 72-1331. (Studies in Dickens, No. 52). 1972. Repr. of 1935 ed. lib. bdg. 52.95x (ISBN 0-8383-1429-5). Haskell.
--Mystery of Edwin Drood. (Classics Ser). (gr. 10 up). pap. 1.50 (ISBN 0-8049-0114-7, CL-114). Airmont.
--The Mystery of Edwin Drood. LC 75-42303. (Studies in Dickens, No. 52). 1974. lib. bdg. 49.95x (ISBN 0-8383-1962-9). Haskell.
--Mystery of Edwin Drood. (Illus.). 1972. 42.00x (ISBN 0-19-812439-2). Oxford U Pr.
--The Mystery of Edwin Drood. (Illus., Concluded by Leon Garfield). 1981. 12.95 (ISBN 0-394-51918-3). Pantheon.
--The Mystery of Edwin Drood. (English Library Ser.). 320p. 1974. pap. 3.95 (ISBN 0-14-043092-X). Penguin.
--The Mystery of Edwin Drood. rev. ed. Grant, Mary L., ed. 1914. 30.00 (ISBN 0-8274-2782-4). R West.
--The Mystery of Edwin Drood. Cardwell, Margaret, ed. (World's Classics Ser.). (Illus.). 1982. pap. 3.50 (ISBN 0-19-281593-8). Oxford U Pr.
--The Mystery of Edwin Drood. 288p. 1984. pap. 4.95 (ISBN 0-452-00688-0, Mer). NAL.
--The Mystery of Edwin Drood. 15.95 (ISBN 0-88411-276-4, Pub. by Aeonian Pr). Amereon Ltd.
--The New Oxford Illustrated Dickens, 21 vols. Incl. The Old Curiosity Shop. Cattermole, George & Phiz, illus. (Illus.). 1951. 22.50x (ISBN 0-19-254506-X); Our Mutual Friend. Stone, Marcus, illus. (Illus.). 1952. 24.50x (ISBN 0-19-254510-8); The Personal History of David Copperfield. (Illus.); The Posthumous Papers of the Pickwick Club. (Illus.). 1947. 22.50x (ISBN 0-19-254501-9); Sketches by Boz: Illustrative of Every-Day Life & Every-Day People. Cruickshank, George, illus. (Illus.). 1957. 22.50x (ISBN 0-19-254518-3); A Tale of Two Cities. (Illus.). 1949; The Uncommercial Traveller, & Reprinted Pieces, Etc. Pinwell, G. J., et al, illus. (Illus.). 1958. 22.50x (ISBN 0-19-254521-3); The Adventures of Oliver Twist. Cruickshank, George, illus. 1949. 19.95x (ISBN 0-19-254505-1); American Notes & Pictures from Italy. Stone, Marcus, et al, illus. 1957. 21.95x (ISBN 0-19-254519-1); Barnaby Rudge: A Tale of the Riots of 'eighty. Cattermole, George & Browne, H. K., illus. 1954. 22.50x (ISBN 0-19-254513-2); Bleak House. Phiz, illus. 1948; Christmas Books. Farjeon, Eleanor, intro. by. (Illus.). 1954; Christmas Stories. Dalziel, E. G., et al, illus. 1956. 21.00x (ISBN 0-19-254517-5); Dealings with the Firm of Dombey, & Son, Wholesale, Retail, & for Exploration. Phiz, illus. 1950; Great Expectations. Pailthrope, F. W., illus. 1953. 17.95x (ISBN 0-19-254511-6); Hard Times for These Times. Walker, F. & Greiffenhagen, Maurice, illus. 1955. 17.95x (ISBN 0-19-254515-9); The Life & Adventures of Martin Chuzzlewit. Phiz, illus. 1951; The Life & Adventures of Nicholas Nickleby. Phiz, illus. 1950; Little Dorrit. Phiz, illus. 1953. 23.50x (ISBN 0-19-254512-4); Master Humphrey's Clock & a Child's History of England. Hudson, Derek, intro. by. 1958. 19.95x (ISBN 0-19-254520-5); The Mystery of Edwin Drood. Fildes, Luke & Collins, Charles, illus. 1956. 17.95x (ISBN 0-19-254516-7). (Illus.). (gr. 7 up). 1947. Boxed Set Ecrase. 695.00x (ISBN 0-19-195252-4). Oxford U Pr.
--Nicholas Nickelby. 1977. (Evman); pap. 3.95x (ISBN 0-460-01238-X, Evman). Biblio Dist.
--Nicholas Nickleby. Slater, Michael, ed. (English Library). 1978. pap. 4.95 (ISBN 0-14-043113-6). Penguin.
--Nicholas Nickleby. 1982. 37.50 (ISBN 0-85967-668-4, Pub. by Scolar England). State Mutual Bk.
--Nicholas Nickleby. (Illus.). 1982. pap. 5.95 (ISBN 0-19-281368-4, GB 699, GB). Oxford U Pr.
--Nicholas Nickleby. (Bantam Classics Ser.). 816p. (YA) (gr. 10-12). 1983. pap. 4.50 (ISBN 0-553-21086-6). Bantam.
--Nicolas Nickleby & Livres De Noel. 1456p. 42.95 (ISBN 0-686-56499-5). French & Eur.
--Old Curiosity Shop. 1977. Repr. of 1907 ed. 12.95x (ISBN 0-460-00173-6, Evman). Biblio Dist.
--The Old Curiosity Shop. Easson, A., ed. (English Library Ser). 1972. pap. 4.95 (ISBN 0-14-043075-X). Penguin.
--Oliver Twist. (Classics Ser). (gr. 9 up). 1964. pap. 2.95 (ISBN 0-8049-0009-4, CL-9). Airmont.
--Oliver Twist. (Literature Ser). (gr. 10-12). 1970. pap. text ed. 5.25 (ISBN 0-87720-747-X). AMSCO Sch.
--Oliver Twist. (Bantam Classics Ser.). 432p. (Orig.). (gr. 7-12). 1981. pap. text ed. 2.50 (ISBN 0-553-21102-1). Bantam.
--Oliver Twist. 1978. 12.95x (ISBN 0-460-00233-3, DEL-04273, Evman); pap. 2.95 (ISBN 0-460-10233-8). Biblio Dist.
--Oliver Twist. pap. 8.95x (ISBN 0-86685-138-0). Intl Bk Ctr.
--Oliver Twist. (RL 7). pap. 2.50 (ISBN 0-451-51685-0, CE1685, Sig Classics). NAL.
--Oliver Twist. Tillotson, Kathleen, ed. 1966. 55.00x (ISBN 0-19-811454-0). Oxford U Pr.
--Oliver Twist. (Now Age Illustrated V Ser.). (Illus.). 64p. (gr. 4-12). 1979. text ed. 5.00 (ISBN 0-88301-406-8); pap. text ed. 1.95 (ISBN 0-88301-394-0); student activity bk. 1.25 (ISBN 0-88301-418-1). Pendulum Pr.
--Oliver Twist. Wilson, Angus, ed. (English Library Ser.). 1966. pap. 3.50 (ISBN 0-14-043017-2). Penguin.
--Oliver Twist. Shefter, Harry, ed. (Enriched Classics Edition Ser.). 512p. pap. 3.50 (ISBN 0-671-44242-2). WSP.
--Oliver Twist. 1982. Repr. lib. bdg. 23.95x (ISBN 0-89966-372-9). Buccaneer Bks.
--Oliver Twist. Tillotson, Kathleen, ed. (World's Classics Ser.). (Illus.). 1982. pap. 3.50 (ISBN 0-19-281591-1). Oxford U Pr.
--Oliver Twist. (Illus.). 592p. 1984. 11.95 (ISBN 0-396-08261-0). Dodd.
--Oliver Twist. LC 84-50429. (Classics for Kids Ser.). 1984. 5.96 (ISBN 0-382-06808-4). Silver.
--Oliver Twist. (Book Notes). 1985. pap. 2.50 (ISBN 0-8120-3532-1). Barron.
--Oliver Twist. (Classics for Kids Ser.). 32p. (gr. 8 up). pap. 3.60 (ISBN 0-382-06950-1). Silver.
--Oliver Twist. LC 84-52581. (Classics for Kids Ser.). (Illus.). 32p. (Span.). (gr. 3 up). 1985. pap. 3.60 (ISBN 0-382-09017-9). Silver.
--Our Mutual Friend. 1978. Repr. of 1929 ed. 12.95x (ISBN 0-460-00294-5, Evman). Biblio Dist.

--Our Mutual Friend. Tarner, Margaret & Milne, John, eds. (Heinemann Guided Readers). 1978. pap. text ed. 2.50x (ISBN 0-435-27051-6). Heinemann Ed.

--Our Mutual Friend. (RL 8). pap. 4.50 (ISBN 0-451-51863-2, CE1863, Sig Classics). NAL.

--Our Mutual Friend. Gill, Stephen, ed. (English Library Ser.). 1971. pap. 4.95 (ISBN 0-14-043060-1). Penguin.

--Personal History, Adventures, Experience, & Observation of David Copperfield, the Younger, of Blunderstone Rookery, 20 Nos. in 1 Vol. LC 72-1651. (Illus.). Repr. of 1850 ed. 45.00 (ISBN 0-404-09139-3). AMS Pr.

--La Petite Dorrit et Un Conte de deux Villes. 1392p. 39.95 (ISBN 0-686-56500-2). French & Eur.

--Pickwick Papers. (Picture Aids to World Geography Ser.). (gr. 10 up). 1968. pap. 2.95 (ISBN 0-8049-0191-0, CL-191). Airmont.

--Pickwick Papers. 1977. (Evman); pap. 3.50x (ISBN 0-460-01235-5, Evman). Biblio Dist.

--Pickwick Papers. (YA) (RL 9). pap. 4.95 (ISBN 0-451-51756-3, CE1756, Sig Classics). NAL.

--Pickwick Papers. Patten, Robert L., ed. (English Library Ser.). (Illus.). 960p. (Orig.). 1973. pap. 4.95 (ISBN 0-14-043078-4). Penguin.

--The Pickwick Papers. 495p. 1983. Repr. lib. bdg. 22.95x (ISBN 0-89966-314-1). Buccaneer Bks.

--The Pickwick Papers. 1983. pap. 4.95 (ISBN 0-553-21123-4). Bantam.

--Pickwick Papers & Oliver Twist. 1488p. 42.95 (ISBN 0-686-56497-9). French & Eur.

--Pictures from Italy. (Illus.). 272p. 1973. 16.95 (ISBN 0-233-96383-9, Pub. by A Deutsch England). David & Charles.

--The Poems & Verses of Charles Dickens. Kitton, F. G., ed. LC 77-6981. 1977. Repr. of 1903 ed. lib. bdg. 25.00 (ISBN 0-89341-172-8). Longwood Pub Group.

--The Portable Charles Dickens. Wilson, Angus, ed. 800p. 1983. pap. 6.95 (ISBN 0-14-015099-4). Penguin.

--The Public Readings. Collins, Philip, ed. 1975. 69.00x (ISBN 0-19-812501-1). Oxford U Pr.

--The Religious Sentiments of Charles Dickens: Collected from His Writings. McKenzie, C., ed. LC 73-7504. (Studies in Dickens, No. 52). 1973. Repr. of 1884 ed. lib. bdg. 39.95x (ISBN 0-8383-1697-2). Haskell.

--Reprinted Pieces. 1970. Repr. of 1921 ed. 12.95x (ISBN 0-460-00744-0, Evman). Biblio Dist.

--Selected Short Fiction. Thomas, Deborah, ed. (English Library Ser.). 432p. 1976. pap. 3.95 (ISBN 0-14-043103-9). Penguin.

--The Signalman. LC 81-19819. (Illus.). 32p. (gr. 5-10). 1982. PLB 9.79 (ISBN 0-89375-630-X); pap. text ed. 2.50 (ISBN 0-89375-631-8). Troll Assocs.

--Sikes & Nancy & Other Public Readings. Collins, Philip, ed. (The World's Classics-Paperback Ser.). 1983. pap. 6.95 (ISBN 0-19-281617-9). Oxford U Pr.

--The Story of the Life of the World's Favorite Author. 1927. 20.00 (ISBN 0-8274-3525-8). R West.

--Tale of Two Cities. (Classics Ser). (gr. 9 up). 1964. pap. 2.50 (ISBN 0-8049-0021-3, CL-21). Airmont.

--Tale of Two Cities. (Literature Ser). (gr. 7-12). 1969. pap. text ed. 5.42 (ISBN 0-87720-716-X). AMSCO Sch.

--A Tale of Two Cities. (Bantam Classics Ser.). 352p. (gr. 9-12). 1981. pap. 2.25 (ISBN 0-553-21176-5). Bantam.

--A Tale of Two Cities. 1979. 10.95x (ISBN 0-460-00102-7, DEL-04393, Evman); pap. 2.95x (ISBN 0-460-01102-2, Evman). Biblio Dist.

--A Tale of Two Cities. (Reader's Request Ser.). 1980. lib. bdg. 14.95 (ISBN 0-8161-3075-2, Large Print Bks). G K Hall.

--Tale of Two Cities. (Illus.). (gr. 4-6). 1948. pap. 5.95 (ISBN 0-448-11023-7, G&D); deluxe ed. 11.95 (ISBN 0-448-06023-X). Putnam Pub Group.

--A Tale of Two Cities. Eyre, A. G., ed. (Longman Simplified English Ser.). 143p. 1947. pap. 1.95x (ISBN 0-582-52821-6). Longman.

--Tale of Two Cities. (RL 7). 1960. pap. 2.25 (ISBN 0-451-51959-0, CJ1776, Sig Classics). NAL.

--A Tale of Two Cities. new ed. Farr, Naunerle, ed. (Now Age Illustrated Ser., No. 2). (Illus.). 64p. (gr. 5-10). 1974. 5.00 (ISBN 0-88301-217-0); pap. text ed. 1.95 (ISBN 0-88301-134-4). Pendulum Pr.

--Tale of Two Cities. Woodcock, George, ed. (English Library Ser). 1970. pap. 2.25 (ISBN 0-14-043054-7). Penguin.

--Tale of Two Cities. Clare, Andrea M., ed. LC 73-80400. (Pacemaker Classics Ser). (Illus., Abridged & adapted to grade 2 reading level). 1973. pap. 4.92 (ISBN 0-8224-9228-8); tchrs' manual free. Pitman Learning.

--A Tale of Two Cities. LC 79-24746. (Raintree Short Classics). (Illus.). (gr. 4 up). 1980. PLB 15.15 (ISBN 0-8172-1658-8). Raintree Pubs.

--Tale of Two Cities. Shefter, Harry, et al, eds. 528p. (YA) pap. 3.95 (ISBN 0-671-54312-1, Re). WSP.

--A Tale of Two Cities. 1982. Repr. lib. bdg. 24.95x (ISBN 0-89966-371-0). Buccaneer Bks.

--A Tale of Two Cities. Krapesh, Patricia, adapted by. LC 79-24746. (Raintree Short Classics Ser.). (Illus.). 48p. (gr. 4-12). 1983. pap. 9.27 (ISBN 0-8172-2022-4). Raintree Pubs.

--A Tale of Two Cities. LC 83-63341. (Illus.). 400p. 1984. 12.95 (ISBN 0-89577-179-9). RD Assn.

--A Tale of Two Cities. Woolsey, Kris, tr. (Illus.). 384p. 1985. 11.95 (ISBN 0-396-08535-0). Dodd.

--A Tale of Two Cities. Date not set. price not set. S&S.

--A Tale of Two Cities. LC 81-83604. (Silver Classic Ser.). 288p. (gr. 6 up). 1985. pap. 3.67 (ISBN 0-382-09993-1). Silver.

--The Tale of Two Cities. 20.95 (ISBN 0-8488-0076-1, Pub. by Amereon Hse). Amereon Ltd.

--Tale of Two Cities with Reader's Guide. (Amsco Literature Program). (gr. 10-12). 1971. pap. text ed. 6.25 (ISBN 0-87720-813-1); tchrs. ed. 4.00 (ISBN 0-87720-913-8). AMSCO Sch.

--Unpublished Letters of Charles Dickens: To Mark Lemon. LC 76-155146. (Studies in Dickens, No. 52). 1971. Repr. of 1927 ed. lib. bdg. 49.95x (ISBN 0-8383-1281-0). Haskell.

--Wit & Wisdom from Dickens. LC 77-24723. 1977. Repr. of 1912 ed. lib. bdg. 30.00 (ISBN 0-8414-4305-X). Folcroft.

--The Writings of Charles Dickens: First Edition. 1978. Repr. of 1913 ed. lib. bdg. 30.00 (ISBN 0-8495-1132-1). Arden Lib.

Dickens, Charles & Hearn, Michael P. The Annotated Christmas Carol. (Illus.). 1977. pap. 4.95 (ISBN 0-380-01722-9, 34108-5). Avon.

Dickens, Charles & Sanders, Andrew. A Christmas Carol. ltd. ed. (Illus.). 156p. 1983. hand bound leather 192.00 (ISBN 0-904351-25-4). Genesis Pubns.

--The Cricket on the Hearth. ltd. ed. (Illus.). 156p. 1981. hand bound leather 170.00 (ISBN 0-904351-21-1). Genesis Pubns.

Dickens, Charles see Allen, W. S.

Dickens, Charles see Eyre, A. G.

Dickens, Charles see Howe, D. H.

Dickens, Charles see Swan, D. K.

Dickens, Charles, et al. A Christmas Carol & Other Victorian Fairy Tales. 1983. pap. 2.95 (ISBN 0-553-21126-9). Bantam.

--Classic Ghost Stories. LC 74-12599. 330p. (Orig.). 1975. pap. 5.95 (ISBN 0-486-20735-8). Dover.

--London Crimes. Aisenberg, Nadya, ed. LC 81-84723. (Mystery Ser.: No. 1). (Illus.). 142p. (Orig.). 1982. pap. 8.95 (ISBN 0-937672-05-X). Rowan Tree.

--The Letters of Charles Dickens. 48.00 (ISBN 0-8369-7100-0, 7934). Ayer Co Pubs.

Dickens, Charles, Jr. Reminiscences of My Father. LC 72-6292. (Studies in Dickens, No. 52). (Illus.). 1972. Repr. of 1908 ed. lib. bdg. 39.95x (ISBN 0-8383-1626-3). Haskell.

Dickens, Deborah S., ed. see Dickens, Nathaniel A.

Dickens, E. Larry. An Introduction to Texas Government: An Outline. 3rd ed. pap. text ed. 6.95 (ISBN 0-88408-102-8). Sterling Swift.

Dickens, E. Larry & Bertone, Pamela S. Fundamentals of Texas Government. 2nd ed. LC 76-2572. (Illus.). 149p. (Orig.). 1985. lib. bdg. 7.95 o. p. (ISBN 0-88408-046-3); pap. text ed. 8.95 (ISBN 0-88408-400-0). Sterling Swift.

Dickens, Floyd, Jr. & Dickens, Jacqueline B. The Black Manager: Making It in the Corporate World. LC 81-69377. (Illus.). 352p. 1982. 13.95 (ISBN 0-8144-5678-2); pap. 10.95 (ISBN 0-8144-7564-7). AMACOM.

Dickens, Frank. Albert Herbert Hawkins: The Naughtiest Boy in the World. LC 72-149044. (Illus.). 32p. (ps-3). 6.95 (ISBN 0-87592-000-4). Scroll Pr.

--A Curl up & Die Day. 1981. 29.00x (ISBN 0-7206-0573-3, Pub. by Owen England). State Mutual Bk.

Dickens, Frank, et al, eds. Carbohydrate Metabolism & Its Disorders, 2 Vols. 1968. Vol. 1. 84.50 (ISBN 0-12-214901-7); Vol. 2. 66.50 (ISBN 0-12-214902-5). Acad Pr.

Dickens, Henry F. Memories of My Father. LC 72-3169. (Studies in Dickens, No. 52). 1972. Repr. of 1929 ed. lib. bdg. 29.95x (ISBN 0-8383-1509-7). Haskell.

Dickens, Homer. The Films of Barbara Stanwyck. (Illus.). 256p. 1984. 19.95 (ISBN 0-8065-0932-5). Citadel Pr.

--Films of Gary Cooper. 1971. Repr. of 1970 ed. 10.00 (ISBN 0-8065-0010-7). Citadel Pr.

--The Films of Gary Cooper. (Illus.). 288p. 1983. pap. 9.95x (ISBN 0-8065-0279-7). Citadel Pr.

--The Films of James Cagney. (Illus.). 256p. 1983. pap. 9.95 (ISBN 0-8065-0277-0). Citadel Pr.

--The Films of Katharine Hepburn. (Illus.). 256p. 1973. pap. 7.95 (ISBN 0-8065-0361-0). Citadel Pr.

--Films of Marlene Dietrich. (Illus.). 1970. pap. 7.95 (ISBN 0-8065-0007-7). Citadel Pr.

--What a Drag! Female & Male Impersonation in Film. 224p. 1982. 30.00x (ISBN 0-207-14819-8, Pub. by Angus & Robertson). State Mutual Bk.

--What a Drag: Men As Women & Women As Men in the Movies. (Illus.). 280p. (Orig.). 1984. pap. 10.95 (ISBN 0-688-02626-5, Quill NY). Morrow.

Dickens, Homer C. The Films of Ginger Rogers. (Illus.). 256p. 1975. 14.00 (ISBN 0-8065-0496-X). Citadel Pr.

--The Films of Ginger Rogers. (Illus.). 256p. 1984. pap. 9.95 (ISBN 0-8065-0681-4). Citadel Pr.

Dickens, Jacqueline B., jt. auth. see Dickens, Floyd, Jr.

Dickens, Linda, et al. Dismissed: A Study of Unfair Dismissal & the Industrial Tribunal System. 304p. 1985. 34.95x (ISBN 0-631-13925-7). Basil Blackwell.

Dickens, M. My Father As I Recall Him. LC 73-21523. (Studies in Dickens, No. 52). 1974. lib. bdg. 49.95x (ISBN 0-8383-1814-2). Haskell.

Dickens, Mamie. Charles Dickens. LC 76-52967. (Studies in Dickens, No. 52). 1977. lib. bdg. 39.95x (ISBN 0-8383-2174-7). Haskell.

Dickens, Milton. Speech: Dynamic Communication. 3rd ed. 400p. 1974. text ed. 17.95 (ISBN 0-15-583193-3, HC); instructor's manual avail. (ISBN 0-15-583194-1). HarBraceJ.

Dickens, Milton & McBath, James H. Guidebook for Speech Communication. 183p. 1973. pap. text ed. 12.95 (ISBN 0-15-530006-7, HC). HarBraceJ.

Dickens, Monica. Miracles of Courage: How Families Meet the Challenge of a Child's Critical Illness. 256p. 1985. 14.95 (ISBN 0-396-08554-7). Dodd.

--An Open Book. (Illus.). 1978. 10.00 (ISBN 0-8317-6620-4, Mayflower Bks). Smith Pubs.

Dickens, Nathaniel A. The Gospel Singer. Dickens, Deborah S., ed. LC 84-90448. (Orig.). 1985. pap. write for info. (ISBN 0-916191-01-X). Gunther Pubs.

--The Official District of Columbia Book of Numbers. Lipkowitz, Brenda, ed. LC 83-90486. (Illus.). 90p. (Orig.). 1984. pap. 4.00 (ISBN 0-916191-00-1). Gunther Pubs.

Dickens, P. & McConville, S. Penal Policy & Prison Architecture. Fairweather, L., ed. 96p. 1978. 30.00x (ISBN 0-85992-133-6, Pub. by B Rose Pub). State Mutual Bk.

Dickens, Peter, et al. Housing, States & Localities. 320p. 1985. text ed. 39.95 (ISBN 0-416-73780-3, 9551). Methuen Inc.

Dickens, Roy S., Jr. Cherokee Prehistory: The Pisgah Phase in the Appalachian Summit Region. LC 76-1972. 1976. 19.95x (ISBN 0-87049-193-8). U of Tenn Pr.

Dickens, Roy S., Jr., ed. Archaeology of Urban America: The Search for Pattern & Process. (Studies in Historical Archaeology). 1982. 42.50 (ISBN 0-12-214980-7). Acad Pr.

Dickens, Roy S., Jr. & Ward, H. Trawick, eds. Structrue & Process in Southeastern Archaelology. LC 84-23. (Illus.). 336p. 1985. 35.00 (ISBN 0-8173-0216-6). U of Ala Pr.

Dickensheet, Dean W., ed. Great Crimes of San Francisco. 192p. (Orig.). 1974. pap. 2.50 (ISBN 0-89174-033-3). Comstock Edns.

Dickenson. Last Master. 2.95 (ISBN 0-317-31861-6). Tor Bks.

Dickenson, A. F. see Trotman-Dickenson, A. F. & Parfitt, G. D.

Dickenson, Celia. Too Many Boys. (Loveswept Ser.: No. 71). 160p. (Orig.). 1984. pap. 2.25 (ISBN 0-553-24355-1). Bantam.

Dickenson, Colin & Lucas, John. Encyclopaedia of Mushrooms. 1981. 60.00x (ISBN 0-686-78778-1, Pub. by RHS Ent England). State Mutual Bk.

Dickenson, D. I. Trotman see Trotman-Dickenson, D. I.

Dickenson, Donna. Emily Dickinson. (Women's Ser.). (Illus.). 144p. (Orig.). 1985. pap. 5.95 (ISBN 0-907582-69-9, Pub. by Berg Pubs). Longwood Pub Group.

Dickenson, Emily. For Love of Her. 1974. pap. 4.95 (ISBN 0-517-51488-5, C N Potter Bks). Crown.

Dickenson, J. P. & Clarke, C. G. A Geography of the Third World. LC 83-7927. 1983. pap. 11.95 (ISBN 0-416-74170-3, NO. 3909). Methuen Inc.

Dickenson, John P. Brazil: An Industrial Geography. (Special Studies in Industrial Geography). 1978. 28.50x (ISBN 0-89158-832-9, Dawson). Westview.

Dickenson, Kate L. William Blake's Anticipation of the Individualistic Revolution. LC 72-193732. 1974. Repr. of 1915 ed. lib. bdg. 10.00 (ISBN 0-8414-3789-0). Folcroft.

Dickenson, Luella. Reminiscences of a Trip Across the Plains in 1846 & Early Days in California. 1977. 12.00 (ISBN 0-87770-180-6). Ye Galleon.

Dickenson, Mary. Democracy in Trade Unions: Studies in Membership Participation & Control. LC 82-2065. (Policy, Politics, & Administration Ser.). (Illus.). 249p. 1983. text ed. 32.50x (ISBN 0-7022-1666-6). U of Queensland Pr.

Dickenson, Richard B., jt. ed. see Nell, Varney R.

Dickenson, Rosalind E. Communication Nil! 1979. 5.00 (ISBN 0-682-49346-5). Exposition Pr FL.

--Who Laughs Last. 64p. 1982. 5.00 (ISBN 0-682-49847-5). Exposition Pr FL.

Dickenson, Sylvia. The Andromeda Vein. 1984. 10.95 (ISBN 0-533-05893-7). Vantage.

Dicker, jt. auth. see Greene.

Dicker, George. Dewey's Theory of Knowledge. 72p. 1976. pap. 19.95 (ISBN 0-87722-115-4). Temple U Pr.

Dicker, Herman. Creativity, Holocaust, Reconstruction: Jewish Life in Wuertemberg, Past & Present. (Illus.). 1984. 18.50 (ISBN 0-87203-118-7). Hermon.

--Piety & Perseverance: Jews from the Carpathian Mountains. LC 80-54595. (Illus.). 252p. 1981. 14.95 (ISBN 0-87203-094-6); pap. 8.95 (ISBN 0-87203-098-9). Hermon.

Dicker, Laverne M. The Chinese in San Francisco: A Pictorial History. LC 79-50669. (Illus.). 1980. pap. 6.00 (ISBN 0-486-23868-7). Dover.

--The Chinese in San Francisco: A Pictorial History. (Illus.). 16.50 (ISBN 0-8446-5748-4). Peter Smith.

Dicker, Leo. Facilitating Manual Communication. 210p. 1978. pap. text ed. 16.95 (ISBN 0-9602220-0-6). RID Pubns.

Dicker, Ralph L. & Syracuse, Victor R. A Consultation with a Plastic Surgeon. LC 74-30176. (Illus.). 273p. 1975. 19.95 (ISBN 0-88229-201-3). Nelson-Hall.

Dicker, Terence F. Computer Programs for the Kitchen. (Illus.). 304p. 1984. 18.95 (ISBN 0-8306-0707-2, 1707); pap. 13.50 (ISBN 0-8306-1707-8). TAB Bks.

Dickerhoff, Heinrich. Wege ins Alte Testament - und Zurueck: Vom Sinn und den Moeglichkeiten einer "Theologie mit dem Alten Testament" in der Arbeit mit Erwachsenen, Vol 211. (European University Studies: No. 23). 409p. (Ger.). 1979. 40.55 (ISBN 3-8204-7734-9). P Lang Pubs.

Dickerhoof, Edward, jt. auth. see Kallio, Edwin.

Dickerman, Alexandra & Dickerman, John. Discovering Hydroponic Gardening: Beginner's Guide to the Pleasures of Soil-Less Gardening. LC 75-17274. (Illus.). 160p. (Orig.). 1975. pap. 5.95 (ISBN 0-912800-19-4). Woodbridge Pr.

Dickerman, Edmund H. Bellievre & Villeroy: Power in France under Henry III & Henry IV. LC 70-127365. (Illus.). 212p. 1971. 18.00x (ISBN 0-87057-131-1). U Pr of New Eng.

Dickerman, John, jt. auth. see Dickerman, Alexandra.

Dickerman, Pat. Farm, Ranch, & Country Vacations. (Illus.). 1983. pap. 8.95 (ISBN 0-913214-04-3). Farm & Ranch.

Dickerman, Philip J., ed. see Symposium on Optical Spectrometric Measurements of High Temparatures.

Dickerman, Sherwood E., ed. see Salinger, John P.

Dickerson, et al. Chemical Principles. 4th ed. 1984. 37.95 (ISBN 0-8053-2422-4); By Samuels. study guide 13.95 (ISBN 0-8053-2424-0); Relevant Problems by Butler & Grosser. 13.95 (ISBN 0-8053-1230-7). By Chastain. instrs' guide 6.95 (ISBN 0-8053-2423-2). Benjamin-Cummings.

Dickerson, Beverly, jt. auth. see Short, J. Rodney.

Dickerson, Donna L. Florida Media Law. LC 82-1976. xii, 194p. 1982. pap. 15.00 (ISBN 0-8130-0719-4). U Presses Fla.

Dickerson, F. Reed. Fundamentals of Legal Drafting (1965) 1965. 18.00 (ISBN 0-316-18394-6). Little.

--The Interpretation & Application of Statutes. 312p. 1975. 22.50 (ISBN 0-316-18396-2). Little.

--Legal Drafting Materials on. LC 81-1359. (American Casebook Ser.). 425p. 1981. text ed. 16.95 (ISBN 0-314-58615-6). West Pub.

--Legislative Drafting. LC 77-8392. 149p. 1977. Repr. of 1954 ed. lib. bdg. 25.00 (ISBN 0-8371-9688-4, DILD). Greenwood.

Dickerson, Florence S. James Stewart Family. 1966. 9.00 (ISBN 0-87012-028-X). McClain.

Dickerson, Grace. Jesus. 1985. 5.50 (ISBN 0-533-03936-3). Vantage.

Dickerson, Gregory W., tr. see Sophocles.

Dickerson, J. W., jt. auth. see Bryce-Smith, D.

Dickerson, Jan. Training Your Own Young Horse. LC 74-9444. (Illus.). 1978. 12.95 (ISBN 0-385-02222-0). Doubleday.

Dickerson, John W. & Booth, Elizabeth M. Clinical Nutrition for Nurses, Dieticians & Other Health Care Professionals. LC 85-4455. 260p. (Orig.). 1985. pap. 17.95 (ISBN 0-571-13426-2). Faber & Faber.

Dickerson, John W. T. & McGurk, Harry, eds. Brain & Behavioural Development: Interdisciplinary Perspectives on Structure & Function. (Illus.). 266p. 1982. 69.95x (ISBN 0-903384-27-2). Intl Ideas.

Dickerson, Lonna J., jt. auth. see Dickerson, Wayne B.

Dickerson, M. O., et al, eds. Problems of Change in Urban Government. 249p. 1980. pap. text ed. 12.00x (ISBN 0-88920-089-0, Pub. by Wilfred Laurier U Pr Canada). Humanities.

Dickerson, Marilyn K. Lord Hap. 176p. 1980. pap. 1.95 (ISBN 0-380-75572-6, 75572). Avon.

Dickerson, Martha U. Our Four Boys: Foster Parenting Retarded Teenagers. 1978. pap. 9.95x (ISBN 0-8156-0155-7). Syracuse U Pr.

--Social Work Practice with the Mentally Retarded. Turner, Francis J. & Strean, Herbert S., eds. LC 80-2316. (Fields of Practice Ser.). 1981. text ed. 18.95 (ISBN 0-02-907430-4). Free Pr.

Dickerson, Mary C. Frog Book. (Illus.). 1969. pap. 8.95 (ISBN 0-486-21973-9). Dover.

--The Frog Book: North American Toads & Frogs, with a Study of the Habits & Life Histories of Those of the Northeastern States. (Illus.). 18.00 (ISBN 0-8446-0582-4). Peter Smith.

Dickerson, O. M. The Navigation Acts & the American Revolution. LC 71-120248. xv, 344p. 1974. Repr. of 1951 ed. lib. bdg. 27.50x (ISBN 0-374-92162-8). Octagon.

Dickerson, Oliver M. The Navigation Acts & the American Revolution. LC 51-13206. 344p. 1974. pap. 9.95x (ISBN 0-8122-1077-8). U of Pa Pr.

Dickerson, Oliver M., ed. Boston under Military Rule 1768-1769. LC 70-118029. (Era of the American Revolution Ser). 1970. Repr. of 1936 ed. 22.50 (ISBN 0-306-71943-6). Da Capo.

--Music & the Higher Education. (Educational Ser.). Repr. 20.00 (ISBN 0-8482-3689-0). Norwood Edns.

--Music in the History of the Western Church. LC 77-127454. Repr. of 1902 ed. 14.50 (ISBN 0-404-02127-1). AMS Pr.

--Music in the History of the Western Church, with an Introduction in Religious Music Among the Primitive & Ancient Peoples. LC 69-13884. Repr. of 1902 ed. lib. bdg. 19.75x (ISBN 0-8371-1062-9, DIMW). Greenwood.

--Music in the History of the Western Church, with an Introduction in Religious Music Among the Primitive & Ancient Peoples. 1977. Repr. 19.00 (ISBN 0-403-08194-7). Scholarly.

--The Spirit of Music. 59.95 (ISBN 0-8490-1111-6). Gordon Pr.

--The Spirit of Music: How to Find It & How to Share It. (Select Bibliographies Reprint Ser.). Repr. of 1925 ed. 18.00 (ISBN 0-8369-6683-X). Ayer Co Pubs.

--The Spirit of Music: How to Find It & How to Share It. 218p. 1982. Repr. of 1927 ed. lib. bdg. 25.00 (ISBN 0-8495-1142-9). Arden Lib.

--The Study of the History of Music. 59.95 (ISBN 0-8490-1155-8). Gordon Pr.

Dickinson, Edwin D. The Equality of States in International Law. LC 72-4270. (World Affairs Ser.: National & International Viewpoints). 440p. 1972. Repr. of 1920 ed. 26.50 (ISBN 0-405-04566-2). Ayer Co Pubs.

--The Equality of States in International Law. LC 21-99. (Harvard Studies in Jurisprudence: Vol. 3). xiii, 424p. 1979. Repr. of 1920 ed. lib. bdg. 35.00 (ISBN 0-89941-138-X). W S Hein.

Dickinson, Elizabeth, et al. Public Employee Compensation: A Twelve City Comparison. 152p. 1980. pap. 10.00x (ISBN 0-317-06396-0, 28900). Urban Inst.

Dickinson, Elizabeth M., jt. ed. see Harvey, John F.

Dickinson, Emily. Acts of Light: Emily Dickinson. Langton, Jane, ed. 188p. 1980. o. p. 24.95 (ISBN 0-8212-1098-X, 006505); deluxe ed. 75.00 (ISBN 0-8212-1118-8, 006513DXLE). NYGS.

--Bolts of Melody: New Poems of Emily Dickinson. Bingham, Millicent T. & Todd, Mabel L., eds. (Illus.). 1945. 8.95i (ISBN 0-06-011035-X, HarpT). Har-Row.

--Choice of Emily Dickinson's Verse. Hughes, Ted, ed. 68p. 1968. pap. 5.95 (ISBN 0-571-08218-1). Faber & Faber.

--The Complete Poems of Emily Dickinson. Johnson, Thomas H., ed. 1960. 24.50 (ISBN 0-316-18414-4); pap. 10.45 (ISBN 0-316-18413-6). Little.

--Emily Dickinson. 160p. pap. 1.75 (ISBN 0-440-32304-5, LE). Dell.

--Emily Dickinson: Selected Letters. Johnson, Thomas H., ed. LC 78-129120. 1971. Repr. of 1958 ed. 25.00x (ISBN 0-674-25060-5, Belknap Pr). Harvard U Pr.

--An Emily Dickinson Year Book. LC 76-52440. 1977. lib. bdg. 15.00 (ISBN 0-8414-2959-6). Folcroft.

--Final Harvest: Emily Dickinson's Poems. Johnson, Thomas H., ed. 1962. 14.95 (ISBN 0-316-18416-0); pap. 6.70 (ISBN 0-316-18415-2). Little.

--I'm Nobody! Who Are You? The Poems of Emily Dickinson. LC 78-6828. (Illus.). 96p. (gr. 1 up). 1978. 17.95 (ISBN 0-916144-21-6); pap. 9.95 (ISBN 0-916144-22-4). Stemmer Hse.

--Letters, 3 vols. Johnson, Thomas H. & Ward, Theodora, eds. LC 58-5594. (Illus.). 1958. boxed set 55.00 (ISBN 0-674-52625-2, Belknap Pr). Harvard U Pr.

--Love Poems. 4.95 (ISBN 0-88088-132-1). Peter Pauper.

--Love Poems & Others. (Classics Ser.). 1982. 8.95 (ISBN 0-88088-907-1). Peter Pauper.

--The Manuscript Books of Emily Dickinson: A Facsimile Edition, 2 vols. Franklin, Ralph W., ed. LC 80-17861. 1442p. 1981. 100.00x (ISBN 0-674-54828-0, Belknap Pr). Harvard U Pr.

--Poems by Emily Dickinson. rev. ed. Bianchi, Martha D. & Hampson, Alfred L., eds. 1957. 16.45i (ISBN 0-316-18417-9). Little.

--Poems, Eighteen Ninety to Eighteen Ninety-Six, 3 Vols. in 1. LC 67-25640. 1967. 75.00x (ISBN 0-8201-1014-0). Schol Facsimiles.

--Poems for Youth. Hampson, Alfred L., ed. (Illus.). (gr. 7-10). 1934. 10.45i (ISBN 0-316-18418-7). Little.

--Poems of Emily Dickinson. Plotz, Helen, ed. LC 64-12111. (Poets Ser.). (Illus.). (gr. 4 up). 1964. 11.49i (ISBN 0-690-63365-3). Crowell Jr Bks.

--Poems of Emily Dickinson, 3 Vols. Johnson, Thomas H., ed. (Illus.). 1350p. (Incl. Variant Readings Critically Compared with All Known Manuscripts). 1955. Set. boxed 55.00 (ISBN 0-674-67600-9, Belknap Pr). Harvard U Pr.

--Selected Poems & Letters of Emily Dickinson. LC 59-12052. pap. 5.95 (ISBN 0-385-09423-X, Anch). Doubleday.

Dickinson, Fidelia, jt. auth. see Gwinup, Thomas.

Dickinson, G. C. Maps & Air Photographs: Images of Earth. 2nd ed. LC 78-31287. 348p. 1979. pap. 17.95 (ISBN 0-470-26641-4). Halsted Pr.

Dickinson, G. Lowes. Causes of International War. LC 84-12797. 110p. 1984. Repr. of 1920 ed. lib. bdg. 27.50x (ISBN 0-313-24565-7, DICI). Greenwood.

--The Greek View of Life. 1915. 15.00 (ISBN 0-686-20095-0). Quality Lib.

--Letters from a Chinese Official: Being an Eastern View of Western Civilization. 1907. Repr. 8.50 (ISBN 0-8274-2829-4). R West.

--A Modern Symposium. 1978. Repr. of 1930 ed. lib. bdg. 10.00 (ISBN 0-8495-1018-X). Arden Lib.

Dickinson, G. Lowes & Meredith, H. O., eds. Temple Greek & Latin Classics, 5 Vols. Repr. of 1907 ed. Set. 120.00 (ISBN 0-404-07900-8). AMS Pr.

Dickinson, G. M., jt. auth. see Cockerell, H. A.

Dickinson, George. The Dynamic Principle of Historical Growth & the Vico Theory. (Illus.). 1978. 88.75 (ISBN 0-89266-089-9). Am Classical Coll Pr.

Dickinson, George S. A Handbook of Style in Music. 2nd ed. LC 72-90211. (Music Reprint Ser). 1969. Repr. of 1965 ed. 32.50 (ISBN 0-306-71820-0). Da Capo.

Dickinson, George T. Jeremiah: The Iron Prophet. (Horizon Ser.). 1978. pap. 5.95 (ISBN 0-8127-0183-6). Review & Herald.

Dickinson, Georgianna M., jt. auth. see Miller, Jean M.

Dickinson, Goldsworthy L. The Greek View of Life. LC 78-12661. 1979. Repr. of 1958 ed. lib. bdg. 24.75x (ISBN 0-313-21195-7, DIGV). Greenwood.

Dickinson, H. T. British Radicalism & the French Revolution. (Historical Association Studies). 96p. 1985. pap. 6.95 (ISBN 0-631-13945-1). Basil Blackwell.

--Caricatures & the Constitution, 1760-1832. LC 85-5957. (English Satirical Print Ser.). 194p. 1985. lib. bdg. 48.00 (ISBN 0-85964-171-6). Chadwyck-Healey.

--Liberty & Property: Political Ideology in Eighteenth-Century Britain. LC 77-13477. 369p. 1978. text ed. 49.50x (ISBN 0-8419-0351-4). Holmes & Meier.

Dickinson, H. T., ed. Politics & Literature in the Eighteenth Century. (Rowman & Littlefield University Library). 234p. 1974. 9.50x (ISBN 0-87471-405-2); pap. 4.00x (ISBN 0-87471-400-1). Rowman.

Dickinson, H. W., jt. auth. see Jenkins, R.

Dickinson, Helena. A Study of Henry D. Thoreau. 59.95 (ISBN 0-8490-1152-3). Gordon Pr.

--A Treasury of Worship. 59.95 (ISBN 0-8490-1230-9). Gordon Pr.

Dickinson, Henry D. Economics of Socialism. (Select Bibliographies Reprint Ser.). Repr. of 1939 ed. 19.00 (ISBN 0-8369-5834-9). Ayer Co Pubs.

--Institutional Revenue. LC 66-21368. Repr. of 1932 ed. 27.50x (ISBN 0-678-00160-X). Kelley.

Dickinson, Henry W. Robert Fulton, Engineer & Artist. facsimile ed. LC 77-148879. (Select Bibliographies Reprint Ser). Repr. of 1913 ed. 26.50 (ISBN 0-8369-5649-4). Ayer Co Pubs.

Dickinson, Hugh. Myth on the Modern Stage. LC 68-18204. 359p. 1969. 24.95x (ISBN 0-252-78400-6). U of Ill Pr.

Dickinson, J. Letters from a Farmer in Pennsylvania to the Inhabitants of the British Colonies. Repr. of 1903 ed. 22.00 (ISBN 0-527-22660-2). Kraus Repr.

Dickinson, J. C. The Later Middle Ages: From the Norman Conquest to the Eve of the Reformation. (Ecclesiastical History of England Ser.). 487p. 1979. text ed. 30.00x (ISBN 0-06-491678-2). B&N Imports.

Dickinson, James & Russell, Robert, eds. Family, Economy & State: The Social Reproduction Process under Capitalism. 288p. 1985. 32.50 (ISBN 0-312-28045-9). St Martin.

Dickinson, Jan. Complete Guide to Family Relocation. LC 83-91431. 246p. 1983. pap. 9.95 (ISBN 0-9613011-0-4). Wheatherstone Pr.

Dickinson, Jane. All about Trees. LC 82-17382. (Question & Answer Bks.). (Illus.). 32p. (gr. 3-6). 1983. PLB 9.59 (ISBN 0-89375-892-2); pap. text ed. 1.95 (ISBN 0-89375-893-0). Troll Assocs.

--Wonders of Water. LC 82-17388. (Question & Answer Bks.). (Illus.). 32p. (gr. 3-6). 1983. PLB 9.59 (ISBN 0-89375-874-4); pap. text ed. 1.95 (ISBN 0-89375-875-2). Troll Assocs.

Dickinson, Janice, ed. see DeJesu, Gil.

Dickinson, Janice, ed. see Edgerly, Webster & DeJesu, Gil.

Dickinson, Joan Y., ed. The Role of the Immigrant Woman in the U.S. Labor Force 1890-1910. Cordasco, Francesco. LC 80-852. (American Ethnic Groups Ser.). 1981. lib. bdg. 24.50x (ISBN 0-405-13415-0). Ayer Co Pubs.

Dickinson, Joanne. Boss Cocky. 1982. 7.95 (ISBN 0-533-04854-0). Vantage.

Dickinson, John. A Behavioural Analysis of Sport. 216p. 1977. pap. text ed. 4.95x (ISBN 0-86019-014-5). Princeton Bk Co.

--Letters from a Farmer in Pennsylvania to the Inhabitants of the British Colonies. LC 3-20873. 1903. 29.00 (ISBN 0-403-00186-2). Scholarly.

--Political Writings of John Dickinson, 1764-1774. Ford, P. L., ed. LC 70-119061. (Era of the American Revolution). 1970. Repr. of 1895 ed. lib. bdg. 49.50 (ISBN 0-306-71950-9). Da Capo.

--Proprioceptive Control of Human Movement. 209p. 1980. 12.00x (ISBN 0-86019-002-1, Pub. by Kimpton). State Mutual Bk.

Dickinson, John C. Monastic Life in Medieval England. LC 78-25804. (Illus.). 1979. Repr. of 1961 ed. lib. bdg. 24.75x (ISBN 0-313-20774-7, DIML). Greenwood.

Dickinson, John K., tr. see Heiber, Helmut.

Dickinson, John N. Andrew Johnson, Eighteen Hundred Eight to Eighteen Seventy-Five: Chronology, Documents, Bibliographical Aids. LC 79-116064. (Presidential Chronology Ser.). 84p. 1970. 8.00 (ISBN 0-379-12075-5). Oceana.

--To Build a Canal: Sault Ste. Marie, 1853-1854 & After. LC 80-27693. (Illus.). 222p. 1981. 21.50 (ISBN 0-8142-0309-4). Ohio St U Pr.

Dickinson, John T., jt. ed. see Conley, John.

Dickinson, Joycelyne G. The Congress of Arras, Fourteen Thirty-Five. 1973. Repr. of 1955 ed. 15.00x (ISBN 0-8196-0281-7). Biblo.

Dickinson, June M., ed. & intro. by. Reminiscences of Clara Schumann as Found in the Diary of Her Grandson Ferdinand Schumann. (Illus.). 1974. pap. 12.00 (ISBN 0-913000-49-3). Musical Scope.

Dickinson, Kate L. William Blake's Anticipation of the Individualistic Revolution. 56p. 1980. Repr. of 1915 ed. lib. bdg. 10.00 (ISBN 0-8495-1055-4). Arden Lib.

Dickinson, L., et al. The Immigrant School Learner: A Study of Pakistani Pupils in Glasgow. 200p. 1975. 17.00x (ISBN 0-85633-062-0, Pub. by NFER Nelson UK). Taylor & Francis.

Dickinson, Leo. Filming the Impossible. (Illus.). 288p. 1982. 22.95 (ISBN 0-224-02015-3, Pub. by Jonathan Cape). Merrimack Pub Cir.

Dickinson, Leon T. A Guide to Literary Study. 1959. pap. text ed. 11.95 (ISBN 0-03-008270-6, HoltC). HR&W.

Dickinson, Lura B., jt. auth. see Dickinson, Robert.

Dickinson, M. & Purvey, P. F. British Tokens & Their Values. (Illus.). 1984. lib. bdg. 11.00 (ISBN 0-900652-65-9, Pub. by B A Seaby England). S J Durst.

Dickinson, Margaret & Street, Sarah. Cinema & State: The Film Industry & the British Government 1927-1984. (Illus.). 284p. 1985. 33.95x (ISBN 0-85170-160-4); pap. 16.95 (ISBN 0-85170-161-2). U of Ill Pr.

Dickinson, Mary. Alex & Roy. (Illus.). 32p. (ps-2). 1982. 9.95 (ISBN 0-233-97347-8). Andre Deutsch.

--Alex & the Baby. (Illus.). 32p. (ps-1). 1983. 9.95 (ISBN 0-233-97465-2). Andre Deutsch.

--Alex's Bed. (Illus.). (ps-1). 1980. 7.95 (ISBN 0-233-97207-2). Andre Deutsch.

--Alex's Outing. (Illus.). 32p. (ps-2). 1983. 8.95 (ISBN 0-233-97558-6). Andre Deutsch.

--New Clothes for Alex. LC 84-71670. (Alex Ser.: No. 5). (Illus.). 32p. (ps-2). 1984. 8.95 (ISBN 0-233-97685-X, Andre Deutsch). Dutton.

Dickinson, Mary, et al. Jilly, You Look Terrible. Royds, Pamela, ed. (Illus.). 32p. (ps-2). 1985. 9.95 (ISBN 0-233-97780-5). Andre Deutsch.

Dickinson, Michael, jt. auth. see Purvey, P. Frank.

Dickinson, Mike. My Brother's Silly. (Illus.). 32p. (ps-1). 1983. 9.95 (ISBN 0-233-97531-4). Andre Deutsch.

--My Dad Doesn't Even Notice. (Illus.). 32p. (gr. k-2). 1982. 18.95 (ISBN 0-233-97385-0). Andre Deutsch.

Dickinson, O. P., jt. auth. see Simpson, R. H.

Dickinson, O. T. The Origins of Mycenaean Civilization. (Studies in Mediterranean Archaeology: No. XLIX). (Illus.). 1977. pap. text ed. 45.50x (ISBN 91-85058-74-2). Humanities.

Dickinson, Pamela I. Music with ESN Children. 176p. 1976. 13.00x (ISBN 0-85633-085-X, Pub. by NFER Nelson UK). Taylor & Francis.

Dickinson, Patric, ed. see Newbolt, Henry.

Dickinson, Patric, tr. see Virgil.

Dickinson, Peter. Annerton Pit. (gr. 7 up). 1977. 7.95 (ISBN 0-316-18430-6, Atlantic-Little, Brown). Little.

--The Blue Hawk. (YA) (gr. 7 up). 1976. 9.95 (ISBN 0-316-18429-2, Pub. by Atlantic Monthly Pr). Little.

--Death of a Unicorn. LC 84-42700. 1984. 13.45 (ISBN 0-394-53947-8). Pantheon.

--Giant Cold. (Illus.). 64p. (gr. 4-7). 1984. 10.95 (ISBN 0-525-44073-9, 01063-320, Unicorn Bk). Dutton.

--The Gift. 192p. (gr. 7-12). 1974. 8.95 (ISBN 0-316-18427-6, Pub. by Atlantic Monthly Pr.). Little.

--The Glass-Sided Ant's Nest. 1981. pap. 2.95 (ISBN 0-14-005864-8). Penguin.

--Healer. LC 84-17454. 192p. (gr. 7 up). 1985. 14.95 (ISBN 0-385-29372-0). Delacorte.

--Hepzibah. LC 80-65425. (Illus.). 32p. (gr. 2-7). 1980. 8.95 (ISBN 0-87923-334-6). Godine.

--Hindsight. LC 83-42816. (International Crime Ser.). 200p. 1983. 12.45 (ISBN 0-394-53182-5); pap. 2.95 (ISBN 0-394-72603-0). Pantheon.

--The Iron Lion. LC 83-19715. (Illus.). 32p. (gr. 2-6). 1984. 10.95 (ISBN 0-911745-18-1, Bedrick Blackie). P Bedrick Bks.

--King & Joker. 1983. pap. 2.95 (ISBN 0-394-71600-0). Pantheon.

--The Last Houseparty. LC 82-47982. 224p. 1982. 12.45 (ISBN 0-394-51795-4). Pantheon.

--The Lively Dead. 1982. pap. 2.95 (ISBN 0-394-73317-7). Pantheon.

--The Seventh Raven. 192p. (gr. 7 up). 1981. 11.50 (ISBN 0-525-39150-9, 01117-330, Unicorn Bk). Dutton.

--Travel & Retirement Edens Abroad. (Illus.). 352p. 1983. 19.95 (ISBN 0-525-93274-7, 01937-580); pap. 12.95 (ISBN 0-525-93273-9, 01258-370). Dutton.

--Tulku. (MagicQuest Ser.: No. 5). 224p. 1984. pap. 2.25 (ISBN 0-441-82630-X, Pub. by Tempo). Ace Bks.

Dickinson, Peter & Anderson, Wayne. The Flight of Dragons. LC 78-22450. (Illus.). 1979. 17.50i (ISBN 0-06-011074-0, HarpT). Har-Row.

Dickinson, Peter A. The Complete Retirement Planning Book. 1984. 17.95 (ISBN 0-525-93304-2, 01743-520). Dutton.

--Retirement Edens: Outside the Sunbelt. LC 80-22629. 288p. 1981. 15.50 (ISBN 0-525-93173-2, 01505-450); pap. 9.25 (ISBN 0-525-93174-0, 0898-270). Dutton.

--Sunbelt Retirement: The Complete State-By-State Guide to Retiring in the South & West of the United States. 2nd ed. (Illus.). 1980. pap. 8.95 (ISBN 0-525-93107-4, 0869-290). Dutton.

Dickinson, Peter H. Surgical Procedures: Subtotal Thyroidectomy, Vol. 5. (Single Surgical Procedures Ser.). 100p. (Orig.). 1983. 25.95 (ISBN 0-87489-504-9). Med Economics.

Dickinson, R. F., jt. auth. see Harmon, G. L.

Dickinson, Robert & Dickinson, Lura B. The Single Woman: A Medical Study in Sex Education. Rothman, David J. & Rothman, Sheila M., eds. (Women & Children First Ser.). Date not set. 60.00 (ISBN 0-8240-7656-7). Garland Pub.

Dickinson, Robert E. The Population Problem of Southern Italy: An Essay in Social Geography. LC 76-49087. (Illus.). 1977. Repr. of 1955 ed. lib. bdg. 15.50x (ISBN 0-8371-9337-0, DIPP). Greenwood.

Dickinson, Robert E. & Howarth, O. J. R. The Making of Geography. LC 75-38379. 1976. Repr. of 1933 ed. lib. bdg. 22.50x (ISBN 0-8371-8669-2, DIMG). Greenwood.

Dickinson, Robert L. Atlas of Human Sex Anatomy. LC 50-5564. (Illus.). 382p. 1970. Repr. of 1949 ed. 37.50 (ISBN 0-88275-014-3). Krieger.

Dickinson, Robert L. & Beam, Lura. Thousand Marriages: A Medical Study of Sex Adjustment. LC 76-95093. Repr. of 1931 ed. lib. bdg. 19.75x (ISBN 0-8371-3085-9, DIMA). Greenwood.

Dickinson, Roger A. Retail Management. LC 81-80597. (Illus.). 695p. 1981. text ed. 19.95 (ISBN 0-914872-17-6). Austin Pr.

Dickinson, Rudolph E. The Broad Soviet Strategy for the Conquest of Asia. (The Great Currents of History Library). (Illus.). 115p. 1981. 79.65x (ISBN 0-930008-88-X). Inst Econ Pol.

Dickinson, S. P. Penguin in the Shrubbery. 1984. 22.00x (ISBN 0-317-14522-3, Pub. by Selecteditions). State Mutual Bk.

Dickinson, Sharon. An Administrative Secretary: Simulation - Dallas Oil, Inc. (gr. 9-12). 1985. 4.65 (ISBN 0-538-25950-7, Y95). SW Pub.

Dickinson, T., jt. ed. see Covington, A. K.

Dickinson, Thomas H. Chief Contemporary Dramatists: Twenty-Two Plays from the Recent Drama of England, Ireland, America, Germany, France, Belgium, Norway, Sweden & Russia. 1979. Repr. of 1915 ed. lib. bdg. 30.00 (ISBN 0-8492-4207-X). R West.

--The Insurgent Theatre. LC 72-83277. Repr. of 1917 ed. 20.00 (ISBN 0-405-08445-5). Ayer Co Pubs.

--An Outline of Contemporary Drama. LC 70-88059. 1969. Repr. of 1927 ed. 12.00x (ISBN 0-8196-0249-3). Biblo.

--Playrights of the New American Theatre. 1981. Repr. lib. bdg. 30.00 (ISBN 0-403-00943-X). Scholarly.

--Playwrights of the New American Theater. facs. ed. LC 67-26731. (Essay Index Reprint Ser). 1925. 21.50 (ISBN 0-8369-0373-0). Ayer Co Pubs.

Dickinson, Thomas H., ed. Chief Contemporary Dramatists. LC 76-6588. Repr. of 1915 ed. 47.50 (ISBN 0-404-15281-3). AMS Pr.

--Chief Contemporary Dramatists. LC 76-6590. (Second Series). Repr. of 1921 ed. 47.50 (ISBN 0-404-15282-1). AMS Pr.

--Chief Contemporary Dramatists. 734p. 1982. Repr. of 1921 ed. lib. bdg. 50.00 (ISBN 0-89987-167-4). Darby Bks.

--Chief Contemporary Dramatists, Second Series: Eighteen Plays from the Recent Drama of England, Ireland, America, France, Germany, Austria, Italy, Spain, Russia, & Scandinavia. 734p. Date not set. Repr. of 1921 ed. lib. bdg. 50.00 (ISBN 0-317-17328-6). Darby Bks.

Dickinson, Thorold & De La Roche, Catherine. Soviet Cinema. Manvell, Roger, ed. LC 77-169327. (National Cinema Series). (Illus.). 140p. 1972. Repr. of 1948 ed. 18.00 (ISBN 0-405-03891-7). Ayer Co Pubs.

Dickinson, W. Calvin. James Harrington's Republic. LC 82-24749. 126p. (Orig.). 1983. lib. bdg. 21.00 (ISBN 0-8191-3019-2); pap. text ed. 9.25 (ISBN 0-8191-3020-6). U Pr of Amer.

Dickinson, W. Croft. Scotland from the Earliest Times to 1603. 3rd ed. Duncan, Archibald A., ed. (Illus.). 1977. text ed. 49.95x (ISBN 0-19-822453-2). Oxford U Pr.

Dickinson, W. J. & Sullivan, D. T. Gene-Enzyme Systems in Drosophila. LC 74-17430. (Results & Problems in Cell Differentiation: Vol. 6). (Illus.). xii, 163p. 1975. 37.00 (ISBN 0-387-06977-1). Springer-Verlag.

Dickinson, William. A Glossary of Words & Phrases Pertaining to the Dialect of Cumberland. (English Dialect Society (Series C: VIII) Publications: Nos. 20 & 24). pap. 16.00 (ISBN 0-317-15745-0). Kraus Repr.

Dickinson, Zenas C. Economic Motives: A Study in the Psychological Foundation of Economic Theory. LC 79-51859. 1980. Repr. of 1922 ed. 24.75 (ISBN 0-88355-952-8). Hyperion Conn.

Dickison, Mary E. Dickison & His Men: Reminiscences of the War in Florida. rev. ed. (Illus.). 287p. 1984. Repr. of 1890 ed. 19.00 (ISBN 0-317-19335-X). San Marcos Bk.

Dickison, S. K., jt. auth. see Schaub, J. H.

Dickison, William C., jt. ed. see White, Richard A.

Dick-Larkam, R. Profit Improvement Techniques. (Illus.). 204p. 1973. 22.00x (ISBN 0-8464-0767-1). Beekman Pubs.

Dick-Larkham, Richard. Cutting Energy Costs. 1977. 24.95x (ISBN 0-8464-0309-9). Beekman Pubs.

Dickler, Howard. The dBASE III Trail Guide. 350p. 1985. pap. 29.95 incl. disk (ISBN 0-912677-56-2). Ashton-Tate Bks.

Dickman, A. I., ed. see Sisk, B. F.

Dickman, Andreas & Mitter, Peter, eds. Stochastic Modelling of Social Processes. 1984. 30.00 (ISBN 0-12-215490-8). Acad Pr.

Dickman, Byron A. You're Fired. LC 76-73206. 1978. write for info. (ISBN 0-932984-00-2). Gracelaine.

Dickman, Daryl, compiled by. Abstract Index to ASA Annual Meeting Papers, 1960-1974. 94p. 1976. pap. 10.00 (ISBN 0-918456-04-5). African Studies Assn.

Dickman, Irving R. Making Life More Livable. LC 83-6412. 89p. 1983. pap. 7.00 (ISBN 0-89128-115-0, PAL115). Am Foun Blind.

--Winning the Battle for Sex Education. LC 82-61000. 64p. (Orig.). 1982. pap. 6.00 (ISBN 0-9609212-0-6). SIECUS.

Dickman, Irving R., ed. Sex Education & Family Life for Visually Handicapped Children & Youth: A Resource Guide. 1975. pap. 5.00 (ISBN 0-89128-053-7, PEP053). Am Foun Blind.

Dickman, J. Fred, et al, eds. Counseling the Troubled Person in Industry: A Guide to the Organization, Implementation, & Evaluation of Employee Assistance Programs. 312p. 1985. 31.75x (ISBN 0-398-05020-1). C C Thomas.

Dickman, Marvin J. Tax Opportunities for Owners of Closely Held Companies. LC 85-5728. 68p. 1985. 50.00 (ISBN 0-932648-65-7). Boardroom.

Dickman, R. F., ed. see Virginia Polytechnic Institute & State University, March 22-24, 1973.

Dickman, R. Thomas. Corporate Body. LC 82-90980. 1983. 9.95 (ISBN 0-87212-168-2). Libra.

--In God We Should Trust. LC 76-53146. 1977. 6.95 (ISBN 0-87212-071-6). Libra.

Dickman, Thelma. Toronto in Your Pocket. (City in Your Pocket Ser.). 144p. 1984. pap. 2.95 (ISBN 0-8120-2836-8). Barron.

Dickman, Thomas. Some Light Remarks. LC 79-92087. 1980. 7.95 (ISBN 0-87212-120-8). Libra.

Dickman, Tom, tr. see Beaud, Michel.

Dickman, William J. Battery Rodgers. 35p. 1980. pap. 4.50x (ISBN 0-89126-094-3). MA-AH Pub.

Dickmeyer, Lowell & Humphreys, Martha. A. J. Goes to Germany. (Soccer Adventure Ser.). (Illus.). 96p. (gr. 5 up). 1983. PLB 8.95 (ISBN 0-87518-246-1, Gemstone Bks). Dillon.

--The Adams See Australia. (Soccer Adventure Ser.). (Illus.). 112p. (gr. 4 up). 1984. pap. 4.95 (ISBN 0-87518-257-7, Gemstone Bks). Dillon.

--The Eagles Fly to Scotland. (Soccer Adventure Ser.). (Illus.). 96p. (gr. 4 up). 1984. pap. 4.95 (ISBN 0-87518-256-9, Gemstone Bks). Dillon.

--Hana Discovers Japan: Soccer Adventure Ser. (Illus.). 112p. (gr. 4 up). 1984. pap. 4.95 (ISBN 0-87518-258-5, Gemstone Bks). Dillon.

--Lyndsey Sees the Midnight Sun. (Soccer Adventure Ser.). (Illus.). 96p. (gr. 5 up). 1983. PLB 8.95 (ISBN 0-87518-251-8, Gemstone Bks). Dillon.

--Paul Meets the Masters. (Soccer Adventure Ser.). (Illus.). 96p. (gr. 5 up). 1983. PLB 8.95 (ISBN 0-87518-250-X, Gemstone Bks). Dillon.

Dickmeyer, Lowell A. Baseball Is for Me. LC 77-92299. (Sports for Me Books). (Illus.). (gr. k-4). 1978. PLB 7.95 (ISBN 0-8225-1079-0). Lerner Pubns.

--Basketball Is for Me. LC 79-16954. (Sports for Me Bks.). (Illus.). (gr. 2-5). 1980. PLB 7.95 (ISBN 0-8225-1089-8). Lerner Pubns.

--Football Is for Me. LC 79-15445. (Sports for Me Bks.). (Illus.). (gr. 2-5). 1979. PLB 7.95 (ISBN 0-8225-1087-1). Lerner Pubns.

--Hockey Is for Me. LC 78-54362. (The Sports for Me Bks). (Illus.). (gr. 2-5). 1978. PLB 7.95 (ISBN 0-8225-1080-4). Lerner Pubns.

--Skateboarding Is for Me. LC 78-54361. (The Sports for Me Bks). (Illus.). (gr. 5 up). 1978. PLB 7.95 (ISBN 0-8225-1081-2). Lerner Pubns.

--Soccer Is for Me. LC 77-92294. (Sports for Me Books). (Illus.). (gr. k-4). 1978. PLB 7.95 (ISBN 0-8225-1076-6). Lerner Pubns.

--Swimming Is for Me. LC 80-15366. (Sports for Me Bks.). (Illus.). (gr. 2-5). 1980. PLB 7.95 (ISBN 0-8225-1084-7). Lerner Pubns.

--Track Is for Me. LC 79-1508. (Sports for Me Bks.). (Illus.). (gr. 2-5). 1979. PLB 7.95 (ISBN 0-8225-1083-9). Lerner Pubns.

Dickmeyer, Lowell A. & Chappell, Annette Jo. Tennis Is for Me. LC 77-92300. (Sports for Me Books). (Illus.). (gr. k-4). 1978. PLB 7.95 (ISBN 0-8225-1077-4). Lerner Pubns.

Dickmeyer, Lowell A. & Humphreys, Martha. Teamwork. (Easy-Read Sports Books Ser.). (Illus.). 48p. (gr. 1-3). 1984. 8.60 (ISBN 0-531-04713-X). Watts.

--Winning & Losing. (Easy-Read Sports Book Ser.). (Illus.). (gr. 1-3). 1984. lib. bdg. 8.60 (ISBN 0-531-04714-8). Watts.

Dickmeyer, Lowell A. & Rolens, Lin. Ice Skating Is for Me. LC 79-20465. (Sports for Me Bks.). (Illus.). (gr. 2-5). 1980. PLB 7.95 (ISBN 0-8225-1088-X). Lerner Pubns.

Dickmeyer, Nathan & Hughes, K. Scott. Financial Self-Assessment: A Workbook for Colleges. 72p. 1980. pap. text ed. 20.00, 1 copy (ISBN 0-915164-11-6); pap. text ed. 17.50 each, 2-4 copies; pap. text ed. 12.50 each, 5 or more copies. Natl Assn Coll.

Dickmeyer, Nathan, et al. Institutionally Funded Student Financial Aid. 1981. 15.00 (ISBN 0-8268-1459-X). ACE.

Dickneider, William C., Jr. & Kaplan, David. Choice & Change: An Introduction to Economics. (Illus.). 1978. pap. text ed. 16.95 (ISBN 0-8299-0165-5); test bank avail. (ISBN 0-8299-0475-1). West Pub.

Dickos, Andrew. Intrepid Laughter: Preston Sturges & the Movies. LC 85-2512. 186p. 1985. 15.00 (ISBN 0-8108-1815-9). Scarecrow.

Dick-Read, Grantly. Childbirth Without Fear. Wessel, Helen & Ellis, Harlan, eds. LC 83-48340. (Illus.). 416p. 1984. 17.26 (ISBN 0-06-015221-4, HarpT). Har-Row.

--Childbirth Without Fear: The Original Approach to Natural Childbirth. 5th ed. Wessel, Helen & Ellis, Harlan, eds. LC 83-48340. (Illus.). 384p. 1985. pap. 8.95 (ISBN 0-06-091284-7, PL 1284, PL). Har-Row.

Dicks, B., jt. ed. see Gordon, G.

Dicks, Brian. The Isle of Wight. LC 78-74082. 1979. 14.95 (ISBN 0-7153-7657-8). David & Charles.

--The Israelis: How They Live & Work. LC 74-30350. 156p. 1975. text ed. 9.95 (ISBN 0-275-26040-2, HoltC). HR&W.

--Rhodes. (Islands Ser.). 1974. 14.95 (ISBN 0-7153-6571-1). David & Charles.

Dicks, D. R. Early Greek Astronomy to Aristotle. LC 76-109335. (Aspects of Greek & Roman Life Ser.). (Illus.). 272p. (Orig.). 1985. pap. text ed. 9.95x (ISBN 0-8014-9310-2). Cornell U Pr.

Dicks, G. R., ed. Sources of World Financial & Banking Information. LC 80-28654. 720p. 1981. lib. bdg. 125.00 (ISBN 0-313-22966-X, DSW/). Greenwood.

Dicks, Henry V. Marital Tensions: Clinical Studies Towards a Psychological Theory of Interaction. 368p. 1984. pap. 9.95 (ISBN 0-7102-0037-4). Routledge & Kegan.

Dicks, Terrance. The Baker Street Irregulars in the Case of the Blackmail Boys. (gr. 4 up). 1980. 7.95 (ISBN 0-525-66710-5). Lodestar Bks.

--The Baker Street Irregulars in the Case of the Cop Catchers. 128p. (gr. 5-9). 1982. 9.95 (ISBN 0-525-66765-2, 0966-290). Lodestar Bks.

--The Baker Street Irregulars in the Case of the Crooked Kids. (gr. 4 up). 1980. 7.95 (ISBN 0-525-66711-3). Lodestar Bks.

--The Baker Street Irregulars in the Case of the Cinema Swindle. 128p. (gr. 4 up). 1981. 9.25 (ISBN 0-525-66728-8, 0898-270). Lodestar Bks.

--The Baker Street Irregulars in the Case of the Ghost Grabbers. 128p. (gr. 4 up). 1981. 9.25 (ISBN 0-525-66729-6, 0898-270). Lodestar Bks.

--The Baker Street Irregulars in the Case of the Missing Masterpiece. LC 79-18861. (gr. 4 up). 1979. 7.95 (ISBN 0-525-66656-7). Lodestar Bks.

--Dr. Who & the Android Invasion. (Dr. Who Ser.: No. 9). (Orig.). 1981. pap. 1.95 (ISBN 0-523-42506-6). Pinnacle Bks.

--Doctor Who & the Android Invasion. 10.95 (ISBN 0-8488-0150-4, Pub. by Amereon Hse). Amereon Ltd.

--Dr. Who & the Day of the Daleks. (Dr. Who Ser.: No. 1). 1979. pap. 1.95 (ISBN 0-523-42496-5). Pinnacle Bks.

--Doctor Who & the Day of the Daleks. 10.95 (ISBN 0-8488-0151-2, Pub. by Amereon Hse). Amereon Ltd.

--Dr. Who & the Genesis of the Daleks. (The Dr. Who Ser.: No. 4). 1982. pap. 1.95 (ISBN 0-523-42361-6). Pinnacle Bks.

--Doctor Who & the Genesis of the Daleks. 10.95 (ISBN 0-8488-0152-0, Pub. by Amereon Hse). Amereon Ltd.

--Doctor Who & the Giant Robot. 9.95 (ISBN 0-8488-0153-9, Pub. by Amereon Hse). Amereon Ltd.

--Doctor Who & the Image of the Fendall. 10.95 (ISBN 0-8488-0154-7, Pub by Amereon Hse). Amereon Ltd.

--Dr. Who & the Loch Ness Monster. (Dr. Who Ser.: No. 6). 1981. pap. 1.95 (ISBN 0-523-41791-8). Pinnacle Bks.

--Doctor Who & the Loch Ness Monster. 10.95 (ISBN 0-8488-0155-5, Pub. by Amereon Hse). Amereon Ltd.

--Dr. Who & the Revenge of the Cybermen. (Dr. Who Ser.: No. 5). 1979. pap. 1.95 (ISBN 0-523-42501-5). Pinnacle Bks.

--Doctor Who & the Revenge of the Cybermen. 10.95 (ISBN 0-8488-0156-3, Pub. by Amereon Hse). Amereon Ltd.

--Doctor Who & the Talons of Weng-Chang. (Doctor Who Ser.: No. 7). 1979. pap. 1.75 (ISBN 0-523-42503-1). Pinnacle Bks.

Dicks, W. Groups, Trees & Projective Modules. (Lecture Notes in Mathematics: Vol. 790). 127p. 1980. pap. 13.00 (ISBN 0-387-09974-3). Springer-Verlag.

Dicksee, Lawrence R. Advanced Accounting: Appendix on the Law Relating to Accounts by J. E. G. Dep Montmorency. LC 75-18464. (History of Accounting Ser.). (Illus.). 1976. Repr. of 1903 ed. 29.00x (ISBN 0-405-07547-2). Ayer Co Pubs.

--Auditing: Practical Manual for Auditors, Authorized American Edition. Montgomery, Robert H., ed. LC 75-18466. (History of Accounting Ser.). 1976. Repr. of 1902 ed. 26.50x (ISBN 0-405-07549-9). Ayer Co Pubs.

--Business Methods & the War: The Fundamentals of Manufacturing Costs: & Published Balance Sheets & Window Dressing, 3 vols. in 1. Brief, Richard P., ed. LC 80-1487. (Dimensions of Accounting Theory & Practice Ser.). 1981. Repr. of 1927 ed. lib. bdg. 18.00x (ISBN 0-686-73167-0). Ayer Co Pubs.

--Business Methods & the War with the Fundamentals of Manufacturing Costs & Published Balance Sheets & Window Dressing. 21.00 (ISBN 0-405-13517-3). Ayer Co Pubs.

--Business Organisation. Brief, Richard P., ed. LC 80-1488. (Dimensions of Accounting Theory & Practice Ser.). 1981. Repr. of 1910 ed. lib. bdg. 28.50x (ISBN 0-405-13518-1). Ayer Co Pubs.

--Depreciation, Reserves, & Reserve Funds. LC 75-18467. (History of Accounting Ser.). (Illus.). 1976. Repr. 14.00x (ISBN 0-405-07550-2). Ayer Co Pubs.

--Fraudulent Accounting. 17.00 (ISBN 0-405-13519-X). Ayer Co Pubs.

--Fraudulent Accounting & Fraud in Accounts, 2 vols. in one. Brief, Richard P., ed. LC 80-1489. (Dimensions of Accounting Theory & Practice Ser.). 1981. Repr. of 1925 ed. lib. bdg. 15.00x (ISBN 0-686-73168-9). Ayer Co Pubs.

--Goodwill & Its Treatment in Accounts. 2nd ed. LC 75-18468. (History of Accounting Ser.). (Illus.). 14.00x (ISBN 0-405-07551-0). Ayer Co Pubs.

Dickson. Apple Teaches Language Arts. (Illus.). 250p. 1984. 17.95 (ISBN 0-8359-0077-0). Reston.

--Man from Earth. 2.95 (ISBN 0-317-31863-2). Tor Bks.

--Pritcher Mass. 2.75 (ISBN 0-317-31884-5). Tor Bks.

--Scottish Capitalism. 1980. text ed. 25.25x (ISBN 0-85315-482-1). Humanities.

Dickson & Wright. Musculoskeletal Disease. (Integrated Clinical Science Ser.). 1984. 22.95 (ISBN 0-8151-9370-X). Year Bk Med.

Dickson, jt. auth. see Bova.

Dickson, jt. auth. see Laumer.

Dickson, Albert A. Fascination of Faith. Keith, Gerald, ed. 268p. (Orig.). 1980. pap. 4.95x (ISBN 0-9604080-0-2). Gloria Pubs.

Dickson, Anna H. Where's My Blankie? LC 83-83278. (Sesame Street Growing-Up Bks.). (Illus.). 32p. (ps). 1984. 2.50 (ISBN 0-307-12013-9, 12013, Golden Bks). Western Pub.

Dickson, Anne. A Woman in Your Own Right: Assertiveness & You. (Illus.). 160p. 1983. 5.95 (ISBN 0-7043-3420-8, Pub. by Quartet Bks). Merrimack Pub Cir.

Dickson, Antonia, jt. auth. see Dickson, W. K.

Dickson, Arthur. Valentine & Orson, a Study in Late Medieval Romance. LC 75-153315. Repr. of 1929 ed. 22.50 (ISBN 0-404-02128-X). AMS Pr.

Dickson, Bruce J., jt. ed. see Downen, Robert L.

Dickson, Carter. Curse of the Bronze Lamp. 260p. 1984. pap. 3.50 (ISBN 0-88184-101-3). Carroll & Graf.

--Death in Five Boxes. 1977. pap. 1.50 (ISBN 0-505-51203-3, Pub. by Tower Bks). Dorchester Pub Co.

--The Department of Queer Complaints. 1981. 14.50 (ISBN 0-8398-2739-3, Gregg). G K Hall.

--A Graveyard to Let. 1978. pap. 1.50 (ISBN 0-505-51222-X, Pub. by Tower Bks). Dorchester Pub Co.

--Skeleton in the Clock. 1977. pap. 1.50 (ISBN 0-505-51194-0, Pub. by Tower Bks). Dorchester Pub Co.

Dickson, D., jt. ed. see Devine, T. M.

Dickson, D. Bruce. Prehistoric Pueblo Settlement Patterns: The Arroyo Hondo, New Mexico, Site Survey. LC 79-21542. (Arroyo Hondo Archaeological Ser.: Vol. 2). (Illus.). 151p. 1980. pap. 8.00 (ISBN 0-933452-02-0). Schol Am Res.

Dickson, D. G. Expansions in Series of Solutions of Linear Difference-Differential & Infinite Order Differential Equations with Constant Coefficients. LC 52-42839. (Memoirs: No. 23). 72p. 1982. pap. 12.00 (ISBN 0-8218-1223-8, MEMO-23). Am Math.

Dickson, David. A Commentary on the Psalms, 2 vols. 1980. 32.50 (ISBN 0-86524-017-5, 1901). Klock & Klock.

--Matthew. (Geneva Ser. Commentaries). Orig. Title: A Brief Exposition of the Evangel of Jesus Christ According to Matthew. 416p. 1981. 14.95 (ISBN 0-85151-319-0). Banner of Truth.

--The Politics of Alternative Technology. LC 75-7919. 1977. pap. 4.50x (ISBN 0-87663-917-1). Universe.

--United States Foreign Policy Towards Sub-Saharan Africa: Change, Continuity, & Restraint. LC 85-9044. (American Values Projected Abroad Ser.: Vol. XVIII). 216p. 1985. lib. bdg. 22.50 (ISBN 0-8191-4727-3); pap. text ed. 11.25 (ISBN 0-8191-4728-1). U Pr of Amer.

Dickson, David R. & Maue, Wilma M. Human Vocal Anatomy. (Illus.). 172p. 1977. 18.75x (ISBN 0-398-00449-8). C C Thomas.

Dickson, David R. & Maue-Dickson, Wilma. Anatomical & Physiological Bases of Speech. 1982. 26.95 (ISBN 0-316-18431-4). Little.

Dickson, Douglas, ed. Business & Its Public: Harvard Business Review. LC 83-23487. (Harvard Business Review Executive Book Ser.). 468p. 1985. 24.95 (ISBN 0-471-88749-8). Wiley.

Dickson, Douglas N. Corporate Political Action Committees. 225p. 1984. cancelled (ISBN 0-88410-839-2). Ballinger Pub.

Dickson, E. M. & Harben, P. W., eds. Phosphates: What Prospects for Growth. 357p. (Orig.). 1984. pap. text ed. 35.00 (ISBN 0-913333-03-4). Metal Bulletin.

Dickson, Elaine. Say No, Say Yes to Change. LC 81-67375. 1982. 6.95 (ISBN 0-8054-5210-9). Broadman.

Dickson, Elizabeth. The Englishwoman's Bedroom. LC 84-52248. (Illus.). 160p. 1985. 26.95 (ISBN 0-88162-087-4, Pub. by Salem Hse Ltd). Merrimack Pub Cir.

Dickson, Elizabeth & Colver, Margaret. Laura Ashley Book of Home Decorating. 1984. 24.95 (ISBN 0-517-54610-8, Harmony); pap. 14.95 (ISBN 0-517-55450-X, Harmony). Crown.

Dickson, Elizabeth & Colvin, Margaret. The Laura Ashley Book of Home Decorating. (Illus.). 160p. 1982. lib. bdg. 24.95 (ISBN 0-517-54610-8, Harmony). Crown.

Dickson, Elizabeth & Peterson, George. Public Employee Compensation: A Twelve City Comparison. 2nd ed. LC 81-53060. 213p. 1981. pap. text ed. 12.00x (ISBN 0-87766-310-6, URI 32800). Urban Inst.

Dickson, Elizabeth, et al. The Laura Ashley Book of Home Decorating. rev. ed. 1985. 24.95 (ISBN 0-517-55686-3). Crown.

Dickson, F. P. Australian Stone Hatchets: A Study in Design & Dynamics. LC 81-67867. (Studies in Archaeological Science). 240p. 1981. 35.00 (ISBN 0-12-215220-4). Acad Pr.

Dickson, Frank & Smythe, Sandra, eds. Handbook of Short Story Writing. LC 73-100315. 238p. 1981. pap. 6.95 (ISBN 0-89879-049-2). Writers Digest.

Dickson, Frank A. One Thousand One Article Ideas. LC 79-11602. 270p. 1979. 10.95 (ISBN 0-911654-64-X). Writers Digest.

Dickson, G. A Jerusalem Christian Treatise on Astrology. 1982. 30.00x (ISBN 0-686-45724-2, Pub. by Palestine Explo England). State Mutual Bk.

Dickson, G. R., ed. Methods of Calcified Tissue Preparation. 765p. 1984. 157.50 (ISBN 0-444-80580-X). Elsevier.

Dickson, G. W. & Smith, H. R. Introduction to FORTRAN IV Programming: A Self-Paced Approach. LC 74-189809. 1972. pap. text ed. 17.95 (ISBN 0-03-088088-2, HoltC). HR&W.

Dickson, G. W. & Wetherbe, J. The Management of Information Systems. 512p. 1984. 00387323x 31.95 (ISBN 0-07-016825-3). McGraw.

Dickson, G. W. & Wetherbe, J. C. The Management of Information Systems Casebook. 248p. 1984. 16.95 (ISBN 0-07-016827-X). McGraw.

Dickson, Gary, ed. see Clowes, Kenneth W.

Dickson, Gary, ed. see Gremillion, Lee L.

Dickson, Gary, ed. see Jenkins, A. Milton.

Dickson, Gary, ed. see Selig, Gad J.

Dickson, Gary L. Resident Assistant Stress Inventory: Manual & Inservice Education Guide. rev. ed. iv, 43p. 1981. pap. 3.95 (ISBN 0-943872-68-5). Andrews Univ Pr.

Dickson, George L. The Direct Way: A Programmed Study of the English Sentence. 108p. (Orig.). 1979. pap. text ed. 4.95x (ISBN 0-89641-023-4). American Pr.

Dickson, Gordon. Dorsai. 1985. pap. 2.95 (ISBN 0-441-16021-2) (ISBN 0-317-31747-4). Ace Bks.

--The Outposter. 256p. (Orig.). 1982. pap. 2.95 (ISBN 0-523-48580-8). Pinnacle Bks.

--The Pritcher Mass. 256p. 1983. pap. 2.75 (ISBN 0-523-48556-5). Pinnacle Bks.

--Secrets of the Deep. 192p. (Orig.). 1985. pap. 2.95 (ISBN 0-931773-29-6). Critics Choice Paper.

--The Space Swimmers. 256p. 1982. pap. 2.25 (ISBN 0-441-77767-8). Ace Bks.

--Time Storm. 432p. 1985. pap. 3.50 (ISBN 0-553-25146-5). Bantam.

Dickson, Gordon, ed. Nebula Winners Twelve. LC 66-20974. 1978. 12.45i (ISBN 0-06-011078-3, HarpT). Har-Row.

Dickson, Gordon R. Alien Art & Arcturus Landing. 352p. 1982. pap. 2.75 (ISBN 0-441-01685-5). Ace Bks.

--Beyond the Dar Al-Harb. 256p. (Orig.). 1985. pap. 2.95 (ISBN 0-8125-3550-2, Dist. by Warner Pub Services & St. Martin). Tor Bks.

--Combat SF. 288p. 1984. pap. 2.75 (ISBN 0-441-11534-9). Ace Bks.

--Dickson! 193p. 1984. 13.00 (ISBN 0-915368-27-7). New Eng SF Assoc.

--Dorsai! 1982. pap. 2.75 (ISBN 0-441-16012-3). Ace Bks.

--Dorsai. 1984. pap. 3.25 (ISBN 0-441-16021-2). Ace Bks.

--The Dragon & the George. 1978. pap. 2.25 (ISBN 0-345-29514-5). Ballantine.

--The Far Call. 416p. 1983. pap. 2.75 (ISBN 0-441-22799-6). Ace Bks.

--The Final Encyclopedia. (The Childe Cycle Ser.). 684p. 1984. 18.95 (ISBN 0-312-93241-3). Tor Bks.

--The Finial Encyclopedia. 704p. 1985. pap. 4.95 (ISBN 0-441-23776-2) (ISBN 0-317-31752-0). Ace Bks.

--Home from the Shore. 1979. pap. 2.25 (ISBN 0-441-34256-6). Ace Bks.

--Hour of the Horde. (Science Fiction Ser). 1978. pap. 1.95 (ISBN 0-87997-689-6, UE1689). DAW Bks.

--Hour of the Horde. 1984. pap. 2.95 (ISBN 0-671-55905-2, Pub. by Baen Bks). PB.

--The Last Master. 320p. (Orig.). 1984. pap. 2.95 (ISBN 0-8125-3562-6, Pinnacle Bks). Tor Bks.

--Lost Dorsai. 288p. 1981. pap. 2.95 (ISBN 0-441-49300-9). Ace Bks.

--Love Not Human. 256p. 1981. pap. 2.50 (ISBN 0-441-50414-0). Ace Bks.

--Masters of Everon. Baen, Jim, ed. 1980. pap. 4.95 (ISBN 0-441-52115-0). Ace Bks.

--Mission to Universe. 224p. 1982. pap. 2.25 (ISBN 0-345-30654-6, Del Rey). Ballantine.

--Mutants. 224p. 1983. pap. 2.95 (ISBN 0-87997-809-0). Daw Bks.

--Necromancer. 1985. pap. 2.75 (ISBN 0-441-56854-8). Ace Bks.

--No Room for Man. 2nd ed. (Necromancer). 1974. pap. 0.75 (ISBN 0-532-95367-3). Woodhill.

--The Outposter. 256p. 1985. pap. 2.95 (ISBN 0-8125-3564-2, Dist. by Warner Pub Services & St. Martin). Tor Bks.

--Sleepwalker's World. 256p. (Orig.). 1982. pap. 2.50 (ISBN 0-523-48537-9). Pinnacle Bks.

--Sleepwalker's World. 256p. (Orig.). 1985. pap. 2.95 (ISBN 0-8125-3556-1, Dist. by Pinnacle Bks, Warner Pub Services & St. Martin). Tor Bks.

--Soldier Ask Not. 1984. pap. 2.95 (ISBN 0-441-77421-0). Ace Bks.

--Space Winners. 256p. 1986. pap. 2.95 (ISBN 0-8125-3558-8, Dist. by Warner Pub Services & St. Martin). Tor Bks.

--Spacepaw. 1983. pap. 2.50 (ISBN 0-441-77759-7, Pub. by Ace Science Fiction). Ace Bks.

--Special Delivery. 1983. pap. 1.95 (ISBN 0-441-77749-X, Pub. by Ace Science Fiction). Ace Bks.

--The Spirit of Dorsai. 1985. pap. 2.75 (ISBN 0-441-77804-6). Ace Bks.

--Star Road. (Science Fiction Ser.). pap. 2.25 (ISBN 0-87997-711-6). DAW Bks.

--Steel Brother. 256p. (Orig.). 1985. pap. 2.95 (ISBN 0-8125-3552-9, Dist. by Warner Pub Services & St. Martin). Tor Bks.

--Survival! (Orig.). 1984. pap. 2.75 (ISBN 0-671-55927-3). PB.

--Tactics of Mistake. 352p. 1984. pap. 2.50 (ISBN 0-441-79972-8). Ace Bks.

--Time to Teleport-Delusion World. 256p. 1982. pap. 2.50 (ISBN 0-441-81237-6). Ace Bks.

Dickson, Gordon R. & Green, Roland. Jamie the Red. 1984. pap. 3.25 (ISBN 0-441-38245-2, Pub. by Ace Science Fiction). Ace Bks.

Dickson, Gordon R. & Laumer, Keith. Planet Run. 288p. 1982. pap. 2.75 (ISBN 0-523-48525-5). Pinnacle Bks.

Dickson, Gordon R., jt. auth. see Anderson, Poul.

Dickson, Gordon R., jt. auth. see Bova, Ben.

Dickson, H. Climate & Weather. 1976. lib. bdg. 59.95 (ISBN 0-8490-1638-X). Gordon Pr.

Dickson, H., et al, eds. Thin Plate Working, Vol. 1. 2nd ed. (Illus.). 1977. 37.50x (ISBN 0-686-65561-3) (ISBN 0-85083-387-6). Intl Ideas.

--Thin Plate Working, Vol. 2. (Engineering Craftsmen: No. D22). (Illus.). 1969. spiral bdg. 37.50x (ISBN 0-85083-033-8). Intl Ideas.

Dickson, H. R. The Arab of the Desert. abr. ed. Wilson, Robert & Freeth, Zahra, eds. (Illus.). 256p. 1983. 24.50 (ISBN 0-04-016106-4). Allen Unwin.

Dickson, Harold E. John Wesley Jarvis, American Painter. LC 49-50388. xx, 476p. 1949. 15.00x (ISBN 0-685-73902-3, New York Historical Society). U Pr of Va.

--The Land Grant Frescoes at the Pennsylvania State University by Henry Varnum Poor. (Illus.). 24p. 1981. brochure 1.00 (ISBN 0-911209-22-0). Penn St Art.

--Masterworks by Pennsylvania Painters in Pennsylvania Collections: Exhibition Catalogue. (Illus.). 72p. 1972. pap. 6.00 (ISBN 0-911209-00-X). Penn St Art.

--Portraits U. S. A. 1776-1976. (Illus.). 133p. 1976. pap. 10.00 exhibition catalogue (ISBN 0-911209-07-7). Penn St Art.

Dickson, Harold E., jt. auth. see Porter, Richard.

Dickson, Harris. Story of King Cotton. LC 79-107513. Repr. of 1937 ed. 19.75x (ISBN 0-8371-3760-8, DKC&, Pub. by Negro U Pr). Greenwood.

Dickson, Irving R. Outreach to the Aging Blind: Some Strategies for Community Action. 168p. 1977. pap. 3.00 (ISBN 0-89128-078-2, PAP078). Am Foun Blind.

Dickson, J. Plantarum Cryptogamicarum Britanniae. (Illus.). 160p. (Latin.). 1976. Repr. of 1785 ed. 67.25x (ISBN 0-916422-28-3, Pub. by Richmond Pub Co). Mad River.

Dickson, J. F., 3rd & Brown, J. H., eds. Future Goals of Engineering in Biology & Medicine: Proceedings. 1969. 73.50 (ISBN 0-12-215250-6). Acad Pr.

Dickson, J. H. see Bowen, D. Q.

Dickson, James F., jt. ed. see Brown, J. H.

Dickson, James F., 3rd see Kenedi, R. M.

Dickson, James G. The Politics of the Texas Sheriff: From Frontier to Bureaucracy. (Texas History Ser.). (Illus.). 68p. (Orig.). 1983. pap. text ed. 2.95x (ISBN 0-89641-131-1). American Pr.

Dickson, James G., et al, eds. The Role of Insectivorous Birds in Forest Ecosystems. LC 79-12111. 1979. 55.00 (ISBN 0-12-215350-2). Acad Pr.

Dickson, Joanne, ed. Manuel Neri: Sculpture & Drawings. LC 80-71065. (Illus.). 28p. (Orig.). 1981. pap. 6.95 (ISBN 0-932216-11-0). Seattle Art.

Dickson, John. Victoria Hotel. LC 78-1215. 1979. 10.00 (ISBN 0-914090-63-1); pap. 5.95 (ISBN 0-914090-64-X). Chicago Review.

Dickson, K., jt. auth. see Bessant, J.

Dickson, K. E., jt. auth. see Bessant, J. R.

Dickson, K. L., jt. ed. see Cairns, John, Jr.

Dickson, K. L., et al, eds. Analyzing the Hazard Evaluation Process. 159p. 1979. 15.00 (ISBN 0-913235-24-5); members 12.00 (ISBN 0-317-32532-9). Am Fisheries Soc.

Dickson, Katharine. Stockman-Gallison Ancestral Lines: 114 Lines of Early New England Settlers & the Descendants, As of 1984 of John Gallison & Martha Moore. (Illus.). xxii, 285p. 1985. 30.00 (ISBN 0-9613959-0-7). Brown Katharine.

Dickson, Keith A. Towards Utopia: A Study of Brecht. 1978. 49.95x (ISBN 0-19-815750-9). Oxford U Pr.

Dickson, Kenneth L. & Maki, Alan W., eds. Modeling the Fate of Chemicals in the Aquatic Environment. LC 82-71527. (Illus.). 413p. 1982. 45.00 (ISBN 0-250-40552-0). Butterworth.

Dickson, Kenneth L., jt. ed. see Cairns, John, Jr.

Dickson, Kwesi A. Theology in Africa. LC 84-5154. 240p. (Orig.). 1984. pap. 9.95 (ISBN 0-88344-508-5). Orbis Bks.

Dickson, L. E. Linear Algebras. (Cambridge Tracts in Mathematics & Mathematical Physics Ser.: No. 16). 1969. Repr. of 1914 ed. 7.95x (ISBN 0-02-843920-1). Hafner.

Dickson, Lance E. & Chiang, Win-Shin S. Legal Bibliography Index (1978, 1979, 1980, 1981, 1982, 1983, 1984) (Legal Bibliography Index Series, Baton Rouge). 289p. pap. 35.00 (ISBN 0-317-14840-0). LSU Paul M Hebert Law Cen Pub Inst.

Dickson, Lance E. & Simpson, Joseph L., eds. Louisiana State University Law Library Dictionary Card Catalog. 526p. 1980. microfiche 150.00 (ISBN 0-940448-07-6). LSU Paul M Hebert Law Cen Pub Inst.

Dickson, Lance E., intro. by. Treatise of Femme Coverts: Or, the Lady's Law. viii, 280p. 1974. Repr. of 1732 ed. text ed. 22.50x (ISBN 0-8377-2129-6). Rothman.

Dickson, Leonard E. Collected Mathematical Papers, 5 vols. Albert, A. Adrian, ed. LC 69-19943. 3300p. 1975. Set. text ed. 195.00 set (ISBN 0-8284-0273-6). Chelsea Pub.

--Collected Mathematical Papers, Vol. VI. Albert, A. Adrian, ed. LC 69-19943. 1983. lib. bdg. 55.00 (ISBN 0-8284-0306-6). Chelsea Pub.

--History of the Theory of Numbers, 3 Vols. LC 66-26932. 49.50 (ISBN 0-8284-0086-5). Chelsea Pub.

--Plane Trigonometry with Practical Applications. LC 70-114597. (Illus.). (gr. 10-12). 1970. Repr. of 1922 ed. text ed. 9.95 (ISBN 0-8284-0230-2). Chelsea Pub.

--Researches on Waring's Problem. LC 35-19856. (Carnegie Institution of Washington Publication Ser.: No. 464). pap. 66.30 (ISBN 0-317-09159-X, 2015710). Bks Demand UMI.

--Studies in the Theory of Numbers. LC 61-13494. 13.95 (ISBN 0-8284-0151-9). Chelsea Pub.

Dickson, Leonard E; see Sierpinski, Waclaw, et al.

Dickson, Margaret. Maddy's Song. 310p. 1985. 15.95 (ISBN 0-395-36077-3). HM.

--Octavia's Hill. LC 82-15830. 384p. 1983. 14.95 (ISBN 0-395-33159-5). HM.

--Octavia's Hill. 400p. 1985. pap. 3.50 (ISBN 0-425-08082-X). Berkley Pub.

Dickson, Martin B. & Welch, S. Carey, eds. The Houghton Shahnameh: A Limited Facsimile Edition of the Shahnameh (Book of Kings) 1982. text ed. 2000.00x Set (ISBN 0-674-40854-3). Vol. I, 312pp., Historical Background. Vol. II, 564pp., Text. Harvard U Pr.

Dickson, Mimi & Robitscher, Jean. Learning Joy: A Book for Parents & Teachers Who Want to Help Children Find Themselves--& Joy. LC 77-76833. (Illus.). 1977. 4.95 (ISBN 0-87426-045-0). Whitmore.

Dickson, Mora. The Aunts. 144p. 1981. 29.00x (ISBN 0-7152-0491-2, Pub. by St Andrew Pr England). State Mutual Bk.

Dickson, Murray. Where There Is No Dentist. Blake, Michael, ed. LC 82-84067. (Illus.). 192p. (Orig.). 1983. pap. 6.00 (ISBN 0-942364-05-8). Hesperian Found.

Dickson, Naida. Biography of a Honeybee. LC 73-11976. (General Juvenile Bks). (Illus.). 48p. (gr. 1-4). 1974. PLB 5.95g (ISBN 0-8225-0292-5). Lerner Pubns.

Dickson, Nicholas. The Bible in Waverley. 1973. Repr. of 1884 ed. write for info. (ISBN 0-8274-1586-9). R West.

--Bible in Waverley: Or, Sir Walter Scott's Use of the Sacred Scripture. 311p. 1980. Repr. of 1884 ed. lib. bdg. 30.00 (ISBN 0-8495-1123-2). Arden Lib.

--Or, Sir Walter Scott's Use of Sacred Scriptures. 1979. Repr. of 1884 ed. lib. bdg. 30.00 (ISBN 0-8414-3830-7). Folcroft.

Dickson, P. Kissinger & the Meaning of History. LC 78-5633. 1978. 32.50 (ISBN 0-521-22113-7). Cambridge U Pr.

Dickson, Paul. The Electronic Battlefield. LC 75-31342. 256p. 1976. 17.50x (ISBN 0-253-12158-2). Ind U Pr.

--The Future File: A Guide for People with One Foot in the 21st Century. LC 77-76998. 1977. 12.95 (ISBN 0-89256-031-2). ETC Pubns.

--The Great American Ice Cream Book. LC 72-78284. (Illus.). 1978. pap. 4.95 (ISBN 0-689-70572-7, 240). Atheneum.

--Jokes: Outrageous Bits, Atrocious Puns, & Ridiculous Routines for Those Who Love Jests. (Illus.). 256p. 1984. 13.95 (ISBN 0-385-29333-X). Delacorte.

--The Official Explanations. 1981. pap. 5.95 (ISBN 0-440-56449-2, Dell Trade Pbks). Dell.

--The Official Rules. 1981. pap. 3.75 (ISBN 0-440-16684-5). Dell.

--The Official Rules. 1980. pap. 4.95 (ISBN 0-440-56684-3, Dell Trade Pbks). Dell.

--Toasts. (Orig.). 1982. pap. 7.95 (ISBN 0-440-58741-7, Dell Trade Pbks). Dell.

--Words. 384p. 1983. pap. 7.95 (ISBN 0-440-59260-7, Dell Trade Pbks). Dell.

Dickson, Paul & Goulden, Joseph. There Are Alligators in Our Sewers: And Other American Credos. 176p. 1983. 11.95 (ISBN 0-385-29052-7). Delacorte.

Dickson, Paul & Goulden, Joseph C. There Are Alligators in Our Sewers & Other American Credos. 1984. pap. 5.95 (ISBN 0-440-58952-5, Dell Trade Pbks). Dell.

Dickson, Peter W. Kissinger & the Meaning of History. LC 78-5633. pap. 51.80 (ISBN 0-317-28006-6, 2025581). Bks Demand UMI.

Dickson, R. A Lepidopterist's Handbook. 136p. 1976. 40.00x (ISBN 0-686-75579-0, Pub. by Amateur Entomol Soc). State Mutual Bk.

Dickson, R. Gary. Divorce Guide for Alberta. 4th ed. 87p. 1984. 9.95 (ISBN 0-88908-233-2); forms 12.95 (ISBN 0-88908-227-8). Self Counsel Pr.

Dickson, RA & Bradford, David S. BIMR Orthopedics 2: Management of Spinal Deformities. 256p. 1984. text ed. 39.95 (ISBN 0-407-02347-X). Butterworth.

Dickson, Robert. Robert's Dinner for Six. LC 78-64486. 1978. 6.00 (ISBN 0-937684-05-8). Tradd St Pr.

Dickson, Roger. Millennial Mistake. 2.50 (ISBN 0-89315-160-2). Lambert Bk.

Dickson, Ron C. The Great American Moon Pie Handbook. LC 85-60339. (Illus.). 128p. (Orig.). 1985. pap. 5.95 (ISBN 0-931948-67-3). Peachtree Pubs.

Dickson, Ron R. Weather & Flight: An Introduction to Meteorology for Pilots. 186p. 1982. 16.95 (ISBN 0-13-947119-7); pap. 7.95 (ISBN 0-13-947101-4). P-H.

Dickson, Ronald S. Organometallic Chemistry of Rhodium & Tridium. (Organometallic Chemistry Ser.). 1983. 85.00 (ISBN 0-12-215480-0). Acad Pr.

Dickson, Samuel. Tales of San Francisco. 1955. 16.95 (ISBN 0-8047-0488-0). Stanford U Pr.

Dickson, Stanley. Communication Disorders: Remedial Principles & Practices. 2nd ed. 1984. text ed. 27.10x (ISBN 0-673-15629-X). Scott F.

Dickson, T. R. Introduction to Chemistry. 4th ed. LC 82-10856. 540p. 1983. text ed. 30.95x (ISBN 0-471-09954-6). lab experiments 16.95 (ISBN 0-471-87192-3); transparencies o.p. 8.00 (ISBN 0-471-04757-0); study guide 12.95 (ISBN 0-471-87191-5); tchrs. manual o.p. 10.00 (ISBN 0-471-04750-3). Wiley.

Dickson, Ted & Harben, Peter, eds. Raw Materials for the Pulp & Paper Industry. 100p. (Orig.). 1984. pap. text ed. 38.50 (ISBN 0-913333-01-8). Metal Bulletin.

Dickson, Tony, ed. Capital & Class in Scotland. 286p. 1982. text ed. 34.25x (ISBN 0-85976-065-0, Pub. by Donald Scotland). Humanities.

--Scottish Capitalism: Class, State & Nation from Before the Union to the Present. 1980. 40.00x (ISBN 0-85315-482-1, Pub. by Lawrence & Wishart England). State Mutual Bk.

Dickson, W. K. & Dickson, Antonia. History of the Kinetograph, Kinetoscope & Kinetophonograph. LC 79-124005. (Literature of Cinema, Ser. 1). Repr. of 1895 ed. 11.95 (ISBN 0-405-01611-5). Ayer Co Pubs.

Dickson, W. Patrick, ed. Children's Oral Communication Skills. (Developmental Psychology Ser.). 1981. 39.50 (ISBN 0-12-215450-9). Acad Pr.

Dickson, Wayne & Raymond, Mike. The Language Arts-Computer Book: A How-to Guide for Teachers. (Illus.). 1983. text ed. 21.95 (ISBN 0-8359-3942-1); pap. 17.95 (ISBN 0-8359-3941-3). Reston.

Dickson, William. Letters on Slavery. LC 79-111573. Repr. of 1789 ed. 17.50x (ISBN 0-8371-4598-8, DLS&, Pub. by Negro U Pr). Greenwood.

Dickson, William, ed. Mitigation of Slavery. facs. ed. LC 78-79013. (Black Heritage Library Collection Ser). 1814. 21.50 (ISBN 0-8369-8655-5). Ayer Co Pubs.

Dickstein, Morris. Gates of Eden: American Culture in the Sixties. LC 76-7684. (Illus.). 1978. pap. 6.95 (ISBN 0-465-09731-6, TB-5081). Basic.

--Keats & His Poetry: A Study in Development. LC 74-136019. 288p. 1974. pap. 4.25x (ISBN 0-226-14796-7, P599, Phoen). U of Chicago Pr.

Dickstein, Morris, jt. ed. see Braudy, Leo.

DiClemente, Carlo C., jt. auth. see Prochaska, James O.

Diclerico, Robert & Hammock, Allan. Points of View. 3rd ed. 352p. 1986. pap. text ed. 11.00 (ISBN 0-394-35408-7, RanC). Random.

DiClerico, Robert & Hammock, Allan S. Points of View: Readings in American Government. 2nd ed. 352p. 1983. pap. text ed. 8.95 (ISBN 0-394-34944-X, RanC). Random.

Di Conversino da Ravenna, Giovanni. Dragmalogia de eligibili vitae genere (1404) Eaker, Helen L. & Kohl, Benjamin G., eds. 1980. 24.50 (ISBN 0-318-11900-5). Renaissance Soc Am.

Di Coppo, Giovanni. Legend of the Holy Fina, Virgin of Santo Gemignano. Mansfield, M., tr. LC 66-25699. (Medieval Library). (Illus., It. & Eng.). Repr. of 1926 ed. 15.00x (ISBN 0-8154-0054-3). Cooper Sq.

DiCosmo, F., jt. auth. see Nag Raj, T. R.

DiCrescenza, Frances. Annihilation or Salvation? Date not set. 8.95 (ISBN 0-8062-2505-X). Carlton.

Di Curcio, Robert A. Art on Nantucket: The History of Painting on Nantucket Island. 1st ed. Kelsey, Susan & Coffin, Elizabeth, eds. LC 81-83847. (Illus.). xvi, 272p. 1982. 250.00 (ISBN 0-9607340-0-7). Nantucket Hist Assn.

Dicus, Alexis. Mexican Cookery. Larsen, Madelyn, ed. (Illus.). 224p. (Orig.). 1980. pap. 4.95 (ISBN 0-346-12447-6). Cornerstone.

DiCyan, Erwin. A Beginner's Introduction to Trace Minerals. Mindell, Earl & Passwater, Richard A., eds. (Good Health Guides Ser.). 26p. 1984. pap. 1.45 (ISBN 0-87983-362-9). Keats.

--The Vitamins in Your Life. 1975. (Fireside); pap. 5.95 (ISBN 0-671-22010-1, Fireside). S&S.

Di Cyan, Erwin, jt. auth. see Moser, Robert H.

Diczfalusy, E., ed. Pharmacology of Reproduction, Vol. 2. LC 67-19416. 1968. 37.00 (ISBN 0-08-012368-6). Pergamon.

Diczfalusy, Egon, jt. ed. see Benagiano, Giuseppe.

Didactic Systems. Understanding Aging & Human Needs. 72p. 1978. 14.95 (ISBN 0-686-85781-X). Van Nos Reinhold.

Didactic Systems, Inc. Management in the Fire Service. Tower, K. & Dean, A. E., eds. LC 7-76527. 1977. text ed. 16.50 (ISBN 0-87765-097-7, TXT-3). Natl Fire Prot.

Didactic Systems Staff. Appraisal by Objectives: Coaching & Appraising. (Simulation Game Ser.). 1970. pap. 24.90 (ISBN 0-89401-003-4); pap. 21.50 two or more (ISBN 0-685-78131-3). Didactic Syst.

--Assigning Work. (Simulation Game Ser.). 1973. pap. 24.90 (ISBN 0-89401-006-9); pap. 21.50 two or more (ISBN 0-685-78097-X); pap. 24.90 french ed. (ISBN 0-89401-096-4); pap. 21.50 two or more (ISBN 0-685-78098-8). Didactic Syst.

--Communicating for Results. (Sumulation Game Ser.). 1969. pap. 24.90 (ISBN 0-89401-007-7); pap. 21.50 ea. two or more; pap. 24.90 french ed. (ISBN 0-89401-097-2); pap. 21.50 ea. two or more french eds. Didactic Syst.

--Constructive Discipline. 2nd ed. (Simulation-Game Ser.). 1978. pap. 24.90 (ISBN 0-89401-123-5); Two Or More Sets. 21.50 (ISBN 0-685-08735-2). Didactic Syst.

--Effective Delegation. Euro-Training & Garcia De Leon, Luis, trs. (Simulation Game Ser.). 1971. pap. 24.90 (ISBN 0-89401-145-6); pap. 21.50 two or more (ISBN 0-686-77274-1); pap. 24.90 french ed. (ISBN 0-89401-017-4); pap. 21.50 ea. two or more; pap. 24.90 spanish ed. (ISBN 0-89401-018-2); pap. 21.50 ea. two or more spanish eds. Didactic Syst.

--Effective Supervision. 1973. pap. 24.90 (ISBN 0-89401-022-0); pap. 21.50 two or more (ISBN 0-685-73203-7); pap. 24.90 spanish ed. (ISBN 0-89401-023-9); pap. 21.50 two or more (ISBN 0-685-73204-5). Didactic Syst.

--Grievance Handling: Industrial. 1970. pap. 24.90 (ISBN 0-89401-027-1); pap. 21.50 two or more (ISBN 0-685-78105-4); pap. 24.90 french ed. (ISBN 0-89401-028-X); pap. 21.50 ea. two or more french eds. Didactic Syst.

--Grievance Handling: Non-Industrial. 1971. pap. 24.90 (ISBN 0-89401-029-8); pap. 21.50 two or more (ISBN 0-685-78107-0); pap. 24.90 french ed. (ISBN 0-89401-030-1); pap. 21.50 ea. two or more french eds. Didactic Syst.

--Handling Conflict in Law Enforcement Management: Conflict Among Peers. (Simulation Game Ser.). 1978. pap. 24.90 (ISBN 0-89401-144-8); pap. 21.50 two or more (ISBN 0-685-89725-7); leader's guide 0.50 (ISBN 0-685-89726-5). Didactic Syst.

--Handling Conflict in Law Enforcement Management: Superior Subordinate Conflict. (Simulation Game Ser.). 1978. pap. 24.90 (ISBN 0-685-89727-3); pap. 21.50 two or more (ISBN 0-685-89728-1); leader's guide 0.50 (ISBN 0-685-89729-X). Didactic Syst.

--The Instructor As Manager of Learning Experiences. (Simulation Game Ser.). 1975. pap. 24.90 (ISBN 0-89401-044-1); pap. 21.50 two or more (ISBN 0-685-78124-0). Didactic Syst.

--Job Enrichment: Redesigning Jobs for Motivation. (Simulation Game Ser.). 1971. pap. 6.00 (ISBN 0-89401-045-X); leader's guide & tape avail. (ISBN 0-685-78125-9). Didactic Syst.

--Long Range Planning. (Simulation Game Ser.). 1971. pap. 24.90 (ISBN 0-89401-049-2); pap. 21.50 two or more (ISBN 0-686-57893-7). Didactic Syst.

--Management by Objectives. (Simulation Game Ser.). 1970. pap. 24.90 (ISBN 0-89401-051-4); pap. 21.50 two or more (ISBN 0-685-78111-9); pap. 24.90 portuguese ed. (ISBN 0-89401-053-0); pap. 21.50 ea. two or more portuguese eds. Didactic Syst.

--Management by Objectives. 2nd ed. 1978. pap. 24.90 (ISBN 0-89401-142-1). Didactic Syst.

--Management by Objectives for Insurance Companies. (Simulation Game Ser.). 1972. pap. 24.90 (ISBN 0-89401-054-9); pap. 21.50 two or more (ISBN 0-685-78128-3). Didactic Syst.

--Management for Supervisors. 1970. pap. 24.90 (ISBN 0-89401-056-5); pap. 21.50 per set for 2 or more sets (ISBN 0-685-73201-0); pap. 24.90 french ed. (ISBN 0-89401-057-3); pap. 24.90 portuguese ed. (ISBN 0-89401-058-1); pap. 0.50 leader guide (ISBN 0-685-73202-9). Didactic Syst.

--Management in Government. (Simulation Game Ser.). 1971. pap. 24.90 (ISBN 0-89401-059-X); pap. 21.50 two or more (ISBN 0-685-78144-5). Didactic Syst.

--Managing in a Foreign Culture. (Simulation Game Ser.). 1974. pap. 24.90 (ISBN 0-89401-062-X). pap. 21.50 ea. two or more. Didactic Syst.

--Managing the Manufacturing & Industrial Engineering Functions. (Simulation Game Ser.). 1970. pap. 24.90 (ISBN 0-89401-064-6); pap. 21.50 two or more (ISBN 0-685-78143-7). Didactic Syst.

--Managing the Quality Control Function. 1970. pap. 24.90 (ISBN 0-89401-065-4); pap. 21.50 two or more (ISBN 0-685-78142-9). Didactic Syst.

--Managing Through Face-to-Face Communication. (Didactic Simulation Game Ser.). 1969. pap. 24.90 (ISBN 0-89401-066-2); pap. 24.90 portuguese (ISBN 0-89401-067-0); pap. 21.50 for 2 or more (ISBN 0-685-79479-2); pap. 0.50 leader's guide (ISBN 0-685-79480-6). Didactic Syst.

--Market Planning. (Simulation Game Ser.). 1972. pap. 24.90 (ISBN 0-89401-068-9); pap. 21.50 two or more (ISBN 0-685-78137-2). Didactic Syst.

--Market Strategy. (Simulation Game Ser.). 1970. pap. 24.90 (ISBN 0-89401-069-7); pap. 21.50 two or more (ISBN 0-685-78138-0); pap. 24.90 portuguese ed. (ISBN 0-89401-118-9). Didactic Syst.

--Office Management. (Simulation Game Ser.). 1970. pap. 24.90 (ISBN 0-89401-070-0); pap. 21.50 two or more (ISBN 0-685-78139-9). Didactic Syst.

--Optimum Delegation. (Simulation Game Ser.). 1973. pap. 24.90 (ISBN 0-89401-019-0); pap. 21.50 two or more (ISBN 0-685-78122-4). Didactic Syst.

--Physical Distribution Management. (Simulation Game Ser.). 1970. pap. 24.90 (ISBN 0-89401-071-9); pap. 21.50 two or more (ISBN 0-685-78140-2); pap. 24.90 portuguese ed. (ISBN 0-89401-119-7). Didactic Syst.

--Planned Maintenance. (Simulation Game Ser.). 1969. pap. 24.90 (ISBN 0-89401-072-7); pap. 21.50 two or more (ISBN 0-685-78141-0). Didactic Syst.

--Planning & Assigning Work. (Study Units Ser.). 1978. pap. 9.00 (ISBN 0-89401-121-9). Didactic Syst.

--Planning for Growth. (Simulation Game Ser.). 1972. pap. 24.90 (ISBN 0-89401-074-3); pap. 21.50 two or more (ISBN 0-686-57895-3). Didactic Syst.

--Positive Discipline. (Study Units Ser.). 1978. pap. 9.00 (ISBN 0-89401-122-7). Didactic Syst.

--Principles of Effective Insurance Agents. (Didactic Simulation Game Ser). 1973. pap. 24.90 (ISBN 0-685-77372-8); pap. 21.50 for 2 or more (ISBN 0-686-57883-X); pap. 24.90 spanish ed. (ISBN 0-89401-102-2); pap. 21.50 for 2 or more (ISBN 0-686-57884-8); pap. 0.50 leader's guide (ISBN 0-685-77375-2). Didactic Syst.

--Procurement Management. (Simulation Game Ser.). 1975. pap. 24.90 (ISBN 0-89401-080-8); pap. 21.50 two or more (ISBN 0-685-78134-8). Didactic Syst.

--Productivity - Improving Performance. (Simulation Game Ser.). 1975. pap. 24.90 (ISBN 0-89401-081-6); pap. 21.50 two or more (ISBN 0-685-78135-6). Didactic Syst.

--Recruiting Effective Insurance Agents. (Didactic Simulation Game Ser.). 1973. pap. 24.90 (ISBN 0-89401-082-4); pap. 24.90 french ed. (ISBN 0-89401-083-2); pap. 21.50 for 2 or more (ISBN 0-685-77370-1); pap. 0.50 leader's guide (ISBN 0-685-77371-X). Didactic Syst.

--Sales Promotion. (Simulation Game Ser.). 1969. pap. 24.90 (ISBN 0-89401-084-0). Didactic Syst.

--Sales Strategy. (Didactic Simulation Game Ser.). 1968. pap. 21.50 for 2 or more (ISBN 0-89401-085-9); pap. 24.90 spanish (ISBN 0-685-77368-X); pap. 0.50 leader guide (ISBN 0-685-77369-8). Didactic Syst.

--Selecting Effective Insurance Agents. (Simulation Game Ser.). 1973. pap. 24.90 (ISBN 0-89401-090-5); pap. 21.50 two or more (ISBN 0-685-78096-1); pap. 24.90 french ed. (ISBN 0-89401-091-3). Didactic Syst.

--Selecting Effective People. (Simulation Game Ser.). 1970. pap. 24.90 (ISBN 0-89401-087-5); pap. 21.50 two or more (ISBN 0-685-78133-X); pap. 24.90 portuguese ed. (ISBN 0-89401-089-1). Didactic Syst.

Didato, Salvatore V. Psychotechniques. LC 81-81978. 304p. 1982. pap. 3.50 (ISBN 0-87216-941-3). Jove Pubns.

Diday, et al. Data Analysis & Informatics III. 1984. 74.00 (ISBN 0-444-87555-7, I-344-84). Elsevier.

Diday, E., et al, eds. Data Analysis & Informatics. 790p. 1980. 89.50 (ISBN 0-444-86005-3, North-Holland). Elsevier.

Didday, Rich & Page, Rex. FORTRAN for Humans. 4th ed. (Illus.). 480p. 1984. pap. text ed. 24.95 (ISBN 0-314-77887-X); intrs.' manual avail. (ISBN 0-314-77889-6). West Pub.

--FORTRAN for Humans (International Edition) 4th ed. (Illus.). 480p. 1984. 17.00 (ISBN 0-314-77891-8). West Pub.

Didday, Rich L., et al. FORTRAN for Business People. (Illus.). 1978. pap. text ed. 21.95 (ISBN 0-8299-0101-9). West Pub.

Didday, Richard & Page, Rex. FORTRAN for Humans. 3rd ed. (Illus.). 450p. 1981. pap. text ed. 20.50 (ISBN 0-8299-0356-9). West Pub.

--Using BASIC. 542p. 1981. pap. text ed. 20.50 (ISBN 0-8299-0357-7). West Pub.

--Using BASIC. 2nd ed. (Illus.). 525p. 1984. pap. text ed. 23.95 (ISBN 0-314-77885-3). West Pub.

Didday, Richard, jt. auth. see Page, Rex.

Didday, Richard L., jt. auth. see Page, Rex L.

Diddee, Dolly, tr. see Rajneesh, Bhagwan S.

Diddens, A. N., et al see Hellwege, K. H.

Didelot, Mary, ed. see Asterita, Mary F. & Macchia, Donald D.

Diderot. Salons. Seznec, Jean & Adhemar, Jean, eds. Incl. Vol. 1. 1759, 1761, 1763. 2nd ed. 1975. 52.00x (ISBN 0-19-817181-1); Vol. 2. 1765. 2nd ed. 1979. 72.00x (ISBN 0-19-817354-7); Vol. 3. 1767. 2nd ed. 1983. 137.00x (ISBN 0-19-817372-5); Vol. 4. 1769, 1771, 1775, 1781. 1967. Oxford U Pr.

Diderot & D'Alembert, eds. Encyclopedie, 18 vols. (Fr., 12 vols. of plates & 6 texts). 1971-1979. Set. 3450.00. Pergamon.

--Encyclopedie; Ou, Dictionnaire Raisonne Des Sciences, Des Arts et Des Metiers, 35 Vols. 1751. Repr. 4750.00 (ISBN 0-8277-3054-3). Pergamon.

Diderot, jt. ed. see D'Holbach, Paul T.

Diderot, Denis. Anatomie-Chirurgie Encyclopedie Ou Dictionnaire Raissonne des Sciences. 2nd ed. (Fr.). 1977. 46.00 (ISBN 3-88210-002-8, M-7053). French & Eur.

--Correspondance Complete de Diderot, 16 vols. Incl. Vol. 1, 1713-1757. 15.95 (ISBN 0-686-57368-4); Vol. 2, 1757-1759. 15.95 (ISBN 0-686-57369-2); Vol. 3, 1759-1761. 15.95 (ISBN 0-686-57370-6); Vol. 4, 1762-1764. 15.95 (ISBN 0-686-57371-4); Vol. 5, 1765-1766. 17.95 (ISBN 0-686-57372-2); Vol. 6, 1766. 24.95 (ISBN 0-686-57373-0); Vol. 7, 1767. 15.95 (ISBN 0-686-57374-9); Vol. 8, 1768. 15.95 (ISBN 0-686-57375-7); Vol. 9, 1769. 15.95 (ISBN 0-686-57376-5); Vol. 10, 1770-1771. 15.95 (ISBN 0-686-57377-3); Vol. 11, 1771. 9.95 (ISBN 0-686-57378-1); Vol. 12, 1772-1773. 15.95 (ISBN 0-686-57379-X); Vol. 13, 1773-1774. 15.95 (ISBN 0-686-57380-3); Vol. 14, 1774-1776. 15.95 (ISBN 0-686-57381-1); Vol. 15, 1776-1784. 15.95 (ISBN 0-686-57382-X); Vol. 16. Complement, Corrections, Listes et Index General. 15.95 (ISBN 0-686-57383-8). 1955-70. French & Eur.

--De la poesie dramatique. new ed. (Nouveaux Classiques Larousse). (Illus.). 1976. pap. 2.95 (ISBN 0-685-66282-9, 86). Larousse.

--Dialogues. LC 78-118409. 1971. Repr. of 1927 ed. 21.00x (ISBN 0-8046-1186-6, Pub. by Kennikat). Assoc Faculty Pr.

--Diderot, Interpreter of Nature: Selected Writings. Kemp, Jonathon, ed. Stewart, Jean & Kemp, Jonathon, trs. from Fr. LC 78-65607. 1981. Repr. of 1937 ed. 29.15 (ISBN 0-88355-841-6). Hyperion Conn.

--Diderot Pictorial Encyclopedia of Trades & Industry, 2 Vols. Gillispie, Charles C., ed. 1959. 25.00 ea. Vol. 1 (ISBN 0-486-22284-5). Vol. 2 (ISBN 0-486-22285-3). Dover.

--Diderot's Early Philosophical Works. Jourdain, Margaret, ed. LC 70-147967. Repr. of 1916 ed. 15.00 (ISBN 0-404-08219-X). AMS Pr.

--Diderot's Early Philosophical Works. Jourdain, Margaret, ed. (Illus.). 246p. 1972. Repr. of 1916 ed. lib. bdg. 20.50 (ISBN 0-8337-4076-8). B Franklin.

--Diderot's Thoughts on Art & Style. Tollemache, Beatrix, tr. LC 77-168922. (Philosophy Monographs: No. 72). 1971. Repr. of 1893 ed. lib. bdg. 17.00 (ISBN 0-8337-4077-6). B Franklin.

--Diderot's Writings on the Theatre. Green, F. C., ed. LC 76-43916. (Music & Theatre in France in the 17th & 18th Centuries). Repr. of 1936 ed. 26.00 (ISBN 0-404-60157-X). AMS Pr.

--L' Encyclopedia. 192p. 1967. 2.95 (ISBN 0-686-56004-3). French & Eur.

--Entretiens Sur le Fils Naturel: Avec: Paradoxe sur le Comedien. 192p. 1967. 3.95 (ISBN 0-686-56005-1). French & Eur.

--Essai sur les Regnes de Claude et de Neron, 2 vols. 1972. 7.95 ea. French & Eur.

--Fils naturel: Les Entretiens. (Documentation thematique). (Fr). pap. 2.95 (ISBN 0-685-13921-2, 84). Larousse.

--Jack the Fatalist & His Master: A New Translation from the French of Denis Diderot. Camp, Wesley D., et al, trs. from Fr. Raymond, Agnes. (American University Studies II: Vol. 8). 225p. 1984. pap. text ed. 21.60 (ISBN 0-8204-0076-9). P Lang Pubs.

--Jacques le Fataliste. 320p. 1970. 4.50 (ISBN 0-686-56007-8). French & Eur.

--Jacques le Fataliste. Walter-Leutrat, ed. 1967. pap. 4.50 (ISBN 0-685-11267-5, 403). French & Eur.

--Jacques the Fatalist & His Master. Loy, J. Robert, tr. 1979. pap. 6.95 (ISBN 0-393-00903-3, N895, Norton Lib). Norton.

--The Letter of the Blind for the Benefit of Those Who See. (The Most Meaningful Classics in World Culture Ser.). (Illus.). 101p. 1983. 66.85 (ISBN 0-89266-383-9). Am Classical Coll Pr.

--Lettre sur les Aveugles a l'Usage de ceux qui Voient. 2nd ed. 124p. 1973. 4.95 (ISBN 0-686-56009-4). French & Eur.

--Neveu De Rameau. D'Adam, ed. (Coll. G.F). 1966. pap. 4.95 (ISBN 0-685-11419-8, 1653). French & Eur.

--Neveu de rameau. (Documentation thematique). (Fr). pap. 2.95 (ISBN 0-685-13999-9, 85). Larousse.

--Neveu De Rameau. Geary, Edward J., ed. (Integral Eds Ser). pap. text ed. 2.75x (ISBN 0-685-20241-0). Schoenhof.

--The Nun. Tancock, Leonard, tr. (Classics Ser). 1974. pap. 4.95 (ISBN 0-14-044300-2). Penguin.

--Oeuvres, 2 tomes. Incl. Les Bijoux Indiscrets; La Religieuse. 1935. Set. deluxe ed. 500.00 (ISBN 0-685-36024-5). French & Eur.

--Oeuvres: Avec: Les Bijoux Indiscrets. 1480p. 1935. 39.95 (ISBN 0-686-56011-6). French & Eur.

--Oeuvres Completes: Avec: La Religieuse, Vol. 11. 468p. 1975. 135.00 (ISBN 0-686-56018-3). French & Eur.

--Oeuvres Completes: Avec: Pensees Philosophiques, Vol. 2. 476p. 1975. 99.50 (ISBN 0-686-56013-2). French & Eur.

--Oeuvres Completes: Le Modele Anglais, Vol. 1. 468p. 1975. 99.50 (ISBN 0-686-56012-4). French & Eur.

--Oeuvres Esthetiques. Verniere, ed. 1959. 16.95 (ISBN 0-685-11473-2). French & Eur.

--Oeuvres Philosophiques. Verniere, ed. 1961. 14.95 (ISBN 0-685-11458-9). French & Eur.

--Oeuvres Politiques. Verniere, ed. 1963. 9.95 (ISBN 0-685-11463-5). French & Eur.

--Oeuvres Romanesques. Benac, ed. 1962. 14.95 (ISBN 0-685-11465-1). French & Eur.

--Opinions et Paradoxes. 220p. 1963. 14.95 (ISBN 0-686-56019-1). French & Eur.

--Le Paradoxe sur le Comedien: Avec: Danaud, Jean-Claude. Un Ouvrage de Dames. (Illus.). 49p. 1977. 4.95 (ISBN 0-686-56020-5). French & Eur.

--Paradoxe Sur le Comedien: Paris, 1902. facsimile ed. 211p. 1968. 65.00 (ISBN 0-686-56021-3). French & Eur.

--Pensees Philosophiques. 3rd ed. 75p. 1965. 5.95 (ISBN 0-686-56022-1). French & Eur.

--Pensees sur l'interpretation de la Nature: Avec: Varloot, Jean. La Pensee de Diderot dans l'Encyclopedie. 2nd ed. 4.95 (ISBN 0-686-56023-X). French & Eur.

--Philosophical Thought of Diderot. (Meaningful Classics in World Culture Ser.). (Illus.). 129p. 1982. 69.75 (ISBN 0-89266-348-0). Am Classical Coll Pr.

--Poesie dramatique. (Nouveaux Classiques Larousse). (Fr). pap. 2.95 (ISBN 0-685-14048-2, 86). Larousse.

--Quatre Contes. 212p. 1964. 5.95 (ISBN 0-686-56026-4). French & Eur.

--Rameau's Nephew & D'Alembert's Dream. (Classics Ser). 1976. pap. 5.95 (ISBN 0-14-044173-5). Penguin.

--Rameau's Nephew & Other Works. Barzun, Jacques & Bowen, Ralph, trs. LC 55-9755. 1964. pap. write for info. (ISBN 0-02-306550-8, LLA200). Macmillan.

--Rameau's Nephew & Other Works. Barzun, Jacques & Brown, Ralph H., trs. from Fr. LC 55-9755. 1964. 26.50x (ISBN 0-672-51089-8). Irvington.

--La Religieuse. (Folio 57). 1972. 4.95 (ISBN 0-686-56027-2). French & Eur.

--Sur l'Art et les Artistes. 220p. 1967. 8.95 (ISBN 0-686-56032-9). French & Eur.

Diderot, Denis & Adam, Antoine. Les Bijoux Indiscrets. 320p. 1968. 4.50 (ISBN 0-686-56002-7). French & Eur.

--Supplement Au Voyage de Bougainville: Avec: Pensees Philosophiques, Lettre sur les Aveugles. 192p. 1972. 3.95 (ISBN 0-686-56030-2). French & Eur.

Diderot, Denis & Desne, R. Les Salons. 2nd ed. 3.95 (ISBN 0-686-56029-9). French & Eur.

Diderot, Denis & Huster, F. Les Amours De Jacques le Fataliste. 9.95 (ISBN 0-686-56001-9). French & Eur.

Diderot, Denis & Jean-Pierre. Essais sur la Peinture. 4.95 (ISBN 0-686-56006-X, 0885145). French & Eur.

Diderot, Denis & Perol, Lucette. Contes et Entretiens. 245p. 1977. 4.50 (ISBN 0-686-56003-5). French & Eur.

Diderot, Denis & Proust, Jacques. Sur la Liberte de la Presse. 1975. 5.95 (ISBN 0-686-56031-0). French & Eur.

Diderot, Denis & Varloot, Jean. Le Reve d'Alembert. 2nd ed. 248p. 1962. 6.95 (ISBN 0-686-56028-0). French & Eur.

Diderot, Denis & Verniere, Paul. Memoires pour Catherine II. (Illus.). 420p. 1966. 14.95 (ISBN 0-686-56010-8). French & Eur.

Diderot, Denis & D'Alembert, eds. Encyclopedie ou dictionnaire raisonne des sciences, des arts et des metiers, 35 Vols. (Illus.). 1967. Repr. of 1751 ed. Set. 4208.75x (ISBN 3-7728-0116-1). Adlers Foreign Bks.

Diderot, Denis, et al. Le Pour et le Contre: Correspondance Polemique sur le Respect de la Posterite. Pline et les Anciens Auteurs qui ont Parle de Peinture et de Sculpture. (Illus.). 384p. 1958. 12.95 (ISBN 0-686-56025-6). French & Eur.

--Le Pour et le Contre: Lettres Sur la Posterite. 384p. 1958. 7.50 (ISBN 0-686-56024-8). French & Eur.

--Jacques le Fataliste et Son Maitre: Texte et Variantes Establis sur le ms de Leingrad. 664p. 1976. 14.95 (ISBN 0-686-56008-6). French & Eur.

--Oeuvres Completes: Encyclopedie I (Lettre A, Vol. 5. 564p. 1977. 115.00 (ISBN 0-686-56014-0). French & Eur.

--Oeuvres Completes: Encyclopedie II (Lettres B-C, Vol. 6. (Illus.). 564p. 1977. 115.00 (ISBN 0-686-56015-9). French & Eur.

--Oeuvres Completes: Encyclopedie III (Lettres D-L, Vol. 7. 728p. 1977. 150.00 (ISBN 0-686-56016-7). French & Eur.

--Oeuvres Completes: Encyclopedie IV (Lettres M-Z, Vol. 8. 564p. 1977. 135.00 (ISBN 0-686-56017-5). French & Eur.

Didi, Dolli, tr. see Rajneesh, Bhagwan S.

Didier, Beatrice, jt. auth. see Stendhal.

Didier, Beatrice, ed. see Sade, Donatien Alphonse Francois de.

Didier, Charles. Sojourn with the Grand Sharif of Makkah. Boulind, Richard, tr. from Fr. (Arabian Past & Present Ser.: Vol. 18). (Illus.). 176p. 1985. 33.00 (ISBN 0-906672-11-2). Oleander Pr.

Didier, Charles, jt. auth. see Paternoster, Lewis M.

Didier, E. L. Life & Poems of Edgar Allen Poe. LC 73-16344. (Studies in Poe, No. 23). 1974. lib. bdg. write for info. (ISBN 0-8383-1726-X). Haskell.

Didier, Eugene L. Poe Cult & Other Poe Papers. LC 72-190662. 1909. lib. bdg. 20.00 (ISBN 0-8414-0808-4). Folcroft.

Didier, J. Diccionario de Filosofia. (Span.). 1980. write for info. (S-33104). French & Eur.

--Granites & Their Enclaves. LC 76-179999. (Developments in Petrology Ser.: Vol. 3). 412p. 1973. 93.75 (ISBN 0-444-40974-2). Elsevier.

DiDio, L. J., ed. Basic, Clinical & Surgical Nephrology. Motta, P. M. (Developments in Nephrology Ser.). 1985. lib. bdg. 69.50 (ISBN 0-318-04536-2, Pub. by Martinus Nijhoff Netherlands). Kluwer Academic.

Didio, L. J., jt. ed. see Motta, P. M.

Didion, Joan. A Book of Common Prayer. 288p. 1983. pap. 3.95 (ISBN 0-671-49589-5). PB.

--Democracy. 1984. 13.95 (ISBN 0-671-41977-3). S&S.

--Democracy. 1985. pap. 3.95 (ISBN 0-671-54633-3). PB.

--Play It as It Lays. 266p. 1983. pap. 3.95 (ISBN 0-671-49590-9). PB.

--Run River. 1961. 12.95 (ISBN 0-8392-1094-9). Astor-Honor.

--Run River. 256p. 1978. pap. 2.95 (ISBN 0-671-44258-9). WSP.

--Salvador. 1983. pap. 5.95 (ISBN 0-671-50174-7). WSP.

--Slouching Towards Bethlehem. 240p. 1983. pap. 2.95 (ISBN 0-671-42210-3). WSP.

DiDomenico, Joseph M. Investigative Technique for the Retail Security Investigator. LC 79-12097. 1979. 15.95 (ISBN 0-86730-530-4). Lebhar Friedman.
DiDonato, Georgia. Woman of Justice. 1981. pap. 2.50 (ISBN 0-380-55798-3, 55798). Avon.
Di Donato, Georgia. Woman of Justice. (General Ser.). 1980. lib. bdg. 15.95 (ISBN 0-8161-3132-5, Large Print GBks). G K Hall.
DiDonno, Lupe & Sperling, Phyllis. How to Design & Build Your Own House. (Illus.). 1978. pap. 11.95 (ISBN 0-394-73416-5). Knopf.
Didsbury, Howard. The World of Work: Careers & the Future. 1983. 14.50 (ISBN 0-930242-21-1). World Future.
Didsbury, Howard F., Jr., ed. Communications & the Future. 400p. 14.50 (ISBN 0-930242-16-5). World Future.
Didsbury, Howard, Jr., ed. Creating a Global Agenda: Assessments, Solutions, & Action Plans. LC 84-50980. 346p. 1984. 14.50 (ISBN 0-930242-25-4). World Future.
Diebel, Don. The Complete Guide to Meeting Women. 180p. 1983. pap. 8.95 (ISBN 0-937164-01-1). Gemini Pub Co.
--How to Pick up Women in Discos. LC 80-67924. (Illus.). 128p. 1981. pap. 6.95 (ISBN 0-937164-00-3). Gemini Pub Co.
Diebener, Wilhelm. Monograms & Decorations from the Art Nouveau Period. (Pictorial Archive Ser.). (Illus.). 144p. 1982. pap. 6.00 (ISBN 0-486-24347-8). Dover.
Diebener, Wilhelm, ed. Monograms & Decorations from the Art Nouveau Period. 1983. 14.00 (ISBN 0-8446-6007-8). Peter Smith.
Diebert, Linda, jt. auth. see Tremper, Andra.
Diebold, Bernhard. Anarchie Im Drama: Einfuhrung Von Klaus Kilian, 1972. 1972. Repr. of 1928 ed. 40.00 (ISBN 0-384-11735-X). Johnson Repr.
Diebold Europe SA. A Methodology to Evaluate Word Processing Text Preparation Equipment. (Illus.). 67p. (Orig.). 1978. pap. 102.50x (ISBN 0-85012-252-X). Intl Pubns Serv.
Diebold Group. Automatic Data Processing Handbook. (Illus.). 1977. 64.95 (ISBN 0-07-016807-5). McGraw.
Diebold, John. Automation. 224p. 1983. 14.95 (ISBN 0-8144-5756-8). AMACOM.
--Business in the Age of Information. LC 84-45782. 144p. 1985. 14.95 (ISBN 0-8144-5792-4). Amacom.
--Making the Future Work: Unleashing Our Powers of Innovation for the Decades Ahead. 470p. 1984. 18.95 (ISBN 0-671-45657-1). S&S.
--Managing Information: The Challenge & the Opportunity. LC 84-45223. 144p. 1985. 14.95 (ISBN 0-8144-5793-2). AMACOM.
--The Role of Business in Society. LC 82-71322. pap. 36.00 (ISBN 0-317-26958-5, 2023576). Bks Demand UMI.
Diebold, William, Jr. Dollars, Jobs, Trade & Aid. LC 72-93265. (Headline Ser.: No. 213). (Illus., Orig.). 1972. pap. 3.00 (ISBN 0-87124-019-X). Foreign Policy.
--Industrial Policy As an International Issue. (Nineteen Eighty's Project (Council on Foreign Relations)). 1979. text ed. 17.95 (ISBN 0-07-016809-1); pap. 8.95 (ISBN 0-07-016810-5). McGraw.
--Industrial Policy for the United States. 256p. 26.95t (ISBN 0-03-069253-9); pap. text ed. 9.95t00932904x (ISBN 0-03-069256-3). Praeger.
Diebold, William, Jr., jt. auth. see Caldwell, Lawrence.
Diebold, William, Jr., jt. auth. see Camps, Miriam.
Diebolt, Thomas, et al. California Elections Code. rev. ed. 570p. 1985. pap. text ed. 25.00 (ISBN 0-686-33177-X). DFM Assoc.
Dieck, Tom T., jt. auth. see Brocker, T.
Dieckmann, Ed, Jr. The Secret of Jonestown: The Reason Why. 176p. (Orig.). 1982. pap. 6.00 (ISBN 0-939482-02-9). Noontide.
Dieckmann, Edward A. Practical Homicide Investigation. 96p. 1961. 15.75X (ISBN 0-398-00450-1). C C Thomas.
Dieckmann, H., et al, eds. Kreativitaet des Unbewussten. (Journal: Analytische Psychologie: Vol. 11, No. 3). (Illus.). 216p. 1980. pap. 12.50 (ISBN 3-8055-1543-X). S Karger.
Dieckmann, Jane M. Use It All: The Leftovers Cookbook. LC 81-15215. (Illus.). 369p. 1981. 22.95x (ISBN 0-89594-061-2); pap. 11.95x (ISBN 0-89594-062-0). Crossing Pr.
Dieckmann, U., et al. Male & Female, Feminine & Masculine. pap. 2.00 (ISBN 0-317-13546-5). C G Jung Frisco.
Diederich, Paul B. Measuring Growth in English. LC 74-84480. 103p. 1974. pap. 4.75 (ISBN 0-8141-3109-3). NCTE.
Diedericks-Verschoor. An Introduction to Air Law, Nineteen Eighty-Three. 220p. pap. 36.00 (ISBN 90-65-44097-6). Kluwer Academic.
Diederiks-Verschoor, I. H. & Heere, W. P., eds. Air Law. 1983. Subscrpition price. 74.00 (ISBN 0-686-40937-X, Pub. by Kluwer Law Netherlands); Incl. bound ed., Jan.-Dec. 38.00 (ISBN 0-686-40938-8). Kluwer Academic.
Diedrich, William M. & Bangert, Jeff. Articulation Learning. LC 80-18405. (Illus.). 368p. 1980. text ed. 24.50 (ISBN 0-933014-59-7). College-Hill.
Diedrich, William M. & Youngstrom, Karl A. Alaryngeal Speech. (Illus.). 232p. 1977. 28.50x (ISBN 0-398-00451-X). C C Thomas.
Diedrichs, Gary, jt. auth. see Ried, Andrea.
Diefenbach, Gabriel. Common Mystic Prayer. 1978. 2.50 (ISBN 0-8198-0527-0); pap. 1.95 (ISBN 0-8198-0528-9). Dghtrs St Paul.
Diefenbach, Karl. The World of Cockatoos. (Illus.). 208p. 1985. text ed. 24.95 (ISBN 0-86622-034-8, H-1072). TFH Pubns.
Diefenbeck, James A. A Celebration of Subjective Thought. LC 83-20109. (Philosophical Explorations Ser.). 280p. 1984. 24.95x (ISBN 0-8093-1088-0). S Ill U Pr.
Diefenderfer, James. Principles of Electronic Instrumentation. 2nd ed. 1979. text ed. 42.95 (ISBN 0-7216-3076-6, CBS C). SCP.
Diefendorf, B. B. Paris City Councillors in the Sixteenth Century: The Politics of Patrimony. 1982. 33.00 (ISBN 0-691-05362-6). Princeton U Pr.
Diefendorf, David. Word Warps: A Glossary of Unfamiliar Terms. (Illus.). 128p. (Orig., Includes index). 1984. pap. 6.95 (ISBN 0-913589-02-0). Williamson Pub Co.
Diefendorf, Jeffry M. Businessmen & Politics in the Rhineland, 1789-1834. LC 79-3200. 1980. 35.00x (ISBN 0-691-05298-0). Princeton U Pr.
Diegel, Leo, jt. auth. see Dante, Jim.
Diegel, Virginia & Hunnisett, Henry S. Retirement in the Pacific Northwest. 253p. 1978. 4.95 (ISBN 0-88908-902-7). Self Counsel Pr.
Diegmueller, Karen S., jt. auth. see Schoenfeld, A. Clay.
Diego, Fernando De see De Diego, Fernando.
Diego, Jose De see De Diego, Jose.
Diehi, William. Hooligans. 448p. 1985. pap. 3.95 (ISBN 0-345-31201-5). Ballantine.
Diehl, Carl. Americans & German Scholarship, 1770-1870. LC 77-12931. (Historical Publications Ser.: No. 115). (Illus.). 1978. 24.50x (ISBN 0-300-02079-1). Yale U Pr.
Diehl, Charles. Afrique Byzantine, 2 vols. LC 72-80217. 1968. lib. bdg. 43.00 (ISBN 0-8337-0858-9). B Franklin.
--Byzantium: Greatness & Decline. Walford, Naomi, tr. (Byzantine Ser.). 1960. pap. 15.00x (ISBN 0-8135-0328-0). Rutgers U Pr.
--Etudes Byzantines. (Illus.). 1905. 29.50 (ISBN 0-8337-0859-7). B Franklin.
--Etudes sur l'Administration Byzantine dans l'Exarchat de Ravenne (568-751) LC 60-1146. 421p. 1972. Repr. of 1888 ed. 29.50 (ISBN 0-8337-0854-6). B Franklin.
--History of the Byzantine Empire. LC 76-91295. Repr. of 1925 ed. 18.00 (ISBN 0-404-02129-8). AMS Pr.
--Justinien Et La Civilization Byzantine Au Seizieme Siecle, 2 Vols. LC 70-80743. (Research & Source Works Ser: No. 1). 1969. Repr. of 1901 ed. Set. lib. bdg. 47.00 (ISBN 0-8337-0862-7). B Franklin.
Diehl, Charles F. A Compendium of Research & Theory on Stuttering. 344p. 1958. 28.75x (ISBN 0-398-04243-8). C C Thomas.
--Introduction to the Anatomy & Physiology of the Speech Mechanisms. (Illus.). 192p. 1968. 14.75x (ISBN 0-398-00452-8). C C Thomas.
Diehl, Digby. Front Page Eighteen Eighty-One to Nineteen Eighty-One: One Hundred Years of the Los Angeles Times. (Illus.). 288p. 1981. 25.00 (ISBN 0-8109-0925-1). Abrams.
Diehl, E. W. Heterocera Sumatrana. 1982. 99.00x (ISBN 0-317-07093-2, Pub. by EW Classey UK). State Mutual Bk.
Diehl, Edith. Bookbinding: Its Background & Technique. (Illus.). 748p. 1980. pap. 12.00 (ISBN 0-486-24020-7). Dover.
--Bookbinding: Its Background & Technique, 2 vols. LC 79-84536. (Illus.). 1979. Repr. of 1946 ed. lib. bdg. 60.00 (ISBN 0-87817-255-6). Hacker.
Diehl, Gaston. Derain. (QLP Art Ser.). 9.95 (ISBN 0-517-03720-3). Crown.
--Fernand Leger. (QLP Art Ser.). (Illus.). 96p. 1985. 9.95 (ISBN 0-517-54711-2). Crown.
--Joan Miro. (Q L P Ser.). (Illus.). 87p. 1974. 9.95 (ISBN 0-517-51671-3). Crown.
--Max Ernst. (Q L P Art Ser.). (Illus.). 96p. 1973. 9.95 (ISBN 0-517-50004-3). Crown.
--Modigliani. LC 76-93407. (Q L P Art Ser). (Illus.). 1969. 9.95 (ISBN 0-517-50798-6). Crown.
--Pascin. (Q L P Art Ser.). (Illus.). 1968. 9.95 (ISBN 0-517-09890-3). Crown.
--Picasso. (Q L P Art Ser.). (Illus.). 1960. 9.95 (ISBN 0-517-00501-8). Crown.
--Van Dongen. (Q L P Art Ser.). (Illus.). 9.95 (ISBN 0-517-02408-X). Crown.
--Vasarely. (Q L P Art Ser.). (Illus.). 96p. 1972. 9.95 (ISBN 0-517-50800-1). Crown.
Diehl, George M. Machinery Acoustics. LC 73-12980. 204p. 1973. 39.95x (ISBN 0-471-21360-8, Pub. by Wiley-Interscience). Wiley.
Diehl, Harold S., et al. Health & Safety for You. 5th ed. 1979. text ed. 22.64 (ISBN 0-07-016863-6). McGraw.
Diehl, Helmut. Atheismus Im Religionsunterricht. (European University Studies Thirty-Three: Vol. 6). 622p. (Ger.). 1982. 46.30 (ISBN 3-8204-6280-5). P Lang Pubs.
Diehl, James M. Paramilitary Politics in Weimar Germany. LC 77-74438. 416p. 1978. 25.00x (ISBN 0-253-34292-9). Ind U Pr.
Diehl, Joanne F. Dickinson & the Romantic Imagination. LC 81-47121. 240p. 1981. 22.50 (ISBN 0-691-06478-4). Princeton U Pr.
Diehl, Judith R. A Woman's Place. write for info. Fortress.
--A Woman's Place: Equal Partnership in Daily Ministry. LC 84-47915. 128p. 1985. pap. 5.95 (ISBN 0-8006-1791-6, 1-1791). Fortress.
Diehl, Katharine S. Batavia: Sixteen Hundred to Eighteen Fifty. (Printers & Printing in the East Indies to 1850 Ser.: Vol. I). 600p. 1985. 90.00 (ISBN 0-89241-390-5). Caratzas.
--Bombay Presidency & the Printing Press. (Printers & Printing in the East Indies to 1850 Ser.: Vol. IV). write for info. (ISBN 0-89241-393-X). Caratzas.
--A Comprehensive & Systematic Bibliography. (Printers & Printing in the East Indies to 1850 Ser.: Vol. IX). write for info. (ISBN 0-89241-398-0). Caratzas.
--Europeans & Ceylon, from Fifteen Hundred Five. (Printers & Printing in the East Indies to 1850 Ser.: Vol. II). 1985. write for info. (ISBN 0-89241-391-3). Caratzas.
--Four Studies: Madrasis, Armenians, Words, Music, Printers & Printing in the East Indies to 1850. (Printers & Printing in the East Indies to 1850 Ser.). Date not set. price not set (ISBN 0-89241-397-2). Caratzas.
--Four Studies: Madrasis, Armenians, Words, Music. (Printers & Printing in the East Indies to 1850 Ser.: Vol. VIII). write for info. (ISBN 0-89241-397-2). Caratzas.
--Jesuits, Lutherans, & the Printing Press in South India. (Printers & Printing in the East Indies to 1850 Ser.: Vol. III). write for info. (ISBN 0-89241-392-1). Caratzas.
--Persian, Arabic, & Urdu Printing in Bengal, from 1778. (Printers & Printing in the East Indies to 1850 Ser.: Vol. V). write for info. (ISBN 0-89241-394-8). Caratzas.
--The Press Beyond Calcutta-North & East. (Printers & Printing in the East Indies to 1850 Ser.: Vol. VI). write for info. (ISBN 0-89241-395-6). Caratzas.
--Printers & Printing in the East Indies to 1850, 9 vols. Set. write for info. (ISBN 0-89241-384-0). Caratzas.
--Scholarship & Education in Bengal. (Printers & Printing in the East Indies to 1850 Ser.: Vol. VII). write for info. (ISBN 0-89241-396-4). Caratzas.
Diehl, Kathryn & Hodenfield, G. K. Johnny Still Can't Read... But You Can Teach Him at Home. 75p. 2.50 (ISBN 0-318-16333-0). Reading Reform Found.
--Johnny Still Can't Read...but You Can Teach Him at Home. 5th ed. (Illus.). 75p. 1979. pap. 3.50 (ISBN 0-9603552-0-0). K Diehl.
Diehl, Kemper & Jarboe, Jan. Cisneros: Portrait of a New American. LC 84-72834. (Illus.). 214p. 1985. 16.95 (ISBN 0-931722-35-7); pap. 7.95 (ISBN 0-931722-37-3). Corona Pub.
Diehl, L. Late Great Pennsylvania Station. 1986. cancelled (ISBN 0-442-21967-9). Van Nos Reinhold.
Diehl, L. W., jt. ed. see Berner, P.
Diehl, Lorraine B. The Late Great Pennsylvania Station. LC 85-3988. (Illus.). 190p. 1985. 19.95 (ISBN 0-8281-1181-2, Dist. by H M). Am Heritage.
--The Late Great Pennsylvania Station. (Illus.). 190p. 1985. 19.95 (ISBN 0-8281-1181-2). HM.
Diehl, Marcy O. & Fordney, Marilyn T. Medical Transcribing: Techniques & Procedures. LC 78-52727. (Illus.). 1979. pap. text ed. 21.95 (ISBN 0-7216-3079-0). Saunders.
--Medical Typing & Transcribing: Techniques & Procedures. 2nd ed. (Illus.). 450p. 1984. pap. 24.95 (ISBN 0-7216-1274-1). Saunders.
Diehl, Mary Ellen. How to Produce a Fashion Show. LC 76-20221. (Illus.). 160p. 1976. 12.50 (ISBN 0-87005-159-8). Fairchild.
Diehl, P. & Khetrapel, C. L. N M R Studies of Molecules Oriented in the Nematic Phase of Liquid Crystals. Bd. with The Use of Symmetry in Nuclear Magnetic Resonance. Jones, R. G. (NMR Basic Principles & Progress: Vol. 1). (Illus.). v, 174p. 1969. 32.00 (ISBN 0-387-04665-8). Springer-Verlag.
Diehl, P., ed. see Kanert, O. & Mehring, M.
Diehl, P., et al. Computer Assistance in the Analysis of High-Resolution NMR Spectra. (NMR Basic Principles & Progress: Vol. 6). (Illus.). 100p. 1972. 24.00 (ISBN 0-387-05532-0). Springer-Verlag.
Diehl, P., et al, eds. Natural & Synthetic High Polymers: Lectures Presented at the 7th Colloquium on NMR Spectroscopy. LC 70-94160. (NMR, Basic Principles & Progress: Vol. 4). (Illus.). 1971. 46.10 (ISBN 0-387-05221-6). Springer-Verlag.
--Van der Waals Forces & Schielding Effects. LC 75-15821. (NMR - Basic Principles & Progress: Vol. 10). (Illus.). 140p. 1975. 36.00 (ISBN 0-387-07340-X). Springer-Verlag.
Diehl, P., et al, eds. see Forsen, S., et al.
Diehl, Patrick S. The Medieval Religious Lyric. LC 83-6557. 475p. 1984. text ed. 32.00x (ISBN 0-520-04673-0). U of Cal Pr.
Diehl, Patrick S., tr. see Dante.
Diehl, Richard, et al, eds. Tzeltal Tales of Demons & Monsters. Stross, Brian, tr. LC 78-622530. (Museum Briefs Ser.: No. 24). 1978. pap. 2.00 (ISBN 0-913134-24-4). Mus Anthro Mo.
Diehl, Richard A. Tula: The Toltec Capital of Ancient Mexico. LC 82-51256. (Illus.). 1983. 29.95 (ISBN 0-500-39018-5). Thames Hudson.
Diehl, Richard A., jt. auth. see Coe, Michael D.
Diehl, William. Chameleon. LC 80-40228. 1982. 14.50 (ISBN 0-394-51961-2). Random.
--Chameleon. 490p. 1982. pap. 3.95 (ISBN 0-345-29445-9). Ballantine.
--Hooligans. 1984. 15.95 (ISBN 0-394-53049-7). Random.
--Sharky's Machine. 1981. pap. 3.50 (ISBN 0-440-18292-1). Dell.
Diehl, William E. Christianity & Real Life. LC 76-7860. 128p. 1976. pap. 4.50 (ISBN 0-8006-1231-0, 1-1231). Fortress.
--Thank God, It's Monday! LC 81-71390. 192p. 1982. pap. 6.95 (ISBN 0-8006-1656-1, 1-1656). Fortress.
Diehm, William J. Finding Your Life Partner. 128p. 1984. pap. 7.95 (ISBN 0-8170-1028-9). Judson.
--Staying in Love. 128p. (Orig.). 1986. pap. 7.95 (ISBN 0-8066-2191-5, 10-5996). Augsburg.
Diehr, George, et al. BASIC Programming for the VAX & PDP-11. LC 83-21689. 473p. 1984. pap. text ed. 23.50 (ISBN 0-471-86817-5); write for info. tchr's. ed. (ISBN 0-471-80224-7). Wiley.
Diejomaoh, V. P., jt. ed. see Bienen, Henry.
Diejomaoh, Victor P., jt. auth. see Damachi, Ukandi G.
Dieke, Gerhard H. Spectra & Energy Levels of Rare Earth Ions in Crystals. Crosswhite, H. M. & Crosswhite, Hannah, eds. LC 67-29453. pap. 103.30 (ISBN 0-317-09061-5, 2011960). Bks Demand UMI.
Diekelman, Nancy. Primary Health Care of the Well Adult. (Illus.). 1977. pap. text ed. 24.00 (ISBN 0-07-016879-2). McGraw.
Diekelmann, John & Schuster, Robert M. Natural Landscaping: Designing with Native Plant Communities. (Illus.). 264p. 1983. 33.50 (ISBN 0-07-016813-X). McGraw.
Diekelmann, Nancy & Broadwell, Martin M. The New Hospital Supervisor. (Illus.). 1977. pap. text ed. 11.95 (ISBN 0-201-00773-8). Addison-Wesley.
Diekelmann, Nancy, et al. Fundamentals of Nursing. (Illus.). 1979. text ed. 34.00 (ISBN 0-07-016885-7). McGraw.
Diekelmann, Nancy L., jt. auth. see Knopke, Harry J.
Diekmahns, E. C., jt. ed. see Spedding, C. R.
Diekman, Bernard A., jt. auth. see Metzger, Bert L.
Diekman, John R. Human Connections: How to Make Communications Work. (Illus.). 118p. 1982. 10.95 (ISBN 0-13-444570-8); pap. 4.95 (ISBN 0-13-444562-7). P-H.
Diekman, Norman & Pile, John. Drawing Interior Architecture: A Guide to Rendering & Presentation. 176p. 1983. 32.50 (ISBN 0-8230-7159-6, Whitney Lib). Watson-Guptill.
--Sketching Interior Architecture. (Illus.). 176p. 1985. 32.50 (ISBN 0-8230-7450-1, Whitney Lib); pap. 19.95 (ISBN 0-8230-7459-5). Watson-Guptill.
Diekmayer, Ulrich, jt. auth. see Kirst, Werner.
Diekmeyer, Ulrich, jt. auth. see Kirst, Werner.
Diekstra, Frans. Early & Middle English Literature. (Dutch Quarterly Review of Anglo-American Letters: Vol. 11, 1981/4). 80p. 1981. pap. text ed. 9.75x (ISBN 90-6203-933-2, Pub. by Rodopi England). Humanities.
Diel, Paul. Symbolism in Greek Mythology: Human Desire & Its Transformations. Stuart, Vincent, et al, trs. from Fr. LC 79-67686. 240p. 1980. 20.00 (ISBN 0-87773-178-0, 51083-6). Shambhala Pubns.
--Symbolism in the Bible: Its Psychological Significance. 240p. 1985. 17.95 (ISBN 0-86683-475-3). Winston Pr.
Dieleman, Dale. Our Life & Times. 1985. pap. 5.95 (ISBN 0-8010-2951-1). Baker Bk.
Dieleman, Dale, compiled by. The Go Book. (Good Things for Youth Leaders). 64p. 1982. pap. 4.50 (ISBN 0-8010-2929-5). Baker Bk.
--The Praise Book. 1984. pap. 5.95 (ISBN 0-8010-2947-3). Baker Bk.
--Taking Charge. (Good Things for Youth Leaders Ser.). pap. 3.45 (ISBN 0-8010-2911-2). Baker Bk.
Dielman, Heinz J. Kreditsicherung in den U. S. A. 170p. (Ger.). 1985. pap. 20.00 (ISBN 0-86640-018-4). German Am Chamber.
Dielman, Louis H., ed. see Marine, William M.
Dielman, P. J. & Trafford, D. B. Drainage Testing. (Irrigation & Drainage Papers: No. 28). (Illus.). 185p. (Eng., Fr. & Span.). 1976. pap. 12.00 (ISBN 92-5-100016-6, F998, FAO). Unipub.
Dielman, Ted & Barton, Keith. Child Personality Structure & Development: Multivariate Theory & Research. LC 82-16583. 224p. 1983. 33.95x (ISBN 0-03-061957-2). Praeger.
Dielman, Terry E. Pooled Data for Financial Markets. Dufey, Gunter, ed. LC 80-22508. (Research for Business Decisions: No. 31). 176p. 1980. 44.95 (ISBN 0-8357-1130-7). UMI Res Pr.

Diels, Paul. Die Stellung Des Verbums in der Alteren Althoch-Deutschen Prosa. 1906. 27.00 (ISBN 0-384-11745-7); pap. 22.00 (ISBN 0-384-11746-5). Johnson Repr.

DiElsi, John, et al. Programming Apple BASIC. 1984. 19.95 (ISBN 0-03-063733-3). HR&W.

DiElsie, et al. Programming Macintosh BASIC. 350p. 1985. pap. text ed. write for info. (ISBN 0-8087-6404-7). Burgess.

Diem, Aubrey. Western Europe: A Geographical Analysis. LC 77-24617. 543p. 1979. text ed. 43.00 (ISBN 0-471-21400-0). Wiley.

Diem, H. G., jt. ed. see Dommergues, Y.

Diem, Hermann. Kierkegaard's Dialectic of Existence. Knight, Harold, tr. from German. LC 77-18886. 1978. Repr. of 1959 ed. lib. bdg. 22.50x (ISBN 0-313-20220-6, DIKD). Greenwood.

Diem, Liselott. Children Learn Physical Skills, 2 vols. 1978. pap. 8.35x ea.; Vol. 1. Birth to 3 Years (ISBN 0-88314-040-3); Vol. 2. Ages 3-5 8.35x (ISBN 0-88314-039-X). AAHPERD.

--Who Can. 1977. 2.95x (ISBN 0-88314-211-2, 245-26074). AAHPERD.

Diem, Richard. How to Use Computers as a Resource. (Social Studies Skills Ser.). 96p. (YA) (gr. 7 up). 1983. lib. bdg. 9.40 (ISBN 0-531-04676-1). Watts.

Dieman, Kurt. O Ye Millions, I Embrace Ye: The New Year's Concerts of the Vienna Philharmonic. Kowanda, Edwin, tr. from Ger. (Illus.). 208p. (Orig.). 1983. 25.00 (ISBN 3-215-05122-2, Pub. by Osterreichischer Bundes-Verlag Austria). Heinman.

Diemann, E., jt. auth. see Mueller, A.

Diemer, Alwin, ed. Sixteenth World Congress of Philosphy, 1978. 477p. 1983. write for info. (ISBN 3-8204-5812-3). P Lang Pubs.

Diemer, Ferdinand, et al, eds. Advanced Concepts in Ocean Measurements for Marine Biology. LC 79-24802. (Belle Baruch Library Ser.: Vol. 10). (Illus.). xvi, 572p. 1980. text ed. 39.95x (ISBN 0-87249-388-1). U of SC Pr.

Diemer, Ferdinand P., jt. ed. see Vernberg, F John.

Diemer, Hugo. Factory Organization & Administration, 2 vols. in 1. Chandler, Alfred D., ed. LC 79-7542. (History of Management Thought & Practice Ser.). 1980. Repr. of 1935 ed. lib. bdg. 67.00x (ISBN 0-405-12326-4). Ayer Co Pubs.

--Industrial Organization & Management. LC 73-6736. (Management History Ser.: No. 61). (Illus.). 315p. 1973. Repr. of 1915 ed. 22.50 (ISBN 0-87960-064-0). Hive Pub.

Diemer, J. Nature & Miracle. 1977. pap. 1.95 (ISBN 0-88906-015-0). Wedge Pub.

Dien, Albert E. Pei Ch'i Shu Forty-Five: Biography of Yen Chih-T'ui. (Wurzburger Sino-Japonica Ser.: Vol. 6). 184p. 1976. 24.80 (ISBN 3-261-01756-2). P Lang Pubs.

Diener, Carolyn S., et al. Energy: A Curriculum Unit for Three, Four & Five Year Olds. LC 81-83050. (Illus.). 80p. 1982. pap. 9.95 (ISBN 0-89334-069-3). Humanics Ltd.

Diener, Edward. Reinterpreting American History. LC 75-378. 217p. 1975. 11.50 (ISBN 0-8022-2166-1). Philos Lib.

Diener, Edward & Crandall, Rick. Ethics in Social & Behavioral Research. LC 78-8881. 1978. lib. bdg. 20.00x (ISBN 0-226-14823-8). U of Chicago Pr.

--Ethics in Social & Behavioral Research. LC 78-8881. 1979. pap. 4.50x (ISBN 0-226-14824-6, P857, Phoen). U of Chicago Pr.

Diener, Royce. How to Finance Your Growing Business. 416p. 1981. pap. 8.95 (ISBN 0-13-406546-8, Spec). P-H.

Diener, Theodor O. Viroids & Viroid Diseases. LC 78-21681. 252p. 1979. 37.50x (ISBN 0-471-03504-1, Pub. by Wiley-Interscience). Wiley.

Diener, Thomas. Growth of an American Invention: A Documentary History of the Junior & Community College Movement. LC 85-9832. (Illus.). 256p. 1985. lib. bdg. 29.95 (ISBN 0-313-24993-8, DGR/). Greenwood.

Dienes, Andre de see De Dienes, Andre.

Dienes, Andre De see De Dienes, Andre.

Dienes, C. Thomas. Law, Politics, & Birth Control. LC 71-182195. 381p. 1972. 27.50x (ISBN 0-252-00200-8). U of Ill Pr.

Dienes, C. Thomas, jt. auth. see Barron, Jerome A.

Dienes, G. J. Studies in Radiation Effects in Solids, 3 vols. LC 66-24006. 992p. Set. 63.50 (ISBN 0-685-58276-0, 450001). Am Nuclear Soc.

Dienes, G. J., jt. auth. see Damask, A. C.

Dienes, G. J., et al, eds. Molecular Crystals & Liquid Crystals: Proceedings of the International Conference on Low-Dimensional Conductors, Boulder, Colorado, August 1981. (Molecular Crystals & Liquid Crystals Ser.: Vols. 77, 79, 81, 83, 85, & 86). 2078p. 1982. Set. 620.00 (ISBN 0-677-16405-X). Gordon.

Dienes, Leslie. Locational Factors & Locational Developments in the Soviet Chemical Industry. LC 69-18023. (Research Papers: No. 119). 285p. 1969. pap. 10.00 (ISBN 0-89065-027-6). U Chicago Dept Geog.

Dienes, Leslie & Shabad, Theodore. The Soviet Energy System: Resource Use & Policies. LC 78-20814. (Scripta Series in Geography). 298p. 1979. 21.95x (ISBN 0-470-26629-5). Halsted Pr.

Dienes, Thomas, jt. auth. see Barron, Jerome.

Dienes, Z. P. Mathematics Through the Senses: Games, Dance & Art. 146p. 1973. 14.00x (ISBN 0-901225-87-8, Pub. by NFER Nelson UK). Taylor & Francis.

--The Six Stages in the Process of Learning Mathematics. Seaborne, P. L., tr. 56p. 1970. 5.00x (ISBN 0-85633-022-1, Pub. by NFER Nelson UK). Taylor & Francis.

Dienes, Z. P., tr. see Peter, Rozsa.

Dienes, Zoltan, jt. auth. see Holt, Michael.

Dienhart, Charlotte M. Basic Human Anatomy & Physiology. 3rd ed. LC 78-64706. (Illus.). 1979. pap. text ed. 13.50 (ISBN 0-7216-3082-0). Saunders.

Dienhart, John W. A Cognitive Approach to the Ethics of Counseling Psychology. LC 82-17393. 152p. (Orig.). 1983. lib. bdg. 21.50 (ISBN 0-8191-2817-1); pap. text ed. 9.50 (ISBN 0-8191-2818-X). U Pr of Amer.

Dienhart, Ligita, jt. auth. see Pinsel, E. Melvin.

Diening, J. A. On Reasonable Liability. 452p. pap. 32.00 (ISBN 90-60-0025-04). Kluwer Academic.

Dienst, Charles F. Administration of Endowments, with Special Reference to the Public Schools & Institutional Trusts of Idaho. LC 74-176707. (Columbia University. Teachers College. Contributions to Education: No. 560). Repr. of 1933 ed. 22.50 (ISBN 0-404-55560-8). AMS Pr.

Dienst, J. Douglas A-26 B26 Variants: Minigraph 18. write for info. (ISBN 0-942548-23-X). Aerofax.

--McDonnell F-4E: Minigraph 19. write for info. (ISBN 0-942548-24-8). Aerofax.

--North American P-51s'in Latin American Service: Minigraph 16. write for info. (ISBN 0-942548-21-3). Aerofax.

--North American P-82 F-82 Variants: Minigraph 17. write for info. (ISBN 0-942548-22-1). Aerofax.

Dienstag, Jacob I. Eschatology in Maimonidean Thought: Messianism, Resurrection, & the World to Come-Jacob I. LC 82-17303. cxx, 281p. 1982. 59.50x (ISBN 0-87068-706-9). Ktav.

--Maimonides & St. Thomas Aquinas. 1974. 39.50x (ISBN 0-87068-249-0). Ktav.

Dienstbier, Richard A., ed. Nebraska Symposium on Motivation, 1978: Human Emotion. LC 53-11655. (Nebraska Symposia on Motivation Ser.: Vol. 26). xxvi, 321p. 1979. 25.50x (ISBN 0-8032-2306-4); pap. 8.95x (ISBN 0-8032-7203-0). U of Nebr Pr.

Dienstbier, Richard A., jt. ed. see Cole, James K.

Dienstbier, Sharon & Hendricks, Sybil D. Natural Foods Storage Bible: Secrets of Storing Cooking & Enjoying Natural Foods. LC 76-29308. (Illus.). 1976. 13.95 (ISBN 0-88290-066-8). Horizon Utah.

Dienstein, Dianne H., ed. see Cox, Meridith B.

Dienstein, William. How to Write a Narrative Investigation Report. 128p. 1975. 14.75x (ISBN 0-398-00454-4). C C Thomas.

--Technics for the Crime Investigator. 2nd ed. 272p. 1974. 28.50x (ISBN 0-398-03112-6). C C Thomas.

Dienstfrey. Protides of the Biological Fluids: Proceedings, Colloquium on Protides of the Biological Fluids, 25th. LC 58-5908. 1978. text ed. 165.00 (ISBN 0-08-021524-6). Pergamon.

Dienstfrey, Pat, ed. see Frank, Thaisa.

Dienstfrey, Patricia. Newspaper Stories & Other Poems. 36p. (Orig.). 1979. pap. 3.75 (ISBN 0-917658-11-6). BPW & P.

Diep, Bridgette. Trip Through Cambodia. LC 73-159478. (Illus.). 32p. (ps-3). 6.95 (ISBN 0-87592-054-3). Scroll Pr.

Diepersloot, Jan. The Tao of the Species: Investigations into the Psychohistory of Western Man. LC 84-70589. 1984. 9.95 (ISBN 0-9608792-1-8). Apprentices.

Dieppe, P. & Calvert, P. Crystals & Joint Disease. LC 83-23445. (Illus.). 180p. 1983. 49.95x (ISBN 0-412-22150-0, NO. 6782, Pub by Chapman & Hall). Methuen Inc.

Dieppe, Paul A., et al. Atlas of Clinical Rheumatology. (Illus.). 360p. 1985. 75.00 (ISBN 0-8121-0903-1). Lea & Febiger.

Dierauf, E., Jr. & Court, J. Unified Concepts in Applied Physics. 1979. 28.95 (ISBN 0-13-938753-6). P-H.

Diercksen, G. H. & Wilson, S., eds. Methods in Computational Molecular Physics. 1983. lib. bdg. 48.00 (ISBN 90-2771-638-2, Pub. by Reidel Holland). Kluwer Academic.

Diercksen, G. H., ed. see Nato Advanced Study Institute, C15, Ramsau, Germany, 1974.

Dierdorf, Stephen F., jt. ed. see Stoelting, Robert K.

Dieren, Bernard Van see Van Dieren, Bernard.

Dieren, W Van see Van Dieren, W. & Hummelinck, M. W.

Dierich, Manfred P., jt. ed. see Ferrone, Soldano.

Dieringer, Peter B., ed. Workplace Perspectives on Education & Training. 176p. 1982. 17.50 (ISBN 0-686-33358-6). Kluwer Nijhoff.

Dierker, Paul F., jt. auth. see Campbell, Howard E.

Dierkes, Henry. Robert Frost: A Friend to a Younger Poet. 80p. 1984. 12.00x (ISBN 0-915739-03-8). Armstrong Pr.

Dierkes, Meinolf, et al, eds. Technological Risk: Its Perception & Handling in the European Community. LC 80-18899. 160p. 1980. text ed. 35.00 (ISBN 0-89946-059-3). Oelgeschlager.

Dierks, Paul A., jt. auth. see Vargo, Richard J.

Dierksmeyer, John, tr. see Boff, Leonardo.

Dierl, Wolfgang. Insects. LC 78-323335. (Nature Guides Ser.). (Illus.). 144p. 1979. pap. 5.95 (ISBN 0-7011-2379-6, Pub. by Chatto & Windus). Merrimack Pub Cir.

Diernisse, Villy. Retort Pouch: New Growth Industry. (Illus.). 191p. 1981. 950.00x (ISBN 0-910211-00-0). Laal Co.

--Word Processors & Typewriters Worldwide: Opportunities & Pitfalls. (Illus.). 270p. 1984. 1500.00x (ISBN 0-910211-01-9). Laal Co.

Dierolf, S., jt. auth. see Roelcke, W.

Dierrsen, Gunther, jt. auth. see Frickelton, Annelise.

Diers, Donna. Research in Nursing Practice. LC 79-878. 1979. text ed. 23.50x (ISBN 0-397-54221-6, 64-01723, Lippincott Nursing). Lippincott.

Dierschke, Hartmut. Internationale Vereinigung Fuer Vegetationskunde: Berichte der Internationalen Symposien: Syntaxonomie (1980) (Illus.). 614p. (Ger.). 1981. lib. bdg. 56.00x (ISBN 3-7682-1309-9). Lubrecht & Cramer.

Dierschke, Hartmut, ed. Struktur und Dynamik von Waeldern: Rinteln, April 1981, Berichte der Internationalen Symposien der Intern'len Vereinigung fuer Vegetationskunde. (Illus.). 600p. (Orig., Ger.). 1983. lib. bdg. 56.00 (ISBN 3-7682-1334-X). Lubrecht & Cramer.

Diers Rau, Henrietta A. Healing with Herbs: Nature's Way to Better Health. LC 75-23579. 240p. 1976. pap. 2.95 (ISBN 0-668-03878-0). Arco.

Dies, Auguste. Autour de Platon: Essais de Critique et d'Histoire. facsimile ed. LC 75-13261. (History of Ideas in Ancient Greece Ser.). (Fr.). 1976. Repr. of 1927 ed. 38.50x (ISBN 0-405-07303-8). Ayer Co Pubs.

Dies, Edward J. Behind the Wall Street Curtain. facs. ed. LC 73-86745. (Essay Index Reprint Ser). 1952. 17.00 (ISBN 0-8369-1178-4). Ayer Co Pubs.

--The Plunger: A Tale of the Wheat Pit. facsimile ed. McCurry, Dan C. & Rubenstein, Richard E., eds. LC 74-30627. (American Farmers & the Rise of Agribusiness Ser.). (Illus.). 1975. Repr. of 1929 ed. 23.50x (ISBN 0-405-06789-5). Ayer Co Pubs.

--Titans of the Soil: Great Builders of Agriculture. LC 76-49613. (Illus.). 1977. Repr. of 1949 ed. lib. bdg. 24.75x (ISBN 0-8371-9329-X, DITS). Greenwood.

Dies, Martin. The Trojan Horse in America. Grob, Gerald, ed. LC 76-46072. (Anti-Movements in America). 1977. Repr. of 1940 ed. lib. bdg. 29.00x (ISBN 0-405-09945-2). Ayer Co Pubs.

Dies, Robert R. & MacKenzie, K. Roy, eds. Advances in Group Psychotherapy: Integrating Research & Practice. LC 83-206. (Monographs of the American Group Psychotherapy Association). xvii, 226p. 1985. text ed. 22.50 (ISBN 0-8236-0107-2, 00107). Intl Univs Pr.

Diesburg, D. E., ed. see Symposium, 112th TMS-AIME Annual Meeting, Atlanta, Georgia, March 9, 1983.

Diesburg, D. E., ed. see TMS-AIME 112th Annual Meeting, Atlanta, March 9, 1983.

Diesburg, Daniel E., ed. Case-Hardened Steel: Microstructural & Residual Stress Effects; Proceedings, AIME Annual Meeting, Atlanta, Georgia, 1983. LC 83-63326. (Illus.). 237p. 1984. 54.00 (ISBN 0-89520-471-1). Metal Soc.

Diesendorf, Margaret & Amanuddin, Syed, eds. New Poetry from Australia. 40p. 1973. pap. 2.00 (ISBN 0-912206-55-1). Poetry Eastwest.

Diesendorf, Mark. Energy & People: Social Implications of Different Energy Futures. LC 80-670075. 176p. (Orig.). 1980. pap. 13.95x (ISBN 0-909509-12-3, Pub. by Soc Res Sci Australia). Intl Spec Bk.

Diesendorf, Mark, ed. The Magic Bullet: Social Implications & Limitations of Modern Medicine, an Environmental Approach. 153p. (Orig.). 1977. pap. 7.95x (ISBN 0-909509-09-3, Pub. by Soc Res Sci Australia). Intl Spec Bk.

Diesfeld, H. J. & Hecklau, H. K. Kenya - A Geomedical Monograph. (Geomedical Monograph: Vol. 5). (Illus.). 1978. 46.10 (ISBN 0-387-08729-X). Springer-Verlag.

Diesfeld, Hans-Jochen. Health Research in Developing Countries. (Medicine in Developing Countries Ser.: Vol. 11). 238p. 1982. 15.25 (ISBN 3-8204-7110-3). P Lang Pubs.

Diesing, Paul. Reason in Society: Five Types of Decisions & Their Social Conditions. LC 72-11328. 262p. 1973. lib. bdg. 29.75x (ISBN 0-8371-6660-8, DIRS); pap. 4.95 (ISBN 0-8371-8941-1, DIR). Greenwood.

--Science & Ideology in the Policy Sciences. 1982. lib. bdg. 39.95x (ISBN 0-202-30301-2); pap. text ed. 18.95x (ISBN 0-202-30302-0). Aldine Pub.

Diesing, Paul, jt. auth. see Snyder, Glenn H.

Diesing, Paul R. Patterns of Discovery in the Social Sciences. LC 72-106978. 360p. 1971. 26.95x (ISBN 0-202-30101-X). Aldine Pub.

Diesner, Hans-Joachim. The Great Migration. (Illus.). 255p. 1982. 35.00 (ISBN 0-88254-640-6). Hippocrene Bks.

Diessenhaus, H. I., jt. auth. see Millon, T.

Diestel, J. Sequences & Series in Banach Spaces. (Graduate Texts in Mathematics Ser.: Vol. 92). 280p. 1984. 38.00 (ISBN 0-387-90859-5). Springer-Verlag.

Diestel, J. & Uhl, J. J. Vector Measures. LC 77-9625. (Mathematical Surveys Ser.: No. 15). 322p. 1979. pap. 36.00 (ISBN 0-8218-1515-6, SURV15). Am Math.

Diet-Heart Review Panel. Mass Field Trials of the Diet-Heart Question. (AHA Monograph Ser.: Vol. 28). pap. text ed. 4.00 (ISBN 0-87493-008-1, 73-020A). Am Heart.

Diet, Tim. Tales of the Sea. Jack, Susan, ed. 160p. 1983. pap. 7.95 (ISBN 0-930096-51-7). G Gannett.

Dietary Allowances Comm. & Food & Nutrition Board. Recommended Dietary Allowances. 9th ed. (Illus.). 1980. pap. 8.00. Natl Acad Pr.

Dieten, Ioannes Van see Van Dieten, Ioannes.

Dieten, Jan-Louis Van see Van Dieten, Jan-Louis.

Dieter, G. E., ed. Workability Testing Techniques. 1984. 70.00 (ISBN 0-87170-174-X). ASM.

Dieter, George. Engineering Design: A Materials & Processing Approach. (Materials Science & Engineering Ser.). (Illus.). 608p. 1983. text ed. 44.00 (ISBN 0-07-016896-2). McGraw.

--Mechanical Metallurgy. 2nd ed. (Illus.). 1976. text ed. 45.00 (ISBN 0-07-016891-1). McGraw.

Dieter, Melvin E. The Holiness Revival of the Nineteenth Century. LC 80-17259. (Studies in Evangelicalism: No. 1). 366p. 1980. 24.00 (ISBN 0-8108-1328-9). Scarecrow.

Dieter, Melvin E. & Berg, Daniel N., eds. Church. (Wesleyan Theological Perspectives Ser.: Vol. IV). 1984. 14.95 (ISBN 0-87162-406-0, D4853). Warner Pr.

Dieter, William. Beyond the Mountain. LC 84-45052. 320p. 1985. 13.95 (ISBN 0-689-11477-X). Atheneum.

--Hunter's Orange. LC 82-73280. 256p. 1983. 13.95 (ISBN 0-689-11379-X). Atheneum.

--Hunter's Orange. 256p. 1984. pap. 2.95 (ISBN 0-380-68684-8). Avon.

Dieterich, Daniel, ed. Teaching about Doublespeak. LC 76-4139. 200p. 1976. pap. 6.15 (ISBN 0-8141-5027-6); pap. 5.00 members. NCTE.

Dieterich, Genoveva. Pequeno Diccionario De Teatro Mundial. 294p. (Span.). 1976. pap. 5.25 (ISBN 84-7090-028-5, S-31395). French & Eur.

Dieterich, T., et al. Assessing Comprehension in a School Setting. Griffin, Peg, ed. LC 78-59785. (Linguistics & Reading Ser.: No. 3). 116p. 1978. pap. text ed. 14.95x (ISBN 0-15-599077-2). Ctr Appl Ling.

Dieterich, Thomas G. & Freeman, Cecilia. A Linguistic Guide to English Proficiency Testing in Schools. (Language in Education Ser.: No. 23). 53p. 1979. pap. 5.95x (ISBN 0-15-599057-8). Ctr Appl Ling.

Dieterle, Gwendolyn. M'lady Gets a Beastie. 48p. (gr. 3-5). 1981. 5.95 (ISBN 0-89962-203-8). Todd & Honeywell.

Dieterlen, F. Zur Phaenologie des aequatorialen Regenwaldes im Ost-Zaire (Kivu) nebst Planzenliste und Klimadaten. (Dissertations Botanica: No. 47). (Illus.). 1979. pap. 10.00x (ISBN 3-7682-1215-7). Lubrecht & Cramer.

Dieterlen, G. & Cisse, Y. Les Fondemonts de la Societe D'initiation Du Komo. (Cahiers De L'homme, Nouvelle Ser.: No. 10). (Illus.). 1972. pap. 21.60x (ISBN 90-2797-012-2). Mouton.

Dieterlen, Germaine, ed. see International African Seminar - 3rd - Salisburg - Southern Rhodesia.

Dieth, Eugen. Vademekum der Phonetik. 2nd ed. (Ger.). 1968. 30.00 (ISBN 3-7720-0292-7, M-7135). French & Eur.

Dieth, Eugen, jt. ed. see Orton, Harold.

Diethelm, Oskar. Medical Dissertations of Psychiatric Interest. 1971. 18.00 (ISBN 3-8055-1201-5). S Karger.

Diethelm, Walter. Visual Transformation: New Creative Trends in Art, Technology, Information & Graphic Design. (Visual Communications Ser.). (Illus.). 180p. 1982. 72.50 (ISBN 0-8038-7768-4). Hastings.

Diethelm, Walter J. Signet-Signal-Symbol. (Visual Communication Bks.). 1976. 72.50 (ISBN 0-8038-6739-5). Hastings.

Diethrich, Edward. The Heart Test: The Arizona Heart Institute Program for the Detection, Prevention & Treatment of Heart Disease. 224p. (Orig.). 1981. pap. 6.95 (ISBN 0-346-12551-0). Cornerstone.

Diethrich, Edward B., ed. Noninvasive Assessment of the Cardiovascular System. LC 82-4785. (Illus.). 432p. 1982. text ed. 47.00 (ISBN 0-7236-7019-6). PSG Pub Co.

Dietiker, S. & Burger, G. Allo la France. 256p. (Orig.). 1985. pap. text ed. 15.95 (ISBN 0-8384-1292-0). Heinle & Heinle.

Dietiker, Simone. Franc Parler. 14.95x (ISBN 0-669-96628-2); instructor's manual free (ISBN 0-669-97915-5); wkbk. 4.95x (ISBN 0-669-97725-X); tapes, 10 reels 50.00 (ISBN 0-669-97907-4); 10 cassettes 50.00 (ISBN 0-669-98350-0). Heath.

Dietiker, Simone R. En Bonne Forme. pap. text ed. 9.95x (ISBN 0-669-00863-X); wkbk. 4.95 (ISBN 0-669-00864-8); cassettes 30.00 (ISBN 0-669-00865-6). Heath.

--En Bonne Forme. 3rd ed. 416p. 1983. pap. 15.95 (ISBN 0-669-05255-8); wkbk. 8.95 (ISBN 0-669-05257-4); reels 60.00 (ISBN 0-669-05259-0); cassettes 1.95 (ISBN 0-669-05258-2); demo tape 1.95 (ISBN 0-669-05260-4); transcript 1.95 (ISBN 0-669-05261-2). Heath.

--Franc-Parler. 2nd ed. 1980. text ed. 23.95x (ISBN 0-669-02491-0); instrs.' guide 1.95 (ISBN 0-669-02494-5); wkbk. 9.95 (ISBN 0-669-02492-9); tapes-reels 60.00 (ISBN 0-669-02496-1); cassettes 35.00 (ISBN 0-669-02497-X); demo tape 1.95 (ISBN 0-669-02498-8); tapescript 1.95 (ISBN 0-669-02495-3). Heath.

Dietl, C. Woerterbuch des Wirtschafts, Rechts und Handelssprache. (Eng. & Ger., Dictionary of Economic, Legal & Commercial Terms). 1970. 33.00 (ISBN 3-87527-003-7, M-6939). French & Eur.

Dietl, L. Kay & Neff, Marsha J. Human Needs & Social Welfare Curriculum Project. Incl. Unit I. To Promote the General Welfare? An Introduction to the United States Social Welfare System. 4.95x (ISBN 0-8077-6070-6); tchr's. manual 4.95x (ISBN 0-8077-6071-4); Unit II. Aging Americans-Profiles, Programs & Possibilities. 6.50x (ISBN 0-8077-6072-2); tchr's. manual 5.50x (ISBN 0-8077-6073-0); Youth-Search for Identity. 9.95x (ISBN 0-8077-6074-9); tchr's. manual 7.95x (ISBN 0-8077-6075-7); Unit IV. Single Parent Families: Choice or Chance? 7.95x (ISBN 0-8077-6076-5); tchr's. manual 5.50x (ISBN 0-8077-6077-3); New Directions: Alternatives to the United States Social Welfare System. 4.95x (ISBN 0-8077-6078-1); tchr's. manual 3.95x (ISBN 0-8077-6079-X). 1983. Tchrs Coll.

Dietl, Walter. Standortgemasse Verbesserung und Bewirtschaftung Von Alpenweiden. (Tierhaltung: No. 7). (Illus.). 67p. (Ger.). 1979. pap. 15.95x (ISBN 0-8176-1028-6). Birkhauser.

Dietl, Wilhelm. Holy War. Humphreys, Martha, tr. 384p. 1985. 19.95 (ISBN 0-02-531530-7). Macmillan.

Dietmann, J. L. Radiodiagnosis of the Skull. Wackenheim, M. T., tr. from Fr. (Exercises in Radiological Diagnosis). (Illus.). 200p. 1985. pap. 19.50 (ISBN 0-387-13266-X). Springer-Verlag.

Dietmeyer. Logic Design of Digital Systems. 2nd ed. 1978. text ed. 42.89 (ISBN 0-205-05960-0, EDP 285960). Allyn.

Dietrich, Anton, intro. by. Russian Popular Tales. (Folklore Ser.). 1857. 15.00 (ISBN 0-8482-7750-3). Norwood Edns.

Dietrich, B. C. The Origins of Greek Religion. 314p. 1973. 64.00x (ISBN 3-11-003982-6). De Gruyter.

Dietrich, D., jt. ed. see Zamrik, S. Y.

Dietrich, D. E., ed. Pressure Vessels & Piping - Computer Program Evaluation & Qualification, Series PVP-PB-024. 1977. pap. text ed. 16.00 (ISBN 0-685-86875-3, G00124). ASME.

Dietrich, D. E. see International Computers in Engineering Conference & Exhibit, 1983.

Dietrich, Daniel J. The Rites of Writing. 112p. 1982. 6.50 (ISBN 0-8141-4173-0). NCTE.

Dietrich, Deborah, jt. auth. see Aitelli, Peter.

Dietrich, Debra M., jt. auth. see Aitelli, Peter.

Dietrich, Donald J. The Goethezeit & the Metamorphosis of Catholic Theology in the Age of Idealism: Theology, Vol. 128. (European University Studies: Ser. 23). 261p. 1979. pap. 26.25 (ISBN 3-261-04703-8). P Lang Pubs.

Dietrich, Emerson, ed. see Elliott, Ralph N.

Dietrich, Frank H., II & Kearns, Thomas. Basic Statistics. 1983. text ed. 26.95 (ISBN 0-02-329540-6). Dellen Pub.

Dietrich, Frank H., II & Shafer, Nancy J. Business Statistics. (Illus.). 815p. 1984. 24.95 (ISBN 0-02-329510-4). Dellen Pub.

Dietrich, Frank H., II, jt. auth. see McClave, James T.

Dietrich, Gunther, et al. General Oceanography: An Introduction. 2nd ed. LC 80-12919. 626p. 1980. 74.95x (ISBN 0-471-02102-4, Pub. by Wiley-Interscience). Wiley.

Dietrich, I., ed. Superconducting Electron-Optic Devices. LC 76-20466. (International Cryogenics Monograph Ser.). (Illus.). 140p. 1976. 39.50x (ISBN 0-306-30882-7, Plenum Pr). Plenum Pub.

Dietrich, Irvine T. & Hove, John. Conservation of Natural Resources: North Dakota. LC 62-63204. (Illus.). (gr. 7 up). 1962. 3.00 (ISBN 0-911042-06-7). N Dak Inst.

Dietrich, John & Waggoner, Susan. The Complete Health Club Handbook. (Orig.). 1983. pap. 9.95 (ISBN 0-671-47027-2). S&S.

Dietrich, John E. & Duckwall, Ralph. Play Direction. 2nd ed. (Illus.). 400p. 1983. 26.95 (ISBN 0-13-683334-9). P-H.

Dietrich, Marlene. Marlene Dietrich's ABC. rev. ed. (Illus.). 200p. 1984. pap. 7.95 (ISBN 0-8044-6117-1); signed ed. avail. Ungar.

Dietrich, Martin O. & Lehmann, Helmut T., eds. Luther's Works: Devotional Writings I, Vol. 42. LC 55-9893. (Prog. Bk.). 1969. 16.95 (ISBN 0-8006-0342-7, 1-342). Fortress.

Dietrich, R. F. Portrait of the Artist As a Young Superman: A Study of Shaw's Novels. LC 75-77613. (Illus.). 1969. 10.00 (ISBN 0-8130-0277-X). U Presses Fla.

Dietrich, R. F. & Sundell, Roger H., eds. The Art of Fiction. 4th ed. 453p. 1983. pap. text ed. 14.95 (ISBN 0-03-060546-6). HR&W.

Dietrich, R. V. Stones: Their Collection, Identification, & Uses. LC 79-24760. (Geology Ser.). (Illus.). 145p. 1980. pap. text ed. 11.95 (ISBN 0-7167-1139-7). W H Freeman.

Dietrich, R. V. & Wicander, E. Reed. Minerals, Rock & Fossils. LC 82-20220. (Self-Teaching Guides Ser.). 212p. 1983. pap. text ed. 9.95 (ISBN 0-471-89883-X, Pub. by Wiley Pr). Wiley.

Dietrich, Richard V. Geology & Virginia. LC 76-110752. (Illus.). xiv, 213p. 1971. 16.95x (ISBN 0-8139-0289-4). U Pr of Va.

--The Tourmaline Group. (Illus.). 228p. 1985. 29.95 (ISBN 0-442-21857-5). Van Nos Reinhold.

Dietrich, Richard V. & Skinner, Brian J. Rocks & Rock Minerals. LC 79-12111. 319p. 1979. pap. 28.50 (ISBN 0-471-02934-3). Wiley.

Dietrich, Richard V. & Dutro, J. Thomas, eds. AGI Data Sheets for the Geologist in the Field, Laboratory & Office. 150p. 1982. pap. 12.95 (ISBN 0-913312-38-X). Am Geol.

Dietrich, Robbi R. Local Income Taxes: One Solution to Fiscal Dilemmas Facing Local Govenments Today. (Discussion Papers: No. 106). 1976. pap. 3.25 (ISBN 0-686-32272-X). Regional Sci Res Inst.

Dietrich, Suzanne. Matthew. LC 59-10454. (Layman's Bible Commentary Ser.: Vol. 16). 1961. pap. 4.95 (ISBN 0-8042-3076-5). John Knox.

Dietrich, Suzanne De see De Dietrich, Suzanne.

Dietrich, T. Stanton. Florida's Older Population Revisited. (Illus.). vi, 78p. (Orig.). 1978. pap. 6.00 (ISBN 0-8130-0686-4). U Presses Fla.

Dietrich, Wendell, ed. see Kane, John F.

Dietrich, Wendell, ed. see Orr, Robert P.

Dietrich, Wendell S., ed. see Smith, David L.

Dietrich, Wolf. Bibliografia Da Lingua Portugesa Do Brasil. (Tuebinger Beitraege Zur Liquistik Ser.: No. 120). (Illus.). 324p. (Orig., Port.). 1979. pap. 37.00x (ISBN 3-87808-120-0). Benjamins North Am.

Dietrich-Boorsch, Dorothea. German Drawings of the Sixties. (Illus.). 100p. (Orig.). 1982. pap. 5.00x. Yale Art Gallery.

Dietrichsen. English-Norse, Norse-English Pocket Dictionary. 9.00 (ISBN 0-317-19065-2, N407). Vanous.

Dietrichsen & Overland-Gabrielsen, eds. English-Norwegian- Pocket Dictionary. 4th, rev. ed. 462p. 1983. pap. 9.75 (ISBN 0-317-18997-2, N407). Vanous.

Dietrick, Ronald W., jt. auth. see Adams, Gene M.

Dietsch, Deborah & Steeneken, Sue, eds. Architecture in the Public Realm: Precis III. (Illus.). 96p. 1981. pap. 12.00 (ISBN 0-8478-5345-4). Rizzoli Intl.

Dietsche, Doreen, jt. auth. see Gerrick, David J.

Dietschmann, Hans J., ed. Representation & Exchange of Knowledge As a Basis of Information Processes: Proceedings of the 5th International Research Forum in Information Science (IRFIS 5) Heidelberg, 5-7 Sept., 1983. 434p. 1984. 55.75 (ISBN 0-444-87563-8, I-302-84, North Holland). Elsevier.

Dietschy, John M., ed. Disorders of the Gastrointestinal Tract; Disorders of the Liver; Nutritional Disorders. LC 75-45266. (The Science & Practice of Clinical Medicine Ser.). (Illus.). 432p. 1976. 47.50 (ISBN 0-8089-0716-6, 791037). Grune.

Dietterlin, Wendel. Fantastic Engravings of Wendel Dietterlin. Orig. Title: Architectura. 1968. pap. 8.50 (ISBN 0-486-21944-5). Dover.

--The Fantastic Engravings of Wendel Dietterlin: The 203 Plates & Text of His Architecture. (Illus.). 11.50 (ISBN 0-8446-1981-7). Peter Smith.

Dietz. Andre. (Illus.). (gr. 2-3). 1979. pap. 6.95 (ISBN 0-89272-052-2). Down East.

Dietz & Goodridge. A Seal Called Andre. 1980. pap. 8.95 (ISBN 0-89272-076-X). Down East.

Dietz, A. & Thayer, W. D., eds. Actinomycete Taxonomy: Special Publ. No. 6. 380p. 1980. 30.00 (ISBN 0-318-16572-4); members 25.00 (ISBN 0-318-16573-2). Soc Indus Micro.

Dietz, A. A. & Grannis, G. F., eds. Aging - Its Chemistry: Proceedings of the Third Arnold O. Beckman Conference in Clinical Chemistry. LC 80-65825. 448p. 1980. AACC members 25.00 (ISBN 0-915274-10-8); non-members 35.00. Am Assn Clinical Chem.

Dietz, Albert A., ed. Genetic Disease: Diagnosis & Treatment. 317p. 1983. 35.00 (ISBN 0-915274-20-5). Am Assn Clinical Chem.

Dietz, Albert G. Dwelling House Construction. rev., 4th ed. (Illus.). 528p. 1974. pap. text ed. 9.95 (ISBN 0-262-54033-9). MIT Pr.

Dietz, Albert G., ed. Composite Engineering Laminates. 1969. 45.00x (ISBN 0-262-04017-4). MIT Pr.

Dietz, Albert G. & Cutler, Laurence S., eds. Industrialized Building Systems for Housing. 1971. 37.50x (ISBN 0-262-04034-4). MIT Pr.

Dietz, August, Sr. Presidents of the United States: Portraits & Biographies. 2.00 (ISBN 0-685-47902-1). Dietz.

Dietz, Beverley. Birdseye Word Skills: World of Words. LC 84-62440. 1983. pap. 5.95 (ISBN 0-8224-0725-6). Pitman Learning.

--Birdseye Writing Skills: Punctuation. LC 83-62439. (gr. 4-6). 1983. pap. 5.95 (ISBN 0-8224-0723-X). Pitman Learning.

--Birdseye Writing Skills: Sentences. LC 83-62441. (gr. 4-6). 1983. pap. 5.95 (ISBN 0-8224-0722-1). Pitman Learning.

Dietz, Brian, ed. The Part & Trade of Early Elizabethan London: Documents. 1972. 50.00x (ISBN 0-686-96612-0, Pub by London Rec Soc England). State Mutual Bk.

Dietz, Chris, ed. see Bisbee Press Collective.

Dietz, Chris, ed. see Granlund, Marvin.

Dietz, Chris, ed. see Patterson, Tom.

Dietz, Chris, ed. see Thornton, Elizabeth.

Dietz, Chris, et al. Bozko. (Binturong Ser.: No. 3). 30p. (Orig.). 1984. pap. 3.00x (ISBN 0-938196-06-5). Bisbee Pr.

Dietz, Craig, jt. auth. see Doan, William.

Dietz, David. Science in Hawaii. (Illus.). 1968. 0.50 (ISBN 0-941200-03-5). Aquarius.

Dietz, Dennis. Mountain Memories, Vol. II. LC 83-80178. (Illus.). 150p. 1983. 5.00 (ISBN 0-934750-18-1). Jalamap.

Dietz, Dennis A. Iowa Legal Forms-Commercial Real Estate. 1983. looseleaf 29.50 (ISBN 0-86678-194-3). Butterworth MN.

Dietz, Donald T. The "Auto Sacramental" & the Parable in the Sixteenth & Seventeenth Centuries. (Studies in the Romance Languages & Literatures: No. 132). 205p. 1973. pap. 11.50x (ISBN 0-8078-9132-0). U of NC Pr.

Dietz, Frederick C. English Government Finance, Fourteen Eighty-Five to Fifteen Fifty-Eight. Repr. of 1920 ed. 14.00 (ISBN 0-384-11750-3). Johnson Repr.

--The Industrial Revolution. LC 73-7193. 111p. 1973. Repr. of 1927 ed. lib. bdg. 15.00x (ISBN 0-8371-6917-8, DIIR). Greenwood.

Dietz, Fredrick C. English Public Finance. Incl. Vol. 1. English Government Finance, 1485-1558. 210p. 1964. Repr. of 1921 ed. 35.00x (ISBN 0-7146-1299-5); Vol. 2. English Government Finance, 1558-1641. 478p. 1964. Repr. of 1932 ed. 42.50x (ISBN 0-7146-1300-2). 1964 (F Cass Co). Biblio Dist.

Dietz, H., jt. ed. see Brock, M.

Dietz, H., et al, eds. Extra-Intracranial Vascular Anastomoses: Microsurgery at the Edge of the Tentorium. (Advances in Neurosurgery Ser.: Vol. 13). (Illus.). 380p. 1985. pap. 39.50 (ISBN 0-387-15615-1). Springer Verlag.

Dietz, Henry A. Poverty & Problem-Solving under Military Rule: The Urban Poor in Lima, Peru. LC 79-620013. (Latin American Monographs: No. 51). 300p. 1980. text ed. 22.50x (ISBN 0-292-76460-X). U of Tex Pr.

Dietz, Henry A. & Moore, Richard J. Political Participation in a Non-Electoral Setting: The Urban Poor in Lima, Peru. LC 79-14218. (Papers in International Studies: Latin America Ser.: No. 6). 1979. pap. 9.00x (ISBN 0-89680-085-7, 82-92575, Ohio U Ctr Intl). Ohio U Pr.

Dietz, J. B., Jr., jt. auth. see Yalisove, I. L.

Dietz, J. Herbert, Jr. Rehabilitation Oncology. LC 80-22911. 194p. 1981. 32.50 (ISBN 0-471-08414-X). Krieger.

Dietz, James M. Ecology & Social Organization of the Maned Wolf (Chrysocyon Brachyurus) LC 83-600292. (Smithsonian Contributions to Zoology: No. 392). pap. 20.00 (ISBN 0-317-19847-5, 2023009). Bks Demand UMI.

Dietz, James S. Price Guide & Introduction to Movie Posters & Movie Memorabilia. 2nd ed. 175p. 1985. pap. 11.95 (ISBN 0-910041-02-4). Baja Pr.

Dietz, Lew. The Allagash. LC 78-8326. 264p. 1978. pap. 8.95 (ISBN 0-89621-000-6). Thorndike Pr.

Dietz, Lois, jt. auth. see Parker, William.

Dietz, Marjorie. ABC's of Gardening Indoors & Outdoors. LC 84-13819. (Illus.). 256p. 1985. 12.95 (ISBN 0-385-18544-8). Doubleday.

Dietz, Marjorie, ed. The Complete Guide to Successful Gardening. LC 78-23734. (Illus.). 1979. 14.95 (ISBN 0-8317-1625-8, Mayflower Bks). Smith Pubs.

Dietz, Marjorie, ed. see Brookes, John.

Dietz, Marjorie J., ed. Ten Thousand Garden Questions Answered by Twenty Experts. 4th ed. LC 80-2738. (Illus.). 1440p. 1982. 19.95 (ISBN 0-385-18509-X). Doubleday.

Dietz, Mary L. Killing for Profit: The Social Organization of Felony Homicide. LC 82-24571. (Illus.). 240p. 1983. text ed. 23.95X (ISBN 0-8304-1008-2). Nelson-Hall.

Dietz, Norman D. Fables & Vaudevilles & Plays: Theatre More-or-Less at Random. LC 68-16685. 176p. (Orig.). 1968. pap. 4.95 (ISBN 0-936520-00-0). Norman & Sandra.

--The Life Guard & the Mermaid, & Other American Fables. LC 75-38194. 79p. (Orig.). 1976. pap. 3.95 (ISBN 0-8170-0702-4). Norman & Sandra.

Dietz, O. & Wiesner, E., eds. Handbuch der Pferdekrankheiten fuer Wissenschaft und Praxis, 3 vols. in 1. (Illus.). 1388p. 1982. 127.00 (ISBN 3-8055-2627-X). S Karger.

Dietz, Park, jt. auth. see Hazelwood, Robert R.

Dietz, Park E., ed. see Frank, Jerome D.

Dietz, Peter. Pension Funds: Measuring Investment Performance. LC 66-12080. 1966. 8.95 (ISBN 0-02-907410-X). Free Pr.

Dietz, Rosalie G., intro. by. History of the Independent Loudoun Virginia Rangers, U. S. Vol. Cav. (Scouts) 1862-65. 234p. 1985. Repr. of 1896 ed. text ed. 19.60 (ISBN 0-913419-28-1). Butternut Pr.

Dietz, Ruth M. Spanish-English Housekeeping. (Illus.). 156p. (Eng. & Span.). 1983. pap. 7.95 (ISBN 0-89015-379-5). Eakin Pubns.

Dietz, Sarah S. Easter Activity Book. (Stick-Out-Your Neck Ser.). (Illus.). 32p. (gr. 3 up). 1984. pap. 1.59 (ISBN 0-88724-067-4, CD-8051). Carson-Dellos.

Dietz, Sarah S. & Brokaw, David. Valentine Activity Book. (Stick-Out-Your-Neck Ser.). (Illus.). 32p. (gr. 4 up). 1984. pap. 1.79 (ISBN 0-88724-065-8, CD-8045). Carson-Dellos.

Dietz, Susan. The Correct Waitress. 2nd ed. 1978. pap. 3.95 (ISBN 0-8104-9468-X). Hayden.

Dietz, Thomas, jt. auth. see McEvoy, James.

Dietz, Tim. Tales of Whales. Jack, Susan, ed. (Illus.). 160p. (Orig.). 1982. pap. 7.95 (ISBN 0-930096-33-9). G Gannett.

Dietz, Ulysses G. The Newark Collection of American Art Pottery. Sweeney, Mary S., ed. (Illus.). 128p. (Orig.). 1984. pap. 19.95 (ISBN 0-932828-19-1). Newark Mus.

--The Newark Museum Collection of American Art Pottery. (Illus.). 128p. 1984. pap. 19.95 (ISBN 0-87905-166-3, Peregrine Smith). Gibbs M Smith.

Dietz, Ulysses G. & Newark Museum Quarterly. Century of Revivals, Vol. 31. (No. 2-3). (Illus.). 64p. 1983. 4.00 (ISBN 0-686-39826-2). Newark Mus.

Dietze, Charles E. The Henderson Crusade. (Illus.). 164p. (Orig.). 1983. pap. 4.95 (ISBN 0-9610198-0-8). G G L Pub Co.

Dietze, Gottfried. America's Political Dilemma: From Limited to Unlimited Democracy. LC 68-12902. 310p. 1968. 28.50x (ISBN 0-8018-0167-2). Johns Hopkins.

--America's Political Dilemma: From Limited to Unlimited Democracy. 310p. 1985. pap. text ed. 12.75 (ISBN 0-8191-4788-5). U Pr of Amer.

--The Federalist: A Classic of Federalism & Free Government. LC 76-57682. 1977. Repr. of 1960 ed. lib. bdg. 22.25x (ISBN 0-8371-9466-0, DIFED). Greenwood.

--The Federalist: A Classic on Federalism & Free Government. 388p. 1960. pap. 7.95x (ISBN 0-8018-0169-9). Johns Hopkins.

--Liberalism Proper & Proper Liberalism. LC 84-7847. 1984. text ed. 27.50x (ISBN 0-8018-3220-9). Johns Hopkins.

Dietze, Gunther, jt. ed. see Fritz, Hans.

Dietzen, John J. The New Question Box. rev., 2nd ed. 444p. 1985. pap. 5.95 (ISBN 0-940518-01-5). Guildhall Pubs.

Dietzgen, Joseph. Nature of Human Brain Work: An Introduction to Dialectics. Untermann, Ernest, tr. from Ger. 127p. (Orig.). 1984. pap. 7.00 (ISBN 0-317-18558-6). Left Bank.

--The Nature of Human Brain Work: An Introduction to Dialectics. 127p. 1984. Repr. of 1906 ed. lib. bdg. 19.95 (ISBN 0-88286-105-0). C H Kerr.

Dietzler, Andrew J. Time Sharing Task Control for a Hybrid Computer Simulation Laboratory. LC 75-128003. 172p. 1969. 19.00 (ISBN 0-403-04494-4). Scholarly.

Dietzmann, Harry E. Emissions Measurement Manual for Natural Gas Pipeline Compressor Engines. 137p. 1976. pap. 8.00 (ISBN 0-318-12606-0, L22278). Am Gas Assn.

Dieudonne, J. History of Functional Analysis. (Mathematics Studies: Vol. 49). 312p. 1981. pap. 39.50 (ISBN 0-444-86148-3, North-Holland). Elsevier.

--Introduction to the Theory of Formal Groups. (Pure & Applied Mathematics Ser: Vol. 20). 288p. 1973. 55.00 (ISBN 0-8247-6011-5). Dekker.

Dieudonne, J. A. Treatise on Analysis, 6 vols. Incl. Vol. 1. 1960. 33.75 (ISBN 0-12-215550-5); Vol. 2. rev. ed. 1970. 67.50 (ISBN 0-12-215502-5); Vol. 3. 1972. 68.50 (ISBN 0-12-215503-3); Vol. 4. 1974. 67.50 (ISBN 0-12-215504-1); Vol. 5. 1977. 49.50 (ISBN 0-12-215505-X); Vol. 6. 1978. 47.50 (ISBN 0-12-215506-8). (Pure & Applied Mathematics Ser.). Acad Pr.

Dieudonne, J. A. & Carrell, James B. Invariant Theory: Old & New. 1971. 23.00 (ISBN 0-12-215540-8). Acad Pr.

Dieudonne, J. A., et al. How to Write Mathematics. LC 72-13840. 1983. pap. 10.00 (ISBN 0-8218-0055-8, HWM). Am Math.

Dieudonne, Jean. History of Algebraic Geometry. Sally, Judith, tr. from Fr. (Mathematics Ser.). 350p. 1985. write for info. (ISBN 0-534-03723-2). Wadsworth Pub.

--A Panorama of Pure Mathematics: As Seen by N. Bourbaki. Macdonald, I., tr. LC 80-2330. (Pure & Applied Mathematics Ser.). 1982. 37.50 (ISBN 0-12-215560-2). Acad Pr.

--Special Functions & Linear Representations of Lie Groups. LC 79-22180. (CBMS Regional Conference Ser. in Mathematics: No. 42). 59p. 1982. pap. 11.00 (ISBN 0-8218-1692-6, CBMS-42). Am Math.

Dieudonne, Jean & Hua, L. K. On the Automorphisms of the Classical Groups. LC 52-42839. (Memoirs: No. 2). 123p. 1980. pap. 13.00 (ISBN 0-8218-1202-5, MEMO-2). Am Math.

Dieulesaint, E. & Royer, D. Elastic Waves in Solids: Applications to Signal Processing. LC 80-49980. 511p. 1981. 74.95x (ISBN 0-471-27836-X, Pub. by Wiley-Interscience). Wiley.

Diez, E. Die Kunst der Islamischen Volker. (Handbuch der Kunstwissenschaft Ser.). (Illus.). xxii, 218p. (Ger.). Repr. of 1917 ed. lib. bdg. 150.00x (ISBN 0-89241-144-9). Caratzas.

Diez Mateo, Felix. Diccionario Espanol Etimologico. 396p. (Span.). 1972. 6.95 (ISBN 84-300-5794-3, S-12291). French & Eur.

--Diccionario Manual Aleman-Espanol, Espanol-Aleman. 952p. (Ger. & Span.). 1978. pap. 12.95 (ISBN 84-239-4766-1, S-50383). French & Eur.

Diez Mateo, Felix & Hochleitner, Frida. Diccionario Manual Frances-Espanol, Espanol-Frances. 992p. (Span. & Fr.). 1971. 9.95 (ISBN 84-239-4721-1, S-50389). French & Eur.

--Diccionario Manual Ingles-Espanol, Espanol-Ingles. 1008p. (Eng. & Span.). 1971. 9.95 (ISBN 84-239-4720-3, S-50351). French & Eur.

Di Fabio, Anthony. Rheumatoid Diseases Cured at Last. 3rd ed. LC 82-72042. (Illus.). 136p. (Orig.). 1984. pap. 9.95 (ISBN 0-931150-12-4). Authors Co-op.

DiFate, Vincent & Summers, Ian. Difate's Catalog of Science Fiction Hardware. LC 80-51612. (Illus.). 160p. 1980. 17.95 (ISBN 0-89480-127-9, 321); pap. 8.95 (ISBN 0-89480-126-0, 425). Workman Pub.

DiFazio, William. Longshoremen: Community & Resistance on the Brooklyn Waterfront. (Critical Studies in Work & Community). 208p. 1985. text ed. 24.95 (ISBN 0-89789-065-5). Bergin & Garvey.

DiFederico, Frank. The Mosaics of Saint Peter's: Decorating the New Basilica. LC 82-42777. (Illus.). 176p. 1983. 42.50x (ISBN 0-271-00344-8). Pa St U Pr.

--The Mosaics of the National Shrine of the Immaculate Conception. (Illus.). 96p. 1981. 16.95 (ISBN 0-916276-09-0). Decatur Hse.

Di Ferrante, R. K. Trace Metals: Exposure & Health Effects. 1979. 48.00 (ISBN 0-08-022446-6). Pergamon.

Diffendal, Kim J. & Johnson, Kasia. The Complete Capital Runner's Guide. 99p. (Orig.). 1985. pap. 6.95 (ISBN 0-9614260-0-4). Diffendal & Johnson.

Diffenderffer, Frank R. The German Immigration into Pennsylvania Through the Port of Philadelphia from 1700 to 1775, & the Redemptioners. LC 77-77782. (Illus.). 328p. 1979. Repr. of 1900 ed. 17.50 (ISBN 0-8063-0776-5). Genealog Pub.

Diffey. Ultraviolet Radiation in Medicine. (Medical Physics Handbook Ser.: No. 11). 1981. 29.00 (ISBN 0-9960022-4-3, Pub. by Inst Physics England). Heyden.

Diffey, Norman R. Jakob Michael Reinhold Lenz & Jean-Jacques Rousseau. (Studien zur Germanistik, Anglistik und Komparatistik: Vol. 104). 284p. 1981. 27.00x (ISBN 3-416-01643-2, Pub. by Bouvier Verlag W Germany). Benjamins North Am.

Diffey, T. J. Tolstoy's "What Is Art?". An Essay in the Philosophy of Art. 240p. 1985. 26.00 (ISBN 0-7099-0891-1, Pub. by Croom Helm Ltd). Longwood Pub Group.

Diffie, Bailey W. Prelude to Empire: Portugal Overseas Before Henry the Navigator. 11.25 (ISBN 0-8446-5705-0). Peter Smith.

--Prelude to Empire: Portugal Overseas before Henry the Navigator. LC 60-14301. (Illus.). xii, 129p. 1960. pap. 3.25x (ISBN 0-8032-5049-5, BB 108, Bison). U of Nebr Pr.

Diffie, Bailey W. & Winius, George D. Foundations of the Portuguese Empire, 1415-1850. Shafer, Boyd C., ed. LC 76-7880. (Europe & the World in the Age of Expansion Ser.: Vol. 1). (Illus.). 1977. 25.00x (ISBN 0-8166-0782-6); pap. 5.95x (ISBN 0-8166-0850-4). U of Minn Pr.

Diffrient, Niels, et al. Humanscale Four-Five-Six. 1981. 39.95 (ISBN 0-262-04059-X). MIT Pr.

--Humanscale Seven-Eight-Nine. 1981. 39.95 (ISBN 0-262-04061-1). MIT Pr.

--Humanscale One-Two-Three. 1974. 39.95 (ISBN 0-262-04042-5). MIT Pr.

Di Fiore, Frank R. It's Stunning Kid. LC 78-65136. 1978. 7.95 (ISBN 0-932896-00-6). Westcliff Pubns.

--You Can Conquer Your Headaches. (Illus.). 66p. (Orig.). 1980. pap. 10.00 (ISBN 0-932896-03-0). Westcliff Pubns.

Di Fiore, Mariano S. Atlas of Human Histology. 5th ed. LC 81-8164. (Illus.). 267p. 1981. text ed. 21.50 (ISBN 0-8121-0756-X). Lea & Febiger.

DiFiori, Larry. If I Had a Little Airplane. (Little Sturdy Shape Bks.). (Illus.). 14p. (ps). 1985. 2.95 (ISBN 0-307-12306-5, Pub. by Golden Bks). Western Pub.

--If I Had a Little Boat. (Little Sturdy Shape Bks.). (Illus.). 14p. (ps-2). 1985. 2.95 (ISBN 0-307-12307-3, Pub. by Golden Bks). Western Pub.

--If I Had a Little Car. (Little Sturdy Shape Bks.). (Illus.). 14p. (ps). 1985. 2.95 (ISBN 0-307-12305-7, Pub. by Golden Bks). Western Pub.

--If I Had a Little Train. (Little Sturdy Shape Bks.). (Illus.). 14p. (ps). 1985. 2.95 (ISBN 0-307-12304-9, Pub. by Golden Bks). Western Pub.

DiFiori, Lawrence. My Toys. (Illus.). 26p. (ps). 1983. 2.95 (ISBN 0-02-730600-3). Macmillan.

Di Fiori, Lawrence. My Toys, My First Book, Baby Animals, the Farm, 20 bk. set. Incl. My Toys, 5 bks. 26p. pap. 2.95 (ISBN 0-02-730600-3); My First Book, 5 bks. 2.95 (ISBN 0-02-730610-0); Baby Animals, 5 bks. 2.95 (ISBN 0-02-730620-8); The Farm, 5 bks. 2.95 (ISBN 0-02-730630-5). (Block Books Ser.). (Illus.). (ps-6). 1983. of 20, 5 of ea. 59.00 set (ISBN 0-02-730640-2). Macmillan.

DiFiori, Lawrence. The Truck Book. LC 83-83106. (Golden Sturdy Shape Bks.). (Illus.). (ps). 1984. 2.95 (ISBN 0-307-12299-9, Golden Bks). Western Pub.

DiFonzo, Luigi. A Good Place to Live & Die. 1986. price not set (ISBN 0-87795-778-9). Arbor Hse.

--St. Peter's Banker. 272p. 1983. 15.95 (ISBN 0-531-09889-3). Watts.

Di Francesca, Sal. Straight A's. Solano, Ric, ed. LC 84-82154. (Illus.). 150p. 1985. 24.95 (ISBN 0-931657-00-8). Learning Proc Ctr.

--Straight A's. Solano, Ric, ed. (Illus.). 250p. 1985. pap. 18.50 (ISBN 0-931657-01-6). Learning Proc Ctr.

Di Francis. Cat Country: The Quest for the British Big Cat. (Illus.). 160p. 1983. 12.50 (ISBN 0-7153-8425-2). David & Charles.

DiFranco, Anthony. Italy: Balanced on the Edge of Time. (Discovering Our Heritage Ser.). (Illus.). 112p. (gr. 5 up). 1983. PLB 10.95 (ISBN 0-87518-229-1). Dillon.

--Pope John Paul II: Bringing Love to a Troubled World. (Taking Part Ser.). (Illus.). 48p. (gr. 3 up). 1983. PLB 8.95 (ISBN 0-87518-241-0). Dillon.

--Streets of Paradise. 352p. (Orig.). 1984. pap. 3.50 (ISBN 0-553-24430-2). Bantam.

DiFranco, Anthony & DiFranco, JoAnn. Mister Rogers: Good Neighbor to America's Children. (Taking Part Ser.). (Illus.). 48p. (gr. 3 up). 1983. PLB 8.95 (ISBN 0-87518-245-3). Dillon.

DiFranco, J. V. & Rubin, W. L. Radar Detection. (Illus.). 654p. 1980. Repr. of 1968 ed. text ed. 61.00 (ISBN 0-89006-092-4). Artech Hse.

DiFranco, JoAnn. Walt Disney: When Dreams Come True. (Taking Part Bks.). (Illus.). 64p. (gr. 3 up). 1985. PLB 8.95 (ISBN 0-87518-281-X). Dillon.

DiFranco, JoAnn, jt. auth. see DiFranco, Anthony.

Difusco, John, et al. Tracers: A Play. (Illus.). 128p. 1985. 12.95 (ISBN 0-8090-9412-6, Pub. by Hill & Wang); pap. 7.95 (ISBN 0-8090-1250-2). FS&G.

DiGaetani, John L. Richard Wagner & the Modern British Novel. 179p. 1978. 18.50 (ISBN 0-8386-1955-X). Fairleigh Dickinson.

DiGaetani, John L. & Harbert, Earl N. Writing Out Loud: A Self-Help Guide to Clear Business Writing. LC 82-73623. 190p. 1983. 14.95 (ISBN 0-87094-374-X). Dow Jones-Irwin.

DiGaetani, John L., jt. auth. see Harbert, Earl N.

DiGaetani, John L., ed. Penetrating Wagner's Ring: An Anthology. (Music Reprint Ser.). 453p. 1983. Repr. of 1978 ed. lib. bdg. 45.00 (ISBN 0-306-76205-6). Da Capo.

Di Gammateo, F., jt. ed. see Lacalamita, M.

Digan, Kathleen E. Herman Hesse's Narcissus & Goldmund: A Phenomenological Study. 1975. lib. bdg. 59.95 (ISBN 0-87700-238-X). Revisionist Pr.

Digan, Parig. Churches in Contestation: Asian Christian Social Protest. LC 83-19338. 224p. (Orig.). 1984. pap. 10.95 (ISBN 0-88344-102-0). Orbis Bks.

Digance. Another Animal Alphabet. 9.95 (ISBN 0-7181-2197-X, Pub. by Michael Joseph). Merrimack Pub Cir.

Digance, Richard. Animal Alphabet. (Illus.). 78p. 1981. 9.95 (ISBN 0-7181-1960-6, Pub. by Michael Joseph). Merrimack Pub Cir.

--Backwater. (Illus.). 190p. 1983. pap. 7.95 (ISBN 0-7181-2103-1, Pub. by Michael Joseph). Merrimack Pub Cir.

DiGangi, Mariano. I Believe in Mission. 1979. pap. 2.95 (ISBN 0-87552-255-6). Presby & Reformed.

Di Gangi, Mariano. Twelve Prophetic Voices. 168p. 1985. pap. 5.95 (ISBN 0-89693-536-1). Victor Bks.

Digby, Anne. The Ghostbusters Storybook. (Illus.). 64p. (Orig.). (gr. 2 up). 1985. pap. 3.95 (ISBN 0-590-33684-3). Scholastic Inc.

--A Horse Called September. 128p. 1982. 8.95 (ISBN 0-312-39143-9). St Martin.

--Madness, Morality & Medicine: A Study of the York Retreat, 1796-1914. (History of Medicine Ser.). (Illus.). 320p. Date not set. price not set (ISBN 0-521-26067-1). Cambridge U Pr.

--The Quicksilver Horse. 96p. 1982. 8.95 (ISBN 0-312-66083-9). St Martin.

Digby, Anne & Searby, Peter. Children, School & Society in Nineteenth Century England. 258p. 1981. (Pub. by Macmillan England); pap. text ed. 16.50x (ISBN 0-333-24679-9). Humanities.

Digby, Ian. California. LC 79-7593. (International Showcase Ser.). (Illus.). 1979. 24.95 (ISBN 0-8317-1150-7, Mayflower Bks). Smith Pubs.

Digby, Joan, jt. auth. see Brier, Bob.

Digby, Joan, jt. auth. see Digby, John.

Digby, John. Miss Liberty? LC 84-72571. (Illus.). Date not set. 14.95 (ISBN 0-500-23428-0). Thames Hudson.

--Sailing into Night. 1978. pap. 3.00 (ISBN 0-686-65479-X). Kayak.

--The Structure of Bifocal Distance. 1974. sewn in wrappers 3.95 (ISBN 0-685-78874-1, Pub. by Anvil Pr). Small Pr Dist.

Digby, John & Digby, Joan. The Collage Handbook. LC 84-52179. 140p. 1985. 19.45 (ISBN 0-500-23427-2). Thames Hudson.

Digby, John, tr. see Epicurus.

Digby, K. H. Lawyer in the Wilderness. 123p. 1980. 5.75 (ISBN 0-87727-114-3, DP 114). Cornell SE Asia.

Digby, Kenelm. Journal of a Voyage into the Mediterranean A.D. 1628. 1868. 19.00 (ISBN 0-384-11770-8). Johnson Repr.

Digby, Kenelm, ed. Journal of a Voyage into the Mediterranean, 1628. LC 72-164832. (Camden Society, London. Publications, First Ser.: No. 96). Repr. of 1868 ed. 19.00 (ISBN 0-404-50196-6). AMS Pr.

Digby, Kenelm E. The History of the Law of Real Property. Mersky, Roy M. & Jacobstein, J. Myron, eds. (Classics in Legal History Reprint Ser.: Vol. 12). 408p. 1972. Repr. of 1875 ed. lib. bdg. 35.00 (ISBN 0-89941-011-1). W S Hein.

Digby, Kenelm H. The Broad Stone of Honour: Or, the True Sense & Practice of Chivalry, 2 vols. 411p. 1981. Repr. of 1866 ed. Set. lib. bdg. 85.00 (ISBN 0-89760-138-6). Telegraph Bks.

Digby, Sir Kenelme. Two Treatises: In the One of Which the Nature of Bodies; In the Other the Nature of Man's Soule is Look'd into the Way of Discovery of the Immortality of Reasonable Souls. Wellek, Rene, ed. LC 75-11217. (British Philosophers & Theologians of the 17th & 18th Centuries Ser.). 514p. 1978. lib. bdg. 51.00 (ISBN 0-8240-1771-4). Garland Pub.

Digby, M. & Gretten, R. Agricultural Cooperative Marketing. (Economic & Social Development Papers: No. 8). 80p. (6th Printing 1978). 1955. pap. 7.25 (ISBN 92-5-100477-3, F1460, FAO). Unipub.

Digby, Michael F. Municipal Electric Utility Systems in Virginia. LC 83-622657. 1982. pap. 3.50 (ISBN 0-318-01108-5). U VA Inst Gov.

DiGennaro, Joseph. Individualized Exercise & Optimal Physical Fitness: A Review Workbook for Men & Women. LC 73-9614. pap. 38.00 (ISBN 0-317-28608-0, 2055420). Bks Demand UMI.

--The New Physical Fitness: Exercise for Everybody. (Illus.). 1983. pap. text ed. 8.95X (ISBN 0-89582-097-8). Morton Pub.

Di Gennaro, Judith. Hysterikos. (Poetry Ser.: No. 1). (Illus.). 1975. 12.50x (ISBN 0-89363-000-4); pap. 4.00x (ISBN 0-89363-001-2). Woolf Quarterly.

--Sue the Bastards. 1975. pap. 1.50 (ISBN 0-89363-004-7). Woolf Quarterly.

Digerness, David S. The Mineral Belt: Georgetown, Mining, Colorado Central Railroad, Vol. III. (Illus.). 416p. 49.00 (ISBN 0-686-84503-X). Sundance.

--The Mineral Belt: Georgetown, Mining, Colorado Central Railroad, Vol. III. (Illus.). 416p. 49.00 (ISBN 0-913582-23-9). Sundance.

--The Mineral Belt: Old South Park-Across the Great Divide, Vol. 2. (Illus.). 416p. 49.00 (ISBN 0-913582-21-2). Sundance.

--Mineral Belt: Old South Park-Denver to Leadville, Vol. 1. (Illus.). 416p. 1977. 49.00 (ISBN 0-913582-20-4). Sundance.

Digges, Dudley. The Defence of Trade, in a Letter to Sir T. Smith. LC 68-54640. (English Experience Ser.: No. 26). 52p. 1968. Repr. of 1615 ed. 9.50 (ISBN 90-221-0026-X). Walter J Johnson.

Digges, Jeremiah. In Great Waters: The Story of Portugese Fishermen. 1977. lib. bdg. 59.95 (ISBN 0-8490-2043-3). Gordon Pr.

--In Great Waters: The Story of the Portuguese Fishermen. Cortes, Carlos E., ed. LC 79-6202. (Hispanics in the United States Ser.). 1981. Repr. of 1941 ed. lib. bdg. 26.50x (ISBN 0-405-13153-4). Ayer Co Pubs.

Digges, Jeremiah see Berger, Josef, pseud.

Digges, Leonard. A Prognostication Everlastinge of Righte Good Effecte: Lately Corrected & Augmented by Thomas Digges, His Sonne. LC 74-28846. (English Experience Ser.: No. 727). 1975. Repr. of 1576 ed. 9.50 (ISBN 90-221-0727-2). Walter J Johnson.

Digges, Leonard & Digges, Thomas. An Arithmeticall Militarie Treatise, Named Stratioticos. LC 68-27478. (English Experience Ser.: No. 71). 192p. 1968. Repr. of 1579 ed. 21.00 (ISBN 90-221-0071-5). Walter J Johnson.

Digges, Leonard, tr. see Cespedes y Meneses, Gonzalo.

Digges, Thomas, jt. auth. see Digges, Leonard.

Digges, Thomas A. Adventures of Alonso. LC 74-104439. Repr. of 1775 ed. lib. bdg. 14.00 (ISBN 0-8398-0362-1). Irvington.

--Adventures of Alonso: Containing Some Striking Anecdotes of the Present Minister of Portugal. LC 43-13609. (Monograph Ser.: No. 18). 1943. Repr. of 1775 ed. 12.00x (ISBN 0-930060-01-6). US Cath Hist.

Diggins, Dean & Huber, Jack. The Human Personality. 1976. pap. text ed. 9.95 (ISBN 0-316-37830-5); tchr's manual free (ISBN 0-316-37831-3). Little.

Diggins, John P. The Bard of Savagery: Thorstein Veblen & Modern Social Theory. LC 77-13319. 1978. 14.95 (ISBN 0-8264-0069-8). Continuum.

--The Lost Soul of American Politics: Virtue, Self-Interest & the Foundations of Liberalism. LC 83-46079. 409p. 1984. 23.95 (ISBN 0-465-04243-0). Basic.

--Mussolini & Fascism: The View from America. LC 78-153845. (Illus.). 1972. 42.50 (ISBN 0-691-04604-2); pap. 12.95 (ISBN 0-691-00581-8). Princeton U Pr.

Diggins, John P. & Kann, Mark E., eds. The Problem of Authority in America. 255p. 1981. 34.95 (ISBN 0-87722-220-7). Temple U Pr.

Diggins, Julia E. String, Straightedge & Shadow: The Story of Geometry. (Illus.). (gr. 4-9). 1965. 9.95 (ISBN 0-670-67858-9). Viking.

Diggle, J. Euripides Fabulae, Vol. I. (Oxford Classical Texts Ser.). 1984. 14.95x (ISBN 0-19-814594-2). Oxford U Pr.

Diggle, J. & Goodyear, F. R., eds. Flavii Cresconii Corippi Iohannidos Seu del Bellis Libycis Libri 8. LC 78-85717. 1970. 39.00 (ISBN 0-521-07626-9). Cambridge U Pr.

Diggle, James. Studies on the Text of Euripides. 1981. 42.00x (ISBN 0-19-814019-3). Oxford U Pr.

Diggle, John & Vijh, Ashok K., eds. Oxides & Oxide Films, Vol. 3. (The Anodic Behavior of Metals & Semiconductors Ser.). 352p. 1976. 75.00 (ISBN 0-8247-6314-9). Dekker.

--Oxides & Oxide Films, Vol. 4. (The Anodic Behavior of Metals & Semiconductors Ser.). 1976. 75.00 (ISBN 0-8247-6315-7). Dekker.

Diggle, John W. Religious Doubt: Its Nature, Treatment, Causes, Difficulties, Consequences & Dissolution. 1978. Repr. of 1895 ed. lib. bdg. 25.00 (ISBN 0-8495-1030-9). Arden Lib.

Diggle, John W., ed. Oxides & Oxide Films. LC 72-83120. (Anodic Behavior of Metals & Semiconductors Ser.: Vol. 1). Repr. of 1972 ed. 106.40 (ISBN 0-8357-9090-8, 2055082). Bks Demand UMI.

--Oxides & Oxide Films, Vol. 2. (Anodic Behavior of Metals & Semiconductors Ser.). 416p. 1973. 75.00 (ISBN 0-8247-6066-2). Dekker.

Diggle, Peter J. Statistical Analysis of Spatial Point Patterns. (Mathematics in Biology Ser.). 1984. 27.50 (ISBN 0-12-215850-4). Acad Pr.

Diggory, Peter & McEwan, John. Planning or Prevention: The New Face of Family Planning. (Ideas in Progress Ser.). 128p. 1978. 11.95 (ISBN 0-7145-2552-9, Dist by Scribner); pap. 6.95 (ISBN 0-7145-2553-7). M Boyars.

Diggory, Peter, jt. auth. see Potts, Malcolm.

Diggory, Terrence. Yeats & American Poetry: The Traditional of the Self. LC 82-15070. 280p. 1983. 29.50x (ISBN 0-691-06558-6). Princeton U Pr.

Diggs, B. J. The State, Justice, & the Common Good: An Introduction to Social & Political Philosophy. 1974. pap. 8.65x (ISBN 0-673-05198-6). Scott F.

Diggs, Bernard J. Love & Being: An Investigation into the Metaphysics of St. Thomas Aquinas. 180p. 1947. 6.75 (ISBN 0-913298-45-X). S F Vanni.

Diggs, Dorothy C. Working Manual for Altar Guilds. rev. ed. (Orig.). 1957. pap. 3.95 (ISBN 0-8192-1028-5). Morehouse.

Diggs, Ellen I. Black Chronology: From 4000 B.C. to the Abolition of the Slave Trade. 1983. lib. bdg. 37.50 (ISBN 0-8161-8543-3, Hall Reference). G K Hall.

Dight, J. L. Breaking the Secretary Barrier: How to Get out from Behind the Typewriter & into a Management Job. 320p. 1985. price not set (ISBN 0-07-016905-5). McGraw.

Di Giacomo, James. When Your Teenager Stops Going to Church. LC 80-65401. (When Books). (Illus.). 96p. (Orig.). 1980. pap. 2.45 (ISBN 0-87029-165-3, 20260-6). Abbey.

DiGiacomo, James, jt. auth. see Shannon, Thomas A.

DiGiacomo, James, jt. auth. see Walsh, John.

Digiacomo, James, et al. The Longest Step: Searching for God. (The Encounter Ser.). (Illus.). 1977. pap. text ed. 4.50 (ISBN 0-86683-180-0, 315); resource manual 1.95 (ISBN 0-86683-181-9, 316). Winston Pr.

--Meet the Lord: Encounters with Jesus. (The Encounter Ser.). 1977. pap. 3.98 (ISBN 0-03-021281-2, 317); resource manual 1.95 (ISBN 0-03-021866-7, 318). Winston Pr.

Digiacomo, James J. & Wakin, Edward. Understanding Teenagers: A Guide for Parents. LC 83-70289. 148p. (Orig.). 1983. pap. 5.95 (ISBN 0-89505-129-X). Argus Comm.

DiGiacomo, Kathy & Bergquist, Barbara J. Maltese. (Illus.). 128p. 1983. 4.95 (ISBN 0-87666-720-5, KW-111). TFH Pubns.

DiGiammarino, Frank & Johnson, Donald. Microcomputer Use & Software Design. (Illus.). 64p. (gr. 3-12). 1982. tchr's guide 5.00 (ISBN 0-88049-007-1). Milton Bradley.

DiGioia, L. Paul. Luke Miles. 1982. 5.95 (ISBN 0-533-05462-1). Vantage.

Di Giorgio Martini, Francesco see Martini, Francesco di Giorgio.

DiGiovanni. Flat & Corrugated Diapharm Design Handbook. (Mechanical Engineering Ser.: Vol. 9). 424p. 1982. 65.00 (ISBN 0-8247-1281-1). Dekker.

DiGiovanni, Cleto, Jr. Crisis in Central America. (Monographs in International Affairs). 1982. pap. text ed. 6.95 (ISBN 0-686-84670-2). AISI.

--The Inter-American Foundation: A Mandate for Leadership Report. LC 81-85319. 89p. 1981. 4.00 (ISBN 0-317-07529-2). Heritage Found.

Di Giovanni, George & Harris, H. S., trs. Between Kant & Hegel: Texts in the Development of Post-Kantian Idealism. (Hegelian Studies). 462p. 1985. lib. bdg. 39.50x (ISBN 0-87395-984-1); pap. text ed. 19.95x (ISBN 0-87395-983-3). State U NY Pr.
Di Giovanni, Norman, tr. see Borges, Jorge L.
Di Giovanni, Norman T., tr. see Borges, Jorge L.
Di Giovanni, Norman T., tr. see Borges, Jorge L. & Bioy-Cesares, Adolfo.
Di Giovanni, Norman T., tr. see Costantini, Humberto.
Di Girolamo, Costanzo. A Critical Theory of Literature. 160p. 1981. 19.50x (ISBN 0-299-08120-6). U of Wis Pr.
Digirolamo, E. L. How to Choose a Husband. 1.98 (ISBN 0-931138-01-9). Maiden Bks.
--A Med Cruise. 1978. pap. 1.50 (ISBN 0-931138-02-7). Maiden Bks.
--Win Trots & Flats. 2.00 (ISBN 0-931138-00-0). Maiden Bks.
Digirolamo, Eduardo L. Tear Drops of Love. 1978. 15.00 (ISBN 0-931138-03-5). Maiden Bks.
Digit Magazine Editors. Ace Your Grades with Your Computer. 1985. pap. 8.95 (ISBN 0-671-53060-7, Pub. by Computer Bks). S&S.
Digit Magazine Editors & Bonnett, Kendra. Everyone Can Build a Robot Book. 1984. pap. 8.95 (ISBN 0-671-53059-3, Pub. by Computer Bks). S&S.
Digital Research Staff, jt. auth. see Que Staff.
Digital Signal Processing Committee, ed. Programs for Digital Signal Processing. LC 79-89028. 1979. 48.85 (ISBN 0-87942-127-4, PC01180); tape version 62.95 (ISBN 0-686-96748-8). Inst Electrical.
--Selected Papers in Digital Signal Processing, II. LC 75-22925. 1976. 34.25 (ISBN 0-87942-059-6, PC00562). Inst Electrical.
Digman, Lester A. Strategic Management & Policy. Date not set. price not set (ISBN 0-256-03256-4). Business Pubns.
Dignaga. Dignaga, on Perception, Being the Pratyaksapariccheda of Dignaga's Pramanasamuccaya from the Sanskrit Fragments & the Tibetan Versions. Hattori, Masaaki, tr. LC 68-14256. (Oriental Ser: No. 47). 276p. 1968. 18.50x (ISBN 0-674-20600-2). Harvard U Pr.
Dignan, Don. Di: The Indian Revolutionary Problem in British Diplomacy 1914-1919. 1985. 16.00x (ISBN 0-8364-1267-2, Pub. by Allied India). South Asia Bks.
Dignan, Mark & Levy, Marvin. Life & Health. 4th ed. 632p. 1984. text ed. 22.00 (ISBN 0-394-33077-3, RanC). Random.
Dignan, Mark B. & Carr, Patricia A. Introduction to Program Planning: A Basic Text for Community Health Education. LC 81-865. (Illus.). 156p. 1981. text ed. 13.00 (ISBN 0-8121-0787-X). Lea & Febiger.
Dignan, Patrick J. A History of the Legal Incorporation of Catholic Church Property in the United States (1784-1932) LC 73-3569. (Catholic University of America. Studies in American Church History: No. 14). Repr. of 1933 ed. 31.00 (ISBN 0-404-57764-4). AMS Pr.
D'Ignazio. Apple Building Blocks. 1985. 12.95 (ISBN 0-8104-6323-7). Hayden.
D'Ignazio, F. How to Get Intimate with Your Computer: A Ten Step Program for Relieving Computer Anxiety. LC 83-9874. 155p. 1984. pap. 6.95 (ISBN 0-07-016901-2, BYTE Bks). McGraw.
--Programming Your Texas Instruments Computer in TI BASIC. 256p. 1984. pap. 9.95 (ISBN 0-07-016897-0, BYTE Bks). McGraw.
D'Ignazio, Fred. The Atari Playground. 130p. (ps-4). 1983. pap. 9.95 (ISBN 0-8104-5771-7, 5770); cassette & documentation 19.95 (7851). Hayden.
--Chip Mitchell: The Case of the Chocolate-Covered Bugs. Brosnan, Rosemary, ed. (Chip Mitchell Computer Mystery Ser.). (Illus.). 128p. (gr. 5-9). 1985. 10.95 (ISBN 0-525-67168-4). Lodestar Bks.
--Chip Mitchell: The Case of the Robot Warriors. LC 83-13529. (Illus.). 128p. (gr. 5-9). 1984. 9.95 (ISBN 0-525-67140-4, 0966-290). Lodestar Bks.
--Chip Mitchell: The Case of the Stolen Computer Brains. (Illus.). 128p. (gr. 5-9). 1982. 8.95 (ISBN 0-525-66790-3, 0869-260). Lodestar Bks.
--Commodore 64. (Playground Ser.). (ps-4). 1983. incl. cassette 19.95 (ISBN 0-317-04656-X). Hayden.
--Commodore 64 in Wonderland. 144p. pap. 9.95 (6308); cassette & documentation 29.95 (7602). Hayden.
--The Commodore 64 Playground. 130p. pap. 9.95 (6307); cassette & documentation 29.95 (7601). Hayden.
--The Computer Parade. (Illus.). 44p. 1983. lib. bdg. 9.95 (ISBN 0-916688-46-1, 9P). Creative Comp.
--Computers in Wonderland Series. (ps-5). 1983. 19.95 (ISBN 0-317-04632-2). Hayden.
--Computing Together: A Parents & Teachers Guide to Computing with Young Children. 320p. (Orig.). 1984. pap. 12.95 (ISBN 0-942386-51-5). Compute Pubns.
--The Crazy Robot. (The World Inside the Computer Ser.: Bk. 3). (Illus.). 40p. (Orig.). (gr. 3-8). pap. cancelled (ISBN 0-916688-47-X, 47-X). Creative Comp.
--The Creative Kid's Guide to Home Computers. LC 79-6860. (Illus.). 144p. (gr. 6). 1981. 10.95a (ISBN 0-385-15313-9); PLB (ISBN 0-385-15314-7). Doubleday.
--Electronic Games. (First Bks). (Illus.). 72p. (gr. 4 up). 1982. PLB 8.90 (ISBN 0-531-04396-7). Watts.
--Invent Your Own Computer Games. (Computer Awareness Ser.). (Illus.). 72p. (gr. 4-6). 1983. PLB 8.90 (ISBN 0-531-04637-0). Watts.
--Katie & the Computer. LC 78-74960. (Illus.). 42p. (gr. 1-4). 1979. lib. bdg. 8.95 (ISBN 0-916688-11-9, 12A). Creative Comp.
--Messner's Introduction to the Computer. LC 82-42881. (Illus.). 288p. (gr. 7 up). 1984. PLB 10.29 (ISBN 0-671-42267-7). Messner.
--The New Astronomy: Probing the Secrets of Space. (First Bks). (Illus.). 72p. (gr. 4 up). 1982. PLB 8.90 (ISBN 0-531-04386-X). Watts.
--Small Computers. LC 80-85049. (gr. 9 up). 1981. 9.60 (ISBN 0-531-04269-3). Watts.
--The Star Wars Question & Answer Book about Computers. LC 82-19030. (Illus.). 64p. (gr. 4-8). 1983. pap. 4.95 (ISBN 0-394-85686-4). Random.
--TI in Wonderland. 144p. pap. 9.95 (7952); cassette & documentation 19.95 (6415). Hayden.
--TI Microcomputer. (Playground Ser.). (ps-4). 1983. incl. cassette 19.95 (ISBN 0-317-04654-3). Hayden.
--The TI Playground. 130p. pap. 9.95 (7951); cassette & documentation 19.95 (6414). Hayden.
--VIC. (Playground Ser.). (ps-4). 1983. incl. cassette 19.95 (ISBN 0-317-04655-1). Hayden.
--VIC in Wonderland. 144p. pap. 9.95 (7503); cassette & documentation 29.95 (6505). Hayden.
--The VIC Playground. 130p. pap. 9.95 (7502); cassette & documentation 29.95 (6504). Hayden.
--Working Robots. (Illus.). 160p. (gr. 7 up). 1981. 11.50 (ISBN 0-525-66740-7, 01117-330). Lodestar Bks.
D'Ignazio, Fred & PC World Editors. Learning & Having Fun with the IBM PC & PCjr. 244p. 1985. pap. 16.95 (ISBN 0-671-49281-0, Pub. by Computer Bks). S&S.
D'Ignazio, Fred & Wold, Allen L. The Science of Artificial Intelligence. (Computer-Awareness First Books Ser.). 96p. (gr. 5 up). 1984. lib. bdg. 8.90 (ISBN 0-531-04703-2). Watts.
Digrande, Joseph. The Stone & the Candle. (Illus.). 60p. 1983. 20.00 (ISBN 0-936204-33-8); pap. 10.00 (ISBN 0-936204-34-6). Jelm Mtn.
Digrappa, Carol, ed. Architecture: Theory. 132p. (Orig.). 1985. 17.95 (ISBN 0-912810-48-3). Lustrum Pr.
Di Grappa, Carol, ed. Landscape: Theory. LC 80-81182. (Illus.). 176p. 1982. 35.00 (ISBN 0-912810-27-0); pap. 19.95 (ISBN 0-912810-32-7). Lustrum Pr.
Di Grappa, Carol, et al, eds. Fashion: Theory. LC 80-81181. (Illus.). 176p. 1982. 35.00 (ISBN 0-912810-28-9); pap. 19.95 (ISBN 0-912810-29-7). Lustrum Pr.
Di Grassi, Giacomo see Jackson, James L.
Di Grazia, Thomas, jt. auth. see Clifton, Lucille.
Di Gregorio, Mario A. T. H. Huxley's Place in Natural Science. LC 84-2375. 280p. 1984. 25.00x (ISBN 0-300-03062-2). Yale U Pr.
Diguet, Edouard J. Les Annamites. LC 71-179191. (Illus.). Repr. of 1906 ed. 27.50 (ISBN 0-404-54821-0). AMS Pr.
--Les Montagnards du Tonkin. LC 77-87484. (Illus.). 176p. Repr. of 1908 ed. 32.00 (ISBN 0-404-16811-6). AMS Pr.
Diguet, Leon, jt. auth. see Grant, Campbell.
Di Guglielmo, L., et al. Xeroradiography in Otorhinolaryngology. 188p. (Eng. & Ital.). 1978. 127.75 (ISBN 0-444-90009-8, Excerpta Medica). Elsevier.
Dihle, Albrecht. The Theory of Will in Classical Antiquity. LC 81-7472. (Sather Classical Lectures Ser.: Vol. 48). 288p. 1982. 28.50x (ISBN 0-520-04059-7). U of Cal Pr.
Dihlmann, Wolfgang. Diagnostic Radiology of the Sacroiliac Joints. 2nd ed. (Illus.). 140p. 1980. 49.95 (ISBN 0-8151-2458-9). Year Bk Med.
Dihlmann, Wolfgang & Stiasny, Gottfried. Joints & Vertebral Connections. (Illus.). 672p. 1985. text ed. 75.00 (ISBN 0-86577-161-8). Thieme Stratton.
DiIorio. Watching Through Tall Windows. 144p. 1982. 7.50 (ISBN 0-682-49841-6, Banner). Exposition Pr FL.
Di'Itri, F. M. Conservation Tillage. (Illus.). 345p. 1985. 39.95 (ISBN 0-87371-024-X). Lewis Pubs Inc.
Di Jeso, Fernando, jt. ed. see Porcellati, Giuseppe.
Dijk, J. J. Van see Hallo, William W. & Van Dijk, J. J.
Dijk, J. P. Van see Wallenburg, H. C. S.
Dijk, J. van see Van Dijk, J.
Dijk, Jan van see Van Dijk, Jan, et al.
Dijk, P. van & Hoof, F. van. Theory & Practice of the European Convention. 1984. pap. 54.00 (ISBN 90-654-4079-8, Pub. by Kluwer Law Netherlands). Kluwer Academic.
Dijk, P. van see Van Dijk, P.
Dijk, Pieter van see Van Dijk, Pieter.
Dijk, Robert van see Van Ham, Laurent & Van Dijk, Robert.
Dijk, T. A. Van see Van Dijk, T. A.
Dijk, T. A. Van see Van Dijk, T. A. & Petoefi, J.
Dijk, Teun A. van. Studies in the Pragmatics of Discourse. (Janua Linguarum Series Maior: No. 101). 332p. 1981. 34.00x (ISBN 90-279-3249-2). Mouton.
Dijk, Teun A. van see Van Dijk, Teun A.
Dijk, Teun A. Van see Van Dijk, Teun A.
Dijk, Teuna. Van see Van Dijk, Teun A.
Dijk, Tuen A. Van see Van Dijk, Tuen A. & Kintsch, Walter.
Dijkema, K. S. & Wolff, W. J., eds. Flora & Vegetation of the Wadden Sea Islands & Coastal Areas: Final Report of the Section "Flora & Vegetation of the Island's of the Wadden Sea Working Group, Report 9. 413p. 1983. lib. bdg. 28.00 (ISBN 90-6191-059-5, Pub. by Balkema RSA). IPS.
Dijkhuizen, N. Van see Van Dijkhuizen, N.
Dijksman, E. A. Motion Geometry of Mechanisms. LC 75-3977. (Illus.). 250p. 1976. 47.50 (ISBN 0-521-20841-6). Cambridge U Pr.
Dijkstra, Bram. Hieroglyphics of a New Speech: Cubism, Stieglitz, & the Early Poetry of William Carlos Williams. LC 69-18054. 1969. 26.00 (ISBN 0-691-06169-6); Abridged Ed. pap. 6.95x (ISBN 0-691-01345-4). Princeton U Pr.
Dijkstra, Bram, ed. see Williams, William C.
Dijkstra, E. W. A Primer of ALGOL 60 Programming: Together with Report on the Algorithmic Language ALGOL 60. 1962. 29.50 (ISBN 0-12-216250-1). Acad Pr.
Dijkstra, Edsger W. Selected Writings on Computing: A Personal Perspective. (Texts & Monographs in Computer Science Ser.). (Illus.). 272p. 1982. 32.00 (ISBN 0-387-90652-5). Springer-Verlag.
Dijkstra, Edward W. A Discipline of Programming. (Illus.). 240p. 1976. 35.00x (ISBN 0-13-215871-X). P-H.
Dijkstra, Gerald. Self-Steering for Yachts. 128p. 1981. 30.00x (ISBN 0-686-81324-3, Pub. by Nautical England). State Mutual Bk.
Dijkstra, Gerard. Self-Steering for Sailboats. (Illus.). 128p. 1979. 15.95 (ISBN 0-914814-17-6). Sail Bks.
Dijkstra, T. K., ed. Misspecification Analysis. (Lecture Notes in Economics & Mathematical Systems Ser.: Vol. 237). v, 129p. 1984. pap. 12.00 (ISBN 0-387-13893-5). Springer-Verlag.
Dijkstra, W. & Van Der Zouwen, J., eds. Response Behaviour in the Survey Interview. 1982. 36.50 (ISBN 0-12-216260-9). Acad Pr.
Dik, Simon. Functional Grammar. 230p. 1982. 28.70x (ISBN 90-70176-41-6); pap. 18.70 (ISBN 90-70176-42-4). Foris Pubns.
--Studies in Functional Grammar. 1981. 47.00 (ISBN 0-12-216350-8). Acad Pr.
Dikaois, Porphyrios, et al. Sotira. (University Museum Monographs: No. 23). (Illus.). xiii, 252p. 1961. soft bound 18.75 (ISBN 0-934718-15-6). Univ Mus of U PA.
Dike, Catherine. Cane Curiosa: From Gun to Gadget. LC 83-670069. (Illus.). 378p. 1983. 68.00 (ISBN 2-85917-027-8, Pub. Editions de l'Amateur). Cane Curiosa.
Dike, Donald A., ed. see Schwarta, Delmore.
Dike, Fatima. The First South African. (Ravan Playscripts Ser.: No. 4). 44p. 1979. pap. 5.00 (ISBN 0-86975-086-0, Pub. by Ravan Pr South Africa). Three Continents.
Dike, Kenneth O. Trade & Politics in the Niger Delta, 1830-1885: An Introduction to the Economic & Political History of Nigeria. LC 81-13381. (Oxford Studies in African Affairs). vi, 250p. 1982. Repr. of 1956 ed. lib. bdg. 29.75x (ISBN 0-313-23297-0, DITR). Greenwood.
Dike, R. Architectural Common Sense Site, Vol. 1. 1983. 22.95 (ISBN 0-442-21364-6); pap. 14.95 (ISBN 0-442-21805-2). Van Nos Reinhold.
Dike, Sarah T. Capital Punishment in the United States: A Consideration of the Evidence. LC 82-216071. 1982. write for info. Natl Coun Crime.
Dikepa, Kalio H., jt. auth. see Lieber, Michael D.
Diket, A. L. Senator John Slidell & the Community He Represented in Washington, 1853-1861. LC 81-43676. 278p. (Orig.). 1982. lib. bdg. 26.00 (ISBN 0-8191-2547-4); pap. text ed. 13.25 (ISBN 0-8191-2548-2). U Pr of Amer.
Dikmen, M. Theory of Thin Elastic Shells. (Surveys & Reference Works in Mathematics Ser.: No. 8). 384p. 1982. text ed. 71.95 (ISBN 0-273-08431-3). Pitman Pub MA.
Dikobe, Modikwe. The Marabi Dance. (African Writers Ser.). 1973. pap. text ed. 4.50x (ISBN 0-435-90124-9). Heinemann Ed.
Dikshit, D. P. Political History of the Chalukyas of Badami. 1980. 26.00x (ISBN 0-8364-0645-1, Pub. by Abhinav India). South Asia Bks.
Dikshit, Kiranmani A., et al. Rural Radio: Programme Format. (Monographs on Communication Technology & Utilization: No. 5). 94p. 1979. pap. 5.00 (ISBN 92-3-101616-4, U893, UNESCO). Unipub.
Dikshit, Sudhakar S., ed. see Maharaj, Nisargadatta.
Dikson, K. J. & Mez'er, A. V. Bibliografice Ukazateli Perevodnoj Belletristiki. 224p. 1971. 40.00x (ISBN 0-902089-19-6, Pub. by Variorum). State Mutual Bk.
Dikstein, S., ed. see International Society for Eye Research, 2nd Meeting, Jerusalem, September 12-17, 1976.
Dikty, Alan S. The American Boys' Book Series Bibliography, 1895-1935. LC 83-8747. 170p. 1983. Repr. lib. bdg. 22.95x (ISBN 0-89370-741-4). Borgo Pr.
Dikty, Alan S. & Cottone, Vincent. The Compleat Microbrewer: A Detailed Handbook for the Production, Marketing, & Distribution of Microbrewery & Specialized Beers. (Malt & Vine Reference Resource Library: No. 1). 256p. Repr. lib. bdg. cancelled (ISBN 0-89370-990-5). Borgo Pr.
Dikty, Alan S., ed. The Boys' Book Collector, 1969-1973, Nos. 1-13. 416p. 1983. Repr. lib. bdg. 19.95x (ISBN 0-89370-742-2). Borgo Pr.
Dikty, T. E., jt. ed. see Bleiler, E. F.
Dikty, Thaddeus & Reginald, R. The Work of Julian May: An Annotated Bibliography & Guide. LC 84-21705. (Bibliographies of Modern Authors Ser.: No. 3). 64p. 1985. lib. bdg. 19.95x (ISBN 0-89370-382-6); pap. text ed. 9.95x (ISBN 0-89370-482-2). Borgo Pr.
Dil, A. S., ed. Aspects of Chinese Sociolinguistics: Essays by Yuen Ren Chao. (Language Science and National Development Ser.). 416p. 1976. 27.50x (ISBN 0-8047-0909-2). Stanford U Pr.
Dil, A. S., ed. see Haugen, Einar.
Dil, Anwar, jt. auth. see Fuller, Buckminster.
Dil, Anwar S., ed. see Bright, William.
Dil, Anwar S., ed. see Emeneau, Murray B.
Dil, Anwar S., ed. see Ervin-Tripp, Susan M.
Dil, Anwar S., ed. see Ferguson, Charles A.
Dil, Anwar S., ed. see Fishman, Joshua A.
Dil, Anwar S., ed. see Frake, Charles O.
Dil, Anwar S., ed. see Friedrich, Paul.
Dil, Anwar S., ed. see Greenberg, Joseph H.
Dil, Anwar S., ed. see Grimshaw, Allen D.
Dil, Anwar S., ed. see Gumperz, John J.
Dil, Anwar S., ed. see Haas, Mary R.
Dil, Anwar S., ed. see Lambert, Wallace E.
Dil, Anwar S., ed. see Lieberson, Stanley.
Dil, Anwar S., ed. see McDavid, Raven I., Jr.
Dil, Anwar S., ed. see McQuown, Norman A.
Dil, Anwar S., ed. see Nida, Eugene A.
Dil, Anwar S., ed. see Polome, Edgar C.
Di Lampedusa, Giuseppe. The Leopard. (Modern Classics Ser.). 1982. pap. text ed. 6.95 (ISBN 0-394-74949-9). Pantheon.
Di Lasso, Orlando. Saemtliche Werke, Alte Reihe, von Orlando di Lasso, 21 vols. Sandberger, Adolf & Haberl, Franz, eds. Incl. Vol. 1. Lateinische Gesaenge Fuer 2, 3 und 4 Stimmen, 1. Theil (ISBN 0-8450-1901-5); Vol. 2. Madrigale, erster Theil (ISBN 0-8450-1902-3); Vol. 3. Lateinische Gesaenge fuer 4 und 5 Stimmen, Theil II (ISBN 0-8450-1903-1); Vol. 4. Madrigale, zweiter Theil (ISBN 0-8450-1904-X); Vol. 5. Lateinische Gesaenge fuer 5 Stimmen, Theil III (ISBN 0-8450-1905-8); Vol. 6. Madrigale, dritter Theil (ISBN 0-8450-1906-6); Vol. 7. Lateinische Gesaenge fuer 5 Stimmen,Theil IV (ISBN 0-8450-1907-4); Vol. 8. Madrigale, vierter Theil (ISBN 0-8450-1908-2); Vol. 9. Lateinische Gesaenge fuer 5 Stimmen, Theil V (ISBN 0-8450-1909-0); Vol. 10. Madrigale, fuenfter Theil (ISBN 0-8450-1910-4); Vol. 11. Lateinische Gesaenge fuer 5 und 6 Stimmen, Theil VI (ISBN 0-8450-1911-2); Vol. 12. Komposition mit franzoesichen Text I, nos. 1-56 (ISBN 0-8450-1912-0); Vol. 13. Lateinische Gesaenge fuer 6 Stimmen, Theil VII (ISBN 0-8450-1913-9); Vol. 14. Kompositionen mit franzoesischen Text, I, No. 57-93, Zweiter Theil (ISBN 0-8450-1914-7); Vol. 15. Lateinische Gesaenge fuer 6 Stimmen, Theil VIII (ISBN 0-8450-1915-5); Vol. 16. Kompositionen mit franzoesischen Text, II, No. 1-18; III, No. 1-19; IV, No. 1-5, Theil III (ISBN 0-8450-1916-3); Vol. 17. Lateinische Gesaenge fuer 6 Stimmen, Theil IX (ISBN 0-8450-1917-1); Vol. 18. Kompositionen mit deutschem Text, I, No. 1-15; II, No. 1-15; III, No. 1-11, Erster Theil (ISBN 0-8450-1918-X); Vol. 19. Lateinische Gesaenge fuer 6, 7 und 8 Stimmen, Theil X (ISBN 0-8450-1919-8); Vol. 20. Kompositionen mit deutschem Text, IV, No. 1-11; V, No. 1-7; VI, No. 1-25; VII, No. 1-9, Zweiter Theil (ISBN 0-8450-1920-1); Vol. 21. Lateinische Gesaenge fuer 8, 9, 10 und 12 Stimmen, Theil XI (ISBN 0-8450-1921-X). (Repr. of 1894-1926 ed.). 1973. pap. 975.00x set (ISBN 0-8450-1900-7); pap. 65.00x ea. Broude.
Dilatush, V. E., et al, eds. A KWIC Index & Bibliography of Operations Research & Related Topics in the Paper & Pulp Industry. 151p. 1966. 4.95 (ISBN 0-317-36016-7, 01-01-R009). TAPPI.
Dilauro, Stephen, et al. Burhan Dogancay. (Illus.). 256p. 1984. 85.00 (ISBN 0-88168-009-5). Alpine Bk Co.
Dilavore, Philip. Energy: Insights from Physics. LC 83-19840. 414p. 1984. text ed. 30.95 (ISBN 0-471-89683-7); write for info. (ISBN 0-471-88494-4). Wiley.
Dilcher, D. L. & Taylor, T. N., eds. Biostratigraphy of Fossil Plants: Sucessional & Paleoecological Analyses. LC 79-24187. 259p. 1980. 34.50 (ISBN 0-87933-373-1). Van Nos Reinhold.
Dilcher, Gerhard & Hoke, Rudolf. Grundrechte Im 19. Jahrhundert. (Rechtshist. Reiche Ser.: Vol. 19). 283p. (Ger.). 1982. 25.25 (ISBN 3-8204-7100-6). P Lang Pubs.
Dilday, Russell H., Jr. Personal Computer: A New Tool for Ministers. 1985. pap. 8.95 (ISBN 0-8054-3111-X). Broadman.

Di Lella, Alexander A., jt. auth. see Hartman, Louis F.

Di Lello, Richard. The Longest Cocktail Party: An Insider's Diary of the Beatles. LC 72-85965. (Rock & Roll Remembrances Ser.: No. 2). (Illus.). 1983. individuals 19.50 (ISBN 0-87650-155-2); institutions 29.50. Pierian.

Dilendik, John R. Independent Mastery Test System for Writing Skills: Implementation Manual. Brett, Jennifer & Schenk, Brian, eds. 64p. 1984. pap. 9.26 (ISBN 0-8428-9813-1). Cambridge Bk.

--Independent Mastery Testing System for Math Skills: Implementation Manual. Brett, Jennifer & Schenk, Brian, eds. 64p. 1984. pap. 9.26 (ISBN 0-8428-9814-X). Cambridge Bk.

Di Leo, Joseph. Physical Factors in Growth & Development: A Manual for Educators, Nurses, & Social Workers. LC 75-106235. 1970. pap. 3.50x (ISBN 0-8077-1244-2). Tchrs Coll.

Di Leo, Joseph H. Children's Drawings As Diagnostic Aids. LC 73-79882. (Illus.). 240p. 1980. pap. 16.95 (ISBN 0-87630-249-5). Brunner-Mazel.

DiLeo, Joseph H. Interpreting Children's Drawings. LC 83-2516. (Illus.). 240p. 1983. 25.00 (ISBN 0-87630-327-0); pap. 16.95 (ISBN 0-87630-331-9). Brunner-Mazel.

DiLeo, Michael & Smith, Eleanor. Two Californias: The Truth about the Split-State Movement. (Illus.). 250p. (Orig.). 1983. pap. 10.95 (ISBN 0-933280-16-5). Island CA.

Di Leonardo, Micaela. The Varieties of Ethnic Experience: Kinship, Class, & Gender among California Italian-Americans. LC 83-45929. 272p. 1984. 29.95x (ISBN 0-8014-1632-9); pap. 9.95x (ISBN 0-8014-9278-5). Cornell U Pr.

Dilfer, Carol. Your Baby, Your Body. (Illus.). 1977. 8.95 (ISBN 0-517-52855-X); pap. 5.95 (ISBN 0-517-52856-8). Crown.

Dilger, Robert J. American Intergovernmental Relations Today: Perspectives & Controversies. (Illus.). 320p. 1986. pap. text ed. 18.95 (ISBN 0-13-027624-3). P-H.

--The Sunbelt-Snowbelt Controversy: The War over Federal Funds. 256p. 1982. 35.00x (ISBN 0-8147-1774-8); pap. 15.00 (ISBN 0-8147-1775-6). NYU Pr.

--The Sunbelt-Snowbelt Controversy: The War over Federal Funds. 240p. 1984. pap. 12.00x (ISBN 0-8147-1775-6). NYU Pr.

DiLiello, L. R. Methods in Food & Dairy Microbiology. (Illus.). 1982. lab manual 19.50 (ISBN 0-87055-411-5). AVI.

DiLiello, Leo R. Clinical Microbiology. (Illus.). 1979. pap. text ed. 13.50 (ISBN 0-87055-325-9). AVI.

Di Liscia, Eleanora see Liscia, Eleanora di.

Dilisio, James E. Maryland: A Geography. (Geographies of the United States Ser.). 256p. 1983. lib. bdg. 36.00x (ISBN 0-86531-092-0); pap. text ed. 18.50x (ISBN 0-86531-474-8). Westview.

Dilka, Karen L., jt. ed. see Hull, Raymond H.

Dilke, Emilia F. Book of the Spiritual Life. LC 70-37689. (Illus., With a memoir of the author by the Rt. Hon. Sir Charles W. Dilke). Repr. of 1905 ed. 26.00 (ISBN 0-404-56743-6). AMS Pr.

--The Renaissance of Art in France, 2 vols. LC 78-16227. 1978. Repr. of 1879 ed. lib. bdg. 65.00 (ISBN 0-89341-362-3). Longwood Pub Group.

Dilke, O. A. Greek & Roman Maps. LC 84-72221. (Aspects of Greek & Roman Life Ser.). (Illus.). 224p. 1985. Repr. text ed. 25.00x (ISBN 0-8014-1801-1). Cornell U Pr.

Dilke, O. A., ed. Horace: Epistles I. (Classical Texts Ser.). 198p. pap. 9.95x (ISBN 0-423-78490-0). Basil Blackwell.

Dilke, O. A., jt. ed. see Connor, W. R.

Dilker, Barbara. Stage Management Forms & Formats. LC 79-16689. (Illus.). 192p. (Orig.). 1982. pap. text ed. 13.95x (ISBN 0-910482-85-3). Drama Bk.

Dilks, David. Curzon in India, 2 vols. Incl. Vol. 1. Achievement (ISBN 0-8008-2106-8); Vol. 2. Frustration (ISBN 0-8008-2107-6). LC 70-88619. 10.00 ea. Taplinger.

--Neville Chamberlain: Pioneering & Reform, 1869-1929, Vol. 1. (Illus.). 660p. 1985. 29.95 (ISBN 0-521-25724-7). Cambridge U Pr.

Dilks, David, ed. Retreat from Power: Studies in Britain's Foreign Policy of the 20th Century, 2 vols. 630p. 1981. (Pub. by Macmillan England); Vol. 1, 1906-36. pap. text ed. 13.50x (ISBN 0-333-28910-2). Vol. 2, 1939 & After (ISBN 0-333-29319-3). Humanities.

Dilks, David, jt. ed. see Andrew, Christopher.

Dill, Alonzo T. Carter Braxton, Virginia Signer: A Conservative in Revolt. LC 83-6513. (Illus.). 306p. (Orig.). 1983. lib. bdg. 26.75 (ISBN 0-8191-3223-3); pap. text ed. 13.75 (ISBN 0-8191-3224-1). U Pr of Amer.

Dill, D. B. The Hot Life of Man & Beast. (Illus.). 176p. 1985. 19.50x (ISBN 0-398-05106-2). C C Thomas.

Dill, J. Wiltshire Songs & Carols. (Folklore Ser.). Repr. 10.00 (ISBN 0-8482-7756-2). Norwood Edns.

Dill, J. F., ed. see American Society of Mechanical Engineers, Lubrication Division.

Dill, L. V. The Obstetrical Forceps. (Illus.). 175p. 1953. 24.50x (ISBN 0-398-00457-9). C C Thomas.

Dill, Marshall, Jr. Germany: A Modern History. rev. ed. LC 60-13891. (History of the Modern World Ser). (Illus.). 1970. 18.50x (ISBN 0-472-07101-7). U of Mich Pr.

Dill, Robert, jt. auth. see Shepard, Francis.

Dill, S. Roman Society from Nero to Marcus Aurelius. 75.00 (ISBN 0-87968-059-8). Gordon Pr.

--Roman Society in the Last Century of Western Empire. 75.00 (ISBN 0-87968-060-1). Gordon Pr.

Dill, Samuel. Roman Society from Nero to Marcus Aurelius. 1905. 65.00 (ISBN 0-8482-3696-3). Norwood Edns.

--Roman Society in Gaul in the Merovingian Age. 1926. 65.00 (ISBN 0-8482-3697-1). Norwood Edns.

--Roman Society in Gaul in the Merovingian Age. 566p. 1970. Repr. of 1926 ed. 22.50x (ISBN 0-87471-319-6). Rowman.

--Roman Society in the Last Century of the Western Empire. 1979. Repr. of 1898 ed. lib. bdg. 50.00 (ISBN 0-8492-4201-0). R West.

Dill, Stephen H. Integrated Studies: Challenges to the College Curriculum. LC 82-17511. (Illus.). 158p. (Orig.). 1983. lib. bdg. 22.25 (ISBN 0-8191-2794-9); pap. text ed. 10.25 (ISBN 0-8191-2795-7). U Pr of Amer.

Dill, W. A., jt. ed. see Pillay, T.

Dill, William R. Running the American Corporation. LC 78-16922. (American Assembly Ser.). 1978. (Spec); pap. 4.95 (ISBN 0-13-783886-7). P-H.

Dill, William R. & Popov, G. Organization for Forecasting & Planning: Experience in the Soviet Union & the United States. LC 78-13620. (IIASA Internatiional Series on Applied Systems Analysis). 256p. 1979. 51.95 (ISBN 0-471-99720-X, Pub. by Wiley-Interscience). Wiley.

Dilla, Harriette M. Politics of Michigan 1865-1878. (Columbia University Studies in the Social Sciences: No. 118). Repr. of 1912 ed. 21.50 (ISBN 0-404-51118-X). AMS Pr.

Dilla, Marvin A. van see Van Dilla, Marvin A., et al.

Dillahunt, et al. Field Hockey for Teachers. 1976. 8.95 (ISBN 0-686-17810-6). Sauk.

Dillane, Christina & Dusharme, Susan. The Wonderful World of "Whey Lovers". Parkhill, Joe M., rev. by. 160p. (Orig.). 1983. pap. text ed. 6.95 (ISBN 0-936744-08-1). Country Bazaar.

Dillard. Insurance Coverage Disputes. 1987. price not set (ISBN 0-471-82656-1). Wiley.

Dillard, et al. How to Score with English. 336p. 1984. pap. text ed. 18.95 (ISBN 0-8403-3508-3). Kendall-Hunt.

Dillard, Annie. Encounters with Chinese Writers. viii, 106p. 1985. pap. 6.95 (ISBN 0-8195-6156-8). Wesleyan U Pr.

--Holy the Firm. LC 77-6883. 76p. 1984. pap. 4.76i (ISBN 0-06-091098-4, CN 1098, CN). Har-Row.

--Living by Fiction. LC 81-47882. 160p. 1982. 13.41i (ISBN 0-06-014960-4, HarpT). Har-Row.

--Living by Fiction. LC 81-47882. 192p. 1983. pap. 4.76i (ISBN 0-06-091044-5, CN 1044, CN). Har-Row.

--Pilgrim at Tinker Creek. LC 73-18655. 232p. 1974. 11.49i (ISBN 0-06-121980-0). Har-Row.

--Pilgrim at Tinker Creek: Winner of the Pulitzer Prize. LC 85-42561. (Illus.). 272p. 1985. pap. 5.95 (ISBN 0-06-091279-0, PL 1279, PL). Har-Row.

--Teaching a Stone to Talk: Expeditions & Encounters. LC 82-47520. 192p. 1982. 12.45i (ISBN 0-06-015030-0, HarpT). Har-Row.

--Teaching a Stone to Talk: Expeditions & Encounters. LC 82-47520. 176p. 1983. pap. 6.68i (ISBN 0-06-091072-0, CN1072, CN). Har-Row.

--Tickets for a Prayer Wheel. LC 73-86759. (Breakthrough Bks). 1983. Repr. of 1974 ed. 8.95x (ISBN 0-8262-0156-3). U of Mo Pr.

Dillard, Clyde R. & Goldberg, David E. Chemistry: Reactions, Structure, & Properties. 2nd ed. (Illus.). 1978. write for info. (ISBN 0-02-329580-5). Macmillan.

Dillard, David H. & Miller, Donald W., Jr. Atlas of Cardiac Surgery. 1983. write for info. (ISBN 0-02-329530-9). Macmillan.

Dillard, David H., jt. auth. see Mohri, Hitoshi.

Dillard, Dudley. Economic Development of the North Atlantic Community: Historical Introduction to Modern Economics. 1967. text ed. 31.95 (ISBN 0-13-223305-3). P-H.

Dillard, Dudley D. The Economics of John Maynard Keynes: The Theory of a Monetary Economy. LC 82-9219. xviii, 364p. 1983. Repr. of 1948 ed. lib. bdg. 42.50x (ISBN 0-313-23628-3, DIEK). Greenwood.

Dillard, Gavin. Notes from a Marriage. LC 83-60443. 80p. (Orig.). 1983. pap. 4.95 (ISBN 0-933322-10-0). Sea Horse.

--Writing of the Virgin. LC 85-2145. 75p. (Orig.). 1985. pap. 5.95 (ISBN 0-933322-22-4). Sea Horse.

Dillard, Heath. Daughters of the Reconquest: Women in Castilian Town Society, 1100-1300. (Iberian & Latin American Studies). (Illus.). 275p. 1985. 49.50 (ISBN 0-521-25922-3). Cambridge U Pr.

Dillard, J. L. Black English. LC 72-102330. 1972. 10.00 (ISBN 0-394-46760-4). Random.

--Black English: Its History & Usage in the United States. (YA) 1973. pap. 4.95 (ISBN 0-394-71872-0, V872, Vin). Random.

--Black Names. Fishman, Joshua A., ed. (Contributions to the Sociology of Language Ser.: No. 13). 1976. pap. text ed. 10.00x (ISBN 90-2797-602-3). Mouton.

--Lexicon of Black English. LC 76-30389. 1977. pap. 6.95 (ISBN 0-8264-0125-2). Continuum.

Dillard, J. L., ed. Perspectives on American English. (Contributions to the Sociology of Language Ser.: No. 29). 468p. 1980. 55.00 (ISBN 90-279-3367-7). Mouton.

--Perspectives on Black English. (Contributions to the Sociology of Language Ser: No. 4). 391p. 1975. text ed. 24.00x (ISBN 90-2797-811-5). Mouton.

Dillard, J. L., ed. see Marckwardt, Albert H.

Dillard, Jack. Heart Stop: No Death at All. (Illus.). 42p. (Orig.). 1982. pap. write for info. (ISBN 0-940588-08-0). Hazlett Print.

Dillard, John. Lifelong & Career Planning. 228p. 1985. 13.95 (ISBN 0-675-20348-1). Merrill.

Dillard, John E., Jr., jt. auth. see Davis, Grant M.

Dillard, John M. Multicultural Counseling: Toward Ethnic & Cultural Relevance in Human Encounters. LC 82-24651. 352p. 1983. lib. bdg. 26.95x (ISBN 0-88229-714-7); pap. 13.95x (ISBN 0-88229-830-5). Nelson-Hall.

Dillard, Leroy F. Pedagogia Ilustrada: Using the Lecture in Teaching & Training, Tomo 3. Maria, Ana, tr. from Eng. 136p. (Sp.). 1983. pap. 3.25 (ISBN 0-311-11027-4). Casa Bautista.

Dillard, Mabel M., jt. auth. see Benson, Brian J.

Dillard, R. H. The First Man on the Sun: A Novel. LC 82-18649. 287p. 1983. 19.95 (ISBN 0-8071-1090-6); pap. 8.95 (ISBN 0-8071-1098-1). La State U Pr.

--The Greeting: New & Selected Poems. (University of Utah Press Poetry Ser.). 1982. 14.95 (ISBN 0-87480-200-8). U of Utah Pr.

Dillard, Tom W. & Thwing, Valerie. Researching Arkansas History: A Beginner's Guide. (Illus.). 64p. 1980. pap. 4.95 (ISBN 0-914546-25-2). Rose Pub.

Dillard, William L. Invasion from Outer Space. 1983. 7.95 (ISBN 0-8062-2079-1). Carlton.

Dillavou, Essel R., jt. auth. see Simpson, Laurence.

Dillaway, Newton. Consent. new ed. 1967. pap. 2.95 (ISBN 0-87159-018-2). Unity School.

--Gospel of Emerson. new ed. 1968. Repr. 4.95 (ISBN 0-87159-046-8). Unity School.

--Prophet of America: Emerson & the Problems of Today. LC 80-2530. Repr. of 1936 ed. 44.50 (ISBN 0-404-19254-8). AMS Pr.

Dillaye, Frederic. La Theorie, la Pratique et L'art En Photographie Avec le Procede Au Gelatino Bromure D'argent. Bunnell, Peter C. & Sobieszek, Robert A., eds. LC 76-23053. (Sources of Modern Photography Ser.). (Illus., Fr.). 1979. Repr. of 1891 ed. lib. bdg. 44.00x (ISBN 0-405-09618-6). Ayer Co Pubs.

Dille, Carolyn, jt. auth. see Belsinger, Susan.

DIlle, Glen F., ed. La Comedia Llamada Serafina: An Anonymous Humanistic Comedy of 1521. LC 78-18308. 141p. 1979. 7.95x (ISBN 0-8093-0866-5). S Ill U Pr.

Dillehunte, Hal, jt. auth. see Stone, Karen.

Dillen, J. C. Van see Van Dillen, J. C.

Dillen, J. G. Van see Van Dillen, J. G.

Dillenberger, Jane. Style & Content in Christian Art: From the Catacombs to the Chapel Designed by Matisse at Vence, France. LC 65-22293. pap. 80.50 (ISBN 0-317-10399-7, 2001274). Bks Demand UMI.

Dillenberger, John. Benjamin West: The Context of His Life's Work. LC 76-42004. (Illus.). 238p. 1977. 25.00 (ISBN 0-911536-65-5). Trinity U Pr.

--Protestant Thought & Natural Science: A Historical Interpretation. LC 77-7200. 1977. Repr. of 1960 ed. lib. bdg. 22.75x (ISBN 0-8371-9670-1, DIPT). Greenwood.

--The Visual Arts & Christianity in America: The Colonial Period Through the Nineteenth Century. LC 84-3897. (Scholars Press Studies in the Humanities). 1984. 29.25 (ISBN 0-89130-734-6, 00 01 05); pap. 19.50 (ISBN 0-89130-761-3). Scholars Pr GA.

Dillenberger, John & Welch, Claude. Protestant Christianity. 340p. 1976. pap. text ed. price not set (ISBN 0-02-330470-7, Pub. by Scribner). Macmillan.

Dillenberger, John, ed. John Calvin: Selections from His Writings. LC 75-26875. (American Academy of Religion. Aids for the Study of Religion). 590p. 1975. pap. 9.95 (ISBN 0-89130-025-2, 010302). Scholars Pr GA.

Dillenberger, John, ed. see Luther, Martin.

Diller, jt. auth. see Haltenorth.

Diller, Angela. First Theory Book. 1921. pap. 10.95 (ISBN 0-02-870720-6). Schirmer Bks.

--Keyboard Harmony Course, 2 bks. 1937. pap. 2.95 ea. Bk. I (ISBN 0-02-870730-3). Bk. II (ISBN 0-02-870740-0). Schirmer Bks.

Diller, Anne-Marie. La Pragmatique des Questions et des Reponses. (Tuebinger Beitraege zur Linguistik: No. 243). 162p. (Orig., Fr.). 1984. pap. 19.00x (ISBN 3-87808-243-6, Pub. by G N Verlag Germany). Benjamins North Am.

Diller, Aubrey. Race Mixture among the Greeks Before Alexander. LC 70-95094. Repr. of 1937 ed. lib. bdg. 22.50x (ISBN 0-8371-3086-7, DIRM). Greenwood.

Diller, Edward. A Mythic Journey: Gunter Grass's Tin Drum. LC 73-86402. pap. 56.00 (ISBN 0-317-27671-9, 2019516). Bks Demand UMI.

Diller, Edward, jt. auth. see Wishard, Armin.

Diller, Edward, jt. ed. see Wishard, Armin.

Diller, George E., jt. auth. see Bagley, Charles R.

Diller, Hans J., et al. Constance Byron Symposium 1977 & Manuscript Revision in Byron's Childe Harold's Pilgrimage Canto IV, 1-29. (SSEL Romantic Reassessment Ser.: No. 80). 1979. pap. text ed. 25.50x (ISBN 0-391-01579-6). Humanities.

Diller, J., ed. see Proof Theory Symposium, Kiel, 1974.

Diller, Jerry V. Ancient Roots & Modern Meanings. LC 77-99196. 1978. 12.50 (ISBN 0-8197-0457-1); pap. 7.95 (ISBN 0-685-27177-3). Bloch.

Diller, Karl C. Individual Differences & Universals in Language Learning Aptitude. (Orig.). 1981. pap. text ed. 17.95 (ISBN 0-88377-164-0). Newbury Hse.

--The Language Teaching Controversy. rev ed. LC 78-7021. 1978. pap. text ed. 10.95 (ISBN 0-88377-114-4). Newbury Hse.

Diller, M. & Mallone, V., eds. Guidance Function & Counseling Roles in Adult Ed. 1978. pap. 4.00 (ISBN 0-686-08767-4, 751-01392). Natl Assn Con Adult Ed.

Diller, Robert. Farm Ownership, Tenancy, & Land Use in the Nebraska Community. Bruchey, Stuart, ed. LC 78-56629. (Management of Public Lands in the U. S. Ser.). 1979. Repr. of 1932 ed. lib. bdg. 17.00x (ISBN 0-405-11339-0). Ayer Co Pubs.

Diller, S. Investor's Guide to Fixed Income Security. 1986. cancelled (ISBN 0-442-21954-7). Van Nos Reinhold.

Dillett, Eric S. What Is Man? 1985. 6.50 (ISBN 0-682-40254-0). Exposition Pr FL.

--Why Were We Born? 1980. 6.00 (ISBN 0-682-49534-4). Exposition Pr FL.

Dilley, Clyde H. Photography & Philosophy of Wynn Bullock. LC 81-65881. (Illus.). 129p. 1984. 30.00 (ISBN 0-87982-042-X). Art Alliance.

Dilley, Frank B. Teacher Certification in Ohio & a Proposed Plan of Reconstruction. LC 73-176720. (Columbia University. Teachers College. Contributions to Education: No. 630). Repr. of 1935 ed. 22.50 (ISBN 0-404-55630-2). AMS Pr.

Dilley, Marjorie R. British Policy in Kenya Colony. 2nd ed. 300p. 1966. 30.00x (ISBN 0-7146-1655-9, F Cass Co). Biblio Dist.

Dilley, Romilda. Mrrarr & Me. (Illus.). 48p. 1982. 20.00 (ISBN 0-88014-062-3). Mosaic Pr OH.

--Snared by Snarling S's. (Illus.). 48p. 1982. 20.00 (ISBN 0-88014-048-8). Mosaic Pr OH.

Dilliard, Irving, ed. see Hand, Learned.

Dilligan, Robert J., et al. A Concordance to Ezra Pound's Cantos. LC 77-83375. (Garland Reference Library of the Humanities: No. 106). 1981. lib. bdg. 121.00 (ISBN 0-8240-9837-4). Garland Pub.

Dilling, E. The Plot Against Christianity: A Study of the Talmud. 1982. lib. bdg. 69.95 (ISBN 0-87700-359-9). Revisionist Pr.

Dilling, Elizabeth. The Jewish Religion: Its Influence Today. (Illus.). 300p. 1983. pap. 8.00 (ISBN 0-939482-07-X). Noontide.

--Plot Against Christianity. 310p. 12.00 (ISBN 0-913022-33-0). Angriff Pr.

--The Roosevelt Red Record & Its Background. 1985. lib. bdg. 79.95 (ISBN 0-87700-654-7). Revisionist Pr.

Dilling, Elizabeth K. The Red Network: A "Who's Who" & Handbook of Radicalism for Patriots. LC 76-46073. (Anti-Movements in America). 1977. Repr. of 1935 ed. lib. bdg. 27.50x (ISBN 0-405-09946-0). Ayer Co Pubs.

Dilling, Yvonne & Rogers, Ingrid. In Search of Refuge. LC 84-9012. 296p. (Orig.). 1984. pap. 9.95 (ISBN 0-8361-3364-1). Herald Pr.

--In Search of Refuge. LC 84-9012. (Illus.). 296p. 1984. pap. 9.95 (ISBN 0-317-31412-2). Herald Pr.

Dilling, Yvonne & Wheaton, Philip, eds. Nicaragua: A People's Revolution. (Illus.). 103p. 1980. pap. text ed. 4.25 (ISBN 0-918346-04-5). EPICA.

Dillinger, James. Adrenaline. 1985. pap. 3.50 (ISBN 0-451-13563-6, Sig). NAL.

Dillingham, Louise B. The Creative Imagination of Theophile Gautier: A Study in Literary Psychology. Bd. with An Experimental Study of Affects & Associations Due to Certain Odors. Kenneth, J. H. Repr. of 1927 ed; Individual Differences in Imagery. Griffitts, C. H. Repr. of 1927 ed. (Psychological Monographs General & Applied: Vol. 27). pap. 44.00 (ISBN 0-317-15638-1). Kraus Repr.

Dillingham, Steven D., jt. auth. see Montgomery, Reid H., Jr.

Dillingham, William B. An Artist in the Rigging: The Early Work of Herman Melville. LC 79-156038. 172p. 1972. 15.00x (ISBN 0-8203-0276-7). U of Ga Pr.

--Frank Norris: Instinct & Art. LC 69-15257. x, 179p. 1969. 16.50x (ISBN 0-8032-0039-0). U of Nebr Pr.

--Melville's Short Fiction, 1853-1856. LC 76-28922. 400p. 1977. 28.00x (ISBN 0-8203-0411-5). U of Ga Pr.

Dillingham, William B., jt. ed. see Cohen, Hennig.

Dillingham, William B., jt. auth. see Watkins, Floyd C.

Dillingham, William P., jt. auth. see United States Immigration Commission, 1907-1910.
Dillion-Peterson, Betty, ed. Staff Development - Organization Development: ASCD 1981 Yearbook. 149p. 1981. pap. text ed. 9.75 (ISBN 0-87120-104-6). Assn Supervision.
Dilliston, William H. Bank Note Reporters & Counterfeit Detectors 1826-1866. (Numismatic Notes & Monographs: 114). (Illus.). 175p. 1949. pap. 10.00 (ISBN 0-89722-016-1). Am Numismatic.
Dillistone, Frederick. Traditional Symbols & the Contemporary World. LC 73-164751. (Bampton Lectures: 1968). 1973. text ed. 15.00x (ISBN 0-8401-0546-0). A R Allenson.
Dillman, jt. auth. see Barber.
Dillman, Don. A. Mail & Telephone Surveys: The Total Design Method. LC 78-581. 325p. 1978. 42.95x (ISBN 0-471-21555-4, Pub. by Wiley-Interscience). Wiley.
Dillman, Don A., jt. auth. see Tremblay, Kenneth R., Jr.
Dillman, Don A. & Hobbs, Daryl J., eds. Rural Society: Issues for the Nineteen Eighties. (Royal Sociological Society Ser.). 400p. 1982. lib. bdg. 30.00x (ISBN 0-86531-100-5); pap. text ed. 11.50x (ISBN 0-86531-263-X). Westview.
Dillman, Karin J. The Subject in Rimbaud: From Self to "Je". (American University Studies II (Romance Languages & Literature): Vol. 23). 155p. 1984. text ed. 20.00 (ISBN 0-8204-0200-1). P Lang Pubs.
Dillman, Richard W. Introduction to Problem Solving with BASIC. 1983. pap. text ed. 20.95 (ISBN 0-03-061981-5). HR&W.
--Problem Solving with FORTRAN 77. 1985. pap. text ed. 23.95 (ISBN 0-03-063734-1). HR&W.
Dillmont, Th. de see De Dillmont, Th.
Dillmont, Therese De see De Dillmont, Therese.
Dillner, Martha H. & Olson, Joanne P. Personalizing Reading Instruction in Middle Junior & Senior High Schools. 2nd ed. 544p. 1982. pap. text ed. write for info. (ISBN 0-02-329780-8). Macmillan.
Dillner, Martha H., jt. auth. see Olson, Joanne P.
Dillon, Andrew, tr. see Shingo, Shigeo.
Dillon, Andrew P., tr. see Japan Management Association Staff.
Dillon, Ann, jt. auth. see Bix, Cynthia.
Dillon, Anne F., jt. auth. see Samson, Patricia M.
Dillon, Anne F., et al. The Complete St. Louis Guide. (Brussels Walk Guide). (Illus.). pap. 4.95 (ISBN 0-911891-03-X). Dillon-Donnelly.
Dillon, Barbara. The Beast in the Bed. LC 80-15069. (Illus.). 32p. (gr. k-3). 1981. 11.25 (ISBN 0-688-22254-4); PLB 11.88 (ISBN 0-688-32254-9). Morrow.
--The Good-Guy Cake. (Skylark Ser.). 64p. 1982. pap. 1.95 (ISBN 0-553-15250-5, Skylark). Bantam.
--Mr. Chill. (Illus.). 96p. (gr. 2-5). 1985. 10.25 (ISBN 0-688-04980-X, Morrow Junior Books); lib. bdg. 10.88 (ISBN 0-688-04981-8). Morrow.
--The Teddy Bear Tree. LC 82-2301. (Illus.). 80p. (gr. 4-6). 1982. 10.25 (ISBN 0-688-01447-X); lib. bdg. 10.88 (ISBN 0-688-01450-X). Morrow.
--What's Happened to Harry? LC 81-11153. (Illus.). 128p. 1982. 10.25 (ISBN 0-688-00763-5). Morrow.
--Who Needs a Bear? LC 80-26530. (Illus.). 64p. (gr. k-3). 1981. 10.00 (ISBN 0-688-00445-8); PLB 10.88 (ISBN 0-688-00446-6). Morrow.
Dillon, Barbara, jt. auth. see Dillon, Douglas.
Dillon, Bert, ed. A Malory Handbook. 1978. lib. bdg. 20.00 (ISBN 0-8161-7964-6, Hall Reference). G K Hall.
Dillon, Brian. Salinas de los Nueve Cerros Guatemala: Preliminary Archaeological Investigations. (No. 2). 1977. pap. 7.95 (ISBN 0-87919-070-1). Ballena Pr.
Dillon, Brian D., ed. Practical Archaeology: Field & Laboratory Techniques & Archaeological Logistics. (Archaeological Research Tools: Vol. 2). 100p. 1982. pap. 8.50 (ISBN 0-917956-38-9). UCLA Arch.
--The Student's Guide to Archaeological Illustrating. rev. ed. (Archaeological Research Tools Ser.: Vol. 1). (Illus.). 154p. Date not set. pap. 8.50x (ISBN 0-917956-38-9). UCLA Arch.
Dillon, C. P., ed. Forms of Corrosion Recognition & Prevention. (NACE Handbook 1). (Illus.). 116p. 1981. 30.00 (ISBN 0-317-35087-0); NACE members 24.00 (ISBN 0-317-35088-9). Natl Corrosion Eng.
Dillon, David. Wallace Stegner: An Interview. (New London Interviews). 1978. signed ltd. ed. 10.00 (ISBN 0-89683-006-3); pap. 3.95 (ISBN 0-89683-005-5). New London Pr.
Dillon, David, jt. auth. see Tomlinson, Doug.
Dillon, Debbie. Collector's Guide to Sheet Music. rev. ed. 78p. 1985. pap. 6.95 (ISBN 0-89145-284-2). Wallace-Homestead.
Dillon, Dorothy R. New York Triumvirate: A Study of the Legal & Political Careers of William Livingston, John Morin Scott, & William Smith Jr. LC 68-58567. (Columbia University Studies in the Social Sciences: No. 548). Repr. of 1949 ed. 18.50 (ISBN 0-404-51548-7). AMS Pr.
Dillon, Douglas & Dillon, Barbara. An Explosion of Being: An American Family's Journey into the Psychic. 213p. 1983. 6.95 (ISBN 0-13-297945-4, Parker). P-H.
Dillon, E. J. Count Leo Tolstoy. LC 72-700. (Studies in European Literature, No. 56). 1972. Repr. of 1933 ed. lib. bdg. 49.95x (ISBN 0-8383-1420-1). Haskell.
--Mexico on the Verge. 1976. lib. bdg. 59.95 (ISBN 0-8490-0631-7). Gordon Pr.
--Sceptics of the Old Testament. LC 73-16064. (Studies in Comparative Literature, No. 35). 1974. Repr. of 1895 ed. lib. bdg. 51.95x (ISBN 0-8383-1723-5). Haskell.
Dillon, E. S., jt. auth. see Dillon, L. S.
Dillon, Edward. The Art of Japan. (Illus.). 202p. 1980. lib. bdg. 35.00 (ISBN 0-8495-1115-1). Arden Lib.
Dillon, Eilis. The Bitter Glass. 220p. 1981. pap. 4.95 (ISBN 0-907085-07-5, Pub. by Ward River Pr Ireland). Irish Bks Media.
--Blood Relations. 1979. pap. 2.25 (ISBN 0-449-24043-6, Crest). Fawcett.
--The Head of the Family. 218p. 1982. pap. 4.95 (ISBN 0-907085-27-X, Pub. by Ward River Pr Ireland). Irish Bks Media.
--Inside Ireland. (Illus.). 208p. 1984. 17.95 (ISBN 0-340-26342-3). Beaufort Bks NY.
--Wild Geese. 320p. 1981. pap. 2.75 (ISBN 0-449-24404-0, Crest). Fawcett.
Dillon, Eilis, et al, eds. The Lucky Bag. (Illus.). 220p. (gr. 3-11). 1985. 12.95 (ISBN 0-86278-064-0, Pub. by O'Brien Pr Ireland). Irish Bks Media.
Dillon, Elizabeth & Dillon, Lawrence. A Manual of Common Beetles of Eastern North America, 2 vols. (Illus.). 1972. pap. 8.95 ea. Vol. 1 (ISBN 0-486-61180-9). Vol. 2 (ISBN 0-486-61190-6). Dover.
Dillon, Elizabeth S. & Lawrence, S. A Manual of Common Beetles of Eastern North America, 2 vols. (Illus.). Set. 33.50 (ISBN 0-8446-4538-9). Peter Smith.
Dillon, Emile J. Mexico on the Verge. LC 78-111712. (American Imperialism: Viewpoints of United States Foreign Policy, 1898-1941). 1970. Repr. of 1921 ed. 20.00 (ISBN 0-405-02013-9). Ayer Co Pubs.
Dillon, G. M. Dependence & Deterrence. 206p. 1983. text ed. 32.95x (ISBN 0-566-00588-3). Gower Pub Co.
Dillon, Gadis J. The Role of Accounting in the Stock Market Crash of 1929. 200p. 1984. Spiral. 35.00 (ISBN 0-88406-170-1). Ga St U BUsn Pub.
Dillon, George, tr. see Racine, Jean B.
Dillon, George E. Freemasonry Unmasked. Fuhley, Denis, pref. by. 114p. 1984. pap. 6.00 (ISBN 0-89562-095-2). Sons Lib.
Dillon, George L. Constructing Texts: Elements of a Theory of Composition & Style. LC 80-8377. 224p. 1981. 19.50x (ISBN 0-253-13113-8). Ind U Pr.
--Introduction to Contemporary Linguistic Semantics. LC 76-4183. 1977. pap. 13.95 (ISBN 0-13-479469-9). P-H.
--Language Processing & the Reading of Literature: Toward a Model of Comprehension. LC 77-9861. 240p. 1978. 17.50x (ISBN 0-253-33195-1). Ind U Pr.
Dillon, J. F. The Law & Jurisprudence of England & America. LC 75-99475. (American Constitutional & Legal History Ser). 1970. Repr. of 1894 ed. lib. bdg. 49.50 (ISBN 0-306-71854-5). Da Capo.
Dillon, J. T. Teaching & the Art of Questioning. LC 83-61781. (Fastback Ser.: No. 194). 50p. 1983. pap. 0.75 (ISBN 0-87367-194-5). Phi Delta Kappa.
Dillon, Jacquelyn, jt. auth. see Kriechbaum, Casimer, Jr.
Dillon, James. Light My Fire, Vol. 1. (My Private Eye Ser.). 150p. (Orig.). 1984. pap. 4.80x (ISBN 0-915153-08-4). Gold Star Pr.
--Spanish Autumn, 2 vols, Vol. 1. 150p. (Orig.). 1984. pap. 5.76x (ISBN 0-915153-04-1). Gold Star Pr.
--Tears in the Rain. (My Private Eye Ser.). 100p. (Orig.). 1985. pap. 4.80 (ISBN 0-915153-11-4). Gold Star Pr.
Dillon, Jane M. School for Young Riders. (Illus.). (YA) 8.95 (ISBN 0-668-02605-7). Arco.
Dillon, Janette. Shakespeare & the Solitary Man. 200p. 1981. 26.50x (ISBN 0-8476-6254-3). Rowman.
Dillon, John. Inventory of the Ornaments, Reliques, Jewels, Vestments, Books, Etc. Belonging to the Cathedral Church of Glasgow. LC 76-168150. (Maitland Club, Glasgow. Publications: No. 13). Repr. of 1831 ed. 15.00 (ISBN 0-404-52945-3). AMS Pr.
Dillon, John, jt. auth. see Heady, Earl O.
Dillon, John, jt. auth. see Winston, David.
Dillon, John A. Foundations of General Systems Theory. (Systems Inquiry Ser.). 300p. 1982. pap. 14.95x (ISBN 0-914105-05-1). Intersystems Pubns.
Dillon, John B. History of Indiana from Its Earliest Exploration by Europeans to the Close of Territorial Government in 1816. LC 73-146392. (First American Frontier Ser.). (Illus.). 1971. Repr. of 1859 ed. 40.00 (ISBN 0-405-02845-8). Ayer Co Pubs.
--Notes on Historical Evidence in Reference to Adverse Theories of the Government of the Origin & Nature of the United States of America. 141p. 1985. Repr. of 1871 ed. lib. bdg. 22.50x (ISBN 0-8377-0521-5). Rothman.
Dillon, John F. Removal of Causes from State Courts to Federal Courts, with Forms Adapted to the Several Acts of Congress on the Subject. 3rd ed. xxiii, 168p. 1981. Repr. of 1881 ed. lib. bdg. 22.00x (ISBN 0-8377-0514-2). Rothman.
Dillon, John L. The Analysis of Response in Crop & Livestock Production. 2nd ed. 1968. pap. text ed. 14.00 (ISBN 0-08-021115-1). Pergamon.
Dillon, John L. & Hardaker, J. Brian. Farm Management Research for Small Farmer Development. (Agricultural Services Bulletins: No. 41). 155p. (Eng. & Span., 2nd Printing 1981). 1980. pap. 12.75 (ISBN 92-5-100822-1, F2119, FAO). Unipub.
Dillon, John M. Edgar Allan Poe. LC 74-3420. (Studies in Poe, No. 23). 1974. lib. bdg. 49.95x (ISBN 0-8383-2069-4). Haskell.
--Edgar Allan Poe: His Genius & Character. LC 73-480. 1972. Repr. of 1911 ed. lib. bdg. 20.00 (ISBN 0-8414-1334-7). Folcroft.
Dillon, John M., jt. auth. see O'Hehir, Brendan.
Dillon, K. V., ed. see Prange, G. W.
Dillon, Karen & Brown, Gail. Sew a Beautiful Wedding. 1980. pap. 6.95 (ISBN 0-935278-05-2). Palmer-Pletsch.
Dillon, Kenneth J. King & Estates in the Bohemian Lands, 1526-1564. 206p. 1982. 21.05. P Lang Pubs.
--Scholars' Guide to Washington D. C. for Central & East European Studies. LC 80-607019. (Scholars' Guide to Washington D. C. Ser.: No. 5). 329p. 1980. text ed. 25.00x (ISBN 0-87474-368-0); pap. text ed. 9.95x (ISBN 0-87474-367-2). Smithsonian.
Dillon, Kristine E., ed. see Linnell, Robert.
Dillon, L. S. The Genetic Mechanism & the Origin of Life. LC 78-4478. (Illus.). 573p. 1978. 55.00 (ISBN 0-306-31090-2, Plenum Pr). Plenum Pub.
Dillon, L. S. & Dillon, E. S. Cerambycidae of the Fiji Islands. (BMB Ser.). 1952. 14.00 (ISBN 0-527-02314-0). Kraus Repr.
Dillon, Lacy. They Died for King Coal. 200p. 1983. pap. 9.95 (ISBN 0-934750-45-9). Jalamap.
--They Died in the Darkness. (Illus.). 280p. 1979. 9.95. Jalamap.
Dillon, Lawrence, jt. auth. see Dillon, Elizabeth.
Dillon, Lawrence S. Animal Variety: An Evolutionary Account. 4th ed. 325p. 1980. pap. text ed. write for info. (ISBN 0-697-04590-0). Wm C Brown.
--The Inconstant Gene. 590p. 1983. 65.00x (ISBN 0-306-41084-2, Plenum Pr). Plenum Pub.
--Ultrastructure, Macromolecules, & Evolution. LC 80-20550. 716p. 1981. 69.50x (ISBN 0-306-40528-8, Plenum Pr). Plenum Pub.
Dillon, Lester R., Jr. American Artillery in the Mexican War, Eighteen Forty-Six to Eighteen Forty-Seven. (Illus.). 1975. 7.95 (ISBN 0-686-25782-0). Presidial.
Dillon, Lowell I. & Lyon, Edward E. Indiana: Crossroads of America. (Regional Geography Ser.). (Illus.). 1978. pap. text ed. 11.95 (ISBN 0-8403-1893-6). Kendall-Hunt.
Dillon, Marian. Wide Awake Billy. (Illus.). 48p. (gr. 2-5). 1984. 3.95 (ISBN 0-241-10984-1, Pub. by Hamish Hamilton England). David & Charles.
Dillon, Mark. American Race Car Drivers. LC 73-22511. (Superwheels & Thrill Sports Bks.). (Illus.). (gr. 5-10). 1974. PLB 8.95 (ISBN 0-8225-0409-X). Lerner Pubns.
Dillon, Mark & Haigh, Frank. International Race Car Drivers. LC 73-22514. (Superwheels & Thrill Sports Bks.). (Illus.). 52p. (gr. 5-10). 1974. PLB 8.95 (ISBN 0-8225-0413-8). Lerner Pubns.
Dillon, Mary E., ed. see Berle, Peter A.
Dillon, Mary E., ed. see Davis, James W.
Dillon, Mary E., ed. see Metz, Joseph G.
Dillon, Mary Earhart. Wendell Wilkie, Eighteen Ninety-Two to Nineteen Fourty-Four. LC 71-39040. (FDR & the Era of the New Deal Ser.). 378p. 1972. Repr. of 1952 ed. lib. bdg. 45.00 (ISBN 0-306-70456-0). Da Capo.
Dillon, Merton L. The Abolitionists: The Growth of a Dissenting Minority. LC 73-15096. (American Minorities Ser). (Illus.). 298p. 1974. 12.00 (ISBN 0-87580-044-0). N Ill U Pr.
--The Abolitionists: The Growth of a Dissenting Minority. 1979. pap. 4.95 (ISBN 0-393-00957-2). Norton.
--Benjamin Lundy & the Struggle for Negro Freedom. LC 66-15473. pap. 55.70 (ISBN 0-8357-9663-9, 2015497). Bks Demand UMI.
--Elijah P. Lovejoy, Abolitionist Editor. LC 80-11000. ix, 190p. 1980. Repr. of 1961 ed. lib. bdg. 24.75x (ISBN 0-313-22352-1, DIEJ). Greenwood.
--Ulrich Bonnell Phillips: Historian of the Old South. Cooper, William J., Jr., ed. (Southern Biography Ser.). 200p. 1985. text ed. 20.00 (ISBN 0-8071-1206-2). La State U Pr.
Dillon, Michael. China Profiles. 1985. 29.50x (ISBN 0-7146-3152-3, BHA-03152, F Cass Co). Biblio Dist.
--A Dictionary of Chinese History. 240p. 1979. 27.50x (ISBN 0-7146-3107-8, F Cass Co). Biblio Dist.
Dillon, Millicent. A Little Original Sin: The Life & Work of Jane Bowles. LC 80-25879. (Illus.). 480p. 1981. 18.95 (ISBN 0-03-058317-9). HR&W.
--A Little Original Sin: The Life & Work of Jane Bowles. 1982. pap. 9.95 (ISBN 0-03-062027-9, Owl Bks). HR&W.
Dillon, Millicent, ed. Out in the World: Selected Letters of Jane Bowles, 1935-1970. (Illus.). 321p. 1985. signed, ed. 30.00 (ISBN 0-87685-627-X); 20.00 (ISBN 0-87685-626-1); pap. 12.50 (ISBN 0-87685-625-3). Black Sparrow.
Dillon, Myles. The Cycles of the Kings. LC 73-15541. (On Irish Sages). 1946. lib. bdg. 20.00 (ISBN 0-8414-3691-6). Folcroft.
--Early Irish Literature. LC 48-6027. 1948. 13.00x (ISBN 0-226-14918-8). U of Chicago Pr.
Dillon, Myles & Croinin, D. O. Teach Yourself Irish. (Teach Yourself Ser.). pap. 4.95 (ISBN 0-679-10183-7). McKay.
Dillon, Myles, ed. Irish Sagas. 4th ed. (Thomas Davis Lecture Ser.). 175p. 1985. pap. 6.95 (ISBN 0-85342-736-4, Pub. by Mercier Pr Ireland). Irish Bks Media.
Dillon, Ray. Zero Base Budgeting for Health Care Institutions. LC 79-15046. 255p. 1979. text ed. 37.00 (ISBN 0-89443-150-1). Aspen Systems.
Dillon, Richard. Fool's Gold: The Decline & Fall of Captain John Sutter of California. (Illus.). 380p. 1981. pap. 7.95 (ISBN 0-934136-15-7). Western Tanager.
--North American Indian Wars. (Illus.). 256p. 29.95 (ISBN 0-87196-641-7). Facts on File.
--North Beach: The Italian Heart of San Francisco. Davis, Lynn L., ed. (Illus.). 229p. 1985. 35.00 (ISBN 0-89141-187-9). Presidio Pr.
--We Have Met the Enemy: The Life of Commodore Oliver Hazard Perry. LC 77-17039. 1978. 12.95 (ISBN 0-07-016981-0). McGraw.
Dillon, Richard, et al. High Steel. LC 78-72833. 176p. 1984. pap. 16.95 (ISBN 0-89087-409-3). Celestial Arts.
--High Steel. LC 78-72833. (Illus.). 1979. 25.00 (ISBN 0-89087-191-4). Celestial Arts.
Dillon, Richard H. Embarcadero. LC 70-139131. 1971. Repr. of 1959 ed. lib. bdg. 15.00x (ISBN 0-8371-5747-1, DIEM). Greenwood.
--The Hatchet Men. LC 62-14747. 270p. 1977. pap. 2.50 (ISBN 0-89174-027-9). Comstock Edns.
--Humbugs & Heroes: A Gallery of California Pioneers. (Illus.). 389p. 1983. pap. 9.95 (ISBN 0-911819-00-2). Yosemite D.
--San Francisco: Adventurers & Visionaries. new ed. Mason, Sharon, ed. LC 83-70414. (American Portrait Ser.). (Illus.). 240p. 1983. 29.95 (ISBN 0-932986-35-8). Continent Herit.
Dillon, Richard H., ed. A Cannoneer in Navajo Country: Journal of Private Josiah M. Rice, 1851. (Illus.). 1970. limited ed. 16.50 (ISBN 0-912094-15-X). Old West.
Dillon, Richard H., ed. see Harris, Benjamin B.
Dillon, Richard S. Handbook of Endocrinology: Diagnosis & Management of Endocrine & Metabolic Disorders. 2nd ed. LC 79-10531. (Illus.). 760p. 1980. text ed. 52.00 (ISBN 0-8121-0642-3). Lea & Febiger.
Dillon, Robert. The River. Bauer, Stephen, adapted by. 272p. 1984. pap. 2.95 (ISBN 0-425-07447-1). Berkley Pub.
Dillon, Robert J. Reality & Value Judgment in Policymaking: A Study of Expert Judgments about Alternative Energy Technologies. Bruchey, Stuart, ed. LC 78-22674. (Energy in the American Economy Ser.). (Illus.). 1979. lib. bdg. 16.00x (ISBN 0-405-11977-1). Ayer Co Pubs.
Dillon, Ronna F. Individual Differences in Cognition, Vol. 2. Date not set. 39.50 (ISBN 0-12-216402-4). Acad Pr.
Dillon, Ronna F. & Schmeck, Ronald R., eds. Individual Differences in Cognition, Vol. 1. 1983. 36.50 (ISBN 0-12-216401-6). Acad Pr.
Dillon, Roy. Working with Animal Supplies & Services. Lee, Jasper S., ed. (Career Preparation for Agriculture-Agribusiness Ser.). (Illus.). 1980. pap. text ed. 11.68 (ISBN 0-07-016951-9). McGraw.
Dillon, T. S. & Forward, J. Microcomputer Systems: A Compendium. 400p. 1983. write for info. Elsevier.
Dillon, W. R., jt. auth. see Goldstein, M.
Dillon, William. Business Mathematics. LC 84-16987. 320p. 1985. pap. text ed. 14.80 spiral-bound (ISBN 0-8273-2346-8); instr's. guide 9.80 (ISBN 0-8273-2347-6); business simulation 8.80 (ISBN 0-8273-2349-2). Delmar.
Dillon, William R. & Goldstein, Matthew. Multivariate Analysis: Methods & Application. LC 84-3584. (Probability & Mathematical Statistics-Applied Probability & Statistics Section Ser.: 1-346). 587p. 1984. text ed. 37.95x (ISBN 0-471-08317-8, Pub. by Wiley Interscience). Wiley.
Dillon-Peterson, Elizabeth & Greenawald, G. Dale. Staff Development for the Social Studies Teacher. LC 80-11118. 102p. 1980. 9.95 (ISBN 0-89994-243-1). Soc Sci Ed.
Dillow, Jeffrey. Circle of Truth. 1984. pap. 13.95 (ISBN 0-8359-0793-7). Reston.
Dillow, Joseph C. Solomon on Sex. LC 77-1049. 1982. pap. 4.95 (ISBN 0-8407-5813-8). Nelson.
Dillow, Linda. Creative Counterpart. LC 76-30387. 1977. pap. 4.95 (ISBN 0-8407-5617-8). Nelson.
--Creative Counterpart Bible Study & Project Guide. LC 78-675. 1978. pap. 2.50 (ISBN 0-8407-5648-8). Nelson.
--La Esposa Virtuosa. 160p. 1981. 2.75 (ISBN 0-88113-064-8). Edit Betania.

Dimbleby, G. W. The Development of British Heathlands & their Soils. 1962. 45.00x (ISBN 0-686-45495-2, Pub. by For Lib Comm England). State Mutual Bk.

Dimbleby, G. W., ed. see Grayson, Donald K.

Dimbleby, Geoffey W. Palynology of Archaeological Sites. 1985. 45.00 (ISBN 0-12-216480-6). Acad Pr.

Dimbleby, Geoffrey W. Plants & Archeology. 2nd ed. LC 67-23020. (Illus.). 1978. 15.50x (ISBN 0-391-00926-5). Humanities.

Dimbleby, Jonathan. The Palestinians. 25.00 (ISBN 0-7043-2205-6, Pub. by Quartet England). Charles River Bks.

--The Palestinians. (Illus.). 256p. 1984. 25.00 (ISBN 0-7043-2256-0, Pub. by Quartet Bks); pap. 12.95 (ISBN 0-7043-3322-8). Merrimack Pub Cir.

Dimbleby, Richard. Elizabeth Our Queen. LC 78-12304. (Illus.). 1979. Repr. of 1953 ed. lib. bdg. 24.75x (ISBN 0-313-21096-9, DIEQ). Greenwood.

Dimbleby, Richard & Burton, Graeme. More Than Words: An Introduction to Communication. (Illus.). 1985. 25.00 (ISBN 0-416-38060-3, 9573); pap. 9.95 (ISBN 0-416-38070-0, 9574). Methuen Inc.

Dimcock, James F., ed. Adam of Eynsham: Magna Vita S. Hugonsi, Episcopi Lincolniensis. (Rolls Ser.: No. 37). Repr. of 1864 ed. 44.00 (ISBN 0-317-16684-0). Kraus Repr.

Dim Delobson, A. A. Les Secrets des sorciers noirs. LC 74-15028. Repr. of 1934 ed. 18.00 (ISBN 0-404-12035-0). AMS Pr.

Di Meglio, Clara, jt. auth. see Valentini, Norberto.

DiMeglio, John. Vaudeville U. S. A. LC 73-78161. 1973. 9.95 (ISBN 0-87972-053-0); pap. 4.95 (ISBN 0-87972-054-9). Bowling Green Univ.

DiMella, Nancy, jt. auth. see Bershad, Carol.

Dimen, Muriel & Friedl, Ernestine, eds. Regional Variation in Modern Greece & Cyprus: Toward a Perspective on the Ethnography of Greece. (Annals of the New York Academy of Sciences: Vol. 268). 465p. 1976. 32.00x (ISBN 0-89072-022-3). NY Acad Sci.

Dimendberg, David C., jt. auth. see Bowers, Warner F.

Dimen-Schein, Muriel. The Anthropological Imagination. (McGraw-Hill Paperbacks Ser.). 1977. pap. 4.95 (ISBN 0-07-016985-3). McGraw.

Diment, Eunice. Kidnapped! (Illus.). 80p. 1976. pap. 2.50 (ISBN 0-85364-199-4). Attic Pr.

Diment, J. A., et al. Catalogue of the Natural History Drawings Commissioned by Joseph Banks on the Endeavour Voyage, Part 1: Botany - Australia. (Illus.). 183p. 1984. pap. text ed. 60.00x (ISBN 0-565-09000-3, Pub. by Brit Mus Nat Hist England). Sabbot Natural Hist Bks.

Diment, Judith, et al. Catalogue of the Natural History Drawings Commissioned by Joseph Banks on the Endeavour Voyage 1768-1771 Held in the British Museum (Natural History) Botany - Australia, Pt. 1. 250p. 1984. lib. bdg. 75.00 (ISBN 0-930466-92-6). Meckler Pub.

DiMento, Joseph F. The Consistency Doctrine & the Limits of Planning. LC 80-12981. 192p. 1980. text ed. 35.00 (ISBN 0-89946-036-4). Oelgeschlager.

Dimic, Milan V., ed. see Hutcheon, Linda.

Di Michael, Eleanor M., jt. auth. see King, Robert G.

Dimick, Kenneth & Krause, Frank. Practicum Manual for Counseling & Psychotherapy. 4th rev. ed. LC 79-53417. 324p. 1980. pap. 12.95x (ISBN 0-915202-26-3). Accel Devel.

Dimick, Kenneth M. Ladies in Waiting: Behind Prison Walls. LC 78-72315. 182p. 1979. pap. text ed. 8.95x (ISBN 0-915202-17-4). Accel Devel.

Dimick, M. T. Memphis, the City of the White Wall. (Illus.). 29p. 1956. pap. 2.50 (ISBN 0-318-01019-4). Univ Mus of U PA.

Dimier. Recueil de Plans d'Eglises Cisterciennes, 2 tomes. Set. 100.75 (ISBN 0-685-34012-0). French & Eur.

Dimier, Louis. French Painting in the Sixteenth Century. LC 74-88821. (Art Histories Collection Ser.). Repr. of 1904 ed. 18.00 (ISBN 0-405-02226-3). Ayer Co Pubs.

Dimitrakopoulou, M. I. Studies in Philodemus' Aesthetic Theories. (London Studies in Classical Philology). 1982. pap. text ed. write for info. (ISBN 0-391-01154-5). Humanities.

Dimitriev, P. P., jt. auth. see Gusev, N. G.

Dimitrijevic, Dimitrije & Macesich, George. Money & Finance in Contemporary Yugoslavia. LC 72-92889. (Special Studies in International Economics & Development). 1973. 37.50x (ISBN 0-275-28725-4); pap. text ed. 19.50x (ISBN 0-89197-857-7). Irvington.

--Money & Finance in Yugoslavia: A Comparative Analysis. LC 84-21162. 220p. 1983. text ed. 27.95 (ISBN 0-03-069561-9). Praeger.

Dimitrijevic, George D., ed. see Altaras, Jakob.

Dimitrijevic, M. R., jt. ed. see Eccles, John.

Dimitriv, Nikolay V. & Nodine, John H., eds. Drugs & Hematologic Reactions: The Twenty-Ninth Hahnemann Symposium. 416p. 1974. 87.50 (ISBN 0-8089-0812-X, 791048). Grune.

Dimitroff, Georgi. The United Front. 287p. 1975. pap. text ed. 5.95 (ISBN 0-89380-004-X). Proletarian Pubs.

Dimitropoulos, C. J. The Nightmare & the Discovery. (Illus.). 1982. 6.95 (ISBN 0-533-04987-3). Vantage.

Dimitrov, Georgi. The Working Class Against Fascism. LC 78-63662. (Studies in Fascism: Ideology & Practice). Repr. of 1935 ed. 21.00 (ISBN 0-404-16925-2). AMS Pr.

Dimitrov, L., jt. ed. see Ionescu, V.

Dimitrov, Th. World Bibliography on International Documentation, 2 vols. LC 80-5653. 846p. 1981. Set. 95.00 (ISBN 0-89111-010-0). UNIFO Pubs.

Dimitrov, Th., ed. see World Symposium on International Documentation, Second, Brussels, 1980.

Dimitrovsky, H. Z. S'ridei Bavli: Spanish Incunabula Fragments of the Babylonian Talmud. 375.00x (ISBN 0-87334-007-8, Pub. by Jewish Theol Seminary). Ktav.

Dimitry of Rostov, St. Angels & the Other Heavenly Bodiless Powers. pap. 0.25 (ISBN 0-686-05638-8). Eastern Orthodox.

Dimitt, Richard. Red & the Green. (Orig.). (ps-3). 1.75 (ISBN 0-8198-0131-3). Dghtrs St Paul.

Dimler, G. Richard. Friedrich Spee Trutznachtigall: Faksimiledruck Nach der Ausgabe Von 1649. LC 80-5639. 438p. (Orig., Ger.). 1982. lib. bdg. 32.00 (ISBN 0-8191-2042-1); pap. text ed. 18.00 (ISBN 0-8191-2043-X). U Pr of Amer.

--Friedrich Spee's "Trutznachtigall". (Germanic Studies in America: Vol. 13). 158p. 1973. 20.90 (ISBN 3-261-00848-2). P Lang Pubs.

Dimmack, Max. Art Techniques for Amateurs. LC 75-97777. (Illus.). 1970. 9.95 (ISBN 0-670-13713-8, Studio). Viking.

--Noel Counihan. (Illus.). 1977. 55.00x (ISBN 0-522-84060-4, Pub. by Melbourne U Pr). Intl Spec Bk.

Dimmette, Celia. Ocean Carry Us Far. 1978. 5.00 (ISBN 0-8233-0283-0). Golden Quill.

--Take Me Home Again. 1979. 8.00. M Jones.

--The Winds Blow Promise. LC 75-95851. 1969. 4.00 (ISBN 0-8233-0142-7). Golden Quill.

Dimmick, Mary L. The Rolling Stones: An Annotated Bibliography. LC 78-53599. 1978. 12.95 (ISBN 0-8229-3384-5). U of Pittsburgh Pr.

Dimmick, Ralph E., tr. see Ramos, Graciliano.

Dimmitt, Cornelia, ed. Classical Hindu Mythology: A Reader in the Sanskrit Puranas. Van Buitenen, J. A., tr. LC 77-92643. 388p. 1978. 34.95 (ISBN 0-87722-117-0); pap. 12.95x (ISBN 0-87722-122-7). Temple U Pr.

Dimmitt, Richard B. Title Guide to the Talkies, 2 Vols. LC 65-13556. 2133p. 1965. Set. 77.50 (ISBN 0-8108-0171-X). Scarecrow.

Dimmock, N. J., jt. auth. see Primrose, S. B.

Dimnet, Ernes. What We Live by. 309p. 1985. Repr. of 1932 ed. lib. bdg. 25.00 (ISBN 0-8482-3701-3). Norwood Edns.

Dimnet, Ernest. The Art of Thinking. 1929. lib. bdg. 27.50 (ISBN 0-8414-9109-7). Folcroft.

--The Bronte Sisters. 1927. 20.00 (ISBN 0-8274-1979-1). R West.

--The Bronte Sisters. Sill, Louise M., tr. from Fr. 256p. Date not set. Repr. of 1984 ed. lib. bdg. 50.00 (ISBN 0-8495-1147-X). Arden Lib.

--Paul Bourget. 1913. Repr. 15.00 (ISBN 0-8274-3108-2). R West.

--What We Live by. 1978. Repr. of 1932 ed. lib. bdg. 15.00 (ISBN 0-8495-1035-X). Arden Lib.

Dimo, P. Nodal Analysis of Power Systems. 1975. 33.00 (ISBN 0-9961002-4-5, Pub. by Abacus England). Heyden.

Dimock, Anthony Weston & Dimock, Julian A. Florida Enchantments. LC 74-13789. (Illus.). 318p. 1975. Repr. of 1908 ed. 43.00x (ISBN 0-8103-4061-5). Gale.

Dimock, E., et al. Introduction to Bengali, Part 1. 1976. Repr. 16.00x (ISBN 0-88386-858-X). South Asia Bks.

Dimock, Edward C., Jr., ed. & tr. Thief of Love: Bengali Tales from Court & Village. LC 63-11396. xiv, 306p. 1975. pap. 3.95x (ISBN 0-226-15236-7, P624, Phoen). U of Chicago Pr.

Dimock, Edward C., Jr. & Levertov, Denise, trs. In Praise of Krishna: Songs from the Bengali. (Illus.). xii, 96p. 1981. 4.95 (ISBN 0-226-15231-6, Phoen). U of Chicago Pr.

Dimock, Edward C., Jr., tr. see Gangarama.

Dimock, Edward C., Jr., et al. The Literatures of India: An Introduction. LC 73-87300. 1978. pap. 6.95x (ISBN 0-226-15233-2, P768, Phoen). U of Chicago Pr.

Dimock, Elna M. Pass the CBEST. 2nd ed. LC 84-13794. (Illus.). 156p. (Orig.). 1984. pap. 14.50 (ISBN 0-914763-01-6). Educ Development.

--Teacher Competency Tests. 160p. 1985. pap. 7.95 (ISBN 0-668-06231-2). Arco.

Dimock, George E., Jr., tr. see Euripides.

Dimock, Giles, jt. ed. see Alexander, Jon.

Dimock, Gladys O. Home Ground: Living in the Country. 160p. 1985. 14.95 (ISBN 0-88150-049-6); pap. 9.95 (ISBN 0-88150-035-6). Countryman.

Dimock, Julian A., jt. auth. see Dimock, Anthony Weston.

Dimock, M. The New American Political Economy. LC 73-16736. 306p. 1974. Repr. of 1962 ed. lib. bdg. 15.00x (ISBN 0-8371-7220-9, DIPE). Greenwood.

Dimock, M. E., jt. ed. see Haines, C. G.

Dimock, Marshall E. Center of My World: An Autobiography. 200p. 1980. 12.95 (ISBN 0-914378-60-0). Countryman.

--Congressional Investigating Committees. LC 72-155626. Repr. of 1929 ed. 12.50 (ISBN 0-404-02134-4). AMS Pr.

--Free Enterprise & the Administrative State. LC 76-142856. 179p. 1972. Repr. of 1951 ed. lib. bdg. 15.50x (ISBN 0-8371-5955-5, DIFE). Greenwood.

--Law & Dynamic Administration. LC 80-12863. 176p. 1980. 33.95 (ISBN 0-03-057367-X); text ed. 16.95 (ISBN 0-03-057396-3). Praeger.

Dimock, Marshall E., jt. ed. see Haines, Charles G.

Dimock, Marshall E., et al. Public Administration. 5th ed. 1983. pap. text ed. 29.95 (ISBN 0-03-056212-0). HR&W.

Dimock, Stuart J., jt. ed. see Sethi, Amarjit S.

Dimoff, Eleanor. Explorations of Visual Phenomena: A Curriculum for Young Children, Integrating Math, Art & Science. (Illus.). 1973. pap. 0.75 (ISBN 0-918374-06-5). Workshop Ctr.

Dimon, jt. auth. see Carton.

Dimon, Cecile, jt. auth. see Carton, Jo-Anne.

Dimon, Joseph H., jt. auth. see Donahoo, Clare A., Jr.

DiMona, Joe. To the Eagle's Nest. LC 79-25496. 320p. 1980. 10.95 (ISBN 0-688-03653-8). Morrow.

Dimona, Joseph. To the Eagle's Nest. 448p. 1981. pap. 3.50 (ISBN 0-440-18944-6). Dell.

Dimona, Joseph, jt. auth. see Haldeman, H. R.

DiMona, Joseph, jt. auth. see Noguchi, Thomas.

DiMona, Joseph, jt. auth. see Noguchi, Thomas T.

Dimond, E. Grey. Digitalis. (Illus.). 246p. 1957. 24.50x (ISBN 0-398-04244-6). C C Thomas.

--Inside China Today: A Western View. 1983. 16.50 (ISBN 0-393-01711-7). Norton.

--Inside China Today: A Western View. (Illus.). 272p. 1984. pap. 5.95 (ISBN 0-393-30215-6). Norton.

--More Than Herbs & Acupuncture. 224p. 1975. 7.95 (ISBN 0-393-06400-X). Norton.

Dimond, Jasper. Dinosaurs. (Illus.). 48p. (gr. 3-7). 1985. 8.95 (ISBN 0-13-214628-2). P-H.

--Noah's Ark. (Illus.). 48p. (gr. k-3). 1983. 7.95 (ISBN 0-13-622951-4). P-H.

Dimond, Margaret & Jones, Susan. Chronic Illness Across the Life Span. (Illus.). 288p. 1982. pap. 15.95x (ISBN 0-8385-1122-8). ACC.

Dimond, Paul R. Beyond Busing: Inside the Challenge to Urban Segregation. 424p. 1985. text ed. 29.95x (ISBN 0-472-10062-9). U of Mich Pr.

Dimond, Stanley E. & Pfieger, Elmer F. Our American Government: Supplement. 32p. 1975. pap. 3.16 (ISBN 0-397-40243-0). Har-Row.

Dimond, Stanley E., et al. Civics for Citizens. rev. ed. 1970. 20.32 (ISBN 0-397-40174-4); tchrs' ed. 12.08 (ISBN 0-397-40175-2); unit texts 1.76 (ISBN 0-397-40176-0). Har-Row.

--Our American Government. rev. ed. 1973. 24.28 (ISBN 0-397-40216-3); tchrs' ed. 14.96 (ISBN 0-397-40217-1); unit tests 1.92 (ISBN 0-397-40218-X). Har-Row.

Dimond, Stuart J. Introducing Neuropsychology: A Study of Brain & Mind. (Illus.). 236p. 1978. 25.75x (ISBN 0-398-03794-9). C C Thomas.

Dimond, Stuart J. & Blizard, David, eds. Evolution & Lateralization of the Brain, Vol. 299. (Annals of the New York Academy of Sciences). 501p. 1977. 42.00x (ISBN 0-89072-045-2). NY Acad Sci.

Dimondstein, Geraldine. Children Dance in the Classroom. 1971. text ed. write for info. (ISBN 0-02-329670-4, 32967). Macmillan.

Dimont, Max. The Jews in America. 1980. 6.95 (ISBN 0-671-25412-X, Touchstone). S&S.

Dimont, Max I. The Amazing Adventures of the Jewish People. 175p. 1984. pap. 3.95 (ISBN 0-87441-391-5). Behrman.

--The Indestructible Jews. 480p. 1973. pap. 4.95 (ISBN 0-451-13878-3, Sig). NAL.

--Jews, God & History. 1972. pap. 3.95 (ISBN 0-451-12181-3, AE2181, Sig). NAL.

Dimov-Bogoev, Christo, jt. ed. see Decsy, Gyula.

D'Imperio, A. see Halpern, M., et al.

D'Imperio, Dan. Flea Market Treasure. (Illus.). 336p. (Orig.). 1984. 15.95 (ISBN 0-8306-0738-2); pap. 9.95 (ISBN 0-8306-1738-8, 1738). TAB Bks.

D'Imperio, M E. The Voynich Manuscript: An Elegant Enigma. 140p. 1976. pap. text ed. 16.80 (ISBN 0-89412-038-7). Aegean Park Pr.

Dimples, Dolly, pseud. The Greatest Diet in the World. rev. ed. LC 74-15778. Orig. Title: Diet or Die. (Illus.). 239p. 1975. pap. 3.95 (ISBN 0-88435-002-9). Chateau Pub.

Dimroth, K. Delocalized Phosphorus-Carbon Double Bonds: Phosphamethin-Cyanines Lambda to the Third Power - Phosphorins & Lambda to the Fifth Power - Phosphorins. LC 51-5497. (Topics in Current Chemistry: Vol. 38). (Illus.). 170p. 1973. pap. 30.70 (ISBN 0-387-06164-9). Springer-Verlag.

Dimsdale, Joel E., ed. Survivors, Victims & Perpetrators: Essays on the Nazi Holocaust. LC 79-24834. (Illus.). 474p. 1980. text ed. 42.50 (ISBN 0-89116-145-7); pap. text ed. 32.95 (ISBN 0-89116-351-4). Hemisphere Pub.

Dimsdale, Marcus S. A History of Latin Literature. (Select Bibliographies Reprint Ser.). Repr. of 1915 ed. 27.50 (ISBN 0-8369-6684-8). Ayer Co Pubs.

Dimsdale, Parks B., jt. auth. see Wright, John S.

Dimsdale, Thomas J. Vigilantes of Montana. LC 53-9887. (Western Frontier Library: No. 1). 1978. pap. 6.95 (ISBN 0-8061-1379-0). U of Okla Pr.

Dimson, Colleen, jt. auth. see Imrie, David.

Din. English Translations of German Standard Catalog. 240p. 1983. pap. 13.00 (Pub. by DIN Germany). Heyden.

Din, tr. from Ger. Din Handbook: Welding I-Standards on Filler Metals, Manufacture, Quality & Testing, No. 8. 420p. 1983. pap. 76.00 (ISBN 3-41011-584-6, Pub. by DIN Germany). Heyden.

Din, Gilbert C. & Nasatir, Abraham P. The Imperial Osages: Spanish-Indian Diplomacy in the Mississippi Valley. LC 82-40449. (The Civilization of the American Indian Ser.: Vol. 161). (Illus.). 432p. 1983. 39.95 (ISBN 0-8061-1834-2). U of Okla Pr.

Din, M. R., jt. auth. see Malik, Imam.

Dinaburg, Kathy & Akel, D'Ann. Nutrition Survival Kit: A Wholefoods Recipe & Reference Guide. LC 76-28772. (Illus.). 256p. 1976. 12.95 (ISBN 0-915572-18-4); pap. 6.95 (ISBN 0-915572-17-6). Panjandrum.

Dinamarca, Maria L., et al. Biological Effect of DDT in Lower Organisms. LC 73-12476. 238p. 1974. text ed. 29.50x (ISBN 0-8422-7120-1). Irvington.

Dinan. Scientific Basis of Psychology. 1986. price not set (ISBN 0-7236-0704-4). PSG Pub Co.

Dinan, Carolyn. The Lunch Box Monster. LC 83-1694. (Illus.). 32p. (ps-1). 1983. pap. 6.95 (ISBN 0-571-13153-0). Faber & Faber.

--Skipper & Sam. LC 84-3988. (Illus.). 96p. (gr. k-2). 1984. 8.95 (ISBN 0-571-13154-9). Faber & Faber.

Dinan, Dennis, ed. see Finn, Molly.

Dinan, Joan. Selected Annotated Bibliography of the Humanistic Needs of Nursing Home Residents. Reed, R., ed. Bowker, Lee. LC 81-85318. (Orig.). 1982. 24.95 (ISBN 0-88247-643-2); pap. 17.95 (ISBN 0-88247-638-6). R & E Pubs.

Dinan, John A. The Pulp Western: A Popular History of the Western Fiction Magazine in America. LC 81-21697. (I. O. Evans Studies in the Philosophy & Criticism of Literature: Vol. 2). (Illus.). 128p. 1983. lib. bdg. 14.95x (ISBN 0-89370-161-0); pap. text ed. 6.95x (ISBN 0-89370-261-7). Borgo Pr.

Di Napoli, Peter J. Homework in New York City Elementary Schools. LC 77-176721. (Columbia University. Teachers College. Contributions to Education: No. 719). Repr. of 1937 ed. 22.50 (ISBN 0-404-55719-8). AMS Pr.

Dinar, N., jt. ed. see Kaplan, H.

Dinardo, C. T., ed. Computers & Security, Vol. III. (The Information Technology Ser.). (Illus.). 247p. 1977. pap. 23.00 (ISBN 0-88283-016-3). AFIPS Pr.

Di Nardo, Tom. Movies on Tape: Reviews & Ratings of over 500 Movies You Can Buy or Rent. 128p. (Orig.). 1984. pap. 3.95 (ISBN 0-89471-267-5); lib. bdg. 12.90 (ISBN 0-89471-268-3). Running Pr.

Dinca, F. & Teodosiu, C. Nonlinear & Random Vibrations. (Eng.). 1974. 76.50 (ISBN 0-12-216750-3). Acad Pr.

Dincauze, Dena F. Cremation Cemeteries in Eastern Massachusetts. LC 68-2247. (Peabody Museum Papers: Vol. 59, No.1). 1968. pap. 5.00x (ISBN 0-87365-171-5). Peabody Harvard.

--The Neville Site: 8,000 Years at Amoskeag. LC 75-40771. (Peabody Museum Monographs: No. 4). (Illus.). 1976. pap. 12.00x (ISBN 0-87365-903-1). Peabody Harvard.

Dince, Robert R., jt. auth. see Greene, Mark R.

Dincher, Judith R., jt. auth. see Hood, Gail H.

Dinda, R. J., tr. Luther's Works, Vol. 18. 1980. 16.95 (ISBN 0-570-06418-X, 15-001760). Concordia.

Dinda, R. J., jt. tr. see Miller, W. M.

Dindorf, F., ed. see Demosthenes.

Dindorf, G., et al, eds. Tragoediae, Sophocles. cvi, 366p. 15.00 (ISBN 0-89005-425-8). Ares.

Dindot, Victor. You Too Can Understand the Bible: Matthew. 1981. 4.25 (ISBN 0-89536-467-0, 2504). CSS of Ohio.

Dindub, L. Brief History of Mongolia in the Autonomous Period: Mongolian Text with an Introduction & Index in English by John G. Hangin. (Special Papers Ser.: No. 6). spiral bdg. 10.00x (ISBN 0-910980-26-8). Mongolia.

D'Indy, Vincent. Beethoven. Baker, Theodore, tr. LC 74-107808. (Select Bibliographies Reprint Ser). 1913. 18.00 (ISBN 0-8369-5184-0). Ayer Co Pubs.

--Beethoven: A Critical Biography. LC 72-125054. (Music Ser). (Illus.). 1970. Repr. of 1913 ed. lib. bdg. 18.50 (ISBN 0-306-70019-0). Da Capo.

D'Indy, Vincent, ed. see Catel, Charles-Simon.

D'Indy, Vincent, ed. see De Lalande, Michel-Richard & Destouches, Andre-Cardinal.

D'Indy, Vincent, ed. see Franck, Cesar.

D'Indy, Vincent see Rameau, Jean Philippe.

Dine, Jim & Krens, Thomas. Jim Dine Prints, 1970-1977. LC 77-3758. (Icon Editions Ser.). (Illus.). 1977. pap. 14.95i (ISBN 0-06-430083-8, IN-83, HarpT). Har-Row.

Dine, Jim, jt. auth. see Beal, Graham.

Dine, Jim, illus. The Temple of Flora. (Illus.). 136p. 1984. 2,000.00 (ISBN 0-910457-04-2). Arion Pr.

Dine, S. S. Van see Van Dine, S. S.

Dineen, Peter & Hildick-Smith, Gavin, eds. The Surgical Wound. LC 81-8163. (Illus.). 222p. 1981. text ed. 28.00 (ISBN 0-8121-0799-3). Lea & Febiger.

Dineen, S. Complex Analysis in Locally Convex Spaces. (Mathematical Studies Ser.: Vol. 57). 492p. 1982. 59.75 (ISBN 0-444-86319-2, North Holland). Elsevier.

Dineen, S., jt. ed. see Aron, R. M.

Dineley, D. Aspects of Stratigraphical System: The Devonian. 223p. 1984. 34.95 (ISBN 0-470-20086-3). Halsted Pr.

DiNenno, Philip J. Simplified Radiation Heat Transfer Calculations from Large Open Hydrocarbon Fires. 1982. 5.35 (ISBN 0-686-37674-9, TR 82-9). Society Fire Protect.

Diner, Hasia R. Erin's Daughters in America: Irish Immigrant Women in the Nineteenth Century. LC 83-183. (Studies in Historical & Political Science: No. 2). 224p. 1983. pap. 9.95 (ISBN 0-8018-2872-4). Johns Hopkins.

--In the Almost Promised Land: American Jews & Blacks, 1915-1935. LC 76-46767. (Contributions in American History: No. 59). 1977. lib. bdg. 29.95 (ISBN 0-8371-9400-8, DIA/). Greenwood.

Diner, Hasia R., ed. Women & Urban Society: A Guide to Information Sources. LC 78-13109. (Urban Studies Information Guide Ser.: Vol. 7). 1979. 60.00x (ISBN 0-8103-1425-8). Gale.

Diner, Steven J. A City & Its Universities: Public Policy in Chicago, 1892-1919. LC 79-16834. xi, 263p. 1980. 22.50 (ISBN 0-8078-1409-1). U of NC Pr.

Diner, Steven J., jt. ed. see Breul, Frank R.

Dinerman, Miriam, ed. Social Work in a Turbulent Word: Proceedings of Seventh NASW Professional Symposium. LC 83-8216. 208p. 1983. text ed. 15.95 (ISBN 0-87101-108-5). Natl Assn Soc Wkrs.

Dinerman, Miriam & Geisman, Ludwig, eds. Quarter Century of Social Work Education. 300p. 1984. 16.95 (ISBN 0-87101-124-7). Natl Assn Soc Wkrs.

Dinerstein, Herbert S. Fifty Years of Soviet Foreign Policy. LC 68-22278. (Washington Center of Foreign Policy Research Studies in International Affairs: No. 6). pap. 20.80 (ISBN 0-317-08607-3, 2004955). Bks Demand UMI.

--The Making of a Missile Crisis: October 1962. LC 75-36943. 1978. pap. text ed. 8.95x (ISBN 0-8018-2146-0). Johns Hopkins.

--War & the Soviet Union. LC 75-45031. 268p. 1976. Repr. of 1962 ed. lib. bdg. 22.50x (ISBN 0-8371-8658-7, DIWS). Greenwood.

Dinerstein, Nelson. Winning the Information Systems Game: A Manager's Survival Guide. LC 85-70191. 225p. 1985. 25.00 (ISBN 0-87094-642-0). Dow Jones-Irwin.

Dinerstein, Nelson T. Creative Business Applications with dBASE II: A Beginner's Introduction. 160p. 1984. pap. 15.95 (ISBN 0-673-15957-4). Scott F.

--Database & File Management Systems for the Microcomputer. 1984. pap. 15.95 (ISBN 0-673-18088-3). Scott F.

--The dBASE II for the Programmer: A How-to-Do-It Book. 1984. pap. 17.95 (ISBN 0-673-15956-6). Scott F.

--The dBASE III for the Programmer: A How-to-Do-It-Book. 1985. pap. 19.95 (ISBN 0-673-18180-4). Scott F.

--The Dynamics of Framework. 300p. 1985. pap. cancelled (ISBN 0-87094-671-4). Dow Jones-Irwin.

Dines, Aaron, jt. auth. see Institute for Continuing Legal Education (New Jersey) Staff.

Dines, David M., jt. ed. see Goldman, Amy Beth.

Dines, Elaine & Howe, Graham, eds. Paul Outerbridge: A Singular Aesthetic: Photographs & Drawings 1921-1941, a Catalogue Raisonne. (Illus.). 240p. 1981. 115.00 (ISBN 0-87685-540-0). Black Sparrow.

Dines, Glen. Sir Cecil & the Bad Blue Beast. LC 70-125868. (Illus.). (gr. k-2). 1970. 10.95 (ISBN 0-87599-175-0). S G Phillips.

Dinescu, T. A. & Radulescu, C. Slip Form Techniques. 1982. 71.00 (ISBN 0-9961005-4-7, Pub. by Abacus England). Heyden.

Dinesen, Betzy, ed. Rediscovery: Three Hundred Years of Stories by & about Women. 272p. 1982. pap. 3.50 (ISBN 0-380-60756-5, 60756-5, Bard). Avon.

Dinesen, Isak. Anecdotes of Destiny. LC 74-5323. (YA) 1974. pap. 3.95 (ISBN 0-394-71177-7, Vin). Random.

--The Angelic Avengers. LC 75-12973. viii, 304p. 1975. Repr. of 1947 ed. 8.95 (ISBN 0-226-15290-1). U of Chicago Pr.

--Carnival: Entertainments & Posthumous Tales. LC 77-5666. 1979. pap. 9.95 (ISBN 0-226-15304-5, P851). U of Chicago Pr.

--Carnival: Entertainments & Posthumous Tales. Mitchell & Paden, trs. from Danish. LC 77-5666. 1977. 10.00 (ISBN 0-226-15303-7). U of Chicago Pr.

--Daguerreotypes & Other Essays. Mitchell, P. M. & Paden, W. D., trs. LC 78-27543. 1979. pap. 12.95x (ISBN 0-226-15305-3). U of Chicago Pr.

--Daguerreotypes & Other Essays. Mitchell, P. M. & Paden, W. D., trs. LC 78-27543. xxvi, 230p. 1984. pap. 6.95 (ISBN 0-226-15306-1). U of Chicago Pr.

--Ehrengard. LC 74-17033. (YA) 1975. pap. 1.95 (ISBN 0-394-71431-8, Vin). Random.

--Isak Dinesen's Africa: Images of the Wild Continent from the Writer's Life & Words. LC 85-8366. (Illus.). 160p. 1985. 35.00 (ISBN 0-87156-821-7). Sierra.

--Last Tales. 1957. 8.95 (ISBN 0-394-43254-1). Random.

--Last Tales. LC 75-9828. (YA) 1975. pap. 4.95 (ISBN 0-394-71752-X, Vin). Random.

--Letters from Africa, Nineteen Fourteen to Nineteen Thirty-One. Lasson, Frans, ed. Born, Anne, tr. LC 80-25856. (Phoenix). (Illus.). xliii, 474p. 1984. pap. 9.95 (ISBN 0-226-15311-8). U of Chicago Pr.

--Letters from Africa, 1914 to 1931. Lasson, Frans, ed. Born, Anne, tr. LC 80-25856. 1981. 25.00x (ISBN 0-226-15309-6). U of Chicago Pr.

--Out of Africa. 416p. 1972. pap. 4.95 (ISBN 0-394-71740-6, V740, Vin). Random.

--Out of Africa. LC 83-42696. 389p. 8.95 (ISBN 0-394-60498-9). Modern Lib.

--Out of Africa. Bd. with Shadows on the Grass. 1985. 4.95 (ISBN 0-394-74211-7, Vin). Random.

--Seven Gothic Tales. 1972. pap. 4.95 (ISBN 0-394-71807-0, V807, Vin). Random.

--Seven Gothic Tales. LC 39-27353. 6.95 (ISBN 0-394-60496-2). Modern Lib.

--Shadows on the Grass. 160p. 1961. pap. 2.95 (ISBN 0-394-71062-2, Vin). Random.

--Shadows on the Grass. pap. 6.95x (ISBN 0-226-15301-0). U of Chicago Pr.

--Winter's Tales. 1961. pap. 4.95 (ISBN 0-394-70205-0, V205, Vin). Random.

Diness, Madelynne. Northern Oregon Cascades Topographic Atlas. LC 82-84631. (Illus.). 106p. 1983. pap. 12.95 (ISBN 0-916473-00-7). Flying Pubns.

Diness, Madelynne, jt. auth. see Casali, Dan.

Dinger, Charlotte. Art of the Carousel. LC 82-90507. (Illus.). 223p. 1984. 40.00 (ISBN 0-914507-00-1). Carousel Art.

Dingerkus, Guido. The Shark Watcher's Guide. (Illus.). 176p. (gr. 7 up). 1985. 9.79 (ISBN 0-671-50234-4). Messner.

Dingerson, Arthur G. & Dingerson, Marilyn R. Practice Management in Preventive Dentistry. (Illus.). 194p. 1973. 21.50 (ISBN 0-397-50317-2). Har-Row.

Dingerson, Marilyn R., jt. auth. see Dingerson, Arthur G.

Dinges, H., ed. see Conference on Martingales, Oberwolfach Germany, 1970.

Dinges, John & Landau, Saul. Assassination on Embassy Row. (McGraw-Hill Paperbacks Ser.). 432p. 1981. pap. 5.95 (ISBN 0-07-016998-5). McGraw.

Dinges, W. Ray. Natural Systems for Water Pollution Control. (Environmental Engineering Ser.). 352p. 1981. 28.95 (ISBN 0-442-20166-4). Van Nos Reinhold.

Dingle, A. E. The Campaign for Prohibition in Victorian England: The United Kingdom Alliance Eighteen Seventy-Two to Eighteen Ninety-Five. 240p. 1980. 25.00x (ISBN 0-8135-0909-2). Rutgers U Pr.

Dingle, Aylward E. Pipe All Hands! LC 74-101279. (Short Story Index Reprint Ser.). 1935. 20.00 (ISBN 0-8369-3216-1). Ayer Co Pubs.

Dingle, Edwin J. China's Revolution, Nineteen Eleven to Nineteen Twelve. LC 72-3486. (World History Ser., No. 48). (Illus.). 1972. Repr. of 1912 ed. lib. bdg. 59.95x (ISBN 0-8383-1565-8). Haskell.

Dingle, H. & Hegmann, J. P. Evolution & Genetics of Life Histories. (Proceedings in Life Science Ser.). (Illus.). 256p. 1982. 39.50 (ISBN 0-686-97803-X). Springer-Verlag.

Dingle, H., jt. ed. see Denno, R. F.

Dingle, Herbert. Science & Literary Criticism. LC 74-16039. 1974. Repr. of 1949 ed. lib. bdg. 15.00 (ISBN 0-8414-3799-8). Folcroft.

--Science & Literary Criticism. 184p. 1980. Repr. of 1949 ed. lib. bdg. 20.00 (ISBN 0-8492-4212-6). R West.

--Scientific Adventure. facs. ed. LC 71-121462. (Essay Index Reprint Ser). 1953. 24.50 (ISBN 0-8369-1749-9). Ayer Co Pubs.

--Wordsworth in "Science & Literary Criticism". 1949. Repr. 20.00 (ISBN 0-8274-3756-0). R West.

Dingle, J. T., ed. Lysosomes: A Laboratory Handbook. 2nd ed. 324p. 1977. 85.00 (ISBN 0-7204-0627-7, Biomedical Pr). Elsevier.

Dingle, J. T & Fell, H. B., eds. Lysosomes in Biology & Pathology, Vols. 1-6. (Frontiers in Biology Ser.: Vols. 14, 29, 43, 45, 48). 1969-77. Repr. Vol. 1. 128.50 (ISBN 0-444-10501-8, Biomedical Pr); Vol. 2. 146.00 (ISBN 0-444-10502-6); Vol. 3. 122.75 (ISBN 0-444-10405-4); Vol. 4. 155.50 (ISBN 0-444-10810-6); Vol. 5. 113.75 (ISBN 0-444-11204-9); Vol. 6. 146.00 (ISBN 0-7204-0668-4). Elsevier.

Dingle, J. T. & Gordon, J. L., eds. Cellular Interactions. (Research Monographs in Cell & Tissue Physiology: Vol. 6). 296p. 1981. 86.50 (ISBN 0-444-80330-0, Biomedical Pr). Elsevier.

Dingle, J. T., et al. Lysosomes in Biology & Pathology, Vol. 7. 1984. 125.00 (ISBN 0-444-80523-0, I-174-84). Elsevier.

Dingle, R. V., et al. Mesozoic & Tertiary Geology of Southern Africa. 384p. 1983. lib. bdg. 39.50 (ISBN 90-6191-099-4, Pub. by Balkema RSA). IPS.

Dingledine, Raymond, ed. Brain Slices. 437p. 1984. 50.00x (ISBN 0-306-41437-6, Plenum Pr). Plenum Pub.

Dingler, Helen, jt. auth. see Hughes, Harry.

Dingley, Fay, et al. Fidelity of Protein Synthesis & Transfer RNA During Aging. LC 74-5496. 174p. 1975. text ed. 34.50x (ISBN 0-8422-7220-8). Irvington.

Dingley, Robert. Proposals for Establishing a Public Place of Reception for Penitent Prostitutes. LC 83-48597. (Marriage, Sex & the Family in England Ser.). 454p. 1984. lib. bdg. 55.00 (ISBN 0-8240-5921-2). Garland Pub.

--Prostitution Reform. LC 83-48597. 454p. 1985. lib. bdg. 55.00 (ISBN 0-317-19435-6). Garland Pub.

Dingley, Thomas. History from Marble, 2 Vols. LC 70-164834. (Camden Society, London. Publications, First Ser.: Nos. 94 & 97). Repr. of 1868 ed. Set. 74.00 (ISBN 0-404-50210-5). AMS Pr.

--History from Marble Comp. in the Reign of Charles II, 2 Vols. 1867-1868. 74.00 (ISBN 0-384-11780-5). Johnson Repr.

Dingli-Attard, Marcel. The Family of Inguanez. rev., 2nd ed. LC 82-670117. 85p. 1979. pap. 7.50 (Pub. by A C Aquilina). Intl Univ MO.

Dingli-Attard-Iguanez, Marcel V. The Family of Inguanez. 2nd ed. LC 82-670117. (Illus.). 85p. 1979. pap. 25.00. U Intel Data Bank.

Dingli-Attard-Inguanez, Marcel V. Einstein on Peace, Congress, Malta, 1984. 39p. (Orig.). 1984. pap. 25.00 (ISBN 0-9610740-4-3). U Intel Data Bank.

--The International Armorial Register. (Illus.). 380p. 1984. 27.50 (ISBN 0-9610740-0-0). U Intel Data Bank.

Dingli-Attard-Inguanez, Marcel V., ed. International Register of Biographies. LC 83-80106. (Illus.). 364p. 1984. 103.50 (ISBN 0-9610740-1-9). U Intel Data Bank.

Dingli-Attard-Inguanez, Marcel V., ed. see Bosredon de Ransijat, Chevalier.

Dingman, Beth, ed. see Schwarz, Judith.

Dingman, Larry. Bibliography of Limited & Signed Editions in Literature, Twentieth Century American Authors. 1973 ed. 15.00 (ISBN 0-87018-069-X). Ross.

Dingman, Reed O. & Natvig, Paul. Surgery of Facial Fractures. LC 63-14507. (Illus.). 1964. 47.00 (ISBN 0-7216-3085-5). Saunders.

Dingman, Richard. Patterns. (Illus.). 450p. (Orig.). 1984. pap. 32.00 (ISBN 0-9613432-0-6). Mind-Dog.

Dingman, Roger. Power in the Pacific: The Origins of Naval Arms Limitation, 1914-1922. LC 75-36402. 1976. lib. bdg. 22.50x (ISBN 0-226-15331-2). U of Chicago Pr.

Dingman, S. Lawrence. Fluvial Hydrology. 1983. text ed. 31.95 (ISBN 0-7167-1452-3); pap. text ed. write for info (ISBN 0-7167-1453-1). W H Freeman.

Dings, John G. The Mind in Its Place: Wordsworth, "Michael" & the Poetry of 1800. (Salzburg Studies in English Literature, Romantic Reassessment: No.8). 1973. pap. text ed. 25.50x (ISBN 0-391-01361-0). Humanities.

Dingus, Anne, ed. The Book of Texas Lists. 1982. 220 pp. 15.00, (ISBN 0-932012-17-5); pap. 6.95, 208 pp. (ISBN 0-932012-41-8). Texas Month Pr.

Dingus, L. R; see Whiting, B. J.

Dingus, Rick. The Photographic Artifacts of Timothy O'Sullivan. (Illus.). 224p. 1982. 45.00 (ISBN 0-8263-0607-1, P-52). U of NM Pr.

Dingus, S. D., jt. auth. see McCorkle, Ruth M.

Dingwall, E. J. Ghosts & Spirits in the Ancient World. 59.95 (ISBN 0-8490-0233-8). Gordon Pr.

Dingwall, Eric J. The American Woman: A Historical Study. 1976. Repr. of 1957 ed. lib. bdg. 20.00x (ISBN 0-374-92190-3). Octagon.

--Racial Pride & Prejudice. LC 78-32177. 1979. Repr. of 1946 ed. lib. bdg. 21.25x (ISBN 0-8371-5940-7, DIR&). Greenwood.

Dingwall, Eric J., jt. auth. see Angoff, Allan.

Dingwall, Eric J., jt. auth. see Price, Harry.

Dingwall, James, tr. see Menger, Carl.

Dingwall, Robert. Aspects of Illness. LC 76-39652. 1977. 22.50 (ISBN 0-312-05687-7). St Martin.

--The Social Organization of Health Visitor Training. 249p. 1977. 30.00x (ISBN 0-85664-432-3, Pub. by Croom Helm Ltd). Longwood Pub Group.

Dingwall, Robert & Lewis, Philip. The Sociology of the Professions. LC 82-3352. 244p. 1983. 25.00x (ISBN 0-312-74075-1). St Martin.

Dingwall, Robert, et al. The Protection of Children: State Intervention & Family Life. 296p. 1985. 49.95x (ISBN 0-631-13105-1); pap. 9.95 (ISBN 0-631-13608-8). Basil Blackwell.

Dingwall, Robert, et al, eds. Health Care & Health Knowledge. LC 76-55745. 1977. lib. bdg. 22.50 (ISBN 0-88202-113-3). Watson Pub Intl.

Dingwall, Robert J. The Garden Answers. LC 77-93696. (Illus.). 1978. pap. 6.95 (ISBN 0-87445-001-2). Cadillac.

Dingwall, William O. Language & the Brain, 2 vols. LC 80-8491. 1981. lib. bdg. 121.00 (ISBN 0-8240-9495-6). Garland Pub.

Dingwaney, Manjari, jt. ed. see Patnaik, Utes.

Dingwell, Eric J. Abnormal Hypnotic Phenomena, a Survey of Nineteenth-Century Cases, Vol. 1: France. LC 68-85483. pap. 86.00 (ISBN 0-317-10970-7, 2003094). Bks Demand UMI.

Dingwell, Eric J., ed. see Zorab, G., et al.

Dingwell, Joyce. L' Annee du Dragon. (Harlequin Romantique Ser.). 192p. 1983. pap. 1.95 (ISBN 0-373-41203-7). Harlequin Bks.

--Brother Wolf. (Harlequin Romances Ser.). 192p. 1984. pap. 1.75 (ISBN 0-373-02600-5). Harlequin Bks.

--Lumiere D'Or. (Harlequin Romantique Ser.). 192p. 1983. pap. 1.95 (ISBN 0-373-41214-2). Harlequin Bks.

--Melodie du Vent. (Harlequin Romantique). 192p. 1983. pap. 1.95 (ISBN 0-373-41180-4). Harlequin Bks.

--Red Ginger Blossom, Wife to Sim: The Pool of Pink Lilies. (Harlequin Romances Ser.). 576p. 1982. pap. 3.50 (ISBN 0-373-20057-9). Harlequin Bks.

--A Thousand Candles: The Mutual Look & There Were Three Princes. (Harlequin Romances Ser.: 3 vols. in 1). 576p. 1983. pap. 3.95 (ISBN 0-373-20074-9). Harlequin Bks.

--La Vallee des Promesses. (Harlequin Romantique Ser.). 192p. 1983. pap. 1.95 (ISBN 0-373-41197-9). Harlequin Bks.

Dinh, Hinh T. Oil & Gas Policies in Tunisia: A Macroeconomic Analysis. (Staff Working Paper: No. 674). 88p. 1985. 5.00 (ISBN 0-318-11905-6, WP 0674). World Bank.

Dinh, Tran Van see Van Dinh, Tran.

Dinha, V. R. The European Freshwater Eel. 134p. 1975. 50.00x (ISBN 0-85323-190-7, Pub. by Liverpool Univ England). State Mutual Bk.

Dinham, Barbara & Hines, Colin. Agribusiness in Africa. (Illus.). 224p. 1983. pap. 9.95 (ISBN 0-317-02666-6). Inst Food & Develop.

Dinham, Barbara, et al. Agribusiness in Africa. 224p. 29.95 (ISBN 0-86543-003-9); pap. text ed. 9.95 (ISBN 0-86543-004-7). Africa Res.

Dini, Gary. The Heart That Followed Me Home. (Illus.). 32p. (gr. 2-5). 1983. pap. 1.95 (ISBN 0-8091-6548-1). Paulist Pr.

Dini, Massimo, ed. Renzo Piano: Buildings & Projects 1964-1983. LC 83-42993. (Illus.). 252p. 1984. pap. 25.00 (ISBN 0-8478-0513-1). Rizzoli Intl.

DiNicola, Albert. Dear David: Prisons & Capital Punishment: A Needed, Balanced Fresh Approach. LC 83-91068. 68p. (Orig.). 1983. write for info (ISBN 0-9611722-1-5); pap. write for info. (ISBN 0-9611722-0-7). Lumen Series.

--Dear David: Prisons & Capital Punishment-A Needed, Balanced Fresh Approach. 2nd ed. (Orig.). 1986. price not set; pap. price not set. Lumen Series.

--Take a Break, Vol. 1. 44p. (Orig.). 1984. pap. 4.00 (ISBN 0-9611722-2-3). Lumen Series.

--Take a Break, Vol. 1. 2nd ed. (Orig.). 1986. pap. price not set. Lumen Series.

DiNicola, D. Dante, jt. auth. see DiMatteo, M. Robin.

Dinin, Denise, ed. see Ritch, Barbara A. & Ficke, Mary M.

Dinin, Samuel. Judaism in a Changing Civilization. LC 70-176722. (Columbia University. Teachers College. Contributions to Education: No. 563). Repr. of 1933 ed. 22.50 (ISBN 0-404-55563-2). AMS Pr.

DiNitto, Diana M. & Dye, Thomas R. Social Welfare Politics & Public Policy. (Illus.). 352p. 1983. text ed. 27.95 (ISBN 0-13-819474-2). P-H.

Dinitz, Simon, jt. auth. see Conrad, John P.

Dinitz, Simon, jt. auth. see Reckless, Walter C.

Dinitz, Simon, jt. auth. see Miller, Stuart J.

Dinitz, Simon, et al, eds. Deviance: Studies in Definition, Management, & Treatment. 2nd ed. (Illus.). 1975. pap. 13.95x (ISBN 0-19-501924-5). Oxford U Pr.

Dinkel, Alvin L. Glass Cutting Techniques. (Illus., Orig.). 1978. pap. 2.00 (ISBN 0-916552-18-7). Acoma Bks.

Dinkel, John J. & Kochenberger, Gary A. Using Management Science: A Workbook, Vol. 1. LC 79-67422. (Illus.). 234p. (Orig.). 1980. 10.95x (ISBN 0-931920-15-9). Dame Pubns.

Dinkelspiel, John R. & Uchenick, Joel. Condominiums: The Effects of Conversion on a Community. LC 80-39894. 224p. 1981. 24.95 (ISBN 0-86569-059-6). Auburn Hse.

Dinkin, Eleanor & Urbont, Rosalind. Parallel Play: A Guide to Playground Exercise. LC 78-23450. (Illus.). 208p. 1978. 18.95x (ISBN 0-88229-424-5). Nelson-Hall.

Dinkin, Robert J. Voting in Provincial America: A Study of Elections in the Thirteen Colonies, 1689-1776. LC 77-71861. (Contributions in American History: No. 64). (Illus.). 1977. lib. bdg. 29.95 (ISBN 0-8371-9543-8, DIV/). Greenwood.

--Voting in Revolutionary America: A Study of Elections in the Original Thirteen States, 1776-1789. LC 81-13266. (Contributions in American History Ser.: No. 99). (Illus.). x, 184p. 1982. lib. bdg. 29.95 (ISBN 0-313-23091-9, DVR/). Greenwood.

Dinkins, James. By an Old Johnnie. (Illus.). 1975. Repr. 15.00 (ISBN 0-89029-024-5). Pr of Morningside.

Dinkins, Lloyd. From Patch to Pot. 1977. spiral bdg. 4.95 (ISBN 0-918544-01-7). Wimmer Bks.

Dinkle, John. The Royal Pavilion, Brighton. LC 83-14676. (Illus.). 144p. 1983. 19.95 (ISBN 0-86565-035-7). Vendome.

Dinklocker, Christina. Typing for Tots. (Illus.). 24p. (gr. 1-9). 1983. pap. 3.95 Tchr Enrichment Bk (ISBN 0-88047-019-4, 8305). DOK Pubs.

Dinkmeyer, Don & Dreikurs, Rudolf. Encouraging Children to Learn. LC 79-84205. 1979. pap. 4.95 (ISBN 0-8015-2333-8, Hawthorn). Dutton.

Dinkmeyer, Don & Losoncy, Lewis E. The Encouragement Book: Becoming a Positive Person. 336p. 1980. 12.95 (ISBN 0-13-274647-6); pap. 7.95 (ISBN 0-13-274639-5). P-H.
Dinkmeyer, Don & McKay, Gary. Padres Eficaces con Entrenamiento Sistematico (PECES) Libro de los padres. De Barranco, Clara, tr. from Eng. (Illus., Span.). 1981. pap. text ed. 8.50 (ISBN 0-913476-78-1). Am Guidance.
--Systematic Training for Effective Teaching (STET) Leader's Manual. 149p. 1980. Vinyl Cover 26.50 (ISBN 0-913476-74-9). Am Guidance.
Dinkmeyer, Don & McKay, Gary D. Padres Eficaces con Entrenamiento Sistematico (PECES) (Span.). leaders manual 28.00 (ISBN 0-913476-87-0). Am Guidance.
--The Parents Guide: The Step Approach to Parenting Your Teens. LC 82-74294. (Illus.). 192p. 1984. pap. 7.95 (ISBN 0-394-72771-1). Random.
--The Parent's Handbook: Systematic Training for Effective Parenting (STEP) (Illus.). 120p. 1982. pap. 8.50 (ISBN 0-913476-80-3). Am Guidance.
--The Parent's Handbook: Systematic Training for Effective Parenting (STEP) 1982. pap. 6.95 (ISBN 0-394-71031-2). Random.
--Raising a Responsible Child: Practical Steps to Successful Family Relationships. LC 72-86989. 1973. 11.95 (ISBN 0-671-21445-4). S&S.
Dinkmeyer, Don, et al. Consultation in Schools. 350p. Date not set. pap. text ed. cancelled (ISBN 0-915202-42-5). Accel Devel.
--Systematic Training for Effective Teaching: Teacher's Handbook. (Illus.). 291p. (Orig.). 1980. pap. text ed. 14.50 (ISBN 0-913476-75-7). Am Guidance.
--Systematic Training for Effective Parenting of Teens-Step-Teen: The Parents Guide. LC 82-74394. (Illus.). 160p. 1983. pap. text ed. 8.50 (ISBN 0-913476-82-X). Am Guidance.
--Systematic Training for Effective Parenting of Teens-Step-Teen: Leader's Guide. 135p. 1983. pap. text ed. 25.50 (ISBN 0-913476-83-8). Am Guidance.
--Systematic Training for Effective Teaching (STET) Teacher's Resource Book: Activities for Teachers & Students. (Illus.). 161p. (Orig.). 1980. pap. 8.25 (ISBN 0-913476-76-5). Am Guidance.
Dinkmeyer, Don C. & Carlson, Jon. Consultation: A Book of Readings. LC 74-34048. Repr. of 1975 ed. 59.90 (ISBN 0-8357-9866-6, 2016465). Bks Demand UMI.
Dinkmeyer, Don C., jt. auth. see Muro, James J.
Dinkmeyer, Don Dr. & McKay, Gary Dr. Raising a Responsible Child: Practical Steps to a Successful Family Relationships. 256p. 1982. pap. 7.50 (ISBN 0-671-44749-1, Fireside). S&S.
Dinkmeyer, Don, Sr., et al. PREP for Effective Family Living. (YA) 1985. 79.50 (ISBN 0-88671-225-4). Am Guidance.
--PREP for Effective Family Living: Student Handbook. (PREP Ser.). 1985. pap. 6.95 (ISBN 0-88671-226-2); pap. text ed. 14.95 (ISBN 0-88671-227-0); tchr's. ed. 24.95 (ISBN 0-88671-229-7); activity bk 4.25 (ISBN 0-88671-228-9). Am Guidance.
Dinman, Bertram D. The Nature of Occupational Cancer: A Critical Review of Present Problems. 112p. 1974. 15.75x (ISBN 0-398-02907-5). C C Thomas.
Dinn, Freda. Early Music for Recorders: An Introduction & Guide to Its Interpretation, & History, for Amateurs. 1974. pap. 12.00 (ISBN 0-901938-07-6, 75 A 11155). Eur-Am Music.
Dinnage, James, jt. auth. see Parry, Anthony.
Dinnar, Uri. Cardiovascular Fluid Dynamics. 264p. 1981. 79.00 (ISBN 0-8493-5573-7). CRC Pr.
Dinneen. Irish-English Dictionary. (Irish & Eng.). 25.00x (ISBN 0-686-12048-5). Colton Bk.
Dinneen, Betty. The Family Howl. LC 80-25385. (Illus.). 96p. (gr. 4-7). 1981. 8.95 (ISBN 0-02-732150-9). Macmillan.
--Striped Horses: The Story of a Zebra Family. LC 82-7786. (Illus.). 96p. (gr. 4-6). 1982. 9.95 (ISBN 0-02-732200-9). Macmillan.
Dinneen, F. P., ed. Georgetown University Round Table on Languages & Linguistics: Linguistics-Teaching & Interdisciplinary Relations. LC 58-31607. (Georgetown Univ. Round Table Ser.: 1974). 197p. (GURT 1974). 1974. pap. 4.95 (ISBN 0-87840-109-1). Georgetown U Pr.
Dinneen, Francis P. An Introduction to General Linguistics. LC 78-1323. 452p. 1978. pap. text ed. 12.95 (ISBN 0-87840-172-5). Georgetown U Pr.
Dinneen, Joseph. Ward Eight. LC 76-6335. (Irish Americans Ser). 1976. Repr. of 1936 ed. 26.50 (ISBN 0-405-09331-4). Ayer Co Pubs.
Dinneen, L. Titles of Addresses in Christian Greek Epistolography. 114p. 1980. 15.00 (ISBN 0-89005-376-6). Ares.
Dinneen, Patrick S. English-Irish Dictionary. rev. ed. Murcava, L. O., ed. (Eng. & Irish.). 24.50 (ISBN 0-87559-072-1); thumb indexed 29.50 (ISBN 0-87559-040-3). Shalom.
Dinneen, Patrick S., ed. see O'Rahilly, Egan.
Dinneen, Patrick S., rev. by. Irish-English Dictionary. (Irish & Eng.). 26.50 (ISBN 0-87559-070-5); thumb indexed 31.50 (ISBN 0-685-32982-8, 071-3). Shalom.
Dinner, Joan, jt. auth. see Riddle, Janet T.

Dinnerstein, Dorothy. The Mermaid & the Minotaur: Sexual Arrangements & Human Malaise. LC 72-23879. 1977. pap. 6.68i (ISBN 0-06-090587-5, CN 587, CN). Har-Row.
Dinnerstein, Harvey. Harvey Dinnerstein: Artist at Work. (Illus.). 144p. 1978. 19.95 (ISBN 0-8230-2210-2). Watson-Guptill.
Dinnerstein, Leonard. America & the Survivors of the Holocaust. LC 81-15443. (Contemporary American History Ser.). 222p. 1982. 24.00x (ISBN 0-231-04176-4). Columbia U Pr.
Dinnerstein, Leonard & Reimers, David M. Ethnic Americans: A History of Immigration & Assimilation. 2nd ed. 174p. 1981. pap. text ed. 11.50 scp (ISBN 0-06-041647-5, HarpC). Har-Row.
--Ethnic Americans: A History of Immigration & Assimilation. LC 77-4352. 184p. 1977. 22.00x (ISBN 0-8147-1762-4). NYU Pr.
Dinnerstein, Leonard & Jackson, Kenneth T., eds. American Vistas: 1600-1877. 4th ed. 1983. pap. 9.95x (ISBN 0-19-503164-4). Oxford U Pr.
--American Vistas: 1877 to the Present. 4th ed. 1983. pap. 9.95 (ISBN 0-19-503166-0). Oxford U Pr.
Dinnerstein, Leonard & Palsson, Mary D., eds. Jews in the South. LC 72-89114. viii, 392p. 1973. 32.50x (ISBN 0-8071-0226-1). La State U Pr.
Dinnerstein, Leonard, et al. Natives & Strangers: Ethnic Groups & the Building of America. LC 78-2415. (Illus.). 1979. 22.50x (ISBN 0-19-502426-5); pap. text ed. 7.95x (ISBN 0-19-502427-3). Oxford U Pr.
Dinninger, Donald. Shield of Faith Behind Badge 88. 1985. 3.95 (ISBN 0-89536-949-4, 7557). CSS of Ohio.
Dinnis, Enid M. Traveller's Tales. LC 72-5908. (Short Story Index Reprint Ser.). Repr. of 1927 ed. 13.50 (ISBN 0-8369-4211-6). Ayer Co Pubs.
Dinno, Mumtaz A. & Callahan, Arthur B. Membrane Biophysics: Structure & Function in Epithelia. LC 81-14318. (Progress in Clinical & Biological Research Ser.: Vol. 73). 332p. 1981. 33.00 (ISBN 0-8451-0073-4). A R Liss.
Dinno, Mumtaz A., et al. Membrane Biophysics: Vol. II: Physical Methods in the Study of Epithelia. LC 83-9862. (Progress in Clinical & Biological Research Ser.: Vol. 126). 392p. 1983. 48.00 (ISBN 0-8451-0126-9). A R Liss.
Dinnsen, Daniel A., ed. Current Approaches to Phonological Theory. LC 78-3241. 352p. 1979. 25.00x (ISBN 0-253-31596-4). Ind U Pr.
Dinoff, Michael, jt. auth. see Rickard, Henry C.
Dinoff, Michael, jt. ed. see Divic, Josif M.
Dinoff, Michael, et al. Psychotherapy: the Promised Land. LC 77-324. 142p. 1977. 11.00 (ISBN 0-8173-2730-4). U of Ala Pr.
Dinoff, Michael L. & Jacobson, Douglas L., eds. Neglected Problems in the Community Mental Health. LC 80-22984. xii, 231p. 1981. text ed. 25.00 (ISBN 0-8173-0061-9). U of Ala Pr.
Di Nola, Alfonso, ed. Prayers of Man. 1960. 20.00 (ISBN 0-8392-1152-X). Astor-Honor.
Dinoso, Vicente P., jt. ed. see Clearfield, Harris R.
DiNoto, Andrea. Art Plastic: Designed for Living. LC 83-73418. (Illus.). 228p. 1984. 45.00 (ISBN 0-89659-437-8). Abbeville Pr.
Dinsdale, Alfred. First Principles of Television. LC 76-161141. (History of Broadcasting: Radio to Television Ser). (Illus.). 1971. Repr. of 1932 ed. 25.50 (ISBN 0-405-03562-4). Ayer Co Pubs.
Dinsdale, J., jt. auth. see Nicolello, L. G.
Dinsdale, Tim. Loch Ness Monster. 4th ed. (Illus.). 208p. (Orig.). 1982. pap. 7.95 (ISBN 0-7100-9022-6). Routledge & Kegan.
Dinsker, Syewart B., et al, eds. The Unstable Spine: Thoracic, Lumbar, & Sacral Regions. LC 79-1095. 1985. price not set (ISBN 0-8089-1757-9). Grune.
Dinsmoor, W. Bell. The Architecture of Ancient Greece. LC 73-12401. 1973. 24.00x (ISBN 0-8196-0283-3). Biblo.
Dinsmoor, William B. Architecture of Ancient Greece. (Illus.). 424p. 1975. pap. 16.95 (ISBN 0-393-00781-2, Norton Lib). Norton.
--Athenian Archon List in the Light of Recent Discoveries. LC 74-114512. (Illus.). 274p. 1974. Repr. of 1939 ed. lib. bdg. 20.75x (ISBN 0-8371-4735-2, DIAA). Greenwood.
Dinsmoor, William B., Jr. The Propylaia to the Athenian Akropolis Vol. 1: The Predecessors. LC 79-9232. (Illus.). 1980. 12.50x (ISBN 0-87661-940-5). Am Sch Athens.
Dinsmoor, William B., Jr., jt. auth. see Camp, John M., II.
Dinsmore, Charles A. Atonement in Literature & Life. 1973. Repr. of 1906 ed. 25.00 (ISBN 0-8274-1637-7). R West.
--Dante: Teachings & Aids, 2 vols. 250.00 (ISBN 0-87968-994-3). Gordon Pr.
--The English Bible as Literature. 1931. Repr. 30.00 (ISBN 0-8274-3832-X). R West.
--Great Poets & the Meaning of Life. facs. ed. LC 68-58786. (Essay Index Reprint Ser.). 1937. 18.00 (ISBN 0-8369-0109-6). Ayer Co Pubs.
--The Great Poets & the Meaning of Life. 1937. Repr. 15.50 (ISBN 0-8274-2447-7). R West.
--Teachings of Dante. facs. ed. (Select Bibliographies Reprint Ser.). 1901. 17.00 (ISBN 0-8369-5521-8). Ayer Co Pubs.

Dinsmore, Charles A., compiled by. Aids to the Study of Dante. 1903. 25.50 (ISBN 0-8337-4078-4). B Franklin.
Dinsmore, Herman. The Bleeding of America. 3rd ed. 1977. pap. 3.00 (ISBN 0-88279-126-5). Western Islands.
Dinsmore, James J., et al. Iowa Birds. (Illus.). 356p. 1984. 27.95 (ISBN 0-8138-0206-7). Iowa St U Pr.
Dinsmore, John. The Inheritance of Presupposition. (Pragmatics & Beyond Ser.: II: 1). 98p. (Orig.). 1981. pap. 16.00 (ISBN 90-272-2511-7, Pub. by Benjamins Holland). Benjamins North Am.
Dinsmore, M. H. What Really Happened When Christ Died. LC 79-52539. 1979. pap. 4.95 (ISBN 0-89636-025-3). Accent Bks.
Dinsmore, Timothy G. The Jesse Livermore's Stock Market Games & Tricks for Maximal Speculative Profits. (Illus.). 117p. 1982. 67.85x (ISBN 0-86654-025-3). Inst Econ Finan.
Dinsmore, William. Hear Me, White Man! 1985. 8.95 (ISBN 0-533-06621-2). Vantage.
Dinstein, Yoram, ed. Models of Autonomy. LC 81-11479. 303p. 1982. 39.95 (ISBN 0-87855-435-1). Transaction Bks.
Dintenfass, L. Blood Viscosity. 1985. lib. bdg. 65.00 (ISBN 0-85200-413-3, Pub. by MTP Pr England). Kluwer-Academic.
Dintenfass, L. & Dintenfass, L., eds. Blood Viscosity in Heart Disease & Cancer: Proceedings. (Illus.). 192p. 1981. 40.00 (ISBN 0-08-024954-X). Pergamon.
Dintenfass, Leopold. Hyperviscosity in Hypertension. (Illus.). 192p. 1981. 42.00 (ISBN 0-08-024816-0). Pergamon.
Dintenfass, Mark. Old World, New World. LC 81-14044. 480p. 1982. 14.50 (ISBN 0-688-00811-9). Morrow.
--Old World, New World. 416p. (Orig.). 1985. pap. 3.95 (ISBN 0-553-23023-9). Bantam.
Dinter, E. & Griffith, P. Not Over by Christmas: NATO's Central Front in World War III. (Illus.). 216p. 1983. 17.95 (ISBN 0-88254-876-X, Pub. by A Bird England). Hippocrene Bks.
Dinter, Wolfgang. Waldgesellschaften der Neiderrheinischen Sandplatten, No. 64. (Dissertationes Botanicae). (Illus.). 112p. 1982. pap. text ed. 17.50x (ISBN 3-7682-1325-0). Lubrecht & Cramer.
Dintiman, George & Greenberg, Jerrold. Health Through Discovery. 3rd ed. 508p. 1986. pap. text ed. 19.95 (ISBN 0-394-35426-5). Random.
Dintiman, George, jt. auth. see Unitas, John.
Dintiman, George, et al. Discovering Lifetime Fitness: Concepts of Excercise & Weight Control. 350p. 1984. pap. text ed. 16.95 (ISBN 0-314-69646-6); instrs.' manual avail. (ISBN 0-314-77895-0). West Pub.
Dintiman, George B. How to Run Faster. LC 82-81448. (Illus.). 160p. (Orig.). 1984. pap. 9.95 (ISBN 0-88011-057-0). Leisure Pr.
--How to Run Faster: A Do-It-Yourself Book for Athletes in All Sports. LC 76-54436. (Illus.). 60p. 1979. text ed. 3.25 (ISBN 0-686-70704-4). Champion Athle.
Dintiman, George B. & Greenberg, Jerrold S. Health Through Discovery. 608p. 1983. pap. text ed. 20.95 (ISBN 0-394-34879-6, RanC). Random.
Dintiman, George B., et al. A Comprehensive Manual of Foundations & Physical Education Activities for Men & Women. (Orig.). 1979. pap. text ed. 18.95x (ISBN 0-8087-0486-9). Burgess.
--Doctor Tennis: A Complete Guide to Conditioning & Injury Prevention for All Ages. LC 80-65623. (Illus.). 106p. (Orig.). 1980. text ed. 4.95 (ISBN 0-938074-00-8). Champion Athlete.
Dintino, Justin J. & Martens, Frederick T. Police Intelligence Systems in Crime Control: Maintaining a Delicate Balance in a Liberal Democracy. (Illus.). 176p. 1983. 19.75x (ISBN 0-398-04830-4). C C Thomas.
DiNunzio, Michael G. Adirondack Wildguide: A Natural History of the Adirondack Park. 2nd ed. Kastner, Joseph, ed. (Illus.). 160p. 1984. 24.50 (ISBN 0-9613403-0-4); pap. 17.95 (ISBN 0-9613403-1-2). Adiron Conserv.
DiNunzio, Sylvester L. The Priesthood & Humanity. 1984. 8.50 (ISBN 0-8062-2379-0). Carlton.
Dinwiddie, Dottie, jt. ed. see Shurden, Kay W.
Dinwiddie, Elza, jt. auth. see Erwin, Bette J.
Dinwiddie, Robert. The Official Records of Robert Dinwiddie, Vols. 1 & 2. LC 77-164836. (Illus.). Repr. of 1883 ed. Set. 60.00 (ISBN 0-404-02135-2). AMS Pr.
Dinwiddy, Caroline. Elementary Mathematics for Economists. 1967. pap. 8.95x (ISBN 0-19-644047-5). Oxford U Pr.
Dinwiddy, J. R. The Correspondence of Jeremy Bentham: January 1798 to December 1801, Vol. 6. (The Collected Works of Jeremy Bentham Ser.). 1984. 64.00x (ISBN 0-19-822613-6). Oxford U Pr.
Dio Cassius. Roman History, 9 vols. Incl. Vol. 1 (ISBN 0-674-99036-6); Vol. 2 (ISBN 0-674-99041-2); Vol. 3 (ISBN 0-674-99059-5); Vol. 4 (ISBN 0-674-99073-0); Vol. 5 (ISBN 0-674-99091-9); Vol. 6 (ISBN 0-674-99092-7); Vol. 7 (ISBN 0-674-99193-1); Vol. 8 (ISBN 0-674-99195-8); Vol. 9 (ISBN 0-674-99196-6). (Loeb Classical Library: No. 32, 37, 53, 66, 82, 83, 175-177). 12.50x ea. Harvard U Pr.

Dio Chrysostom. Discourses, 5 Vols. (Loeb Classical Library: No. 257, 339, 358, 376, 385). 12.50x ea. Vol. 1 (ISBN 0-674-99283-0). Vol. 2 (ISBN 0-674-99374-8). Vol. 3 (ISBN 0-674-99395-0). Vol. 4 (ISBN 0-674-99414-0). Vol. 5 (ISBN 0-674-99424-8). Harvard U Pr.
Dio Chrysoston see Hadas, Moses.
Diodorus, jt. auth. see Xenophon.
Diodorus Siculus. Library of History, 12 vols. Incl. Vol. 1 (ISBN 0-674-99307-1); Vol. 2 (ISBN 0-674-99334-9); Vol. 3 (ISBN 0-674-99375-6); Vol. 4 (ISBN 0-674-99413-2); Vol. 5 (ISBN 0-674-99422-1); Vol. 6 (ISBN 0-674-99439-6); Vol. 7 (ISBN 0-674-99428-0); Vol. 8 (ISBN 0-674-99464-7); Vol. 9 (ISBN 0-674-99415-9); Vol. 10 (ISBN 0-674-99429-9); Vol. 11 (ISBN 0-674-99450-7); Vol. 12 (ISBN 0-674-99465-5). (Loeb Classical Library: No. 279, 303, 340, 375, 377, 384, 389, 390, 399, 409, 422, 423). 12.50x ea. Harvard U Pr.
Diogenes, Laertius. La Vie De Pythagore De Diogene Laerce. Vlastos, Gregory, ed. LC 78-19342. (Morals & Law in Ancient Greece Ser.). 1979. Repr. of 1922 ed. lib. bdg. 21.00x (ISBN 0-405-11537-7). Ayer Co Pubs.
Diogenes, the Cynic, jt. auth. see Heraclitus of Ephesius.
Diogenes Laertius. Lives of Eminent Philosophers, 2 Vols. (Loeb Classical Library: No. 184-185). 12.50x ea. Vol. 1 (ISBN 0-674-99203-2). Vol. 2 (ISBN 0-674-99204-0). Harvard U Pr.
Dioguardi, Nicola, ed. see European Symposium on Medical Enzymology - 1st - Milan - 1960.
Diole, Philippe. The Forgotten People of the Pacific. Bernard, Jack, tr. from Fr. LC 77-6830. 1978. 12.95 (ISBN 0-8120-5129-7). Barron.
Diole, Philippe, jt. auth. see Cousteau, Jacques-Yves.
Diomedi, Alexander. Sketches of Indian Life in the Pacific Northwest. 1978. 12.00 (ISBN 0-87770-199-7). Ye Galleon.
Dion, Bernard A. Locally Least-Cost Error Correctors for Context-Free & Context-Sensitive Parsers. Stone, Harold, ed. LC 82-8397. (Computer Science: Systems Programming Ser.: No. 14). 102p. 1982. 34.95 (ISBN 0-8357-1358-X). UMI Res Pr.
Dion, Gerard. Dictionnaire Canadien des Relations du Travail: Francais-Anglais. 682p. (Eng. & Fr.). 1976. 49.95 (ISBN 0-686-57118-5, M-6163). French & Eur.
--Vocabulaire Francais-Anglais Des Relations Professionnelles. 2nd ed. 350p. (Fr.-Eng.). 1975. 7.95 (ISBN 0-686-57266-1, M-4655). French & Eur.
Dion, Leon. Quebec: The Unfinished Revolution. rev. & enl. ed. 1976. text ed. 20.00x (ISBN 0-7735-0242-4); pap. 8.95 (ISBN 0-7735-0279-3). McGill-Queens U Pr.
Dionetti, Michelle. Drums Do Beat at Night. 1985. price not set (ISBN 0-670-80780-X). Viking.
Dionigi, R., jt. ed. see Bozzetti, F.
Dionigi, R., et al, eds. European Surgical Research, 17th Congress, Stresa, May 1982: Abstracts. (Journal: European Surgical Research: Vol. 14, No. 2). (Illus.). 120p. 1982. pap. 29.25 (ISBN 3-8055-3558-9). S Karger.
Dionisopoulos, P. Allan. Rebellion, Racism, & Representation: The Adam Clayton Powell Case & Its Antecedents. LC 76-125335. 175p. 1970. 8.50 (ISBN 0-87580-018-1); pap. 3.50 (ISBN 0-87580-504-3). N Ill U Pr.
Dionne, J. Robert. The Papacy & the Church: A Study of Praxis & Reception in Ecumenical Perspective. LC 85-9319. 1985. 29.95 (ISBN 0-8022-2494-6). Philos Lib.
Dionne, James R. Pascal & Nietzsche: Etude Historique & Comparee. LC 74-3300. (Fr.). 1976. lib. bdg. 18.00 (ISBN 0-89102-032-2). B Franklin.
Dionne, Leah. Love Notes. 160p. 1984. pap. 1.95 (ISBN 0-441-49702-0). Ace Bks.
Dionne, Narcisse E. Inventaire Chronologique des Ouvrages Publies a l'Etranger en Diverses Langues sur Quebec et la Nouvelle France, 5 vols. in 2. 1969. 45.50 (ISBN 0-8337-0866-X). B Franklin.
--Inventaire chronologique des livres, 5 pts. in 1 vol. LC 70-164837. Repr. of 1912 ed. 45.00 (ISBN 0-404-02138-7). AMS Pr.
Dionne, Rene & Fitzgerald, Michael. Catalysts. 308p. 1980. 5.95 (ISBN 0-318-14910-9). Missionaries Africa.
Dionne, Roger, jt. auth. see Sklansky, David.
Dionnet, Georges. Le Neomercantilisme Au Dix-Huitieme Siecle et Au Debut Du Dix-Neuvieme Siecle. LC 73-146140. (Research & Source Works Ser.: No. 625). 1971. Repr. of 1901 ed. lib. bdg. 21.00 (ISBN 0-8337-0867-8). B Franklin.
Dionysius Of Fourna. Manuel d'iconographie Chretienne, Grecque et Latine. Durand, Paul, tr. 1963. Repr. of 1845 ed. 32.00 (ISBN 0-8337-0868-6). B Franklin.
Dionysius Of Halicarnassus. Critical Essays, Vol. I. Usher, Stephen, tr. from Gr. (Loeb Classical Library: No. 465). 640p. (Eng.). 1974. text ed. 12.50x (ISBN 0-674-99512-0). Harvard U Pr.
--Dionysius of Halicarnassus On Literary Composition. Roberts, W. Rhys, ed. & tr. LC 75-41075. Repr. of 1910 ed. 27.00 (ISBN 0-404-14533-7). AMS Pr.

--Roman Antiquities, Vols. 1-7. (Loeb Classical Library: No. 319, 347, 357, 364, 372, 378, 388). 12.50x ea. Vol. 1 (ISBN 0-674-99352-7). Vol. 2 (ISBN 0-674-99382-9). Vol. 3 (ISBN 0-674-99394-2). Vol. 4 (ISBN 0-674-99401-9). Vol. 5 (ISBN 0-674-99410-8). Vol. 6 (ISBN 0-674-99416-7). Vol. 7 (ISBN 0-674-99427-2). Harvard U Pr.

Diop, Aliou, jt. auth. see Kat, Jan.

Diop, C. A. Pre-Colonial Black Africa. Salemson, Harold & Wimby, Diedre, trs. from Fr. 1985. 16.95 (ISBN 0-88208-187-X); pap. 7.95 (ISBN 0-88208-188-8). Lawrence Hill.

Diop, Cheikh A. The African Origin of Civilization: Myth or Reality. Cook, Mercer, ed. & tr. from Fr. LC 73-81746. (Illus.). 317p. 1974. 16.95 (ISBN 0-88208-021-0); pap. 9.95 (ISBN 0-88208-022-9). Lawrence Hill.

--Black Africa: Economic & Cultural Basis for a Federated State. Salemson, Harold J., tr. LC 78-62368. 132p. 1978. pap. 4.95 (ISBN 0-88208-095-4). Lawrence Hill.

Diop, David. Hammer Blows. (African Writers Ser.). 1975. pap. text ed. 5.50x (ISBN 0-435-90174-5). Heinemann Ed.

DiOrio. Borrowed Time. 9.95 (ISBN 0-89471-111-3); 19.80 (ISBN 0-89471-110-5). Running Pr.

DiOrio, Al. Barbara Stanwyck: A Biography. LC 83-14358. (Illus.). 300p. 1984. 15.95 (ISBN 0-698-11247-4, Coward). Putnam Pub Group.

--Barbara Stanwyck: A Biography. 256p. 1985. pap. 3.50 (ISBN 0-425-07749-7). Berkley Pub.

DiOrio, Al, Jr. Borrowed Time: The Thirty-Seven Years of Bobby Darin. LC 80-20720. (Illus.). 1980. 9.95 (ISBN 0-89471-111-3); lib. bdg. 19.80 (ISBN 0-89471-110-5). Running Pr.

DiOrio, Dorothy M. Leconte De Lisle: A Hundred & Twenty Years of Criticism, 1850-1970. (Romance Monographs: No. 1). 1972. 20.00x (ISBN 0-686-17909-9); pap. 15.00x (ISBN 0-686-17910-2). Romance.

DiOrio, Louis P. Clinical Preventive Dentistry. 352p. 1983. 34.50 (ISBN 0-8385-1144-9). ACC.

Diorio, MaryAnn L. Dating Etiquette for Christian Teens. (Illus.). 48p. (Orig.). (gr. 6-12). 1984. pap. 3.95 (ISBN 0-930037-00-6). Daystar Comm.

DiOrio, Ralph A. Called to Heal. LC 82-45354. (Illus.). 264p. 1982. 14.95 (ISBN 0-385-18226-0). Doubleday.

--Called to Heal: Releasing the Transforming Power of God. LC 82-45354. (Illus.). 264p. 1984. pap. 7.95 (ISBN 0-385-19704-7, Im). Doubleday.

--The Healing Power of Affirmation: Accepting God & Goodness in Your Life. LC 84-25903. 1985. 13.95 (ISBN 0-385-18227-9). Doubleday.

--Miracle to Proclaim: First-Hand Experience of Healing. LC 83-18218. 224p. 1984. pap. 4.50 (ISBN 0-385-19241-X, Im). Doubleday.

DiOrio, Ralph A. & Gropman, Donald. The Man Beneath the Gift: The Story of My Life. LC 80-17619. (Illus.). 239p. 1981. 9.95 (ISBN 0-688-03740-2); pap. 6.95 (ISBN 0-688-00795-3). Morrow.

Diosdado, Ana. Olvida los Tambores. Maroto, Angel R., ed. 112p. (Orig.). (gr. 11-12). 1974. pap. text ed. 4.50x (ISBN 0-88334-063-1). Ind Sch Pr.

Diosdi, Gy. Contract in Roman Law. 230p. 1981. 79.00x (ISBN 0-569-08695-7, Pub. by Collet's). State Mutual Bk.

Dioszegi, V., ed. Popular Beliefs & Folklore Tradition in Siberia. (Uralic & Altaic Ser.: No. 57). 1968. text ed. 40.80x (ISBN 0-686-22621-6). Mouton.

Diot, A., jt. auth. see Gregory, David D.

Diotima. Dialectics of Diotima: Dialogues in the Greek Mode. 1969. 7.50x (ISBN 0-87556-079-2). Saifer.

Dioudonnat, Pierre-Marie & Bragadir, Sabine. Dictionnaire des 10,000 Dirigeants Politiques Francais. 756p. (Fr.). 1978. 69.50 (ISBN 0-686-56727-7, M-6164). French & Eur.

Dioumoulen, I. I., et al. For a Restructuring of International Economic Relations. 182p. 1983. pap. 2.95 (ISBN 0-8285-2592-7, Pub. by Progress Pubs USSR). Imported Pubns.

Di Palma, Giuseppe. Political Syncretism in Italy: Historical Coalition Strategies & the Present Crisis. LC 78-620042. (Policy Papers in International Affairs Ser.: No. 7). 1978. pap. 3.95x (ISBN 0-87725-507-5). U of Cal Intl St.

DiPalma, Guiseppe. Surviving Without Governing: The Italian Parties in Parliament. LC 75-46035. 1977. 36.00x (ISBN 0-520-03195-4). U of Cal Pr.

DiPalma, Joseph R. Basic Pharmacology in Medicine. 2nd ed. (Illus.). 640p. 1981. text ed. 34.00 (ISBN 0-07-017011-8). McGraw.

DiPalma, Ray. The Gallery Goers. 24p. 1971. 1.50 (ISBN 0-87886-002-9). Ithaca Hse.

--January Zero. (Morning Coffee Chapbook Ser.). (Illus.). 24p. (Orig.). 1984. pap. 7.50 (ISBN 0-915124-95-5). Coffee Hse.

--Soli. LC 73-91970. 65p. 1974. 5.95 (ISBN 0-87886-026-6); pap. 2.95 (ISBN 0-87886-027-4). Ithaca Hse.

Di Paolo, J. A. see Ts'o, P. O.

DiPaolo, J. A. see Ts'o, P. O.

DiPaolo-Healey, Antonette, ed. The Old English Vision of St. Paul. LC 77-89928. 1978. 11.00x (ISBN 0-910956-76-6, SAM 2); pap. 5.00x (ISBN 0-910956-62-6). Medieval Acad.

DiPasquale, Dominic & Delius, Jean. Jewelry Making: An Illustrated Guide to Technique. (Creative Handcrafts Ser). 1975. 10.95 (ISBN 0-13-509836-X, Spec); pap. 4.95 (ISBN 0-13-509828-9, Spec). P-H.

Di Pasquale, Emanuel P. The Dynamics of Student Writing. 208p. 1984. pap. text ed. 12.95 (ISBN 0-8403-3349-8). Kendall Hunt.

DiPaul, H. Bert. Focusing Industrial Arts on Career Education. LC 79-53500. (Illus.). 143p. (Orig.). (gr. 9-12). 1979. pap. 2.95x (ISBN 0-9605418-0-2). DiPaul.

Dipboye, Robert L., jt. auth. see Howell, William C.

DiPego, Gerald. Shadow of the Beast. 1984. pap. 3.50 (ISBN 0-451-12952-0, Sig). NAL.

DiPerna, Paula. Cluster Mystery: Epidemic & the Children of Woburn, Mass. 1985. 13.95 (ISBN 0-8016-1301-9). Mosby.

--The Complete Travel Guide to Cuba. LC 78-19436. (Illus.). 1978. pap. 4.95 (ISBN 0-312-15863-7). St Martin.

--Juries on Trial: Faces of American Justice. LC 84-9406. 1984. 17.50 (ISBN 0-934878-43-9, Dist. by Norton). Dembner Bks.

DiPeso, Charles C. Casas Grandes: A Fallen Trading Center of the Gran Chichimeca, 8 vols. LC 74-82018. (Illus.). 1974. Set. 260.00 (ISBN 0-685-99080-X); Vols. 1-3. 75.00 (ISBN 0-685-99081-8); Vols. 4-8. 185.00 (ISBN 0-87358-056-7). Northland.

--Casas Grandes & the Gran Chichimeca. (Illus.). 1972. pap. 1.25 (ISBN 0-89013-019-1). Museum NM Pr.

Di Piero, W. S. Early Light. (Poetry Ser.). 80p. (Orig.). 1985. pap. 7.95 (ISBN 0-87480-189-3). U of Utah Pr.

DiPiero, W. S. Solstice. (Porch Chapbook Ser.: No. 5). (Illus.). 1980. pap. 3.00 (ISBN 0-932968-15-5); signed & numbered ed. 5.00 (ISBN 0-686-96856-5). Porch Pubns.

Di Piero, W. S., tr. see Leopardi, Giacomo.

Di Piero, W. S., tr. see Penna, Sandro.

DiPierro, John C. Structures in Beckett's Watt. 116p. 1981. 11.95 (ISBN 0-917786-22-X). Summa Pubns.

DiPietre, Dennis D., jt. auth. see Kimmins, Peter H.

DiPietro, Marylou, ed. Flowers in Your Path. (Illus.). 68p. 1982. pap. 3.50 (ISBN 0-934830-28-2). Ten Penny.

Di Pietro, Robert, ed. Ethnic Perspectives in American Literature: Selected Essays on the European Contribution. Ifcovic, Edward, et al. LC 82-14265. 333p. 1983. 27.50x (ISBN 0-87352-126-9); pap. 13.50x (ISBN 0-87352-127-7). Modern Lang.

DiPietro, Robert, ed. see Williams, Stephanie.

DiPietro, Robert J. Linguistics & the Professions. Freedle, Roy O., ed. LC 81-22905. (Advances in Discourse Processes Ser.: Vol. 8). 275p. (Orig.). 1982. text ed. 39.50x (ISBN 0-89391-092-9); pap. 24.50 (ISBN 0-89391-120-8). Ablex Pub.

Di Pietro, Robert J., jt. auth. see Agard, Frederick B.

Di Pietro, Robert J., ed. see Linguistic Association of Canada & the U.S.

Di Pietro, Robert J., et al, eds. The First Delaware Symposium on Language Studies: Selected Papers. LC 80-71116. 420p. 1981. 39.50 (ISBN 0-87413-190-1). U Delaware Pr.

Dipl-Ling, V. & Bensch, Erhard. Dictionary of Shipbuilding, Shipping & Fisheries. 784p. 1980. vinyl 150.00x (ISBN 0-686-30016-5, Pub. by Collet's). State Mutual Bk.

Dipl-Ing, W. H. Cement Data Book: International Process Engineering in the Cement Industry, Vol. 2. (Illus.). 456p. 1983. 105.00 (ISBN 0-9915000-3-2, Pub. by Brauverag Germany). Heyden.

Dipl-Ing, W. H. & Czernin, W. H. C. Cement Chemistry & Physics for Civil Engineers. 2nd ed. (Illus.). 196p. 1980. 24.00 (ISBN 0-9915000-1-6, Pub. by Brauverag Germany). Heyden.

Dipoko, M. S. Because of Women. (African Writers Ser.). 1970. pap. text ed. 4.00x (ISBN 0-435-90057-9). Heinemann Ed.

Dipoko, Mbella S. Black & White in Love. (African Writers Ser.). 1972. pap. text ed. 5.50x (ISBN 0-435-90107-9). Heinemann Ed.

--A Few Nights & Days. (African Writers Ser.). 1970. pap. text ed. 5.50x (ISBN 0-435-90082-X). Heinemann Ed.

Di Porto, Paolo, jt. auth. see Crosignani, Bruno.

Dippel, Horst. Germany & the American Revolution: A Sociohistorical Investigation of Late Eighteenth-Century Political Thinking. Uhlendorf, Bernhard A., tr. LC 77-367. (Institute of Early American History & Culture Ser.). (Illus.). xxiv, 448p. 1977. 30.00 (ISBN 0-8078-1301-X). U of NC Pr.

Dippie, Brian W. Remington & Russell: The Sid Richardson Collection. (Illus.). 188p. 1982. 29.95 (ISBN 0-292-77027-8). U of Tex Pr.

--The Vanishing American: White Attitudes & U. S. Indian Policy. LC 82-2804. (Illus.). 432p. 1982. 27.95 (ISBN 0-8195-5056-6). Wesleyan U Pr.

Dippie, Brian W., ed. Nomad: George A. Custer in "Turf, Field & Farm". (John Fielding & Lois Lasater Maher Ser: No. 3). (Illus.). 192p. 1980. text ed. 22.50x (ISBN 0-292-75519-8). U of Tex Pr.

Dippie, Brian W., ed. see Russell, Charles.

Dipple, Elizabeth. Iris Murdoch: Work for the Spirit. LC 81-52553. 366p. 1981. lib. bdg. 30.00x (ISBN 0-226-15363-0). U of Chicago Pr.

--Plot. (Critical Idiom Ser.: Vol. 12). 1970. pap. 5.50x (ISBN 0-416-19780-9, NO. 2165). Methuen Inc.

Dipple, Richard. Cracks in the Image. (Gay Modern Classics Ser.). 132p. (Orig.). 1981. pap. 5.50 (ISBN 0-907040-07-1, Pub. by GMP England). Alyson Pubns.

Dipple, Richard, ed. Cracks in the Image: Stories by Gay Men. 136p. 1981. pap. 5.50 (ISBN 0-907040-08-X). Gay Mens Pr.

Dippman, Gerda. Practical Review of German Grammar. 514p. 1986. text ed. price not set (ISBN 0-02-329610-0). Macmillan.

Di Prampero, P. E. & Poortsmans, J., eds. Physiological Chemistry of Exercise & Training. (Medicine & Sport: Vol. 13). (Illus.). viii, 216p. 1981. 41.75 (ISBN 3-8055-2028-X). S Karger.

Di Prete, John. TV Ad Trivia Quiz Book. LC 80-15375. (Illus.). 96p. 1981. pap. 3.95 (ISBN 0-498-02464-4). A S Barnes.

Di Prima, Diane. Dinners & Nightmares. new ed. 1974. pap. 3.50 (ISBN 0-87091-029-9). Corinth Bks.

--Loba. LC 78-50779. 1978. 15.00 (ISBN 0-914728-21-0); signed ed. 35.00 (ISBN 0-914728-22-9). Wingbow Pr.

--Revolutionary Letters. LC 78-134224. (Pocket Poets Ser.: No. 27). 1971. pap. 3.50 (ISBN 0-87286-059-0). City Lights.

--Selected Poems: Nineteen Fifty-Six to Nineteen Seventy-Six. LC 76-39890. 1977. 40.00 (ISBN 0-913028-48-7). North Atlantic.

Di Prima, Diane & Jones, LeRoi, eds. The Floating Bear: A Newsletter, Nos. 1-37, 1961-1969. LC 72-79790. (Introduction & notes adapted from interviews with Diane di Prima). 1973. pap. 20.00 (ISBN 0-910938-54-7); lib. bdg. 30.00 (ISBN 0-910938-29-6). McGilvery.

Diprima, R. C., jt. auth. see Boyce, W. E.

DiPrima, Richard. The City & Its Problems. LC 80-70425. 89p. (Orig.). 1980. pap. text ed. 4.95 (ISBN 0-86652-004-X). Know Unltd.

--The First Amendment. LC 81-65895. (Orig.). (gr. 6-12). 1982. pap. text ed. 4.95 (ISBN 0-86652-012-0). Know Unltd.

--The Great Whales: Endangered Monarchs of the Deep. 155p. (Orig.). 1981. pap. text ed. 7.95 (ISBN 0-86652-042-2). Know Unltd.

--Headline History of the Sixties. LC 80-71081. 73p. (Orig.). (gr. 6-12). pap. text ed. 4.95 (ISBN 0-86652-011-2). Know Unltd.

--Perspective On... Inflation. LC 80-70424. 181p. (Orig.). 1980. pap. text ed. 5.95 (ISBN 0-86652-005-8). Know Unltd.

Di Prima, Richard C., jt. auth. see Boyce, William E.

DiPrima, Richard C., jt. auth. see Boyce, William E.

DiPrima, Richard O., ed. Modern Modeling of Continuum Phenomena. LC 77-9041. (Lectures in Applied Mathematics Ser.: Vol. 16). 251p. 1982. pap. 50.00 (ISBN 0-8218-1116-9, LAM-16). Am Math.

Di Prisco, C. A., ed. Methods in Mathematical Logic. (Lecture Notes in Mathematics: Vol. 1130). vii, 407p. 1985. pap. 25.80 (ISBN 0-387-15236-9). Springer-Verlag.

Di Prisco, Joseph. Wit's End. LC 75-25719. 64p. 1976. 6.95 (ISBN 0-8262-0193-8). U of Mo Pr.

Diqs, Isaak. A Bedouin Boyhood. LC 83-10451. 176p. 1983. Repr. of 1969 ed. 10.40x (ISBN 0-87663-430-7). Universe.

Dirac, P. The Development of Quantum Theory: J. Robert Oppenheimer Memorial Prize Acceptance Speech. 76p. 1971. 22.00 (ISBN 0-677-02970-5). Gordon.

Dirac, P. A. The Principles of Quantum Mechanics. 4th ed. (International Series of Monographs on Physics). 1958. pap. text ed. 19.95x (ISBN 0-19-852011-5). Oxford U Pr.

--Spinors in Hilbert Space. LC 74-18371. 91p. 1974. 22.50x (ISBN 0-306-30798-7, Plenum Pr). Plenum Pub.

Dirac, Pam, et al. Directions in Physics: Lectures Delivered During a Visit to Australia & New Zealand, August & September, 1975. LC 77-24892. 95p. 1978. 24.50x (ISBN 0-471-02997-1, Pub. by Wiley-Interscience). Wiley.

Dirac, Paul A. General Theory of Relativity. LC 75-8690. 71p. 1975. 28.95 (ISBN 0-471-21575-9, Pub. by Wiley-Interscience). Wiley.

Dircks, Henry. Naturalistic Poetry. 1872. 20.00 (ISBN 0-686-17680-4). Quaker City.

--Naturalistic Poetry, Selected from Psalms & Hymns of the Last Three Centuries: In Four Essays, Developing the Progress of Nature-Study, in Connection with Sacred Song. 1979. Repr. of 1872 ed. lib. bdg. 20.00 (ISBN 0-8482-0622-3). Norwood Edns.

Dircks, Phillis T. David Garrick. (English Authors Ser.: No. 403). 1985. lib. bdg. 18.95 (ISBN 0-8057-6893-9, Twayne). G K Hall.

Dircks, Richard J. Henry Fielding. (English Authors Ser.). 170p. 1983. lib. bdg. 13.50 (ISBN 0-8057-6768-1, Twayne). G K Hall.

Dircks, W. H. Cavalier & Courtier Lyrists. 15.00 (ISBN 0-686-17679-0). Quaker City.

--Cavalier & Courtier Lyrists: An Anthology of 17th Century Minor Verse. 1977. lib. bdg. 20.00 (ISBN 0-8482-0557-X). Norwood Edns.

Dirckx, John. The Language of Medicine: Its Evolution, Structure, Dynamics. 2nd ed. 206p. 1983. 24.95 (ISBN 0-03-063961-1). Praeger.

Direccion General de Correos Staff. Itinerarios de los Dias en Que Se Recibe y Despacha Correspondencia, No. 2. Ubico, Emilio, ed. 24p. 1984. pap. 3.25 (ISBN 0-913129-04-6). La Tienda.

Direct Marketing Association, Washington Office Staff. Compendium of Government Issues Affecting Direct Marketing, 1985. 4th ed. 65p. 1985. pap. text ed. 20.00 (ISBN 0-933641-01-X). Direct Mktng Assn.

Direct Marketing Creative Guild. Direct Marketing Design. LC 84-25502. (Illus.). 256p. 1985. 47.50 (ISBN 0-86636-006-9). PBC Intl Inc.

Director, Aaron, jt. auth. see Douglas, Paul H.

Director, Anne. The Standard Wine Cookbook. (Culinary Arts Ser.). (Illus.). 192p. 1979. 8.95 (ISBN 0-89496-014-8); pap. 4.95 (ISBN 0-686-77351-9). Ross Bks.

Director General to the World Health Assembly & to the United Nations. Official Records of the World Health Organization; Work of WHO: Reports. Incl. No. 164. 1967. pap. o. p. (ISBN 0-686-16937-9); No. 172. 1968. pap. o. p. (ISBN 0-686-16938-7); No. 180. 1969. 1970. pap. 3.60 (ISBN 92-4-160180-9, 1693); No. 188. 1970. 1971. pap. 4.80 (ISBN 0-686-16939-5, 1694); No. 197. 1971. 1972. pap. 6.00 (ISBN 92-4-160197-3); No. 205. 1972. 1973. pap. 6.00 (ISBN 92-4-160205-8); No. 213. 1973. 1974. pap. 4.80 (ISBN 92-4-160213-9); No. 221. 1974. 1975. pap. 7.20 (ISBN 92-4-160221-X); No. 229. 1975. 1976. pap. 6.00 (ISBN 92-4-160229-5). (Also avail. in French, Russian & Spanish). pap. World Health.

Director, Mark D., jt. auth. see Ginsburg, Douglas H.

Director, S. W. Circuit Theory: The Computational Approach. LC 75-2016. 679p. 1975. text ed. 48.50 (ISBN 0-471-21580-5); tchrs manual 10.00 (ISBN 0-471-21582-1). Wiley.

Director, S. W., ed. Computer-Aided Circuit Design: Simulation & Optimization. LC 73-16060. (Benchmark Papers in Electrical Engineering & Computer Science: Vol. 5). 380p. 1974. 51.95 (ISBN 0-87933-068-6). Van Nos Reinhold.

Director, Steven M. Strategic Planning for Human Resources. (Work in America Productivity Studies: No. 42). 50p. 1985. pap. 35.00 (ISBN 0-08-029516-9, Pub. by Aberdeen Scotland). Pergamon.

Directorate General of Antiguities, Baghdad, ed. Texts in the Iraq Museum: Cuneiform Texts, 7 vols. Incl. Vol. 7. Old Babylonian Contracts & Administrative Documents from Tell Ed der Near Sippar. Edzard, D. O. (Illus.). 76p. 1971. 32.50x (ISBN 3-447-01358-3). LC 68-143534. Intl Pubns Serv.

Directories from InfoSource Inc. Business Software for the CP-M Computers: An Applications Directory. LC 83-45379. 256p. (Orig.). 1984. pap. 12.95 (ISBN 0-8019-7434-8). Chilton.

--Business Software for the IBM PC: An Applications Directory. LC 83-45380. 336p. (Orig.). 1984. pap. 12.95 (ISBN 0-8019-7432-1). Chilton.

Directories from InfoSource, Inc. Business Software for the TRS-80: An Applications Directory. LC 83-45381. 168p. (Orig.). 1984. pap. 12.95 (ISBN 0-8019-7433-X). Chilton.

--Micro Software for Business: An Applications Directory. LC 83-45396. 656p. (Orig.). 1984. pap. 19.95 (ISBN 0-8019-7430-5). Chilton.

Directories from InfoSource Inc. Staff. Business Software for the Apple II: An Applications Directory. LC 83-45382. 176p. (Orig.). 1984. pap. 12.95 (ISBN 0-8019-7431-3). Chilton.

Directors Guild of America. Byron Haskin. Adamson, Joe, contrib. by. LC 84-14080. (Illus.). 334p. 1984. 22.50 (ISBN 0-8108-1740-3). Scarecrow.

Directors of National Research Institutions in Education Colloquy, 3rd, Hamburg, 12-14 September 1978. Equality of Opportunity Reconsidered: Values in Education for Tomorrow, Proceedings. Carelli, M. Dino & Morris, John G., eds. 234p. 1979. pap. text ed. 14.00 (ISBN 90-265-0296-6, Pub. by Swets & Zeitlinger Netherlands). Hogrefe Intl.

Directory Center for Self Sufficency, Research Division. Directory of Alternative Schools & Teachers for the Arts, Crafts & Other Back to Basic Topics. 1985. pap. 1.00 (ISBN 0-910811-79-2, Pub. by Center Self Suff). Prosperity & Profits.

Di Renzo, Giancarlo & Hawkins, Denis F., eds. Perinatal Medicine: Problems & Controversies. 250p. 1984. text ed. 47.00 (ISBN 8-88503-747-X). Raven.

Di Renzo, Gordon J. Personality, Power & Politics. (Illus.). 1967. 6.95x (ISBN 0-268-00205-3). U of Notre Dame Pr.

DiRenzo, Gordon J., ed. We, the People: American Character & Social Change. LC 76-51926. (Contributions in Sociology Ser.: No. 24). (Illus.). 1977. lib. bdg. 29.95 (ISBN 0-8371-9481-4, DWP/). Greenwood.

Dirickx, Yvo M. & Jennergren, L. Peter. Systems Analysis by Multilevel Methods: With Applications to Economics & Management. LC 79-40639. (International Ser. on Applied Systems Analysis). 217p. 1979. 57.95 (ISBN 0-471-27626-X, Pub. by Wiley-Interscience). Wiley.

Diringer, D. History of the Alphabet. (Illus.). 1983. 16.50 (ISBN 0-946095-03-5). Newbury Bks.

Diringer, David. The Book Before Printing. 1983. 18.00 (ISBN 0-8446-5926-6). Peter Smith.

--The Book Before Printing; Ancient, Medival & Oriental. (Illus.). 604p. pap. 10.00 (ISBN 0-486-24243-9). Dover.

Diringer, David & Freeman, H. A History of the Alphabet. 78p. 1978. casebound ed. 35.00x (ISBN 0-905418-12-3, Pub. by Gresham Bks England). State Mutual Bk.

Dirkes, M. A. Writing Activites to Develop Mathematical Thinking. 116p. 12.50 (ISBN 0-89824-049-2). Trillium Pr.

Dirkes, M. Ann. Learning Through Creative Thinking. (Illus.). 48p. (Orig.). (gr. 4-12). 1984. 4.95 (ISBN 0-88047-035-6, 7706). DOK Pubs.

--Learning to Think--to Learn. LC 80-65613. 145p. 1981. perfect bdg. 11.50 (ISBN 0-86548-032-X). R & E Pubs.

--Math Through Creative Thinking. Zilliox, Elaine, ed. (Illus.). 44p. (Orig.). (gr. 4-12). 1984. 4.75 (ISBN 0-88047-034-8, 7707). DOK Pubs.

Dirks, Gerald E. Canada's Refugee Policy: Indifference or Opportunism? 1978. lib. bdg. 23.00 (ISBN 0-7735-0296-3). McGill-Queens U Pr.

Dirks, John E. Critical Theology of Theodore Parker. LC 70-100156. Repr. of 1948 ed. lib. bdg. 15.00x (ISBN 0-8371-3682-2, DITP). Greenwood.

Dirks, Ray. Heads You Win, Tails You Win. LC 78-27174. 1979. 10.95 (ISBN 0-8128-2581-0). Stein & Day.

Dirksen, A. J. Microcomputers, What They Are & How to Put Them to Productive Use. (Illus.). 392p. 1982. pap. 11.95 (ISBN 0-8306-1406-0, 1406). TAB Bks.

Dirksen, Charles J. & Kroeger, Arthur. Advertising Principles & Problems. 6th ed. 1983. 27.95x (ISBN 0-256-02646-7). Irwin.

Dirksen, D. J. & Reeves, R. A. Recreation Lakes of California. 6th ed. 224p. 1983. pap. 9.95 (ISBN 0-943798-06-X). Sail Sale Pub.

--Recreation on the Colorado River. 112p. (Orig.). 1985. pap. 9.95 (ISBN 0-943798-07-8). Sail Sale Pub.

Dirksen, Ellen R., et al, eds. Cell Reproduction: In Honor of Daniel Mazia. (ICN-UCLA Symposia on Molecular & Cellular Biology, 1978 Ser.: Vol. 12). 1978. 65.00 (ISBN 0-12-217850-5). Acad Pr.

Dirksen, H A. & Linden, H R. Autohydrogenation of Oil Gases. (Research Bulletin Ser.: No. 25). iv, 75p. 1955. 5.00 (ISBN 0-317-34301-7). Inst Gas Tech.

--Pipeline Gas from Coal by Methanation of Synthesis Gas. (Research Bulletin Ser.: No. 31). vi, 137p. (B). 1963. 10.00 (ISBN 0-317-34310-6). Inst Gas Tech.

Dirkson, Carolyn. Teen Talent: Creative Writing Manual. LC 77-77026. 1977. pap. 1.00 (ISBN 0-87148-838-8). Pathway Pr.

Dirlam, Joel B. & Kahn, Alfred E. Fair Competition: The Law & Economics of Antitrust Policy. LC 73-100157. 307p. Repr. of 1954 ed. lib. bdg. 15.00x (ISBN 0-8371-2971-0, DIFC). Greenwood.

Dirlik, Arif. Revolution & History: Origins of Marxist Historiography in China, 1919-1937. LC 77-80469. 1978. 38.50x (ISBN 0-520-03541-0). U of Cal Pr.

Di Rocco, C., ed. Brain Tumors in Children. (Journal: Child's Brain: Vol. 9, No. 3-4). (Illus.). 176p. 1982. softcover 40.00 (ISBN 3-8055-3529-5). S Karger.

DiRosa, Veronica. Napa Town & Country Fair Red Hot Chili Cook off. (Illus., Orig.). 1981. pap. 5.95 (ISBN 0-935360-04-2). Napa Landmarks.

Dirr, Michael. All about Evergreens. Smith, Michael D., ed. LC 84-61504. (Illus.). 96p. (Orig.). 1985. pap. 5.95 (ISBN 0-89721-030-1). Ortho.

--Manual of Woody Landscape Plants. 3rd ed. (Illus.). 1983. 29.80x (ISBN 0-87563-231-9); pap. text ed. 22.80x (ISBN 0-87563-226-2). Stipes.

--Photographic Manual for Woody Landscape Plants. (Illus.). 1978. text ed. 24.00x (ISBN 0-87563-156-8); pap. text ed. 16.40 (ISBN 0-87563-153-3). Stipes.

Dirsh, V. A. Morphometrical Studies on Phases of the Desert Locust (Schistocerca Gregaria Forskal) 1953. 35.00x (ISBN 0-85135-066-6, Pub. by Centre Overseas Research). State Mutual Bk.

Dirsh, V. M. The African Genera of Acridoidea. 579p. 1965. 60.00x (ISBN 0-521-04837-0, Pub. by Centre Overseas Research). State Mutual Bk.

--Classification of the Acridomorphoid Insects. 178p. 1975. 60.00x (ISBN 0-317-07056-8, Pub. by EW Classey UK). State Mutual Bk.

Dirsmith, Mark W. & Simon, Abraham J. Local Government Internal Controls: A Guide for Public Officials. 177p. 1983. 19.95 (ISBN 0-916450-45-7). Coun on Municipal.

Dirven, Rene & Radden, Guenter, eds. Issues in the Theory of Universal Grammar. (Tuebinger Beitraege zur Linguistik Ser.: No. 196). 196p. (Orig.). 1982. pap. 19.00x (ISBN 3-87808-565-6). Benjamins North Am.

Dirven, Rene, et al. The Scene of Linguistic Action & its Perspectivization by SPEAK, TALK, SAY & TELL. (Pragmatics & Beyond: III-6). 160p. (Orig.). 1983. pap. 21.00 (ISBN 90-272-2528-1). Benjamins North Am.

Dirvin, Joseph I. St. Catherine Laboure of the Miraculous Medal. LC 84-50466. 245p. 1984. pap. 7.50 (ISBN 0-89555-242-6). TAN Bks Pubs.

Dirzo, Rodolfo & Sarukhan, Jose, eds. Perspectives on Plant Population Ecology. LC 83-20182. (Illus.). 450p. 1984. text ed. 47.50x (ISBN 0-87893-142-2); pap. text ed. 28.75x (ISBN 0-87893-143-0). Sinauer Assoc.

D'Isa, Frank A. Mechanics of Metals. 1968. 21.95 (ISBN 0-201-01550-1). Addison-Wesley.

Di Sabato, Giovanni, et al, eds. Methods in Enzymology: Immunochemical Techniques, Vol. 108, Pt. G. 1984. 69.50 (ISBN 0-12-182008-4). Acad Pr.

DiSaia, Philip J. & Creasman, William T. Clinical Gynecologic Oncology. LC 80-18687. (Illus.). 478p. 1981. text ed. 39.50 (ISBN 0-8016-1314-0). Mosby.

DiSaisa, Philip J., jt. auth. see Brown, Stephen G.

DiSalvo, Arthur F., ed. Occupational Mycoses. LC 83-765. (Illus.). 247p. 1983. text ed. 24.50 (ISBN 0-8121-0885-X). Lea & Febiger.

DiSalvo, Jackie. War of Titans: Blake's Critique of Milton & the Politics of Religion. LC 82-11136. 403p. 1983. 35.00x (ISBN 0-8229-3804-9). U of Pittsburgh Pr.

Disalvo, Vincent. Business & Public Professional Communication: Basic Skills & Principles. (Speech & Drama Ser.). 1977. text ed. 22.95 (ISBN 0-675-08486-5). Additional supplements may be obtained from publisher. Merrill.

Di San Lazzaro, G., ed. Twentieth Century Art-No. 34: Panorama '70. (Illus., Fr & Eng.). 19.95 (ISBN 0-8148-0488-8). L Amiel Pub.

--Twentieth Century Art-No. 35: Panorama '70. (Illus., Fr & Eng.). 19.95 (ISBN 0-8148-0493-4). L Amiel Pub.

--Twentieth Century Art-No. 38: Panorama '72. (Illus., Fr., Abridged English trans). 1972. 19.95 (ISBN 0-8148-0539-6). L Amiel Pub.

Di San Lazzaro, G. see San Lazzaro, G. Di.

DiSante, Theodore. How to Select & Use Medium-Format Cameras. 192p. 1981. 12.95 (ISBN 0-89586-046-5). H P Bks.

Disbrow, Mildred A., et al. Maternity Nursing Case Studies. 1976. spiral bdg. 14.50 (ISBN 0-87488-036-X). Med Exam.

DiScala, Spencer. Dilemmas of Italian Socialism: The Politics of Filippo Turati. LC 79-10274. 224p. 1980. lib. bdg. 17.50x (ISBN 0-87023-285-1). U of Mass Pr.

Discenza, Richard, jt. auth. see Elbert, Norbert.

Disch, Joanne M. Diagnostic Procedures for Cardiovascular Disease. (CECN Ser.). (Illus.). 100p. 1979. pap. 6.95x (ISBN 0-8385-1701-3). ACC.

Disch, Lizann, tr. see Aas, Kjell.

Disch, Lizann, tr. see Thorsen, Kjell.

Disch, Robert & Schwartz, Barry N. Hard Rains: Conflict & Conscience in America. 10.25 (ISBN 0-8446-0585-9). Peter Smith.

Disch, Robert, ed. Ecological Conscience: Values for Survival. LC 71-130009. 1970. pap. 2.45 (ISBN 0-13-222810-6, Spec). P-H.

Disch, Thomas, et al. Burning with a Vision: Poetry of Science & the Fantastic. Frazier, Robert, ed. 138p. 1984. 14.75 (ISBN 0-913896-22-5); pap. 8.75 (ISBN 0-913896-23-3). Owlswick Pr.

Disch, Thomas M. ABCDEFGHIJKLMNOPWRSTUVWXYZ. 79p. 1981. pap. 6.95 (ISBN 0-686-72558-1). Small Pr Dist.

--The Businessman: A Tale of Terror. LC 83-48811. 352p. 1984. 13.94 (ISBN 0-06-015292-3, HarpT). Har-Row.

--The Early Science Fiction Stories of Thomas M. Disch (1963-1966) 1977. lib. bdg. 13.95 (ISBN 0-8398-2370-3, Gregg). G K Hall.

--Getting into Death & Other Stories. LC 75-30998. 227p. 1976. 15.00 (ISBN 0-394-49803-8). Ultramarine Pub.

--On Wings of Song. 368p. (Orig.). 1985. pap. 3.50 (ISBN 0-553-25076-0). Bantam.

--On Wings of Song. LC 78-21411. 359p. 1979. 17.50 (ISBN 0-312-58466-0). Ultramarine Pub.

--Orders of the Retina. LC 82-4728. 48p. 1982. (Pub. by Toothpaste); pap. 7.50 (ISBN 0-915124-61-0). Coffee Hse.

--The Right Way to Figure Plumbing. 75p. (Orig.). 1972. pap. 5.95 (ISBN 0-913560-05-7). Ultramarine Pub.

--Ringtime. LC 82-19279. (Singularities Ser.). (Illus.). 48p. (Orig.). 1983. (Pub. by Toothpaste); pap. 10.00 (ISBN 0-915124-71-8). Coffee Hse.

--Torturing Mr. Amberwell. (Illus.). 80p. (Orig.). 1985. cancelled traycased, signed, numbered, casebound publisher's ed. 200.00 (ISBN 0-941826-13-9); signed, numbered slipcased, casebound, collector's ed. 75.00 (ISBN 0-941826-12-0). Cheap St.

Disch, Thomas M. & Naylor, Charles. Neighboring Lives. LC 80-19021. 351p. 1981. 15.00 (ISBN 0-684-16644-5). Ultramarine Pub.

Disch, Thomas M., ed. Bad Moon Rising. LC 72-9167. 1973. 15.00 (ISBN 0-06-011046-5). Ultramarine Pub.

--The New Improved Sun: An Anthology of Utopian S-F. LC 74-15866. (Illus.). 216p. (YA) 1975. 8.95i (ISBN 0-06-011052-X, HarpT). Har-Row.

Disch, Thomas M. & Naylor, Charles, eds. Strangeness. 1983. pap. 2.50 (ISBN 0-380-41434-1, 41434). Avon.

Disch, Thomas M., ed. see Lupoff, Richard.

Discher, Clarence A. Modern Inorganic Pharmaceutical Chemistry. LC 64-14986. pap. 160.00 (ISBN 0-317-07903-4, 2006347). Bks Demand UMI.

Dischert, Dave, jt. auth. see Keen, Dan.

Discipio, William, ed. The Behavioral Treatment of Psychotic Illness. LC 73-18292. 240p. 1974. text ed. 26.95 (ISBN 0-87705-131-3). Human Sci Pr.

Disciples of Donato the Christ. Healing: A Thought Away, Vol. 2. 438p. 1981. pap. 10.00 (ISBN 0-935146-61-X). Morningland.

Disciples of Morningland. The Way to Oneness. 4th ed. 1979. pap. 3.95 (ISBN 0-935146-00-8). Morningland.

Disciples of the Master Donato the Christ. Healing: As It Is, Vol. 4. 418p. (Orig.). pap. 10.00 (ISBN 0-935146-65-2). Morningland.

Disco, Cornelis, ed. see Gouldner, Alvin W.

Dise, Craig A., ed. see PreTest Services, Inc.

Disease Control Centers, for Atlanta, Georgia. Author-Title & Subject Catalogs of the Centers for Disease Control Library. 1983. lib. bdg. 780.00 (ISBN 0-8161-0395-X, Hall Library). G K Hall.

Disend, Michael. Stomping the Goyim. LC 73-77370. 1969. 5.00 (ISBN 0-685-79019-3). Small Pr Dist.

DiSessa, Andrea, jt. auth. see Abelson, Harold.

DiSessa, Thomas G., jt. auth. see Hagan, Arthur D.

Disfarmer, et al. Aperture, No. 78. 1977. pap. 12.50 on boards (ISBN 0-89381-014-2). Aperture.

Disher, Dorothy R., ed. A Black Swamp Family. LC 81-90497. 1983. 8.95 (ISBN 0-533-05214-9). Vantage.

Disher, M. W. Blood & Thunder. LC 73-21683. (English Literature Ser., No. 33). 1974. lib. bdg. 49.95x (ISBN 0-8383-1761-8). Haskell.

Disher, Maurice W. Clowns & Pantomimes. LC 68-21211. (Illus.). 1968. Repr. of 1925 ed. 21.50 (ISBN 0-405-08446-3, Blom Pubns). Ayer Co Pubs.

Dishner, Ernest K., et al. Reading in the Content Areas: Improving Classroom Instruction. 304p. 1981. pap. text ed. 10.95 (ISBN 0-8403-2409-X). Kendall-Hunt.

Dishon, Daniel, ed. Middle East Record, 4 vols. Incl. Vol. 1. 1960; Vol. 2. 826p. 1961 (ISBN 0-87855-165-4); Vol. 3. 668p. 1967; Vol. 4. 920p. 1968 (ISBN 0-87855-167-0). vols. 2-4 69.95 ea.; Set. casebound o. p. 200.00 (ISBN 0-87855-223-5). Transaction Bks.

--Middle East Record, 1969-70, 2 vols in one, Vol. 5-6. 1414p. text ed. 89.95 (ISBN 0-87855-218-9) (ISBN 0-87855-219-7). Transaction Bks.

Dishon, Dee & O'Leary, Pat W. A Guidebook for Cooperative Learning: A Technique for Creating More Effective Schools. LC 83-83183. 224p. 1985. 19.95 (ISBN 0-918452-58-9). Learning Pubns.

Dishon, Dee, jt. auth. see Moorman, Chick.

Disimone, Marian A. A Genuine Smile: The Positive Approach to Mastectomy. (Illus.). 145p. 1982. 14.95 (ISBN 0-943964-00-8). VinMar Agency.

DiSimoni, Frank. Logbook for the Speech-Language Pathologist. rev. ed. 1981. text ed. 7.95x (ISBN 0-8134-2188-8). Interstate.

Diska, Pat & Jenkyns, Chris. Andy Says Bonjour. LC 54-11522. (Illus.). 48p. (gr. 1-3). 1954. 10.95 (ISBN 0-8149-0297-9). Vanguard.

Diskalkar, D. B. Selections from Sanskrit Inscriptions. 1977. 18.00x (ISBN 0-686-22673-9). Intl Bk Dist.

Diskin, Lahna. Reader's Guide to Theodore Sturgeon. Schlobin, Roger C., ed. LC 80-21423. (Starmont Reader's Guides to Contemporary Science Fiction & Fantasy Author Ser.: Vol. 7). (Illus., Orig.). 1981. 13.95x (ISBN 0-916732-66-5-3); pap. text ed. 5.95x (ISBN 0-916732-09-6). Starmont Hse.

--Theodore Sturgeon. LC 81-21639. (Starmont Reader's Guide Ser.: No. 7). 80p. 1981. Repr. lib. bdg. 13.95x (ISBN 0-89370-038-X). Borgo Pr.

--Theodore Sturgeon: A Primary & Secondary Bibliography. 1979. lib. bdg. 18.00 (ISBN 0-8161-8046-6, Hall Reference). G K Hall.

Diskin, Martin, ed. Trouble in Our Backyard: Central America & the United States in the Eighties. LC 83-52810. 19.50 (ISBN 0-394-52295-8); pap. 9.95 (ISBN 0-394-71589-6). Pantheon.

Diskin, Martin, jt. ed. see Cook, Scott.

Diskit, K. R., ed. Contributions to Indian Geography: Geomorphology, Vol. 2. 1983. 37.50x (ISBN 0-8364-1038-6, Pub. by Heritage India). South Asia Bks.

Diskul, M. Subhadrarus, ed. The Art of Srivijaya. (Illus.). 1980. 45.00x (ISBN 0-19-580433-3). Oxford U Pr.

Disley, John. Orienteering. rev. 2nd ed. LC 67-22990. (Illus.). 176p. 1979. lib. bdg. 8.95 (ISBN 0-8117-2023-3). Stackpole.

Dismukes, Key & Sekular, Robert. Aging & Human Visual Functions. LC 82-7172. (Modern Aging Research Ser.: Vol. 2). 366p. 1982. 54.00 (ISBN 0-8451-2301-7). A R Liss.

Disney, A. R. Twilight of the Pepper Empire: Portuguese Trade in Southwest India in the Early Seventeenth Century. LC 77-17376. (Harvard Historical Studies: No. 95). 1978. 18.50x (ISBN 0-674-91429-5). Harvard U Pr.

Disney, Diane M., et al. Partners in Public Service: Government & the Nonprofit Sector in Rhode Island. 164p. (Orig.). 1984. pap. text ed. 14.95x (ISBN 0-87766-344-0). Urban Inst.

Disney, Doris D. At Some Forgotten Door. 224p. 1975. pap. 1.25 (ISBN 0-532-12304-2). Woodhill.

Disney, Doris M. Fire at Will. 1976. pap. 1.25 (ISBN 0-532-12377-8). Woodhill.

--The Magic Grandfather. Repr. lib. bdg. 13.95 (ISBN 0-88411-842-8, Pub. by Aeonian Pr). Amereon Ltd.

--The Magic Grandfather. 192p. 1975. pap. 1.25 (ISBN 0-532-12305-0). Woodhill.

--Only Couples Need Apply. Repr. lib. bdg. 11.95x (ISBN 0-88411-841-X, Pub. by Aeonian Pr). Amereon Ltd.

--Shadow of a Man. Repr. lib. bdg. 13.95x (ISBN 0-88411-840-1, Pub. by Aeonian Pr). Amereon Ltd.

Disney, Michael. The Hidden Universe. 256p. 1985. 17.95 (ISBN 0-02-531670-2). Macmillan.

Disney, R. & Ott, T., eds. Applied Probability--Computer Science: The Interface, 2 Vols. (Progress in Computer Science Ser.). 1982. text ed. 39.95x ea. Vol. 2, 532pp (ISBN 0-8176-3067-8). Vol. 3, 514pp (ISBN 0-8176-3093-7). Birkhauser.

Disney, R. H. A Key to the Larvae, Pupae & Adults of the British Dixidae (Diptera) 1975. 20.00x (ISBN 0-900386-23-1, Pub. by Freshwater Bio). State Mutual Bk.

Disney, R. L., jt. auth. see Clarke, A. B.

Disney, Ralph L., jt. auth. see Clarke, A. Bruce.

Disney, Richard, jt. auth. see Creedy, John.

Disney Studio Staff, ed. see Dickens, Charles.

Disney Studios. Mickey Mouse Says I Can, Can You? Klimo, Kate, ed. (Illus.). 6p. 1982. 9.95 (ISBN 0-671-45821-3, Little Simon). S&S.

Disney, Walt. Cinderella. (Disney Movie-Go-Round Bks.). (Illus.). 10p. (ps-3). 1982. bds. 8.95 (ISBN 0-671-44898-6). Windmill Bks.

--Diccionario Disney. 112p. (Span.). 1973. pap. 5.95 (ISBN 84-305-0601-2, S-24118). French & Eur.

--Pinocchio. (Disney-Movie-Go-Round Bks.). (Illus.). 10p. (ps-3). 1982. bds. 8.95 (ISBN 0-671-44899-4). Windmill Bks.

--Snow White & the Seven Dwarfs. (gr. 2 up). 1979. pap. 0.95 (ISBN 0-448-15923-6, G&D). Putnam Pub Group.

--Snow White & the Seven Dwarfs. (Disney Movie-Go-Round Bks.). (Illus.). 10p. (ps-3). 1982. bds. 8.95 (ISBN 0-671-44897-8). Windmill Bks.

Dison, Norma. Simplified Drugs & Solutions for Nurses, Including Arithmetic. 8th ed. (Illus.). 150p. 1984. pap. text ed. 10.95 (ISBN 0-8016-1313-2). Mosby.

Disque, Jerry. In Between: The Adolescents' Struggle for Independence. (Fastback Ser.: No. 31). (Orig.). 1973. pap. 0.75 (ISBN 0-87367-031-0). Phi Delta Kappa.

Disque, Robert O. Applied Plastic Design in Steel. LC 77-10512. 256p. 1978. Repr. of 1971 ed. lib. bdg. 16.50 (ISBN 0-88275-312-6). Krieger.

--Applied Plastic Design in Steel. LC 79-153190. pap. 63.80 (ISBN 0-317-11073-X, 2007244). Bks Demand UMI.

Disraeli, Benjamin. Coningsby. 1979. lib. bdg. 69.95 (ISBN 0-87700-296-7). Revisionist Pr.

--Coningsby. Braun, Thom, ed. (Penguin English Library). 528p. 1983. pap. 5.95 (ISBN 0-14-043192-6). Penguin.

--Coningsby: Or, the New Generation. Smith, Shelia M., ed. (World's Classics Ser.). 1982. pap. 5.95 (ISBN 0-19-281580-6). Oxford U Pr.

--Coningsby or the New Generation. 440p. Date not set. Repr. of 1905 ed. lib. bdg. 25.00 (ISBN 0-8492-4228-2). R West.

--Lothair. LC 75-98810. Repr. of 1906 ed. lib. bdg. 19.75x (ISBN 0-8371-2846-3, BELO). Greenwood.

--Lothair. LC 78-115230. 1971. Repr. 16.00x (ISBN 0-403-00458-6). Scholarly.

--Sybil. Smith, Sheila, ed. (World's Classics Paperback Ser.). 1981. pap. 5.95 (ISBN 0-19-281551-2). Oxford U Pr.

--Sybil. Braun, Thom, ed. (English Library). 1980. pap. 5.95 (ISBN 0-14-043134-9). Penguin.

--Sybil, Or the Two Nations. (World's Classics Ser.). 14.95x (ISBN 0-19-250291-3). Oxford U Pr.

--Tancred: Or, the New Crusade. LC 79-98811. Repr. of 1877 ed. lib. bdg. 24.75x (ISBN 0-8371-3072-7, BATA). Greenwood.

--The Works of Benjamin Disraeli, Earl of Beaconsfield, 20 vols. Incl. Vols. 1-2. Vivian Grey: A Romance of Youth. LC 76-12451; Vols. 3-4. The Young Duke, etc. LC 76-12450; Vols. 5-6. Contarini Fleming: A Psychological Romance, etc. LC 76-12449; Vol. 7. Alroy: Or, the Prince of the Captivity. LC 76-12448; Vols. 8-9. Henrietta Temple: A Love Story, etc. LC 76-12447; Vols. 10-11. Venetia, etc. LC 76-12445; Vols. 12-13. Coningsby: Or, the New Generation & Selected Speeches. LC 76-12444; Vols. 17-18. Lothair & Letters to His Sister. LC 76-12443; Vols. 19-20. Endymion, Miscellania. LC 76-12442; Vols. 14-16. Sybil; Tancred. LC 76-148746. (Illus.). Repr. of 1904 ed. Set. 800.00 (ISBN 0-404-08800-7); 40.00 ea. AMS Pr.

--The Young Duke: A Moral Tale, Though Gay. 1853. lib. bdg. 20.00 (ISBN 0-8414-2473-X). Folcroft.

D'Israeli, I. Curiosities of Literature. 582p. Date not set. Repr. of 1787 ed. lib. bdg. 45.00 (ISBN 0-89987-183-6). Darby Bks.

Disraeli, Isaac. Amenities of Literature, Consisting of Sketches & Characters of English Literature, 2 vols. 1973. Repr. of 1859 ed. 30.00 (ISBN 0-8274-1639-3). R West.

--The Calamities & Quarrels of Authors with Some Inquiries Respecting Their Moral & Literary Characters. 1973. Repr. of 1860 ed. 24.75 (ISBN 0-8274-1638-5). R West.

D'Israeli, Isaac. Calamities of Authors: Including Some Inquiries Respecting Their Moral & Literary Character, 2 Vols. Repr. of 1812 ed. 45.00 (ISBN 0-384-11810-0). Johnson Repr.

Disraeli, Isaac. The Literary Character: Or the History of Men of Genius. 1973. Repr. of 1868 ed. 40.00 (ISBN 0-8274-1696-2). R West.

--Miscellanies of Literature: A New Edition, Revised & Corrected. 1973. Repr. of 1840 ed. 50.00 (ISBN 0-8274-1640-7). R West.

D'Israeli, Isaac. Quarrels of Authors: Or Some Memoirs for Our Literary History, 3 vols. 1814. Set. 70.00 (ISBN 0-384-11870-4). Johnson Repr.

Dissanayake, Wimal, jt. auth. see Arno, Andrew.

Dissanayake, Wimal, jt. auth. see Wang, Georgette.

Disselkoen, Laura, ed. Semana de la Pasion, Muerte y Resurreccion: Muerte y Resurreccion. 75p. 1981. pap. 2.25 (ISBN 0-311-08501-6). Casa Bautista.

Dissemination Center for Bilingual-Bicultural Education. Guide to Title VII ESEA Bilingual Bicultural Projects: 1973-1974. Cordasco, Francesco, ed. LC 77-90544. (Bilingual Bicultural Education in the U. S. Ser.). 1978. Repr. of 1974 ed. lib. bdg. 24.50x (ISBN 0-405-11084-7). Ayer Co Pubs.

Dissemination Center For Bilingual Bicultural Education. Proceedings: National Conference on Bilingual Education. Cordasco, Francesco, ed. LC 77-90556. (Bilingual-Bicultural Education in the U. S. Ser.). 1978. Repr. of 1975 ed. lib. bdg. 31.00x (ISBN 0-405-11094-4). Ayer Co Pubs.

Dissent (Periodical) Voices of Dissent. LC 77-99630. (Essay Index Reprint Ser.). 1958. 27.50 (ISBN 0-8369-1405-8). Ayer Co Pubs.

Dissere, Jean. Dictionnaire Encyclopedique Des Citations. 395p. (Fr.). 1970. 15.00 (ISBN 0-686-56876-1, M-6654). French & Eur.

Diss-Greis, Theresa. The Decline of Annual Hours Worked in the United States Since 1947. (Manpower & Human Resources Studies: No. 10). 350p. 1984. 30.00 (ISBN 0-89546-044-0). Indus Res Unit-Wharton.

Dissinger, Katherine. Old, Poor, Alone, & Happy: How to Live Nicely on Nearly Nothing. LC 79-23731. 272p. 1980. 19.95 (ISBN 0-88229-629-9). Nelson-Hall.

Disston, Harry. Beginning the Rest of Your Life. LC 78-75301. (Business Ser.). 160p. (Orig.). 1980. pap. 4.95 (ISBN 0-87000-518-9). Dame Inc.

--Know All about Horses. 1975. pap. 3.00 (ISBN 0-87980-294-4). Wilshire.

--Riding Rhymes for Young Riders. (Illus.). (gr. 1-6). 1951. pap. 1.95 (ISBN 0-87027-100-8). Cumberland Pr.

Distad, Audree. Come to the Fair. LC 77-3812. (Illus.). (gr. 3-7). 1977. PLB 10.89 (ISBN 0-06-021687-5). HarpJ.

--The Dream Runner. LC 72-80365. 1978. pap. 1.95 (ISBN 0-06-440091-3, Trophy). HarpJ.

Distad, N. Merrill. Guessing at Truth: The Life of Julius Charles Hare 1795-1855. LC 78-11625. xiv, 258p. 1979. 23.50x (ISBN 0-915762-07-2). Patmos Pr.

Distant, W. L. Rhynchota: Heteroptera, Vol. 1. (Fauna of British India Ser,). xxxviii, 438p. 1977. Repr. of 1902 ed. 25.00 (ISBN 0-88065-048-6, Pub. by Messers Today & Tomorrows Printers & Publishers India). Scholarly Pubns.

--Rhynchota: Heteroptera, Vol. 2. (Fauna of British India Ser.). xviii, 504p. 1977. Repr. of 1902 ed. 25.00 (ISBN 0-88065-049-4, Pub. by Messers Today & Tomorrows Printers & Publishers India). Scholarly Pubns.

--Rhynchota: Heteroptera - Appendix, Vol. 5. (Fauna of British India Ser.). xii, 362p. 1977. Repr. of 1910 ed. 20.00 (ISBN 0-88065-077-X, Pub. by Messers Today & Tomorrows Printers & Publishers India). Scholarly Pubns.

--Rhynchota: Heteroptera-Homoptera, Vol. 3. (Fauna of British India Ser.). iiv, 504p. 1977. Repr. of 1906 ed. 25.00 (ISBN 0-88065-075-3, Pub. by Messers Today & Tomorrows Printers & Publishers India). Scholarly Pubns.

--Rhynchota: Homoptera - Appendix, Vol. 4. (Fauna of British India Ser.). xiv, 502p. 1977. Repr. of 1908 ed. 25.00 (ISBN 0-88065-076-1, Pub. by Messers Today & Tomorrows Printers & Publishers India). Scholarly Pubns.

--Rhynchota: Homoptera - Appendix, Vol. 6. (Fauna of British India Ser.). viii, 250p. 1977. Repr. of 1916 ed. 15.00 (ISBN 0-88065-078-8, Pub. by Messers Today & Tomorrows Printers & Publishers India). Scholarly Pubns.

--Rhynchota: Homoptera - Appendix, Heteroptera - Addenda, Vol. 7. (Fauna of British India Ser.). viii, 212p. 1977. Repr. of 1918 ed. 15.00 (ISBN 0-88065-079-6, Pub. by Messers Today & Tomorrows Printers & Publishers India). Scholarly Pubns.

Distant, William L. Synonymic Catalogue of Homoptera, Pt. 1, Cicadidae. 1906. 19.00 (ISBN 0-384-11870-4). Johnson Repr.

Di Stasi, Lawrence. Mal Occhio: The Underside of Vision. LC 81-7. (Illus.). 160p. 1981. 17.50 (ISBN 0-86547-033-2). N Point Pr.

DiStasio, J., jt. ed. see Silverman, R.

DiStasio, J. I., ed. Chemicals for Oil Field Operations: Recent Developments. LC 81-11052. (Chem. Tech. Rev. 195: Energy Tech. Rev. 69). (Illus.). 307p. 1982. 48.00 (ISBN 0-8155-0861-1). Noyes.

--Epoxy Resin Technology: Developments Since 1979. LC 81-18926. (Chemical Technology Review Ser.: No. 204). (Illus.). 366p. (Orig.). 1982. 48.00 (ISBN 0-8155-0888-3). Noyes.

--Surfactants, Detergents & Sequestrants: Developments since 1979. LC 81-38360. (Chem. Tech. Rev. 192). 353p. 1981. 48.00 (ISBN 0-8155-0856-5). Noyes.

--Ultrasonics as a Medical Diagnostic Tool. LC 79-26029. (Radiology Review Ser.: No. 1). (Illus.). 330p. 1980. 32.00 (ISBN 0-8155-0785-2). Noyes.

DiStefano, J. J., et al. Feedback & Control Systems. (Schaum's Outline Ser.). (Orig.). 1967. pap. 9.95 (ISBN 0-07-017045-2). McGraw.

Distefano, Nestor. Nonlinear Processes in Engineering: Dynamic Programming, Invariant Imbedding, Quasilinearization, Finite Element, System Identification & Optimization. 1974. 80.00 (ISBN 0-12-218050-X). Acad Pr.

Distefano, Philip, et al. Elementary Language Arts. LC 84-2224. 423p. 1984. text ed. 29.95 (ISBN 0-471-86658-X). Wiley.

Distel, Ann. Andre Dunoyer de Segonzac. (QLP Ser.). (Illus.). 96p. 1980. 9.95 (ISBN 0-517-54004-5). Crown.

Distelberger, Rudolf, jt. auth. see Leithe-Jasper, Manfred.

Distelhorst, David. How to Prepare for the Texas Real Estate Exam. 1984. pap. 14.95 (ISBN 0-88462-496-X). Caroline Hse.

Distelhorst, David F. How to Prepare for the Texas Real Estate Exam: A Study Manual for Brokers & Salespeople. 3rd ed. LC 84-2138. 252p. (Orig.). 1984. pap. 14.95 (ISBN 0-88462-496-X, 1970-03, Real Estate Ed). Longman USA.

Disterheft, Dorothy. The Syntactic Development of the Infinitive in Indo-European. 220p. (Orig.). 1980. pap. 14.95 (ISBN 0-89357-058-3). Slavica.

Distler, A., jt. ed. see Philip, T.

Distler, Bette. Timothy Tuneful. LC 68-11270. (ps-3). 1968. 3.50g (ISBN 0-685-16349-0, CCPr). Macmillan.

District Judges Association-Fifth Circuit, Committee on Pattern Jury Instructions. Pattern Jury Instructions (Civil Cases) LC 84-153433. ix, 183p. Date not set. price not set. West Pub.

District of Colombia Bar Association. Administrative Practice Manual. 1983. write for info. looseleaf. DC Bar Assn.

Dita, P. & Georgescu, V., eds. Gauge Theories: Fundamentals Interactions & Rigorous Results. (Progress in Physics Ser.: Vol. 5). 389p. 1982. 22.50x (ISBN 0-8176-3095-3). Birkhauser.

Ditchburn, R. W. Light, 3 vols. 3rd. ed. 1977. Vol. 2, 1976. pap. 33.00 (ISBN 0-12-218102-6); Vol. 3. 70.00 (ISBN 0-12-218150-6). Acad Pr.

Ditchfield, P. H. Books Fatal to Their Authors. 1973. lib. bdg. 20.00 (ISBN 0-8414-2474-8). Folcroft.

--Books Fatal to Their Authors. 1977. lib. bdg. 59.95 (ISBN 0-8490-1536-7). Gordon Pr.

--The Cathedrals of Great Britain: Their History & Architecture. (Illus.). 1979. Repr. of 1916 ed. lib. bdg. 45.00 (ISBN 0-8495-1112-7). Arden Lib.

--Old English Customs Extant at the Present Time. LC 68-21765. 1968. Repr. of 1896 ed. 40.00x (ISBN 0-8103-3427-5). Gale.

--The Old-Time Parson. 342p. 1980. Repr. of 1908 ed. lib. bdg. 35.00 (ISBN 0-89760-130-0). Telegraph Bks.

--Vanishing Old Castles in England. (A Philosophy of History Library). (Illus.). 109p. 1981. 85.50 (ISBN 0-86650-003-0). Gloucester Art.

Ditchfield, P. H., jt. ed. see Fishwick.

Ditchfield, Peter H. Books Fatal to Their Authors. LC 71-125019. (Research & Source Ser.: No. 495). 1970. Repr. of 1895 ed. lib. bdg. 18.50 (ISBN 0-8337-0869-4). B Franklin.

--Old English Sports: Pastimes & Customs. (Illus.). 1977. Repr. of 1891 ed. 11.50x (ISBN 0-8277-3272-4). Charles River Bks.

Ditella, Guido. Argentina under Peron, 1973-76: The Nation's Experience with a Labor-Based Government. LC 81-23281. 256p. 1983. 26.00x (ISBN 0-312-04871-8). St Martin.

Di Tella, Guido & Platt, D. C., eds. The Political Economy of Argentina: 1880-1946. 256p. 1985. 30.00 (ISBN 0-312-62252-X). St Martin.

Di Tella, Guido, jt. ed. see Platt, D. C.

Ditewig, William, jt. auth. see Brinkmann, William.

Ditfurth, Hoimar. The Origins of Life: Evolution As Creation. Heinegg, Peter, tr. from Ger. LC 82-47757. (Illus.). 220p. 1982. 14.37i (ISBN 0-06-250909-8, HarpR). Har-Row.

Ditfurth, Hoimar Von see Von Ditfurth, Hoimar.

Dithmar, Edward A. John Drew. 137p. 1982. Repr. of 1900 ed. lib. bdg. 35.00 (ISBN 0-89760-143-2). Telegraph Bks.

DiTillio, Larry, et al. Demon Magic: The Second Stormbringer Companion. Willis, Lynn & Peterson, Sandy, eds. (Illus.). 80p. 1985. pap. 10.00 (ISBN 0-933635-22-2). Chaosium.

Ditlea, Steve. The Osborne-McGraw-Hill Home Computer Guide. 1983. 11.95 (ISBN 0-07-881107-4). Mcgraw.

--The Osborne McGraw-Hill Home Computer Software Guide. (Illus.). 200p. (Orig.). 1983. pap. 11.95 (ISBN 0-07-881107-4, 107-4). Osborne-McGraw.

Ditlea, Steve, ed. Digital Deli: The Lunch Group. LC 83-40030. (Illus.). 373p. 1984. pap. 12.95 (ISBN 0-89480-591-6, 591). Workman Pub.

Ditlevsen, Ove. Uncertainty Modeling: With Applications to Multidimensional Civil Engineering. (Illus.). 448p. 1981. text ed. 80.00 (ISBN 0-07-017046-0). McGraw.

Ditlevsen, Tove. Complete Freedom & Other Stories. Brondum, Jack, tr. LC 81-15124. 96p. 1982. pap. 7.00 (ISBN 0-915306-24-7). Curbstone.

--Early Spring. Nunnally, Tina, tr. from Danish. Orig. Title: Childhood & Youth. 260p. (Orig.). 1985. 14.95 (ISBN 0-931188-29-6); pap. 8.95 (ISBN 0-931188-28-8). Seal Pr Feminist.

Ditmars, Raymond L. Confessions of a Scientist. facs. ed. LC 75-121463. (Essay Index Reprint Ser). 1934. 20.00 (ISBN 0-8369-1800-2). Ayer Co Pubs.

Ditmas, C. A. Historic Homesteads of Kings County. 59.95 (ISBN 0-8490-0306-7). Gordon Pr.

Ditmore, Esteban, tr. see Sisson, Richard, et al.

Dito, William R., jt. ed. see Baer, Daniel M.

DiTomasso, A., jt. ed. see Sih, G. C.

Di Tommaso, Andrea. Structure & Ideology in Boiardo's "Orlando Innamorato". (Studies in the Romance Languages & Literatures: No. 123). 102p. 1972. pap. 7.50x (ISBN 0-8078-9123-1). U of NC Pr.

D'Itri. PCB's: Human & Environmental Hazards. 1983. text ed. 49.95 (ISBN 0-250-40598-9). Butterworth.

D'itri, F. M., jt. auth. see D'itri, P. A.

D'Itri, F. M., jt. auth. see Prince, H. H.

D'Itri, Frank, et al, eds. Municipal Wastewater in Agriculture. 1982. 55.00 (ISBN 0-12-214880-0). Acad Pr.

D'Itri, Frank M. Artificial Reefs: U. S. & Japan. (Illus.). 489p. 1985. 49.95 (ISBN 0-87371-010-X). Lewis Pubs Inc.

D'Itri, Frank M., ed. Wastewater Renovation & Reuse: Proceedings of the International Conference on the Renovation & Reuse of Wastewater Through Aquatic & Terrestrial Systems. LC 76-54588. (Pollution Engineering & Technology: Vol. 3). pap. 120.00 (ISBN 0-317-08391-0, 2055036). Bks Demand UMI.

D'itri, P. A. & D'itri, F. M. Mercury Contamination: A Human Tragedy. LC 76-58478. 311p. (Orig.). 1977. 28.95 (ISBN 0-471-02654-9). Krieger.

D'Itri, Patricia W. Damon Runyon. (United States Authors Ser.). 1982. lib. bdg. 13.50 (ISBN 0-8057-7336-3, Twayne). G K Hall.

Ditsky, John. Friend & Lover: Poems. LC 80-84832. (Ontario Review Press Poetry Ser.). 70p. 1981. 10.95 (ISBN 0-86538-011-2); pap. 6.95 (ISBN 0-86538-012-0). Ontario Rev NJ.

--The Onstage Christ: Studies in the Persistence of a Theme. (Critical Studies Ser.). 188p. 1980. 28.50x (ISBN 0-389-20059-X). B&N Imports.

Ditta, Joseph M. Natural & Conceptual Design: Radical Confusion in Critical Theory. LC 84-47541. (American University Studies IV (English Language & Literature): Vol. 9). 201p. 1984. text ed. 30.00 (ISBN 0-8204-0119-6). P Lang Pubs.

Dittberner, Job L. The End of Ideology & American Social Thought: 1930-1960. Berkhofer, Edward, ed. LC 78-27771. (Studies in American History & Culture: No. 1). 370p. 1979. 49.95 (ISBN 0-8357-0972-8). UMI Res Pr.

Dittburner, Delos A., jt. auth. see Gervais, Robert L.

Dittenhaver, Sarah L., et al. Tune Time, 2 pts. rev. ed. Goss, Louise, ed. (Frances Clark Library for Piano Students). 48p. (gr. k-6). 1973. pap. text ed. 7.95 Pt. A (ISBN 0-87487-194-8); pap. text ed. 7.95 Pt. B (ISBN 0-87487-195-6). Birch Tree Gr.

Dittenhofer, Mortimer & Klemm, Rebecca. Ethics & the Internal Auditor. Holman, Richard, ed. (Illus.). 1983. pap. text ed. 12.00 (ISBN 0-89413-103-6, 517). Inst Inter Aud.

Dittenhofer, Mortimer A., ed. Concepts of Government Auditing: A Book of Readings from the Internal Auditor. 1977. pap. text ed. 10.00 (ISBN 0-89413-059-5). Inst Inter Aud.

Ditters, Carl, jt. auth. see Dittersdorf, Von.

Dittersdorf, Karl D. see Von Dittersdorf, Karl D.

Dittersdorf, Karl D. Von see Von Dittersdorf, Karl D.

Dittersdorf, Von & Ditters, Carl. Die Liebe im Narrenbaus (Vienna, 1787) Bauman, Thomas, ed. (German Opera Ser., 1770-1800). 95.00 (ISBN 0-8240-8864-6). Garland Pub.

Dittert, Alfred E., Jr. & Plog, Fred. Generations in Clay: Pueblo Pottery of the American Southwest. LC 80-81831. (Illus.). 168p. 1980. pap. 14.95 (ISBN 0-87358-270-5). Northland.

Dittes, James E. The Male Predicament: On Being a Man Today. LC 84-47719. 256p. 1985. 14.37i (ISBN 0-06-061924-4, HarpT). Har-Row.

--Minister on the Spot. LC 79-114051. 1970. pap. 3.95 (ISBN 0-8298-0155-3). Pilgrim NY.

Dittman, Antia. Trapped in Hitler's Hell. Markell, Jan, as told to. LC 84-82493. 176p. (Orig.). 1985. 3.95 (ISBN 0-88243-529-9). Gospel Pub.

Dittman, Richard & Schmieg, Glenn. Physics in Everyday Life. Rogers, Janice L. & Zappa, C. R., eds. LC 78-13381. (Schaum's Outline Seri). (Illus.). 1979. text ed. 28.95 (ISBN 0-07-017056-8). McGraw.

Dittman, Richard, jt. auth. see Zemansky, Mark.

Dittmann, Laura L., ed. The Infants We Care for. rev ed. LC 87-635070. (Illus.). 112p. 1984. pap. text ed. 3.50 (ISBN 0-912674-21-0). Natl Assn Child Ed.

Dittmann, Laura L. & Ramsey, Marjorie, eds. Their Future Is Now: Today Is for Children. LC 82-22716. (Illus.). 48p. 1982. pap. 6.90 (ISBN 0-87173-102-9). ACEI.

Dittmann, Reidar. Eros & Psyche: Strindberg & Munch in the 1890s. Foster, Stephen, ed. LC 82-4923. (Studies in the Fine Arts: The Avant-Garde: No. 27). 232p. 1982. 39.95 (ISBN 0-8357-1319-9). UMI Res Pr.

Dittmar, Heinrich. Aischines von Sphettos: Studien zur Literaturgeschichte der Sokratiker. facsimile ed. LC 75-13262. (History of Ideas in Ancient Greece Ser.). (Ger.). 1976. Repr. of 1912 ed. 21.00x (ISBN 0-405-07304-6). Ayer Co Pubs.

Dittmar, Lucy. Caribbean Tropical Nature Guide. (Illus.). 64p. pap. 5.95 (ISBN 0-686-75259-7). Banyan Bks.

Dittmar, Mark. Jumbo Art Yearbook: Grade 3 & 4. (Jumbo Art Ser.). 96p. (gr. 3-4). 1981. wkbk. 14.00 (ISBN 0-8209-0046-X, JAY-34). ESP.

--Jumbo Art Yearbook: Grade 5 & 6. (Jumbo Art Ser.). 96p. (gr. 5-6). 1981. wkbk. 14.00 (ISBN 0-8209-0047-8, JAY-56). ESP.

--Jumbo Art Yearbook: Grade 7 & 8. (Jumbo Art Ser.). 96p. (gr. 7-8). 1982. wkbk. 14.00 (ISBN 0-8209-0048-6, JAY-78). ESP.

--Math Montana & Friends. (gr. 4-6). 1982. 5.95 (ISBN 0-86653-084-3, GA 430). Good Apple.

Dittmar, N., jt. auth. see Klein, W.

Dittmar, Norbert. A Critical Survey of Sociolinguistics: Theory & Application. LC 76-27160. (Illus.). 320p. 1977. 35.00 (ISBN 0-312-17500-0). St Martin.

Dittmar, P. Woerterbuch der Chinesischen Revolution. 224p. (Ger.). 1975. pap. 5.95 (ISBN 0-686-56644-0, M-7035). French & Eur.

Dittmer, Dorothy S., jt. ed. see Altman, Philip L.

Dittmer, Howard J., ed. see Coulter, Merle C.

Dittmer, Ingeborg. James Marion Sims. (De Medicinae Rebus Ser.: Vol. 2). 120p. (Ger.). 1983. 12.50 (ISBN 0-931902-36-3). Inst Mediaeval Mus.

Dittmer, John. Black Georgia in the Progressive Era, 1900-1920. LC 77-24249. (Blacks in the New World Ser). 251p. 1977. 19.50x (ISBN 0-252-00306-3); pap. 6.95 (ISBN 0-252-00813-8). U of Ill Pr.

Dittmer, Kalogreant S. Etude d'une Methode Non-invasive d'Enregistrement des Potentiels Hisiens et Pre-P. (De Medicinae Rebus Ser.: No. 1). 160p. (Fr., Lat., Eng. & Ger.). pap. 12.50 (ISBN 0-912024-19-4). Inst Mediaeval Mus.

Dittmer, Lowell. Liu Shao-Ch'i & the Chinese Cultural Revolution: The Politics of Mass Criticism. LC 73-85786. (Center for Chinese Studies). 1975. 34.00x (ISBN 0-520-02574-1). U of Cal Pr.

--Liu Shao-Ch'i & the Chinese Cultural Revolution: The Politics of Mass Criticism. 400p. 1982. pap. 9.95x (ISBN 0-520-02957-7, CAMPUS 286). U of Cal Pr.

Dittmer, Lowell & Ruoxi, Chen. Ethics & Rhetoric of the Chinese Cultural Revolution. LC 81-82595. (Current Chinese Language Project Ser.: No. 19). 1981. pap. 4.00x (ISBN 0-912966-47-5). IEAS.

Dittmer, Luther, ed. Oxford Latin Litug. (Veroffentlichungen Mittelalterlicher Musikhandschriften - Publications of Mediaeval Musical Manuscripts Ser.: Vol. 6). (Eng. & Ger.). 1961. pap. 24.00 (ISBN 0-912024-06-2). Inst Mediaeval Mus.

--Paris, Nouv. Arc. Frg. 13531. (Veroffentlichungen Mittelaltlicher Musikhandschriften-Publications of Mediaeval Musical Ma nuscripts Ser.: Vol. 4). (Eng. & Ger.). 1961. pap. 15.00 (ISBN 0-912024-04-6). Inst Mediaeval Mus.

--Robert De Handlo. (Musical Theorists in Translation Ser.: Vol. 2). 1961. pap. 14.00 (ISBN 0-912024-22-4). Inst Mediaeval Mus.

--Wolfenbuttel 1099 Helmst (1206) (Veroffentlichungen Mittelalterlicher Musikhandschriften-Publications of Mediaeval Musical Manuscripts: Vol. 2). (Eng. & Ger.). 1961. lib. bdg. 100.00 (ISBN 0-912024-02-X). Inst Mediaeval Mus.

--Worcester, Add. 68. (Veroffentlichungen Mittelalterlicher Musikhandschriften - Publications of Mediaeval Musical Manuscripts Ser.: Vol. 4). (Eng. & Ger.). 1961. pap. 18.00 (ISBN 0-912024-05-4). Inst Mediaeval Mus.

Dittmer, Luther, jt. ed. see Anderson, Gordon A.

Dittmer, Luther, ed. see Firenze.

Dittmer, Luther, ed. see Goudimel.

Dittmer, Luther, ed. see Ludwig, Friedrich.

Dittmer, Paul. Accounting Practices for Hotels, Motels, & Restaurants. LC 79-142507. 1971. text ed. 26.01 scp (ISBN 0-672-96062-1); tchr's manual o.p. 6.67 (ISBN 0-672-26064-6); scp wkbk., 1972 14.47 (ISBN 0-672-96063-X). Bobbs.

Dittmer, Terry. Creating Contemporary Worship. 80p. (Orig.). 1985. pap. 6.95 (ISBN 0-570-03954-1, 12-2889). Concordia.

Ditto, Tanya. The Longest Street: A History of Lafourche Parish & GrandIsle. Woolfolk, Doug, ed. (Illus.). 136p. 1980. 13.00 (ISBN 0-86518-013-X). Moran Pub Corp.

Ditton, Jason, ed. The View from Goffman. LC 79-25202. 1980. 27.50x (ISBN 0-312-84598-7). St Martin.

Ditton, Pam, jt. auth. see Bell, Diane.

Ditton, Richard P., et al. Yosemite Road Guide. (Illus.). 77p. 1981. pap. 1.89 (ISBN 0-939666-24-3). Yosemite Natl Hist.

Dittrich, F. L. Biophysics of the Ear. (Illus.). 136p. 1963. 16.75x (ISBN 0-398-00461-7). C C Thomas.

Dittrich, John E. & Zawacki, Robert A. People & Organizations: Cases in Management & Organizational Behavior. 2nd ed. 1985. pap. 16.95x (ISBN 0-256-03257-2). Business Pubns.

Dittrich, Ludwig O., jt. auth. see Ott, Attiat F.

Dittrich, R. Juggling Made Easy. 3.00x (ISBN 0-685-38464-0). Wehman.

Dittrich, Rudolf. Juggling Made Easy. pap. 3.00 (ISBN 0-87980-086-0). Wilshire.

Dittrich, W. & Reuter, M. Effective Lagrangians in Quantum Electrodynamics. (Lecture Notes in Physics: Vol. 220). v, 244p. 1985. pap. 14.60 (ISBN 0-387-15182-6). Springer-Verlag.

Dittrich, W., ed. Recent Developments in Particle & Field Theory. 1979. casebound 47.50 (ISBN 0-9940012-0-7, Pub. by Vieweg & Sohn Germany). Heyden.

Dittrick, Mark, ed. Design Crochet. LC 78-53411. 1979. 14.95 (ISBN 0-8015-2019-3, Hawthorn). Dutton.

Di Tullio, Benigno. Horizons in Clinical Criminology. (New York University Criminal Law Education & Research Center Monograph: No. 3). xvi, 232p. (Orig.). 1969. pap. 20.00x (ISBN 0-8377-0501-0). Rothman.

Ditzel, J., ed. see Conference on Microcirculation, 6th, Aalborg, 1970.

Ditzel, J., ed. see Conference on Microcirculation, 6th European, Aalborg, 1970.

Ditzel, J., ed. see European Conference on Microcirculation, 7th, Aberdeen, Aug.-Sept. 1972, Part I.

Ditzenberger, Roger & Kidney, John R. Selling. (gr. 9-12). 1984. text ed. 4.95 (ISBN 0-538-19160-0, S16). SW Pub.

Diubaldo, Richard J. Stefansson & the Canadian Arctic. (Illus.). 1978. 21.95 (ISBN 0-7735-0324-2). McGill-Queens U Pr.

Diulio, Eugene. Macroeconomic Theory. 256p. (Orig.). 1974. pap. text ed. 8.95 (ISBN 0-07-017049-5). McGraw.

Diulio, Eugene, jt. auth. see Salvatore, Dominick.

Div. of Communications. The Rights of Fair Trial & Free Press: The American Bar Association Standards. 60p. 1981. pap. 1.00 (ISBN 0-686-47949-1). Amer Bar Assn.

Div. of Earth Sciences. Geographical Perspectives & Urban Growth. (Illus.). 120p. 1973. pap. 9.50 (ISBN 0-309-02106-5). Natl Acad Pr.

Divakaran, S. Animal Blood Processing & Utilization: Processing & Utilization. (Agricultural Services Bulletins: No. 32). 107p. (Eng. & Span.). 1982. pap. 7.75 (ISBN 92-5-100491-9, F2315, FAO). Unipub.

Divale, William. Matrilocal Residence in Pre-Literate Society. Kottak, Conrad, ed. LC 83-24146. (Studies in Cultural Anthropology: No. 4). 264p. 1984. 39.95 (ISBN 0-8357-1489-6). UMI Res Pr.

Di Valmarana, Mario, ed. Building by the Book I. (Palladian Studies in America: No. I). (Illus.). 110p. 1984. text ed. 20.00x (ISBN 0-8139-1022-6). U Pr of Va.

Divari, Nikolai B., ed. Atmospheric Optics, Vol. VI. Dresner, Stephen B., tr. from Russian. LC 69-18138. pap. 46.00 (ISBN 0-317-08298-1, 2020682). Bks Demand UMI.

--Atmospheric Optics, Vol. 2. LC 67-10534. 164p. 1972. 35.00x (ISBN 0-306-17172-4, Consultants). Plenum Pub.

Divas, Mireille. I'm a Year Old Now. (Illus.). 166p. 1983. 15.95 (ISBN 0-13-451344-4); pap. 7.95 (ISBN 0-13-451336-3). P-H.

Dively, George S. Power of Professional Management. LC 77-151052. 1971. 12.95 (ISBN 0-8144-5188-8). AMACOM.

--The Power of Professional Management. LC 77-151052. pap. 47.80 (ISBN 0-317-28127-5, 2055740). Bks Demand UMI.

Diven, T. Aztecs & Mayas. 1976. lib. bdg. 59.95 (ISBN 0-8490-1465-4). Gordon Pr.

Diver, Bradford B. van. Roadside Geology of New York. (Roadside Geology Ser.). (Illus.). 320p. 1985. pap. 9.95 (ISBN 0-87842-180-7). Mountain Pr.

Diver, Bradford B. Van see Van Diver, Bradford B.

Diver, Katherine H. Royal India. facs. ed. LC 76-142620. (Essay Index Reprint Ser). 1942. 22.00 (ISBN 0-8369-2152-6). Ayer Co Pubs.

Diver, Keith. Focus on Profitability: A Handbook for the Policymaker. 80p. 1982. 35.00x (ISBN 0-686-45856-7, Pub. by Pubns Sec Templegate Pr England). State Mutual Bk.

Diver, Maud. Royal India. (Essay Index Reprint Ser.). (Illus.). 288p. Repr. of 1942 ed. lib. bdg. 19.00 (ISBN 0-8290-0780-6). Irvington.

--Siege Perilous, & Other Stories. LC 78-122694. (Short Story Index Reprint Ser). 1924. 17.00 (ISBN 0-8369-3527-6). Ayer Co Pubs.

DiVesta, Francis J. & Thompson, George G. Educational Psychology: Instruction & Behavioral Change. 2nd ed. LC 72-109527. (Century Psychology Ser.). (Illus.). 1970. text ed. 19.95x (ISBN 0-89197-133-5). Irvington.

Divett, Robert T. Medicine & the Mormons. LC 81-84588. 230p. 1981. pap. 9.95 (ISBN 0-88290-194-X, 2050). Horizon Utah.

Divic, Josif M. & Dinoff, Michael, eds. Aspects of Community Psychiatry: Review & Preview. LC 78-3427. (POCA Ser.: No. 7). 187p. 1978. 14.00 (ISBN 0-8173-2731-2). U of Ala Pr.

Divien, Emmanuel, jt. auth. see Scholberg, Henry.

Divilbiss, J. L., ed. Clinic on Library Applications of Data Processing, Proceedings: 1977: Negotiating for Computer Services. LC 78-13693. 117p. 1978. 9.00x (ISBN 0-87845-048-3). U of Ill Lib Info Sci.

Divilbiss, J. L., ed. see Boss, Richard W., et al.

Divilbiss, J. L., ed. see Clinic on Library Applications of Data Processing Proceedings, 1976.

Divilkovsky, S. & Ognetov, I. The Road to Victory. 270p. 1980. pap. 5.45 (ISBN 0-8285-1841-6, Pub. by Progress Pubs USSR). Imported Pubns.

DiVincenti, Marie. Administering Nursing Service. 2nd ed. 350p. 1977. 19.95 (ISBN 0-316-18651-1). Little.

Divine, Donna R., jt. auth. see Bourque, Susan C.

Divine, J. A. & Blachford, G. Stained Glass Craft. 115p. 1972. pap. 2.50 (ISBN 0-486-22812-6). Dover.

--Stained Glass Craft. (Illus.). 14.00 (ISBN 0-8446-4539-7). Peter Smith.

Divine, James & Divine, Judy. Strategies for Taking Tests. 1982. pap. 8.95 (ISBN 0-8120-2565-2). Barron.

Divine, James & Kylen, David. How to Beat Test Anxiety & Score Higher on Your Exams. LC 79-14251. (gr. 11-12). 1979. pap. 3.50 (ISBN 0-8120-2091-X). Barron.

Divine, James H. & Kylen, David W. How to Beat Test Anxiety & Score Higher on the SAT & all Other Exams. 176p. (gr. 10-12). 1982. pap. 4.95 (ISBN 0-8120-2583-0). Barron.

Divine, John E. Eighth Virginia Infantry. (The Virginia Regimental Histories Ser.). (Illus.). 89p. 1983. 16.45 (ISBN 0-930919-05-X). H E Howard.

--Thirty-Fifth Battalion Cavalry. (The Virginia Regimental Histories Ser.). (Illus.). 1985. 16.45 (ISBN 0-930919-19-X). H E Howard.

Divine, Judy, jt. auth. see Divine, James.

Divine, M. J. The Peace Mission Movement. LC 82-90163. (Illus.). 192p. (Orig.). 1982. 7.00 (ISBN 0-9609078-0-7); pap. 5.00 (ISBN 0-9609078-1-5). Palace Mission.

Divine, Robert A. American Immigration Policy Nineteen Twenty-Four to Nineteen Fifty-Two. LC 70-166323. (Civil Liberties in American History Ser). 200p. 1972. Repr. of 1957 ed. lib. bdg. 27.50 (ISBN 0-306-70244-4). Da Capo.

--Blowing on the Wind: The Nuclear Test Ban Debate, 1954-1960. LC 77-25057. 1978. 22.50x (ISBN 0-19-502390-0). Oxford U Pr.

--Eisenhower & the Cold War. (Illus.). 1981. 17.50x (ISBN 0-19-502823-6). Oxford U Pr.

--Eisenhower & the Cold War. 1981. pap. 5.95 (ISBN 0-19-502824-4, 621, GB). Oxford U Pr.

--The Illusion of Neutrality. LC 62-10993. pap. 95.50 (ISBN 0-317-09678-8, 2020057). Bks Demand UMI.

--The Reluctant Beligerent: American Entry into World War II. 2nd ed. 179p. 1979. pap. text ed. 7.95 (ISBN 0-394-34171-6, RanC). Random.

--The Reluctant Belligerent: American Entry into World War II. LC 75-31695. (America in Crisis Ser.). 186p. 1976. Repr. of 1965 ed. 9.50 (ISBN 0-88275-346-0). Krieger.

--Roosevelt & World War Two. LC 69-13655. (Albert Shaw Lectures on Diplomatic History Ser). (Illus.). 117p. 1969. 12.00x (ISBN 0-8018-1079-5). Johns Hopkins.

--Roosevelt & World War Two. 1970. pap. 4.95 (ISBN 0-14-021191-8, Pelican). Penguin.

--Second Chance: The Triumph of Internationalism in America During World War Two. LC 67-14101. 1967. pap. text ed. 3.45x (ISBN 0-689-70267-1, 175). Atheneum.

--Since 1945: Politics & Foreign Policy in Recent American History. 2nd ed. 278p. 1979. pap. text ed. 9.95 (ISBN 0-394-34172-4, RanC). Random.

Divine, Robert A. & Breen, T. H. America: Past & Present, Vol. I. 1984. pap. text ed. 18.60x (ISBN 0-673-15882-9). Scott F.

Divine, Robert A., ed. & intro. by. The Cuban Missile Crisis. LC 70-157090. 247p. 1970. pap. text ed. 8.95x (ISBN 0-8129-6146-3). Wiener Pub Inc.

Divine, Robert A., ed. Exploring the Johnson Years. (Illus.). 288p. 1981. text ed. 24.95 (ISBN 0-292-72031-9). U of Tex Pr.

Divine, Robert A., et al. America: Past & Present, Vol. II. 1984. pap. text ed. 18.60x (ISBN 0-673-15883-7). Scott F.

--America: Past & Present. 1984. text ed. 28.95x (ISBN 0-673-15420-3). Scott F.

--America: Past & Present. 1985. pap. text ed. 18.95x brief ed. (ISBN 0-673-18137-5). Scott F.

--America: Past & Present, Vol. II. brief ed. 1985. pap. text ed. 12.95x (ISBN 0-673-18139-1). Scott F.

Divine, Thomas F. Interest, an Historical & Analytical Study in Economics & Modern Ethics. 1959. 13.95 (ISBN 0-87462-405-3). Marquette.

Divis, B., ed. see Mahler, K.

Divis, Karel. Kommunikative Strukturen im Tschechischen Drama der 60er Jahre. (Symboloe Slavicae Ser.: Vol. 16). 220p. (Ger.). 1983. write for info. (ISBN 3-8204-7314-9). P Lang Pubs.

Division of Biology & Agriculture. Degradation of Synthetic Organic Molecules in the Biosphere. (Illus.). 352p. 1972. pap. 20.95 (ISBN 0-309-02046-8). Natl Acad Pr.

Division of Biology and Agriculture - Agricultural Board. Principles of Plant & Animal Pest Control, Vol. 4, Control Of Plant Parasitic Nematodes. 1968. pap. 11.50 (ISBN 0-309-01696-7). Natl Acad Pr.

Division of Building Research, ed. Testing Timber for Moisture Content. (Illus.). 31p. 1977. pap. 1.50x (ISBN 0-643-01073-4, Pub. by CSIRO). Intl Spec Bk.

Division of Chemistry & Chemical Technology. Critical Evaluation of Chemical & Physical Structural Information. LC 74-4164. (Illus.). 624p. 1974. pap. 37.95 (ISBN 0-309-02146-4). Natl Acad Pr.

--Specifications & Criteria for Biochemical Compounds. 3rd ed. 224p. 1972. 22.25 (ISBN 0-309-01917-6). Natl Acad Pr.

Division of Chemistry and Chemical Technology. Survey of Chemical Notation Systems. 1964. pap. 8.00 (ISBN 0-309-01150-7). Natl Acad Pr.

Division of Communications, jt. auth. see ABA Special Committee on Centennial.

Division of Earth Sciences. Rock-Mechanics Research in the U. S. (Illus.). 1966. pap. 5.25 (ISBN 0-309-01466-2). Natl Acad Pr.

Division Of Earth Sciences, jt. auth. see Geophysics Research Board.

Division of Health Sciences Policy, Institute of Medicine National Research Council. Toxic Shock Syndrome. 1982. pap. text ed. 10.50 (ISBN 0-309-03286-5). Natl Acad Pr.

Division of Mathematics - Committee on Support of Research in Mathematical Sciences. Mathematical Sciences: A Report. pap. 8.25 (ISBN 0-309-01681-9). Natl Acad Pr.

Division of Medical Sciences. Contraception: Science, Technology & Application. 1979. pap. 17.50 (ISBN 0-309-02892-2). Natl Acad Pr.

--Phototherapy in the Newborn: An Overview. LC 74-31207. 1975. pap. 13.95 (ISBN 0-309-02313-0). Natl Acad Pr.

Division of Medical Sciences, Assembly of Life Sciences, National Research Council. Chlorine & Hydrogen Chloride. LC 76-39940. (Medical & Biological Effects of Environmental Pollutants Ser.). 282p. 1976. pap. 11.50 (ISBN 0-309-02519-2). Natl Acad Pr.

Division of Medical Sciences, National Research Council. Copper. LC 76-57888. (Medical & Biologic Effects of Environmental Pollutants Ser.). 115p. 1977. pap. 8.50 (ISBN 0-309-02536-2). Natl Acad Pr.

Division of Mental Health & Behavioral Medicine, Institute of Medicine, National Research Council. Behavior, Health Risks & Social Disadvantage, Report No. 6. 198p. 1982. pap. text ed. 16.50 (ISBN 0-309-03295-4). Natl Acad Pr.

--Biobehavioral Factors in Sudden Cardiac Death, Report No. 3. 144p. 1981. pap. text ed. 12.25 (ISBN 0-309-03292-X). Natl Acad Pr.

--Combining Psychosocial & Drug Therapy, Report No. 2. 1982. pap. text ed. 13.50 (ISBN 0-309-03291-1). Natl Acad Pr.

--Health, Behavior & Aging, Report No. 5. 1982. pap. text ed. 9.95 (ISBN 0-309-03294-6). Natl Acad Pr.

Division of Mental Health & Behavioral Medicine, Institute of Medicine, National Research Counicil. Infants at Risk for Developmental Dysfunction, Report No. 4. 1982. pap. text ed. 11.50 (ISBN 0-309-03293-8). Natl Acad Pr.

Division of Mental Health & Behavioral Medicine, Institute of Medicine, National Research Council. Smoking & Behavior, Report No. 1. 1982. pap. text ed. 8.50 (ISBN 0-309-03290-3). Natl Acad Pr.

Division of Near Eastern Affairs, U. S. Department of State. The Palestine Mandate. Orig. Title: Mandate for Palestine. 1977. Repr. of 1927 ed. lib. bdg. 27.95x (ISBN 0-89712-061-2). Documentary Pubns.

Division of Physical Sciences. Physics in Perspective, Vol. 1. (Illus.). 1024p. 1974. pap. 28.50 (ISBN 0-309-02037-9). Natl Acad Pr.

--Research in Solid State Sciences: Opportunities & Relevance to National Needs. LC 8-61848. 1968. pap. 5.75 (ISBN 0-309-01600-2). Natl Acad Pr.

Division of Science Information, National Science Foundation. Current Research on Scientific & Technical Information Transfer. LC 77-9216. (Micropapers Editions Ser). 1977. 12.95x (ISBN 0-88432-007-3). J Norton Pubs.

Division of Soils Commenwealth Scientific & Industrial Research Organization, Australia, ed. Soils: An Australian View Point. 1983. 89.00 (ISBN 0-12-654240-6). Acad Pr.

Division of Statistics on Culture & Communication, Office of Statistics, UNESCO. Statistics on Radio & Television 1960-1976. (Statistical Reports & Studies: No. 23). (Illus.). 124p. 1979. pap. 5.25 (ISBN 92-3-101681-4, U929, UNESCO). Unipub.

Division of Statistics on Education, Office of Statistics. Statistics of Students Abroad: 1974-1978. (Statistical Reports & Studies: No. 27). (Illus.). 275p. (Eng. & Fr.). 1982. pap. 12.25 (ISBN 92-3-002050-8, U1253, UNESCO). Unipub.

Divita, S. F., ed. Advertising & the Public Interest. LC 74-82870. 300p. 1974. 16.00 (ISBN 0-87757-047-7). Am Mktg.

--Advertising & the Public Interest: Selected Papers from the Conference on Advertising & the Public Interest Held in Washington D.C., May 1973. LC 74-82870. pap. 70.00 (ISBN 0-317-28855-5, 2017780). Bks Demand UMI.

Divita, Sal & McLaughlin, Frank, eds. Consumer Complaints - Public Policy Alternatives. LC 75-43405. 1975. pap. 9.95 (ISBN 0-87491-064-1). Acropolis.

DiVitto, Barbara A., jt. auth. see Goldberg, Susan.

DIVO Institut fuer Wirtschaftsforschung, Sozialforschung und Angewandte Mathematik. German Election Study, October 1965. 1975. codebk. write for info. (ISBN 0-89138-109-0). ICPSR.

Divoky, Diane & Schrag, Peter. The Myth of the Hyperactive Child: And Other Means of Child Control. LC 75-10359. 320p. 1975. 10.00 (ISBN 0-394-49555-1). Pantheon.

Divort, Joan E. Van see Van Divort, Joan E.

Divry, D. C. Divry's Greek-English Dialogues. 1947. pocket ed. 7.00 (ISBN 0-685-09028-0). Divry.

Divry, G. C. Modern English-Greek-English Desk Dictionary with Thumb Index. 768p. (Gr. & Eng.). 1979. 19.95 (ISBN 0-686-97405-0, M-9443). French & Eur.

--New English-Greek-English Handy Dictionary. 511p. (Eng. & Gr.). 1978. 9.95 (ISBN 0-686-92414-2, M-9439). French & Eur.

Divry, George C. Divry's English-To-Greek Phrase & Conversation Pronouncing Manual. 1966. flexible bdg. 7.00 (ISBN 0-685-09027-2). Divry.

--Divry's New Modern Greek-English & English-Greek Handy Dictionary. (Greek & Eng.). 1983. pocket ed. 4.80 (ISBN 0-317-02288-1); thumb index 7.00 (ISBN 0-317-02289-X); lea. 9.00 (ISBN 0-317-02290-3). Divry.

--Divry's New Self Taught English Method for Greeks. 1983. 7.00 (ISBN 0-685-09032-9). Divry.

--Greek Made Easy. 3rd ed. 1953. 7.00 (ISBN 0-685-09037-X). Divry.

Diwakar, R. R. Mahayogi: Life, Sadhana & Teachings of Sri Aurobindo. 292p. 1976. pap. 6.00 (ISBN 0-89744-240-7, Pub. by Bharatiya Vidya Bhavan India). Auromere.

Diwaker, R. R., et al. Mohandas Karamchand Gandhi: A Bibliography. LC 75-901382. cancelled (ISBN 0-8364-0490-4, Orient Longman). South Asia Bks.

Diwal Kul. Intermediate Studies of the Human Aura. Prophet, Elizabeth C., ed. LC 75-19605. (Illus.). 139p. (Orig.). 1976. pap. 5.95 (ISBN 0-916766-13-6). Summit Univ.

Dix, Brian F., jt. auth. see Steane, John M.

Dix, C. Hewitt. Seismic Prospecting for Oil. 2nd ed. LC 80-84573. (Illus.). 422p. 1981. Repr. of 1952 ed. text ed. 36.00 (ISBN 0-934634-06-8). Intl Human Res.

Dix, Carol. D. H. Lawrence & Women. 126p. 1980. 18.75x (ISBN 0-8476-6196-2). Rowman.

--New Mother Syndrome: Coping with Post-Partum Stress & Depression. LC 85-1638. 312p. 1985. 17.95 (ISBN 0-385-27986-8, Dial). Doubleday.

Dix, Carol, jt. auth. see Scher, Jonathan.

Dix, Colin. Accommodation Operations: Front Office. 2nd ed. (Illus.). 166p. 1984. pap. text ed. 15.95x (ISBN 0-7121-0185-3). Trans-Atlantic.

--Accomodation Operations. 176p. 1979. pap. text ed. 15.95x (ISBN 0-7121-0174-8, Pub. by Macdonald & Evans). Trans-Atlantic.

Dix, David, ed. see Llewellyn Publications Staff.

Dix, Dom G. Power of God. 96p. 1984. pap. 5.95 (ISBN 0-8192-1334-9). Morehouse.

--The Shape of the Liturgy. 816p. 1982. 24.50 (ISBN 0-8164-2418-7, Pub. by Seabury). Winston Pr.

Dix, Dorothea L. On Behalf of the Insane Poor: Selected Reports 1843-1852. LC 78-137163. (Poverty U.S.A. Historical Record Ser). 1971. Repr. of 1843 ed. 27.50 (ISBN 0-405-03101-7). Ayer Co Pubs.

--Remarks on Prison & Prison Discipline in the United States. 2nd ed. LC 84-7714. (Patterson Smith Series in Criminology, Law Enforcement, & Social Problems: Publication No. 4). iv, 113p. 1984. Repr. of 1845 ed. lib. bdg. 13.50 (ISBN 0-87585-705-1). Patterson Smith.

--Remarks on Prisons & Prison Discipline in the United States. LC 67-24731. (Criminology, Law Enforcement, & Social Problems Ser.: No. 4). 1967. Repr. of 1845 ed. 10.00x (ISBN 0-87585-004-9). Patterson Smith.

Dix, Dorothy, pseud. How to Win & Hold a Husband. LC 74-3939. (Women in America Ser). 288p. 1974. Repr. of 1939 ed. 22.00x (ISBN 0-405-06086-6). Ayer Co Pubs.

Dix, Ernest R. Catalogue of Early Dublin Printed Books, 1601-1700, 4 vols in 2. LC 71-132673. 1971. Repr. of 1898 ed. Set. lib. bdg. 47.00 (ISBN 0-8337-0873-2). B Franklin.
--Printing in Dublin Prior to 1601. 2nd ed. LC 75-132674. 1971. Repr. of 1932 ed. lib. bdg. 14.50 (ISBN 0-8337-0874-0). B Franklin.
Dix, Frank L. Royal River Highway. (Illus.). 336p. 1985. 35.00 (ISBN 0-7153-8005-2). David & Charles.
Dix, George E. & Sharlot, M. Michael. Basic Criminal Law, Cases & Materials, Criminal Justice Ser. 2nd ed. 650p. 1980. text ed. 27.95 (ISBN 0-8299-0318-6); instrs.' manual avail. (ISBN 0-8299-0588-X). West Pub.
--Criminal Law Cases & Materials. 2nd ed. LC 79-16929. (American Casebook Ser.). 764p. 1979. text ed. 20.95 (ISBN 0-8299-2056-0). West Pub.
Dix, George E., jt. auth. see Dawson, Robert O.
Dix, George E., jt. ed. see Dahl, Richard C.
Dix, Gregory, ed. Apostoliki Paradosis: The Treatise on the Apostolic Tradition of St. Hippolytus of Rome, Bishop & Martyr, Vol. 1. (Church Historical Society, London, New Ser.: No. 24). pap. 23.00 (ISBN 0-317-15598-9). Kraus Repr.
Dix, H. M. Environmental Pollution: Atmosphere, Land, Water & Noise. LC 80-40287. (Institution of Environmental Sciences Ser.). 286p. 1981. 57.95x (ISBN 0-471-27797-5, Pub. by Wiley-Interscience); pap. 28.95x (ISBN 0-471-27905-6). Wiley.
Dix, Isabel. Cast a Tender Shadow. (Harlequin Presents Ser.). 192p. 1982. pap. 1.50 (ISBN 0-373-02491-6). Harlequin Bks.
Dix, J. Harlan. Allergy & Clinical Immunology: Continuing Education Review. 1981. pap. text ed. 24.00 (ISBN 0-87488-435-7). Med Exam.
Dix, John A. Sketch of the Resources of the City of New York: With a View of Its Municipal Government, Population, Etc. LC 79-112538. (Rise of Urban America). 1970. Repr. of 1827 ed. 17.00 (ISBN 0-405-02447-9). Ayer Co Pubs.
Dix, M. C. & Layzell, A. D. Road Users & the Police. (Illus.). 152p. 1983. 27.00 (ISBN 0-7099-2059-8, Pub. by Croom Helm Ltd); pap. 13.00 (ISBN 0-7099-2060-1). Longwood Pub Group.
Dix, M. C., et al. Car Use: A Social & Economic Study. LC 83-14177. 265p. 1983. text ed. 35.50 (ISBN 0-566-00666-9). Gower Pub Co.
Dix, M R. & Hood, J P. Vertigo. 491p. 1984. 60.00x (ISBN 0-471-90261-6, Pub by Wiley Med). Wiley.
Dix, O. R. & Jackson, M. P. Lithology, Microstructures, Fluid Inclusions, & Geochemistry of Rock Salt & of the Cap-Rock Contact in Oakwood Dome East Texas: Significance for Nuclear Waste Storage. (Report of Investigations: RI 120). (Illus.). 59p. 1982. 3.00 (ISBN 0-318-03261-9). Bur Econ Geology.
Dix, Otto. Der Krieg. LC 71-147682. (Library of War & Peace; Artists on War). 1972. lib. bdg. 42.00 (ISBN 0-8240-0439-6). Garland Pub.
--Der Krieg: Twenty Four Offsetdruke Nach Originden Aus Dem Radierwerk. Cook, Blanche W. & Chatfield, Charles, eds. (Library of War & Peace). 46.00 (ISBN 0-317-26265-3). Garland Pub.
Dix, Samuel M. The Cost of Future Freedom: Energy Economics. 1982. 15.95 (ISBN 0-918998-05-0). Energy Educ.
--Energy: A Critical Decision for the United States Economy. LC 77-78403. (Illus.). 1977. 12.95 (ISBN 0-918998-01-8); pap. text ed. 5.95 (ISBN 0-918998-02-6). Energy Educ.
Dix, Suzan. The Phantom Light. 224p. (Orig.). (gr. 7 up). 1983. pap. 1.95 (ISBN 0-590-32534-5, Windswept Bks). Scholastic Inc.
Dix, William, ed. see American Library Association Committee On Intellectual Freedom-1st Conference-New York-1952.
Dixhoorn, J. van see Van Dixhoorn, J. & Karnopp, D.
Dixhoorn, Jan J. Van see Karnopp, Dean, et al.
Dixin, Xu, et al. China's Search for Economic Growth. (Illus.). 217p. (Orig.). 1982. pap. 5.95 (ISBN 0-8351-0974-7); 8.95 (ISBN 0-8351-1030-3). China Bks.
Dixit, A. & Norman, V. D. Theory of International Trade. (Cambridge Economic Handbooks). 250p. 1980. 42.50 (ISBN 0-521-23481-6); pap. 17.95 (ISBN 0-521-29969-1). Cambridge U Pr.
Dixit, A. K. Optimization in Economic Theory. (Illus.). 1976. pap. 9.95x (ISBN 0-19-877103-7). Oxford U Pr.
Dixit, Avinash. The Theory of Equilibrium Growth. (Illus.). 1976. text ed. 15.95x (ISBN 0-19-877080-4); pap. text ed. 10.95x (ISBN 0-19-877081-2). Oxford U Pr.
Dixit, Prabha. Communalism: A Struggle for Power. 248p. 1981. 30.00x (ISBN 0-86125-039-7, Pub. by Orient Longman India). State Mutual Bk.
Dixit, R. K. Political History of Chandalas. 1977. 16.00x (ISBN 0-8364-0446-7). South Asia Bks.
Dixler. Red Badge of Courage (Crane) (Book Notes Ser.). 1984. pap. 2.50 (ISBN 0-8120-3438-4). Barron.
Dixmier, J. C Algebras. (Mathematical Library Studies: 15). 492p. 1977. 68.00 (ISBN 0-7204-0762-1, North-Holland). Elsevier.
--Enveloping Algebras. (North Holland Mathematical Library: Vol. 14). 376p. 1977. 55.50 (ISBN 0-7204-0430-4, North-Holland). Elsevier.
--General Topology. Berberian, S. K., tr. from Fr. (Undergraduate Texts in Mathematics Ser.). 125p. 1984. 19.80 (ISBN 0-387-90972-9). Springer Verlag.
--Von Neumann Algebras. (Mathematical Library: Vol. 27). 438p. 1981. 57.50 (ISBN 0-444-86308-7, North-Holland). Elsevier.
Dixon. Advances in Immunology, Vol. 35. 1984. 40.00 (ISBN 0-12-022435-6). Acad Pr.
Dixon, et al, trs. see Insingel, Mark, et al.
Dixon, A. C. Beyond the Sunset. pap. 1.25 (ISBN 0-8010-2801-9). Baker Bk.
Dixon, A. F. Aphid Ecology. 168p. 1985. text ed. 39.95 (ISBN 0-412-00411-9, NO. 5047, Pub. by Chapman & Hall England). Methuen Inc.
Dixon, A. F., jt. auth. see Carter, N.
Dixon, Adrian K. Body C. T. (Illus.). 176p. (Orig.). 1983. pap. text ed. 24.00 (ISBN 0-443-02956-3). Churchill.
Dixon, Adrienne, tr. see Boon, Louis P.
Dixon, Adrienne, tr. see Insingel, Mark.
Dixon, Adrienne, tr. see Michiels, Ivo.
Dixon, Adrienne, tr. see Montyn, Jan.
Dixon, Adrienne, tr. see Nooteboom, Cees.
Dixon, Alan C. Network Analysis. LC 72-90475. 1973. text ed. 28.95 (ISBN 0-675-09024-5). Merrill.
Dixon, Andrew D. & Sarnat, Bernard G., eds. Factors & Mechanisms Influencing Bone Growth. LC 82-13115. (Progress in Clinical & Biological Research Ser.: Vol. 101). 680p. 1982. 96.00 (ISBN 0-8451-0101-3). A R Liss.
Dixon, B. R. & Renowden, P. I Can Manage. 1983. write for info (ISBN 0-07-072902-6). McGraw.
Dixon, Bashford. Biology of the Rhodophyta. (University Reviews of Botany: No. 4). (Illus.). 285p. 1977. pap. text ed. 17.50x (ISBN 3-87429-124-3). Lubrecht & Cramer.
Dixon, Bernard. Beyond the Magic Bullet: The Real Story of Medicine. LC 77-11811. 1978. 12.45i (ISBN 0-06-011062-7, HarpT). Har-Row.
--Magnificent Microbes. LC 75-14678. 1979. pap. 4.95 (ISBN 0-689-70589-1, 250). Atheneum.
Dixon, Billy R., et al, eds. see Morant, Mack B.
Dixon, Bob. Searching for Aboriginal Languages: Memoirs of a Field Worker. LC 83-5919. (Illus.). 330p. 1984. text ed. 29.95 (ISBN 0-7022-1713-1); pap. 14.95 (ISBN 0-7022-1933-9). U of Queensland Pr.
Dixon, Browning M. Chatterton. 1930. 10.00 (ISBN 0-8492-0656-1). R West.
Dixon, C. W. Society, Schools & Progress in Scandinavia. 1965. 30.00 (ISBN 0-08-011405-9); pap. 13.75 (ISBN 0-08-011404-0). Pergamon.
Dixon, C. Willis. Colonial Administration of Sir Thomas Maitland. 1968. Repr. of 1939 ed. 27.50x (ISBN 0-7146-1469-6, F Cass Co). Biblio Dist.
--Colonial Administrations of Sir Thomas Maitland. LC 74-94534. Repr. of 1939 ed. lib. bdg. 27.50x (ISBN 0-678-05099-6). Kelley.
Dixon, Canon, jt. auth. see Lock, John.
Dixon, Carol. Language Experience Approach to Reading (& Writing) (Illus.). 136p. 1983. pap. text ed. 11.95 (ISBN 0-88084-037-4). Alemany Pr.
Dixon, Charles. Advanced Calculus. LC 80-41382. 147p. 1981. 39.95 (ISBN 0-471-27913-7, Pub. by Wiley-Interscience); pap. 25.95 (ISBN 0-471-27914-5). Wiley.
Dixon, Colin J. Atlas of Economic Mineral Deposits. (Illus.). 143p. 1979. 125.00x (ISBN 0-8014-1231-5). Cornell U Pr.
Dixon, Conrad. Basic Astro Navigation. (Illus.). 119p. 1973. 9.95x (ISBN 0-8464-0173-8). Beekman Pubs.
--Basic Astro Navigation. (Illus.). 119p. (Orig.). 1985. pap. 7.95 (ISBN 0-229-11740-6, Pub. by Adlard Coles). Sheridan.
--Basic Coastal Navigation. (Illus.). 96p. 1973. 6.95x (ISBN 0-8464-0174-6). Beekman Pubs.
--Basic Coastal Navigation. (Illus.). 96p. 1985. pap. text ed. 6.95 (ISBN 0-229-11739-2, Pub. by Adlard Coles). Sheridan.
--Navigation by Pocket Calculator. (Illus.). 80p. (Orig.). 1983. pap. 4.95 (ISBN 0-229-11691-4, Pub. by Adlard Coles). Sheridan.
--Start to Navigate. (Illus.). 120p. 1977. 9.95x (ISBN 0-8464-1139-3). Beekman Pubs.
--Start to Navigate. 2nd ed. (Illus.). 128p. (Orig.). 1983. pap. 9.95 (ISBN 0-229-11706-6, Pub. by Adlard Coles). Sheridan.
Dixon, D. N. & Glover, J. A. Counseling: A Problem Solving Approach. 239p. 1984. 20.95 (ISBN 0-471-88877-X). Wiley.
Dixon, Daphne, jt. auth. see Francis, Dorothy.
Dixon, Diana & Hills, Philip. Talking about Your Research. 1981. 25.00x (ISBN 0-906083-19-2, Pub. by Primary Com England). State Mutual Bk.
Dixon, Diana, jt. auth. see Madden, Lionel.
Dixon, Dorothy. Leather & Lace, No. 1: The Lavender Blossom. (Orig.). 1982. pap. 2.50 (ISBN 0-8217-1029-X). Zebra.
--Leather & Lace, No. 2: The Trembling Heart. (Orig.). 1982. pap. 2.50 (ISBN 0-686-97467-0). Zebra.
--Leather & Lace, No. 3: The Belle of the Rio Grande. (Orig.). 1982. pap. 2.50 (ISBN 0-8217-1059-1). Zebra.
--Leather & Lace, No. 4: Flame of the West. 1982. pap. 2.50 (ISBN 0-8217-1091-5). Zebra.
--Leather & Lace, No. 5: Cimarron Rose. 1982. pap. 2.50 (ISBN 0-8217-1106-7). Zebra.
--Leather & Lace, No. 7: Diamond Queen. 1983. pap. 2.50 (ISBN 0-8217-1138-5). Zebra.
--Teaching Children to Care. (Illus.). 306p. (Orig.). (gr. k-3). tchrs. ed. 19.95x (ISBN 0-89622-144-X). Twenty-Third.
--Yellowstone Jewel. (Leather & Lace Ser.: Vol. 9). 1983. pap. 2.50 (ISBN 0-8217-1237-3). Zebra.
Dixon, Dougal. After Man: A Zoology of the Future. LC 81-50345. (Illus.). 128p. 1981. 14.95 (ISBN 0-312-01163-6). St Martin.
--After Man: A Zoology of the Future. (Illus.). 128p. 1983. pap. 9.95 (ISBN 0-312-01162-8). St Martin.
--A Closer Look at Prehistoric Reptiles. (A Closer Look at... Ser.). (Illus.). 32p. (gr. 4 up). 1984. lib. bdg. 8.90 (ISBN 0-531-03480-1, Gloucester Pr). Watts.
--Deserts & Wastelands. (Picture Atlas Ser.). (Illus.). 40p. (gr. 4 up). 1985. lib. bdg. 10.90 (ISBN 0-531-04921-3). Watts.
--Forests. LC 84-51225. (Picture Atlas Ser.). (Illus.). 40p. 1984. lib. bdg. 9.90 (ISBN 0-531-04834-9). Watts.
--Geography. (Science World Ser.). 40p. (gr. 4 up). 1984. lib. bdg. 9.90 (ISBN 0-531-04744-X). Watts.
--Geology. (Science World Ser.). (Illus.). 40p. (gr. 4 up). 1983. PLB 9.90 (ISBN 0-531-04582-X). Watts.
--Mountains. LC 84-51226. (Picture Atlas Ser.). (Illus.). 38p. (gr. 4-6). 1984. PLB 10.90 (ISBN 0-531-04834-9). Watts.
Dixon, Dougal, jt. auth. see Burton, Jane.
Dixon, Dwight R. & Dixon, Paul B. Photography: Experiments & Projects. (Illus.). 1976. pap. text ed. write for info. (ISBN 0-02-329840-5). Macmillan.
Dixon, E. J. see Taliaferro, W. H. & Humphrey, J. H.
Dixon, Edward L., Jr., ed. The Franchise Annual Directory 1985. 277p. 1985. pap. text ed. 19.95. Info Pr NY.
Dixon, Eileen. The Theatre Nurse & the Law. 144p. (Orig.). 1984. pap. 14.50 (ISBN 0-7099-0818-0, Pub. by Croom Helm Ltd). Longwood Pub Group.
--Theatre Technique. 5th ed. (Illus.). 304p. 1983. pap. 9.95 (ISBN 0-7216-0804-3, Pub. by Bailliere-Tindall). Saunders.
Dixon, Eustace A. New Jersey: Environment & Cancer. Vivian, V. Eugene, ed. (Illus.). 410p. 1982. 19.95 (ISBN 0-942848-00-4); pap. 12.95 (ISBN 0-942848-01-2). Eureka Pubns.
Dixon, Eustace A., ed. see Lipfert, Frederick W.
Dixon, F. J., Jr. see Taliaferro, W. H. & Humphrey, J. H.
Dixon, Frank & Fisher, David W. Immunopathology. 1980. text ed. write for info. HP Pub Co.
Dixon, Frank, jt. ed. see Kunkel, Henry.
Dixon, Frank H. State Railroad Control with a History of Its Development in Iowa. Bruchey, Stuart, ed. LC 80-1303. (Railroads Ser.). 1981. Repr. of 1896 ed. lib. bdg. 22.00x (ISBN 0-405-13772-9). Ayer Co Pubs.
Dixon, Frank J. & Miescher, Peter A. Immunopathology: Eighth International Symposium. 1982. 65.00 (ISBN 0-12-218320-7). Acad Pr.
Dixon, Frank J., ed. Advances in Immunology, Vol. 36. 1984. 36.50 (ISBN 0-12-022436-4). Acad Pr.
--Advances in Immunology, Vol. 37. 1985. 49.50 (ISBN 0-12-022437-2). Acad Pr.
Dixon, Frank J. & Fisher, David W., eds. Biology of Immunologic Disease. LC 83-4780. (Illus.). 399p. 1983. text ed. 32.50x (ISBN 0-87893-148-1). Sinauer Assoc.
Dixon, Frank J. & Kunkel, Henry G., eds. Advances in Immunology, Vol. 34. (Serial Publication Ser.). 1983. 45.00 (ISBN 0-12-022434-8). Acad Pr.
Dixon, Franklin W. Arctic Patrol Mystery. LC 69-12166. (Hardy Boys Ser: Vol. 48). (Illus.). (gr. 4-7). 1969. 2.95 (ISBN 0-448-08948-3, G&D). Putnam Pub Group.
--Bombay Boomerang. LC 70-100116. (Hardy Boys Ser.: Vol. 49). (Illus.). (gr. 5-9). 1970. 2.95 (ISBN 0-448-08949-1, G&D). Putnam Pub Group.
--The Clue in the Embers. LC 74-181843. (Hardy Boys Ser.: Vol. 35). (Illus.). 196p. (gr. 5-9). 1956. 2.95 (ISBN 0-448-08935-1, G&D). Putnam Pub Group.
--Clue of the Broken Blade. LC 73-119043. (Hardy Boys Ser: Vol. 21). (Illus.). (gr. 5-9). 1942. 2.95 (ISBN 0-448-08921-1, G&D). Putnam Pub Group.
--The Clue of the Hissing Serpent. new ed. (Hardy Boys Ser.: Vol. 53). (Illus.). 196p. (gr. 5-9). 1974. 2.95 (ISBN 0-448-08953-X, G&D). Putnam Pub Group.
--Clue of the Screeching Owl. (Hardy Boys Ser: Vol. 41). (Illus.). (gr. 5-9). 1962. 2.95 (ISBN 0-448-08941-6, G&D). Putnam Pub Group.
--The Crimson Flame. Barish, Wendy, ed. (Hardy Boys Ser.: No. 77). 192p. (gr. 3-7). 1983. 8.95 (ISBN 0-671-42366-5); pap. 2.95 (ISBN 0-671-42367-3). Wanderer Bks.
--Crisscross Shadow. rev. ed. (Hardy Boys Ser: Vol. 32). (gr. 5-9). 1953. 2.95 (ISBN 0-448-08932-7, G&D); PLB 3.29 (ISBN 0-448-18932-1, G&D). Putnam Pub Group.
--Danger on Vampire Trail. LC 70-130337. (Hardy Boys Ser.: Vol. 50). (Illus.). (gr. 5-9). 1971. 2.95 (ISBN 0-448-08950-5, G&D). Putnam Pub Group.
--Disappearing Floor. (Hardy Boys Ser: Vol. 19). (gr. 5-9). 1940. 2.95 (ISBN 0-448-08919-X, G&D). Putnam Pub Group.
--Figure in Hiding. (Hardy Boys Ser: Vol. 16). (gr. 5-9). 1937. 2.95 (ISBN 0-448-08916-5, G&D); PLB 3.29 (ISBN 0-448-18916-X, G&D). Putnam Pub Group.
--The Firebird Rocket. LC 77-76131. (Hardy Boys Ser.: Vol. 57). (Illus.). (gr. 5-9). 1978. 2.95 (ISBN 0-448-08957-2, G&D). Putnam Pub Group.
--Flickering Torch Mystery. (Hardy Boys Ser: Vol. 22). (gr. 5-9). 1943. 2.95 (ISBN 0-448-08922-X, G&D); PLB 3.29 (ISBN 0-448-18922-4, G&D). Putnam Pub Group.
--Footprints under the Window. (Hardy Boys Ser: Vol. 12). (gr. 5-9). 1933. 3.29 (ISBN 0-448-18912-7, G&D). Putnam Pub Group.
--Ghost at Skeleton Rock. rev. ed. (Hardy Boys Ser: Vol. 37). (gr. 5-9). 1958. 2.95 (ISBN 0-448-08937-8, G&D). Putnam Pub Group.
--Great Airport Mystery. (Hardy Boys Ser: Vol. 9). (gr. 5-9). 1930. 2.95 (ISBN 0-448-08909-2, G&D). Putnam Pub Group.
--Hardy Boys: Billion Dollar Ransom. Barish, Wendy, ed. (Hardy Boys Ser.: 73). (Illus.). 192p. (gr. 3-7). 1982. 8.95 (ISBN 0-671-42352-5); pap. 2.75 (ISBN 0-671-42355-X). Wanderer Bks.
--The Hardy Boys: Demon's Den. Barish, Wendy, ed. (The Hardy Boys Ser.: No. 81). (Illus.). 208p. (gr. 3 up). 1984. 9.95 (ISBN 0-671-49724-3); pap. 2.95 (ISBN 0-671-49723-5). Wanderer Bks.
--The Hardy Boys: Ghost Stories. Schwartz, Betty, ed. (The Hardy Boys Ser.). (Illus.). 160p. (Orig.). (gr. 3-7). 1984. pap. 2.95 (ISBN 0-671-50808-3). Wanderer Bks.
--The Hardy Boys Gift Set, 3 vols. Boxed Set. pap. 8.55 (ISBN 0-317-12424-2). Wanderer Bks.
--Hardy Boys: Mystery of Smugglers Cove. (The Hardy Boys Ser.: No. 64). 192p. (gr. 3-7). 1980. PLB 8.95 (ISBN 0-671-41117-9); pap. 2.95 (ISBN 0-671-41112-8). Wanderer Bks.
--The Hardy Boys No. 75: Trapped at Sea. Schneider, Meg, ed. (Illus.). 192p. (gr. 3-7). 1982. 8.95 (ISBN 0-671-42362-2); pap. 2.95 (ISBN 0-671-42363-0). Wanderer Bks.
--The Hardy Boys Number Seventy-Six: Game Plan for Disaster. Schneider, Meg, ed. (Illus.). 208p. (gr. 3-7). 1982. 8.95 (ISBN 0-671-42364-9); pap. 2.95 (ISBN 0-671-42365-7). Wanderer Bks.
--Hardy Boys: The Apeman's Secret. (Hardy Boys Ser.: No. 62). (Illus.). 192p. (Orig.). (gr. 3-7). 1980. 8.95 (ISBN 0-671-95530-6); pap. 2.95 (ISBN 0-671-95482-2). Wanderer Bks.
--The Hardy Boys: The Blackwing Puzzle. (Hardy Boys Ser.: No. 82). 1984. 8.95 (ISBN 0-671-49726-X, Juveniles); pap. 2.95 (ISBN 0-671-49725-1). S&S.
--Hardy Boys: The Demon's Den. (Hardy Boys Ser.: No. 81). 1984. 8.95 (ISBN 0-671-49724-3, Juveniles); pap. 2.95 (ISBN 0-671-49723-5). S&S.
--Hardy Boys: The Infinity Clue. (The Hardy Boys Ser.: No. 70). (Illus.). 192p. (Orig.). (gr. 3-7). 1981. 8.95 (ISBN 0-671-42342-8); pap. 2.95 (ISBN 0-671-42343-6). Wanderer Bks.
--Hardy Boys: The Mummy Case. (The Hardy Boys Ser.: No. 63). 192p. (gr. 3-7). 1980. PLB 8.95 (ISBN 0-671-41116-0); pap. 2.95 (ISBN 0-671-41111-X). Wanderer Bks.
--Hardy Boys: The Outlaw's Silver. (The Hardy Boys Ser.: No. 67). 192p. (Orig.). (gr. 3-7). 1981. 8.95 (ISBN 0-671-42336-3); pap. 2.95 (ISBN 0-671-42337-1). Wanderer Bks.
--Hardy Boys: The Pentagon Spy. (Hardy Boys Ser.: No. 61). (Illus.). (gr. 3-7). 1980. lib. bdg. 8.95 (ISBN 0-671-95562-4); pap. 2.95 (ISBN 0-671-95570-5). Wanderer Bks.
--The Hardy Boys: The Skyfire Puzzle. Arico, Diane, ed. (The Hardy Boys Mystery Stories Ser.: No. 85). 160p. (gr. 3-7). 1985. 9.95 (ISBN 0-671-49732-4); pap. 3.50 (ISBN 0-671-49731-6). Wanderer Bks.
--Hardy Boys: The Stone Idol. (Hardy Boys Ser.: No. 65). (Illus.). 192p. (gr. 3-7). 1981. 8.95 (ISBN 0-671-42289-8); pap. 2.95 (ISBN 0-671-42290-1). Wanderer Bks.
--Hardy Boys: The Submarine Caper. (Hardy Boys Ser.: No. 68). (Illus.). 192p. (Orig.). (gr. 3-7). 1981. 8.95 (ISBN 0-671-42338-X); pap. 2.95 (ISBN 0-671-42339-8). Wanderer Bks.
--The Hardy Boys: The Swamp Monster. Arico, Diane, ed. (The Hardy Boys Mystery Stories Ser.). 192p. (gr. 8-12). 1985. 9.95 (ISBN 0-671-55054-3); pap. 3.50 (ISBN 0-671-55048-9). Wanderer Bks.
--Hardy Boys: The Vanishing Thieves. (Hardy Boys Ser.: No. 66). (Illus.). 176p. (Orig.). (gr. 3-7). 8.95 (ISBN 0-671-42291-X); pap. 2.95 (ISBN 0-671-42292-8). Wanderer Bks.
--Hardy Boys: Tic-Tac Terror. (The Hardy Boys Ser.: No. 74). (Illus.). 192p. (gr. 3-7). 1982. 8.95 (ISBN 0-671-42356-8); pap. 2.95 (ISBN 0-671-42357-6). Wanderer Bks.
--Hardy Boys: Track of the Zombie. (The Hardy Boys Ser.: No. 71). (Illus.). 192p. (gr. 3-7). 1982. 8.95 (ISBN 0-671-42348-7); pap. 2.95 (ISBN 0-671-42349-5). Wanderer Bks.
--Hardy Boys: Voodoo Plot. (The Hardy Boys Ser.: No. 72). (Illus.). 192p. (gr. 3-7). 1982. 8.95 (ISBN 0-671-42350-9); pap. 2.95 (ISBN 0-671-42351-7). Wanderer Bks.
--Haunted Fort. (Hardy Boys Ser: Vol. 44). (gr. 5-9). 1964. 2.95 (ISBN 0-448-08944-0, G&D). Putnam Pub Group.

--Hidden Harbor Mystery. (Hardy Boy Ser: Vol. 14). (gr. 5-9). 1935. 2.95 (ISBN 0-448-08914-9, G&D). Putnam Pub Group.
--Hooded Hawk Mystery. rev. ed. (Hardy Boys Ser: Vol. 34). (Illus.). (gr. 5-9). 1955. 2.95 (ISBN 0-448-08934-3, G&D); PLB 3.29 (ISBN 0-448-18934-8, G&D). Putnam Pub Group.
--House on the Cliff. (Hardy Boys Ser: Vol. 2). (gr. 5-9). 1927. 2.95 (ISBN 0-448-08902-5, G&D). Putnam Pub Group.
--Hunting for Hidden Gold. (Hardy Boys Ser.: Vol. 5). (gr. 5-9). 1928. 2.95 (ISBN 0-448-08905-X, G&D). Putnam Pub Group.
--The Jungle Pyramid. LC 76-14297. (Hardy Boys Ser.: Vol. 56). (Illus.). (gr. 5-9). 1977. 2.95 (ISBN 0-448-08956-4, G&D). Putnam Pub Group.
--Mark on the Door. rev. ed. (Hardy Boys Ser: Vol. 13). (gr. 5-9). 1934. 2.95 (ISBN 0-448-08913-0, G&D). Putnam Pub Group.
--The Masked Monkey. (Hardy Boys Ser.: Vol. 51). (Illus.). 196p. (gr. 5-9). 1972. 2.95 (ISBN 0-448-08951-3, G&D). Putnam Pub Group.
--Melted Coins. rev. ed. LC 78-86722. (Hardy Boys Ser.: Vol. 23). (Illus.). (gr. 5-9). 1944. 2.95 (ISBN 0-448-18923-2, G&D). Putnam Pub Group.
--Missing Chums. rev. ed. (Hardy Boys Ser: Vol. 4). (gr. 5-9). 1930. 2.95 (ISBN 0-448-08904-1, G&D); PLB 3.29 (ISBN 0-448-18904-6). Putnam Pub Group.
--The Mysterious Caravan. new ed. LC 74-10463. (Hardy Boys Ser.: Vol. 54). (Illus.). 196p. (gr. 5-9). 1975. 2.95 (ISBN 0-448-08954-8, G&D). Putnam Pub Group.
--Mystery at Devil's Paw. (Hardy Boys Ser.: Vol. 38). (Illus.). 192p. (gr. 5-9). 1959. Repr. 2.95 (ISBN 0-448-08938-6, G&D). Putnam Pub Group.
--Mystery of Cabin Island. (Hardy Boys Ser: Vol. 8). (gr. 5-9). 1929. 2.95 (ISBN 0-448-08908-4, G&D). Putnam Pub Group.
--Mystery of the Aztec Warrior. (Hardy Boys Ser: Vol. 43). (gr. 5-9). 1964. 2.95 (ISBN 0-448-08943-2, G&D). Putnam Pub Group.
--Mystery of the Chinese Junk. (Hardy Boys Ser.: Vol. 39). (gr. 5-9). 1959. 3.29 (ISBN 0-448-18939-9, G&D). Putnam Pub Group.
--Mystery of the Desert Giant. (Hardy Boys Ser.: Vol. 40). (Illus.). (gr. 5-9). 1960. PLB 3.29 (ISBN 0-448-18940-2, G&D). Putnam Pub Group.
--Mystery of the Flying Express. LC 73-106327. (Hardy Boys Ser.: Vol. 20). (Illus.). (gr. 5-9). 1941. 2.95 (ISBN 0-448-08920-3, G&D). Putnam Pub Group.
--The Mystery of the Samurai Sword. (The Hardy Boys Ser.: No. 60). (Illus.). (gr. 3-6). 1979. 7.95 (ISBN 0-671-95506-3); pap. 2.95 (ISBN 0-671-95497-0). Wanderer Bks.
--Mystery of the Samurai Sword. (The Hardy Boys Boxed Gift Set Ser.: No. 60). (gr. 2-7). 1984. 8.85 (ISBN 0-671-93296-9). Wanderer Bks.
--Mystery of the Spiral Bridge. (Hardy Boys Ser: Vol. 45). (Illus.). (gr. 5-9). 1966. 2.95 (ISBN 0-448-08945-9, G&D). Putnam Pub Group.
--Mystery of the Whale Tattoo. (Hardy Boys Ser: Vol. 47). (gr. 5-9). 1967. 2.95 (ISBN 0-448-08947-5, G&D). Putnam Pub Group.
--Night of the Werewolf. (The Hardy Boys Ser.: No. 59). (Illus.). (gr. 3-6). 1979. 8.95 (ISBN 0-671-95498-9); pap. 2.95 (ISBN 0-671-95520-9). Wanderer Bks.
--Night of the Werewolf. (The Hardy Boys Boxed Gift Set Ser.: No. 59). (gr. 2-7). 1984. 8.85 (ISBN 0-671-93296-9). Wanderer Bks.
--The Pentagon Spy. (The Hardy Boys Boxed Gift Set Ser.: No. 61). (gr. 2-7). 1984. 8.85 (ISBN 0-671-93296-9). Wanderer Bks.
--Phantom Freighter. rev. ed. LC 75-115957. (Hardy Boys Ser.: Vol. 26). (Illus.). (gr. 5-9). 1947. 2.95 (ISBN 0-448-08926-2, G&D); PLB 3.29 (ISBN 0-448-18926-7). Putnam Pub Group.
--The Roaring River Mystery. Schwartz, Betty, ed. (The Hardy Boys Ser.: No. 80). (Illus.). 192p. (Orig.). (gr. 3-7). 1984. 8.95 (ISBN 0-671-49722-7); pap. 2.95 (ISBN 0-671-49721-9). Wanderer Bks.
--Secret Agent on Flight 101. (Hardy Boys Ser: Vol. 46). (gr. 5-9). 1967. 2.95 (ISBN 0-448-08946-7, G&D). Putnam Pub Group.
--The Secret of Pirates' Hill. rev. ed. (Hardy Boys Ser.: Vol. 36). (Illus.). 196p. (gr. 5-9). 1957. 2.95 (ISBN 0-448-08936-X, G&D). Putnam Pub Group.
--Secret of Skull Mountain. (Hardy Boys Ser: Vol. 27). (gr. 5-9). 1948. 2.95 (ISBN 0-448-08927-0, G&D). Putnam Pub Group.
--Secret of the Caves. rev. ed. (Hardy Boys Ser: Vol. 7). (gr. 5-9). 1929. 2.95 (ISBN 0-448-08907-6, G&D). Putnam Pub Group.
--Secret of the Lost Tunnel. rev. ed. (Hardy Boys Ser: Vol. 29). (Illus.). (gr. 5-9). 1950. 2.95 (ISBN 0-448-08929-7, G&D). Putnam Pub Group.
--Secret of the Old Mill. (Hardy Boys Ser: Vol. 3). (gr. 5-9). 1927. 2.95 (ISBN 0-448-08903-3, G&D). Putnam Pub Group.
--Secret of Wildcat Swamp. (Hardy Boys Ser: Vol. 31). (gr. 5-9). 1952. 2.95 (ISBN 0-448-08931-9, G&D). Putnam Pub Group.
--Secret Panel. rev. ed. LC 74-86693. (Hardy Boys Ser.: Vol. 25). (Illus.). (gr. 5-9). 1946. 2.95 (ISBN 0-448-08925-4, G&D). Putnam Pub Group.
--Secret Warning. (Hardy Boys Ser: Vol. 17). (gr. 5-9). 1938. 2.95 (ISBN 0-448-08917-3, G&D). Putnam Pub Group.
--The Shattered Helmet. LC 72-90825. (Hardy Boys Ser.: Vol. 52). (Illus.). 196p. (gr. 5-9). 1973. 2.95 (ISBN 0-448-08952-1, G&D); PLB 3.29 (ISBN 0-448-18952-6). Putnam Pub Group.
--Shore Road Mystery. (Hardy Boys Ser: Vol. 6). (Illus.). (gr. 5-9). 1964. 2.95 (ISBN 0-448-08906-8, G&D). Putnam Pub Group.
--Short-Wave Mystery. rev. ed. (Hardy Boys Ser: Vol. 24). (gr. 5-9). 1928. 2.95 (ISBN 0-448-08924-6, G&D); PLB 3.29 (ISBN 0-448-18924-0). Putnam Pub Group.
--Sign of the Crooked Arrow. rev ed. LC 71-100119. (Hardy Boys Ser.: Vol. 28). (Illus.). (gr. 5-9). 1949. 2.95 (ISBN 0-448-08928-9, G&D); PLB 3.29 (ISBN 0-448-18928-3, Putnam). Putnam Pub Group.
--Sinister Sign Post. (Hardy Boys Ser: Vol. 15). (gr. 5-9). 1936. 2.95 (ISBN 0-448-08915-7, G&D); PLB 3.29 (ISBN 0-448-18915-1). Putnam Pub Group.
--The Sting of the Scorpion. LC 78-57930. (Hardy Boys Ser.: Vol. 58). (Illus.). (gr. 3-7). 1979. 2.95 (ISBN 0-448-08958-0, G&D). Putnam Pub Group.
--Tower Treasure. (Hardy Boys Ser: Vol. 1). (gr. 5-9). 1927. 2.95 (ISBN 0-448-08901-7, G&D). Putnam Pub Group.
--Twisted Claw. rev. ed. LC 77-86667. (Hardy Boys Ser.: Vol. 18). (Illus.). (gr. 5-9). 1939. 2.95 (ISBN 0-448-08918-1, G&D). Putnam Pub Group.
--Viking Symbol Mystery. (Hardy Boys Ser: Vol. 42). (gr. 5-9). 1963. 2.95 (ISBN 0-448-08942-4, G&D). Putnam Pub Group.
--Wailing Siren Mystery. rev. ed. (Hardy Boys Ser: Vol. 30). (Illus.). (gr. 5-9). 1951. 2.95 (ISBN 0-448-08930-0, G&D); PLB 3.29 (ISBN 0-448-18930-5). Putnam Pub Group.
--What Happened at Midnight. (Hardy Boys Ser: Vol. 10). (gr. 5-9). 1931. 2.95 (ISBN 0-448-08910-6, G&D). Putnam Pub Group.
--While the Clock Ticked. (Hardy Boys Ser: Vol. 11). (gr. 5-9). 1932. 2.95 (ISBN 0-448-08911-4, G&D). Putnam Pub Group.
--The Witchmaster's Key. LC 75-17392. (Hardy Boys Ser.: Vol. 55). (Illus.). 196p. (gr. 5-9). 1976. 2.95 (ISBN 0-448-08955-6, G&D). Putnam Pub Group.
--Yellow Feather Mystery. (Hardy Boys Ser: Vol. 33). (gr. 5-9). 1954. 2.95 (ISBN 0-448-08933-5, G&D); PLB 3.29 (ISBN 0-448-18933-X). Putnam Pub Group.
Dixon, Franklin W. & Barish, Wendy. Cave-In. (The Hardy Boys Ser.: No. 78). (Illus.). 192p. (Orig.). (gr. 3-7). 1983. 8.95 (ISBN 0-671-42368-1); pap. 2.95 (ISBN 0-671-42369-X). Wanderer Bks.
--Sky Sabotage. (The Hardy Boys Ser.: No. 79). (Illus.). 192p. (Orig.). (gr. 3-7). 1983. 8.95 (ISBN 0-671-47556-8); pap. 2.95 (ISBN 0-671-47557-6). Wanderer Bks.
Dixon, Franklin W. & Keene, Carolyn. The Secret of the Knight's Sword. Schwartz, Betty, ed. (Nancy Drew & The Hardy Boys Be a Detective Mystery Stories Ser.: No. 1). (Illus.). 128p. (Orig.). (gr. 3-7). 1984. pap. 2.95 (ISBN 0-671-49919-X). Wanderer Bks.
Dixon, Franklin W. & Link, Sheila. Hardy Boys Handbook: Seven Stories of Survival. (Illus.). 144p. (gr. 3-7). 1980. PLB 8.95 (ISBN 0-671-95705-8); pap. 3.95 (ISBN 0-671-95602-7). Wanderer Bks.
Dixon, Franklin W. & Spina, D. A. Hardy Boys Detective Handbook. rev. ed. (Hardy Boys Ser.). (Illus.). 224p. (gr. 4-7). 1972. 3.95 (ISBN 0-448-01990-6, G&D); PLB 3.29 (ISBN 0-448-03227-9, G&D). Putnam Pub Group.
Dixon, Franklin W., jt. auth. see Keene, Carolyn.
Dixon, G. M. Heritage of Anglican Crafts. 1984. 20.00x (ISBN 0-906791-11-1, Pub. by Minimax Bks UK). State Mutual Bk.
Dixon, G. M. & Rippon, J. Wings Over Eastern England. 1984. 20.00x (ISBN 0-906791-09-X, Pub. by Minimax Bks UK). State Mutual Bk.
Dixon, G. M., jt. auth. see Harland, M.
Dixon, G. R. Plant Pathogens & Their Control in Horticulture. (Sciences in Horticulture Ser.). (Illus.). 265p. (Orig.). 1984. pap. text ed. 16.50x (ISBN 0-333-35912-7). Scholium Intl.
--Vegetable Crop Diseases. American ed. 1981. pap. text ed. 35.00 (ISBN 0-87055-390-9). AVI.
Dixon, Geoffrey M. Folk Tales & Legends of Kent. (Illus.). 1984. 20.00x (ISBN 0-906791-27-8, Pub. by Minimax Bks UK). State Mutual Bk.
--Folk Tales & Legends of Norfolk. (Illus.). 1984. 20.00x (ISBN 0-906791-10-3, Pub. by Minimax Bks UK). State Mutual Bk.
--Folk Tales & Legends of Suffolk. (Illus.). 1984. 20.00x (ISBN 0-906791-18-9, Pub. by Minimax Bks UK). State Mutual Bk.
--For Those in Peril. 96p. 1984. 20.00x (ISBN 0-906791-14-6, Pub. by Minimax Bks UK). State Mutual Bk.
--Traditional Norfolk Recipes. 1984. 15.00x (ISBN 0-906791-24-3, Pub. by Minimax Bks UK). State Mutual Bk.
Dixon, Geraldine B. Guidelines to Microwave Cooking. (Illus., Orig.). 1980. pap. 6.95 (ISBN 0-89305-028-8). Anna Pub.
Dixon, Hollis M., tr. see Hubner, Kurt.
Dixon, Hugh, jt. auth. see Walker, Brian.
Dixon, J. A. Surgical Application of the Laser. (Illus.). 1983. 44.95 (ISBN 0-8151-2514-3). Year Bk Med.
Dixon, J. B. & Weed, S. B., eds. Minerals in Soil Environments. 1977. 25.00 (ISBN 0-89118-765-0). Soil Sci Soc Am.
Dixon, J. C., ed. Continuing Education in the Later Years. LC 53-12339. (Center for Gerontological Studies & Programs Ser.: No. 12). 1963. pap. 5.00 (ISBN 0-8130-0062-9). U Presses Fla.
Dixon, J. E. & Robertson, A. H., eds. The Geological Evolution of the Eastern Mediterranean. (Illus.). 848p. 1985. text ed. 84.00x (ISBN 0-632-01144-0). Blackwell Pubns.
Dixon, J. H. Whittingham Vale, Northumberland. (Folklore Ser.). Repr. 20.00 (ISBN 0-8482-7755-4). Norwood Edns.
Dixon, J. I., jt. auth. see Boggs, R. S.
Dixon, J. S., jt. auth. see Gosling, J. A.
Dixon, James G., III, jt. auth. see Franklin, Miriam A.
Dixon, James M. English Idioms. LC 73-163172. vi, 288p. 1975. Repr. of 1927 ed. 48.00x (ISBN 0-8103-3986-2). Gale.
--Matthew Arnold. LC 72-197297. 1974. Repr. of 1906 ed. lib. bdg. 20.00 (ISBN 0-8414-3795-5). Folcroft.
Dixon, James R. The Neotropical Colubrid Snake Genus Liophis. I. The Generic Concept. 40p. 1980. 3.25 (ISBN 0-89326-055-X). Milwaukee Pub Mus.
--A Systematic Review of the Teiid Lizards, Genus Bachia, with Remarks on Heterodactlus & Anotosaura. (Miscellaneous Publications: No. 57). 47p. 1973. pap. 2.50 (ISBN 0-686-79839-2). U of KS Mus Nat Hist.
Dixon, James W. Reading the Bible As History. 605p. 1985. 21.90 (ISBN 0-533-06192-X). Vantage.
Dixon, Jay R. A Practical Guide to Personal Protection & Security. LC 84-1043. 192p. 1984. lib. bdg. 21.95x (ISBN 0-8304-1034-1). Nelson-Hall.
Dixon, Jeane. Jeane Dixon's Astrological Cookbook. LC 76-21798. 1976. 6.95 (ISBN 0-688-03091-2). Morrow.
Dixon, Jeannette. Welsh Ghosts. 2.00 (ISBN 0-913714-11-9). Legacy Bks.
Dixon, Jennie C. How to Make Ends Meet. LC 83-51734. 108p. 1984. 4.95 (ISBN 0-916315-00-2). Swansea.
Dixon, Jesse T. Adapting Activities for Therapeutic Recreation Service: Concepts & Applications. (Illus.). 37p. (Orig.). 1981. pap. 8.00 (ISBN 0-916304-48-5). SDSU Press.
Dixon, Joe C. Defeat & Disarmament: Allied Diplomacy & the Politics of Military Affairs in Austria, 1918-1922. LC 82-49193. 208p. 1984. 21.50 (ISBN 0-87413-221-5). U Delaware Pr.
Dixon, John. The Chinese Welfare System, Nineteen Forty-Nine to Nineteen Seventy-Nine. LC 81-2822. 462p. 1981. 52.95x (ISBN 0-03-059046-9). Praeger.
--Pocket Examiner in Orthopaedics. 160p. (Orig.). 1984. pap. text ed. 8.50 (ISBN 0-272-79691-3, Pub. by Pitman Bks Ltd UK). Urban & S.
Dixon, John, jt. auth. see Cowan, Henry J.
Dixon, John & Kim, Hyung S., eds. Social Welfare in Asia. LC 85-40076. 352p. 1985. 37.50 (ISBN 0-312-73556-1). St Martin.
Dixon, John D. Problems in Group Theory. LC 72-76597. 1973. pap. 4.00 (ISBN 0-486-61574-X). Dover.
Dixon, John E., jt. auth. see Esmay, Merle L.
Dixon, John P. The Spatial Child. (Illus.). 248p. 1983. 28.75x (ISBN 0-398-04821-5). C C Thomas.
Dixon, John R. A Programmed Introduction to Probability. LC 78-25984. 420p. 1979. pap. text ed. 18.50 (ISBN 0-88275-825-X). Krieger.
Dixon, John W., Jr. Art & Theological Imagination. (Illus.). 1978. 12.95 (ISBN 0-8164-0397-X, Pub. by Seabury). Winston Pr.
Dixon, K. C. Cellular Defects in Disease. (Illus.). 504p. 1982. text ed. 36.50 (ISBN 0-632-00734-6, B 1321-3). Mosby.
Dixon, L. C. Numerical Optimization of Dynamic Systems. 410p. 1980. 64.00 (ISBN 0-444-85494-0, North-Holland). Elsevier.
Dixon, L. C. & Szego, G. P., eds. Towards Global Optimisation, Vols. I & II. LC 74-28195. 1975-78. Vol. I. 68.00 (ISBN 0-444-10955-2, North-Holland); Vol. II. 68.00 (ISBN 0-444-85171-2). Elsevier.
Dixon, L. C., et al, eds. Nonlinear Optimization, Theory & Algorithms. 492p. 1980. 35.00x (ISBN 0-8176-3020-1). Birkhauser.
Dixon, L. W., ed. Optimization in Action: Proceedings. 1977. 76.50 (ISBN 0-12-218550-1). Acad Pr.
Dixon, Laurinda S. Alchemical Imagery in Bosch's "Garden of Delights". Seidel, Linda, ed. LC 81-14673. (Studies in Fine Arts: Iconography: No. 2). 250p. 1981. 49.95 (ISBN 0-8357-1247-8). UMI Res Pr.
Dixon, Lawrence. Project Turn-Around. LC 84-61674. 61p. 1985. Three ring notebook. 49.95 (ISBN 0-914607-20-0). Master Tchr.
--Wills, Death, & Taxes: Basic Principles for Protecting Estates. 184p. 1968. pap. 1.00 (ISBN 0-318-02948-0). Biblio Dist.
Dixon, Lawrence W. Wills, Death & Taxes: Basic Principles for Protecting Estates. LC 77-21380. (Quality Paperback: No. 228). 184p. (Orig.). 1977. pap. 1.00 (ISBN 0-8226-0228-8). Littlefield.
--Wills, Death & Taxes: Basic Principles for Protecting Estates. rev. ed. 184p. 1979. Repr. of 1968 ed. 9.50x (ISBN 0-8476-6019-2). Rowman.
Dixon, Linda K. & Johnson, Ronald C. The Roots of Individuality: A Survey of Human Behavior Genetics. LC 79-26601. 1980. pap. text ed. 12.00 pub net (ISBN 0-8185-0376-9). Brooks-Cole.
Dixon, Maceo, et al. Which Way for Teachers. 1974. pap. 0.50 (ISBN 0-87348-340-5). Path Pr NY.
Dixon, Malcolm. In the Factory. LC 83-71638. (Young Engineer Bks.). (Illus.). 32p. (gr. 3-6). 1983. PLB 8.90 (ISBN 0-531-04701-6). Watts.
Dixon, Malcolm & Webb, Edwin. The Enzymes. 3rd ed. 1980. 64.95 (ISBN 0-12-218358-4). Acad Pr.
Dixon, Malcom. Young Engineer in Communication. (Young Engineers Ser.). (gr. 4-6). 1984. PLB 8.90 (ISBN 0-531-04700-8). Watts.
--Young Engineer on the Road. LC 83-71639. (Young Engineer Bks.). (Illus.). 32p. 1983. lib. bdg. 8.90 (ISBN 0-531-04702-4). Watts.
Dixon, Marlene. The Future of Women. LC 83-607. 220p. (Orig.). 1983. 14.95 (ISBN 0-89935-031-3, 83-607); pap. 7.95 (ISBN 0-89935-021-6). Synthesis Pubns.
Dixon, Marlene, ed. Health Care in Crisis: Essays on Health Services Under Capitalism. 2nd ed. Bodenheimer, Thomas. LC 79-90213. 76p. 1980. pap. 3.95 (ISBN 0-89935-012-7). Synthesis Pubns.
--Omens of Darkness: The Rise of Reaction in the United States. 304p. (Orig.). 1985. 23.95 (ISBN 0-89935-045-3); pap. 9.95 (ISBN 0-89935-044-5). Synthesis Pubns.
--On Trial: Reagan's War Against Nicaragua. 300p. 1985. 23.95 (ISBN 0-89935-043-7); pap. 9.95 (ISBN 0-89935-042-9). Synthesis Pubns.
Dixon, Marlene & Jonas, Susanne, eds. Revolution & Intervention in Central America. rev. ed. LC 83-5068. (Contemporary Marxism Ser.). 350p. (Orig.). 1983. 19.95 (ISBN 0-89935-029-1); pap. 10.95 (ISBN 0-89935-027-5). Synthesis Pubns.
Dixon, Melvin. Change of Territory. Rowell, Charles H., ed. (Callaloo Poetry Ser.). (Illus.). 62p. (Orig.). pap. 5.00 (ISBN 0-912759-04-6). Callaloo Journ.
Dixon, Melvin, tr. see Fabre, Genevieve.
Dixon, Michael B., et al. Striking Out! (Orig.). 1984. pap. 3.00 (ISBN 0-87602-252-2). Anchorage.
Dixon, Mim. What Happened to Fairbanks? The Effects of the Trans-Alaska Oil Pipeline on the Community of Fairbanks, Alaska. (Social Impact Assessment Ser.: No. 1). (Illus.). 337p. 1980. pap. text ed. 11.50x (ISBN 0-89158-961-9). Westview.
Dixon, N. Rex & Martin, Thomas B., eds. Automatic Speech & Speaker Recognition. LC 78-65703. 1979. 41.55 (ISBN 0-87942-117-7, PC01149). Inst Electrical.
--Automatic Speech & Speaker Recognition. LC 78-65703. 433p. 1979. 39.95 (ISBN 0-471-05833-5); pap. 25.95x (ISBN 0-471-05834-3, Pub. by Wiley-Interscience). Wiley.
Dixon, Nan. We'll All Have Soup. 98p. 1981. 8.95 (ISBN 0-939796-00-7). Recipe Pr.
Dixon, Nancy P. Children of Poverty with Handicapping Conditions: How Teachers Can Cope Humanistically. 164p. 1981. 19.75x (ISBN 0-398-04478-3). C C Thomas.
Dixon, Norm F. On the Psychology of Military Incompetence. 448p. 1984. 16.95 (ISBN 0-224-01161-8, Pub. by Jonathan Cape). Merrimack Pub Cir.
Dixon, Norman. Georgian Pistols: The Art & Craft of the Flintlock Pistol, 1715-1840. LC 72-166147. 184p. 1972. casebound 22.50 (ISBN 0-87387-046-8). Shumway.
Dixon, Norman F. Preconscious Processing. LC 80-42012. 313p. 1981. 44.95x (ISBN 0-471-27982-X, Pub. by Wiley-Interscience). Wiley.
Dixon, P. The Theory of Joint Maximization. LC 74-24348. (Contributions to Economic Analysis: Vol. 91). 212p. 1975. 51.00 (ISBN 0-444-10792-4, North-Holland). Elsevier.
Dixon, P. B., et al. Notes & Problems in Microeconomic Theory. (Advanced Textbooks in Economics: Vol. 15). 320p. 1980. text ed. 32.00 (ISBN 0-444-85325-1, North Holland). Elsevier.
--ORANI: A Multisectoral Model of the Australian Economy. (Contributions to Economic Analysis Ser.: Vol. 142). 356p. 1982. 68.00 (ISBN 0-444-86294-3, North-Holland). Elsevier.
Dixon, P. F., et al, eds. High Pressure Liquid Chromatography in Clinical Chemistry. 1976. 42.00 (ISBN 0-12-218450-5). Acad Pr.
Dixon, P. S. & Price, J. H. The Genus Callithamnion Rhodophyta: Ceramiaceae in the British Isles. 59.00x (ISBN 0-686-78657-2, Pub. by Brit Mus Pubns England). State Mutual Bk.
Dixon, Paige. May I Cross Your Golden River. LC 75-6943. 256p. (gr. 7 up). 1975. 8.95 (ISBN 0-689-30466-8). Atheneum.
--The Search for Charlie. LC 75-23187. 96p. (gr. 5-8). 1976. 6.95 (ISBN 0-689-30500-1). Atheneum.
--Silver Wolf. 112p. (gr. 4-7). 1973. pap. 1.95 (ISBN 0-689-70422-4, A-53, Aladdin). Atheneum.
--Skipper. LC 79-10420. 132p. (gr. 5-9). 1979. 8.95 (ISBN 0-689-30706-3). Atheneum.
--Summer of the White Goat. LC 76-25848. (Illus.). 128p. (gr. 3-7). 1977. 5.95 (ISBN 0-689-30552-4). Atheneum.
--Walk My Way. LC 79-23291. 156p. (gr. 6-9). 1980. 7.95 (ISBN 0-689-30738-1). Atheneum.

Dixon, Pamela. Ginseng. 102p. 1976. 16.00 (ISBN 0-7156-1006-6, Pub. by Duckworth England); pap. 4.50 (ISBN 0-7156-1007-4, Pub. by Duckworth England). Biblio Dist.

Dixon, Pamela, jt. auth. see Whisker, R. G.

Dixon, Paul B. Reversible Readings: Ambiguity in Four Modern Latin American Novels. LC 83-5070. (Illus.). 176p. 1985. 19.95x (ISBN 0-8173-0192-5). U of Ala Pr.

Dixon, Paul B., jt. auth. see Dixon, Dwight R.

Dixon, Paul R., tr. see Hubner, Kurt.

Dixon, Paul R., Jr., tr. see Hubner, Kurt.

Dixon, Penelope. Photographers of the Farm Security Administration: An Annotated Bibliography. LC 81-49120. (Reference Library of the Humanities: Vol. 373). (Illus.). 265p. 1983. lib. bdg. 33.00. Garland Pub.

Dixon, Peter. The Olympian. LC 83-63198. 265p. 1984. 13.95 (ISBN 0-915677-00-8). Roundtable Pub.

--Rhetoric. (Critical Idiom Ser.: Vol. 19). 1971. pap. 5.25x (ISBN 0-416-66760-0, NO. 2166). Methuen Inc.

Dixon, Peter, ed. Writers & Their Background: Alexander Pope. LC 72-85534. (Writers & Their Background Ser.). xx, 324p. 1972. 20.00x (ISBN 0-8214-0113-0, 82-81164); pap. 10.00x (ISBN 0-8214-0114-9, 82-81172). Ohio U Pr.

Dixon, Peter, ed. & pref. by see Farquhar, George.

Dixon, Peter, jt. ed. see Rudrum, Alan.

Dixon, Peter, ed. see Swift, Jonathan.

Dixon, Peter, ed. see Vanbrugh, John & Cibber, Colley.

Dixon, Peter S. & Irvine, Linda M. Seaweeds of the British Isles; Vol. 1, Rhodophyta: Pt. 1, Introduction, Nemeliales, Gigartinales. (Illus.). 1977. pap. 31.00x (ISBN 0-565-00781-5, Pub. by Brit Mus Nat Hist). Sabbot-Natural Hist Bks.

Dixon, Philip. Discoveries at Crickley Hill. 100p. 1983. 10.00x (ISBN 0-85224-444-4, Pub. by Edinburgh U Pr Scotland). Columbia U Pr.

Dixon, R., tr. see Pisarev, Dimitri I.

Dixon, R. A. Spain. LC 79-89189. (A Rand McNally Pocket Guide). (Illus., Orig.). 1980. pap. 3.95 (ISBN 0-528-84292-7). Rand.

Dixon, R. A., jt. auth. see Dey, P. M.

Dixon, R. A., ed. Plant Cell Culture: A Practical Approach. (A Practical Approach Ser.). (Illus.). 250p. (Orig.). 1985. pap. 25.00 (ISBN 0-947946-22-5). IRL Pr.

Dixon, R. G., et al. Right of Privacy: A Symposium. LC 75-147833. (Symposia on Law & Society Ser). 1971. Repr. of 1965 ed. lib. bdg. 22.50 (ISBN 0-306-70114-6). Da Capo.

Dixon, R. J. & Thirlwall, A. P. Regional Growth & Unemployment in the United Kingdom. 251p. 1975. text ed. 42.50x (ISBN 0-8419-5010-5). Holmes & Meier.

Dixon, R. L. The McGraw-Hill Thirty-Six Hour Accounting Course. 2nd ed. 1982. 34.50 (ISBN 0-07-017091-6). McGraw.

Dixon, R. M. The Dyirbal Language of North Queensland: Studies in Linguistics. LC 78-190415. (No. 9). (Illus.). 448p. 1973. 64.50 (ISBN 0-521-08510-1); pap. 19.95 (ISBN 0-521-09748-7). Cambridge U Pr.

--A Grammar of Yidin. LC 76-27912. (Cambridge Studies in Linguistics: No. 19). (Illus.). 1977. 79.50 (ISBN 0-521-21462-9). Cambridge U Pr.

--The Languages of Australia. LC 79-21353. (Cambridge Language Surveys Ser.). (Illus.). 400p. 1980. 74.50 (ISBN 0-521-22329-6); pap. 22.95 (ISBN 0-521-29450-9). Cambridge U Pr.

Dixon, R. M., ed. Grammatical Categories in Australian Languages. (AIAS Linguistic Ser.: No. 22). 768p. 1976. text ed. 58.00x (ISBN 0-391-00694-0); pap. text ed. 34.25x (ISBN 0-391-00695-9). Humanities.

Dixon, R. M. & Blake, B. J., eds. Handbook of Australian Languages, Vol. I. xiv, 392p. 1979. 60.00x (ISBN 90-272-0512-4). Benjamins North Am.

--Handbook of Australian Languages, Vol. II. xxiv, 427p. 1982. 60.00x (ISBN 90-272-2004-2). Benjamins North Am.

Dixon, R. M. W. Where Have All the Adjectives Gone & Other Essays on Semantics & Syntax. (Janua Linguarum Series Maior: No. 107). 256p. 1982. text ed. 27.20 (ISBN 90-279-3309-X). Mouton.

Dixon, R. M. W. & Blake, B. J., eds. Handbook of Australian Languages, Vol. III. (Illus.). xxiv, 531p. 1983. 60.00x (ISBN 90-272-2002-6). Benjamins North Am.

Dixon, R. N. & Thomson, C., eds. Theoretical Chemistry, Vols. 1-3. LC 73-92911. Vol. 1 1974. 1973 literature 29.00 (ISBN 0-85186-754-5); Vol. 2 1975. 32.00 (ISBN 0-85186-764-2); Vol. 3 1978. 34.00 (ISBN 0-85186-774-X). Am Chemical.

Dixon, Reginald A. Portugal. LC 83-62036. (Pocket Guide Ser.). (Illus.). 1984. pap. 4.95 (ISBN 0-528-84890-9). Rand.

Dixon, Rhonda. Corrie's Cat Ring. 192p. 1985. 13.95 (ISBN 0-8027-0829-3). Walker & Co.

--Man Around the House. LC 83-40433. 192p. 1984. 12.95 (ISBN 0-8027-0773-4). Walker & Co.

Dixon, Richard, ed. see Marx, Karl & Engels, Friedrich.

Dixon, Richard E., ed. Nosocomial Infections. LC 81-50243. (Illus.). 344p. 1981. text ed. 35.00 (ISBN 0-914316-24-9); pap. text ed. 22.00 (ISBN 0-914316-29-X). Yorke Med.

Dixon, Richard W. The Last Poems of Richard Watson Dixon. Bridges, Robert, ed. 1905. 20.00 (ISBN 0-8274-2802-2). R West.

Dixon, Robert. El Ingles en Accion-See It & Say It in English. 1982. pap. 3.50 (ISBN 0-451-12101-5, AE2101, Sig). NAL.

--Physical Science: A Dynamic Approach. (Illus.). 1979. 30.95 (ISBN 0-13-669820-4). P-H.

Dixon, Robert C. Spread Spectrum Systems. 2nd ed. 422p. 1984. text ed. 37.50x (ISBN 0-471-88309-3, Wiley-Interscience). Wiley.

Dixon, Robert G. Benchwork. LC 80-66607. (Machine Trades-Machine Shop Ser.). (Illus.). 211p. 1981. pap. text ed. 11.60 (ISBN 0-8273-1743-3); instr's. guide 2.85 (ISBN 0-8273-1744-1). Delmar.

Dixon, Robert G., ed. American Government: Basic Documents & Materials. LC 70-141281. (Illus.). 420p. 1972. Repr. of 1950 ed. lib. bdg. 28.25x (ISBN 0-8371-5878-8, DIAG). Greenwood.

Dixon, Robert G., Jr. Standards Development in the Private Sector: Thoughts on Interest Representation & Procedural Fairness. Dean, Amy E., ed. LC 78-50058. 1978. pap. text ed. 3.00 (ISBN 0-87765-118-3, STD-CSS). Natl Fire Prot.

Dixon, Robert L. Executive's Accounting Primer. 2nd ed. 1982. 29.95 (ISBN 0-07-017079-7). McGraw.

--Perspectives in Toxicology, Vol. 1. Date not set. write for info. (ISBN 0-89004-436-8, 496). Raven.

Dixon, Robert L., jt. auth. see Paton, William A.

Dixon, Robert L., ed. Reproductive Toxicology. (Target Organ Toxicology Ser.). 368p. 1985. text ed. 69.50 (ISBN 0-89004-474-0). Raven.

Dixon, Robert S. & Sonneborn, George. A Master List of Nonstellar Optical Astronomical Objects. LC 79-27627. (Illus.). 74p. 1980. 30.00x (ISBN 0-8142-0250-0). Ohio St U Pr.

Dixon, Robert T. Dynamic Astronomy. 4th ed. (Illus.). 544p. pap. text ed. 32.95 (ISBN 0-13-221333-8). P-H.

--The Dynamic World of Physics. 512p. 1984. text ed. 24.95 (ISBN 0-675-20093-8). Additional supplements may be obtained from publisher. Merrill.

--Physical Science: A Dynamic Approach. 2nd ed. (Illus.). 480p. 1986. text ed. 29.95 (ISBN 0-13-669847-6). P-H.

Dixon, Roger & Muthesius, Stefan. Victorian Architecture. (World of Art Ser.). (Illus.). 208p. 1985. pap. text ed. 9.95 (ISBN 0-500-20160-9). Thames Hudson.

Dixon, Roland. The Racial History of Man, 2 vols. Set. 250.00 (ISBN 0-87968-273-6). Gordon Pr.

Dixon, Roland B. The Building of Cultures. LC 76-44709. 328p. Repr. of 1928 ed. 35.00 (ISBN 0-404-15917-6). AMS Pr.

--The Building of Cultures. 1977. lib. bdg. 59.95 (ISBN 0-8490-1560-X). Gordon Pr.

--Maidu Texts. LC 73-3539. (American Ethnological Society. Publications: No. 4). Repr. of 1912 ed. 22.00 (ISBN 0-404-58154-4). AMS Pr.

--The Northern Maidu. LC 76-43692. (AMNH. Bulletin: Vol. XVII, Pt. 3). 152p. 1983. Repr. of 1905 ed. 31.50 (ISBN 0-404-15523-5). AMS Pr.

--Oceanic Mythology, Vol. 9. LC 63-19094. (Mythology of All Races Ser). (Illus.). 1964. Repr. of 1932 ed. 30.00 (ISBN 0-8154-0059-4). Cooper Sq.

--The Shasta. LC 76-43689. (AMNH. Bulletin: Vol. XVII, Pt. 5). 256p. 1983. Repr. of 1907 ed. 26.50 (ISBN 0-404-15524-3). AMS Pr.

Dixon, Ruth B. Rural Women at Work: Strategies for Development in South Asia. LC 78-5825. (Resources for the Future Ser). 1978. text ed. 18.50x (ISBN 0-8018-2124-X). Johns Hopkins.

--Rural Women at Work: Strategies for Development in South Asia. 245p. 1978. 18.50 (ISBN 0-8018-2124-X). Resources Future.

Dixon, S. L. Fluid Mechanics & Thermodynamics of Turbomachinery: In SI-Metric Units. 3rd ed. 44.00 (ISBN 0-08-022721-X); pap. 15.00 (ISBN 0-08-022722-8). Pergamon.

--Worked Examples in Turbomachinery: Fluid Mechanics & Thermodynamics. LC 75-9757. 116p. 1975. text ed. 22.00 (ISBN 0-08-019797-3); pap. text ed. 10.00 (ISBN 0-08-019700-0). Pergamon.

Dixon, Samuel, jt. auth. see Trojanowicz, Robert.

Dixon, Samuel L. Working with People in Crisis: Theory & Practice. LC 78-31227. (Illus.). 204p. 1979. pap. text ed. 14.95 (ISBN 0-8016-1320-5). Mosby.

Dixon, Solon. The Dixon Legend. LC 82-60023. 1982. 9.95 (ISBN 0-87397-208-2). Strode.

Dixon, Stephen. Fall & Rise. 256p. 1985. 17.75 (ISBN 0-86547-192-4). N Point Pr.

--Fourteen Stories. LC 80-14911. (Johns Hopkins Poetry & Fiction Program). 160p. 1980. 12.50 (ISBN 0-8018-2445-1). Johns Hopkins.

--Movies: Seventeen Stories. 176p. (Orig.). 1983. 11.50 (ISBN 0-86547-129-0). N Point Pr.

--Time to Go. LC 83-22624. 192p. 1984. 12.50 (ISBN 0-8018-3234-9). Johns Hopkins.

Dixon, Susan B. History of the Missouri Compromise & Slavery in American Politics. Repr. of 1903 ed. 45.00 (ISBN 0-384-11885-2). Johnson Repr.

Dixon, T. A., tr. see Sighart, Joachim.

Dixon, Terence & Buzan, Tony. The Evolving Brain. 1978. professional ed. 16.95 (ISBN 0-03-044581-7, HoltC). HR&W.

Dixon, Terence & Lucas, Martin. The Human Race. LC 82-14280. (New Press Ser.). 256p. 1982. 24.95 (ISBN 0-07-017080-0). McGraw.

Dixon, Thomas. The Clansman. 1973. Repr. of 1905 ed. lib. bdg. 75.00 (ISBN 0-87968-194-2). Gordon Pr.

--The Fall of a Nation: Sequel to the Birth of a Nation. LC 74-15965. (Science Fiction Ser). (Illus.). 372p. 1975. Repr. of 1916 ed. 26.50x (ISBN 0-405-06286-9). Ayer Co Pubs.

Dixon, Thomas B. The Enemy Fought Splendidly: Being the 1914-1915 Diary of the Battle of the Falklands & Its Aftermath. (Illus.). 120p. 1983. 8.95 (ISBN 0-7137-1326-7, Pub. by Blandford Pr England). Sterling.

Dixon, Thomas, Jr. The Clansman: An Historical Romance of the Ku Klux Klan. LC 71-104761. (Novel As American Social History Ser.). 392p. 1970. pap. 10.00x (ISBN 0-8131-0126-3). U Pr of Ky.

--The Leopard's Spots: A Romance of the White Man's Burden. LC 67-29265. (Americans in Fiction Ser.). (Illus.). 481p. 1979. Repr. of 1902 ed. lib. bdg. 47.50 (ISBN 0-8398-0366-4). Irvington.

Dixon, Thomas W. Chesapeake & Ohio. (Illus.). 128p. 1984. pap. 15.95 (ISBN 0-911868-49-6, C49). Carstens Pubns.

Dixon, Thomas W., Jr. Chesapeake & Ohio H7 Series. LC 79-51795. (Classic Power Ser.: No. 1). (Illus.). 53p. 1979. pap. 6.95 (ISBN 0-934088-00-4). NJ Intl Inc.

Dixon, Thomas W., Jr. & Million, Arthur B. Pere Marquette Power. Shaver, Carl W., ed. LC 85-70004. (Illus.). 224p. (Orig.). 1984. pap. 23.95 (ISBN 0-87012-472-2). Ches & OH Hist.

--Pere Marquette Power. (Illus.). 256p. 1985. 23.95 (ISBN 0-318-17773-0). Ches & OH Hist.

Dixon, Trudy, ed. see Suzuki, Shunryu.

Dixon, W. G. Special Relativity. LC 77-83991. (Illus.). 1978. 57.50 (ISBN 0-521-21871-3). Cambridge U Pr.

--Special Relativity: The Foundation of Macroscopic Physics. LC 77-83991. (Illus.). 261p. 1982. pap. 22.95 (ISBN 0-521-27241-6). Cambridge U Pr.

Dixon, W. J. & Nicholson, W. L. Exploring Data Analysis: The Computer Revolution in Statistics. LC 73-85786. 1974. 34.50x (ISBN 0-520-02470-2). U of Cal Pr.

Dixon, W. J., ed. BMD: Biomedical Computer Programs. new ed. Orig. Title: BMD & BMD: X-Series Supplement (2 Books) (Orig.). 1973. pap. 14.95x (ISBN 0-520-02426-5). U of Cal Pr.

Dixon, W. J. & Brown, M. B., eds. BMDP Statistical Software 1983 Manual. rev. ed. LC 80-53770. 744p. 1983. pap. text ed. 17.50x (ISBN 0-686-04408-8). U of Cal Pr.

Dixon, W. M. Primer of Tennyson. LC 70-130255. (Studies in Tennyson, No. 27). 1971. Repr. of 1896 ed. lib. bdg. 45.95x (ISBN 0-8383-1147-4). Haskell.

Dixon, W. M. & Price, Susan M., eds. Aspects of Occupational Health. (Illus.). 208p. (Orig.). 1984. pap. 11.95 (ISBN 0-571-13203-0). Faber & Faber.

Dixon, W. Macneile. An Apology for the Arts (Chatterton, English & Scottish Ballads, Wordsworth, Scott, Thomas Campbell, Tolstoy) LC 76-17899. 1973. lib. bdg. 17.50 (ISBN 0-8414-3734-3). Folcroft.

--English Epic & Heroic Poetry. LC 65-15894. (Studies in Poetry, No. 38). 1969. Repr. of 1912 ed. lib. bdg. 75.00x (ISBN 0-8383-0540-7). Haskell.

--English Poetry from Blake to Browning. LC 72-6118. lib. bdg. 17.50 (ISBN 0-8414-0070-9). Folcroft.

--The Human Situation. 438p. 1981. Repr. lib. bdg. 50.00 (ISBN 0-89987-161-5). Darby Bks.

--The Human Situation. 1973. lib. bdg. 40.00 (ISBN 0-8414-2476-4). Folcroft.

--The Human Situation. 75.00 (ISBN 0-87968-062-8). Gordon Pr.

Dixon, W. Macneile, ed. The Edinburgh Book of Scottish Verse, 1300-1900. facsimile ed. LC 75-37012. (Granger Index Reprint Ser.). Repr. of 1910 ed. 51.00 (ISBN 0-8369-6311-3). Ayer Co Pubs.

--The Edinburgh Book of Scottish Verse, 1300-1900. LC 75-37012. (Granger Index Reprint Ser.). 939p. Repr. of 1910 ed. 34.00 (ISBN 0-8290-0510-2). Irvington.

Dixon, W. Macneile, ed. see Dixon, William M.

Dixon, W. T. Theory & Interpretation of Magnetic Resonance Spectra. LC 73-180922. 168p. 1972. 29.50x (ISBN 0-306-30567-4, Plenum Pr). Plenum Pub.

Dixon, Walter M. The Psychological Vivisection of Contemporary Man. (Illus.). 167p. 1984. 77.85 (ISBN 0-89920-107-5). Am Inst Psych.

Dixon, Wilfred J. & Massey, Frank J. Introduction to Statistical Analysis. 4th ed. (Illus.). 624p. 1983. 34.95 (ISBN 0-07-017073-8). McGraw.

Dixon, William C. Pointed Tales. LC 80-81102. 98p. (Orig.). (gr. 1-4). 1980. pap. 4.50 (ISBN 0-8192-1270-9). Morehouse.

Dixon, William C., jt. auth. see Detwiler-Zapp, Diane.

Dixon, William H. The London Prisons. LC 83-49227. (Crime & Punishment in England 1850-1922 Ser.). 425p. 1984. lib. bdg. 50.00 (ISBN 0-317-11884-6). Garland Pub.

--New America, 2 vols. LC 79-134428. Repr. of 1867 ed. Set. 36.50 (ISBN 0-404-08468-0). Vol. 1 (ISBN 0-404-08469-9). Vol. 2. AMS Pr.

--Personal History of Lord Bacon. 424p. 1984. Repr. of 1841 ed. lib. bdg. 82.50 (ISBN 0-8495-1146-1). Arden Lib.

--Spiritual Wives, Vol. 1 & 2. LC 72-134428. Repr. of 1868 ed. Set. 49.50 (ISBN 0-404-08471-0). AMS Pr.

--White Conquest, 2 Vols. facsimile ed. LC 70-138335. (Black Heritage Library Collection Ser.). 1876. Set. 38.25 (ISBN 0-8369-8727-6). Ayer Co Pubs.

Dixon, William M. An Apology for the Arts. 215p. 1980. pap. 22.50 (ISBN 0-8495-1056-2). Arden Lib.

--Edinburgh Book of Scottish Verse, 1300-1900. Dixon, W. Macneile, ed. LC 76-164841. Repr. of 1910 ed. 52.50 (ISBN 0-404-08632-2). AMS Pr.

--English Epic & Heroic Poetry. LC 76-144503. (Channels of English Literature: No. 2). Repr. of 1912 ed. 34.50 (ISBN 0-404-07812-5). AMS Pr.

--Tragedy. LC 74-194357. 1974. Repr. of 1924 ed. lib. bdg. 15.00 (ISBN 0-8414-3798-X). Folcroft.

Dixon-Gough, R. W., jt. auth. see Bullard, R. K.

Dixon-Hunt, John & Holland, Faith M., eds. The Ruskin Polygon. (Illus.). 266p. 1982. 30.00 (ISBN 0-7190-0834-4, Pub. by Manchester Univ Pr). Longwood Pub Group.

Dixon-Scott, James. John Bunyan's England. LC 76-58374. 1977. Repr. of 1928 ed. lib. bdg. 10.00 (ISBN 0-8414-3423-9). Folcroft.

Dixson & Fox. Mi Primer Diccionario Illustrado De Ingles. rev. ed. 67p. (gr. 3-6). 1974. pap. 4.50 (ISBN 0-88345-232-4, 18130). Regents Pub.

Dixson, jt. auth. see Boggs.

Dixson, A. F. The Natural History of the Gorilla. (Illus.). 202p. 1981. 24.00 (ISBN 0-231-05318-5). Columbia U Pr.

--The Natural History of the Gorilla. 202p. 1985. pap. 10.95 (ISBN 0-231-05319-3). Columbia U Pr.

Dixson, Anne, jt. auth. see Pinkus, Charles E.

Dixson, Robert. Modern Short Stories. 1984. pap. text ed. 4.25 (ISBN 0-88345-539-0). Regents Pub.

Dixson, Robert J. Complete Course in English Series, 4 bks. rev. ed. (Illus.). (gr. 9-12). 1972. Bk. 1. pap. text ed. 3.75 (ISBN 0-88345-028-3, 17994); Bk. 2. pap. text ed. 3.75 (ISBN 0-88345-029-1, 17995); Bk. 3. pap. text ed. 3.75 (ISBN 0-88345-030-5, 17996); Bk. 4. pap. text ed. 3.75 (ISBN 0-88345-031-3, 17997); cassettes, each level 120.00 (ISBN 0-685-19786-7). Regents Pub.

--Curso Completo de Ingles, 4 bks. (gr. 9-12). 1973. Bk. 1. pap. text ed. 3.75 (ISBN 0-88345-035-6, 17998); Bk. 2. pap. text ed. 3.75 (ISBN 0-88345-036-4, 17999); Bk. 3. pap. text ed. 3.75 (ISBN 0-88345-037-2, 18118); Bk. 4. pap. text ed. 3.50 (ISBN 0-88345-038-0, 18119). cassettes 120.00 (ISBN 0-685-04772-5). Regents Pub.

--Easy Reading Selections in English. rev. ed. (Illus.). 112p. 1983. pap. text ed. 4.25 (ISBN 0-88345-538-2, 21395). Regents Pub.

--Elementary Reader in English. rev. ed. (Illus.). 112p. 1983. pap. text ed. 4.25 (ISBN 0-88345-537-4, 21410). Regents Pub.

--English in Action. (gr. 7 up). 1960. pap. text ed. 3.50 (ISBN 0-88345-045-3, 17857). Regents Pub.

--Essential Idioms in English. rev. ed. (Illus.). 208p. 1983. pap. 5.25 (ISBN 0-88345-532-3, 21143). Regents Pub.

--Everyday Dialogues in English. rev. ed. (Illus.). 208p. 1983. pap. text ed. 4.25 (ISBN 0-88345-536-6, 21369). Regents Pub.

--Exercises in English Conversation, 2 Bks. (Illus., Orig.). (YA) (gr. 7 up). 1971. Bk. 1. pap. text ed. 3.75 (ISBN 0-88345-052-6, 18011); Bk. 2. pap. text ed. 3.75 (ISBN 0-88345-053-4, 18012); cassettes 60.00 ea.; tapes o.p. 35.00 ea. Regents Pub.

--Graded Exercises in English. rev. ed. 208p. 1983. pap. text ed. 4.95 (ISBN 0-88345-535-8, 21357). Regents Pub.

--El Ingles en Accion. (Illus.). 1977. pap. text ed. 4.50 (ISBN 0-88345-295-2, 18490). cassettes 70.00 (ISBN 0-685-77025-7, 38492). Regents Pub.

--Ingles Practico Sin Maestro, 2 vols. (gr. 9 up). 1972. One-vol. Ed. pap. text ed. 7.95 (ISBN 0-88345-068-2, 18102); Vol. 1. pap. text ed. 4.50 (ISBN 0-88345-069-0, 18103); Vol. 2. pap. text ed. 4.50 (ISBN 0-88345-070-4, 18104). ea cassettes 70.00. Regents Pub.

--Modern American English, 2 bks. (gr. 7-12). 1977. pap. text ed. 4.65 ea. (18720); Bk. 1. pap. text ed. 3.25 (ISBN 0-88345-308-8, 18726) (ISBN 0-88345-314-2, 18726). Bk. 2. pap. text ed. (ISBN 0-88345-309-6, 18721); wkbk. 3.25 (ISBN 0-88345-315-0, 18727); cassette 90.00 ea. Regents Pub.

--Modern American English, Bk. 3. (Illus.). (gr. 7-12). 1977. pap. text ed. 4.65 (ISBN 0-88345-310-X, 18722); wkbk. 3.25 (ISBN 0-88345-316-9, 18728); cassettes 90.00 (ISBN 0-686-68052-9). Regents Pub.

--Modern American English, Bk. 4. 1978. pap. text ed. 4.65 (ISBN 0-88345-311-8, 18723); tchr's manual 1 7.25 (ISBN 0-88345-319-3, 18732); tchr's manual 2 7.25 (ISBN 0-88345-321-5, 18733); wkbk. 4 3.25 (ISBN 0-88345-317-7, 18729). Regents Pub.
--Modern American English, Bk. 5. (Illus.). 167p. (gr. 7-12). 1980. pap. text ed. 4.95 (ISBN 0-88345-312-6, 18724); tchr's manual 7.25 (ISBN 0-88345-324-X, 18736); wkbk. 3.25 (ISBN 0-88345-318-5, 18730). Regents Pub.
--Modern American English, Bk. 6. (Illus.). 167p. (gr. 9-12). 1981. pap. text ed. 4.95 (ISBN 0-88345-313-4, 18725); tchr's manual 7.25 (ISBN 0-88345-325-8, 18737); wkbk 3.25 (ISBN 0-88345-320-7, 18731). Regents Pub.
--Modern American English Skillbooks, Bks. 1, 2, & 4. new ed. (Modern American English Ser.). (gr. 7 up). 1974. 1.25 ea. Bk. 1 (ISBN 0-88345-233-2). Bk. 2 (ISBN 0-88345-234-0). Bk. 4 (ISBN 0-88345-236-7). Regents Pub.
--Modern American English: Teacher's Manual 3. (Modern American English Ser.). (Illus.). 187p. 1978. pap. text ed. 7.25 (ISBN 0-88345-322-3, 18734). Regents Pub.
--Modern American English: Teacher's Manual, No. 4. new ed. (Illus.). 187p. 1979. pap. text ed. 7.25 (ISBN 0-88345-323-1, 18735). Regents Pub.
--Oral Pattern Drills in Fundamental English. (gr. 9 up). 1963. pap. text ed. 4.50 (ISBN 0-88345-124-7, 17410); with cassettes 90.00 (ISBN 0-685-04777-6, 58454). Regents Pub.
--Practical Guide to the Teaching of English As a Foreign Language. 1975. pap. text ed. 3.75 (ISBN 0-88345-244-8, 18132). Regents Pub.
--Practice Exercises in Everyday English. (Orig.). (gr. 9 up). 1957. pap. text ed. 4.25 (ISBN 0-88345-131-X, 17414); answer key 1.50 (ISBN 0-685-19801-4, 17415). Regents Pub.
--Regents English Workbooks, 3 Bks. (gr. 6 up). 1956-1969. pap. text ed. 4.25 ea.; Bk. 1. pap. text ed. (ISBN 0-88345-139-5, 17420); Bk. 2. pap. text ed. (ISBN 0-88345-140-9, 17421); Bk. 3. pap. text ed. (ISBN 0-88345-141-7, 17742); answer key, bk 1, 2 1.50 (ISBN 0-685-19803-0, 17422). Regents Pub.
--Second Book in English. 128p. 1983. pap. text ed. 4.25 (ISBN 0-317-02317-9, 21179). Regents Pub.
--The U. S. A. Vol. 1, the Land & the People. rev. ed. (Illus.). 169p. (gr. 7 up). 1975. pap. 3.75 (ISBN 0-88345-240-5, 18435). Regents Pub.
Dixson, Robert J. & Andujar, Julio I. Resumen Practico de la Gramatica Inglesa. (Orig.). (gr. 9 up). 1967. pap. text ed. 2.95 (ISBN 0-88345-142-5, 17423). Regents Pub.
Dixson, Robert J. & Fox, Herbert. The U. S. A. Vol. 2, Men & History. rev. ed. (Illus.). 179p. 1975. pap. 3.75 (ISBN 0-88345-241-3, 18436). Regents Pub.
Dixson, Robert J., jt. auth. see Andujar, Julio I.
Dixson, Robert J., jt. auth. see Clarey, Elizabeth M.
Dixson, Robert J., jt. auth. see Clarey, M. Elizabeth.
Dixson, Robert J., jt. auth. see Fisher, Isobel Y.
Dixson, Robert J., jt. auth. see Whitford, Harold C.
Dixson, Robert J., ed. Dos Mil Palabras Usadas Con Mas Frecuencia En Ingles. (Orig.). (gr. 9 up). 1956. pap. text ed. 2.50 (ISBN 0-88345-178-6, 17399). Regents Pub.
Dixson, Robert J., ed. see Cooper, James F.
Dixson, Robert J., ed. see Crane, Stephen.
Dixson, Robert J., ed. see Eggleston, Edward.
Dixson, Robert J., ed. see Harte, Bret.
Dixson, Robert J., ed. see Hawthorne, Nathaniel.
Dixson, Robert J., ed. see Howells, William D.
Dixson, Robert J., ed. see James, Henry.
Dixson, Robert J., ed. see Melville, Herman.
Dixson, Robert J., ed. see Poe, Edgar Allan.
Dixson, Robert J., ed. see Twain, Mark.
Dixson, Robin J. Assessment of the Pulmonary Patient. Youtsey, John W., ed. LC 84-43158. (Faculty Lecture Series in Respiratory Care). (Illus.). 182p. (Orig.). 1985. text ed. 18.95x (ISBN 0-940122-17-0). Multi Media Co.
Dixson, Zella. Comprehensive Subject Index to Universal Prose Fiction. LC 72-13508. 1897. lib. bdg. 30.00 (ISBN 0-8414-1203-0). Folcroft.
--A Comprehensive Subject Index to Universal Prose Fiction. 59.95 (ISBN 0-87968-920-X). Gordon Pr.
Dixson, Zella A. The Comprehensive Subject Index to Universal Prose Fiction. 421p. 1983. Repr. of 1897 ed. lib. bdg. 30.00 (ISBN 0-8492-4223-1). R West.
Dixter, Charles, et al. Pediatric Radiographic Interpretation. LC 79-67303. (Exercises in Dental Radiology Ser.: Vol. 3). (Illus.). 271p. 1980. pap. 18.50 (ISBN 0-7216-3095-2). Saunders.
DiYanni, Robert. Introduction to Literature. 1350p. 1986. text ed. 17.95 (ISBN 0-394-33774-3, RanC). Random.
Di Yanni, Robet. Connections: Writing, Reading, & Thinking. LC 84-16825. 320p. (Orig.). 1985. pap. text ed. 11.75x (ISBN 0-86709-049-9). Boynton Cook Pubs.
Diyasena, W. Pre-Vocational Education in Sri Lanka: Study Prepared for the Asian Centre of Educational Innovation for Development. (Experiments & Innovations in Education: No. 28). 50p. 1977. pap. 2.50 (ISBN 92-3-101404-8, U743, UNESCO). Unipub.
Diz, Marta A., ed. Patronio y Lucanor: La Lectura Inteligente "en el Tiempo Que Es Turbio". LC 83-51708. (Scripta Humanistica Ser.). (Span.). 1984. 26.00 (ISBN 0-916379-01-9). Scripta.
Dizard, W. P. The Comming Information Age: An Overview of Technology, Economics, & Politics. 2nd ed. LC 84-12625. 224p. 1984. pap. text ed. 13.95x (ISBN 0-582-28522-4). Longman.
DiZazzo, Ray, jt. auth. see Parrish, Darrell.
DiZazzo, Raymond. Clovin's Head. 1976. pap. 2.50 (ISBN 0-88031-027-8). Invisible-Red Hill.
Dizazzo, Raymond, jt. auth. see Parrish, Darrell.
Dizenfeld, Bruce, et al, eds. see UCLA Moot Court Honors Program.
Dizeno, Patricia. Why Me? The Story of Jenny. (gr. 7 up). 1976. pap. 2.50 (ISBN 0-380-00563-8, 90002-5, Flare). Avon.
Dizer, John T., Jr. Tom Swift & Company: Boys' Books by Stratemeyer & Others. LC 81-1559. (Illus.). 192p. 1982. lib. bdg. 17.95x (ISBN 0-89950-024-2). McFarland & Co.
Dizick, Missy & Bly, Mary. Dogs Are Better Than Cats. LC 83-25506. (Illus.). 80p. 1985. pap. 3.95 (ISBN 0-385-19212-6, Dolp). Doubleday.
Dizik, A. Allen. The Estimator. 12.95 (ISBN 0-938614-03-7). Stratford Hse.
--The Style Wheel of Furniture & Decoration. (Illus.). 12.95 (ISBN 0-686-86777-7). Stratford Hse.
Dizikes, John. Britain, Roosevelt & the New Deal: British Opinion, 1932-1938. LC 78-63282. (Modern American History Ser.: Vol. 7). 330p. 1979. lib. bdg. 36.00 (ISBN 0-8240-3631-X). Garland Pub.
Dizon, Andrew E., jt. ed. see Sharp, Gary D.
Djabbaroff, Ruby, jt. auth. see Hodgman, Ann.
Djairo Guedes De Figuerido, ed. Functional Analysis-Proceedings of the Sao Paulo Symposium. (Lecture Notes in Pure & Applied Mathematics Ser.: Vol. 18). 1976. 59.75 (ISBN 0-8247-6334-3). Dekker.
Djait, Hichem. Europe & Islam. Heinegg, Peter, tr. LC 84-8786. 1985. 30.00x (ISBN 0-520-05040-1). U of Cal Pr.
Djaladiningrat, Idrus N. The Beginnings of the Indonesian-Dutch Negotiations & the Hoge Veluwe Talks. LC 60-4142. (Cornell University Modern Indonesia Project Monograph Ser.). pap. 34.50 (ISBN 0-317-09545-5, 2010638). Bks Demand UMI.
Djamour, Judith. Malay Kinship & Marriage in Singapore. (London School of Economics, Monographs on Social Anthropology: No.21). 155p. 1965. pap. 16.95 (ISBN 0-485-19621-2, Pub. by Athlone Pr Ltd). Longwood Pub Group.
--The Muslim Matrimonial Court in Singapore. (London School of Economics Monographs on Social Anthropology: No.31). 191p. 1966. 28.50 (ISBN 0-485-19531-3, Pub. by Athlone Pr Ltd). Longwood Pub Group.
Djamson. The Dynamics of Euro-African Co-Operation. 1976. lib. bdg. 55.00 (ISBN 90-247-1841-4, Pub. by Martinus Nijhoff Netherlands). Kluwer Academic.
Djang Chu, ed. & tr. see Huang Lui-hung.
Djanikian, Gregory. The Man in the Middle. LC 84-70176. (Poetry Ser.). 79p. 1984. pap. 6.95 (ISBN 0-88748-002-0). Carnegie-Mellon.
Djaparidze, David, ed. Mediaeval Slavic Manuscripts: A Bibliography of Printed Catalogues. LC 57-9659. 1957. 7.50x (ISBN 0-910956-38-3). Medieval Acad.
Djavakhishvili, A., jt. auth. see Ghlonti, L.
Djeddah, Eli. Moving up. rev. ed. LC 75-16692. (Illus.). 192p. 1978. pap. 4.95 (ISBN 0-913668-83-4). Ten Speed Pr.
Dje Dje, Jacqueline C. Distribution of the One String Fiddle in West Africa. LC 80-54180. (Monograph Series in Ethnomusicology: No. 2). (Illus.). 43p. (Orig.). 1980. pap. text ed. 6.00 (ISBN 0-88287-014-9). Progm Ethnom.
Dje Dje, Jacqueline C., jt. ed. see Nketia, J. H.
Djega-Mariadassou, G., jt. auth. see Boudart, Michel.
Djenev, Kiril, jt. auth. see Katzarova-Kukudova, Raina.
Djerassi, Carl. The Politics of Contraception: Birth Control in the Year 2001. LC 81-5460. (Illus.). 282p. 1981. 23.95 (ISBN 0-7167-1341-1); pap. 13.95 (ISBN 0-7167-1342-X). W H Freeman.
--The Politics of Contraception, Nineteen Eighty. (Illus.). 1980. 12.95 (ISBN 0-393-01264-6). Norton.
Djerassi, Carl, jt. auth. see Budzikiewicz, Herbert.
Djerassi, Norma L. Glimpses of China from a Galloping Horse (a Woman's Journal). LC 74-19098. 1975. 9.75 (ISBN 0-08-018215-1). Pergamon.
Djilas, Milovan. Conversations with Stalin. Petrovich, Michael B., tr. LC 62-14470. 1963. pap. 5.95 (ISBN 0-15-622591-3, Harv). HarBraceJ.
--Land Without Justice. LC 58-8574. 1972. pap. 8.95 (ISBN 0-15-648117-0, Harv). HarBraceJ.
--Montenegro. Johnstone, Kenneth, tr. LC 63-8090. 1963. 9.95 (ISBN 0-15-162102-0). HarBraceJ.
--The New Class: An Analysis of the Communist System. LC 82-48032. 224p. 1982. 4.95 (ISBN 0-15-665489-X, Harv). HarBraceJ.
--Rise & Fall. Loud, John, tr. 382p. 1985. 24.95 (ISBN 0-15-177572-9). HarBraceJ.
--Tito: The Story from Inside. LC 80-23040. 1980. 9.95 (ISBN 0-15-190474-X). HarBraceJ.
--The Unperfect Society: Beyond the New Class. Cooke, Dorian, tr. LC 70-76568. 1970. pap. 5.95 (ISBN 0-15-693125-7, Harv). HarBraceJ.
--Wartime. LC 80-16174. 1980. 7.95 (ISBN 0-15-694712-9, Harv). HarBraceJ.
Djin, Nodar, intro. by. Kniga Evreiskikh Aforizmov. LC 84-60080. 406p. (Orig., Rus.). 1984. pap. 16.00 (ISBN 0-89830-082-7). Russica Pubs.
Djindjian, R. & Merland, J. J. Super-Selective Arteriography of the External Carotid Artery. LC 77-2949. (Illus.). 1977. 275.00 (ISBN 0-387-08118-6). Springer-Verlag.
Djindjian, R., jt. ed. see Pia, H. W.
Djiteye, M. A., jt. ed. see Penning de Vries, F. W.
Djokovic, D. Z. & Malzan, Jerry. Products of Reflections in U (P.Q) LC 81-20544. (Memoirs Ser.: No. 259). 86p. 1982. pap. 9.00 (ISBN 0-8218-2259-4, MEMO-259). Am Math.
Djoleto, Amu. Money Galore. (African Writers Ser.). Heinemann Ed.
--The Strange Man. (African Writers Ser.). 1968. pap. text ed. 5.00x (ISBN 0-435-90041-2). Heinemann Ed.
Djonovich, Dusan. United Nations Resolutions: Series II, Security Council, Vol. 1. 1985. lib. bdg. 45.00 (ISBN 0-379-14320-8). Oceana.
Djonovich, Dusan J. United Nations Resolutions, 16 vols. LC 72-13009. 1977. 50.00 ea. (ISBN 0-379-14260-0). Oceana.
Djonovich, Dusan J., ed. Legal Education, a Selective Bibliography. LC 73-21942. (Annual Survey of American Law Ser). 500p. 1970. 35.00 (ISBN 0-379-12229-4). Oceana.
Djordevich, L., jt. auth. see Gregory, D. P.
Djordjevic, Dmitrije & Fischer-Galati, Stephen. The Balkan Revolutionary Tradition. LC 80-24039. 272p. 1981. 26.00x (ISBN 0-231-05098-4). Columbia U Pr.
Djordjevich, Michael. About Happy Living. LC 84-21555. 184p. 1985. 9.95 (ISBN 0-917569-00-8); pap. 5.95 (ISBN 0-917569-01-6). Bks With Ideas.
Djubek, Jozef, et al. Limit State of the Plate Elements of Steel Structures. 216p. 1984. text ed. 34.95 (ISBN 0-8176-1478-8). Birkhauser.
Djukanovic, V. & Mach, E. P., eds. Alternative Approaches to Meeting Basic Health Needs in Developing Countries: A Joint UNICEF-WHO Study. (Also avail. in French). 1975. pap. 9.60 (ISBN 92-4-156048-7). World Health.
Djung, Lu-Dzai. History of Democratic Education in Modern China. (Studies in Chinese History & Civilization). 258p. 1977. Repr. of 1934 ed. 19.00 (ISBN 0-89093-080-5). U Pubns Amer.
Djunkovskoy, E. De see Lacroix & De Djunkovskoy, E.
Djurfeldt, Linberg S. Pills Against Poverty: A Study of the Introduction of Western Medicine in a Tamil Village. 1981. 11.00x (ISBN 0-8364-0681-8, Pub. by Macmillan India). South Asia Bks.
Djuric, Mihailo. Nietzsche und Die Metaphysik. (Monographien und Texte zur Nietzsche-Forschung: Band 16). viii, 326p. (Ger.). 1985. 61.60x (ISBN 3-11-010169-6). De Gruyter.
Djuvera, Neagu M. Civilisations et Lois Historiques: Essai d'Etude des Civilisations et. 446p. 1975. pap. text ed. 28.00x (ISBN 90-2797-705-4). Mouton.
Djwa, Sandra & St. J. Macdonald, R., eds. On F. R. Scott: Essays on His Contributions to Law, Literature, & Politics. 256p. 1983. 25.00x (ISBN 0-7735-0397-8); pap. 8.95 (ISBN 0-7735-0398-6). McGill-Queens U Pr.
Dlab, V. & Gabriel, P., eds. Representation Theory I. (Lecture Notes in Mathematics Ser.: Vol. 831). 373p. 1980. pap. 26.00 (ISBN 0-387-10263-9). Springer-Verlag.
--Representation Theory II. (Lecture Notes in Mathematics: Vol. 832). 673p. 1980. pap. 43.00 (ISBN 0-387-10264-7). Springer-Verlag.
Dlab, V., ed. see International Conference, Ottawa, 1974.
Dlab, Vlastimil & Ringel, Claus M. Indecomposable Representations of Graphs & Algebras. LC 76-18784. (Memoirs: No. 173). 57p. 1976. pap. 12.00 (ISBN 0-8218-1873-2, MEMO-173). Am Math.
Dlamini, Moses. Robben Island, Hell-Hole: Reminiscences of a Political Prisoner in South Africa. LC 84-72593. 202p. 1985. text ed. 25.95 (ISBN 0-86543-008-X); pap. 8.95 (ISBN 0-86543-009-8). Africa Res.
D'Larmessin, jt. auth. see Valck, G.
Dlatt, Jacqueline P., jt. auth. see Maglio, Rudolph.
D'Lima, Hazel. Women in Local Government: A Study in Maharashtra. 211p. 1983. text ed. 16.25x (ISBN 0-391-03077-9, Pub. by Concept India). Humanities.
Dlouhy, Z. Disposal of Radioactive Wastes. (Studies in Environmental Science: Vol. 15). 246p. 1982. 59.75 (ISBN 0-444-99724-5). Elsevier.
Dlugatch, Irving. Dynamic Cost Reduction. LC 78-21078. (Systems & Controls for Financial Management Ser.). 195p. 1979. 50.95x (ISBN 0-471-03565-3, Pub. by Wiley-Interscience). Wiley.
Dlugokinski, Eric. Thoughts from a Friend. LC 83-60342. 60p. 1983. 7.95 (ISBN 0-938232-31-2). Winston-Derek.
Dlugolenski, Y. Que Sabes Del Reloj? 26p. (Span.). 1982. pap. 1.99 (ISBN 0-8285-2497-1, Pub. by Progress Pubs USSR). Imported Pubns.
Dlugolensky, Yakov. Clocks & Watches. Bobrova, Raissa, tr. from Rus. 26p. (gr. k-3). 1983. pap. 2.00 (ISBN 0-8285-2292-8, Pub. by Progress Pubs USSR). Imported Pubns.
Dlugosch, Sharon. Folding Table Napkins: A New Look at a Traditional Craft. rev. ed. LC 77-70868. 64p. 1980. pap. 4.95 (ISBN 0-918420-06-7). Brighton Pubns.
--Table Setting Guide. 1980. tchrs. manual 8.00 (ISBN 0-918420-05-9). Brighton Pubns.
--Table Setting Guide. LC 82-74344. 64p. (Orig.). 1982. pap. 4.95 (ISBN 0-918420-07-5). Brighton Pubns.
Dlugosch, Sharon & Battcher, Joyce. Food Processor Recipes for Conventional & Microwave Cooking. LC 78-74899. 1979. pap. 3.95 (ISBN 0-918420-03-2); pap. 12.00 tchrs' manual (ISBN 0-918420-04-0). Brighton Pubns.
Dlugosch, Sharon & Nelson, Florence. Games for Wedding Shower Fun. LC 83-73600. 112p. 1985. pap. 4.95 (ISBN 0-918420-12-1). Brighton Pubns.
--Wedding Shower Fun. LC 83-72952. (Illus.). 144p. (Orig.). 1984. pap. 5.95 (ISBN 0-918420-22-9). Brighton Pubns.
Dluhosch, Eric, tr. see Egorov, Iurii A.
Dluhosch, Eric, tr. see Lissitzky, El.
Dluhy, Milan J. Changing the System: Political Advocacy for Disadvantaged Groups. (Sage Human Services Guides Ser.: Vol. 24). 119p. 1981. pap. 7.95 (ISBN 0-8039-1726-0). Sage.
Dluhy, Robert, ed. Dictionary for Marine Technology, 2 vols. (Ger. & Eng.). 1974. 89.75x ea.; Vol. 1. (ISBN 3-7788-1220-3); Vol. 2. (ISBN 3-7788-1221-1). Adlers Foreign Bks.
DLW Corporation. My Computer Guide: An Introduction to the IBM-PC. 1984. write for info. (ISBN 0-07-031740-2). McGraw.
Dmitriev, I. S. Molecules Without Chemical Bonds. 155p. 1981. pap. 3.50 (ISBN 0-8285-2021-6, Pub. by Mir Pubs USSR). Imported Pubns.
--Symmetry in World of Molecules. 148p. 1979. pap. 4.45 (ISBN 0-8285-1519-0, Pub. by Mir Pubs USSR). Imported Pubns.
Dmitriev, V. K. & Nuti, D. M. Economic Essays on Value: Competition & Utility. LC 73-77176. (Illus.). 280p. 1974. 47.50 (ISBN 0-521-20253-1). Cambridge U Pr.
Dmitriev, Valentine. Time to Begin. 248p. (Orig.). 1983. 30.00 (ISBN 0-911163-00-X); pap. 20.00 (ISBN 0-911163-01-8). Caring.
Dmitriyev, Y. Man & Animals. 311p. 1984. 9.95 (ISBN 0-8285-2916-7, Pub. by Raduga Pubs USSR). Imported Pubns.
Dmytrenko, Maria. Mykhailyk. Skorkhid, W. Nicholson, tr. from Ukraianian. (Illus.). 64p. 1983. 7.95 (ISBN 0-89962-290-9). Todd & Honeywell.
Dmytrshyn, Basil, jt. ed. see Letiche, John M.
Dmytryk, Edward. On Film Editing. (Illus.). 152p. (Orig.). 1984. pap. 9.95 (ISBN 0-240-51738-5). Focal Pr.
--On Screen Directing. (Illus.). 160p. (Orig.). 1983. pap. 9.95 (ISBN 0-240-51716-4). Focal Pr.
--On Screen Writing. 192p. 1985. pap. 10.95 (ISBN 0-240-51753-9). Focal Pr.
Dmytryk, Edward & Dmytryk, Jean P. On Screen Acting. 152p. 1984. pap. text ed. 9.95 (ISBN 0-240-51739-3). Focal Pr.
Dmytryk, Jean P., jt. auth. see Dmytryk, Edward.
Dmytryshyn, Basil. A History of Russia. (Illus.). 1977. 28.95 (ISBN 0-13-392134-4). P-H.
--Imperial Russia: A Source Book 1700-1917. 2nd ed. LC 73-4179. 1974. text ed. 19.95 (ISBN 0-03-089237-6, HoltC). HR&W.
--U. S. S. R. A Concise History. 4th ed. (The Scribner Press Ser.). (Illus.). 672p. 1984. 30.00 (ISBN 0-684-18083-9, ScribT). Scribner.
--U. S. S. R. A Concise History. 4th ed. (Illus.). 697p. 1984. pap. text ed. 18.95 (ISBN 0-02-330430-8, Pub. by Scribner). Macmillan.
Dmytryshyn, Basil, ed. Medieval Russia: A Source Book, 900-1700. 2nd ed. LC 70-18214. (Dryden Press). 1973. pap. text ed. 18.95 (ISBN 0-03-086441-0, HoltC). HR&W.
Dmytryshyn, Basil & Crownhart-Vaughan, E. A., trs. Colonial Russian America: Kyrill T. Khlebnikov's Reports, 1817-1832. LC 76-43154. (North Pacific Studies Ser.: No. 2). (Illus.). 158p. 1976. 21.95 (ISBN 0-87595-053-1); pap. 12.95 (ISBN 0-87595-139-2). Oreg Hist Soc.
Dmytryshyn, Basil, tr. see Golovin, Pavel N.
Dmytryshyn, Basil, tr. see Khlebnikov, Kyrill T.
Dmytryshyn, Basil, tr. see Letiche, John M.
DNB Design, tr. see Ebel, H., et al.
Dnyansagar, V. R., et al, eds. Recent Trends & Contacts Between Cytogenetics Embryology & Morphology, 1976. (Current Trends in Life Sciences Ser.: Vol. 5). xiv, 592p. 1977. 50.00 (ISBN 0-88065-081-8, Pub. by Messers Today & Tomorrows Printers & Publishers India). Scholarly Pubns.
Do, ed. see Malyala, Panduranga R.
Do it Yourself Magazine Editors. Do It Yourself Guide to Glass, Timber & Tiles. (Illus.). 96p. 1985. 9.95 (ISBN 0-7137-1512-X, Pub. by Blandford Pr England). Sterling.
Doak, Cecilia C., et al. Teaching Patients with Low Literary Skills. LC 64-4016. (Illus.). 192p. 1985. pap. text ed. 9.95 (ISBN 0-397-54498-7, Lippincott Nursing). Lippincott.

Doak, George D. & Freedman, Leon D. Organometallic Compounds of Arsenic, Antimony, & Bismuth. LC 75-120703. 509p. 1970. 42.50 (ISBN 0-471-21650-X, Pub. by Wiley). Krieger.

Doak, Henry A., jt. auth. see Doak, Mary E.

Doak, Mary E. & Doak, Henry A. Sentence & Paragraph Technique. 1978. Repr. of 1931 ed. lib. bdg. 25.00 (ISBN 0-8492-0655-3). R West.

Doak, Wade. Dolphin Dolphin. (Illus.). 298p. 1982. 19.95 (ISBN 0-911378-43-X). Sheridan.

Doan, Cortland C. Design, Drafting, & Construction Practices for Electronics. LC 77-6064. 1985. pap. text ed. 18.00 (ISBN 0-534-04722-X). Breton Pubs.

Doan, Daniel. Fifty Hikes in the White Mountains: Walks, Day Hikes & Backpacking Trips in the High Peaks Region of New Hampshire. 3rd, rev. ed. LC 83-2602. (Fifty Hikes Ser.). (Illus.). 208p. 1983. pap. 8.95 (ISBN 0-942440-12-9). Backcountry Pubns.

--Fifty More Hikes in New Hampshire: Day Hikes & Backpacking Trips from the Coast to Coos County. rev. ed. LC 82-20665. (Fifty Hikes Ser.). (Illus.). 208p. 1983. pap. 8.95 (ISBN 0-942440-06-4). Backcountry Pubns.

Doan, Edward N. The La Follettes & the Wisconsin Idea. LC 83-45744. Repr. of 1947 ed. 29.50 (ISBN 0-404-20081-8). AMS Pr.

Doan, Eleanor, compiled by. The Speaker's Sourcebook. 1978. pap. 9.95 (ISBN 0-310-23781-5). Zondervan.

Doan, James. The Romance of Cearbhall & Fearbhlaidh. (Dolmen Texts Ser.: No.7). Orig. Title: Bas Chearbhaill agus Fhearbhlaidhe. 80p. (Irish.). 1985. text ed. 14.75x (ISBN 0-85105-409-9, Dolmen Pr.). Humanities.

Doan, Marilyn. Hiking Light. 1983. 14.50 (ISBN 0-8446-6046-9). Peter Smith.

Doan, Marlyn. Hiking Light. (Illus.). 204p. 1982. pap. 8.95 (ISBN 0-89886-036-9). Mountaineers.

--Starting Small in the Wilderness: The Sierra Club Outdoors Guide for Families. LC 79-748. (Outdoor Activities Guides Ser.). (Illus.). 288p. 1979. pap. 6.95 (ISBN 0-87156-253-7). Sierra.

Doan, Peter, et al. Local Institutional Development for Natural Resource Management. (Special Series on Local Institutional Development: No. 2). 66p. (Orig.). 1985. pap. 6.50 (ISBN 0-86731-109-6). RDC Ctr Intl Stud.

Doan, Rachel N., jt. auth. see Nieland, Robert G.

Doan, Rebecca M., et al. Local Institutional Development for Primary Health Care. (Special Series on Local Institutional Development: No. 4). 61p. 1985. pap. text ed. 6.50 (ISBN 0-86731-111-8). RDC Ctr Intl Stud.

--Mobilizing & Managing Economic Resources for Local Institutional Development. (Special Series on Local Institutional Development: No. 8). 59p. (Orig.). 1985. pap. text ed. 6.25 (ISBN 0-86731-115-0). RDC Ctr Intl Stud.

Doan, Robert L. Arts & Crafts Achievement Activities. (Early Childhood Achievement Units Ser.). 1979. pap. 6.40x (ISBN 0-87628-282-6). Ctr Appl Res.

--Body Management Achievement Activities. (Early Childhood Achievement Units Ser.). 1979. pap. 6.40x (ISBN 0-87628-284-2). Ctr Appl Res.

--Early Childhood Achievement Units. 1979. 6.40x ea. Ctr Appl Res.

--Language Development Achievement Activities. (Early Childhood Achievement Units Ser.). 1979. pap. 6.40x (ISBN 0-87628-281-8). Ctr Appl Res.

--Number Readiness Achievement Activities. (Early Childhood Achievement Units Ser.). 1979. pap. 6.40x (ISBN 0-87628-283-4). Ctr Appl Res.

--Science Discovery Achievement Activities. (Early Childhood Achievement Units Ser.). 1979. pap. 6.40x (ISBN 0-87628-285-0). Ctr Appl Res.

--Social Living Achievement Activities. (Early Childhood Achievement Unit Ser.). 1979. pap. 6.40x (ISBN 0-87628-286-9). Ctr Appl Res.

Doan, William & Dietz, Craig. Photoflexion: A History of Bodybuilding Photography. (Illus.). 128p. 1984. 19.95 (ISBN 0-312-60834-9). St Martin.

Doane, Alger N. Genesis A: A New Edition. LC 77-77437. 430p. 1978. 45.00x (ISBN 0-299-07430-7). U of Wis Pr.

Doane, Benjamin K., ed. The Limbic System: Functional Organization & Clinical Disorders. 1985. text ed. price not set (ISBN 0-88167-134-7). Raven.

Doane, D. V., ed. see TMS-AIME Fall Meeting, Chicago, 1977.

Doane, Donald C. Needs of Youth: An Evaluation for Curriculum Purposes. LC 74-176723. (Columbia University. Teachers College. Contributions to Education: No. 848). Repr. of 1942 ed. 22.50 (ISBN 0-404-55848-8). AMS Pr.

Doane, Doris. Book of Cape Cod Houses. LC 78-107080. (Illus.). 1970. 12.95 (ISBN 0-85699-011-6). Chatham Pr.

--Exploring Old Cape Cod. rev. ed. (Illustrated Guide Ser.). (Illus.). 1985. pap. 5.95 (ISBN 0-85699-003-5). Chatham Pr.

Doane, Doris C. Astrology - Thirty Years Research. 328p. 1956. 11.00 (ISBN 0-86690-070-5, 1065-01). Am Fed Astrologers.

--Horoscopes of the U.S. Presidents. 160p. 1971. 6.25 (ISBN 0-86690-071-3, 1066-01). Am Fed Astrologers.

--How to Prepare & Pass an Astrologer Certification Exam. 56p. 1973. 5.00 (ISBN 0-86690-072-1, 1067-01). Am Fed Astrologers.

--Progressions in Action. 256p. 1977. Repr. 11.00 (ISBN 0-86690-074-8, 1869-01). Am Fed Astrologers.

--Time Changes in Canada & Mexico. 80p. 1980. 8.00 (ISBN 0-86690-075-6, 1070-01). Am Fed Astrologers.

--Time Changes in the U.S.A. 200p. 1981. 10.00 (ISBN 0-86690-076-4, 1071-01). Am Fed Astrologers.

--Time Changes in the World. 112p. 1980. 9.00 (ISBN 0-86690-077-2, 1072-01). Am Fed Astrologers.

--Vocational Selection & Counseling, 2 vols. Vol. 1, 158p. 13.50 (ISBN 0-86690-011-X, 1073-01); Vol. 2, 176p. 13.50 (ISBN 0-86690-012-8, 1074-01). Am Fed Astrologers.

Doane, Doris C. & Keyes, King. How to Read Tarot Cards. (Illus.). 208p. 1979. pap. 4.76i (ISBN 0-06-463481-7, EH 481, EH). B&N NY.

Doane, E. Aquarian Age Philosophy. 128p. 1969. 5.95 (ISBN 0-86690-242-2, 1075-01). Am Fed Astrologers.

Doane, Edith R. County Systems of R. F. D. 1977. 15.00 (ISBN 0-916170-05-5). J-B Pub.

Doane, George W. The Goodly Heritage of Jerseymen: The First Annual Address before the New Jersey Historical Society at Their Meeting in Trenton, on Thursday, January 15, 1846. 2nd ed. 32p. 1971. pap. 2.00 (ISBN 0-686-81822-9). NJ Hist Soc.

Doane, Gerald G. Hostage Negotiator's Manual. (Illus.). pap. 24.95 (ISBN 0-89415-005-7). Police Pr.

Doane, Gilbert H. & Bell, James B. Searching for Your Ancestors: The How & Why of Geneaology. 5th ed. 1980. 12.95 (ISBN 0-8166-0934-9). U of Minn Pr.

Doane, Gilbert H. & Doane, Gilbert J., eds. The Doane Family, Vol. 2. 587p. 1976. text ed. 30.00 (ISBN 0-686-32800-0). Vail Ballou.

Doane, Gilbert J., jt. ed. see Doane, Gilbert H.

Doane, Jim. Great Smoky Mountains Picture Book. Castaldo, George, ed. (Color Pictorial of Great Smoky Mountains Ser.: No. 1). (Illus.). 72p. (Orig.). 1981. 10.95 (ISBN 0-936672-13-7); pap. 7.50 (ISBN 0-936672-14-5). Aerial Photo.

--North Carolina: From the Mountains to the Sea. LC 80-80955. 72p. 1980. 10.95 (ISBN 0-936672-01-3); pap. text ed. 7.50 (ISBN 0-936672-00-5). Aerial Photo.

Doane, Mary A., et al, eds. Re-Vision: Essays in Feminist Film Criticism. 220p. 1983. 25.00 (ISBN 0-89093-585-8); pap. 10.00. U Pubns Amer.

Doane, Nancy L. Indian Doctor Book. 54p. pap. text ed. 2.00 (ISBN 0-936672-15-3). Aerial Photo.

Doane, R. Michael. The Legends of Jesse Dark. LC 84-47809. 356p. 1984. 16.95 (ISBN 0-394-53748-3). Knopf.

Dobai, Johannes, jt. auth. see Novotny, Fritz.

Dobai, Peter. Budapest in Seventy-One Colour Photographs. (Illus.). 32p. 1982. 14.95 (ISBN 0-8044-5330-6). Ungar.

Dobak, Annelies, tr. see Waechter, Friederich K.

Dobash, R. E. & Dobash, Russell. Violence Against Wives. LC 79-7181. 1979. 19.95 (ISBN 0-02-907320-0). Free Pr.

Dobash, R. Emerson & Dobash, Russell. Violence Against Wives: A Case Against the Patriarchy. 352p. 1980. 39.00x (ISBN 0-7291-0153-3, Pub. by Open Bks England). State Mutual Bk.

Dobash, R. Emerson & Dobash, Russell P. Violence Against Wives. 1979. 8.95x (ISBN 0-02-907810-5). Free Pr.

Dobash, Russell, jt. auth. see Dobash, R. E.

Dobash, Russell, jt. auth. see Dobash, R. Emerson.

Dobash, Russell P., jt. auth. see Dobash, R. Emerson.

Dobb, Maurice. Capitalism, Yesterday & Today. 64p. 1958. pap. 4.50x (ISBN 0-8464-0234-3). Beekman Pubs.

--Political Economy & Capitalism: Some Essays in Economic Tradition. LC 76-108389. 357p. 1972. Repr. of 1945 ed. lib. bdg. 29.75x (ISBN 0-8371-3812-4, DOPE). Greenwood.

--Studies in the Development of Capitalism. rev. ed. LC 74-13744. 415p. (Orig.). 1964. pap. 4.95 (ISBN 0-7178-0197-7). Intl Pubs Co.

--Theories of Value & Distribution since Adam Smith. LC 72-88619. (Illus.). 264p. 1973. 47.50 (ISBN 0-521-20100-4); pap. 17.95 (ISBN 0-521-09936-6). Cambridge U Pr.

--Welfare Economics & the Elements of Socialism. LC 69-16280. (Illus.). 1969. 49.50 (ISBN 0-521-07462-2); pap. 17.95 (ISBN 0-521-09937-4). Cambridge U Pr.

Dobb, Maurice, ed. see Marx, Karl.

Dobb, Maurice, ed. see Ricardo, David.

Dobb, Maurice, et al. The Transition from Feudalism to Capitalism. 1978. (Pub by NLB); pap. 6.25 (ISBN 0-86091-701-0). Schocken.

Dobb, Maurice H. Capitalist Enterprise & Social Progress. LC 79-1577. 1981. Repr. of 1925 ed. 31.00 (ISBN 0-88355-883-1). Hyperion Conn.

--Wages. LC 82-994. (Cambridge Economic Handbooks). (Illus.). xv, 201p. 1982. Repr. of 1966 ed. lib. bdg. 22.50x (ISBN 0-313-23483-3, DOWA). Greenwood.

Dobberpuhl, Daniel W., jt. auth. see Glaser, Lance A.

Dobbert, Guido A. The Disintegration of an Immigrant Community: The Cincinnati Germans, 1870-1920. Cordasco, Francesco, ed. LC 80-853. (American Ethnic Groups Ser.). 1981. lib. bdg. 43.00x (ISBN 0-405-13416-9). Ayer Co Pubs.

Dobbert, John A. If Being a Christian Is So Great, Why Do I Have the Blahs? LC 79-65420. 160p. 1980. pap. 4.95 (ISBN 0-8307-0729-8, 5413206). Regal.

Dobbert, Marion L. Ethnographic Research: Theory & Application for Modern Schools & Societies. Rist, Ray C., ed. LC 81-23387. (Praeger Studies in Ethnographic Perspectives on American Education). 410p. 1982. 39.95 (ISBN 0-03-061473-2). Praeger.

--Ethnographic Research: Theory & Application for Modern Schools & Societies. LC 81-23387. (Praeger Special Studies in Ethnographic Perspectives on American Education). 1984. pap. 16.95 (ISBN 0-03-071543-1). Praeger.

Dobberteen, Sara, ed. Eleventh Annual Exhibition: National Academy of Western Art, 1983. (Illus.). 80p. (Orig.). 1983. pap. 12.95 (ISBN 0-932154-13-1). Natl Cowboy Hall of Fame.

--National Academy of Western Art: Thirteenth Annual Exhibition. (Illus.). 93p. 1985. pap. 15.00 (ISBN 0-932154-16-6). Natl Cowboy Hall of Fame.

--Twelfth Annual Exhibition: National Academy of Western Art, 1984. (Illus.). 100p. (Orig.). 1984. pap. 15.00 (ISBN 0-932154-14-X). Natl Cowboy Hall of Fame.

Dobbie, Elliot V., ed. The Anglo-Saxon Minor Poems. LC 43-1513. (Anglo-Saxon Poetic Records Ser.). 220p. 1942. 22.50x (ISBN 0-231-08770-5). Columbia U Pr.

Dobbin, Christine. Islamic Revivalism in a Changing Peasant Economy: Central Sumatra, 1784-1847. 328p. 1981. 40.00x (ISBN 0-7007-0155-9, Pub. by Curzon England). State Mutual Bk.

--Islamic Revivalism in a Changing Peasant Economy: Central Sumatra, 1784-1847. (Scandinavian Institute of Asian Studies, Monograph Ser.: No. 47). 300p. 1983. pap. text ed. 14.75x (ISBN 0-7007-0155-9, Pub. by Curzon Pr England). Humanities.

Dobbin, Leonard, tr. see Scheele, K. W.

Dobbin, Muriel. Joe's World. LC 83-45060. (Illus.). 128p. 1983. 10.95 (ISBN 0-689-11426-5). Atheneum.

Dobbing, Herbert. Cause for Concern: A Quaker's View of the Palestine Problem. 70p. 1970. 2.75 (ISBN 0-88728-108-7). Inst Palestine.

Dobbing, John, ed. Maternal Nutrition & Lactational Infertility. (Nestle Nutrition Workshop Ser.: Vol. 9). 170p. 1985. text ed. 23.50 (ISBN 0-88167-100-2). Raven.

--Maternal Nutrition in Pregnancy: Eating for Two? LC 80-41611. 1981. 40.00 (ISBN 0-12-218850-0). Acad Pr.

--Prevention of Spina Bifida & Other Neural Tube Defects. 1983. 33.00 (ISBN 0-12-218860-8). Acad Pr.

Dobbing, John, et al, eds. Scientific Studies in Mental Retardation. (Illus.). 400p. 1984. text ed. 99.50x (ISBN 0-333-35454-0). Sheridan Med Bks.

Dobbins, Austin C. Milton & the Book of Revelation: The Heavenly Cycle. LC 73-22715. (Studies in the Humanities Ser.: No. 7). 176p. 1975. o. p. 12.50 (ISBN 0-8173-7320-9); pap. 4.95 (ISBN 0-8173-7321-7). U of Ala Pr.

Dobbins, Bill & Prague, Ken. The Gold's Gym Weight Training Book. 256p. 1985. pap. 3.50 (ISBN 0-425-07491-9). Berkley Pub.

Dobbins, Bill & Sprague, Ken. The Gold's Gym Weight Training Book. 1981. pap. 3.50 (ISBN 0-425-06382-8). Berkley Pub.

Dobbins, Bill, jt. auth. see Jenner, Bruce.

Dobbins, Bill, jt. auth. see Schwarzenegger, Arnold.

Dobbins, Bill, jt. auth. see Schwarzenegger, Arnold.

Dobbins, Bill, jt. auth. see Sprague, Ken.

Dobbins, Frank A. The Contributions of Mohammedanism to the Historical Growth of Mankind & Its Future Prospects. (Illus.). 103p. Repr. of 1883 ed. 97.75 (ISBN 0-89901-111-X). Found Class Reprints.

Dobbins, G. S. Aprenda a Ser Lider. Molina, S. P., tr. from Eng. Orig. Title: Learning to Lead. 126p. (Span.). 1980. pap. 2.50 (ISBN 0-311-17013-7). Casa Bautista.

Dobbins, Gaines S. Churchbook. 1951. 11.95 (ISBN 0-8054-2502-0). Broadman.

--Learning to Lead. LC 68-12342. (Orig.). 1968. pap. 4.25 (ISBN 0-8054-3208-6). Broadman.

--Ministering Church. LC 60-9530. 1960. 9.50 (ISBN 0-8054-2505-5). Broadman.

Dobbins, Joann H. Pineapple Gold. LC 83-90001. 304p. 1983. pap. 10.95 (ISBN 0-9610540-0-X). J H Dobbins.

Dobbins, John, ed. see Hegel, G. W.

Dobbins, M. F. Vette Vues Factbook of the 1963-1967 Stingray. 6th ed. (Vette Vues Factbook Ser.). (Illus.). 312p. 1984. 24.95x (ISBN 0-9607176-3-3). M F Dobbins.

Dobbins, M. F. & Incremona, F. J. Camaro Factbook, 1967-1969. (Illus.). 238p. 1984. 19.95x (ISBN 0-9607176-4-1). M F Dobbins.

Dobbins, Mike, ed. see Dobbins, Peggy P.

Dobbins, Peggy P. From Kin to Class. rev. 4th ed. Weston, Judith & Dobbins, Mike, eds. (Illus.). 100p. (Orig.). 1981. pap. 7.00 (ISBN 0-9605774-0-8). Signmaker.

Dobbins, R. & Witt, S. C. Portfolio Theory & Investment Management. 176p. 1984. 34.95x (ISBN 0-85520-620-9); pap. 14.95x (ISBN 0-85520-621-7). Basil Blackwell.

Dobbins, Richard & McRae, Thomas W. Institutional Shareholders. 1975. 59.00x (ISBN 0-903763-34-6, Pub. by MCB Pubns). State Mutual Bk.

Dobbins, Richard & Pettman, Barrie O. Disclosing Financial Information to Employees. 1978. 80.00x (ISBN 0-905440-43-9, Pub. by MCB Pubns). State Mutual Bk.

--Managerial Finance. 1977. 90.00x (ISBN 0-905440-25-0, Pub. by MCB Pubns). State Mutual Bk.

Dobbins, Richard & Witt, Stephen. An Introduction to Portfolio Management. 1979. 95.00x (ISBN 0-86176-019-0, Pub. by MCB Pubns). State Mutual Bk.

Dobbins, Richard, jt. auth. see McRae, Thomas.

Dobbins, Richard, jt. auth. see Pettman, Barrie O.

Dobbins, Richard, et al. Financial Objectives, Ownership & Control. 1978. 90.00x (ISBN 0-905440-70-6, Pub. by MCB Pubns). State Mutual Bk.

Dobbins, Richard A. Atmospheric Motion & Air Pollution: An Introduction for Students of Engineering & Science. LC 79-952. (Environmental Science & Technology: Texts & Monographs). 323p. 1979. 60.00 (ISBN 0-471-21675-5, Pub. by Wiley-Interscience). Wiley.

Dobbins, Richard D. Venturing into a Child's World. 160p. 1985. 8.95 (ISBN 0-8007-1404-0). Revell.

--You Can Find a Good Mate. 0.75 (ISBN 0-8010-2913-9). Baker Bk.

--Your Spiritual & Emotional Power. 160p. (Orig.). 1984. pap. 4.95Bks (ISBN 0-8007-5136-1, Power Bks). Revell.

Dobbins, Robert R. If & Only If in Analysis. 1977. pap. text ed. 11.25 (ISBN 0-8191-0344-6). U Pr of Amer.

Dobbs. Bankruptcy: Reorganizations under Chapter 11 of the Bankruptcy Code. incl. latest pocket part supplement 39.95 (ISBN 0-686-90671-3); separate pocket part supplement, 1983 14.95. Harrison Co GA.

--Enforcement of Security Interests in Personal Property. (The Law in Georgia Ser.). incl. latest pocket part supplement 24.95 (ISBN 0-686-90390-0); separate pocket part supplement, 1983 (foruse in 1984) 13.95 (ISBN 0-686-90391-9). Harrison Co GA.

Dobbs, A. L., jt. auth. see McBride, M. W.

Dobbs, Annie C. Dictionnaire Abrege du Surrealisme. (Fr.). pap. 23.95 (ISBN 0-686-57119-3, M-6165). French & Eur.

Dobbs, Archibald E. Education & Social Movements 1700-1850. LC 68-55702. Repr. of 1919 ed. 27.50x (ISBN 0-678-00501-X). Kelley.

Dobbs, Arthur. An Account of the Counties Adjoining to Hudson's Bay, in the Northwest Part of America. 1744. 17.00 (ISBN 0-384-12045-8). Johnson Repr.

Dobbs, Betty J. The Foundation of Newton's Alchemy; or, "The Hunting of the Greene Lyon". LC 74-31795. (Illus.). 320p. 1976. 49.50 (ISBN 0-521-20786-X). Cambridge U Pr.

--The Foundations of Newton's Alchemy: Or "The Hunting of the Greene Lyon". LC 74-31795. (Cambridge Paperback Library). (Illus.). 300p. 1983. pap. 16.95 (ISBN 0-521-27381-1). Cambridge U Pr.

Dobbs, Brian & Dobbs, Judy. Dante Gabriel Rossetti: An Alien Victorian. 1977. text ed. 21.25x (ISBN 0-686-86085-3). Humanities.

Dobbs, Charles M. The Unwanted Symbol: American Foreign Policy, the Cold War, & Korea, 1945-1950. LC 81-6261. (Illus.). 250p. 1981. 20.00x (ISBN 0-87338-258-7). Kent St U Pr.

Dobbs, D. E. Cech Cohomological Dimensions for Commutative Rings. LC 78-131545. (Lecture Notes in Mathematics: Vol. 147). 1970. pap. 11.00 (ISBN 0-387-04936-3). Springer-Verlag.

Dobbs, Dan B. Problems in Remedies. 137p. 1974. pap. write for info. West Pub.

--Remedies. (Hornbook Ser.). 1067p. 1973. 21.95 (ISBN 0-317-00040-3). West Pub.

--Torts & Compensation: Personal Accountability & Social Responsibility for Injury. LC 84-26950. (American Casebook Ser.). 1233p. 1985. text ed. 30.95 (ISBN 0-314-93140-6). West Pub.

Dobbs, David & Hanks, Robert. A Modern Course on the Theory of Equations. LC 80-13487. 1980. 15.00x (ISBN 0-936428-03-1). Polygonal Pub.

Dobbs, E. R. Electricity & Magnetism. (Student Physics Ser.). (Illus.). 128p. 1984. pap. 9.95x (ISBN 0-7102-0157-5). Routledge & Kegan.

Dobbs, Elizabeth. Pushes & Pulls. 7.50x (ISBN 0-392-08264-0, SpS). Sportshelf.

Dobbs, Farrell. Revolutionary Continuity: Birth of the Communist Movement, 1918-1922, Vol. 2. Barnes, Jack, ed. LC 80-84850. 1983. lib. bdg. 22.00 (ISBN 0-913460-92-3); pap. 5.95 (ISBN 0-913460-93-1). Monad Pr.

--Teamster Bureaucracy. LC 76-52771. (Illus.). 1977. 23.00 (ISBN 0-913460-52-4); pap. 6.95 (ISBN 0-913460-53-2). Monad Pr.

--Teamster Politics. LC 75-17324. (Illus.). 256p. 1975. 23.00 (ISBN 0-913460-38-9); pap. 6.95 (ISBN 0-913460-39-7). Monad Pr.

--Teamster Power. LC 73-78115. 256p. 1973. 23.00 (ISBN 0-913460-20-6, Dist. by Path Pr NY); pap. 6.95 (ISBN 0-913460-21-4). Monad Pr.

--Teamster Rebellion. LC 78-186690. (Illus.). 192p. 1972. 20.00 (ISBN 0-913460-02-8, Dist. by Path Pr NY); pap. 5.95 (ISBN 0-913460-03-6). Monad Pr.

Dobbs, Farrell, intro. by see Trotsky, Leon.

Dobbs, Horace. Follow the Wild Dolphins. LC 82-5712. (Illus.). 292p. 1982. 15.95 (ISBN 0-312-29752-1). St Martin.

Dobbs, Jeannine, et al. Three Some Poems. LC 75-23819. 88p. 1976. pap. 6.95 (ISBN 0-914086-11-1). Alicejamesbooks.

Dobbs, Judy, jt. auth. see Dobbs, Brian.

Dobbs, Larry & Farr, Donald. How to Restore Your Mustang. 1980. 14.95 (ISBN 0-941596-01-X). Mustang Pubns.

Dobbs, Larry, et al. Mustang Recognition Guide, Nineteen Sixty Four-and-a-Half to Nineteen Seventy-Three. LC 81-84075. (Illus.). 1981. pap. text ed. 16.95 (ISBN 0-941596-00-1). Mustang Pubns.

Dobbs, Leonard. Shakespeare Revealed. Kingsmill, Hugh, ed. 222p. 1984. Repr. of 1984 ed. lib. bdg. 35.00 (ISBN 0-89984-169-4). Century Bookbindery.

Dobbs, M., et al. Poland-Solidarity-Walesa. 1981. pap. 9.95 (ISBN 0-07-006681-7). McGraw.

Dobbs, Mary Lou. Cinderella Salesman: An Inspiring Success Story for Every Woman Who Seeks a Fascinating Career. LC 82-82418. 1982. pap. 7.95 (ISBN 0-910580-28-6). Farnswth Pub.

Dobbs, Michael, et al. Poland Solidarity Walesa. (Illus.). 128p. 1981. 17.50 (ISBN 0-08-028147-8). Pergamon.

Dobbs, Paul. To Baruch - a Responsum. LC 75-39329. 128p. 1976. 6.00 (ISBN 0-8022-2177-7). Philos Lib.

Dobbs, Roland. Electromagnetic Waves. (Student Physics Ser.). (Illus.). 128p. (Orig.). 1985. pap. 9.95x (ISBN 0-7102-0506-6). Routledge & Kegan.

Dobbs, Rose, ed. see Brothers Grimm.

Dobbs, Stephen M., ed. Arts Education & Back to Basics. 1979. pap. 12.50 (ISBN 0-937652-09-1). Natl Art Ed.

Dobbs, Zygmund. Keynes at Harvard. rev. & enl ed. 3.75 (ISBN 0-685-46997-2). Veritas.

Dobby, Alan. Conservation & Planning. (The Built Environment Ser.). 173p. 1978. pap. 10.00 (ISBN 0-09-132271-5, Pub. by Hutchinson Educ). Longwood Pub Group.

Dobbyn, John F. Injunctions. (Nutshell Ser.). 264p. 1974. pap. 7.95. West Pub.

--Insurance Law in a Nutshell. LC 81-7468. (Nutshell Ser.). 315p. 1981. pap. text ed. 7.95 (ISBN 0-314-59851-0). West Pub.

--So You Want to Go to Law School. LC 76-19202. 1976. pap. 6.95 (ISBN 0-685-71466-7). West Pub.

Dobelis, M. C. Anonymous & Pseudononymous Publications of Twentieth Century Authors. Date not set. 16.95x (ISBN 0-918230-06-3). Barnstable.

--Bridging the Gap Between Computer Technicians & Users. (Illus.). 1976. pap. 0.50 (ISBN 0-918230-05-5). Barnstable.

--The Three-Day Week-Offshoot of an EDP Operation. (Illus.). 1976. pap. 0.50 (ISBN 0-918230-04-7). Barnstable.

Dobell, Bertram. Catalogue of Books Printed for Private Circulation. LC 66-25693. 1966. Repr. of 1906 ed. 35.00x (ISBN 0-8103-3303-1). Gale.

--Laureate of Pessimism. LC 77-105781. 1970. Repr. of 1910 ed. 14.50x (ISBN 0-8046-1013-4, Pub. by Kennikat). Assoc Faculty Pr.

--Laureate of Pessimism. 1973. Repr. of 1910 ed. 8.50 (ISBN 0-8274-1657-1). R West.

--Sidelights on Charles Lamb. LC 76-43277. 1976. Repr. of 1903 ed. lib. bdg. 30.00 (ISBN 0-8414-3702-5). Folcroft.

Dobell, Bertram, ed. see Goldsmith, Oliver.

Dobell, Bertram, ed. see Leopardi, Giacomo.

Dobell, Bertram, ed. see Shelley, Percy B.

Dobell, Bertram, jt. ed. see Wilson, J. D.

Dobell, Peter. Travels in Kamtchatka & Siberia: With a Narrative of a Residence in China. LC 78-115529. (Russia Observed Ser., No. 1). 1970. Repr. of 1830 ed. 33.00 (ISBN 0-405-03021-5). Ayer Co Pubs.

Dobelstein, A. Politics, Economics, & the Public Welfare. 1980. 27.95 (ISBN 0-13-683979-7). P-H.

Dobelstein, Andrew J. & Johnson, Ann. Serving Older Adults: Policy, Programs, & Professional Activities. (Illus.). 272p. 1985. text ed. 26.95 (ISBN 0-13-806860-7). P-H.

Dobelstein, Andrew W. Politics, Economics & Public Welfare. 2nd ed. (Illus.). 240p. 1986. pap. text ed. 20.95 (ISBN 0-13-684101-5). P-H.

Dober, Richard P. Environmental Design. LC 75-11961. 288p. 1975. Repr. of 1969 ed. 24.50 (ISBN 0-88275-331-2). Krieger.

Dobereiner, J., et al, eds. Limitations & Potentials for Biological Nitrogen Fixation in the Tropics. LC 77-28218. (Basic Life Sciences Ser.: Vol. 10). 412p. 1978. 52.50x (ISBN 0-306-36510-3, Plenum Pr). Plenum Pub.

Dobereiner, Peter. The Book of Golf Disasters. LC 83-45491. (Illus.). 180p. 1984. 12.95 (ISBN 0-689-11453-2). Atheneum.

--Down the Nineteenth Fairway. LC 82-73279. (Illus.). 256p. 1983. 13.95 (ISBN 0-689-11380-3). Atheneum.

--Golf Rules Explained. 144p. 1984. 12.95 (ISBN 0-7153-8623-9). David & Charles.

Doberer, Kurt K. The Goldmakers: Ten Thousand Years of Alchemy. Dickes, E. W., tr. LC 72-597. (Illus.). 301p. 1972. Repr. of 1948 ed. lib. bdg. 19.75x (ISBN 0-8371-6355-2, DOGM). Greenwood.

Doberkat, E. E. Stochastic Automata: Stability, Nondeterminism, & Prediction. (Lecture Notes in Computer Science Ser.: Vol. 113). 135p. 1981. pap. 12.00 (ISBN 0-387-10835-1). Springer-Verlag.

Doberstein, Dick. Communications Made Easy for Pilots. (Illus.). 78p. 1980. pap. text ed. 5.95x (ISBN 0-685-55702-2, Simplified). Aviation.

--Communications Made Easy for Pilots. Date not set. 5.95 (ISBN 0-9607866-3-5). Simplified Reg.

--Navigation Made Easy for Pilots. (Illus.). 98p. 1976. pap. text ed. 5.95x (ISBN 0-685-55701-4, Pub. by Simplified). Aviation.

--Navigation Made Easy for Pilots. 1984. pap. text ed. 5.95 (ISBN 0-9607866-2-7). Simplified Reg.

--Regulations Made Easy for Commercial Pilots. 1984. pap. text ed. 5.95 (ISBN 0-9607866-0-0). Simplified Reg.

--Regulations Made Easy for Instrument Pilots. 1984. pap. text ed. 5.95 (ISBN 0-9607866-1-9). Simplified Reg.

--Regulations Made Easy for Private Pilots. 1984. pap. text ed. 5.95 (ISBN 0-9607866-4-3). Simplified Reg.

Doberstein, J. W., tr. see Thielicke, Helmut.

Doberstein, John, ed. & tr. see Thielicke, Helmut.

Doberstein, John W., jt. ed. see Lehmann, Helmut T.

Doberstein, John W., tr. see Lehmann, Helmut T. & Doberstein, John W.

Doberstein, John W., tr. see Schubert, Kurt.

Doberstein, John W., tr. see Thielicke, Helmut.

Dobias, B., et al. New Developments, Vol. 56. (Structure & Bonding). (Illus.). 160p. 1984. 34.00 (ISBN 0-387-13106-X). Springer-Verlag.

Dobie, Ann B. & Hirt, Andrew J. Comprehension & Composition: An Introduction to the Essay. (Illus.). 1980. pap. text ed. write for info. (ISBN 0-02-329920-7). Macmillan.

--Comprehension & Composition: An Introduction to the Essay. 2nd ed. 528p. 1986. pap. price not set (ISBN 0-02-330320-4). Macmillan.

Dobie, Charles C. San Francisco Adventures. LC 70-101800. (Short Story Index Reprint Ser.). 1937. 17.00 (ISBN 0-8369-3188-2). Ayer Co Pubs.

Dobie, Edith. Malta's Road to Independence. LC 67-15591. Repr. of 1967 ed. 77.00 (ISBN 0-8357-9733-3, 2016210). Bks Demand UMI.

--The Political Career of Stephen Mallory White. LC 74-155605. (Stanford University. Stanford Studies in History, Economics, & Political Science: Vol. 2, Pt. 1). Repr. of 1927 ed. 24.50 (ISBN 0-404-50963-0). AMS Pr.

Dobie, G. Vera. Alphonse Daudet. LC 74-19263. 1974. Repr. of 1949 ed. lib. bdg. 25.00 (ISBN 0-8414-3712-2). Folcroft.

Dobie, J. F. The Flavor of Texas. 176p. (YA) 1975. 12.50 (ISBN 0-8363-0130-7). Jenkins.

Dobie, J. Frank. Apache Gold & Yaqui Silver. (Illus.). 380p. 1985. pap. 8.95 (ISBN 0-292-70381-3). U of Tex Pr.

--Ben Lilly Legend. (Illus.). 1950. 14.45 (ISBN 0-316-18792-5). Little.

--The Ben Lilly Legend. 253p. 1981. pap. 6.95 (ISBN 0-292-70728-2). U of Tex Pr.

--Coronado's Children: Tales of Lost & Buried Treasures of the Southwest. 367p. 1982. Repr. of 1931 ed. lib. bdg. 50.00 (ISBN 0-89987-170-4). Darby Bks.

--Coronado's Children: Tales of Lost Mines & Buried Treasures of the Southwest. (Barker Texas History Center Ser.: No. 3). (Illus.). 351p. 1978. 14.95 (ISBN 0-292-71050-X); pap. 8.95 (ISBN 0-292-71052-6). U of Tex Pr.

--Cow People. (Illus.). 1964. 12.95 (ISBN 0-316-18793-3). Little.

--Cow People. (Illus.). 317p. 1981. pap. 7.95 (ISBN 0-292-71060-7). U of Tex Pr.

--I'll Tell You a Tale. 1960. 11.95 (ISBN 0-316-18794-1). Little.

--I'll Tell You a Tale: An Anthology. (Illus.). 378p. 1981. pap. 8.95 (ISBN 0-292-73821-8). U of Tex Pr.

--J. Frank Dobie on Libraries. (Illus.). 8p. 1970. pap. 3.00 (ISBN 0-87959-031-9). U of Tex H Ransom Ctr.

--John C. Duval: First Texas Man of Letters: His Life & Some of His Unpublished Writings. LC 40-5152. (Illus.). 1965. Repr. of 1939 ed. 9.95 (ISBN 0-87074-038-5). SMU Press.

--Legends of Texas, 2 vols. Incl. Vol. 1. Lost Mines & Buried Treasures. 132p (ISBN 0-88289-085-9); Vol. 2. Pirates Gold & Other Tales. 144p (ISBN 0-88289-086-7). 1975. pap. 3.95 ea. Pelican.

--The Longhorns. (Illus.). 1941. 17.45i (ISBN 0-316-18796-8). Little.

--The Longhorns. LC 79-67706. (Illus.). 440p. 1980. pap. 9.95 (ISBN 0-292-74627-X). U of Tex Pr.

--The Mustangs. (Illus.). 1952. pap. 8.70i (ISBN 0-316-18798-4). Little.

--The Mustangs. (Illus.). 392p. 1984. pap. 8.95 (ISBN 0-292-75081-1). U of Tex Pr.

--Out of the Old Rock. 1972. 9.95 (ISBN 0-316-18789-5). Little.

--Out of the Old Rock. 247p. 1982. pap. 7.95 (ISBN 0-292-76013-2). U of Tex Pr.

--Prefaces. 212p. 1982. pap. 6.95 (ISBN 0-292-76461-8). U of Tex Pr.

--Rattlesnakes. 1965. 14.45 (ISBN 0-316-18799-2). Little.

--Rattlesnakes. 207p. 1982. pap. 6.95 (ISBN 0-292-77023-5). U of Tex Pr.

--Some Part of Myself. 1967. 10.95 (ISBN 0-316-18790-9). Little.

--Some Part of Myself. LC 79-67708. (Illus.). 292p. 1980. pap. 7.95 (ISBN 0-292-77558-X). U of Tex Pr.

--Tales of Old-Time Texas. 1955. 15.45 (ISBN 0-316-18801-8); pap. 8.70i (ISBN 0-316-18802-6). Little.

--Tales of Old-Time Texas. (Illus.). 350p. 1984. pap. 8.95 (ISBN 0-292-78069-9). U of Tex Pr.

--A Texan in England. (Illus.). 301p. 1980. pap. 7.95 (ISBN 0-292-78034-6). U of Tex Pr.

--Tongues of the Monte. 319p. 1980. pap. 7.95 (ISBN 0-292-78035-4). U of Tex Pr.

--A Vaquero of the Brush Country. (Illus.). 320p. 1981. pap. 7.95 (ISBN 0-292-78704-9). U of Tex Pr.

--The Voice of the Coyote. LC 49-8879. (Illus.). xx, 386p. 1961. pap. 6.95 (ISBN 0-8032-5050-9, BB 109, Bison). U of Nebr Pr.

Dobie, J. Frank & Dykes, Jeff C. Forty Four Range Country Books & 44 More Range Country Books. 35p. 1972. Repr. 15.00 (ISBN 0-88426-003-8). Encino Pr.

Dobie, J. Frank, jt. auth. see Goddard, Ruth.

Dobie, J. Frank, ed. Coffee in the Gourd. (Texas Folklore Society Publications Ser.: No. 2). 1969. Repr. of 1923 ed. 9.95 (ISBN 0-87074-039-3). SMU Press.

--Follow De Drinkin' Gou'd. LC 33-1132. (Texas Folklore Society Publications: No. 7). 1965. Repr. of 1928 ed. 9.95 (ISBN 0-87074-040-7). SMU Press.

--Guide to Life & Literature of the Southwest: Revised & Enlarged in Both Knowledge & Wisdom. LC 52-11834. (Illus.). 230p. 1952. 15.95 (ISBN 0-87074-036-9); pap. 9.95 (ISBN 0-87074-037-7). SMU Press.

--Happy Hunting Ground. (Texas Folklore Society Publications: No. 4). (Illus.). 1964. Repr. of 1925 ed. 9.95 (ISBN 0-87074-149-7). SMU Press.

--Legends of Texas. LC 76-17825. (Texas Folklore Society Publications: No. 3). (Illus.). 1964. Repr. of 1924 ed. 15.95 (ISBN 0-87074-156-X). SMU Press.

--Man, Bird, & Beast. LC 33-1132. (Texas Folklore Society Publications: No. 8). (Illus.). 1965. Repr. of 1930 ed. 9.95 (ISBN 0-87074-131-4). SMU Press.

--Puro Mexicano. LC 35-1517. (Texas Folklore Society Publication Ser.: No. 12). 276p. 1969. Repr. of 1935 ed. 9.95 (ISBN 0-87074-041-5). SMU Press.

--Rainbow in the Morning. LC 74-32243. (Texas Folklore Society Publications: No. 5). 1965. Repr. of 1926 ed. 9.95 (ISBN 0-87074-150-0). SMU Press.

--Southwestern Lore. LC 33-1134. (Texas Folklore Society Publications: No. 9). 1965. Repr. of 1931 ed. 9.95 (ISBN 0-87074-042-3). SMU Press.

--Spur-Of-The-Cock. LC 34-1434. (Texas Folklore Society Publications Ser.: No. 11). 1965. Repr. of 1933 ed. 9.95 (ISBN 0-87074-043-1). SMU Press.

--Straight Texas. (Texas Folklore Society Publications: No. 13). 1966. Repr. of 1937 ed. 15.95 (ISBN 0-87074-164-0). SMU Press.

--Texas & Southwestern Lore. LC 33-1131. (Texas Folklore Society Publications Ser.: No. 6). 1967. Repr. of 1927 ed. 9.95 (ISBN 0-87074-044-X). SMU Press.

--Tone the Bell Easy. LC 33-1135. (Texas Folklore Society Publications: No. 10). (Illus.). 1965. Repr. of 1932 ed. 9.95 (ISBN 0-87074-045-8). SMU Press.

Dobie, J. Frank, et al, eds. Coyote Wisdom. LC 40-499. (Texas Folklore Society Publications: No. 14). (Illus.). 1965. Repr. of 1938 ed. 15.95 (ISBN 0-87074-046-6). SMU Press.

--Mustangs & Cow Horses. 2nd ed. LC 65-3030. (Texas Folklore Society Publications: No. 16). (Illus.). 1965. Repr. of 1940 ed. 16.95 (ISBN 0-87074-047-4). SMU Press.

--Texian Stomping Grounds. LC 41-4871. (Texas Folklore Society Publications: No. 17). 1967. Repr. of 1941 ed. 9.95 (ISBN 0-87074-048-2). SMU Press.

--In the Shadow of History. (Texas Folklore Society Publication Ser.: No. 15). 192p. 1966. Repr. of 1939 ed. 9.95 (ISBN 0-87074-173-X). SMU Press.

Dobie, M. R., tr. see Grenier, Albert.

Dobie, M. R., tr. see Jarde, Auguste.

Dobie, M. R., tr. see Toutain, Jules.

Dobie, Norman. Odalisque in White. (Porch Chapbook Ser.: No. 1). (Illus.). 1978. pap. 3.00 (ISBN 0-932968-01-5). Porch Pubns.

Dobieski, Alex. Basic Principles of Computer Systems. (Illus.). 555p. (Orig.). 1985. pap. 10.95x (ISBN 0-933039-01-8). Fountain Valley Pub.

Dobihal, Edward F., Jr. & Stewart, Charles W. When a Friend Is Dying: A Guide to Caring for the Terminally Ill & Bereaved. 224p. 1984. pap. 10.95 (ISBN 0-687-44972-3). Abingdon.

Dobija, Jane, jt. auth. see Brereton, John.

Dobin, Joel C. The Astrological Secrets of the Hebrew Sages: To Rule Both Day & Night. LC 77-8288. 256p. 1983. pap. 8.95 (ISBN 0-89281-052-1). Inner Tradit.

Dobinson, Charles H., ed. Education in a Changing World. facs. ed. LC 78-117783. (Essay Index Reprint Ser). 1951. 17.00 (ISBN 0-8369-1801-0). Ayer Co Pubs.

Dobinson, I., jt. auth. see Tomasic, R.

Dobkin, A. B., ed. Developments of New Volatile Inhalation Anaesthetics. (Monographs in Anaesthesiology Ser.: Vol. 6). 1979. 85.00 (ISBN 0-444-80064-6, Excerpta Medica). Elsevier.

Dobkin, Kaye. Desire & Dream. 352p. 1984. pap. 3.50 (ISBN 0-380-89342-8, 89342-8). Avon.

--The Red Room. 160p. (Orig.). (gr. 7 up). 1982. pap. 1.95 (ISBN 0-590-32441-1, Windswept). Scholastic Inc.

--A Valentine for Betsy. (Turning Points Ser.: No. 3). (gr. 5-9). 1984. pap. 2.50 (ISBN 0-451-14075-3, Sig Vista). NAL.

Dobkin, Marjorie H., ed. The Making of a Feminist: Early Journals & Letters of M. Carey Thomas. LC 79-88605. (Illus.). 314p. 1980. 18.00x (ISBN 0-87338-232-3); pap. 6.95 (ISBN 0-87338-237-4). Kent St U Pr.

Dobkin de Rios, Marlene. Visionary Vine: Hallucinogenic Healing in the Peruvian Amazon. (Illus.). 161p. 1984. pap. text ed. 7.95x (ISBN 0-88133-093-0). Waveland Pr.

Dobkins, David H. & Kneller, Richard. Workbook for Speech Fundamentals. 128p. 1980. pap. text ed. 7.25 (ISBN 0-8403-2257-7). Kendall-Hunt.

Dobkowski, Michael N. The Politics of Indifference: A Documentary History of Holocaust Victims in America. LC 81-40867. 486p. (Orig.). 1982. lib. bdg. 33.75 (ISBN 0-8191-2576-8); pap. text ed. 19.75 (ISBN 0-8191-2577-6). U Pr of Amer.

Dobkowski, Michael N. & Wallimann, Isidor, eds. Towards the Holocaust: The Social & Economic Collapse of the Weimar Republic. LC 82-18388. (Illus.). 440p. 1983. lib. bdg. 29.95 (ISBN 0-313-22795-0, DHO/). Greenwood.

Doble, G. H. Lives of the Welsh Saints. Evans, D. Simon, ed. 258p. 1984. text ed. 15.25x (ISBN 0-7083-0870-8, Pub. by Univ of Wales Pr England). Humanities.

Doble, Gilbert H. Saints of Cornwall: Midcornwall. pap. 7.50 (ISBN 0-686-05862-3). British Am Bks.

Doble, Henry F., Jr. Medical Office Design: Territory & Conflict. 200p. 1982. 42.50 (ISBN 0-87527-243-6). Green.

Dobler, Dean D. & Lee, Lamar. Purchasing & Materials Management: Texts & Cases. 4th ed. (Management & Marketing Ser.). (Illus.). 736p. 1984. text ed. 37.95 (ISBN 0-07-037042-7). McGraw.

Dobler, Donald W., jt. auth. see Lee, Lamar, Jr.

Dobler, Lavinia. Customs & Holidays Around the World. LC 62-8222. (Around the World Ser.). (Illus.). (gr. 7-12). 1962. 10.95 (ISBN 0-8303-0043-0). Fleet.

--I Didn't Know That. (gr. 7 up). 1978. pap. 1.75 (ISBN 0-590-03302-6). Scholastic Inc.

--The Land & People of Uruguay. new rev. ed. LC 72-3741. (Portraits of the Nations Ser.). (Illus.). (gr. 6 up). 1972. PLB 10.89 (ISBN 0-397-31391-8). Lipp Jr Bks.

--National Holidays Around the World. LC 66-16525. (Around the World Ser.). (Illus.). (gr. 7-12). 1968. 10.95 (ISBN 0-8303-0044-9). Fleet.

Dobler, Max. Ionophores & Their Structures. LC 81-4373. 379p. 1981. 81.50 (ISBN 0-471-05270-1, Pub. by Wiley-Interscience). Wiley.

Dobler, Peggy R. Sincerely Peg. (Illus.). 1976. pap. 4.95 (ISBN 0-686-17611-1). New Expressions.

Dobler, Roslyn. Opportunities in Fashion. (VGM Career Bks.). (Illus.). 160p. 1983. 7.95 (ISBN 0-8442-6643-4, 6643-4, Passport Bks.); pap. 5.95 (ISBN 0-8442-6644-2, 6644-2). Natl Textbk.

Doblhofer, Ernst. Voices in Stone. Savill, Mervyn, tr. LC 71-122076. Repr. of 1961 ed. lib. bdg. 35.00x (ISBN 0-678-03152-5). Kelley.

--Voices in Stone. (Illus.). 327p. 1982. pap. 6.95 (ISBN 0-586-08119-4, Pub. by Granada England). Academy Chi Pubs.

Doblin, Alfred. Berlin, Alexanderplatz. Jolas, Eugene, tr. LC 58-8957. 1958. pap. 9.95 (ISBN 0-8044-6120-1). Ungar.

--Berlin Alexanderplatz: The Story of Franz Biberkopf. Jolas, Eugene, tr. 1984. pap. 9.95 (ISBN 0-8044-6121-X). Ungar.

--Karl & Rosa: November 1918 A German Revolution. Woods, John E., tr. from German. LC 83-16461. 560p. (English.). 1983. 19.95 (ISBN 0-88064-010-3); pap. 10.95 (ISBN 0-88064-011-1). Fromm Intl Pub.

--A People Betrayed: November Nineteen Eighteen, A German Revolution. Woods, John E., tr. from Gr. LC 82-25133. 656p. 1983. 19.95 (ISBN 0-88064-007-3). Fromm Intl Pub.

--Tales of a Long Night. Kimber, Robert & Kimber, Rita, trs. LC 84-18798. 496p. 1984. 18.95 (ISBN 0-88064-016-2); pap. 12.95 (ISBN 0-88064-017-0). Fromm Intl Pub.

Doblin, F. Men's Garment Designing & Grading. rev. ed. (Illus.). Date not set. 25.00 (ISBN 0-686-30449-7). Master Design.

--The Modern Mitchell System on Men's Garment Designing & Grading. 1984. 20.00 (ISBN 0-318-01022-4). Master Design.

Doblin, Jay. Perspective: A New System for Designers. (Illus.). 68p. 1956. 14.95 (ISBN 0-8230-7419-6, Whitney Lib). Watson-Guptill.

Dobneck, Johann. Commentaria. 372p. 1549. text ed. 102.50x (ISBN 0-576-99121-X, Pub. by Gregg Intl Pubs England). Gregg Intl.

Dobney, Frederick J., ed. see Clayton, William.

Dobo. Fifth Tihany Symposium on Radiation Chemistry: Proceedings. 87.00 (ISBN 0-9910000-1-3, Pub. by Akademiai Kaido Hungary). Heyden.

Dobos, David E. & Martin, Betty H. Family Portrait: A Study of Contemporary Lifestyles (30 Lessons) 3rd ed. 192p. 1983. pap. write for info. (ISBN 0-534-02733-4). Wadsworth Pub.

Dobos, David E. & Mastin, Betty H. Family Portrait: A Study of Contemporary Lifestyles (45 Lessons) 3rd ed. 264p. 1983. pap. write for info. (ISBN 0-534-02732-6). Wadsworth Pub.

Doboson, E. J., jt. ed. see D'Ardenne, S. R.

Dobovsky, jt. auth. see Tauxe.

Dobratz, Betty A., jt. auth. see Kourvetaris, George A.

Dobratz, Betty A., jt. auth. see Kourvetaris, Geroge E.

Dobratz, Betty A., jt. ed. see Kourvetaris, George A.

Dobree, Bonamy. Alexander Pope. LC 72-94604. Repr. of 1951 ed. lib. bdg. 18.75x (ISBN 0-8371-2459-X, DOAP). Greenwood.

--Amateur & the Theatre. LC 72-12988. 1947. lib. bdg. 6.00 (ISBN 0-8414-1006-2). Folcroft.

--As Their Friends Saw Them. facs. ed. LC 67-30183. (Essay Index Reprint Ser). 1933. 15.00 (ISBN 0-8369-0375-7). Ayer Co Pubs.

--The Broken Cistern. LC 72-6790. (Studies in Comparative Literature, No. 35). 1972. Repr. of 1955 ed. lib. bdg. 48.95x (ISBN 0-8383-1664-6). Haskell.

--Byron's Dramas. LC 76-30810. 1962. lib. bdg. 6.00 (ISBN 0-8414-3808-0). Folcroft.

--English Essayists. LC 73-12886. 1973. lib. bdg. 10.00 (ISBN 0-8414-3674-6). Folcroft.

--English Literature in the Early Eighteenth Century, 1700-1740. (Oxford History of English Literature Ser.). 1959. 42.00x (ISBN 0-19-812205-5). Oxford U Pr.

--Essays in Biography, Sixteen Eighty to Seventeen Twenty-Six. facs. ed. LC 67-23203. (Essay Index Reprint Ser). 1925. 20.00 (ISBN 0-8369-0376-5). Ayer Co Pubs.

--Histriophone: A Dialogue on Dramatic Diction. LC 76-27892. 1925. lib. bdg. 8.50 (ISBN 0-8414-3710-6). Folcroft.

--John Wesley. LC 74-7428. 1973. lib. bdg. 12.50 (ISBN 0-8414-3739-4). Folcroft.

--Milton to Ouida: A Collection of Essays. 198p. 1970. 26.00x (ISBN 0-7146-2393-8, F Cass Co). Biblio Dist.

--Modern Prose Style. 2nd ed. LC 77-25320. 1978. Repr. of 1964 ed. lib. bdg. 32.50x (ISBN 0-313-20124-2, DOMP). Greenwood.

--Restoration Comedy 1660 to 1720. 182p. 1983. lib. bdg. 40.00 (ISBN 0-89984-165-1). Century Bookbindery.

--Restoration Comedy, 1660-1720. LC 81-1230. 182p. 1981. Repr. of 1924 ed. lib. bdg. 22.50x (ISBN 0-313-22722-5, DORC). Greenwood.

--Rochester: A Conversation Between Sir George Etherege & Mister Fitzjames. LC 73-13531. 1926. lib. bdg. 8.50 (ISBN 0-8414-3672-X). Folcroft.

--Theme of Patriotism in the Poetry of the Early Eighteenth Century. 1949. lib. bdg. 9.00 (ISBN 0-8414-2478-0). Folcroft.

--Three Eighteenth Century Figures: Sarah Churchill, John Wesley, Giacomo Casanova. LC 80-19398. xi, 248p. 1981. Repr. of 1962 ed. lib. bdg. 25.00x (ISBN 0-313-22682-2, DOTF). Greenwood.

--The Unacknowledged Legislator. LC 73-13656. 1973. lib. bdg. 6.50 (ISBN 0-8414-3656-8). Folcroft.

--Variety of Ways. LC 73-12773. 1932. lib. bdg. 8.00 (ISBN 0-8414-3668-1). Folcroft.

--Variety of Ways: Discussion on Six Authors. facs. ed. LC 67-23204. (Essay Index Reprint Ser). 1932. 12.00 (ISBN 0-8369-0377-3). Ayer Co Pubs.

--William Congreve: A Conversation Between Swift & Gay. LC 73-12881. 1929. lib. bdg. 6.00 (ISBN 0-8414-3675-4). Folcroft.

--William Penn, Quaker & Pioneer. LC 78-15258. 1978. Repr. of 1932 ed. lib. bdg. 35.00 (ISBN 0-8414-3790-4). Folcroft.

--William Penn: Quaker & Pioneer. 346p. 1980. Repr. of 1932 ed. lib. bdg. 35.00 (ISBN 0-8482-0643-6). Norwood Edns.

--William Penn, Quaker & Pioneer. 346p. 1983. Repr. of 1932 ed. lib. bdg. 35.00 (ISBN 0-8492-4227-4). R West.

Dobree, Bonamy, jt. auth. see Manwaring, G. E.

Dobree, Bonamy, jt. auth. see Manwaring, George E.

Dobree, Bonamy, ed. Five Heroic Plays. LC 78-14410. 1979. Repr. of 1960 ed. lib. bdg. 32.50x (ISBN 0-313-21051-9, DOFH). Greenwood.

--Five Restoration Tragedies. LC 83-45430. Repr. of 1928 ed. 40.00 (ISBN 0-404-20082-6). AMS Pr.

--From Anne to Victoria: Essays by Various Hands. facs. ed. LC 67-30184. (Essay Index Reprint Ser). 1937. 27.50 (ISBN 0-8369-0378-1). Ayer Co Pubs.

Dobree, Bonamy, ed. see Beljame, Alexandre.

Dobree, Bonamy, ed. see Pope, Alexander.

Dobree, Bonamy, ed. see Radcliffe, Ann.

Dobree, Bonamy, ed. see Vanbrugh, John.

Dobree, Bonamy, et al, eds. see Blackstone, Bernard.

Dobree, Bonamy, et al, eds. see Bloomfield, Paul.

Dobree, Bonamy, et al, eds. see Bradbrook, M. C.

Dobree, Bonamy, et al, eds. see Doughty, Oswald.

Dobree, Bonamy, et al, eds. see Muir, Kenneth.

Dobree, Bonamy, et al, eds. see Swan, Michael.

Dobree, John H. & Boulter, Eric. Blindness & Visual Handicap: The Facts. (Facts Ser.). (Illus.). 1982. 13.95x (ISBN 0-19-261328-6). Oxford U Pr.

Dobretsov, L. N. & Gomoyunova, M. V. Emission Electronics. 433p. 69.95x (ISBN 0-470-21680-8). Halsted Pr.

Dobrev, V. K., et al. Harmonic Analysis. (Lecture Notes in Physics: Vol. 63). 1977. pap. 18.00 (ISBN 0-387-08150-X). Springer-Verlag.

Dobrez, L. A. The Existential & Its Exits: Literary & Philosophical Perspectives in the Works of Beckett, Ionesco, Genet, & Pinter. 320p. 1985. 32.50 (ISBN 0-312-27502-1). St Martin.

Dobrez, L. A., ed. Australia: Annual Volume Review of National Literatures. 256p. 1980. pap. 20.00 (ISBN 0-918680-16-6). Griffon Hse.

Dobrian, Walter A. Conversational Spanish. (Illus.). 1966. text ed. 22.50 scp (ISBN 0-06-041666-1, HarpC); scp tapes 275.00 (ISBN 0-06-041667-X). Har-Row.

Dobriansky, A. F., ed. see Pinkevich, A. & Amelin, B.

Dobriansky, Lev E. U. S. A. & the Soviet Myth. 9.50 (ISBN 0-8159-7005-6). Devin.

Dobrilla, G., et al, eds. Current Therapy of Gastrointestinal Disorders. 250p. 1983. text ed. 67.00. Raven.

Dobrin, Arnold. Josephine's 'Magination. (Illus.). (gr. k-3). 1975. pap. 1.95 (ISBN 0-590-10008-4). Scholastic Inc.

--Peter Rabbit's Natural Foods Cookbook. LC 76-45309. (Illus.). 1977. 8.95 (ISBN 0-7232-6142-3). Warne.

Dobrin, Arthur. Gentle Spears. Barkan, Stanley H., ed. (Cross-Cultural Review Chapbook 3: American Poetry 2). 16p. 1980. pap. 2.00 (ISBN 0-89304-802-X). Cross Cult.

--Little Heroes. (Ethical Humanist Society Monograph: No. 1). (Illus.). 1977. pap. 2.50x (ISBN 0-89304-200-5, CCC111). Cross Cult.

--Saying My Name Out Loud. (Illus.). 1978. pap. 2.50 (ISBN 0-918870-05-4); signed & numbered ed. 3.50 (ISBN 0-918870-06-2). Pleasure Dome.

--Sunbird. 64p. signed ed. 15.00 (ISBN 0-89304-046-0); pap. 3.95 (ISBN 0-89304-012-6). Cross Cult.

Dobrin, Arthur, ed. Lace: Poetry from the Poor, the Homeless, the Aged, the Physically & Emotionally Disabled. LC 79-90011. (Orig.). 1979. 15.00x (ISBN 0-89304-036-3, CCC123); pap. 7.95x (ISBN 0-89304-037-1). Cross Cult.

Dobrin, Arthur, et al. Convictions: Political Prisoners-Their Stories. LC 80-2787. 128p. (Orig.). 1981. pap. 5.95 (ISBN 0-88344-089-X). Orbis Bks.

Dobrin, Milton. Introduction to Geophysical Prospecting. 3rd ed. LC 75-37603. 1976. text ed. 44.95 (ISBN 0-07-017195-5). McGraw.

Dobrin, Ronald L. Cheap Sex. 1985. 15.95 (ISBN 0-87949-244-9). Ashley Bks.

Dobriner, William M. Class in Suburbia. LC 81-19070. xii, 166p. 1982. Repr. of 1963 ed. lib. bdg. 17.50x (ISBN 0-313-23145-1, DOCS). Greenwood.

Dobrinsky, Hebert. A Treasury of Sephardic Laws & Customs. 25.00x (ISBN 0-88125-031-7). Ktav.

Dobrish, Cecelia, et al. Hiring the Right Person for the Right Job. 320p. 1984. 15.95 (ISBN 0-531-09576-2). Watts.

Dobritzhoffer, Martin. An Account of the Abipones, An Equestrian People of Paraguay, 3 Vols. in 1. LC 3-21856. (Landmarks in Anthropology Ser.). 1970. Repr. of 1822 ed. 85.00 (ISBN 0-384-12055-5). Johnson Repr.

Dobroczki, L. & Kirshenblatt-Gimblett, B. Image Before My Eyes: A Photographic History of Jewish Life in Poland, 1864-1939. (Illus.). 1977. 25.00; pap. text ed. 15.00 (ISBN 0-914512-38-2). Yivo Inst.

Dobrof, Rose, ed. Gerontological Social Work in Home Health Care. LC 84-10924. (Journal of Gerontological Social Work Ser.: Vol. 7, No. 4). 114p. 1984. 22.95 (ISBN 0-86656-337-7, B337). Haworth Pr.

Dobroliubov, Aleksandr M. Iz knigi nevidimoi. Grossman, Joan D., ed. (Modern Russian Literature & Culture, Studies & Texts: Vol. (Eleven)). 230p. (Orig., Rus.). 1983. pap. 15.00 (ISBN 0-933884-34-6). Berkeley Slavic.

--Natura Naturans, Natura Naturata; Sobranie Stikhov. (Modern Russian Literature & Culture, Studies & Texts: Vol. 10). 211p. (Rus.). 1981. pap. 10.00 (ISBN 0-933884-20-6). Berkeley Slavic.

Dobroliubov, Nikolai A. Selected Philosophical Essays. Finberg, J., tr. LC 79-2899. 659p. 1981. Repr. of 1956 ed. 51.70 (ISBN 0-8305-0070-7). Hyperion Conn.

Dobrolyubov, N. A. Selected Philosophical Russian Contemporary Essays. 174p. 1985. 89.45x (ISBN 0-86722-090-2). Inst Econ Pol.

Dobroski, H. Edward, jt. auth. see Norton, Joseph J.

Dobroszycki, Lucjan & Kirshenblatt-Gimblett, Barbara. Image Before My Eyes: A Photographic History of Jewish Life in Poland, 1864-1939. LC 75-35448. (Illus.). 1977. 29.95 (ISBN 0-8052-3607-4). Schocken.

--Image Before My Eyes: A Photographic History of Jewish Life in Poland, 1864-1939. LC 75-35448. (Illus.). 1979. pap. 19.95 (ISBN 0-8052-0634-5). Schocken.

Dobroszycki, Lucjan, ed. The Chronicle of the Lodz Ghetto, 1941-1944. LC 84-3614. (Illus.). 603p. 1984. 35.00x (ISBN 0-300-03208-0). Yale U Pr.

Dobrota, M. see Work, T. S. & Work, E.

Dobrotworsky, N. V. Mosquitoes of Victoria. 1965. 25.00x (ISBN 0-522-83584-8, Pub. by Melbourne U Pr). Intl Spec Bk.

Dobrova, L. Yelena Belova. 48p. 1979. pap. 2.95 (ISBN 0-8285-1753-3, Pub. by Progress Pubs USSR). Imported Pubns.

Dobrovitz, Peter. Rochestrivia: An Illuminating Look at Rochester. (Illus.). 226p. (Orig.). 1984. pap. 9.95 (ISBN 0-930249-00-3). Big Kids Pub.

Dobrovolny, J. S., et al. Problems in Engineering Drawing & Geometry, Series 12, 13, 15, 16, 21. 1964. pap. 6.80x ea. Stipes.

Dobrovolny, Jerry S. & O'Bryant, David C. Graphics for Engineers: Visualization, Communication, & Design. 2nd. ed. LC 84-3547. 608p. 1984. 35.95 (ISBN 0-471-87124-9). Wiley.

Dobrovol'skii, Andreevich. Prepodobny Feodor, Igumen Studiisky, 2 vols. in 1. LC 80-2355. Repr. of 1913 ed. 115.00 (ISBN 0-404-18907-5). AMS Pr.

Dobrow, Larry. When Advertising Tried Harder: The Sixties: The Golden Age of American Advertising. LC 83-82058. (Illus.). 205p. 1984. 35.00 (ISBN 0-914919-00-8). Friendly Pr NY.

Dobrozemsky, R., ed. Vacuum-Industry-Energy: Proceedings of Second Joint Meeting of the Roland Eotvos Physical Society (Vacuum Physics & Thin Films Section) & the Austrian Vacuum Society, held Niederosterreich, Austria, 27-29 October, 1981. 128p. 1983. 28.00 (ISBN 0-08-029993-8). Pergamon.

Dobrushin & Sinai. Multicomponent Random Systems. (Advances in Probability Ser.: Vol. 6). 84.50 (ISBN 0-8247-6831-0). Dekker.

Dobry, Ricardo, jt. ed. see O'Neill, Michael W.

Dobryshin, R. L., et al, eds. Locally Interacting Systems & Their Application in Biology: Proceedings of the School - Seminar on Markov Interaction Processes in Biology, Held in Pushchino, Moscow Region, March, 1976. (Lecture Notes in Mathematics Ser.: Vol. 653). 1978. pap. 16.00 (ISBN 0-387-08450-9). Springer-Verlag.

Dobryshman, E. M. Review of Forecast Verification Techniques. (Technical Note Ser.: No. 120). x, 52p. 1972. pap. 10.00 (ISBN 0-685-34863-6, W106, WMO). Unipub.

Dobrzycki, Jerzy, ed. see Symposium of 'Nicolas Copernicus Committee of International Union of History & Philosophy of Science, Torum, Poland, 1973.

Dobschutz, Ernst Von. Christian Life in the Primitive Church. 1977. lib. bdg. 59.95 (ISBN 0-8490-1615-0). Gordon Pr.

Dobson, A. J. An Introduction to Statistical Modelling. LC 83-7495. (Illus.). 200p. 1983. 25.00 (ISBN 0-412-24850-6, NO. 6864); pap. 14.95 (ISBN 0-412-24860-3, NO. 6865). Methuen Inc.

Dobson, A. J. & Stokoe, J. Self-Paced Introductory Mathematics. LC 78-73315. 339p. 1983. pap. text ed. 17.95 (ISBN 0-7081-1199-8, 1616, Pub. by ANUP Australia). Australia N U P.

Dobson, Alban. Bibliography of the First Editors of Published & Privately Printed Books & Pamphlets by Austin Dobson. 1925. 18.00 (ISBN 0-8274-1937-6). R West.

Dobson, Alban, ed. Bibliography of the First Editions of Published & Privately Printed Books & Pamphlets by Austin Dobson. LC 73-123509. (Bibliography & Reference Ser.: No. 354). 1970. Repr. of 1925 ed. 18.50 (ISBN 0-8337-0875-9). B Franklin.

Dobson, Austin. At Prior Park & Other Papers. facsimile ed. LC 73-105007. (Essay Index Reprint Ser.). 1925. 20.00 (ISBN 0-8369-1567-4). Ayer Co Pubs.

--At the Sign of the Lyre. 1890. lib. bdg. 15.00 (ISBN 0-8414-2480-2). Folcroft.

--Austin Dobson: An Anthology of Prose & Verse. 1922. lib. bdg. 15.00 (ISBN 0-8414-2482-9). Folcroft.

--A Bookman's Budget. 1979. Repr. of 1927 ed. lib. bdg. 20.00 (ISBN 0-8495-1043-0). Arden Lib.

--Collected Poems. 567p. 1980. Repr. of 1907 ed. lib. bdg. 25.00 (ISBN 0-89984-151-1). Century Bookbindery.

--Collected Poems. 1978. Repr. of 1899 ed. lib. bdg. 20.00 (ISBN 0-8492-0667-7). R West.

--Complete Poetical Works. LC 70-115236. 1971. Repr. of 1923 ed. 59.00 (ISBN 0-403-00421-7). Scholarly.

--Eighteenth Century Studies. 1978. Repr. lib. bdg. 15.00 (ISBN 0-8482-0630-4). Norwood Edns.

--Eighteenth Century Vignettes, 3 vols. 1892. lib. bdg. 60.00 (ISBN 0-8414-2485-3). Folcroft.

--Eighteenth Century Vignettes, 3 Vols. LC 73-115237. (Illus.). 1971. Repr. of 1923 ed. Set. 57.00x (ISBN 0-686-57480-X); 19.00 ea. Scholarly.

--Eighteenth Century Vignettes, First, Second & Third Series, 3 Vols. LC 67-29812. (Illus.). 1968. Repr. of 1896 ed. Set. 50.00 (ISBN 0-405-08447-1, Pub. by Blom); Vol. 1. 22.00 (ISBN 0-686-66382-9); Vol. 2. 22.00 (ISBN 0-405-08448-X); Ser. 3. 22.00 (ISBN 0-405-08449-8). Ayer Co Pubs.

--Fanny Burney: Madame D'arblay. 1977. Repr. of 1904 ed. lib. bdg. 15.00 (ISBN 0-8495-1004-X). Arden Lib.

--Fanny Burney (Madame D'Arblay) 1978. Repr. of 1904 ed. lib. bdg. 12.50 (ISBN 0-8414-3828-5). Folcroft.

--Fielding. Morley, John, ed. LC 73-100820. (English Men of Letters). Repr. of 1889 ed. 12.50 (ISBN 0-404-51708-0). AMS Pr.

--Fielding. 210p. 1980. Repr. of 1902 ed. lib. bdg. 15.00 (ISBN 0-89987-153-4). Darby Bks.

--Fielding. 1889. lib. bdg. 15.00 (ISBN 0-8482-9951-5). Norwood Edns.

--Four Frenchwomen. LC 72-6853. (Essay Index Reprint Ser.). 1972. Repr. of 1893 ed. 20.00 (ISBN 0-8369-7269-4). Ayer Co Pubs.

--Four Frenchwomen. LC 72-6853. (Essay Index Reprint Ser.). 212p. Repr. of 1893 ed. lib. bdg. 11.50 (ISBN 0-8290-0523-4). Irvington.

--A Handbook of English Literature. 1897. lib. bdg. 20.00 (ISBN 0-8414-2490-X). Folcroft.

--Horace Walpole: A Memoir. 4th, rev. & enl. ed. (Select Bibliographies Reprint Ser.). Repr. of 1927 ed. 26.50 (ISBN 0-8369-5883-7). Ayer Co Pubs.

--Horace Walpole: A Memoir. LC 72-160127. (English Biography Ser., No. 31). 1971. Repr. of 1890 ed. lib. bdg. 49.95x (ISBN 0-8383-1267-5). Haskell.

--Later Essays Nineteen Seventeen to Nineteen Twenty. facs. ed. LC 68-22910. (Essay Index Reprint Ser). 1921. 15.00 (ISBN 0-8369-0379-X). Ayer Co Pubs.

--Later Essays: Nineteen Seventeen to Nineteen Twenty. 1921. lib. bdg. 17.50 (ISBN 0-8414-2487-X). Folcroft.

--Life of Oliver Goldsmith. LC 72-38350. (Select Bibliographies Reprint Ser.). Repr. of 1888 ed. 18.00 (ISBN 0-8369-6767-4). Ayer Co Pubs.

--Life of Oliver Goldsmith. 1973. Repr. of 1888 ed. 15.50 (ISBN 0-8274-1365-3). R West.

--Miscellanies. LC 73-100820. (Second Ser). Repr. of 1901 ed. 12.00 (ISBN 0-404-02140-9). AMS Pr.

--Miscellanies. 1889. Repr. 10.00x (ISBN 0-403-00250-8). Scholarly.

--Miscellanies: Second Series. facs. ed. LC 67-28749. (Essay Index Reprint Ser). 1901. 18.00 (ISBN 0-8369-0380-3). Ayer Co Pubs.

--Miscellanies: Second Series. LC 79-108474. 1970. Repr. of 1901 ed. 16.00x (ISBN 0-403-00206-0). Scholarly.

--Old Kensington Palace, & Other Papers. facs. ed. LC 68-54344. (Essay Index Reprint Ser). 1926. 18.00 (ISBN 0-8369-0110-X). Ayer Co Pubs.

--Poems on Several Occasions, 2 vols. 1983. Repr. of 1891 ed. Set. lib. bdg. 50.00 (ISBN 0-89760-145-9). Telegraph Bks.

--Richard Steele. 1973. 15.00 (ISBN 0-8274-0064-0). R West.

--Richard Steele. Long, Andrew, ed. LC 72-108475. 1970. Repr. of 1888 ed. 39.00x (ISBN 0-403-00229-X). Scholarly.

--Rosalba's Journal & Other Papers. LC 71-111827. (Essay Index Reprint Ser.). 1915. 24.00 (ISBN 0-8369-1605-0). Ayer Co Pubs.

--Samuel Richardson. LC 67-23877. 1968. Repr. of 1902 ed. 35.00x (ISBN 0-8103-3055-5). Gale.

--Samuel Richardson. 1973. Repr. of 1902 ed. 10.50 (ISBN 0-8274-1778-0). R West.

--Samuel Richardson. 1902. 7.00 (ISBN 0-403-00018-1). Scholarly.

--Selected Poems. rev & enl ed. LC 77-112323. 247p. 1924. Repr. lib. bdg. 18.75x (ISBN 0-8371-4711-5, DOPO). Greenwood.

--Side-Walk Studies. (Mrs. Delany, Goldsmith, Johnson, Addison, Walton). 1902. lib. bdg. 20.00 (ISBN 0-8414-2488-8). Folcroft.

--Thomas Bewick & His Pupils. LC 69-17340. 1968. Repr. of 1884 ed. 35.00x (ISBN 0-8103-3523-9). Gale.

Dobson, Austin, ed. Old English Songs. LC 70-116398. (Granger Index Reprint Ser). 1894. 16.00 (ISBN 0-8369-6139-0). Ayer Co Pubs.

Dobson, Austin. A Handbook of English Literature. 384p. 1981. Repr. lib. bdg. 35.00 (ISBN 0-8495-1963-2). Arden Lib.

Dobson Books Ltd., ed. The Sacred Bridge: Supplementary Volume. 256p. 1981. 75.00x (ISBN 0-234-77038-4, Pub. by Dobson Bks England). State Mutual Bk.

Dobson, C. B. Stress: The Hidden Adversary. 280p. 1983. 34.95 (ISBN 0-942068-05-X). Bogden & Son.

--Stress: The Hidden Adversary. 1983. lib. bdg. 29.00 (ISBN 0-85200-381-1, Pub. by MTP Pr England). Kluwer Academic.

Dobson, C. B., jt. auth. see Burns, R. B.

Dobson, C. R. Masters & Journeyman: A Prehistory of Industrial Relations 1717 to 1800. LC 80-491631. 212p. 1980. 24.75x (ISBN 0-8476-6768-5). Rowman.

Dobson, Christopher & Payne, Ronald. Counterattack: The West's Battle Against the Terrorists. 224p. 1982. 14.95 (ISBN 0-87196-526-7). Facts on File.

--Counterattack: The West's Battle Against the Terrorists. 224p. 1984. pap. 6.95 (ISBN 0-87196-878-9). Facts-on-File.

--The Terrorists: Their Weapons, Leaders & Tactics. rev. & updated ed. 272p. 1982. 14.95 (ISBN 0-87196-669-7); pap. 6.95 (ISBN 0-87196-668-9). Facts on File.

--The Terrorists: Their Weapons, Leaders & Tactics. 1979. lib. bdg. 14.95 (ISBN 0-87196-406-6). Facts on File.

--Who's Who in Espionage. 240p. 1985. 15.95 (ISBN 0-312-87432-4). St Martin.

Dobson, Danae. Woof! 1985. pap. 4.95 (ISBN 0-8499-3024-3, 3024-3). Word Bks.

Dobson, David. Directory of Scottish Settlers in North America, 1625-1825, Vol. II. LC 83-82470. 216p. 1984. 17.50 (ISBN 0-8063-1074-X). Genealog Pub.

--Directory of Scottish Settlers in North America, 1625-1825, Vol. III. LC 83-82470. 194p. 1984. 17.50 (ISBN 0-8063-1087-1). Genealog Pub.

--Directory of Scottish Settlers in North America, 1625-1825, Vol. IV. LC 83-82470. 161p. 1985. 17.50 (ISBN 0-8063-1105-3). Genealog Pub.

--Directory of Scottish Settlers in North America, 1625-1825, Vol. V. LC 83-82470. 312p. 1985. 20.00 (ISBN 0-8063-1124-X). Genealog Pub.

--Directory of Scottish Settlers in North America, 1625-1825, Vol. 1. LC 83-82470. 267p. 1985. 20.00 (ISBN 0-8063-1054-5). Genealog Pub.

--Directory of the Scots Banished to the American Plantations, 1650-1775. LC 83-81052. 239p. 1984. 17.50 (ISBN 0-8063-1035-9). Genealog Pub.

Dobson, Dorothy. The Parting. 1980. 7.00 (ISBN 0-682-49502-6). Exposition Pr FL.

Dobson, E. J. & Harrison, F. L., eds. Medieval English Songs. LC 79-51498. 1980. 54.50 (ISBN 0-521-22912-X). Cambridge U Pr.

Dobson, Edward. In Search of Unity. 176p. 1985. pap. 4.95 (ISBN 0-8407-5989-4). Nelson.

Dobson, Edward D. Commodities: A Chart Anthology. rev. ed. LC 79-112544. (Illus.). 394p. 1981. 29.95 (ISBN 0-934380-02-3). Traders Pr.

--Commodity Spreads, Vol. 2. (Illus.). 1981. 22.50 (ISBN 0-934380-01-5). Traders Pr.

--Commodity Spreads: A Historical Chart Perspective. Rev. ed. LC 79-112547. (Illus.). 128p. 1983. 29.95 (ISBN 0-934380-00-7). Traders Pr.

--Dobson's Guide to Short Term Stock Index Trading. 120p. 1984. cancelled (ISBN 0-934380-07-4). Traders Pr.

--The Trading Rule That Can Make You Rich: Precision Bid Commodity Trading. LC 79-64620. (Illus.). 1979. pap. 25.00 (ISBN 0-934380-03-1). Traders Pr.

--Understanding Fibonacci Numbers. 16p. 1984. pap. 5.00 (ISBN 0-934380-08-2). Traders Pr.

Dobson, Eileen. New Zealand Ways with Flowers. 84p. 1980. pap. 4.50 (ISBN 0-85467-012-2, Pub. by Viking Sevenseas New Zealand). Intl Spec Bk.

Dobson, Eugene, tr. see Burgin, Hans & Mayer, Hans-Otto.

Dobson, F., et al, eds. Air-Sea Interaction: Instruments & Methods. LC 80-17895. 815p. 1980. 59.50x (ISBN 0-306-40543-1, Plenum Pr). Plenum Pub.

Dobson, Frank. Lichens: An Illustrated Guide. 1981. 37.00x (ISBN 0-686-78773-0, Pub. by RHS Ent England). State Mutual Bk.

--Lichens: An Illustrated Guide. (Illus.). 320p. 1981. pap. text ed. 25.25x (ISBN 0-916422-34-8, Pub. by Richmond Pub Co). Mad River.

Dobson, G. E. Catalogue of the Chiroptera in the Collection of the British Museum. (Illus.). 1966. 35.00 (ISBN 3-7682-0300-X). Lubrecht & Cramer.

Dobson, Hubert E. Power to Excel. 273p. 1982. 10.95 (ISBN 0-9607256-0-1); pap. 4.95x (ISBN 0-9607256-1-X). Rich Pub Co.

Dobson, J. F. The Greek Orators. 336p. 1974. 10.00 (ISBN 0-89005-050-3). Ares.

Dobson, James. Dare to Discipline. 1982. pap. 2.75 (ISBN 0-553-20346-0). Bantam.

--Dare to Discipline. 1973. pap. 5.95 (ISBN 0-8423-0631-5). Tyndale.

--Dare to Discipline. 1977. pap. 3.50 mass (ISBN 0-8423-0635-8). Tyndale.

--Discipline with Love. 1972. pap. 1.95 (ISBN 0-8423-0665-X). Tyndale.

--Dr. Dobson Answers Your Questions. 1982. 16.95 (ISBN 0-8423-0652-8). Tyndale.

--Emotions: Can You Trust Them? LC 79-91703. 144p. 1984. pap. 4.95 (ISBN 0-8307-0996-7, 5418350); pap. text ed. 3.50 (ISBN 0-8307-0866-9, 5017909). Regal.

--Emotions: Can You Trust Them? LC 79-91703. 144p. 1980. text ed. 7.95 (ISBN 0-8307-0730-1, 5109108). Regal.

--Esto Es Ser Hombre: Conversaciones Francas Con los Hombres y Sus Esposas. Almanza, Francisco, tr. from Eng. Orig. Title: Straight Talk to Men & Wives. 240p. 1983. pap. 7.50 (ISBN 0-311-46096-8, Edit Mundo). Casa Bautista.

--Hide or Seek. expanded & updated ed. 192p. 1974. 11.95 (ISBN 0-8007-1070-3); pap. 6.95 (ISBN 0-8007-5146-9). Revell.

--Preparemonos para la Adolescencia. 192p. 1981. 2.95 (ISBN 0-88113-253-5). Edit Betania.

--Preparing for Adolescence. 160p. 1980. pap. 3.50 (ISBN 0-553-24231-8). Bantam.

--Preparing for Adolescence. LC 78-57673. 192p. 1980. pap. 2.95 (ISBN 0-88449-045-9, A324551); 5.95 (ISBN 0-88449-111-0, A424717). Vision Hse.

--Prescription for a Tired Housewife. 1978. pap. 1.95 (ISBN 0-8423-4878-6). Tyndale.

--Straight Talk to Men & Their Wives. (QP Proven-Word Ser.). 224p. 1984. pap. 5.95 (ISBN 0-8499-2981-4). Word Bks.

--The Strong-Willed Child. 1978. 9.95 (ISBN 0-8423-0664-1). Tyndale.

--What Wives Wish Their Husbands Knew about Women. 1975. 9.95 (ISBN 0-8423-7890-1). Tyndale.

--What Wives Wish Their Husbands Knew about Women. 1977. pap. 4.95 (ISBN 0-8423-7889-8). Tyndale.

Dobson, James C. How to Preserve Your Marriage. 1985. price not set (ISBN 0-8499-0505-2, 0505-2). Word Bks.

--Straight Talk to Men & Their Wives. 1980. 9.95 (ISBN 0-8499-0260-6). Word Bks.

--The Strong-Willed Child. 240p. pap. 6.95 (ISBN 0-8423-6661-X). Tyndale.

Dobson, John, intro. by. Tennessee Beginnings. new ed. Bd. with A Short Description of the Tennessee Government (1793) Smith, Daniel; The Constitution of the State of Tennessee, (1796; A Catechetical Exposition of the Constitution of the State of Tennessee, (1803) Blount, Willie. LC 74-583. (Illus.). 144p. 1974. 16.50 (ISBN 0-87152-152-0). Reprint.

Dobson, John F. Ancient Education & Its Meaning for Us. LC 63-10297. (Our Debt to Greece & Rome Ser.). Repr. of 1930 ed. 17.50 (ISBN 0-8154-0060-8). Cooper Sq.

--Greek Orators. facs. ed. LC 67-23205. (Essay Index Reprint Ser.). 1919. 19.00 (ISBN 0-8369-0381-1). Ayer Co Pubs.

Dobson, John M. America's Ascent: The United States Becomes a Great Power, 1880-1914. LC 77-90754. (Illus.). 251p. 1978. 17.50 (ISBN 0-87580-070-X); pap. 6.00 (ISBN 0-87580-523-X). N Ill U Pr.

Dobson, Joseph A. The Dobson Fourteen-Day Method of Dog Training. LC 80-26724. 160p. 1981. 14.95 (ISBN 0-8329-3346-5, Pub. by Winchester Pr). New Century.

--Training Guard & Protection Dogs. LC 83-26620. (Illus.). 208p. 1984. 16.95 (ISBN 0-668-05830-7, 5830). Arco.

Dobson, Judith, jt. auth. see Dobson, Russell.

Dobson, Julia. Mountbatten, Sailor Head. (Julia MacRae Blackbird Bks.). (Illus.). 48p. (gr. k-3). 1982. 5.95 (ISBN 0-531-04431-9, MacRae). Watts.

Dobson, Julia M. & Hawkins, Gerald S. Conversation in English: Professional Careers. (Illus.). 108p. (gr. 9-12). 1978. pap. 7.50 (ISBN 0-88018-077-3). Heinle & Heinle.

Dobson, Julia M. & Sedwick, Frank. Conversation in English: Points of Departure. 2nd ed. (Illus.). 112p. 1981. pap. text ed. 7.50 (ISBN 0-88018-076-5). Heinle & Heinle.

Dobson, Margaret. Cactus Rose. (Candlelight Ecstasy Ser.: No. 145). (Orig.). 1983. pap. 1.95 (ISBN 0-440-11290-7). Dell.

--Eventide. (Candlelight Ecstasy Supreme Ser.: No. 30). 288p. (Orig.). 1984. pap. 2.50 (ISBN 0-440-12031-4). Dell.

--Restless Wind. (Candlelight Ecstasy Ser.: No. 173). 192p. (Orig.). 1983. pap. 1.95 (ISBN 0-440-17378-7). Dell.

--Stand Still the Moment. (Candlelight Ecstasy Romance Ser.: No. 300). 192p. (Orig.). 1985. pap. 1.95 (ISBN 0-440-18197-6). Dell.

--Tender Journey. (Candlelight Ecstasy Ser.: No. 211). 192p. (Orig.). 1984. pap. 1.95 (ISBN 0-440-18556-4). Dell.

Dobson, Margaret J. & Sisley, Becky L. Softball for Girls. LC 79-24256. 232p. 1980. Repr. of 1971 ed. lib. bdg. 12.50 (ISBN 0-89874-103-3). Krieger.

Dobson, P. J., ed. Interdisciplinary Surface Science: Proceedings of the ISSC6 Conference, Warwick, UK, 18-21 April 1983, Vol. VI. 250p. 1983. pap. 41.25 (ISBN 0-08-031146-6). Pergamon.

Dobson, P. N. & Peterson, V. Z., eds. Proceedings of the Fifth Hawaii Topical Conference in Particle Physics (1973) LC 73-92867. 719p. (Orig.). 1974. pap. text ed. 20.00x (ISBN 0-8248-0327-2). UH Pr.

Dobson, P. N., Jr., et al, eds. Proceedings of the Sixth Hawaii Topical Conference in Particle Physics (1975) 1976. pap. text ed. 20.00x (ISBN 0-8248-0464-3). UH Pr.

Dobson, Peter N., jt. ed. see Yount, David.

Dobson, R. & Donaghey, S. The History of Clementhrope Nunnery. (The Archaeology of York - Historical Sources for York Archaeology after AD 1100,). 40p. 1984. pap. text ed. 11.00x (ISBN 0-906780-40-3, Pub. by Coun Brit Archaeology England). Humanities.

Dobson, R. B. The Peasants' Revolt of Thirteen Eighty-One. 460p. 1982. text ed. 30.50x (ISBN 0-333-25504-6, Pub. by Macmillan England); pap. text ed. 14.50x (ISBN 0-333-25505-4, Pub. by Macmillan England). Humanities.

Dobson, R. B. & Taylor, J. Rymes of Robyn Hood: An Introduction to the English Outlaw. LC 75-31564. (Illus.). 1976. 27.95 (ISBN 0-8229-1126-4). U of Pittsburgh Pr.

Dobson, R. B., ed. The Church, Politics & Patronage in the Fifteenth Century. LC 84-15102. 245p. 1985. 25.00 (ISBN 0-312-13481-9). St Martin.

Dobson, R. L., et al, eds. Bactroban. (Current Clinical Practice Ser.: Vol. 16). 1985. 83.50 (ISBN 0-444-90407-7). Elsevier.

Dobson, Richard B. Durham Priory, Fourteen Hundred to Fourteen Fifty. LC 72-89809. (Cambridge Studies in Medieval Life & Thought, Third Ser.: vol. 6). pap. 110.50 (ISBN 0-317-28398-7, 2022444). Bks Demand UMI.

Dobson, Richard L. The Practice of Dermatology. (Illus.). 350p. 1985. pap. text ed. 32.50 (ISBN 0-06-140697-X, Harper Medical). Lippincott.

Dobson, Richard L., ed. Year Book of Dermatology, 1981. 1981. 44.95 (ISBN 0-8151-2667-0). Year Bk Med.

--Year Book of Dermatology 1983. 1983. 44.95 (ISBN 0-8151-2669-7). Year Bk Med.

--Year Book of Dermatology, 1984. 1984. 44.95 (ISBN 0-8151-2670-0). Year Bk Med.

Dobson, Richard L. & Thiers, Bruce H., eds. Year Book of Dermatology, 1982. (Illus.). 425p. 1982. 44.95 (ISBN 0-8151-2668-9). Year Bk Med.

Dobson, Rosemary & Campbell, David, trs. from Russian. Seven Russian Poets: Imitations. 1980. 9.95x (ISBN 0-7022-1418-3). U of Queensland Pr.

Dobson, Russell & Dobson, Judith. The Language of Schooling. LC 81-40594. 86p. (Orig.). 1982. lib. bdg. 21.00 (ISBN 0-8191-1876-1); pap. text ed. 8.00 (ISBN 0-8191-1877-X). U Pr of Amer.

Dobson, Russell, et al. Staff Development: A Humanistic Approach. LC 80-67254. 175p. 1980. pap. text ed. 10.00 (ISBN 0-8191-1131-7). U Pr of Amer.

--Looking at, Talking about, & Living with Children: Reflections on the Process of Schooling. 142p. (Orig.). 1985. lib. bdg. 19.75 (ISBN 0-8191-4786-9); pap. text ed. 7.75 (ISBN 0-8191-4787-7). U Pr of Amer.

Dobson, Terry. Safe & Alive. LC 81-9045. (Illus.). 154p. 1981. pap. 4.95 (ISBN 0-87477-189-7). J P Tarcher.

Dobson, Theodore. How to Pray for Spiritual Growth: A Practical Handbook of Inner Healing. LC 81-83182. 176p. (Orig.). 1982. pap. 6.95 (ISBN 0-8091-2419-X). Paulist Pr.

--Inner Healing: God's Great Assurance. LC 78-65129. 216p. 1978. pap. 5.95 (ISBN 0-8091-2161-1). Paulist Pr.

Dobson, Theodore E. Say but the Word: How the Lord's Supper Can Transform Your Life. 144p. (Orig.). 1984. pap. 6.95 (ISBN 0-8091-0355-9). Paulist Pr.

Dobson, Theodoree. Inner Healing. 384p. 1985. 12.95 (ISBN 0-8027-2488-4). Walker & Co.

Dobson, Vernon G., jt. auth. see Rose, David.

Dobson, W. A. Dictionary of the Chinese Particles, with a Prolegomenon in Which the Problems of the Particles are Considered & They are Classified by Their Grammaticel Functions. LC 73-91242. (Chinese.). 1974. 75.00x (ISBN 0-8020-2119-0). U of Toronto Pr.

--Early Archaic Chinese: A Descriptive Grammar. LC 63-1488. 1962. 30.00x (ISBN 0-8020-5106-5). U of Toronto Pr.

--The Language of the Book of Songs. LC 68-92657. (Illus.). pap. 87.80 (ISBN 0-317-10173-0, 2020473). Bks Demand UMI.

--Late Archaic Chinese: A Grammatical Study. LC 59-38059. pap. 70.50 (ISBN 0-317-09817-9, 2055464). Bks Demand UMI.

--Late Han Chinese: A Study of the Archaic-Han Shift. LC 65-976. 1964. 25.00x (ISBN 0-8020-1308-2). U of Toronto Pr.

--Mencius. LC 63-23889. (UNESCO Ser.). pap. 58.30 (ISBN 0-317-08766-5, 2014187). Bks Demand UMI.

Dobson, W. G. Engineering Problem Solving with Spreadsheet Programs. Wolff, A. K., ed. (Illus.). 125p. 1984. 79.95 (ISBN 0-932217-00-1). Binary Eng Assocs.

Dobson, W. T. The Classic Poets: Their Lives & Their Times with the Epics Epitomised. 1879. 30.00 (ISBN 0-8274-3946-6). R West.

Dobson, Wendy, jt. auth. see Carmichael, Edward A.

Dobson, William, tr. see Schleiermacher, Friedrich E.

Doby, John T. Introduction to Social Psychology. (Illus.). 1966. 24.50x (ISBN 0-89197-245-5). Irvington.

Doby, John T., et al. Introduction to Social Research. 2nd ed. LC 67-15984. (Illus.). 1981. pap. text ed. 19.95x (ISBN 0-8290-0262-6). Irvington.

Dobyns, et al, eds. Year Book of Hand Surgery, 1985. 1985. 39.95 (ISBN 0-8151-2636-0). Year Bk Med.

Dobyns, Henry F. Native American Historical Demography: A Critical Bibliography Ser. LC 76-12371. (The Newberry Library Center for the History of the American Indian Bibliographical). 104p. 1976. pap. 4.95 (ISBN 0-253-33974-X). Ind U Pr.

--Spanish Colonial Tucson: A Demographic History. LC 75-10344. 246p. 1976. 14.95x (ISBN 0-8165-0546-2); pap. 8.95 (ISBN 0-8165-0438-5). U of Ariz Pr.

--Their Number Become Thinned: Native American Population Dynamics in Eastern North America. LC 83-5952. (Native American Historic Demography Ser.). 396p. 1983. text ed. 29.95x (ISBN 0-87049-400-7); pap. text ed. 14.95x (ISBN 0-87049-401-5). U of Tenn Pr.

Dobyns, Henry F. & Doughty, Paul L. Peru: A Cultural History. LC 76-9224. (Latin American Histories). (Illus.). 1976. 22.50x (ISBN 0-19-502089-8); pap. 9.95x (ISBN 0-19-502091-X). Oxford U Pr.

Dobyns, Kenneth W. & Thorpe, Margaret S. Daniel Dobyns of Colonial Virginia: His English Ancestry & American Descendants. LC 73-20318. pap. 47.00 (ISBN 0-317-08867-X, 2005247). Bks Demand UMI.

Dobyns, L. R. Money: It Comes in Many Packages. LC 73-6710. (Illus.). 92p. Date not set. 7.95 (ISBN 0-913842-03-6); pap. 5.95 (ISBN 0-913842-07-9). Correlan Pubns.

Dobyns, L. R., jt. auth. see Anderson, Richard C.

Dobyns, Stephen. The Balthus Poems. LC 81-70061. 80p. 1982. 11.95 (ISBN 0-689-11278-5); pap. 6.95 (ISBN 0-689-11279-3). Atheneum.

--Black Dog, Red Dog. (The National Poetry Ser.). 84p. 1984. 7.95 (ISBN 0-03-071077-4). HR&W.

--Cold Dog Soup. 1985. 14.95 (ISBN 0-670-80840-7). Viking.

--Griffon. LC 76-10213. 96p. 1976. pap. 4.95 (ISBN 0-689-10736-6). Atheneum.

--Heat Death. LC 79-55592. 1980. 10.00 (ISBN 0-689-11034-0); pap. 5.95 (ISBN 0-689-11063-4). Atheneum.

--Saratoga Headhunter. 201p. 1985. 13.95 (ISBN 0-670-80488-6). Viking.

--Saratoga Swimmer. 224p. 1983. pap. 2.95 (ISBN 0-14-006357-9). Penguin.

Dobyns, Zipporah. Expanding Astrology's Universe. 256p. (Orig.). 1983. pap. 9.95 (ISBN 0-917086-49-X). A C S Pubns Inc.

Dobyns, Zipporah & Wrobel, William. Seven Paths to Understanding. (Illus., Orig.). 1985. pap. 9.95 (ISBN 0-917086-46-5). A C S Pubns Inc.

Dobzhansky, T., et al. Evolutionary Biology, 6 vols. Incl. Vol. 1. 455p. 1967 (ISBN 0-306-50011-6); Vol. 2. 463p. 1968 (ISBN 0-306-50012-4); Vol. 3. 317p. 1969 (ISBN 0-306-50013-2); Vol. 4. 321p. 1970 (ISBN 0-306-50014-0); Vol. 5. 326p. 1972 (ISBN 0-306-50015-9); Vol. 6. 458p. 1972 (ISBN 0-306-50016-7). LC 67-11961. 35.00x ea. (Plenum Pr). Plenum Pub.

Dobzhansky, T., et al, eds. Evolutionary Biology, Vol. 7. LC 67-11961. (Illus.). 324p. 1974. 35.00x (ISBN 0-306-35407-1, Plenum Pr). Plenum Pub.

--Evolutionary Biology, Vol. 8. (Illus.). 405p. 1975. 39.50x (ISBN 0-306-35408-X, Plenum Pr). Plenum Pub.

Dobzhansky, Theodosius. Dobzhansky's Genetics of Natural Populations: I-XLIII. Lewontin, R. C., et al, eds. 1024p. 1982. 60.00x (ISBN 0-231-05132-8). Columbia U Pr.

--Genetic Diversity & Human Equality. LC 73-76262. 1973. pap. 3.95x (ISBN 0-465-09710-3, TB-5075). Basic.

--Genetics & the Origin of Species. Eldredge, Niles & Gould, Stephen Jay, eds. (Classics of Modern Evolution Ser.). 416p. 1982. pap. 18.00x (ISBN 0-231-05475-0). Columbia U Pr.

--Genetics of the Evolutionary Process. LC 72-127363. 505p. 1971. 40.00x (ISBN 0-231-02837-7); pap. 17.00x (ISBN 0-231-08306-8). Columbia U Pr.

--Mankind Evolving: The Evolution of the Human Species. (Silliman Memorial Lectures Ser.). (Illus.). 1962. 33.00x (ISBN 0-300-00427-3); pap. 8.95x 1964 (ISBN 0-300-00070-7, Y116). Yale U Pr.

Dobzhansky, Theodosius & Boesiger, Ernest. Human Culture: A Moment in Evolution. Wallace, Bruce, ed. LC 82-22172. (Illus.). 175p. 1983. 20.00 (ISBN 0-231-05632-X). Columbia U Pr.

Dobzhansky, Theodosius, jt. ed. see Ayala, Francisco.

Dobzhansky, Theodosius, et al. Evolution. LC 77-23284. (Illus.). 572p. 1977. text ed. 34.95 (ISBN 0-7167-0572-9). W H Freeman.

Do Carmo, Manfredo. Differential Geometry of Curves & Surfaces. 1976. 37.95 (ISBN 0-13-212589-7). P-H.

Do Carmo, Pamela B. & Patterson, Angelo T. First Aid Principles & Procedures. (Illus.). 256p. 1976. pap. text ed. 17.95 (ISBN 0-13-317933-8). P-H.

Doche, Viviane. Cedars by the Mississippi: The Lebanese-Americans in the Twin-Cities. LC 77-81012. 1978. soft cover 13.00 (ISBN 0-88247-488-X). R & E Pubs.

Docherty, Charles. Steel & Steelworkers: The Sons of Vulcan. (Illus.). x, 247p. 1983. text ed. 30.00x (ISBN 0-435-82196-2). Gower Pub Co.

Docherty, George. I've Seen the Day. 304p. 1984. 19.95 (ISBN 0-8028-3591-0). Eerdmans.

Docherty, Thomas. Reading (Absent) Character: Towards a Theory of Characterization in Fiction. LC 83-12197. 1983. 34.95x (ISBN 0-19-812822-3). Oxford U Pr.

Docherty, Tommy. Better Soccer for Boys. (Better Bks.). (Illus.). 96p. 1984. text ed. 17.95x (ISBN 0-7182-0144-2, SpS). Sportshelf.

Dochniak, Jim. A Simple Exchange. (Poetry Chapbook Ser.: No. 4). 8p. (Orig.). 1985. pap. 1.50x (ISBN 0-937724-05-X). Shadow Pr.

Dochniak, Jim, ed. see Davalos, Armando H. & Union of Writers & Artists of Cuba.

Dochniak, Jim, ed. see McAnally, Mary E.

Dochterman, Delores. The Art of Taking Minutes. LC 82-42639. 208p. 1982. 12.95 (ISBN 0-9609526-0-8). Snyder Pub Co.

Dock, Lavinia. A Lavinia Dock Reader. James, Janet & Reverby, Susan, eds. LC 83-49183. (The History of American Nursing Ser.). 320p. 1985. lib. bdg. 40.00 (ISBN 0-8240-6512-3). Garland Pub.

Dock, V. Thomas. Structured BASIC: Programming for Business. 2nd ed. (Illus.). 144p. 1982. pap. text ed. 17.95 (ISBN 0-314-63167-4). West Pub.

--Structured BASIC Programming for Business. 3rd ed. (Illus.). 140p. 1984. pap. text ed. 18.95 (ISBN 0-314-85230-1). West Pub.

--Structured COBOL: American National Standard. (The West Series in Data & Information Systems). (Illus.). 1978. pap. text ed. 18.50 (ISBN 0-8299-0181-7). West Pub.

--Structured COBOL: American National Standard. 2nd ed. (Illus.). 300p. 1984. pap. text ed. 23.95 (ISBN 0-314-77896-9). West Pub.

--Structured COBOL: American National Standard. 2nd ed. 90p. 1984. write for info. instr's manual (ISBN 0-314-77897-7). West Pub.

--Structured FORTRAN IV Programming. (Data Processing & Information System Ser.). (Illus.). 1979. pap. text ed. 22.95 (ISBN 0-8299-0249-X). West Pub.

Dock, V. Thomas & Essick, Edward. Principles of Business Data Processing. 4th ed. 544p. 1981. text ed. 23.95 (ISBN 0-574-21295-7, 13-4295); instr's guide avail. (ISBN 0-574-21296-5, 13-4296); transparency masters avail. (ISBN 0-574-21303-1, 13-4303); study guide 10.95 (ISBN 0-574-21297-3, 13-4297). SRA.

--Principles of Business Data Processing with MIS...including BASIC. 4th ed. 640p. 1981. text ed. 25.95 (ISBN 0-574-21305-8, 13-4305); instructor's guide avail. (ISBN 0-574-21301-5, 13-4301); study guide 10.95 (ISBN 0-574-21302-3, 13-4302). SRA.

--Principles of Business Data Processing with MIS...including BASIC: MIS Edition, Language Free. 4th ed. 544p. 1981. 25.95 (ISBN 0-574-21300-7, 13-4300). SRA.

Dock, V. Thomas, jt. auth. see Luchsinger, Vincent P.

Dock, V. Thomas, et al, eds. MIS: A Managerial Perspective. LC 77-7063. 1977. pap. text ed. 16.95 (ISBN 0-574-21050-4, 13-4050). SRA.

Dock, William. Prevention of Obstruction of Coronary & Vital Arteries. LC 79-50185. 200p. 1983. 42.50 (ISBN 0-87527-202-9). Green.

Dockens, William S., jt. ed. see Thompson, Travis.

Dockery, F. A., jt. auth. see Whittle, Elizabeth.

Dockes, Pierre. Medieval Slavery & Liberation. Goldhammer, Arthur, tr. from Fr. LC 81-11594. 1982. lib. bdg. 27.00x (ISBN 0-226-15482-3). U of Chicago Pr.

Dockhorn, Jean. Essentials of Social Work Programs in Hospitals. rev. ed. LC 81-20613. 48p. 1982. 15.00 (ISBN 0-87258-353-8, AHA-187103, Pub. by AHPI). Am Hospital.

Dockhorn, Klaus. Die Staatsphilosophie des Englischen Idealismus. 1937. pap. 20.00 (ISBN 0-384-12065-2). Johnson Repr.

Dockhorn, Robert J., jt. auth. see Speer, Frederic.

Docking, Jim. Controlling Discipline in Schools. 1980. text ed. 18.35 (ISBN 0-06-318152-5, IntlDept); pap. text ed. 10.45 (ISBN 0-06-318153-3). Har-Row.

Dockray, G. J., jt. ed. see De Belleroche, J.

Dockrell, W. B., jt. auth. see Black, H. D.

Dockrell, W. B., ed. An Attitude of Mind. (SCRE Ser.: No. 83). 172p. 1984. pap. text ed. 16.25x (ISBN 0-901116-90-4, Pub. by Scottish Coun Res UK). Humanities.

Dockrey, Karen. Friends: Finding & Keeping Them. 1985. pap. 4.50 (ISBN 0-8054-5343-1). Broadman.

--Getting to Know God. LC 84-1702. (Orig.). (gr. 9-12). 1984. pap. 4.50 (ISBN 0-8054-5341-5, 4253-41). Broadman.

Dockrill, D. W. & Mortley, R., eds. The Via Negativa. 211p. 1983. pap. text ed. 31.00x (ISBN 0-85668-915-7, Pub. by Aris & Phillips England). Humanities.

Dockrill, M. L., jt. auth. see Paskins, B. A.

Dockrill, Michael & Goold, Douglas. Peace Without Promise: Britain & the Peace Conferences 1919-1923. 287p. 1981. 25.00 (ISBN 0-208-01909-X, Archon). Shoe String.

Docks, L. R. American Premium Record Guide (1915-1965) 3rd ed. 354p. (Orig.). 1985. pap. 14.95 (ISBN 0-89689-054-6). Bks Americana.

Dockser, Cheryl B. A Nation of Immigrants. (Illus.). 40p. (Orig., Prog. Bk.). 1984. pap. text ed. 2.99 (ISBN 0-940712-25-3). Dahlstrom & Co.

Dockstader, Frederick J. The American Indian in Graduate Studies: A Bibliolgrapy of Theses & Dissertations, 2 vols. 1973. Set. pap. 18.00 (ISBN 0-934490-06-6); Vol. 1. pap. 10.00 (ISBN 0-934490-07-4); Vol. 2. pap. 10.00 (ISBN 0-934490-08-2). Mus Am Ind.

--Indian Art of the Americas. LC 73-89979. (Illus., Orig.). 1973. 5.00x (ISBN 0-934490-09-0). Mus Am Ind.

--The Kachina & the White Man: The Influence of White Culture on the Hopi Kachina Cult. rev. ed. (Illus.). 224p. 1985. 19.95 (ISBN 0-8263-0789-2); pap. 10.95 (ISBN 0-8263-0790-6). U of NM Pr.

Dockstader, Frederick J. & Krevolin, Lewis. Naked Clay: Three Thousand Years of Unadorned Pottery of the American Indian. (Illus.). 96p. (Orig.). 1972. 3.50 (ISBN 0-934490-10-4). Mus Am Ind.

Dockx, S., ed. see Symposium, Brussels.

Docs, Diane L. Visual Defects. (Illus.). 1978. 20.00 (ISBN 0-916750-79-5). Dayton Labs.

Doc Smith & Eklund, Gordon. Lord Tedric III: Black Knight of the Iron Sphere. (Lord Tedric Ser.). 224p. (Orig.). 1981. pap. 2.25 (ISBN 0-441-49256-8). Ace Bks.

Docter, Richard F., jt. auth. see Holmen, Milton G.

Dr. Williams' Library, London. Early Nonconformity, 1566-1800: A Catalogue of Books in Dr. Williams' Library, London, 3 pts. Incl. Pt. 1. Author Catalogue, 5 vols. Set. 495.00 (ISBN 0-8161-0797-1); Pt. 2. Subject Catalogue, 5 vols. Set. 495.00 (ISBN 0-8161-0174-4); Pt. 3. Chronological Catalogue, 2 vols. Set. 198.00 (ISBN 0-8161-0173-6). 1968 (Hall Library). G K Hall.

Doctoroff, Michael. Synergistic Management: Creating the Climate for Superior Performance. (Illus.). 1978. 13.95 (ISBN 0-8144-5445-3). AMACOM.

Doctorow, E. L. The Book of Daniel. 1984. pap. 3.95 (ISBN 0-553-23632-6). Bantam.

--The Book of Daniel. 1971. 14.95 (ISBN 0-394-46271-8). Random.

--The Book of Daniel. LC 83-42866. 303p. 8.95 (ISBN 0-394-60501-2). Modern Lib.

--Drinks Before Dinner. LC 78-21794. 1979. 8.95 (ISBN 0-394-40092-5). Random.

--Lives of the Poets: Six Stories & a Novella. LC 84-42513. 224p. 1984. 14.45 (ISBN 0-394-52530-2). Random.

--Ragtime. 384p. 1981. pap. 4.50 (ISBN 0-553-24520-1). Bantam.

--Ragtime. LC 75-9613. 288p. 1975. 12.95 (ISBN 0-394-46901-1). Random.

--Welcome to Hard Times. 224p. 1975. pap. 7.95 (ISBN 0-394-73107-7). Random.

--World's Fair. 1985. 17.95 (ISBN 0-394-52528-0). Random.

Doctors, Samuel, et al. Educating the Innovative Public Manager. LC 80-39481. 160p. 1981. text ed. 30.00 (ISBN 0-89946-079-8). Oelgeschlager.

Doctors, Samuel I. Technology Transfer by State & Local Government. LC 81-11194. 280p. 1981. text ed. 35.00 (ISBN 0-89946-050-X). Oelgeschlager.

Doczi, Gyorgy. The Power of Limits: Proportional Harmonies in Nature, Art, & Architecture. LC 77-90883. (Illus.). 224p. 1981. pap. 14.95 (ISBN 0-87773-193-4). Shambhala Pubns.

Dod, Charles. Electoral Facts from 1832-1853, Impartially Stated. A Complete Political Gazetteer. Hanham, H. J., ed. 388p. 1972. Repr. of 1853 ed. 25.00x (ISBN 0-8476-6051-6). Rowman.

Doda, Nancy. Teacher to Teacher. 63p. 1981. 5.95 (ISBN 0-318-15787-X, NMSA007). Natl Middle Schl.

Dodd, et al. Solitions & Nonlinear Wave Equations. 1984. 25.00 (ISBN 0-317-12003-4). Academie Pr.

Dodd, A. H. Life in Wales. 1972. 17.95 (ISBN 0-7134-1463-4, Pub. by Batsford England). David & Charles.

--Studies in Stuart Wales. 2nd ed. 251p. 1971. text ed. 15.75x (ISBN 0-900768-85-1, Pub. by Univ of Wales Pr England). Humanities.

Dodd, A. J. The Core Model. LC 81-17989. (London Mathematical Society Lecture Note Series 61). 272p. 1982. 27.95 (ISBN 0-521-28530-5). Cambridge U Pr.

Dodd, Bella V. School of Darkness. 1963. pap. 6.95 (ISBN 0-8159-6804-3). Devin.

Dodd, C. Crisis of Turkish Democracy. 132p. 1983. text ed. 19.00x (Pub. by Eothen Pr England); pap. text ed. 12.00x (ISBN 0-906719-05-4). Humanities.

Dodd, C. H. A Course of Study Outlines for Bible Class Leaders. 59.95 (ISBN 0-87968-954-4). Gordon Pr.

--Democracy & Development in Turkey. 1980. text ed. 24.00x (ISBN 0-906719-01-1); pap. text ed. 13.00x o. p. (ISBN 0-906719-00-3). Humanities.

--The Parables of the Kingdom. 176p. 1977. pap. text ed. price not set (ISBN 0-02-330460-X, Pub. by Scribner). Macmillan.

--Politics & Government in Turkey. LC 78-85453. 1969. 36.00x (ISBN 0-520-01430-8). U of Cal Pr.

Dodd, Carley H. Dynamics of Intercultural Communication. 300p. 1982. pap. text ed. write for info. (ISBN 0-697-04191-3); instr's manual avail. (ISBN 0-697-04209-X). Wm C Brown.

Dodd, Carol S. The Richardson Years: Nineteen Sixty-Six to Nineteen Eighty-Two. (Illus.). 168p. 1985. text ed. 14.95X (ISBN 0-8248-0988-2). UH Pr.

Dodd, Charles. Dodd's Church History of England, 1500-1688, 5 Vols. Tierney, M. A., ed. LC 75-119152. Repr. of 1843 ed. Set. 262.00 (ISBN 0-404-02150-6); 52.50 ea. Vol. 1 (ISBN 0-404-02151-4). Vol. 2 (ISBN 0-404-02152-2). Vol. 3 (ISBN 0-404-02153-0). Vol. 4 (ISBN 0-404-02154-9). Vol. 5 (ISBN 0-404-02155-7). AMS Pr.

Dodd, Charles H. Historical Tradition in the Fourth Gospel. 1975. pap. 16.95x (ISBN 0-521-29123-2). Cambridge U Pr.

--Interpretation of the Fourth Gospel. 67.50 (ISBN 0-521-04848-6); pap. text ed. 17.95 (ISBN 0-521-09517-4, 517). Cambridge U Pr.

Dodd, Christopher, ed. Boating. (Small Oxford Bks.). (Illus.). 1983. 9.95 (ISBN 0-19-214138-4). Oxford U Pr.

Dodd, Craig. The Performing World of the Dancer. LC 81-50298. (The Performing World Ser.). 114p. (gr. 7 up). 15.20 (ISBN 0-382-06590-5). Silver.

--Rudolf Nureyev. (Profile Ser.). (Illus.). 64p. (gr. 3-6). 1982. 7.95 (ISBN 0-241-10849-7, Pub. by Hamish Hamilton England). David & Charles.

--Young Person's Guide to the Ballet. (Masterworks of Opera Ser.). 160p. (gr. 6 up). 15.96 (ISBN 0-382-06445-3). Silver.

Dodd, Damon C. All of Mine for Him. 1977. pap. 2.50 (ISBN 0-89265-045-1). Randall Hse.

--The Book of Revelation, Study Guide. 1973. pap. 2.75 (ISBN 0-89265-013-3). Randall Hse.

Dodd, Donald B. Historical Atlas of Alabama. LC 73-36. (Illus.). 173p. 1974. 11.00 (ISBN 0-8173-5226-0). U of Ala Pr.

Dodd, Donald B. & Dodd, Wynelle S. Historical Statistics of the United States, 1790-1970, Vol. 2: The Midwest. LC 75-23482. 80p. 1976. 9.50 (ISBN 0-8173-9701-9). U of Ala Pr.

Dodd, E. E. Atlas of Histology. 1979. 45.00 (ISBN 0-07-017230-7). McGraw.

Dodd, Ed, jt. auth. see Osler, Tom.

Dodd, Edward, ed. see Martin, Henry B.

Dodd, Edward H. The Rape of Tahiti: The Ring of Fire, Vol. IV. LC 82-21997. 1983. 14.95 (ISBN 0-396-08114-2). Dodd.

Dodd, Edwin M. American Business Corporations Until 1860 with Special Reference to Massachusetts. LC 53-9043. 1954. 32.50x (ISBN 0-674-02000-6). Harvard U Pr.

Dodd, Erica C. & Khairallah, Shereen. The Image of the Word: A Study of Quranic Verses in Islamic Architecture, 2 vols. (Illus.). 434p. 1982. 95.00x (ISBN 0-8156-6061-8, Am U Beirut). Syracuse U Pr.

Dodd, Fred W. Number Theory in the Quadratic Field with Golden Section Unit. LC 83-17799. (Examples of Mathematical Structures: Vol. 3). 159p. 1984. 16.95x (ISBN 0-936428-08-2). Polygonal Pub.

Dodd, G. G. & Rossol, L., eds. Computer Vision & Sensor-Based Robots. LC 79-18698. (General Motors Symposia Ser.). 363p. 1979. 55.00x (ISBN 0-306-40305-6, Plenum Pr). Plenum Pub.

Dodd, George. Days at the Factories. LC 67-18569. (Illus.). Repr. of 1843 ed. 45.00x (ISBN 0-678-00262-2). Kelley.

--Days at the Factories: Manufacturing in the Nineteenth Century. (Illus.). 408p. 1975. Repr. of 1843 ed. 16.95x (ISBN 0-8464-0313-7). Beekman Pubs.

--Days at the Factories: Or, The Manufacturing Industry of Great Britain Described. (Illus.). 1978. Repr. of 1843 ed. 18.00x (ISBN 0-7158-1076-6). Charles River Bks.

--Days at the Factories; or, the Manufacturing Industry of Great Britain, Described & Illustrated by Numerous Engravings of Machines & Processes. (Illus.). 408p. 1975. Repr. of 1843 ed. 18.50x (ISBN 0-87471-620-9). Rowman.

--The Food of London. LC 75-27635. (World Food Supply Ser). 1976. Repr. of 1856 ed. 41.00x (ISBN 0-405-07777-7). Ayer Co Pubs.

Dodd, Gerard R. & Sample, Tim. Management Workbooks for Self-Employed People, 5 wkbks. 2nd, rev. ed. Bd. with The Business Review (ISBN 0-930205-01-4); The Business Plan (ISBN 0-930205-02-2); Basic Finances (ISBN 0-930205-03-0); Basic Marketing (ISBN 0-930205-04-9); Managing Time & Personnel (ISBN 0-930205-05-7). (Illus.). 1984. Set. wkbk. 18.00 (ISBN 0-930205-00-6). Dodd-Blair Assocs.

Dodd, Harold & Cockett, Frank B. The Pathology & Surgery of the Veins of the Lower Limb. LC 75-599. (Illus.). 1976. text ed. 62.50 (ISBN 0-443-01292-X). Churchill.

Dodd, Henry P. Epigrammatists: A Selection from the Epigrammatic Literature of Ancient, Mediaeval & Modern Times. LC 69-16801. 1969. Repr. of 1876 ed. 51.00x (ISBN 0-8103-3524-7). Gale.

--The Epigrammatists: A Selection from the Epigrammatic Literature of Ancient, Medieval & Modern Times. 1977. lib. bdg. 59.95 (ISBN 0-8490-1782-3). Gordon Pr.

Dodd, James. The Ideas of Particle Physics: An Introduction for Scientists. LC 83-15227. (Illus.). 270p. 1984. 44.50 (ISBN 0-521-25338-1); pap. 17.95 (ISBN 0-521-27322-6). Cambridge U Pr.

Dodd, James, jt. auth. see Wiener, Harvey S.

Dodd, James B. Fee-Based Information Centers in Libraries. (Professional Librarian). 150p. cancelled (ISBN 0-86729-049-8); pap. cancelled (ISBN 0-86729-048-X). Knowledge Indus.

Dodd, John D. Course Book in General Botany. (Illus.). 1977. text ed. 16.95x (ISBN 0-8138-0690-9). Iowa St U Pr.

Dodd, K. N. Computer Programming & Languages. LC 70-80822. 148p. 1969. 9.95x (ISBN 0-306-30660-3, Plenum Pr). Plenum Pub.

Dodd, Lamar. Lamar Dodd: A Retrospective Exhibition. LC 71-133620. 138p. 1970. pap. 10.00x (ISBN 0-8203-0307-0). U of Ga Pr.

Dodd, Lawrence C. Coalitions in Parliamentary Government. LC 75-2986. 184p. 1975. 32.00x (ISBN 0-691-07564-6). Princeton U Pr.

Dodd, Lawrence C. & Schott, Richard L. Congress & the Administrative State. LC 79-14347. (Viewpoints on American Politics Ser.). 364p. 1979. pap. text ed. 15.95 (ISBN 0-471-21741-7). Wiley.

Dodd, Lawrence C., et al. Congress Reconsidered. 3rd ed. 460p. 1985. pap. 14.95 (ISBN 0-87187-332-X). Congr Quarterly.

Dodd, Loring H. see Robinson, Fred C.

Dodd, Maxine K. Call for Volunteers: The Life of Colonel Warren E. Dodd. (Illus.). 48p. 1984. 5.95 (ISBN 0-89962-390-5). Todd & Honeywell.

Dodd, Michael, jt. auth. see Kissiah, Gary F.

Dodd, Nigel & Hickson, Winifred, eds. Drama & Theatre in Education. 1971. pap. text ed. 9.50x (ISBN 0-435-18271-4). Heinemann Ed.

Dodd, Philip, ed. The Art of Travel: Essays on Travel Writing. 172p. 1982. text ed. 17.50x (ISBN 0-7146-3205-8, F Cass Co). Biblio Dist.

--Walter Pater: An Imaginative Sense of Fact. 104p. 1981. 17.50x (ISBN 0-7146-3183-3, F Cass Co). Biblio Dist.

Dodd, Philip & Colls, Robert, eds. The Idea of Englishness: National Identity in Arts, Politics & Society 1880-1920. 224p. 1985. 29.00 (ISBN 0-7099-0849-0, Pub. by Croom Helm Ltd). Longwood Pub Group.

Dodd, Randall M., jt. auth. see Wells, E. Hazard.

Dodd, Robert J. & Stanton, Robert J., Jr. Paleoecology, Concepts & Applications. LC 80-19623. 559p. 1981. 49.95x (ISBN 0-471-04171-8, Pub. by Wiley-Interscience). Wiley.

Dodd, Robert T. Meteorites: A Chemical-Petrologic Synthesis. LC 80-25327. (Illus.). 368p. 1981. 27.95 (ISBN 0-521-22570-1). Cambridge U Pr.

--The Survivors: An Introduction to Meteroites. 224p. 1985. pap. 18.95 (ISBN 0-02-949220-3). Macmillan.

Dodd, Robert V. Faith Is for Sharing. 1977. pap. text ed. 3.50 (ISBN 0-89536-075-6). CSS of Ohio.

--Helping Children Cope with Death. LC 84-6713. 56p. (Orig.). 1984. pap. 1.95 (ISBN 0-8361-3368-4). Herald Pr.

--Praying the Name of Jesus. 96p. (Orig.). 1985. pap. 4.95 (ISBN 0-8358-0514-X). Upper Room.

--Speck of Sawdust in My Eye. LC 79-56164. 96p. (Orig.). 1979. pap. 2.95x (ISBN 0-8358-0396-1). Upper Room.

--Your Church's Ministry of Prayer. 1981. 3.00 (ISBN 0-89536-476-X). CSS of Ohio.

Dodd, Roger Y. & Barker, Lewellys F. Infection, Immunity, & Blood Transfusion. LC 85-6866. (Progress in Clinical & Biological Research Ser.: Vol. 182). 490p. 1985. 68.00 (ISBN 0-8451-5032-4). A R Liss.

Dodd, Sandra, jt. auth. see Esmiol, Barbara.

Dodd, Stuart C. Social Relations in the Near East. 2nd, rev. & enl. ed. LC 75-180333. Repr. of 1940 ed. 62.50 (ISBN 0-404-56239-6). AMS Pr.

Dodd, Sue. Cataloging Machine-Readable Data Files: An Interpretive Manual. LC 82-11597. 268p. 1982. pap. text ed. 35.00x (ISBN 0-8389-0365-7). ALA.

Dodd, Sue A. & Fox, Ann M. S. Cataloging Microcomputer Files: A Manual of Interpretation for AACR2. LC 85-1359. 228p. 1985. text ed. 40.00 (ISBN 0-8389-0401-7). ALA.

Dodd, Sue A. & Sandberg-Fox, Ann M. Cataloging Microcomputer Files: A Manual of Interpretation for AACR2. 228p. 1985. 40.00 (ISBN 0-8389-0401-7). ALA.

Dodd, Susan M. Old Wives' Tales. LC 84-8879. (Iowa Short Fiction Award Ser.: No. 15). 181p. (Orig.). 1984. pap. 9.95 (ISBN 0-87745-133-8). U of Iowa Pr.

Dodd, T. F. Sales Forecasting: How to Prepare & Use Market Data & Sales Forecasts in Profit Planning. 220p. 1974. text ed. 44.50x (ISBN 0-7161-0233-1). Gower Pub Co.

Dodd, Virginia A. Henry County, Virginia, Marriage Bonds 1778-1849. LC 75-34714. 132p. 1976. Repr. of 1953 ed. 12.50 (ISBN 0-8063-0702-1). Genealog Pub.

Dodd, W. E., ed. see Wilson, Woodrow.

Dodd, W. F. Modern Constitutions, 2 vols. 1977. lib. bdg. 250.00 (ISBN 0-8490-2265-7). Gordon Pr.

--Revision & Amendment of State Constitutions. LC 73-120854. (American Constitutional & Legal History Ser). 1970. Repr. of 1910 ed. lib. bdg. 42.50 (ISBN 0-306-71959-2). Da Capo.

Dodd, Walter A., Jr. Final Year Excavations at the Evans Mound Site. (Anthropological Papers: No. 106). 160p. (Orig.). 1982. pap. 10.00 (ISBN 0-87480-207-5). U of Utah Pr.

Dodd, Walter F. The Revision & Amendment of State Constitutions. LC 78-64273. (Johns Hopkins University. Studies in the Social Sciences. Extra Volumes-New Ser.: 1). Repr. of 1910 ed. 19.00 (ISBN 0-404-61374-8). AMS Pr.
Dodd, Wayne. The General Mule Poems, Juniper Bk. 37. 1981. 4.00 (ISBN 0-686-79782-5). Juniper Pr WI.
--The Names You Gave It. LC 80-14240. x, 62p. 1980. 13.95x (ISBN 0-8071-0665-8); pap. 4.95 (ISBN 0-8071-0666-6). La State U Pr.
--A Time of Hunting. LC 75-4779. 128p. (gr. 6 up). 1975. 6.95 (ISBN 0-395-28903-3, Clarion). HM.
Dodd, Wayne D., ed. The Ohio Review, No. 30. 280p. 1983. 13.95 (ISBN 0-942148-00-2). Ohio Review.
Dodd, William. Beauties of Shakespeare, 2 vols. (Eighteenth Century Shakespeare Ser.: Vol. 9). 1971. Repr. of 1752 ed. 55.00x set (ISBN 0-7146-2528-0, F Cass Co). Biblio Dist.
--Beauties of Shakespeare, 2 Vols. LC 79-96352. (Eighteenth Century Shakespeare). Repr. of 1752 ed. lib. bdg. 50.00x (ISBN 0-678-05109-7). Kelley.
--Factory System Illustrated. 3rd ed. 319p. 1968. Repr. of 1842 ed. 30.00x (ISBN 0-7146-1389-4, F Cass Co.). Biblio Dist.
--Factory System Illustrated. LC 67-28260. (Illus.). Repr. of 1842 ed. 27.50x (ISBN 0-678-05043-0). Kelley.
--Labouring Classes of England. LC 68-55703. Repr. of 1847 ed. 22.50x (ISBN 0-678-00961-9). Kelley.
Dodd, William, jt. auth. see Presley, John.
Dodd, William C. The Tai Race, Elder Brother of the Chinese. 1976. lib. bdg. 59.95 (ISBN 0-8490-2726-8). Gordon Pr.
Dodd, William E. Cotton Kingdom. 1919. 8.50x (ISBN 0-686-83514-X). Elliots Bks.
--Life of Nathaniel Macon 1757-1837. LC 78-130600. (Research & Source Works: No. 537). 1970. lib. bdg. 26.50 (ISBN 0-8337-0876-7). B Franklin.
--Robert J. Walker: Imperialist. 1914. 7.75 (ISBN 0-8446-1157-3). Peter Smith.
--Woodrow Wilson & His Work. 1958. 11.25 (ISBN 0-8446-1156-5). Peter Smith.
Dodd, William E see Johnson, Allen & Nevins, Allan.
Dodd, William G. Courtly Love in Chaucer & Gower. 59.95 (ISBN 0-87968-956-0). Gordon Pr.
Dodd, Wynelle S., jt. auth. see Dodd, Donald B.
Dodder, Laura, jt. auth. see Muhlbauer, Gene.
Dodderidge, Esme. New Gulliver. LC 79-65728. 1979. 9.95 (ISBN 0-8008-5506-X). Taplinger.
Doddridge, Ben F. & Howard, J. Rodney. Operation Encounter. 1975. pap. text ed. 13.00x (ISBN 0-673-16121-8). Scott F.
Doddridge, John. A Compleat Parson: Or, a Description of Advowsons. LC 73-6119. (English Experience Ser.: No. 586). 95p. 1973. Repr. of 1630 ed. 10.50 (ISBN 90-221-0586-5). Walter J Johnson.
--The English Lawyer, Describing a Method for the Managing of the Lawes of This Land. LC 72-5973. (English Experience Ser.: No. 503). 280p. 1973. Repr. of 1631 ed. 30.00 (ISBN 90-221-0503-2). Walter J Johnson.
--The History of the Ancient & Moderne Estate of the Principality of Wales. LC 73-6120. (English Experience Ser.: No. 587). 142p. 1973. Repr. of 1630 ed. 15.00 (ISBN 90-221-0587-3). Walter J Johnson.
Doddridge, Joseph. Notes on the Settlement & Indian Wars. 1976. Repr. of 1824 ed. 15.00 (ISBN 0-87012-001-8). McClain.
Doddridge, Philip. Some Remarkable Passages in the Life of the Honorable Col. James Gardiner, 1747. Shugrue, Michael F., ed. (The Flowering of the Novel, 1740-1775 Ser: Vol. 19). 1975. lib. bdg. 61.00 (ISBN 0-8240-1118-X). Garland Pub.
Dodds, Annie E. The Romantic Theory of Poetry: An Examination in the Light of Croce's Aesthetic. LC 75-28996. Repr. of 1926 ed. 22.50 (ISBN 0-404-14007-6). AMS Pr.
Dodds, Dennis R. Oriental Rugs from the Robert A. Fisher Collection in the Virginia Museum. LC 85-2954. (Illus.). 175p. (Orig.). 1985. pap. 27.50 (ISBN 0-917046-15-3). Va Mus Arts.
Dodds, E. R. Missing Persons: An Autobiography. (Illus.). 1977. 22.50x (ISBN 0-19-812086-9). Oxford U Pr.
--Pagan & Christian in an Age of Anxiety: Some Aspects of Religious Experience from Marcus Aurelius to Constantine. 1970. pap. 5.95 (ISBN 0-393-00545-3, Norton Lib). Norton.
--Select Passages Illustrating Neoplatonism. 128p. 1980. 12.50 (ISBN 0-89005-302-2). Ares.
Dodds, E. R., ed. see Euripides.
Dodds, E. R., jt. ed. see MacNeice, Louis.
Dodds, E. R., ed. see Plato.
Dodds, Eric R. The Greeks & the Irrational. (Sather Classical Lectures: No. 25). 1951. pap. 7.95 (ISBN 0-520-00327-6, CAL74). U of Cal Pr.
Dodds, George. Voice Placing & Training Exercise, 2 vols. Incl. Contralto & Baritone (ISBN 0-19-322141-1); Soprano & Tenor (ISBN 0-19-322140-3). (YA) (gr. 9up). 1927. pap. 7.00 ea. Oxford U Pr.
Dodds, Gideon S., jt. auth. see Van Liere, Edward J.
Dodds, Gordan B. Hiram Martin Chittenden: His Public Career. LC 72-91664. 232p. 1973. 20.00x (ISBN 0-8131-1283-4). U Pr of Ky.
Dodds, Gordon B. Oregon: A History. (States & the Nation Ser.). (Illus.). 1977. 14.95 (ISBN 0-393-05632-5, Co-Pub. by AASLH). Norton.
Dodds, Harold W. Out of This Nettle, Danger. LC 78-99631. (Essay Index Reprint Ser.). 1943. 14.00 (ISBN 0-8369-1406-6). Ayer Co Pubs.
Dodds, Harold W., et al. The Academic President: Educator or Caretaker? LC 77-5574. (Carnegie Ser. in American Education). 1977. Repr. of 1962 ed. lib. bdg. 22.75x (ISBN 0-8371-9644-2, DOAC). Greenwood.
Dodds, J. C. The Investment Behaviour of British Life Insurance Companies. 193p. 1979. 50.00x (ISBN 0-7099-0058-9, Pub. by Croom Helm Ltd). Longwood Pub Group.
Dodds, J. C., jt. auth. see Bridge, John.
Dodds, J. W. Thomas Southerne Dramatist. 237p. 1980. Repr. of 1933 ed. lib. bdg. 30.00 (ISBN 0-89984-154-6). Century Bookbindery.
Dodds, Jack. The Writer in Performance. 737p. 1986. text ed. 14.00 (ISBN 0-02-330380-8). Macmillan.
Dodds, James E. The Gentleman from Heaven. 123p. 1962. Repr. of 1948 ed. 3.50 (ISBN 0-87516-464-1). De Vorss.
Dodds, John H. & Roberts, Lorin W. Experiments in Plant Tissue Culture. LC 81-6106. (Illus.). 192p. 1982. 34.50 (ISBN 0-521-23477-8); pap. 12.95 (ISBN 0-521-29965-9). Cambridge U Pr.
Dodds, John H., ed. Plant Genetic Engineering. 208p. Date not set. price not set. (ISBN 0-521-25966-5). Cambridge U Pr.
Dodds, John W. Thomas Southerne: Dramatist. LC 78-91179. (Yale Studies in English Ser.: No. 81). iv, 232p. 1970. Repr. of 1933 ed. 18.50 (ISBN 0-208-00912-4, Archon). Shoe String.
Dodds, John W., jt. ed. see Durham, Willard H.
Dodds, Josiah. A Child Psychotherapy Primer: Suggestions for the Beginning Therapist. 128p. 1985. 16.95 (ISBN 0-89885-240-4). Human Sci Pr.
Dodds, Lois. How Do I Look from Up There? LC 80-51160. 143p. (gr. 9-12). 1981. pap. 3.95 (ISBN 0-88207-584-5). Victor Bks.
Dodds, Madeleine H. & Dodds, Ruth. Pilgrimage of Grace, 1536-1537 & the Exeter Conspiracy, 1538, 2 vols. 1971. Repr. of 1915 ed. 62.50x set (ISBN 0-7146-1470-X, F Cass Co). Biblio Dist.
Dodds, Maggie, ed. Ghana Talks. LC 76-46239. (Illus., Orig.). 1976. cased 10.00 (ISBN 0-914478-35-4). Three Continents.
Dodds, Margaret K. Easy-to-Build Wooden Chairs for Children: Measured Drawings & Illustrated Step-by-Step Instructions for Traditional Chairs. (Woodworking Ser.). (Illus.). 32p. (Orig.). 1984. pap. 2.00 (ISBN 0-486-24579-9). Dover.
Dodd's Parliamentary Companion Ltd., ed. The Official Handbook of the European Parliament. 700p. 1981. 100.00x (ISBN 0-686-79451-6, Pub. by Dodd's). State Mutual Bk.
Dodds, Robert H. Writing for Technical & Business Magazines. LC 80-23843. (Illus.). 208p. 1982. Repr. of 1969 ed. text ed. 14.95 (ISBN 0-89874-237-4). Krieger.
Dodds, Ruth, jt. auth. see Dodds, Madeleine H.
Dodds, Vera W., jt. auth. see Perloff, Harvey S.
Dodds, W. Jean & Orlans, F. Barbara, eds. Scientific Perspectives in Animal Welfare: Symposium. LC 82-24375. 1983. 19.00 (ISBN 0-12-219140-4). Acad Pr.
Dodds, William F., jt. auth. see Gallagher, Sr. Vera.
Doder, Dusko. The Yugoslavs. 1978. 10.00 (ISBN 0-394-42538-3). Random.
--The Yugoslavs. LC 79-5027. 1979. pap. 4.95 (ISBN 0-394-74158-7, Vin). Random.
Doderidge, Esme. The New Gulliver. LC 79-65728. 220p. 1980. pap. 3.95 (ISBN 0-8008-5507-8). Taplinger.
Dodes, I. Numerical Analysis for Computer Science. 618p. 1978. text ed. 30.00 (ISBN 0-444-00238-3, North-Holland). Elsevier.
--Numerical Analysis for Computer Science. 618p. 1980. 32.00 (ISBN 0-317-30899-8, North-Holland). Elsevier.
Dodes, Irving A. Finite Mathematics with BASIC: A Liberal Arts Approach. Rev. ed. LC 78-31505. (Illus.). 372p. 1981. Repr. of 1970 ed. lib. bdg. 21.00 (ISBN 0-88275-862-4). Krieger.
--Mathematics: A Liberal Arts Approach with Basic. 2nd. ed. LC 79-131. 464p. 1980. lib. bdg. 21.50 (ISBN 0-88275-892-6). Krieger.
Dodge. Sampling Inspection Tables: Single & Double Sampling. 2nd ed. 224p. 40.95 (ISBN 0-318-13245-1, P46). Am Soc QC.
Dodge, et al. Marketing Research. 561p. 1982. text ed. 28.95 (ISBN 0-675-09847-5). Additional supplements may be obtained from publisher. Merrill.
Dodge, A. J., jt. auth. see Myers, E.
Dodge, Arthur F. Occupational Ability Patterns. LC 78-176724. (Columbia University. Teachers College. Contributions to Education: No. 658). Repr. of 1935 ed. 22.50 (ISBN 0-404-55658-2). AMS Pr.
Dodge, Bayard. Al-Azhar: A Millennium of Muslim Learning. (Illus.). 1974. 7.95 (ISBN 0-916808-11-4). Mid East Inst.
--Muslim Education in Medieval Times. LC 63-144. 1962. 3.75 (ISBN 0-916808-02-5). Mid East Inst.
Dodge, Bayard, tr. Fihrist of al-Nadim: A Tenth-Century Survey of Muslim Culture, 2 vols. LC 68-8874. (Records of Civilization Ser.). 114p. 1970. Set. 100.00x (ISBN 0-231-02925-X). Columbia U Pr.
Dodge, Bertha S. Cotton: The Plant That Would Be King. LC 83-23333. (Illus.). 187p. 1984. 14.95 (ISBN 0-292-76487-1). U of Tex Pr.
--The Road West: Saga of the Thirty Fifth Parallel. LC 79-21051. (Illus.). 222p. 1980. 15.95 (ISBN 0-8263-0526-1). U of NM Pr.
--Tales of Vermont Ways & People. LC 84-61170. (Illus.). 192p. 1984. pap. 5.95 (ISBN 0-933050-22-4). New Eng Pr VT.
Dodge, Bertha S., ed. Marooned. LC 78-24058. (Illus.). 278p. 1979. 14.95 (ISBN 0-8048-1481-3). C E Tuttle.
Dodge, C. W. Some Lichens of Tropical Africa IV: Dermatocarpaceae to Pertusariaceae. 1964. pap. 28.00 (ISBN 3-7682-5412-7). Lubrecht & Cramer.
--Some Lichens of Tropical Africa V: Lecanoraceae to Physiaceae. 1971. pap. 35.00 (ISBN 3-7682-5438-0). Lubrecht & Cramer.
Dodge, Calvert R., et al. Executive Communication Development, 2 Vols. (Illus.). 150p. 1983. Vol. 1. write for info. (ISBN 0-915159-00-7); Vol. 2. write for info. (ISBN 0-915159-01-5); facilitators guide avail. (ISBN 0-915159-02-3). Human Equat.
Dodge, Carroll W. Lichen Flora of the Antarctic Continent & Adjacent Islands. LC 73-82976. 496p. 1973. 40.00 (ISBN 0-914016-01-6). Phoenix Pub.
Dodge, Charlyne, ed. see Frederic, Harold.
Dodge, Clayton W. Numbers & Mathematics. 2nd ed. LC 74-31133. 1975. text ed. write for info. (ISBN 0-87150-180-5, PWS 1481, Prindle). PWS Pubs.
Dodge, Cole P. & Wiebe, Paul D., eds. Crisis in Uganda: The Breakdown of Health Services. (Illus.). 240p. 1985. 19.50 (ISBN 0-08-032682-X, Pub. by Aberdeen Scotland); pap. 11.00 (ISBN 0-08-032683-8, Pub. by Aberdeen Scotland). Pergamon.
Dodge, D. O. & Kyriss, S. E. Seamanship: Fundamentals for the Deck Officer. 2nd ed. LC 80-5684. (Fundamentals of Naval Science: Vol. 2). 272p. 1981. text ed. 16.95x (ISBN 0-87021-613-9). Naval Inst Pr.
Dodge, Daniel, jt. auth. see Griffen, Edmund.
Dodge, David L. War Inconsistent with the Religion of Jesus Christ. LC 75-137540. (Peace Movement in America Ser). xxiv, 168p. 1972. Repr. of 1905 ed. lib. bdg. 13.95x (ISBN 0-89198-067-9). Ozer.
Dodge, David L. & Martin, Walter T. Social Stress & Chronic Illness: Mortality Patterns in Industrial Society. LC 79-122051. 1970. 19.95x (ISBN 0-268-00435-8). U of Notre Dame Pr.
Dodge, David O. & Kyriss, S. E. Seamanship: Fundamentals for the Deck Officer. 2nd ed. (Illus.). 272p. 1981. 16.95 (ISBN 0-87021-613-9); bulk rates avail. Naval Inst Pr.
Dodge, Doris J. Agricultural Policy & Performance in Zambia: History, Prospects, & Proposals for Change. LC 77-620042. (Research Ser.: No. 32). (Illus.). 1977. pap. 4.95x (ISBN 0-87725-132-0). U of Cal Intl St.
Dodge, Douglas C., jt. auth. see Greenwood, Michael.
Dodge, Ed. Dau. 288p. 1984. pap. 3.50 (ISBN 0-425-07324-6). Berkley Pub.
--Dau: A Novel of Vietnam. 288p. 1984. 13.95 (ISBN 0-02-531990-6). Macmillan.
Dodge, Ernest S. Catalogue: Special Exhibition of the Saltonstall Family Portraits. 1962. pap. 1.00 (ISBN 0-87577-022-3). Peabody Mus Salem.
--Hawaiian & Other Polynesian Gourds. 1978. 5.00 (ISBN 0-914916-34-3). Topgallant.
--Islands & Empires: Western Impact on the Pacific & East Asia. LC 74-83131. (Europe & the World in the Age of Expansion Ser). 1978. pap. 5.95x (ISBN 0-8166-0853-9). U of Minn Pr.
--Islands & Empires: Western Inpact on the Pacific & East Asia. Shafer, Boyd, ed. LC 74-83131. (Europe & the World in the Age of Expansion Ser: Vol. 7). (Illus.). 1976. 17.50x (ISBN 0-8166-0788-5). U of Minn Pr.
--Morning Was Starlight: My Maine Boyhood. LC 80-82791. (Illus.). 216p. 1981. pap. 8.95 (ISBN 0-87106-047-7). Globe Pequot.
Dodge, Ernest S., ed. Thirty Years of the American Neptune. LC 72-82988. 1972. 20.00x (ISBN 0-674-88465-5). Harvard U Pr.
Dodge, Frederick W. How to Develop a Big Money-Making Export Business. (Illus.). 127p. 1984. 59.75x (ISBN 0-86654-108-X); pap. 19.75x (ISBN 0-86654-109-8). Inst Econ Finan.
Dodge, George A. A Whaling Voyage in the Pacific Ocean & Its Incidents. 30p. 1982. pap. 3.50 (ISBN 0-87770-243-8). Ye Galleon.
Dodge, Guy H. Benjamin Constant's Philosophy of Liberalism: A Study in Politics & Religion. LC 79-26784. xii, 194p. 1980. 18.00x (ISBN 0-8078-1433-4). U of NC Pr.
--The Political Theory of the Huguenots of the Dispersion. LC 79-159178. ix, 287p. 1971. Repr. of 1947 ed. lib. bdg. 20.00x (ISBN 0-374-92213-6). Octagon.
Dodge, Guy H., ed. Jean-Jacques Rousseau: Authoritarian Libertarian? LC 77-158944. (Problems in Political Science Ser.). 1972. pap. text ed. 2.95x (ISBN 0-669-74534-0). Heath.
Dodge, Gwen H., jt. auth. see Kneedler, Julia A.
Dodge, Harold F. & Romig, Harry G. Sampling Inspection Tables: Single & Double Sampling. 2nd ed. LC 59-6763. (Ser. in Probability & Mathematical Statistics). (Illus.). 224p. 1959. 40.95 (ISBN 0-471-21747-6, Pub. by Wiley-Interscience). Wiley.
Dodge, Howard. How to Prepare for the College Board Achievement Test - Mathematics Level II. LC 78-8655. 1979. pap. 7.95 (ISBN 0-8120-0325-X). Barron.
Dodge, J. A., ed. Topics in Paediatric Nutrition. 254p. 1983. text ed. 39.50 (ISBN 0-272-79699-9, Pitman Med. UK). Urban & S.
--Topics in Pediatric Gastroenterology. (Illus.). 1976. pap. text ed. 27.95x (ISBN 0-8464-0931-3). Beekman Pubs.
Dodge, James W., ed. Other Words, Other Worlds: Language in Culture. 1972. pap. 7.95x (ISBN 0-915432-72-2). NE Conf Teach Foreign.
--Sensitivity in the Foreign Language Classroom. Incl. Individualization of Instruction. Gougher, Ronald L; Interraction in the Foreign Language Class. Moskowitz, Gertrude; Teaching Spanish to the Native Spanish Speaker. LaFontaine, Herman. 142p. 1973. pap. 7.95x (ISBN 0-915432-73-0). NE Conf Teach Foreign.
Dodge, Jim. FUP. 1984. 7.95 (ISBN 0-671-50910-1). S&S.
Dodge, Joseph M. Cases & Materials on Federal Income Taxation: Principles, Policy & Planning. (American Casebook Ser.). 917p. 1985. text ed. 27.95 (ISBN 0-314-90283-X). West Pub.
--Federal Income Taxation: Principles, Policy & Planning, Cases & Materials on Teacher's Manual to Accompany. C ed. (American Casebook). 370p. 1985. pap. text ed. write for info. (ISBN 0-314-95572-0). West Pub.
--Federal Taxation of Estates, Trusts & Gifts, Principles & Planning. LC 81-11602. (American Casebook Ser.). 771p. 1981. 22.95 (ISBN 0-314-59848-0); supplement avail. (ISBN 0-314-69793-4). West Pub.
Dodge, Kirsten, et al, eds. Government & Business: Prospects for Partnership. (Symposia Ser.). 238p. 1980. pap. 8.50 (ISBN 0-89940-409-X). LBJ Sch Pub Aff.
Dodge, Louise, jt. auth. see Preston, Harriet W.
Dodge, Lowell, jt. auth. see Nader, Ralph.
Dodge, Marshall. Frost, You Say? A Yankee Monologue. LC 80-69082. (Illus.). 128p. 1980. pap. 7.95 (ISBN 0-89272-105-7). Down East.
Dodge, Marshall & Bryan, Robert. Bert I: Other Stories form Down East. Babbidge, Homer D., intro. by. (Illus.). 140p. (Orig.). 1981. 13.95 (ISBN 0-9607546-0-1); pap. 9.95. Bert & I Bks.
Dodge, Marshall J. & Howe, Walter. Frost, You Say? A Yankee Monologue. LC 73-83355. (Illus.). 128p. 1973. 12.95 (ISBN 0-85699-078-7). Chatham Pr.
Dodge, Martin, jt. auth. see Dodge, Venus.
Dodge, Mary A. Twelve Miles from a Lemon. facsimile ed. LC 76-37512. (Essay Index Reprint Ser). Repr. of 1873 ed. 20.00 (ISBN 0-8369-2544-0). Ayer Co Pubs.
--Wool-Gathering. text ed. 18.25 (ISBN 0-8369-9241-5, 9095). Ayer Co Pubs.
Dodge, Mary A., jt. auth. see Todd, John.
Dodge, Mary L. Sticks & Stones. (Orig.). 1979. pap. 1.75 (ISBN 0-532-23279-8). Woodhill.
Dodge, Mary M. Hans Brinker. (Illus.). (gr. 4-6). 1945-63. deluxe ed. 9.95 (ISBN 0-448-06011-6, G&D); Companion Lib. Ed. o.p. 2.95 (ISBN 0-448-05462-0). Putnam Pub Group.
--Hans Brinker. 1985. pap. 2.25 (ISBN 0-14-035042-X). Penguin.
--Hans Brinker. (gr. k-6). 1985. pap. 4.95 (ISBN 0-440-43446-7, Pub. by Yearling Classics). Dell.
--Hans Brinker, Or the Silver Skates. 15.95 (ISBN 0-89190-548-0, Pub. by Am Repr). Amereon Ltd.
--Hans Brinker: The Silver Skates. (Classics Ser). (gr. 5 up). pap. 1.50 (ISBN 0-8049-0099-X, CL-99). Airmont.
--Hans Brinker: The Silver Skates. 1982. Repr. lib. bdg. 16.95x (ISBN 0-89966-389-3). Buccaneer Bks.
--Mary Anne. LC 83-980. (Illus.). (ps-1). 1983. 10.25 (ISBN 0-688-02087-9); PLB 10.88 (ISBN 0-688-02089-5). Lothrop.
Dodge, Michael J. Star Trek: Voyage into Adventure. (A Which Way Bks.: No. 15). 128p. (Orig.). (gr. 3-6). 1984. pap. 2.95 (ISBN 0-671-50989-6). Archway.
Dodge, Nancy C. Thumpy's Story: A Story of Love & Grief Shared. LC 84-61293. (Illus.). 24p. (gr. k-12). 1985. pap. 5.95 (ISBN 0-918533-33-3). Prairie Lark.
Dodge, Natt N. One Hundred Desert Wildflowers in Natural Color. 8th ed. LC 63-13471. (Popular Ser.: No. 10). (Illus.). 1963. pap. 3.50 (ISBN 0-911408-42-8). SW Pks Mnmts.
--One Hundred Roadside Wildflowers of Southwest Uplands in Natural Color. 4th ed. LC 67-30422. (Popular Ser.: No. 12). (Illus.). 1967. pap. 3.50 (ISBN 0-911408-03-7). SW Pks Mnmts.
--Poisonous Dwellers of the Desert. 17th ed. LC 75-187220. (Popular Ser.: No. 3). 1976. pap. 2.00 (ISBN 0-911408-26-6). SW Pks Mnmts.
Dodge, Natt N. & Janish, Jeanne R. Flowers of the Southwest Deserts. 10th ed. LC 72-92509. (Popular Ser.: No. 4). (Illus.). 1976. pap. 2.50 (ISBN 0-911408-45-2). SW Pks Mnmts.

Dodge, Nicholas A. A Climbing Guide to Oregon. LC 75-16654. (Illus.). 1975. pap. 8.95 (ISBN 0-911518-33-9). Touchstone Pr Ore.

Dodge, Norton & Hilton, Alison, eds. New Art from the Soviet Union: The Known & the Unknown. LC 77-13442. (Illus.). 1977. 24.50 (ISBN 0-87491-209-1). Acropolis.

Dodge, Norton T. Women in the Soviet Economy: Their Role in Economic, Scientific, & Technical Development. LC 76-57945. (Illus.). 1977. Repr. of 1966 ed. lib. bdg. 25.75x (ISBN 0-8371-9467-9, DOWS). Greenwood.

Dodge, Peter, ed. A Documentary Study of Hendrik De Man, Socialist Critic of Marxism. LC 78-70288. 1979. 38.00 (ISBN 0-691-03123-1). Princeton U Pr.

Dodge, R. N., jt. auth. see Clark, S. K.

Dodge, Raymond. Conditions & Consequences of Human Variability. 1931. 49.50x (ISBN 0-685-69812-2). Elliots Bks.

Dodge, Raymond & Kahn, Eugen. The Craving for Superiority. 1931. 32.50 (ISBN 0-686-51366-5). Elliots Bks.

Dodge, Raymond see Rowland, Eleanor H.

Dodge, Richard, jt. auth. see Casty, Alan.

Dodge, Richard H. How to Read & Write in College: A Complete Course, 4 forms. (Orig.). Form 2, 1964. pap. text ed. 12.00 scp (ISBN 0-06-041661-0, HarpC); Form 4, 1970. pap. text ed. 12.80 scp (ISBN 0-06-041663-7); Form 5, 1973. pap. text ed. 14.00 scp (ISBN 0-06-041664-5); Form 6, 1980. pap. text ed. 13.00 scp (ISBN 0-06-041657-2); pap. text ed. achievement tests & short quizzes avail. Har-Row.

--How to Read & Write in College: A Complete Course. (Second Ser.: Form 1). 264p. 1983. pap. text ed. 11.50 scp (ISBN 0-06-041668-8, HarpC); master key avail. (ISBN 0-06-361689-0); Ach Test M avail. (ISBN 0-06-361688-2); Ach Test N avail. (ISBN 0-06-361687-4). Har-Row.

Dodge, Richard I. Black Hills. (Illus.). Repr. 8.75 (ISBN 0-87018-014-2). Ross.

--Our Wild Indians: Thirty Three Years' Personal Experience Among the Red Men of the Great West. (Select Bibliographies Reprint Ser). 1882. 55.00 (ISBN 0-8369-5230-8). Ayer Co Pubs.

--Our Wild Indians: Thirty Three Years Personal Experience Among the Red Men of the Great West. 657p. 1978. Repr. of 1883 ed. 24.95 (ISBN 0-87928-089-1). Corner Hse.

Dodge, Robert J. Isolated Splendor: Put-in-Bay & South Bass Island. (YA) 1975. 10.00 (ISBN 0-682-48233-1, Lochinvar). Exposition Pr FL.

Dodge, Robert K. & McCullough, Jos. B. New & Old Voices of Wah'Kon-Tah. LC 85-14445. 176p. 1985. pap. 4.95 (ISBN 0-7178-0629-4); 9.50 (ISBN 0-7178-0630-8). Intl Pubs Co.

Dodge, Robert K. & McCullough, Joseph B., eds. Voices from Wah'kon-Tah: Contemporary Poetry of Native Americans. LC 74-1321. 144p. 1974. pap. 2.75 (ISBN 0-7178-0417-8). Intl Pubs Co.

Dodge, Roy L. Michigan Ghost Towns, Vol. 1. (Illus.). 191p. (Orig.). 5.00 (ISBN 0-934884-01-3). Glenson Pub.

--Michigan Ghost Towns, Vol. 2. (Illus.). 120p. (Orig.). 5.50 (ISBN 0-934884-03-X). Glenson Pub.

--Michigan Ghost Towns, Vol. 3. (Orig.). write for info. (ISBN 0-934884-02-1). Glenson Pub.

Dodge, Steve. Abaco: The History of an Out Island & Its Cays. LC 83-70072. 182p. 1984. pap. 12.50 (ISBN 0-932265-00-6). White Sound.

Dodge, Steve & Malone, Vernon. A Guide & History of Hope Town. (Illus.). 56p. (Orig.). 1985. pap. 3.95 (ISBN 0-932265-01-4). White Sound.

Dodge, Theodore A. Napoleon: A History of the Art of War, 4 Vols. Repr. of 1907 ed. Set. 140.00 (ISBN 0-404-02160-3); 35.00 ea. Vol. 1 (ISBN 0-404-02161-1). Vol. 2 (ISBN 0-404-02162-X). Vol. 3 (ISBN 0-404-02163-8). Vol. 4 (ISBN 0-404-02164-6). AMS Pr.

Dodge, Tom. A Literature of Sports. 1980. pap. text ed. 14.95 (ISBN 0-669-02744-8). Heath.

Dodge, Venus. Making Old-Fashioned Dolls. LC 84-26788. (Illus.). 160p. 1985. 19.95 (ISBN 0-317-17085-6); pap. 9.95 (ISBN 0-8069-7974-7). Sterling.

Dodge, Venus & Dodge, Martin. The Doll's House Do-It Yourself Book. LC 82-19486. (Illus.). 224p. 1983. pap. 9.95 (ISBN 0-8069-7710-8). Sterling.

Dodge, Venus A. Making Collector's Dolls. (Illus.). 168p. 1984. 18.95 (ISBN 0-8069-5506-6); pap. 9.95 (ISBN 0-8069-7800-7). Sterling.

Dodge, Walter P. Piers Gaveston: A Chapter of Early Constitutional History. LC 74-173161. (Illus.). Repr. of 1899 ed. 20.00 (ISBN 0-405-08451-X, Blom Pubns). Ayer Co Pubs.

Dodge, William. Skilled Labour Supply Imbalances: The Canadian Experience. LC 77-93071. (British-North American Committee Ser.). 56p. 1977. 3.00 (ISBN 0-902594-31-1). Natl Planning.

Dodge, Y. Analysis of Experiments with Missing Data. (Probability & Mathematical Statistics Ser.). 492p. 1985. write for info. (ISBN 0-471-88736-6). Wiley.

Dodge, Yadolah, jt. auth. see Arthanari, Subramanyam.

Dodgeson, K. S., et al, eds. Sulfates of Microbial Origin, Vols. 1 & 2. 1982. Vol. 1, 216p. 59.00 (ISBN 0-8493-6035-8); Vol. 2, 208p. 59.00 (ISBN 0-8493-6036-6). CRC Pr.

Dodgshon, R. A. & Butlin, R. A., eds. An Historical Geography of England & Wales. 1978. 55.00 (ISBN 0-12-219250-8); pap. 24.00 (ISBN 0-12-219252-4). Acad Pr.

Dodgshon, Robert A. Land & Society in Early Scotland. (Illus.). 1982. 57.00x (ISBN 0-19-822660-8). Oxford U Pr.

--The Origin of British Field Systems: An Interpretation. LC 80-49987. 1980. 35.00 (ISBN 0-12-219260-5). Acad Pr.

Dodgson, Campbell. Albrecht Durer: Engravings & Etchings. LC 67-27451. (Graphic Art Ser). 1967. Repr. of 1926 ed. 29.50 (ISBN 0-306-70976-7). Da Capo.

Dodgson, Charles L. The Diaries of Lewis Carroll, 2 vols. Green, Roger L., ed. & suppl. by. LC 74-110268. (Illus.). Repr. of 1954 ed. lib. bdg. 55.00x (ISBN 0-8371-4494-9, DOLC). Greenwood.

--Lewis Carroll Picture Book: A Selection from the Unpublished Writings & Drawings of Lewis Carroll, Together with Reprints from Scarce & Unacknowledged Work. LC 70-159931. (Tower Bks). (Illus.). 1971. Repr. of 1899 ed. 40.00x (ISBN 0-8103-3915-3). Gale.

Dodgson, Charles L. see Carroll, Lewis, pseud.

Dodgson, Charles L. see Carrol, Lewis.

Dodgson, Hazel, jt. auth. see Payne, Christian.

Dodi, Andrea, jt. auth. see Giusti-Lanham, Hedy.

Dodin, Jean-Daniel. Enter. Jarett, Keith, ed. Dodin, Mary-Denise, tr. from Fr. LC 84-51380. 142p. 1984. pap. text ed. 12.95 (ISBN 0-9612174-2-1). Synthetix.

--Inside the HP-41. Holes, W. W., ed. Dodin, Mary D., tr. from Fr. LC 84-51921. 256p. 1985. pap. text ed. 18.95 (ISBN 0-9612174-4-8). Synthetix.

Dodin, Mary D., tr. see Dodin, Jean-Daniel.

Dodin, Mary-Denise, tr. see Dodin, Jean-Daniel.

Dodrill, Charles T. Heritage of a Pioneer. 1967. 18.00 (ISBN 0-87012-029-8). McClain.

Dodrill, William. Moccasin Tracks & Other Imprints. 1974. Repr. of 1915 ed. 16.00 (ISBN 0-87012-157-X). McClain.

Dods, John B. Philosophy of Electrical Psychology. (Hypnosis & Altered States of Consciousness Ser.). 252p. 1982. Repr. of 1850 ed. lib. bdg. 29.50 (ISBN 0-306-76077-0). Da Capo.

Dods, Marcus. Bible. (Select Bibliographies Reprint Ser.). 1972. Repr. of 1905 ed. 18.00 (ISBN 0-8369-6876-X). Ayer Co Pubs.

--Forerunners of Dante. 275p. 1981. Repr. of 1903 ed. lib. bdg. 35.00 (ISBN 0-89987-162-3). Darby Bks.

--Later Letters of Marcus Dods, D. D. 1895-1909. 1911. 25.00 (ISBN 0-932062-46-6). Sharon Hill.

--The Prayer That Teaches to Pray. LC 80-82323. (Shepherd Illustrated Classics Ser.). (Illus.). 1980. pap. 5.95 (ISBN 0-87983-232-0). Keats.

Dods, Marcus, tr. see St. Augustine.

Dodsley, Robert. A Collection of Poems, 6 vols. LC 78-144978. 1972. Repr. 40.00 ea.; Set. 195.00x (ISBN 0-686-66734-4). Scholarly.

Dodsley, Robert, ed. Select Collection of Old English Plays, 15 Vols. in 7. LC 64-14702. Repr. of 1876 ed. Set. 305.00 (ISBN 0-405-08452-8, Blom Pubns); 44.00 ea. Vol. 1 (ISBN 0-405-08453-6). Vol. 2 (ISBN 0-405-08454-4). Vol. 3 (ISBN 0-405-08455-2). Vol. 4 (ISBN 0-405-08456-0). Vol. 5 (ISBN 0-405-08457-9). Vol. 6 (ISBN 0-405-08458-7). Vol. 7 (ISBN 0-405-08459-5). Ayer Co Pubs.

Dodsley, Robert, ed. see Aesopus.

Dodson, Bert. Keys to Drawing. (Illus.). 224p. 1985. 19.95 (ISBN 0-89134-113-7). North Light Pub.

Dodson, Bert, illus. Lazy Jack. LC 78-18070. (Illus.). 32p. (gr. k-4). 1979. PLB 7.89 (ISBN 0-89375-123-5); pap. 1.95 (ISBN 0-89375-101-4). Troll Assocs.

Dodson, C. T. & Poston, T. Tensor Geometry: The Geometric Viewpoint & Its Uses. (Reference Works in Mathematics Ser.: No. 1). (Illus.). 620p. 1979. pap. 33.95 (ISBN 0-273-01040-9). Pitman Pub MA.

Dodson, Calaway H., jt. auth. see Van Der Pijl, L.

Dodson, Carleen, jt. auth. see McAdam, Robert E.

Dodson, Carolyn see Arnberger, Leslie P.

Dodson, Carolyn, ed. see Meketa, Charles & Meketa, Jacqueline.

Dodson, Carolyn, ed. see Trimble, Stephen.

Dodson, Carolyn, ed. see Viele, Catherine W.

Dodson, Carolyn R. Horoscopes of U.S. States & Cities. 216p. 1976. 9.95 (ISBN 0-86690-079-9, 1077-01). Am Fed Astrologers.

--Rising Signs. 120p. 1979. 8.00 (ISBN 0-86690-034-9, 2405-01). Am Fed Astrologers.

Dodson, Dan W. New Challenges to Social Agency Leadership. Grossman, Arnold H., ed. LC 76-330. (Groupwork Today Seminar Series). 75p. 1976. pap. text ed. 4.45 (ISBN 0-916068-02-1). Groupwork Today.

Dodson, Daniel B. Dancers in the Dark. 288p. 1983. 15.95 (ISBN 0-396-08148-7). Dodd.

--Malcolm Lowry. LC 70-126542. (Columbia Essays on Modern Writers Ser.: No. 51). 48p. (Orig.). 1970. pap. 2.50 (ISBN 0-231-03244-7). Columbia U Pr.

Dodson, E. O. The Phenomenon of Man Revisited: A Biological Viewpoint on Teilhard de Chardin. (Illus.). 288p. 1984. 25.00x (ISBN 0-231-05850-0). Columbia U Pr.

Dodson, Edward O. & Dodson, Peter. Evolution: Process & Product. 3rd ed. 1985. text ed. write for info. (ISBN 0-87150-826-5, 40N4601, Prindle). PWS Pubs.

Dodson, Fitzhugh. Give Your Child a Head Start in Reading. 192p. 1981. pap. 6.95 (ISBN 0-671-43641-4, Fireside). S&S.

--How to Discipline with Love. 1978. pap. 3.95 (ISBN 0-451-12211-9, AE2211, Sig). NAL.

--How to Father. 1975. pap. 4.50 (ISBN 0-451-13361-7, AE2701, Sig). NAL.

--How to Parent. 444p. 1973. pap. 3.95 (ISBN 0-451-11908-8, AE1908, Sig). NAL.

--I Wish I Had a Computer That Makes Waffles: Teaching Your Child with Modern Nursery Rhymes. LC 78-13178. (Illus.). 1978. Oak Tree Pubns.

Dodson, Fitzhugh & Alexander, Ann. Your Child: Pregnancy Through Preschool. (Illus.). 416p. 1983. pap. 12.95 (ISBN 0-671-45894-9, Fireside). S&S.

Dodson, Fitzhugh & Reuben, Paul. How to Grandparent. 1982. pap. 6.95 (ISBN 0-452-25329-2, Plume). NAL.

Dodson, Fitzhugh & Reuben, Paula. The Carnival Kidnap Caper. LC 79-20260. (gr. 5-9). 1979. 7.95 (ISBN 0-916392-40-6). Oak Tree Pubns.

--How to Grandparent. 1984. pap. 3.95 (ISBN 0-451-13129-0, Sig). NAL.

Dodson, Fitzhugh & Ruben, Paula. How to Grandparent. LC 80-7849. 304p. 1981. 13.41i (ISBN 0-690-01874-6, HarpT). Har-Row.

Dodson, George R. Bergson & the Modern Spirit. 1976. lib. bdg. 59.95 (ISBN 0-8490-1489-1). Gordon Pr.

Dodson, Guy, et al, eds. Structural Studies on Molecules of Biological Interest: A Volume in Honour of Professor Dorothy Hodgkin. (Illus.). 1981. 42.50x (ISBN 0-19-855362-5). Oxford U Pr.

Dodson, James. The Accountant, Or, the Method of Bookkeeping Deducted from Clear Principles, & Illustrated by a Variety of Examples. LC 82-48383. (Accounting History & the Development of a Profession Ser.). 230p. 1984. lib. bdg. 30.00 (ISBN 0-8240-6323-6). Garland Pub.

Dodson, Jualynne E. An Afrocentric Educational Manual: Toward a Non-Deficit Perspective in Services to Families & Children. 169p. 10.00 (ISBN 0-686-40917-5). U of Tenn Sch.

Dodson, Laura S. & Kurpius, DeWayne. Family Counseling: A Systems Approach. LC 76-46908. 158p. 1977. 9.95x (ISBN 0-915202-08-5). Accel Devel.

Dodson, Leonidas. Alexander Spotswood, Governor of Colonial Virginia, 1710-22. LC 76-91784. (BCL Ser. I). (Illus.). Repr. of 1932 ed. 24.50 (ISBN 0-404-02141-7). AMS Pr.

Dodson, Margery. The Cup of My Hand. (Contemporary Poets of Dorrance Ser.). 64p. 1982. 6.95 (ISBN 0-8059-2832-4). Dorrance.

Dodson, Owen. Boy at the Window. 212p. 1972. Repr. of 1951 ed. 7.50x (ISBN 0-911860-10-X). Chatham Bkseller.

--The Confession Stone. (Heritage Ser). 1970. pap. 2.50x (ISBN 0-685-26075-5). Broadside.

Dodson, Pat, ed. see Campbell, Richard L.

Dodson, Peter, jt. auth. see Dodson, Edward O.

Dodson, Reynolds. Urban Renewal. LC 82-45103. 312p. 1984. 15.95 (ISBN 0-385-18194-9). Doubleday.

Dodson, Rita. Life, Love & God. 1982. 4.95 (ISBN 0-533-04647-5). Vantage.

Dodson, Susan. The Creep. (gr. 7-9). 1980. pap. 1.95 (ISBN 0-671-56087-5). Archway.

--Medical Office Applications Using Your Epson. 1985. pap. 19.95 (ISBN 0-8359-4492-1). Reston.

--Shadows Across the Sand. LC 83-5469. (Illus.). 224p. (gr. 6 up). 1983. 10.25 (ISBN 0-688-02426-2). Lothrop.

--Shadows Across the Sand. (gr. 7 up). pap. 2.25 (ISBN 0-317-13276-8, Juniper). Fawcett.

Dodson, Susanne. Microform Research Collections. 2nd ed. 800p. 1984. 125.00 (ISBN 0-930466-66-7). Meckler Pub.

Dodson, Suzanne C. Microform Research Collections: A Guide. (Microform Review Series in Library Micrographics Management: No. 8). 1978. 35.00x (ISBN 0-913672-21-1). Microform Rev.

Dodsworth, Martin. Hamlet Closely Observed. LC 85-6151. 322p. 1985. 36.00 (ISBN 0-485-11283-3, Pub. by Athlone Pr Ltd). Longwood Pub Group.

Dodsworth, Roger. Glass & Glass Making. (Shire Album Ser.: No. 83). (Illus.). 32p. 1982. pap. 2.95 (ISBN 0-85263-585-0, Pub. by Shire Pubns England). Seven Hills Bks.

Dodsworth, T. L. Beef Production. 100p. 1972. pap. text ed. 8.50 (ISBN 0-08-017017-X). Pergamon.

Dodu, Gaston J. Histoire des institutions monarchiques dans le Royaume latin de Jerusalem, 1099-1291. LC 76-29820. (Fr.). Repr. of 1894 ed. 32.50 (ISBN 0-404-15415-8). AMS Pr.

Dodwell, Barbara, ed. Feet of Fines for the County of Norfolk for the 10th Year of the Reign of Richard, 1198-1199, & for the First Four Years of the Reign of King John, 199-1202. (Pipe Roll Society, London, Ser.: No. 2, Vol. 27). Repr. of 1952 ed. 48.00 (ISBN 0-317-16217-9). Kraus Repr.

--Feet of Fines for the County of Norfolk, 1201-1215 & Suffolk, 1199-1214. (Pipe Roll Society, London, Ser.: No. 2, Vol. 32). Repr. of 1958 ed. 60.00 (ISBN 0-317-16224-1). Kraus Repr.

Dodwell, C. R. Anglo-Saxon Art: A New Perspective. (Illus.). 368p. 1982. 49.50x (ISBN 0-8014-1516-0). Cornell U Pr.

--Anglo-Saxon Art: A New Perspective. LC 82-71592. (Illus.). 368p. (Orig.). 1985. pap. text ed. 19.95x (ISBN 0-8014-9300-5). Cornell U Pr.

Dodwell, C. R. see Malone, Kemp & Schibsbye, Knud.

Dodwell, G. T. Encyclopedia of Canaries. (Illus.). 288p. 1976. 19.95 (ISBN 0-87666-952-6, H-967). TFH Pubns.

--The Lizard Canary & Other Rare Breeds. 200p. 1983. 15.95 (ISBN 0-86230-052-5). Triplegate.

Dodwell, Henry. Dupleix & Clive: Beginning of Empire. new ed. 277p. 1967. 29.50x (ISBN 0-7146-1125-5, F Cass Co). Biblio Dist.

Dodwell, Henry H. The Founder of Modern Egypt. LC 74-15029. (BCL Ser. II). Repr. of 1931 ed. 22.50 (ISBN 0-404-12036-9). AMS Pr.

Dodwell Marketing Consultants. Industrial Groupings in Japan, 1982-83. rev. ed. LC 78-324735. (Illus.). 529p. 1982. pap. 335.00x (ISBN 0-8002-3032-9). Intl Pubns Serv.

Dodwell, P. C. Painting in Europe 800-1200. (Pelican History of Art Ser.: No. 34). (Illus.). 1971. 50.00 (ISBN 0-670-53632-6, Pelican). Viking.

Dodwell, Peter C. & Caelli, Terrence M., eds. Figural Synthesis. 320p. 1984. 34.95 (ISBN 0-89859-382-4). L Erlbaum Assocs.

Dody, Sandford, jt. auth. see Hayes, Helen.

Doe, Andrew, jt. auth. see Tobler, John.

Doe, B. R. & Smith, D. K., eds. Studies in Mineralogy & Precambrian Geology: A Volume in Honor of John W. Gruner. LC 70-190173. (Geological Society of America Memoir Ser.: No. 135). pap. 93.00 (ISBN 0-317-30052-0, 2025029). Bks Demand UMI.

Doe, Brian D. Monuments of South Arabia. (Arabia Past & Present Ser: Vol. 12). (Illus.). 320p. 1984. 75.00 (ISBN 0-900891-17-3). Oleander Pr.

Doe, Bruce R. Lead Isotopes. LC 70-124067. (Minerals, Rocks & Inorganic Materials: Vol. 3). (Illus.). 1970. 26.00 (ISBN 0-387-05205-4). Springer-Verlag.

Doe, Jane. Alcoholism-One Family's Story. 1978. pap. 4.50 (ISBN 0-8309-0231-7). Herald Hse.

Doe, Maryann & Warlum, Michael. Business Mathematics: A Positive Approach. 1982. pap. text ed. 20.60x (ISBN 0-673-16011-4). Scott F.

Doe, Paul. Tallis. 2nd ed. (Oxford Studies of Composers). (Illus.). 1976. pap. 8.95x (ISBN 0-19-314122-1). Oxford U Pr.

Doe, Paula. A Warbler's Song in the Dusk: The Life & Writings of Otomo Yakamochi. LC 80-29236. 180p. (Japanese.). 1982. 30.00x (ISBN 0-520-04346-4). U of Cal Pr.

DOE Technical Information Center. Acid Precipitation: A Compilation of Worldwide Literature-A Bibliography. 732p. 1983. pap. 30.00 (ISBN 0-87079-500-7, DOE/TIC-3399); microfiche 4.50 (ISBN 0-87079-501-5, DOE/TIC-3399). DOE.

--Appropriate Technology: A Bibliography. 59p. 1981. 10.00 (ISBN 0-87079-137-0, DOE/TIC-3385); microfiche 4.50 (ISBN 0-87079-406-X, DOE/TIC-3385). DOE.

--Carbon Dioxide & Climate: A Bibliography, July 1976 through June 1981. 170p. 1981. 12.25 (ISBN 0-87079-391-8, DOE/TIC-3382-R1); microfiche 4.50 (ISBN 0-87079-408-6, DOE/TIC-3382-R1). DOE.

--Coal Desulfurization: A Bibliography. 510p. 1983. pap. 24.75 (ISBN 0-87079-514-7, DOE/TIC-3400); microfiche 4.50 (ISBN 0-87079-515-5, DOE/TIC-3400). DOE.

--Coal Processing: Production & Properties-A Bibliography. 570p. 1976. pap. 40.00 (ISBN 0-87079-386-1, TID-3349-S1P2); microfiche 4.50 (ISBN 0-87079-450-7, TID-3349-S1P2). DOE.

--Coal Production Expansion: A Selected Bibliography. 55p. 1980. pap. 10.00 (ISBN 0-87079-166-4, DOE/TIC-3381); microfiche 4.50 (ISBN 0-87079-411-6, DOE/TIC-3381). DOE.

--Computer Codes: A Bibliography. 925p. 1981. pap. 25.00 (ISBN 0-87079-394-2, DOE/TIC-3386); microfiche 4.50 (ISBN 0-87079-412-4, DOE/TIC-3386). DOE.

--Cooling Towers: A Bibliography, Supplement 4. 120p. 1980. pap. 13.00 (ISBN 0-87079-173-7, DOE/TIC-3360 (SUPPL. 4)); microfiche 4.50 (ISBN 0-87079-414-0, DOE/TIC-3360 (SUPPL. 4)). DOE.

--Cooling Towers: A Bibliography, Supplement 5. 88p. 1981. pap. 11.50 (ISBN 0-87079-174-5, DOE/TIC-3360 (SUPPL. 5)); microfiche 4.50 (ISBN 0-87079-415-9, DOE/TIC-3360 (SUPPL. 5)). DOE.

--Electric Batteries: A Bibliography. 779p. 1978. pap. 31.50 (ISBN 0-87079-185-0, TID-3361); microfiche 4.50 (ISBN 0-87079-416-7, TID-3361). DOE.

--Energy: Social & Economic Aspects: A Bibliography. (DOE Technical Information). 956p. 1980. 36.00 (ISBN 0-87079-192-3, DOE/TIC-3383); microfiche 4.50 (ISBN 0-87079-418-3, DOE/TIC-3383). DOE.

--Engineering Materials: A Bibliography. 57p. 1982. pap. 10.00 (ISBN 0-87079-488-4, DOE/TIC-4628); microfiche 4.50 (ISBN 0-87079-489-2, DOE/TIC-4628). Doe.

--Fuel Cells: A Bibliography, June 1977 to June 1980. 243p. 1980. pap. 16.00 (ISBN 0-87079-211-3, DOE/TIC-3359 (SUPPL. 1)); microfiche 4.50 (ISBN 0-87079-421-3, DOE/TIC-3359 (SUPPL. 1)). DOE.

--Fuel Cells: A Bibliography, Mid-Sixties through 1976. 416p. 1977. 31.00 (ISBN 0-87079-210-5, TID-3359); microfiche 4.50 (ISBN 0-87079-420-5, TID-3359). DOE.

--Gas-Cooled Reactor Technology: A Bibliography July 1976 Through December 1977. 393p. 1978. pap. 19.75 (ISBN 0-87079-239-3, TID-3339-S2); microfiche 4.50 (ISBN 0-87079-422-1, TID-3339-S2). DOE.

--Gas-Cooled Reactor Technology: A Bibliography January 1978 Through June 1981. 763p. 1981. pap. 31.00 (ISBN 0-87079-363-2, DOE/TIC-3339 (SUPPL. 3)); microfiche 4.50 (ISBN 0-87079-423-X, DOE/TIC-3339 (SUPPL. 3)). DOE.

--Hydrogen Fuels: A Bibliography: Supplement 1. 701p. 1981. pap. 29.50 (ISBN 0-87079-242-3, DOE/TIC-3358 (SUPPL. 1)); microfiche 4.50 (ISBN 0-87079-426-4, DOE/TIC-3358 (SUPPL. 1)). DOE.

--Liquid Metal Fast Breeder Reactors: A Bibliography, January to December 1977. 518p. 1978. pap. 25.00 (ISBN 0-87079-362-4, TID-3333-S5); microfiche 4.50 (ISBN 0-87079-427-2, TID-3333-S5). DOE.

--Liquid Metal Fast Breeder Reactors: A Bibliography, Supplement 6, January 1978 to August 1980, 2 vols. 1196p. 1980. pap. 42.00 (ISBN 0-87079-361-6, DOE/TIC-3333 (SUPPL. 6)); microfiche 4.50 (ISBN 0-87079-428-0, DOE/TIC-3333 (SUPPL. 6)). DOE.

--Low-Level Radiation: Biological Interactions, Risks & Benefits, A Bibliography. 731p. 1978. pap. 30.25 (ISBN 0-87079-360-8, TID-3373); microfiche 4.50 (ISBN 0-87079-429-9, TID-3373). DOE.

--Nuclear Medicine: A Bibliography, 2 vols. 1978. Vol. 1, 677p. pap. 29.00 microfiche (ISBN 0-87079-365-9, TID-3319-58-P1); Vol. 2, 665p. pap. 28.75 (ISBN 0-87079-366-7); microfiche 4.50 (ISBN 0-87079-434-5, TID-3319-58-P1). DOE.

--Nuclear Quality Assurance: A Bibliography. 80p. 1978. pap. 11.50 (ISBN 0-87079-392-6, TID-3374); microfiche 4.50 (ISBN 0-87079-435-3, TID-3374). DOE.

--Nuclear Raw Materials: A Selected Bibliography. 48p. 1976. pap. 8.50 (ISBN 0-87079-367-5, TID-3357); microfiche 4.50 (ISBN 0-87079-436-1, TID-3357). DOE.

--Occupational Health Aspects of Uranium: A Selected Bibliography, 1948 to 1976. 129p. 1977. pap. 14.50 (ISBN 0-87079-368-3, TID-3352); microfiche 4.50 (ISBN 0-87079-437-X, TID-3352). DOE.

--Oil Shales & Tar Sands: A Bibliography. 744p. 1977. 30.50 (ISBN 0-87079-369-1, TID-3367); microfiche 4.50 (ISBN 0-87079-439-6, TID-3367). DOE.

--Oil Shales & Tar Sands: A Bibliography. 973p. 1981. pap. 36.25 (ISBN 0-87079-390-X, DOE/TIC-3367 (SUPPL. 1)); microfiche 4.50 (ISBN 0-87079-440-X, DOE/TIC-3367 (SUPPL. 1)). DOE.

--Oil Shales: Selected Bibliography of DOE Sponsored Research. 126p. 1980. pap. 14.50 (ISBN 0-87079-370-5, DOE/TIC-3378); microfiche 4.50 (ISBN 0-87079-438-8, DOE/TIC-3378). DOE.

--Patents (DOE) Available for Licensing: A Bibliography Covering January 1974 Through December 1980. 284p. 1982. pap. 17.00 (ISBN 0-87079-445-0, DOE/TIC-3398); microfiche 4.50 (ISBN 0-87079-456-6, DOE/TIC-3398). DOE.

--Patents (DOE) Available for Licensing: A Bibliography for the Period 1966-1974. 60p. 1983. pap. 9.25 (ISBN 0-87079-512-0, DOE/TIC-3398 SUPPL. 1); microfiche 4.50 (ISBN 0-87079-513-9, DOE/TIC-3398 SUPPL. 1). DOE.

--Radioactive Waste Management: Airborne Radioactive Effluents: Releases & Processing: A Bibliography. 244p. 1982. pap. 16.00 (ISBN 0-87079-479-5, DOE/TIC-3397); microfiche 4.50 (ISBN 0-87079-480-9, DOE/TIC-3397). DOE.

--Radioactive Waste Management: Decontamination & Decommissioning: Bibliography. 126p. 1982. pap. 13.00 (ISBN 0-87079-484-1, DOE/TIC-3391); microfiche 4.50 (ISBN 0-87079-485-X, DOE/TIC-3391). DOE.

--Radioactive Waste Management: Formerly Utilized Sites-Remedial Action: A Bibliography. 47p. 1982. pap. 8.50 (ISBN 0-87079-486-8, DOE/TIC-3392); microfiche 4.50 (ISBN 0-87079-487-6, DOE/TIC-3392). DOE.

--Radioactive Waste Management: High-Level Radioactive Wastes: A Bibliography. 246p. 1982. pap. 16.25 (ISBN 0-87079-475-2, DOE/TIC-3389); microfiche 4.50 (ISBN 0-87079-476-0, DOE/TIC-3389). DOE.

--Radioactive Waste Management: Low-Level Radioactive Waste: A Bibliography Covering January Through December 1982. 144p. 1983. pap. 14.50 (ISBN 0-87079-502-3, DOE/TIC-3387 (SUPPL. 1)); microfiche 4.50 (ISBN 0-87079-503-1, DOE/TIC-3387 (SUPPL. 1)). DOE.

--Radioactive Waste Management: Low-Level Radioactive Waste: A Bibliography. 183p. 1984. pap. 12.50 (ISBN 0-87079-524-4, DOE-TIC-3387 SUPPL. 2); microfiche 4.50 (ISBN 0-87079-525-2, DOE-TIC-3387 SUPPL. 2). DOE.

--Radioactive Waste Management: Nuclear Fuel Cycle Reprocessing: A Bibliography. 248p. 1982. pap. 16.25 (ISBN 0-87079-506-6, DOE/TIC-3396); microfiche 4.50 (ISBN 0-87079-507-4, DOE/TIC-3396). DOE.

--Radioactive Waste Management: Radioactive Waste Inventories & Projections: A Bibliography. 18p. 1982. pap. 7.00 (ISBN 0-87079-490-6, DOE/TIC-3394); microfiche 4.50 (ISBN 0-87079-491-4, DOE/TIC-3394). DOE.

--Radioactive Waste Management: Spent Fuel Storage: A Bibliography. 154p. 1982. pap. 12.00 (ISBN 0-87079-477-9, DOE/TIC-3395); microfiche 4.50 (ISBN 0-87079-478-7, DOE/TIC-3395). DOE.

--Radioactive Waste Management: Transuranic Wastes: A Bibliography. 146p. 1982. pap. 14.50 (ISBN 0-87079-481-7, DOE/TIC-3390); microfiche 4.50 (ISBN 0-87079-482-5, DOE/TIC-3390). DOE.

--Radioactive Waste Management: Uranium Mill Tailings: A Bibliography. 105p. 1982. pap. 13.00 (ISBN 0-87079-492-2, DOE/TIC-3393); microfiche 4.50 (ISBN 0-87079-493-0, DOE/TIC-3393). DOE.

--Radioactive Waste Management: Waste Isolation: A Bibliography. 295p. 1982. pap. 17.50 (ISBN 0-87079-504-X, DOE/TIC-3388); microfiche 4.50 (ISBN 0-87079-505-8, DOE/TIC-3388). DOE.

--Radioactive Waste Processing & Disposal: A Bibliography Covering June 1976 Through August 1978. 942p. 1980. pap. 35.50 (ISBN 0-87079-371-3, NUREG-0643 (TID-3311-S8)); microfiche 4.50 (ISBN 0-87079-441-8, NUREG-0643 (TID-3311-S8)). DOE.

--Radioactive Waste Processing & Disposal: A Bibliography Covering January 1981 Through December 1981. 855p. 1982. pap. 33.50 (ISBN 0-87079-395-0, DOE/TIC-3311-S11); microfiche 4.50 (ISBN 0-87079-460-4, DOE/TIC-3311-S11). DOE.

--Radioactive Waste Processing & Disposal: A Bibliography Covering January 1982 Through December 1982. 1122p. 1983. pap. 40.00 (ISBN 0-87079-508-2, DOE/TIC-311-S12); microfiche 4.50 (ISBN 0-87079-509-0, DOE/TIC-3311-S12). DOE.

--Radioactive Waste Processing & Disposal: A Bibliography Covering November 1979 Through December 1980. 900p. 1981. 34.50 (ISBN 0-87079-372-1, NUREG-0644(TID-3311-S9)); microfiche 4.50 (ISBN 0-87079-442-6, NUREG-0644(TID-3311-S9)). DOE.

--Radioactive Waste Processing & Disposal: A Bibliography Covering September 1978 Through November 1979. 883p. 1980. 34.00 (ISBN 0-87079-373-X, DOE/TIC-3311-S10); microfiche 4.50 (ISBN 0-87079-443-4, DOE/TIC-3311-S10). DOE.

--Reactor Safety: A Bibliography Covering June 1977 Through June 1980. 743p. 1980. pap. 30.50 (ISBN 0-87079-374-8, DOE/TIC-3525 (REV. 5)(SUPPL. 12)); microfiche 4.50 (ISBN 0-87079-444-2, DOE/TIC-3525 (REV. 5)(SUPPL. 12)). DOE.

--Solar Energy: A Bibliography & Indexes. 400p. 1976. pap. 29.50 (ISBN 0-87079-377-2, TID-3351-R1P2); microfiche 4.50 (ISBN 0-87079-446-9, TID-3351-R1P2). DOE.

--Wood & Energy: A Bibliography. 213p. 1980. pap. 15.25 (ISBN 0-87079-381-0, DOE/TIC-3380); microfiche 4.50 (ISBN 0-87079-448-5, DOE/TIC-3380). DOE.

DOE Technical Information Center see Hanna, Steven R., et al.

DOE Technical Information Center see Hanson, Wayne C.

DOE Technical Information Center, jt. auth. see Kocher, David C.

DOE Technical Information Center see Shifrine, Moshe & Wilson, Floyd D.

DOE Technical Information Center, jt. auth. see Taylor, Lauriston S.

DOE Technical Information Center Staff. Coal Processing: Gasification, Liquefaction, Desulfurization. A Bibliography, 1930-1974. 763p. 1974. pap. 32.00 (ISBN 0-87079-165-6, TID-3349); microfiche 4.50 (ISBN 0-87079-409-4, TID-3349). DOE.

Doebele, William A. Land Readjustment: A Different Approach to Financing Urbanization. LC 82-47967. 256p. 1982. 31.00x (ISBN 0-669-05723-1). Lexington Bks.

Doebele-Fluegel, Verena. Die Lerche Motivgeschichtliche Untersuchung Zur Deutschen Literatur, Insbesondere Zur Deutschen Lyrik. 1977. 46.40x (ISBN 3-11-005909-6). De Gruyter.

Doebelin, E. O. System Dynamics: Modeling & Response. LC 77-187802. 448p. 1972. 36.95 (ISBN 0-675-09120-9). Merrill.

Doebelin, Ernest O. Control System Principles & Design. 624p. Date not set. price not set (ISBN 0-471-08815-3). Wiley.

--Measurement Systems: Application & Design. 3rd ed. (Illus.). 896p. 1982. text ed. 45.00 (ISBN 0-07-017337-0). McGraw.

--System Modeling & Response: Theoretical & Experimental Approaches. LC 79-27609. 587p. 1980. text ed. 52.45 (ISBN 0-471-03211-5). Wiley.

Doebler, Bettie A. The Quickening Seed: Death in the Sermons of John Donne. (Salzburg Studies in English Literature, Elizabethan & Renaissance Studies: No. 30). 304p. 1974. pap. text ed. 25.50x (ISBN 0-391-01362-9). Humanities.

Doebler, John, ed. see Beaumont, Francis.

Doebner, H., jt. ed. see DeNardo, G.

Doebner, H. D., ed. Differential Geometric Methods in Mathematical Physics: Proceedings. (Lecture Notes in Physics Ser.: Vol. 139). 329p. 1981. pap. 22.00 (ISBN 0-387-10578-6). Springer-Verlag.

Doebner, H. D. & Palev, T. D., eds. Twistor Geometry & Non-Linear Systems: Proceedings, Primorsko, Bulgaria, 1980. (Lecture Notes in Mathematics Ser.: Vol. 970). 216p. 1982. pap. 14.00 (ISBN 0-387-11972-8). Springer-Verlag.

Doebner, H. D., jt. ed. see Andersson, S. I.

Doeff, Annick M., jt. auth. see Barker, William F.

Doehaerd. Early Middle Ages in the West: Economy & Society. (Europe in the Middle Ages Ser.: Vol. 13). 308p. 1978. 59.75 (ISBN 0-444-85091-0, North-Holland). Elsevier.

Doehring, Donald, et al. Reading Disabilities: The Interaction of Reading, Leading & Neuropsychological Deficits. LC 81-10932. (Perspectives in Neurolinguistics, Neuropsychology & Psycholinguistics Ser.). 1981. 35.00 (ISBN 0-12-219180-3). Acad Pr.

Doehring, Donald O., ed. Geomorphology in Arid Regions. (Binghamton Symposia in Geomorphology: International Ser.: No. 8). (Illus.). 276p. 1980. pap. text ed. 30.00x (ISBN 0-04-551041-5). Allen Unwin.

Doehring, M. Gene. Cashier Clerk. (gr. 9-12). 1983. text ed. 6.10 (ISBN 0-538-04320-2, D32). SW Pub.

Doeing, Dennis, jt. auth. see Allen, Douglas.

Doeker, Gunther. Federal Republic of Germany & German Democratic Republic in International Relations, Vols. 1-3. LC 79-1334. 1979. Set. lib. bdg. 135.00 (ISBN 0-379-20329-4). Oceana.

Doel, Van Den H. see Van Den Doel, H.

Doelken, Dr. Theodor, jt. ed. see Strute, Karl.

Doelken, Theodor Dr., jt. ed. see Strute, Karl.

Doelle, H. W. Bacterial Metabolism. 2d ed. 1975. 77.50 (ISBN 0-12-219352-0). Acad Pr.

Doelle, H. W., ed. Microbial Metabolism. LC 73-16370. (Benchmark Papers in Microbiology: Vol. 5). 424p. 1974. 59.95 (ISBN 0-87933-063-5). Van Nos Reinhold.

Doelling, Norman, jt. auth. see Bennett, John B.

Doellinger, Johann J. Beitrage Zur Sektengenchichte des Mittelalter, 2 vols in 1. LC 91-26634. (Social Science Ser). (Ger). 1970. Repr. of 1890 ed. Set. lib. bdg. 57.50 (ISBN 0-8337-0880-5). B Franklin.

Doelp, Alan. Autumn's Children: A Dramatic Account of High-Risk Pregnancy. 288p. 1985. 15.95 (ISBN 0-02-532010-6). MacMillan.

Doelp, Alan, jt. auth. see Franklin, Jon.

Doenecke, Justus D. The Literature of Isolationism: Non-Interventionist Scholarship 1930-1972. LC 72-80272. 90p. 1972. pap. 1.85 (ISBN 0-87926-016-5). R Myles.

--Not to the Swift: The "Old" Isolationists in the Cold War Era. LC 76-1030. 289p. 1978. 26.50 (ISBN 0-8387-1940-6). Bucknell U Pr.

--The Presidencies of James A. Garfield & Chester A. Arthur. LC 80-18957. (The American Presidency Ser.). 232p. 1981. 19.95x (ISBN 0-7006-0208-9). U Pr of KS.

--When the Wicked Rise. LC 82-45619. 192p. 1984. 24.50 (ISBN 0-8387-5048-6). Bucknell U pr.

Doenecke, Justus D., compiled by. The Diplomacy of Frustration: The Manchurian Crisis of 1931-1933 As Revealed in the Papers of Stanley K. Hornbeck. (Publication Ser.: No. 231). 1981. 22.95x (ISBN 0-8179-7311-7). Hoover Inst Pr.

Doenges, Byron, ed. see Pacific Northwest Conference on Higher Education, 1971.

Doenges, E. Marilynn, et al. Nursing Care Plans: Diagnoses in Planning Patient Care. LC 83-25211. 697p. 1984. pap. text ed. 25.00 (ISBN 0-8036-2660-6). Davis Co.

Doenges, Marilynn & Moorhouse, Mary. Nurse's Pocket Guide: Nursing Diagnoses with Interventions. 160p. 1985. 11.95 (ISBN 0-8036-2663-0, 2663-0). Davis Co.

Doenges, Norman A. The Letters of Themistokles. rev. ed. Connor, W. R., ed. LC 80-2648. (Monographs in Classical Studies). 1981. lib. bdg. 55.00 (ISBN 0-405-14035-5). Ayer Co Pubs.

Doenhoff, Albert E. Von see Abbott, Ira H. & Von Doenhoff, Albert E.

Doenicke, A., ed. Etomidate: An Intravenous Hypnotic Agent. First Report on Clinical & Experimental Experience. (Anesthesiology & Resuscitation Ser.: Vol. 106). (Illus.). 1977. pap. 24.80 (ISBN 0-387-08485-1). Springer-Verlag.

Doenitz, Karl. Memoirs: Ten Years & Twenty Days. 1977. pap. 1.95 (ISBN 0-8439-0493-3, Leisure Bks). Dorchester Pub co.

Doeppers, Daniel F. Social Change in a Late Colonial Metropolis: Manila Nineteen Hundred to Nineteen Forty-One. LC 84-50326. (Monograph Ser.: No. 27). (Illus.). 194p. 1985. pap. 14.00x (ISBN 0-938692-06-2). Yale U SE Asia.

Doer, Bruno. Die Romische Namengebung: Ein Historischer Versuch. LC 75-7317. (Roman History Ser.). (Ger.). 1975. Repr. 18.00x (ISBN 0-405-07081-0). Ayer Co Pubs.

Doerblin, Alfred. The Living Thoughts of Confucius. 182p. 1983. Repr. of 1940 ed. lib. bdg. 25.00 (ISBN 0-89987-173-9). Darby Bks.

Doeren, Stephen E. & Hageman, Mary J. Community Corrections. LC 81-70991. (Illus.). 350p. 1982. 16.95 (ISBN 0-87084-187-4). Anderson Pub Co.

Doerfer, Gerhard. Khalaj Materials. LC 70-630301. (Uralic & Altaic Ser: Vol. 115). (Illus., Orig.). 1971. pap. text ed. 10.50x (ISBN 0-87750-150-5). Res Ctr Lang Semiotic.

Doerfer, Jane A. The Pantry Gourmet. Hupping, Carol, ed. (Illus.). 304p. 1984. 15.95 (ISBN 0-87857-506-5); pap. 9.95 (ISBN 0-87857-520-0). Rodale Pr Inc.

Doerffler, Alfred. The Burden Made Light. abr. ed. LC 74-34213. 128p. 1981. pap. 5.50 (ISBN 0-570-03026-9, 6-1154). Concordia.

--God at My Sickbed. 1966. 1.50 (ISBN 0-570-03062-5, 6-1114). Concordia.

--The Mind at Ease. rev. ed. LC 75-43869. (Large Print Ser.). 104p. 1976. pap. 5.50 (ISBN 0-570-03040-4, 6-1163). Concordia.

--Open the Meeting with Prayer. LC 55-7442. 1955. 3.50 (ISBN 0-570-03147-8, 12-2531). Concordia.

--The Yoke Made Easy. LC 75-2344. 128p. 1974. pap. 5.50 (ISBN 0-570-03027-7, 6-1155). Concordia.

Doerffler, W., ed. The Molecular Biology of Adenoviruses 1. (Current Topics in Microbiology & Immunity Ser.: Vol. 109). (Illus.). 240p. 1983. 42.50 (ISBN 0-387-13034-9). Springer-Verlag.

Doerfler, W., ed. The Molecular Biology of Adenoviruse 3: Thirty Years of Adenovirus Research 1953-1983. (Current Topics in Microbiology & Immunology Ser.: Vol. 111). (Illus.). 130p. 1984. 24.50 (ISBN 0-387-13138-8). Springer-Verlag.

--The Molecular Biology of Adenoviruses 2: Thirty Years of Adenovirus Research 1953-1983. (Current Topics in Microbiology & Immunology: Vol. 110). (Illus.). 290p. 1984. 49.00 (ISBN 0-387-13127-2). Springer-Verlag.

Doerge, Robert F., ed. Wilson & Gisvold's Textbook of Organic Medicinal & Pharmaceutical Chemistry. 8th ed. (Illus.). 960p. 1982. text ed. 49.50 (ISBN 0-397-52092-1, 65-05903, Lippincott Medical). Lippincott.

Doering, Bernard. Jacques Maritain & the French Catholic Intellectuals. LC 82-40377. 288p. 1983. text ed. 22.95. U of Notre Dame Pr.

Doering, Charles H., tr. see Kruskemper, Hans L.

Doering, Henry, ed. see Considine, Tim.

Doering, Jeanne. The Power of Encouragement. 176p. (Orig.). 1983. pap. 5.95 (ISBN 0-8024-0146-5). Moody.

--Your Power of Encouragement. (Moody Press Electives Ser.). (Orig.). 1985. pap. text ed. 3.95 (ISBN 0-8024-0687-4); leader's guide 2.50 (ISBN 0-8024-0688-2). Moody.

Doering, Mildred & Rhodes, Susan R. The Aging Worker: Research & Recommendations. 352p. 1983. 29.95 (ISBN 0-8039-1949-2). Sage.

Doering, Susan G., jt. auth. see Entwisle, Doris B.

Doering, Susan G., et al, eds. Your Toddler. (Illus.). 304p. 1984. 12.95 (ISBN 0-02-077840-6). Macmillan.

Doeringer, Peter & Vermeulen, Bruce. Jobs & Training in the Eighties: Vocational Policy & the Labor Market. (Boston Studies in Applied Economics). 240p. 1981. lib. bdg. 21.00 (ISBN 0-89838-062-6). Kluwer-Nijhoff.

Doeringer, Peter B. & Piore, Michael J. Internal Labor Markets & Manpower Analysis. LC 85-2063. 224p. (Orig.). 1985. 30.00 (ISBN 0-87332-351-3); pap. 13.95 (ISBN 0-87332-332-7). M E Sharpe.

Doeringer, Peter B., ed. Industrial Relations in International Perspective. LC 79-13690. 425p. 1981. text ed. 39.50x (ISBN 0-8419-0525-8). Holmes & Meier.

--Workplace Perspectives on Education & Training. (Boston Studies in Applied Economics). 184p. 1981. lib. bdg. 17.50 (ISBN 0-89838-054-5, Pub. by Martinus Nijhoff). Kluwer Academic.

Doerken, Maurine. Classroom Combat: Teaching & Television. LC 82-25125. 336p. 1983. 27.95 (ISBN 0-87778-186-9). Educ Tech Pubns.

Doerksen, Nan. Bears for Breakfast: The Thiessen Family Adventures. (Kinderbook Ser.). (Illus.). 34p. (gr. 4-8). 1983. pap. 2.40 (ISBN 0-317-31840-3). Herald Pr.

Doerksen, Vernon C., rev. by see Thiessen, Henry C.

Doerkson, Margaret. Jazzy: A Novel. LC 81-1156. 248p. 1981. 13.95 (ISBN 0-8253-0039-8). Beaufort Bks NY.

Doerkson, Vernon. James. (Everyman's Bible Commentaries Ser.). (Orig.). 1983. pap. 5.95 (ISBN 0-8024-0242-9). Moody.

Doern, G. Bruce. Canadian Nuclear Policies. 1980. pap. text ed. 14.95x (ISBN 0-920380-25-5, Pub. by Inst Res Pub Canada). Brookfield Pub Co.

--Government Intervention in the Canadian Nuclear Industry. 1980. pap. text ed. 8.95x (ISBN 0-920380-46-8, Pub. by Inst Res Pub Canada). Brookfield Pub Co.

--Science & Politics in Canada. LC 79-180255. pap. 63.00 (ISBN 0-317-26055-3, 2023842). Bks Demand UMI.

Doern, G. Bruce & Maslove, Allan M. Public Evaluation of Government Spending. 192p. 1979. pap. text ed. 10.95x (ISBN 0-920380-19-0, Pub. by Inst Res Pub Canada). Brookfield Pub Co.

Doern, G. Bruce & Phidd, Richard W. Canadian Public Policy: Ideas, Structure, Process. LC 83-219798. 624p. cancelled (ISBN 0-458-94850-0). Methuen Inc.

Doern, G. Bruce, jt. auth. see Prince, Michael J.

Doern, G. Bruce, jt. ed. see Tupper, Allan.

Doerner, Klaus. Madmen & the Bourgeoisie: A Social History of Insanity & Psychiatry. Neugroschel, Joachim & Steinberg, Jean, trs. 368p. 1981. text ed. 45.00x (ISBN 0-631-10181-0). Basil Blackwell.

--Madmen & the Bourgeoisie: A Social History of Insanity & Psychiatry. 368p. 1984. pap. 12.95 (ISBN 0-631-13715-7). Basil Blackwell.

Doerner, Max. The Materials of the Artist & Their Use in Painting with Notes of the Techniques of the Old Masters. rev. ed. Neuhaus, Eugen, tr. (Illus.). 480p. 1984. pap. 10.95 (ISBN 0-15-657716-X, Harv). HarBraceJ.

Doerper, John. Eating Well: A Guide to Foods of the Pacific Northwest. 320p. 1984. pap. 12.95 (ISBN 0-914718-88-6). Pacific Search.

--The Eating Well Cookbook. 204p. (Orig.). 1984. pap. 9.95 (ISBN 0-914718-93-2). Pacific Search.

--Shellfish Cookery: Absolutely Delicious Recipes from the West Coast. 200p. (Orig.). pap. 12.95 (ISBN 0-931397-01-4). Pacific Search.

Doerr, Christine. Microcomputers & the Three R's. 2nd ed. 192p. pap. 9.95 (6300). Hayden.

Doerr, Harriet. Stones for Ibarra. LC 83-47861. 215p. 1984. 14.95 (ISBN 0-670-19203-1). Viking.

--Stones for Ibarra. large print ed. LC 84-6535. 338p. 1984. Repr. of 1984 ed. 14.95 (ISBN 0-89621-535-0). Thorndike Pr.

--Stones for Ibarra. 214p. 1985. pap. 4.95 (ISBN 0-14-007562-3). Penguin.

Doerr, Juergen C., jt. auth. see Buse, Dieter K.

Doerr, Robert. Grace in the Plaza. 86p. 1984. 6.95 (ISBN 0-911819-03-7). Yosemite D.

Doerries, Hermann. Constantine & Religious Liberty. 1960. 39.50x (ISBN 0-686-51363-0). Elliots Bks.

Doerschel, Birgit & Herforth, Lieselott. Neutronen - Personendosimetrie. (Physikalische Reihe: No. 7). (Illus.). 364p. (Ger.). 1980. 57.95x (ISBN 0-8176-1037-5). Birkhauser.

Doerschuk, Bob, ed. Rock Keyboard. LC 84-60757. (Illus.). 1985. pap. 12.95 (ISBN 0-688-02961-2, Quill). Morrow.

Doery, A. C., jt. auth. see Croll, R. D.

Doeser, Linda & Richardson, Rosamond. The Little Garlic Book. (Illus.). 64p. 1983. 5.95 (ISBN 0-312-48864-5). St Martin.

--The Little Green Avocado Book. (Illus.). 64p. 1983. 5.95 (ISBN 0-312-48862-9). St Martin.

Doessel, D. P., jt. auth. see Bulter, J. R.

Doetsch, G. Einfuhrung in Theorie und Anwendung der Laplace-Transformation. rev. 3rd ed. (Mathematische Reihe Ser.: No. 24). 351p. (Ger.). 1976. 69.95x (ISBN 0-8176-0784-6). Birkhauser.

--Handbuch der Laplace Transformation, 3 vols. Incl. Vol. 1. Theorie der Laplace Transformation. 581p. 92.95x (ISBN 0-8176-0083-3); Vol. 2. Anwendungen der Laplace Transformation, 1, Abteilung. 436p. 72.95x (ISBN 0-8176-0653-X); Vol. 3. Anwendungen der Laplace Transformation, 2, Abteilung. 2nd ed. 299p. 49.95 (ISBN 0-8176-0674-2). (Mathematische Reihe Ser.: Nos. 14, 15 & 19). (Ger.). 1971-73. Birkhauser.

--Introduction to the Theory & Application of the Laplace Transformation. Nader, W., ed. & tr. LC 73-10661. (Illus.). 340p. 1974. 45.00 (ISBN 0-387-06407-9). Springer-Verlag.

Doetsch, G., jt. auth. see Voelker, D.

Doetsch, Raymond N. Journey to the Green & Golden Lands: The Epic of Survival on the Wagon Trail. 1976. 11.50 (ISBN 0-8046-9142-8, Pub. by Kennikat). Assoc Faculty Pr.

Doetz, Karl H., et al. Transition Metal Carbene Complexes: Dedicated to Professor E. O. Fischer. 264p. 1983. 60.00x (ISBN 0-89573-073-1). VCH Pubs.

Doezema, Linda P., ed. Dutch Americans: A Guide to Information Sources. LC 79-13030. (Ethnic Studies Information Guide Ser.: Vol. 3). 1979. 60.00x (ISBN 0-8103-1407-X). Gale.

D'Offay, Danielle & Lionnet, Guy. Diksyonner Kreol-Franse: Dictionnaire Creole Seychellois-Francais. (Kreolische Bibliothek Band 3). 422p. (French.). 1982. 26.00x (ISBN 3-87118-569-8, Pub. by Helmut Buske Verlag Hamburg). Benjamins North Am.

Dofny, Jacques & Akiwowo, Akinsola, eds. National & Ethnic Movements. LC 80-40177. (Sage Studies in International Sociology: Vol. 19). 177p. 1980. 28.00 (ISBN 0-8039-9820-1); pap. 14.00 (ISBN 0-8039-9821-X). Sage.

Dofny, Jacques, jt. ed. see Haug, Marie R.

Dogan, Mattei & Pelassy, Dominique. How to Compare Nations: Strategies in Comparative Politics. LC 83-20997. 192p. 1984. pap. text ed. 11.95x (ISBN 0-934540-20-9). Chatham Hse Pubs.

Dogan, Mattei, ed. The Mandarins of Western Europe: The Political Role of Top Civil Servants. LC 75-8734. 314p. 1975. 18.50 (ISBN 0-470-21749-9, Pub. by Wiley). Krieger.

Dogan, Peter, jt. auth. see Professional Instrument Courses, Inc.

Doganis, Rigas. Flying off Course: The Economics of International Airlines. 300p. 1985. text ed. 22.50x (ISBN 0-04-387004-X). Allen Unwin.

Dogen. Moon in a Dewdrop. Tanahashi, Kazuaki, ed. 288p. 1985. 25.00 (ISBN 0-86547-185-1); pap. 12.50 (ISBN 0-86547-186-X). N Point Pr.

--A Primer of Soto Zen: A Translation of Dogen's Shobogenzo Zuimonki. Masunaga, Reiho, tr. from Japanese. LC 76-126044. 1971. text ed. 7.50x (ISBN 0-8248-0094-X, Eastwest Ctr). UH Pr.

--A Primer of Soto Zen: A Translation of Dogen's Shobogenzo Zuimonki. Masunaga, Reiho, tr. from Japanese. LC 76-126044. 128p. 1975. pap. text ed. 5.95x (ISBN 0-8248-0357-4, Eastwest Ctr). UH Pr.

Doggeral Press, ed. see Szerlip, Barbara, et al.

Doggett, Frank. Cigarette Cards & Novelties. (Illus.). 96p. 1982. pap. 11.95 (ISBN 0-7181-2141-4, Pub. by Michael Joseph). Merrimack Pub Cir.

--Stevens' Poetry of Thought. 240p. (Orig.). 1966. pap. 5.95x (ISBN 0-8018-0174-5). Johns Hopkins.

--Wallace Stevens: The Making of the Poem. 160p. 1980. 16.50x (ISBN 0-8018-2324-2). Johns Hopkins.

Doggett, Frank & Buttel, Robert, eds. Wallace Stevens: A Celebration. LC 79-18877. 1980. 35.00x (ISBN 0-691-06414-8). Princeton U Pr.

Doggett, H., et al, eds. Striga: Biology & Control. LC 84-12877. (Symposium Ser.: No. 2). 1984. write for info. (ISBN 0-930357-01-9). ICSU Pr.

Doggett, Joella, jt. auth. see Scheick, William J.

Doggett, L. L. Life of Robert R. McBurney. Repr. of 1902 ed. 15.00 (ISBN 0-686-19861-1). Ridgeway Bks.

Doggett, R. G., ed. Pseudomonas Aeruginosa: Clinical Manifestations of Infection & Current Therapy. 1979. 66.00 (ISBN 0-12-219550-7). Acad Pr.

Dogherty, Marian A. Literature in the Schools. (Educational Ser.). 1927. Repr. 10.00 (ISBN 0-8482-3684-X). Norwood Edns.

Dogin, Yvette. Help Yourself to a Job, 3 pts. (Illus.). (gr. 7 up). Set. text ed. 11.25 (ISBN 0-912486-00-7); Pt. 1, 1977. text ed. 3.75 (ISBN 0-912486-32-5); Pt. 2, 1980. text ed. 3.75 (ISBN 0-912486-02-3); Pt. 3, 1978. text ed. 3.75 (ISBN 0-912486-03-1). Finney Co.

--Jobs from "A" to "Z". 1982. pap. 3.00x (ISBN 0-88323-183-2, 147). Richards Pub.

--Lots of Things, 2 Vols. (Illus.). (gr. 4 up). Set. wkbk 7.50 (ISBN 0-912486-04-X); Bk. 1, 1978. wkbk 3.75 (ISBN 0-912486-37-6); Bk. 2, 1972. wkbk. 3.75 (ISBN 0-912486-06-6). Finney Co.

--Teen-Agers at Work. rev. ed. 1983. pap. 3.25x (ISBN 0-88323-184-0, 164). Richards Pub.

Dogo, G. Guide to Artistic Italy. (Illus.). 1981. 65.00 (ISBN 0-686-46739-6). Heinman.

Dogo, G., jt. ed. see May, S. R.

Dogoloff, Lee, ed. see Peterson, Robert C., et al.

Dogra, Sneh Kumar & Dogra, Sulekha. Physical Chemistry Through Problems. LC 83-12819. 674p. 1984. 29.95x (ISBN 0-470-27491-3). Halsted Pr.

Dogra, Sulekha, jt. auth. see Dogra, Sneh Kumar.

Dogramaci, A. Productivity Analysis: A Range of Perspectives. (Studies in Productivity Analysis: Vol. 1). 208p. 1980. lib. bdg. 19.95 (ISBN 0-89838-039-1, Pub. by Martinus Nijhoff Netherlands). Kluwer Academic.

Dogramaci, Ali. Developments in Econometric Analyses of Productivity. (Studies in Productivity Analysis). 1982. lib. bdg. 30.00 (ISBN 0-89838-101-0). Kluwer-Nijhoff.

Dogramaci, Ali & Adam, Nabil R. Aggregate & Industry-Level Productivity Analysis. (Productivity Analysis Studies: Vol. 2). 204p. 1981. lib. bdg. 25.00 (ISBN 0-89838-037-5, Pub. by Martinus Nijhoff Netherlands). Kluwer Academic.

Dogramaci, Ali, jt. ed. see Adam, Nabil R.

Doh, Herman. Fortune by Land & Sea. LC 79-54335. (Renaissance Drama Ser.). 340p. 1982. lib. bdg. 45.00 (ISBN 0-8240-4453-3). Garland Pub.

Doh, Joon C. The Planning-Programming-Budgeting Systems in Three Federal Agencies. LC 74-149965. (Special Studies in U.S. Economic, Social, & Political Issues). 1971. 29.00x (ISBN 0-89197-887-9). Irvington.

Dohan, Mary H. Mr. Roosevelt's Steamboat. LC 81-5488. (Illus.). 224p. 1981. 10.95 (ISBN 0-396-07983-0). Dodd.

Dohan, Michael & Hewett, Edward. Two Studies in Soviet Terms of Trade, (1918-1970) (Studies in East European & Soviet Planning, Development, & Trade: No. 21). 1973. pap. text ed. 3.00 (ISBN 0-89249-001-2). Intl Development.

Dohanian, Diran D. The Mahayana Buddhist Sculpture of Ceylon. LC 76-23613. (Outstanding Dissertations in the Fine Arts). (Illus.). 1977. Repr. of 1964 ed. lib. bdg. 58.00 (ISBN 0-8240-2685-3). Garland Pub.

Dohanos, Stevan. American Realist. LC 80-13884. (Illus.). 128p. 1980. 22.50 (ISBN 0-89134-027-0). North Light Pub.

Doheman, Warren. The Alchemy of Intelligence: A Rationale for Learning. (The U. W. W. Ser.). (Illus.). 274p. (Orig.). 1984. 18.00 (ISBN 0-943920-24-8); pap. 10.00 (ISBN 0-943920-04-3). Metamorphous Pr.

Doheny, James, ed. Mertens Code Commentary: 1954, 3 vols. Set. 245.00 (ISBN 0-317-11932-X); Suppl., 1982. 200.00; Suppl., 1983. 210.00. Callaghan.

--Mertens Law of Federal Income Taxation: 1954-1983, 59 vols. LC 75-27726. Set. 1195.00 (ISBN 0-317-11931-1). Callaghan.

Doheny, John R., ed. see Wright, James.

Doheny, Margaret. The Discipline of Nursing: An Introduction. LC 81-18114. 224p. 1982. pap. text ed. 15.95 (ISBN 0-89303-058-9). Brady Comm.

Doherty. Tempo Junior Scrambled Word Find Anthologies, Nos. 1-6. 128p. (gr. 4-8). 1975. pap. 0.75 ea. (Tempo). Ace Bks.

Doherty, Barbara. I Am What I Do: Contemplation & Human Experience. 226p. 1982. pap. 7.95 (ISBN 0-88347-129-9). Thomas More.

--Make Yourself an Ark. 1984. 10.95 (ISBN 0-88347-162-0). Thomas More.

Doherty, Catherine. Lubov: The Heart of the Beloved. (Illus.). 112p. (Orig.). 1985. pap. 5.95 (ISBN 0-914544-60-8). Living Flame Pr.

Doherty, Catherine D. Dear Father: A Message of Love to Priests. LC 78-31389. 1979. pap. 3.50 (ISBN 0-8189-0377-5). Alba.

--Doubts, Loneliness & Rejection. LC 81-19115. (Illus.). 93p. 1982. pap. 4.50 (ISBN 0-8189-0419-4). Alba.

--The Gospel of a Poor Woman. 6.95 (ISBN 0-87193-151-6). Dimension Bks.

--Journey Inward: Interior Conversations 1960 to the Present. LC 84-443. 116p. (Orig.). 1984. pap. 6.95 (ISBN 0-8189-0468-2). Alba.

--Molchanie: The Silence of God. 112p. 1982. 8.95 (ISBN 0-8245-0407-0). Crossroad NY.

--Poustinia. LC 74-19961. 216p. 1975. pap. 3.95 (ISBN 0-87793-083-X). Ave Maria.

--Sobornost. LC 77-89078. 112p. 1977. pap. 2.45 (ISBN 0-87793-141-0). Ave Maria.

Doherty, Catherine de Hucck. Molchanie: The Silence of God. 128p. 1984. pap. 7.95 (ISBN 0-8245-0672-3). Crossroad NY.

Doherty, Catherine de Hueck. Coming Home. 3.95 (ISBN 0-87193-081-1). Dimension Bks.

--Fragments of My Life. LC 79-56889. (Illus.). 208p. (Orig.). 1979. pap. 3.95 (ISBN 0-87793-194-1). Ave Maria.

--Urodivoi: Fools for Good. LC 82-23530. 112p. 1983. 9.95 (ISBN 0-8245-0553-0). Crossroad NY.

Doherty, Catherine de Hueck see De Hueck Doherty, Catherine.

Doherty, Catherine de Hueck see Doherty, Catherine D.

Doherty, Cecilia & Ilyin, Donna. Technical Manual for ELSA: English Language Skills Assessment in a Reading Context. (ELSA Tests Ser.). 1981. pap. 3.95 (ISBN 0-88377-226-4). Newbury Hse.

Doherty, Eddie. True Devotion to Mary. pap. 2.00 (ISBN 0-910984-02-6). Montfort Pubns.

--Wisdom's Fool. 4.95 (ISBN 0-910984-08-5); pap. 2.95 (ISBN 0-910984-09-3). Montfort Pubns.

Doherty, Filomena, jt. auth. see T. F. H. Staff.

Doherty, H., tr. see Fourier, Francois M.

Doherty, Herbert J., Jr. The Whigs of Florida, Eighteen Forty Five-Eighteen Fifty Four. LC 59-62570. (University of Florida Social Sciences Monographs: No. 1). 1959. 3.50 (ISBN 0-8130-0064-5). U Presses Fla.

Doherty, Herbert J., Jr., intro. by see Williams, John L.

Doherty, Ivy D. Rainbows of Promise. Wheeler, Gerald, ed. (A Banner Bk.). (Illus.). 92p. (Orig.). (gr. 2 up). 1984. pap. 5.95 (ISBN 0-8280-0213-4). Review & Herald.

Doherty, J. C., jt. auth. see Porter, Douglas R.

Doherty, J. E., jt. auth. see Hickey, D. J.

Doherty, John. Praying in the Home. 2nd. ed. LC 83-61212. 54p. 1984. pap. text ed. 1.95 (ISBN 0-911905-04-9). Past & Mat Rene Ctr.

Doherty, Jon & Hoehn, Robert G. The Magic of Thinking Big in Selling. 224p. 1983. 16.95 (ISBN 0-13-545285-6); pap. 7.95 (ISBN 0-13-545210-4). P-H.

Doherty, Jonathan, compiled by see International Museum of Photography at George Eastman House.

Doherty, Jonathan L., ed. see Hine, Lewis W.

Doherty, Joseph C. Growth Management in Countryfied Cities, Vol. 1: Change & Response. Doherty, Kristan & Grieg, Margot, eds. LC 84-51900. (Illus.). 100p. (Orig.). 1984. pap. 6.95 (ISBN 0-9613980-1-9). Vert Milon Pr.

--Growth Management in Countryfied Cities, Vol. 2: Six Perspectives. LC 84-51900. (Growth Management in Countryfied Cities Ser.). (Illus.). 170p. 1985. pap. 7.00 (ISBN 0-9613980-2-7). Vert Milon Pr.

Doherty, Joseph L., Jr. & Meyer, Andrew C., Jr. Massachusetts Legal Forms-Personal. 250p. Date not set. price not set looseleaf. Butterworth Legal Pubs.

Doherty, Katherine M., ed. History Highlights: Bridgewater, Massachusetts, a Commemorative Journal. LC 76-2972. (Illus.). 1976. 12.00 (ISBN 0-88492-014-3). W S Sullwold.

Doherty, Kristan, ed. see Doherty, Joseph C.

Doherty, Lillian, tr. see DeRomilly, Jacqueline.

Doherty, Linda. Tempo Scrambled Word Find Puzzles, No. 1. 1982. pap. 1.50 (Pub. by Tempo). Ace Bks.

--Tempo Word Find Puzzles, No. 4. 1982. pap. 1.50 (ISBN 0-448-05572-4, Pub. by Tempo). Ace Bks.

--Word Find Puzzles, No. 1. pap. 1.75 (ISBN 0-448-17199-6, Pub. by Tempo). Ace Bks.

--Word Find Puzzles, No. 3. 128p. (gr. 5 up). 1974. pap. 1.25 (ISBN 0-448-05720-4, Pub. by Tempo). Ace Bks.

--Word Find Puzzles, No. 5. 128p. (Orig.). (gr. 5 up). 1975. pap. 1.50 (ISBN 0-448-05774-3, Pub. by Tempo). Ace Bks.

--Word Find Puzzles, No. 6. pap. 1.50 (ISBN 0-448-07523-7, Pub. by Tempo). Ace Bks.

Doherty, Liz, jt. auth. see Yorke, Harvey.

Doherty, M. Stephen. Dynamic Still Lifes in Watercolor: Sondra Freckelton's Approach to Color, Composition, & Control of the Medium. (Illus.). 144p. 1983. 23.50 (ISBN 0-8230-1583-1). Watson-Guptill.

--Paul Ortlip: His Heritage & His Art. LC 82-16686. (Illus.). 152p. 1983. 45.00 (ISBN 0-914016-91-1). Phoenix Pub.

Doherty, Michael E. & Shemberg, Kenneth M. Asking Questions about Behavior: An Introduction to What Psychologists Do. 2nd ed. 1978. pap. 9.40x (ISBN 0-673-15043-7). Scott F.

Doherty, N. Corporate Risk Management. LC 84-17095. (Insurance Ser.). 480p. 1985. 31.95 (ISBN 0-07-017360-5). McGraw.

Doherty, P. D., jt. auth. see Martin, J. W.

Doherty, Paul. The Arrival of Halley's Comet, 1985-1986. 1985. pap. 8.95 (ISBN 0-8120-3632-8). Barron.

Doherty, Paul G., jt. auth. see Mann, Stephen G.

Doherty, R. D., jt. auth. see Martin, J. W.

Doherty, Robert. Society & Power: Five New England Towns, 1800-1860. LC 77-73477. (Illus.). 128p. 1977. 11.00x (ISBN 0-87023-242-8). U of Mass Pr.

Doherty, Robert, jt. auth. see Hurley, F. Jack.

Doherty, Robert E. Industrial & Labor Relations Terms: A Glossary. 4th rev. ed. LC 79-18839. (ILR Bulletin: No. 44). 40p. 1979. pap. 2.50 (ISBN 0-87546-075-5). ILR Pr.

--Labor Relations Primer: An Introduction to Collective Bargaining Through Documents. rev. ed. LC 84-10859. (ILR Bulletin Ser.: No. 54). (Illus.). 56p. 1984. pap. text ed. 4.95 (ISBN 0-87546-105-0). ILR Pr.

Doherty, Robert E., jt. auth. see Aboud, Grace S.

Doherty, Robert E., ed. Public Access: Citizens & Collective Bargaining in the Public Schools. LC 79-13189. 112p. 1979. pap. 7.95 (ISBN 0-87546-073-9). ILR Pr.

Doherty, Robert E., jt. ed. see Adler, Joseph.

Doherty, Stephen M., jt. ed. see Commager, Henry S.

Doherty, Steve S. The Boats They Sailed In. (Illus.). 1985. 24.95 (ISBN 0-393-03299-X). Norton.

Doherty, Terence. The Anatomical Works of George Stubbs. LC 74-15259. (Illus.). 356p. 1975. 125.00 (ISBN 0-87923-117-3). Godine.

Doherty, W. T., jt. auth. see Zaba, Joseph.

Doherty, William J. & Baird, Macaran A. Family Therapy & Family Medicine. LC 82-3135. (Family Therapy Ser.). 285p. 1983. text ed. 25.00 (ISBN 0-89862-041-4, 2041). Guilford Pr.

Doherty, William T. West Virginia Studies, Our Heritage. Buckalew, Marshall, ed. (Illus.). 306p. (gr. 8). 1984. 20.00 (ISBN 0-914498-04-5). Educ Found.

--West Virginia University. LC 82-62028. 384p. 1982. 25.00 (ISBN 0-937058-16-5). West Va U Pr.

Dohm, Hedwig. Women's Nature & Privilege. Campbell, C., tr. from Ger. LC 75-743. (Pioneers of the Woman's Movement: an International Perspective Ser.). 151p. 1976. Repr. of 1876 ed. 16.50 (ISBN 0-88355-280-9). Hyperion Conn.

Dohm, Richard R. see Hardy, Richard J.

Dohnal, Karal. Yukon Solo. LC 83-70953. (Illus.). 240p. 1984. pap. 8.95 (ISBN 0-8323-0421-2). Binford.

Dohr, Donald A. El Camino Hacia el Amor. rev. ed. LC 81-71328. Orig. Title: Beginning Your Marriage. 128p. 1982. pap. 1.95 (ISBN 0-915388-14-6). Buckley Pubns.

Dohr, Gerhard. Applied Geophysics: Introduction to Geophysical Prospecting. 2nd ed. LC 80-28695. (Geology of Petroleum Ser.). 231p. 1981. pap. 23.95x (ISBN 0-470-99102-X). Halsted Pr.

Dohren, Hans van see Kleinkauf, Horst & Van Dohren, Hans.

Dohrenwend, Barbara S. & Dohrenwend, Bruce P. Stressful Life Events: Their Nature & Effects. LC 74-6369. 340p. 1974. 45.95x (ISBN 0-471-21753-0, Pub. by Wiley-Interscience). Wiley.

Dohrenwend, Barbara S., jt. auth. see Dohrenwend, Bruce P.

Dohrenwend, Barbara S. & Dohrenwend, Bruce P., eds. Stressful Life Event & Their Contexts. (Monographs in Psychsocial Epidemiology). 287p. 1984. pap. text ed. 14.95 (ISBN 0-8135-1004-X). Rutgers U Pr.

Dohrenwend, Bruce P. Mental Illness in the United States: Epidemiological Estimates. LC 79-18725. 182p. 1980. 29.95 (ISBN 0-03-053506-9). Praeger.

Dohrenwend, Bruce P. & Dohrenwend, Barbara S. Social Status & Psychological Disorder: A Casual Inquiry. LC 72-88310. (Personality Processes Ser). Repr. of 1969 ed. 42.40 (ISBN 0-8357-9978-6, 2012570). Bks Demand UMI.

Dohrenwend, Bruce P., jt. auth. see Dohrenwend, Barbara S.

Dohrenwend, Bruce P., jt. ed. see Dohrenwend, Barbara S.

Dohrenwenwend, Barbara S., jt. ed. see Ricks, David F.

Dohrman, H. T. California Cult: The Story of Mankind United. LC 76-42724. Repr. of 1958 ed. 15.00 (ISBN 0-404-60059-X). AMS Pr.

Dohrs, Fred E. & Sommers, Lawrence M. World Regional Geography: A Problem Approach. LC 76-3748. pap. 160.00 (ISBN 0-317-20533-1, 2022841). Bks Demand UMI.

Doi, A. R. Hadith: An Introduction. 1980. pap. 6.50 (ISBN 0-686-64661-4). Kazi Pubns.

--Non-Muslims Under Shari'ah. 1981. 6.50 (ISBN 0-686-97861-7). Kazi Pubns.

--Shari'ah & Family Law. 9.95 (ISBN 0-686-97873-0). Kazi Pubns.

Doi, Kochi, ed. Select Letters of English Poets. 1978. Repr. of 1935 ed. lib. bdg. 40.00 (ISBN 0-8495-1031-7). Arden Lib.

Doi, Mary L., et al. Pacific-Asian American Research: An Annotated Bibliography. LC 81-4086. (Bibliography Ser.: No.1). xvi, 269p. (Orig.). 1981. pap. 6.95 (ISBN 0-934584-11-7). Pacific-Asian.

Doi, Masaru. Cook Japanese. LC 65-10171. (Illus.). 128p. 1964. 15.95 (ISBN 0-87011-121-3). Kodansha.

Doi, T., ed. The Intellectual Property Law of Japan. 352p. 1980. 65.00x (ISBN 90-286-0649-1). Sijthoff & Noordhoff.

Doi, Takeo. The Anatomy of Dependence. Bester, John, tr. LC 72-76297. 170p. 1982. pap. 4.25 (ISBN 0-87011-494-8, 0340982). Kodansha.

Doi, Teruo & Shattuck, Warren L., eds. Patent & Know-How Licensing in Japan & the United States. LC 76-7785. (Asian Law Ser.: No.5). 444p. 1977. 40.00x (ISBN 0-295-95513-9). U of Wash Pr.

Doi, Tsugiyoshi. Momoyama Decorative Painting. LC 76-44338. (Illus.). 1976. 17.50 (ISBN 0-8348-1024-7). Weatherhill.

Doi Chrysostomus. Orationes, Vol. 1. Bude, Guy de, ed. 441p. 1985. Repr. of 1916 ed. 15.00 (ISBN 0-89005-540-8). Ares.

Doidge, Spencer. Fingerpicking Joplin. 1984. pap. 7.95 (ISBN 0-8256-2310-3, Pub by Amsco Music). Music Sales.

Doig, Alison, tr. see Berg, Claude.

Doig, Alison G., jt. auth. see Kendall, Maurice G.

Doig, Allan. The Architectural Drawings Collection of King's College, Cambridge. (Illus.). 160p. 1980. 50.00 (ISBN 0-86127-501-2). Eastview.

--The Architectural Drawings Collection of King's College, Cambridge. 160p. 1979. text ed. 57.50x (ISBN 0-86127-501-2, Pub. by Avebury England). Humanities.

Doig, Caroline M. Surgical Procedures: Inguinal Hernias & Hydroceles in Infants & Children, Vol. 3. (Single Surgical Procedures Ser.). 100p. (Orig.). 1983. 25.95 (ISBN 0-87489-502-2). Med Economics.

Doig, Desmond. Mother Teresa: Her Work & Her People. LC 75-39857. (Illus.). 176p. 1980. pap. 11.49 (ISBN 0-06-061941-4, RD336, HarpR). Har-Row.

Doig, Ivan. English Creek. LC 84-45051. 352p. 1984. 15.95 (ISBN 0-689-11478-8). Atheneum.

--Inside This House of Sky. LC 83-45079. (Illus.). 112p. 1983. 27.50 (ISBN 0-689-11405-2). Atheneum.

--The Sea Runners. LC 82-45174. (Illus.). 288p. 1982. 13.95 (ISBN 0-689-11302-1). Atheneum.

--The Sea Runners. 288p. 1983. pap. 4.95 (ISBN 0-14-006780-9). Penguin.

--The Streets We Have Come Down: Literature of the City. 224p. 1975. pap. text ed. 6.00x (ISBN 0-8104-5823-3). Boynton Cook Pubs.

--This House of Sky: Landscapes of a Western Mind. LC 79-18783. 1980. pap. 5.95 (ISBN 0-15-689982-5, Harv). HarBraceJ.

--Winter Brothers: A Season at the Edge of America. LC 80-7933. (Illus.). 252p. 1982. pap. 5.95 (ISBN --15-697215-8, Harv). HarBraceJ.

Doig, Jameson, ed. Issues & Realities in Corrections: A Symposium. 1982. pap. 8.00 (ISBN 0-918592-58-5). Policy Studies.

Doig, Jameson W. Criminal Corrections: Ideals & Realities. LC 81-48633. (Policy Studies Organization Bk.). 240p. 1982. 28.50x (ISBN 0-669-05467-4). Lexington Bks.

--Metropolitan Transportation Politics & the New York Region. LC 66-16768. (Metropolitan Politics Ser.). (Illus.). 327p. 1966. 35.00x (ISBN 0-231-02791-5). Columbia U Pr.

Doig, Jameson W., jt. auth. see Danielson, Michael N.

Doig, P, ed. Electron Microscopy & Analysis 1983. (Institute of Physics Conference Ser.: No. 68). 1984. 60.00 (ISBN 0-9903800-0-9, Pub. by A Hilger England). Heyden.

Doight Du Nez. The Complete Book of Nose Etiquette. 77p. 1983. 3.95 (ISBN 0-934126-45-3). Randall Bk Co.

Doinas, Stefan A. Alibi & Other Poems. Jay, Peter & Nemoianu, Virgil, trs. from Romanian. (International Bks.). 31p. pap. 1.50 (ISBN 0-317-04121-5). U of Iowa Pr.

Doiron, Daniel R. & Gomer, Charles J. Porphyrin Localization & Treatment of Tumors. (Progress in Clinical & Biological Research Ser.: Vol. 170). 908p. 1984. 98.00 (ISBN 0-8451-5020-0). A R Liss.

Doiron, David, et al. Anger: Issues of Emotional Living in an Age of Stress for Clergy & Religious. Riordan, Brendan P., ed. LC 84-29031. 144p. 1985. pap. 8.00 (ISBN 0-89571-022-6). Affirmation.

Doiron, John & Hyde, Cornelius J., III. Louisiana Supplement to Modern Real Estate Practice. 96p. (Orig.). 1982. pap. text ed. 8.95 (ISBN 0-88462-296-7, 1510-40, Real Estate Ed). Longman USA.

Doise, W. & Douglas, G. Groups & Individuals. LC 77-84800. (Illus.). 1978. 34.50 (ISBN 0-521-21953-1); pap. 12.95 (ISBN 0-521-29320-0). Cambridge U Pr.

Doise, W. & Mugny, G. The Social Development of the Intellect. St. James, A. & Emler, N., trs. LC 84-9227. (International Series in Experimental Social Psychology: Vol. 10). 196p. 1984. 33.00 (ISBN 0-08-030209-2); pap. 17.50 (ISBN 0-08-030215-7). Pergamon.

Doise, Willem & Palmonari, Augusto. Social Interaction in Individual Development. (European Studies in Social Psychology). 287p. 1984. 49.50 (ISBN 0-521-25024-2). Cambridge U Pr.

Doise, Willem & Moscovici, Serge, eds. Current Issues in European Social Psychology, Vol. 1. (European Studies in Social Psychology Ser.). 335p. 1984. 69.50 (ISBN 0-521-24239-8). Cambridge U Pr.

Doisneau, Robert. Three Seconds from Eternity: Photographs by Robert Doisneau. 144p. 1980. 32.50 (ISBN 0-8212-1096-3, 749540). NYGS.

Doisneau, Robert & Sage, James D. The Boy & the Dove. LC 77-18427. (Illus.). 1978. pap. 3.95 (ISBN 0-89480-027-2). Workman Pub.

Doj, A. R. Quran, an Introduction. pap. 5.50 (ISBN 0-686-63911-1). Kazi Pubns.

Doke, C. M. English & Zulu Dictionary: English-Zulu, Zulu-English. (Zulu & Eng.). 1958. pap. 12.00x (ISBN 0-85494-010-3). Intl Learn Syst.

Doke, C. M., ed. Zulu-English, English-Zulu Dictionary. rev. ed. (Zulu & Eng.). pap. 20.00 (ISBN 0-85494-010-3). Heinman.

Doke, Clement M. English-Lamba Dictionary. (Eng. & Lamba.). 24.00 (ISBN 0-87559-055-1). Shalom.

--Lamba Folklore. LC 28-18358. (American Folklore Society Memoirs). Repr. of 1927 ed. 58.00 (ISBN 0-527-01072-3). Kraus Repr.

--Lambas of Northern Rhodesia: A Study of Their Customs & Beliefs. LC 74-107473. (Illus.). Repr. of 1931 ed. 23.00x (ISBN 0-8371-3751-9, DOL&, Pub. by Negro U Pr). Greenwood.

Dokey, Richard. August Heat. (Illus.). 160p. 1982. 10.50 (ISBN 0-931704-09-X); pap. 3.95 (ISBN 0-931704-08-1). Story Pr.

--Funeral: A Play. (Pikestaff Review Ser.: No. 3). 80p. (Orig.). 1982. pap. 3.00 (ISBN 0-936044-03-9). Pikestaff Pr.

--Sanchez & Other Stories. (Regional Ser.). 125p. (Orig.). 1981. pap. 4.75 (ISBN 0-933906-14-5). Gusto Pr.

Doksum, K. A., jt. auth. see Bickel, P. J.

Doksum, Kjell, jt. ed. see Bickel, Peter J.

Doktor & Slevin, eds. Implementation of Management Science, Vol. 13. (TIMS Studies in the Management Sciences). 242p. 29.50 (ISBN 0-318-14457-3). Inst Mgmt Sci.

Doktor, R., et al, eds. The Implementation of Management Science. (TIMS Studies in Management Science: Vol. 13). 246p. 1980. 32.50 (ISBN 0-444-85376-6, North Holland). Elsevier.

Dokulil, M., et al, eds. Shallow Lakes: Contributions to Their Limnology. (Developmrnts in Hydrobiology Ser.: No. 3). 218p. 1981. PLB 59.50 (ISBN 0-686-28842-4, Pub. by Junk Pubs Netherlands). Kluwer Academic.

Dokumentationsring Padagogik & GFD, eds. Bibliographie Padagogik. viii, 911p. 1984. lib. bdg. 61.50 (ISBN 0-317-18602-7). K G Saur.

Dolaghan, Thomas & Scates, David R. The Navajos Are Coming to Jesus. LC 78-3609. (Illus.). 1978. pap. 4.95 (ISBN 0-87808-162-3). William Carey Lib.

Dolan. The Bermuda Triangle & Other Mysteries of Nature. LC 79-22798. (Triumph Bks.). 1980. PLB 8.90 (ISBN 0-531-04113-1, A23). Watts.

Dolan, A. G., jt. auth. see Balman, F. E.

Dolan, A. P., tr. see Buhlmann, Walbert.

Dolan, A. T., jt. ed. see Ahsen, Akhter.

Dolan, C. Terrence, ed. Subcutaneous Mycoses: Clinical Mycology V. LC 80-720448. (Atlases of Clinical Mycology: 5). 27p. 1976. text & slides 80.00 (ISBN 0-89189-043-2, 15-7-009-00); microfiche ed. 12.00 (ISBN 0-89189-091-2, 17-7-009-00). Am Soc Clinical.

--Systemic Mycoses - Deep Seated: Clinical Mycology II. LC 75-736235. (Atlases of Clinical Mycology: 2). (Illus.). 20p. 1975. text & slides 80.00 (ISBN 0-89189-040-8, 15-7-003-00); microfiche ed. 12.00 (ISBN 0-89189-088-2, 17-7-003-00). Am Soc Clinical.

Dolan, D. & Williamson, J. Teaching Problem-Solving Strategies. (Resource Bk.). 1982. 18.50 (ISBN 0-201-10231-5, Sch-Div). Addison-Wesley.

Dolan, Doug & Parsons, Wayne. Hill of Beans: A Trivia Workout Book. 304p. 1985. pap. 2.95 (ISBN 0-345-32096-4). Ballantine.

Dolan, Edward. Bicycle Touring & Camping. (Illus.). 192p. (gr. 8 up). 1982. pap. 5.95 (ISBN 0-671-44544-8). Wanderer Bks.

Dolan, Edward & Finney, Shan. The New Japan. (Illus.). 128p. (YA) (gr. 7 up). 1983. PLB 8.90 (ISBN 0-531-04665-6). Watts.

Dolan, Edward F. The Julian Messner Sports Question & Answer Book. (Illus.). 256p. (gr. 3 up). 1984. PLB 10.79 (ISBN 0-671-53134-4). Messner.

--Let's Make Magic. LC 79-8014. (Illus.). 96p. (gr. 2-6). 1981. PLB 7.95 (ISBN 0-385-15193-4). Doubleday.

Dolan, Edward F., Jr. Adolf Hitler: A Portrait in Tyranny. (Illus.). 240p. (gr. 7 up). 1981. PLB 10.95 (ISBN 0-396-07982-2). Dodd.

--Anti-Semitism. (Illus.). (gr. 7-12). 1985. PLB 10.90 (ISBN 0-531-10068-5). Watts.

--Basic Football Strategy. 1978. pap. 2.95 (ISBN 0-346-12344-5). Cornerstone.

--Be Your Own Man: A Step-by-Step Guide to Thinking & Acting Independently. 146p. 1984. 12.95 (ISBN 0-13-071571-9); pap. 6.95 (ISBN 0-13-071563-8). P-H.

--Bicycle Touring & Camping. LC 81-21962. 192p. (gr. 7 up). 1982. PLB 9.79 (ISBN 0-671-42876-4). Messner.

--Calling the Play: A Beginner's Guide to Amateur Sports Officiating. LC 81-66014. (Illus.). 256p. 1984. pap. 6.95 (ISBN 0-689-70676-6, 316). Atheneum.

--Go Fly a Kite: The Complete Guide to Making & Flying Kites. (Illus.). 1979. pap. 2.95 (ISBN 0-346-12376-3). Cornerstone.

--Great Moments in the Indy 500. (Triumph Bks.). (Illus.). (gr. 6 up). 1982. PLB 8.90 (ISBN 0-531-04407-6). Watts.

--Great Moments in the NBA Championships. (Triumph Bks.). (Illus.). 96p. (gr. 5 up). 1982. PLB 8.90 (ISBN 0-531-04406-8). Watts.

--Great Moments in the Superbowl. (Triumph Bks.). (Illus.). 96p. (gr. 5 up). 1982. PLB 8.90 (ISBN 0-531-04408-4). Watts.

--Great Moments in the World Series. (Triumph Bks.). (Illus.). 96p. (gr. 5 up). 1982. PLB 8.90 (ISBN 0-531-04409-2). Watts.

--Great Mysteries of the Air. (Illus.). (gr. 4 up). 1983. 8.95 (ISBN 0-396-08185-1). Dodd.

--Great Mysteries of the Ice & Snow. (High Interest, Low Vocabulary Ser.). (Illus.). 128p. (gr. 4-9). 1985. PLB 8.95 (ISBN 0-396-08642-X). Dodd.

--Great Mysteries of the Sea. (High Interest, Low Vocabulary Ser.). (Illus.). 128p. (gr. 4 up). 1984. PLB 8.95 (ISBN 0-396-08461-3). Dodd.

--The Insanity Plea. (Impact Ser.). (gr. 7 up). 1984. lib. bdg. 9.90 (ISBN 0-531-04756-3). Watts.

--International Drug Traffic. (Single Title Ser.). 112p. 1985. lib. bdg. 10.90 (ISBN 0-531-04937-X). Watts.

--It Sounds Like Fun: How to Use & Enjoy Your Tape Recorder & Stereo. LC 81-296. (Illus.). 192p. (gr. 7 up). 1981. PLB 9.79 (ISBN 0-671-34053-0). Messner.

--Matters of Life & Death. (Impact Bks.). (Illus.). 112p. (gr. 7 up). 1982. PLB 9.90 (ISBN 0-531-04497-1). Watts.

--Matthew Henson, Black Explorer. LC 79-52053. (Illus.). (gr. 7 up). 1979. 8.95 (ISBN 0-396-07728-5). Dodd.

--Protect Your Legal Rights: A Handbook for Teenagers. LC 83-8162. (Teen Survival Library). 128p. (YA) (gr. 7 up). 1983. lib. bdg. 9.29 (ISBN 0-671-46121-4); pap. 4.95 (ISBN 0-671-49566-6). Messner.

--The Simon & Schuster Sports Question & Answer Book. Arico, Diane, ed. (Illus.). 256p. (gr. 3 up). 1984. 8.95 (ISBN 0-671-47749-8). Wanderer Bks.

--Starting Soccer. 1978. pap. 3.00 (ISBN 0-87980-352-5). Wilshire.

--Starting Soccer: A Handbook for Boys & Girls. LC 76-3838. (Illus.). (gr. 4-8). 1976. PLB 10.89 (ISBN 0-06-021683-2). HarpJ.

Dolan, Edward F., Jr. & Finney, Shan. Youth Gangs. 144p. (gr. 7 up). 1984. lib. bdg. 9.79g (ISBN 0-671-46524-4). Messner.

Dolan, Edward F., Jr. & Lyttle, Richard B. Archie Griffin. (Illus.). (gr. 4 up). 1978. pap. 1.25 (ISBN 0-671-29904-2). Archway.

--Janet Guthrie: First Woman Driver at Indianapolis. LC 77-12848. (Signal Bks.). (gr. 4-7). 1978. 7.95 (ISBN 0-385-12526-7). Doubleday.

--Kyle Rote, Jr. American-Born Soccer Star. LC 78-18561. 1979. 7.95 (ISBN 0-385-14098-3). Doubleday.

Dolan, Edward V. TV or CATV? A Struggle for Power. LC 83-12264. 1984. 12.50x (ISBN 0-8046-9329-3). Assoc Faculty Pr.

Dolan, Edwin, intro. by. The Foundations of Modern Austrian Economics. LC 76-5894. (Studies in Economic Theory). 238p. 1976. 25.00x (ISBN 0-8362-0653-3); pap. 12.00x (ISBN 0-8362-0654-1). NYU Pr.

Dolan, Edwin G. Basic Economics. 3rd ed. LC 82-72173. 1983. text ed. 31.95x (ISBN 0-03-062381-2); instr's. Manual 19.95 (ISBN 0-03-062399-5); study guide 13.95 (ISBN 0-03-062401-0). Dryden Pr.

--Basic Macroeconomics. 3rd ed. LC 82-72175. 400p. 1983. pap. text ed. 19.95x (ISBN 0-03-062407-X). Dryden Pr.

--Basic Microeconomics. 3rd ed. LC 82-72174. 464p. 1983. pap. text ed. 19.95x (ISBN 0-03-062406-1). Dryden Pr.

--TANSTAAFL: The Economic Strategy for Environmental Crisis. LC 73-147846. (Dryden Press). 1971. pap. text ed. 10.95 (ISBN 0-03-086315-5, HoltC). HR&W.

Dolan, Edwin G., jt. auth. see Goodman, John C.

Dolan, Edwin G., jt. auth. see Stoner, James A.

Dolan, Eleanor F. Half a Life to Live. 96p. 1978. pap. 10.00 (ISBN 0-318-12412-2). Am Assn Univ Women.

Dolan, Eleanor F. & Gropp, Dorothy M. The Mature Woman in America: A Selected Annotated Bibliography, 1979-1982. LC 84-3292. ix, 122p. (Orig.). 1984. pap. 10.00 (ISBN 0-910883-02-5). Natl Coun Aging.

Dolan, G. Keith. Athletes & Athletics: Sports Almanac-U. S. A. 383p. 1984. pap. 14.95 (ISBN 0-9613548-0-1); text ed. 8.95 (ISBN 0-317-11586-3). Footprint Pub.

Dolan, Grace M., jt. ed. see Dolan, Paul J.

Dolan, Jack. I Wonder Who's in Charge. LC 79-64095. 1979. pap. 4.95 (ISBN 0-8356-0529-9, Quest). Theos Pub Hse.

Dolan, Jay P. American Catholic Experience: A History from Colonial Times to the Present. LC 84-26026. 504p. 1985. 19.95 (ISBN 0-385-15206-X). Doubleday.

--Catholic Revivalism: The American Experience, 1830-1900. LC 77-89755. 1979. pap. text ed. 4.95x (ISBN 0-268-00729-2). U of Notre Dame Pr.

--Catholic Revivalism: The American Experience, 1830-1900. LC 77-89755. 1978. text ed. 19.95x (ISBN 0-268-00722-5). U of Notre Dame Pr.

--The Immigrant Church: New York's Irish & German Catholics. LC 75-12552. pap. 59.30 (ISBN 0-317-08406-2, 2019817). Bks Demand UMI.

--The Immigrant Church: New York's Irish & German Catholics, 1815-1865. LC 82-23827. (Illus.). xiv, 221p. 1983. pap. text ed. 7.95x (ISBN 0-268-01151-6, 85-11511). U of Notre Dame Pr.

Dolan, Jay P., ed. Heritage of Seventy-Six. LC 76-739. (Illus.). 160p. 1976. 9.95 (ISBN 0-268-01065-X). U of Notre Dame Pr.

Dolan, John, jt. ed. see Jedin, Hubert.

Dolan, John, ed. see More, Thomas.

Dolan, John F. Law of Letters of Credit. 1984. 77.00 (ISBN 0-88712-003-2). Warren.

Dolan, John, Jr. Bills of Particulars in New York: 1969-1984, 1 vol. LC 84-17489. 85.00. Callaghan.

Dolan, John P. Catholicism. LC 67-28536. (Orig.). 1968. pap. text ed. 5.95 (ISBN 0-8120-0273-3). Barron.

Dolan, John P. & Adams-Smith, William N. Health & Society: A Documentary History of Medicine. LC 77-13478. 1978. 12.95 (ISBN 0-8264-0112-0). Continuum.

Dolan, John P., ed. see De Cusa, Nicolas.

Dolan, John P., jt. ed. see Jedin, Hubert.

Dolan, John P., tr. see Erasmus, Desiderius.

Dolan, Joseph, tr. see Buttner, Gottfried.

Dolan, Joseph P. & Holladay, Lloyd J. First-Aid Management: Athletics, Physical Education, Recreation. LC 73-85694. (Illus.). 564p. 1974. text ed. 8.95x (ISBN 0-8134-1604-3, 1604). Interstate.

Dolan, Josephine A., et al. Nursing in Society: A Historical Perspective. 15th ed. (Illus.). 432p. 1983. 19.95 (ISBN 0-7216-3135-5). Saunders.

Dolan, Jr. Child Abuse. LC 79-26266. (gr. 7 up). 1980. PLB 10.90 (ISBN 0-531-02864-X, A29). Watts.

Dolan, Kathleen. Business Computer Systems Design. 336p. 1984. pap. text ed. 13.95x (ISBN 0-938188-20-8). Mitchell Pub.

Dolan, Maryanne. Collecting Rhinestone Jewelry. (Illus.). 248p. (Orig.). 1984. pap. 10.95 (ISBN 0-89689-049-X). Bks Americana.

--Vintage Clothing-Eighteen Eighty to Nineteen Sixty: Identification & Value Guide. 304p. 1983. pap. 10.95 (ISBN 0-89689-039-2). Bks Americana.

Dolan, Patricia G., jt. auth. see Carter, Dilford C.

Dolan, Paul. The Organization of State Administration in Delaware. LC 78-64211. (Johns Hopkins University. Studies in the Social Sciences. Sixty-Eighth Ser. 1950: 1). Repr. of 1951 ed. 18.00 (ISBN 0-404-61316-0). AMS Pr.

Dolan, Paul J. Of War & War's Alarms: Fiction & Politics in the Modern World. LC 75-11287. (Illus.). 1976. 9.95 (ISBN 0-02-907500-9). Free Pr.

Dolan, Paul J., jt. auth. see Quinn, Edward G.

Dolan, Paul J. & Bennett, Joseph T., eds. Introduction to Fiction. LC 73-18250. Repr. of 1974 ed. 133.30 (ISBN 0-8357-9915-8, 2012360). Bks Demand UMI.

Dolan, Paul J. & Dolan, Grace M., eds. Introduction to Drama. LC 73-18343. pap. 120.00 (ISBN 0-317-10084-X, 2012359). Bks Demand UMI.

Dolan, Paul J. & Quinn, Edward, eds. The Sense of the Seventies: A Rhetorical Reader. 1978. pap. 9.95x (ISBN 0-19-502309-9). Oxford U Pr.

Dolan, Pavel, tr. see Tondl, Ales.

Dolan, Pavel, tr. see Vojtasek, S. & Janac, K.

Dolan, Richard C. Fresh Starts: Charting Your New Career. 224p. 1984. 19.95 (ISBN 0-931028-50-7). Pluribus Pr.

Dolan, Robert, jt. ed. see Fisher, John S.

Dolan, Steve. Decision at Burlington. 1978. 6.95 (ISBN 0-87839-034-0). North Star.

Dolan, T. P., jt. ed. see Dunning, Thomas.

Dolan, Terrence R., jt. auth. see Mayzner, Mark S.

Dolan, Terrence R., jt. ed. see Mayzner, Mark S.

Dolan, Thomas J. Fusion Research, 3 vols. LC 80-18383. 1000p. Set. 130.00 (ISBN 0-08-025565-5); Vol. I. pap. 25.00 (ISBN 0-08-025566-3); Vol. II. pap. 28.00 (ISBN 0-08-025567-1); Vol. III. pap. 28.00 (ISBN 0-08-028817-0). Pergamon.

Dolan, Walter. The Classical World Bibliography of Greek & Roman History. LC 76-52511. (Library of Humanities Reference Bks.: No. 94). 247p. 1978. lib. bdg. 36.00 (ISBN 0-8240-9879-X). Garland Pub.

--The Classical World Bibliography of Greek Drama & Poetry. LC 76-52510. (Library of Humanities Reference Bks.: No. 93). 350p. 1978. lib. bdg. 48.00 (ISBN 0-8240-9880-3). Garland Pub.

--The Classical World Bibliography of Philosophy, Religion, & Rhetoric. LC 76-52512. (Library of Humanities Reference Bks.: No. 95). 396p. 1978. lib. bdg. 51.00 (ISBN 0-8240-9878-1). Garland Pub.

Dolan, Yvonne. A Path with a Heart: Ericksonian Utilization with Chronic & Resistant Clients. 220p. 1985. 25.00 (ISBN 0-87630-389-0). Brunner-Mazel.

Doland, Edmund, tr. see Duhem, Pierre.

Dolar-Mantuani, Ludmila. Handbook of Concrete Aggregates: A Petrographic & Technological Evaluation. LC 83-12180. (Illus.). 345p. 1984. 48.00 (ISBN 0-8155-0951-0). Noyes.

Dolbeare, K. M. American Public Policy: A Citizen's Guide. 1982. 18.95x (ISBN 0-07-017405-9). McGraw.

Dolbeare, Kenneth & Medcalf, Linda J. Neopolitics: Today's Political Ideas. 320p. 1985. pap. text ed. 8.95 (ISBN 0-394-33565-1, RanC). Random.

Dolbeare, Kenneth, jt. auth. see Medcalf, Linda.

Dolbeare, Kenneth, et al. Institutions, Policies, & Goals: A Reader in American Politics. 1973. pap. text ed. 6.95x (ISBN 0-669-82511-5). Heath.

Dolbeare, Kenneth M. American Political Thought. rev. ed. LC 84-19927. 576p. 1984. pap. text ed. 14.95x (ISBN 0-934540-36-5). Chatham Hse Pubs.

--Democracy at Risk: The Politics of Economic Renewal. LC 84-19928. (Chatham House Series on Change in American Politics). 256p. 1984. 20.00 (ISBN 0-934540-27-6); pap. text ed. 11.95x (ISBN 0-934540-26-8). Chatham Hse Pubs.

Dolbeare, Kenneth M. & Dolbeare, Patricia. American Ideologies. 3rd ed. 1976. pap. 16.50 (ISBN 0-395-30795-3). HM.

Dolbeare, Kenneth M. & Edelman, Murray J. American Politics: Policies, Power, & Change. 4th ed. 592p. 1981. pap. text ed. 17.95 (ISBN 0-669-03348-0); student guide 6.95 (ISBN 0-669-03957-8); instr's guide 1.95 (ISBN 0-669-03701-X). Heath.

Dolbeare, Kenneth M. & Hammond, Philip E. School Prayer Decisions: From Court Policy to Local Practice. LC 70-140461. 1971. 8.00x (ISBN 0-226-15515-3). U of Chicago Pr.

Dolbeare, Kenneth M., jt. auth. see Davis, James W., Jr.

Dolbeare, Kenneth M., ed. Public Policy Evaluation. LC 75-14631. (Sage Yearbooks in Politics & Public Policy: Vol. 2). 286p. 1975. 28.00 (ISBN 0-8039-0268-9); pap. 14.00 (ISBN 0-8039-0312-X). Sage.

Dolbeare, Patricia, jt. auth. see Dolbeare, Kenneth M.

Dolben, Digby M. The Poems of Digby Mackworth Dolben. Bridges, Robert, ed. & memoir by. 1915. 25.00 (ISBN 0-8274-3152-X). R West.

Dolby & Tukey. The Statistics CumIndex, Vol. 1. LC 72-86074. 1973. 43.00 (ISBN 0-88274-000-8). R & D Pr.

Dolby, A. E., et al. Introduction to Oral Immunology. (Illus.). 1982. 11.95 (ISBN 0-7216-3130-4). Saunders.

Dolby, G. L. Charles Dickens As I Knew Him. LC 79-130252. (English Literature Ser., No. 33). 1970. Repr. of 1885 ed. lib. bdg. 54.95x (ISBN 0-8383-1142-3). Haskell.

Dolby, J. L. Evaluation of the Utility & Cost of Computerized Library Catalogues. 1969. 27.50x (ISBN 0-262-04023-9). MIT Pr.

Dolby, Thomas. The Shakespeare Dictionary: Forming a General Index to All the Popular Expressions, & Most Striking Passages in the Works of Shakespeare. 1982. Repr. of 1832 ed. lib. bdg. 100.00 (ISBN 0-89760-144-0). Telegraph Bks.

Dolby, William, tr. Eight Chinese Plays: From the Thirteenth Century to the Present. LC 77-15601. 1978. 17.00x (ISBN 0-231-04488-7). Columbia U Pr.

Dolce, Donald & Devellard, Jean-Paul. The Consumer's Guide to Menswear. (Illus.). 1983. pap. 9.95 (ISBN 0-89696-188-5). Lodestar Bks.

Dolce, Philip C., jt. ed. see Coppa, Frank J.

Dolcetta, I. C., et al, eds. Recent Mathematical Methods in Dynamic Programming. (Lecture Notes in Mathematics: Vol. 1119). vi, 202p. 1985. pap. 14.40 (ISBN 0-387-15217-2). Springer-Verlag.

Dolch, Edward W. Psychology & Teaching of Reading. LC 76-97327. Repr. of 1951 ed. lib. bdg. 20.00x (ISBN 0-8371-3087-5, DOPR). Greenwood.

Dolch, Edward W. & Dolch, M. P. Aesop's Stories. (Pleasure Reading Ser.). (Illus.). (gr. 3-12). 1951. PLB 7.29 (ISBN 0-8116-2602-4). Garrard.

--Andersen Stories. (Pleasure Reading Ser.). (Illus.). (gr. 3-12). 1956. PLB 7.29 (ISBN 0-8116-2601-6). Garrard.

--Animal Stories. (Basic Vocabulary Ser.). (Illus.). (gr. 1-6). 1952. PLB 7.29 (ISBN 0-8116-2501-X). Garrard.

--Bear Stories. (Basic Vocabulary Ser.). (gr. 1-6). 1957. PLB 7.29 (ISBN 0-8116-2510-9). Garrard.

--Big, Bigger, Biggest. (First Reading Bks.). (gr. 1-4). 1959. PLB 5.58 (ISBN 0-8116-2807-8). Garrard.

--Circus Stories. (Basic Vocabulary Ser.). (gr. 1-6). 1956. PLB 7.29 (ISBN 0-8116-2512-5). Garrard.

--Dog Stories. (Basic Vocabulary Ser.). (gr. 1-6). 1954. PLB 7.29 (ISBN 0-8116-2508-7). Garrard.

--Elephant Stories. (Basic Vocabulary Ser.). (gr. 1-6). 1956. PLB 7.29 (ISBN 0-8116-2509-5). Garrard.

--Fairy Stories. (Pleasure Reading Ser.). (gr. 3-12). 1950. PLB 7.29 (ISBN 0-8116-2600-8). Garrard.

--Famous Stories. (Pleasure Reading Ser.). (gr, 3-12). 1955. PLB 7.29 (ISBN 0-8116-2603-2). Garrard.

--Far East Stories. (Pleasure Reading Ser.). (gr. 3-12). 1953. PLB 7.29 (ISBN 0-8116-2606-7). Garrard.

--Folk Stories. (Basic Vocabulary Ser.). (gr. 1-6). 1952. PLB 7.29 (ISBN 0-8116-2500-1). Garrard.

--Friendly Birds. (First Reading Bks.). (gr. 1-4). 1959. PLB 5.58 (ISBN 0-8116-2805-1). Garrard.

--Gospel Stories. (Pleasure Reading Ser.). (gr. 3-12). 1951. PLB 7.29 (ISBN 0-8116-2608-3). Garrard.

--Greek Stories. (Pleasure Reading Ser.). (gr. 3-12). 1955. PLB 7.29 (ISBN 0-8116-2607-5). Garrard.

--Gulliver's Stories. (Pleasure Reading Ser.). (gr. 3-12). 1960. PLB 7.29 (ISBN 0-8116-2611-3). Garrard.

--Horse Stories. (Basic Vocabulary Ser.). (gr. 1-6). 1958. PLB 7.29 (ISBN 0-8116-2514-1). Garrard.

--I Like Cats. (First Reading Books Ser). (gr. 1-4). 1959. PLB 5.58 (ISBN 0-8116-2809-4). Garrard.

--In the Woods. (First Reading Bks.). (gr. 1-4). 1958. PLB 5.58 (ISBN 0-8116-2800-0). Garrard.

--Irish Stories. (Basic Vocabulary Ser.). (gr. 1-6). 1958. PLB 7.29 (ISBN 0-8116-2513-3). Garrard.

--Ivanhoe. (Pleasure Reading Ser.). (gr. 3-12). 1961. PLB 7.29 (ISBN 0-8116-2612-1). Garrard.

--Lion & Tiger Stories. (Basic Vocabulary Ser.). (gr. 1-6). 1957. PLB 7.29 (ISBN 0-8116-2511-7). Garrard.

--Lodge Stories. (Basic Vocabulary Ser.). (gr. 1-6). 1957. PLB 7.29 (ISBN 0-8116-2506-0). Garrard.

--Monkey Friends. (Dolch First Reading Bks.). (gr. 1-4). 1958. PLB 5.58 (ISBN 0-8116-2803-5). Garrard.

--More Dog Stories. (Dolch Basic Vocabulary Ser.). (gr. 1-6). 1962. PLB 7.29 (ISBN 0-8116-2515-X). Garrard.

--Navaho Stories. (Dolch Basic Vocabulary Ser.). (Illus.). (gr. 1-6). 1957. PLB 7.29 (ISBN 0-8116-2507-9). Garrard.

--Old World Stories. (Dolch Pleasure Reading Ser.). (gr. 3-12). 1952. PLB 7.29 (ISBN 0-8116-2605-9). Garrard.

--Once There Was a Bear. (First Reading Bks.). (Illus.). (gr. 1-4). 1962. PLB 5.58 (ISBN 0-8116-2814-0). Garrard.

--Once There Was a Cat. (Dolch First Reading Bks.). (gr. 1-4). 1961. PLB 5.58 (ISBN 0-8116-2812-4). Garrard.

--Once There Was a Dog. (First Reading Bks.). (gr. 1-4). 1962. PLB 5.58 (ISBN 0-8116-2815-9). Garrard.

--Once There Was a Monkey. (Dolch First Reading Bks.). (Illus.). (gr. 1-4). 1962. PLB 5.58 (ISBN 0-8116-2813-2). Garrard.

--Once There Was a Rabbit. (Dolch First Reading Bks.). (gr. 1-4). 1961. PLB 5.58 (ISBN 0-8116-2811-6). Garrard.

--Once There Was an Elephant. (Dolch First Reading Bks.). (gr. 1-4). 1961. PLB 5.58 (ISBN 0-8116-2810-8). Garrard.

--Pueblo Stories. (Basic Vocabulary Ser.). (gr. 1-6). 1956. PLB 7.29 (ISBN 0-8116-2503-6). Garrard.

--Robin Hood Stories. (Dolch Pleasure Reading Ser.). (gr. 3-12). 1957. PLB 7.29 (ISBN 0-8116-2604-0). Garrard.

--Robinson Crusoe. (Dolch Pleasure Reading Ser.). (gr. 3-12). 1958. PLB 7.29 (ISBN 0-8116-2610-5). Garrard.

--Some Are Small. (Dolch First Reading Bks.). (gr. 1-4). 1959. PLB 5.58 (ISBN 0-8116-2808-6). Garrard.

--Stories from Alaska. (Dolch Folklore of the World Ser.). (gr. 2-8). 1961. PLB 8.25 (ISBN 0-8116-2554-0). Garrard.

--Stories from Canada. (Dolch Folklore of the World Ser.). (gr. 2-8). 1964. PLB 8.28 (ISBN 0-8116-2561-3). Garrard.

--Stories from France. (Dolch Folklore of the World Ser.). (Illus.). (gr. 2-8). 1963. PLB 8.28 (ISBN 0-8116-2557-5). Garrard.

--Stories from Hawaii. (Dolch Folklore of the World Ser.). (Illus.). (gr. 2-8). 1960. PLB 8.28 (ISBN 0-8116-2550-8). Garrard.

--Stories from India. (Dolch Folklore of the World Ser.). (Illus.). (gr. 2-8). 1961. PLB 8.28 (ISBN 0-8116-2553-2). Garrard.

--Stories from Italy. (Dolch Folklore of the World Ser.). (Illus.). (gr. 2-8). 1962. PLB 8.28 (ISBN 0-8116-2556-7). Garrard.

--Stories from Japan. (Dolch Folklore of the World Ser.). (Illus.). (gr. 2-8). 1960. PLB 8.28 (ISBN 0-8116-2552-4). Garrard.

--Stories from Mexico. (Dolch Folklore of the World Ser.). (Illus.). (gr. 2-8). 1960. PLB 8.28 (ISBN 0-8116-2551-6). Garrard.

--Stories from Old China. (Dolch Folklore of the World Ser.). (Illus.). (gr. 2-8). 1964. PLB 8.28 (ISBN 0-8116-2558-3). Garrard.

--Stories from Old Egypt. (Dolch Folklore of the World Ser.). (Illus.). (gr. 2-8). 1964. PLB 8.28 (ISBN 0-8116-2559-1). Garrard.

--Stories from Old Russia. (Dolch Folklore of the World Ser.). (Illus.). (gr. 2-8). 1964. PLB 7.29 (ISBN 0-8116-2560-5). Garrard.

--Stories from Spain. (Dolch Folklore of the World Ser.). (Illus.). (gr. 2-8). 1962. PLB 8.28 (ISBN 0-8116-2555-9). Garrard.

--Tommy's Pets. (Dolch First Reading Bks.). (gr. 1-4). 1958. PLB 5.58 (ISBN 0-8116-2802-7). Garrard.

--Why Stories. (Dolch Basic Vocabulary Ser.). (gr. 1-6). 1958. PLB 7.29 (ISBN 0-8116-2502-8). Garrard.

--Wigwam Stories. (Dolch Basic Vocabulary Ser.). (gr. 1-6). 1956. PLB 7.29 (ISBN 0-8116-2505-2). Garrard.

--Zoo Is Home. (First Reading Books Ser.). (gr. 1-4). 1958. PLB 5.58 (ISBN 0-8116-2801-9). Garrard.

Dolch, M. P., jt. auth. see Dolch, Edward W.

Dolch, Marguerite P. Animal Stories from Africa. LC 75-8862. (Dolch Folklore of the World Ser.). (Illus.). 176p. (gr. 2-8). 1975. PLB 8.28 (ISBN 0-8116-2563-X). Garrard.

--Once There Was a Coyote. LC 75-2124. (Dolch First Reading Bks.). (Illus.). 64p. (gr. 1-4). 1975. PLB 5.58 (ISBN 0-8116-2816-7). Garrard.

--True Cat Stories. LC 75-2146. (Dolch Basic Vocabulary Ser.). (Illus.). 176p. (gr. 1-6). 1975. PLB 7.29 (ISBN 0-8116-2516-8). Garrard.

Dolci, Danilo. Creature of Creatures: Selected Poems. Vitiello, Justin, ed. (Stanford French & Italian Studies: No. 22). Orig. Title: Creatura Di Creature, Poesie, 1949-1978. xxviii, 104p. 1980. pap. 25.00 (ISBN 0-915838-17-6). Anma Libri.

--A New World in the Making. Munroe, R., tr. from It. LC 75-3990. 327p. 1976. Repr. of 1965 ed. lib. bdg. 19.25x (ISBN 0-8371-7419-8, DONW). Greenwood.

--Sicilian Lives. 1982. 16.00 (ISBN 0-394-51536-6); pap. 6.95 (ISBN 0-394-74938-3). Pantheon.

Dolciani, Mary P., et al. Intermediate Algebra for College Students. LC 71-146721. 1971. text ed. 24.95 (ISBN 0-395-12072-1); tchrs. ed. & key 8.50 (ISBN 0-395-12074-8). HM.

--Modern Introductory Analysis. 2nd ed. (gr. 11-12). 1980. text ed. 21.76 (ISBN 0-395-28697-2); tchrs.' ed. 23.30 (ISBN 0-395-28696-4); progress tests 3.96 (ISBN 0-395-19857-7). HM.

Dold, A. Lectures on Algebraic Topology. LC 79-79062. (Grundlehren der Mathematischen Wissenschaften Ser.: Vol. 200). (Illus.). 377p. 1980. 42.00 (ISBN 0-387-10369-4). Springer-Verlag.

Dold, A. & Eckmann, B., eds. Cylindric Set Algebras. (Lecture Notes in Mathematics, Ser.: Vol. 883). 323p. 1981. pap. 20.00 (ISBN 0-387-10881-5). Springer-Verlag.

Dold, A., ed. see Bloom, F.

Dold, A., ed. see Haley, D. K.

Dold, A., ed. see Zielke, R.

Dold, Graham. Dear Graham. 1984. 14.95 (ISBN 0-533-05788-4). Vantage.

Dolder, Eugene J. & Durrer, Gustav T. The Bar Joint Denture. (Illus.). 150p. 1978. 48.00 (ISBN 0-931386-02-0). Quint Pub Co.

Dolder, Willi, jt. auth. see Rothermund, Dietmar.

Dole, Anita S. Bible Study Notes, Vols. 1-3. Woofenden, William R., ed. LC 76-24081. 1976-78. lib. bdg. write for info. (ISBN 0-685-92171-9). Vol 1 (ISBN 0-917426-01-0). Vol. 2 (ISBN 0-917426-02-9). Vol. 3 (ISBN 0-917426-03-7). Am New Church Sunday.

--Bible Study Notes, Vol. 4. Woofenden, William R., ed. LC 76-24081. 1979. write for info. (ISBN 0-917426-04-5). Am New Church Sunday.

--Bible Study Notes, Vol. 5. Woofenden, William R., ed. LC 76-24081. 1979. write for info (ISBN 0-917426-05-3). Am New Church Sunday.

--Bible Study Notes, Vol. 6. Woofenden, William R., ed. LC 76-24081. 1979. write for info (ISBN 0-917426-06-1). Am New Church Sunday.

Dole, Charles E. Flight Theory & Aerodynamcs: A Practical Guide for Operational Safety. LC 81-3009. 299p. 1981. 42.95x (ISBN 0-471-09152-9, Pub. by Wiley-Interscience). Wiley.

--Flight Theory for Pilots. (Illus.). 244p. 1984. pap. 9.95 (ISBN 0-9614216-0-6). Aviation.

Dole, D. J., intro. by. Agricultural Engineering, 1980: Agricultural Conferences. 290p. (Orig.). 1980. pap. text ed. 45.00x (ISBN 0-85825-138-8, Pub. by Inst Engineering Australia). Brookfield Pub Co.

Dole, Daniel, tr. see Barrot, Theodore-Adolphe.

Dole, Edmund P. Hiwa, a Tale of Ancient Hawaii. (Illus.). 1977. pap. 1.00 (ISBN 0-912180-31-5). Petroglyph.

Dole, George. Introduction to Swedenborg's Theological Latin. 140p. pap. 8.95 (ISBN 0-87785-125-5). Swedenborg.

--A View from Within: A Compendium of Swedenborg's Thought. LC 85-50799. 128p. pap. 5.95 (ISBN 0-87785-128-X). Swedenborg.

Dole, George F., tr. see Swedenborg, Emanuel.

Dole, Malcolm, ed. The Radiation Chemistry of Macromolecules, 2 vols. 1972. Vol. 1. 73.50 (ISBN 0-12-219801-8). Acad Pr.

Dole, Nathan H. Famous Composers. facsimile ed. LC 68-24848. (Essay Index Reprint Ser). Orig. Title: Score of Composers. (Illus.). 1936. Repr. of 1891 ed. 40.00 (ISBN 0-8369-0382-X). Ayer Co Pubs.

--Teacher of Dante, & Other Studies in Italian Literature. facs. ed. LC 67-26733. (Essay Index Reprint Ser). 1908. 16.00 (ISBN 0-8369-0383-8). Ayer Co Pubs.

--The Wisdom of Marcus Aurelius. (Illus.). 145p. Repr. of 1903 ed. 87.15 (ISBN 0-89901-055-5). Found Class Reprints.

Dole, Nathan H., ed. see Rambaud, Alfred N.

Dole, Nathan H., tr. see Dupuy, Ernest.

Dole, Nathan H., tr. see Tolstoy, Leo N.

Dole, Nathan Haskell. The Life of Count Lyof N. Tolstoi. 1911. 30.00 (ISBN 0-8274-2882-0). R West.

Dole, Richard F., jt. auth. see Alderman, Richard.

Dolecheck, Carolyn C. & Murphy, Danny W. Applied Word Processing. 1983. text ed. 13.50 (ISBN 0-538-23760-0, W76). SW Pub.

Dolejs, Ladislaw, jt. auth. see Sorm, Frantisek.

Dolejsi, Robert. Modern Viola Technique. LC 72-8343. (Music Ser.). (Illus.). viii, 133p. 1973. Repr. of 1939 ed. lib. bdg. 25.00 (ISBN 0-306-70552-4). Da Capo.

Doleman, Edgar. Tools of War. Dreyfus, Paul, ed. LC 84-72888. (Vietnam Experience Ser.: Vol. XIII). (Illus.). 176p. 1984. 16.95 (ISBN 0-939526-13-1). Boston Pub Co.

Doleschal, Eugene. Prevention of Crime & Delinquency. LC 83-82948. (Dialogue Bks.). 1984. 12.75 (ISBN 0-89881-017-5). Intl Dialogue Pr.

Doleschal, Eugene & Newton, Anne. A Guide to the Literature on Organized Crime: An Annotated Bibliography Covering the Years 1967-81. 182p. 1981. 21.50 (ISBN 0-318-15365-3). Natl Coun Crime.

Dolesh, Daniel J. & Lehman, Sherelynn. Love Me, Love Me Not: How to Survive Infidelity. 256p. 1985. 16.95 (ISBN 0-07-017394-X). McGraw.

Doleski, Teddi. The Hurt. (Illus.). 32p. (gr. 2-5). 1983. pap. 1.95 (ISBN 0-8091-6551-1). Paulist Pr.

Doleys, Daniel M., et al, eds. Behavioral Psychology in Medicine & Rehabilitation: Assessment & Treatment Strategies. LC 81-23376. 647p. 1982. 47.50 (ISBN 0-306-40841-4, Plenum Pr). Plenum Pub.

Dolezal, Hubert. Living in a World Transformed: Perceptual & Performatory Adaptation to Visual Distortion. LC 81-14856. (Cognition & Perception Ser.). 1981. 49.50 (ISBN 0-12-219950-2). Acad Pr.

Dolezal, Ivan. Asian & African Studies, Vol. 17. 360p. 1981. 35.00x (ISBN 0-7007-0145-1, Pub. by Curzon England). State Mutual Bk.

--Asian & African Studies, Vol. 18. 323p. 1982. text ed. 15.50x (ISBN 0-7007-0156-7, 41190, Pub. by Curzon Pr England). Humanities.

Dolezal, Ivan, ed. Asian & African Studies, Vol. 15. 1979. text ed. 15.50x (ISBN 0-7007-0130-3). Humanities.

--Asian & African Studies, Vol. 16. 360p. 1980. text ed. 15.50x (ISBN 0-7007-0137-0). Humanities.

--Asian & African Studies, Vol. 17. 360p. 1981. text ed. 15.50x (ISBN 0-7007-0145-1, Pub. by Curzon Pr England). Humanities.

Dolezal, R. & Varcop, L. Process Dynamics: Automatic Control of Steam Generation Plant. (Illus.). 460p. 1970. 26.00 (ISBN 0-444-20042-8, Pub. by Elsevier Applied Sci England). Elsevier.

Dolezal, V. Nonlinear Networks. 156p. 1977. 42.75 (ISBN 0-444-41571-8). Elsevier.

Dolezal, V. J. Monotone Operators & Applications in Control & Network Theory. (Studies in Automation & Control: Vol. 2). 174p. 1979. 42.75 (ISBN 0-444-41791-5). Elsevier.

Dolezalek, H. The Application of Atmospheric Electricity Concepts & Methods to Other Parts of Meteorology. (Technical Note Ser.: No. 162). 130p. 1978. pap. 20.00 (ISBN 92-63-10507-3, W414, WMO). Unipub.

Dolezel, L., et al, eds. Language & Literary Theory. (Papers in Slavic Philology Ser.: No. 5). 1985. 15.00 (ISBN 0-930042-59-X). Mich Slavic Pubns.

Dolezelova-Velingerova, Milena, ed. The Chinese Novel at the Turn of the Century. (Modern East Asian Studies). 1980. 35.00x (ISBN 0-8020-5473-0). U of Toronto Pr.

Dolfino, Pietro see Brown, Howard M.

Dolgachev, I., ed. Algebraic Geometry. (Lecture Notes in Mathematics Ser.: Vol. 1008). 138p. 1983. pap. 10.00 (ISBN 0-387-12337-7). Springer-Verlag.

Dolgan, Robert. The Polka King: The Life of Frankie Yankovic. LC 77-72539. (Illus.). 1977. 8.95 (ISBN 0-913228-23-0). Dillon-Liederbach.

Dolge, Alfred. Men Who Have Made Piano History. (Illus.). 242p. 1980. 15.00 (ISBN 0-911572-18-X). Vestal.

--Pianos & Their Makers. (Illus.). 581p. 1972. pap. 7.00 (ISBN 0-486-22856-8). Dover.

--Pianos & Their Makers: A Comprehensive History of the Development of the Piano from the Monochord to the Concert Grand Player Piano. (Illus.). 13.25 (ISBN 0-8446-4540-0). Peter Smith.

Dolger, Franz J. Der Exorzismus Im Altchristlichen Taufritual. 1909. pap. 15.00 (ISBN 0-384-12090-3). Johnson Repr.

--Sphragis. 1911. pap. 15.00 (ISBN 0-384-12095-4). Johnson Repr.

Dolger, Henry & Seeman, Bernard. How to Live with Diabetes. 3rd ed. LC 70-159453. 1972. 6.50 (ISBN 0-393-06378-X). Norton.

--How to Live with Diabetes. 4th ed. 1977. 10.95 (ISBN 0-393-06424-7). Norton.

--How to Live with Diabetes. 4th ed. LC 78-54397. 1978. pap. 5.95 (ISBN 0-8052-0603-5). Schocken.

--How to Live with Diabetes. 5th ed. 1985. 15.95 (ISBN 0-393-01917-9). Norton.

Dolgin, Janet L. Jewish Identity & the JDL. LC 76-325. 1976. 22.50 (ISBN 0-691-09368-7). Princeton U Pr.

Dolgin, Janet L., et al, eds. Symbolic Anthropology: A Reader in the Study of Symbols & Meanings. LC 77-3176. 523p. 1977. text ed. 42.00x (ISBN 0-231-04032-6); pap. 18.00x (ISBN 0-231-04033-4). Columbia U Pr.

Dolgin, Robert M. The Bank Income Tax Return Manual with Specimen Filled-in Returns. 1984. 72.00 (80-54680). Warren.

Dolgoff, Ralph & Feldstein, Donald. Understanding Social Welfare. 2nd ed. LC 83-20003. 400p. 1984. pap. text ed. 19.95 (ISBN 0-582-28462-7). Longman.

Dolgoff, Ralph, jt. auth. see Loewenberg, Frank.

Dolgoff, Ralph, jt. auth. see Loewenberg, Frank M.

Dolgopolov, Y. Army & the Revolutionary Transformation of Society. 112p. 1981. pap. 2.50 (ISBN 0-8285-2186-7, Pub. by Progress Pubs USSR). Imported Pubns.

Dolgopolva, Z., ed. Russia Dies Laughing: Jokes from Soviet Russia. (Illus.). 126p. 1983. 9.95 (ISBN 0-233-97402-4, Pub by Salem Hse Ltd). Merrimack Pub Cir.

Dolgov, K. M., et al. Marxist-Leninist Aesthetics & the Arts. 1980. 8.95 (ISBN 0-8285-1839-4, Pub. by Progress Pubs USSR). Imported Pubns.

D'Olier, J. & Delmas, B. Planning National Infrastructures for Documentation, Libraries, & Archives. (Documentation, Libraries & Archives: Studies & Research: No. 4). 328p. 1975. pap. 14.50 (ISBN 92-3-101144-8, U454, UNESCO). Unipub.

Dolin, Anton. Dolin: Friends & Memories. Wheatcroft, Andrew, ed. (Illus.). 192p. 1984. pap. 14.95 (ISBN 0-7102-0237-7). Routledge & Kegan.

--Friends & Memories. Wheatcroft, Andrew, compiled by. (Illus.). 192p. 1984. 29.95 (ISBN 0-7100-9199-0); pap. 14.95 (ISBN 0-7102-0237-7). Routledge & Kegan.

--Pas de Deux: The Art of Partnering. LC 68-17403. (Illus.). 1969. pap. 2.95 (ISBN 0-486-22038-9). Dover.

Dolin, Armin. Buy-Sell-Merge-Affiliate: Insurance Agency Manual & Workbook, 2 vols. LC 82-81856. 626p. 1982. Set. 75.00 (ISBN 0-87218-319-X). Vol. I, 490p. Vol. II, 136p. Natl Underwriter.

Dolin, Arnold, jt. ed. see Geiser, Elizabeth.

Dolin, Edwin, ed. see Aeschylus & Sophocles.

Dolin, John, Jr. Examination Before Trial & Other Disclosure Devices, 1984. LC 84-1903. 85.00 (ISBN 0-317-12203-7). Callaghan.

Dolinar, F. & Schmitt, S. The Osborne-McGraw-Hill 16-Bit CP-M User's Guide. (Osborne Books). 500p. 1984. pap. 18.95 (ISBN 0-88134-130-4). McGraw.

Dolinato, Gerardo Reichel see Reichel-Dolmatoff, Gerardo.

Doliner, Roy. The Twelfth of April. 320p. 1985. 16.95 (ISBN 0-517-55735-5). Crown.

Doling, J. F., jt. auth. see Hobbs, F. D.

Doling, John & Davies, Mary. Public Control of Privately Rented Housing: Studies in Urban & Regional Policy, 2. 184p. 1984. text ed. 36.50x (ISBN 0-566-00732-0). Gower Pub Co.

Dolinsky, Mike. A Corporate Affair. (Orig.). 1981. pap. 2.95 (ISBN 0-440-11435-7). Dell.

Dolit, Alan. You Can Lose Weight. 130p. 1980. 7.95 (ISBN 0-8290-1571-X). Irvington.

Dolitsky, Marlene. Under the Tumtum Tree: From Nonsense to Sense. LC 84-28471. (Pragmatics & Beyond Ser.: Vol. 1). vii, 119p. (Orig.). 1984. pap. 18.00x (ISBN 0-915027-39-9). Benjamins North Am.

Dolive, Linda L. Electoral Politics at the Local Level in the German Federal Republic. LC 76-26473. (University of Florida Social Sciences Monographs: No. 56). (Illus.). 1976. pap. 4.00 (ISBN 0-8130-0554-X). U Presses Fla.

D'Oliveira, H. U., ed. Netherlands Reports to the Eleventh International Congress of Comparative Law. 465p. 1982. pap. 34.00 (ISBN 90-65-4407-39). Kluwer Academic.

--Netherlands Reports to the Tenth International Congress of Comparative Law, Budapest. 380p. 1978. pap. 36.00 (ISBN 90-26-81008-3). Kluwer Academic.

D'Oliveira, Manuela, jt. auth. see Greene, Judith.

D'Olivet, Fabre. The Hebraic Tongue Restored. Redfield, Louise N., tr. 1976. 35.00 (ISBN 0-87728-332-X). Weiser.

Dolkart, Ronald, jt. ed. see Falcoff, Mark.

Doll, Dixon R. Data Communications: Facilities, Networks, & System Design. LC 77-12508. 493p. 1978. 49.95x (ISBN 0-471-21768-9, Pub by Wiley-Interscience). Wiley.

--Data Communications: Facilities, Networks & System Design. 493p. 1978. 34.50 (ISBN 0-686-98099-9). Telecom Lib.

Doll, Howard D. Oral Interpretation of Literature: An Annotated Bibliography with Multimedia Listings. LC 82-3344. 505p. 1982. 35.00 (ISBN 0-8108-1538-9). Scarecrow.

Doll, John & George, Terry. The On-Your-Own Guide to Asia. 5th, rev. ed. 383p. 1981. 6.95 (ISBN 0-8048-1353-1). Appropriate Techn Proj.

Doll, John P. & Orazem, Frank. Production Economics: Theory with Applications. Esposito, R., ed. LC 76-41478. (Agricultural Economics Ser.). 406p. 1978. text ed. 33.95x (ISBN 0-471-87001-3). Wiley.

--Production Economics: Theory with Applications. 2nd ed. LC 83-21575. 470p. 1984. text ed. 34.95 (ISBN 0-471-87470-1). Wiley.

Doll, R., ed. see IARC Meeting, Primosten, Yugoslavia. Aug. 27-Sept. 2, 1972.

Doll, Richard & Peto, Richard. The Causes of Cancer: Quantitative Estimates of Avoidable Risks of Cancer in the U. S. Today. 1981. pap. text ed. 14.95x (ISBN 0-19-261359-6). Oxford U Pr.

Doll, Richard, ed. see Royal Society of London.

Doll, Ronald C. Curriculum Improvement: Decision Making & Process. 5th ed. 500p. 1981. text ed. 33.22 (ISBN 0-205-07558-4, 237558). Allyn.

--Supervision for Staff Development: Ideas & Application. 450p. 1983. scp 31.43 (ISBN 0-205-07854-0, 237854). Allyn.

Doll, Thomas E. Flying Leathernecks in World War Two. LC 79-123469. (Aero Pictorial Ser.: Vol. 4). (Illus., Orig.). 1971. pap. 4.95 (ISBN 0-8168-0312-9). Aero.

Doll, Thomas E., jt. auth. see Jackson, B. R.

Doll, Thomas E., et al. Navy Air Colors, Vol. 1. (Aircraft Special Ser.: No. 6156). (Illus.). 96p. 1983. 8.95 (ISBN 0-89747-143-1). Squad Sig Pubns.

Doll, Tom, jt. auth. see Maloney, Edward.

Doll, Tom, jt. auth. see Weber, Eberhard D.

Dollar, Alta & Burnett, Mary J. Business English: A Guide for Successful Communication. 440p. 1983. scp 22.00 (ISBN 0-205-07786-2, 067786); instr's. manual avail. Allyn.

Dollar, Alta, jt. auth. see Burnett, Mary J.

Dollar, Bruce. Learning & Growing through Tutoring. 130p. 1974. pap. 4.00 (ISBN 0-912041-07-2). Natl Comm Res Youth.

Dollar, Bruce & Kleinbard, Peter. Thinking about the Work Experience. 65p. 1981. pap. write for info. (ISBN 0-912041-11-0). Natl Comm Res Youth.

--Youth Participation in Documenting CETA Youth Employment Programs. 62p. 1981. pap. 5.00 (ISBN 0-912041-10-2). Natl Comm Res Youth.

Dollar, Charles M. America, 2 vols. Incl. Vol. 1. Changing Times to 1877. study guide, 264 p. 7.95 (ISBN 0-471-05908-0); Vol. 2. Changing Times Since 1865. study guide avail. (ISBN 0-471-05907-2). LC 78-12242. 1979. Wiley.

Dollar, Charles M., et al. America: Changing Times, A Brief History. 729p. 1984. pap. text ed. 17.95 (ISBN 0-394-34209-7, RanC). Random.

Dollar, Michele. The Fabulous Frog Book. (Illus.). 96p. (Orig.). 1984. pap. text ed. 4.95 (ISBN 0-88693-076-6). Banbury Bks.

Dollar, William E. Effective Purchasing & Inventory Control for Small Business. 160p. 1983. Comb-bound 22.95 (ISBN 0-8436-0893-5). Van Nos Reinhold.

Dollard, Jerry. Toward Spirituality: The Inner Journey. 20p. 1983. pap. 0.85 (ISBN 0-89486-193-X). Hazelden.

Dollard, John. Criteria for the Life History. 11.25 (ISBN 0-8446-1158-1). Peter Smith.

--Criteria for the Life History, with Analyses of Six Notable Documents. (Select Bibliographies Reprint Ser.). Repr. of 1935 ed. 20.00 (ISBN 0-8369-6685-6). Ayer Co Pubs.

--Fear in Battle. LC 75-41076. Repr. of 1944 ed. 9.50 (ISBN 0-404-14714-3). AMS Pr.

Dollard, John & Horton, Donald. Fear in Battle. LC 77-2970. 1977. Repr. of 1944 ed. lib. bdg. 24.75x (ISBN 0-8371-9579-9, DOFB). Greenwood.

Dollard, John, jt. auth. see Miller, Neal E.

Dollard, John, et al. Frustration & Aggression. LC 79-26458. 1980. Repr. of 1939 ed. lib. bdg. 27.50x (ISBN 0-313-22201-0, DOFR). Greenwood.

Dollard, John D. & Friedman, Charles N. Encyclopedia of Mathematics & Its Applications: Product Integration with Applications to Differential Equations, Vol. 10. 1984. 39.50 (ISBN 0-521-30230-7). Cambridge U Pr.

Dollarhide, Kenneth. Nichiren's Senji-sho: An Essay on the Selection of Proper Time. LC 82-21687. (Studies in Asian Thought & Religion: Vol. 1). 184p. 1983. 39.95x (ISBN 0-88946-051-5). E Mellen.

Dollarhide, Kenneth, tr. Micheren's Senji-sho: An Essay on the Selection of the Proper Time. LC 82-21687. (Studies in Asian Thought & Religion: Vol. 1). 176p. 1983. 29.95x (ISBN 0-88946-051-5). Voter Ed Proj.

Dollarhide, Louis. Of Art & Artists: Selected Reviews of the Arts in Mississippi, 1955-1976. LC 80-52629. (Illus.). 166p. 1981. 4.95 (ISBN 0-87805-144-9). U Pr of Miss.

Dollarhide, Louis D., jt. ed. see Abadie, Ann J.

Dollberg, Donald D. & Verstuyft, Allen W., eds. Analytical Techniques in Occupational Health Chemistry. LC 79-28460. (ACS Symposium Ser.: No. 120). 1980. 39.95 (ISBN 0-8412-0539-6). Am Chemical.

Dolleans, Edouard. Histoire du Mouvement Ouvrier, 3 vols. in two. Mayer, J. P., ed. LC 78-67350. (European Political Thought Ser.). (Fr.). 1979. Repr. of 1953 ed. Set. lib. bdg. 84.00x (ISBN 0-405-11693-4); Vols. 1 & 2. lib. bdg. 42.00x (ISBN 0-405-11694-2); Vol. 3. 36.00x (ISBN 0-405-11696-9). Ayer Co Pubs.

Dollen, Charles. Civil Rights. (Magister Paperback Ser). (Orig.). 1964. pap. 1.00 (ISBN 0-8198-0031-7). Dghtrs St Paul.

--Jesus Lord. (Orig.). 1964. 3.00 (ISBN 0-8198-0066-X); pap. 2.00 (ISBN 0-8198-0067-8). Dghtrs St Paul.

--John F. Kennedy. American. (Illus., Orig.). 1965. 5.00 (ISBN 0-8198-0068-6); pap. 4.00 (ISBN 0-8198-0069-4). Dghtrs St Paul.

--Prayer Book of the Saints. LC 84-60749. 1984. pap. 6.95 (ISBN 0-87973-717-4, 717). Our Sunday Visitor.

--Prayers for the Third Age: A Devotion for the Mature Catholic. LC 85-60889. 200p. (Orig.). 1985. pap. 7.95 (ISBN 0-87973-837-5, 837). Our Sunday Visitor.

--Ready or Not. LC 67-29164. 1969. 3.00 (ISBN 0-8198-0130-5). Dghtrs St Paul.

Dollenmayer, David, et al. Neue Horizonte. 544p. 1984. text ed. 23.95 (ISBN 0-669-04534-9). Heath.

Dollerup, Cay. Denmark, Hamlet & Shakespeare, 2 vols. (Salzburg Studies in English Literature, Elizabethan & Renaissance Studies Ser.: No. 47). 347p. (Orig.). 1975. Set. pap. text ed. 50.75x (ISBN 0-391-01363-7). Humanities.

Dollery, Colin. The End of an Age of Optimism: Medical Science in Retrospect & Prospect. 104p. 1978. 30.00x (ISBN 0-900574-29-1, Pub. by Nuffield England). State Mutual Bk.

Dolley, M. The Norman Conquest & the English Coinage. 1966. 3.00 (ISBN 0-685-51535-4, Pub by Spink & Son England). S J Durst.

Dolley, M., jt. auth. see Brown, I. D.

Dolley, Michael. Anglo-Norman Ireland, Vol. 3. (Gill History of Ireland). (Illus.). 210p. 1973. pap. 7.95 (ISBN 0-7171-0560-1). Irish Bk Ctr.

Dollfus, Charles & Bouche, Henri. Histoire de l'Aeronautique: The History of Aeronautics. Gilbert, James, ed. LC 79-7246. (Flight: Its First Seventy-Five Years Ser.). (Illus., Fr.). 1979. Repr. of 1942 ed. lib. bdg. 229.00x (ISBN 0-405-12158-X). Ayer Co Pubs.

Dollfus, Jean. France: Its Geography & Growth. 128p. 1972. 15.25 (ISBN 0-7195-1898-9). Transatlantic.

Dollimore, jt. auth. see European Symposium on Thermal Analysis.

Dollimore, D. Thermal Analysis: European Symposium 2nd, Proceedings. 1981. 71.95 (ISBN 0-471-25661-7, Pub. by Wiley Heyden). Wiley.

Dollimore, D., jt. auth. see Keattch, C. J.

Dollimore, Jonathan. Radical Tragedy: Religion, Ideology, & Power in the Drama of Shakespeare & His Contemporaries. LC 83-18290. viii, 312p. 1984. 22.50x (ISBN 0-226-15538-2). U of Chicago Pr.

Dollimore, Jonathan & Sinfield, Alan, eds. Political Shakespeare: New Essays in Cultural Materialism. LC 84-72950. 256p. 1985. text ed. 29.95x (ISBN 0-8014-1794-5); pap. text ed. 9.95x (ISBN 0-8014-9325-0). Cornell U Pr.

Dollimore, Jonathan, ed. see Webster, John.

Dollinger, A., ed. Dictionary of Metallurgy. 767p. (Eng., Fr., Ger., Rus., Pol. & Slovene.). 1974. 150.00 (ISBN 0-686-92409-6, M-9893). French & Eur.

Dollinger, Hans. The Decline & Fall of Nazi Germany & Imperial Japan. (Illus.). 1968. 7.98 (ISBN 0-517-01313-4). Outlet Bk Co.

Dollinger, Johann J. Von. Lectures on the Reunion of the Churches. LC 74-131579. (Sources in the History of Interpretation: No. 2). 1973. 15.00x (ISBN 0-8401-0567-3). A R Allenson.

Dollinger, Johann J. Von. see Von Dollinger, Johann J.

Dollinger, John J. The First Age of Christianity & the Church. 1977. lib. bdg. 59.95 (ISBN 0-8490-1840-4). Gordon Pr.

Dollinger, Philippe. The German Hansa. Ault, D. S. & Steinberg, S. H., trs. from Ger. LC 77-120697. 1970. 30.00x (ISBN 0-8047-0742-1). Stanford U Pr.

Dollot, Rene. L' Afghanistan. LC 75-179192. (Illus.). Repr. of 1937 ed. 24.50 (ISBN 0-404-54822-9). AMS Pr.

Dolman, Anthony J. Resources, Regimes, World Order. (Pergamon Policy Studies on International Development Ser.). 425p. 1981. 41.00 (ISBN 0-08-028080-3); pap. 10.95 (ISBN 0-08-028079-X). Pergamon.

Dolman, Anthony J., ed. Global Planning & Resource Management: Toward International Decision Making in a Divided World. (Pergamon Policy Studies on International Development). 272p. 1980. 24.00 (ISBN 0-08-026309-7); pap. 9.25 (ISBN 0-08-026320-8). Pergamon.

Dolman, Bernard. The Dictionary of Contemporary British Artists, 1929. 551p. 1981. 39.50 (ISBN 0-902028-99-5). Antique Collect.

--Dictionary of Contemporary British Artists 1929. 561p. 1985. 39.50 (ISBN 0-902028-99-5). Apollo.

Dolman, C. L. Ultrastructure of Brain Tumors & Biopsies: A Diagnostic Atlas. LC 84-3469. (Methods in Laboratory Medicine Ser.: Vol. 5). 272p. 1984. 34.95 (ISBN 0-03-068897-3). Praeger.

Dolman, Dirk H. The Tabernacle. 525p. 1982. Repr. lib. bdg. 19.75 smythe sewn (ISBN 0-86524-152-X, 0203). Klock & Klock.

Dolman, Frederick. Municipalities at Work: The Municipal Policy of Six Great Towns & Its Influence On... Lees, Lynn H. & Lees, Andrew, eds. LC 84-48287. (The Rise of Urban Britain Ser.). 1985. Repr. of 1895 ed. lib. bdg. 30.00 (ISBN 0-8240-6289-2). Garland Pub.

Dolman, John. Art of Acting. LC 79-109289. Repr. of 1949 ed. lib. bdg. 32.50x (ISBN 0-8371-3832-9, DOAA). Greenwood.

Dolman, Sue, illus. Brambly Hedge Pattern Book. (Illus.). 64p. 1985. 14.95 (ISBN 0-399-21194-2, Philomel). Putnam Pub Group.

Dolmatoff, Gerardo Reichel see Reichel-Dolmatoff, Gerardo.

Dolmatz, M., jt. auth. see Wong, H.

Dolmatz, Malvin, jt. auth. see Wong, Harry.

Dolmetsch, A., ed. Select English Songs & Dialogues of the 16th & 17th Centuries, 2 vols. in 1. LC 74-24070. Repr. of 1898 ed. 34.50 (ISBN 0-404-12897-1). AMS Pr.

Dolmetsch, Arnold. Interpretation of the Music of the Seventeenth & Eighteenth Centuries. LC 76-75611. (Illus.). 512p. 1969. pap. 8.95x (ISBN 0-295-78578-0, WP51); 2 Stereo Cassettes 20.00 13.50 (ISBN 0-295-75007-3). U of Wash Pr.

Dolmetsch, Carl R., ed. see Hansford, Charles.

Dolmetsch, Christopher. The German Press of the Shenandoah Valley, 1789-1854. LC 81-69881. (Studies in German Literature, Linguistics, & Culture: Vol. 4). (Illus.). 157p. 1984. 19.00x (ISBN 0-938100-01-7). Camden Hse.

Dolmetsch, Joan D. Eighteenth Century Prints in Colonial America: To Educate & Decorate. LC 78-25921. (Illus.). xviii, 206p. 1979. Repr. of 1980 ed. 11.95x (ISBN 0-87935-049-0). U Pr of Va.

--Rebellion & Reconciliation: Satirical Prints on the Revolution at Williamsburg. LC 75-41443. (Illus.). viii, 221p. 1976. 12.95x (ISBN 0-87935-032-6, Williamsburg Decorative Arts Ser.). U Pr of Va.

Dolmetsch, Mabel. Dances of England & France from 1450-1600: With Their Music & Authentic Manner of Performance. LC 74-34449. (Ser. in Dance). (Illus.). xii, 163p. 1975. lib. bdg. 22.50 (ISBN 0-306-70725-X); pap. 6.95 (ISBN 0-306-80025-X). Da Capo.

--Dances of Spain & Italy from 1400 to 1600. LC 74-28450. (Series in Dance). (Illus.). xii, 174p. 1975. Repr. of 1954 ed. lib. bdg. 22.50 (ISBN 0-306-70726-8). Da Capo.

--Personal Recollections of Arnold Dolmetsch. (Music Reprint Ser.). (Illus.). 1980. Repr. of 1957 ed. lib. bdg. 25.00 (ISBN 0-306-76022-3). Da Capo.

Dolmetsch, Paul & Shih, Alexa. Kid's Book about Single Parent Families. LC 84-21156. 216p. 1985. pap. 7.95 (ISBN 0-385-19279-7, Dolp). Doubleday.

Dolney, Pam C., jt. auth. see Ito, Robert.

Dolnick, Sandy, ed. Friends of Libraries Sourcebook. LC 80-24643. 176p. 1980. pap. 7.00x (ISBN 0-8389-3245-2). ALA.

Dologite, Dorothy. Using Small Business Computers. (Illus.). 448p. 1984. text ed. 24.95 (ISBN 0-13-940156-3). P-H.

Dologite, Dorothy G. Using Small Business Computers with Lotus 1-2-3, dBASE II & Wordstar. 1985. text ed. 24.95 (ISBN 0-13-940230-6). P-H.

Dolon, Bill, jt. auth. see Warner, Karen.

Dolores, Carmen. Aunt Zeze's Tears. Goldberg, Isaac, ed. & tr. (International Pocket Library). pap. 4.00 (ISBN 0-8283-1426-8). Branden Pub Co.

Dolot, Miron. Execution by Hunger: The Hidden Holocaust. LC 84-16568. 1985. 16.95 (ISBN 0-393-01886-5). Norton.

Dolphin, D., et al. Pyridoxal Phosphate: Chemical, Biochemical & Medical Aspects, 2 vols. 1985. Vol. 1, Pt. A. 150.00 (ISBN 0-471-09785-3); Vol. 1, Pt. B. 200.00 (ISBN 0-471-09783-7). Wiley.

Dolphin, D., jt. auth. see Dunford, H. B.

Dolphin, David. B-12, 2 vols. LC 81-10300. 1176p. 1982. Set of Vols. 1 & 2. 154.95x (ISBN 0-471-03655-2, Pub. by Wiley-Interscience). Wiley.

--BTwelve, Vols. 1 & 2. Chemistry, Vol. 1, 671p. 85.95 (ISBN 0-471-80846-6); Biochemistry & Medicine, Vol. 2, 505p. 85.95 (ISBN 0-471-80844-X); Two vol. set, 1176p. 165.95 (ISBN 0-471-03655-2). Wiley.

Dolphin, David & Wick, Alexander. Tabulation of Infared Spectral Data. LC 76-48994. 566p. 1977. 31.50 (ISBN 0-471-21780-8). Krieger.
Dolphin, David, ed. The Porphyrins. Incl. Vol. 1, Pt. A. 1978. 78.00 (ISBN 0-12-220101-9); Physical Chemistry. 1978. Vol. 3, Pt. A. 90.00 (ISBN 0-12-220103-5); Vol. 4, Pt. B, 1979. 65.00 (ISBN 0-12-220104-3); Vol. 5, Pt. C. 77.50 (ISBN 0-12-220105-1). LC 77-14197. 1978-79. Acad Pr.
--The Porphyrins: Biochemistry, Vol. 6, Pt. A. 1979. 95.00 (ISBN 0-12-220106-X); o.p. 83.50 set. Acad Pr.
--The Porphyrins Vol. 7: Biochemistry Part B. 1979. 69.50 (ISBN 0-12-220107-8). Acad Pr.
Dolphin, David, et al, eds. Biomimetic Chemistry. LC 80-22864. (ACS Advances in Chemistry Ser.: No. 191). 1980. 59.95 (ISBN 0-8412-0514-0). Am Chemical.
Dolphin, Deon K. Rune Magic. 20p. 1982. pap. 5.00 (ISBN 0-9613157-3-3). D K Dolphin.
Dolphin, Philippa, et al. The London Region: An Annotated Geographical Bibliography. 396p. 1981. 61.00x (ISBN 0-7201-1598-1). Mansell.
Dolphin, Richard. The Principles of Data Communications. 1983. write for info. (ISBN 0-935506-15-2). Carnegie Pr.
Dolph Owings, W. A. The Sarajevo Trial, 2 vols. Pribic, E. & Pribic, N., eds. 1984. 49.95x (ISBN 0-89712-122-8). Documentary Pubns.
Dols, M. W. The Black Death in the Middle East. 1976. 42.00x (ISBN 0-691-03107-X). Princeton U Pr.
Dols, Michael W. Medieval Islamic Medecine: Ibn Ridwan's Treatise "On the Prevention of Bodily Ills in Egypt". Gamal, Adil S., ed. Dols, Michael W., tr. from Arabic. LC 83-5017. (Comparative Studies of Health Systems & Medical Care). 250p. 1984. lib. bdg. 35.00x (ISBN 0-520-04836-9). U of Cal Pr.
Dols, Michael W., tr. see Dols, Michael W.
Dolson, Bobbie J. Van see Aaen, Bernhard.
Dolson, Bobbie J. Van see Armistead, Charles.
Dolson, Bobbie J. Van see Baerg, Harry J.
Dolson, Bobbie J. Van see Degering, Etta B.
Dolson, Bobbie J. Van see Dewees, Eleanor.
Dolson, Bobbie J. Van see Hills, Desmond B.
Dolson, Bobbie J. Van see Irland, Nancy B.
Dolson, Bobbie J. Van see Johnston, Madeline.
Dolson, Bobbie J. Van see Jones, Lucile.
Dolson, Bobbie J. Van see Loller, Sherry G.
Dolson, Bobbie J. Van see Osman, Jack & Van Dolson, Bobbie J.
Dolson, Bobbie J. Van see Todd, Sharon.
Dolson, Bobbie J. Van see Van Dolson, Leo & Van Dolson, Robbie.
Dolson, Bobbie J. Van see Vollmer, Marion W. & Sonnenberg, Lydia.
Dolson, Bobbie J. Van see Willis, Mary.
Dolson, Frank. Always Young: A Biography. LC 75-20961. (Illus.). 206p. (Orig.). 1975. pap. 3.95 (ISBN 0-89037-072-9); handbk. 4.95 (ISBN 0-89037-073-7). Anderson World.
--Beating the Bushes: Life in the Minor Leagues. (Illus.). 296p. 1983. 13.95 (ISBN 0-89651-055-7). Icarus.
--The Philadelphia Story: A City of Winners. (Illus.). 336p. 1981. 12.95 (ISBN 0-89651-600-8). Icarus.
Dolson, Gina, ed. Lisa & the Magic Doll: Russian & Ukrainian Fairy Tales. Mandeville, Jerry & Brodsky, Anna, trs. from Rus. & Ukrainian. (Folk Tales from Russia Ser.). (Illus.). 56p. (Orig.). (gr. 4-10). 1985. pap. 4.50x (ISBN 0-914265-07-5). New Eng Pub MA.
Dolson, John. Black Canyon of the Gunnison: A Guide & Reference Book. LC 82-531. (Illus.). 80p. (Orig.). 1982. pap. 4.95 (ISBN 0-87108-622-0). Pruett.
Dolson, Leo Van see Van Dolson, Leo.
Dolstra, O. Synthesis & Fertility of Brassicoraphanus & Ways of Transferring Raphanus Characters to Brassica. (Agricultural Research Reports: No. 917). 98p. 1982. pap. 14.50 (ISBN 90-220-0805-3, PDC256, PUDOC). Unipub.
Dolukhanov, Paul M. Ecology & Economy in Neolithic Eastern Europe. (Illus.). 1979. 29.95x (ISBN 0-312-22613-6). St Martin.
Dolzall, Donnette & Model Railroader Staff, eds. ABC's of Model Railroading. LC 78-55680. 1978. pap. 6.75 (ISBN 0-89024-536-3). Kalmbach.
Dolzall, Donnette, ed. see Model Railroader Staff.
Dolzall, Gary & Dolzall, Stephen. Diesel From Eddystone: The Story of Baldwin Diesel Locomotives. Hayden, Bob, ed. (Illus.). 152p. (Orig.). 1984. pap. 18.95 (ISBN 0-89024-052-3). Kalmbach.
Dolzall, Stephen, jt. auth. see Dolzall, Gary.
Dolzer, Rudolf. Property & Environment: The Social Obligation Inherent in Ownership. (Environmental Policy & Law Papers: No. 12). 72p. 1976. pap. 10.00 (ISBN 2-88032-082-8, IUCN41, IUCN). Unipub.
Domagala, R., jt. auth. see Rostoker, W.
Domalain, Jean-Yves. The Animal Connection: The Confessions of an Ex-Wild Animal Trafficker. Barnett, Marguerite, tr. from Fr. (Illus.). 250p. 1978. 17.50x (ISBN 0-8464-1181-4). Beekman Pubs.
Doman. Teach Your Baby to Read Book. 9.95 (ISBN 0-224-60064-8, Pub. by Jonathan Cape). Merrimack Pub Cir.
Doman, Bruce K. Goodbye, Mommy. LC 77-79632. (The Gentle Revolution Ser.). (Illus.). 86p. 1982. 7.95 (ISBN 0-936676-00-0). Better Baby.
Doman, Glenn. How to Multiply Your Baby's Intelligence. LC 83-9026. (Illus.). 336p. 1984. 15.95 (ISBN 0-385-18880-3). Doubleday.
--How to Teach Your Baby How to Read. 160p. 1975. pap. 4.50 (ISBN 0-385-11161-4, Dolp). Doubleday.
--How to Teach Your Baby to Read. rev. ed. LC 80-70032. (The Gentle Revolution Ser.). 166p. 1983. 9.50 (ISBN 0-936676-01-9). Better Baby.
--Nose Is Not Toes. LC 81-67340. (Gentle Revolution Ser.). (Illus.). 84p. 1963. 7.95 (ISBN 0-936676-12-4). Better Baby.
--Teach Your Baby Math. 112p. 1982. pap. 2.75 (ISBN 0-671-41615-4). PB.
--The Teach Your Baby to Read Kit. 160p. 1980. 9.95 (ISBN 0-224-60064-8, Pub. by Jonathan Cape); instruction kit 7.95 (ISBN 0-224-60081-8, Pub. by Jonathan Cape). Merrimack Pub Cir.
--What to Do about Your Brain Injured Child. LC 72-92202. (Illus.). 312p. 1974. 14.95 (ISBN 0-385-02139-9). Doubleday.
Doman, Glenn & Armentrout, J. Michael. The Universal Multiplication of Intelligence. LC 80-66236. (The Gentle Revolution Ser.). 223p. 1980. 12.50 (ISBN 0-936676-02-7). Better Baby.
Doman, Glenn, et al. How to Give Your Baby Encyclopedic Knowledge. LC 83-73584. (The Gentle Revolution Ser.). (Illus.). 325p. 1984. 14.95 (ISBN 0-936676-34-5). Better Baby.
--How to Give Your Baby Encyclopedic Knowledge. LC 84-28701. 312p. 1985. 15.95 (ISBN 0-385-19974-0). Doubleday.
Domandi, Agnes K. & Guilloton, D. S. Deutsche Literatur Von Heute: An Intermediate German Course. 1974. text ed. 19.95 (ISBN 0-03-005626-8, HoltC). HR&W.
Domandi, Agnes K., ed. Modern German Literature, 2 vols. LC 70-160436. (Library of Literary Criticism Ser.). Set. 100.00 (ISBN 0-8044-3075-6). Ungar.
Domandi, Mario, tr. see Cassirer, Ernst.
Domanska, Janina. Busy Monday Morning. LC 83-25362. (Illus.). 32p. (ps-1). 1985. 13.00 (ISBN 0-688-03833-6); PLB 12.88 (ISBN 0-688-03834-4). Greenwillow.
--Din Dan Don It's Christmas. LC 75-8509. (Illus.). 32p. (ps-3). 1975. 11.75 (ISBN 0-688-80003-3). Greenwillow.
--King Krakus & the Dragon. LC 78-12934. (Illus.). 32p. (gr. k-3). 1979. 13.00 (ISBN 0-688-80189-7); PLB 12.88 (ISBN 0-688-84189-9). Greenwillow.
--Marek, the Little Fool. LC 81-6966. (Illus.). 32p. (gr. k-3). 1982. 11.75 (ISBN 0-688-00912-3); PLB 11.88 (ISBN 0-688-00913-1). Greenwillow.
--A Scythe, a Rooster, & a Cat. LC 80-17445. (Illus.). 32p. (gr. k-3). 1981. 11.75 (ISBN 0-688-80308-3); PLB 11.88 (ISBN 0-688-84308-5). Greenwillow.
--Spring Is. LC 75-25953. (Illus.). 32p. (gr. k-3). 1976. PLB 11.88 (ISBN 0-688-84026-4). Greenwillow.
--What Do You See? LC 73-6052. (Illus.). 32p. (gr. k-2). 1974. 9.95 (ISBN 0-02-732830-9, 73283). Macmillan.
--What Happens Next? LC 82-24219. (Illus.). 32p. (gr. k-3). 1983. 11.50 (ISBN 0-688-01748-7); PLB 11.88 (ISBN 0-688-01749-5). Greenwillow.
Domanski, Don. Cape Breton Book of the Dead. (House of Anansi Poetry Ser.: No. 34). 60p. 1975. 2.00 (ISBN 0-88784-035-3, Pub. by Hse Anansi Pr Canada); pap. 3.95 (ISBN 0-88784-135-X). U of Toronto Pr.
--Heaven. (House of Anansi Poetry Ser.: No. 37). 62p. (Orig.). 1978. pap. 5.95 (ISBN 0-88784-069-8, Pub. by Hse Anansi Pr Canada). U of Toronto Pr.
--War in an Empty House. (House of Anansi Poetry Ser.: No. 41). 72p. (Orig.). 1982. pap. 6.95 (ISBN 0-88784-094-9, Pub. by Hse Anansi Pr Canada). U of Toronto Pr.
Domar, Evsey D. Essays in the Theory of Economic Growth. LC 82-6262. x, 272p. 1982. Repr. of 1957 ed. lib. bdg. 35.00x (ISBN 0-313-23592-9, DOET). Greenwood.
Domart, Andre & Bourneuf, Jacques. Larousse de la Medecine, 3 vols. 1728p. 1971. Set. 225.00 (ISBN 0-686-57120-7, M-6166). French & Eur.
Domart, Andre, ed. Petit Larousse De la Medecine. Bourneuf, Jacques. 852p. (Fr.). 1976. 42.50 (ISBN 0-686-57075-8, M-6448). French & Eur.
Domart, Andre & Bourneuf, Jacques, eds. Larousse de la Medecine, 2. 515p. (Fr.). 87.50 (ISBN 0-686-56993-8, M-6333). French & Eur.
Domaszewski, Alfred von see Von Domaszewski, Alfred.
Domat, Jean. The Civil Law in Its Natural Order, 2 vols. Cushing, Luther S., ed. Strahan, William, tr. from Fr. 1763p. 1981. Repr. of 1850 ed. Set. lib. bdg. 97.50x (ISBN 0-8377-0511-8). Rothman.
Domb, C. & Lebowitz, J. L. Phase Transitions & Critcal Phenomena, Vol. 9. LC 77-170760. 1984. 60.00 (ISBN 0-12-220309-7). Acad Pr.
Domb, C. & Green, M., eds. Phase Transitions & Critical Phenomena. Vol. 1. 1973. 83.00 (ISBN 0-12-220301-1); Vol. 2. 1972. 84.50 (ISBN 0-12-220302-X); Vol. 5a. 1976. 69.50 (ISBN 0-12-220305-4); Vol. 5B. 1976. 69.50 (ISBN 0-12-220351-8); Vol. 6. 1977. 99.50 (ISBN 0-12-220306-2). Acad Pr.
--Phase Transitions & Critical Phenomena: Series Expansion for Lattice Models, Vol. 3. 1974. 99.00 (ISBN 0-12-220303-8). Acad Pr.
Domb, C. M. & Lebowitz, Joel L., eds. Phase Transitions & Critical Phenomena, Vol. 7. 1983. 60.00 (ISBN 0-12-220307-0). Acad Pr.
Domb, Cyril, jt. ed. see Carmell, Aryeh.
Domb, Risa. The Arab in Hebrew Prose 1911-1948. 192p. 1982. text ed. 27.50x (ISBN 0-85303-203-3, Pub. by Vallentine Mitchell England). Biblio Dist.
Dombal, E. T. De see IFIP TC Four Working Conference & De Dombal, E. T.
Dombal, F. T. see Rozen, P. & De Dombal, F. T.
Dombal, F. T. De see De Dombal, F. T.
Dombal, Robert W. Residential Condominiums: A Guide to Analysis & Appraisal. 77p. 1976. pap. 10.00 (ISBN 0-911780-37-8). Am Inst Real Estate Appraisers.
Domberger, Simon & Murphy, Philip. Industrial Structure, Pricing & Inflation. LC 83-13993. 208p. 1983. 27.50 (ISBN 0-312-41567-2). St Martin.
Dombradi, Z. S. & Fenyes, T. In Beam Nuclear Spectroscopy. 820p. 1984. 75.00 (ISBN 9-63053-993-4, Pub. by Akademiai Kiado Hungary). Heyden.
Dombrady, Dora T. Orko. 1977. 10.00 (ISBN 0-918570-06-9). Karpat.
Dombroff, Mark A. Dombroff on Demonstrative Evidence. LC 83-6514. 238p. 1983. 75.00x (ISBN 0-471-87112-5, Pub. by Wiley Law Pubns). Wiley.
--Dombroff on Demonstrative Evidence: 1985 Supplement. (Trial Practice Library). 1985. pap. 25.00 (ISBN 0-471-82937-4). Wiley.
--Dombroff on Direct & Cross-Examination. LC 85-9321. (Trial Practice Library Ser.: No. 1-676). 1985. 75.00 (ISBN 0-471-82034-2). Wiley.
--Dombroff on Unfair Tactics. (Trial Practice Library Ser.: No. 1-676). 300p. 1984. text ed. 75.00 (ISBN 0-471-88463-4, Wiley Law Pubns). Wiley.
--Dynamic Closing Arguments. LC 85-9335. write for info. (ISBN 0-13-221391-5). P-H.
--Key Trial Control Tactics: A Guide to Winning the Ultimate Verdict. rev., enl. ed. LC 84-8099. 1984. 99.50 (ISBN 0-13-515073-6). Exec Reports.
--Litigation Organization & Management: Effective Tactics & Techniques. LC 84-1257. 1984. 60.00 (ISBN 0-15-004369-4, #H43694, Law & Business). HarBraceJ.
--Personal Injury Defense Reporter. 1985. looseleaf incl. one year's service 150.00 (571); looseleaf annual renewal 150.00. Bender.
--U. S. A. Products Liability Litigation Institute. LC 85-139119. (Illus.). Date not set. price not set. Lawyers Co-op.
Dombrovsky, A. In the White Stone's Shadow. 1979. 4.95 (ISBN 0-8285-1909-9, Pub. by Progress Pubs USSR). Imported Pubns.
Dombrowski, Daniel A. The Philosophy of Vegetarianism. LC 83-18125. 192p. 1984. lib. bdg. 20.00x (ISBN 0-87023-430-7); pap. 9.95 (ISBN 0-87023-431-5). U of Mass Pr.
Dombrowski, Eric. German Leaders of Yesterday & Today. facs. ed. LC 67-23206. (Essay Index Reprint Ser). 1920. 20.00 (ISBN 0-8369-0384-6). Ayer Co Pubs.
Dombrowski, James. Early Days of Christian Socialism in America. 1966. lib. bdg. 19.50x (ISBN 0-374-92223-3). Octagon.
Dombrowski, Sharon A. A Concise Manual on the Theory of Music. (Illus.). 64p. (Orig.). 1983. 5.00 (ISBN 0-9610658-0-X). Blue Note.
Domcroft, Mark A. & Practice Law Institute. Aircraft Crash Litigation 1984. LC 83-62215. (Litigation Course Handbook Ser.: No. 267). (Illus.). 349p. 1984. 35.00. PLI.
Domench, Dan. Three American One-Act Monologues: Frontier Trailer Court, Caliber of Faith, Covered Bridge. 39p. (Orig.). 1983. pap. 3.95 (ISBN 0-913341-00-2). Coyote Love.
Domencich, T. Urban Travel Demand. LC 74-30936. (Contributions to Economic Analysis Ser.: Vol. 93). 215p. 1975. 51.00 (ISBN 0-444-10830-0, North-Holland). Elsevier.
Domenech, Margie, ed. Oxbridge Directory of Newsletters 1985-86. 4th rev. ed. 400p. 1985. pap. 95.00 (ISBN 0-917460-13-8). Oxbridge Comm.
Domenet, J. G., jt. ed. see Mitchell, J. R.
Domenico, Joseph M. Di see DiDomenico, Joseph M.
Domer, Larry R., jt. auth. see Snyder, Thomas L.
Domer, Larry R., ed. see Snyder, Thomas L. & Bauer, Jeffrey C.
Domer, Larry R., et al. Dental Practice Management: Concepts & Application. LC 80-15309. (Illus.). 376p. 1980. text ed. 29.95 (ISBN 0-8016-1422-8). Mosby.
Domergue, Denise. Artists Design Furniture. (Illus.). 176p. 1984. 35.00 (ISBN 0-8109-0932-4). Abrams.
Domes, Jurgen. China after the Cultural Revolution. Goodman, David, tr. from Ger. 1977. 33.00x (ISBN 0-520-03064-8). U of Cal Pr.
--The Government & Politics of the PRC: A Time for Transition. 300p. 1985. 42.50x (ISBN 0-86531-565-5); pap. text ed. 17.95x (ISBN 0-86531-566-3). Westview.
--P'eng Te-Huai: A Political Biography. LC 85-50942. 224p. 1986. 25.00x (ISBN 0-8047-1303-0). Stanford U Pr.
--Socialism in the Chinese Countryside. 1980. 32.50x (ISBN 0-7735-0532-6). McGill-Queens U Pr.
Domesdav Commemoration, 1886. Domesday Studies, 2 Vols. Dove, P. Edward, ed. 1965. Repr. of 1891 ed. 57.50 (ISBN 0-8337-0895-3). B Franklin.
Domhoff, G. William. The Bohemian Grove & Other Retreats: A Study in Ruling-Class Cohesiveness. abr. ed. 128p. 1975. pap. 4.95xi (ISBN 0-06-131880-9, TB1880, Torch). Har-Row.
--Higher Circles: The Governing Class in America. 1971. pap. 3.95 (ISBN 0-394-71671-X, Vin). Random.
--The Mystique of Dreams: A Search for Utopia Through Senoi Dream Therapy. LC 85-970. 1975. 14.95 (ISBN 0-520-05504-7). U of Cal Pr.
--The Powers That Be: Process of Ruling Class Domination in America. LC 78-55633. 1979. pap. 5.95 (ISBN 0-394-72649-9, Vin). Random.
--Who Really Rules? New Have & Community Power Reexamined. 190p. 1978. text ed. 29.95 (ISBN 0-87855-228-6). Transaction Bks.
--Who Rules America Now? A View for the Eighties. 230p. (Orig.). (YA) (gr. 9-12). 1983. 15.95 (ISBN 0-13-958413-7, Spec); pap. 6.95 (ISBN 0-13-958405-6, Spec). P-H.
Domhoff, G. William, ed. Power Structure Research. (Sage Focus Editons: No. 17). (Illus.). 270p. 1980. 28.00 (ISBN 0-8039-1431-8). Sage.
Domhoff, G. William, jt. ed. see Ballard, Hoyt B.
Domhoff, William G., ed. see Zweigenhaft, Richard L.
Domholdt, L. C., jt. auth. see Tuve, George L.
Domico, Terry. Western Wild Harvest: Edible Plants of The Pacific Northwest. (Illus.). 88p. 1979. pap. 6.95 (ISBN 0-88839-022-X). Hancock House.
Domingo, Placido. My First Forty Years. LC 83-48100. (Illus.). 1983. 15.95 (ISBN 0-394-52329-6). Knopf.
--My First Forty Years. (Illus.). 288p. 1984. pap. 7.95 (ISBN 0-14-007367-1). Penguin.
Domingo, Willis, tr. see Adorno, Theodor.
Domingo, Zenaida T. The Community Advisory Board as the Grass Roots Planning Arm of Broadcasting in the Philippines. (Institute of Culture & Communication Case Studies: No. 10). (Illus.). xii, 137p. (Orig.). 1984. pap. 5.00 (ISBN 0-86638-041-8). E W Center HI.
Domingo De Guzman, Saint The Life of St. Dominie in Old French Verse. Manning, Warren F., ed. (Harv Studies in Romance Languages). 1944. 32.00 (ISBN 0-527-01118-5). Kraus Repr.
Dominguez. Economic Issues & Political Conflict: U. S.- Latin America Relation. 1982. text ed. 49.95. Butterworth.
Dominguez, G. S., ed. Guidebook: Toxic Substances Control Act. 448p. 1977. 66.00 (ISBN 0-8493-5321-1). CRC Pr.
Dominguez, George S. The Business Guide to Tosca: Effects & Actions. LC 79-20054. 365p. 1980. 45.95 (ISBN 0-471-05371-6, Pub. by Wiley Interscience). Wiley.
--The Business Guide to Tosca: Effects & Actions. LC 79-20054. pap. 95.80 (ISBN 0-317-26169-X, 2025187). Bks Demand UMI.
--Government Relations: A Hanbook of Developing & Conducting the Company Program. LC 81-11500. 420p. 1982. 50.50 (ISBN 0-471-06421-1, Pub. by Wiley-Interscience). Wiley.
--Government Relations: A Handbook for Developing & Conducting the Company Program. LC 81-11500. (A Wiley-Interscience Publication). pap. 109.50 (ISBN 0-317-26182-7, 2025182). Bks Demand UMI.
--Marketing in a Regulated Environment. LC 77-22099. (Marketing Management Ser.). Repr. of 1978 ed. 89.80 (ISBN 0-8357-9525-X, 2055255). Bks Demand UMI.
Dominguez, Henry. The Ford Agency: A Pictorial History. 1981. pap. 14.95 (ISBN 0-87938-095-0). Motorbooks Intl.
Dominguez, Jorge I. U. S. Interests & Policies in the Caribbean & Central America. 1982. pap. 4.75 (ISBN 0-8447-1097-0). Am Enterprise.
Dominguez, Jorge I., jt. auth. see Dominguez, Virginia R.
Dominguez, Jorge I., ed. Cuba: Internal & International Affairs. (Sage Focus Editions). (Illus.). 224p. 1982. 24.00 (ISBN 0-8039-1843-7); pap. 12.00 (ISBN 0-8039-1844-5). Sage.
Dominguez, Jorge L. Cuba: Order & Revolution. LC 78-8288. 1978. 35.00x (ISBN 0-674-17925-0, Belknap Pr). Harvard U Pr.
Dominguez, Luis, ed. The Conquest of the River Plate (1535-1555) LC 73-281410. (Hakluy Soc. First Ser.: No. 81). 282p. 1891. Repr. 30.50 (ISBN 0-8337-0881-3). B Franklin.
Dominguez, Richard H. Complete Book of Sports Medicine. 1980. pap. 6.95 (ISBN 0-446-38181-0). Warner Bks.
Dominguez, Richard H. & Gajda, Robert. Total Body Training. (Illus.). 256p. 1982. 14.95 (ISBN 0-684-17320-4, ScribT). Scribner.
Dominguez, Richard H. & Gajda, Robert J. Total Body Training. 288p. 1983. pap. 8.95 (ISBN 0-446-38279-5). Warner Bks.
Dominguez, Sylvia. La Comadre Maria. LC 73-86204. 1973. pap. 5.95 (ISBN 0-913632-05-8). Am Univ Artforms.
--La Comadre Maria Instruction Production System. 1976. pap. 64.00 (ISBN 0-913632-12-0). Am Univ Artforms.

Dominguez, Virginia R. & Dominguez, Jorge I. The Caribbean: Its Implications for the United States. LC 81-65441. (Headline Ser.: No. 253). (Illus.). 80p. (Orig.). 1981. pap. 3.00 (ISBN 0-87124-068-8). Foreign Policy.

Dominguez, Xorge A., tr. see McNair, Harold M.

Domini, Amy L. & Kinder, Peter D. Ethical Investing. LC 84-2783. (Illus.). 256p. 1984. 17.95 (ISBN 0-201-10803-8, 1726). Addison-Wesley.

Domini, John. Bedlam. LC 81-71002. 135p. (Orig.). 1981. pap. 6.95 (ISBN 0-931362-03-2). Fiction Intl.

Dominiak, Geraldine J. & Louderback, Joseph G. Managerial Accounting. 4th ed. LC 84-23395. 816p. 1984. text ed. write for info. (ISBN 0-534-04185-X). Kent Pub Co.

Dominiak, Pati, jt. ed. see Sheldon, Roger.

Dominian, B. The Frontiers of Language & Nationality in Europe. 1917. 30.00 (ISBN 0-8274-2385-3). R West.

Dominian, J. Marital Breakdown. 1969. 5.95 (ISBN 0-8199-0151-2, L38436). Franciscan Herald.

Dominian, Jack. The Capacity to Love. 176p. (Orig.). 1985. text ed. 5.95 (ISBN 0-8091-2726-1). Paulist Pr.

--The Growth of Love & Sex. LC 84-1573. pap. 23.80 (ISBN 0-317-30137-3, 2025320). Bks Demand UMI.

--Make or Break: A Guide to Marriage Counselling. (Pastoral Help Bks.: Vol. 1). 1985. pap. 8.95 (ISBN 0-89453-473-4). M Glazier.

--Marriage, Faith & Love. 288p. 1982. 14.95 (ISBN 0-8245-0425-9). Crossroad NY.

Dominic, Annette V. Why Didn't He Tell Me? 28p. 1985. 6.95 (ISBN 0-533-06329-9). Vantage.

Dominic, J. F., jt. ed. see Frederiksen, C. H.

Dominic, Joseph F., jt. ed. see Frederiksen, Carl H.

Dominic, R. B. The Attending Physician. LC 79-1702. (A Harper Novel for Suspense Ser.). 1980. 11.49i (ISBN 0-06-011073-2, HarpT). Har-Row.

--Unexpected Developments. 225p. 1983. 11.95 (ISBN 0-312-83278-8, J Kahn). St Martin.

Dominic, Randolph & Barry, William. Pyrrhus Venture. 416p. 1983. 17.45i (ISBN 0-316-18934-0, Pub. by Atlantic Monthly Pr.). Little.

Dominican Fathers of the Province of St. Joseph, ed. The Maritain Volume of "The Thomist", Dedicated to Jacques Maritain on the Occasion of His 60th Anniversary. LC 77-92509. (Essay Index in Reprint Ser.). 1978. Repr. 24.50x (ISBN 0-8486-3003-3). Core Collection.

Dominican Nuns of the Perpetual Rosary, tr. see Alonso, Joaquin M.

Dominicis, F., ed. see Cusatelli, G. & Brunacci, G.

Dominicis, M. C. & Cussen, J. Casos y Cosas. LC 80-15371. 1981. text ed. 11.00 (ISBN 0-394-33286-5, RanC). Random.

--Casos y Cosas. 2nd ed. 1985. pap. text ed. 11.95 (ISBN 0-394-33663-1, RanC). Random.

Dominicis, Maria C. Don Juan En el Teatro Espanol Del Siglo XX. LC 77-89033. 1978. pap. 10.00 (ISBN 0-89729-180-8). Ediciones.

--Escenas Cotidianas. 246p. 1983. pap. text ed. 12.00 (ISBN 0-394-33420-5, RanC). Random.

Dominick, Bayard. Joe, a Porpoise. (Illus.). (gr. 3-5). 1968. 7.95 (ISBN 0-8392-3067-2). Astor-Honor.

--Sam, a Goat. (Illus.). (gr. 3-5). 1968. 7.95 (ISBN 0-8392-3062-1). Astor-Honor.

Dominick, John J. St. Cloud: The Triplet City. (Illus.). 192p. 1983. 22.95 (ISBN 0-89781-091-0). Windsor Pubns Inc.

Dominick, Joseph. The Dynamics of Mass Communication. 512p. 1983. pap. text ed. 19.95 (ISBN 0-394-35004-9, RanC). Random.

Dominick, Joseph R., jt. auth. see Wimmer, Roger D.

Dominick, Joseph R. & Fletcher, James E., eds. Broadcasting Research Methods. 1985. text ed. 35.73 net (ISBN 0-205-08307-2, 488307). Allyn.

Dominick, Mary F., ed. Human Rights & the Helsinki Accord. LC 81-80195. x, 411p. 1981. Repr. lib. bdg. 30.00 (ISBN 0-89941-095-2). W S Hein.

Dominick, Raymond H., III. Wilhelm Liebknecht & the Founding of the German Social Democratic Party. LC 81-16329. xiv, 551p. 1982. 25.00x (ISBN 0-8078-1510-1). U of NC Pr.

Dominik, Mark. William Shakespeare & the Birth of Merlin. LC 84-20694. 213p. 1985. 19.95 (ISBN 0-8022-2469-5). Philos Lib.

Dominioni, Valerie. Cooking with Italian Cheese. (Cucina Classica Italiana Ser.). (Illus.). 160p. 1985. 14.95 (ISBN 0-86573-081-4). Cy De Cosse.

Dominique, C. Rene. The Economic Analysis of the Dynamics of Food Crop Production. (European University Studies: Series 5, Economics: Vol. 188). 139p. 1979. 17.70 (ISBN 3-261-02455-0). P Lang Pubs.

Dominique, Jean Leopold. Vibrancy or the Weight of Inertia: A Testimonial to Haitian Original Creative Expression Across Endogenous or Exogenous Constraints. 14p. 1982. pap. 5.00 (ISBN 92-808-0270-4, TUNU200, UNU). Unipub.

Dominique-Rene de Lerma. Bibliography of Black Music: Geographical Studies, Vol. 3. LC 80-24681. (Encyclopedia of Black Music Ser.). xiv, 284p. 1982. lib. bdg. 35.00 (ISBN 0-313-23510-4, DBI/03). Greenwood.

Dominitz, Ben. How to Find the Love of Your Life: Ninety Days to a Permanent Relationship. 200p. (Orig.). 1985. pap. 8.95 (ISBN 0-914629-03-4). Prima Pub Comm.

Dominitz, Ben & Dominitz, Nancy. Travel Free! How to Start & Succeed in Your Own Travel Consultant Business. LC 83-63113. (Illus.). 209p. 1984. 19.95 (ISBN 0-914629-00-X, Pub. by Prima Pub). Interbook.

Dominitz, Ben & Dominitz, Nancy D. Travel Free! How to Start & Succeed in Your Own Travel Consultant Business. LC 83-63113. (Illus.). 209p. 1984. 19.95 (ISBN 0-914629-00-X). Prima Pub Comm.

Dominitz, Nancy, jt. auth. see Dominitz, Ben.

Dominitz, Nancy D., jt. auth. see Dominitz, Ben.

Domino, E. F., ed. PCP (Phencyclidine) Historical & Current Perspectives. LC 80-81498. (Illus.). 537p. 1981. 40.00x (ISBN 0-916182-03-7). NPP Bks.

Domino, E. F. & Davis, J. M., eds. Neurotransmitter Balances Regulating Behavior. LC 75-21131. 240p. 1975. 30.00x (ISBN 0-916182-00-2). NPP Bks.

Domino, F. A., ed. Energy from Solid Waste-Recent Developments. LC 79-84428. (Energy Tech. Rev. No. 42, Pollution Tech. Rev. No. 56). (Illus.). 321p. 1979. 36.00 (ISBN 0-8155-0750-X). Noyes.

Domino, Ruth. Search. 1983. pap. 5.00x (ISBN 0-87574-052-9, 052). Pendle Hill.

Dominowski, R. Research Methods. 1980. 28.95 (ISBN 0-13-774315-7). P-H.

Dominquez, Jorge I. Insurrection of Loyalty: The Breakdown of the Spanish-American Empire. LC 78-8288. 319p. 1980. text ed. 29.50x (ISBN 0-674-45635-1). Harvard U Pr.

Dominy. Judo: Beginner to Black Belt. 8.95 (ISBN 0-685-21999-2). Wehman.

Dominy, E. Camping. (Teach Yourself Ser.). 1974. pap. 3.95 (ISBN 0-679-10456-9). McKay.

Dominy, Eric. Judo: Contest Techniques & Tactics. (Illus.). 181p. 1969. pap. 3.95 (ISBN 0-486-22310-8). Dover.

--Judo Techniques & Tactics: Contest Judo. (Illus.). 13.00 (ISBN 0-8446-0586-7). Peter Smith.

--Teach Yourself Judo. (Illus.). 1962. 9.95 (ISBN 0-87523-140-3). Emerson.

--Teach Yourself Karate. (Illus.). 1968. 9.95 (ISBN 0-87523-163-2). Emerson.

--Teach Yourself Self-Defense. (Illus.). 1963. 9.95 (ISBN 0-87523-150-0). Emerson.

Domitrz, Joseph. Money & Banking. 138p. 1983. 14.95 (ISBN 0-318-17595-9). Credit Union Natl Assn.

Domiyama, M., jt. auth. see Bender, M. L.

Domjan, Evelyn A. Edge of Paradise: A Collection of Color Woodcuts. Emig, Jane, ed. LC 78-73442. (Illus.). 1979. 20.00x (ISBN 0-933652-14-3). Domjan Studio.

--Eternal Wool. Brogan, Peggy, ed. (Illus.). 160p. 1980. 25.00 (ISBN 0-933652-15-1). Domjan Studio.

--Pavologia: A Celebration of Peacocks Past. Stein, Rose & Skewerer, Lory, eds. (Illus.). 200p. 1984. 25.00 (ISBN 0-933652-17-8). Domjan Studio.

Domjan, Evelyn A., jt. auth. see Domjan, Joseph.

Domjan, Joseph & Domjan, Evelyn A. Pacatus, a Trade-Mark from Antiquity. Emig, Jane, ed. LC 78-73444. (Illus.). 1979. 15.00 (ISBN 0-933652-13-5). Domjan Studio.

Domjan, Michael & Burkhard, Barbara. The Principles of Learning & Behavior. LC 81-10205. (Psychology Ser.). 572p. 1981. text ed. 21.00 pub net (ISBN 0-8185-0466-8). Brooks-Cole.

Domjan, Micheal P. & Burkhard, Barbara. The Principles of Learning & Behavior. LC 85-5276. (Psychology Ser.). 500p. 1985. text ed. 18.50 (pub net) (ISBN 0-534-05208-8). Brooks-Cole.

Domke, Martin & Wilner, Gabriel M. Domke on Commercial Arbitration: The Law & Practice of Commercial Arbitration. rev. ed. LC 83-26207. 1983. 95.00. Callaghan.

Domke, Martin, ed. International Trade Arbitration: A Road to World-wide Cooperation. LC 73-11852. 320p. 1974. Repr. of 1958 ed. lib. bdg. 55.00x (ISBN 0-8371-7075-3, DOTA). Greenwood.

Domke, Todd. Grounded. LC 81-14267. 192p. (gr. 4-7). 1982. PLB 9.99 (ISBN 0-394-95163-8); pap. 9.95 (ISBN 0-394-85163-3). Knopf.

Domling, Wolfgang, jt. ed. see Schwendowius, Barbara.

Dommanget, Maurice. Auguste Blanqui & la Revolution de 1848. 1972. pap. 20.00x (ISBN 90-2796-939-6). Mouton.

--Auguste Blanqui, au Debut de la IIIe Republique (1871-80) Derniere Prison et Ultimes Combats. 1971. pap. 9.20x (ISBN 90-2796-272-3). Mouton.

Dommel, Paul R. The Politics of Revenue Sharing. LC 74-376. (Illus.). Repr. of 1974 ed. 55.80 (ISBN 0-8357-9235-8, 2017617). Bks Demand UMI.

Dommel, Paul R., et al. Decentralizing Urban Policy: Case Studies in Community Development. LC 81-70465. 300p. 1982. 26.95 (ISBN 0-8157-1888-8); pap. 9.95 (ISBN 0-8157-1887-X). Brookings.

Dommen, Arthur J. Laos: The Keystone of Indochina. (Westview Profiles-Nations of Contemporary Asia Ser.). 135p. 1985. 26.50x (ISBN 0-86531-771-2). Westview.

Dommen, Edward, ed. Islands. (Illus.). 135p. 1981. 22.00 (ISBN 0-08-026799-8). Pergamon.

Dommen, Edward & Hein, Philippe, eds. States, Microstates & Islands. 226p. 1985. 29.00 (ISBN 0-7099-0862-8, Pub. by Croom Helm Ltd). Longwood Pub Group.

Dommergues, Y. & Diem, H. G., eds. Microbiology of Tropical Soils & Plant Productivity. 1982. 69.50 (ISBN 90-247-2405-8, Pub. by Martinus Nijhoff Netherlands). Kluwer Academic.

Dommergues, Y. R., tr. see Krupa, S. V.

Dommermuth, William P. Promotion: Analysis, Creativity & Strategy. LC 84-970. 768p. 1984. text ed. write for info. (ISBN 0-534-03106-4). Kent Pub Co.

--The Use of Sampling in Marketing Research. LC 75-8843. 40p. 1975. pap. 7.00 (ISBN 0-87757-065-5). Am Mktg.

Dommerques, Y. & Krupa, S. V. Interactions Between Non-Pathogenic Soil Microorganisms & Plants. (Developments in Agricultural & Managed-Forest Ecology: Vol. 4). 476p. 1978. 117.00 (ISBN 0-444-41638-2). Elsevier.

Dommeyer, Frederick C. Current Philosophical Issues: Essays in Honor of Curt John Ducasse. (Illus.). 288p. 1966. 24.50x (ISBN 0-398-00465-X). C C Thomas.

Dommisse, G. F. Arteries & Veins of the Human Spinal Cord from Birth. (Illus.). 112p. 1975. text ed. 33.00 (ISBN 0-443-01219-9). Churchill.

Domning, Daryl. Sirenian Evolution in the North Pacific Ocean. (Publications in Geological Science Ser.: Vol. 118). 1978. 18.00x (ISBN 0-520-09581-2). U of Cal Pr.

Domning, Joan. Lahti's Apple. (Loveswept Ser.). 208p. (Orig.). 1984. pap. text ed. 2.25 (ISBN 0-553-21634-1). Bantam.

Domnitz, Linda D. John Lennon Conversations. (Illus.). 286p. (Orig.). 1984. pap. 16.00 (ISBN 0-942494-85-7). Coleman Pub.

Domokos, G. & Kovesi-Domokos, S. Lattice Gauge Theory-Supersymmetry & Grand Unification: Proceedings of the 7th Johns Hopkins Workshop on Current Problems in Particle Theory, Bad Honnef-Bonn, June 21-23, 1983. 350p. 1983. 40.00x (ISBN 9971-950-63-4, Pub. by World Sci Singapore); pap. 21.00x (ISBN 9971-950-62-6, Pub. by World Sci Singapore). Taylor & Francis.

Domokos, G. & Kovesi-Domokos, S., eds. Particles & Gravity: Proceedings of the Johns Hopkins Workshop on Current Problems in Particle Theory, John Hopkins University, June 20-22, 1984. 400p. 1984. 44.00x (ISBN 9971-966-90-5, Pub. by World Sci Singapore); pap. 30.00x (ISBN 9971-966-91-3, Pub. by World Sci Singapore). Taylor & Francis.

--Particles & Gravity: Proceedings of the Johns Hopkins Workshop on Current Problems in Particle Theory, June 8, 1984. 400p. 1984. 44.00x (ISBN 9971-966-78-6, Pub. by World Sci Singapore). Taylor & Francis.

Domokos, Varga. Hungary in Greatness & Decline: The Fourteenth & Fifteenth Centuries. Szacsvay, Martha, tr. Ertavy-Barath, Joseph M., ed. LC 81-81143. (History Ser.). (Illus.). 160p. 1982. 14.90 (ISBN 0-914648-11-X). Hungarian Cultural.

Domolki, B. & Gergely, T., eds. Mathematical Logic in Computer Science. (Colloquia Mathematica Societatis Janos Bolyai Ser.: Vol. 26). 758p. 1982. 117.00 (ISBN 0-444-85440-1, North-Holland). Elsevier.

Domonkos, Anthony N. & Arnold, Harry L., Jr. Andrew's Diseases of the Skin. 7th ed. (Illus.). 1100p. 1982. 74.00 (ISBN 0-7216-3138-X). Saunders.

Domotor, Tekla. Hungarian Folk Beliefs. LC 82-48163. (Illus.). 324p. 1983. 20.00x (ISBN 0-253-32876-4). Ind U Pr.

Domsch, K. L., et al. Compendium of Soil Fungi, 2 vols. LC 80-41403. 1981. Set. 1. 192.00 (ISBN 0-12-220420-4); Vol. 1, 1981. 120.00 (ISBN 0-12-220401-8); Vol. 2, 1984. 55.50 (ISBN 0-12-220402-6). Acad Pr.

Domschke, Eliane, jt. auth. see Goyer, Doreen S.

Domschke, W. & Drexl, A. Location & Layout Planning. (Lecture Notes in Economics & Mathematical Systems Ser.: Vol. 238). iv, 134p. 1985. pap. 12.30 (ISBN 0-387-13908-7). Springer-Verlag.

Domsky, I. & Perry, J., eds. Recent Advances in Gas Chromatography. 1971. 85.00 (ISBN 0-8247-1146-7). Dekker.

Domson, Charles & Cohen, I. Bernard, eds. Nicolas Fatio De Duillier & the Prophets of Paris. LC 80-2086. (Development of Science Ser.). (Illus.). 1981. lib. bdg. 15.00 (ISBN 0-405-13852-0). Ayer Co Pubs.

Domson, Joanne F., jt. ed. see Al-Doory, Yousef.

Domuret, Allan J., et al. Encyclopedia for the TRS-80, Vol. 3. Putnam, Katherine & Comiskey, Kate, eds. (Illus.). 265p. 1981. text ed. 19.95 (ISBN 0-88006-031-X, EN8103); pap. text ed. 10.95 (ISBN 0-88006-032-8, EN8083). Green Pub Inc.

Domvile, Barry. From Admiral to Cabin Boy. 2nd ed. 163p. pap. 8.00 (ISBN 0-89562-099-5). Sons Lib.

Domville, Barry. From Admiral to Cabin Boy. 1982. lib. bdg. 69.00 (ISBN 0-87700-453-6). Revisionist Pr.

Domville, Eric, ed. A Concordance to the Plays of W. B. Yeats, 2 vols. LC 71-162547. (Concordances Ser). 2300p. 1972. Set. 85.00x (ISBN 0-8014-0663-3). Cornell U Pr.

--Editing British & American Literature: 1880-1920. LC 76-7323. (Conference on Editorial Problems Ser.). 1976. lib. bdg. 22.00 (ISBN 0-8240-2409-5). Garland Pub.

Domville-Fife, C. This Is Germany. 59.95 (ISBN 0-8490-1195-7). Gordon Pr.

Domville-Fife, Charles W. The United States of Brazil. 1976. lib. bdg. 59.95 (ISBN 0-8490-1243-0). Gordon Pr.

Don, Frank. Color Your World. 189p. 1983. pap. 5.95 (ISBN 0-89281-048-3). Destiny Bks.

--Earth Changes Ahead: The Coming of Great Catastrophies. 256p. 1983. pap. 2.75 (ISBN 0-686-33184-2). Destiny Bks.

Don, Sarah. Fair Isle Knitting: A Practical Handbook of Traditional Designs. LC 82-63014. (Illus.). 124p. 1983. 9.95 (ISBN 0-312-27960-4). St Martin.

Don White Consultants Staff. EMC Technology: 1982 Anthology. (Illus.). 200p. 1984. text ed. 42.00 (ISBN 0-932263-24-0). White Consult.

Donabedian, Avedis. Aspects of Medical Care Administration: Specifying Requirements for Health Care. LC 72-93948. (Commonwealth Fund Publications Ser). 800p. 1973. 45.00x (ISBN 0-674-04980-2). Harvard U Pr.

--Benefits in Medical Care Programs. 432p. 1976. 30.00x (ISBN 0-674-06580-8). Harvard U Pr.

--The Criteria & Standards of Quality, Vol. II. LC 81-6873. (Explorations in Quality Assessment & Monitoring Ser.). (Illus.). 522p. 1981. text ed. 30.00x (ISBN 0-914904-67-1); pap. text ed. 25.00x (ISBN 0-914904-68-X). Health Admin Pr.

--The Definition of Quality & Approaches to Its Assessment, Vol. 1. LC 80-15173. (Explorations in Quality Assessment & Monitoring Ser.). (Illus.). 178p. 1980. text ed. 17.95x (ISBN 0-914904-47-7); pap. text ed. 12.95x (ISBN 0-914904-48-5). Health Admin Pr.

--The Methods & Findings of Quality Assessment & Monitoring: An Illustrated Analysis. LC 83-18397. (Explorations in Quality Assessment & Monitoring Ser.: Vol. 3). (Illus.). 546p. 1985. text ed. 40.00 (ISBN 0-914904-89-2, 00859); pap. text ed. 35.00 (ISBN 0-914904-88-4, 00888). Health Admin Pr.

Donabedian, Avedis & Axelrod, Solomon J., eds. Medical Care Chartbook. (Illus.). 420p. 1980. pap. text ed. 22.50 (ISBN 0-914904-62-0); 42.50 (ISBN 0-914904-61-2, 1162). Healthcare Fin Mgmt Assn.

Donabedian, Avedis & Wyszewianski, Leon, eds. Medical Care Chartbook. 7th ed. LC 80-69098. (Illus.). 440p. 1980. text ed. 29.50x (ISBN 0-914904-61-2). Health Admin Pr.

Donachie, M. J., Jr., ed. Superalloys: Source Book. 1983. 54.00 (ISBN 0-87170-170-7). ASM.

Donachie, Matthew, Jr., ed. Titanium & Titanium Alloys: Source Book. 1982. 54.00 (ISBN 0-87170-140-5). ASM.

Donagan, Alan. Human Ends & Human Actions: An Exploration in St. Thomas's Treatment. LC 84-63124. (Aquinas Lectcure Series). 50p. 1985. 7.95 (ISBN 0-87462-153-4). Marquette.

--The Later Philosophy of R. G. Collingwood. 352p. 1985. pap. 16.00x (ISBN 0-226-15568-4). U of Chicago Pr.

--Theory of Morality. LC 76-25634. 1979. pap. 7.95x (ISBN 0-226-15567-6, P838, Phoen). U of Chicago Pr.

--The Theory of Morality. LC 76-25634. 1977. 20.00x (ISBN 0-226-15566-8). U of Chicago Pr.

Donaghey, John. An Architect: The First Ten Years. LC 80-66726. (Illus.). 96p. (Orig.). (gr. 12 up). 1980. pap. text ed. 5.00x (ISBN 0-9604298-0-8). J Donaghey.

Donaghey, Lee F., et al, eds. see International Conference on Chemical Vapor Deposition.

Donaghey, Robert & Ruddel, JoAnna. Fundamentals of Algebra: An Integrated Text-Workbook. (Illus.). 559p. 1978. pap. text ed. 19.95 (ISBN 0-15-529420-2, HC); instructor's manual with test resources avail. (ISBN 0-15-529421-0). HarBraceJ.

Donaghey, S., jt. auth. see Dobson, R.

Donaghue, Denis, pref. by see Blackmur, R. P.

Donaghue, Jeffrey J., tr. see Shawq, Navvab M.

Donaghue, Patricia, ed. see O'Laughlin, Michael C.

Donaghy, Henry. Graham Greene: An Introduction to his Writings. (Costerus New Ser.: No. 38). 120p. 1983. pap. text ed. 13.45x (ISBN 9-062-03535-3, Pub. by Rodopi Holland). Humanities.

Donaghy, Henry J. James Clarence Mangan. (English Authors Ser.). 1974. lib. bdg. 15.95 (ISBN 0-8057-1370-0, Twayne). G K Hall.

Donaghy, John, ed. To Proclaim Peace: Religious Communities Speak Out On the Arms Race. 2nd Rev. ed. 53p. 1983. 2.75 (ISBN 0-317-36578-9); 25 or more copies 1.25 ea. Fellowship of Recon.

Donaghy, Peter. In Search of Life. 1976. 3.95 (ISBN 0-8199-0596-8). Franciscan Herald.

Donaghy, Thomas J. Liverpool & Manchester Railway Operations 1831-1845. (Illus.). 184p. 1973. 7.95 (ISBN 0-7153-5705-0). David & Charles.

Donaghy, William C. The Interview: Skills & Applications. 1984. pap. text ed. 14.10x (ISBN 0-673-15736-9). Scott F.

--Our Silent Language: An Introduction to Nonverbal Communication. (Comm Comp). (Illus.). 54p. 1980. pap. text ed. 2.95x (ISBN 0-89787-304-1). Gorsuch Scarisbrick.

Donaghy, William C., jt. auth. see Emmert, Philip.

Donahey, William. The Teenie Weenies Book. LC 84-80569. (Illus.). 90p. (Orig.). Date not set. pap. write for info. (ISBN 0-88138-035-0, Star & Elephant Bks.). Green Tiger Pr.

Donahoe, Bernard. Private Plans & Public Dangers: The Story of FDR's Third Nomination. 1965. 15.95x (ISBN 0-268-00217-7). U of Notre Dame Pr.

Donahoe, Betty J. How to Boil Water. 148p. 1973. pap. 6.95 (ISBN 0-938400-00-2). Donahoe Pubs.

Donahoe, James J. Dream Reality: The Conscious Creation of Dream & Paranormal Experience. rev. ed. LC 75-35014. 1979. 8.95 (ISBN 0-916534-01-4); pap. 4.95 (ISBN 0-916534-07-3). Bench Pr.

--Enigma: Psychology, the Paranormal & Self-Transformation. LC 79-12874. (Illus.). 1979. 11.95 (ISBN 0-916534-08-1); pap. 6.95 (ISBN 0-916534-09-X). Bench Pr.

Donahoe, John W. & Wessells, Michael G. Learning, Language, & Memory. (Illus.). 1979. text ed. 24.00 scp (ISBN 0-06-041685-8, HarpC); instructor's manual avail. (ISBN 0-06-361699-8). Har-Row.

Donahoe, Mary. You Are Mountain. 32p. 1984. chapbook 6.00 (ISBN 0-911051-11-2). Plain View.

Donahoo, Clare A., Jr. & Dimon, Joseph H. Orthopedic Nursing. 1977. 14.95 (ISBN 0-316-18940-5). Little.

Donahue, Bob & Donahue, Marilyn. Don't Be a Puppet on a String. 1983. pap. 3.95 (ISBN 0-8423-0610-2). Tyndale.

--Getting Your Act Together. (No. 4). 108p. (gr. 7-9). 1983. pap. 3.95 (ISBN 0-8423-1005-3). Tyndale.

--How to Make People Like You When You Know They Don't. 1982. pap. 4.95 (ISBN 0-8423-1531-4). Tyndale.

--Things That Go Bump in the Night, & Other Fears. (YA) 1983. pap. 3.95 (ISBN 0-8423-7083-8). Tyndale.

Donahue, Bud. The Language of Layout. LC 78-6949. (Art & Design Ser.). 1978. 19.95 (ISBN 0-13-522953-7, Spec); pap. 11.95 (ISBN 0-13-522961-8). P-H.

Donahue, Charles, Jr., et al. Property: An Introduction to the Concept & Institution Cases & Materials. 2nd ed. LC 83-6529. (American Casebook Ser.). 1362p. 1983. 28.95 (ISBN 0-314-72904-6); pap. text ed. tchr's. manual avail. (ISBN 0-314-79129-9). West Pub.

Donahue, Hugh C., jt. auth. see Green, James R.

Donahue, Jack. The Finest in the Land. LC 84-4645. 352p. 1984. 19.95x (ISBN 0-87201-284-0). Gulf Pub.

--Hack Donavon of the Press & the Purification of Houston. 256p. 1984. pap. 9.95 (ISBN 0-940672-25-1). Shearer Pub.

--The Lady Loved Too Well. 1978. 8.95 (ISBN 0-07-017541-1). McGraw.

--Wildcatter: The Story of Michel T. Halbouty & the Search for Oil. LC 83-10781. 270p. 1983. Repr. of 1979 ed. 18.95x (ISBN 0-87201-915-2). Gulf Pub.

Donahue, Jack & Halbouty, Michel T. Grady Barr. LC 81-66961. 352p. 1981. 12.95 (ISBN 0-87795-329-5). Arbor Hse.

Donahue, James, et al, trs. see Nunis, Doyce B., Jr.

Donahue, James L., jt. auth. see Lincoln, James H.

Donahue, John C. & Jenkins, Linda W., eds. Five Plays from the Children's Theatre Company of Minneapolis. LC 73-91051. pap. 67.50 (ISBN 0-317-27932-7, 2055855). Bks Demand UMI.

Donahue, John D., jt. auth. see Reich, Robert B.

Donahue, John N., jt. ed. see Bastien, Joseph W.

Donahue, John R. The Theology & Setting of Discipleship in the Gospel of Mark. LC 83-60749. (Pere Marquette Lecture Ser.). 1983. 7.95 (ISBN 0-87462-538-6). Marquette.

Donahue, John R., ed. see Bailey, Lloyd R., Sr.

Donahue, John R., ed. see Brueggemann, Walter.

Donahue, John R., ed. see Hamerton-Kelly, Robert.

Donahue, John R., ed. see Harrelson, Walter.

Donahue, John R., ed. see Harrington, Daniel J.

Donahue, John R., ed. see Johnson, Luke T.

Donahue, John R., ed. see Patrick, Dale.

Donahue, John R., ed. see Westermann, Claus.

Donahue, John R., tr. see Klein, Ralph W.

Donahue, Joseph A. Tin Cans & Other Ships. (Illus.). 1979. 7.50 (ISBN 0-8158-0378-8). Chris Mass.

Donahue, Kenneth, ed. see Pignatti, Terisio.

Donahue, Leo O. Encyclopedia of Batik Designs. LC 80-67118. (Illus.). 520p. 1982. 60.00 (ISBN 0-87982-035-7). Art Alliance.

--Encyclopedia of Batik Designs. LC 80-67121. (Illus.). 640p. 1981. 60.00 (ISBN 0-8453-4729-2). Cornwall Bks.

Donahue, Lois. Dear Moses: Letters to Saints & Other Prominent People. LC 84-60743. (Illus.). 104p. 1984. pap. 4.95 (ISBN 0-87973-699-2, 699). Our Sunday Visitor.

--That Taste In My Mouth Is Foot. 106p. 1982. pap. 4.95 (ISBN 0-9610104-0-1). F & L Assocs.

Donahue, Lou A. Noritake Collectibles. (Illus.). pap. 5.95 (ISBN 0-87069-282-8); price guide 1.50 (ISBN 0-87069-290-9). Wallace-Homestead.

Donahue, Lou Ann. Noritake Collectibles. 96p. 1985. pap. 5.95 (ISBN 0-87069-282-8); price guide 1.50 (ISBN 0-87069-290-9). Wallace-Homestead.

Donahue, Marilyn. The Crooked Gate. (Pennypincher Ser.). 127p. (gr. 5-10). 1984. pap. 2.25 softcover (ISBN 0-89191-830-2). Cook.

--To Catch a Golden Ring. (gr. 4-9). 1980. pap. 2.95 (ISBN 0-89191-330-0). Cook.

--To Catch a Golden Ring. rev. ed. (Pennypincher Ser.). 127p. (gr. 5-10). 1984. pap. 2.25 softcover (ISBN 0-89191-831-0). Cook.

Donahue, Marilyn, jt. auth. see Donahue, Bob.

Donahue, Marilyn C. Music Play Past Midnight. (Pennypincher Bks.). 132p. (gr. 4-7). 1983. 2.25 (ISBN 0-89191-756-X, 57562). Cook.

--Straight along a Crooked Road. (Illus.). 128p. (YA) (gr. 10 up). 1985. 12.95 (ISBN 0-8027-6585-8). Walker & Co.

--Violets Grow in Secret Places. (Pennypincher Ser.). 128p. (gr. 5-9). 1984. pap. 2.25 (ISBN 0-89191-885-X, 58859). Cook.

Donahue, Marilyn C., jt. auth. see Sinclair, Marti.

Donahue, Moraima. Figuras y Contrafiguras en la obra poetica de Fernando Alegria. Miller, Yvette E., ed. LC 80-54902. 141p. 1981. pap. 7.95 (ISBN 0-935480-05-6). Lat Am Lit Rev Pr.

--La Poesia de Manuel Duran. Miller, Yvette E., ed. 242p. (Orig., Span.). 1977. pap. 8.50. Lat Am Lit Rev Pr.

Donahue, Moraima D. Blas de Otero en su Poesia. (Studies in the Romance Languages & Literatures: No.189). 224p. (Orig.). 1978. pap. 14.50x (ISBN 0-8078-9189-4). U of NC Pr.

Donahue, P. J., ed. see O'Laughlin, Michael C.

Donahue, Parnell & Capellaro, Helen. Germs Make Me Sick: A Health Handbook for Kids. LC 74-15309. (Illus.). 96p. (gr. 4 up). 1975. PLB 5.99 (ISBN 0-394-92909-8). Knopf.

Donahue, Paulette. Take the Bull by the Horns. 1981. 4.95 (ISBN 0-8062-1767-7). Carlton.

Donahue, Phil. The Human Animal. 234p. 1985. 19.95 (ISBN 0-671-54696-1). S&S.

Donahue, Phil, et al. Donahue: My Own Story. 288p. 1981. pap. 2.95 (ISBN 0-449-24358-3, Crest). Fawcett.

Donahue, Robert. Thirty Two Canons for Keyboard Instruments. 1975. pap. 3.25 (ISBN 0-934286-57-4). Kenyon.

Donahue, Roy & Miller, John. Soils: An Introduction to Soils & Plant Growth. 5th ed. (Illus.). 656p. 1983. text ed. 34.95 (ISBN 0-13-822288-6). P-H.

Donahue, Roy, jt. auth. see Arakeri, H. R.

Donahue, Roy L., et al. Our Soils & Their Management (Increasing Production Through Environmental Soil & Water Conservation. 5th ed. LC 82-82462. xv, 622p. 1983. 23.00 (ISBN 0-8134-2251-5); text ed. 18.00x. Interstate.

Donahue, Thomas J. The Theater of Fernando Arrabal: A Garden of Earthly Delights. LC 79-2598. (The Gotham Library). 1980. 30.00x (ISBN 0-8147-1771-3); pap. 15.00x (ISBN 0-8147-1772-1). NYU Pr.

Donahue, Thomas R., jt. auth. see Daly, John.

Donahue, William H. & Cohen, I. Bernard, eds. The Dissolution of the Celestial Sphere. LC 80-2087. (Development of Science Ser.). (Illus.). 1981. lib. bdg. 28.00x (ISBN 0-405-13853-9). Ayer Co Pubs.

Donahue, Wilma, et al. Free Time: Challenge to Later Maturity. Stein, Leon, ed. LC 79-8667. (Growing Old Ser.). 1980. Repr. of 1958 ed. lib. bdg. 17.00x (ISBN 0-405-12807-X). Ayer Co Pubs.

Donahue, Wilma, et al, eds. see Conference on the Aging, 4th, University of Michican, 1951.

Donahue-Gandy, Marlene M. Teaching Basic Aquatics...Especially to Those Who Have Difficulty Learning. LC 84-71097. (Illus.). 104p. (Orig.). 1984. pap. 10.00 (ISBN 0-9613514-0-3). M M Donahue Gandy.

Donahue-Gaudet. Le Vocalisme et le Consonantisme Francais. 14.95 (ISBN 0-685-36654-5). French & Eur.

Donakowski, Conrad L. A Muse for the Masses: Ritual & Music in an Age of Democratic Revolution, 1770-1870. LC 77-6228. 1977. lib. bdg. 27.50x (ISBN 0-226-15621-4). U of Chicago Pr.

Donald. Endocrine Disorders. (Basic & Clinical Endocrinology Ser.). 464p. 1983. 85.00 (ISBN 0-8247-1913-1). Dekker.

--Practical Obstetric Problems. 5th ed. (Illus.). 1071p. 1979. text ed. 57.50 (ISBN 0-397-58247-1, 65-72457, Lippincott Medical). Lippincott.

Donald, A. D., et al. Epidemiology & Control of Gastrointestinal Parasites of Sheep in Australia. 152p. 1982. 30.00x (ISBN 0-643-00301-0, Pub. by CSIRO Australia). State Mutual Bk.

Donald, A. G. Management, Information & Systems. 2nd ed. 1979. text ed. 44.00 (ISBN 0-08-021271-9); pap. text ed. 14.50 (ISBN 0-08-021270-0). Pergamon.

Donald, A. K., ed. see Scott, Alexander.

Donald, A. L. Mac see Mac Donald, A. L.

Donald, Aida D. see Adams, Charles F.

Donald, Alexander G., jt. ed. see Shah, Nandkumar S.

Donald, Alexander K., ed. see Jean D'Arras.

Donald, D. W. Compound Interest & Annuities--Certain. 1975. 21.50 (ISBN 0-434-90366-3, Pub. by W Heinemann Ltd). David & Charles.

Donald, David. Charles Sumner & the Coming of the Civil War. LC 81-11612. 1981. pap. 12.50x (ISBN 0-226-15633-8). U of Chicago Pr.

--Lincoln Reconsidered. 1956. pap. 5.95 (ISBN 0-394-70190-9). Knopf.

--Lincoln Reconsidered: Essays on the Civil War Era. pap. 5.95 (ISBN 0-394-70190-9, V-190, Vin). Random.

--The Politics of Reconstruction: 1863-1867. 128p. 1984. pap. text ed. 4.95x (ISBN 0-674-68953-4). Harvard U Pr.

Donald, David, jt. auth. see Randall, James G.

Donald, David, compiled by. The Nation in Crisis, Eighteen Sixty-One to Eighteen Seventy-Seven. LC 74-79169. (Goldentree Bibliographies in American History Ser.). 112p. 1969. pap. 6.95x (ISBN 0-88295-511-X). Harlan Davidson.

Donald, David, ed. Why the North Won the Civil War. 1962. pap. 2.95 (ISBN 0-02-031660-7, Collier). Macmillan.

Donald, David see Adams, Charles F.

Donald, David, ed. see Chase, Salmon P.

Donald, David H. Liberty & Union. 1978. pap. text ed. 12.95x (ISBN 0-669-01152-5). Heath.

--Liberty & Union. LC 78-54090. (Illus.). 1978. 12.50 (ISBN 0-316-18949-9). Little.

--Lincoln Reconsidered: Essays on the Civil War Era. LC 80-22804. (Illus.). xiii, 200p. 1981. Repr. of 1956 ed. lib. bdg. 23.50x (ISBN 0-313-22575-3, DOLR). Greenwood.

--The Politics of Reconstruction, 1863-1867. LC 82-1015. (The Walter Lynnwood Fleming Lectures in Southern History). 105p. 1982. Repr. of 1967 ed. lib. bdg. 17.50x (ISBN 0-313-23481-7, DONP). Greenwood.

Donald, David H., ed. see Wiltse, Charles M. & Mayfield, John.

Donald, Elsie B., ed. The Book of Creative Crafts. (Octopus Book). (Illus.). 1978. 19.95 (ISBN 0-7064-0757-1). Smith Pubs.

Donald, G. H. Cooking for Your Children Cookbook. 17.50 (ISBN 0-87559-125-6). Shalom.

Donald, Gertrude. Men Who Left the Movement. facs. ed. LC 67-23207. (Essay Index Reprint Ser). 1933. 20.00 (ISBN 0-8369-0385-4). Ayer Co Pubs.

Donald, Gordon, Jr. U. S. Foreign Aid & the National Interest. (Committee on Changing International Realities Ser.). 32p. (Orig.). 1983. pap. 4.00 (ISBN 0-89068-067-1). Natl Planning.

Donald, H. P., jt. auth. see Lerner, I. M.

Donald, Henderson H. Negro Freedman: Life Conditions of the American Negro in the Early Years After Emancipation. LC 70-160846. 1971. Repr. of 1952 ed. lib. bdg. 22.50 (ISBN 0-8154-0388-7). Cooper Sq.

Donald, Ian. Practical Obstetric Problems. 5th ed. (Illus.). 1979. text ed. 57.50i (ISBN 0-397-58247-1). Har-Row.

Donald, Ian, jt. auth. see Canter, David.

Donald, K. M. Marine Steam Turbines. (Marine Engineering Design & Installation Ser.). (Illus.). 1978. pap. 18.75x (ISBN 0-900976-58-6, Pub. by Inst Marine Eng). Intl Spec Bk.

--Marine Steam Turbines. 146p. 1981. 52.00x (ISBN 0-900976-58-6, Pub. by Marine Mgmt England). State Mutual Bk.

Donald, Kathleen & Holloway, Elizabeth. Self Hypnosis to Self-Improvement. 300p. (Orig.). 1984. pap. text ed. 16.95 (ISBN 0-915202-37-9). Accel Devel.

Donald, L. & MacDonald, W. S., eds. Roll of Graduates of the University of Aberdeen, 1956-1970: With Supplement 1860-1955. 1982. 82.80 (ISBN 0-08-028469-8). Pergamon.

Donald, Mary Ellen. Doumbec Delight. 2nd ed. Munro, Jane, ed. (Illus.). 111p. (Orig.). 1976. pap. text ed. 9.95 (ISBN 0-9606602-0-8). Mary Ellen Bks.

Donald, Maryann. The Palladium Book of Contemporary Weapons. Marciniszyn, Alex, ed. (Weapons Ser.: No. 5). (Illus.). 48p. 1984. pap. 4.95 (ISBN 0-916211-01-0, 408). Palladium Bks.

Donald, Miles. American Novel in the Twentieth Century. (Comparative Literature Ser.). 215p. 1978. text ed. 24.50x (ISBN 0-06-491742-8). B&N Imports.

Donald, Paul J. Head & Neck Cancer: Management of the Difficult Case. (Illus.). 480p. 1984. 70.00 (ISBN 0-7216-3141-X). Saunders.

Donald, R. B., et al. Models for Clear Writing. (Illus.). 400p. 1984. pap. text ed. 11.95 (ISBN 0-13-586249-3). P-H.

Donald, Robert & Moore, James. Writing Clear Paragraphs. 2nd ed. (Illus.). 272p. 1983. pap. text ed. 14.95 (ISBN 0-13-970004-8). P-H.

Donald, Robert B. & Morrow, Betty R. Writing Clear Essays. (Illus.). 384p. 1983. pap. text ed. 14.95 (ISBN 0-13-970145-1). P-H.

Donald, Robyn. The Gates of Rangitatau. (Harlequin Presents Ser.). 192p. 1984. pap. 1.95 (ISBN 0-373-10665-3). Harlequin Bks.

--The Guarded Heart. (Harlequin Presents Ser.). 192p. 1983. pap. 1.95 (ISBN 0-373-10623-8). Harlequin Bks.

--Mansion for My Love. (Harlequin Presents Ser.). 192p. 1983. pap. 1.75 (ISBN 0-373-10567-3). Harlequin Bks.

--An Old Passion. (Harlequin Presents Ser.). 192p. 1983. pap. 1.95 (ISBN 0-373-10649-1). Harlequin Bks.

--Return to Yesterday. (Harlequin Presents Ser.). 192p. 1983. pap. 1.95 (ISBN 0-373-10631-9). Harlequin Bks.

--Sous la Lune des Tropiques. (Collection Harlequin). 192p. 1983. pap. 1.95 (ISBN 0-373-49323-1). Harlequin Bks.

--Summer at Awakopu. (Harlequin Presents Ser). (Orig.). 1979. pap. 1.25 (ISBN 0-373-70785-1). Harlequin Bks.

Donald, Ted M. Laugh - It's Good for the Jaws. 1985. 10.95 (ISBN 0-533-06534-8). Vantage.

Donaldson, A. M., jt. ed. see Steltz, W. E.

Donaldson, Alfred G. Some Comparative Aspects of Irish Law. LC 57-8815. (Duke University, Commonwealth-Studies Center, Publication: No. 3). pap. 76.80 (ISBN 0-317-20096-8, 2023376). Bks Demand UMI.

Donaldson, Alfred L. History of the Adirondacks, 2 vols. LC 77-12661. (Illus.). 1977. Repr. of 1921 ed. Set. 45.00 (ISBN 0-916346-26-9). Harbor Hill Bks.

Donaldson, Ann. Scottish Highland Games in America. (Orig.). 1985. write for info. (ISBN 0-88289-474-9). Pelican.

Donaldson, Aug. B. Five Great Oxford Leaders. (Victorian Age Ser). 1900. Repr. 20.00 (ISBN 0-8482-3667-X). Norwood Edns.

Donaldson, Augustas B. Five Great Oxford Leaders: Keble, Newman, Pusey, Liddon & Church. 1978. Repr. of 1900 ed. lib. bdg. 35.00 (ISBN 0-8495-1036-8). Arden Lib.

Donaldson, B. Dutch Reference Grammar. 324p. 1982. 25.00 (ISBN 90-247-2354-X, Pub. by Martinus Nijhoff Netherlands). Kluwer Academic.

Donaldson, B. C. Dutch: A Linguistic History of Holland & Belgium. lib. bdg. 14.50 (ISBN 0-318-00842-4, Pub. by Martinus Nijhoff Netherlands). Kluwer Academic.

Donaldson, Bess A. The Wild Rue. LC 73-6277. (The Middle East Ser.). Repr. of 1938 ed. 17.00 (ISBN 0-405-05332-0). Ayer Co Pubs.

Donaldson, Bruce. Dutch Vocabulary. 96p. pap. 10.00 (ISBN 0-86787-025-7, Pub. by Australasian Educa Pr). Heinman.

Donaldson, C. D., ed. see Bird, R. B., et al.

Donaldson, Christine F., jt. auth. see Flynn, Elizabeth A.

Donaldson, Christopher. Martin of Tours: Parish Priest, Mystic & Exorcist. (Illus.). 171p. 1985. pap. 8.95 (ISBN 0-7102-0682-8). Routledge & Kegan.

Donaldson, Cyril & Le Cain, George. Tool Design. 3rd ed. (Illus.). 840p. 1973. text ed. 37.55 (ISBN 0-07-017531-4). McGraw.

Donaldson, D. & Panton, G. A., eds. The Gest Hystoriale of the Destruction of Troy: Parts I & II. 1869-1873. (EETS, OS Ser.: Nos. 39, 56). 42.00 (ISBN 0-527-00035-3). Kraus Repr.

Donaldson, David, ed. see Jamieson, John.

Donaldson, Dwight M. The Shi, Its Religion: A History of Islam in Persia & Iraq. 1976. lib. bdg. 59.95 (ISBN 0-8490-2598-2). Gordon Pr.

--The Shi'ite Religion: A History of Islam in Persia & Irak. LC 80-1933. 49.50 (ISBN 0-404-18959-8). AMS Pr.

Donaldson, E. C. Enhanced Oil Recovery, 1: Fundamentals & Analyses. (Developments in Petroleum Science Ser.: Vol. 17A). 1985. 65.00 (ISBN 0-444-42206-4, I-456-84). Elsevier.

Donaldson, E. T., ed. Chaucer's Poetry: An Anthology for the Modern Reader. 2nd ed. LC 74-22536. 1975. text ed. 32.55 (ISBN 0-673-15667-2). Scott F.

Donaldson, E. Talbert. Speaking of Chaucer. 190p. 1983. pap. 7.95x (ISBN 0-939464-15-2). Labyrinth Pr.

Donaldson, E. Talbot. The Swan at the Well: Shakespeare Reading Chaucer. LC 84-21913. 192p. 1985. text ed. 15.00 (ISBN 0-300-03349-4). Yale U Pr.

Donaldson, E. Talbot, jt. ed. see Kane, George.

Donaldson, E. Talbot, tr. Beowulf: A New Translation. (Orig.). 1966. pap. 2.95x (ISBN 0-393-09687-4, NortonC). Norton.

Donaldson, E. Talbot, tr. see Tuso, Joseph F.

Donaldson, Frances. The British Council: The First Fifty Years. (Illus.). 365p. 1985. 24.95 (ISBN 0-224-02041-2, Pub. by Jonathan Cape). Merrimack Pub Cir.

--P. G. Wodehouse: A Biography. LC 81-48111. 1982. 18.50 (ISBN 0-394-50580-8). Knopf.

Donaldson, Frances & Usborne, Richard. P. G. Wodehouse 1881-1981: Addresses Given by Frances Donaldson & Richard Usborne. (Wodehouse Monograph: No. 2). 44p. (Orig.). 1982. pap. 14.50 (ISBN 0-87008-101-2). Heineman.

Donaldson, Fred. Crooked Trail. 208p. (Orig.). 1982. pap. 2.25 (ISBN 0-8439-1134-4, Pub. by Leisure Bks). Dorchester Pub Co.

--Crooked Trail. 208p. 1983. pap. 2.25 (ISBN 0-8439-2008-4, Leisure Bks). Dorchester Pub Co.

Donaldson, G. The Scottish Reformation. 49.50 (ISBN 0-521-08675-2). Cambridge U Pr.

Donaldson, Gerald. The Grand Prix of Canada. 128p. 1984. pap. 14.95 (ISBN 0-380-87080-0, 87080-0). Avon.

Donaldson, Gordon. All the Queen's Men: Power & Politics in Mary Stewart's Scotland. LC 83-653. 190p. 1983. 21.95 (ISBN 0-312-02009-0). St Martin.

--A Dictionary of Scottish History. 1980. pap. text ed. 11.00x (ISBN 0-85976-018-9). Humanities.

--Eighteen Men. 2nd, rev. ed. LC 89-28656. 336p. 1985. 16.95 (ISBN 0-385-23037-0). Doubleday.

--The First Trial of Mary, Queen of Scots. LC 83-18334. (Illus.). 254p. 1983. Repr. of 1969 ed. lib. bdg. 35.00x (ISBN 0-313-22931-7, DOFT). Greenwood.

--Managing Corporate Wealth: The Operation of a Comprehensive Financial Goals System. LC 84-4779. 208p. 1984. 24.95 (ISBN 0-03-063414-8); pap. 10.95 (ISBN 0-03-063416-4). Praeger.

--Northwards by Sea. (Illus.). 1978. 21.00x (ISBN 0-8464-0677-2). Beekman Pubs.
--Scotland: Shaping of a Nation. rev. ed. 272p. 1980. 24.50 (ISBN 0-7153-7975-5). David & Charles.
--The Scots Overseas. LC 75-36360. (Illus.). 1976. Repr. of 1966 ed. lib. bdg. 18.25x (ISBN 0-8371-8625-0, DOTSO). Greenwood.
--Strategy for Financial Mobility. LC 73-94406. 1969. 21.95x (ISBN 0-87584-078-7). Harvard Busn.
--Strategy for Financial Mobility. 343p. 1985. pap. 12.95 (ISBN 0-87584-127-9). Harvard Busn.
Donaldson, Gordon & Lorch, Jay W. Decision Making at the Top: The Shaping of Strategic Direction. LC 83-70753. 224p. 1985. pap. 6.95 (ISBN 0-465-01586-7, CN-5137). Basic.
Donaldson, Gordon & Lorsch, Jay W. Decision Making at the Top: The Shaping of Strategic Direction. LC 83-70753. 208p. 1983. 16.95 (ISBN 0-465-01584-0). Basic.
Donaldson, Gordon & Morpeth, Robert S. A Dictionary of Scottish History. 234p. 1982. 29.00x (ISBN 0-85976-018-9, Pub. by Donald Pubs Scotland). State Mutual Bk.
Donaldson, Graham. Forestry. (Sector Policy Paper). 63p. 1978. pap. 5.00 (ISBN 0-686-36066-4, PP-7804). World Bank.
Donaldson, Hamish. A Guide to the Successful Management of Computer Projects. LC 78-16180. 266p. 1978. 44.95x (ISBN 0-470-26472-1). Halsted Pr.
Donaldson, Harvey. Yours Truly, Harvey Donaldson. Wolfe, Dave, ed. 271p. text ed. 19.50 (ISBN 0-935632-01-8). Wolfe Pub Co.
Donaldson, Ian. The Rapes of Lucretia: A Myth & Its Transformations. (Illus.). 1982. 29.95x (ISBN 0-19-812638-7). Oxford U Pr.
Donaldson, Ian, ed. Ben Johnson. (Oxford Authors Ser.). 750p. 1985. 24.95x (ISBN 0-19-254178-1). Oxford U Pr.
--Transformations in Modern European Drama. 240p. 1983. text ed. 27.50x (ISBN 0-391-02486-8); pap. 10.50x. Humanities.
Donaldson, Ian & Donaldson, Tamsin, eds. Seeing the First Australians. (Illus.). 216p. 1985. text ed. 32.00 (ISBN 0-86861-689-3); pap. 15.00 (ISBN 0-86861-697-4). Allen Unwin.
Donaldson, Ian, ed. see Jonson, Ben.
Donaldson, Ivan & Cramer, Frederick. Fishwheels of the Columbia. LC 76-173928. (Illus.). 1971. 10.00 (ISBN 0-8323-0007-1). Binford.
Donaldson, J., ed. see Ante-Nicene Fathers.
Donaldson, J. A., jt. auth. see Donaldson, T. H.
Donaldson, James. Woman: Her Position & Influence in Ancient Greece & Rome & Among the Early Christians. 69.95 (ISBN 0-87968-065-2). Gordon Pr.
Donaldson, James & Roberts, Alexander, trs. Martyrdom of St. Polycarp: The Encyclical Epistle of the Church at Smyrna Concerning the Martyrdom of the Holy Polycarp. pap. 1.50 (ISBN 0-317-11392-5). Eastern Orthodox.
Donaldson, James A., jt. auth. see Anson, Barry.
Donaldson, James H. Casualty Claim Practice. 3rd ed. 1976. 28.95x (ISBN 0-256-01878-2). Irwin.
Donaldson, James O. Neurology of Pregnancy. LC 76-58600. (Major Problems in Neurology: Vol. 7). (Illus.). 1978. text ed. 31.95 (ISBN 0-7216-3139-8). Saunders.
Donaldson, Janet M., ed. see Bingham, Marjorie W. & Gross, Susan H.
Donaldson, Janet M., ed. see Gross, Susan H. & Bingham, Marjorie W.
Donaldson, Jim. The Official Fantasy Football League Manual: 1985. rev. ed. LC 8092005126000004. (Illus.). 160p. (Orig.). 1985. pap. 7.95 (ISBN 0-8092-5145-0). Contemp Bks.
Donaldson, John. International Economic Relations: A Treatise on World Economy & World Politics. LC 82-48301. (The World Economy Ser.). 674p. 1983. lib. bdg. 72.00 (ISBN 0-8240-5356-7). Garland Pub.
--State Administration in Maryland. LC 78-63959. (Johns Hopkins University. Studies in the Social Sciences. Thirty-Fourth Ser. 1916: 4). Repr. of 1916 ed. 19.50 (ISBN 0-404-61206-7). AMS Pr.
Donaldson, John & Philby, Pamela. Pay Differentials: An Integration of Theories, Evidence & Policies. 268p. 1985. text ed. 34.50 (ISBN 0-566-00838-6). Gower Pub Co.
Donaldson, John W. The Theatre of the Greeks. LC 72-2095. (Studies in Drama, No. 39). 1972. Repr. of 1890 ed. lib. bdg. 56.95x (ISBN 0-8383-1495-3). Haskell.
Donaldson, John W., jt. auth. see Muller, Karl O.
Donaldson, Judith E. Doodles, Diddles, Puzzles, Quizzies & Fun Stuff, Vol. 2. (Illus.). 144p. (Orig.). (YA) 1981. pap. 2.25 (ISBN 0-939942-00-3). Larkspur.
--Travel Games: Vol. 2, Five to Ten Years. Brown, George H., ed. (Illus.). 36p. (gr. k-5). pap. text ed. 1.50 (ISBN 0-939942-06-2). Larkspur.
Donaldson, Judith E. & Brown, George H. Travel Games: Vol. 1, Family. (Illus.). 36p. (Orig.). pap. text ed. 1.50 (ISBN 0-939942-05-4). Larkspur.
Donaldson, Judith E., ed. see Brown, George H.
Donaldson, Judy P. Transcultural Education Model: Developing ESL-LEP-Bilingual Curriculum & Programs. 176p. (Orig.). 1985. pap. text ed. 22.95 (ISBN 0-918452-60-0). Learning Pubns.
--Transcultural Picture Word List: For Teaching English to Children from Any of Twenty One Language Backgrounds, Vol. I. LC 78-58532. 1980. pap. text ed. 21.95x (ISBN 0-918452-10-4). Learning Pubns.
--Transcultural Picture Word List: For Teaching English to Children from any of Twelve Language Backgrounds, Vol. II. LC 78-58532. 204p. (Orig.). pap. text ed. 15.95x (ISBN 0-918452-38-4). Learning Pubns.
Donaldson, Kloyd & Edington, Everett D. Exemplary Career Guidance Programs. 90p. 1979. 6.25 (ISBN 0-318-15468-4, RD158). Natl Ctr Res Voc Ed.
Donaldson, L. J., jt. auth. see Donaldson, R. J.
Donaldson, Les. Behavioral Supervision: Practical Ways to Change Unsatisfactory Behavior & Increase Productivity. LC 79-25100. 1980. pap. text ed. 10.95 (ISBN 0-201-01473-4). Addison-Wesley.
--Conversational Magic: Key to Poise, Popularity & Success. 1982. pap. 4.95 (ISBN 0-13-172098-8, Reward). P-H.
Donaldson, Les & Scannell, Edward. Human Resource Development: The New Trainer's Guide. 1978. pap. text ed. 12.95 (ISBN 0-201-03081-0). Addison-Wesley.
Donaldson, Lex. In Defence of Organization Theory: A Reply to the Critics. (Illus.). 250p. Date not set. price not set (ISBN 0-521-26869-9); pap. price not set (ISBN 0-521-31539-5). Cambridge U Pr.
Donaldson, Lorraine. Economic Development: Analysis & Policy (International Edition) (Illus.). 500p. 1984. 17.00 (ISBN 0-314-80462-5). West Pub.
--Economics Development: Analysis & Policy. 500p. 1984. text ed. 26.95 (ISBN 0-314-77898-5). West Pub.
Donaldson, Margaret. Children's Minds. (Illus.). 1979. pap. 4.95x (ISBN 0-393-95101-4). Norton.
--Journey into War. (Illus.). (gr. 2-6). 1980. 7.95 (ISBN 0-233-97109-2). Andre Deutsch.
--The Moon's on Fire. LC 80-65664. (Illus.). 152p. (gr. 2-7). 1980. pap. 9.95 (ISBN 0-233-97249-8). Andre Deutsch.
Donaldson, Margaret, ed. Early Childhood Education. 1985. pap. 12.50 (ISBN 0-89862-633-1, 2633). Guilford Pr.
Donaldson, Margaret, et al. Early Childhood Development & Education. 335p. 1983. 25.00 (ISBN 0-89862-631-5); pap. 12.50 (ISBN 0-89862-633-1). Guilford Pr.
Donaldson, Norman. In Search of Dr. Thorndyke. 300p. 1971. pap. 3.95 (ISBN 0-87972-014-X). Bowling Green Univ.
Donaldson, P. S., ed. A Machiavellian Treatise by Stephen Gardiner. LC 74-12963. (Studies in the History & Theory of Politics). 204p. 1976. 44.50 (ISBN 0-521-20593-X). Cambridge U Pr.
Donaldson, Peter. Guide to the British Economy. 1965. lib. bdg. 13.50x (ISBN 0-88307-079-0). Gannon.
Donaldson, R. J. Parasites & Western Man. (Illus.). 232p. 1979. text ed. 32.00 (ISBN 0-8391-1432-X). Univ Park.
Donaldson, R. J. & Donaldson, L. J. Essential Community Medicine: Including Relevant Social Services. 600p. 1983. text ed. write for info. (ISBN 0-85200-373-0, Pub by MTP Pr England). Kluwer Academic.
Donaldson, Robert H. The Soviet-Indian Alignment: Quest for Influence. (Monograph Series in World Affairs: Vol. 16, 1978-79, Bks. 3 & 4). 70p. (Orig.). 1979. 5.95 (ISBN 0-87940-059-5). Monograph Series.
--Soviet Policy Toward India: Ideology & Strategy. LC 73-89708. (Russian Research Center Studies: No. 74). 352p. 1974. text ed. 20.00x (ISBN 0-674-82776-7). Harvard U Pr.
--Soviet Policy Toward India: Ideology & Strategy. LC 73-89708. (Russian Research Center. Studies: No. 74). pap. 88.80 (ISBN 0-317-09565-X, 2021769). Bks Demand UMI.
Donaldson, Robert H., jt. auth. see Nogee, Joseph L.
Donaldson, Robert H., ed. The Soviet Union in the Third World: Success & Failures. (Special Studies in International Relations). 458p. 1980. lib. bdg. 35.00x (ISBN 0-89158-974-0); pap. text ed. 13.50x (ISBN 0-86531-158-7). Westview.
Donaldson, Robert M. How to Select a Career or Manage a Job Change. 1983. pap. text ed. 6.95 (ISBN 0-9611386-0-2). D B Assoc.
--Managing Your Career: How to Choose or Change Your Job. Lyon, Jack, ed. 123p. 1985. 7.95 (ISBN 0-87747-723-X). Deseret Bk.
Donaldson, Scott. Conversations with John Cheever. (Literary Conversations Ser.). 1987. 17.95 (ISBN 0-87805-276-3); pap. 9.95 (ISBN 0-87805-277-1). U Pr of Miss.
--Critical Essays on F. Scott Fitzgerald's "The Great Gatsby". (Critical Essays on American Literature Ser.). 304p. 1984. lib. bdg. 29.00 (ISBN 0-8161-8679-0). G K Hall.
--Poet in America: Winfield Townley Scott. (Illus.). 414p. 1972. 22.50x (ISBN 0-292-76400-6). U of Tex Pr.
--The Suburban Myth. LC 77-79191. 1969. 26.00x (ISBN 0-231-03192-0); pap. 11.00x (ISBN 0-231-08659-8). Columbia U Pr.
Donaldson, Scott, ed. see Kerouac, Jack.
Donaldson, Stanley S. Test Papers in Technical Drawing. 2nd ed. (Illus.). 104p. 1981. pap. text ed. 18.95x (ISBN 0-291-39488-4). Intl Ideas.
Donaldson, Stephen. The One Tree. (The Second Chronicles of Thomas Covenant: Bk. 2). 1982. 14.50 (ISBN 0-345-29898-5, Del Rey). Ballantine.
Donaldson, Stephen R. Chronicles of Thomas Covenant, 3 vols. 1982. pap. 8.85 (ISBN 0-345-30072-6, Del Rey). Ballantine.
--The Chronicles of Thomas Covenant, 3 vols. Incl. Lord Foul's Bane; The Illearth War; The Power That Preserves. 1983. Boxed Set. 23.85 (ISBN 0-345-31328-3). Ballantine.
--The Chronicles of Thomas Covenant: The Unbeliever, 3 vols. LC 77-73868. 1977. 14.95 ea.; Vol. 1: Lord Foul's Bane. (ISBN 0-03-022771-2); Vol. 2: The Illearth War. (ISBN 0-03-022776-3); Vol. 3: The Power that Preserves. (ISBN 0-03-022781-X). HR&W.
--Daughter of Regals & Other Tales. 304p. 1985. pap. 14.95 (ISBN 0-345-31442-5, Del Rey). Ballantine.
--The Ill-Earth War: The Chronicles of Thomas Covenant, the Unbeliever, Vol. 2. (A Del Rey Bk.). 1979. pap. 3.50 (ISBN 0-345-25717-0). Ballantine.
--Lord Foul's Bane: The Chronicles of Thomas Covenant, the Unbeliever, Vol. 1. (A Del Rey Bk.). 1978. pap. 3.95 (ISBN 0-345-32603-2). Ballantine.
--The One Tree. (The Second Chronicles of Thomas Covenant: Bk. 2). 496p. 1983. pap. 3.50 (ISBN 0-345-30550-7, Del Rey). Ballantine.
--The Power That Preserves. 1979. pap. 2.95 (ISBN 0-345-29658-3, Del Rey Bks.). Ballantine.
--The Second Chronicle of Thomas Covenant, 3 vols. Boxed Set. pap. 10.95 (ISBN 0-345-32088-3, Del Rey). Ballantine.
--White Gold Wielder. (The Second Chronicles of Thomas Covenant Ser.: Bk. 3). 480p. 1983. 14.95 (ISBN 0-345-30307-5, Del Rey). Ballantine.
--White Gold Wielder. 1984. pap. 3.95 (ISBN 0-345-31699-1, Del Rey). Ballantine.
--The Wounded Land: Book One of the Second Chronicles of Thomas Covenant. 512p. 1981. 12.95 (ISBN 0-345-28647-2); pap. 2.95 (ISBN 0-345-27831-3). Ballantine.
Donaldson, Sven. A Sailor's Guide to Sails. (Illus.). 192p. 1984. 14.95 (ISBN 0-396-08190-8); pap. 8.95 (ISBN 0-396-08199-1). Dodd.
Donaldson, T. Issues in Moral Philosophy. 560p. 1986. pap. text ed. price not set (ISBN 0-07-017534-9). McGraw.
--Ngiyambaa: The Language of the Wangaaybuwan. LC 79-7646. (Cambridge Studies in Linguistics: No. 29). (Illus.). 320p. 1980. 69.50 (ISBN 0-521-22524-8). Cambridge U Pr.
Donaldson, T. H. Lending in International Commercial Banking. LC 79-15566. (International Banking Ser.). 187p. 1979. 33.95x (ISBN 0-470-26793-3). Halsted Pr.
--Understanding Corporate Credit: The Lending Banker's Viewpoint. LC 83-16156. 256p. 1983. 27.50 (ISBN 0-317-13190-7). St Martin.
Donaldson, T. H. & Donaldson, J. A. The Medium-Term Loan Market. LC 82-42619. 176p. 1982. 25.00x (ISBN 0-312-52820-5). St Martin.
Donaldson, Tamsin, jt. ed. see Donaldson, Ian.
Donaldson, Terence L. Jesus on the Mountain: A Study in Matthean Theology. (JSNT Supplement Ser.: No. 8). 290p. 1985. text ed. 28.50x (ISBN 0-905774-74-4, Pub. by JSOT Pr England); pap. text ed. 13.50x (ISBN 0-905774-75-2, Pub. by JSOT Pr England). Eisenbrauns.
Donaldson, Thomas. Case Studies in Business Ethics. (Illus.). 256p. 1984. pap. text ed. 15.95 (ISBN 0-13-116079-6). P-H.
--Corporations & Morality. 288p. 1982. pap. 14.95 (ISBN 0-13-177006-3); 18.95 (ISBN 0-13-177014-4). P-H.
--A Laplace Transform Calculus for Partial Differential Operators. LC 74-7370. (Memoirs: No. 143). 166p. 1974. pap. 11.00 (ISBN 0-8218-1843-0, MEMO-143). Am Math.
--The Public Domain, Its History, with Statistics. (History of American Economy Ser.). 1970. Repr. of 1884 ed. 54.00 (ISBN 0-384-12305-8). Johnson Repr.
--Walt Whitman: The Man. LC 73-9633. Repr. of 1896 ed. lib. bdg. 25.00 (ISBN 0-8414-1883-7). Folcroft.
Donaldson, Thomas & Werhane, Patricia H. Ethical Issues in Business. 2nd ed. (Illus.). 416p. 1983. pap. 21.95 (ISBN 0-13-290148-X). P-H.
Donaldson, Wayne, jt. ed. see Tulving, Endel.
Donaldson, Weber D. French Reflexive Verbs: A Case Grammar Description. (Janua Linguarum Ser. Practica: No. 194). 1973. pap. text ed. 20.80x (ISBN 90-2792-503-8). Mouton.
Donaldson, William. The Life & Adventures of Sir Bartholomew Sapskull Baronet, 1768, 2 vols. in 1. LC 74-26834. (Novel in England, 1700-1775 Ser). 1975. lib. bdg. 61.00 (ISBN 0-8240-1183-X). Garland Pub.
Donaldson, William B. How Rich Do You Want To Be? 206p. (Orig.). 1981. pap. write for info. (ISBN 0-942882-00-8). Lindbrook Pr.
Donaldson-Evans, Lancelot K. Love's Fatal Glance: A Study of Eye Imagery in the Poets of the Ecole lyonnaise. LC 80-10415. (Romance Monographs: No. 39). 155p. 1980. 16.00 (ISBN 84-499-3694-2). Romance.
Donaldy, Ernestine, jt. ed. see Norton, Andre.
Donarico, Elnora. Nurse Jessica's Cruise. (YA) 1980. 8.95 (ISBN 0-686-59796-6, Avalon). Bouregy.
--Nurse Vicky's Love. (YA) 1979. 8.95 (ISBN 0-685-59935-3, Avalon). Bouregy.
Donaruma, L. Guy & Vogl, Otto, eds. Polymeric Drugs. 1978. 49.50 (ISBN 0-12-220750-5). Acad Pr.
Donaruma, L. Guy, et al. Anionic Polymeric Drugs. LC 80-11364. (Polymers in Biology & Medicine Ser. of Monographs: Vol. 1). 356p. 1980. 64.50x (ISBN 0-471-05530-1, Pub. by Wiley-Interscience). Wiley.
Donat, Alexander. The Holocaust Kingdom. LC 77-89067. 361p. (Orig.). 1963. pap. 9.95 (ISBN 0-89604-001-1). Holocaust Pubns.
--The Holocaust Kingdom: A Memoir. LC 77-89067. 1978. pap. 5.95 (ISBN 0-8052-5001-8, Pub by Holocaust Library). Schocken.
--The Holocaust Kingdom: A Memoir. 368p. pap. 5.95 (ISBN 0-686-95070-4). ADL.
Donat, Alexander, ed. The Death Camp Treblinka. LC 79-53471. (Illus.). 320p. (Orig.). 1979. 11.95 (ISBN 0-89604-008-9); pap. 8.95 (ISBN 0-89604-009-7). Holocaust Pubns.
--The Death Camp Treblinka: A Documentary. LC 78-71296. (Illus.). 1979. 9.95 (ISBN 0-8052-5009-3, Pub. by Holocaust Library); pap. 4.95 (ISBN 0-89604-500-5). Schocken.
Donatelli, Gary, jt. auth. see Armentani, Andy.
Donath. Approx Positions of Asteroids, Eighteen Fifty One to Two Thousand Fifty. 8.00 (ISBN 0-318-01835-7). Am Fed Astrologers.
Donath, A. & Righetti, A., eds. Cardiovascular Nuclear Medicine. (Progress in Nuclear Medicine: Vol. 6). (Illus.). viii, 228p. 1980. 63.00 (ISBN 3-8055-0618-X). S Karger.
Donath, A., jt. ed. see Juge, O.
Donath, Emma B. Asteroids in Midpoints. 160p. 1982. 12.00 (ISBN 0-86690-242-2, 2291-01). Am Fed Astrologers.
--Asteroids in Synastry. 96p. 1977. 6.50 (ISBN 0-86690-082-9, 1080-02). Am Fed Astrologers.
--Asteroids in the Birthchart. 104p. 1979. 6.50 (ISBN 0-86690-081-0, 1079-02). Am Fed Astrologers.
--Asteroids in the USA. 144p. 1979. 9.80 (ISBN 0-86690-083-7, 1081-02). Am Fed Astrologers.
--Minor Aspects Between Natal Planets. 168p. 1982. 10.00 (ISBN 0-86690-013-6, 1082-01). Am Fed Astrologers.
--Patterns of Professions. 112p. 1984. 9.00 (ISBN 0-86690-243-0, 2299-01). Am Fed Astrologers.
Donati, Maria B., jt. ed. see Coccheri, S.
Donati, Maria B., et al, eds. Malignancy & the Hemostatic System. (Monographs of the Mario Negri Institute for Pharmacological Research). 148p. 1981. text ed. 25.50 (ISBN 0-89004-463-5). Raven.
Donati, Robert M., jt. auth. see Newton, William T.
Donato, Anthony. Preparing Music Manuscript. LC 77-4024. (Illus.). 1977. Repr. of 1963 ed. lib. bdg. 20.50x (ISBN 0-8371-9587-X, DOPM). Greenwood.
Donato, Eugenio, jt. ed. see Macksey, Richard.
Donato, Georgia di see Di Donato, Georgia.
Donato, Gopi G. Lord Uranus. Morningland Publications, Inc., ed. (Astrology Ser.). (Illus.). 341p. (Orig.). 1981. pap. 6.95 spiral bdg. (ISBN 0-935146-52-0). Morningland.
Donato, Gopi G., jt. auth. see Donato, Sri.
Donato, Gopi G., jt. auth. see Morningland Publications, Inc.
Donato, Luigi A., ed. Frontiers in Cardiology for the Eighties. L'Abbate, Antonio. 1984. 49.00 (ISBN 0-12-220680-0). Acad Pr.
Donato, Sri. The Day of Brahma. Morningland Publications, Inc., ed. (Illus.). 377p. 1981. pap. 10.00 (ISBN 0-935146-20-2). Morningland.
--The Unicorn. Morningland Publications, Inc., ed. (Illus.). 207p. (Orig.). 1981. pap. 10.00 (ISBN 0-935146-16-4). Morningland.
Donato, Sri & Donato, Gopi G. Oneness, Vol. III. Morningland Publications, Inc., ed. 167p. 1981. pap. 7.95 spiral bdg. (ISBN 0-935146-58-X). Morningland.
Donato, Vince & Poole, Gary. How to Laugh & Be Well. (Illus.). 105p. (Orig.). 1982. pap. 5.95 (ISBN 0-942106-00-8). FEELGREAT.
Donatucci, Frederich, et al. Motivational Activities for Child Involvement in Mathematics. 2nd ed. (Illus.). 40p. (gr. 3-7). 1982. pap. 8.75 (ISBN 0-937138-03-7). FABMATH.
Donatucci, Frederich J., et al. Motivational Activities for Child Involvement in Mathematics. (Illus.). 40p. (gr. 3-6). 1980. pap. 6.95 (ISBN 0-937138-00-2). Fabmath.
Donatus, Cornelius. How to Anticipate the Business Future Without the Need of Computers, 2 vols. in 1. (The Study Center for Economic Psychology Ser.). (Illus.). 1978. deluxe ed. 79.75x (ISBN 0-918968-04-6). Inst Econ Finan.
--How to Anticipate the Business Future Without the Use of Computers. (Illus.). 47p. 1974. 69.50 (ISBN 0-913314-27-7). Am Classical Coll Pr.

Donlan, Walter, intro. by. The Classical World Bibliography of Roman Drama & Poetry & Ancient Fiction. LC 76-52516. (Library of Humanities Reference Bks.: No. 97). lib. bdg. 50.00 (ISBN 0-8240-9876-5). Garland Pub.
--The Classical World Bibliography of Vergil. LC 76-52514. (Library of Humanities Reference Bks.: No. 96). lib. bdg. 25.00 (ISBN 0-8240-9877-3). Garland Pub.
Donleavy, Al. The Counter Revolution for Peace: Words of Warning & Love from the Virgin Mary. LC 76-16324. 1976. 6.00 (ISBN 0-87212-067-8). Libra.
Donleavy, C. Douglas. Advanced Management Accountancy. (Illus.). 393p. 24.95 (ISBN 0-7121-0181-0). Trans-Atlantic.
Donleavy, Douglas & Metcalfe, Mike. How to Manage Money. (Building Your Business Ser.). 222p. 1984. text ed. 19.95x (ISBN 0-09-151820-2, Pub. by Busn Bks England). Brookfield Pub Co.
Donleavy, J. P. De Alfonce Tennis: The Superlative Game of Eccentric Champions - Its History, Accoutrements, Rules, Conduct & Regimen. (Illus.). 240p. 1985. 16.95 (ISBN 0-525-24324-0, 01646-490). Dutton.
--Destinies of Darcy Dancer, Gentlemen. 1978. pap. 12.95 (ISBN 0-385-28216-8, Delta). Dell.
--The Ginger Man. 1970. pap. 2.50 (ISBN 0-440-32886-1). Dell.
--Leila. LC 83-1970. 440p. 1983. 17.50 (ISBN 0-385-29260-0, Sey Lawr). Delacorte.
--Meet My Maker, the Mad Molecule. pap. 2.50 (ISBN 0-440-35937-6). Dell.
--The Onion Eaters. pap. 2.75 (ISBN 0-440-36643-7). Dell.
--Schultz. (Orig.). 1981. pap. 3.95 (ISBN 0-440-18102-X). Dell.
Donleavy, James P. Ginger Man. 1958. 10.00 (ISBN 0-8392-1037-X); pap. 6.95 (ISBN 0-8392-5007-X). Astor-Honor.
--Singular Man. 1968. pap. 2.50 (ISBN 0-440-37941-5, LE). Dell.
Donley, Carol, jt. auth. see Freidman, A. J.
Donley, Diana, jt. ed. see Burkhalter, Pamela.
Donley, Michael. Atlas of California. LC 79-84439. (Illus.). 192p. 1979. 29.95 (ISBN 0-943226-02-3, Pub. by Academic Book Ctr). Prof Bk Ctr Inc.
Donley, Michael B. The SALT Handbook. 1979. pap. text ed. 3.00 (ISBN 0-686-50012-1). Heritage Found.
Donley, R. Tucker. Law of Coal, Oil & Gas in Virginia & West Virginia. 1951. with 1972 suppl. 25.00 (ISBN 0-87215-084-4). Michie Co.
Donlon, Edward T. & Burton, Louise F., eds. The Severely & Profoundly Handicapped: A Practical Approach to Teaching. LC 76-17293. 272p. 1976. 42.00 (ISBN 0-8089-0952-5, 791058). Grune.
Donlon, Patrick T. & Schaffer, Charles B. A Manual of Psychotropic Drugs. LC 83-2660. (Illus.). 304p. 1983. pap. 15.95 (ISBN 0-89303-650-1). Brady Comm.
Donlon, T. A. & Echternacht, G. A Feasibility Study of the SAT Performance of High-Ability Students from 1960 to 1974(Valedictorian Study) 1977. 3.00 (ISBN 0-87447-044-7, 251711). College Bd.
Donn. Pediatric Transillumination. 1982. 31.50 (ISBN 0-8151-2733-2). Year Bk Med.
Donn, Clifford B. The Australian Council of Trade Unions: History & Economic Policy. LC 83-15951. 400p. 1984. lib. bdg. 27.25 (ISBN 0-8191-2728-0); pap. text ed. 14.75 (ISBN 0-8191-2729-9). U Pr of Amer.
Donn, Elizabeth R. Spanish-English Comparative Dictionary of Cognates: Diccionario Comparativo de Cognados en Espanol e Ingles. Camacho de Rodas, Isabel & Lyle, Jean K., eds. LC 85-90321. (Illus.). 212p. (Orig., Eng. & Span.). 1985. pap. 12.95 (ISBN 0-932058-02-7). RoDonn Pub.
Donn, Patsy, jt. auth. see Hollis, Joseph.
Donn, William. The Earth: Our Physical Environment. LC 79-37431. Repr. of 1972 ed. 158.00 (ISBN 0-8357-9875-5, 2055110). Bks Demand UMI.
Donn, William L. Meteorology. 4th ed. (Illus.). 608p. 1975. text ed. 36.55 (ISBN 0-07-017599-3). McGraw.
Donn, William L. & Shimer, John A. Graphic Methods in Structural Geology. LC 58-5315. (The Century Earth Science Ser.). pap. 45.00 (ISBN 0-317-26222-X, 2055684). Bks Demand UMI.
Donna, Natalie. The Peanut Cookbook. LC 75-33709. (Illus.). 56p. (gr. 3-7). 1976. 11.25 (ISBN 0-688-41729-9); PLB 11.88 (ISBN 0-688-51729-3). Lothrop.
Donnachie, A. & Shaw, G., eds. Electromagnetic Interactions of Hadrons. LC 77-17811. (Nuclear Physics Monographs). (Illus.). 1978. Vol. 1, 458 Pp. 65.00x (ISBN 0-306-31052-X, Plenum Pr); Vol. 2, 590 Pp. 85.00x (ISBN 0-306-31106-2). Plenum Pub.
Donnachie, Ian. A History of the Brewing Industry in Scotland. 1979. text ed. 39.50x (ISBN 0-85976-032-4). Humanities.
Donnachie, Ian & MacLeod, Innes. Victorian & Edwardian Scottish Lowlands from Historic Photographs. (Illus.). 120p. 1980. 19.95 (ISBN 0-7134-1297-6, Pub. by Batsford England). David & Charles.
Donnan, Christopher B. & McClelland, Donna. Burial Theme in Moche Iconography. LC 79-63727. (Studies in Pre-Columbian Art & Archeology: No. 21). (Illus.). 1979. pap. 5.00x (ISBN 0-88402-084-3). Dumbarton Oaks.
Donnan, Christopher B., ed. Early Ceremonial Architecture in the Andes. LC 84-10291. (Illus.). 300p. 1985. 15.00x (ISBN 0-88402-135-1). Dumbarton Oaks.
Donnan, Elizabeth, ed. see Bayard, James A.
Donnan, Frederick G. & Haas, Arthur, eds. Commentary on the Scientific Writings of Josiah-Willard Gibbs: A Propos de la Publication Des Ses Memories Scientifiques, 3 vols. in 2. LC 79-7963. (Three Centuries of Science in America Ser.). 1980. Repr. of 1936 ed. Set. lib. bdg. 115.00x (ISBN 0-405-12544-5); lib. bdg. 57.50x ea. Vol. 1 (ISBN 0-405-12611-5). Vol. 2 (ISBN 0-405-12612-3). Ayer Co Pubs.
Donn-Byrne, Brian O. see Byrne, Donn B., pseud.
Donne, Brian K. Christ Ascended: A Study in the Significance of the Ascension of Jesus Christ in the New Testament. 1982. pap. text ed. 8.95 (ISBN 0-85364-336-9). Attic Pr.
Donne, Charles E. Essay on the Tragedy of Arden of Feversham. LC 77-164773. Repr. of 1873 ed. 14.00 (ISBN 0-404-02143-3). AMS Pr.
Donne, John. Biathanatos. Kastenbaum, Robert, ed. LC 76-19567. (Death & Dying Ser.). 1977. Repr. of 1930 ed. lib. bdg. 23.50x (ISBN 0-405-09563-5). Ayer Co Pubs.
--The Complete English Poems: John Donne. Smith, A. J., ed. (Poets Ser.). 1977. pap. 7.95 (ISBN 0-14-042209-9). Penguin.
--Complete Poems. 1976. 9.95x (ISBN 0-460-00867-6, Evman); pap. 3.50x (ISBN 0-460-01867-1). Biblio Dist.
--Complete Poems. Bennett, Roger, ed. 336p. 1973. pap. 4.45 (ISBN 0-87532-103-8). Hendricks House.
--The Complete Poetry & Selected Prose of John Donne. Coffin, Charles M., ed. LC 52-5874. 1952. 6.95 (ISBN 0-394-60440-7). Modern Lib.
--Deaths Duel. Keynes, Geoffrey, ed. LC 72-75133. (Illus.). 64p. 1973. 20.00x (ISBN 0-87923-050-9); deluxe ed. 40.00 O.s.i. (ISBN 0-87923-051-7). Godine.
--Devotions upon Emergent Occasions. LC 72-10115. 1973. lib. bdg. 27.50 (ISBN 0-8414-0650-2). Folcroft.
--Devotions Upon Emergent Occasions. Bd. with Death's Duel. 1959. pap. 6.95 (ISBN 0-472-06030-9, 30, AA). U of Mich Pr.
--Devotions upon Emergent Occasions. Raspa, Anthony, ed. LC 76-361973. pap. 62.00 (ISBN 0-317-26281-5, 2024263). Bks Demand UMI.
--The Divine Poems. 2nd ed. Gardner, Helen, ed. (Oxford English Texts Ser.). 1979. 45.00x (ISBN 0-19-812745-6); pap. 11.95x (ISBN 0-19-871100-X). Oxford U Pr.
--Donne: Concordance to the Poems. Combs, Homer C. & Sullins, Z. R., eds. Date not set. price not set (ISBN 0-87532-036-8). Hendricks House.
--Donne: Selected Poems. Shaaber, Matthias A., ed. LC 58-12942. (Crofts Classics Ser.). 1958. pap. text ed. 3.75x (ISBN 0-88295-032-0). Harlan Davidson.
--Donne: Selected Poems. Hayward, John, ed. (Poets Ser.). (Orig.). (gr. 9 up). 1950. pap. 4.95 (ISBN 0-14-042013-4). Penguin.
--Donne's Prebend Sermons. Mueller, Janel M., ed. LC 77-143229. pap. 94.30 (ISBN 0-8357-9156-4, 2014652). Bks Demand UMI.
--Elegies, & the Songs & Sonnets. Gardner, Helen, ed. (Oxford English Texts Ser). 1965. 54.00x (ISBN 0-19-811835-X). Oxford U Pr.
--The Epithalamions, Anniversaries & Epicedes. Milgate, W., ed. (Elglish Texts Ser.). (Illus.). 1978. 49.00x (ISBN 0-19-812729-4). Oxford U Pr.
--John Donne's Poetry: An Annotated Text with Critical Essays. Clements, Arthur L., ed. (Critical Editions Ser). (Orig.). 1966. pap. 6.95x (ISBN 0-393-09642-4, NortonC). Norton.
--John Donne's Sermons on the Psalms & Gospels: With a Selection of Prayers & Meditations. Simpson, Evelyn M., ed. & intro. by. LC 63-16249. 1963. pap. 6.95 (ISBN 0-520-00340-3, CAL84). U of Cal Pr.
--Juvenilia: Or, Certaine Paradoxes & Probleme. LC 70-25438. (English Experience Ser.: No. 239). 64p. 1970. Repr. of 1633 ed. 9.50 (ISBN 90-221-0239-4). Walter J Johnson.
--Letters to Several Persons of Honour. LC 77-10078. 352p. 1977. Repr. of 1651 ed. lib. bdg. 50.00x (ISBN 0-8201-1296-8). Schol Facsimiles.
--The Love Poems of John Donne. Fawkes, Charles, ed. 128p. 1982. 8.95 (ISBN 0-312-49944-2). St Martin.
--Paradoxes & Problems. Peters, Helen, ed. (Oxford English Texts Ser.). (Illus.). 1980. 47.50x (ISBN 0-19-812753-7). Oxford U Pr.
--Poems. Grierson, Herbert J., ed. (Oxford Standard Authors Ser.). 1933. 29.95 (ISBN 0-19-254123-4); pap. 9.95x (ISBN 0-19-281113-4). Oxford U Pr.
--Poems, 2 vols. Grierson, Herbert J., ed. (Oxford English Texts Ser.). 1912. Set. 89.00x (ISBN 0-19-811809-0). Oxford U Pr.
--Poems: With Elegies on the Author's Death. LC 72-191. (English Experience Ser.: No. 240). 408p. 1970. Repr. of 1633 ed. 35.00 (ISBN 90-221-0240-8). Walter J Johnson.
--Poetry & Prose. Warnke, Frank J., ed. (Modern Library College Editions). 400p. 1967. pap. 5.00x (ISBN 0-394-30989-8, T89, RanC). Random.
--Poetry & Prose, with Izaac Walton's Life, Appreciations by Ben Jonson, Dryden, Coleridge & Others. LC 75-41077. Repr. of 1960 ed. 17.00 (ISBN 0-404-14769-0). AMS Pr.
--The Prayers of John Donne. Umbach, Herbert H., ed. (Orig.). 1962. pap. 5.95x (ISBN 0-8084-0252-8). New Coll U Pr.
--Pseudo-Martyr. LC 74-16215. 450p. 1974. 60.00x (ISBN 0-8201-1140-6). Schol Facsimiles.
--Satires, Epigrams & Verse Letters. Milgate, W., ed. (Oxford English Texts Series). (Illus.). 1967. 54.00x (ISBN 0-19-811842-2). Oxford U Pr.
--Selected Poems. Hayward, John, ed. (Penguin Poetry Ser.). 192p. 1950. pap. 4.95 (ISBN 0-14-042013-4). Penguin.
--Some Poems & a Devotion of John Donne. LC 76-21761. 1976. Repr. of 1941 ed. lib. bdg. 18.50 (ISBN 0-8414-3732-7). Folcroft.
--Suicide. Clebsch, William A., ed. LC 83-4466. (SP Studies in the Humanities). 134p. 1983. pap. 8.95 (ISBN 0-89130-624-2). Scholars Pr GA.
Donne, John, II. Biathanatos, Sullivan, Ernest W., ed. LC 80-66387. 352p. 1984. 38.50 (ISBN 0-87413-175-8). U Delaware Pr.
Donne, Sr. John. Devotions upon Emergent Occasions: A Critical Edition with an Introduction & Commentary, 2 vols. Savage, Elizabeth, ed. (Salzburg Studies in English Literature, Elizabethan & Renaissance Studies Ser.: No. 21). 392p. (Orig.). 1975. Set. pap. text ed. 50.75x (ISBN 0-391-01364-5). Humanities.
Donne, Michael, et al. Per Ardua Ad Astra: Seventy Years of the RFC & the RAF. (Illus.). 191p. 1983. 26.95 (ISBN 0-584-11022-7, Pub. by Salem Hse Ltd). Merrimack Pub Cir.
Donne, Robert C. Determinants of Value: An Annotated Bibliography. (Bibliographic Ser.: No.1). 48p. 1976. 11.00 (ISBN 0-88329-045-6). Intl Assess.
Donne, W. B., ed. Correspondence of King George the Third with Lord North, 1768-1783. LC 76-154697. (Era of the American Revolution Ser). 1971. Repr. of 1867 ed. lib. bdg. 95.00 (ISBN 0-306-70155-3). Da Capo.
Donne, William B. Tacitus. 1978. Repr. of 1873 ed. 20.00 (ISBN 0-8492-0688-X). R West.
Donnell, Annie H. Rebecca Mary. LC 72-4455. (Short Story Index Reprint Ser). Repr. of 1905 ed. 20.00 (ISBN 0-8369-4173-X). Ayer Co Pubs.
Donnell, Ezekiel J. Chronological & Statistical History of Cotton. LC 72-89084. (Rural America Ser.). 1973. Repr. of 1872 ed. 41.00 (ISBN 0-8420-1482-9). Scholarly Res Inc.
Donnell, John D. Corporate Counsel: A Role Study. LC 78-633785. (Business Study Ser: No. 40). 1971. 15.00 (ISBN 0-685-03851-3, IBS40). Ind U Busn Res.
Donnell, John D., et al. Law for Business. rev. ed. 1983. 28.50x (ISBN 0-256-02804-4). Irwin.
Donnell, Lloyd H. Beams, Plates & Shells. (Engineering Societies Monograph Ser.). 1976. text ed. 60.00 (ISBN 0-07-017593-4). McGraw.
Donnell, Nils. It's Not the Same Old Me. 1975. pap. 2.00 (ISBN 0-88027-007-1). Firm Foun Pub.
Donnellan, Anne, ed. Classic Readings in Autism. (Special Education Ser.). 456p. 1985. pap. 29.95x (ISBN 0-8077-2774-1). Tchrs Coll.
Donnellan, Brendan. Nietzsche & the French Moralists. 1982. 39.00x (ISBN 3-416-01667-X, Pub. by Bouvier Verlag Ger). State Mutual Bk.
--Nietzsche & the French Moralists. (Modern German Studies: Vol. 9). 210p. 1982. 22.00x (ISBN 3-416-01667-X, Pub. by Bouvier Verlag W Germany). Benjamins North Am.
Donnellan-Walsh, Anne, jt. auth. see LaVigna, Gary W.
Donnelley, Elfie. So Long Grandpa. Bell, Anthea, tr. LC 81-3241. (Illus.). 95p. (gr. 3-5). 1981. 8.95 (ISBN 0-517-54423-7). Crown.
Donnelley, Paul, ed. see Duncan, W. Jack.
Donnell-Kotrozo, Carl. Critical Essays on Post Impressionism. LC 81-65879. (Illus.). 176p. 1983. 32.50 (ISBN 0-87982-041-1). Art Alliance.
Donnelly. Coping with Stress: RN's Survival Sourcebook. 116p. 1983. 11.95 (ISBN 0-87489-299-6). Med Economics.
Donnelly, et al. Perspectives on Management. 5th ed. 1984. 13.95 (ISBN 0-256-03059-6). Business Pubns.
Donnelly, Alton S., ed. see Tikhmenev, P. A.
Donnelly, Alton S., tr. from Rus. & Quileute. The Wreck of the SV. Nikolai. Owens, Kenneth S., intro. by. (North Pacific Studies: Vol. 8). (Illus.). 128p. 1985. text ed. 14.95 (ISBN 0-87595-124-4). Oreg Hist Soc.
Donnelly, Alton S., tr. see Tikhmenev, P. A.
Donnelly, Austin S. The Three Rs of Investing: Return, Risk & Relativity. LC 84-72830. 1985. 17.95 (ISBN 0-87094-557-2). Dow Jones-Irwin.
Donnelly, Denis, ed. The Computer Culture: A Symposium to Explore the Computer's Impact on Society. LC 83-49215. (Illus.). 176p. 1985. 24.50 (ISBN 0-8386-3220-3). Fairleigh Dickinson.
Donnelly, Dody. Team. LC 77-74584. 168p. (Orig.). 1977. pap. 5.95 (ISBN 0-8091-2013-5). Paulist Pr.
Donnelly, Doris. Learning to Forgive. (Festival Ser.). 144p. 1982. pap. 3.25 (ISBN 0-687-21323-1). Abingdon.
--Putting Forgiveness into Practice. LC 82-71967. 192p. 1982. 5.95 (ISBN 0-89505-087-0). Argus Comm.
Donnelly, Dorothy. God & the Apple of His Eye. 1973. pap. 2.00 (ISBN 0-913382-05-1, 101-6). Prow Bks-Franciscan.
--Kudzu & Other Poems. (Pourboire Ser.). 1979. pap. 6.00 (ISBN 0-930900-57-X). Burning Deck.
Donnelly, Dorothy H. Radical Love: Toward a Sexual Spirituality. 144p. 1984. pap. 6.95 (ISBN 0-86683-817-1, AY8407). Winston Pr.
Donnelly, E. L. Electrical Installation Theory & Practice. 2nd ed. (Illus.). 1972. pap. text ed. 23.50x (ISBN 0-245-51007-9). Intl Ideas.
Donnelly, Elfie. Offbeat Friends. Bell, Anthea, tr. from Ger. LC 82-7995. 128p. (gr. 3-5). 1982. 8.95 (ISBN 0-517-54617-5). Crown.
Donnelly, Elizabeth A., jt. auth. see Beckmann, David M.
Donnelly, Elizabeth Anne, jt. auth. see Beckman, David.
Donnelly, Francis P. Literary Art & Modern Education. 328p. 1981. Repr. of 1927 ed. lib. bdg. 35.00 (ISBN 0-89987-175-5). Darby Bks.
--Literature the Leading Educator. LC 79-107694. (Essay Index Reprint Ser.). 1938. 19.00 (ISBN 0-8369-1497-X). Ayer Co Pubs.
Donnelly, G. F., et al. The Nursing System: Issues, Ethics & Politics. LC 80-12402. 224p. 1980. pap. 16.00 (ISBN 0-471-04441-5). Wiley.
Donnelly, Gloria F., jt. ed. see Sutterley, Doris C.
Donnelly, Hallie & Fletcher, Janet K. Appetizers & Hors d'Oeuvres. Smith, Sally W., ed. LC 85-70881. (California Culinary Academy Ser.). (Illus.). 128p. (Orig.). 1985. pap. 7.95 (ISBN 0-89721-055-7). Ortho.
Donnelly, Honoria & Billings, Richard. Sara & Gerald. 1983. 17.95 (ISBN 0-8129-1030-3). Times Bks.
Donnelly, Honoria M. & Billings, Richard N. Sara & Gerald: Villa America & after. 1984. pap. 7.95 (ISBN 0-03-069831-6, Owl Bks.). HR&W.
Donnelly, Hugh. Desert Jungle. Ashton, Sylvia, ed. LC 77-80279. 1977. 10.95 (ISBN 0-87949-091-8). Ashley Bks.
Donnelly, Ignatius. The American People's Money. LC 75-311. (The Radical Tradition in America Ser). 186p. 1975. Repr. of 1895 ed. 18.70 (ISBN 0-88355-215-9). Hyperion Conn.
--Atlantis: Antediluvian World. LC 80-8340. (Library of Spiritual Wisdom). (Illus.). 512p. 1981. pap. 9.57i (ISBN 0-06-061960-0, CN4006, HarpR). Har-Row.
--Atlantis: The Antediluvian World. Bleiler, E. F., ed. LC 76-24138. 518p. 1976. pap. 6.95 (ISBN 0-486-23371-5). Dover.
--Atlantis: The Antediluvian World. lib. bdg. 100.00 (ISBN 0-87968-055-5). Krishna Pr.
--Caesar's Column: A Story of the Twentieth Century. LC 76-42811. Repr. of 1890 ed. 36.00 (ISBN 0-404-60060-3). AMS Pr.
--Doctor Huguet. LC 75-92230. (American Negro: His History & Literature, Ser. No 3). 1970. Repr. of 1891 ed. 18.00 (ISBN 0-405-01920-3). Ayer Co Pubs.
--The Golden Bottle. LC 68-57523. (The Muckrakers Ser.). Repr. of 1892 ed. lib. bdg. 19.50 (ISBN 0-8398-0368-0). Irvington.
--The Golden Bottle. 1968. Repr. of 1892 ed. 25.00 (ISBN 0-384-12315-5). Johnson Repr.
--Great Cryptogram, 2 vols. LC 72-135730. Repr. of 1888 ed. Set. 75.00 (ISBN 0-404-02144-1). AMS Pr.
Donnelly, J., jt. auth. see Marks, D. J.
Donnelly, Jack. The Concept of Human Rights. LC 84-22863. 160p. 1985. 22.50 (ISBN 0-312-15941-2). St Martin.
Donnelly, James H. & George, William R., eds. Marketing of Services: Proceedings. (Proceedings Ser.). (Illus.). 244p. (Orig.). 1981. pap. text ed. 24.00 (ISBN 0-87757-148-1). Am Mktg.
Donnelly, James H., et al. Fundamentals of Management. 5th ed. 1984. 28.95 (ISBN 0-256-03057-X); 9.50 (ISBN 0-256-03058-6); study guide 9.50 (ISBN 0-256-03058-8). Business Pubns.
Donnelly, James H., Jr., jt. auth. see Peter, J. Paul.
Donnelly, James H., Jr., et al. Marketing Financial Services: A Strategic Vision. LC 84-72996. 1985. 25.00 (ISBN 0-87094-517-3). Dow Jones-Irwin.
Donnelly, James S., Jr., jt. ed. see Clark, Samuel.
Donnelly, Jane. Call Up the Storm. (Harlequin Romances Ser.). 192p. 1983. pap. 1.75 (ISBN 0-373-02552-1). Harlequin Bks.
--Diamond Cut Diamond. (Harlequin Romances Ser.). 192p. 1982. pap. 1.50 (ISBN 0-373-02510-6). Harlequin Bks.
--Face the Tiger. (Harlequin Romance Ser.). 192p. 1983. pap. 1.75 (ISBN 0-373-02576-9). Harlequin Bks.
--Flash Point. 192p. 1982. pap. 1.50 (ISBN 0-373-02456-8). Harlequin Bks.
--Il Neigeait sur la lande. (Harlequin Romantique Ser.). 192p. 1983. pap. 1.95 (ISBN 0-373-41202-9). Harlequin Bks.
--Le Jardinier De Tir Glyn. (Harlequin Romantique Ser.). 192p. 1983. pap. 1.95 (ISBN 0-373-41191-X). Harlequin Bks.

--The Mill in the Meadow, A Stranger Came, The Long Shadow. (Harlequin Romances Ser.). 576p. 1982. pap. 3.50 (ISBN 0-373-20062-5). Harlequin Bks.
--Un Parfum De Pluie. (Collection Harlequin Ser.). 192p. 1983. pap. 1.95 (ISBN 0-373-49370-3). Harlequin Bks.
--Ride Out the Storm. (Romances Ser.). 1975. pap. 0.95 (ISBN 0-373-01882-7, 51882). Harlequin Bks.
--Le Talisman Chinois. (Collection Harlequin Ser.). 192p. 1983. pap. 1.95 (ISBN 0-373-49357-6). Harlequin Bks.
Donnelly, John, ed. Language, Metaphysics, & Death. LC 76-18463. viii, 244p. 1978. pap. 10.00x (ISBN 0-8232-1017-0). Fordham.
Donnelly, John & Lyons, Leonard, eds. Conscience. new ed. LC 72-6720. 249p. (Orig.). 1973. pap. 4.95 (ISBN 0-8189-0259-0). Alba.
Donnelly, John, tr. see More, Thomas.
Donnelly, Joseph E. Living Anatomy. LC 81-82448. (Illus.). 207p. 1982. pap. 14.95x spiral (ISBN 0-931250-22-6, BDON0022). Human Kinetics.
Donnelly, Joseph P. Jacques Marquette, S. J., Sixteen Thirty-Seven to Sixteen Seventy-Five. LC 68-9498. 1968. 8.95 (ISBN 0-8294-0024-9). Loyola.
--Jean De Brebeuf: 1593-1649. LC 75-5682. 1976. 6.95 (ISBN 0-8294-0233-0). Loyola.
--Pierre-Gibault, Missionary, Seventeen Thirty-Seven to Eighteen Hundred Two. LC 77-156371. 1971. 8.95 (ISBN 0-8294-0203-9). Loyola.
--Thwaites' Jesuit Relations, Errata & Addenda. LC 66-27701. (The American West Ser). 1967. 6.95 (ISBN 0-8294-0025-7). Loyola.
Donnelly, Judy. True-Life Treasure Hunts. LC 84-4777. (Step-up Bks.). (Illus.). 72p. (gr. 2-5). 1984. 4.95 (ISBN 0-394-86801-3, Pub. by BYR); PLB 5.99 (ISBN 0-394-96801-8). Random.
Donnelly, Judy, ed. see Penner, Lucille R.
Donnelly, K., ed. see Mecking, P. R.
Donnelly, Katherine F. Recovering from the Loss of a Child. 224p. 1982. 13.50 (ISBN 0-02-532150-1). Macmillan.
Donnelly, Kerry. Doberman Pinschers. (Illus.). 1979. 4.95 (ISBN 0-87666-698-5, KW-009). TFH Pubns.
--Poodles. (Illus.). 1979. 4.95 (ISBN 0-87666-699-3, KW-010). TFH Pubns.
--Yorkshire Terriers. (Illus.). 1979. 4.95 (ISBN 0-87666-696-9, KW-007). TFH Pubns.
Donnelly, Kerry V., jt. auth. see Bruette, William A.
Donnelly, Linda, jt. auth. see Lee, Kaiman.
Donnelly, Marian. A Short History of Observatories. LC 73-175209. 1973. 7.50 (ISBN 0-87114-058-6). U of Oreg Bks.
Donnelly, Marian C. New England Meeting Houses of the Seventeenth Century. LC 68-27546. (Illus.). 1968. 18.50x (ISBN 0-8195-3092-1). Wesleyan U Pr.
Donnelly, Mary G. The King's Advocate. 1942. 10.00 (ISBN 0-932062-45-8). Sharon Hill.
--Skills for Consumer Success. (gr. 9-12). 1981. text ed. 5.20 wkbk. (ISBN 0-538-08100-7, H10). SW Pub.
Donnelly, Mary L. Arnold Livers Family in America (Lyvers, Lievers) LC 77-852223. (Illus.). 362p. 1977. 21.00 (ISBN 0-939142-02-3). Donnelly.
--The Buckman Family of Maryland & Kentucky. LC 79-90465. (Illus.). 530p. 1979. 32.00 (ISBN 0-939142-04-X). Donnelly.
--Craycrofts of Maryland & Kentucky Kin. LC 82-90280. (Illus.). 336p. 1982. 25.00 (ISBN 0-939142-06-6). Donnelly.
--Genealogy: A Step-by-Step Approach for Beginners, Ages 10 to 80. LC 83-71116. (Illus.). 64p. 1983. 4.00 (ISBN 0-939142-08-2). Donnelly.
--Maryland Elder Family & Kin. LC 76-351164. 330p. 1975. 15.00 (ISBN 0-939142-01-5). Donnelly.
--Rapier, Hayden & Allied Families: Colonial Maryland & Kentucky. LC 78-656670. (Illus.). 595p. 1978. 30.00 (ISBN 0-939142-03-1). Donnelly.
--Willett Family of Maryland, Colonial Pewters, Kentucky Pioneers. LC 82-74006. (Illus.). 712p. 1983. 40.00 (ISBN 0-939142-07-4). Donnelly.
Donnelly, Mary Louise. Imprints Sixteen Hundred Eight to Nineteen Eighty, Hamilton, Allied Families. LC 80-84574. (Illus.). 660p. 1980. 38.00 (ISBN 0-939142-05-8). Donnelly.
Donnelly, Michael. Managing the Mind: A Study of Medical Psychology in Early 19th-Century Britain. LC 83-4748. 200p. 1983. 19.95 (ISBN 0-422-78380-3, NO. 3809). Methuen Inc.
Donnelly, Milly L. Me Spik English. 31p. soft bdg. 1.95 (ISBN 0-930492-08-0). Hawaiian Serv.
Donnelly, Morwenna. Founding the Life Divine. 176p. 1976. Repr. of 1976 ed. write for info. Auromere.
--Founding the Life Divine: An Introduction to the Integral Yoga of Sri Aurobindo. LC 74-2430. 250p. 1976. pap. 7.95 (ISBN 0-913922-13-7). Dawn Horse Pr.
Donnelly, Patricia J. Manual & Dissection Guide for Mammalian Anatomy. (Illus.). 116p. 1972. pap. text ed. 10.95x (ISBN 0-8036-2680-0); instructor's guide, 20 slides 15.00 set incl. (ISBN 0-8036-2681-9). Davis Co.
Donnelly, Patricia J. & Wistreich, George A. Laboratory Manual for Anatomy & Physiology: With Cat Dissection. 636p. 1982. pap. text ed. 20.50 scp (ISBN 0-06-046644-8, HarpC); instr's manual avail. (ISBN 0-06-361701-3). Har-Row.
Donnelly, Paul, jt. auth. see Williams, Kenneth.
Donnelly, Paul, ed. see Anderson, Rolph & Hair, Joseph.
Donnelly, Paul, ed. see Ben-Horim, Moshe & Levy, Haim.
Donnelly, Paul, ed. see Ben-Horin, Moshe & Levy, Haim.
Donnelly, Paul S., ed. see Boone, Louis E. & Kurtz, David L.
Donnelly, Paul S., ed. see Fay, Charles & Wallace, Marc J., Jr.
Donnelly, Paul S., ed. see Gellerman, Saul.
Donnelly, Peter, jt. ed. see Theberge, Nancy.
Donnelly, Richard W. Project Development for Gas Processing Plants & Facilities. 2nd ed. Stelzner, Karen L., ed. (Illus.). 347p. (Orig.). 1982. pap. write for info binder (ISBN 0-88698-047-X, 3.80010). PETEX.
Donnelly, Robert M. Guidebook to Planning: Strategic Planning & Budgeting Basics for the Growing Firm. 1984. 24.95 (ISBN 0-442-22256-4). Van Nos Reinhold.
Donnelly, Russell J. Experimental Superfluidity. LC 66-23686. (Illus., Orig.). 1967. pap. 7.00x (ISBN 0-226-15757-1). U of Chicago Pr.
Donnelly, Shirley. The Hatfield - McCoy Feud Reader. 1971. pap. 3.50 (ISBN 0-87012-115-4). McClain.
Donnelly, Susan. Eve Names the Animals. (Samuel French Morse Poetry Prize Ser.: Vol. 1). 80p. (Orig.). 1984. pap. 4.95x (ISBN 0-930350-64-2). NE U Pr.
Donnelly, Thomas C., jt. auth. see Peel, Roy V.
Donnelly, Thomas D., ed. see Caribbean Geological Conference (5th: 1968: St. Thomas, Virgin Islands) Staff.
Donnelly, Thomas R. & Ciosek, Karen. To Those That Have Ears. LC 82-62455. 100p. 1982. 9.95 (ISBN 0-9610268-0-4). Seventh Trumpet.
Donnelly, Thomas W., ed. Earth Sciences: Problems & Progress in Current Research. LC 63-20901. 1963. 12.50x (ISBN 0-226-15656-7). U of Chicago Pr.
Donnelly, Tom, jt. auth. see Thoms, David.
Donnelly, William F., ed. American Economic Growth. LC 73-10339. 1973. 28.50x (ISBN 0-8422-5110-3); pap. text ed. 12.50x (ISBN 0-8422-0309-5). Irvington.
Donnelly, William J., jt. auth. see Meyer, Howard.
Donner, Ethyl, et al. Eleventh Year Math. (Regents Review Ser.). 288p. (Orig.). (gr. 9-12). 1984. pap. 3.95 (ISBN 0-668-05982-6). Arco.
Donner, Florinda. Shabono. 1983. pap. 3.95 (ISBN 0-440-38276-9, LE). Dell.
--Shabono: A Visit to a Remote & Magical World in the Heart of the South American Jungle. 1982. 14.95 (ISBN 0-385-28894-8). Delacorte.
--The Witch's Dream. 280p. 1985. 16.95 (ISBN 0-671-55198-1). S&S.
Donner, Frank J. The Age of Surveillance: The Aims & Methods of America's Political Intelligence System. LC 79-3479. 1980. 17.95 (ISBN 0-394-40298-7). Knopf.
--The Age of Surveillance: The Aims & Methods of America's Political Intelligence System. LC 81-40086. 576p. 1981. pap. 7.95 (ISBN 0-394-74771-2, Vin). Random.
Donner, Fred M. The Early Islamic Conquests. LC 80-8544. (Princeton Studies on the Near East). (Illus.). 328p. 1981. 44.00 (ISBN 0-691-05327-8). Princeton U Pr.
Donner, Frederick W., Jr. A Preliminary Glossary of Chinese Linguistic Terminology. (Orig., Chinese.). 1977. pap. 6.50 (ISBN 0-89644-521-6). Chinese Materials.
Donner, H. W. Introduction to Utopia. 59.95 (ISBN 0-8490-0421-7). Gordon Pr.
Donner, H. W., ed. see Beddoes, Thomas L.
Donner, Henry W. Introduction to Utopia. LC 78-94268. (Select Bibliographies Reprint Ser.). 1946. 18.00 (ISBN 0-8369-5042-9). Ayer Co Pubs.
Donner, Joan. Personal Vision of Ingmar Bergman. x1964 ed. (Biography Index Reprint Ser.). pap. 4.95 (ISBN 0-8290-1760-7). Irvington.
Donner, Jorn. The Films of Ingmar Bergman: From Torment to All These Women. Lundbergh, Holger, tr. from Swedish. Orig. Title: The Personal Vision Ingmar Bergman. (Illus.). 276p. 1972. pap. 6.95 (ISBN 0-486-20093-0). Dover.
--Personal Vision of Ingmar Bergman. Lundbergh, Holger, tr. (Biography Index Reprint Ser.). Repr. of 1964 ed. 20.25 (ISBN 0-8369-8119-7). Ayer Co Pubs.
--The Personal Vision of Ingmar Bergman. (Biography Index Reprint Ser.). (Illus.). 276p. Repr. of 1964 ed. lib. bdg. 18.25 (ISBN 0-8290-0832-2). Irvington.
Donner, K. Extension of Positive Operators & Korovkin Theorems. (Lecture Notes in Mathematics Ser.: Vol. 904). 182p. 1982. pap. 14.00 (ISBN 0-387-11183-2). Springer-Verlag.
Donner, M. W. & Heuck, F., eds. Radiology Today. A Multinational Series, Vol. 1. (Illus.). 431p. 1981. 79.50 (ISBN 0-387-10099-7). Springer-Verlag.
Donner, M. W. & Heuck, F. H., eds. Radiology Today, Vol. 2. (Illus.). 420p. 1983. 69.00 (ISBN 0-387-11754-7). Springer-Verlag.
--Radiology Today, Vol. 3. (Illus.). 256p. 1985. 55.00 (ISBN 0-387-13438-7). Springer-Verlag.
Donner, Michael. How to Beat the SAT. LC 80-54619. 135p. (gr. 11-12). 1981. pap. 3.95 (ISBN 0-89480-154-6, 460). Workman Pub.
Donner, Michael & Bramesco, Norton J. The Illustrated Encyclopedia of Crossword Words. LC 82-60067. (Illus.). 384p. 1982. pap. 9.95 (ISBN 0-89480-221-6). Workman Pub.
Donner, N., tr. see Kanakura, Y.
Donner, Neal, tr. see Sueno, Akira.
Donner, Stanley T., ed. The Meaning of Commercial Television. 171p. 1967. pap. 4.95x (ISBN 0-292-73181-7). U of Tex Pr.
Donnersberger, Anne, et al. A Manual of Anatomy & Physiology: Lab Animal the Cat. 2nd ed. 1980. pap. text ed. 17.95 (ISBN 0-669-02481-3); answer key 1.95 (ISBN 0-669-03168-2). Heath.
Donnersberger, Anne B., et al. A Manual of Anatomy & Physiology. fetal pig ed. 1978. pap. text ed. 17.95 (ISBN 0-669-01490-7); answer key 1.95 (ISBN 0-669-01632-2). Heath.
Donnerstein, Edward, jt. auth. see Malamuth, Neil M.
Donnerstein, Edward, jt. ed. see Geen, Russell.
Donnet, Jean B., et al. Carbon Black: Physics, Chemistry, & Elastomer Reinforcement. LC 75-16753. (Illus.). pap. 90.80 (ISBN 0-317-08000-8, 2020283). Bks Demand UMI.
Donnison, David. Social Policy & Administration Revised Studies in the Development of Social Services at the Local Level. 1970. 30.00x (ISBN 0-317-05808-8, Pub. by Natl Inst Social Work). State Mutual Bk.
Donnison, David & Soto, Paul. The Good City: A Study of Urban Development Policy in Britain. (Centre for Environmental Studies Ser.). 1980. 44.00x (ISBN 0-435-85216-7). Gower Pub Co.
Donnison, David V. & Eversley, David, eds. London: Urban Patterns, Problems, & Policies. LC 73-80440. (Centre for Environmental Studies Ser.: Vol. 2). pap. 116.00 (ISBN 0-317-29595-0, 2021888). Bks Demand UMI.
Donnithorne, Audrey. China's Economic System (2nd Imp.) 592p. 1981. 75.00x (ISBN 0-905838-61-0, Pub. by C Hurst & Co UK). State Mutual Bk.
Donnithorne, Audrey G. China's Economic System. LC 67-23967. pap. 148.00 (ISBN 0-317-29979-4, 2051762). Bks Demand UMI.
Donnithorne, Audrey G., jt. auth. see Allen, George C.
Donno, Daniel, ed. see Machiavelli, Niccolo.
Donno, Daniel J., ed. see Campanella, Tommaso.
Donno, Daniel J., tr. see Boccaccio, Giovanni.
Donno, Elizabeth S., ed. Andrew Marvell: The Critical Heritage. (The Critical Heritage Ser.). 1978. 29.95x (ISBN 0-7100-8791-8). Routledge & Kegan.
--Elizabethan Minor Epics. LC 63-20343. Repr. of 1963 ed. 68.60 (ISBN 0-8357-9064-9, 2013727). Bks Demand UMI.
--Twelfth Night. (The New Cambridge Shakespeare Ser.). 200p. Date not set. price not set. (ISBN 0-521-22752-6); pap. price not set. (ISBN 0-521-29633-1). Cambridge U Pr.
Donno, Elizabeth S., ed. see Marvell, Andrew.
Donocik, Rudolf. Theory of Phase-Controlled Oscillations. (Illus.). 296p. 1971. 40.00x (ISBN 0-7165-1314-5, Pub. by Irish Academic Pr Ireland). Biblio Dist.
Donoghue, Charles. Light Your Own Fire to Bigger Sales. LC 79-88425. (Illus.). 1979. 8.75 (ISBN 0-87218-006-9). Natl Underwriter.
Donoghue, D. Jonathan Swift. LC 77-79053. 1969. 49.50 (ISBN 0-521-07564-5). Cambridge U Pr.
Donoghue, Denis. The Arts Without Mystery: The BBC Reith Lectures. LC 83-824223. 195p. 1983. 15.95 (ISBN 0-316-18981-2). Little.
--Emily Dickinson. (Pamphlets on American Writers Ser: No. 81). (Orig.). 1969. pap. 1.25x (ISBN 0-8166-0543-2, MPAW81). U of Minn Pr.
--The Sovereign Ghost: Studies in Imagination. LC 75-27923. 1977. 25.00x (ISBN 0-520-03134-2). U of Cal Pr.
Donoghue, Denis, ed. Seven American Poets from Macleish to Nemerov: An Introduction. LC 74-22560. (Library on American Writers: Vol. 9). 320p. 1975. 16.95 (ISBN 0-8166-0739-7). U of Minn Pr.
Donoghue, Denis, ed. see Blackmure, R. P.
Donoghue, Denis, et al. PRATT Series on the Arts, Vol. I. 300p. 1984. pap. 15.00x (ISBN 0-930586-20-4). Haven Pubns.
Donoghue, Dennis. Connoisseurs of Chaos: Ideas of Order in Modern American Poetry. 1984. 26.00x (ISBN 0-317-14031-0); pap. 9.00x (ISBN 0-317-14032-9). Columbia U Pr.
--Ferocious Alphabets. 211p. 1984. pap. 9.00 (ISBN 0-231-05823-3). Columbia U Pr.
Donoghue, E. A., ed. Safety Code for Elevators & Escalators: Handbook on A17.1. 372p. 1981. 50.00 (A00112). ASME.
Donoghue, Gerald. My Friend, the Arabian Horse. 24.95 (ISBN 0-87505-328-9). Borden.
Donoghue, John. Alexander Jackson Davis, Romantic Architect, 1803-1892. 50.00 (ISBN 0-405-14078-9). Ayer Co Pubs.
Donoghue, John D. Pariah Persistence in Changing Japan: A Case Study. 1977. pap. text ed. 9.50 (ISBN 0-8191-0170-2). U Pr of Amer.
Donoghue, Mildred R. The Child & the English Language Arts. 3rd ed. 536p. 1979. text ed. write for info. (ISBN 0-697-06185-X). Wm C Brown.
--The Child & the English Language Arts. 4th ed. 592p. 1985. pap. text ed. write for info. (ISBN 0-697-00416-3). Wm C Brown.
Donoghue Organization, ed. see Donoghue, William E.
Donoghue, Quentin & Shapiro, Linda. Bless Me, Father, For I Have Sinned: Catholics Speak out about Confession. LC 84-81332. 303p. 1984. 17.95 (ISBN 0-917657-02-0). D I Fine.
--Bless Me Father, for I Have Sinned: Catholics Speak out about Confession. LC 84-81332. 303p. 1985. pap. 8.95 (ISBN 0-917657-44-6). D I Fine.
Donoghue, W. F., Jr. Monotone Matrix Functions & Analytic Continuation. LC 73-15293. (Grundlehren der Mathematischen Wissenschaften: Vol. 207). 210p. 1974. 31.00 (ISBN 0-387-06543-1). Springer-Verlag.
Donoghue, William E. Donoghue's Mutual Funds Almanac, Vol. 16. LC 83-646298. (Illus.). 140p. (Orig.). 1985. pap. 19.18i (ISBN 0-06-091264-2, CN 1264, CN). Har-Row.
--Donoghue's Mutual Funds Almanac, 1984. 15th ed. Donoghue Organization, ed. (Illus.). 1984. pap. 23.00 (ISBN 0-913755-01-X). Donoghue Organ Inc.
--William E. Donoghue's Guide to Finding Money to Invest: Building a Lifetime Savings Program with Your Hidden Cash Resources. LC 84-48155. (Illus.). 192p. 1985. 14.37 (ISBN 0-06-015393-8, HarpT). Har-Row.
Donoghue, William E. & Tilling, Thomas. William E. Donoghue's Complete Money Market Guide. LC 80-8200. (Illus.). 256p. 1981. 3.50i (ISBN 0-690-02008-2, HarpT). Har-Row.
--William E. Donoghue's No-Load Mutual Fund Guide: How to Take Advantage of the Investment Opportunity of the '80s. LC 82-48116. (Illus.). 224p. 1983. 13.41i (ISBN 0-06-015096-3, HarpT). Har-Row.
--William E. Donoghue's No-Load Mutual Fund Guide. 256p. 1984. pap. 3.95 (ISBN 0-553-25235-6). Bantam.
Donoghue, William F. Distributions & Fourier Transforms. (Pure & Applied Mathematics Ser.: Vol. 32). 1969. 68.50 (ISBN 0-12-220650-9). Acad Pr.
Donohue, Agnes M. Hawthorne: Calvin's Ironic Stepchild. LC 84-12550. 351p. 1985. 27.50x (ISBN 0-87338-310-9). Kent St U Pr.
Donohue, Brian. How to Buy an Office Computer or Word Processor. (Illus.). 232p. 1983. 17.95 (ISBN 0-13-403113-X); pap. 8.95 (ISBN 0-13-403105-9). P-H.
Donohue, Christine N. & Urdang, Laurence, eds. Prefixes & Other Word-Initial Elements of English. LC 83-20662. 533p. 1983. 68.00x (ISBN 0-8103-1548-3). Gale.
Donohue, Christine N., jt. ed. see Urdang, Laurence.
Donohue, Daniel P. An Analysis of Radiographic Quality: Lab Manual & Workbook. 2nd ed. (Illus.). 378p. 1984. pap. text ed. 19.00 (ISBN 0-8391-1988-7, 20885). Univ Park.
--An Analysis of Radiographic Quality, Manual. (Illus.). 278p. 1979. pap. text ed. 16.95 (ISBN 0-8391-1446-X). Univ Park.
Donohue, David A. & Ertekin, Turqay. Gaswell Testing: Theory, Practice & Regulation. LC 81-80726. (Illus.). 214p. 1981. text ed. 35.00 (ISBN 0-934634-10-6); pap. text ed. 26.00 (ISBN 0-934634-12-2). Intl Human Res.
Donohue, Dina. Mr. Harty Comes for Christmas. 1978. pap. 1.95 (ISBN 0-8170-0771-7). Judson.
Donohue, James F. Spitballs & Holy Water. 1977. pap. 1.75 (ISBN 0-380-01655-9, 33233). Avon.
Donohue, Jerry. The Structures of the Elements. LC 80-15363. 448p. 1982. Repr. of 1974 ed. lib. bdg. 29.50 (ISBN 0-89874-230-7). Krieger.
Donohue, John J. & Esposito, John L., eds. Islam in Transition: Muslim Perspectives. 1982. 26.00x (ISBN 0-19-503022-2); pap. 11.95x (ISBN 0-19-503023-0). Oxford U Pr.
Donohue, John K. Baffling Eyes of Youth. LC 74-9578. 251p. 1974. Repr. of 1957 ed. lib. bdg. 15.00x (ISBN 0-8371-7601-8, DOBY). Greenwood.
Donohue, John M. Beyond the Rate Card-Radio. 150p. 1984. pap. text ed. 39.00 (ISBN 0-943382-01-7). RadioResource Corp.
--The Radio Account Executive: Designs for Radio Advertising Campaign Sales. LC 82-7583. (Illus.). 825p. 1984. 3 ring binder 89.00 (ISBN 0-943382-00-9). RadioResource Corp.
Donohue, John P. Testis Tumors. (IPU: Vol. 7). (Illus.). 324p. 1983. lib. bdg. 46.50 (ISBN 0-683-02613-5). Williams & Wilkins.
Donohue, John W. Work & Education. LC 59-15751. (Jesuit Studies). 1959. 2.95 (ISBN 0-8294-0026-5). Loyola.
Donohue, Joseph W., Jr., ed. Theatrical Manager in Britain & America: Players of a Perilous Game. LC 72-154992. (Illus.). 1972. 22.50x (ISBN 0-691-06188-2). Princeton U Pr.
Donohue, William A. The Politics of the American Civil Liberties Union. 390p. 1985. 29.95 (ISBN 0-88738-021-2); pap. 14.95 (ISBN 0-87855-983-3). Transaction Bks.

onohue, Wilma, ed. see Conference on Aging, 2nd, University of Michigan.

Donohugh, Donald L. The Middle Years. 448p. 1983. pap. 3.95 (ISBN 0-425-06323-2). Berkley Pub.

Donoso, Anton. Julian Marias. (World Author Ser.). 1982. lib. bdg. 17.95 (ISBN 0-8057-6486-0, Twayne). G K Hall.

Donoso, Ephraim. Cardiac Arrhythmia. 1973. pap. 5.00 (ISBN 0-87493-036-7, 73-029A). Am Heart.

Donoso, Ephraim, ed. Symposium on Cardiac Arrhythmias. (AHA Monograph: No. 40). 200p. 1973. pap. 5.00 (ISBN 0-87493-040-5, 73-029A). Am Heart.

Donoso, Jose. The Boom in Spanish-American Literature: A Personal History. LC 76-53747. (Center for Inter-American Relations). 122p. 1977. pap. 11.00x (ISBN 0-231-04165-9). Columbia U Pr.

--Charleston & Other Stories. Conrad, Andree, tr. from Spanish. LC 76-19449. 1977. 12.95 (ISBN 0-87923-197-1); limited ed. 25.00x (ISBN 0-87923-206-4). Godine.

--A House in the Country. Levine, Suzanne J., tr. LC 82-11975. 352p. 1984. 16.95 (ISBN 0-394-50949-8). Knopf.

--A House in the Country. (Aventura Ser.). 1985. pap. 8.95 (ISBN 0-394-73657-5, Vin). Random.

--The Obscene Bird of Night. St. Martin, Hardie & Mades, Leonard, trs. from Span. LC 79-88419. 448p. 1979. pap. 9.95 (ISBN 0-87923-191-2, Nonpareil Bks.). Godine.

Donoso Cortes, Juan. An Essay on Catholicism, Authority & Order Considered in Their Fundamental Principles. Goddard, Madeleine V., tr. LC 78-59018. 1979. Repr. of 1925 ed. 28.00 (ISBN 0-88355-692-8). Hyperion Conn.

Donougher, Christine, tr. see Sagan, Francoise.

Donoughue, Carol, et al. In-Service: The Teacher & the School. 220p. 1981. 25.00 (ISBN 0-89397-109-X). Nichols Pub.

Donovan. Fabric Filtration for Combustion Sources. (Mechanical Engineering Ser.). 352p. 1985. write for info. (ISBN 0-8247-7452-3). Dekker.

--A Gift from a Flower to a Garden. pap. 3.50 (ISBN 0-686-09059-4). Peer-Southern.

--Greatest Hits. pap. 3.50 (ISBN 0-686-09060-8, Pub. by Peer-Southern). Columbia Pictures.

--The Hurdy Gurdy Man. pap. 3.50 (ISBN 0-686-09057-8, Pub. by Peer-Southern). Columbia Pictures.

--Open Road. pap. 3.50 (ISBN 0-686-09058-6, Pub. by Peer-Southern). Columbia Pictures.

Donovan, A. Philosophical Chemistry. 343p. 1983. 24.00x (ISBN 0-85224-281-6, Pub. by Edinburgh U Pr Scotland). Columbia U Pr.

Donovan, Arthur & Prentiss, Joseph. James Hutton's Medical Dissertation. LC 80-65850. (Transaction Ser.: Vol. 70). 1980. 8.00 (ISBN 0-87169-706-8). Am Philos.

Donovan, Bonnie. The Cesarean Birth Experience. rev. ed. LC 85-47520. 240p. 1985. pap. 8.95 (ISBN 0-8070-2701-4, BP 703). Beacon Pr.

Donovan, Bruce E. Euripides Papyri I: Texts from Oxyrhynchus. 104p. 1969. 10.50 (ISBN 0-88866-005-7, 31-00-05). Scholars Pr GA.

--Euripides Papyri 1: Texts from Oxyrhynelius. (American Society of Papyrology Ser.). 10.50 (ISBN 0-89130-698-6, 31-00-05). Scholars Pr GA.

Donovan, Caroline, jt. auth. see Rohan, Patrick J.

Donovan, Carrie. Living Well: The New York Times Book of Home Design & Decoration. LC 81-50088. (Illus.). 256p. 1981. 37.50 (ISBN 0-8129-0993-3). Times Bks.

Donovan, Chester D. Medical Devices & Equipment: Standards, Design, Failures & Safety: Medical Subject Analysis & Research Index with Bibliography. LC 83-71665. 120p. 1984. 29.95 (ISBN 0-88164-048-4); pap. 21.95 (ISBN 0-88164-049-2). ABBE Pubs Assn.

--Reducing Diet & Medical Processes: A Research Subject Analysis with Bibliography. LC 84-45734. 150p. 1985. 29.95 (ISBN 0-88164-246-0); pap. 21.95 (ISBN 0-88164-247-9). ABBE Pubs Assn.

Donovan, D. Once a Warrior King: Memories of an Officer in Vietnam. 384p. 1985. 15.95 (ISBN 0-07-017592-6). McGraw.

Donovan, D. T. Synoptic Supplement to T. Wright's Monograph on the Lias Ammonites of the British Islands. 1954. pap. 12.00 (ISBN 0-384-12325-2). Johnson Repr.

Donovan, D. T., ed. see Fourteenth Inter-University Geological Congress.

Donovan, Dennis G. & Herman, Magaretha G. Sir Thomas Browne & Robert Burton: A Reference Guide. 1981. lib. bdg. 42.00 (ISBN 0-8161-8018-0, Hall Reference). G K Hall.

Donovan, Dolores A. Prosecutorial & Judicial Misconduct. LC 79-53126. (California Criminal Law Practice Ser.). xi, 148p. 1979. 30.00 (ISBN 0-88124-062-1). Cal Cont Ed Bar.

Donovan, Edward. The Natural History of British Fishes: Scientific & General Descriptions of the Most Interesting Species, 2 vols. Sterling, Keir B., ed. LC 77-81091. (Biologists & Their World Ser.). (Illus.). 1978. Repr. of 1808 ed. Set. lib. bdg. 62.00x (ISBN 0-405-10668-8); lib. bdg. 31.50x ea. Vol. 1 (ISBN 0-405-10669-6). Vol. 2 (ISBN 0-405-10670-X). Ayer Co Pubs.

Donovan, Frances R. The Saleslady. LC 74-3942. (Women in America Ser.). 278p. 1974. Repr. of 1929 ed. 23.50x (ISBN 0-405-06088-2). Ayer Co Pubs.

--The Schoolma'am. LC 74-3943. (Women in America Ser). 368p. 1974. Repr. of 1938 ed. 27.00x (ISBN 0-405-06087-4). Ayer Co Pubs.

--The Woman Who Waits. facsimile ed. LC 74-3941. (Women in America Ser.: From Colonial Times to the 20th Century). 228p. 1974. Repr. of 1920 ed. 18.00x (ISBN 0-405-06089-0). Ayer Co Pubs.

Donovan, Frank & Henry, Seth. Headlights & Markers. LC 68-8776. (Illus.). 1968. 17.95 (ISBN 0-87095-006-1). Golden West.

Donovan, Frank P., Jr. Harry Bedwell, Last of the Great Railroad Storytellers. (Illus.). 3.75 (ISBN 0-87018-016-9). Ross.

Donovan, Frank R. & Kendrick, T. D. Vikings. LC 64-17106. (Horizon Caravel Bks.). (Illus.). (gr. 6 up). 1964. PLB 12.89 o.p (ISBN 0-06-021716-2). HarpJ.

Donovan, Gregory. Land Boom! An Amateur's Guide to Professional Wealth or... Your Inalienable Right to Your Own Eldorado! LC 83-80389. (Illus.). 76p. (Orig.). 1985. pap. 10.00 (ISBN 0-317-28185-2). Gregg Inc.

Donovan, Hedley. Roosevelt to Reagan: A Reporter's Encounters with Nine Presidents. LC 84-48592. 480p. 1985. 23.99 (ISBN 0-06-039042-5, C&M Bessie Bk). Har-Row.

Donovan, Herbert D. The Barnburners. LC 73-16337. (Perspectives in American History Ser.: No. 5). (Illus.). 140p. 1974. Repr. of 1925 ed. lib. bdg. 17.50x (ISBN 0-87991-337-1). Porcupine Pr.

Donovan, J. Democracy at the Crossroads: An Introduction to American Government & Politics. LC 74-5584. 1978. pap. text ed. 17.95 (ISBN 0-275-85580-5). HR&W.

Donovan, J. B. Bill Speed-Special Squad. 1971. pap. 1.95 (ISBN 0-87508-645-4). Chr Lit.

Donovan, J. J., ed. Recruitment & Selection in the Public Service. 1967. 8.00 (ISBN 0-87373-001-1). Intl Personnel Mgmt.

Donovan, J. J., jt. ed. see Warner, Kenneth O.

Donovan, J. W. Skill in Trials: Containing a Variety of Civil & Criminal Cases Won by the Art of Advocates; 173p. 1982. Repr. of 1891 ed. lib. bdg. 20.00x (ISBN 0-8377-0515-0). Rothman.

--Tact in Court Containing Sketches of Cases Won by Skill, Wit, Art, Tact, Courage & Eloquence with Practical Illustrations in Letters of Lawyers Giving Their Best Rules for Winning Cases. 3rd rev. ed. 135p. 1983. Repr. of 1886 ed. lib. bdg. 20.00x (ISBN 0-8377-0517-7). Rothman.

Donovan, Jerry J., jt. auth. see Blake, Judith.

Donovan, Joan, et al. The Nurse Assistant. 2nd ed. (Illus.). 1977. pap. text ed. 29.00 (ISBN 0-07-017675-2). McGraw.

Donovan, John. Bittersweet Temptation. (Orig.). 1979. pap. 2.50 (ISBN 0-89083-445-8). Zebra.

--Eichmann: Mastermind of the Holocaust. 1978. pap. 1.95 (ISBN 0-89083-406-7). Zebra.

--Good Old James. LC 74-20387. (An Ursula Nordstrom Bk.). (Illus.). (gr. 1 up). 1975. PLB 6.89 (ISBN 0-06-021704-9). HarpJ.

--I'll Get There: It Better Be Worth the Trip. LC 69-15539. (gr. 7 up). 1969. PLB 11.89 (ISBN 0-06-021718-9). HarpJ.

--Remove Protective Coating a Little at a Time. LC 73-4977. 112p. (gr. 7 up). 1973. 9.57i (ISBN 0-06-021719-7); PLB 11.89 (ISBN 0-06-021720-0). HarpJ.

--Systems Programming. LC 79-172263. (Computer Science Ser). (Illus.). 480p. 1972. text ed. 45.95 (ISBN 0-07-017603-5). McGraw.

--Wild in the World. (gr. 7 up). 1974. pap. 1.25 (ISBN 0-380-01625-7, 29264). Avon.

--Wild in the World. LC 74-159044. (gr. 5 up). 1971. 11.89 (ISBN 0-06-021702-2). HarpJ.

Donovan, John, jt. auth. see Madnick, Stuart.

Donovan, John, et al. People, Power & Politics. 2nd ed. 1986. pap. text ed. 14.00 (ISBN 0-394-35286-6, RanC). Random.

Donovan, John A. The Dog in Philosophy. LC 85-1579. (Other Dog Bks). (Illus.). 1985. 9.95 (ISBN 0-87714-090-1). Denlingers.

--The Dogs in Shakespeare. LC 79-55728. (Illus.). 1980. 11.95 (ISBN 0-87714-074-X). Denlingers.

--Gaelic Names for Celtic Dogs. LC 78-56243. (Other Dog Bks.). (Illus.). 1980. 11.95 (ISBN 0-87714-067-7). Denlingers.

--You & Your Irish Wolfhound. LC 76-20960. (Other Dog Bks.). (Illus.). 1977. 24.95 (ISBN 0-87714-053-7). Denlingers.

Donovan, John C. The Cold Warriors: A Policy-Making Elite. 1974. 8.95x (ISBN 0-669-83931-0). Heath.

--The Nineteen Sixties: Politics & Public Policy. LC 80-5757. 142p. 1980. lib. bdg. 18.50 (ISBN 0-8191-1189-9); pap. text ed. 7.50 (ISBN 0-8191-1190-2). U Pr of Amer.

Donovan, John C., et al. People, Power & Politics: An Introduction to Political Science. (Illus.). 384p. 1981. pap. text ed. 16.95 (ISBN 0-394-34928-8, RanC). Random.

Donovan, Joseph P. Pelagius & the Fifth Crusade. LC 76-29822. Repr. of 1950 ed. 18.50 (ISBN 0-404-15416-6). AMS Pr.

Donovan, Josephine. Feminist Theory: The Intellectual Traditions of American Feminism. 250p. 1985. 17.95 (ISBN 0-8044-2151-X); pap. 9.95 (ISBN 0-8044-6122-8). Ungar.

--New England Local Color Literature: A Women's Tradition. LC 82-40252. 158p. 1983. 12.95 (ISBN 0-8044-2138-2). Ungar.

Donovan, Josephine, ed. Feminist Literary Criticism: Explorations in Theory. LC 75-12081. 96p. 1975. pap. 5.00x (ISBN 0-8131-1334-2). U Pr of Ky.

Donovan, Josephine L. Sarah Orne Jewett. LC 80-5334. (Literature and Life Ser.). 175p. 1980. 12.95 (ISBN 0-8044-2137-4). Ungar.

Donovan, Karen & Stuart, Kiel, eds. Island Women. 140p. (Orig.). 1984. pap. 3.95 (ISBN 0-915675-00-5). Women Writers Alliance.

Donovan, Sr. M. Denise. Parents & the First Grade. LC 74-103703. 1971. pap. 2.95 (ISBN 0-913228-00-1). Dillon-Liederbach.

Donovan, Marilee & Richardson, S. G. Cancer Care Nursing. 2nd ed. (Illus.). 592p. 1984. pap. 29.95 (ISBN 0-8385-1032-9). ACC.

Donovan, Mary E., jt. auth. see Sanford, Linda.

Donovan, Mary E., jt. auth. see Sanford, Linda T.

Donovan, Mary S., jt. auth. see Ment, David.

Donovan, Michael. Official Grants & Financial Aids to Business in Western Europe. 400p. 1977. 40.00x (ISBN 0-86010-057-X, Pub. by Graham & Trotman England). State Mutual Bk.

--Official Grants & Finanial Aids to Business in Western Europe: Basic Volume with the First Two Updating Supplements (1978 & 1979) 400p. 1979. 66.00x (ISBN 0-686-64024-1, Pub. by Graham & Trotman England). State Mutual Bk.

Donovan, Michael & Appleby, Harrison. Planning & Controlling Manufacturing Resources. 1979. pap. 10.00 (ISBN 0-8144-2235-7). AMACOM.

Donovan, P. F. At the Other End of Australia: The Commonwealth & the Northern Territory 1911-1978. LC 83-21746. (Illus.). 277p. 1985. 35.00 (ISBN 0-7022-1914-2). U of Queensland Pr.

--A Land Full of Possibilities: A History of South Australia's Northern Territory. (Illus.). xxii, 267p. 1982. text ed. 24.50x (ISBN 0-7022-1606-2). U of Queensland Pr.

Donovan, Pete. Carol Johnston: The One-Armed Gymnast. LC 82-4499. (Sports Stars Ser.). (Illus.). (gr. 2-8). 1982. PLB 9.25 (ISBN 0-516-04323-4); pap. 2.95 (ISBN 0-516-44323-2). Childrens.

Donovan, Peter. The Red Army in Kiangsi: 1931-1934. (East Asia Papers: No. 10). 216p. 1976. 6.00 (ISBN 0-318-04617-2). Cornell China-Japan Pgm.

Donovan, Peter & Oxford University Press Englaish Language Teaching Development Unit. Basic English for Science. (Illus.). 1978. pap. text ed. 8.50x students ed. (ISBN 0-19-457180-7); pap. text ed. 10.95x teacher's ed. (ISBN 0-19-457181-5). Oxford U Pr.

Donovan, Peter, et al. Chinese Communist Materials at the Bureau of Investigation Archives, Taiwan. (Michigan Monographs in Chinese Studies: No. 24). 105p. 1976. pap. 5.00 (ISBN 0-89264-024-3). U of Mich Ctr Chinese.

Donovan, Priscilla, jt. auth. see Wonder, Jacquelyn.

Donovan, Robert, jt. auth. see Bignell, James.

Donovan, Robert, et al. Mostly Mine. (Illus.). 1978. pap. 2.95 (ISBN 0-685-87716-7). Orovan Bks.

Donovan, Robert J. Conflict & Crisis: The Presidency of Harry S. Truman, 1945-1948. (Illus.). 1977. 19.95 (ISBN 0-393-05636-8); pap. 10.95 (ISBN 0-393-00924-6). Norton.

--Nemesis: Truman & Johnson in the Coils of War in Asia. 256p. 1984. 14.95 (ISBN 0-312-56370-1, Pub. by Marek). St Martin.

--Tumultuous Years: The Presidency of Harry S. Truman, 1949-1953. (Illus.). 1982. 19.95 (ISBN 0-393-01619-6). Norton.

--Tumultuous Years: The Presidency of Harry S. Truman, 1949-1953. (Illus.). 448p. 1984. pap. 9.95 (ISBN 0-393-30164-8). Norton.

Donovan, Robert J., intro. by see Truman, Harry S.

Donovan, Robert K., ed. Current Research in British Studies. 8th ed. 82p. 1980. pap. 14.00x (ISBN 0-89126-084-6). MA-AH Pub.

Donovan, Robert O. The Bible Back in Our Schools. LC 72-80782. 80p. 1972. pap. 1.50 (ISBN 0-913748-01-3). Orovan Bks.

--Her Door of Faith. LC 79-172385. (Illus.). 112p. 1971. pap. 1.95 (ISBN 0-913748-02-1). Orovan Bks.

Donovan, Ronald & Orr, Marsha J. Subcontracting in the Public Sector: The New York State Experience. LC 82-6379. (IPE Monograph: No. 10). 44p. 1982. pap. 4.95 (ISBN 0-87546-095-X). ILR Pr.

Donovan, Suzanne & Bannon, William J. Volunteers & Ministry: A Manual for Developing Parish Volunteers. LC 82-62963. 112p. 1983. pap. 5.95 (ISBN 0-8091-2545-5). Paulist Pr.

Donovan, Terence. Glances. LC 84-61057. (Illus.). 132p. 1984. cancelled (ISBN 0-394-54249-5, GP946). Grove.

--Glances. (Illus.). 160p. 1985. 24.95 (ISBN 0-7181-2375-1, Pub. by Michael Joseph). Merrimack Pub Cir.

Donovan, Thomas. English Historical Plays: Shakespeare, Marlowe. Peele, Heywood, Fletcher & Ford. 1978. Repr. of 1896 ed. lib. bdg. 100.00 set (ISBN 0-8495-1033-3). Arden Lib.

Donovan, Timothy P. Historical Thought in America: Postwar Patterns. LC 72-9272. 300p. 1973. 14.95x (ISBN 0-8061-1078-3); pap. text ed. 6.95x (ISBN 0-8061-1504-1). U of Okla Pr.

Donovan, Timothy P. & Gatewood, Willard B., Jr., eds. The Governors of Arkansas: Essays in Political Biography. LC 81-50374. 320p. 1981. text ed. 20.00x (ISBN 0-938626-00-0). U of Ark Pr.

Donovan, Vincent J. Christianity Rediscovered. rev. ed. LC 81-18992. 208p. 1982. pap. 8.95 (ISBN 0-88344-096-2). Orbis Bks.

Donow, Herbert S., ed. A Concordance to the Poems of Sir Philip Sidney. LC 73-20816. (The Concordances Ser.). 637p. 1975. 50.00x (ISBN 0-8014-0805-9). Cornell U Pr.

Donow, Herbert S., compiled by. The Sonnet in England & America: A Bibliography of Criticism. LC 82-929. xxii, 477p. 1982. lib. bdg. 49.95 (ISBN 0-313-21336-4, DSE/). Greenwood.

Donowitz, Mark & Sharp, Geoffrey W. Mechanisms of Intestinal Electrolyte Transport & Regulation by Calcium: Proceedings of Kroc Foundation Conference, Santa Ynez Valley, California, September 26-30, 1983. LC 84-17127. (Kroc Foundation Ser.: Vol. 17). 388p. 1984. 78.00 (ISBN 0-8451-0307-5). A R Liss.

Don Pascual de Gayangos. Catalogue of the Manuscripts in the Spanish Language in the British Library, 4 vols. Incl. Vol. 1. 833p. Repr. of 1875 ed; Vol. 2. 824p. Repr. of 1877 ed; Vol. 3. 819p. Repr. of 1881 ed; Vol. 4. 345p. Repr. of 1893 ed. 1976. Repr. Set. 142.50 (ISBN 0-7141-0491-4, Pub. by British Lib). Longwood Pub Group.

Donsbach, Kurt. Metabolic Cancer Therapies. 1981. 1.95x (ISBN 0-686-37945-4). Cancer Control Soc.

--Passport to Good Health. 191p. 5.95 (ISBN 0-318-15682-2). Natl Health Fed.

--Passport to Good Health: Preventive Organic Medicine. 1.95x (ISBN 0-686-29910-8). Cancer Control Soc.

--Superhealth. 1980. 8.95x (ISBN 0-686-32628-8). Cancer Control Soc.

Donsbach, Kurt & Walker, Morton. Chelation. 1981. 1.95x (ISBN 0-686-36341-8). Cancer Control Soc.

--DMSO. 1981. 1.25x (ISBN 0-686-36344-2); 10.95. Cancer Control Soc.

Donsbach, Kurt W. Dr. Donsbach's Guide to Good Health. (Orig.). 1985. pap. text ed. 9.95 (ISBN 0-671-47294-1, Long Shadow Bks). PB.

--Preventive Organic Medicine. LC 76-2979. (Pivot Health Book). 1976. pap. 2.50 (ISBN 0-87983-122-7). Keats.

Donsker, M. D., ed. see Kac, Mark.

Donski, A. V., et al. Physics & Technology of Low-Temperature Plasmas. Dresvin, S. V. & Eckert, H. U., eds. Cheron, T., tr. from Rus. (Illus.). 1977. text ed. 25.00x (ISBN 0-8138-1950-4). Iowa St U Pr.

Donskis, M., tr. see Bartol'd, Vasilii V.

Donsky, Joanne, jt. auth. see Bone, Barry.

Donson, Alexandra. Healing Herbs for Arthritis & Rheumatism. LC 81-85031. (Illus.). 144p. (Orig.). 1982. pap. 6.95 (ISBN 0-8069-7578-4). Sterling.

Donson, Theodore B. Prints & the Print Markets: A Handbook for Buyers, Collectors, & Connoisseurs. LC 76-14487. (Illus.). 1977. 23.99i (ISBN 0-690-01160-1). T Y Crowell.

Dont, J. Etudes & Caprices for Violin. (Carl Fischer Music Library: No. 306). (Illus.). 1903. pap. 6.00 (ISBN 0-8258-0040-4). Fischer Inc NY.

--Twenty Progressive Exercises for Violin, Op. 38a. (Carl Fischer Music Library: No. 357). 1964. pap. 6.00 (ISBN 0-8258-0044-7, L357). Fischer Inc NY.

Dontchev, A. L. Perturbations, Approximations, & Sensitivity Analysis of Optimal Control Systems. (Lecture Notes in Control & Information Sciences Ser.: Vol. 52). 162p. 1983. pap. 13.00 (ISBN 0-387-12463-2). Springer-Verlag.

Donway, Roger, jt. auth. see Kelley, David.

Dony, J. G. Flora of Bedfordshire. 532p. 1953. 60.00x (ISBN 0-7158-1337-4, Pub. by EP Pub England). State Mutual Bk.

Dony, John G. & Dyer, James. The Story of Luton. 160p. 1982. 35.00x (ISBN 0-900804-11-4, Pub. by White Crescent England). State Mutual Bk.

Don-Yehiya, Eliezer, jt. auth. see Liebman, Charles S.

Donze, Sr. M. Terese. The Kingdom Lost & Found: A Fable for Everyone. LC 82-71983. (Illus.). 64p. (Orig.). 1982. pap. 3.95 (ISBN 0-87793-253-0). Ave Maria.

Donze, Mary T. Down Gospel By Ways: Eighteen Stories of People Who Met Jesus. 80p. 1984. pap. 2.95 (ISBN 0-89243-198-9). Liguori Pubns.

--In My Heart Room. 64p. 1982. pap. 1.50 (ISBN 0-89243-161-X). Liguori Pubns.

--Teresa of Avila. LC 81-85380. 176p. (Orig.). 1982. pap. 5.95 (ISBN 0-8091-2434-3). Paulist Pr.

--Touching a Child's Heart: An Innovative Guide to Becoming a Good Storyteller. LC 85-71557. 88p. (Orig.). 1985. pap. 3.95 (ISBN 0-87793-290-5). Ave Maria.

Donze, Terese. In My Heart Room Coloring Book. Murphy, Mary, tr. 32p. 1982. pap. 1.50 (ISBN 0-89243-169-5). Liguori Pubns.

Donzelot, Jacques. The Policing of Families. LC 79-1888. 1980. 10.00 (ISBN 0-394-50338-4); pap. 4.95 (ISBN 0-394-73752-0). Pantheon.

Doob, Anthony, jt. auth. see Freedman, Jonathan N.

Doob, J. L. Classical Potential Theory & Its Probabilistic Counterpart. (Grundelehren der Mathematischen Wissenchaften Ser.: Vol. 262). 750p. 1984. 64.00 (ISBN 0-387-90881-1). Springer-Verlag.

Doob, J. L., ed. see Symposia in Pure Mathematics.

Doob, Joseph L. Stochastic Processes. LC 52-11857. (Wiley Series in Probability & Mathematical Statistics). 654p. 1953. 52.50x (ISBN 0-471-21813-8, Pub. by Wiley-Interscience). Wiley.

Doob, Leonard W. Becoming More Civilized, a Psychological Exploration. LC 73-6211. 333p. 1973. Repr. of 1960 ed. lib. bdg. 17.50x (ISBN 0-8371-6893-7, DOMC). Greenwood.

--Communication in Africa: A Search for Boundaries. LC 78-27557. (Illus.). 1979. Repr. of 1961 ed. lib. bdg. 37.50 (ISBN 0-313-20789-5, DOCA). Greenwood.

--Panorama of Evil: Insights from the Behavioral Sciences. LC 77-87964. (Contributions in Philosophy Ser.: No. 10). 1978. lib. bdg. 27.50 (ISBN 0-313-20030-0, DPE/). Greenwood.

--Pathways to People. LC 74-29716. (Illus.). 320p. 1975. 33.00x (ISBN 0-300-01843-6). Yale U Pr.

--Patriotism & Nationalism: Their Psychological Foundations. LC 76-42309. (Illus.). 1976. Repr. of 1964 ed. lib. bdg. 22.00x (ISBN 0-8371-8978-0, DOPN). Greenwood.

--Patterning of Time. LC 72-97346. pap. 121.50 (ISBN 0-317-10352-0, 2007547). Bks Demand UMI.

--Personality, Power & Authority: A View from the Behavioral Sciences. LC 83-1688. (Contributions in Psychology Ser.: No. 1). xiii, 218p. 1983. lib. bdg. 29.95 (ISBN 0-313-23920-7, DPA/). Greenwood.

--Plans of Men. xix, 411p. 1968. Repr. of 1940 ed. 25.00 (ISBN 0-208-00126-3, Archon). Shoe String.

--Public Opinion & Propaganda. 2nd ed. x, 612p. 1966. 32.50 (ISBN 0-208-00513-7, Archon). Shoe String.

--The Pursuit of Peace. LC 80-1201. x, 335p. 1981. lib. bdg. 35.00 (ISBN 0-313-22630-X, DPO/). Greenwood.

--Social Psychology: An Analysis of Human Behavior. LC 79-136063. 1971. Repr. of 1952 ed. lib. bdg. 23.50x (ISBN 0-8371-5213-5, DOSP). Greenwood.

Doob, Leonard W., ed. Ezra Pound Speaking: Radio Speeches of World War II. LC 77-91288. (Contributions in American Studies: No. 37). 1978. lib. bdg. 35.00 (ISBN 0-313-20057-2, DEP/). Greenwood.

--Resolving Conflict in Africa: The Fermeda Workshop. LC 71-123396. pap. 57.00 (ISBN 0-317-11303-8, 2021995). Bks Demand UMI.

Doob, Penelope B. Nebuchadnezzar's Children: Conventions of Madness in Middle English Literature. LC 73-86890. pap. 66.30 (ISBN 0-317-29584-5, 2021994). Bks Demand UMI.

Doody, Francis S., jt. auth. see Clemence, Richard V.

Doody, Margaret. Aristotle Detective. LC 79-1703. (A Harper Novel of Suspense Ser.). 288p. 1980. 10.95i (ISBN 0-06-011086-4, HarpT). Har-Row.

Doody, Margaret A. The Daring Muse: Augustan Poetry Reconsidered. (Illus.). 320p. 1985. 44.50 (ISBN 0-521-25825-1); pap. 12.95 (ISBN 0-521-27723-X). Cambridge U Pr.

Doody, Terrence. Confession & Community in the Novel. LC 79-26388. viii, 248p. 1980. 22.50x (ISBN 0-8071-0662-3). La State U Pr.

D'Ooge, Martin L., tr. see Nicomachus, Gerasenus.

Dooghe, Gilbert & Helander, Jan, eds. Family Life in Old Age. (Netherlands Demographic Institute & the Population & Family Study Center Ser.: No. 8). 1979. lib. bdg. 31.00 (ISBN 90-247-2207-1, Pub. by Martinus Nijhoff Netherlands). Kluwer Academic.

Doohan, Leonard. The Lay-Centered Church: Theology & Spirituality. 204p. 1984. pap. 8.95 (ISBN 0-86683-808-2, AY8403). Winston Pr.

--Luke: The Perennial Spirituality. LC 82-71449. 321p. (Orig.). 1982. pap. 11.95 (ISBN 0-939680-03-3). Bear & Co.

--Luke: The Perennial Spirituality. 240p. (Orig.). 1985. pap. 9.95 (ISBN 0-939680-24-6). Bear & Co.

--Matthew: Spirituality for the 80's & 90's. 220p. (Orig.). 1985. pap. 9.95 (ISBN 0-939680-19-X). Bear & Co.

Doohovskoy, A. P., tr. see Landkof, N. S.

Doohovskoy, A. P., tr. see Mal'cev, A. I.

Dookeran, Winston, jt. ed. see Brereton, Bridget.

Doolan, Brian. Principles of Irish Law. 1981. 37.50x (ISBN 0-7171-1124-5, Pub. by Gill & Macmillan Ireland). State Mutual Bk.

Doole, Louise E. Herbs for Health: How to Grow & Use Them. pap. 4.00 (ISBN 0-87980-052-6). Wilshire.

Dooley, Agnes W. Promises to Keep. (Illus.). 272p. 1962. 5.95 (ISBN 0-374-23808-1). FS&G.

Dooley, Beth, jt. auth. see Anton, Liz.

Dooley, Betty, jt. auth. see Dooley, Claude.

Dooley, Brian J., jt. auth. see Blumberg, Donald F.

Dooley, Claude & Dooley, Betty. Why Stop? 2nd ed. 600p. (Orig.). 1985. pap. 9.95x (ISBN 0-88415-922-1, Lone Star Bks). Gulf Pub.

Dooley, D. J. The Art of Sinclair Lewis. LC 65-17173. xvi, 286p. 1967. pap. 6.50x (ISBN 0-8032-5051-7, BB 199, Bison). U of Nebr Pr.

Dooley, D. J., jt. auth. see Morriss, Margaret.

Dooley, D. J., ed. Data Conversion Integrated Circuits. LC 80-10541. 1980. 34.25 (ISBN 0-87942-131-2, PC01263). Inst Electrical.

Dooley, Daniel J. Data-Conversion Integrated Circuits. (IEEE Press Selected Reprint Ser.). 298p. 1980. 32.95x (ISBN 0-471-08154-X, Pub. by Wiley-Interscience); pap. 21.50x (ISBN 0-471-08155-8). Wiley.

Dooley, David. Social Research Methods. (Illus.). 400p. 1984. text ed. 28.95 (ISBN 0-13-818121-7). P-H.

Dooley, David, jt. auth. see Goodman, Gerald.

Dooley, Dennis. Dashiell Hammett. (Recognitions Ser.). 1984. 11.95 (ISBN 0-8044-2141-2); pap. 6.95 (ISBN 0-8044-6124-4). Ungar.

Dooley, Dennis A., ed. Index to State Bar Association Reports & Proceedings. LC 76-48816. xii, 640p. 1976. Repr. of 1942 ed. lib. bdg. 38.50 (ISBN 0-930342-30-5). W S Hein.

Dooley, Eliza B. Old San Juan. LC 70-76348. 1969. 3.75 (ISBN 0-87272-006-3). Brodart.

Dooley, Fern P. Joey's Ghost Pumpkin. LC 81-69695. (gr. 3-6). 1982. 6.95 (ISBN 0-8054-4515-3). Broadman.

Dooley, H. H. Last Rights. 224p. 1981. pap. 2.50 (ISBN 0-449-24392-3, Crest). Fawcett.

Dooley, James. Modern Tort Law: 1977-1983, 3 vols. LC 77-10972. Set. 250.00 (ISBN 0-317-12045-X). Callaghan.

Dooley, Mrs. James H. Dem Good Ole Times. LC 72-6486. (Black Heritage Library Collection Ser.). 1972. Repr. of 1906 ed. 17.25 (ISBN 0-8369-9166-4). Ayer Co Pubs.

Dooley, James W. Inside Huntsville Prison. 160p. (Orig.). 1981. pap. 5.95 (ISBN 0-9605576-0-1). Grace Pub House.

Dooley, John, jt. auth. see Tanis, James.

Dooley, John, ed. see Carroll, Lewis.

Dooley, Kate. The Saints Book: Stories for Children. LC 80-82814. 48p. (Orig.). (gr. k-3). 1981. pap. 2.95 (ISBN 0-8091-6547-3). Paulist Pr.

Dooley, Kate C. The Jesus Book. LC 82-61422. 48p. (Orig.). 1983. pap. 2.95 (ISBN 0-8091-2514-5). Paulist Pr.

Dooley, Ken. Forty Plus: The Manager's Guide to Avoididng Age Discrimination Claims. 250p. 1985. write for info. 3-ring looseleaf binding (ISBN 0-86604-191-5). Hamilton Inst.

Dooley, L. M. That Motherly Mother of Guadalupe. 2.25 (ISBN 0-8198-0634-X); pap. 1.25 (ISBN 0-8198-0635-8). Dghtrs St Paul.

Dooley, Michael P., et al, eds. The Political Economy of Policy-Making: Essays in Honor of Will E. Mason. LC 78-25960. (Comparative Political Economy & Public Policy Ser.: Vol. 4). (Illus.). pap. 62.00 (ISBN 0-317-09719-9, 2021889). Bks Demand UMI.

Dooley, Patricia, ed. The First Steps. 148p. 1985. 17.50 (ISBN 0-318-17736-6). Childrens Lit.

--Scandinavian Folk & Fairy Tales. 666p. 1984. 7.98 (ISBN 0-517-43620-5). Outlet Bk Co.

Dooley, Patrick K. Pragmatism As Humanism: The Philosophy of William James. LC 73-86935. 232p. 1974. 21.95x (ISBN 0-88229-125-4). Nelson-Hall.

Dooley, Peter C. Elementary Price Theory. 2nd ed. (Illus., Orig.). 1973. pap. text ed. 14.95 (ISBN 0-13-259531-1). P-H.

Dooley, Roger. From Scarface to Scarlett: American Films in the 1930s. 704p. 1984. pap. 14.95 (ISBN 0-15-633998-6, Harv). HarBraceJ.

Dooley, Susan, jt. auth. see Hirsch, Abby.

Dooley, Thomas W. Buy Now! How Alternative Financing Can Work For You. 48p. (Orig.). 1982. pap. 2.95 (ISBN 0-88462-444-7, 1995-02, Real Estate Ed). Longman USA.

--Real Estate Brokerage in the Eighties: Survival among the Giants. 1980. 16.95 (ISBN 0-88462-364-5, 1978-01, Real Estate Ed). Longman USA.

Dooley, Virginia, ed. Nudes & Foods: Gorman Goes Gourmet. (Illus.). 100p. 1981. pap. 14.95 (ISBN 0-87358-294-2); ltd. ed. 200.00 (ISBN 0-87358-295-0). Northland.

Doolin, Dennis & North, Robert C. Chinese People's Republic. LC 65-19769. (Studies Ser.: No. 14). 1966. pap. 3.00x (ISBN 0-8179-3142-2). Hoover Inst Pr.

Doolin, Dennis & Ridley, Charles. A Chinese-English Dictionary of Communist Chinese Terminology. LC 70-170210. (Publications Ser.: No. 124). 569p. (Chinese & Eng.). 1973. 30.00x (ISBN 0-8179-6241-7). Hoover Inst Pr.

Doolin, Dennis J. Territorial Claims in the Sino-Soviet Conflict: Documents & Analysis. LC 65-19766. (Studies Ser.: No. 7). 1965. pap. 4.95x (ISBN 0-8179-3072-8). Hoover Inst Pr.

Doolin, Dennis J., tr. Communist China: The Politics of Student Opposition. LC 64-16879. (Studies Ser.: No. 2). 1964. pap. 4.50x (ISBN 0-8179-3022-1). Hoover Inst Pr.

Doolin, James H. Auto Air Conditioning. 48p. 1982. pap. 15.00 (ISBN 0-914626-03-5). Doolco Inc.

--La Biblia Doolin Para el Tecnico Reparador. 500p. 1973. 35.00 (ISBN 0-914626-01-9). Doolco Inc.

--Commercial Refrigeration. 72p. 1982. pap. 15.00 (ISBN 0-914626-08-6). Doolco Inc.

--Doolin's Trouble Shooters Bible. 500p. 1963. 35.00 (ISBN 0-914626-00-0). Doolco Inc.

--Frost Free & Conventional Refrigerators. 70p. 1982. pap. 15.00 (ISBN 0-914626-09-4). Doolco Inc.

--Residential Cooling, 2 pts. 1982. pap. 15.00 ea. Pt. 1: 50p (ISBN 0-914626-04-3). Pt. 2: 91p (ISBN 0-914626-05-1). Doolco Inc.

--Residential Gas Heating. 75p. 1982. pap. 15.00 (ISBN 0-914626-06-X). Doolco Inc.

--Window Units. 39p. 1982. pap. 15.00 (ISBN 0-914626-08-6). Doolco Inc.

Doolin, James P. Eighteen Ninety-Three Columbian Exposition, Admission & Concession Tickets. 22p. 1981. soft cover 10.00 (ISBN 0-914626-02-7). Doolco Inc.

Dooling, John, ed. Great Personalities One As Reported in the New York Times: Program Guide. (Illus.). 101p. (gr. 7-12). 1979. pap. 7.95 wkbk (ISBN 0-667-00603-6). Microfilming Corp.

Dooling, John & Violano, Michael, eds. Great Events One As Reported in the New York Times: Program Guide. (Illus.). 101p. (gr. 7-12). 1978. pap. 7.95 wkbk. (ISBN 0-667-00604-4). Microfilming Corp.

Doolittle, David W. Life's Guarantees. LC 84-52211. (Illus.). 218p. 1985. 15.00 (ISBN 0-932417-00-0). Sierra Pub CA.

Doolittle, Fred C., jt. auth. see Nathan, Richard P.

Doolittle, H. D. Priest & A Dead Priestess Speaks. (Illus.). 38p. 1983. 90.00x (ISBN 0-914742-79-5). Copper Canyon.

Doolittle, Hilda. Bid Me to Live. (Imagist Ser.). (Illus.). 220p. 1983. 20.00 (ISBN 0-933806-19-1). Black Swan CT.

--Hedylus. rev. ed. LC 79-22495. (Imagist Ser). (Illus.). 160p. 1980. 17.50 (ISBN 0-933806-00-0). Black Swan CT.

--Hippolytus Temporizes. (Imagist Ser.). (Illus.). 132p. 1985. 20.00 (ISBN 0-933806-23-X). Black Swan CT.

--Ion. (Imagist Ser.). (Illus.). 120p. 1985. 20.00 (ISBN 0-933806-24-8). Black Swan CT.

--Notes on Thought & Vision. 44p. (Orig.). 1983. 9.95 (ISBN 0-87286-142-2); pap. 4.00 (ISBN 0-87286-141-4). City Lights.

Doolittle, Hilda see H. D.

Doolittle, Hilda see H. D., pseud.

Doolittle, Jan. The City of London & It's Livery Companies. 1982. 45.00x (ISBN 0-905868-11-0, Pub. by Gavin Pr). State Mutual Bk.

Doolittle, Jesse S. Energy-a Crisis, a Dilemma, or Just Another Problem. 2nd ed. 316p. pap. 16.95 (ISBN 0-916460-33-9). Matrix Pub.

Doolittle, Jesse S. & Hale, Francis J. Thermodynamics for Engineers. LC 82-7052. 588p. 1983. text ed. 37.50 (ISBN 0-471-05805-X). Wiley.

--Thermodynamics for Engineers. 582p. 1984. SI version 34.95 (ISBN 0-471-87384-5). Wiley.

Doolittle, Robert. Professionally Speaking: A Concise Guide. (PROCOM Ser.). 1984. pap. 9.95 (ISBN 0-673-15548-X). Scott F.

Doolittle, Rosalie & Tiedebohl, Harriet. Southwest Gardening. rev. ed. LC 52-11535. (Illus.). 222p. 1967. pap. 7.50 (ISBN 0-8263-0027-8). U of NM Pr.

Doolittle, Russell F., jt. ed. see Mosesson, Michael W.

Doolottle. Only in Maine: The Second Down East Reader. Repr. 7.95 (ISBN 0-89272-002-6). Down East.

Doomkamp, J. C., et al, eds. Geology, Geomorphology & Pedology of Bahrain. 443p. 150.00x (ISBN 0-86094-021-7, Pub. by GEO Abstracts England). State Mutual Bk.

Doona, Mary E. Travelbee's Intervention in Psychiatric Nursing. 2nd ed. LC 78-23472. 281p. 1979. 14.00x (ISBN 0-8036-2671-1). Davis Co.

Doonan, Gladys. From My Jewel Box. LC 83-4439. 1983p. pap. 3.95 (ISBN 0-87227-092-0). Reg Baptist.

Doonan, Helen. Leadership in Paul. (Good News Studies Ser.: Vol. 11). 1984. pap. 7.95 (ISBN 0-89453-435-1). M Glazier.

Dooner, M. G. The Lost Post. 446p. 1981. 70.00 (ISBN 0-903754-92-4, Picton England). State Mutual Bk.

Dooner, W. Pierton. Last Days of the Republic. Daniels, Roger, ed. LC 78-54814. (Asian Experience in North America Ser.). 1979. Repr. of 1880 ed. lib. bdg. 19.00x (ISBN 0-405-11270-X). Ayer Co Pubs.

Dooner, William & Proctor, William. How to Go From Rags to Riches in Real Estate: A Guide to Turning Depressed, Neglected, or Little-Known Property Investments into Millions in the 1980's. LC 82-2201. 256p. 1982. 13.50 (ISBN 0-688-00998-0). Morrow.

Doonican, Val. The Special Years: An Autobiography. (Illus.). 192p. 1981. 17.95 (ISBN 0-241-10499-8, Pub. by Hamish Hamilton England). David & Charles.

Doore, Diana & Johnson, Debra. Sultana & Miriam: Two Hundred Fifty Creative Writing Ideas. LC 83-62301. 75p. (Orig.). 1985. pap. text ed. 4.95 (ISBN 0-88247-718-8). R & E Pubs.

Dooren, Ingrid van see Pinxten, Rik & Van Dooren, Ingrid.

Doorenbos, H., ed. Non-Surgical Treatment of Malignant Diseases. (The Jonxis Lectures Ser.: Vol. 5). 316p. 1981. 44.25 (ISBN 0-444-90179-5, Excerpta Medica). Elsevier.

Doorlag, Donald H., jt. auth. see Lewis, Rena B.

Doorly, Eleanor. Insect Man. (New Windmill Ser). (Illus.). (gr. 6-8). 1968. 5.00 (ISBN 0-435-12011-5). Dufour.

Doorn, Cornelis V. Investigation into the Character of Jonathan Swift. 1931. lib. bdg. 15.00 (ISBN 0-8414-2493-4). Folcroft.

Doorn, Cornelius Van see Van Doorn, Cornelius.

Doorn, E. A. Van see Van Doorn, E. A.

Doorn, Jacques van see Van Doorn, Jacques.

Doorn, Jacques Van see Van Doorn, Jacques.

Doorn, Robert J. A Blueprint for a New Nation: The Structure of the Na-Griamel Federation. 1979. 9.95 (ISBN 0-682-49365-1). Exposition Pr FL.

Doorn, Willem V. Theory & Practice of English Narrative Verse since Eighteen Thirty-Three. 253p. 1980. Repr. of 1833 ed. lib. bdg. 25.00 (ISBN 0-8492-4220-7). R West.

Doorn, Willem Van see Van Doorn, Willem.

Doorn, William Van see Van Doorn, William.

Doornbos, Daniel, ed. Farm Tractor 1985: Self Propelled Implement Lubrication Guide. rev. ed. (Illus.). 384p. 1984. pap. 37.85 wkbk. (ISBN 0-88098-060-5). H M Gousha.

Doornekamp, Rinke, jt. auth. see Blanchet, Francoise.

Doornik, N. Van see Van Doornik, N.

Doornink, Jon, jt. auth. see Bettis, Stan.

Doornkamp, J. C., jt. ed. see Johnston, R. J.

Doornkamp, John C., jt. auth. see Cooke, Ronald U.

Doory Yousef, Al see Al-Doory, Yousef & Domson, Joanne F.

Doos, B. R. Numerical Experimentation Related to GARP. (GARP Publications Ser.: No. 6). (Illus.). xiv, 68p. (Orig.). 1970. pap. 10.00 (ISBN 0-685-04920-5, W295, WMO). Unipub.

Dooyeweerd, Herman. In the Twilight of Western Thought. 1960. pap. 3.95 (ISBN 0-934532-09-5). Presby & Reformed.

--Roots of Western Culture: Pagan, Secular & Christian Options. 1979. 12.95x (ISBN 0-88906-104-1). Radix Bks.

Dop, D. van, jt. ed. see Nieuwstadt, F. T. M.

Dop, H. Van see Nieuwstadt, F. T. & Van Dop, H.

Dopfer, Kurt. The New Political Economy of Development: Integrated Theory & Asian Experience. LC 79-13396. 1980. 37.50x (ISBN 0-312-56869-X). St Martin.

Dophlin, Patricia & Hotzclaw, Barbara. Continuing Education in Nursing: Strategies for Lifelong Learning. 1983. text ed. 14.95 (ISBN 0-8359-1011-3). Reston.

Dopp, Katharine E. The Place of Industries in Elementary Education. (Educational Ser.). 1908. Repr. 15.00 (ISBN 0-8482-3692-0). Norwood Edns.

Dopp, Peggy H. & Vroman, Barbara F. Tomorrow Is a River. LC 76-52054. 390p. 1977. 14.95 (ISBN 0-931762-00-6). Phunn Pubs.

--Tomorrow Is a River. LC 76-52054. 390p. (Orig.). 1986. pap. 9.95 (ISBN 0-931762-01-4). Phunn Pubs.

Doppelt, Jerome E. Organization of Mental Abilities in the Age Range Thirteen to Seventeen. LC 71-176725. (Columbia University. Teachers College. Contributions to Education: No. 962). Repr. of 1950 ed. 22.50 (ISBN 0-404-55962-X). AMS Pr.

Doppman, John L., et al. Selective Arteriography of the Spinal Cord. LC 68-58106. (Illus.). 248p. 1969. 14.50 (ISBN 0-87527-006-9). Green.

Doppo, Kunikida. River Mist & Other Stories. Chibbett, David G., tr. from Japanese. LC 82-84515. 182p. 1983. 14.95 (ISBN 0-87011-591-X). Kodansha.

Dopsch, Alfons. Economic & Social Foundations of European Civilization. 59.95 (ISBN 0-8490-0079-3). Gordon Pr.

Dopuch, Nicholas, et al. Cost Accounting: Accounting Data for Management's Decisions. 3rd ed. 726p. 1982. text ed. 33.95 (ISBN 0-15-514201-1, HC); solutions manual avail. (ISBN 0-15-514202-X). HarBraceJ.

Dopyera, John E., jt. auth. see Lay-Dopyera, Margaret Z.

Dor, I., jt. ed. see Por, F. D.

Dor, Moshe. Maps of Time. 1978. pap. 4.00 (ISBN 0-685-50204-X, Pub. by Menard Pr). Small Pr Dist.

Dora, E., ed. see Kovach, A. G., et al.

Dora, J. Della, et al, eds. Numerical Methods in the Study of Critical Phenomena: Proceedings. (Springer Series in Synergetics: Vol. 9). (Illus.). 269p. 1981. 31.00 (ISBN 0-387-11009-7). Springer Verlag.

Dorais, Lucie. James Wilson Morrice. (Canadian Artists Ser.: No. 8). (Illus.). 80p. 1985. pap. 7.95 (ISBN 0-317-30255-8, Pub. by Natl Mus Canada). U of Chicago Pr.

Dorais, Lucie, ed. J. W. Morrice. (Illus.). 80p. 1985. pap. 7.95 (ISBN 0-226-56426-6). U of Chicago Pr.

Doraiswamy, L. K. & Mashelkar, R. A. Frontiers in Chemical Reaction Engineering. Vol. 1, 697p. 43.50 (ISBN 0-470-20038-3); Vol. 2, 463p. 43.50 (ISBN 0-470-20039-1); Set, 1160p. 87.00 (ISBN 0-470-20041-3). Halsted Pr.

Doraiswamy, L. K. & Sharma, M. M. Heterogeneous Reactions: Analysis, Examples & Reactor Design, 2 vols. LC 82-19968. 538p. 1984. Vol. 1, Gas-solid & Solid-solid reactions, 624pgs. 66.95x (ISBN 0-471-05368-6, Pub. by Wiley-Interscience); Vol. 2, Fluid-Fluid-Solid Reactions, 650pgs. 59.95x (ISBN 0-471-05367-8, Pub. by Wiley-Interscience). Wiley.

Doraiswamy, L. K., ed. Recent Advances in the Engineering Analysis of Chemically Reacting Systems. 611p. 1984. 49.95 (ISBN 0-470-20026-X). Halsted Pr.

Doran, Adelaide L. Pieces of Eight Channel Islands: A Bibliographical Guide & Source Book. LC 80-66447. (Illus.). 341p. 1981. 26.50 (ISBN 0-87062-132-7). A H Clark.

Doran, Carol & Troeger, Thomas H. Open to Glory. 160p. 1983. pap. 9.50 (ISBN 0-8170-0981-7). Judson.

Doran, Charles. Forgotten Partnership: U. S.-Canada Relations Today. LC 83-48052. 304p. 1983. 29.95x (ISBN 0-8018-3033-8). Johns Hopkins.

Doran, Charles F. Economic Interdependence, Autonomy, & Canadian-American Relations. 86p. (Orig.). 1983. pap. text ed. 5.00x (ISBN 0-920380-91-3, Pub. by Inst Res Pub Canada). BrookField Pub Co.

--Forgotten Partnership: U. S.-Canada Relations Today. LC 83-48052. 304p. 1985. pap. text ed. 10.95x (ISBN 0-8018-3001-X). Johns Hopkins.

--Myth, Oil & Politics: Introduction to the Political Economy of Petroleum. LC 77-4571. (Illus.). 1979. pap. text ed. 8.95 (ISBN 0-02-907710-9). Free Pr.

--Myth, Oil & Politics: Introduction to the Political Economy of Petroleum. LC 77-4571. (Illus.). 1977. 14.95 (ISBN 0-02-907580-7). Free Pr.

--The Politics of Assimilation: Hegemony & Its Aftermath. LC 77-148241. pap. 59.30 (ISBN 0-317-20650-8, 2024137). Bks Demand UMI.

Doran, Charles F. & Sigler, John H. Canada & the United States: Enduring Friendship, Persistant Stress. (Illus.). 264p. 1985. 15.95 (ISBN 0-13-113812-X); pap. 7.95 (ISBN 0-13-113804-9). P-H.

Doran, Charles F. & Modelski, Goerge, eds. North-South Relations: Studies of Dependency Reversal. LC 83-13657. 240p. 1983. text ed. 31.95 (ISBN 0-03-062822-9). Praeger.

Doran, Edwin, Jr. Wangka: Austronesian Canoe Origins. LC 80-6108. (Illus.). 112p. 1981. 15.00x (ISBN 0-89096-107-7). Tex A&M Univ Pr.

Doran, Frances. Words from Tikal. 1978. pap. 1.50 (ISBN 0-532-15341-3). Woodhill.

Doran, Genevieve, ed. see Fielding, Mantle.

Doran, George T. How to Be a Better Manager in Ten Easy Steps. 128p. 1983. 6.95 (ISBN 0-671-49388-4). Monarch Pr.

Doran, J. S. Turn Up the Lamp: Tales of a Mourne Childhood. (Illus.). 140p. 1981. 11.95 (ISBN 0-904651-73-8, Pub. by Appletree Pr). Irish Bks Media.

Doran, James E. & Hodson, Frank R. Mathematics & Computers in Archaeology. (Illus.). 371p. 1975. text ed. 22.50x (ISBN 0-674-55455-8). Harvard U Pr.

Doran, James M. Erroll Garner: The Most Happy Piano. LC 84-17886. (Studies in Jazz: No. 3). (Illus.). 500p. 1985. 29.50 (ISBN 0-8108-1745-4). Scarecrow.

Doran, Jeff. This Guest of Summer. 114p. (Orig.). 1984. pap. 6.95 (ISBN 0-88978-151-6). Left Bank.

Doran, Jeffry W. Search on Mount St. Helens. Pica, George, ed. LC 80-84501. (Illus.). 96p. (Orig.). 1981. pap. 7.95 (ISBN 0-938700-00-6). Imagesmith.

Doran, John. History of Court Fools. LC 68-3844. (Studies in Comparative Literature, No. 35). 1969. Repr. of 1858 ed. lib. bdg. 49.95x (ISBN 0-8383-0656-X). Haskell.

--In & About Drury Lane, 2 vols. Set. 40.00 (ISBN 0-8482-3670-X). Norwood Edns.

--Lady of the Last Century: Mrs. Elizabeth Montague. 2nd ed. LC 75-37690. (Illus.). Repr. of 1873 ed. 28.00 (ISBN 0-404-56744-4). AMS Pr.

--Lady of the Last Century: Mrs. Elizabeth Montagu. 1873. Repr. 19.50 (ISBN 0-8274-2791-3). R West.

--London in the Jacobite Times. Repr. 35.00 (ISBN 0-8482-3685-8). Norwood Edns.

--Their Majesties' Servants: Or Annals of the English Stage, 3 Vols. Lowe, R. W., ed. LC 68-58985. Repr. of 1888 ed. Set. 125.00 (ISBN 0-404-02170-0). AMS Pr.

Doran, Madeleine. Endeavors of Art: A Study of Form in Elizabethan Drama. (Illus.). 496p. 1954. pap. text ed. 10.95x (ISBN 0-299-01084-8). U of Wis Pr.

--Henry Sixth, Parts Two & Three. LC 77-929. lib. bdg. 15.00 (ISBN 0-8414-3682-7). Folcroft.

--Shakespeare's Dramatic Language. LC 75-32072. 264p. 1976. 29.50x (ISBN 0-299-07010-7). U of Wis Pr.

--Something about Swans: Essays. 134p. 1973. 7.50x (ISBN 0-299-06170-1). U of Wis Pr.

--Text of King Lear. LC 74-164775. (Stanford University. Stanford Studies in Language & Literature: Vol. 4, Pt. 2). 1931. 21.00 (ISBN 0-404-51807-9). AMS Pr.

--Text of King Lear. LC 74-7224. 1931. lib. bdg. 15.50 (ISBN 0-8414-3758-0). Folcroft.

Doran, Madeleine, ed. see Shakespeare, William.

Doran, Pat, et al. The Redhead's Handbook. (Illus.). 1984. pap. 5.95 (ISBN 0-452-25509-0, Plume). NAL.

Doran, R. S. & Wichmann, J. Approximate Identities & Factorization in Banach Modules. (Lecture Notes in Mathematics: Vol. 768). 305p. 1979. pap. 23.00 (ISBN 0-387-09725-2). Springer-Verlag.

Doran, R. W. Computer Architecture: A Structured Approach. (A. P. I. C. Studies in Data Processing Ser.). 1979. 49.50 (ISBN 0-12-220850-1). Acad Pr.

Doran, Robert. Temple Propaganda: The Purpose & Character of 2 Maccabees. LC 81-10084. (Catholic Biblical Quarterly Monographs). ix, 156p. 1981. pap. 4.50 (ISBN 0-915170-11-6). Catholic Biblical.

Doran, Robert M. Psychic Conversion & Theological Foundations: Toward a Reorientation of the Human Sciences. LC 81-9360. (American Academy of Religion Studies in Religion Ser.). 1981. pap. 9.95 (ISBN 0-89130-522-X, 01-00-25). Scholars Pr GA.

Doran, Rodney L. Basic Measurement & Evaluation of Science Instruction. (Illus., Orig.). 1980. pap. 5.00 (ISBN 0-87355-016-1). Natl Sci Tchrs.

Doran, Thomas J., Jr., jt. auth. see Kubeck, James J.

Doran, Verda C., tr. see Philippe, Thomas.

Doran, William. Trinity of Terror. 48p. (Orig.). 1980. pap. 2.95 (ISBN 0-89288-045-7). Maverick.

Dorati, Antal. Notes of Seven Decades. Rev. ed. LC 80-27568. (Illus.). 382p. 1981. 22.50 (ISBN 0-8143-1685-9). Wayne St U Pr.

Doray, Maya. J Is for Jump: Moving into Language Skills. (ps-2). 1982. pap. 7.95 (ISBN 0-8224-4004-0). Pitman Learning.

Doray, S. J. Gateway to Islam, 4. pap. 9.50 (ISBN 0-686-18395-9). Kazi Pubns.

D'Orazio, Leo, jt. auth. see Snook, I. Donald, Jr.

Dorazio, Mary, jt. auth. see Dorazio, Ralph.

Dorazio, Ralph & Dorazio, Mary. Wooden Toys, Puzzles & Games. Roundtable Press Editors, ed. LC 85-3839. (Illus.). 160p. (Orig.). 1985. 19.95 (ISBN 0-932944-78-7); pap. 7.95 (ISBN 0-932944-77-9). Creative Homeowner.

Dor Bahadur Bista. People of Nepal. 4th ed. (Illus.). 210p. (gr. 9-12). 1980. 29.95x (ISBN 0-940500-20-5). Asia Bk Corp.

Dorbe, Gustave, ed. see Coleridge, Samuel Taylor.

Dorbes, Daniel. The Rapist. 1982. pap. 2.95 (ISBN 0-440-17294-2). Dell.

D'Orbessan, Marez E., compiled by. Walter Muir Whitehill, Director & Librarian, Boston Athenaeum, 1946-1973: A Bibliography & Verses by Friends Presented on His Retirement. (Illus.). 36p. (Orig.). 1974. pap. 0.50 (ISBN 0-934552-30-4). Boston Athenaeum.

D'Orbigny, A. see Orbigny, A. D'.

D'Orbigny, Alcide. Cours Elementaire de Paleontologie et de Geologie Stratgraphiques, Vol. 2, Pt. 2. (Fr.). 33.00 (ISBN 0-405-12744-8). Ayer Co Pubs.

D'Orbigny, Alcide D. Cours Elementaire de Paleontologie et de Geologie Stratigraphiques: Beginning Course in Paleontology & Stratigraphic Geology, 2 vols. in 3. Gould, Stephen J., ed. LC 79-8339. (The History of Paleontology Ser.). (Illus., Fr.). 1980. Repr. of 1849 ed. Set. lib. bdg. 98.00x (ISBN 0-405-12725-1); Vol. 1. 33.00 (ISBN 0-405-12726-X); Vol. 2. 33.00 (ISBN 0-405-12727-8). Ayer Co Pubs.

Dorbin, Philip B., jt. auth. see Abramson, David I.

Dorchester, Daniel. The Liquor Problem in All Ages. Grob, Gerald N., ed. LC 80-1268. (Addiction in America Ser.). (Illus.). 1981. Repr. of 1884 ed. lib. bdg. 65.00x (ISBN 0-405-13582-3). Ayer Co Pubs.

Dorchester, Guy C. Condition of the Indian Trade in North America, 1767: As Described in a Letter to Sir William Johnson. (Historical Printing Club. Publications: No. 37). 16p. 1972. Repr. of 1890 ed. 11.00 (ISBN 0-8337-0474-5). B Franklin.

Dorchester, Wendy, jt. auth. see Redmann, Ruth E.

Dorcy, Jean. Mime. 1961. pap. 4.95 (ISBN 0-8315-0045-X). Speller.

Dorcy, Mary J. Saint Dominic. LC 82-50978. 173p. 1982. pap. 5.00 (ISBN 0-89555-195-0). TAN Bks Pubs.

--St. Dominic's Family. LC 83-70219. 631p. 1983. pap. 20.00 (ISBN 0-89555-208-6). TAN Bks Pubs.

Dordevic, Mihailo. Serbian Poetry & Milutin Bojic. (East European Monographs: No. 4). 113p. 1977. 20.00x (ISBN 0-914710-27-3). East Eur Quarterly.

Dordevic, Mihailo, ed. Anthology of Serbian Poetry. LC 84-7672. 206p. 1984. 19.95 (ISBN 0-8022-2467-9). Philos Lib.

Dordevic, Tikhomir R. Macedonia. LC 77-87529. Repr. of 1918 ed. 23.50 (ISBN 0-404-16586-9). AMS Pr.

Dordick, B. F., jt. ed. see Babb, Janice B.

Dordick, H. S. Understanding Modern Telecommunications. 336p. 1986. price not set (ISBN 0-07-017662-0). McGraw.

Dordick, Herbert, jt. auth. see Williams, Frederick.

Dordillon, Ildefonse. Dictionnaire de la Langue des Iles Marquises. 598p. (Fr. & Marquise.). 1932. 27.50 (ISBN 0-686-56819-2, M-6597). French & Eur.

D'Ordonez, Carlo. Seven Symphonies. Brown, Peter & Brook, Barry S., eds. LC 79-12057. (The Symphony 1720-1840, Ser. B: Vol. IV). 255p. 1980. lib. bdg. 90.00 (ISBN 0-8240-3800-2). Garland Pub.

Dore, Anita, ed. The Premier Book of Major Poets. 336p. 1977. pap. 2.50 (ISBN 0-449-30855-3, Prem). Fawcett.

Dore, Anita W. & Gotlin, Stanley. Distrust of Authority: An Anthology on Dissent. 144p. (Orig.). 1981. pap. text ed. 6.25x (ISBN 0-317-19852-1). Boynton Cook Pubs.

Dore, Barbara Y., compiled by. Jasper County, Texas Marriages: 1837-1900. 100p. 1985. pap. price not set. M S Wright.

Dore, Clement. Theism. 1984. lib. bdg. 34.50 (ISBN 0-318-00886-6, Pub. by Reidel Holland). Kluwer Academic.

Dore, Elizabeth W. The Peruvian Mining Industry: Growth, Stagnation & Crisis. (WVSS on Latin America & the Caribbean Ser.). 195p. 1985. pap. 21.00x (ISBN 0-8133-7061-2). Westview.

Dore, Gustave. Dore Bible Illustrations. (Illus.). 256p. 1974. pap. 8.95 (ISBN 0-486-23004-X). Dover.

--The Dore Bible Illustrations. (Illus.). 14.50 (ISBN 0-8446-5023-4). Peter Smith.

--The Dore Illustrations for Dante's Divine Comedy. LC 75-17176. 1976. lib. bdg. 15.00x (ISBN 0-88307-605-5). Gannon.

--Dore's Illustrations for Ariosto's "Orlando Furioso". 208 Illustrations by Gustave Dore. (Illus., Orig.). 1980. pap. 6.95 (ISBN 0-486-23973-X). Dover.

--Dore's Illustrations for Dante's Divine Comedy. LC 75-17176. (Illus., Orig.). 1976. pap. 5.00 (ISBN 0-486-23231-X). Dover.

--Dore's Illustrations for Don Quixote: A Selection of 190 Illustrations by Gustave Dore. (Illus.). 160p. 1982. pap. 6.00 (ISBN 0-486-24300-1). Dover.

--Dore's Illustrations for Rabelais. LC 78-51529. 1978. lib. bdg. 13.50x (ISBN 0-88307-643-8). Gannon.

--Dore's Illustrations for Rabelais: A Selection of 252 Illustrations. (Illus.). 1978. pap. 6.50 (ISBN 0-486-23656-0). Dover.

--The Rime of the Ancient Mariner. (Illus.). 1970. pap. 4.95 (ISBN 0-486-22305-1). Dover.

Dore, Gustave & Jerrold, Blanchard. London: A Pilgrimage. LC 68-56513. (Illus.). 1968. Repr. of 1872 ed. 44.00 (ISBN 0-405-08460-9, Blom Pubns). Ayer Co Pubs.

--London: A Pilgrimage. (Illus.). 1970. pap. 7.00 (ISBN 0-486-22306-X). Dover.

Dore, Ian. Fresh Seafood: The Commercial Buyer's Guide. Dore, Yvonne, ed. LC 84-5174. (Seafood Handbooks Ser.). 1984. 58.00x (ISBN 0-943738-07-5). Osprey Bks.

--Seafood Exporter's Handbook. (Osprey Seafood Handbooks). 1984. cancelled (ISBN 0-943738-06-7). Osprey Bks.

Dore, Ian, ed. Frozen Seafood-the Buyer's Handbook: A Guide to Profitable Buying for Commercial Users. LC 82-12513. (Osprey Seafood Handbks.). 308p. 1982. text ed. 48.00x (ISBN 0-943738-00-8). Osprey Bks.

--The Seafood Industry's Almanac. (Osprey Seafood Handbooks Ser.). (Orig.). 1986. price not set (ISBN 0-943738-14-8); pap. price not set (ISBN 0-943738-15-6). Osprey Bks.

Dore, Ian, ed. see Coons, Kenelm.

Dore, Ian, ed. see Nettleton, Joyce.

Dore, Isaak I. International Law & the Superpowers: Normative Order in a Divided World. LC 83-9738. 210p. 1984. 30.00 (ISBN 0-8135-1014-7). Rutgers U Pr.

--The International Mandate System & Namibia. (A Westview Replica Edition-Softcover). 260p. 1985. softcover 22.00x (ISBN 0-86531-879-4). Westview.

Dore, M. H. Dynamic Investment Planning. 176p. 1978. text ed. 29.50x (ISBN 0-8419-5511-5). Holmes & Meier.

Dore, R. P., tr. see Fukutake, Tadashi.

Dore, Ronald & Mars, Zoe, eds. Community Development: Comparative Case Studies in India, Republic of Korea, Mexico & the United Republic of Tanzania. 446p. (Co-published with Croom Helm Ltd., London). 1981. 63.25 (ISBN 92-3-101877-9, U1118, UNESCO). Unipub.

Dore, Ronald P. British Factory-Japanese Factory: The Origins of National Diversity in Employment Relations. LC 72-78948. 1973. 34.00x (ISBN 0-520-02268-8); pap. 9.95x (ISBN 0-520-02495-8, CAMPUS96). U of Cal Pr.

--City Life in Japan: A Study of a Tokyo Ward. (Illus.). 1958. pap. 5.95x (ISBN 0-520-00343-8, CAMPUS49). U of Cal Pr.

--Shinohata: Portrait of a Japanese Village. (Pantheon Village Ser.). 1980. pap. 5.95 (ISBN 0-394-73843-8). Pantheon.

Dore, Ronald P., tr. see Fukutake, Tadashi.

Dore, Wade Van see Van Dore, Wade.

Dore, Yvonne, ed. see Dore, Ian.

Doreian, P. & Hummon, N. P. Modeling Social Processes. 27.50 (ISBN 0-444-41465-7, DMS/, Pub. by Elsevier). Greenwood.

Dorell, J. R., tr. see Erofeev, Benedict.

Doremus, R. H. Rates of Phase Transformations. Date not set. 29.00 (ISBN 0-12-220530-8). Acad Pr.

Doremus, Robert H. Glass Science. LC 73-4713. (Science & Technology of Materials Ser). 349p. 1973. 46.95x (ISBN 0-471-21900-2, Pub. by Wiley-Interscience). Wiley.

Doren, A., ed. see Salimbene Ognibene Di Guido Di Adamo.

Doren, Alan, ed. The Punch Book of Dogs. (Illus.). 160p. 1985. pap. 4.95 (ISBN 0-88186-828-0). Parkwest Pubns.

Doren, Arnold Van see Van Doren, Arnold.

Doren, Carl C. Van see Van Doren, Carl C.

Doren, Carl Van see Lazarillo de Tormes.

Doren, Carl van see Prokosch, Frederic.

Doren, Carl Van see Swift, Jonathan.

Doren, Carl Van see Van Doren, Carl.

Doren, Carl Van see Van Doren, Carl C.

Doren, Carl Van see Van Doren, Carl & Van Doren, Mark.

Doren, Carl Van see Van Doren, Carl.

Doren, Charles Van see Adler, Mortimer J. & Van Doren, Charles.

Doren, Charles Van see Roske, Ralph J. & Van Doren, Charles.

Doren, D. M. Van see Unger, P. W. & Van Doren, J. M., Jr.

Doren, Dorothy van see Twentieth Century Fund.

Doren, Dorothy Van see Van Doren, Dorothy.

Doren, M. Van see Van Doren, M.

Doren, M. Van see Van Doren, M. Q.

Doren, Mark Van see Bartram, William.

Doren, Mark Van see Bergendoff, Conrad & Van Doren, Mark.

Doren, Mark Van see Spencer, Theodore & Van Doren, Mark.

Doren, Mark Van see Van Doren, Carl & Van Doren, Mark.

Doren, Mark Van see Van Doren, Mark.

Doren, Mark Van see Whitman, Walt.

Doren, Mark Van see Wordsworth, William.

Doren, Mark Van see Todd, Mabel L. & Van Doren, Mark.

Doren, Mark Van see Van Doren, Mark.

Doren, V. E. Van see Devreese, J. T. & Van Doren, V. E.

Doren, V. Van see Devreeese, J. T. & Van Doren, V.

Doren, W. H. Van see Van Doren, W. H.

Dorenkamp, Angela G., et al. Images of Women in American Popular Culture. 462p. 1985. pap. text ed. 15.95x (ISBN 0-15-540600-0, HC). HarBraceJ.

Dorenlot, Francoise & Braun, Micheline T., eds. Andre Malraux: Metamorphosis & Imagination. LC 77-18629. (New York Literary Forum Ser.). (Illus., Orig.). 1979. pap. text ed. 15.00 (ISBN 0-931196-02-7). NY Lit Forum.

Dorer, Frances, jt. auth. see Dorer, Nancy.

Dorer, Francis & Dorer, Nancy. Deadman's Rest. 1978. pap. 1.50 (ISBN 0-532-15354-5). Woodhill.

--God of the Forest. 1978. pap. 1.50 (ISBN 0-532-15345-6). Woodhill.

Dorer, Nancy. Sentinel Point. 1978. pap. 1.50 (ISBN 0-532-15346-4). Woodhill.

Dorer, Nancy & Dorer, Frances. The Bundle of Firewood. (Orig.). 1979. pap. 1.95 (ISBN 0-532-23238-0). Woodhill.

--By Daybreak the Eagle. (Orig.). 1979. pap. 1.95 (ISBN 0-686-64016-0). Woodhill.

--The Cry of the Night Hawk. 1979. pap. 1.50 (ISBN 0-532-15389-8). Woodhill.

--From the Unknown. (Orig.). 1979. pap. 1.95 (ISBN 0-532-23225-9). Woodhill.

--Journey at Dawn. (Orig.). 1980. pap. 1.95 (ISBN 0-532-23179-1). Woodhill.

--Return of the Eagle. (Orig.). 1979. pap. 1.95 (ISBN 0-532-23267-4). Woodhill.

--Terra Incognita. (Orig.). 1980. pap. 1.95 (ISBN 0-532-23178-3). Woodhill.

--Two Came Calling. (Orig.). 1980. pap. 1.95 (ISBN 0-532-23226-7). Woodhill.

--Where No Man Had Trod. (Orig.). 1979. pap. 1.95 (ISBN 0-532-23155-4). Woodhill.

--The Wings of the Eagle. (Orig.). 1979. pap. 1.95 (ISBN 0-532-23287-9). Woodhill.

--You Will Like It Here. (Orig.). 1979. pap. 1.95 (ISBN 0-532-23257-7). Woodhill.

Dorer, Nancy, jt. auth. see Dorer, Francis.

Doreski, Carole, ed. Massachusetts Officers & Soldiers in the Seventeenth-Century Conflicts. 260p. 1982. pap. 14.95 (ISBN 0-88082-002-0, F63.M35). New Eng Hist.

Doreski, William. Half of the Map. (Burning Deck Poetry Ser.). 30p. (Orig.). 1980. pap. 3.00 (ISBN 0-930900-83-9). Burning Deck.

--The Testament of Israel Potter. LC 76-8902. (Illus.). 72p. 7.95 (ISBN 0-913282-06-5); signed limited ed. 60.00 (ISBN 0-913282-08-1); pap. 3.75 (ISBN 0-913282-07-3). Seven Woods Pr.

Doreski, William, ed. Earth That Sings: On the Poetry of Andrew Glaze. (American Poets Profile Ser.). (Illus.). 120p. (Orig.). 1985. pap. 9.95 (ISBN 0-918644-16-X). Thunder City.

Doress, Irvin, jt. auth. see Porter, Jack N.

Doresse, Jean. The Secret Books of the Egyptian Gnostics. LC 79-153316. Repr. of 1960 ed. 27.50 (ISBN 0-404-04646-0). AMS Pr.

Dorf, Martin E. The Role of the Major Histocompatibility Complex in Immunobiology. LC 80-772. 525p. 1981. lib. bdg. 66.00 (ISBN 0-8240-7129-8). Garland Pub.

Dorf, Richard C. Computers & Man. 3rd ed. LC 82-70804. 560p. 1982. pap. text ed. 17.50x (ISBN 0-87835-121-3). Boyd & Fraser.

--The Energy Answer. 200p. (Orig.). 1982. pap. 8.95 (ISBN 0-931790-33-6). Brick Hse Pub.

--The Energy Factbook. Dembofsky, Thomas J., ed. (Illus.). 256p. 1981. pap. 7.95 (ISBN 0-07-017629-9). McGraw.

--The Energy Factbook. 1980. 25.00 (ISBN 0-07-017623-X). McGraw.

--Energy, Resources & Policy. LC 76-45151. 1978. text ed. 26.95 (ISBN 0-201-01673-7); instr's guide o.p. 2.50. Addison-Wesley.

--A Guide to the Best Business Software for the IBM PC. (Illus.). 192p. 1983. pap. 12.95 (ISBN 0-201-10256-0). Addison-Wesley.

--Introduction to Computers & Computer Science. 3rd ed. LC 81-66059. (Illus.). 632p. 1981. text ed. 25.00x (ISBN 0-87835-113-2); write for info. solutions manual. Boyd & Fraser.

--Investment Management with Microcomputers. 1984. 16.95 (ISBN 0-8359-3301-6). Reston.

--Investment Management with Microcomputers. (Illus.). 230p. 15.95 (ISBN 0-317-13072-2). P-H.

--Investment Management with Your Personal Computer. Compute Editors, ed. (Orig.). 1985. pap. 14.95 (ISBN 0-87455-005-X). Compute Pubns.

--Modern Control Systems. 2nd ed. LC 73-7664. 1974. 38.95 (ISBN 0-201-01258-8); ans. bk avail. (ISBN 0-201-01259-6). Addison-Wesley.

--The New Mutual Fund Investment Advisor. 225p. 1985. 18.95 (ISBN 0-917253-13-2). Probus Pub Co.

--Robotics & Automated Manufacturing. 208p. 1983. text ed. 27.95 (ISBN 0-8359-6686-0). Reston.

Dorf, Richard C. & Hunter, Yvonne, eds. Appropriate Visions. LC 78-9045. 1978. 16.00x (ISBN 0-87835-072-1); pap. 12.50 (ISBN 0-87835-069-1). Boyd & Fraser.

Dorfer, Ingemar. Arms Deal: The Selling of the F-16. LC 82-13132. 304p. 1983. 36.95 (ISBN 0-03-062369-3). Praeger.

Dorff, Elliot. Jewish Law & Modern Ideology. 1970. pap. 6.50x (ISBN 0-8381-0209-3). United Syn Bk.

Dorff, Pat. File...Don't Pile. LC 79-66751. (Illus.). 200p. (Orig.). 1983. pap. 6.95 (ISBN 0-9603648-1-1). Willowtree Pr.

Dorff, Ralph. Marketing for the Small Manufacturer. (Illus.). 193p. 1983. 18.95 (ISBN 0-13-557298-3); pap. 10.95 (ISBN 0-13-557280-0). P-H.

Dorff, Robert H., jt. auth. see Steiner, Jurg.

Dorfles, Gillo. Kitsch: The World of Bad Taste. LC 78-93950. (Illus.). 320p. 1967. pap. 4.95 (ISBN 0-87663-911-2). Universe.

Dorfman, Albert, ed. see Conference on Antenatal Diagnosis (1970: University of Chicago).

Dorfman, Ariel. The Empire's Old Clothes: What the Lone Ranger Babar, & Other Innocent Heroes do to Our Minds. Hansen, Clark, tr. LC 82-148954. 225p. 1983. 14.45 (ISBN 0-394-52723-2); pap. 9.95 (ISBN 0-394-71486-5). Pantheon.

--Hacia la Liberacion del Lector Latinoamericano. 286p. (Span.). 1984. pap. 10.00 (ISBN 0-910061-21-1, 1503). Ediciones Norte.

--Widows. LC 84-40224. 160p. 1984. pap. 6.95 (ISBN 0-394-71108-4, Vin). Random.

Dorfman, Ariel & Mattelart, Armand. How to Read Donald Duck: Imperialist Ideology in the Disney Comic. 2nd, enl. ed. Kunzle, David, tr. from Span. (Illus.). 120p. 1984. pap. 6.00 (ISBN 0-88477-023-0). Intl General.

Dorfman, Bruce K., jt. auth. see Cobleigh, Ira U.

Dorfman, Ellen J., jt. auth. see Ramsdale, David A.

Dorfman, Gerald A. British Trade Unionism Against the Trades Union Congress. LC 82-83300. (Hoover Press Publication Ser.: No. 281). vii, 165p. 1983. 24.95 (ISBN 0-8179-7811-9). Hoover Inst Pr.

--Government Versus Trade Unionism in British Politics Since 1968. LC 78-70886. (Publication 224 Ser.). 187p. 1979. 13.95x (ISBN 0-8179-7241-2). Hoover Inst Pr.

Dorfman, Gerald A., jt. ed. see Schmidt, Steffen W.

Dorfman, J., ed. see Mitchell, Wesley C.

Dorfman, J. R., jt. auth. see Kestin, Joseph.

Dorfman, John. Family Investment Guide. 272p. 1984. pap. 3.50 (ISBN 0-515-07647-3). Jove Pubns.

Dorfman, John, et al. Well-Being: An Introduction to Health. 1980. pap. text ed. 16.80x (ISBN 0-673-15088-7). Scott F.

Dorfman, Joseph. Economic Mind in American Civilization, 1606-1933, 5 Vols. LC 64-7764. 1946-59. Set. 150.00x (ISBN 0-678-00111-1). Vol. 1. 37.50x (ISBN 0-678-04004-4); Vol. 2. 37.50x (ISBN 0-678-04005-2); Vol. 3. 37.50x (ISBN 0-678-00539-7); Vol. 4. 27.50 (ISBN 0-678-04007-9); Vol. 5. 27.50 (ISBN 0-678-04008-7). Kelley.

--Thorstein Veblen & His America. LC 64-7662. (Illus.). Repr. of 1934 ed. 37.50x (ISBN 0-678-00007-7). Kelley.

Dorfman, Joseph & Tugwell, Rexford G. Early American Policy. LC 72-6758. (Essay Index Reprint Ser.). 1972. Repr. of 1960 ed. 26.50 (ISBN 0-8369-7268-6). Ayer Co Pubs.

Dorfman, Joseph, ed. see Adams, Henry C.

Dorfman, Joseph, ed. see Mitchell, Wesley C.

Dorfman, Joseph, ed. see Veblen, Thorstein B.

Dorfman, L. Cavalcade of American Ballroom Dancing. (Ballroom Dance Ser.). 1985. lib. bdg. 79.95 (ISBN 0-87700-764-0). Revisionist Pr.

Dorfman, Leon. Student Biologist Explores Ecology. LC 75-14158. (Student Scientist Ser.). (gr. 7-12). 1975. PLB 8.97 (ISBN 0-8239-0327-3). Rosen Group.

Dorfman, Leslie J., ed. see Proceedings of a Workshop, Palo Alto, California, July 1979, et al.

Dorfman, Mark S. Introduction to Insurance. 2nd ed. (P-H Series in Security & Insurance). (Illus.). 496p. 1982. text ed. 28.95 (ISBN 0-13-485367-9). P-H.

Dorfman, Mary, jt. ed. see Abelson, Philip H.

Dorfman, Myron H., ed. Geopressured-Geothermal Energy: Proceedings of the Sixth U. S. Gulf Coast Geopressured-Geothermal Energy Conference, Austin, Texas, February 1985. (Illus.). 380p. 1985. 75.00 (ISBN 0-08-032784-2, Pub. by Aberdeen Scotland). Pergamon.

Dorfman, Nancy. Who Bears the Cost of Pollution Control? 120p. 10.00 (ISBN 0-318-16316-0, C-3). Public Int Econ.

Dorfman, Nancy & Jones, Norman. Incidence of Alternative Financing Methods for the Municipal Treatment Facilities Program. 126p. 3.00 (ISBN 0-318-16285-7, C-6). Public Int Econ.

Dorfman, Nancy & Dorfman, Robert, eds. Economics of the Environment, Selected Readings. 2nd ed. LC 76-58542. (Illus.). 1977. pap. text ed. 13.95x (ISBN 0-393-09137-6). Norton.

Dorfman, Ralph, ed. Methods in Hormone Research: A Multi-Volume Work, 5 vols. Incl. Vol. 3. Steroidal Activity in Experimental Animals & Man: Part a. 1964. 74.50 (ISBN 0-12-221103-0); Vol. 4. Steroidal Activity in Experimental Animals & Man: Part B. 1965. 65.00 (ISBN 0-12-221104-9); Vol. 5. Steroidal Activity in Experimental Animals & Man: Part C. 1966. 65.00 (ISBN 0-12-221105-7); Vol. 1. 2nd ed. 1969. 78.00 (ISBN 0-12-221161-8); Vol. 2a. 2nd ed. 1969. 78.00 (ISBN 0-12-221162-6). Acad Pr.

Dorfman, Ralph & Ungar, F., eds. Metabolism of Steroid Hormones. 1965. 95.00 (ISBN 0-12-221150-2). Acad Pr.

Dorfman, Ralph I., et al, eds. Biogenesis & Action of Steroid Hormones: Report of a Symposium at Kaike Spa, Yonago, Japan, Aug. 16-17, 1967. LC 68-54863. (Illus.). 1968. text ed. 8.50x (ISBN 0-87672-000-9). Geron-X.

Dorfman, Robert. Prices & Markets. 3rd ed. LC 77-26772. (Foundations of Modern Economics Ser.). 1978. pap. 14.95 ref. (ISBN 0-13-699611-6). P-H.

Dorfman, Robert, ed. Measuring Benefits of Government Investments. LC 79-28577. (Brookings Institution, National Committee on Government Finance, Studies of Government Finance). (Illus.). xv, 429p. 1980. Repr. of 1965 ed. lib. bdg. 37.50x (ISBN 0-313-22307-6, DOMB). Greenwood.

--Measuring Benefits of Government Investments: Papers Presented at a Conference of Experts: November 7-9, 1963. LC 65-18313. (Brookings Institutions Studies of Government Finance). pap. 111.30 (ISBN 0-317-20803-9, 2025372). Bks Demand UMI.

Dorfman, Robert, jt. ed. see Dorfman, Nancy.

Dorfman, Robert, et al, eds. Models for Managing Regional Water Quality. LC 72-87770. (Illus.). 512p. 1973. 27.50x (ISBN 0-674-57825-2). Harvard U Pr.

Dorfman, Ron & Fuller, Harry, Jr., eds. Reporting, Writing, Editing: The QUILL Guides to Journalism. LC 82-83109. 1982. pap. 6.50 (ISBN 0-317-28296-4). Soc Pro.

Dorfman, Wilfred & Cristofar, Leo, eds. Psychosomatic Illness Review. LC 84-45192. 192p. 1985. 22.50 (ISBN 0-669-08970-2). Lexington Bks.

Dorgan, C. Energy Management Manual. 1986. cancelled (ISBN 0-442-23877-0). Van Nos Reinhold.

Dorgan, Ethel J. Luther Halsey Gulick: 1865-1918. LC 75-176726. (Columbia University. Teachers College. Contributions to Education Ser.: No. 635). Repr. of 1934 ed. 22.50 (ISBN 0-404-55635-3). AMS Pr.

Dorgan, Howard, jt. ed. see Logue, Cal M.

D'Orgeix, Le Chevalier. Horse in the Blood. 15.00x (ISBN 0-392-03274-0, SpS). Sportshelf.

Dorham, David P., ed. see Paton, George Whitecross.

Doria, Charles. The Game of Europe: A Comedy of High Gothic Romance Frankly Rendered Out of the Senseless. LC 82-7851. 150p. 1983. lib. bdg. 19.95x (ISBN 0-8040-0409-9, 82-75539, Pub. by Swallow); pap. 10.95 (ISBN 0-8040-0410-2, 82-75547, Pub. by Swallow). Ohio U Pr.

--Short. 50p. (Orig.). limited ed, signed & lettered 15.00 (ISBN 0-915066-47-5); pap. 3.00 (ISBN 0-915066-48-3). Assembling Pr.

--Short R. 45p. (Orig.). 1983. pap. 15.00 limited edition, signed & lettered (ISBN 0-915066-54-8); pap. 3.00 (ISBN 0-317-06987-X). Assembling Pr.

--Shortend. 40p. (Orig.). 1984. pap. 15.00 limited edition, signed & lettered (ISBN 0-915066-59-9); pap. 3.00 (ISBN 0-915066-58-0). Assembling Pr.

Doria, Charles, ed. Origins: Creation Texts from the Ancient Mediterranean - A Chrestomathy. Lenowitz, Harris. LC 74-18844. 1976. lib. bdg. 32.50 (ISBN 0-404-14849-2). AMS Pr.

--The Tenth Muse: Classical Drama in Translation. LC 77-88695. vi, 587p. 1980. 25.00x (ISBN 0-8040-0781-0, 82-75844, Pub by Swallow). Ohio U Pr.

Doria, G. & Eshkol, A. The Immune System: Functions & Therapy of Dysfunction. LC 79-41519. (Serono Symposia Ser.: No.27). 1980. 44.00 (ISBN 0-12-220550-2). Acad Pr.

Dorian, A. & Osenton, J. Fachwoerterbuch der Luftfahrt. (Eng., Fr., Span., Ital., Port & Ger., Dictionary of Aviation). 1964. 75.00 (ISBN 3-486-30971-4, M-7389, Pub. by R. Oldenbourg). French & Eur.

Dorian, A. F. Dictionary of Science & Technology: English-German. 2nd., rev. ed. 1402p. 1978. 138.50 (ISBN 0-444-41649-8). Elsevier.

--Dictionary of Science & Technology: German-English. 2nd ed. 1120p. 1981. 121.50 (ISBN 0-444-41997-7). Elsevier.

--Elsevier's Dictionary of Chemistry Including Terms from Biochemistry. 686p. (Eng., Fr., Span., Ital. & Ger.). 1983. 125.75 (ISBN 0-444-42230-7). Elsevier.

--Elsevier's Dictionary of Industrial Chemistry, 2 vols. (Eng., Fr., Ital., Ger. & Dutch., Polyglot). 1964. 149.00 (ISBN 0-444-40753-7). Elsevier.

Dorian, A. F. & Osenton, J. Elsevier's Dictionary of Aeronautics. 842p. (Eng., Fr., Span., Ital., Port., & Ger., Polyglot). 1964. 117.00 (ISBN 0-444-40177-6). Elsevier.

Dorian, A. F., ed. Dictionary of Science & Technology, 2 Vols. 1979. Vol. I: Eng. & Fr. 138.50 (ISBN 0-444-41829-6); Vol. II: Fr. & Eng. 138.50 (ISBN 0-444-41911-X). Elsevier.

Dorian, D. Instant Magic Tricks. 174p. 1985. 28.50 (ISBN 0-317-19966-8). Porter.

Dorian, Donald C. English Diodatis. LC 74-92175. (BCL Ser. I). Repr. of 1950 ed. 21.50 (ISBN 0-404-02146-8). AMS Pr.

Dorian, Edith M. High-Water Cargo. (Illus.). 1965. pap. 8.95 (ISBN 0-8135-0473-2). Rutgers U Pr.

Dorian, Emil. The Quality of Witness: A Romanian Diary, 1937-1944. Dorian, Marguerite, ed. Vamos, Mara S., tr. from Romanian. 352p. 1983. 19.95 (ISBN 0-8276-0211-1). Jewish Pubns.

Dorian, Frederick. History of Music in Performance. (Illus.). 1966. pap. 7.95 (ISBN 0-393-00369-8, Norton Lib). Norton.

--The History of Music in Performance: The Art of Musical Interpretation from the Renaissance to Our Day. LC 80-28028. (Illus.). 387p. 1981. Repr. of 1971 ed. lib. bdg. 29.75x (ISBN 0-313-22893-0, DOHM). Greenwood.

--Musical Workshop. LC 77-138109. (Illus.). 1971. Repr. of 1947 ed. lib. bdg. 19.75x (ISBN 0-8371-5685-8, DOMW). Greenwood.

Dorian, Marguerite, ed. see Dorian, Emil.

Dorian, Marguerite, tr. see Caraion, Ion.

Dorian, Nancy. Language Death: The Life Cycle of a Scottish Gaelic Dialect. 1980. text ed. 30.00x (ISBN 0-8122-7785-6); pap. text ed. 14.95 (ISBN 0-8122-1111-1). U of Pa Pr.

Dorian, Nancy C. The Tyranny of Tide: An Oral History of the East Sutherland Fisherfolk. (Illus.). 145p. 1984. pap. 10.50 (ISBN 0-89720-062-4). Karoma.

Doriani, Daniel. David the Anointed. (Orig.). 1984. pap., text ed. 4.95 (ISBN 0-934688-09-5); leader's guide 3.95 (ISBN 0-934688-10-9). Great Comm Pubns.

Dorill, J. F. & Harwell, C. W. Models & Methods: Guide to Effective Composition. (Illus.). 352p. 1976. pap. 11.95 O.P. (ISBN 0-13-586040-7). P-H.

Dorin & Salisbury. Train Watcher's Log. 64p. 1981. pap. 2.95 (ISBN 0-686-98187-1). Superior Pub.

Dorin, Pat. Lake Superior Iron Ore Railroads. encore ed. LC 77-77686. (Illus.). 1969. 9.95 (ISBN 0-87564-501-1). Superior Pub.

Dorin, Patrick. Canadian Pacific Railroad. LC 74-75664. (Illus.). 192p. 1974. 19.95 (ISBN 0-87564-520-8). Superior Pub.

Dorin, Patrick C. Amtrak Trains & Travel. LC 79-22566. (Illus.). 1980. 19.95 (ISBN 0-87564-533-X). Superior Pub.

--The Chesapeake & Ohio Railway: George Washington's Railroad. (Illus.). 256p. 1981. 24.95 (ISBN 0-87564-537-2). Superior Pub.

--Commuter Railroads. encore ed. LC 72-113615. 1970. 9.95 (ISBN 0-87564-507-0). Superior Pub.

--The Great Northern Railway: Lines East. (Illus.). 192p. 1983. 24.95 (ISBN 0-87564-541-0). Superior Pub.

--The Ontario Northland Railway. (Illus.). 192p. 1982. 24.95 (ISBN 0-87564-539-9). Superior Pub.

--Yesterday's Trains. LC 81-3696. (Superwheels & Thrill Sports Bks.). (Illus.). (gr. 4 up). 1981. PLB 7.95 (ISBN 0-8225-0439-1, ASTERISKS). Lerner Pubns.

--Yesterday's Trucks. LC 81-20717. (Superwheels & Thrill Sports Bks.). (Illus.). (gr. 4 up). 1982. PLB 8.95 (ISBN 0-8225-0502-9). Lerner Pubns.

--The Young Railroaders Book of Steam. LC 77-3625. (Illus.). (gr. 4 up). 1977. pap. 2.95 (ISBN 0-87564-527-5). Superior Pub.

Doring, G. & Rudolphi. Tiefkuhl Lexikon. 239p. (Ger.). 10.95 (ISBN 3-87150-020-8, M-7666, Pub. by Deutscher Fachverlag). French & Eur.

Doring, Herbert & Smith, Gordon. Party Government & Political Culture in Western Germany. 1982. 27.50x (ISBN 0-312-59760-6). St Martin.

Doring, P. F. Learn German for English Speakers. pap. 12.50 (ISBN 0-87557-027-5, 027-6). Saphrograph.

Doring, R., jt. auth. see Knapp, H.

Dorinson, A. & Ludema, K. C. Mechanics & Chemistry in Lubrication. (Tribology Ser.: No. 9). 650p. 1985. 120.50 (ISBN 0-444-42492-X). Elsevier.

Dorio, Evelyn. Pigalee Pink. 96p. 1979. 4.50 (ISBN 0-9603118-4-X). MD Bks.

--Pigalee Pink & Other Stories. LC 79-56540. (Illus.). 95p. (gr. 3-6). 1979. 7.50 (ISBN 0-9603118-5-8); pap. text ed. 3.50x (ISBN 0-9603118-4-X). Davenport.

Dorio, M. M. & Freed, J. A., eds. Multiple Electron Resonance Spectroscopy. LC 78-27381. (Illus.). 524p. 1979. 69.50x (ISBN 0-306-40123-1, Plenum Pr). Plenum Pub.

Dorion, Henri & Poirier, Jean. Lexique Des Termes Utiles a L'etude Des Noms De Lieux. 162p. (Fr.). 1975. pap. 12.95 (ISBN 0-686-57121-5, M-6168). French & Eur.

Doriot, G., tr. see See, Henri.

Doris. Listen...The Speaking Heart. LC 79-50254. 1979. pap. 3.75 (ISBN 0-87516-361-0). De Vorss.

Doris, John, jt. auth. see Sarason, Seymour B.

Doris, Lillian & Miller, Bessemoy. Complete Secretary's Handbook. 5th ed. 596p. 1970. 24.95 (ISBN 0-13-163410-0, Busn). P-H.

Doris, Liz, ed. see Broadcast Information Bureau,.

Doris, Liz, ed. see Broadcast Information Bureau.

Doris, Liz, ed. see Broadcast Information Bureau, Inc.

Doris, Liz, ed. see Broadcast Information Bureau Staff.

Doriss, Barbara B. The Little Sister Jacket & Vest Book. (Illus.). 32p. 1985. pap. 6.00 (ISBN 0-932946-17-8). Yours Truly.

--The Original Log Cabin Jacket & Vest Book. (Illus.). 48p. (Orig.). (gr. 10-12). 1983. pap. 9.00 (ISBN 0-932946-11-9). Yours Truly.

Dority, G. K. A Guide to Reference Books for Small & Medium-Sized Libraries, 1970-1982. 1983. lib. bdg. 28.50 (ISBN 0-87287-403-6). Libs Unl.

Dority, Kim, ed. see Block, Betsy & Henry, Sue S.

Dorival, Bernard. Georges Rouault. (QLP Art Ser.). 9.95 (ISBN 0-517-54870-4). Crown.

Dorizas, H. Workbook for Aesop's Fables Reader. 1976. 2.50 (ISBN 0-685-73008-5). Divry.

--Workbook for Greek Children Reader. 1976. 2.50 (ISBN 0-685-79097-5). Divry.

Dorjahn, Alfred P. Political Forgiveness in Old Athens: The Amnesty of 403 B.C. (Northwestern University. Humanities Ser.: No. 13). Repr. of 1946 ed. 18.00 (ISBN 0-404-50713-1). AMS Pr.

Dorjahn, Alfred P., jt. ed. see Guinagh, Kevin.

Dorjahn, Vernon R. & Isaac, Barry L., eds. Essays on the Economics Anthropology of Liberia & Sierra Leone. (Liberian Studies Monograph Ser.: No. 6). 17.00 (ISBN 0-686-33173-7). Liberian Studies.

Dorje, Rinjing. Food in Tibetan Life. (Illus.). 120p. 1985. 15.95x (ISBN 0-907325-22-X, Pub. by Prospect England); pap. 10.95x (ISBN 0-317-19751-7, Pub. by Prospect England). U Pr of Va.

--Tales of Uncle Tompa: The Legendary Rascal of Tibet. LC 75-18105. (Illus.). 80p. 1975. pap. 10.00 (ISBN 0-915880-02-4). Dorje Ling.

Dorken Herbert, & Associates. The Professional Psychologist Today: New Developments in Law, Health Insurance, & Health Practice. LC 75-24011. (Social & Behavioral Science Ser.). (Illus.). 1976. 23.95x (ISBN 0-87589-271-X). Jossey-Bass.

Dorken, Hildegard. Lord Byron's Subjektivismus in Seinem Verhalten Zur Geschichte. 1929. pap. 12.00 (ISBN 0-384-12265-5). Johnson Repr.

Dorkin, C. M., jt. auth. see Munden, D. L.

Dorland, Gilbert N. & Van Der Wal, John. The Business Idea: From Birth to Profitable Company. 208p. 1982. pap. 11.95 (ISBN 0-442-22165-7). Van Nos Reinhold.

--The Business Idea from Birth to Profitable Company. 1978. 14.95 (ISBN 0-442-22163-0). Van Nos Reinhold.

Dorland, James R., intro. by. When You're Teaching Adults. rev. ed. LC 59-15148. 1970. pap. text ed. 1.00 (ISBN 0-686-00786-7, 751-00798). Natl Assn Con Adult Ed.

Dorland, Wayne E. & Rogers, James A. The Fragrance & Flavor Industry. (Illus.). 1977. 30.00 (ISBN 0-9603250-1-8). Dorland Pub Co.

D'Orleans, Pierre J. History of the Two Tartar Conquerors of China. LC 75-162706. 1963. Repr. of 1668 ed. 26.00 (ISBN 0-8337-3630-2). B Franklin.

Dorling, Ian P., ed. see International Symposium on Stability in Coal Mining, First, Vancouver, B. C., Canada, 1978.

Dorling Kindersley, Ltd. Pattern Library: Rugs & Wall Hangings. (Illus.). 1984. pap. 5.95 (ISBN 0-345-31867-6). Ballantine.

Dorling Kindersley Ltd., ed. see Beckett, Kenneth A.

Dorling, T. A. Activated Carbon Adsorption in Odour Control: The Adsorption of Styrene Vapour. 1979. 1981. 65.00x (ISBN 0-686-97008-X, Pub. by W Spring England). State Mutual Bk.

--Activated Carbon in Odour Control, 1979. 1981. 75.00x (ISBN 0-686-91578-X, Pub. by W Spring England). State Mutual Bk.

Dorling, T. A. & Sullivan, E. J. Airborne Particulate Lead Levels in Central London, 1980: Nineteen Seventy-Three to Seventy-Nine. 1981. 50.00x (ISBN 0-686-97019-5, Pub. by W Spring England). State Mutual Bk.

Dormael, Armand Van see Van Dormael, Armand.

Dorman, C. C. North Western Album. (Illus.). 20.50x (ISBN 0-392-04067-0, SpS). Sportshelf.

Dorman, C. C., jt. auth. see Casserly, H. C.

Dorman, Harry G. Toward Understanding Islam: Contemporary Apologetic of Islam & Missionary Policy. LC 79-176727. (Columbia University. Teachers College. Contributions to Education: No. 940). Repr. of 1948 ed. 22.50 (ISBN 0-404-55940-9). AMS Pr.

Dorman, James E. Recorded Dylan: A Critical Review & Discography. LC 82-60706. (Illus., Orig.). 1982. pap. 6.95 (ISBN 0-943564-00-X). Soma Pr Cal.

Dorman, John, jt. auth. see Paschal, John.

Dorman, John F. Index to the Virginia Genealogist, Vols. 1-20. LC 81-83768. 941p. 1981. cloth 50.00x (ISBN 0-89157-032-2). GBIP.

--The Prestons of Smithfield & Greenfield in Virginia. LC 80-2841. (Filson Club Publications, Second Ser.: No. 3). (Illus.). 441p. 1982. 28.75 (ISBN 0-9601072-1-5). Filson Club.

Dorman, L. I., ed. Cosmic Rays. 675p. 1974. 91.50 (ISBN 0-444-10480-1, North-Holland). Elsevier.

Dorman, Lesley & Zussman, Mark. The Secret Life of Girls. (Illus.). 128p. 1984. pap. 3.95 (ISBN 0-452-25508-2, Plume). NAL.

Dorman, Marcus R. Journal of a Tour in the Congo Free State. LC 75-106775. (Illus.). Repr. of 1905 ed. cancelled (ISBN 0-8371-3531-1, DCS&, Pub. by Negro U Pr). Greenwood.

Dorman, Marsha & Klein, Diane. How to Stay Two When Baby Makes Three. LC 83-62191. 156p. 1984. 17.95 (ISBN 0-87975-231-9); pap. 8.95 (ISBN 0-87975-253-X). Prometheus Bks.

--How to Stay Two When Baby Makes Three. 208p. 1985. pap. 3.50 (ISBN 0-345-32352-1). Ballantine.

Dorman, Peter J., ed. The Book of Hearts. LC 83-13957. (Illus.). 1983. lib. bdg. 12.90 (ISBN 0-89471-230-6); pap. 4.95 (ISBN 0-89471-229-2). Running Pr.

Dorman, Sonya. The Far Traveller. (Juniper Bks: No. 31). 1980. pap. 4.00 (ISBN 0-686-61799-1). Juniper Pr WI.

--Palace of Earth. Hunting, Constance, ed. 60p. 1984. pap. 5.95 (ISBN 0-913006-31-9). Puckerbrush.

--A Paper Raincoat. 60p. 1979. pap. 3.50 (ISBN 0-913006-09-2). Puckerbrush.

--Poems. LC 74-109104. 1970. 5.00 (ISBN 0-8142-0137-7). Ohio St U Pr.

--Stretching Fence. LC 75-14550. 61p. 1975. 8.95 (ISBN 0-8214-0188-2, 82-81891); pap. 4.95 (ISBN 0-8214-0209-9, 82-81909). Ohio U Pr.

Dormandy, J. A., ed. Red Cell Deformability & Filterability. (Developments in Hematology & Immunology Ser.). 1983. lib. bdg. 40.00 (ISBN 0-89838-578-4, Pub. by Martinus Nijhoff Netherlands). Kluwer Academic.

Dormandy, James, jt. auth. see Tesi, Marcello.

Dormandy, John, ed. Blood Filtration & Blood Cell Deformability. 1985. pap. text ed. 22.00 (ISBN 0-89838-714-0, Pub. by Martinus Nijhoff Netherlands). Kluwer Academic.

Dormann, Genevieve. Colette: A Passion for Life. (Illus.). 320p. Date not set. 39.95 (ISBN 0-89659-583-8). Abbeville Pr.

Dormant, Diane. Rolemaps. Langdon, Danny G., ed. LC 79-23398. (Instructional Design Library). 128p. 1980. 19.95 (ISBN 0-87778-153-2). Educ Tech Pubns.

Dorment, Richard. Alfred Gilbert. LC 84-52241. (Illus.). 320p. 1985. 29.95 (ISBN 0-300-03388-5). Yale U pr.

Dormer, Albert, jt. auth. see Reese, Terence.

Dormer, Francis J. Vengeance as a Policy in Afrikanderland, a Plea for a New Departure. LC 79-106776. Repr. of 1901 ed. cancelled (ISBN 0-8371-3532-X). Greenwood.

Dormer, K. J. Fundamental Tissue Geometry. LC 79-50235. (Illus.). 1980. 47.50 (ISBN 0-521-22326-1). Cambridge U Pr.

Dormer, Kenneth J. Shoot Organization in Vascular Plants. LC 70-39412. (Illus.). 256p. 1972. text ed. 22.95x (ISBN 0-8156-5032-9). Syracuse U Pr.

Dormer, Peter & Turner, Ralph. The New Jewelry: Trends & Traditions. LC 84-52518. (Illus.). 1985. 35.00f (ISBN 0-500-23406-X, Dist by Norton). Thames Hudson.

D'Ormesson, Jean, et al. Grand Hotel: An Architectural & Social History. (Illus.). 256p. 45.00 (ISBN 0-86565-040-3). Vendome.

D'Ormesson, Jean, jt. auth. see Dubois, Jacques.

Dormon, Caroline. Bird Talk. 1969. 4.95 (ISBN 0-87511-024-X). Claitors.

--Flowers Native to the Deep South. 1958. 15.00 (ISBN 0-87511-025-8). Claitors.

--Natives Preferred. 1965. 12.50 (ISBN 0-87511-026-6). Claitors.

--Southern Indian Boy. (Illus.). 1967. 3.95 (ISBN 0-87511-027-4). Claitors.

Dormon, James H. The People Called Cajuns: Introduction to an Ethnohistory. LC 83-71493. (Illus.). 110p. 1983. 7.95 (ISBN 0-940984-09-1). U of SW LA Ctr LA Studies.

Dormon, James H. & Jones, Robert R. The Afro-American Experience: A Cultural History Through Emancipation. LC 73-16475. (Illus.). pap. 54.00 (ISBN 0-317-10002-5, 2013075). Bks Demand UMI.

Dormon, James J., Jr. Theater in the Ante Bellum South, Eighteen Fifteen to Eighteen Sixty-One. xvi, 322p. 1967. 27.50 (ISBN 0-8078-1047-9). U of NC Pr.

Dormstadt, Jennifer, et al. From Some Kids. Wiggens, Dorothy & Schneider, Andrea, eds. (Illus.). 16p. (Orig.). 1984. pap. 8.95 (ISBN 0-318-02990-1). Gifted Child Prog.

Dorn. Rules & Racial Equality. LC 79-64228. 1979. 24.50x (ISBN 0-300-02362-6). Yale U Pr.

Dorn, Al. One-Minute Photo Lessons. (Illus.). 136p. 1980. (Amphoto); pap. 7.95 (ISBN 0-8174-2179-3). Watson-Guptill.

Dorn, Alfred, ed. see Vrbovska, Anca.

Dorn, Alfred, jt. ed. see Vrbovska, Anca.

Dorn, B., tr. see Ni'Mat, Allah.

Dorn, Edward. By the Sound. (Illus.). 200p. (Orig.). 1971. pap. 3.00 (ISBN 0-686-05068-1). Frontier Press Calif.

--Collected Poems: 1956-1974. LC 74-27227. (Writing Ser.: No. 34). 288p. 1975. 15.00 (ISBN 0-87704-030-3); pap. 10.00 (ISBN 0-87704-029-X). Four Seasons Foun.

--The Cycle. (Illus.). 32p. (Orig.). 1971. pap. 2.00 (ISBN 0-686-05054-1). Frontier Press Calif.

--Geography. 1964. 7.50 (ISBN 0-89760-133-5). Telegraph Bks.

--Gunslinger. LC 74-80868. 1975. pap. 5.00 (ISBN 0-914728-05-9). Wingbow Pr.

--Gunslinger One & Two. 1970. 15.00 (ISBN 0-89760-134-3). Telegraph Bks.

--Hands Up. Jones, LeRoi, ed. 46p. (Orig.). 1964. pap. 1.50 (ISBN 0-87091-033-7). Corinth Bks.

--Hello, La Jolla. LC 78-50780. 1978. 12.50 (ISBN 0-914728-24-5); signed ed 35.00 (ISBN 0-914728-25-3); pap. 3.50 (ISBN 0-914728-23-7). Wingbow Pr.

--Interviews, 1961-1978. Allen, Donald, ed. LC 78-6100. (Writing: 38). 126p. 1980. pap. 5.00 (ISBN 0-87704-038-9). Four Seasons Foun.

--The North Atlantic Tribune. 1967. 7.50 (ISBN 0-89760-135-1). Telegraph Bks.

--Recollections of Gran Apacheria. (New World Writing Ser.). 1975. 12.00 (ISBN 0-913666-17-3); pap. 2.00 (ISBN 0-913666-03-3). Turtle Isl Foun.

--Selected Poems. Allen, Donald, ed. LC 78-2925. 108p. 1978. pap. 3.50 (ISBN 0-912516-32-1). Grey Fox.

--Some Business Recently Transacted in the White World. 83p. (Orig.). 1971. pap. 2.00 (ISBN 0-686-05069-X). Frontier Press Calif.

--Songs, Set Two: A Short Count. 28p. (Orig.). 1970. pap. 1.00 (ISBN 0-686-05052-5). Frontier Press Calif.

--Twenty-Four Love Songs. 1969. pap. 2.00 (ISBN 0-686-18964-7). Frontier Press Calif.

--Views. Allen, Donald, ed. LC 79-25498. (Writing 40 Ser.). 144p. 12.00 (ISBN 0-87704-050-8); pap. 5.95 (ISBN 0-87704-051-6). Four Seasons Foun.

--Yellow Lola. LC 80-68260. 132p. 1981. signed ltd. ed. 20.00 (ISBN 0-932274-14-5); pap. 6.00 (ISBN 0-686-85759-3). Cadmus Eds.

Dorn, Frank. Appointment with Yesterday. 1978. pap. 1.50 (ISBN 0-532-15379-0). Woodhill.

--Safari. (Orig.). 1979. pap. 1.95 (ISBN 0-532-23175-9). Woodhill.

--The Silent Whisper. (Orig.). 1979. pap. 1.75 (ISBN 0-686-71740-6). Woodhill.

--Sunwatch. (Orig.). 1980. pap. 1.95 (ISBN 0-532-23239-9). Woodhill.

--When Next I Wake. 1978. pap. 1.75 (ISBN 0-532-17199-3). Woodhill.

Dorn, Fred. Publishing for Professional Development. 1985. 13.95 (ISBN 0-915202-46-8). Accel Devel.

Dorn, Fred J. Counseling As Applied Social Psychology: An Introduction to the Social Influence Model. 192p. 1984. 19.75x (ISBN 0-398-04951-3). C C Thomas.

Dorn, Fredric Van see Van Dorn, Fredric.

Dorn, Georg & Weingartner, P., eds. Foundations of Logic & Linguistics. 728p. 1985. 95.00x (ISBN 0-306-41916-5, Plenum Pr). Plenum Pub.

Dorn, Jacob H. Washington Gladden: Prophet of the Social Gospel. LC 67-17173. (Illus.). 501p. 1968. 8.00 (ISBN 0-8142-0045-1). Ohio St U Pr.

Dorn, James M. & Hopkins, Barbara. Thanatochemistry: A Survey of General, Organic & Biochemistry for Funeral Service Professionals. 1985. text ed. 38.95 (ISBN 0-8359-7640-8). Reston.

Dorn, Karen. Players & Painted Stage: The Theatre of W. B. Yeats. LC 83-7140. (Illus.). 143p. 1984. 24.95x (ISBN 0-389-20413-7, 07298). B&N Imports.

Dorn, Lois & Eldredge-Martin, Penni. Peace in the Family: A Workbook of Ideas & Actions. LC 83-42823. 192p. 1983. pap. 8.95 (ISBN 0-394-71580-2). Pantheon.

Dorn, Marybeth. Minnesota Family Law Digest. LC 83-184316. 1983. looseleaf 70.00 (ISBN 0-86678-038-6). Butterworth MN.

Dorn, Michael. Tycoons in the Kitchen: A Cookbook. gift boxed 15.00 (ISBN 0-87497-169-1). Assoc Bk.

Dorn, Nicholas. Alcohol, Youth & the State: Drinking Practices, Controls & Health Education. 280p. 1983. 35.00 (ISBN 0-7099-0243-3, Pub. by Croom Helm Ltd). Longwood Pub Group.

Dorn, Nicholas & South, Nigel. Helping Drug Users: Social Work, Advice Giving, Referral & Training Services of Three London 'Street Agencies' 246p. 1985. text ed. 29.95x (ISBN 0-566-00797-5). Gower Pub Co.

--Message in a Bottle. 192p. 1983. text ed. 29.95x (ISBN 0-566-00621-9). Gower Pub Co.

Dorn, Raymond. Tabloid Design for the Organizational Press: A Compendium of Design. (Illus.). 63p. (Orig.). 1983. pap. 15.00 (ISBN 0-931368-14-6). Ragan Comm.

--Twenty Problems--Twenty Solutions: The Basic Design Workbook. (Illus.). 88p. 1980. pap. 10.00 (ISBN 0-931368-03-0). Ragan Comm.

--The Universal Layout Sheet. (Illus.). 14p. 1983. pap. text ed. 20.00 (ISBN 0-931368-13-8). Ragan Comm.

Dorn, Sylvia O. Insider's Guide to Antiques, Art & Collectibles. 1977. pap. 3.95 (ISBN 0-346-12277-5). Cornerstone.

Dorn, William G. Van see Van Dorn, William G.

Dorn, William S. & McCracken, Daniel D., eds. Numerical Methods with FORTRAN IV Case Studies. LC 77-37365. 477p. 1972. 44.50 (ISBN 0-471-21918-5). Wiley.

Dornan, Edward A., et al. The Brief English Handbook. 1984. Student edition 11.95 (ISBN 0-316-19013-6). Little.

Dornan, James E., Jr. U. S. War Machine: An Encyclopedia of American Military. 272p. 1981. pap. 10.95 (ISBN 0-517-54552-7). Crown.

--The U. S. War Machine: An Illustrated Encyclopedia of American Military Equipment & Strategy. rev. ed. 1983. pap. 10.95 (ISBN 0-517-54984-0). Crown.

Dornan, James E., Jr., ed. United States National Security Policy in the Decade Ahead. LC 77-90924. 304p. 1978. 17.95x (ISBN 0-8448-1302-8). Crane-Russak Co.

Dornan, Peter. Sporting Injuries: A Trainer's Guide. (Illus.). 69p. 1980. pap. 5.00 (ISBN 0-7022-1448-5). U of Queensland Pr.

Dornberg, John. Eastern Europe: A Communist Kaleidoscope. LC 79-72202. (Illus.). (gr. 7 up). 1980. 10.95 (ISBN 0-8037-2208-7). Dial Bks Young.

--The Two Germanys. LC 73-15446. (Illus.). 288p. (gr. 7 up). 1974. 8.95 (ISBN 0-8037-8757-X). Dial bKs Young.

Dornblatt, Leah. Tova's Happy Purim: In Yerusholayim. (Illus.). (ps-4). 0.99 (ISBN 0-87306-989-7). Feldheim.

Dornbrand, Laurie, et al. Manual of Clinical Problems in Adult Ambulatory Care: With Annotated Key References. (Spiral Manual Ser.). 600p. 1985. spiral bdg. 18.95 (ISBN 0-316-19016-0). Little.

Dornburgh, Henry. Why the Wilderness Is Called Adirondack: The Earliest Account of Founding of the MacIntyre Mine. LC 79-25055. 1980. pap. 3.95 (ISBN 0-916346-39-0). Harbor Hill Bks.

Dornbusch, Charles E. Charles King, American Army Novelist: A Bibliography. 1963. pap. 3.00 (ISBN 0-910746-05-2). Hope Farm.

Dornbusch, Charles E. & Paszek, Lawrence J. Unit Histories of the United States Air Forces: Including Privately Printed Personal Narratives & United States Air Force History: a Guide to Documentary Sources. Gilbert, James, ed. LC 79-7247. (Flight: Its First Seventy-Five Years Ser.). (Illus.). 1979. Repr. of 1958 ed. lib. bdg. 28.50x (ISBN 0-405-12159-8). Ayer Co Pubs.

Dornbusch, Charles E., ed. Military Bibliography of the Civil War: Regimental Publications & Personal Narratives of the Civil War a Checklist Northern States, Vol. 1. LC 61-15574. 1983. Repr. of 1961 ed. 25.00 (ISBN 0-87104-504-4). NY Pub Lib.

--Military Bibliography of the Civil War: Regimental Publications & Personal Narratives: Southern, Border, & Western States & Territories, Federal Troops & the Union & Confederate Biographies, Vol. 2. LC 72-137700. 1975. Repr. of 1967 ed. 20.00 (ISBN 0-87104-514-1). NY Pub Lib.

--Military Bibliography of the Civil War, Vol. 3: General References, Armed Forces, & Campaigns & Battle, Vol. 3. LC 72-137700. xv, 224p. 1982. Repr. of 1972 ed. 20.00 (ISBN 0-87104-117-0). NY Pub Lib.

Dornbusch, R. David. DFaster DBetter. 100p. 1984. looseleaf 35.00 (ISBN 0-930627-12-1). Micro db Sys.

Dornbusch, Rudiger. Open Economy Macroeconomics. LC 80-66308. (Illus.). 293p. 1980. text ed. 21.95x (ISBN 0-465-05286-X). Basic.

Dornbusch, Rudiger & Fischer, Stanley. Macroeconomics. 3rd ed. 752p. 1984. text ed. 31.95c (ISBN 0-07-017770-8). McGraw.

Dornbusch, Rudiger, jt. auth. see Aspe-Armella, Pedro.

Dornbusch, Rudiger, jt. auth. see Fischer, Stanley.

Dornbusch, Rudiger & Frenkel, Jacob A., eds. International Economic Policy: Theory & Evidence. 1979. pap. 10.95x (ISBN 0-8018-2133-9); 18.50 (ISBN 0-8018-2132-0). Johns Hopkins.

Dornbusch, Sanford M. & Scott, W. Richard. Evaluation & the Exercise of Authority: A Theory of Control Applied to Diverse Organizations. LC 74-9344. (Social & Behavioral Science Ser.). (Illus.). 368p. 1975. 23.95x (ISBN 0-87589-247-7). Jossey-Bass.

Dornbush, Rhea L., et al, eds. Chronic Cannabis Use, Vol. 282. (Annals of the New York Academy of Sciences). 430p. 1976. 32.00x (ISBN 0-89072-028-2). NY Acad Sci.

Dorne, David. Easy-to-Do Leathercraft Projects with Full-Size Templates. 32p. 1976. pap. 3.50 (ISBN 0-486-23319-7). Dover.

Dornemann, Rudolph H. The Archaeology of the Transjordan in the Bronze & Iron Ages, No. 10. LC 83-61718. (Publications in Anthropology & History: No. 4). (Illus.). 288p. 1983. pap. text ed. 50.00 (ISBN 0-89326-053-3). Milwaukee Pub Mus.

Dorner, Alexander. The Way Beyond "Art". rev. ed. LC 59-3452. pap. 39.00 (ISBN 0-317-10179-X, 2050282). Bks Demand UMI.

Dorner, B. Coherent Inelastic Neutron Scattering in Lattices Dynamics. (Springer Tracts in Modern Physics Ser.: Vol. 93). (Illus.). 120p. 1982. 24.00 (ISBN 0-387-11049-6). Springer-Verlag.

Dorner, Isaak A. Geschichte Der Protestantischen Theologie. 1867. 55.00 (ISBN 0-384-12385-6). Johnson Repr.

--History of Protestant Theology, 2 Vols. LC 72-133823. Repr. of 1871 ed. Set. 87.50 (ISBN 0-404-02147-6). AMS Pr.

Dorner, Jane. Cortes & the Aztecs. Reeves, Marjorie, ed. (Then & There Ser.). (Illus.). 112p. (YA) (gr. 7-12). 1972. pap. text ed. 3.40 (ISBN 0-582-20529-8). Longman.

Dorner, Joe. Assembly Language Routines for the IBM PC. (Illus.). 192p. 1985. pap. 17.95 (ISBN 0-89303-409-6). Brady Comm.

Dorner, Peter, ed. Cooperative & Commune: Group Farming in the Economic Development of Agriculture. LC 76-53651. 408p. 1977. 35.00x (ISBN 0-299-07380-7). U of Wis Pr.

Dorner, Peter & El-Shafie, Mahmoud A., eds. Resources & Development: Natural Resource Policies & Economic Development in an Interdependent World. (Illus.). 516p. 1980. 29.50x (ISBN 0-299-08250-4). U of Wis Pr.

Dorner, Rita C., ed. From Ashes to Easter. 1979. pap. 9.95 (ISBN 0-918208-99-8). Liturgical Conf.

Dornette, W. Stuart & Cross, Robert R. Federal Judiciary Almanac. LC 83-21880. (Wiley Federal Practice & Law Ser.: 1703). 1087p. 1984. 75.00x (ISBN 0-471-80269-7, Pub. by Wiley Law). Wiley.

Dornette, William H., ed. Monitoring in Anesthesia. (Illus.). 428p. 1973. text ed. 25.00x (ISBN 0-8036-2725-4). Davis Co.

Dornette, William H. L. Stedman's Medical Dictionary: Fifth Unabridged Lawyers' Edition. 1678p. 1982. 52.50. Anderson Pub Co.

Dorney, Cay, jt. auth. see Frooks, Dorothy.

Dornfeld, A. A. Behind the Front Page: The Story of the City News Bureau of Chicago. (Illus.). 350p. 1983. 17.95 (ISBN 0-89733-070-6). Academy Chi Pubs.

Dornfeld, Ernst. Butterflies of Oregon. LC 80-51936. 275p. 1980. 24.95 (ISBN 0-917304-58-6). Timber.

Dornfeldt, Jeanne & Knights of the Square Table. Inside Insight. 83p. (Orig.). 1982. pap. 4.95. Tech Data.

Dornfield, D. A., ed. Automation in Manfacturing: Systems, Processes, & Aids. (PED Ser.: Vol. 4). 176p. 1981. 30.00 (ISBN 0-686-34504-5, H00211). ASME.

Dornfield, D. A., jt. ed. see De Vries, W. R.

Dornhaus, R., et al. Narrow-Gap Semiconductors. (Springer-Gap Tracts in Modern Physics: Vol. 98). (Illus.). 320p. 1983. 49.50 (ISBN 0-387-12091-2). Springer-Verlag.

Dornhoff, L. Group Representation Theory, Pt. A: Ordinary Representation Theory. (Pure & Applied Mathematics Ser: Vol. 7). 362p. 1971. 45.00 (ISBN 0-8247-1147-5). Dekker.

--Group Representation Theory, Pt. B: Modular Representation Theory. (Pure & Applied Mathematics Ser: Vol. 7). 280p. 1972. 45.00 (ISBN 0-8247-1148-3). Dekker.

Dornhoff, Larry L. & Hohn, Franz E. Applied Modern Algebra. (Illus.). 1978. write for info. (ISBN 0-02-329980-0). Macmillan.

Dornic, S., ed. Attention & Performance: Reaction Time, Vol. VI, Part I. 800p. 1977. 49.95x (ISBN 0-89859-427-8). L Erlbaum Assocs.

Dornic, Stanislav. Attention & Performance: International Symposium on Attention & Performance, Vol. 6. LC 77-9284. 777p. 1977. 29.95x (ISBN 0-470-99120-8). Halsted Pr.

Dornin, May, jt. auth. see Pickerell, Albert G.

Dornoy, Myriam. Politics in New Caledonia. (Illus.). 302p. 1984. text ed. 52.00x (ISBN 0-424-00101-2, Pub. by Sydney U Pr Australia). Intl Spec Bk.

Dornseiff, F. & Hansen, Bernard. Reverse Lexicon of Greek Proper Names. (Gr.). 1978. 30.00 (ISBN 0-89005-251-4); pap. 25.00. Ares.

Dornseiff, Franz. Der Deutsche Wortschatz nach Sachgruppen. 7th ed. (Ger). 1983. 35.20x (ISBN 3-11-000287-6). De Gruyter.

Dorny, C. Nelson. A Vector Space Approach to Models & Optimization. LC 80-12423. 620p. 1980. lib. bdg. 34.50 (ISBN 0-89874-210-2). Krieger.

Doro, Marion E. Rhodesia-Zimbabwe: A Bibliographic Guide to the Nationalist Period. 1984. lib. bdg. 50.00 (ISBN 0-8161-8275-2, Hall Reference). G K Hall.

Doroff, Larry, jt. auth. see Doroff, Steven.

Doroff, Steven & Doroff, Larry. WordStar in English I. (English I Computer Tutorials Ser.). (Illus.). 184p. pap. 12.95 (ISBN 0-915869-01-2). Eng Comp Tut.

Doroghazi, R. M. & Slater, E. E. Aortic Dissection. 352p. 1983. 45.00 (ISBN 0-07-017767-8). McGraw.

Doron, Gideon. The Smoking Paradox: Public Regulation in the Cigarette Industry. LC 79-50400. 1979. text ed. 18.00 (ISBN 0-89011-531-1). Abt Bks.

--The Smoking Paradox: Public Regulation in the Cigarette Industry. (Illus.). 158p. 1984. Repr. of 1979 ed. lib. bdg. 18.50 (ISBN 0-8191-4089-9). U Pr of Amer.

Doron, P. Nehemiah Kalomiti's War of Truth. 25.00x. Ktav.

Doron, Pinchas. Interpretations of Difficult Passages in Rashi, Vol. I. (Hebrew.). 1985. text ed. 20.00x (ISBN 0-88125-080-5). Ktav.

Doron, William D. Legislating for the Wilderness: Rare II & the California National Forests. 160p. 1985. text ed. 16.00 (ISBN 0-86733-070-8). Assoc Faculty Pr.

Dorosh, G., jt. auth. see Kennedy, P.

Doroshenko, Dmytro. Het'man Petro Dorohenko. Omelchenko, William, ed. (Illus.). 520p. (Ukrainian.). 1985. 35.00 (ISBN 0-916381-03-X). Ukrainian St.

Doroshinskaya, Y. & Kruchina-Bogdanov, V. Leningrad & Its Environs: A Guide. 1979. 8.45 (ISBN 0-8285-1781-9, Pub. by Progress Pubs USSR). Imported Pubns.

Doroshkin, Milton. Yiddish in America: Social & Cultural Foundations. LC 72-78612. (Illus.). 281p. 1970. 26.50 (ISBN 0-8386-7453-4). Fairleigh Dickinson.

Doroszewski, Witold. Elements of Lexicology & Semiotics. Taylor, Iain, tr. from Pol. (Approaches to Semiotics Ser.: No. 46). 314p. 1973. text ed. 19.20x (ISBN 90-2792-699-9). Mouton.

Dorotheus, Abba. Dushepoljezniya Poichjenija. 300p. 15.00 (ISBN 0-317-28897-0); pap. 10.00 (ISBN 0-317-28898-9). Holy Trinity.

Dorotheus Of Gaza. Dorotheos of Gaza: Discourses & Sayings. LC 77-4295. (Cistercian Studies Ser: No. 33). 1977. 7.00 (ISBN 0-87907-933-9). Cistercian Pubns.

Dorp, Rolf Von see Myrdal, Jan.

Dorp, W. G. Van, jt. auth. see Lintermans, J. P.

Dorpalen, Andreas. Heinrich Von Treitschke. LC 72-85312. 360p. 1973. Repr. of 1957 ed. 37.50x (ISBN 0-8046-1693-0, Pub. by Kennikat). Assoc Faculty Pr.

--World of General Haushofer: Geopolitics in Action. LC 66-21393. 1942. Repr. 25.00x (ISBN 0-8046-0112-7, Pub. by Kennikat). Assoc Faculty Pr.

Dorpat, Paul. Seattle Now & Then. (Illus.). 288p. (Orig.). 1984. 25.00 (ISBN 0-9614357-0-4); pap. 12.95 (ISBN 0-9614357-1-2). Tartu Pubns.

Dorpat, Theodore L. Denial & Defense in the Therapeutic Situation. LC 84-24257. 304p. 1984. 30.00 (ISBN 0-87668-755-9). Aronson.

Dorr. Revision of Total Hip & Knee. (Illus.). 192p. 1983. text ed. 40.00 (ISBN 0-8391-1849-X, 20125). Univ Park.

Dorr, A. T. & Fritz, W. L. Cancer Chemotherapy Handbook. 786p. 1980. 59.50 (ISBN 0-444-00330-4, Biomedical Pr); pap. 34.00 (ISBN 0-444-00343-6). Elsevier.

Dorr, B. F. The Surveyor's Guide. 1978. pap. 8.50 (ISBN 0-686-25542-9, 514). CARBEN Survey.

Dorr, Darwin, et al. The Psychology of Discipline: Six Approaches to Discipline. LC 81-20775. xi, 253p. 1981. text ed. 27.50 (ISBN 0-8236-5581-4). Intl Univs Pr.

Dorr, Donal. Option for the Poor: A Hundred Years of Vatican Social Teaching. 333p. (Orig.). 1983. pap. 11.95 (ISBN 0-88344-365-1). Orbis Bks.

--Spirituality & Justice. 264p. (Orig.). 1985. pap. 10.95 (ISBN 0-88344-449-6). Orbis Bks.

Dorr, Eugene, ed. see Bikkie, James A.

Dorr, Eugene, ed. see Crawford, Lucy.

Dorr, Eugene, ed. see Ely, Vivian & Barnes, Michael.

Dorr, Eugene, ed. see Hiserodt, Donald.

Dorr, Eugene, et al. Merchandising. 2nd ed. (Occupational Manuals & Projects in Marketing Ser.). 1977. pap. text ed. 8.68 (ISBN 0-07-017615-9). McGraw.

Dorr, Eugene L., ed. see Antrim, William.

Dorr, Eugene L., ed. see Ertel, Kenneth & Walsh, Lawrence.

Dorr, Eugene L., ed. see Harris, E. Edward.

Dorr, Eugene L., ed. see Klaurens, Mary.

Dorr, Eugene L., ed. see Logan, William.

Dorr, J. Bermuda. 1976. lib. bdg. 59.95 (ISBN 0-8490-1490-5). Gordon Pr.

Dorr, John A., Jr. & Eschman, Donald F. Geology of Michigan. LC 69-17351. (Illus.). 1970. 19.95x (ISBN 0-472-08280-9). U of Mich Pr.

Dorr, John A., Jr., et al. Deformation & Deposition Between a Foreland Uplift & an Impinging Thrust Belt: Hoback Basin, Wyoming. LC 77-70022. (Special Paper: No. 177). (Illus.). 1977. pap. 10.00 (ISBN 0-8137-2177-6). Geol Soc.

Dorr, Lawrence D., ed. The Knee: Papers of the First Scientific Meeting of the Knee Society. 176p. 1985. text ed. 40.00 (ISBN 0-8391-2076-1, 22012). Univ Park.

Dorr, Nell & Hardee, Covington. Life Dance: A Photography Album. (Illus.). 72p. 1975. pap. 9.75 (ISBN 0-911726-21-7). Alleluia Pr.

Dorr, R. L. What Eight Million Women Want. LC 10-28964. Repr. of 1910 ed. 28.00 (ISBN 0-527-24600-X). Kraus Repr.

Dorr, Rheta C. Inside the Russian Revolution. LC 72-115530. (Russia Observed, Series I). (Illus.). 1970. Repr. of 1918 ed. 19.00 (ISBN 0-405-03022-3). Ayer Co Pubs.

--Susan B. Anthony, The Woman Who Changed the Mind of a Nation. LC 74-100519. Repr. of 1928 ed. 47.50 (ISBN 0-404-00626-4). AMS Pr.

--The Theory of the Child That Is Different & What to Do About It. (Illus.). 1977. 45.35 (ISBN 0-89266-085-6). Am Classical Coll Pr.

--A Woman of Fifty. Baxter, Annette K., ed. LC 79-8787. (Signal Lives Ser.). 1980. Repr. of 1924 ed. lib. bdg. 46.00x (ISBN 0-405-12835-5). Ayer Co Pubs.

Dorr, Robert. McDonnell Douglas F-4 Phantom II. (Osprey Air Combat Ser.). (Illus.). 192p. 1984. 19.95 (ISBN 0-85045-587-1, Pub. By Osprey England). Motorbooks Intl.

Dorr, Robert T. & Fritz, William L. Cancer Chemotherapy Handbook. 784p. members 28.90 (ISBN 0-317-33266-X, P155). Am Soc Hosp Pharm.

Dorr, Roberta. Bathsheba. 368p. 1984. pap. 7.95 (ISBN 0-310-60731-0, Pub by Chosen Bks). Zondervan.

--David & Bathsheba. 1982. pap. 4.50 (ISBN 0-8423-0618-8). Tyndale.

Dorr, Steven R. Scholar's Guide to Washington, D. C. for Middle Eastern Studies. LC 81-607073. (Scholar's Guides to Washington, D. C. Ser.: No. 7). 540p. 1981. text ed. 29.95x (ISBN 0-87474-372-9); pap. text ed. 15.00x (ISBN 0-87474-371-0). Smithsonian.

Dorra, Henri. Art in Perspective: A Brief History. (Illus.). 334p. (Orig.). 1973. pap. text ed. 21.95 (ISBN 0-15-503475-8, HC); o.p. instr's. manual (ISBN 0-15-503477-4). HarBraceJ.

Dorram, Peter. The Expert Witness. LC 82-71941. 112p. (Orig.). 1982. pap. 16.95 (ISBN 0-918286-27-1). Planners Pr.

--The Expert Witness. (Illus.). 113p. 1982. pap. 16.95 (ISBN 0-318-17094-9); pap. 14.95 members & PAS subscribers (ISBN 0-318-17095-7). Am Plan Assn.

Dorrance & Co. Editors, ed. Modern American Short Stories 1982. (Anthology Ser.). 1982. 9.95 (ISBN 0-8059-2850-2). Dorrance.

Dorrance, G. S. National Monetary & Financial Analysis. LC 77-82744. (Illus.). 1978. 24.00 (ISBN 0-312-55946-1). St Martin.

Dorrance, Graeme S., jt. ed. see Black, John.

Dorrance, Ward. A Man About the House: A Novella. LC 72-79643. 116p. 1972. 8.95 (ISBN 0-8262-0128-8); pap. 5.95 (ISBN 0-8262-0127-X). U of Mo Pr.

Dorre, E., et al. Alumina: Processing, Properties & Applications. (Materials Research & Engineering Ser.). (Illus.). 330p. 1984. 36.00 (ISBN 0-387-13576-6). Springer-Verlag.

Dorri, Jacobs. A Guide for the Employee Who is to be Relocated. (Change; How to Live with, Manage, Create & Enjoy It Ser.). 21p. 1982. wkbk spiral bound 7.95 (ISBN 0-9606012-5-2). Progs on Change.

Dorrie, Heinrich. One Hundred Great Problems of Elementary Mathematics: Their History & Solution. Antin, David, tr. from Ger. 393p. 1965. pap. 5.95 (ISBN 0-486-61348-8). Dover.

Dorrington, Ward, jt. auth. see Fekete, Irene.

Dorris, C. E see Gospel Advocate.

Dorris, George E. Paolo Rolli & the Italian Circle in London, 1715-1744. (Studies in Italian Literature: No. 2). (Orig.). 1967. pap. text ed. 26.00x (ISBN 90-2790-329-8). Mouton.

Dorris, Jonathon T. Pardon & Amnesty Under Lincoln & Johnson: The Restoration of the Confederates to Their Rights & Privileges, 1861-1898. LC 77-5940. 459p. 1953. 27.75 (ISBN 0-8371-9646-9). Greenwood.

Dorris, Paul. Pocket Irish Phrase Book. 71p. (Orig.). 1983. pap. 3.95 (ISBN 0-86281-010-8, Pub. by Appletree Pr). Irish Bks Media.

Dorros, Arthur. Alligator Shoes. LC 82-2409. (Illus.). 24p. (ps-k). 1982. 3.95 (ISBN 0-525-44001-1, 0383-120). Dutton.

--Pretzels. LC 81-1021. (Read-Alone Bks.). (Illus.). 56p. (gr. 1-3). 1981. 8.75 (ISBN 0-688-00668-X); PLB 8.88 (ISBN 0-688-00669-8). Greenwillow.

Dorros, Sidney. Parkinson's: A Patient's View. 240p. 1981. 14.95 (ISBN 0-932020-08-9); pap. 9.95 (ISBN 0-932020-09-7). Seven Locks Pr.

--Parkinson's: A Patient's View. 240p. 1985. pap. 3.95 (ISBN 0-446-32837-5). Warner Bks.

Dorrough, Ardith. The Real Christmas Tree. 48p. (Orig.). 1983. pap. 2.50 (ISBN 0-88144-020-5, CPS/020). Christian Pub.

Dorry, Gertrude N. Games for Second Language Learning. 1966. 3.00 (ISBN 0-07-017653-1). McGraw.

Dorsaneo, William V. & Crump, David. Texas Civil Procedure: Pretrial Litigation. LC 84-115769. (Analysis & Skills Ser.). Date not set. price not set. Bender.

D'Orsay, Laurence R. Stories You Can Sell. LC 79-101280. (Short Story Index Reprint Ser.). 1935. 18.00 (ISBN 0-8369-3217-X). Ayer Co Pubs.

Dorsch, F. Psychologisches Woerterbuch. 9th ed. 784p. (Ger.). 1976. 75.00 (ISBN 3-456-80320-6, M-7595, Pub. by H. Huber). French & Eur.

Dorsch, Friedrich. Diccionario De Psicologia. 3rd ed. 756p. (Span.). 1978. 59.95 (ISBN 84-254-1026-6). French & Eur.

Dorsch, T. S., ed. see Lord Byron.

Dorsch, T. S., ed. see Shakespeare, William.

Dorsch, T. S., tr. Classical Literary Criticism. Incl. Poetics. Aristotle; Ars Poetica. Horace; On the Sublime. Longinus. (Classics Ser.). 1965. pap. 4.95 (ISBN 0-14-044155-7). Penguin.

Dorschner, Jon P. Alcohol Consumption in a Village in North India. Kottak, Conrad, ed. LC 83-4987. (Studies in Cultural Anthropology Ser.: No. 1). 262p. 1983. 39.95 (ISBN 0-8357-1449-7). UMI Res Pr.

Dorsen, Norman. Political & Civil Rights in the United States: 1982 Supplement to Volume I. 1982. pap. 10.95 (ISBN 0-316-19052-7). Little.

Dorsen, Norman, jt. auth. see Gillers, Stephen.

Dorsen, Norman, ed. Our Endangered Rights: The ACLU Report on Civil Liberties Today. LC 83-43146. 1984. 22.00 (ISBN 0-394-53261-9); pap. 11.95 (ISBN 0-394-72229-9). Pantheon.

Dorsen, Norman, et al. Emerson, Haber & Dorsen's Political & Civil Rights in the United States, Vol. I. 4th ed. 1976. lawyers ed. 50.00 (ISBN 0-316-23624-1); students ed 34.00 (ISBN 0-316-19046-2). Little.

--Emerson, Haber & Dorsen's Political & Civil Rights in the United States, Vol. 2. 4th ed. 1979. text ed. 34.00 student ed. (ISBN 0-316-19049-7); lawyers ed. 50.00 (ISBN 0-316-23627-6). Little.

--Political & Civil Rights in the U. S. 1981 Supplement. suppl. ed. LC 78-69780. 337p. 1981. text ed. 10.95 (ISBN 0-316-23628-4). Little.

Dorsen, Richard M., ed. see Busk, Rachel H.

Dorsen, Richard M., ed. see Christiansen, Reidar T.

Dorsen, Richard M., ed. see Clouston, William A.

Dorsen, Richard M., ed. see Colcord, Joanna C.

Dorsen, Richard M., ed. see Increase, Mather.

Dorsen, Richard M., ed. see MacDougall, James.

Dorset, Gerald. Adventure in the Rich Port. 2nd ed. 68p. 1983. pap. 4.95 (ISBN 0-317-11802-1). New England Pr.

--Aristocrat of Intellect. (Studies in Poe, No. 23). 1970. pap. 22.95x (ISBN 0-8383-0089-8). Haskell.

--Cloud Four Shadows. 1977. pap. 3.00 (ISBN 0-931060-49-4). New England Pr.

--Cute & Cutty Cut-Ups: Piece of the Action. LC 79-88224. (Illus.). 1979. pap. 4.95x (ISBN 0-931060-15-X). New England Pr.

--Hawks & Doves. 1976. pap. 3.00 (ISBN 0-931060-04-4). New England Pr.

--How to Write Love Letters: Poems. 1977. pap. 3.00 (ISBN 0-931060-03-6). New England Pr.

--Inscriptions & Appellations. LC 79-88225. (Illus.). 1979. pap. 3.95x (ISBN 0-931060-19-2). New England Pr.

--Little Joys, Big Joys. LC 79-87829. (Illus.). text ed. 9.95 (ISBN 0-931060-20-6); pap. 5.00 (ISBN 0-931060-13-3). New England Pr.

--Love You. 2nd. ed. LC 79-88227. Orig. Title: How-to Write Love Letters. (Illus.). 1979. pap. 3.95x (ISBN 0-931060-10-9). New England Pr.

--The Mysterious Mr. Poe; & Other Essays. (Illus.). 1979. 5.95 (ISBN 0-931060-11-7). New England Pr.

--New York Geographical Poems. 1978. pap. text ed. 3.50 (ISBN 0-931060-06-0). New England Pr.

--Poetry Reading. (Illus.). 6.95 (ISBN 0-931060-21-4); pap. 4.95 (ISBN 0-931060-14-1). New England Pr.

--Time Music. 2nd ed. 39p. 1984. pap. 3.00 (ISBN 0-317-11800-5). New England Pr.

--Video Tapes. (Illus.). 20p. 1978. pap. 1.50 (ISBN 0-931060-09-5). New England Pr.

Dorsett, Cora M. The Mississippi Delta. LC 83-14375. 150p. 1983. pap. 15.00 (ISBN 0-8389-0395-9). ALA.

Dorsett, Cora Matheny see Laughlin, Mildred.

Dorsett, Joseph L. Integrated Algebra & Trigonometry. 2nd ed. 1977. pap. text ed. 16.95 (ISBN 0-8403-1699-2). Kendall-Hunt.

Dorsett, Joseph L., jt. auth. see Rice, William.

Dorsett, Judy. Bulletin Board Builders, No. 2. (Illus.). 64p. 1985. 3.95 (ISBN 0-87239-918-4, 3288). Standard Pub.

--Handbook of Creativity. (Illus.). 128p. 1985. pap. 7.95 (ISBN 0-87239-729-7, 3226). Standard Pub.

Dorsett, Loyd G. Audio-Visual Teaching Machines. LC 71-125871. (Illus.). 128p. 1971. pap. 11.95 (ISBN 0-87778-009-9). Educ Tech Pubns.

Dorsett, Lyle W. And God Came In: The Extraordinary Story of Joy Davidman-Her life & Marriage to C.S. Lewis. (Illus.). 192p. 1983. 14.95 (ISBN 0-02-532250-8). Macmillan.

--And God Came In: The Extraordinary Story of Joy Davidman; Her Life & Marriage to C. S. Lewis. (Illus.). 192p. 1984. pap. 2.95 (ISBN 0-345-31787-4). Ballantine.

--The Pendergast Machine. LC 80-11581. (Illus.). xvi, 163p. 1980. 15.50x (ISBN 0-8032-1655-6); pap. 3.95 (ISBN 0-8032-6554-9, BB 744, Bison). U of Nebr Pr.

--The Queen City: A History of Denver. LC 77-7327. (The Western Urban History Ser.). (Illus.). 1977. 14.95 (ISBN 0-87108-098-2). Pruett.

--The Queen City: A History of Denver. (The Western Urban History Ser.). (Illus.). 350p. 1980. pap. 8.50 (ISBN 0-87108-567-4). Pruett.

Dorsett, Lyle W., jt. auth. see Brown, A. Theordore.

Dorsett, Lyle W., ed. & compiled by see Lewis, C. S.

Dorsett, Mary, ed. see MacDonald, George.

Dorsey, Anne G., jt. auth. see Sciarra, Dorothy J.

Dorsey, Bernard. The Drummer Percussionist: Musically-Physically-Professionally, Vol. 1. 1983. 4.95 (ISBN 0-8062-2182-8). Carlton.

Dorsey, David F., et al, eds. Design & Intent in African Literature. LC 82-50450. 137p. 1982. 22.00 (ISBN 0-89410-354-7); pap. 14.00 (ISBN 0-89410-355-5). Three Continents.

Dorsey, Frances & Williams, Wendy. Creative Ice Skating: Ice Dancing, Freestyle, & Pair Skating. (Illus.). 86p. 1980. pap. 6.95 (ISBN 0-8092-7106-0). Contemp Bks.

Dorsey, G. A. The Arapaho Sun Dance, the Ceremony of the Offerings Lodge. (Chicago Field Museum of Natural History Fieldiana Anthropology Ser.). 1903. 80.00 (ISBN 0-527-01864-3). Kraus Repr.

--Cheyenne. enl. ed. (Chicago Field Museum of Natural History Fieldiana Anthropology Ser). 1905. 31.00 (ISBN 0-527-01869-4). Kraus Repr.

--Traditions of the Skidi Pawnee. LC 4-28964. (American Folklore Society Memoirs). Repr. of 1904 ed. 31.00 (ISBN 0-527-01060-X). Kraus Repr.

Dorsey, G. A. & Kroeber, A. L. Traditions of the Arapaho. (Chicago Field Museum of Natural History Fieldiana Anthropology Ser). 1903. 44.00 (ISBN 0-527-01865-1). Kraus Repr.

Dorsey, G. A. & Voth, H. R. Oraibi Soyal Ceremony, & Oraibi Powamu Ceremony, & Mishongnovi Ceremonies of the Snake & Antelope Fraternities, & Oraibi Summer Snake Ceremony, 4 wks. in 1 vol. 1901-03. (Chicago Field Museum of Natural History). 70.00 (ISBN 0-527-01863-5). Kraus Repr.

Dorsey, George A. The Cheyenne. 1975. 9.95 (ISBN 0-87770-157-1). Ye Galleon.

--The Evolution of Charles Darwin. 1973. Repr. of 1927 ed. 20.00 (ISBN 0-8274-1404-8). R West.

--Hows & Whys of Human Behavior. 298p. 1984. Repr. of 1929 ed. lib. bdg. 35.00 (ISBN 0-89760-178-5). Telegraph Bks.

--Indians of the Southwest. LC 74-7952. (Illus.). Repr. of 1903 ed. 19.50 (ISBN 0-404-11841-0). AMS Pr.

--Traditions of the Caddo. LC 74-7956. Repr. of 1905 ed. 16.50 (ISBN 0-404-11845-3). AMS Pr.

--Traditions of the Osage. LC 74-7957. Repr. of 1904 ed. 12.50 (ISBN 0-404-11846-1). AMS Pr.

--Why We Behave Like Human Beings. 1978. Repr. of 1925 ed. lib. bdg. 25.00 (ISBN 0-8495-1009-0). Arden Lib.

Dorsey, Gray L. American Freedoms. LC 74-20856. 1974. lib. bdg. 15.00 (ISBN 0-930342-25-9); pap. text ed. 10.00 (ISBN 0-930342-26-7). W S Hein.

Dorsey, J. Employee-Employer Rights: A Guide for the British Columbia Work Force. 7th ed. 137p. 1984. 6.95 (ISBN 0-88908-152-2). Self Counsel Pr.

Dorsey, James E. Footprints Along the Hoopee: A History of Emanuel County, 1812-1900. LC 78-12908. 1978. 15.00 (ISBN 0-87152-291-8). Reprint.

--Georgia Genealogy & Local History: A Bibliography. LC 82-7594. 416p. 1983. 27.50 (ISBN 0-87152-359-0); pap. 20.00 (ISBN 0-87152-363-9). Reprint.

Dorsey, James E. & Davis, Robert S., Jr. Lincoln County Genealogy & History. LC 84-63066. 325p. 1985. 25.00 (ISBN 0-916369-01-3). Magnolia Pr.

Dorsey, James E. & Derden, John K. Montgomery County, Georgia: A Source Book of Genealogy & History. LC 83-1880. 304p. 1983. 25.00 (ISBN 0-87152-377-9); pap. 20.00 (ISBN 0-87152-376-0). Reprint.

Dorsey, James E., jt. auth. see Rowland, Arthur R.

Dorsey, James O. Omaha & Ponka Letters. Repr. of 1891 ed. 29.00x (ISBN 0-403-03675-5). Scholarly.

--Omaha Sociology. LC 16-5488. 1971. Repr. of 1884 ed. 18.00 (ISBN 0-384-12395-3). Johnson Repr.

--Study of Siouan Cults. (Illus.). 208p. pap. 11.95 (ISBN 0-8466-4055-4, I55). Shorey.

Dorsey, Joan. Introducing Your Kids to the Outdoors. rev. ed. LC 82-80135. (Illus.). 156p. 1982. pap. 8.95 (ISBN 0-913276-34-0). Stone Wall Pr.

Dorsey, John. Mount Vernon Place: An Anecdotal Essay. LC 83-60810. (Illus.). 97p. 1983. 13.95 (ISBN 0-940776-06-5). Maclay Assoc.

Dorsey, John & Dilts, James D. A Guide to Baltimore Architecture. 2nd ed. LC 80-27243. (Illus.). 382p. 1981. pap. 4.95 (ISBN 0-87033-272-4). Tidewater.

Dorsey, John, ed. On Mencken. LC 80-7639. 320p. 1980. 15.00 (ISBN 0-394-51253-7). Knopf.

Dorsey, John M. American Government: Conscious Self Sovereignty. 139p. 1969. 4.95x (ISBN 0-8143-1637-9). Wayne St U Pr.

--American Psychiatrist in Vienna, 1935-1937 & His Sigmund Freud. 213p. 1976. 12.90 (ISBN 0-8143-1644-1). Wayne St U Pr.

--Illness or Allness: Conversations of a Psychiatrist. LC 65-10770. 638p. 1965. 16.50x (ISBN 0-8143-1249-7). Wayne St U Pr.

--The Psychic Nature of Physiology. 135p. 1977. 7.90 (ISBN 0-8143-1642-5). Wayne St U Pr.

--Psychology of Emotion. 174p. 1971. 6.95x (ISBN 0-8143-1638-7). Wayne St U Pr.

--Psychology of Ethics. 2617p. 1974. 8.00x (ISBN 0-8143-1639-5). Wayne St U Pr.

--Psychology of Language. 195p. 1971. 6.95x (ISBN 0-8143-1640-9). Wayne St U Pr.
--Psychology of Political Science. 262p. 1973. 15.00 (ISBN 0-8143-1641-7). Wayne St U Pr.
--Selected Essays. 508p. 1976. 16.00 (ISBN 0-8143-1643-3). Wayne St U Pr.
--University Professor John M. Dorsey. LC 79-25046. (Illus.). 280p. 1980. 12.00 (ISBN 0-8143-1645-X). Wayne St U Pr.
Dorsey, John M. & Seegers, Walter H. Living Consciously: The Science of Self. LC 59-12400. 183p. 1959. 7.95x (ISBN 0-8143-1118-0). Wayne St U Pr.
Dorsey, Mary E. Reading Games & Activities. LC 72-80026. 1972. pap. 6.95 (ISBN 0-8224-5810-1). Pitman Learning.
Dorsey, Michael, jt. auth. see Calabrese, Edward.
Dorsey, Noah E. Properties of Ordinary Water-Substances in All Its Phases: Water-Vapor, Water, & All the Ices. LC 68-19563. (American Chemical Society Monograph Ser.: No. 81). pap. 160.00 (ISBN 0-317-09001-1, 2015237). Bks Demand UMI.
Dorsey, Stephen. American Military Cartridge Belts & Related Equipment. 10.95 (ISBN 0-913150-49-5). Pioneer Pr.
D'Orsi, Carl J. & Wilsson, Richard. Carcinoma of the Breast. 1983. 35.00 (ISBN 0-316-16780-0). Little.
Dorsky, Susan. Women of Camran: A Middle Eastern Ethnographic Study. (Illus.). 216p. 1985. 22.50x (ISBN 0-87480-250-4). U of Utah Pr.
Dorso, Richard. Thicker Than Water. LC 79-3357. 288p. 1980. 10.95 (ISBN 0-15-189586-4). HarBraceJ.
Dorson, Edward, jt. ed. see Ives, Edward D.
Dorson, Richard, ed. America Begins: Early American Writings. LC 72-5802. (Folklore of the World Ser.). (Illus.). 1980. Repr. of 1950 ed. lib. bdg. 39.00x (ISBN 0-8369-2986-1). Ayer Co Pubs.
Dorson, Richard, ed. see Gomme, George L.
Dorson, Richard, ed. see Hector, Lee H.
Dorson, Richard, ed. see Palmer, Abram S.
Dorson, Richard, ed. see Von Sydow, Carl W.
Dorson, Richard M. America in Legend: Folklore from the Colonial Period to the Present. LC 73-7018. (Illus.). 1973. pap. 12.95 (ISBN 0-394-70926-8). Pantheon.
--American Folklore. LC 59-12283. (Chicago History of American Civilization Ser.). 4.50 (ISBN 0-226-15859-4, CHAC 4). U of Chicago Pr.
--Bloodstoppers & Bearwalkers: Folk Traditions of the Upper Peninsula. LC 52-5394. (Illus.). xvi, 305p. 1952. pap. 7.95x (ISBN 0-674-07665-6). Harvard U Pr.
--British Folklorists: A History. LC 68-16689. (Folktales of the World Ser). 1969. 27.50x (ISBN 0-226-15863-2). U of Chicago Pr.
--Buying the Wind: Regional Folklore in the United States. LC 63-13010. 1964. 27.50x (ISBN 0-226-15861-6). U of Chicago Pr.
--Buying the Wind: Regional Folklore in the United States. LC 63-13010. 573p. 1972. pap. 12.00x (ISBN 0-226-15862-4, Phoen). U of Chicago Pr.
--Folk Legends of Japan. LC 60-11972. (Illus.). (YA) (gr. 9 up). 1962. pap. 5.95 (ISBN 0-8048-0191-6). C E Tuttle.
--Folklore & Fakelore: Essays Toward a Discipline of Folk Studies. 368p. 1976. 22.50x (ISBN 0-674-30715-1). Harvard U Pr.
--Folklore of the Santal Parganas. Bompas, Cecil H., tr. LC 77-70579. (International Folklore Ser.). 1977. Repr. of 1909 ed. lib. bdg. 37.50x (ISBN 0-405-10080-9). Ayer Co Pubs.
--Folklore: Selected Essays. LC 72-76944. Repr. of 1972 ed. 79.80 (ISBN 0-8357-9212-9, 2015454). Bks Demand UMI.
--Folktales Told Around the World. (Illus.). xxvi, 622p. 1978. pap. 15.00x (ISBN 0-226-15874-8, P781, Phoen). U of Chicago Pr.
--Land of the Millrats. LC 81-2944. (Illus.). 336p. 1981. text ed. 22.50x (ISBN 0-674-50855-6). Harvard U Pr.
--Man & Beast in American Comic Legend. LC 81-48622. (Illus.). 208p. 1983. 20.00 (ISBN 0-253-33665-1). Ind U Pr.
--Negro Folktales in Michigan. LC 73-21099. (Illus.). 245p. 1974. Repr. of 1956 ed. lib. bdg. 17.25x (ISBN 0-8371-5989-X, DONF). Greenwood.
--Negro Tales from Pine Bluff, Arkansas & Calvin, Michigan. LC 58-63484. (Indiana University Folklore Ser: No. 12). 1958. 26.00 (ISBN 0-527-24650-6). Kraus Repr.
Dorson, Richard M., ed. Davy Crockett: American Comic Legend. LC 77-70590. (International Folklore Ser.). (Illus.). 1977. Repr. of 1939 ed. lib. bdg. 15.00x (ISBN 0-405-10091-4). Ayer Co Pubs.
--Davy Crockett American Comic Legend. LC 77-2876. (Illus.). 1977. Repr. of 1939 ed. lib. bdg. 15.75x (ISBN 0-8371-9517-9, DOCR). Greenwood.
--Egyptian Tales & Romances: Pagan, Christian & Muslim. Budge, Ernest A., tr. from Egyptian. LC 80-739. (Folklore of the World Ser.). (Illus.). 1980. Repr. of 1931 ed. lib. bdg. 45.00x (ISBN 0-405-13304-9). Ayer Co Pubs.
--Folklore & Folklife: An Introduction. LC 77-189038. viii, 562p. 1982. pap. 10.00x (ISBN 0-226-15871-3). U of Chicago Pr.
--Folklore & Traditional History. (Studies in Folklore Ser.: Vol. 1). 1973. pap. text ed. 11.60x (ISBN 90-2792-473-2). Mouton.
--Folklore of the World Series, 38 bks. 1980. Set. lib. bdg. 1516.00x (ISBN 0-405-13300-6). Ayer Co Pubs.
--Handbook of American Folklore. LC 82-47574. (Illus.). 608p. 1983. 35.00x (ISBN 0-253-32706-7). Ind U Pr.
--International Folklore Series, 48 bks. (Illus.). 1977. Repr. 1460.00 (ISBN 0-405-10077-9). Ayer Co Pubs.
--Peasant Customs & Savage Myths Selections from the British Folklorists, 2 Vols. LC 68-16690. (avail. only as set). 1969. Set. lib. bdg. 60.00x (ISBN 0-226-15867-5); Vol. 1. 13.50xo.s.i (ISBN 0-226-15865-9). U of Chicago Pr.
--Sixty Folk-Tales from Exclusively Slavonic Sources. Wratislaw, Albert H., tr. LC 77-70629. (International Folklore Ser.). 1977. Repr. of 1889 ed. lib. bdg. 24.50x (ISBN 0-405-10133-3). Ayer Co Pubs.
--Studies in Folk Life: Essays in Honor of Iorwerth C. Peate, John G. Jenkins. LC 77-70603. (International Folklore Ser.). 1977. lib. bdg. 30.00x (ISBN 0-405-10102-3). Ayer Co Pubs.
--Studies in Japanese Folklore. LC 80-744. (Folklore of the World Ser.). (Illus.). 1980. Repr. of 1963 ed. lib. bdg. 34.50x (ISBN 0-405-13310-3). Ayer Co Pubs.
--Tales of the Sun: Folklore of Southern India. LC 77-70604. (International Folklore Ser.). 1977. Repr. of 1890 ed. lib. bdg. 24.50x (ISBN 0-405-10103-1). Ayer Co Pubs.
Dorson, Richard M., ed. see Allies, Jabez.
Dorson, Richard M., jt. ed. see Almquist, Bo.
Dorson, Richard M., ed. see Arewa, Erastus O.
Dorson, Richard M., ed. see Beck, E. C.
Dorson, Richard M., ed. see Briggs, Katherine M.
Dorson, Richard M., ed. see Campbell, Charles G.
Dorson, Richard M., ed. see Carey, George.
Dorson, Richard M., jt. ed. see Carpenter, Inta G.
Dorson, Richard M., ed. see Carpenter, Inta G.
Dorson, Richard M., ed. see Childers, J. Wesley.
Dorson, Richard M., ed. see Christiansen, Reider T.
Dorson, Richard M., ed. see Davids, Rhys.
Dorson, Richard M., ed. see Dawkins, Richard M.
Dorson, Richard M., ed. see Degh, Linda.
Dorson, Richard M., ed. see Delarue, Paul.
Dorson, Richard M., jt. ed. see Douglas, George B.
Dorson, Richard M., ed. see Eberhard, Wolfram.
Dorson, Richard M., ed. see Elwin, Verrier.
Dorson, Richard M., ed. see Flowers, Helen L.
Dorson, Richard M., ed. see Gardner, E. E.
Dorson, Richard M., ed. see Georges, Robert A.
Dorson, Richard M., ed. see Gill, William W.
Dorson, Richard M., ed. see Gizelis, Gregory.
Dorson, Richard M., ed. see Grimm, Jacob & Grimm, Wilhelm.
Dorson, Richard M., ed. see Groome, Francis H.
Dorson, Richard M., ed. see Hambruch, Paul.
Dorson, Richard M., ed. see Hardwick, Charles.
Dorson, Richard M., ed. see Henri, Gaidoz & Sebillot, Paul.
Dorson, Richard M., ed. see Jansen, William H.
Dorson, Richard M., ed. see Kirtley, Bacil F.
Dorson, Richard M., ed. see Klein, Barbro S.
Dorson, Richard M., ed. see Klymasz, Robert B.
Dorson, Richard M., ed. see Knowles, James H.
Dorson, Richard M., ed. see Kongas-Maranda, Elli Kaija.
Dorson, Richard M., ed. see McNair, John F. & Barlow, Thomas L.
Dorson, Richard M., ed. see McPherson, Joseph M.
Dorson, Richard M., ed. see Mattfield, Julius.
Dorson, Richard M., ed. see Menez, Herminia Q.
Dorson, Richard M., ed. see Miller, Hugh.
Dorson, Richard M., ed. see Muller, Friedrich Max.
Dorson, Richard M., ed. see Parker, Henry.
Dorson, Richard M., ed. see Parkinson, Thomas.
Dorson, Richard M., jt. ed. see Parry, Adam.
Dorson, Richard M., ed. see Penzer, Norman M.
Dorson, Richard M., ed. see Perrault, Charles.
Dorson, Richard M., jt. ed. see Perry, Ben E.
Dorson, Richard M., ed. see Rael, Juan B.
Dorson, Richard M., ed. see Ralston, William S.
Dorson, Richard M., ed. see Ricks, George R.
Dorson, Richard M., ed. see Rooth, Anna Birgitta.
Dorson, Richard M., ed. see Sebillot, Paul.
Dorson, Richard M., ed. see Stern, Stephen.
Dorson, Richard M., ed. see Taliaferro, Harden E.
Dorson, Richard M., ed. see Taylor, Archer.
Dorson, Richard M., ed. see Temple, Richard C.
Dorson, Richard M., ed. see Teske, Robert T.
Dorson, Richard M., ed. see Thigpen, Kenneth A.
Dorson, Richard M., ed. see Tully, Marjorie F. & Rael, Juan B.
Dorson, Richard M., ed. see Winner, Thomas G.
Dorson, Richard M., ed. see Yates, Norris W.
Dorson, Ron. The Indy Five Hundred. (Illus.). 1974. 9.95 (ISBN 0-87880-025-5). Norton.
--Stay Tuned for the Greatest Spectacle in Racing. (Illus.). 260p. 1980. lib. bdg. 9.95 (ISBN 0-915088-21-5). C Hungness.
Dorst & Dandelot. A Field Guide to the Larger Mammals of Africa. 24.95 (ISBN 0-00-219294-2, Collins Pub England). Greene.
Dorst, Jean. The Life of Birds, 2 vols. (Illus.). 717p. 1974. 85.00x (ISBN 0-231-03909-3). Columbia U Pr.
Dorst, T. Toller. Jacobs, M., ed. (German Texts Ser.). 116p. (Ger.). 1975. pap. text ed. 5.95 (ISBN 0-7190-0602-3, Pub. by Manchester Univ Pr). Longwood Pub Group.
Dorsten, J. A. Poets, Patrons & Professors. (Publications of Sir Thomas Brown Institute Ser: No. 2). 1962. lib. bdg. 24.00 (ISBN 90-6021-060-3, Pub. by Leiden Univ. Holland). Kluwer Academic.
--The Radical Arts. (Publications of Sir Thomas Browne Institute Ser.: No. 4). 1973. lib. bdg. 24.00 (ISBN 90-6021-001-8, Pub. by Leiden Univ Holland). Kluwer Academic.
--Ten Studies in Anglo-Dutch Relations. (Publications of Sir Thomas Browne Institute Ser: No. 5). 1974. lib. bdg. 34.00 (ISBN 90-6021-217-7, Pub. by Leiden Univ. Holland). Kluwer Academic.
--Tomas Basson. (Publications of Sir Thomas Browne Institute Ser.: No. 1). 1961. lib. bdg. 18.00 (ISBN 90-6021-063-8, Pub. by Leiden Univ Holland). Kluwer Academic.
Dorszynski, ed. see Eisen, Jon, et al.
Dorszynski, ed. see Eisen, Jon & Fine, David.
Dorszynski, Alexia, ed. see Carr, John D.
Dorszynski, Alexia, ed. see Howe, Irving.
Dorter, Kenneth. Plato's 'Phaedo' An Interpretation. 256p. 1982. 30.00x (ISBN 0-8020-5550-8). U of Toronto Pr.
Dorter, Tom & Armbruster, Greg, eds. The Art of Electronic Music. LC 85-60142. (Illus.). 320p. 1985. 25.00 (ISBN 0-688-03105-6). Morrow.
--The Art of Electronic Music. LC 84-24955. (Illus.). 320p. 1985. pap. 15.95 (ISBN 0-688-03106-4, Quill). Morrow.
Dorth, Cassandra. In Passion's Tempest. (Orig.). 1981. pap. 2.25 (ISBN 0-505-51634-9, Pub. by Tower Bks). Dorchester Pub Co.
Dortha. Fit for Fashion: A Sewing Handbook. Halsey, Alexandra & Meadow, Jane, eds. 324p. (Orig.). 1985. pap. 17.95 (ISBN 0-915643-12-X). Santa Barb Pr.
D'Ortigue, J. L. Dictionnaire Liturgique, Historique, et Theorique de Plain Chantet de Musique Religieuse. Migne, J. P., ed. (Nouvelle Encyclopedie Theologique Ser.: Vol. 29). 782p. (Fr.). Date not set. Repr. of 1860 ed. lib. bdg. 99.00x (ISBN 0-89241-272-0). Caratzas.
D'Ortigue, M. J. Dictionnaire Liturgique, Historique et Theorique de Plainchant et de Musique d'Eglise. LC 79-155353. (Music Ser). (Fr.). 1971. Repr. of 1854 ed. lib. bdg. 85.00 (ISBN 0-306-70165-0). Da Capo.
Dortland, R. J. Toxicological Evaluation of Parathion & Azinphosmethyl in Freshwater Model Ecosystems. (Agricultural Research Reports: No. 898). 120p. 1980. pap. 20.75 (ISBN 90-220-0732-4, PDC210, PUDOC). Unipub.
Dorward, Barbara & Barraga, Natalie. Teaching Aids for Blind & Visually Handicapped Children. 132p. 1968. 5.00 (ISBN 0-89128-062-6, PEP062). Am Foun Blind.
Dorward, David. Scotland's Place Names. 61p. 1981. 10.00x (ISBN 0-85158-132-3, Pub. by Blackwood & Sons England). State Mutual Bk.
--Scottish Surnames. 70p. 1981. 10.00x (ISBN 0-85158-126-9, Pub. by Blackwood & Sons England). State Mutual Bk.
Dorward, Douglas. Wild Australia: A View of Birds & Men. (Illus.). 128p. 20.95x (ISBN 0-00-211446-1, Pub. by W Collins Australia). Intl Spec Bk.
Dorwart, Harold L. Configurations: Number Puzzles & Patterns for All Ages. 7.00 (ISBN 0-911624-32-5). Wffn Proof.
--The Geometry of Incidence. pap. 4.00 (ISBN 0-911624-34-1). Wffn Proof.
Dorwart, Jeffery M. Conflict of Duty: U. S. Navy's Intelligence Dilemma 1919-1945. 228p. 1983. 18.95 (ISBN 0-87021-685-6). Naval Inst Pr.
--The Office of Naval Intelligence: Birth of America's First Intelligence Agency, 1865-1918. LC 79-84925. 216p. 1979. 18.95x (ISBN 0-87021-498-5). Naval Inst Pr.
--The Pigtail War: American Involvement in the Sino-Japanese War of 1894-1895. LC 75-8446. (Illus.). 168p. 1975. 12.50x (ISBN 0-87023-183-9). U of Mass Pr.
Dorwart, Jeffrey M. The Office of Naval Intelligence, 1865-1918. (Illus.). 216p. 1979. 18.95 (ISBN 0-87021-498-5); bulk rates avail. Naval Inst Pr.
Dorwart, R. A. & Meyers, W. R. Citizen Participation in Mental Health. 194p. 1981. 19.75x (ISBN 0-398-04522-4). C C Thomas.
Dorwart, Reinhold A. Administrative Reforms of Frederick William First of Prussia. LC 70-138221. 1971. Repr. of 1953 ed. lib. bdg. 22.50x (ISBN 0-8371-5578-9, DOAR). Greenwood.
--Prussian Welfare State Before 1740. LC 77-134954. (Illus.). 1971. 20.00x (ISBN 0-674-71975-1). Harvard U Pr.
Dorwick, T., jt. auth. see Knorre, M.
Dorwick, Thalia. Que Tal? LC 82-21434. 1983. text ed. 25.00 (ISBN 0-394-33099-4, RanC); wkbk. 10.00 (ISBN 0-394-33141-3); lab manual 10.00 (ISBN 0-394-33142-7). Random.
Dory, John P. The Domestic Diversifying Acquisition Decision. Dufey, Gunter, ed. LC 78-24529. (Research for Business Decisions Ser.: No. 2). 262p. 1978. 49.95 (ISBN 0-8357-0954-X). UMI Res Pr.
Dosa, Marta L., tr. Libraries in the Political Scene: Georg Leyh & German Librarianship, 1933-53. LC 72-5218. (Contributions in Librarianship & Information Science: No. 7). 256p. 1973. lib. bdg. 29.95 (ISBN 0-8371-6443-5, DGL/). Greenwood.
Dosanjh, Darshan S., ed. Modern Optical Methods in Gas Dynamic Research. LC 75-155352. 295p. 1971. 45.00 (ISBN 0-306-30537-2, Plenum Pr). Plenum Pub.
Dosch, Donald F. The Old Courthouse: Americans Build a Forum on the Frontier. Murphy, Dan, ed. LC 79-66506. (The Gateway Ser.). (Illus.). 1979. pap. 3.95 (ISBN 0-931056-02-0). Jefferson Natl.
Dosch, Hans-Michael, jt. ed. see Gelfand, Erwin W.
Dosch, J. C. Trauma. (Radiology of the Spine Ser.). (Illus.). xiii, 94p. 1985. 48.50 (ISBN 0-387-13767-X). Springer-Verlag.
Doscher, Paul, et al. Intensive Gardening Round the Year. LC 80-21921. (Illus.). 224p. 1981. pap. 10.95 (ISBN 0-8289-0399-9). Greene.
Doscherholmen, Alfred. Studies in the Metabolism of Vitamin B12. LC 65-12097. pap. 69.80 (ISBN 0-317-27930-0, 2055856). Bks Demand UMI.
Dose, K., et al, eds. The Origin of Life & Evolutionary Biochemistry. LC 74-10703. 484p. 1974. 59.50x (ISBN 0-306-30811-8, Plenum Pr). Plenum Pub.
--Origins of Life: Proceedings of the Seventh International Conference, Mainz, July 10-15, 1983 (A Special Issue of a Journal) 1984. lib. bdg. 109.00 (ISBN 90-277-1694-3, Pub. by Reidel Holland). Kluwer Academic.
Dose, Klaus, jt. auth. see Fox, Sidney W.
Doshay, Lewis J. Boy Sex Offender & His Later Career. LC 69-14921. (Criminology, Law Enforcement, & Social Problems Ser.: No. 59). 1969. Repr. of 1943 ed. 12.00x (ISBN 0-87585-059-6). Patterson Smith.
Doshi, Malvi. Sundowner: The Cuisines of Kenya. (Illus.). 240p. (Orig.). 1986. pap. 9.95 (ISBN 0-89407-055-X). Strawberry Hill.
--A Surti Touch: Adventures in Indian Cooking. LC 80-21487. (Illus., Orig.). 1980. pap. 7.95 (ISBN 0-89407-042-8). Strawberry Hill.
Doshi, Nagin. Guidance from Sri Aurobindo: Letters to a Young Disciple, Vol. 2. 1976. pap. 4.50 (ISBN 0-89071-265-4). Matagiri.
Doshi, Nagin, ed. see Ghose, Aurobindo.
Doshi, S., ed. The Performing Arts. 156p. 1983. text ed. 35.50x (ISBN 0-391-02917-7). Humanities.
--Shivaji & Facets of Maratha Culture. 202p. 1983. text ed. 46.50x (ISBN 0-391-02918-5). Humanities.
Doshi, S., et al, eds. Pageant of Indian Art. 173p. 1983. text ed. 60.50x (ISBN 0-391-03289-5, Pub. by Marg Pubns India). Humanities.
Doshi, S. L. Processes of Tribal Unification & Integration: Case Study of the Bhils. 1978. 11.00x (ISBN 0-8364-0291-X). South Asia Bks.
Doshi, Saryu. Homage to Shravana Belgola. 176p. 1981. text ed. 43.50x (ISBN 0-391-02518-X, Pub. by UBS India). Humanities.
Doshi, Sayru. Symbols & Manifestations of Indian Art. 136p. 30.00 (ISBN 0-89410-512-4, Pub. by UBSPD India). Three Continents.
Dosi, Giovanni. Technical Change & Industrial Transformation. LC 83-16017. 338p. 1984. 29.95 (ISBN 0-312-78775-8). St Martin.
Dosi, Giovanni, jt. auth. see Soete, Luc.
Dosker, Henry E., ed. The Dutch Anabaptists: Stone Lectures Delivered at Princeton Theological Seminary, 1918-1919. LC 83-45610. Date not set. Repr. of 1921 ed. 36.50 (ISBN 0-404-19828-7). AMS Pr.
Doskey, John S., jt. auth. see Rosenberg, Kenyon C.
Doskow, Minna. William Blake's Jerusalem. LC 81-65463. (Illus.). 388p. 1982. 37.50 (ISBN 0-8386-3090-1). Fairleigh Dickinson.
Dosman, James A. & Cotton, David J., eds. Occupational Pulmonary Disease: Focus on Grain Dust & Health. 1980. 60.00 (ISBN 0-12-221240-1). Acad Pr.
Dos Passos, John. Big Money. 1969. pap. 4.95 (ISBN 0-451-51981-7, Sig Classics). NAL.
--The Big Money. 14.95 (ISBN 0-88411-534-8, Pub. by Aeonian Pr). Amereon Ltd.
--Brazil on the Move. LC 74-42. (Illus.). 205p. 1974. Repr. of 1963 ed. lib. bdg. 15.00x (ISBN 0-8371-7356-6, DOBM). Greenwood.
--Century's Ebb. LC 75-920. (Thirteenth Chronicle Ser.). 448p. 1975. 9.95 (ISBN 0-87645-089-3, Pub. by Gambit). Harvard Common Pr.
--Chosen Country. 23.95 (ISBN 0-317-27925-4, Pub. by Aeonian Pr). Amereon Ltd.
--Facing the Chair: Story of the Americanization of Two Foreign-Born Workmen. LC 72-104066. (Civil Liberties in American History Ser.). 1970. Repr. of 1927 ed. 19.50 (ISBN 0-306-71871-5). Da Capo.
--First Encounter. LC 83-45746. Repr. of 1945 ed. 19.50 (ISBN 0-404-20083-4). AMS Pr.
--The Forty Second Parallel. 1983. pap. 3.95 (Sig Classics). NAL.
--The Forty Second Parallell. 14.95 (ISBN 0-88411-344-2, Pub. by Aeonian Pr). Amereon Ltd.
--Journeys Between Wars. 1980. lib. bdg. 27.50x (ISBN 0-374-92251-9). Octagon.
--Manhattan Transfer. LC 79-10459. 1980. Repr. of 1953 ed. lib. bdg. 16.50x (ISBN 0-8376-0433-8). Bentley.
--Manhattan Transfer. 1963. pap. 7.95 (ISBN 0-395-08375-3, 26, SenEd). HM.

--Nineteen Nineteen. pap. 3.50 (ISBN 0-451-51508-0, CE1508, Sig Classics). NAL.
--The Prospect Before Us. LC 72-10716. (Illus.). 375p. 1973. Repr. of 1950 ed. lib. bdg. 18.75 (ISBN 0-8371-6626-8, DOPB). Greenwood.
--State of the Nation. LC 73-718. (Illus.). 333p. 1973. Repr. of 1944 ed. lib. bdg. 17.25x (ISBN 0-8371-6782-5, DOSN). Greenwood.
--Theme Is Freedom. facsimile ed. LC 71-99632. (Essay Index Reprint Ser). 1956. 22.00 (ISBN 0-8369-1460-0). Ayer Co Pubs.
--Three Soldiers. 1964. pap. 12.95 (ISBN 0-395-08389-3, 40, SenEd). HM.
--U. S. A. The Forty-Second Parallel, Nineteen Nineteen, The Big Money. (Illus.). 1963. 20.00 (ISBN 0-395-07627-7). HM.

Dos Passos, John see Dos Passos, John.

Dos Passos, John R. Commercial Trusts: The Growth & Rights of Aggregated Capital. An Argument Delivered Before the Industrial Commission at Washington, D. C., December 12, 1899. LC 77-38275. (The Evolution of Capitalism Ser.). 152p. 1972. Repr. of 1901 ed. 15.00 (ISBN 0-405-04118-7). Ayer Co Pubs.

Dos Remedios, Cristobal G. & Barden, Julian A., eds. ACTIN: Structure & Function in Muscle & Non-Muscle Cells. 336p. 1983. 47.50 (ISBN 0-12-221180-4). Acad Pr.

Doss, M., ed. see International Porphyrin Meeting, 1st, Freiburg, Germany, May, 1975.

Doss, Manfred, ed. see International Research Conference, Marburg an der Lahn, June 28 - July 1, 1973.

Doss, Margot P. The Bay Area at Your Feet: Walks with San Francisco's Margot Patterson Doss. rev. ed. LC 80-20540. (Illus.). 284p. 1981. pap. 7.95 (ISBN 0-89141-097-X). Presidio Pr.
--San Francisco at Your Feet: The Great Walks in a Walker's Town. rev. ed. LC 79-6170. (Illus.). 204p. 1980. pap. 5.95 (ISBN 0-394-17863-7, E639, Ever). Grove.

Doss, Margot Patterson. A Walker's Yearbook: Fifty-Two Seasonal Walks in the San Francisco Bay Area. (Illus.). 288p. (Orig.). 1983. pap. 8.95 (ISBN 0-89141-154-2). Presidio Pr.

Doss, Martha M., ed. The Directory of Special Opportunities for Women. LC 80-85274. (Illus.). 293p. (Orig.). 1981. pap. 19.00 (ISBN 0-686-72163-2). Garrett Pk.

Doss, Vernon L. Survival. (Orig.). 1981. pap. 2.50 (ISBN 0-505-51727-2, Pub. by Tower Bks). Dorchester Pub Co.

Dossani, Nazir G. Duality Theories in Linear, Quadratic & Convex Programming: A Survey. (Discussion Paper Ser.: No. 44). 1971. pap. 4.50 (ISBN 0-686-32213-4). Regional Sci Res Inst.

Dossani, Nazir G., jt. auth. see Miller, Ronald E.

Dos Santos, Jose, Jr. Occlusion: Principles & Concepts. (Illus.). 212p. 1985. pap. text ed. 22.50 (ISBN 0-912791-18-7). Ishiyaku Euro.

Dos Santos, Joyce A. Giants of Smaller Worlds: Drawn in Their Natural Sizes. LC 82-45993. (Illus.). 48p. (gr. 2-5). 1983. 12.95 (ISBN 0-396-08143-6). Dodd.
--Henri & the Loup-Garou. LC 81-9445. (Illus.). 40p. (ps-2). 1982. 8.95 (ISBN 0-394-84950-7); PLB 8.99 (ISBN 0-394-94950-1). Pantheon.
--Sand Dollar, Sand Dollar. LC 79-3019. (Illus.). (gr. k-3). 1980. 7.95i (ISBN 0-397-31891-X); (JBL-J). Lipp Jr Bks.

Dos Santos, S. M., jt. auth. see Barney, G. C.

Dossat, Roy J. Principles of Refrigeration. 2nd ed. LC 78-2938. 603p. 1978. text ed. 35.95x (ISBN 0-471-03550-5); solutions manual 8.00 (ISBN 0-471-03771-0). Wiley.
--Principles of Refrigeration: SI Version. 2nd ed. LC 80-16918. 612p. 1981. 36.95 (ISBN 0-471-06219-7). Wiley.

Dossat, Yves. Eglise et Heresie en France au XIIIe Siecle. 364p. 1982. 70.00x (ISBN 0-86078-094-5, Pub. by Variorum). State Mutual Bk.
--Englise et Heresie en France au XIII e siecle. 365p. 1982. 75.00x (ISBN 0-86078-094-5, Pub. by Variorum England). State Mutual Bk.

Dossenbach, Hans, jt. auth. see Dossenbach, Monique.

Dossenbach, Hans D., jt. auth. see Dossenbach, Monique.

Dossenbach, Monique & Dossenbach, Hans. Irish Horses. (Illus.). 1978. 22.00x (ISBN 0-8464-0532-6). Beekman Pubs.

Dossenbach, Monique & Dossenbach, Hans D. The Noble Horse. Orig. Title: Konig Pferd. (Illus.). 440p. (Ger.). 1985. price not set. G K Hall.

Dosser, Douglas & Gowland, David. The Collaboration of Nations. LC 81-21434. 1982. 25.00 (ISBN 0-312-14722-8). St Martin.

Dossey, Larry. Beyond Illness: Discovering the Experience of Health. LC 84-5487. (New Science Library). 207p. 1984. 14.95 (ISBN 0-87773-295-7). Shambhala Pubns.
--Beyond Illness: Discovering the Experience of Health. LC 85-8323. 208p. 1985. pap. 9.95 (ISBN 0-87773-336-8, 74192-7, Pub. by New Sci Lib-Shambhala). Shambhala Pubns.
--Space, Time & Medicine. LC 81-84449. 300p. 1982. p. 15.95o. (ISBN 0-87773-222-1); pap. 9.95 (ISBN 0-87773-224-8). Shambhala Pubns.

Dossick, Jesse J. Doctoral Research on Russia & the Soviet Union: 1960-1975. LC 75-5115. (Reference Library of Social Science: Vol. 7). 200p. 1975. lib. bdg. 47.00 (ISBN 0-8240-1079-5). Garland Pub.

Dossman, Sterly, ed. see Speck, Pat K.

Doss-Quinby, Eglal. Les Refrains chez les trouveres du XIIe siecle au debut du XIVe. LC 84-47878. (American University Studies II (Romance Languages & Literature): Vol. 17). 316p. 1984. text ed. 32.00 (ISBN 0-8204-0153-6). P Lang Pubs.

Dostal, J. Operational Amplifiers. (Studies in Electrical & Electronic Engineering Ser.: Vol. 4). 488p. 1981. 83.00 (ISBN 0-444-99760-1). Elsevier.

Dostal, John, jt. auth. see Gillette, Ned.

Dostal, M. A., jt. auth. see Berenstein, C. A.

Dostal, Rudolf. On Integration in Plants. Thimann, Kenneth V., ed. Kiely, Jana M., tr. LC 67-27083. (Illus.). 1967. 16.50x (ISBN 0-674-63450-0). Harvard U Pr.

Doster, et al. Barron's How to Prepare for the CLEP Subject Exams: English Composition-Freshman English. LC 78-664. (Illus.). 1979. pap. text ed. 5.95 (ISBN 0-8120-0622-4). Barron.
--How to Prepare for the CLEP General Exam. 4th ed. LC 78-32129. 1983. 8.95 (ISBN 0-8120-2447-8). Barron.

Doster, Alexis, ed. White-Tails & Whooping Cranes. A Smithsonian Magazine Wildlife Collection. (Illus.). Date not set. 27.50 (ISBN 0-89599-011-3). Norton.

Doster, Rebecca J., jt. auth. see Whordley, Derek.

Dostert, Dennis, jt. auth. see Farr, Naunerle.

Dostert, P., jt. ed. see Tipton, Keith.

Dostert, Pierre E., ed. see Thompson, Wayne C.

Dosti, Rose. Middle Eastern Cooking. (Illus.). 192p. 1982. pap. 12.95 (ISBN 0-89586-184-4). H P Bks.

Dosti, Rose, et al. Light Style: The New American Cuisine, the Low Calorie, Low Salt, Low Fat Way to Good Food & Good Health. LC 79-1771. (Illus.). 312p. 1982. 14.95i (ISBN 0-06-250485-1, CN-4040, HarpT); pap. 9.57i (ISBN 0-06-250487-8). Har-Row.

Dostoevski, Fedor see Dostoyevsky, Fedor.

Dostoevski, Fyodor. A Gentle Spirit. Hitchcock, D. R., ed. (Library of Russian Classics). 98p. pap. text ed. 9.95x (ISBN 0-631-13865-X). Basil Blackwell.

Dostoevsky, Fedor see Dostoyevsky, Fyodor.

Dostoevsky, Fyodor. The Adolescent. MacAndrew, Andrew R., tr. 608p. 1981. pap. 11.95 (ISBN 0-393-00995-5). Norton.
--The Brothers Karamazov. Matlaw, Ralph, ed. Garnett, Constance, tr. (Critical Edition Ser). 1000p. 1976. 17.50x (ISBN 0-393-04426-2); pap. 10.95x (ISBN 0-393-09214-3). Norton.
--Crime & Punishment. rev. ed. Gibian, George, ed. (Critical Editions Ser). (gr. 9-12). 1975. pap. 8.95x (ISBN 0-393-09292-5, 9633, NortonC). Norton.
--The Gambler & The Diary of Polina Suslova. Wasiolek, Edward, ed. Terras, Victor, tr. 1972. pap. 2.95 (ISBN 0-226-15972-8, P470, Phoen). U of Chicago Pr.
--Notebooks for a Raw Youth. Wasiolek, Edward, ed. Terras, Victor, tr. LC 75-84588. 1969. 15.00x (ISBN 0-226-15965-5). U of Chicago Pr.
--The Notebooks for "Crime & Punishment". Wasiolek, Edward, ed. & tr. from Rus. LC 66-23702. viii, 246p. 1974. pap. 3.95x (ISBN 0-226-15960-4, P600, Phoen). U of Chicago Pr.
--Notebooks for the Possessed. Wasiolek, Edward, ed. Terras, Victor, tr. LC 68-26723. 1968. 12.50x (ISBN 0-226-15963-9). U of Chicago Pr.
--The Notebooks of "The Idiot". Wasiolek, Edward, ed. Strelsky, Katherine, tr. LC 67-25513. 1973. pap. 2.95x (ISBN 0-226-15962-0, P559, Phoen). U of Chicago Pr.

Dostoievski, see Dostoyevsky, Fyodor.

Dostoievsky, Feodor. Diary of a Writer. Brasol, Boris, tr. from Rus. LC 78-32010. 1100p. 1985. pap. 14.95 (ISBN 0-87905-046-2, Peregrine Smith). Gibbs M Smith.

Dostoyevsky, Aimee. Feodor Dostoyevsky. A Study. LC 72-1329. (Studies in European Literature, No. 56). 1972. Repr. of 1922 ed. lib. bdg. 49.95x (ISBN 0-8383-1438-4). Haskell.

Dostoyevsky, F. M. see Dostoyevsky, Fyodor.

Dostoyevsky, Fedor see Dostoyevsky, Fyodor.

Dostoyevsky, Fyodor. L' Adolescent, Les Nuits Blanches, Le Sous-Sol, Le Joueur, L'Eternel Mari. 1168p. 35.95 (ISBN 0-686-56505-3). French & Eur.
--Best Short Stories. Magarshack, David, tr. (YA) 1964. pap. 6.95x (ISBN 0-394-60477-6, T66, Mod LibC). Modern Lib.
--The Best Short Stories of Dostoyevsky. Magarshack, David, tr. LC 54-10655. 1950. 6.95 (ISBN 0-394-60477-6). Modern Lib.
--Brothers Karamazov. (Classics Ser). (gr. 11 up). pap. 2.50 (ISBN 0-8049-0128-7, CL-128). Airmont.
--The Brothers Karamazov. MacAndrew, Andrew, tr. from Rus. (Classic Ser.). 936p. (gr. 9-12). 1981. pap. 2.95 (ISBN 0-553-21163-3). Bantam.
--Brothers Karamazov. Garnett, Constance, tr. (Modern Library College Editions Ser.). (YA) 1950. pap. 6.00x (ISBN 0-394-30912-X, T12, RanC). Random.
--Brothers Karamazov. Komroff-Hill, Manuel, ed. 1971. pap. 2.75 (ISBN 0-451-51464-5, CE1464, Sig Classics). NAL.
--Brothers Karamazov. (Russian Library Ser). 1955. pap. 6.95 (ISBN 0-394-70722-2, V722, Vin). Random.
--The Brothers Karamazov. Garnett, Constance, tr. LC 38-5761. 1933. 9.95 (ISBN 0-394-60415-6). Modern Lib.
--The Brothers Karamazov. 595p. 1983. Repr. lib. bdg. 31.95x (ISBN 0-89966-315-X). Buccaneer Bks.
--The Complete Brothers Karamazov. 1982. pap. 5.95 (ISBN 0-14-044416-5). Penguin.
--Complete Letters, Vol. 1. Lowe, David & Meyer, Ronald, eds. 275p. 1985. 35.00 (ISBN 0-88233-897-8). Ardis Pubs.
--Crime & Punishment. (Classics Ser). (Illus.). (gr. 11 up). pap. 2.95 (ISBN 0-8049-0145-7, CL-145). Airmont.
--Crime & Punishment. (Literature Ser). (gr. 9-12). 1969. pap. text ed. 5.25 (ISBN 0-87720-705-4). AMSCO Sch.
--Crime & Punishment. Garnett, Constance, tr. from Rus. (Bantam Classics Ser.). 472p. (gr. 10-12). 1981. pap. 2.50 (ISBN 0-553-21175-7). Bantam.
--Crime & Punishment. Garnett, Constance, tr. 1977. (Evman); pap. 3.75x (ISBN 0-460-01501-X, DEL-04072). Biblio Dist.
--Crime & Punishment. Garnett, Constance, tr. LC 50-13714. 1950. 6.95 (ISBN 0-394-60450-4). Modern Lib.
--Crime & Punishment. Monas, Sidney, tr. pap. 2.25 (ISBN 0-451-51745-8, CE1745, Sig Classics). NAL.
--Crime & Punishment. Coulson, Jessie, tr. from Rus. (World's Classics Paperback Ser.). 1981. pap. 3.95 (ISBN 0-19-281549-0). Oxford U Pr.
--Crime & Punishment. (Now Age Illustrated V Ser.). (Illus.). 64p. (gr. 4-12). 1979. text ed. 5.00 (ISBN 0-686-26918-7); pap. text ed. 1.95 (ISBN 0-88301-386-X); student activity bk. 1.25 (ISBN 0-88301-410-6). Pendulum Pr.
--Crime & Punishment. Magarshack, David, tr. (Classics Ser.). (Orig.). 1952. pap. 3.95 (ISBN 0-14-044023-2). Penguin.
--Crime & Punishment. Garnett, Constance, tr. (Modern Library College Editions). 1955. pap. text ed. 5.95 (ISBN 0-394-70721-4, RanC). Random.
--Crime & Punishment. 1982. Repr. lib. bdg. 29.95 (ISBN 0-89966-397-4). Buccaneer Bks.
--Crime & Punishment with Reader's Guide. (Amsco Literature Program). (gr. 10-12). 1970. pap. text ed. 7.50 (ISBN 0-87720-805-0); tchr's ed. 3.90 (ISBN 0-87720-905-7). AMSCO Sch.
--Crime et Chatiment, Journal de Raskolnikov, Souvenirs de la Maison des Morts. 1280p. 39.95 (ISBN 0-686-56501-0). French & Eur.
--The Crocodile, an Extraordinary Event. Cioran, S. D., tr. from Rus. Orig. Title: Krokodil. 1984. 15.00 (ISBN 0-88233-590-1); 3.50 (ISBN 0-88233-588-X). Ardis Pubs.
--Les Demons (Les Possedes) & Les Rauvres Gens. 1384p. 39.95 (ISBN 0-686-56504-5). French & Eur.
--Devils. Magarshack, David, tr. (Classics Ser.). (Orig.). 1954. pap. 5.95 (ISBN 0-14-044035-6). Penguin.
--Dostoevsky: Letters & Reminiscences. Koteliansky, S. S. & Murray, J. Middleton, trs. (Select Bibliographies Reprint Ser.). Repr. of 1923 ed. 23.00 (ISBN 0-8369-5835-7). Ayer Co Pubs.
--The Double. Harden, Evelyn, tr. from Rus. 1985. 19.50 (ISBN 0-88233-756-4); pap. 6.50 (ISBN 0-88233-757-2). Ardis Pubs.
--Les Freres Karamazov & Nietotchka Niezvanov. 1296p. 37.50 (ISBN 0-686-56502-9). French & Eur.
--The Gambler. MacAndrew, Andrew R., tr. 192p. 1981. pap. 3.95 (ISBN 0-393-00044-3). Norton.
--Gambler-Bobok: A Nasty Story. Coulson, Jesse, tr. Bd. wit. (Classics Ser.). (Orig.). 1966. pap. 3.95 (ISBN 0-14-044179-4). Penguin.
--The Grand Inquisitor. LC 56-7503. (Milestones of Thought Ser.). pap. 2.45 (ISBN 0-8044-6125-2). Ungar.
--Grand Inquisitor on the Nature of Man. Garnett, Constance, tr. 1948. pap. 4.79 scp (ISBN 0-672-60237-7, LLA63). Bobbs.
--Great Short Works of Fyodor Dostoevsky. Hingley, Ronald, ed. Bird, George, et al, trs. 754p. 1968. pap. 3.80i (ISBN 0-06-083081-6, P3081, PL). Har-Row.
--An Honest Thief, & Other Stories. Garnett, Constance, tr. LC 74-15163. 404p. 1975. Repr. of 1919 ed. lib. bdg. 42.50 (ISBN 0-8371-7807-X, DOHT). Greenwood.
--House of the Dead. 1975. 12.95x (ISBN 0-460-00533-2, Evman); pap. 3.95x (ISBN 0-460-01533-8, Evman). Biblio Dist.
--The Idiot. Garnett, Constance, tr. from Rus. (Bantam Classic Ser.). 597p. (gr. 7-12). 1981. pap. 3.50 (ISBN 0-553-21136-6). Bantam.
--The Idiot, 2 vols. 709p. Set. 8.45 (ISBN 0-8285-0955-7, Pub. by Progress Pubs USSR). Imported Pubns.
--Idiot. (Classic Ser.). 1969. pap. 2.25 (ISBN 0-451-51799-7, CE1799, Sig Classics). NAL.
--Idiot. Magarshack, David, tr. (Classics Ser.). (Orig.). 1956. pap. 5.95 (ISBN 0-14-044054-2). Penguin.
--Idiot. Strahan, John W., tr. (Orig.). (gr. 9-12). pap. 1.25 (ISBN 0-671-48122-3). WSP.
--The Idiot. Garnett, Constance, tr. LC 82-42864. 10.95 (ISBN 0-394-60434-2). Modern Lib.
--L' Idiot & Humilies et Offenses. 1400p. 39.95 (ISBN 0-686-56503-7). French & Eur.
--The Insulted & Injured. Garnett, Constance, tr. from Rus. LC 75-19182. 333p. 1975. Repr. of 1955 ed. lib. bdg. 32.50x (ISBN 0-8371-8248-4, DOII). Greenwood.
--The Insulted & the Humiliated. 406p. 1976. 6.95 (ISBN 0-8285-0958-1, Pub. by Progress Pubs USSR). Imported Pubns.
--Journal d'un Ecrivain. 1648p. 42.95 (ISBN 0-686-56507-X). French & Eur.
--Karamazov Brothers, 2 vols. 1173p. 1980. Set. 15.95 (ISBN 0-8285-2244-8, Pub. by Progress Pubs USSR). Imported Pubns.
--Letters from the Underworld: The Gentle Maiden, & the Landlady. 1971. 12.95x (ISBN 0-460-00654-1, Evman); pap. 3.95x (ISBN 0-460-01654-7, Evman). Biblio Dist.
--Letters of Dostoevsky. Mayne, Ethel C., tr. from Rus. LC 61-8505. (Illus.). 384p. pap. 11.50 (ISBN 0-8180-1136-X). Horizon.
--Memoirs from the House of the Dead. Hingley, Ronald, ed. Coulson, Jessie, tr. (The World's Classics Ser.). 1983. pap. 4.95 (ISBN 0-19-281613-6). Oxford U Pr.
--New Dostoyevsky Letters. Koteliansky, S., tr. LC 73-20335. (Studies in Dostoyevsky, No. 86). 1974. lib. bdg. 49.95x (ISBN 0-8383-1824-X). Haskell.
--Notes from Underground. Ginsburg, Mirra, tr. from Russian. (Bantam Classics Ser.). 192p. (gr. 9-12). 1981. pap. 2.50 (ISBN 0-553-21144-7). Bantam.
--Notes from Underground. Matlaw, Ralph E., tr. Bd. with Grand Inquisitor. 1960. pap. 4.95 (ISBN 0-525-47050-6, 0481-140). Dutton.
--Notes from Underground. Durgy, Robert G., ed. Shishkoff, Serge, tr. from Russian. LC 82-45080. 288p. 1982. pap. text ed. 12.25 (ISBN 0-8191-2415-X). U Pr of Amer.
--Notes from Underground & Selected Stories: White Nights, Dream of a Ridiculous Man, House of the Dead. MacAndrew, Andrew R., tr. pap. 2.25 (ISBN 0-451-51823-3, CE1823, Sig Classics). NAL.
--Notes from Underground & the Double. Coulson, Jessie, tr. (Classics Ser.). 1972. pap. 2.95 (ISBN 0-14-044252-9). Penguin.
--Poor Folk. Dessaix, Robert, tr. from Rus. (Eng.). 1982. 19.50 (ISBN 0-88233-754-8); pap. 4.50 (ISBN 0-686-78410-3). Ardis Pubs.
--Poor Folk & the Gambler. Hogarth, C. J., tr. Bd. with The Gambler. 1974. 9.95x (ISBN 0-460-00711-4, Evman); pap. 4.95x (ISBN 0-460-01711-X, Evman). Biblio Dist.
--Possessed. MacAndrew, Andrew R., tr. (Orig.). 1962. pap. 4.95 (ISBN 0-451-51918-3, Sig Classics). NAL.
--The Possessed. Garnett, Constance, tr. Yarmolinsky, Avrham, ed. LC 36-3324. 1936. 7.95 (ISBN 0-394-60441-5). Modern Lib.
--Recits, Chroniques et Polemiques. 1872p. 45.00 (ISBN 0-686-56506-1). French & Eur.
--Stavrogin's Confession & the Plan of the Life of a Great Sinner. LC 72-2556. (Studies in Fiction: No. 34). 1972. Repr. of 1922 ed. lib. bdg. 48.95x (ISBN 0-8383-1494-5). Haskell.
--Stories. 374p. 1981. pap. 4.00 (ISBN 0-8285-2190-5, Pub. by Progress Pubs USSR). Imported Pubns.
--The Unpublished Dostoevsky: Diaries & Notebooks 1860-1881, Vol. 1. Proffer, Carl R., ed. (Illus.). 1972. 25.00 (ISBN 0-88233-016-0). Ardis Pubs.
--The Unpublished Dostoevsky: Diaries & Notebooks 1860-1881, Vol. 2. Proffer, Carl & Boyer, Arline, trs. from Russ. 1975. 25.00 (ISBN 0-88233-018-7). Ardis Pubs.
--Unpublished Dostoevsky, Vol. 3: Diaries & Notebooks, 1876-1881. Lapeza, David & Boyer, Arline, trs. from Rus. (Eng.). 1976. 25.00 (ISBN 0-88233-020-9). Ardis Pubs.
--The Village of Stepanchikovo & Its Inhabitants. Cioran, S. D., tr. from Rus. Orig. Title: Selo Stepanchikovo. 1985. 17.50 (ISBN 0-88233-975-3). Ardis Pubs.
--Zapiski iz Podpolia. 1982. 15.00 (ISBN 0-88233-779-3); pap. 3.50 (ISBN 0-88233-777-7). Ardis Pubs.

Dostrovsky, S., jt. auth. see Cannon, J. T.

Doswell, Andrew. Office Automation. LC 82-6988. (Wiley Series Information Processing). 283p. 1983. 29.95 (ISBN 0-471-10457-4, Pub. by Wiley-Interscience). Wiley.

Doswell, Andrew, ed. Foundations of Business Information Systems. (Approaches to Information Technology Ser.). 236p. 1985. pap. 18.95x (ISBN 0-306-41796-0). Plenum Pub.

Doswell, R. Word Processing Security. 150p. 1982. pap. 20.75 (ISBN 0-471-89432-X). Wiley.
--Word Processing: Security Guidelines. 29p. 1983. 12.50x (ISBN 0-85012-361-5). Intl Pubns Serv.

Dotan, Aron. Ben Asher's Creed: A Study of the History of the Controversy. LC 76-27649. (Society of Biblical Literature. Masoretic Studies). 1977. pap. 9.95 (ISBN 0-89130-084-8, 06-05-03). Scholars Pr GA.

Dotevall, Gerhard. Stress & Common Gastrointestinal Disorders: A Comprehensive Approach. LC 85-6565. (Gastroenterology Ser.: Vol. 3). 192p. 1985. 32.95 (ISBN 0-03-002762-4). Praeger.

Dothan, Trude. The Philistines & Their Material Culture. LC 80-22060. 352p. 1982. 52.00x (ISBN 0-300-02258-1). Yale U Pr.
Dotoyevsky, Feodor see Dostoyevsky, Fyodor.
D'Otrange, Marie-Louise, jt. auth. see Mastai, Boleslaw.
Dotsenko, Paul. The Struggle for a Democracy in Siberia, 1917-1920: Eyewitness Account of a Contemporary. (Publication Ser.: No. 277). (Illus.). 195p. 1983. lib. bdg. 16.95 (ISBN 0-8179-7771-6). Hoover Inst Pr.
Dotson, Bill, et al. Concepts in Coaching Wrestling. LC 83-25635. (Illus.). 160p. 1984. pap. 9.95 (ISBN 0-88011-188-7). Leisure Pr.
Dotson, Bob. In Pursuit of the American Dream. LC 85-47600. 288p. 1985. 15.95 (ISBN 0-689-11628-4). Atheneum.
Dott, Robert H. & Shaver, Robert H., eds. Modern & Ancient Geosynclinal Sedimentation: Proceedings of a Symposium Dedicated to Marshall Key & Held at Madison, Wisconsin, 1972. LC 74-175858. (Society of Economic Paleontologists & Mineralogists, Special Publication: No. 19). pap. 97.30 (ISBN 0-317-27152-0, 2024742). Bks Demand UMI.
Dott, Robert H., Jr. & Batten, Roger L. Evolution of the Earth. 3rd ed. (Illus.). 576p. 1980. text ed. 37.95 (ISBN 0-07-017625-6). McGraw.
Dott, Robert H., Jr., jt. ed. see Siegfried, Robert.
Dotter, C. T., et al, eds. Percutaneous Transluminal Angioplasty. (Illus.). 380p. 1983. pap. 35.00 (ISBN 0-387-12654-6). Springer-Verlag.
Dotterer, Ray H. Philosophy by Way of the Sciences: An Introductory Textbook. (Select Bibliographies Reprint Ser). Repr. of 1929 ed. 26.50 (ISBN 0-8369-6642-2). Ayer Co Pubs.
--Philosophy by Way of the Sciences: An Introductory Textbook. 484p. Repr. of 1929 ed. lib. bdg. 23.00 (ISBN 0-8290-0823-3). Irvington.
Dottin, Erskine S., jt. ed. see Jones, Alan H.
Dottin, G., ed. see Marguerite D'Angouleme, Reine de Navarre.
Dottin, Paul. Life & Strange & Surprising Adventures of Daniel DeFoe. LC 70-154663. 1971. Repr. of 1929 ed. lib. bdg. 24.50x (ISBN 0-374-92257-8). Octagon.
--Robinson Crusoe: Examin'd & Criticis'd on A New Edition of Charles Gildon's Famous Pamphlet. LC 74-5071. 1923. lib. bdg. 25.00 (ISBN 0-8414-3754-8). Folcroft.
Dottori, D. Mathematics for Today & Tomorrow. 2nd ed. 1975. 11.32 (ISBN 0-07-082244-1). McGraw.
Dotts, Linda. Love Your Microwave Cookbook: A Gourmet Guide. 210p. 1982. spiral bdg. 8.95 (ISBN 0-89896-023-1). Larksdale.
Dotts, Maryann J. The Church Resource Library: How to Start It & Make It Grow. LC 75-28087. 1976. pap. 3.95 (ISBN 0-687-08345-1). Abingdon.
--When Jesus Was Born. LC 79-3958. (Illus.). (ps-3). 1979. 10.95 (ISBN 0-687-45020-9). Abingdon.
Dotts, Maryann J., jt. auth. see Franklin, M.
Doty. Cardiac Surgery. 1985. 195.00 (ISBN 0-8151-2760-X). Year Bk Med.
Doty, Betty. Break the Anger Trap. LC 85-71508. (Illus.). 90p. (Orig.). 1985. pap. 19.95 (ISBN 0-930822-06-4). Bookery.
--Marriage Insurance. LC 77-92285. (Illus.). 1978. pap. 8.95 (ISBN 0-930822-01-3). Bookery.
--Publish Your Own Handbound Books. LC 80-67947. (Illus.). 127p. 1980. 8.95 (ISBN 0-930822-01-3); lib. bdg. 7.95 (ISBN-0-930822-03-X). Bookery.
Doty, Brant L. Numbers. (The Bible Study Textbook Ser.). 1973. 13.80 (ISBN 0-89900-008-8). College Pr Pub.
Doty, C. Stewart. The First Franco-Americans: New England Life Histories from the Federal Writers' Project 1938-1939. (Illus.). 163p. 1985. text ed. 20.00 (ISBN 0-89101-063-7); pap. 9.95 (ISBN 0-89101-062-9). U Maine Orono.
--From Cultural Rebellion to Counterrevolution: The Politics of Maurice Barres. LC 75-15337. 294p. 1976. 16.00x (ISBN 0-8214-0191-2, 82-81941). Ohio U Pr.
Doty, Carolyn. A Day Late. 232p. 1980. 10.95 (ISBN 0-670-25923-3). Viking.
--What She Told Him. 312p. 1985. 16.95 (ISBN 0-670-71087-3). Viking.
Doty, Charles R., et al. Review & Synthesis of Research & Development in Technical Education. 126p. 1980. 8.25 (ISBN 0-318-15550-8, IN206). Natl Ctr Res Voc Ed.
Doty, Charlotte L., jt. auth. see Keen, A. Myra.
Doty, Gladys, jt. auth. see Ross, Janet.
Doty, Gladys G. & Ross, Janet. Language & Life in the USA: Communicating in English, Vol. I. 4th ed. (Illus.). 448p. 1981. pap. text ed. 12.25 scp (ISBN 0-06-041693-9, HarpC). Har-Row.
--Language & Life in the USA: Reading English, Vol. II. 4th ed. (Illus.). 192p. 1981. pap. text ed. 10.95 scp (ISBN 0-06-041694-7, HarpC). Har-Row.
Doty, Gresdna A. Career of Mrs. Anne Brunton Merry in the American Theatre. LC 74-166970. (University Studies: Humanities Vol. 21). xiv, 170p. 1971. 20.00x (ISBN 0-8071-0947-9). La State U Pr.
Doty, Harry. Prayer Meetings. LC 78-10622. 1979. pap. 6.00 (ISBN 0-8309-0228-7). Herald Hse.
Doty, James. Journal of Operations. 12.00 (ISBN 0-87770-204-7). Ye Galleon.
Doty, Jean S. Can I Get There by Candlelight? LC 79-24466. (Illus.). 128p. (gr. 5-9). 1980. 9.95 (ISBN 0-02-732670-5). Macmillan.
--The Crumb. LC 75-33648. 128p. (gr. 5-9). 1976. PLB 11.88 (ISBN 0-688-84035-3). Greenwillow.
--Dark Horse. LC 82-21651. (Illus.). 122p. (gr. 4-6). 1983. PLB 10.75 (ISBN 0-688-01703-7). Morrow.
--If Wishes Were Horses. LC 84-882. 132p. (gr. 5-9). 1984. 10.95 (ISBN 0-02-733020-6). Macmillan.
--Monday Horses. (gr. 5-7). 1979. pap. 1.75 (ISBN 0-671-41856-4). Archway.
--Summer Pony. LC 74-20801. (gr. 3-7). 1976. pap. 1.95 (ISBN 0-02-042950-9, 04295, Collier). Macmillan.
--The Valley of the Ponies. LC 81-19381. (Illus.). 96p. (gr. 3-6). 1982. 8.95 (ISBN 0-02-732790-6). Macmillan.
--Yesterday's Horses. LC 84-42981. 120p. (gr. 5-9). 1985. 9.95 (ISBN 0-02-733040-0). Macmillan.
Doty, Jean Slaughter. Summer Pony. LC 74-20802. (Illus.). 128p. (gr. 3-6). pap. 1.95x (ISBN 0-02-042950-9). Macmillan.
Doty, Keith L. Fundamental Principles of Microcomputer Architecture. (Illus.). 680p. 1979. 33.95 (ISBN 0-916460-13-4). Matrix Pub.
Doty, M. R. An Alphabet. (Illus.). 1979. pap. 3.50 (ISBN 0-934184-00-3). Alembic Pr.
--An Introduction to the Geography of Iowa. 3.50 (ISBN 0-686-15306-5). Great Raven Pr.
Doty, Mark A. Tell Me Who I Am: James Agee's Search for Selfhood. LC 80-22440. xvi, 144p. 1981. 15.95x (ISBN 0-8071-0758-1). La State U Pr.
Doty, Pamela. Guided Change of the American Health System: Where the Levers Are. LC 80-12484. (Center for Policy Research, Monograph Ser.: Vol. II). 299p. 1980. 29.95 (ISBN 0-87705-472-X). Human Sci Pr.
Doty, Paul, jt. ed. see Boutwell, Jeffrey D.
Doty, R. H. Indecent Deception. LC 84-90095. 158p. 1985. 10.00 (ISBN 0-533-06169-5). Vantage.
Doty, Richard G. The Macmillan Encyclopedic Dictionary of Numismatics. LC 81-18632. (Illus.). 416p. 1982. 34.95 (ISBN 0-02-532270-2). Macmillan.
Doty, Richard G., jt. ed. see Newman, Eric P.
Doty, Richard L., ed. Mammalian Olfaction: Reproducive Processes, & Behavior. 1976. 55.00 (ISBN 0-12-221250-9). Acad Pr.
Doty, Robert. Photo-Secession: Stieglitz & the Fine Art Movement in Photography. LC 77-20467. (Illus.). 1978. pap. 5.95 (ISBN 0-486-23588-2). Dover.
Doty, Robert & Watts, Melvin, eds. Eagles, Urns, & Columns: Decorative Arts in the Federal Period. LC 79-54956. (Illus.). Date not set. 27.50 (ISBN 0-87923-303-6). Godine.
Doty, Robert M. Will Barnet. LC 84-396. (Illus.). 172p. 1984. 45.00 (ISBN 0-8109-0731-3). Abrams.
Doty, Robert M., ed. New Hampshire Photographs: The Portrait & the Environment. (Illus.). 72p. (Orig.). 1985. pap. text ed. 10.00 (ISBN 0-914339-07-9). P E Randall Pub.
Doty, Roy. Eye Fooled You. (Illus.). 48p. (gr. 3-7). 1983. pap. 2.95 (ISBN 0-02-042980-0, Collier). Macmillan.
--Gunga Your Din Din Is Ready & Pinocchio Was Nosey. (Illus.). (gr. 3-5). 1978. pap. 1.50 (ISBN 0-671-29856-9). Archway.
--Gunga, Your Din-Din Is Ready: Son of Puns, Gags, Quips & Riddles. LC 75-24624. 64p. (gr. 4-7). 1976. PLB 4.95 (ISBN 0-385-11522-9). Doubleday.
--Pinocchio Was Nosy: Grandson of Puns, Gags, Quips & Riddles. LC 76-57873. (gr. 4-6). 1977. PLB 5.95 (ISBN 0-385-12920-3). Doubleday.
--Tinkerbell Is a Ding-a-Ling. LC 79-6973. (Illus.). 64p. (gr. 4-6). 1980. PLB 6.95 (ISBN 0-385-13491-6). Doubleday.
Doty, Roy & Reuther, David. Fun to Go: A Take-Along Activity Book. (Illus.). 64p. (gr. 2-6). 1982. pap. 4.95 (ISBN 0-02-042960-6) (ISBN 0-686-86315-1). Macmillan.
Doty, Russel L., Jr. Poles Apart: The Politics of Opposing Montana Power's Rate Increase of 1969. pap. 6.00 (ISBN 0-318-00810-6). U of MT Pubns Hist.
Doty, W. D., jt. auth. see Stout, R. D.
Doty, Walter & Sinnes, A. Cort. All about Tomatoes. Susan Lammers, ed. LC 76-29249. (Illus.). 96p. (Orig.). 1981. pap. 5.95 (ISBN 0-917102-97-5). Ortho.
Doty, Walter, jt. auth. see Burke, Ken.
Doty, William G. Letters in Primitive Christianity. Via, Dan O., Jr., ed. LC 72-87058. (Guides to Biblical Scholarship: New Testament Ser.). 96p. 1973. pap. 3.95 (ISBN 0-8006-0170-X, 1-170). Fortress.
Doty, William G., tr. see Guttgemans, Erhard T.
Doty, William G., tr. see Petersen, Norman R.
Doty, William L. One Season Following Another: A Cycle of Faith. 1968. 4.50 (ISBN 0-8199-0152-0, L38573). Franciscan Herald.
Dotzauer, J. J. Sixty Two Select Studies for Violoncello, Bk. 2. Girard, F., ed. (Carl Fischer Music Library: No. 456). 1914. pap. 6.00 (ISBN 0-8258-0181-8, L456). Fischer Inc NY.
Dotzenko, Grisha. Enku: Master Carver. LC 75-11396. (Illus.). 156p. 1976. 29.95 (ISBN 0-87011-251-1). Kodansha.
Dotzler, Frederick J. The Marketing Idea Generator. (Illus.). 76p. (Orig.). 1982. pap. 11.95 (ISBN 0-9609906-0-7). Innovex.
Dou, Alberto. Lectures on Partial Differential Equations of First Order. LC 74-186519. 248p. 1972. pap. 9.95x (ISBN 0-268-00468-4). U of Notre Dame Pr.
Douady, Jules. Liste chronologique des oeuvres de William Hazlitt. LC 78-164776. Repr. of 1906 ed. 12.50 (ISBN 0-686-77062-5). AMS Pr.
Douais, Celestin. Les Albigeois. 2nd ed. LC 78-63182. (Heresies of the Early Christian & Medieval Era: Second Ser.). Repr. of 1879 ed. 47.50 (ISBN 0-404-16221-5). AMS Pr.
Douarche, Aristide. Les Tribunaux civils de Paris pendant la Revolution: 1791-1800, 2 vols. LC 71-164777. (Collection de documents relatifs a l'histoire de Paris pendant la Revolution francaise). Repr. of 1907 ed. Set. 140.00 (ISBN 0-404-52553-9); 70.00 ea. Vol. 1 (ISBN 0-404-52554-7). Vol. 2 (ISBN 0-404-52555-5). AMS Pr.
Douarin, N. Le see Le Douarin, N. & Monroy, A.
Douassot, Jean. La Gana. Trocchi, Alexander, tr. from Fr. 1980. 15.95 (ISBN 0-7145-0327-4). Riverrun NY.
Doubiago, Sharon. Hard Country. 250p. (Orig.). 1982. pap. 9.95 (ISBN 0-931122-25-2). West End.
Double, Don. Life in a New Dimension. 1979. pap. 3.50 (ISBN 0-88368-083-1). Whitaker Hse.
Doubleday, Abner. Reminiscences of Forts Sumter & Moultrie in 1860-61. LC 76-4786. (Illus.). 184p. 1976. Repr. of 1876 ed. 12.50 (ISBN 0-87152-231-4). Reprint.
Doubleday, Ellen. Counterpoint: French School. pap. 5.00 (ISBN 0-8283-1134-X). Branden Pub Co.
--Manual of Chords. pap. 5.00 (ISBN 0-8283-1133-1). Branden Pub Co.
--Two-Part Writing. (Orig.). pap. 5.00 (ISBN 0-8283-1135-8). Branden Pub Co.
Doubleday, Neal F. Variety of Attempt: British & American Fiction in the Early Nineteenth Century. LC 75-38057. viii, 218p. 1976. 17.95x (ISBN 0-8032-0876-6). U of Nebr Pr.
Doubleday, Thomas. Financial, Monetary & Statistical History of England, from the Revolution of 1688 to the Present Time. LC 68-28626. 1968. Repr. of 1847 ed. lib. bdg. 22.50x (ISBN 0-8371-0388-6, DOFM). Greenwood.
--True Law of Population: Shown to Be Connected with the Food of the People. 2nd ed. LC 67-17492. Repr. of 1847 ed. 35.00x (ISBN 0-678-00244-4). Kelley.
Doubrovsky, Serge. The New Criticism in France. Coltman, Derek, tr. from Fr. 1973. 20.00x (ISBN 0-226-16040-8). U of Chicago Pr.
Doubtfire, Dianne. The Craft of Novel Writing. 1981. pap. 5.95 (ISBN 0-8052-8087-1, Pub. by Allison & Busby England). Schocken.
Doubtfire, Stanley. Make Your Own Classical Guitar. LC 82-16860. (Illus.). 128p. 1983. Repr. of 1981 ed. 17.95 (ISBN 0-8052-3833-6). Schocken.
Douce, Francis. Illustrations of Shakespeare & of Ancient Manners. LC 68-58465. (Research & Source Ser.: No. 329). (Illus.). 1969. Repr. of 1839 ed. 21.50 (ISBN 0-8337-0892-9). B Franklin.
Douce, R. & Day, D. A., eds. Higher Plant Cell Respiration. (New Encyclopedia of Plant Physiology Ser.: Vol. 18). (Illus.). 525p. 1985. 104.50 (ISBN 0-387-13935-4). Springer-Verlag.
Douce, Roland. Mitochondria in Higher Plants. (American Society of Plant Physiologists Monograph). 1985. 48.00 (ISBN 0-12-221280-0). Acad Pr.
Doucet, Carol J. La Charrue. (Editions de la Nouvelle Acadie Ser.). (Illus.). 55p. (Fr.). 1982. pap. 3.50 (ISBN 0-940984-04-0). U of SW LA Ctr LA Studies.
Doucet, Friedrich W. Diccionario de Psicoanalisis Clasico. 232p. (Span.). 1974. pap. 15.75 (ISBN 0-686-57337-4, S-50069). French & Eur.
Doucet, Jacques. Catalogue de Fonds Speciaux de la Bibliotheque Litteraire Jacques Doucet, (Paris, France) (Fonds Valery). 1972. 100.00 (ISBN 0-8161-0952-4, Hall Library). G K Hall.
--Catalogue de Fonds Speciaux de la Bibliotheque Litteraire Jacques Doucet, (Paris, France) (Fonds Mauriac et Fonds Jouhandeau). 1972. 100.00 (ISBN 0-8161-0954-0, Hall Library). G K Hall.
--Catalogue de Fonds Speciaux de la Bibliotheque Litteraire Jacques Doucet, (Paris, France) (Lettres a Andre Gide). 1972. 100.00 (ISBN 0-8161-0951-6, Hall Library). G K Hall.
--Catalogue de Manuscrits de la Bibliotheque Litteraire Jacques Doucet, (Paris, France) 1972. 105.00 (ISBN 0-8161-0950-8, Hall Library). G K Hall.
Doucet, Lorraine. Medical Technology Review. (Illus.). 446p. 1981. pap. text ed. 15.00 (ISBN 0-397-50459-4, 65-06000, Lippincott Nursing). Lippincott.
Doucet, Lorraine D. & Packard, Albert E. Medical Technology Examination Review. 2nd ed. LC 65-8154. (Illus.). 340p. 1984. pap. text ed. 16.50 (ISBN 0-397-54486-3, Lippincott Medical). Lippincott.
Doucet, Louis. The Caribbean Today. (Illus.). 256p. 1977. 14.95 (ISBN 2-85258-062-4, Pub. by J A Editions France). Hippocrene Bks.
Doucet, Michel. Woerterbuch der Deutschen und Franzoesischen Rechtssprache, Vol. 1. 2nd ed. (Ger. & Fr.). 1966. 28.00 (ISBN 3-406-00969-7, M-7030). French & Eur.
--Woerterbuch der Deutschen und Franzoesischen Rechtssprache, Vol. 2. 2nd ed. (Ger. & Fr.). 1977. 54.00 (ISBN 3-406-01196-9, M-7029). French & Eur.
Doucette, John & Freedman, Ruth. Progress Tests for the Developmentally Disabled: An Evaluation. LC 79-55773. 319p. 1980. 27.50 (ISBN 0-89011-539-7). Brookline Book.
Doucette, Joseph & Collins, Charles. Collecting Antique Toys: A Practical Guide. (Illus.). 146p. 1981. 17.95 (ISBN 0-02-533010-1). Macmillan.
Doucette, Leonard E. Theatre in French Canada: Laying the Foundations 1606-1867. (Romance Ser.: No. 52). 304p. 1984. 30.00x (ISBN 0-8020-5579-6). U of Toronto Pr.
Doud, Mildred L. Your Miniature Schnauzer. LC 73-84514. (Your Dog Bk.). (Illus.). 160p. 1974. 12.95 (ISBN 0-87714-015-4). Denlingers.
Doud, Richard K. & Quimby, Ian M. G. Winterthur Portfolio, No. 6. (A Winterthur Bk.). (Illus.). 1970. 15.00x (ISBN 0-226-92132-8). U of Chicago Pr.
Doud, Richard K., ed. Winterthur Portfolio, No. 4. (A Wintherthur Bk.). (Illus.). 1968. 15.00x (ISBN 0-226-92129-8). U of Chicago Pr.
--Winterthur Portfolio No. 5: Thematic Issue on Maryland. (Winterthur Bk.). (Illus.). 1969. 15.00 (ISBN 0-226-92126-3). U of Chicago Pr.
Douday, Jules. Vie De William Hazlitt L'essayiste. 1973. Repr. of 1907 ed. 50.00 (ISBN 0-8274-0065-9). R West.
Doudera, A. Edward & Peters, J. Douglas, eds. Legal & Ethical Aspects of Treating Critically & Terminally Ill Patients. LC 81-20523. 370p. 1982. text ed. 27.00x (ISBN 0-914904-76-0). Health Admin Pr.
Doudera, A. Edward & Swazey, Judith P., eds. Refusing Treatment in Mental Health Institutions-Values in Conflict. LC 82-1615. 230p. 1982. text ed. 24.00x (ISBN 0-914904-77-9). Health Admin Pr.
Doudera, A. Edward, jt. ed. see Cranford, Ronald E.
Doudera, A. Edward, jt. ed. see Shaw, Margery W.
Doudera, A. Edward, jt. ed. see Shepard, Ira M.
Doudna, Lyn. The Odds Against Them. 1985. 11.95 (ISBN 0-533-06574-7). Vantage.
Doudna, Martin K. Concerned about the Planet: The Reporter Magazine & American Liberalism, 1949-1968. LC 77-10048. (Contributions in American Studies: No. 32). 1977. lib. bdg. 27.50 (ISBN 0-8371-9698-1, DCA/). Greenwood.
Doudoroff, Michael J. Moros y Cristianos in Zacatecas: Text of a Mexican Folk Play. LC 81-1558. 66p. (Orig.). 1981. pap. text ed. 5.00 (ISBN 0-939448-00-9). Amadeo Concha.
Doudoroff, Peter. A Critical Review of Recent Literature on Toxicity of Cyanides to Fish. LC 80-68588. 71p. (Orig.). 1980. pap. 3.60 (ISBN 0-89364-039-5, API 847-87000). Am Petroleum.
Douet D'Arcq, L., ed. see De Monstrelet, Enguerrend.
Douet-D'Arcq, Louis C. Comptes De l'Hotel Des Rois De France Au Quatorzieme et Quinzieme Siecles. 1865. 43.00 (ISBN 0-384-12421-6); pap. 39.00 (ISBN 0-384-12420-8). Johnson Repr.
Douet-d'Arcq, Louis C., ed. Choix de Pieces Inedites Relatives au Regne de Charles Six, 2 Vols. 1863-1864. 77.00 (ISBN 0-384-12400-3); pap. 65.00 (ISBN 0-384-12401-1). Johnson Repr.
--Comptes De L'argenterie Des Rois De France Au Quatorzieme Siecle. 1851. 34.00 (ISBN 0-384-12410-0); pap. 28.00 (ISBN 0-384-12411-9). Johnson Repr.
Dougal, John, tr. see Born, Max.
Dougall, Charles S. The Burns Country. 1979. Repr. of 1904 ed. lib. bdg. 35.00 (ISBN 0-8414-3831-5). Folcroft.
--The Burns Country. 1973. Repr. of 1925 ed. 20.00 (ISBN 0-8274-1652-0). R West.
Dougall, E. G., jt. ed. see Finch, J. H.
Dougall, Herbert E. & Gaumnitz, Jack E. Capital Markets & Institutions. 4th ed. (Foundations of Finance Ser.). (Illus.). 1980. pap. text ed. 16.95 (ISBN 0-13-113670-4). P-H.
--Capital Markets & Institutions. 5th ed. (Illus.). 256p. 1986. pap. text ed. 14.95 (ISBN 0-13-113713-1). P-H.
Dougall, J. A., jt. ed. see Koerner, R. M.
Dougall, Lucy. War & Peace in Literature. 128p. 1981. 5.00 (ISBN 0-318-16880-4). World Without War.
Dougall, Neil. Horses & Ponies on Small Areas. (Illus.). pap. 1.50 (ISBN 0-85131-273-X, NL51, Dist. by Miller). J A Allen.
--Stallions: Their Management & Handling. pap. 5.95 (ISBN 0-85131-256-X, NL51, Dist. by Miller). J A Allen.
Dougan. TET: The Crucial Year of Nineteen Sixty-Eight. Boston Publishing Company, ed. (Vietnam Experience Ser.). (Illus.). 192p. 1983. 16.95 (ISBN 0-201-11326-0). Addison-Wesley.
Dougan, Carol W., jt. auth. see Dougan, Michael B.
Dougan, Charles W. The Shanghai Postal System. 200p. 1981. 27.00 (ISBN 0-933580-06-1). Am Philatelic Society.
Dougan, Clark & Fulghum, David. The Fall of the South. Manning, Robert, ed. (Vietman Experience Ser.: Vol. XV). (Illus.). 192p. 1985. 16.95 (ISBN 0-939526-16-6). Boston Pub Co.

Douglas, Bodie & Hollingworth, Charles A. Introduction to Applications of Symmetry to Bonding & Spectra. Date not set. 39.00 (ISBN 0-12-221340-8). Acad Pr.

Douglas, Bodie & Saito, Yoshihiko, eds. Stereochemistry of Optically Active Transition Metal Compounds. LC 80-10816. (ACS Symposium Ser.: No. 119). 1980. 44.95 (ISBN 0-8412-0538-8). Am Chemical.

Douglas, Bodie, et al. Concepts & Models of Inorganic Chemistry. 2nd ed. LC 82-2606. 816p. 1982. text ed. 41.50 (ISBN 0-471-21984-3). Wiley.

Douglas, Brodie E., ed. Inorganic Syntheses, Vol. 18. LC 39-23015. (Inorganic Syntheses Ser.). 238p. 1977. 45.95x (ISBN 0-471-03393-6, Pub. by Wiley-Interscience). Wiley.

Douglas, C. E. When All Hell Breaks Loose. 1974. pap. 4.95 (ISBN 0-9601124-0-5). Tusayan Gospel.

Douglas, C. H. The Big Idea. 59.95 (ISBN 0-87968-747-9). Gordon Pr.

--The Brief for the Prosecution. 59.95 (ISBN 0-87968-787-8). Gordon Pr.

--Collected Writings. 600.00 (ISBN 0-87968-901-3). Gordon Pr.

--The Control & Distribution of Production. 59.95 (ISBN 0-87968-942-0). Gordon Pr.

--Credit Power & Democracy. 59.95 (ISBN 0-87968-960-9). Gordon Pr.

--The Development of World Dominion. 59.95 (ISBN 0-8490-0021-1). Gordon Pr.

--Economic Democracy. 69.95 (ISBN 0-8490-0081-5). Gordon Pr.

--Fifty Years of Social Credit. 59.95 (ISBN 0-8490-0162-5). Gordon Pr.

--The Land for the Chosen People Racket. 1982. lib. bdg. 55.00 (ISBN 0-87700-415-3). Revisionist Pr.

--Money & the Price System. 59.95 (ISBN 0-8490-0659-7). Gordon Pr.

--The Monopoly of Credit. 59.95 (ISBN 0-8490-0664-3). Gordon Pr.

--Programme for the Third World War. 59.95 (ISBN 0-8490-0896-4). Gordon Pr.

--A Reply to J. A. Hobson. 59.95 (ISBN 0-8490-0945-6). Gordon Pr.

--Social Credit. 69.95 (ISBN 0-87968-107-1). Gordon Pr.

Douglas, C. L. Thunder on the Gulf. 1973. Repr. of 1936 ed. 9.95 (ISBN 0-88342-027-9). Old Army.

Douglas, C. N., ed. see Keller, Helen.

Douglas, Carol. Working in Retailing. 1982. 26.00x (ISBN 0-7134-2361-7, Pub. by Careers Con England). State Mutual Bk.

Douglas, Carol A. To the Cleveland Station. 300p. (Orig.). 1982. pap. 6.95 (ISBN 0-930044-27-4). Naiad Pr.

Douglas, Carole N. Azure Days, Quicksilver Nights. (Loveswept Ser.: No. 92). 208p. (Orig.). 1985. pap. 2.25 (ISBN 0-553-21705-4). Bantam.

--The Best Man. (Love & Life Ser.). 176p. 1983. pap. 1.75 (ISBN 0-345-30914-6). Ballantine.

--Exiles of the Rynth. 193p. 1984. pap. 2.95 (ISBN 0-345-30836-0, Del Rey). Ballantine.

--Her Own Person. (Love & Life Romance Ser.). 176p. (Orig.). 1982. pap. 1.75 (ISBN 0-345-30733-X). Ballantine.

--In Her Prime. (Love & Life Romance Ser.). 160p. (Orig.). 1982. pap. 1.75 (ISBN 0-345-30523-X). Ballantine.

--Lady Rogue. (Orig.). 1983. pap. 3.50 (ISBN 0-345-31136-1). Ballantine.

--Probe. 384p. 1985. pap. 6.95 (ISBN 0-8125-3585-5, Dist. by St. Martin). Tor Bks.

--Six of Swords. 288p. 1984. pap. 2.95 (ISBN 0-345-31810-2, Del Rey). Ballantine.

Douglas, Caroline, jt. auth. see Norris, Anne.

Douglas, Casey. Le Cavalier Infidele. (Harlequin Seduction Ser.). 332p. 1983. pap. 3.25 (ISBN 0-373-45020-6, Pub. by Worldwide). Harlequin Bks.

--Dance-Away Lover. (Superromances Ser.). 384p. 1983. pap. 2.95 (ISBN 0-373-70075-X, Pub. by Worldwide). Harlequin Bks.

--Proud Surrender. (Super Romances Ser.). 384p. 1983. pap. 2.95 (ISBN 0-373-70056-3, Pub. by Worldwide). Harlequin Bks.

Douglas, Charles. John Stuart Mill: A Study of His Philosophy. LC 73-11056. Repr. of 1895 ed. lib. bdg. 20.00 (ISBN 0-8414-1885-3). Folcroft.

--Natural History Notebook, 2 bks. (Illus.). 1977. No. 1. pap. 2.50 (ISBN 0-660-00092-X, 56440-1, Pub. by Natl Mus Canada); No. 2. pap. 2.50 (ISBN 0-660-00094-6, 56442-8). U of Chicago Pr.

--Natural History Notebook, No. 3. (Illus.). iv, 54p. 1980. pap. 2.50 (ISBN 0-660-10341-9, 56444-4, Pub. by Natl Mus Canada). U of Chicago Pr.

--Natural History Notebook, No. 4. (National Museum of Natural Science Ser.). (Illus.). iv, 56p. 1981. pap. 2.50 (ISBN 0-660-10321-4, 56445-2, Pub. by Natl Mus Canada). U of Chicago Pr.

Douglas, Charles G. Family Law. LC 83-146097. (New Hampshire Practice Ser.: Vol. 3). (Illus.). xxv, 680p. Date not set. price not set. Equity Pub NH.

Douglas, Charles H. Basic Music Theory. McKenzie, Wesley M., ed. 1970. pap. 3.45 (ISBN 0-910842-01-9, GE11, Pub. by GWM). Kjos.

--The Financial History of Massachusetts. 59.95 (ISBN 0-8490-0167-6). Gordon Pr.

--Financial History of Massachusetts from the Organization of the Massachusetts Bay Colony to the American Revolution. LC 71-82251. (Columbia University, Studies in the Social Sciences Ser.: No. 4). 1968. Repr. of 1892 ed. 10.00 (ISBN 0-404-51004-3). AMS Pr.

Douglas, Charles L. Comparative Ecology of Pinyon Mice & Deer Mice in Mesa Verde National Park, Colorado. (Museum Ser.: Vol. 18, No. 5). 84p. 1969. pap. 4.50 (ISBN 0-686-80275-6). U of KS Mus Nat Hist.

Douglas, Charles N. Uncle Charlie's Poems. 1977. Repr. 25.00 (ISBN 0-403-08367-2). Scholarly.

Douglas, Charlotte, ed. see Khlebnikov, Velimir.

Douglas, Charlotte C. Swans of Other Worlds: Kazimir Malevich & the Origins of Abstraction in Russia. Foster, Stephen, ed. LC 80-13165. (Studies in the Fine Arts: The Avant-Garde, No. 2). 148p. 1980. 39.95 (ISBN 0-8357-1058-0). UMI Res Pr.

Douglas Co. Legal Aid Society, Inc. Staff. Kansas Attorney Practice Manual. 1981. 60.00 (ISBN 0-318-04138-3). KS Bar CLE.

Douglas, Colin. Bleeders Come First. LC 79-64156. 1979. 8.95 (ISBN 0-8008-0816-9). Taplinger.

--The Greatest Breakthrough Since Lunchtime. LC 78-27167. 1979. 8.95 (ISBN 0-8008-3649-9). Taplinger.

--The Houseman's Tale. LC 78-57603. 1978. 8.95 (ISBN 0-8008-3952-8). Taplinger.

--The Intern's Tale. LC 82-47995. 192p. 1982. pap. 7.95 (ISBN 0-394-17996-X, E831, Ever). Grove.

--Sickness & Health: A Novel. LC 80-28316. 200p. cancelled (ISBN 0-8008-7178-2). Taplinger.

Douglas, Crerar, ed. Autobiography of Augustus Hopkins Strong. 352p. 1981. 25.00 (ISBN 0-8170-0916-7). Judson.

Douglas, D. Biographical History of Sir William Blackstone. 489p. 1971. Repr. of 1782 ed. 35.00x (ISBN 0-8377-2025-7). Rothman.

Douglas, D. C., ed. Feudal Documents from the Abbey of Bury St. Edmunds. (British Academy, London, Records of the Social & Economic History of England & Wales: Vol. 8). pap. 45.00 (ISBN 0-317-16223-3). Kraus Repr.

Douglas, David. Douglas of the Forests: The North American Journals of David Douglas. Davies, John, ed. LC 80-12535. (Illus.). 194p. 1980. 16.95x (ISBN 0-295-95707-7). U of Wash Pr.

--English Scholars, Sixteen Sixty to Seventeen Thirty. LC 75-3865. (Illus.). 291p. 1975. Repr. of 1951 ed. lib. bdg. 22.50x (ISBN 0-8371-8093-7, DOES). Greenwood.

--Journal Kept by David Douglas During His Travels in North America, 1823-27. Repr. of 1959 ed. text ed. 22.50 (ISBN 0-934454-54-X). Lubrecht & Cramer.

Douglas, David, jt. ed. see Auer, Peter L.

Douglas, David C. The Norman Achievement: 1050-1100. LC 74-88028. 1969. 36.50x (ISBN 0-520-01383-2). U of Cal Pr.

--The Norman Fate, 1100-1154. LC 75-13155. 350p. 1976. 46.00x (ISBN 0-520-03027-3). U of Cal Pr.

--William the Conqueror: The Norman Impact upon England. (English Monarchs Ser.). 1964. 42.50x (ISBN 0-520-00348-9); pap. 9.95 (ISBN 0-520-00350-0, CAL131). U of Cal Pr.

Douglas, Donald, jt. auth. see Gaddie, Ronald E.

Douglas, Donald M. Many Brave Hearts. 150p. 1985. pap. 3.50 (ISBN 0-88184-122-6). Carroll & Graf.

--Rebecca's Pride. 224p. 1984. pap. 3.50 (ISBN 0-88184-070-X). Carroll & Graf.

Douglas, Dorothy, jt. auth. see Roth, Julius.

Douglas, Drake. Creature. 400p. (Orig.). 1985. pap. 3.75 (ISBN 0-8439-2256-7, Leisure Bks). Dorchester Pub Co.

--Undertow. 400p. (Orig.). 1984. pap. 3.75 (ISBN 0-8439-2121-8, Leisure Bks). Dorchester Pub Co.

Douglas, E. H., tr. see Palacios, Miguel A.

Douglas, Edward M. Boundaries, Areas, Geographic Centers & Altitudes in the U. S. 1981. Repr. lib. bdg. 39.00 (ISBN 0-403-00575-2). Scholarly.

Douglas, Eileen. Eileen Douglas's New York Inflation Fighters' Guide. LC 82-20378. (Illus.). 256p. (Orig.). 1983. pap. 8.70 (ISBN 0-688-01851-3, Quill NY). Morrow.

Douglas, Ellen. A Lifetime Burning. 224p. 1982. 13.95 (ISBN 0-394-52719-4). Random.

--The Rock Cried Out. LC 79-87474. 1979. 10.95 (ISBN 0-15-178322-5). HarBraceJ.

Douglas, Emily T. Margaret Sanger: Pioneer of the Future. LC 75-29862. (Illus.). 298p. 1975. 8.50 (ISBN 0-912048-75-1); pap. 6.95 (ISBN 0-685-63962-2). Garrett Pk.

Douglas, Erika, ed. The Family Circle Hints Book. 1982. 15.95 (ISBN 0-8129-1016-8). Times Bks.

Douglas, Eva M., ed. see Marshall, Oscar S.

Douglas, Evan J. Intermediate Microeconomic Analysis: Theory & Applications. (Illus.). 576p. 1982. text ed. 29.95 (ISBN 0-13-470708-7). P-H.

--Managerial Economics: Theory, Practice, & Problems. 2nd ed. (Illus.). 544p. 1983. 29.95 (ISBN 0-13-550210-1). P-H.

Douglas, Evelyn, pseud. Phantasmagoria. Fletcher, Ian & Stokes, John, eds. Bd. with Love Sonnets. LC 82-49104. (Degeneration & Regeneration: Texts of the Pre-Modern Era Ser.). 150p. 1984. lib. bdg. 25.00 (ISBN 0-8240-5567-5). Garland Pub.

Douglas, F. Reflections on Celibacy & Marriage in Four Letters to a Friend. LC 83-48585. (Marriage, Sex & the Family in England Ser.). 87p. 1984. lib. bdg. 20.00 (ISBN 0-8240-5907-7). Garland Pub.

Douglas, F. C. Land Value Rating. 76p. 1961. pap. 1.00 (ISBN 0-911312-60-9). Schalkenbach.

Douglas, F. Gordon. How to Profitably Sell or Buy a Company or Business. 320p. 1981. 24.95 (ISBN 0-442-23336-1). Van Nos Reinhold.

Douglas, Frederic H. & D'Harnoncourt, Rene. Indian Art of the United States. LC 74-86425. (Museum of Modern Art Publications in Reprint Ser). (Illus.). 1970. Repr. of 1941 ed. 20.00 (ISBN 0-405-01534-8). Ayer Co Pubs.

Douglas, Frederick. My Bondage & My Freedom. LC 68-28994. (American Negro: His History & Literature Ser., No. 1). (Illus.). 480p. 1968. Repr. of 1855 ed. 34.00 (ISBN 0-405-01813-4). Ayer Co Pubs.

Douglas, G., jt. auth. see Doise, W.

Douglas, G., et al. Quasars & High Energy Astronomy. 504p. 1969. 144.50 (ISBN 0-677-11520-2). Gordon.

--Systematic New Product Development. 2nd ed. 196p. 1983. text ed. 33.00x (ISBN 0-566-02412-8). Gower Pub Co.

Douglas, G. H., ed. The Teaching of Business Communication. 1978. pap. 6.60 (ISBN 0-931874-00-9). Assn Busn Comm.

Douglas, Garvin. The Palis of Honoure. LC 77-6155. (English Experience Ser.: No. 89). 80p. 1969. Repr. of 1553 ed. 13.00 (ISBN 90-221-0089-8). Walter J Johnson.

Douglas, Gavin. Poetical Works of Gavin Douglas, Bishop of Dunkeld, 4 vols. Small, J., ed. (Illus.). 1970. Repr. of 1874 ed. Set. 121.00x (ISBN 3-4870-3095-0). Adlers Foreign Bks.

Douglas, Gavin, tr. see Coldwell, David F.

Douglas, Gawin. Palice of Honour. Kinnear, John G., ed. LC 70-144417. (Bannatyne Club, Edinburgh. Publications: No. 17). Repr. of 1827 ed. 17.50 (ISBN 0-404-52717-5). AMS Pr.

Douglas, Gawin, tr. see Virgil.

Douglas, Gawyn. The Palice of Honour. Kinnear, John, ed. Repr. of 1827 ed. 25.00 (ISBN 0-384-12440-2). Johnson Repr.

Douglas, George. James Hogg. LC 74-9780. 1899. 17.50 (ISBN 0-8414-3762-9). Folcroft.

--Scottish Poetry: Drummond of Hawthornden to Fergusson. LC 74-13044. 1973. lib. bdg. 25.00 (ISBN 0-8414-3777-7). Folcroft.

Douglas, George A. Writing for Public Relations. (Marketing & Management Ser.). 192p. 1980. pap. text ed. 13.50 (ISBN 0-675-08171-8). Merrill.

Douglas, George B. The Book of Scottish Poetry. LC 77-144506. Repr. of 1911 ed. 49.50 (ISBN 0-404-08635-7). AMS Pr.

--Contemporary Scottish Verse. LC 70-144504. (Canterbury Poets Ser.). Repr. of 1893 ed. 26.00 (ISBN 0-404-08633-0). AMS Pr.

Douglas, George B., ed. Poems of the Scottish Minor Poets. LC 73-144505. Repr. of 1891 ed. 26.00 (ISBN 0-404-08634-9). AMS Pr.

Douglas, George B. & Dorson, Richard M., eds. Scottish Fairy & Folk Tales. LC 77-70591. (International Folklore Ser.). (Illus.). 1977. Repr. of 1901 ed. lib. bdg. 23.00x (ISBN 0-405-10092-2). Ayer Co Pubs.

Douglas, George H. Edmund Wilson's America. LC 83-19696. (Illus.). 272p. 1983. 23.00x (ISBN 0-8131-1494-2). U Pr of Ky.

--H. L. Mencken: Critic of American Life. 248p. 1978. 19.50 (ISBN 0-208-01693-7, Archon). Shoe String.

--Rail City: Chicago, U. S. A. LC 81-6361. (Illus.). 288p. 1981. 27.50 (ISBN 0-8310-7150-8). Howell-North.

--Skyscraper Odyssey: An Informal History of Tall Buildings in America. (Illus.). 320p. 1984. 29.95 (ISBN 0-317-11483-2). Hastings.

Douglas, George H. & Hildebrandt, Herbert W., eds. Studies in the History of Business Writing. 224p. (Orig.). 1985. pap. text ed. write for info. (ISBN 0-931874-16-5). Assn Busn Comm.

Douglas, George H., jt. ed. see Holland, G. Pepper.

Douglas, Gertrude. Linked Lives. Wolff, Robert L., ed. (Victorian Fiction Ser.). 1975. Repr. of 1876 ed. lib. bdg. 73.00 (ISBN 0-8240-1537-1). Garland Pub.

Douglas, Gilean. The Protected Place. (Illus.). 190p. 1979. pap. 7.95 (ISBN 0-88826-080-6). Superior Pub.

Douglas, Gina. The Ganges. LC 78-62983. (Rivers of the World Ser.). (Illus.). 68p. (gr. 4 up). 1978. PLB 13.96 (ISBN 0-382-06205-1). Silver.

Douglas, Gregory. The Rite. (Orig.). 1979. pap. 2.50 (ISBN 0-89083-529-2). Zebra.

Douglas, Gregory A. The Nest. 1980. pap. 2.75 (ISBN 0-89083-662-0). Zebra.

--The Unholy Smile. 1981. pap. 2.50 (ISBN 0-89083-796-1). Zebra.

Douglas, Harriet C. Handweaver's Instruction Manual. LC 76-24020. (Shuttle Craft Guild Monograph: No. 34). (Illus.). 41p. 1949. pap. 8.45 (ISBN 0-916658-30-9). HTH Pubs.

Douglas, Henry K. The Douglas Diary: Student Days at Franklin & Marshall College 1856-1858. Klein, Frederic S. & Carrill, John H., eds. LC 73-89382. (Illus.). 1973. 7.95 (ISBN 0-910626-00-6). Franklin & Marsh.

--I Rode with Stonewall. 1983. pap. 2.95 (ISBN 0-89176-027-X). Mockingbird Bks.

--I Rode with Stonewall. xiii, 401p. 1940. 17.50 (ISBN 0-8078-0337-5). U of NC Pr.

Douglas, Herb, ed. see Anderson, R. A.

Douglas, Howard. A Treatise on Naval Gunnery, Eighteen Fifty-Five. 672p. 1982. 60.00x (ISBN 0-85177-275-7, Pub. by Conway Marit England). State Mutual Bk.

Douglas, Hugh M., jt. auth. see Crowe, Jaon M.

Douglas, I. J. Audit & Control of Mini & Microcomputers. 145p. 1982. 25.00x (ISBN 0-85012-368-2). Taylor & Francis.

--Security & Audit of Database Systems. 23p. (Orig.). 1980. 15.00x (ISBN 0-85012-279-1). Intl Pubns Serv.

Douglas, I. J., jt. auth. see Thomas, A. J.

Douglas, Ian. Humid Landforms. (Illus.). 1977. text ed. 22.50x (ISBN 0-262-04054-9). Mit Pr.

--The Urban Environment: A Biophysical Approach. 275p. 1984. pap. text ed. 18.95 (ISBN 0-7131-6392-5). E Arnold.

Douglas, Ian & Spencer, Tom, eds. Environmental Change & Tropical Geomorphology. (Illus.). 400p. 1985. text ed. 45.00x (ISBN 0-04-551074-1). Allen Unwin.

Douglas, J. B. Analysis with Standard Contagious Distributions. (Statistical Distributions in Scientific Work Ser.: Vol. 4). 530p. 1980. 35.00 (ISBN 0-89974-012-X). Intl Co-Op.

Douglas, J. D., ed. The New Bible Dictionary. 1344p. 1982. 24.95 (ISBN 0-8423-4667-8). Tyndale.

Douglas, J. D. & Cairns, Earle E., eds. The New International Dictionary of the Christian Church. rev. ed. 1978. 29.95 (ISBN 0-310-23830-7). Zondervan.

Douglas, J. D. & Johnson, J. M., eds. Existential Sociology. LC 76-47198. 1977. 47.50 (ISBN 0-521-21515-3); pap. 15.95 (ISBN 0-521-29225-5). Cambridge U Pr.

Douglas, J. F., et al. Fluid Mechanics. (Civil Engineering Ser.). 721p. 1979. 37.95 (ISBN 0-273-00461-1). Pitman Pub MA.

Douglas, J. Fielding, ed. Carcinogenesis & Mutagenesis Testing. LC 84-12820. (Contemporary Biomedicine Ser.). 352p. 1984. 49.50 (ISBN 0-89603-042-3). Humana.

Douglas, J. G., et al. Fluid Mechanics. 2nd ed. 768p. 1985. pap. text ed. 24.95 (ISBN 0-273-02134-6). Pitman Pub MA.

Douglas, J., Jr. & Dupont, T. Collocation Methods for Parabolic Equations in a Single Space Variable: Based on C to the First Power-Piecewise-Polynomial Spaces. (Lecture Notes in Mathematics: Vol. 385). v, 147p. 1974. pap. text ed. 12.00 (ISBN 0-387-06747-7). Springer-Verlag.

Douglas, J. M. & Lomo, A., eds. Divry's New Spanish-English & English-Spanish Handy Dictionary. (Span. & Eng.). 1965. pocket size, flexible 4.00 (ISBN 0-685-09033-7); thumb indexed 6.00 (ISBN 0-685-09034-5). Divry.

Douglas, J. N., jt. ed. see Boal, F. W.

Douglas, J. Sholto. Hydroponics: The Bengal System with Notes on Other Methods of Soil Cultivation. 5th ed. 1975. 7.95x (ISBN 0-19-560566-7). Oxford U Pr.

Douglas, J. Sholto & Hart, Robert A. Forest Farming: Towards a Solution to Problems of World Hunger & Conservation. 2nd ed. (Illus.). 207p. (Orig.). 1984. pap. 11.50x (ISBN 0-946688-30-3, Pub. by Intermediate Tech England). Intermediate Tech.

--Forest Farming: Towards a Solution to Problems of World Hunger & Conservation. 207p. 1985. pap. 15.95 (ISBN 0-8133-0331-1). Westview.

Douglas, Jack. The Sociology of Deviance. 325p. 1984. pap. 21.43 (ISBN 0-205-08003-0, 818003). Allyn.

Douglas, Jack D. Creative Interviewing. LC 84-23715. 159p. 1985. 24.00 (ISBN 0-8039-2409-7); pap. 12.00 softcover (ISBN 0-8039-2408-9). Sage.

--Investigative Social Research: Individual & Team Field Research. LC 76-21663. (Sage Library of Social Research: Vol. 29). 1976. 24.00 (ISBN 0-8039-0675-7); pap. 12.00 (ISBN 0-8039-0676-5). Sage.

--Observations of Deviance. 350p. 1981. pap. text ed. 13.25 (ISBN 0-8191-1819-2). U Pr of Amer.

--Social Meanings of Suicide. 1967. pap. 9.95x (ISBN 0-691-02812-5). Princeton U Pr.

Douglas, Jack D. & Waksler, Frances C. The Sociology of Deviance: An Introducton. 1982. text ed. 23.95 (ISBN 0-316-19111-6); test bank avail. (ISBN 0-316-19112-4). Little.

Douglas, Jack D., ed. Crime & Justice in American Society. LC 74-126302. 1971. 32.50x (ISBN 0-672-51377-3). Irvington.

--Impact of Sociology: Readings in the Social Sciences. LC 76-119991. (Orig.). 1970. pap. text ed. 4.95x (ISBN 0-89197-228-5). Irvington.

--Introduction to Sociology: Situations & Structures. LC 75-163608. 1973. text ed. 21.95 (ISBN 0-02-907540-8). Free Pr.

Douglas, James. Gundog Training. (Illus.). 144p. 1983. 14.95 (ISBN 0-7153-8336-1). David & Charles.

--North City Traffic, Straight Ahead. (The Irish Play Ser.). Date not set. pap. 1.25x (ISBN 0-912262-09-5). Proscenium.

--Robert Browning. LC 72-12897. 1973. lib. bdg. 10.00 (ISBN 0-8414-1031-3). Folcroft.

--The Savages. (Irish Play Ser.). 6.95x (ISBN 0-912262-60-5); pap. 2.95x (ISBN 0-912262-61-3). Proscenium.
--The Sporting Gun. (Illus.). 240p. 1983. 23.50 (ISBN 0-7153-8324-8). David & Charles.
--Theodore Watts-Dunton: Dunton-Poet, Novelist, Critic. 1973. Repr. of 1904 ed. 17.75 (ISBN 0-8274-1392-0). R West.
--Theodore Watts-Dunton: Poet, Novelist, Critic. LC 72-1509. (English Literature Ser., No. 33). (Illus.). 1972. Repr. of 1904 ed. lib. bdg. 63.95x (ISBN 0-8383-1447-3). Haskell.
--Why Charity? The Case for a Third Sector. LC 83-3363. 181p. 1983. 17.95 (ISBN 0-8039-2003-2). Sage.
Douglas, James & Rice, Terry. Basic Banking Forms. 1984. 75.00 (ISBN 0-88712-131-4). Warren.
Douglas, James, et al. Modern Construction & Development Forms: Cumulative Supplementation. 2nd ed. LC 82-50345. (Modern Real Estate & Mortgage Forms Ser.). 1983. 72.00 (ISBN 0-88262-775-9). Warren.
Douglas, James A & McNee, R. P. Estate & Gift Digest. LC 84-51092. 396p. Date not set. price not set (ISBN 0-88712-106-3). Warren.
Douglas, James A., jt. auth. see Launer, Deborah J.
Douglas, James A., et al. Real Estate Tax Digest: Federal Income, Estate & Gift Taxes. LC 83-51782. 1984. 68.00 (ISBN 0-88712-008-3). Warren.
Douglas, James S. Advanced Guide to Hydroponics. (Illus.). 333p. 1980. 19.95 (ISBN 0-7207-0830-3, Pub. by Michael Joseph). Merrimack Pub Cir.
--Advanced Guide to Hydroponics. (Illus.). 368p. 1985. Repr. 17.95 (ISBN 0-7207-1571-7, Pub. by Michael Joseph). Merrimack Pub Cir.
--Beginner's Guide to Hydroponics: Soilless Gardening. (Illus.). 156p. 1984. 14.95 (ISBN 0-7207-1507-5, Pub. by Michael Joseph). Merrimack Pub Cir.
Douglas, Janet, jt. auth. see Hanson, A. H.
Douglas, Jeannine G. Don't Drown in the Mainstream: Unexpurgated Edition. 66p. (Orig.). 1981. pap. text ed. 4.95 (ISBN 0-9607872-0-8). Vail Pub.
Douglas, Joel M. Issues in Collective Bargaining for Nurses. 17p. 1981. 4.50 (ISBN 0-88737-096-9, 23-1874). Natl League Nurse.
Douglas, Joel M., jt. ed. see Lipsky, David B.
Douglas, John. Bacteriophages. 1975. (Pub. by Chapman & Hall); pap. 11.50 (ISBN 0-412-12640-0, NO.6088). Methuen Inc.
--Milton No Plagiary; or a Detection of the Forgeries. LC 72-187954. Repr. of 1756 ed. lib. bdg. 10.00 (ISBN 0-8414-0508-5). Folcroft.
--Parent Power! LC 77-85881. 1977. pap. 1.75 (ISBN 0-915106-11-6, Enterprise Pubns). Newspaper Ent.
Douglas, John, jt. auth. see Massie, Joseph L.
Douglas, John, jt. auth. see Peterson, Roger T.
Douglas, John, et al. The Strategic Managing of Human Resources. (Management Ser.: I-309). 619p. 1985. text ed. 28.95x (ISBN 0-471-05315-5); student manual 12.95 (ISBN 0-471-89128-2); study guide avail. (ISBN 0-471-81815-1). Wiley.
Douglas, John H. & Grolier Editors. The Future World of Energy. LC 84-10886. (Epcot Center Ser.). (Illus.). 112p. (gr. 7-9). 1984. PLB 11.90 (ISBN 0-531-04881-0). Watts.
Douglas, John S. Story of the Oceans. LC 78-106686. Repr. of 1952 ed. lib. bdg. 26.00x (ISBN 0-8371-3357-2, DOSO). Greenwood.
Douglas, Johnson E. Successful Seed Programs: A Planning & Management Guide. (IADS Development - Oriented Literature Ser.). 353p. 1980. pap. 17.00x (ISBN 0-89158-793-4). Westview.
Douglas, K. Joyce Mansour. (Collection Monographique Rodopi en Litterature Francais Contemporaine: Vol. 3). Orig. Title: Fr. 144p. 1985. pap. text ed. 11.50x (ISBN 90-6203-806-9, Pub. by Rodopi Holland). Humanities.
--A Prose Miscellany. 144p. 1985. text ed. 20.45x (ISBN 0-85635-526-7, Pub. by Carcanet New Pr England). Humanities.
Douglas, Kate. Captive of the Heart. 1982. pap. 2.75 (ISBN 0-380-81125-1, 81125-1). Avon.
Douglas, Kathryn. Amelia. 256p. (Orig.). 1985. pap. 2.95 (ISBN 0-345-31103-5). Ballantine.
--Vivian of Cavendish Square. 416p. 1982. pap. 2.95 (ISBN 0-345-28923-4). Ballantine.
Douglas, Keith. Alamein to Zem Zem. Graham, Desmond, intro. by. (Oxford Paperback Bks). 1979. pap. 7.95x (ISBN 0-19-281267-X). Oxford U Pr.
Douglas, Kenneth, ed. see De Cervantes, Miguel.
Douglas, Kenneth, tr. see Tsogyal, Yeshe.
Douglas, Kenneth, tr. see Wagner, Jean.
Douglas, Kenneth D., jt. auth. see Teglovic, Steve.
Douglas, Koppel. Real Estate Financing Forms Manual. 1985. 64.00 (ISBN 0-88712-271-X). Warren.
Douglas, Lee, Jr. Winning Blackjack Made Easy. LC 82-80758. (Illus.). 52p. (Orig.). 1982. pap. 3.95 (ISBN 0-88083-001-8). Poverty Hill Pr.
Douglas, Lewis W. The Liberal Tradition: A Free People & a Free Economy. LC 77-171382. (FDR & the Era of the New Deal Ser). 136p. 1972. Repr. of 1935 ed. lib. bdg. 19.50 (ISBN 0-306-70376-9). Da Capo.
Douglas, Lillie B. Cape Town to Cairo. LC 64-15394. (Illus.). 348p. 6.95 (ISBN 0-87004-035-9). Caxton.
Douglas, Lloyd. Disputed Passage. 22.95 (ISBN 0-88411-535-6, Pub. by Aeonian Pr). Amereon Ltd.
--Forgive Us Our Trespasses. 19.95 (ISBN 0-88411-536-4, Pub. by Aeonian Pr). Amereon Ltd.
--Magnificent Obsession. 1982. lib. bdg. 18.95x (ISBN 0-89966-387-7). Buccaneer Bks.
--White Banners. 20.95 (ISBN 0-88411-537-2, Pub. by Aeonian Pr). Amereon Ltd.
Douglas, Lloyd C. Big Fisherman. 1948. 15.95 (ISBN 0-395-07630-7). HM.
--Magnificent Obsession. 1938. 17.95 (ISBN 0-395-07634-X). HM.
--Robe. 1942. 12.95 (ISBN 0-395-07635-8). HM.
Douglas, Lloyd V., et al. Teaching Business Subjects. 3rd ed. (Illus.). 1973. ref. ed. 32.95 (ISBN 0-13-891457-5). P-H.
Douglas, Louis H., jt. auth. see Rohrer, Wayne.
Douglas, Marilyn K., jt. auth. see Shinn, Julie A.
Douglas, Marjory S. The Everglades: River of Grass. 1981. pap. 2.75 (ISBN 0-89176-029-6, 6029). Mockingbird Bks.
Douglas, Mark, jt. auth. see Moore, Marcia.
Douglas, Martha C. Go for It! How to Get Your First Good Job. LC 83-70111. 208p. (Orig.). (gr. 9 up). 1983. pap. 5.95 (ISBN 0-89815-090-6). Ten Speed Pr.
Douglas, Martin, jt. auth. see Brandes, Joseph.
Douglas, Mary. Cultural Bias. (RIA Occasional Paper Ser.: No. 35). 1978. pap. text ed. 7.00x (ISBN 0-391-01110-3). Humanities.
--Implicit Meanings: Essays in Anthropology. (Illus.). 1978. pap. 9.95x (ISBN 0-7100-0047-2). Routledge & Kegan.
--In the Active Voice. 280p. 1982. 26.95x (ISBN 0-7100-9065-X). Routledge & Kegan.
--Natural Symbols: Explorations in Cosmology. 1972. pap. 5.95 (ISBN 0-394-71105-X, VG42, Vin). Random.
--Natural Symbols: Explorations in Cosmology. 1982. pap. 5.95 (ISBN 0-394-71105-X). Pantheon.
--Purity & Danger: An Analysis of the Concepts of Pollution & Taboo. 196p. 1984. pap. 6.95 (ISBN 0-7448-0011-0, Ark Paperbks). Routledge & Kegan.
--Risk Acceptability According to the Social Sciences. (Social Research Perspectives: Occasional Reports on Current Topics Ser.). 160p. (Orig.). 1985. pap. text ed. 6.95x (ISBN 0-87154-211-0). Russell Sage.
Douglas, Mary & Isherwood, Baron. The World of Goods: An Anthropologist's Perspective. LC 78-54498. 1979. 12.95x (ISBN 0-465-09228-4). Basic.
--The World of Goods: Towards an Anthropology of Consumption. 1982. pap. 4.95 (ISBN 0-393-30022-6). Norton.
Douglas, Mary & Wildavsky, Aaron. Risk & Culture: An Essay on the Selection of Technological & Environmental Dangers. LC 81-16318. 224p. 1982. 17.95 (ISBN 0-520-04491-6). U of Cal Pr.
--Risk & Culture: An Essay on the Selection of Technological & Enviornmental Dangers. 229p. 1983. pap. 6.95 (ISBN 0-520-05063-0). U of Cal Pr.
Douglas, Mary, ed. Essays in the Sociology of Perception. 288p. (Orig.). 1982. pap. 17.95x (ISBN 0-7100-0881-3). Routledge & Kegan.
--Food in the Social Order: Studies of Food & Festivities in Three American Communities. LC 84-60262. 304p. 1984. 27.50x (ISBN 0-87154-210-2). Russell Sage.
Douglas, Mary & Tipton, Steven M., eds. Religion & America: Spirituality in a Secular Age. LC 82-72500. 256p. 1983. 25.00x (ISBN 0-8070-1106-1, BP 648); pap. 12.95x (ISBN 0-8070-1107-X). Beacon Pr.
Douglas, Mary A. The Secretarial Dental Assistant. LC 75-19522. 1976. pap. 14.00 (ISBN 0-8273-0349-1); instr.'s guide 3.00 (ISBN 0-8273-0350-5). Delmar.
--Secretarial Dental Assistant. 304p. 1981. 17.95 (ISBN 0-442-21860-5). Van Nos Reinhold.
Douglas, Mary L., jt. auth. see Bates, Frank.
Douglas, Mary P. Primary School Library & Its Services. (Manuals for Libraries: No. 12). 104p. (Orig., 4th Printing 1968). 1961. pap. 5.00 (ISBN 92-3-100462-X, U481, UNESCO). Unipub.
--Pupil Assistant in the School Library. LC 57-9534. 68p. 1957. pap. 4.00x (ISBN 0-8389-0050-X). ALA.
Douglas, Michael, jt. auth. see Passafiume, John.
Douglas, Molly. Teen Girl Talk: A Guide to Beauty, Fashion & Health. (Illus.). 1980. pap. 4.95 (ISBN 0-87491-412-4). Acropolis.
Douglas, Nancy E. & Baum, Nathan. Library Research Guide to Psychology. (Library Research Guides Ser.: No. 7). 1984. 19.50 (ISBN 0-87650-156-0); pap. 12.50 (ISBN 0-87650-175-7). Pierian.
Douglas, Nathan, et al. The Defiant Ones: A Screen Adaptation of the Story of "The Long Road". Garrett, George, et al, eds. LC 71-135273. (Film Scripts Ser.). 1971. pap. text ed. 12.95x (ISBN 0-89197-725-2). Irvington.
Douglas, Neil H. Freshwater Fishes of Louisiana. 1974. 12.95 (ISBN 0-87511-028-2). Claitors.
Douglas, Nik. Tibetan Tantric Charms & Amulets: 230 Examples Reproduced from Original Woodblocks. LC 77-70855. 1978. lib. bdg. 18.50x (ISBN 0-88307-646-2). Gannon.
--Tibetan Tantric Charms & Amulets: 230 Examples Reproduced from Original Woodblocks. (Illus.). 22.00 (ISBN 0-8446-5749-2). Peter Smith.
Douglas, Nik & Slinger, Penny. The Pillow Book: The Erotic Sentiment & the Paintings of India, Nepal, China, & Japan. LC 81-9760. (Illus.). 144p. 1981. 29.95 (ISBN 0-89281-012-2). Destiny Bks.
--The Pillow Book: The Erotic Sentiment & the Paintings of India, Nepal, China & Japan. (Illus.). 144p. (Orig.). 1984. pap. 12.95 (ISBN 0-89281-037-8). Destiny Bks.
--The Secret Dakini Oracle. (Illus.). 224p. 1979. pap. 6.95 (ISBN 0-89281-005-X). Destiny Bks.
--Sexual Secrets, the Alchemy of Ecstasy. LC 79-9479. (Illus.). 384p. 1979. 24.95 (ISBN 0-89281-010-6); limited signed ed. 250.00 (ISBN 0-89281-009-2); pap. 14.95 (ISBN 0-89281-011-4). Destiny Bks.
Douglas, Norman. Birds & Beasts of the Greek Anthology. LC 78-173162. Repr. of 1927 ed. 22.00 (ISBN 0-405-08461-7, Blom Pubns). Ayer Co Pubs.
--D. H. Lawrence & Maurice Magnus. LC 72-8663. (Studies in D. H. Lawrence, No. 20). 1973. Repr. of 1924 ed. lib. bdg. 29.95x (ISBN 0-8383-1673-5). Haskell.
--Good-Bye to Western Culture: Some Footnotes on East & West. LC 70-184841. 241p. 1930. Repr. lib. bdg. 22.50x (ISBN 0-8371-6330-7, DOWC). Greenwood.
--In the Beginning. LC 76-144980. 1971. Repr. of 1927 ed. 39.00x (ISBN 0-403-00946-4). Scholarly.
--Late Harvest. LC 75-41082. Repr. of 1946 ed. 16.00 (ISBN 0-404-14717-8). AMS Pr.
--London Street Games. 2nd ed. LC 68-31089. 1968. Repr. of 1931 ed. 30.00x (ISBN 0-8103-3477-1). Gale.
--London Street Games. 2nd rev. & enl. ed. (Folklore & Society Ser). 1969. Repr. of 1931 ed. 14.00 (ISBN 0-384-12445-3). Johnson Repr.
--Looking Back. LC 70-144981. 1971. Repr. of 1934. ed. 49.00x (ISBN 0-403-00795-X). Scholarly.
--Old Calabria. 352p. 1983. lib. bdg. 23.95 (ISBN 0-7126-0112-0). Hippocrene Bks.
--Siren Land. 208p. 1983. 13.95 (ISBN 0-436-13204-4, Pub. by Secker & Warburg UK). David & Charles.
--South Wind. LC 73-144982. 1971. Repr. of 1931 ed. 39.00x (ISBN 0-403-00947-2). Scholarly.
--South Wind. 416p. 1982. pap. 5.95 (ISBN 0-486-24361-3). Dover.
Douglas, P. German Market Survey. 1977. 39.50x (ISBN 0-8464-0450-8). Beekman Pubs.
Douglas, Patricia, ed. see Pacific Northwest Conference on Higher Education, 1975.
Douglas, Paul. The Handbook of Tennis. LC 81-48125. (Illus.). 288p. 1982. 19.95 (ISBN 0-394-52373-3). Knopf.
--Monetary, Credit, & Fiscal Policies. LC 82-48221. (Gold, Money, Inflation & Deflation Ser.). 300p. 1982. lib. bdg. 71.00 (ISBN 0-8240-5268-4). Garland Pub.
Douglas, Paul H. American Apprenticeship & Industrial Education. LC 68-56652. (Columbia University Studies in the Social Sciences: No. 216). Repr. of 1921 ed. 24.50 (ISBN 0-404-51216-X). AMS Pr.
--Ethics in Government. LC 74-138222. 114p. 1972. Repr. of 1952 ed. lib. bdg. 15.00x (ISBN 0-8371-5579-7, DOEG). Greenwood.
--Know America: Its Ills & Cures. 1933. pap. 6.00x (ISBN 0-686-17412-7). R S Barnes.
--Real Wages in the United States, 1890-1926. LC 66-21671. (Illus.). Repr. of 1930 ed. 47.50x (ISBN 0-678-00171-5). Kelley.
--Social Security in the United States. LC 75-136527. 384p. 1972. Repr. of 1936 ed. lib. bdg. 17.50x (ISBN 0-8371-5448-0, DOSS). Greenwood.
--Social Security in the United States: An Analysis & Appraisal of the Federal Social Security Act. LC 71-137164. (Poverty U.S.A. Historical Record Ser). 1971. Repr. of 1936 ed. 21.00 (ISBN 0-405-03102-5). Ayer Co Pubs.
--Social Security in the United States: An Analysis & Appraisal of the Federal Social Security Act. 2nd ed. LC 70-167847. (FDR & the Era of the New Deal). 1971. Repr. of 1939 ed. lib. bdg. 55.00 (ISBN 0-306-70323-8). Da Capo.
--Theory of Wages. LC 64-22237. Repr. of 1934 ed. 45.00x (ISBN 0-678-00062-X). Kelley.
Douglas, Paul H. & Director, Aaron. The Problem of Unemployment. LC 75-17217. (Social Problems & Social Policy Ser.). (Illus.). 1976. Repr. of 1931 ed. 38.50x (ISBN 0-405-07488-3). Ayer Co Pubs.
Douglas, Paul H., et al. The Worker in Modern Economic Society. LC 70-89730. (American Labor, from Conspiracy to Collective Bargaining Ser., No. 1). 929p. 1969. Repr. of 1923 ed. 42.00 (ISBN 0-405-02117-8). Ayer Co Pubs.
Douglas, Peter & Helm, Clive. The Ideal Home Book of Interiors. (Illus.). 128p. 1985. 6.98 (ISBN 0-317-20552-8, Pub. by New Orchard England). Sterling.
Douglas, Philip. Saint of Philadelphia: The Life of Bishop John Neumann. 1977. 7.95 (ISBN 0-911218-07-6); pap. 3.95 (ISBN 0-911218-08-4). Ravengate Pr.
Douglas, Philip A. & Stroud, Richard H., eds. A Symposium on the Biological Significance of Estuaries. 1971. 4.00 (ISBN 0-686-21854-X). Sport Fishing.
Douglas, R. Confucianism & Taoism. 59.95 (ISBN 0-87968-930-7). Gordon Pr.
Douglas, R. Alan. John Prince, Seventeen Ninety-Six to Eighteen Seventy: A Collection of Documents. (Champlain Society Ontario Ser.). 350p. 1980. 25.00x (ISBN 0-8020-2378-9). U of Toronto Pr.
Douglas, R. G. Banach Algebra Techniques in the Theory of Toeplitz Operators. LC 73-1021. (CBMS Regional Conference Ser. in Mathematics: No. 15). 53p. 1980. pap. 15.00 (ISBN 0-8218-1665-9, CBMS-15). Am Math.
Douglas, R. G., ed. see Kurpel, N. S.
Douglas, R. G., jt. auth. see Choppin, P. W.
Douglas, R. Gordon, jt. auth. see Reese, Richard E.
Douglas, R. Gordon, Jr., jt. auth. see Mandell, Gerald L.
Douglas, R. W. & Ellis, Bryan, eds. Amorphous Materials: Papers Presented to the Third International Conference on the Physics of Non-Crystalline Solids, Sheffield University, September 1970. LC 77-162326. pap. 142.00 (ISBN 0-317-08992-7, 2016152). Bks Demand UMI.
Douglas, Randall C., III. The Joy of Stuffed Preppies. 1982. pap. 3.95 (ISBN 0-03-061596-8, Owl Bks). HR&W.
Douglas, Richard. The Rig. 1982. 15.00x (ISBN 0-7274-0258-7, Pub. by Severn Hse). State Mutual Bk.
Douglas, Robert B., ed. & tr. see De Pontgibaud, Chevalier.
Douglas, Robert C. Freedom in Christ. Thomas, J. D., ed. LC 72-140290. (Twentieth Century Sermons Ser). 1970. 11.95 (ISBN 0-89112-305-9). Bibl Res Pr.
--Selected Indices of Industrial Characteristics for U. S. SMSA. (Discussion Paper Ser.: No. 20). 1967. pap. 5.75 (ISBN 0-686-32189-8). Regional Sci Res Inst.
Douglas, Robert K. Li-Hung-Chang. (Studies in Chinese History & Civilization). 1977. Repr. of 1895 ed. 19.75 (ISBN 0-89093-110-0). U Pubns Amer.
Douglas, Robert W. John Paul II: The Pilgrim Pope. LC 79-24930. (Picture-Story Biographies Ser.). (Illus.). 32p. (gr. k up). 1980. PLB 10.60 (ISBN 0-516-03563-0). Childrens.
Douglas, Robin, jt. auth. see Payne, Chris.
Douglas, Ronald G. Banach Algebra Techniques in Operator Theory. (Pure & Applied Mathematics Ser). 1972. 44.00 (ISBN 0-12-221350-5). Acad Pr.
--C-Algebra Extensions & K-Homology. LC 80-424. (Annals of Mathematics Studies: No. 95). (Illus.). 87p. 1980. 16.50x (ISBN 0-691-08265-0); pap. 7.95x (ISBN 0-691-08266-9). Princeton U Pr.
Douglas, Ronald G. & Schochet, Claude, eds. Operator Algebras & K-Theory. LC 82-4094. (Contemporary Mathematics: Vol. 10). 204p. 1982. pap. 15.00 (ISBN 0-8218-5011-3, CONM-10). Am Math.
Douglas, Ronald M. The Scots Book: A Miscellany of Poems, Etc. 1979. Repr. of 1935 ed. PLB 45.00 (ISBN 0-8495-1109-7). Arden Lib.
Douglas, Rose A. The V. A. Syndrome. 1981. 8.95 (ISBN 0-8062-1734-0). Carlton.
Douglas, Roy. Advent of War, 1939-1940. LC 78-12266. 1979. 24.95 (ISBN 0-312-00650-0). St Martin.
--From War to Cold War: 1942-48. 1981. 26.00x (ISBN 0-312-30862-0). St Martin.
--The History of the Liberal Party: 1895-1970. LC 70-169814. 331p. 1971. 25.00 (ISBN 0-8386-1056-0). Fairleigh Dickinson.
--In the Year of Munich. LC 77-82823. (Illus.). 1978. 25.00 (ISBN 0-312-41179-0). St Martin.
--New Alliances, Nineteen Forty to Forty-One. LC 81-9283. 1982. 22.50 (ISBN 0-312-56481-3). St Martin.
--Nineteen Thirty-Nine: A Retrospect Forty Years after. 107p. 1983. 19.50 (ISBN 0-208-02020-9, Archon Bks). Shoe String.
Douglas, S. W. & Williamson, H. D. Principles of Veterinary Radiography. 3rd ed. (Illus.). 304p. 1980. 37.50 (ISBN 0-7216-0786-1, Pub. by Bailliere-Tindall). Saunders.
--Veterinary Radiological Interpretation. (Illus.). 303p. 1970. text ed. 17.00 (ISBN 0-8121-0300-9). Lea & Febiger.
Douglas, Sara, ed. see Sa'di of Shiraz.
Douglas, Shawhan. Physics with the Computer. (Orig.). 1981. tchr's ed. 24.95 (ISBN 0-87567-037-7); student's ed. 14.95; incl. diskettes 150.00. Entelek.
--Physics with the Computer: Teacher's Edition. 288p. (Orig.). 1981. 24.95 (ISBN 0-87567-037-7). Entelek.
Douglas, Shelia. The Uncertain Heart. (Harlequin Romance Ser.). 1982. pap. 1.75 (ISBN 0-373-02517-3). Harlequin Bks.
Douglas, Stephen, jt. auth. see Lincoln, Abraham.
Douglas, Stephen A. Political Socialization & Student Activism in Indonesia. LC 73-94394. (Studies in Social Science, Vol. 57). 234p. 1970. 17.50x (ISBN 0-252-00074-9). U of Ill Pr.
Douglas, Sue. Earth Music. 64p. 1981. 8.95 (ISBN 0-9607090-0-2); pap. 4.95 (ISBN 0-9607090-1-0). D&S Pubns.
Douglas, Susan P. & Craig, C. Samuel. International Marketing Research. 384p. 1983. 28.95 (ISBN 0-13-473140-9). P-H.

Douglas, Thomas. The Gehlen Portfolio. (Orig.). 1981. pap. 2.25 (ISBN 0-505-51654-3, Pub. by Tower Bks). Dorchester Pub Co.
Douglas, Thorne. Calhoon. 1978. pap. 1.75 (ISBN 0-449-13935-2, GM). Fawcett.
--Killraine. 1979. pap. 1.50 (ISBN 0-449-14227-2, GM). Fawcett.
--The Mustang Men. 192p. 1981. pap. 1.75 (ISBN 0-449-13918-2, GM). Fawcett.
Douglas, Tom. Basic Groupwork. LC 78-61491. 208p. 1978. text ed. 22.50 (ISBN 0-8236-0450-0). Intl Univs Pr.
--Group Processes in Social Work: A Theoretical Synthesis. LC 78-8401. 236p. 1979. 48.95x (ISBN 0-471-99676-9, Pub. by Wiley-Interscience). Wiley.
--Groups: Understanding People Gathered Together. LC 83-406. 252p. 1983. 22.00 (ISBN 0-422-77660-2, NO.3856, Pub. by Tavistock); pap. 9.95 (ISBN 0-422-77670-X, NO. 3857). Methuen Inc.
--Groupwork Practice. LC 76-1316. 217p. 1976. 25.00 (ISBN 0-8236-2270-3). Intl Univs Pr.
Douglas, Virginia. The Roadrunner(and His Cuckoo Cousin) 48p. 1984. 9.95 (ISBN 0-87961-146-4); pap. 3.95 (ISBN 0-87961-147-2). Naturegraph.
Douglas, W. B. Carpentry & Joinery. 22.50 (ISBN 0-87559-109-4). Shalom.
Douglas, W. C. Pastoral Elegy in English. LC 77-1729. 1934. lib. bdg. 9.50 (ISBN 0-8414-3820-X). Folcroft.
Douglas, W. H. Illustrated Topical Dictionary of the Western Desert Language: 1959. 2nd rev. ed. (AIAS Research Regional Studies: No. 11). 1977. pap. text ed. 4.25x (ISBN 0-85575-061-8). Humanities.
Douglas, Walter B. Manuel Lisa. Nasatir, Abraham P., ed. (Illus.). 1964. Repr. of 1911 ed. 12.50 (ISBN 0-87266-006-0). Argosy.
Douglas, Wilfrid H. Aboriginal Languages of the Southwest of Australia. 2nd ed. (Research & Regional Studies: No. 9). 1976. pap. text ed. 7.75x (ISBN 0-85575-050-2). Humanities.
Douglas, William D. An Almanac of Liberty. LC 73-10752. 409p. 1973. Repr. of 1954 ed. lib. bdg. 19.75x (ISBN 0-8371-7019-2, DOAL). Greenwood.
Douglas, William L., et al. Garden Design: History, Principles, Elements, Practice. LC 84-1319. 224p. 1984. 35.00 (ISBN 0-671-47993-8). S&S.
Douglas, William O. America Challenged. 1960. 16.50x (ISBN 0-691-09200-1). Princeton U Pr.
--Being an American. facsimile ed. LC 77-134071. (Essay Index Reprint Ser). Repr. of 1948 ed. 16.00 (ISBN 0-8369-2223-9). Ayer Co Pubs.
--The Court Years: Nineteen Thirty-Nine to Nineteen Seventy-Five. LC 81-40191. (Illus.). 464p. 1981. pap. 5.95 (ISBN 0-394-74902-2, Vin). Random.
--Court Years, Nineteen Thirty-Nine to Nineteen Seventy-Five: The Autobiography of William O. Douglas. LC 80-5297. (Illus.). 1980. 16.95 (ISBN 0-394-49240-4). Random.
--Douglas of the Supreme Court: A Selection of His Opinions. Countryman, Vern, ed. LC 73-719. 401p. 1973. Repr. of 1959 ed. lib. bdg. 24.25x (ISBN 0-8371-6790-6, DODS). Greenwood.
--Go East, Young Man. 1974. 10.00 (ISBN 0-394-48834-2). Random.
--Go East, Young Man: The Early Years. LC 81-4196. (Illus.). 544p. pap. 7.95 (ISBN 0-394-71165-3, Vin). Random.
--A Living Bill of a Rights. 72p. pap. 0.75 (ISBN 0-686-95045-3). ADL.
--Of Men & Mountains. (Illus.). 1981. pap. 7.95 (ISBN 0-915112-15-9). Seattle Bk.
--Of Men & Mountains. 1981. 7.95 (ISBN 0-915112-15-9). Superior Pub.
--The Right of the People. LC 80-19135. 238p. 1980. Repr. of 1958 ed. lib. bdg. 24.75x (ISBN 0-313-22640-7, DORP). Greenwood.
--Supreme Court & the Bicentennial. LC 77-77835. (The Leverton Lecture Ser: No. 4). 99p. 1978. 12.00 (ISBN 0-8386-2064-7). Fairleigh Dickinson.
--The Three Hundred Year War: A Chronicle of Ecological Disease. LC 72-2713. 1972. 5.95 (ISBN 0-394-47224-1). Random.
Douglas, William O., jt. auth. see UCLA Law Review.
Douglas, William O., jt. ed. see Weinberg, Arthur.
Douglas, William S., ed. see Lockhart, John G.
Douglas-Hamilton, James. The Air Battle for Malta. 212p. 1981. 40.00x (ISBN 0-906391-20-2, Pub. by Mainstream). State Mutual Bk.
--Motive For a Mission: The Story Behind Rudolf Hess' Flight to Britain. (Illus.). 330p. 1982. 15.95 (ISBN 0-906391-05-9, Pub. by Mainstream Pub Scotland). Presidio Pr.
Douglas-Home, William & Muggeridge, Malcolm. P. G. Wodehouse: Three Talks & a Few Words at a Festive Occasion. (Wodehouse Monograph: No. 4). 48p. (Orig.). 1983. pap. 16.50 limited ed. (ISBN 0-87008-103-9). Heineman.
Douglas-Irving, Helen. Extracts Relating to Medieval Markets & Fairs in England. 1978. Repr. of 1912 ed. lib. bdg. 15.00 (ISBN 0-8274-4184-3). R West.
Douglas-Morris, K. J., jt. auth. see Perkins, Roger.
Douglass, jt. auth. see Gillings.
Douglass, A. E. Climatic Cycle & Tree Growth, 3 vols. in one. (Vols. 1 & 2, A Study of the Annual Rings of Trees in Relation to Climate & Solar Activity; Vol. 3, A Study of Cycles). 1971. 52.50 (ISBN 3-7682-0720-X). Lubrecht & Cramer.
Douglass, Amanda H. Charlotte. 1978. pap. 1.95 (ISBN 0-505-51271-8, Pub. by Tower Bks). Dorchester Pub Co.
--Christabel. 1978. pap. 2.25 (ISBN 0-505-51310-2, Pub. by Tower Bks). Dorchester Pub Co.
--The Heavens Blaze Forth. (Inflation Fighters Ser.). 192p. 1982. pap. write for info. (ISBN 0-8439-1136-0, Leisure Bks). Dorchester Pub Co.
--The Heavens Blaze Forth. 1978. pap. 1.75 (ISBN 0-505-51252-1, Pub. by Tower Bks). Dorchester Pub Co.
--Jamaica. 1977. pap. 1.75 (ISBN 0-8439-0492-5, Leisure Bks). Dorchester Pub Co.
--Jamaica. (Inflation Fighter Ser.). 208p. 1982. pap. 1.50 (ISBN 0-8439-1147-6, Leisure Bks). Dorchester Pub Co.
--McCormack's Mountain. 1980. pap. 2.25 (ISBN 0-8439-0835-1, Pub. by Nordon Pubns). Dorchester Pub Co.
--Sugar Hill. 1979. pap. 2.25 (ISBN 0-505-51412-5, Pub. by Tower Bks). Dorchester Pub Co.
Douglass, Barbara. The Chocolate Chip Cookie Contest. (Illus.). 32p. (gr. k-3). 1985. PLB 12.88 (ISBN 0-688-04044-6); 13.00 (ISBN 0-688-04043-8). Lothrop.
--Good As New. LC 80-21406. (Illus.). 32p. (ps-1). 1982. 11.75 (ISBN 0-688-41983-6); PLB 11.88 (ISBN 0-688-51983-0). Lothrop.
--THe Great Town & Country Bicycle Balloon Chase. LC 83-14877. (Illus.). 32p. (gr. k-3). 1984. 11.00 (ISBN 0-688-02231-6); PLB 10.08 (ISBN 0-688-02232-4). Lothrop.
--Sizzle Wheels. LC 80-39750. (Illus.). 174p. (gr. 3-6). 1981. 9.95 (ISBN 0-664-32680-3). Westminster.
--Skateboard Scramble. LC 78-12480. (Illus.). 92p. (gr. 3-6). 1979. 8.95 (ISBN 0-664-32641-2). Westminster.
Douglass, Bruce P. Applications Programming in IBM BASIC. LC 84-45166. 390p. (Orig.). 1985. pap. 29.95 (ISBN 0-8019-7622-7). Chilton.
--BASIC Applications Programming for the IBM PC. LC 84-45166. 250p. (Orig.). 1985. pap. 17.95 (ISBN 0-8019-7524-7). Chilton.
--Numerical BASIC. LC 83-50711. 224p. 1983. pap. text ed. 12.95 (ISBN 0-672-22048-2, 22048). Sams.
--Numerical BASIC. 1984. write for info. Bobbs.
Douglass, D. H., ed. Superconductivity in D-& F-Band Metals. LC 76-46953. 648p. 1976. 95.00x (ISBN 0-306-30994-7, Plenum Pr). Plenum Pub.
Douglass, D. H., ed. see AIP Conference, Univ. of Rochester, 1971.
Douglass, D. L. The Metallurgy of Zirconium. (Illus.). 470p. (Orig.). 1972. pap. 32.50 (ISBN 92-0-159071-7, IAER/S71, IAEA). Unipub.
Douglass, D. L. & Kunz, F. W., eds. Columbium Metallurgy: Proceedings. LC 61-9442. (Metallurgy Society Conferences Ser.: Vol. 10). pap. 160.00 (ISBN 0-317-10234-6, 2000673). Bks Demand UMI.
Douglass, David & Krieger, Joel. A Miner's Life. 116p. (Orig.). 1983. pap. 9.95x (ISBN 0-7100-9473-6). Routledge & Kegan.
Douglass, David H., ed. see Braginsky, V. B. & Manukin, A. B.
Douglass, Donna N. Choice & Compromise: A Woman's Guide to Balancing Family & Career. 208p. (Orig.). 1983. 14.95 (ISBN 0-8144-5746-0); pap. 8.95 (ISBN 0-8144-7604-X). AMACOM.
Douglass, Donna N., jt. auth. see Douglass, Merrill E.
Douglass, E. P. Rebels & Democrats. LC 77-160853. (Era of the American Revolution Ser.). 368p. 1971. Repr. of 1955 ed. 45.00 (ISBN 0-306-70402-1). Da Capo.
Douglass, Fenner. Language of the Classical French Organ: A Musical Tradition Before 1800. LC 72-81415. (Studies in the History of Music Ser.: No. 5). (Illus.). 1969. 27.00x (ISBN 0-300-01117-2). Yale U Pr.
Douglass, Frederick. A Black Diplomat in Haiti: The Diplomatic Correspondence of U.S. Minister Frederick Douglass from Haiti, 1889-1891, 2 vols. Brown, Norma, ed. 1977. lib. bdg. 44.95x set (ISBN 0-89712-049-3). Documentary Pubns.
--The Frederick Douglass Papers: Series 1: Speeches, Debates, & Interviews Vol. I: 1841-1846. Blassingame, John W., ed. 1979. 52.00x (ISBN 0-300-02246-8). Yale U Pr.
--The Frederick Douglass Papers, Series 1: Speeches, Debates, & Interviews, Vol. 2, 1847-54. Blassingame, John W., ed. LC 78-16687. 608p. 1982. text ed. 52.00 (ISBN 0-300-02661-7). Yale U Pr.
--Frederick Douglass: The Narrative & Selected Writings. 1981. pap. 4.95 (Mod LibC). Modern Lib.
--Frederick Douglass: The Narrative & Selected Writings. Meyer, Michael, ed. (Modern Library College Editions). 448p. 1983. pap. text ed. 4.95 (ISBN 0-394-32981-3, RanC). Random.
--Life & Times. 16.25 (ISBN 0-8446-1992-2). Peter Smith.
--Life & Times of Frederick Douglass. 514p. 1984. 20.00 (ISBN 0-8065-0873-6); pap. 8.95 (ISBN 0-8065-0865-5). Citadel Pr.
--Life & Times of Frederick Douglass: The Complete Autobiography. LC 62-12834. 640p. 1962. pap. 9.95 (ISBN 0-02-002350-2, Collier). Macmillan.
--The Life & Writings of Frederick Douglass, 5 vols. Foner, Philip S., ed. Incl. Vol. 1. Early Years. 448p; Vol. 2. Pre-Civil War Decade. 576p; Vol. 3. The Civil War. 448p; Vol. 4. Reconstruction & After. 574p; Vol. 5. Supplementary Volume, 1844-1860. 564p. LC 50-7654. 1975. Set. 60.00 (ISBN 0-7178-0119-5); Set. pap. 30.00 (ISBN 0-7178-0118-7). Intl Pubs Co.
--The Life & Writings of Frederick Douglass: Supplementary Volume: 1844-1860, Vol. 5. Foner, Philip S., ed. 1975. pap. 5.95 (ISBN 0-7178-0454-2). Intl Pubs Co.
--Mind & Heart of Frederick Douglass: Excerpts from Speeches of the Great Negro Orator. Ritchie, Barbara, ed. LC 68-13587. (gr. 7 up). 1968. 11.49i (ISBN 0-690-54206-2). Crowell Jr Bks.
--My Bondage & My Freedom. (Black Rediscovery Ser). 1969. pap. 6.95 (ISBN 0-486-22457-0). Dover.
--My Bondage & My Freedom. (Ebony Classic Ser). 7.95 (ISBN 0-87485-034-7). Johnson Chi.
--My Bondage & My Freedom. 14.50 (ISBN 0-8446-0588-3). Peter Smith.
--Narrative of the Life of Frederick Douglass, An American Slave. 128p. (YA) (RL 7). 1968. pap. 2.25 (ISBN 0-451-13448-6, Sig). NAL.
--Narrative of the Life of Frederick Douglass, an American Slave. Baker, Houston A., Jr., ed. (Penguin American Library). 160p. 1982. pap. 3.95 (ISBN 0-14-039012-X). Penguin.
--Narrative of the Life of Frederick Douglass, an American Slave, Written by Himself. Quarles, Benjamin, ed. LC 59-11516. (The John Harvard Library). (Illus.). 1960. 10.00x (ISBN 0-674-60100-9); pap. 3.95x (ISBN 0-674-60101-7). Harvard U Pr.
--Narrative of the Life of Frederick Douglass. pap. 3.50 (ISBN 0-385-00705-1, Anch). Doubleday.
Douglass, Gladys. Oh Grandma, You're Kidding. (Illus.). 110p. (Orig.). 1983. pap. 6.95 (ISBN 0-934904-00-6). J & L Lee.
Douglass, Gordon K., ed. Agricultural Sustainability in a Changing World Order. (Westview Special Studies in Agriculture Science & Policy). 280p. 1983. hardcover 26.50x (ISBN 0-86531-669-4). Westview.
Douglass, H. E. Hello Neighbor. (Outreach Ser.). 16p. 1983. pap. 0.99 (ISBN 0-8163-0523-4). Pacific Pr Pub Assn.
Douglass, Harl R. Modern Methods in High School Teaching. 544p. 1981. Repr. lib. bdg. 25.00 (ISBN 0-8495-1061-9). Arden Lib.
Douglass, Harl R., jt. auth. see Gruhn, William.
Douglass, Harlan P. Little Town: Especially in Its Rural Relationships. LC 75-112553. (Rise of Urban America). (Illus.). 1970. Repr. of 1919 ed. 22.00 (ISBN 0-405-02448-7). Ayer Co Pubs.
--The Little Town; Especially in Its Rural Relationships. (Select Bibliographies Reprint Ser). Repr. of 1919 ed. 22.00 (ISBN 0-8369-6643-0). Ayer Co Pubs.
--St. Louis Church Survey: A Religious Investigation with a Social Background. LC 77-112540. (Rise of Urban America). (Illus.). 1970. Repr. of 1924 ed. 21.00 (ISBN 0-405-02449-5). Ayer Co Pubs.
--Suburban Trend. LC 73-124478. (Rise of Urban America). 1970. Repr. of 1925 ed. 23.50 (ISBN 0-405-02450-9). Ayer Co Pubs.
--The Suburban Trend. LC 25-8827. (American Studies). 1970. Repr. of 1925 ed. 25.00 (ISBN 0-384-12465-8). Johnson Repr.
Douglass, Herb, jt. auth. see Walton, Lew.
Douglass, Herbert. Faith-Saying Yes to God. (Waymark Ser.). 1978. pap. 5.95 (ISBN 0-8127-0173-9). Review & Herald.
--Parable of the Hurricane. (Uplook Ser.). 1980. pap. 0.79 (ISBN 0-8163-0356-8). Pacific Pr Pub Assn.
Douglass, J. H., et al. Units in Woodworking. LC 79-8737. (Industrial Arts Ser.). 320p. 1981. text ed. 18.20 (ISBN 0-8273-1332-2); pap. text ed. 14.40 (ISBN 0-8273-1333-0); comprehensive tests 2.80 (ISBN 0-8273-1335-7); instr's guide 2.85 (ISBN 0-8273-1334-9). Delmar.
Douglass, J. Harvey. Projects in Wood Furniture. rev. ed. LC 67-21721. (Illus.). (gr. 7 up). 1967. text ed. 16.64 (ISBN 0-87345-027-2). McKnight.
Douglass, James W. Lightning East to West: Jesus, Gandhi & the Nuclear Age. 112p. 1983. pap. 6.95 (ISBN 0-8245-0587-5). Crossroad NY.
Douglass, Joseph D., jt. auth. see Livingstone, Neil C.
Douglass, Joseph D., Jr. & Hoeber, Amoretta M. Conventional War & Escalation: The Soviet View. LC 81-3265. (NSIC Strategy Paper Ser.: No. 37). 80p. 1981. pap. text ed. 5.95x (ISBN 0-8448-1390-7). Crane-Russak Co.
--Soviet Strategy for Nuclear War. Staar, Richard F., ed. LC 79-1787. (Publications 208 Ser.). 1979. pap. 8.95x (ISBN 0-8179-7082-7). Hoover Inst Pr.
Douglass, Laura M. The Effective Nurse: Leader & Manager. 2nd ed. LC 83-6796. (Illus.). 288p. 1984. pap. text ed. 14.95 (ISBN 0-8016-1449-X). Mosby.
--Review of Leadership in Nursing. 2nd ed. LC 76-41258. 174p. 1977. pap. text ed. 12.95 (ISBN 0-8016-1442-2). Mosby.
Douglass, Leslie S. Women in Business: How to Make Yourself Marketable. (Illus.). 192p. 1980. 10.95 (ISBN 0-13-962019-2, Spec); pap. 4.95 (ISBN 0-13-962001-X). P-H.
Douglass, Malcolm P., ed. Reading Reading: Fiftieth Anniversary Perspectives. (Claremont Reading Conference Yearbook Ser.). 241p. 1983. pap. 12.00 (ISBN 0-941742-01-6). Claremont Grad.
--Writing & Reading in a Balanced Curriculum. (Claremont Reading Conference Yearbook Ser.). 222p. (Orig.). 1982. pap. 11.00 (ISBN 0-941742-00-8). Claremont Grad.
Douglass, Melvin I. Black Winners: History of Springarm Medalists, 1915-1983. 160p. 1984. 7.95 (ISBN 0-912444-31-2). Gaus.
Douglass, Merrill E. & Douglass, Donna N. Manage Your Time, Manage Your Work, Manage Yourself. LC 79-55062. 278p. 1985. pap. 8.95 (ISBN 0-8144-7632-5). Amacom.
--Mangage Your Time, Manage Your Work, Manage Yourself. 304p. 1980. 16.95 (ISBN 0-8144-5597-2). AMACOM.
Douglass, Merrill E. & Goodwin, Phillip H. Successful Time Management for Hospital Administrators. LC 79-55063. pap. 37.50 (ISBN 0-317-26716-7, 2023519). Bks Demand UMI.
Douglass, R. C. Steps to Pass from Individual to Cosmic Consciousness, 2 vols. (Illus.). 350p. 1984. Set. 225.85 (ISBN 0-89920-102-4). Am Inst Psych.
Douglass, Ralph. Calligraphic Lettering. 3rd ed. 112p. 1975. 12.95 (ISBN 0-8230-0551-8); write for info. spiral ed. Watson-Guptill.
Douglass, Robert W. Forest Recreation. 3rd. ed. (Illus.). 336p. 1982. 22.50 (ISBN 0-08-028804-9, K110). Pergamon.
Douglass, Stephen B. Managing Yourself. LC 78-70647. 1978. pap. 4.95 (ISBN 0-918956-49-8). Campus Crusade.
Douglass, Stephen B. & Roddy, Lee. Making the Most of Your Mind. 250p. (Orig.). 1982. pap. 6.95 (ISBN 0-86605-109-0). Heres Life.
Douglass, Steve. Managing Yourself Leaders Guide. 150p. (Orig.). 1981. pap. 6.95 (ISBN 0-918956-69-2). Campus Crusade.
Douglass, Steve, et al. Ministry of Management Workbook. rev. ed. 1981. pap. text ed. 16.95 (ISBN 0-686-73039-9). Campus Crusade.
Douglass, Vonda & Baer, Richard. CAMS Expressive Language Program. Casto, Glendon, ed. LC 79-88181. (Curriculum & Monitoring System Ser.). 80p. (For use with early-childhood handicapped). 1979. pap. text ed. 11.90 (ISBN 0-8027-9063-1). Walker & Co.
Douglass, William. Emigration in a South Italian Town: An Anthropological History. 344p. 1984. text ed. 32.00 (ISBN 0-8135-0984-X). Rutgers U Pr.
--Sermons Preached in the African Protestant Episcopal Church of St. Thomas' Philadelphia. facs. ed. LC 79-157366. (Black Heritage Library Collection Ser). 1854. 20.00 (ISBN 0-8369-8804-3). Ayer Co Pubs.
--Summary, Historical & Political, of the First Planting, Progressive Improvements, & Present State of the British Settlements in North-America. LC 74-141084. (Research Library of Colonial Americana). 1971. Repr. of 1749 ed. 79.50 (ISBN 0-405-03279-X). Ayer Co Pubs.
Douglass, William A. Basque Sheepherders of the American West: A Photodocumentary. (Basque Book Ser.). (Illus.). 184p. 1985. 19.50 (ISBN 0-87417-089-3). U of Nev Pr.
Douglass, William A. & Bilbao, Jon. Amerikanuak: Basques in the New World. LC 75-30830. (Basque Bk. Ser.). (Illus.). xiv, 519p. 1975. 16.00 (ISBN 0-87417-043-5). U of Nev Pr.
Douglass, William A., jt. auth. see Aceves, Joseph.
Douglass, William A. & Etulain, Richard W., eds. Basque Americans: A Guide to Information Sources. (Ethnic Studies Information Guide Ser.: Vol. 6). 175p. 1981. 60.00x (ISBN 0-8103-1469-X). Gale.
Douglass, William A., as told to see Paris, Beltran.
Douglass, William C., jt. auth. see Walker, Morton.
Douglass, William S. Echalar & Murelaga: Opportunity & Rural Exodus in Two Spanish Basque Villages. LC 74-28932. 200p. 1975. 27.50 (ISBN 0-312-22540-7). St Martin.
Douglass, Winsome. Decorative Stuffed Toys for the Needle-Worker. (Sewing & Related Miscellaneous Ser.). 224p. 1984. pap. 6.95 (ISBN 0-486-24638-8). Dover.
--Decorative Stuffed Toys for the Needleworker. Date not set. 15.25 (ISBN 0-8446-6137-6). Peter Smith.
Douglas-Wilson, J. & McLachlan, Gordon, eds. Health Service Prospects: An International Survey. 358p. 1973. 35.00x (ISBN 0-686-96986-3, Pub. by Nuffield England). State Mutual Bk.
Douglas-Young, John. Complete Guide to Electronic Test Equipment & Troubleshooting Techniques. 256p. cancelled 17.95 (ISBN 0-13-160085-0, Parker). P-H.
--Complete Guide to Reading Schematic Drawings. 2nd ed. 303p. 1972. pap. 8.95 (ISBN 0-13-160424-4, Reward). P-H.
--Illustrated Encyclopedic Dictionary of Electronics. LC 80-23639. 512p. 1981. 39.95 (ISBN 0-13-450791-6, Parker). P-H.
--Illustrated Encyclopedic Dictionary of Electronic Circuits. LC 82-23067. 444p. 1983. 29.95 (ISBN 0-13-450734-7). P-H.
--Practical Oscilloscope Handbook. (Illus.). 1979. 14.95 (ISBN 0-13-693549-4, Parker). P-H.

Dow, Frances. Radicalism in the English Revolution. (Historical Association Studies). 112p. 1985. pap. 6.95 (ISBN 0-631-13943-5). Basil Blackwell.
Dow, George. The Great Central Eighteen Sixty Four to Eighteen Ninety Nine. 29.50x (ISBN 0-392-15442-0, SpS). Sportshelf.
Dow, George F. Arts & Crafts in New England. 1704-1775. LC 67-2035. (Architecture & Decorative Art Ser). (Illus.). 1967. Repr. of 1927 ed. lib. bdg. 39.50 (ISBN 0-306-70955-4). Da Capo.
--Domestic Life in New England in the Seventeenth Century. LC 72-83087. (Illus.). Repr. of 1925 ed. 17.00 (ISBN 0-405-08462-5, Blom Pubns). Ayer Co Pubs.
--Everyday Life in the Massachusetts Bay Colony. LC 67-13326. (Illus.). Repr. of 1935 ed. 22.00 (ISBN 0-405-08463-3, Blom Pubns). Ayer Co Pubs.
--Slave Ships & Slaving. LC 68-57116. (Illus.). 399p. 1968. 10.00 (ISBN 0-87033-112-4). Cornell Maritime.
--Slave Ships & Slaving. LC 71-109323. Repr. of 1927 ed. 20.00x (ISBN 0-8371-3589-3, DSL&). Greenwood.
--Slave Ships & Slaving. LC 76-92426. 1927. 39.00 (ISBN 0-403-00159-5). Scholarly.
--Whale Ships & Whaling. (Illus.). 1967. Repr. of 1925 ed. 35.00 (ISBN 0-87266-007-9). Argosy.
--Whale Ships & Whaling: A Pictorial History. (Antiques Ser.: Transportation). 288p. 1985. pap. 8.95 (ISBN 0-486-24808-9). Dover.
Dow, George F. & Edmonds, John H. Pirates of the New England Coast 1630-1730. (Illus.). 1968. Repr. of 1923 ed. 27.50 (ISBN 0-87266-008-7). Argosy.
Dow, Gwyneth. Learning to Teach: Teaching to Learn. (Education Bks.). 1985. pap. 10.95x (ISBN 0-7102-0542-2). Routledge & Kegan.
Dow, Gwyneth, ed. Teacher Learning. (Routledge Education Bks.). 110p. 1982. pap. 12.95x (ISBN 0-7100-9020-X). Routledge & Kegan.
Dow, Gwyneth M. Samuel Terry: The Botany Bay Rothschild. (Illus.). 256p. 1975. 23.00x (ISBN 0-424-06820-6, Pub. by Sydney U Pr). Intl Spec Bk.
Dow, J. Kamal. Colombia's Foreign Trade & Economic Integration in Latin America. LC 71-631067. (University of Florida Latin American Monographs: No. 9). 1971. 9.00 (ISBN 0-8130-0308-3). U Presses Fla.
Dow, J. W., jt. auth. see Chasen, S. H.
Dow, James E. A Prussian Liberal: The Life of Eduard Von Simson. LC 81-40312. 226p. (Orig.). 1982. lib. bdg. 24.00 (ISBN 0-8191-1984-9); pap. text ed. 11.75 (ISBN 0-8191-1985-7). U Pr of Amer.
Dow, James R. & Lixfeld, Hannjost, eds. German Volkskunde: A Decade of Theoretical Confrontation, Debate, & Reorientation (1967-1977) Dow, James R. & Lixfeld, Hannjost, trs. from Ger. LC 84-43175. (Folklore Studies in Translation). (Illus.). 448p. 1985. 35.00 (ISBN 0-253-32577-3). Ind U Pr.
Dow, James R., tr. see Dow, James R. & Lixfeld, Hannjost.
Dow, John G. Selections from the Poems of Robert Burns. 1979. Repr. of 1898 ed. lib. bdg. 20.00 (ISBN 0-8495-1111-9). Arden Lib.
Dow Jones & Company Staff. The Dow Jones News Retrieval Membership Kit. 330p. 1985. 29.95 (ISBN 0-87128-650-5). Dow Jones-Irwin.
Dow, Mary-Lou M., jt. auth. see Maynard, Mary.
Dow, Michael & Cook, Elizabeth, eds. Annals of Nyingma Lineage in America, Vol. III. 255p. (Orig.). 1985. 12.00 (ISBN 0-913546-99-2). Dharma Pub.
Dow, Michael & Endemann, Carl T., eds. Voices of the Wineland. (Illus.). 48p. (Orig.). 8.50 (ISBN 0-931926-07-6); pap. 3.75 (ISBN 0-931926-08-4). Alta Napa.
Dow, Miroslava W., ed. A Variorum Edition of Elizabeth Barrett Browning's Sonnets from the Portuguese. LC 37-1751. 201p. 1980. 12.50x (ISBN 0-87875-179-3). Whitston Pub.
Dow, Norman D., Jr. The Word Was Made Flesh. 1977. pap. 2.25 (ISBN 0-89536-146-9). CSS of Ohio.
Dow, Paul E. Criminal Law. LC 84-23205. (Criminal Justice Ser.). 400p. 1985. text ed. 21.00 pub net (ISBN 0-534-04716-5). Brooks-Cole.
--Discretionary Justice: A Critical Inquiry. LC 81-1565. 314p. 1981. prof ref 35.00 (ISBN 0-88410-835-X). Ballinger Pub.
Dow, Philip. Paying Back the Sea. LC 78-71891. (Poetry Ser.). 1979. 8.95 (ISBN 0-915604-54-X); pap. 4.50 (ISBN 0-915604-55-8). Carnegie-Mellon.
Dow, Philip, ed. Nineteen New American Poets of the Golden Gate. LC 83-6124. 455p. 1984. 26.95 (ISBN 0-15-136418-4). HarBraceJ.
--Nineteen New American Poets of the Golden Gate. pap. 14.95 (ISBN 0-15-636101-9, Harv). HarBraceJ.
Dow, R. Changing Societal Roles & Teaching. LC 76-39645. 1977. pap. 2.50 (ISBN 0-686-21734-9, 261-08428). Home Econ Educ.
Dow, Richard A. & Mowbray, E. Andrew. Newport. LC 76-23489. (Illus.). 1976. pap. 4.00 (ISBN 0-917218-05-1). Mowbray.
Dow, Robert & Moruzzi, Giuseppe. The Physiology & Pathology of the Cerebellum. LC 58-8343. pap. 160.00 (ISBN 0-317-27914-9, 2055857). Bks Demand UMI.
Dow, Robert A. Ministry with Single Adults. LC 76-48518. 1977. pap. 6.95 (ISBN 0-8170-0693-1). Judson.
Dow, Roger W. Business English. LC 78-18253. 451p. 1979. pap. 22.95 (ISBN 0-471-36661-7); wkbk., 250p. 11.95 (ISBN 0-471-04959-X); avail. tchrs. manual (ISBN 0-471-05251-5). Wiley.
Dow, Sheila C. Macroeconomic Thought. 256p. 1985. 29.95x (ISBN 0-631-14084-0). Basil Blackwell.
Dow, Sheila C. & Earl, Peter E. Money Matters: A Keynesian Approach to Monetary Economics. LC 82-11380. (Illus.). 280p. 1982. text ed. 29.50x (ISBN 0-389-20323-8). B&N Imports.
Dow, Sterling. Fifty Years of Sathers: The Sather Professorship of Classical Literature in the University of California, Berkeley, 1913-14-1963-64. LC 65-17449. 1965. 16.95x (ISBN 0-520-00353-5); pap. 12.95x (ISBN 0-520-00354-3). U of Cal Pr.
Dow, Sterling T. Maine Postal History & Postmarks. LC 75-1790. (Illus.). 256p. 1976. Repr. 25.00x (ISBN 0-88000-065-1). Quarterman.
Dow, Steven. Breeding Angelfish. (Illus.). 1977. pap. 4.95 (ISBN 0-668-04055-6). Arco.
Dow, T. I. Confucianism vs. Marxism. 200p. 1977. pap. text ed. 12.25 (ISBN 0-8191-0183-4). U Pr of Amer.
Dow, T. W. The Moon Has No Rotation. 1958. pap. 1.00 (ISBN 0-910340-01-3). Celestial Pr.
--Repeal Kepler's Laws. LC 60-13372. 1960. 5.00 (ISBN 0-910340-02-1). Celestial Pr.
--Reshape Newton's Laws. LC 64-19218. 1965. 5.00 (ISBN 0-910340-03-X). Celestial Pr.
--Truth of Creation. LC 67-31148. (Illus.). 1968. 5.00 (ISBN 0-910340-04-8). Celestial Pr.
Dowaliby, Margaret. Practical Aspects of Ophthalmic Optics. 2nd ed. LC 72-173927. 1980. 26.00, leatherette (ISBN 0-87873-010-9). Prof Press.
Dowaliby, Margaret & Dowaliby, Pauline. Healthy Eyes for Your Children. LC 81-80235. 1981. pap. 8.95 (ISBN 0-87873-027-3). Prof Press.
Dowaliby, Pauline, jt. auth. see Dowaliby, Margaret.
Dowall, David E. The Surburban Squeeze: Land Conversion & Regulation in the San Francisco Bay Area. LC 83-17945. (Series in Urban Development). 264p. 1984. text ed. 24.50x (ISBN 0-520-04968-3). U of Cal Pr.
Dowall, David E. & Mingilton, Jesse. Effects of Environmental Regulations on Housing Costs. (CPL Bibliographies: No. 6). 67p. 1979. pap. 7.00 (ISBN 0-86602-006-3). CPL Biblios.
Doward, Jan S. The Moment to Decide. Woolsey, Raymond H., ed. (Daily Devotional Ser.). 384p. 1984. 7.95 (ISBN 0-8280-0234-7). Review & Herald.
--Voices from the Sky. (Anch Ser.). 1985. pap. 5.95 (ISBN 0-8163-0598-6). Pacific Pr Pub Assn.
Dowben, Robert M. & Shay, Jerry W., eds. Cell & Muscle Motility, Vol. 1. 414p. 1981. 45.00x (ISBN 0-306-40703-5, Plenum Pr). Plenum Pub.
--Cell & Muscle Motility, Vol. 2. 327p. 1982. text ed. 39.50 (ISBN 0-306-40798-1, Plenum Pr). Plenum Pub.
--Cell & Muscle Motility, Vol. 3. 296p. 1983. 39.50x (ISBN 0-306-41157-1, Plenum Pr). Plenum Pub.
--Cell & Muscle Motility, Vol. 4. 320p. 1983. 39.50x (ISBN 0-306-41227-6, Plenum Pr). Plenum Pub.
Dowbenko, Uri. Marijuana Double-Take. 2nd ed. 64p. (Orig.). 1982. pap. 3.95 (ISBN 0-686-36145-8). Sirius Pubns.
Dowd, jt. auth. see Alpin.
Dowd, Ben, ed. Some Dimensions of the Formal Organization. 121p. 1972. pap. text ed. 7.95x (ISBN 0-8422-0205-6). Irvington.
Dowd, D. W., et al, eds. Medical, Moral & Legal Implications of Recent Medical Advances: A Symposium. LC 71-152124. (Symposia on Law & Society Ser). 1971. Repr. of 1968 ed. lib. bdg. 19.50 (ISBN 0-306-70128-6). Da Capo.
Dowd, David L. Pageant-Master of the Republic. facs. ed. LC 72-75507. (Select Bibliographies Reprint Ser). 1948. 22.00 (ISBN 0-8369-5005-4). Ayer Co Pubs.
Dowd, Douglas & Nichols, Mary, eds. Step by Step. (Illus.). 1965. pap. 1.45 (ISBN 0-393-00317-5, Norton Lib). Norton.
Dowd, Douglas F., ed. Thorstein Veblen: A Critical Reappraisal-Lectures & Essays Commemorating the Hundredth Anniversary of Veblen's Birth. LC 77-9623. 1977. Repr. of 1958 ed. lib. bdg. 26.75x (ISBN 0-8371-9714-7, DOTV). Greenwood.
Dowd, E. Thomas. Leisure Counseling: Concepts & Applications. (Illus.). 332p. 1984. 29.75x (ISBN 0-398-04824-X). C C Thomas.
Dowd, J. E., jt. auth. see Glasunov, I. S.
Dowd, James P. Built Like A Bear. 190p. 1979. 16.00 (ISBN 0-87770-212-8). Ye Galleon.
--Custer Lives! 264p. 19.95 (ISBN 0-87770-268-3). Ye Galleon.
Dowd, Jerome. Negro in American Life. LC 68-56331. Repr. of 1926 ed. 29.00x (ISBN 0-8371-0389-4, DON&, Pub. by Negro U Pr). Greenwood.
--Negro Races: A Sociological Study. LC 70-99368. 1969. Repr. of 1907 ed. lib. bdg. 25.00 (ISBN 0-8411-0039-X). Metro Bks.
Dowd, John. Sea Kayaking: A Manual for Long-Distance Touring. rev. ed. LC 81-186. (Illus.). 240p. 1983. pap. 8.95 (ISBN 0-295-96047-7). U of Wash Pr.
Dowd, John C. You Cannot Hold Back the Dawn. LC 74-75619. 1974. 4.95 (ISBN 0-8198-0320-0); pap. 3.95 (ISBN 0-8198-0321-9). Dghtrs St Paul.
Dowd, John D., jt. auth. see Wilkens, Ernest C.
Dowd, Merle E. How to Earn Tax-Free SuperIncome. LC 84-16728. 240p. (Orig.). 1984. pap. 9.95 (ISBN 0-913539-00-7). Backwater Corp.
--How to Live Better & Spend Twenty Percent Less. 320p. 1980. pap. 2.50 (ISBN 0-345-29135-2). Ballantine.
Dowd, Merle E., jt. auth. see Garrison, William E.
Dowd, Steven. Kuntaw: Filipino Fighting. Date not set. pap. 5.95 (ISBN 0-86635-027-6). Koinonia Prods.
Dowd, Thomas, jt. auth. see Franks, Ronald.
Dowdall, John. Traditionary Anecdotes of Shakespeare. Collier, J. Payne, ed. LC 70-164782. Repr. of 1838 ed. 19.00 (ISBN 0-404-02165-4). AMS Pr.
Dowdall, Mike & Welch, Pat. Humans. (Illus.). 128p. 1984. 15.95 (ISBN 0-671-53257-X). S&S.
--Humans. 1985. pap. 8.95 (ISBN 0-671-60277-2, Fireside). S&S.
Dowdell, D. Secrets of the ABCs. LC 65-22301. (Illus.). (gr. 2 up). 1968. PLB 9.26 (ISBN 0-87783-035-5). Oddo.
DowDell, Del. Spearmen of Arn. 1978. pap. 1.75 (ISBN 0-505-51326-9, Pub. by Tower Bks). Dorchester Pub Co.
Dowdell, Dorothy. Glory Land. 384p. (Orig.). 1981. pap. 2.75 (ISBN 0-449-14404-6, GM). Fawcett.
--Golden Flame. 384p. (Orig.). 1985. pap. 3.95 (ISBN 0-449-18048-4, Pub. by GM). Fawcett.
--Hawk Over Hollyhedge Manor. 1973. pap. 0.75 (ISBN 0-380-01242-1, 15040). Avon.
--Hibiscus Lagoon. (Orig.). 1981. pap. 1.50 (ISBN 0-440-14494-9). Dell.
--A Woman's Empire. 480p. (Orig.). 1984. pap. 3.50 (ISBN 0-449-12447-9, GM). Fawcett.
Dowdell, John & Zakia, Richard. Zone Systemizer. LC 73-87272. 63p. 1973. 14.95 (ISBN 0-87100-040-7). Morgan.
Dowdell, Rodger B., ed. see Symposium on Flow, Its Measurement & Control in Science & Industry, Pittsburgh, Pa., 1971.
Dowden, Ann O. Look at a Flower. LC 63-12650. (Illus.). (gr. 5 up). 1963. 10.95 (ISBN 0-690-50656-2). Crowell Jr Bks.
Dowden, Anne O. The Blossom on the Bough: A Book of Trees. LC 74-6192. (Illus.). (gr. 5 up). 1975. 12.02i (ISBN 0-690-00384-6). Crowell Jr Bks.
--From Flower to Fruit. LC 83-46163. (Illus.). 64p. (YA) (gr. 7 up). 1984. 12.98i (ISBN 0-690-04402-X); PLB 12.89g (ISBN 0-690-04403-8). Crowell Jr Bks.
--State Flowers. LC 78-51927. (Illus.). (gr. 5 up). 1978. 9.95i (ISBN 0-690-01339-6); PLB 9.89 (ISBN 0-690-03884-4). Crowell Jr Bks.
Dowden, C. James. Community Associations: A Guide for Public Officials. 87p. 1980. pap. 19.00; pap. 14.25 members. Urban Land.
--Creating a Community Association: The Developer's Role in Condominium & Homeowner Associations. LC 76-56982. 78p. 1977. 19.00 (ISBN 0-87420-574-3); members 14.25. Urban Land.
Dowden, E. Mr. Tennyson & Mr. Browning in Studies in Literature: 1789-1877. 1878. Repr. 35.00 (ISBN 0-8274-2769-7). R West.
Dowden, E., ed. see Shelley, Percy B.
Dowden, Edward. Correspondence of Henry Taylor. LC 74-10771. 1888. 50.00 (ISBN 0-8414-3764-5). Folcroft.
--Correspondence of Sir Henry Taylor. 1888. Repr. 35.00 (ISBN 0-8274-3840-0). R West.
--Essays, Modern & Elizabethan. facs. ed. LC 71-117784. (Essay Index Reprint Ser). 1910. 19.50 (ISBN 0-8369-1647-6). Ayer Co Pubs.
--Fragments from Old Letters, E. D. to E. D. 1978. Repr. lib. bdg. 25.00 (ISBN 0-8482-0627-4). Norwood Edns.
--The French Revolution & English Literature. LC 76-22533. Repr. of 1897 ed. lib. bdg. 25.00 (ISBN 0-8414-3714-9). Folcroft.
--French Revolution & English Literature. LC 67-27592. Repr. of 1901 ed. 21.00x (ISBN 0-8046-0114-3, Pub. by Kennikat). Assoc Faculty Pr.
--A History of French Literature. (Select Bibliographies Reprint Ser). Repr. of 1897 ed. 24.50 (ISBN 0-8369-6644-9). Ayer Co Pubs.
--A History of French Literature. 1973. lib. bdg. 30.00 (ISBN 0-8414-2498-5). Folcroft.
--Introduction to Shakespeare. LC 73-130989. Repr. of 1893 ed. 10.00 (ISBN 0-404-02166-2). AMS Pr.
--Introduction to Shakespeare. facsimile ed. (Select Bibliographies Reprint Ser). 1907. 17.00 (ISBN 0-8369-5254-5). Ayer Co Pubs.
--Introduction to Shakespeare. 1973. lib. bdg. 10.00 (ISBN 0-8414-2499-3). Folcroft.
--Life of Percy Bysshe Shelley. lib. bdg. 40.00 (ISBN 0-8414-3851-X). Folcroft.
--Michel De Montaigne. 1977. Repr. of 1905 ed. lib. bdg. 25.00 (ISBN 0-8495-1002-3). Arden Lib.
--Michel De Montaigne. Jessup, Alexander, ed. 383p. 1981. Repr. of 1905 ed. lib. bdg. 25.00 (ISBN 0-89987-164-X). Darby Bks.
--Michel de Montaigne. 1905. lib. bdg. 30.00 (ISBN 0-8414-3852-8). Folcroft.
--Michel De Montaigne. LC 77-153266. 1971. Repr. of 1905 ed. 23.50x (ISBN 0-8046-1562-4, Pub. by Kennikat). Assoc Faculty Pr.
--Milton in the Eighteenth Century, 1701-1750. 1908. lib. bdg. 8.50 (ISBN 0-8414-3853-6). Folcroft.
--New Studies in Literature. 1973. lib. bdg. 50.00 (ISBN 0-8414-3854-4). Folcroft.
--Puritan & Anglican: Studies in Literature. facs. ed. LC 67-23208. (Essay Index Reprint Ser). 1901. 20.00 (ISBN 0-8369-0386-2). Ayer Co Pubs.
--Robert Browning. 59.95 (ISBN 0-8490-0960-X). Gordon Pr.
--Robert Browning. LC 70-103185. 1970. Repr. of 1904 ed. 28.50x (ISBN 0-8046-0822-9, Pub. by Kennikat). Assoc Faculty Pr.
--Shakespeare: A Critical Study of His Mind. 59.95 (ISBN 0-8490-1029-2). Gordon Pr.
--A Shakespeare Primer. 1877. lib. bdg. 10.00 (ISBN 0-8414-3855-2). Folcroft.
--The Sonnets of William Shakespeare. LC 79-14590. 1881. lib. bdg. 27.50 (ISBN 0-8414-3829-3). Folcroft.
--Southey. Morley, John, ed. LC 68-58377. (English Men of Letters). Repr. of 1888 ed. lib. bdg. 12.50 (ISBN 0-404-51709-9). AMS Pr.
--Southey. 1973. Repr. of 1880 ed. lib. bdg. 12.00 (ISBN 0-8414-3856-0). Folcroft.
Dowden, Edward, ed. A Woman's Reliquary. 124p. 1971. Repr. of 1913 ed. 12.50x (ISBN 0-7165-1345-5, BBA 02048, Pub. by Cuala Press Ireland). Biblio Dist.
Dowden, R. Rosemary, ed. Fluid Flow Measurement Bibliography. 1972. microfiche 24.00x (ISBN 0-900983-21-3, Dist. by Air Science Co.). BHRA Fluid.
Dowden, Tony, jt. auth. see Tymes, Elna.
Dowden, Wilfred S. Joseph Conrad: The Imaged Style. LC 74-112936. 1970. 11.95x (ISBN 0-8265-1153-8). Vanderbilt U Pr.
Dowden, Wilfred S., ed. The Journal of Thomas Moore, Vol. 1. LC 79-13541. (Illus.). 400p. 1983. 50.00 (ISBN 0-87413-145-6). U Delaware Pr.
Dowden, Wilfrid S., ed. The Journal of Thomas Moore, Vol. 2. LC 79-13541. (Illus.). 488p. 1984. 50.00 (ISBN 0-87413-245-2). U Delaware Pr.
Dowdey, Clifford. Bugles Blow No More. LC 37-27301. 497p. 1971. Repr. of 1937 ed. 16.95 (ISBN 0-910220-07-7). Berg.
--Experiment in Rebellion. facs. ed. LC 75-111828. (Essay Index Reprint Ser). 1946. 29.00 (ISBN 0-8369-1648-4). Ayer Co Pubs.
--The Land They Fought for. LC 73-19499. (Mainstream of America Ser). (Illus.). 438p. 1974. Repr. of 1955 ed. lib. bdg. 28.25x (ISBN 0-8371-7328-0, DOLA). Greenwood.
Dowdey, Clifford, jt. auth. see Manarin, Louis H.
Dowdey, Landon G., ed. Journey to Freedom: A Casebook with Music. LC 70-84899. 106p. 1969. 7.95 (ISBN 0-8040-0174-X, 82-71116, Pub. by Swallow); pap. 4.50x (ISBN 0-8040-0175-8, 82-71124, Pub. by Swallow). Ohio U Pr.
Dowding, Charles H. Blast Vibration Monitoring & Control. (Illus.). 256p. 1985. text ed. 49.95 (ISBN 0-13-078197-5). P-H.
Dowding, Charles H. & Singh, Madan M., eds. Rock Mechanics in Productivity & Production. LC 84-70738. (Twenty-Fifth Symposium on Rock Mechanics Ser.). (Illus.). 1222p. 1984. 50.00x (ISBN 0-89520-424-X, 424-X). Soc Mining Eng.
Dowding, Muriel. Psychic Life of Muriel the Lady Dowding. LC 81-23260. (Illus.). 284p. 1982. pap. 6.95 (ISBN 0-8356-0564-7, Quest). Theos Pub Hse.
Dowdle, Anthony, jt. auth. see Dowdle, Vincent P.
Dowdle, Vincent P. & Dowdle, Anthony. The Philadelphia Sampler. 80p. (Orig.). 1982. pap. 4.95 (ISBN 0-9611304-0-7). Earpacker Pr.
Dowdle, Wade. One Hundred & One Ideas to Help You Sell More Typesetting. (Illus.). 147p. 28.50 (ISBN 0-318-03249-X); members 14.25 (ISBN 0-318-03250-3). Print Indus Am.
Dowdle, Walter & La Patra, Jack. Informed Consent: Influenza Facts & Myths. LC 83-4099. 208p. 1983. lib. bdg. 22.95x (ISBN 0-88229-741-4). Nelson-Hall.
Dowdney, Donna, ed. see Conner, Terri & Sanderson, Joyce.
Dowdy, Gerald S., Jr. The Biliary Tract. LC 73-78536. (Illus.). Repr. of 1969 ed. 82.50 (ISBN 0-8357-9396-6, 2014541). Bks Demand UMI.
Dowdy, Mac. The Book of Ely. 1981. 40.00x (ISBN 0-86023-117-8, Pub. by Barracuda England). State Mutual Bk.
Dowdy, R. H., et al, eds. Chemistry in the Soil Environment. (Illus.). 1981. pap. 10.00 (ISBN 0-89118-065-6). Am Soc Agron.
Dowdy, S. & Wearden, S. Statistics for Research. (Probability & Mathematical Statistics Ser.). 537p. 1983. 36.95 (ISBN 0-471-08602-9); solutions manual 6.95 (ISBN 0-471-88394-8). Wiley.
Dowdy, William L. & Trood, Russell, eds. The Indian Ocean: Perspectives on a Strategic Arena. (Policy Studies). (Illus.). 630p. 1985. 40.00x (ISBN 0-8223-0649-2); pap. 19.95x (ISBN 0-8223-0691-3). Duke.

Dowell, Arlene T. AACR Two Headings: A Five-Year Projection of Their Impact on Catalogs. (Research Studies in Library Science: No. 17). 146p. 1982. lib. bdg. 25.00 (ISBN 0-87287-330-7). Libs Unl.

--Cataloging with Copy: A Decision-Makers Handbook. LC 76-1844. (Illus.). 295p. 1976. lib. bdg. 22.50 (ISBN 0-87287-153-3). Libs Unl.

Dowell, Arlene T., ed. see Frost, Carolyn O.

Dowell, Cassius. Military Aid to the Civil Power. Kavass, Igor I. & Sprudzs, Adolf, eds. LC 72-75030. (International Military Law & History Ser.: Vol. 1). 1972. Repr. of 1925 ed. lib. bdg. 30.00 (ISBN 0-930342-38-0). W S Hein.

Dowell, Coleman. Island People. LC 75-34150. 320p. 1976. 12.50 (ISBN 0-8112-0604-1). New Directions.

--Mrs. October Was Here. LC 73-89479. 224p. 1974. 9.25 (ISBN 0-8112-0518-5); pap. 3.75 (ISBN 0-8112-0519-3, NDP368). New Directions.

--White on Black on White. 251p. 1983. 14.95 (ISBN 0-88150-000-3). Countryman.

Dowell, David E. & Mingilton, Jesse. Effects of Environmental Regulations on Housing Costs. (CPL Bibliographies Ser.: No. 6). 67p. 1979. 7.00 (ISBN 0-86602-006-3). Coun Plan Librarians.

Dowell, E. H. Aeroelasticity of Plates & Shells. (Mechanics: Dynamical System Ser.: No. 1). 154p. 1974. 25.00x (ISBN 90-286-0404-9). Sijthoff & Noordhoff.

Dowell, E. H. & Curtiss, H. C., Jr. A Modern Course in Aeroelasticity. (Mechanics: Dynamical Systems Ser.: No. 4). 479p. 1978. 85.00x (ISBN 90-286-0057-4); pap. 25.00x (ISBN 90-286-0737-4). Sijthoff & Noordhoff.

Dowell, Eldridge F. A History of Criminal Syndicalism Legislation in the United States. LC 78-64174. (Johns Hopkins University. Studies in the Social Sciences. Fifty-Seventh Ser. 1939: 1). Repr. of 1939 ed. 24.50 (ISBN 0-404-61283-0). AMS Pr.

--History of Criminal Syndicalism Legislation in the United States. LC 73-87517. (American History, Politics & Law Ser.). 1969. Repr. of 1939 ed. lib. bdg. 25.00 (ISBN 0-306-71426-4). Da Capo.

Dowell, Ian, jt. auth. see Hoorweg, Jan.

Dowell, L. Handbook of Teaching & Coaching Points for Basic Physical Education Skills. 288p. 1974. pap. 14.50x (ISBN 0-398-03194-0). C C Thomas.

Dowell, Linus J. Didactic Strategies in Physical Education. (Illus.). 232p. (Orig.). 1980. pap. text ed. 11.95x (ISBN 0-89641-047-1). American Pr.

--Principles of Mechanical Kinesiology. 2nd ed. (Illus.). 357p. 1983. pap. text ed. 19.95x (ISBN 0-89641-133-8). American Pr.

Dowell, Linus J. & Grice, William A. Racquetball. 2nd ed. (Illus.). 128p. pap. text ed. 4.95x (ISBN 0-89641-123-0). American Pr.

Dowell, Linus J. & Mamaliga, Emil. Anaerobics. (Illus.). 298p. 1982. pap. text ed. 6.95x (ISBN 0-89641-086-2). American Pr.

Dowell, Lynne. The Vinegar Year. Lott, Clarinda H., ed. (New Poet Ser.: Vol 7). (Illus.). 50p. 1980. pap. 2.95 (ISBN 0-932616-05-4). New Poets.

Dowell, Richard W., et al, eds. An Amateur Laborer: Theodore Dreiser. LC 83-3616. (Illus.). 256p. (Orig.). 1984. pap. 9.95 (ISBN 0-8122-1174-X). U of Pa Pr.

Dowell, Richard W., et al. eds. see Dreiser, Theodore.

Dowell, Spright. Columbus Roberts: Christian Steward Extraordinary. LC 83-887. xvi, 171p. 13.95x (ISBN 0-86554-071-3, H67). Mercer Univ Pr.

Dowell, Stephen. History of Taxation & Taxes in England, 4 vols. 3rd, rev. ed. 1965. Repr. of 1888 ed. 275.00x set (ISBN 0-7146-1303-7, BHA-01303, F Cass Co). Biblio Dist.

--History of Taxation & Taxes in England, 4 Vols. 2nd ed. LC 67-5737. Repr. of 1884 ed. 250.00x (ISBN 0-678-05167-4). Kelley.

Dowell, Susan S., jt. auth. see Kitching, Frances.

Dowen, Edward. Studies in Literature 1789-1877. 523p. 1981. Repr. of 1902 ed. lib. bdg. 65.00 (ISBN 0-8495-1135-6). Arden Lib.

Dowen, Ken, ed. Sour Grapes, an Anthology of Work in Progress. (Illus., Orig.). 1985. pap. 5.00 (ISBN 0-933967-01-2). North Am Edit.

Dower, Catherine. Puerto Rican Music Following the Spanish American War: 1898, the Aftermath of the Spanish American War & Its Influence on the Musical Culture of Puerto Rico. LC 83-10290. (Illus.). 212p. (Orig.). 1983. lib. bdg. 25.50 (ISBN 0-8191-3333-7); pap. text ed. 11.75 (ISBN 0-8191-3334-5). U Pr of Amer.

Dower, J. W. Empire & Aftermath: Yoshida Shigeru & the Japanese Experience, 1878-1954. (Harvard East Asian Monographs: No. 84). 1979. text ed. 30.00x (ISBN 0-674-25125-3). Harvard U Pr.

Dower, John. The Elements of Japanese Design: A Handbook of Family Crests, Heraldry & Symbolism. LC 73-139688. (Illus.). 176p. 1971. 20.00 (ISBN 0-8348-0143-4). Weatherhill.

Dower, John, ed. Origins of the Modern Japanese State: Selected Writings of E. H. Norman. LC 74-4773. 512p. 1975. pap. 8.95 (ISBN 0-394-70927-6). Pantheon.

Dower, John W. Japanese History, Politics & Society: A Bibliographic Guide. LC 84-51129. (History Ser.). 250p. 1985. 29.95x (ISBN 0-910129-20-7). Wiener Pub Inc.

--Japanese History, Politics & Society: A Bibliographical Guide. LC 84-51129. 250p. 1985. pap. text ed. 19.95x (ISBN 0-317-18634-5). Wiener Pub Inc.

Dower, John W. & Junkerman, John. The Hiroshima Murals: The Art of Iri Maruki & Toshi Maruki. LC 85-40041. (Illus.). 128p. 1985. 29.95 (ISBN 0-87011-735-1). Kodansha.

Dowers, Patrick. One Day Scene Through a Leaf. (Star & Elephant Ser.). (Illus.). 44p. (Orig.). (gr. 1-4). pap. 4.95 (ISBN 0-317-19810-6, Start Elephant Bks). Green Tiger Pr.

Dowie, J. Iverne. Prairie Grass Dividing. LC 60-2575. (Augustana Historical Society Ser.: Vol. 18). xvi, 262p. 1959. pap. 7.50 (ISBN 0-910184-18-6). Augustana.

Dowie, J. Iverne & Tredway, J. Thomas, eds. Immigration of Ideas: Studies in the North Atlantic Community. LC 68-28713. (Augustana Historical Society Publication Ser.: No. 21). ix, 214p. 1968. 5.95 (ISBN 0-910184-21-6). Augustana.

Dowie, Jack & Lefrere, Paul, eds. Risk & Chance. 320p. 1980. pap. 19.00x (ISBN 0-335-00262-5, Pub. by Open Univ Pr). Taylor & Francis.

Dowie, Robin. General Practioners & Consultants: A Study of Outpatient Referrals. 1983. 19.95x (ISBN 0-19-724624-9). Oxford U Pr.

Dowland, Robert. Varietie of Lute Lessons. Hunt, Edgar, ed. 1958. 24.00 (ISBN 0-901938-45-9, 75-A10441). Eur-Am Music.

--Varietie of Lute Lessons. LC 79-84102. (English Experience Ser.: No. 921). 76p. 1979. Repr. of 1610 ed. lib. bdg. 14.00 (ISBN 90-221-0921-6). Walter J Johnson.

Dowlatshahi, Ali. Persian Designs & Motifs for Artists & Craftsmen. (Illus.). 1979. pap. 5.00 (ISBN 0-486-23815-6). Dover.

Dowle, A. & Finn, P. The Guide Book to the Coinage of Ireland. 1969. 6.00 (ISBN 0-685-51508-7, Pub by Spink & Son England). S J Durst.

Dowlen, Shane. Prowl. 50p. pap. 4.95 (ISBN 0-931926-14-9). Gondwana Bks.

Dowler, Bryan, jt. auth. see Arneil, Steve.

Dowler, Louise B. & Dowler, Warren L. Lake Powell & Rainbow Bridge: Gems of the Southwest. LC 78-51820. (Illus.). 1982. 16.00 (ISBN 0-930188-10-1); softcover 7.00 (ISBN 0-930188-09-8). W L Dowler.

--Lake Powell Boat & Tour Guide. LC 77-80564. (Illus.). 1983. 14.00 (ISBN 0-930188-11-X); softcover 7.00 (ISBN 0-930188-10-1). W L Dowler.

Dowler, Warren L., jt. auth. see Dowler, Louise B.

Dowler, Wayne. Dostoevsky, Grigor'ev, & Native Soil Conservatism. 240p. 1982. 27.50x (ISBN 0-8020-5604-0). U of Toronto Pr.

Dowley, Tim. Bach: His Life & Times. 144p. 1982. 40.00x (Pub. by Midas Bks England). State Mutual Bk.

--Eerdmans' Handbook to the History of Christianity. LC 77-5616. 1977. 24.95 (ISBN 0-8028-3450-7). Eerdmans.

--J. S. Bach: His Life & Times. expanded ed. (Life & Times Ser.). (Illus.). 192p. 1981. 12.95 (ISBN 0-87666-584-9, Z-53). Paganiniana Pubns.

--The Rolling Stones. (Illus.). 156p. (gr. 6 up). 1984. 10.95 (ISBN 0-88254-734-8). Hippocrene Bks.

--Schumann: His Life & Times. (Life & Times Ser.). 160p. 1982. 16.95x (ISBN 0-85936-150-0, Pub. by Midas Bks England). Hippocrene Bks.

Dowley, Tim, ed. Schumann: His Life & Times. (Illus.). 192p. 1981. 12.95 (ISBN 0-87666-634-9, Z-64). Paganiniana Pubns.

Dowley, Timothy. Bach: His Life & Times. (Midas-Composer Life & Times Ser.). (Illus.). 144p. 1983. 16.95x (ISBN 0-85936-145-4, Pub. by Midas Bks England). Hippocrene Bks.

Dowliing, Marion & Dauncey, Elizabeth. Teaching Three to Nine Year Olds: Theory into Practice. (Ward Lock Educational Ser.). 29.00x (ISBN 0-7062-4338-2, Pub. by Ward Lock Educational England). State Mutual Bk.

Dowlin, Kenneth E. The Electronic Library: The Promise & the Process. (Applications in Information Management & Technology Ser.). (Illus.). 199p. 1984. pap. 27.95 (ISBN 0-918212-75-8). Neal-Schuman.

Dowling. Musculoskeletal Disease: Staged for Rapid Comparison. 1985. 39.95 (ISBN 0-8151-2791-X). Year Bk Med.

Dowling, Ann & Williams, John e. Sound & Sources of Sound. LC 82-15687. 321p. 1983. 64.95x (ISBN 0-470-27370-4); pap. 26.95x (ISBN 0-470-27388-7). Halsted Pr.

Dowling, Barbara T. & McDougal, Marianne. Business Concepts for English Practice. 193p. 1982. pap. text ed. 10.95 (ISBN 0-88377-240-X); 3.50. Newbury Hse.

Dowling, Christopher, ed. see Allen, Louis.

Dowling, Christopher, ed. see Bond, Brian.

Dowling, Christopher, ed. see Callahan, Raymond A.

Dowling, Christopher, ed. see Cruickshank, Charles.

Dowling, Christopher, ed. see Jackson, William.

Dowling, Christopher, ed. see Upton, Anthony F.

Dowling, Christopher, ed. see Warner, Geoffrey.

Dowling, Colette. The Cinderella Complex: Women's Hidden Fear of Independence. 304p. 1982. pap. 3.95 (ISBN 0-671-44834-X). PB.

--The Cinderella Complex: Women's Hidden Fear of Independence. 288p. 1981. 15.95 (ISBN 0-671-40052-5). Summit Bks.

Dowling, David. Bloomsbury Aesthetics & the Novels of Forster & Woolf. LC 83-40124. 249p. 1985. 22.50 (ISBN 0-312-08517-6). St Martin.

Dowling, David, ed. Novelists on Novelists. LC 83-28. 283p. 1983. text ed. 27.50x (ISBN 0-391-02485-X). Humanities.

Dowling, Edward T., jt. auth. see Salvatore, Dominick.

Dowling, Emilia & Osborne, Elsie. The Family & the School: A Joint Systems Approach to Problems with Children. 208p. 1985. 24.95x (ISBN 0-7102-0613-5); pap. 14.95x (ISBN 0-7102-0166-4). Routledge & Kegan.

Dowling, Gregory. Double Take. 224p. 1985. 13.95 (ISBN 0-312-21831-1). St Martin.

Dowling, Harry F. The City Hospitals: The Undercare of the Underprivileged. 280p. 1982. text ed. 22.50x (ISBN 0-674-13197-5). Harvard U Pr.

--Fighting Infection: Conquests of the Twentieth Century. LC 77-8307. 1977. 20.00x (ISBN 0-674-30075-0, Commonwealth Fund Book). Harvard U Pr.

Dowling, J. P., jt. auth. see Allen, D. E.

Dowling, John. War-Peace Film Guide. 3rd ed. 188p. 1980. pap. 5.00 (ISBN 0-686-64878-1). World Without War.

Dowling, John E., jt. ed. see Cone, Richard A.

Dowling, John R. Developing & Administering an Industrial Training Program. LC 79-10713. (Illus.). 200p. 1979. pap. 14.95 (ISBN 0-8436-0777-7). Van Nos Reinhold.

Dowling, M. & Glahe, F. R., eds. Readings in Econometric Theory. LC 79-128867. 1970. pap. 15.00 (ISBN 0-87081-004-9). Colo Assoc.

Dowling, Marion. The Modern Nursery. (Longman Early Childhood Education Ser.). 1977. pap. text ed. 6.95x (ISBN 0-582-25005-6). Longman.

Dowling, Michael J. Health Care & the Church. Koenig, Robert E., ed. LC 77-1242. (Doing the Word Resource Ser.). (Orig.). 1977. pap. text ed. 3.95 (ISBN 0-8298-0333-5). Pilgrim NY.

Dowling, P. J. The Hedge Schools of Ireland. 3rd ed. 126p. 1985. pap. 5.50 (ISBN 0-85342-064-5, Pub. by Mercier Pr Ireland). Irish Bks Media.

--A History of Irish Education: A Study of Conflicting Loyalties. 192p. 1971. pap. 5.95 (ISBN 0-85342-232-X, Pub. by Mercier Pr Ireland). Irish Bks Media.

Dowling, P. J., et al, eds. Steel Plated Structures: An International Symposium. 1977. text ed. 50.00x (ISBN 0-8464-0884-8). Beekman Pubs.

--Offshore Structures Engineering, Vol. 3: Buckling of Shells in Offshore Structures. LC 81-83737. (Offshore Structures Engineering Ser.). 582p. 1982. 49.95x (ISBN 0-87201-611-0). Gulf Pub.

Dowling, R. H. & Hofmann, A. F. The Medical Treatment of Gallstones. 400p. 1982. text ed. write for info. (ISBN 0-85200-206-8, Pub. by MTP Pr England). Kluwer Academic.

Dowling, R. H., jt. auth. see Robinson, J. W.

Dowling, Seward T. Schaum's Outline of Mathematics for Economists. (Illus., Orig.). 1979. pap. 9.95 (ISBN 0-07-017760-0). McGraw.

Dowling, Shirley. Love Needs No Reason. 368p. 1985. pap. 3.50 (ISBN 0-380-89500-5). Avon.

Dowling, Theodore E. Armenian Church. LC 71-131511. Repr. of 1910 ed. 16.00 (ISBN 0-404-02167-0). AMS Pr.

Dowling, Tom. Coach: A Season with Lombardi. (Illus.). 1970. 7.50 (ISBN 0-393-08622-4). Norton.

Dowling, William. Poets & Statesmen: Their Homes & Memorials in the Neighborhood of Windsor & Elton-Milton, Cowley, Denham, Waller, Pope. 1973. Repr. of 1856 ed. 50.00 (ISBN 0-8274-1698-9). R West.

Dowling, William, ed. Effective Management & the Behavioral Sciences. 1982. 8.95 (ISBN 0-8144-7569-8). AMACOM.

Dowling, William C. The Boswellian Hero. LC 78-5886. 222p. 1979. 19.00x (ISBN 0-8203-0461-1). U of Ga Pr.

--Jameson, Althusser, Marx: An Introduction to "The Political Unconscious". LC 84-7032. 152p. 1984. 24.95x (ISBN 0-8014-1714-7); pap. 6.95x (ISBN 0-8014-9284-X). Cornell U Pr.

--Language & Logos in Boswell's Life of Johnson. LC 80-8545. 232p. 1981. 20.00 (ISBN 0-691-06455-5). Princeton U Pr.

Dowling, William F. & Sayles, Leonard R. How Managers Motivate. 2nd ed. 1978. text ed. 30.95 (ISBN 0-07-017668-X). McGraw.

Dowling, William F., ed. Effective Management & the Behavioral Sciences: Conversations from Organizational Dynamics. LC 78-6695. pap. 72.80 (ISBN 0-317-26909-7, 2023553). Bks Demand UMI.

Dowling, William L. Prospective Rate Setting. LC 77-18700. 157p. 1977. text ed. 38.95 (ISBN 0-89443-028-9). Aspen Systems.

Dowman, Keith, ed. Sky Dancer: The Secret Life & Songs of the Lady Yeshe Tsogyel. (Illus.). 350p. (Orig.). 1984. pap. 14.95 (ISBN 0-7100-9576-7). Routledge & Kegan.

Dowman, Kieth, tr. The Divine Madman. 180p. 1982. pap. 7.95 (ISBN 0-913922-75-7). Dawn Horse Pr.

Down, Edith. What's to Eat? 1981. text ed. 14.64 (ISBN 0-02-666150-0); tchr's. ed. 9.32 (ISBN 0-02-666160-8). Bennett IL.

Down, Goldie. Feed Me Well, Ilona. (Dest Two Ser.). 1985. pap. 4.95 (ISBN 0-8163-0575-7). Pacific Pr Pub Assn.

--More Lives Than a Cat. LC 79-17814. (Crown Ser.). 1979. pap. 5.95 (ISBN 0-8127-0243-3). Review & Herald.

--Saga of An Ordinary Man. (Dest Two Ser.). 1984. pap. 4.95 (ISBN 0-8163-0554-4). Pacific Pr Pub Assn.

--You Never Can Tell When You May Meet a Leopard. Davis, Tom, ed. 128p. 1980. pap. 5.95 (ISBN 0-8280-0026-3). Review & Herald.

Down, Jack. Basic Statistics for High School. 2nd, rev. ed. (Illus.). 194p. (Orig.). 1985. pap. text ed. 12.50x (ISBN 0-918907-00-4). Golden Poplar Pr.

--Basic Statistics for Non-Math People. 2nd ed. (Illus.). 194p. (Orig.). 1984. pap. text ed. 13.50 (ISBN 0-918907-01-2). Golden Poplar Pr.

Down, P. G. Heating & Cooling Load Calculations. 1969. 31.00 (ISBN 0-08-013001-1). Pergamon.

Down, P. J. Fault Diagnosis in Data Communications Systems. LC 78-30112. (Illus.). 1982. pap. 35.00 (ISBN 0-85012-186-8). Intl Pubns Serv.

Down, P. J. & Taylor, F. E. Why Distributed Computing? An NCC Review of Potential & Experience in UK. LC 77-363488. 168p. 1976. pap. 32.50x (ISBN 0-85012-170-1). Intl Pubns Serv.

Downame, John. The Christian Warfare. LC 74-80174. (English Experience Ser.: No. 653). 674p. 1974. Repr. of 1604 ed. 67.00 (ISBN 90-221-0653-5). Walter J Johnson.

Downard, William L. Dictionary of the History of the American Brewing & Distilling Industries. LC 79-6826. (Illus.). xxv, 268p. 1980. lib. bdg. 49.95 (ISBN 0-313-21330-5, DOD/). Greenwood.

Downen, Robert. Of Grave Concern: U. S.-Taiwan Relations on the Threshold of the 1980's. LC 81-69544. (Significant Issues Ser.: Vol. 3, No. 4). 67p. 1981. 1.50 (ISBN 0-89206-032-8). CSI Studies.

Downen, Robert, jt. auth. see Chiu, Hungdah.

Downen, Robert, ed. Northeast Asia in the Nineteen Eighties: Challenge & Opportunity for Constructive Action Conference Proceedings July 28-29, 1982. LC 83-5492. (Significant Issues Ser.: Vol. 5, No. 2). 169p. 1983. 5.95 (ISBN 0-89206-043-3). CSI Studies.

Downen, Robert L. Bridging the Taiwan Strait. (Journal of Social Political & Economic Studies Monograph). 128p. (Orig.). 1984. pap. text ed. 12.00 (ISBN 0-930690-17-6). Coun Am Affairs.

--The Tattered China Card. (Journal of Social Political & Economic Studies Monograph). 128p. pap. text ed. 12.00 (ISBN 0-930690-16-8). Coun Am Affairs.

Downen, Robert L. & Dickson, Bruce J., eds. The Emerging Pacific Community: A Regional Perspective. (Replica Edition). 260p. 1984. softcover 17.50 (ISBN 0-86531-864-6). Westview.

Downer, Alan S. British Drama: A Handbook & Brief Chronicle. (Illus.). 1950. 39.50x (ISBN 0-89197-047-9); pap. text ed. 19.50x (ISBN 0-89197-048-7). Irvington.

--Eminent Tragedian: William Charles Macready. LC 66-14441. (Illus.). 1966. 27.50x (ISBN 0-674-25100-8). Harvard U Pr.

Downer, Alan S., ed. American Drama & Its Critics: A Collection of Critical Essays. LC 65-24424. (Midway Reprint Ser). 1965. pap. 15.00x (ISBN 0-226-16061-0). U of Chicago Pr.

Downer, Alan S., ed. see Columbia University. English Institute.

Downer, Alan S., ed. & tr. see Ibsen, Henrik.

Downer, Alan S., ed. see Jefferson, Joseph.

Downer, Alan S., ed. see Sheridan, Richard B.

Downer, Alan S., ed. see Tarkington, Booth.

Downer, Ann H. Physical Therapy for Animals: Selected Techniques. (Illus.). 196p. 1978. 14.75x (ISBN 0-398-03702-7). C C Thomas.

--Physical Therapy Procedures: Selected Techniques. 3rd ed. (Illus.). 320p. 1981. 17.75x (ISBN 0-398-03840-6). C C Thomas.

Downer, Arthur C. Odes of Keats. LC 72-194427. 1897. lib. bdg. 8.50 (ISBN 0-8414-3858-7). Folcroft.

Downer, Charles A. Frederic Mistral: Poet & Leader in Provence. LC 74-164783. (Columbia University. Studies in Romance Philology & Literature: No. 2). Repr. of 1901 ed. 19.75 (ISBN 0-404-50602-X). AMS Pr.

Downer, R. G., ed. Energy Metabolism in Insects. LC 81-11839. 256p. 1981. 37.50x (ISBN 0-306-40697-7, Plenum Pr). Plenum Pub.

Downer, Roger G. & Laufer, Hans. Endocrinology of Insects. LC 82-24987. (Invertebrate Endocrinology Ser.: Vol. 1). 724p. 1983. 146.00 (ISBN 0-8451-2900-7). A R Liss.

Downes, Brian W., ed. see Fielding, Henry.

Downes, David & Rock, Paul. Understanding Deviance: A Guide to the Sociology of Crime & Rule Breaking. 1982. pap. 14.95x (ISBN 0-19-876087-6). Oxford U Pr.

Downes, David & Rock, Paul, eds. Deviant Interpretations. 176p. 1979. text ed. 25.00x (ISBN 0-06-491759-2). B&N Imports.

Downes, David A. The Great Sacrifice: Studies in Hopkins. LC 83-3619. 132p. (Orig.). 1983. lib. bdg. 21.50 (ISBN 0-8191-3142-3); pap. text ed. 9.25 (ISBN 0-8191-3143-1). U Pr of Amer.
--Hopkins' Sanctifying Imagination. LC 85-11071. 134p. (Orig.). 1985. lib. bdg. 19.75 (ISBN 0-8191-4755-9); pap. text ed. 8.75 (ISBN 0-8191-4756-7). U Pr of Amer.
--Ruskin's Landscape of Beatitude. LC 83-48767. (American University Studies IV (English Language & Literature): Vol. 4). 247p. 1984. pap. text ed. 24.75 (ISBN 0-8204-0049-1). P Lang Pubs.
--Temper of Victorian Belief: Studies in the Religious Novels of Pater, Kingsley, & Newman. LC 76-147189. 159p. 1972. text ed. 26.50x (ISBN 0-8290-0209-X). Irvington.
Downes, Edward. The Guide to Symphonic Music. LC 76-13813. (Illus.). 1058p. 1981. pap. 19.95 (ISBN 0-8027-7177-7). Walker & Co.
--New York Philharmonic Guide to the Symphony. LC 76-13813. 1976. 25.00 (ISBN 0-8027-0540-5). Walker & Co.
Downes, Edward, tr. see Werfel, Franz & Stefan, Paul.
Downes, Galen. Language Development & the Disadvantaged Child. 91p. 1978. 25.00x (ISBN 0-7157-1631-X, Pub. by H McDougall UK). State Mutual Bk.
Downes, John. Roscius Anglicanus. Summers, Montague, ed. LC 68-20220. 1968. Repr. of 1929 ed. 22.00 (ISBN 0-405-08464-1). Ayer Co Pubs.
Downes, John, jt. auth. see Goodman, Jordan E.
Downes, John see Wright, James.
Downes, Kathleen. The Man Next Door. (Loveswept Ser.: No. 49). 192p. 1984. pap. 2.25 (ISBN 0-553-21660-0). Bantam.
--Practice Makes Perfect. (Loveswept Ser.: No. 93). 208p. (Orig.). 1985. pap. 2.25 (ISBN 0-553-21697-X). Bantam.
Downes, Kerry. The Architecture of Wren. LC 82-8425. (Illus.). 256p. 1982. text ed. 40.00x (ISBN 0-87663-395-5). Universe.
--Hawksmoor. 2nd. ed. 1980. 70.00x (ISBN 0-262-04060-3). MIT Pr.
--Rubens. (Art Ser.). (Illus.). 288p. 1984. 29.50 (ISBN 0-906379-04-0, Pub. by Jupiter Bks England). Hippocrene Bks.
--Rubens. 208p. 1981. 44.00x (ISBN 0-906379-04-0, Pub. by Jupiter England). State Mutual Bk.
Downes, Olin. Symphonic Masterpieces. LC 72-5560. (Essay Index Reprint Ser). 1972. Repr. of 1935 ed. 22.00 (ISBN 0-8369-2987-X). Ayer Co Pubs.
Downes, Olin, jt. auth. see Siegmeister, Elie.
Downes, Paul & Layton, Marjorie. Seek Student Activity Booklet. 20p. (Orig.). 1982. 1.00 (ISBN 0-912578-54-8); tchrs guide 5.50 (ISBN 0-912578-55-6). Chron Guide.
Downes, Paul, ed. Chronicle Career Index. rev. ed. 160p. 1985. pap. 12.50 (ISBN 0-912578-78-5). Chron Guide.
--Chronicle Four-Year College Databook. rev. ed. 1985. pap. 15.50 (ISBN 0-912578-75-0). Chron Guide.
--Chronicle Student Aid Annual, 1985. rev. ed. 410p. 1985. pap. 16.50 (ISBN 0-912578-76-9). Chron Guide.
--Chronicle Two-Year College Databook, 1985. rev. ed. 350p. 1985. pap. 14.45 (ISBN 0-912578-74-2). Chron Guide.
--Chronicle Vocational School Manual, 1985. rev. ed. 350p. 1985. pap. 14.00 (ISBN 0-912578-77-7). Chron Guide.
Downes, R. & Hellmers, H. Controlled Climate & Plant Research. (Technical Note Ser.: No. 143). 60p. (Report of the CMAG Rapporteurs on Controlled Climates). 1976. pap. 12.00 (ISBN 0-685-68368-0, W197, WMO). Unipub.
Downes, R. P. John Ruskin: A Study. LC 73-7768. 1890. lib. bdg. 17.50 (ISBN 0-8414-1872-1). Folcroft.
Downes, Randolph C. Council Fires on the Upper Ohio. LC 40-34394. (Illus.). 1969. pap. 6.95 (ISBN 0-8229-5201-7). U of Pittsburgh Pr.
--Rise of Warren Gamaliel Harding, 1865-1920. LC 68-31421. (Illus.). 744p. 1970. 17.50 (ISBN 0-8142-0140-7). Ohio St U Pr.
Downes, Robert P. Hours with the Immortals: A Series of Popular Sketches & Appreciations of Distinguished Foreign Poets. Repr. of 1973 ed. 25.00 (ISBN 0-8274-1697-0). R West.
--Hours with the Immortals-British Poets: William Cowper to E. B. Browning. 1973. 25.00 (ISBN 0-8274-1444-7). R West.
--Seven Supreme Poets: Homer, Aeschylus, Sophocles, Vergil, Dante, Shakespeare, Milton. 1973. 25.00 (ISBN 0-8274-1701-2). R West.
--Woman: Charm & Power. 1974. lib. bdg. 69.95 (ISBN 0-685-51378-5). Revisionist Pr.
Downes, Stephen. The New Compleat Angler. (Illus.). 176p. 1983. 24.95 (ISBN 0-8117-1011-4). Stackpole.
Downes, William H. The Life & Works of Winslow Homer. LC 72-81983. 1974. Repr. of 1911 ed. lib. bdg. 25.50 (ISBN 0-8337-5127-1). B Franklin.
Downeth, Robert L. To Bridge the Taiwan Strait. 1982p. 1982. pap. 15.00 (ISBN 0-930690-17-6). Coun Soc Econ.
Downey. Lennon & McCartney. (Illus.). 156p. 1982. 9.95 (ISBN 0-88254-652-X, Pub. by Midas Bks England). Hippocrene Bks.
Downey, Bill. Black Viking. 320p. (Orig.). 1981. pap. 2.50 (ISBN 0-449-14393-7, GM). Fawcett.
--Right Brain-Write On: Overcoming Writer's Block & Achieving Your Creative Potential. (Illus.). 212p. 1984. 14.95 (ISBN 0-13-780990-5); pap. 6.95 (ISBN 0-13-780982-4). P-H.
--Uncle Sam Must Be... Losing the War: Black Marines of the 51st. LC 82-5879. (Illus.). 224p. (Orig.). 1982. pap. 7.95 (ISBN 0-89407-050-9). Strawberry Hill.
Downey, Bob. V-Bombers. (Warbirds Illustrated Ser.). (Illus.). 72p. (Orig.). 1985. pap. 5.95 (ISBN 0-85368-740-4, Pub. by Arms & Armour). Sterling.
Downey, David G. Modern Poets & Christian Teaching: Richard Watson Gilder, Edwin Markham, Edward Rowland Sill. 1973. Repr. of 1906 ed. 25.00 (ISBN 0-8274-1700-4). R West.
--Modern Poets & Christian Teaching: Richard Watson Gilder, Edwin Markham, Edward Rowland Sill. 183p. 1982. Repr. lib. bdg. 40.00 (ISBN 0-89984-013-2). Century Bookbindery.
Downey, Douglas W., et al, eds. see Standard Educational Corporation.
Downey, Durbin H. The Gift & the Promise: In the Fourth Dimension. LC 82-90787. (Illus.). 176p. (Orig.). 1983. pap. 9.95 (ISBN 0-9610006-0-0). Four D Pub Co.
Downey, Earl. How to Fish for Snook. (Orig.). pap. 1.95 (ISBN 0-8200-0104-X). Great Outdoors.
Downey, Edmund. Twenty Years Ago: A Book of Anecdote Illustrating Literary Life in London-Hardy, Etc. 1973. Repr. of 1905 ed. 25.00 (ISBN 0-8274-1699-7). R West.
Downey, Edward H. & Balk, Walter L. Employee Innovation & Government Productivity: A Study of Suggested Systems in the Public Sector. 90p. 1976. pap. 6.00 (ISBN 0-686-81166-6). Intl Personnel Mgmt.
Downey, Fairfax. The Color-Bearers. (Illus.). 24.95 (ISBN 0-8488-0014-1, Pub. by J M C & Co); Note Cards 2.95 (ISBN 0-317-28529-7). Amereon Ltd.
--It Happened in New Hampshire. LC 81-11397. (Illus.). 93p. (Orig.). 1981. pap. 4.95 (ISBN 0-936988-04-5). Tompson & Rutter.
--It Happened in New Hampshire. LC 81-11397. (Illus.). 92p. 1981. pap. 4.95 (ISBN 0-936988-04-5, Pub. by Tompson & Rutter). Shoe String.
--Richard Harding Davis & His Day. 1933. 25.00 (ISBN 0-8274-3279-8). R West.
Downey, Fairfax D. Our Lusty Forefathers: Being Diverse Chronicles of the Fervors, Frolics, Fights, Festivities, & Failings of Our American Ancestors. LC 74-179725. (Biography Index Reprint Ser). Repr. of 1947 ed. 21.50 (ISBN 0-8369-8093-X). Ayer Co Pubs.
Downey, Glanville. Antioch in the Age of Theodosius the Great. 1st ed. LC 62-16481. (The Centers of Civilization Ser.: No. 6). pap. 44.00 (ISBN 0-317-08141-1, 2010090). Bks Demand UMI.
--Constantinople in the Age of Justinian. LC 60-13473. (The Centers of Civilization Ser.: Vol. 3). (Illus.). 181p. 1981. pap. 7.95x (ISBN 0-8061-1708-7). U of Okla Pr.
--The Late Roman Empire. LC 76-15145. (Berkshire Studies). 158p. 1976. pap. 6.95 (ISBN 0-88275-441-6). Krieger.
Downey, H. Kirk, et al. Organizational Behavior: A Reader. (Illus.). 1977. pap. text ed. 18.95 (ISBN 0-8299-0137-X). West Pub.
Downey, J., jt. auth. see Dryer, R.
Downey, J., jt. auth. see Slosson, Edwin E.
Downey, J. A. U. S. Federal Official Publications: The International Dimension. 1978. 69.50 (ISBN 0-08-021839-3). Pergamon.
Downey, Jake. Better Badminton Ball for All. 3rd ed. 256p. pap. 9.95 (ISBN 0-7207-1438-9, Pub. by Michael Joseph). Merrimack Pub Cir.
--Winning Badminton Doubles. (Illus.). 224p. (Orig.). 1985. pap. 7.95 (ISBN 0-7136-2655-0, Pub. by A & C Black UK). Sterling.
--Winning Badminton Singles. (Illus.). 160p. 1983. 14.95 (ISBN 0-7158-0823-0, Pub by EP Publishing England). Sterling.
Downey, James. Them & Us. (Illus.). 258p. 1983. pap. 8.95 (ISBN 0-907085-57-1, Pub. by Ward River Pr Ireland). Irish Bks Media.
Downey, James & Rindsberg, Don. Timex-Sinclair Interfacing: Tested Interfacing Projects for the ZX-80, ZX-81 & the Timex-Sinclair 1000. (Illus.). 176p. 1983. 17.95 (ISBN 0-13-921759-2); pap. 10.95 (ISBN 0-13-921742-8). P-H.
Downey, James & Rindsberg, Donald. Easy Interfacing Projects for the Commodore 64. (Illus.). 208p. 1985. pap. 10.95 (ISBN 0-13-223553-6). P H.
Downey, James, ed. see Thomas Gray Bicentenary Conference, 1971.
Downey, James, et al. Easy Interfacing Projects for the VIC-20. 160p. 1984. 19.95 (ISBN 0-13-223439-4); pap. 12.95 (ISBN 0-13-223421-1). P-H.
Downey, James M. & Rogers, Steven M. PET Interfacing. LC 81-50568. 264p. 1981. pap. 16.95 (ISBN 0-672-21795-3). Sams.
Downey, Jean, ed. see Longfellow, Henry W.
Downey, Jean, ed. see Whitman, Walter.
Downey, Joan M., jt. auth. see Irvin, Judith L.
Downey, Joel. Winning Election to Public Office: The ABC's of Conducting a Local Political Campaign. LC 77-89897. (Illus.). 1977. pap. 12.50 (ISBN 0-9601284-1-7). J Downey.
Downey, John A. Stroke: A Guide for Patient & Family. Date not set. text ed. price not set (ISBN 0-89004-637-9). Raven.
Downey, John A. & Low, Niels L. The Child with Disabling Illness: Principles of Rehabilitation. LC 73-77937. (Illus.). Repr. of 1974 ed. 159.30 (ISBN 0-8357-9535-7, 2012285). Bks Demand UMI.
Downey, John A. & Low, Niels L., eds. The Child with Disabling Illness. 700p. 1982. text ed. 64.00 (ISBN 0-89004-664-6). Raven.
Downey, John A., et al, eds. Bereavement of Physical Disability: Recommitment to Life, Health & Function. 18.00 (ISBN 0-405-14214-5). Ayer Co Pubs.
Downey, John C. & Kelly, James L. Biological Illustration: Techniques & Exercises. (Illus.). 126p. 1982. pap. text ed. 11.75x (ISBN 0-8138-0201-6). Iowa St U Pr.
Downey, June E. Control Process in Modified Handwriting. Bd. with No. 5. Iowa University Studies in Psychology. Seashore, C. E., ed. Repr. of 1908 ed (ISBN 0-317-15634-9); Combination Tones & Other Related Auditory Phenomena. Peterson, Joseph. Repr. of 1906 ed. (Psychological Monographs General & Applied: Vol. 9). Repr. of 1908 ed. 29.00. Kraus Repr.
Downey, Kathleen, et al. Advances in Gene Technology: Molecular Genetics of Plants & Animals. LC 83-21371. 1984. 55.00 (ISBN 0-12-221480-3). Acad Pr.
Downey, Lawrence L. Water Resources Policy & the Nineteen Seventy-Seven South Dakota Legislature. 1977. write for info. U of SD Gov Res Bur.
Downey, M. E. & Kelly, A. V. Theory & Practice of Education. 2nd ed. 1979. text ed. 16.95 (ISBN 0-06-318113-4, IntlDept); pap. text ed. 10.45 (ISBN 0-06-318114-2). Har-Row.
Downey, Matthew & Metcalf, Fay. Colorado: Crossroads of the West. LC 76-25857. (Illus.). 200p. (gr. 4-6). 1976. pap. text ed. 6.95 (ISBN 0-87108-202-0); tchr's ed. 6.00x (ISBN 0-87108-204-7). Pruett.
Downey, Matthew, jt. auth. see Metcalf, Fay.
Downey, Matthew T., jt. auth. see Metcalf, Fay D.
Downey, Matthew T., ed. History in the Schools. LC 84-63085. 53p. 1985. 5.95 (ISBN 0-87986-049-9). Nat Coun Soc Studies.
--Teaching American History: New Directions. LC 81-86080. 115p. (Orig.). 1982. pap. 7.25 (ISBN 0-87986-043-X). Nat Coun Soc Studies.
Downey, Matthew T., jt. ed. see Linden, Glenn M.
Downey, Meriel. Interpersonal Judgments in Education. 1977. (IntlDept); pap. text ed. 7.80 (ISBN 0-06-318052-9, IntlDept). Har-Row.
Downey, Meriel, jt. auth. see Kelly, A. V.
Downey, Michael, ed. In Praise of the Irish. LC 84-72951. 160p. (Orig.). 1985. pap. 7.95 (ISBN 0-8264-0354-9). Continuum.
Downey, Murray W. Art of Soul Winning. 1957. pap. 5.95 (ISBN 0-8010-2820-5). Baker Bk.
Downey, Richard. Critical & Constructive Essays. facs. ed. LC 68-8455. (Essay Index Reprint Ser). 1968. Repr. of 1934 ed. 17.00 (ISBN 0-8369-0387-0). Ayer Co Pubs.
--Some Errors of H. G. Wells. LC 74-13585. 1933. lib. bdg. 12.50 (ISBN 0-8414-3709-2). Folcroft.
Downey, Robert, jt. auth. see Roth, Jordan.
Downey, Robert J. & Roth, Jordan T. Baton Techniques for Officer Survival. (Illus.). 304p. 1983. pap. 29.75x spiral (ISBN 0-398-04781-2). C C Thomas.
--Weapon Retention Techniques for Officer Survival. (Illus.). 120p. 1981. 17.50x (ISBN 0-398-04108-3). C C Thomas.
Downey, Susan B. The Excavations at Dura-Europos: The Stone & Plaster Sculpture (Final Report III, Part I, Fascicle 2) LC 77-88106. (Monumenta Archaeologica: No. 5). (Illus.). 375p. 1978. 46.00x (ISBN 0-917956-04-4). UCLA Arch.
--The Heracles Sculpture: Final Report III, Part 1, Fascicle 1. LC 43-2669. pap. 22.50 (ISBN 0-685-71741-0). J J Augustin.
Downey, W. David & Trocke, John K. Agribusiness Management. (Illus.). 480p. 1980. text ed. 31.95 (ISBN 0-07-017645-0). McGraw.
Downey, W. David, et al. Agri Selling. 2nd ed. LC 82-73827. 238p. 1984. 21.95 (ISBN 0-930264-50-9). Century Comm.
Downey, W. K., ed. Food Quality & Nutrition: Research Priorities for Thermal Processing. (Illus.). 712p. 1980. 63.00 (ISBN 0-85334-803-0, Pub. by Elsevier Applied Sci England). Elsevier.
Downhower, Jerry F. & Hall, E. Raymond. The Pocket Gopher in Kansas. (Miscellaneous Ser.: No. 44). 32p. 1966. pap. 1.75 (ISBN 0-686-80276-4). U of KS Mus Nat Hist.
Downie. Cash's Textbook of General Medical & Surgical Conditions for Physiotherapists. LC 65-73216. 1984. 18.75 (ISBN 0-397-58292-7, Lippincott Medical). Lippincott.
--Cash's Textbook of Orthopaedics & Rheumatology for Physiotherapists. LC 65-73208. 1984. 19.75 (ISBN 0-397-58293-5, Lippincott Medical). Lippincott.
Downie, C. H. Acritarchs in British Stratigraphy. (Illus.). 28p. 1984. pap. text ed. 11.95x (ISBN 0-632-01225-0). Blackwell Pubns.
Downie, Don. Cockpit Navigation Guide. 1962. 8.95 (ISBN 0-8306-9939-2); pap. 4.95 (ISBN 0-8306-2208-X, 2208). TAB Bks.
Downie, Don & Downie, Julia. Air Camping. (Illus.). 160p. (Orig.). 1985. pap. 12.95 (ISBN 0-8306-2380-9, 2380). TAB Bks.
--Complete Guide to Rutan Aircraft. 2nd ed. (Illus.). 352p. 1984. pap. 13.50 (ISBN 0-8306-2360-4, 2360). TAB Bks.
--The Oshkosh Fly-In. (Illus.). 224p. 1982. pap. 9.95 (ISBN 0-8306-2315-9, 2315). TAB Bks.
--Your Mexican Flight Plan. (Illus.). 272p. (Orig.). 1983. pap. 12.95 (ISBN 0-8306-2337-X, 2337). TAB Bks.
Downie, Don & Downie, Julie. The Complete Guide Aeroncas, Citabrias, & Decathlons. (Illus.). 256p. 1984. pap. 15.50 (ISBN 0-8306-2317-5, 2317). TAB Bks.
Downie, Don, rev. by. Flight Facts for Private Pilots. 2nd ed. Rodney, Morgan R. 1983. pap. 10.95 (ISBN 0-8168-5804-7). Aero.
Downie, Freda. Plainsong. 1981. 11.50 (ISBN 0-436-13251-6, Pub. by Secker & Warburg UK). David & Charles.
Downie, J. A. Jonathan Swift: Political Writer. 352p. 1984. 50.00x (ISBN 0-7100-9645-3). Routledge & Kegan.
--Robert Harley & the Press. LC 78-67810. 1979. 42.50 (ISBN 0-521-22187-0). Cambridge U Pr.
Downie, John. High Fidelity. 48p. 1981. pap. 2.50 (ISBN 0-86212-002-0). Falling Wall.
--Mary Ann; an Elegy. 128p. 1981. pap. 5.95 (ISBN 0-86212-000-4). Falling Wall.
Downie, Julia, jt. auth. see Downie, Don.
Downie, Julie, jt. auth. see Downie, Don.
Downie, Mary A. & Hamilton, Mary. And Some Brought Flowers: Plants in a New World. (Illus.). 160p. 1980. 24.95 (ISBN 0-8020-2363-0). U of Toronto Pr.
Downie, Mary A. & Robetson. The New Wind Has Wings. (Illus.). 112p. 1985. 11.95 (ISBN 0-19-540431-9, Pub. by Oxford U Pr Childrens). Merrimack Pub Cir.
Downie, N. M. & Heath, Robert W. Basic Statistical Methods. 5th ed. 384p. 1983. text ed. 23.95 scp (ISBN 0-06-041728-5, HarpC); scp study guide 9.95 (ISBN 0-06-041723-4). Har-Row.
--Metodos Estadisticos Aplicados. (Sp.). 1971. pap. 12.80 (ISBN 0-06-310074-6, IntlDept). Har-Row.
Downie, P., ed. see Hughes, Beatrix & Boothroyd, Rodney.
Downie, Patricia A. Cancer Rehabilitation: An Introduction for Physiotherapist & the Allied Professions. (Illus.). 208p. 1978. pap. 8.95 (ISBN 0-571-11163-7). Faber & Faber.
Downie, Patricia A. & Kennedy, Pat. Lifting, Handling & Helping Patients. (Illus.). 160p. 1981. pap. 8.95 (ISBN 0-571-11631-0). Faber & Faber.
Downie, Patricia A., ed. Cash's Textbook of Chest, Heart & Vascular Disorders for Physiotherapists. 3rd ed. (Illus.). 493p. 1983. pap. text ed. 18.75 (ISBN 0-397-58285-4, 65-73133, Lippincott Medical). Lippincott.
--Cash's Textbook of Neurology for Physiotherapists. 3rd ed. 464p. 1981. pap. text ed. 18.75 (ISBN 0-397-58281-1, 65-73091, Lippincott Nursing). Lippincott.
Downie, R. S. Roles & Values. 1979. pap. 10.95x (ISBN 0-416-14920-0, NO. 2167). Methuen Inc.
Downie, R. S. & Telfer, Elizabeth. Caring & Curing: A Philosophy of Medicine & Social Work. LC 80-40246. 180p. 1980. 24.00x (ISBN 0-416-71800-0, NO.2063). Methuen Inc.
Downie, Robert A., ed. see Frazer, James G.
Downing. Algebra the Easy Way. (Easy Way Ser.). 1983. 7.95 (ISBN 0-8120-2716-7). Barron.
--Encyclopedia of Math Terms. Date not set. pap. price not set (ISBN 0-8120-2641-1). Barron.
--Trigonometry the Easy Way. (Easy Way Ser.). 225p. 1984. pap. 7.95 (ISBN 0-8120-2717-5). Barron.
Downing, A. F. & Scully, V. J., Jr. Architectural Heritage of Newport, Rhode Island: 1640-1915. 2nd ed. (Illus.). 1967. 7.98 (ISBN 0-517-09719-2, American Legacy pr.). Crown.
Downing, A. J. The Architecture of Country Houses. (Illus.). 16.00 (ISBN 0-8446-0592-1). Peter Smith.
Downing, Alfred. The Region of the Upper Columbia River & How I Saw It. 50p. 1980. 7.50 (ISBN 0-686-98303-3); pap. 4.95 (ISBN 0-87770-234-9). Ye Galleon.
Downing, Andrew J. Architecture of Country Houses. LC 68-16230. (Architecture & Decorative Art Ser). (Illus.). 1968. Repr. of 1850 ed. 55.00 (ISBN 0-306-71034-X). Da Capo.
--Architecture of Country Houses. 1969. pap. 7.95 (ISBN 0-486-22003-6). Dover.
--Rural Essays. Curtis, George W., ed. LC 69-13713. (Architecture & Decorative Art Ser.). 640p. 1975. Repr. of 1854 ed. lib. bdg. 55.00 (ISBN 0-306-71035-8). Da Capo.
--A Treatise on the Theory & Practice of Landscape Gardening Adapted to North America. (Illus.). 1976. Repr. of 1875 ed. 20.00 (ISBN 0-913728-23-3). Theophrastus.

--Victorian Cottage Residences. Harney, George E., ed. (Illus.). 352p. 1981. pap. 6.00 (ISBN 0-486-24078-9). Dover.

--Victorian Cottage Residences. 1982. 13.00 (ISBN 0-8446-5883-9). Peter Smith.

Downing, C. T. The Fan-Qui in China in 1836-7, 3 vols. (Illus.). 980p. 1972. Repr. of 1838 ed. 84.00 set (ISBN 0-7165-2026-5, BBA 02125, Pub. by Irish Academic Pr Ireland). Biblio Dist.

Downing, Charles. Armenian Folk-Tales & Legends. Papas, William, ed. (Oxford Myths & Legends Ser.). (Illus.). (gr. 6 up). 1972. 14.95 (ISBN 0-19-274117-9). Oxford U Pr.

--The Messiahship of Shakespeare. LC 76-57998. (Studies in Shakespeare, No. 24). 1977. lib. bdg. 39.95x (ISBN 0-8383-2172-0). Haskell.

--Russian Tales & Legends. (Oxford Myths & Legends Ser.). (gr. 6-12). 1978. Repr. of 1956 ed. 14.95 (ISBN 0-19-274106-3). Oxford U Pr.

Downing, Christine. The Goddess: Mythological Images of the Feminine. 256p. 1984. pap. 9.95 (ISBN 0-8245-0624-3). Crossroad NY.

Downing, D. & Clark, J. Statistics the Easy Way. (Easy Way Ser.). 368p. 1983. pap. 7.95 (ISBN 0-8120-2666-7). Barron.

Downing, Danna. Sub Survival: A Handbook for the Substitute Elementary Teacher. 150p. 1981. pap. text ed. 9.95 (ISBN 0-918452-30-9). Learning Pubns.

Downing, David. The Devil's Virtuoso. LC 79-89963. (World War II Ser.). 272p. 1985. pap. 2.95 (ISBN 0-515-07294-X). Jove Pubns.

--Jack Nicholson: A Biography. LC 83-40363. (Illus.). 208p. 1984. 14.95 (ISBN 0-8128-2953-0). Stein & Day.

--Marlon Brando. LC 84-40244. (Illus.). 212p. 1984. 17.95 (ISBN 0-8128-2981-6). Stein & Day.

--Robert Redford. (Illus.). 224p. 1983. pap. 11.95 (ISBN 0-312-68747-8). St Martin.

--Russian Revolution Nineteen Eighty-Five. 235p. 1984. 14.95 (ISBN 0-450-06002-0, New Eng Lib). David & Charles.

Downing, Donald O. & Mackenzie, Brian W. Public Policy Aspects of Information Exchange in Canadian Mineral Exploration. 60p. (Orig.). 1979. pap. text ed. 4.00x (ISBN 0-686-63138-2, Pub. by Ctr Resource Stud Canada). Brookfield Pub Co.

Downing, Douglas. Calculus. (The Easy Way Ser.). 1982. pap. 7.95 (ISBN 0-8120-2588-1). Barron.

--Calculus by Discovery. 224p. (gr. 10-12). 1982. 12.95 (ISBN 0-8120-5451-2). Barron.

--Computer Programming in BASIC the Easy Way. (Easy Way Ser.). 225p. 1983. pap. 8.95 (ISBN 0-8120-2626-8). Barron.

--Computer Programming in Pascal the Easy Way. (Easy Way Ser.). 256p. 1984. pap. 8.95 (ISBN 0-8120-2799-X). Barron.

--Encyclopedia of Computer Terms. LC 82-11350. 160p. 1983. pap. 6.95 (ISBN 0-8120-2519-9). Barron.

Downing, Douglas & Clark, Jeff. Business Statistics. (Business Review Ser.). 288p. 1985. pap. 8.95 (ISBN 0-8120-3576-3). Barron.

Downing, Elisabeth. Keeping Pigs. (Illus.). 128p. 1985. pap. 6.95 (ISBN 0-7207-0987-3, Pub. by Michael Joseph). Merrimack Pub Cir.

Downing, Elizabeth. Keeping Goats. (Illus.). 128p. 1984. pap. 6.95 (ISBN 0-7207-1515-6, Pub. by Michael Joseph). Merrimack Pub Cir.

--Keeping Goats. (Illus.). 127p. 11.95 (ISBN 0-317-11560-X). Diamond Farm Bk.

--Keeping Rabbits. (Illus.). 144p. 1984. pap. 6.95 (ISBN 0-7207-1513-X, Pub. by Michael Joseph). Merrimack Pub Cir.

Downing, Francis G. Church & Jesus. LC 78-3050. (Studies in Biblical Theology, 2nd Ser.: No. 10). 1968. pap. 10.00x (ISBN 0-8401-3060-0). A R Allenson.

Downing, Frank & Bardoff, O. The Hollywood Emergency Diet. LC 80-70950. 192p. 1981. 9.95 (ISBN 0-8119-0419-9, Pegasus Rex). Fell.

Downing, George. Massage & Meditation. 1974. pap. 4.95 (ISBN 0-394-70648-X). Random.

--Massage Book. 1972. pap. 8.95 (ISBN 0-394-70770-2, Co-Pub by Random). Bookworks.

Downing, George, jt. ed. see Robbins, Daniel.

Downing, George D. Professional Sales Management. LC 81-4694. (Marketing Ser.). 620p. 1983. text ed. 34.95 (ISBN 0-471-84157-9, Pub. by Grid). Wiley.

Downing, Henry F. The American Cavalryman: A Liberian Romance. LC 78-164784. Repr. of 1917 ed. 24.00 (ISBN 0-404-00148-3). AMS Pr.

Downing, J. & Valtin, R., eds. Language Awareness & Learning to Read. (Series in Language & Communication: Vol. 17). (Illus.). 385p. 1984. 37.00 (ISBN 0-387-90890-0). Springer-Verlag.

Downing, J. A. & Rigler, F. H., eds. A Manual on Methods for the Assessment of Secondary Productivity in Fresh Waters. 2nd ed. (Illus.). 500p. 1984. text ed. 55.00x (ISBN 0-632-00616-1). Blackwell Pubns.

Downing, Jim. Meditation: The Bible Tells You How. LC 76-24064. 96p. 1976. pap. 2.95 (ISBN 0-89109-422-9, 14225). NavPress.

Downing, Jim, jt. auth. see Bendt, Ingela.

Downing, Joan. Baseball Is Our Game. LC 82-4418. (Sports Primers Ser.). (Illus.). (gr. k-3). 1982. PLB 10.60 (ISBN 0-516-03402-2); pap. 2.95 o. p. (ISBN 0-516-43402-0). Childrens.

Downing, Joan J. The Gypsy & the Yachtsman. (Longswept Ser.: No. 54). 192p. (Orig.). 1984. pap. 2.25 (ISBN 0-553-21653-8). Bantam.

Downing, John. The Coast of Puget Sound: Its Processes & Development. (A Puget Sound Bk.). (Illus.). 142p. (Orig.). 1983. pap. 8.95 (ISBN 0-295-95944-4, Pub. by Wash Sea Grant). U of Wash Pr.

--Radical Media: The Political Experience of Alternative Communication. LC 83-61475. 350p. 1984. 20.00 (ISBN 0-89608-192-3); pap. 8.00 (ISBN 0-89608-191-5). South End Pr.

Downing, John & James, Frederick. Pediatric Cardiology Case Studies. 1981. pap. text ed. 29.00 (ISBN 0-87488-028-9). Med Exam.

Downing, John & Leong, Che Kan. Psychology of Reading. 1982. text ed. write for info. (ISBN 0-02-330020-5). Macmillan.

Downing, John, jt. auth. see Gross, Ira.

Downing, John D., ed. Third World Cinema: Film, Politics & Aesthetics. Date not set. price not set. Praeger.

Downing, John G. The Cutaneous Manifestations of Systemic Diseases. (Illus.). 152p. 1954. photocopy ed. spiral 14.50X (ISBN 0-398-04246-2). C C Thomas.

Downing, Lester N. Counseling Theories & Techniques: Summarized & Critiqued. LC 74-23725. 264p. 1975. 21.95x (ISBN 0-88229-203-X); pap. 10.95x (ISBN 0-88229-502-0). Nelson-Hall.

Downing, M. E. Landscape Construction. 1977. 28.00x (ISBN 0-419-10890-4, NO. 6089, Pub. by E & FN Spon). Methuen Inc.

Downing, Mildred H. Introduction to Cataloging & Classification. 5th ed. LC 80-20299. (Illus.). 240p. 1981. lib. bdg. 15.95x (ISBN 0-89950-017-X). McFarland & Co.

Downing, Niki. The Wings of the Morning. 1983. 10.95 (ISBN 0-533-05581-4). Vantage.

Downing, Paul, ed. Cross-National Comparisons in Environmentals Protection. (Orig.). 1982. pap. 8.00 (ISBN 0-918592-57-7). Policy Studies.

Downing, Paul B. Environmental Economics & Policy. 1984. text ed. 25.95 (ISBN 0-316-19180-9). Little.

Downing, Paul B. & Hanf, Kenneth. International Comparisons in Implementing Pollution Laws. 1983. lib. bdg. 26.00 (ISBN 0-89838-110-X). Kluwer Nijhoff.

Downing, Paul B., ed. Air Pollution & the Social Sciences: Formulating & Implementing Control Programs. LC 75-153390. (Special Studies in U. S. Economic, Social & Political Issues). 1971. 34.50x (ISBN 0-89197-652-3). Irvington.

Downing, Peggy. Help! I'm Drowning. (Making Choices Ser.). 124p. (gr. 4-8). 1985. pap. 2.50 (ISBN 0-89191-964-3, 59642, Chariot Bks). Cook.

Downing, Robert E., jt. auth. see Beall, James R.

Downing, Rosie. Meet the Moodies. LC 84-62008. (Cuddle Shape Bks.). (Illus.). 14p. (ps-1). 1985. pap. 3.95 (ISBN 0-394-87248-7, BYR). Random.

Downing, Sybil & Barker, Jane V. Florence Rena Sabin. (Illus.). 80p. (Orig.). (gr. 5-6). 1981. pap. 5.50 (ISBN 0-87108-237-3). Pruett.

Downing, Sybil, jt. auth. see Barker, Jane V.

Downing, T. The Mexican Earth. 1976. lib. bdg. 59.95 (ISBN 0-8490-2234-7). Gordon Pr.

Downing, Theodore E. & Gibson, McGuire, eds. Irrigation's Impact on Society. LC 74-15602. (Anthropological Papers: No. 25). 181p. 1974. pap. text ed. 5.95x (ISBN 0-8165-0419-9). U of Ariz Pr.

Downing, Warwick. The Player. 184p. 1974. 2.95 (ISBN 0-933472-11-0). Johnson Bks.

Downings, Sybil, jt. auth. see Barker, Jane V.

Downs. Magic Coin Tricks Anyone Can Do. 1.00 (ISBN 0-685-02621-3, 00545314). Stein Pub.

Downs, jt. auth. see Fawcett.

Downs, A. J., et al, eds. Essays in Structural Chemistry. LC 76-144136. 479p. 1971. 55.00x (ISBN 0-306-30525-9, Plenum Pr). Plenum Pub.

Downs, Anthony. Economic Theory of Democracy. 1965. pap. text ed. 11.50 scp (ISBN 0-06-041750-1, HarpC). Har-Row.

--Inside Bureaucracy. 292p. 1967. pap. 12.95 (ISBN 0-316-19193-0). Little.

--Neighborhoods & Urban Development. LC 81-66190. 250p. 1981. 26.95 (ISBN 0-8157-1920-5); pap. 9.95 (ISBN 0-8157-1919-1). Brookings.

--Opening up the Suburbs: An Urban Strategy for America. LC 76-158984. 224p. 1973. 24.50x (ISBN 0-300-01464-3); pap. 7.95x (ISBN 0-300-01455-4, Y275). Yale U Pr.

--Rental Housing in the Nineteen Eighties. LC 83-10124. 225p. 1983. 26.95 (ISBN 0-8157-1922-1); pap. 9.95 (ISBN 0-8157-1921-3). Brookings.

--Urban Problems & Prospects. 2nd ed. 1976. pap. 19.95 (ISBN 0-395-30590-X). HM.

--Who Are the Urban Poor? rev ed. LC 77-133484. 64p. 1970. pap. 1.50 (ISBN 0-87186-226-3). Comm Econ Dev.

Downs, Anthony see Bradbury, Katharine L.

Downs, Anthony, jt. auth. see Bradbury, Katharine L.

Downs, Anthony, jt. auth. see Bradbury, Katherine L.

Downs, Art. Paddlewheels on the Frontier. (Illus.). 160p. 11.95 (ISBN 0-88826-033-4). Superior Pub.

Downs, Barnabus. A Brief and Remarkable Narrative on the Life & Extreme Suffering of Barnabus Downs. facsimile ed. 24p. 1972. pap. 2.95 (ISBN 0-940160-01-3). Parnassus Imprints.

Downs, Barry. Sacred Places: Religious Architecture of the 18th & 19th Centuries in British Columbia. LC 81-670050. (Illus.). 160p. 1980. 29.95 (ISBN 0-295-95774-3, Pub. by Douglas & McIntyre Canada). U of Wash Pr.

Downs, Brian W. Ibsen: The Intellectual Background. LC 74-86275. 1969. Repr. of 1946 ed. lib. bdg. 17.00x (ISBN 0-374-92261-6). Octagon.

Downs, Brian W., jt. auth. see Mortensen, Brita M.

Downs, Cal W., et al. The Organizational Communicator. (Illus.). 1977. text ed. 20.95 scp (ISBN 0-06-041734-X, HarpC); instructor's manual avail. (ISBN 0-06-361742-0). Har-Row.

--Professional Interviewing. (Illus.). 432p. 1980. (HarpC); pap. text ed. 13.95 scp (ISBN 0-06-041736-6). Har-Row.

Downs, Chugger & Buz, E. Z. The Complete Book of Drinking Games. LC 84-8496. (Illus., Orig.). 1984. pap. 4.95 (ISBN 0-943392-58-6). Tribeca Comm.

Downs, Donald A. Nazis in Skokie: Freedom, Community, & the First Amendment. LC 84-40294. 272p. 1985. text ed. 20.00 (ISBN 0-268-00968-6, 85-09689). U of Notre Dame Pr.

Downs, Dorothy. Excavations at Esna Nineteen Hundred Five to Nineteen Hundred Six. 136p. 1974. text ed. 50.50x (ISBN 0-85668-006-0, Pub. by Aris & Phillips England). Humanities.

Downs, E. V. English Literature: The Rudiments of Its Art & Craft. 295p. 1981. Repr. of 1932 ed. lib. bdg. 40.00 (ISBN 0-8495-1064-3). Arden Lib.

--English Literature: The Rudiments of Its Art & Craft. 1973. lib. bdg. 12.50 (ISBN 0-8414-3859-5). Folcroft.

Downs, Eliza & Crooks. American Humor. 1938. 10.00 (ISBN 0-8495-6256-2). Arden Lib.

Downs, Elizabeth C., jt. auth. see Downs, Robert B.

Downs, Fane & Flukinger, Roy. Abilene: An American Centennial. LC 82-60427. (Illus.). 110p. 1982. 24.50 (ISBN 0-292-70364-3, Pub. by R N Richardson Pr). U of Tex Pr.

Downs, Florence & Brooten, Dorothy. New Careers in Nursing. LC 82-18449. (Illus.). 192p. 1983. pap. 7.95 (ISBN 0-668-05260-0). Arco.

Downs, Florence S. A Sourcebook of Nursing Research. 3rd ed. LC 83-14295. (Illus.). 236p. 1983. pap. 13.95x (ISBN 0-8036-2792-0). Davis Co.

Downs, Florence S. & Fleming, Juanita W., eds. Issues in Nursing Research. 200p. 1979. pap. 13.95x (ISBN 0-8385-4436-3). ACC.

Downs, Floyd L., jt. ed. see Pfingsten, Ralph.

Downs, Frederick. Aftermath. 256p. 1985. pap. 3.50 (ISBN 0-425-07564-8). Berkley Pub.

--The Killing Zone: My Life in the Vietnam War. 1978. 13.95 (ISBN 0-393-07531-1). Norton.

--The Killing Zone: My Life in the Vietnam War. 288p. 1985. pap. 3.50 (ISBN 0-425-06534-0). Berkley Pub.

Downs, Frederick, Jr. Aftermath: A Soldier's Return from Vietnam. LC 83-42659. 224p. 1984. 12.95 (ISBN 0-393-01769-9). Norton.

Downs, Gary E., jt. auth. see Boyd, K. T.

Downs, Gary E. & Gerlovich, Jack A., eds. Science Safety for Elementary Teachers. (Illus.). 102p. 1983. pap. text ed. 8.95x (ISBN 0-8138-1641-6). Iowa St U PR.

Downs, George & Larkey, Patrick. Government Efficiency. 275p. 1986. pap. text ed. 9.00 (ISBN 0-394-35213-0, RanC). Random.

Downs, H. R. Rhythns of a Himilayan Village. LC 79-2983. 1980. 9.95i (ISBN 0-686-46178-9, CN 4001, CN). Har-Row.

Downs, Harold. Alphabet of Attributes. LC 72-107695. (Essay Index Reprint Ser.). 1931. 18.00 (ISBN 0-8369-1498-8). Ayer Co Pubs.

--Appraising a Play. LC 80-18347. (Practical Stage Handboob Ser.). (Illus.). 96p. 1980. Repr. of 1955 ed. lib. bdg. 22.50x (ISBN 0-313-22539-7, DOAAP). Greenwood.

--Theatregoing. 1951. 10.00 (ISBN 0-8482-7753-8). Norwood Edns.

Downs, Harold, ed. Theatre & Stage: An Encyclopedic Guide to the Performance of All Amateur Dramatic, Operatic, & Theatrical Work, 2 vols. LC 77-28803. (Illus.). 1978. Repr. of 1951 ed. lib. bdg. 137.50x (ISBN 0-313-20222-2, DOTS). Greenwood.

Downs, Hugh & Roll, Richard J. Hugh Downs' the Best Years Book. 1982. pap. 8.95 (ISBN 0-440-53901-3, Dell Trade Pbks). Dell.

Downs, Hugh R. Rhythms of a Himalayan Village. LC 79-2983. (Illus.). 240p. (Orig.). 1980. pap. 9.95i (ISBN 0-06-250240-9, CN 4001). Har-Row.

Downs, James F. The Navajo. (Illus.). 136p. 1984. pap. text ed. 6.95x (ISBN 0-88133-037-X). Waveland Pr.

--Two Worlds of the Washo: An Indian Tribe of California & Nevada. LC 66-13592. (Case Studies in Cultural Anthropology). (Orig.). 1966. pap. text ed. 9.95 (ISBN 0-03-056610-X, HoltC). HR&W.

Downs, James, Jr. Principles of Real Estate Management. 12th ed. Kirk, Nancye J., ed. LC 79-92870. (Illus.). 386p. 1980. 30.00 (ISBN 0-912104-43-0, 852). Inst Real Estate.

Downs, Janet, jt. ed. see Williams, Janice L.

Downs, Kathy. I Care... Do You? LC 81-50999. (Illus.). 16p. (Orig.). (gr. k-3). 1981. pap. 0.98 (ISBN 0-87239-474-3, 2872). Standard Pub.

--I'm Not Afraid. LC 81-51000. (Illus.). 16p. (Orig.). (gr. k-3). 1981. pap. 0.98 (ISBN 0-87239-475-1, 2873). Standard Pub.

--My ABC Zoo Book. (Happy Day Bks.). (Illus.). 24p. (ps-2). 1983. 1.39 (ISBN 0-87239-642-8, 3562). Standard Pub.

Downs, Kathy see Stortz, Diane, et al.

Downs, Marion P., jt. auth. see Northern, Jerry L.

Downs, Marion P., jt. auth. see Roeser, Ross J.

Downs, Philip G. Classical Music. write for info. (ISBN 0-393-95191-X). Norton.

Downs, R. G. & Hellmers, H. Environment & the Experimental Control of Plant Growth. (Experimental Botany Ser.). 1975. 31.50 (ISBN 0-12-221450-1). Acad Pr.

Downs, Robert B. Australian & New Zealand Library Resources. 164p. 1979. 43.00x (ISBN 0-7201-0913-2). Mansell.

--Books & History. LC 74-620006. (Monograph: No. 13). 83p. 1974. 5.00x (ISBN 0-87845-039-4). U of Ill Lib Info Sci.

--Books That Changed the South. (Quality Paperback Ser.: NO. 326). 292p. 1977. pap. 3.95 (ISBN 0-8226-0326-8). Littlefield.

--Books That Changed the South. LC 76-13181. (Illus.). xvii, 292p. 1977. 17.50x (ISBN 0-8078-1286-2). U of NC Pr.

--Books that Changed the World. 2nd ed. LC 78-13371. 1978. text ed. 20.00x (ISBN 0-8389-0270-7). ALA.

--Books That Changed the World. 1971. pap. 4.50 (ISBN 0-451-62407-6, ME2250, Ment). NAL.

--Famous American Books. LC 72-172256. 394p. 1971. 18.00 (ISBN 0-07-017665-5). McGraw.

--Famous Books: Great Writings in the History of Civilization. (Quality Paperback Ser.: No. 297). 278p. (Orig.). 1975. pap. 4.95 (ISBN 0-8226-0297-0). Littlefield.

--In Search of New Horizons. LC 78-13656. 1978. lib. bdg. 20.00x (ISBN 0-8389-0269-3). ALA.

--Landmarks in Science: Hippocrates to Carson. LC 82-154. 305p. 1982. lib. bdg. 23.50 (ISBN 0-87287-295-5). Libs Unl.

--Perspectives on the Past: An Autobiography. LC 84-5589. 240p. 1984. 17.50 (ISBN 0-8108-1703-9). Scarecrow.

Downs, Robert B. & Downs, Elizabeth C. British & Irish Library Resources. 2nd ed. 448p. 1982. 82.00 (ISBN 0-7201-1604-X). Mansell.

Downs, Robert B. & Keller, Clara D. How to Do Library Research. 2nd ed. LC 74-28301. pap. 76.50 (ISBN 0-317-10545-0, 2022780). Bks Demand UMI.

Downs, Robert B., ed. American Library Resources: A Bibliographical Guide Supplement, 1971-1980. 224p. 1981. text ed. 30.00x (ISBN 0-8389-0342-8). ALA.

--Bear Went over the Mountain: Tall Tales of American Animals. LC 73-148835. 1971. Repr. of 1964 ed. 40.00x (ISBN 0-8103-3279-5). Gale.

Downs, Robert B. & Jenkins, Frances B., eds. Bibliography: Current State & Future Trends. LC 67-21851. (Illinois Contributions to Librarianship Ser.: No. 8). pap. 154.80 (ISBN 0-317-10248-6, 2019015). Bks Demand UMI.

Downs, Robert B. & McCoy, Ralph E., eds. The First Freedom Today: Critical Issues Relating to Censorship & to Intellectual Freedom. LC 84-461. 342p. 1984. lib. bdg. 40.00x (ISBN 0-8389-0412-2). ALA.

Downs, Robert B., et al. Memorable Americans. 400p. 1983. lib. bdg. 23.50 (ISBN 0-87287-360-9). Libs Unl.

--More Memorable Americans, Seventeen Fifty to Nineteen Fifty. 375p. 1985. lib. bdg. 30.00 (ISBN 0-87287-421-4). Libs Unl.

Downs, Robert C. Living Together. 256p. 1983. 13.95 (ISBN 0-312-49025-9, Pub. by Marek). St Martin.

Downs, Robert J. Controlled Environments for Plant Research. LC 74-20878. (Illus.). 175p. 1975. 27.50x (ISBN 0-231-03561-6). Columbia U Pr.

Downs, Robert J., jt. auth. see Smith, Lyman B.

Downs, Rose G. Dietary Policy & Procedure Manual. LC 79-16595. 1979. pap. 7.00 (ISBN 0-87125-058-6). Cath Health.

Downs, T. Nelson. The Art of Magic. Hilliard, John N., ed. 352p. 1980. pap. 5.00 (ISBN 0-486-24005-3). Dover.

--The Art of Magic. Hilliard, John N., ed. 11.50 (ISBN 0-8446-5753-0). Peter Smith.

Downs, Theodore. Fossil Vertebrates of Southern California. LC 68-26065. (California Natural History Guides: No. 23). (Illus., Orig.). 1968. pap. 1.75 (ISBN 0-520-00352-7). U of Cal Pr.

Downs, Thomas. The Career Girl Killings. (True Crime Ser.: No. 3). (Orig.). 1985. pap. 2.95 (ISBN 0-440-11062-9). Dell.

--The Door-to-Door Killer. (True Crime Ser.: No. 1). 176p. (Orig.). 1984. pap. 3.25 (ISBN 0-440-12132-9). Dell.

--Murder Man. (True Crime Ser.: No. 2). (Orig.). 1984. pap. 3.25 (ISBN 0-440-15995-4). Dell.

--The Parish As Learning Community. LC 78-70816. 128p. 1979. pap. 2.95 (ISBN 0-8091-2172-7). Paulist Pr.

Downs, Tim. Downstown. (Illus.). 128p. (Orig.). 1986. pap. cancelled (ISBN 0-88289-490-0). Pelican.

Downs, W. G., jt. auth. see Theiler, Max.

Downsbrough, Peter. Around. LC 78-65770. (Illus.). 1978. pap. text ed. 4.50 (ISBN 0-9602192-0-X). P Downsbrough.
--As to Place. LC 78-65771. (Illus.). 1979. pap. 5.00 (ISBN 0-9602192-1-8). P Downsbrough.
--Notes on Location 1. 3.00 (ISBN 0-931106-08-7). TVRT.
--Notes on Location 2. 3.00 (ISBN 0-931106-09-5). TVRT.
Downstate Medical Center Conference, Brooklyn, 1971. Basic Thalamic Structure & Function: Proceedings. Riss, W., et al, eds. (Brain, Behavior & Evolution: Vol. 6, Nos. 1-6). (Illus.). 350p. 1972. pap. 49.50 (ISBN 3-8055-1491-3). S Karger.
Downs-Taylor, Carol & Landon, Eleanor M. Collaboration in Special Education: Children, Parents, Teachers, & the IEP. LC 80-84187. 1981. pap. 9.95 (ISBN 0-8224-1607-7). Pitman Learning.
Downton. Computer Systems. 1986. cancelled (ISBN 0-317-12944-9). Van Nos Reinhold.
Downton, James V., Jr. Sacred Journeys: Conversion & Commitment to Divine Light Mission. LC 79-546. (Illus.). 1979. 25.00x (ISBN 0-231-04198-5). Columbia U Pr.
Dowrick. Tales of the Supernatural. pap. 1.95 (ISBN 0-686-32313-0, Evman). Biblio Dist.
Dowrick, F. E. Human Rights. 232p. 1979. text ed. 37.95x (ISBN 0-566-00281-7). Gower Pub Co.
Dowrick, Peter & Biggs, Simon J., eds. Using Video: Psychological & Social Applications. LC 82-20058. 239p. 1983. 31.95x (ISBN 0-471-90093-1, Pub. by Wiley-Interscience). Wiley.
Dowrick, Stephanie, ed. Great Tales of the Supernatural. 1978. pap. 1.95x (ISBN 0-460-01266-5, Evman). Biblio Dist.
Dowrick, Stephanie & Grundberg, Sibyl, eds. Why Children? LC 80-84688. 1981. 12.95 (ISBN 0-15-196324-X). HarBraceJ.
--Why Children? LC 80-84688. 1981. pap. 6.95 (ISBN --15-696362-0, Harv). HarBraceJ.
Dowrie, George W. The Development of Banking in Illinois, 1817-1863. 1913. 15.00 (ISBN 0-384-12485-2). Johnson Repr.
Dowse, R. E., ed. see Hardie, James K.
Dowse, Sara. Silver City. 1985. pap. 3.95 (ISBN 0-14-007636-0). Penguin.
Dowsett, B. O., jt. auth. see Chormack, D.
Dowsett, David J., jt. auth. see Ennis, Joseph T.
Dowsett, Dick. God, That's Not Fair. 1982. pap. 2.95 (ISBN 0-85363-148-4). OMF Bks.
--Is God Really Fair? 1985. pap. 3.95 (ISBN 0-8024-3277-8). Moody.
Dowsett, Norman & Jayaswal, Sita R. Dimensions of Spiritual Education. (Integral Education Ser.: No.4). (Illus.). 91p. 1975. pap. 2.50 (ISBN 0-89071-216-6). Matagiri.
Dowsett, Norman & Jayaswal, Sitaram, eds. Education of the Future. (Integral Education Ser.: No. 5). 1976. pap. 2.50 (ISBN 0-89071-262-X). Matagiri.
Dowsett, Norman C. & Jayaswal, Sita R., eds. The True Teacher. (Integral Education Ser.: No. 3). 72p. (Orig.). 1975. pap. 2.55 (ISBN 0-89071-210-7). Matagiri.
Dowsett, Norman C. & Jayaswal, Sitaram, eds. Yoga & Education. (Integral Educaion Ser.: No. 6). 1977. pap. 2.25 (ISBN 0-89071-273-5). Matagiri.
Dowsett, Rosemary. Let's Look at the Phillipines. 1974. pap. 1.50 (ISBN 0-85363-103-4). OMF Bks.
Dowsing & Infotech. Microcomputer Systems, 2 vols. Set. 125.00x (ISBN 0-08-028519-8). Pergamon.
Dowson, Duncan. A History of Tribology. (Illus.). 1979. text ed. 90.00x (ISBN 0-582-44766-6). Longman.
Dowson, Duncan & Higginson, Gordon R. Elasto-Hydrodynamics Lubrication: SI Edition. 2nd ed. 1977. o.p, 35.00 (ISBN 0-08-021303-0); pap. 15.50 (ISBN 0-08-021302-2). Pergamon.
Dowson, Duncan, jt. auth. see Hamrock, Bernard J.
Dowson, Ernest. The Letters of Ernest Dowson. Flower, Desmond & Maas, Henry, eds. LC 67-29136. (Illus.). 470p. 1968. 40.00 (ISBN 0-8386-6747-3). Fairleigh Dickinson.
--The Stories of Ernest Dowson. Longaker, Mark, ed. 1977. lib. bdg. 59.95 (ISBN 0-8490-2672-5). Gordon Pr.
Dowson, Ernest C. Complete Poems. 1980. Repr. of 1928 ed. 29.00x (ISBN 0-403-00576-0). Scholarly.
--Dilemmas: Stories & Studies in Sentiment. facsimile ed. LC 71-157774. (Short Story Index Reprint Ser.). Repr. of 1895 ed. 13.00 (ISBN 0-8369-3886-0). Ayer Co Pubs.
--Poetical Works. 1980. Repr. of 1934 ed. 29.00x (ISBN 0-403-00948-0). Scholarly.
Dowson, H., jt. auth. see Berrios, G. E.
Dowson, H. R. Spectral Theory of Linear Operators. 1978. 75.00 (ISBN 0-12-220950-8). Acad Pr.
Dowson, John. A Classical Dictionary of Hindu Mythology & Religion, Geography, History & Literature. 11th ed. 26.95 (ISBN 0-7100-1302-7). Routledge & Kegan.
--A Classical Dictionary of Hindu Mythology. 10th ed. 1968. Repr. of 1961 ed. 27.00 (ISBN 0-7100-1302-7). Routledge & Kegan.
Dowson, John, ed. see Elliot, Henry M.
Dowson, V. H. & Aten, A. Dates: Handling, Processing & Packing. (Plant Production & Protection Papers: No. 13). (Orig., 2nd Printing 1978). 1962. pap. 16.25 (ISBN 92-5-100456-0, F111, FAO). Unipub.
Dowst, Somerby R. Basics for Buyers: A Practical Guide to Better Purchasing. LC 74-156479. (Illus.). 224p. 1971. 17.95 (ISBN 0-8436-1301-7). Van Nos Reinhold.
--More Basics for Buyers. LC 79-11755. 261p. 1979. 17.95 (ISBN 0-8436-0780-7). Van Nos Reinhold.
Dowty, Alan. Middle East Crisis: U. S. Decision-Making in 1958, 1970 & 1973. LC 83-1396. (International Crisis Behavior Ser.: Vol. 3). (Illus.). 1984. 42.50 (ISBN 0-520-04809-1). U of Cal Pr.
Dowty, David R. Word Meaning & Montague Grammar. (Synthese Language Library: No. 7). 1979. lib. bdg. 47.00 (ISBN 90-277-1008-2, Pub. by Reidel Holland); pap. 18.00 (ISBN 90-277-1009-0). Kluwer Academic.
Dowty, David R., et al, eds. Natural Language Parsing: Psychological, Computational, & Theoretical Perspectives. (Studies in Natural Language Processing). (Illus.). 408p. 1985. 49.50 (ISBN 0-521-26203-8). Cambridge U Pr.
Dowty, Stuart, jt. auth. see Goldwasser, Janet.
Dowven, Robert L. The Tattered China Card. 1984. pap. 15.00 (ISBN 0-318-03038-1). Coun Soc Econ.
Dox, Diane. Pulses, Pulses, Pulses. (Illus.). 1978. 20.00 (ISBN 0-916750-47-7). Dayton Labs.
Dox, Ida. Melloni's Illustrated Medical Dictionary. 2nd ed. Melloni, Biagio J., ed. (Illus.). 560p. 1985. text ed. 22.50 (ISBN 0-683-02641-0). Williams & Wilkins.
Dox, Victor L. What the World Needs. LC 67-31068. 3.50 (ISBN 0-8198-0328-6); pap. 2.50 (ISBN 0-8198-0329-4). Dghtrs St Paul.
Doxey, D. L. Clinical Pathology & Diagnostic Procedures. 2nd ed. (Illus.). 320p. 1983. 38.00 (ISBN 0-7216-0810-8, Pub. by Bailliere-Tindall). Saunders.
Doxey, G. V. The Industrial Colour Bar in South Africa. LC 73-11865. 205p. 1974. Repr. of 1961 ed. lib. bdg. 15.00x (ISBN 0-8371-7099-0, DOCB). Greenwood.
Doxey, Margaret P. Economic Sanctions & International Enforcement. 2nd ed. (RIIA Ser.). 1980. 24.95x (ISBN 0-19-520200-7). Oxford U Pr.
Doxey, W. S. A Winter in the Woods. (Illus.). pap. 3.00 (ISBN 0-686-12232-1). Doxey.
--A Winter in the Woods. 1975. 1.00 (ISBN 0-685-67936-5). Windless Orchard.
Doxey, William. Bye-Bye, Lonesome Blues. (Orig.). 1981. pap. 2.50 (ISBN 0-505-51652-7, Pub. by Tower Bks). Dorchester Pub Co.
--Countdown. 352p. (Orig.). 1986. pap. 3.50 (ISBN 0-8439-2321-0, Lesiure Bks). Dorchester Pub Co.
--Cousins to the Kudzu. LC 84-21317. 288p. 1985. 16.95 (ISBN 0-8071-1225-9). La State U Pr.
--Dead Wrong. 1980. pap. 1.75 (ISBN 0-505-51455-9, Pub. by Tower Bks). Dorchester Pub Co.
--Espionage. 256p. 1984. pap. 3.50 (ISBN 0-8439-2147-1, Leisure Bks). Dorchester Pub Co.
Doxey, William S. E.S.P. Ionage. 1979. pap. 1.95 (ISBN 0-505-51363-3, Pub. by Tower Bks). Dorchester Pub Co.
Doxiadis, C. A. Anthropopolis: City for Human Development. (Illus.). 398p. 1975. pap. 5.95x (ISBN 0-393-08737-9). Norton.
Doxiadis, Calliope. Visions of the King. 1966. pap. 4.00 (ISBN 0-685-62614-8). Atlantis Edns.
Doxiadis, Constantinos A. Architectural Space in Ancient Greece. 1972. pap. 9.95 (ISBN 0-262-54030-4). MIT Pr.
--Emergence & Growth of an Urban Region: The Developing Urban Detroit Area Vol. 3A Concept for Future Development. LC 66-29622. 399p. 1969. 20.00x (ISBN 0-8143-1506-2). Wayne St U Pr.
--Emergence & Growth of an Urban Region: The Developing Urban Detroit Area, Vol. 2, Future Alternatives. LC 66-29622. 408p. 1969. 20.00x (ISBN 0-8143-1505-4). Wayne St U Pr.
Doxiadis, Spyros, ed. see Institute of Child Health Athens International Symposium 2-8, July 1978 Athens, Greece.
Doyal, Guy T., jt. auth. see Freidman, Ronald J.
Doyal, Lesley & Pennell, Imogen. The Political Economy of Health. LC 80-85406. 360p. 1981. 20.00 (ISBN 0-89608-048-X); pap. 6.50 (ISBN 0-89608-047-1). South End Pr.
Doyama, Masa & Yoshida, Sho, eds. Progress in the Study of Point Defects. 440p. 1977. 64.50x (ISBN 0-86008-185-0, Pub. by U of Tokyo Japan). Columbia U Pr.
Doyle, jt. auth. see Kammerman.
Doyle, A. C. Bimbo the Bumble Bee & Rose the Rose Bud. 20p. 1982. 3.50 (ISBN 0-939476-74-6, Pub. by Biblio Pr GA). Prosperity & Profits.
--Energized Color Framable Art Book with Tear out Pages. LC 83-90742. 25p. Date not set. pap. text ed. 12.95 (ISBN 0-913597-00-7, Pub. by Alpha Pyramis). Prosperity & Profits.
--I Am, I Am, I Am. 60p. 1984. pap. 1.50 (ISBN 0-913597-63-5, Pub. by Alpha Pyramis). Prosperity & Profits.
--I Can, I Shall, I Will. 50p. 1983. pap. text ed. 2.95 (ISBN 0-939476-54-1, Pub. by Biblio Pr GA). Prosperity & Profits.
--The Ingredient Substitution Recipe Book One. 30p. 1984. pap. 4.95 (ISBN 0-318-00206-X, Pub. by Cookbk Consort). Prosperity & Profits.
--The Multi-Charity Benefit Greeting Card Concept: A Series of Suggestions. 1984. pap. text ed. 1.00 (ISBN 0-913597-58-9, Pub. by Alpha Pyramis). Prosperity & Profits.
--Murphy the Mistletoe: Adventures from the Garden of Eden to the Garden of Nede. 30p. 1984. pap. text ed. 3.00 (ISBN 0-913597-64-3, Pub. by Alpha Pyramis). Prosperity & Profits.
--Poetry for the Peace Movement. 17p. 1984. pap. text ed. 2.00 (ISBN 0-913597-56-2, Pub. by Alpha Pyramis). Prosperity & Profits.
--Posie the Positive Train: Illustrated Edition. 60p. 1983. pap. 9.95 (ISBN 0-939476-96-7, Pub. by Biblio Pr GA). Prosperity & Profits.
--Prayerful Poetry. 16p. 1984. pap. text ed. 1.25 (ISBN 0-917593-05-7, Pub. by Intl Partners). Prosperity & Profits.
--Seeds As Food Use, 2 vols. 1984. pap. 1.95 ea. (ISBN 0-913597-70-8, Pub. by Alpha Pyramis). Vol. 1. Vol. 2. Prosperity & Profits.
--Seeds for Use As Medicine, Sprouts, Oils, Teas, Imitation Coffee, Teas, Spices, Beauty, Food, etc. Formula & Recipe Book. 25p. 1984. pap. text ed. 7.95 (Pub. by Center Self Suff). Prosperity & Profits.
--Soy: A Sprouting Story Poem. 12p. 1984. pap. text ed. 2.50 (ISBN 0-913597-65-1, Pub. by Alpha Pyramis). Prosperity & Profits.
--Survival Suggestions for Libraries. 1982. pap. 2.00 (ISBN 0-939476-48-7, Pub. by Biblio Pr GA). Prosperity & Profits.
--There Will Always Be a Day That the Creator Will Bless Me. 16p. 1985. pap. text ed. 0.75 (ISBN 0-917593-06-5, Pub. by Intl Partners). Prosperity & Profits.
Doyle, A. C., compiled by. Posie, Positive History: Reference Guide. 1983. pap. 6.95 (ISBN 0-317-00636-3, Pub. by Biblio Pr GA). Prosperity & Profits.
Doyle, A. E., jt. auth. see Lovell, R. R.
Doyle, A. E., ed. Clinical Pharmacology of Antihypertensive Drugs. (Handbook of Hypertension Ser.: Vol. 5). 428p. 1984. 96.50 (ISBN 0-444-90354-2). Elsevier.
Doyle, A. E. & Mendelsohn, F. A., eds. Receptors, Membranes & Transport Mechanisms in Medicine: Proceedings of the Symposium Held in Heidelberg, Australia, 22-23 March, 1984. (International Congress Ser.: Vol. 660). 288p. 1984. 65.00 (ISBN 0-444-80631-8). Elsevier.
Doyle, Alan, jt. auth. see Moo, Eunice W.
Doyle, Alfreda. The Creator or Almighty Always Has an Answer. 1986. (Pub. by Biblio Pr GA); pap. text ed. 2.95 (ISBN 0-939476-23-1). Prosperity & Profits.
--How to Make Simple Potpourri to Give as Gifts. 35p. 1983. pap. 3.95 (ISBN 0-939476-61-4, Pub. by Biblio Pr GA). Prosperity & Profits.
--Just As It Was Given to Me, Bk. 1. 50p. 1983. pap. text ed. 1.95 (ISBN 0-939476-55-X, Pub. by Biblio Pr GA). Prosperity & Profits.
--Obey Your Signal Only. Date not set. 1.95 (ISBN 0-939476-20-7, Pub. by Biblio Pr GA). Prosperity & Profits.
--Posie the Positive Train: Story Edition. Date not set. 6.95 (ISBN 0-939476-27-4, Pub. by Biblio Pr GA); pap. 4.95 (ISBN 0-939476-28-2). Prosperity & Profits.
--Posie the Positive Train Workbook. 60p. 1983. 4.95 (ISBN 0-939476-63-0, Pub. by Biblio Pr GA). Prosperity & Profits.
--Starting a Self Sufficiency Library; Suggested Places to Look for Used & Inexpensive Books. 25p. 1983. pap. text ed. 4.00 (ISBN 0-910811-32-6, Pub. by Center Self Suff). Prosperity & Profits.
--Unusual & Different Greeting Cards & Forms to Duplicate. 45p. 1983. pap. text ed. 9.95 (ISBN 0-939476-59-2, Pub. by Biblio Pr GA). Prosperity & Profits.
Doyle, Alfreda C. Another Batch of Greeting Card Ideas. 20p. 1984. pap. text ed. 8.95 (ISBN 0-913597-55-4, Pub. by Alpha Pyramis). Prosperity & Profits.
--Just As It Was Given to Me: Bk. 2. 31p. 1984. pap. text ed. 3.75 (ISBN 0-913597-51-1, Pub. by Alpha Pyramis). Prosperity & Profits.
--Rhyming Affirmations, Prayer, & Philosophy Poetry, Bk. 1. 32p. 1984. pap. text ed. 3.95 (ISBN 0-913597-47-3, Pub. by Alpha Pyramis). Prosperity & Profits.
--Suggestions for Becoming Self Sufficient. LC 83-90723. 90p. 1983. pap. text ed. 15.95 (ISBN 0-910811-29-6, Pub. by Center Self Suff). Prosperity & Profits.
--Survival Suggestions for Libraries (Continued...) 25p. 1983. pap. 2.00 (ISBN 0-939476-93-2, Pub. by Biblio Pr GA). Prosperity & Profits.
Doyle, Arthur. Green Flag & Other Stories of War & Sport. facsimile ed. LC 70-101468. (Short Story Index Reprint Ser.). 1900. 19.00 (ISBN 0-8369-3201-3). Ayer Co Pubs.
--Man from Archangel & Other Tales of Adventure. facsimile ed. LC 73-101801. (Short Story Index Reprint Ser.). 1925. 17.00 (ISBN 0-8369-3189-0). Ayer Co Pubs.
Doyle, Arthur C. Conan Doyle Stories. 1200p. 1985. 14.95 (ISBN 0-86136-887-8, Pub. by Hamlyn Pub Group England). Hippocrene Bks.
--The History of Spiritualism, 2 vols. in 1. LC 75-7375. (Perspectives in Psychical Research Ser.). (Illus.). 1975. Repr. of 1926 ed. 22.00x (ISBN 0-405-07025-X). Ayer Co Pubs.
--Sir Nigel. 19.95 (ISBN 0-88411-538-0, Pub. by Aeonian Pr). Amereon Ltd.
--Strange Studies from Life & Other Narratives: The Complete True Crime Writings of Sir Arthur Conan Doyle. (Conan Doyle Centennial Ser.). 96p. 1985. 12.95 (ISBN 0-934468-49-4). Gaslight.
Doyle, Arthur Conan. Adventures of Sherlock Holmes. (Classics Ser.). (gr. 5 up). pap. 1.95 (ISBN 0-8049-0097-3, CL-97). Airmont.
--Adventures of Sherlock Holmes. 1901. Repr. of 1892 ed. 13.41i (ISBN 0-06-011070-8, HarpT). Har-Row.
--Adventures of Sherlock Holmes. 288p. 1962. pap. 4.95 (ISBN 0-02-019600-8, Collier). Macmillan.
--The Adventures of Sherlock Holmes. 288p. 1981. pap. 3.50 (ISBN 0-14-005724-2). Penguin.
--Adventures of Sherlock Holmes. 1982. lib. bdg. 16.95x (ISBN 0-89966-385-0). Buccaneer Bks.
--The Adventures of Sherlock Holmes. (gr. 10 up). 1984. pap. 2.50 (ISBN 0-425-07501-X, Medallion). Berkley Pub.
--The Adventures of Sherlock Holmes. 1985. pap. 3.50 (ISBN 0-440-10049-6). Dell.
--The Adventures of Sherlock Holmes. 304p. 1985. pap. 2.50 (ISBN 0-425-08089-7). Berkley Pub.
--Adventures of Sherlock Holmes. Date not set. price not set. S&S.
--The Adventures of Sherlock Holmes. 288p. (Orig.). 1985. pap. 2.50 (ISBN 0-553-24996-7). Bantam.
--The Adventures of Sherlock Holmes, Bk. 1. (Illus.). 140p. (Orig.). (gr. 4-7). 1981. pap. 2.25 (ISBN 0-380-78089-5, 85589-5, Camelot). Avon.
--The Adventures of Sherlock Holmes, Bk. 2. 156p. (Orig.). (gr. 4-7). 1981. pap. 2.25 (ISBN 0-380-78097-6, 85597-6, Camelot). Avon.
--The Adventures of Sherlock Holmes, Bk. 3. (Illus.). 112p. (Orig.). (gr. 4-7). 1981. pap. 2.50 (ISBN 0-380-78105-0, 89383, Camelot). Avon.
--The Adventures of Sherlock Holmes, Bk. 4. (Illus.). 112p. (Orig.). (gr. 4-7). 1981. pap. 2.25 (ISBN 0-380-78113-1, 84749-3, Camelot). Avon.
--Annotated Sherlock Holmes, 2 Vols. Baring-Gould, William S., ed., pseud. (Illus.). 1967. Set. 39.95 (ISBN 0-517-50291-7, C N Potter Bks). Crown.
--Best Supernatural Tales of Arthur Conan Doyle. Bleiler, E. F., ed. LC 78-66710. (Illus.). 256p. 1979. pap. 4.95 (ISBN 0-486-23725-7). Dover.
--Captain of the Polestar, & Other Tales. LC 70-116950. (Short Story Index Reprint Ser). 1894. 19.00 (ISBN 0-8369-3453-9). Ayer Co Pubs.
--Case Book of Sherlock Holmes. (gr. 10 up). 1984. pap. 2.50 (ISBN 0-425-07175-8, Medallion). Berkley Pub.
--The Case of the Five Orange Pips. Pauk, Walter & Harris, Raymond, eds. (Jamestown Classics Ser.). (Illus.). 41p. (gr. 6-12). 1976. pap. text ed. 3.00x (ISBN 0-89061-062-2, 545); tchrs. ed. 4.00 (ISBN 0-89061-063-0, 547). Jamestown Pubs.
--The Case of the Six Napoleons. Pauk, Walter & Harris, Raymond, eds. (Jamestown Classics Ser.). (Illus.). 45p. (gr. 6-12). 1976. pap. text ed. 3.00x (ISBN 0-89061-058-4, 537); tchrs. ed. 4.00 (ISBN 0-89061-059-2, 539). Jamestown Pubs.
--The Casebook of Sherlock Holmes. 1985. pap. 2.50 (ISBN 0-425-07175-8). Berkley Pub.
--Complete Professor Challenger Stories. 1952. 20.00 (ISBN 0-7195-0360-4). Transatlantic.
--Complete Sherlock Holmes. LC 65-6074. 15.95 (ISBN 0-385-00689-6); 2 vols. 19.95 (ISBN 0-385-04591-3). Doubleday.
--Doings of Raffles Haw, & Other Stories. facsimile ed. LC 72-103507. (Short Story Index Reprint Ser.). 1891. 12.50 (ISBN 0-8369-3249-8). Ayer Co Pubs.
--The Edinburgh Stories of Arthur Conan Doyle. Edwards, Owen D., compiled by. 88p. 1983. 10.95 (ISBN 0-904919-49-8, Pub. by Salem Hse Ltd). Merrimack Pub Cir.
--Essays on Photography. Gibson, Michael J. & Green, Richard L., eds. (The Unknown Conan Doyle Ser.). 224p. 1983. 18.95 (ISBN 0-436-13302-4, Pub. by Secker & Warburg UK). David & Charles.
--Exploits of Brigadier Gerard. 15.95 (ISBN 0-7195-3227-2). Transatlantic.
--The Great Adventures of Sherlock Holmes. Platt, Kin, ed. (Now Age Illustrated Ser.: No. 2). (Illus.). 64p. (gr. 5-10). 1974. 5.00 (ISBN 0-88301-205-7); pap. text ed. 1.95 (ISBN 0-88301-137-9). Pendulum Pr.
--His Last Bow. (gr. 10 up). 1984. pap. 2.50 (ISBN 0-425-07502-8, Medallion). Berkley Pub.
--Hound of the Baskervilles. (Classics Ser.). (gr. 8 up). pap. 1.50 (ISBN 0-8049-0062-0, CL-62). Airmont.
--Hound of the Baskervilles. lib. bdg. 14.95x (ISBN 0-89966-229-3). Buccaneer Bks.
--Hound of the Baskervilles. 224p. (gr. 5 up). 1959. pap. 2.50 (ISBN 0-440-93758-2, LFL). Dell.
--The Hound of the Baskervilles. Eyre, A. G., ed. (Longman Simplified English Ser.). 72p. 1976. pap. 1.95x (ISBN 0-582-52910-7). Longman.
--The Hound of the Baskervilles. (Oxford Progressive English Readers Ser.). (Illus.). (gr. k-6). 1979. pap. text ed. 3.50x (ISBN 0-19-581211-5). Oxford U Pr.

--Hound of the Baskervilles. new & abr. ed. Fago, John N., ed. (Now Age Illustrated III Ser.). (Illus.). (gr. 4-12). 1977. text ed. 5.00 (ISBN 0-88301-276-6); pap. text ed. 1.95 (ISBN 0-88301-264-2). Pendulum Pr.

--The Hound of the Baskervilles. 1981. pap. 2.50 (ISBN 0-14-000111-5). Penguin.

--The Hound of the Baskervilles. (Madhuban Abridge Classics Ser.). 104p. (gr. 7-8). 1983. pap. text ed. 3.95x (ISBN 0-7069-2470-3, Pub by Vikas India). Advent NY.

--The Hound of the Baskervilles. (gr. 10 up). 1983. pap. 2.50 (ISBN 0-425-08090-0). Berkley Pub.

--The Hound of the Baskervilles. Goodenough, Simon, ed. (Illus.). 192p. 1984. pap. 19.45i (ISBN 0-316-32002-1). Little.

--The Hound of the Baskervilles. 200p. 1985. deluxe ed. 300.00 limited ed. (ISBN 0-910457-06-9). Arion Pr.

--The Illustrated Sherlock Holmes. (Illus.). 832p. 1985. pap. 6.95 (ISBN 0-517-55660-X, C N Potter). Crown.

--Letters to the Press. Gibson, John M. & Green, Richard L., eds. (The Unknown Conan Doyle Ser.). 352p. 1985. 28.00 (ISBN 0-436-13303-2, Pub. by Secker & Warburg UK). David & Charles.

--The Lost World. lib. bdg. 15.95x (ISBN 0-89966-233-1). Buccaneer Bks.

--Masterworks of Crime & Mystery. Tracy, Jack, ed. 320p. 1982. 14.95 (ISBN 0-385-27688-5, Dial). Doubleday.

--The Memoirs of Sherlock Holmes. 288p. 1985. pap. 2.95 (ISBN 0-345-32714-4). Ballantine.

--Memoirs of Sherlock Holmes. (gr. 10 up). 1984. pap. 2.50 (ISBN 0-425-07315-7, Medallion). Berkley Pub.

--Memoirs of Sherlock Holmes. 1951. pap. 2.95 (ISBN 0-14-000785-7). Penguin.

--The Memoirs of Sherlock Holmes. 1982. Repr. lib. bdg. 16.95x (ISBN 0-89966-428-8). Buccaneer Bks.

--Memories & Adventures. 408p. 1983. Repr. of 1924 ed. lib. bdg. 50.00 (ISBN 0-89987-180-1). Darby Bks.

--The Musgrave Ritual. Pauk, Walter & Harris, Raymond, eds. (Jamestown Classics Ser.). (Illus.). 39p. (gr. 6-12). 1976. pap. text ed. 3.00x (ISBN 0-89061-056-8, 533); tchrs. ed. 4.00 (ISBN 0-89061-057-6, 535). Jamestown Pubs.

--My Friend the Murderer: & Other Mysteries & Adventures. facsimile ed. LC 76-37267. (Short Story Index Reprint Ser.). Repr. of 1893 ed. 16.00 (ISBN 0-8369-4078-4). Ayer Co Pubs.

--The New Revelation. 122p. 1983. pap. 6.50 (ISBN 0-89540-103-7, SB-103). Sun Pub.

--The Red-Headed League. Pauk, Walter & Harris, Raymond, eds. (Jamestown Classics Ser.). (Illus.). 47p. (gr. 6-12). 1976. pap. text ed. 3.00x (ISBN 0-89061-060-6, 541); tchrs. ed. 4.00x (ISBN 0-89061-061-4, 543). Jamestown Pubs.

--Refugees: A Tale of Two Continents. 8.95 (ISBN 0-685-20618-1). Transatlantic.

--The Return of Gerard. 192p. (Orig.). 1982. pap. 2.25 (ISBN 0-515-05531-X). Jove Pubns.

--Return of Sherlock Holmes. 1982. pap. 2.95 (ISBN 0-14-005708-0). Penguin.

--The Return of Sherlock Holmes. (gr. 10 up). 1983. pap. 2.50 (ISBN 0-425-07125-1, Medallion). Berkley Pub.

--The Return of Sherlock Holmes. 320p. 1985. pap. 2.50 (ISBN 0-425-08005-6). Berkley Pub.

--Round the Red Lamp. facsimile ed. LC 77-101802. (Short Story Index Reprint Ser.). 1894. 16.00 (ISBN 0-8369-3190-4). Ayer Co Pubs.

--Sherlock Holmes. LC 79-24106. (Raintree Short Classics). (Illus.). (gr. 4 up). 1980. PLB 15.15 (ISBN 0-8172-1657-X). Raintree Pubs.

--Sherlock Holmes. Stewart, Diana, adapted by. LC 79-24106. (Raintree Short Classics). (Illus.). 48p. (gr. 4-12). 1983. pap. 9.27 (ISBN 0-8172-2021-6). Raintree Pubs.

--Sherlock Holmes: A Study in Scarlet. (Bambi Classics Ser.). (Illus.). 204p. (Orig.). 1981. pap. 3.95 (ISBN 0-89531-055-4, 0221-48). Sharon Pubns.

--Sherlock Holmes, Master Detective. LC 80-54136. (Silver Classics Ser.). 288p. (gr. 6 up). 1985. pap. 3.67 (ISBN 0-382-09992-3). Silver.

--The Sherlock Holmes Mysteries. 1985. pap. 2.95 (ISBN 0-451-51901-9, Sig Classics). NAL.

--Sherlock Holmes: Selected Stories. (World's Classics Ser.). 1980. pap. 3.95 (ISBN 0-19-281530-X). Oxford U Pr.

--Sherlock Holmes: The Published Apocrypha. Tracy, Jack, ed. LC 80-16328. 325p. 1980. 15.95 (ISBN 0-317-11704-1). Gaslight.

--Sherlock Holmes: The Published Apocrypha. Tracy, Jack, ed. 335p. 1985. 13.95 (ISBN 0-317-30097-0). Vanguard.

--The Sign of Four: pb. Goodenough, Simon, ed. (Illus.). 192p. 1985. pap. 19.45i (ISBN 0-316-32009-9). Little.

--Sign of the Four. lib. bdg. 15.95x (ISBN 0-89966-230-7). Buccaneer Bks.

--The Sign of the Four. new ed. LC 60-6582. (Illus.). 160p. (YA) 1979. lib. bdg. 5.98 (ISBN 0-87460-218-1); pap. 1.95 (ISBN 0-87460-219-X). Lion Bks.

--The Sign of the Four. 1982. pap. 2.95 (ISBN 0-14-005855-9). Penguin.

--Six Notable Adventures of Sherlock Holmes. 512p. (gr. 3 up). 1982. pap. 6.95 (ISBN 0-448-41101-6, G&D). Putnam Pub Group.

--The Stark Munro Letters. LC 79-8259. Repr. of 1895 ed. 44.50 (ISBN 0-404-61840-5). AMS Pr.

--The Stark Munro Letters. LC 80-67705. (Conan Doyle Centennial Ser.). (Illus.). 220p. 1982. 14.95 (ISBN 0-934468-46-X). Gaslight.

--A Study in Scarlet. 192p. 1981. pap. 2.25 (ISBN 0-441-79076-3, Pub. by Charter Bks). Ace Bks.

--A Study in Scarlet. lib. bdg. 15.95x (ISBN 0-89966-231-5). Buccaneer Bks.

--Study in Scarlet. 1982. pap. 2.95 (ISBN 0-14-005707-2). Penguin.

--A Study in Scarlet & the Sign of Four. (gr. 10 up). 1983. pap. 2.25 (ISBN 0-425-05209-5). Berkley Pub.

--A Study in Scarlet & the Sign of the Four. 256p. 1985. pap. 2.50 (ISBN 0-425-08004-8). Berkley Pub.

--Tales of Terror & Mystery. (Illus.). 1979. pap. 3.50 (ISBN 0-14-004878-2). Penguin.

--Tales of Terror & Mystery. 1982. Repr. lib. bdg. 16.95x (ISBN 0-89966-429-6). Buccaneer Bks.

--Uncle Bernac: A Memory of the Empire. 9.95 (ISBN 0-7195-0392-2). Transatlantic.

--Uncollected Stories: The Unknown Conan Doyle. Gibson, John M. & Green, Richard L., eds. LC 83-45159. 480p. 1984. 14.95 (ISBN 0-385-19028-X). Doubleday.

--Valley of Fear. lib. bdg. 15.95x (ISBN 0-89966-232-3). Buccaneer Bks.

--The Valley of Fear. 176p. 1985. pap. 2.50 (ISBN 0-425-07140-5). Berkley Pub.

Doyle, Arthur Conan & Carr, John D. Exploits of Sherlock Holmes. facsimile ed. LC 75-157775. (Short Story Index Reprint Ser.). Repr. of 1954 ed. 21.00 (ISBN 0-8369-3887-9). Ayer Co Pubs.

Doyle, Arthur Conan see Allen, W. S.

Doyle, Arthur Conan see Doyle, Arthur Conan.

Doyle, Arthur Conan see Eyre, A. G.

Doyle, Arthur Conan see Howe, D. H.

Doyle, Arthur Conan see Swan, D. K.

Doyle, Austin, ed. Anti-Hypertensive Drugs. (International Encyclopedia of Pharmacology & Therapeutics: Section 109). (Illus.). 260p. 1981. 61.00 (ISBN 0-08-028849-9). Pergamon.

Doyle, Austin E. Pharmacological & Therapeutic Aspects of Hypertension. LC 78-27898. 232p. 1980. Vol. 1, 224p. 71.00 (ISBN 0-8493-5385-8); Vol. 2, 256p. 76.00 (ISBN 0-8493-5386-6). CRC Pr.

Doyle, Austin E. & Bearn, Alexander G., eds. Hypertension & the Angiotensin System: Therapeutic Approaches (MEDAC 1983) (Illus.). 320p. 1984. text ed. 48.00 (ISBN 0-89004-309-4). Raven.

Doyle, Barbara. The Hunted Heart. (Velvet Glove Ser.: No. 9). 192p. (Orig.). 1984. pap. 2.25 (ISBN 0-380-89458-0). Avon.

Doyle, Bertram W. Etiquette of Race Relations in the South. LC 68-25198. 1968. Repr. of 1937 ed. 19.50x (ISBN 0-8046-0115-1, Pub. by Kennikat). Assoc Faculty Pr.

Doyle, Brendan. Meditations with TM Julian of Norwich. LC 82-73955. (Meditations with TM). (Illus.). 135p. (Orig.). 1983. pap. 6.95 (ISBN 0-939680-11-4). Bear & Co.

Doyle, Brian, ed. The Who's Who of Children's Literature. LC 68-28904. (Illus.). 1971. Repr. 14.00x (ISBN 0-8052-3290-7). Schocken.

Doyle, Brian B. & Scheiber, Stephen C., eds. The Impaired Physician. 230p. 1983. 24.50x (ISBN 0-306-41081-8, Plenum Pr). Plenum Pub.

Doyle, Cassie, jt. auth. see McClain, Janet.

Doyle, Charles. Wallace Stevens: The Critical Heritage. (The Critical Heritage Ser.). 500p. 1985. 34.95x (ISBN 0-7100-9647-X). Routledge & Kegan.

--William Carlos Williams & the American Poem. LC 81-8925. 224p. 1982. 20.00x (ISBN 0-312-88064-2). St Martin.

--William Carlos Williams: The Critical Heritage. (The Critical Hertigage Ser.). 1980. 30.00x (ISBN 0-7100-8987-2). Routledge & Kegan.

Doyle, Charles H. Fifty Funeral Homilies. 110p. 1984. pap. 10.00 spiral bdg. (ISBN 0-87061-094-5). Chr Classics.

Doyle, Charles H. & Stewart, Terrell. Stand in the Door. Phillips, James M., ed. LC 79-13509. (Illus.). 15.00x (ISBN 0-932572-09-X). Phillips Pubns.

Doyle, Conan. Adventure of the Speckled Band & Other Stories of Sherlock Holmes. 1985. pap. 1.95 (ISBN 0-451-51642-7, Sig Classics). NAL.

Doyle, Conan A. Beyond the City. LC 80-67703. (Conan Doyle Centennial Ser.). (Illus.). 177p. 1982. 12.95 (ISBN 0-934468-44-3). Gaslight.

--The Doings of Raffles Haw. LC 80-67702. (Conan Doyle Centennial Ser.). (Illus.). 147p. 1981. 12.95 (ISBN 0-934468-43-5). Gaslight.

--A Duet with an Occasional Chorus. LC 80-67707. (Conan Doyle Centennial Ser.). (Illus.). 260p. 1985. 16.95 (ISBN 0-934468-48-6). Gaslight.

--The Firm of Girdlestone. LC 80-65205. (Conan Doyle Centennial Ser.). (Illus.). 364p. 1981. 16.95 (ISBN 0-934468-42-7). Gaslight.

--The Mystery of Cloomber. LC 80-65206. (Conan Doyle Centennial Ser.). (Illus.). 195p. 1980. 12.95 (ISBN 0-934468-41-9). Gaslight.

--The Tragedy of the Korosko. LC 80-67706. (Conan Doyle Centennial Ser.). (Illus.). 202p. 1983. 12.95 (ISBN 0-934468-47-8). Gaslight.

Doyle, D. M. Efficient Accounting & Record Keeping. 123p. 1977. 8.00 (ISBN 0-686-48194-1, 0811). T-C Pubns CA.

Doyle, Darrell J., jt. ed. see Segal, Harold.

Doyle, David N. Ireland, Irishmen & Revolutionary America, 1760-1820. (Illus.). 257p. (Orig.). 1981. 12.50 (ISBN 0-85342-590-6, Pub. by Mercier Pr Ireland). Irish Bk Ctr.

--Irish-Americans, Native Rights & National Empires: The Structure, Divisions, & Attitudes of the Catholic Minority in the Decade of Expansion, 1890-1901. LC 76-6336. (Irish Americans Ser). 1976. 26.50 (ISBN 0-405-09332-2). Ayer Co Pubs.

Doyle, David N. & Edwards, Owen D., eds. America & Ireland, Seventeen Seventy-Six to Nineteen Seventy-Six: The American Identify & the Irish Connection. LC 79-7066. 1980. lib. bdg. 29.95 (ISBN 0-313-21119-1, DOA/). Greenwood.

Doyle, Deborah, ed. The Chicago Architectural Journal, 1984, Vol. 4. LC 82-641459. (Illus.). 136p. 1984. 17.50x (ISBN 0-9614052-0-1). Chicago Arch.

Doyle, Denis P. The Brain Race: The Failure of American Education; Lessons for Tomorrow. 1983. 13.95 (ISBN 0-88015-012-2). Empire Bks.

Doyle, Dennis. The Complete Series Six Study Book. 5th ed. (Illus.). 350p. (Orig.). 1984. pap. text ed. 25.00 (ISBN 0-914234-63-3). Human Res Dev Pr.

Doyle, Dennis M. Efficient Accounting & Record Keeping. LC 78-2474. (Wiley Series The Small Business). 116p. 1977. pap. 7.95 (ISBN 0-471-05044-X, Pub. by Wiley Pr). Wiley.

Doyle, Derek. Coping With a Dying Relative. 1983. 30.00x (ISBN 0-86334-028-8, Pub. by Macdonald Pub UK); pap. 20.00x (ISBN 0-86334-026-1). State Mutual Bk.

Doyle, Dickie. Diary by Dickie Doyle. pap. 8.95 (ISBN 0-317-02545-7). Faber & Faber.

Doyle, Don H. Nashville in the New South: 1880-1930. LC 84-11976. 312p. 1985. 19.95 (ISBN 0-87049-446-5). U of Tenn Pr.

--Nashville since the Nineteen Twenties. LC 85-3262. (Illus.). 1985. 23.50 (ISBN 0-87049-470-8). U of Tenn Pr.

--The Social Order of a Frontier Community: Jacksonville, Illinois, Eighteen Twenty-Five to Eighteen Seventy. LC 78-5287. 304p. 1978. 22.50x (ISBN 0-252-00685-2); pap. 8.95x (ISBN 0-252-01036-1). U of Ill Pr.

Doyle, Edward & Lipsman, Samuel. America Takes over the Big Build-Up (1965-1967) (Vietnam Experience Ser.). (Illus.). 192p. 1983. 16.95 (ISBN 0-201-11328-7). Addison-Wesley.

--The Vietnam Experience, 3 vols. Boston Publishing Co. & Manning, Robert, eds. (Illus.). 1982. 16.95 ea. Vol. I: Setting The Stage (pre-1946) 192p (ISBN 0-201-11260-4). Vol. II: Passing The Torch (1946-1960) 208p. (ISBN 0-201-11261-2); Vol. III: Raising The Stakes (1960-1965) 192p. (ISBN 0-201-11262-0). Addison-Wesley.

Doyle, Edward & Maitland, Terrence. Aftermath. Manning, Robert, ed. (Vietnam Experience Ser.: Vol. 17). (Illus.). 192p. 1985. 16.95 (ISBN 0-939526-17-4). Boston Pub Co.

Doyle, Edward & Weiss, Stephen. A Collision of Cultures. Manning, Robert, ed. LC 84-72041. (Vietnam Experience Ser.: Vol. XII). (Illus.). 192p. 1984. 16.95 (ISBN 0-939526-12-3). Boston Pub Co.

Doyle, Edward, jt. auth. see Weiss, Stephen.

Doyle, Edward G. & Lipsman, Samuel. Setting the Stage, Vol. I. LC 81-65796. (Vietnam Experience Ser.). (Illus.). 192p. 1981. 16.95 (ISBN 0-939526-00-X). Boston Pub Co.

Doyle, Edward G. & Lipsman, Samuel L. America Takes Over, Vol. 4. Manning, Robert, ed. LC 82-61227. (Vietnam Experience Ser.). (Illus.). 192p. 1982. 16.95 (ISBN 0-939526-03-4). Boston Pub Co.

--Fighting for Time, Vol. 7. Manning, Robert, ed. LC 83-72005. (Vietnam Experience Ser.). (Illus.). 192p. 1983. 16.95 (ISBN 0-939526-07-7). Boston Pub Co.

Doyle, Edward G., tr. see Scottus, Sedulius.

Doyle, Edward G., et al. Passing the Torch, Vol II. Manning, Robert, ed. LC 81-68920. (Vietnam Experience Ser.). (Illus.). 208p. 1981. 16.95 (ISBN 0-939526-01-8). Boston Pub Co.

Doyle, Elizabeth. Strawberry Shortcake & the Birthday Surprise. (Strawberry Shortcake Ser.). (Illus.). 40p. (ps-3). 1983. cancelled 5.95 (ISBN 0-910313-11-3). Parker Bro.

Doyle, Elizabeth, ed. Yankee Magazines' Travel Guide to New England: Summer-Fall 1985. (Illus.). 240p. 1985. pap. 2.95 (ISBN 0-89909-073-7). Yankee Bks.

Doyle, Eric. The Disciple & the Master. 1983. 15.00 (ISBN 0-8199-0842-8). Franciscan Herald.

--Saint Francis & the Song of Brotherhood. 1981. pap. 5.95 (ISBN 0-8164-2300-8, Pub. by Seabury). Winston Pr.

Doyle, Esther M. & Floyd, Virginia H., eds. Studies in Interpretation, No. 2. 375p. 1977. pap. text ed. 28.25x (ISBN 90-6203-070-X). Humanities.

Doyle, F. H. Lectures Delivered Before the University of Oxford: Matthew Arnold Etc. 1973. Repr. of 1869 ed. 30.00 (ISBN 0-8274-1692-X). R West.

Doyle, F. L., jt. ed. see Tolson, J. S.

Doyle, G. A., ed. see Research Seminar on Promisian Biology (1972: London University).

Doyle, Georgina R. Roxanne, Does Your Husband Travel? The Corporate Wife: for Bitters or Wurst. 196p. 1985. pap. write for info. (ISBN 0-931515-07-6). Triumph Pr.

Doyle, H. C. & Kliment, C. K. Czechoslovak Armoured Fighting Vehicles. 160p. pap. 7.95 (ISBN 0-85242-628-3). Aztex.

Doyle, Harrison. Golden Chia, Ancient Indian Energy Food. new ed. Doyle, R. H., ed. (Illus.). 7.75 (ISBN 0-918462-00-2). Hillside.

Doyle, Helen M. Doctor Nellie: The Autobiography of Dr. Helen MacKnight Doyle. LC 83-5720. (Illus.). 384p. 0.17.50 (ISBN 0-931378-07-9, Dist. by W. Kaufmann Inc.); pap. 9.95 (ISBN 0-931378-06-0). Genny Smith Bks.

Doyle, Hilary L., jt. auth. see Chamberlain, Peter.

Doyle, I. A., intro. by. The Vernon Manuscript: Bodleian Library MS. English poet a.l. (Illus.). 704p. 1986. facsimile 375.00 (ISBN 0-85991-200-0, Pub. by Boydell & Brewer). Longwood Pub Group.

Doyle, J. Introduction to Electrical Wiring. 2nd ed. (Illus.). 1980. text ed. 24.95 (ISBN 0-8359-3185-4). Reston.

Doyle, J. G. Louis Moreau Gottschalk. LC 75-24917. (Bibliographies in American Music). 219p. 1983. 25.00 (ISBN 0-89990-015-1). Info Coord.

Doyle, Jack. Altered Harvest: Agriculture, Genetics & the Fate of the World's Food Supply. 512p. 1985. 22.95 (ISBN 0-670-12697-7). Viking.

Doyle, James, jt. ed. see Campbell, Jane.

Doyle, James A. Catholic Press Directory. 184p. 1985. pap. 25.00 (ISBN 0-686-30366-0). Cath Pr Assn.

--The Male Experience. 336p. 1983. pap. text ed. write for info. (ISBN 0-697-06553-7). Wm C Brown.

--Sex & Gender: The Human Experience. 432p. 1985. pap. text ed. write for info. (ISBN 0-697-00304-3); instr's. manual avail. (ISBN 0-697-00571-2). Wm C Brown.

Doyle, Jean M. & Dennis, Robert L. The Complete Handbook for Medical Secretaries & Assistants. 2nd ed. 1978. pap. text ed. 18.95 (ISBN 0-316-18082-3, Little Med Div). Little.

Doyle, Joan, jt. auth. see Reilly, Nancy.

Doyle, John. Auto Repair. 381p. 1983. write for info. (ISBN 0-89434-031-X). Ferguson.

Doyle, John A. The English in America, 5 vols. Incl. Vol. 1. Puritan Colonies, Pt. 1 (ISBN 0-404-02181-6); Vol. 2. Puritan Colonies, Pt. 2 (ISBN 0-404-02182-4); Vol. 3. The Middle Colonies (ISBN 0-404-02183-2); Vol. 4. Virginia, Maryland & the Carolinas (ISBN 0-404-02184-0); Vol. 5. The Colonies Under the House of Hanover (ISBN 0-404-02185-9). (Illus.). Repr. of 1907 ed. Set. 34.50 ea.; 172.50 (ISBN 0-404-02180-8). AMS Pr.

Doyle, John R., Jr. Arthur Shearly Cripps. (World Authors Ser.). 1975. lib. bdg. 16.95 (ISBN 0-8057-6216-7, Twayne). G K Hall.

--Poetry of Robert Frost: An Analysis. LC 84-39902. 1965. 10.95x (ISBN 0-02-843990-2). Hafner.

Doyle, Joseph B. Frederick William Von Steuben & the American Revolution. LC 74-114827. (Research & Source Works: No. 432). 1970. Repr. of 1913 ed. text ed. 26.50 (ISBN 0-8337-0897-X). B Franklin.

Doyle, Judith. Transcript. 12p. (Orig.). 1981. pap. 3.00 (ISBN 0-917061-08-X). Top Stories.

Doyle, Kathleen, ed. see Read, Jenny.

Doyle, Kathleen E. & Hoover, Jan. Cooperative Law for California Retail Consumer Co-ops. 316p. 1982. pap. text ed. free avail. (ISBN 0-686-82421-0). Calif Dept Co.

Doyle, Kenneth O., Jr. Evaluating Teaching. LC 79-9673. 192p. 1983. 22.50 (ISBN 0-669-03613-7). Lexington Bks.

Doyle, Kenneth O., Jr., jt. auth. see Arnold, Darlene B.

Doyle, L. E., et al. Manufacturing Processes & Materials for Engineers. 2nd ed. 1969. text ed. 37.95 (ISBN 0-13-555862-X). P-H.

Doyle, Larry R., et al. Living with the West Florida Shore. (Living with the Shore Ser.). 1984. 24.75 (ISBN 0-8223-0516-X); pap. 11.75 (ISBN 0-8223-0517-8). Duke.

Doyle, Lauren. Information Retrieval & Processing. LC 75-1179. (Information Science Ser.). 410p. 1975. 49.95 (ISBN 0-471-22151-1, Pub. by Wiley-Interscience). Wiley.

Doyle, Lawrence E., et al. Manufacturing Processes & Materials for Engineers. 3rd ed. (Illus.). 960p. 1985. text ed. 36.95 (ISBN 0-13-555921-9). P-H.

Doyle, Lynn. The Ballygullion Bus. 142p. 1983. 18.95 (ISBN 0-85640-287-7, Pub. by Blackstaff Pr). Longwood Pub Group.

Doyle, M. P., jt. auth. see Neckers, D. C.

Doyle, M. P. & West, C. T., eds. Stereoselective Reductions. (Benchmark Papers in Organic Chemistry: Vol. 6). 1976. 71.00 (ISBN 0-12-786368-0). Acad Pr.

Doyle, Marion. The Heart Turns Back. LC 77-79576. 1978. 5.95 (ISBN 0-87212-080-5). Libra.

Doyle, Marjorie, ed. see Kirk, Paul L.

Doyle, Marvyl & Mittwer, Marie. Basic Reading Patterns: Words & Sentences. (gr. 10 up). 1969. pap. text ed. 16.95 (ISBN 0-13-068031-1). P-H.

Doyle, Mary E. The Sympathetic Response: George Eliot's Fictional Rhetoric. LC 80-65908. (Illus.). 192p. 1981. 19.50 (ISBN 0-8386-3065-0). Fairleigh Dickinson.

Doyle, Mary L., ed. see Mead, Sidney E.

Doyle, Sr. Mary P. Study of Play Selection in Women's Colleges. LC 72-176728. (Columbia University. Teachers College. Contributions to Education: No. 648). Repr. of 1935 ed. 12.50 (ISBN 0-404-55648-5). AMS Pr.

Doyle, Michael. The Sound of Rock: The History of Marshall Valve (Tube) Amplifiers. Clinton, George, ed. (Illus.). 67p. 1983. 12.95 (ISBN 0-86175-330-5, Pub. by Mus New Serv Ltd England). Bold Strummer Ltd.

Doyle, Michael & Straus, David. How to Make Meetings Work. 320p. pap. 3.95 (ISBN 0-515-08308-9). Jove Pubns.

Doyle, Michael, et al, eds. see Anderson-Sannes, Barbara.

Doyle, Michael E. Color Drawing: A Marker-Colored-Pencil Approach. LC 79-15640. (Illus.). 320p. 1981. 39.95 (ISBN 0-442-22184-3). Van Nos Reinhold.

Doyle, Michael P. & Mungall, William S. Experimental Organic Chemistry. LC 79-18392. 490p. 1980. pap. text ed. 31.50 (ISBN 0-471-03383-9); avail. tchrs. manual (ISBN 0-471-08053-5). Wiley.

Doyle, Michael V. Gerald R. Ford Selected Speeches. 1973. pap. 3.95 (ISBN 0-87948-029-7). Beatty.

Doyle, Nora. Word Building One. Fischer, Jean, ed. (Golden Step Ahead Workbooks). 36p. (gr. 1). 1984. 1.95 (ISBN 0-307-23542-4, Golden Bks). Western Pub.

--Word Building Two. Fischer, Jean, ed. (Golden Step Ahead Workbooks). (Illus.). 36p. (gr. 2). 1984. 1.95 (ISBN 0-307-23550-5, Golden Bks). Western Pub.

Doyle, Owen, et al. Analysis Manual for Hospital Information Systems. LC 80-13875. (Illus.). 472p. (Orig.). 1980. pap. text ed. 42.50x (ISBN 0-914904-41-8). Health Admin Pr.

--Analysis Manual for Hospital Information Systems. 463p. 1980. 45.50 (ISBN 0-914904-41-8, 1115). Healthcare Fin Mgmt Assn.

Doyle, P. A. Guide to Basic Information Sources in English Literature. LC 75-43260. (Information Resources Ser). 1976. 10.95x (ISBN 0-470-15011-4, Dist. by Halsted). J Norton Pubs.

Doyle, P. J., ed. Glass-Making Today. 343p. 1981. 79.00x (ISBN 0-86108-047-5, Pub. by Portcullio Pr). State Mutual Bk.

Doyle, Patrick J. & Banta, James E. New Traveller's Health Guide. LC 82-1797. 1982. pap. 4.95 (ISBN 0-87491-193-1). Acropolis.

--Travelers' Health Guide: How to Stay Fit Whenever & Wherever You Go in the U.S. & Around the World. LC 78-6773. (Illus.). 1978. 9.95 (ISBN 0-87491-192-3); pap. 4.95 (ISBN 0-87491-193-1). Acropolis.

Doyle, Paul A. Liam O'Flaherty: An Annotated Bibliography. LC 71-161085. 1972. 7.50x (ISBN 0-87875-017-7). Whitston Pub.

--Paul Vincent Carroll. LC 70-126005. (Irish Writers Ser.). 115p. 1971. 4.50 (ISBN 0-8387-7764-3); pap. 1.95 (ISBN 0-8387-7659-0). Bucknell U Pr.

--Pearl S. Buck. rev. ed. (United States Authors Ser.). 1980. lib. bdg. 13.50 (ISBN 0-8057-7325-8, Twayne). G K Hall.

Doyle, Peter. Analytical Marketing Management. (European Marketing Ser.). 1975. 12.80 (ISBN 0-06-318018-9, IntlDept); pap. 6.60 (ISBN 0-06-318017-0, IntlDept). Har-Row.

Doyle, Peter & Hart, Norman. Case Studies in International Marketing. 272p. (Orig.). 1982. pap. 19.95 (ISBN 0-434-90370-1, Pub. by W Heinemann Ltd); pap. 16.95 tchr's manual (ISBN 0-434-90371-X). David & Charles.

Doyle, Phyllis B., et al. Helping the Severely Handicapped Child: A Guide for Parents & Teachers. LC 78-3300. (John Day Book in Special Education). (Illus.). 1979. 12.45i (ISBN 0-381-90063-0). T Y Crowell.

Doyle, Polly. Grief Counseling & Sudden Death: A Manual & Guide. (Illus.). 352p. 1980. 35.75x (ISBN 0-398-04060-5). C C Thomas.

Doyle, R. H., ed. see Doyle, Harrison.

Doyle, R. J. & Ciardi, J. E., eds. Glucosyltransferases, Glucans, Sucrose & Dental Caries: NIDR Proceedings. (Illus.). 286p. 1983. pap. 33.00 (ISBN 0-917000-10-2). IRL Pr.

Doyle, Richard. The Foreign Tour of Messrs Brown, Jones & Robinson: Being the History of What They Saw & Did in Belgium, Germany, Switzerland, & Italy. LC 74-177503. (Illus.). Repr. of 1854 ed. 17.00 (ISBN 0-405-08465-X, Blom Pubns). Ayer Co Pubs.

Doyle, Richard E. Ate: Its Use & Meaning. x, 190p. 1984. 45.00x (ISBN 0-8232-1062-6). Fordham.

Doyle, Richard F. Divorce: What Everyone Should Know to Beat the Racket. 4th, rev. ed. (Illus.). 21p. 1984. pap. 3.45 (ISBN 0-917212-02-9). Poor Richards.

--A Manifesto of Men's Liberation. 4th, rev. ed. 1985. pap. 3.45 (ISBN 0-917212-03-7). Poor Richards.

--The Rape of the Male. LC 76-3141. (Illus.). 286p. 1976. pap. 4.95 (ISBN 0-917212-01-0). Poor Richards.

Doyle, Robert J. Gainsharing & Productivity: A Guide to Planning, Implementation & Development. 288p. 1983. 24.95 (ISBN 0-8144-5764-9). AMACOM.

Doyle, Rodger P. The Medical Wars. LC 83-16742. (Illus.). 256p. 1983. FPT 13.95 (ISBN 0-688-02216-2). Morrow.

Doyle, Rodger P. & Redding, James L. The Complete Food Handbook. LC 79-52123. (Illus.). 320p. (Revised & Updated ed.). 1980. pap. 3.50 (ISBN 0-394-17398-8, B431, BC). Grove.

Doyle, Roger. The Vegetarian Handbook. 1979. 10.00 (ISBN 0-517-53470-3); pap. 6.95 (ISBN 0-517-53471-1). Crown.

Doyle, Sr. Rosa. Catholic Atmosphere in Marie Von Ebner Eschenbach: Its Use As a Literary Device. LC 70-140040. (Catholic University Studies in German Ser.: No. 6). Repr. of 1936 ed. 18.00 (ISBN 0-404-50226-1). AMS Pr.

Doyle, Ruth L., compiled by. Victor Hugo's Drama: An Annotated Bibliography, 1900 to 1980. LC 80-29680. x, 217p. 1981. lib. bdg. 39.95 (ISBN 0-313-22884-1, DVH/). Greenwood.

Doyle, Ruth M. Soft Toys Made with Love...& the Help of 30 Full-Size Patterns. LC 74-82109. pap. 5.95 (ISBN 0-87299-018-4). East Dennis.

--Soft Toys Made with Love...& the Help of 30 Full Size Patterns. LC 74-82109. 1975. pap. 5.95 (ISBN 0-87299-018-4). Howard Doyle.

Doyle, Stephen. The Pilgrim's New Guide to the Holy Land. 1985. pap. 7.95 (ISBN 0-89453-440-8). M Glazier.

Doyle, Stephen C. Covenant Renewal in Religious Life: Biblical Reflections. 140p. 1976. 6.95 (ISBN 0-8199-0585-2). Franciscan Herald.

Doyle, Suzanne. Sweeter for the Dark. 56p. 1982. pap. 5.00 (ISBN 0-941150-04-6). Barth.

Doyle, Suzanne J. Domestic Passions. 12p. (Orig.). 1984. pap. 4.00 (ISBN 0-941150-20-8). Barth.

Doyle, Teresa A., ed. see Adams, Daniel J.

Doyle, Thomas P. Rights & Responsibilities. 64p. (Orig.). 1983. pap. 2.50 (ISBN 0-916134-58-X). Pueblo Pub Co.

Doyle, Thomas P., ed. Marriage Studies: Reflections in Canon Law & Theology, Vol. 1. 155p. (Orig.). 1980. pap. 4.00 (ISBN 0-943616-03-4). Canon Law Soc.

--Marriage Studies: Reflections in Canon Law & Theology, Vol. 2. 202p. (Orig.). 1982. pap. 4.50 (ISBN 0-943616-04-2). Canon Law Soc.

--Marriage Studies, Vol. 3: Reflections in Canon Law & Theology. (Orig.). 1985. pap. write for info. (ISBN 0-943616-25-5). Canon Law Soc.

Doyle, Walter & Good, Thomas L., eds. Focus on Teaching: Readings from the Elementary School Journal. 290p. 1983. lib. bdg. 22.00x (ISBN 0-226-16177-3); pap. 8.95x (ISBN 0-226-16178-1). U of Chicago Pr.

Doyle, William. Old European Order Sixteen Sixty to Eighteen Hundred. (Short Oxford History of the Modern World Ser.). (Illus.). 1978. 39.95x (ISBN 0-19-913073-6); pap. 15.95x (ISBN 0-19-913131-7). Oxford U Pr.

--Origins of the French Revolution. 1980. pap. 19.95x (ISBN 0-19-873021-7). Oxford U Pr.

Doyle, William, jt. ed. see Milburn, Josephine.

Doyle, William, tr. see Chaussinand-Nogaret, Guy.

Doyle, William J., Jr. Using SuperCalc-The Next Generation: A Self-Teaching Guide. 1985. pap. 16.95 (ISBN 0-471-80828-8); Book with program disk. 46.95 (ISBN 0-471-82606-5). Wiley.

Doyle, Winifred. Up the I. R. A. (Illus.). 289p. 1983. 15.50 (ISBN 0-682-49924-2). Exposition Pr FL.

D'Oyley, Elizabeth. An Anthology of Animal Lovers. 1977. Repr. of 1927 ed. 20.00 (ISBN 0-89984-179-1). Century Bookbindery.

--English Diaries. 1930. Repr. 10.00 (ISBN 0-8274-2255-5). R West.

--English Essays. 1925. Repr. 10.00 (ISBN 0-8274-2257-1). R West.

--Great Travel Stories of All Nations. 1932. 35.00 (ISBN 0-932062-44-X). Sharon Hill.

D'Oyley, Elizabeth, ed. Great Travel Stories from All Nations. 1979. Repr. of 1932 ed. lib. bdg. 40.00 (ISBN 0-8495-1047-3). Arden Lib.

D'Oyley, Enid. Between Sea & Sky. (Illus.). 144p. 1982. cased 15.00 (ISBN 0-88795-002-7, Pub. by Williams-Wallace Canada); pap. 8.00 (ISBN 0-88795-003-5). Three Continents.

D'Oyley, Maud. Great Travel Stories of All Nations. Repr. of 1922 ed. lib. bdg. 30.00 (ISBN 0-8414-3860-9). Folcroft.

D'Oyley, Vincent, jt. auth. see Ray, Douglas.

D'Oyly-Watkins, C., jt. ed. see Butlin, A. G.

Doyno, Victor, ed. Mark Twain: Selected Writings of an American Skeptic. LC 82-60382. 450p. 1982. 25.95 (ISBN 0-87975-189-4); pap. 13.95 (ISBN 0-87975-190-8). Prometheus Bks.

Doyon, Roy, jt. auth. see Suckling, Philip.

Doz, Y. Multinational Strategic Management. (Illus.). 240p. 1985. 25.00 (ISBN 0-08-031808-8); pap. 14.00 (ISBN 0-08-031807-X). Pergamon.

Doz, Yves L. Government Power & Multinational Strategic Management: Power Systems & Telecommunication Equipment. LC 79-11793. (Praeger Special Studies Ser.). 298p. 1979. 39.95 (ISBN 0-03-049476-1). Praeger.

Dozer, Donald. The Monroe Doctrine: Its Modern Significance. LC 75-38904. 274p. 1976. Repr. 6.50x (ISBN 0-87918-026-9). ASU Lat Am St.

Dozer, Donald M. Are We Good Neighbors? xi, 456p. 1972. Repr. of 1959 ed. 40.00 (ISBN 0-384-12515-8). Johnson Repr.

--Portrait of the Free State. LC 76-47023. (Illus.). 653p. 1976. 17.50 (ISBN 0-87033-226-0). Tidewater.

Dozier, Craig L. Nicaragua's Mosquito Shore: The Years of British & American Presence. LC 84-237. (Illus.). x, 276p. 1985. 32.75 (ISBN 0-8173-0226-3). U of Ala Pr.

Dozier, Edward P. Hano: A Tewa Indian Community in Arizona. LC 65-26674. (Case Studies in Cultural Anthropology). (Orig.). 1966. pap. text ed. 9.95 (ISBN 0-03-055115-3, HoltC). HR&W.

--The Kalinga of Northern Luzon, Philippines. Spindler, George & Spindler, Louise, eds. (Case Studies in Cultural Anthropology). (Illus.). 112p. 1983. pap. text ed. 6.95x (ISBN 0-8290-0279-0). Irvington.

--Mountain Arbiters: The Changing Life of a Philippine Hill People. LC 66-18530. (Illus.). pap. 79.80 (ISBN 0-317-11066-7, 2055373). Bks Demand UMI.

--Pueblo Indians of North America. Spindler, George & Spindler, Louise, eds. (Case Studies in Cultural Anthropology). (Illus.). 1982. pap. text ed. 8.95x (ISBN 0-8290-0601-X). Irvington.

--The Pueblo Indians of North America. (Illus.). 224p. 1983. pap. text ed. 7.95x (ISBN 0-88133-059-0). Waveland Pr.

Dozier, Grady. The Bell. 120p. (Orig.). Date not set. 11.95 (ISBN 0-931290-92-9). Alchemy Bks.

--False Echoes. 244p. (Orig.). (YA) 1984. pap. 5.95x (ISBN 0-931290-84-8). Alchemy Bks.

Dozier, Howard D. History of the Atlantic Coast Line Railroad. LC 68-27846. Repr. of 1920 ed. 25.00x (ISBN 0-678-00753-5). Kelley.

Dozier, Jeff, jt. auth. see Marsh, William.

Dozier, Jeffrey, jt. auth. see Marsh, William.

Dozier, Robert R. For King, Constitution & Country: The English Loyalists & the French Revolution. LC 83-1221. 224p. 1983. 22.00x (ISBN 0-8131-1490-X). U Pr of Ky.

Dozier, Zoe. Home Again, My Love. (YA) 1978. 8.95 (ISBN 0-685-86408-1, Avalon). Bouregy.

--The Warm Side of the Island. (YA) 1978. 8.95 (ISBN 0-685-53394-8, Avalon). Bouregy.

Dozois. Alternatives to Conventional Ileostomy. 1985. 49.95 (ISBN 0-8151-2815-0). Year Bk Med.

Dozois, Gardener, jt. auth. see Dann, Jack.

Dozois, Gardner. The Fiction of James Tiptree, Jr. 1977. pap. 2.50 (ISBN 0-916186-04-0). Algol Pr.

--The Fiction of James Tiptree, Jr. LC 83-14374. 36p. 1983. Repr. lib. bdg. 12.95x (ISBN 0-89370-752-X). Borgo Pr.

Dozois, Gardner, jt. auth. see Dann, Jack.

Dozois, Gardner, ed. The Year's Best Science Fiction: First Annual Collection. (The Year's Best Science Fiction Ser.: No. 1). 576p. 1984. lib. bdg. 17.95 (ISBN 0-312-94482-9); pap. 9.95 (ISBN 0-312-94483-7). Bluejay Bks.

--The Year's Best Science Fiction: Second Annual Collection. 576p. 1985. 19.95 (ISBN 0-312-94484-5, Dist. by St. Martin); pap. 10.95 (ISBN 0-312-94485-3, Dist. by St. Martin). Bluejay Bks.

Dozois, Gardner, ed. see Dann, Jack.

Dozon, A. Contes Albanais. LC 78-20111. (Collection de contes et de chansons populaires: Vol. 3). Repr. of 1881 ed. 21.50 (ISBN 0-404-60353-X). AMS Pr.

Dozoretz, Eileen & Pearl, Shirley. California Personal Injury, a Guide for Law Office Paper Work & Procedure: With 1977 Supplement. LC 74-83831. 1974. 15.00x (ISBN 0-910874-33-6). Legal Bk Co.

Dozy, R. Dictionaire Detaille des Noms de Vetements Chez Les Arabes. (Arabic & Fr.). 20.00x. Intl Bk Ctr.

--Glossaire des Mots Espagnols et Portugais Derives de L'arabe. (Span., Port. & Arabic.). 1974. 20.00x (ISBN 0-86685-105-4). Intl Bk Ctr.

--Supplement Aux Dictionnaire Arabe (Arabic-French, 2 vols. (Arabic & Fr.). 1969. 80.00x (ISBN 0-86685-106-2). Intl Bk Ctr.

Dozy, Reinhart. Spanish Islam: History of the Moslems in Spain. 770p. 1972. Repr. of 1913 ed. 45.00x (ISBN 0-7146-2128-5, F Cass Co). Biblio Dist.

Drabbe, P. Spraakkunst Van Het Marind. 1955. 28.00 (ISBN 0-384-12595-6). Johnson Repr.

Drabbel, Phil. What Price the Countryside? (Illus.). 224p. 1985. 14.95 (ISBN 0-7181-2345-X, Pub. by Michael Joseph). Merrimack Pub Cir.

Drabble, Margaret. For Queen & Country: Victorian England. LC 78-9782. (Illus.). (gr. 6 up). 1979. 8.95 (ISBN 0-395-28960-2, Clarion). HM.

--The Garrick Year. 1984. pap. 6.95 (ISBN 0-452-25590-2, Plume). NAL.

--The Ice Age. 1985. 6.95 (ISBN 0-452-25680-1, Plume). NAL.

--The Middle Ground. LC 80-7630. 288p. 1980. 10.95 (ISBN 0-394-51224-3). Knopf.

--The Millstone. LC 83-62868. 144p. 1984. pap. 5.95 (ISBN 0-452-25516-3, Plume). NAL.

--The Needle's Eye. 1972. 11.95 (ISBN 0-394-47966-1). Knopf.

--A Writer's Britain: Landscape in Literature. LC 79-2117. (Illus.). 1979. 22.50 (ISBN 0-394-50819-X). Knopf.

Drabble, Margaret, ed. The Oxford Companion to English Literature. 5th ed. 1985. 35.00 (ISBN 0-19-866130-4). Oxford U Pr.

Drabble, Margaret, ed. see Austen, Jane.

Drabble, Phil. Country Matters. (Illus.). 216p. 1983. 15.95 (ISBN 0-7181-2177-5, Pub by Michael Joseph). Merrimack Pub Cir.

--One Man & His Dog. (Illus.). 152p. 1984. pap. 11.95 (ISBN 0-7181-2416-2, Pub. by Michael Joseph). Merrimack Pub Cir.

--One Man & His Dog. (Illus.). 185p. 17.95 (ISBN 0-317-11564-2). Diamond Farm Bk.

Drabeck, Bernard A., et al. Structures for Composition. 2nd ed. LC 77-77675. (Illus.). 1978. pap. text ed. 17.95 (ISBN 0-395-25567-8); instrs.' manual 0.50 (ISBN 0-395-25568-6). HM.

--Exploring Literature. LC 81-82566. 1982. 17.95 (ISBN 0-395-31694-4); instr's manual 1.00 (ISBN 0-395-31695-2). HM.

Drabek, Anne G. & Knapp, Wilfred. The Politics of African & Middle Eastern States: An Annotated Bibliography. LC 76-26649. 1977. pap. text ed. 13.50 (ISBN 0-08-020583-6). Pergamon.

Drabek, Gordon, jt. ed. see Sinha, Radha.

Drabek, Thomas E. Disaster in Aisle Thirteen. pap. 4.50x (ISBN 0-87776-201-5, D1). Ohio St U Admin Sci.

--Laboratory Simulation of a Police Communications System Under Stress. 1970. pap. 4.50x (ISBN 0-87776-202-3, D2). Ohio St U Admin Sci.

Drabek, Thomas E. & Key, William H. Conquering Disaster: Family Recovery & Long Term Consequences. 485p. 1985. text ed. 49.50x (ISBN 0-8290-1000-9); pap. text ed. 29.50x (ISBN 0-8290-1536-1). Irvington.

Drabek, Thomas E., jt. auth. see Haas, J. Eugene.

Drabelle, Dennis, jt. auth. see Reed, Nathaniel P.

Drabick, Lawrence W., ed. Interpreting Education: A Sociological Approach. LC 77-153388. 1971. 23.00x (ISBN 0-89197-235-8); pap. text ed. 6.95x (ISBN 0-89197-236-6). Irvington.

Drabik, Harry. The Spirit of Canoe Camping. (Illus.). 126p. 1981. pap. 5.95 (ISBN 0-931714-11-7). Nodin Pr.

--The Spirit of Winter Camping. (Illus.). 104p. (Orig.). 1985. pap. 5.95 (ISBN 0-931714-24-9). Nodin Pr.

Drabkin, David L. Fundamental Structure: Nature's Architecture. LC 74-19577. 96p. 1975. 30.00x (ISBN 0-8122-7685-X); pap. 20.00x (ISBN 0-8122-1082-4). U of Pa Pr.

Drabkin, I. E., jt. tr. see Drake, Stillman.

Drabkin, Israel E., jt. auth. see Cohen, Morris R.

Drabkin, Marjorie. Word Mastery: A Guide to the Understanding of Words. Bromberg, Murray, ed. LC 75-34906. 1978. pap. 6.95 (ISBN 0-8120-0526-0). Barron.

Drach, Ivan. Orchard Lamps. Kunitz, Stanley, ed. LC 77-95136. 71p. 1978. 9.95 (ISBN 0-8180-1538-1); pap. 3.95 (ISBN 0-8180-1544-6). Sheep Meadow.

Drach, Robert F., jt. auth. see Herzfeld, Thomas J.

Drache, Hiram M. Beyond the Furrow: Some Keys to Successful Farming in the Twentieth Century. LC 76-29489. 560p. 1976. 14.95 (ISBN 0-8134-1858-5). Interstate.

--The Challenge of the Prairie. LC 70-632775. 260p. 1970. text ed. 14.95 (ISBN 0-8134-1994-8). Interstate.

--The Day of the Bonanza. LC 64-65044. (Illus.). 239p. 1964. text ed. 12.95 (ISBN 0-8134-1995-6, 1995). Interstate.

--Koochiching: Pioneering along the Rainy River Frontier. (Illus.). 350p. 1983. 14.95x (ISBN 0-8134-2287-6). Interstate.

--Tomorrow's Harvest. LC 78-57250. 1978. 14.95 (ISBN 0-8134-2032-6, 2032). Interstate.

Drache, Hiram R. Plowshares to Printouts. (Illus.). 263p. 1985. 14.95 (ISBN 0-8134-2459-3, 2459). Interstate.

Drachkovitch, Milorad, jt. auth. see Lazitch, Branko.

Drachkovitch, Milorad, ed. East Central Europe: Yesterday, Today, Tomorrow. (Publication Ser.: No. 240). 417p. 1982. 25.95x (ISBN 0-686-86067-5). Hoover Inst Pr.

Drachkovitch, Milorad M., ed. Fifty Years of Communism in Russia. LC 68-8178. 1968. 24.95x (ISBN 0-271-00068-6). Pa St U Pr.

--Marxism in the Modern World. 1965. 25.00x (ISBN 0-8047-0254-3). Stanford U Pr.

--Marxist Ideology in the Contemporary World-Its Appeals & Paradoxes. LC 72-13359. (Essay Index Reprint Ser.). (Published for the Hoover Institution on War, Revolution, & Peace, Stanford University). Repr. of 1966 ed. 18.75 (ISBN 0-8369-8154-5). Ayer Co Pubs.

--The Revolutionary Internationals, 1864-1943. 1966. 20.00x (ISBN 0-8047-0293-4). Stanford U Pr.

Drachler, Jacob, ed. Black Homeland - Black Diaspora: Cross Currents of the African Relationship. LC 74-80066. 1975. 23.50x (ISBN 0-8046-9077-4, Pub. by Kennikat). Assoc Faculty Pr.

Drachler, Jacob, ed. see Drachler, Rose.

Drachler, Rose. The Choice. LC 77-70787. 1977. pap. 3.00 (ISBN 0-686-19541-8). Tree Bks.

--The Collected Poems of Rose Drachler. Drachler, Jacob & Ratner, Rochelle, eds. (Illus.). 240p. 1983. 20.00 (ISBN 0-915066-49-1); pap. 10.00 (ISBN 0-915066-50-5). Assembling Pr.

Drachman, A. Atheism in Pagan Antiquity. 1977. 12.50 (ISBN 0-89005-201-8). Ares.

Drachman, Bermard, tr. see Hirsch, Samson R.

Drachman, Bernard. From the Heart of Israel. LC 72-110183. (Short Story Index Reprint Ser.). 1905. 23.50 (ISBN 0-8369-3334-6). Ayer Co Pubs.

--Looking at America. LC 76-107696. (Essay Index Reprint Ser.). 1934. 20.00 (ISBN 0-8369-1499-6). Ayer Co Pubs.

Drachman, Bernard, tr. see Hirsch, Somson R.

Drachman, Edward R. United States Policy Toward Vietnam 1940-1945. LC 71-86293. 470p. 1970. 18.00 (ISBN 0-8386-7535-2). Fairleigh Dickinson.

Drachman, Theodore S. The Deadly Dream. 224p. 1982. 9.95 (ISBN 0-8397-1900-0). Eriksson.

Drachman, Virginia & Harvey-Felder, Zena, eds. Women's History: A Literature of Struggle Program Guide. (MicroSources: Social Science Skills Development Program Ser.). 67p. (gr. 9-12). 1980. pap. text ed. 7.95 (ISBN 0-667-00618-4). Microfilming Corp.

Drachman, Virginia G. Hospital with a Heart: Women Doctors & the Paradox of Separatism at the New England Hospital, 1862-1969. LC 83-45930. (Illus.). 256p. 1984. 19.95x (ISBN 0-8014-1624-8). Cornell U Pr.

Drachmann, A. B. Atheism in Pagan Antiquity. 69.95 (ISBN 0-87968-675-8). Gordon Pr.

Drachmann, A. G. The Mechanical Technology of Greek & Roman Antiquity. (Illus.). 1963. 7.50 (ISBN 0-934454-61-2). Lubrecht & Cramer.

Drachsler, Julius. Democracy & Assimilation: The Blending of Immigrant Heritages in America. LC 72-132073. Repr. of 1920 ed. cancelled (ISBN 0-8371-3669-5, DDA&, Pub. by Negro U Pr). Greenwood.

--Intermarriage in New York City: A Statistical Study of the Amalgamation of European Peoples. (Columbia University. Studies in the Social Sciences: No. 213). 7.50 (ISBN 0-404-51213-5). AMS Pr.

--Intermarriage in New York City: A Statistical Study of the Amalgamation of European Peoples. LC 74-145477. (The American Immigration Library). 204p. 1971. Repr. of 1921 ed. lib. bdg. 12.95x (ISBN 0-89198-009-1). Ozer.

Drachsler, Leo M. & Torczyner, Harry, eds. Forgery in Art & the Law. 61p. 1956. pap. 5.00 (ISBN 0-87945-012-6). Fed Legal Pubn.

Drackett, Phil. All Color World of Cars. (Illus.). 1979. 5.98 (ISBN 0-7064-1007-6, Mayflower Bks). Smith Pubs.

--The Book of Cromer. 1981. 40.00x (ISBN 0-86023-144-5, Pub. by Barracuda England). State Mutual Bk.

--Car Makers. LC 80-51161. (Careers Ser.). lib. style bind 12.68 (ISBN 0-382-06414-3). Silver.

--The Story of the RAC International Rally. 18.95 (ISBN 0-85429-270-5, F270). Haynes Pubns.

Drackett, Phil, ed. Encyclopedia of the Motor Car. (Illus.). 1979. 12.98 (ISBN 0-517-53833-4). Crown.

Dracop, Joseph F. & Kelley, Carl F. Horizontal Controls as Applied to Local Surveying Needs. 126p. 1978. Repr. 9.00 (ISBN 0-317-32458-6, S200). Am Congrs Survey.

Dracott, Alice E. Simla Village Tales, or, Folk Tales from the Himalayas. 1976. lib. bdg. 59.95 (ISBN 0-8490-2606-7). Gordon Pr.

Dracup, Joseph F. & Kelley, Carl F. Surveying Instrumentation & Coordinate Computation Workshop Lecture Notes. 3rd ed. 208p. 1979. 15.00 (ISBN 0-317-32471-3, S260). Am Congrs Survey.

Draeger, jt. auth. see Kiong.

Draeger, Alain. Rio, Fantastic Carnival. LC 83-80852. (Illus.). 208p. 1983. 51.50 (ISBN 0-86710-061-3). Edns Vilo.

Draeger, Don. Budo: Classical. 1975. 15.00x. Wehman.

--Bujutso: Classical. 1973. 17.95x (ISBN 0-685-83519-7). Wehman.

Draeger, Donn. Ninjutsu: The Art of Invisibility. 2nd ed. (Illus.). 1980. pap. 4.95 (ISBN 0-914778-19-6). Phoenix Bks.

Draeger, Donn, jt. auth. see Warner, Gordon.

Draeger, Donn F. Classical Budo. LC 73-6613. (Martial Arts & Ways of Japan Ser: Vol. 2). (Illus.). 136p. 1973. 15.00 (ISBN 0-8348-0086-1). Weatherhill.

--Classical Bujutsu. LC 72-78593. (Martial Arts & Ways of Japan Ser: Vol. 1). (Illus.). 120p. 1973. 15.00 (ISBN 0-8348-0071-3). Weatherhill.

--Modern Bujutsu & Budo. LC 74-76779. (Martial Arts of Japan Ser: Vol. 3). (Illus.). 192p. 1974. 17.95 (ISBN 0-8348-0099-3). Weatherhill.

Draeger, Donn F. & Chambers, Quintin. Javanese Silat: The Fighting Art of Perisai Diri. LC 78-60969. (Illus.). 128p. 1979. pap. 7.95 (ISBN 0-87011-353-4). Kodansha.

Draeger, Donn F. & Chambers, Quintin T. Shantung Black Tiger: A Shaolin Fighting Art of North China. LC 76-18800. 152p. 1976. 8.95 (ISBN 0-8348-0127-2). Weatherhill.

Draeger, Donn F. & Nakayama, Masatoshi. Practical Karate, 6 vols. LC 63-11828. (Illus.). 1963-65. Vol. 1. pap. 5.95 (ISBN 0-8048-0481-8); Vol. 2. pap. 5.95 (ISBN 0-8048-0482-6); Vol. 3. pap. 5.95 (ISBN 0-8048-0483-4); Vol. 4. pap. 5.95 (ISBN 0-8048-0484-2); Vol. 5. pap. 4.75 (ISBN 0-8048-0485-0); Vol. 6. pap. 4.75 (ISBN 0-8048-0486-9). C E Tuttle.

Draeger, Donn F. & Otaki, Tadao. Judo Formal Techniques: A Complete Guide to Kodokan Randori No Kata. LC 82-50095. (Illus.). 1983. 35.00 (ISBN 0-8048-1187-3). C E Tuttle.

Draeger, Donn F. & Smith, Robert. Comprehensive Asian Fighting Arts. (Illus.). 1969. 12.50x (ISBN 0-685-21878-3, Pub. by Kodansha). Wehman.

Draeger, Donn F. & Smith, Robert W. Comprehensive Asian Fighting Arts. LC 80-82527. (Illus.). 207p. 1981. pap. 12.50 (ISBN 0-87011-436-0). Kodansha.

Draeger, Donn F. & Warner, Gordon. Japanese Swordsmanship: Technique & Practice. (Illus.). 224p. 1982. 29.95 (Pub. by John Weatherhill Inc Japan). C E Tuttle.

Draeger, Donn F., jt. auth. see Cheong Cheng Leong.

Draeger, Donn F., jt. auth. see Khim, P'Ng C.

Draeger, Donn F., jt. auth. see Nakayama, Masatoshi.

Draeger, J. Corneal Sensitivity: Measurement & Clinical Importance. (Illus.). 160p. 1984. 27.00 (ISBN 0-387-81794-8). Springer-Verlag.

Draeger, O. Theodor Mundt und Seine Beziehungen Zum Jungen Deutschland. 1909. pap. 9.00 (ISBN 0-384-12605-7). Johnson Repr.

Draenos, Stan. Freud's Odyssey: Psychoanalysis & the End of the Metaphysics. LC 82-1961. 192p. 1982. 23.50x (ISBN 0-300-02791-5). Yale U Pr.

Draf, W. Endoscopy of the Paranasal Sinuses: Technique-Typical Findings-Therapeutic Possibilities. Pohl, W. E., tr. from Ger. (Illus.). 102p. 1983. 29.50 (ISBN 0-387-11258-8). Springer-Verlag.

Draffan, I. W. & Poole, F., eds. Distributed Data Bases. LC 80-40399. 400p. 1981. 37.50 (ISBN 0-521-23091-8). Cambridge U Pr.

Drafts, Gene. Bloodwhispers, Blacksongs. 1974. pap. 1.50 (ISBN 0-685-42552-5); tape 5.00 (ISBN 0-685-42553-3). Broadside.

Drag Reduction, 2nd International Conference. Proceedings. pap. 54.00x (ISBN 0-900983-71-X, Dist. by Air Science Co.). BHRA Fluid.

Dragadze, Tamara. Kinship & Marriage in the Soviet Union. 200p. 1984. 39.95x (ISBN 0-7100-0995-X). Routledge & Kegan.

Draganic, Ivan G. & Draganic, Zorica D. The Radiation Chemistry of Water. (Physical Chemistry Ser.: Vol. 26). 1971. 65.00 (ISBN 0-12-221650-4). Acad Pr.

Draganic, Zorica D., jt. auth. see Draganic, Ivan G.

Dragastin, S. E. & Elder, G. H., Jr., eds. Adolescence in the Life Cycle: Psychological Change & the Social Context. LC 74-22002. Repr. of 1975 ed. 84.00 (ISBN 0-8357-9146-7, 2050705). Bks Demand UMI.

Drage, Charles, ed. Respiratory Medicine for Primary Care Physicians. LC 82-6870. 222p. 1983. 33.00 (ISBN 0-12-788165-4). Acad Pr.

Drage, Charles W., jt. ed. see Gong, Henry, Jr.

Dragendorff, Georg. Die Heilpflanzen der verschiedenen Voelker & Zeiten: Ihre Anwendung wesentlichen Bestanteile und Geschichte. 1967. Repr. of 1898 ed. 40.00 (ISBN 0-934454-47-7). Lubrecht & Cramer.

Draghi, Suzanne C., jt. auth. see Flach, Frederic F.

Dragnich, Alex N. The Development of Parliamentary Government in Serbia. (East European Monographs: No. 44). 138p. 1978. 20.00x (ISBN 0-914710-37-0). East Eur Quarterly.

--The First Yugoslavia: Search for a Viable Political System. (Publication Ser.: No. 284). (Illus.). 186p. 1983. 24.95 (ISBN 0-8179-7841-0). Hoover Inst Pr.

Dragnich, Alex N. & Rasmussen, Jorgen S. Major European Governments. 6th ed. 1982. 30.00x (ISBN 0-256-02738-2). Dorsey.

Dragnich, Alex N. & Todorovich, Slavko. The Saga of Kosovo: Focus on Serbian-Albanian Relationships. (East European Monographs). 1985. 22.50 (ISBN 0-317-18452-0). Brooklyn Coll Pr.

Dragnich, Alex N., et al. Politics & Government: A Brief Introduction. LC 81-21726. 208p. (Orig.). 1982. pap. 8.95x (ISBN 0-934540-13-6). Chatham Hse Pubs.

--Politics & Government: A Brief Introduction. 2nd ed. 256p. 1985. pap. 11.95x (ISBN 0-934540-43-8). Chatham Hse Pubs.

Drago, jt. auth. see Bertini.

Drago, Edmund L. Black Politicians & Reconstruction in Georgia: A Splendid Failure. LC 82-232. 204p. 1982. text ed. 20.00x (ISBN 0-8071-1021-3). La State U Pr.

Drago, Gail, jt. auth. see Ruff, Ann.

Drago, Harry S. The Great Range Wars: Violence on the Grasslands. LC 84-23432. (Illus.). xii, 323p. 1985. pap. 9.95 (ISBN 0-8032-6563-8, BB 918, Bison). U Of Nebr Pr.

Drago, John J. Hydraulics: A New Approach. LC 78-67464. (Illus.). 1978. pap. 3.00x (ISBN 0-89368-301-9). Davis Pub Co.

Drago, R. S; see Dunitz, J. D., et al.

Drago, Russell, jt. ed. see Bertini, Ivano.

Drago, Russell S. Physical Methods in Chemistry. 2nd ed. 1977. text ed. 37.95 (ISBN 0-7216-3184-3, CBS C). SCP.

Dragomir, V., jt. auth. see Gheorghiu, A.

Dragomir, V. C., et al. Theory of the Earth's Shape. (Developments in Solid Earth Geophysics Ser.: Vol. 13). 694p. 1982. 110.75 (ISBN 0-444-99705-9). Elsevier.

Dragonas, Phyllis. The High School Goes Abroad: International Homestay Exchange Programs. (Language in Education Ser.: No. 55). 1983. pap. 6.95 (ISBN 0-15-599058-6) Ctr Appl Ling.

Dragone, Carol. Out of Absence. Hettich, M. & Ahern, Colleen, eds. 25p. 1978. 1.50 (ISBN 0-686-38057-6). MoonsQuilt Pr.

Dragonetti, Roger. La Technique Poetique des Trouveres dans la Chanson Courtouise: Contribution a l'Etude de la Rhetorique Medievale. LC 80-2163. Repr. of 1960 ed. 76.00 (ISBN 0-404-19029-4). AMS Pr.

Dragonwagon, Crescent. Always, Always. LC 83-22199. (Illus.). 32p. (gr. k-4). 1984. PLB 10.95 (ISBN 0-02-733080-X). Macmillan.

--Coconut. LC 83-47691. (Illus.). 32p. (ps-3). 1984. 12.98i (ISBN 0-06-021759-6); PLB 13.89g (ISBN 0-06-021760-X). HarpJ.

--The Dairy Hollow House Cookbook. (Illus.). 200p. 1985. cancelled (ISBN 0-935304-85-1). August Hse.

--I Hate My Brother Harry. LC 82-47706. (Illus.). 32p. (ps-3). 1983. 10.53i (ISBN 0-06-021757-X); PLB 10.89 (ISBN 0-06-021758-8). HarpJ.

--If You Call My Name. LC 78-22480. (Illus.). 32p. (gr. k-4). 1981. 9.13i (ISBN 0-06-021743-X); PLB 9.89 (ISBN 0-06-021744-8). HarpJ.

--Jemima Remembers. LC 84-855. (Illus.). 32p. (gr. 1-3). 1984. 12.95 (ISBN 0-02-733070-2). Macmillan.

--Katie in the Morning. LC 82-47709. (Illus.). 32p. (ps-3). 1983. 10.53i (ISBN 0-06-021729-4); PLB 10.89g (ISBN 0-06-021730-8). HarpJ.

--Messsage from the Avocadoes. LC 81-85357. 72p. 1982. 10.95 (ISBN 0-941780-10-4); pap. 5.95 (ISBN 0-941780-03-1). Parkhurst-Little.

--When Light Turns into Night. LC 74-2634. (Illus.). 32p. (ps-3). 1975. PLB 11.89 (ISBN 0-06-021740-5). HarpJ.

--Will It Be Okay? LC 76-48859. (Illus.). (gr. k-3). 1977. PLB 10.89 (ISBN 0-06-021738-3). HarpJ.

--Wind Rose. LC 75-25414. (Illus.). 32p. (ps-3). 1976. 10.53i (ISBN 0-06-021741-3). HarpJ.

--The Year It Rained: A Novel. LC 84-42980. 228p. (gr. 8 up). 1985. 11.95 (ISBN 0-02-733110-5). Macmillan.

--Your Owl Friend. LC 76-58725. (gr. k-3). 1977. 8.61i (ISBN 0-06-021731-6). HarpJ.

Dragonwagon, Crescent & Zindel, Paul. To Take a Dare. LC 80-8441. 256p. (YA) (gr. 7 up). 1982. 11.06i (ISBN 0-06-026858-1); PLB 10.89 (ISBN 0-06-026859-X). HarpJ.

--To Take a Dare. (Bantam Starfire Bks.). 240p. (YA) 1984. pap. 2.50 (ISBN 0-553-23864-7). Bantam.

Dragoo, Alva W. General Shop Metalwork. rev. ed. (gr. 8-9). 1964. pap. text ed. 6.64 (ISBN 0-87345-109-0). McKnight.

Dragoo, Don W. Mounds for the Dead. (Annals of Carnegie Museum of Natural History Ser.: Vol. 37). (Illus.). 315p. 1963. pap. 10.00 (ISBN 0-911239-09-X). Carnegie Board.

Dragoo, M. M., jt. auth. see Mitchell, B. J.

Dragoo, Mick R. Regeneration of the Periodontal Attachment in Humans. LC 81-1649. (Illus.). 200p. 1981. text ed. 35.00 (ISBN 0-8121-0786-1). Lea & Febiger.

Dragos, L. Magneto-Fluid Dynamics. 1975. 43.00 (ISBN 0-9961001-6-4, Pub. by Abacus England). Heyden.

Dragos, Stephen F., jt. auth. see Beckley, Robert M.

Dragoumis, Julia D. Tales of a Greek Island. LC 76-110184. (Short Story Index Reprint Ser.). 1912. 21.00 (ISBN 0-8369-3335-4). Ayer Co Pubs.

Dragovic, J. English-Russian-Serbocroatian Aviations Dictionary. 460p. (Eng., Rus. & Serbocroation.). 1973. Leatherette 35.00 (ISBN 0-686-92266-2, M-9632). French & Eur.

Dragovic, M B., jt. auth. see Popovic, B. D.

Drags, Harry S. Top Hand with a Gun. 9.95 (ISBN 0-89190-162-0, Pub. by Am Repr). Amereon Ltd.

Dragt, Donald, tr. see Chudakov, A. P.

Draguns, jt. auth. see Triandis.

Dragunsky, D. Soldier's Life. 280p. 1977. 4.95 (ISBN 0-8285-1569-7, Pub. by Progress Pubs USSR). Imported Pubns.

--Soldier's Memoirs. 296p. 1983. pap. 4.95 (ISBN 0-8285-2579-X, Pub. by Progress Pubs USSR). Imported Pubns.

Dragunsky, V. The Adventures of Dennis. 237p. 1981. 7.00 (ISBN 0-8285-1983-8, Pub. by Progress Pubs USSR). Imported Pubns.

Dragutan, A. T., et al. Olefin Metathesis & Ring-Opening Polymerization of Cyclo-Olefins. 400p. 1985. text ed. 64.95 (ISBN 0-471-90267-5, Pub. by Wiley-Interscience). Wiley.

Draheim, Joachim von & Wille, Guenther. Horaz-Vertonungen vom Mittelalter bis zur Gegenwart eine Anthologie. (Heuremata Studien zu Literatur, Sprachen und Kultur der Antike: Vol. 7A). iv, 221p. (Orig., Ger.). 1985. pap. 32.00x (ISBN 90-6032-180-4, Pub. by B R Gruener Nethrlands). Benjamins North Am.

Drahmann, Theodore. The Catholic School Principal: An Outline for Action. 50p. 1981. 4.00 (ISBN 0-686-39893-9). Natl Cath Educ.

Drahms, August. Criminal, His Personnel & Environment: A Scientific Study. LC 72-108231. (Criminology, Law Enforcement, & Social Problems Ser.: No. 114). (With intro. added). 1971. Repr. of 1900 ed. lib. bdg. 20.00x (ISBN 0-87585-114-2). Patterson Smith.

Drahos, Mary. To Touch the Hem of His Garment. 224p. (Orig.). 1983. pap. 7.95 (ISBN 0-8091-2548-X). Paulist Pr.

Drain, Cecil B. & Shipley, Susan B. The Recovery Room. (Illus.). 608p. 1979. 24.00 (ISBN 0-7216-3186-X). Saunders.

Drain, L. E. The Laser Doppler Technique. LC 79-40638. 241p. 1980. text ed. 69.95 (ISBN 0-471-27627-8). Wiley.

Draine, Betsy. Substance under Pressure: Artistic Coherence & Evolving Form in the Novels of Doris Lessing. LC 82-70556. 240p. 1983. 20.00x (ISBN 0-299-09230-5). U of Wis Pr.

Drais, John H. Index to the Source of Measures. LC 81-50203. (Secret Doctrine Reference Ser.). 76p. 1982. pap. 5.00 (ISBN 0-913510-44-0). Wizards.

Draitser, Emil. Peshchera Neozhidannostei ("The Fun House") LC 83-63368. 160p. (Rus.). 1984. pap. 7.50 (ISBN 0-911971-03-3, Pub. by Effect Pub Co). Maxim Bk Pubs.

Draitser, Emil, ed. Forbidden Laughter. Pariser, Jon, tr. LC 79-89635. (Soviet Underground Jokes Ser.: No. 1). (Illus., Orig., Rus. & Eng.). 1980. pap. 5.95 (ISBN 0-89626-045-3, Pub. by Almanac Press). Maxims Bks.

Drakakis, John, ed. Alternative Shakespeares. 272p. (Orig.). 1985. 23.00 (ISBN 0-416-36850-6, 9456); pap. 9.95 (ISBN 0-416-36860-3, 9457). Methuen Inc.

--British Radio Drama. 300p. 1981. 54.50 (ISBN 0-521-22183-8); pap. 16.95 (ISBN 0-521-29383-9). Cambridge U Pr.

Drakakis-Smith, David. Urbanization, Housing & the Development Process. 256p. 1980. 36.00 (ISBN 0-312-83519-1). St Martin.

Drakakis-Smith, David W., jt. ed. see Rimmer, Peter J.

Drakard, David & Holdway, Paul. Spode Printed Ware. (Illus.). 240p. 1983. text ed. 100.00 (ISBN 0-582-50314-0). Longman.

Drake. Dragon Lord. 2.95 (ISBN 0-317-31843-8). Tor Bks.

--Forlorn Hope. pap. 2.95 (ISBN 0-317-31849-7). Tor Bks.

--Heart of Darkness. 2.95 (ISBN 0-317-31855-1). Tor Bks.

--Time Safari. 2.75 (ISBN 0-317-31907-8). Tor Bks.

Drake & Roe. The Principalship. 3rd ed. 604p. 1986. text ed. 22.50 write for info. (ISBN 0-02-330420-0). Macmillan.

Drake, A., ed. Mastering Reading: Comp. II. 156p. 1985. 5.65 (ISBN 0-317-31630-3); instr's. key, 16p 1.30 (ISBN 0-317-31631-1). Cambridge Bk.

--Mastering Reading: Comp. 1. 156p. 1985. 5.65 (ISBN 0-317-31627-3); instr's key, 24 1.30 (ISBN 0-317-31628-1). Cambridge Bk.

Drake, Albert. Beyond the Pavement. LC 80-53525. 175p. 1981. 9.95 (ISBN 0-917976-10-X). White Ewe.

--The Big Little GTO Book. (Illus.). 185p. 1982. pap. 14.95 (ISBN 0-87938-112-4). Motorbooks Intl.

--I Remember the Day James Dean Died & other Stories. LC 82-51027. 189p. (Orig.). 1983. pap. 7.95 (ISBN 0-917976-17-7). White Ewe.

--In the Time of Surveys & Other Stories of Americans Abroad. LC 78-53998. 1978. pap. 3.00 (ISBN 0-917976-02-9). White Ewe.

--One Summer. LC 79-63672. 1979. pap. 5.00 (ISBN 0-917976-06-1). White Ewe.

--Pomes. 1972. 2.50 (ISBN 0-936892-01-3). Stone Pr MI.

--The Postcard Mysteries & Other Stories. (Illus.). 1976. pap. 2.50 (ISBN 0-936892-10-2). Stone Pr MI.

--Riding Bike. (Illus.). 1973. 2.00 (ISBN 0-936892-02-1). Stone Pr MI.

--Rod & Custom Builders Wish Book, 1950's. (Illus.). 1985. pap. 9.95 (ISBN 0-936892-13-7). Stone Pr Mi.

--Street was Fun in Fifty-One. 1982. pap. 8.00 (ISBN 0-936892-11-0). Stone Pr MI.

--Tillamook Burn. LC 77-14012. 1977. pap. 2.00 (ISBN 0-685-86165-1). Fault Pubns.

--Tillamook Burn. (Illus.). 1977. pap. 2.50 (ISBN 0-930646-15-0). Stone Pr MI.

Drake, Alvin W. Fundamentals of Applied Probability Theory. (Illus.). 1967. text ed. 48.00 (ISBN 0-07-017815-1). McGraw.

Drake, Alvin W., et al. The American Blood Supply: Issues & Policies of Blood Donation. (Health & Public Policy Ser.). 224p. 1982. 30.00x (ISBN 0-262-04070-0). MIT Pr.

Drake, Alvin W., et al, eds. Analysis of Public Systems. 480p. 1972. 37.50x (ISBN 0-262-04038-7). MIT Pr.

Drake, Angela J. & Noble, Mark I., eds. Cardiac Metabolism. (Developments in Cardiopulmonary Research Ser.: I-642). 568p. 1983. 75.00 (ISBN 0-471-10249-0, Pub. by Wiley Med). Wiley.

Drake, Asa. Crimson Kisses. 304p. 1981. pap. 2.50 (ISBN 0-380-77131-4, 77131-4). Avon.

--Warrior Witch of Hel. 240p. 1985. pap. 2.95 (ISBN 0-445-20039-1, Popular Lib). Warner Bks.

Drake, Barbara. Life in a Gothic Novel. (WEP Poetry Ser.: No. 4). 24p. (Orig.). 1981. pap. 2.50 (ISBN 0-917976-09-6). White Ewe.

--Love at the Egyptian Theatre. LC 78-50183. 1978. pap. 2.50 (ISBN 0-686-09378-X). Red Cedar.

--Women in Trade Unions: A Classic Account of Women & Trade Unionism. 256p. 1984. pap. 8.95 (ISBN 0-86068-405-9, Pub. by Virago Pr). Merrimack Pub Cir.

--Writing Poetry. 312p. 1983. pap. text ed. 13.95 (ISBN 0-15-597990-6, HC). HarBraceJ.

Drake, Benjamin. Life of Tecumseh & of His Brother the Prophet: With a Historical Sketch of the Shawanoe Indians. LC 78-90173. (Mass Violence in America Ser). Repr. of 1841 ed. 14.00 (ISBN 0-405-01307-8). Ayer Co Pubs.

Drake, Benjamin, jt. auth. see Todd, Charles S.

Drake, Betty. Alabama Eighteen Forty Census Index: Vol. 1, The Counties Formed from the Creek & Cherokee Sessions of the 1830s. 93p. 1983. Repr. of 1973 ed. 13.50 (ISBN 0-89308-331-3). Southern Hist Pr.

Drake, Bill. Cultivators Handbook of Marijuana. rev ed. (Illus.). 224p. (Orig.). pap. 10.95 (ISBN 0-914728-44-X). Wingbow Pr.

--The Cultivator's Handbook of Natural Tobacco. (Illus.). 1981. pap. 3.95 (ISBN 0-686-32843-4). Cultivators Res Serv.

--Marijuana Cultivation: A Handbook of Essential Techniques. 1984. 10.95 (ISBN 0-686-78527-4). Wingbow Pr.

Drake, Bonnie. Amber Enchantment. (Candlelight Ecstasy Ser.: No. 101). (Orig.). 1982. pap. 1.95 (ISBN 0-440-10842-X). Dell.

--The Ardent Protector. (Candlelight Ecstasy Ser.: No. 42). (Orig.). 1982. pap. 1.75 (ISBN 0-440-10273-1). Dell.

--Gemstone. (Candlelight Ecstacy Romance Ser.: No. 186). (Orig.). 1983. pap. 1.95 (ISBN 0-440-12827-7). Dell.

--Lilac Awakening. (Candlelight Ecstasy Ser.: No. 85). (Orig.). 1982. pap. 1.95 (ISBN 0-440-14588-0). Dell.

--Lover from the Sea. (Candlelight Ecstasy Ser.: No. 114). (Orig.). 1983. pap. 1.95 (ISBN 0-440-14888-X). Dell.

--Moment to Moment. (Candlelight Ecstasy Ser.: No. 219). 192p. (Orig.). 1984. pap. 1.95 (ISBN 0-440-15791-9). Dell.

--Passion & Illusion. (Candlelight Ecstasy Ser.: No. 146). (Orig.). 1983. pap. 1.95 (ISBN 0-440-16816-3). Dell.

--Sensuous Burgundy. (Candlelight Ecstasy Ser.: No. 32). 224p. (Orig.). 1981. pap. 1.75 (ISBN 0-440-18427-4). Dell.

--The Silver Fox. (Candlelight Ecstacy Ser.: No. 132). (Orig.). 1983. pap. 1.95 (ISBN 0-440-18139-9). Dell.

--Whispered Promise. (Candlelight Ecstasy Ser.: No. 70). 1982. pap. 1.95 (ISBN 0-440-17673-5). Dell.

Drake, C. L., jt. ed. see Burk, C. A.

Drake, C. L., jt. ed. see Knopoff, L.

Drake, Charles A. A Study of an Interest Test & Affectivity Test in Forecasting Freshman Success in College. LC 76-176729. (Columbia University. Teachers College. Contributions to Education: No. 504). Repr. of 1931 ed. 22.50 (ISBN 0-404-55504-7). AMS Pr.

Drake, Charles D. Union & Anti-Slavery Speeches. facs. ed. LC 77-83961. (Black Heritage Library Collection Ser). 1864. 18.00 (ISBN 0-8369-8552-4). Ayer Co Pubs.

--Union & Anti Slavery Speeches, Delivered During the Rebellion. LC 72-97421. Repr. of 1864 ed. 25.00x (ISBN 0-8371-2734-3, DRU&). Greenwood.

Drake, Christine, ed. see Befu, Harumi, et al.

Drake, D. Mind & Its Place in Nature. LC 26-1041. Repr. of 1925 ed. 16.00 (ISBN 0-527-25120-8). Kraus Repr.

Drake, D., et al. Essays in Critical Realism. LC 67-30877. 1967. Repr. of 1920 ed. 10.00x (ISBN 0-87752-028-3). Gordian.

Drake, Dana. Don Quijote (1894-1970) A Selective Annotated Bibliography, Vol. 1. (Studies in the Romance Languages & Literatures: No. 138). 267p. 1974. pap. 14.50x (ISBN 0-8078-9138-X). U of NC Pr.

Drake, Dana & Madrigal, Jose A. Studies in the Spanish Golden Age: Cervantes & Lope De Vega. LC 78-53263. 1978. pap. 10.00 (ISBN 0-89729-175-1). Ediciones.

Drake, Dana B. Cervantes' Novelas Ejemplares: A Selective, Annotated Bibliography. 2nd,rev. ed. LC 80-8492. 250p. 1981. lib. bdg. 43.00 (ISBN 0-8240-9473-5). Garland Pub.

--Don Quijote, Eighteen Ninety-Four to Nineteen Seventy: A Selective & Annotated Bibliography, Vol. 2. LC 74-8503. 1978. pap. 20.00 (ISBN 0-89729-186-7). Ediciones.

--Don Quixote in World Literature: A Selective, Annotated Bibliography. LC 79-7926. 292p. 1980. lib. bdg. 43.00 (ISBN 0-8240-9542-1). Garland Pub.

Drake, Dana B. & Vina, Frederick. Don Quijote, 1894-1970: A Selective Annotated Bibliography (Volume IV extended to 1979) LC 83-51009. 260p. 1984. pap. 35.00 (ISBN 0-89295-026-9). Society Sp & Sp Am.

Drake, Daniel. Malaria in the Interior Valley of North America: A Selection from A Treatise, Historical, Etiological, & Practical, on the Principal Diseases of the Interior Valley of North America As They Appear in the Caucasion, African, Indian, & Esquimaux Varieties of Its Population. Levine, Norman D., ed. LC 64-14806. (Facsimile Reprints in the History of Science Ser: No. 3). Repr. of 1964 ed. 76.50 (ISBN 0-8357-9687-6, 2011137). Bks Demand UMI.

--Physician to the West: Selected Writings of Daniel Drake on Science & Society. Shapiro, Henry D. & Miller, Zane L., eds. LC 73-94071. (Illus.). 464p. 1970. 25.00x (ISBN 0-8131-1197-8). U Pr of Ky.

--Systematic Treastise, Historical, Etiological & Practical on the Principal Diseases of the Interior Valley of North America, 8 Pts. in 2 Vols. 1971. Repr. of 1850 ed. lib. bdg. 89.00 (ISBN 0-8337-0907-0). B Franklin.

Drake, David. At Any Price. 288p. 1985. pap. 3.50 (ISBN 0-317-27052-4, Pub. by Baen Bks). PB.

--Birds of Prey. 320p. 1984. 14.95 (ISBN 0-671-55909-5, Baen Enterprises); pap. 7.95 (ISBN 0-671-55912-5). S&S.

--Birds of Prey. 352p. 1985. pap. 2.95 (ISBN 0-8125-3612-6). Tor Bks.

--Bridgehead. 320p. (Orig.). 1986. pap. 3.50 (ISBN 0-8125-3616-9, Dist. by Warner Pub Services & St. Martin). Tor Bks.

--Cross the Stars. 352p. (Orig.). 1984. pap. 2.95 (ISBN 0-8125-3614-2). Tor Bks.

--The Dragon Lord. 320p. 1983. pap. 2.95 (ISBN 0-523-48552-2). Pinnacle Bks.

--The Forlorn Hope. 320p. (Orig.). 1984. pap. 2.95 (ISBN 0-8125-3610-X, Pinnacle Bks). Tor Bks.

--From the Heart of Darkness. 320p. (Orig.). 1983. pap. 2.95 (ISBN 0-8125-3607-X, Pinnacle Bks). Tor Bks.

--Hammer's Slammers. 288p. 1983. pap. 2.75 (ISBN 0-441-31599-2). Ace Bks.

--Skyripper. 352p. 1986. pap. 2.95 (ISBN 0-8125-3618-5, Dist. by Warner Pub Services & St. Martin). Tor Bks.

--Skyripper. 3.50 (ISBN 0-317-31888-8). Tor Bks.

--Strangers & Lovers. 512p. (Orig.). 1985. pap. 3.95 (ISBN 0-8439-2277-X, Leisure Bks). Dorchester Pub Co.

--Time Safari. 288p. (Orig.). 1982. pap. 2.75 (ISBN 0-523-48541-7, Pinnacle Bks). Tor Bks.

Drake, David, jt. auth. see Morris, Janet.

Drake, Durant. Problems of Religion: An Introductory Survey. LC 68-19268. Repr. of 1916 ed. lib. bdg. 19.75x (ISBN 0-8371-0062-3, DRPR). Greenwood.

Drake, Ellen, ed. History of Geology. (DNAG Special Volumes Ser.: Vol. 1). (Illus.). 1985. write for info. Geol Soc.

Drake, Ellen A., jt. auth. see Cantor, Dorothy W.

Drake, F. R., et al, eds. Recursion Theory: Its Generalisations & Applications, Proceedings of Logic Colloquim '79, Leeds, Aug. 1979. (London Mathematical Society Lecture Notes Ser.: No. 45). 300p. 1980. pap. 27.95 (ISBN 0-521-23543-X). Cambridge U Pr.

Drake, Francis. The World Encompassed & Analagous Contemporary Documents Concerning Sir Francis Drake's Circumnavigation of the World. LC 78-75030. (Illus.). 28.50 (ISBN 0-8154-0307-0). Cooper Sq.

--The World Encompassed by Sir F. Drake, Being His Next Voyage to That to Nombre De Dios. LC 78-26252. (English Experience Ser.: No. 103). 108p. 1969. Repr. of 1628 ed. 16.00 (ISBN 90-221-0103-7). Walter J Johnson.

--World Encompassed by Sir Francis Drake. Vaux, W. S., ed. (Hakluyt Soc., First Ser.: No. 16). Repr. of 1854 ed. 32.00 (ISBN 0-8337-0909-7). B Franklin.

Drake, Francis S. Dictionary of American Biography Including Men of the Time. LC 73-11061. 1974. Repr. of 1872 ed. 95.00x (ISBN 0-8103-3731-2). Gale.

--Tea Leaves: Being a Collection of Letters & Documents Relating to the Shipment of Tea to the American Colonies in the Year 1773, by the East India Tea Company. LC 77-95778. (Illus.). 1970. Repr. of 1884 ed. 40.00x (ISBN 0-8103-3577-8). Gale.

Drake, Frank R. Set Theory: An Introduction to Large Cardinals. (Studies in Logic & the Foundation of Mathematics Ser: Vol. 76). 352p. 1974. 53.25 (ISBN 0-444-10535-2, North-Holland). Elsevier.

Drake, Fred W. China Charts the World: Hsu Chi-Yu & His Geography of 1848. (Harvard East Asian Monographs: N0. 64). 320p. 1975. text ed. 20.00x (ISBN 0-674-11643-7). Harvard U Pr.

Drake, Fred W., ed. see Hemenway, Ruth V.

Drake, Frederick C. The Empire of the Seas: A Biography of Rear Admiral Robert Wilson Shufeldt, USN. LC 84-66. (Illus.). 483p. 1984. text ed. 29.95x (ISBN 0-8248-0846-0). UH Pr.

Drake, Frederick S., ed. Historical Archaeological & Linguistic Studies on Southern China, South East Asia & the Hong Kong Region: Symposium Papers Presented at Meetings Held in Sept. 1961. LC 68-100453. pap. 111.80 (ISBN 0-317-11279-1, 2017724). Bks Demand UMI.

Drake, George. Small Gas Engines: Maintenance, Troubleshooting & Repair. 500p. 1981. text ed. 21.95 (ISBN 0-8359-7014-0); soln. manual avail. (ISBN 0-8359-7015-9). Reston.

Drake, George A. see Brauer, Jerald C.

Drake, Gertrude, ed. Latin Readings. 112p. 1984. 8.00x (ISBN 0-318-01229-4); pap. 4.00x (ISBN 0-86516-044-9). Bolchazy Carducci.

--More Latin Readings. 112p. 1984. 8.00x (ISBN 0-318-01230-8); pap. 4.00 (ISBN 0-86516-046-5). Bolchazy Carducci.

Drake, Gertrude C., ed. see Vida, Marco G.

Drake, Glendon F. The Role of Prescriptivism in American Linguistics 1820-1970. x, 130p. 1977. 21.00x (ISBN 90-272-0954-5, SIHOL 13). Benjamins North Am.

Drake, H. A. In Praise of Constantine: A Historical Study of Eusebius' Tricennial Orations. LC 75-62009. (Library Reprint Ser.: No. 93). 1978. 22.50x (ISBN 0-520-03694-8). U of Cal Pr.

Drake, Hal, et al, eds. see Pacific Stars & Stripes Newspaper.

Drake, Harold L. Humanistic Radio Production. LC 81-40943. 126p. (Orig.). 1982. lib. bdg. 22.25 (ISBN 0-8191-2250-5); pap. text ed. 9.25 (ISBN 0-8191-2251-3). U Pr of Amer.

Drake, J. B., jt. auth. see Bourhill, E. J.

Drake, J. W. & Koch, R. E., eds. Mutagenesis. LC 75-43761. (Benchmark Papers in Genetics Ser: Vol. 4). 384p. 1976. 59.50 (ISBN 0-12-786375-3). Acad Pr.

Drake, Jacqueline. Corporate Planning & Libraries. 1979. 90.00x (ISBN 0-86176-023-9, Pub. by MCB Pubns). State Mutual Bk.

Drake, Jacqueline, et al. Management & Organization Development Bibliography. 3rd ed. 1979. 90.00x (ISBN 0-86176-040-9, Pub. by MCB Pubns). State Mutual Bk.

Drake, James. The Antient & Modern Stages Surveyed. LC 70-170446. (The English Stage Ser.: Vol. 32). lib. bdg. 61.00 (ISBN 0-8240-0615-1). Garland Pub.

--Antient & Modern Stages Surveyed, or Mr. Collier's View of the Immorality & Profaneness of the English Stage Set in a True Light. LC 74-126668. Repr. of 1699 ed. 28.00 (ISBN 0-404-02176-X). AMS Pr.

Drake, James A., jt. auth. see Laforse, Martin W.

Drake, James A., jt. auth. see Ponselle, Rosa.

Drake, Jamesa. Teaching Critical Thinking. LC 75-30309. 1976. pap. 8.75x (ISBN 0-8134-1774-0, 1774). Interstate.

Drake, John. Radio Control Helicopter Models. rev. ed. (Illus.). 144p. 1983. pap. 9.95 (Pub. by Argus). Aztex.

Drake, John D. Effective Interviewing: A Guide for Managers. LC 81-69360. 288p. 1983. pap. 8.95 (ISBN 0-8144-7600-7). AMACOM.

--Interviewing for Managers: A Complete Guide to Employment Interviewing. Rev. ed. 1982. 19.95 (ISBN 0-8144-5737-1). AMACOM.

Drake, Jonathan, jt. auth. see Drew, Dennis.

Drake, Julia A. & Orndorff, J. R. From Millwheel to Plowshare: Orndorff Family Genealogy. 271p. 1938. 10.00 (ISBN 0-686-36497-X). Md Hist.

Drake, Kay N., jt. auth. see Day, Barbara D.

Drake, Kenneth. The Sonatas of Beethoven: As He Played & Taught Them. LC 80-8608. (Midland Bks.: No. 262). 224p. 1981. 17.50x (ISBN 0-253-12869-2); pap. 7.95x (ISBN 0-253-20262-0). Ind U Pr.

Drake, Lewis E. & Oetting, Eugene R. MMPI Codebook for Counselors. LC 59-10187. 1959. 10.95x (ISBN 0-8166-0187-9). U of Minn Pr.

Drake, Lisa & Perzler, Otto. The Medical Center Murders. (Whodunit Mystery Ser.: No. 2). (Orig.). 1984. pap. 3.50 (ISBN 0-671-52362-7). PB.

Drake, M. Gastro-Esophageal Cytology. (Monographs in Clinical Cytology: Vol. 10). (Illus.). xii, 268p. 1985. 52.50 (ISBN 3-8055-3931-2). S Karger.

Drake, M., tr. see Sundt, Eilert.

Drake, Madeline & Biebuych, Tony. Policy & Provision for the Single Homeless: Research Paper. 1977. 22.00x (ISBN 0-317-05797-9, Pub. by Natl Inst Social Work). State Mutual Bk.

Drake, Marsha. The Proverbs Thirty-One Lady & Other Impossible Dreams. LC 84-6453. 192p. (Orig.). 1984. pap. 4.95 (ISBN 0-87123-595-1). Bethany Hse.

Drake, Marvia, jt. auth. see Drake, Terrance.

Drake, Maurice. Saints & Their Emblems. 1971. Repr. of 1916 ed. lib. bdg. 24.50 (ISBN 0-8337-0902-X). B Franklin.

Drake, Michael. Population & Society in Norway, 1735-1865. LC 69-14393. (Cambridge Studies in Economic History). pap. 69.00 (ISBN 0-317-26008-1, 2024445). Bks Demand UMI.

Drake, Michael, ed. Applied Historical Studies. 1973. pap. 9.50x (ISBN 0-416-79110-7, NO.2171). Methuen Inc.

Drake, Michael, jt. ed. see Barker, Theo.

Drake, Miriam A. User Fees: A Practical Perspective. LC 81-6032. 142p. 1981. lib. bdg. 22.50 (ISBN 0-87287-244-0). Libs Unl.

Drake, Nathan. Essays: Biographical, Critical & Historical Illustrative of the Rambler, Adventurer & Idler, 2 Vols. (Belles Lettres in English Ser). 1969. Repr. of 1810 ed. Set. 80.00 (ISBN 0-384-12650-2). Johnson Repr.

--Essays: Biographical, Critical & Historical, Illustrative of the Tatler, Spectator, & Guardian, 3 vols. (Belles Letters in English Ser). 1969. Repr. of 1805 ed. Set. 110.00 (ISBN 0-384-12700-2). Johnson Repr.

--Memorials of Shakespeare. LC 76-164789. Repr. of 1828 ed. 34.00 (ISBN 0-404-02177-8). AMS Pr.

--Shakespeare & His Times, 2 vols in 1. LC 68-58458. (Research & Source Ser: No. 332). 1969. Repr. of 1838 ed. 35.50 (ISBN 0-8337-0901-1). B Franklin.

Drake, Oliver, jt. auth. see Canutt, Yakima.

Drake, P. J., jt. ed. see Nieuwenhuysen, J. P.

Drake, Paul W. Socialism & Populism in Chile, Nineteen Thirty-Two to Nineteen Fifty-Two. LC 77-17414. 416p. 1977. 25.00x (ISBN 0-252-00657-7). U of Ill Pr.

Drake, Peter & Burrell, Sidney. Amiable Renegade: The Memoirs of Captain Peter Drake, 1671-1753. (Illus.). 1960. 35.00x (ISBN 0-8047-0022-2). Stanford U Pr.

Drake, Peter J. Money, Finance & Development. LC 80-14964. 244p. 1980. 33.95x (ISBN 0-470-26992-8). Wiley.

Drake, Phyllis E. How to Succeed in Selling Real Estate: A Guide for Real Estate Rookies. (Illus.). 112p. (Orig.). 1982. pap. 3.50 (ISBN 0-914846-12-4). Golden West Pub.

Drake, R. A. R., ed. Instrumentation & Control of Water & Wastewater Treatment & Transport Systems: Proceedings of the 4th IAWPRC Workshop Held in Houston & Denver, USA, 27 April - 4 May 1985. (Advances in Water Pollution Control Ser.). (Illus.). 766p. 1985. 130.00 (ISBN 0-08-032591-2, Pub. by P P L). Pergamon.

Drake, R. M., jt. auth. see Eckert, Ernest R.

Drake, Raleigh M. Abnormal Psychology. rev. ed. (Quality Paperback Ser.: No. 101). 1972. pap. 4.95 (ISBN 0-8226-0101-X). Littlefield.

Drake, Raymond L., jt. auth. see Grimstad, Bill.

Drake, Richard. Byzantium for Rome: The Politics of Nostalgia in Umbertian Italy, 1878-1900. LC 79-16578. xxvii, 308p. 1980. 27.00 (ISBN 0-8078-1405-9). U of NC Pr.

--Revelations of a Slave Smuggler. LC 74-99369. (Illus.). xi, 109p. 1972. Repr. of 1860 ed. lib. bdg. 12.00 (ISBN 0-8411-0040-3). Metro Bks.

Drake, Richard, ed. Let Us Have Music for Flute. (Illus.). 79p. 1963. pap. 5.95 (ISBN 0-8258-0156-7, 0-4077). Fischer Inc NY.

Drake, Robert. Amazing Grace. LC 80-16873. Repr. of 1980 ed. 42.00 (ISBN 0-8357-9121-1, 2019320). Bks Demand UMI.

--The Burning Bush & Other Stories. LC 73-93410. 200p. 1975. 5.95 (ISBN 0-87695-171-X). Aurora Pubs.

--The Home Place: A Memory & a Celebration. LC 80-24110. (Illus.). 192p. 1980. 14.95 (ISBN 0-87870-198-2). Memphis St Univ.

--Single Heart. LC 75-148010. 1971. 4.95 (ISBN 0-87695-142-6). Aurora Pubs.

Drake, Rollen H. A Comparative Study of the Mentality & Achievement of Mexican & White Children. LC 74-147297. pap. 10.95 (ISBN 0-88247-185-6). R & E Pubs.

Drake, S. A. The Border Wars of New England. 305p. 1973. Repr. of 1897 ed. 16.95 (ISBN 0-87928-045-X). Corner Hse.

Drake, St. Clair. Redemption of Black Religion. 1980. pap. 2.95 (ISBN 0-88378-017-8). Third World.

Drake, Samuel A. Book of New England Legends & Folk Lore. LC 76-157254. (Illus.). (YA) (gr. 9 up). 1971. pap. 7.95 (ISBN 0-8048-0990-9). C E Tuttle.

--Burgoyne's Invasion of 1777; Etc. 1977. Repr. 29.00x (ISBN 0-403-06301-9). Scholarly.

--The Heart of the White Mountains: Their Legend & Scenery. Repr. of 1882 ed. 30.00 (ISBN 0-8482-3669-6). Norwood Edns.

--The Heroical Book of American Colonial Homes. (Illus.). 109p. 1983. Repr. of 1894 ed. 117.50 (ISBN 0-89901-104-7). Found Class Reprints.

--Historic Mansions & Highways Around Boston. LC 73-157256. (Illus.). 1971. pap. 3.75 (ISBN 0-8048-0992-5). C E Tuttle.

--Nooks & Corners of the New England Coast. LC 69-19883. 1969. Repr. of 1875 ed. 43.00x (ISBN 0-8103-3827-0). Gale.

--Old Boston Taverns & Tavern Clubs. LC 78-162511. 132p. 1971. Repr. of 1917 ed. 40.00x (ISBN 0-8103-3293-0). Gale.

--Old Landmarks & Historic Personages of Boston. LC 70-157258. (Illus.). 1971. pap. 3.95 (ISBN 0-8048-0993-3). C E Tuttle.

--Old Landmarks & Historic Personages of Boston. LC 76-99068. (Illus.). 1970. Repr. of 1900 ed. 43.00x (ISBN 0-8103-3582-4). Gale.

Drake, Samuel G. Annals of Witchcraft in New England & Elsewhere in the United States from Their First Settlement. LC 67-13327. 1967. Repr. of 1869 ed. 20.00 (ISBN 0-405-08466-8, Blom Pubns). Ayer Co Pubs.

--Annals of Witchcraft in New England, & Elsewhere in the United States. LC 73-161683. (Woodward's Historical Ser.: No. 8). 306p. 1972. Repr. of 1869 ed. lib. bdg. 23.50 (ISBN 0-8337-0898-8). B Franklin.

--Annals of Witchcraft in New England & Elsewhere in the United States. 69.95 (ISBN 0-87968-641-3). Gordon Pr.

--The Book of the Indians. LC 74-7960. Repr. of 1841 ed. 49.00 (ISBN 0-404-11848-8). AMS Pr.

--Indian Captivities: Or, Life in the Wigwam. LC 74-7961. Repr. of 1851 ed. 27.50 (ISBN 0-404-11849-6). AMS Pr.

--Particular History of the Five Years French & Indian War in New England & Parts Adjacent. facs. ed. (Select Bibliographies Reprint Ser). 1870. 19.00 (ISBN 0-8369-5575-7). Ayer Co Pubs.

--A Particular History of the Five Years French & Indian War. 312p. 1984. 25.00 (ISBN 0-917890-42-6). Heritage Bk.

--Witchcraft Delusion in New England, 3 vols. LC 79-120720. (Research & Source Works Ser.: No. 471). 1970. Repr. of 1866 ed. lib. bdg. 62.00 (ISBN 0-8337-0908-9). B Franklin.

Drake, Samuel G., ed. The Old Indian Chronicle. LC 74-7963. Repr. of 1867 ed. 26.00 (ISBN 0-404-11850-X). AMS Pr.

Drake, Shannon. Tomorrow the Glory. 368p. (Orig.). 1985. pap. 6.95 (ISBN 0-523-42354-3). Pinnacle Bks.

Drake, Stan, jt. auth. see Star, Leonard.

Drake, Stan, jt. auth. see Starr, Leonard.

Drake, Stillman. Cause, Experiment, & Science: A Galilean Dialogue Incorporating a New English Translation of Galileo's Bodies That Stay Atop Water, or Move in It. LC 81-2974. (Illus.). 288p. 1981. 20.00 (ISBN 0-226-16228-1); pap. 9.95 (ISBN 0-226-16230-3). U of Chicago Pr.

--Galileo. (Past Masters Ser.). 1980. pap. 3.95 (ISBN 0-19-287526-4). Oxford U Pr.

--Galileo at Work: His Scientific Biography. LC 78-5239. xxiv, 536p. 1981. pap. 9.95 (ISBN 0-226-16227-3). U of Chicago Pr.

--Telescopes, Tides, & Tactics: A Galilean Dialogue about the "Starry Messenger" & Systems of the World. LC 82-24790. 256p. 1983. lib. bdg. 22.50x (ISBN 0-226-16231-1). U of Chicago Pr.

Drake, Stillman, tr. from Lat. Galileo Galilei: "Two New Sciences". 366p. 1974. 27.50x (ISBN 0-299-06400-X). U of Wis Pr.

Drake, Stillman & Drabkin, I. E., trs. Mechanics in Sixteenth-Century Italy: Selections from Tartaglia, Benedetti, Guido Ubaldo, & Galileo. (Medieval Science Publications: No. 13). (Illus.). 442p. 1969. 30.00x (ISBN 0-299-05100-5). U of Wis Pr.

Drake, Stillman, tr. from Ital. see Galilei, Galileo.

Drake, Stillman, tr. see Galilei, Galileo.

Drake, Terrance & Drake, Marvia. Teaching Your Child about Sex. LC 83-71726. 60p. 1983. 5.95 (ISBN 0-87747-951-8). Deseret Bk.

Drake, Thelbert L., jt. auth. see Roe, William H.

Drake, W. Homer & Morris, Jeffrey W. Chapter Thirteen Practice & Procedure. (Bankruptcy Publications). 768p. 1983. write for info. (Pub. By Shepards-McGraw). McGraw.

Drake, W. Homer, Jr. & Herzog, Richard B. Bankruptcy: A Concise Guide for Creditors & Debtors. LC 82-8834. (Illus.). 160p. 1983. 14.95 (ISBN 0-668-05256-2); pap. 9.95 (ISBN 0-668-05261-9). Arco.

Drake, W. Magruder, ed. see King, Edward.

Drake, William, ed. see Teasdale, Sara.

Drake, William A. Contemporary European Writers. 69.95 (ISBN 0-87968-937-4). Gordon Pr.

Drake, William A., ed. American Criticism, Nineteen Twenty-Six. facs. ed. LC 67-28734. (Essay Index Reprint Ser.). 1926. 20.00 (ISBN 0-8369-0389-7). Ayer Co Pubs.

Drake, William A., ed. see Goldoni, Carlo.

Drake, William A., tr. see Istrati, Panait.

Drake, William A., tr. see Schnitzler, Arthur.

Drake, William A., tr. see Tarasov-Rodionov, Aleksandr I.

Drake, William E. Betrayal on Mt. Parnassus. 1983. 21.95 (ISBN 0-8022-2416-4). Philos Lib.

Drake, Willmarth W. The New Frontier: Based on American Regionalism by Howard W. Odum & Harry E. Moore. 1939. 10.00 (ISBN 0-8482-3691-2). Norwood Edns.

Drake-Brockman, D. L. Mathura: A Gazetteer. 1985. Repr. of 1911 ed. 32.00x (ISBN 0-8364-1324-5, Pub. by Usha). South Asia Bks.

Drake Del Castillo, E. Illustrationes Florae Insularum Maris Pacifici. 1977. Repr. of 1892 ed. 87.50 (ISBN 3-7682-1130-4). Lubrecht & Cramer.

Drakeford, J. W. Psicologia y Religion. 384p. 1980. pap. 10.95 (ISBN 0-311-46035-6, Edit Mundo). Casa Bautista.

Drakeford, John W. The Awesome Power of the Healing Thought. LC 80-70915. 1981. 8.95 (ISBN 0-8054-5294-X). Broadman.

--The Awesome Power of the Listening Heart. 192p. 1982. pap. 5.95 (ISBN 0-310-70261-5). Zondervan.

--A Christian View of Homosexuality. LC 76-41474. 1977. pap. 3.50 (ISBN 0-8054-5620-1). Broadman.

--Counseling for Church Leaders. LC 61-12412. 1961. 8.50 (ISBN 0-8054-2405-9). Broadman.

--Growing Old-Feeling Young. 1985. pap. 7.95 (ISBN 0-8054-5009-2). Broadman.

--Hechos el Uno Para el Otro. De Plou, Dafne C., tr. (Sexo en la Vida Cristiana Ser.). 1980. pap. 3.50 (ISBN 0-311-46256-1). Casa Bautista.

--Integrity Therapy. LC 67-19396. 1974. pap. 6.50 (ISBN 0-8054-6702-5). Broadman.

--It's Your Move: How to Motivate Yourself & Your Family. 192p. 1985. 10.95 (ISBN 0-8007-1425-3). Revell.

--A Proverb a Day Keeps the Troubles Away. 140p. 1976. pap. 4.95 (ISBN 0-8054-5143-9). Broadman.

--Psychology in Search of a Soul. LC 64-15096. 1964. 11.95 (ISBN 0-8054-6701-7). Broadman.

--Wisdom for Today's Family. LC 77-94449. 1978. pap. 5.50 (ISBN 0-8054-5592-2). Broadman.

Drakeford, John W. & Drakeford, Robina. Mothers Are Special. LC 78-73137. 1979. 8.95 (ISBN 0-8054-5636-8). Broadman.

Drakeford, Robina, jt. auth. see Drakeford, John W.

Drakin, S., jt. auth. see Karapetyants, M.

Drakontides, Anna B., et al. Anatomy & Physiology: Workbook & Laboratory Manual. (Illus.). 1977. pap. text ed. write for info. (ISBN 0-02-330050-7, 33005). Macmillan.

Draley, J. E. & Weeks, J. R. Corrosion by Liquid Metals. LC 75-119057. 615p. 1970. 49.50x (ISBN 0-306-30482-1, Plenum Pr). Plenum Pub.

Dralle, Elizabeth. Angel in the Tower. (Illus.). 101p. (gr. 7 up). 1962. 2.75 (ISBN 0-374-30330-4). FS&G.

Dramann, Ann. The Last Victim. (Orig.). 1980. pap. text ed. 1.95 (ISBN 0-505-51595-4, Pub. by Tower Bks). Dorchester Pub Co.

Dramer, jt. auth. see Kravitz.

Dramer, Dan. Disasters! (Illus.). 160p. (Orig.). (gr. 6-10). 1982. pap. text ed. 7.20x (ISBN 0-89061-247-1, 760). Jamestown Pubs.

--Literary Tales. 240p. (Orig.). (gr. 9 up). 1980. pap. text ed. 7.20x (ISBN 0-89061-233-1, 761). Jamestown Pubs.

--Monsters. (Illus.). 160p. (gr. 6 up). 1985. pap. text ed. 7.20x (ISBN 0-89061-451-2). Jamestown Pubs.

Dramer, Dan, jt. auth. see Kravitz, Alvin.

Drance, Stephen, jt. auth. see Reed, Howard.

Drance, Stephen M. & Anderson, Douglas, eds. Automatic Perimetry in Glaucoma: A Practical Guide. 208p. 1985. 49.50 (ISBN 0-8089-1705-6, 791062). Grune.

Drance, Stephen M. & Neufeld, Arthur H., eds. Glaucoma: Applied Pharmacology of Medical Treatment. 608p. 1984. 89.50 (ISBN 0-8089-1660-2, 791061). Grune.

Drane, James. A New American Reformation. LC 73-82161. 159p. 1974. 7.50 (ISBN 0-8022-2123-8). Philos Lib.

--Your Emotional Life & What You Can Do about It. 204p. 1984. 9.95 (ISBN 0-88347-157-4). Thomas More.

Drane, James F. A New American Reformation: A Study of Youth Culture & Religion. (Quality Paperback Ser.: No. 293). 166p. 1974. pap. 2.95 (ISBN 0-8226-0293-8). Littlefield.

--The Possibility of God. (Quality Paperback Ser.: No. 321). 194p. 1976. pap. 3.50 (ISBN 0-8226-0321-7). Littlefield.

Drane, John. The Early Christians: Life in the First Years of the Church, an Illustrated Documentary. LC 81-47835. (Illus.). 144p. (Orig.). 1982. pap. 9.57i (ISBN 0-06-062067-6, RD 378, HarpR). Har-Row.

--Jesus & the Gospels. LC 77-20448. 1979. pap. 9.57i (ISBN 0-06-062066-8, RD264, HarpR). Har-Row.

--The Old Testament Story: An Illustrated Documentary. LC 83-48402. 192p. (Orig.). 1984. pap. 10.53 (ISBN 0-06-062068-4, RD 504, HarpR). Har-Row.

--Paul: An Illustrated Documentary on the Life & Writings. LC 76-62918. (Illus.). 1977. pap. text ed. 9.57i (ISBN 0-06-062065-X, RD 208, HarpR). Har-Row.

Drane, Keat B. Convert Your Car to Alcohol. LC 80-81750. (Illus.). 64p. (Orig.). 1980. lib. bdg. 12.95 (ISBN 0-915216-61-2); pap. 4.95 (ISBN 0-915216-54-X). Marathon Intl Pub Co.

Drange, Theodore. Type Crossings: Sentential Meaninglessness in the Border Area of Linguistics & Philosophy. (Janua Linguarum, Ser. Minor: No. 44). (Orig.). 1966. pap. text ed. 19.20x (ISBN 90-2790-578-9). Mouton.

Dranov, Paula. Inside the Music Publishing Industry. LC 80-13304. (Communications Library). 185p. 1980. professional 29.95 (ISBN 0-914236-40-7, 413-BW). Knowledge Indus.

Dranov, Paula, et al. Video in the 80s: Emerging Uses for Television in Business, Education, Medicine & Government. LC 80-15745. 186p. 1980. pap. 19.95 professional (ISBN 0-86729-065-X, 516-BW). Knowledge Indus.

Dranow, Ralph. The Woman Who Knocked out Sugar Ray. Darlington, Sandy & Reynolds, Julie, eds. LC 81-70081. (Illus.). 192p. (Orig.). 1982. pap. 4.95 (ISBN 0-9604152-5-4). Arrowhead Pr.

Dransfield, John E. Administration of Enrichment to Superior Children in a Typical Classroom. LC 70-176730. (Columbia University. Teachers College. Contributions to Education: NO. 558). Repr. of 1933 ed. 22.50 (ISBN 0-404-55558-6). AMS Pr.

Dransfield, Michael. The Second Month of Spring. Hall, Rodney, ed. 83p. 1980. 14.95x (ISBN 0-7022-1512-0); pap. 8.95x (ISBN 0-7022-1513-9). U of Queensland Pr.

--Voyage into Solitude. Hall, Rodney, intro. by. 1979. 14.95x (ISBN 0-7022-1245-8); pap. 8.95x (ISBN 0-7022-1246-6). U of Queensland Pr.

Dransfield, P. Hydraulic Control Systems: Design & Analysis of the Dynamics. (Lecture Notes in Control & Information Sciences Ser.: Vol. 33). 227p. 1981. pap. 18.00 (ISBN 0-387-10890-4). Springer-Verlag.

Dransfield, Peter. Introducing Root Locus: A Programmed Instruction Text. pap. 34.00 (ISBN 0-317-20849-7). Bks Demand UMI.

Drant, Thomas H., tr. see Horatius Flaccus, Quintus.

Drapela, Victor J. The Counselor As Consultant & Supervisor. (Illus.). 228p. 1983. 23.75x (ISBN 0-398-04789-8). C C Thomas.

--Guidance & Counseling Around the World. LC 79-64966. 344p. 1981. lib. bdg. 25.25 (ISBN 0-8191-1384-0); pap. text ed. 13.50 (ISBN 0-8191-0777-8). U Pr of Amer.

Draper. Analytic Methods in Communicative Algebra. (Lecture Notes in Pure & Applied Mathematics Ser.: Vol. 68). 1982. 45.00 (ISBN 0-8247-1282-X). Dekker.

--Caring for Children. 1979. text ed. 19.40 (ISBN 0-02-662810-4); tchr's. guide 11.20 (ISBN 0-02-662840-6); student guide 5.08 (ISBN 0-02-662820-1). Bennett IL.

--Studying Children: Observing & Participating. 1977. pap. text ed. 13.32 (ISBN 0-02-665770-8). Bennett IL.

Draper & Bailey. Steps in Clothing Skills. (gr. 7-9). 1978. text ed. 19.48 (ISBN 0-02-665710-4); tchr's guide 2.00 (ISBN 0-02-665720-1). Bennett IL.

Draper, jt. auth. see Mitchell.

Draper, A. B., jt. auth. see Niebel, B. W.

Draper, Alec. Electrical Circuits: Including Machines. 2nd ed. LC 73-173070. (Electrical Engineering Ser.). pap. 106.30 (ISBN 0-317-10117-X, 2006385). Bks Demand UMI.

--Electrical Machines. 2nd ed. LC 67-98866. (Electrical Engineering Ser.). pap. 101.00 (ISBN 0-317-27852-5, 2025256). Bks Demand UMI.

Draper, C. G. Great American Stories: An ESL-EFL Reader. (Illus.). 112p. 1985. pap. text ed. 4.50 (ISBN 0-13-363748-4). P-H.

Draper, C. R., ed. see Ross, W. MacLeod.

Draper, Cena C. The Worst Hound Around. LC 78-25687. 118p. (gr. 5-8). 1979. 8.95 (ISBN 0-664-32643-9). Westminster.

Draper, E. Linn, Jr., ed. Technology of Controlled Thermonuclear Fusion Experiments & the Engineering Aspects of Fusion Reactors: Proceedings. LC 74-600044. (AEC Symposium Ser.). 1052p. 1974. pap. 34.25 (ISBN 0-87079-221-0, CONF-721111); microfiche 4.50 (ISBN 0-87079-222-9, CONF-721111). DOE.

Draper, Edythe. Cool: How a Kid Should Live. 1974. kivar 5.95 (ISBN 0-8423-0435-5). Tyndale.

--In Touch. 1983. deluxe ed. 8.95 gift ed. (ISBN 0-8423-1711-2); christmas ed. 8.95 (ISBN 0-8423-1712-0); deluxe graduation ed. 8.95 (ISBN 0-8423-1713-9); kivar 5.95 (ISBN 0-8423-1710-4). Tyndale.

--Living Light. Incl. Large Print Edition. 1976. kivar 4.95 (ISBN 0-8423-2652-9). 1972. leatherette o.p. 8.95 (ISBN 0-8423-2651-0); kivar o.p. 5.95 (ISBN 0-8423-2650-2); pap. 8.95 (ISBN 0-8423-2490-9). Tyndale.

--Stretch. (gr. 5-9). 1983. kivar, girls' ed. 5.95 (ISBN 0-8423-6673-3). Tyndale.

--Stretch. (gr. 5-9). 1983. kivar, boys' ed. 5.95 (ISBN 0-8423-6668-7). Tyndale.

--Wonder. 448p. (gr. 1-4). 1984. 5.95 (ISBN 0-8423-8385-9). Tyndale.

Draper, George & Sather, Edgar. It's All in a Day's Work. LC 76-57146. 1977. pap. text ed. 9.95 (ISBN 0-88377-067-9). Newbury Hse.

Draper, George, et al. Human Constitution in Clinical Medicine. (Psychology Ser). 1969. Repr. of 1914 ed. 24.00 (ISBN 0-384-12755-X). Johnson Repr.

Draper, H. H., ed. Advances in Nutritional Research, Vols. 1-3. Incl. Vol. 1. 362p. 1977. 39.50x (ISBN 0-306-34321-5); Vol. 2. 264p. 1979. 39.50x (ISBN 0-306-40213-0); Vol. 3. 378p. 1980. 39.50x (ISBN 0-306-40415-X). Plenum Pub. (Illus., Plenum Pr). Plenum Pub.

--Advances in Nutritional Research, Vol. 4. 358p. 1982. 39.50 (ISBN 0-306-40786-8, Plenum Pr). Plenum Pub.

--Advances in Nutritional Research, Vol. 5. 272p. 1983. 39.50x (ISBN 0-306-41095-8, Plenum Pr). Plenum Pub.

--Advances in Nutritional Research, Vol. 6. 352p. 1984. 49.50x (ISBN 0-306-41811-8, Plenum Pr). Plenum Pub.

Draper, Hal. The Complete Poems of Heinrich Heine: A Modern English Version. 1050p. 1982. 29.95 (ISBN 3-518-03048-5, Pub. by Insel Verlag Germany). Suhrkamp.

--Karl Marx's Theory of Revolution: The State & Bureaucracy, Vol. 1. LC 76-40467. 748p. 1978. pap. 9.50 (ISBN 0-85345-461-2, PB-4612). Monthly Rev.

--Karl Marx's Theory of Revolution, Vol. III: The "Dictatorship of the Proletariat". 480p. 1985. 28.00 (ISBN 0-85345-673-9); pap. 13.50 (ISBN 0-85345-674-7). Monthly Rev.

--Karl Marx's Theory of Revolution Vol. 2: The Politics of Social Classes. LC 76-40467. 756p. 1981. 20.00 (ISBN 0-85345-439-6); pap. 12.95 (ISBN 0-85345-566-X). Monthly Rev.

--The Marx-Engels Register: A Complete Bibliography of Marx & Engels' Individual Writings. (Marx-Engels Cyclopedia Ser.: Vol. II). 288p. 1985. 28.50x (ISBN 0-8052-3975-8). Schocken.

Draper, Hal & Center for Socialist History, eds. The Marx-Engels Chronicle: A Day-by-Day Chronology of Marx & Engel's Life & Activity, Vol. 1. LC 84-3013. (Marx-Engels Cyclopedia Ser.). 320p. 1985. 28.50x (ISBN 0-8052-3909-X). Schocken.

Draper, Hal, tr. The Complete Poems of Heinrich Heine: A Modern English Version. 1050p. 1984. pap. 19.95 (ISBN 3-518-03062-0). Suhrkamp.

Draper, Henry. The Caring Parent. 1983. text ed. 18.60 (ISBN 0-02-662850-3). Bennett IL.

Draper, Hilary. Private Police. 1978. text ed. 20.00x (ISBN 0-391-00852-8). Humanities.

Draper, J. Everett. Putting People in Your Paintings. (Illus.). 160p. 1985. 22.50 (ISBN 0-89134-162-5). North Light Pub.

Draper, James. Colossians: A Portrait of Christ. 1982. pap. 3.95 (ISBN 0-8423-0358-8); leader's guide 2.95 (ISBN 0-8423-0359-6). Tyndale.

Draper, James, jt. auth. see Brooks, James.

Draper, James D. European Terracottas from the Arthur M. Sackler Collections. Shultz, Ellen, ed. (Illus.). 32p. (Orig.). 1981. pap. 2.95 (ISBN 0-87099-265-1). Metro Mus Art.

Draper, James D., ed. see Bode, Wilhelm.

Draper, James T. The Conscience of a Nation. LC 82-73420. 1983. pap. 7.95 (ISBN 0-8054-1530-0). Broadman.

--What to Do until the Lord Comes. (Studies in First & Second Thessalonians). 1983. 6.95 (ISBN 0-8423-7878-2); leader's guide 2.95 (ISBN 0-8423-7879-0). Tyndale.

Draper, James T., Jr. Authority: The Critical Issue for Southern Baptists. 128p. 1984. 7.95 (ISBN 0-8007-1389-3). Revell.

--The Church Christ Approves. LC 73-89856. pap. 6.95 (ISBN 0-8054-1922-5). Broadman.

--Discover Joy: Studies in Philippians. 1983. pap. 4.95 (ISBN 0-8423-0606-4); leader's guide 2.95 (ISBN 0-8423-0607-2). Tyndale.

--Faith that Works: Studies in James. 1983. pap. 5.95 (ISBN 0-8423-0872-5); Leader's Guide 2.95 (ISBN 0-8423-0873-3). Tyndale.

--Foundations of Biblical Faith. LC 78-67001. 1979. 8.50 (ISBN 0-8054-1951-9). Broadman.

--Live up to Your Faith: Studies in Titus. 1983. pap. 3.95 (ISBN 0-8423-3687-7); leader's guide 2.95 (ISBN 0-8423-3688-5). Tyndale.

--Proverbs: Practical Directions for Living. (Living Studies). pap. 4.95 (ISBN 0-8423-4922-7); leader's guide 2.95 (ISBN 0-8423-4923-5). Tyndale.

--The Unveiling. LC 83-25229. 1984. pap. 7.95 (ISBN 0-8054-1504-1). Broadman.

Draper, James T., Jr. & Watson, Forrest E. If the Foundations Be Destroyed. LC 84-1067. 224p. 1984. 11.95 (ISBN 0-8407-9027-9); pap. 6.95 (ISBN 0-8407-9525-4). Nelson.

Draper, Jean. Mathematics Para Administration y Economia. new ed. 1976. text ed. 17.00x (ISBN 0-06-310100-9, IntlDept). Har-Row.

Draper, Jo. Post-Medieval Pottery, 1650-1800. (Shire Archaeology Ser.: No. 40). (Illus.). 70p. (Orig.). 1984. pap. 5.95 (ISBN 0-85263-681-4, Pub. by Shire Pubns England). Seven Hills Bks.

Draper, Joan E., jt. auth. see Zukowsky, John.

Draper, John E., ed. Napoleon's Thoughts on History, Politics & the Management of Men. (Illus.). 1980. deluxe ed. 59.75 (ISBN 0-89266-232-8). Am Classical Coll Pr.

Draper, John S. Shams or Uncle Ben's Experience with Hypocrites. LC 71-166712. (Illus.). 1971. Repr. of 1898 ed. 29.00x (ISBN 0-403-01430-1). Scholarly.

Draper, John W. Funeral Elegy & the Rise of English Romanticism. 1967. lib. bdg. 23.00x (ISBN 0-374-92299-3). Octagon.

--Funeral Elegy & the Rise of English Romanticism. LC 67-30902. 1967. Repr. of 1929 ed. 10.00x (ISBN 0-87753-013-0). Phaeton.

--History of the American Civil war, 3 vols. 117.00 (ISBN 0-8369-7159-0, 7991). Ayer Co Pubs.

--History of the Conflict Between Religion & Science. 394p. 1875. text ed. 62.10x (ISBN 0-318-12114-X, Pub. by Gregg Intl Pubs England). Gregg Intl.

--Humors & Shakespeare's Characters. LC 77-142248. Repr. of 1945 ed. 16.00 (ISBN 0-404-02178-6). AMS Pr.

--Othello of Shakespeare's Audience. 1967. lib. bdg. 19.00x (ISBN 0-374-92338-8). Octagon.

--Scientific Memoirs. LC 72-9194. (The Literature of Photography Ser.). Repr. of 1878 ed. 32.00 (ISBN 0-405-04904-8). Ayer Co Pubs.

--Stratford to Dogberry: Studies in Shakespeare's Earlier Plays. (Select Bibliographies Reprint Ser). 1961. 29.00 (ISBN 0-8369-5255-3). Ayer Co Pubs.

--The Tempo-Patterns of Shakespeare's Plays. 163p. 1957. 24.00x (ISBN 3-5330-0958-0). Adlers Foreign Bks.

--Thoughts on the Future Civil Policy of America. Incl. Memoir of John William Draper, 1811-1882. Barker, George F. (The Neglected American Economists Ser.). 1975. lib. bdg. 61.00 (ISBN 0-8240-1017-5). Garland Pub.

--The Twelfth Night of Shakespeare's Audience. 1972. lib. bdg. 21.50x (ISBN 0-374-92277-2). Octagon.

Draper Lab Inc., ed. Flexible Manufacturing Systems Handbook. LC 84-4097. (Illus.). 392p. 1984. 48.00 (ISBN 0-8155-0983-9). Noyes.

Draper, Lyman C. King's Mountain & Its Heroes: History of the Battle of King's Mountain, October 7th 1780 & the Events Which Led to It. LC 67-25801. (Illus.). 1967. Repr. of 1881 ed. 25.00 (ISBN 0-87152-035-4). Reprint.
--King's Mountain & Its Heroes: History of the Battle of King's Mountain, October 7th, 1780, & the Events Which Led to It. LC 67-28623. (Illus.). 612p. 1983. Repr. of 1881 ed. 25.00 (ISBN 0-8063-0097-3). Genealog Pub.
Draper, M. W. & Nissenson, R. A., eds. Parathyroid Hormone. (Journal: Mineral & Electrolyte Metabolism: Vol. 8, No. 3-4). (Illus.). vi, 124p. 1982. pap. 33.25 (ISBN 3-8055-3550-3). S Karger.
Draper, Maurice L. Credo: I Believe. 1983. pap. 14.00 (ISBN 0-8309-0366-6). Herald Hse.
--Isles & Continents. (Orig.). 1982. pap. 14.00 (ISBN 0-8309-0343-7). Herald Hse.
--Restoration Studies, Vol. II. 1983. pap. 13.00 (ISBN 0-8309-0362-3). Herald Hse.
Draper, Maurice L., ed. Restoration Studies, 1980, Vol. 1. 1980. pap. 13.00 (ISBN 0-8309-0292-9). Herald Hse.
Draper, Nancy-Carroll. The Great Dane: Dogdom's Apollo. LC 81-6404. (Illus.). 203p. 1982. 15.95 (ISBN 0-87605-162-X). Howell Bk.
Draper, Norman R. & Smith, Harry. Applied Regression Analysis. 2nd ed. LC 80-17951. (Probability & Mathematical Statistics Ser.). 709p. 1981. 36.95x (ISBN 0-471-02995-5). Wiley.
Draper, Norman R., jt. auth. see Box, George E.
Draper, Paul & Stevens, James. The Investment Market in the U. K. 150p. 1986. text ed. price not set (ISBN 0-566-05064-1). Gower Pub Co.
Draper, Perry L. Parents, Take Charge! 1982. pap. 4.95 (ISBN 0-8423-4822-0); leader's guide 2.95 (ISBN 0-8423-4823-9). Tyndale.
Draper, R., jt. auth. see Brown, A.
Draper, R. P. Lyric Tragedy. 192p. 1985. 25.00 (ISBN 0-312-50053-X). St Martin.
Draper, R. P., ed. D. H. Lawrence: The Critical Heritage. (Critical Heritage Ser.). 1970. text ed. 35.00x (ISBN 0-7100-6591-4). Routledge & Kegan.
Draper, Raymond, jt. auth. see Brown, Alex.
Draper, Richard & Draper, Ann, illus. The AA Three Mile Road Altas. (Illus.). 336p. 1985. 35.00 (ISBN 0-86156-259-3, Pub. by Auto Assn-British Tourist Authority England). Merrimack Pub Cir.
--The AA Three Mile Road Atlas. (Illus.). 336p. 1985. 35.00 (ISBN 0-86145-259-3, Pub by Auto Assn-British Tourist Authority England). Merrimack Pub Cir.
Draper, Robert. Huey Lewis & the News. 160p. 1986. pap. 2.95 (ISBN 0-345-33028-5). Ballantine.
--ZZ Top. 1985. pap. 2.95 (ISBN 0-345-32230-4). Ballantine.
Draper, Ronald P. D. H. Lawrence. (English Authors Ser.). 1964. lib. bdg. 13.50 (ISBN 0-8057-1320-4, Twayne). G K Hall.
Draper, Rosalind, jt. ed. see Campbell, David.
Draper, Samuel. Simple Guide to Research Papers. rev. ed. 1978. 6.95 (ISBN 0-89529-040-5). Avery Pub.
Draper, Sarah. Once Upon the Main Line. 1980. 5.75 (ISBN 0-8062-1399-X). Carlton.
Draper, Stephen, jt. auth. see Norman, Donald A.
Draper, Theodore. American Communism & Soviet Russia. LC 76-51212. 1977. Repr. of 1960 ed. lib. bdg. 40.00x (ISBN 0-374-92334-5). Octagon.
--The Eighty-Fourth Infantry Division in the Battle of Germany. (Divisional Ser.: No. 24). (Illus.). 260p. 1985. Repr. of 1946 ed. 25.00 (ISBN 0-89839-069-9). Battery Pr.
--Present History: On Nuclear War, Detente & Other Controversies. 1984. pap. 9.95 (ISBN 0-394-72371-6, Vin). Random.
--The Roots of American Communism. LC 76-51210. 1977. Repr. lib. bdg. 37.50x (ISBN 0-374-92342-6). Octagon.
Draper, Thomas, ed. Emerging China. (Reference Shelf Ser.). 1980. 8.00 (ISBN 0-8242-0644-4). Wilson.
--Human Rights. (Reference Shelf Ser.: Vol. 54: No. 1). 154p. 1982. pap. text ed. 8.00 (ISBN 0-8242-0665-7). Wilson.
--Israel & the Middle East. 233p. (Reference Shelf Service). 1983. 8.00 (ISBN 0-8242-0683-5). Wilson.
Draper, Verden R., jt. auth. see Irving, Robert H.
Draper, Wanetta W., jt. auth. see Hunt, Inez.
Draper, William. The Growth of European Culture & the Age of Faith. (Illus.). 167p. 1985. 137.45 (ISBN 0-89266-543-2). Am Classical Coll Pr.
Draper, William H. Petrarch's Secret. LC 74-16342. 1974. Repr. of 1911 ed. lib. bdg. 28.50 (ISBN 0-8414-3801-3). Folcroft.
--Petrarch's Secret or the Soul's Conflict with Passion. 1973. Repr. of 1911 ed. 28.50 (ISBN 0-8274-1390-4). R West.
Draper, William H., tr. see Petrarca, Francesco.
Drar, M., jt. auth. see Tackholm, V.
Drasar, D. R. & Hill, M. J. Human Intestinal Flora. 1975. 49.50 (ISBN 0-12-221750-0). Acad Pr.
Drasdo, Harold, jt. ed. see Tobias, Michael.
Drasdo, Harold, jt. ed. see Tobias, Michael C.
Drashek, Thomas S. Von see Von Drashek, Thomas S.
Draskau, Jennifer, ed. Taw & Other Thai Stories. (Writing in Asia Ser.). 1975. pap. text ed. 6.50x (ISBN 0-686-65344-0, 00215). Heinemann Ed.
Draskhanakertetsi, Hovhannes. Patmowt'iwn Hayots' History of the Armenians. Maksoudian, Krikor, ed. LC 79-24542. 1980. Repr. of 1912 ed. 50.00x (ISBN 0-88206-028-7). Caravan Bks.
Draskovich, Slobodan. Will America Surrender? 480p. 1972. 12.95 (ISBN 0-8159-7211-3). Devin.
--Will America Surrender? 1976. pap. 1.95 (ISBN 0-8159-7217-2). Devin.
Drassler, Melvin. Treasure Hunting Around the World. 140p. (Orig.). 1985. pap. text ed. 14.95 (ISBN 0-89769-088-5, Dist. by Caroline Hse). Pine Mntn.
Dratch, Gladys I., compiled by. Childs Gallery, Boston: Exhibition Chronology & Publications, 1937-1980. 1985. pap. 5.00 (ISBN 0-317-13415-9). Boston Public Lib.
Drate, Stanley, ed. see Chirgotis, William G.
Drath, Viola & Moeller, Jack. Noch Dazu! LC 79-64140. (Sequential German Readers Ser.: Bk. II). (gr. 9-12). 1980. pap. text ed. 5.76 (ISBN 0-395-27930-5). HM.
Drath, Wilfred H. & Kaplan, Robert E. The Looking Glass Experience: A Story of Learning Through Action & Reflection. (Special Report Ser.: No. 6). 175p. 1984. pap. 15.00 (ISBN 0-912879-55-6). Ctr Creat Leader.
Drath, Wilfred H., et al. High Hurdles: The Challenge of Executive Self-Development. (Technical Report: No. 25). 25p. 1985. pap. 7.00 (ISBN 0-912879-23-8). Ctr Creat Leader.
Drath, Wilfred H., III, ed. A Miscellany of Issues & Observations. (Special Report: No. 7). 68p. 1985. pap. 15.00 (ISBN 0-912879-56-4). Ctr Creat Leader.
Draudt, Susan B. Food Processor Cookery. (Illus.). 175p. 1981. pap. 8.95 (ISBN 0-89586-122-4). H P Bks.
--Thirty Minute Meals. (Illus.). 160p. 1984. pap. 6.95 (ISBN 0-89586-308-1). H P Bks.
Drauglis, E., et al. Molecular Processes on Solid Surfaces. (Materials Science & Engineering Ser.). 1969. text ed. 77.50 (ISBN 0-07-017827-5). McGraw.
Drauglis, Edmund & Jaffee, Robert I., eds. The Physical Basis for Heterogeneous Catalysis. LC 75-41427. 596p. 1975. 85.00 (ISBN 0-306-30912-2, Plenum Pr). Plenum Pub.
Draus, Franciszek, ed. see Aron, Raymond.
Draves, Bill. The Free University: A Model for Lifelong Learning. 314p. 1980. 12.95 (ISBN 0-318-14138-8, Association Press). Free Univ Network.
Draves, Cornelia P. Summer Hum. Baker, Cornelia D., ed. LC 84-60279. (Illus.). 160p. 1984. lib. bdg. 11.95 (ISBN 0-916335-00-3). Mimosa Pubns.
Draves, Debra J. Anatomy of the Lower Extremity. (Illus.). 350p. 1985. 45.00 (ISBN 0-683-02651-8). Williams & Wilkins.
Draves, Pamela, ed. Citizens Media Directory. 1977. pap. 3.50 (ISBN 0-9603466-3-5); 1980 update avail. T R A C.
Draves, William A. How to Teach Adults. LC 83-82761. 110p. 1984. 12.95 (ISBN 0-914951-21-1); pap. 7.95 (ISBN 0-914951-20-3). Learn Net Res.
Dravich, Jay. Tales for a Child's Heart. LC 80-50009. (Illus.). 136p. (Orig.). (gr. k-6). 1980. 12.00 (ISBN 0-686-27348-6); pap. 5.00 (ISBN 0-686-27349-4). Tari Bk Pubs.
Dravich, Jay E. Dreams of Cloud Dancing. (Illus.). 150p. (Orig.). (gr. 4-12). 1982. 15.00 (ISBN 0-9604258-2-9); pap. 6.00 (ISBN 0-9604258-3-7). Tari Bk Pubs.
Dravid, R. R. The Problem of Universals in Indian Philosophy. 1972. 12.50 (ISBN 0-89684-486-2). Orient Bk Dist.
Dravida dasa, ed. see Svarupa dasa, Ravindra.
Dravnieks, Dzintar E., et al, eds. IBM Personal Computer Handbook. LC 83-9953. (Illus.). 448p. (Orig.). 1983. pap. 19.95 (ISBN 0-915904-66-7). And-Or Pr.
Drawbaugh, Charles C. Time & Its Use: A Self Management Guide for Teachers. 1984. pap. text ed. 11.95x (ISBN 0-8077-2706-7). Tchrs Coll.
Drawbaugh, Charles C. & Hull, William L. Agricultural Education: Approaches to Learning & Teaching. LC 71-132866. 1971. text ed. 23.95 (ISBN 0-675-09274-4). Merrill.
Drawbaugh, Susan M. What Pet Will I Get? LC 77-83881. 1977. 5.95 (ISBN 0-89430-017-2). Palos Verdes.
Drawford, Mary C. The Story of the City & of Its People During the 19th Century. 1979. Repr. of 1910 ed. lib. bdg. 30.00 (ISBN 0-8495-0943-2). Arden Lib.
Drawing Board Greeting Cards, illus. God's in His Heaven: A Coloring Book. (God's in His Heaven Bks.). (Illus.). 64p. (ps-3). 1984. pap. 2.95 (saddle-stitched) (ISBN 0-394-86884-6, Pub. by BYR). Random.
Drawson. Do Something Special on Your Birthday. (ps-3). pap. 1.25 (ISBN 0-590-05799-5, Schol Pap). Scholastic Inc.
--I Like Hats. (ps-3). pap. 1.95 (ISBN 0-590-05800-2, Schol Pap). Scholastic Inc.
Drawson, Maynard C. Treasures of the Oregon Country: No. IV. (Illus.). 1977. pap. 9.95 (ISBN 0-934476-03-9). Dee Pub Co.
--Treasures of the Oregon Country: No. V. (Historical Travel Ser.). (Illus., Orig.). 1979. pap. 9.95 (ISBN 0-934476-04-7). Dee Pub Co.
Draxe, Thomas. Bibliotheca Scholastica Instructissima: Or a Treasure of Ancient Adagies. LC 76-57378. (English Experience Ser.: No. 796). 1977. Repr. lib. bdg. 24.00 (ISBN 90-221-0796-5). Walter J Johnson.
Draxl, Peter K. Skew Fields. LC 82-22036. (London Mathematical Society Lecture Note Ser.: No. 81). 194p. 1983. pap. 22.95 (ISBN 0-521-27274-2). Cambridge U Pr.
Draxten, Nina. Kristofer Janson in America. (International Studies & Translations Program Ser.). 1976. lib. bdg. 12.50 (ISBN 0-8057-9000-4, Twayne). G K Hall.
Dray, Philip, jt. auth. see Cagin, Seth.
Dray, William. Perspectives on History. 192p. 1980. 23.95x (ISBN 0-7100-0569-5); pap. 10.00 (ISBN 0-7100-0570-9). Routledge & Kegan.
Dray, William H. Laws & Explanation in History. LC 78-25936. 1979. Repr. of 1957 ed. lib. bdg. 24.75x (ISBN 0-313-20790-9, DRLE). Greenwood.
--Philosophy of History. (Orig.). 1964. pap. 13.95x ref. ed. (ISBN 0-13-663849-X). P-H.
Dray, William H., ed. Philosophical Analysis & History. LC 77-26206. 1978. Repr. of 1966 ed. lib. bdg. 34.00x (ISBN 0-313-20068-8, DRPA). Greenwood.
Dray, Williams, jt. ed. see Pampa, Leon.
Drayson, James E. Herd Bull Fertility. (Illus.). 160p. (Orig.). 1982. pap. 9.95 (ISBN 0-934318-08-5). Falcon Pr MT.
Drayton, Daniel. Personal Memoirs of Daniel Drayton. LC 76-97422. Repr. of 1855 ed. 15.00 (ISBN 0-8371-2711-4, DRI&). Greenwood.
Drayton, Geoffrey. Christopher. (Caribbean Writers Ser.). 1972. pap. text ed. 4.00x (ISBN 0-435-98235-4). Heinemann Ed.
Drayton, Geoffrey, jt. auth. see Wilson, David.
Drayton, Grace. Dolly Dingle Paper Dolls. (Illus.). 1978. pap. 3.50 (ISBN 0-486-23711-7). Dover.
Drayton, Grace & Fontana, Frank. Dolly Dingle Coloring Book. (Coloring Bks.). (Illus.). 32p. (Orig.). (gr. 2 up). 1983. pap. 2.00 (ISBN 0-486-24416-4). Dover.
Drayton, Grace G. Adventures of Dolly Dingle Paper Dolls: Sixteen Antique Plates in Full Color. 1985. 3.50 (ISBN 0-486-24809-7). Dover.
--More Dolly Dingle Paper Dolls. 32p. 1979. pap. 2.95 (ISBN 0-486-23848-2). Dover.
Drayton, John. Memoirs of the American Revolution, 2 Vols. Decker, Peter, ed. LC 77-76244. (Eyewitness Accounts of the American Revolution Ser., No. 2). 1969. Repr. of 1821 ed. Set. 45.50 (ISBN 0-405-01149-0); 17.00 ea. Vol. 1 (ISBN 0-405-01150-4). Vol. 2 (ISBN 0-405-01151-2). Ayer Co Pubs.
Drayton, Julia, et al, trs. see Trotsky, Leon.
Drayton, Mary. All Our Secrets. 384p. (Orig.). 1981. pap. 2.95 (ISBN 0-449-14391-0, GM). Fawcett.
Drayton, Michael. The Barons' Wars. 1887. 15.00 (ISBN 0-8274-1913-9). R West.
--The Battle of Agincourt. 1979. Repr. of 1893 ed. lib. bdg. 40.00 (ISBN 0-8495-1046-5). Arden Lib.
--Michael Drayton: A Selection of Shorter Poems. Cole, G. D. & Cole, M. I., eds. 1927. 17.50 (ISBN 0-8274-2731-X). R West.
--Minor Poems. (Select Bibliographies Reprint Ser). 1972. Repr. of 1907 ed. 19.00 (ISBN 0-8369-6853-0). Ayer Co Pubs.
--Muses Elizium. (Spencer Soc.: No. 5). 1966. 29.50 (ISBN 0-8337-0913-5). B Franklin.
--Poemes, Lyrick, & Pastorall. (Spencer Soc.: No. 4). 1605. 26.00 (ISBN 0-8337-0914-3). B Franklin.
--Poems, 2 vols. (Spencer Soc.: Nos. 45-46). 1966. Repr. of 1888 ed. 52.00 (ISBN 0-8337-0915-1). B Franklin.
--Poly-Olbion: A Chronologic Description of Great Britain, 3 Vols. in One. (Spencer Soc.: Nos. 1-3). (Illus.). 1966. 78.50 (ISBN 0-8337-0921-6). B Franklin.
--A Selection of Shorter Poems. LC 77-18727. 1927. 10.00 (ISBN 0-8414-0109-8). Folcroft.
--To the Majestie of King James, a Gratulatorie Poem. LC 71-25832. (English Experience Ser.: No. 169). 16p. 1969. Repr. of 1603 ed. 7.00 (ISBN 90-221-0169-X). Walter J Johnson.
Drayton, Michael, et al. Sir John Oldcastle. LC 72-133657. (Tudor Facsimile Texts. Old English Plays: No. 89). Repr. of 1911 ed. 49.50 (ISBN 0-404-53389-2). AMS Pr.
Drayton, William H. The Letters of Freeman, Etc. LC 75-31089. Repr. of 1771 ed. 19.50 (ISBN 0-404-13507-2). AMS Pr.
Drazan, Joseph G. The Nightmare: A Checklist of the World Literature to 1976. LC 78-68457. 1979. perfect bdg. 9.95 (ISBN 0-88247-560-6). R & E Pubs.
--The Pacific Northwest: An Index to People & Places in Books. LC 79-16683. 176p. 1979. 15.00 (ISBN 0-8108-1234-7). Scarecrow.
--The Unknown Eric: A Selection of Documents for the General Library. LC 80-25975. 239p. 1981. lib. bdg. 15.00 (ISBN 0-8108-1402-1). Scarecrow.
Drazan, Joseph G., compiled by. An Annotated Bibliography of ERIC Bibliographies, 1966-1980. LC 82-6151. (Illus.). xiv, 520p. 1982. lib. bdg. 49.95 (ISBN 0-313-22688-1, DRE/). Greenwood.
Drazan, P. J. Robot Systems. 320p. 1985. cancelled (ISBN 0-246-11703-6, Pub. by Granada England). Sheridan.
Draze, Dianne. Above & Beyond, Bk. 1. (Illus.). (gr. 5 up). 1978. wkbk 5.00 (ISBN 0-931724-03-1). Dandy Lion.
--Above & Beyond, Bk. 2. (Illus.). 1978. wkbk. 5.00 (ISBN 0-931724-04-X). Dandy Lion.
--Above & Beyond, Bk. 3. (Illus.). 1978. wkbk. 5.00 (ISBN 0-931724-08-2). Dandy Lion.
--Alphabet Soup. (Illus.). 1978. pap. text ed. 6.00 (ISBN 0-931724-07-4). Dandy Lion.
--The Anywhere, Anytime Individualized Speller. (Illus.). (gr. 3 up). 1978. pap. 5.00 (ISBN 0-931724-02-3). Dandy Lion.
--Asking Questions, Finding Answers. (Illus., Orig.). (gr. 2-9). 1979. pap. 7.50 (ISBN 0-931724-10-4). Dandy Lion.
--Connections, Advanced. Bachelis, Faren, ed. (Illus.). 32p. 1983. pap. 5.00 (ISBN 0-931724-22-8). Dandy Lion.
--Design-a-Project. Schnare, Sharon, ed. (Illus.). 48p. (gr. 4-10). 1980. tchrs ed 12.00 (ISBN 0-931724-11-2). Dandy Lion.
--Experiences in the Fourth Dimension. (Illus.). 64p. (gr. 4-8). 1980. tchrs'. ed. 6.50 (ISBN 0-931724-12-0). Dandy Lion.
--The Future Traveler. Ryder, Dixie, ed. (Illus.). 96p. tchrs. ed. 10.00 (ISBN 0-931724-26-0). Dandy Lion.
--Options: A Guide for Creative Decision Making. Bachelis, Faren, ed. (Illus.). 72p. 1982. 8.50 (ISBN 0-931724-18-X). Dandy Lion.
--Patchwork (Activities in Flexible Thinking) (Illus., Orig.). 1980. pap. text ed. 7.00 (ISBN 0-931724-13-9); tchr's ed. avail. Dandy Lion.
--Pot Pourri. (Illus.). (gr. 3-8). 1978. pap. 7.00 (ISBN 0-931724-01-5). Dandy Lion.
--Think Tank. (Illus.). 1978. tchrs'. ed. 7.50 (ISBN 0-931724-09-0). Dandy Lion.
Draze, Dianne, ed. see Aiken, Dawn.
Draze, Dianne, ed. see Neff, Carolyn & Verett, Dotty.
Draze, Dianne, ed. see Powell, Carolyn.
Draze, Dianne, ed. see Risby, Bonnie.
Draze, Dianne L. The Last Word Book. (Illus.). (gr. 4-8). 1978. pap. 6.00 (ISBN 0-931724-00-7). Dandy Lion.
Drazil, J. V. Quantities & Units of Measurement: A Dictionary & Handbook. 240p. 1983. 33.00x (ISBN 0-7201-1665-1). Mansell.
Drazin, Israel. Targum Onkelos on Deuteronomy. 1981. 45.00x (ISBN 0-87068-755-7). Ktav.
Drazin, Judith. Stage Fever. 94p. (gr. 7-10). 1984. 5.95 (ISBN 0-241-11073-4, Pub. by Hamish Hamilton England). David & Charles.
Drazin, P. G. Solitons. LC 83-7170. (London Mathematical Society Lecture Note Ser. No. 85). 136p. 1983. pap. 16.95 (ISBN 0-521-27422-2). Cambridge U Pr.
Drazin, P. G. & Reid, W. H. Hydrodynamic Stability. LC 80-40273. (Cambridge Monographs on Mechanics & Applied Mathematics). (Illus.). 600p. 1981. 95.00 (ISBN 0-521-22798-4). Cambridge U Pr.
--Hydrodynamic Stability. LC 80-40273. (Cambridge Monographs on Mechanics & Applied Mathematics). (Illus.). 539p. 1982. pap. 27.95 (ISBN 0-521-28980-7). Cambridge U Pr.
Draznin, Boris. Marshmellowterra: The Land of Marshmallow People & Whimsical Animals. (Illus.). 96p. (gr. 7-12). 1982. 6.50 (ISBN 0-682-49914-5). Exposition Pr FL.
Dreamer, Sue. Circus ABC. (Illus.). (ps up). 1985. pap. 3.70 (ISBN 0-316-19196-5). Little.
--Circus 1-2-3. (Illus.). (ps up). 1985. pap. 3.95 (ISBN 0-316-19195-7). Little.
Drebin, Allan R. Advanced Accounting. 1982. text ed. 24.20 (ISBN 0-538-01580-2, A58). SW Pub.
Drebin, Allan R. & Chan, James L. Objectives of Accounting & Financial Reporting by Governmental Units: A Research Study, 2 vols. Incl. Vol. I. (Illus.). 128p. pap.; Vol. II. (Illus.). 200p. pap. 7.50 (ISBN 0-686-84260-X). 1981. pap. Municipal.
Drebin, Allan R., jt. auth. see Bierman, Harold, Jr.
Drechsel, D., jt. ed. see Arenhovel, H.
Drechsel, Robert. Newsmaking in the Trial Courts. LC 81-17202. (Professional Studies in Political Communication & Policy). 224p. 1982. 22.50x (ISBN 0-582-28319-1). Longman.
Dreckamer, John M., tr. see Walther, C. F.
Dredging Technology, 2nd International Conference. Proceedings, 2 vols. Stephens, H. S., ed. 1979. Set. pap. 62.00x (ISBN 0-900983-76-0, Dist. by Air Science Co). BHRA Fluid.
Dreeben, Robert, jt. auth. see Barr, Rebecca.
Dreeben, Robert & Thomas, J. Alan, eds. Issues in Microanalysis. LC 79-62118. (Analysis of Educational Productivity Ser.: Vol. 1). 288p. 1980. prof ref 35.00 (ISBN 0-88410-191-6). Ballinger Pub.
Dreele, W. H. Von see Von Dreele, W. H.
Dreer, Herman. The Immediate Jewel of His Soul. LC 72-144596. Repr. of 1919 ed. 23.50 (ISBN 0-404-00149-1). AMS Pr.
Drees, L., ed. see Middleton, Thomas.
Drees, Thomas. Blood Plasma: The Promise & the Politics. LC 82-11617. (Illus.). 1983. 25.00 (ISBN 0-87949-225-2). Ashley Bks.
Dreese, G. Richard, et al. Guidelines for Attracting Private Capital to Corps of Engineers Projects. 208p. 1977. avail. Assn U Busn & Econ Res.

Dreesman, Gordon R. & Bronson, Judith Gunn, eds. High-Technology Route to Virus Vaccines. 175p. 1985. pap. 27.00 (ISBN 0-914826-81-6). Am Soc Microbio.

Dreger, Carol, jt. auth. see Patterson, Barbara.

Dreger, Carol H. The Complete Guide to MultiMate. 250p. 1984. pap. 15.95 (ISBN 0-89588-229-9). SYBEX.

Dreger, Georgia E. A Different Dream. LC 81-67750. (gr. 5-9). 1982. pap. 6.95 (ISBN 0-8054-4806-3, 4248-06). Broadman.

Dreger, Ralph. Multivariate Personality Research. 1972. 17.50x (ISBN 0-87511-029-0). Claitors.

Dreger, Ralph M., jt. ed. see Miller, Kent S.

Dreghorn, William. Geology Explained in the Severn Vale & Cotswolds. (Illus.). 192p. 1974. 14.95 (ISBN 0-7153-4102-2). David & Charles.

Dregne, H. E. Desertification of Arid Lands. LC 83-83969. (Advances in Desert & Arid Land Technology & Development Ser.: Vol. 3). (Illus.). 228p. 1983. 33.25 (ISBN 3-7186-0168-0). Harwood Academic.

Dregne, H. E. & Willis, W. O., eds. Dryland Agriculture. (Illus.). 1983. 35.00 (ISBN 0-89118-075-3). Am Soc Agron.

Dregni, Meredith S. Experiencing More with Less. LC 83-80954. 88p. (Orig.). 1983. pap. 4.95 (ISBN 0-8361-3334-X). Herald Pr.

Dreher, Barbara B. & Gervase, Charles J. Phonetics: Instructional Aid in Language Arts. 1976. perfect bdg. 6.95 (ISBN 0-8403-1310-1). Kendall-Hunt.

Dreher, Denise. From the Neck Up: An Illustrated Guide to Hatmaking. LC 80-83507. (Illus.). 206p. 1982. pap. 20.00 (ISBN 0-941082-00-8). Madhatter.

Dreher, Diane E. The Fourfold Pilgrimage: The Estates of Innocence, Misery, & Glory in Seventeenth-Century Literature. LC 81-40829. (Illus.). 176p. (Orig.). 1982. lib. bdg. 25.00 (ISBN 0-8191-2177-0); pap. text ed. 11.75 (ISBN 0-8191-2178-9). U Pr of Amer.

Dreher, E. Der Mensch Zwischen Anschauungen und Abstraktion. Bd. with Genie und Irrsinn: Ein ueberholtes Begriffspaar. Simson, G. (Schriftenreihe des Instituts fuer Konfliktforschung: Vol. 8). x, 54p. 1982. pap. 6.50 (ISBN 3-8055-3489-2). S Karger.

Dreher, E., ed. Schweizerische Gesellschaft fuer Gynaekologie, Bericht ueber die Jahresversammlung, Montreux, Juni 1979. (Journal: Gynaekologische Rundschau: Vol. 19, Suppl. 2). 1980. pap. 14.25 (ISBN 3-8055-0456-X). S Karger.

--Schweizerische Gesellschaft fuer Gynaekologie Bericht ueber die Jahresversammlung, St. Gallen. J 1980. (Journal: Gynaekologische Rundschau: Vol. 20, No. 1). (Illus.). iv, 144p. 1981. pap. 14.25 (ISBN 3-8055-2126-X). S Karger.

--Schweizerische Gesellschaft fuer Gynaekologie und Geburtshilfe, Bericht ueber die Jahresversammlung, Lausanne, Juni 1983. (Journal: Gynaekologische Rundschau: Vol. 23, Suppl. 4). (Illus.). iv, 116p. 1984. pap. 14.25 (ISBN 3-8055-3815-4). S Karger.

--Schweizerische Gesellschaft fuer Gynaekologie und Geburtshilfe: Societe Suisse de Gynecologie et Obstetrique, Bericht ueber die Jahresversammlung, St. Moritz, April 1984. (Journal: Gynaekologische Rundschau: Vol. 24, Suppl. 1). iv, 160p. 1985. pap. 20.50 (ISBN 3-8055-3964-9). S Karger.

--Schweizerische Gesellschaft fuer Gynaekologie und Geburtshilfe unter Mitkirkung der Schweizerischen Gesellschaft fuer Medizinische Genetik. Bericht ueber die Jahresversammlung, Zuerich, 1982. (Journal-Gynaekologische Rundschau: Vol. 22, Suppl. 3). (Illus.). xiv, 104p. 1983. pap. 16.75 (ISBN 3-8055-3656-9). S Karger.

--Societe Suisse de Gynecologie, Bericht ueber die Jahresversammlung, Genf, 1981. (Gynaekologische Rundschau Journal: Vol. 21, Suppl. 3). (Illus.). iv, 88p. 1981. pap. 12.50 (ISBN 3-8055-3479-5). S Karger.

Dreher, E., ed. see Schweizerische Gesellschaft fuer Gynaekologie, Bericht Ueber die Jahresversammlung, Lugano, Juni 30 - Juli 2, 1977.

Dreher, E., ed. see Schweizerische Gesellschaft fuer Gynaekologie, Bericht ueber die Jahresversammlung, Lugano, Juni 30 - Juli 2, 1977.

Dreher, G. K., ed. see Peele, George.

Dreher, George F. & Sackett, Paul R. Perspectives on Employee Staffing & Selection: Readings & Commentary. 1983. 18.95x (ISBN 0-256-02948-2). Irwin.

Dreher, Jean. Iron Horses-Iron Men. (Illus.). 130p. 1984. 12.95 (ISBN 0-912113-20-0); pap. 5.95 (ISBN 0-912113-21-9). Railhead Pubns.

Dreher, Melanie C. Working Men & Ganja: Marijuana Use in Rural Jamaica. LC 81-6872. (Illus.). 232p. 1982. text ed. 21.00 (ISBN 0-89727-025-8). ISHI PA.

Dreher, Sarah. Stoner McTavish. 200p. 1985. pap. 7.95 (ISBN 0-934678-06-5). New Victoria Pubs.

Drehle, Dave Von see Von Drehle, Dave.

Dreiblatt, Lorraine, jt. auth. see Beckelman, Florance.

Dreier, Patricia, ed. Beginnings. (Reader's Digest Words of Gold Ser.). (Illus.). 96p. 1985. 8.00 (ISBN 0-8378-1807-9). Gibson.

Dreier, Patricia, compiled by. The Gold of Friendship: A Bouquet of Special Thoughts. (Illus.). 1980. 6.95 (ISBN 0-8378-5049-5). Gibson.

--Happiness Is a Journey. (Illus.). 1983. boxed 8.00 (ISBN 0-8378-1804-4). Gibson.

Dreier, Patricia, ed. A Mother's World. (A Reader's Digest-C. R. Gibson Bk.). (Illus.). 96p. 1984. 8.00 (ISBN 0-8378-1805-2). Gibson.

--Pocketful of Joys. (Reader's Digest Words of Gold Ser.). (Illus.). 96p. 1985. 8.00 (ISBN 0-8378-1808-7). Gibson.

Dreier, William A. & Castner, Jane F. Guidebook to Chancery Practice in New Jersey (1984) 2nd ed. LC 83-182286. (Illus.). 287p. 1985. looseleaf 45.00. NJ Inst Cle.

Dreier, William A. & Goldman, Hannah G. Products Liability Law in New Jersey: A Practitioner's Guide (1983) LC 84-179016. 500p. 1985. looseleaf 45.00. NJ Inst CLE.

Dreifort, John E. Yvon Delbos at the Quai D'Orsay: French Foreign Policy During the Popular Front, 1936-1938. LC 72-85252. (Illus.). 256p. 1973. 25.00x (ISBN 0-7006-0094-9). U Pr of KS.

Dreifus, Claudia, ed. Seizing Our Bodies: The Politics of Women's Health Care. 1978. pap. 5.95 (ISBN 0-394-72360-0, Vin). Random.

Dreifus, J. J., jt. ed. see Baertschi, A. J.

Dreifus, Leonard S. Pacemaker Therapy. LC 83-1949. (Cardiovascular Clinics Ser.: Vol. 14, No. 2). (Illus.). 287p. 1983. text ed. 45.00x (ISBN 0-8036-2901-X). Davis Co.

Dreifus, Leonard S. & Brest, Albert N., eds. Cardiac Arrhythmias: Electrophysiologic Techniques & Management. LC 70-6558. (Cardiovascular Clinics Ser.: Vol. 16, No. 1). (Illus.). 370p. 1985. 50.00 (ISBN 0-8036-2903-6). Davis Co.

--Clinical Applications of Cardiovascular Drugs. (Developments in Cardiovascular Medicine Ser.: No. 5). (Illus.). 275p. 1980. 50.00 (ISBN 9-0247-2295-0, Pub. by Martinus Nijhoff Netherlands); pap. 31.50 (ISBN 9-0247-2369-8, Pub. by Martinus Nijhoff Netherlands). Kluwer Academic.

Dreifus, Leonard S., jt. ed. see Watanabe, Yoshio.

Dreifuss. Pediatric Epileptology. 1983. text ed. 39.50 (ISBN 0-7236-7039-0). PSG Pub Co.

Dreifuss, Fritz & Lee, Soo Ik. Epilepsy Case Studies. 1981. pap. text ed. 22.50 (ISBN 0-87488-095-5). Med Exam.

Dreifuss, Fritz E., et al. Pediatric Epileptology: Classification & Management of Seizures in the Child. LC 83-1257. (Illus.). 314p. 1983. 39.50 (ISBN 0-7236-7039-0). PSG Pub Co.

Dreifuss, Jerome. Catherine & Potemkin: An Imperial Romance. 1978. Repr. of 1937 ed. lib. bdg. 30.00 (ISBN 0-8495-1037-6). Arden Lib.

Dreifuss, Kurt. America's Brave Call for an Occupational Democracy. 1985. 1.75 (ISBN 0-9614149-1-X). Soc Wld Serv.

--The Endangered Human Animal. LC 84-52235. (First Serial Rights Ser.). 320p. 23.50 (ISBN 0-9614149-0-1). Soc Wld Serv.

--Other Side of the Universe. 1961. 12.95 (ISBN 0-8084-0231-5). New Coll U Pr.

--What Debs Means to America. 1982. write for info. Soc Wld Serv.

Dreikausen, Margret. Aerial Perception. LC 82-65880. (Illus.). 1985. 30.00 (ISBN 0-87982-040-3). Art Alliance.

Dreikorn, Kurt, jt. auth. see Marberger, Michael.

Dreikups, Rudolf. Social Equality. LC 83-72318. 1971. pap. 6.95x (ISBN 0-918560-30-6). A Adler Inst.

Dreikurs, Rudolf. Adult-Child Relations. 1972. pap. 6.00x (ISBN 0-918560-13-6). A Adler Inst.

--The Challenge of Child Training. 1972. pap. 4.50 (ISBN 0-8015-1146-1, Hawthorn). Dutton.

--Challenge of Marriage. 1978. pap. 7.95 (ISBN 0-8015-1177-1, 0772-230, Hawthorn). Dutton.

--Challenge of Parenthood. 1979. (Hawthorn); pap. 5.95 (ISBN 0-8015-1183-6, 0577-180). Dutton.

--Character Education & Spiritual Values in an Anxious Age. (AAI Monograph Ser.: No. 1). 1971. pap. 2.00x (ISBN 0-918560-16-0). A Adler Inst.

--Child Guidance & Education: Collected Papers. pap. 6.50x (ISBN 0-918560-11-X). A Adler Inst.

--Coping with Children's Misbehavior. 1972. pap. 6.95 (ISBN 0-8015-1764-8, 0674-210, Hawthorn). Dutton.

--Fundamentals of Adlerian Psychology. pap. 6.00x (ISBN 0-918560-08-X). A Adler Inst.

--Psychodynamics, Psychotherapy & Counseling: Collected Papers. LC 68-2060. pap. 10.00x (ISBN 0-918560-12-8). A Adler Inst.

--Psychology in the Classroom: A Manual for Teachers. rev., enl. ed. 1968. pap. text ed. 15.95 scp (ISBN 0-06-041756-0, HarpC). Har-Row.

Dreikurs, Rudolf & Grey, Loren. Logical Consequences: A New Approach to Discipline. LC 68-28720. 1968. 9.95 (ISBN 0-8015-4638-9, Hawthorn); pap. 7.95 (ISBN 0-8015-4632-X, 0772-230, Hawthorn). Dutton.

--Parent's Guide to Child Discipline. 1970. pap. 6.50 (ISBN 0-8015-5736-4, 0631-190, Hawthorn). Dutton.

Dreikurs, Rudolf & Soltz, Vicki. Children: The Challenge. 1964. pap. 6.95 (ISBN 0-8015-1249-2, 0674-210, Hawthorn). Dutton.

Dreikurs, Rudolf, jt. auth. see Dinkmeyer, Don.

Dreikurs, Rudolf, et al. Maintaining Sanity in the Classroom: Classroom Management Techniques. 2nd ed. 353p. 1982. pap. text ed. 15.95 scp (ISBN 0-06-041761-7, HarpC). Har-Row.

--Multiple Psychotherapy. LC 84-71164. 146p. (Orig.). 1984. pap. 10.00x (ISBN 0-918560-31-4). A Adler Inst.

Dreikurs, Rudolph. Discipline Without Tears. 1974. pap. 5.25 (ISBN 0-8015-2132-7, 0510-150, Hawthorn). Dutton.

Dreisbach, Robert H. Handbook of Poisoning: Prevention, Diagnosis, & Treatment. 11th ed. LC 82-83909. 632p. 1983. lexotone cover 11.00 (ISBN 0-87041-075-X). Lange.

--Handbook of Poisoning: Prevention, Diagnosis & Treatment. 10th ed. (Illus.). 578p. 1982. pap. 13.95 (ISBN 0-684-17504-5, ScribT). Scribner.

Dreisbach, Robert R. Physical Properties of Chemical Compounds, 3 vols. Incl. Vol. 1. 536p. 1955; Vol. 2. 491p. 1959. 37.95 (ISBN 0-8412-0023-8); Vol. 3. 489p. 1961. 39.95 (ISBN 0-8412-0030-0). LC 55-2887. (Advances in Chemistry Ser: Nos. 15, 22, 29). Am Chemical.

--Physical Properties of Chemical Compounds. LC 55-2887. (American Chemical Society Advances in Chemistry Ser.: No. 15). pap. 135.00 (ISBN 0-317-09629-X, 2011699). Bks Demand UMI.

Dreiser, Peter, jt. auth. see Matcham, Jonathan.

Dreiser, T. The Best Short Stories of Theodore Dreiser. 18.95 (ISBN 0-88411-539-9, Pub. by Aeonian Pr). Amereon Ltd.

--Fine Furniture. LC 75-22164. (Studies in Fiction, No. 34). 1975. lib. bdg. 29.95x (ISBN 0-8383-2107-0). Haskell.

Dreiser, Theodore. An Amateur Laborer. Dowell, Richard W., et al, eds. LC 83-3616. (Illus.). 256p. 1983. 25.00x (ISBN 0-8122-7890-9). U of Pa Pr.

--An American Tragedy. LC 78-55741. 1978. Repr. of 1948 ed. lib. bdg. 22.50x (ISBN 0-8376-0424-9). Bentley.

--An American Tragedy. 832p. 1973. pap. 3.95 (ISBN 0-451-51696-6, CE1696, Sig Classics). NAL.

--Financier. 1967. pap. 3.95 (ISBN 0-451-51719-9, CE1719, Sig Classics). NAL.

--Fine Furniture. LC 76-28778. 1973. lib. bdg. 15.00 (ISBN 0-8414-3708-4). Folcroft.

--Free & Other Stories. LC 70-144984. 1971. Repr. of 1918 ed. 49.00x (ISBN 0-403-00949-9). Scholarly.

--The Genius. 1981. pap. 5.95 (ISBN 0-452-00753-4, Mer). NAL.

--A Hoosier Holiday. LC 73-16642. (Illus.). 513p. 1974. Repr. of 1916 ed. lib. bdg. 24.75x (ISBN 0-8371-7211-X, DRHH). Greenwood.

--Jennie Gerhardt. LC 81-84117. 380p. 1982. pap. 8.95 (ISBN 0-8052-0692-2). Schocken.

--Newspaper Days. (Amer. Newspapermen Ser.: 1790-1933). 502p. 1974. Repr. of 1931 ed. 21.50x (ISBN 0-8464-0023-5). Beekman Pubs.

--Notes on Life. Tjader, Marguerite & McAleer, John J., eds. LC 73-41. 352p. 1974. 25.75 (ISBN 0-8173-8555-X). U of Ala Pr.

--Plays of the Natural & Supernatural. LC 73-97893. 1969. Repr. of 1916 ed. 18.00 (ISBN 0-404-02179-4). AMS Pr.

--Plays of the Natural & the Supernatural. LC 74-131690. Repr. of 1916 ed. 49.00x (ISBN 0-403-00577-9). Scholarly.

--Sister Carrie. (Classics Ser). (YA) (gr. 11 up). pap. 2.50 (ISBN 0-8049-0147-3, CL-147). Airmont.

--Sister Carrie. (Literature Ser). (gr. 10-12). 1970. pap. text ed. 5.17 (ISBN 0-87720-739-9). AMSCO Sch.

--Sister Carrie. (Bantam Classics Ser.). 432p. (gr. 9-12). 1982. pap. 2.25 (ISBN 0-553-21058-0). Bantam.

--Sister Carrie. LC 78-183140. 472p. 1971. Repr. lib. bdg. 15.00x (ISBN 0-8376-0401-X). Bentley.

--Sister Carrie. Salzman, Jack, ed. LC 69-16530. 1970. pap. 6.65 scp (ISBN 0-672-61014-0). Bobbs.

--Sister Carrie. LC 69-13798. (Merrill Standard Ser). 6.00 (ISBN 0-675-09527-1); pap. 4.00 (ISBN 0-675-09528-X). Brown Bk.

--Sister Carrie. Simpson, Claude, ed. LC 59-1819. (YA) (gr. 9 up). 1959. pap. 5.50 (ISBN 0-395-05134-7, RivEd). HM.

--Sister Carrie. Lynn, Kenneth S., ed. (Rinehart Editions Ser.). 1957. pap. text ed. 10.95 (ISBN 0-03-009075-X, HoltC). HR&W.

--Sister Carrie. abr. ed. (Belles Lettres in English Ser). 1969. Repr. of 1901 ed. 24.00 (ISBN 0-384-12780-0). Johnson Repr.

--Sister Carrie. 557p. 1980. Repr. of 1907 ed. lib. bdg. 23.95 (ISBN 0-89968-207-3). Lightyear.

--Sister Carrie. 1962. pap. 2.95 (ISBN 0-451-51725-3, CE1725, Sig Classics). NAL.

--Sister Carrie. Pizer, Donald, ed. (Critical Editions). 1970. pap. text ed. 9.95x (ISBN 0-393-09949-0). Norton.

--Sister Carrie. (Penguin American Library). 488p. 1981. pap. 3.95 (ISBN 0-14-039002-2). Penguin.

--Sister Carrie: The Pennsylvania Edition. West, James L., et al, eds. 1981. 45.00x (ISBN 0-8122-7784-8); pap. 16.95x (ISBN 0-8122-1110-3). U of Pa Pr.

--The Stoic. 1981. pap. 3.95 (ISBN 0-451-51549-8, CE1549, Sig Classics). NAL.

--Theodore Dreiser: A Selection of Uncollected Prose. Pizer, Donald, ed. LC 77-771. 296p. 1977. 15.95x (ISBN 0-8143-1569-0). Wayne St U Pr.

--Titan. 1965. pap. 4.95 (ISBN 0-452-00756-9, Mer). NAL.

--The Titan. LC 83-45747. Repr. of 1946 ed. 27.50 (ISBN 0-404-20084-2). AMS Pr.

--Twelve Men. LC 74-144985. 1971. Repr. of 1919 ed. 49.00x (ISBN 0-403-00914-6). Scholarly.

Dreiser, Theodore, et al. Harlan Miners Speak: Report on Terrorism in the Kentucky Coal Fields. LC 70-107410. (Civil Liberties in American History Ser.). 1970. Repr. of 1932 ed. lib. bdg. 32.50 (ISBN 0-306-71889-8). Da Capo.

Dreiser, Theordore. The Genius. 463p. 1980. Repr. of 1917 ed. lib. bdg. 24.95 (ISBN 0-89968-206-5). Lightyear.

Dreiss, Joseph G. Gari Melchers: His Works in the Belmont Collection. LC 83-19775. (Illus.). 350p. 1984. text ed. 37.50x (ISBN 0-8139-0999-6); pap. text ed. 19.95x (ISBN 0-8139-1024-2). U Pr of Va.

Dreissig, Georg. The Hunchback & the Princess. Adams, Neville, tr. from Ger. (Illus.). 32p. 1985. 9.95 (ISBN 0-89281-108-0). Inner Tradit.

Dreist, Edward R. Van see AAS - AAAS Symposium - Montreal - 1964.

Dreisziger, Nandor F., jt. ed. see Kiraly, Bela.

Dreizen, Laverne, jt. auth. see Audet, Thelma.

Dreizler, Reiner M. & Da Providencia, Joo, eds. Density Functional Methods in Physics. (NATO ASI Series B Physics: Vol. 123). 542p. 1985. 85.00x (ISBN 0-306-41926-2, Plenum Pr). Plenum Pub.

Drekmeier, Charles. Kingship & Community in Early India. LC 62-9565. 1962. 27.50x (ISBN 0-8047-0114-8). Stanford U Pr.

Drell, S. D., jt. auth. see Bjorken, James D.

Drell, Sidney D. Facing the Threat of Nuclear Weapons: With an Open Letter on the Danger of Thermonuclear War from Andrei Sakharov. LC 83-6580. (The Jessie & John Danz Lecture Ser.). 130p. 1983. 10.00x (ISBN 0-295-96082-5); pap. 4.95 (ISBN 0-295-96083-3). U of Wash Pr.

Drell, Sidney D., et al. The Reagan Strategic Defense Initiative: A Technical, Political, & Arms Control Assessment. 168p. 1985. pap. 12.95x professional reference (ISBN 0-88730-064-2). Ballinger Pub.

Dreman, David. The New Contrarian Investment Strategy: The Psychology of Stock Market Success. LC 78-21820. 1983. 16.95 (ISBN 0-394-52364-4). Random.

Dreman, David N. Psychology & the Stock Market. new ed. LC 76-49986. 1977. 14.95 (ISBN 0-8144-5429-1). AMACOM.

Dremann, Craig C. Chili Peppers in California. 2nd ed. (Illus.). 49p. (Orig.). 1985. pap. 2.50 (ISBN 0-933421-00-1). Redwood Seed.

Dremiere, P. Y. & Nedelec, C. Data on Fishing Vessels & Gear in the Mediterranean. (General Fisheries Council of the Mediterranean (GFCM): Studies & Reviews: No. 56). (Illus.). 188p. (Eng. & Fr.). 1977. pap. 12.00 (ISBN 92-5-000350-1, F1257, FAO). Unipub.

Drendel, Lou. Air War in Viet Nam. (Illus., Orig.). 1969. pap. 5.95 (ISBN 0-668-01817-8). Arco.

--Air War over Southeast Asia, Vol. I. (Illus.). 80p. 1982. softcover 8.95 (ISBN 0-89747-134-2, 6034). Squad Sig Pubns.

--Air War over Southeast Asia, Vol. III. (Vietnam Studies Group: No. 6037). (Illus.). 80p. 1984. 8.95 (ISBN 0-89747-148-2). Squad Sig Pubns.

--Air War over Southeast Asia, Vol. II. (Vietnam Studies Group Ser.). (Illus.). 80p. 1983. 8.95 (ISBN 0-89747-140-7). Squad Sig Pubns.

--Aircraft of the Vietnam War. LC 79-113405. (Famous Aircraft Ser.). (Illus.). 64p. 1980. pap. 6.95 (ISBN 0-8168-5651-6). Aero.

--And Kill MIGs. pap. 6.95 (ISBN 0-89747-056-7). Squad Sig Pubns.

--Century Series. (Specials Ser.: No. 6039). (Illus.). 96p. 1983. pap. 8.95 (ISBN 0-89747-097-4). Squad Sig Pubns.

--F-Sixteeen Falcon in Action. (Aircraft in Action Ser.). (Illus.). 50p. 1982. saddlestitch 4.95 (ISBN 0-89747-133-4). Squad Sig Pubns.

--F-15 Eagle in Action. (Aircraft in Action Ser.). (Illus.). 1984. pap. 4.95 (ISBN 0-89747-023-0, 1024). Squad Sig Pubns.

--HUEY. (Modern Military Aircraft Ser.: No. 5001). (Illus.). 64p. 1983. saddlestitch 6.95 (ISBN 0-89747-145-8). Squad Sig Pubns.

--SR-71 Blackbird in Action. (Illus.). 50p. 1982. 4.95 (ISBN 0-89747-136-9, 1055). Squad Sig Pubns.

--TAC: A Pictorial History of the USAF Tactical Air Forces 1970-1977. (Aircraft Special Ser.: No. 6012). (Illus.). 64p. 1983. 6.95 (ISBN 0-89747-064-8). Squad Sig Pubns.

Drengson, Alan R., jt. ed. see Beehler, Roger.

Drenick, R. F. & Kozin, F., eds. System Modeling & Optimization, New York 1981: Proceedings. (Lecture Notes in Control & Information Sciences: Vol. 38). 894p. 1982. pap. 57.00 (ISBN 0-387-11691-5). Springer-Verlag.

Drennan, James. Oswald Mosley & British Fascism. 1976. lib. bdg. 69.95 (ISBN 0-8490-2388-2). Gordon Pr.

Drennan, James C., jt. auth. see Campen, Henry.

Drennan, James C., ed. Orthopaedic Management of Neuromuscular Disorders. (Illus.). 384p. 1983. text ed. 47.50 (ISBN 0-397-50469-1, 65-06109, Lippincott Medical). Lippincott.

Drennan, Mathew P. Modeling Metropolitan Economies for Forecasting & Policy Analysis. 256p. text ed. 40.00x (ISBN 0-8147-1781-0). NYU Pr.

Drennan, Robert D. Excavations at Quachilco: A Report on the 1977 Season of the Palo Blanco Project. (Technical Reports Ser.: No. 7). (Illus., Eng. & Span., Contribution 3 in Research Reports in Archaeology). 1977. pap. 4.00x (ISBN 0-932206-73-5). U Mich Mus Anthro.

--Fabrica San Jose & Middle Formative Society in the Valley of Oaxaca. New ed. Flannery, Kent V., ed. (Memoirs, No. 8, Prehistory & Human Ecology of the Valley of Oaxaca: Vol. 4). (Illus., Orig.). 1976. pap. 8.00x (ISBN 0-932206-70-0). U Mich Mus Anthro.

Drennan, Robert D., ed. Prehistoric Social, Political, & Economic Development in the Area of the Tehuacan Valley: Some Results of the Palo Blanco Project. (Technical Reports Ser.: No. 11; Contribution 6 in Research Reports in Archaeology). (Illus., Orig.). 1979. pap. 6.50x (ISBN 0-932206-82-4). U Mich Mus Anthro.

Drennan, Robert E., ed. The Algonquin Wits. 180p. 1985. pap. 5.95 (ISBN 0-8065-0947-3). Citadel Pr.

Drennan, Susan R. Where to Find Birds in New York State: The Top 500 Sites. LC 81-16744. (York State Bks.). (Illus.). 532p. 1981. text ed. 38.00x (ISBN 0-8156-2250-3); pap. 18.95 (ISBN 0-8156-0173-5). Syracuse U Pr.

Drennen, D. A. Barron's Simplified Approach to Descartes. LC 68-31477. 1969. pap. text ed. 1.95 (ISBN 0-8120-0359-4). Barron.

Drentea, Cornell. Radio Communications Receivers. (Illus.). 288p. (Orig.). 1982. o.p 19.95 (ISBN 0-8306-2393-0, 1393); pap. 14.50 (ISBN 0-8306-1393-5). TAB Bks.

Drenth, P. J., jt. auth. see Cronbach, L. J.

Drenth, P. J., et al, eds. Handbook of Work & Organizational Psychology, 2 vols. 600p. 1984. Vol. 1. 64.95x (ISBN 0-471-90400-7); Vol. 2. text ed. 64.95x (ISBN 0-471-90401-5); Set. 129.00 (ISBN 0-471-90344-2). Wiley.

Drenth, Wiendelt & Kwart, Harold. Kinetics Applied to Organic Reactions. (Studies in Organic Chemistry Ser.: Vol. 9). 224p. 1980. 23.50 (ISBN 0-8247-6889-2). Dekker.

Dreosti, Ivor E. & Smith, Richard M., eds. Neurobiology of the Trace Elements: Neurotoxicology & Neuropharmacology, Vol. 2. LC 83-8413. (Contemporary Neuroscience Ser.). 320p. 1983. 49.50 (ISBN 0-89603-047-4). Humana.

--Neurobiology of the Trace Elements: Vol. 1, Trace Element Neurobiology & Deficiencies. LC 83-8412. (Contemporary Neuroscience Ser.). 384p. 1983. 49.50 (ISBN 0-89603-046-6). Humana.

Dreosti, Ivor E., jt. ed. see Prasad, Ananda S.

Drepperd, C. Pioneer Arts & Artists. LC 70-121195. 1970. 12.00 (ISBN 0-87282-026-2). CHB-ALF.

Drepperd, Carl. Treasures in Truck & Trash. LC 78-86067. (Essay & General Literature Index Reprint Ser). 1969. Repr. of 1950 ed. 19.50x (ISBN 0-8046-0592-0, Pub by Kennikat). Assoc Faculty Pr.

Drepperd, Carl W. Pioneer America: Its First Three Centuries. LC 71-190546. (Illus.). vi, 311p. 1972. Repr. of 1949 ed. lib. bdg. 29.50 (ISBN 0-8154-0415-8). Cooper Sq.

Drerup, Engelbert. Aus Einer Alten Advokatenrepublik. 1916. pap. 15.00 (ISBN 0-384-12800-9). Johnson Repr.

--Demosthenes Im Urteile Des Altertums. 1923. pap. 19.00 (ISBN 0-384-12805-X). Johnson Repr.

--Der Humanismus in Seiner Geschichte. 1934. pap. 12.00 (ISBN 0-384-12815-7). Johnson Repr.

--Kulturprobleme Des Klassischen Griechentums. 1933. pap. 12.00 (ISBN 0-384-12820-3). Johnson Repr.

--Die Schulaussprache Des Griechischen Von der Renaissance Bis Zur Gegenwart, 2 Vols. 1930-32. Vol. 6. pap. 37.00 (ISBN 0-384-12825-4); Vol. 7. pap. 41.00 (ISBN 0-384-12830-0). Johnson Repr.

Drerup, Heinrich. Die Datierung der Mumienportrats. 1933. pap. 7.00 (ISBN 0-384-12835-1). Johnson Repr.

Dresang, Dennis L. Public Personnel Management & Public Policy. 1984. text ed. 25.95 (ISBN 0-316-19320-8). Little.

Dresang, Dennis L., jt. ed. see Holden, Matthew, Jr.

Dresang, Eliza T. The Land & People of Zambia. LC 74-23108. (Portraits of the Nations Ser). (gr. 7 up). 1975. PLB 10.89 (ISBN 0-397-31561-9). Lipp Jr Bks.

Dresch, Stephen P. An Economic Perspective on the Evolution of Graduate Education: A Technical Report Presented to the National Board on Graduate Education. 88p. 1974. pap. text ed. 3.50 (ISBN 0-309-02221-5). Natl Acad Pr.

Drescher, Betty, jt. auth. see Drescher, John.

Drescher, Dennis G., ed. Auditory Biochemistry. (Illus.). 536p. 1985. 64.50x (ISBN 0-398-05122-4). C C Thomas.

Drescher, H. & Kemmler, J. Skiing on the Level. 1978. pap. 2.95 (ISBN 0-346-12375-5). Cornerstone.

Drescher, Henrik. Look-alikes. LC 85-225. (Illus.). 32p. (gr. k-3). 1985. 13.00 (ISBN 0-688-05816-7); PLB 12.88 (ISBN 0-688-05817-5). Lothrop.

--Looking for Santa Claus. LC 84-4419. (Illus.). 32p. (ps-1). 1984. 13.00 (ISBN 0-688-02997-3); lib. bdg. 11.47 (ISBN 0-688-02999-X). Lothrop.

--Simon's Book. LC 82-24931. (Illus.). 32p. (gr. k-3). 1983. 11.75 (ISBN 0-688-02085-2); lib. bdg. 11.88 (ISBN 0-688-02086-0). Lothrop.

--The Strange Appearance of Howard Cranebill Jr. (Illus.). (ps-3). 1982. 11.75 (ISBN 0-688-00961-1); PLB 11.88 (ISBN 0-688-00962-X). Lothrop.

Drescher, Henrik & Zeit, Calvin. True Paranoid Facts. LC 82-61411. (Illus.). 64p. (Orig.). 1982. pap. 3.70 (ISBN 0-688-01854-8, Quill NY). Morrow.

Drescher, Horst W., ed. Thomas Carlyle, 1981: Papers Given at the International Thomas Carlyle Centenary Symposium. (Scottish Studies: Vol 1). 420p. 1982. pap. 36.30 (ISBN 3-8204-7327-0). P Lang Pubs.

Drescher, Joan. I'm in Charge. (Illus.). (gr. 1-3). 1981. 9.95 (ISBN 0-316-19330-5, Pub. by Atlantic Pr). Little.

--Max & Rufus. (Illus.). (gr. k-3). 1982. PLB 9.20 (ISBN 0-395-32435-1); write for info. HM.

--Your Family, My Family. (Illus.). 32p. (gr. 2-5). 1980. 7.95 (ISBN 0-8027-6382-0); PLB 8.85 (ISBN 0-8027-6383-9). Walker & Co.

Drescher, John & Drescher, Betty. If We Were Starting Our Marriage Again. 96p. (Orig.). 1985. pap. 5.95 (ISBN 0-687-18672-2). Abingdon.

Drescher, John, jt. auth. see Drescher, Sandra.

Drescher, John M. If I Were Starting My Family Again. LC 78-13278. (Festival Ser.). (Illus.). 1979. pap. 2.50 (ISBN 0-687-18674-9). Abingdon.

--Meditations for the Newly Married. LC 69-10835. 142p. 1969. gift-boxed 8.95 (ISBN 0-8361-1571-6). Herald Pr.

--Now Is the Time to Love. LC 73-123411. 144p. 1970. pap. 1.50 (ISBN 0-8361-1641-0). Herald Pr.

--Seven Things Children Need. LC 76-2879. 152p. 1976. pap. 2.95 (ISBN 0-8361-1798-0). Herald Pr.

--Siete Necesidades Basicas Del Nino. 128p. (Span.). 1985. pap. 4.50 (ISBN 0-311-46085-2). Casa Bautista.

--Spirit Fruit. rev. ed. LC 73-21660. 352p. 1978. pap. 6.95 (ISBN 0-8361-1867-7). Herald Pr.

--When Opposites Attract. LC 79-53272. (When Bks.). (Illus., Orig.). 1979. pap. 2.45 (ISBN 0-87029-153-X, 20239-0). Abbey.

--Why I Am a Conscientious Objector. LC 82-894. (Christian Peace Shelf Ser.). 73p. (Orig.). 1982. pap. 3.95 (ISBN 0-8361-1993-2). Herald Pr.

--You Can Know It's True Love. 1.25 (ISBN 0-8010-2932-5). Baker Bk.

--You Can Learn to Communicate as Husband-Wife. 1.25 (ISBN 0-8010-2933-3). Baker Bk.

--You Can Plan a Good Marriage. 1.25 (ISBN 0-8010-2907-4). Baker Bk.

Drescher, Sandra. Dear Jesus, Love Sandy. 112p. 1982. pap. 3.95 (ISBN 0-310-44841-7); gift ed. o. p. 7.95 (ISBN 0-310-44840-9). Zondervan.

--Just Between God & Me. 1977. girls 9.95 (ISBN 0-310-23940-0); boys 9.95 (ISBN 0-310-23950-8); pap. 4.95 (ISBN 0-310-23941-9). Zondervan.

Drescher, Sandra & Drescher, John. When You Think You're in Love. LC 81-65208. (When Bks.). 96p. 1981. pap. 2.45 (ISBN 0-87029-174-2, 20270-5). Abbey.

Drescher, Seymour. Dilemmas of Democracy: Tocqueville & Modernization. LC 76-12725. pap. 79.00 (ISBN 0-317-26641-1, 2025437). Bks Demand UMI.

--Econocide: British Slavery in the Era of Abolition. LC 76-50887. 1977. 24.95x (ISBN 0-8229-3344-6). U of Pittsburgh Pr.

Drescher, Seymour, ed. & tr. see De Tocqueville, Alexis & De Beaumont, Gustave.

Drescher, Seymour, et al, eds. Political Symbolism in Modern Europe: Essays in Honor of George L. Mosse. LC 80-26544. (Illus.). 310p. 1982. 49.95 (ISBN 0-87855-422-X). Transaction Bks.

Drescher, Seymour I. Tocqueville & England. LC 63-20764. (Historical Monographs Ser: No. 55). 1964. 16.50x (ISBN 0-674-89430-8). Harvard U Pr.

Dresden, Donald. Donald Dresden's Guide to Dining Out in Washington, D.C. LC 77-84325. 1977. pap. 3.95 (ISBN 0-87491-189-3). Acropolis.

Dresher, Bezalel E. Old English & the Theory of Phonology. (Outstanding Dissertations in Linguistics Ser.). 166p. 1985. 35.00 (ISBN 0-8240-5425-3). Garland Pub.

Dresher, Melvin. The Mathematics of Games of Strategy: Theory & Applications. viii, 184p. 1982. pap. 4.00 (ISBN 0-486-64216-X). Dover.

Dresher, Melvin, et al, eds. Advances in Game Theory. (Annals of Mathematics Studies, Vol. 52). (Orig.). 17.50 (ISBN 0-691-07902-1). Princeton U Pr.

Dresher, Seymour, jt. auth. see Bolt, Christine.

Dreskin, Wendy & Dreskin, William. The Day Care Decision: What's Best for You & Your Child. 192p. 1983. 13.95 (ISBN 0-87131-418-5). M Evans.

Dreskin, William, jt. auth. see Dreskin, Wendy.

Dresner, Joanne, ed. It's up to You. (English As a Second Language Bk.). (Illus.). 1979. pap. text ed. 5.95x (ISBN 0-582-79727-6); cassette 12.75x (ISBN 0-582-79728-4); plastic tote (book & cassette) 15.75x (ISBN 0-582-79771-3). Longman.

Dresner, Joanne, ed. see Kimbrough, Victoria, et al.

Dresner, Joanne, ed. see Kimbrough, Victoria & Palmer, Michael.

Dresner, L. Similarity Solutions of Nonlinear Partial Differential Equations. (Research Notes in Mathematics: No. 88). 136p. 1983. pap. text ed. 18.95 (ISBN 0-273-08621-9). Pitman Pub MA.

Dresner, Samuel. Prayer, Humility & Compassion. 4.95 (ISBN 0-87677-006-5). Hartmore.

Dresner, Samuel & Sherwin, Byron. Judaism: The Way of Sanctification. 1978. text ed. 6.50 (ISBN 0-8381-0222-0). United Syn Bk.

Dresner, Samuel & Siegel, Seymour. Jewish Dietary Laws. rev. ed. LC 83-235401. 110p. pap. 2.95x (ISBN 0-8381-2105-5). United Syn Bk.

Dresner, Samuel H. Between the Generations. pap. 1.75 (ISBN 0-87677-042-1). Hartmore.

--Between the Generations: A Jewish Dialogue. new ed. LC 79-172413. 80p. (YA) 1971. pap. 1.75 (ISBN 0-87677-042-1, Hartmore). Prayer Bk.

--God, Man & Atomic War. 6.95 (ISBN 0-87677-007-3). Hartmore.

--Sabbath. 1970. pap. 2.95 (ISBN 0-8381-2114-4). United Syn Bk.

--Zaddik: The Doctrine of the Zaddik According to the Writings of Rabbi Yaakov Yosef of Polnoy. LC 60-7228. 312p. 1974. pap. 4.95 (ISBN 0-8052-0437-7). Schocken.

Dresner, Samuel H., ed. see Heschel, Abraham J.

Dresner, Stephen. Units of Measurement: An Encyclopaedic Dictionary of Units, Both Scientific & Popular, & the Quantities They Measure. LC 72-187346. pap. 75.80 (ISBN 0-317-26195-9, 2052071). Bks Demand UMI.

Dresner, Stephen B., tr. see Divari, Nikolai B.

Dresnick, Stephen J., jt. auth. see Meislin, Harvey W.

Dressa, Connie M., et al. Food Consumption Profiles of White & Black Persons Aged 1-74 Years: United States, 1971-4. (Series II: No. 210). (Illus.). 1978. pap. text ed. 1.95 (ISBN 0-8406-0143-3). Natl Ctr Health Stats.

Dressel, G. Organization & Management of a Construction Company. 192p. 1969. 102.95 (ISBN 0-677-61470-5). Gordon.

Dressel, Paul L. Administrative Leadership: Effective & Responsive Decision Making in Higher Education. LC 81-81962. (Higher Education Ser.). 1981. text ed. 18.95x (ISBN 0-87589-500-X). Jossey-Bass.

--Handbook of Academic Evaluation: Assessing Institutional Effectiveness, Student Progress, & Professional Performance for Decision Making in Higher Education. LC 75-44881. (Higher Education Ser.). (Illus.). 1976. 27.95x (ISBN 0-87589-276-0). Jossey-Bass.

--Improving Degree Programs: A Guide to Curriculum Development, Administration, & Review. LC 80-82376. (Higher Education Ser.). 1980. text ed. 19.95x (ISBN 0-87589-486-0). Jossey-Bass.

Dressel, Paul L. & Faricy, William H. Return to Responsibility: Constraints on Autonomy in Higher Education. LC 70-186574. (Jossey-Bass Higher Education Ser.). pap. 47.90 (ISBN 0-8357-9344-3, 2013936). Bks Demand UMI.

Dressel, Paul L. & Marcus, Dora. On Teaching & Learning in College: Reemphasizing the Roles of Learners & the Disciplines. LC 82-48077. (Higher Education Ser.). 1982. text ed. 18.95x (ISBN 0-87589-543-3). Jossey Bass.

Dressel, Paul L. & Mayhew, Lewis B. Higher Education As a Field of Study: The Emergence of a Profession. LC 73-21073. (Higher Education Ser). 1974. 19.95x (ISBN 0-87589-226-4). Jossey-Bass.

Dressel, Paul L. & Pratt, Sally R. The World of Higher Education: An Annotated Guide to the Major Literature. LC 71-158562. (Jossey-Bass Series in Higher Education). pap. 64.00 (ISBN 0-317-10873-5, 2013934). Bks Demand UMI.

Dressel, Paul L. & Thompson, Mary M. Independent Study: A New Interpretation of Concepts, Practices, & Problems. LC 73-50. (Jossey-Bass Higher Education Ser.). pap. 44.00 (ISBN 0-8357-9327-3, 2013755). Bks Demand UMI.

Dressel, Paul L., et al. The Confidence Crisis: An Analysis of University Departments. LC 70-110642. (Jossey-Bass Higher Education Ser.). Repr. of 1970 ed. 71.50 (ISBN 0-8357-9309-5, 2013948). Bks Demand UMI.

Dressel, Paula. The Service Trap: From Altruism to Dirty Work. 178p. 1984. pap. 16.75x (ISBN 0-398-04975-0). C C Thomas.

Dresselhaus, G., jt. ed. see Dresselhaus, M. S.

Dresselhaus, M. S. & Dresselhaus, G., eds. Intercalated Graphite. (Materials Research Society Symposia Proceedings Ser.: Vol. 20). 428p. 1983. 77.00 (ISBN 0-444-00781-4, North Holland). Elsevier.

Dresselhaus, Richard. Your Sunday School at Work. 78p. 1980. pap. 2.50 (ISBN 0-88243-793-3, 02-0793). Gospel Pub.

Dresselhaus, Richard L. The Deacon & His Ministry. LC 77-73518. 1977. pap. 2.25, 2.00 for 6 or more (ISBN 0-88243-493-4, 02-0493). Gospel Pub.

--The Joy of Belonging. LC 78-66868. (Radiant Life Ser.). 128p. 1978. pap. 2.50 (ISBN 0-88243-526-4, 02-0526); tchr's ed. 2.95 (ISBN 0-88243-186-2, 32-0186). Gospel Pub.

--Teaching for Decision. LC 73-75502. 124p. 1973. pap. 1.25 (ISBN 0-88243-616-3, 02-0616). Gospel Pub.

Dressell, H. Funf Gold Medaillons Aus Dem Funde Von Abukir Nineteen Hundred Six. (Alexander the Great Ser.). (Illus.). 112p. 1981. 40.00 (ISBN 0-916710-90-4). Obol Intl.

Dresser, Christopher. Art of Decorative Design. (Library of Victorian Culture). (Illus.). 1977. pap. text ed. 12.00 (ISBN 0-89257-030-X). Am Life Foun.

--Modern Ornamentation, Being a Series of Original Designs. (Library of Victorian Culture). (Illus.). 1976. pap. 7.00 (ISBN 0-89257-011-3). Am Life Foun.

Dresser, Ginny, ed. see Andrews, Janice H.

Dresser, Horatio W., ed. The Quimby Manuscripts. 2nd ed. 480p. 1984. pap. 9.95 (ISBN 0-8065-0913-9). Citadel Pr.

Dresser, Louisa. Background of Colonial American Portraiture. 1966. pap. 6.00x (ISBN 0-912296-20-8, Dist. by U Pr of Va). Am Antiquarian.

Dresser, Louisa, ed. Catalogue of European Paintings in the Worcester Art Museum, 2 vols. LC 73-90538. (Illus.). 696p. 1974. Set. 35.00x (ISBN 0-87023-169-3). U of Mass Pr.

Dresser, Peter Van see Van Dresser, Peter.

Dressler, Claus P., jt. auth. see Jahn, Janheinz.

Dressler, David. Practice & Theory of Probation & Parole. 2nd ed. LC 74-89861. 347p. 1969. 21.50x (ISBN 0-231-02956-X). Columbia U Pr.

--Readings in Criminology & Penology. 2nd ed. LC 75-181783. 743p. 1972. 45.00x (ISBN 0-231-03429-6); pap. 18.00x (ISBN 0-231-08672-5). Columbia U Pr.

Dressler, Gallus. Siebzehn Motetten zu vier & fuenf Stimmen. Eitner, Robert, ed. (Publikation aelterer praktischer und theoretischer Musikwerke Ser.: Vol. XXIV). (Ger., Lat.). 1967. Repr. of 1900 ed. write for info. (ISBN 0-8450-1724-1). Broude.

Dressler, Hermigild, jt. auth. see McGuire, Martin R.

Dressler, Isidore. Algebra I. (gr. 9). 1966. text ed. 12.83 (ISBN 0-87720-208-7). AMSCO Sch.

--Algebra One Review Guide. (Illus., Orig.). (gr. 9). 1966. pap. text ed. 6.83 (ISBN 0-87720-207-9). AMSCO Sch.

--Current Mathematics: A Work-Text. (gr. 7 up). 1977. Bk. I. wkbk. 10.67 (ISBN 0-87720-239-7). AMSCO Sch.

--Geometry. (Orig.). (gr. 10-12). 1973. text ed. 15.42 (ISBN 0-87720-235-4); pap. text ed. 10.25 (ISBN 0-87720-234-6). AMSCO Sch.

--Geometry Review Guide. (gr. 10-12). 1973. pap. text ed. 7.25 (ISBN 0-87720-215-X). AMSCO Sch.

--Preliminary Mathematics. (gr. 8). 1981. text ed. 17.50 (ISBN 0-87720-243-5). AMSCO Sch.

--Preliminary Mathematics. (Orig.). 1981. pap. text ed. 12.25 (ISBN 0-87720-242-7). AMSCO Sch.

--Preliminary Mathematics Review Guide. (Illus.). (gr. 8-10). 1965. pap. text ed. 6.75 (ISBN 0-87720-205-2). AMSCO Sch.

--Review Text in Preliminary Mathematics. (Illus.). (gr. 7-9). 1962. text ed. 12.75 (ISBN 0-87720-203-6); pap. text ed. 9.17 (ISBN 0-87720-202-8). AMSCO Sch.

Dressler, Isidore & Dressler, Robert. Introductory Algebra for College Students. (Orig.). 1976. pap. text ed. 9.47 (ISBN 0-87720-975-8). AMSCO Sch.

Dressler, Isidore & Keenan, Edward P. Integrated Mathematics: Course I. (Orig.). (gr. 9). 1980. text ed. 20.25 (ISBN 0-87720-249-4); pap. text ed. 12.92 (ISBN 0-87720-248-6). AMSCO Sch.

Dressler, Isidore & Rich, Barnett. Algebra Two & Trigonometry: A Modern Integrated Course. (gr. 11-12). 1972. text ed. 15.00 (ISBN 0-87720-221-4); pap. text ed. 9.75 (ISBN 0-87720-220-6). AMSCO Sch.

--Modern Algebra Two. (Orig.). (gr. 11-12). 1973. text ed. 14.17 (ISBN 0-87720-233-8); pap. text ed. 8.33 (ISBN 0-87720-232-X). AMSCO Sch.

--Trigonometry. (gr. 10-12). 1975. pap. text ed. 7.65 (ISBN 0-87720-219-2). AMSCO Sch.

Dressler, Isidore, jt. auth. see Keenan, Edward P.

Dressler, Isidore, et al. Intermediate Algebra for College Students. 1977. pap. text ed. 9.47 (ISBN 0-87720-977-4). AMSCO Sch.

Dressler, Robert, jt. auth. see Dressler, Isidore.

Dressler, Robert E. & Stromberg, Karl. Techniques of Calculus. (Orig.). (gr. 12 up). 1982. text ed. 25.00 (ISBN 0-87720-979-0); pap. text ed. 17.50 (ISBN 0-87720-978-2). AMSCO Sch.

Dressler, Robert L. The Orchids: Natural History & Classification. LC 80-24561. (Illus.). 352p. 1981. text ed. 30.00x (ISBN 0-674-87525-7). Harvard U Pr.

Dressler, Thomas. The First Northerns: Northern Pacific A Class 4-8-4. LC 80-85076. (Classic Power Ser.: No. 4). (Illus.). 100p. 1981. pap. 12.95 (ISBN 0-934088-03-9). NJ Intl Inc.

--USRA 2-8-8-2 Series. rev. & exp. ed. LC 80-81576. (Classic Power Ser.: No. 3). (Illus.). 150p. 1985. pap. 18.95 (ISBN 0-934088-02-0). NJ Intl Inc.

Dressler, W., jt. auth. see De Beaugrande, R.

Dressler, William. Clinical Aids in Cardiac Diagnosis. LC 74-82556. 256p. 1970. 62.00 (ISBN 0-8089-0120-6, 791077). Grune.

Dressler, William W. Hypertension & Culture Change: Acculturation & Disease in the West Indies. vii, 158p. (Orig.). 1982. pap. text ed. 13.65 (ISBN 0-913178-70-5). Redgrave Pub Co.

Dressler, Wolfgang U. Morphonology: The Dynamics of Derivation. (Linguistica Extranea: Studia: No. 12). 250p. 1984. 14.50 (ISBN 0-89720-034-9); pap. 10.50 (ISBN 0-89720-035-7). Karoma.

Dressler, Wolfgang U., ed. Current Trends in Textlinguistics. (Research in Text Theory: Vol. 2). 1978. 28.80x (ISBN 3-11-006518-5). De Gruyter.

Dressler, Wolfgang U., et al. Leifmotifs in Natural Morphology. (Studies in Language Companion: No. 10). 400p. (Orig.). 1986. 48.00x (ISBN 90-272-3009-9). Benjamins North Am.

Dressman, Denny. Gerry Faust: Notre Dame's Man in Motion. LC 81-3592. (Illus.). 224p. 1981. 12.95 (ISBN 0-498-02573-X). A S Barnes.

Dressman, John. On the Cliffs of Acoma. Ortega, Pedro R., tr. from Span. LC 83-20177. (Illus.). 32p. (gr. 2-4). 1984. pap. 5.95 (ISBN 0-86534-021-8). Sunstone Pr.

Dressner, Howard R., jt. auth. see Janis, J. Harold.

Dresvin, S. V., ed. see Donski, A. V., et al.

Dretke, James P. A Christian Approach to Muslims: Reflections from West Africa. LC 79-11912. (Islamic Studies). 1979. pap. 3.95 (ISBN 0-87808-432-0). William Carey Lib.

Dretske, Fred I. Knowledge & the Flow of Information. LC 81-21633. (Illus.). 288p. 1981. text ed. 30.00x (ISBN 0-262-04063-8, Pub. by Bradford); pap. 9.95x (ISBN 0-262-54038-X). MIT Pr.

--Seeing & Knowing. pap. write for info. (ISBN 0-226-16245-1). U of Chicago Pr.

Dreuihe. Dictionnaire Anglais-Francais et Lexique Francais-Anglais des termes Politiques Juridiques et Economiques. (Eng. & Fr.). 1981. pap. 22.95 (ISBN 0-686-92584-X, M-9628). French & Eur.

Dreux, William B. No Bridges Blown. LC 72-165994. pap. 84.00 (ISBN 0-317-26695-0, 2024369). Bks Demand UMI.

Drevdahl, Elmer R. Fundamentals of Excavation Equipment for Engineering & Technology. 10.50x (ISBN 0-89741-004-1). Roadrunner Tech.

--Profitable Use of Excavation Equipment. 14.95x (ISBN 0-89741-009-2); pap. 11.25 (ISBN 0-686-96875-1). Roadrunner Tech.

Drever, James. Dictionary of Psychology. rev. ed. (Reference Ser.). (Orig.). (gr. 11 up). 1952. pap. 6.95 (ISBN 0-14-051005-2). Penguin.

Drever, James I. The Geochemistry of Natural Waters. (Illus.). 400p. 1982. 37.95 (ISBN 0-13-351403-X). P-H.

Drever, James I., ed. The Chemistry of Weathering. 1985. lib. bdg. 44.00 (ISBN 90-277-1962-4, Pub. by Reidel Holland). Kluwer Academic.

--Sea Water: Cycles of the Major Elements. (Bench Mark Papers in Geology Ser.). 1977. 61.50 (ISBN 0-12-786383-4). Acad Pr.

Dreves, G. M., ed. see Von Lilienfeld, Christian.

Dreves, Guido M., ed. Cantiones Bohemicae. 1886. 60.00 (ISBN 0-384-12860-2). Johnson Repr.

--Cantiones et Muteti, 3 vols. (Illus.). 1895-1904. 60.00 ea. (ISBN 0-384-12865-3). Johnson Repr.

--Historiae Rhythmicae, 8 Vols. 1889-1904. 60.00 ea. (ISBN 0-384-12880-7). Johnson Repr.

--Hymni Inediti, 7 Vols. 1888-1903. 60.00 ea. Johnson Repr.

--Hymnodia Hiberica: Liturgische Reimofficien, Aus Spanischen Brevieren. (Illus.). 1894. 60.00 (ISBN 0-384-12915-3). Johnson Repr.

--Hymnodia Hiberica: Spanische Hymnen Des Mittelalters. 1894. 60.00 (ISBN 0-384-12920-X). Johnson Repr.

--Pia Dictamina, 7 Vols. 1893-1905. 60.00 ea. (ISBN 0-384-12950-1). Johnson Repr.

--Psalteria Rhythmica, 2 Vols. 1900-01. 60.00 ea. (ISBN 0-384-12960-9) (ISBN 0-384-12961-7). Johnson Repr.

--Sequentiae Ineditae, 9 Vols. 1890-1904. 60.00 ea. (ISBN 0-384-12981-1). Johnson Repr.

Dreves, Guido M., ed. see Scacabarotius, Orricus.

Dreves, Guido M., ed. see Stocklin, Ulrich V.

Drevet. Bibliographie de la Litterature Francaise (1940-1948) 85.95 (ISBN 0-685-35967-0). French & Eur.

Drew, Benjamin. North-Side View of Slavery. LC 68-55881. Repr. of 1856 ed. 19.75x (ISBN 0-8371-0393-2, DRN&, Pub. by Negro U Pr). Greenwood.

--North-Side View of Slavery - the Refugee: Or the Narratives of Fugitive Slaves in Canada. 1969. Repr. of 1856 ed. 20.00 (ISBN 0-384-13015-1). Johnson Repr.

Drew, Charles S. An Account of the Origin & Early Prosecution of the Indian War in Oregon. 48p. 1973. Repr. of 1860 ed. Ye Galleon.

Drew, Christopher, jt. auth. see Berry, Newton.

Drew, Clifford J. Introduction to Designing & Conducting Research. 2nd. ed. LC 79-25403. (Illus.). 1980. 22.95 (ISBN 0-8016-1460-0). Mosby.

Drew, Clifford J. & Hardman, Michael L. Designing & Conducting Behavioral Research. (Pergamon General Psychology Ser.: No. 134). (Illus.). 352p. 1985. 45.00 (ISBN 0-08-031941-6); pap. 19.50 (ISBN 0-08-031940-8). Pergamon.

Drew, Daniel. The Book of Daniel Drew. 8.50 (ISBN 0-686-24068-5); pap. 3.50 (ISBN 0-686-24069-3). Frontier Press Calif.

Drew, David. Man-Environment Processes. (Processes in Physical Geography Ser.: No. 6). (Illus.). 152p. 1983. pap. text ed. 9.95x (ISBN 0-04-551063-6). Allen Unwin.

Drew, David E. Strengthening Academic Science. LC 85-6471. 300p. 1985. write for info. (ISBN 0-03-071574-1). Praeger.

Drew, Dennis & Drake, Jonathan. Boys for Sale. 1969. 10.00 (ISBN 0-910294-01-1). Brown Bk.

Drew, Donald B. Uncle Don's Down East Cookbook. LC 77-1458. 1977. 8.95 (ISBN 0-8128-2275-7). Stein & Day.

Drew, E. A., et al, eds. Underwater Research. 1976. 68.00 (ISBN 0-12-221950-3). Acad Pr.

Drew, Edwin P. The Complete Light-Pack Camping & Trail-Food Cookbook. (Orig.). 1977. pap. 4.95 (ISBN 0-07-017843-7). McGraw.

Drew, Elizabeth. Campaign Journal: The Political Events of 1983-1984. 783p. 1985. 24.95 (ISBN 0-02-533510-3). Macmillan.

--Politics & Money: The New Road to Corruption. 176p. 1983. 11.95 (ISBN 0-02-533520-0). Macmillan.

--Politics & Money: The New Road to Corruption. 176p. 1984. pap. 5.95 (ISBN 0-02-072840-9, Collier). Macmillan.

--Washington Journal: The Events of 1973-1974. 448p. 1984. pap. 9.95 (ISBN 0-02-072850-6, Collier). Macmillan.

Drew, Elizabeth A. Discovering Poetry. 1933. 8.95x (ISBN 0-393-04159-X, Norton Lib). Norton.

--Jane Welsh & Jane Carlyle. LC 72-3641. (English Literature Ser., No. 33). 1972. Repr. of 1928 ed. lib. bdg. 52.95x (ISBN 0-8383-1555-0). Haskell.

Drew, Elizabeth A. & Sweeney, J. L. Directions in Modern Poetry. LC 67-30307. 1967. Repr. of 1940 ed. 12.50x (ISBN 0-87752-029-1). Gordian.

Drew, Fraser. John Masefield's England: A Study of the National Themes in His Work. LC 72-415. (Illus.). 261p. 1973. 24.50 (ISBN 0-8386-1020-X). Fairleigh Dickinson.

Drew, Garfield A. New Methods for Profits in the Stock Market. 1966. Repr. of 1955 ed. flexible cover 14.00 (ISBN 0-87034-020-4). Fraser Pub Co.

Drew, George. The Beatitudes: Attitudes for a Better Future. 63p. (Orig.). 1980. pap. 6.95 (ISBN 0-940754-03-7). Ed Ministries.

--Making the Bible Our Own. 65p. 1985. pap. 6.95 (ISBN 0-940754-29-0). Ed Ministries.

--The Original Ideas of Jesus That Are Changing the World. 45p. (Orig.). 1980. pap. 5.45 (ISBN 0-940754-05-3). Ed Ministries.

--The Parables in Depth. 55p. (Orig.). 1982. pap. 6.95 (ISBN 0-940754-18-5). Ed Ministries.

--The Prophets Speak to Our Time. 62p. (Orig.). 1981. pap. 6.95 (ISBN 0-940754-09-6). Ed Ministries.

--St. Paul. 60p. (Orig.). 1984. pap. 6.95 (ISBN 0-940754-22-3). Ed Ministries.

--The Ten Commandments in Today's World. 48p. (Orig.). 1979. pap. 6.95 (ISBN 0-940754-00-2). Ed Ministries.

Drew, J., et al. Networking in Organizations: The Rank Xerox Experiment. 145p. 1985. text ed. write for info. (ISBN 0-566-02599-X). Gower Pub Co.

Drew, James M. Blacksmithing. facs. ed. (Shorey Lost Arts Ser.). 119p. pap. 7.95 (ISBN 0-8466-6037-7, U37). Shorey.

Drew, Jane, jt. auth. see Fry, Maxwell.

Drew, John H. The Stock Market Trading Practices of the Great Speculators of the Late 19th Century & How to Gain a Major Success in the Market by Following Them, 2 vols. 356p. 1984. Set. 177.35x (ISBN 0-86654-117-9). Inst Econ Finan.

Drew, John K. Pictorial Guide to Hardy Perennials. (Illus.). 96p. 1984. text ed. 14.95 (ISBN 0-89484-091-6); pap. text ed. 8.95 (ISBN 0-89484-092-4). Merchants Pub Co.

Drew, Joseph W. & Hague, W. Creation of Full Human Personality. pap. 0.75 (ISBN 0-8199-0247-0, L38115). Franciscan Herald.

Drew, Katherine F. The Lombard Laws. (Middle Ages Ser). 240p. 1973. 18.00x (ISBN 0-8122-7661-2); pap. 9.95x (ISBN 0-8122-1055-7, Pa Paperbacks). U of Pa Pr.

Drew, Katherine F., ed. The Barbarian Invasions: Catalyst of a New Order. LC 77-8450. (European Problem Studies Ser.). 144p. 1977. pap. text ed. 5.95 (ISBN 0-88275-572-2). Krieger.

Drew, Katherine F & Lear, Floyd S., eds. Perspectives in Medieval History. LC 63-20902. Repr. of 1963 ed. 26.30 (ISBN 0-8357-9653-1, 2015753). Bks Demand UMI.

Drew, Katherine F., tr. Burgundian Code: Book of Constitutions or Law of Gundobad & Additional Enactments. LC 70-182499. (Middle Ages Ser.). (Orig.). 1972. 15.00x (ISBN 0-8122-7654-X); pap. 8.95x (ISBN 0-8122-1035-2, Pa Paperbks). U of Pa Pr.

Drew, Katherine F., et al. Studies in History. (Rice University Studies: Vol. 58, No. 4). 155p. 1972. pap. 10.00x (ISBN 0-89263-214-3). Rice Univ.

Drew, Leslie. Haida-Their Art & Culture. (Illus.). 112p. 12.95 (ISBN 0-88839-160-9); pap. 5.95 (ISBN 0-88839-132-3). Hancock House.

Drew, Louise C., jt. ed. see Miller, Max B.

Drew, Mary. Acton, Gladstone & Others. facs. ed. LC 68-20294. (Essay Index Reprint Ser). 1924. 14.00 (ISBN 0-8369-0390-0). Ayer Co Pubs.

--Acton, Gladstone & Others. LC 68-16292. 1968. Repr. of 1924 ed. 19.50x (ISBN 0-8046-0118-6, Pub. by Kennikat). Assoc Faculty Pr.

Drew, Mary Anne. The Diabolist. (Orig.). 1975. pap. 0.95 (ISBN 0-380-00235-3, 21451). Avon.

Drew, P. The Meaning of Freedom. 500p. 1982. text ed. 35.50x (ISBN 0-08-025743-7, Pub. by Aberdeen Pr Scotland). Humanities.

Drew, Philip. The Architecture of Arata Isozaki. LC 81-48061. (Illus.). 206p. 1982. 33.65i (ISBN 0-06-431550-9, HarpT). Har-Row.

Drew, Rad A., jt. auth. see Mikuleckye, Larry.

Drew, Ralph. Professional Ophthalmic Dispensing. LC 73-120180. 1970. leatherette 23.00 (ISBN 0-87873-007-9). Prof Press.

Drew, Richard H., jt. ed. see Arena, Jay M.

Drew, Rodney. Microcomputers for Financial Planning. 116p. 1983. pap. 38.50x (ISBN 0-566-03443-3). Gower Pub Co.

Drew, Thomas, compiled by. The John Brown Invasion: An Authentic History of the Harper's Ferry Tragedy. LC 72-8568. (Black Heritage Library Collection Ser.). 1972. Repr. of 1859 ed. 15.50 (ISBN 0-8369-9188-5). Ayer Co Pubs.

Drew, Thomas B. & Hoopes, John W. Advances in Chemical Engineering, Vol. 10. (Serial Publication Ser.). 1978. 85.00 (ISBN 0-12-008510-0). Acad Pr.

Drew, Thomas B. & Hoopes, John W., Jr., eds. Advances in Chemical Engineering. Incl. Vol. 1. 1956. 85.00 (ISBN 0-12-008501-1); Vol. 2. 1958. 85.00 (ISBN 0-12-008502-X); Vol. 3. Drew, Thomas B., et al, eds. 1962. 85.00 (ISBN 0-12-008503-8); Vol. 4. 1964. 85.00 (ISBN 0-12-008504-6); Vol. 5. 1964. 85.00 (ISBN 0-12-008505-4); Vol. 6. 1966. 85.00 (ISBN 0-12-008506-2); Vol. 7. 1968. 85.00 (ISBN 0-12-008507-0); Vol. 8. 1970. 85.00 (ISBN 0-12-008508-9); Vol. 9. 1974. 85.00 (ISBN 0-12-008509-7). Acad Pr.

Drew, Thomas B., et al, eds. Advances in Chemical Engineering, Vol. 11. LC 56-6600. (Serial Publication Ser.). 1981. 85.00 (ISBN 0-12-008511-9). Acad Pr.

Drew, W. Lawrence. Viral Infections: A Clinical Approach. LC 76-10599. 301p. 1976. pap. text ed. 17.00x (ISBN 0-8036-2898-6). Davis Co.

Drew, Walter F., et al. Motivating Today's Students. LC 74-16805. (Learning Handbooks Ser.). 1974. pap. 5.95 (ISBN 0-8224-1908-4). Pitman Learning.

Drew, Wayland. Dragonslayer. (Orig.). 1985. pap. 2.75 (ISBN 0-345-32306-8, Del Rey). Ballantine.

--The Gaian Expedient. (The Erthring Cycle Ser.: Pt. 2). 272p. (Orig.). 1985. pap. 2.95 (ISBN 0-345-30888-3, Del Rey). Ballantine.

--The Memoirs of Alcheringia. (Earthring Cycle Ser.: Pt. 1). 256p. 1985. pap. 2.75 (Del Rey). Ballantine.

Drew, Wayland, jt. auth. see Litteljohn, Bruce.

Drewal, Henry J. African Artistry: Technique & Aesthetics in Yoruba Sculpture. Morris, Kelly, ed. LC 80-81184. (Illus.). 100p. (Orig.). 1980. pap. 7.00 (ISBN 0-939802-03-1). High Mus Art.

--The Traditional Art of the Nigerian Peoples: The Ratner Collection. (Illus.). 1977. 7.00 (ISBN 0-686-25965-3). Mus African Art.

Drewal, Henry J. & Drewal, Margaret T. Gelede: Art & Female Power among the Yoruba. LC 82-48388. (Traditional Arts of Africa Ser.). (Illus.). 352p. 1983. 35.00x (ISBN 0-253-32569-2). Ind U Pr.

Drewal, Margaret T., jt. auth. see Drewal, Henry J.

Drew-Bear, Annette. Rhetoric in Ben Jonson's Middle Plays: A Study of Ethos, Character Portrayal & Persuasion. (Salzburg Studies in English Literature, Jacobean Drama Studies: No.24). 1973. pap. text ed. 25.50x (ISBN 0-391-01365-3). Humanities.

Drew-Bear, Marie. Le Nome Hermopolite. LC 78-13005. (American Studies in Papyrology: No. 21). 45.00x (ISBN 0-89130-258-1, 310021). Scholars Pr GA.

Drew-Bear, Thomas, jt. auth. see Stroud, Ronald.

Drew Connor, Melody, et al. Dynamics of Utilization Management. Kinsworthy, Geraldine S., ed. 304p. (Orig.). 1984. 49.95 (ISBN 0-939450-49-6, 001113). AHPI.

Drewe, Robert. The Bodysurfers. 170p. (Orig.). 1984. pap. 6.95 (ISBN 0-571-13389-4). Faber & Faber.

Drewery, Benjamin. Origen & the Doctrine of Grace. LC 61-19395. 1960. text ed. 17.50x (ISBN 0-8401-0579-7). A R Allenson.

Drewery, Benjamin, jt. ed. see Cunliffe-Jones, Hubert.

Drewery, Benjamin, jt. ed. see Rupp, E. G.

Drewery, Mary. Hamid & the Palm Sunday Donkey. LC 67-26848. (Illus.). (gr. 4-6). 1968. 6.95g (ISBN 0-8038-2962-0); PLB 7.95 (ISBN 0-8038-2963-9). Hastings.

--William Carey: A Biography. 224p. 1984. pap. 5.95 (ISBN 0-310-38851-1). Zondervan.

Drewes, C. F. Introduction to the Books of the Bible. 1929. 4.95 (ISBN 0-570-03185-0, 12-2110). Concordia.

Drewes, Marilyn. Your Bull Terrier. LC 77-92121. (Your Dog Bk.). (Illus.). 1978. 12.95 (ISBN 0-87714-043-X). Denlingers.

Drewes, S. E. Chroman & Related Compounds. LC 73-84458. (Progress in Mass Spectrometry: Vol. 2). (Illus.). 145p. 1974. 48.80x (ISBN 3-527-25494-3). VCH Pubs.

Drewett, John. Surrey. (Shire County Guide Ser.: No. 8). 1985. pap. 4.95 (ISBN 0-85263-741-1, Pub by Shire Pubns England). Seven Hills Bks.

Drewett, R., jt. auth. see Drewitt, M.

Drewfs, Sharon B. Woodcarving in Relief. (Illus.). 76p. (Orig.). 1978. pap. 6.50 (ISBN 0-917119-11-8, 45-1029). Priscillas Pubns.

Drewin, F. J. Construction Productivity: Measurement & Improvement Through Work Study. 176p. 1982. 28.50 (ISBN 0-444-00619-2). Elsevier.

Drewitt, M. & Drewett, R. Nature of Settle Structure & Change: A European View. cancelled (ISBN 0-08-028138-9). Pergamon.

Drewitz, jt. auth. see Richling.

Drewnowski, Jan, ed. Crisis in the East European Economy: The Spread of the Polish Disease. LC 82-42560. 1982. 25.00 (ISBN 0-312-17314-8). St Martin.

Drewry, David J. Glacial Geologic Processes. 288p. 1985. pap. text ed. write for info. (ISBN 0-7131-6390-9). E Arnold.

Drewry, Gavin, jt. auth. see Burton, Ivor.

Drewry, Gavin, jt. auth. see Parliament Group Study.

Drewry, Gavin, jt. ed. see Blom-Cooper, Louis.

Drewry, Gavin, jt. ed. see Englefield, Dermot.

Drewry, John E. Concerning the Fourth Estate. 2nd ed. LC 42-18567. pap. 44.50 (ISBN 0-317-29264-1, 2055537). Bks Demand UMI.

--Writing Book Reviews. LC 73-17951. 230p. 1974. Repr. of 1966 ed. lib. bdg. 22.50x (ISBN 0-8371-7285-3, DRWB). Greenwood.

Drewry, William S. Southampton Insurrection. (Illus.). 1968. Repr. of 1900 ed. 15.00 (ISBN 0-930230-21-3). Johnson NC.

Drews, Arthur. The Witnesses to the Historicity of Jesus. McCabe, Joseph, tr. LC 70-161327. (Atheist Viewpoint Ser.). 332p. 1972. Repr. of 1912 ed. 23.50 (ISBN 0-405-03811-9). Ayer Co Pubs.

--The Witnesses to the Historicity of Jesus. 69.95 (ISBN 0-8490-1313-5). Gordon Pr.

Drews, Elizabeth M. The Higher Levels of Human Growth. LC 79-83602. 1979. 11.95 (ISBN 0-8022-2242-0). Philos Lib.

--Learning Together: How to Foster Creativity, Self-Fulfillment & Social Awareness in Today's Students & Teachers. LC 70-172679. 264p. 1972. 7.95 (ISBN 0-13-527036-7). P-H.

Drews, J., ed. R-Factors: Their Properties & Possible Control: Symposium, Baden Near Vienna, April 27-29, 1977. (Topics in Infectious Diseases: Vol. 2). 1977. 39.00 (ISBN 0-387-81455-8). Springer-Verlag.

Drews, Robert. Basileus: The Evidence for Kingship in Geometric Greece. LC 82-10915. (Yale Classical Monographs: No. 4). 160p. 1983. text ed. 21.00x (ISBN 0-300-02831-8). Yale U Pr.

--In Search of the Shroud of Turin: New Light on Its History & Origins. LC 83-24586. (Illus.). 148p. 1984. 17.95x (ISBN 0-8476-7349-9). Rowman & Allanheld.

Drews, Robert C., jt. ed. see Steele, Arthur.

Drews, Toby R. Get Rid of Anxiety & Stress. LC 82-61228. 1982. pap. 4.95 (ISBN 0-88270-537-7). Bridge Pub.

--Getting Them Sober, Vol. 1. LC 80-82751. (Orig.). 1980. pap. 2.95 (ISBN 0-88270-460-5, Pub. by Logos). Bridge Pub.

--Getting Them Sober, Vol. 2. LC 80-82751. 1983. 2.95 (ISBN 0-88270-560-1). Bridge Pub.

--Getting Them Sober Action Guide, Vol. 1. 1983. 1.95 (ISBN 0-88270-559-8). Bridge Pub.

--Getting Them Sober Complete. LC 80-82751. 1984. 19.95 (ISBN 0-88270-576-8). Bridge Pub.

Drexel, Henry W., tr. see Raeder, Erich.

Drexel Institute of Technology. Sheet Formability of Alpha-Brass: Effect of Material Properties, Anisotrophy, & Processing Parameters. 127p. 1973. 19.05 (ISBN 0-317-34545-1, 129). Intl Copper.

Drexelius, Jeremias. Heliotropium: Conformity of the Human Will to the Divine. LC 84-51597. 416p. 1985. pap. 8.50 (ISBN 0-89555-245-0). Tan Bks Pubs.

Drexl, A., jt. auth. see Domschke, W.

Drexler, Arthur. Architecture of Japan. LC 55-5987. (Museum of Modern Art - Publications in Repr. Ser). (Illus.). Repr. of 1955 ed. 15.00 (ISBN 0-405-01516-X). Ayer Co Pubs.

--Charles Eames: Furniture from the Design Collection. LC 73-76672. (Illus.). 56p. 1973. pap. 4.50 (ISBN 0-87070-314-5). Museum Mod Art.

--The Miles Van Der Rohe Archive, Pt. I: 1907-1938, Vol. 2. Date not set. 187.50 (ISBN 0-8240-4026-0). Garland Pub.

--The Miles Van Der Rohe Archive, Pt. I: 1907-1938, Vol. 3. Date not set. 187.50 (ISBN 0-8240-4027-9). Garland Pub.

--The Miles Van Der Rohe Archive, Pt. I: 1907-1938, Vol. 4. Date not set. 187.50 (ISBN 0-8240-4028-7). Garland Pub.

--Transformations in Modern Architecture. LC 79-62956. (Illus.). 1980. pap. 18.95 (ISBN 0-87070-608-X, 852244). NYGS.

Drexler, Arthur & Hines, Thomas. The Architecture of Richard Neutra: From International Style to California Modern. LC 82-81426. (Illus.). 112p. 1982. pap. 10.00 (ISBN 0-87070-506-7). Museum Mod Art.

Drexler, Arthur, ed. The Architecture of the Ecole des Beaux-Arts. 1977. 60.00 (ISBN 0-262-04053-0). MIT Pr.

--The Miles Van Der Rohe Archive, Pt. I: 1907-1938, Vol. 1. Date not set. 187.50 (ISBN 0-8240-4025-2). Garland Pub.

Drexler, G., jt. auth. see Wachsmann, F.

Drexler, Rosalyn. The Cosmopolitan Girl. LC 74-23526. 192p. 1975. 6.95 (ISBN 0-87131-169-0). M Evans.

Drey, Rudolph E. Apothecary Jars: Pharmaceutical Pottery & Porcelain in Europe & the East 1150-1850. (Illus.). 257p. 1978. 49.95 (ISBN 0-571-09965-3). Faber & Faber.

Dreyer, Angela E. Taboo. LC 83-62045. 87p. 1983. pap. 3.95 (ISBN 0-914241-00-1). Macanna-Rose.

Dreyer, Edward L. Early Ming China: A Political History, 1355-1435. LC 80-51646. 336p. 1982. 32.50x (ISBN 0-8047-1105-4). Stanford U Pr.

Dreyer, Frederick A. Burke's Politics: A Study in Whig Orthodoxy. 93p. 1979. text ed. 13.25x (ISBN 0-88920-077-7, Pub. by Wilfred Laurier U Pr Canada). Humanities.

Dreyer, Herbert E. & Scheel, Randall L. Recognizing & Using TRENDS. (Audio Cassette Learning Program Ser.). 70p. 1983. audio cassettes pession 87.50 (ISBN 0-915375-01-X). Strategic Moves.

Dreyer, Jacob S. Composite Reserve Assets in the International Monetary System, Vol. 2. Altman, Edward I. & Walter, Ingo, eds. LC 76-5757. (Contemporary Studies in Economic and Financial Analysis). 325p. 1977. lib. bdg. 34.50 (ISBN 0-89232-003-6). Jai Pr.

Dreyer, Jacob S., et al, eds. International Monetary System: A Time of Turbulence. 1982. 25.95 (ISBN 0-8447-2228-6); pap. 14.95 (ISBN 0-8447-2227-8). Am Enterprise.

--Exchange Rate Flexibility. 1978. 15.25 (ISBN 0-8447-2124-7); pap. 7.25 (ISBN 0-8447-2123-9). Am Enterprise.

Dreyer, John L. History of Astronomy from Thales to Kepler. pap. 8.50 (ISBN 0-486-60079-3). Dover.

--History of Astronomy from Thales to Kepler. 15.50 (ISBN 0-8446-1997-3). Peter Smith.

--Tycho Brahe: A Picture of Scientific Life & Work in the Sixteenth Century. (Illus.). 13.25 (ISBN 0-8446-1996-5). Peter Smith.

Dreyer, June. China's Forty Millions. (East Asian Ser.: No. 87). 1977. 20.00x (ISBN 0-674-11964-9). Harvard U Pr.

Dreyer, O. Cultural Changes in Developing Countries. 295p. 1976. 3.95 (ISBN 0-8285-0220-X, Pub. by Progress Pubs USSR). Imported Pubns.

Dreyer, Peter. A Gardener Touched with Genius: The Life of Luther Burbank. Date not set. price not set. U of Cal Pr.

Dreyer, Peter & Stackpole, Edouard. Nantucket in Color. (Profiles of America Ser). (Illus.). 1974. 8.95 (ISBN 0-8038-5030-1). Hastings.

Dreyer, Philip H., jt. ed. see Havighurst, Robert J.

Dreyer, Regina A. Career Directions for Dental Hygienists. LC 85-70408. 214p. (Orig.). 1985. pap. text ed. 12.50x (ISBN 0-933163-00-2). Career Directions.

Dreyer, Sharon, et al. Guide to Nursing Management of Psychiatric Patients. 2nd ed. LC 78-31432. 248p. 1979. pap. text ed. 15.95 (ISBN 0-8016-0832-5). Mosby.

Dreyer, Sharon S. Bookfinder, Vol. 3. 1985. 44.50 (ISBN 0-913476-48-X); pap. 17.95 (ISBN 0-913476-49-8); Set. 115.00 (ISBN 0-913476-47-1). Am Guidance.

--The Bookfinder: A Guide to Children's Literature about the Needs & Problems of Youth Aged 2 to 15, 3 vols. 1981. Set. text ed. 115.00 (ISBN 0-913476-47-1); Vol. 1. text ed. 44.50 (ISBN 0-913476-45-5); Vol. 2. text ed. 44.50 (ISBN 0-913476-48-X). Am Guidance.

Dreyer, W. Underground Storage of Oil & Gas in Salt Deposits & Other Non-Hard Rocks. (Geology of Petroleum Ser.). 207p. 1982. pap. 21.95 (ISBN 0-470-27138-8). Halsted Pr.

Dreyfack, Ray. Customers: How to Get Them, How to Serve Them, How to Keep Them. 1983. 91.50 (ISBN 0-85013-140-5). Dartnell Corp.

Dreyfack, Raymond. The Complete Book of Walking. LC 80-26185. (Illus.). 288p. 1981. pap. 5.95 (ISBN 0-668-05167-1, 5167). Arco.

--The Complete Book of Walking. LC 79-84700. (Illus.). 1979. 9.95 (ISBN 0-87863-188-7). Farnswth Pub.

--How to Develop a Successful Zero-Base Budgeting Program. 1978. 75.50 (ISBN 0-85013-092-1). Dartnell Corp.

--Making It In Management the Japanese Way. LC 82-5175. 228p. 1982. 14.95 (ISBN 0-87863-006-6). Farnswth Pub.

--Profitable Salesmanship in the Eighties. LC 80-50317. 180p. 1980. pap. 7.95 (ISBN 0-8019-6943-3). Chilton.

Dreyfus, Alfred. Five Years of My Life. Mortimer, James, tr. (Select Bibliographies Reprint Ser). Repr. of 1901 ed. 24.00 (ISBN 0-8369-5836-5). Ayer Co Pubs.

--Five Years of My Life: The Diary of Captain Alfred Dreyfus. (Illus.). 253p. 1977. 18.75x (ISBN 0-8464-1184-9). Beekman Pubs.

Dreyfus, Alfred & Dreyfus, Pierre. Dreyfus Case. 1937. 49.50x (ISBN 0-686-83527-1). Elliots Bks.

Dreyfus, B. Hematologie. (Illus.). 950p. (Fr.). 1984. lib. bdg. 99.00 (ISBN 2-257-12526-6). S M P F Inc.

Dreyfus, Herbert L., tr. see Merleau-Ponty, Maurice.

Dreyfus, Hubert & Dreyfus, Stuart. Mind Over Machine: The Power of Human Intuition & Expertise in the Era of the Computer. 250p. 16.95 (ISBN 0-02-908060-6). Free Pr.

--Mind Over Machine: The Power of Human Intuition & Expertise in the Era of the Computer. 250p. 1985. 16.95 (ISBN 0-02-908060-6). Free Pr.

Dreyfus, Hubert L. What Computers Can't Do: A Critique of Artificial Reason. 1979. pap. 7.64i (ISBN 0-06-090613-8, CN 613, CN). Har-Row.

Dreyfus, Hubert L. & Hall, Harrison. Husserl, Intentionality & Cognitive Science. 256p. 1984. pap. text ed. 9.95 (ISBN 0-262-54041-X). MIT Pr.

Dreyfus, Hubert L. & Rabinow, Paul. Michel Foucault: Beyond Structuralism & Hermeneutics. 2nd ed. LC 83-9316. (Illus.). 232p. 1983. lib. bdg. 25.00x (ISBN 0-226-16311-3); pap. 9.95 (ISBN 0-226-16312-1). U of Chicago Pr.

Dreyfus, Hubert L. & Hall, Harrison, eds. Husserl, Intentionality & Cognitive Science. (Bradford Bks.). 256p. 1982. 35.00x (ISBN 0-262-04065-4); pap. 9.95x (ISBN 0-262-54041-X). MIT Pr.

Dreyfus, Jack. A Remarkable Medicine Has Been Overlooked. rev. ed. 1983. pap. 4.95 (ISBN 0-671-47673-4). PB.

Dreyfus, Jean-Claude & Schapira, Georges. Biochemistry of Hereditary Myopathies. (Illus.). 160p. 1962. 15.50x (ISBN 0-398-00475-7). C C Thomas.

Dreyfus, Kay, jt. auth. see Grainger, Percy.

Dreyfus, Patrica A, tr. see Merleau-Ponty, Maurice.

Dreyfus, Paul, ed. see Doleman, Edgar.

Dreyfus, Paul, ed. see Morrocco, John.

Dreyfus, Pierre, jt. auth. see Dreyfus, Alfred.

Dreyfus, Rene & Kimes, Beverly R. My Two Lives: Race Driver to Restauranteur. (Illus.). 192p. 1983. 19.95 (ISBN 0-89404-080-4). Aztex.

Dreyfus, S., jt. auth. see Bellman, Richard E.

Dreyfus, Stuart, jt. auth. see Dreyfus, Hubert.

Dreyfus, Stuart E. The Art & Theory of Dynamic Programming. (Mathematics in Science & Engineering Ser.). 1977. 19.25i (ISBN 0-12-221860-4). Acad Pr.

--Dynamic Programming & the Calculus of Variations. (Mathematics in Science & Engineering Ser.: Vol. 21). 1965. 55.00 (ISBN 0-12-221850-7). Acad Pr.

Dreyfuss, Barbara, ed. Prospective Payments: Health Care Revolution. 565p. (Orig.). 1984. pap. text ed. 72.00 (ISBN 0-914176-25-0). Wash Busn Info.

Dreyfuss, Carl. Occupation & Ideology of the Salaried Employee. Stein, Leon, ed. LC 77-70490. (Work Ser.). 1977. Repr. of 1938 ed. lib. bdg. 42.00x (ISBN 0-405-10162-7). Ayer Co Pubs.

Dreyfuss, Henry. Symbol Sourcebook: An Authoritative Guide to International Graphic Symbols. LC 83-12514. (Illus.). 292p. 1984. pap. 19.95 (ISBN 0-442-21806-0). Van Nos Reinhold.

Dreyfuss, Henry, ed. Symbol Sourcebook: An Authoritative Guide to International Graphic Symbols. LC 71-172261. (Illus.). 320p. 1972. 63.95 (ISBN 0-07-017837-2). McGraw.

Dreyfuss, Joel & Lawrence, Charles, III. The Bakke Case: The Politics of Inequality. LC 78-22249. 1979. pap. 3.95 (ISBN 0-15-616782-4, Harv). HarBraceJ.

Dreyfuss, P. Poly (Tetrahydrofuran, Vol. 8. (Polymer Monographs). 320p. 1982. 63.00 (ISBN 0-677-03330-3). Gordon.

Dreyfuss, Robert. Hostage to Khomeini. LC 80-24288. (Illus.). 241p. (Orig.). 1981. pap. 4.25 (ISBN 0-933488-11-4). New Benjamin.

Dreyfuss, Robert, jt. ed. see Bush, George P.

Drez, D., jt. auth. see D'Ambrosia, R.

Drezner, Stephen M. & McCurdy, William B. A Planning Guide for Voluntary Human Service Delivery Agencies. 2nd ed. LC 78-26125. 1979. pap. 14.95 (ISBN 0-87304-167-4). Family Serv.

Driben, Paul. We Are Metis: The Ethnography of a Halfbreed Community in Northern Alberta. LC 83-45353. (Immigrant Communities & Ethnic Minorities in the U. S. & Canada Ser.: No. 2). (Illus.). 190p. 1985. 32.50 (ISBN 0-404-19406-0). AMS Pr.

Driben, Paul & Trudeau, Robert S. When Freedom Is Lost: The Dark Side of the Relationship Between Government & the Fort Hope Band. 128p. 1983. 15.00x (ISBN 0-8020-2506-4); pap. 6.95 (ISBN 0-8020-6526-0). U of Toronto Pr.

Driberg, J. H. The Lango: A Nilotic Tribe of Uganda. LC 78-66496. (Classics of Anthropology). 488p. 1985. lib. bdg. 85.00 (ISBN 0-8240-9641-X). Garland Pub.

Driberg, Jack H. People of the Small Arrow. LC 72-3367. (Short Story Index Reprint Ser.). Repr. of 1930 ed. 21.50 (ISBN 0-8369-4146-2). Ayer Co Pubs.

Driberg, Tom. Ruling Passions. LC 76-49058. 1978. pap. 4.95 (ISBN 0-8128-6027-6). Stein & Day.

Drickamer, H. G. Electronic Transitions & the High Pressure Chemistry & Physics of Solids. (Studies in Chemical Physics). 1973. 35.00x (ISBN 0-412-11650-2, NO.6090, Pub. by Chapman & Hall). Methuen Inc.

Drickamer, Lee & Vessey, Steve. Animal Behavior: Concepts, Processes & Methods. 528p. 1982. text ed. write for info. (ISBN 0-87150-751-X, 4371, Pub. by Willard Grant Pr). PWS Pubs.

Dridzo, Solomon A. Marx & the Trade Unions. LC 75-22758. 1976. Repr. of 1942 ed. lib. bdg. 22.50x (ISBN 0-8371-8352-9, DRMT). Greenwood.

Drieberg, T. Towards Closer Indo-Soviet Cooperation. 1974. 10.50 (ISBN 0-686-20322-4). Intl Bk Dist.

Driel, G. J. Van see Van Driel, G. J., et al.

Drier, Patricia, compiled by. The Blessings of Friendship. 1979. 6.95 (ISBN 0-8378-5060-6). Gibson.

Driere, Mimi L. La see La Driere, Mimi L. & Pikunis, Justin.

Dries, Bob. Manual of Electrical Contracting. 224p. (Orig.). 1983. pap. 17.00 (ISBN 0-910460-33-7). Craftsman.

Dries, R. R., jt. ed. see Wuttke, W.

Driesbach, Janice, jt. ed. see Showalter, J. Camille.

Driesch, Angela von den. A Guide to the Measurement of Animal Bones from Archaeological Sites. LC 76-49773. (Peabody Museum Bulletins: No. 1). (Illus.). 1976. pap. text ed. 10.00x (ISBN 0-87365-950-3). Peabody Harvard.

Driesch, Hans. Psychical Research: The Science of the Super-Normal. Besterman, Theodore, tr. LC 75-7376. (Perspectives in Psychical Research Ser.). 1975. Repr. of 1933 ed. 20.00x (ISBN 0-405-07026-8). Ayer Co Pubs.

Driesch, Hans A. The Science & Philosophy of the Organism, 2 vols. LC 77-27217. (Gifford Lectures: 1907-08). Repr. of 1908 ed. Set. 70.00 (ISBN 0-404-60500-1). AMS Pr.

Driesen, W., et al, eds. Computerized Tomography-Brain Metabolism-Spinal Injuries. (Advances in Neurosurgery Ser.: Vol. 10). (Illus.). 420p. 1982. pap. 54.00 (ISBN 0-387-11115-8). Springer-Verlag.

Driessen, E. J., jt. auth. see De Boer, S. P.

Driessen, Gerald J., jt. auth. see Driessen, Henry J.

Driessen, Henry J. & Driessen, Gerald J. Henry's History. 2nd ed. (Illus.). 191p. 1983. pap. 9.95 (ISBN 0-912495-03-0). San Diego Pub Co.

Driessens, F. C. Mineral Aspects of Dentistry. (Monographs in Oral Science: Vol. 10). (Illus.). xvi, 216p. 1982. 63.00 (ISBN 3-8055-3469-8). S Karger.

Drieux, Jean P. & Jarlaud, Alain. Let's Talk D. P. Computer Lexicon. 116p. (Eng., Amer. & Fr.). 1977. pap. 11.95 (ISBN 0-686-57123-1, M-6171). French & Eur.

Driever, Dorothea. Aspects of a Case Grammer of Mombasa Swahili. (Hamburger Philologische Studien: No. 43). 253p. (Orig.). 1976. pap. text ed. 18.00 (ISBN 3-87118-245-1, Pub. by Helmut Buske Verlag Hamburg). Benjamins North Am.

Drifte, R., jt. ed. see Chapman, J. W.

Driggers, Joann, jt. auth. see Leet, Donald.

Driggs, Don, jt. auth. see Bushnell, Eleanore.

Driggs, Frank & Lewine, Harris. Black Beauty, White Heat: A Pictorial History of Classic Jazz, 1920-1950. LC 82-60449. 360p. 1982. 50.45 (ISBN 0-688-03771-2). Morrow.

Driggs, Howard R., jt. auth. see McConnell, William J.

Driggs, Howard R., ed. see Cook, James H.

Driggs, M. F. Problem-Directed & Medical Information Systems. 1979. 27.50 (ISBN 0-8151-2855-X). Year Bk Med.

Drigotas, Frank M., Jr., jt. auth. see Dunlop, Bill.

Drijvers, H. J. Cults & Beliefs at Edessa. (Illus.). 204p. 1980. text ed. 55.25x (ISBN 90-04-06050-2). Humanities.

Driljvers, H. J., jt. ed. see Van Baaren, T. P.

Drill, V. A. & Lazar, Paul, eds. Cutaneous Toxicity. 1977. 45.00 (ISBN 0-12-222050-1). Acad Pr.

Drill, Victor A., ed. Current Concepts in Cutaneous Toxicity. LC 79-21172. 1980. 44.00 (ISBN 0-12-222052-8). Acad Pr.

Drill, Victor A. & Lazar, Paul, eds. Cutaneous Toxicity. (Target Organ Toxicology Ser.). 288p. 1984. text ed. 58.50 (ISBN 0-89004-933-5). Raven.

Drillien, Cecil M. & Drummond, Margaret. Developmental Screening & the Child with Special Needs. (Clinics in Developmental Medicine: No. 86). 294p. 1984. text ed. 26.75 (ISBN 0-433-07810-3). Lippincott.

Drillock, David & Erickson, John, eds. The Divine Liturgy. 368p. 1982. text ed. 30.00 (ISBN 0-913836-95-8); pap. 20.00 (ISBN 0-913836-93-1). St Vladimirs.

Drillock, David, et al. Pascha: The Resurrection of Christ. (Music Ser.). 274p. 1980. pap. 15.00 (ISBN 0-913836-50-8); 20.00 (ISBN 0-913836-65-6). St Vladimirs.

--Holy Week. (Music Ser.: Vol. I). 186p. (Orig.). 1980. 18.00 (ISBN 0-913836-67-2); pap. 14.00 (ISBN 0-913836-66-4). St Vladimirs.

Drilon, J. D., ed. Agribusiness Management Resource Materials. Incl. Vol. 1. Introduction to Agribusiness Management. LC 72-170364. 236p. 1973. 13.50 (ISBN 0-685-56587-4, APO1); Vol. 2, Pt. 2. Agribusiness (Asian Case Studies) 444p. 1971. 13.50 (ISBN 0-685-56589-0, APO8); Vol. 3. Southeast Asia Agribusiness. 326p. 1975. 29.00 (ISBN 0-685-56590-4, APO10). APO). Unipub.

Drimmer, Frederick. Body Snatchers, Stiffs & Other Ghouls. (Illus.). 1981. pap. 2.75 (ISBN 0-449-14432-1, GM). Fawcett.

--The Elephant Man. (gr. 6 up). 1985. 13.95 (ISBN 0-399-21262-0, Putnam). Putnam Pub Group.

Drimmer, Frederick, ed. Captured by the Indians: Fifteen Firsthand Accounts, 1750-1870. 384p. 1985. pap. 6.95 (ISBN 0-486-24901-8). Dover.

Drimmer, Frederick, compiled by. A Friend Is Someone Special. LC 75-16038. 44p. 1976. 4.95 (ISBN 0-8378-2101-0). Gibson.

Drinan, Ann, ed. see International Joint Conference on Artificial Intelligence, 7th, Vancouver, BC, Aug. 1981.

Drinan, Robert F. Beyond the Nuclear Freeze. 160p. (Orig.). 1983. pap. 7.95 (ISBN 0-8164-2406-3, Pub. by Seabury). Winston Pr.

--God & Caesar on the Potomac: A Pilgrimage of Conscience. 1985. 15.00 (ISBN 0-89453-458-0). M Glazier.

--Religion, the Courts, & Public Policy. LC 78-6124. 261p. 1978. Repr. of 1963 ed. lib. bdg. 20.75x (ISBN 0-313-20444-6, DRRE). Greenwood.

Dring, D. M. Contributions Toward a Rational Arrangement of the Clthraceae. (Illus.). 96p. 1979. pap. 8.00 (ISBN 0-318-11896-3). Lubrecht & Cramer.

Dring, Gerald J., et al. Fundamental & Applied Aspects of Bacterial Spores. Date not set. 49.50 (ISBN 0-12-222080-3). Acad Pr.

Dring, M. J. The Biology of Marine Plants. 208p. 1983. pap. text ed. 18.95 (ISBN 0-7131-2860-7). E Arnold.

Drinka, George F. The Birth of Neurosis: Myth, Malady & the Victorians. (Illus.). 400p. 1984. 21.95 (ISBN 0-671-44999-0). S&S.

Drinker, Frederick E. Booker T. Washington: The Master Mind of a Child of Slavery. LC 77-100288. Repr. of 1915 ed. 22.50x (ISBN 0-8371-2939-7, DRW&). Greenwood.

Drinker, Henry S. Legal Ethics. LC 80-11445. (Legal Studies of the William Nelson Cromwell Foundation). xxii, 448p. 1980. Repr. of 1953 ed. lib. bdg. 42.50x (ISBN 0-313-22321-1, DRLG). Greenwood.

Drinker, Henry S., tr. see Schubert, Franz.

Drinker, Henry S., Jr. The Chamber Music of Johannes Brahms. LC 73-7698. (Illus.). 130p. 1974. Repr. of 1932 ed. lib. bdg. 15.00x (ISBN 0-8371-6941-0, DRJB). Greenwood.

Drinker, Sophie, jt. auth. see Leonard, Eugenie A.

Drinker, Sophie L. Music & Women: The Story of Women in Their Relation to Music. LC 75-35730. 1976. Repr. of 1948 ed. 17.95 (ISBN 0-89201-011-8). Zenger Pub.

Drinkrow, John. Mozart. (Evergreen Lives Ser.). (Illus.). 128p. 1985. 6.95 (ISBN 0-312-55076-6). St Martin.

Drinkwater, J. F. Roman Gaul. LC 83-45143. (Illus.). 272p. 1983. 25.00x (ISBN 0-8014-1642-6). Cornell U Pr.

Drinkwater, John. Discovery, Being the Second Book of an Autobiography. LC 78-131691. 435p. 1983. Repr. of 1933 ed. lib. bdg. 13.00x (ISBN 0-403-00578-7). Scholarly.

--English Poetry: An Unfinished History. 1979. Repr. of 1938 ed. lib. bdg. 30.00 (ISBN 0-8495-1105-4). Arden Lib.

--English Poetry: An Unfinished History. 18.00 (ISBN 0-8369-5837-3, 6901). Ayer Co Pubs.

--The Life & Adventures of Carl Laemmle. Jowett, Garth S., ed. LC 77-11374. (Aspects of Film Ser.). 1978. Repr. of 1931 ed. lib. bdg. 37.50x (ISBN 0-405-11130-4). Ayer Co Pubs.

--The Muse in Council. 255p. 1984. Repr. lib. bdg. 35.00 (ISBN 0-8482-3700-5). Norwood Edns.

--The Muse in Council: John Milton, B. Shelley, Johnson. 255p. 1982. Repr. of 1925 ed. lib. bdg. 30.00 (ISBN 0-89987-168-2). Darby Bks.

--Patriotism in Literature. 1980. Repr. of 1924 ed. lib. bdg. 25.00 (ISBN 0-8482-0649-5). Norwood Edns.

--Robert Burns. 1973. Repr. of 1925 ed. 10.00 (ISBN 0-8274-1648-2). R West.

--Shakespeare. 1933. lib. bdg. 15.00 (ISBN 0-8482-9954-X). Norwood Edns.

Drinkwater, John, ed. Way of Poetry. facs. ed. LC 73-116399. (Granger Index Reprint Ser.). 1922. 16.00 (ISBN 0-8369-6140-4). Ayer Co Pubs.

Drinkwater, John, ed. see Fellows of the Royal Society of Literature of the U.K.

Drinnon, Anna M., ed. see Goldman, Emma.

Drinnon, Richard. Facing West: The Metaphysics of Indian-Hating & Empire-Building. 1980. pap. 10.95 (ISBN 0-452-00632-5, F632, Mer). NAL.

--Facing West: The Metaphysics of Indian-Hating & Empire-Building. (Illus.). 544p. 1980. 20.00 (ISBN 0-8166-0978-0). U of Minn Pr.

--Rebel in Paradise. LC 82-8531. (Phoenix). (Illus.). xvi, 350p. 1983. pap. 9.95 (ISBN 0-226-16364-4). U of Chicago Pr.

Drinnon, Richard, ed. see Goldman, Emma.

Dripps, Robert D., et al. Introduction to Anesthesia: The Principles of Safe Practice. 6th ed. LC 76-51011. (Illus.). 1982. text ed. 27.95 (ISBN 0-7216-3194-0). Saunders.

Driscoll. Handbook of Family Practice. 1985. 14.95 (ISBN 0-8151-2883-5). Year Bk Med.

--Instrumental Evaluation in Biomedical Science. (Clinical & Biochemical Analysis Ser.). 312p. 1984. 59.75 (ISBN 0-8247-7184-2). Dekker.

Driscoll, Charles B. The Life of O. O. McIntyre. (American Newspapermen 1790-1933 Ser.). (Illus.). 344p. 1974. Repr. of 1938 ed. 17.50x (ISBN 0-8464-0022-7). Beekman Pubs.

Driscoll, Daniel J., tr. The Sworn Book of Honourius the Magician. LC 76-57011. 1983. 20.00 (ISBN 0-935214-00-3). Heptangle.

Driscoll, Dennis M., jt. auth. see Griffiths, John F.

Driscoll, Donald C. & Davey, Homer C. The Practice of Real Estate in California. (Illus.). 304p. 1981. 27.95 (ISBN 0-13-693606-7). P-H.

Driscoll, Dorothy L., et al. The Nursing Process in Later Maturity. (Illus.). 1980. text ed. 28.95 (ISBN 0-13-627570-2). P-H.

Driscoll, E. F. Industrial Electronics: Devices, Circuits & Applications. (Illus.). 420p. 1976. text ed. 22.50 (ISBN 0-8269-1625-2). Am Technical.

Driscoll, Edward, jt. auth. see Musil, Thomas.

Driscoll, Edward J & Musil, Thomas A. Minnesota Supplement for Modern Real Estate Practice. 4th ed. LC 85-1956. (Illus.). 248p. 1985. pap. 9.95 (ISBN 0-88462-491-9, 1510-22, Real Estate Ed). Longman USA.

Driscoll, Edwin. Alf & the Red-Eyed Yellow Monster. 1985. 3.50 (ISBN 0-89536-942-7, 7559). CSS of Ohio.

Driscoll, Eileen R. The Selection & Appointment of School Heads. 3rd. ed. 1982. pap. 7.75 (ISBN 0-934338-47-7). NAIS.

Driscoll, F. F., jt. auth. see Coughlin, R. F.

Driscoll, Fred & Coughlin, Robert F. Solid State Devices & Applications. (Illus.). 384p. 1975. 31.95 (ISBN 0-13-822106-5). P-H.

Driscoll, Frederick F. Microprocessor-Microcomputer Technology. 1983. text ed. write for info. (ISBN 0-534-01326-0, Pub. by Breton Pubs). Wadsworth Pub.

--Microprocessor-Microcomputer Technology. 520p. 1983. 29.95 (ISBN 0-442-21827-3). Van Nos Reinhold.

Driscoll, Frederick F., Jr., jt. auth. see Coughlin, Robert F.

Driscoll, Frederick, Jr. Analysis of Electric Circuits. LC 72-3691. (Illus.). 544p. 1973. text ed. 31.95 (ISBN 0-13-032912-6). P-H.

Driscoll, H. T. Filter Aids & Materials-Technology & Applications. LC 77-71926. (Chemical Technology Review Ser.: No. 86). (Illus.). 307p. 1977. 39.00 (ISBN 0-8155-0658-9). Noyes.

Driscoll, J. R., tr. see Rommel, Erwin.

Driscoll, J. Walter, jt. auth. see Gurdjieff Foundation of California.

Driscoll, Jack. Fishing the Backwash. LC 84-3843. 71p. 1984. pap. 5.00 (ISBN 0-87886-123-8). Ithaca Hse.

Driscoll, James G., ed. see Hernandez, Ernie.

Driscoll, James P. Identity in Shakespearean Drama. LC 81-72027. 208p. 1983. 25.00 (ISBN 0-8387-5024-9). Bucknell U Pr.

Driscoll, Jeanne W., ed. see Nursing Mother's Council of the Boston Association for Childbirth Education.

Driscoll, John. The China Cantos of Ezra Pound. (Studia Anglistica Upsaliensia: No. 46). 166p. 1983. pap. text ed. 15.50x (ISBN 91-554-1396-X, Pub. by Almqvist & Wiksell Sweden). Humanities.

Driscoll, John P. American Paintings from the Collection of Daniel J. Terra: Exhibition Catalogue. (Illus.). 38p. 1977. pap. 2.50 (ISBN 0-911209-10-7). Penn St Art.

--Communicating on Film. 124p. 1983. pap. text ed. 5.80x (ISBN 0-87563-238-6). Stipes.

--John F. Kensett Drawings: Exhibition Catalogue. (Illus.). 104p. 1978. pap. 4.00 (ISBN 0-911209-13-1). Penn St Art.

--Works by Arthur B. Davies: From the Collection of Mr. & Mrs. Herbert Brill. (Illus.). 36p. 1979. pap. 3.00 exhibition catalogue (ISBN 0-911209-15-8). Penn St Art.

Driscoll, John P., jt. auth. see Howat, John R.

Driscoll, Laura A., jt. auth. see Goodwin, William L.

Driscoll, Mark J. Research Within Reach: Elementary School Mathematics. 141p. 1981. pap. 6.25 (ISBN 0-87353-194-9). NCTM.

Driscoll, Mary C. Cash Management: Corporate Strategies for Profit. 243p. 1983. 28.95x (ISBN 0-471-87409-4, Pub. by Wiley-Interscience). Wiley.

Driscoll, Maryanne, jt. auth. see Fromberg, Doris.

Driscoll, P., et al. Decimals. West, K. & Johnston, D., eds. (Math Skills for Daily Living Ser.). (Illus.). 32p. (gr. 7-12). 1979. pap. text ed. 4.20x (ISBN 0-87453-093-8, 82093). Denoyer.

--Fractions. West, K. & Johnston, D., eds. (Math Skills for Daily Living Ser.). (Illus.). 40p. (gr. 7-12). 1979. pap. text ed. 4.20x (ISBN 0-87453-092-X, 82092). Denoyer.

--Ratio, Proportion & Percent. West, K. & Johnston, D., eds. (Math Skills for Daily Living Ser.). (Illus.). 32p. (gr. 7-12). 1979. pap. text ed. 4.20x (ISBN 0-87453-094-6). Denoyer.

--Whole Numbers. West, K. & Johnston, D., eds. (Math Skills for Daily Living Ser.). (Illus.). 32p. (gr. 7-12). 1979. pap. text ed. 4.20x (ISBN 0-87453-091-1, 82091). Denoyer.

Driscoll, R. B. Annex to Unified Theory of Ether, Field & Matter. 83p. 1985. pap. 5.00x (ISBN 0-317-19556-5). R B Driscoll.

--Unified Theory of Ether, Field & Matter. 3rd ed. 310p. 1966. pap. 10.00x (ISBN 0-9601374-1-6). R B Driscoll.

Driscoll, Richard. Pragmatic Psychotherapy. LC 83-10422. 266p. 1984. 26.95 (ISBN 0-442-21983-0). Van Nos Reinhold.

Driscoll, Robert E., ed. National Industrial Policies. Behrman, Jack N. LC 83-25054. 1984. 30.00 (ISBN 0-89946-180-8). Oelgeschlager.

Drisdale, Tommy & Hanes, Steven. The Ultralight Aviator's Handbook. (Illus.). 336p. (Orig.). 1982. pap. 16.95 (ISBN 0-912185-00-7). Skyflight Intl.

Driskell, Jeanette. A Guide to Tutoring. LC 77-83053. 32p. 1977. 1.95 (ISBN 0-89301-050-2). U Pr of Idaho.

Driskell, L. R. Control Valve Sizing. 192p. 1982. pap. text ed. 29.95x (ISBN 0-87664-620-8); pap. text ed. 10.00x instr's guide (ISBN 0-87664-621-6). Instru Soc.

--Introduction to Control Valves. LC 81-80513. 142p. 1982. Instr's Guide: 40. pap. text ed. 10.00x (ISBN 0-87664-617-8); Student Text: 142. pap. text ed. 24.95x (ISBN 0-87664-616-X). Instru Soc.

Driskell, Leon V. Passing Through: A Fiction. 239p. 1983. 13.95 (ISBN 0-912697-00-8). Algonquin Bks.

Driskell, Leslie R. Control Valve Selection & Sizing: An Independent Learning Module of the Instrument Society of America. LC 82-48157. 520p. 1983. text ed. 59.95x (ISBN 0-87664-628-3). Instru Soc.

Driskell, Ursula, tr. see Richter, Lydia.

Driskill, Frank. Davy Crockett: The Untold Story. 1981. 5.95 (ISBN 0-89015-298-5). Eakin Pubns.

--Free the North Wind. 1980. 11.95 (ISBN 0-89015-237-3). Eakin Pubns.

Driskill, Frank & Grisham, Noel. A Tour Guide to Historic San Antonio & the Border Country. 1982. 7.95 (ISBN 0-89015-357-4). Eakin Pubns.

Driskill, Frank A. & Casad, Dede. Admiral of the Hills: Biography of Chester W. Nimitz. (Illus.). 312p. 1983. 12.95 (ISBN 0-89015-364-7). Eakin Pubns.

Driskill, Frank A. & Grisham, Noel. Historic Churches of Texas. (Illus.). 400p. 1980. 16.95 (ISBN 0-89015-267-5). Eakin Pubns.

Driskill, Linda & Simpson, Margaret. Decisive Writing: An Improvement Program. (Illus.). 1978. pap. text ed. 10.95x (ISBN 0-19-502121-5). Oxford U Pr.

Drisko, R. L., jt. ed. see Cowan, D. O.

Driskoll, L. R. Selection of Control Valves. 1982. Instr's Guide: 56p. pap. text ed. 10.00x (ISBN 0-87664-619-4); Student Text: 142p. pap. text ed. 24.95x (ISBN 0-87664-618-6). Instru Soc.

Driss Ben Hames Charhadi, see Layachi, Larbi, pseud.

Driven, Rene & Goosens, Louis. The Scene of Linguistic Action & Its Perspectivization by Speak, Talk, Say, & Tell. 1983. 16.00 (ISBN 90-272-2528-1). Benjamins North Am.

Driver, B. L. Elements of Outdoor Recreation Planning. 316p. 1974. pap. text ed. 5.95x (ISBN 0-472-08284-1). U of Mich Pr.

Driver, C. J. Patrick Duncan. text ed. 65.00x (ISBN 0-435-96200-0). Heinemann Ed.

Driver, Cecil H. Tory Radical - the Life of Richard Oastler. LC 75-120249. 1970. Repr. of 1946 ed. lib. bdg. 40.00x (ISBN 0-374-92348-5). Octagon.

Driver, Christopher & Berriedale-Johnson, Michelle, eds. Pepys at Table. LC 84-40346. (Illus.). 240p. 1984. 10.95 (ISBN 0-520-05386-9). U of Cal Pr.

Driver, Clive E. The Art of Claud Lovat Fraser. 1971. pap. 6.50 (ISBN 0-939084-01-5). Rosenbach Mus and Lib.

--Early American Maps & Views. pap. 3.95x (ISBN 0-939084-12-0, Pub. by Rosenbach Mus & Lib). U Pr of Va.

--Passing Through: Letters & Documents Written in Philadelphia by Famous Vistors. (Illus.). 144p. 1983. pap. 10.00 (ISBN 0-939084-14-7, Dist. by U Pr of VA). Rosenbach Mus Lib.

--A Selection from Our Shelves: Books, Manuscripts & Drawings from the Rosenbach Foundation Museum. 1972. pap. 12.50x (ISBN 0-939084-08-2, Pub by Rosenbach Museum & Library). U Pr of Va.

Driver, Clive E., compiled by. Passing Through: Letters & Documents Written in Philadelphia by Famous Visitors. (Illus.). 196p. 1983. 35.00 (ISBN 0-939084-14-7); pap. 9.95 (ISBN 0-317-01413-7). U Pr of Va.

Driver, Clive E., jt. ed. see Feldman, Evelyn.

Driver, David Miller. The Indian in Brazilian Literature. 182p. 2.90 (ISBN 0-318-14275-9). Hispanic Inst.

Driver, Edwin D. Differential Fertility in Central India. 1963. 19.00 (ISBN 0-691-09314-8). Princeton U Pr.

--The Sociology & Anthropology of Mental Illness: A Reference Guide. rev. ed. LC 71-103476. 504p. 1972. pap. 20.00x (ISBN 0-87023-062-X). U of Mass Pr.

Driver, Edwin D., ed. see Du Bois, W. E. B.

Driver, G. R. Semitic Writing: From Pictograph to Alphabet. (British Academy, London, Schweich Lectures on Biblical Archaeology Series, 1944). Repr. of 1948 ed. 21.00 (ISBN 0-317-15908-9). Kraus Repr.

Driver, G. R., tr. see Nestorius Patriarch Of Constantinople.

Driver, Godfrey. Semitic Writing: From Pictograph to Alphabet. 3rd ed. (Schweich Lectures). (Illus.). 1976. 49.95x (ISBN 0-19-725917-0). Oxford U Pr.

Driver, Harold E. Indians of North America. 2nd rev. ed. LC 79-76207. (Illus.). 1969. 25.00x (ISBN 0-226-16466-7, Phoen); pap. 15.95 (ISBN 0-226-16467-5, P388). U of Chicago Pr.

Driver, Harold E. & Coffin, James L. Classification & Development of North American Indian Cultures: A Statistical Analysis of the Driver-Massey Sample. LC 75-2609. (Transactions Ser: Vol. 65, Pt. 3). (Illus.). 1975. pap. 7.00 (ISBN 0-87169-653-3). Am Philos.

Driver, Harold E. & Driver, Wilhelmine. Ethnography & Acculturation of the Chichimeca-Jonaz of Northeast Mexico. LC 63-62521. (General Publications Ser: Vol. 26). 1963. pap. text ed. 5.50x (ISBN 0-87750-116-5). Res Ctr Lang Semiotic.

Driver, J. E., tr. see Stein, R. A.

Driver, Jessica S. Speak for Yourself. rev. ed. LC 55-11267. (Essentials of Speaking & Reading Aloud Ser.: No. 193-96). (Illus.). 245p. pap. 11.95 (ISBN 0-9614864-0-6). Speak Yourself.

Driver, John. Community & Commitment. LC 76-41463. 96p. 1976. pap. 3.95 (ISBN 0-8361-1802-2). Herald Pr.

--Comunidad y Compromiso. 90p. 1979. pap. 2.95x (ISBN 0-8361-1215-6). Herald Pr.

--Kingdom Citizens. LC 80-16171. 160p. 1980. pap. 6.95 (ISBN 0-8361-1935-5). Herald Pr.

--Kingdom Citizens. LC 80-16171. 160p. 1980. pap. 6.95 (ISBN 0-8361-1935-5). Herald Hse.

Driver, John & Foxall, Gordon. Advertising: Policy & Practice. LC 84-40336. 172p. 1984. 25.00 (ISBN 0-312-00731-0). St Martin.

Driver, John, jt. auth. see Escobar, Samuel.

Driver, Leota S. Fanny Kemble. LC 76-97449. Repr. of 1933 ed. 18.75x (ISBN 0-8371-2697-5, DRF&, Pub. by Negro U Pr). Greenwood.

Driver, R. Ordinary & Delay Differential Equations. LC 76-58452. (Applied Mathematical Sciences Ser.: Vol. 20). 1977. pap. 25.00 (ISBN 0-387-90231-7). Springer-Verlag.

Driver, R., jt. auth. see Annino, R.

Driver, R. D. Why Math? (Undergraduate Texts in Mathematics Ser.). (Illus.). 220p. 1984. 24.00 (ISBN 0-387-90973-7). Springer Verlag.

Driver, Robienetta & Feeley, Mary A. The Revolution in Medical Technology Education. 68p. 1974. 12.75x (ISBN 0-398-02960-1). C C Thomas.

Driver, Rosalind, ed. The Pupil As Scientist? 128p. 1983. pap. 14.00x (ISBN 0-335-10178-X, Pub. by Open Univ Pr). Taylor & Francis.

Driver, S. R. Introduction to the Literature of the Old Testament. 16.50 (ISBN 0-8446-1998-1). Peter Smith.

--Isaiah: His Life & Times. 228p. 1981. Repr. lib. bdg. 20.00 (ISBN 0-89984-158-9). Century Bookbindery.

--Modern Research as Illustrating the Bible. (British Academy, London, Schweich Lectures on Biblical Archaeology, 1908). pap. 19.00 (ISBN 0-317-16233-0). Kraus Repr.

--Notes on the Hebrew Text of Samuel. 1984. 24.95 (ISBN 0-88469-163-2). BMH Bks.

Driver, Tom F. Christ in a Changing World: Toward an Ethical Christology. LC 81-5552. 224p. 1981. 12.95 (ISBN 0-8245-0105-5). Crossroad NY.

--Jean Genet. LC 66-26003. (Essays on Modern Writers Ser.: No. 20). (Orig.). 1966. pap. 2.50 (ISBN 0-231-02942-X). Columbia U Pr.

--Patterns of Grace: Human Experience As Word of God. 214p. 1985. pap. text ed. 9.75 (ISBN 0-8191-4637-4). U Pr of Amer.

--Romantic Quest & Modern Query: A History of the Modern Theater. LC 80-5756. 510p. 1980. lib. bdg. 23.50 (ISBN 0-8191-1217-8); pap. text ed. 12.25 (ISBN 0-8191-1218-6). U Pr of Amer.

--The Sense of History in Greek & Shakespearean Drama. LC 59-15146. 1960. pap. 11.00x (ISBN 0-231-08576-1). Columbia U Pr.

Driver, Walter E. Plastics Chemistry & Technology. LC 78-24011. 1979. 26.50 (ISBN 0-442-22156-8). Van Nos Reinhold.

Driver, Wilhelmine, jt. auth. see Driver, Harold E.

Drivers License Guide Co. Drivers License Guide, 1985. (Illus.). 96p. 1985. pap. 15.95 (ISBN 0-938964-08-9). Drivers License.

--U. S. Identification Manual. (Illus.). 700p. 1985. text ed. 99.50 (ISBN 0-938964-09-7). Drivers License.

Drizari, Nelo. Albanian-English, English-Albanian Dictionary. LC 57-9330. (Albanian & Eng.). 20.00 (ISBN 0-8044-0130-6). Ungar.

Drizd, Terence A., jt. auth. see O'Brien, Richard J.

Drlica, Karl. Understanding DNA & Gene Cloning: A Guide for the Curious. LC 84-3518. 205p. 1984. pap. text ed. 12.50 (ISBN 0-471-87942-8). Wiley.

Drnevich & Gray, eds. Acoustic Emissions in Geotechnical Engineering Practice - STP 750. 218p. 1981. 25.00 (ISBN 0-8031-0788-9, 04-750000-38). ASTM.

Drob, Harold A., jt. auth. see Merrill, Irving R.

Drob, Ralph E. Number Mastery. Smith, Donald E., ed. (Michigan Tracking Ser.). 1974. pap. text ed. 2.45x (ISBN 0-914004-46-8). Ulrich.

Drobena, Thomas J. & Kucharek, Wilma S. Heritage of the Slavs: The Christianization of the Great Moravian Empire. (Illus.). xviii, 174p. 1979. pap. 5.95 (ISBN 0-915887-01-0). Kosovo Pub Co.

Drobni. Surgery of the Intestines. 1975. 35.00 (ISBN 0-9960008-1-X, Pub. by Akademiai Kaido Hungary). Heyden.

Drobni, S. Surgery of the Intestines. 1977. 35.00x (ISBN 963-05-0632-7). Intl Pubns Serv.

Drobnic, Karl, et al. Sci Tech: Reading & Writing the English of Science & Technology. 132p. (Orig.). (gr. 10-12). 1981. pap. text ed. 4.95 (ISBN 0-89285-156-2). English Lang.

Drobnig, Ulrich. American-German Private International Law. LC 79-132281. (Bilateral Studies in Private International Law Ser.: No. 4). 516p. 1972. lib. bdg. 20.00 (ISBN 0-379-11418-6). Oceana.

Drobnik, J., et al. Polymers in Medicine. (Advances in Polymer Science Ser.: Vol. 57). (Illus.). 190p. 1984. 44.00 (ISBN 0-387-12796-8). Springer-Verlag.

Drobot, Eva. Class Acts: Etiquette for Today. 1984. pap. 3.95 (ISBN 0-380-68270-2, 68270-2). Avon.

Drobot, Eve. Class Acts: Etiquette for Today. 160p. 1982. 12.95 (ISBN 0-442-29663-0). Van Nos Reinhold.

Drochner, Karl Heinz & Foehr, Dieter. Eindruecke-Einblicke. 112p. 9.25 (ISBN 3-468-49785-7); Arbeitsbuch 128p. pap. 5.25 (ISBN 3-468-49786-5); Hoertexte und Diktate 24p. 2.75 (ISBN 3-468-49787-3); cassette 14.95 (ISBN 3-468-84765-3). Langenscheidt.

Drochner, Karl-Heinz & Drochner-Kirchberg, Erika, eds. Deutsche Fragen, Texte zur juengsten Vergangenheit. 207p. pap. 9.95 (ISBN 3-468-49460-2). Langenscheidt.

Drochner-Kirchberg, Erika, jt. ed. see Drochner, Karl-Heinz.

Droege, Thomas A. Faith Passages & Patterns. LC 82-48544. (Lead Bks.). 128p. 1983. pap. 4.95 (ISBN 0-8006-1602-2, 1-1602). Fortress.

Droegkamp, Janis & Munger, Fredi. Women Centered Training: Responding to Issues & Ideas for Women in Development. (Illus.). 51p. (Orig.). 1980. pap. 4.00 (ISBN 0-932288-56-1). Ctr Intl Ed U of MA.

Droessler, Judith B. Craniometry & Biological Distance. LC 81-11009. (Research Ser.: No. 1). (Illus.). 270p. 1981. 17.50 (ISBN 0-942118-11-1, E78.13D76); pap. 12.00 (ISBN 0-942118-12-X). Ctr Amer Arche.

Droge & Glander-Bandyk. Woman's Day Book of Calligraphy. 1980. 12.95 (ISBN 0-671-25018-3, 25018). S&S.

Droge, Dennis, jt. auth. see Bandyk-Glander, Janice.

Drogheda, Lord, et al. The Covent Garden Album: Two Hundred Fifty Years of Theatre, Opera & Ballet. 1982. 35.00 (ISBN 0-7100-0880-5); pap. 16.95 (ISBN 0-7100-9336-5). Routledge & Kegan.

Drogin, Marc. Anathema! The History of Book Curses. (Medieval Scribes & Books). (Illus.). 135p. 1983. 15.95 (ISBN 0-8390-0301-3, Allanheld & Schram). Abner Schram Ltd.

--Medieval Calligraphy: Its History & Technique. (Illus.). 1980. 29.50 (ISBN 0-8390-0211-4, Allanheld & Schram). Abner Schram Ltd.

--Medieval Calligraphy: Its History & Technique. 1980. 29.50 (ISBN 0-8390-0211-4, Allanheld & Schram). Rowman & Allanheld.

--Yours Truly, King Arthur: How Medieval People Wrote... & How You Can, Too! LC 79-66643. (Illus.). 95p. 1983. pap. 9.95 (ISBN 0-8008-8766-2, Pentalic). Taplinger.

Droh, R., et al, eds. Anaesthesia: Innovations in Management. (Illus.). 220p. 1985. pap. 31.50 (ISBN 0-387-13961-3). Springer-Verlag.

Drohan, Francis B. Jesus Who? The Greatest Mystery Never Told. LC 84-16654. 270p. 1985. 15.00 (ISBN 0-8022-2475-X). Philos Lib.

Droke, Maxwell. Speaker's Handbook of Humor. LC 56-9669. 1956. 16.95i (ISBN 0-06-110270-9, HarpT). Har-Row.

Drolet, Cindy. Unipix: Universal Language of Pictures. Drolet, Ken, ed. LC 82-90721. (Illus.). 58p. (Orig.). 1982. pap. 8.95 (ISBN 0-9609464-0-3). Imaginart Pr.

Drolet, Ken, ed. see Drolet, Cindy.

Drollet, A., jt. auth. see Viller, M.

Drollinger, William C. Tax Shelters & Tax-Free Income for Everyone. Special Edition ed. LC 81-125456. 1981. 14.95 (ISBN 0-914244-08-6). Epic Pubns.

--Tax Shelters & Tax-Free Income for Everyone, Vol. 1. 4th ed. LC 81-125456. 1981. 21.95 (ISBN 0-914244-04-3). Epic Pubns.

Drollinger, William C. & Drollinger, William C. Jr. Tax Shelters & Tax-Free Income for Everyone, Vol II. 4th ed. LC 81-125456. 1981. 24.95 (ISBN 0-914244-06-X). Epic Pubns.

Drollinger, William C. & Drollinger, William C., Sr. You Are a Money Brain. LC 81-67503. 1981. write for info. (ISBN 0-914244-07-8). Epic Pubns.

Drollinger, William C. Jr., jt. auth. see Drollinger, William C.

Dromey, R. How to Solve It by Computer. 1983. pap. 24.95 (ISBN 0-13-434001-9). P-H.

Dromgoole, Dick, ed. see Stopple, Libby.

Dromgoole, R. H., ed. see McPhillips, Lawrence.

Dromgoole, R. H., ed. see Stopple, Libby.

Dromgoole, Will A. Heart of Old Hickory & Other Stories of Tennessee. LC 72-113658. (Short Story Index Reprint Ser.). 1895. 15.00 (ISBN 0-8369-3387-7). Ayer Co Pubs.

Droms, William C., jt. auth. see Amling, Frederick.

Droms, William G. The Dow Jones-Irwin Mutual Fund Yearbook, 1985. 1985. 35.00 (ISBN 0-87094-633-1). Dow Jones-Irwin.
--Finance & Accounting For Non-Financial Managers. (Illus.). 1983. 17.95 (ISBN 0-201-10359-1). Addison-Wesley.
Droms, William G., jt. auth. see Amling, Frederick.
Dronamraju, K. R., ed. Haldane: The Life & Work of J. B. S. Haldane with Special Reference to India. (Illus.). 224p. 1985. 16.50 (ISBN 0-08-032436-3, Pub by AUP). Pergamon.
Dronberger, Ilse. Political Thought of Max Weber: In Quest of Statesmanship. LC 70-133904. (Orig.). 1971. 39.00x (ISBN 0-89197-349-4); pap. text ed. 9.95x (ISBN 0-89197-350-8). Irvington.
Drone, Eaton S. A Treatise on the Law of Property in Intellectual Productions in Great Britain & the United States. liv, 774p. 1972. Repr. of 1879 ed. lib. bdg. 45.00x (ISBN 0-8377-2027-3). Rothman.
Drone, Jeanette M. Index to Opera, Operetta & Musical Comedy Synopses in Collections & Periodicals. LC 77-25822. 177p. 1978. 17.50 (ISBN 0-8108-1100-6). Scarecrow.
Drongowski, Paul J. A Graphical Engineering Aid for VLSI Systems. Stone, Harold, ed. LC 85-1041. (Computer Science Series: Computer Architecture & Design: No. 4). 226p. 1985. 44.95 (ISBN 0-8357-1656-2). UMI Res Pr.
Dronke, Peter. Medieval Latin & the Rise of the European Love Lyric, 2 Vols. 2nd ed. (Latin). 1968. Set. 63.00x (ISBN 0-19-814346-X). Oxford U Pr.
--Women Writers of the Middle Ages: A Critical Study of Texts from Perpetua (203) to Marguerite Porete (1310) LC 83-7456. 1984. 54.50 (ISBN 0-521-25580-5); pap. 15.95 (ISBN 0-521-27573-3). Cambridge U Pr.
Dronke, Ursula, ed. Poetic Edda Vol. 1: Heroic Poems. 1969. 32.50x (ISBN 0-19-811497-4). Oxford U Pr.
Droogers, Andre. The Dangerous Journey: Symbolic Aspects of Boys' Initiation Among the Wagenia of Kisangani, Zaire. (Change & Continuity in Africa Ser.). 1979. pap. text ed. 23.60x (ISBN 90-279-3357-X). Mouton.
Drooker, Penelope B. Samplers You Can Use. LC 84-80008. (Illus.). 94p. 1984. spiral bdg. 15.00 (ISBN 0-934026-13-0). Interweave.
Droop, M. & Wood, F., eds. Advances in Microbiology of the Sea, Vol. 1. 1968. 50.00 (ISBN 0-12-027801-4). Acad Pr.
Droop, M. R. & Jannasch, H. W., eds. Advances in Aquatic Microbiology, Vol. 1. (Serial Publication Ser.). 1977. 70.00 (ISBN 0-12-003001-2). Acad Pr.
--Advances in Aquatic Microbiology, Vol. 2. LC 76-5988. (Serial Publication Ser.). 1980. 60.00 (ISBN 0-12-003002-0). Acad Pr.
--Advances in Aquatic Microbiology, Vol. 3. (Serial Publication). Date not set. price not set (ISBN 0-12-003003-9). Acad Pr.
Drooyan & Wooton. Intermediate Algebra. 6th ed. 488p. write for info. (ISBN 0-534-01433-X); write for info study guide 263p. Wadsworth Pub.
Drooyan, et al. Essentials of Trigonometry. 4th ed. 385p. 1986. text ed. 26.95 (ISBN 0-02-330570-3). Macmillan.
Drooyan, I. & Hadel, W. Elementary Algebra: Structure & Skills. 5th ed. 351p. 1981. 28.45 (ISBN 0-471-08286-4); student ed. 14.00 (ISBN 0-471-08503-0). Wiley.
Drooyan, Irving & Rosen, William. Elementary Arithmetic: A Problem Solving Approach. 480p. 1985. text ed. 20.95x (ISBN 0-471-80814-8). Wiley.
--Intermediate Algebra: A Guided Wordtext. 656p. 1983. pap. text ed. write for info. (ISBN 0-534-01172-1). Wadsworth Pub.
Drooyan, Irving & Wooton, William. Beginning Algebra: A Modular Approach, 8 Vols. LC 75-29776. Vol. 1. pap. 20.00 (ISBN 0-317-11109-4, 2012437); Vol. 2. pap. 26.00 (ISBN 0-317-11110-8); Vol. 3. pap. 24.30 (ISBN 0-317-11111-6); Vol. 4. pap. 20.30 (ISBN 0-317-11112-4); Vol. 5. pap. 35.80 (ISBN 0-317-11113-2); Vol. 6. pap. 35.80 (ISBN 0-317-11114-0); Vol. 7. pap. 20.50 (ISBN 0-317-11115-9); Vol. 8. pap. 26.50 (ISBN 0-317-11116-7). Bks Demand UMI.
--Beginning Algebra: An Individualized Approach. LC 78-625. 420p. 1978. 29.00x (ISBN 0-471-03877-6). Wiley.
--Elementary Algebra for College Students. 6th ed. LC 83-3556. 432p. 1984. text ed. 28.50 (ISBN 0-471-87387-X); student solution manual 10.50x (ISBN 0-471-88573-8); test avail. (ISBN 0-471-88595-9). Wiley.
--Elementary Algebra with Geometry. 2nd ed. 467p. 1984. text ed. 26.95 (ISBN 0-471-09825-6, Pub by Wiley); write for info. solutions manual (ISBN 0-471-88070-1). Wiley.
Drooyan, Irving, jt. auth. see Carico, Charles C.
Drooyan, Irving, jt. auth. see Hyatt, Herman R.
Drooyan, Irving, et al. Essentials of Trigonometry. 3rd ed. 1981. text ed. 20.95x (ISBN 0-02-330270-4); pap. text ed. write for info. (ISBN 0-02-330280-1). Macmillan.
--Trigonometry: An Analytic Approach. 4th ed. 370p. 1982. text ed. write for info. (ISBN 0-02-330350-6). Macmillan.
--Introductory Algebra: A Guided Worktext. LC 81-99. 410p. 1982. text ed. 30.95 (ISBN 0-471-06318-5); text suppl. avail. (ISBN 0-471-86591-5). Wiley.
Drop, Paul A. Santa Goes to Heaven. 22p. (Orig.). 1985. pap. text ed. 6.95x (ISBN 0-9615147-0-1). Mr Padco Pubns.
Dropkin, Ruth, ed. Changing Schools: Open Corridors & Teaching Centers. 1978. pap. 3.50 (ISBN 0-918374-02-2). Workshop Ctr.
--Cumulative Index to Notes from Workshop Center for Open Education. 1979. pap. 1.00 (ISBN 0-918374-04-9). Workshop Ctr.
--The Teacher As Learner: Highlights of Work at the Center & Summer Institutes. (Illus.). 1977. pap. 3.50 (ISBN 0-918374-15-4). Workshop Ctr.
--Teachers with Children: Curriculum in Open Classrooms. (Illus.). 68p. 1976. pap. 3.50 (ISBN 0-918374-16-2). Workshop Ctr.
Dropkin, Ruth & Tobier, Arthur, eds. Roots of Open Education in America: Reminiscences & Reflections on the Ways Americans Have Educated Themselves, in & Out of Schools. LC 76-53146. (Illus.). 1976. pap. 5.00 (ISBN 0-918374-01-4). Workshop Ctr.
Dropkin, Ruth, jt. ed. see Alberty, Beth.
Dropkin, Victor H. Introduction to Plant Nematology. LC 80-13556. 293p. 1980. 32.50x (ISBN 0-471-05578-6, Pub. by Wiley Interscience). Wiley.
Dropper, G. Outlines of Economic History in the 19th. Century. 1977. lib. bdg. 59.95 (ISBN 0-8490-2396-3). Gordon Pr.
Dror, Yehezkel. Crazy States: A Counterconventional Strategic Problem. LC 80-81613. 1980. Repr. lib. bdg. 22.00 (ISBN 0-527-25140-2). Kraus Repr.
--Policymaking under Adversity. 450p. 1985. 39.95 (ISBN 0-87855-488-2). Transaction Bks.
--Public Policymaking Reexamined. LC 83-351. (Illus.). 415p. 1983. pap. text ed. 19.95x (ISBN 0-87855-928-0). Transaction Bks.
Dror, Yehezkel see Crenshaw, Martha.
Droscher, Elke. The Victorian Sticker Postcard Book. (Illus.). 136p. (Orig.). (gr. k up). pap. 5.95 (ISBN 0-89471-384-1). Running Pr.
--The World of Dolls: A Postcard Book. (Illus.). 176p. (Orig.). (gr. k up). 1985. pap. 5.95 (ISBN 0-89471-383-3). Running Pr.
Droske, Susan C. & Francis, Sally. Pediatric Diagnostic Procedures: With Guidelines for Preparing Children for Clinical Tests. LC 80-22920. 293p. 1981. pap. 18.50x (ISBN 0-471-04928-X, Pub. by Wiley Med). Wiley.
Drosnin, Michael. Citizen Hughes: In His Own Words-How Howard Hughes Tried to Buy America. LC 84-25211. 1985. 18.95 (ISBN 0-03-041846-1). HR&W.
Drossin, Julius, jt. auth. see Martin, William R.
Drossman, Douglas A., ed. Manual of Gastroenterologic Procedures. 214p. 1982. pap. text ed. 16.50 spiral (ISBN 0-89004-790-1). Raven.
Drossman, Evan, jt. ed. see Knappman, Edward W.
Drossman, Melvyn, jt. auth. see Belove, Charles.
Drost, Walter H. David Snedden & Education for Social Efficiency. (Illus.). 254p. 1967. 22.50x (ISBN 0-299-04460-2). U of Wis Pr.
Droste, R. L., jt. ed. see Schiller, E. J.
Drost-Hansen, W., ed. Cell-Associated Water. 1979. 55.00 (ISBN 0-12-222250-4). Acad Pr.
Drotar, David L. Hiking: Pure & Simple. LC 83-51087. (Illus.). 136p. (Orig.). 1984. pap. 7.95 (ISBN 0-913276-47-2). Stone Wall Pr.
--Microsurgery: Revolution in the Operating Room. LC 81-3850. (Illus.). 128p. 1982. 10.95 (ISBN 0-8253-0056-8). Beaufort Bks NY.
Drotar, David L., jt. auth. see Madison, Arnold.
Drotning, Phillip T. Five Hundred Ways for Small Charities to Raise Money. 1981. pap. 16.00 (ISBN 0-686-31964-8). Public Serv Materials.
--You Can Buy a Home Now. 160p. 1982. 11.95 (ISBN 0-8092-5735-1). Contemp Bks.
Drotning, Phillip T. & Smith, Wesley. Up from the Ghetto. 1971. pap. 0.95 (ISBN 0-671-47838-9). WSP.
Drotning, Phillip T., jt. auth. see Kaplan, Melvin J.
Drott, M. Carl, jt. auth. see Mancall, Jacqueline C.
Drotts, Wallace D. Take up Your Cross: Invitation to Abundant Life. LC 84-61032. 80p. (Orig.). 1985. pap. 3.95 (ISBN 0-8091-2655-9). Paulist Pr.
Drouet, F. Revision of the Nostocaceae with Constricted Trichomes. (Beihefte zur Nova Hedwigia: No. 57). (Illus.). 1978. text ed. 35.00 (ISBN 3-7682-5457-7). Lubrecht & Cramer.
--Revision of the Stigonemataceae: With a Summary of the Classification of Blue-Green Algae. (Nova Hedwigia Beiheft: No. 66). (Illus.). 300p. 1981. lib. bdg. 42.00x (ISBN 3-7682-5466-6). Lubrecht & Cramer.
Drouet, Francais. Summary of the Classification of Blue-Green Algae. (Illus.). 1981. pap. text ed. 7.00x (ISBN 3-7682-1293-9). Lubrecht & Cramer.
Drouet, Francis. Revision of Nostocaceae with Cylindrical Trichomes. new ed. (Illus.). 256p. 1973. 18.95x (ISBN 0-02-844060-9). Hafner.
--Revision of the Classification of the Oscillatoriaceae. (Monograph: No. 15). (Illus.). 370p. 1968. lib. bdg. 18.00 (ISBN 0-910006-23-7). Acad Nat Sci Phila.
Drought, A. Bernard, ed. see Teller, Edward, et al.
Droughton, John, jt. auth. see Stamper, Eugene.
Drouillard, Anne & Keefe, William F. How to Earn Twenty-Five Thousand Dollars a Year or More Typing at Home. rev. ed. LC 73-80454. 176p. 1980. 9.95 (ISBN 0-8119-0222-6). Fell.
Drouillard, Richard, jt. auth. see Raynor, Sherry.
Drouillard, T. F. Acoustic Emission: A Bibliography with Abstracts. LC 79-268. (IFI Data Base Library). 805p. 1979. 135.00x (ISBN 0-306-65179-3, IFI Plenum). Plenum Pub.
Drouin, R., jt. ed. see Knystautas, E. J.
Drouse Assoc. Staff. CAD on a Personal Computer: Technology & Applications, Software & Systems, Suppliers & Costs. 85p. 1985. 179.00 (ISBN 0-914849-03-4). TBC Inc.
Drov, Yehezkel, jt. auth. see Akzin, Benjamin.
Drover, jt. auth. see Dawson.
Drover, Glenn, jt. ed. see Moscovitch, Allan.
Drowatzky, John & Armstrong, Charles. Physical Education: Career Perspectives & Professional Foundations. (Illus.). 400p. 1984. 23.95 (ISBN 0-13-668285-5). P-H.
Drowatzky, John N. Legal Issues in Sport & Physical Education Management. Zeigler, Earle F., ed. (Monograph Series on Sport & Physical Education Management). (Illus.). 44p. 1984. pap. text ed. 3.20x (ISBN 0-87563-253-X). Stipes.
--Motor Learning: Principles & Practices. 2nd ed. LC 80-69551. 1981. text ed. 14.95x (ISBN 0-8087-0495-8). Burgess.
--Physical Education for the Mentally Retarded. LC 70-157467. (Health Education, Physical Education, & Recreational Ser.). (Illus.). pap. 50.30 (ISBN 0-317-09951-5, 2055419). Bks Demand UMI.
Drower, Ethel S. By Tigris & Euphrates. LC 77-87642. (Illus.). Repr. of 1923 ed. 29.50 (ISBN 0-404-16424-2). AMS Pr.
--Folk-Tales of Iraq. LC 78-63226. (Illus.). 30.50 (ISBN 0-404-16165-0). AMS Pr.
--Peacock Angel: Being Some Account of Votaries of a Secret Cult & Their Sanctuaries. LC 77-87643. Repr. of 1941 ed. 20.00 (ISBN 0-404-16425-0). AMS Pr.
--Water into Wine: A Study of Ritual Idiom in the Middle East. LC 77-87663. Repr. of 1956 ed. 23.50 (ISBN 0-404-16401-3). AMS Pr.
Drower, G. M. Neil Kinnock: The Path to Leadership. (Illus.). 176p. 1984. pap. 9.95x (ISBN 0-297-78522-2, GWN 05238, Pub. by Weidenfeld & Nicolson England). Biblio Dist.
Drown, Ruth B. Wisdom from Atlantis. 153p. 1981. pap. 8.00 (ISBN 0-686-78074-4, SB-098). Sun Pub.
Drown, Simeon DeWitt. The Peoria Directory for 1844. 1978. Repr. of 1844 ed. 6.95x (ISBN 0-930358-02-3). Spoon River.
Drowner, Margaret S. Flinders Petrie: A Life in Archaeology. (Illus.). 512p. 1985. 52.00 (ISBN 0-575-03667-2, Pub. by Gollancz England). David & Charles.
Drowning, Niki. Two Novels: No More Pricking Brier & the Dew of Thy Youth. 1984. 12.95 (ISBN 0-533-06154-7). Vantage.
Droz, Eugene, jt. auth. see Klebs, Arnold C.
Droz, Eugenie, et al, eds. Trois Chansonniers Francais Du XV Siecle. (Music Reprint Ser.). 1978. Repr. of 1927 ed. lib. bdg. 32.50 (ISBN 0-306-77561-1). Da Capo.
Droz, Jacques. Europe Between Revolutions, Eighteen Fifteen to Eighteen Forty-Eight. LC 80-66909. (History of Europe Ser.; Cornell Paperbacks Ser.). 288p. 1980. pap. 6.95x (ISBN 0-8014-9206-8). Cornell U Pr.
Droz, M., jt. auth. see Gunton, J. D.
Droz, R. & Rahmy, M. Understanding Piaget. Diamanti, Joyce, tr. from Fr. LC 75-18509. Orig. Title: Lire Piaget. 212p. 1976. text ed. 22.50 (ISBN 0-8236-6690-5). Intl Univs Pr.
Drozd, J. Chemical Derivatization in Gas Chromatography. (Journal of Chromatography Library: Vol. 19). 232p. 1981. 57.50 (ISBN 0-444-41917-9). Elsevier.
Drozd, L. & Seibicke, W. Deutsche Fach und Wissenschaftssprache. Bestandsaufnahme Theorie Geschichte. x, 207p. (Ger.). 1973. 14.00x (ISBN 3-87097-058-8, Pub. by O Branstetter W Germany). Benjamins North Am.
Drozd, Taras, tr. see Olhovych, Orest.
Drozd, V. N. & Zefirov, N. S. Sigmatropic Additions & Cyclosubstitutions in Five-Membered Heterocyclic Compounds Containing Exocyclic Double Bonds. (Sulfur Reports Ser.). 45p. 1981. flexicover 16.50 (ISBN 3-7186-0081-1). Harwood Academic.
Drozda, Tom, ed. Manufacturing Engineering Reviews Grinding. LC 82-50273. 208p. 1982. text ed. 18.50 (ISBN 0-87263-082-X). SME.
Drozdov, V. & Korkeshkin, A. The Soviet Soldier. 180p. 1980. pap. 4.45 (ISBN 0-8285-1666-9, Pub. by Progress Pubs USSR). Imported Pubns.
Drozdowski, Marian M. Ignacy Jan Paderewski: A Political Biography in Outline. (Illus.). 288p. 1983. pap. 7.50 (ISBN 83-223-1771-9). Hippocrene Bks.
Droze, Wilmon H. High Dams & Slack Waters: TVA Rebuilds a River. LC 65-14533. pap. 46.00 (ISBN 0-317-09202-2, 2007179). Bks Demand UMI.
Dr. Seuss. And to Think That I Saw It on Mulberry Street. LC 37-38873. (gr. k-3). 6.95 (ISBN 0-8149-0387-8). Vanguard.
--Bartholomew & the Oobleck. (Illus.). (gr. k-3). 1949. 6.95 (ISBN 0-394-80075-3, BYR); PLB 6.99 (ISBN 0-394-90075-8); pap. 2.95 (ISBN 0-394-84539-0). Random.
--Cat in the Hat. LC 56-5470. (Illus.). (gr. 1-2). 1957. 4.95 (ISBN 0-394-80001-X); PLB 5.99 (ISBN 0-394-90001-4). Beginner.
--Cat in the Hat Comes Back. LC 58-9017. (Illus.). (gr. k-3). 1958. 4.95 (ISBN 0-394-80002-8); PLB 5.99 (ISBN 0-394-90002-2). Beginner.
--The Cat in the Hat in English & Spanish. Rivera, Carlos, tr. (Spanish Beginner Bks: No. 1). (gr. 1-2). 1967. 6.95 (ISBN 0-394-81626-9). Beginner.
--Cat in the Hat Songbook. LC 67-21921. (Illus.). (gr. k-3). 1967. Beginner.
--The Cat's Quizzer. LC 76-753. (A Big Beginner Bk). (Illus.). (gr. k-4). 1976. 4.95 (ISBN 0-394-83296-5); PLB 5.99 (ISBN 0-394-93296-X). Beginner.
--Did I Ever Tell You How Lucky You Are? (Illus.). (ps-4). 1973. (BYR); PLB 7.99 (ISBN 0-394-92719-2). Random.
--Dr. Seuss's ABC. LC 63-9810. (Illus.). (gr. k-3). 1963. 4.95 (ISBN 0-394-80030-3); PLB 5.99 (ISBN 0-394-90030-8). Beginner.
--Dr. Seuss's Sleep Book. (Illus.). (gr. 3-7). 1962. 6.95 (ISBN 0-394-80091-5, BYR); PLB 6.99 (ISBN 0-394-90091-X). Random.
--Five Hundred Hats of Bartholomew Cubbins. LC 38-30610. (Illus.). (gr. k-3). 6.95 (ISBN 0-8149-0388-6). Vanguard.
--Foot Book. LC 68-28462. (Bright & Early Bk.). (Illus.). (ps-1). 1968. 4.95 (ISBN 0-394-80937-8, BYR); PLB 5.99 (ISBN 0-394-90937-2). Random.
--Fox in Socks. LC 65-10484. (Illus.). (gr. k-3). 1965. 4.95 (ISBN 0-394-80038-9); PLB 5.99 (ISBN 0-394-90038-3). Beginner.
--Great Day for up! LC 74-5517. (Bright & Early Bk.). (Illus.). 36p. (ps-1). 1974. 4.95 (ISBN 0-394-82913-1, BYR); PLB 5.99 (ISBN 0-394-92913-6). Random.
--Green Eggs & Ham. LC 60-13493. (Illus.). (gr. 1-2). 1960. 4.95 (ISBN 0-394-80016-8); PLB 5.99 (ISBN 0-394-90016-2). Beginner.
--Happy Birthday to You. (Illus.). (gr. 1-5). 1959. 6.95 (ISBN 0-394-80076-1, BYR); PLB 7.99 (ISBN 0-394-90076-6). Random.
--Hop on Pop. LC 63-9810. (gr. 1-2). 1963. 4.95 (ISBN 0-394-80029-X); PLB 5.99 (ISBN 0-394-90029-4). Beginner.
--Horton Hatches the Egg. (Illus.). (gr. k-3). 1940. 7.95 (ISBN 0-394-80077-X, BYR); PLB 7.99 (ISBN 0-394-90077-4). Random.
--Horton Hears a Who. (Illus.). (gr. k-3). 1954. 7.95 (ISBN 0-394-80078-8, BYR); PLB 7.99 (ISBN 0-394-90078-2). Random.
--How the Grinch Stole Christmas. (Illus.). (gr. k-3). 1957. 5.95 (ISBN 0-394-80079-6, BYR); PLB 6.99 (ISBN 0-394-90079-0). Random.
--Hunches in Bunches. (Illus.). 48p. (gr. 1-5). 1982. PLB 7.99 (ISBN 0-394-95502-1); pap. 5.95 (ISBN 0-394-85502-7). Random.
--I Can Lick Thirty Tigers Today! & Other Stories. LC 71-86940. (Dr. Seuss Paperback Classics Ser.). (Illus.). 64p. (gr. k-3). 1980. pap. 3.95 (ISBN 0-394-84543-9). Random.
--I Can Lick Thirty Tigers Today & Other Stories. (Illus.). (gr. k-3). 1969. 7.95 (ISBN 0-394-80094-X, BYR); PLB 7.99 (ISBN 0-394-90094-4). Random.
--I Can Read with My Eyes Shut! LC 78-7193. (A Beginner Bk.). (Illus.). (gr. 1-3). 1978. 4.95 (ISBN 0-394-83912-9); PLB 5.99 (ISBN 0-394-93912-3). Beginner.
--I Had Trouble in Getting to Solla Sollew. LC 65-23994. (Dr. Seuss Paperback Classics Ser.). (Illus.). 64p. (gr. k-3). 1980. pap. 2.95 (ISBN 0-394-84542-0). Random.
--I Had Trouble in Getting to Solla Sollew. (Illus.). (ps-3). 1965. (BYR); PLB 7.99 (ISBN 0-394-90092-8). Random.
--If I Ran the Circus. LC 56-9469. (Dr. Seuss Paperback Classics Ser.). (Illus.). 64p. (gr. k-3). 1980. pap. 3.95 (ISBN 0-394-84546-3). Random.
--If I Ran the Circus. (Illus.). (gr. k-3). 1956. 5.95 (ISBN 0-394-80080-X, BYR); PLB 7.99 (ISBN 0-394-90080-4). Random.
--If I Ran the Zoo. LC 50-10185. (Illus.). 64p. (gr. k-3). 1980. pap. 2.95 (ISBN 0-394-84545-5). Random.
--If I Ran the Zoo. (Illus.). (gr. k-3). 1950. 7.95 (ISBN 0-394-80081-8, BYR); PLB 7.99 (ISBN 0-394-90081-2). Random.
--King's Stilts. (Illus.). (gr. k-3). 1939. 7.95 (ISBN 0-394-80082-6, BYR); PLB 7.99 (ISBN 0-394-90082-0). Random.
--Lorax. (Illus.). 1971. 6.95 (ISBN 0-394-82337-0, BYR); PLB 6.99 (ISBN 0-394-92337-5). Random.
--McElligot's Pool. (Illus.). (gr. k-3). 1947. 7.95 (ISBN 0-394-80083-4, BYR); PLB 7.99 (ISBN 0-394-90083-9). Random.
--Marvin K. Mooney, Will You Please Go Now. (Bright & Early Book Ser: No. 13). (Illus.). (ps-2). 1972. 4.95 (ISBN 0-394-82490-3, BYR); PLB 5.99 (ISBN 0-394-92490-8). Random.
--Mister Brown Can Moo, Can You. (Bright & Early Book Ser). (Illus.). (ps-1). 1970. 4.95 (ISBN 0-394-80622-0, BYR); PLB 5.99 (ISBN 0-394-90622-5). Random.
--My Book About Me. LC 75-85289. (Illus.). (gr. k-4). 1969. 6.95 (ISBN 0-394-80093-1). Beginner.

--Oh, Say Can You Say? LC 78-20716. (Illus.). (gr. 1-4). 1979. 4.95 (ISBN 0-394-84255-3, BYR); PLB 5.99 (ISBN 0-394-94255-8). Beginner.
--Oh! the Thinks You Can Think! LC 75-1602. (ps-1). 1975. 4.95 (ISBN 0-394-83129-2); PLB 5.99 (ISBN 0-394-93129-7). Beginner.
--On Beyond Zebra! LC 55-9321. (Dr. Seuss Paperback Classics Ser.). (Illus.). 64p. (gr. k-3). 1980. pap. 3.95 (ISBN 0-394-84541-2). Random.
--On Beyond Zebra. (ps-3). 1955. 7.95 (ISBN 0-394-80084-2, BYR); PLB 7.99 (ISBN 0-394-90084-7). Random.
--One Fish Two Fish Red Fish Blue Fish. LC 60-7180. (Illus.). (gr. 1-2). 1960. 4.95 (ISBN 0-394-80013-3); PLB 5.99 (ISBN 0-394-90013-8). Beginner.
--Scrambled Eggs Super! LC 53-5013. (Dr. Seuss Paperback Classics Ser.). (Illus.). 64p. (gr. k-3). 1980. pap. 3.95 (ISBN 0-394-84544-7). Random.
--Scrambled Eggs Super. (Illus.). (gr. k-3). 1953. PLB 7.99 (ISBN 0-394-90085-5). Random.
--Sneetches & Other Stories. (Illus.). (gr. k-4). 1961. 6.95 (ISBN 0-394-80089-3, BYR); PLB 7.99 (ISBN 0-394-90089-8). Random.
--There's a Wocket in My Pocket! LC 74-5516. (Bright & Early Book Ser). (Illus.). 36p. (ps-1). 1974. 4.95 (ISBN 0-394-82920-4, BYR); PLB 5.99 (ISBN 0-394-92920-9). Random.
--Thidwick, the Big-Hearted Moose. LC 48-8129. (Dr. Seuss Paperback Classics Ser.). (Illus.). 48p. (gr. k-3). 1980. pap. 3.95 (ISBN 0-394-84540-4). Random.
--Thidwick: The Big-Hearted Moose. (Illus.). (gr. k-3). 1948. 6.95 (ISBN 0-394-80086-9, BYR); PLB 7.99 (ISBN 0-394-90086-3). Random.
--Yertle the Turtle & Other Stories. (Illus.). (gr. k-3). 1958. 8.95 (ISBN 0-394-80087-7, BYR); PLB 6.99 (ISBN 0-394-90087-1). Random.

Dr. Seuss, see Seuss, Dr.

Dru, Alexander, ed. & tr. see Kierkegaard, Soren.

Dru, Alexander, tr. see Burckhardt, Jakob.

Druash, Denis. Alapin's Opening. 50p. (Orig.). 1984. pap. 3.50 (ISBN 0-931462-33-9). Chess Ent Inc.

Drub, Gendun. Bridging the Sutras & Tantras. Mullin, Glen H., tr. from Tibetan. LC 81-86166. 176p. 1982. lib. bdg. 14.00 (ISBN 0-937938-12-2); pap. 9.95 (ISBN 0-937938-11-4). Snow Lion.

Druck, Ken & Simmons, Jim. Secrets Men Keep. LC 85-6744. 216p. 1985. 15.95 (ISBN 0-385-23092-3). Doubleday.

Druck, Kitty, jt. ed. see Groth, Patricia C.

Druck, Mark. The Final Mission. (Orig.). 1978. pap. 2.25 (ISBN 0-89083-386-9). Zebra.

Drucker, D. B. Microbiological Applications of Gas Chromatography. LC 80-40447. 300p. 1981. 110.00 (ISBN 0-521-22365-2). Cambridge U Pr.

Drucker, Daniel. Exceptional Lie Algebras & the Structure of Hermitian Symmetric Spaces. LC 78-15619. (Memoirs: No. 208). 207p. 1982. pap. 18.00 (ISBN 0-8218-2208-X). Am Math.

Drucker, Daniel C. & Gilman, J. J., eds. Fracture of Solids: Proceedings of an International Conference, Maple Valley, Washington, August 21-24, 1962. LC 63-13590. (Metallurgical Society Conferences Ser.: Vol. 20). pap. 160.00 (ISBN 0-317-11259-7, 2001508). Bks Demand UMI.

Drucker, H. M., ed. Multi-Party Britain. LC 79-52940. (Praeger Special Studies). 256p. 1980. 36.95 (ISBN 0-03-053446-1). Praeger.

Drucker, Harvey & Wildung, Raymond E., eds. Biological Implications of Metals in the Environment: Proceedings. LC 77-1039. (ERDA Symposium Ser.). 692p. 1977. pap. 25.25 (ISBN 0-87079-104-4, CONF-750929); microfiche 4.50 (ISBN 0-87079-149-4, CONF-750929). DOE.

Drucker, Henry, et al, eds. Developments in British Politics. LC 83-8642. 290p. 1983. 25.00 (ISBN 0-312-19745-4). St Martin.

Drucker, Henry M. & Brown, Gordon. The Politics of Nationalism & Devolution. LC 79-41025. pap. 36.00 (ISBN 0-317-27702-2, 2025219). Bks Demand UMI.

Drucker, Henry M. & Clarke, Michael G., eds. The Scottish Government Year Book, 1978. 208p. 1978. 22.50x (ISBN 0-87471-878-3). Rowman.

Drucker, Henry M. & Drucker, N. L., eds. The Scottish Government Yearbook, 1979. 269p. 1978. 27.50x (ISBN 0-8476-6114-8). Rowman.

Drucker, Howard. The Organization & Management of the Resource Room: A Cookbook Approach. (Illus.). 184p. 1976. 19.75x (ISBN 0-398-03538-5). C C Thomas.

Drucker, Lucy see Steel, David & Steel, Judith.

Drucker, Malka. Celebrating Life: Jewish Rites of Passage. LC 84-4684. (Illus.). 112p. (gr. 5 up). 1984. reinforced bdg. 11.95 (ISBN 0-8234-0539-7). Holiday.
--Hanukkah: Eight Nights, Eight Lights. LC 80-15852. (A Jewish Holidays Book). (Illus.). 96p. (gr. 5 up). 1980. reinforced bdg. 11.95 (ISBN 0-8234-0377-7). Holiday.
--Passover: A Season of Freedom. LC 80-8810. (Jewish Holidays Bks.). (Illus.). 96p. (gr. 5 up). 1981. reinforced bdg. 10.95 (ISBN 0-8234-0389-0). Holiday.
--Rosh Hashanah & Yom Kippur: Sweet Beginnings. LC 81-2928. (A Jewish Holidays Bk.). (Illus.). 96p. (gr. 5 up). 1981. reinforced bdg. 8.95 (ISBN 0-8234-0427-7). Holiday.
--Shabbat: A Peaceful Island (a Jewish Holidays Book) LC 83-7900. (Illus.). 96p. (gr. 5up). 1983. reinforced bdg. 11.95 (ISBN 0-8234-0500-1). Holiday.
--Sukkot: A Time to Rejoice. LC 82-80814. (A Jewish Holidays Bk.). (Illus.). 96p. (gr. 5 up). 1982. Reinforced bdg. 10.95 (ISBN 0-8234-0466-8). Holiday.

Drucker, Malka & Foster, George. The George Foster Story. rev. ed. LC 80-11437. (Illus.). 128p. (gr. 5 up). 1980. 8.95 (ISBN 0-8234-0413-7). Holiday.

Drucker, Malka & James, Elizabeth. Series TV: How a Show Is Made. LC 83-2119. (Illus.). 112p. (gr. 4up). 1983. 11.95 (ISBN 0-89919-142-8, Clarion). HM.

Drucker, Mark, ed. Urban Decision Making...a Guide to Information Sources. LC 80-19252. (Urban Studies Information Guide Series. Part of the Gale Information Guide Library: Vol. 13). 200p. 1981. 60.00x (ISBN 0-8103-1481-9). Gale.

Drucker, N. L., jt. ed. see Drucker, Henry M.

Drucker, Peter. People & Performance: The Best of Peter Drucker on Management. 1977. pap. text ed. 14.50 scp (ISBN 0-06-166400-6, HarpC). Har-Row.

Drucker, Peter F. Adventures of a Bystander. LC 78-2120. 1979. 14.37i (ISBN 0-06-011101-1, HarpT). Har-Row.
--Age of Discontinuity. 1978. pap. 8.95xi (ISBN 0-06-131973-2, TB1973, Torch). Har-Row.
--Age of Discontinuity: Guidelines to Our Changing Society. LC 68-28192. 1969. 14.37i (ISBN 0-06-011093-7, HarpT). Har-Row.
--America's Next Twenty Years. LC 72-6759. (Essay Index Reprint Ser.). 1972. Repr. of 1957 ed. 16.00 (ISBN 0-8369-7267-8). Ayer Co Pubs.
--The Changing World of the Executive. LC 81-52566. 288p. 1982. 18.95 (ISBN 0-8129-0932-1). Times Bks.
--The Changing World of the Executive. LC 84-40427. 296p. 1985. pap. 9.95 (ISBN 0-8129-1165-2). Times Bks.
--The Concept of the Corporation. LC 72-74. (John Day Bk.). 352p. 1972. 13.41i (ISBN 0-381-98093-6, A16190). T Y Crowell.
--Concept of the Corporation. 1983. pap. 3.95 (ISBN 0-451-62197-2, ME2197, Ment). NAL.
--Effective Executive. LC 67-11341. 1967. 14.37i (ISBN 0-06-031825-2, HarpT). Har-Row.
--The Effective Executive. LC 84-48156. 192p. 1985. pap. 6.68i (ISBN 0-06-091209-X, CN1209, CN). Har-Row.
--The Future of Industrial Man: A Conservative Approach. LC 77-28895. 1978. Repr. of 1942 ed. lib. bdg. 22.75x (ISBN 0-313-20227-3, DRFI). Greenwood.
--Innovation & Entrepreneurship: Practice & Principles. LC 84-48593. 256p. 1985. 19.95 (ISBN 0-06-015428-4, HarpT). Har-Row.
--An Introductory View of Management. 1978. text ed. 25.50 scp (ISBN 0-06-166402-2, HarpC); scp casebk 13.95 (ISBN 0-06-166403-0); inst. manual avail. (ISBN 0-06-166404-9). Har-Row.
--The Last of All Possible Worlds: A Novel. LC 81-48034. 288p. 1982. 13.41i (ISBN 0-06-014974-4, HarpT). Har-Row.
--Management. abr. & rev. ed. LC 84-48157. 576p. 1985. pap. 10.53i (ISBN 0-06-091207-3, CN1207, CN). Har-Row.
--Management: Tasks, Practices, Responsibilities. LC 72-79655. 854p. 1974. 23.95i (ISBN 0-06-011092-9, HarpT). Har-Row.
--Managing for Results. LC 64-12670. 1964. 15.34i (ISBN 0-06-031830-9, HarpT). Har-Row.
--Managing in Turbulent Times. LC 79-33389. 1980. 14.37i (ISBN 0-06-011094-5, HarpT). Har-Row.
--Managing in Turbulent Times. LC 79-3389. 266p. 1985. pap. 6.68i (ISBN 0-06-091208-1, CN1208, CN). Har-Row.
--Men, Ideas & Politics. LC 73-138719. 1971. 13.41i (ISBN 0-06-011091-0, HarpT). Har-Row.
--The New Society: The Anatomy of the Industrial Order. LC 81-20312. ix, 356p. 1982. Repr. of 1950 ed. lib. bdg. 25.00x (ISBN 0-313-23359-4, DRNS). Greenwood.
--Practice of Management. LC 54-8946. 1954. 18.22i (ISBN 0-06-011095-3, HarpT). Har-Row.
--Toward the Next Economics & Other Essays. LC 80-8370. 256p. 1981. 14.37i (ISBN 0-06-014828-4, HarpT). Har-Row.
--The Unseen Revolution: How Pension Fund Socialism Came to America. LC 75-34795. 160p. 1976. 12.45i (ISBN 0-06-011097-X, HarpT). Har-Row.

Drucker, Peter F., et al. Power & Democracy in America. D'Antonio, William V. & Ehrlich, Howard J., eds. LC 79-28576. xviii, 181p. 1980. Repr. of 1961 ed. lib. bdg. 22.50x (ISBN 0-313-22319-X, PDAM). Greenwood.

Drucker, Philip. Archaelogical Survey of the Northern Northwest Coast. (Shorey Indian Ser.). (Illus.). 133p. pap. 9.95 (ISBN 0-8466-4061-9, I61). Shorey.
--Cultures of the North Pacific Coast. (Culture Area Studies Ser.). (Illus., Orig.). 1965. pap. text ed. 13.50 scp (ISBN 0-8102-0087-2, HarpC). Har-Row.
--Indians of the Northwest Coast. pap. 4.50 (ISBN 0-385-02443-6, B3, AMS). Natural Hist.
--The Native Brotherhoods: Modern Inter-Tribal Organizations on the Northwest Coast. Repr. of 1958 ed. 29.00x (ISBN 0-403-03657-7). Scholarly.
--The Northern & Central Nootkan Tribes. Repr. of 1951 ed. 39.00 (ISBN 0-403-03666-6). Scholarly.

Drucker, Phillip. Indians of the Northwest Coast. (Illus.). 1963. 4.50 (ISBN 0-385-02443-6). Doubleday.

Drucker, S., jt. auth. see Georgia Technical Research Institute.

Drucker, Saul & Hexter, Maurice-Beck. Children Astray. LC 74-1681. (Children & Youth Ser.: Vol. 28). 450p. 1974. Repr. of 1923 ed. 33.00x (ISBN 0-405-05959-0). Ayer Co Pubs.

Drucker, Trudy, ed. see Lillo, George.

Drucker-Brown, Susan, ed. see Malinowski, Bronislaw.

Drucker-Brown, Susan, ed. see Malinowski, Bronislaw & De La Fuente, Julio.

Drucker- Colin, R. R. & McGaugh, J. L. Neurobiology of Sleep & Memory. 1977. 55.00 (ISBN 0-12-222350-0). Acad Pr.

Drucker-Colin, R. R., jt. ed. see Myers, R. D.

Drucker-Colin, Rene, jt. ed. see Bayon, Alejandro.

Drucker-Colin, Rene, et al, eds. The Functions of Sleep. LC 78-25669. 1979. 40.00 (ISBN 0-12-222340-3). Acad Pr.

Druckman, Daniel, ed. Negotiations: Social-Psychological Perspectives. LC 76-58353. (Illus.). 416p. 1977. 37.50 (ISBN 0-8039-0829-6). Sage.

Druckner, Peter F. The Temptation to Do Good. LC 83-48341. 160p. 1984. 13.94i (ISBN 0-06-015253-2, HarpT). Har-Row.

Druckrey, Timothy & Gillett, Marnie. Reasoned Space. (Illus.). 71p. 1980. pap. 5.00 (ISBN 0-938262-02-5). U Ariz Ctr Photog.

Dructor, Robert M. Guide to Geneological Sources at the Pennsylvania State Archives. (Illus.). 129p. (Orig.). 1980. pap. 5.95 (ISBN 0-89271-011-X). Pa Hist & Mus.

Dructor, Robert M., compiled by. Guide to the Microfilmed Harmony Society Records, 1786-1951 in the Pennsylvania State Archives. 77p. 1983. pap. 3.00 (ISBN 0-89271-025-X). Pa Hist & Mus.

Drud, Arne & Grais, Wafik. Thailand: An Analysis of Structural & Non-Structural Adjustments. LC 82-10890. (World Bank Staff Working Papers: No. 513). (Orig.). 1982. pap. text ed. 5.00 (ISBN 0-8213-0023-7). World Bank.

Drude, O., jt. ed. see Engler, A.

Drude, Oscar. Handbuch der Pflanzengeographie: Handbook of Phytogeography. Egerton, Frank N., 3rd, ed. LC 77-74213. (History of Ecology Ser.). (Illus.). 1978. Repr. of 1890 ed. lib. bdg. 46.50x (ISBN 0-405-10384-0). Ayer Co Pubs.

Drudy, P. J. Agrarian Change & Labour Mobility. 1981. 45.00x (ISBN 0-686-87262-2, Pub. by Geographical Pubns). State Mutual Bk.

Drudy, P. J., ed. Anglo Irish Studies, No. 4. 1979. text ed. 17.50x (ISBN 0-391-01178-2). Humanities.
--Anglo-Irish Studies, No. 3. 1977. text ed. 13.00x (ISBN 0-391-00820-X). Humanities.
--Ireland: Land, Politics & People. LC 81-18044. (Irish Studies: Vol. 2). (Illus.). 250p. 1982. 54.50 (ISBN 0-521-24577-X). Cambridge U Pr.
--Irish Studies, Vol. 1. LC 80-40084. 192p. 1981. 34.50 (ISBN 0-521-23336-4). Cambridge U Pr.

Drue, Thomas. Bloody Banquet. (Tudor Facsimile Texts. Old English Plays: N0. 142). Repr. of 1914 ed. 49.50 (ISBN 0-404-53442-2). AMS Pr.

Druee, Hermann. Psychologie Aus Dem Begriff. 1976. 58.40 (ISBN 3-11-004603-2). De Gruyter.

Druesedow, John E., Jr. Library Research Guide to Music: Illustrated Search Strategy & Sources. LC 81-86634. (Library Research Guides Ser.: No. 6). 1982. 19.50 (ISBN 0-87650-138-2); pap. 12.50 (ISBN 0-87650-139-0). Pierian.

Druett, Joan. Exotic Intruders: The Introduction of Plants & Animals into New Zealand. (Illus.). 291p. 1984. 24.95x (ISBN 0-86863-397-6, Pub. by Heinemann Pub New Zealand). Intl Spec Bk.

Druffel, Ann & Marcotte, Armand. The Psychic & the Detective, Vol. 3. (Inner Visions Ser.). 140p. 1984. pap. 7.95 (ISBN 0-917086-53-8). A C S Pubns Inc.

Drug Abuse Council. The Facts About "Drug Abuse". LC 79-54668. (Illus.). 1980. 16.95 (ISBN 0-02-907720-6). Free Pr.

Drugulin, Wilhelm E. Allgemeiner Portrait Katalog. (Ger.). Repr. of 1860 ed. 80.00 (ISBN 3-601-00374-0). Kraus Repr.

Druhe, David N. Soviet Russia & Indian Communism. 1959. 14.95x (ISBN 0-8084-0385-0). New Coll U Pr.

Druick, Douglas & D'Argencourt, Louise, eds. The Other Nineteenth Century: Paintings & Sculpture in the Collection of Mr. & Mrs. Joseph M. Tanebaum. (Illus.). 1978. 29.95 (ISBN 0-88884-348-8, 56451-7, Pub. by Natl Gallery Canada). U of Chicago Pr.

Druist, Miriam. Wildlife on the Farm. 1977. 5.80 (ISBN 0-686-23334-4). Rod & Staff.

Druitt, Herbert. A Manual of Costume As Illustrated by Monumental Brasses. LC 74-126136. (Illus.). 384p. 1970. Repr. of 1906 ed. lib. bdg. 20.00 (ISBN 0-8063-0428-6). Genealog Pub.

Drujan, Boris D. & Laufer, Miguel, eds. The S-Potential. LC 82-20394. (Progress in Clinical & Biological Research Ser.: Vol. 113). 364p. 1982. 60.00 (ISBN 0-8451-0113-7). A R Liss.

Druke, Mary, ed. Iroquois Indians: A Documentary History-Guide to the Mircofilm Collection. 718p. 1985. lib. bdg. 180.00 (ISBN 0-89235-088-1). Res Pubns Conn.

Drukker, J. W., jt. ed. see Wagener, J.

Drukker, Joan, jt. auth. see Knuppel, Robert A.

Drukker, W. & Parsons, F, eds. Replacement of Renal Function by Dialysis. 2nd ed. lib. bdg. 160.00 (ISBN 0-89838-553-9, Pub. by Martinus Nijhoff Netherlands). Kluwer Academic.

Drukker, William, et al, eds. Replacement of Renal Function by Dialysis. (Illus.). 1978. lib. bdg. 115.80 (ISBN 90-247-2042-7, Pub. by Martinus Nijhoff Netherlands); pap. 49.50 (ISBN 0-686-28552-2). Kluwer Academic.

Druks, Herbert. The Failure to Rescue. 1977. 9.50 (ISBN 0-8315-0175-8); pap. 5.95 (ISBN 0-685-87594-6). Speller.
--Jewish Resistance During the Holocaust. LC 83-14. 132p. 1983. text ed. 14.95x (ISBN 0-8290-1295-8). Irvington.
--Not in Vain: A Holocaust Documentary. 125p. 1984. text ed. 14.95x (ISBN 0-8290-1499-3). Irvington.
--Truman & the Russians. 1981. pap. 12.50 (ISBN 0-8315-0183-9). Speller.
--The U. S. & Israel. 1979. pap. 7.95 (ISBN 0-8315-0147-2). Speller.

Druley, Ray M. & Ordway, Gerald L. Toxic Substances Control Act. rev. ed. LC 81-12811. 416p. 1981. pap. 21.00 (ISBN 0-87179-362-8). BNA.

Druley, Ray M., jt. auth. see Cohen, Annette R.

Drullinsky, Rafael. Labiega y el Labrador. Slusa, ed. 72p. (Orig., Span.). 1985. pap. 9.00 (ISBN 0-917129-01-6). SLUSA.

Drum, David J. & Figler, Howard E. Outreach in Counseling: Applying the Growth & Prevention Model in Schools & Colleges. LC 77-8091. 1973. pap. 8.50x (ISBN 0-910328-11-0). Carroll Pr.

Drum, David J. & Knott, J. Eugene. Structured Groups for Facilitating Development: Acquiring Life Skills, Resolving Life Themes, & Making Life Transitions. Walz, Gary & Libby, Benjamin B., eds. LC 77-1947. (New Vistas in Counseling Ser.: Vol. I). 284p. 1977. 24.95 (ISBN 0-87705-308-1). Human Sci Pr.

Drum, Karl. Airpower & Russian Partisan Warfare. LC 68-22553. (German Air Force in World War 2 Ser.). (Illus.). 1968. Repr. of 1962 ed. 13.00 (ISBN 0-405-00041-3). Ayer Co Pubs.

Drum, Priscilla A., jt. ed. see Calfee, Robert C.

Drum, William O., jt. auth. see Clark, James F.

Drumann, W. Die Arbeiter und Communisten in Griechenland und Rom, Nach den Quellen. (Ger.). 1860. text ed. 31.00x (ISBN 90-6090-101-0). Humanities.

Drumheller, Dan. Uncle Dan Drumheller Tells Thrills of Western Trails in 1854. (Illus.). 131p. pap. 4.95 (ISBN 0-8466-0234-2, S234). Shorey.

Drumheller, Sidney J. Handbook of Curriculum Design for Individualized Instruction: A Systems Approach (How to Develop Curriculum Materials from Rigorously Defined Behavioral Objectives). LC 79-122812. 116p. 1971. pap. 24.95 (ISBN 0-87778-004-8). Educ Tech Pubns.
--Teacher's Handbook for a Functional Behavior-Based Curriculum: Communicable Models & Guides for Classroom Use. LC 72-933. 138p. 1972. pap. 16.95 (ISBN 0-87778-036-6). Educ Tech Pubns.

Drumm, D. B. Border War. (Traveler Ser.: No. 6). (Orig.). 1985. pap. 2.50 (ISBN 0-440-10762-8). Dell.
--First, You Fight. (Traveller Ser.: No. 1). 192p. (Orig.). 1984. pap. 2.25 (ISBN 0-440-12551-0). Dell.
--Kingdom Come. (Traveler Ser.: No. 2). (Orig.). 1984. pap. 2.25 (ISBN 0-440-14559-7). Dell.
--The Road Ghost. (Traveler Ser.: No. 7). (Orig.). 1985. pap. 2.50 (ISBN 0-440-17469-4). Dell.
--Road War. (Traveler Ser.: No. 5). (Orig.). 1985. pap. 2.25 (ISBN 0-440-17471-6). Dell.
--The Stalkers. (Traveler Ser.: No. 3). 176p. (Orig.). 1984. pap. 2.25 (ISBN 0-440-18107-0). Dell.
--Terminal Road. (Traveler Ser.: No. 8). (Orig.). 1986. pap. 2.50 (ISBN 0-440-18651-X). Dell.
--To Kill a Shadow. (Traveler Ser.: No. 4). (Orig.). 1984. pap. 2.25 (ISBN 0-440-18705-2). Dell.

Drumm, David E. The Computer in Training & Development. (Illus.). 176p. 1985. pap. 25.00 (ISBN 0-934634-77-7). Intl Human Res.

Drumm, Stella M., ed. see Magoffin, Susan S.

Drummond. Pascal Supplement. 2nd ed. 1985. write for info. (ISBN 0-07-054716-5). McGraw.
--The Western Hemisphere. (Our World Today Ser.). (gr. 5-8). 1978. text ed. 20.80 (ISBN 0-205-05856-6, 7758561); tchr's guide 24.40 (ISBN 0-205-05857-4, 775857). Allyn.

Drummond, jt. ed. see Freestone, John.

Drummond, A. H., Jr. Complete Guide to Sailing. 1980. pap. 4.95 (ISBN 0-346-12400-X). Cornerstone.

Drummond, A. J. & Thekaekara, M. P. The Extraterrestrial Solar Spectrum. 1973. pap. text ed. 12.00 (ISBN 0-915414-43-0). Inst Environ Sci.

Drummond, A. J. & Thekaekara, M. P., eds. The Extraterrestrial Solar Spectrum. 169p. non-members 12.00 (ISBN 0-915414-43-0); member 9.60 (ISBN 0-317-36254-2). Inst Environ Sci.

Drummond, A. M. & Coles-Mogford, A. M. Applied Typing. 4th ed. 240p. 1983. write for info. (ISBN 0-07-084650-2). McGraw.

Drummond, A. M. & Gard, Robert E., eds. The Lake Guns of Seneca & Cayuga & Eight Other Plays of Upstate New York. LC 72-86786. (Empire Historical Publications Ser: No. 98). 288p. 1972. Repr. of 1942 ed. 21.00 (ISBN 0-8046-8098-1). Friedman.

Drummond, Alfred & Shiffman, Yvette. Saving Homes for the Poor: Low Income Tenants Can Own Their Apartments (with Case Summaries) 21p. (Orig.). 1984. pap. 2.00 (ISBN 0-88156-017-0). Comm Serv Soc NY.

Drummond, Andrew H. American Opera Librettos. LC 72-8111. 1973. 15.00 (ISBN 0-8108-0553-7). Scarecrow.

Drummond, Andrew L. The Churches in English Fiction. 1950. 30.00 (ISBN 0-8495-6277-5). Arden Lib.

Drummond, Ann E., jt. auth. see Clifford, Margaret A.

Drummond, Anthony, ed. see Schleit, Phillip.

Drummond, Anthony, ed. see Weeks, Christopher.

Drummond, Audrey. Honor Thy Womanself. 1982. pap. 7.50 (ISBN 0-933840-12-8). Unitarian Univ.

Drummond, David A. & Perkins, G. Dictionary of Russian Obscenities. rev. ed. 79p. (Rus. & Eng.). 1980. pap. text ed. 3.50 (ISBN 0-933884-17-6). Berkeley Slavic.

Drummond, David D. Today We Think of Our Tomorrows. 1945. 2.00 (ISBN 0-685-09013-2). Dietz.

Drummond, Don & Wignell, Edna. Reading: A Source Book. LC 79-670405. (Orig.). 1979. pap. text ed. 13.50x (ISBN 0-435-10261-3). Heinemann Ed.

Drummond, Donald. Mountain. LC 74-150763. 63p. 1971. 5.95 (ISBN 0-8040-0519-2, 82-72569, Pub. by Swallow); pap. 3.25 (ISBN 0-8040-0619-9, 82-72577, Pub. by Swallow). Ohio U Pr.

Drummond, Donald F. No Moat, No Castle. LC 73-179801. (New Poetry Ser.). Repr. of 1949 ed. 16.00 (ISBN 0-404-56001-6). AMS Pr.

--Passing of American Neutrality, Nineteen Thirty-Seven to Nineteen Forty-One. LC 68-54416. (Illus.). 1968. Repr. of 1955 ed. lib. bdg. 18.25x (ISBN 0-8371-0394-0, DRAN). Greenwood.

Drummond, Emma. Beyond All Frontiers. 472p. 1983. 13.95 (ISBN 0-312-07773-4). St Martin.

--Beyond All Frontiers. 448p. 1985. pap. 3.95 (ISBN 0-312-90077-5). St Martin.

--Forget the Glory. 480p. 1985. 16.95 (ISBN 0-312-29892-7). St Martin.

--Scarlet Shadows. 1978. pap. 2.25 (ISBN 0-440-17812-6). Dell.

Drummond, G. I., et al, eds. see International Conference on Cyclic Amp, 2nd, July, 1974.

Drummond, George I. Cyclic Nucleotides in the Nervous System. 135p. 1984. pap. text ed. 19.00 (ISBN 0-88167-015-4). Raven.

Drummond, Gordon D. The German Social Democrats in Opposition, 1949-1960. LC 82-2731. 384p. 1982. 27.50x (ISBN 0-8061-1730-3). U of Okla Pr.

Drummond, H. J., compiled by. A Short-Title Catalogue of Books Printed on the Continent of Europe, Fifteen Hundred to Sixteen Hundred, in Aberdeen University Library. 1979. text ed. 69.00x (ISBN 0-19-714106-4). Oxford U Pr.

Drummond, Harold D. & Hughes, James. The Western Hemisphere. (gr. 7-12). 1982. 20.80 (ISBN 0-205-07666-1, 7776667); tchr's ed. 24.40 (ISBN 0-205-07667-X, 7776675); wkbk. 6.40 (ISBN 0-205-07668-8, 7776683); tchr's ed. wkbk. 7.84 (ISBN 0-205-07669-6, 7776691). Allyn.

Drummond, Harold D. & Hughes, James W. The Eastern Hemisphere. LC 77-76624. (Geography Drummond Ser.). (gr. 7-12). 1982. 20.80 (ISBN 0-205-07662-9, 77762); tchr's ed. 24.40 (ISBN 0-205-07663-7, 7776632); wkbk. 6.40 (ISBN 0-205-07664-5, 7776640); tchr's ed. wkbk. 7.84 (ISBN 0-205-07665-3, 7776659). Allyn.

--The Eastern Hemisphere. (Our World Today Ser.). (gr. 7-12). 1980. text ed. 20.80 (ISBN 0-205-06627-5, 7766270); 24.40 (ISBN 0-205-06628-3, 776628); wkbk 6.40 (ISBN 0-205-06629-1, 776629). Allyn.

--A Journey Through Many Lands. (Our World Today Ser.). (gr. 5-8). 1981. text ed. 18.44 (ISBN 0-205-07196-1, 7771967); tchr's guide 21.72 (ISBN 0-205-07197-X, 777197); wkbk. 6.40 (ISBN 0-205-07198-8, 777198). Allyn.

--Journeys Through the Americas. (Our World Today Ser.). (gr. 5-8). 1981. text ed. 18.44 (ISBN 0-205-07200-3, 7772009); tchr's guide 21.72 (ISBN 0-205-07202-X, 777202); wkbk. 6.40 (ISBN 0-205-07201-1, 777201). Allyn.

Drummond, Harold P. Attempted Suicide: Guidebook for Medicine, Reference & Research. LC 83-46100. 150p. 1985. 29.95 (ISBN 0-88164-132-4); pap. 21.95 (ISBN 0-88164-133-2). ABBE Pubs Assn.

--Psychology of Attempted Suicide: A Medical Subject Analysis with Reference Bibliography. 150p. (Orig.). 1986. 29.95 (ISBN 0-88164-434-X); pap. 21.95 (ISBN 0-88164-435-8). ABBE Pubs Assn.

--Sex Offenses: Medical & Psychological Subject Analysis with Research Index & Bibliography. LC 84-45994. 150p. 1985. 29.95 (ISBN 0-88164-310-6); pap. 21.95 (ISBN 0-88164-311-4). ABBE Pubs Assn.

--Sexual Deviations Paraphilias: Medical Analysis Index with Research Bibliography. LC 85-47570. 150p. 1985. 29.95 (ISBN 0-88164-314-9); pap. 21.95 (ISBN 0-88164-315-7). ABBE Pubs Assn.

Drummond, Helga, tr. see Spuler, Bertold.

Drummond, Henry. The Doctrine of Immortality & the Conquest of Eternal Life. (An Essential Knowledge Library Bk.). (Illus.). 137p. 1983. Repr. of 1886 ed. 77.75 (ISBN 0-89901-102-0). Found Class Reprints.

--The Greatest Thing in the World. Bd. with The Skeleton in the Closet. Darrow, Clarence. pap. 3.00 (ISBN 0-8283-1438-1, IPL). Branden Pub Co.

--Greatest Thing in the World. (Illus.). 1981. gift ed. 4.95 (ISBN 0-915720-52-3). Brownlow Pub Co.

--Greatest Thing in the World. 1959. 3.95 (ISBN 0-399-12828-X, G&D). Putnam Pub Group.

--Greatest Thing in the World. (Inspirational Classic Ser.). 64p. 1968. 6.95 (ISBN 0-8007-1144-0); (Spire Bks). Revell.

--The Greatest Thing in the World. 64p. 1981. pap. 2.95 (ISBN 0-88368-100-5). Whitaker Hse.

--Natural Law in the Spiritual World. 371p. 1981. pap. 18.50 (ISBN 0-89540-082-0, SB-082). Sun Pub.

--Peace Be with You. (Illus.). 1978. 4.95 (ISBN 0-915720-44-2). Brownlow Pub Co.

--The Treatise on Biogenesis by Henry Drummond. (Illus.). 129p. 1982. Repr. of 1886 ed. 79.95 (ISBN 0-89901-069-5). Found Class Reprints.

--Tropical Africa. LC 69-18651. (Illus.). Repr. of 1890 ed. 15.00x (ISBN 0-8371-2266-X, DRT&). Greenwood.

Drummond, Henry, et al. Inspiration Three, Vol. 2: Three Famous Classics in One Book. LC 73-80032. (Pivot Family Reader Ser.). 128p. 1973. pap. 2.50 (ISBN 0-87983-042-5). Keats.

Drummond, Hugh. Dr. Drummond's Spirited Guide to Health Care in a Dying Empire. LC 80-994. 352p. 1980. pap. 3.95 (ISBN 0-394-17674-X, B447, BC). Grove.

Drummond, Ian. The Floating Pound & the Sterling Area, 1931-1939. LC 80-14539. 352p. 1981. 54.50 (ISBN 0-521-23165-5). Cambridge U Pr.

Drummond, J., ed. Onward & Upward: Extracts from the Magazine of the Onward & Upward Association Founded by Lady Aberdeen for the Material, Mental & Moral Elevation of Women. pap. 6.50 (ISBN 0-08-030354-4). Pergamon.

Drummond, James. Via, Veritas, Vita: Lectures on "Christianity in Its Most Simple & Intelligible Form". 2nd ed. LC 77-27160. (Hibbert Lectures: 1894). Repr. of 1895 ed. 25.00 (ISBN 0-404-60412-9). AMS Pr.

Drummond, John. Memoirs of Sir Ewen Cameron. Macknight, James, ed. LC 72-983. (Maitland Club. Glasgow. Publications: No. 59). Repr. of 1842 ed. 45.00 (ISBN 0-404-53049-4). AMS Pr.

Drummond, John D. Opera in Perspective. (Illus.). 369p. 1980. 25.00 (ISBN 0-8166-0848-2). U of Minn Pr.

Drummond, John K. Thy Sting, O' Death: A Matilda Worthing Mystery. 240p. 1985. 14.95 (ISBN 0-312-80419-9). St Martin.

Drummond, June. Drop Dead. rev. ed. 1984. pap. 2.95 (ISBN 0-8027-3089-2). Walker & Co.

--Funeral Urn. (British Mysteries Ser.). 1984. pap. 2.95 (ISBN 0-8027-3048-5). Walker & Co.

--Slowly the Poison. (British Mysteries Ser.). 1983. pap. 2.95 (ISBN 0-8027-3038-8). Walker & Co.

Drummond, Laura W. Youth & Instruction in Marriage & Family Living. LC 74-176731. (Columbia University. Teachers College. Contributions to Education: No. 856). Repr. of 1942 ed. 22.50 (ISBN 0-404-55856-9). AMS Pr.

Drummond, Lewis. Leading Your Church in Evangelism. LC 75-30135. 168p. 1976. pap. 5.50 (ISBN 0-8054-6210-4). Broadman.

--The Life & Ministry of Charles Finney. 272p. 1985. pap. 5.95 (ISBN 0-87123-818-7). Bethany Hse.

Drummond, Lewis A. The Awaking That Must Come. LC 78-59239. 1979. pap. 4.50 (ISBN 0-8054-6535-9). Broadman.

--The Revived Life. LC 82-71217. 1982. pap. 6.50 (ISBN 0-8054-5205-2). Broadman.

Drummond, Lewis A. & Baxter, Paul R. How to Respond to a Skeptic. (Orig.). 1986. pap. 5.95 (ISBN 0-8024-7703-8). Moody.

Drummond, Lorena, ed. see Texas University.

Drummond, M., tr. see Haberlandt, G.

Drummond, M. F. Principles of Economic Appraisal in Health Care. (Illus.). 1980. pap. 15.95x (ISBN 0-19-261273-5). Oxford U Pr.

--Studies in Economic Appraisal in Health Care. 1981. text ed. 35.00x (ISBN 0-19-261274-3). Oxford U Pr.

Drummond, Maldwin & Rodhouse, Paul. The Yachtsman's Naturalist. 1981. 27.00 (ISBN 0-686-72937-4, Pub. by Angus & Robertson). State Mutual Bk.

Drummond, Margaret, jt. auth. see Drillien, Cecil M.

Drummond, Pippa. The German Concerto: Five Eighteenth Century Studies. (Oxford Monographs on Music). (Illus.). 1980. 79.00x (ISBN 0-19-816122-0). Oxford U Pr.

Drummond, Richard H. Toward a New Age in Christian Theology. LC 85-5155. 272p. 1985. pap. 12.95 (ISBN 0-88344-514-X). Orbis Bks.

--Unto the Churches: Jesus Christ, Christianity, & the Edgar Cayce Readings. 1978. pap. 7.95 (ISBN 0-87604-102-0). ARE Pr.

Drummond, Robert R. Early German Music in Philadelphia. LC 72-1596. Repr. of 1910 ed. 11.50 (ISBN 0-404-09917-3). AMS Pr.

--Early German Music in Philadelphia. LC 74-125068. (Music Ser). 1970. Repr. of 1910 ed. lib. bdg. 18.50 (ISBN 0-306-70005-0). Da Capo.

Drummond, W. Poetical Works of William Drummond of Hawthornden, 2 Vols. Kastner, L. E., ed. LC 68-24906. (Studies in Poetry, No. 38). 1969. Repr. of 1913 ed. lib. bdg. 79.95x (ISBN 0-8383-0157-6). Haskell.

Drummond, W. H., ed. see Leslie, David.

Drummond, William. Academical Questions. LC 84-13925. 1985. Repr. of 1805 ed. 60.00x (ISBN 0-8201-1398-0). Schol Facsimiles.

--Flowres of Sion: To Which Is Adjoyned His Cypresse Grove. LC 73-6124. (English Experience Ser.: No. 590). 80p. 1973. Repr. of 1623 ed. 8.00 (ISBN 90-221-0590-3). Walter J Johnson.

--Forth Feasting: A Panegyricke to the Kings Most Excellent Majestie. LC 79-25570. (English Experience Ser.: No. 138). 16p. 1969. Repr. of 1617 ed. 7.00 (ISBN 90-221-0138-X). Walter J Johnson.

--Poems. Maitland, Thomas, ed. LC 77-144419. (Maitland Club. Glasgow. Publications: No. 18). Repr. of 1832 ed. 35.00 (ISBN 0-404-52956-9). AMS Pr.

--Poems. LC 76-6156. (English Experience Ser.: No. 83). 128p. 1969. Repr. of 1616 ed. 16.00 (ISBN 90-221-0083-9). Walter J Johnson.

--Poems of William Drummond of Hawthornden. Repr. of 1832 ed. 46.00 (ISBN 0-384-13070-4). Johnson Repr.

--The Poems of William Drummond of Hawthornden, 2 vols. Ward, William C., ed. 1894. 65.00 set (ISBN 0-8274-3157-0). R West.

Drumwright, Huber L. An Introduction to New Testament Greek. 2nd ed. LC 78-59982. 1980. 11.95 (ISBN 0-8054-1368-5). Broadman.

Drumwright, Huber L. & Vaughan, Curtis, eds. New Testament Studies: Essays in Honor of Ray Summers in His Sixty-fifth Year. LC 75-29815. 195p. 1975. 7.95 (ISBN 0-918954-15-0). Baylor Univ Pr.

Drury, Allen. Advise & Consent. LC 59-9137. 1959. 16.95 (ISBN 0-385-05419-X). Doubleday.

--Capable of Honor. LC 66-20961. 1966. 15.95 (ISBN 0-385-01028-1). Doubleday.

--Come Nineveh, Come Tyre. LC 73-9347. 480p. 1973. 17.95 (ISBN 0-385-04392-9). Doubleday.

--Decision. 544p. (Orig.). 1984. pap. 3.95 (ISBN 0-523-42258-X). Pinnacle Bks.

--Egypt, the Eternal Smile: Reflections on a Journey. LC 78-20069. (Illus.). 288p. 1980. 45.00 (ISBN 0-385-00193-2). Doubleday.

--The Hill of Summer. LC 80-1849. 504p. 1981. 15.95 (ISBN 0-385-00234-3). Doubleday.

--The Hill of Summer. 576p. 1985. pap. 3.95 (ISBN 0-523-42649-6). Pinnacle Bks.

--Preserve & Protect. LC 68-26725. 1968. 14.95 (ISBN 0-385-01030-3). Doubleday.

--The Promise of Joy. LC 74-18774. 456p. 1975. 14.95 (ISBN 0-385-04396-1). Doubleday.

--Return to Thebes. 1978. pap. 2.25 (ISBN 0-440-17296-9). Dell.

--The Roads of Earth. LC 82-45393. 384p. 1984. 16.95 (ISBN 0-385-00219-X). Doubleday.

--The Roads of Earth. 496p. 1985. pap. 4.50 (ISBN 0-523-42611-9). Pinnacle Bks.

--A Senate Journal, Nineteen Forty-Three to Nineteen Forty-Five. LC 76-38824. (FDR & the Era of the New Deal Ser.). 1972. Repr. of 1963 ed. lib. bdg. 59.50 (ISBN 0-306-70448-X). Da Capo.

--Shade of Difference. LC 62-8838. 1962. 15.95 (ISBN 0-385-02389-8). Doubleday.

Drury, Barbara M., ed. Pricare's Computer Primer: For Health Professionals Managing Office Computers. LC 83-63347. 88p. (Orig.). 1984. pap. text ed. 24.95 (ISBN 0-9613095-6-3). Pricare.

Drury, C. G., ed. Human Reliability in Quality Control. Fox, J. G. LC 75-11695. (Illus.). 250p. 1975. 33.00x (ISBN 0-85066-088-2). Taylor & Francis.

Drury, Clifford. Nine Years with Spokane Indians: Diary of Elkanah Walker. (Illus.). 1976. 26.50 (ISBN 0-87062-117-3). A H Clark.

Drury, Clifford M. Chief Lawyer of the Nez Perce Indians, Seventeen Ninety-Six to Eighteen Seventy-Six. LC 78-67267. (Northwest Historical Ser.: 14). (Illus.). 1979. 22.75 (ISBN 0-87062-127-0). A H Clark.

--My Road from Yesterday: An Autobiography. LC 83-73402. (Illus.). 350p. 1984. 25.00 (ISBN 0-87062-154-8). A H Clark.

Drury, Donald W. The Art of Computer Programming. (Illus.). 312p. (Orig.). 1982. o.p 16.95 (ISBN 0-8306-0455-3); pap. 10.95 (ISBN 0-8306-1455-9, 1455). TAB Bks.

--Learning MS-BASIC on the TI Professional Computer. LC 84-8698. (Illus.). 240p. (Orig.). 1984. 21.95 (ISBN 0-8306-0815-X); pap. 15.95 (ISBN 0-8306-1815-5, 1815). TAB Bks.

Drury, Elizabeth & Bridgeman. The Last Word. 224p. 1982. 18.95 (ISBN 0-233-97474-1). Andre Deutsch.

--The Last Word. 224p. 1982. 18.95 (ISBN 0-233-97474-1, Pub. by A Deutsch England). David & Charles.

Drury, G. Thorn, ed. see Waller, Edmund.

Drury, George. The Train-Watcher's Guide to North American Railroads. Hayden, Bob, ed. (Illus.). 230p. (Orig.). 1983. pap. 10.95 (ISBN 0-89024-061-2). Kalmbach.

Drury, Horace B. Scientific Management. 2nd rev. ed. LC 68-56654. (Columbia University. Studies in the Social Sciences: No. 157). 1922. 21.00 (ISBN 0-404-51157-0). AMS Pr.

Drury, Horace B., jt. auth. see Nourse, Edwin G.

Drury, Ian, intro. by. Hard Lines. (Illus.). 1983. pap. 4.95 (ISBN 0-571-13073-9). Faber & Faber.

Drury, J., jt. auth. see Falconer, P.

Drury, James W. The Government of Kansas. 3rd rev. ed. LC 77-86624. (Illus.). 600p. 1980. pap. 17.95x (ISBN 0-7006-0205-4). U Pr of KS.

Drury, John. Historic Midwest Houses. LC 77-78084. (Illus.). 1977. pap. 6.95 (ISBN 0-226-16551-5). U of Chicago Pr.

--Old Chicago Houses. (Illus.). xviii, 518p. 1975. pap. 6.95 (ISBN 0-226-16555-8). U of Chicago Pr.

--Old Illinois Houses. (Illus.). 1977. pap. 3.95 (ISBN 0-226-16552-3). U of Chicago Pr.

--Parables in Gospels. LC 84-27652. 192p. 1985. 14.95 (ISBN 0-8245-0655-3). Crossroad NY.

Drury, John, ed. & tr. see Bellini, Enzo, et al.

Drury, John, ed. & tr. see Bellini, Enzo.

Drury, John, ed. & tr. see Bellini, Enzo, et al.

Drury, John, tr. see Alves, Rubem.

Drury, John, tr. see Boff, Leonardo.

Drury, John, tr. see Camps, Arnulf.

Drury, John, tr. see Christo, Carlos A.

Drury, John, tr. see Comblin, Jose.

Drury, John, tr. see Cosmao, Vincent.

Drury, John, tr. see Cussianovich, Alejandro.

Drury, John, tr. see Eagleson, John.

Drury, John, tr. see Ellacuria, Ignacio.

Drury, John, tr. see Fierro, Alfredo.

Drury, John, tr. see Frei, Eduardo.

Drury, John, tr. see Gibellini, Rosino.

Drury, John, tr. see Miranda, Jose P.

Drury, John, tr. see Motte, Gonzague.

Drury, John, tr. see Perez-Esclarin, Anthony.

Drury, John, tr. see Segundo, Jean L.

Drury, John, tr. see Segundo, Juan L.

Drury, John, tr. see Slijper, Everhard J.

Drury, John, tr. see Sobrino, Jon.

Drury, John, tr. see Thielcke, Gerhard.

Drury, John, tr. see Torres, Sergio & Eagleson, John.

Drury, Jolyon, ed. Factories: Planning & Design. (Illus.). 320p. 1981. 150.00 (ISBN 0-89397-113-8). Nichols Pub.

Drury, K. This Is the Newfoundland. 17.95 (ISBN 0-87666-340-4, PS-666). TFH Pubns.

Drury, M. The Danger of Words. (Studies in Philosophical Psychology). 136p. 1973. text ed. 18.00x (ISBN 0-391-00277-5). Humanities.

Drury, M. & Hull, Robin. Introduction to General Practice: Concise Medical Textbook. (Illus.). 1979. pap. text ed. 13.95 (ISBN 0-7216-0721-7, Pub. by Bailliere-Tindall). Saunders.

Drury, Michael. The Adventure of Spiritual Healing. 304p. 1985. pap. 9.95 large print ed. (ISBN 0-8027-2493-0). Walker & Co.

--Advice to a Young Wife from an Old Mistress. LC 68-22668. 1968. 9.95 (ISBN 0-385-03632-9). Doubleday.

Drury, Michael, jt ed. see Hull, Helen R.

Drury, Nevill. Don Juan, Mescalito & Modern Magic: The Mythology of Inner Space. 256p. 1985. pap. 8.95 (ISBN 1-85063-015-1, Ark Paperbacks). Routledge & Kegan.

--Encyclopedia of Mysticism & the Occult. LC 84-48215. (Illus.). 544p. (Orig.). 1985. 28.80 (ISBN 0-06-062093-5, HarpR); pap. 14.37 (ISBN 0-06-062094-3). Har-Row.

--The Healing Power: A Handbook of Alternative Medicine & Natural Health in Australia & New Zealand. (Illus.). 235p. 1982. pap. 12.95 (ISBN 0-938190-10-5). North Atlantic.

--Inner Health: The Health Benefits of Relaxation, Meditation, & Visualization. (Illus.). 211p. 1985. pap. 10.95 (ISBN 0-907061-73-7, Pub. by Prism Pr). Interbook.

--Music for Inner Space: Techniques for Meditation & Visualization. 200p. 1985. pap. 9.95 (ISBN 0-907061-74-5, Pub. by Prism Pr). Interbook.

--The Shaman & the Magician: Journeys Between the Worlds. 156p. (Orig.). 1982. pap. 8.95 (ISBN 0-7100-0910-0). Routledge & Kegan.

Drury, P. J. Excavations at Melbourne Street, Southhampton, 1971-1976. (Chelmsford Excavation Committee Report Ser.: No. 26). 148p. 1978. pap. text ed. 48.50x (ISBN 0-900312-64-5, Pub. by Coun Brit Archaeology). Humanities.

Drury, P. J., jt. auth. see Cunningham, C. M.

Drury, Rebecca. Blue Glory. (Women at War Ser.: Bk. 6). 352p. 1982. pap. 3.25 (ISBN 0-440-00456-X, Emerald). Dell.

--Darkness at Dawn. (Women at War Ser.: No. 11). (Orig.). 1983. pap. 3.25 (ISBN 0-440-01663-0, Emerald). Dell.

--Splendid Victory. (Woman at War Ser.: No. 10). 352p. (Orig.). 1983. pap. 3.25 (ISBN 0-440-08016-9, Emerald). Dell.

Drury, Richard S. My Secret War. LC 79-50359. (Illus.). 1979. 12.95 (ISBN 0-8168-6841-7). Aero.

Duane, Drake & Leong, Che K., eds. Understanding Learning Disabilities: International & Multidisciplinary Views. 286p. 1985. 42.50x (ISBN 0-306-41900-9, Plenum Pr). Plenum Pub.

Duane, Edward A., jt. ed. see Bridgeland, William M.

Duane, James E. Media About Media: An Annotated Listing of Media Software. LC 80-21339. (The Instructional Media Library: Vol. 6). 232p. 1981. 27.95 (ISBN 0-87778-166-4). Educ Tech Pubns.

Duane, James E., ed. Individualized Instruction - Programs & Materials. LC 72-11990. 440p. 1973. 27.95 (ISBN 0-87778-043-9). Educ Tech Pubns.

Duane, James E., ed. see Baker, Dan & Weisgerber, Bill.

Duane, James E., ed. see Beatty, LaMond F.

Duane, James E., ed. see Bullough, Sr. Robert V.

Duane, James E., ed. see Cluff, E. Dale.

Duane, James E., ed. see Flanagan, Cathleen C.

Duane, James E., ed. see Kueter, Roger A. & Miller, Janeen.

Duane, James E., ed. see Schneider, Edward W. & Bennion, Junius L.

Duane, James E., ed. see Soulier, J. Steven.

Duane, James E., ed. see Sparks, Jerry D.

Duane, James E., ed. see Wood, Rulon K.

Duane, Kit. Mother Earth Father Time. 58p. 1979. 4.50 (ISBN 0-932716-04-0). Kelsey St Pr.

Duane, Thomas, ed. see Loose Leaf Reference Service.

Duane, Thomas D. & Jaeger, Edward A., eds. Biomedical Foundations of Opthalmology, 3 vols. (Illus.). 1982. 300.00 (ISBN 0-06-148001-0, Harper Medical); revision pages 25.00. Lippincott.

Duane, William, ed. Letters to Benjamin Franklin, from His Family & Friends, 1751-1790. facs. ed. (Select Bibliographies Reprint Ser). 1858. 18.00 (ISBN 0-8369-5325-8). Ayer Co Pubs.

Duane, William, jt. ed. see Marshall, Christopher.

Duane, William, tr. see Blanchard, Claude.

Duane, William J. Letters Addressed to the People of Pennsylvania. LC 68-18218. 1968. Repr. of 1811 ed. 25.00x (ISBN 0-678-00381-5). Kelley.

--Letters Addressed to the People of Pennsylvania Respecting the Internal Improvement of the Commonwealth: By Means of Roads & Canals. (American Classics in History & Social Science Ser.: No. 22). 1968. 16.00 (ISBN 0-8337-0923-2). B Franklin.

--Narrative & Correspondence Concerning the Removal of the Deposites, & Occurences Connected Therewith. 1966. Repr. of 1838 ed. 17.00 (ISBN 0-8337-0924-0). B Franklin.

Duarte, Alex. Cataract Breakthrough. 1982. 8.95 (ISBN 0-86664-034-7). Cancer Control Soc.

Duarte, Cristobal G. Renal Function Tests. (Laboratory Medicine Ser.). 1980. text ed. 32.50 (ISBN 0-316-19398-4). Little.

DuArte, Jack, jt. auth. see Joynes, St. Leger.

Du'Arte, Jack, jt. auth. see Joynes, St. Leger M.

Duarte, R. L., jt. auth. see Duarte, Salvador R.

Duarte, Salvador R. & Duarte, R. L. Electronics Assembly & Fabrication Methods. 2nd ed. LC 72-6495. 1973. text ed. 18.25 (ISBN 0-07-017880-1). McGraw.

Dua-Sharma, Shushil & Sharma, K. N. Human Physiology: Mechanism of Functions & Clinical Co-Relates. 560p. Date not set. text ed. 50.00x (ISBN 0-7069-1232-2, Pub. by Vikas India). Advent NY.

Duax, jt. ed. see Griffin, J. F.

Duax, William L. & Norton, Dorita A., eds. Atlas of Steroid Structure, Vol. 1. LC 75-22419. 586p. 1975. 85.00x (ISBN 0-306-66101-2, IFI Plenum). Plenum Pub.

Duax, William L., et al, eds. Atlas of Steroid Structure, Vol. 2. 765p. 1983. 140.00x (ISBN 0-306-66102-0, IFI Plenum). Plenum Pub.

Dub, M., ed. Organometallic Compounds: Methods of Synthesis, Physical Constants & Chemical Reactions, 3 vols. Incl. Vol. 1. Compounds of Transition Metals. 2nd ed. xviii, 828p. 1966. 83.00 (ISBN 0-387-03632-6); Vol. 2. Compounds of Germanium, Tin & Lead, Including Biological Activity & Commercial Application. 2nd ed. Weiss, R. W., ed. xx, 627p. 1967. 83.00 (ISBN 0-387-03948-1); 91.00 (ISBN 0-387-06304-8); Vol. 3. Compounds of Arsenic, Antimony & Bismuth. 2nd ed. xx, 925p. 1968. 83.00 (ISBN 0-387-04296-2); Formula Index to Volumes 1-3. 2nd ed. vii, 343p. 1970. 57.00 (ISBN 0-387-04985-1). LC 66-28249. Springer-Verlag.

Dub, M., ed. see Bauer, K. & Haller, G.

Dubach, C., ed. see Angieski, S.

Dubach, U. & Schmidt, U. Diagnostic Significance of Enzymes & Proteins in Urine. 385p. 1979. 65.00 (ISBN 3-456-80689-2, Pub. by Holdan Bk Ltd UK). State Mutual Bk.

Dubach, U C. & Schmidt, U. Recent Advances in Quantitative Histo & Cytochemistry. 363p. 90.00 (ISBN 3-456-00038-3, Pub. by Holdan Bk Ltd UK). State Mutual Bk.

Dubach, U. C., jt. ed. see Obrecht, J. B.

Dubacher, H., ed. see Ladewig, D. & Hobi, V.

Dubal, David. Reflections from the Keyboard: The World of the Concert Pianist. (Illus.). 384p. 1984. 19.95 (ISBN 0-671-49240-3). Summit Bks.

Duban, James. Melville's Major Fiction: Politics, Theology, & Imagination. LC 83-2432. (Illus.). 284p. 1983. 25.00 (ISBN 0-87580-086-6). N Ill U Pr.

Duban, Jeffrey M. Ancient & Modern Images of Sappho: Translations & Studies in Archaic Greek Love Lyric. (Classical World Special Ser.: Vol. 2). 188p. (Orig.). 1984. lib. bdg. 23.50 (ISBN 0-8191-3560-7); pap. text ed. 11.25 (ISBN 0-8191-3561-5). U Pr of Amer.

DuBane, Janet & Friend, Diane, eds. Country-Style Decorating Ideas. (Illus.). 64p. (Orig.). 1982. pap. 2.50 (ISBN 0-918178-27-4). Simplicity.

--Kid Crafts. (Illus.). 64p. (Orig.). 1984. pap. 2.95 (ISBN 0-918178-23-1). Simplicity.

--Needlework Plus. (Illus.). 96p. 1980. pap. 2.50 (ISBN 0-918178-18-5). Simplicity.

DuBane, Janet & Kuman, Alexandra, eds. Americana Crafts. (Illus.). 64p. (Orig.). 1980. pap. 2.00 (ISBN 0-918178-22-3). Simplicity.

--Pillow Ideas. (Illus.). 64p. (Orig.). 1980. pap. 2.50 (ISBN 0-918178-19-3). Simplicity.

--Quick & Quilted Projects. (Illus.). 64p. (Orig.). 1981. pap. 2.50 (ISBN 0-918178-26-6). Simplicity.

Dubanevich, Arlene. Pig William. LC 85-5776. (Illus.). 32p. (ps-2). 1985. PLB 12.95 (ISBN 0-02-733200-4). Bradbury Pr.

Dubar, Jules R. Stratigraphy & Paleontology of the Late Neogene Strata of the Caloosahatchee River Area of Southern Florida. (Illus.). 267p. 1958. 1.00 (ISBN 0-318-17300-X, B 40). FL Bureau Geology.

DuBar, Jules R., jt. ed. see Oaks, Robert Q., Jr.

Dubard, Etoile. Teaching Aphasics & Other Language Deficient Children: Theory & Application of the Association Method. rev. ed. LC 83-1284. (Illus.). 1983. 20.00x (ISBN 0-87805-182-1). U Pr of Miss.

DuBarry, Michele. Into Passion's Dawn. (The Loves of Angela Carlyle Ser.: No. 1). 1981. pap. 2.50 (ISBN 0-8439-0902-1, Pub. by Leisure Bks). Dorchester Pub Co.

--Into Passion's Dawn. (Loves of Angela Carlyle Ser.: Vol. 1). 320p. 1985. pap. 3.50 (ISBN 0-8439-2186-2, Leisure Bks). Dorchester Pub Co.

--Loves of Angela Carlyle: Across Captive Seas, Vol. II. (Angela Carlyle Ser.). 320p. 1985. pap. 3.50 (ISBN 0-8439-2211-7, Leisure Bks). Dorchester Pub Co.

--The Loves of Angela Carlyle: Toward Love's Horizon, Vol. III. (Angela Carlyle Ser.). 320p. 1985. pap. 3.50 (ISBN 0-8439-2239-7, Leisure Bks). Dorchester Pub Co.

--Toward Love's Horizon: The Loves of Angela Carlyle, Vol. III. 320p. 1981. pap. 2.50 (ISBN 0-8439-0957-9, Leisure Bks). Dorchester Pub Co.

DuBarry, Michelle. Across Captive Seas, No. 2. (The Loves of Angela Carlyle Ser.). 1981. pap. 2.50 (ISBN 0-8439-0932-3). Dorchester Pub Co.

Du Bartas, Guillaume D. Bartas: His Devine Weekes & Workes. LC 65-10398. 1965. Repr. of 1605 ed. lib. bdg. 90.00x (ISBN 0-8201-1265-8). Schol Facsimilies.

Du Bartas, Sieur, jt. auth. see Du Saluste, Guillaume.

Dubas, M., jt. auth. see Schumann, W.

Dubasov, Yu V., jt. auth. see Vdovenko, V. M.

Du Bay, Bill, tr. see Rovin, Jeff.

Dubay, Guy F. Chez-Nous: The St. John Valley. LC 83-61808. (Illus.). 114p. 1983. pap. 7.95 (ISBN 0-913764-17-5). Maine St Mus.

Dubay, Robert W. John Jones Pettus, Mississippi Fire-Eater: His Life & Times, 1813-1867. LC 74-33923. 1975. 3.00x (ISBN 0-87805-066-3). U Pr of Miss.

DuBay, Sandra. The Claverleigh Curse. (Orig.). 1982. pap. 2.50 (ISBN 0-89083-958-1). Zebra.

--Crimson Conquest. 320p. 1984. pap. 3.50 (ISBN 0-8439-2153-6, Leisure Bks). Dorchester Pub Co.

--Fidelity's Flight. 448p. (Orig.). 1982. pap. write for info. (ISBN 0-505-51825-2, Pub. by Tower Bks). Dorchester Pub Co.

--Fidelity's Flight. 464p. 1983. pap. 3.75 (ISBN 0-8439-2031-9, Leisure Bks). Dorchester Pub Co.

--Flame of Fidelity. 288p. (Orig.). 1981. pap. 2.50 (ISBN 0-505-51741-8, Pub. by Tower Bks). Dorchester Pub Co.

--In Passion's Shadow. 480p. (Orig.). 1984. pap. 3.95 (ISBN 0-8439-2164-1, Leisure Bks). Dorchester Pub Co.

--Mistress of the Sun King. (Orig.). 1980. pap. 2.25 (ISBN 0-505-51495-8, Pub. by Tower Bks). Dorchester Pub Co.

--Where Passion Dwells. 480p. (Orig.). 1985. pap. 3.95 (ISBN 0-8439-2245-1, Leisure Bks). Dorchester Pub Co.

--Whispers of Passion. 416p. 1984. pap. 3.75 (ISBN 0-8439-2101-3). Dorchester Pub Co.

Dubay, Thomas. Authenticity. 4.95 (ISBN 0-87193-143-5). Dimension Bks.

--Dawn of a Consecration. 1964. 4.00 (ISBN 0-8198-0034-1). Dghtrs St Paul.

--Faith & Certitude. LC 84-80910. 258p. (Orig.). 1985. pap. 9.95 (ISBN 0-89870-054-X). Ignatius Pr.

--Happy Are You Poor. 5.95 (ISBN 0-87193-141-9). Dimension Bks.

--Philosophy of the State As Educator. LC 78-6256. 1978. Repr. of 1959 ed. lib. bdg. 22.50x (ISBN 0-313-20416-0, DUPH). Greenwood.

--What is Religious Life? 5.95 (ISBN 0-87193-116-8). Dimension Bks.

DuBay, W. The Trap. (Golden Super Adventure Bks.). (Illus.). 24p. (gr. k-3). 1983. pap. 1.95 (ISBN 0-307-11795-2, 11795, Golden Bks). Western Pub.

Dubbe, Marguerite. Beginner's Recorder Method Based on the Pentatonic Scale for Use with Orff Instruments. 1971. pap. 2.25 (ISBN 0-918812-01-1). MMB Music.

Dubbelman, C. Disturbances in the Linear Model: Estimation & Hypothesis Testing. 1978. pap. 16.00 (ISBN 90-207-0772-8, Pub. by Martininus Nijhoff Netherlands). Kluwer Academic.

Dubberstein, Waldo H. Babylonian Chronology, 626 B. C. - A. D. 75. (Brown University Studies: No. 19). 1956. write for info. U Pr of New Eng.

Dubbert, Joe L. A Man's Place: Masculinity in Transition. 1979. text ed. 11.95 (ISBN 0-13-552059-2, Spec); pap. text ed. 5.95 (ISBN 0-13-552042-8). P-H.

Dubbey, J. M. Development of Modern Mathematics. LC 72-88125. 153p. 1975. pap. 8.75x (ISBN 0-8448-0656-0). Crane-Russak Co.

--The Mathematical Work of Charles Babbage. LC 77-71409. (Illus.). 1978. 57.50 (ISBN 0-521-21649-4). Cambridge U Pr.

Dubbs, Chris. Ms. Faust. 1985. 16.95 (ISBN 0-931933-04-8). Richardson & Steirman.

Dubbs, Chris & Heberle, Dave. The Easy Art of Smoking Food. LC 77-4893. 1978. pap. 10.95 (ISBN 0-8329-2641-8, Pub. by Winchester Pr). New Century.

Dubbs, Patrick J. & Whitney, Daniel P. Cultural Contexts: An Introduction to the Anthropological Perspective. 320p. 1980. pap. text ed. 13.97 (ISBN 0-205-06871-5, 6668712); instrs' manual free (ISBN 0-205-06872-3). Allyn.

Dubcek, Alexander. Czechoslovakia's Blueprint for Freedom. Ello, Paul, ed. LC 68-58075. 1968. pap. text ed. 6.95 (ISBN 0-87491-106-0). Acropolis.

Dube, Anthony & Franson, J. Earl. Structure & Meaning: An Introduction to Literature. 2nd ed. LC 82-83173. 1296p. 1983. text ed. 21.95 (ISBN 0-395-32570-6); instr's manual 2.00 (ISBN 0-395-32571-4). HM.

Dube, H. C. An Introduction to Fungi. 616p. 1983. text ed. 45.00x (ISBN 0-7069-1896-7, Pub. by Vikas India). Advent NY.

Dube, H. C., jt. auth. see Bilgrami, K. S.

Dube, Lawrence E., Jr., jt. auth. see Kruchko, John G.

Dube, Normand. Le Nuage de ma pensee. (Illus.). 91p. (Fr.). (gr. 11-12). 1981. pap. 2.50 (ISBN 0-911409-12-2). Natl Mat Dev.

Dube, Pierre H. & Davidson, Hugh M. A Concordance to Pascal's "Les Provinciales". LC 79-54323. (Garland Reference Library of the Humanities). 1000p. 1980. lib. bdg. 121.00 (ISBN 0-8240-9536-7). Garland Pub.

Dube, Pierre H., jt. ed. see Davidson, Hugh M.

Dube, R. C., jt. auth. see Bilgrami, K. S.

Dube, R. K., jt. auth. see Upadhyaya, G. S.

Dube, Rani. The Evil Within. 9.95 (ISBN 0-7043-2161-0, Pub. by Quartet England). Charles River Bks.

Dube, S. C. Contemporary India & Its Modernization. 1974. 7.50 (ISBN 0-686-20207-4). Intl Bk Dist.

--Development Perspectives for the 1980s. 127p. 1983. text ed. 9.50x (ISBN 0-391-02947-9). Humanities.

--On Crisis & Commitment in the Social Sciences. 108p. 1983. text ed. 10.25x (ISBN 0-391-02852-9, Pub. by Abhinav India). Humanities.

Dube, S. C., ed. Public Services & Social Responsibility. 277p. 1979. 14.00x (ISBN 0-7069-0669-1, Pub. by Vikas India). Advent NY.

Dube, S. C. & Basilov, V. N., eds. Secularization in Multi-Religious Societies: Indo-Soviet Perspectives. 322p. 1983. text ed. 17.75x (ISBN 0-391-02987-8, Pub. by Concept India). Humanities.

Dube, S. N. Cross Currents in Early Buddhism. 1981. 22.50x (ISBN 0-8364-0686-9, Pub. by Manohar India). South Asia Bks.

Dube, Shiv K. & Pierog, Sophie H., eds. Immediate Care of the Sick & Injured Child. LC 78-763. 1978. pap. 29.50 (ISBN 0-8016-1459-7). Mosby.

Dube, Wolf-Dieter. The Expressionists. (World of Art Ser.). (Illus.). 216p. 1985. pap. 9.95 (ISBN 0-500-20123-4). Thames Hudson.

Dube, Wolf-Dieter & Skira-Rizzoli. Expressionists & Expressionism. LC 83-42910. (Illus.). 172p. 1983. 75.00 (ISBN 0-8478-0494-1). Rizzoli Intl.

Du Bec-Crespin, Jean. The Historie of the Great Emperour Tamerlan. LC 68-54630. (English Experience Ser.: No. 38). 266p. 1968. Repr. of 1597 ed. 35.00 (ISBN 90-221-0038-3). Walter J Johnson.

Dubeck, Leroy W., jt. auth. see Meisinger, Richard J., Jr.

Dubeck, Paula J & Miller, Zane L., eds. Urban Professionals & the Future of the Metropolis. (National University Publications, Interdisciplinary Urban Ser.). 134p. 1980. 13.50x (ISBN 0-8046-9261-0, Pub by Kennikat). Assoc Faculty Pr.

Dubeif, H., jt. auth. see Bernard, P.

Dubelaar, Thea. Maria. Bell, Anthea, tr. LC 82-2134. (Illus.). 160p. (gr. 4-6). 1982. 10.75 (ISBN 0-688-01062-8). Morrow.

Du Bellay, Guillaume. Fragments de la Premiere Ogdoade. 177p. 1905. 14.95 (ISBN 0-686-56033-7). French & Eur.

Du Bellay, Jean. Correspondance, 2 vols. 549p. 1969. Vol. 1, 1529-1535. 39.95 (ISBN 0-686-56034-5); Vol. 2, 1535-Dec. 1536. 39.95 (ISBN 0-686-56035-3). French & Eur.

Du Bellay, Joachim. Les Antiquities de Rome: Avec: Les Regrets, La Defense et Illustration de la Langue Francaise. 1975. 4.50 (ISBN 0-686-56036-1). French & Eur.

--La Defence et Illustration De la Langue Francoyse. 13.95 (ISBN 0-685-34183-6). French & Eur.

--Defense et illustration de langue francaise. (Documentation thematique). 2.95 (ISBN 0-685-36191-8, 101). Larousse.

--Poemes Choisis. (Illus.). 56p. 1973. 7.95 (ISBN 0-686-56040-X). French & Eur.

--Poesies. 96p. 1978. 18.95 (ISBN 0-686-56041-8). French & Eur.

--Les Regrets et autres oeuvres poetiques. Jolliffe, ed. Bd. with Antiquitez de Rome Plus un Songe ou Vision sur le Mesme Subject. (Textes Litteraires Francais). 8.75 (ISBN 0-685-34184-4). French & Eur.

Du Bellay, Joachim & Caldarini, E. L' Olive. 180p. 1975. 20.00 (ISBN 0-686-56039-6). French & Eur.

Du Bellay, Joachim & Nolhac, Pierre de. Lettres, Paris, 1883. facsimile ed. (Illus.). 104p. 1974. 25.00 (ISBN 0-686-56038-8). French & Eur.

Du Bellay, Joachim & Saulnier, V. L. Divers Jeux Rustiques. new ed. 232p. 1965. 12.00 (ISBN 0-686-56037-X). French & Eur.

Du Bellay, Joachim see Bellay, Joachim Du.

Dubelle, Stanley T., Jr., et al. Misbehavin' LC 84-50299. 110p. 1984. pap. 12.95 (ISBN 0-87762-346-5). Technomic.

Du Bellet, Louise Pecquet. Some Prominent Virginia Families, 4 vols. in 2. LC 76-13286. (Illus.). 1715p. 1976. Repr. of 1907 ed. 72.50 set (ISBN 0-8063-0722-6). Genealog Pub.

Dubendorf, Donald R. & Storey, M. John. The Insider Buyout. LC 84-52258. 225p. 1985. 19.95 (ISBN 0-88266-387-9, Pub. by Storey Publishing). Garden Way Pub.

Du Berg, Peter, tr. see Duras, Marguerita.

Duberman, Lucile. Marriage & Other Alternatives. 2nd ed. LC 75-36200. 239p. 1977. pap. text ed. 13.95 (ISBN 0-275-85500-7, HoltC). HR&W.

--Reconstituted Family: A Study of Remarried Couples & Their Children. LC 75-8840. 200p. 1975. 19.95x (ISBN 0-88229-168-8). Nelson-Hall.

Duberman, Lucile, et al. Gender & Sex in Society. LC 73-10658. 274p. 1975. pap. text ed. 13.95 (ISBN 0-275-85070-6, HoltC). HR&W.

Duberman, Lucille. Sociology: Focus on Society. LC 78-68634. 1979. text ed. 24.00 (ISBN 0-394-33327-6, RanC); wkbk 6.95 (ISBN 0-394-33328-4). Random.

Duberman, Martin. Charles Francis Adams, 1807-1886. LC 68-13742. (Illus.). 1961. 35.00x (ISBN 0-8047-0625-5); pap. 10.95 (ISBN 0-8047-0626-3, SP84). Stanford U Pr.

--The Uncompleted Past. Winks, Robin W., ed. LC 83-49169. (History & Historiography Ser.). 356p. 1985. lib. bdg. 35.00 (ISBN 0-8240-6359-7). Garland Pub.

--Uncompleted Past. 1971. pap. 2.45 (ISBN 0-525-47290-8). Dutton.

Duberman, Martin, ed. Antislavery Vanguard: New Essays on the Abolitionists. 1965. 38.00x (ISBN 0-691-04505-4); pap. 12.95 (ISBN 0-691-00552-4). Princeton U Pr.

Dubern, Roger, jt. auth. see McGowan, John.

DuBern, Roger, jt. auth. see McGowan, John.

Dubernard, Jean-Michel, jt. ed. see Traeger, Jules.

Duberstein, Helen. Changes. 1977. pap. 1.50 (ISBN 0-686-20606-1). Ghost Dance.

--The Voyage Out. LC 77-92495. 1978. pap. 2.00x (ISBN 0-931598-04-4). Fallen Angel.

Dubey, Deepak. Praise to the Morning Koel. 8.00 (ISBN 0-89253-477-X); flexible cloth 4.00 (ISBN 0-89253-478-8). Ind-US Inc.

--Stories for Ramu. 10.00 (ISBN 0-89253-794-9); flexible cloth 5.00 (ISBN 0-89253-795-7). Ind-US Inc.

Dubey, Leon B., Jr. No Need to Count. LC 79-23884. (Illus.). 176p. 1981. pap. 7.95 (ISBN 0-498-02465-2). A S Barnes.

DuBey, R. E., et al. A Practical Guide for Dynamic Conferences. LC 80-6083. (Illus.). 180p. 1982. lib. bdg. 25.25 (ISBN 0-8191-2152-5); pap. text ed. 11.25 (ISBN 0-8191-2153-3). U Pr of Amer.

DuBey, Robert E., et al. Performance-Based Guide to Student Teaching. 2nd ed. 1975. pap. text ed. 6.50x (ISBN 0-8134-1713-9, 1713). Interstate.

Dubey, S. M., et al. Family Marriage & Social Change on the Indian Fringe. 283p. 1980. 22.00 (ISBN 0-89684-259-2, Pub. by Cosmo Pubns India). Orient Bk Dist.

Dubey, S. N. Administration of Social Welfare Programs in India. 1973. 13.25 (ISBN 0-89684-530-3). Intl Bk Dist.

Dubey, Vinod & Faruqi, Shakil. Turkey: Policies & Prospects for Growth. xxxi, 316p. 1980. pap. 10.00 (ISBN 0-686-36123-7, RC-8003). World Bank.

Dubie, Norman. Alehouse Sonnets. LC 76-151506. (Pitt Poetry Ser). 1971. pap. 5.95 (ISBN 0-8229-5223-8). U of Pittsburgh Pr.

--The Illustrations. LC 76-16637. 1977. 6.95 (ISBN 0-8076-0857-2); pap. 3.95 (ISBN 0-8076-0858-0). Braziller.

--Selected & New Poems. LC 83-42686. 160p. 1983. 14.95 (ISBN 0-393-01817-2); pap. 5.95 (ISBN 0-393-30140-0). Norton.

Dubie, William. Closing the Moviehouse. 1981. pap. 2.95 (ISBN 0-939736-23-3). Wings ME.

Dubiel, Hulmet. Theory & Politics: Studies in the Development of Critical Theory. Gregg, Benjamin, tr. from Ger. (German Social Thought Ser.). (Illus.). 188p. 1985. text ed. 20.00x (ISBN 0-262-04080-8). MIT Pr.

Dubillard, Roland. The House of Bones. 1981. pap. 4.95 (ISBN 0-7145-0767-9). Riverrun NY.

--The Swallows. Wright, Barbara, tr. from Fr. 1981. pap. 4.95 (ISBN 0-7145-0648-6). Riverrun NY.

Dubin, A. see Rafelson, M. E.

Dubin, Burt & Milhander, Marc. Achievement Handbook. LC 81-82014. 316p. 1981. 60.00 (ISBN 0-9606744-0-3). Personal Achievement Inst.

Dubin, Dale. Rapid Interpretation of EKG's. 3rd ed. 1974. pap. 17.00 (ISBN 0-912912-00-6). Cover Pub.

Dubin, F. & Margol, M. It's Time to Talk: Communication Activities for Learning English As a New Language. 1977. pap. text ed. 13.95 (ISBN 0-13-507103-8); tchr's man. o.p. free. P-H.

Dubin, F. & Olshtain, E. Reading by All Means. 1981. 13.95 (ISBN 0-201-10077-0, World Language Div). Addison-Wesley.

Dubin, Fraida & Olshtain, Elite. Facilitating Language Learning: A Guidebook for the ESL-EFL Teacher. Davis, Winifred, ed. (Illus.). 249p. 1977. pap. 9.00x (ISBN 0-07-017877-1). McGraw.

Dubin, Fred S. & Long, Chalmers G., Jr. Energy Conservation Standards: For Building Design, Construction & Operation. 432p. 1982. 21.50 (ISBN 0-07-017884-4). McGraw.

Dubin, Harry N., et al. Coping Successfully: A How-To Manual for Operational Improvement. 238p. (Orig.). 1981. text ed. 24.50x (ISBN 0-8290-0262-6); pap. text ed. 12.95x (ISBN 0-8290-0270-7). Irvington.

Dubin, J. A. Consumer Durable Choice & the Demand for Electricity: Contributions to Economic Analysis. (Vol. 155). 284p. 1985. 49.50 (ISBN 0-444-87766-5, North-Holland). Elsevier.

Dubin, Marc. Backpacker's Greece. LC 81-17046. (Backpacker's Guide Ser.). (Illus.). 144p. 1982. pap. 9.95 (ISBN 0-933982-25-9). Bradt Ent.

Dubin, Michael. Foreign Acquisitions & the Spread of the Multinational Firm. Bruchey, Stuart, ed. LC 80-572. (Multinational Corporations Ser.). (Illus.). 1980. lib. bdg. 22.00x (ISBN 0-405-13366-9). Ayer Co Pubs.

Dubin, N. A Stochastic Model for Immunological Feedback in Carcinogenesis: Analysis & Approximations. (Lecture Notes in Biomathematics: Vol. 9). 1976. soft cover 14.00 (ISBN 0-387-07786-3). Springer-Verlag.

Dubin, Reese P. Telecult Power: The Amazing New Way to Psychic & Occult Wonders. (Illus.). 1970. 12.95 (ISBN 0-13-902437-9, Reward); pap. 4.95 (ISBN 0-13-902411-5). P-H.

Dubin, Robert. Theory Building. rev. ed. LC 77-90010. (Illus.). 1978. text ed. 24.95 (ISBN 0-02-907620-X). Free Pr.

Dubin, Samuel S., et al, eds. Maintaining Professional & Technical Competence of the Older Engineer: Engineering & Psychological Aspects. 246p. 1974. 4.00 (ISBN 0-317-33259-7). Am Soc Ag Eng.

Dubin, W. R. & Stolberg, R. Emergency Psychiatry for the House Officer. (Illus.). 166p. (Orig.). 1981. pap. text ed. 15.00 (ISBN 0-89335-149-0). SP Med & Sci Bks.

Dubinin, Y. V., jt. auth. see Borisov, C. B.

Dubins, Lester E. & Savage, Leonard J. Inequalities for Stochastic Processes. LC 75-25001. 288p. 1976. pap. 6.95 (ISBN 0-486-63283-0). Dover.

Dubinskaya, L. Moscow-Leningrad-Kiev: A Guide. 215p. 1981. 7.45 (ISBN 0-8285-2356-8, Pub. by Progress Pubs USSR). Imported Pubns.

Dubinski, Roman R., ed. see Brome, Alexander.

Dubinskii, Ju. A., et al. Nine Papers on Functional Analysis & Partial Differential Equations. (Translations Ser.: No. 2, Vol. 67). 1968. 36.00 (ISBN 0-8218-1767-1, TRANS 2-67). Am Math.

Dubinsky, Alan J. Sales Training: An Analysis of Field Sales Techniques. Dufey, Gunter, ed. LC 80-39882. (Research for Business Decisions Ser.: No. 35). 410p. 1981. 49.95 (ISBN 0-8357-1149-8). UMI Res Pr.

Dubinsky, Alan J., jt. auth. see Comer, James M.

Dubinsky, E. The Structure of Nuclear Frechet Spaces. (Lecture Notes in Mathematics: Vol. 720). 1979. pap. 14.00 (ISBN 0-387-09504-7). Springer-Verlag.

Dubinsky, Ed & Ramanujan, M. S. On Lambda Nuclearity. LC 72-4515. (Memoirs: No. 128). 101p. 1972. pap. 10.00 (ISBN 0-8218-1828-7, MEMO-128). Am Math.

Dubinsky, Irwin. Reform in Trade Union Discrimination in the Construction Industry: Operation Dig & Its Legacy. LC 72-12974. (Special Studies in U. S. Economic, Social, & Political Issues). 1973. 39.50x (ISBN 0-275-07080-8). Irvington.

Dubis, Mark. The Pennsylvania Bachelor Book. 60p. (Orig.). 1982. pap. 4.95 (ISBN 0-942076-00-1). Dubis Assoc.

Dubisch, Roy. Basic Concepts of Mathematics for Elementary Teachers. 2nd ed. LC 80-19446. (Mathematics Ser.). (Illus.). 483p. 1981. 26.95 (ISBN 0-201-03170-1); wkbk. 7.95 (ISBN 0-201-03156-6); instr's.manual 3.50 (ISBN 0-201-03173-6). Addison-Wesley.

--Basic Mathematics with Hand-Held Calculator. LC 78-57267. 1979. text ed. 29.95 (ISBN 0-8053-2341-4); instr's guide 4.95 (ISBN 0-8053-2344-9). Benjamin-Cummings.

--Teaching of Mathematics from Intermediate Algebra Through First Year Calculus. LC 74-23520. 136p. 1975. Repr. of 1963 ed. 7.50 (ISBN 0-88275-198-0). Krieger.

--Trigonometry. LC 55-6084. pap. 102.50 (ISBN 0-317-08418-6, 2012451). Bks Demand UMI.

Dubisch, Roy & Hood, Vernon. Elementary Algebra. LC 76-3846. 1977. text ed. 27.95 (ISBN 0-8053-2338-4); instr's guide o.p. 4.95 (ISBN 0-8053-2339-2). Benjamin-Cummings.

Dubisch, Roy, jt. auth. see Fitting, Marjorie A.

Dubitsky, Cora M. Building the Faith Community. LC 74-12632. 192p. 1975. pap. 2.95 (ISBN 0-8091-1848-3). Paulist Pr.

Duble, Richard & Kell, J. Carroll. Southern Lawns & Groundcovers. LC 77-73533. (Illus.). 96p. (Orig.). 1977. pap. 6.95x (ISBN 0-88415-426-2, Pub. by Pacesetter Pr). Gulf Pub.

Dubler, N. & Melnick, V., eds. Alzheimer's Dementia: Dilemmas in Clinical Research. LC 85-11740. (Contemporary Issues in Biomedicine, Ethics, & Society Ser.). 344p. 1985. 34.50 (ISBN 0-89603-067-9). Humana.

Dublin, Arthur B., jt. auth. see Dublin, William B.

Dublin, Jack. Credit Unions: Theory & Practice. 2nd ed. LC 66-19830. (Waynebooks Ser: No. 20). 180p. (Orig.). 1971. pap. 5.95x (ISBN 0-8143-1442-2). Wayne St U Pr.

Dublin, Jack & Dublin, Selma M. Credit Unions in a Changing World: The Tanzania-Kenya Experience. 1983. 19.95 (ISBN 0-8143-1742-1); pap. 9.95 (ISBN 0-8143-1743-X). Wayne St U Pr.

Dublin, Louis I. & Lotka, Alfred J. The Money Value of a Man. Rosenkrantz, Barbara G., ed. LC 76-25659. (Public Health in America Ser.). (Illus.). 1977. Repr. of 1930 ed. lib. bdg. 24.50x (ISBN 0-405-09814-6). Ayer Co Pubs.

Dublin, Selma M., jt. auth. see Dublin, Jack.

Dublin, Stanley W., jt. auth. see Stamper, Eugene.

Dublin, Thomas. Farm & Factory: The Mill Experience & Women's Lives in New England, Eighteen Thirty to Eighteen Sixty. LC 80-28084. 220p. 1981. 26.00x (ISBN 0-231-05118-2); pap. 11.00x (ISBN 0-231-05119-0). Columbia U Pr.

--Women at Work: The Transformation of Work & Community in Lowell, Massachusetts, 1826-1860. LC 79-10701. 360p. 1981. 26.00x (ISBN 0-231-04166-7); pap. 11.00x (ISBN 0-231-04167-5). Columbia U Pr.

Dublin University. Catalogue of Fifteenth Century Books in the Library of Trinity College, Dublin, & in Marsh's Library, Dublin, with a Few from Other Collections. Abbott, T. K., ed. LC 70-128846. (Bibliography & Reference Ser.: No. 360). 1970. Repr. of 1905 ed. lib. bdg. 21.00 (ISBN 0-8337-0001-4). B Franklin.

--John Millington Synge, Eighteen Seventy-One to Nineteen Hundred & Nine: A Catalogue of an Exhibition Held at Trinity College Library, Dublin on the Occasion of the 50th Anniversary of His Death. 53p. 1980. Repr. of 1959 ed. lib. bdg. 17.50 (ISBN 0-8492-8117-2). R West.

Dublin, William B. Fundamentals of Vestibular Pathology. 380p. 1985. 32.50 (ISBN 0-87527-203-7). Green.

Dublin, William B. & Dublin, Arthur B. Atlas of Neuroanatomy for Radiologists: Surface & Sectional-with CT Scanning Correlation. LC 79-50199. (Illus.). 250p. 1982. 62.50 (ISBN 0-87527-204-5). Green.

Dublois, Jacques. Histoire monastique en Franc au XIIe siecle: Les institutions monastiques et leur evolution. 342p. 1982. 75.00x (ISBN 0-86078-109-7, Pub. by Variorum England). State Mutual Bk.

Dubna Conference on the Mossbauer Effect. Proceedings of the Dubna Conference on the Mossbauer Effect. 271p. 1963. 42.50x (ISBN 0-306-10662-0, Consultants). Plenum Pub.

Dubnau, David A. The Molecular Biology of the Bacilli, Vol 1. LC 81-22815. (Molecular Biology Ser.). 1982. 60.00 (ISBN 0-12-222701-8). Acad Pr.

--The Molecular Biology of the Bacilli, Vol. 2. (Molecular Biology Ser.). Date not set. 49.00 (ISBN 0-12-222702-6). Acad Pr.

Dubner. The Law of Territorial Waters of Midocean Archipelagos & Archipelagic States. 1977. pap. 24.00 (ISBN 90-247-1893-7, Pub. by Martinus Nijhoff Netherlands). Kluwer Academic.

Dubner, Barry H. The Law of International Sea Piracy. (Developments in International Law Ser.: No. 2). lib. bdg. 34.00 (ISBN 90-247-2191-1, Pub. by Martinus Nijhoff Netherlands). Kluwer Academic.

Dubner, R., jt. ed. see Yokota, T.

Dubner, Ronald see Kawamura, Yojiro.

Dubner, Ronald & Kawamura, Yojiro, eds. Oral-Facial Sensory & Motor Mechanisms. LC 75-135617. 384p. 1971. 32.50x (ISBN 0-306-50018-3, Plenum Pr). Plenum Pub.

Dubner, Ronald, et al, eds. The Neural Basis of Oral & Facial Function. LC 78-4048. (Illus.). 495p. 1978. 55.00x (ISBN 0-306-31094-5, Plenum Pr). Plenum Pub.

Dubnick, M. J. & Bardes, B A. Thinking about Public Policy: A Problem Solving Approach. LC 82-21782. 283p. 1983. pap. 16.95 (ISBN 0-471-86464-1). Wiley.

Dubnick, Mel & Gitelson, Alan, eds. Regulatory Policy Analysis. (Orig.). 1982. pap. 8.00 (ISBN 0-918592-51-8). Policy Studies.

Dubnick, Randa. The Structure of Obscurity: Gertrude Stein, Language, & Cubism. LC 83-3603. (Illus.). 184p. 1984. 19.95x (ISBN 0-252-00909-6). U of Ill Pr.

Dubnov, Simon. History of the Jews, Vol. 1. 18.00 (ISBN 0-8453-6410-3). Cornwall Bks.

--History of the Jews, Vol. 2. 18.00 (ISBN 0-8453-6659-9). Cornwall Bks.

--History of the Jews, Vol.3. 18.00 (ISBN 0-8453-6822-2). Cornwall Bks.

--History of the Jews, Vol. 4. 18.00 (ISBN 0-8453-7537-7). Cornwall Bks.

--History of the Jews, Vol. 5. 18.00 (ISBN 0-8453-7691-8). Cornwall Bks.

Dubnow, Semen M. Jewish History: An Essay in the Philosophy of History. LC 72-5481. (Select Bibliographies Reprint Ser.). 1972. Repr. of 1903 ed. 16.00 (ISBN 0-8369-6903-0). Ayer Co Pubs.

Duboc, Greg. Mathematics Worksheets Generation: Apple II. 1984. 49.95. Sterling Swift.

DuBoff, Leonard D. Art Law in a Nutshell. LC 84-5236. (Nutshell Ser.). 335p. 1984. pap. 11.95 (ISBN 0-314-82347-6). West Pub.

--Book Publishers' Legal Guide. 363p. 1983. 50.00 (ISBN 0-409-20436-6). Butterworth Legal Pubs.

--The Law (in Plain English) for Craftspeople. Scott, Michael, ed. LC 84-7886. 152p. (Orig.). 1984. pap. 7.95 (ISBN 0-88089-003-7). Madrona Pubs.

DuBoff, Leonard D., ed. Art Law, Domestic & International. LC 75-7668. (Illus.). x, 627p. 1975. text ed. 27.50x (ISBN 0-8377-0503-7). Rothman.

DuBoff, Richard B. Electric Power in American Manufacturing, Eighteen Eighty-Nine to Nineteen Fifty-Eight. Bruchey, Stuart, ed. LC 78-22675. (Energy in the American Economy). (Illus.). 1979. lib. bdg. 23.00x (ISBN 0-405-11978-X). Ayer Co Pubs.

Dubofsky, Melvyn. Industrialism & the American Worker: 1865-1920. LC 74-7326. (American History Ser.). 1975. pap. 7.95x (ISBN 0-88295-726-0). Harlan Davidson.

--Industrialism & the American Worker, 1865-1920. 2nd ed. Franklin, John H. & Eisenstadt, Abraham, eds. (The American History Ser.). 176p. 1985. pap. text ed. 8.95 (ISBN 0-88295-831-3). Harlan Davidson.

--When Workers Organize: New York City in the Progressive Era. LC 68-19669. 1968. 13.50x (ISBN 0-87023-042-5). U of Mass Pr.

Dubofsky, Melvyn & Theoharis, Alan. Imperial Democracy: The United States since 1945. (Illus.). 288p. 1983. pap. 19.95 (ISBN 0-13-451740-7). P-H.

Dubofsky, Melvyn & Van Tine, Warren. John L. Lewis: A Biography. (Illus.). 640p. 1977. 20.00x (ISBN 0-252-01050-7). U of Ill Pr.

Dubofsky, Melvyn, jt. auth. see Dulles, Foster R.

Dubofsky, Melvyn, et al. United States in the Twentieth Century. LC 77-13246. (Illus.). 1978. pap. 25.95 ref. ed. (ISBN 0-13-938712-9). P-H.

Dubois, Andre & Castell, Donald, eds. Esophageal & Gastric Emptying. LC 84-1895. 168p. 1984. 56.00 (ISBN 0-8493-6367-5). CRC Pr.

DuBois, Annette M. Belly of the Beholder. (Famous Last Words Ser.: No. V). (Orig.). 1985. pap. 2.50 (ISBN 0-916331-00-8). Famous Last Wds.

DuBois, Armand B. English Business Company after the Bubble Act, 1720-1800. LC 72-159179. 1971. Repr. of 1938 ed. lib. bdg. 34.50x (ISBN 0-374-92362-0). Octagon.

Du Bois, Arthur E. The Beginnings of Tragic Comedy in the Drama of the Nineteenth Century. 1934. lib. bdg. 8.50 (ISBN 0-8414-3862-5). Folcroft.

DuBois, Bessie W. History of Juno Beach & Juno, Florida. (Illus.). 21p. pap. 2.95 (ISBN 0-317-19709-6). Florida Classics.

--History of Jupiter Lighthouse. (Illus.). 29p. pap. 2.95 (ISBN 0-317-19707-X). Florida Classics.

--History of the Loxahatchee River. (Illus.). 29p. pap. 2.95 (ISBN 0-317-19708-8). Florida Classics.

--Shipwrecks in the Vicinity of Jupiter Inlet. (Illus.). 31p. 1981. pap. 2.95 (ISBN 0-317-19706-1). Florida Classics.

Dubois, Betty L. & Crouch, Isabel. Regulatory Language Behavior. (Edward Sapir Monograph Series in Language, Culture, & Cognition: No. 13). xii, 96p. (Orig.). 1985. pap. 8.00x (ISBN 0-933104-19-7). Jupiter Pr.

Dubois, C. Pluri Dictionnaire. new ed. (Illus., Fr.). 1974. 31.50x (ISBN 2-03-020124-3, 3677). Larousse.

Dubois, D. W. & Recio, T., eds. Ordered Fields & Real Algebraic Geometry. LC 82-3951. (Contemporary Mathematics: Vol. 8). 368p. 1982. pap. 22.00 (ISBN 0-8218-5007-5, CONM-8). Am Math.

Dubois, Daniel, jt. auth. see Fronval, George.

Dubois, David G. And Bid Him Sing. 224p. 1975. 8.95 (ISBN 0-87867-041-6). Ramparts.

Dubois, Diana, ed. & intro. by. My Harvard, My Yale. 292p. 1982. 15.00 (ISBN 0-394-51920-5). Random.

Dubois, Didier & Prade, Henri. Fuzzy Sets & Systems: Theory & Applications. LC 79-6952. (Mathematics in Science & Engineering Ser.). 1980. 75.00 (ISBN 0-12-222750-6). Acad Pr.

Dubois, Donald E. The Odyssey & Other Adventures. 1983. 5.95 (ISBN 0-8062-2221-2). Carlton.

Dubois, Edmund L. Lupus Erythematosus: A Review of the Current Status of Discoid & Systemic Lupus Erythematosus & Their Variants. rev. 2nd ed. LC 73-86882. 1976. 39.50 (ISBN 0-88474-000-5). U of S Cal Pr.

Dubois, Edward N. Essential Methods in Business Statistics. (Illus.). 1979. text ed. 31.95 (ISBN 0-07-017889-5). McGraw.

Dubois, Ellen, ed. Elizabeth Cady Stanton-Susan B. Anthony: Correspondence, Writings, Speeches. LC 80-6190. (Studies in the Life of Women Ser.). 1981. 17.95x (ISBN 0-8052-3759-3); pap. 6.95 (ISBN 0-8052-0672-8). Schocken.

DuBois, Ellen C. Feminism & Suffrage: The Emergence of an Independent Women's Movement in America 1848-1869. 224p. 1978. 29.95x (ISBN 0-8014-1043-6); pap. 7.95x 1980 ed. (ISBN 0-8014-9182-7). Cornell U Pr.

DuBois, Ellen C., et al. Feminist Scholarship: Kindling in the Groves of Academe. LC 84-2589. 240p. 1985. 19.95x (ISBN 0-252-00957-6). U of Ill Pr.

Dubois, Eugene. Pithecanthropus erectus, eine menschenaehnliche Uebergangsform aus Java. LC 78-72693. Repr. of 1894 ed. 18.50 (ISBN 0-404-18264-X). AMS Pr.

Dubois, F. & Werny, P. Dictionnaire Francais-Allemand des Locutions. (Fr. & Ger.). 1976. 23.95 (ISBN 0-686-57124-X, M-6172). French & Eur.

Dubois, Felix. Timbuctoo the Mysterious. White, Diana, tr. LC 70-94475. (Illus.). Repr. of 1896 ed. 25.00x (ISBN 0-8371-2372-0, DTI&). Greenwood.

Dubois, J. L' Assommoir de Zola. (La Collection Themes & Textes Ser.). 224p. (Orig., Fr.). 1973. pap. 6.75 (ISBN 2-03-035018-4, 2647). Larousse.

--Dictionnaire du Francais Contemporain. 1263p. (Fr.). 1980. 19.95 (ISBN 2-03-320101-5, M-9357). French & Eur.

Dubois, J. & Giacomo, M. Dictionnaire de Linguistique. 516p. (Fr.). 1974. 27.50 (ISBN 2-03-020299-1, 1002). Larousse.

Dubois, J. B., et al, eds. Immunopharmacologic Effects of Radiation Therapy. (European Organization for Research on Treatment of Cancer (EORTC) Monographs: Vol. 8). 568p. 1981. 89.00 (ISBN 0-89004-531-3). Raven.

DuBois, J. Harry. Plastics History, U. S. A. LC 79-156480. (Illus.). 464p. 1972. 24.95 (ISBN 0-8436-1203-7). Van Nos Reinhold.

DuBois, J. Harry, jt. auth. see Levy, Sidney.

Dubois, Jacques & D'Ormesson, Jean. Versailles: A Garden in Four Seasons. Wheeler, Daniel, tr. from Fr. LC 83-14697. (Illus.). 222p. 1983. 85.00 (ISBN 0-86565-039-X). Vendome.

Dubois, Jacques, ed. see Zola, Emile.

Dubois, Jacques, et al. Rhetorique Generale. (Langue et langage). (Fr). 1970. pap. 12.25 (ISBN 0-685-14067-9, 3638). Larousse.

--A General Rhetoric. Burrell, Paul B. & Slotkin, Edgar M., trs. from Fr. LC 80-24495. (Illus.). 288p. 1981. text ed. 26.50x (ISBN 0-8018-2326-9). Johns Hopkins.

Dubois, Jean. Diccionario de Linguistica. (Span.). 1979. pap. pns (S-50086). French & Eur.

--Grammaire de Base. new ed. (Orig., Fr.). 1976. pap. 7.25 (ISBN 2-03-040166-8). Larousse.

--Grammaire Structurale du Francais, 3 vols. Incl. Vol. 1. Nom et pronom. 192p (3630); Vol. 2. Verbe. 192p (3631); Vol. 3. Phrase et transformations. 180p (3632). (Fr.). pap. 14.50 ea. Larousse.

--Patchwork Quilting with Wool. (Quilting, Patchwork, Applique Ser.). 192p. 1985. pap. 5.95 (ISBN 0-486-24821-6). Dover.

--Vocabulaire Politique et Social en France de 1869 a 1872. (Fr). pap. 11.95x (ISBN 0-685-14095-4). Larousse.

Dubois, Jean & Lagane, Rene. Dictionnaire du Francais Classique. 608p. (Fr.). 1971. 22.50 (ISBN 0-686-57298-X, F-133960). French & Eur.

--La Nouvelle Grammaire du francais. 272p. (Orig., Fr.). 1973. pap. 9.95 (ISBN 2-03-040165-X, 3772). Larousse.

Dubois, Jean, ed. Lexis: Dictionnaire De la Langue Francaise. 2032p. (Fr.). 1975. 47.50 (ISBN 0-686-57019-7, M-6376). French & Eur.

--Lexis-Dictionnaire de la langue francaise. 1939p. (Fr.). 1975. 56.25 (ISBN 2-03-020285-1, 3924). Larousse.

--Lexis-Dictionnaire de la Langue Francaise. (Fr.). 1979. 56.25 (ISBN 0-686-60644-2, 2427). Larousse.

Dubois, Jean-Paul, jt. auth. see Bird, Eric.

DuBois, Jill. Reap the Bitter Wind. 432p. 1985. pap. 3.50 (ISBN 0-345-32166-9). Ballantine.

DuBois, June. Indiana Artists George Jo & Evelynne Bernloehr Mess: A Story of Devotion. (Illus., Orig.). 1985. pap. 13.95 (ISBN 0-87195-000-6). Ind Hist Soc.

--William R. Leigh: the Definitive Illustrated Biography. LC 77-15343. 1977. 40.00 (ISBN 0-913504-42-4). Lowell Pr.

Dubois, Marguerite-Marie. Dictionnaire de Locutions, Francais-Anglais. 392p. (Fr. & Eng.). 1973. 22.50 (ISBN 0-686-57125-8, M-6173). French & Eur.

Dubois, Marie-Marguerite. Dictionnaire Moderne Saturne: Francais-Anglais, Anglais-Francais. 10th ed. 1552p. (Fr. & Eng.). 1972. 29.95 (ISBN 0-686-57126-6, M-6174). French & Eur.

Dubois, Michel. Dictionnaire de Sigles Nationaux et Internationaux. 479p. (Fr.). 1977. pap. 50.00 (ISBN 0-686-56831-1, M-6609). French & Eur.

DuBois, Nelson, et al. Educational Psychology & Instructional Decisions. LC 78-70013. 1979. pap. text ed. 27.00x (ISBN 0-256-02056-6). Dorsey.

Dubois, P. Le Baroque. new ed. (Collection themes et textes). 256p. (Orig., Fr.). 1973. pap. 6.75 (ISBN 2-03-035016-8). Larousse.

Dubois, P. & Brighton, C. A. Plastics in Agriculture. (Illus.). 1978. text ed. 20.50 (ISBN 0-85334-776-X, Pub. by Elsevier Applied Sci England). Elsevier.

DuBois, Page. Centaurs & Amazons: Women & the Pre-History of the Great Chain of Being. (Women & Culture Ser.). (Illus.). 192p. 1982. text ed. 8.95x (ISBN 0-472-10021-1). U of Mich Pr.

--History, Rhetorical Description & the Epic: From Homer to Spenser. 131p. 1982. text ed. 22.50 (ISBN 0-85991-093-8, BAB-04699). Boydell & Brewer.

--History, Rhetorical Description & the Epic: From Homer to Spenser. 131p. 1982. 22.50 (ISBN 0-317-19409-7, Pub. by Boydell & Brewer). Longwood Pub Group.

DuBois, Paul. The Hospice Way of Death. LC 79-12326. 223p. 1980. bds. 24.95 (ISBN 0-87705-415-0). Human Sci Pr.

DuBois, Paul M. Modern Administrative Practices in Human Services. 144p. 1981. 20.50x (ISBN 0-398-04164-4). C C Thomas.

Du Bois, Pene. Gentleman Bear. Date not set. lib. bdg. 12.95 (ISBN 0-374-32533-2). FS&G.

Dubois, Philip, ed. Judicial Reform. (Orig.). 1982. pap. 8.00 (ISBN 0-918592-56-9). Policy Studies.

Dubois, Philip L. The Analysis of Judicial Reform. LC 80-8947. (Policy Studies Organization Bk.). 224p. 1982. 27.50x (ISBN 0-669-04480-6). Lexington Bks.

--From Ballot to Bench: Judicial Elections & the Quest for Accountability. LC 80-12728. 332p. 1980. text ed. 25.00x (ISBN 0-292-72028-9). U of Tex Pr.

Dubois, Philip L., ed. The Politics of Judicial Reform. LC 80-8948. (A Policy Studies Organization Bk.). 208p. 1982. 27.50x (ISBN 0-669-04478-4). Lexington Bks.

Dubois, Pierre. Bio-Bibliographie De Victor Hugo De 1802 a 1825. 1971. Repr. of 1913 ed. lib. bdg. 22.50 (ISBN 0-8337-0929-1). B Franklin.

DuBois, Rachel. Handbook for Leaders of Quaker Dialogue. (FGC). 52p. 1964. 1.00 (ISBN 0-318-14147-7). Friends Genl Conf.

DuBois, Rachel D. All This & Something More: Pioneering in Intercultural Education. 320p. 1984. 14.95 (ISBN 0-317-02678-X). Dorrance.

Du Bois, Rachel D. & Schweppe, Emma. The Germans in American Life. 13.75 (ISBN 0-8369-6928-6, 7809). Ayer Co Pubs.

Dubois, Rochelle. The Invisible Dog. (Illus.). 64p. 18.00 (ISBN 0-88014-023-2). Mosaic Pr OH.

DuBois, Rochelle H. Timelapse. LC 83-9883. (Contemporary Poetry Ser.: No. 1). 80p. (Orig.). 1983. pap. 6.50 (ISBN 0-938136-08-9). Lunchroom Pr.

--Timesharing: A Consumer's Guide to a New Vacation Concept. 32p. (Orig.). 1982. pap. 3.00 (ISBN 0-9603950-4-0). Somrie Pr.

Dubois, Rochelle H. & Kenny, Adele. Dialogue of Days. 40p. 1983. pap. 3.75 (ISBN 0-934536-16-3). Merging Media.

Dubois, Sally. The Marriage Season. (Candlelight Ecstasy Ser.: No. 13). (Orig.). 1981. pap. 1.75 (ISBN 0-440-16058-8). Dell.

Dubois, Shirley G. Gamal Abdel Nasser: Son of the Nile. (Illus.). 250p. 1972. 8.95 (ISBN 0-89388-048-5). Okpaku Communications.

--His Day Is Marching on: Memoirs of W. E. B. DuBois. LC 71-146693. 1971. 10.00 (ISBN 0-89388-156-2); pap. 5.95 (ISBN 0-89388-157-0). Okpaku Communications.

Du Bois, Shirley G. Pictorial History of W. E. B. Du Bois. 14.95 (ISBN 0-87485-081-9). Johnson Chi.

DuBois, Shirley G. Zulu Heart: A Novel. LC 73-92801. 1973. 8.95 (ISBN 0-89388-132-5). Okpaku Communications.

Dubois, Theodora & Smith, Dorothy V. Staten Island Patroons. (Illus.). 1961. pap. 1.50 (ISBN 0-686-23393-X). Staten Island.

DuBois, W. Burghardt. Negro. 1970. pap. 5.95 (ISBN 0-19-501262-3, 333, GB). Oxford U Pr.

Du Bois, W. E. Black Reconstruction in America, 1860-1880. LC 68-1237. (Studies in American Negro Life). 1969. pap. text ed. 8.95x (ISBN 0-689-70063-6, NL20). Atheneum.

--Economic Co-operation among Negro Americans. (Atlanta Univ. Publ. Ser.: No. 12). (Orig.). 1907. pap. 16.00 (ISBN 0-527-03113-5). Kraus Repr.

--The Education of Black People: Ten Critiques, 1906-1960. Aptheker, Herbert, ed. LC 72-90495. 176p. 1975. pap. 4.50 (ISBN 0-85345-363-2). Monthly Rev.

--The Education of Black People: Ten Critiques, 1906-1960. Aptheker, Herbert, ed. LC 72-90495. 184p. 1973. 12.00x (ISBN 0-87023-130-8). U of Mass Pr.

DuBois, W. E. Quest of the Silver Fleece. facs. ed. LC 71-83922. (Black Heritage Library Collection Ser). (Illus.). 1911. 21.00 (ISBN 0-8369-8553-2). Ayer Co Pubs.

Du Bois, W. E. Quest of the Silver Fleece: A Novel. LC 70-92742. Repr. of 1911 ed. 27.50x (ISBN 0-8371-2066-7, DSF&). Greenwood.

--The Souls of Black Folk. (Great Illustrated Classics). (gr. 7 up). 1979. 8.95 (ISBN 0-396-07757-9). Dodd.

Dubois, W. E. Souls of Black Folk. 1970. pap. 1.25 (ISBN 0-671-47833-8). WSP.

--Suppression of the African Slave Trade to the United States of America, 1638-1870. 325p. 1970. Repr. of 1896 ed. 16.50 (ISBN 0-87928-011-5). Corner Hse.

Dubois, W. E., jt. auth. see Washington, Booker T.

DuBois, W. E., jt. auth. see Washington, Booker T.

DuBois, W. E., ed. Atlanta University Publications, Nos. 1-11, 2 Vols. 1968. Set. lib. bdg. 34.00x (ISBN 0-374-92356-6). Octagon.

Du Bois, W. E., ed. Negro American Family. LC 68-55882. (Illus.). Repr. of 1908 ed. 19.75x (ISBN 0-8371-1342-3, DUF&, Pub. by Negro U Pr). Greenwood.

Du Bois, W. E. B. Africa: Its Geography, People & Products, 2 vols. in 1. Aptheker, Herbert, ed. & intro. by. Bd. with Its Place in Modern History. LC 76-53579. 1977. Repr. of 1930 ed. lib. bdg. 8.00x (ISBN 0-527-25260-3). Kraus Intl.

DuBois, W. E. B. Against Racism: Unpublished Essays, Papers, Addresses, 1887-1961. Aptheker, Herbert, ed. LC 84-16173. (Illus.). 352p. 1985. lib. bdg. 25.00x (ISBN 0-87023-134-0). U of Mass Pr.

Du Bois, W. E. B. The Autobiography of W. E. B. Du Bois: A Soliloquy on Viewing My Life from the Last Decade of Its First Century. LC 68-14103. 1976. Repr. 20.00 (ISBN 0-527-25262-X). Kraus Intl.

--The Bkack Flame: A Trilogy, 3 Vols. Incl. Bk. 1. The Ordeal of Mansart. LC 57-13796. 1957. 19.00 (ISBN 0-527-25270-0); Bk. 2. Mansart Builds a School. LC 59-65207. 22.00 (ISBN 0-527-25271-9); Bk. 3. Worlds of Color. LC 61-3560. 1961. 21.00 (ISBN 0-527-25272-7). 1976. Set. 55.00 (ISBN 0-317-19749-5). Kraus Intl.

--Black Folk Then & Now: An Essay in the History & Sociology of the Negro Race. LC 75-28300. 1975. Repr. of 1939 ed. 24.00 (ISBN 0-527-25275-1). Kraus Intl.

--Black North in 1901: A Social Study. LC 70-92229. (American Negro: His History & Literature, Ser. No. 3). 1970. Repr. of 1901 ed. 7.00 (ISBN 0-405-01921-1). Ayer Co Pubs.

--Black Reconstruction: An Essay Toward a History of the Part Which Black Folk Played in the Attempt to Reconstruct Democracy in America, 1860-1880. LC 35-8545. 746p. 1976. Repr. of 1935 ed. lib. bdg. 35.00x (ISBN 0-527-25280-8). Kraus Intl.

--Color & Democracy: Colonies & Peace. LC 75-28190. 1975. Repr. of 1945 ed. 10.00 (ISBN 0-527-25290-5). Kraus Intl.

--The Correspondence of W. E. B. Du Bois: Selections, 1877-1934. Aptheker, Herbert, ed. LC 72-90496. (Correspondence of W.E.B. Du Bois: Vol. 1). (Illus.). 510p. 1973. 27.50x (ISBN 0-87023-131-6). U of Mass Pr.

--The Correspondence of W. E. B. Du Bois: Selections, 1934-1944, Vol. 2. Aptheker, Herbert, ed. LC 72-90496. (Illus.). 1976. 27.50x (ISBN 0-87023-132-4). U of Mass Pr.

--The Correspondence of W. E. B. Du Bois: Vol. 3, Selections, 1944-1963. Aptheker, Herbert, ed. LC 72-90496. (Illus.). 1978. lib. bdg. 27.50x (ISBN 0-87023-133-2). U of Mass Pr.

--Creative Writings by W. E. B. Du Bois: A Pageant, Poems, Short Stories & Playlets. (The Complete Published Works of W. E. B. Du Bois). 1985. lib. bdg. 42.00 (ISBN 0-527-25346-4). Kraus Intl.

--Dark Princess: A Romance. LC 74-7248. 340p. 1975. Repr. of 1928 ed. lib. bdg. 18.00 (ISBN 0-527-25295-6). Kraus Intl.

--Darkwater: Voices from Within the Veil. LC 75-1429. 1975. Repr. of 1920 ed. 17.00 (ISBN 0-527-25300-6). Kraus Intl.

--Dusk of Dawn: An Essay Toward an Autobiography of a Race Concept. LC 75-28189. 1975. Repr. of 1940 ed. 20.00 (ISBN 0-527-25305-7). Kraus Intl.

DuBois, W. E. B. Dusk of Dawn: An Essay Toward an Autobiography of a Race Concept. (Black Classics in Social Science Ser.). 355p. 1983. pap. 19.95 (ISBN 0-87855-917-5). Transaction Bks.

Du Bois, W. E. B. Efforts for Social Betterment Among Negro Americans. (Atlanta Univ. Publ. Ser.: No. 14). (Orig.). 1909. Repr. of 1909 ed. 15.00 (ISBN 0-527-03115-1). Kraus Repr.

--The Gift of Black Folk: The Negroes in the Making of America. LC 75-1447. 1975. Repr. of 1924 ed. 21.00 (ISBN 0-527-25310-3). Kraus Intl.

--In Battle for Peace: The Story of My 83rd Birthday. LC 52-3784. 1976. Repr. of 1952 ed. 13.00 (ISBN 0-527-25265-4). Kraus Intl.

--John Brown. Repr. of 1909 ed. 25.00 (ISBN 0-527-25285-9). Kraus Intl.

--The Negro. LC 74-7274. 1975. Repr. of 1915 ed. 17.00 (ISBN 0-527-25315-4). Kraus Intl.

--The Negro American Family. (Atlanta Univ. Publ. Ser.: No. 13). (Orig.). 1908. pap. 15.00 (ISBN 0-527-03114-3). Kraus Repr.

--The Negro Artisan. (Atlanta Univ. Publ. Ser.: No. 7). (Orig.). 1902. pap. 16.00 (ISBN 0-527-03110-0). Kraus Repr.

DuBois, W. E. B. Pamphlets & Leaflets by W. E. B. DuBois. (The Complete Published Works of W. E. B. DuBois Ser.). 1985. lib. bdg. write for info. (ISBN 0-527-25348-0). Kraus Intl.

Du Bois, W. E. B. The Philadelphia Negro: A Social Study. Together with a Special Report on Domestic Service by Isabel Eaton. 520p. 1973. Repr. of 1899 ed. 31.00 (ISBN 0-527-25320-0). Kraus Intl.

--Prayers for Dark People. Aptheker, Herbert, ed. LC 80-12234. 88p. 1980. lib. bdg. 12.00x (ISBN 0-87023-302-5); pap. 5.95 (ISBN 0-87023-303-3). U of Mass Pr.

--Quest of the Silver Fleece. LC 73-86658. (American Negro: His History & Literature, Series No. 3). 1970. Repr. of 1911 ed. 21.00 (ISBN 0-405-01922-X). Ayer Co Pubs.

--The Quest of the Silver Fleece. LC 74-7364. 451p. 1975. Repr. of 1911 ed. lib. bdg. 26.00 (ISBN 0-527-25325-1). Kraus Intl.

--Some Notes on Negro Crime Particularly in Georgia. (Atlanta Univ. Publ. Ser.: No. 9). (Orig.). 1904. pap. 14.00 (ISBN 0-527-03111-9). Kraus Repr.

--Souls of Black Folk: Essays & Sketches. 264p. 1973. Repr. of 1953 ed. 17.00 (ISBN 0-527-25330-8). Kraus Intl.

--The Suppression of the African Slave Trade to the United States of America, 1638-1870. 335p. 1973. Repr. of 1896 ed. 20.00 (ISBN 0-527-25335-9). Kraus Intl.

--W. E. B. Du Bois on Sociology & the Black Community. Green, Dan S. & Driver, Edwin D., eds. LC 78-770. 1980. pap. 5.50x (ISBN 0-226-16760-7, 866, Phoen). U of Chicago Pr.

--The World & Africa: An Inquiry into the Part Which Africa Has Played in World History. Repr. of 1965 ed. 21.00 (ISBN 0-527-25340-5). Kraus Intl.

--Writings in Periodicals Edited by W. E. B. Du Bois: Selections from The Horizon. (The Complete Published Works of W. E. B. Du Bois Ser.). 1985. lib. bdg. 40.00 (ISBN 0-527-25350-2). Kraus Intl.

Du Bois, W. E. B., ed. The College-Bred Negro American. (Atlanta Univ. Publ. Ser.: No. 15). (Orig.). pap. 14.00 (ISBN 0-527-03116-X). Kraus Repr.

--The Common School & the Negro American. (Atlanta Univ. Publ. Ser.: No. 16). (Orig.). 1911. pap. 15.00 (ISBN 0-527-03117-8). Kraus Repr.

--Morals & Manners Among Negro Americans. (Atlanta Univ. Publ. Ser.: No. 18). (Orig.). 1914. pap. 15.00 (ISBN 0-527-03119-4). Kraus Repr.

--The Negro-American Artisan. (Atlanta Univ. Publ. Ser.: No. 17). (Orig.). 1912. pap. 15.00 (ISBN 0-527-03118-6). Kraus Repr.

--A Select Bibliography of the Negro American. (Atlanta Univ. Publ. Ser.: No. 10). (Orig.). 1905. pap. 14.00 (ISBN 0-527-03112-7). Kraus Repr.

Du Bois, William E. ABC of Color. 216p. (Orig.). 1970. pap. 2.25 (ISBN 0-7178-0391-0). Intl Pubs Co.

--Autobiography of W. E. Burghardt Du Bois: A Soliloquy on Viewing My Life from the Last Decade of Its First Century. Aptheker, Herbert, ed. LC 68-14103. (Illus.). 448p. 1968. 17.00 (ISBN 0-7178-0235-3); pap. 4.75 (ISBN 0-7178-0234-5). Intl Pubs Co.

Dubois, William E. Darkwater: Voices from Within the Veil. LC 70-91785. Repr. of 1920 ed. 12.50 (ISBN 0-404-00151-3). AMS Pr.

--The Gift of Black Folk. LC 70-144598. Repr. of 1924 ed. 15.00 (ISBN 0-404-00152-1). AMS Pr.

Du Bois, William E. John Brown. 2nd, rev. ed. LC 62-21668. 312p. (Orig.). 1974. pap. 2.25 (ISBN 0-7178-0375-9). Intl Pubs Co.

--John Brown. LC 79-99370. 406p. 1972. Repr. of 1909 ed. lib. bdg. 19.00 (ISBN 0-8411-0041-1). Metro Bks.

Dubois, William E. Negro in Business. LC 70-153098. Repr. of 1899 ed. 12.50 (ISBN 0-404-00153-X). AMS Pr.

Du Bois, William E. Quest of the Silver Fleece. LC 73-144599. Repr. of 1911 ed. 12.50 (ISBN 0-404-00154-8). AMS Pr.

--Quest of the Silver Fleece. pap. 3.95 (ISBN 0-685-16795-X, N261P). Mnemosyne.

--Souls of Black Folk. (Classic Ser). (Orig.). 1969. pap. 3.95 (ISBN 0-451-51953-1, CE1820, Sig Classics). NAL.

--Suppression of the African Slave Trade, 1638 to 1870. LC 65-18803. xx, 336p. 1970. pap. text ed. 7.95x (ISBN 0-8071-0149-4). La State U Pr.

--World & Africa: Inquiry into the Part Which Africa Has Played in World History. rev. ed. LC 65-16392. (Illus., Orig.). 1965. pap. 5.25 (ISBN 0-7178-0221-3). Intl Pubs Co.

Du Bois, William E; see Franklin, John H.

Du Bois, William E., jt. auth. see Washington, Booker T.

Du Bois, William P. Mother Goose for Christmas. (Picture Puffins Ser.). (Illus.). 32p. 1979. pap. 3.50 (ISBN 0-14-050329-3, Puffin). Penguin.

Du Bois, William Pene see Pene Du Bois, William.

Du Bois, William Pene see Pene du Bois, William.

Du Bois, William Pene see Strand, Mark.

Dubois, William R. & Nisbet-Snyder Drama Collection, Northern Illinois University Libraries, eds. English & American Stage Productions: An Annotated Checklist of Prompt Books, 1800-1900. 1973. lib. bdg. 23.50 (ISBN 0-8161-1035-2, Hall Reference). G K Hall.

DuBois, William W. & Hodik, Barbara J. A Guide to Photographic Design. (Illus.). 128p. 1983. pap. 12.95 (ISBN 0-13-370346-0). P-H.

Dubois-Charlier, F., et al. Dictionnaire d'Anglais. 868p. (Fr.). 1975. pap. text ed. 11.50 (ISBN 2-03-040531-0). Larousse.

Dubois-Charlier, Francoise. Comment d'Initier a la Linguistique, 5 livrets in 1 vol. 319p. (Fr.). 1975. pap. 19.95 (ISBN 2-03-041307-0, 4541). Larousse.

Dubois-Dalco, M., et al. Assembly of Enveloped RNA Viruses. Kingsbury, D. W., ed. (Illus.). 250p. 1984. 49.50 (ISBN 0-387-81802-2). Springer-Verlag.

DuBois-Reymond, E; see Brodie, Benjamin.

DuBois-Reymond, E. see Whytt, Robert.

Du Bos, Charles. Byron & the Need of Fatality. LC 78-95423. (Studies in Byron, No. 5). 1970. Repr. of 1932 ed. lib. bdg. 49.95x (ISBN 0-8383-0971-2). Haskell.

--What Is Literature? LC 76-40044. Repr. of 1940 ed. lib. bdg. 15.00 (ISBN 0-8414-3810-2). Folcroft.

Dubos, Jean B. Critical Reflections on Poetry, Painting & Music, 3 vols. LC 78-3659. (Music & Theatre in France in the 17th & 18th Centuries). Repr. of 1748 ed. Set. 87.50 (ISBN 0-404-60170-7). AMS Pr.

Dubos, Reme. Celebrations of Life. 276p. 1982. pap. 5.95 (ISBN 0-07-017894-1). McGraw.

Dubos, Rene. Beast or Angel? Choices That Make Us Human. LC 74-10737. (The Scribner Library of Contemporary Classics). 240p. 1984. pap. 7.95 (ISBN 0-684-14436-0, ScribT). Scribner.

--Celebrations of Life. 1981. 12.95 (ISBN 0-07-017893-3). McGraw.

--A God Within. LC 76-37224. 320p. 1972. text ed. 29.50x (ISBN 0-684-12768-7). Irvington.

--A God Within. LC 76-37224. 320p. 1973. pap. 8.95 (ISBN 0-684-13506-X, SL 458, ScribT). Scribner.

--Man Adapting. enl. ed. LC 80-16492. (Silliman Lectures Ser.). (Illus.). 527p. 1980. 36.00x (ISBN 0-300-02580-7); pap. 9.95 (ISBN 0-300-02581-5, Y-197). Yale U Pr.

--Of Human Diversity. LC 73-78352. (Heinz Werner Lec. Ser.: No. 7). 1974. 3.00x (ISBN 0-517-51739-6). Clark U Pr.

--The Professor, the Institute, & DNA. LC 76-26812. (Illus.). 262p. 1976. 15.00x (ISBN 0-87470-022-1). Rockefeller.

--The Resilience of Ecosystems. (Illus.). 1978. pap. 2.50x (ISBN 0-87081-107-X). Colo Assoc.

--So Human an Animal. LC 68-27794. (The Scribner Library of Contemporary Classics). 228p. 1984. pap. 7.95 (ISBN 0-684-71753-0, SL195, ScribT). Scribner.

--The Wooing of Earth. 1980. pap. 6.95 encore ed. (ISBN 0-684-16951-7, ScribT). Scribner.

Dubos, Rene, jt. auth. see Ward, Barbara.

Dubos, Rene J. The Dreams of Reason: Science & Utopias. LC 61-11753. (George B. Pegram Lecture Ser.). 167p. 1961. 21.00x (ISBN 0-231-02493-2); pap. 9.50x (ISBN 0-231-08544-3). Columbia U Pr.

--Reason Awake: Science for Man. LC 70-111327. 280p. 1970. 26.00x (ISBN 0-231-03181-5); pap. 11.00x (ISBN 0-231-08629-6). Columbia U Pr.

Du Bosc, Jacques. The Compleat Woman. LC 68-54642. (English Experience Ser.: No. 12). 88p. 1968. Repr. of 1639 ed. 16.00 (ISBN 90-221-0012-X). Walter J Johnson.

Duboscq, Genevieve. My Longest Night. Woodward, Richard S., tr. from Fr. LC 80-23169. (Illus.). 288p. 1981. 13.95 (ISBN 0-394-51590-0). Seaver Bks.

Dubose, Anita, jt. auth. see Pearlman, Daniel.

DuBose, Estelle & DuBose, LaRocque. Cyrano De Bergerac Notes. (Orig.). 1971. pap. 3.25 (ISBN 0-8220-0346-5). Cliffs.

DuBose, Francis M. God Who Sends. LC 83-70002. 1983. 10.95 (ISBN 0-8054-6331-3). Broadman.

Dubose, Francis M., ed. Classics of Christian Missions. LC 78-53147. 1979. pap. 12.95 (ISBN 0-8054-6313-5). Broadman.

DuBose, Fred. The Total Tomato. LC 83-48342. (Illus.). 224p. 1985. pap. 8.61 (ISBN 0-06-091105-0, CN). Har-Row.

Du Bose, Heyward. Mamba's Daughters. 311p. Date not set. Repr. of 1929 ed. lib. bdg. 25.00 (ISBN 0-8495-2406-7). Arden Lib.

--Mamba's Daughters. 17.95 (ISBN 0-89190-749-1, Pub. by Am Repr). Amereon Ltd.

Du Bose, J. W. The Life & Times of William Lowndes Yancey, 2 vols. Set. 26.00 (ISBN 0-8446-1161-1). Peter Smith.

DuBose, Larocque. Barron's Simplified Approach to Maugham's Of Human Bondage. LC 67-31236. 1968. pap. text ed. 1.95 (ISBN 0-8120-0279-2). Barron.

--For Whom the Bell Tolls Notes. (Orig.). 1967. pap. 2.75 (ISBN 0-8220-0497-6). Cliffs.

DuBose, LaRocque, jt. auth. see DuBose, Estelle.

DuBose, Sybil. The Pastors' Wives Cookbook. Buford, Janine, ed. 1978. pap. 9.95 (ISBN 0-918544-13-0). Wimmer Bks.

DuBose, William P. A DuBose Reader. Armentrout, Donald S., ed. LC 84-51878. 256p. 1984. pap. 10.95 (ISBN 0-918769-06-X). Univ South.

--The Ecumenical Councils. 1977. lib. bdg. 59.95 (ISBN 0-8490-1751-3). Gordon Pr.

Dubost, G. Flat Radiating Dipoles & Applications to Arrays. (Electronic & Electrical Engineering Research Studies: Research Studies on Antennas Ser.). 103p. 1981. 38.95x (ISBN 0-471-10050-1, Pub. by Res Stud Pr). Wiley.

Du Boulay, F. R. Germany in the Later Middle Ages. LC 83-2903. 220p. 1984. 30.00x (ISBN 0-312-32625-4). St Martin.

DuBoulay, G. H., ed. Considerations about the Use of Computers in Radiodiagnostic Departments. 1980. 50.00x (ISBN 0-686-69947-5, Pub. by Brit Inst Radiology England). State Mutual Bk.

DuBoulay, G. H., ed. see European Seminar on Computerized Axial Tomography in Clinical Practice, 1st.

DuBoulay, Juliet. Portrait of a Greek Mountain Village. (Oxford Monographs on Social Anthropology). (Illus.). 1974. 14.95x (ISBN 0-19-823198-9). Oxford U Pr.

Du Boulay, Shirley. Cicley Saunders: Founder of the Modern Hospice Movement. LC 84-70585. (Illus.). 268p. 1984. 17.95 (ISBN 0-943276-05-5). Amaryllis Pr.

DuBourg, George. The Violin. LC 77-75186. 1977. Repr. of 1852 ed. lib. bdg. 45.00 (ISBN 0-89341-090-X). Longwood Pub Group.

Dubov, Irving, ed. Contemporary Agricultural Marketing. LC 67-29414. pap. 69.50 (ISBN 0-317-29906-9, 2021775). Bks Demand UMI.

Dubovik, A. S. Photographic Recording of High-Speed Processes. 1968. 72.00 (ISBN 0-08-012017-2). Pergamon.

Dubovsky, E. V., et al. Nuclear Medicine Technology Continuing Education Review. 2nd ed. 1981. 19.00 (ISBN 0-87488-331-8). Med Exam.

Dubovsky, Steven L. Psychotherapeutics in Primary Care. 240p. 1981. 30.50 (ISBN 0-8089-1337-9, 791090). Grune.

Dubovsky, Steven L. & Feiger, Allan D. Psychiatric Decision Making. (Decision Making Ser.). 300p. 1984. text ed. 36.00 (ISBN 0-941158-16-0, D1483-X). Mosby.

Dubovsky, Steven L. & Weissberg, Michael P. Clinical Psychiatry in Primary Care. 2nd ed. (Illus.). 292p. 1982. pap. text ed. 15.50 (ISBN 0-683-02672-0). Williams & Wilkins.

Dubovy, Andrew. Pilgrims of the Prairie. Bloch, Marie H., tr. from Ukrainian. Date not set. price not set. Ukrainian Cult Inst.

--Pilgrims of the Prairie: Pioneer Ukrainian Baptists in North Dakota. Bloch, Marie H., ed. (Illus.). 72p. (Orig.). 1983. lib. bdg. 8.50; pap. 4.50. Ukrainian Cult Inst.

Dubovy, Joseph. Complete Guide to Amateur Radio. 1982. pap. 5.95 (ISBN 0-13-159798-1, Reward). P-H.

DuBovy, Joseph L. Introduction to Biomedical Electronics. (Illus.). 1978. text ed. 25.15 (ISBN 0-07-017895-X). McGraw.

DuBow, Fredric, jt. auth. see Podolefsky, Aaron.

DuBow, Michael S. Bacteriophage Assembly. LC 81-8224. (Progress in Clinical & Biological Research Ser.: Vol. 64). 574p. 1981. 57.00 (ISBN 0-8451-0064-5). A R Liss.

Dubowitz, Libby & Dubowitz, Victor. Neurological Assessment of the Pre-Term & Full Term Newborn Infant. (Clinics in Developmental Medicine Ser.: Vol. 79). 112p. 1981. text ed. 28.75 (Pub. by Spastics Intl England). Lippincott.

Dubowitz, Victor. Muscle Biopsy: A Practical Approach. 2nd ed. (Illus.). 415p. Date not set. price not set (Pub. by Bailliere-Tindall). Saunders.

--Muscle Disorders in Childhood. LC 77-23997. (Major Problems in Clinical Pediatrics Ser.: Vol. 16). (Illus.). 1978. text ed. 15.00 (ISBN 0-7216-3210-6). Saunders.

Dubowitz, Victor, jt. auth. see Dubowitz, Libby.

Dubowitz, Victor, ed. The Floppy Infant. 2nd ed. (Clinics in Developmental Medicine Ser.: Vol. 76). 158p. 1980. 29.75 (ISBN 0-433-07902-9, Pub. by Spastics Intl England). Lippincott.

Dubowski, Cathy E. Escape to Third Earth: A Thundercats Adventure. LC 85-1990. (Illus.). 32p. (gr. 5-8). 1985. bds. 4.95 (ISBN 0-394-87467-6, BYR). Random.

Du Boys, Albert. Catherine of Aragon & the Sources of the English Reformation, 2 vols in 1. Yonge, Charlotte M., ed. 1969. Repr. of 1881 ed. 35.50 (ISBN 0-8337-0931-3). B Franklin.

Dubpernell, George. Electrodeposition of Chromium from Chromic Acid Solutions. LC 77-549. 1977. text ed. 19.00 (ISBN 0-08-021925-X). Pergamon.

Dubray, Charles A. see Judd, Charles H.

DuBreuil, Linda. Housewife Hustlers. (Orig.). 1976. pap. 1.50 (ISBN 0-685-64009-4, LB334DK, Leisure Bks). Dorchester Pub Co.

Dubreton, J. Lucas. Samuel Pepys: A Portrait in Miniature. Stenning, H. F., tr. 280p. 1980. Repr. lib. bdg. 25.00 (ISBN 0-89984-150-3). Century Bookbindery.

Du Breuil, Alice. Novel of Democracy in America. LC 72-195477. 1923. lib. bdg. 15.00 (ISBN 0-8414-3863-3). Folcroft.

Dubreuil, Hyacinth. Robots or Men: French Workman's Experience in American Industry. Stein, Leon, ed. LC 77-70491. (Work Ser.). 1977. Repr. of 1930 ed. lib. bdg. 24.50x (ISBN 0-405-10163-5). Ayer Co Pubs.

DuBreuil, Linda. Crooked Letter. 1979. pap. 1.75 (ISBN 0-505-51385-4, Pub. by Tower Bks). Dorchester Pub Co.

--Deadly Party. 1979. pap. 1.50 (ISBN 0-505-51374-9, Pub. by Tower Bks). Dorchester Pub Co.

--Divorce Las Vegas Style. 1976. pap. 1.50 (ISBN 0-685-72566-9, Leisure Bks). Dorchester Pub Co.

--Double Standard. 1980. pap. 2.25 (ISBN 0-8439-0801-7, Pub. by Nordon Pubns). Dorchester Pub Co.

--Follow the Leader. 1979. pap. 2.25 (ISBN 0-505-51433-8, Pub. by Tower Bks). Dorchester Pub Co.

--The Girl Who Writes Dirty Books. 1975. pap. 1.75 (ISBN 0-685-51413-7, LB225KK, Leisure Bks). Dorchester Pub Co.

--Heyday. 1978. pap. 1.95 (ISBN 0-532-19212-5). Woodhill.

--Kept Men. (Orig.). 1976. pap. 1.50 (ISBN 0-685-64010-8, LB341DK, Leisure Bks). Dorchester Pub Co.

--Mirror Image. 1979. pap. 1.75 (ISBN 0-505-51393-5, Pub. by Tower Bks). Dorchester Pub Co.

--Only on Sunday. 1977. pap. 1.50 (ISBN 0-8439-0459-3, Leisure Bks). Dorchester Pub Co.

--Poppy. 1976. pap. 1.50 (ISBN 0-685-69146-2, LB357ZK, Leisure Bks). Dorchester Pub Co.

--Sex Clinic. 1975. pap. 1.50 (ISBN 0-685-59193-X, LB307DK, Leisure Bks). Dorchester Pub Co.

--So Dear, So Deadly. 1979. pap. 1.75 (ISBN 0-8439-0657-X, Leisure Bks). Dorchester Pub Co.

--Some Call It Perjury. 1979. pap. 1.75 (ISBN 0-8439-0633-2, Leisure Bks). Dorchester Pub Co.

--The Sunday Seducer. 1975. pap. 1.50 (ISBN 0-685-52173-7, LB246DK, Leisure Bks). Dorchester Pub Co.

--The Trial. 1975. pap. 1.50 (ISBN 0-685-52172-9, LB245DK, Leisure Bks). Dorchester Pub Co.

Du Breuil, Linda. Ultimate Sex. 1976. pap. 1.50 (ISBN 0-8439-0347-3, Leisure Bks). Dorchester Pub Co.

Dubreuil, Linda. Without a Man of Her Own. (Orig.). 1975. pap. 1.50 (ISBN 0-685-53906-7, LB282DK, Leisure Bks). Dorchester Pub Co.

DuBreuil, Linda, jt. auth. see Anderson, Kristen.

Dubreuil, P. Recueil Quadrilingue de Mots Usuels en Hydrologie. 113p. (Quadrilingual Collection of Commonly Used Words in Hydrology). 1969. pap. 9.95 (ISBN 0-686-56767-6, M-6176). French & Eur.

DuBrey, Rita J. Promoting Wellness in Nursing Practice: A Step-by-Step Approach in Patient Education. LC 81-22321. (Illus.). 387p. 1982. pap. text ed. 15.95 (ISBN 0-8016-1480-5). Mosby.

DuBrin. Contemporary Applied Management. 2nd ed ed. 1985. 16.95t (ISBN 0-256-03258-0). Business Pubns.

--Essentials of Management. 1986. pap. text ed. price not set (ISBN 0-538-07631-3, G63). SW Pub.

Dubrin, A. J. Casebook of Organizational Behavior. flexi-cover 10.50 (ISBN 0-08-020502-X). Pergamon.

Dubrin, Andrew. Effective Business Psychology. 2nd ed. 1985. text ed. 25.95 (ISBN 0-8359-1570-0); instr's. manual avail. Reston.

DuBrin, Andrew J. Bouncing Back: How to Handle Setbacks in Work & Personal Life. 185p. 1982. 11.95 (ISBN 0-13-080366-9); pap. 5.95 (ISBN 0-13-080358-8). P-H.

--Foundations of Organizational Behavior: An Applied Perspective. (Illus.). 528p. 1984. 28.95 (ISBN 0-13-329367-X). P-H.

--Human Relations: A Job Oriented Approach. 3rd ed. text ed. 25.95 (ISBN 0-8359-2954-X); instr's manual avail. (ISBN 0-8359-2952-3). Reston.

--Human Relations for Career & Personal Success. 1983. text ed. 22.95 (ISBN 0-8359-3011-4); instr's. manual free (ISBN 0-8359-3012-2). Reston.

--The Last Straw. 240p. 1984. 9.95 (ISBN 0-89697-190-2). Intl Univ Pr.

--The New Husbands & How to Become One. LC 76-15359. 228p. 1976. 18.95 (ISBN 0-88229-358-3). Nelson-Hall.

Du Brin, Andrew J. The Practice of Managerial Psychology. 1972. pap. 14.50 (ISBN 0-08-018126-0). Pergamon.

Dubrin, Andrew J. The Practice of Supervision: Achieving Results Through People. 1980. 24.95x (ISBN 0-256-02272-0). Business Pubns.

--Survival in the Office: How to Move Ahead Or Hang On. LC 76-54768. 330p. 1977. 11.50 (ISBN 0-442-80447-4). Krieger.

--Winning at Office Politics. 1980. pap. 2.95 (ISBN 0-345-29532-3). Ballantine.

--Winning at Office Politics. 1978. 16.95 (ISBN 0-442-22187-8). Van Nos Reinhold.

Dubroff. The United States Tax Court, an Historical Analysis. 504p. pap. 12.50 (ISBN 0-317-04241-6). Commerce.

Du Broff, Sidney. Still Water Fly Fishing for Young People. (Illus.). 111p. (gr. 4-7). 1983. 9.95 (ISBN 0-7182-2280-6, Pub. by Kaye & Ward). David & Charles.

Dubroff, Susanne, tr. see Becquer, Gustavo A.

Dubrov, A. P. The Geomagnetic Field & Life: Geomagnetobiology. LC 78-1705. (Illus.). 335p. 1978. 55.00x (ISBN 0-306-31072-4, Plenum Pr). Plenum Pub.

Dubrov, A. P. & Pushkin, V. N. Parapsychology & Contemporary Science. LC 82-2335. 228p. 1982. 39.50x (ISBN 0-306-10973-5, AACR2, Consultants). Plenum Pub.

Dubrova, Sara K. Vitreous Lithium Silicates: Their Properties & Field of Application. 46p. 1964. 20.00x (ISBN 0-306-10679-5, Consultants). Plenum Pub.

Dubrovin, B. A., et al. Modern Geometry: Methods & Applications Pt. I: The Geometry of Surface, of Transformation Groups & of Fields. Burns, R. G., tr. (Graduate Texts in Mathematics Ser.: Vol. 93). (Illus.). 495p. (Rus.). 1984. 48.00 (ISBN 0-387-90872-2). Springer-Verlag.

Dubrovin, M. I. A Book of Russian Idioms Illustrated. LC 79-40433. (Illus.). 328p. 1981. text ed. 8.00 (ISBN 0-08-023594-8). Pergamon.

--Book of Russian Idioms Illustrated. 349p. 1980. 7.95 (ISBN 0-8285-1890-4, Pub. by Rus Lang Pubs USSR). Imported Pubns.

Dubrovin, Vivian. Baseball Just for Fun. LC 74-10867. (Summer Fun, Winter Fun Ser.). (gr. 3-6). 1974. pap. 3.95 (ISBN 0-88436-137-3). EMC.

--A Better Bit & Bridle. LC 75-20346. (Saddle up Ser.). (Illus.). 40p. (gr. 4-9). 1975. PLB 6.95 (ISBN 0-88436-201-9, 35555); pap. 3.95 (ISBN 0-88436-202-7). EMC.

--A Chance to Win. LC 75-20081. (Saddle Ser.). (Illus.). 40p. (gr. 4-9). 1975. PLB 6.95 (ISBN 0-88436-203-5, 35556); pap. 3.95 (ISBN 0-88436-204-3). EMC.

--The Magic Bowling Ball. LC 74-10869. (Summer Fun, Winter Fun Ser.). (gr. 3-6). 1974. pap. 3.95 (ISBN 0-88436-131-4). EMC.

--Open the Gate. LC 75-20026. (Saddle up Ser.). (Illus.). 40p. (gr. 4-9). 1975. PLB 6.95 (ISBN 0-88436-207-8, 35558); pap. 3.95 (ISBN 0-88436-208-6). EMC.

--Rescue on Skis. LC 74-11004. (Summer Fun, Winter Fun Ser.). (gr. 3-6). 1974. pap. 3.95 (ISBN 0-88436-135-7, ELA 129054). EMC.

--The Track Trophy. LC 74-10931. (Summer Fun, Winter Fun Ser). (gr. 3-6). 1974. pap. 3.95 (ISBN 0-88436-133-0). EMC.

--Trailering Troubles. LC 75-20362. (Saddle up Ser.). (Illus.). 40p. (gr. 4-9). 1975. PLB 6.95 (ISBN 0-88436-205-1, 35557); pap. 3.95 (ISBN 0-88436-206-X). EMC.

--Write Your Own Story. (First Bks.). 72p. 1984. lib. bdg. 8.90 (ISBN 0-531-04739-3). Watts.

Dubrovnin, Vivian. Running a School Newspaper. (First Bk.). (gr. 4-6). 1985. PLB 9.40 (ISBN 0-531-10046-4). Watts.

Dubrovsky, V. B. Construction of Nuclear Power Plants. 279p. 1981. 11.00 (ISBN 0-8285-2023-2, Pub. by Mir Pubs USSR). Imported Pubns.

Dubrow, Eileen, jt. auth. see Dubrow, Richard.

Dubrow, Heather. Genre. (Critical Idiom Ser.). 120p. 1982. pap. 5.50 (ISBN 0-416-74690-X, NO. 3658). Methuen Inc.

Dubrow, Richard & Dubrow, Eileen. American Furniture of the Nineteenth Century, 1840-1880. LC 82-50615. (Illus.). 248p. 1983. 30.00 (ISBN 0-916838-68-4). Schiffer.

--American Furniture of the 19th Century: 1840-1880. (Illus.). 224p. 1983. 30.00 (ISBN 0-686-47035-4). Apollo.

--Furniture Made in America: 1875-1905. LC 82-50617. (Illus.). 320p. (Orig.). 1982. pap. 17.95 (ISBN 0-916838-66-8). Schiffer.

DuBroy. Canadian Directorship Practices: Compensation. 5th ed. 91p. 1983. 125.00 (ISBN 0-317-36596-7, CS-74); members 25.00 (ISBN 0-317-36597-5). Conference Bd.

Dubrul & Menekratis. The Physiology of Oral Reconstruction. 1981. 46.00 (ISBN 0-931386-47-0). Quint Pub Co.

DuBrul, E. Lloyd. Evolution of the Speech Apparatus. (Illus.). 116p. 1958. 12.75x (ISBN 0-398-00479-X). C C Thomas.

--Sicher's Oral Anatomy. 7th ed. LC 80-15943. (Illus.). 578p. 1980. text ed. 33.95 (ISBN 0-8016-4605-7). Mosby.

DuBrul, E. Lloyd & Sicher, Harry. The Adaptive Chin. (Illus.). 120p. 1954. photocopy ed. spiral 14.50x (ISBN 0-398-04248-9). C C Thomas.

DuBrul, Paul, jt. auth. see Newfield, Jack.

Dubs, H. H., tr. see Ku, Pan.

Dubs, Homer H., tr. see Hsun-Tzu.

Dubsky, Dora. Sing & Dance. 1977. 4.25 (ISBN 0-913650-51-X). Columbia Pictures.

Dubsky, Mario. Tom Pilgrim's Progress among the Consequences of Christianity. (Illus.). 84p. (Orig.). 1981. pap. 9.95 (ISBN 0-907040-09-8, Pub. by GMP England). Alyson Pubns.

--Tom Pilgrim's Progress among the Consquences of Christianity & Other Drawings. (Illus.). 84p. 1981. pap. 9.95 (ISBN 0-686-87069-7). Gay Mens Pr.

Dubuc, E. J. Kan Extensions in Enriched Category Theory. LC 77-131542. (Lecture Notes in Mathematics: Vol. 145). 1970. pap. 11.00 (ISBN 0-387-04934-7). Springer-Verlag.

DuBuque, Jean H. & Gleckner, Robert F. The Development of the Heavy Bomber, 1918-1944. (USAF Historical Studies: No. 6). 188p. 1951. pap. text ed. 19.00x (ISBN 0-89126-030-7). MA-AH Pub.

Du Bury, Richard. The Love of Books: The Philobiblon of Richard Du Bury. Thomas, E. C., tr. 1903. Repr. 20.00 (ISBN 0-8274-3001-9). R West.

Dubus, Andre. Adultery & Other Choices. LC 77-78392. 192p. 1977. 13.95 (ISBN 0-87923-213-7); pap. 7.95 (ISBN 0-87923-284-6). Godine.

--Finding a Girl in America. LC 79-90371. 192p. 1981. 13.95 (ISBN 0-87923-311-7); pap. 7.95 (ISBN 0-87923-393-1). Godine.

--Land Where My Fathers Died. LC 84-51505. 50p. 1984. signed, ltd. 30.00 (ISBN 0-913773-13-1). S Wright.

--Separate Flights. LC 74-25955. 216p. 1975. 13.95x (ISBN 0-87923-122-X). Godine.

--Separate Flights. LC 74-25955. 216p. 1977. 13.95 (ISBN 0-87923-122-X); pap. 7.95 (ISBN 0-87923-123-8). Godine.

--The Times Are Never So Bad. LC 82-48703. 192p. 1983. 14.95 (ISBN 0-87923-459-8). Godine.

--Voices from the Moon. 1985. pap. 6.95 (ISBN 0-517-55846-7). Crown.

--We Don't Live Here Anymore. 1984. pap. 7.95 (ISBN 0-517-55362-7). Crown.

Dubus, Andre & Godine, David R. Voices from the Moon: A Novel. LC 84-47652. 160p. 1984. 12.95 (ISBN 0-87923-532-2). Godine.

Dubus, Elizabeth N. Marguerite Tanner. 304p. (Orig.). 1982. pap. 2.95 (ISBN 0-8439-1037-2, Leisure Bks). Dorchester Pub Co.

--Marguerite Tanner. 304p. 1985. pap. 3.50 (ISBN 0-8439-2279-6, Leisure Bks). Dorchester Pub Co.

--Where Love Rules. LC 84-24919. 352p. 1985. 17.95 (ISBN 0-399-13019-5). Putnam Pub Group.

Duby, G. Histoire de la France. 1978. pap. text ed. 33.95 (ISBN 2-03-079951-3, 3916). Larousse.

Duby, Georges. The Age of the Cathedrals: Art & Society, 980-1420. Levieux, Eleanor & Thompson, Barbara, trs. LC 80-22769. (Illus.). vi, 312p. 1981. 26.00x (ISBN 0-226-16769-0); pap. 11.95 (ISBN 0-226-16770-4). U of Chicago Pr.

--The Chivalrous Society. Postan, Cynthia, tr. from Fr. LC 74-81431. 254p. 1978. pap. 5.95 (ISBN 0-520-04271-9, CAL 471). U of Cal Pr.

--The Early Growth of the European Economy: Warriors & Peasants from the Seventh to the Twelfth Century. Clarke, Howard B., tr. from Fr. LC 73-16955. (World Economic History Ser.). 292p. 1978. pap. 7.95x (ISBN 0-8014-9169-X). Cornell U Pr.

--Hommes & Structures Du Moyen Age: Racueil d'articles. (Le Savoir Historique: No. 1). (Illus.). 1973. pap. 42.40x (ISBN 90-2797-191-9). Mouton.

--The Knight, the Lady & the Priest: The Making of Modern Marriage in Medieval France. Bray, Barbara, tr. from Fr. LC 83-4000. 311p. 1984. 16.45 (ISBN 0-394-52445-4). Pantheon.

--Medieval Marriage: Two Models from Twelfth-Century France. Forster, Elborg, tr. from Fr. LC 77-17255. (Johns Hopkins Symposia in Comparative History: No. 11). (Illus.). 1978. text ed. 14.50x (ISBN 0-8018-2049-9). Johns Hopkins.

--Rural Economy & Country Life in the Medieval West. Postan, Cynthia, tr. LC 68-20530. Orig. Title: Economie Rurale et la Vie Des Campagnes Dans l'Occident Medieval. (Illus.). xvi, 612p. 1968. pap. 9.95x (ISBN 0-87249-347-4). U of SC Pr.

--The Three Orders: Feudal Society Imagined. Goldhammer, Arthur, tr. LC 80-13158. 432p. 1980. lib. bdg. 32.00x (ISBN 0-226-16771-2, PHOEN); pap. 11.95 (ISBN 0-226-16772-0). U of Chicago Pr.

Duc, Don R. Le see LeDuc, Don R.

Duc, Robert. Renald, the Adventurer. Ashton, Sylvia, ed. LC 77-70428. 1977. 12.95 (ISBN 0-87949-069-1). Ashley Bks.

Duc, Thomas Le see Le Duc, Thomas.

Duc, William G. Le see Le Duc, William G.

Du Camp, Maxime. Convulsions De Paris, 1878-1879, 4 Vols. LC 78-164792. Repr. of 1881 ed. Set. 110.00 (ISBN 0-404-07180-5); 27.50 ea. AMS Pr.

--Theophile Gautier. 1893. 30.00 (ISBN 0-8495-6280-5). Arden Lib.

--Theophile Gautier. Gordon, J. E., tr. (Select Bibliographies Reprint Ser.). Repr. of 1893 ed. 18.00 (ISBN 0-8369-5732-6). Ayer Co Pubs.

--Theophile Gautier. Gordon, J. E., tr. LC 74-153268. 1971. Repr. of 1893 ed. 21.00x (ISBN 0-8046-1564-0, Pub by Kennikat). Assoc Faculty Pr.

--Theophile Gautier. Gordon, J. E., tr. 1883. 25.00 (ISBN 0-8274-3592-4). R West.

Ducan, James P. & Mair, Susan G. Sculptured Surfaces in Engineering & Medicine. LC 82-1116. (Illus.). 400p. 1983. 82.50 (ISBN 0-521-23450-6). Cambridge U Pr.

Ducan, Starkey, Jr., et al. Interaction Structure & Strategy. (Studies in Emotion & Social Interaction). (Illus.). 320p. Date not set. price not set (ISBN 0-521-30154-8). Cambridge U Pr.

Du Cane, Edmund. The Punishment & Prevention of Crime. LC 83-49247. (Crime & Punishment in England, 1850-1922 Ser.). 231p. 1984. lib. bdg. 30.00 (ISBN 0-8240-6212-4). Garland Pub.

Du Cane, Hubert, tr. see Prussia.

Du Cange, Charles D. Les Familles d'Outre-Mer. LC 70-173996. (Research & Source Works Ser.: No. 864). 1006p. (Fr.). 1972. Repr. of 1869 ed. lib. bdg. 47.50 (ISBN 0-8337-0932-1). B Franklin.
--Histoire De L'empire De Constantinople Sous les Empereurs Francais, 2 vols. 2nd ed. Buchon, J. A., ed. LC 73-175147. (Research & Source Works Ser.: No. 861). (Fr.). 1972. Repr. of 1826 ed. 62.50 (ISBN 0-8337-0935-6). B Franklin.
Du Cange, Charles D. Du Fresne see Du Cange, Charles D.
Ducanis, Alex J. & Golin, Anne K. Interdisciplinary Health Care Team: A Handbook. LC 79-21028. 201p. 1980. text ed. 27.95 (ISBN 0-89443-167-6). Aspen Systems.
Ducanis, Alex J., jt. auth. see Golin, Anne K.
DuCann, C. G. Adventures in Antiques. 17.50x (ISBN 0-392-10032-0, SpS). Sportshelf.
Du Cann, Charles G. The Love-Lives of Charles Dickens. LC 72-6192. 288p. 1972. Repr. of 1961 ed. lib. bdg. 23.50x (ISBN 0-8371-6464-8, DULL). Greenwood.
DuCann, Charlotte, et al, eds. The Dirty Weekend Book. Duncan, Emma & Greenwood, Gillian. (Illus.). 192p. 1985. pap. 9.95 (ISBN 0-7043-3464-X, Pub. by Quartet Bks). Merrimack Pub Cir.
Ducasse, C. J. Critical Examination of the Belief in a Life after Death. 336p. 1974. pap. 35.75x spiral (ISBN 0-398-03037-5). C C Thomas.
--Nature, Mind & Death. (Paul Carus Lecture Ser.). xix, 533p. 1951. 29.95x (ISBN 0-87548-102-7). Open Court.
--Paranormal Phenomena, Science, & Life After Death. LC 79-76282. (Parapsychological Monographs No. 8). 1969. pap. 2.25 (ISBN 0-912328-12-6). Parapsych Foun.
Ducasse, Curt J. Philosophy As a Science, Its Matter & Its Method. LC 72-12326. Repr. of 1941 ed. lib. bdg. 15.00x (ISBN 0-8371-6730-2, DUPT). Greenwood.
Ducasse, Curt J., et al. Philosophy in American Education, Its Tasks & Opportunities. LC 75-3317. Repr. of 1945 ed. 21.50 (ISBN 0-404-59297-X). AMS Pr.
Ducasse, Isidore see De Lautreamont, Comte, pseud.
Ducasse, Isidore L. see De Lautreamont, Comte, pseud.
Du Castel, Christine. Here Begynneth the Boke of the Fayt of Armes & of Chyualrye. Caxton, William, tr. LC 78-6332. (English Experience Ser.: No. 13). 1968. Repr. of 1489 ed. 49.00 (ISBN 90-221-0013-8). Walter J Johnson.
--Here Begynneth the Booke Which Is Called "the Body of Polycye". LC 72-184. (English Experience Ser.: No. 304). 180p. 1971. Repr. of 1521 ed. 28.00 (ISBN 90-221-0304-8). Walter J Johnson.
--The Morale Proberbes of Christyne. LC 73-25783. (English Experience Ser.: No. 241). 8p. 1970. Repr. of 1478 ed. 14.00 (ISBN 90-221-0241-6). Walter J Johnson.
Ducat, jt. auth. see Chase.
Ducat, C., ed. see Corwin, E. S.
Ducat, Craig R. Modes of Constitutional Interpretation. LC 78-8496. 299p. 1978. pap. text ed. 7.95 (ISBN 0-8299-2009-9). West Pub.
Ducat, Craig R. & Chase, Harold W. Constitutional Interpretation. 3rd ed. 1550p. 1983. text ed. 32.95 (ISBN 0-314-69640-7). West Pub.
--Constitutional Interpretation: 1983 Supplement. 3rd ed. 100p. 1983. pap. text ed. 9.95 (ISBN 0-314-77899-3). West Pub.
Ducat, Craig R., ed. see Corwin, Edward S.
Ducat, Lee & Cohen, Sherry S. Diabetes. LC 82-48661. 320p. (Orig.). 1985. pap. 7.64i (ISBN 0-06-091281-2, PL 1281, PL). Har-Row.
--Diabetes: A New & Complete Guide to Healthier Living for Parents, Children, & Young Adults Who Have Insulin-Dependent Diabetes. LC 82-48661. 224p. 1983. 13.41i (ISBN 0-06-015153-6, HarpT). Har-Row.
Du Caurroy, Eustache see Expert, Henry.
Duce, R. A. Implementation Plan for the Determination of the Atmospheric Contribution on Petroleum Hydrocarbons to the Oceans. (Special Environmental Reports: No. 12). x, 49p. 1979. pap. 10.00 (ISBN 92-63-10504-9, W430, WMO). Unipub.
Duce, Richard & Ziegler, Olive. The Washington Supplement for Modern Real Estate Practice. 1978. pap. 8.95 (ISBN 0-88462-331-9, 1510-33, Real EState Ed). Longman USA.
D'Ucel, Jeanne. Berber Art: An Introduction. (Illus.). pap. 56.80 (ISBN 0-317-10500-0, 2004772). Bks Demand UMI.
Ducey, Agnes C. A Family Lifeline. LC 80-820. (Ducey Bks.). (Illus.). 160p. 1981. 9.95x (ISBN 0-9605110-0-8); pap. 7.50x (ISBN 0-9605110-1-6). World Issues.
Ducey, Jean. Out of This Nettle. (Voyager Ser.). (Orig.). 1983. pap. 3.50 (ISBN 0-8010-2927-9). Baker Bk.
Ducey, Michael H. Sunday Morning: Aspects of Urban Ritual. LC 76-25342. 1977. 17.00 (ISBN 0-02-907640-4). Free Pr.
Ducey, Mitchell F. & Microfilming Corporation of America. The Women's International League for Peace & Freedom Papers, 1915-1978: A Guide to the Microfilm Edition. LC 83-183902. vii, 130p. Date not set. price not set (ISBN 0-667-00696-6). Microfilming Corp.
Duchac, Rene. La Sociologie Des Migrations Aux Etats-Unis Societe, Mouvements Sociaux & Ideologies. (Premier Serie, Etudes: No. 15). 1974. pap. 25.60 (ISBN 90-2797-191-9). Mouton.
Duchacek, Ivo D. Nations & Men: An Introduction to International Politics. 3rd ed. LC 81-40916. 608p. 1982. pap. text ed. 22.00 (ISBN 0-8191-2260-2). U Pr of Amer.
Du Chaillu, Paul. Explorations & Adventures in Equatorial Africa. LC 74-97364. (Illus.). Repr. of 1861 ed. 25.00x (ISBN 0-8371-2407-7, DUE&, Pub. by Negro U Pr). Greenwood.
--Land of the Long Night. LC 75-159938. (Tower Bks). (Illus.). (gr. 5 up). 1971. Repr. of 1899 ed. 40.00x (ISBN 0-8103-3905-6). Gale.
--Lost in the Jungle. LC 79-159939. 1971. Repr. of 1872 ed. 40.00x (ISBN 0-8103-3766-5). Gale.
Du Chaillu, Paul B. Explorations & Adventures in Equatorial Africa. rev. & enl. ed. Repr. of 1871 ed. 35.00 (ISBN 0-384-13180-8). Johnson Repr.
--A Journey to Ashango-Land & Further Penetration into Equatorial Africa. LC 5-9143. 1971. Repr. of 1867 ed. 23.00 (ISBN 0-384-13185-9). Johnson Repr.
--Viking Age, 2 vols. LC 75-118628. Repr. of 1889 ed. Set. 85.00 (ISBN 0-404-02187-5). AMS Pr.
Du Chaillu, Paul E. Country of the Dwarfs. LC 75-88406. (Illus.). Repr. of 1872 ed. 19.75x (ISBN 0-8371-1840-9, DUC&, Pub. by Negro U Pr). Greenwood.
Duchaine, Nina. The Literature of Police Corruption. A Selected, Annotated Bibliography, Vol. II. LC 76-30895. 1979. 12.50x (ISBN 0-89444-008-X). John Jay Pr.
Duchambge, Pauline, et al. Anthology of Songs. (Women Composers Ser.: No. 22). 130p. 1985. Repr. of 1820 ed. lib. bdg. 27.50 (ISBN 0-306-76287-0). Da Capo.
Duchan & Schultheis. Comparative Filing Practices. (gr. 9-12). 1983. text ed. 4.30 wkbk. (ISBN 0-538-25150-6, Y15). SW Pub.
Duchan, Judith F., jt. auth. see Lund, Nancy J.
Duchan, Simon & Schultheis, Robert. Filing Business Names. (gr. 9-12). 1983. text ed. 4.30 wkbk. (ISBN 0-538-25140-9, Y14). SW Pub.
--Filing Names of People. (gr. 9-12). 1983. text ed. 4.30 wkbk. (ISBN 0-538-25130-1, Y13). SW Pub.
Duchane, Emma, ed. User's Manual, Advanced FORTRAN IV Utilities for Data General Computers. (Illus.). viii, 223p. 1980. pap. 20.00 (ISBN 0-938876-03-1). Entropy Ltd.
Ducharme, Bruno, jt. auth. see Boidman, Nathan.
DuCharme, Gail, jt. auth. see Ducharme, Jerry.
DuCharme, Jerome. Readers Proclaim the Word. 1976. Vols. For Cycle C Of The Liturgical Cycles. pap. 2.95 ea. (ISBN 0-8199-0579-8). Franciscan Herald.
Du Charme, Jerome, tr. see Roguet, A. M.
DuCharme, Jerome J. The Reader's Guide to Proclamation: For Sundays & Major Feasts in Cycle A. 160p. 1974. pap. 2.95 (ISBN 0-8199-0577-1). Franciscan Herald.
Ducharme, Jerry & DuCharme, Gail. Lector Becomes Proclaimer. 80p. (Orig.). 1985. pap. 4.95 (ISBN 0-89390-059-1). Resource Pubns.
Ducharme, Raymond A., jt. ed. see Fink, Lawrence A.
Ducharme, Robert. Art & Idea in the Novels of Bernard Malamud: Toward "The Fixer". (Studies in American Literature: No. 13). 1974. pap. text ed. 14.00x (ISBN 90-2793-212-3). Mouton.
Ducharte, P. L. The Italian Comedy. (Illus.). 16.75 (ISBN 0-8446-2002-5). Peter Smith.
Ducharte, Pierre L. Italian Comedy: The Improvisation, Scenarios, Lives, Attributes, Portraits & Masks of the Illustrious Characters of the Commedia Dell'arte. 1965. pap. 9.95 (ISBN 0-486-21679-9). Dover.
DuChateau, Paul. The Cauchy-Goursat Problem. LC 52-42839. (Memoirs: No. 118). 60p. 1972. pap. 9.00 (ISBN 0-8218-1818-X, MEMO-118). Am Math.
Duchaufour, Philippe. Ecological Atlas of Soils of the World. De Kimpe, C. R., tr. from Fr. LC 77-94822. (Illus.). 178p. 1978. 43.00x (ISBN 0-89352-012-8). Masson Pub.
Duchaufour, R. Pedology. Paton, T. R., tr. from French. (Illus.). 480p. 1982. text ed. 50.00x (ISBN 0-04-631015-0); pap. text ed. 24.95x (ISBN 0-04-631016-9). Allen Unwin.
Duche, Jean, jt. auth. see Bryan, Anne-Marie.
Duchein, Michel. Archive Buildings & Equipment. (ICA Handbook Ser.). 201p. 1977. pap. text ed. 17.00 (ISBN 3-7940-3780-4). K G Saur.
Duchein, Michel, ed. Archival Legislation, Nineteen Seventy to Nineteen Eighty. (Archivum, International Review on Archives Ser.). 447p. 1981. pap. text ed. 28.00 (ISBN 3-598-21228-3). K G Saur.
--Archives, Libraries, Museums & Information Centers with Index Archivum: Volumes 1-29. (Archivum, International Review on Archives). 250p. 1984. text ed. 28.00 (ISBN 3-598-21230-5). K G Saur.
--International Congress on Archives, 9th, London, 1980: Proceedings. (Archivum, International Review on Archives Ser.). 204p. 1981. pap. text ed. 28.00 (ISBN 3-598-21229-1). K G Saur.
--Labour & Trade Union Archives. (Archivum, International Review on Archives Ser.). 190p. 1980. pap. text ed. 25.00 (ISBN 3-598-21227-5). K G Saur.
Duchemin. Chateaubriand: Essais de Critique et d'Histoire. 23.75 (ISBN 0-685-34885-7). French & Eur.
Duchene, ed. see De Sevigne, Marie.
Duchene, A., ed. see ICRP.
Duchene, Francois, et al. New Limits on European Agriculture: Politics & the Common Agricultural Policy. (Atlantic Institute Research Ser.). 220p. 1985. 45.00x (ISBN 0-8476-7375-8). Rowman & Allanheld.
Duchesne, Edmond J., jt. auth. see Mayrand, Lionel E., Jr.
Duchesne, J., ed. Physico-Chemical Properties of Nucleic Acids, 3vols. Incl. Vol.1. Electrical, Optical & Magnetic Properties of Nucleic Acids & Components. 1973. 49.50 (ISBN 0-12-222901-0); Vol.2. Structural Studies on Nucleic Acids & Other Biopolymers. 1973. 69.00 (ISBN 0-12-222902-9); Vol.3. Intra - Intermolecular Interactions, Radiation Effects in Dnacells & Repair Mechanisms. 1974. 41.50 (ISBN 0-12-222903-7). 1973. Acad Pr.
Du Chesne, Joseph. The Practise of Chymicall, & Hermeticall Physicke, for the Preservation of Health. Timme, T., tr. from Lat. LC 74-28847. (English Experience Ser.: No. 728). 1975. Repr. of 1605 ed. 15.00 (ISBN 90-221-0728-0). Walter J Johnson.
Duchesneau, Francois. La Physiologie des Lumieres: Empirisme, Modeles et Theories. 640p. 1981. 97.00 (ISBN 90-247-2500-3, Pub. by Martinus Nijhoff Netherlands). Kluwer Academic.
Duchesneau, Vicki L. & Casey, Judy I. Blueberry Summer Cookbook. (Illus.). 100p. (Orig.). 1982. pap. 6.95 (ISBN 0-9608432-0-5). Valley View.
Duchesne-Guillemin, J. The Western Response to Zoroaster. LC 72-9593. 112p. 1973. Repr. of 1958 ed. lib. bdg. 15.00x (ISBN 0-8371-6590-3, DUWR). Greenwood.
Duchess of Devonshire. The House: Living at Chatsworth. (Illus.). 1982. 30.00 (ISBN 0-03-062428-2). HR&W.
Ducheyne, P. G., et al, eds. Biomaterials & Biomechanics, 1983: Proceedings of the 4th European Conference on Biomaterials, Leuven, Belgium, Aug. 31-Sept. 2, 1983. (Advances in Biomaterials Ser.: No. 5). 500p. 1984. 96.50 (ISBN 0-444-42352-4). Elsevier.
Ducheyne, Paul & Hastings, Garth W., eds. Functional Behavior of Orthopedic Biomaterials. LC 83-3737. 1984. Vol. I, 176p. 50.00 (ISBN 0-8493-6265-2); Vol. II, 224p. 57.00 (ISBN 0-8493-6266-0). CRC Pr.
--Metal & Ceramic Biomaterials, Vol. II. 184p. 1984. 66.00 (ISBN 0-8493-6262-8). CRC Pr.
--Metal & Ceramic Biomaterials: Structure, Vol. I. 160p. 1984. 50.00 (ISBN 0-8493-6261-X). CRC Pr.
Ducheyne, Paul, jt. ed. see Hastings, Garth W.
Duchin, Faye, jt. auth. see Leontief, Wassily.
Duchossier, Andre. Fender Stratocaster. (Illus.). 48p. (Fr.). 1985. pap. 5.95 (ISBN 0-88188-388-3). H Leonard Pub Corp.
Duchossoir, Andre. Guitar Identification: Fender - Gibson - Gretsch - Martin. rev. ed. (Illus.). 48p. 1985. pap. 5.95 (ISBN 0-88188-387-5, 183288). H Leonard Pub Corp.
Du Choul, Guillaume. Discours De la Religion Des Anciens Romains Illustre. LC 75-27851. (Renaissance & the Gods Ser.: Vol. 9). (Illus.). 1976. Repr. of 1556 ed. lib. bdg. 88.00 (ISBN 0-8240-2058-8). Garland Pub.
Duchscherer, W., Jr. Geochemical Hydrocarbon Prospecting with Case Histories. 208p. 1984. write for info. (ISBN 0-87814-261-4). PennWell Bks.
Ducibella, Joseph W. Phonology of the Sicilian Dialects. LC 77-94206. (Catholic University of America Studies in Romance Languages & Literatures Ser: No. 10). Repr. of 1934 ed. 43.00 (ISBN 0-404-50310-1). AMS Pr.
Ducic, Jovan. Blue Legends: Contains Serbian Text & Parallel English Translation. Mihailovich, Vasa D., tr. from Serbian. xiv, 104p. 5.00 (ISBN 0-915887-02-9). Kosovo Pub Co.
Duck. Teaching with Charisma. 364p. 1980. text ed. 25.72 (ISBN 0-205-07256-9, 2372568). Allyn.
Duck, E. W. Plastics & Rubbers. 1972. 10.00 (ISBN 0-8022-2076-2). Philos Lib.
Duck, Mike. Using Computer Graphics: Hangman. (Write Your Own Program Bks.). (gr. 4 up). 1984. 9.90 (ISBN 0-531-03483-6). Watts.
Duck, Ralph S. Kinderhook & Its People: Nineteen Thirty-four to Nineteen Sixty-four. (Illus.). 232p. 1984. pap. 18.00x (ISBN 0-932334-74-1). Heart of the Lakes.
Duck, Ruth, jt. auth. see Bausch, Michael.
Duck, Ruth C. Bread for the Journey: Resources for Worship Based on the New Ecumenical Lectionary. LC 81-5046. 96p. 1981. pap. 4.95 (ISBN 0-8298-0423-4). Pilgrim NY.
--Flames of the Spirit. (Orig.). 1985. pap. 6.95 (ISBN 0-8298-0537-0). Pilgrim NY.
Duck, S., ed. Personal Relationships: Vol. 4, Dissolving Personal Relationships. 1982. 36.00 (ISBN 0-12-222804-9). Acad Pr.
Duck, S. & Gilmour, R., eds. Personal Relationships, Vol. 1: Studying Personal Relationships. LC 80-41360. 1981. 33.00 (ISBN 0-12-222801-4). Acad Pr.
--Personal Relationships, Vol. 2: Developing Personal Relationships. LC 80-41360. 1981. 34.00 (ISBN 0-12-222802-2). Acad Pr.
--Personal Relationships: Vol. 3, Personal Relationships in Disorder. LC 80-41360. 1981. 35.00 (ISBN 0-12-222803-0). Acad Pr.
Duck, Stephen W. Personal Relationships & Personal Constructs: A Study of Friendship Formation. LC 73-8193. Repr. of 1973 ed. 45.50 (ISBN 0-8357-9952-2, 2014898). Bks Demand UMI.
Duck, Steve. Friends for Life: The Psychology of Close Relationships. LC 82-25081. 200p. 1984. 19.95x (ISBN 0-312-30564-8). St Martin.
--Personal Relationships, Vol. 5. 1984. 30.00 (ISBN 0-12-222805-7). Acad Pr.
Duck, Steve & Perlman, Daniel. Understanding Personal Relationships. 1985. 29.95 (ISBN 0-8039-9701-9). Sage.
Duck, Steve, ed. Theory & Practice in Interpersonal Attraction. 1977. 69.00 (ISBN 0-12-222850-2). Acad Pr.
Duck, Steve, jt. ed. see Gilmour, Robin.
Duck, Steven. The Study of Acquaintance. 1977. 26.00x (ISBN 0-566-00160-8, 01085-5, Pub. by Saxon Hse England). Lexington Bks.
Ducker, James H. Men of the Steel Rails: Workers on the Atchison, Topeka & Santa Fe Railroad, 1869-1900. LC 82-17541. (Illus.). xiv, 230p. 1983. 17.95x (ISBN 0-8032-1662-9). U of Nebr Pr.
Ducker, S. C. The Genus Chlorodesmis (Chlorophyta) in the Indo-Pacific Region. 1966. pap. 8.00 (ISBN 3-7682-0679-3). Lubrecht & Cramer.
Duckert, A. R., jt. auth. see Cassidy, F. G.
Duckert, Mary. Help: I'm a Sunday School Teacher. LC 77-83133. (Illus.). 126p. 1969. pap. 3.95 (ISBN 0-664-24862-4). Westminster.
Duckert, Mary, jt. auth. see Koenig, Norma E.
Duckert, Mary, ed. see Chenoweth, Linda.
Duckert, Mary J., ed. see Fogle, Jeanne S.
Duckett, Alfred. Raps: Poems by Alfred Duckett. LC 73-77120. 1973. 8.95 (ISBN 0-88229-112-2). Nelson-Hall.
Duckett, Caroline. Heartbeats & Poems. 64p. 1985. pap. 5.95 (ISBN 0-89962-459-6). Todd & Honeywell.
Duckett, Eleanor S. Alfred the Great: The King & His England. LC 56-13050. (Illus.). 1956. 15.00x (ISBN 0-226-16777-1). U of Chicago Pr.
--Alfred the Great: The King & His England. LC 56-13050. 1958. pap. 6.95 (ISBN 0-226-16779-8, P29, Phoen). U of Chicago Pr.
--Anglo-Saxon Saints & Scholars. x, 484p. 1967. Repr. of 1947 ed. 26.00 (ISBN 0-208-00200-6, Archon). Shoe String.
--Catullus in English Poetry. 1925. 25.00 (ISBN 0-8274-2012-9). R West.
Duckett, Graham. Creative Airbrushing: Step-by-Step Guide to Techniques, Skills, & Equipment. (Illus.). 172p. 1985. pap. 10.95 (ISBN 0-02-011260-2, Collier). Macmillan.
Duckett, J. G. & Racey, P. A., eds. The Biology of the Male Gamete: Linnean Society Supplement No. 1 to the Biological Journal, Vol. 7. 1975. 73.00 (ISBN 0-12-223050-7). Acad Pr.
Duckett, J. G., jt. ed. see Amos, W. B.
Duckett, J. G., jt. ed. see Clarke, G. C. S.
Duckett, J. G., jt. ed. see Dyer, A. F.
Duckett, John W., ed. see International Pediatric Urological Seminar, Phila., Pa., Apr. 1976.
Duckett, Kenneth W. Modern Manuscripts: A Practical Manual for Their Management, Care & Use. LC 75-5717. (Illus.). 384p. 1975. 17.00 (ISBN 0-910050-16-3). AASLH Pr.
Duckett, Margaret. Mark Twain & Bret Harte. LC 64-21709. (Illus.). Repr. of 1964 ed. 74.10 (ISBN 0-8357-9734-1, 2010091). Bks Demand UMI.
Duckett, Steven W. Photoelectronic Processes & a Search for Exciton Mobility in Pure & Doped Alkali Halides. LC 79-135074. 145p. 1969. 25.00 (ISBN 0-403-04496-0). Scholarly.
Duckham, A. N., et al, eds. Food Production & Consumption. 542p. 1977. 78.50 (ISBN 0-7204-0396-0, Biomedical Pr). Elsevier.
Duckham, Baron F. Yorkshire Ouse. LC 67-108689. (Illus.). 1967. 17.95x (ISBN 0-678-05628-5). Kelley.
Duckham, Baron F., jt. auth. see Hume, John R.
Duckham, F. & Hume, J. R., eds. Transport History, 2 vols. LC 69-10856. (Illus.). Vol. 1, Nos. 1-3. 1969 19.95x (ISBN 0-678-05594-7); Vol. 2, Nos. 1-3. 1970 19.95x (ISBN 0-678-05668-4). Kelley.
Duckitt, M. & Wragg, H. Selected English Letters: Fifteenth to Nineteenth Centuries. 599p. 1981. Repr. of 1941 ed. lib. bdg. 20.00 (ISBN 0-89987-158-5). Darby Bks.
Duckles, Vincent. Music Reference & Research Materials: An Annotated Bibliography. 3rd ed. LC 73-10697. 1974. text ed. 19.95 (ISBN 0-02-907700-1). Free Pr.
Duckman, Baron F., ed. Transport History, Vol. 3. (Illus.). 360p. 1971. 3.95 (ISBN 0-7153-5166-4). David & Charles.
Ducksbury, Sally. Females. (Illus.). 32p. (Orig.). 1985. pap. 8.95 (ISBN 0-86068-462-8, Pub. by Virago Pr). Merrimack Pub Cir.
Duckwall, Ralph, jt. auth. see Dietrich, John E.

Duckwitz, M., jt. ed. see Warfel, A.

Duckworth. A Creative Approach to Music Fundamentals. 1984. write for info. (ISBN 0-534-03753-4). Wadsworth Pub.

Duckworth, D., jt. auth. see Ormerod, M. B.

Duckworth, Derek, jt. auth. see Philp, Mark.

Duckworth, Eddie, tr. see Frantzeskakis, Ion F.

Duckworth, Eleanor. Learning with Breadth & Depth. 1979. pap. 2.50 (ISBN 0-918374-09-X). Workshop Ctr.

Duckworth, Eleanor, tr. see Piaget, Jean.

Duckworth, Elisabeth, tr. see Kafka, Franz.

Duckworth, F. G. Browning: Background & Conflict. iv, 219p. 1966. Repr. of 1931 ed. 17.50 (ISBN 0-208-00221-9, Archon). Shoe String.

Duckworth, G. Keyboard Musicianship. LC 79-132080. 1970. text ed. 21.95 (ISBN 0-02-907670-6). Free Pr.

Duckworth, George E. Foreshadowing & Suspense. (Studies in Comparative Literature, No. 35). 1970. pap. 22.95x (ISBN 0-8383-0021-9). Haskell.

Duckworth, H. E., ed. see International Conference on Nuclidic Masses.

Duckworth, Henry T. The Church of the Holy Sepulchre. LC 78-63361. (BCL Ser.). Repr. of 1922 ed. 25.50 (ISBN 0-404-17014-5). AMS Pr.

Duckworth, J. R., jt. auth. see Northen, E. E.

Duckworth, Jane. MMPI Interpretation Manual for Counselors & Clinicians. 2nd, rev. ed. LC 79-64500. (Illus.). 316p. 1979. pap. text ed. 14.95x (ISBN 0-915202-22-0). Accel Devel.

Duckworth, John & Duckworth, Liz. The No-Frills Guide to Youth Group Drama. 64p. 1985. pap. 4.95 (ISBN 0-88207-574-8). Victor Bks.

Duckworth, John, et al. Muhammad & the Arab Empire. Yapp, Malcolm & Killingray, Margaret, eds. (World History Ser.). (Illus.). (gr. 10). 1980. lib. bdg. 6.95 (ISBN 0-89908-036-7); pap. text ed. 2.45 (ISBN 0-89908-011-1). Greenhaven.

Duckworth, John E. Forensic Photography. (Illus.). 170p. 1983. 32.50x (ISBN 0-398-04849-5). C C Thomas.

Duckworth, John H. How to Use Auto-Suggestion Effectively. pap. 3.00 (ISBN 0-87980-067-4). Wilshire.

Duckworth, Liz, jt. auth. see Duckworth, John.

Duckworth, Marion. Becoming Complete: Embracing Your Biblical Image. LC 85-10465. 1985. pap. 4.95 (ISBN 0-88070-099-8). Multnomah.

--The Strong Place. 1983. pap. 4.95 (ISBN 0-8423-6663-6). Tyndale.

--When Your Child Becomes Your Friend. LC 81-71998. (When Bk.). 96p. (Orig.). 1982. pap. 2.45 (ISBN 0-87029-183-1, 20275-4). Abbey.

Duckworth, R. B., ed. Water Relations of Foods. (Food Science & Technology Ser.). 1975. 95.00 (ISBN 0-12-223150-3). Acad Pr.

Duckworth, Rita L. see Lucy, Reda, pseud.

Duckworth, Robin. This Is the Word of the Lord: Year B., the Year of the Mark. 1981. pap. 9.95 (ISBN 0-19-826662-6). Oxford U Pr.

--This Is the Word of the Lord: Year C. the Year of Luke. (Orig.). 1982. pap. 9.95 (ISBN 0-19-826666-9). Oxford U Pr.

Duckworth, Robin, ed. This Is the Word of the Lord: Year A: The Year of Matthew. 1980. pap. 9.95 (ISBN 0-19-213248-2). Oxford U Pr.

Duckworth, Roger A. Mechanics of Fluids. LC 76-10368. (Introductory Engineering Ser.). (Illus.). pap. 71.30 (ISBN 0-317-08297-3, 2019602). Bks Demand UMI.

Duckworth, Walter E. & Hoyle, G. Electro-Slag Refining. 1969. 30.00 (ISBN 0-412-09670-6, NO.6091, Pub. by Chapman & Hall). Methuen Inc.

Duckworth, Walter E., et al. A Guide to Operational Research. 3rd ed. 1977. 9.95 (ISBN 0-412-13500-0, NO. 6092, Pub. by Chapman & Hall). Methuen Inc.

Duckworth, William & Brown, Edward. Theoretical Foundations of Music. 1978. text ed. write for info. (ISBN 0-534-00526-8). Wadsworth Pub.

Duclaud-Williams, Roger H. The Politics of Housing in Britain & France. LC 78-323819. (Centre for Environmental Studies Ser.). 1978. text ed. 40.00x (ISBN 0-435-85222-1). Gower Pub Co.

Duclaux, Agnes M. French Ideal. facs. ed. LC 67-23209. (Essay Index Reprint Ser.). 1911. 18.00 (ISBN 0-8369-0393-5). Ayer Co Pubs.

--French Procession. facs. ed. LC 68-8456. (Essay Index Reprint Ser.). 1909. 20.00 (ISBN 0-8369-0394-3). Ayer Co Pubs.

--Twentieth Century French Writers. facs. ed. LC 67-22089. (Essay Index Reprint Ser.). 1920. 20.00 (ISBN 0-8369-1330-2). Ayer Co Pubs.

Duclaux, Mary. Life of Racine. LC 73-153904. 1971. Repr. of 1925 ed. 19.50x (ISBN 0-8046-1595-0, Pub. by Kennikat). Assoc Faculty Pr.

--Life of Racine. 1973. Repr. of 1925 ed. 25.00 (ISBN 0-8274-1782-9). R West.

--Portrait of Pascal. 1927. Repr. 25.00 (ISBN 0-8274-3188-0). R West.

Du Claux, Mary. Twelfth Century French Writers. 258p. 1982. pap. text ed. 14.00x (ISBN 0-8290-0484-X). Irvington.

Duclaux, Mary. Victor Hugo. LC 70-153903. 1971. Repr. of 1921 ed. 22.00x (ISBN 0-8046-1594-2, Pub by Kennikat). Assoc Faculty Pr.

Du Clos, J. Tournyal see Tournyal Du Clos, J.

Duclox, J., jt. ed. see Bisdom, E. B.

Duco, Joyce. Can You Cope with Happiness? LC 83-91233. 99p. (Orig.). 1983. pap. 5.95 (ISBN 0-9612896-0-0). J Duco.

Ducoli, Jane. Three for the Pot. 1981. 4.00 (ISBN 0-87012-413-7). McClain.

Duconte, C. M. & Sabourud, J. A. Pyrenean Mountain Dogs. 96p. 1983. 16.95 (ISBN 0-7182-2290-3, Pub. by Kaye & Ward). David & Charles.

Ducornet, Rikki. The Stain. LC 84-48117. 192p. 1984. 12.95 (ISBN 0-394-54284-3, GP-955). Grove.

Ducote, Darryl, jt. auth. see McKenna, Megan.

Ducote, Kitce. Cloud Station Number Fifty-Two. 64p. (gr. 2-6). 1985. 6.95 (ISBN 0-89962-481-2). Todd & Honeywell.

Ducoudray, Gustave. Les Origines du Parlement de Paris et la Justice aux Treizieme et Quatorzieme Siecles, 2 vols. 1969. 61.50 (ISBN 0-8337-0938-0). B Franklin.

Ducourneau, ed. see De Balzac, Honore.

Ducovny, Amram. Billion Dollar Swindle. LC 74-76029. 1969. pap. 5.95 (ISBN 0-8303-0058-9). Fleet.

--David Ben Gurion: In His Own Words. LC 68-31018. 1968. 7.95 (ISBN 0-8303-0057-0). Fleet.

Du Creux, Francois. History of Canada, or New France, 2 Vols. Conacher, James B., ed. Robinson, Percy J., tr. LC 69-14507. 1969. Repr. of 1951 ed. Vol. 1. lib. bdg. 26.75x (ISBN 0-8371-5070-1, DUHI); Vol. 2. lib. bdg. 25.75x (ISBN 0-8371-5071-X, DUHJ). Greenwood.

Ducrocq, Marie-Pascale. Therese of Lisieux: A Vocation of Love. LC 81-20512. 77p. (Orig.). 1982. pap. 3.95 (ISBN 0-8189-0431-3). Alba.

Ducrocq, Theophile G. Etudes d'Histoire Financiere et Monetaire. LC 75-132536. (Research & Source Works Ser.: No. 559). (Fr). 1970. Repr. of 1887 ed. lib. bdg. 23.50 (ISBN 0-8337-0939-9). B Franklin.

Ducros, Louis. Diderot, l'Homme et l'Ecrivain.; ed. LC 73-166446. (Philosophy Monographs: No. 75). (;fr). 22.50 (ISBN 0-8337-4080-6). B Franklin.

--Encyclopedistes. (Research & Source Works Ser: No. 167). 1968. Repr. of 1900 ed. 23.50 (ISBN 0-8337-0940-2). B Franklin.

--French Society in the Eighteenth Century. De Geijer, W., tr. (Illus.). 1927. 22.50 (ISBN 0-8337-0941-0). B Franklin.

--Jean-Jacques Rousseau, 3 Vols. 1908-18. Set. 75.50 (ISBN 0-8337-0945-3). B Franklin.

Ducrot, H., et al, eds. Computer Aid to Drug Therapy & to Drug Monitoring. 444p. 1978. 61.75 (ISBN 0-444-85188-7, North-Holland). Elsevier.

Ducrot, O. & Todorov, T. Dictionnaire Encyclopedique des Sciences du Langage. 476p. (Fr.). 1972. 26.50 (ISBN 0-686-57296-3, F-132840). French & Eur.

Ducrot, Oswald & Todorov, Tzvetan. Encyclopedic Dictionary of the Sciences of Language. Porter, Catherine, tr. LC 78-23901. 400p. 1979. pap. 10.95x (ISBN 0-8018-2857-0). Johns Hopkins.

Ducsik, Dennis W. Shoreline for the Public: A Handbook of Social, Economic, & Legal Considerations Regarding Public Recreational Use of the Nation's Coastal Shoreline. 1974. 22.50x (ISBN 0-262-04045-X). MIT Pr.

Duczynska, Ilona. Workers in Arms: The Austrian Schutzbund & the Civil War of 1934. LC 77-70970. 1978. 15.00 (ISBN 0-85345-410-8). Monthly Rev.

Duda, Deborah. Coming Home: A Guide to Home Care for the Terminally Ill. rev. ed. (Illus.). 270p. (Orig.). 1984. pap. 8.95 (ISBN 0-912528-39-7). John Muir.

Duda, Frederick, jt. ed. see Creth, Sheila.

Duda, Margaret B. Miniature Shops: How to Design & Make Them. LC 76-10884. (Illus.). 1977. 12.00 (ISBN 0-498-01783-4). A S Barnes.

--Useful Gifts Children Can Make. LC 81-38404. (Illus.). 112p. (Orig.). 1981. pap. 7.95 (ISBN 0-916392-66-X). Oak Tree Pubns.

Duda, Phyllis & Sebranek, Patrick. A Study Skills & Writing Process Workbook. (Illus.). (gr. 9-10). 1983. pap. text ed. 4.50x (ISBN 0-9605312-2-X). Basic Eng Rev.

Duda, Richard O. & Hart, Peter E. Pattern Classification & Scene Analysis. LC 72-7008. 482p. 1973. 58.95x (ISBN 0-471-22361-1, Pub. by Wiley-Interscience). Wiley.

Duda, W. H. Cement Data Book. 2nd ed. (Ger. - Eng.). 1977. 160.00 (ISBN 0-686-56597-5, M-7317, Pub. by Bauverlag). French & Eur.

Dudawaki, B., et al. Russian-Polish Political Dictionary. 726p. (Rus. & Pol.). 1955. leatherette 9.95 (ISBN 0-686-92134-8, M-9114). French & Eur.

Dudden, Arthur P. Joseph Fels & the Single-Tax Movement. LC 77-157738. 308p. 1971. 24.95 (ISBN 0-87722-010-7). Temple U Pr.

Dudden, Faye E. Serving Women: Household Service in Nineteenth-Century America. 352p. 1983. 19.95x (ISBN 0-8195-5072-8); pap. 9.95 (ISBN 0-8195-6109-6). Wesleyan U Pr.

Dudding, Burton, jt. auth. see Cho, Cheng.

Duddington, C. L. Instructions in Biology. (Illus.). (gr. 9 up). 14.50x (ISBN 0-392-03422-0, SpS). Sportshelf.

Duddington, Natalie, tr. see Berdiaev, Nikolai.

Duddington, Natalie, tr. see Pushkin, Alexander.

Duddington, Natalie, tr. see Saltykov-Schedrin, Mikhail Y.

Duddington, Natalie, tr. see Solov'Ev, Vladimir S.

Duddington, Nathalie A., tr. see Chertkov, Vladimir G.

Dudeck, C. V. Hegel's Phenomenology of Mind: Analysis & Commentary. LC 80-67258. 292p. 1981. lib. bdg. 25.25 (ISBN 0-8191-1406-5); pap. text ed. 12.75 (ISBN 0-8191-1407-3). U Pr of Amer.

Dudek, Gerald, jt. auth. see Ault, Addison.

Dudek, Lee. Professional Broadcast Announcing. 336p. 1981. text ed. 27.14 (ISBN 0-205-07660-2, 4876601). Allyn.

Duden, Gottfried. Report on a Journey to the Western States of North America & a Stay of Several Years Along the Missouri: During the Years 1824, '25, '26 & '27. Goodrich, James W., ed. Kellner, George H., et al, trs. from German. LC 79-3335. 384p. 1980. text ed. 26.00x (ISBN 0-8262-0295-0). U of Mo Pr.

Duden, R. Duden-Stilwoerterbuch. 5th rev. ed. (Der Grosse Duden: Vol. 2). (Ger.). 15.95x (ISBN 3-411-00902-0). Adlers Foreign Bks.

Duden, R., ed. Duden-Ausspracheworterbuch. (Der Grosse Duden: Vol. 6). 15.95x (ISBN 3-4110-0916-0). Adlers Foreign Bks.

--Duden-Bedeutungswoerterbuch. (Der Grosse Duden: Vol. 10). 1971. 15.95x (ISBN 3-4110-0910-1). Adlers Foreign Bks.

--Duden-Bildwoerterbuch. 2nd ed. (Der Grosse Duden: Vol. 3). (Illus.). 15.95x (ISBN 3-4110-0913-6). Adlers Foreign Bks.

--Duden-Etymologie. (Der Grosse Duden: Vol. 7). 15.95x (ISBN 3-4110-0907-1). Adlers Foreign Bks.

--Duden-Fremdwoerterbuch. 2nd rev. ed. (Der Grosse Duden: Vol. 5). 15.95x (ISBN 3-4110-0915-2). Adlers Foreign Bks.

--Duden-Grammatik. 2nd rev. ed. (Der Grosse Duden: Vol. 4). 15.95x (ISBN 3-4110-0914-4). Adlers Foreign Bks.

--Duden-Hauptschwierigkeiten der Deutschen Sprache. (Der Grosse Duden: Vol. 9). 15.95x (ISBN 3-4110-0919-5). Adlers Foreign Bks.

--Duden-Rechtschreibung. 16th rev. ed. (Der Grosse Duden: Vol. 1). 1971. 15.95x (ISBN 3-4110-0911-X). Adlers Foreign Bks.

--Duden-Synonymenwoerterbuch. (Der Grosse Duden: Vol. 8). 15.95x (ISBN 3-4110-0918-7). Adlers Foreign Bks.

Dudeney, Charles. A Guide to Executive Re-Employment. (Illus.). 192p. 1980. pap. 12.95x (ISBN 0-7121-1972-8, Pub. by Macdonald & Evans). Trans-Atlantic.

Dudeney, Henry E. Amusements in Mathematics. 1917. pap. 4.50 (ISBN 0-486-20473-1). Dover.

--Five Hundred Thirty-Six Puzzles & Curious Problems. LC 67-15488. 448p. 1983. pap. 9.95 (ISBN 0-684-71755-7, ScribT). Scribner.

Dudenhausen, J. W., jt. auth. see Pschyrembel, W.

Dudenhoeffer, Ferdinand. Mehrheitswahl-Entscheidungen ueber Umweltnutzungen, Vol. 9. (Staatliche Allokationspolitik). 234p. (Ger.). 1983. 28.40 (ISBN 3-8204-7778-0). P Lang Pubs.

Dudenredaktion & German Section Staff, ed. see Pheby, John.

Duderstadt, James & Kikuchi, Chihiro. Nuclear Power: Technology on Trial. 1979. 16.00 (ISBN 0-472-09311-8); pap. 9.95 (ISBN 0-472-06312-X). U of Mich Pr.

Duderstadt, James J. & Hamilton, Louis J. Nuclear Reactor Analysis. LC 75-20389. 650p. 1976. text ed. 54.00 (ISBN 0-471-22363-8). Wiley.

Duderstadt, James J. & Martin, William R. Transport Theory. LC 78-13672. 1979. 59.95x (ISBN 0-471-04492-X, Pub. by Wiley-Interscience). Wiley.

Duderstadt, James J., et al. Principles of Engineering. LC 81-10450. 558p. 1982. text ed. 32.50 (ISBN 0-471-08445-X); study guide 14.45 (ISBN 0-471-09746-2); solns. manual 8.50 (ISBN 0-471-09154-5). Wiley.

Duderstat. Nuclear Power. (Energy, Power, & Environment: A Ser. of Reference Bks.: Vol. 3). 1979. 34.25 (ISBN 0-8247-6829-9). Dekker.

Dudevan, Honore see Sand, George, pseud.

Dudevant, Auroc see Sand, George, pseud.

Dudevant, Jean F. see Sand, Maurice, pseud.

Dudevant, Mme. see Sand, George, pseud.

DuDewicz. Introduction to Statistics & Probability. 512p. 22.95 (ISBN 0-318-13224-9, P 50). Am Soc QC.

Dudewicz, Edward J. Introduction to Statistics & Probability. LC 75-26827. (American Sciences Press Ser. in Mathematical & Management Sciences: Vol. 1). 1976. text ed. 29.95 (ISBN 0-03-086688-X). Am Sciences Pr.

--Solutions in Statistics & Probability. LC 80-68285. (The American Sciences Press Ser. in Mathematical & Management Sciences: Vol. 3). 1980. pap. text ed. 24.95 (ISBN 0-935950-00-1). Am Sciences Pr.

Dudewicz, Edward J. & Karian, Zaven A. Tutorial: Modern Design & Analysis of Discrete-Event Computer Simulations. 500p. 1985. 45.00 (ISBN 0-8186-0597-9); prepub. 36.00 (ISBN 0-317-31782-2). IEEE Comp Soc.

Dudewicz, Edward J. & Koo, Joo O. The Complete Categorized Guide to Statistical Selection & Ranking Procedures. LC 80-68288. (The American Sciences Press Series in Mathematical & Management Sciences: Vol. 6). 1982. text ed. 85.00 (ISBN 0-935950-03-6). Am Sciences Pr.

Dudewicz, Edward J. & Ralley, Thomas G. The Handbook of Random Number Generation & Testing with TESTRAND Computer Code. LC 80-68286. (The American Sciences Press Ser. in Mathematical & Management Sciences: Vol. 4). 1981. text ed. 95.00 (ISBN 0-935950-01-X). Am Sciences Pr.

Dudewicz, Edward J., ed. The Frontiers of Modern Statistical Inference Procedures: Proceedings & Discussions of the IPASRAS Conference (First International Conference on Inference Procedures Associated with Statistical Ranking & Selection, East-West Center, Honolulu, July 1982) LC 83-72590. (Series in Mathematical & Management Sciences: Vol. 10). 1985. for info. 79.95 (ISBN 0-935950-07-9). Am Sciences Pr.

Dudgeon, Dan E. & Mersereau, Russell M. Multidimensional Digital Signal Processing. (Illus.). 448p. 1984. professional 41.95 (ISBN 0-13-604959-1). P-H.

Dudgeon, John A., jt. auth. see Hanshaw, James B.

Dudich, E. Contributions to the History of Geological Mapping: Proceedings. 441p. 1984. text ed. 40.00 (ISBN 0-9910001-6-1, Pub. by Aluminium W Germany). Heyden.

Dudick, Thomas S. Dudick on Manufacturing Cost Controls. LC 84-15090. 331p. 1984. 59.95 (ISBN 0-13-220971-3, Busn). P-H.

--Profile for Profitability: Using Cost Control & Profitability Analysis. LC 72-4353. (Wiley Systems & Controls for Financial Management Ser.). Repr. of 1972 ed. 67.80 (ISBN 0-8357-9963-8, 2015619). Bks Demand UMI.

Dudick, Thomas S. & Cornell, Ross. Inventory Control for the Financial Executive. 251p. 1979. 56.95 (ISBN 0-471-01503-2, Pub. by Wiley-Interscience). Wiley.

Dudick, Thomas S., ed. How to Improve Profitability Through More Effective Planning. LC 75-20445. (Wiley Series on Systems & Controls for Financial Management). (Illus.). pap. 93.80 (ISBN 0-317-09012-7, 2015850). Bks Demand UMI.

Dudick, Thomas S. & Gorski, Robert V., eds. Handbook of Business Planning & Budgeting for Executives with Profit Responsibility. 512p. 1983. 44.50 (ISBN 0-442-22188-6). Van Nos Reinhold.

Dudin, M. Nightingales. 263p. 1981. 5.00 (ISBN 0-8285-2045-3, Pub. by Progress Pubs USSR). Imported Pubns.

Dudits, D. & Farkas, G. L., eds. Cell Genetics in Higher Plants. 1976. 17.00 (ISBN 0-9960002-2-4, Pub. by Akademiai Kaido Hungary). Heyden.

Dudley. An Aid to Clinical Surgery. 3rd ed. (Illus.). 1984. pap. text ed. 14.00 (ISBN 0-443-02684-X). Churchill.

--Emergency Surgery. 10th ed. 1032p. 1977. 83.50 (ISBN 0-7236-0448-7). PSG Pub Co.

--Emergency Surgery. 11th ed. 1985. price not set (ISBN 0-7236-0799-0). PSG Pub Co.

--Hamilton Baileys Emergency Surgery. 11th ed. 1986. price not set (ISBN 0-7236-0799-0). PSG Pub Co.

Dudley, Art. Word Processing Basics: An Introduction for Young People. LC 84-22315. (Illus.). 48p. (gr. 4-9). 1985. PLB 9.95 (ISBN 0-13-963513-0). P-H.

Dudley, B. J. Parties & Politics in Northern Nigeria. 352p. 1968. 30.00x (ISBN 0-7146-1658-3, F Cass Co). Biblio Dist.

Dudley, Billy. An Introduction to Nigerian Government & Politics. LC 82-47926. 384p. (Orig.). pap. 9.95 (ISBN 0-253-33104-8). Ind U Pr.

Dudley, Carl S. Making the Small Church Effective. LC 78-2221. 1983. pap. 7.95 (ISBN 0-687-23044-6). Abingdon.

--Where Have All Our People Gone? New Choices for Old Churches. LC 79-525. (Illus.). 1979. pap. 6.95 (ISBN 0-8298-0359-9). Pilgrim NY.

Dudley, Carl S., ed. Building Effective Ministry: Theory & Practice in the Local Church. LC 82-48411. 256p. 1983. pap. 8.61 (ISBN 0-06-062102-8, RD-418, HarpR). Har-Row.

Dudley, Cliff. The Hidden Christian. LC 80-80657. 160p. 1980. 7.95 (ISBN 0-89221-074-5). New Leaf.

Dudley, Cliff, jt. auth. see Bakker, Tammy.

Dudley, Cliff, jt. auth. see Curtis, Helene.

Dudley, Cliff, jt. auth. see Custodio, Sidney.

Dudley, Cliff, jt. auth. see Harrison, Henry.

Dudley, Cliff, jt. auth. see Hill, Elsie Isensce.

Dudley, Cliff, jt. auth. see Kilpatrick, Paula.

Dudley, Cliff, jt. auth. see McLeod, Mary Alice.

Dudley, Cliff, jt. auth. see Steer, John L.

Dudley, Cliff, jt. auth. see Tari, Mel.

Dudley, Cliff, pref. by. I Gotta Be Me. Bakker, Tammy. LC 78-64670. 142p. (Orig.). 1981. pap. 3.50 (ISBN 0-89221-084-2). New Leaf.

Dudley, Cliff, ed. see Auch, Ron.

Dudley, Cliff, ed. see Godman, Henry.

Dudley, D. R. A History of Cynicism. 224p. 1937. 15.00 (ISBN 0-89005-365-0). Ares.

--A History of Cynicism from Diogenes to the Sixth Century A. D. 69.95 (ISBN 0-87968-137-3). Gordon Pr.

Dudley, D W. Handbook of Practical Gear Design. rev. ed. 656p. 1984. 59.50 (ISBN 0-07-017951-4). Mcgraw.

Dudley, Darle W., ed. Gear Handbook: The Design, Manufacture & Application of Gears. (Illus.). 1962. 81.00 (ISBN 0-07-017902-6). McGraw.

Dudley, Dean, jt. auth. see Jones, Ray G.

Dudley, Donald R. Civilization of Rome. (Orig.). 1960. pap. 4.95 (ISBN 0-452-00759-3). NAL.
Dudley, Dorothy. Forgotten Frontiers. LC 77-119663. (BCL Ser. I). Repr. of 1932 ed. 20.00 (ISBN 0-404-02188-3). AMS Pr.
--Forgotten Frontiers: Drieser & the Land of the Free. LC 75-144988. 485p. 1972. Repr. of 1932 ed. 18.00x (ISBN 0-403-00917-0). Scholarly.
--Theatrum Majorum, the Cambridge of 1776: Diary of Dorothy Dudley. LC 73-140861. (Eyewitness Accounts of the American Revolution Ser., No. 3). (Illus.). 1970. Repr. of 1876 ed. 13.00 (ISBN 0-405-01228-4). Ayer Co Pubs.
Dudley, Dorothy H., et al. Museum Registration Methods. 3rd ed. (Illus.). 437p. 21.00 (ISBN 0-317-32313-X); members 17.00 (ISBN 0-317-32314-8); pap. 15.00 (ISBN 0-317-32315-6); pap. 12.00 members (ISBN 0-317-32316-4). Am Assn Mus.
Dudley, E. P., et al. Curriculum Change for the Nineties: A Report of the Curriculum Development Project on Library & Information Work. Moore, N. E., ed. (LIR Report: No. 14). 80p. (Orig.). 1983. pap. 13.50 (ISBN 0-7123-3018-6, Pub. by British Lib). Longwood Pub Group.
Dudley, Earl C., jt. auth. see Arkin, Stanley S.
Dudley, Edward & Heller, Peter. American Attitudes Toward Foreign Languages & Foreign Cultures. (Modern German Studies: Vol. 12). 146p. 1983. 20.00 (ISBN 3-416-01773-0, Pub. by Bouvier Verlag W Germany). Benjamins North Am.
Dudley, Edward, jt. auth. see Crow, John A.
Dudley, Edward & Novak, Maximillian E., eds. The Wild Man Within: An Image in Western Thought from the Renaissance to Romanticism. LC 72-77191. (Illus.). 1972. 29.95x (ISBN 0-8229-3246-6). U of Pittsburgh Pr.
Dudley, Ernest. For Love of a Wild Thing. LC 74-80816. 224p. 1974. 10.00 (ISBN 0-8397-2325-3). Eriksson.
Dudley, Fred A., ed. The Relations of Literature & Science: A Selected Bibliography, 1930-1949. LC 50-4895. pap. 36.50 (ISBN 0-317-10401-2, 2000294). Bks Demand UMI.
Dudley, Geoffrey. Increase Your Learning Power. pap. 3.00 (ISBN 0-87980-085-2). Wilshire.
Dudley, Geoffrey A. Dreams, Their Mysteries Revealed. (Paths to Inner Power Ser). 1972. pap. 2.50 (ISBN 0-85030-175-0). Weiser.
--How to Understand Your Dreams. pap. 3.00 (ISBN 0-87980-066-6). Wilshire.
Dudley, Gordon A., jt. auth. see Tiedeman, David V.
Dudley, Gordon H., jt. auth. see Sumich, James L.
Dudley, Guilford, 3rd. Religion on Trial: Mircea Eliade & His Critics. LC 77-77644. 191p. 1977. 27.95 (ISBN 0-87722-102-2). Temple U Pr.
Dudley, Hugh. Alimentary Tract & Abdominal Wall (Upper GI, Pt. 2. 4th ed. (Operative Surgery Ser.). 336p. 1983. text ed. 130.00 (ISBN 0-686-40643-5). Mosby.
--The Presentation of Original Work in Medicine & Biology. LC 76-30629. (Illus.). 1977. pap. text ed. 10.75 (ISBN 0-443-01583-X). Churchill.
Dudley, Hugh, ed. Alimentary Tract & Abdominal Wall (Upper GI, Pt. 1. 4th ed. (Operative Surgery Ser.). 496p. 1983. text ed. 175.00 (ISBN 0-407-00651-6). Mosby.
Dudley, J. W., ed. Seventy Generations of Selection for Oil & Protein in Maize. 1974. 10.00 (ISBN 0-89118-502-X). Crop Sci Soc Am.
Dudley, James R. Living with Stigma: The Plight of the People Who We Label Mentally Retarded. 146p. 1983. 14.75x (ISBN 0-398-04831-2). C C Thomas.
Dudley, Jim. Promoting the Organization: A Guide to Low Budget Publicity. 1975. 24.95x (ISBN 0-7002-0259-5). Intl Ideas.
Dudley, L. Architectural Illustration. 1976. 34.95 (ISBN 0-13-044610-6). P-H.
Dudley, Linda. Going Through Changes. 36p. 1977. pap. 3.00 (ISBN 0-686-19056-4). Dudley.
Dudley, Lofton L. The School & the Community. (Harvard Studies in Education: Vol. 22). 1933. pap. 19.00 (ISBN 0-384-13190-5). Johnson Repr.
Dudley, Louise. Art of Lytton Stachey. 1929. Repr. 20.00 (ISBN 0-8274-1887-6). R West.
Dudley, Louise, et al. The Humanities. 6th ed. (Illus.). 1978. text ed. 28.95 (ISBN 0-07-017971-9). McGraw.
Dudley, Michael. Roasted Chestnuts. 24p. 1979. 10.00 (ISBN 0-913719-11-0); pap. 3.50 (ISBN 0-913719-10-2). High-Coo Pr.
--Through the Green Fuse. 32p. 1983. 10.00 (ISBN 0-913719-24-2); pap. 3.50 (ISBN 0-913719-23-4). High-Coo Pr.
Dudley, N. A., jt. ed. see Muramatsu, R.
Dudley, Owen Francis. Will Men Be Like Gods? Humanitarianism of Human Happiness. 1979. 5.95 (ISBN 0-8199-0766-9). Franciscan Herald.
Dudley, Patricia L. Development & Systematics of Some Pacific Marine Symbiotic Copepods: A Study of the Biology of the Notodelphyidae, Associates of Ascidians. LC 66-29836. (University of Washington Publications in Biology Ser.: No. 21). (Illus.). 282p. 1966. 20.00x (ISBN 0-295-73765-4). U of Wash Pr.
Dudley, Phil. Salt Box. (Illus.). 128p. (Orig.). 1982. pap. 5.95 (ISBN 0-933614-18-7). Peregrine Pr.
Dudley, R. M. Lectures in Modern Analysis & Applications - Three. Taam, C. T., ed. LC 64-54683. (Lecture Notes in Mathematics: Vol. 170). 1970. pap. 14.00 (ISBN 0-387-05284-4). Springer-Verlag.
Dudley, R. M., et al. Ecole d'Ete de Probabilities de Saint-Flour XII, 1982. (Lecture Notes in Mathematics Ser.: Vol. 1097). x, 396p. 1984. pap. 22.50 (ISBN 0-387-13897-8). Springer-Verlag.
Dudley, Robert. A Briefe Report of the Militaire Services Done in the Low Countries by the Erle of Leicester. LC 72-192. (English Experience Ser.: No. 201). 36p. 1969. Repr. of 1587 ed. 7.00 (ISBN 90-221-0201-7). Walter J Johnson.
--Correspondence of Robert Dudley. 1844. 35.00 (ISBN 0-384-32130-5). Johnson Repr.
Dudley, Robert J. Think Like a Lawyer: How to Get What You Want by Using Advocacy Skills. LC 79-26488. 234p. 1980. 19.95x (ISBN 0-88229-571-3). Nelson-Hall.
Dudley, Roger L. & Cummings, Des, Jr. Adventures in Church Growth. Wheeler, Gerald, ed. LC 83-16089. (Illus.). 160p. (Orig.). 1983. pap. 8.95 (ISBN 0-8280-0228-2). Review & Herald.
Dudley, Rosemary & Rowland, Wade. How to Find Relief from Migraines. LC 81-10216. 175p. 1982. 12.95 (ISBN 0-8253-0077-0). Beaufort Bks NY.
Dudley, T. R., ed. see Swartley, John.
Dudley, Underwood. Elementary Number Theory. 2nd ed. LC 78-5661. (Mathematical Sciences Ser.). (Illus.). 249p. 1978. text ed. 25.95 (ISBN 0-7167-0076-X); instrs.' guide avail. W H Freeman.
Dudley, William C. Letters to Our Son: The AG Teacher. 108p. 1983. pap. text ed. 8.95x (ISBN 0-8134-2288-4). Interstate.
Dudley-Edwards, Owen. The Quest for Sherlock Holmes: A Biographical Study of Arthur Conan Doyle. LC 83-6011. 380p. 1983. text ed. 28.50x (ISBN 0-389-20402-1, 07278). B&N Imports.
Dudley-Evans, Tony, jt. ed. see Bates, Martin.
Dudley-Smith, Timothy. Lift Every Heart. 306p. (Orig.). 1984. pap. 8.95 (ISBN 0-916642-21-6). Hope Pub.
--Someone Who Beckons. LC 78-18548. 1978. pap. 3.95 (ISBN 0-87784-731-2). Inter-Varsity.
Dudman, Helge. Street People. (Illus.). 263p. 1982. 14.95 (ISBN 965-220-039-5, Carta Pub Israel). Hippocrene Bks.
Dudman, Jane. International Music Guide: 1984. (Tantivy). (Illus.). 288p. 1983. pap. 11.95 (ISBN 0-900730-07-2). NY Zoetrope.
Dudman, Jane, ed. International Music Guide 1983. (International Music Guide Ser.). (Illus.). 304p. 1983. pap. 10.95 (ISBN 0-900730-05-6). NY Zoetrope.
--International Music Guide: 1985. (Illus.). 288p. 1985. pap. 12.95 (ISBN 0-900730-08-0, Pub. by Tantivy). NY Zoetrope.
Dudman, Richard. Forty Days with the Enemy. LC 70-157097. (Illus.). 1972. pap. 2.45 (ISBN 0-87140-259-9). Liveright.
Dudok, G. A. Development of English Prose in the Nineteenth Century. (English Literature Ser., No. 33). 1970. pap. 11.95x (ISBN 0-8383-0022-7). Haskell.
Dudon, Paul. St. Ignatius of Loyola. Young, William J., tr. LC 83-45591. Date not set. Repr. of 1949 ed. 49.50 (ISBN 0-404-19884-8). AMS Pr.
Dudovitz, R. L., ed. Women in Academe. 118p. 1983. 17.50 (ISBN 0-08-030819-8, 26/13). Pergamon.
Dudrick, Stanley J., jt. ed. see Miller, Thomas A.
Dudukovic, Milorad P. & Mills, Patrick L., eds. Chemical & Catalytic Reactor Modeling. LC 83-22378. (ACS Symposium Ser.: No. 237). 426p. 1983. lib. bdg. 59.95 (ISBN 0-8412-0815-8). Am Chemical.
Dudycha, George J. Psychology for Law Enforcement Officers. (Illus.). 416p. 1982. 18.75x (ISBN 0-398-00482-X). C C Thomas.
Dudyche, George J. Applied Psychology. LC 63-13748. (Illus.). 390p. pap. 119.50 (ISBN 0-317-10428-4, 2012553). Bks Demand UMI.
Dudzinski, M. L., jt. auth. see Arnold, G. W.
Due, Jean M. Costs, Returns & Repayment Experience of Ujamaa Villages in Tanzania, 1973-1976. LC 80-490. 167p. 1980. text ed. 22.50 (ISBN 0-8191-1019-1); pap. text ed. 11.00 (ISBN 0-8191-1020-5). U Pr of Amer.
Due, John F. Indirect Taxation in Developing Economies: The Role & Structure of Customs Duties, Excises, & Sales Taxes. LC 70-119108. 201p. 1970. 17.50x (ISBN 0-8018-1167-8). Johns Hopkins.
Due, John F. & Friedlaender, Ann F. Government Finance: Economics of the Public Sector. 7th ed. 1981. text ed. 26.95x (ISBN 0-256-02492-8). Irwin.
Due, John F. & Mikesell, John L. Sales Taxation: State & Local Structure & Administration. LC 82-13968. 352p. 1983. text ed. 35.00x (ISBN 0-8018-2842-2). Johns Hopkins.
Due, John F., jt. auth. see Hilton, George W.
Due, Linnea A. Give Me Time. LC 84-6677. 396p. 1984. 15.95 (ISBN 0-688-03926-X). Morrow.
--High & Outside. LC 79-3406. 192p. 1980. 9.95i (ISBN 0-06-011102-X, HarpT). Har-Row.
--High & Outside. 1983. pap. 2.25 (ISBN 0-553-23618-0). Bantam.
Duea, K. P., jt. auth. see Goeldner, C. R.
Duea, Karen. Ski Rental Shop Survey. 38p. 1983. pap. text ed. 25.00 (ISBN 0-89478-101-4). U Co Busn Res Div.
Duea, Karen, jt. auth. see Goeldner, C. R.
Duea, Karen, jt. auth. see Goeldner, Charles R.
Dueber, Julianne, jt. auth. see Holt, Marion P.
Duecker, Werner W. & West, James R. The Manufacture of Sulfuric Acid. LC 59-15498. (A C S Ser: No. 144). 526p. 1974. Repr. of 1959 ed. 34.50 (ISBN 0-88275-015-1). Krieger.
Duecker, Werner W. & West, James R., eds. The Manufacture of Sulfuric Acid. LC 59-15498. (ACS Monographs: No. 144). 1959. 34.50 (ISBN 0-8412-0283-4). Am Chemical.
Duedall, I. W., et al. Wastes in the Ocean: Energy Wastes in the Ocean, Vol. 4. (Environmental Science & Technology Ser.). 816p. 1985. 95.00 (ISBN 0-471-89332-3). Wiley.
--Wastes in the Ocean: Industrial & Sewage Wastes in the Ocean, Vol. 1. (Environmental Science & Technology Ser.). 431p. 1983. 69.95 (ISBN 0-471-09772-1); Set. 180.00 (ISBN 0-471-82054-7). Wiley.
Duedall, Iver. W., et al, eds. Biological Processes & Wastes in the Ocean. LC 84-29733. (Oceanic Processes in Marine Pollution Ser.: Vol. 1). 1985. lib. bdg. price not set (ISBN 0-89874-810-0). Krieger.
Duedall, Iver W., et al, eds. Physicochemical Processes & Wastes in the Ocean. LC 84-29746. (Oceanic Processes in Marine Pollution Ser.: Vol. 2). 1986. lib. bdg. price not set (ISBN 0-89874-811-9). Krieger.
--Scientific Considerations of Marine Waste Management. LC 84-29691. (Oceanic Processes in Marine Pollution Ser.: Vol. 3). 1985. lib. bdg. price not set (ISBN 0-89874-812-7). Krieger.
--Scientific Monitoring Strategies for Ocean Waste Disposal. LC 84-29701. (Oceanic Processes in Marine Pollution Ser.: Vol. 4). 1986. lib. bdg. price not set (ISBN 0-89874-813-5). Krieger.
Duedney, Daniel. Space: The High Frontier in Perspective. LC 82-50920. (Worldwatch Papers). 1982. pap. 2.00 (ISBN 0-916468-49-6). Worldwatch Inst.
Due-Gundersen, Gunnar, jt. auth. see Prince, Betty.
Dueker, Christopher W. Scuba Diving Safety. LC 78-55789. 200p. 1979. pap. 5.95 (ISBN 0-89037-135-0). Anderson World.
Dueker, Marilynn, jt. auth. see Spirer, Herbert F.
Dueland, Joy. Barn Kitten, House Kitten. (Illus.). 1978. pap. 3.50 (ISBN 0-931942-00-4). Phunn Pubs.
--The Blessings of Jesus. (Illus.). 1979. 8.95 (ISBN 0-931942-02-0). Phunn Pubs.
--Dear Tabby. (Illus.). 1978. pap. 2.50 (ISBN 0-931942-02-0). Phunn Pubs.
--God's Great Adventure. (Illus.). 111p. 1980. 8.95. Phunn Pubs.
--Kitten in the Manger. (Illus.). 1981. pap. 6.95. Phunn Pubs.
Duelberg, Peter. Erweitern Sie Ihren Wortschatz. 160p. (Ger.). 1971. pap. 2.95 (ISBN 3-581-66170-5). Langenscheidt.
Duell, Donna, jt. auth. see Smith, Sandra F.
Duell, J. & Lawson, F. Damp Proof Course Detailing. (Illus.). 64p. 1983. 18.80x (ISBN 0-85139-150-8, Pub. by Architectural Pr England); pap. text ed. 12.50x (ISBN 0-85139-149-4). Humanities.
Duelli-Klein, R., ed. So Far, So Good, So What? Women's Studies in the UK. 100p. 1983. pap. 17.50 (ISBN 0-08-030816-3). Pergamon.
Duelli-Klein, Renate, jt. ed. see Bowles, Gloria.
Duellman, W. E. Biology of Amphibians. (Illus.). 623p. 1985. 40.00 (ISBN 0-07-017977-8). McGraw.
Duellman, William E. The Biology of an Equatorial Herpetofauna in Amazonian Ecuador. (Miscellaneous Publications Ser.: No. 65). 352p. 1978. pap. 15.00 (ISBN 0-686-80352-3). U of KS Mus Nat Hist.
--Centrolenid Frogs from Peru. (Occasional Papers: No. 52). 11p. 1976. pap. 1.25 (ISBN 0-686-80349-3). U of KS Mus Nat Hist.
--Description of New Hylid Frogs from Mexico & Central America. (Museum Ser.: Vol. 17, No. 13). 20p. 1968. pap. 1.25 (ISBN 0-686-80341-8). U of KS Mus Nat Hist.
--Descriptions of Two Species of Frogs, Genus Ptychohyla: Studies of American Hylid Frogs, Vol. V. (Museum Ser.: Vol. 13, No. 8). 9p. 1961. pap. 1.25 (ISBN 0-686-80336-1). U of KS Mus Nat Hist.
--A Distributional Study of the Amphibians of the Isthmus of Tehuantepec, Mexico. (Museum Ser.: Vol. 13, No.2). 54p. 1960. pap. 3.00 (ISBN 0-686-79840-6). U of KS Mus Nat Hist.
--The Genera of Phyllomedusine Frogs (Anura Hylidae) (Museum Ser.: Vol. 18, No. 1). 10p. 1968. pap. 1.25 (ISBN 0-686-80342-6). U of KS Mus Nat Hist.
--A New Species of Fringed-Limbed Tree Frog, Genus Hyla, from Darien, Panama. (Museum Ser.: Vol. 17, No. 5). 6p. 1966. 1.25 (ISBN 0-317-04850-3). U of KS Mus Nat Hist.
--A New Subspecies of Lizard, Cnemidophorus Sacki, from Michoacan, Mexico. (Museum Series: Vol. 10, No. 9). 12p. 1960. 1.25 (ISBN 0-317-04846-5). U of KS Mus Nat Hist.
--On the Classification of Frogs. (Occasional Papers: No. 42). 14p. 1975. 1.25 (ISBN 0-317-04852-X). U of KS Mus Nat Hist.
--A Reassessment of the Taxonomic Status of Some Neotropical Hylid Frogs. (Occasional Papers: No. 27). 27p. 1974. pap. 1.50 (ISBN 0-686-80348-5). U of KS Mus Nat Hist.
--A Review of the Frogs of the Hyla Bistincta Group. (Museum Ser.: Vol. 15, No. 9). 23p. 1964. pap. 1.25 (ISBN 0-686-80338-8). U of KS Mus Nat Hist.
--A Review of the Neotropical Frogs of the Hyla Bogotensis Group. (Occasional Papers: No. 11). 31p. 1972. pap. 1.75 (ISBN 0-686-80345-0). U of KS Mus Nat Hist.
--A Systematic Review of the Marsupial Frogs (Hylidae Gastrotheca) of the Andes of Ecuador. (Occasional Papers: No. 22). 27p. 1974. pap. 1.50 (ISBN 0-686-80347-7). U of KS Mus Nat Hist.
--Systematic Status of the Colubrid Snake: Leptodeira Discolor Gunther. (Museum Ser.: Vol. 11, No.1). 9p. 1958. 1.25 (ISBN 0-317-04849-X). U of KS Mus Nat Hist.
--Taxonomic Notes on Some Mexican & Central American Hylid Frogs. (Museum Ser.: Vol. 17, No. 6). 17p. 1966. pap. 1.25 (ISBN 0-686-80339-6). U of KS Mus Nat Hist.
--A Taxonomic Review of South American Hylid Frogs, Genus Phrynohyas. (Occasional Papers: No. 4). 21p. 1971. pap. 1.25 (ISBN 0-686-80343-4). U of KS Mus Nat Hist.
--A Taxonomic Study of the Middle American Snake: Pituophis Deppei. (Museum Ser.: Vol. 10, No. 10). 12p. 1960. 1.25 (ISBN 0-317-04847-3). U of KS Mus Nat Hist.
--Three New Species of Centrolenid Frogs from the Pacific Versant of Ecuador & Colombia. (Occasional Papers: No. 88). 9p. 1981. 1.25 (ISBN 0-317-04856-2). U of KS Mus Nat Hist.
Duellman, William E. & Crump, Martha L. Speciation in Frogs of the Hyla Parviceps Group in the Upper Amazon Basin. (Occasional Papers: No. 23). 40p. 1974. pap. 2.25 (ISBN 0-686-32527-3). U of KS Mus Nat Hist.
Duellman, William E. & Foquette, M. J., Jr. Middle American Frogs of the Hyla Microcephala Group. (Museum Ser.: Vol. 17, No. 12). 41p. 1968. pap. 2.25 (ISBN 0-686-80340-X). U of KS Mus Nat Hist.
Duellman, William E. & Fritts, Thomas H. A Taxonomic Review of the Southern Andean MarsupialFrogs (Hylidae Gastrotheca) (Occasional Papers: No. 9). 37p. 1972. pap. 2.00 (ISBN 0-686-80344-2). U of KS Mus Nat Hist.
Duellman, William E. & Leseure, Jean. Life History & Ecology of the Hylid Frog Osteocephalus Taurinus, with Observations on Larval Behavior. (Occasional Papers: No. 13). 12p. 1973. pap. 1.25 (ISBN 0-686-80346-9). U of KS Mus Nat Hist.
Duellman, William E. & Pyles, Rebecca A. A New Marsupial Frog (Hylidae: Gastrotheca) from the Andes of Ecuador. (Occasional Papers: No. 84). 13p. 1980. 1.25 (ISBN 0-317-04854-6). U of KS Mus Nat Hist.
Duellman, William E. & Trueb, Linda. The Systematic Status & Relationships of the Hylid Frog Nyctimantis Rugiceps Boulenger. (Occasional Papers: No. 58). 14p. 1976. pap. 1.25 (ISBN 0-686-80350-7). U of KS Mus Nat Hist.
Duellman, William E. & Velosom, Alberto. Phylogeny of Pleurodema (Anura Leptodactylidae) A Biogeographic Model. (Occasional Papers: No. 64). 46p. 1977. pap. 2.50 (ISBN 0-686-80351-5). U of KS Mus Nat Hist.
Duellman, William E., jt. auth. see Lynch, John D.
Duellman, William E., jt. auth. see Trueb, Linda.
Duellman, William E., jt. auth. see Walker, Charles F.
Duellman, William E., et al, eds. The South American Herpetofauna: Its Origin, Evolution & Dispersal. (U of KS Museum of Nat. Hist. Monograph: No. 7). (Illus.). 485p. 1979. 30.00 (ISBN 0-89338-009-1); pap. 15.00 (ISBN 0-89338-008-3). U of KS Mus Nat Hist.
Duelo, Gerardo. Diccionario de Grupos, Fuerzas, y Partidos Politicos Espanoles. 128p. (Span.). 1977. pap. 5.25 (ISBN 84-7080-940-7, S-50175). French & Eur.
Duenas. Curso Basico de Correspondencia Comercial. 120p. 1982. 6.76 (ISBN 0-07-017995-6). McGraw.
--Curso Basico de Matematicas Comerciales. 172p. 1982. 5.60 (ISBN 0-07-017994-8). McGraw.
--Curso Basico de Mecanografia. 84p. 1982. 6.68 (ISBN 0-07-017991-3). McGraw.
--Curso Basico de Practicas Secretariales. 120p. 1982. 6.64 (ISBN 0-07-017992-1). McGraw.
Duenewald, Doris, ed. see Elliott, Joan.
Duenewald, Doris, ed. see Fujikawa, Guyo.
Duenewald, Doris, ed. see Hoch, Edward D.
Duenewald, Doris, ed. see Mumford, Thad & Muntean, Michaela.
Duenewald, Doris, ed. see Rushnell, Elaine.
Duenhoelter, Johann H., ed. Greenhill's Office Gynecology. 10th ed. (Illus.). 448p. 1983. 41.95 (ISBN 0-8151-2930-0). Year Bk Med.
Duenk, et al. Auto Body Repair. (gr. 9-12). 1984. text ed. 21.28 (ISBN 0-02-662340-4). Bennett Il.
Duenk, Lester G., et al. Autobody Repair. 1977. student guide 5.00 (ISBN 0-02-662320-X). Bennett IL.

Duensing, Edward, jt. auth. see Carr, James H.
Duensing, Edward E., jt. ed. see Carr, James H.
Duer, David. To Bread. (Morning Coffee Chapbks.). (Illus.). 16p. 1985. pap. 7.50 (ISBN 0-918273-16-1). Coffee Hse.
Duer, John. The Law & Practice of Marine Insurance, Deduced from a Critical Examination of the Adjudged Cases, the Nature & Analogies of the Subject, & the General Usage of Commercial Nations, 2 vols. LC 72-37972. (American Law Ser.: The Formative Years). 1650p. 1972. Repr. of 1846 ed. Set. 92.50 (ISBN 0-405-04010-5); Vol. 1. 46.50 (ISBN 0-405-04011-3); Vol. 2. 46.50 (ISBN 0-405-04012-1). Ayer Co Pubs.
Duer, William A. Course of Lectures on the Constitutional Jurisprudence of the U. S. 2nd ed. LC 79-173993. (Research & Source Works Ser.: No. 844). 1971. Repr. of 1856 ed. lib. bdg. 29.50 (ISBN 0-8337-0946-1). B Franklin.
Duerden, C. Noise Abatement. LC 77-164907. (Illus.). 1971. 15.00 (ISBN 0-8022-2061-4). Philos Lib.
Duerden, Dennis. A Concise Handbook of African Art: Ancient, Modern, & Contemporary. (Illus.). 360p. 1986. lib. bdg. 82.50 (ISBN 3-598-10543-6). K G Saur.
Duerden, Dennis, jt. ed. see Pieterse, Cosmo.
Duerden, Frank. The Complete Rambler: A Guide to Every Aspect of Walking in Britain. (Illus.). 317p. 1983. pap. 4.95 (ISBN 0-686-46181-9, Pub. by Granada England). Academy Chi Pubs.
Duerden, P., jt. auth. see Ambrose, W.
Duerden, Richard. The Air's Nearly Perfect Elasticity. 1979. pap. 3.50 (ISBN 0-939180-08-1). Tombouctou.
Duerfeldt, Pryse H., ed. see O'Dell, Richard F.
Duerichen, Norbert. Woodburning Stoves. (Illus.). 112p. pap. 7.95 (ISBN 0-88839-133-1). Hancock House.
Duerksen, Christena. Come with Me. LC 75-156751. (gr. 1-6). 1971. pap. 1.50 (ISBN 0-87303-208-X). Faith & Life.
Duerksen, Christopher J. Dow vs California: A Turning Point in the Envirobusiness Struggle. LC 82-19942. (Illus.). 150p. (Orig.). 1982. pap. 10.00 (ISBN 0-89164-076-2). Conservation Foun.
--Environmental Regulation Of Industrial Plant Siting: How to Make it Work Better. LC 83-20901. 232p. 1983. pap. 15.00 (ISBN 0-89164-078-9). Conservation Foun.
Duerksen, Christopher J., et al. A Handbook on Historic Preservation Law. LC 83-7699. 1983. 50.00 (ISBN 0-89164-074-6); pap. 30.00 (ISBN 0-89164-079-7). Conservation Foun.
Duerksen, Roland A., ed. see Shelley, Percy B.
Duerlinger, James P., ed. Ultimate Reality & Spiritual Discipline. (God Ser.). 240p. (Orig.). 1984. text ed. 17.95 (ISBN 0-913757-09-8, Pub. by New Era Bks); pap. text ed. 12.95 (ISBN 0-913757-08-X). Paragon Hse.
Duermueller, Urs. Towards a Varieties Grammar of English. 238p. 1982. pap. 25.80 (ISBN 3-261-05027-6). P Lang Pubs.
Duerr, Charles. One Hundred Double-Acrostics. 1984. pap. 4.95 (ISBN 0-517-55197-7, Harmony). Crown.
Duerr, Edwin. Radio & Television Acting: Criticism, Theory & Practice. LC 78-138223. 417p. 1972. Repr. of 1950 ed. lib. bdg. 32.50x (ISBN 0-8371-5580-0, DURT). Greenwood.
Duerr, Hans P. Dreamtime. 448p. 24.95 (ISBN 0-631-13375-5). Basil Blackwell.
--Dreamtime: Concerning the Boundary Between Wilderness & Civilization. 448p. 1985. 24.95 (ISBN 0-631-13375-5). Basil Blackwell.
Duerr, Hans-Peter, jt. auth. see Breitenlohner, Peter.
Duerr, Michael G. Are Today's Schools Preparing Tomorrow's Business Leaders? A Worldwide Survey of Chief Executives. (Report Ser: No. 622). 30p. (Orig.). 1974. pap. 10.00 (ISBN 0-8237-0002-X). Conference Bd.
--Impact of Commodity Shortages: A World Survey. (Report Ser.: No. 648). 28p. (Orig.). 1975. pap. 20.00 (ISBN 0-8237-0067-4); pap. 4.00 member. Conference Bd.
Duerr, Michael G., jt. auth. see Basche, James R., Jr.
Duerr, W. A. Forest Resource Management 1982. text ed. 19.95x (ISBN 0-88246-036-6). Oreg St U Bkstrs.
Duerr, William A. Economic Problems of Forestry in the Appalachian Region. LC 49-8873. (Economic Studies: No. 84). (Illus.). 1949. 18.50x (ISBN 0-674-22950-9). Harvard U Pr.
Duerr, William A., ed. Timber! Problems, Prospects, Policies. LC 72-1160. 260p. 1973. 10.95x (ISBN 0-8138-1700-5). Iowa St U Pr.
Duerschner, Arthur E., jt. auth. see McKee, James L.
Duesberg, Peter, et al. Rous Sarcoma: Current Research I. LC 72-10910. (Illus.). 220p. 1973. text ed. 29.00x (ISBN 0-8422-7063-9). Irvington.
Duesen, Nancy Van see Van Deusen, Nancy.
Duesen, Robert V. Christian Garve & English Belles-Lettres. (European University Studies: Series 18, Comparative Literature, Vol. 1). 200p. 1970. pap. 25.00 (ISBN 3-261-00221-2). P Lang Pubs.
Duesenberry, James. Money & Credit: Impact & Control. 3rd ed. LC 70-173310. (Foundations of Modern Economics Ser.). (Illus.). 160p. 1972. pap. 14.95 ref. ed. (ISBN 0-13-600304-4). P-H.
Duesenberry, James S. Business Cycles & Economic Growth. LC 77-24362. (Economics Handbook Ser.). (Illus.). 1977. Repr. of 1958 ed. lib. bdg. 24.25x (ISBN 0-8371-9751-1, DUBU). Greenwood.
--Income, Saving & the Theory of Consumer Behavior. LC 49-50134. (Economic Studies: No. 87). (Illus.). 1949. 7.95x (ISBN 0-674-44750-6). Harvard U Pr.
Duespohl, T. Audean, jt. auth. see Carpenito, Lynda J.
Duespohl, T. Audean, ed. Nursing in Transition. LC 82-13946. 259p. 1982. 24.50 (ISBN 0-89443-837-9). Aspen Systems.
Duet, Clyde P., jt. auth. see Villere, Maurice F.
Duetsch, H. U., ed. Influence of the Biosphere on the Atmosphere. (Contributions to Current Research in Geophysics: No. 5). 376p. 1978. 67.95x (ISBN 0-8176-1017-0). Birkhauser.
Dueuker, R. Sheldon. Tensions in the Connection. 128p. 1983. pap. 4.95 (ISBN 0-687-41243-9). Abingdon.
Dueuzeide, H., jt. auth. see Becker, H. A.
Duey, Phillip A. Bel Canto & Its Golden Age. (Music Reprint Ser.: 1980). 1980. Repr. of 1951 ed. lib. bdg. 27.50 (ISBN 0-306-76021-5). Da Capo.
Dufau, Maria & Means, Anthony, eds. Hormone Binding & Target Cell Activation in the Testis. LC 74-23709. (Current Topics in Molecular Endocrinology: Vol. 1). 380p. 1974. 47.50x (ISBN 0-306-34001-1, Plenum Pr). Plenum Pub.
Dufau, Maria L., jt. ed. see Catt, K. J.
Dufau, Micheline & D'Alelio, Ellen. Decouverte du Poeme: Introduction a l'Explication de Textes. 172p. (Orig., Fr.). 1967. pap. text ed. 12.95 (ISBN 0-15-517290-5, HC). HarBraceJ.
Dufau, Micheline see Bishop, G. Reginald, Jr.
Dufau, Micheline, jt. auth. see D'Alelio, Ellen.
Dufau, Micheline, tr. see Quinn, Esther C.
Dufaucon, Marguerite, tr. see Vignant, Jean-Francois.
Dufault, Joan. Vintage: The Bold Survivors. LC 78-1754. (Illus.). 256p. 1978. 12.95 (ISBN 0-8298-0356-4). Pilgrim NY.
Dufey, Gunter, ed. see Abbey, Augustus.
Dufey, Gunter, ed. see Brock, James L.
Dufey, Gunter, ed. see Bryan, E. Lewis.
Dufey, Gunter, ed. see Butler, David H.
Dufey, Gunter, ed. see Cunningham, Gary M.
Dufey, Gunter, ed. see Davidson, William H.
Dufey, Gunter, ed. see DeAngelo, Linda E.
Dufey, Gunter, ed. see Dielman, Terry E.
Dufey, Gunter, ed. see Dory, John P.
Dufey, Gunter, ed. see Dubinsky, Alan J.
Dufey, Gunter, ed. see Euh, Yoon-dae.
Dufey, Gunter, ed. see Fast, Norman D.
Dufey, Gunter, ed. see Frieder, Larry A.
Dufey, Gunter, ed. see Giroux, Gary & Rose, Peter S.
Dufey, Gunter, ed. see Glasgo, Philip W.
Dufey, Gunter, ed. see Goehle, Donna G.
Dufey, Gunter, ed. see Jilling, Michael.
Dufey, Gunter, ed. see Kelly, Marie W.
Dufey, Gunter, ed. see Kennedy, William F.
Dufey, Gunter, ed. see Kilpatrick, John A.
Dufey, Gunter, ed. see Klein, Hans E.
Dufey, Gunter, ed. see Landeau, Jean-Francois.
Dufey, Gunter, ed. see Leonard, Paul A.
Dufey, Gunter, ed. see Ligon, Helen H.
Dufey, Gunter, ed. see Lundsten, Lorman L.
Dufey, Gunter, ed. see McLeod, Robert W.
Dufey, Gunter, ed. see Morsicato, Helen G.
Dufey, Gunter, ed. see Olson, Margrethe H.
Dufey, Gunter, ed. see O'Neill, Hugh M.
Dufey, Gunter, ed. see Oppenheimer, Henry R.
Dufey, Gunter, ed. see Pence, Christine C.
Dufey, Gunter, ed. see Picard, Jacques L.
Dufey, Gunter, ed. see Rader, James.
Dufey, Gunter, ed. see Sanger, Gary C.
Dufey, Gunter, ed. see Schillereff, Ronald L.
Dufey, Gunter, ed. see Shimaguchi, Mitsuaki.
Dufey, Gunter, ed. see Siegel, Michael H.
Dufey, Gunter, ed, see Smith, Charles H.
Dufey, Gunter, ed. see Smith, Francis G.
Dufey, Gunter, ed. see Stephens, Ray G.
Dufey, Gunter, ed. see Swary, Itzhak.
Dufey, Gunter, ed. see Tewari, Harish C.
Dufey, Gunter, ed. see Tong, Hsin-Min.
Dufey, Gunter, ed. see Tran, Vinh Quang.
Dufey, Gunter, ed. see Van Breda, Michael F.
Dufey, Gunter, ed. see Vonderembse, Mark A.
Dufey, Gunter, ed. see Wakabayashi, Mitsuru.
Dufey, Gunter, ed. see Williamson, Nicholas C.
Dufey, Gunter, ed. see Wilson, Brent D.
Dufey, Gunter, ed. see Wilson, Mollie H.
Dufey, Gunter, ed. see Yahr, Robert B.
Dufey, Gunther, ed. see Crim, John W.
Duff. A Century of the English Book Trade. 1978. Repr. of 1948 ed. lib. bdg. 30.00 (ISBN 0-8495-1015-5). Arden Lib.
--Century of the English Book Trade. LC 72-188912. 1948. lib. bdg. 25.00 (ISBN 0-8414-3864-1). Folcroft.
Duff, jt. ed. see Baruth.
Duff, A. M., ed. see Duff, John W.
Duff, Alan, jt. auth. see Maley, Alan.
Duff, Alan, tr. see Touraine, Alain.
Duff, Alan, tr. see Varady, Tibor.
Duff, Annis, jt. auth. see Adshead, Gladys L.
Duff, Arlie. Ya'll Come. 200p. 1983. pap. 9.95 (ISBN 0-89015-404-X). Eakin Pubns.
Duff, C. Introducing the Macintosh. 1984. pap. 14.95 (ISBN 0-07-018024-5, BYTE Bks). McGraw.
Duff, Charles. The Basis & Essentials of French. (Quality Paperback Ser.: No. 247). 122p. (Orig.). 1972. pap. 2.95 (ISBN 0-8226-0247-4). Littlefield.
--French for Beginners. 1955. pap. 5.29 (ISBN 0-06-463252-0, EH 252, EH). B&N NY.
--A Handbook on Hanging. 192p. 1974. Repr. of 1961 ed. 10.00x (ISBN 0-87471-459-1). Rowman.
--Italian for Beginners. 2nd rev ed. 1959. pap. 6.95i (ISBN 0-06-463214-8, EH 214, EH): B&N NY.
--James Joyce & the Plain Reader. LC 72-194752. 1932. lib. bdg. 15.00 (ISBN 0-8414-3713-0). Folcroft.
--James Joyce & the Plain Reader. LC 78-164027. (Studies in Irish Literature, No. 16). 1971. Repr. of 1932 ed. lib. bdg. 32.95x (ISBN 0-8383-1329-9). Haskell.
--Spanish for Beginners. (Orig.). 1958. pap. 5.72i (ISBN 0-06-463271-7, EH 271, EH). B&N NY.
Duff, Charles & Freund, Richard. The Basis & Essentials of German. (Quality Paperback Ser.: No. 248). 117p. 1972. pap. 2.95 (ISBN 0-8226-0248-2). Littlefield.
Duff, Charles & Makaroff, Dmitri. Russian for Beginners. 1962. pap. 5.72i (ISBN 0-06-463287-3, EH 287, EH). B&N NY.
Duff, Charles & Stamford, Paul. German for Beginners. 2nd rev. ed. 1960. pap. 5.29i (ISBN 0-06-463217-2, EH 217, EH). B&N NY.
Duff, Charles, ed. see Quevedo y Villegas, Francisco G. de.
Duff, Clarence W. Cords of Love. 1980. pap. 7.50 (ISBN 0-87552-248-3). Presby & Reformed.
--God's Higher Ways. 1978. pap. 7.50 kivar (ISBN 0-87552-257-2). Presby & Reformed.
Duff, D., jt. ed. see Craig, G. Y.
Duff, David. Hessian Tapestry: The Hesse Family & British Royalty. (Illus.). 1979. 28.00 (ISBN 0-7153-7838-4). David & Charles.
--Queen Mary. (Illus.). 1985. 17.95 (ISBN 0-00-217240-2, Pub. by Salem Hse Ltd). Merrimack Pub Cir.
--Victoria & Albert. LC 72-2203. 1972. 9.95 (ISBN 0-8008-7967-8). Taplinger.
Duff, David, ed. Queen Victoria's Highland Journals. (Illus.). 240p. 1981. 22.50 (ISBN 0-03-059828-1). Webb & Bower.
--Queen Victoria's Highland Journals. (Illus.). 240p. 1983. pap. 10.95 (ISBN 0-03-063549-7). HR&W.
Duff, E. Gordon. Early English Printing: A Series of Facsimilies of All the Types Used in England During the 15th Century. 1969. Repr. of 1896 ed. 23.50 (ISBN 0-8337-0947-X). B Franklin.
--Early Printed Books. LC 68-25309. (Bibliophile Ser., No. 83). (Illus.). 1968. Repr. of 1843 ed. lib. bdg. 51.95x (ISBN 0-8383-0936-4). Haskell.
--The Printers, Stationers, & Book-Binders of Westminster & London from 1476 to 1535. LC 78-172540. (Illus.). Repr. of 1906 ed. 22.00 (ISBN 0-405-08467-6, Blom Pubns). Ayer Co Pubs.
--William Caxton, Fourteen Twenty-Two to Fourteen Ninety-One. LC 79-128840. (Bibliography & Reference Ser.: No. 359). 1970. Repr. of 1905 ed. lib. bdg. 22.50 (ISBN 0-8337-0948-8). B Franklin.
Duff, E. Gordon, ed. Information for Pilgrims Unto the Holy Land. LC 78-63464. Repr. of 1893 ed. 16.50 (ISBN 0-404-16536-2). AMS Pr.
Duff, E. Grant. Ernest Renan in Memoriam. 320p. 1981. Repr. of 1893 ed. lib. bdg. 40.00 (ISBN 0-89987-163-1). Darby Bks.
Duff, Edward G. A Century of English Book Trade. xxxv, 200p. Date not set. Repr. lib. bdg. 39.00 (ISBN 0-932051-46-4). Am Repr Serv.
--Fifteen Century English Books. LC 74-14846. 1974. Repr. of 1917 ed. lib. bdg. 25.00 (ISBN 0-8414-3779-3). Folcroft.
--Fifteenth Century English Books: A Bibliography of Books & Documents Printed in England & of Books for the English Market Printed Abroad. LC 18-6817. (Bibliographical Society, London, Illustrated Monographs: No. 18). (Illus.). pap. 33.00 (ISBN 0-317-09313-4, 2055409). Bks Demand UMI.
Duff, Ernest A. Leader & Party in Latin America. (Special Studies on Latin America & the Caribbean). 150p. 1985. softcover 17.50x (ISBN 0-8133-7019-1). Westview.
Duff, Ernest A. & McCamant, John F. Violence & Repression in Latin America: A Quantitative & Historical Analysis. LC 75-16645. (Illus.). 1976. 22.95 (ISBN 0-02-907690-0). Free Pr.
Duff, Frank. Miracles on Tap. 5.00 (ISBN 0-910984-14-X); pap. 3.50 (ISBN 0-910984-15-8). Montfort Pubns.
--Robert Bradshaw. 8.95 (ISBN 0-910984-53-0); pap. 5.95 (ISBN 0-317-20160-3). Montfort Pubns.
Duff, Gail. The Barbecue Book. (Illus.). 1985. pap. 9.95 (ISBN 0-907061-70-2). Interbook.
--A Book of Pot-Pourri: New & Old Ideas for Fragrant Flowers & Herbs. 128p. 1985. 14.95 (ISBN 0-8253-0296-X). Beaufort Bks NY.
Duff, George F. Partial Differential Equations. LC 56-4187. (Mathematical Expositions: No. 9). pap. 64.50 (ISBN 0-317-08885-8, 2014193). Bks Demand UMI.
Duff, George F. & Naylor, D. Differential Equations of Applied Mathematics. LC 65-26844. pap. 82.30 (ISBN 0-317-08714-2, 2012598). Bks Demand UMI.
Duff, Gerald. Calling Collect. LC 82-2819. (University of Central Florida Contemporary Poetry Ser.). 1982. 8.95 (ISBN 0-8130-0711-9). U Presses Fla.
--Indian Giver. LC 83-47829. 288p. 1983. 12.95 (ISBN 0-253-13999-6). Ind U Pr.
--William Cobbett & the Politics of Earth. (Salzburg Studies in English Literature, Romantic Reassessment: No. 24). 143p. 1972. pap. text ed. 25.50x (ISBN 0-391-01366-1). Humanities.
Duff, Gerald, ed. see Cobbett, William.
Duff, Hector L. Nyasaland under the Foreign Office. LC 70-78369. (Illus.). Repr. of 1903 ed. 21.75x (ISBN 0-8371-1341-5, DNY&, Pub. by Negro U Pr). Greenwood.
Duff, Howard. Astrological Types. 52p. 1948. 1.50 (ISBN 0-86690-084-5, 1083-02). Am Fed Astrologers.
Duff, I., ed. Sparse Matrices & Their Uses. LC 80-42355. 1981. 49.50 (ISBN 0-12-223280-1). Acad Pr.
Duff, I. S. & Stewart, G. W., eds. Sparse Matrix Proceedings 1978. LC 79-88001. xvi, 334p. 1979. text ed. 25.00 (ISBN 0-89871-160-6). Soc Indus-Appl Math.
Duff, J., tr. see Aksakov, Sergei T.
Duff, J. B. & Greene, Larry A., eds. Slavery: Its Origins & Legacy. LC 74-22308. (Problem Studies in American History Ser.). 1975. pap. 7.95x (ISBN 0-88295-727-9). Harlan Davidson.
Duff, J. D., ed. see Juvenal.
Duff, J. D., tr. see Aksakov, Sergei.
Duff, J. D., tr. see Hertzen, Alexander.
Duff, J. D., tr. see Herzen, Alexander.
Duff, J. D., tr. see Rostovtsev, Mikhail.
Duff, J. D., tr. see Rostovtzeff, Mikhail I.
Duff, James. Home Front. 1985. pap. 3.35 (ISBN 0-317-27154-7). Dramatists Play.
Duff, James D. History of the Mahrattas, 2 vols. 1971. 65.00 set (ISBN 0-686-20243-0). Intl Bk Dist.
Duff, John R. & Kaufman, Milton. Alternating Current Fundamentals. 2nd ed. (Electrical Trades Ser.). (gr. 9-10). 1980. 22.00 (ISBN 0-8273-1133-8); pap. 18.00 (ISBN 0-8273-1142-7). Delmar.
Duff, John W. A Literary History of Rome in the Silver Age: From Tiberius to Hadrian. 3rd ed. Duff, A. M., ed. LC 79-9906. 1979. Repr. of 1964 ed. lib. bdg. 47.50x (ISBN 0-313-20939-1, DULH). Greenwood.
Duff, Jon M. Industrial Technical Illustration. 1982. 26.50 (ISBN 0-442-21957-1). Van Nos Reinhold.
Duff, Karl J. Martial Arts & the Law. Lee, Mike, ed. LC 84-62295. (Ser. 439). 96p. (Orig.). 1985. pap. 6.95 (ISBN 0-89750-126-8). Ohara Pubns.
Duff, Larry J. Audit & Control of Distributed Data Processing Systems. 1983. 33.00 (ISBN 0-89413-104-4); nonmembers 33.00. Inst Inter Aud.
Duff, M., jt. auth. see Kittler, J.
Duff, M. Grant see Grant Duff, M. E.
Duff, M. J. & Isham, C. J., eds. Quantum Structure of Space & Time: Proceedings of the Nuffield Workshop, Imperial College, London, August 3-21, 1981. LC 82-9732. 420p. 1983. 52.50 (ISBN 0-521-24732-2). Cambridge U Pr.
Duff, M. J. & Leviadi, S., eds. Languages & Architectures for Image Processing. LC 81-67909. 1981. 49.50 (ISBN 0-12-223320-4). Acad Pr.
Duff, Maggie. Dancing Turtle. LC 80-24683. (Illus.). 32p. (gr. k-3). 1981. PLB 8.95 (ISBN 0-02-733010-9). Macmillan.
--The Princess & the Pumpkin. LC 79-24060. (Illus.). 32p. (gr. 1-3). 1980. PLB 9.95 (ISBN 0-02-733000-1). Macmillan.
--Rum Pum Pum. LC 77-12389. 32p. (gr. k-3). 1978. 9.95 (ISBN 0-02-732950-X, 73295). Macmillan.
Duff, Margaret, tr. see Simenon, Georges.
Duff, Michael J., jt. auth. see Preston, Kendall, Jr.
Duff, Michael J., ed. Computing Structures for Image Processing. 1983. 33.00 (ISBN 0-12-223340-9). Acad Pr.
Duff, Moira. The Vocation of Pearl Duncan. 180p. (Orig.). 1984. pap. 6.95 (ISBN 0-7043-3897-1, Pub. by Quartet Bks). Merrimack Pub Cir.
Duff, Mountstuart E. Grant see Grant Duff, Mountstuart E.
Duff, O. French Reader & Vocabulary. (Illus.). 1985. 25.00 (ISBN 0-89835-056-5). Abaris Bks.
Duff, P. M. & Smith, A. J. Geology of England & Wales, 3 Vols. 600p. 1985. 49.95x (ISBN 0-470-27261-9). Halsted Pr.
Duff, Patrick W. Personality in Roman Private Law. LC 70-138536. 241p. Repr. of 1938 ed. lib. bdg. 22.50x (ISBN 0-678-04544-5). Kelley.
--Personality in Roman Private Law. xiii, 241p. 1971. Repr. of 1938 ed. 12.50x (ISBN 0-8377-2026-5). Rothman.
Duff, Peter. British Ships & Shipping. 1977. lib. bdg. 59.95 (ISBN 0-8490-1556-1). Gordon Pr.
Duff, Peter, et al. Cyclic Sedimentation. (Developments in Sedimentology Ser.: Vol. 10). 280p. 1967. 81.00 (ISBN 0-444-40183-0). Elsevier.
Duff, R. A. Trials & Punishments. LC 85-15128. (Cambridge Studies in Philosophy). Date not set. price not set (ISBN 0-521-30818-6). Cambridge U Pr.
Duff, R. E., jt. auth. see Swick, Kevin.
Duff, R. Eleanor, jt. auth. see Swick, Kevin J.

Duff, R. Eleanor, et al. Building Successful Parent-Teacher Partnerships. LC 79-91107. 81p. (Orig.). 1980. pap. 9.95 (ISBN 0-89334-053-7). Humanics Ltd.

Duff, Robert A. Spinoza's Political & Ethical Philosophy. LC 71-108858. Repr. of 1903 ed. lib. bdg. 37.50x (ISBN 0-678-00615-6). Kelley.

--Spinoza's Political & Ethical Philosophy. 1973. Repr. of 1903 ed. 14.00 (ISBN 0-8274-1391-2). R West.

Duff, Stella F., jt. auth. see Cappon, Lester J.

Duff, Susan. Miss Universe Beauty Book. (Illus.). 240p. 1983. 15.95 (ISBN 0-698-11195-8, Coward). Putnam Pub Group.

--Secrets of Beautiful Eyes. 1984. pap. 6.95 (ISBN 0-671-50175-5, Wallaby). PB.

Duff, Susan, jt. auth. see Woman's Day Editors.

Duff, Thomas A. Monarch Notes on Defoe's Robinson Crusoe. (Orig.). pap. 2.95 (ISBN 0-671-00821-8). Monarch Pr.

Duff, William. Critical Observations on the Writings of the Most Celebrated Original Geniuses in Poetry (1770) LC 73-9526. 400p. 1973. Repr. lib. bdg. 55.00x (ISBN 0-8201-1119-8). Schol Facsimiles.

--An Essay on Original Genius & Its Various Modes of Exertion in Philosophy & the Fine Arts. LC 64-10669. 1978. Repr. of 1767 ed. 55.00x (ISBN 0-8201-1261-5). Schol Facsimiles.

--The History of Rhedi, the Hermit of Mount Ararat: An Oriental Tale, 1773. (The Flowering of the Novel, 1740-1775 Ser: Vol. 101). 1974. lib. bdg. 61.00 (ISBN 0-8240-1200-3). Garland Pub.

Duff, William G. Mobile Communications. 2nd ed. (Illus.). 296p. 1980. text ed. 43.00 (ISBN 0-932263-09-7). White Consult.

Duff, William G., jt. auth. see White, Donald R.

Duffala, Sharon L. Rocky Mountain Cache: Western Wild Game Cookbook. LC 82-7542. (Illus.). 72p. (Orig.). 1982. pap. 5.95 (ISBN 0-87108-630-1). Pruett.

Duffany, Brett. An Illustrated Voice. 1975. pap. 3.00 (ISBN 0-317-11869-2). Mathom.

--Until Telepathy. 1976. pap. 3.00 (ISBN 0-317-11871-4). Mathom.

Duffee, David & Fitch, Robert. An Introduction to Corrections: A Policy & Systems Approach. LC 75-19931. 1976. text ed. 19.95 (ISBN 0-394-33372-1, RanC). Random.

Duffee, David E. Correctional Management: Change & Control in Correctional Organizations. (Criminal Justice Ser.). (Illus.). 1980. text ed. 25.95 (ISBN 0-13-178400-5). P-H.

--Explaining Criminal Justice: Community Theory & Criminal Justice Reform. LC 80-17465. 288p. 1980. text ed. 30.00 (ISBN 0-89946-058-5). Oelgeschlager.

Duffee, David E., jt. auth. see Hussey, Frederick A.

Duffell, Roy, tr. see Harder, Erik.

Duffels, J. P. & Van der Laan, P. A. Catalogue of the Cicadoidea (Homoptera, Auchenorhyncha) 1956-1980. 1985. lib. bdg. 65.00 (ISBN 90-6193-522-9, Pub. by Junk Pub Netherlands). Kluwer-Academic.

Duffendack, Stanley D. Effective Management Through Work Planning. 1971. 28.95 (ISBN 0-932078-00-1). GE Tech Prom & Train.

Duffer, H. F., Jr., tr. see Maston, T. B.

Duffer, Hiram F., Jr., tr. see Bunyan, Juan & Leavell, L. P.

Dufferin & Ava. Dufferin - Carnarvon Correspondence, 1874-1878. Hamilton-Temple-Blackwood, Frederick T., et al, eds. LC 69-14508. 1969. Repr. of 1955 ed. lib. bdg. 29.50x (ISBN 0-8371-5073-6, DUDC). Greenwood.

Duffet, Michel, jt. auth. see Aveline, Claude.

Duffett, John. Boatowner's Guide to Modern Maintenance: Protecting Your Floating Investment. LC 82-18787. (Illus.). 208p. 1985. 19.95 (ISBN 0-393-03279-5). Norton.

--Modern Marine Maintenance. 256p. 1973. 9.95 (ISBN 0-910990-15-8). Hearst Bks.

Duffett-Smith, Peter. Astronomy on Your Personal Computer. (Illus.). 240p. Date not set. price not set (ISBN 0-521-26620-3); pap. price not set (ISBN 0-521-31976-5). Cambridge U Pr.

--Practical Astronomy with Your Calculator. 2nd ed. LC 81-6191. 200p. 1981. 37.50 (ISBN 0-521-24059-X); pap. 10.95 (ISBN 0-521-28411-2). Cambridge U Pr.

Duffey, Bernard. Poetry in America: Expression & Its Values in the Times of Bryant, Whitman & Pound. LC 77-81281. xiv, 357p. 1978. 25.00 (ISBN 0-8223-0392-2). Duke.

Duffey, Bernard, jt. ed. see Williams, Kenny J.

Duffey, Bernard I. The Chicago Renaissance in American Letters: A Critical History. LC 72-6193. 285p. 1972. Repr. of 1956 ed. lib. bdg. 55.00x (ISBN 0-8371-6461-3, DUCR). Greenwood.

Duffey, David M. Expert Advice on Gun Dog Training. rev. ed. 288p. 1985. 15.95 (ISBN 0-8329-0412-0, Pub. by Winchester Pr). New Century.

Duffey, Eliza B. The Relations of the Sexes. LC 73-20619. (Sex, Marriage & Society Ser.). 320p. 1974. Repr. of 1876 ed. 24.50x (ISBN 0-405-05824-1, Blom Pubns). Ayer Co Pubs.

--What Women Should Know: Information for Wives & Mothers. LC 73-20620. (Sex, Marriage & Society Ser.). 324p. 1974. Repr. of 1873 ed. 22.00x (ISBN 0-405-05825-X). Ayer Co Pubs.

Duffey, Eric, jt. auth. see Muir, Richard.

Duffey, George H. A Development of Quantum Mechanics. 1983. lib. bdg. 60.00 (ISBN 90-277-1587-4, Pub. by Reidel Holland). Kluwer Academic.

--Theoretical Physics: Classical & Modern Views. LC 79-23794. 704p. 1980. Repr. of 1973 ed. lib. bdg. 34.50 (ISBN 0-89874-062-2). Krieger.

Duffey, Rick & Stephenson, Harry. Fifth House. 1979. 1.50 (ISBN 0-942582-01-2). Erie St Pr.

Duff-Gordon, C. L., jt. auth. see Symonds, M.

Duff-Gordon, Lucie. Letters from Egypt, 1863-65. 2nd ed. LC 75-164794. (BCL Ser. I). Repr. of 1865 ed. 27.50 (ISBN 0-404-02189-1). AMS Pr.

Duffie, John A. & Beckman, William A. Solar Energy Thermal Processes. LC 74-12390. 386p. 1974. 44.95 (ISBN 0-471-22371-9, Pub. by Wiley-Interscience). Wiley.

--Solar Engineering of Thermal Processes. LC 80-13297. 762p. 1980. 36.95 (ISBN 0-471-05066-0, Pub. by Wiley-Interscience). Wiley.

Duffie, John A., jt. ed. see Boer, Karl W.

Duffie, John A., jt. ed. see Daniels, Farrington.

Duffie, Mary A. So-You Are Ready to Cook. 4th ed. LC 72-76094. (Illus.). 320p. 1974. spiral bdg. 10.95 (ISBN 0-8087-0412-5). Burgess.

Duffield, A. J. Don Quixote: His Critics & Commentators. 155p. 1980. Repr. of 1881 ed. lib. bdg. 17.50 (ISBN 0-8414-3778-5). Folcroft.

--Don Quixote: His Critics & Commentators. 1973. Repr. of 1881 ed. 25.00 (ISBN 0-8274-1415-3). R West.

Duffield, B. S., jt. auth. see Coppock, J. T.

Duffield, C. G., jt. auth. see Welch, W.

Duffield, G. E., ed. Thomas Cramer. 416p. 1981. 90.00x (ISBN 0-686-79494-X, Pub. by Sutton Courtenay). State Mutual Bk.

Duffield, Guy P. Handbook of Bible Lands. 192p. 1985. pap. 5.95 (ISBN 0-8010-2948-1). Baker Bk.

Duffield, Mark. Maiurno: Capitalism & Rural Life in Sudan. (Sudam Studies: No. 5). (Illus.). 350p. 1981. 25.00 (ISBN 0-903729-79-2, Pub. by Ithaca England). Evergreen Dist.

Duffield, Mary R. & Jones, Warren D. Plants for Dry Climates: How to Select, Grow & Enjoy. LC 80-82535. (Illus.). 176p. 1981. pap. 7.95 (ISBN 0-89586-042-2). H P Bks.

Duffield, Robert. Rogue Bull: The Story of Lang Hancock King of the Pilbara. 231p. 1982. 20.95x (ISBN 0-00-216423-X, Pub. by W. Collins Australia); pap. 8.95x (ISBN 0-00-634515-8). Intl Spec Bk.

Duffield, Robert, jt. auth. see Murrell, Kenneth L.

Duffield, Robert H., jt. auth. see Murrell, Kenneth L.

Duffield, Samuel W. English Hymns: Their Authors & History. 1980. Repr. of 1886 ed. lib. bdg. 60.00 (ISBN 0-89341-441-7). Longwood Pub Group.

--The Latin Hymn-Writers & Their Hymns. 1980. Repr. of 1889 ed. lib. bdg. 50.00 (ISBN 0-89341-440-9). Longwood Pub Group.

Duffield, William. The Art of Flower Painting. (The Library of the Arts). (Illus.). 1977. 47.50 (ISBN 0-89266-070-8). Am Classical Coll Pr.

Duffieux, P. M. The Fourier Transform & Its Applications to Optics. 2nd ed. LC 82-20302. (Pure & Applied Optics Ser.). 197p. 1982. 36.50 (ISBN 0-471-09589-3, Pub. by Wiley-Interscience). Wiley.

Duffin, H. C. Walter De La Mare, a Study of His Poetry. LC 71-95424. (Studies in Poetry, No. 38). 1970. Repr. of 1949 ed. lib. bdg. 48.95x (ISBN 0-8383-0972-0). Haskell.

Duffin, Henry C. The Quintessence of Bernard Shaw. LC 75-34135. 1975. Repr. of 1920 ed. lib. bdg. 25.00 (ISBN 0-8414-3748-3). Folcroft.

--Thomas Hardy: A Study of the Wessex Novels, the Poems, & the Dynasts. LC 77-17945. 1978. Repr. of 1937 ed. lib. bdg. 37.50x (ISBN 0-313-20109-9, DUTH). Greenwood.

--Walter De La Mare, a Study of His Poetry. (Select Bibliographies Reprint Ser.). 1949. 21.00 (ISBN 0-8369-5043-7). Ayer Co Pubs.

--Walter De La Mare, A Study of His Poetry. 1973. lib. bdg. 15.00 (ISBN 0-8414-3866-8). Folcroft.

--Way of Happiness: A Reading of Wordsworth. LC 72-192021. 1947. lib. bdg. 12.50 (ISBN 0-8414-3726-2). Folcroft.

Duffin, James. Physics for Anaesthetists. (Illus.). 296p. 1976. 30.75x (ISBN 0-398-03451-6). C C Thomas.

Duffin, Lorna, ed. Women & Work in Pre-Industrial Britain. LC 85-14950. 224p. 1985. 29.00 (ISBN 0-7099-0814-8, Pub. by Croom Helm Ltd); pap. 13.50 (ISBN 0-7099-0856-3). Longwood Pub Group.

Duffin, Lorna, jt. ed. see Delamont, Sara.

Duffin, W. J., tr. see Guinier, A.

Duffner. The Sorrowful & Immaculate Heart of Mary. 47p. 0.90 (ISBN 0-911988-24-6). AMI Pr.

Duffner, Patricia K., jt. auth. see Cohen, Michael E.

Duffus, C. M. & Duffus, J. H. Carbohydrate Metabolism in Plants. LC 82-22855. (Illus.). 192p. (Orig.). 1984. 13.95 (ISBN 0-582-44642-2). Longman.

Duffus, C. M. & Slaughter, J. C. Seeds & Their Uses. LC 80-40283. 154p. 1980. 44.95x (ISBN 0-471-27799-1, Pub. by Wiley-Interscience); pap. 14.95 (ISBN 0-471-27798-3). Wiley.

Duffus, Gordon D. Clan Campbell. 16p. 1984. pap. 1.95 (ISBN 0-912951-14-1). Scotpr.

--Clan Sutherland: The Story. write for info. (ISBN 0-912951-10-9). Scotpr.

Duffus, J. H., jt. auth. see Duffus, C. M.

Duffus, John H. Environmental Toxicology. LC 80-82387. (Resource & Environmental Science Ser.). 164p. 1980. pap. 19.95x (ISBN 0-470-27051-9). Halsted Pr.

Duffus, R. L. Santa Fe Trail. (Illus.). 1971. Repr. of 1930 ed. 39.00x (ISBN 0-403-00918-9). Scholarly.

Duffus, Robert L. American Renaissance. LC 70-105679. Repr. of 1928 ed. 24.50 (ISBN 0-404-02214-6). AMS Pr.

--The Innocents at Cedro: A Memoir Thorstein Veblen & Some Others. LC 74-182193. 163p. Repr. of 1944 ed. lib. bdg. 22.50x (ISBN 0-678-00885-X). Kelley.

Duffus, Robert L. & Holt, L. Emmett, Jr. L. Emmett Holt: Pioneer of a Children's Century. LC 74-1683. (Children & Youth Ser.: Vol. 25). 310p. 1974. Repr. of 1940 ed. 25.50x (ISBN 0-405-05960-4). Ayer Co Pubs.

Duffy, A. R. & Battelle Columbus Laboratories. Study of Feasibility of Basing Natural Gas Pipeline Operating Pressure on Hydrostatic Test Pressure. 100p. 1968. softcover 10.00 (ISBN 0-318-12706-7, L30050). Am Gas Assn.

Duffy, A. R., jt. auth. see Kiefner, J. F.

Duffy, Ben. Advertising Media & Markets. LC 84-46057. (History of Advertising Ser.). 453p. 1985. lib. bdg. 50.00 (ISBN 0-8240-6751-7). Garland Pub.

Duffy, Benedict J. & Wallace, M. Jean. Biological & Medical Aspects of Contraception. LC 70-79611. 1969. 9.95x (ISBN 0-268-00361-0). U of Notre Dame Pr.

Duffy, Cameron & Woolcock, Richard, eds. Commodore 16 Games Book. (Illus.). 228p. (Orig.). (gr. 6up). 1984. pap. 12.95 (ISBN 0-86161-185-3). Melbourne Hse.

Duffy, Charles & Petit, Henry. Dictionary of Literary Terms. rev. ed. pap. 2.00 (ISBN 0-910294-02-X). Brown Bk.

Duffy, Charles G. Young Ireland: A Fragment of Irish History, 1840-1850. LC 71-127257. (Europe 1815-1945 Ser.). 796p. 1973. Repr. of 1881 ed. lib. bdg. 79.50 (ISBN 0-306-71119-2). Da Capo.

Duffy, Charles G., ed. The Ballad Poetry of Ireland. LC 72-13882. 256p. 1973. Repr. of 1869 ed. lib. bdg. 40.00x (ISBN 0-8201-1116-3). Schol Facsimiles.

Duffy, Christopher. The Fortress in the Age of Vauban & Frederick the Great, 1660-1789. (Siege Warfare Ser.: Vol. II). (Illus.). 400p. 1985. 50.00x (ISBN 0-7100-9648-8). Routledge & Kegan.

--The Military Life of Frederick the Great. LC 84-45618. 384p. 1986. 19.95 (ISBN 0-689-11548-2). Atheneum.

--Russia's Military Way to the West: Origins & Nature of Russian Military Power 1700-1800. 320p. 1985. 37.50x (ISBN 0-7100-0797-3); pap. 12.95 (ISBN 0-7102-0535-X). Routledge & Kegan.

--Siege Warfare: The Fortress in the Early Modern World, 1494-1660. (Illus.). 1979. 30.00 (ISBN 0-7100-8871-X). Routledge & Kegan.

Duffy, Clinton T. San Quentin Story, As Told to Dean Jennings. LC 68-54417. (Illus.). 1968. Repr. of 1950 ed. lib. bdg. 22.50x (ISBN 0-8371-0395-9, DUSQ). Greenwood.

Duffy, Cynthia L. & Meyer, Linda. Responsible Childbirth: How to Give Birth Normally & Avoid a Cesarean Section. LC 83-62295. 120p. (Orig.). 1984. pap. text ed. 7.95 (ISBN 0-88247-713-7). R & E Pubs.

Duffy, Dave, jt. auth. see Lamb, Tony.

Duffy, David L. Survey of the United States Government's Investment in Africa. 1978. pap. 10.00 (ISBN 0-918456-22-3, Crossroads). African Studies Assn.

Duffy, David M. Hunting Dog Know-How. LC 83-5727. (Illus.). 208p. 1983. pap. 8.95 (ISBN 0-8329-0287-X, Pub. by Winchester Pr). New Century.

Duffy, Dennis. Gardens, Convenants, Exiles: Loyalism in the Literature of Upper Canada-Ontario. 176p. 1982. 27.50x (ISBN 0-8020-5561-3); pap. 10.95 (ISBN 0-8020-6477-9). U of Toronto Pr.

Duffy, Dick, jt. auth. see Jones, Jeanne.

Duffy, E. A. A Monograph of the Immature Stages of Australasian Timber Beetles - Cerambycidae. (Illus.). 235p. 1963. 34.00x (ISBN 0-565-00577-4, Pub. by Brit Mus Nat Hist England). Sabbot-Natural Hist Bks.

--A Monograph of the Immature Stages of African Timber Beetles (Cerambycidae) (Illus.). vii, 338p. 1957. 43.00x (ISBN 0-565-00094-2, Pub. by Brit Mus Nat Hist). Sabbot-Natural Hist Bks.

--A Monograph of the Immature Stages of African Timber Beetles (Cerambycidae) Supplement. (Illus.). 186p. 1980. pap. 28.00x (ISBN 0-85198-473-8, Pub. by Brit Mus Nat Hist England). Sabbot-Natural Hist Bks.

--A Monograph of the Immature Stages of Neotropical Timber Beetles (Cerambycidae) (Illus.). v, 327p. 1960. 42.00x (ISBN 0-565-00109-4, Pub. by Brit Mus Nat Hist). Sabbot-Natural Hist Bks.

--A Monograph of the Immature Stages of Oriental Timber Beetles (Cerambycidae) (Illus.). 434p. 1968. 50.00x (ISBN 0-565-00667-3, Pub. by Brit Mus Nat Hist England). Sabbot-Natural Hist Bks.

--A Monograph of the Immature Stages of the African Timber Beetles (Cerambycidae) Supplement. 186p. 1980. 89.00x (ISBN 0-85198-473-8, Pub. by CAB Bks England). State Mutual Bk.

Duffy, Edward. Rousseau in England: The Context for Shelley's Critique of the Enlightenment. LC 78-57307. 1979. 23.00x (ISBN 0-520-03695-6). U of Cal Pr.

Duffy, Francis, et al. Planning Office Space. (Illus.). 1976. 98.50 (ISBN 0-85139-505-8, Pub. by Architectural Pr). Nichols Pub.

Duffy, Frank, ed. see Klein, Judy G.

Duffy, George H., ed. see Duffy, Nicholas.

Duffy, Gerald G., ed. Reading in the Middle School. LC 74-23428. (Perspectives in Reading Ser.). 212p. 1974. pap. 6.50 (ISBN 0-87207-118-9, 118). Intl Reading.

Duffy, Gerald G. & Roehler, Laura R., eds. Comprehensive Instruction: Perspectives & Suggestions. LC 82-23944. 352p. 1983. 29.95x (ISBN 0-582-28406-6). Longman.

Duffy, Gerald G., et al. How to Teach Reading Systematically. 2nd ed. 1977. pap. text ed. 16.50 scp (ISBN 0-06-041784-6, HarpC). Har-Row.

Duffy, Gloria, ed. see Stanford Arms Control Group.

Duffy, Ian P. Bankruptcy & Insolvency in London During the Industrial Revolution. LC 84-45999. 420p. 1985. lib. bdg. 45.00 (ISBN 0-8240-6679-0). Garland Pub.

Duffy, J. C. Moot Points: Deranged Drawings. (Illus.). 128p. 1981. pap. 3.95 (ISBN 0-201-03968-0). Addison-Wesley.

Duffy, J. I. Printing Inks: Developments Since 1975. LC 79-16231. (Chemical Technology Review Ser.: No. 139). (Illus.). 1980. 42.00 (ISBN 0-8155-0772-0). Noyes.

Duffy, J. I., ed. Chemicals by Enzymatic & Microbial Processes: Recent Advances. LC 80-16150. (Chemical Technology Review: No. 161). (Illus.). 386p. 1980. 48.00 (ISBN 0-8155-0805-0). Noyes.

--Electrodeposition Processes, Equipment & Compositions. LC 82-2235. (Chemical Tech. Rev.: No. 206). (Illus.). 308p. 1982. 42.00 (ISBN 0-8155-0898-0). Noyes.

--Electroless & Other Nonelectrolytic Plating Techniques: Recent Developments. LC 80-19494. (Chemical Tech. Rev. 171). (Illus.). 366p. 1981. 45.00 (ISBN 0-8155-0818-2). Noyes.

--Electroplating Technology: Recent Developments. LC 81-2365. (Chemical Technology Review: No. 187). (Illus.). 349p. 1981. 45.00 (ISBN 0-8155-0844-1). Noyes.

--Glass Technology: Developments Since 1978. LC 80-26045. (Chemical Tech. Rev.: 184). (Illus.). 323p. 1981. 48.00 (ISBN 0-8155-0838-7). Noyes.

--Refractory Materials: Developments Since 1977. LC 80-21945. (Chemical Technology Review: No. 178). (Illus.). 367p. 1981. 42.00 (ISBN 0-8155-0827-1). Noyes.

--Snack Food Technology: Recent Developments. LC 81-16757. (Food Technical Review: No. 55). (Illus.). 255p. 1982. 36.00 (ISBN 0-8155-0873-5). Noyes.

--Treatment, Recovery, & Disposal Processes for Radioactive Wastes: Recent Advances. LC 82-22260. (Pollution Technology Review No.95, Chemical Technology Review No. 216). (Illus.). 287p. 1983. 39.00 (ISBN 0-8155-0922-7). Noyes.

Duffy, James. The Revolt of the Teddy Bears: A May Gray Mystery. LC 84-15522. (Illus.). 80p. (gr. 5 up). 1985. 7.95 (ISBN 0-517-55533-6). Crown.

Duffy, James, et al. International Directory of Scholars & Specialists in Third World Studies. 564p. 1981. 70.00 (ISBN 0-918456-40-1). Crossroads MA.

Duffy, James, et al, eds. International Directory of Scholars & Specialists in African Studies. 1978. 35.00 (ISBN 0-918456-20-7, Crossroads). African Studies Assn.

Duffy, James E. Modern Automotive Mechanics. 1985. text ed. 24.00 (ISBN 0-87006-479-7); tchr's. ed. 18.00. Goodheart.

Duffy, James P. How to Earn a College Degree Without Going to College. LC 81-40337. 192p. 1981. 14.95 (ISBN 0-8128-2820-8); pap. 8.95 (ISBN 0-8128-6139-6). Stein & Day.

--How to Earn an Advanced Degree Without Going to Graduate School. LC 84-40615. 208p. 1985. 16.95 (ISBN 0-8128-3008-3). Stein & Day.

Duffy, James P., jt. auth. see Czajka, Peter A.

Duffy, John. Epidemics in Colonial America. LC 53-9904. x, 274p. 1971. pap. text ed. 7.95x (ISBN 0-8071-0205-9). La State U Pr.

--The Healers: A History of American Medicine. LC 78-27222. 385p. 1979. pap. 7.50x (ISBN 0-252-00743-3). U of Ill Pr.

--The Songs & Motets of Alfonso Ferrabosco, the Younger (1575-1628) Buelow, George, ed. LC 80-22513. (Studies in Musicology: No. 20). 435p. 1980. 49.95 (ISBN 0-8357-1110-2). UMI Res Pr.

--The Tulane University Medical Center: One Hundred & Fifty Years of Medical Education. (Illus.). 253p. 1985. text ed. 22.50x (ISBN 0-8071-1195-3). La State U Pr.

--Under the Goldwood Tree. 64p. 1982. 5.00 (ISBN 0-682-49869-6). Exposition Pr FL.

--Vermont: An Illustrated History. 296p. 1985. 24.95 (ISBN 0-89781-159-3). Windsor Pubns Inc.

Duffy, John, ed. Coleridge's American Disciples: Selected Correspondence of James Marsh. LC 72-90497. 280p. 1973. 17.50x (ISBN 0-87023-121-9). U of Mass Pr.

--Synodicon Vetus. Parker, John. LC 79-52935. (Dumbarton Oaks Texts: Vol. 5). 209p. 1979. 35.00x (ISBN 0-88402-088-6). Dumbarton Oaks.

Duffy, John C. Child Psychiatry. 3rd ed. (Medical Examination Review Bks.: Vol. 23). 1977. spiral bdg. 23.00 (ISBN 0-87488-126-9). Med Exam.

--Emotional Issues in the Lives of Physicians. 104p. 1970. 11.75x (ISBN 0-398-00483-8). C C Thomas.

Duffy, John C. & Gemelli, Ralph J. Child Psychiatry & Behavioral Pediatrics. 3rd ed. (Medical Outline Ser.). 1984. pap. text ed. write for info. (ISBN 0-87488-315-6). Med Exam.

Duffy, John C. & Litin, Edward M. The Emotional Health of Physicians. (Illus.). 100p. 1967. 11.75x (ISBN 0-398-00484-6). C C Thomas.

Duffy, John C. & Gerber, Lane A., eds. Psychiatry Continuing Education Review. 2nd. ed. LC 79-91844. 1980. text ed. 19.50 (ISBN 0-87488-352-0). Med Exam.

Duffy, John J. & Muller, H. Nicholas, III. An Anxious Democracy: Aspects of the 1830s. LC 81-6387. (Contributions in American Studies: No. 58). xii, 172p. 1982. lib. bdg. 29.95 (ISBN 0-313-22727-6, DUA/). Greenwood.

Duffy, Joseph. Analysis of Mechanisms & Robot Manipulators. 419p. 1980. 135.95x (ISBN 0-470-27002-0). Halsted Pr.

--Power: Prime Mover of Technology. rev. ed. (gr. 11-12). 1972. text ed. 21.97 (ISBN 0-87345-420-0). McKnight.

Duffy, Karen L., jt. ed. see Rankin, Sally.

Duffy, Kevin. Children of Forest. (Illus.). 224p. 1984. 14.95 (ISBN 0-396-08430-3). Dodd.

Duffy, M., ed. The Military Revolution & the State 1500-1800. (Exeter Studies in History: No. 1). 96p. 1980. pap. text ed. 4.50x (ISBN 0-85989-111-9, Pub. by U Exeter England). Humanities.

Duffy, Mary E., jt. auth. see Wolf, Margaret S.

Duffy, Maureen. Capital. LC 75-42406. 222p. 1976. 6.95 (ISBN 0-8076-0817-3). Braziller.

--Collected Poems. 320p. 1985. 19.95 (ISBN 0-241-11595-7, Pub. by Hamish Hamilton England); pap. 10.95 (ISBN 0-241-11667-8, Pub. by Hamish Hamilton England). David & Charles.

--The Erotic World of Faery. 1980. pap. 3.50 (ISBN 0-380-48108-1, 48108-1, Discus). Avon.

--Memorials of the Quick & the Dead. 1979. 14.95 (ISBN 0-241-10316-9, Pub. by Hamish Hamilton England). David & Charles.

--The Passionate Shepherdess. 1979. pap. 2.95 (ISBN 0-380-41863-0, Discus). Avon.

--That's How it Was. LC 83-72527. 224p. 1984. pap. 6.95 (ISBN 0-385-27955-8, Virago). Doubleday.

Duffy, Michael. The Englishman & the Foreigner. LC 85-5943. (The English Satirical Print Ser.). 208p. 1985. lib. bdg. 50.00 (ISBN 0-85964-173-2). Chadwyck-Healey.

Duffy, Michelle. Self-Instructional Introduction to Searching the OCLC on-Line Union Catalog. 2nd ed. (Amigos Training Ser.: No. 2). 53p. pap. 7.50 (ISBN 0-938288-01-6). AMIGOS Biblio.

Duffy, Michelle, ed. see Juergens, Bonnie.

Duffy, Natalie. Modern Dance: An Adult Beginner's Guide. (Illus.). 182p. 1982. 16.95 (ISBN 0-13-590935-X); pap. 8.95 (ISBN 0-13-590927-9). P-H.

Duffy, Neil & Assad, Mike. Information Management: An Executive Approach. (Illus.). 1980. 37.50x (ISBN 0-19-570190-9). Oxford U Pr.

Duffy, Nellie, jt. auth. see Goodwin, E. H.

Duffy, Nicholas. Poems from the Eighteen-Thirties by a Poor Son of Ireland. Duffy, George H., ed. 1977. 6.50 (ISBN 0-682-48834-8). Exposition Pr FL.

Duffy, Nona K. I Love Trees. LC 85-71312. (Illus.). 68p. (Orig.). 1985. pap. 5.95 (ISBN 0-931494-70-2). Brunswick Pub.

--Poems of Devotion & Inspiration, Bk. I. 55p. 1985. 3.25 (ISBN 0-89697-237-2). Intl Univ Pr.

--Poems of Devotion & Inspiration, Bk. II: Doors Will Open. 57p. 1985. 3.25 (ISBN 0-89697-238-0). Intl Univ Pr.

Duffy, Patrick G. The Official Mixer's Manual. 7th, rev. & enl. ed. Misch, Robert J., rev. by. LC 82-45452. (Illus.). 216p. 1983. 10.95 (ISBN 0-385-18307-0). Doubleday.

Duffy, Philip E. Astrocytes: Normal, Reactive, & Neoplastic. 236p. 1983. text ed. 45.50 (ISBN 0-89004-996-3). Raven.

Duffy, Regis. Real Presence: Worship, Sacraments, & Commitment. LC 81-47877. 192p. 1982. pap. 8.61i (ISBN 0-06-062105-2, RD 383, HarpR). Har-Row.

Duffy, Regis, et al. Initiation & Conversion. Johnson, Lawrence, ed. 88p. 1985. pap. 4.95 (ISBN 0-8146-1431-0). Liturgical Pr.

Duffy, Regis A. On Becoming a Catholic: The Challenge of Christian Initiation. LC 84-47721. 176p. (Orig.). 1984. pap. 7.64 (ISBN 0-06-062106-0, RD 525, HarpR). Har-Row.

--A Roman Catholic Theology of Pastoral Care. LC 83-48006. (Theology & Pastoral Care Ser.). 128p. 1983. pap. 6.95 (ISBN 0-8006-1727-4, 1-1727). Fortress.

Duffy, Richard. Brother Earth, Sister Sky. 1981. 1.50 (ISBN 0-942582-03-9). Erie St Pr.

Duffy, Ron. Effective Listening Facilitator Guide. rev., 2nd ed. 116p. 1982. pap. text ed. 15.00 (ISBN 0-943000-03-3). Telstar Inc.

Duffy, Thomas. Let's Write a Feature, 1969. (Lucas Text Ser). text ed. 4.00x perfect bdg. (ISBN 0-87543-056-2). Lucas.

Duffy, Thomas & Waller, Robert, eds. Designing Usable Texts. (Educational Technology Ser.). 1985. 48.00 (ISBN 0-12-223260-7). Acad Pr.

Duffy, Thomas J. & Vergeer, Paul P. California Toxic Fungi. LC 77-76180. (Toxicology Monograph: No. 1). (Illus.). 1977. 2.00 (ISBN 0-918942-00-4). Mycological.

Duffy, Thomas P. The Best System: Basic Recordkeeping for a Small Business. LC 84-70087. 116p. 1984. 35.00 (ISBN 0-916115-00-3). Challenge Pub Co.

Duffy, Tony, jt. auth. see Powell, Steve.

Duffy, William. Sugar Blues. pap. 3.95x (ISBN 0-686-29913-2). Cancer Control Soc.

Duffy, Yvonne. All Things Are Possible. LC 81-83657. (Illus.). 1981. pap. 8.95 (ISBN 0-9607252-0-2). A J Garvin.

Dufort. Dictionnaire de Biographie Francaise, Fasc. 61-69. 13.95ea. (ISBN 0-685-35953-0). French & Eur.

Dufort, Anthony. Ballet Steps: Practice to Performance. (Illus.). 160p. (gr. 7 up). 1985. 12.95 (ISBN 0-517-55522-0, C N Potter Bks). Crown.

Du Fossat, Guy. Synopsis of the History of Louisiana. 1975. 7.50 (ISBN 0-686-20898-6). Polyanthos.

Dufour, Barry, jt. auth. see Lawton, Denis.

Dufour, Charles, ed. see Hermann, Bernard M.

Dufour, Leon. Vocabulario De Teologia Biblica. 9th ed. 976p. (Espn.). 1977. pap. 29.25 (ISBN 84-254-0808-3, S-50204). French & Eur.

--Vocabulario De Teologila Biblica. 9th ed. 976p. 1977. 35.95 (ISBN 84-254-0809-1, S-50205). French & Eur.

Dufour, R., ed. see Colloque du Club Jules Gonin, 7th & Assemblee de la Societe Suisse d'ophtalmologie, 63rd, Lausanne, 1970.

Dufour, Theophile A. Recherches Bibliographiques sur les Oeuvres Imprimes De J. J. Rousseau, 2 vols. in 1. 1925. 35.50 (ISBN 0-8337-0949-6). B Franklin.

Dufourcq. Le Livre de l'Orgue Francais (1589-1789, 2 tomes. Set. 218.75 (ISBN 0-685-35984-0). French & Eur.

Dufourcq, N., ed. Musique, 2 Vols. (Illus., Fr.). 62.50x ea. Vol. 1 (ISBN 2-03-014110-0). Vol. 2 (ISBN 2-03-014120-8). Larousse.

Dufournet. Une Heure Avec Peguy. pap. 3.40 (ISBN 0-685-37048-8). French & Eur.

Dufournet, Jean, ed. see Villon, Francois.

Dufrene, Maurice. Three Hundred & Five Authentic Art Nouveau Jewelry Designs. 48p. 1985. pap. 3.95 (ISBN 0-486-24904-2). Dover.

Dufrenne, M. Jalons. (Phaenomenologica Ser: No. 20). 1966. lib. bdg. 24.00 (ISBN 90-247-0252-6, Pub. by Martinus Nijhoff Netherlands). Kluwer Academic.

Dufrenne, Mikel. Language & Philosophy. Veatch, Henry B., tr. LC 68-55630. (Illus.). 1968. Repr. of 1963 ed. lib. bdg. 18.75x (ISBN 0-8371-0396-7, DULP). Greenwood.

--The Notion of the A Priori. Casey, E. S., tr. (Studies in Phenomenology & Existential Philosophy). 1966. 13.95 (ISBN 0-8101-0082-7). Northwestern U Pr.

--The Phenomenology of Aesthetic Experience. Casey, Edward S. & Anderson, Albert A., trs. from Fr. LC 73-76806. (Studies in Phenomenology & Existential Philosophy). 1974. text ed. 26.95 (ISBN 0-8101-0426-1); pap. 13.50 (ISBN 0-8101-0591-8). Northwestern U Pr.

Dufrenne, Mikel, ed. Main Trends in Aesthetics & the Sciences of Art. LC 79-12758. (Main Trends in the Social & Human Sciences Ser.). 418p. 1979. pap. text ed. 21.00x (ISBN 0-8419-0507-X). Holmes & Meier.

Dufresne, Ed. Faithfulness. 57p. 1981. pap. 1.95 (ISBN 0-89274-212-7). Harrison Hse.

--Healing for God's Glory. 60p. 1981. pap. 1.75 (ISBN 0-89274-196-1). Harrison Hse.

--Praying God's Word. 96p. (Orig.). 1983. pap. 2.25 (ISBN 0-89274-276-3). Harrison Hse.

Du Fresne, Florine see Fresne, Florine Du.

DuFresne, Jim. Isle Royale National Park: Foot Trails & Water Routes. (Illus.). 136p. (Orig.). 1984. pap. 7.95 (ISBN 0-89886-082-2). Mountaineers.

Du Fresne, Jim. Tramping in New Zealand. (Lonely Planet Travel Ser.). (Illus.). 144p. (Orig.). 1982. pap. 6.95 (ISBN 0-88254-675-9, Pub. by Lonely Planet Australia). Hippocrene Bks.

Du Fresnoy, Charles A. Art of Painting. LC 76-88819. (Art Histories Collection Ser). Repr. of 1783 ed. 14.00 (ISBN 0-405-02221-2). Ayer Co Pubs.

Du Fresnoy, Nicolas Lenglet see Lenglet Du Fresnoy, Nicolas.

Duft, Ken. Principles of Management in Agribusiness. (Illus.). 1979. text ed. 21.95 (ISBN 0-8359-5595-8); instrs'. manual avail. (ISBN 0-8359-5596-6). Reston.

Dufton, Henry. Narrative of a Journey Through Abyssinia in 1862 & 1863. LC 76-106778. Repr. of 1867 ed. 25.00x (ISBN 0-8371-3534-6, DUA&, Pub. by Negro U Pr). Greenwood.

Dufty, N. E., ed. The Sociology of the Blue Collar Worker. (International Studies in Sociology & Social Anthropology). 1969. text ed. 26.75x (ISBN 90-040-1054-8). Humanities.

Dufty, William. Sugar Blues. 256p. 1976. pap. 3.95 (ISBN 0-446-30512-X). Warner Bks.

Dufty, William, jt. auth. see Holiday, Billie.

Dufualt, Paul. Sanatorium. (Novels by Franco-Americans in New England 1850-1940 Ser.). 153p. (Fr.). (gr. 10 up). 1982. pap. 4.50 (ISBN 0-911409-23-8). Natl Mat Dev.

Dufwa, Jacques. Winds from the East: A Study In the Art of Manet, Degas, Monet & Whistler. 300p. 1981. text ed. 40.75x (ISBN 0-391-02334-9, Pub. by Almqvist & Wiksell Sweden). Humanities.

Dufwa, Thamar E. Transcontinental Railroad Legislation, 1835-1862. Bruchey, Stuart, ed. LC 80-1279. (Railroads Ser.). 1981. lib. bdg. 18.00x (ISBN 0-405-13754-0). Ayer Co Pubs.

Dugan, Alan. New & Collected Poems: Nineteen Sixty-One to Nineteen Eighty-Three. LC 83-14014. (American Poetry Ser.: No. 29). 210p. 1983. 17.50 (ISBN 0-88001-030-4). Ecco Pr.

--New & Collected Poems, Nineteen Sixty-One to Nineteen Eighty-Three, No. 29. LC 38-14014. (American Poetry Ser.). 210p. 1985. pap. 9.50 (ISBN 0-88001-085-1). Ecco Pr.

--Poems of Alan Dugan. LC 79-144761. (Yale Series of Younger Poets: No. 57). Repr. of 1961 ed. 18.00 (ISBN 0-404-53857-6). AMS Pr.

Dugan, Dick. How To Know You'll Live Forever. LC 84-70727. 176p. 1984. pap. 3.50 (ISBN 0-87123-312-6). Bethany Hse.

Dugan, Jack. The Deep Kill. 208p. 1984. pap. 2.95 (ISBN 0-441-14224-9). Ace Bks.

Dugan, John R. Illusion & Reality: A Study of Descriptive Techniques in the Works of Guy de Maupassant. (De Proprietatibus Litterarum Ser. Pratica: No. 59: No. 59). 1973. pap. text ed. 17.60x (ISBN 90-2792-445-7). Mouton.

Dugan, Kathleen M. The Vision Quest of the Plains Indians: Its Spiritual Significance. (Studies in American Religion: Vol. 16). 264p. 1985. lib. bdg. 49.95x (ISBN 0-88946-659-9). E Mellen.

Dugan, Ken. Winning Baseball: How-To Secrets for Every League. 288p. 1980. pap. write for info (ISBN 0-13-960773-0, Reward). P-H.

Dugan, LeRoy. Help Yourself to a Healthier Mind. 112p. (Orig.). 1980. 4.95 (ISBN 0-87123-205-7, 210205). Bethany Hse.

--Heroes of the Old Testament. 96p. (Orig.). (ps-4). 1981. No. 1. pap. 1.95 oversized, saddle stitched (ISBN 0-87123-704-0, 220704); No. 2. pap. 1.95 (ISBN 0-87123-705-9, 220705). Bethany Hse.

--The Uncomplicated Christian. LC 78-66886. 128p. 1978. pap. 2.50 (ISBN 0-87123-572-2, 200572). Bethany Hse.

Dugan, LeRoy, illus. Heroes of the New Testament Coloring Book. 96p. (Orig.). (gr. k-4). 1981. saddle-stitched 1.95 (ISBN 0-87123-701-6). Bethany Hse.

--Heroes of the Old Testament, No. 3. 96p. (Orig.). (gr. k-4). 1981. pap. 1.95 saddle stitched (ISBN 0-87123-703-2). Bethany Hse.

Dugan, Patrick. Biochemical Ecology of Water Pollution. LC 74-26780. 170p. 1975. pap. text ed. 12.95x (ISBN 0-306-20012-0, Rosetta). Plenum Pub.

Dugan, Patrick R. Biochemical Ecology of Water Pollution. LC 72-167676. 170p. 1972. 29.50x (ISBN 0-306-30540-2, Plenum Pr). Plenum Pub.

Dugan, Richard L. Building Christian Commitment. (Trinity Bible Ser.). 107p. (Orig.). 1982. wkbk. 3.50 (ISBN 0-87123-280-4, 240280). Bethany Hse.

Dugan, Thomas. A Modern Bestiary. (Illus.). 58p. (Orig.). 1982. pap. 9.95 (ISBN 0-940170-06-X). Station Hill Pr.

Dugan, Tom. Photography Between Covers: Interviews with Photo Book Makers. LC 79-9260. (Illus.). 1979. 15.00 (ISBN 0-87992-012-2). Light Impressions.

Duganne, Augustine J. Parnassus in Pillory. LC 76-122648. 1971. Repr. of 1851 ed. 19.00x (ISBN 0-8046-1296-X, Pub. by Kennikat). Assoc Faculty Pr.

Dugard, John. Human Rights & the South African Legal Order. LC 77-85536. 1978. text ed. 48.00 (ISBN 0-691-09236-2). Princeton U Pr.

Dugard, John, ed. The South West Africa-Namibia Dispute: Documents & Scholarly Writings on the Controversy Between South Africa & the United Nations. LC 76-142052. (Perspectives on Southern Africa: No. 9). 1973. pap. 19.50x (ISBN 0-520-02614-4). U of Cal Pr.

Dugard, Marie. Ralph Waldo Emerson: Sa Vie et Son Oeuvre. LC 76-100530. (Illus.). Repr. of 1907 ed. 31.50 (ISBN 0-404-02215-4). AMS Pr.

--Ralph Waldo Emerson: Sa Vie et Son Oeuvre. 1973. 16.45 (ISBN 0-8274-0066-7). R West.

Du Gard, Rene C. Une Affaire de Coeur. Rev., 2nd ed. Chantal, tr. (Illus.). 356p. (Fr.). 1983. 19.00 (ISBN 0-939586-10-X). Edns Des Deux Mondes.

--Dictionary of Spanish Place Names, Vol. V. 210p. 1986. 39.00 (ISBN 0-939586-05-3). Edns Des Deux Mondes.

Du Gard, Rene Coulet see Coulet du Gard, Rene & Western, Dominique.

Du Gard, Roger M. Notes on Andre Gide. Russell, John, tr. 1953. 15.00 (ISBN 0-8274-3049-3). R West.

Du Gard, Roger Martin see Martin Du Gard, Roger.

Dugard, Simon. The Marriages of Cousin Germans Vindicated. LC 83-48580. (Marriage, Sex & the Family in England Ser.). 368p. 1984. lib. bdg. 42.00 (ISBN 0-8240-5903-4). Garland Pub.

Dugas, Andre, jt. auth. see Paillet, Jean-Pierre.

Du Gas, Beverly W. Introduction to Patient Care: A Comprehensive Approach to Nursing. 4th ed. LC 82-42568. (Illus.). 1983. text ed. 26.95 (ISBN 0-7216-3227-0). Saunders.

Dugas, H. & Penney, C. Bioorganic Chemistry: A Chemical Approach to Enzyme Action. (Springer Advanced Texts in Chemistry Ser.). (Illus.). 508p. 1981. 32.50 (ISBN 0-387-90491-3). Springer-Verlag.

Dugas, Ludovic. Le Amitie Antique D'apres les Moeurs Populaires & les Theories Des Philosophes. facsimile ed. LC 75-13263. (History of Ideas in Ancient Greece Ser.). (Fr.). 1976. Repr. of 1894 ed. 29.00x (ISBN 0-405-07305-4). Ayer Co Pubs.

Dugdale, Blanche E. Arthur James Balfour, First Earl of Balfour. LC 70-97328. Repr. of 1936 ed. lib. bdg. 36.00x (ISBN 0-8371-2893-5, DUI&). Greenwood.

--Arthur James Balfour, First Earl of Balfour. 1936. Repr. 27.50 (ISBN 0-8482-3673-4). Norwood Edns.

Dugdale, D. S. Elements of Elasticity. 1968. 25.00 (ISBN 0-08-012634-0); pap. 11.25 (ISBN 0-08-012633-2). Pergamon.

Dugdale, Kathleen. A Manual of Form for Theses & Term Reports. 5th ed. 59p. 1972. pap. 5.00x (ISBN 0-9600028-2-0). Dugdale.

--Manual on Writing Research. 2nd ed. 48p. 1967. pap. 5.00x (ISBN 0-9600028-1-2). Dugdale.

Dugdale, Norman. Running Repairs. 64p. (Orig.). 1983. pap. 7.95 (ISBN 0-85640-283-4, Pub. by Blackstaff Pr). Longwood Pub Group.

Dugdale, Richard L. The Jukes. LC 79-38664. (Foundations of Criminal Justice Ser.). Repr. of 1895 ed. 11.50 (ISBN 0-404-09173-3). AMS Pr.

--Jukes: A Study in Crime, Pauperism, Disease, & Heredity. LC 74-112542. (Rise of Urban America). (Illus.). 1970. Repr. of 1877 ed. 16.00 (ISBN 0-405-02451-7). Ayer Co Pubs.

Dugdale, S. Electrical Properties of Metals & Alloys. (Structure & Properties of Solids Ser.). 304p. 1977. pap. text ed. 17.50 (ISBN 0-7131-2524-1). E Arnold.

Duggal, Heidi, jt. auth. see Ashley, Richard.

Duggal, K. S. Twice Born Twice Dead: A Novel. 1980. text ed. 10.00x (ISBN 0-7069-0714-0, Pub. by Vikas India). Advent NY.

Duggal, Kartar S. Death of a Song & Other Stories. (Indian Short Stories Ser.). 186p. 1974. 4.95 (ISBN 0-88253-458-0). Ind-US Inc.

--The Sikh Gurus. 240p. 1980. text ed. 22.50x (ISBN 0-7069-0995-X, Pub. by Vikas India). Advent NY.

Duggan, Alfred. Historical Fiction. 1957. lib. bdg. 10.00 (ISBN 0-8414-3868-4). Folcroft.

Duggan, Ann S., et al. The Folk Dance Library, 5 vols. LC 79-7758. (Dance Ser.). (Illus.). 1980. Repr. of 1948 ed. Set. lib. bdg. 105.00x (ISBN 0-8369-9305-5). Ayer Co Pubs.

Duggan, Anne. Thomas Becket: A Textual History of His Letters. 1980. 52.00x (ISBN 0-19-822486-9). Oxford U Pr.

Duggan, Anne S. Comparative Study of Undergraduate Women Majors & Non-Majors in Physical Education with Respect to Certain Personal Traits. LC 78-176732. (Columbia University. Teachers College. Contributions to Education: No. 682). Repr. of 1936 ed. 22.50 (ISBN 0-404-55682-5). AMS Pr.

--The Complete Tap Dance Book. 1977. pap. text ed. 9.00 (ISBN 0-8191-0137-0). U Pr of Amer.

Duggan, C. R. The GG 2 Deception. (Orig.). 1981. pap. 2.50 (ISBN 0-505-51619-5, Pub. by Tower Bks). Dorchester Pub Co.

Duggan, Charles. Canon Law in Medieval England: The Becket Dispute & Decretal Collections. 338p. 1982. 75.00x (ISBN 0-86078-103-8, Pub. by Variorum England). State Mutual Bk.

--Twelfth-Century Decretal Collections & Their Importance in English History. 220p. 1963. 75.00 (ISBN 0-485-13112-9, Pub. by Athlone Pr Ltd). Longwood Pub Group.

Duggan, Ed. The Impact of Industrialization on an Urban Labor Market: Birmingham, England 1770-1860. Mathias, Peter & Bruchey, Stuart, eds. LC 84-46000. (British Economic History Ser.). 245p. 1985. lib. bdg. 25.00 (ISBN 0-8240-6680-4). Garland Pub.

Duggan, Ervin S. & Wattenberg, Ben J. Against All Enemies. 1979. pap. 2.50 (ISBN 0-380-41723-5, 41723). Avon.

Duggan, Francis X. Paul Elmer Moore. LC 66-24144. (United States Authors Ser.). 1966. lib. bdg. 15.95 (ISBN 0-8057-0524-4). Irvington.

--Paul Elmer More. (Twayne's United States Authors Ser). 1966. pap. 5.95x (ISBN 0-8084-0240-4, T106, Twayne). New Coll U Pr.

Duggan, George C. Stage Irishman. LC 70-91899. (Illus.). 1937. 20.00 (ISBN 0-405-08468-4, Blom Pubns). Ayer Co Pubs.

Duggan, Hayden A. Crisis Intervention: Theory & Practice. LC 79-2976. (Illus.). 160p. 1984. 21.50x (ISBN 0-669-03302-2). Lexington Bks.

Duggan, Janie P. Child of the Sea: A Chronicle of Puerto Rico. 1976. lib. bdg. 69.95 (ISBN 0-8490-1600-2). Gordon Pr.

Duggan, Joseph J. A Concordance of the "Chanson De Roland.". LC 79-92337. 430p. 1970. 12.50 (ISBN 0-8142-0011-7). Ohio St U Pr.

--The Song of Roland: Formulaic Style & Poetic Craft. LC 75-186101. (Center for Medieval & Renaissance Studies, UCLA Publications: No. 6). 1973. 30.00x (ISBN 0-520-02201-7). U of Cal Pr.

Duggan, Lawrence G. Bishop & Chapter: The Governance of the Bishopric of Speyer to 1552. 1978. 30.00x (ISBN 0-8135-0857-6). Rutgers U Pr.

Duggan, M. A. Law & Computer. new ed. LC 72-84755. 1973. 9.95 (ISBN 0-02-468470-8). Macmillan Info.

Duggan, Maurice. Falter Tom & the Water Boy. LC 59-12200. (Illus.). (gr. 3-6). 1959. 8.95 (ISBN 0-87599-027-4). S G Phillips.

Duggan, Michael. Antitrust & the U. S. Supreme Court, 1980-1982: Supplement. 20p. 1983. 10.00 (ISBN 0-317-06385-5). Fed Legal Pubn.

Duggan, Michael A., et al, eds. The Computer Utility: Implications for Higher Education. LC 75-12104. 1969. 28.00x (ISBN 0-89197-708-2); pap. text ed. 14.95x (ISBN 0-89197-709-0). Irvington.

Duggan, Robert, ed. Conversion & the Catechumenate. 1984. pap. 7.95 (ISBN 0-8091-2614-1). Paulist Pr.

Duggan, Stephen P. Eastern Question. LC 76-120209. (Columbia University Studies in the Social Sciences: No. 39). Repr. of 1902 ed. 12.50 (ISBN 0-404-51039-6). AMS Pr.

--A Professor at Large. LC 72-4507. (Essay Index Reprint Ser.). Repr. of 1943 ed. 27.50 (ISBN 0-8369-2942-X). Ayer Co Pubs.

Duggan, Timothy, ed. see Reid, Thomas.

Duggan, William. The Great Thirst. 1985. 16.95 (ISBN 0-385-29387-9). Delacorte.

Duggan, William R. Our Neighbors Upstairs: The Canadians. LC 79-1308. 360p. 1979. 26.95x (ISBN 0-88229-530-6); pap. 13.95x (ISBN 0-88229-667-1). Nelson-Hall.

--A Socioeconomic Profile of South Africa. LC 72-91715. (Special Studies in International Economics & Development). 1973. 39.50x (ISBN 0-275-28653-3). Irvington.

Duggan-Cronin, Alfred M. The Bantu Tribes of South Africa, 4 vols. in 12 pts. LC 74-15033. Repr. of 1935 ed. Set. 450.00 (ISBN 0-404-12050-4); 37.50 ea. AMS Pr.

Duggar, B. M. Cultivation of Mushrooms. facs. ed. (Shorey Lost Arts Ser.). 24p. Repr. of 1904 ed. pap. 1.95 (ISBN 0-8466-6038-5, U38). Shorey.

Duggar, Gordon E. Jehovah's Witness: Not Just Another Denomination. (Illus.). 144p. 1982. 8.00 (ISBN 0-682-49874-2). Exposition Pr FL.

--Jehovah's Witnesses: Not Just Another Denomination. 144p. 1985. pap. 5.95 (ISBN 0-8010-2955-4). Baker Bk.

Duggar, John W. Girl with a Missionary Heart. (Illus.). 104p. 1975. pap. 1.95 (ISBN 0-89114-074-3). Baptist Pub Hse.

Duggar, Lillie. A. J. Tomlinson. 1964. 13.95 (ISBN 0-934942-00-5). White Wing Pub.

Dugger, James G. The New Professional: An Introduction for the Human Service Worker. 2nd ed. LC 80-13324. 200p. 1980. text ed. 17.00 pub net (ISBN 0-8185-0393-9). Brooks-Cole.

Dugger, Mack, ed. Air Pollution Effects on Plant Growth. LC 74-26543. (ACS Symposium Ser.: No. 3). 1974. 19.95 (ISBN 0-8412-0223-0). Am Chemical.

Dugger, Ronnie. On Reagan: The Man & His Presidency. LC 83-9833. 1983. 19.95 (ISBN 0-07-017974-3). McGraw.

--The Politician: The Life & Times of Lyndon Johnson. (Illus.). 544p. 1982. 18.95 (ISBN 0-393-01598-X). Norton.

Dugger, Ronnie, ed. Three Men in Texas: Bedichek, Webb, & Dobie. LC 67-22307. 307p. 1967. pap. 7.95 (ISBN 0-292-78014-1). U of Tex Pr.

Dugger, Shepherd M. The Balsam Groves of Grandfather Mountain. (Illus.). 1974. 6.00 (ISBN 0-686-15218-2). Puddingstone.

--The War Trails of the Blue Ridge. (Illus.). 1974. 6.00 (ISBN 0-686-15219-0). Puddingstone.

Dugger, W. E., Jr., jt. auth. see Gerrish, H. H.

Dugger, W., Jr., jt. auth. see Gerrish, H.

Dugger, William E., Jr., jt. auth. see Gerrish, Howard H.

Dugger, William M. An Alternative to Economic Retrenchment. 1984. 24.95 (ISBN 0-89433-231-7). Petrocelli.

--An Alternative to Economic Retrenchment. (Illus.). 394p. 1984. 24.95. Van Nos Reinhold.

Duggins, Kay. Heartwarming Soft Toys. 128p. (Orig.). 1985. pap. 9.95 (ISBN 0-938432-30-3). Mother Earth.

Duggins, Lydia A. Developing Children's Perceptual Skills in Reading. 2nd ed. LC 70-81156. (Illus.). 122p. 1968. 9.50 (ISBN 0-912056-00-2). Mediax.

Dugmore, C. W., ed. see Cargill Thompson, W. D.

DuGran, Claurene. Wordsmanship: A Dictionary. 1982. Repr. pap. 2.95 (ISBN 0-671-45468-4). WSP.

DuGuay, G. E., jt. auth. see Treyz, G. I.

Duguay, Jean. How to Import a European Car: The Official Gray Market Guide. Williamson, Susan, ed. 192p. (Orig.). 1985. pap. 12.95 (ISBN 0-913589-18-7). Williamson Pub Co.

Dugue, D., ed. Analytical Methods in Probability Theory: Proceedings. (Lecture Notes in Mathematics Ser.: Vol. 861). 183p. 1981. pap. 14.00 (ISBN 0-387-10823-8). Springer-Verlag.

DuGuerny, J. Migration & Rural Development: Selected Topics for Teaching & Research. (Economic & Social Development Papers: No. 3). 69p. (Eng., Fr. & Span.). 1978. pap. 7.50 (ISBN 92-5-100611-3, F1513, FAO). Unipub.

Du Gue Trapier, Elizabeth. Goya & His Sitters. (Illus.). 1964. 10.00 (ISBN 0-87535-101-8). Hispanic Soc.

--Valdes Leal, Spanish Baroque Painter. (Illus.). 1960. 10.00 (ISBN 0-87535-112-3). Hispanic Soc.

--Velazquez. (Illus.). 1948. 15.00 (ISBN 0-87535-062-3). Hispanic Soc.

Duguid, J. P., et al, eds. Medical Microbiology, Vol. 1. 13th ed. (Illus.). 1979. text ed. 35.00 (ISBN 0-443-01787-5); pap. text ed. 29.75 (ISBN 0-443-01788-3). Churchill.

Dugundji, James. Topology. 1966. text ed. 45.72 (ISBN 0-205-00271-4, 5602718). Allyn.

Duguy, R., ed. see International Conference on the Mediterranean Monk Seal, 1st, Rhodes, Greece, 1978.

Duhaime, Irene M. The Divestment Behavior of Large Diversified Firms. (Research Ser.). 126p. 1984. pap. 12.00 (ISBN 0-912841-21-4). Planning Forum.

--The Divestment Behavior of Large Diversified Firms. (Research Ser.). 126p. 12.00 (ISBN 0-317-36916-4). Planning Forum.

Duhamel, Georges. America, the Menace: Scenes from the Life of the Future. Thompson, Charles M., tr. LC 73-13126. (Foreign Travelers in America, 1810-1935 Ser.). 236p. 1974. Repr. 20.00x (ISBN 0-405-05450-5). Ayer Co Pubs.

--Chronique des Pasquier, 10 tomes. Incl. Le Notaire du Havre. pap. 7.50 (ISBN 0-685-36025-3); Le Jardin des betes sauvages. pap. 7.50 (ISBN 0-685-36026-1); Vue de la Terre Promise. pap. 7.50 (ISBN 0-685-36027-X); La Nuit de la Saint-Jean. pap. 7.50 (ISBN 0-685-36028-8); Le Desert de Bievres. pap. 7.50 (ISBN 0-685-36029-6); Les Maitres. pap. 7.50 (ISBN 0-685-36030-X); Cecile Parmi Nous. pap. 7.50 (ISBN 0-685-36031-8); Le Combat Contre les Ombres. pap. 7.50 (ISBN 0-685-36032-6); Suzanne et les Jeunes Hommes. pap. 7.50 (ISBN 0-685-36033-4); La Passion de Joseph Pasquier. pap. 5.25 (ISBN 0-685-36034-2). 1957-63. pap. French & Eur.

--La Chronique des Pasquier: Cecile Parminous, Vol. 7. 1976. 3.95 (ISBN 0-686-55161-3). French & Eur.

--La Chronique des Pasquier: La Passion de Joseph Pasquier, Vol. 10. 276p. 1977. 3.95 (ISBN 0-686-55165-6). French & Eur.

--La Chronique des Pasquier: La Pierre d'Horeb, Vol. 4. 248p. 1974. 3.95 (ISBN 0-686-55162-1). French & Eur.

--La Chronique des Pasquier: Le Combat Contre les Ombres, Vol. 8. 304p. 1976. 3.95 (ISBN 0-686-55163-X). French & Eur.

--La Chronique des Pasquier: Le Desert de Bievres, Vol. 5. 1973. 3.95 (ISBN 0-686-55159-1). French & Eur.

--La Chronique des Pasquier: Le Jardin des Betes Sauvages, Vol. 2. 192p. 1972. 3.95 (ISBN 0-686-55157-5). French & Eur.

--La Chronique des Pasquier: Le Notaire du Havre, Vol. 1. 1972. 3.95 (ISBN 0-686-55156-7). French & Eur.

--La Chronique des Pasquier: Les Maitres, Vol. 6. 256p. 3.95 (ISBN 0-686-55160-5). French & Eur.

--La Chronique des Pasquier: Suzanne et les Jeunes Hommes, Vol. 9. 374p. 1977. 3.95 (ISBN 0-686-55164-8). French & Eur.

--La Chronique des Pasquier: Vue de la Terre Promise, Vol. 3. 1973. 3.95 (ISBN 0-686-55158-3). French & Eur.

--Chronique des Saisons Ameres. 232p. 1949. 6.95 (ISBN 0-686-55166-4). French & Eur.

--Civilization, Nineteen Fourteen to Nineteen Seventeen. Brooks, E. S., tr. 1978. Repr. of 1919 ed. lib. bdg. 20.00 (ISBN 0-8492-0672-3). R West.

--Le Club des Lyonnais. 11.50 (ISBN 0-685-37288-X). French & Eur.

--Les Compagnons de l'Apocalypse. 1956. 7.95 (ISBN 0-686-55167-2). French & Eur.

--Le Complexe de Theophile. 228p. 1958. 7.95 (ISBN 0-686-55168-0). French & Eur.

--Confession de Minuit: Vie et Aventures de Salavin. 160p. 1973. 3.95 (ISBN 0-686-55169-9). French & Eur.

--Consultation aux Pays d'Islam. 128p. 1947. 6.95 (ISBN 0-686-55170-2). French & Eur.

--Cri des Profodeurs. 240p. 1951. 9.95 (ISBN 0-686-55171-0). French & Eur.

--Deux Hommes. 7.95 (ISBN 0-685-37289-8). French & Eur.

--Deux Hommes. 320p. 3.95 (ISBN 0-686-55172-9). French & Eur.

--Discours aux Nuages. 276p. 1947. 5.95 (ISBN 0-686-55173-7). French & Eur.

--Fables de Mon Jardin. 1961. 10.95 (ISBN 0-686-55174-5). French & Eur.

--Histopathologie Clinique de la Moelle Osseuse. (Illus.). 256p. 1974. 125.00 (ISBN 0-686-55175-3). French & Eur.

--In Defence of Letters. LC 68-16293. 1968. Repr. of 1939 ed. 20.50x (ISBN 0-8046-0121-6, Pub. by Kennikat). Assoc Faculty Pr.

--In Defense of Letters. 1973. 10.00 (ISBN 0-8274-1728-4). R West.

--Israel, Clef de l'Orient. 112p. 1957. 7.95 (ISBN 0-686-55176-1). French & Eur.

--Le Japon. 176p. 1953. 9.95 (ISBN 0-686-55177-X). French & Eur.

--Journal de Salavin. 11.95 (ISBN 0-685-37290-1). French & Eur.

--Les Jumeaux de Vallangoujard. 2.50 (ISBN 0-686-55178-8). French & Eur.

--Lieu d'Asile. 144p. 1948. 6.95 (ISBN 0-686-55179-6). French & Eur.

--Les Livres du Bonheur. 256p. 1957. 11.95 (ISBN 0-686-55180-X). French & Eur.

--Lumieres sur ma Vie: Biographies de mes Fantomer (1901-1906), Vol. 2. 1949. 7.95 (ISBN 0-686-55182-6). French & Eur.

--Lumieres sur ma Vie: Inventaire de l'Aimbe (1884-1901), Vol. 1. 1949. 7.95 (ISBN 0-686-55181-8). French & Eur.

--Lumieres sur ma Vie: La Pesee des Ames (1914-1919), Vol. 4. 1949. 7.95 (ISBN 0-686-55184-2). French & Eur.

--Lumieres sur ma Vie: Le Temps de la Recherche (1906-1914), Vol. 3. 7.95 (ISBN 0-686-55183-4). French & Eur.

--Lumieres sur ma Vie: Les Espoirs et les Epreuves (1919-1928), Vol. 5. 1928. 7.95 (ISBN 0-686-55185-0). French & Eur.

--Nouvelles du Sombre Empire. 206p. 1960. 7.95 (ISBN 0-686-55187-7). French & Eur.

--La Nuit d'Orage. 262p. 1928. 7.95 (ISBN 0-686-55188-5). French & Eur.

--La Pierre d'Horeb. 286p. 1947. 6.95 (ISBN 0-686-55189-3). French & Eur.

--La Possession du Monde. 1963. 11.95 (ISBN 0-686-55190-7). French & Eur.

--Problemes de Civilisation: Avec: Traite de Depart, Fables de ma Vie, La Medicine au 20e Siecle. 232p. 1961. 8.95 (ISBN 0-686-55191-5). French & Eur.

--Querelles de Famille. 224p. 1959. 7.95 (ISBN 0-686-55192-3). French & Eur.

--Recits des Temps de Guerre, 2 vols. 554p. 1952. Set. 16.95 (ISBN 0-686-55193-1). French & Eur.

--Remarques sur les Memoires Imaginaires. 96p. 1934. 4.95 (ISBN 0-686-55194-X). French & Eur.

--Salavin. 144p. 1972. 4.95 (ISBN 0-686-55195-8). French & Eur.

--Souvenirs de la Vie du Paradis. 204p. 6.95 (ISBN 0-686-55196-6). French & Eur.

--Tel Qu'en Lui-Meme. 1973. 3.95 (ISBN 0-686-55197-4). French & Eur.

--Trois Nouvelles. 25.00 (ISBN 0-686-55198-2). French & Eur.

--Vie et Aventures de Salavin. (Illus.). 522p. 1959. 29.95 (ISBN 0-686-55199-0). French & Eur.

--Vie et Aventures de Salavin: Le Journal Salavin. 320p. 1970. pap. 3.95 (ISBN 0-686-55200-8). French & Eur.

--Voyage de Candide. 15.00 (ISBN 0-686-55201-6). French & Eur.

--Le Voyage de Patrice Periot. 256p. 1969. 3.95 (ISBN 0-686-55202-4). French & Eur.

--Vues sur Rimbaud. 256p. 1952. 25.00 (ISBN 0-686-55203-2). French & Eur.

Duhamel, Georges & Vildrac, Charles. Notes sur la Technique Poetique. 50p. 1925. 25.00 (ISBN 0-686-55186-9). French & Eur.

Duhamel, Georges, jt. auth. see Vildrac, Charles.

Duhamel, Jean M. Lehrbuch der Analytischen Mechanik. Schloemilch, O., ed. (Bibliotheca Mathematica Teubneriana Ser: No. 37). (Ger). 1969. Repr. of 1861 ed. 55.00 (ISBN 0-384-13230-8). Johnson Repr.

Duhamel, P. Albert. After Strange Fruit: Changing Literary Tastes in Post-World-War II Boston. 1980. 4.00 (ISBN 0-89073-063-6). Boston Public Lib.

Duhe, Camille, jt. auth. see Von Furstenberg, Egon.

Duhem, Pierre. Aim & Structure of Physical Theory. LC 53-6383. 1962. pap. text ed. 5.95x (ISBN 0-689-70064-4, 13). Atheneum.

--Medieval Cosmology: Theories of Infinity, Place, Time, Void, & the Plurality of Worlds. Ariew, Roger, tr. LC 85-8115. 632p. 1985. lib. bdg. 40.00x (ISBN 0-226-16922-7). U of Chicago Pr.

--To Save the Phenomena: An Essay on the Idea of Physical Theory from Plato to Galileo. Doland, Edmund & Maschler, Chaninah, trs. LC 71-77978. xxvi, 120p. 1985. pap. text ed. 9.00x. U of Chicago Pr.

Duhem, Pierre M. The Evolution of Mechanics. Oravas, G. A., ed. (Genesis & Method Ser.: No. 1). Orig. Title: L' Evolution de la Mecanique. 234p. 1980. Repr. 47.50x (ISBN 90-286-0688-2). Sijthoff & Noordhoff.

Duhl, Bunny S. From the Inside Out & Other Metaphors: Creative & Integrative Approaches to Training in Systems Thinking. LC 82-24428. 320p. 1983. 30.00 (ISBN 0-87630-328-9). Brunner-Mazel.

Duhl, Leonard J. & Leopold, Robert L., eds. Mental Health & Urban Social Policy: A Casebook of Community Action. LC 68-54942. (Jossey-Bass Behavioral Science Ser.). Repr. of 1968 ed. 65.80 (ISBN 0-8357-9334-6, 2013787). Bks Demand UMI.

Duigan, Peter, jt. auth. see Gann, L. H.

Duignan, P. & Gann, L. H., eds. Colonialism in Africa, 1870-1960, 5 vols. Incl. Vol. 1. History & Politics of Colonialism, 1870-1914. 84.50 (ISBN 0-521-07373-1); Vol. 2. History & Politics of Colonialism, 1914-1960. 84.50 (ISBN 0-521-07732-X); Vol. 3. 1975. 74.50 (ISBN 0-521-07844-X); Vol. 4. The Economics of Colonialism. 1975. 99.50 (ISBN 0-521-08641-8); Vol. 5. Bibliography. 84.50 (ISBN 0-521-07859-8). Cambridge U Pr.

Duignan, Peter. Handbook of American Resources for African Studies. LC 66-20901. (Bibliographical Ser.: No. 29). 1966. 9.95 (ISBN 0-8179-2291-1). Hoover Inst Pr.

Duignan, Peter & Clendenen, Clarence. The United States & the African Slave Trade, 1619-1862. LC 77-20159. (Hoover Institution Studies). 1978. Repr. of 1963 ed. lib. bdg. 15.00x (ISBN 0-313-20009-2, DUUS). Greenwood.

Duignan, Peter & Gann, L. H. The Middle East & North Africa: The Challenge to Western Security. (Publication Ser.: No.239). 180p. 1981. pap. 9.95x (ISBN 0-8179-7392-3). Hoover Inst Pr.

Duignan, Peter & Gann, Lewis H. The United States & Africa: A History. (Illus.). 450p. 1984. 29.95 (ISBN 0-521-26202-X). Cambridge U Pr.

Duignan, Peter, jt. auth. see Gann, L. H.

Duignan, Peter, jt. auth. see Gann, Lewis H.

Duignan, Peter, ed. The Library of the Hoover Institution on War, Revolution & Peace. (Publication Ser.: No. 316). 176p. 1985. lib. bdg. 22.95 (ISBN 0-8179-8161-6); pap. text ed. 14.95 (ISBN 0-8179-8162-4); deluxe ed. 35.95 (ISBN 0-8179-8163-2). Hoover Inst Pr.

Duignan, Peter & Rabushka, Alvin, eds. The United States in the 1980's. LC 79-5475. (Publication Ser.: No. 228). 1980. 20.00 (ISBN 0-8179-7281-1). Hoover Inst Pr.

Duignan, Peter, jt. ed. see Gann, L. H.

Duignan, Peter, ed. see University of the State of New York, Foreign Area Materials Center.

Duignan, Peter, et al. African & Middle East Collections: A Survey of Holdings at the Hoover Institution of War, Revolution & Peace. LC 73-142945. (Library Survey Ser.: No. 4). 37p. 1971. pap. 2.00x (ISBN 0-8179-5042-7). Hoover Inst Pr.

Duignan, Peter J., jt. auth. see Gann, Lewis H.

Duijker, Hubert C. Dictionnaire de Psychologie en Trois Langues, Vol. 2. (Fr., Ger. & Eng.). 1978. pap. 39.95 (ISBN 0-686-57264-5, M-4660). French & Eur.

Duijker, Hubert C. & Van Sijswijk, Maria. Dictionnaire de Psychologie en 3 Langues, 3 vols. (Eng., Fr. & Ger., Dictionary of Psychology in 3 Languages). pap. 40.00 (ISBN 0-686-56801-X, M-4661). French & Eur.

Duijn, Jacob J. The Long Wave in Economic Life. 240p. 1983. text ed. 29.50x (ISBN 0-04-330330-7); pap. text ed. 12.50x (ISBN 0-04-330331-5). Allen Unwin.

Duijvestijn, A. & Lockemann, P. C., eds. Trends in Information Processing Systems: Proceedings. (Lecture Notes in Computer Science: Vol 123). 349p. 1981. pap. 22.00 (ISBN 0-387-10885-8). Springer-Verlag.

Duiker, William. The Communist Road to Power in Vietnam. LC 80-22098. (Westview Special Studies on South & Southeast Asia). 375p. 1982. lib. bdg. 35.00x (ISBN 0-89158-794-2); pap. 13.50x (ISBN 0-86531-505-1). Westview.

--Vietnam since the Fall of Saigon. rev., 2nd ed. 300p. 1985. pap. text ed. 12.00x (ISBN 0-89680-133-0, Ohio U Ctr Intl). Ohio U Pr.

Duiker, William J. Ts'ai Yuan-P'ei: Educator of Modern China. LC 76-43212. (Penn State Studies: No. 41). 1977. pap. 5.95x (ISBN 0-271-00504-1). Pa St U Pr.

--Vietnam: A Nation in Revolution. LC 82-21946. (Nations of Contemporary Asia Ser.). 171p. 1983. lib. bdg. 20.00x (ISBN 0-86531-336-9). Westview.

--Vietnam: Nation in Revolution. LC 82-21946. (Illus.). 171p. 1983. 10.95 (ISBN 0-86531-731-3). Westview.

Duin, Edgar C., tr. see Bachmann, Bertha.

Duin, Nancy E. Wanda Gag: Author & Illustrator of Childrens Books. Rahmas, D. Steve, ed. (Outstanding Personalities Ser.: No. 57). 32p. 1972. lib. bdg. 3.50 incl. catalog cards (ISBN 0-87157-546-9); pap. 1.95 vinyl laminated covers (ISBN 0-87157-046-7). SamHar Pr.

Duing, Walter. Monsoon Regime of the Currents in the Indian Ocean. LC 76-104320. (International Indian Ocean Expedition Oceanographic Monographs: No. 1). (Illus.). 68p. 1970. 14.00x (ISBN 0-8248-0092-3, Eastwest Ctr). UH Pr.

Duinker, J. C., jt. ed. see Kramer, C. J.

Duis, Perry. Chicago: Creating New Traditions. LC 76-45167. (Illus.). 1976. 12.50 (ISBN 0-913820-03-2); pap. 7.95 (ISBN 0-913820-05-9). Chicago Hist.

--The Saloon: Public Drinking in Chicago & Boston, 1880-1920. LC 83-6971. (Illus.). 392p. 1983. 24.95x (ISBN 0-252-01010-8). U of Ill Pr.

Duisit, Lionel. Satire, Parodie, Calembour: Esquisse d'une Theorie des Devalues. (Stanford French & Italian Studies: No. 11). vi, 164p. (Fr.). 1978. pap. 25.00 (ISBN 0-915838-26-5). Anma Libri.

Duizend, Richard Van see Saks, Michael J. & Van Duizend, Richard.

Dujardin, Edouard. Mallarme par un des Siens. LC 77-10259. Repr. of 1936 ed. 27.50 (ISBN 0-404-16314-9). AMS Pr.

--We'll to the Woods No More. Gilbert, Stuart, tr. LC 67-13317. 1957. 5.00 (ISBN 0-8112-0268-2). New Directions.

Du Jardin, Rosamond. Boy Trouble. (gr. 4-9). 1953. 14.47i (ISBN 0-397-30229-0). Lipp Jr Bks.

--Practically Seventeen. (gr. 4-9). 1949. 12.89 (ISBN 0-397-30153-7). Lipp Jr Bks.

--Practically Seventeen. 208p. (gr. 7 up). 1982. pap. 1.95 (ISBN 0-590-02397-7, Vagabond). Scholastic Inc.

Du Jardin, Rosamond see Du Jardin, Rosamond.

Dujarier, Michel. A History of the Catechumenate. 144p. 1982. pap. 4.95 (ISBN 0-8215-9327-7). Sadlier.

--The Rites of Christian Initiation. 244p. 1982. pap. 4.95 (ISBN 0-8215-9328-5). Sadlier.

Dujcev, Ivan. Bdinski Zbornik: Old Slavonic Menologium A. D. 1360 Facsimile Edition Codex Gandavesis 408. 484p. 1972. 30.00x (ISBN 0-902089-40-4, Pub. by Variorum). State Mutual Bk.

Dujcev, Ivan, illus. Cartulary A of St. John Prodromos Monastery: Facsimile of the Prague Manuscript XXV.C.9 (605) 280p. 1972. 50.00x (ISBN 0-902089-23-4, Pub. by Variorum). State Mutual Bk.

Dujning, William A., compiled by. Studies in Southern History & Politics. 1964. Repr. of 1914 ed. 22.50x (ISBN 0-8046-0451-7, Pub. by Kennikat). Assoc Faculty Pr.

Du Jonchay, Yvan. Handbook of World Transport. 221p. 1980. 20.00 (ISBN 0-87196-393-0). Facts on File.

Dukas, Helen & Hoffman, Banesh, eds. Albert Einstein, the Human Side: New Glimpses from His Archives. 1979. 19.50x (ISBN 0-691-08231-6); pap. 5.95 (ISBN 0-691-02368-9). Princeton U Pr.

Dukas, Paul see Rameau, Jean Philippe.

Dukas, Peter. Hotel Front Office Management & Operation. 3rd ed. 192p. 1970. text ed. write for info. (ISBN 0-697-08400-0); solutions manual avail. (ISBN 0-697-08414-0). Wm C Brown.

--Planning Profits in the Food and Lodging Industry. 192p. 1976. 16.95 (ISBN 0-8436-2080-3). Van Nos Reinhold.

Dukas, Vytas, ed. & tr. from Rus. Twelve Contemporary Russian Stories. LC 74-4969. 130p. 1977. 16.50 (ISBN 0-8386-1491-4). Fairleigh Dickinson.

Duke, A. C. & Tamse, C. A., eds. Britain & the Netherlands: War & Society. (Britain & the Netherland Ser: Vol. VI.). 1978. lib. bdg. 26.00 (ISBN 90-247-2012-5, Pub. by Martinus Nijhoff Netherlands). Kluwer Academic.

Duke, Basil W. History of Morgan's Cavalry. LC 60-8607. (Indiana University Civil War Centennial Ser.). (Illus.). 1968. Repr. of 1960 ed. 50.00 (ISBN 0-527-25500-9). Kraus Repr.

--History of the Bank of Kentucky, 1792-1895. Bruchey, Stuart, ed. LC 80-1183. (The Rise of Commercial Banking Ser.). (Illus.). 1981. Repr. of 1895 ed. lib. bdg. 14.00x (ISBN 0-405-13647-1). Ayer Co Pubs.

--Reminiscences of General Basil W. Duke, C. S. A. (Select Bibliographies Reprint Ser). 1911. 33.00 (ISBN 0-8369-5150-6). Ayer Co Pubs.

Duke, Benjamin C. Japan's Militant Teachers: A History of the Left-Wing Teachers' Movement. 352p. 1973. 15.00x (ISBN 0-8248-0237-3, Eastwest Ctr). UH Pr.

Duke, Betty la see La Duke, Betty.

Duke, Bill, jt. auth. see Lyon, William.

Duke, C. B. Tunneling in Solids. (Solid State Physics, Suppl. 10). 1969. 76.00 (ISBN 0-12-607770-3). Acad Pr.

Duke, Carolyn van see Van Dyke, Carolynn.

Duke, Charles R. Writing Through Experience: A Process Approach. 1983. 12.95 (ISBN 0-316-19484-0) (ISBN 0-316-19485-9). Little.

Duke, Charles R., ed. Writing Exercises from "Exercise Exchange", Vol. II. 335p. (Orig.). 1984. pap. 13.00 (ISBN 0-8141-5908-7); pap. 10.00 members. NCTE.

Duke, Charles R. & Jacobsen, Sally A., eds. Reading & Writing Poetry: Successful Approaches for the Student & Teacher. 288p. 1983. pap. 22.50x (ISBN 0-89774-031-9). Oryx Pr.

Duke, Chris, ed. Combatting Poverty Through Adult Education: National Development Strategies. LC 84-23777. (Series in International Adult Education). 256p. 1985. 31.00 (ISBN 0-7099-0861-X, Pub. by Croom Helm). Longwood Pub Group.

Duke, Cordia S. & Frantz, Joe B. Six Thousand Miles of Fence: Life on the XIT Ranch of Texas. (M. K. Brown Range Life Ser.: No. 1). (Illus.). 285p. 1981. pap. 6.95 (ISBN 0-292-77564-4). U of Tex Pr.

Duke, D. W. & Owens, J. F., eds. Perturbative Quantum Chromodynamics: Tallahassee, 1981. (AIP Conference Proceedings: No. 74). 477p. 1981. lib. bdg. 34.75 (ISBN 0-88318-173-8). Am Inst Physics.

Duke, Daniel. Managing Student Behavior Problems. LC 80-10443. 1980. pap. 13.95x (ISBN 0-8077-2583-8). Tchrs Coll.

Duke, Daniel L. Decision Making in an Era of Fiscal Instability. LC 84-61198. (Fastback Ser.: No. 212). 50p. 1984. pap. 0.75 (ISBN 0-87367-212-7). Phi Delta Kappa.

--The Retransformation of the School: The Emergence of Contemporary Alternative Schools in the United States. LC 77-25257. 212p. 1978. 21.95x (ISBN 0-88229-294-3). Nelson-Hall.

--Teaching: The Imperiled Profession. 268p. 1983. 34.50x; pap. 8.95x (ISBN 0-317-05031-1). State U NY Pr.

Duke, Daniel L. & Mekel, Adrienne M. Teacher's Guide to Classroom Management. 160p. 1983. pap. text ed. 7.95 (ISBN 0-394-32690-3, RanC). Random.

Duke, Daniel L., ed. Helping Teachers Manage Classrooms. LC 82-70273. 163p. 1982. pap. text ed. 8.50 (ISBN 0-87120-113-5). Assn Supervision.

Duke, David A. Christ's Coming-Satan's Kingdom. 220p. (Orig.). 1981. pap. 2.95 (ISBN 0-9605056-0-1). D A Duke.

Duke, David C. Distant Obligations: Modern American Writers & Foreign Causes. 1983. 30.00x (ISBN 0-19-503221-7). Oxford U Pr.

Duke, David N. The Biblical View of Reality: The Bible & Christian Ethics. ii, 59p. 1985. pap. text ed. 6.95 (ISBN 0-932269-05-2). Wyndham Hall.

Duke, Donald. Pacific Electric Railway. LC 56-12943. (Illus.). 64p. pap. 7.95 (ISBN 0-87095-030-4). Golden West.

--Southern Pacific Steam Locomotives. LC 62-6982. (Illus.). 88p. 13.95 (ISBN 0-87095-012-6). Golden West.

Duke, Donald & Kistler, Stan. Santa Fe: Steel Rails Through California. LC 63-23869. (Illus.). 184p. 1963. 22.95 (ISBN 0-87095-009-6). Golden West.

Duke, Dulcie. Lincoln: The Growth of a Medieval City. LC 73-80476. (Introduction to the History of Mankind Ser). (Illus.). 48p. (gr. 9-12). 1974. pap. text ed. 4.50 (ISBN 0-521-08712-0). Cambridge U Pr.

Duke, Elizabeth see Mallis, Jackie.

Duke, Francis, tr. see Baudelaire, Charles.

Duke, Gaylon. Potboilers. 64p. 1980. pap. text ed. 15.00 (ISBN 0-87879-251-1). Acad Therapy.

Duke, James. Handbook of Medicinal Herbs. 704p. 1985. 180.00 (ISBN 0-8493-3630-9). CRC Pr.

Duke, James, tr. see Schleiermacher, Friedrich.

Duke, James A. Culinary Herbs: A Potpourri. (Trado-Madic Bks). 191p. 1984. 15.95 (ISBN 0-932426-32-8); pap. 10.00x (ISBN 0-932426-33-6). Conch Mag.

--Culinary Herbs: A Potpourri. (Illus.). 196p. 1984. 15.95x (ISBN 0-932426-33-6); pap. 10.00x (ISBN 0-932426-33-6). Trado-Medic.

--Handbook of Legumes of World Economic Importance. LC 80-16421. (Illus.). 356p. 1981. 55.00x (ISBN 0-306-40406-0, Plenum Pr). Plenum Pub.

--Medicinal Plants of the Bible. (Traditional Healing Ser.: No. 10). (Illus.). 300p. 1983. lib. bdg. 49.95 (ISBN 0-932426-23-9). Trado-Medic.

Duke, James A. & Ayensu, Edward S. Medicinal Plants of China, 2 vols. (Medicinal Plants of the World Ser.: No. 4). (Illus.). 1985. Set. 94.95 (ISBN 0-917256-20-4); Vol. 1, 352 pgs., not available separately (ISBN 0-917256-26-3); Vol. 2, 352 pgs. not available separately (ISBN 0-917256-27-1). Ref Pubns.

Duke, James O. Horace Bushnell: On the Vitality of Biblical Language. LC 83-16312. (SBL-Biblical Schlolarship in North America). 138p. 1984. pap. 13.50 (ISBN 0-89130-650-1, 06 11 09). Scholars Pr GA.

Duke, James T. Issues in Sociological Theory: Another Look at the "Old Masters". LC 83-14631. 408p. 1983. lib. bdg. 32.75 (ISBN 0-8191-3455-4); pap. text ed. 17.75 (ISBN 0-8191-3456-2). U Pr of Amer.

Duke, Jerry. Clog Dance in the Appalachians. (Illus.). 96p. (Orig.). (gr. 9-12). 1984. pap. 7.95 (ISBN 0-9613727-0-2). Duke Pub Co.

Duke, Judith S. Children's Books & Magazines: A Market Study. LC 78-24705. (Communications Library). (Illus.). 1979. text ed. 29.95 professional ed. (ISBN 0-914236-17-2, 405-BW). Knowledge Indus.

--Religious Publishing & Communications. LC 80-17694. (Communications Library). 274p. 1980. professional 29.95 (ISBN 0-914236-61-X, 416-BW). Knowledge Indus.

--The Technical, Scientific & Medical Publishing Market. LC 84-26163. (Communications Library). 218p. 1985. professional 29.95 (ISBN 0-86729-084-6, 424-BW). Knowledge Indus.

Duke, Judith S., ed. Knowledge Industry Two Hundred: America's Two Hundred Largest Media Companies. 1st ed. 500p. 1982. 155.00x (ISBN 0-8103-1624-2, Pub. by Knowledge Indus). Gale.

--U. S. Book Publishing Yearbook & Directory, 1981-82. 319p. 1981. pap. 60.00 professional (ISBN 0-914236-99-7, 419-BW). Knowledge Indus.

Duke, Kate. The Guinea Pig ABC. LC 83-1410. (Illus.). 32p. (ps-1). 1983. 9.95 (ISBN 0-525-44058-5, 0966-290). Dutton.

--Guinea Pigs Far & Near. LC 84-1580. (Illus.). 24p. (ps-1). 1984. 9.95 (ISBN 0-525-44112-3, 0966-290). Dutton.

--Seven Froggies Went to School. LC 84-1371. (Illus.). 32p. (ps-1). 1985. 11.95 (ISBN 0-525-44160-3, 01160-350). Dutton.

Duke, Kenneth L., jt. auth. see Mossman, Harland W.

Duke, Madelaine. Bormann Receipt. LC 77-93993. 8.95 (ISBN 0-8128-2479-2). Stein & Day.

Duke, Marshall & Nowicki, Steven. Abnormal Psychology: Perspectives on Being Different. LC 78-7584. (Illus.). 1978. text ed. 23.25 pub net (ISBN 0-8185-0274-6). Brooks-Cole.

Duke, Maurice. James Branch Cabell: A Reference Guide. 1979. lib. bdg. 16.00 (ISBN 0-8161-7838-0, Hall Reference). G K Hall.

Duke, Maurice & Jordan, Daniel P., eds. A Richmond Reader, Seventeen Seventy-Three to Nineteen Eighty-Three. LC 82-21921. (Illus.). xvii, 446p. 1983. 19.95 (ISBN 0-8078-1546-2). U of NC Pr.

Duke, Maurice, et al, eds. American Women Writers: Bibliographical Essays. LC 82-6156. 464p. 1983. lib. bdg. 39.95 (ISBN 0-313-22116-2, DAW/). Greenwood.

Duke, Michael S. Blooming & Contending: Chinese Literature in the Post-Mao Era. LC 84-48641. (Studies in Chinese Literature & Society). 304p. 1985. 22.50x (ISBN 0-253-31202-7). Ind U Pr.

Duke, Micheal S., ed. Contemporary Chinese Literature. 125p. 1985. 25.00 (ISBN 0-87332-339-4); pap. 12.95 (ISBN 0-87332-340-8). M E Sharpe.

Duke, Neville & Lanchbery, Edward. Sound Barrier: The Story of High-Speed Flight. Gilbert, James, ed. LC 79-7248. (Flight: Its First Seventy-Five Years Ser.). (Illus.). 1979. Repr. of 1955 ed. lib. bdg. 14.00x (ISBN 0-405-12160-1). Ayer Co Pubs.

Duke Of Bedford. Parrots & Parrot-Like Birds. 14.95 (ISBN 0-87666-428-1, H-931). TFH Pubns.

Duke, Paul D. Irony in the Fourth Gospel. LC 85-42822. pap. 11.95 (ISBN 0-8042-0242-7). John Knox.

Duke, Philip S. The Law of Karma with Biblical Quotations & a Karmic Bibliography. 1978. pap. 2.00 (ISBN 0-685-59611-7). Duke Pr IL.

Duke, Richard D. & Greenblat, Cathy S. Game-Generating-Games: A Trilogy of Games for Community & Classroom. LC 79-15721. (Illus.). 183p. 1979. pap. 15.00 (ISBN 0-8039-1282-X). Sage.

Duke, Richard D., jt. auth. see Greenblatt, Cathy.

Duke, Robert E. Holistic Health. 272p. 1985. 14.95 (ISBN 0-88282-011-7). New Horizon NY.

--How to Create a Successful School Atmosphere: A Treasury of Innovative School Programs. 1985. text ed. 17.95 (ISBN 0-8290-1323-7). Irvington.

--How to Lose Weight & Stop Smoking Through Self-Hypnosis. 140p. text ed. cancelled (ISBN 0-8290-1276-1). Irvington.

--Hypnotherapy for Troubled Children. 220p. 1984. text ed. 24.95x incl. audio cassette (ISBN 0-8290-1030-0). Irvington.

--Why Children Fail: And How You Can Help Them. 130p. 1985. 16.95x (ISBN 0-8290-1277-X). Irvington.

Duke, Robert W. The Sermon As God's Word: Theologies for Preaching. LC 80-18094. (Abingdon Preacher's Library). 128p. (Orig.). 1980. pap. 6.50 (ISBN 0-687-37520-7). Abingdon.

Duke, S. C. English-Spanish Workbook II: Taller de la Gramatica Espanola II. (Illus.). 1983. write for info. (ISBN 0-9609446-1-3). Research Lang.

Duke, Salcacion C. English-Spanish Workbook I: Taller de la Gramatica Espanola I. (Illus.). 237p. (Orig.). 1983. write for info. (ISBN 0-9609446-0-5); Workbook avail. (ISBN 0-9609446-2-1). Research Lang.

Duke, Stephen O., ed. Weed Physiology, Vols. I & II. 480p. 1985. 57.00 (ISBN 0-8493-6313-6); 86.00 (ISBN 0-8493-6314-4). CRC Pr.

Duke, Thomas S. Celebrated Criminal Cases of America. LC 79-172594. (Criminology, Law Enforcement, & Social Problems Ser.: No. 184). (Illus.). Date not set. 22.50x (ISBN 0-87585-184-3). Patterson Smith.

Duke University. Financing Health Care: Competition vs. Regulation. Yaggy, Duncan & William, Anlyan G., eds. LC 81-20629. 264p. 1982. prof ref 35.00 (ISBN 0-88410-737-X). Ballinger Pub.

--In Memoriam, William Kenneth Boyd. LC 74-115997. (Trinity College Historical Papers Ser.: No. 22). pap. 24.50 (ISBN 0-404-51772-2). AMS Pr.

--Trinity College Historical Society Historical Papers, Series 1-32. LC 74-115989. Repr. of 1956 ed. Set. 735.00 (ISBN 0-404-51750-1); 24.50 ea. AMS Pr.

--Trinity College Historical Society Papers, Series 1: Reconstruction & State Biography. Repr. of 1897 ed. 24.50 (ISBN 0-404-51751-X). AMS Pr.

--Trinity College Historical Society Papers, Series 11: 1915. Repr. 24.50 (ISBN 0-404-51761-7). AMS Pr.

--Trinity College Historical Society Papers, Series 15: 1925. Repr. 24.50 (ISBN 0-404-51765-X). AMS Pr.

--Trinity College Historical Society Papers, Series 14: 1922. Repr. 24.50 (ISBN 0-404-51764-1). AMS Pr.

--Trinity College Historical Society Papers, Series 10: 1914. Repr. 24.50 (ISBN 0-404-51760-9). AMS Pr.

--Trinity College Historical Society Papers, Series 13: 1919. Repr. 24.50 (ISBN 0-404-51763-3). AMS Pr.

--Trinity College Historical Society Papers, Series 12: 1916. Repr. 24.50 (ISBN 0-404-51762-5). AMS Pr.

--Trinity College Historical Society Papers, Series 2: Legal & Biographical Studies. Repr. of 1898 ed. 24.50 (ISBN 0-404-51752-8). AMS Pr.

--Trinity College Historical Society Papers, Series 3: Gov. W. W. Holden & Revolutionary Documents. Repr. of 1899 ed. 24.50 (ISBN 0-404-51753-6). AMS Pr.

--Trinity College Historical Society Papers, Series 4: 1900. Repr. 24.50 (ISBN 0-404-51754-4). AMS Pr.

--Trinity College Historical Society Papers, Series 5: 1905. Repr. 24.50 (ISBN 0-404-51755-2). AMS Pr.

--Trinity College Historical Society Papers, Series 6: 1906. Repr. 24.50 (ISBN 0-404-51756-0). AMS Pr.

--Trinity College Historical Society Papers, Series 7: 1907. Repr. 24.50 (ISBN 0-404-51757-9). AMS Pr.

--Trinity College Historical Society Papers, Series 8: 1908-1909. Repr. 24.50 (ISBN 0-404-51758-7). AMS Pr.

--Trinity College Historical Society Papers, Series 9: 1912. Repr. 24.50 (ISBN 0-404-51759-5). AMS Pr.

Duke University Center for International Studies Publications see Kornberg, Allan & Clarke, Harold D.

Duke University Commonwealth-Studies Center. The American Economic Impact of Canada. LC 81-4163. xviii, 176p. 1981. Repr. of 1959 ed. lib. bdg. 23.50x (ISBN 0-313-23056-0, AIAI). Greenwood.

Duke University - Durham - North Carolina - Americana Club. American Studies in Honor of William Kenneth Boyd. facs. ed. Jackson, D. K., ed. LC 68-20295. (Essay Index Reprint Ser). 1940. 20.00 (ISBN 0-8369-0395-1). Ayer Co Pubs.

Duke University Hospital Nursing Services, ed. Guidelines for Nursing Care: Process & Outcomes. (Illus.). 496p. 1983. pap. text ed. 18.75 (ISBN 0-397-54436-7, 64-03778, Lippincott Nursing). Lippincott.

Duke University Library. Dante Gabriel Rossetti. Baum, Paull F., ed. LC 31-11769. Repr. of 1931 ed. 9.00 (ISBN 0-404-05414-5). AMS Pr.

Duke, Vernon. Listen Here. 1963. 8.95 (ISBN 0-685-06621-5); pap. 5.95 (ISBN 0-8392-5010-X). Astor-Honor.

Duke Des Cars, ed. Memoirs of the Duchess De Tourzel: Governess to the Children of France During the Years 1789, 1790, 1791, 1792, 1793 & 1795, 2 vols. 1977. Repr. of 1886 ed. lib. bdg. 65.00 (ISBN 0-8495-1003-1). Arden Lib.

Duke-Elder, Stewart, ed. System of Ophthalmology Series. Incl. Vol. 1. The Eye in Evolution. (Illus.). 843p. 1958. 65.00 (ISBN 0-8016-8282-7); Vol. 2. The Anatomy of the Visual System. (Illus.). 901p. 1961. 67.50 (ISBN 0-8016-8283-5); Vol. 3, Pt. 1. Normal & Abnormal Development: Embryology. (Illus.). 330p. 1963. 51.50 (ISBN 0-8016-8285-1); Vol. 3, Pt. 2. Normal & Abnormal Development: Congenital Deformities. (Illus.). 1190p. 1964. 72.50 (ISBN 0-8016-8286-X); Vol. 4. The Physiology of the Eye & of Vision. (Illus.). xx, 734p. 1968. 79.50 (ISBN 0-8016-8296-7); Vol. 5. Ophthalmic Optics & Refraction. (Illus.). xix, 879p. 1970; Vol. 7. The Foundations of Ophthalmology: Heredity, Pathology, Diagnosis & Therapeutics. (Illus.). 829p. 1962. 69.50 (ISBN 0-8016-8284-3); Vol. 8. Diseases of the Outer Eye: Conjunctiva, Cornea & Sclera, 2 vols. (Illus.). 1242p. 1965. 100.00 (ISBN 0-8016-8287-8); Vol. 9. Diseases of Uveal Tract. (Illus.). xvi, 978p. 1966. 85.00 (ISBN 0-8016-8290-8); Vol. 10. Diseases of the Retina. (Illus.). xv, 878p. 1967. 85.00 (ISBN 0-8016-8295-9); Vol. 11. Diseases of the Lens & Vitreous: Glaucoma & Hypotony. (Illus.). xx, 779p. 1969. 85.00 (ISBN 0-8016-8297-5); Vol. 12. Neuro-Ophthalmology. (Illus.). xxi, 994p. 1971. 89.50 (ISBN 0-8016-8299-1); Vol. 14. Injuries, 2 vols. 1357p. 1972. Set. 125.00 (ISBN 0-8016-8300-9). Mosby.

Dukek, W., jt. auth. see Bustin, W.

Dukelow, Richard W., jt. auth. see Erwin, Joe.

Dukelow, Samuel G. Improving Boiler Efficiency. 144p. 1981. pap. text ed. 19.95x (ISBN 0-87664-615-1). Instru Soc.

Dukelow, W. Richard. Graduate Student Survival. (Illus.). 88p. 1980. pap. 11.50x spiral (ISBN 0-398-04068-0). C C Thomas.

Dukelow, W. Richard, ed. Nonhuman Primate Models for Human Diseases. 208p. 1983. 65.50 (ISBN 0-8493-6466-3). CRC Pr.

Dukelow, W. Richard, et al. Laparoscopic Techniques in Studies of Reproductive Physiology. 1977. text ed. 32.50x (ISBN 0-8422-7232-1). Irvington.

Dukelskaya, L. English Art in the Hermitage. 1981. 90.00x (ISBN 0-686-73051-8, Pub. by Collet's). State Mutual Bk.

Dukeminier, Jesse & Johanson, Stanley. Wills, Trusts & Estates. 3rd ed. LC 83-82694. 1140p. 1984. text ed. 33.00 (ISBN 0-316-19514-6). Little.

Dukeminier, Jesse & Krier, James E. Property. LC 80-84030. 1507p. 1981. text ed. 34.00 (ISBN 0-316-19510-3); Supplement, 1985. text ed. write for info. (ISBN 0-316-19516-2). Little.

--Property: 1985 Supplement. 1985. pap. text ed. write for info. Little.

Dukeminier, Jesse, Jr. Perpetuities Law in Action: Kentucky Case Law & the 1960 Reform Act. LC 62-13459. (Illus.). 180p. 1962. 16.00x (ISBN 0-8131-1070-X). U Pr of Ky.

Duke Of Beaufort. Fox Hunting. LC 79-56043. (Illus.). 236p. 1980. 29.95x (ISBN 0-7153-7896-1). David & Charles.

Duke of Bedford. The Neglected Issue: Some Essays on the Need for Monetary Reform. 1982. lib. bdg. 59.95 (ISBN 0-87700-355-6). Revisionist Pr.

--Straight Speaking from a Pacifist to a Militarist. 1982. lib. bdg. 59.95 (ISBN 0-87700-337-8). Revisionist Pr.

Duke of Northumberland. The First Jewish Bid for World Power. 1982. lib. bdg. 59.95 (ISBN 0-87700-360-2). Revisionist Pr.

Dukepoo, Frank. The Elder American Indian. LC 77-83494. (Elder Minority Ser). 1978. 3.50x (ISBN 0-916304-33-7). SDSU Press.

Duker, A. G. Studies in Polish-Jewish History & Relations. 35.00x (ISBN 0-87068-293-8). Ktav.

Duker, Abraham G. & Ben Hurin, Meir. Emancipation & Counter Emancipation. LC 70-147927. 420p. 1974. text ed. 25.00x (ISBN 0-87068-160-5). Ktav.

Duker, Jan, jt. auth. see Gilberstad, Harold.

Duker, Jan, jt. auth. see Gilberstadt, Harold.

Duker, Jan, jt. auth. see White, Mary A.

Duker, Sam. Individualized Reading. 288p. 1971. 22.50x (ISBN 0-398-02274-7). C C Thomas.

Duker, William F. A Constitutional History of Habeas Corpus. LC 79-6834. (Contributions in Legal Studies Ser.: No. 13). 349p. 1980. lib. bdg. 35.00 (ISBN 0-313-22264-9, DHC/). Greenwood.

Dukert, Joseph M. A Short Energy History of the United States & Some Thoughts About the Future. (Decisionmakers Bookshelf Ser.: Vol. 7). (Illus.). 88p. (Orig.). 1980. pap. 2.50 (ISBN 0-931032-07-5). Edison Electric.

Dukert, Joseph M., jt. auth. see Landsberg, Hans H.

Dukes, Ashley. Modern Dramatists. facs. ed. LC 67-23210. (Essay Index Reprint Ser). 1912. 18.00 (ISBN 0-8369-0396-X). Ayer Co Pubs.

--Modern Dramatists. LC 76-23463. lib. bdg. 13.00 (ISBN 0-8414-3782-3). Folcroft.

--Youngest Drama. LC 77-646. 1924. lib. bdg. 27.00 (ISBN 0-8414-3804-8). Folcroft.

Dukes, Ashley, et al. Plays of Today, Vol. 3. facs. ed. LC 76-132137. (Play Anthology Reprint Ser). 1930. 18.75 (ISBN 0-8369-8216-9). Ayer Co Pubs.

Dukes, Graham. The Effects of Drug Regulation. LC 84-23394. 1985. lib. bdg. 42.50 (ISBN 0-85200-879-1, Pub. by MTP Pr England). Kluwer-Academic.

Dukes, Helen, jt. auth. see Hoffmann, Banesh.

Dukes, M. N. Encyclopedia of Adverse Reactions & Interactions, Vol. 10. (Side Effects of Drugs Ser.). 1984. 107.50 (ISBN 0-444-90323-2). Elsevier.

--Side Effects of Drugs, 1984. 1984. 67.50 (ISBN 0-444-90339-9, I-196-84). Elsevier.

Dukes, M. N., ed. Side Effect of Drugs, Vol. 9. 9th ed. 860p. 1980. 123.50 (ISBN 0-444-90102-7, Excerpta Medica). Elsevier.

--Side Effects of Drugs: Annual. 9th ed. 500p. 1985. 70.50 (ISBN 0-444-90394-1). Elsevier.

--Side Effects of Drugs Annual: No. 3, 1979. 470p. 1979. 74.50 (ISBN 0-444-90055-1, Excerpta Medica). Elsevier.

--Side Effects of Drugs: Annual 4, 1980. 376p. 1980. 74.50 (ISBN 0-444-90130-2, Excerpta Medica). Elsevier.

--Side Effects of Drugs: Annual 6, 1982. 478p. 1982. 74.50 (ISBN 0-444-90211-2, Excerpta Medica). Elsevier.

--Side Effects of Drugs: Annual 7, 1983. 500p. 1983. 74.50 (ISBN 0-444-90279-1, Excerpta Medica). Elsevier.

Dukes, Norman. The Reckless Sleeper. Kaplan, Peter, ed. LC 75-23871. 1975. 2.00x (ISBN 0-915176-11-4). Pourboire.

Dukes, Paul. Catherine the Great & the Russian Nobility: A Study Based on the Materials of the Legislative Commission of 1767. LC 67-13802. pap. 70.30 (ISBN 0-317-20839-X, 2024441). Bks Demand UMI.

--The Making of Russian Absoulutism Sixteen Thirteen to Eighteen One. LC 81-8333. (History of Russia Ser.). 197p. 1982. text ed. 30.00x (ISBN 0-582-48684-X); 12.95x (ISBN 0-582-48685-8). Longman.

--October & the World: Perspectives on the Russian Revolution. LC 79-15143. 1979. 20.00x (ISBN 0-312-58096-7). St Martin.

--Russia under Catherine the Great, 2 vols. 1978. 24.00 set (ISBN 0-89250-104-9); Vol. 1. 12.00 ea. (ISBN 0-89250-106-5). Vol. 2 (ISBN 0-89250-105-7). pap. set o. p. (ISBN 0-89250-107-3). Orient Res Partners.

Dukes, Roland E. An Empirical Investigation of the Effects of Statement of Financial Accounting Standards No. 8 on Security Return Behavior. LC 78-74875. (The Financial Accounting Standards Board Research Report). (Illus.). 102p. (Orig.). 1978. pap. 3.00 (ISBN 0-910065-07-1). Finan Acct.

Dukler, A. E. Gas Liquid Flow in Pipelines: I-Research Results. 200p. 1969. pap. 5.00 (ISBN 0-318-12631-1, L20169). Am Gas Assn.

Dukor, P., et al, eds. Cell Mediated Reactions, Miscellaneous Topics: PAR, Vol. 3 Pseudo-Allergic Reactions. Involvement of Drugs & Chemicals. (Illus.). viii, 160p. 1982. 33.75 (ISBN 3-8055-0960-X). S Karger.

--Cytotoxic & Complement Mediated Reactions. (Par Pseudo-Allergic Reactions. Involvement of Drugs & Chemicals: Vol. 2). (Illus.). viii, 144p. 1980. 27.75 (ISBN 3-8055-0666-X). S Karger.

--Genetic Aspects Anaphylactoid Reactions. (Par Pseudo-Allergic Reactions. Involvement of Drugs & Chemicals: Vol. 1). (Illus.). xiv, 310p. 1980. 55.50 (ISBN 3-8055-0537-X). S Karger.

--Idiopathic & Food or Drug-Induced PAR. (PAR. Pseudo-Allergic Reactions. Involvement of Drugs & Chemicals: Vol. 4). (Illus.). viii, 196p. 1985. 51.25 (ISBN 3-8055-3798-0). S Karger.

Dukore, B. F. Dramatic Theory & Criticism. LC 73-9778. 1974. text ed. 21.95 (ISBN 0-03-091152-4, HoltC). HR&W.

Dukore, Bernard, jt. ed. see Cohn, Ruby.

Dukore, Bernard, ed. see Shaw, G. B.

Dukore, Bernard, ed. see Shaw, George B.

Dukore, Bernard F. Bernard Shaw, Playwright: Aspects of Shavian Drama. LC 72-92204. 325p. 1973. 23.00x (ISBN 0-8262-0146-6). U of Mo Pr.

--Harold Pinter. LC 81-84705. 160p. 1982. pap. 7.95 (ISBN 0-394-17964-1, E797, Ever). Grove.

--Money & Politics in Ibsen, Shaw, & Brecht. LC 79-5380. 224p. 1980. text ed. 17.00x (ISBN 0-8262-0294-2). U of Mo Pr.

--The Theatre of Peter Barnes. LC 81-81246. (Orig.). 1981. pap. text ed. 11.00x (ISBN 0-435-18280-3). Heinemann Ed.

--Where Laughter Stops: Pinter's Tragicomedy. LC 76-15590. (Literary Frontiers Ser.). 96p. 1976. pap. 7.95 (ISBN 0-8262-0208-X). U of Mo Pr.

Dukore, Bernard F., ed. American Dramatists Nineteen Eighteen to Nineteen Forty. (Modern Dramatists Ser.). 224p. 1984. 19.50 (ISBN 0-394-54293-2, GP948). Grove.

--American Dramatists 1918-1945. (Modern Dramatists Ser.). 224p. 1984. pap. 7.95 (ISBN 0-394-62340-1, E-963, Ever). Grove.

Dukore, Bernard F., compiled by. Bernard Shaw's "Arms & the Man". A Composite Production Book. LC 80-29681. (Special Issues Ser.). (Illus.). 216p. 1982. 22.50x (ISBN 0-8093-1017-1). S Ill U Pr.

Dukore, Bernard F., ed. see Shaw, Bernard.

DuKore, Jesse. Breaking the Boy Barrier. 176p. (Orig.). (gr. 7up). 1985. pap. 2.25 (ISBN 0-590-33431-X, Wildfire). Scholastic Inc.

--Never Love a Cowboy. (Sweet Dreams Ser.). 163p. (gr. 6-12). 1983. pap. 2.25 (ISBN 0-553-24313-6). Bantam.

Dukore, Margaret M. Bloom: A Novel. 368p. 1985. 17.95 (ISBN 0-531-09708-0). Watts.

--A Novel Called Heritage. 288p. 1982. 12.95 (ISBN 0-684-17428-6, ScribT). Scribner.

--A Novel Called Heritage. 288p. 1983. pap. 3.95 (ISBN 0-440-36109-5, LE). Dell.

Duk Song Son & Clark, Robert J. Black Belt Korean Karate. LC 81-8625. (Illus.). 240p. 1983. 14.95 (ISBN 0-13-077669-6). P-H.

Dula, Andrew S. America's Manifesto. 336p. 1982. 12.95 (ISBN 0-89962-248-8). Todd & Honeywell.

Dula, Lucile N. The Pelican Guide to Hillsborough: Historic Orange County, North Carolina. LC 78-26081. (The Pelican Guide Ser). (Illus.). 124p. 1979. pap. 4.95 (ISBN 0-88289-208-8). Pelican.

Dulabaum, Nina. Dulcimers. (Illus.). 48p. 1982. 18.00 (ISBN 0-88014-036-4). Mosaic Pr OH.

Dulac, Colette. Shortcut to French. (gr. 9 up). 1977. pap. text ed. 5.45 (ISBN 0-88345-300-2, 18441); cassettes 25.00 (ISBN 0-685-79306-0, 58442). Regents Pub.

Dulac, Colette, jt. auth. see Madrigal, Margarita.

Dulac, Collette, jt. auth. see Madrigal, Margarita.

Dulac, Edmund. The Metropolitan Museum of Art Book of Names & Addresses. (Illus.). 174p. 1981. 9.95 (ISBN 0-8109-0705-4). Abrams.

Dulacskai, E., jt. auth. see Kollar, L.

Dulaing, Donncha O. Voices of Ireland. (Illus.). 176p. 1984. (Pub. by O'Brien Pr Ireland); pap. 10.95 (ISBN 0-86278-064-0). Irish Bks Media.

Dulakis, Carrie C. Freedom Plays the Flute: A Selection from the Folk Poetry of Modern Greece. 144p. 1982. 7.50 (ISBN 0-682-49867-X). Exposition Pr FL.

Dulaney, Paul S. The Architecture of Historic Richmond. 2nd ed. LC 68-14089. (Illus.). 218p. 1976. pap. 5.95 (ISBN 0-8139-0709-8). U Pr of Va.

Dulaure, Jacques-Antoine. The Gods of Generation. LC 72-9635. Repr. of 1934 ed. 24.50 (ISBN 0-404-57433-5). AMS Pr.

Dulay, Heidi, et al. The Language Two. (Illus.). 1982. text ed. 14.95x (ISBN 0-19-502552-0); pap. text ed. 10.95x (ISBN 0-19-502553-9). Oxford U Pr.

Dulay, Heidi C., ed. see Teachers of English to Speakers of Other Languages.

Dulbecco, Renato & Ginsberg, Harold. Virology. (Illus.). 408p. 1980. 23.50 (ISBN 0-06-140725-9, 14-07253, Harper Medical). Lippincott.

Dulcy, Faye H., ed. Aquatics: A Revived Approach to Pediatric Management. LC 83-85. (Physical & Occupational Therapy in Pediatrics Ser.: Vol. 3, No. 1). 92p. 1983. text ed. 19.95 (ISBN 0-86656-215-X, B215). Haworth Pr.

Duldt, Bonnie W. & Giffin, Kim. Theoretical Perspectives for Nursing. 1985. pap. text ed. 15.95 (ISBN 0-316-19528-6). Little.

Duldt, Bonnie W., et al. Interpersonal Communication in Nursing. LC 83-5213. 285p. 1983. 12.95x (ISBN 0-8036-2936-2). Davis Co.

Duleba, Wladyslaw. Wieniawski: Life & Times Ser. Czerny, Grazyna, tr. from Polish. (Illus.). 175p. 19.95 (ISBN 0-86622-017-8). Paganiniana Pubns.

Duleba, Wladyslaw & Sokolowska, Zofia. Ignacy Paderewski. Litwinski, Wiktor, tr. from Polish. (Library of Polish Studies: Vol. VII). (Illus.). text ed. 9.00 (ISBN 0-917004-14-0). Kosciuszko.

Dulek, Ronald E., jt. auth. see Fielden, John S.

Duley, W. W. Laser Processing & Analysis of Materials. LC 82-18611. 476p. 1983. 65.00x (ISBN 0-306-41067-2, Plenum Pr). Plenum Pub.

Duley, W. W., ed. Carbon Dioxide Lasers: Effects & Applications. 1976. 74.50 (ISBN 0-12-223350-6). Acad Pr.

Duley, Walter W. & Williams, David A. Interstellar Chemistry. 1984. 49.50 (ISBN 0-12-223360-3). Acad Pr.

Duley-Morrow, Margot & Edwards, Mary I., eds. The Cross-Cultural Study of Women: A Comprehensive Guide. 320p. (Orig.). 1985. 29.95 (ISBN 0-935312-45-5); pap. 12.95 (ISBN 0-935312-02-1). Feminist Pr.

Dulfano, Celia. Families, Alcoholism & Recovery. 163p. 1982. 7.95 (ISBN 0-89486-148-4). Hazelden.

Dulfano, Mauricio J., ed. Sputum: Fundamentals & Clinical Pathology. (Illus.). 648p. 1973. 48.50x (ISBN 0-398-02737-4). C C Thomas.

Dulfer, E. Operational Efficiency of Agricultural Cooperatives in Developing Countries. (Agricultural Development Papers: No. 96). (Illus.). 188p. (2nd Printing 1977). 1975. pap. 13.25 (ISBN 92-5-100203-7, F306, FAO). Unipub.

Du Liban, Libr. A Comprehensive English-Arabic Dictionary. 1983. 15.00 (ISBN 0-86685-356-1). Intl Bk Ctr.

--My First Dictionary of the Zoo in Arabic & English. 4.95x (ISBN 0-317-20271-5). Intl Bk Ctr.

Du Liban, Librarie. Spoken Arabic of the Arabian Gulf. 1976. pap. 3.95x (ISBN 0-86685-042-2). Intl Bk Ctr.

Dulieu, Jean. Paulus & the Dragon. Visser, Vivien, tr. LC 77-17090. (Children's Stories Ser.). (Illus.). 80p. (gr. 2-5). 1977. PLB 12.95 (ISBN 0-912278-96-X); pap. 5.95 (ISBN 0-912278-97-8). Crossing Pr.

Dulin, John, jt. auth. see Veley, Victory.

Dulin, John J., jt. auth. see Veley, Victor F.

Dulin, Mark. Fish Diseases. 1979. 4.95 (ISBN 0-87666-524-5, KW-066). TFH Pubns.

Dulin, Mark P. Diseases of Marine Aquarium Fishes. (Illus.). 1976. pap. 7.95 (ISBN 0-87666-099-5, PS-731). TFH Pubns.

Dulin, Robert O., Jr. & Garzke, William H., Jr. Battleships: Allied Battleships of World War Two. LC 79-90551. (Battleships Ser.: Vol. 2). (Illus.). 352p. 1980. 39.95 (ISBN 0-87021-100-5). Naval Inst Pr.

--Battleships: United States Battleships in World War II. (Illus.). 267p. 1976. 36.95 (ISBN 0-87021-099-8); bulk rates avail. Naval Inst Pr.

Dulin, Robert O., Jr., jt. auth. see Garzke, William H., Jr.

Dulin, Robert O., Jr., jt. auth. see Garzke, William, Jr.

Duling, Dennis C. Jesus Christ Through History. 324p. 1979. pap. text ed. 13.95 (ISBN 0-15-547370-0, HC). HarBraceJ.

Duling, Dennis C., jt. auth. see Perrin, Norman.

Duling, Gretchen A. Adopting Joe: A Black Vietnamese Child. LC 76-20946. (Illus.). 1977. pap. 2.95 (ISBN 0-8048-1203-9). C E Tuttle.

--Creative Problem Solving for an Eency Weency Spider. (Illus.). 24p. (Orig.). 1983. pap. text ed. 3.95 teacher enrichment (ISBN 0-88047-025-9). DOK Pubs.

--Creative Problem Solving for the Fourth Little Pig. (Illus.). 28p. (Orig.). (gr. 4-6). 1984. 4.95 (ISBN 0-88047-043-7, 8412). DOK Pubs.

Duling, Jean S. Wing Songs. 80p. Date not set. 6.50 (ISBN 0-8233-0412-4). Golden Quill.

Duling, Paul. Love: Until the Sun Goes Down. 72p. (Orig.). pap. 3.95 (ISBN 0-317-06305-7). NY Lit Pr.

Dull, Elaine & Sekowsky, Jo Anne. Teach Us to Pray. (Aglow Bible Study Book Enrichment: E-2). 64p. 1980. pap. 2.95 (ISBN 0-930756-49-5, 522002). Aglow Pubns.

Dull, Jack, ed. see Hsu, Cho-yun.

Dull, Jack L., ed. see Ch'u, T'ung-tsu.

Dull, James. The Politics of American Foreign Policy. (Illus.). 1985. pap. text ed. 18.95 (ISBN 0-13-684291-7). P-H.

Dull, Jonathan. A Diplomatic History of the American Revolution. LC 85-5306. (Illus.). 224p. 1985. 15.95x (ISBN 0-300-03419-9). Yale U Pr.

Dull, Jonathan R. Franklin the Diplomat: The French Mission. LC 81-68191. (Transactions Ser.: Vol. 72, Pt. 1). 1982. 10.00 (ISBN 0-87169-721-1). Am Philos.

--The French Navy & American Independence: A Study of Arms & Diplomacy, 1774-1787. LC 75-2987. 448p. 1975. 45.00 (ISBN 0-691-06920-4). Princeton U Pr.

Dull, Lloyd W. Educational Supervision: A Handbook. (Illus.). 504p. 1981. text ed. 26.95 (ISBN 0-675-08060-6). Merrill.

Dull, Paul S. A Battle History of the Imperial Japanese Navy: 1941-1945. LC 77-77933. 402p. 1978. 24.95 (ISBN 0-87021-097-1). Naval Inst Pr.

--A Battle History of the Imperial Japanese Navy, 1941-1945. (Illus.). 402p. 1978. 24.95 (ISBN 0-87021-097-1); bulk rates avail. Naval Inst Pr.

Dullemeijer, P., et al, eds. Morphology: Its Place & Meaning. 100p. 1983. pap. text ed. 16.00 (ISBN 90-265-0470-5, Pub. by Swets Pub Serv Holland). Swets North Am.

Duller, Edward & Gutzkow, Karl, eds. Phonix: Fruhlings-Zeitung Fur Deutschland, 2 vols. 1973. Repr. of 1835 ed. vol. 1 nos. 1-309 77.00 (ISBN 0-384-46413-0). Johnson Repr.

Duller, H. J. Development Technology. (International Library of Anthropology). 192p. (Orig.). 1982. pap. 14.95x (ISBN 0-7100-0990-9). Routledge & Kegan.

Dulles, Allen. The Boer War: A History. 79.95 (ISBN 0-87968-184-5). Gordon Pr.

--The Craft of Intelligence. LC 76-57671. (Illus.). 1977. Repr. of 1963 ed. lib. bdg. 32.50 (ISBN 0-8371-9452-0, DUCI). Greenwood.

--The Craft of Intelligence. (Westview Encore Edition Ser.). (Illus.). 296p. 1985. 25.00 (ISBN 0-8133-0285-4). Westview.

--Great True Spy Stories. 1982. pap. 3.50 (ISBN 0-345-30181-1). Ballantine.

Dulles, Allen, ed. Great Spy Stories from Fiction. LC 69-15272. 1969. 11.95i (ISBN 0-06-011124-0, HarpT). Har-Row.

Dulles, Allen W. Germany's Underground. LC 78-746. 1978. Repr. of 1947 ed. lib. bdg. 22.50x (ISBN 0-313-20287-7, DUGU). Greenwood.

Dulles, Allen W. & Armstrong, Hamilton F. Can We Be Neutral? facsimile ed. (Select Bibliographies Reprint Ser). Repr. of 1936 ed. 17.00 (ISBN 0-8369-6686-4). Ayer Co Pubs.

Dulles, Avery. Apologetics & the Biblical Christ. LC 63-22027. 88p. (Orig.). 1963. pap. 3.95 (ISBN 0-8091-1505-0). Paulist Pr.

--Church Membership As a Catholic & Ecumenical Problem. (Pere Marquette Theology Lectures). 1974. 7.95 (ISBN 0-87462-506-8). Marquette.

--Church to Believe In. 1982. 14.95 (ISBN 0-8245-0426-7). Crossroad NY.

--A Church to Believe In: Discipleship & the Dynamics of Freedom. LC 81-17520. 208p. 1983. pap. 8.95 (ISBN 0-8245-0593-X). Crossroad NY.

--Dimensions of the Church. LC 67-20429. 128p. 1967. 3.50 (ISBN 0-8091-0031-2); pap. 2.95 (ISBN 0-8091-1543-3). Paulist Pr.

--Models of Revelation. LC 82-45243. 360p. 1983. 16.95 (ISBN 0-385-17975-8). Doubleday.

--Models of Revelation. LC 82-45243. 360p. 1985. pap. 8.95 (ISBN 0-385-23235-7, Im). Doubleday.

--Models of the Church. LC 77-11246. 1978. pap. 3.95 (ISBN 0-385-13368-5, Im). Doubleday.

--The Survival of Dogma: Faith, Authority & Dogma in a Changing World. (Crossroad Paperback Ser.). 240p. 1982. pap. 7.95 (ISBN 0-8245-0427-5). Crossroad NY.

Dulles, Avery & Granfield, Patrick. The Church: A Bibliography. (Theology & Life Ser.: Vol. 14). 1985. 15.00 (ISBN 0-89453-449-1); pap. 7.95 (ISBN 0-89453-470-X). M Glazier.

Dulles, Eleanor L. The French Franc: 1914-1928. Wilkins, Mira, ed. LC 78-3910. (International Finance Ser.). (Illus.). 1978. Repr. of 1929 ed. lib. bdg. 48.50x (ISBN 0-405-11214-9). Ayer Co Pubs.

--One Germany or Two: The Struggle at the Heart of Europe. LC 70-96725. (Publications Ser.: No. 86). 1970. 10.95x (ISBN 0-8179-1861-2). Hoover Inst Pr.

Dulles, Foster R. America in the Pacific. LC 73-86595. (American Scene Ser). 1969. Repr. of 1932 ed. 37.50 (ISBN 0-306-71431-0). Da Capo.

--American Policy Toward Communist China, 1949-1969. LC 70-184974. 1972. pap. 13.95x (ISBN 0-88295-728-7). Harlan Davidson.

--American Red Cross, a History. LC 71-138110. 1971. Repr. of 1950 ed. lib. bdg. 26.00x (ISBN 0-8371-5686-6, DUAR). Greenwood.

--America's Rise to World Power, 1898-1954. LC 55-6575. (New American Nation Ser.). (Illus.). 1955. 15.00xi (ISBN 0-06-011115-1, HarpT). Har-Row.

--China & America: The Story of Their Relations Since 1784. LC 81-16. vii, 277p. 1981. Repr. of 1946 ed. lib. bdg. 25.00x (ISBN 0-313-22146-4, DUCA). Greenwood.

--Civil Rights Commission Nineteen Fifty-Seven to Nineteen Sixty-Five. xiii, 274p. 1968. 7.50 (ISBN 0-87013-118-4). Mich St U Pr.

--Eastward Ho! LC 73-90632. (Essay Index Reprint Ser). 1931. 19.00 (ISBN 0-8369-1256-X). Ayer Co Pubs.

--A History of Recreation: America Learns to Play. 2nd ed. LC 65-25489. (Illus.). 1965. 39.50x (ISBN 0-89197-498-9). Irvington.

--Labor in America: A History. 3rd ed. LC 66-19224. 1968. pap. 13.95x (ISBN 0-88295-729-5). Harlan Davidson.

--Old China Trade. LC 70-111470. Repr. of 1930 ed. 32.50 (ISBN 0-404-02216-2). AMS Pr.

Dulles, Foster R. & Dubofsky, Melvyn. Labor in America. 4th rev ed. (Illus.). 472p. 1984. text ed. 25.95 (ISBN 0-88295-824-0); pap. text ed. 15.95 (ISBN 0-88295-825-9). Harlan Davidson.

Dulles, John W. Anarchists & Communists in Brazil, 1900-1935. LC 73-4913. (Illus.). 623p. 1973. 30.00x (ISBN 0-292-70302-3). U of Tex Pr.

--Brazilian Communism, 1935-1945: Repression During World Upheaval. (Illus.). 311p. 1983. text ed. 25.00x (ISBN 0-292-70741-X). U of Tex Pr.

--Castello Branco: The Making of a Brazilian President. LC 77-99279. (Illus.). 544p. 1978. 27.50x (ISBN 0-89096-043-7). Tex A&M Univ Pr.

--President Castello Branco: Brazilian Reformer. LC 79-5281. (Illus.). 568p. 1981. 27.50x (ISBN 0-89096-092-5). Tex A&M Univ Pr.
--The Sao Paulo Law School & the Anti-Vargas Resistance, 1938-1945. (Illus.). 312p. 1986. text ed. 30.00x (ISBN 0-292-77599-7). U of Tex Pr.
--The Sao Paulo Law School & the Anti-Vargas Resistance 1938-1945. 312p. 1985. 30.00 (ISBN 0-292-77599-7). U of Tex Pr.
--Unrest in Brazil: Political Military Crises, 1955-1964. (Illus.). 465p. 1970. 27.50x (ISBN 0-292-70006-7). U of Tex Pr.
--Vargas of Brazil: A Political Biography. (Illus.). 409p. 1967. 25.00x (ISBN 0-292-73655-X). U of Tex Pr.
--Yesterday in Mexico: A Chronicle of the Revolution, 1919-1936. (Illus.). 821p. 1961. 24.50x (ISBN 0-292-78361-2). U of Tex Pr.
Dullien, F. A. Transport Phenomena in Porous Media & Pore Structure. LC 79-52794. 1979. 55.00 (ISBN 0-12-223650-5). Acad Pr.
Dullum, Kare B., jt. auth. see Stonehill, Arthur I.
Dulmatovskaya, G. & Shilova, I. Who's Who in Soviet Cinema. 685p. 1982. 12.50 (ISBN 0-8285-1553-0, Pub. by Progress Pubs USSR). Imported Pubns.
Dulong, Marthe, jt. auth. see Moore, Philip S.
Duls, L. D. Richard II in the Early Chronicles. LC 73-80355. (Studies in English Literature: No. 79). 274p. 1975. pap. text ed. 24.00x (ISBN 90-2793-326-X). Mouton.
Dulsey, Bernard M., tr. see Icaza, Jorge.
Dultz, Ron. The Collected Poetry of Ron Dultz. Towbin, Ruth, ed. LC 84-91082. (Illus.). 165p. 1984. 12.00 (ISBN 0-9601636-2-X); pap. 7.00 (ISBN 0-9601636-3-8). R Dultz.
--Educating the Entire Person. Towbin, Ruth, ed. LC 78-52911. 108p. 1984. pap. 6.00 (ISBN 0-9601636-0-3); 10.00 (ISBN 0-9601636-1-1). R Dultz.
--Hainesville. Towbin, Ruth, ed. LC 84-91137. 195p. 1984. 11.00 (ISBN 0-9601636-5-4); pap. 6.00 (ISBN 0-9601636-4-6). R Dultz.
DuLuca, Charles J., jt. auth. see Tinker, Spencer W.
Duly, Leslie C. British Land Policy at the Cape, Seventeen Ninety-Five to Eighteen Forty-Four: A Study of Administrative Procedures in the Empire. LC 67-29574. Repr. of 1968 ed. 61.50 (ISBN 0-8357-9097-5, 2017900). Bks Demand UMI.
Dumaine, Deborah. Write to the Top: Writing for Corporate Success. LC 82-40145. Date not set. pap. price not set (ISBN 0-394-52505-1). Random.
Dumais, et al. Investigating Inservice: Program Policy & Project Practices. 1982. Tchr's Ed. 2.50 (ISBN 0-318-00399-6). Assn Tchr Ed.
Duman, D. The Judical Bench in England Seventeen Twenty-Seven to Eighteen Seventy-Five: The Reshaping of a Professional Elite. 1982. 65.00 (ISBN 0-901050-80-6, Royal Hist Soc England). State Mutual Bk.
Duman, Daniel. The English & Colonial Bars in the Nineteenth Century. (Illus.). 228p. 1983. 30.00 (ISBN 0-85664-468-4, Pub. by Croom Helm Ltd). Longwood Pub Group.
--The Judicial Bench in England. (Royal Historical Society-Studies in History: No. 29). 208p. 1982. text ed. 34.25x (ISBN 0-901050-80-6, Pub. by Swiftbks England). Humanities.
Dumarcay, Jacques. Borobudur. Smithies, Michael, ed. (Illus.). 1978. pap. text ed. 6.95x (ISBN 0-19-580379-5). Oxford U Pr.
Dumarest, Noel. Notes on Cochiti, New Mexico. LC 20-23196. (Amer Anthro Assn Memories). 1919. 11.00 (ISBN 0-527-00526-6). Kraus Repr.
DuMars, Charles T., et al, eds. Pueblo Indian Water Rights: Struggle for a Precious Resource. LC 84-2490. 183p. 1984. 22.50x (ISBN 0-8165-0832-1). U of Ariz Pr.
Dumas, ed. see Eluard, Paul.
Dumas, ed. see Hugo, Victor.
Dumas, Alecandre. The Vicomte de Bragelonne or Ten Years Later, 5 vols. 1981. Set. lib. bdg. 100.00 (ISBN 0-8495-1129-1). Arden Lib.
Dumas, Alexander. The Crimes of the Borgias, 2 vols. Burham, I. H., tr. (Illus.). 276p. 1984. Repr. of 1895 ed. Set. 178.75 (ISBN 0-89901-157-8). Found Class Reprints.
--The Son of Monte-Cristo. 190p. 1983. Repr. of 1894 ed. lib. bdg. 17.95x (ISBN 0-89966-476-8). Buccaneer Bks.
--The Son of Porthos. 287p. 1983. Repr. lib. bdg. 19.95x (ISBN 0-89966-316-8). Buccaneer Bks.
--The Three Musketeers. LC 84-50433. (Classics for Kids Ser.). 1984. 5.96 (ISBN 0-382-06812-2). Silver.
--The Three Musketeers. (Classics for Kids Ser.). 32p. (gr. 2 up). 1985. pap. 3.60 (ISBN 0-382-06955-2). Silver.
--Los Tres Mosqueteros. LC 84-52574. (Classics for Kids Ser.). (Illus.). 32p. (Span.). (gr. 3 up). 1985. pap. 3.60 (ISBN 0-382-09022-5). Silver.
--Les Trois Mousquetaires. Samaran, ed. (Coll. Prestige). 35.00 (ISBN 0-685-34892-X). French & Eur.
Dumas, Alexandre. Adventures in Caucasia. Murch, A. E., ed. LC 75-16415. (Illus.). 205p. 1975. Repr. of 1962 ed. lib. bdg. 27.50x (ISBN 0-8371-8187-9, DUAC). Greenwood.
--Alexandre Dumas' Adventures in Czarist Russia. Murch, Alma E., ed. LC 75-11422. (Illus.). 208p. 1975. Repr. of 1961 ed. lib. bdg. 27.50x (ISBN 0-8371-8188-7, DUCZR). Greenwood.
--Ange Pitou. 5.95 (ISBN 0-686-55834-0). French & Eur.
--Ascanio. (Illus.). 600p. 1956. 7.95 (ISBN 0-686-55835-9). French & Eur.
--Aventures de John Davys. 378p. 1975. 5.95 (ISBN 0-686-55836-7). French & Eur.
--Les Barricades de Juillet: Avec: 20 Pages du Petit Journal Illustre. 192p. 1975. 7.95 (ISBN 0-686-55837-5). French & Eur.
--Les Blancs et les Bleus. 5.95 (ISBN 0-686-55838-3). French & Eur.
--Camille. 1972. pap. 3.50 (ISBN 0-451-51933-7, Sig Classics). NAL.
--Le Capitaine Pamphile. 230p. 1977. 15.95 (ISBN 0-686-55807-3). French & Eur.
--Chicot the Jester. 1968. Repr. of 1910 ed. 9.95x (ISBN 0-460-00421-2, Evman). Biblio Dist.
--Le Collier de la Reine. 1973. 12.95 (ISBN 0-686-55808-1). French & Eur.
--Les Compagnons de Jehu. 8.95 (ISBN 0-686-55809-X). French & Eur.
--Le Comte de Monte-Cristo, 3 vols. 1973. 4.95 ea. French & Eur.
--Le Comte de Monte-Cristo, 2 tomes. Bornecque, ed. (Class. Garnier). Set. pap. 19.90 (ISBN 0-685-34891-1). French & Eur.
--Le Contesse de Charny, 2 vols. Set. 8.95 (ISBN 0-686-55810-3). French & Eur.
--Corsican Brothers. 321p. 1983. Repr. lib. bdg. 12.95 (ISBN 0-89966-317-6). Buccaneer Bks.
--The Count of Monte Cristo. abr. ed. Blair, Lowell, tr. from Fr. (Classics Ser.). 441p. (gr. 6 up). 1981. pap. 3.50 (ISBN 0-553-21187-0). Bantam.
--Count of Monte Cristo. 1976. lib. bdg. 23.95x (ISBN 0-89968-147-6). Lightyear.
--The Count of Monte Cristo. (Regents Illustrated Classics Ser.). (gr. 7-12). 1982. pap. text ed. 2.50 (ISBN 0-88345-472-6, 20557). Regents Pub.
--The Count of Monte Cristo. (Illus.). 496p. 1984. 12.95 (ISBN 0-396-08255-6). Dodd.
--Les Crimes Celebres. 320p. 1961. 3.95 (ISBN 0-686-55811-1). French & Eur.
--La Dame de Monsoreau. (Illus.). 256p. 1972. 9.95 (ISBN 0-686-55812-X). French & Eur.
--Le Destin du San Felice. 5.95 (ISBN 0-686-55813-8). French & Eur.
--Le Docteur Mysterieux. 8.95 (ISBN 0-686-55814-6). French & Eur.
--Dumas on Food. Davidson, Alan & Davidson, Jane, trs. (Illus.). 327p. (Fr.). 1982. 14.95 (ISBN 0-7181-1842-1). U Pr of Va.
--La Fille du Marquis. 8.95 (ISBN 0-686-55815-4). French & Eur.
--Fille du Regent. 8.95 (ISBN 0-686-55816-2). French & Eur.
--Forty-Five. 1968. Repr. of 1907 ed. 9.95x (ISBN 0-460-00420-4, Evman). Biblio Dist.
--Georges. 512p. 4.95 (ISBN 0-686-55817-0). French & Eur.
--The Great Lover & Other Plays. Shaw, Barnett, tr. from Fr. LC 78-20925. 1979. 15.00 (ISBN 0-8044-2147-1). Ungar.
--La Guerre des Femmes. 8.95 (ISBN 0-686-55818-9). French & Eur.
--Histoire de la Cuisine. (Illus.). 176p. 1967. 5.95 (ISBN 0-686-55819-7). French & Eur.
--Joseph Balsamo: Illustre de Photos du Film Televise, 2 vols. (Illus.). 1972. Set. 19.95 (ISBN 0-686-55820-0). French & Eur.
--Journal of Madame Giovanni. Wilbur, M. E., tr. (Black & Gold Lib). 1945. 6.95 (ISBN 0-87140-947-X, Co-Pub with Tudor). Liveright.
--Man in the Iron Mask. (Classics Ser.). (gr. 9 up). 1967. pap. 2.50 (ISBN 0-8049-0150-3, CL-150). Airmont.
--Man in the Iron Mask. 1976. lib. bdg. 22.95x (ISBN 0-89968-146-8). Lightyear.
--The Man in the Iron Mask. Farr, Naunerle, ed. (Now Age Illustrated IV Ser.). (Illus.). (gr. 4-12). 1978. text ed. 5.00 (ISBN 0-88301-328-2); pap. text ed. 1.95 (ISBN 0-88301-316-9); activity bk. 1.25 (ISBN 0-88301-340-1). Pendulum Pr.
--Mes Memoires, 5 vols. 1954-68. Vol. 1. 16.50 (ISBN 0-686-55821-9); Vol. 2. 7.95 (ISBN 0-686-55822-7); Vol. 3. 14.95 (ISBN 0-686-55823-5); Vol. 4. 16.50 (ISBN 0-686-55824-3); Vol. 5. 16.50 (ISBN 0-686-55825-1). French & Eur.
--Mille et un Fantomes. 448p. 1975. 7.95 (ISBN 0-686-55826-X). French & Eur.
--Les Mohicans de Paris. 1973. 4.95 (ISBN 0-686-55827-8). French & Eur.
--My Memoirs. Bell, A. Craig, ed. & tr. from Fr. LC 75-17781. (Illus.). 257p. 1975. Repr. of 1961 ed. lib. bdg. 19.75x (ISBN 0-8371-8186-0, DUMM). Greenwood.
--The Nutcracker. Munro, Douglas, tr. from Fr. (Illus.). (gr. 6-9). 1978. 12.95 (ISBN 0-19-271379-5). Oxford U Pr.
--Les Oeuvres Completes d'Alexandre Dumas, 48 vols. Set. 1000.00 (ISBN 0-686-55828-6). French & Eur.
--Oeuvres Illustrees, 29 tomes. Incl. Les Trois Mousquetaires, 2 tomes. Set. pap. 11.90 (ISBN 0-685-36035-0); Vingts Ans Apres, 2 tomes. Set. pap. 11.90 (ISBN 0-685-36036-9); Le Vicomte de Bragelonne, 6 tomes. Set. pap. 37.50 (ISBN 0-685-36037-7); La Reine Margot, 2 tomes. Set. pap. 11.90 (ISBN 0-685-36038-5); La Dame de Monsoreau, 3 tomes. Set. pap. 17.85 (ISBN 0-685-36039-3); Joseph Balsamo, 5 tomes. Set. pap. 23.80 (ISBN 0-685-36040-7); Le Collier de la Reine, 3 tomes. Set. pap. 17.85 (ISBN 0-685-36041-5); Le Chevalier de Maison-Rouge, 2 tomes. Set. pap. 11.90 (ISBN 0-685-36042-3); La Fille du Regent. pap. 5.95 (ISBN 0-685-36043-1); Le Chevalier d'Harmenthal, 2 tomes. pap. write for info. (ISBN 0-685-36044-X). 1922-35. pap. French & Eur.
--Le Pape Devant les Evangiles: L'Histoire et la Raison Humaine. 216p. 1960. 4.95 (ISBN 0-686-55829-4). French & Eur.
--Les Quarante-Cinq. 12.50 (ISBN 0-686-55830-8). French & Eur.
--La Reine Margot. 1973. 4.95 (ISBN 0-686-55833-2). French & Eur.
--Robin des Bois. 580p. 1966. 5.95 (ISBN 0-686-55204-0). French & Eur.
--Salvator, 4 vols. 1976. pap. 3.95 ea. French & Eur.
--Short Stories, 10 vols. in 1. LC 72-5898. (Short Story Index Reprint Ser.). Repr. of 1927 ed. 50.00 (ISBN 0-8369-4212-4). Ayer Co Pubs.
--Le Sphinx Rouge. 533p. 1966. 5.95 (ISBN 0-686-55205-9). French & Eur.
--Theatre Complet, Vol. 1. (Illus.). 588p. 1974. 42.00 (ISBN 0-686-55211-3). French & Eur.
--Theatre Complet: Christine ou Stockholm, Fontainebleau et Rome, Vol. 1, Pt. 6. 186p. 1976. 15.00 (ISBN 0-686-55210-5). French & Eur.
--Theatre Complet: Flesque de Lavagna, Vol. 1, Pt. 4. 166p. 1976. 12.50 (ISBN 0-686-55208-3). French & Eur.
--Theatre Complet: Henry III et sa Cour, Vol. 1, Pt. 5. 152p. 1976. 12.50 (ISBN 0-686-55209-1). French & Eur.
--Theatre Complet: La Chasse et l'Amour, La Noce et l'Enterrement, Vol. 1, Pt. 2. 126p. 1976. 12.50 (ISBN 0-686-55207-5). French & Eur.
--Three Musketeers. (Classics Ser). (gr. 8 up). pap. 2.95 (ISBN 0-8049-0127-9, CL-127). Airmont.
--Three Musketeers. 1977. Repr. of 1906 ed. 14.95x (ISBN 0-460-00081-0, Evman). Biblio Dist.
--Three Musketeers. (Illustrated Junior Library). (Illus.). (gr. 4-6). 1953-59. pap. 5.95 (ISBN 0-448-11024-5, G&D); deluxe ed. 10.95 (ISBN 0-448-06024-8). Putnam Pub Group.
--The Three Musketeers. 1976. lib. bdg. 18.95 (ISBN 0-89968-148-4). Lightyear.
--The Three Musketeers. Farr, Naunerle, ed. (Now Age Illustrated Ser., No. 2). (Illus.). 64p. (Orig.). (gr. 5-10). 1974. 5.00 (ISBN 0-88301-218-9); pap. text ed. 1.95 (ISBN 0-88301-133-6). Pendulum Pr.
--The Three Musketeers. 1982. pap. 5.95 (ISBN 0-14-044025-9). Penguin.
--The Three Musketeers. (Regents Illustrated Classics Ser.). 62p. (gr. 7-12). 1982. pap. text ed. 2.75 (ISBN 0-88345-479-3, 20533). Regents Pub.
--The Three Musketeers. 1984. Repr. lib. bdg. 18.95x (ISBN 0-89966-486-5). Buccaneer Bks.
--The Three Musketeers. (Illus.). 608p. 1984. 11.95 (ISBN 0-396-08355-2). Dodd.
--The Three Musketeers. Bair, Lowell, tr. from Fr. (Bantam Classics Ser.). 1984. pap. 3.95 (ISBN 0-553-21147-1). Bantam.
--Trois Maitres. 288p. 1977. 19.95 (ISBN 0-686-55212-1). French & Eur.
--Les Trois Mousquetaires, 2 vols. 1973. pap. 4.95 ea. French & Eur.
--Les Trois Mousquetaires, 3 vols. (Illus.). 950p. 1974. Set. 160.00 (ISBN 0-686-55214-8). French & Eur.
--Les Trois Mousquetaires & Vingt Ans Apres. 1800p. 45.00 (ISBN 0-686-56508-8). French & Eur.
--Les Trois Mousquetaires: Avec Vingt Ans Apres. 1800p. 1962. 35.00 (ISBN 0-686-55213-X). French & Eur.
--Le Trou de l'Enfer. 1975. 4.95 (ISBN 0-686-55215-6). French & Eur.
--La Tulipe Noire. (Illus.). 1973. 10.95 (ISBN 0-686-55216-4). French & Eur.
--Twenty Years After. 1979. Repr. of 1907 ed. 14.95x (ISBN 0-460-00175-2, Evman). Biblio Dist.
--Twenty Years After. 467p. 1981. Repr. lib. bdg. 21.95 (ISBN 0-89968-229-4). Lightyear.
--Vingt Ans Apres, 2 vols. 1975. pap. 4.95 ea. French & Eur.
--Vingt Ans Apres. Samaran, ed. (Class. Garnier). pap. 12.95 (ISBN 0-685-34893-8). French & Eur.
--Vingt Ans Apres. Samaran, ed. (Coll. Prestige). 12.95 (ISBN 0-685-34894-6). French & Eur.
Dumas, Alexandre & Bassan, Fernande. Theatre Complet: Comment je devins Auteur Dramatique. Ivanhoe, Vol. 1, Pt. 1. 144p. 1976. 12.50 (ISBN 0-686-55206-7). French & Eur.
Dumas, Alexandre & Raffalli, Bernard. La Dame aux Camelias. 1975. 4.95 (ISBN 0-686-55217-2). French & Eur.
Dumas, Alexandre see Eyre, A. G.
Dumas, Alexandre see Peyrazat, Jean E.
Dumas, Alexandre see Swan, D. K.
Dumas, Alexandre, et al. Quinze Chasses au Tresor. (Illus.). 224p. 1974. 7.95 (ISBN 0-686-55832-4). French & Eur.
--Quinze Aventures de Mousquetaires. 256p. 1976. 7.95 (ISBN 0-686-55831-6). French & Eur.
Dumas, Alexandre, fils see Stanton, Stephen S.
Dumas, Alexandre, Jr. Camille. facsimile ed. Heron, Matilde, tr. from Fr. LC 76-170697. (Black Heritage Library Collection). Repr. of 1856 ed. 11.50 (ISBN 0-8369-8887-6). Ayer Co Pubs.
Dumas, Alexandre, Sr. Trois Mousquetaires. Samaran, ed. 1961. pap. 9.95 (ISBN 0-685-11605-0). French & Eur.
--Vingt Ans Apres, 2 tomes. (Coll. GF). 1961. Set. pap. 9.00 (ISBN 0-685-11621-2). French & Eur.
Dumas, C., ed. see Sartre, Jean-Paul.
Dumas, Charles E. Effects of Government Deficits: A Comparative Analysis of Crowding Out. (Essays in International Finance Ser.: No. 157). 1985. pap. text ed. 2.50x (ISBN 0-88165-064-1). Princeton U Int Finan Econ.
Dumas, Edith B. The Least of These. 128p. 1982. 7.95 (ISBN 0-89962-261-5). Todd & Honeywell.
Dumas, Emma P. Mirbah. (Novels by Franco-Americans in New England 1850-1940 Ser.). 246p. (Fr.). (gr. 10 up). 1979. pap. 4.50 (ISBN 0-911409-20-3). Natl Mat Dev.
Dumas, Enoch, et al. Arithmetic Charts Handbook. 1960. pap. 3.95 (ISBN 0-8224-0400-1). Pitman Learning.
Dumas, Frederic, jt. auth. see Cousteau, Jacques-Yves.
Dumas, Gerald. Rabbits Rafferty. (Illus.). 204p. (gr. 3-7). 1981. pap. 1.95 (ISBN 0-380-53348-0, 53348-0, Camelot). Avon.
Dumas, Glenda. The Rootworker. (Orig.). 1983. pap. 1.95 (ISBN 0-87067-711-X, BH711). Holloway.
Dumas, Jacques. Registering Title to Land: A Series of Lectures Delivered at Yale. 106p. 1985. Repr. of 1900 ed. lib. bdg. 20.00x (ISBN 0-8377-0522-3). Rothman.
Dumas, Jean-Louis R., jt. auth. see Poirier, Jacques.
Dumas, Lloyd J. The Political Economy of Arms Reduction: Reversing Economic Delay. LC 82-60041. (AAAS Selected Symposium 80 Ser.). 162p. 1982. pap. 18.50x (ISBN 0-86531-405-5). Westview.
Dumas, Marie-Claire, jt. auth. see Desnos, Robert.
Dumas, Philippe. Caesar, Cock of the Village. J. M. Dent & Sons, Ltd., tr. from Fr. (Illus.). (gr. k-4). 1980. PLB 7.95 (ISBN 0-13-110189-7). P-H.
--Laura, Alice's New Puppy. (Illus.). 64p. (ps-3). 1979. 9.95 (ISBN 0-575-02568-9, Pub. by Gollancz England). David & Charles.
--Laura Loses Her Head. (Illus.). 64p. (ps-3). 1981. 9.95 (ISBN 0-575-03016-X, Pub. by Gollancz England). David & Charles.
--The Lippizaners: And the Spanish Riding School of Vienna. (gr. 3-7). 1981. 10.95 (ISBN 0-13-537068-X). P-H.
Dumas, R. & Fulachier, L., eds. Structure of Complex Turbulent Shear Flow: Marseille, France, 1982, Proceedings. (IUTLM Symposium). (Illus.). 444p. 1983. 42.00 (ISBN 0-387-12156-0). Springer-Verlag.
Dumas, T. & Bulani, W. Oxidation of Petrochemicals: Chemistry & Technology. (Illus.). 186p. 1974. 33.50 (ISBN 0-85334-589-9, Pub. by Elsevier Applied Sci England). Elsevier.
Dumas, Wayne & Lee, William B. Social Studies in West German Schools: Firsthand Perspectives for Educators. LC 77-87587. (Illus.). 144p. 1978. 11.00x (ISBN 0-8262-0238-1). U of Mo Pr.
Dumas Ribadeau, Francois. These Moderns: Some Parisian Closeups. LC 71-113308. 1971. Repr. of 1932 ed. 25.00x (ISBN 0-8046-1357-5, Pub by Kennikat). Assoc Faculty Pr.
Du Maurier. Trilby, a Novel. 1977. Repr. of 1895 ed. lib. bdg. 25.00 (ISBN 0-8414-1857-8). Folcroft.
Du Maurier, Daphne. Breaking Point. 1973. pap. 1.25 (ISBN 0-380-01072-0, 15479). Avon.
--Don't Look Now. 320p. 1985. pap. 3.95 (ISBN 0-440-12122-1). Dell.
DuMaurier, Daphne. Echoes from the Macabre: Selected Stories. 18.95 (ISBN 0-88411-543-7, Pub. by Aeonian Pr). Amereon Ltd.
--Flight of the Falcon. 288p. 1985. pap. 3.95 (ISBN 0-380-69868-4). Avon.
Du Maurier, Daphne. Frenchman's Creek. pap. 1.95 (ISBN 0-380-00979-X, 32565). Avon.
--Frenchman's Creek. LC 70-184730. 320p. 1971. Repr. lib. bdg. 14.00x (ISBN 0-8376-0412-5). Bentley.
--Frenchman's Creek. 1984. pap. 3.95 (ISBN 0-440-12688-6). Dell.
--Gerald, a Portrait. 1978. Repr. of 1934 ed. 12.50 (ISBN 0-8492-0686-3). R West.
--The Glass-Blowers. (General Ser.). 491p. 1983. lib. bdg. 17.95 (ISBN 0-8161-3491-X, Large Print Bks). G K Hall.
--Golden Lads: Sir Frances Bacon, Anthony Bacon & Their Friends. 15.95 (ISBN 0-88411-544-5, Pub. by Aeonian Pr). Amereon Ltd.
--The House on the Strand. 1976. pap. 3.95 (ISBN 0-380-00643-X, 60317-9). Avon.
--Hungry Hill. LC 78-184732. 416p. 1971. Repr. of 1945 ed. lib. bdg. 14.00x (ISBN 0-8376-0414-1). Bentley.
--Hungry Hill. (General Ser.). 1984. lib. bdg. 19.95 (ISBN 0-8161-3490-1, Large Print). G K Hall.

--Jamaica Inn. 1971. pap. 3.50 (ISBN 0-380-00072-5, 65078-9). Avon.
--Jamaica Inn. 1979. Repr. lib. bdg. 17.95x (ISBN 0-89966-432-6). Buccaneer Bks.
--The King's General. 1978. pap. 3.50 (ISBN 0-380-00210-8, 60316-0). Avon.
--The Loving Spirit. 1973. pap. 1.25 (ISBN 0-380-01337-1, 10686). Avon.
--The Loving Spirit. LC 71-184733. 384p. 1971. Repr. lib. bdg. 14.00x (ISBN 0-8376-0415-X). Bentley.
--Mary Anne. LC 76-184729. 352p. 1971. Repr. of 1954 ed. lib. bdg. 14.00x (ISBN 0-8376-0411-7). Bentley.
--My Cousin Rachel. LC 74-184731. 352p. 1971. Repr. lib. bdg. 14.00x (ISBN 0-8376-0413-3). Bentley.
DuMaurier, Daphne. Myself When Young: The Shaping of a Writer. (General Ser.). 1978. lib. bdg. 10.95 (ISBN 0-8161-6611-0, Large Print Bks). G K Hall.
Du Maurier, Daphne. The Parasites. LC 72-184728. 320p. 1971. Repr. of 1950 ed. lib. bdg. 14.00x (ISBN 0-8376-0410-9). Bentley.
DuMaurier, Daphne. The Parasites. (General Ser.). 1983. lib. bdg. 18.95 (ISBN 0-8161-3489-8, Large Print Bks). G K Hall.
Du Maurier, Daphne. Rebecca. 1971. pap. 3.95 (ISBN 0-380-00917-X, 60315-7). Avon.
--Rebecca. 1948. 15.95 (ISBN 0-385-04380-5). Doubleday.
--Rule Britannia. 1974. pap. 1.50 (ISBN 0-380-00062-8, 19547). Avon.
--The Scapegoat. 1977. Repr. of 1957 ed. lib. bdg. 19.95x (ISBN 0-89244-037-6). Queens Hse.
--The Winding Stair. 1978. pap. 2.25 (ISBN 0-380-01848-9, 36459-X). Avon.
--The Winding Stair: Sir Francis Bacon, His Rise & Fall. 14.95 (ISBN 0-88411-545-3, Pub. by Aeonian Pr). Amereon Ltd.
Du Maurier, Daphne, jt. auth. see Couch, Anthony Q.
Du Maurier, Daphne, jt. auth. see Couch, Arthur Q.
Du Maurier, Daphne, ed. The Young George du Maurier: A Selection of his Letters, 1869-67. 307p. 1982. Repr. of 1951 ed. lib. bdg. 30.00 (ISBN 0-89987-586-6). Darby Bks.
Du Maurier, Daphne, ed. see Du Maurier, George L.
Du Maurier, George. L. P. B. Trilby. 1977. 12.95 (ISBN 0-460-00863-3, DEL 04575, Evman); pap. 3.95 (ISBN 0-460-01863-9, DEL 04417, Evman). Biblio Dist.
--Martian. LC 77-144991. (Illus.). 1971. Repr. of 1897 ed. 23.00x (ISBN 0-403-00919-7). Scholarly.
--The Martian: A Novel. 477p. 1980. Repr. of 1897 ed. lib. bdg. 25.00 (ISBN 0-89984-153-8). Century Bookbindery.
--Trilby. 1977. 9.95x (ISBN 0-460-00863-3, Evman); pap. 3.95x (ISBN 0-460-01863-9). Biblio Dist.
Du Maurier, George, ed. Peter Ibbetson with an Introduction by His Cousin Lady ("Madge Plunket") 1979. Repr. of 1891 ed. lib. bdg. 25.00 (ISBN 0-8495-1044-9). Arden Lib.
Du Maurier, George L. Peter Ibbetson. 1971. Repr. of 1932 ed. 23.00x (ISBN 0-403-00920-0). Scholarly.
--Young George Du Maurier: A Selection of His Letters, 1860-67. Du Maurier, Daphne, ed. LC 73-97329. Repr. of 1951 ed. lib. bdg. 22.50x (ISBN 0-8371-2830-7, DUDU). Greenwood.
Dumazedier, Joffre & Guinchat, Claire. La Sociologie Du Loisir: Tendances Actuelles De la Recherche & Bibliographie (1945-65) (Current Sociology-la Sociologie Contemporaine: No. 16-1). 1969. pap. 9.60x (ISBN 90-2796-576-5). Mouton.
Dumbach, Annette E., jt. auth. see Newborn, Jud.
Dumbarton Oaks Collection. Pre-Columbian Art. Benson, Elizabeth P., ed. LC 76-8176. 1976. 25.00 (ISBN 0-226-68981-6, Chicago Visual Lib); 1 colorfiche incl. U of Chicago Pr.
Dumbaugh, Kerry & Serota, Gary. Capitol Jobs: An Insider's Guide to Finding a Job in Congress. LC 82-50885. 120p. (Orig.). 1982. pap. 5.95 (ISBN 0-9605750-4-9). Tilden Pr.
Dumbauld, Edward. The Bill of Rights & What It Means Today. LC 78-12307. (Illus.). xv, 242p. 1979. Repr. of 1957 ed. lib. bdg. 32.50 (ISBN 0-313-21215-5, DUBR). Greenwood.
--Constitution of the United States. LC 64-11324. (Illus.). Repr. of 1964 ed. 99.00 (ISBN 0-8357-9722-8, 2016211). Bks Demand UMI.
--Declaration of Independence & What It Means Today. (Illus.). 1968. Repr. of 1950 ed. 10.95x (ISBN 0-8061-0214-4). U of Okla Pr.
--The Declaration of Independence & What it Means Today. pap. 52.00 (ISBN 0-317-27970-X, 2052153). Bks Demand UMI.
--Thomas Jefferson & the Law. LC 78-5742. (Illus.). 1978. 29.50x (ISBN 0-8061-1441-X). U of Okla Pr.
Dumbauld, Edward, ed. see Jefferson, Thomas.
Dumbauld, Edward H. Thomas Jefferson, American Tourist. (American Exploration & Travel Ser.: No. 9). (Pap. ed. 1978 reprint of 1946 ed.). 1976. 17.95x (ISBN 0-8061-1345-6); pap. 8.95 (ISBN 0-8061-1353-7). U of Okla Pr.
Dumbleton, J. H. The Tribology of Natural & Artificial Joints. (Tribology Ser.: Vol. 3). 460p. 1981. 74.50 (ISBN 0-444-41898-9). Elsevier.
Dumbleton, John, jt. auth. see Black, Jonathan.
Dumbleton, John H. & Black, Jonathan. An Introduction to Orthopaedic Materials. (Illus.). 268p. 1975. 31.00x (ISBN 0-398-03368-4). C C Thomas.
Dumbleton, Peter, jt. auth. see Williams, Brian.
Dumbleton, Susanne. In & Around Albany Calendar & Chronicle of Past Events. (Illus.). 28p. (Orig.). 1982. pap. 8.95 (ISBN 0-9605460-2-2). Wash Park.
Dumbleton, Susanne & Older, Anne. In & Around Albany: A Guide for Residents, Students & Visitors. (Illus.). 183p. (Orig.). 1980. pap. 4.50 (ISBN 0-9605460-0-6). Wash Park.
Dumbleton, Susanne, et al. St. Margaret's House & Hospital for Babies: A Celebration. (Illus.). 80p. (Orig.). 1983. pap. 6.95 (ISBN 0-9611828-0-6). St Marg Hse Hosp.
Dumbleton, William A. Ireland: Life & Land in Literature. 192p. 1984. 29.95x (ISBN 0-87395-783-0); pap. 9.95x (ISBN 0-87395-782-2). State U NY Pr.
--James Cousins. (English Authors Ser.). 1980. 15.95 (ISBN 0-8057-6745-2, Twayne). G K Hall.
Dumbreck, J. C., ed. see Forbes, Nevill.
Dumbrell, R. Understanding Antique Wine Bottles. (Illus.). 340p. 1983. 29.50 (ISBN 0-907462-14-6). Antique Collect.
--Understanding Antique Wine Bottles. (Illus.). 340p. 1985. 29.50 (ISBN 0-907462-14-6). Apollo.
Dumenil, Lynn. Freemasonry & American Culture: Eighteen Eighty to Nineteen Thirty. LC 84-42594. (Illus.). 320p. 1984. text ed. 30.00x (ISBN 0-691-04716-2). Princeton U Pr.
Dumeril, Auguste H., et al. Mission Scientifique Au Mexique et Dans L'Amerique Centrale,....Recherches Zoologiques: Etude Sur les Reptiles, Avec Atlas, 2 vols. Sterling, Keir B., ed. LC 77-81098. (Biologists & Their World Ser.). (Illus., Fr.). 1978. Repr. of 1909 ed. lib. bdg. 110.00x (ISBN 0-405-10680-7). Ayer Co Pubs.
Dumery, Henry. Phenomenology & Religion: Structures of the Christian Institution. Barrett, Paul, tr. LC 73-94443. (Hermeneutics Series: Studies in the History of Religion). 1975. 25.00x (ISBN 0-520-02714-0). U of Cal Pr.
Dumesil, Carla D., jt. auth. see Evans, Helen M.
Dumesnil. Gustave Flaubert, l'Homme et l'Oeuvre. 23.50 (ISBN 0-685-34907-1). French & Eur.
Dumesnil, ed. see Flaubert, Gustave.
Dumesnil, Maurice. Claude Debussy: Master of Dreams. LC 78-23438. 1979. Repr. of 1940 ed. lib. bdg. 24.75x (ISBN 0-313-20775-5, DUCB). Greenwood.
Du Mesnil-Marigny, Jules. Histoire De l'Economie Politique Des Anciens Peuples De l'Inde, De l'Egypte, De la Judee et De la Grece, 3 Vols. 3rd ed. 1967. Repr. of 1878 ed. 69.50 (ISBN 0-8337-4800-9). B Franklin.
Dumezil, Georges. Archaic Roman Religion, 2 Vols. Krapp, Philip, tr. from Fr. LC 76-116981. 1971. Set. 45.00x (ISBN 0-226-16968-5). U of Chicago Pr.
--Camillus: A Study of Indo-European Religion As Roman History. Strutynski, Udo, ed. Aronowicz, Annette, et al, trs. from Fr. LC 80-36771. 250p. 1980. 22.00x (ISBN 0-520-02841-4). U of Cal Pr.
--Deesses Latines et Mythes Vediques. Bolle, Kees W., ed. LC 77-79121. (Mythology Ser.). (Fr.). 1978. Repr. of 1956 ed. lib. bdg. 17.00x (ISBN 0-405-10533-9). Ayer Co Pubs.
--Destiny of a King. Hiltebeitel, Alf, tr. 1973. 15.00x (ISBN 0-226-16975-8). U of Chicago Pr.
--Destiny of the Warrior. Hiltebeitel, Alf, tr. LC 75-113254. 1971. 15.00x (ISBN 0-226-16970-7). U of Chicago Pr.
--From Myth to Fiction. Coltman, Derek, tr. from Fr. 1973. 22.00x (ISBN 0-226-16972-3). U of Chicago Pr.
--Gods of the Ancient Northmen. Haugen, Einar, ed. & tr. (Study of Comparative Folklore & Mythology, No. 3). 1974. 34.00x (ISBN 0-520-02044-8); CAL 371. pap. 3.95 (ISBN 0-520-03507-0). U of Cal Pr.
--Horace et les Curiaces. Bolle, Kees W., ed. (Mythology Ser.). (Fr.). 1978. Repr. of 1942 ed. lib. bdg. 17.00x (ISBN 0-405-10534-7). Ayer Co Pubs.
--The Stakes of the Warrior. Puhvel, Jaan, ed. Weeks, David, tr. from Fr. LC 82-13384. 128p. 1983. text ed. 19.95x (ISBN 0-520-04834-2). U of Cal Pr.
Dumia, Mariano A. The Ifugao World. Edades, Jean, ed. (Illus.). 1979. pap. 6.00x (ISBN 0-686-24953-4, Pub. by New Day Pub). Cellar.
Dumicich, John, ed. Picture It. (Illus.). 194p. (gr. 10-12). 1981. pap. text ed. 5.75 (ISBN 0-88345-413-0, 18677). Regents Pub.
Dumitrescu, Ion & Kenyon, Julian N. Electrographic Methods in Medicine & Biology. 288p. 1983. 35.00x (ISBN 0-85435-045-4, Pub. by Neville Spearman Ltd England). State Mutual Bk.
Dumitrescu, Maria, ed. see Amerie De Belenoi.
Dumitriu, A. History of Logic, 4 vols. 1977. Set. 99.00 (ISBN 0-9961000-7-5, Pub. by Abacus England). Heyden.
--History of Logic, Vol. 1: Logic in Non-European Cultures. 1977. 26.00 (ISBN 0-9961000-8-3, Pub. by Abacus England). Heyden.
--History of Logic, Vol. 2: Scholastic Logic; Renaissance Logic. 1977. 26.00 (ISBN 0-9961000-9-1, Pub. by Abacus England). Heyden.
--History of Logic, Vol. 3: Methodological Logic; Development of Modern Logic. 1977. 26.00 (ISBN 0-9961001-0-5, Pub. by Abacus England). Heyden.
--History of Logic, Vol. 4: Mathematical Logic. 1977. 26.00 (ISBN 0-686-40610-9, 996100113H, Pub. by Abacus England). Heyden.
Dumitriu, Petru. To the Unknown God. Kirkup, James, tr. from Fr. LC 82-5722. 256p. 1982. pap. 11.95 (ISBN 0-8164-2424-1, Pub. by Seabury). Winston Pr.
Dummelow, John. The Wax Chandlers of London: A Short History of the Worshipful Company of Wax Chandlers of London. (Illus.). 204p. 1973. 47.50x (ISBN 0-8476-1381-X). Rowman.
Dummelow, John R. Commentary on the Holy Bible. 1909. 19.95 (ISBN 0-02-533770-X). Macmillan.
Dummer, G. W. Electronic Inventions & Discoveries: Electronics from Its Earliest Beginnings to the Present Day. 3rd, rev. ed. 220p. 1983. 40.00 (ISBN 0-08-029354-9); pap. 18.00 (ISBN 0-08-029353-0). Pergamon.
Dummer, G. W. & Wells, Malvern, eds. Semiconductor & Microprocessor Technology 1980: Selected Papers Presented at the Annual SEMINEX Technical Seminar & Exhibition, London, UK. 190p. 1981. pap. 44.00 (ISBN 0-08-028674-7). Pergamon.
Dummer, G. W. A., ed. Semiconductor & Microprocessor Technology 1981: Selected Papers Presented at the 1981 Annual Seminex Technical Seminar & Exhibition, London, UK. 144p. 1982. pap. 43.00 (ISBN 0-08-028722-0). Pergamon.
Dummer, G. W. A., ed. see SEMINEX Technical Seminar & Exhibition, London, England, March 26-30, 1979.
Dummer, Geoffrey W. Electronic Reliability Electronics. Griffin, N. B., ed. 1966. 19.00 (ISBN 0-08-011448-2). Pergamon.
--Semiconductor Technology 1975. pap. 32.00 (ISBN 0-08-019976-3). Pergamon.
--Semiconductor Technology 1977. pap. 39.00 (ISBN 0-08-022148-3). Pergamon.
--Semiconductor Technology 1978. pap. 52.00 (ISBN 0-08-024205-7). Pergamon.
Dummer, Geoffrey W. & Winton, R. C. An Elementary Guide to Reliability. 2nd ed. LC 73-16199. 66p. 1974. pap. text ed. 7.75 (ISBN 0-08-017821-9). Pergamon.
Dummer, Geoffrey W., ed. Semiconductor Technology 1976. 1977. pap. text ed. 32.00 (ISBN 0-08-020983-1). Pergamon.
Dummer, Jeremiah. Defence of the New-England Charters. LC 71-141122. (Research Library of Colonial Americana). 1972. Repr. of 1721 ed. 18.00 (ISBN 0-405-03333-8). Ayer Co Pubs.
Dummett, Clifton O. Community Dentistry: Contributions to New Directions. (Illus.). 232p. 1974. 23.50x (ISBN 0-398-02882-6). C C Thomas.
Dummett, Michael. Frege Philosophy of Language. LC 80-29692. 752p. 1981. text ed. 40.00x (ISBN 0-674-31930-3). Harvard U Pr.
--The Game of Tarot. (Illus.). 600p. 1980. 39.95 (ISBN 0-7156-1014-7). US Games Syst.
--The Interpretation of Frege's Philosophy. LC 77-12777. 1981. text ed. 40.00x (ISBN 0-674-45975-X). Harvard U Pr.
--Truth & Other Enigmas. LC 77-12777. 528p. 1978. 35.00x (ISBN 0-674-91075-3); pap. 12.50x (ISBN 0-674-91076-1). Harvard U Pr.
--Twelve Tarot Games. (Illus.). 242p. 1980. 14.95 (ISBN 0-7156-1485-1); pap. 9.95 (ISBN 0-7156-1488-6). US Games Syst.
--Voting Procedures. (Illus.). 1985. 34.50 (ISBN 0-19-876188-0). Oxford U Pr.
Dummett, Michael & Minio, Robert. Elements of Intuitionism. (Oxford Logic Guides Ser.). 1977. text ed. 39.95x (ISBN 0-19-853158-3). Oxford U Pr.
Dummett, Nanci L. Self-Paced Business Mathematics. 2nd ed. LC 81-23626. 425p. 1982. pap. text ed. write for info. (ISBN 0-534-01155-1). Kent Pub Co.
Dumochel, Robert. European Housing Rehabilitation Experience: A Summary & Analysis. (Illus.). 94p. 1978. 9.00 (ISBN 0-318-14938-9, N595); members 7.00 (ISBN 0-318-14939-7). NAHRO.
Dumoga, John. Africa Between East & West. LC 76-77360. (Background Ser.). 1969. 7.95 (ISBN 0-8023-1214-4). Dufour.
Dumon, Jean-Francois, et al. Yag Laser Bronchoscopy. LC 84-26310. 128p. 1985. 23.00 (ISBN 0-03-071877-5). Praeger.
Du Moncel, Theodore A. The Telephone, the Microphone, & the Phonograph. LC 74-4673. (Telecommunications Ser). (Illus.). 282p. 1974. Repr. of 1879 ed. 23.50x (ISBN 0-405-06039-4). Ayer Co Pubs.
Dumond, Annie H. Annie Nelles. Baxter, Annette K., ed. LC 79-8788. (Signal Lives Ser.). 1980. Repr. of 1868 ed. lib. bdg. 39.00x (ISBN 0-405-12836-3). Ayer Co Pubs.
Dumond, Don E. The Eskimos & Aleuts. (Illus.). 1977. 19.95 (ISBN 0-500-02089-2). Thames Hudson.
Dumond, Dwight L. Antislavery Origins of the Civil War in the United States. LC 80-12505. vii, 133p. 1980. Repr. of 1959 ed. lib. bdg. 19.75x (ISBN 0-313-22378-5, DUAO). Greenwood.
--Antislavery: The Crusade for Freedom in America. (Illus.). 1966. pap. 2.45x (ISBN 0-393-00370-1, Norton Lib). Norton.
--A Bibliography of Antislavery in America. LC 81-4220. 119p. 1981. Repr. of 1961 ed. lib. bdg. 32.50x (ISBN 0-313-23075-7, DUBA). Greenwood.
--A Bibliography of Antislavery in America. LC 61-9306. pap. 32.50 (ISBN 0-317-10569-8, 2051081). Bks Demand UMI.
--Secession Movement, Eighteen Sixty to Eighteen Sixty-One. LC 68-55883. Repr. of 1931 ed. 19.75x (ISBN 0-8371-0398-3, DUS&). Greenwood.
--Secession Movement, Eighteen Sixty to Eighteen Sixty-One. 1963. lib. bdg. 24.50x (ISBN 0-374-92375-2). Octagon.
Dumond, Dwight L., ed. Southern Editorials on Secession. 1964. 16.50 (ISBN 0-8446-1162-X). Peter Smith.
Dumond, Dwight L., jt. ed. see Barnes, Gilbert H.
Dumond, Dwight L., ed. see Birney, James G.
DuMond, Jesse W., ed. see Millikan, Robert A.
Dumond, Michael. Coping with the Dating Game. 1985. 8.97 (ISBN 0-8239-0637-X). Rosen Group.
Dumond, Michael, ed. Coping with Life after High School. (Personal Adjustment Ser.). 1983. lib. bdg. 8.97 (ISBN 0-8239-0606-X). Rosen Group.
Dumond, Val. Sheit: A No-Nonsense Guidebook to Writing & Using Nonsexist Language. 60p. (Orig.). 1984. pap. 8.95 (ISBN 0-9613673-0-X). V Dumond.
--Visiting Olympia. (Color-a-Story Ser.). (Illus.). 24p. (Orig.). (gr. 1-4). 1983. pap. 2.75 (ISBN 0-933992-39-4). Coffee Break.
Dumonde, D. C. & Path, M. R. Infection & Immunology in the Rheumatic Diseases. (Blackwell Scientific Pubns.). (Illus.). 1976. 90.00 (ISBN 0-8016-1495-3). Mosby.
Dumont, Bernard. Functional Literacy in Mali: Training for Development. LC 73-77353. (Educational Studies & Documents: No. 10). (Illus.). 67p. (Orig.). 1973. pap. 5.00 (ISBN 92-3-101113-8, U257, UNESCO). Unipub.
Dumont, Fernand. Vigil of Quebec. LC 72-97423. 1974. pap. 6.95 (ISBN 0-8020-6184-2). U of Toronto Pr.
Dumont, Francis M. French Grammar. 2nd ed. 1969. pap. 5.95i (ISBN 0-06-460035-1, CO 35, COS). B&N NY.
Dumont, Gabriel P. Parallele de Plans des Plus Belles Salles de Spectacles d'Italie et de France. LC 68-17155. (Illus., Fr.). 1968. Repr. 49.50 (ISBN 0-405-08469-2, Blom Pubns). Ayer Co Pubs.
Dumont, H. J. & Tundisi, J. G. Tropical Zooplankton. (Developments in Hydrobiology Ser.: No. 23). 344p. 1984. 84.00 (ISBN 90-6193-774-4, Pub. by Junk Pubs Netherlands). Kluwer Academic.
Dumont, H. J. & Green, J., eds. Rotatoria. (Developments in Hydrobiology Ser.: No. 1). 268p. 1980. lib. bdg. 79.00 (ISBN 90-6193-754-X, Pub. Junk Pubs Netherlands). Kluwer Academic.
Dumont, H. J., et al, eds. Limnology & Marine Biology in the Sudan. (Developments in Hydrobiology Ser.). 1984. lib. bdg. 84.00 (ISBN 90-6193-772-8, Pub. by Junk Pubs Netherlands). Kluwer Academic.
Du Mont, J. The Basis of Combination in Chess. (Illus.). 1978. pap. 4.50 (ISBN 0-486-23644-7). Dover.
Du Mont, J., jt. auth. see Tartakower, A.
Du Mont, J., jt. auth. see Tartakower, S.
Dumont, J. & Nunez, J., eds. Hormones & Cell Regulation, Vol. 6. 320p. 1982. 66.00 (ISBN 0-444-80419-6, Biomedical Pr). Elsevier.
Du Mont, J., tr. see Lasker, Edward.
Dumont, J. E. & Nunez, J. Hormones & Cell Regulation. (European Symposium Ser.: Vol. 8). 1984. 68.00 (ISBN 0-444-80583-4, I-253-84). Elsevier.
Dumont, J. E., jt. ed. see Boeynaems, J. J.
Dumont, J. E., et al, eds. Hormones & Cell Regulation, Vol. 7. 360p. 1983. 64.00 (ISBN 0-444-80500-1, Biomedical Pr). Elsevier.
Dumont, Jacques E., jt. ed. see Swillens, Stephane.
Dumont, Jacques E., et al, eds. Cyclic Nucleotides: Proceedings of the Fourth International Conference, Brussels, Belgium. (Advances in Cyclic Nucleotide Research: Vol. 14). 756p. 1981. text ed. 113.50 (ISBN 0-89004-546-1). Raven.
--Eukariotic Cell Function & Growth: Regulation by Intracellular Cyclic Nucleotides. LC 76-10784. (NATO ASI Series A, Life Sciences: Vol. 9). 860p. 1976. 89.50x (ISBN 0-306-35609-0, Plenum Pr). Plenum Pub.
Dumont, Jean, et al, eds. Corps Universel Diplomatique du Droit des Gens, 8 Vols. LC 72-164796. Repr. of 1731 ed. Set. lib. bdg. 600.00 (ISBN 0-404-01810-6); lib. bdg. 75.00 ea. AMS Pr.
--Corps Universel Diplomatique: Supplement, 5 Vols. LC 72-953. Repr. of 1739 ed. Set. lib. bdg. 375.00 (ISBN 0-404-01820-3); lib. bdg. 75.00 ea. AMS Pr.
Dumont, Jean-Paul. The Headman & I: Ambiguity & Ambivalence in the Fieldworking Experience. (Texas Pan American Ser.). (Illus.). 229p. 1978. text ed. 14.95x (ISBN 0-292-73007-1). U of Tex Pr.
DuMont, John S. American Engraved Powder Horns: The Golden Age 1755-1783. LC 78-25546. (Illus.). 1979. 29.50 (ISBN 0-914016-57-1). Phoenix Pub.
Dumont, K. P. Sclerotinaceae Two: Lambertella, Vol. 22(1) (Memoirs of the New York Botanical Garden Ser.). 178p. 1971. 14.00 (ISBN 0-317-35529-5). NY Botanical.

Dumont, Lora L. Consonant Articulation Drills. 2nd ed. 268p. 1980. pap. text ed. 7.95x (ISBN 0-8134-2129-2, 2129). Interstate.

Dumont, Louis. Affinity As a Value: Marriage Alliance in South India with Comparative Essays on Austrailia. LC 82-13468. (Illus.). 248p. 1983. lib. bdg. 22.00x (ISBN 0-226-16964-2). U of Chicago Pr.

--Dravidien et Kariera: L'Alliance De Marriage Dans L'Inde Du Sud et En Australie. (Texts de Sciences Sociales Ser.: No. 14). 148p. 1975. pap. text ed. 15.20x (ISBN 90-2797-715-1). Mouton.

--From Mandeville to Marx: The Genesis & Triumph of Economic Ideology. LC 76-8087. (Midway Reprint Ser.). 236p. 1977. pap. 10.00x (ISBN 0-226-16966-9). U of Chicago Pr.

--Homo Hierarchicus: The Caste System & Its Implications. rev. ed. Gulati, Basia, tr. LC 80-16480. 1981. 36.00x (ISBN 0-226-16962-6); pap. 15.00x (ISBN 0-226-16963-4, P601, Phoen). U of Chicago Pr.

--Religion, Politics & History in India: Collected Papers in Indian Sociology. (Le Monde D'outre Mer Passe et Present Etudes: No.34). 1970. text ed. 11.20x (ISBN 90-2791-571-7). Mouton.

--Une Sous-Caste De L'Inde Du Sud: Organisation Sociale et Religion Des Pramalai Kallar. (Le Monde D'outre Mer Passe et Present Etudes: No. 1). (Fr.). 1957. pap. text ed. 21.60x (ISBN 0-686-22530-9). Mouton.

Dumont, M. A Treatise on Judicial Evidence, Extracted from the Manuscripts of Jeremy Bentham. xvi, 366p. 1981. Repr. of 1825 ed. lib. bdg. 35.00x (ISBN 0-8377-0318-2). Rothman.

Dumont, Raymond A. & Lannon, John M. Business Communications. 1984. text ed. 25.95 (ISBN 0-316-19533-2); tchr's. ed. avail. Little.

Dumont, Rene. Is Cuba Socialist? 160p. 1974. 12.95 (ISBN 0-670-40192-7). Viking.

--Utopia or Else... LC 74-32587. 188p. 1975. 10.00x (ISBN 0-87663-218-5). Universe.

Dumont, Rene & Cohen, Nicholas. The Growth of Hunger: Concerning a New Politics of Agriculture. (Ideas in Progress). 240p. 1980. 15.00 (ISBN 0-7145-2641-X, Dist by Scribner); pap. 7.95 (ISBN 0-7145-2642-8). M Boyars.

Dumont, Rene & Mottin, Marie-France. Strangehold on Africa. 272p. 1984. 27.50x (ISBN 0-389-20466-8, 08027). B&N Imports.

DuMont, Rosemary R. Reform & Reaction: The Big City Public Library in American Life. LC 77-71864. (Contributions in Librarianship & Information Science: No. 21). 1977. lib. bdg. 27.50 (ISBN 0-8371-9540-3, DRR/). Greenwood.

Dumont, T. Q. Personal Magnetism. 15.00x (ISBN 0-685-22069-9). Wehman.

Dumont, Theron. Art & Science of Personal Magnetism. 7.00 (ISBN 0-911662-38-3). Yoga.

--Power of Concentration. 7.00 (ISBN 0-911662-39-1). Yoga.

--Solar Plexus. pap. 1.00 (ISBN 0-911662-40-5). Yoga.

Dumont, Theron Q. Advanced Course in Personal Magnetism. 281p. 1972. Repr. of 1916 ed. 7.00 (ISBN 0-911662-46-4). Yoga.

--The Master Mind: The Key to Mental Power, Development & Efficiency. 276p. 1980. Repr. of 1918 ed. 7.00 (ISBN 0-911662-66-9). Yoga.

--Mental Therapeutics. 235p. 1972. Repr. of 1914 ed. 7.00 (ISBN 0-911662-47-2). Yoga.

Dumont, William & Bryan, Mary. Passports Issued by Governors of Georgia, 1810 to 1820. 112p. 7.00 (ISBN 0-915156-28-8, 28). Natl Genealogical.

Dumont, William H. Colonial Georgia Genealogical Data 1748-1783. 77p. 6.50 (ISBN 0-915156-36-9). Natl Genealogical.

Dumortier, F., et al. Germs of Diffeomorphisms in the Plane. (Lecture Note in Mathematics: Vol. 902). 197p. 1981. pap. 16.00 (ISBN 0-387-11177-8). Springer-Verlag.

Dumoulin, Heinrich. Christianity Meets Buddhism. Maraldo, John C., tr. from Ger. LC 73-82783. (Religious Encounter: West Meets East Ser., Vol. 1). 212p. 1974. 19.95 (ISBN 0-87548-121-3). Open Court.

--Zen Enlightenment. LC 78-27310. 1979. pap. 7.95 (ISBN 0-8348-0141-8). Weatherhill.

Dumoulin, J. & Moisi, D. The Historian Between the Ethnologist & the Futurologist. (New Babylon Studies in the Social Sciences: No. 13). 1973. text ed. 18.80x (ISBN 90-2797-230-3). Mouton.

Dumoulin, Jerome & Moisi, Dominique, eds. L' Historian Entre L'ethnologue & le Futurologue: Actes Du Seminaire International Organise Sous les Auspices De L'association Internationale Pour la Liberte De la Culture, la Fondation Giovanni Agnelli & la Fondation Giongio Cini, Venice, 2-8 Avril 1971. Actes Du Seminaire International Organise Sous les Auspices De L'association Internationale Pour la Liberte De la Culture, la Fondation Giovanni Agnelli & la Fondation Giorgio Cini, Venice, 2-8 Avril 1971. (Le Savoir Historique Ser.: No. 4). 1973. pap. 12.80x (ISBN 90-2797-157-9). Mouton.

Du Moulin, Yvonne. Creative Watercolor Techniques. 80p. 1982. pap. 8.95 (ISBN 0-442-21876-1). Van Nos Reinhold.

Dumpe, Bert. Using the Wang for Business: The Technician's Perspective. 346p. 1984. pap. text ed. 28.70 scp (ISBN 0-06-041801-X, HarpC); instr's. manual avail. (ISBN 0-06-361782-X). Har-Row.

Dumpert, Klaus. The Social Biology of Ants. Johnson, K. C., tr. LC 79-25013. (Pitman International Series in Bio Science). 298p. 1981. text ed. 59.95 (ISBN 0-273-08479-8). Pitman Pub MA.

Dumpleton, John. Law & Order: The Story of the Police. (Junior Ref. Ser). (Illus.). (gr. 3-7). 1983. Repr. of 1963 ed. 8.95 (ISBN 0-7136-1079-4). Dufour.

--Make Your Own Booklet. LC 79-3815. 1980. pap. 2.95 (ISBN 0-8008-5058-0, Pentalic). Taplinger.

Dumpleton, John L. Handwriting. pap. 3.50 (ISBN 0-8008-3809-2, Pentalic). Taplinger.

Dumur, Guy. Histoire des Spectacles. (Historique Ser.). 2040p. 48.95 (ISBN 0-686-56460-X). French & Eur.

--Nicolas De Stael. (Q. L. P. Ser.). (Illus.). 1976. 9.95 (ISBN 0-517-52611-5). Crown.

Dumville, David, jt. auth. see Grabowski, Kathryn.

Dumville, David, ed. The Historia Brittonum: The Vatican Recension, Vol. 3. 122p. 1985. 33.75 (ISBN 0-85991-203-5, Pub. by Boydell & Brewer). Longwood Pub Group.

Dumville, David & Lapidge, Michael, eds. The Anglo-Saxon Chronicle-A Collaborative Edition: The Annals of St. Noets with Vita Prima Sancti Neoti, No. 17. (Anglo-Saxon Chronicle Ser.: No. 17). 160p. 1985. 29.50 (ISBN 0-85991-117-9, Pub. by Boydell & Brewer). Longwood Pub Group.

--The Anglo-Saxon Chronicle Seventeen: The Annals of St. Neots. 108p. 1983. text ed. 30.00x (ISBN 0-85991-117-9, BAB-04769, Pub. by Boydell & Brewer). Biblio Dist.

--Gildas: New Approaches. (Studies in Celtic History: No. 5). 256p. 1985. 37.50 (ISBN 0-85115-403-4, Pub. by Boydell & Brewer). Longwood Pub Group.

Dumville, David, ed. see Hughes, Kathleen.

Dun & Bradstreet. Dun's Employment Opportunities Directory, 1983-1984: The Career Guide. 4256p. 1983. 295.00 (ISBN 0-318-00213-2). Dun.

Dun, John & Higonnet, Rene. The Banking Institutions, Bullion Reserves, & Non Legal Tender Note Circulation of the United Kingdom Statistically Investigated. Bd. with Bank Deposits in the United Kingdom, 1870-1914. LC 82-48219. (Gold, Money, Inflation & Deflation Ser.). 227p. 1982. lib. bdg. 22.00 (ISBN 0-8240-5229-3). Garland Pub.

Dun, Smith. Memoirs of the Four-Foot Colonel, Data Paper No. 113. 125p. 1980. 6.00 (ISBN 0-87727-113-5). Cornell SE Asia.

Duna, Bill & Duna, Lois. Let's Play--Right Away with Play-Along Tape, Bk. 1. (Illus.). 32p. (Orig.). (gr. k up). 1981. pap. 12.95 (ISBN 0-942928-00-8). Duna Studios.

--Let's Play--Right Away with Play-Along Tape, Bk. 2. (Let's Play--Right Away Ser.). (Illus.). 30p. (Orig.). (gr. k-9). 1981. pap. 12.95 (ISBN 0-942928-01-6). Duna Studios.

--Let's Play & Play & Play... Practice & Assignment Book. (Let's Play-Right Away Ser.). (Illus.). 56p. (ps up). 1983. pap. 6.95 (ISBN 0-942928-02-4). Duna Studios.

Duna, Lois, jt. auth. see Duna, Bill.

Duna, Lois R. Professional Musician's Business Kit. 180p. 1984. 3-ring binder 29.95 (ISBN 0-942928-03-2). Duna Studios.

Dunae, Patrick. Gentlemen Emigrants: From the British Public Schools to the Canadian Frontier. LC 82-106614. (Illus.). 286p. 1981. 16.95x (ISBN 0-295-95862-6, Pub. by Douglas & McIntyre Canada). U of Wash Pr.

Dunaev, M. Smolensk: A Guide. 102p. 1982. 5.95 (ISBN 0-8285-2320-7, Pub. by Progress Pubs USSR). Imported Pubns.

Dunahoo, Kermit L., jt. auth. see Berger, Peter W.

Dunaif-Hattis, Janet. Doubling the Brain: On the Evolution of Brain Lateralization & Its Implications for Language. LC 83-48765. (American University Studies XI (Anthropology & Sociology): Vol. 3). (Illus.). 215p. (Orig.). text ed. 27.00 (ISBN 0-8204-0056-4). P Lang Pubs.

Dunakey, David D. Iowa Legal Forms-Residential Real Estate. LC 83-135870. 1982. looseleaf 27.50 (ISBN 0-86678-105-6). Butterworth MN.

Dunand-Henry, A. Doctrines et la Politique Economiques Du Comte De Cavour. LC 78-146353. (Research & Source Works Ser.: No. 74). 1971. Repr. of 1902 ed. lib. bdg. 21.00 (ISBN 0-8337-0956-9). B Franklin.

Dunant, Peter. Exterminating Angels. 194p. 1984. 14.95 (ISBN 0-233-97590-X, Pub. by A Deutsch England). David & Charles.

Dunar, Andrew J. The Truman Scandals & the Politics of Morality. LC 84-2205. 1984. 24.00 (ISBN 0-8262-0443-0). U of Mo Pr.

Dunas, Jeff. Mademoiselle, Mademoiselle. LC 82-48005. 112p. 1982. 27.95 (ISBN 0-394-52832-8, GP856). Grove.

--Mademoiselle, Mademoiselle! LC 83-61058. (Illus.). 112p. 1984. pap. 14.95 (ISBN 0-394-62262-6, E962, Ever). Grove.

Dunas, Jeff, photos by. Captured Women. LC 81-83035. (Illus.). 112p. 1981. 24.95 (ISBN 0-394-52341-5, GP-849). Grove.

--Captured Women. (Illus.). 96p. pap. 12.95 (ISBN 0-394-62466-1, Ever). Grove.

--The Voyeur. LC 83-48405. 96p. 1983. slipcased 29.95 (ISBN 0-394-53348-8, GP 887). Grove.

Dunaway, Baxter. The Law of Distressed Real Estate. 1985. 85.00 (ISBN 0-317-20548-X). Boardman.

--The Law of Distressed Real Estate: Foreclosure, Workouts, Procedures. write for info. Amer Bar Assn.

Dunaway, D. K. How Can I Keep from Singing: Pete Seeger. 1981. 14.95 (ISBN 0-07-018150-0). McGraw.

Dunaway, David K. How Can I Keep from Singing: Pete Seeger. (Illus.). 1982. pap. 9.95 (ISBN 0-07-018151-9). McGraw.

Dunaway, David K. & Baum, Willa K. Oral History: An Interdisciplinary Anthology. 436p. 1984. 29.50 (ISBN 0-910050-70-8); pap. 17.95 (ISBN 0-317-17699-4). AASLH Pr.

Dunaway, Diane. Desert Hostage. (Orig.). 1982. pap. 3.95 (ISBN 0-440-11963-4). Dell.

--Desire & Conquer. (Candlelight Ecstasy Ser.: No. 158). (Orig.). 1983. pap. 1.95 (ISBN 0-440-11779-8). Dell.

Dunaway, John. Simon Weil. (World Authors Ser.: No. 723). 1984. lib. bdg. 18.95 (ISBN 0-8057-6570-0, Twayne). G K Hall.

Dunaway, John M. The Metamorphoses of the Self: The Mystic, the Sensualist, & the Artist in the Works of Julien Green. LC 78-88007. (Studies in Romance Languages: No. 19). 128p. 1978. 12.00x (ISBN 0-8131-1364-4). U Pr of Ky.

Dunaway, Kate A., jt. auth. see Knopf, Howard.

Dunaway, Patricia. Beyond the Distant Shadows. 208p. (Orig.). 1984. pap. 4.95 (ISBN 0-87123-446-7). Bethany Hse.

--A Distant Call. (Promise Romance Ser.: No. 16). 192p. 1985. pap. 2.25 (ISBN 0-8407-7367-6). Nelson.

--Irish Lace. (Promise Romance Ser.: No. 1). 192p. (Orig.). 1984. pap. 2.25 (ISBN 0-8407-7350-1). Nelson.

--Lessons in Love. (Promise Romance Ser.: No. 7). 192p. (Orig.). 1984. pap. 2.25 (ISBN 0-8407-7357-9). Nelson.

--No Limits on Love. (Promise Romance Ser.). 192p. 1985. pap. 2.25 (ISBN 0-8407-7378-1). Nelson.

Dunaway, Robert M. How to Plan Your Estate. 192p. pap. 7.95 (ISBN 0-87069-408-1). Wallace-Homestead.

Dunaway, Robert M. & Morrow, Alvin. Farm Lease Guide. (Illus.). 176p. pap. 6.95 (ISBN 0-87069-357-3). Wallace-Homestead.

Dunaway, Vic. Vic Dunaway's Complete Book of Baits, Rigs & Tackle. 5th, rev. ed. (Illus.). 224p. 1984. pap. 5.95 (ISBN 0-936240-01-6). Wickstrom.

Dunaway, Wayland F. History of the James River & Kanawha Company. (Columbia University. Studies in the Social Sciences: No. 236). Repr. of 1922 ed. 21.00 (ISBN 0-404-51236-4). AMS Pr.

--The Scotch-Irish of Colonial Pennsylvania. LC 79-52943. 273p. 1985. Repr. of 1944 ed. 17.50 (ISBN 0-317-31640-0). Genealog Pub.

Du Nay, Andre. The Early History of the Rumanian Language. LC 79-115770. (Edward Sapir Monograph Series in Language, Culture, & Cognition: No. 3). (Illus.). xii, 275p. (Orig.). 1977. pap. 7.00x (ISBN 0-933104-03-0). Jupiter Pr.

Dunayavskaya, Raya. Rosa Luxemburg, Women's Liberation & Marx's Philosophy of Revolution. 260p. 1982. text ed. 20.45x (ISBN 0-391-02569-4, Pub. by Harvester England); pap. text ed. 11.45x (ISBN 0-391-02793-X). Humanities.

Dunayevskaya, Raya. Marxism & Freedom: From 1776 Until Today. 378p. 1982. pap. text ed. 11.45x (ISBN 0-391-02624-0, Harvester England). Humanities.

--Marx's Capital & Today's Global Crisis. 108p. (Orig.). 1978. pap. 2.00x (ISBN 0-686-32889-2). News & Letters MN.

--Nationalism, Communism, Marxist-Humanism & the Afro-Asian Revolutions. 3rd ed. 48p. 1984. pap. 1.25 (ISBN 0-914441-06-X). News & Letters.

--New Essays: Post-Mao China, Dialectics of Liberation, Trotsky as Theoretician. (Illus.). 50p. (Orig.). 1977. pap. 2.00x (ISBN 0-686-32890-6). News & Letters MN.

--Philosophy & Revolution: From Hegel to Sartre & from Marx to Mao. 372p. 1982. pap. text ed. 11.45x (ISBN 0-391-02648-8, Harvester England). Humanities.

--Russia As State-Capitalist Society: The Original Historical Analysis. 27p. (Orig.). 1973. pap. 1.00x (ISBN 0-686-32892-2). News & Letters MN.

--State Capitalism & Marx's Humanism, or Philosophy & Revolution: China, Russia, U. S. A. 62p. (Orig.). 1967. pap. 0.50x (ISBN 0-686-32894-9). News & Letters MN.

--Twenty-Five Years of Marxist-Humanism in the U. S. A History of Worldwide Revolutionary Developments. (Illus.). 30p. (Orig.). 1980. pap. 1.50x (ISBN 0-686-33365-9). News & Letters.

Dunayevskaya, Raya, jt. auth. see Phillips, Andy.

Dunayevskaya, Raya, jt. auth. see Savio, Mario.

Dunbabin, J. P. Rural Discontent in 19th Century Britain. LC 73-94070. 320p. 1975. text ed. 35.00x (ISBN 0-8419-0146-5). Holmes & Meier.

Dunbabin, Jean. France in the Making, Eight Hundred Forty-Three to Eleven Hundred Eighty. (Illus.). 520p. 1985. 37.50x (ISBN 0-19-873030-6); pap. 17.95x (ISBN 0-19-873031-4). Oxford U Pr.

Dunbabin, Katherine M. The Mosaics of Roman North Africa: Studies in Iconography & Patronage. (Monographs on Classical Archaeology). (Illus.). 1978. 89.00x (ISBN 0-19-813217-4). Oxford U Pr.

Dunbabin, T. J. The Greeks & Their Eastern Neighbours. (Illus.). 96p. 1979. 15.00 (ISBN 0-89005-317-0). Ares.

--The Western Greeks. 504p. 1979. 40.00 (ISBN 0-89005-300-6). Ares.

Dunbabin, Thomas J. The Greeks & Their Eastern Neighbours: Studies in the Relations Between Greece & the Countries of the Near East in the Eighth & Seventh Centuries B. C. Boardman, John, ed. LC 78-24477. (Illus.). 1979. Repr. of 1957 ed. lib. bdg. 22.50x (ISBN 0-313-20791-7, DUGR). Greenwood.

Dunbar, Alice. The Goodness of St. Rocque. facsimile ed. LC 77-161258. (Black Heritage Library Collection). Repr. of 1899 ed. 19.25 (ISBN 0-8369-8817-5). Ayer Co Pubs.

Dunbar, Alice M., ed. Masterpieces of Negro Eloquence: The Best Speeches Delivered by the Negro from the Days of Slavery to the Present Day. 1970. Repr. of 1914 ed. 28.00 (ISBN 0-384-13275-8). Johnson Repr.

Dunbar, Anthony P. Against the Grain: Southern Radicals & Prophets, 1929-1959. LC 81-1782. (Illus.). ix, 306p. 1981. 17.95x (ISBN 0-8139-0892-2). U Pr of Va.

Dunbar, Bonnie J., ed. Advances in Ceramics: Material Processing in Space, Vol. 5. (Advances in Ceramics Ser.). (Illus.). text ed. 45.00 (ISBN 0-916094-51-0). Am Ceramic.

Dunbar, Carl O. & Waage, Karl M. Historical Geology. 3rd ed. LC 72-89681. (Illus.). 556p. 1969. text ed. 39.95x (ISBN 0-471-22507-X). Wiley.

Dunbar, Charles F. Chapters on the Theory & History of Banking. Bruchey, Stuart, ed. LC 80-1145. (The Rise of Commercial Banking Ser.). 1981. Repr. of 1891 ed. lib. bdg. 18.00x (ISBN 0-405-13648-X). Ayer Co Pubs.

--Economic Essays. 16.75 (ISBN 0-8369-6971-5, 7852). Ayer Co Pubs.

Dunbar, Charles F., ed. Laws of the United States Relating to Currency, Finance & Banking from 1789 to 1891. LC 68-28627. 309p. Repr. of 1893 ed. lib. bdg. 20.25x (ISBN 0-8371-4585-6, DULU). Greenwood.

Dunbar, Charles F., compiled by. Laws of the United States Relating to Currency Finance & Banking 1789-1896. rev. ed. LC 69-16856. 1897. 35.00x (ISBN 0-678-00476-5). Kelley.

Dunbar, Clement. A Bibliography of Shelley Studies: 1823-1950. LC 75-24093. (Reference Library of the Humanities: Vol. 32). 363p. 1976. lib. bdg. 43.00 (ISBN 0-8240-9980-X). Garland Pub.

Dunbar, Donald R. How to Walk Through Walls (& Stop Fighting with the Kids) 216p. 1982. 12.95 (ISBN 0-89182-051-5). Charles River Bks.

Dunbar, Elton. Primer for Clients (Humor) 1972. pap. 0.50 (ISBN 0-911214-47-X). Rational Isl.

Dunbar, Florence W., jt. auth. see Kerr, Willard A.

Dunbar, Gary S. Elisee Reclus: Historian of Nature. (Illus.). 193p. 1978. 17.50 (ISBN 0-208-01746-1, Archon). Shoe String.

--The History of Modern Geography: An Annotated Bibliography of Selected Works. LC 83-48277. (Reference Library of the Humanities, Bibliographies of the History of Science & Technology Ser.). 398p. 1985. lib. bdg. 53.50 (ISBN 0-8240-9066-7). Garland Pub.

Dunbar, Gary S., intro. by see Martonne, E., et al.

Dunbar, George. History of India from Earliest Times to 1939, 2 vols. 1949. Set. 64.50x (ISBN 0-391-01989-9). Humanities.

--A History of India: From the Earliest Times to the Present Day. (Illus.). 632p. 1981. Repr. of 1936 ed. text ed. 65.00x (ISBN 0-391-02433-7, Pub. by Concept India). Humanities.

Dunbar, Georgia, jt. auth. see Barzun, Jacques.

Dunbar, Georgia, jt. auth. see Rorabacher, Louise.

Dunbar, Georgia, jt. auth. see Rorabacher, Louise E.

Dunbar, H. H. Dramatic Career of Arthur Murphy. (MLA RFS Ser.). 1946. 29.00 (ISBN 0-527-25600-5). Kraus Repr.

Dunbar, Helen F. Emotions & Bodily Changes: A Survey of Literature on Psychosomatic Interrelationships, 1910-1953. 4th ed. LC 75-16699. (Classics in Psychiatry Ser.). 1976. Repr. of 1954 ed. 90.50x (ISBN 0-405-07426-3). Ayer Co Pubs.

--Psychosomatic Diagnosis. (Psychology Ser). 1968. Repr. of 1948 ed. 48.00 (ISBN 0-384-13285-5). Johnson Repr.

Dunbar, Henry. Complete Concordance to the Comedies & Fragments of Aristophanes. 1968. Repr. of 1883 ed. 93.75x (ISBN 3-4870-5017-X). Adlers Foreign Bks.

--Complete Concordance to the Odyssey of Homer. 408p. Repr. of 1880 ed. 73.50x (ISBN 3-4870-4030-1). Adlers Foreign Bks.

Dunbar, Howard H. The Dramatic Career of Arthur Murphy. 339p. 1981. Repr. of 1946 ed. lib. bdg. 40.00 (ISBN 0-89984-159-7). Century Bookbindery.

Dunbar, Ian. Dog Behavior. (Illus.). 223p. 1979. 12.95 (ISBN 0-87666-671-3, H-1016). TFH Pubns.
Dunbar, J. Telfar. The Costume of Scotland. (Illus.). 216p. 1981. 42.00 (ISBN 0-7134-2534-2, Pub. by Batsford England). David & Charles.
Dunbar, James, jt. auth. see Dunbar, Joyce.
Dunbar, Janet. The Early Victorian Woman: Some Aspects of Her Life, 1837-1857. LC 78-59019. (Illus.). 1979. Repr. of 1953 ed. 23.00 (ISBN 0-88355-693-6). Hyperion Conn.
Dunbar, John & Allis, Samuel. The Dunbar-Allis Letters on the Pawnee. Wedel, Waldo R., ed. LC 83-47638. (The North American Indian Ser.). 214p. 1985. lib. bdg. 30.00 (ISBN 0-8240-5889-5). Garland Pub.
Dunbar, John B., jt. ed. see Tarazi, Robert C.
Dunbar, John R. The Combat at the Barrier. (Illus.). 1967. 12.50 (ISBN 0-910330-13-1). Grant Dahlstrom.
Dunbar, John T. Highland Costume. 62p. 1981. 10.00x (ISBN 0-85158-122-6, Pub. by Blackwood & Sons England). State Mutual Bk.
--The Life & Photographs of M. E. M. Donaldson. 80p. 1981. 20.00x (ISBN 0-85158-133-1, Pub. by Blackwood & Sons England). State Mutual Bk.
Dunbar, John T. & Pottinger, Don. The Official Tartan Map. (Illus.). 1976. pap. 3.95 (ISBN 0-517-52652-2). Crown.
Dunbar, Joyce & Dunbar, James. Jugg. 1980. 9.90 (ISBN 0-85967-596-3). Scolar.
Dunbar, Leslie W., ed. Minority Report: What's Happened to Blacks, Hispanics, American Indians, & Other American Minorities in the 1980's. LC 84-42670. 256p. 1984. pap. 8.95 (ISBN 0-394-72513-1). Pantheon.
Dunbar, Louise B. A Study of "Monarchical" Tendencies in the United States from 1776 to 1801. LC 23-4276. (Illinois Studies in the Social Sciences: Vol. 10). 1970. Repr. of 1923 ed. 12.00 (ISBN 0-384-13295-2). Johnson Repr.
Dunbar, M. J. Environment & Good Sense. (Environmental Damage & Control in Canada Ser.: Vol. 1). 1971. pap. 3.95 (ISBN 0-7735-0126-6). McGill-Queens U Pr.
Dunbar, M. J., ed. Marine Production Mechanisms. LC 77-78675. (International Biological Programme Ser: No. 20). (Illus.). 1979. 77.50 (ISBN 0-521-21937-X). Cambridge U Pr.
Dunbar, Margaret. Joystick. (Illus.). 128p. (Orig.). 1986. pap. 8.95 (ISBN 0-937966-17-7). Dog Ear.
Dunbar, Margaret, jt. auth. see Porter, Bern.
Dunbar, Maria. Miracle Survival under Communism & Hitlerism. Date not set. 6.75 (ISBN 0-8062-2510-6). Carlton.
Dunbar, Maury. Books & Collectors. 208p. 1980. text ed. 11.95 (ISBN 0-686-27441-5). Book Nest.
Dunbar, Michael. Antique Woodworking Tools: A Guide to the Purchase, Restoration & Use of Old Tools for Today's Shop. (Illus.). 1977. 12.50 (ISBN 0-8038-5821-3). Hastings.
--Make a Windsor Chair with Michael Dunbar. LC 83-50681. (Illus.). 176p. 1984. pap. 13.95 (ISBN 0-918804-21-3, Dist. by W W Norton). Taunton.
Dunbar, Newell. Phillip Brooks: The Man, the Preacher, & the Author. 1978. Repr. of 1893 ed. lib. bdg. 35.00 (ISBN 0-8492-0668-5). R West.
Dunbar, P. L. Life & Works: Containing His Complete Poetical Works, His Best Short Stories, Numerous Anecdotes & a Complete Biography. LC 7-13414. Repr. of 1911 ed. 37.00 (ISBN 0-527-25620-X). Kraus Repr.
Dunbar, Pamela. William Blake's Illustrations to the Poetry of Milton. (Illus.). 1980. 59.00x (ISBN 0-19-817345-8). Oxford U Pr.
Dunbar, Patsy, jt. auth. see Dunbar, R.
Dunbar, Paul L. Candle-Lightin' Time. LC 76-164797. (Illus.). Repr. of 1901 ed. 12.50 (ISBN 0-404-00030-4). AMS Pr.
--Collected Works. 600.00 (ISBN 0-87968-888-2). Gordon Pr.
--The Complete Poems of Paul Laurence Dunbar. LC 80-16651. 1980. pap. 4.95 (ISBN 0-396-07895-8). Dodd.
--Fanatics. facs. ed. LC 70-81110. (Black Heritage Library Collection Ser). 1901. 15.00 (ISBN 0-8369-8555-9). Ayer Co Pubs.
--Fanatics. LC 70-84687. Repr. of 1901 ed. 22.50x (ISBN 0-8371-1264-8, DUT&, Pub. by Negro U Pr). Greenwood.
--Fanatics. pap. 2.95 (ISBN 0-685-16783-6, N262P). Mnemosyne.
--Folks from Dixie. LC 72-101281. (Short Story Index Reprint Ser.). 1898. 18.00 (ISBN 0-8369-3218-8). Ayer Co Pubs.
--Folks from Dixie. facs. ed. LC 73-81111. (Black Heritage Library Collection Ser). (Illus.). 1922. 13.75 (ISBN 0-8369-8699-7). Ayer Co Pubs.
--Folks from Dixie. LC 72-75531. (Illus.). Repr. of 1898 ed. cancelled (ISBN 0-8371-1098-X, Pub. by Negro U Pr). Greenwood.
--Folks from Dixie. LC 78-78572. (Illus.). 263p. lib. bdg. 9.00 (ISBN 0-8398-0371-0). Irvington.
--Heart of Happy Hollow. LC 77-110597. (Short Story Index Reprint Ser.). 1904. 19.00 (ISBN 0-8369-3318-4). Ayer Co Pubs.
--Heart of Happy Hollow. LC 79-88407. Repr. of 1904 ed. 22.50x (ISBN 0-8371-1811-5, DUH&, Pub. by Negro U Pr). Greenwood.
--Howdy, Honey, Howdy. LC 73-164799. (Illus.). Repr. of 1905 ed. 12.50 (ISBN 0-404-00035-5). AMS Pr.
--Howdy Honey Howdy. facs. ed. LC 79-78993. (Black Heritage Library Collection Ser). (Illus.). 1905. 12.00 (ISBN 0-8369-8556-7). Ayer Co Pubs.
--In Old Plantation Days. LC 70-88429. Repr. of 1903 ed. cancelled (ISBN 0-8371-1886-7, DUP&, Pub. by Negro U Pr). Greenwood.
--Joggin'erlong. facs. ed. LC 78-83921. (Black Heritage Library Collection Ser). (Illus.). 1906. 12.00 (ISBN 0-8369-8557-5). Ayer Co Pubs.
--Li'l Gal. LC 73-164800. (Illus.). Repr. of 1904 ed. 12.50 (ISBN 0-404-00034-7). AMS Pr.
--Li'l'gal. facs. ed. LC 75-78992. (Black Heritage Library Collection Ser). (Illus.). 1904. 12.00 (ISBN 0-8369-8558-3). Ayer Co Pubs.
--Love of Landry. facs. ed. LC 70-81113. (Black Heritage Library Collection Ser). 1900. 14.25 (ISBN 0-8369-8559-1). Ayer Co Pubs.
--Love of Landry. LC 72-88408. Repr. of 1900 ed. 18.75x (ISBN 0-8371-1810-7, DUL&, Pub. by Negro U Pr). Greenwood.
--The Love of Landry. LC 76-104442. 200p. Repr. of 1900 ed. lib. bdg. 12.25 (ISBN 0-8398-0372-9). Irvington.
--Love of Landry. pap. 2.95 (ISBN 0-685-16790-9, N265P). Mnemosyne.
--Love of Landry. 200p. 1984. pap. 1.95 (ISBN 0-8290-1564-7). Irvington.
--Lyrics of a Lowly Life. LC 69-18587. (American Negro: His History & Literature Ser.: No. 2). 1969. Repr. of 1899 ed. 9.25 (ISBN 0-405-01858-4). Ayer Co Pubs.
--Lyrics of a Lowly Life. LC 71-78573. 239p. lib. bdg. 8.50 (ISBN 0-8398-0373-7). Irvington.
--Lyrics of Lonely Life. 224p. 1984. pap. 5.95 (ISBN 0-8065-0922-8). Citadel Pr.
--Lyrics of Lowly Life. facs. ed. LC 70-78996. (Black Heritage Library Collection Ser). 1896. 9.25 (ISBN 0-405-01858-4). Ayer Co Pubs.
--Lyrics of Sunshine & Shadow. LC 77-164801. Repr. of 1905 ed. 12.50 (ISBN 0-404-00038-X). AMS Pr.
--Lyrics of Sunshine & Shadow. facs. ed. LC 70-83919. (Black Heritage Library Collection Ser). 1905. 10.75 (ISBN 0-8369-8561-3). Ayer Co Pubs.
--Lyrics of the Hearthside. LC 70-164802. Repr. of 1899 ed. 10.50 (ISBN 0-404-00037-1). AMS Pr.
--Lyrics of the Hearthside. facs. ed. LC 74-83920. (Black Heritage Library Collection Ser). 1899. 14.25 (ISBN 0-8369-8562-1). Ayer Co Pubs.
--Majors & Minors: Poems. facs. ed. LC 76-83918. (Black Heritage Library Collection Ser.). 1896. 10.00 (ISBN 0-8369-8563-X). Ayer Co Pubs.
--Poems of Cabin & Field. LC 74-164803. (Illus.). Repr. of 1899 ed. 12.50 (ISBN 0-404-00041-X). AMS Pr.
--Poems of Cabin & Field. facs. ed. LC 72-83917. (Black Heritage Library Collection Ser). (Illus.). 1899. 12.00 (ISBN 0-8369-8564-8). Ayer Co Pubs.
--Speakin' O' Christmas & Other Christmas & Special Poems. LC 73-18574. (Illus.). Repr. of 1914 ed. 12.50 (ISBN 0-404-11385-0). AMS Pr.
--Sport of the Gods. LC 69-18588. (American Negro: His History & Literature Ser., No. 2). 1969. Repr. of 1902 ed. 21.00 (ISBN 0-405-01859-2). Ayer Co Pubs.
--Sport of the Gods. pap. 2.95 (ISBN 0-685-16798-4, N266P). Mnemosyne.
--Strength of Gideon & Other Stories. LC 69-18589. (American Negro: His History & Literature Ser., No. 2). 1969. Repr. of 1899 ed. 17.00 (ISBN 0-405-01860-6). Ayer Co Pubs.
--Uncalled. LC 78-164804. Repr. of 1898 ed. 10.00 (ISBN 0-404-00042-8). AMS Pr.
--Uncalled. facs. ed. LC 71-81116. (Black Heritage Library Collection Ser). 1901. 17.00 (ISBN 0-8369-8567-2). Ayer Co Pubs.
--The Uncalled. LC 70-104443. Repr. of 1898 ed. lib. bdg. 9.50 (ISBN 0-8398-0374-5). Irvington.
--Uncalled. pap. 2.95 (ISBN 0-685-16799-2, N268P). Mnemosyne.
--Uncalled: A Novel. LC 70-100262. Repr. of 1898 ed. 19.75x (ISBN 0-8371-2854-4, DUU&). Greenwood.
--When Malindy Sings. LC 71-164805. (Illus.). Repr. of 1903 ed. 12.50 (ISBN 0-404-00039-8). AMS Pr.
--When Malindy Sings. facs. ed. LC 79-83916. (Black Heritage Library Collection Ser.). (Illus.). 1903. 14.25 (ISBN 0-8369-8568-0). Ayer Co Pubs.
Dunbar, R. & Dunbar, Patsy. Social Dynamics of Gelada Baboons. (Contributions to Primatology: Vol. 6). (Illus.). 176p. 1975. 38.00 (ISBN 3-8055-2137-5). S Karger.
Dunbar, R. I. Reproductive Decisions: An Economic Analysis of Gelada Baboon Social Strategies. LC 84-42584. (Monographs in Behavior & Ecology). (Illus.). 256p. 1984. text ed. 40.00x (ISBN 0-691-08360-6); pap. text ed. 14.50x (ISBN 0-691-08361-4). Princeton U Pr.
Dunbar, Robert E. A Doctor Discusses a Man's Sexual Health. (Illus.). 1979. pap. 2.99 (ISBN 0-685-64313-1). Budlong.
--A Doctor Discusses Learning to Cope with Arthritis Rheumatism & Gout. (Illus., Orig.). 1973. pap. 2.99 (ISBN 0-685-35675-2). Budlong.
--Heart & Circulatory System. (Projects for Young Scientists Ser.). (Illus.). 128p. (YA) 1984. lib. bdg. 9.90 (ISBN 0-531-04766-0). Watts.
--Heredity. (First Bks.). (Illus.). (gr. 4 up). 1978. PLB 8.90 s&l (ISBN 0-531-01408-8). Watts.
--Mental Retardation. (First Bks). (Illus.). (gr. 4-6). 1978. PLB 8.90 (ISBN 0-531-01491-6). Watts.
Dunbar, Robert G. Forging New Rights in Western Waters. LC 82-13421. (Illus.). xvi, 278p. 1983. 21.50x (ISBN 0-8032-1663-7). U of Nebr Pr.
Dunbar, Ronald W. & Hieke, Adolf E. Building Fluency in English: Conversation Management. (Illus.). 250p. 1985. pap. text ed. 9.95 (ISBN 0-13-086117-0). P-H.
Dunbar, Ronald W., jt. auth. see Hieke, Adolf E.
Dunbar, Rowland, compiled by. Guide to the General Correspondence of Louisiana: 1678-1763. 1975. 15.00 (ISBN 0-686-20871-4). Polyanthos.
Dunbar, Seymour. History of Travel in America, 4 Vols. LC 68-23283. (Illus.). 1968. Repr. of 1915 ed. Set. lib. bdg. 81.75x (ISBN 0-8371-0063-1, DUHT). Greenwood.
Dunbar, William. Dunbar: Being a Selection from the Poems of an Old Maker, Adapted for Modern Readers by Hugh Haliburton. 1895. 25.00 (ISBN 0-8274-2207-5). R West.
--The Poems, 3 vols. Small, John, ed. Repr. of 1893 ed. Set. 102.00x (ISBN 3-4870-4650-4). Adlers Foreign Bks.
--Poems. 1979. Repr. of 1890 ed. lib. bdg. 50.00 (ISBN 0-8495-1110-0). Arden Lib.
--Poems of William Dunbar, 3 vols. in 2. Small, John, ed. LC 71-144463. Repr. of 1893 ed. Set. 67.50 (ISBN 0-404-08554-7). AMS Pr.
--The Poems of William Dunbar. Kinsley, James, ed. (Oxford English Texts Ser.). 1979. 79.00x (ISBN 0-19-811888-0). Oxford U Pr.
--The Poems of William Dunbar. LC 70-161970. Repr. of 1950 ed. 29.00x (ISBN 0-403-01321-6). Scholarly.
--Poems of William Dunbar: From the Obsolete. Mackean, William, ed. 1890. 35.00 (ISBN 0-8274-3158-9). R West.
--William Dunbar Poems. LC 74-161966. 159p. 1958. Repr. 29.00x (ISBN 0-403-01339-9). Scholarly.
Dunbar, Willis F. Michigan: A History of the Wolverine State. rev. ed. May, George S., rev. by. (Illus.). 24.95 (ISBN 0-8028-7043-0). Eerdmans.
Dunbaugh, Edwin L. The Era of the Joy Line: A Saga of Steamboating on Long Island Sound. LC 81-6293. (Contributions in Economics & Economic History Ser.: No. 43). (Illus.). xxv, 363p. 1982. lib. bdg. 29.95 (ISBN 0-313-22888-4, DEJ/). Greenwood.
Duncan. Brimstone. pap. 2.95 (ISBN 0-317-31804-7). Tor Bks.
--Fifth Generation Challenge. Date not set. write for info. (ISBN 0-444-87661-8). Elsevier.
--Quality Control & Industrial Statistics. 1012p. 27.50 (ISBN 0-318-13233-8, P 48). Am Soc QC.
Duncan & Hollander. Retailing. 3rd ed. (Plain Ser.). 1979. 9.95 (ISBN 0-256-02245-3). Dow Jones-Irwin.
Duncan, jt. ed. see MacDougall.
Duncan, A. B. Rydberg Series in Atoms & Molecules. (Physical Chemistry Ser, Vol. 23). 1971. 45.00 (ISBN 0-12-223950-4). Acad Pr.
Duncan, A. M., tr. see Kepler, Johannes.
Duncan, A. S., et al, eds. Dictionary of Medical Ethics. 496p. 1981. 24.50x (ISBN 0-8245-0038-5). Crossroad NY.
Duncan, Acheson J. Quality Control & Industrial Statistics. 4th ed. 1974. 34.50x (ISBN 0-256-01558-9). Irwin.
Duncan, Aileen. Teaching Mathematics to Slow Learners. 160p. 1981. 35.00x (ISBN 0-7062-3666-1, Pub. by Ward Lock Ed England). State Mutual Bk.
Duncan, Alastair. Art Deco Furniture: The French Designers. LC 84-81003. (Illus.). 192p. 1984. 35.00 (ISBN 0-03-000099-8). HR&W.
--Art Nouveau Furniture. (Illus.). 1982. 10.98 (ISBN 0-517-54786-4, C N Potter Bks). Crown.
Duncan, Alastair & De Bartha, Georges. Glass by Galle. (Illus.). 224p. 1984. 40.00 (ISBN 0-8109-0986-3). Abrams.
Duncan, Alistair. The Noble Heritage: Jerusalem & Christianity - a Portrait of the Church of the Resurrection. 1974. 12.95x (ISBN 0-86685-011-2). Intl Bk Ctr.
Duncan, Archibald A., ed. see Dickinson, W. Croft.
Duncan, Barbara. The Single Mother's Survival Manual. LC 83-62294. 180p. 1984. pap. 12.95 (ISBN 0-88247-707-2). R & E Pubs.
Duncan, Barbara & Bayon, Damian. Recent Latin American Drawings 1969-1976: Lines of Vision. LC 77-71639. (Illus.). 80p. (Orig.). 1977. pap. 6.00 (ISBN 0-88397-000-7, Pub. by Intl Exhibit Foun). C E Tuttle.
Duncan, Barbara, intro. by. Latin American Paintings & Drawings from the Collection of John & Barbara Duncan. 1970. pap. 2.00 (ISBN 0-913456-10-1, Pub. by Ctr Inter-Am Rel). Interbk Inc.
Duncan, Ben. Soothing Food: Gourmet Cooking for Ulcers & Difficult Stomachs. 180p. 1983. pap. 7.95 (ISBN 0-88254-798-4). Hippocrene Bks.
Duncan, Beverly & Duncan, Otis D. Sex Typing & Social Roles: A Research Report. (Quantitative Studies in Social Relations Ser.). 1978. 34.50 (ISBN 0-12-223850-8). Acad Pr.
Duncan, Beverly, jt. auth. see Duncan, Otis D.
Duncan, C. H., et al. College Keyboarding-Typewriting. 11th ed. 1985. 16.95 (ISBN 0-538-20750-7, T75). SW Pub.
Duncan, C. J. & Hopkins, C. R., eds. Secretory Mechanisms. LC 79-10003. (Society for Experimental Biology Symposium: No. 33). (Illus.). 1980. 82.50 (ISBN 0-521-22684-8). Cambridge U Pr.
Duncan, C. Tovey. Review & Essays in English Literature. 187p. 1980. Repr. of 1897 ed. lib. bdg. 30.00 (ISBN 0-8492-8427-9). R West.
Duncan, Charles. The Art of Classical Guitar Playing. (The Art of Ser.). (Illus.). 132p. (Orig.). 1980. pap. text ed. 19.95 (ISBN 0-87487-079-8). Birch Tree Gr.
Duncan, Christopher, tr. see Guglielmi, Joseph.
Duncan, Colin, et al. Low Pay: Its Causes & the Post-War Trade Union Response. (Social Policy Research Monographs). 159p. 1981. 52.95x (ISBN 0-471-10052-8, Pub. by Res Stud Pr). Wiley.
Duncan, Cora, et al. Guide for Board Members of Voluntary Family Service Agencies. 1975. pap. 4.50 (ISBN 0-87304-136-4). Family Serv.
Duncan, Darlene, jt. auth. see Duncan, T. Roger.
Duncan, David. The Life & Letters of Herbert Spencer. 1908. Repr. 65.00 (ISBN 0-8274-2869-3). R West.
--Pedaling the Ends of the Earth. 1985. 17.95 (ISBN 0-671-49289-6). S&S.
--The World of Allah. 35.00x (ISBN 0-86685-370-7). Intl Bk Ctr.
Duncan, David & Gold, Robert. Drugs & the Whole Person. LC 81-15984. 272p. 1982. pap. 18.45 (ISBN 0-471-04120-3). Wiley.
Duncan, David, jt. auth. see Litwiller, Bonnie.
Duncan, David D. The World of Allah. 1982. 40.00 (ISBN 0-395-32504-8). HM.
Duncan, David D. & Forss, George. New York - New York: Masterworks of a Street Peddler. (Illus.). 1984. 19.95 (ISBN 0-07-018208-6). McGraw.
Duncan, David J. The River Why. LC 82-5508. 320p. (Orig.). 1983. 12.95 (ISBN 0-87156-321-5). Sierra.
--The River Why. 352p. 1984. pap. 6.95 (ISBN 0-553-34192-8). Bantam.
Duncan, Delbert J., et al. Modern Retailing Management. 10th ed. 1983. 26.95x (ISBN 0-256-02532-0). Irwin.
Duncan, Denis. Victorious Living: A Thought & a Prayer a Day at a Time. LC 81-16478. 96p. (Orig.). 1982. pap. 3.95 (ISBN 0-664-24406-8). Westminster.
--The Way of Love: A Thought & a Prayer a Day at a Time. LC 81-15925. 96p. 1982. Westminster.
Duncan, Doris G. & Aviel, S. David. Computers & Remote Computing Services. LC 82-20094. (Illus.). 258p. (Orig.). 1983. lib. bdg. 25.50 (ISBN 0-8191-2881-3); pap. text ed. 13.00 (ISBN 0-8191-2882-1). U Pr of Amer.
Duncan, Edmondstoune. Story of Minstrelsy. LC 69-16802. (Music Story Ser). 1968. Repr. of 1907 ed. 40.00x (ISBN 0-8103-4240-5). Gale.
Duncan, Edmonstoune. Opera Stories of Today & Yesterday. LC 77-75231. 1977. Repr. of 1923 ed. lib. bdg. 15.00 (ISBN 0-89341-083-7). Longwood Pub Group.
Duncan, Edmonstoune, ed. Lyrics from Old Song Books. facsimile ed. LC 77-168780. (Granger Index Reprint Ser.). Repr. of 1927 ed. 28.00 (ISBN 0-8369-6300-8). Ayer Co Pubs.
Duncan, Elmer H. Soren Kierkegaard. Patterson, Bob E., ed. LC 76-2862. (Markers of the Modern Theological Mind Ser.). 1976. 7.95 (ISBN 0-87680-463-6, 80463). Word Bks.
Duncan, Elwin R., ed. Dimensions of World Food Problems. (Illus.). 1977. pap. text ed. 11.95x (ISBN 0-8138-1870-2). Iowa St U Pr.
Duncan, Emma see DuCann, Charlotte, et al.
Duncan, Eric. Fifty-Seven Years in the Comox Valley: 1980 Edition. (Illus.). 1979. pap. 3.75 (ISBN 0-912276-17-7). Comox.
Duncan, Erika. Those Giants: Let Them Rise! 176p. 1985. 14.95 (ISBN 0-8052-4000-4). Schocken.
--Unless Soul Clap Its Hands: Portraits & Passages. 160p. 1984. 17.95 (ISBN 0-8052-3916-2). Schocken.
Duncan, F. Microprocessor Programming & Software Development. 1980. 35.00 (ISBN 0-13-581405-7). P-H.
Duncan, Frances. Finding Home. 192p. 1982. pap. 2.75 (ISBN 0-380-80143-4, 80143-4, Flare). Avon.
Duncan, Frances S. Around the World Alone. (Illus.). 1982. 8.95 (ISBN 0-533-04998-9). Vantage.
Duncan, Francis, jt. auth. see Hewlett, Richard G.
Duncan, Fraser, tr. see Arsac, Jacques.
Duncan, G. Marx & Mill: Two Views of Social Conflict & Social Harmony. 416p. 1973. 44.50 (ISBN 0-521-20257-4); pap. 12.95 (ISBN 0-521-29130-5). Cambridge U Pr.
Duncan, Gary W., jt. auth. see Wells, Charles E.
Duncan, George. Every Day with Jesus. 288p. 1984. pap. 6.95 (ISBN 0-89066-059-X). World Wide Pubs.
Duncan, George, ed. Mechanisms of Cataract Formation the Human Lens. 1981. 48.00 (ISBN 0-12-223750-1). Acad Pr.
Duncan, George B. Preacher among the Prophets. 176p. 1985. pap. 5.95 (ISBN 0-930577-00-0). N Burleson.
Duncan, Glenn. The Timber Beast, Vol. 2. 84p. 1983. pap. 5.95 (ISBN 0-939116-10-3). Creative Comm.

Duncan, Glenn R. The Timber Beast. (Illus.). 117p. 1979. pap. 6.95 (ISBN 0-939116-02-2). Creative Comm.

Duncan, Gordon W., et al, eds. Female Sterilization: Prognosis for Qualified Outpatient Procedures. (Illus.). 1972. 39.00 (ISBN 0-12-224050-2). Acad Pr.

--Fertility Control Methods. 1973. 35.00 (ISBN 0-12-224060-X). Acad Pr.

Duncan, Graeme, ed. Democratic Theory & Practice. LC 82-14653. 296p. 1983. 42.50 (ISBN 0-521-24209-6); pap. 11.95 (ISBN 0-521-28526-7). Cambridge U Pr.

Duncan, Greg J., jt. auth. see Morgan, James N.

Duncan, Greg J. & Morgan, James N., eds. Five Thousand American Families--Patterns of Economic Progress: Analyses of the First Thirteen Years of the Panel Study of Income Dynamics, Vol. 10. (Five Thousand American Families--Patterns of Economic Progress Ser.). (Illus.). 448p. 1983. 25.00x (ISBN 0-87944-286-7); (10-volume set) 160.00 (ISBN 0-87944-289-1). Inst Soc Res.

Duncan, Greg J., jt. ed. see Morgan, James N.

Duncan, Greg J., et al. Years of Poverty, Years of Plenty: The Changing Economic Fortunes of American Workers & Families. LC 83-12923. (Illus.). 184p. 1984. 24.00x (ISBN 0-87944-285-9); pap. 14.00x (ISBN 0-87944-298-0). Inst Soc Res.

--A Validation Study of Economic Survey Date. 136p. (Orig.). 1985. pap. text ed. 18.00x except research reports (ISBN 0-87944-303-0). Inst Soc Res.

Duncan, Hannibal G. Race & Population Problems. LC 77-89031. Repr. of 1929 ed. 19.75x (ISBN 0-8371-1903-0, DUR&). Greenwood.

Duncan, Harry. Doors of Perception. 1983. 150.00x. W T Taylor.

Duncan, Horace G., jt. auth. see Club Managers Association.

Duncan, Hugh D. Communication & Social Order. 486p. 1985. pap. 14.95x (ISBN 0-87855-971-X). Transaction Bks.

Duncan, Ida R. The Complete Book of Needlecraft. LC 61-15020. (Illus.). 1972. pap. 3.95 (ISBN 0-87140-265-3). Liveright.

--Complete Book of Progressive Knitting. rev. ed. LC 70-149630. 1971. pap. 9.95 (ISBN 0-87140-243-2). Liveright.

Duncan, Irma. Duncan Dancer. LC 79-7759. (Dance Ser.). 1980. Repr. of 1966 ed. lib. bdg. 33.00x (ISBN 0-8369-9288-1). Ayer Co Pubs.

Duncan, Isadora. Isadora Speaks. (Illus.). 132p. (Orig.). 1981. 12.95 (ISBN 0-87286-134-1); pap. 5.95 (ISBN 0-87286-133-3). City Lights.

--My Life. (Black & Gold Lib). (Illus.). 1955. pap. 7.95 (ISBN 0-87140-274-2). Liveright.

Duncan, J., jt. auth. see Bonsall, F. F.

Duncan, J. A. & Gumaer, J. Developmental Groups for Children. (Illus.). 440p. 1980. 50.50x (ISBN 0-398-04025-7). C C Thomas.

Duncan, J. L., jt. auth. see Ogbourne, C. P.

Duncan, J. Robert & Prasse, Keith W. Veterinary Laboratory Medicine: Clinical Pathology. 2nd ed. 192p. 1985. text ed. 26.95x (ISBN 0-8138-1915-6). Iowa St U Pr.

Duncan, J. W. Statistical Services in Ten Years' Time. 53.00 (ISBN 0-08-022416-4). Pergamon.

Duncan, James P., Jr. Your Future in Foreign Service Careers. (Careers in Depth Ser.). (gr. 7-12). 1979. PLB 8.97 (ISBN 0-8239-0460-1). Rosen Group.

Duncan, James S., ed. Housing & Identity: Cross-Cultural Perspectives. LC 81-4837. 250p. 1981. text ed. 25.00 (ISBN 0-8419-0701-3). Holmes & Meier.

Duncan, Jane. Brave Janet Reachfar. LC 74-8693. 32p. (ps-3). 1975. 7.95 (ISBN 0-8164-3130-2, Clarion). HM.

--Janet Reachfar & the Kelpie. LC 75-44166. (Illus.). 32p. (ps-3). 1976. 7.50 (Clarion). HM.

Duncan, Jeffrey L. The Power & Form of Emerson's Thought. LC 73-85043. xiv, 105p. 1974. 10.95x (ISBN 0-8139-0510-9). U Pr of Va.

--Writing from Start to Finish: A Rhetoric with Readings. 474p. 1985. pap. text ed. 13.95 (ISBN 0-15-598260-5, HC); instr's manual avail. (ISBN 0-15-598261-3). HarBraceJ.

Duncan, Jim, jt. auth. see Rubin, Louis D., Sr.

Duncan, John. The Elements of Complex Analysis. pap. 80.80 (ISBN 0-317-09164-6, 2016025). Bks Demand UMI.

--Travels in Western Africa in 1845 & 1846, 2 vols. 1968. Repr. of 1847 ed. 85.00x set (ISBN 0-7146-1804-7, F Cass Co). Biblio Dist.

--Travels in Western Africa, in 1845 & 1846, 2 Vols. (Illus.). 1847. 50.00 (ISBN 0-384-13300-2). Johnson Repr.

Duncan, John, jt. auth. see Webb, Brian.

Duncan, John D., Jr. A Crimson Fountain for Harlingscourt. Ashton, Sylvia, ed. LC 75-774. 1976. 13.95 (ISBN 0-87949-038-1). Ashley Bks.

Duncan, Joseph E. Milton's Earthly Paradise: A Historical Study of Eden. LC 71-187167. (Monographs in the Humanities Ser: No. 5). (Illus.). 320p. 1972. 12.50x (ISBN 0-8166-0633-1). U of Minn Pr.

--Revival of Metaphysical Poetry. LC 79-75991. 1969. Repr. of 1959 ed. lib. bdg. 19.00x (ISBN 0-374-92394-9). Octagon.

Duncan, Juanita. Nothing's Wrong with Me! Penoi, Mary, ed. LC 85-60543. 180p. (Orig.). 1985. pap. 4.75 (ISBN 0-942316-09-6). Pueblo Pub Pr.

Duncan, Judith. Birdseed. (Illus.). 1978. pap. 1.00 (ISBN 0-933006-00-4). Birdseed.

--Hold Back the Dawn. (Superromances Ser.). 384p. 1983. pap. 2.95 (ISBN 0-373-70077-6, Pub. by Worldwide). Harlequin Bks.

--Tender Rhapsody. (Superromances Ser.). 384p. 1983. pap. 2.50 (ISBN 0-373-70051-2, Pub. by Worldwide). Harlequin Bks.

Duncan, Judith A., illus. The Sermon on the Mount: From the Translation Prepared at Cambridge in 1611 for King James I. LC 81-211201. (Illus.). 1978. 15.00 (ISBN 0-9606844-0-9). Mac Col MN.

Duncan, Judy & McCance, Allison. Clock Watcher's Cookbook. LC 82-63133. (Illus.). 128p. (Orig.). 1983. pap. 8.95 (ISBN 0-89909-013-3). Yankee Bks.

Duncan, Julian S. Public & Private Operation of Railways in Brazil. (Columbia University. Studies in the Social Sciences: No. 367). Repr. of 1932 ed. 20.00 (ISBN 0-404-51367-0). AMS Pr.

Duncan, Karen, ed. Information Technology & Health Care: The Critical Issues. 200p. 1980. 25.00 (ISBN 0-88283-031-7). AFIPS Pr.

Duncan, Kenn. Red Shoes. (Illus.). 96p. 1984. 17.50 (ISBN 0-87663-444-7). Universe.

Duncan, Kenneth, et al, eds. Land & Labour in Latin America: Essays on the Development of Agrarian Capitalism in the Nineteenth & Twentieth Centuries. LC 76-11076. (Cambridge Latin American Studies: No. 26). pap. 137.30 (ISBN 0-317-20619-2, 2024573). Bks Demand UMI.

Duncan, Leland L., jt. ed. see Phillimore, W. P.

Duncan, Leo. Coke Smoke on Stumpy Row. 1984. 12.95 (ISBN 0-8062-2265-4). Carlton.

Duncan, Leonard C. Greek Roots. (Illus.). 82p. (Orig.). (gr. 6-12). 1982. pap. 10.00 (ISBN 0-941414-01-9). LCD.

--An Introduction to Greek Roots. (Illus.). 67p. (gr. 6-12). 1983. pap. 10.00 (ISBN 0-941414-05-1). LCD.

--Learn to Read with Phonetic & Non-Phonetic Words. Incl. Bk. 1. 97p; Bk. 2. 85p (ISBN 0-941414-12-4); Bk. 3. 99p (ISBN 0-941414-13-2); Bk. 4. 110p (ISBN 0-941414-14-0); Bk. 5. Nursery Rhymes. 109p. (Illus., Orig.). (gr. 1-3). pap. 10.00 (ISBN 0-317-11632-0). LCD.

Duncan, Lois. Chapters: My Growth as a Writer. 276p. (gr. 7 up). 1982. 12.45i (ISBN 0-316-19552-9). Little.

--Daughters of Eve. 272p. (YA) (gr. 7 up). 1980. pap. 2.50 (ISBN 0-440-91864-2, LFL); tchr's. guide by Lou Stanek 0.50. Dell.

--Daughters of Eve. LC 79-14918. (gr. 7 up). 1979. 14.45i (ISBN 0-316-19550-2). Little.

--Down a Dark Hall. 192p. (gr. 7 up). 1974. 12.45i (ISBN 0-316-19547-2). Little.

--Down a Dark Hall. 192p. (YA) (gr. 5-9). 1983. pap. 2.50 (ISBN 0-440-91805-7, LFL). Dell.

--From Spring to Spring: Poems & Photographs. LC 82-11100. (Illus.). 96p. (gr. 3-7). 1982. 10.95 (ISBN 0-664-32695-1). Westminster.

--A Gift of Magic. (gr. 5-7). 1981. pap. 2.25 (ISBN 0-671-43932-4). Archway.

--A Gift of Magic. (Illus.). (gr. 4-6). 1971. 9.95 (ISBN 0-316-19545-6). Little.

--Horses of Dreamland. (Illus.). 32p. (ps-3). 1985. 12.95 (ISBN 0-316-19554-5). Little.

--Hotel for Dogs. (Illus.). (gr. 1-3). 1972. pap. 1.95 (ISBN 0-380-01258-8, 62133-9, Camelot). Avon.

--How to Write & Sell Your Personal Experiences. LC 79-17407. 226p. 1979. 10.95 (ISBN 0-911654-74-7). Writers Digest.

--I Know What You Did Last Summer. (gr. 7 up). 1985. pap. 2.50 (ISBN 0-671-55713-0). Archway.

--I Know What You Did Last Summer. (gr. 7 up). 1973. 12.45i (ISBN 0-316-19546-4). Little.

--Killing Mr. Griffin. 224p. (YA) (gr. 7 up). 1980. pap. 2.50 (ISBN 0-440-94515-1, LFL); tchr's. guide by Lou Stanek 0.50. Dell.

--Killing Mr. Griffin. (gr. 7 up). 1978. 13.45i (ISBN 0-316-19549-9). Little.

--Locked in Time. 240p. (gr. 7 up). 1985. 12.95 (ISBN 0-316-19555-3). Little.

--Ransom. 144p. (gr. 7-12). 1984. pap. 2.50 (ISBN 0-440-97292-2, LFL). Dell.

--Stranger with My Face. (gr. 8 up). 1981. 14.45i (ISBN 0-316-19551-0). Little.

--Stranger with My Face. 176p. (gr. 7 up). 1982. pap. 2.50 (ISBN 0-440-98356-8, LFL); tchr's. guide by Lou Stanek 0.50. Dell.

--Summer of Fear. 224p. (YA) (gr. 7 up). 1977. pap. 2.50 (ISBN 0-440-98324-X, LFL). Dell.

--Summer of Fear. 252p. (gr. 7-12). 1976. PLB 12.45i (ISBN 0-316-19548-0). Little.

--Terrible Tales of the Happy Days School. LC 82-82623. (Illus.). 32p. (gr. 3-6). 1983. PLB 9.70i (ISBN 0-316-19541-3). Little.

--They Never Came Home. 192p. 1980. pap. 2.50 (ISBN 0-380-50229-1, 60045-5, Flare). Avon.

--The Third Eye. (gr. 7up). 1984. 13.45i (ISBN 0-316-19553-7). Little.

--The Third Eye. (gr. k-12). 1985. pap. 2.75 (ISBN 0-440-98720-2, LFL). Dell.

Duncan, Louis C. The Medical Department of the U. S. in the Civil War. 400p. 1985. Repr. of 1910 ed. 28.50 (ISBN 0-913419-30-3). Butternut Pr.

--Medical Men in the American Revolution 1775-1783. LC 76-95629. (Illus.). Repr. of 1931 ed. 35.00x (ISBN 0-678-03756-6). Kelley.

Duncan, M. C. Masonic Ritual. rev. ed. 10.95x (ISBN 0-685-22033-8). Wehman.

Duncan, MacDonald B. Development of Muslin Theology, Jurisprudence, & Constitutional Theory. LC 65-2183. 386p. 1903. Repr. of 1973 ed. 14.00xcancelled (ISBN 0-686-43336-X). Intl Pubns Serv.

Duncan, Malcolm. Masonic Ritual & Monitor, 2 Pts. 1946. 8.50 ea.; 1 vol. ed. 12.50 (ISBN 0-685-19489-2). Powner.

Duncan, Malcolm C. Duncan's Masonic Ritual & Monitor. new ed. 288p. 1976. pap. 4.95 (ISBN 0-679-50626-8). McKay.

Duncan, Mark. On Target with Mark Duncan: An Illustrated Pocket Guide to Handgun Accuracy. (Illus.). 52p. (Orig.). 1984. pap. 4.95 (ISBN 0-9613502-0-2). Duncan Gun.

Duncan, Marti. Being & Breakfast. 1975. 1.00 (ISBN 0-686-71049-5). Windless Orchard.

Duncan, Norman. Australian Byways. Repr. of 1915 ed. 10.00 (ISBN 0-8482-3672-6). Norwood Edns.

--Battles Royal Down North. LC 70-125209. (Short Story Index Reprint Ser). (Illus.). 1918. 17.00 (ISBN 0-8369-3576-4). Ayer Co Pubs.

--Harbor Tales Down North. LC 72-121536. (Short Story Index Reprint Ser.). (Illus.). 1918. 19.00 (ISBN 0-8369-3492-X). Ayer Co Pubs.

--Way of the Sea. LC 76-121537. (Short Story Index Reprint Ser). 1903. 20.00 (ISBN 0-8369-3493-8). Ayer Co Pubs.

Duncan, Otis D. An Examination of the Problem of Optimum City Size. Zuckerman, Harriet & Merton, Robert K., eds. LC 79-8994. (Dissertations on Sociology). (Illus.). 1980. lib. bdg. 25.50x (ISBN 0-405-12965-3). Ayer Co Pubs.

--Notes on Social Measurement: Historical & Critical. LC 83-62503. 272p. 1984. 14.50x (ISBN 0-87154-219-6). Russell Sage.

Duncan, Otis D. & Duncan, Beverly. Negro Population of Chicago. LC 57-5271. Repr. of 1957 ed. 99.80 (ISBN 0-8357-9651-5, 2015754). Bks Demand UMI.

Duncan, Otis D., jt. auth. see Blau, Peter M.

Duncan, Otis D., jt. auth. see Duncan, Beverly.

Duncan, Otis D., jt. ed. see Goldberger, Arthur.

Duncan, Otis D., jt. auth. see Hauser, Philip M.

Duncan, Otis D., ed. see Ogburn, William F.

Duncan, Otis D., et al. Statistical Geography: Problems in Analyzing Areal Data. LC 77-7890. (Illus.). 1977. Repr. of 1961 ed. lib. bdg. 17.75x (ISBN 0-8371-9676-0, DUSG). Greenwood.

--Introduction to Structural Equation Models. (Studies in Population Ser.). 1975. 24.50 (ISBN 0-12-224150-9). Acad Pr.

--Socioeconomic Background & Achievement. LC 72-88537. (Studies in Population Ser). 1972. 39.50 (ISBN 0-12-785174-7). Acad Pr.

--Social Change in a Metropolitan Community. LC 73-76764. 136p. 1973. pap. 4.50x (ISBN 0-87154-216-1). Russell Sage.

--Metropolis & Region. LC 77-86393. (Resources for the Future Ser.). (Illus.). 608p. Repr. of 1960 ed. 64.50 (ISBN 0-404-60331-9). AMS Pr.

Duncan, P. B. Literary Conglomerate: A Combination of Various Thoughts & Facts on Various Subjects. 1978. Repr. of 1839 ed. lib. bdg. 50.00 (ISBN 0-8492-0691-X). R West.

--Literary Conglomerate; or a Combination of Various & Facts on Various Thoughts. 1973. Repr. of 1839 ed. 45.00 (ISBN 0-8274-1693-8). R West.

Duncan, Patricia D. Tallgrass Prairie: The Inland Sea. LC 78-60177. (Illus.). 1979. 20.00 (ISBN 0-913504-44-0). Lowell Pr.

Duncan, Paul. Who Is Sun Myung Moon? 21p. (Orig.). 1981. pap. text ed. 1.25 (ISBN 0-87148-914-7). Pathway Pr.

Duncan, Peter. Winemaking with Concentrates. 2nd. ed. (Illus.). 98p. Date not set. pap. 3.95 (ISBN 0-900841-44-3, Pub. by Aztex Corp). Argus Bks.

Duncan, Peter & Acton, Bryan. Progressive Winemaking. (Illus.). 430p. Date not set. pap. 11.95 (ISBN 0-900841-23-0, Pub. by Aztex Corp). Argus Bks.

Duncan, Peter, jt. auth. see Acton, Bryon.

Duncan, Peter, jt. auth. see Aston, Bryan.

Duncan, Phillip K., ed. Current Topics in Organizational Behavior Management. LC 82-11685. (Journal of Organizational Behavior Management Ser.: Vol. 3, No. 3). 111p. 1982. text ed. 22.95 (ISBN 0-86656-198-6, B198); pap. text ed. 12.95 (ISBN 0-86656-172-2). Haworth Pr.

Duncan, R. & Weston-Smith, M., eds. The Encyclopaedia of Medical Ignorance: The Mind & Body in Health & Disease. LC 83-4785. (Illus.). 240p. 1983. 17.95 (ISBN 0-08-024515-3, 37). Pergamon.

--The Encyclopedia of Ignorance, Vol. 1 & 2. 1977. 21.00. Pergamon.

Duncan, R. M., ed. see Sender, Ramon J.

Duncan, R. S. A History of the Baptists in Missouri. 1981. Repr. of 1882 ed. 38.00 (ISBN 0-686-77695-X). Church History.

Duncan, Ray. IBM PC-DOS Programmer's Reference Guide. Date not set. pap. price not set postponed (ISBN 0-89303-523-8). Brady Comm.

Duncan, Raymond W., ed. Soviet Policy in Developing Countries. 2nd ed. LC 78-20847. 262p. 1981. 13.50 (ISBN 0-88275-846-2). Krieger.

Duncan, Riana. A Nutcracker in a Tree. LC 80-67492. (Illus.). 32p. (ps-3). 1981. 8.95 (ISBN 0-318-12068-2). Delacorte.

--A Nutcracker in a Tree: A Book of Riddles. LC 80-67492. (Illus.). 32p. (gr. k-3). 1981. 8.95 (ISBN 0-385-28732-1); PLB 8.95 (ISBN 0-385-28733-X). Delacorte.

Duncan, Richard R., compiled by. Theses & Dissertations on Virginia History: A Bibliography. 1985. price not set (ISBN 0-88490-135-1); pap. price not set (ISBN 0-88490-136-X). VA State Lib.

Duncan, Robert. Bending the Bow. LC 68-15879. 1968. 6.50 (ISBN 0-8112-0269-0); pap. 4.95 (ISBN 0-8112-0033-7, NDP255). New Directions.

--Derivations. 1968. 10.00 (ISBN 0-89760-132-7). Telegraph Bks.

--Faust Foutu. (Illus.). 56p. 1985. pap. 8.95 (ISBN 0-88268-019-6). Station Hill Pr.

--Fictive Certainties. LC 85-11417. 320p. 1985. 17.95 (ISBN 0-8112-0944-X); pap. 11.95 (ISBN 0-8112-0949-0, NDP598). New Directions.

--Ground Work: Before the War. LC 84-4889. 192p. 1984. 19.50 (ISBN 0-8112-0895-8); pap. 10.95 (ISBN 0-8112-0896-6, NDP571); limited ed. 50.00 (ISBN 0-8112-0915-6). New Directions.

--The Noise: Notes from a Rock 'n' Roll Era. LC 84-8558. 288p. 1984. 16.95 (ISBN 0-89919-168-1); pap. 8.95 (ISBN 0-89919-326-9). Ticknor & Fields.

--Only the Good Die Young. 1985. 7.95 (ISBN 0-517-55757-6). Crown.

--Opening of the Field. rev. ed. LC 72-93976. 96p. 1973. pap. 4.95 (ISBN 0-8112-0480-4, NDP356). New Directions.

--Peiping Municipality & the Diplomatic Quarter. LC 78-74355. (Modern Chinese Economy Ser.). 146p. 1980. lib. bdg. 20.00 (ISBN 0-8240-4271-9). Garland Pub.

--The Regulators. 56p. (Orig.). 1985. 19.95; pap. 8.95 (ISBN 0-88268-019-6). Station Hill Pr.

--Roots & Branches. LC 64-24233. 1969. pap. 4.95 (ISBN 0-8112-0034-5, NDP275). New Directions.

--The Story of the Edinburgh Burns Relics with Fresh Facts About Burns & His Family. LC 75-42242. 1976. Repr. of 1910 ed. lib. bdg. 20.00 (ISBN 0-8414-3722-X). Folcroft.

--Writing, Writing. (Orig.). 1971. pap. 3.00 (ISBN 0-932264-15-8). Trask Hse Bks.

--The Years As Catches. 1977. sewn in wrappers 3.00 (ISBN 0-685-80007-5). Oyez.

Duncan, Robert & Meltzer, David. Wallace Berman Retrospective. (Illus.). 118p. (Orig.). 1978. pap. write for info. (ISBN 0-911291-03-2). Fellows Cont Art.

Duncan, Robert & Spicer, Jack. An Ode & Arcadia. (Illus.). 1974. perfect bound in wrappers 4.00 (ISBN 0-685-79018-5). Small Pr Dist.

Duncan, Robert, jt. auth. see Zaltman, Gerald.

Duncan, Robert, et al. The Male Muse: Gay Poetry Anthology. Young, Ian, ed. LC 73-77318. (Contemporary Anthologies Ser.). 128p. (Orig.). 1973. 16.95 (ISBN 0-912278-35-8); pap. 6.95 (ISBN 0-912278-34-X). Crossing Pr.

Duncan, Robert C. & Knapp, Rebecca G. Introductory Biostatistics for the Health Sciences. 2nd ed. LC 82-23822. 249p. 1983. pap. 18.50 (ISBN 0-471-07869-7, Wiley Med). Wiley.

Duncan, Robert G., ed. see Marder, William & Marder, Estelle.

Duncan, Robert I. Architectural Drawing Problems. 3rd ed. 1977. pap. text ed. 12.95 (ISBN 0-8403-1756-5). Kendall-Hunt.

--Architectural Graphics & Communication. (Illus.). 1980. pap. text ed. 10.95 (ISBN 0-8403-2711-0, 40271101). Kendall-Hunt.

--Architectural Graphics & Communication Problems. 144p. 1982. pap. text ed. 12.95 (ISBN 0-8403-2764-1). Kendall-Hunt.

Duncan, Robert J., jt. auth. see Estes, Ross.

Duncan, Robert L. Brimstone. 352p. 1982. pap. 2.95 (ISBN 0-523-48025-3). Pinnacle Bks.

--In the Blood. (Orig.). 1984. pap. 3.95 (ISBN 0-440-14025-0). Dell.

--In the Enemy Camp. LC 84-23011. 312p. 1985. 15.95 (ISBN 0-385-29388-7). Delacorte.

--The Queen's Messenger. 1983. pap. 3.95 (ISBN 0-440-17540-2). Dell.

Duncan, Roger. Frienship Sloops. LC 84-947757. (Illus.). 208p. 1985. 35.00 (ISBN 0-87742-172-2). Intl Marine.

Duncan, Roger F. Fog Sailing: A Primer on Seamanship. (Illus.). 112p. 1986. pap. 9.95 (ISBN 0-87742-208-7). Intl Marine.

Duncan, Roger F. & Ware, John P. A Cruising Guide to the New England Coast. Rev. ed. (Illus.). 1983. 24.95 (ISBN 0-396-08166-5). Dodd.

Duncan, Ronald. The Collected Poems, Nineteen Nineteen to Nineteen Eighty. 160p. 1982. 24.95 (ISBN 0-434-98022-6, Pub. by W Heinemann Ltd). David & Charles.

Duncan, Ronald & Smith, Miranda W. The Encyclopedia of Ignorance. 1979. pap. 8.95 (ISBN 0-671-79087-0, Wallaby). PB.

Duncan, Ronald & Weston-Smith, Miranda. The Encyclopedia of Delusions. 256p. 1981. pap. 6.95 (ISBN 0-671-42391-6, Wallaby). S&S.

Duncan, Ronald, ed. Rochester. (Pocket Poet Ser.). 1959. pap. 2.00 (ISBN 0-289-27752-3). Dufour.

Duncan, Ronald C., jt. auth. see Akiyama, Takamasa.

Duncan, Ronald J., ed. Investigacion Social En Puerto Rico. LC 80-23445. 289p. 1980. text ed. 13.00 (ISBN 0-913480-45-2); pap. 8.00 (ISBN 0-913480-44-4). Inter Am U Pr.

Duncan, Ronald J. & Richardson, Edward, eds. Social Research in Puerto Rico: Science, Humanism & Society. LC 83-12635. 255p. 1984. pap. 8.00 (ISBN 0-913480-57-6). Inter Am U Pr.

Duncan, Ronald J., et al. Manual De Tecnicas De Investigacion Social. LC 80-23411. (Illus.). 73p. 1980. 5.00 (ISBN 0-913480-46-0). Inter Am U Pr.

Duncan, S. Blackwell. The Build-it Book of Cabinets & Built-Ins. (Illus.). 1979. pap. 12.50 (ISBN 0-8306-1002-2, 1002). TAB Bks.

--How to Build Your Own Log Home & Cabin from Scratch. (Illus.). 1978. 17.95 (ISBN 0-8306-9874-4); pap. 8.95 (ISBN 0-8306-1081-2, 1081). TAB Bks.

Duncan, S. S., ed. Qualitative Change in Human Geography. (Illus.). 127p. 1981. 32.00 (ISBN 0-08-025222-2). Pergamon.

Duncan, Sara J. The Pool in the Desert. (Fiction Ser.). 224p. 1985. pap. 5.95 (ISBN 0-14-007457-0). Penguin.

Duncan, Simon, jt. ed. see Anderson, James.

Duncan, Starkey & Fiske, Donald W. Face-To-Face Interaction: Research, Methods, & Theory. 362p. 1977. text ed. 36.00 (ISBN 0-89859-118-X). L Erlbaum Assocs.

Duncan, Sylvia, jt. auth. see Freese, Marjorie.

Duncan, T. Exploring Physics, Vol. 1. (gr. 11-12). pap. text ed. 7.50 (ISBN 0-7195-2043-6). Transatlantic.

Duncan, T. Bentley. Atlantic Islands: Madeira, the Azores, & the Cape Verdes in Seventeenth Century Commerce & Navigation. LC 72-80157. (Studies in the History of Discoveries Ser). (Illus.). 320p. 1972. 25.00x (ISBN 0-226-17001-2). U of Chicago Pr.

Duncan, T. Roger & Duncan, Darlene. You're Divorced, but Your Children Aren't. 1979. text ed. 10.95 (ISBN 0-13-981902-9, Spec); pap. 4.95 (ISBN 0-13-981894-4). P-H.

Duncan, Tannis. Reaching for Excellence. 67p. (Orig.). 1982. pap. text ed. 2.50 (ISBN 0-87148-737-3). Pathway Pr.

Duncan, Theodore. Exercise over Fifty-Five. (Illus.). 400p. 1985. write for info (ISBN 0-89168-057-8). L Erlbaum Assocs.

Duncan, Theodore G., ed. Over Fifty-Five: A Handbook on Health. 633p. 1982. 19.95 (ISBN 0-89168-031-4). L Erlbaum Assocs.

Duncan, Thomas. Electronics & Nuclear Physics. (gr. 9-12). text ed. 14.95 (ISBN 0-7195-2003-7). Transatlantic.

--A Taxonomic Study of the Ranunculus Hispidus. (U.-C. Publications in Botany V Ser.: Vol. 77). 1980. 14.00x (ISBN 0-520-09617-7). U of Cal Pr.

Duncan, Thomas & Stuessy, Tod F. Cladistic Theory & Methodology. (Illus.). 450p. 1985. 47.50 (ISBN 0-442-21845-1). Van Nos Reinhold.

--Cladistics: Perspectives on the Reconstruction of Evolutionary History. (Illus.). 368p. 1984. 35.00 (ISBN 0-231-05430-0). Columbia U Pr.

Duncan, Thomas R. How to Buy & Restore Wicker Furniture. LC 82-73902. (Illus.). 166p. 1983. lib. bdg. 22.95 (ISBN 0-9609480-0-7); pap. 14.95 (ISBN 0-9609480-1-5). Duncan-Holmes.

Duncan, Thomas S. Domestic Crisis Intervention for Law Enforcement Officers. LC 85-70682. (Illus.). 180p. 1985. 17.95 (ISBN 0-931494-63-X); pap. 10.95 (ISBN 0-931494-62-1). Brunswick Pub.

Duncan, Tom, et al. Alaska Place Names Pronunciation Guide. (The Elmer E. Rasmuson Library Occasional Papers Ser.: No. 4). 29p. 1975. pap. text ed. 2.00x (ISBN 0-937592-00-5). U Alaska Rasmuson Lib.

Duncan, U. K. Flora of East Ross-Shire. 272p. 1980. 37.00x (ISBN 0-317-07066-5, Pub. by EW Classey UK). State Mutual Bk.

--Introduction to British Lichens. (Illus.). 292p. 1970. 24.95x (ISBN 0-916422-48-8). Mad River.

Duncan, W., ed. Experimental Model Systems in Toxicology & Their Significance in Man. (International Congress Ser.). (Proceedings). 1974. pap. 77.75 (ISBN 0-444-15106-0). Elsevier.

--Lung Cancer. (Recent Results in Cancer Research Ser.: Vol. 92). (Illus.). 160p. 1984. 36.50 (ISBN 0-387-13116-7). Springer-Verlag.

--Paediatric Oncology. (Recent Results in Cancer Research Ser.: Vol. 88). (Illus.). 170p. 1983. 37.00 (ISBN 0-387-12349-0). Springer-Verlag.

--Prostate Cancer. (Recent Results in Cancer Research Ser.: Vol. 78). (Illus.). 192p. 1981. 48.00 (ISBN 0-387-10676-6). Springer-Verlag.

Duncan, W., et al. Thyroid Cancer. (Recent Results in Cancer Research Ser.: Vol. 73). (Illus.). 190p. 1980. 40.00 (ISBN 0-387-09328-1). Springer-Verlag.

Duncan, W. A., jt. ed. see Plaa, Gabriel L.

Duncan, W. Jack. Essentials of Management. 2nd ed. LC 77-81236. 1978. text ed. 29.95x (ISBN 0-03-039826-6). Dryden Pr.

--Management. Donnelley, Paul, ed. 1983. pap. 10.95 (ISBN 0-394-33531-7, RanC); study guide avail. Random.

--Organizational Behavior. 2nd ed. LC 80-82460. (Illus.). 464p. 1981. text ed. 29.50 (ISBN 0-395-29640-4). HM.

Duncan, W. P. & Susan, A. B. Synthesis & Applications of Isotopically Labelled Compounds. 1983. 110.75 (ISBN 0-444-42152-1, I-472-82). Elsevier.

Duncan, W. R. The Queen's Messenger. 1982. 14.95 (ISBN 0-385-28818-2). Delacorte.

Duncan, W. Raymond. Soviet Policy in the Third World. (Policy Studies). 1980. 42.00 (ISBN 0-08-025125-0). Pergamon.

--The Soviet Union & Cuba: Interests & Influences. Rubinstein, Alvin, ed. LC 84-26296. 240p. 1985. 28.95 (ISBN 0-03-064111-X); pap. 12.95 (ISBN 0-03-064109-8). Praeger.

Duncan, Walter J. Atlas of Pediatric Two-Dimensional Echocardiography. (Illus.). 180p. 1981. 19.75x (ISBN 0-398-04128-8). C C Thomas.

Duncan, Wilbur H. Guide to Georgia Trees. LC 41-11394. 64p. 1941. pap. 3.50x (ISBN 0-8203-0214-7). U of Ga Pr.

--Woody Vines of the Southeastern United States. LC 74-13511. 84p. 1975. pap. 6.95x (ISBN 0-8203-0348-8). U of Ga Pr.

Duncan, Wilbur H. & Foote, Leonard E. Wildflowers of the Southeastern United States. LC 74-75940. (Illus.). 304p. 1975. 16.50 (ISBN 0-8203-0347-X). U of Ga Pr.

Duncan, Wilbur H. & Kartesz, John T. Vascular Flora of Georgia: An Annotated Checklist. LC 80-22014. 158p. 1981. pap. 6.00x (ISBN 0-8203-0538-3). U of Ga Pr.

Duncan, William C., ed. Contact: An Anthology of Contemporary Poetry. 1978. 10.00 (ISBN 0-930266-02-1). Contemporary Lit.

--Cornucopia: An Anthology of Contemporary Poetry. 1978. 10.00 (ISBN 0-930266-00-5). Contemporary Lit.

--Variations: An Anthology of Contemporary Poetry. 1978. 10.00 (ISBN 0-930266-01-3). Contemporary Lit.

Duncan, William J., ed. Miscellaneous Papers, Principally Illustrative of Events in the Reigns of Queen Mary & King James Sixth. LC 79-164807. (Maitland Club. Glasgow. Publications: No. 26). Repr. of 1834 ed. 17.50 (ISBN 0-404-52981-X). AMS Pr.

--Notices & Documents Illustrative of the Literary History of Glasgow During the Greater Part of Last Century. (Maitland Club. Glasgow. Publications: No. 14). Repr. of 1831 ed. 18.00 (ISBN 0-404-52947-X). AMS Pr.

Duncan-Clark, S. J. Progressive Movement, Its Principles & Its Programme. LC 72-164808. Repr. of 1913 ed. 24.00 (ISBN 0-404-02217-0). AMS Pr.

Duncan-Eaves, T. C., ed. see Richardson, Samuel.

Duncan-Jones, Arthur S. The Struggle for Religious Freedom in Germany. LC 78-63664. (Studies in Fascism: Ideology & Practice). Repr. of 1938 ed. 34.00 (ISBN 0-404-16927-9). AMS Pr.

Duncan-Jones, C. M. A London Sparrow & Mignonette. Repr. lib. bdg. 10.00 (ISBN 0-8414-3870-6). Folcroft.

Duncan-Jones, Caroline M. Miss Mitford & Mr. Harkness: Records of a Friendship. 1955. Repr. 17.50 (ISBN 0-8274-2744-1). R West.

--Miss Mitford & Mr. Harness: Records of a Friendship. 1955. 20.00 (ISBN 0-932062-43-1). Sharon Hill.

Duncan-Jones, Katherine, ed. see Sidney, Philip.

Duncan-Jones, Katherine, ed. see Sidney, Phillip.

Duncan-Jones, Richard. The Economy of the Roman Empire: Quantitative Studies. 2nd ed. LC 81-21564. (Illus.). 432p. 1982. pap. 19.95 (ISBN 0-521-28793-6). Cambridge U Pr.

Duncann, C. G. Teach Yourself to Live. 12.50x (ISBN 0-392-07034-0, LTB). Sportshelf.

Duncann, Geraldine. Some Like It Hotter. LC 85-334. (Illus.). 192p. (Orig.). 1985. pap. 9.95 (ISBN 0-89286-245-9). One Hund One Prods.

Duncanson, Dennis. Changing Qualities of Chinese Life. 125p. 1983. 19.50x (ISBN 0-8448-1404-0). Crane-Russak Co.

Dunckel, Jacqueline & Parnham, Elizabeth. The Business Guide to Effective Speaking: Making Presentations, Using Audio-Visuals, & Dealing with the Media. 192p. 1984. pap. 6.95 (ISBN 0-88908-591-9, 9528, Pub. by Intl Self-Counsel Pr). TAB Bks.

Duncker, Karl. On Problem-Solving. Lees, Lynne S., tr. LC 73-138621. (Illus.). 113p. 1972. Repr. of 1945 ed. lib. bdg. 18.75x (ISBN 0-8371-5733-1, DUPS). Greenwood.

Duncomb, J. see Skeat, W. W.

Duncombe, Alice E. Handbook for Telephone Ministry. Rev. ed. 7.95 (ISBN 0-89985-110-X). Christ Nations.

Duncombe, Beverly. A Matter of Love. 1983. 5.95 (ISBN 0-533-05091-X). Vantage.

--Need I Say More. LC 83-90386. 45p. 1985. 5.95 (ISBN 0-533-05888-0). Vantage.

Duncombe, Charles. Duncombe's Free Banking. LC 68-27852. Repr. of 1841 ed. 35.00x (ISBN 0-678-00530-3). Kelley.

Duncombe, Giles. Tryals Per Pais, or the Law Concerning Juries by Nisi Prius. Helmholz, R. H. & Reams, Bernard D., Jr., eds. LC 79-91755. (Historical Writings in Law & Jurisprudence Ser.: No. 2, Bk. 2). xxii, 486p. 1980. Repr. of 1725 ed. lib. bdg. 32.50 (ISBN 0-89941-041-3). W S Hein.

Duncombe, Herbert S. Modern County Government. LC 77-80607. (Illus.). 1977. 10.95 (ISBN 0-911754-01-6); pap. 7.95 (ISBN 0-686-77333-0). Natl Assn Counties.

Duncombe, R. L., ed. Methods in Astrodynamics & Celestial Mechanics. LC 66-21326. (Illus.). 436p. 1966. 30.00 (ISBN 0-317-36820-6); members 15.00 (ISBN 0-317-36821-4). AIAA.

Duncombe, R. L., et al. The Stability of Planetary Systems: Reprinted from Celestial Mechanics, Vol. 34, Nos. 1-4. 1985. lib. bdg. 96.00 (ISBN 90-277-1961-6, Pub. by Reidel Holland). Kluwer Academic.

Duncombe, Raynor L., ed. Dynamics of the Solar System. (I. A. U. Symposia Ser.: No. 81). 1979. lib. bdg. 45.00 (ISBN 90-277-0976-9, Pub. by Reidel Holland); pap. 28.95 (ISBN 90-277-0977-7, Pub. by Reidel Holland). Kluwer Academic.

Duncombe, S., et al, eds. Idaho Tomorrow Book. 1975. 1.95 (ISBN 0-89301-024-3). U Pr of Idaho.

Duncombe, Sydney & Weisel, Robert. State & Local Government in Idaho & the Nation. LC 84-50973. 157p. (Orig.). 1984. pap. text ed. 9.95 (ISBN 0-89301-099-5). U Pr of Idaho.

Duncombe, Sydney, et al. Idaho State & Local Government. LC 77-155358. (Illus.). 1971. 3.00 (ISBN 0-87004-224-6). Caxton.

Dundas, Charles. African Crossroads. LC 76-45443. 1977. Repr. of 1955 ed. lib. bdg. 21.00x (ISBN 0-8371-9089-4, DUAF). Greenwood.

--Kilimanjaro & Its People. (Illus.). 349p. 1968. Repr. of 1924 ed. 32.50x (ISBN 0-7146-1659-1, F Cass Co). Biblio Dist.

Dundas, George, ed. see Virgil.

Dundas, James L. Heating Service. (Illus.). 1978. text ed. 19.95 (ISBN 0-8403-1866-9). Kendall-Hunt.

Dundas, Judith. The Spider & the Bee: The Artistry of Spenser's Faerie Queene. LC 83-18253. (Illus.). 248p. 1985. 12.95x (ISBN 0-252-01118-X). U of Ill Pr.

Dundass, Samuel R. & Keller, George. Crossing the Plains to California in 1849 & Crossing the Plains to California in 1850. 1983. 12.00 (ISBN 0-87770-291-8). Ye Galleon.

Dundee, Angelo & Winters, Mike. I Only Talk Winning. LC 84-27474. (Illus.). 304p. 1985. 16.95 (ISBN 0-8092-5303-8). Contemp Bks.

Dundee, John G. Letters. Smythe, George, ed. LC 76-164808. (Bannatyne Club, Edinburgh. Publications: No. 15). Repr. of 1826 ed. 17.50 (ISBN 0-404-52715-9). AMS Pr.

Dundee, John W. Intravenous Anesthetic Agents. (Current Topics in Anesthesia Ser.: Vol. 1). (Illus.). 1979. 34.95 (ISBN 0-8151-2943-2). Year Bk Med.

Dundes, Alan. Analytic Essays in Folklore. (Studies in Folklore Ser.: No. 2). 1975. pap. text ed. 21.60x (ISBN 90-279-3231-X). Mouton.

--Cinderella: A Casebook. LC 81-43334. (Garland Folklore Casebooks Ser.). 325p. 1982. lib. bdg. 39.00 (ISBN 0-8240-9295-3). Garland Pub.

--The Evil Eye: A Folklore Casebook. 1981. lib. bdg. 43.00 (ISBN 0-8240-9471-9). Garland Pub.

--Folklore Theses & Dissertations in the United States. LC 75-29244. (American Folklore Society Bibliographical & Special Ser: No. 27). 628p. 1976. 27.50x (ISBN 0-292-72413-6). U of Tex Pr.

--Interpreting Folklore. LC 79-2969. (Midland Bks.: No. 240). 320p. 1980. 25.00x (ISBN 0-253-14307-1); pap. 10.95x (ISBN 0-253-20240-X). Ind U Pr.

--Life Is Like a Chicken Coop Ladder: A Portrait of German Culture Through Folklore. LC 83-7540. (Illus.). 176p. 1984. 18.50x (ISBN 0-231-05494-7). Columbia U Pr.

--Study of Folklore. (Illus.). 1965. text ed. 22.95 (ISBN 0-13-858944-5). P-H.

Dundes, Alan & Falassi, Alessandro. La Terra in Piazza: An Interpretaion of the Palio of Siena. (Illus.). 325p. 1983. 40.00x (ISBN 0-520-02681-0); pap. 11.95 (ISBN 0-520-04771-0). U of Cal Pr.

Dundes, Alan & Pagter, Carl R. Work Hard & You Shall Be Rewarded: Urban Folklore from the Paperwork Empire. LC 77-74429. (Midland Bks: No. 207). (Illus.). 248p. 1978. pap. 6.95 (ISBN 0-253-20207-8). Ind U Pr.

Dundes, Alan, jt. auth. see Mieder, Wolfgang.

Dundes, Alan, ed. Cinderalla: A Casebook. 320p. 1985. pap. 12.95 (ISBN 0-939544-15-6, 9664). Methuen Inc.

--Cinderella: A Folklore Casebook. LC 83-70454. xix, 311p. 1983. pap. 12.95x (ISBN 0-939544-15-6). Wildman Pr.

--Mother Wit from the Laughing Barrel: Readings in the Interpretation of Afro-American Folklore. LC 80-8528. 688p. 1981. lib. bdg. 46.00 (ISBN 0-8240-9456-5). Garland Pub.

--Sacred Narrative: Readings in the Theory of Myth. LC 83-17921. (Illus.). ix, 352p. 1985. 24.50x (ISBN 0-520-05156-4, CAL 699); pap. 9.95 (ISBN 0-520-05192-0). U of Cal Pr.

Dundes, Alan, jt. ed. see Hasan-Rokem, Galit.

Dundes, Alan, ed. see Jones, Steven S.

Dundes, Alan, ed. see Samuelson, Sue.

Dundes, Allan, jt. auth. see Edmunds, Lowell.

Dundon, H. Dwyer, ed. Occupational Therapy Examination Review, Vol. 1. 4th ed. 1983. pap. text ed. 14.00 (ISBN 0-87488-475-6). Med Exam.

Dundon, Mary L. The Cooperative Health Statistics System: Its Mission & Program. Cox, Klaudia, ed. (Ser. 4: No. 19). 1977. pap. text ed. 1.75 (ISBN 0-8406-0092-5). Natl Ctr Health Stats.

Dundon, Mary L. & Gay, George A. The Nineteen Seventy-Eight Revision of the U. S. Standard Certificates. Olmstead, Mary, tr. (Ser. 4: No. 23). 45p. 1982. pap. 1.75 (ISBN 0-8406-0268-5). Natl Ctr Health Stats.

Dundy, Elaine. Elvis & Gladys. 320p. 1985. 18.95 (ISBN 0-02-553910-8). Macmillan.

Dunedin Youth Guild. Suncoast Seasons. (Illus.). 430p. 1984. 13.95 (ISBN 0-9613858-0-4). Dunedin Youth.

Dunegan, H. L., jt. auth. see Hartman, W. F.

Duner, Anders, ed. Research into Personal Development: Educational & Vocational Choice. 192p. 1978. pap. text ed. 11.75 (ISBN 90-265-0284-2, Pub. by Swets & Zeitlinger Netherlands). Hogrefe Intl.

Duner, Bertil. Military Intervention in Civil Wars, the 1970's. LC 84-9921. 200p. 1985. 25.95 (ISBN 0-312-53237-7). St Martin.

Dunes of Dare Garden Club. Wildflowers of the Outer Banks: Kitty Hawk to Hatteras. LC 79-18927. (Illus.). xvii, 165p. 1980. pap. 6.95 (ISBN 0-8078-4061-0). U of NC Pr.

Dunfee, Maxine, jt. auth. see Crump, Claudia.

Dunfee, Maxine, ed. Eliminating Ethnic Bias in Instructional Materials: Comment & Bibliography. new ed. LC 74-81684. 52p. 1974. pap. text ed. 3.25 (ISBN 0-87120-021-X, 611-74020). Assn Supervision.

Dunfee, Thomas & Blackburn, John. Modern Business Law. 1000p. 1984. text ed. 29.95 (ISBN 0-394-32888-4, RanC). Random.

Dunfee, Thomas W. & Bellace, Janice. Business & Its Legal Environment. (Illus.). 688p. 1983. text ed. 29.95 (ISBN 0-13-101006-9). P-H.

Dunfee, Thomas W. & Gibson, Frank F. Antitrust & Trade Regulation: Cases & Materials. 2nd ed. LC 85-12480. price not set (ISBN 0-471-87030-7). Wiley.

--Introduction to Contracts. 2nd ed. LC 84-7364. 392p. 1984. pap. text ed. 20.95 (ISBN 0-471-87031-5). Wiley.

--Legal Aspects of Government Regulation of Business. 3rd ed. LC 83-21879. 335p. 1984. pap. 19.45 (ISBN 0-471-87029-3). Wiley.

Dunfee, Thomas W., jt. auth. see Whitman, Douglas.

Dunfee, Thomas W. & Reitzel, J. David, eds. Business Law: Key Issues & Concepts. LC 78-17091. (Grid Series in Law). pap. 42.00 (ISBN 0-317-29933-6, 2021722). Bks Demand UMI.

Dunfee, Thomas W., et al. Modern Business Law: An Introduction to the Legal Environment. LC 77-71017. (Law Ser.). 346p. 1982. pap. text ed. 20.95 (ISBN 0-471-87018-8). Wiley.

Dunford, Christopher, jt. auth. see Pulliam, H. Ronald.

Dunford, Elizabeth P. The Hawaiians of Old. Rayson, Ann, ed. (Illus.). 220p. (gr. 4 up). 1980. text ed. 14.45 (ISBN 0-935848-00-2); pap. text ed. 11.95 (ISBN 0-935848-01-0); wkbk 4.00 (ISBN 0-935848-08-8); tchr's. manual 5.00 (ISBN 0-935848-09-6). Bess Pr.

Dunford, H. B. & Dolphin, D. The Biological Chemistry of Iron. 1982. 59.50 (ISBN 90-277-1444-4, Pub. by Reidel Holland). Kluwer Academic.

Dunford, Jill. Teach Me, Mommy. 2nd ed. 290p. (Orig.). 1985. pap. 11.95 (ISBN 0-89879-187-1, 2204). Writers Digest.

Dunford, Martin & Holland, Jack. Rough Guide to Amsterdam & Holland. (The Routledge Rough Guides Ser.). 192p. (Orig.). 1984. pap. 7.95 (ISBN 0-7102-0158-3). Routledge & Kegan.

Dunford, Michael & Perrons, Diane. The Arena of Capital. (Critical Human Geography Ser.). 410p. 1983. 37.50 (ISBN 0-312-04857-2). St Martin.

Dunford, Nelson & Schwartz, Jacob T. Linear Operators, 3 pts. Incl. Pt. 1. General Theory. 872p. 1958. 77.95x (ISBN 0-470-22605-6); Pt. 2. Spectral Theory, Self Adjoint Operators in Hilbert Space. 1072p. 1963. 101.95 (ISBN 0-470-22638-2); Pt. 3. Spectral Operators. 667p. 1971. 85.95x (ISBN 0-471-22639-4). LC 57-10545. (Pure & Applied Mathematics Ser). Set. 225.00 (ISBN 0-471-86913-9, Pub. by Wiley-Interscience). Wiley.

Dunford, Nelson J. Handbook for Technical Typists. 144p. 1964. 19.75 (ISBN 0-677-40010-1). Gordon.

Dung, Van Tien. Our Great Spring Victory: An Account of the Liberation of South Vietnam. Speagens, John, tr. LC 76-58106. 275p. 1977. 15.00 (ISBN 0-85345-409-4). Monthly Rev.

--Our Great Spring Victory: An Account of the Liberation of South Vietnam. Spragens, John, Jr., tr. LC 76-58106. 1978. pap. 4.95 (ISBN 0-85345-455-8). Monthly Rev.

Dungan, David L., jt. auth. see Cartlidge, David R.

Dungan, Dougal. My Sons, My England. 320p. 1981. pap. 2.75 (ISBN 0-449-24441-5, Crest). Fawcett.

Dungen, Peter van den see Van den Dungen, Peter.

Dunglison, Robley. Human Health. Rosenkrantz, Barbara G., ed. LC 76-25660. (Public Health in America Ser.). 1977. Repr. of 1844 ed. lib. bdg. 35.50x (ISBN 0-405-09815-4). Ayer Co Pubs.

Dunham, Aileen. Political Unrest in Upper Canada, 1815-1836. LC 74-3751. 210p. 1975. Repr. of 1927 ed. lib. bdg. 15.50x (ISBN 0-8371-7474-0, DUPU). Greenwood.

Dunham, Arthur & Nusberg, Charlotte. Planning for the Aging in Local Communities: An International Perspective. 49p. 4.00 (ISBN 0-318-14567-7). Intl Fed Ageing.

--Toward Planning for the Aging in Local Communities: An International Perspective. LC 81-210416. 49p. (Orig.). 1978. pap. text ed. 4.00 (ISBN 0-910473-05-6). Intl Fed Ageing.

Dunham, Arthur L. Anglo-French Treaty of Commerce of 1860. LC 77-159180. 1971. Repr. of 1930 ed. lib. bdg. 27.50x (ISBN 0-374-92411-2). Octagon.

Dunham, C. W., jt. auth. see Bockrath, J.

Dunham, Caroll, et al. Bochner, Leva, Rockburne, Tuttle. (Illus.). 1976. pap. 10.00 (ISBN 0-917562-02-X). Contemp Arts.

Dunham, Clarence, et al. Contracts, Specifications & Law for Engineers. 3rd ed. (Illus.). 1979. text ed. 42.00 (ISBN 0-07-018236-1). McGraw.

Dunham, Clarence W. & Bockrath, Joseph T. Dunham & Young's Contracts, Specifications, & Law for Engineers. 4th ed. LC 85-16571. Date not set. price not set (ISBN 0-07-018237-X). McGraw.

Dunham, Daniel C. Building For the Maritime Desert: Energy, Climate, and Construction in Djibouti. 65p. (Avail. in Eng. & Fr.). 1983. 7.95 (ISBN 0-86619-168-2, E-11077); in French 7.95 (ISBN 0-86619-169-0, F-19077). Vols Tech Asst.

Dunham, David M. & Hilhorst, J. G., eds. Issues in Regional Planning: A Selection of Seminar Papers. LC 76-169994. (Publications of the Institute of Social Studies Paperback Ser.: No. 4). 275p. 1971. text ed. 12.00x (ISBN 0-686-22494-9). Mouton.

Dunham, David W., jt. ed. see Rebach, Steve.

Dunham, Geoffrey, jt. auth. see Biostim Inc. Clinical & Engineering Research Group.

Dunham, H. Warren. Social Realities & Community Psychiatry. LC 74-10967. 252p. 1976. 29.95 (ISBN 0-87705-215-8). Human Sci Pr.

--Social Systems & Schizophrenia: Selected Papers. LC 80-14193. 332p. 1980. 41.95 (ISBN 0-03-056134-5). Praeger.

Dunham, H. Warren & Weinberg, S. Kirson. The Culture of the State Mental Hospital. LC 59-114720. 307p. 1960. 9.95x (ISBN 0-8143-1123-7). Wayne St U Pr.

Dunham, H. Warren, jt. auth. see Faris, Robert E.

Dunham, Harold H. Government Handout: A Study in the Administration of the Public Lands 1875-1891. LC 79-87564. (American Scene Ser). 1970. Repr. of 1941 ed. lib. bdg. 42.50 (ISBN 0-306-71433-7). Da Capo.

Dunham, Jack. Stress in Teaching. 200p. 1984. 25.00 (ISBN 0-89397-198-7). Nichols Pub.

Dunham, James H. Religion of Philosophers. facs. ed. LC 78-80386. (Essay Index Reprint Ser). 1947. 21.50 (ISBN 0-8369-1059-1). Ayer Co Pubs.

Dunham, Judith, jt. auth. see Brown, Christopher.

Dunham, Katharine. Kasamance: A Fantasy. LC 73-92612. (gr. 7 up). 1974. 6.95 (ISBN 0-89388-128-7). Okpaku Communications.

Dunham, Katherine. Dances of Haiti. LC 83-14328. (CAAS Special Publications Ser.). (Illus.). 103p. 1983. 22.50x (ISBN 0-934934-17-7); pap. 14.50x (ISBN 0-934934-11-8). Ctr Afro-Am Stud.

--Katherine Dunham's Journey to Accompong. LC 78-135595. (Illus.). 162p. 1972. Repr. of 1946 ed. lib. bdg. 17.50x (ISBN 0-8371-5187-2, DJA&). Greenwood.

--A Touch of Innocence. LC 79-7760. (Dance Ser.). 1980. Repr. of 1959 ed. lib. bdg. 28.00x (ISBN 0-8369-9289-X). Ayer Co Pubs.

--A Touch of Innocence. LC 59-10256. 312p. 1969. pap. 1.45 (ISBN 0-15-690771-2, Harv). HarBraceJ.

Dunham, Lowell. Romulo Gallegos: An Oklahoma Encounter & the Writing of the Last Novel. LC 73-19391. (Illus.). 100p. (Orig.). 1974. pap. 5.95x (ISBN 0-8061-1188-7). U of Okla Pr.

Dunham, Lowell & Ivask, Ivar. The Cardinal Points of Borges. LC 76-163635. (Illus.). 1971. 13.95x (ISBN 0-8061-0983-1); pap. 6.95x (ISBN 0-8061-0984-X). U of Okla Pr.

Dunham, Lowell, tr. see Caso, Alfonso.

Dunham, Lowell, tr. see Zea, Leopoldo.

Dunham, Randall, jt. auth. see Smith, Frank J.

Dunham, Randall B. Organizational Behaviour: People & Processes in Management. 1984. 27.95x (ISBN 0-256-02627-0). Irwin.

Dunham, Randall B., jt. auth. see Cummings, L. L.

Dunham, Russell. Episode on Hill Six Sixteen: Memoirs of Congressional Medal of Honor Recipient Russell Dunham. 1982. 12.50 (ISBN 0-916445-02-X). Crossroads Comm.

Dunham, Sam C. The Alaskan Gold Fields. (Illus.). 64p. 1984. pap. 5.95 (ISBN 0-88240-260-9). Alaska Northwest.

Dunham, Terry. TFH Book of Finches. (Illus.). 96p. 1983. 6.95 (ISBN 0-87666-818-X, HP-011). TFH Pubns.

Dunham, Tracy. Morgan's Land. LC 83-42729. (Western Ser.). 192p. 1983. 12.95 (ISBN 0-8027-4021-9). Walker & Co.

Dunham, Vera S. In Stalin's Time. LC 75-10238. 368p. 1976. pap. 13.95 (ISBN 0-521-29650-1). Cambridge U Pr.

Dunham, W. H., jt. ed. see Morris, W. A.

Dunham, William H. & Pargellis, Stanley M. Complaint & Reform in England, 1436-1714. 1967. lib. bdg. 52.00x (ISBN 0-374-92413-9). Octagon.

Dunham, William H., Jr. Lord Hastings' Indentured Retainers, 1461-1483: The Lawfulness of Livery & Retaining Under the Yorkists & Tudors. (Connecticut Academy of Arts & Sciences Transactions: Vol. 39). (Illus.). 175p. 1970. pap. 19.50 (ISBN 0-208-00989-2, Archon). Shoe String.

Dunham, William J., jt. auth. see Connors, Richard J.

Dunham, Wm. H. Fane Fragment of the 1461 Lord's Journal. (Yale Historical Pubs., Manuscripts & Edited Texts: No. XIV). 1935. 49.50x (ISBN 0-685-69813-0). Elliots Bks.

Dunhill, Thomas F. Chamber Music. (Select Bibliographies Reprint Ser.). 1972. Repr. of 1913 ed. 15.25 (ISBN 0-8369-9935-5). Ayer Co Pubs.

--Mozart's String Quartets. LC 77-104260. Repr. of 1927 ed. lib. bdg. 15.00x (ISBN 0-8371-3919-8, DUMQ). Greenwood.

--Sullivan's Comic Operas: A Critical Appreciation. (Music Ser.). 256p. 1981. Repr. of 1928 ed. lib. bdg. 27.50 (ISBN 0-306-76080-0). Da Capo.

Dunhouse, Mary B., ed. International Directory of Children's Literature: A Directory of Children's Literature. LC 73-91215. 164p. 1985. 24.95 (ISBN 0-914746-45-6); pap. 20.95 (ISBN 0-914746-44-8). G Kurian.

Duniec, M. L., jt. auth. see Davids, Kenneth.

Dunifon, jt. auth. see Cohn.

Dunigan, Jack. The Pastor's Handbook. (Orig.). 1985. pap. 6.95 (ISBN 0-932943-00-4). Life Lines.

Dunigan, Opal. Training Budgerigars to Talk. (Illus.). 128p. 1981. 8.95 (ISBN 0-87666-845-7, PS-791). TFH Pubns.

Dunin, Elsie I. South Slavic Dances in California: A Compendium for the Years 1924-1977. LC 79-63063. 1979. 10.00 (ISBN 0-918660-11-4). Ragusan Pr.

Dunin, Elsie I. & Ruyter, Nancy L. Yugoslav Dance: An Introduction & List of Sources Available in United States Libraries. LC 80-51688. 100p. 1981. perfect bound 10.00 (ISBN 0-918660-11-4). Ragusan Pr.

Duniphan, Steve. A Simple Man in a Complicated World. (Illus.). 1985. 10.00 (ISBN 0-934426-08-2). Napsac Reprods.

Dunitz, et al, eds. Structure & Bonding, Vol. 17. LC 67-11280. (Illus.). 260p. 1973. 43.00 (ISBN 0-387-06458-3). Springer-Verlag.

Dunitz, J. D., et al. Bonding Problems. (Structure & Bonding Ser.: Vol.43). (Illus.). 220p. 1981. 60.00 (ISBN 0-387-10407-0). Springer-Verlag.

--Inorganic Chemistry & Spectroscopy. (Structure & Bonding: Vol. 36). (Illus.). 1979. 51.00 (ISBN 0-387-09201-3). Springer-Verlag.

Dunitz, J. D., et al, eds. Alkali Metal Complexes with Organic Ligands. LC 67-11280. (Structure & Bonding Ser.: Vol. 16). (Illus.). iii, 189p. 1973. pap. 40.00 (ISBN 0-387-06423-0). Springer-Verlag.

--Biochemistry. (Structure & Bonding Ser.: Vol. 40). (Illus.). 160p. 1980. 52.00 (ISBN 0-387-09816-X). Springer-Verlag.

--Biochemistry. LC 67-11280. (Structure & Bonding Ser.: Vol. 23). (Illus.). iv, 193p. 1975. 46.00 (ISBN 0-387-07332-9). Springer-Verlag.

--Biochemistry. LC 67-11280. (Structure & Bonding: Vol. 29). (Illus.). 1976. 42.00 (ISBN 0-387-07886-X). Springer-Verlag.

--Coordinative Interactions. Incl. Metal Complexes of Chelating Olefin-Group V Ligands. Williams, R. J., et al.; Structural Radii, Electron-Cloud Radii, Ionic Radii & Solvation. Baughan, E. C; Quantitative Evaluation & Prediction of Donor-Acceptor Interactions. Drago, R. S; Redox Properties: Changes Affected by Coordination. Gutmann, V; Thermodynamics of the Stepwise Formation of Metal-Ion Complexes in Aqueous Solution. Ahrland, S. (Structure & Bonding Ser.: Vol. 15). (Illus.). 189p. 1973. pap. 40.00 (ISBN 0-387-06410-9). Springer-Verlag.

--Electrons in Oxygen & Sulphur-Containing Ligands. (Structure & Bonding: Vol. 28). (Illus.). 1976. 30.00 (ISBN 0-387-07753-7). Springer-Verlag.

--Inorganic Chemistry. (Structure & Bonding Ser.: Vol. 14). (Illus.). iii, 176p. 1973. pap. 38.00 (ISBN 0-387-06162-2). Springer-Verlag.

--Luminescence & Energy Transfer. (Structure & Bonding Ser.: Vol. 42). (Illus.). 133p. 1980. 45.00 (ISBN 0-387-10395-3). Springer-Verlag.

--Novel Aspects. LC 67-11280. (Structure & Bonding: Vol. 34). 1978. 48.00 (ISBN 0-387-08676-5). Springer-Verlag.

Dunitz, Jack D. X-Ray Analysis & the Structure of Organic Molecules. LC 78-15588. (George Fisher Baker Non-Resident Lectureship Ser.). 528p. 1979. 79.50x (ISBN 0-8014-1115-7). Cornell U Pr.

Duniway, A. S. Path Breaking, an Autobiographical History of the Equal Suffrage Movement in Pacific Coast States. LC 14-17220. Repr. of 1914 ed. 23.00 (ISBN 0-527-25700-1). Kraus Repr.

Duniway, Abigail S. Path Breaking: An Autobiographical History of the Equal Suffrage Movement in the Pacific Coast States. 2nd ed. LC 79-162285. (Studies in the Life of Women). 1971. pap. 5.50 (ISBN 0-8052-0322-2). Schocken.

Duniway, Clyde A. The Development of Freedom of the Press in Massachusetts. LC 68-58770. 202p. 1906. Repr. 21.00 (ISBN 0-8337-0957-7). B Franklin.

Duniway, David. Glimpses of Historic South Salem. 56p. (Orig.). 1982. pap. 3.95 (ISBN 0-9610326-0-X). S Salem News.

Dunk, Gillean. Ferns: For the Home & Garden. (Illus.). 130p. 1983. pap. 12.95 (ISBN 0-207-14675-6, Pub. by Salem Hse Ltd). Merrimack Pub Cir.

Dun Karm. Poet of Malta. Arberry, Arthur J. & Grech, P., eds. (University of Cambridge Oriental Pubns.). 1961. 39.50 (ISBN 0-521-04040-X). Cambridge U Pr.

Dunkel, jt. auth. see Virgo.

Dunkel, Harold B. Herbart & Education. 12.00 (ISBN 0-8446-2007-6). Peter Smith.

Dunkel, Harold B. & Pillet, Roger A. French in the Elementary School: Five Years Experience. LC 62-12631. pap. 39.00 (ISBN 0-317-09674-5, 2019962). Bks Demand UMI.

Dunkel, Patricia, jt. auth. see Pialorsi, Frank.

Dunkel, Patty L. Curriculum for Educators in Health Care Institutions: Proceedings & Recommendations of an Invitational Conference. 85p. 1978. 10.00 (ISBN 0-87914-046-1, 9620). Hosp Res & Educ.

--Curriculum for Educators in Health Care Institutions: Proceedings & Recommendations of an Invitational Conference. LC 77-26933. (Illus.). 1978. pap. 10.00 (ISBN 0-87914-046-1, 549620). Hosp Res & Educ.

Dunkel, Wilbur D. Sir Arthur Pinero, a Critical Biography with Letters. LC 67-27594. 1941. Repr. 15.00x (ISBN 0-8046-0123-2, Pub. by Kennikat). Assoc Faculty Pr.

Dunkelberg, William C., jt. auth. see Shay, Robert P.

Dunkelberg, William C., jt. auth. see Sonquist, John A.

Dunkell, Samuel. Lovelives: How We Make Love. (Illus.). 1980. pap. 3.50 (ISBN 0-451-12716-1, AE2716, Sig). NAL.

Dunkelman, Mark H. & Winey, Michael J. The Hardtack Regiment: An Illustrated History of the 154th Regiment, New York State Infantry Volunteers. LC 79-64502. (Illus.). 220p. 1981. 19.50 (ISBN 0-8386-3007-3). Fairleigh Dickinson.

Dunkels, Marjorie. Donkey Wrinkles & Tales. (Illus.). pap. 2.75 (ISBN 0-85131-274-8, NL51). J A Allen.

--Donkey Wrinkles & Tales: Donkey Discipline & Training. 1977. 10.00 (ISBN 0-87556-622-7). Saifer.

--Training Your Donkey. pap. write for info. (ISBN 0-85131-048-6, NL51, Dist. by Miller). J A Allen.

Dunker, George F., Jr., ed. California Legal Systems: Personal Injury. 1983. write for info. (089). Bender.

--California Personal Injury System. 1984. Updates avail. Incl. Disks 1695.00 (089); looseleaf 1984 150.00. Bender.

Dunker, Marilee P. Days of Glory, Seasons of Night. rev. ed. 176p. 1984. pap. text ed. 6.95 (ISBN 0-310-45501-4, 12040P, Pub. by Minister Res Lib). Zondervan.

Dunkerley, David, jt. auth. see Clegg, Stewart.

Dunkerley, Gary B. A Basic Atlas of the Human Nervous System. LC 75-14044. (Illus.). 216p. 1975. pap. text ed. 9.95x (ISBN 0-8036-2940-0). Davis Co.

Dunkerley, Harold B. & Whitehead, Christine M. E. Urban Land Policy: Issues & Opportunities. LC 82-20247. 224p. 1983. 22.50 (ISBN 0-19-520403-4, OX 520403). World Bank.

Dunkerley, Harold B., ed. Urban Land Policy: Issues & Opportunities. (Illus.). 1983. 22.50x (ISBN 0-19-520403-4). Oxford U Pr.

Dunkerley, James. The Long War: Dictatorship & Revolution in El Salvador. 264p. 1983. pap. 10.95 (ISBN 0-8052-7166-X, Pub. by NLB England). Schocken.

--Rebellion in the Veins: Political Struggle in Bolivia, 1952-82. (Illus.). 400p. 1984. 30.00 (ISBN 0-8052-7211-9, Pub. by Verso England); pap. 9.50 (ISBN 0-8052-7212-7, Pub. by Verso England). Schocken.

Dunkerley, Joy. International Comparisons of Energy Consumption. LC 78-4334. 256p. 1978. pap. 7.50x. (ISBN 0-8018-2129-0). Johns Hopkins.

Dunkerley, Joy & Alterman, Jack. Trends in Energy Use in Industrial Countries. LC 80-8022. (Resources for the Future Research Ser.: Paper R-19). (Illus., Orig.). 1980. pap. text ed. 8.00x (ISBN 0-8018-2487-7). Johns Hopkins.

Dunkerley, Joy, ed. International Comparisons of Energy Consumption. 259p. 1978. 7.50 (ISBN 0-8018-2129-0). Resources Future.

--International Energy Strategies: Proceedings of the 1979 IAEE-RFF Conference. LC 80-16503. 512p. 1980. pap. text ed. 30.00 (ISBN 0-89946-061-5). Oelgeschlager.

Dunkerley, Joy, et al. Energy Strategies for Developing Nations. LC 80-8774. (Resources for the Future Ser.). (Illus.). 288p. 1981. text ed. 24.00x (ISBN 0-8018-2596-2); pap. text ed. 9.50x (ISBN 0-8018-2597-0). Johns Hopkins.

Dunkerly, W. A. see Oxenham, John.

Dunkin, M. & Biddle, J. The Study of Teaching. 1982. Repr. of 1974 ed. text ed. cancelled (ISBN 0-8290-0603-6). Irvington.

Dunkin, Michael J. & Biddle, Bruce J. The Study of Teaching. LC 81-40903. (Illus.). 508p. 1982. pap. text ed. 18.50 (ISBN 0-8191-2259-9). U Pr of Amer.

Dunkin, Naomi. Psychology for Physiotherapists. (Psychology for Professional Groups Ser.). 350p. 1981. text ed. 23.75x (ISBN 0-333-31857-9, Pub. by Macmillan England); pap. text ed. 9.75x (ISBN 0-333-31884-6). Humanities.

Dunkin, Paul. How to Catalog a Rare Book. 2nd, rev. ed. LC 72-6515. pap. 29.30 (ISBN 0-317-30447-X, 2024922). Bks Demand UMI.

Dunkin, Steve. Church Advertising: A Practical Guide. LC 81-17562. (Creative Leadership Ser.). 128p. (Orig.). 1982. pap. 5.95 (ISBN 0-687-08140-8). Abingdon.

Dunkl, C. F. & Ramirez, D. E. Representations of Communicative Semitopological Semigroups. (Lecture Notes in Mathematics Ser.: Vol. 435). vi, 181p. 1975. pap. 14.00 (ISBN 0-387-07132-6). Springer-Verlag.

Dunkl, Charles F. & Ramirez, Donald E. Topics in Harmonic Analysis. LC 73-153387. (Century Mathematics Ser.). 1971. 34.50x (ISBN 0-89197-454-7); pap. text ed. 16.95x (ISBN 0-89197-969-7). Irvington.

Dunkle, David S. Guide to Pension & Profit Sharing Plans: Taxation, Selection, & Design. (Commercial Law Publications). 500p. 1984. write for info. (Pub. By Shepards-McGraw). McGraw.

Dunkle, Ruth E. & Haug, Marie R. Communications Technology & the Elderly: Issues & Forecasts. 256p. 1984. text ed. 31.00 (ISBN 0-8261-4060-2). Springer Pub.

Dunkle, Ruth E., jt. auth. see Hooper, Celia R.

Dunkle, W., Jr. Splendor of Gods Glory. 1978. 4.00 (ISBN 0-89536-351-8). CSS of Ohio.

Dunkley, Peter. The Crisis of the Old Poor Law in England, 1795-1834: An Interpretative Essay. Stansky, Peter & Hume, Leslie, eds. LC 81-48357. (Modern British History Ser.). 240p. 1982. lib. bdg. 34.00 (ISBN 0-8240-5153-X). Garland Pub.

Dunklin, Howard T. Prevention of Failure in First Grade Reading by Means of Adjusted Instruction. LC 71-176733. (Columbia University. Teachers College. Contributions to Education: No. 802). Repr. of 1940 ed. 22.50 (ISBN 0-404-55802-X). AMS Pr.

Dunkling, L see Allen, W. S.

Dunkling, Leslie. Our Secret Names: What Names Reveal & Conceal. 140p. 1982. 11.95 (ISBN 0-13-644443-1); pap. 5.95 (ISBN 0-13-644435-0). P-H.

Dunkling, Leslie & Gosling, William. The New American Dictionary of First Names. 1985. pap. 3.95 (ISBN 0-451-13872-4, Sig). NAL.

Dunkling, Leslie A. First Names First. 290p. 1982. Repr. of 1977 ed. 70.00x (ISBN 0-8103-0184-9). Gale.

Dunkman, William E. Qualitative Credit Control. (Columbia University. Studies in the Social Sciences: No. 395). Repr. of 1933 ed. 24.50 (ISBN 0-404-51395-6). AMS Pr.

Dunlap, jt. auth. see Belford.

Dunlap, A. Basic Cases in Public International Law. 1971. pap. text ed. 14.95x (ISBN 0-8290-1388-1). Irvington.

--Readings on National & Regional Foreign Policies. 1971. pap. text ed. 7.95x (ISBN 0-8290-1175-7). Irvington.

Dunlap, A. M. Behind the Bamboo Curtain. LC 72-14086. (Illus.). 208p. 1973. Repr. of 1956 ed. lib. bdg. 15.00x (ISBN 0-8371-6752-3, DUBC). Greenwood.

Dunlap, A. R. Dutch & Swedish Place-Names in Delaware. LC 57-62613. 66p. pap. 2.50 (ISBN 0-87413-110-3). U Delaware Pr.

Dunlap, Alice. Hospital Literature Subject Headings. 2nd ed. LC 77-519. 200p. 1977. pap. 31.25 (ISBN 0-87258-202-7, AHA-121006). Am Hospital.

Dunlap, Alice & Kiger, Anne F., eds. Hospital Literature Index: 1981 Cumulative Annual, Vol. 37. 612p. 1982. 125.00 (ISBN 0-87258-370-8, AHA 121370). Am Hospital.

Dunlap, Alice, et al, eds. Hospital Literature Index: 1980 Cumulative Annual, Vol. 36. 704p. 1981. 125.00 (ISBN 0-87258-348-1, AHA-121360). Am Hospital.

Dunlap, Alice, et al, eds. see American Hospital Association.

Dunlap, B. D., et al see Shenoy, G. K.

Dunlap, Carla & Dayton, Laura. Building the Perfect Body. (Illus.). 160p. 1986. 17.95 (ISBN 0-02-533980-X); pap. 8.95 (ISBN 0-02-028410-1). MacMillan.

Dunlap, Carol. California People. LC 82-10495. (Illus.). 240p. 1982. (Peregrine Smith); pap. 9.95 (ISBN 0-87905-091-8). Gibbs M Smith.

Dunlap, G. D., jt. auth. see Shufeldt, H. H.

Dunlap, George A. One Hectic Summer. 64p. 1981. 4.95 (ISBN 0-8059-2784-0). Dorrance.

Dunlap, Howard G. Social Aspects of a Verb Form: Native Atlanta Fifth-Grade Speech--the Present Tense of "Be". (Publications of the American Dialect Society: Nos. 61 & 62). 120p. 1974. pap. 9.35 (ISBN 0-8173-0661-7). U of Ala Pr.

Dunlap, Howard G., jt. auth. see Daniel, Wanda R.

Dunlap, J. Diseases of Racial & Ethnic Groups. 1978. 10.00 (ISBN 0-686-00962-2). World Intl.

--Diseases of Racial & Ethnic Groups. (Illus.). 1979. pap. 2.75 (ISBN 0-686-23755-2). World Intl.

--Medical Negligence Malpractice: The Uncontrolled Killer. 1976. 8.95 (ISBN 0-686-17451-8). World Intl.

--Medical Negligence: The Uncontrolled Killer. 1978. pap. 2.95 (ISBN 0-686-10225-8). World Intl.

--Medical Negligence: The Uncontrolled Killer. rev. ed. 1979. 10.75 (ISBN 0-686-24851-1). World Intl.

Dunlap, J., et al. Nazis Will Rule the World. 1979. 8.95 (ISBN 0-686-14563-1). World Intl.

Dunlap, J. Carlisle. Fitness for the Busy Executive in Only Ten Minutes per Day. 96p. 1985. 10.95 (ISBN 0-89896-247-1). Larksdale.

Dunlap, James. Diseases Caused by Discrimination. 1977. 7.95 (ISBN 0-686-17553-0). World Intl.

--The Health Food Store Can Save Your Life. 1977. 7.95 (ISBN 0-686-17625-1). World Intl.

--Intermarriage Prevents Disease. 1977. 8.95 (ISBN 0-686-17626-X). World Intl.

--Intermarriage Prevents Disease. 1978. pap. 2.50 (ISBN 0-686-22704-2). World Intl.

--Malpractice of Dentists, Psychiatrists & Chiropractors. 1978. pap. 2.25 (ISBN 0-686-22705-0). World Intl.

--Malpractice of Dentists, Psychiatrists, Chiropractors. 1977. 8.95 (ISBN 0-686-18980-9). World Intl.

Dunlap, James & Koken, Nickolas. World Nazism Grows. 1978. 8.95 (ISBN 0-686-20931-1). World Intl.

Dunlap, Jane B., jt. auth. see Pfeiffer, Isobel L.

Dunlap, Knight. Habits: Their Making & Unmaking. LC 77-184102. 336p. 1949. pap. 3.95 (ISBN 0-87140-267-X). Liveright.

--Mysticism, Freudianism & Scientific Psychology. facsimile ed. (Select Bibliographies Reprint Ser). Repr. of 1920 ed. 17.00 (ISBN 0-8369-5838-1). Ayer Co Pubs.

--Religion: Its Functions in Human Life: A Study of Religion from the Point of View of Psychology. LC 77-100158. Repr. of 1946 ed. lib. bdg. 17.75x (ISBN 0-8371-3716-0, DURE). Greenwood.

Dunlap, Leslie W. American Historical Societies: 1790-1860. LC 73-16331. (Perspectives in American History Ser.: No. 7). 238p. Repr. of 1944 ed. lib. bdg. 19.50x (ISBN 0-87991-343-6). Porcupine Pr.

Dunlap, Lloyd A., ed. see Scripps, John L.

Dunlap, Lois C. Mental Health Concepts Applied to Nursing. 256p. 1978. pap. 25.50 (ISBN 0-471-04360-5). Wiley.

Dunlap, Mary J. Children Hour. 1984. 4.95 (ISBN 0-8062-2188-7). Carlton.

Dunlap, Mary M., et al, eds. A Catalog of the South Caroliniana Collection of J. Rion McKissick. LC 77-3552. (The South Caroliniana Ser.: Bibliographical & Textual, No. 1). (Illus.). 1977. 21.00 (ISBN 0-87152-250-0). Reprint.

Dunlap, Orrin E. Radio's One Hundred Men of Science. facs. ed. LC 70-128235. (Essay Index Reprint Ser). 1944. 25.00 (ISBN 0-8369-1916-5). Ayer Co Pubs.

Dunlap, Orrin E., Jr. Marconi: The Man & His Wireless. rev. ed. LC 72-161142. (History of Broadcasting: Radio to Television Ser). 1971. Repr. of 1937 ed. 32.00 (ISBN 0-405-03563-2). Ayer Co Pubs.

Dunlap, R. Bruce, ed. Immobilized Biochemicals & Affinity Chromatography. LC 74-7471. (Advances in Experimental Medicine & Biology Ser.: Vol. 42). 388p. 1974. 59.50x (ISBN 0-306-39042-6, Plenum Pr). Plenum Pub.

Dunlap, Rhodes, ed. see Carew, Thomas.

Dunlap, Roy. The Gunowner's Book of Care, Repair & Maintenance. LC 73-92404. (Outdoor Life). (Illus.). 320p. 1974. 12.95i (ISBN 0-06-011137-2, HarpT). Har-Row.

Dunlap, Roy F. Gunsmithing. LC 63-21755. (Illus.). 848p. 1963. 27.95 (ISBN 0-8117-0770-9). Stackpole.

Dunlap, Shirlee. Circle of Light. (Illus.). 183p. (Orig.). 1982. pap. 7.95 (ISBN 0-942494-19-9). Coleman Pub.

Dunlap Society. Biennial Reports of the Treasurer & Secretary of the Dunlap Society. LC 71-130084. (Drama Ser). 1970. Repr. of 1888 ed. 16.50 (ISBN 0-8337-4083-0). B Franklin.

Dunlap, Susan. As a Favor. 192p. 1984. 12.95 (ISBN 0-312-05594-3). St Martin.

--An Equal Opportunity Death: A Mystery. 192p. 1984. 12.95 (ISBN 0-312-25775-9). St Martin.

--Not Exactly a Brahmin: A Jill Smith Mystery. 192p. 1985. 12.95 (ISBN 0-312-57947-0). St Martin.

Dunlap, Thomas R. DDT: Scientists, Citizens, & Public Policy. LC 80-8546. 304p. 1981. 32.00x (ISBN 0-691-04680-8); pap. 10.95 (ISBN 0-691-00592-3). Princeton U Pr.

Dunlap, Virginia & Winchester, Barbara. Vocal Chamber Music: A Selected Bibliography. LC 83-49309. (Library of the Humanities). 178p. 1985. lib. bdg. 26.00 (ISBN 0-8240-9003-9). Garland Pub.

Dunlap, W. Crawford, ed. see International Conference on Hot Electrons in Semiconductors, Denton, TX, 6-8 Jul. 1977.

Dunlap, William. Andre: A Tragedy in Five Acts. LC 74-130082. (Dunlap Society Ser.: No. 4). 1970. Repr. lib. bdg. 16.50 (ISBN 0-8337-0960-7). B Franklin.

--Diary of William Dunlap, 3 Vols. in 1. LC 78-84204. 1930. 44.00 (ISBN 0-405-08474-9, Blom Pubns). Ayer Co Pubs.

--Father, or American Shandyism: A Comedy. LC 77-130080. (Dunlap Society Ser.: No. 2). 1970. Repr. of 1887 ed. lib. bdg. 16.50 (ISBN 0-8337-0959-3). B Franklin.

--Four Plays, 1789-1812. LC 76-46978. 300p. 1976. lib. bdg. 45.00x (ISBN 0-8201-1283-6). Schol Facsimiles.

--A History of the American Theatre. 59.95 (ISBN 0-8490-0351-2). Gordon Pr.

--History of the American Theatre & Anecdotes of the Principal Actors, 3 vols. in 1. 2nd ed. Incl. A Narrative of His Connection with the Old American Company 1792-1797. Hodgkinson, John. LC 11-19430. 1832. Repr. 36.50 (ISBN 0-8337-0964-X). B Franklin.

--History of the New Netherlands, Province of New York, & State of New York, to the Adoption of the Federal Constitution, 2 Vols. LC 70-130594. 1970. Repr. of 1839 ed. Set. 48.00 (ISBN 0-8337-0963-1). B Franklin.

--History of the Rise & Progress of the Arts of Design in the United States, 3 vols. rev. ed. Bayley, Frank W., et al, eds. LC 65-16236. (Illus.). 1964. Set. 82.50 (ISBN 0-405-08470-6, Blom Pubns); 27.50 ea. Vol. 1 (ISBN 0-405-08471-4). Vol. 2 (ISBN 0-405-08472-2). Vol. 3 (ISBN 0-405-08473-0). Ayer Co Pubs.

--A History of the Rise & Progress of the Arts of Design in the U. S, 2 vols. bound as 3. Weiss, Rita, ed. (Illus.). Repr. of 1834 ed. 45.00 (ISBN 0-8446-0598-0). Peter Smith.

--The Life of Charles Brockden Brown, 2 vols. 1977. Repr. 75.00 (ISBN 0-403-08555-1). Scholarly.

--Musical Works. LC 79-24504. 1979. 45.00x (ISBN 0-8201-1348-4). Schol Facsimiles.

--Thirty Years Ago, or the Memoirs of a Water Drinker, 2 Vols. Repr. of 1836 ed. 28.00 (ISBN 0-384-13324-X). Johnson Repr.

Dunlavy, John. Manifesto, or a Declaration of the Doctrines & Practice of the Church of Christ. LC 74-134416. Repr. of 1818 ed. 34.50 (ISBN 0-404-08460-5). AMS Pr.

Dunlay, Thomas W. Wolves for the Blue Soldiers: Indian Scouts & Auxiliaries with the United States Army, 1860-90. LC 81-16326. (Illus.). xii, 316p. 1982. 23.95x (ISBN 0-8032-1658-0). U of Nebr Pr.

Dunleavy, jt. ed. see Ashe.

Dunleavy, Aidan O. & Miracle, Andrew W., eds. Studies in the Sociology of Sport. LC 82-16807. 420p. 1982. pap. 15.00x (ISBN 0-912646-78-0). Tex Christian.

Dunleavy, Gareth. Douglas Hyde. (Irish Writers Ser.). 92p. 1974. 4.50 (ISBN 0-8387-7883-6); pap. 1.95 (ISBN 0-8387-7975-1). Bucknell U Pr.

Dunleavy, Janet E. George Moore: The Artist's Vision, the Storyteller's Art. LC 75-125793. 156p. 1973. 16.50 (ISBN 0-8387-7757-0). Bucknell U Pr.

Dunleavy, Janet E., ed. George Moore in Perspective. LC 83-3722. (Irish Literary Studies: No. 16). (Illus.). 174p. 1983. text ed. 28.50x (ISBN 0-389-20395-5). B&N Imports.

Dunleavy, Patrick. The Politics of Mass Housing in Britain, 1945-1975: A Study of Corporate Power & Professional Influence in the Welfare State. (Illus.). 1981. 43.50x (ISBN 0-19-827426-2). Oxford U Pr.

--Urban Political Analysis: The Politics of Collective Consumption. 176p. 1980. text ed. 23.00x (ISBN 0-333-23948-2). Humanities.

Dunleavy, Patrick & Husbands, Christopher T. British Democracy at the Crossroads: Voting & Party Competition in the 1980's. (Illus.). 320p. 1985. text ed. 25.00x (ISBN 0-04-324010-0); pap. text ed. 13.50x (ISBN 0-04-324011-9). Allen Unwin.

Dunleavy, Steve. The Very First Lady. 1982. pap. 3.50 (ISBN 0-440-19314-1). Dell.

Dunlevy, Marion B., jt. auth. see Maxwell, Alice S.

Dunlop, Bill & Drigotas, Frank M., Jr. One Man Alone: Across the Atlantic in a Nine-Foot Boat. (Illus.). 128p. 1983. pap. 8.95 (ISBN 0-89272-182-0, 520). Down East.

Dunlop, Burton, jt. auth. see Durman, E. C.

Dunlop, Burton D. The Growth of Nursing Home Care. LC 78-14715. 1979. 26.50x (ISBN 0-669-02704-9). Lexington Bks.

Dunlop, Charles E., ed. Philosophical Essays on Dreaming. LC 77-4582. 372p. 1977. 24.95x (ISBN 0-8014-1015-0); pap. 9.95x (ISBN 0-8014-9862-7). Cornell U Pr.

Dunlop, D. M., ed. Muntakhab Siwan Al-Hikmah of Abu Sulaiman As-Sijistani. (Near & Middle East Monographs: No. 4). (Arabic.). 1979. text ed. 38.00x (ISBN 90-279-3377-4). Mouton.

Dunlop, David J., ed. Origin of Thermoremanent Magnetization. 1979. 24.50x (ISBN 0-89955-133-5, Pub. by Japan Sci Soc Japan). Intl Spec Bk.

Dunlop, David L. & Sigmund, Thomas F. Problem Solving with a Programmable Calculator: Puzzles, Games, & Simulations with Math & Science Applications. (Illus.). 227p. 1982. 19.95 (ISBN 0-13-721340-9); pap. 10.95 (ISBN 0-13-721332-8). P-H.

Dunlop, David W., jt. ed. see Mushkin, Selma J.

Dunlop, Douglas. Arab Civilization to A.D. 1500. (Arab Background Ser.). 1971. 20.00x (ISBN 0-86685-012-0). Intl Bk Ctr.

Dunlop, Eileen. The Maze Stone. LC 82-22232. (gr. 6 up). 1983. 10.95 (ISBN 0-698-20587-1, Coward). Putnam Pub Group.

Dunlop, Eileen & Kamm, Antony, eds. A Book of Old Edinburgh. 1983. 59.00x (ISBN 0-86334-012-1, Pub. by Macdonald Pub UK). State Mutual Bk.

Dunlop, Emma E. & Paris, Pat. Have You Snuzzled A Wuzzle Today? LC 85-2141. (Illus.). 32p. (gr. 4-8). 1985. bds. 4.95 (ISBN 0-394-87495-1, BYR). Random.

Dunlop, Francis. The Education of Feeling & Emotion. (Introductory Studies in Philosophy of Education). 144p. 1984. text ed. 14.95x (ISBN 0-04-370132-9); pap. text ed. 7.50x (ISBN 0-04-370133-7). Allen Unwin.

Dunlop, G. D. Successful Celestial Navigation with H. O. 229. LC 76-8771. pap. 40.00 (ISBN 0-317-27601-8, 2025072). Bks Demand UMI.

Dunlop, Geoffrey, tr. see Roth, Joseph.

Dunlop, Geoffrey, tr. see Werfel, Franz.

Dunlop, I. & Schrand, H. Communication for Business: Materials for Reading Comprehension & Discussion. (Materials for Language Practice Ser.). (Illus.). 110p. 1982. pap. 4.50 (ISBN 0-08-029438-3). Pergamon.

Dunlop, Ian. The Cathedrals' Crusade. 256p. 1981. 50.00x (ISBN 0-241-10689-3, Pub. by Hamish Hamilton England). State Mutual Bk.

--The Cathedrals' Crusade. LC 81-14431. (Illus.). 256p. 1982. 20.00 (ISBN 0-8008-1316-2). Taplinger.

--Degas. LC 79-1660. (Illus.). 1979. 37.50i (ISBN 0-06-011111-9, HarpT). Har-Row.

--Edvard Munch. LC 77-71078. (Art for All Ser.). 1977. pap. 5.95 (ISBN 0-312-23822-3). St Martin.

--Royal Palaces of France. 1985. 35.00 (ISBN 0-393-02222-6). Norton.

Dunlop, J. & Smith, D. G. Telecommunications Engineering. 1985. pap. 19.95 (ISBN 0-442-30586-9). Van Nos Reinhold.

Dunlop, Jean. The British Fisheries Society 1786-1893. 280p. 1982. 40.00x (ISBN 0-85976-026-X, Pub. by Donald Pubs Scotland). State Mutual Bk.

Dunlop, Jocelyn & Denman, R. P. English Apprenticeship & Child Labor: A History. 1976. lib. bdg. 59.95 (ISBN 0-8490-1770-X). Gordon Pr.

Dunlop, John, ed. Labor in the Twentieth Century. (Studies in Labor Economics Ser.). 1978. 27.50 (ISBN 0-12-224350-1). Acad Pr.

Dunlop, John B. The Faces of Contemporary Russian Nationalism. LC 83-42554. 363p. 1983. 32.50x (ISBN 0-691-05390-1). Princeton U Pr.

--The Recent Activities of the Moscow Patriarchate Abroad & in the USSR. 2nd ed. Holy Transfiguration Monastery, ed. 235p. (Orig.). 1986. pap. 7.50x (ISBN 0-913026-58-1). St Nectarios.

Dunlop, John B., et al, eds. Solzhenitsyn in Exile: Critical Essays & Documentary Materials. (Publication Ser.: No. 305). xv, 416p. 1985. lib. bdg. 19.95 (ISBN 0-8179-8051-2). Hoover Inst Pr.

Dunlop, John C. History of Prose Fiction, 2 Vols. Wilson, Henry, ed. LC 71-95396. 1969. Repr. of 1906 ed. Set. 32.50 (ISBN 0-404-02218-9). Vol. 1 (ISBN 0-404-02219-7). Vol. 2 (ISBN 0-404-02220-0). AMS Pr.

--History of Roman Literature. 72.25 (ISBN 0-8369-7266-X, 8065). Ayer Co Pubs.

Dunlop, John C., ed. History of Prose Fiction, 2 Vols. new ed. 1970. text ed. 34.50 (ISBN 0-8337-0967-4). B Franklin.

Dunlop, John T. Business & Public Policy. LC 80-81866. (Harvard Business School Publications Ser.). 144p. 1981. 8.95 (ISBN 0-87584-119-8). Harvard U Pr.

--Dispute Resolution: Negotiation & Consensus Building. LC 83-27531. 320p. 1984. 24.95 (ISBN 0-86569-123-1). Auburn Hse.

--The Secular Outlook: Wages & Prices. 1957. 2.00 (ISBN 0-89215-046-7). U Cal LA Indus Rel.

--Wage Determination Under Trade Unions. LC 50-58147. Repr. of 1944 ed. 25.00x (ISBN 0-678-00137-5). Kelley.

Dunlop, John T. & Brown, Irving. Labor & International Affairs: Two Views. LC 84-80548. 44p. (Orig.). 1984. pap. 3.00 (ISBN 0-934742-27-8, Inst Study Diplomacy). Geo U Sch For Serv.

Dunlop, John T. & Fedor, Kenneth J., eds. The Lessons of Wage & Price Controls--the Food Sector. LC 77-86591. 1978. 24.95x (ISBN 0-87584-117-1). Harvard Busn.

Dunlop, John T., ed. see Slichter, Sumner H.

Dunlop, Laurence. Patterns of Prayer in the Psalms. 160p. (Orig.). 1982. pap. 9.95 (ISBN 0-8164-2377-6, Pub. by Seabury). Winston Pr.

Dunlop, Philip, tr. see Tibullus.

Dunlop, Richard. Donovan: America's Master Spy. (Illus.). 576p. 1982. 19.95 (ISBN 0-528-81117-7). Rand.

Dunlop, Robert. Daniel O'Connell & the Revival of National Life in Ireland. LC 73-14439. (Heroes of the Nations Ser.). Repr. of 1900 ed. 30.00 (ISBN 0-404-58258-3). AMS Pr.

Dunlop, S., tr. see Hoffmeister, C., et al.

Dunlop, Storm. Macmillan Practical Guides: Astronomy. Lippman, ed. (Illus.). 192p. 1985. pap. 8.95 (ISBN 0-02-079650-1, Collier). Macmillan.

Dunlop, Storm, jt. auth. see Ronan, Colin.

Dunman, Jack. Agriculture: Capitalist & Socialist. 1975. text ed. 13.00x (ISBN 0-85315-330-2). Humanities.

Dunmire, Reba. Toys of Early America: You Can Make. (Illus.). 64p. (Orig.). 1983. pap. text ed. 6.00 (ISBN 0-87006-441-X). Goodheart.

Dunmore. The Stalinist Command Economy. LC 79-26712. 224p. 1980. 26.00 (ISBN 0-312-75516-3). St Martin.

Dunmore, Charles W. Selections from Ovid. rev. ed. LC 63-12153. 1969. pap. text ed. 12.50x (ISBN 0-582-28131-8). Longman.

Dunmore, Charles W. & Fleischer, Rita M. Medical Terminology: Exercise in Etymology. 327p. 1977. pap. text ed. 13.95x (ISBN 0-8036-2945-1). Davis Co.

Dunmore, Charles W. & Fleisher, Rita M. Medical Terminology: Exercises in Etymology. 2nd ed. 350p. 1985. pap. text ed. 16.95 (ISBN 0-8036-2946-X, 2946-X). Davis Co.

Dunmore, John. The Expedition of the St. Jean-Baptiste to the Pacific, 1769-1770. 1981. 50.00x (ISBN 0-904180-11-5, Pub. by Hakluyt Soc England). State Mutual Bk.

Dunmore, Spencer. Collision. 1981. pap. 2.50 (ISBN 0-89083-720-1). Zebra.

--The Sound of Wings. Date not set. price not set. MacMillan.

--The Sounds of Wings. LC 84-21355. 288p. 1985. 13.95 (ISBN 0-02-533910-9). Macmillan.

Dunmore, Timothy. Soviet Politics, Nineteen Forty-Five to Nineteen Fifty-Three. LC 83-40702. 176p. 1984. 27.50 (ISBN 0-312-74869-8). St Martin.

Dunn. The Sun Also Rises (Hemingway) (Book Notes Ser.). 1984. pap. 2.50 (ISBN 0-8120-3443-0). Barron.

Dunn, jt. auth. see Alter.

Dunn, et al. Rural Housing: Competition & Choice. (Urban & Regional Studies: No. 9). (Illus.). 28p. 1981. pap. text ed. 37.50x (ISBN 0-04-309105-9, 2652). Allen Unwin.

Dunn, A. J., jt. ed. see Nemeroff, C. B.

Dunn, A. M., jt. auth. see Hinton, H. E.

Dunn, A. S. Rubber & Rubber Elasticity, No. 48. (Journal of Polymer Science: Polymer Symposia). 232p. 1974. pap. 15.00 (ISBN 0-685-88107-5, Pub. by Wiley). Krieger.

Dunn, Alan, jt. auth. see Thorpe, Denis.

Dunn, Albert H. & Johnson, Eugene M. Managing Your Sales Team. (Illus.). 224p. 1980. 13.95 (ISBN 0-13-550905-X, Spec); pap. 6.95 (ISBN 0-13-550897-5). P-H.

Dunn, Allan J. The Flower of Fate. Reginald, R. & Melville, Douglas, eds. LC 77-84219. (Lost Race & Adult Fantasy Ser.). 1978. Repr. of 1928 ed. lib. bdg. 24.50x (ISBN 0-405-10974-1). Ayer Co Pubs.

Dunn, Angela. Mathematical Bafflers. rev. ed. (Illus.). 217p. 1980. pap. 3.75 (ISBN 0-486-23961-6). Dover.

--Second Book of Mathematical Bafflers. (Puzzles, Amusements, Recreations Ser.). (Illus.). 192p. (Orig.). 1983. pap. 3.95 (ISBN 0-486-24352-4). Dover.

Dunn, Arthur W. From Harrison to Harding, 2 Vols. LC 78-137908. (American History & Culture in the Nineteenth Century Ser). 1971. Repr. of 1922 ed. Set. 67.50x (ISBN 0-8046-1476-8, Pub. by Kennikat). Assoc Faculty Pr.

--Gridiron Nights: Humorous & Satirical Views of Politics & Statesmen, Presented by the Dining Club. LC 73-19141. (Politics & People Ser.). (Illus.). 402p. 1974. Repr. 27.50x (ISBN 0-405-05866-7). Ayer Co Pubs.

Dunn, Brian, ed. see Runyan, Scot T.

Dunn, Bruce. Make the Most of Your Internship. 46p. (Orig.). 1983. pap. 5.95 (ISBN 0-939296-07-1). Bond Pub Co.

Dunn, C. D., ed. Current Concepts in Erythropoiesis. 415p. 1983. 60.00 (ISBN 0-471-90033-8, Pub. by Wiley Med). Wiley.

Dunn, C. J. & Yanoda, S. Teach Yourself Japanese. (Teach Yourself Ser.). pap. 5.95 (ISBN 0-679-10185-3). McKay.

Dunn, Carola. Angel. LC 83-19693. 192p. 1984. 12.95 (ISBN 0-8027-0756-4). Walker & Co.

--Angel. 208p. 1985. pap. 2.50 (ISBN 0-446-32797-2). Warner Bks.

--Lavender Lady. 1983. 11.95 (ISBN 0-8027-0734-3). Walker & Co.

--Lavender Lady. 224p. 1985. pap. 2.50 (ISBN 0-446-32799-9). Warner Bks.

--The Miser's Sister. 192p. 1984. 13.95 (ISBN 0-8027-0804-8). Walker & Co.

Dunn, Charles. American Democracy Debated: An Introduction to American Government. 2nd ed. 1982. text ed. 22.75x (ISBN 0-673-15547-1). Scott F.

--The Upstream Christian in a Downstream World. LC 79-65191. 155p. 1979. pap. 4.95 (ISBN 0-88207-789-9). Victor Bks.

Dunn, Charles, tr. see Kaiko, Takeshi.

Dunn, Charles J. Everyday Life in Traditional Japan. (Illus.). 1977. pap. 5.25 (ISBN 0-8048-1229-2). C E Tuttle.

Dunn, Charles W. American Political Theology: Historical Perspective & Theoretical Analysis. LC 84-13308. 208p. 1984. 29.95x (ISBN 0-03-071843-0); pap. 12.95x (ISBN 0-03-071844-9). Praeger.

--Highland Settler: A Portrait of the Scottish Gael in Nova Scotia. LC 53-7025. 1953. pap. 7.95 (ISBN 0-8020-6094-3). U of Toronto Pr.

Dunn, Charles W., ed. The Actors' Analects. LC 79-8837. (Studies in Oriental Culture Ser). (Illus.). 306p. 1970. 26.00x (ISBN 0-231-03391-5). Columbia U Pr.

--Chaucer Reader: Selections from the Canterbury Tales. 225p. 1952. pap. text ed. 13.95 (ISBN 0-15-506411-8, HC). HarBraceJ.

Dunn, Charles W., ed. see Geoffrey of Monmouth.

Dunn, Charleta J. & Payne, Bill F. World of Work. 1971. 4.95x (ISBN 0-685-22703-0); vocational bks. kit avail. (ISBN 0-685-22704-9). Leslie Pr.

Dunn, Clarice & Lewis, Gen, eds. We Were Children Then, Vol. II. LC 76-22961. 249p. 1982. pap. 10.95 (ISBN 0-88361-085-X). Stanton & Lee.
Dunn, D. Try Giving Yourself Away. 3rd ed. LC 74-102032. 1970. deluxe ed. 7.95 (ISBN 0-13-932467-4); pap. 2.95 (ISBN 0-13-932442-9). P-H.
Dunn, D. A. Models of Particles & Moving Media. 1971. 59.50 (ISBN 0-12-224250-5). Acad Pr.
Dunn, Dalmer D. Financing Presidential Campaigns. LC 72-64. (Brookings Institution Studies in Presidential Selection). pap. 46.00 (ISBN 0-317-20807-1, 2025373). Bks Demand UMI.
Dunn, Daphne F. The Clownfish Sea Anemones. LC 80-68486. (Transactions Ser.: Vol. 71, Pt. 1). 1981. 12.00. Am Philos.
Dunn, David. Sky Drift. LC 80-80806. (Illus.). 90p. 1979. soft wrap-around cover 13.50 (ISBN 0-939044-27-7). Lingua Pr.
Dunn, David, jt. auth. see Gaburo, Kenneth.
Dunn, David H. The Myth Behind the Man. 136p. 1981. 7.95 (ISBN 0-8059-2806-5). Dorrance.
Dunn, Dennis J. The Catholic Church & the Soviet Government. (East European Monographs: No. 30). 267p. 1977. 25.00x (ISBN 0-914710-23-0). East Eur Quarterly.
Dunn, Dennis J., ed. Religion & Communist Society: Selected Papers from the Second World Congress for Soviet & East European Studies. 165p. (Orig.). 1983. pap. 14.00 (ISBN 0-933884-29-X). Berkeley Slavic.
Dunn, Diane. Short but Sweet. LC 84-90050. 45p. 1984. 5.95 (ISBN 0-533-06128-8). Vantage.
Dunn, Donald J., Jr. & Flynn, Kathlee M. Immigration & Nationality Law Review, 1976-84, 7 vols. LC 76-43517. Vol. 1. lib. bdg. 35.00; Vol. 2. lib. bdg. 35.00; Vol. 3. lib. bdg. 35.00; Vol. 4, 1980-81. lib. bdg. 35.00; lib. bdg. 35.00; lib. bdg. 230.00 (ISBN 0-930342-68-2); Vol. 6. lib. bdg. 38.50; Vol. 7. lib. bdg. 38.50. W S Hein.
Dunn, Douglas. Elegies. LC 84-25880. 64p. 1985. 15.95 (ISBN 0-571-13570-6); pap. 8.95 (ISBN 0-571-13469-6). Faber & Faber.
--Secret Villages. 224p. 1985. 15.95 (ISBN 0-396-08606-3). Dodd.
--Terry Street. 62p. 1971. pap. 3.95 (ISBN 0-571-09713-8). Faber & Faber.
Dunn, Douglas, ed. The Poetry of Scotland. (Illus.). 127p. 1980. 15.50 (ISBN 0-7134-1414-6, Pub. by Batsford England). David & Charles.
--Two Decades of Irish Writing: A Critical Survey. LC 75-7932. 1975. 18.95 (ISBN 0-8023-1253-5). Dufour.
Dunn, Douglas, ed. see Byron, Lord.
Dunn, E. Catherine, et al, eds. The Medieval Drama & Its Claudelian Revival. LC 79-121385. 72p. 1970. pap. 5.95x (ISBN 0-8132-0505-0). Cath U Pr.
Dunn, Edgar S. Social Information Processing & Statistical Systems-Change & Reform. LC 74-5289. pap. 64.00 (ISBN 0-317-10338-5, 2051570). Bks Demand UMI.
Dunn, Edgar S., Jr. The Development of the U. S. Urban System: Concepts, Structures, Regional Shifts, Vol. I & II. (Resources for the Future Ser.). 1980. text ed. 115.00x (ISBN 0-8018-3150-4). Johns Hopkins.
--The Development of the U.S. Urban System: Concepts, Structures, Regional Shifts, Vol. I. 240p. 1980. 65.00 (ISBN 0-8018-2196-7). Resources Future.
--Economic & Social Development: A Process of Social Learning. LC 70-134691. (Resources for the Future Ser). 342p. 1971. 24.50x (ISBN 0-8018-1198-8). Johns Hopkins.
--Economic & Social Development: A Process of Social Learning. 342p. 1971. 24.50 (ISBN 0-8018-1198-8). Resources Future.
--Recent Southern Economic Development as Revealed by the Changing Structure of Employment. LC 62-63139. (University of Florida Social Sciences Monographs: No. 14). (Illus.). 1962. pap. 3.50 (ISBN 0-8130-0067-X). U Presses Fla.
Dunn, Edmond J. Missionary Theology: Foundations in Development. LC 80-67259. 409p. 1980. lib. bdg. 27.50 (ISBN 0-8191-1209-7); pap. text ed. 16.50 (ISBN 0-8191-1210-0). U Pr of Amer.
Dunn, Edward C. Dawn at PM: A History of the Patrician Movement. (Illus.). 1984. 12.95 (ISBN 0-89015-466-X). Eakin Pubns.
Dunn, Eleanor, ed. Let's Cook Today. (gr. k-3). 1974. 3.95x (ISBN 0-933892-03-9). Child Focus Co.
--Lexikits. (gr. k-3). 1973. 6.95 (ISBN 0-933892-04-7). Child Focus Co.
--Lexilogs. (gr. k-3). 1973. 6.95 (ISBN 0-933892-05-5). Child Focus Co.
Dunn, Esther C. Ben Jonson's Art. 159p. 1980. Repr. of 1925 ed. lib. bdg. 30.00 (ISBN 0-8495-1122-4). Arden Lib.
--Literature of Shakespeare's England. LC 68-58513. Repr. of 1936 ed. 25.00 (ISBN 0-8154-0273-2). Cooper Sq.
--Shakespeare in America. LC 68-21212. (Illus.). 1968. Repr. of 1939 ed. 18.00 (ISBN 0-405-08475-7, Blom Pubns). Ayer Co Pubs.
--Shakespeare in America. 310p. Repr. of 1939 ed. lib. bdg. 50.00 (ISBN 0-89984-170-8). Century Bookbindery.
Dunn, F. S. The Diplomatic Protection of Americans in Mexico. (MLA MS). Repr. of 1933 ed. 28.00 (ISBN 0-527-25750-8). Kraus Repr.
--Protection of Nationals. Repr. of 1932 ed. 20.00 (ISBN 0-527-25760-5). Kraus Repr.
Dunn, Fannie W. Interest Factors in Primary Reading Material. LC 79-177602. (Columbia University. Teachers College. Contributions to Education: No. 113). Repr. of 1921 ed. 22.50 (ISBN 0-404-55113-0). AMS Pr.
Dunn, Finlay. American Farming & Food. 1980. lib. bdg. 75.00 (ISBN 0-8490-3185-0). Gordon Pr.
Dunn, Forrest D. Butte County Place Names. (ANCRR Occasional Paper: No. 3). 122p. 1977. 6.00 (ISBN 0-686-38932-8). Assn NC Records.
Dunn, Frank. Paul's Later Life & Letters. pap. 1.00 (ISBN 0-88027-101-9). Firm Foun Pub.
Dunn, Frank E. The Ministering Teacher. 112p. 1982. pap. 5.95 (ISBN 0-8170-0958-2). Judson.
Dunn, Frank T., compiled by. A Cumulative Analytic Index to the Dickensian 1905-1974: Together with an Index to the Illustrations Compiled by Mary Ford & Michael Slater. 212p. 1976. text ed. 60.50x (ISBN 0-85527-049-7). Humanities.
Dunn, Frederick S. Peace-Making & the Settlement with Japan. LC 81-6223. xviii, 210p. 1981. Repr. of 1963 ed. lib. bdg. 23.50x (ISBN 0-313-23076-5, DUPM). Greenwood.
--Practice & Procedure of International Conferences. LC 70-158959. Repr. of 1929 ed. 14.50 (ISBN 0-404-02221-9). AMS Pr.
--War & the Minds of Men. LC 79-131371. xvi, 115p. 1971. Repr. of 1950 ed. 12.00 (ISBN 0-208-00945-0, Archon). Shoe String.
Dunn, G. & Everitt, B. S. An Introduction to Mathematical Taxonomy. LC 81-7658. (Cambridge Studies in Mathematical Biology: No. 5). 120p. 1982. 34.50 (ISBN 0-521-23979-6); pap. 13.95 (ISBN 0-521-28388-4). Cambridge U Pr.
Dunn, G., jt. auth. see Everitt, B. S.
Dunn, G. H., jt. ed. see Maerk, T. D.
Dunn, G. P., et al. Some Properties of the Bank Model. (Bank of England, Discussion Papers, Technical Ser.: No. 9). pap. 28.80 (ISBN 0-317-26529-6, 2023978). Bks Demand UMI.
Dunn, George E. A Gilbert & Sullivan Dictionary. LC 72-10177. 1972. Repr. of 1936 ed. lib. bdg. 25.00 (ISBN 0-8414-0683-9). Folcroft.
Dunn, George E., ed. Gilbert & Sullivan Dictionary. LC 72-125070. (Music Ser). 1971. Repr. of 1936 ed. lib. bdg. 22.95 (ISBN 0-306-70007-7). Da Capo.
Dunn, H. H. The Crimson Jester: Zapata of Mexico. 1976. lib. bdg. 59.95 (ISBN 0-87968-964-1). Gordon Pr.
Dunn, H. L. High Level Wellness. LC 61-17851. 1977. pap. 8.95 (ISBN 0-87948-030-0). Slack Inc.
Dunn, Halbert L. High Level Wellness. 7th ed. (Positive Health Bookshelf Ser., Vol. 1). 1972. 9.95 (ISBN 0-87948-002-5); pap. 6.95 (ISBN 0-685-06827-7). Beatty.
--Your World & Mine. 1970. 5.95 (ISBN 0-87948-001-7). Beatty.
Dunn, Hampton. Yesterday's Tampa. LC 72-82937. (Illus.). 1977. pap. 5.95 (ISBN 0-912458-92-5). E A Seemann.
Dunn, Henry. Guatimala, or the Republic of Central America, in 1827-8: Being Sketches & Memorandums Made During a Twelve-Months Residence. LC 80-25556. 1981. Repr. of 1829 ed. 25.00. Ethridge.
Dunn, Henry T. Recollections of Dante Gabriel Rossetti & His Circle. Pedrick, Gale, ed. LC 73-129379. Repr. of 1904 ed. 12.00 (ISBN 0-404-02222-7). AMS Pr.
Dunn, Hilda B. The Art of Reading Spanish. 167p. 1984. pap. text ed. 10.95x (ISBN 0-89917-426-4). Tichenor Pub.
Dunn, Irving S., et al. Fundamentals of Geotechnical Analysis. LC 79-13583. 414p. 1980. text ed. 42.50x (ISBN 0-471-03698-6); solutions manual avail. (ISBN 0-471-04997-2). Wiley.
Dunn, J. Allan. Treasure of Atlantis. (Time-Lost Ser.). (Illus.). 1971. 5.00 (ISBN 0-87818-006-0); pap. 0.75 (ISBN 0-87818-002-8). Centaur.
Dunn, J. D. & Rachel, F. Wage & Salary Administration: Total Compensation Systems. 1970. text ed. 33.95 (ISBN 0-07-018291-4). McGraw.
Dunn, J. F. & Wakefield, G. L. Exposure Manual. 3rd ed. 1978. text ed. 16.95 (ISBN 0-85242-361-6, Pub. by Fountain). Morgan.
--Exposure Manual. 2nd ed. (Illus.). 240p. 1981. text ed. 16.95 (ISBN 0-85242-762-X, 3361). Morgan.
Dunn, J. Michael & Epstein, George, eds. Modern Uses of Multiple-Valued Logic. (Episteme: No. 2). 1977. lib. bdg. 55.00 (ISBN 90-277-0747-2, Pub. by Reidel Holland). Kluwer Academic.
Dunn, Jacob P. Indiana: A Redemption from Slavery. new & enl. ed. LC 72-3754. (American Commonwealths: No. 12). Repr. of 1905 ed. 40.00 (ISBN 0-404-57212-X). AMS Pr.
Dunn, James A., Jr. Miles to Go: European & American Transportation Politics. (Transportation Studies). 288p. 1981. 30.00x (ISBN 0-262-04062-X). MIT Pr.
Dunn, James D. Baptism in the Holy Spirit: A Re-Examination of the New Testament Teaching on the Gift of the Spirit in Relation to Pentacostalism Today. LC 77-3995. 256p. 1977. pap. 8.95 (ISBN 0-664-24140-9). Westminster.
--Christology in the Making: A New Testament Inquiry into the Origins of the Doctrine of the Incarnation. LC 80-16968. 462p. 1980. pap. 24.50 (ISBN 0-664-24356-8). Westminster.
--Jesus & the Spirit: A Study of the Religious & Charismatic Experience of Jesus & the First Christians as Reflected in the New Testament. LC 75-9802. 528p. 1979. Repr. of 1975 ed. pap. 15.95 (ISBN 0-664-24290-1). Westminster.
--Unity & Diversity in the New Testament: An Inquiry into the Character of Earliest Christianity. LC 77-22598. 488p. 1977. Westminster.
--Unity & Diversity in the New Testament: An Inquiry into the Character of Earliest Christianity. LC 77-22598. 488p. 1984. pap. 14.95 (ISBN 0-664-24525-0). Westminster.
Dunn, James P., jt. auth. see Mendeloff, Albert.
Dunn, James T. The St. Croix: Midwest Border River. LC 79-52970. (Illus.). 310p. 1979. pap. 7.95 (ISBN 0-87351-141-7). Minn Hist.
--St. Paul's Schubert Club: A Century of Music 1882-1982. 103p. 1983. 5.00 (ISBN 0-912373-02-4). Schubert.
Dunn, James T., jt. ed. see Poatgieter, A. Hermina.
Dunn, Jane. Moon in Eclipse: A Life of Mary Shelley. LC 78-850. 1978. 20.00 (ISBN 0-312-54692-0). St Martin.
Dunn, Jay. The Tigers of Princeton, Old Nassau Football. LC 76-24240. (College Sports Ser.). (Illus.). 1977. 10.95 (ISBN 0-87397-107-8). Strode.
Dunn, Jean. Astronomy for the Younger Set. 1984. 7.95 (ISBN 0-533-05825-2). Vantage.
Dunn, Jean, ed. Seeds of Consciousness: The Wisdom of Sri Nisargadatta Maharaj. LC 81-47636. 224p. 1982. pap. 9.95 (ISBN 0-394-17939-0, E785, Ever). Grove.
Dunn, Jean, ed. see Maharaj, Nisargadatta.
Dunn, Jeffrey D. Reappraising Social Security: Toward an Alternative System. 244p. 1982. pap. 5.95 (ISBN 0-89940-850-8). LBJ Sch Pub Aff.
Dunn, Jerry G. Alcoholic Victorious. (Moody Acorn Ser.). pap. 5.95 pkg. of 10 (ISBN 0-8024-0200-3). Moody.
--God Is for the Alcoholic. LC 65-24232. 1967. pap. 2.95 (ISBN 0-8024-3020-1). Moody.
Dunn, Jimmy, jt. auth. see Manocchio, Anthony J.
Dunn, Joan. Retreat from Learning: Why Teachers Can't Teach, a Case History. LC 75-16609. 224p. 1975. Repr. of 1955 ed. lib. bdg. 22.50x (ISBN 0-8371-8252-2, DURL). Greenwood.
Dunn, John. Identity, Modernity & the Claim to Know Better: Project on Socio-Cultural Development Alternatives in a Changing World: Sub-project on the Transformation of the World. 22p. 1982. pap. 5.00 (ISBN 92-808-0441-3, TUNU203, UNU). Unipub.
--Locke. (Past Master Ser.). (Illus.). 1984. 12.95x (ISBN 0-19-287561-2); pap. 3.95 (ISBN 0-19-287560-4). Oxford U Pr.
--Modern Revolutions: An Introduction to the Analysis of a Political Phenomenon. LC 72-177942. 352p. 1972. 39.50 (ISBN 0-521-08441-5); pap. 13.95 (ISBN 0-521-09698-7). Cambridge U Pr.
--Political Obligation in Its Historical Context. LC 80-40037. (Illus.). 360p. 1980. 42.50 (ISBN 0-521-22890-5). Cambridge U Pr.
--Political Thought of John Locke. 1969. 39.50 (ISBN 0-521-07408-8). Cambridge U Pr.
--The Political Thought of John Locke: An Historical Account of the Argument of the 'Two Treatises of Government' 306p. 1983. pap. 13.95 (ISBN 0-521-27139-8). Cambridge U Pr.
--The Politics of Socialism: An Essay in Political Theory. (Themes in the Social Sciences Ser.). 140p. 1984. 29.95 (ISBN 0-521-26736-6); pap. 8.95 (ISBN 0-521-31840-8). Cambridge U Pr.
--Rethinking Modern Political Theory: Essays 1979-1983. 248p. 1985. 34.50 (ISBN 0-521-30130-0); pap. 12.95 (ISBN 0-521-31695-2). Cambridge U Pr.
--Western Political Theory in the Face of the Future. LC 78-25625. (Themes in the Social Sciences Ser.). 1979. 32.50 (ISBN 0-521-22619-8); pap. 9.95 (ISBN 0-521-29578-5). Cambridge U Pr.
Dunn, John & Robertson, A. F. Independence & Opportunity: Political Change in Ahafo. LC 73-79303. (African Studies, No. 8). (Illus.). 420p. 1974. 49.50 (ISBN 0-521-20270-1). Cambridge U Pr.
Dunn, John, ed. How to Play Cricket Australian Style. (Illus.). 1977. 10.95 (ISBN 0-285-62200-5, Pub. by Souvenir Pr). Intl Spec Bk.
--West African States. LC 77-80832. (African Studies Ser.). (Illus.). 1978. 42.50 (ISBN 0-521-21801-2); pap. 14.95 (ISBN 0-521-29283-2). Cambridge U Pr.
Dunn, John F., ed. see Krieger, Richard.
Dunn, John M., jt. auth. see Fait, Hollis F.
Dunn, John P. Ornamentation in the Works of Frederick Chopin. LC 78-125069. (Music Ser). (Illus.). 1971. Repr. of 1921 ed. lib. bdg. 17.50 (ISBN 0-306-70006-9). Da Capo.
Dunn, Joseph. Grammar of the Portuguese Language. 1977. Repr. of 1928 ed. 6.50 (ISBN 0-87535-023-2). Hispanic Soc.
--The Real Race. 272p. 1985. 10.95 (ISBN 0-8423-5276-7). Tyndale.
Dunn, Joseph, jt. auth. see Wilkins, Alfred T., Jr.
Dunn, Joseph, ed. see Kyle, Louisa V.
Dunn, Joseph W. Jr. & Lyle, Barbara S. Virginia Beach: Wish You Were Here. LC 83-8903. (Illus.). 128p. 1984. pap. 16.95 (ISBN 0-89865-292-8). Donning Co.
Dunn, Joy B., ed. see Holt, Edgar A.
Dunn, Joy B., ed. see Livingood, James W.
Dunn, Joy B., ed. see Mason, Robert L.
Dunn, Joyce E. Riding on a School Bus. LC 84-90496. 56p. 1985. 4.95 (ISBN 0-533-06378-7). Vantage.
Dunn, Judy. Distress & Comfort. (Developing Child Ser.). 1977. 7.95x (ISBN 0-674-21284-3); pap. 3.95 (ISBN 0-674-21285-1). Harvard U Pr.
--The Little Duck. LC 75-36467. (Picturebacks Ser). (Illus.). 32p. (ps-1). 1976. pap. 1.50 (ISBN 0-394-83247-7, BYR). Random.
--The Little Goat. LC 77-91658. (Picturebacks Ser.). (Illus.). (ps-1). 1979. PLB 4.99 (ISBN 0-394-93872-0, BYR); pap. 1.50 (ISBN 0-394-83872-6). Random.
--The Little Kitten. LC 82-16711. (Picturebacks Ser.). (Illus.). 32p. (ps-4). 1983. PLB 4.99 (ISBN 0-394-95818-7); pap. 1.95 (ISBN 0-394-85818-2). Random.
--The Little Lamb. LC 76-24167. (Pictureback Library Editions). (ps-2). 1978. PLB 4.99 (ISBN 0-394-93455-5, BYR). Random.
--The Little Lamb. LC 76-24167. (Picturebacks Ser). (Illus.). (ps-1). 1977. pap. 1.50 (ISBN 0-394-83455-0, BYR). Random.
--The Little Puppy. LC 84-2031. (Picturebacks Ser.). (Illus.). 32p. (ps-3). 1984. pap. 1.95 saddle-stitched (ISBN 0-394-86595-2, Pub. by BYR); lib. bdg. 4.99 GLB (ISBN 0-394-96595-7). Random.
--The Little Rabbit. LC 79-5241. (Picturebacks Ser.). (Illus.). 32p. (ps). 1980. PLB 4.99 (ISBN 0-394-94377-5, BYR); pap. 1.95 (ISBN 0-394-84377-0). Random.
--Sisters & Brothers. LC 84-19343. (The Developing Child Ser.). (Illus.). 182p. 1985. text ed. 10.00x (ISBN 0-674-80980-7); pap. 4.95 (ISBN 0-674-80981-5). Harvard U Pr.
Dunn, Judy & Kendrick, Carol. Siblings: Love, Envy, & Understanding. LC 81-7251. (Illus.). 304p. 1982. text ed. 18.50x (ISBN 0-674-80735-9). Harvard U Pr.
Dunn, Judy, jt. auth. see Dunn, Phoebe.
Dunn, Judy, jt. auth. see Shaffer, David.
Dunn, Judy, jt. ed. see Plomin, Robert.
Dunn, Keith A. & Staudenmaier, William O., eds. Alternative Military Strategies for the Future. (Studies in International Security Affairs & Military Strategy). 210p. 1985. hardcover 26.50x (ISBN 0-8133-0065-7). Westview.
--Military Strategy in Transition: Defense & Deterrence in the 1980's. (SSI Studies in International Security Affairs & Military Strategy). 160p. 1984. lib. bdg. 26.00x (ISBN 0-86531-789-5). Westview.
Dunn, Kenneth & Dunn, Rita. Situational Leadership for Principals: The School Administrator in Action. LC 82-11211. 228p. 1983. 17.50x (ISBN 0-686-84595-1, Parker). P-H.
--Teaching Students Through Their Individual Learning Styles: A Practical Approach. (Illus.). 1978. pap. 21.95 (ISBN 0-87909-808-2). Reston.
Dunn, Kenneth J., jt. auth. see Dunn, Rita.
Dunn, L. & Capobianco, R. J. Studies of Reading & Arithmetic in Mentally Retarded Boys. (SRCD M Ser.). 1954. pap. 13.00 (ISBN 0-527-01560-1). Kraus Repr.
Dunn, L. C. Anthropometric Study of Hawaiians of Pure & Mixed Blood. Tozzer, A. M., ed. (HU PMP Ser.). 1928. pap. 15.00 (ISBN 0-527-01220-3). Kraus Repr.
Dunn, Leslie C. Heredity & Evolution in Human Populations. rev. ed. LC 65-11617. (Books in Biology: No. 1). (Illus.). 1965. 8.95x (ISBN 0-674-38950-6). Harvard U Pr.
Dunn, Lesoie C. Race & Biology. (Race Question in Modern Science). 48p. (7th Printing 1965). 1965. pap. 5.00 (ISBN 92-3-100436-0, U505, UNESCO). Unipub.
Dunn, Lewis. Influence at the Margin: Alternative Institutional Options for Global Nuclear Activities. 136p. 1979. 18.00 (ISBN 0-318-14345-3, HI3109RR). Hudson Inst.
--U. S. Defense Planning for a More Proliferated World. 248p. 1979. 20.00 (ISBN 0-318-14358-5, HI29562RR). Hudson Inst.
Dunn, Lewis A. Controlling the Bomb: Nuclear Proliferation in the 1980's. LC 81-16086. (Fastsback Ser.: No. 25). 224p. 1982. 24.00x (ISBN 0-300-02820-2); pap. 7.95x (ISBN 0-300-02821-0, YF-25). Yale U Pr.
Dunn, Linwood. The ASC Treasury of Visual Effects. (Illus.). 297p. 29.95 (ISBN 0-935578-03-X). ASC Holding.
Dunn, Lloyd M., ed. Exceptional Children in the Schools: Special Education in Transition. 2nd ed. LC 73-813. 1973. text ed. 26.95 (ISBN 0-03-086293-0, HoltC). HR&W.
Dunn, Lois, tr. see Freeman, Lory.

Dunn, Lynn P. Asian-Americans: A Study Guide & Source Book. LC 74-31620. 1975. soft bdg. 8.00 (ISBN 0-88247-304-2). R & E Pubs.
--Black Americans: A Study Guide & Source Book. LC 74-31621. 1975. soft bdg. 8.00 (ISBN 0-88247-306-9). R & E Pubs.
--Chicanos: A Study Guide & Source Book. LC 74-31537. 1975. soft bdg 8.00 (ISBN 0-88247-307-7). R & E Pubs.
Dunn, M. H., jt. auth. see Maitland, Arthur.
Dunn, M. J., jt. ed. see Horton, R.
Dunn, Marsh L. Pre-Writing Skills. (Skill Starters for Motor Development Ser.). 96p. 1982. pap. text ed. 12.95 (ISBN 0-88450-822-6, 2089-B). Communication Skill.
Dunn, Marsha L. Pre-Dressing Skills. (Skill Starters for Motor Development Ser.). 100p. 1983. pap. text ed. 14.95 (ISBN 0-88450-868-4, 4689-B). Communication Skill.
--Pre-Scissor Skills. (Skill Starters for Motor Development Ser.). (Illus.). 1979. pap. text ed. 10.95 (ISBN 0-88450-701-7, 3101-B). Communication Skill.
--Pre-Sign Language Motor Skills. (Skill Starters for Motor Development Ser.). 106p. 1982. pap. text ed. 14.95 (ISBN 0-88450-821-8, 2085-B). Communication Skill.
Dunn, Martha D. Fundamentals of Nutrition. (Illus.). 580p. 1983. text ed. 19.95 (ISBN 0-8436-2284-9). Van Nos Reinhold.
Dunn, Marvin, jt. auth. see Porter, Bruce.
Dunn, Mary. William Penn: Politics & Conscience. 1967. 21.00x (ISBN 0-691-04574-7). Princeton U Pr.
Dunn, Mary, ed. Lady Addle Remembers: Being the Memoirs of Lady Addle of Eigg. (Illus.). 118p. 1985. 7.95 (ISBN 0-86072-070-5, Pub. by Quartet Bks). Merrimack Pub Cir.
Dunn, Mary L., jt. auth. see Maguire, John G.
Dunn, Mary M., ed. The Papers of William Penn: Vol. III, 1684-1699. Date not set. price not set. U of Pa Pr.
--The Papers of William Penn: Vol. IV, 1699-1718. Date not set. price not set. U of Pa Pr.
Dunn, Mary M., ed. see Penn, William.
Dunn, Mary M., et al, eds. see Penn, William.
Dunn, Marylois & Mayhar, Ardath. The Absolutely Perfect Horse. LC 82-47726. 192p. (gr. 5 up). 1983. 10.53i (ISBN 0-06-021773-1); PLB 10.89g (ISBN 0-06-021774-X). HarpJ.
Dunn, Michael. Walking Through the Lake District. (Illus.). 224p. 1984. 16.95 (ISBN 0-7153-8443-0). David & Charles.
Dunn, Michael, III. Easy Going: Vilas & Oneida Counties. LC 78-908. (Easy Going Ser.). (Illus., Orig.). 1978. pap. 5.00 (ISBN 0-915024-16-0). Tamarack Pr.
Dunn, Michael J. & Patrono, Carlo, eds. Prostaglandins & the Kidney: Biochemistry, Physiology, Pharmacology, & Clinical Applications. 438p. 1983. 49.50 (ISBN 0-306-41054-0, Plenum Med Bk). Plenum Pub.
Dunn, Millard. Engraved on Air. LC 83-620027. 32p. 1983. pap. 4.00 (ISBN 0-939058-02-2). Kentucky Arts.
Dunn, Miriam. Kim & Ting. 1981. pap. 1.95 (ISBN 0-85363-137-9). OMF Bks.
--Let's Look at Malaysia. pap. 1.50 (ISBN 0-85363-096-8). OMF Bks.
Dunn, Nell. Steaming. 1984. pap. 6.95 (ISBN 0-87910-215-2). Limelight Edns.
Dunn, Olive J. Basic Statistics: A Primer for the Biomedical Sciences. 2nd ed. LC 77-9328. (Probability & Mathematical Statistics: Applied Probability & Statistics Section). 218p. 1977. 29.95x (ISBN 0-471-22744-7, Pub. by Wiley-Interscience). Wiley.
Dunn, Olive J. & Clark, Virginia A. Applied Statistics: Analysis of Variance & Regression. LC 73-13683. (Probability & Mathematical Statistics Ser.). 387p. 1974. 35.50x (ISBN 0-471-22700-5, Pub. by Wiley-Interscience). Wiley.
Dunn, P., jt. ed. see Sharp, F.
Dunn, P. D. & Reay, D. A. Heat Pipes. 3rd ed. text ed. 54.00 (ISBN 0-08-029356-5); 20.00 (ISBN 0-08-029355-7). Pergamon.
Dunn, P. H. Proceedings of the Second International Symposium on Biological Control of Weeds. 220p. 1973. 40.00x (ISBN 0-85198-299-9, Pub. by CAB Bks England). State Mutual Bk.
Dunn, P. N., ed. Calderon de la Barca: El Lcade de Zalemea. 1966. pap. 5.80 (ISBN 0-08-011548-9). Pergamon.
Dunn, Patrick R. Mr. Austin's Commercial Bartending Basics. Orig. Title: Professional Bartending Basics. (Illus.). 62p. (Orig.). 1985. pap. 4.95 (ISBN 0-9613869-1-6). Texas Cedar Pr.
Dunn, Paul D., jt. auth. see Schuller, Robert H.
Dunn, Paul H. Anxiously Engaged. 1974. 6.95 (ISBN 0-87747-546-6). Deseret Bk.
--Discovering the Quality of Success. LC 73-77365. 102p. 1973. 6.95 (ISBN 0-87747-493-1). Deseret Bk.
Dunn, Peter. The Goatkeeper's Veterinary Book. (Illus.). 192p. 18.95 (ISBN 0-85236-121-1, Pub. by Farming Pr UK). Diamond Farm Bk.
Dunn, Peter M. The First Vietnam War. LC 84-17842. 400p. 1985. 29.95 (ISBN 0-312-29314-3). St Martin.
Dunn, Peter M. & Watson, Bruce W., eds. American Intervention in Grenada: The Implications of Project "Urgent Fury". 140p. 1985. softcover 15.00x (ISBN 0-86531-868-9). Westview.
Dunn, Peter M., jt. ed. see Watson, Bruce.
Dunn, Peter M., jt. ed. see Watson, Bruce W.
Dunn, Philip. The Cabal, No. 2: The Black Moon. (Orig.). 1982. pap. 2.95 (ISBN 0-425-05194-3). Berkley Pub.
Dunn, Phoebe. Animal Friends. LC 85-2254. (Knee-High Books). (Illus.). 24p. (ps-1). 1985. bds. 3.95 (ISBN 0-394-87304-1, BYR); PLB 4.99 (ISBN 0-394-97304-6). Random.
Dunn, Phoebe & Dunn, Judy. The Animals of Buttercup Farm. LC 81-4892. (Illus.). 48p. (ps-1). 1981. 5.95 (ISBN 0-394-84798-9). Random.
Dunn, R. Software Defect Removal. 368p. 1984. 29.95 (ISBN 0-07-018313-9). McGraw.
Dunn, R. D., ed. see Camden, William.
Dunn, Richard, ed. The English Novel: Twentieth Century Criticism, Defoe Through Hardy, Vol. 1. LC 76-17741. 202p. 1976. 20.00x (ISBN 0-8040-0742-X, 82-74110, Pub. by Swallow). Ohio U Pr.
Dunn, Richard, tr. see Zampaglione, Gerardo.
Dunn, Richard, et al, trs. see Freund, Gisele.
Dunn, Richard J. David Copperfield: An Annotated Bibliography. LC 80-9023. (Dickens Bibliography Ser.). 284p. 1981. lib. bdg. 52.00 (ISBN 0-8240-9322-4). Garland Pub.
Dunn, Richard J., ed. Approaches to Teaching Dickens' David Copperfield. (Approaches to Teaching Masterpieces of World Literature Ser.: No. 5). 162p. 1985. 25.00x (ISBN 0-87352-483-7); pap. 12.50x (ISBN 0-87352-484-5). Modern Lang.
Dunn, Richard J., ed. see Bronte, Charlotte.
Dunn, Richard M., jt. auth. see Babuscio, Jack.
Dunn, Richard S. Age of Religious Wars, Fifteen Fifty-Nine to Seventeen Fifteen. 2nd ed. (Illus.). 1979. pap. text ed. 7.95x (ISBN 0-393-09021-3). Norton.
--Sugar & Slaves: The Rise of the Planter Class in the English West Indies, 1624-1713. (Illus.). 384p. 1973. pap. 8.95 (ISBN 0-393-00692-1). Norton.
--Sugar & Slaves: The Rise of the Planter Class in the English West Indies, 1624-1713. (Institute of Early American History & Culture Ser.). xx, 359p. 1972. 30.00 (ISBN 0-8078-1192-0). U of NC Pr.
Dunn, Richard S. see Gilbert, Felix.
Dunn, Richard S., ed. see Penn, William.
Dunn, Richard S., jt. ed. see Soderlund, Jean R.
Dunn, Rita & Dunn, Kenneth J. Administrator's Guide to New Programs for Faculty Management & Evaluation. 1976. 18.95 (ISBN 0-13-008623-1, Parker). P-H.
Dunn, Rita, jt. auth. see Dunn, Kenneth.
Dunn, Robert. Quo, Musa, Tendis? (Illus.). 64p. (Orig.). 1983. pap. 4.95 (ISBN 0-914339-02-8). P E Randall Pub.
Dunn, Robert & Ullman, Richard. Quality Assurance for Computer Software. (Illus.). 1982. 32.95 (ISBN 0-07-018312-0). McGraw.
Dunn, Robert, jt. auth. see Howard, Sidney.
Dunn, Robert L. Recovery of Damages for Lost Profits. 2nd ed. LC 81-81470. 438p. 1981. 65.00 (ISBN 0-915544-09-1). Lawpress Ca.
Dunn, Robert M., Jr. The Canada: U. S. Capital Market. LC 78-71657. (Canadian: U. S. Prospect Ser.). 148p. 1978. 6.00 (ISBN 0-88806-046-7). Natl Planning.
--Canada-U.S. Capital Market: The/Intermediation, Integration, & Policy Independence. (Canada-U.S. Prospects: No. 2). 139p. 1978. 6.00 (ISBN 0-88806-046-7). Inst C D Howe.
--The Many Disappointments of Flexible Exchange Rates. LC 83-26543. (Essays in International Finance Ser.: No. 154). 1983. pap. text ed. 2.50x (ISBN 0-88165-061-7). Princeton U Int Finan Econ.
Dunn, Robert M., Jr. & Neftci, Salih N. Economic Growth among Industrialized Countries: Why the United States Lags. LC 80-81478. (Committee on Changing International Realities Ser.). 77p. 1980. 5.50 (ISBN 0-89068-053-1). Natl Planning.
Dunn, Robert W. American Foreign Investments. Richt, Adrian, ed. LC 76-5003. (American Business Abroad Ser.). 1976. Repr. of 1926 ed. 35.50x (ISBN 0-405-09272-5). Ayer Co Pubs.
--The Americanization of Labor. LC 74-22740. (The Labor Movement in Fiction & Non-Fiction Ser.). Repr. of 1927 ed. 22.00 (ISBN 0-404-58492-6). AMS Pr.
Dunn, Ronald. The Faith Crisis. LC 83-51675. 224p. 1984. pap. 6.95 (ISBN 0-8423-0838-5). Tyndale.
--The Faith Crisis. Chao, Lorna Y., tr. (Chinese.). 1985. pap. write for info. (ISBN 0-941598-30-6). Living Spring Pubns.
--Victory. LC 83-51646. 144p. 1984. pap. 4.95 (ISBN 0-8423-7819-7). Tyndale.
Dunn, S. & Gennard, J. Closed Shop in British Industry. 232p. 1984. text ed. 37.50x (ISBN 0-333-26202-6, Pub. by Macmillan England); pap. text ed. 15.25x (ISBN 0-333-26203-4, Pub. by Macmillan England). Humanities.
Dunn, S. Watson & Barban, Arnold M. Advertising: Its Role in Modern Marketing. 5th ed. LC 81-67231. 710p. 1982. text ed. 34.95x (ISBN 0-03-060049-9); instr's manual with transparencies & test bank 20.00 (ISBN 0-03-060051-0). Dryden Pr.
Dunn, S. Watson, et al. How Fifteen Transnational Corporations Manage Public Affairs. LC 79-52256. (Orig.). 1979. pap. text ed. 10.95 (ISBN 0-87251-041-7). Crain Bks.
Dunn, Samuel, compiled by see Calvin, John.
Dunn, Samuel W. & Lorimar, E. S., eds. International Advertising & Marketing. LC 78-6802. (Grid Series in Advertising & Journalism). pap. 147.30 (ISBN 0-317-29934-4, 2021721). Bks Demand UMI.
Dunn, Sarah S. Noah & the Golden Turtle: Stories from the East & West for the ESL Student. (Illus.). 256p. 1985. pap. text ed. 9.95 (ISBN 0-13-622945-X). P-H.
Dunn, Seamus & Morgan, Valerie. The Apple IIe Personal Computer for Beginners. 260p. 17.95 (ISBN 0-13-038969-2). P-H.
--The Apple Personal Computer for Beginners. 1983. 17.95 (ISBN 0-13-039131-X). P-H.
--BBC Microcomputer for Beginners. 1984. pap. 15.95 (ISBN 0-13-069328-6). P-H.
--The IBM Personal Computer for Beginners. (Illus.). 320p. 1984. pap. 15.95 (ISBN 0-13-448259-X). P-H.
--The PET Personal Computer for Beginners. 1983. pap. 19.95 (ISBN 0-13-661827-8). P-H.
--The PET Personal Computer for Beginners. 1982. 25.99 (ISBN 0-13-661835-9). P-H.
Dunn, Sharon, ed. The Agni Review. 1985. 4.00. Agni Review.
Dunn, Si. The Challenge of One Hundred-Sixty (160) Force, Richard C., ed. 54p. 1977. pap. 4.95 (ISBN 0-88006-003-4, BK 7309). Green Pub Inc.
Dunn, Si, ed. see Daniel, Timothy M.
Dunn, Stephen. A Circus of Needs. LC 78-59800. (Poetry Ser). 1978. 14.95; pap. 6.95 (ISBN 0-915604-15-9). Carnegie-Mellon.
--The Fall & Rise of the Asiatic Mode of Production. 240p. (Orig.). 1982. pap. 12.95x (ISBN 0-7100-9053-6). Routledge & Kegan.
--Full of Lust & Good Usage. LC 76-12129. (Poetry Ser.). 1985. pap. 6.95 (ISBN 0-915604-07-8). Carnegie-Mellon.
--Looking for Holes in the Ceiling. LC 73-93172. 72p. 1974. lib. bdg. 7.50x (ISBN 0-87023-154-5); pap. 4.00 (ISBN 0-87023-155-3). U of Mass Pr.
--Not Dancing. LC 84-70175. (Poetry Ser.). 77p. 1984. 14.95 (ISBN 0-88748-000-4); pap. 6.95 (ISBN 0-88748-001-2). Carnegie-Mellon.
--Work & Love. LC 81-69796. 1981. 14.95 (ISBN 0-915604-60-4); pap. 6.95 (ISBN 0-915604-61-2). Carnegie-Mellon.
Dunn, Stephen P., ed. see Klibanov, A. I.
Dunn, Stephen P., tr. see Yanov, Alexander.
Dunn, Stephen P., tr. see Zdravomyslov, A. G., et al.
Dunn, Thomas, ed. Renaissance Singer. LC 75-20077. 1976. 7.50 (ISBN 0-911318-10-0). E C Schirmer.
Dunn, Thomas F. Financially Surviving the 1980's. (Illus.). 100p. spiral bdg. 14.95 (ISBN 0-686-31584-7). R&D Pubs.
Dunn, Thomas P. & Erlich, Richard D., eds. The Mechanical God: Machines in Science Fiction. LC 81-13429. (Contributions to the Study of Science Fiction & Fantasy Ser.: No. 1). xiv, 284p. 1982. lib. bdg. 29.95 (ISBN 0-313-22274-6, DME/). Greenwood.
Dunn, Thomas P., jt. ed. see Erlich, Richard D.
Dunn, Tom, jt. auth. see Pike, Frank.
Dunn, W. Public Policy Analysis: An Introduction. 1981. pap. 27.95 (ISBN 0-13-737957-9). P-H.
Dunn, W. E. The Sex Tax: A Political Fantasy. 1979. 6.00 (ISBN 0-682-49463-1). Exposition Pr FL.
Dunn, W. L., jt. auth. see Douthwaite, G. K.
Dunn, Waldo H. English Biography. (Channels of English Literature: No. 3). Repr. of 1916 ed. 34.50 (ISBN 0-404-07813-3). AMS Pr.
--Froude & Carlyle: A Study of the Froude-Carlyle Controversy. LC 68-26221. 1969. Repr. of 1933 ed. 29.00x (ISBN 0-8046-0124-0, Pub. by Kennikat). Assoc Faculty Pr.
--R. D. Blackmore: The Author of "Lorna Doone"; a Biography. LC 73-19573. (Illus.). 316p. 1974. Repr. of 1956 ed. lib. bdg. 24.75x (ISBN 0-8371-7286-1, DUBL). Greenwood.
Dunn, Walter S. A Red Army Microcosm. 1985. pap. 3.00 (ISBN 0-317-19915-3). Intl Inst Adv Stud.
Dunn, Walter S., Jr. Second Front Now: Nineteen Forty-Three. LC 78-32063. (Illus.). 327p. 1980. 22.50 (ISBN 0-8173-0008-2). U of Ala Pr.
Dunn, Wendy & Morey, Janet. Who's News! World Personalities. (Illus.). 128p. (gr. 5 up). 1985. 9.29 (ISBN 0-671-54436-5). Messner.
Dunn, William. I Stand by Sand Creek. LC 84-62056. (Illus.). 1985. 7.95 (ISBN 0-88342-249-2). Old Army.
Dunn, William, ed. Social Values & Public Policy. (Orig.). 1981. pap. 8.00 (ISBN 0-918592-44-5). Policy Studies.
Dunn, William E. Spanish & French Rivalry in the Gulf Region of the U. S., 1678-1702: The Beginnings of Texas & Pensacola. facsimile ed. (Select Bibliographies Reprint Ser). Repr. of 1917 ed. 18.00 (ISBN 0-8369-5792-X). Ayer Co Pubs.
Dunn, William H. The Sale of a Small Business. (Orig.). 1982. 1984 supplement 65.00 (ISBN 0-933808-02-X). Busn Sale Inst.
Dunn, William H., et al. Strength Training & Conditioning for Basketball: Featuring Ralph Sampson's Training Program. (Illus.). 112p. 1984. pap. 9.95 (ISBN 0-8092-5375-5). Contemp Bks.
Dunn, William N., ed. Values, Ethics & the Practice of Policy Analysis. LC 82-47929. (Policy Studies Organization Bk.). 256p. 1982. 31.00x (ISBN 0-669-05707-X). Lexington Bks.
Dunn, William N. & Obradovic, Josip, eds. Worker's Self-Management & Organizational Power in Yugoslavia. LC 78-16307. 1978. pap. text ed. 16.95x (ISBN 0-8229-8261-7, Pub. by U Ctr Intl St). U of Pittsburgh Pr.
Dunn, William P. Sir Thomas Browne. 1950. 7.50x (ISBN 0-8166-0058-9). U of Minn Pr.
Dunn, William R. Fighter Pilot: The First American Ace of World War II. LC 82-40172. (Illus.). 272p. 1982. 18.00 (ISBN 0-8131-1465-9). U Pr of Ky.
Dunnagan, Cecil G. Grinnin', Dusty, Fightin' Men. (Illus.). 97p. 1985. price not set (ISBN 0-9615188-0-4). Shelley Bks.
Dunnagan, William R. A Survey of Lubbock's Growth As a Medical Center, 1909-1954. 65p. 1980. 5.00 (ISBN 0-911618-05-8). West Tex Mus.
Dunnahoo, Terry. Break Dancing. (First Bk.). (Illus.). 72p. (gr. 4-6). 1985. lib. bdg. 9.40 (ISBN 0-531-04883-7). Watts.
Dunnam, Maxie. Jesus' Claims-Our Promise: A Study of the "I Am" Sayings of Jesus. LC 84-51831. 128p. (Orig.). 1984. pap. 5.95 (ISBN 0-8358-0502-6). Upper Room.
--The Sanctuary for Lent, 1985. 48p. (Orig.). 1985. pap. 30.00 per 100 (ISBN 0-687-36847-2). Abingdon.
--Workbook on Spiritual Disciplines. LC 83-51402. 160p. 1984. wkbk. 4.50 (ISBN 0-8358-0479-8). Upper Room.
Dunnam, Maxie, ed. Our Journey: A Wesleyan View of the Christian Way. LC 84-72237. 104p. (Orig.). Date not set. DR013B. pap. 5.95 (ISBN 0-88177-013-2). Discipleship Res.
Dunnam, Maxie D. Alive in Christ: The Dynamic Process of Spiritual Formation. LC 81-20631. 160p. 1982. 8.75 (ISBN 0-687-00993-6). Abingdon.
--Workbook of Intercessory Prayer. LC 78-65617. 1979. pap. 3.95x (ISBN 0-8358-0382-1). Upper Room.
--The Workbook of Living Prayer. 1975. 3.95x (ISBN 0-8358-0323-6). Upper Room.
Dunnan, Nancy. Financial Savvy for Singles: New Ways to Multiply Your Money in the '80s if You Are Unmarried, Widowed or Divorced. LC 82-42692. 256p. 1983. 15.95 (ISBN 0-89256-227-7); pap. 7.95 (ISBN 0-89256-243-9). Rawson Assocs.
--How to Invest Fifty-Five Thousand Dollars. 128p. 1985. pap. 5.72i (ISBN 0-06-464100-7, BN 4100). B&N NY.
Dunnan, Nancy, jt. auth. see Boehm, Helen F.
Dunne, Agnes C., jt. auth. see Le Gros, Clark F.
Dunne, Carrin. Buddha & Jesus: Conversations. 1975. pap. 4.95 (ISBN 0-87243-057-X). Templegate.
Dunne, Dominick. The Two Mrs. Grenvilles. LC 85-445. 1985. 14.95 (ISBN 0-517-55713-4). Crown.
--The Winners: Part II of Joyce Haber's "The Users". 464p. 1983. pap. 3.95 (ISBN 0-446-30221-X). Warner Bks.
Dunne, Edward F. Cardiac Radiology. (Illus.). pap. 67.00 (ISBN 0-317-10366-0, 2055421). Bks Demand UMI.
Dunne, Finley P. Dissertations by Mr. Dooley. 1977. Repr. 27.00 (ISBN 0-403-08561-6). Scholarly.
--Mister Dooley in Peace & in War. 1968. Repr. of 1898 ed. 13.00x (ISBN 0-403-00095-5). Scholarly.
--Mr. Dooley in Peace & War. 69.95 (ISBN 0-87968-249-3). Gordon Pr.
--Mr. Dooley in the Hearts of His Countrymen. 69.95 (ISBN 0-87968-248-5). Gordon Pr.
--Mister Dooley in the Hearts of His Countrymen. 1968. Repr. of 1899 ed. 13.00x (ISBN 0-403-00096-3). Scholarly.
--Mr. Dooley's Opinions. 69.95 (ISBN 0-87968-161-6). Gordon Pr.
--Mr. Dooley's Opinions. 1977. Repr. 9.00 (ISBN 0-403-08562-4). Scholarly.
--Mr. Dooley's Philosophy. (Illus.). 1978. Repr. of 1900 ed. lib. bdg. 20.00 (ISBN 0-8495-1027-9). Arden Lib.
--Mr. Dooley's Philosophy. LC 73-10444. (The American Humorists Ser.). 267p. Repr. of 1900 ed. lib. bdg. 17.00 (ISBN 0-8398-0376-1). Irvington.
--Observations by Mr. Dooley. 1906. lib. bdg. 20.00 (ISBN 0-8414-3874-9). Folcroft.
--Observations by Mr. Dooley. 69.95 (ISBN 0-8490-0746-1). Gordon Pr.
--Observations by Mr. Dooley. LC 69-13889. Repr. of 1902 ed. lib. bdg. 18.75x (ISBN 0-8371-1636-8, DUOB). Greenwood.
--Observations by Mr. Dooley. 1968. Repr. of 1902 ed. 13.00x (ISBN 0-403-00094-7). Scholarly.
Dunne, George H. Generation of Giants. 1962. 19.95 (ISBN 0-268-00109-X). U of Notre Dame Pr.
Dunne, Gerald T. Grenville Clark: Public Citizen. 320p. 1985. 19.95 (ISBN 0-374-16683-8). FS&G.
--Hugo Black & the Judicial Revolution. 1977. text ed. 24.50x (ISBN 0-8290-0344-4). Irvington.
Dunne, Hope. The Art of Teaching Reading: A Language & Self Concept Approach. LC 72-80163. 1972. pap. text ed. 9.95 (ISBN 0-675-09075-X). Merrill.
Dunne, J. W. An Experiment with Time. 3rd. rev. ed. 1958. pap. text ed. 7.45x (ISBN 0-571-05996-1). Humanities.
Dunne, Jim, jt. auth. see Norbye, Jan.

Dunne, Jim, jt. auth. see Norbye, Jan P.
Dunne, John. The House of Wisdom. LC 84-48767. 224p. 1985. 15.34 (ISBN 0-317-18550-0, HarpR). Har-Row.
--How God Created. pap. 2.00 (ISBN 0-268-00120-0). U of Notre Dame Pr.
Dunne, John F., jt. ed. see Coulston, Frederick.
Dunne, John G. Dutch Shea, Jr. 1983. pap. 3.95 (ISBN 0-671-46170-2). PB.
--Qunitana & Friends. 304p. 1980. pap. 3.95 (ISBN 0-671-83241-7). WSP.
--Studio. 272p. 1985. 7.95 (ISBN 0-87910-031-1). Limelight Edns.
--True Confessions. 1983. pap. 3.95 (ISBN 0-671-49809-6). PB.
Dunne, John J. & O'Connor, Lawrence. Haunted Ireland: Her Romantic & Mysterious Ghosts. (Illus.). 115p. pap. 8.95 (ISBN 0-904651-30-4, Pub. by Salem Hse Ltd). Merrimack Pub Cir.
Dunne, John S. The Church of the Poor Devil. 160p. 1982. 14.95 (ISBN 0-02-533960-5). Macmillan.
--The Church of the Poor Devil: Reflections on a Riverboat Voyage & a Spiritual Journey. LC 83-14548. 1983. pap. text ed. 6.95 (ISBN 0-268-00746-2, 85-07469). U of Notre Dame Pr.
--The City of the Gods: A Study in Myth & Mortality. LC 78-2588. 1978. Repr. of 1965 ed. text ed. 4.95x (ISBN 0-268-00725-X). U of Notre Dame Pr.
--The Reasons of the Heart: A Journey into Solitude & Back Again into the Human Circle. 1979. pap. 5.95 (ISBN 0-268-01606-2). U of Notre Dame Pr.
--A Search for God in Time & Memory. LC 76-20165. 1977. text ed. 15.95x (ISBN 0-268-01689-5); pap. 6.95 (ISBN 0-268-01673-9). U of Notre Dame Pr.
--Time & Myth. LC 74-32289. 128p. 1975. pap. 4.95 (ISBN 0-268-01828-6). U of Notre Dame Pr.
--The Way of All the Earth: Experiments in Truth & Religion. LC 78-1575. 1978. text ed. 19.95x (ISBN 0-268-01927-4); pap. 7.95 (ISBN 0-268-01928-2). U of Notre Dame Pr.
Dunne, Karolyn J. Lady Enhanced. 1983. 7.75 (ISBN 0-8062-1938-6). Carlton.
Dunne, Lavon J., jt. auth. see Kirschmann, John D.
Dunne, Mary C. Return to Timberlake. (YA) 1981. 8.95 (ISBN 0-686-73949-3, Avalon). Bouregy.
Dunne, Mary Collins. The Secret of Cliffsedge. (YA) 1979. 8.95 (ISBN 0-685-93874-3, Avalon). Bouregy.
Dunne, Patrick & Obenhouse, Susan. Product Management: A Reader. LC 80-22355. 174p. 1980. pap. 22.00 (ISBN 0-87757-147-3). Am Mktg.
Dunne, Patrick M. & Obenhouse, Susan. Product Management: A Reader. LC 80-22355. pap. 45.50 (ISBN 0-317-26622-5, 2025427). Bks Demand UMI.
Dunne, Patrick M., ed. see Theory Conference, Phoenix, Arizona, February, 1980.
Dunne, Peter M. Black Robes in Lower California. (California Library Reprint Ser.: No. 3). (Illus.). 1968. Repr. 37.50x (ISBN 0-520-00362-4). U of Cal Pr.
Dunne, Philip. Take Two: A Life in Movies & Politics. (Illus.). 1980. 14.95 (ISBN 0-07-018306-6). McGraw.
Dunne, Robert L. & Sterman, Donna. Egg Carton Critters. LC 78-4319. (Illus.). (gr. 1-4). 1978. PLB 7.85 (ISBN 0-8027-6335-9). Walker & Co.
Dunne, Tad. We Cannot Find Words. casebound 8.95 (ISBN 0-87193-138-9). Dimension Bks.
Dunne, Thomas & Leopold, Luna B. Water in Environmental Planning. LC 78-8013. (Illus.). 818p. 1978. text ed. 47.95 (ISBN 0-7167-0079-4). W H Freeman.
Dunne, Thomas A. Do This in Memory of Me. LC 81-67927. (Illus.). 237p. (Orig.). (gr. 10-12). 1981. pap. text ed. 4.95x (ISBN 0-89944-056-8); tchr's manual 2.95x (ISBN 0-89944-057-6). Don Bosco Multimedia.
Dunne, Tom. Gerard Manley Hopkins: A Comprehensive Bibliography. LC 81-81582. 396p. 1983. 35.00 (ISBN 0-906795-21-4). U Pr of Va.
Dunne, William P. Is It a Saint's Name? 1977. pap. 1.25 (ISBN 0-89555-024-5). TAN Bks Pubs.
Dunnell, Karen. Health Service Planning. 120p. 1976. 39.00x (ISBN 0-900889-61-6, Pub. by Pitman Bks England). State Mutual Bk.
Dunnell, Karen, ed. Health Services Planning. 1977. 17.00x (ISBN 0-8464-0474-5). Beekman Pubs.
Dunnell, R. C. The Prehistory of Fishtrap, Kentucky. LC 72-90078. (Publications in Anthropology: No. 75). 1972. pap. 7.00 (ISBN 0-913516-08-2). Yale U Anthro.
Dunnell, Robert C. & Hall, Edwin C. Archaeological Essays in Honor of Irvin B. Rouse. 1979. 23.20x (ISBN 90-279-7834-4). Mouton.
Dunnell, Robert C. & Grayson, Donald K., eds. Lulu Linear Punctated: Essays in Honor of George Irving Quimby. (Anthropological Papers: No. 72). (Illus.). 354p. 1983. pap. 12.00x (ISBN 0-932206-94-8). U Mich Mus Anthro.
Dunner, Donald R. Patent Law Perspectives, 6 vols. 2nd ed. LC 82-61193. 1970. A Year's Service. 560.00; Annual Renewal. 460.00; looseleaf 1983 375.00; looseleaf 1984 425.00. Bender.
Dunner, Peter M. Pioneer Jesuits in Northern Mexico. LC 78-10566. (Illus.). 1979. Repr. of 1944 ed. lib. bdg. 24.75x (ISBN 0-313-20653-8, DUPJ). Greenwood.
Dunnet, Dorothy. Checkmate. 736p. 1984. pap. 4.95 (ISBN 0-446-31301-7). Warner Bks.
Dunnet, Fiona & King, Aileen. The Home Book of Scottish Cookery. 124p. (Orig.). 1973. pap. 4.95 (ISBN 0-571-10332-4). Faber & Faber.
Dunnet, G. M. & Mardon, D. K. A Monograph of Australian Fleas: Siphonaptera. (Illus.). 273p. 1974. pap. 7.50x (ISBN 0-686-32815-9, Pub. by Brit Mus Nat Hist England). Sabbot-Natural Hist Bks.
Dunnett, Dorothy. Checkmate. 425p. 1983. lib. bdg. 21.95x (ISBN 0-89966-319-2). Buccaneer Bks.
--Disorderly Knights. 334p. 1981. Repr. lib. bdg. 21.95x (ISBN 0-89966-295-1). Buccaneer Bks.
--The Disorderly Knights. 576p. 1984. pap. 3.95 (ISBN 0-446-31290-8). Warner Bks.
--Dolly & the Bird of Paradise. LC 83-48851. 1984. 14.95 (ISBN 0-394-52377-6). Knopf.
--Dolly & the Cooky Bird. LC 82-400143. 288p. 1982. pap. 2.95 (ISBN 0-394-71164-5, Vin). Random.
--Dolly & the Doctor Bird. LC 82-40016. 288p. 1982. pap. 2.95 (ISBN 0-394-71163-7, Vin). Random.
--Dolly & the Nanny Bird. LC 82-47814. 260p. 1982. 12.95 (ISBN 0-394-52376-8). Knopf.
--Dolly & the Nanny Bird. LC 83-5782. 272p. 1983. pap. 3.95 (ISBN 0-394-71723-6, Vin). Random.
--Dolly & the Singing Bird. LC 82-40044. 288p. 1982. pap. 2.95 (ISBN 0-394-71162-9, Vin). Random.
--Dolly & the Starry Bird. LC 82-40045. 288p. 1982. pap. 2.95 (ISBN 0-394-71158-0, Vin). Random.
--The Game of Kings. 425p. 1983. lib. bdg. 21.95x (ISBN 0-89966-318-4). Buccaneer Bks.
--The Game of Kings. 512p. 1984. pap. 3.95 (ISBN 0-446-31282-7). Warner Bks.
--King Hereafter. LC 81-48122. 1982. 16.95 (ISBN 0-394-52378-4). Knopf.
--Pawn in Frankencense. 576p. 1984. pap. 3.95 (ISBN 0-446-31294-0). Warner Bks.
--Pawn in Frankincense. 425p. 1983. Repr. lib. bdg. 21.95x (ISBN 0-89966-321-4). Buccaneer Bks.
--Queen's Play. 425p. 1983. Repr. lib. bdg. 20.95x (ISBN 0-89966-320-6). Buccaneer Bks.
--Queens Play. 512p. 1984. pap. 3.95 (ISBN 0-446-31288-6). Warner Bks.
--The Ringed Castle. 425p. 1983. Repr. lib. bdg. 22.95x (ISBN 0-89966-322-2). Buccaneer Bks.
--The Ringed Castle. 640p. 1984. pap. 4.95 (ISBN 0-446-31296-7). Warner Bks.
Dunnett, Peter J. The Decline of the British Motor Industry: The Effects of Government Policy, 1945-1979. 208p. 1980. 28.50 (ISBN 0-7099-0012-0, Pub. by Croom Helm Ltd). Longwood Pub Group.
Dunnett, W. M. Sintesis del Nuevo Testamento. Blanch, Jose M., tr. from Eng. (Curso Para Maestros Cristianos: No. 3). 128p. (Span.). 1972. pap. 3.50 (ISBN 0-89922-012-6). Edit Caribe.
Dunnett, Walter. Outline of New Testament Survey. (Orig.). 1960. pap. 4.95 (ISBN 0-8024-6245-6). Moody.
Dunnett, Walter M. The Book of Acts. (Shield Bible Study Ser.). 144p. (Orig.). 1981. pap. 3.95 (ISBN 0-8010-2915-5). Baker Bk.
--The Interpretation of Holy Scripture. 224p. 1984. pap. 6.95 (ISBN 0-8407-5923-1). Nelson.
--New Testament Survey. LC 63-7410. 96p. 1963. pap. text ed. 4.95 (ISBN 0-910566-03-8); Perfect bdg. instr's. guide 4.95 (ISBN 0-910566-19-4). Evang Tchr.
Dunnett, Walter M., rev. by see Tenney, Merrill C.
Dunnette, Marvin D. Personnel Selection & Placement. (Behavioral Science in Industry Ser). (Orig.). 1966. pap. text ed. 7.25 pub net (ISBN 0-8185-0311-4). Brooks-Cole.
Dunnette, Marvin D., ed. Handbook of Industrial & Organizational Psychology. LC 83-42702. 1740p. 1983. 74.95x (ISBN 0-471-88642-4, Pub. by Wiley-Interscience). Wiley.
Dunnette, Marvin D. & Fleishman, Edwin A., eds. Human Capability Assessment. (Human Performance & Productivity Ser.: Vol. 1). 304p. 1982. 29.95x (ISBN 0-89859-085-X). L Erlbaum Assocs.
Dunney, Joseph A. Church History in the Light of the Saints. LC 74-2196. (Essay Index Reprint Ser.). Repr. of 1944 ed. 25.00 (ISBN 0-518-10162-2). Ayer Co Pubs.
Dunnhaupt, Gerhard, ed. The Martin Luther Quincentennial. LC 84-15239. 315p. 1985. 22.00 (ISBN 0-8143-1774-X). Wayne St U Pr.
Dunnicliff, John & Deere, Don U., eds. Judgement in Geotechnical Engineering: The Professional Legacy of Ralph B. Peck. LC 83-23261. 332p. 1984. 49.95x (ISBN 0-471-89767-1, Pub. by Wiley-Interscience). Wiley.
Dunnigan, Ann, tr. see Chekhov, Anton.
Dunnigan, Ann, tr. see Ferrucci, Franco.
Dunnigan, Ann, tr. see Tolstoy, Leo.
Dunnigan, Brian L. The British Army at Mackinac, Eighteen Twelve to Eighteen Fifteen. Armour, David A., ed. (Reports in Mackinac History & Archaelogy Ser.: No. 7). (Illus.). 56p. (Orig.). 1981. pap. 5.00 (ISBN 0-911872-40-X). Mackinac Island.
--Fort Holmes. Armour, David A., ed. (Reports in Mackinac History & Archaeology: No. 10). (Illus.). 40p. (Orig.). 1984. pap. 5.00 (ISBN 0-911872-51-5). Mackinac Island.
--King's Men at Mackinac: The British Garrisons, 1780-1796. Armour, David A., ed. LC 74-172729. (Reports in Mackinac History & Archaeology Ser: No. 3). (Illus.). 38p. (Orig.). 1973. pap. 3.00 (ISBN 0-911872-19-1). Mackinac Island.
Dunnigan, Dorothy & Rowley, Patricia D. Help! Company's Coming: For Brides, Bachelors, & Busy People. LC 81-90658. (Illus.). 216p. 1982. 9.95 (ISBN 0-9607954-0-5). D Dunnigan.
Dunnigan, James, ed. The War Against Hitler: Europe, North Africa, Southeast Asia, 1939-1945. (Illus.). 200p. 1983. 22.50 (ISBN 0-88254-631-7). Hippocrene Bks.
Dunnigan, James F. The Complete Wargames Handbook: How to Play, Design, & Find Them. (Illus.). 256p. 1980. pap. 7.95 (ISBN 0-688-08649-7, Quill NY). Morrow.
--How to Make War: A Comprehensive Guide to Modern Warfare. (Illus.). 416p. 1982. 14.50 (ISBN 0-688-00780-5). Morrow.
--How to Make War: A Comprehensive Guide to Modern Warfare. rev., upd. ed. LC 82-23065. (Illus.). 444p. 1983. pap. 8.95 (ISBN 0-688-01975-7, Quill NY). Morrow.
Dunnigan, James F. & Bay, Austin. A Quick & Dirty Guide to War: Briefings on Present & Potential Wars. LC 84-22797. (Illus.). 384p. 1985. 17.95 (ISBN 0-688-04199-X). Morrow.
Dunnigan, John, jt. auth. see Barter, Tanya.
Dunnill, M. S. Pulmonary Pathology. (Illus.). 496p. 1982. text ed. 75.00 (ISBN 0-443-01996-7). Churchill.
Dunnill, Mary. Siamese Cats. (Pet Care Ser.). 1984. pap. 5.95 (ISBN 0-8120-2924-0). Barron.
Dunnill, Mary, jt. auth. see Pond, Grace.
Dunnill, Michael, jt. auth. see Aherne, William.
Dunnill, Peter, et al, eds. Enzymic & Non-Enzymic Catalysis. LC 79-40784. 249p. 1980. 79.95x (ISBN 0-470-26773-9). Halsted Pr.
Dunning & Hammons. Let's Talk About Rocks. 3.95 (ISBN 0-87505-125-1). Borden.
Dunning, A. Electrostimulation of the Carotid Sinus Nerve in Angina Pectoris. 1971. 13.75 (ISBN 90-219-2061-1, Excerpta Medica). Elsevier.
Dunning, Al. Reining. Close, Pat, ed. (Illus.). 144p. 1983. pap. 9.95 (ISBN 0-911647-02-3). Western Horseman.
Dunning, Albert. Count Unico Wilhelm van Wassenaer 1692-1766: A Master Unmasked or The Pergolesi-Ricciotti Puzzle Solved. (Illus.). 1980. 75.00 (ISBN 9-06027-400-8). Heinman.
Dunning, Chester S., ed. & tr. see Margeret, Jacques.
Dunning, D., jt. ed. see Whelan, A.
Dunning, David, jt. auth. see Dunning, Mary.
Dunning, Eric & Sheard, Kenneth. Barbarians, Gentlemen & Players: A Sociological Study of the Development of Rugby Football. LC 78-70471. 1979. 23.50x (ISBN 0-8147-1765-9). NYU Pr.
Dunning, Eric, jt. auth. see Williams, John.
Dunning, F. B., jt. ed. see Stebbings, R. F.
Dunning, F. W. & Mykura, W., eds. Mineral Deposits of Europe: Vol. 2-Southeast Europe. 304p. 1982. text ed. 100.00x (ISBN 0-900488-63-8). IMM North Am.
Dunning, Glenna. The American Amusement Park: An Annotated Bibiography. (Architecture Ser.: Bibliography A 1318). 48p. 1985. pap. 7.50 (ISBN 0-89028-268-4). Vance Biblios.
Dunning, Glenna, jt. ed. see Johnson, Julia.
Dunning, H. Ray. Fruit of the Spirit. 1982. pap. 1.95 (ISBN 0-8341-0806-2). Beacon Hill.
Dunning, H. Ray, jt. auth. see Greathouse, William.
Dunning, Harold. Trade Unions & Vocational Training: A Workers' Education Guide. International Labour Office Staff, ed. ii, 83p. (Orig.). 1984. pap. 5.70 (ISBN 92-2-103522-0). Intl Labour Office.
Dunning, Harrison C. Water Allocation in California: Legal Rights & Reform Needs. LC 82-6110. (IGS Research Papers). 62p. 1982. pap. 4.50x (ISBN 0-87772-288-9). Inst Gov Stud Berk.
Dunning, J. H. Multinational Enterprises: Economic Structure & International Competitiveness. (IRM Series in Multinationals). 1986. price not set (ISBN 0-471-90700-6). Wiley.
Dunning, James B. Ministries: Sharing God's Gifts. LC 80-52058. (Illus.). 136p. (Orig.). 1980. pap. 5.95 (ISBN 0-88489-123-2). St Marys.
--New Wine: New Wineskins. 128p. (Orig.). 1981. pap. 4.95 (ISBN 0-8215-9807-4). Sadlier.
Dunning, James B. & Ready, William J., eds. Christian Initiation Resources, Vol. IV. 300p. 1983. 45.00 (ISBN 0-8215-9866-X). Sadlier.
Dunning, James B. & Reedy, William J., eds. Christian Initiation Resources, Vol. I. (Illus.). 300p. 1980. 45.00 (ISBN 0-8215-9800-7). Sadlier.
--Christian Initiation Resources, Vol. II. (Illus.). 300p. 1981. 45.00 (ISBN 0-8215-9813-9). Sadlier.
Dunning, James M. Dental Care for Everyone: Problems & Proposals. 224p. 1976. 15.00x (ISBN 0-674-19790-9). Harvard U Pr.
--Principles of Dental Public Health. 3rd ed. LC 78-14328. (Illus.). 1979. text ed. 30.00x (ISBN 0-674-70549-1). Harvard U Pr.
Dunning, Jennifer. But First a School. 1985. 17.95 (ISBN 0-670-80407-X). Viking.
Dunning, Joan. The Loon: Voice of the Wilderness. Taylor, Sandra J., ed. LC 85-50055. (Illus.). 144p. 1985. 15.95 (ISBN 0-89909-080-X). Yankee Bks.
Dunning, John. Arbor House Treasure of True Crime. 1985. 18.95 (ISBN 0-87795-679-0). Arbor Hse.
--Deadline. 224p. (Orig.). 1981. pap. 2.50 (ISBN 0-449-14398-8, GM). Fawcett.
--Looking for Ginger North. 1980. pap. 1.95 (ISBN 0-449-14317-1, GM). Fawcett.
--Tune in Yesterday: The Ultimate Encyclopedia of Old-Time Radio, 1925-1976. LC 76-28369. 1979. pap. 8.95 (ISBN 0-13-932608-1). P-H.
Dunning, John & Stopford, John. World Directory of Multinational Enterprises, 2 vols. 1500p. 1980. 195.00 set (ISBN 0-87196-649-2); Vol. 1. (ISBN 0-87196-440-6); Vol. 2. (ISBN 0-87196-441-4). Facts on File.
Dunning, John H. American Investment in British Manufacturing Industry. Bruchey, Stuart & Bruchey, Eleanor, eds. LC 76-5004. (American Business Abroad Ser.). (Illus.). 1976. 30.00x (ISBN 0-405-09273-3). Ayer Co Pubs.
--International Production & the Multinational Enterprise. (Illus.). 416p. 1981. text ed. 40.00x (ISBN 0-04-330319-6); pap. text ed. 18.50x (ISBN 0-04-330320-X). Allen Unwin.
Dunning, John H. & Pearce, Robert D. World's Largest Industrial Enterprises, 1962-1983. 2nd ed. 200p. 1985. 55.00 (ISBN 0-312-89278-0). St Martin.
Dunning, John H., ed. The Multinational Enterprise. 1971. text ed. 36.00x (ISBN 0-04-330189-4). Allen Unwin.
Dunning, John H., jt. ed. see Black, John.
Dunning, John H., jt. ed. see Stopford, John M.
Dunning, John S. South American Land Birds: A Photographic Aid to Identification. Ridgely, Robert S., ed. LC 82-9351. (Illus.). 400p. 1982. 37.50 (ISBN 0-915180-21-9); pap. 27.50 (ISBN 0-915180-22-7). Harrowood Bks.
Dunning, Kenneth A. Getting Started in General Purpose Simulation System. LC 80-28281. 117p. (Orig.). 1981. pap. 8.95x (ISBN 0-910554-34-X). Engineering.
Dunning, Lawrence. Keller's Bomb. 1978. pap. 1.95 (ISBN 0-380-40873-2, 40873). Avon.
--Taking Liberty. 496p. 1981. pap. 2.95 (ISBN 0-380-77297-3, 77297). Avon.
Dunning, Marcy, jt. auth. see Houghton-Alico, Doann.
Dunning, Mary & Dunning, David. Good Apple & Wonderful Word Games. (gr. 3-7). 1981. 9.95 (ISBN 0-86653-053-3, GA 254). Good Apple.
Dunning, N. A. & McCurry, Dan C., eds. The Farmers' Alliance History & Agricultural Digest. facsimile ed. LC 74-30629. (American Farmers & the Rise of Agribusiness Ser.). (Illus.). 1975. Repr. of 1891 ed. 71.50x (ISBN 0-405-06798-4). Ayer Co Pubs.
Dunning, R. A. Pest & Disease Control in Vegetables, Potatoes & Sugar Beet. 97p. 1980. 35.00x (Pub. by CAB Bks England). State Mutual Bk.
Dunning, R. A., et al. Pest & Disease Control in Vegetables, Potatoes & Sugar Beet. 97p. (Orig.). 1981. pap. 9.95x (ISBN 0-901436-59-3, Pub. by B C P C England). Intl Spec Bk.
Dunning, R. W. Social & Economic Change among the Northern Ojibwa. LC 60-50269. 1959. pap. 6.95 (ISBN 0-8020-6131-1). U of Toronto Pr.
Dunning, R. W., ed. A History of the Counties of Somerset, Vol. 5. (The Victoria History of the Counties of England Ser.). (Illus.). 256p. 1985. 105.00 (ISBN 0-19-722764-3). Oxford U Pr.
--Somerset, Vol. IV. (Victoria History of the Counties of England Ser.). (Illus.). 1979. 99.00x (ISBN 0-19-722747-3). Oxford U Pr.
Dunning, Stephen. Do You Fear No One. (Illus.). 32p. (Orig.). 1982. pap. 4.95 (ISBN 0-942908-05-8). Pancake Pr.
--Teaching Literature to Adolescents: Poetry. 1966. pap. 10.80 (ISBN 0-673-05544-2). Scott F.
--Teaching Literature to Adolescents: Short Stories. 1968. pap. 10.80 (ISBN 0-673-05843-3). Scott F.
Dunning, Stephen, et al, eds. Reflections on a Gift of Watermelon Pickle & Other Modern Verse. LC 66-8763. (Illus.). (gr. 7 up). 1966. 12.50 (ISBN 0-688-41231-9); PLB 12.88 (ISBN 0-688-51231-3). Lothrop.
--Some Haystacks Don't Even Have Any Needle: And Other Complete Modern Poems. (Illus.). (gr. 7 up). 1969. 12.50 (ISBN 0-688-41445-1). Lothrop.
Dunning, Stephen N. Kierkegaard's Dialectic of Inwardness: A Structural Analysis of the Theory of Stages. LC 85-3443. 315p. 1985. text ed. 32.00x (ISBN 0-691-07299-X). Princeton U Pr.
--The Tongues of Men: Hegel & Hamann on Religious Language & History. LC 79-10729. (American Academy of Religion, Dissertation Ser.: No. 27). 1979. 14.00 (ISBN 0-89130-283-2, 010127); pap. 9.95 (ISBN 0-89130-302-2). Scholars Pr GA.
Dunning, T. P. Piers Plowman: An Interpretation of the A-Text. LC 72-186986. 1937. lib. bdg. 25.00 (ISBN 0-8414-3876-5). Folcroft.
Dunning, T. P., jt. ed. see Bliss, A. J.
Dunning, Thomas & Dolan, T. P., eds. Piers Plowman: An Interpretation of the A Text. 2nd ed. 1980. 39.95x (ISBN 0-19-812446-5). Oxford U Pr.

Dunning, Thomas P. Piers Plowman: An Interpretation of the A-Text. LC 73-95095. 1971. Repr. of 1937 ed. lib. bdg. 18.75x (ISBN 0-8371-3088-3, DUPP). Greenwood.

Dunning, W. J. & Robin, L. P. Home Planning & Architectural Drawing: An Illustrated Guide. LC 76-13029. 92p. 1976. Repr. of 1966 ed. text ed. 8.50 (ISBN 0-88275-400-9). Krieger.

Dunning, William A. British Empire & the United States. LC 14-18567. 1969. Repr. of 1914 ed. 24.00 (ISBN 0-527-25800-8). Kraus Repr.

--Essays on the Civil War & Reconstruction. facsimile ed. LC 79-37151. (Essay Index Reprint Ser). Repr. of 1897 ed. 24.50 (ISBN 0-8369-2494-0). Ayer Co Pubs.

--Essays on the Civil War & Reconstruction. 13.25 (ISBN 0-8446-0600-6). Peter Smith.

--A History of Political Theories, 3 vols. Repr. of 1902 ed. Vol. 1 Ancient & Medieval,1902. 120.00 ea. (ISBN 0-384-13340-1). Vol. 2 From Luther To Montesquieu, 1905. Vol. 3, From Rousseau To Spencer, 1920. Johnson Repr.

Dunning-Davies, J. Mathematical Methods for Mathematicians, Physical Scientists & Engineers. 425p. 1982. 64.95x (ISBN 0-470-27322-4). Halsted Pr.

Dunninger. One Hundred Classic Houdini Tricks You Can Do. LC 74-14200. (Illus.). 144p. 1975. pap. 3.50 (ISBN 0-668-03617-6). Arco.

Dunninger, J. Monument to Magic. 1974. 14.95 (ISBN 0-8184-0160-5). Lyle Stuart.

Dunninger, Joseph. Dunninger's Complete Encyclopedia of Magic. (Illus.). 1967. 20.00 (ISBN 0-8184-0029-3). Lyle Stuart.

Dunnings, Thomas, jt. ed. see Gregory, James.

Dunnington, Ann L. Hellcoal Annual, No. 4. 1978. pap. 3.00 (ISBN 0-916912-11-6). Hellcoal Pr.

Dunnington, Ann L., ed. Hellcoal Annual, No. 5. 1979. pap. text ed. 3.00 (ISBN 0-685-91298-1). Hellcoal Pr.

--Hellcoal Review, Vol. 5, No. 1. 1978. pap. text ed. 2.50 (ISBN 0-685-91299-X). Hellcoal Pr.

--Prose & Poetry, Vol. 4, No. 1. 1978. pap. 2.50 (ISBN 0-916912-33-7). Hellcoal Pr.

Dunnington, Tom, jt. auth. see Punnett, Dick.

Dunnington, Tom, illus. Animals. LC 83-25213. (The Shape of Poetry Ser.). (Illus.). 32p. (gr. k-3). 1984. PLB 7.45 (ISBN 0-89565-264-1). Childs World.

Dunn-Meynell, Hugo, jt. auth. see Salmon, Alice W.

Dunnom, D., ed. Health Effects of Synthetic Silica Particulates-STP 732. 223p. 1981. 24.00 (ISBN 0-8031-0734-X, 04-732000-17). ASTM.

Dunn-Pattison, R. P. Napoleon's Marshals. (Illus.). 373p. 1977. Repr. of 1909 ed. 26.50x (ISBN 0-8476-6060-5). Rowman.

Dunn-Rankin, Peter. Scaling Methods. (Illus.). 448p. 1983. text ed. 36.00x (ISBN 0-89859-203-8). L Erlbaum Assocs.

Dunoyer, Alphonse. The Public Prosecutor of the Terror: Antoine Quentin Fouquier-Tinville. 1977. lib. bdg. 59.95 (ISBN 0-8490-2489-7). Gordon Pr.

Dunphy, D. C. & Dick, B. Organizational Change by Choice. 312p. 1981. 21.00 (ISBN 0-07-072947-6). McGraw.

Dunphy, J. Englebert & Botsford, Thomas W. Physical Examination of the Surgical Patient: An Introduction to Clinical Surgery. 4th ed. LC 74-4557. (Illus.). 435p. 1975. text ed. 26.00 (ISBN 0-7216-3267-X). Saunders.

Dunphy, Jack. First Wine: A Novel. LC 82-7326. 213p. 1982. 16.95 (ISBN 0-8071-1046-9). La State U Pr.

--John Fury: A Novel in Four Parts. LC 76-6338. (Irish Americans Ser.). 1976. Repr. of 1946 ed. 23.50 (ISBN 0-405-09333-0). Ayer Co Pubs.

--Nightmovers. 8.95 (ISBN 0-911660-16-X). Yankee Peddler.

Dunphy, Philip W., ed. Career Development for the College Student. 5th ed. LC 80-20933. 128p. 1981. pap. 7.50x (ISBN 0-910328-02-1). Carroll Pr.

Dunphy, Thomas & Cummins, Thomas J., eds. Remarkable Trials of All Countries; Particularly of the United States, Great Britain, Ireland & France: With Notes & Speeches of Counsel. Containing Thrilling Narratives of Fact from the Court-Room, Also Historical Reminiscences of Wonderful Events. 464p. 1981. Repr. of 1867 ed. lib. bdg. 35.00x (ISBN 0-8377-0512-6). Rothman.

Dunraven. The Great Divide: Travels in the Upper Yellowstone in the Summer of 1874. (Illus.). 11.25 (ISBN 0-8446-2011-4). Peter Smith.

Dunraven, Geraldine. Irish Houses, Castles & Gardens: Open to the Public. (Illus.). 34p. 1982. pap. 3.95 (ISBN 0-900346-34-5, Pub. by Salem Hse Ltd.). Merrimack Pub Cir.

Dunrea, Olivier. Eddy B, Pigboy. LC 83-2832. (Illus.). 24p. (gr. k-3). 1983. 8.95 (ISBN 0-689-50277-X, McElderry Bk). Atheneum.

--Fergus & Bridey. LC 84-19828. (Illus.). 36p. (ps-2). 1985. reinforced bdg. 14.95 (ISBN 0-8234-0554-0). Holiday.

--Mogwogs on the March. LC 85-5493. (Illus.). 32p. (ps-1). 1985. reinforced 12.95 (ISBN 0-8234-0578-8). Holiday.

--Ravena. LC 82-23244. (Illus.). 32p. (ps-3). 1984. reinforced bdg. 13.95 (ISBN 0-8234-0487-0). Holiday.

Dun's Marketing Services. Export Documentation Handbook: 1985 Edition. Hurd, Ruth E., compiled by. 200p. 1985. soft-cover handbook 60.00 (ISBN 0-918257-03-4). Dun's Mktg.

Dunsany, Edward. Five Plays. 1917. lib. bdg. 20.00 (ISBN 0-8414-3879-X). Folcroft.

Dunsany, Edward see Brown, Edmund R.

Dunsany, Edward J. Book of Wonder. LC 72-6079. (Short Story Index Reprint Ser.). Repr. of 1918 ed. 19.00 (ISBN 0-8369-4213-2). Ayer Co Pubs.

--Dreamer's Tales. LC 70-101803. (Short Story Index Reprint Ser.). 1910. 17.00 (ISBN 0-8369-3191-2). Ayer Co Pubs.

--Last Book of Wonder. LC 76-101282. (Short Story Index Reprint Ser). (Illus.). 1916. 15.00 (ISBN 0-8369-3219-6). Ayer Co Pubs.

--Time & the Gods. LC 76-113659. (Short Story Index Reprint Ser.). 1913. 16.00 (ISBN 0-8369-3388-5). Ayer Co Pubs.

Dunsany, Lord. The Curse of the Wise Woman. 315p. Repr. of 1933 ed. lib. bdg. 16.60x (ISBN 0-88411-650-6, Pub. by Aeonian Pr). Amereon Ltd.

--A Dreamer's Tales. (Illus.). 1979. 13.95 (ISBN 0-913896-13-6). Owlswick Pr.

--A Dreamer's Tales & Other Stories. 1978. Repr. lib. bdg. 25.00 (ISBN 0-8482-0621-5). Norwood Edns.

--Five Plays. 116p. 1984. Repr. of 1919 ed. lib. bdg. 35.00 (ISBN 0-89760-175-0). Telegraph Bks.

--Ghosts of the Heaviside Layer. (Illus.). 1980. 20.00 (ISBN 0-913896-14-4). Owlswick Pr.

--Gods, Men, & Ghosts. (Illus.). 13.50 (ISBN 0-8446-0081-4). Peter Smith.

--Gods, Men & Ghosts: The Best Supernatural Fiction of Lord Dunsany. Bleiler, E. F., ed. LC 75-164735. (Illus.). 1971. pap. 4.95 (ISBN 0-486-22808-8). Dover.

--The Lost Silk Hat. Brown, Edmund R., ed. (International Pocket Library). pap. 4.00 (ISBN 0-8283-1435-7). Branden Pub Co.

--Plays of Gods & Men. 1979. Repr. of 1917 ed. lib. bdg. 30.00 (ISBN 0-8495-1102-X). Arden Lib.

--Plays of Gods & Men. LC 77-70355. (One-Act Plays in Reprint Ser.). 1977. Repr. of 1917 ed. 16.50x (ISBN 0-8486-2015-1). Core Collection.

--The Sword of Welleran & Other Wonder Tales. 16.50 (ISBN 0-8159-6833-7). Devin.

--Tales of Three Hemispheres. LC 76-8950. (Illus.). 130p. 1976. 13.95 (ISBN 0-913896-04-7). Owlswick Pr.

Dunsany, Lord Edward. The Food of Death: Fifty-One Tales. Reginald, R. & Menville, Douglas, eds. LC 80-19151. (Newcastle Forgotten Fantasy Library: Vol. 3). Orig. Title: Fifty-One Tales. 138p. 1980. Repr. of 1974 ed. lib. bdg. 14.95x (ISBN 0-89370-502-0). Borgo Pr.

Dunsby, Jonathan M. Structural Ambiguity in Brahms: Analytical Approaches to Four Works. Fortune, Nigel, ed. LC 81-24. (British Studies in Musicology: No. 2). 130p. 1981. 34.95 (ISBN 0-8357-1159-5). UMI Res Pr.

Dunscomb, S. Whitney, Jr. Bankruptcy: A Study in Comparative Legislation. LC 78-82250. (Columbia University. Studies in the Social Sciences: No. 6). Repr. of 1893 ed. 16.50 (ISBN 0-404-51006-X). AMS Pr.

Dunsdorfs, Edgars. The Baltic Dilemma. 12.50 (ISBN 0-8315-0148-0). Speller.

Dunseath, T. K. Spenser's Allegory of Justice in Book Five of "The Faerie Queene". LC 78-14441. 1979. Repr. of 1968 ed. lib. bdg. 27.50x (ISBN 0-313-21047-0, DUSA). Greenwood.

Dunseth, William B. An Introduction to Annuity, Charitable Remainder Trust & Bequest Programs. 2nd ed. 37p. 1982. 14.50 (ISBN 0-89964-193-8). Coun Adv & Supp Ed.

Dunsheath, Percy. History of Electrical Power Engineering. 1969. pap. 8.95x (ISBN 0-262-54007-X). MIT Pr.

Dunshee, Marilyn H., jt. auth. see Keithahn, Mary N.

Dunsing, R. You & I Have Simply Got to Stop Meeting This Way. 1981. pap. 5.95 (ISBN 0-317-31403-3). AMACOM.

Dunsing, Richard J. You & I Have Simply Got to Stop Meeting this Way. LC 78-2516. (Illus.). 176p. 1981. 5.95 (ISBN 0-8144-7558-2). Am Mgmt Assns.

Dunsire, Andrew. Control in a Bureaucracy. LC 78-19207. 1979. 30.00 (ISBN 0-312-16897-7). St Martin.

--Implementation in a Bureaucracy. LC 78-19208. 1979. 30.00x (ISBN 0-312-40999-0). St Martin.

Dunsire, Andrew, jt. auth. see Hood, Christopher.

Dunsker, Stewart, ed. Cervical Spondylosis. (Seminars in Neurological Surgery). 229p. 1980. text ed. 36.00 (ISBN 0-89004-421-X). Raven.

Dunsmore, I. R., jt. auth. see Aitchison, J.

Dunson, Josh. Freedom in the Air: Song Movements of the Sixties. LC 80-11678. 127p. 1980. Repr. of 1965 ed. lib. bdg. 24.75 (ISBN 0-313-22393-9, DUFA). Greenwood.

Dunson, W. A. Biology of Sea Snakes. (Illus.). 544p. 1975. pap. text ed. 53.50 (ISBN 0-8391-0819-2). Univ Park.

Dunst, Carl J. A Clinical & Educational Manual for Use with the Uzgiris-Hunt Scales. (Illus.). 128p. 1980. pap. 11.00 (ISBN 0-8391-1571-7). Pro-Ed.

Dunst, Klaus H. Portfolio Management. 1982. 31.20x (ISBN 3-11008-876-2). De Gruyter.

Dunstan, Alan. Interpreting Worship. 102p. 1985. pap. 5.95 (ISBN 0-8192-1357-8). Morehouse.

Dunstan, Bernard. Composing Your Paintings. LC 79-84661. (Start to Paint Ser.). (Illus.). 1979. pap. 3.95 (ISBN 0-8008-1803-2, Pentalic). Taplinger.

--Painting Methods of the Impressionists: Revised Edition Entirely in Color. (Illus.). 176p. 1983. 27.50 (ISBN 0-8230-3711-8). Watson-Guptill.

--Starting to Paint Portraits. LC 79-63840. (Start to Paint Ser.). (Illus.). 1979. pap. 3.95 (ISBN 0-8008-7382-3, Pentalic). Taplinger.

--Starting to Paint Still Life. LC 79-63841. (Start to Paint Ser.). (Illus.). 1979. pap. 3.95 (ISBN 0-8008-7383-1, Pentalic). Taplinger.

Dunstan, Bob. The Book of Falmouth & Penryn. 1977. 40.00x (ISBN 0-86023-002-3). State Mutual Bk.

Dunstan, David. Governing the Metropolis: Politics, Technology & Social Change in a Victorian City - Melbourne 1850-1891. (Illus.). xvii, 362p. 1984. 28.00x (ISBN 0-522-84276-3, Pub. by Melbourne Pr). Intl Spec Bk.

Dunstan, Elizabeth. Twelve Nigerian Languages. LC 70-95611. 185p. (Orig.). 1969. pap. text ed. 9.95x (ISBN 0-8419-0031-0, Africana). Holmes & Meier.

Dunstan, Florence J., tr. see Pena, Carlos G.

Dunstan, G. R., ed. see Kirk, Kenneth E.

Dunstan, J. Leslie, ed. Protestantism. LC 61-15497. (Great Religions of Modern Man Ser). 1961. 8.95 (ISBN 0-8076-0161-6). Braziller.

Dunstan, John. Paths to Excellence & the Soviet School. 302p. 1979. 22.00x (ISBN 0-85633-150-3, Pub. by NFER Nelson UK). Taylor & Francis.

Dunstan, Ralph. A Cyclopaedic Dictionary of Music. LC 72-14060. 642p. 1973. Repr. of 1925 ed. lib. bdg. 65.00 (ISBN 0-306-70559-1). Da Capo.

Dunstan, Reginald, jt. ed. see Ivens, Michael.

Dunstan, Simon. British Army Fighting Vehicles, Nineteen Forty-Five to the Present. (Tanks Illustrated Ser.: Vol. 12). 1984. pap. 7.95 (ISBN 0-85368-669-6, Arms & Armour Pr). Sterling.

--The British Army in Northern Ireland, No. 4. (Uniforms Illustrated Ser.). (Illus.). 72p. 1984. pap. 7.95 (ISBN 0-85368-631-9, Pub. by Arms & Armour Pr). Sterling.

--The Modern British Soldier, No. 2. (Uniforms Illustrated Ser.). (Illus.). 72p. 1984. pap. 7.95 (ISBN 0-85368-630-0, Pub. by Arms & Armour Pr). Sterling.

--Tank War Korea. (Tanks Illustrated Ser.: Vol. 14). 1984. pap. 7.95 (ISBN 0-85368-000-0, Arms & Armour Pr). Sterling.

--Vietnam Tracks: Armor in Battle, 1945-1975. (Illus.). 192p. 1983. 20.00 (ISBN 0-89141-171-2). Presidio Pr.

Dunster, David. Key Buildings of the Twentieth Century: House 1900-1945, Vol. 1. LC 85-42945. (Illus.). 128p. 1985. pap. 14.95 (ISBN 0-8478-0642-1). Rizzoli Intl.

Dunster, David, jt. auth. see Scully, Vincent.

Dunster, David, ed. Alvar Aalto: An Academy Architectural Monograph. (Illus.). 128p. 1984. pap. 19.95 (ISBN 0-312-02150-X). St Martin.

Dunster, Jack. China & Mao Zedong. LC 83-1854. (Cambridge Topic Bks.). (Illus.). 36p. (gr. 5 up). 1983. PLB 7.95 (ISBN 0-8225-1230-0). Lerner Pubns.

--Mao Zedong & China. LC 81-21577. (Cambridge Introduction to the History of Mankind Topic Bk.). 32p. 1982. 4.50 (ISBN 0-521-23148-5). Cambridge U Pr.

Dunster, Mark. Ace. 26p. (Orig.). 1985. pap. 4.00 (ISBN 0-89642-126-0). Linden Pubs.

--Aloes: Poems from Hollywood. 63p. (Orig.). 1985. pap. 6.00 (ISBN 0-89642-119-8). Linden Pubs.

--Amleth. 1979. pap. 4.00 (ISBN 0-89642-056-6). Linden Pubs.

--Angel. 1972. 4.00 (ISBN 0-89642-011-6). Linden Pubs.

--Armin. 22p. (Orig.). 1982. pap. 4.00 (ISBN 0-89642-094-9). Linden Pubs.

--Bicentennials. 1977. pap. 4.00 (ISBN 0-89642-003-5). Linden Pubs.

--Body & Soul. 1979. pap. 4.00 (ISBN 0-89642-057-4). Linden Pubs.

--A Boys Beginning. 17p. 1984. pap. 4.00 (ISBN 0-89642-108-2). Linden Pubs.

--Brandy. (Rin: Part 13). 1977. pap. 4.00 (ISBN 0-89642-000-0). Linden Pubs.

--Bret (Rin, Pt. 23) A Play. LC 77-356479. 1976. 4.00 (ISBN 0-89642-012-4). Linden Pubs.

--Brutus. (Antony Ser.: Pt. 6). (Orig.). 1980. pap. 4.00 (ISBN 0-89642-063-9). Linden Pubs.

--Caesar. (Borgia: Pt. 3). 1979. pap. 4.00 (ISBN 0-89642-049-3). Linden Pubs.

--Caesars Fall: Antony, Pt. 3. 1978. pap. text ed. 4.00 (ISBN 0-89642-045-0). Linden Pubs.

--Caesar's Rise. (Antony Ser.: Pt. 1). 40p. (Orig.). 1986. pap. 5.00 (ISBN 0-89642-134-1). Linden Pubs.

--Cam. LC 74-437961. (Rin Ser: Pt. 47). 1974. 4.00 (ISBN 0-89642-013-2). Linden Pubs.

--Canterville. 19p. (Orig.). 1985. pap. 4.00 (ISBN 0-89642-122-8). Linden Pubs.

--Capers. (Poems from Hollywood Ser.). 64p. (Orig.). 1986. pap. 6.00 (ISBN 0-89642-131-7). Linden Pubs.

--Caravans: Three Books of Poems. 57p. (Orig.). 1981. pap. 4.00 (ISBN 0-89642-071-X). Linden Pubs.

--Catherine. (Borgia Ser.: Pt. 2). 49p. (Orig.). 1980. pap. 4.00 (ISBN 0-89642-067-1). Linden Pubs.

--Catherine. (Henry the 8th Ser.: Pt. 2). 22p. (Orig.). 1984. pap. 4.00 (ISBN 0-89642-111-2). Linden Pubs.

--Chris. (Rin: Pt. 14). (Orig.). 1978. pap. 4.00 (ISBN 0-89642-044-2). Linden Pubs.

--Clay. LC 74-165104. 1973. 4.00 (ISBN 0-89642-014-0). Linden Pubs.

--Cleopatra: Antony, Part 11. 37p. 1984. pap. 4.00 (ISBN 0-89642-115-5). Linden Pubs.

--Corky: Kel, Pt. 2. (Rin: Pt. 29). 82p. (Orig.). 1981. pap. 5.00 (ISBN 0-89642-072-8). Linden Pubs.

--Cory. (Rin Ser.: Pt. 51). 55p. (Orig.). 1984. pap. 4.00 (ISBN 0-89642-117-1). Linden Pubs.

--Crumwell. (Henry the 8th Ser.: Pt. 4). 41p. (Orig.). 1982. pap. 4.00 (ISBN 0-89642-085-X). Linden Pubs.

--Dancers. (Rin Ser.: Pt. 18). 36p. (Orig.). 1986. pap. 4.00 (ISBN 0-89642-133-3). Linden Pubs.

--Dialogue. 15p. (Orig.). 1985. pap. 4.00 (ISBN 0-89642-120-1). Linden Pubs.

--Dit. LC 78-100964. 1978. pap. 4.00 (ISBN 0-89642-004-3). Linden Pubs.

--Dogs, 2 vols. (Animals Ser.: Pt. 1). (Orig.). 1979. pap. 8.00 (ISBN 0-89642-058-2). Linden Pubs.

--Driss. 62p. (Orig.). 1982. pap. 4.00 (ISBN 0-89642-088-4). Linden Pubs.

--Druce. (Rin: Part 2). 1976. pap. 4.00 (ISBN 0-89642-015-9). Linden Pubs.

--Ella. LC 75-212842. 87p. (Orig.). 1975. pap. 4.00 (ISBN 0-89642-016-7). Linden Pubs.

--Emily, Part 1: Charles. 46p. (Orig.). 1975. pap. 4.00 (ISBN 0-89642-017-5). Linden Pubs.

--Enid. 55p. (Orig.). 1975. pap. 4.00 (ISBN 0-89642-018-3). Linden Pubs.

--Erastus. 80p. (Orig.). 1975. pap. 4.00 (ISBN 0-89642-019-1). Linden Pubs.

--Farms. 57p. (Orig.). 1984. pap. 4.00 (ISBN 0-89642-116-3). Linden Pubs.

--Fasces, Bazaars, Ariosos: Three Books of Poems. 1979. pap. 4.00 (ISBN 0-89642-051-5). Linden Pubs.

--Fat Man. 53p. (Orig.). 1981. pap. 4.00 (ISBN 0-89642-081-7). Linden Pubs.

--Fox. 68p. (Orig.). 1980. pap. 4.00 (ISBN 0-89642-064-7). Linden Pubs.

--Gage. 13p. (Orig.). 1985. pap. 4.00 (ISBN 0-89642-130-9). Linden Pubs.

--Gareth. 43p. 1977. pap. 4.00 (ISBN 0-89642-005-1). Linden Pubs.

--Geneva. (Rin: Part 41). 1977. pap. 4.00 (ISBN 0-89642-020-5). Linden Pubs.

--Gotham. 14p. (Orig.). 1985. Linden Pubs.

--Griggs. 47p. 1979. pap. 4.00 (ISBN 0-89642-048-5). Linden Pubs.

--Hash. (Rin, Pt. 12: Fathers. The Village Plays, Pt. 3, Sheridan Square). 59p. (Orig.). 1984. pap. text ed. 5.00 (ISBN 0-89642-109-0). Linden Pubs.

--Haslemere. LC 78-100953. (Rin: Pt. 9). 1978. pap. 4.00 (ISBN 0-89642-001-9). Linden Pubs.

--Herod. (Antony: Pt. 9). 23p. (Orig.). 1983. pap. 4.00 (ISBN 0-89642-105-8). Linden Pubs.

--Heroes. (Rin Ser.: Pt. 21). 25p. (Orig.). 1985. pap. 4.00 (ISBN 0-89642-129-5). Linden Pubs.

--Hollywood Poems. 80p. (Orig.). 1983. pap. 5.00 (ISBN 0-89642-095-7). Linden Pubs.

--Hoop, 2 vols. 140p. (Orig.). 1980. Set. pap. 8.00 (ISBN 0-89642-070-1). Linden Pubs.

--Infare. 23p. (Orig.). 1983. pap. 4.00 (ISBN 0-89642-098-1). Linden Pubs.

--Ish. (Rin Ser.: Pt. 32). 51p. (Orig.). 1984. pap. 4.00 (ISBN 0-89642-113-9). Linden Pubs.

--Jeff. (Rin Ser.: Pt. 30). 23p. (Orig.). 1983. pap. 4.00 (ISBN 0-89642-096-5). Linden Pubs.

--Jiggs. (Rin Ser.: Pt. 49). 82p. (Orig.). 1981. pap. 5.00 (ISBN 0-89642-076-0). Linden Pubs.

--Jipsies, Otherwise, Raphael. 38p. 1984. pap. 4.00 (ISBN 0-89642-110-4). Linden Pubs.

--Joy. 18p. 1985. pap. 4.00 (ISBN 0-317-18631-0). Linden Pubs.

--Joy, Otherwise, Seasong. 19p. 1981. pap. 4.00 (ISBN 0-89642-121-X). Linden Pubs.

--Kansas. (John Brown: Pt. 1). 31p. (Orig.). 1984. pap. 4.00 (ISBN 0-89642-107-4). Linden Pubs.

--Katherine Howard. (Henry the Eighth Ser.: Pt. 5). 1979. pap. 4.00 (ISBN 0-89642-047-7). Linden Pubs.

--Kids, Alias, Haloween. LC 78-314767. (Holiday Ser.: Pt. 1). 1978. pap. 4.00 (ISBN 0-89642-040-X). Linden Pubs.

--Kip. (Rin: Part 33). 79p. (Orig.). 1975. pap. 4.00 (ISBN 0-89642-022-1). Linden Pubs.

--Kit. (Rin: Pt. 45). (Orig.). 1980. pap. 5.00 (ISBN 0-89642-060-4). Linden Pubs.

--Knightwood. 1973. 4.00 (ISBN 0-89642-023-X). Linden Pubs.

--Laramie. 83p. (Orig.). 1975. pap. 4.00 (ISBN 0-89642-024-8). Linden Pubs.

--Les: Kel, Pt. 1. (Rin Ser.: Pt. 28). 60p. 1981. pap. 4.00 (ISBN 0-89642-075-2). Linden Pubs.

--Lint. 24p. (Orig.). 1983. pap. 4.00 (ISBN 0-89642-100-7). Linden Pubs.

--Loris. (Rin Ser.: Pt. 1). (Orig.). 1980. pap. 4.00 (ISBN 0-89642-062-0). Linden Pubs.

--Marga. (Rin Ser.: Pt. 4). 61p. (Orig.). 1982. pap. 4.00 (ISBN 0-89642-086-8). Linden Pubs.

--Mary. LC 78-112416. (Henry the Eighth Ser.: Pt. 3). 1978. pap. 4.00 (ISBN 0-89642-043-4). Linden Pubs.

--Massachusetts. (John Brown: Pt. 2). 1978. pap. 4.00 (ISBN 0-89642-041-8). Linden Pubs.
--Mermaid. 41p. 1982. pap. 4.00 (ISBN 0-89642-087-6). Linden Pubs.
--Miles. LC 75-177113. (Rin Ser.: Pt. 39). 1974. 4.00 (ISBN 0-89642-025-6). Linden Pubs.
--Miser. 2nd, Rev. ed. 39p. (Orig.). 1982. pap. 4.00 (ISBN 0-89642-093-0). Linden Pubs.
--Mr. Jings. 80p. (Orig.). 1975. pap. 4.00 (ISBN 0-89642-027-2). Linden Pubs.
--Moneymakers. (Rin Ser.: Pt. 17). 37p. (Orig.). 1982. pap. 4.00 (ISBN 0-89642-090-6). Linden Pubs.
--Motorcycles. LC 77-155954. (Rin: Pt. 7). 1978. pap. 4.00 (ISBN 0-89642-006-X). Linden Pubs.
--Moviemakers. (Rin Ser.: Pt. 16). 49p. (Orig.). 1982. pap. 4.00 (ISBN 0-89642-089-2). Linden Pubs.
--Myrna: Rin, Pt. 10. 30p. 1982. pap. 4.00 (ISBN 0-89642-084-1). Linden Pubs.
--Myrrhs: A Book of Poems for the Los Angeles Bicentennial. 20p. (Orig.). 1981. pap. 4.00 (ISBN 0-89642-078-7). Linden Pubs.
--The Nan Shan. 1977. pap. 4.00 (ISBN 0-89642-007-8). Linden Pubs.
--Nard. (Poems from Hollywood Ser.). 70p. (Orig.). 1984. pap. 5.00 (ISBN 0-89642-114-7). Linden Pubs.
--Ned. LC 74-172084. (Rin Ser.: Pt. 3). 1973. 4.00 (ISBN 0-89642-028-0). Linden Pubs.
--New York. LC 74-229035. 1973. 4.00 (ISBN 0-89642-029-9). Linden Pubs.
--Octavian: Prolog to Actium, Antony, Pt. 10. 50p. (Orig.). 1981. pap. 4.00 (ISBN 0-89642-074-4). Linden Pubs.
--Ofice. LC 78-105243. 1978. pap. 4.00 (ISBN 0-89642-010-8). Linden Pubs.
--Parthia. (Antony: Pt. 7). (Orig.). 1979. pap. 4.00 (ISBN 0-89642-055-8). Linden Pubs.
--Periapts, Amulets, Inflections: Three Books of Poems. 1978. pap. 4.00 (ISBN 0-89642-002-7). Linden Pubs.
--Pip. (Rin: Pt. 53). 1979. pap. 4.00 (ISBN 0-89642-052-3). Linden Pubs.
--Playboy. (Rin Ser.: Pt. 43). 1974. 4.00 (ISBN 0-89642-030-2). Linden Pubs.
--The Pope. (Borgia Ser.: Pt. 1). 36p. (Orig.). 1984. pap. 4.00 (ISBN 0-89642-112-0). Linden PUbs.
--Portraits. 2nd ed. LC 76-358986. 140p. 1976. pap. 5.00 (ISBN 0-89642-031-0). Linden Pubs.
--Postmortem. 19p. (Orig.). 1983. pap. 4.00 (ISBN 0-89642-099-X). Linden Pubs.
--Ransom. 15p. (Orig.). 1986. pap. 4.00 (ISBN 0-89642-132-5). Linden Pubs.
--Red. (Rin: Pt. 46). 1979. pap. 5.00 (ISBN 0-89642-054-X). Linden Pubs.
--Rinwood. 21p. (Orig.). 1984. pap. 4.00 (ISBN 0-89642-118-X). Linden Pubs.
--Rites & Choruses: Three Books of Poems. 1980. pap. 4.00 (ISBN 0-89642-059-0). Linden Pubs.
--Rock. (Rin: Part 48). 1977. pap. 4.00 (ISBN 0-89642-008-6). Linden Pubs.
--Ror. (Rin Ser.: Pt. 50). 50p. (Orig.). 1981. pap. 4.00 (ISBN 0-89642-080-9). Linden Pubs.
--Ry: A Play. 1977. 4.00 (ISBN 0-89642-032-9). Linden Pubs.
--Scrooge. 16p. (Orig.). 1983. pap. 4.00 (ISBN 0-89642-101-5). Linden Pubs.
--Six Loves. (Rin Ser: Pt. 5). 1978. pap. 4.00 (ISBN 0-89642-046-9). Linden Pubs.
--Skip. LC 74-281770. (Rin Ser.: Pt. 27). 1973. 4.00 (ISBN 0-89642-033-7). Linden Pubs.
--Skitch. 50p. (Orig.). 1982. pap. 4.00 (ISBN 0-89642-092-2). Linden Pubs.
--Sojourner Truth. 12p. (Orig.). 1983. pap. 4.00 (ISBN 0-89642-106-6). Linden Pubs.
--Stig. 1978. pap. 4.00 (ISBN 0-89642-042-6). Linden Pubs.
--Storkwood. rev. ed. (Rin Ser.: Pt. 8). 62p. (Orig.). 1980. pap. 4.00 (ISBN 0-89642-066-3). Linden Pubs.
--Sumner: John Brown, Second Prolog. 1980. pap. 4.00 (ISBN 0-89642-065-5). Linden Pubs.
--Surrey: Henry the Eighth, Pt. 6. 1980. pap. 4.00 (ISBN 0-89642-061-2). Linden Pubs.
--Teacher. 15p. (Orig.). 1985. pap. 4.00 (ISBN 0-89642-127-9). Linden Pubs.
--Tecumseh. 1979. pap. 4.00 (ISBN 0-89642-053-1). Linden Pubs.
--Thief. 24p. (Orig.). 1983. pap. 4.00 (ISBN 0-89642-097-3). Linden Pubs.
--Tib. (The Holiday Ser.: Pt. 6: Easter). 77p. (Orig.). 1981. pap. 5.00 (ISBN 0-89642-077-9). Linden Pubs.
--Tiger. (Holiday Ser.: Pt. 4: New Years Eve). 79p. (Orig.). 1980. pap. 4.00 (ISBN 0-89642-068-X). Linden Pubs.
--Titch. 24p. 1983. pap. 4.00 (ISBN 0-89642-103-1). Linden Pubs.
--Tracy. (Rin Ser.: Pt. 54). (Orig.). 1981. pap. 4.00 (ISBN 0-89642-079-5). Linden Pubs.
--Trent. 33p. (Orig.). 1982. pap. 4.00 (ISBN 0-89642-091-4). Linden Pubs.
--Troy. LC 74-437973. (Rin Ser.: Pt. 31). 1974. 4.00 (ISBN 0-89642-035-3). Linden Pubs.
--Truce. (Drex: Pt. 2). 1979. pap. 4.00 (ISBN 0-89642-050-7). Linden Pubs.
--Tuck. (Holiday Ser.: Pt. 2: Thanksgiving). 55p. (Orig.). 1981. pap. 4.00 (ISBN 0-89642-073-6). Linden Pubs.
--Twins. LC 75-192367. (Rin Ser.: Pt. 35). 1975. 4.00 (ISBN 0-89642-036-1). Linden Pubs.
--Two Men. 18p. 1983. pap. 4.00 (ISBN 0-89642-102-3). Linden Pubs.
--Virginia. (John Brown Ser.: Pt. 3). 34p. (Orig.). 1983. pap. 4.00 (ISBN 0-89642-104-X). Linden Pubs.
--Virginia. (James Ser.: Pt. 4). 79p. (Orig.). 1975. pap. 4.00 (ISBN 0-89642-037-X). Linden Pubs.
--Webster. (John Brown, First Prolog). 1977. pap. 4.00 (ISBN 0-89642-009-4). Linden Pubs.
--Weekend. LC 74-438797. (Rin Ser.: Pt. 6). 1974. 4.00 (ISBN 0-89642-038-8). Linden Pubs.
--Winter. (Rin Ser.: Pt. 36). 47p. (Orig.). 1985. pap. 5.00 (ISBN 0-89642-125-2). Linden Pubs.
--The Winter War: Antony, Part 2. 42p. 1985. pap. 5.00 (ISBN 0-89642-124-4). Linden Pubs.
--Wolsey. (Henry the Eighth: Pt. 1). 54p. (Orig.). 1980. pap. 4.00 (ISBN 0-89642-069-8). Linden Pubs.
--York: Being the Story of Mrs. Osgoods Will. 50p. (Orig.). 1981. pap. 4.00 (ISBN 0-89642-082-5). Linden Pubs.
--Zora. 19p. (Orig.). 1985. pap. 4.00 (ISBN 0-89642-128-7). Linden Pubs.

Dunsterville, G. C. & Garay, L. A. Orchids of Venezuela, 3 vols. 1980. pap. 40.00 (ISBN 0-87544-000-2). Museum Bks.
--Venezuelan Orchids Illustrated, Vol. 6. 1975. 30.00 (ISBN 0-87544-001-0). Museum Bks.

Dunsterville, L. C. Stalky's Reminiscences. 1928. Repr. 20.00 (ISBN 0-8274-3499-5). R West.
--Stalky's Reminiscences (on Kipling) 298p. 1982. Repr. of 1928 ed. lib. bdg. 40.00 (ISBN 0-8495-1137-2). Arden Lib.

Dunston, G. R. Moral Reasoning in Management. 1978. 90.00x (ISBN 0-905440-59-5, Pub. by MCB Pubns). State Mutual Bk.

Dunsworth, Charles E. A Treasury of Old & Historical American & British Furniture. (Illus.). 187p. 1983. 89.75x (ISBN 0-86650-067-7). Gloucester Art.

Dunt, William. The Price Guide to Good Wine. 128p. 1984. pap. 5.95 (ISBN 0-201-11381-3). Addison-Wesley.

Dunteman, George H. Introduction to Multi-Variate Analysis. LC 83-19139. 237p. 1984. 27.50 (ISBN 0-8039-2176-4). Sage.

Duntemann, Jeff. Complete Turbo Pascal. 1985. pap. 19.95 (ISBN 0-673-18111-1). Scott F.

Dunthorne, Gordon. Flower & Fruit Prints of the Eighteenth & Early Nineteenth Centuries. LC 67-25443. (Graphic Art Ser). (Illus.). 1970. Repr. of 1938 ed. lib. bdg. 75.00 (ISBN 0-306-70958-9). Da Capo.

Dunthorne, Kirstine B. Artists Exhibited in Wales, Nineteen Forty-Five to Nineteen Seventy-Four. 344p. 1980. pap. 20.95x (ISBN 0-9500455-8-6, Pub. by Welsh Art Wales). Intl Spec Bk.

Duntiz, J. D., et al, eds. Electrons & Transitions. (Structure & Bonding: Vol. 39). (Illus.). 1980. 42.00 (ISBN 0-387-09787-2). Springer-Verlag.

Dunton, Darlene. Complete Bonsai Handbook. 1978. pap. 12.95 (ISBN 0-8128-6008-X). Stein & Day.

Dunton, Gardner. The Letters of World War I Pilot in the Army Air Corps. 252p. 1977. pap. text ed. 25.00x (ISBN 0-89126-028-5). MA-AH Pub.

Dunton, John. Letters Written from New England Sixteen Eighty-Six. (Prince Soc: No. 4). 1966. 22.50 (ISBN 0-8337-0971-2). B Franklin.
--Life & Errors of John Dunton Citizen of London, 2vols. (Research & Source Works Ser: No. 402). 1970. Repr. of 1818 ed. lib. bdg. 49.50 (ISBN 0-8337-0970-4). B Franklin.
--The Nightwalker: Or, Evening, Rambles in Search of Lewd Women. LC 83-48614. (Marriage, Sex & the Family in England Ser.). 66p. 1985. lib. bdg. 68.00 (ISBN 0-8240-5918-2). Garland Pub.
--Teague Land or a Merry Ramble to the Wild Irish. 78p. 1982. Repr. of 1733 ed. 10.00x (ISBN 0-7165-0291-7, BBA 03642, Pub. by Irish Academic Pr Ireland). Biblio Dist.
--A True Journal of the Sally Fleet, with the Proceedings of the Voyage. LC 71-25745. (English Experience Ser.: No. 242). 26p. 1970. Repr. of 1637 ed. 9.50 (ISBN 90-221-0242-4). Walter J Johnson.

Dunton, Loren, ed. Your Book of Financial Planning. 1983. text ed. 21.95 (ISBN 0-8359-9505-4). Reston.

Dunton, Loren, intro. by see Richard, Paul S.

Dunton, Robert E. Out Where the Day Begins. (Illus.). 200p. 1982. text ed. 10.95 (ISBN 0-9608100-0-5); pap. text ed. 9.95 (ISBN 0-9608100-1-3). Orange Blossom.

Dunton, Sabina & Miller, Kathy A. Counselfile. McNeely, Richard A., ed. LC 82-50626. (Illus.). 150p. (Orig.). 1982. 27.50 (ISBN 0-943562-50-3). Well Aware.

Dunton, Sabina, jt. auth. see Miller, Kathy A.

Dunton, Sabina M. & Fanning, Melody S. Smoking: Facilitator's Manual. McNeely, Richard A., ed. (Well Aware About Health Risk Reduction Ser.). (Illus.). 186p. (Orig.). 1982. 29.95 (ISBN 0-943562-51-1). Well Aware.
--Smoking: Workbook. McNeely, Richard A., ed. (Well Aware About Health Risk Reduction Ser.). (Illus.). 109p. (Orig.). 1982. pap. 7.95 (ISBN 0-943562-52-X). Well Aware.

Dunton, William R. & Licht, Signey. Occupational Therapy: Principles & Practice. 2nd ed. (Illus.). 384p. 1957. 32.50x (ISBN 0-398-04249-7). C C Thomas.

Dunton, William R., Jr. Prescribing Occupational Therapy. 2nd ed. 164p. 1947. 14.75x (ISBN 0-398-04250-0). C C Thomas.

Duntzer, H. Life of Goethe, 2 vols. 250.00 (ISBN 0-8490-0531-0). Gordon Pr.
--Life of Goethe, 2 vols. 1973. 50.00 set (ISBN 0-8274-1366-1). R West.

Dunville, B. The Science of Speech. 1909. 12.50 (ISBN 0-8274-3339-5). R West.

Dunwell, Bruce S. Save That Smile. (Illus.). 72p. (Orig.). 1984. pap. 2.95 (ISBN 0-89407-067-3). Strawberry Hill.

Dunwell, Steve. Connecticut, A Scenic Discovery. Patrick, James B., ed. (Scenic Discovery Ser.). (Illus.). 120p. Repr. of 1980 ed. 27.50 (ISBN 0-89909-050-8). Foremost Pubs.
--Duke: A Portrait. Patrick, James B., ed. (Illus.). 128p. 1984. 30.00 (ISBN 0-917585-00-3). Gothic.
--Massachusetts. Patrick, James B., ed. (Scenic Discovery Ser.). (Illus.). 120p. Repr. of 1979 ed. 25.00 (ISBN 0-940078-04-X). Foremost Pubs.
--Massachusetts: A Scenic Discovery. Patrick, James B., ed. (Scenic Discovery Ser.). (Illus.). 118p. 1985. Repr. of 1979 ed. 27.50 (ISBN 0-89909-051-6). Yankee Bks.
--Rhode Island: A Scenic Discovery. Patrick, James B., ed. (Scenic Discovery Ser.). 120p. 1983. Repr. of 1976 ed. 25.00 (ISBN 0-940078-03-1). Foremost Pubs.
--The Run of the Mill. LC 78-57683. (Illus.). 312p. 1978. 30.00x (ISBN 0-87923-249-8). Godine.

Dunwoody, H. H., et al. Weather Proverbs. 1977. lib. bdg. 69.95 (ISBN 0-8490-2813-2). Gordon Pr.

Duo Publishing Staff. French Farm & Village Holiday Guide. 1985. pap. 12.95 (ISBN 0-906318-14-9). Bradt Ent.

Duong, Danh R. English Grammar for the Vietnamese. LC 76-15646. 400p. 1977. 15.00 (ISBN 0-8044-0137-3); pap. 7.95 (ISBN 0-8044-6127-9). Ungar.

Duong, Pham C. Vietnamese Peasants under French Domination 1861-1945. LC 85-7499. (Monograph Ser.: No. 24). (Illus.). 240p. (Orig.). 1985. lib. bdg. 23.50 (ISBN 0-8191-4714-1, Ctr South & Southeast Asia); pap. 12.00 (ISBN 0-8191-4715-X). U Pr of Amer.

Duong, Quyen Van see Van Duong, Quyen & Coburn, Jewell R.

Duong Thanh Binh, jt. auth. see Gage, William.

Duong Thanh Binh, et al. A Handbook for Teachers of Vietnamese Students: Hints for Dealing with Cultural Differences in Schools. (Vietnamese Refugee Education Ser.: No. 3). 30p. 1975. pap. text ed. 2.25 (ISBN 0-15-599010-1). Ctr Appl Ling.

Duorak, Eileen M. & Kane, Michael, eds. The National Council Licensure Examination for Practical Nurses. 2nd ed. 150p. 1985. pap. 8.95 (ISBN 0-914091-66-2). Chicago Review.

Dupac, Vaclac, ed. see Hajek, Jaroslav.

Dupain, Max & Johnson, Peter. Leslie Wilkinson: A Practical Idealist. (Illus.). 128p. 1983. 50.00 (ISBN 0-9594202-1-5). Allen Unwin.

Dupaquier, J., et al, eds. Marriage & Remarriage in Populations of the Past. (Population & Social Structure Ser.). 1981. 72.00 (ISBN 0-12-224660-8). Acad Pr.

Dupaquier, Jacques & Fauve-Chamoux, A. Malthus Past & Present. LC 82-74008. (Population & Social Structure Ser.). 1983. 49.00 (ISBN 0-12-224670-5). Acad Pr.

Dupasguier, Philippe. The Service Station. (Busy Places Ser.). (Illus.). 24p. (gr. k-1). 1984. pap. 3.95 (ISBN 0-448-21501-2, G&D). Putnam Pub Group.

Dupasquier, A., jt. ed. see Brandtt, W.

Dupasquier, Philippe. The Airport. (Busy Places Ser.). (Illus.). 24p. (gr. k-1). 1984. pap. 3.95 (ISBN 0-448-21503-9, G&D). Putnam Pub Group.
--The Building Site. (Busy Places Ser.). (Illus.). 24p. (gr. k-1). 1984. 3.95 (ISBN 0-448-21502-0, G&D). Putnam Pub Group.
--Dear Daddy. LC 84-27505. (Illus.). 32p. (ps-2). 1985. PLB 12.95 (ISBN 0-02-733170-9). Bradbury Pr.
--The Factory. (Busy Places Ser.). (Illus.). 24p. (ps-1). 1984. 3.95 (ISBN 0-448-19052-4, G&D). Putnam Pub Group.
--The Harbor. (Busy Places Ser.). (Illus.). 24p. (ps-1). 1984. 3.95 (ISBN 0-448-19053-2, G&D). Putnam Pub Group.
--The Train Station. (Busy Places Ser.). (Illus.). 24p. (ps-1). 1984. 3.95 (ISBN 0-448-19051-6, G&D). Putnam Pub Group.

Dupayrat, Jaques. Dictionary of Biomedical Acronyms & Abbreviations. 1984. 14.50 (ISBN 0-471-90582-8). Wiley.

Dupee, F. W. The King of Cats: And Other Remarks on Writers & Writing. Exp. ed. 275p. 1984. 28.00x (ISBN 0-226-17286-4); pap. 12.50 (ISBN 0-226-17287-2). U of Chicago Pr.

Dupee, F. W. see Trotsky, Leon.

Dupee, Frederick W. Henry James. LC 72-9047. (American Men of Letters Ser.). (Illus.). 301p. 1973. Repr. of 1951 ed. lib. bdg. 24.75x (ISBN 0-8371-6566-0, DUHE). Greenwood.

Dupee, Frederick W., ed. Autobiography: Henry James. LC 83-60460. 640p. 1984. 50.00 (ISBN 0-691-06584-5); pap. 12.50 (ISBN 0-691-01408-6). Princeton U Pr.

Dupee, Frederick W., ed. see James, Henry.

Duperly, A. Picturesque Jamaica. 1976. lib. bdg. 59.95 (ISBN 0-8490-2443-9). Gordon Pr.

Duperoux, J. J. & Rabier, J. J. Yearbook of the European Institute for Social Security: 1978-1980 the Retirement Age in Europe. (The Retirement Age in Europe: Pt. 1). 224p. 1980. 20.00 (ISBN 90-312-0134-0, Pub. by Kluwer Law, Netherlands). Kluwer Academic.

Du Perron, E. Country of Origin. Beekman, E. M. & Bulhof, Francis, eds. Daverman, Elizabeth, tr. from Dutch. LC 83-18171. (Library of the Indies Ser.). 480p. 1984. lib. bdg. 30.00x (ISBN 0-87023-429-3). U of Mass Pr.

Dupertius, C. Wesley, jt. auth. see Hooton, E. A.

Du Petit-Thouars, Aubert-Aubert. Histoire Particuliere Des Plantes Orchidees Recueillies sur les Trois Iles Australes d'Afrique. (Orchid Ser.). (Illus.). 1980. Repr. of 1822 ed. text ed. 15.00 (ISBN 0-930576-24-1). E M Coleman Ent.

Dupeux, Georges. French Election Study, 1958. 1974. codebk. write for info. (ISBN 0-89138-100-7). ICPSR.

Dupin, Amandine A. see Sand, George.

Dupin, Aurore see Sand, George, pseud.

Dupin, Henri. La Courtoisie au Moyen Age: (d'apres les textes du XII et du XIII siecle) LC 78-63496. 176p. Repr. of 1931 ed. 26.00 (ISBN 0-404-17144-3). AMS Pr.

Duplan, J. F. & Chapiro, A., eds. Advances in Radiation Research: Biology & Medicine, 3 vols, Pt. 2. LC 72-92724. 1973. Set, 1564p. 249.75 (ISBN 0-677-15770-3); Vol. 1, 490p. 90.25 (ISBN 0-677-30880-9); Vol. 2, 540p. 97.25 (ISBN 0-677-30890-6); Vol. 3, 534p. 97.25 (ISBN 0-677-30900-7). Gordon.
--Advances in Radiation Research: Physics & Chemistry, 2 vols, Pt. 1. LC 72-92724. 1973. Set, 668p. 134.25 (ISBN 0-677-15780-0); Vol. 1, 360p. 79.75 (ISBN 0-677-30640-7); Vol. 2, 308p. 69.50 (ISBN 0-677-30650-4). Gordon.

DuPlessis. Synopsis of Surgical Anatomy. 11th ed. 900p. 1975. 36.00 (ISBN 0-7236-0384-7). PSG Pub Co.

Du Plessis, jt. auth. see Decker.

Duplessis, jt. auth. see Tuchmann.

DuPlessis, D. J. Principles of Surgery. 2nd ed. 192p. 1976. pap. text ed. 16.00 (ISBN 0-7236-0445-2). PSG Pub Co.

Du Plessis, David. Forgiveness: God Has No Grandsons. 1974. 0.95 (ISBN 0-88270-203-3, Pub. by Logos). Bridge Pub.

DuPlessis, David. A Man Called Mr. Pentecost. LC 76-53322. 1977. pap. 5.95 (ISBN 0-88270-184-3, Pub. by Logos). Bridge Pub.
--Spirit Bade Me Go: A Famous Pentecostal Tells His Story. 123p. 1970. pap. 2.50 (ISBN 0-912106-59-X, Pub. by Logos). Bridge Pub.

Duplessis, Laura, jt. auth. see Danesi, Anthony.

DuPlessis, Rachel B. Wells. (Montemora Supplements Ser.). 76p. (Orig.). 1980. pap. 3.00 (ISBN 0-935528-02-4). Montemora Found.
--Writing Beyond the Ending: Narrative Strategies of Twentieth-Century Women Writers. (Every Woman: Studies in History, Literature & Culture). 272p. (Orig.). 1985. 27.50 (ISBN 0-317-14891-5); pap. 12.95 (ISBN 0-253-20345-7). Ind U Pr.

Duplessis, Yves. Surrealism. Capon, Paul, tr. LC 77-17880. 1978. Repr. of 1963 ed. lib. bdg. 18.50x (ISBN 0-313-20110-2, DUSU). Greenwood.

Duplessis, Yvonne. The Paranormal Perception of Color. LC 75-19563. (Parapsychological Monographs: No. 16). 1975. pap. 5.50 (ISBN 0-912328-27-4). Parapsych Foun.

Du Plessix Gray, Francine. October Blood. 256p. 1985. 16.95 (ISBN 0-671-55511-1). S&S.

Du Plou, Dafne C., tr. see Edens, David.

Dupoizat, Marie-France, jt. ed. see Young, Carol M.

Dupon, Duane, ed. see Buist, Linda.

Du Ponceau, Peter S. A Brief View of the Constitution of the United States. LC 72-124893. (American Constitutional & Legal History Ser.). 1974. Repr. of 1834 ed. lib. bdg. 18.50 (ISBN 0-306-71986-X). Da Capo.
--Campanius Holm, Tomas: Description of the Province of New Sweden. LC 1-1320. Repr. of 1834 ed. 21.00 (ISBN 0-527-03241-7). Kraus Repr.
--A Dissertation on the Nature & Extent of the Jurisdiction of the Courts of the U. S., Being a Valedictory Address Delivered... LC 79-37971. (American Law Ser.: The Formative Years). 296p. 1972. Repr. of 1824 ed. 22.00 (ISBN 0-405-04007-5). Ayer Co Pubs.

DuPonceau, Peter S. An Historical Account of the Origin & Formation of the American Philosophical Society. (American Philosophical Society History Ser.). 196p. 1914. 10.00 (ISBN 0-317-33126-4, APS-4). Am Philos.

Du Ponceau, Peter S., tr. see Zeisberger, David.

Dupont, Beatrice. Unequal Education: A Study of Sex Differences in Secondary-School Curricula. (Illus.). 88p. 1981. pap. 7.50 (ISBN 92-3-101823-X, U1175, UNESCO). Unipub.

Dupont, Bo & Good, Robert A., eds. Immunobiology of Bone Marrow Transplantation. (Transplantation Proceedings Reprint Ser.: Vol. I). 352p. 1977. 63.00 (ISBN 0-8089-0982-7, 791100). Grune.

DuPont, Diana, et al. San Francisco Museum of Modern Art: The Painting & Sculpture Collection. LC 84-11844. (Illus.). 404p. 1985. 75.00 (ISBN 0-933920-59-8, Dist. by Viking-Penguin); For museum distribution only. pap. 32.50 (ISBN 0-933920-60-1). Hudson Hills.

Du Pont, Diane. The Emerald Embrance. 1980. pap. 2.50 (ISBN 0-449-14316-3, GM). Fawcett.

DuPont, Elizabeth N. Landscaping with Native Plants in the Middle-Atlantic Region. Williams, Wick, ed. LC 78-21194. (Illus.). 1978. 7.95 (ISBN 0-940540-02-9). Brandywine Conserv.

Dupont, Etienne. La Participation De la Bretagne a la Conquete De l'Angleterre Par les Normands. LC 80-2229. Repr. of 1911 ed. 22.00 (ISBN 0-404-18758-7). AMS Pr.

Dupont, Herbert L. & Pickering, Larry K. Infections of the Gastrointestinal Tract: Microbiology, Pathophysiology & Clinical Features. (Current Topics in Infectious Disease Ser.). (Illus.). 289p. 1980. 35.00x (ISBN 0-306-40409-5, Plenum Med Bk). Plenum Pub.

Dupont, J. L. & Madsen, J. H., eds. Algebraic Topology: Aarhus Nineteen Seventy-Eight. (Lecture Notes in Mathematics: Vol. 763). 695p. 1979. pap. 38.00 (ISBN 0-387-09721-X). Springer-Verlag.

Dupont, Jacqueline. Cholesterol Systems in Insects & Animals. 160p. 1982. 55.00 (ISBN 0-8493-5315-7). CRC Pr.

Dupont, Jacques & McNutly, Frank J. The Salvation of the Gentiles. LC 78-65901. 168p. 1979. pap. 5.95 (ISBN 0-8091-2193-X). Paulist Pr.

DuPont, John E. Philippine Birds. (Delaware Museum of Natural History Monograph: No. 2). (Illus.). 490p. text ed. 35.00x (ISBN 0-913176-03-6). Foris Pubns.

--South Pacific Birds. (Delaware Museum of Natural History Monograph: No. 3). (Illus.). 230p. text ed. 24.95x (ISBN 0-913176-04-4). Foris Pubns.

Du Pont, John E., jt. auth. see Brownlow, Donald G.

DuPont, John E., jt. auth. see Weaver, Clifton S.

DuPont, Marcella M. Definitions & Criteria. LC 65-16526. 1965. 3.50 (ISBN 0-8040-0065-4, 82-70431, Pub. by Swallow). Ohio U Pr.

DuPont, Robert L. Getting Tough on Gateway Drugs: A Guide for the Family. LC 84-14595. 352p. 1984. 16.95x (ISBN 0-88048-035-1, 48-035-1). Am Psychiatric.

DuPont, Robert L., ed. Phobia: A Comprehensive Summary of Modern Treatments. LC 82-9. 300p. 1982. 27.50 (ISBN 0-87630-274-6). Brunner-Mazel.

DuPont, Robert L., jt. ed. see Weissman, James C.

DuPont, Robert L., jt. auth. see De Silva, Robin.

DuPont, Robert L., Jr. Getting Tough on Gateway Drugs: A Guide for the Family. LC 84-14595. 352p. 1985. pap. 7.95x (ISBN 0-88048-046-7, 48-046-7). Am Psychiatric.

Dupont, T., jt. auth. see Douglas, J., Jr.

DuPont, V. John Galsworthy: The Dramatic Artist. LC 76-43253. 1942. lib. bdg. 20.00 (ISBN 0-8414-3812-9). Folcroft.

DuPont, Yves. Catholic Prophecy. (Eng.). 1977. pap. 2.50 (ISBN 0-89555-015-6). TAN Bks Pubs.

Du Pont De Nemours, Victor M. Journey to France & Spain, 1801. David, Charles W., ed. LC 70-153259. (French Civilization Ser). 1971. Repr. of 1961 ed. 19.50x (ISBN 0-8046-1565-9, Pub. by Kennikat). Assoc Faculty Pr.

Du Pontet, R. L., ed. see Caesar.

Dupont-Sommer, A. The Essene Writings from Qumran. Vermes, G., tr. 13.50 (ISBN 0-8446-2012-2). Peter Smith.

DuPorte, E. Melville. Manual of Insect Morphology. LC 76-13005. 236p. 1977. Repr. of 1959 ed. 10.50 (ISBN 0-88275-422-X). Krieger.

Dupotet de Sennevoy, Jean. An Introduction to the Study of Animal Magnetism. LC 75-36837. (Occult Ser.). 1976. Repr. of 1838 ed. 30.00x (ISBN 0-405-07950-8). Ayer Co Pubs.

Duprat, A. M., et al, eds. The Role of Cell Interactions in Early Neurogenesis. (NATO ASI Life Sciences Series: Series A: Vol. 77). 344p. 1984. 55.00x (ISBN 0-306-41716-2, Plenum Pr). Plenum Pub.

DuPrau, Jeanne. Adoption: The Facts, Feelings & Issues of a Double Heritage. LC 81-11007. (Teen Survival Library). 128p. (gr. 7 up). 1981. PLB 9.79 (ISBN 0-671-34067-0); pap. 4.95 (ISBN 0-671-49483-X). Messner.

Du Praw, Ernest J., ed. Advances in Cell & Molecular Biology. Incl. Vol. 1. 1971. 70.00 (ISBN 0-12-008001-X); Vol. 2. 1972. 80.00 (ISBN 0-12-008002-8); Vol. 3. 1975. 70.00 (ISBN 0-12-008003-6). Acad Pr.

Dupre, C., ed. see Lanecki, F.

DuPre, Carole E. Luo of Kenya: An Annotated Bibliography. LC 68-8362. 2.95 (ISBN 0-911976-04-3); pap. 1.95 (ISBN 0-911976-01-1). ICR.

Dupre, Celine, jt. auth. see Lanecki, Francois.

DuPre, Flint O. Your Career in Federal Civil Service. 288p. 1981. pap. 5.95 (ISBN 0-06-463529-5, EH529, EH). B&N NY.

--Your Career in Federal Civil Service. rev. ed. LC 79-2618. 256p. 1980. 11.49i (ISBN 0-06-011103-8, HarpT). Har-Row.

DuPre, Gabrielle. Forget Me Not. 448p. pap. 3.95 (ISBN 0-441-52092-8, Pub. by Charter Bks). Ace Bks.

Dupre, Henri. Purcell. LC 74-24071. Repr. of 1928 ed. 18.50 (ISBN 0-404-12899-8). AMS Pr.

Dupre, Huntley. Lazare Carnot, Republican Patriot. LC 75-29217. (Perspectives in European Hist. Ser.: No. 5). viii, 343p. Repr. of 1940 ed. lib. bdg. 27.50x (ISBN 0-87991-612-5). Porcupine Pr.

Dupre, Irma, et al. The Romance of Dundee. (Illus.). 360p. 1985. 18.50 (ISBN 0-916445-12-7). Crossroads Comm.

Dupre, Louis. Common Life. 96p. 12.95 (ISBN 0-8245-0644-8); pap. 7.95 (ISBN 0-8245-0627-8). Crossroad NY.

--The Deeper Life: A Meditation on Christian Mysticism. 128p. (Orig.). 1981. pap. 4.95 (ISBN 0-8245-0007-5). Crossroad NY.

--Marx's Social Critique of Culture. LC 83-42871. 328p. 1983. 30.00x (ISBN 0-300-03082-7). Yale U Pr.

--Marx's Social Critique of Culture. LC 83-42871. 328p. 1985. pap. 9.95x (ISBN 0-300-03517-9). Yale U Pr.

--Transcendent Selfhood: The Loss & Rediscovery of the Inner Life. 1976. 8.95 (ISBN 0-8164-0306-6, Pub. by Seabury). Winston Pr.

Dupre, M. J. The Classification & Structure of C-Algebra Bundles. LC 79-17975. (Memoirs Ser.: No. 222). 77p. 1979. pap. 10.00 (ISBN 0-8218-2222-5). Am Math.

Dupre, M. J. & Gillette, R. M. Banach Bundles: Banach Modules & Automorphisms of C-Algebras. (Research Notes in Mathematics: No. 92). 120p. 1983. pap. text ed. 16.95 (ISBN 0-273-08626-X). Pitman Pub MA.

Dupre, Paul. Encyclopedie Des Citations. 14th ed. (Fr.). 1959. 37.50 (ISBN 0-686-57274-2, F-C1020). French & Eur.

--Encyclopedie Du Bon Francais Dans L'usage Contemporain, 3 vols. 2900p. (Fr.). 1959. Set. 160.00 (ISBN 0-686-57128-2, M-6179). French & Eur.

Du Pre, Peter D., jt. auth. see Haynes, J. H.

Dupre, Wilhelm. Religion in Primitive Cultures: A Study in Ethnophilosophy. (Religion & Reason: No. 9). 366p. 1975. text ed. 29.60x (ISBN 0-686-22610-0). Mouton.

Dupree, A., jt. ed. see Bonnet, R.

Dupree, A. Hunter. Science in the Federal Government: A History of Policies & Activities to 1940. Cohen, I. Bernard, ed. LC 79-7959. (Three Centuries of Science in America Ser.). (Illus.). 1980. Repr. of 1957 ed. lib. bdg. 39.00x (ISBN 0-405-12540-2). Ayer Co Pubs.

DuPree, Don K., ed. see Harrison, Charles T.

Dupree, Garland C., jt. auth. see Namanny, Dorothy S.

Dupree, Herbert & Dupree, Sherry. Busy Bookworm: Good Conduct Book. (Illus.). 1980. pap. 1.25 (ISBN 0-686-70919-5). Displays Sch.

Dupree, Louis. Afghanistan. LC 76-154993. (Illus.). 672p. 1973. 65.00x (ISBN 0-691-03006-5); pap. 13.50x (ISBN 0-691-00023-9). Princeton U Pr.

Dupree, Nathalie. Cooking of the South. Atcheson, Richard, ed. LC 81-70443. (Great American Cooking Schools Ser.). (Illus.). 84p. 1982. pap. 5.95 (ISBN 0-941034-11-9). I Chalmers.

Dupree, Robert S. Allen Tate & the Augustinian Imagination: A Study of the Poetry. LC 83-7990. (Southern Literary Studies). 288p. 1983. text ed. 25.00x (ISBN 0-8071-1100-7). LA State U Pr.

Dupree, Sherry, jt. auth. see Dupree, Herbert.

DuPree, Sherry S. What You Always Wanted to Know about the Card Catalog But Were Afraid to Ask. rev.1985 ed. LC 77-87133. (Illus.). 1978. pap. 4.95 (ISBN 0-9600962-3-X). Displays Sch.

Dupreez, Peter. The Politics of Identity. 1980. 26.00 (ISBN 0-312-62697-5). St Martin.

Du Prel, Carl. The Philosophy of Mysticism, 2vols. in 1. Massey, C. C., tr. LC 75-36838. (Occult Ser.). 1976. Repr. of 1889 ed. 51.00x (ISBN 0-405-07951-6). Ayer Co Pubs.

--The Philosophy of Mysticism, 2 vols. 1977. lib. bdg. 250.00 (ISBN 0-8490-2434-X). Gordon Pr.

Dupret, S., jt. auth. see Pauchet, V.

Dupret, S., jt. auth. see Pauchet, Victor.

Duprey, Kenneth. Old Houses on Nantucket. (Illus.). 256p. 1984. pap. 18.95 (ISBN 0-8038-5399-8). Hastings.

Du Prey, Pierre De La Ruffiniere. John Soane: The Making of an Architect. LC 81-16453. 1982. 42.50x (ISBN 0-226-17298-8); pap. 19.95 (ISBN 0-226-17299-6). U of Chicago Pr.

Du Prey, Pierre de la Ruffiniere see De la Ruffiniere du Prey, Pierre.

Duprey, Richard. Silver Wings. 224p. 1983. pap. 2.95 (ISBN 0-515-05457-7). Jove Pubns.

Duprey, Richard & O'Leary, Brian. Space Ship Titanic. 192p. 1983. 14.95 (ISBN 0-396-08187-8). Dodd.

DuPriest, Maude W., et al. Cherokee Recollections. DuPriest, Maude W., ed. LC 76-10640. 1976. 10.00 (ISBN 0-914312-08-1). Indian Pocahontas Club.

Dupry, Renee J. The University Teaching of Social Sciences: International Law. 1967. pap. 6.00 (ISBN 92-3-100653-3, U707, UNESCO). Unipub.

Dupuch, Etienne. Tribune Story. (Illus.). 1968. 8.95 (ISBN 0-685-20643-2). Transatlantic.

Dupuis, Adrian M. Philosophy of Education in Historical Perspective. rev. ed. 312p. 1985. pap. text ed. 12.25 (ISBN 0-8191-4729-X). U Pr of Amer.

Dupuis, Adrian M., ed. Nature, Aims, & Policy. LC 70-100373. (Readings in the Philosophy of Education Ser.). pap. 89.50 (ISBN 0-317-08579-4, 2022255). Bks Demand UMI.

Dupuis, Charles. The Origin of All Religious Worship. Feldman, Burton & Richardson, Robert D., eds. LC 78-60897. (Myth & Romanticism Ser.). 1984. lib. bdg. 80.00 (ISBN 0-8240-3558-5). Garland Pub.

Dupuis, H., et al. Lexique de la Fabrication du Refrigerateur: Francais-Anglais. 66p. (Fr. & Eng.). 1975. pap. 5.95 (ISBN 0-686-92434-7, M-9240). French & Eur.

Dupuis, Hector & Legare, Romain. Dictonnaire des Synonymes et des Antonymes. 608p. (Fr.). 1975. 22.50 (ISBN 0-686-57129-0, M-6180). French & Eur.

Dupuis, J., jt. ed. see Neuner, J.

Dupuis, Joseph. Journal of a Residence in Ashanti. new ed. 502p. 1966. 50.00x (ISBN 0-7146-1805-5, F Cass Co). Biblio Dist.

Dupuis, Mary M., ed. Reading in the Content Area: Research for Teachers. 88p. 1984. pap. 6.00 (ISBN 0-317-12553-2). Intl Reading.

DuPuis, Melanie, ed. Corporate Five Hundred: The Directory of Corporate Philanthropy. 3rd ed. 744p. 1984. 245.00x (ISBN 0-916664-35-X). Public Management.

Du Puis, Robert J. The Executive Man's Diet. 210p. (Orig.). 1985. pap. 7.95 (ISBN 0-89769-062-1, Dist. by Caroline Hse). Pine Mntn.

DuPuis, Robert J. The Un-Diet Book. 222p. 1980. pap. 1.95 (ISBN 0-8439-0866-1, Pub. by Nordon Pubns). Dorchester Pub Co.

Dupuy & Crick. Campaigns on the Turkish Front. 109p. 1967. 8.60 (ISBN 0-531-01225-5). Watts.

Dupuy, C. H., ed. Physics of Nonmetallic Thin Films. LC 76-8385. (NATO ASI Series B, Physics: Vol. 14). 510p. 1976. 75.00 (ISBN 0-306-35714-3, Plenum Pr). Plenum Pub.

Dupuy, Chachie. Chachie Dupuy's New Orleans Home Cooking. (Illus.). 192p. 1985. 14.95 (ISBN 0-672-52819-3). Bobbs.

Dupuy, Eliza A. The Cancelled Will. facsimile ed. LC 78-164559. (American Fiction Reprint Ser). Repr. of 1872 ed. 32.00 (ISBN 0-8369-7035-7). Ayer Co Pubs.

--Dethroned Heiress. facs. ed. LC 76-76923. (American Fiction Reprint Ser.). 1873. 18.00 (ISBN 0-8369-7002-0). Ayer Co Pubs.

Dupuy, Ernest. The Great Masters of Russian Literature in the Nineteenth Century. Dole, Nathan H., tr. 1973. Repr. of 1886 ed. 30.00 (ISBN 0-8274-1695-4). R West.

Dupuy, Ernest, ed. see Melick, Arden D.

Dupuy, Ernest R. & Dupuy, Trevor N. An Outline History of the American Revolution. LC 73-1803. (Illus.). 352p. 1975. 12.50i (ISBN 0-06-011127-5, HarpT). Har-Row.

Dupuy, Harold J. The Construction & Utility of Three Indexes of Intellectual Achievement. Stevenson, Taloria, ed. Incl. An Index of Intellectual Development (ID; A Socio-Intellctual-Status (SIS) Index; A Differential-Intellectual-Development (DID) Index (U.S. Children & Youth 6-17 Years. (Ser. 2: No. 74). 1977. pap. text ed. 1.85 (ISBN 0-8406-0106-9). Natl Ctr Health Stats.

Dupuy, J. & Dianioux, A. J., eds. Microscopic Structure & Dynamics of Liquids. LC 78-4197. (NATO ASI Series B, Physics: Vol. 33). 534p. 1978. 79.50x (ISBN 0-306-35733-X, Plenum Pr). Plenum Pub.

Dupuy, J., ed. see NATO Advanced Study Institutes.

Dupuy, J., jt. ed. see Wright, A. F.

Dupuy, Jean, ed. Collective Consciousness: Art Performances in the Seventies. LC 80-83856. (Illus.). 245p. 1980. pap. 12.00 (ISBN 0-933826-27-3). Performing Arts.

Dupuy, R. E. & Dupuy, T. N. Brave Men & Great Captains. (Illus.). 400p. 1984. Repr. of 1959 ed. text ed. 23.95 (ISBN 0-915979-03-9). Hero Books.

Dupuy, R. Ernest & Dupuy, Trevor N. The Encyclopedia of Military History. rev. ed. LC 75-6333. (Illus.). 1488p. 1977. 43.27i (ISBN 0-06-011139-9, HarpT). Har-Row.

--The Encyclopedia Of Military History: From 3500 B. C. to the Present. rev. ed. LC 84-48158. (Illus.). 1500p. 1985. 38.41 (ISBN 0-06-015417-9, HarpT). Har-Row.

--Military Heritage of America. Rev. ed. (Illus.). 885p. 1984. Repr. text ed. 29.95 (ISBN 0-915979-00-4). Hero Books.

Dupuy, R. J. The Right to Development at the International Level. 458p. 1981. 40.00 (ISBN 90-286-0990-3). Sijthoff & Noordhoff.

Dupuy, R. J., ed. The Right to Health As a Human Right: Colloquim 1978 of the Hague Academy of International Law. 513p. 1980. 40.00x (ISBN 90-286-1028-6). Sijthoff & Noordhoff.

Dupuy, Rene J. & Tunkin, Gregory. Comparability of Degrees & Diplomas in International Law: A Study of the Structural & Functional Aspects. (Studies on the Evaluation of Qualifications at the Higher Education Level). 75p. (Orig.). 1973. pap. 5.00 (ISBN 92-3-101057-3, U94, UNESCO). Unipub.

Dupuy, Rene-Jean. The Settlement of Disputes on the New Natural Resources: Workshop 1982. 1983. lib. bdg. 43.50 (ISBN 90-247-2901-7, Pub. by Martinus Nijhoff Netherlands). Kluwer Academic.

Dupuy, Rene-Jean, ed. The Future of International Law in a Multicultural World (Workshop 1983) 1984. lib. bdg. 50.00 (ISBN 90-247-3070-8, Pub. by Martinus Nijhoff Netherlands). Kluwer Academic.

Dupuy, T. N. A Genius for War. (Illus.). 400p. 1984. Repr. of 1977 ed. text ed. 24.95 (ISBN 0-915979-02-0). Hero Books.

--Options of Command. (Illus.). 352p. 1984. 19.95 (ISBN 0-88254-993-6). Hippocrene Bks.

Dupuy, T. N., jt. auth. see Dupuy, R. E.

Dupuy, Trevor N. Elusive Victory: The Arab-Israeli Wars, 1947-1974. LC 78-2119. (Illus.). 1978. 25.00i (ISBN 0-06-011112-7, HarpT). Har-Row.

--Elusive Victory: The Arab-Israeli Wars, 1947-1974. Rev. ed. (Illus.). 696p. 1984. Repr. of 1978 ed. text ed. 28.60 (ISBN 0-915979-01-2). Hero Books.

--The Evolution of Weapons & Warfare. (Illus.). 360p. 1984. Repr. of 1980 ed. text ed. 19.95 (ISBN 0-915979-05-5). Hero Books.

--Numbers, Predictions & War. 262p. 1985. pap. 13.95 (ISBN 0-915979-06-3). Hero Books.

Dupuy, Trevor N. & Martell, Paul. Flawed Victory: The Nineteen Eighty Two War in Lebanon. 256p. 1985. text ed. 24.95 (ISBN 0-915979-07-1). Hero Books.

Dupuy, Trevor N., jt. auth. see Dupuy, Ernest R.

Dupuy, Trevor N., jt. auth. see Dupuy, R. Ernest.

Dupuy, Trevor N., et al, eds. Almanac of World Military Power. 4th ed. LC 80-11844. (Illus.). 432p. 1980. 40.00 (ISBN 0-89141-070-8). Presidio Pr.

DuPuy, William, jt. auth. see Wilbur, Ray L.

Du Puy, William A. Hawaii & Its Race Problem. LC 75-35214. Repr. of 1932 ed. 19.50 (ISBN 0-404-14237-0). AMS Pr.

Dupuy, William A. Our Bird Friends & Foes. (Illus.). 10.75 (ISBN 0-8446-0601-4). Peter Smith.

Du Puynode, M. Gustave. Grandes Crises Financieres de La France. LC 70-166961. (History, Economics & Social Science Ser.: No. 287). (Fr). 1971. Repr. of 1876 ed. lib. bdg. 26.50 (ISBN 0-8337-0973-9). B Franklin.

Duquesne, Terence & Reeves, Julian. A Handbook of Psychoactive Medicines: Tranquilizers--Antidepressants--Sedatives--Stimulants--Narcotics--Psychedilics. 512p. 1982. 45.00 (ISBN 0-7043-2270-6, Pub. by Quartet Bks); pap. 17.50 (ISBN 0-7043-3393-7). Merrimack Pub Cir.

Duquet, Richard. Actively Seeking Nutrition. 27p. 1978. pap. 2.00 (ISBN 0-934332-20-7). L'Epervier Pr.

Duquette, Susan. Sunburst Farm Family Cookbook. rev. ed. LC 78-70916. (Illus.). 256p. (Orig.). 1978. pap. 7.95 (ISBN 0-912800-60-7). Woodbridge Pr.

Duquoc, Christian. Opportunities for Belief & Behavior. LC 67-31523. (Concilium Ser.: Vol. 29). 186p. 1967. 6.95 (ISBN 0-8091-0106-8). Paulist Pr.

--Secularization & Spirituality. LC 76-103390. (Concilium Ser.: Vol. 49). 187p. 6.95 (ISBN 0-8091-0136-X). Paulist Pr.

Duquoc, Christian & Floristan, Casiano. Job & the Silence of God. (Concilium Ser. 1983: Vol. 169). 128p. (Orig.). 1983. pap. 6.95 (ISBN 0-8164-2449-7, Pub. by Seabury). Winston Pr.

Duquoc, Christian, jt. auth. see Floristan, Casiano.

Duquoc, Christian, ed. Spirituality in Church & World. LC 65-28868. (Concilium Ser.: Vol. 9). 174p. 6.95 (ISBN 0-8091-0139-4). Paulist Pr.

--Spirituality in the Secular City. LC 66-30386. (Concilium Ser.: Vol. 19). 192p. 6.95 (ISBN 0-8091-0140-8). Paulist Pr.

Duquoc, Christian & Floristan, Casiano, eds. Discernment of the Spirit & the Spirits. (Concilium Ser.: Vol. 119). (Orig.). 1978. pap. 6.95x (ISBN 0-8245-0280-9). Crossroad NY.

--Models of Holiness. (Concilium Ser.: Vol. 129). 120p. (Orig.). 1980. pap. 6.95 (ISBN 0-8245-0290-6). Crossroad NY.

Duquoc, Christian, jt. ed. see Floristan, Casiano.

Durachko, Michael. Poetry from Heaven. LC 84-90275. 45p. 1985. 5.95 (ISBN 0-533-06310-8). Vantage.

Duraiswami, Pandit M. Sri Pancaratra-Raksha of Vedanta Desika. 2nd ed. 1967. 6.00 (ISBN 0-8356-7482-7, ALS 36). Theos Pub Hse.

Durakovic, Asaf. Nuclear Medicine Technologist's Handbook. 1985. 32.50 (ISBN 0-87527-311-4). Green.

Durall, Wilbur I., jt. auth. see Obert, Leonard.

Duram, James C. A Moderate among Extremists: Dwight D. Eisenhower & the School Desegregation Crisis. LC 81-542. 328p. 1981. text ed. 23.95x (ISBN 0-88229-394-X). Nelson-Hall.

Duran, Bonte. The Adventures of Arthur & Edmund: A Tale of Two Seals. LC 83-71900. (Illus.). 32p. (ps-3). 1984. 10.95 (ISBN 0-689-50295-8, McElderry Bk). Atheneum.

Duran, Carlos, et al, eds. Recent Progress in Mitral Valve Disease. 426p. 1984. text ed. 99.95 (ISBN 0-407-00294-4). Butterworth.

Duran, Cheli, ed. The Yellow Canary Whose Eye Is So Black: Poems from Spanish-Speaking Latin America. LC 77-6354. 352p. (Eng. & Span.). (gr. 6 up). 1977. 14.95 (ISBN 0-02-732910-0, 732910). Macmillan.

Duran, Daniel F. Latino Communication Patterns. Cortes, Carlos E., ed. LC 79-6203. (Hispanics in the United States Ser.). (Illus.). 1981. lib. bdg. 56.50x (ISBN 0-405-13154-2). Ayer Co Pubs.

--Latino Materials: A Multimedia Guide for Children & Young Adults, No. 1. LC 78-18470. (Selection Guide Ser.). 249p. 1979. text ed. 22.95 (ISBN 0-87436-262-8). Neal-Schuman.

Duran Duran. Duran Duran: Arena. (Piano-Vocal-Guitar Ser.). (Illus.). 56p. 1985. pap. 8.95 (ISBN 0-88188-367-0). H Leonard Pub Corp.

Duran, Eduardo. Archetypal Consultation: A Service Delivery Model for Native Americans. (American University Studies VIII: Vol. 2). 168p. (Orig.). 1984. pap. text ed. 16.85 (ISBN 0-8204-0082-3). P Lang Pubs.

Duran, Esperanza, ed. Latin America & the World Recession. (Illus.). 224p. 1985. 37.50 (ISBN 0-521-30271-4). Cambridge U Pr.

Duran, Fr. Diego. Book of the Gods & Rites & the Ancient Calendar. Horcasitas, Fernando & Heyden, Doris, trs. LC 73-88147. (Civilization of the American Indian Ser.: No. 102). (Illus.). 1971. pap. 12.95 (ISBN 0-8061-1201-8). U of Okla Pr.

Duran, G. & Duran, M. Autoretratos y Espejos: Self Portraits & Reflections. 1977. text ed. 13.95 (ISBN 0-13-055533-9); pap. write for info. P-H.

Duran, Gloria. The Archetypes of Carlos Fuentes: From Witch to Androgyne. 240p. 1980. 22.50 (ISBN 0-208-01775-5, Archon). Shoe String.

--Doce historias de la Artamila de Ana Maria Matute. Duran, Manuel & Duran, Gloria, eds. 172p. (Span.). 1965. pap. text ed. 10.95 (ISBN 0-15-517949-7, HC). HarBraceJ.

Duran, Gloria & Duran, Manuel. Vivir Hoy. 2nd ed. 212p. 1981. pap. text ed. 10.95 (ISBN 0-15-594948-9, HC). HarBraceJ.

Duran, Gloria, ed. see Duran, Gloria.

Duran, Helen C. Blonde Chicana Bride's Mexican Cookbook. (Wild & Woolly West Ser.: No. 40). (Illus., Orig.). 1980. 8.00 (ISBN 0-910584-95-8); pap. 2.00 (ISBN 0-910584-96-6). Filter.

--Mexican Recipe Shortcuts or Casserolization of the Classics. (Wild & Woolly West Ser.). (Illus.). 52p. (Orig.). 1983. 8.00 (ISBN 0-86541-012-7); pap. 2.00 (ISBN 0-86541-013-5). Filter.

Duran, Ignacio, jt. auth. see Decker, David R.

Duran, John C. Exercises in Genetics. (EMI Programed Biology Ser). (Orig.). (gr. 9-12). 1969. pap. 3.00 (ISBN 0-88462-022-0, 3304-22, Ed Methods). Longman USA.

Duran, Leo. Plays of Old Japan. LC 73-476. 1973. lib. bdg. 16.50 (ISBN 0-8414-1487-4). Folcroft.

Duran, Leo, ed. Plays of Old Japan. LC 77-94339. (One-Act Plays in Reprint Ser.). 1978. Repr. of 1921 ed. 16.50x (ISBN 0-8486-2037-2). Core Collection.

Duran, M., jt. auth. see Duran, G.

Duran, Manuel. Cervantes. LC 74-7006. (World Authors Ser.). 1974. lib. bdg. 13.50 (ISBN 0-8057-2206-8, Twayne). G K Hall.

--Luis de Leon. LC 79-19352. (World Authors Ser.). 1971. lib. bdg. 15.95 (ISBN 0-8057-2524-5). Irvington.

Duran, Manuel & Safir, Margery. Earth Tones: The Poetry of Pablo Neruda. LC 80-8095. (Illus.). 240p. 1981. 25.00x (ISBN 0-253-16662-4). Ind U Pr.

Duran, Manuel, jt. auth. see Duran, Gloria.

Duran, Manuel, ed. Graded Spanish Reader. 3rd ed. 1978. pap. text ed. 8.95x (ISBN 0-669-00880-X). Heath.

Duran, Manuel, ed. see Duran, Gloria.

Duran, Manuel & Kluback, William, trs. Luis de Leon: Names of Christ. (Classics of Western Spirituality Ser.). 1984. 14.95 (ISBN 0-8091-0346-X); pap. 11.95 (ISBN 0-8091-2561-7). Paulist Pr.

Duran, Manuel, et al. Spoken Spanish for Students & Travelers. 3rd ed. 1978. pap. text ed. 8.95x (ISBN 0-669-00879-6). Heath.

Duran, Manuel, et al, eds. Estudios literarios en honor de Gustavo Correa. (Span.). 25.00 (ISBN 0-317-07674-4). Scripta.

Duran, Richard P. Hispanics' Education & Background: Predictors of College Achievement. (Illus.). 160p. 1983. pap. 12.95 (ISBN 0-87447-157-5, 001575). College Bd.

--Hispanics Education & Background: Predictors of College Achievement. 160p. 1983. 12.95 (ISBN 0-686-87564-8). College Bd.

Duran, Richard P., ed. Latino Language & Communicative Behavior, Vol. 6. (Advances in Discourse Processers Ser.). 384p. 1981. 39.50x (ISBN 0-89391-038-4); pap. text ed. 24.50 (ISBN 0-89391-093-7). Ablex Pub.

Durand, B., ed. Thermal Phenomena in Sedimentary Basins. LC 84-73154. (Illus.). 400p. (Orig.). 1985. pap. 76.95x (ISBN 0-87201-865-2). Gulf Pub.

Durand, Claude. Conscience Ouvriere & Action Syndicale. (Societe, Mouvements Sociaux & Ideologies, Etudes: No. 10). (Illus.). 1971. pap. 10.40x (ISBN 90-2796-875-6). Mouton.

Durand, Dawn. Shanghaied. Gilbert, Jim, ed. 288p. cancelled (ISBN 0-915160-84-6). Seven Seas.

Durand, Dianne. Smocking: Techniques, Projects & Designs. (Illus.). 1979. pap. 2.00 (ISBN 0-486-23788-5). Dover.

Durand, Douglas E., jt. auth. see Chusmir, Leonard H.

Durand, Douglas E., jt. auth. see Schoen, Sterling H.

Durand, Francis, jt. auth. see Burke, Kenneth M.

Durand, H. & Maycock, P., eds. Medium-Size Photovoltaic Power Plants. 1981. 28.95 (ISBN 90-277-1279-4, Pub. by Reidel Holland). Kluwer Academic.

Durand, Harff. La Qualite de la Vie. 1977. 12.80x (ISBN 90-279-7913-8). Mouton.

Durand, J. B. Labor Force in the United States (1890-1960) (Demographic Monographs). 304p. 1968. 56.75 (ISBN 0-677-01550-X). Gordon.

Durand, Jacques, ed. Dependency & Non-Linear Phonology. 300p. 1985. 37.50 (ISBN 0-7099-0894-6, Pub. by Croom Helm Ltd). Longwood Pub Group.

Durand, John. Life & Times of Asher Brown Durand. LC 68-8688. (Library of American Art Ser). 1970. Repr. of 1894 ed. lib. bdg. 29.50 (ISBN 0-306-71167-2). Da Capo.

Durand, John & Miller, A. T. The Business of Trading in Stocks. 1967. Repr. of 1933 ed. flexible cover 7.00 (ISBN 0-87034-019-0). Fraser Pub Co.

DuRand, John, jt. auth. see DuRand, Lance.

Durand, John, tr. see Taine, Hippolyte A.

Durand, John D. The Labor Force in Economic Development: A Comparison of International Census Data, 1946-1966. LC 75-2988. 288p. 1975. 29.00 (ISBN 0-691-04207-1). Princeton U Pr.

DuRand, Lance & DuRand, John. The Affirmative Industry. 320p. 1978. 9.00 (ISBN 0-318-15701-2, 1039). NIMR.

Durand, Loup. The Angkor Massacre. Lane, Helen R., tr. from Fr. LC 82-18818. 416p. 1983. 16.95 (ISBN 0-688-00487-3). Morrow.

Durand, Loyal & Pondrom, Lee G., eds. High Energy Physics, 1980: International Conference, Madison Wisconsin, 2 pts. (AIP Conference Proceedings Ser.: No. 68). 1622p. 1981. lib. bdg. 85.00 (ISBN 0-88318-167-3). Am Inst Physics.

Durand, Maurice & Huan, Nguyen T. An Introduction to Vietnamese Literature. 232p. 1985. 25.00s (ISBN 0-231-05852-7). Columbia U Pr.

Durand, Maurice, jt. auth. see Huard, Pierre A.

Durand, Megan. The Chipmunks Camp Out. LC 84-61693. (Sniffy Bks.). (Illus.). 24p. (ps). 1985. pap. 4.95 (ISBN 0-394-87151-0, BYR). Random.

Durand, P. & O'Brien, J. S., eds. Genetic Errors of Glycoprotein Metabolism. (Illus.). 220p. 1982. 35.50 (ISBN 0-387-12066-1). Springer-Verlag.

Durand, Paul, tr. see Dionysius Of Fourna.

Durand, Pauline & Languirand, Yolande. Brunch: Great Ideas for Planning, Cooking & Serving. LC 77-21616. 1978. pap. text ed. 3.95 (ISBN 0-8120-0726-3). Barron.

Durand, R. A. A Handbook to the Poetry of Rudyard Kipling. Repr. of 1914 ed. 24.00 (ISBN 0-527-25900-4). Kraus Repr.

Durand, Regis, jt. auth. see Couturier, Maurice.

Durand, Robert. The Ages of J. LC 73-76636. (Hip-Pocket Ser.: No. 1). 1973. pap. 2.50 (ISBN 0-87922-020-1). Christopher's Bks.

--J. LC 79-182347. 1971. pap. 2.00 (ISBN 0-87922-005-8). Christopher's Bks.

Durand, T. see Jackson, B. D., et al.

Durand, Ursin, jt. auth. see Martene, Edmond.

Durand, Ursin, jt. ed. see Martene, Edmund.

Durand, W. Fredrick, ed. Aerodynamic Theory: A General View of Progress, 6 vols. Incl. Vol. 1. Mathematical Aids, Fluid Mechanics, Historical Sketch. 16.00 (ISBN 0-8446-0603-0); Vol. 2. General Aerodynamic Theory, Perfect Fluids. 16.00 (ISBN 0-8446-0604-9); Vol. 3. Theory of Single Burbling, Mechanics of Viscous Fluids, Etc. 16.00 (ISBN 0-8446-0605-7); Vol. 4. Applied Airfoil Theory, Airplane Body Drag & Influence, Etc. 16.00 (ISBN 0-8446-0606-5); Vol. 5. Dynamics of the Airplane, Airplane Performance. 16.00 (ISBN 0-8446-0607-3); Vol. 6. Airplanes As a Whole, Aerodynamics of Airships, Etc. 16.00 (ISBN 0-8446-0739-8). Set. 96.00 (ISBN 0-8446-0602-2). Peter Smith.

Durand, William F. Adventures in the Navy, in Education, Science, Engineering & the War: A Life Story. LC 53-2031. pap. 57.00 (ISBN 0-317-08712-6, 2013306). Bks Demand UMI.

Durand-Drouhin, J. L. & Szwengrub, L. M., eds. Rural Community Studies in Europe: Trends, Selected & Annotated Bibliographies, Analyses, Vol. III. (Vienna Centre Ser.). 212p. 1985. 39.50 (ISBN 0-08-031845-2). Pergamon.

Durand-Drouhin, Jean-Louis & Szwengrub, Lili-Marie, eds. Rural Community Studies in Europe: Trends, Selected & Annotated Bibliographies, Analyses, Vol. I. LC 80-41523. (Publications of the Vienna Centre Ser.). (Illus.). 342p. 1981. text ed. 79.00 (ISBN 0-08-021384-7). Pergamon.

Durang, Charles. The Theatrical Rambles of Mr. & Mrs. John Greene. Slout, William L., ed. LC 84-11165. (Clipper Studies in the American Theater: No. 1). 192p. (Orig.). 1985. lib. bdg. 19.95x (ISBN 0-89370-360-5); pap. text ed. 9.95x (ISBN 0-89370-460-1). Borgo Pr.

Durang, Christopher. Christopher Durang Explains It All for You. 240p. 1983. pap. 3.95 (ISBN 0-380-82636-4, 82636-4, Bard). Avon.

Durang, Christopher & Innaurato, Albert. The Idiots Karamazov. pap. 3.35x (ISBN 0-686-73313-4). Dramatists Play.

Durant, Alan. Conditions of Music. 250p. 1985. lib. bdg. 39.50x (ISBN 0-88706-015-3); pap. text ed. 12.95x (ISBN 0-88706-017-X). State U NY Pr.

--Ezra Pound, Identity in Crisis: A Fundamental Reassessment of the Poet & His Work. 216p. 1981. 27.50x (ISBN 0-389-20197-9, 06978). B&N Imports.

Durant, Ariel, jt. auth. see Durant, Will.

Durant, Charles. Exposition: A New Theory of Animal Magnetism. (Hypnosis & Altered States of Consciousness Ser.). 225p. 1982. Repr. of 1837 ed. lib. bdg. 27.50 (ISBN 0-306-76075-4). Da Capo.

Durant, Clarence W. Roman Afternoon: Two Thousand & Nineteen A.D, 3 vols, Vol. 1. 116p. (Orig.). 1984. pap. 5.76X (ISBN 0-915153-03-3). Gold Star Pr.

--Roman Afternoon: Two Thousand & Nineteen A.D, 3 Vols, Vol. 2. 180p. (Orig.). 1984. pap. 5.76X (ISBN 0-915153-07-6). Gold Star Pr.

--Roman Afternoon: Two Thousand & Nineteen A.D, 3 vols, Vol. 3. 220p. (Orig.). 1984. pap. 5.76X (ISBN 0-915153-10-6). Gold Star Pr.

--Stella Rjin. 250p. (Orig.). 1985. pap. 6.98 (ISBN 0-915153-16-5). Gold Star Pr.

Durant, David S. Ann Radcliffe's Novels: Experiments in Setting. Varma, Devendra P., ed. LC 79-8450. (Gothic Studies & Dissertations Ser.). 1980. lib. bdg. 24.50x (ISBN 0-405-12665-4). Ayer Co Pubs.

Durant, Freddie O. The Donaldson Mansion. LC 80-53470. 415p. 1984. 13.95 (ISBN 0-86632-000-8); pap. 3.95 (ISBN 0-317-05215-2). Shane Pub.

Durant, Frederick C., jt. auth. see Miller, Ron.

Durant, Frederick C., III, ed. Between Sputnik & the Shuttle: New Perspectives on American Astronautics, 1957-1980. (American Astronautical Society History Ser.: Vol. 3). (Illus.). 350p. 1981. text ed. 40.00x (ISBN 0-87703-145-2, Pub. by Am Astronaut); pap. text ed. 30.00x (ISBN 0-87703-149-5). Univelt Inc.

Durant, Helen, jt. auth. see Durant, Kenneth.

Durant, Jack D. Richard Brinsley Sheridan: A Reference Guide. 1981. lib. bdg. 33.50 (ISBN 0-8161-8146-2, Hall Reference). G K Hall.

Durant, John. Highlights of the Olympics. 5th ed. (Illus.). (gr. 6 up). 1977. pap. 5.95 (ISBN 0-8038-3038-6). Hastings.

--The Story of Baseball. rev. 3rd ed. (Illus.). 302p. (gr. 6 up). 1973. 10.95 (ISBN 0-8038-6715-8). Hastings.

Durant, John & Etter, Les. Highlights of College Football. (gr. 7 up). 1970. 9.95 (ISBN 0-8038-3013-0). Hastings.

Durant, John, ed. Darwinism & Divinity: Essays on Evolution & Religious Belief. 240p. 1985. 24.95x (ISBN 0-631-14188-X). Basil Blackwell.

Durant, John R. & Smalley, Richard V. The Chronic Leukemias: Chemistry, Pathophysiology & Treatment. (Illus.). 240p. 1972. photocopy ed. 28.50X (ISBN 0-398-02275-5). C C Thomas.

Durant, Kenneth. The Naphtha Launch. (Adirondack Museum Monographs). (Illus.). 31p. 1976. pap. 2.50 (ISBN 0-686-74846-8). Adirondack Mus.

Durant, Kenneth & Durant, Helen. The Adirondack Guide-Boat. (Illus.). xvii, 250p. 1980. 30.00 (ISBN 0-686-75279-1). Adirondack Mus.

Durant, Mary. American Heritage Guide to Antiques. LC 72-111653. 1970. pap. 4.95 (ISBN 0-07-018346-5). McGraw.

--Who Named the Daisy? Who Named the Rose? A Roving Dictionary of North American Wildflowers. LC 83-1781. (Illus.). 224p. 1983. pap. 8.95 (ISBN 0-312-92944-7). Congdon & Weed.

Durant, Mary & Harwood, Michael. On the Road with John James Audubon. LC 79-22734. (Illus.). 576p. 1980. 19.95 (ISBN 0-396-07740-4). Dodd.

--On the Road with John James Audubon. (Illus.). 682p. 1984. pap. 14.95 (ISBN 0-396-08353-6). Dodd.

Durant, Robert F. When Government Regulates Itself: EPA, TVA & Pollution Control in the 1970's. LC 84-22058. 224p. 1985. text ed. 18.95x (ISBN 0-87049-458-9). U of Tenn Pr.

Durant, S. History of Oneida County, 1878. Date not set. Repr. of 1878 ed. deluxe ed. write for info. (ISBN 0-932334-41-5). Heart of the Lakes.

Durant, Will. Age of Faith. (Story of Civilization: Vol. 4). (Illus.). 1950. 32.95 (ISBN 0-671-01200-2). S&S.

--Caesar & Christ: A History of Roman Civilization from Its Beginnings to A.D. 337. (Story of Civilization: Vol. 3). 1944. 29.95 (ISBN 0-671-11500-6). S&S.

--Life of Greece. (Story of Civilization: Vol. 2). (Illus.). 1939. 29.95 (ISBN 0-671-41800-9). S&S.

--Our Oriental Heritage. (Story of Civilization: Vol. 1). 1935. 29.95 (ISBN 0-671-54800-X). S&S.

--The Pleasures of Philosophy. pap. 10.75 (ISBN 0-671-58110-4, Touchstone Bks). S&S.

--Reformation. (Story of Civilization: Vol. 6). (Illus.). 1957. 29.95 (ISBN 0-671-61050-3). S&S.

--Renaissance. (Story of Civilization: Vol. 5). 1953. 29.95 (ISBN 0-671-61600-5). S&S.

--Story of Philosophy. (gr. 11-12). 1961. pap. 10.95 (ISBN 0-671-20159-X, Touchstone Bks). S&S.

--The Story of Philosophy. 576p. 1969. pap. 5.95 (ISBN 0-671-49415-5). WSP.

Durant, Will & Durant, Ariel. Age of Louis Fourteenth. (Story of Civilization Ser.: Vol. 8). (Illus.). 1963. 29.95 (ISBN 0-671-01215-0). S&S.

--The Age of Napoleon. LC 75-6888. (Illus.). 1975. 29.95 (ISBN 0-671-21988-X). S&S.

--Age of Reason Begins. (Story of Civilization: Vol. 7). (Illus.). 1961. 29.95 (ISBN 0-671-01320-3). S&S.

--Age of Voltaire. (Story of Civilization Ser.: Vol. 9). (Illus.). 1965. 29.95 (ISBN 0-671-01325-4). S&S.

--Lessons of History. LC 68-19949. 1968. 13.95 (ISBN 0-671-41333-3). S&S.

--Rousseau & Revolution. (Story of Civilization: Vol. 10). (Illus.). 1967. 32.95 (ISBN 0-671-63058-X). S&S.

Durante, F., et al. Recueil Des Cours De La'academie De Droit International De la Haye: Collected Courses of the Hague Academy of International Law, Vol. 152 (1976-iv) 478p. 1980. 40.00x (ISBN 90-286-0590-8). Sijthoff & Noordhoff.

Durante, Francesco & Rodino, Walter. Western Europe & the Development of the Law of the Sea, 4 binders. LC 79-55008. 1979. looseleaf 45.00 ea. (ISBN 0-379-20286-7). Oceana.

Durantel, J. Saint Thomas et le Pseudo-Denis. (Medieval Studies Ser.). (Fr.). Repr. of 1919 ed. lib. bdg. 45.00x (ISBN 0-697-00036-2). Irvington.

Durantini, Mary F. The Child in Seventeenth Century Dutch Painting. Seidel, Linda, ed. LC 81-21852. (Studies in the Fine Arts: Iconography: No. 7). 406p. 1983. 49.95 (ISBN 0-8357-1292-3). UMI Res Pr.

Durantis, Gulielmus. The Symbolism of Churches & Church Ornaments. 1980. lib. bdg. 64.95 (ISBN 0-8490-3166-4). Gordon Pr.

--Symbolism of Churches & Church Ornaments: A Translation of the First Book of the Rationale Divinorum Officiorum. Neale, John M. & Webb, Benjamin, eds. Repr. of 1843 ed. 28.00 (ISBN 0-404-04653-3). AMS Pr.

Duranty, Louis-Emile. Neighbors. (Silver Series of Puppet Plays). pap. 1.50 (ISBN 0-8283-1259-1). Branden Pub Co.

--Punch Plays Teacher. (Silver Series of Puppet Plays). 1966. pap. 1.50 (ISBN 0-8283-1257-5). Branden Pub Co.

Duranty, Walter. Curious Lottery & Other Tales of Russian Justice. LC 78-101805. (Short Story Index Reprint Ser.). 1929. 17.00 (ISBN 0-8369-3193-9). Ayer Co Pubs.

--Stalin & Co. the Politburo: The Men Who Run Russia. 1979. Repr. of 1949 ed. lib. bdg. 20.00 (ISBN 0-8495-1107-0). Arden Lib.

DuRapau, Gladys W. When You Went Away. LC 84-90174. 51p. 1985. 5.95 (ISBN 0-533-06232-2). Vantage.

Duras, Marguerita. The Little Horses of Tarquinia. Du Berg, Peter, tr. from Fr. 1980. pap. 4.95 (ISBN 0-7145-0348-7). Riverrun NY.

Duras, Marguerite. Abahn. Incl. Sabana; David. (Coll. Soleil). 13.25 (ISBN 0-685-34105-4). French & Eur.

--Amante Anglaise. (Coll. Soleil). 1967. 12.95 (ISBN 0-685-10992-5). French & Eur.

--L' Amour. (Coll. Soleil). 13.25 (ISBN 0-685-34106-2). French & Eur.

--L' Apres-Midi de Monsieur Andesmas. pap. 6.95 (ISBN 0-685-34107-0). French & Eur.

--Barrage Contre le Pacifique. 1950. pap. 4.95 (ISBN 0-685-11035-4). French & Eur.

--Le Camion: Avec: Entretien avec Michele Porte. 136p. 1977. 7.95 (ISBN 0-686-55840-5). French & Eur.

--Des Journees Entieres Dans les Arbres. 238p. 1954. 12.95 (ISBN 0-686-55841-3). French & Eur.

--Detruire, Dit-Elle. pap. 7.95 (ISBN 0-685-34109-7). French & Eur.

--Dix Heures et Demie du Soir en Ete. pap. 14.95 (ISBN 0-685-34110-0). French & Eur.

--L' Eden Cinema. 154p. 1977. 9.95 (ISBN 0-686-55842-1). French & Eur.

--Four Novels. Seaver, Richard, et al, trs. from Fr. Incl. The Afternoon of Mr. Andesmas; Ten-Thirty on a Summer Night; Moderato Cantabile; The Square. 1965. pap. 9.95 (ISBN 0-394-17987-0, E808, Ever). Grove.

--Hiroshima Mon Amour. 1960. pap. 3.95 (ISBN 0-685-11232-2). French & Eur.

--Hiroshima, Mon Amour. Seaver, Richard, tr. from Fr. (Illus., Text for the film). 1961. pap. 7.95 (ISBN 0-394-17227-2, E284, Ever). Grove.

--India Song. 152p. 1973. 11.95 (ISBN 0-686-55843-X). French & Eur.

--India Song. Bray, Barbara, tr. from Fr. LC 75-16763. (Orig.). 1976. pap. 3.95 (ISBN 0-394-17893-9, E647, Ever). Grove.

--The Lover. Bray, Barbara, tr. from Fr. LC 84-26321. 113p. 1985. 11.95 (ISBN 0-394-54588-5). Pantheon.

--The Malady of Death: Five Novels. 1984. cancelled (ISBN 0-394-53866-8, GP909); pap. cancelled (ISBN 0-394-62175-1, E929). Grove.

--Marin de Gibraltar. (Coll. Soleil). 1952. 13.25 (ISBN 0-685-11352-3). French & Eur.

--Le Marin de Gibraltar. 429p. 1977. 4.95 (ISBN 0-686-55846-4). French & Eur.

--Moderato Cantabile. 1958. pap. 5.50 (ISBN 0-685-11399-X). French & Eur.

--Moderato Cantabile. 192p. 1962. 5.50 (ISBN 0-686-55847-2). French & Eur.
--Nathalie Granger. 200p. 1973. 10.95 (ISBN 0-686-55848-0). French & Eur.
--Les Petits Chevaux de Tarquinia. pap. 3.95 (ISBN 0-685-34111-9). French & Eur.
--Ravissement de Lol V. Stein. (Coll. Soleil). 1964. 13.50 (ISBN 0-685-11522-4). French & Eur.
--Le Ravissement de Lol V. Stein. (Folio 810). 1976. 3.95 (ISBN 0-686-55850-2). French & Eur.
--The Sailor from Gibraltar. Bray, Barbara, tr. from Fr. 1980. pap. 6.95 (ISBN 0-7145-0511-0). Riverrun NY.
--The Sea Wall. Briffault, Herma, tr. 288p. 1985. 7.95 (ISBN 0-374-51945-5). FS&G.
--Le Square. 160p. 1955. 8.95 (ISBN 0-686-55851-0). French & Eur.
--Square. Begue, Claude M., ed. (Fr). 1965. pap. text ed. 2.50x (ISBN 0-685-16005-X). Macmillan.
--Theatre: Avec: Les Eaux et Forets, Le Square, La Musica, Vol. 1. 176p. 1956. 11.95 (ISBN 0-686-55852-9). French & Eur.
--Theatre: Avec: Suzanne Andler, Des Journees Entieres dans les Arbres, Yes Peut-Etre?, Le Shape, et, Vol. 2. 298p. 1968. 9.95 (ISBN 0-686-55853-7). French & Eur.
--Les Viaducs de la Seine et Oise. (Coll. le Manteau d'Arlequin). pap. 7.50 (ISBN 0-685-34112-7). French & Eur.
--Vice-Consul. (Coll. Soleil). 1966. 12.25 (ISBN 0-685-11616-6). French & Eur.
--Le Vice-Consul. 216p. 1965. 5.95 (ISBN 0-686-55854-5). French & Eur.
--La Vie Tranquille. 222p. 1944. 5.95 (ISBN 0-686-55855-3). French & Eur.
--Whole Days in the Trees. Barrows, Anita, tr. from Fr. 1984. pap. 5.95 (ISBN 0-7145-3854-X). Riverrun NY.

Duras, Marguerite & Gauthier, Xaviere. Les Parleuses. (Vol. 44). 25p. 1974. 11.95 (ISBN 0-686-55849-9). French & Eur.

Duras, Marguerite & Gerard, Jariot. Une Aussi Longue Absence. 108p. 1961. 3.95 (ISBN 0-686-55839-1). French & Eur.

Duras, Marguerite & Porte, Michelle. Les Lieux de Marguerite Duras. (Illus.). 117p. 1977. 9.95 (ISBN 0-686-55844-8). French & Eur.

Duras, Marguerite & Robbe-Grillet, Alain. Hiroshima Mon Amour & Last Year at Marienbad: Two Screenplays. Resnais, Alain, ed. LC 83-49426. 352p. (Orig.). 1984. cancelled (ISBN 0-394-53867-6); pap. cancelled (ISBN 0-394-62176-X). Grove.

Duras, Marguerite, et al. Marguerite Duras: Etude sur l'Oeuvre Litteraire, Theatrale et Cinematographique de Marguerite Duras. (Illus.). 200p. 1976. 14.95 (ISBN 0-686-55845-6). French & Eur.

Durasoff, Steve. The Russian Protestants: Evangelicals in the Soviet Union. LC 72-76843. (Illus.). 312p. 1969. 27.50 (ISBN 0-8386-7465-8). Fairleigh Dickinson.

Duray, Paul, ed. see Pretest Service Inc.

Durbach, Errol. Ibsen the Romantic: Analogues of Paradise in the Later Plays. LC 81-1249. 250p. 1982. lib. bdg. 21.00x (ISBN 0-8203-0554-5). U of Ga Pr.

Durbach, Errol, ed. Ibsen & the Theatre: The Dramatist in Production. LC 79-47995. 1980. 25.00x (ISBN 0-8147-1773-X). NYU Pr.

Durbahn, W. E. & Putnam, R. E. Fundamentals of Carpentry: Tools, Materials, Practices 1. 407p. 1977. 19.95 (ISBN 0-8269-0554-4, Sterling). Am Technical.

Durbahn, W. E. & Sundberg, E. W. Fundamentals of Carpentry 2: Practical Construction. 5th ed. (Illus.). 1977. 16.95 (ISBN 0-8269-0569-2). Am Technical.

Durban, Pam. All Set about with Fever Trees. LC 84-48749. 224p. 1985. 14.95 (ISBN 0-87923-569-1). Godine.

Durban, T. J., jt. auth. see Hromadka, T. V., II.

Durband, Alan, ed. Hamlet. (Shakespeare Made Easy Ser.). 288p. 1985. pap. 4.95 (ISBN 0-8120-3638-7). Barron.
--King Lear. (Shakespeare Made Easy Ser.). 288p. 1985. pap. 4.95 (ISBN 0-8120-3637-9). Barron.
--The Tempest. (Shakespeare Made Easy Ser.). 288p. 1985. pap. 4.95 (ISBN 0-8120-3603-4). Barron.
--Twelfth Night. (Shakespeare Made Easy Ser.). 288p. 1985. pap. 4.95 (ISBN 0-8120-3604-2). Barron.

Durbin, Elizabeth. New Jerusalem: The Labour Party & the Economics of Democratic Socialism. 320p. 1985. 32.00x (ISBN 0-7100-9650-X). Routledge & Kegan.

Durbin, Elizabeth, jt. auth. see Allison, R. Bruce.

Durbin, Enoch & McGeer, Patrick L., eds. Methane: Fuel for the Future. LC 82-13120. 350p. 1982. 47.50x (ISBN 0-306-41122-9, Plenum Pr). Plenum Pub.

Durbin, Evan F. Politics of Democratic Socialism. LC 71-83799. Repr. of 1940 ed. 35.00x (ISBN 0-678-06513-6). Kelley.
--Problems of Economic Planning. LC 68-29483. Repr. of 1949 ed. 22.50x (ISBN 0-678-06514-4). Kelley.

Durbin, Gail. Wig, Hairdressing, & Shaving Bygones. (Shire Album Ser.: No. 117). (Illus.). 32p. (Orig.). 1984. pap. 2.95 (ISBN 0-85263-663-6, Pub. by Shire Pubns England). Seven Hills Bks.

Durbin, Harold. Color Separation Scanner Comparison Charts: 1985 Edition. Date not set. write for info. (ISBN 0-936786-10-8). Durbin Assoc.
--Interactive Layout System Comparison Charts: 1985 Edition. Date not set. write for info. (ISBN 0-936786-09-4). Durbin Assoc.
--Micro-Computer Word Processing Comparison Charts: 1985 Edition. Date not set. write for info. (ISBN 0-936786-08-6). Durbin Assoc.
--Offset Duplicator Press Comparison Charts: 1985 Edition. Date not set. pap. 25.00 (ISBN 0-936786-11-6). Durbin Assoc.
--Text Processing Computer System Comparison Charts: 1985 Edition. 1985. pap. 25.00 (ISBN 0-936786-04-3). Durbin Assoc.

Durbin, Harold C. Camera Comparison Charts: 1984 Edition. 1984. pap. 25.00 (ISBN 0-936786-03-5). Durbin Assoc.
--Film & Paper Processor Comparison Charts. 1984. pap. 25.00 (ISBN 0-936786-02-7). Durbin Assoc.
--Phototypesetter Comparison Charts: 1985 Edition. 1985. pap. 25.00 (ISBN 0-936786-05-1). Durbin Assoc.
--Printing & Computer Terminology. LC 80-65655. 206p. (Orig.). 1980. pap. 9.50 (ISBN 0-936786-00-0); pap. text ed. 8.50 (ISBN 0-936786-01-9). Durbin Assoc.
--Word Processing Glossary. LC 84-70288. 364p. 1984. pap. 15.00 (ISBN 0-936786-07-8). Durbin Assoc.

Durbin, J. Distribution Theory for Tests Based on the Sample Distribution Function. (CBMS-NSF Regional Conference Ser.: No. 9). (Orig.). 1973. pap. text ed. 8.00 (ISBN 0-89871-007-3). Soc Indus-Appl Math.

Durbin, J. R. College Algebra. 2nd ed. 528p. 1985. 25.95 (ISBN 0-471-81714-7). Wiley.
--Modern Algebra: An Introduction. 2nd ed. 346p. 1985. 29.95 (ISBN 0-471-88487-1). Wiley.

Durbin, John. College Algebra & Trigonometry. LC 83-16829. (Recreational Computing Ser.: 1-704). 688p. 1984. text ed. 27.95 (ISBN 0-471-03367-7); solutions manual avail. (ISBN 0-471-88351-4); test manual avail. (ISBN 0-471-81066-5). Wiley.

Durbin, John R. College Algebra. LC 81-11379. 506p. 1982. text ed. 25.95x (ISBN 0-471-03368-5); student solutions manual 8.00 (ISBN 0-471-86456-0). Wiley.
--Modern Algebra: An Introduction. LC 78-15778. 329p. 1979. text ed. 32.45 (ISBN 0-471-02158-X); tchrs. manual 6.00 (ISBN 0-471-03753-2). Wiley.

Durbin, Mary L. Teaching Techniques: For Retarded & Pre-Reading Students. (Illus.). 276p. 1973. pap. 27.75x spiral (ISBN 0-398-00487-0). C C Thomas.

Durbin, Paul. Research in Philosophy & Technology, Vol. 7. 52.50 (ISBN 0-89232-505-4). Jai Pr.

Durbin, Paul T., ed. A Guide to the Culture of Science, Technology, & Medicine. LC 79-7582. 1980. 65.00 (ISBN 0-02-907820-2). Free Pr.
--A Guide to the Culture of Science, Technology, & Medicine. 784p. 1984. 19.95x (ISBN 0-02-907890-3). Free pr.
--Research in Philosophy & Technology, Vol. 1. 350p. (Orig.). 1979. lib. bdg. 45.00 (ISBN 0-89232-022-2). Jai Pr.
--Research in Philosophy & Technology, Vol. 2. (Orig.). 1979. lib. bdg. 45.00 (ISBN 0-89232-101-6). Jai Pr.
--Research in Philosophy & Technology, Vol. 4. 450p. 1981. 47.50 (ISBN 0-89232-181-4). Jai Pr.

Durbin, Paul T. & Mitcham, Carl, eds. Research in Philosophy & Technology, Vol. 6. 1983. 47.50 (ISBN 0-89232-352-3). Jai Pr.

Durbin, Paul T. & Rapp, Friedrich, eds. Philosophy & Technology. 1983. lib. bdg. 59.00 (ISBN 90-277-1576-9, Pub. by Reidel Holland). Kluwer Academic.

Durbin, Paula, ed. see Jussawalla, Meheroo.

Durbin, R. D., ed. Toxins in Plant Disease. LC 80-70601. (Physiology Ecology Ser.). 1981. 65.00 (ISBN 0-12-225050-8). Acad Pr.

Durbin, Sandra, jt. auth. see Browning, Ruth.

Durburg, Suzanne, jt. auth. see Beyers, Marjorie.

Durcan, J. W., et al. Strikes in Post-War Britain: A Study of Stoppages of Work Due to Industrial Disputes 1946-1973. 456p. 1983. text ed. 37.50x (ISBN 0-04-331093-1). Allen Unwin.

Durcan, Paul. Ark of the North. 1982. 8.95 (ISBN 0-906897-42-4); pap. 4.95 (ISBN 0-906897-41-6). Dufour.
--Jesus, Break His Fall. 62p. 1980. 8.95 (ISBN 0-906897-10-6). Dufour.
--Jumping the Train Tracks with Angela. 97p. 1983. pap. 7.95 (ISBN 0-906897-68-8); 11.95 (ISBN 0-906897-69-6). Dufour.
--The Selected Paul Durcan. Longley, Edna, ed. 141p. 1983. pap. 8.95 (ISBN 0-85640-269-9, Pub. by Blackstaff Pr). Longwood Pub Group.

Durch, William, ed. National Interests & the Military Use of Space. LC 84-9241. 286p. 1984. prof. ref. 28.00 (ISBN 0-88410-974-7). Ballinger Pub.

Durchslag, A., tr. see Lasker-Schuler, Else.

Durckheim, Karlfried G. Way of Transformation. (Unwin Paperbacks). 112p. 1980. pap. 4.95 (ISBN 0-04-291014-5). Allen Unwin.

Durckheim, Karlfried von see Von Duerckheim, Karlfried.

Durdag, M. Some Problems of Development Financing: A Case Study of the Turkish First Five-Year Plan 1963-1967. LC 72-77873. 297p. 1973. lib. bdg. 42.00 (ISBN 90-277-0267-5, Pub. by Reidel Holland). Kluwer Academic.

Durden, Charles. No Bugles, No Drums. (Vietnam Ser.). 240p. 1984. pap. 3.50 (ISBN 0-380-69260-0, 69260). Avon.

Durden, Robert F. The Climax of Populism: The Election of 1896. LC 81-4137. xii, 190p. 1981. Repr. of 1965 ed. lib. bdg. 19.75x (ISBN 0-313-22846-9, DUCP). Greenwood.
--The Climax of Populism: The Election of 1896. LC 65-11824. 208p. 1965. pap. 5.00x (ISBN 0-8131-0103-4). U Pr of Ky.
--The Dukes of Durham, 1850-1929. LC 74-83785. (Illus.). xiv, 295p. 1975. 18.75 (ISBN 0-8223-0330-2). Duke.
--The Gray & the Black: The Confederate Debate on Emancipation. LC 72-79330. xii, 306p. 1972. 27.50x (ISBN 0-8071-0244-X). La State U Pr.
--James Shepherd Pike: Republicanism & the American Negro, 1850-1882. LC 77-26867. (Illus.). 1978. Repr. of 1957 ed. lib. bdg. 19.75x (ISBN 0-313-20168-4, DUJP). Greenwood.
--James Shepherd Pike: Republicanism & the American Negro, 1850-1882. LC 57-6284. pap. 65.80 (ISBN 0-317-28965-9, 2023760). Bks Demand UMI.
--Reconstruction Bonds & Twentieth-Century Politics: South Dakota Versus North Carolina, 1904. LC 62-10051. Repr. of 1961 ed. 55.10 (ISBN 0-8357-9116-5, 2017901). Bks Demand UMI.
--The Self Inflicted Wound: Southern Politics in the Nineteenth Century. LC 84-29173. (New Perspectives on the South). 160p. 1985. 16.00 (ISBN 0-8131-0307-X). U Pr of Ky.

Durden, Robert F., jt. auth. see Crow, Jeffrey J.

Durden, William G., jt. auth. see Fox, Lynn H.

Durden-Smith, Jo & DeSimone, Diane. Sex & the Brain. (Illus.). 1983. 16.95 (ISBN 0-87795-484-4). Arbor Hse.

Durden-Smith, Jo & Simone, Diane de. Sex & the Brain. 352p. 1984. pap. 3.95 (ISBN 0-446-32316-0). Warner Bks.

Dureau, George. George Dureau's New Orleans. (Illus.). 112p. 1985. 24.95 (ISBN 0-907040-83-7, Pub. by GMP England); pap. 13.50 (ISBN 0-907040-47-0). Alyson Pubns.

Dureau, Lorena. Iron Lace. (Tapestry Romance Ser.). (Orig.). 1983. pap. 2.50 (ISBN 0-671-46052-8). PB.
--The Last Casquette Girl. 288p. (Orig.). 1981. pap. 2.50 (ISBN 0-523-41266-5). Pinnacle Bks.
--Lynette. 352p. (Orig.). 1983. pap. 2.95 (ISBN 0-523-41638-5). Pinnacle Bks.

Dureau De La Malle, Adolphe. Economie Politique des Romains, 2 Vols. LC 73-165343. (Research & Source Works Ser.: No. 850). 1971. Repr. of 1840 ed. lib. bdg. 50.50 (ISBN 0-8337-0976-3). B Franklin.

Durel, Lionel C. L' Oeuvre D'Andre Mareschal. 1973. pap. 14.00 (ISBN 0-384-13390-8). Johnson Repr.

Durel, Marie. Speak English: A Practical Course for Foreign Students. (Orig.). 1972. pap. 5.29i (ISBN 0-06-463320-9, EH 320, EH). B&N NY.

Durell, Ann, ed. see Brown, Marc.

Durell, Ann, ed. see Dabcovich, Lydia.

Durell, Ann, ed. see Delton, Judy.

Durell, Ann, ed. see Greaves, Margaret.

Durell, Ann, ed. see Howard, Jane R.

Durell, Ann, ed. see Levinson, Riki.

Durell, Ann, ed. see McPhail, David.

Durell, Ann, ed. see Milne, A. A.

Durell, Ann, ed. see Rockwell, Anne.

Durell, Ann, ed. see Sachs, Marilyn.

Durell, Ann, ed. see Turkle, Brinton.

Durell, W. R. Data Administration: A Practical Guide to Successful Data Management. 192p. 1984. 32.95 (ISBN 0-07-018391-0). McGraw.

Durem, Ray. Take No Prisoners. (Heritage Ser). 1971. pap. 2.50x (ISBN 0-685-26076-3). Broadside.

Duren, Almetris M. & Iscoe, Louise. Overcoming: A History of Black Integration at the University of Texas at Austin. (Illus.). 57p. 1979. text ed. 9.95x (ISBN 0-292-76012-4, Pub. by the U of Tex. at Austin). U of Tex Pr.

Duren, Donald & Andreoni, Jill. Writing Successful Proposals. (Illus.). 144p. 1979. pap. 7.98 (ISBN 0-9604056-0-7). Durand Intl.

Duren, James W. Trekking Across the Mind. LC 85-50087. 54p. 1985. 5.95 (ISBN 0-938232-67-3). Winston-Derek.

Duren, Lista. Frame It: A Complete Do-It-Yourself Guide to Picture Framing. 1976. 12.95 (ISBN 0-395-24765-9); pap. 9.95 (ISBN 0-395-24976-7). HM.

Duren, Lista & McDonald, Billy. Build Your Own Home Darkroom. (Illus.). 160p. 1982. pap. 14.95 (ISBN 0-930764-26-9). Curtin & London.
--Building Your Own Home Darkroom Step-by-Step. 1982. pap. 14.95 (ISBN 0-442-22089-8). Van Nos Reinhold.

Duren, P. L. Univalent Functions. (Grundlehern der Mathematischen Wissenschaften Ser.: Vol. 259). (Illus.). 382p. 1983. 48.00 (ISBN 0-387-90795-5). Springer-Verlag.

Duren, Peter L. Theory of HP Spaces. LC 74-117092. (Pure & Applied Mathematics Ser.: Vol. 38). 1970. 55.00 (ISBN 0-12-225150-4). Acad Pr.

Duren, Ronald Van see Moore, Robin & Van Duren, Ronald.

Duren, Ryne. The Comeback. 169p. 1978. 7.95 (ISBN 0-318-15302-5). Natl Coun Alcoholism.

Duren, Ryne & Drury, Robert F. The Comeback. 1978. 7.95 (ISBN 0-89328-014-3). Lorenz Pr.

Durer, Albrecht. The Complete Engravings, Etchings & Drypoints of Albrecht Durer. Strauss, Walter L., ed. (Illus.). 16.50 (ISBN 0-8446-4624-5). Peter Smith.
--Complete Engravings, Etchings, & Dry Points of Albrecht Durer. Strauss, Walter L., ed. (Illus.). 240p. (Orig.). 1972. pap. 7.50 (ISBN 0-486-22851-7). Dover.
--Complete Woodcuts of Albrecht Durer. Kurth, Willi, ed. (Illus.). 1963. pap. 8.95 (ISBN 0-486-21097-9). Dover.
--Complete Woodcuts of Albrecht Durer. Kurth, Willi, ed. (Illus.). 16.50 (ISBN 0-8446-2015-7). Peter Smith.
--A Course in the Art of Measurement with Compass & Ruler. (Printed Sources of Western Art Ser.). (Illus.). 180p. (Ger.). 1981. pap. 45.00 slipcase (ISBN 0-915346-52-4). A Wofsy Fine Arts.
--Drawings. Woelfflin, H., ed. Appelbaum, Stanley, tr. (Illus.). 1970. pap. 6.00 (ISBN 0-486-22352-3). Dover.
--Drawings of Albrecht Durer: Selected. (Illus.). 11.50 (ISBN 0-8446-0593-X). Peter Smith.
--Drawings of Durer. Longstreet, Stephen, ed. (Master Draughtsman Ser). (Illus., Orig.). treasure trove bdg. 9.95x (ISBN 0-87505-007-7); pap. 4.95 (ISBN 0-87505-160-X). Borden.
--Human Figure: Dresden Sketchbook. Strauss, Walter L., ed. & tr. 1972. pap. 9.95 (ISBN 0-486-21042-1). Dover.
--The Human Figure: The Complete 'Dresden Sketchbook' Strauss, Walter L., ed. & tr. 16.00 (ISBN 0-8446-4542-7). Peter Smith.
--Maximilian's Triumphal Arch: Woodcuts by Albrecht Durer & Others. (Illus.). 13.75 (ISBN 0-8446-4625-3). Peter Smith.
--Of the Just Shaping of Letters. Nichol, tr. 13.25 (ISBN 0-8446-2016-5). Peter Smith.
--Of the Just Shaping of Letters: From the Applied Geometry of Albrecht Durer, Book 3. Nichol, R. T., tr. (Illus.). 1917. pap. 3.00 (ISBN 0-486-21306-4). Dover.

Durer, C., ed. see Witkiewicz, Stanislaw I.

Durer, Ulbrecht. Etchings of Ulbrecht Durer. 81p. 1984. pap. text ed. 25.00 (ISBN 0-87556-376-7). Saifer.

Dures, A. & Dures, K. Poverty. (History in Focus Ser.). (Illus.). 72p. (gr. 7-12). 1984. 14.95 (ISBN 0-7134-4349-9, Pub. by Batsford England). David & Charles.

Dures, Alan & Dures, Katherine. Mao Tse-Tung. (Leaders Ser.). (Illus.). 96p. (YA) (gr. 9-12). 1980. 14.95 (ISBN 0-7134-1923-7, Pub. by Batsford England). David & Charles.
--Riots. (History in Focus Ser.). (Illus.). 72p. (gr. 7-12). 1985. 14.95 (ISBN 0-7134-4350-2, Pub. by Batsford England). David & Charles.

Dures, K., jt. auth. see Dures, A.

Dures, Katherine, jt. auth. see Dures, Alan.

Duret, Theodore. Manet & the French Impressionists. facsimile ed. Crawford Flitch, J. E., tr. (Select Bibliographies Reprint Ser). Repr. of 1910 ed. 24.00 (ISBN 0-8369-6687-2). Ayer Co Pubs.

Durey, Michael. The Return of the Plague: British Society & the Cholera 1831-32. 1979. text ed. 39.50x (ISBN 0-391-01038-7). Humanities.

Durey, Peter. Staff Management in University & College Libraries. Chandler, C., ed. 144p. 1976. text ed. 19.00 (ISBN 0-08-019718-3). Pergamon.

Durey De Noinville, Jacques B. Histoire Du Theatre De l'Academie Royale De Musique En France, Depuis Son Etablissement Jusqu' a Present, 2 vols. in 1. 2nd ed. LC 80-2273. Repr. of 1757 ed. 47.50 (ISBN 0-404-18838-9). AMS Pr.

Durfee. Analytic Philosophy & Phenomenology. 1976. pap. 42.00 (ISBN 90-247-1880-5, Pub. by Martinus Nijhoff Netherlands). Kluwer Academic.

Durfee, Charles A. A Precise Concordance to the Principal Poets of the World Embracing Titles, First Lines, Characters, Subjects & Quotations. 1978. Repr. of 1884 ed. 65.00 (ISBN 0-8492-0674-X). R West.

Durfee, D. A., ed. William H. Harrison, 1773-1841; John Tyler 1790-1862: Chronology, Documents, Bibliographical Aids. LC 76-116058. (Oceana Presidential Chronology Ser.). 160p. 1970. 8.00 (ISBN 0-379-12081-X). Oceana.

Durfee, David A. Power in American Society: Burden or Blessing. Fraenkel, Jack R., ed. (Crucial Issues in American Government Ser.). (gr. 9-12). 1976. pap. text ed. 7.64 (ISBN 0-205-04907-9, 764907X). Allyn.

Durfey, Carolyn, jt. ed. see Cole, Ginny.

D'Urfey, Thomas. Butler's Ghost. LC 84-13916. 1985. Repr. of 1682 ed. 45.00x (ISBN 0-8201-1399-9). Schol Facsimiles.
--Songs of Thomas D'Urfey. Day, Cyrus L., ed. (Harvard Studies in English). 1969. Repr. of 1933 ed. 23.00 (ISBN 0-384-11020-7). Johnson Repr.

Durfield, Richard. How Shall We Escape. 1983. pap. 3.95 (ISBN 0-938612-07-7). Revival Press.

Durgin, F. A; see Joly, B.

Durgin, J., jt. auth. see Bartilucci, A.

Durgin, Jean P., jt. auth. see Ross, Beverly B.

Durgin, Max W. FORTRAN 77. (Illus.). 316p. (Orig.). 1982. pap. text ed. 22.50 (ISBN 0-935920-04-8). Natl Pub Black Hills.
--Subset FORTRAN-77. (Illus.). 320p. (Orig.). 1983. pap. text ed. 22.50 (ISBN 0-935920-11-0). Natl Pub Black Hills.
Durgin, Winslow. Separation Poems. 3.00 (ISBN 0-318-11911-0). Great Raven Pr.
--Traces-Fire. 3.00 (ISBN 0-686-15294-8). Great Raven Pr.
Durgnat, Raymond. Durgnat on Film. (Illus.). 238p. 1976. pap. 7.95 (ISBN 0-571-10656-0). Faber & Faber.
--Franju: Movie Edition. movie ed. LC 68-31139. 144p. 1967. pap. 1.95 (ISBN 0-520-00367-5, CAL 171, CAL171). U of Cal Pr.
--Jean Renoir. LC 72-82221. (Illus.). 1975. 30.00x (ISBN 0-520-02283-1); pap. 4.95 (ISBN 0-520-02743-4). U of Cal Pr.
--Luis Bunuel. expanded rev. ed. LC 76-56661. (Cal Ser.: No. 368). 1978. pap. 4.95 (ISBN 0-520-03424-4). U of Cal Pr.
--The Strange Case of Alfred Hitchcock, or the Plain Man's Hitchcock. LC 74-7239. 1974. pap. 9.95 (ISBN 0-262-54034-7). MIT Pr.
Durgy, Robert G., ed. see Dostoyevsky, Fyodor.
Durham. One Hundred Careers: How to Pick the One That's Best for You. 1977. 9.95 (ISBN 0-13-634717-7, Spec); pap. 4.95 (ISBN 0-13-634709-6). P-H.
Durham, Bill. Canoes & Kayaks of Western America. (Shorey Indian Ser.). 104p. 1974. pap. 9.95 (ISBN 0-8466-4073-2, I 73). Shorey.
Durham, Carolyn A. L' Art Romanesque de Raymond Roussel. 196p. (Fr.). 1982. 14.95 (ISBN 0-917786-25-4). Summa Pubns.
Durham, Charles. Temptation: Help for Struggling Christians. LC 82-153. 164p. (Orig.). 1982. pap. 4.95 (ISBN 0-87784-382-1). Inter-Varsity.
--When You Are Feeling Lonely. LC 84-10499. 180p. (Orig.). 1984. pap. 5.95 (ISBN 0-87784-915-3). Inter-Varsity.
Durham, Eleanor, jt. ed. see Durham, James.
Durham, Floyd E., jt. auth. see Hoffmeister, Donald F.
Durham, Frank. Elmer Rice. (Twayne's U.S. Authors Ser.). 1970. lib. bdg. 12.50 (ISBN 0-8057-0616-X). Irvington.
Durham, Frank & Purrington, Robert D. The Frame of the Universe. (Illus.). 1983. 25.00x (ISBN 0-231-05392-4). Columbia U Pr.
--Frame of the Universe. 284p. 1985. pap. 12.50x (ISBN 0-231-05393-2). Columbia U Pr.
Durham, G. Homer. N. Eldon Tanner: His Life & Service. LC 82-9681. (Illus.). 370p. 1982. 8.95 (ISBN 0-87747-913-5). Deseret Bk.
Durham, George. Taming the Nueces Strip: The Story of McNelly's Rangers. (Illus.). 198p. 1962. pap. 7.95 (ISBN 0-292-78048-6). U of Tex Pr.
Durham, Glenda P. International Export Management Group, Inc. Corporate Capabilities. (Illus.). 32p. (Orig.). 1984. pap. text ed. 4.25 (ISBN 0-89904-084-5). Crumb Elbow Pub.
Durham, Jack L. & Teasley, John I., eds. Chemistry of Particles, Fogs & Rains. (Acid Precipitation Ser.: Vol. 2). 288p. 1984. text ed. 32.50 (ISBN 0-250-40567-9). Butterworth.
Durham, Jackie. In Search of Energy. Pennington, Celeste, ed. (Home Mission Study). (Illus., Orig.). (gr. 4-6). 1984. pap. 1.75 (ISBN 0-937170-27-5). Home Mission.
Durham, Jackie, jt. ed. see Joyner, Nelson T., Jr.
Durham, Jacqueline. Miss Strong Arm: The Story of Annie Armstrong. LC 66-10385. (gr. 4-6). 1966. 6.95 (ISBN 0-8054-4308-8, 4243-08). Broadman.
Durham, James. Song of Solomon. 1981. lib. bdg. 17.25 (ISBN 0-86524-075-2, 2201). Klock & Klock.
--Song of Solomon. (Geneva Ser.). 460p. 1982. Repr. of 1840 ed. 12.95 (ISBN 0-85151-352-2). Banner of Truth.
Durham, James & Durham, Eleanor, eds. Soldier of the Cross-the Civil War Diary & Correspondence of Rev. Andrew Jackson Hartsock. 275p. 1979. pap. 27.50x (ISBN 0-89126-076-5). MA-AH Pub.
Durham, James C. To Write, Write: Writing. 240p. (gr. 9-12). 1981. pap. 6.95x (ISBN 0-88334-144-1). Ind Sch Pr.
Durham, Jimmy. Columbus Day. 88p. 1983. pap. 4.50 (ISBN 0-931122-30-9). West End.
Durham, John G. Lord Durham's Report on the Affairs of British North America, 3 Vols. Lucas, C. P., ed. LC 73-117388. Repr. of 1912 ed. lib. bdg. 87.50x (ISBN 0-678-00647-4). Kelley.
Durham, John I., ed. Southeastern Studies: Toward A.D. 2000. LC 77-80400. (Emerging Directions in Christian Ministry Ser.: Vol. 1). 154p. 1981. 8.95x (ISBN 0-86554-026-8). Mercer Univ Pr.
Durham, John I. & Porter, J. R., eds. Proclamation & Presence: Old Testament Essays in Honor of Gwynne Henton Davies. LC 83-17445. 335p. 1983. 17.95x (ISBN 0-86554-101-9, MUP/H93). Mercer Univ Pr.
Durham, John W. Football's Modular Offense: A Flexible System of Attack. 161p. 1983. 16.95 (ISBN 0-13-324160-2, Parker). P-H.
Durham, Katherine C., jt. auth. see Rush, Susan D.
Durham, Marilyn. Flambard's Confession. LC 82-2978. 784p. 1982. 17.95 (ISBN 0-15-131453-5). HarBraceJ.
Durham, Mary E. High Albania. LC 70-135803. (Eastern Europe Collection Ser.). 1970. Repr. of 1909 ed. 23.50 (ISBN 0-405-02745-1). Ayer Co Pubs.
--Some Tribal Origins, Laws & Customs of the Balkans. LC 76-44710. (Illus.). Repr. of 1928 ed. 27.50 (ISBN 0-404-15856-0). AMS Pr.
Durham, Oren C., jt. auth. see Samter, Max.
Durham, Philip & Jones, Everett L. The Negro Cowboys. LC 83-6446. (Illus.). x, 278p. 1983. pap. 7.95 (ISBN 0-8032-6560-3, BB 857, Bison). U of Nebr Pr.
Durham, Philip & Jones, Everett, eds. Frontier in American Literature. LC 68-31708. 1969. pap. 13.24 scp (ISBN 0-672-63040-0). Odyssey Pr.
Durham, Philip & Jones, Everett L., eds. The Frontier in American Literature. 393p. 1969. pap. text ed. write for info. (ISBN 0-02-330630-0). Macmillan.
Durham, Quentin. Minigroup Science. (Illus.). 230p. (gr. 7-12). 1980. pap. 22.50 (ISBN 0-87879-244-9). Acad Therapy.
--Supermath. 276p. (Orig.). (gr. 6-12). 1981. 27.50 (ISBN 0-87562-070-1). Spec Child.
Durham, Taylor R., jt. auth. see LaPlante, Josephine M.
Durham, Willard H. & Dodds, John W., eds. British & American Plays Eighteen Thirty to Nineteen Forty-Five. (Illus.). 796p. 1981. lib. bdg. 50.00 (ISBN 0-89984-074-4). Century Bookbindery.
Durham, William H. Scarcity & Survival in Central America: Ecological Origins of the Soccer War. LC 78-55318. (Illus.). xx, 209p. 1979. 17.50x (ISBN 0-8047-1000-7); pap. 6.95 (ISBN 0-8047-1154-2, SP5). Stanford U Pr.
Duri, A. A. The Rise of Historical Writing among the Arabs. Conrad, Lawrence I., ed. & tr. from Arabic. LC 82-24028. (Modern Classics in Near Eastern Studies). 192p. 1984. 22.00 (ISBN 0-691-05388-X). Princeton U Pr.
Durie, Alastair. The Scottish Linen Industry in the Eighteenth Century. (Illus.). 1979. text ed. 31.75x (ISBN 0-685-94719-X). Humanities.
Durie, Alistair. Weird Tales. 128p. 1981. 24.00x (ISBN 0-686-72295-7, Pub. by Jupiter England). State Mutual Bk.
Durie, G. M., jt. auth. see Russell, D. H.
Durie, Sheila & Edwards, Rob. Fueling the Nuclear Arms Race: The Links between Nuclear Power & Nuclear Weapons. 129p. (Orig.). 1982. pap. 5.95 (ISBN 0-86104-372-3). Pluto Pr.
Durieux, Philippe. Enciclopedia de la Construccion, 7 vols. 2366p. (Espn.). 1977. Set. 340.00 (ISBN 84-7146-084-X, S-50540). French & Eur.
Durig, J. R., ed. Vibrational Spectra & Structure: A Series of Advances, Vol. 9. 520p. 1981. 130.00 (ISBN 0-444-41943-8). Elsevier.
--Vibrational Spectra & Structure: A Series of Advances, Vol. 10. 498p. 1981. 129.75 (ISBN 0-686-80642-5). Elsevier.
--Vibrational Spectra & Structure: A Series of Advances, Vol. 11. 362p. 1982. 117.00 (ISBN 0-444-42103-3, I-262-82). Elsevier.
--Vibrational Spectra & Structure: A Series of Advances, Vol. 13. 460p. 1984. 115.00 (ISBN 0-444-42394-X). Elsevier.
Durig, James R., ed. Analytical Applications of FT-IR to Molecular & Biological Systems. (NATO Advanced Study Institute Ser. C. - Mathematical & Physical Sciences: No. 57). 607p. 1980. lib. bdg. 68.50 (ISBN 90-277-1145-3, Pub. by Reidel Holland). Kluwer Academic.
--Vibrational Spectra & Structure, Vol. 1. pap. 52.00 (ISBN 0-317-08365-1, 2055083). Bks Demand UMI.
--Vibrational Spectra & Structure: A Series of Advances, Vol. 2. 300p. 1975. 85.00 (ISBN 0-8247-6193-6). Dekker.
--Vibrational Spectra & Structure: A Series of Advances, Vol. 3. 344p. 1975. 85.00 (ISBN 0-8247-6220-7). Dekker.
--Vibrational Spectra & Structure: A Series of Advances, Vols. 4-7. 1981. Vol. 4. 81.00 (ISBN 0-444-41437-1); Vol. 5. 81.00 (ISBN 0-444-41437-1); Vol. 7. 93.75 (ISBN 0-444-41707-9). Elsevier.
Durighello, Joy, jt. auth. see Blass, Laurie.
Durin, Bernard. Insects Etc: An Anthology of Arthropods, Featuring a Bounty of Beetles. Zappler, Georg, tr. from Ger. LC 81-6908. (Illus.). 108p. 1981. 50.00 (ISBN 0-933920-25-3). Hudson Hills.
During, H. J. Taxonomical Revision of the Garovaglioideae (Pterobryaceae, Musci) (Bryophytorum Bibliotheca Ser.: No. 12). (Illus.). 1977. lib. bdg. 21.00x (ISBN 3-7682-1161-4). Lubrecht & Cramer.
During, Ingemar. Aristotle's Chemical Treatise. Meterlolica, Book IV: With an Introduction & Commentary. LC 78-66544. (Ancient Philosophy Ser.). 112p. 1982. lib. bdg. 18.00 (ISBN 0-8240-9601-0). Garland Pub.
--Aristotle's De Partibus Animalium: Critical & Literary Commentaries. LC 78-66546. (Ancient Philosophy Ser.). 223p. 1980. lib. bdg. 26.00 (ISBN 0-8240-9602-9). Garland Pub.
--Die Harmonienlehre des Klaudios Ptolemaios. Bd. with Porphyrios Kommentar zur Harmonienlehre des Ptolemaios. LC 78-66554. (Ancient Philosophy Ser.). 513p. 1982. lib. bdg. 62.00 (ISBN 0-8240-9600-2). Garland Pub.
--Porphyrios Kommentar Zur Harmonielehre Des Ptolemaios. 1980. Repr. of 1932 ed. lib. bdg. 75.00 (ISBN 0-8495-4390-8). Arden Lib.
--Ptolemaios und Porphyrios Uber Die Musik. LC 78-20290. (Ancient Philosophy Ser.). 293p. 1980. lib. bdg. 34.00 (ISBN 0-8240-9599-5). Garland Pub.
During, Ingemar & Owen, G. E., eds. Aristotle & Plato in the Mid-Fourth Century. (Studia Graeaca et Latina). 1960. text ed. 25.50x (ISBN 0-391-00424-7). Humanities.
Durio, Alice & Rice, James. Cajun Columbus. LC 75-20484. (Illus.). 32p. (gr. 2 up). 1975. 10.95 (ISBN 0-88289-074-3). Pelican.
Duris, Gene. Real Endings. 1978. pap. 1.95 (ISBN 0-532-19186-2). Woodhill.
Duris, Jerry. Coming Alive: A Complete Daily Health Guide & Diary. (Skill Builder Ser.). (Illus.). 154p. (Orig.). 1985. 10.00 (ISBN 0-943920-15-9). Metamorphous pr.
--The Shoe That Wouldn't. (Young People Ser.). (Illus.). 60p. (Orig.). 1985. pap. 8.00 (ISBN 0-943920-49-3). Metamorphous Pr.
Durizch, Mary L., jt. ed. see Littleton, Jesse T.
Durka, Gloria & Smith, Joanmarie. Aesthetic Dimensions of Religious Education. LC 78-65903. 252p. 1979. pap. 8.50 (ISBN 0-8091-2164-6). Paulist Pr.
--Family Ministry. 216p. (Orig.). 1980. pap. 7.95 (ISBN 0-86683-762-0). Winston Pr.
Durkacz, Victor. The Decline of the Celtic Languages. 260p. 1983. text ed. 35.00x (ISBN 0-85976-090-1, Pub. by John Donald Scotland). Humanities.
Durkan, John & Kirk, James. The University of Glasgow, 1451-1577. 504p. 1982. 79.00x (ISBN 0-686-96582-5, Pub. by U of Glasgow Pr Scotland). State Mutual Bk.
Durkan, Michael J., jt. auth. see Ayling, Ronald.
Durkee. Durkee Spice & Herb Cookbook. (Illus.). 64p. (Orig.). 1983. pap. 3.50 (ISBN 0-8249-3020-7). Ideals.
Durkee, Cornelius, jt. auth. see Ritchie, Henry.
Durkee, Jean K. Tout de Suite: A la Microwave, 2 vols. Incl. Vol. I. French, Acadian & Creole Recipes, Delicious, Nutrious & Colorful. (Illus.). 224p. 1977. write for info; Vol. II. Mexican, Italian & French Recipes Tested & Tasted by the Author. (Illus.). 236p. 1980. write for info.. (Illus.). 224p. 1977. Tout de Suite.
--Tout de Suite a la Microwave I. LC 77-93096. (Illus.). 224p. 1977. plastic comb bdg. 9.95 (ISBN 0-9605362-0-5). Tout de Suite.
--Tout de Suite a la Microwave II. LC 80-53827. (Illus.). 236p. 1980. plastic comb bdg. 9.95 (ISBN 0-9605362-1-3). Tout de Suite.
--Voila! Lafayette Centennial Cookbook 1884-1984. (Illus.). 264p. 1983. 11.95 (ISBN 0-9605362-2-1). J K Durkee.
Durken, Daniel, ed. Blow the Trumpet at the New Moon: A Sisters Today Jubilee. LC 79-27505. xi, 480p. (Orig.). 1980. pap. 3.00 (ISBN 0-8146-1016-1). Liturgical Pr.
Durken, Daniel, ed. & pref. by. Sin, Salvation, & the Spirit. LC 79-20371. (Illus.). 368p. 1979. text ed. 6.00 (ISBN 0-8146-1078-1); pap. text ed. 10.00 (ISBN 0-8146-1079-X). Liturgical Pr.
Durkheim, Emile. Division of Labor in Society. 1947. 17.00 (ISBN 0-02-907840-7); pap. text ed. 12.95 (ISBN 0-02-907850-4). Free Pr.
--The Division of Labor in Society. Hall, W. D., tr. 350p. 1985. text ed. 9.95x (ISBN 0-02-907960-8); 24.95x (ISBN 0-02-907950-0). Free Pr.
--Education & Sociology. LC 55-11002. 1956. 12.95 (ISBN 0-02-907920-9). Free Pr.
--Elementary Forms of the Religious Life. Swain, Joseph W., tr. 1965. pap. text ed. 14.95 (ISBN 0-02-908010-X). Free Pr.
--The Elementary Forms of the Religious Life. 2nd ed. Swain, Joseph W., tr. LC 76-369730. pap. 117.80 (ISBN 0-317-20057-7, 2023276). Bks Demand UMI.
--Emile Durkheim on Institutional Analysis. Traugott, Mark, ed. LC 77-25105. (Heritage of Sociology). 1978. lib. bdg. 23.00x (ISBN 0-226-17330-5). U of Chicago Pr.
--Emile Durkheim on Morality & Society. Bellah, Robert N., ed. LC 73-76594. (Heritage of Sociology Ser.). lvi, 244p. 1975. pap. 10.00x (ISBN 0-226-17336-4, P565, Phoen). U of Chicago Pr.
--Montesquieu & Rousseau: Forerunners of Sociology. 1960. pap. 7.95x (ISBN 0-472-08291-4, AA). U of Mich Pr.
--Moral Edication: A Study in the Theory & Application of the Sociology of Education. Wilson, Everett K., tr. 288p. pap. 10.95 (ISBN 0-02-908320-6). Free Pr.
--Moral Education: A Study in the Theory & Application of the Sociology of Education. Wilson, Everett K., tr. LC 59-6815. 288p. 1961. 14.95 (ISBN 0-02-908330-3); pap. text ed. 10.95x (ISBN 0-02-908320-6). Free Pr.
--Pragmatism & Sociology. Allcock, John B., ed. Whitehouse, J. C., tr. LC 82-14630. 184p. 1983. 32.50 (ISBN 0-521-24686-5). Cambridge U Pr.
--Professional Ethics & Civic Morals. Brookfield, Cornelia, tr. LC 83-12653. xliv, 228p. 1983. Repr. of 1958 ed. lib. bdg. 45.00x (ISBN 0-313-24114-7, DUPR). Greenwood.
--Rules of Sociological Method. 8th ed. 1950. 12.95 (ISBN 0-02-908490-3); pap. text ed. 13.95 (ISBN 0-02-908500-4). Free Pr.
--The Rules of Sociological Method & Selected Texts on Sociology & Its Method. Lukes, Steven, ed. Halls, W. D., tr. 1982. pap. text ed. 8.95 (ISBN 0-02-907930-6). Free Pr.
--Selected Writings. Giddens, Anthony, ed. 288p. 1972. 44.50 (ISBN 0-521-08504-7); pap. 12.95 (ISBN 0-521-09712-6). Cambridge U Pr.
--Socialism & Saint-Simon (Le Socialisme) Gouldner, Alvin W., ed. LC 58-8736. pap. 70.50 (ISBN 0-317-20142-5, 2023199). Bks Demand UMI.
--Sociology & Philosophy. Pocock, D. F., tr. LC 54-2835. 1974. 14.95 (ISBN 0-02-908570-5); pap. text ed. 7.95 (ISBN 0-02-908580-2). Free Pr.
--Suicide. 1966. 24.95 (ISBN 0-02-908650-7); pap. text ed. 9.95 (ISBN 0-02-908660-4). Free Pr.
Durkheim, Emile & Mauss, Marcel. Primitive Classification. Needham, Rodney, tr. LC 63-9737. 1967. pap. 3.95x (ISBN 0-226-17334-8, P273, Phoen). U of Chicago Pr.
Durkin. Teaching Young Children to Read. 3rd ed. 544p. 1980. text ed. 32.86 (ISBN 0-205-06903-7, 2369036). Allyn.
Durkin, Andrew R. Sergei Aksakov & Russian Pastoral. 421p. 1983. 30.00x (ISBN 0-8135-0954-8). Rutgers U Pr.
Durkin, Barbara W. Oh, You Dundalk Girls, Can't You Dance the Polka? 288p. 14.95 (ISBN 0-688-01930-7). Morrow.
Durkin, Dolores. Children Who Read Early. LC 66-25980. 1966. text ed. 10.95x (ISBN 0-8077-1260-4). Tchrs Coll.
--Getting Reading Started: A Textbook for Early Childhood Educators Responsible for Readiness & Beginning Reading Instruction. 200p. 1981. pap. 16.79 (ISBN 0-205-07559-2, 2375591). Allyn.
--Phonics, Linguistics, & Reading. LC 72-87115. 1972. pap. 6.95x (ISBN 0-8077-1258-2). Tchrs Coll.
--Strategies for Identifying Words: A Workbook for Teachers & Those Preparing to Teach. 2nd ed. 1980. pap. 17.86 (ISBN 0-205-07229-1, 2372290). Allyn.
--Teaching Them to Read. 4th ed. 1983. text ed. 32.50x (ISBN 0-205-07933-4, 2379333). Allyn.
Durkin, Helen. The Group in Depth. LC 64-7550. 378p. (Orig.). 1966. text ed. 32.50 (ISBN 0-8236-2240-1). Intl Univs Pr.
Durkin, Helen E. Group Psychotherapy for Mothers. 144p. 1969. spiral 14.50x (ISBN 0-398-00488-9). C C Thomas.
Durkin, Henry P. Forty-Four Hours to Change Your Life: Marriage Encounter. (Orig.). pap. write for info (ISBN 0-515-09442-0). Jove Pubns.
Durkin, James, ed. see Educational Research Council of America.
Durkin, James E., ed. Living Groups: Group Psychotherapy & General Systems Theory. LC 81-4365. 400p. 1981. 35.00 (ISBN 0-87630-253-3). Brunner-Mazel.
Durkin, Jim. Life with a Purpose: Catching God's Vision for Your Life. 96p. 1982. pap. 2.95 (ISBN 0-89283-105-7). Servant.
--Living the Word: How to Apply Scripture to Your Life. 1979. pap. 2.95 (ISBN 0-89283-069-7). Servant.
Durkin, M., ed. see Eltringham, R., et al.
Durkin, Mary, jt. auth. see Anzia, Joan.
Durkin, Mary, jt. auth. see Greeley, Andrew.
Durkin, Sr. Mary Brian. Dorothy L. Sayers. (English Authors Ser.). 1980. lib. bdg. 13.50 (ISBN 0-8057-6778-9, Twayne). G K Hall.
Durkin, Mary G. Feast of Love. 248p. 1984. 9.95 (ISBN 0-8294-0443-0). Loyola.
Durkin, Mary G., jt. auth. see Greeley, Andrew.
Durkin, Thomas A., jt. auth. see Polakoff, Murray.
Durksen, Hedy. Aling Highways & Hedges. 183p. 1977. pap. 2.95 (ISBN 0-317-31422-X). Herald Pr.
Durlach, Hansi, jt. auth. see Blumin, Stuart.
Durlach, J. & Altura, B. M., eds. Magnesium, Diabetes & Carbohydrate Metabolism: Journal - Magnesium. (Vol. 2, Nos. 4-6). (Illus.). iv, 172p. 1984. pap. 41.75 (ISBN 3-8055-3865-0). S Karger.
Durlach, J., jt. ed. see Halpern, M. J.
Durlach, Jeannette V. Saga of an Ego Trip. 48p. 1976. pap. 1.00 (ISBN 0-87844-038-0). Sandlapper Pub Co.
Durlach, Theresa M. The Relationship Systems of the Tlingit, Haida, & Tsimshian. LC 73-3547. (American Ethnological Society. Publications: No. 11). Repr. of 1928 ed. 27.50 (ISBN 0-404-58161-7). AMS Pr.
Durlacher, Ed. The Play Party Book: Thirty-Seven Singing Games. (Illus.). 38p. (ps-5). 1945. 9.50 (ISBN 0-8159-6505-2). Devin.
Durlacher, J. Direct Mail Databook. 4th ed. 300p. (Orig.). 1983. pap. text ed. 68.50x (ISBN 0-566-02386-5). Gower Pub Co.
Durlacher, Jennifer, jt. ed. see Blauvelt, Euan.
Durland, Frances C. Coping with Widowhood. 1979. pap. 1.50 (ISBN 0-89243-098-2). Liguori Pubns.
--Creative Dramatics for Children: A Practical Manual for Teachers & Leaders. LC 75-1493. 181p. 1975. pap. 4.50x (ISBN 0-87338-175-0). Kent St U Pr.

--I Never Feel Old: An Eighty-Eight-Year-Old Shares Her Positive Approach to the Challenges of Aging. Van Leeuwen, Julie, tr. (Illus.). 83p. 1981. pap. text ed. 2.50 (ISBN 0-912228-78-4). St Anthony Mess Pr.
Durland, William R. No King But Caesar? LC 74-30093. (Christian Peace Shelf Ser.). 184p. 1975. 6.95 (ISBN 0-8361-1757-3); pap. 4.95 (ISBN 0-8361-1927-4). Herald Pr.
Durling, A., jt. auth. see Cuenod, M.
Durling, Allen E., jt. auth. see Childers, Donald G.
Durling, Dwight & Watt, William, eds. Biography: Varieties & Parallels. 1978. Repr. of 1941 ed. lib. bdg. 25.00 (ISBN 0-8492-0673-1). R West.
Durling, R. J., ed. Galenus Latinus I. (Ars Medica: Vol. 6). 1976. text ed. 70.00x (ISBN 3-11-005759-X). De Gruyter.
Durling, Robert M. The Figures of the Poet in Renaissance Epic. LC 65-22060. pap. 73.00 (ISBN 0-317-10089-0, 2002966). Bks Demand UMI.
Durling, Robert M., ed. Petrarch's Lyric Poems. 512p. 1976. 30.00x (ISBN 0-674-66345-4); pap. 9.95x (ISBN 0-674-66348-9). Harvard U Pr.
Durman, E. C. & Dunlop, Burton. Volunteers in Social Services: Consumer Assessment of Nursing Homes. 183p. 1979. pap. text ed. 7.00x (ISBN 0-87766-261-4). Urban Inst.
Durnbaugh, Donald F. The Believers' Church. LC 85-7599. 328p. (Orig.). 1985. pap. 12.95x (ISBN 0-8361-1271-7). Herald Pr.
--The Brethren in Colonial America. (Illus.). 659p. (YA) 1967. 13.95 (ISBN 0-87178-110-7). Brethren.
--European Origins of the Brethren. 463p. 1958. 8.95 (ISBN 0-87178-256-1). Brethren.
Durnbaugh, Donald F., ed. Church of the Brethren Past & Present. 182p. (Orig.). 1971. pap. 6.95 (ISBN 0-87178-146-8). Brethren.
--Every Need Supplied: Mutual Aid & Christian Community in Free Churches, 1525-1675. LC 73-94279. (Documents in Free Church History Ser.: No. 1). (Illus.). 258p. 1974. 19.95 (ISBN 0-87722-031-X). Temple U Pr.
--On Earth Peace. 1978. pap. 9.95 (ISBN 0-87178-660-5). Brethren.
Durnbaugh, Donald F., ed. see Zigler, M. R., et al.
Durnell, Hazel. America of Carl Sandburg: Sandburg Centennial Facsimile of First Edition. 1978. lib. bdg. 7.00 (ISBN 0-685-87861-9); text ed. 5.00 (ISBN 0-685-87862-7). U Pr of Wash.
Durnell, Hazel B. Japanese Cultural Influences on American Poetry & Drama. 324p. 1983. 45.00 (ISBN 0-89346-240-3, Pub. by Hokuseido Pr). Heian Intl.
Durnell, Jane B. & Stevens, Norman D., eds. The Librarian: Selections from the Column of That Name by Edmund L. Pearson. LC 75-35725. 659p. 1976. 30.00 (ISBN 0-8108-0851-X). Scarecrow.
Durney, Carl H. & Johnson, Curtis C. Introduction to Modern Electromagnetics. LC 81-23602. 1982. Repr. of 1969 ed. 27.50 (ISBN 0-89874-333-8). Krieger.
Durney, Carl H., et al. Electric Circuit Theory & Engineering Applications. 1982. pap. text ed. 40.95 (ISBN 0-03-057951-1). HR&W.
Durney, Charles M. Building Free-Form Furniture. (Illus.). 224p. 1982. o.p 15.95 (ISBN 0-8306-1340-4, 1440); pap. 9.95 (ISBN 0-8306-1440-0). TAB Bks.
Durney, Lawrence J. Graham's Electroplating Handbook. 4th ed. 1984. 69.50 (ISBN 0-442-22002-2). Van Nos Reinhold.
Durnin, John. Toward Educational Engineering. LC 81-40101. (Illus.). 134p. (Orig.). 1982. PLB 21.75 (ISBN 0-8191-2435-4); pap. text ed. 9.50 (ISBN 0-8191-2436-2). U Pr of Amer.
Durnin, Richard G., ed. American Education: A Guide to Information Sources. LC 73-17553. (American Studies Information Guide: Vol. 14). 225p. 1982. 60.00x (ISBN 0-8103-1265-4). Gale.
Durning, Mary, jt. auth. see Durning, William.
Durning, William & Durning, Mary. A Guide to Irish Roots. LC 84-62760. (Illus.). 250p. 1985. pap. write for info. (ISBN 0-9601868-1-6). Irish Family Names.
Durning-Lawrence, Edwin. Bacon Is Shake-Speare. LC 78-97330. Repr. of 1910 ed. lib. bdg. 18.75x (ISBN 0-8371-2894-3, DUBS). Greenwood.
Durnovo, L. A. Ornaments of Armenian Manuscripts. 1978. 90.00x (ISBN 0-317-14272-0, Pub. by Collet's). State Mutual Bk.
Duro, A., jt. ed. see Migliorini, B.
Durocher, Joseph F. Practical Ice Carving. 112p. 1981. pap. text ed. 11.95 (ISBN 0-8436-2206-7). Van Nos Reinhold.
Durocher, Joseph F. & Goodman, Raymond J., Jr. The Essentials of Tableside Cookery. (Illus., Orig.). 1978. pap. text ed. 5.00 (ISBN 0-937056-00-6, F&B22). Cornell U Sch Hotel.
DuRocher, Richard J. Milton & Ovid. LC 85-47698. 248p. 1985. text ed. 27.50x (ISBN 0-8014-1812-7). Cornell U Pr.
Durodola, James I. Scientific Insights into Yoruba Traditional Medicine. (Traditional Healing Ser.). 1985. 27.50 (ISBN 0-686-85813-1). Conch Mag.
--Scientific Insights into Yoruba Traditional Medicine. (Traditional Healing Ser.). 1984. 27.50 (ISBN 0-932426-17-4). Trado-Medic.
Duron, J. Langue francaise, langue humaine. (Langue Vivante Ser). (Fr). pap. 8.25 (ISBN 0-685-13956-5, 3626). Larousse.
Duroselle, Jean B. France & the United States: From the Beginnings to the Present Day. Coltman, Derek, tr. from Fr. LC 78-1467. (United States & the World: Foreign Perspectives Ser.). 1978. lib. bdg. 18.00x (ISBN 0-226-17408-5). U of Chicago Pr.
Duroska, Lud, jt. auth. see Schiffer, Don.
Durost, Walter N. Children's Collecting Activity Related to Social Factors. LC 75-176734. (Columbia University. Teachers College. Contributions to Education: No. 535). Repr. of 1932 ed. 22.50 (ISBN 0-404-55535-7). AMS Pr.
Duroux, Paul-Emile. Dictionnaire des Anthropologistes. 336p. (Fr.). 1974. pap. 35.00 (ISBN 0-686-57130-4, M-6182). French & Eur.
Durova, N. Your Turn. 221p. 1980. 7.45 (ISBN 0-8285-1857-2, Pub. by Progress Pubs USSR). Imported Pubns.
Durozi, G. Artaud: L'Alienation et la Folie. new ed. (Collection themes et textes). 232p. (Orig., Fr.). 1972. pap. 6.75 (ISBN 2-03-035009-5, 2664). Larousse.
Durozoi, Gerard & Lecherbonnier, Bernard. Andre Breton: L'Ecriture Surrealiste. (Collection Themes et Textes). 255p. (Orig., Fr.). 1974. pap. 6.75 (ISBN 2-03-035025-7, 2664). Larousse.
Durphy, Michael, jt. auth. see Sonkin, Daniel J.
Durr, Frank, jt. auth. see Greene, Orville.
Durr, Karl. The Propositional Logic of Boethius. LC 80-18931. (Studies in Logic & the Foundations of Mathematics). 79p. 1980. Repr. of 1951 ed. lib. bdg. 19.75x (ISBN 0-313-21102-7, DUPL). Greenwood.
Durr, Kenneth & White, Ralph. A Practical Approach to Writing Business Letters. 1984. pap. 17.50 (ISBN 0-8403-3295-5, 40329501). Kendall Hunt.
Durr, Michael. Networking IBM PCs: A Practical Guide. 320p. 1984. pap. 18.95 (ISBN 0-88022-106-2, 125). Que Corp.
--Using Netware. 250p. 1985. pap. 24.95 (ISBN 0-88022-166-6, 183). Que Corp.
Durr, Ruth E. A Shelter from Compassion. LC 56-6375. (Orig.). 1956. pap. 5.00x (ISBN 0-87574-087-1). Pendle Hill.
Durr, Virginia F. Outside the Magic Circle: Autobiography of Virginia Foster Durr. Barnard, Hollinger F., ed. LC 84-2556. (Illus.). 384p. 1985. 24.50 (ISBN 0-8173-0232-8). U of Ala Pr.
Durr, Volker, et al, eds. Imperial Germany: Monatshefte Occasional, Vol. 3. LC 84-40571. 256p. 1986. text ed. 20.00x (ISBN 0-299-97016-7). U of Wis Pr.
Durran, C. P. Dublin Decorative Plasterwork. 1967. 25.00 (ISBN 0-693-01112-2). Transatlantic.
Durran, I. M., jt. auth. see Cashell, G. T.
Durran, J. H. Statistics & Probability. LC 70-96086. (School Mathematics Project Handbks). 1970. text ed. 27.95 (ISBN 0-521-06933-5). Cambridge U Pr.
Durrance, Joan. Armed for Action: Library Response to Citizen Information Needs. 190p. 1984. 29.95 (ISBN 0-918212-71-5). Neal Schuman.
Durrani, Osman. Faust & the Bible: A Study of Goethe's Use of Scriptural Allusions & Christian Religious Motifs in Faust I & II. (European University Studies: Ser. 1, German Language & Literature: Vol. 208). 247p. 1977. pap. 35.90 (ISBN 3-261-02975-7). P Lang Pubs.
Durrani, Robinson. Geophysical Signal Processing. (Illus.). 560p. 1986. text ed. 46.95 (ISBN 0-13-352667-4). P-H.
Durrani, S. A. & Bull, R. K. Solid State Nuclear Track Detection: Principles, Methods & Applications. (International Series in Natural Philosophy: Vol. 111). (Illus.). 336p. 1985. 50.00 (ISBN 0-08-020605-0). Pergamon.
Durrani, Tariq S. & Greated, Clive A. Laser Systems in Flow Measurments. LC 76-26093. (Illus.). 289p. 1977. 45.00x (ISBN 0-306-30857-6, Plenum Pr). Plenum Pub.
Durrant, A. E. The Garratt Locomotive. LC 80-70298. (Illus.). 176p. 1981. 28.00 (ISBN 0-7153-7641-1). David & Charles.
Durrant, Beryl, jt. auth. see Durrant, Philip J.
Durrant, Christopher J., jt. ed. see Bruzek, Anton.
Durrant, Digby. Addle. 1981. 29.00x (ISBN 0-7206-0555-5, Pub. by Owen England). State Mutual Bk.
Durrant, Geoffrey H. William Wordsworth. (British Authors Ser.). 32.50 (ISBN 0-521-07608-0); pap. 10.95 (ISBN 0-521-09584-0). Cambridge U Pr.
--Wordsworth & the Great System: A Study of Wordsworth's Poetic Universe. LC 78-92247. 1970. 34.50 (ISBN 0-521-07704-4). Cambridge U Pr.
Durrant, John D. & Lovrinic, Jean H. Bases of Hearing Sciences. 2nd ed. 304p. 1984. text ed. 23.00 (ISBN 0-683-02736-0). Williams & Wilkins.
Durrant, Michael. The Logical Status of God. LC 72-93886. (New Studies in the Philosophy of Religion). 132p. 1973. 18.95 (ISBN 0-312-49455-6). St Martin.
Durrant, Philip J. & Durrant, Beryl. Introduction to Advanced Inorganic Chemistry. 2nd ed. LC 76-479352. pap. 160.00 (ISBN 0-317-08779-7, 2007227). Bks Demand UMI.
Durrant, Samuel W. & Peirce, Henry B. History of Saint Lawrence County, New York 1749-1878. LC 84-103114. (Illus.). 914p. 1983. Repr. of 1878 ed. 40.00 (ISBN 0-932334-52-0). Heart of the Lakes.
Durrant, Stephen, jt. auth. see Nowak, Margaret.
Durrant, Stephen D. Mammals of Utah: Taxonomy & Distribution. (Museum Ser.: Vol. 6). 549p. 1952. 25.00 (ISBN 0-686-80278-0). U of KS Mus Nat Hist.
--The Pocket Gophers (Genus Thomomys) of Utah. (Museum Ser.: Vol. 1, No. 1). 82p. 1946. pap. 4.25 (ISBN 0-686-80277-2). U of KS Mus Nat Hist.
Durrant, Stephen D. & Crane, Harold S. Three New Beavers from Utah. (Museum Ser.: Vol. 1, No. 20). 11p. 1948. pap. 1.25 (ISBN 0-317-05005-2). U of KS Mus Nat Hist.
Durrant, Stephen D., et al. Additional Records & Extensions of Known Ranges of Mammals from Utah. (Museum Ser.: Vol 9, No. 2). 12p. 1955. pap. 1.25 (ISBN 0-317-05006-0). U of KS Mus Nat Hist.
Durrant, Stephen D., jt. auth. see Woodbury, Angus M.
Durrant, Tom. The Camellia Story. 168p. 1983. 47.95 (ISBN 0-86863-395-X, Pub. by Heinemann Pub New Zealand). Intl Spec Bk.
Durrant, W. R., et al. Machine Printing. (Library of Printing Technology). 1977. 17.95 (ISBN 0-8038-4671-1). Hastings.
Durrbach, F., ed. Choix D'inscriptions De Delos. 1977. 25.00 (ISBN 0-89005-190-9). Ares.
Durrel, Julie, illus. The Pudgy Book of Toys. (Pudgy Board Bks.). (Illus.). 16p. (ps-3). 1983. pap. 2.95 (ISBN 0-448-10201-3, G&D). Putnam Pub Group.
Durrell, Ann, ed. see Chorao, Kay.
Durrell, Doris. The Critical Years: A Guide for Dedicated Parents. 208p. 1984. 19.95 (ISBN 0-934986-12-6); pap. 9.95 (ISBN 0-934986-07-X). New Harbinger.
Durrell, Fletcher. Fundamental Sources of Efficiency. (Management History Ser.: No. 37). 371p. Repr. of 1914 ed. 22.50 (ISBN 0-87960-040-3). Hive Pub.
Durrell, Gerald. Ark on the Move. 1983. 14.95 (ISBN 0-698-11211-3, Coward). Putnam Pub Group.
--Birds, Beasts, & Relatives. 1977. pap. 3.95 (ISBN 0-14-004385-3). Penguin.
--Birds, Beasts & Relatives. 1983. 12.75 (ISBN 0-8446-6071-X). Peter Smith.
--Golden Bats & Pink Pigeons: A Journey to the Flora & Fauna of a Unique Island. pap. 6.95 (ISBN 0-671-50757-5, Touchstone Bks). S&S.
--How to Shoot an Amateur Naturalist. (Illus.). 205p. 1985. 15.95 (ISBN 0-316-19717-3). Little.
--Menagerie Manor. (Illus.). 176p. 1975. pap. 3.95 (ISBN 0-14-002522-7). Penguin.
--My Family & Other Animals. 1977. pap. 3.95 (ISBN 0-14-001399-7). Penguin.
--My Family & Other Animals. 1983. 12.75 (ISBN 0-8446-6073-6). Peter Smith.
--The Stationary Ark. 1984. pap. 6.95 (ISBN 0-671-50758-3, Touchstone). S&S.
--The Talking Parcel. LC 74-23367. (gr. 4-7). 1975. 12.02i (ISBN 0-397-31608-9). Lipp Jr Bks.
--The Whispering Land. (Illus.). 224p. 1975. pap. 3.95 (ISBN 0-14-002083-7). Penguin.
--The Whispering Land. 1983. 11.50 (ISBN 0-8446-6072-8). Peter Smith.
--A Zoo in My Luggage. 192p. 1976. pap. 3.95 (ISBN 0-14-002084-5). Penguin.
--A Zoo in My Luggage. 1983. 11.50 (ISBN 0-8446-6074-4). Peter Smith.
Durrell, Gerald & Durrell, Lee. The Amateur Naturalist. LC 83-47940. (Illus.). 192p. 1983. 22.50 (ISBN 0-394-53390-9). Knopf.
Durrell, Gerald, frwd. by. The Encyclopedia of Natural History. (Octopus Book). (Illus.). 1978. 16.95 (ISBN 0-7064-0676-1, Mayflower Bks). Smith Pubs.
Durrell, Jacquie. Intimate Relations. LC 76-15196. (Illus.). 1976. 8.95 (ISBN 0-8128-2089-4); pap. 2.50 (ISBN 0-8128-7069-7). Stein & Day.
Durrell, Julie. Mouse Tails. LC 84-12638. (Illus.). 32p. (ps-1). 1985. 6.95 (ISBN 0-517-55592-1). Crown.
--Peek-A-Boo. Bahr, Amy & Klimo, Kate, eds. (Illus.). 8p. (ps). 1982. 3.95 (ISBN 0-671-45546-X, Little Simon). S&S.
Durrell, Julie, illus. The Pudgy Book of Farm Animals. (Pudgy Bks.). (Illus.). 16p. (gr. k). 1984. 2.95 (ISBN 0-448-10211-0, G&D). Putnam Pub Group.
Durrell, L. W., jt. auth. see Harrington, H. D.
Durrell, Lawrence. Alexandria Quartet. Incl. Justine; Balthazar; Mountolive; Clea. 1961. Boxed set. pap. 19.50 (ISBN 0-525-47795-0, 01893-570). Dutton.
--Antrobus Complete. LC 85-6995. (Illus.). 224p. 1985. 16.95 (ISBN 0-571-13602-8). Faber & Faber.
--Balthazar. (Alexandria Quartet Ser.: Vol. 2). 256p. 1982. pap. 3.95 (ISBN 0-671-45102-2). WSP.
--Bitter Lemons. (Illus.). 1959. pap. 7.95 (ISBN 0-525-47044-1, 0772-230). Dutton.
--Clea. 1961. pap. 4.95 (ISBN 0-525-47083-2, 0481-140). Dutton.
--Clea: Alexandria Quartet, Vol. 4. 288p. 1982. pap. 3.95 (ISBN 0-671-45103-0). WSP.
--Collected Poems, Nineteen Thirty-One to Nineteen Seventy-Four. Brigham, James A., ed. 352p. 1980. 22.95 (ISBN 0-670-22792-7). Viking.
--Constance. LC 81-69998. 365p. 1982. 15.95 (ISBN 0-670-23909-7). Viking.
--Constance: Or, Solitary Practices. 416p. 1984. pap. 6.95 (ISBN 0-14-007026-5). Penguin.
--The Dark Labyrinth. 1978. pap. 3.95 (ISBN 0-14-005025-6). Penguin.
--Esprit de Corps: Sketches from Diplomatic Life. (Illus.). 90p. 1981. pap. 4.50 (ISBN 0-571-05667-9). Faber & Faber.
--The Greek Islands. 1980. pap. 14.95 (ISBN 0-14-005661-0). Penguin.
--The Ikons, & Other Poems. 2nd ed. LC 80-17105. (Mediterranean Culture Ser.). (Illus.). 64p. 1981. 15.00 (ISBN 0-933806-01-9). Black Swan CT.
--Justine. 1961. pap. 4.95 (ISBN 0-525-47080-8, 0481-140). Dutton.
--Justine. (The Alexandria Quartet Ser.: Vol. 1). 240p. 1982. pap. 3.95 (ISBN 0-671-45104-9). WSP.
--A Key to Modern British Poetry. 1952. pap. 7.95x (ISBN 0-8061-0919-X). U of Okla Pr.
--Livia. 1979. 12.95 (ISBN 0-670-43447-7). Viking.
--Livia: or, Buried Alive. 272p. 1984. pap. 5.95 (ISBN 0-14-007101-6). Penguin.
--Monsieur. 320p. 1975. 12.95 (ISBN 0-670-48678-7). Viking.
--Monsieur. 320p. 1984. pap. 5.95 (ISBN 0-14-007102-4). Penguin.
--Mount Olive: Alexandria Quartet, Vol. 3. 304p. 1982. pap. 3.95 (ISBN 0-671-45105-7). WSP.
--Mountolive. 1961. pap. 4.95 (ISBN 0-525-47082-4, 0481-140). Dutton.
--Nunquam: A Novel. 1979. pap. 4.95 (ISBN 0-14-005189-9). Penguin.
--Pope Joan. LC 82-81088. (Tusk Bks.). 176p. 1984. 22.50 (ISBN 0-87951-963-0); pap. 7.95 (ISBN 0-87951-964-9). Overlook Pr.
--Quinx, or the Ripper's Tale. 224p. 1985. 15.95 (ISBN 0-670-80658-7). Viking.
--Reflections on a Marine Venus. 1978. pap. 3.95 (ISBN 0-14-004686-0). Penguin.
--Sappho: A Play in Verse. 96p. 1967. pap. 4.95 (ISBN 0-571-08161-4). Faber & Faber.
--Sauve Qui Peut. (Illus.). 82p. 1979. pap. 4.95 (ISBN 0-571-09224-1). Faber & Faber.
--Sebastian: Or Ruling Passions. 216p. 1984. 15.95 (ISBN 0-670-62741-0). Viking.
--Sebastian, or Ruling Passions. rev. ed. (Fiction Ser.). 224p. 1985. pap. 5.95 (ISBN 0-14-007705-7). Penguin.
--Sicilian Carousel. 1977. 13.95 (ISBN 0-670-64362-9). Viking.
--A Smile in the Mind's Eye. LC 81-19864. 96p. 1982. 10.95x (ISBN 0-87663-380-7); pap. 5.95 (ISBN 0-87663-576-1). Universe.
--The Spirit of Place: Letters & Essays on Travel. Thomas, Alan G., ed. 432p. 1984. pap. 8.95 (ISBN 0-918172-17-9). Leetes Isl.
--Stiff Upper Lip. 94p. (Orig.). 1983. pap. 3.95 (ISBN 0-571-06722-0). Faber & Faber.
--Tunc: A Novel. 1979. pap. 4.95 (ISBN 0-14-005184-8). Penguin.
--Vega & Other Poems. LC 73-75122. 58p. 1973. 14.95 (ISBN 0-87951-009-9). Overlook Pr.
--White Eagles Over Serbia. LC 58-7779. 1958. 10.95 (ISBN 0-87599-030-4). S G Phillips.
Durrell, Lawrence, jt. auth. see Gascoyne, David.
Durrell, Lawrence, ed. see Lawrence, D. H.
Durrell, Lawrence, ed. see Miller, Henry.
Durrell, Lee, jt. auth. see Durrell, Gerald.
Durrenberger, E. Paul. Agricultural Production & Household Budgets in a Shan Peasant Village in Northwest Thailand: A Quantitative Description. LC 78-13234. (Papers in International Studies: Southeast Asia Ser.: No. 49). (Illus.). 1978. pap. 9.50x (ISBN 0-89680-071-7, 82-90504, Ohio U Ctr Intl). Ohio U Pr.
Durrenberger, E. Paul, ed. Chayanov Peasants, & Economic Anthropology. (Studies in Anthropology). 1984. 27.50 (ISBN 0-12-225180-6). Acad Pr.
Durrenmatt, Friedrich. Der Besuch der Alten Dame. Ackermann, Paul K., ed. LC 60-3863. (Ger). (gr. 11-12). 1960. pap. text ed. 11.50 (ISBN 0-395-04089-2). HM.
--Drei Horspiele. Regensteiner, Henry, ed. LC 79-22768. (Ger.). 1980. pap. text ed. 9.95x (ISBN 0-8290-0116-6). Irvington.
--The Judge & His Hangman-The Quarry. LC 82-81347. (Double Detective Ser.: No. 2). 256p. (Orig.). 1983. pap. 7.95 (ISBN 0-87923-437-7). Godine.
--The Physicists. Kirkup, James, tr. from Ger. 1964. pap. 3.95 (ISBN 0-394-17246-9, E380, Ever). Grove.
--Die Physiker. Helbling, Robert E., ed. (Illus., Orig., Ger.). 1965. pap. 7.95x (ISBN 0-19-500908-8). Oxford U Pr.
--Play Strindberg. Kirkup, James, tr. 1973. pap. 1.95 (ISBN 0-394-17798-3, E-612, Ever). Grove.
--Plays & Essays. Sander, Volkmar, ed. LC 81-22184. (The German Library: Vol. 89). 315p. 1982. 19.50x (ISBN 0-8264-0257-7); pap. 8.95 (ISBN 0-8264-0267-4). Continuum.
--The Quarry. 2nd ed. Bd. with The Judge & His Hangman. (Double Detective Ser.: No. 2). 256p. 1983. pap. 7.95 (ISBN 0-87923-408-3). Godine.
--Der Richter und Sein Henker. Gillis, William & Neumaier, J. J., eds. 1964. pap. text ed. 11.50 (ISBN 0-395-04499-5). HM.
--The Visit. Bowles, Patrick, tr. from Ger. 1962. pap. 4.95 (ISBN 0-394-17239-6, E344, Ever). Grove.
Durrenmatt, Friedrich see Otten, Anna.
Durrer, Gustav T., jt. auth. see Dolder, Eugene J.

Dusthimer, David & Buehholz, Ted. VIC-20. LC 83-51669. (Tool Kit Ser.). 8.95 (ISBN 0-672-22310-4). Sams.

Dustin, P. Microtubules. 2nd rev. ed. (Illus.). 500p. 1984. 75.00 (ISBN 0-387-13283-X). Springer-Verlag.

Dustin, Richard & George, Rickey. Action Counseling for Behavior Change. 2nd ed. LC 77-8686. 1977. 8.50x (ISBN 0-910328-20-X). Carroll Pr.

Duston, Nettie M. & Musso, Laurie D. Some Tales of Mother Earth & Her Children, 3 vols. LC 83-60494. (Illus.). 412p. (gr. 2-5). 1983. Set. 29.95 (ISBN 0-9610150-0-4) (ISBN 0-9610150-1-2, VOL. I) (ISBN 0-9610150-2-0, VOL. II) (ISBN 0-9610150-3-9, VOL. III). Megans Wld.

Duszhanov, D. The Little Jockey. 22p. 1979. 1.99 (ISBN 0-8285-1575-1, Pub. by Progress Pubs USSR). Imported Pubns.

Dutch, Oswald. The Errant Diplomat: The Life of Franz von Papen. LC 78-63665. (Studies in Fascism: Ideology & Practice). 320p. Repr. of 1940 ed. 34.50 (ISBN 0-404-16928-7). AMS Pr.

Dutch, Oswald, pseud. Hitler's Twelve Apostles. facsimile ed. LC 75-93333. (Essay Index Reprint Ser). 1940. 19.00 (ISBN 0-8369-1286-1). Ayer Co Pubs.

Dutch, R. A., ed. see Roget, Peter M.

Dutcher, Nadine. The Use of First & Second Languages in Primary Education: Selected Case Studies. (World Bank Staff Working Paper: No. 504). iii, 62p. 1982. pap. 3.00 (ISBN 0-686-39727-4, WP-0504). World Bank.

Dutcher, R. M., ed. see International Symposium on Comparative Leukemia Research, 4th, Cherry Hill, N.J., 1969.

Dutcher, R. M., ed. see International Symposium on Comparative Leukemia Research, 5th, Padova-Venice, 1971.

Dutcher, Raymond M., jt. ed. see Dameshek, William.

Dutcher, Salem, jt. auth. see Jones, Charles C., Jr.

Dutchess of St. Albans. Where Time Stood Still: A Portrait of Oman. (Illus.). 160p. 1982. 11.95 (ISBN 0-7043-2247-1, Pub. by Quartet England). Charles River Bks.

Du Terme, Laurence. The Flower De Luce Planted in England, Wherein Is Contained the Pronuntiation & Understanding of the French Tongue. LC 72-5977. (English Experience Ser.: No. 505). 68p. 1973. Repr. of 1619 ed. 6.00 (ISBN 90-221-0505-9). Walter J Johnson.

du Terrage, Marc de Villiers see De Villiers du Terrage, Marc.

Du Terte, Estienne see Expert, Henry.

Duthie, Alexander. The Greek Mythology: A Reader's Handbook. 2nd ed. LC 78-12988. 1979. Repr. of 1949 ed. lib. bdg. 22.50x (ISBN 0-313-21077-2, DUGM). Greenwood.

Duthie, Arthur L. Decorative Glass Processes. (Illus.). 280p. 1982. pap. 4.95 (ISBN 0-486-24270-6). Dover.

--Decorative Glass Processes. 1983. 13.25 (ISBN 0-8446-5925-8). Peter Smith.

Duthie, Enid L. The Themes of Elizabeth Gaskell. 217p. 1980. 29.50x (ISBN 0-8476-6224-1). Rowman.

Duthie, Eric. Tall Stories. 1959. 16.50 (ISBN 0-686-18176-X). Havertown Bks.

Duthie, George I. Bad Quarto of Hamlet. LC 72-194428. 1941. lib. bdg. 15.00 (ISBN 0-8414-3881-1). Folcroft.

--Elizabethan Shorthand & the First Quarto of King Lear. LC 72-169522. 1949. lib. bdg. 10.00 (ISBN 0-8414-3882-X). Folcroft.

--Shakespeare's King Lear: A Critical Edition. LC 76-29726. 1949. lib. bdg. 35.00 (ISBN 0-8414-3730-0). Folcroft.

Duthie, H. C., jt. auth. see Contant, H.

Duthie, J. F. Flora of the Upper Gangetic Plain & of the Adjacent Siwalik & Sub-Himalayan Tracts, 3 vols. in 2. 1978. Repr. Set. 31.20x (ISBN 0-89955-267-6, Pub. by Intl Bk Dist). Intl Spec Bk.

--The Fodder Grasses of Northern India. 1982. 2 Vol. Set 120.00x (ISBN 0-686-45805-2, Pub. by United Bk Traders India). State Mutual Bk.

--The Orchids of the Western Himalaya. (Illus.). 1967. Repr. of 1906 ed. 105.00 (ISBN 3-7682-0465-0). Lubrecht & Cramer.

Duthie, R. B. & Bentley, George, eds. Mercer's Orthopaedic Surgery. 8th ed. (Illus.). 1184p. 1983. text ed. 100.00 (ISBN 0-8391-1806-6, 19828). Univ Park.

Dutile, Fernand N. & Gaffney, Edward M. State & Campus: State Regulation of Religiously Affiliated Higher Education. LC 83-27366. 526p. 1984. pap. 19.95 (ISBN 0-268-01712-3). U of Notre Dame Pr.

Dutile, Fernand N., ed. Legal Education & Lawyer Competency: Curricula for Change. LC 81-50458. 160p. 1981. 16.95 (ISBN 0-268-01264-4). U of Notre Dame Pr.

Dutile, Fernand N. & Foust, Cleon H., eds. Early Childhood Intervention & Juvenile Delinquency: As the Twig Is Bent. LC 81-47973. 224p. 1982. 26.50x (ISBN 0-669-05204-3). Lexington Bks.

Dutile, Fernand N., jt. ed. see Gaffney, Edward M.

Dutka. Membrane Filtration. (Pollution Engineering & Technology Ser.: Vol. 17). 632p. 1981. 85.00 (ISBN 0-8247-1164-5). Dekker.

Dutka, jt. auth. see Liu.

Dutka, JoAnna. Music in the English Mystery Plays. (Early Drama, Art, & Music Ser.). (Illus.). 171p. 1980. pap. 10.95 (ISBN 0-918720-11-7). Medieval Inst.

DuToit, Alexander L. Our Wandering Continents: An Hypothesis of Continental Drifting. LC 76-147217. 366p. 1972. Repr. of 1957 ed. lib. bdg. 24.75x (ISBN 0-8371-5982-2, DUWC). Greenwood.

Du Toit, Andre & Giliomee, Hermann. Afrikaner Political Thought: Analysis & Documents, Volume I; 1780-1850, Vol. 22. LC 82-40090. (Perspectives on Southern Africa Ser.). 320p. 1983. 40.00x (ISBN 0-520-04319-7). U of Cal Pr.

Du Toit, Bettie. Ukubamba Amadolo. 1978. pap. 5.95 (ISBN 0-906383-01-3, Onyx Press). Carrier Pigeon.

Du Toit, Briam M. see Toit, Brian M. du.

Du Toit, Brian M. Drug Use & South African Students. LC 78-21910. (Papers in International Studies: Africa Ser.: No. 35). (Illus.). 1978. pap. 7.50x (ISBN 0-89680-076-8, 82-91866, Ohio U Ctr Intl). Ohio U Pr.

Du Toit, Brian M. & Abdalla, Ismail H., eds. African Healing Strategies. (Traditional Healing Ser.). 400p. 1985. 39.95 (ISBN 0-932426-35-2); pap. 20.00 (ISBN 0-932426-36-0). Trado-Medic.

Du Toit, Darcy. Capital & Labour in South Africa. (Monographs from the African Studies Centre, Leiden). 480p. 1981. 55.00x (ISBN 0-7103-0001-8). Routledge & Kegan.

Dutoit, Ulysse, jt. auth. see Bersani, Leo.

Duton, Mark & Owen, David. The Complete Home Video Handbook. LC 82-5410. (Illus.). 1982. 19.95 (ISBN 0-394-52761-5). Random.

Dutot, Charles. Political Reflections on the Finances & Commerce of France. LC 76-146461. Repr. of 1739 ed. lib. bdg. 45.00x (ISBN 0-678-00842-6). Kelley.

Dutourd, Jean. The Horrors of Love. Chancellor, Robin, tr. from Fr. LC 75-3991. 1976. Repr. of 1967 ed. lib. bdg. 37.50x (ISBN 0-8371-7481-3, DUHL). Greenwood.

Dutre, W. L. A European Transient Simulation Model for Thermal Solar Systems. 1985. lib. bdg. 79.00 (ISBN 90-277-2051-7, Pub. by Reidel Netherlands). Kluwer Academic.

Dutro, J. Thomas, jt. ed. see Dietrich, Richard V.

Dutro, J. Thomas, Jr., ed. Carboniferous of the Northern Rocky Mountains. LC 78-74895. (AGI Selected Guidebook Ser.: No. 3). 1979. pap. 12.00 (ISBN 0-913312-10-X). Am Geol.

Dutson, T. R., jt. auth. see Pearson, A. M.

Dutt, Ashok K. Southeast Asia: Realm of Contrasts. 3rd rev. ed. 275p. 1985. 37.50x (ISBN 0-86531-561-2); pap. text ed. 15.95x (ISBN 0-86531-562-0). Westview.

Dutt, Ashok K. & Geib, Margaret. An Atlas of South Asia. 150p. 1985. 28.00x (ISBN 0-8133-0044-4); pap. 15.00x (ISBN 0-8133-0045-2). Westview.

Dutt, Ashok K., ed. Medical Geography South & Southeast Asia. (Illus.). 78p. 1981. pap. 22.00 (ISBN 0-08-026762-9). Pergamon.

Dutt, Ashok K. & Costa, Frank J., eds. Public Planning in the Netherlands. (Illus.). 1984. 29.95x (ISBN 0-19-823248-9). Oxford U Pr.

Dutt, Ashok K. & Noble, Allan G., eds. India: Cultural Patterns & Processes. (Special Study on South & Southeast Asia). (Illus.). 400p. 1982. 20.00x (ISBN 0-86531-237-0). Westview.

Dutt, C. P., tr. see Frolov, Yuril P.

Dutt, Gautam, jt. auth. see Nisson, J. D.

Dutt, Indu, tr. see Tagore, Rabindranath.

Dutt, Nalinaksha. Buddhist Sects in India. 1978. (Pub. by Motilal Banarsidas India); pap. 7.50 (ISBN 0-89684-044-1). Orient Bk Dist.

--Early History of the Spread of Buddhism & the Buddhist Schools. LC 78-72429. Repr. of 1925 ed. 33.50 (ISBN 0-404-17293-8). AMS Pr.

--Early Monastic Buddhism. 1981. Repr. of 1971 ed. 12.50x (ISBN 0-8364-0815-2, Pub. by Mukhopadhyay). South Asia Bks.

--Mahayana Buddhism. rev. ed. 1978. 12.95 (ISBN 0-89684-032-8, Pub. by Motilal Banarsidass India). Orient Bk Dist.

--Mahayana Buddhism. 1976. Repr. of 1973 ed. 11.00x (ISBN 0-8364-0430-0). South Asia Bks.

Dutt, R. C. Socialism of Jaharwalal Nehru. 1981. 18.50x (ISBN 0-8364-0708-3, Pub. by Abhinav India). South Asia Bks.

Dutt, R. Palme. Facism & Social Revolution. 2nd ed. 318p. 1974. pap. 5.95 (ISBN 0-89380-014-7). Proletarian Pubs.

--George Bernard Shaw: A Memoir. LC 77-4096. 1951. lib. bdg. 8.50 (ISBN 0-8414-3819-6). Folcroft.

--Whither China? 1967. pap. 0.40 (ISBN 0-87898-021-0). New Outlook.

Dutt, Romesh. India in the Victorian Age: An Economic History of the People. 628p. 1985. Repr. of 1904 ed. text ed. 100.00x (ISBN 0-86590-705-6, Pub. by Daya Pub Hse India). Apt Bks.

Dutt, Romesh C. The Economic History of India. Incl. Vol. 1. The Economic History of Early British Rule; Vol. 2. India in the Victorian Age. LC 79-80224. 1902-04. Repr. Set. 46.50 (ISBN 0-8337-0981-X). B Franklin.

--Economic History of India, 2 Vols. 817p. 1976. Set. pap. 12.50x (ISBN 0-89684-384-X). Orient Bk Dist.

--Economic History of India, 2 Vols. 2nd ed. LC 67-30372. Repr. of 1906 ed. 57.50x set (ISBN 0-678-06515-2). Kelley.

--A History of Civilisation in Ancient India, 2 vols. 789p. 1972. Repr. of 1888 ed. Set. 29.50x (ISBN 0-89684-403-X). Orient Bk Dist.

--History of India from the Earliest Times to the Sixth Century, B.C. LC 72-14391. (History of India Ser.: No. 1). Repr. of 1906 ed. 32.00 (ISBN 0-404-09001-X). AMS Pr.

Dutt, Romesh C., tr. The Ramayana. Bd. with The Mahabharata. 1972. 12.95x (ISBN 0-460-00403-4, Evman). Biblio Dist.

Dutt, S. C. The Wild Tribes of India. 278p. 1984. text ed. 31.50x (ISBN 0-391-03301-8, Pub. by Cosmo India). Humanities.

Dutt, Shoshee C. Historical Studies & Recreations, 2 vols. LC 72-13307. (Essay Index Reprint Ser.). Repr. of 1879 ed. Set. 51.50 (ISBN 0-8369-8155-3). Ayer Co Pubs.

Dutt, Subimal. With Nehru in the Foreign Office. 1977. 14.00x (ISBN 0-88386-905-5). South Asia Bks.

Dutt, Sukumar. Supernatural in English Romantic Poetry. LC 72-197457. 1938. lib. bdg. 30.00 (ISBN 0-8414-3883-8). Folcroft.

Dutt, Toru. Ancient Ballads & Legends of Hindustan. 1975. pap. text ed. 6.75 (ISBN 0-88253-495-5). Ind-US Inc.

Dutt, Utpal. Towards a Revolutionary Theatre. 1983. 5.50x (ISBN 0-8364-1022-X, Pub. by MC Sarkar Calcutta). South Asia Bks.

Dutt, V. P. India's Foreign Policy. 432p. 1984. text ed. 35.00x (ISBN 0-7069-2657-9, Pub. by Vikas India); pap. text ed. 15.95x (ISBN 0-7069-2656-0). Advent NY.

Dutt, V. P., ed. China: The Post-Mao View. 1981. 12.00x (ISBN 0-8364-0758-X, Pub. by Allied India). South Asia Bks.

Dutt, Vishnu. Gandhi, Nehru & the Challenge. 1979. 14.00x (ISBN 0-8364-0322-3). South Asia Bks.

Dutt, William A. Some Literary Associations of East Anglia: George Borrow, George Crabbe, John Evelyn, Edward Fitzgerald, Charles Lamb, Lord Tennyson & William Wordsworth. 1978. Repr. of 1907 ed. 35.00 (ISBN 0-8492-0689-8). R West.

Dutta, A. K. Indian Artifacts. (Illus.). 30.00 (ISBN 0-89410-501-9, Pub. by UBSPD India). Three Continents.

Dutta, M. & Hartline, Jessie, eds. Essays in Regional Economic Studies. LC 82-71901. (Economic Communications Ser.: No. 1). xii, 289p. 1983. 33.50x (ISBN 0-89386-005-0). Acorn NC.

Dutta, Manoranjan & Alonso, Irma T. Metodos Econometricos. (Span.). 1982. text ed. 11.30 (ISBN 0-538-22880-6, V88). SW Pub.

Dutta, Manoranjan, ed. Studies in U. S.-Asia Economic Relations. LC 83-70889. (Acorn Economic Communication Ser.: No. 2). xvi, 578p. 1985. 58.50x (ISBN 0-89386-010-7). Acorn NC.

Dutta, R. C. Civilization in the Buddhist Age. 209p. 1981. Repr. of 1908 ed. text ed. 16.75x (ISBN 0-391-02435-3, Pub. by Concept India). Humanities.

Dutta, Reginald. Beginner's Guide to Tropical Fish. Rev. ed. (Illus.). 184p. 1984. 14.95 (ISBN 0-7207-1506-7, Pub. by Michael Joseph). Merrimack Pub Cir.

Dutta, S. & Hemalata. Harishchandra. (Illus.). (gr. 1-8). 1979. pap. 2.00 (ISBN 0-89744-155-9). Auromere.

Dutta, S., jt. auth. see Savitri.

Dutta, S. C. The North-East & the Mughals. 302p. 1984. text ed. 40.00x (ISBN 0-86590-222-4). Apt Bks.

Dutta, Sukanta K., jt. auth. see Mohanty, Sashi B.

Dutta, Upendra. Financing Higher Education in Nepal. 78p. 1964. 4.00 (ISBN 0-318-12879-9, 2). Am-Nepal Ed.

Dutta Majumdar, J. & Das, J. Digital Computer's Memory Technology. 2nd ed. 533p. 1985. 29.95x (ISBN 0-470-27419-0). Halsted Pr.

Dutta-Majumder, D., jt. auth. see Pal, S. K.

Duttmann, Martina, et al. Color in Townscape. LC 81-1145. (Illus.). 191p. 1981. 43.95 (ISBN 0-7167-1310-1); pap. 27.95 (ISBN 0-7167-1405-1). W H Freeman.

Dutton, Allen A. & Bunting, Diane T. Arizona Then & Now. LC 81-90280. (Illus.). 171p. 1981. smyth sewn casebound 59.00 (ISBN 0-9606552-0-4); deluxe ed. 450.00 (ISBN 0-9606552-1-2). Agtwo Pr.

Dutton, Alpha C. see White, George.

Dutton, B. The Rancheria, Ute & Southern Paiote Peoples. 1976. 3.95 (ISBN 0-13-752923-6, Spec). P-H.

Dutton, Bertha P. American Indians of the Southwest. rev. ed. (Illus.). 320p. 1983. pap. 14.95 (ISBN 0-8263-0704-3). U of NM Pr.

Dutton, Bertha P. & Olin, Caroline. Myths & Legends of the Indian Southwest. (Bk 2). (Illus.). 1978. pap. 2.95 (ISBN 0-88388-062-8). Bellerophon Bks.

Dutton, Bertha P., jt. auth. see Hewett, Edgar L.

Dutton, Beth & De Meo, Victoria. The Little Black Book: A Guide to N. Y.'s Most Eligible Men. (Illus.). 256p. 1981. pap. 3.95 (ISBN 0-02-097500-7). Macmillan.

Dutton, Beth & DeMeo, Victoria. The Little Black Book: A Guide to the One Hundred Most Eligible Bachelors in Washington D.C. 200p. 1983. pap. 5.95 (ISBN 0-312-48821-1). St Martin.

--The Little Black Book: A Guide to the One Hundred Most Eligible Bachelors in Beverly Hills. 200p. 1983. pap. 5.95 (ISBN 0-312-48818-1). St Martin.

Dutton, Brian. Catalogo-Indice de la Poesia Cancioneril del Siglo XV, 2 Vols. in 1. (Bibliographical Ser.: No. 3). xv, 294p. 1982. 40.00x (ISBN 0-942260-25-2). Hispanic Seminary.

Dutton, Charles J. The Samaritans of Molokai. facsimile ed. (Select Bibliographies Reprint Ser). Repr. of 1932 ed. 23.50 (ISBN 0-8369-5733-4). Ayer Co Pubs.

Dutton, Clarence E. Tertiary History of the Grand Canyon District, 2 vols. LC 77-15074. (Illus.). 1977. Repr. of 1882 ed. 175.00 set (ISBN 0-87905-031-4, Peregrine Smith). Gibbs M Smith.

Dutton, D. & Krausz, M., eds. The Concept of Creativity in Science & Art. (Martinus Nijhoff Philosophy Library: No. 6). 262p. 1981. 31.00 (ISBN 90-247-2418-X, Pub. by Martinus Nijhoff Netherlands). Kluwer Academic.

Dutton, Davis & Dutton, Judy, eds. Tales of Monterey. 170p. 1974. pap. 1.95 (ISBN 0-89174-016-3). Comstock Edns.

Dutton, Denis. The Forger's Art: Forgery & the Philosophy of Art. LC 82-11029. (Illus.). 250p. 1983. 24.50 (ISBN 0-520-04341-3). U of Cal Pr.

Dutton, F. B., jt. auth. see Alyea, Hubert N.

Dutton, F. H., tr. see Mofolo, Thomas.

Dutton, G. F. Camp One. 1983. 20.00x (ISBN 0-904265-18-8, Pub. by Macdonald Pub UK). State Mutual Bk.

Dutton, G. J. Glucuronidation of Drugs & Other Compounds. 288p. 1980. 86.00 (ISBN 0-8493-5295-9). CRC Pr.

Dutton, Geoffrey. The Eye Opener. LC 81-14633. (Paperback Prose Ser.). 151p. 1982. text ed. 14.95 (ISBN 0-7022-1622-4); pap. 8.50 (ISBN 0-7022-1623-2). U of Queensland Pr.

--Patrick White. LC 74-9788. 1962. 8.50 (ISBN 0-8414-3749-1). Folcroft.

Dutton, Geoffrey, ed. Harvard Papers on Geographic Information Systems, 8 vols. 1979. Set. text ed. 180.00 (ISBN 0-201-03920-6). Addison-Wesley.

Dutton, Geoffrey J., ed. Glucuronic Acid: Free & Combined Chemistry, Biochemistry, Pharmacology & Medicine. 1966. 95.00 (ISBN 0-12-225350-7). Acad Pr.

Dutton, H. I. The Patent System & Inventive Activity During the Industrial Revolution, 1750-1852. LC 83-18803. 232p. 1984. 32.50 (ISBN 0-7190-0997-9, Pub. by Manchester Univ Pr). Longwood Pub Group.

Dutton, H. I. & King, J. E. Ten Per Cent & No Surrender: The Preston Strike, 1853-1854. (Illus.). 288p. 1981. 44.50 (ISBN 0-521-23620-7). Cambridge U Pr.

Dutton, Henry P. Principles of Organization As Applied to Business. (Management History Ser.: No. 33). 325p. Repr. of 1931 ed. 20.00 (ISBN 0-87960-067-5). Hive Pub.

Dutton, Joan P. The Flower World of Williamsburg. rev. ed. LC 62-18751. (Illus.). 131p. (Orig.). 1973. pap. 5.95 (ISBN 0-87935-007-5). Williamsburg.

--Plants of Colonial Williamsburg. LC 76-50633. (Illus.). 193p. 1979. pap. 10.95 (ISBN 0-87935-042-3). Williamsburg.

--They Left their Mark. LC 82-83659. (Illus.). 192p. 1983. 15.95 (ISBN 0-937088-05-6); pap. 9.00 (ISBN 0-937088-06-4). Illum Pr.

Dutton, Joan P., jt. auth. see Booth, Letha.

Dutton, John A. The Scientific Objectives, Philosophy, & Management of the MOCAT Project. LC 77-136104. 141p. 1969. 19.00 (ISBN 0-403-04497-9). Scholarly.

Dutton, John A., jt. auth. see Panofsky, Hans A.

Dutton, John L. How to Be An Outstanding Speaker. (Illus., Orig.). 1986. pap. price not set. Life Skills Pub Co.

Dutton, Judy, jt. ed. see Dutton, Davis.

Dutton, June. The Adventures of the S. S. Happiness Crew: Cap'n Joshua's Super Secret: 3rd Adventure. (Illus.). 1982. 5.95 (ISBN 0-915696-50-9). Determined Prods.

--Fourth Adventure of the S. S. Happiness Crew: Visit to a Magic Mountain. (Illus.). 1983. 5.95 (ISBN 0-915696-64-9). Determined Prods.

Dutton, June & Hill, Eric. The Adventures of the S. S. Happiness Crew: Cap'n Joshua's Dangerous Dilemma: 1st Adventure. (Illus.). 1982. Repr. of 1980 ed. 5.95 (ISBN 0-915696-36-3). Determined Prods.

Dutton, June & Perl, Susan. Faith, Hope & Charity. LC 77-78293. (Illus.). 5.95 (ISBN 0-915696-46-0). Determined Prods.

Dutton, June & Schulz, Charles M. Snoopy & the Gang Out West. LC 82-71284. (Illus.). 1983. 6.95 (ISBN 0-915696-55-X); pap. 4.95 (ISBN 0-915696-82-7). Determined Prods.

Dutton, Leslie P., et al, eds. Frontiers of Biological Energetics: Electrons to Tissues, Vol. 1. (Johnson Foundation Colloquia Ser.). 1979. 75.00 (ISBN 0-12-225401-5). Acad Pr.

--Frontiers of Biological Energetics: Electrons to Tissues, Vol. 2. (Johnson Foundation Colloquia Ser.). 1979. 75.00 (ISBN 0-12-225402-3); Set. 125.00. Acad Pr.

Dutton, Lois, jt. ed. see Skubik, Stephen J.

Dutton, Nancy C. Civil Defense: From Town Hall to the Pentagon. Smith, Linda H., ed. 1980. pap. 4.95 (ISBN 0-936386-07-X). Creative Learning.

Dutton, Phyl. Music Clubs, Festivals & Concerts: How to Organize Them. 128p. 1980. pap. 30.00x (ISBN 0-905418-86-7, Pub. by Gresham England). State Mutual Bk.

Dutton, Richard. Ben Jonson: To the First Folio. LC 83-1819. (British & Irish Authors Ser.). 188p. 1984. 29.95 (ISBN 0-521-24313-0); pap. 9.95 (ISBN 0-521-28596-8). Cambridge U Pr.

Dutton, Richard, ed. Ben Jonson: Epigrams & the Forest. (The Fyfield Ser.). (Illus.). 128p. pap. 7.50 (ISBN 0-85635-523-2). Carcanet.

Dutton, Robert R. Saul Bellow. rev. ed. (United States Authors Ser.). 1982. lib. bdg. 13.50 (ISBN 0-8057-7353-3, Twayne). G K Hall.

Dutton, Roderic. An Arab Family. LC 85-10272. (Families the World over Ser.). (Illus.). 32p. (gr. 2-5). 1985. PLB 8.95 (ISBN 0-8225-1660-8). Lerner Pubns.

Dutton, S. P. Depositional Systems & Hydrocarbon Resource Potential of the Pennsylvanian System, Palo Duro & Dalhart Basins, Texas Panhandle. (Illus.). 49p. 1980. 1.50 (ISBN 0-318-03136-1, GC80-8). Bur Econ Geology.

--Depositional Systems & Hydrocarbon Resource Potential of the Pennsylvanian System, Palo Duro & Dalhart Basins, Texas Panhandle. (Geological Circular: No.80-8). 49p. 1980. 1.50 (ISBN 0-318-13665-1). Bur Econ Geology.

--Petroleum Source Rock Potential & Thermal Maturity, Palo Duro Basin, Texas. (Geological Circular Ser.: GC 80-10). (Illus.). 48p. 1980. 1.50 (ISBN 0-318-03137-X). Bur Econ Geology.

Dutton, S. P., jt. auth. see Kreitler, C. W.

Dutton, S. P., et al. Geology & Geohydrology of the Palo Duro Basin, Texas Panhandle: A Report on the Progress of Nuclear Waste Isolation Feasibility Studies (1978) (Geological Circular Ser.: 79-1). (Illus.). 99p. 1979. 2.50 (ISBN 0-686-29328-2, GC 79-1). Bur Econ Geology.

--Petroleum Potential of the Palo Duro Basin, Texas Panhandle. (Report of Investigations: RI 123). (Illus.). 87p. 1982. 5.00 (ISBN 0-318-03264-3). Bur Econ Geology.

Dutton, Tom. The Hiri in History. (Pacific Research Monograph: No. 8). 159p. (Orig.). 1982. pap. text ed. 12.00 (ISBN 0-909150-63-X, 1258, Pub. by ANUP Australia). Australia N U P.

Dutton, William & Kraemer, Kenneth. Modeling As Negotiating. Voigt, Melvin J., ed. (Communication & Information Science Ser.). 272p. 1985. text ed. 37.50 (ISBN 0-89391-261-1). Ablex Pub.

Dutton, William H., jt. auth. see Danziger, James N.

Duttweiler, Gottlieb. Business Leadership & Social Responsibility. 1960. pap. 2.00 (ISBN 0-87744-012-3). Mich St U Pr.

Dutwin, Phillis & Diamond, Harriet. Writing the Easy Way. (Easy Way Ser.). 224p. Date not set. pap. text ed. 7.95 (ISBN 0-8120-2729-9). Barron.

Dutwin, Phyllis, jt. auth. see Diamond, Harriet.

Dutwin, Physsil, jt. auth. see Diamond, Harriet.

Duty, Guy. Divorce & Remarriage. LC 96-2485. 160p. 1967. 8.95 (ISBN 0-87123-097-6, 230097). Bethany Hse.

--Divorcio y Nuevo Matrimonio. 176p. 1975. 2.75 (ISBN 0-88113-060-5). Edit Betania.

--Escape from the Coming Tribulation. LC 75-17979. 160p. (Orig.). 1975. pap. 3.95 (ISBN 0-87123-131-X, 210131). Bethany Hse.

--If Ye Continue. LC 82-2314. 192p. 1966. pap. 4.95 (ISBN 0-87123-243-X, 210243). Bethany Hse.

Duty, Michael. A Guide to Running in Texas. 128p. (Orig.). pap. cancelled (ISBN 0-88415-782-2, Lone Star Bks). Gulf Pub.

Duuren, B. L. Van see Van Duuren, B. L. & Rubin, B. A.

Duursma, E. K. & Dawson, R., eds. Marine Organic Chemistry: Evolution, Composition, Interactions & Chemistry of Organic Matter in Seawater. (Oceanography Ser.: Vol. 31). 522p. 1981. 98.00 (ISBN 0-444-41892-X). Elsevier.

Duus, Erling. Danish-American Journey. 1971. pap. 2.75 (ISBN 0-686-00051-X). Gauntlet Bks.

Duus, Masayo. Tokyo Rose: Orphan of the Pacific. LC 78-60968. 248p. 1979. 14.95x (ISBN 0-87011-354-2). Kodansha.

--Tokyo Rose: Orphan of the Pacific. Duus, Peter, tr. from Jap. (Illus.). 268p. 1983. pap. 4.95 (ISBN 0-87011-607-X). Kodansha.

Duus, Olaus F. Frontier Parsonage. Scott, Franklyn D., ed. LC 78-15205. (Scandinavians in America Ser.). 1979. Repr. of 1947 ed. lib. bdg. 14.00x (ISBN 0-405-11632-2). Ayer Co Pubs.

Duus, Peter. Feudalism in Japan. 2nd ed. (Studies in World Civilization). 1975. pap. text ed. 8.00x (ISBN 0-394-31076-4, KnopfC). Knopf.

--Party Rivalry & Political Change in Taisho Japan. LC 68-21972. (Harvard East Asian Ser.: No. 35). pap. 82.00 (ISBN 0-317-08420-8, 2005490). Bks Demand UMI.

--The Rise of Modern Japan. LC 75-33416. (Illus.). 304p. 1976. text ed. 22.50 (ISBN 0-395-20665-0). HM.

--Topical Diagnosis in Neurology. (Illus.). 471p. 1983. 15.00 (ISBN 0-86577-138-3). Thieme-Stratton.

Duus, Peter, tr. see Duus, Masayo.

Duva, Nicholas, compiled by. Somebody Real. (Illus.). 192p. (Orig.). (gr. 5-12). 1973. 6.95 (ISBN 0-912834-01-3); pap. 3.95 (ISBN 0-912834-04-8). Am Faculty Pr.

Duval, Arnaud, tr. see Wolman, Arnold.

Du Val, Benjamin S., Jr. The Class Action As an Antitrust Enforcement Device: The Chicago Experience (II) 86p. (Reprinted from 1976 ABF Res. J., No. 4). 1976. 2.50 (ISBN 0-317-33317-8). Am Bar Foun.

--The Class Action as an Antitrust Enforcement Device: The Chicago Experience (I) 86p. (Reprinted from 1976 ABF Res. J., No. 3). 1976. 2.50 (ISBN 0-317-33318-6). Am Bar Foun.

--The Human Subjects Protection Committee: An Experiment in Decentralized Federal Regulation. 118p. (Reprinted from 1979 ABF Res. J., No. 3). 1979. 3.25 (ISBN 0-317-33335-6). Amer Bar Assn.

Duval, C. Dictionnaire de la Chimie et de Ses Applications. 3rd ed. 1100p. (Fr.). 1977. 225.00 (ISBN 0-686-56741-2, M-6183). French & Eur.

Duval, Cynthia. Five Hundred Years of the Decorative Arts from the Ringling Collection: 1350-1850. LC 81-85393. (Illus.). 175p. 1981. pap. 10.00 (ISBN 0-916758-08-7). Ringling Mus A.

Duval, Edwin M. Poesis & Poetic Tradition in the Early Works of Saint-Amant: Four Essays in Contextual Reading. 220p. 1981. 16.95 (ISBN 0-917786-23-8). Summa Pubns.

Duval, Elizabeth W. T. E. Lawrence: A Bibliography. LC 74-185877. (Reference Ser., No. 44). 1972. Repr. of 1938 ed. lib. bdg. 49.95x (ISBN 0-8383-1385-X). Haskell.

Duval, Evelyn M. Por Que Esperar Hasta el Matrimonio? Deiros, Pablo A., tr. from Eng. Orig. Title: Why Wait till Marriage? 160p. 1982. pap. 2.75 (ISBN 0-311-46044-5, Edit Mundo). Casa Bautista.

DuVal, F. Alan, et al. Moderne Deutsche Sprachlehre. 3rd ed. 672p. 1980. text ed. 25.00 (ISBN 0-394-32345-9, RanC); wkbk. 9.00 (ISBN 0-394-32406-4); tapes 200.00 (ISBN 0-394-32407-2); individualized instruction program 5.95 (ISBN 0-394-32434-X). Random.

Duval, Francis Y. & Rigby, Ivan. Early American Gravestone Art in Photographs: 201 Outstanding Examples. 1978. pap. 6.95 (ISBN 0-486-23689-7). Dover.

Duval, Hanson R. Aldous Huxley: A Bibliography. LC 72-190714. 1939. lib. bdg. 25.00 (ISBN 0-8414-0812-2). Folcroft.

Duval, J. H. Svengali's Secrets & Memoirs of the Golden Age. 5.95 (ISBN 0-8315-0014-X). Speller.

Duval, Jean-Jacques. Working with Stained Glass: Fundamental Techniques & Applications. LC 74-184975. (Funk & W Bk.). (Illus.). 144p. 1974. pap. 5.95i (ISBN 0-308-10153-7, F112). T Y Crowell.

DuVal, Jim. The Heart of Selling. 112p. 1984. 19.95 (ISBN 0-8403-3201-7). Kendall Hunt.

DuVal, John, jt. auth. see Eichmann, Raymond.

Duval, John, jt. ed. see Eichmann, Raymond.

DuVal, John, tr. Cuckolds, Clerics & Countrymen: Medieval French Fabliaux. LC 81-14731. 192p. 1982. text ed. 17.00x (ISBN 0-938626-06-X). U of Ark Pr.

Duval, John C. The Adventures of Big-Foot Wallace. Major, Mabel & Lee, Rebecca S., eds. LC 36-334. xxxvi, 353p. 1966. pap. 6.50 (ISBN 0-8032-5053-3, BB 343, Bison). U of Nebr Pr.

Duval, Marguerite. The King's Garden. Tomarken, Annette & Cowen, Claudine, trs. LC 81-15934. Orig. Title: La Planete Des Fleurs. (Illus.). 214p. (Fr.). 1982. 17.95x (ISBN 0-8139-0916-3). U Pr of Va.

Du Val, Miles P. And the Mountains Will Move: The Story of the Building of the Panama Canal. LC 69-10086. (Illus.). 1969. Repr. of 1947 ed. lib. bdg. 22.50x (ISBN 0-8371-0400-9, DUBP). Greenwood.

--Cadiz to Cathay: The Story of the Long Diplomatic Struggle for the Panama Canal. 2nd ed. LC 68-23284. Repr. of 1947 ed. lib. bdg. 30.00x (ISBN 0-8371-0065-8, DUCC). Greenwood.

Duval, Nicole. Passion's Tempest. (Orig.). 1982. pap. 3.95 (ISBN 0-8217-1426-0). Zebra.

Duval, Paul-Marie & Hawkes, Christopher, eds. Celtic Art in Ancient Europe - Five Protohistoric Centuries: Proceedings. 1976. 55.00 (ISBN 0-12-785180-1). Acad Pr.

Duval, Quinton. Dinner Music. LC 84-824. (Lost Roads Ser. No. 25). 56p. (Orig.). 1984. pap. 5.95 (ISBN 0-918786-28-2). Lost Roads.

Duval, Shelley & Duval, Virginia H. Consistency & Cognition: A Theory of Causal Attribution. 176p. 1983. text ed. 19.95x (ISBN 0-89859-220-8). L Erlbaum Assocs.

Duval, Virginia H., jt. auth. see Duval, Shelley.

Duvall, Aimee. After the Rain. (Second Chance at Love Ser.: No. 179). 192p. 1984. pap. 1.95 (ISBN 0-515-07594-9). Jove Pubns.

--Brief Encounter. (Second Chance at Love Ser.: No. 252). 192p. 1985. pap. 1.95 (ISBN 0-425-07977-5). Berkley Pub.

--Lover in Blue. (Second Chance at Love Ser.: No. 84). 1982. pap. 1.75 (ISBN 0-515-06695-8). Jove Pubns.

--The Loving Touch. 192p. 1983. pap. 1.95 (ISBN 0-515-07247-8). Jove Pubns.

--One More Tomorrow. (Second Chance at Love Ser.: No. 211). 192p. 1984. pap. 1.95 (ISBN 0-515-07959-6). Jove Pubns.

--Spring Madness. (Second Chance at Love: No. 299). 192p. 1985. pap. 2.25 (ISBN 0-425-08627-5). Berkley Pub.

--Too Near the Sun, No. 56. (Second Chance at Love Ser.). pap. 1.75 (ISBN 0-317-06914-4, 06575-7). Jove Pubns.

Duvall, Betty. Handwriting Abecedarian. 113p. 1983. pap. text ed. 16.95 (ISBN 0-943024-01-3). Can Do Pubns.

--Learn to Write Italic Style: A Programmed Workbook for the Older Beginner. 49p. 1981. pap. 7.50 (ISBN 0-943024-00-5). Can Do Pubns.

Duvall, Charles R., jt. auth. see Krepel, Wayne J.

Duvall, D. C., jt. auth. see Wissler, Clark.

Du Vall, Dean F. Class Prophecy: Murder. LC 80-65177. (Derek Dax Adventure Ser.: No. 2). 228p. 1982. pap. 6.95 (ISBN 0-931232-25-2). Du Vall Financial.

--The Du Vall Method for Acquiring Great Self-Publishing Wealth. 7th ed. 88p. 1980. pap. 25.00 (ISBN 0-931232-10-4). Du Vall Financial.

--The Enchanted Cottage. LC 80-65176. (Derek Dax Adventure Ser.: No. 1). 228p. 1981. pap. 6.95 (ISBN 0-931232-21-X). Du Vall Financial.

--Exactly How to Build a Fortune in Mail Order. 1978. pap. 10.00 (ISBN 0-931232-18-X). Du Vall Financial.

--Grab Your Share of the Wealth. 1978. 100.00 (ISBN 0-931232-17-1). Du Vall Financial.

--How I'm Creating a Fortune in Real Estate Using Other People's Money, Time & Talent. 1975. pap. 32.50 (ISBN 0-931232-12-0). Du Vall Financial.

--How to Average a Thousand Dollars or More per Week in the Stock Market (Bear or Bull) 2nd. ed. 100p. 1980. pap. text ed. 100.00 (ISBN 0-931232-11-2). Du Vall Financial.

--The Princely Profits of Party Plan. 12th ed. 84p. 1980. pap. 10.00 (ISBN 0-931232-08-2). Du Vall Financial.

Duvall, Evelyn M. Marriage & Family Development. 5th ed. LC 76-30744. 1977. text ed. 24.00 scp (ISBN 0-397-47362-1, HarpC). Har-Row.

Duvall, Evelyn M. & Miller, Brent. Marriage & Family Development. 6th ed. 425p. 1984. text ed. 22.50 scp (ISBN 0-06-041826-5, HarpC); instr's. manual avail. (ISBN 0-06-361790-0). Har-Row.

DuVall, J. Barry, et al. Getting the Message: The Technology of Communication. LC 79-57016. (Technology Ser.). 384p. 1981. text ed. 17.95 (ISBN 0-87192-123-5, 000-6); tchr's guide 19.50 (ISBN 0-87192-125-1, 00-6A); postponed activity manual (ISBN 0-87192-124-3, 00-6B). Davis Mass.

Duvall, Lindsay O. James City County, Virginia 1634-1659, Vol. 4. (Virginia Colonial Abstracts, Series II). 1979. Repr. of 1957 ed. 17.50 (ISBN 0-89308-065-9). Southern Hist Pr.

--Lancaster County, Virginia Records, Vol. 2. (Virginia Colonial Abstracts, Series II). 1979. Repr. 17.50 (ISBN 0-89308-063-2). Southern Hist Pr.

--Northumberland County, Virginia 1678-1713, Vol. 1. (Virginia Colonial Abstracts, Series II). 160p. 1979. pap. 17.50 (ISBN 0-89308-062-4). Southern Hist Pr.

--Prince George County, Virginia, Vol. 6. (Virginia Colonial Abstracts, Series II). 80p. 1978. pap. 17.50 (ISBN 0-89308-067-5). Southern Hist Pr.

--York County, Virginia Wills, Deeds, Orders, 1657-1659, Vol. 5. (Virginia Colonial Abstracts, Series II). 1978. Repr. of 1961 ed. 17.50 (ISBN 0-89308-066-7). Southern Hist Pr.

Duvall, P. F. & Husch, L. S. Embedding Coverings into Bundles with Applications. LC 82-8742. (Memoirs of the American Mathematical Society 263). 55p. pap. 9.00 (ISBN 0-8218-2263-2). Am Math.

Duvall, Patricia. How to Marry Money. (Illus.). 130p. (Orig.). 1984. write for info. (ISBN 0-911405-00-3). Shattuck Pr.

Duvall, Sylvanus M. Men, Women, & Morals. LC 72-12636. 336p. 1973. Repr. of 1952 ed. lib. bdg. 17.50x (ISBN 0-8371-6681-0, DUMW). Greenwood.

--Methodist Episcopal Church & Education up to 1869. LC 79-176735. (Columbia University. Teachers College. Contributions to Education: No. 284). Repr. of 1928 ed. 22.50 (ISBN 0-404-55284-6). AMS Pr.

Duval-Thibault, Anna. Les Deux Testaments. (Novels by Franco-Americans in New England 1850-1940 Ser.). 204p. (Fr.). (gr. 10 up). pap. 4.50 (ISBN 0-911409-15-7). Natl Mat Dev.

Duvant, G. & Lions, J. L. Inequalities in Mechanics & Physics. John, C., tr. from Fr. (Die Grundlehren der Mathematischen Wissenschaften: Vol. 219). (Illus.). 400p. 1976. 60.00 (ISBN 0-387-07327-2). Springer-Verlag.

Duve, Christian de see De Duve, Christian.

Duveau, Georges. Eighteen Forty-Eight: The Making of a Revolution. 288p. 1984. pap. text ed. 6.95x (ISBN 0-674-54348-3). Harvard U Pr.

Duveen, Anneta, jt. auth. see Motz, Lloyd.

Duveen, Dennis I. Supplementary Volume to a Bibliography of the Works of Antoine Lavoisier: 1753-1794. 173p. 1965. 26.50x (ISBN 0-8464-0900-3). Beekman Pubs.

Duveen, Dennis I. & Klickstein, H. S. Bibliography of the Works of Antoine Lavoisier: Bibliography of the Works of Antoine Lavoisier: Seventeen Forty-Three to Seventeen Ninety-Four. (Illus.). 491p. 1954. 37.50x (ISBN 0-8464-0192-4). Beekman Pubs.

Duveneck, Josephine W. Life on Two Levels: An Autobiography. LC 78-17903. (Illus.). 382p. 1978. 14.95 (ISBN 0-913232-56-4). W Kaufmann.

Duvenright, Reginald. The Approaching Arab Control of the World's Capital, 2 vols. (Illus.). 131p. 1981. Set. 147.75x (ISBN 0-930008-90-1). Inst Econ Pol.

Duverger, Christian. L' Esprit du Jeu Chez les Azteques. (Civilisations et Societes Ser.: No. 59). (Illus.). 1978. pap. 26.00 (ISBN 90-279-7664-3). Mouton.

Duverger, Maurice. The French Political System. North, Barbara & North, Robert, trs. LC 58-5538. (The Chicago Library of Comparative Politics Ser.). (Illus.). pap. 59.80 (ISBN 0-317-09093-3, 2011226). Bks Demand UMI.

--Political Parties: Their Organization & Activity in the Modern State. 3rd rev. ed. North, Barbara & North, Robert, trs. 1964. pap. 12.50x (ISBN 0-416-68320-7, NO. 2173). Methuen Inc.

Du Vernet, Christopher. Photography & the Law. 160p. 1985. pap. 6.95 (ISBN 0-88908-615-X, 9539, Pub. by Intl Self-Counsel Pr). TAB Bks.

Duverney, Guichard J. A Treatise of the Organ of Hearing. LC 77-147969. Repr. of 1737 ed. 21.50 (ISBN 0-404-08221-1). AMS Pr.

Duvernoy, Emile & Harmand, Rene. Le Tournoi de Chauvency en 1285: Etude sur la societe et les moeurs chevaleresques au XIII Siecle. LC 79-8361. Repr. of 1905 ed. 13.50 (ISBN 0-404-18343-3). AMS Pr.

Duvernoy, H. M. Human Brainstem Vessels. (Illus.). 1977. 180.00 (ISBN 0-387-08336-7). Springer-Verlag.

--The Superficial Veins of the Human Brain: Veins of the Brain Stem & of the Base of the Brain. (Illus.). viii, 110p. 1975. pap. 52.00 (ISBN 0-387-06876-7). Springer-Verlag.

Duvernoy, J. B. Elementary Studies for Piano. Seifert, Hans T., ed. (Carl Fischer Music Library: No. 506). (Illus.). 1908. pap. 3.50 (ISBN 0-8258-0129-X). Fischer Inc NY.

--The School of Mechanism: Fifteen Etudes for the Piano, Op. 120. Seifert, Hans., ed. (Carl Fischer Music Library: No. 361). 1904. pap. 5.00 (ISBN 0-8258-0112-5, L361). Fischer Inc NY.

Duverus, Delamer. The Golden Reed. 2nd ed. LC 77-75697. 1978. 8.50 (ISBN 0-918700-01-9). Duverus Pub.

--The Next Voice You Hear: Editorial Reprints from The American Sunbeam. 1978. pap. 3.50 (ISBN 0-918700-02-7). Duverus Pub.

--Reflections on a Quiet Scene. (Illus.). 23p. 1979. pap. 3.00 (ISBN 0-918700-03-5). Duverus Pub.

--Somatic Reasoning: Teleological Entelechies Patterns in Time. 2nd ed. 36p. (Orig.). 1981. pap. 3.50 (ISBN 0-918700-11-6). Duverus Pub.

Duveyrier, Henri. Exploration du Sahara: Les Touareg du nord. LC 77-87622. (Illus.). Repr. of 1864 ed. 41.50 (ISBN 0-404-16448-X). AMS Pr.

Duvoisin, Roger. Christmas Whale. (Illus.). (gr. k up). 1945. PLB 7.99 (ISBN 0-394-91024-9). Knopf.

--Easter Treat. (Illus.). (gr. k-3). 1954. PLB 6.99 (ISBN 0-394-91106-7). Knopf.

--The Importance of Crocus. LC 81-5030. (Illus.). (ps). 1981. 9.95 (ISBN 0-394-84957-4); PLB 9.99 (ISBN 0-394-94957-9). Knopf.

--Petunia. (Illus.). (gr. k-3). 1950. PLB 7.99 (ISBN 0-394-90865-1). Knopf.

--Petunia, Beware! (gr. 1-3). 1958. PLB 7.99 (ISBN 0-394-90867-8). Knopf.

--Petunia, I Love You. (Illus.). (gr. k-3). 1965. PLB 6.99 (ISBN 0-394-90870-8). Knopf.

--Petunia's Christmas. (Illus.). (gr. k-3). 1985. PLB 7.99 (ISBN 0-394-90868-6). Knopf.

--Snowy & Woody. LC 79-897. (Illus.). (ps-2). 1979. PLB 6.99 (ISBN 0-394-94241-8). Knopf.

--Transactions of the American Neurological Association 1981, Vol. 106. 448p. 1982. text ed. 45.00 (ISBN 0-8261-0483-5). Springer pub.

--Veronica. (Illus.). (gr. k-3). 1961. PLB 9.99 (ISBN 0-394-91792-8). Knopf.

Duvoisin, Roger C. Parkinson's Disease: A Guide for Patient & Family. 2nd ed. 220p. 1984. 25.50 (ISBN 0-89004-904-1); pap. 14.50 (ISBN 0-89004-177-6). Raven.

Duvoisin, Roger C. & Plaitakis, Andreas, eds. The Olivopontocerebellar Atrophies. (Advances in Neurology Ser.: Vol. 41). 304p. 1984. text ed. 49.50 (ISBN 0-89004-958-0). Raven.

Duvoism, R. C., jt. ed. see Birkmayer, W.

Dux, James P. Handbook of Quality Assurance for the Analytical Chemistry Laboratory. 160p. 1985. 28.50 (ISBN 0-442-21972-5). Van Nos Reinhold.

Dux, John A., ed. A Collection of Letters & Addresses Issued by Great Americans in all Walks of Life at the Time of the Unification of Italy. (An American Culture Library). (Illus.). 167p. 1982. Repr. of 1871 ed. 137.45 (ISBN 0-686-83078-4). Found Class Reprints.

Duxberry & Leach. Drugs in Dentistry. 3rd ed. 1986. price not set. PSG Pub Co.

Duxbury, Alison, jt. auth. see Duxbury, Alun C.

Duxbury, Alun C. & Duxbury, Alison. The World Oceans: An Introduction. (Illus.). 475p. 1984. 29.95 (ISBN 0-201-11348-1); instr's manual 2.00 (ISBN 0-201-11364-3). Addison-Wesley.
Duxbury, Janell R. Rockin' the Classics & Classicizin' the Rock: A Selectively Annotated Discography. LC 84-22419. (Discographies Ser.: No. 14). xix, 188p. 1985. lib. bdg. 29.95 (ISBN 0-313-24605-X, DUR/). Greenwood.
Duxbury, Ken. Lugworm Island Hopping. (Illus.). 122p. 1983. pap. 7.50 (ISBN 0-907746-19-5, Pub. by A Mott Ltd). Longwood Pub Group.
Duyckinck, E. A. Cyclopedia of American Literature, 2 vols. Set. 250.00 (ISBN 0-87968-981-1). Gordon Pr.
Duyckinck, Evert A. & Duyckinck, George L. Cyclopaedia of American Literature, 2 vols. Simons, M. Laird, ed. LC 66-31801. 1965. Repr. of 1875 ed. Set. 99.00x (ISBN 0-8103-3021-0). Gale.
Duyckinck, George L., jt. auth. see Duyckinck, Evert A.
Duyff, R. L., jt. auth. see Ohl, S. S.
Duym, A. V. van see DeJong, Dola.
Duyn, H. Van see Cobb, W. A. & Van Duyn, H.
Duyn, J. Van see Van Duyn, J. A.
Duyn, Julia Van see Van Duyn, Julia.
Duyn, Julia van see Van Duyn, Julia.
Duyn, Mona Van see Van Duyn, Mona.
Duyn, Van see Van Duyn.
Duyne, Carl Van see Van Duyne, Carl.
Duyvendak, Jan J., tr. see Ching-Shan.
Duza, M. Badrud & Baldwin, C. Stephen. Nuptiality & Population Policy: An Investigation in Tunisia, Sri Lanka, & Malaysia. LC 77-23888. 83p. (Orig.). 1977. pap. text ed. 4.50 (ISBN 0-87834-028-9). Population Coun.
Duzee, E. P. Van see Van Duzee, E. P.
Duzee, Mabel Van see Van Duzee, Mabel.
Duzer, Charles H. Van see Van Duzer, Charles H.
Duzer, Henry S. Van see Van Duzer, Henry S.
Duzer, T. Van see Van Duzer, T. & Turner, O.
Dverk, Donna & Campbell, David, eds. The Challenge of Diversity: EDRA Proceedings: 1984. 344p. 1984. 35.00 (ISBN 0-939922-05-3). EDRA.
Dvinov, Boris. Ot Legal 'nostik Podpol'-Iu (From Legality to the Underground) LC 67-19592. (Foreign Language Ser.: No. 2). (Rus). 1968. 12.95x (ISBN 0-8179-4021-9). Hoover Inst Pr.
Dvinsky, E. Moscow & Its Environs: A Guide. 430p. 1981. 12.00 (ISBN 0-8285-2239-1, Pub. by Progress Pubs USSR). Imported Pubns.
Dvir, Ori. Off the Beaten Track in Israel. (Illus.). 224p. (Hebrew.). 1985. 14.95 (ISBN 0-915361-28-0). Adama Pubs Inc.
Dvorak, Eileen M. & Showalter, Ray. NCLEX-LPN Examination. 100p. 1982. pap. 6.95 (ISBN 0-914091-10-7). Chicago Review.
Dvorak, G. J. & Shield, R. T. Mechanics of Material Behavior. (Studies in Applied Mechanics: Vol. 6). 1984. 94.25 (ISBN 0-444-42169-6, I-091-84). Elsevier.
Dvorak, G. J., ed. Mechanics of Composite Materials. 184p. 1983. pap. text ed. 40.00 (ISBN 0-317-02631-3, H00273). ASME.
Dvorak, J., et al, eds. Manual Medicine, 1984. Gilliar, W. G., tr. from Ger. (Illus.). 225p. 1985. 45.00 (ISBN 0-387-15097-8). Springer-Verlag.
Dvorak, Jiri, et al. Manual Medicine. Gilliar, Wolfgang, ed. Greeman, Phillip, tr. (Illus.). 180p. 1985. text ed. 39.00 (ISBN 0-86577-124-3). Thieme Stratton.
Dvorak, John & Smith, Marolee. The Instant Expert's Guide to the IBM PCjr. (Orig.). 1984. pap. 9.95 (ISBN 0-440-54064-X, Dell Trade Pbks). Dell.
Dvorak, John, jt. auth. see Osborne, Adam.
Dvorak, John C., ed. see Bennett, M. A.
Dvorak, John C., ed. see Price, Jonathan.
Dvorak, M. Differentiation of Rat Ova During Cleavage. LC 78-13480. (Advances in Anatomy, Embryology & Cell Biology: Vol. 55, Pt. 2). (Illus.). 1978. pap. 46.00 (ISBN 0-387-08983-7). Springer-Verlag.
Dvorak, Max. The History of Art As a History of Ideas. (Illus.). 256p. (Ger.). 1984. 27.95x (ISBN 0-7100-9969-X). Routledge & Kegan.
Dvorak, Patrisha, jt. auth. see Bretz, Mary L.
Dvorak, Paul F., tr. see Hermlin, Stephan.
Dvorak, S. & Musset, A. BASIC in Action. 176p. 1984. pap. text ed. 29.95 (ISBN 0-408-01395-8). Butterworth.
Dvorak, Trisha, jt. auth. see Valdes, Guadalupe.
Dvorin, Eugene P. Racial Separation in South Africa. (Midway Reprint Ser). 1974. pap. 8.50x (ISBN 0-226-17571-5). U of Chicago Pr.
Dvorine, William. A Dermatologist's Guide to Home Skin Treatment. 160p. 1984. 12.95 (ISBN 0-684-17875-3, ScribT); pap. 6.95 (ISBN 0-684-18206-8). Scribner.
Dvorkin, David. Time for Sherlock Holmes. 224p. 1983. 14.95 (ISBN 0-396-08175-4). Dodd.
--The Trellisane Confrontation: Star Trek. (Orig.). 1984. pap. 2.95 (ISBN 0-671-46543-0). PB.
Dvorkin, Elizabeth, et al. Becoming a Lawyer: A Humanistic Perspective on Legal Education, Professionalism. LC 80-6225. 211p. 1980. pap. text ed. 9.95 (ISBN 0-8299-2126-5). West Pub.
Dvornik, Francis. Byzantium & the Roman Primacy. rev. ed. 176p. 1979. pap. 7.50 (ISBN 0-8232-0701-3). Fordham.
--Early Christian & Byzantine Political Philosophy: Origins & Background, 2 vols. LC 67-4089. (Dumbarton Oaks Studies: Vol. 9). 975p. 1966. 50.00x (ISBN 0-88402-016-9). Dumbarton Oaks.
--The Idea of Apostolicity in Byzantium & the Legend of the Apostle Andrew. (Dumbarton Oaks Studies: Vol. 4). 342p. (LC A58-8640). 1958. 25.00x (ISBN 0-88402-004-5). Dumbarton Oaks.
--Legendes de Constantin et de methode vues de Byzance. (Russian Ser: No. 12). 1969. Repr. of 1933 ed. 35.00 (ISBN 0-87569-009-2). Academic Intl.
--The Making of Central & Eastern Europe, Vol. 3. 2nd ed. Zacek, Joseph F., ed. LC 73-90780. (Central & East European Ser.: Cees 3). (Illus.). xxviii, 351p. 1974. Repr. of 1949 ed. 35.00 (ISBN 0-87569-023-8). Academic Intl.
--Origins of Intelligence Services: The Ancient Near East Persia, Greece, Rome, Byzantium, the Arab Muslim Empires, the Mongol Empire, China, Muscovy. LC 73-17098. (Illus.). pap. 87.50 (ISBN 0-317-08176-4, 2050512). Bks Demand UMI.
--Les Slavs, Byzance et Rome Au Onzieme Siecle. (Russian Ser.: Vol. 13). Repr. of 1926 ed. 35.00 (ISBN 0-87569-016-5). Academic Intl.
--The Slavs in European History & Civilization. 726p. 1975. pap. 20.00x (ISBN 0-8135-0799-5). Rutgers U Pr.
Dwan, Lois. Los Angeles Restaurant Guide. LC 76-24713. 192p. 1982. pap. 6.95 (ISBN 0-87477-226-5). J P Tarcher.
Dwan, Lois & Los Angeles Times Staff, eds. The Los Angeles Times Guide to Dining Out in L. A. 1984. pap. 8.95 (ISBN 0-452-25510-4, Plume). NAL.
Dwaraki, Leela, jt. auth. see Blumberg, Rhoda.
Dward, Jeannette W. I Have a Question, God. LC 80-70521. (gr. 3-7). 5.95 (ISBN 0-8054-4265-0, 4242-65). Broadman.
Dwarkai, Leela, jt. auth. see Blumberg, Rhoda L.
Dwarki, Leela, jt. auth. see Blumberg, Rhoda L.
Dwayne, Craig. Somewhere Under Da Rainbow. 32p. 1982. 14.95 (ISBN 0-943758-00-9). Aloha Pr.
Dweck, Carol S., jt. auth. see Langer, Ellen J.
Dweck, J. S., jt. auth. see Mix, T. W.
Dwek, Joe. Backgammon for Profit. LC 75-37885. (Illus.). 1978. pap. 6.95 (ISBN 0-8128-2313-3). Stein & Day.
Dwek, R. A., jt. auth. see Campbell, I. D.
Dwek, R. A., et al, eds. NMR in Biology. 1977. 56.50 (ISBN 0-12-225850-9). Acad Pr.
Dwek, Raymond, jt. auth. see Price, Nicholas.
Dwek, Raymond A. Nuclear Magnetic Resinance (NMR) in Biochemistry: Applications to Enzyme Systems. (Monographs on Physical Biochemistry Ser.). 1973. 42.50x (ISBN 0-19-854614-9). Oxford U Pr.
Dwelley. Spring Wildflowers of New England. (Illus.). 1973. 10.95 (ISBN 0-89272-008-5). Down East.
--Summer & Fall Wildflowers of New England. (Illus.). 1975. 10.95 (ISBN 0-89272-020-4). Down East.
Dwelley, Charles M. & Dwelley, Helen M., eds. Skagit Memories. (Skagit County Historical Ser.: No. 6). (Illus.). 166p. 1979. 16.50 (ISBN 0-914989-04-9). Skagit Cnty Hist.
Dwelley, Helen M., jt. ed. see Dwelley, Charles M.
Dwelley, Marilyn J. Trees & Shrubs of New England. LC 79-52448. (Illus., Orig.). 1980. pap. 12.95 (ISBN 0-89272-064-6). Down East.
Dwelly. Illustrated Gaelic-English Dictionary. 8th ed. (Illus., Gaelic & Eng.). 35.00x (ISBN 0-686-00868-5). Colton Bk.
Dwier, Lois A. Wilderness Wetlands in Spring: A Canoe Trip in the Pine Barrens of South Jersey. Vivian, V. Eugene, ed. (Illus.). 64p. (gr. 4-12). 1983. 8.95 (ISBN 0-9613007-0-1). Edlo Bks.
Dwigans, Cathy M., et al, eds. A Guide to the Museum of Natural History the University of Kansas. (Illus.). 65p. (Orig.). 1984. pap. 2.90 (ISBN 0-89338-023-7). U of KS Mus Nat Hist.
Dwiggins. The Complete Book of Cockpits. (Illus.). 232p. 1982. 39.95 (ISBN 0-8306-2332-9, 2332). TAB Bks.
Dwiggins, Boyce. Automotive Air Conditioning. 5th ed. LC 82-46007. 480p. 1983. pap. text ed. 18.00 (ISBN 0-8273-1940-1); tchr's. guide 5.70 (ISBN 0-8273-1942-8). Delmar.
Dwiggins, Boyce H. Automotive Electricity. (Illus.). 352p. 1981. text ed. 25.95 (ISBN 0-8359-0268-4); pap. text ed. 19.95 (ISBN 0-8359-0267-6). Reston.
Dwiggins, Clare V. School Days: An Original Compilation. Blackbeard, Bill, ed. LC 76-53039. (Classic American Comic Strips). 1977. 16.45 (ISBN 0-88355-633-2); pap. 10.00 (ISBN 0-88355-632-4). Hyperion Conn.
Dwiggins, Don. The Barnstormers. (Illus.). 144p. 1982. pap. 5.95 (ISBN 0-8306-2297-7, 2297). TAB Bks.
--Build Your Own Sport Plane. 1979. pap. 6.95 (ISBN 0-8015-0971-8, Hawthorn). Dutton.
--The Complete Book of Airships: Dirigibles, Blimps & Hot Air Balloons. (Illus.). 352p. 1982. 16.95 (ISBN 0-8306-9696-2); pap. 9.95 o.p (ISBN 0-8306-9692-X, 2300). TAB Bks.
--Flying the Frontiers of Space. (gr. 6 up). 1982. PLB 10.95 (ISBN 0-396-08041-3). Dodd.
--Flying the Space Shuttles. (Illus.). 64p. (gr. 3 up). 1985. 11.95 (ISBN 0-396-08510-5). Dodd.
--Low-Horsepower Fun Aircraft You Can Build. (Modern Aviation Ser.). (Illus.). 1979. pap. 5.95 (ISBN 0-8306-2267-5, 2267). TAB Bks.
--Man-Powered Aircraft. (Illus.). 1979. 9.95 (ISBN 0-8306-9851-5); pap. 5.95 (ISBN 0-8306-2254-3, 2254). TAB Bks.
--Thirty-One Practical Ultralight Aircraft You Can Build. (Modern Aviation Ser.). (Illus.). 128p. (Orig.). 1980. pap. 7.95 (ISBN 0-8306-2294-2, 2294). TAB Bks.
--Welcome to Flying: A Primer for Pilots. (Illus.). 224p. (Orig.). 1984. pap. 13.50 (ISBN 0-8306-2362-0, 2362). TAB Bks.
Dwiggins, W. A. Marionette in Motion. (Illus.). 1976. 3.00 (ISBN 0-89073-041-5). Boston Public Lib.
Dwight, David W., et al, eds. Photon, Electron, & Ion Probes of Polymer Structure & Properties. LC 81-10816. (ACS Symposium Ser.: No. 162). 1981. 44.95 (ISBN 0-8412-0639-2). Am Chemical.
Dwight, Henry Otis, et al, eds. Encyclopedia of Missions: Descriptive, Historical, Biographical, Statistical. 2nd ed. LC 74-31438. 851p. 1975. Repr. of 1904 ed. 80.00x (ISBN 0-8103-3325-2). Gale.
Dwight, Herbert B. Tables of Integrals & Other Mathematical Data. 4th ed. 1961. write for info. (ISBN 0-02-331170-3, 33117). Macmillan.
Dwight, John, jt. auth. see Perkins, Charles.
Dwight, John A. & Peel, William J. Video Reading Technics, Bk. 1. 1976. pap. text ed. 5.30 (ISBN 0-934902-00-3); tchr's ed. 10.00 (ISBN 0-934902-04-6). Learn Concepts OH.
Dwight, John A. & Speer, Dana C. How to Write a Research Paper. LC 79-3012. (gr. 11-12). 1979. pap. text ed. 12.00 (ISBN 0-934902-01-1); tchr's ed. 30.00 (ISBN 0-934902-02-X); work pad 1.20 (ISBN 0-934902-03-8). Learn Concepts OH.
Dwight, John S. Dwight's Journal of Music, 21 Vols. 1852-1881. Set. 1050.00 (ISBN 0-384-13545-5). Johnson Repr.
Dwight, Jonathan, Jr. The Ipswich Sparrow (Ammodramus Princeps Maynard) & Its Summer Home. (Memoirs: Vol. II). (Illus.). 56p. 1895. 4.00 (ISBN 0-318-16024-2). Nuttall Ornith.
--The Sequence of Plumages & Moults of the Passerine Birds of New York, Vol. 13. (Annals of the New York Academy of Sciences). Repr. of 1900 ed. 10.00x (ISBN 0-89072-004-5). NY Acad Sci.
Dwight, Margaret L., jt. auth. see Sewell, George A.
Dwight, Margaret V. A Journey to Ohio in Eighteen-Ten As Recorded in the Journal of Margaret Van Horn Dwight. Farrand, Max, ed. 1912. 39.50x (ISBN 0-317-27489-9). Elliots Bks.
Dwight, Theodore. History of the Hartford Convention. facs. ed. (Select Bibliographies Reprint Ser). 1833. 27.50 (ISBN 0-8369-5326-6). Ayer Co Pubs.
--History of the Hartford Convention. LC 77-99474. (American Constitutional & Legal History Ser). 1970. Repr. of 1833 ed. 52.50 (ISBN 0-306-71855-3). Da Capo.
--Sketches of Scenery & Manners in the United States. LC 82-10258. 1983. 35.00x (ISBN 0-8201-1383-2). Schol Facsimiles.
Dwight, Theodore W., jt. auth. see Wines, Enoch C.
Dwight, Timothy. Conquest of Canaan. LC 78-129380. Repr. of 1785 ed. 12.50 (ISBN 0-404-02226-X). AMS Pr.
--Conquest of Canaan: A Poem. 1788. 11.00x (ISBN 0-403-00414-4). Scholarly.
--Conquest of Canaan: A Poem in Eleven Books. LC 69-13890. Repr. of 1788 ed. lib. bdg. 19.75x (ISBN 0-8371-3407-2, DWCC). Greenwood.
--Greenfield Hill. LC 73-144600. Repr. of 1794 ed. 12.50 (ISBN 0-404-02227-8). AMS Pr.
--Major Poems: 5 Vols. in 1. LC 68-24207. 1969. 70.00x (ISBN 0-8201-1059-0). Schol Facsimiles.
--Remarks on the Review of Inchiquin's Letters. 1972. Repr. of 1815 ed. text ed. 24.00 (ISBN 0-8422-8040-5). Irvington.
--Theology, 5 vols. LC 75-3132. Repr. of 1819 ed. 200.00 set (ISBN 0-404-59136-1). AMS Pr.
--Travels in New England & New York, 4 Vols. Solomon, Barbara M., ed. LC 69-12735. (The John Harvard Library). (Illus.). 1969. Repr. of 1821 ed. Set. boxed 50.00x (ISBN 0-674-90670-5). Harvard U Pr.
Dwighte, Ronald. Lucilla, the Queen: An Allegory. 1984. 8.95 (ISBN 0-533-05896-1). Vantage.
Dwijendra. Business Communities of India. 1985. 26.00x (ISBN 0-8364-1276-1, Pub. by Manohar). South Asia Bks.
Dwinell, Olive C. Story of Our Money. 1979. lib. bdg. 59.95 (ISBN 0-8490-3009-9). Gordon Pr.
Dwinelle, John W. The Colonial History: City of San Francisco. 4th ed. 497p. 1978. 10.00 (ISBN 0-937106-03-8). Ross Valley.
Dwinger, Philip, jt. auth. see Balbes, Raymond.
Dwivedi, A. N. Essentials of Hinduism, Jainism & Buddhism. 148p. 1979. 12.00 (ISBN 0-88065-083-4, Pub. by Messers Today & Tomorrows Printers & Publishers India). Scholarly Pubns.
--Indian Poetry in English: A Literary History & Anthology. 159p. 1980. text ed. 10.50x (ISBN 0-391-01789-6). Humanities.
--T. S. Eliot's Major Poems: An Indian Interpretation. (Salzburg-Poetic Drama: Vol. 61). 145p. 1982. pap. text ed. 25.50x (ISBN 0-391-02731-X, Pub. by Salzburg Austria). Humanities.
--Toru Dutt. (Indian Writers Ser.: Vol. 15). 168p. 1977. 8.50 (ISBN 0-86578-002-1). Ind-US Inc.
Dwivedi, Basant K., ed. Low Calorie & Special Dietary Foods. (Uniscience Ser.). 1978. 46.95 (ISBN 0-8493-5249-5). CRC Pr.
Dwivedi, D., ed. Readings in Indian Public Finance. 1981. 17.00x (ISBN 0-8364-0805-5, Pub. by Chanakya India). South Asia Bks.
Dwivedi, D. N. Fundamentals of Managerial Economics. (Aima-Vikas Management Ser.). 310p. 1984. pap. text ed. 15.95x (ISBN 0-7069-2717-6, Pub. by Vikas India). Advent NY.
--Managerial Economics. 1980. text ed. 22.50x (ISBN 0-7069-0794-9, Pub. by Vikas India). Advent NY.
--Managerial Economics. 2nd rev. ed. 424p. 1982. 50.00x (ISBN 0-7069-1472-4, Pub. by Garlandfold England); pap. 39.00x (ISBN 0-7069-1473-2). State Mutual Bk.
--Principles in Economics. 922p. 1985. pap. text ed. 25.00x (ISBN 0-7069-2716-8, Pub. by Vikas India). Advent NY.
Dwivedi, O. P., jt. auth. see Hodgetts, J. E.
Dwivedi, O. P., ed. The Administrative State in Canada: Essays in Honour of J. E. Hodgetts. 272p. 1982. 30.00x (ISBN 0-8020-5603-2); pap. 10.95 (ISBN 0-8020-6480-9). U of Toronto Pr.
Dwivedi, R. C. Contributions of Jainism to Indian Culture. 1975. 12.95 (ISBN 0-8426-0953-9). Orient Bk Dist.
Dwivedi, R. C., ed. Principles of Literary Criticism in Sanskrit. 1969. 9.95 (ISBN 0-89684-298-3). Orient Bk Dist.
Dwivedi, R. C., tr. The Poetic Light: Kavya Prakasha of Mammata, Vol. 1. 2nd rev. ed. 1977. pap. 8.50 (ISBN 0-89684-290-8). Orient Bk Dist.
Dwivedi, S. Hindi on Trial. 250p. 1980. text ed. 30.00x (ISBN 0-7069-1210-1, Pub by Vikas India). Advent NY.
Dwivedi, S. N., ed. Robotics & Factories of the Future. 650p. 1985. 50.00 (ISBN 0-387-15015-3). Springer-Verlag.
Dwivedi, Sharada, jt. auth. see Allen, Charles.
Dwivedy, S. Quest for Socialism: Fifty Years of Struggle for India. 373p. 1984. text ed. 36.50x (ISBN 0-391-03156-2, Pub. by Radiant Pub India). Humanities.
D'Wolf, John. Voyage to the North Pacific. 1968. Repr. of 1861 ed. 9.95 (ISBN 0-87770-011-7). Ye Galleon.
Dworacsek, Marian. Grievance Arbitration: A Selective Bibliography. rev. ed. LC 83-137314. (Public Administration Ser.: P-1144). 9p. 1983. 2.00 (ISBN 0-88066-394-4). Vance Biblios.
Dworaczek, Marian. Grievance Procedures: A Bibliography. LC 83-181049. (Public Administration Ser.: P-1230). 22p. 1983. 3.00 (ISBN 0-88066-560-2). Vance Biblios.
--Health & Safety Aspects of Visual Display Terminals: A Bibliography. 2nd ed. (Public Administration Series - Bibliography: P-1421). 66p. 1984. pap. 9.75 (ISBN 0-88066-921-7). Vance Biblios.
--Performance Appraisal: A Bibliography. (Public Administration Ser.: Bibliography P-1302). 51p. 1983. pap. 7.50 (ISBN 0-88066-712-5). Vance Biblios.
--Wages: A Bibliography of Statistical Sources. (Public Administration Ser.: Bibliography P 1631). 1985. pap. 4.50 (ISBN 0-89028-301-X). Vance Biblios.
--Women in Banking: A Bibliography. (Public Administration Ser.: Bibliography P 1634). 1985. pap. 2.00 (ISBN 0-89028-304-4). Vance Biblios.
Dworak, Robert J. Taxpayers, Payers Guide to Revolt: Perspectives on the Taxpayers Revolt. LC 80-135. 272p. 1980. 39.95 (ISBN 0-03-056111-6); pap. 18.95 (ISBN 0-03-056109-4). Praeger.
Dworetzky, John. Introduction to Child Development. (Illus.). 550p. 1981. pap. text ed. 25.95 (ISBN 0-8299-0368-2). West Pub.
Dworetzky, John P. Child Psychology. 2nd ed. 625p. 1984. text ed. 26.95 (ISBN 0-314-77981-7). West Pub.
--Introduction to Child Development. 2nd ed. 200p. 1984. write for info. instr's manual (ISBN 0-314-79137-X). West Pub.
--Introduction to Psychology. (Illus.). 600p. 1982. text ed. 25.95 (ISBN 0-314-63168-2). West Pub.
--Psychology. 2nd ed. (Illus.). 650p. 1985. text ed. 29.95 (ISBN 0-314-85231-X). West Pub.
Dwork, Bernard. Lectures on P-Adic Differential Equations. (Grundlehron der Mathematischen Wissenschaften Ser.: Vol. 253). (Illus.). 304p. 1982. 54.00 (ISBN 0-387-90714-9). Springer-Verlag.
Dworken, Harvey J. Gastroenterology: Pathophysiology & Clinical Applications. 660p. 1981. 49.95 (ISBN 0-409-95021-1). Butterworth.
Dworkin. Developmental Biology of the Bacteria. 1985. write for info. (ISBN 0-8053-2460-7). Benjamin-Cummings.
Dworkin, Andrea. The New Womans Broken Heart: Short Stories. LC 79-55919. 56p. (Orig.). 1980. pap. 3.00 (ISBN 0-9603628-0-0). Frog in Well.
--Right-Wing Women: The Politics of Domesticated Females. 256p. 1983. pap. 8.95 (ISBN 0-399-50671-3, Perigee). Putnam Pub Group.
--Woman Hating: A Radical Look at Sexuality. 217p. 1976. pap. 7.95 (ISBN 0-525-47423-4, 0772-230). Dutton.

Dworkin, Anthony G. & Dworkin, Rosalind J. The Minority Report: An Introduction to Racial, Ethnic, & Gender Relations. 2nd ed. 1982. pap. text ed. 22.95 (ISBN 0-03-055186-2). HR&W.

Dworkin, Daniel, jt. auth. see Baumann, Duane.

Dworkin, Daniel M., jt. ed. see Baumann, Duane D.

Dworkin, Florence, jt. auth. see Dworkin, Stanley.

Dworkin, Floss, jt. auth. see Dworkin, Stan.

Dworkin, Gerald, jt. ed. see Block, N. J.

Dworkin, James B. Owners Versus Players: Baseball & Collective Bargaining. LC 81-3472. 320p. 1981. 24.95 (ISBN 0-86569-072-3). Auburn Hse.

Dworkin, Martin, ed. Dewey on Education: Selections, with an Introduction & Notes. LC 59-15893. (Classics in Education Ser.). (Illus.). 1959. pap. text ed. 6.00x (ISBN 0-8077-1263-9). Tchrs Coll.

Dworkin, Martin S., ed. The Literature of Cinema: Series One, 48 bks. 1970. Set. 2045.00 (ISBN 0-405-01600-X). Ayer Co Pubs.

--Literature of Cinema: Series Two, 15 bks. 1972. Repr. Set. 353.00 (ISBN 0-405-03887-9). Ayer Co Pubs.

Dworkin, Ronald. Taking Rights Seriously. 1977. 18.50x (ISBN 0-674-86710-6); pap. 8.95x (ISBN 0-674-86711-4). Harvard U Pr.

Dworkin, Ronald M. A Matter of Principle. LC 84-25122. 480p. 1985. 25.00 (ISBN 0-674-55460-4). Harvard U Pr.

Dworkin, Ronald M., ed. The Philosophy of Law. (Oxford Readings in Philosophy). 1977. pap. 8.95x (ISBN 0-19-875022-6). Oxford U Pr.

Dworkin, Rosalind J., jt. auth. see Dworkin, Anthony G.

Dworkin, Stan. Jockey Club Cookbook. (Illus.). 1984. 21.95 (ISBN 0-87833-452-1). Taylor Pub.

Dworkin, Stan & Dworkin, Floss. The Apartment Gardener. 280p. (Orig.). 1974. pap. 1.75 (ISBN 0-451-08414-4, E8414, Sig). NAL.

--The Good Goodies. 1979. pap. 2.50 (ISBN 0-449-23964-0, Crest). Fawcett.

Dworkin, Stanley & Dworkin, Florence. Bake Your Own Bread. (Illus.). 224p. 1973. pap. 2.25 (ISBN 0-451-11708-5, AE1708, Sig). NAL.

Dworkin, Susan. Desperately Seeking Susan. 1985. pap. 4.95 (ISBN 0-517-55976-5). Crown.

--Double De Palma: A Film Study with Brian De Palma. (Illus.). 256p. 1984. 14.95 (ISBN 0-937858-42-0); pap. 8.95 (ISBN 0-937858-43-9). Newmarket.

--Making Tootsie: A Film Study With Dustin Hoffman & Sydney Pollack. LC 83-2355. (Illus.). 192p. 1983. pap. 7.95 (ISBN 0-937858-19-6). Newmarket.

Dworkin, Susan, jt. auth. see Cooke, Cynthia W.

Dworman, Thomas, jt. auth. see Schramm, Jack E.

Dworsky, Lawrence N. Modern Transmission Line Theory & Applications. LC 79-9082. 236p. 1979. 34.95x (ISBN 0-471-04086-X, Pub. by Wiley-Interscience). Wiley.

Dworsky, Leonard B., et al, eds. see Symposium on Social & Economic Aspects of Water Resources Development, Ithaca, NY, 1971.

Dwoskin, Robert P. The Rights of the Public Employee. 180p. 1978. 15.00 (ISBN 0-8389-0257-X). ALA.

Dwoskin, Stephen. Film Is: The International Free Cinema. LC 75-7685. (Illus.). 272p. 1985. 10.95 (ISBN 0-87951-036-6); pap. 8.95 (ISBN 0-87951-072-2). Overlook Pr.

Dwyer, Anthony P., jt. auth. see Nelson, Carl L.

Dwyer, Corinne, jt. auth. see Hollatz, Tom.

Dwyer, D. J., ed. China Now: An Introductory Survey with Readings. LC 73-87225. (Illus.). pap. 130.00 (ISBN 0-317-11042-X, 2022526). Bks Demand UMI.

Dwyer, Daisy H. Images & Self-Images: Male & Female in Morocco. (Illus.). 194p. 1978. 21.00x (ISBN 0-231-04302-3); pap. 10.50 (ISBN 0-231-04303-1). Columbia U Pr.

Dwyer, David. Ariana Olisvos: Her Last Works & Days. LC 76-8752. 80p. 1976. lib. bdg. 8.00x (ISBN 0-87023-218-5); pap. 4.50 (ISBN 0-87023-219-3). U of Mass Pr.

Dwyer, De see De Dwyer.

Dwyer, Edward B., jt. auth. see Dwyer, Jane P.

Dwyer, F. P. & Mellor, D. P., eds. Chelating Agents & Metal Chelates. 1964. 76.00 (ISBN 0-12-225950-5). Acad Pr.

Dwyer, Francis G., jt. ed. see Stucky, Galen D.

Dwyer, Frank. Looking Wayward. 1974. pap. 2.00 (ISBN 0-931848-04-0). Dryad Pr.

Dwyer, Fred. Georgian People. 1978. 14.95 (ISBN 0-7134-0045-5, Pub. by Batsford England). David & Charles.

Dwyer, J. & Mason, R., eds. New Perspectives on the Politics & Culture of Early Modern Scotland. 330p. 1982. text ed. 32.00x (ISBN 0-85976-066-9, Pub. by Alan Sutton England). Humanities.

Dwyer, J. M., jt. auth. see PreTest Service, Inc.

Dwyer, James. Private Pilot's Blue Book. LC 76-41837. 1977. 9.95 (ISBN 0-685-81548-X). Macmillan.

--The Private Pilot's Blue Book. 1979. Repr. of 1977 ed. 9.95 (ISBN 0-8128-2146-7). Stein & Day.

Dwyer, James H. Statistical Models for the Social & Behavioral Sciences. (Illus.). 1983. text ed. 39.95x (ISBN 0-19-503145-8). Oxford U Pr.

Dwyer, Jane P. & Dwyer, Edward B. Traditional Art of Africa, Oceania, & the Americas. LC 73-75844. (Illus.). 1973. 5.95 (ISBN 0-88401-014-7); pap. 5.95. Fine Arts Mus.

Dwyer, Jeffrey R., jt. auth. see Madison, Michael T.

Dwyer, Joesph D., ed. Slovenes in the United States & Canada: A Bibliography. LC 81-83551. (IHRC Ethnic Bibliography Ser.: No. 3). (Illus.). xiv, 196p. 1981. pap. text ed. 7.00 (ISBN 0-932833-02-0). Immig His Res.

Dwyer, Johanna, jt. ed. see Mayer, Jean.

Dwyer, John C. Church History: Twenty Centuries of Catholic Christianity. 384p. (Orig.). 1985. pap. 9.95 (ISBN 0-8091-2686-9). Paulist Pr.

--Son of Man & Son of God: A New Language for Faith. 160p. 1983. pap. 7.95 (ISBN 0-8091-2505-6). Paulist Pr.

Dwyer, Joseph D. Russia, the Soviet Union & Eastern Europe: A Survey of Holdings at the Hoover Institution on War, Revolution & Peace. LC 78-70888. (Survey Ser.: No. 6). 245p. 1980. 18.95x (ISBN 0-8179-5011-7). Hoover Inst Pr.

Dwyer, Joyce M. Human Reproduction: The Female System & the Neonate. LC 76-2580. 209p. 1976. text ed. 7.95x (ISBN 0-8036-2970-2). Davis Co.

Dwyer, Judith A., ed. The Catholic Bishops & Nuclear War: A Critique & Analysis of the Pastoral, the Challenge of Peace. 120p. 1984. pap. 6.50 (ISBN 0-87840-409-0). Georgetown U Pr.

--Questions of Special Urgency: The Church in the Modern World Twenty Years after Vatican II. 200p. (Orig.). 1985. pap. 9.95 (ISBN 0-87840-425-2). Georgetown U Pr.

Dwyer, June. The Discipline of Crevices. 64p. (Orig.). 1982. pap. 3.95 (ISBN 0-939666-38-3). Yosemite Natl Hist.

Dwyer, Karen & Brown, Patrika. The Erotic Baker Cookbook. LC 83-8356. (Illus.). 160p. 1983. pap. 6.95 (ISBN 0-452-25439-6, Plume). NAL.

Dwyer, Kevin. Moroccan Dialogues: Anthropology in Question. LC 82-15167. (Illus.). 288p. 1982. text ed. 29.50x (ISBN 0-8018-2759-0). Johns Hopkins.

Dwyer, M. J., ed. The Performance of Off-Road Vehicles & Machines: Proceedings of the 8th International ISTVS Conference, Cambridge, August 1984. 120p. 1984. pap. 30.00 (ISBN 0-08-031655-7). Pergamon.

Dwyer, Margaret A., jt. auth. see Adams, Judith-Anne.

Dwyer, O. E. Boiling Liquid-Metal Heat Transfer. LC 75-11012. (Nuclear Science Technology Ser.). (Illus.). 1976. text ed. 37.95 (ISBN 0-89448-000-6, 300008). Am Nuclear Soc.

Dwyer, P. Siege of Londonderry. 1971. Repr. of 1689 ed. 17.00x (ISBN 0-8464-0847-3). Beekman Pubs.

Dwyer, Peter, et al. Confronting School & Work: Youth & Class Cultures in Australia. (Studies in Society Ser.: No. 23). 188p. 1984. text ed. 30.00x (ISBN 0-86861-279-0). Allen Unwin.

Dwyer, Rex, jt. auth. see Rozycki, William.

Dwyer, Richard A. Boethian Fictions: Narratives in the Medieval French Versions of the Consolatio Philosophiae. LC 75-36477. 1976. 8.00x (ISBN 0-910956-57-X). Medieval Acad.

Dwyer, Richard A. & Lingenfelter, Richard E. Lying on the Eastern Slope: James Townsend's Comic Journalism on the Mining Frontier. LC 84-2251. (Illus.). 175p. 1984. 15.00 (ISBN 0-8130-0780-1). U Presses Fla.

Dwyer, Richard A., jt. ed. see Lingenfelter, Richard E.

Dwyer, Richard E. Labor Education in the U. S. An Annotated Bibliography. LC 77-21572. 292p. 1977. 17.50 (ISBN 0-8108-1058-1). Scarecrow.

Dwyer, Robert J. The Gentile Comes to Utah. 270p. 1971. 7.95 (ISBN 0-914740-05-9). Western Epics.

Dwyer, T. & Critchfield, M. You Just Bought a Personal What? 1980. 11.95 (ISBN 0-07-018492-5). McGraw.

Dwyer, T. Ryle. De Valera's Darkest Hour: In Search of National Independence 1919-1932. 190p. (Orig.). 1982. pap. 8.95 (ISBN 0-85342-676-7, Pub. by Mercier Pr Ireland). Irish Bk Ctr.

--De Valera's Finest Hour: In Search of National Independence 1932-1959. 205p. (Orig.). 1982. pap. 8.95 (ISBN 0-85342-675-9, Pub. by Mercier Pr Ireland). Irish Bk Ctr.

--Eamon de Valera. (Gill's Irish Lives Ser.). 156p. 1980. 15.95 (ISBN 0-7171-1081-8, Pub. by Gill & Macmillan Ireland); pap. 5.95 (ISBN 0-7171-0964-X). Irish Bk Ctr.

--Irish Neutrality & the U.S.A. 1939-1947. 241p. 1977. 20.00x (ISBN 0-87471-994-1). Rowman.

--Michael Collins & the Treaty: His Differences with de Valera. 180p. (Orig.). 1981. pap. 7.50 (ISBN 0-85342-667-8, Pub. by Mercier Pr Ireland). Irish Bk Ctr.

Dwyer, Terence. Teaching Musical Appreciation. 1967. 8.00 (ISBN 0-19-317409-X). Oxford U Pr.

Dwyer, Terrence, et al. Making Electronic Music: A Course for Schools, Bks 1 & 2. (Illus.). (gr. k-6). 1975. Bk. 1. pap. 6.75 (ISBN 0-19-321071-1); Bk. 2. pap. 6.75 (ISBN 0-19-321072-X); tchr. ed. 10.75 (ISBN 0-19-321070-3); source material 1 11.00, incl. 2-45 rpm mono records (ISBN 0-19-321073-8); source material 2 11.00, incl. 2-45 rpm mono records (ISBN 0-19-321074-6). Oxford U Pr.

Dwyer, Thomas & Critchfield, Margot. Bit of BASIC. LC 80-11428. 192p. 1980. pap. text ed. 8.95 (ISBN 0-201-03115-9). Addison-Wesley.

--Pocket Guide to CP-M. pap. 6.95 (ISBN 0-201-10363-X). Addison-Wesley.

Dwyer, Thomas & Kaufman, Michael. A Guided Tour for Computer Programming in BASIC. (Illus.). 1973. 7.60 (ISBN 0-395-14716-6). HM.

Dwyer, Thomas, jt. auth. see Critchfield, Margot.

Dwyer, Thomas A. & Critchfield, Margot A. BASIC & the Personal Computer. (Illus.). 438p. 1978. pap. 15.95 (ISBN 0-201-01589-7). Addison-Wesley.

Dwyer, Thomas A. & Critchfield, Margot. A Bit of Applesoft BASIC. (Illus.). 240p. 1985. pap. 12.95 (ISBN 0-201-11161-6). Addison-Wesley.

--A Bit of IBM BASIC. 240p. 1984. pap. 12.95 (ISBN 0-201-11162-4). Addison-Wesley.

--CP-M & the Personal Computer: Popular. LC 82-20703. (Microcomputer Bks.). 280p. 1983. pap. 19.95 (ISBN 0-201-10355-9). Addison-Wesley.

--Structured Program Design with the TRS-80 BASIC. (Illus.). 352p. 1983. pap. 17.95 (ISBN 0-07-018493-3, BYTE Bks). McGraw.

Dwyer, Thomas A., et al. BASIC: A Guide to Structured Programming. LC 84-61356. 384p. 1984. pap. text ed. 18.95 (ISBN 0-395-35653-9); instr's manual 2.00 (ISBN 0-395-35726-8). HM.

Dwyer, Willaim M. The Day Is Ours! November 1776-January 1777: An Inside View of the Battles of Trenton & Princeton. (Illus.). 512p. 1983. 22.50 (ISBN 0-670-11446-4). Viking.

Dwyer, William J. Bhakti in Kabir. 1983. 20.00x (ISBN 0-8364-0999-X, Pub. by Assoc Bks Indian). South Asia Bks.

Dwyer, William L. The Goldmark Case: An American Libel Trial. LC 84-40326. 304p. 1984. 16.95 (ISBN 0-295-96163-5). U of Wash Pr.

Dwyer, William W. A Study of John Webster's Use of Renaissance Natural & Moral Philosophy. (Salzburg Studies in English Literature, Jacobean Drama Studies: No. 18). 206p. 1973. pap. text ed. 25.50x (ISBN 0-391-01368-8). Humanities.

Dwyer-Joyce, Alice. Gibbet Fen. 1984. 10.95 (ISBN 0-312-32701-3). St Martin.

--The Unwinding Corner. 205p. 1983. 10.95 (ISBN 0-312-83377-6). St Martin.

Dwyre, Bill, ed. Los Angeles Times 1984 Olympic Sports Pages. 1984. 20.00 (ISBN 0-8109-1286-4). Abrams.

Dwyre, Bill, ed. see Los Angeles Times Sports Staff.

Dyachenko, P. & Mirotvorsky, S. Precast Reinforced Concrete. (Russian Monographs). 240p. 1969. 69.50 (ISBN 0-677-20780-8). Gordon.

Dyachenko, P. E., et al. Actual Contact Area Between Touching Surfaces. LC 64-13145. 1964. 22.50x (ISBN 0-306-10678-7, Consultants). Plenum Pub.

Dyachenko, V. F. Basic Computational Math. 125p. 1979. pap. 4.95 (ISBN 0-8285-1593-X, Pub. by Mir Pubs USSR). Imported Pubns.

Dyadkin, Iosif G. Unnatural Deaths in the U. S. S. R., 1928-1954. Deruguine, Tania, tr. from Rus. LC 82-8455. (Illus.). 80p. (Orig.). 1983. pap. text ed. 6.95x (ISBN 0-87855-919-1). Transaction Bks.

Dyak, Miriam. Dying. LC 78-70873. 1978. pap. 3.00 (ISBN 0-934678-00-6). New Victoria Pubs.

--Fire under Water. LC 77-78508. 1977. pap. 3.00 (ISBN 0-934678-01-4). New Victoria Pubs.

Dyal, Carole, jt. auth. see Morrow, Carolyn C.

Dyal, Donald H. Addison Mizner: The Palm Beach Architect. (Architecture Ser.: Bibliography A 1341). 1985. pap. 2.00 (ISBN 0-89028-311-7). Vance Biblios.

Dyal, James A. Study Guide for Basic Economics. 170p. 1985. pap. 8.00 (ISBN 0-317-30109-8). Macmillan.

Dyal, James A. & Karatjas, Nicholas. Basic Economics. 520p. 1985. text ed. write for info. (ISBN 0-02-331200-9). Macmillan.

Dyba, Thomas J. Seventeen Years at Eighth & Jackson. (Illus.). 68p. (Orig.). 1982. pap. 4.00 (ISBN 0-931090-03-2). I B C Pubns.

--The Story of the Only Home Abraham Lincoln Ever Owned. (Illus.). 16p. (Orig.). 1977. pap. 1.70 (ISBN 0-931090-00-8). I B C Pubns.

Dyball, G. E. Mathematics for Technician Engineers: Levels 4 & 5. 384p. 1983. write for info. (ISBN 0-07-084664-2). McGraw.

Dyballa, Cynthia D., et al. The Tug Hill Program: A Regional Planning Option for Rural Areas. LC 81-8999. (Illus.). 208p. 1981. pap. text ed. 11.95x (ISBN 0-8156-2241-4). Syracuse U Pr.

Dybek, Stuart. Brass Knuckles. LC 79-4700. (Pitt Poetry Ser.). 1979. 12.95x (ISBN 0-8229-3399-3); pap. 5.95 (ISBN 0-8229-5307-2). U of Pittsburgh Pr.

--Childhood & Other Neighborhoods. 1980. 9.95 (ISBN 0-670-21618-6). Viking.

Dyboski, Roman. Outlines of Polish History. LC 78-24236. 1979. Repr. of 1941 ed. lib. bdg. 24.75x (ISBN 0-313-20831-X, DYOP). Greenwood.

--Rise & Fall in Shakespeare's Dramatic Art. LC 73-13527. 1923. lib. bdg. 8.50 (ISBN 0-8414-3679-7). Folcroft.

--Seven Years in Russia & Siberia, 1914-1921. Coleman, Marion M., tr. from Polish. LC 79-137001. (Illus., Orig.). 1971. pap. 5.00 (ISBN 0-910366-09-8). Alliance Coll.

--Tennysons Sprache und Stil. 1907. pap. 25.00 (ISBN 0-384-13620-6). Johnson Repr.

Dyboski, Roman, ed. see Hill, Richard.

Dybovskaia, V. & Kirillova, I. Dictionnaire Geologique: Francais-Russe. 406p. (Fr. & Rus.). 1958. leatherette 4.95 (ISBN 0-686-92570-X, M-9099). French & Eur.

Dybowski, C. R., jt. auth. see Gerstein, B. C.

Dybwad, Gunnar. Challenges in Mental Retardation. LC 64-14238. Repr. of 1964 ed. 74.80 (ISBN 0-8357-9059-2, 2011001). Bks Demand UMI.

Dybwad, Gunnar & Dybwad, Rosemary. Severe Mental Retardation. 86p. 1978. 3.50 (ISBN 0-318-15726-8, 1170). NIMR.

Dybwad, Rosemary, jt. auth. see Dybwad, Gunnar.

Dyce, Alexander. A Few Notes on Shakespeare. LC 71-164813. Repr. of 1853 ed. 16.00 (ISBN 0-404-02228-6). AMS Pr.

--Glossary of the Works of William Shakespeare. (Library of Literature, Drama & Criticism). Repr. of 1902 ed. lib. bdg. 48.00 (ISBN 0-384-13635-4). Johnson Repr.

--A Glossary to the Works of William Shakespeare. 69.95 (ISBN 0-8490-0241-9). Gordon Pr.

--Remarks on Mister J. P. Collier's & Mister C. Knight's Editions of Shakespeare. LC 79-164815. Repr. of 1844 ed. 24.00 (ISBN 0-404-02230-8). AMS Pr.

--Reminiscences of Alexander Dyce. Schrader, Richard J., ed. LC 75-157716. (Illus.). 272p. 1972. 11.00 (ISBN 0-8142-0160-1). Ohio St U Pr.

--Strictures on Mr. Colliers New Edition of Shakespeare, 1858. LC 72-164816. Repr. of 1859 ed. 20.00 (ISBN 0-404-02231-6). AMS Pr.

Dyce, Alexander, ed. Timon, a Play. LC 75-16481. Repr. of 1842 ed. 11.50 (ISBN 0-404-02229-4). AMS Pr.

Dyce, Alexander, ed. see Akenside, Mark.

Dyce, Alexander, ed. see Bentley, Richard.

Dyce, Alexander, ed. see Skelton, John.

Dyce, J. R. Patrick White As Playwright. 1974. 19.95x (ISBN 0-7022-0854-X). U of Queensland Pr.

Dyce, James M. Stress & Decision Making in the Dental Practice. (Illus.). 165p. 1973. 24.00 (ISBN 0-931386-72-1). Quint Pub Co.

Dyche, June. Educational Program Development for Employees in Health Care Agencies. 384p. (Orig.). 1982. pap. text ed. 23.50 (ISBN 0-9609732-0-6). Tri-Oak.

Dyche, Thomas. A New General English Dictionary. 1971. Repr. of 1723 ed. 114.25x (ISBN 3-4870-4398-X). Adlers Foreign Bks.

Dychtwald, Ken. Bodymind. 1984. pap. 3.50 (ISBN 0-515-07900-6). Jove Pubns.

Dyck, et al. Computing: An Introduction to Structured Problem Solving Using Pascal. 1981. text ed. 26.95 (ISBN 0-8359-0902-6); instr's. manual free (ISBN 0-8359-0903-4). Reston.

--Introduction to Computing. 1982. 24.95 (ISBN 0-8359-3158-7). Reston.

Dyck, Andrew R., ed. Epimerismi Homerici: Pars Prior: Epimerismos continens qui ad Iliadis librum A pertinent. 340p. (Latin.). 1983. 88.00 (ISBN 3-11-006556-8). De Gruyter.

Dyck, Anthony Van see Van Dyck, Sir Anthony.

Dyck, Arthur J. On Human Care: An Introduction to Ethics. LC 76-52490. (Orig.). 1977. pap. 5.50 (ISBN 0-687-28845-2). Abingdon.

Dyck, C. J. An Introduction to Mennonite History. rev. ed. LC 81-1958. 400p. 1981. 12.95 (ISBN 0-8361-1955-X). Herald Pr.

Dyck, C. J., ed. Something Meaningful for God. LC 80-10975. (MCC Story Ser.: Vol. 4). 408p. (Orig.). 1981. pap. 7.95x (ISBN 0-8361-1244-X). Herald Pr.

Dyck, Cornelius J. From the Files of the MCC. LC 80-10975. (MCC Story Ser.: Vol. 1). 168p. 1980. pap. 3.95x (ISBN 0-8361-1229-6). Herald Pr.

--An Introduction to Mennonite History. LC 81-1958. 400p. 1981. pap. 11.95. Herald Pr.

--Responding to Worldwide Needs. LC 80-10975. (MCC Story Ser.: Vol. 2). 168p. 1980. pap. 3.95x (ISBN 0-8361-1230-X). Herald Pr.

--Something Meaningful for God. LC 80-10975. (Mennonite Central Committee Story Ser.). 408p. 1981. pap. 7.95. Herald Hse.

--Twelve Becoming, Biographies of Mennonite Disciples from the Sixteenth to the Twentieth Century. LC 73-75174. 1973. pap. 4.50 (ISBN 0-87303-865-7). Faith & Life.

--Witness & Service in North America. LC 80-10975. (MCC Story Ser.: Vol. 3). 1980. pap. 3.95x (ISBN 0-8361-1231-8). Herald Pr.

Dyck, J. W. Boris Pasternak. (World Authors Ser.). lib. bdg. 16.95 (ISBN 0-8057-2678-0; Twayne). G K Hall.

Dyck, Martin. Novalis & Mathematics. LC 76-164817. (North Carolina. University. Studies in the Germanic Languages & Literatures: No. 27). Repr. of 1960 ed. 27.00 (ISBN 0-404-50927-4). AMS Pr.

Dyck, Paul. Brule. 2nd ed. LC 75-134924. (Western Classic Bk.). (Illus.). 363p. 1985. Repr. of 1971 ed. 36.00 (ISBN 0-87358-370-1). Northland.

Dyck, Peter, ed. Stereotaxic Biopsy & Brachytherapy of Brain Tumors. LC 83-14500. (Illus.). 240p. 1983. text ed. 64.50 (ISBN 0-8391-1926-7, 20400). Univ Park.

Dyck, Peter, tr. see Gerber, Samuel.

Dyck, Peter J., et al. Peripheral Neuropathy, 2 Vols. 2nd ed. (Illus.). 2491p. 1984. Two Vol. Set. 240.00 (ISBN 0-7216-3275-0); Vol. 1. 120.00 (ISBN 0-7216-3273-4); Vol. 2. 120.00 (ISBN 0-7216-3274-2). Saunders.
Dyck, V. A., et al. FORTRAN 77: A Structured Approach to Problem Solving. 1983. text ed. 25.95 (ISBN 0-8359-3163-3). Reston.
Dyckman & Morse. Efficient Capital Markets & Accounting: A Critical Analysis. 2nd ed. (Illus.). 112p. 1986. pap. text ed. 19.95 (ISBN 0-317-29659-0). P-H.
Dyckman, Katharine M., jt. auth. see Carroll, L. Patrick.
Dyckman, Katherine M. & Carroll, L. Patrick. Solitude to Sacrament. LC 82-252. 128p. (Orig.). 1982. pap. 2.95 (ISBN 0-8146-1255-5). Liturgical Pr.
Dyckman, T. R. Investment Analysis & General Price-Level Adjustments, Vol. 1. (Studies in Accounting Research). 76p. 1969. nonmember 6.00 (ISBN 0-86539-013-4); 4.00. Am Accounting.
Dyckman, Thomas & Thomas, L. Joseph. Algebra & Calculus for Business. (Illus.). 464p. 1974. text ed. 29.95 (ISBN 0-13-021758-1). P-H.
Dyckman, Thomas, et al. Efficient Capital Markets & Accounting: A Critical Analysis. (Contemporary Topics in Accounting Ser.). (Illus.). 144p. 1975. pap. 20.95 (ISBN 0-13-246967-7). P-H.
Dyckman, Thomas R. The Effects of the Issuance of the Exposure Draft & FASB Statement No. 19 on the Security Returns of Oil & Gas Producing Companies. LC 79-50567. (The Financial Accounting Standards Board Research Report). (Illus.). 84p. (Orig.). 1979. pap. 3.00 (ISBN 0-910065-08-X). Finan Acct.
Dyckman, Thomas R. & Swieringa, Robert J. Cases in Financial Accounting, Vol. 1. rev. ed. LC 81-67860. (Illus.). 336p. (Orig.). 1981. pap. text ed. 13.95x (ISBN 0-931920-31-0). Dame Pubns.
Dyckman, Thomas R. & Thomas, L. Joseph. Fundamental Statistics for Business & Economics. 1977. 29.95 (ISBN 0-13-344523-2). P-H.
Dyckman, Thomas R., jt. auth. see Bierman, Harold, Jr.
Dydak, J. & Segal, J. Shape Theory: An Introduction. (Lecture Notes in Mathematics: Vol. 688). 1978. pap. 15.00 (ISBN 0-387-08955-1). Springer-Verlag.
Dyde, J. A. & Smith, R. E. Present State of Thoracic Surgery. 300p. text ed. cancelled (ISBN 0-272-79592-5, Pub. by Pitman Bks Ltd UK). Pitman Pub MA.
Dyde, J. A. & Smih, R. E., eds. Present State of Thoracic Surgery. 300p. 1981. text ed. 48.00x (ISBN 0-8464-1218-7). Beekman Pubs.
Dyde, J. A. & Smith, R. E., eds. Surgery of the Heart. LC 76-14827. 220p. 1976. 29.50x (ISBN 0-306-30944-0, Plenum Med Bk). Plenum Pub.
Dyde, Walter F. Public Secondary Education in Canada. LC 72-176736. (Columbia University. Teachers College. Contributions to Education: No. 345). Repr. of 1929 ed. 22.50 (ISBN 0-404-55345-1). AMS Pr.
D'Ydewalle, Gery & Lens, Willy, eds. Cognition in Human Motivation & Learning. LC 80-23715. 304p. 1981. text ed. 29.95x (ISBN 0-89859-067-1). L Erlbaum Assocs.
Dydo, Stephen & Kirshbaum, Randa, eds. The Norman Rockwell Family Songbook. (Illus.). 256p. 1984. 25.00 (ISBN 0-8109-1561-8). Abrams.
Dye & Frankfort. Spectrum One: Teacher's Edition. (Spectrum Ser.). 158p. 1982. pap. text ed. 9.95 (ISBN 0-88345-513-7, 20103). Regents Pub.
--Spectrum Two: Teacher's Edition. (Spectrum Ser.). 1983. pap. text ed. 9.95 (ISBN 0-88345-514-5, 20266). Regents Pub.
Dye, Alan. IFAI Excise Tax Guide: Contents, Questions & Answers. 1980. 25.00 (ISBN 0-318-01564-1, 24025). Indus Fabrics.
Dye, Carol J., jt. auth. see Brownstone, Jane E.
Dye, Celeste. Assessment & Intervention in Geropsychiatric Nursing. 224p. 1985. 29.50 (ISBN 0-8089-1712-9, 791105). Grune.
Dye, Charles M., ed. The American Educator: Introductory Readings in the Traditions of the Profession. LC 80-5759. 430p. 1980. pap. text ed. 18.00 (ISBN 0-8191-1221-6). U Pr of Amer.
Dye, Daniel S. Chinese Lattice Designs. LC 74-82205. (Illus.). 469p. 1974. pap. 7.95 (ISBN 0-486-23096-1). Dover.
--Chinese Lattice Designs. (Illus.). 11.25 (ISBN 0-8446-5182-6). Peter Smith.
--The New Book of Chinese Lattice Designs. (Pictorial Archive Ser.). (Illus.). 128p. (Orig.). 1981. pap. 4.50 (ISBN 0-486-24128-9). Dover.
Dye, David A., jt. auth. see Tourda, Wayne F.
Dye, Edward. Let's Make a Law. (Illus.). 12p. (gr. 4-12). 1983. 9.95 (ISBN 0-910141-03-7, KP117). Kino Pubns.
--Take Me to Your Leader: A Game about Presidential Elections. (Illus.). 12p. (gr. 4-12). 1982. inc. game 9.95 (ISBN 0-910141-02-9, KP116). Kino Pubns.
Dye, Frank & Dye, Margaret. Ocean Crossing Wayfarer. 1977. 14.95 (ISBN 0-7153-7371-4). David & Charles.
Dye, Gillian. Bobbin Lace Braid. (Illus.). 144p. 1979. 16.95 (ISBN 0-8231-5055-0). Branford.
Dye, Harold. The Touch of Friendship. LC 79-51138. 1979. pap. 4.25 large type (ISBN 0-8054-5422-5). Broadman.
Dye, Harold E. A Daily Miracle. (Orig.). 1986. pap. 3.25 (ISBN 0-8054-5026-2). Broadman.
--No Rocking Chair for Me! LC 75-8325. 154p. 1976. 5.95 (ISBN 0-8054-5234-6). Broadman.
--No Rocking Chair for Me. 1980. pap. 5.50 (ISBN 0-8054-5286-9). Broadman.
Dye, Joan see Warshawsky & Constinett.
Dye, John S. History of the Plots & Crimes of the Great Conspiracy to Overthrow Liberty in America. facs. ed. LC 76-75508. (Select Bibliographies Reprint Ser). 1866. 27.50 (ISBN 0-8369-5006-2). Ayer Co Pubs.
Dye, Joseph M. Ways to Shiva: Life & Ritual in Hindu India. LC 80-25113. (Illus.). 94p. (Orig.). 1980. pap. 4.95 (ISBN 0-87633-038-3). Phila Mus Art.
Dye, Margaret, jt. auth. see Dye, Frank.
Dye, Nancy S. As Equals & As Sisters: Feminism, the Labor Movement, & the Women's Trade Union League of New York. LC 80-16751. 224p. 1980. text ed. 17.50x (ISBN 0-8262-0318-3). U of Mo Pr.
Dye, Sylvia. Sandhill Stories: Life on the Prairie 1875-1925. (Illus.). 183p. (Orig.). 1980. pap. 6.95 (ISBN 0-686-27610-8). Parthenon Pubns.
Dye, Thomas, jt. auth. see Gray, Virginia.
Dye, Thomas R. Policy Analysis: What Governments Do, Why They Do It, & What Difference It Makes. LC 75-37717. 128p. 1976. 8.95 (ISBN 0-8173-4834-4); pap. 5.75 (ISBN 0-8173-4835-2). U of Ala Pr.
--Politics in States & Communities. 5th ed. (Illus.). 512p. 1985. text ed. 27.95 (ISBN 0-13-685199-1). P-H.
--Power & Society: An Introduction to the Social Sciences. 3rd ed. LC 82-14579. (Political Science Ser.). 400p. 1982. pap. text ed. 15.00 pub net (ISBN 0-534-01237-X). Brooks-Cole.
--Understanding Public Policy. 4th ed. (Illus.). 464p. 1981. text ed. 27.95 (ISBN 0-13-936260-6). P-H.
--Who's Running America: The Conservative Years. 4th ed. (Illus.). 304p. 1986. pap. text ed. 16.95 (ISBN 0-13-958505-2). P-H.
--Who's Running America? The Reagan Years. 3rd ed. (Illus.). 272p. 1983. pap. 16.95 (ISBN 0-13-958470-6). P-H.
Dye, Thomas R. & Zeigler, L. Harmon. American Politics in the Media Age. LC 82-17710. (Political Science Ser.). 450p. 1983. text ed. 20.00 pub net (ISBN 0-534-01176-4). Brooks-Cole.
--American Politics in the Media Age. 2nd ed. 450p. 1985. pap. 20.25 (ISBN 0-534-05598-2). Brooks-Cole.
--The Irony of Democracy: An Uncommon Introduction to American Politics. 6th ed. LC 83-15045. (Political Science Ser.). 525p. 1983. pap. text ed. 15.00 pub net (ISBN 0-534-02847-0). Brooks-Cole.
Dye, Thomas R., jt. auth. see DiNitto, Diana M.
Dye, Thomas R., et al. Governing the American Democracy. 624p. 1980. text ed. 24.95x (ISBN 0-312-34104-0); write for info. instructor's manual. St Martin.
Dye, Thomas S., jt. auth. see Bevacqua, Robert F.
Dye, William M. Moslem Egypt & Christian Abyssinia. LC 78-97365. Repr. of 1880 ed. 23.00x (ISBN 0-8371-2432-8, DYM&, Pub. by Negro U Pr). Greenwood.
Dyen, I. Sanskrit Indeclinables of the Hindu Grammarians & Lexicographers. (Language Dissertations: No. 31). 1939. pap. 16.00 (ISBN 0-527-00777-3). Kraus Repr.
Dyen, Isidore. Linguistic Subgrouping & Lexicostatistics. LC 73-82418. (Janua Linguarum, Series Minor: No. 175). (Illus.). 251p. 1975. pap. text ed. 37.00x (ISBN 90-2793-054-6). Mouton.
--A Sketch of Trukese Grammar. (American Oriental Society Essays: 4). 1964. pap. 3.00 (ISBN 0-940490-93-5). Am Orient Soc.
--Spoken Malay. Incl. Units 1-12. v, 192p. pap. 10.00x (ISBN 0-87950-160-X); Bk. 2, Units 13-30. 324p (ISBN 0-87950-161-8); Cassettes, Six Dual Track. 60.00x (ISBN 0-87950-165-0); Cassette Course - Bk. 1 & Cassettes. pap. 65.00x (ISBN 0-87950-166-9). LC 74-176207. (Spoken Language Ser.). (Prog. Bk.). 1974. pap. Spoken Lang Serv.
Dyen, Isidore, ed. Lexicostatistics in Genetic Linguistics: Proceedings of the Yale Conference, Yale University, April 3-4, 1971. (Janua Linguarum Series Maior: No. 69). 1973. 23.20x (ISBN 0-686-21262-2). Mouton.
Dyer, A., ed. Gas Chemistry in Nuclear Reactors & Large Industrial Plant. 281p. 1980. 75.00x (ISBN 0-85501-449-0, Pub. by Brit Nuclear England). State Mutual Bk.
Dyer, A. F., ed. The Experimental Biology of Ferns. (Experimental Biology Ser.). 1979. 99.50 (ISBN 0-12-226350-2). Acad Pr.
Dyer, A. F. & Duckett, J. G., eds. The Experimental Biology of Bryophytes. (Experimental Botany: An International Series Of Monographs). 1984. 68.50 (ISBN 0-12-226370-7). Acad Pr.
Dyer, Alan. James Parker, Colonial Printer: 1715-1770. LC 80-52545. 441p. 1982. 32.50x (ISBN 0-87875-202-1). Whitston Pub.
Dyer, Alan, ed. Gas Chemistry in Nuclear Reactors & Large Industrial Plant: Proceedings of the Conference Held at the University of Salford, UK, 21-24 April 1980. LC 82-104413. pap. 73.80 (ISBN 0-317-30333-3, 2024810). Bks Demand UMI.
Dyer, Albion M. First Ownership of Ohio Lands. LC 69-18897. 85p. 1982. Repr. of 1911 ed. 9.50 (ISBN 0-8063-0098-1). Genealog Pub.
Dyer, Allen R., jt. auth. see Robbins, Dennis A.
Dyer, Alvin R. Challenge. 216p. 1962. 8.95 (ISBN 0-87747-031-6). Deseret Bk.
--The Refiner's Fire. 8.95 (ISBN 0-87747-222-X). Deseret Bk.
Dyer, Anne. Design Your Own Stuffed Toys. LC 75-105680. (Illus.). 1970. 10.50 (ISBN 0-8231-5021-6). Branford.
--Dyes from Natural Sources. 88p. 1976. pap. 7.25 (ISBN 0-8231-5049-6). Branford.
Dyer, Annie I. Administration of Home Economics in City Schools: A Study of Present & Desired Practices in the Organization of the Home Economics Program. LC 76-176737. (Columbia University. Teachers College. Contributions to Education: No. 318). Repr. of 1928 ed. 22.50 (ISBN 0-404-55318-4). AMS Pr.
Dyer, B. Personnel Systems & Records. 3rd ed. 240p. 1979. text ed. 34.00x (ISBN 0-566-02106-4). Gower Pub Co.
Dyer, Barbara, jt. auth. see Vaughan, Roger J.
Dyer, Barbara, ed. see Nothdurft, William E.
Dyer, Barbara, ed. see Smith, Rodney T.
Dyer, Barbara, et al. Agenda for a Dynamic Economy: State Development Policies for Innovations & Entrepreneurship. Date not set. price not set (ISBN 0-934842-23-X). Coun State Plan.
Dyer, Brainerd. The Public Career of William M. Evarts. (Publications of the University of California at Los Angeles in Social Sciences Ser.: Vol. 2). 1933. pap. 12.50x (ISBN 0-686-17390-2). R S Barnes.
--The Public Career of William M. Evarts. LC 72-87565. (American Scene Ser.). 279p. 1969. Repr. of 1933 ed. lib. bdg. 35.00 (ISBN 0-686-42966-4). Da Capo.
Dyer, Brian. The Celtic Queen. 192p. 1976. pap. 1.25 (ISBN 0-532-12372-7). Woodhill.
--The Wayward Heart. 1977. pap. 1.50 (ISBN 0-532-15296-4). Woodhill.
Dyer, C. Pizza Cookery. 224p. 1983. 12.95 (ISBN 0-07-018542-5); pap. 6.95 (ISBN 0-07-018543-3). McGraw.
Dyer, Carole, jt. ed. see Marsh, Judy.
Dyer, Ceil. Best Recipes from the Backs of Boxes, Bottles, Cans & Jars. LC 79-17925. (Illus.). 194p. 1979. 11.95 (ISBN 0-07-018551-4); pap. 5.95 (ISBN 0-07-018550-6). McGraw.
--Chicken Cookery. (Illus.). 160p. 1983. pap. 7.95 (ISBN 0-89586-054-6). H P Bks.
--Great Desserts from Ceil Dyer. 304p. 1985. price not set (ISBN 0-07-018545-X); pap. price not set (ISBN 0-07-018544-1). McGraw.
--More Recipes from the Backs of Boxes, Bottles, Cans & Jars. (McGraw-Hill Paperbacks Ser.). 192p. (Orig.). 1981. text ed. 11.95 (ISBN 0-07-018554-9); pap. 5.95 (ISBN 0-07-018555-7). McGraw.
--More Wok Cookery. LC 82-81010. (Illus.). 160p. 1982. 7.95 (ISBN 0-89586-138-0). H P Bks.
--The Newport Cookbook. rev ed. (Illus.). 256p. pap. 5.95 (ISBN 0-940078-08-2). Foremost Pubs.
--Wok Cookery. 1981. pap. 4.50 (ISBN 0-440-19663-9). Dell.
--Wok Cookery. LC 77-83279. (Illus.). 1977. pap. 7.95 (ISBN 0-912656-75-1). H P Bks.
Dyer, Cell. Even More Recipes from the Backs of Boxes, Bottles, Cans & Jars. 1982. 12.95 (ISBN 0-07-018558-1); pap. 6.95 (ISBN 0-07-018559-X). McGraw.
Dyer, Christopher. Lords & Peasants in a Changing Society: The Estates of the Bishopric of Worcester, 680-1540. LC 79-51225. (Past & Present Publications Ser.). (Illus.). 466p. 1980. 57.50 (ISBN 0-521-22618-X). Cambridge U Pr.
Dyer, Colin. Population & Society in Twentieth Century France. LC 77-2908. (Illus.). 256p. 1978. text ed. 39.50x (ISBN 0-8419-0308-5); pap. text ed. 13.50x (ISBN 0-8419-6209-X). Holmes & Meier.
Dyer, D., et al. Measuring & Improving the Efficiency of Boilers. Gyftopoulos, Elias P. & Cohen, Karen C., eds. (Industrial Energy-Conservation Manuals: No. 3). 120p. 1982. loose-leaf 20.00x (ISBN 0-262-04067-0). MIT Pr.
Dyer, D. G., tr. see Bidermann, Jacob.
Dyer, David L. Darts in Los Angeles. (Illus.). 177p. (Orig.). 1984. lib. bdg. 11.95 (ISBN 0-930103-00-9); pap. 4.95 (ISBN 0-930103-01-7). Travel Guides Pub.
Dyer, Davis, jt. auth. see Lawrence, Paul R.
Dyer, Denys. The Stories of Kleist: A Critical Study. LC 76-58356. 210p. 1977. text ed. 32.50x (ISBN 0-8419-0303-4). Holmes & Meier.
Dyer, Dewey A. So You Want to Start a Restaurant? rev. ed. 160p. 1981. 15.95 (ISBN 0-8436-2199-0). Van Nos Reinhold.
Dyer, Donita. Bright Promise. 176p. 1983. pap. 5.95 (ISBN 0-310-45751-3). Zondervan.
Dyer, E. R., ed. see International Symposium on Solar-Terrestial Physics, Leningrad, 1970.
Dyer, Edwin A., ed. Gas Chemistry in Nuclear Reactors & Large Industrial Plants. 296p. 1980. pap. 57.95x (ISBN 0-471-25663-3, Pub. by Wiley Heyden). Wiley.
Dyer, Esther & Berger, Pam, eds. Public, School & Academic Media Centers: A Guide to Information Sources. LC 74-11554. (Books, Publishing & Libraries Information Guide Ser.: Vol. 3). 350p. 1980. 60.00x (ISBN 0-8103-1286-7). Gale.
Dyer, Esther R. Cooperation in Library Service to Children. LC 77-28190. 160p. 1978. 15.00 (ISBN 0-8108-1111-1). Scarecrow.
--Cultural Pluralism & Children's Media. (School Media Centers: Focus on Trends & Issues: No. 1). 77p. 1978. pap. 6.00x (ISBN 0-8389-3218-5). ALA.
Dyer, Everett D. The American Family: Variety & Change. (Illus.). 1979. text ed. 31.95 (ISBN 0-07-018540-9). McGraw.
--Courtship, Marriage, & Family. 479p. 1983. 27.00x (ISBN 0-256-02413-8). Dorsey.
Dyer, Florence. Dante on Chartres. (Nebraska Review Chapbook Ser.: No. 5). 16p. (Orig.). 1980. pap. 1.00 (ISBN 0-937796-04-2). Nebraska Review.
Dyer, Frederick C. & Dyer, John M. Bureaucracy Vs Creativity: The Dilemna of Modern Leadership. LC 65-25638. (Business & Economic Ser: No. 9). 1965. 7.95x (ISBN 0-87024-134-6). U of Miami Pr.
Dyer, G. W. Democracy in the South Before the Civil War. LC 72-11343. (The American South Ser.). Repr. of 1905 ed. 12.00 (ISBN 0-405-05059-3). Ayer Co Pubs.
Dyer, George. Privileges of the University of Cambridge, 2 Vols. Repr. of 1824 ed. Set. 105.00 (ISBN 0-404-07306-9). AMS Pr.
Dyer, George, ed. An American Catholic Catechism. LC 75-7786. 320p. 1975. (Pub. by Seabury); pap. 7.95 (ISBN 0-8164-2588-4). Winston Pr.
Dyer, Gillian. Advertising as Communication. (Studies in Communication). 250p. 1982. pap. 8.95 (ISBN 0-416-74530-X, NO. 3662). Methuen Inc.
Dyer, Gwynne. War. (Illus.). 1985. 17.95 (ISBN 0-517-55615-4). Crown.
Dyer, Heather. Stories Jesus Told. Incl. The Good Samaritan (ISBN 0-89191-286-X); The Good Shepherd (ISBN 0-89191-283-5); The Great Feast (ISBN 0-89191-284-3); The House Built on Sand (ISBN 0-89191-288-6); The Prodigal Son (ISBN 0-89191-285-1); The Rich Man (ISBN 0-89191-287-8). (Illus.). (gr. 1-4). 1980. Repr. 2.50 ea. Cook.
Dyer, Henry. The Evolution of Industry. LC 72-5044. (Technology & Society Ser.). 322p. 1972. Repr. of 1895 ed. 21.00 (ISBN 0-405-04696-0). Ayer Co Pubs.
--Parents Can Understand Testing. LC 80-80939. 1980. pap. 3.50 (ISBN 0-934460-08-6). NCCE.
Dyer, Ira & Chryssostomidis, C., eds. Arctic Technology & Policy. LC 83-18403. (Illus.). 281p. 1984. text ed. 79.95 (ISBN 0-89116-361-1). Hemisphere Pub.
Dyer, Irwin A., jt. ed. see O'Mary, Clayton C.
Dyer, Isaac W. Bibliography of Thomas Carlyle's Writings & Annotations. 1967. Repr. of 1928 ed. 23.50 (ISBN 0-8337-0985-2). B Franklin.
--Bibliography of Thomas Carlyle's Writings. 1967. lib. bdg. 26.00x (ISBN 0-374-92432-5). Octagon.
Dyer, J. Applications of Absorption Spectroscopy of Organic Compounds. 1965. pap. 23.95 (ISBN 0-13-038802-5). P-H.
Dyer, James. Discovering Archaeology in Denmark. (Discovering Ser.: No. 141). (Illus., Orig.). 1979. pap. 3.50 (ISBN 0-85263-158-8, Pub. by Shire Pubns England). Seven Hills Bks.
--Discovering Archaeology in England & Wales. (Discovering Ser.: No. 46). 1985. pap. 4.95 (ISBN 0-85263-705-5, Pub. by Shire Pubns England). Seven Hills Bks.
--Hillforts of England & Wales. (Shire Archaeology Ser.: No. 16). (Illus.). 64p. 1985. pap. 6.95 (ISBN 0-85263-536-2, Pub. by Shire Pubns England). Seven Hills Bks.
--The Penguin Guide to Prehistoric England & Wales. (Illus.). 400p. 1983. pap. 7.95 (ISBN 0-14-046351-8). Penguin.
--Southern England: An Archaeological Guide. LC 73-76369. (Illus.). 380p. 1974. 16.00 (ISBN 0-8155-5016-2, NP). Noyes.
--Teaching Archaeology in Schools. (Shire Archaeology Ser.: No. 29). (Illus.). 64p. 1983. pap. 5.95 (ISBN 0-85263-622-9, Pub. by Shire Pubns England). Seven Hills Bks.
Dyer, James, jt. auth. see Dony, John G.
Dyer, James A., jt. auth. see Bernstein, Robert A.
Dyer, James S. & Shapiro, Roy D. Management Science-Operations Research: Cases & Readings. LC 81-19703. 388p. 1982. pap. text ed. 24.50x (ISBN 0-471-09757-8) (ISBN 0-471-86554-0). Wiley.
Dyer, Jane, illus. Goldilocks & the Three Bears. (Pudgy Pals Ser.). (Illus.). 16p. (ps). 1984. 3.50 (ISBN 0-448-10213-7, G&D). Putnam Pub Group.
--Little Red Riding Hood. (Pudgy Pal Board Bks.). (Illus.). 18p. (ps). 1985. 3.95 (ISBN 0-448-10227-7, G&D). Putnam Pub Group.
Dyer, Janell G. The Australian Christian Play. 1985. 11.95 (ISBN 0-533-06485-6). Vantage.

Dyer, Jean R. Understanding & Evaluating Educational Research. LC 78-67952. (Education Ser.). (Illus.). 1979. text ed. 23.05 (ISBN 0-201-01184-0, Sch Div). Addison-Wesley.
Dyer, John. Atlas of Extraocular Muscle Surgery. LC 73-113023. pap. 47.00 (ISBN 0-317-26626-8, 20131066). Bks Demand UMI.
--Tracking the Snow-Shoe Itinerant. LC 80-54041. (Illus.). 128p. 1981. text ed. 18.95 (ISBN 0-9605366-0-4); pap. text ed. 11.95 (ISBN 0-9605366-1-2). Snowstorm.
Dyer, John A. & Lee, David A. Atlas of Extraocular Muscle Surgery. 2nd ed. LC 84-18090. 256p. 1984. 35.95x (ISBN 0-03-000837-9). Praeger.
Dyer, John M., jt. auth. see Dyer, Frederick C.
Dyer, Jon C. Handbook of Industrial Wastes Pretreatment. LC 79-25702. 280p. 1980. lib. bdg. 36.00 (ISBN 0-8240-7066-6). Garland Pub.
Dyer, Jon C. & Mignone, Nicholas A. Handbook of Industrial Residues. LC 82-19082. (Environment Engineering Ser.). (Illus.). 453p. 1983. 54.00 (ISBN 0-8155-0924-3, Noyes Pubns). Noyes.
Dyer, Judith & Schram, Frederick. A Manual of Invertebrate Paleontology. (Illus.). 165p. (Orig.). 1983. pap. text ed. 6.80 (ISBN 0-87563-237-8). Stipes.
Dyer, Judith C. Vegetarianism: An Annotated Bibliography. LC 82-3159. 292p. 1982. 16.00 (ISBN 0-8108-1532-X). Scarecrow.
Dyer, K. F. Catching up with the Men: Women in Sport. 1982. 50.00x (ISBN 0-686-45576-2, Pub. by Junct Bks England); pap. 39.00 (ISBN 0-686-45577-0). State Mutual Bk.
--Challenging the Men: Women in Sport. LC 81-21846. (Illus.). 271p. 1982. pap. 14.95 (ISBN 0-7022-1921-5). U of Queensland Pr.
Dyer, K. R., ed. Estuarine Hydrography & Sedimentation. LC 78-67308. (Illus.). 1980. 52.50 (ISBN 0-521-22435-7); pap. 19.95 (ISBN 0-521-29496-7). Cambridge U Pr.
Dyer, Keith R. Estuaries: A Physical Introduction. LC 72-8598. 140p. 1973. 29.95x (ISBN 0-471-22905-9, Pub. by Wiley-Interscience). Wiley.
Dyer, L. S. A Practical Approach to Bank Lending. 2nd ed. 232p. 1981. 25.00x (ISBN 0-85297-056-0, Pub. by Woodhead-Faulkner England). State Mutual Bk.
Dyer, L. S., jt. auth. see Hutchinson, H. H.
Dyer, Lee & Paulson, Gary D. Project Management: An Annotated Bibliography. LC 76-2085. (ILR Bibliography Ser.: No. 13). 48p. 1976. pap. 2.75 (ISBN 0-87546-059-3). ILR Pr.
Dyer, Lee, ed. Careers in Organizations: Individual Planning & Organizational Development. LC 76-49471. (Illus.). 68p. 1976. pap. 7.25 special hard bdg. (ISBN 0-87546-288-X). ILR Pr.
--Merchandising in Action. (Illus.). 13.95 (ISBN 0-911790-07-1). Prog Grocer.
Dyer, Lorna. Ice Dancing Illustrated. Brandt, Harry, ed. (Illus.). 297p. 1980. 35.00 (ISBN 0-9602616-0-5). Moore Pubns.
Dyer, Louis. Machiavelli & the Modern State. 69.95 (ISBN 0-8490-0573-6). Gordon Pr.
Dyer, Louis, ed. see Plato.
Dyer, Louise, tr. see Cossa, Luigi.
Dyer, Marilyn, jt. auth. see Dickerson, Thelma M.
Dyer, Mary L. Practical Bookkeeping for the Small Business. LC 75-32968. (Illus.). 240p. 1976. pap. 12.95 (ISBN 0-8092-8206-2). Contemp Bks.
Dyer, Michael G. In-Depth Understanding: A Computer Model of Integrated Processing for Narrative Comprehension. (Artificial Intelligence Ser.). (Illus.). 458p. 1983. text ed. 37.50x (ISBN 0-262-04073-5). MIT Pr.
Dyer, Mike. Getting into Pro Baseball. (Getting into the Pros Ser.). (Illus.). (gr. 6 up). 1979. PLB 8.40 s&l (ISBN 0-531-01319-7). Watts.
Dyer, Nancy & Homeyer, Pat. A Practical Education Program for the Diabetic Client Within the Rehabilitation Setting. 147p. pap. 5.00 (ISBN 0-89128-970-4, PRP970). Am Foun Blind.
Dyer, Nancy A., jt. auth. see Starr, John B.
Dyer, Oliver. Great Senators of the United States Forty Years Ago. LC 72-8557. (Essay Index Reprint Ser.). 1972. Repr. of 1889 ed. 19.00 (ISBN 0-8369-7344-5). Ayer Co Pubs.
--History of the Battle of Lake Erie. 264p. Date not set. Repr. of 1891 ed. lib. bdg. 34.00 (ISBN 0-932051-81-2). Am Repr Serv.
Dyer, P. & McReynolds, S. R. Computation & Theory of Optimal Control. (Mathematics in Science & Engineering Ser., Vol. 65). 1970. 70.00 (ISBN 0-12-226250-6). Acad Pr.
Dyer, R. A. The Genera of South African Flowering Plants, 2 Vols. Incl. Vol. 1. Dicotyledons. 756p. text ed. 12.50 (ISBN 0-621-02854-1); Vol. 2. Monocotyledons. 284p. text ed. 12.50 (ISBN 0-621-02863-0). 1983 (Pub. by Dept Agriculture & Fish S Africa). Intl Spec Bk.
Dyer, R. Allen, jt. auth. see Reid, C.
Dyer, R. Allen, ed. Ceropegia, Brachystelma & Riocreuxia in Southern Africa. (Illus.). 274p. 1983. lib. bdg. 35.00 (ISBN 90-6191-227-X, Pub. by Balkema RSA). IPS.
Dyer, Raymond. Her Father's Daughter: The Work of Anna Freud. LC 82-11334. 332p. 1983. 25.00 (ISBN 0-87668-627-7). Aronson.
Dyer, Richard. Stars. (British Film Institute Bks.). (Illus.). 204p. 1979. pap. 8.95 (ISBN 0-85170-085-3). U of Ill Pr.
Dyer, Richard, ed. Gays & Film. rev. ed. LC 84-61788. (Illus.). 112p. 1984. pap. 8.95 (ISBN 0-918432-58-8). NY Zoetrope.
Dyer, Ruth. I Remember Well. LC 85-50085. 74p. (Orig.). 1985. pap. 4.95 (ISBN 0-938232-66-5). Winston-Derek.
Dyer, Ruth C. The Indians' Land Title in California: A Case in Federal Equity, 1851-1942. LC 74-31772. 1975. soft bdg. 10.95 (ISBN 0-88247-338-7). R & E Pubs.
Dyer, S. A Common Sense Method of Double Entry Bookkeeping, on First Principles as Suggested by De Morgan: Theoretical. LC 82-48384. (Accounting History & the Development of a Profession Ser.). 135p. 1984. lib. bdg. 20.00 (ISBN 0-8240-6324-4). Garland Pub.
Dyer, Susan K. Manual of Procedures for Private Law Libraries: 1984 Supplement. (AALL Publications Ser.: No. 21). ix, 130p. 1984. 18.50 (ISBN 0-8377-0119-8). Rothman.
Dyer, Susan K., jt. auth. see American Association of Law Librarians.
Dyer, T. A. A Way of His Own. (gr. 5-8). 1981. 7.95 (ISBN 0-395-30443-1). HM.
--The Whipman Is Watching. (gr. 5-9). 1979. 7.95 (ISBN 0-395-28581-X). HM.
Dyer, Thomas, ed. see Lines, Amelia A.
Dyer, Thomas G. Theodore Roosevelt & the Idea of Race. LC 79-20151. x, 198p. 1980. 20.00x (ISBN 0-8071-0658-5). La State U Pr.
--The University of Georgia: A Bicentennial History, 1785-1985. LC 84-232. 435p. 1985. 35.00 (ISBN 0-8203-0725-4). U of Ga Pr.
Dyer, Walter A. Early American Craftsmen. 1971. Repr. of 1915 ed. lib. bdg. 25.50 (ISBN 0-8337-0986-0). B Franklin.
--Gulliver the Great: And Other Dog Stories. LC 72-5906. (Short Story Reprint Ser.). Repr. of 1916 ed. 24.50 (ISBN 0-8369-4214-0). Ayer Co Pubs.
--Many Dogs There Be. LC 71-122695. (Short Story Index Reprint Ser). 1924. 16.00 (ISBN 0-8369-3528-4). Ayer Co Pubs.
Dyer, Wayne. Gifts from Eykis. 224p. 1984. pap. 3.95 (ISBN 0-671-55180-9). PB.
--The Sky's the Limit. 384p. 1984. pap. 4.50 (ISBN 0-671-54757-7). PB.
Dyer, Wayne & Vriend, John. Counseling Techniques that Work. 270p. 1975. nonmembers 10.25 (ISBN 0-911547-26-6, 72044W34); 7.25 (ISBN 0-686-34289-5). Am Assn Coun Dev.
Dyer, Wayne W. Pulling Your Own Strings. 1979. pap. 3.95 (ISBN 0-380-44388-0, 60056-0). Avon.
--Pulling Your Own Strings. LC 77-23368. (Funk & W Bk.). 1978. 8.95i (ISBN 0-308-10336-X). T Y Crowell.
--What Do You Really Want for Your Children? 352p. 1985. 17.95 (ISBN 0-688-04527-8). Morrow.
--Your Erroneous Zones. 1977. pap. 3.95 (ISBN 0-380-01669-9, 60088-9). Avon.
--Your Erroneous Zones. LC 75-35621. (Funk & W Bk.). 256p. 1976. 12.45i (ISBN 0-308-10228-2). T Y Crowell.
Dyer, Wayne W. & Vriend, John. Group Counseling for Personal Mastery. 288p. 1982. pap. 8.95 (ISBN 0-346-12575-8). Cornerstone.
Dyer, Wayne W., jt. ed. see Vriend, John.
Dyer, William G. Choices: A Father's Counsel. LC 80-14692. 116p. 1980. 6.95 (ISBN 0-87747-822-8). Deseret Bk.
--Contemporary Issues in Management & Organization Development. LC 82-8732. 224p. 1982. text ed. 17.95 (ISBN 0-201-10348-6). Addison-Wesley.
--Creating Closer Families: Principles of Positive Family Interaction. LC 75-20169. (Illus.). 144p. 1975. pap. 6.95 (ISBN 0-8425-0726-4). Brigham.
--Modern Theory & Method in Group Training. LC 80-24641. 268p. 1981. Repr. of 1972 ed. text ed. 14.95 (ISBN 0-89874-280-3). Krieger.
--Team Building: Issues & Alternatives. LC 77-76115. 1977. pap. text ed. 10.50 (ISBN 0-201-01191-3). Addison-Wesley.
Dyer, William P. Activities of the Elementary School Principal for the Improvement of Instruction: The Kind of Supervisory Program Which a City Superintendent of Schools Should Set up for His Elementary School Principals. LC 70-176738. (Columbia University. Teachers College. Contributions to Education: No. 274). Repr. of 1927 ed. 22.50 (ISBN 0-404-55274-9). AMS Pr.
Dyet, James T. Getting Through to Adults. LC 79-53294. (Accent Teacher Training Ser.). (Orig.). 1980. pap. 3.95 (ISBN 0-89636-037-7). Accent Bks.
--Paul: Apostle of Steel & Velvet. 3rd. ed. LC 76-9579. 1976. pap. 2.95 (ISBN 0-89636-086-5). Accent Bks.
--Peter: Apostle of Contrast. LC 81-70776. (Chosen Messengers Ser.). 128p. (Orig.). 1982. pap. text ed. 3.50 (ISBN 0-89636-077-6). Accent Bks.
Dygard, Thomas. Halfback Tough. 192p. (gr. 7 up). 1986. 11.50 (ISBN 0-688-05925-2). Morrow.
--Rebound Caper. LC 82-18821. 176p. (gr. 7 up). 1983. 10.75 (ISBN 0-688-01707-X). Morrow.
--Running Scared. LC 76-56862. (gr. 7 up). 1977. 11.25 (ISBN 0-688-22103-3). Morrow.
--Tournament Upstart. LC 83-25039. 208p. (gr. 7 up). 1984. 9.50 (ISBN 0-688-02761-X). Morrow.
--Wilderness Peril. LC 84-25577. 208p. (gr. 7 up). 1985. 10.25 (ISBN 0-688-04146-9, Morrow Junior Books). Morrow.
Dygard, Thomas J. Point Spread. LC 79-24511. 192p. (gr. 7-9). 1980. PLB 11.88 (ISBN 0-688-32222-0). Morrow.
--Quarterback Walk-on. LC 81-18715. 224p. (gr. 7-9). 1982. 11.75 (ISBN 0-688-01065-2). Morrow.
--Quarterback Walk-on. 208p. (gr. 7-12). 1983. pap. 1.95 (ISBN 0-590-32821-2). Scholastic Inc.
--Soccer Duel. LC 81-883. 192p. (gr. 7-9). 1981. 11.25 (ISBN 0-688-00366-4); PLB 11.88 (ISBN 0-688-00367-2). Morrow.
Dygat, Stanislaw. Cloak of Illusion. Welsh, David, tr. 1970. 22.50x (ISBN 0-262-04029-8). MIT Pr.
Dygert, Janice. Red Horse & the Buffalo Robe Man. Gilliland, Hap, ed. (Indian Culture Ser.). (Illus.). (gr. 4-8). 1978. 1.95 (ISBN 0-89992-074-8). Coun India Ed.
Dygert, Warren B. Radio As an Advertising Medium. LC 84-46058. 269p. 1985. PLB 30.00 (ISBN 0-317-19424-0). Garland Pub.
Dyhouse, Carol. Girls Growing up in Late Victorian & Edwardian England. (Studies in Social History). 224p. 1981. 22.95x (ISBN 0-7100-0821-X). Routledge & Kegan.
Dyhr-Nielsen, M. Long-Range Water-Supply Forecasting. (Operational Hydrology Reports: No. 20). 20p. 1982. pap. 6.00 (ISBN 92-63-10587-1, W519, WMO). Unipub.
Dyk, Adrian C. Van see Van Dyk, Adrian C., Jr.
Dyk, Ruth B., jt. auth. see Dyk, Walter.
Dyk, Timothy B. & Practising Law Institute. Campaign Eighty-Four: Advertising & Programming Obligations of the Electronic Media. LC 83-62217. (Patents, Copyrights, Trademarks, & Literary Property Course Handbook Ser.: No. 165). 512p. 1984. 35.00. PLI.
Dyk, Walter & Dyk, Ruth B. Left Handed: A Navajo Autobiography. (Illus.). 624p. 1980. 31.50x (ISBN 0-231-04946-3). Columbia U Pr.
Dyk, Walter, ed. Old Mexican, Navaho Indian: A Navaho Autobiography. 1947. 19.00 (ISBN 0-384-43215-8). Johnson Repr.
--Son of Old Man Hat: A Navaho Autobiography. LC 44-2654. xiv, 378p. 1967. pap. 7.95 (ISBN 0-8032-5054-1, BB 355, Bison). U of Nebr Pr.
Dyke, B. & Morrill, W. T., eds. Genealogical Demography. LC 80-17683. (Population & Social Structure: Advances in Historical Demography Ser.). 1980. 32.50 (ISBN 0-12-226380-4). Acad Pr.
Dyke, Bennett & MacCluer, Jean W. Computer Simulation in Human Population Studies: Proceedings. (Studies in Anthropology). 1974. 55.00 (ISBN 0-12-785185-2). Acad Pr.
Dyke, Bill & Jones, Bill. The Horse Business: An Investor's Guide. (Illus.). 1974. 10.00 (ISBN 0-912830-22-0). Printed Horse.
Dyke, C. Philosophy of Economics. (Foundations of Philosophy Ser.). (Illus.). 200p. 1981. pap. text ed. 13.95 (ISBN 0-13-663336-6). P-H.
Dyke, Donald L. see Mocarski, S. & Pietrocini, T.
Dyke, Henry van. The Story of the Other Wise Man. LC 83-47885. (Illus.). 96p. 1983. 8.61 (ISBN 0-06-068855-6, HarpR). Har-Row.
Dyke, Henry Van see Van Dyke, Henry.
Dyke, Henry van see Van Dyke, Henry.
Dyke, Henry Van see Van Dyke, Henry.
Dyke, Henry van see Van Dyke, Henry.
Dyke, Henry Van see Van Dyke, John C.
Dyke, Henry Van see Van Dyke, Henry.
Dyke, John C. Van see Van Dyke, John C.
Dyke, Jon M. Van see Van Dyke, Jon M.
Dyke, Knox V., ed. Bioluminesence & Chemiluminesence Instruments & Applications, Vols. I & II. 1985. Vol. I, 288 pgs. 83.00 (ISBN 0-8493-5863-9); Vol. II, 320 pgs. 93.00 (ISBN 0-8493-5864-7). CRC Pr.
Dyke, M. Van see Van Dyke, M. & Vincenti, W. G.
Dyke, M. Van see Van Dyke, M. & Wehausen, J. V.
Dyke, Milton Van see Van Dyke, Milton.
Dyke, P. P. & Heaps, N. S., eds. Jonsmod Eighty-Two: A Workshop of the Joint North Sea Modelling Group on Mathematical Models of the North Sea & Surrounding Continental Shelf Seas, 1-3 September 1982, Heriot-Watt University, Edinburgh, UK. 136p. 1984. pap. 23.50 (ISBN 0-08-031425-2). Pergamon.
Dyke, P. P., et al, eds. Offshore & Coastal Modelling. (Lecture Notes on Coastal & Estuarine Studies: Vol. 12). ix, 399p. 1985. pap. 32.80 (ISBN 0-387-96054-6). Springer-Verlag.
Dyke, Paul Van see Van Dyke, Paul.
Dyke, S. E. Thoughts on the American Flintlock Pistol. LC 74-24435. (Illus.). 52p. 1974. pap. 7.50 (ISBN 0-87387-070-0). Shumway.
Dyke, S. F., et al. Organic Spectroscopy: An Introduction. 2nd ed. (Illus.). 1979. pap. text ed. 13.95x (ISBN 0-582-45076-4). Longman.
Dyke, Samuel E. The Pennsylvania Rifle. Walker, Joseph E., ed. LC 74-29189. (Lancaster County During the American Revolution Ser). (Illus.). 64p. 1975. pap. 2.00 (ISBN 0-915010-05-4). Sutter House.
Dyke, Scott Van see Van Dyke, Scott.
Dyke, Stanley F. The Chemistry of Anamines. LC 72-78893. (Cambridge Chemistry Texts Ser.). pap. 25.30 (ISBN 0-317-20838-1, 2024440). Bks Demand UMI.
Dyke, Van Henry. First Christmas Tree. 76p. 1984. 2.95 (ISBN 0-89783-034-2). Larlin Corp.
Dyke, Vernon van see Van Dyke, Vernon.
Dyke, Vernon Van see Van Dyke, Vernon.
Dykema, G., tr. see English, L. & Szczepanowski, N.
Dykema, Greg, tr. see Bartel, Ranier.
Dykema, Greg, tr. see Gerits, Klaus, et al.
Dykema, Greg, tr. see Plenge, Axel.
Dykema, Greg, tr. see Severin, Ranier.
Dykema, Roland W., et al. Modern Practice in Removable Partial Prosthodontics. (Illus.). 417p. 1969. 18.00 (ISBN 0-7216-3290-4). Saunders.
Dykeman, jt. auth. see Elias, Thomas.
Dykeman, Francis C. Forensic Accounting: The Accountant As Expert Witness. LC 81-13001. 236p. 1982. 55.00x (ISBN 0-471-08395-X, Pub. by Wiley-Interscience). Wiley.
Dykeman, Wilma. Explorations. LC 84-52024. 265p. 1984. 12.95 (ISBN 0-9613859-0-1). Wakestone Bks.
--The French Broad. LC 54-9347. (Illus.). 1965. pap. text ed. 7.95 (ISBN 0-03-011491-8). U of Tenn Pr.
--Prophet of Plenty: The First Ninety Years of W. D. Weatherford. LC 66-26067. 1966. 14.95x (ISBN 0-87049-068-0). U of Tenn Pr.
--The Tall Woman. LC 62-11580. 315p. 1982. pap. 8.95 (ISBN 0-9613859-1-X). Wakestone Bks.
--Tennessee. (States & the Nation). (Illus.). 224p. 1975. 14.95 (ISBN 0-393-05555-8, Co-Pub by AASLH). Norton.
--Tennessee. (States & the Nation Ser.). (Illus.). 1984. 7.95 (ISBN 0-393-30144-3). Norton.
Dykeman, Wilma & Stokely, James. Seeds of Southern Change: The Life of Will Alexander. 368p. 1976. pap. 4.95x (ISBN 0-393-00813-4, Norton Lib). Norton.
Dyken, A. R. Van see Silverman, Joseph & Van Dyken, A. R.
Dyker, David A. The Future of the Soviet Economic Planning System. LC 84-27594. 196p. 1985. 25.00 (ISBN 0-87332-324-6). M E Sharpe.
--The Process of Investment in the Soviet Union. LC 82-14600. (Soviet & East European Studies). (Illus.). 240p. 1983. 42.50 (ISBN 0-521-24831-0). Cambridge U Pr.
--Soviet Economy. (Illus.). 173p. 1976. 16.95x (ISBN 0-8464-1138-5). Beekman Pubs.
Dykes, Andrea, tr. see Von Franz, Marie-Louise.
Dykes, J. C., ed. see Latham, Hiram.
Dykes, Jeff C., jt. auth. see Dobie, J. Frank.
Dykes, Jeff C. see Tucker, William.
Dykes, M. T. A Time to Kill. LC 82-6811. 1985. 14.95 (ISBN 0-87949-223-6). Ashley Bks.
Dykes, P. W. & Keighley, M. R., eds. Gastrointestinal Haemorrhage. (Illus.). 448p. 1981. text ed. 62.50 (ISBN 0-7236-0584-X). PSG Pub Co.
Dykes, William R. The Genus Iris. 1975. Repr. of 1913 ed. 30.00 (ISBN 0-486-23037-6). Dover.
--A Handbook of Garden Irises. LC 75-42381. (Illus.). 1976. Repr. of 1924 ed. write for info (ISBN 0-685-78307-3). Theophrastus.
Dykhuizen, George. Life & Mind of John Dewey. LC 73-4602. (Illus.). 472p. 1973. 22.50x (ISBN 0-8093-0616-6). S Ill U Pr.
--Life & Mind of John Dewey. LC 73-4602. 472p. 1978. pap. 5.95 (ISBN 0-8093-0869-X). S Ill U Pr.
Dykstra, Andrew. The Kanji ABC. LC 76-58964. (Illus.). 185p. 1977. pap. 9.95 (ISBN 0-913232-37-8). W Kaufmann.
--Kanji One-Two-Three. LC 82-14007. (Illus.). 150p. (Orig.). 1983. pap. 9.95 (ISBN 0-86576-030-6). W Kaufmann.
Dykstra, Craig. Vision & Character: A Christian Educator's Alternative to Kohlberg. LC 81-82340. 160p. (Orig.). 1981. pap. 5.95 (ISBN 0-8091-2405-X). Paulist Pr.
Dykstra, Darrell I. Egypt in the Nineteenth Century: The Impact of Europe Upon a Non-Western Society. (Orig.). (gr. 9-12). 1979. pap. text ed. 5.00x (ISBN 0-932098-15-0). Ctr for NE & North African Stud.
Dykstra, David C. Computers for Profit. 1983. 25.95 (ISBN 0-8359-0868-2). Reston.
Dykstra, Dennis P. Mathematical Programming for Natural Resource Management. (Illus.). 384p. 1983. text ed. 36.95 (ISBN 0-07-018552-2). McGraw.
Dykstra, Gerald. Composition: Guided - Free Kit Prog. 1-4. 1973. pap. text ed. 17.95x (ISBN 0-8077-2521-8). Tchrs Coll.
Dykstra, Gerald, jt. auth. see Paulston, Christina B.
Dykstra, Gerald, et al. Ananse Tales: A Course in Controlled Composition. (Prog. Bk.). (gr. 9-12). 1966. pap. text ed. 3.75x (ISBN 0-8077-1269-8); tchrs. manual 1.15x (ISBN 0-8077-1272-8); wkbk. 5.00x (ISBN 0-8077-1273-6). Tchrs Coll.
--Composition: Guided - Free Kit Prog. 5-8. 1978. pap. text ed. 17.95x (ISBN 0-8077-2515-3). Tchrs Coll.
--Composition: Guided Free Manual, Programs 5-8. 1978. pap. text ed. 3.95x (ISBN 0-8077-2388-6). Tchrs Coll.
--Composition: Guided Free Program 5. 1978. pap. text ed. 3.50x (ISBN 0-8077-2389-4). Tchrs Coll.
--Composition: Guided Free Program 6. 1978. pap. text ed. 3.50x (ISBN 0-8077-2390-8). Tchrs Coll.
--Composition: Guided Free Program 7. 1978. pap. text ed. 3.50x (ISBN 0-8077-2391-6). Tchrs Coll.
--Composition: Guided Free Program 8. 1978. pap. text ed. 3.50x (ISBN 0-8077-2392-4). Tchrs Coll.

Dykstra, Gerald, et al, eds. Composition: Guided-Free. LC 73-76064. (gr. 1-6). 1974. Program 1. pap. text ed. 3.50x (ISBN 0-8077-2384-3); Program 2. pap. text ed. 3.50x (ISBN 0-8077-2385-1); Program 3. pap. text ed. 3.50x (ISBN 0-8077-2386-X); Program 4. pap. text ed. 3.50x (ISBN 0-8077-2387-8); tchrs. manual 3.95x (ISBN 0-8077-2383-5). Tchrs Coll.
Dykstra, Jari, jt. auth. see Yeagley, Joan.
Dykstra, Robert R. The Cattle Towns. LC 83-6485. (Illus.). xii, 412p. 1983. pap. 9.95 (ISBN 0-8032-6561-1, BB 858, Bison). U of Nebr Pr.
Dykstra, Yohiko K., tr. see Chingen.
Dylan, Bob. Lyrics. Kaplan, Martha, ed. 400p. 1985. pap. 19.95 (ISBN 0-394-54278-9). Knopf.
--The Songs of Bob Dylan, Nineteen Sixty-Six to Nineteen Seveny-Five. 1976. slip cased, spiral bound 19.95 (ISBN 0-394-40888-8); pap. 11.95 (ISBN 0-394-73523-4). Knopf.
--Tarantula. 1977. pap. 4.95 (ISBN 0-14-004572-4). Penguin.
--Writings & Drawings. 1973. 14.95 (ISBN 0-394-48243-3). Knopf.
Dylis, N., jt. auth. see Sukachev, V.
Dym, C. L. Stability Theory & Its Applications to Structural Mechanics. (Mechanics of Elastic Stability Ser.: No. 3). 200p. 1974. 22.50x (ISBN 90-286-0094-9). Sijthoff & Noordhoff.
--Stability Theory & Its Application To Structural Mechanics. 1974. lib. bdg. 22.50 (ISBN 90-28600-94-9, Pub. by Martinus Nijhoff Netherlands). Kluwer Academic.
Dym, C. L., jt. auth. see Shames, I. H.
Dym, Clive L. & Ivey, Elizabeth. Principles of Mathematical Modeling. LC 79-65441. (Computer Science & Applied Mathematics Ser.). 261p. 1980. tchrs' ed. 20.00i (ISBN 0-12-226550-5); solutions manual 2.50i (ISBN 0-12-226560-2). Acad Pr.
Dym, H. & McKean, H. P. Fourier Series & Integrals. (Probability & Mathematical Statistics Ser). 1972. 55.00 (ISBN 0-12-226450-9). Acad Pr.
Dym, H. & McKean, Henry P. Gaussian Processes: Complex Function Theory & the Inverse Spectral Method. (Probability & Mathematical Statistics Ser.). 1976. 59.50 (ISBN 0-12-226460-6). Acad Pr.
Dym, Harry, et al, eds. Topics in Operator Theory Systems & Networks, Vol. 12. (Operator Theory Ser.). 300p. 1984. write for info. (ISBN 3-7643-1550-4). Birkhauser.
Dym, Joseph B. Product Design with Plastics: A Practical Manual. (Illus.). 288p. 1983. 28.95 (ISBN 0-8311-1141-0). Indus Pr.
Dymally, Mervyn M. & Elliot, Jeffrey M. The Black Politician: The New Struggle for Power. (Black Political Studies: No. 2). 160p. 1986. lib. bdg. 19.95x (ISBN 0-89370-847-X); pap. text ed. 9.95x (ISBN 0-89370-947-6). Borgo Pr.
--Cuba in Transition: A New Force in the Western Hemisphere. (Caribbean-American Studies). 160p. 1986. lib. bdg. 19.95x (ISBN 0-89370-849-6); pap. text ed. 9.95x (ISBN 0-89370-949-2). Borgo Pr.
Dymally, Mervyn M. & Reginald, R. Black Politics: Voices from the Past. (Black Political Studies: No. 1). 160p. 1986. lib. bdg. 19.95x (ISBN 0-89370-846-1); pap. text ed. 9.95x (ISBN 0-89370-946-8). Borgo Pr.
Dymally, Mervyn M. & Smith, Stanley H. The Status of Third-World People in the Western Hemisphere. (Caribbean-American Studies). 160p. 1986. lib. bdg. 19.95x (ISBN 0-89370-848-8); pap. text ed. 9.95x (ISBN 0-89370-948-4). Borgo Pr.
Dyment, Clifford. Matthew Arnold: An Introduction & a Selection. 1977. Repr. of 1948 ed. lib. bdg. 25.00 (ISBN 0-8492-0637-5). R West.
Dymock, Eric. The Sprites & Midgets: Collector's Guide. (Illus.). 136p. 1981. 18.95 (ISBN 0-900549-53-X, Pub. by Motor Racing Pubns England). Motorbooks Intl.
Dymock, William, et al. Pharmacographia Indica: A History of Principal Drugs of Vegetable Origin Met with in British India, 3 vols. 1978. Repr. of 1890 ed. Set. 225.00x (ISBN 0-89955-296-X, Pub. by Intl Bk Dist). Intl Spec Bk.
Dymond, David. The Norfolk Landscape: The Making of the English Landscape. (Illus.). 261p. 1985. 18.95 (ISBN 0-340-04332-6, Pub. by Hodder & Stoughton UK). David & Charles.
--Writing Local History: A Practical Guide. 91p. 1981. pap. 8.00x (ISBN 0-7199-1048-X, Pub. by Bedford England). Brookfield Pub Co.
Dymond, David & Betterton, Alec. Lavenham: Seven Hundred Years of Textile Making. (Illus.). 108p. 1982. pap. 13.95 (ISBN 0-85115-164-7, Pub. by Boydell & Brewer). Longwood Pub Group.
Dymond, J. H. & Smith, E. B. The Second Virial Coefficients of Pure Gases & Mixtures: A Critical Compilation. (Oxford Science Research Papers Ser.). (Illus.). 1980. pap. text ed. 79.00x (ISBN 0-19-855361-7). Oxford U Pr.
Dymond, Jonathan. Inquiry into the Accordancy of War with the Principles of Christianity. LC 79-147432. (Library of War & Peace; Proposals for Peace: a History). 1973. lib. bdg. 46.00 (ISBN 0-8240-0222-9). Garland Pub.
--War, An Essay. LC 72-147433. (Library of War & Peace; Proposals for Peace: a History). 1980. lib. bdg. 46.00 (ISBN 0-8240-0480-9). Garland Pub.
--War, an Essay. 59.95 (ISBN 0-8490-1275-9). Gordon Pr.
Dymond, Rosalind F., jt. ed. see Rogers, Carl R.
Dymtryshyn, Basil, tr. see Golovin, Pavel N.
Dynamic Aspects of Cerebral Edema International Workshop, 3rd, Montreal June 25-9, 1976. Dynamics of Brain Edema: Proceedings. Pappius, H. M., et al, eds. (Illus.). 1976. soft cover 31.90 (ISBN 0-387-08009-0). Springer-Verlag.
Dynamic Publications, ed. Canadian Review: 1985 Edition. (Illus.). 112p. 1985. 35.00 (ISBN 0-915569-07-8). Dynamic Pubns.
--Mid-Atlantic Review: 1983 Edition. (Illus.). 158p. 1983. 29.95 (ISBN 0-915569-00-0). Dynamic Pubns.
--Mid-Atlantic Review, 1985. (Illus.). 158p. 1985. 35.00 (ISBN 0-915569-01-9). Dynamic Pubns.
--Northern Review: 1985 Edition. (Illus.). 158p. 1985. 35.00 (ISBN 0-915569-04-3). Dynamic Pubns.
--Regional Review Source Book, 1985, 5 bks. (Illus.). 1985. Set. 125.00 (ISBN 0-915569-06-X). Dynamic Pubns.
--Southwest Review: 1985 Edition. (Illus.). 120p. 1984. 35.00 (ISBN 0-915569-02-7). Dynamic Pubns.
--Western Review, Nineteen Eighty-Five. (Illus.). 188p. 1984. 35.00 (ISBN 0-915569-03-5). Dynamic Pubns.
Dynamic Publications Editorial Staff, ed. New York-New England Review, 1985. (Illus.). 384p. 1985. 35.00 (ISBN 0-915569-05-1). Dynamic Pubns.
Dynamic Publications, Inc. Mid Atlantic Review: 1986 Edition. (Illus.). 344p. 1985. 35.00 (ISBN 0-915569-08-6). Dynamic Pubns.
--New York-New England Review: 1986 Edition. (Illus.). 1985. 45.00 (ISBN 0-915569-12-4). Dynamic Pubns.
--Northern Review: 1986 Edition. (Illus.). 1985. 45.00 (ISBN 0-915569-13-2). Dynamic Pubns.
--Southwest Review: 1986 Edition. (Illus.). 176p. 1985. 35.00 (ISBN 0-915569-09-4). Dynamic Pubns.
--Western Review, Nineteen Eighty-Six. (Illus.). 384p. 1985. 35.00 (ISBN 0-915569-10-8). Dynamic Pubns.
Dynatech Corporation. Electrically Insulating Thermally Conducting Copper Materials. 88p. 1962. 13.20 (ISBN 0-317-34519-2, 14). Intl Copper.
Dynatech R-D Company, jt. auth. see Haines, D. M.
Dynatech R-D Company, jt. auth. see Walker, D. H.
Dyne, George Van see Van Dyne, George.
Dyne, Penny Van see Carter, Sharon & Van Dyne, Penny.
Dyne, Susan R. Van see Schuster, Marilyn R. & Van Dyne, Susan R.
Dyne, Susan Van see Van Dyne, Susan.
Dynes, Russell R., jt. auth. see Anderson, William A.
Dynes, Russell R., jt. ed. see Freeman, Howard E.
Dynes, Wayne. The Illuminations of the Stavelot Bible. LC 77-94693. (Outstanding Dissertations in the Fine Arts Ser.). (Illus.). 1979. lib. bdg. 44.00 (ISBN 0-8240-3225-X). Garland Pub.
Dynkin, E. B. Markov Processes & Related Problems of Analysis. LC 81-38438. (London Mathematical Society Lecture Note Ser.: No. 54). 300p. 1982. pap. 29.95 (ISBN 0-521-28512-7). Cambridge U Pr.
Dynkin, E. B. & Yushkevich, A. A. Markov Processes: Theorems & Problems. LC 69-12529. 237p. 1969. 27.50x (ISBN 0-306-30378-7, Plenum Pr). Plenum Pub.
Dynkin, E. B., jt. auth. see Yushkevich, A. A.
Dynkin, E. B., et al. Eleven Papers on Analysis, Probability & Topology. LC 51-5559. (Translations, Ser.: No. 2, Vol. 12). 1966. Repr. of 1959 ed. 27.00 (ISBN 0-8218-1712-4, TRANS 2-12). Am Math.
--Five Papers on Algebra & Group Theory. LC 51-5559. (Translations Ser.: No. 2, Vol. 6). 1957. 55.00 (ISBN 0-8218-1706-X, TRANS 2-6). Am Math.
--Six Lectures Delivered at the International Congress of Mathematicians in Stockholm, 1962. LC 51-5559. (Translations Ser.: No. 2, Vol. 31). 1963. 15.00 (ISBN 0-8218-1731-0, TRANS 2-31). Am Math.
Dynkin, E. G., et al. Mathematical Problems: An Anthology. (Pocket Mathematical Library). 76p. 1967. 24.50 (ISBN 0-677-20710-7). Gordon.
Dynneson, Thomas L., jt. ed. see Gross, Richard E.
Dynski-Klein, Martha. Color Atlas of Pediatrics. (Year Book Color Atlas Ser.). (Illus.). 415p. 1975. 59.95 (ISBN 0-8151-2983-1). Year Bk Med.
Dyomin, Mikhail. Blatnoi. LC 80-54025. 364p. (Orig., Rus.). 1981. pap. 18.50 (ISBN 0-89830-027-4). Russica Pubs.
--Perekrestki Sudeb: Dve povesti. LC 80-54024. 307p. (Rus.). 1983. 25.00 (ISBN 0-89830-071-1); pap. 17.00 (ISBN 0-89830-033-9). Russica Pubs.
--Taezhnyi Brodiaga. 300p. (Orig.). 1985. write for info. (ISBN 0-89830-093-2); pap. write for info. (ISBN 0-89830-094-0). Russica Pubs.
Dyorak, Max. Idealism & Naturalism in Gothic Art. Klawiter, Randolph J., tr. LC 67-22143. (Illus.). pap. 70.50 (ISBN 0-317-10425-X, 2022072). Bks Demand UMI.
Dyos, H. J. Exploring the Urban Past: Essays in Urban History. Cannadine, David & Reeder, David, eds. LC 82-1209. (Illus.). 320p. 1982. 44.50 (ISBN 0-521-24624-5); pap. 14.95 (ISBN 0-521-28848-7). Cambridge U Pr.
--Study of Urban History. LC 68-29379. (Illus.). 1968. 27.50 (ISBN 0-312-77280-7). St Martin.
Dyos, H. J. & Wolff, Michael. The Victorian City-Images & Realities, Vol. 1: Past & Present & Numbers of People. (Illus.). 1978. pap. 14.95 (ISBN 0-7100-8458-7). Routledge & Kegan.
Dyos, H. J., ed. Urban History Yearbook, 1978. 255p. 1978. pap. 18.75x (ISBN 0-8476-3164-8). Rowman.
Dyos, H. J. & Wolff, Michael, eds. Victorian City: Images & Realities, 2 vols. (Illus.). 1001p. 1973. Set. 110.00 (ISBN 0-7100-7384-4); Vol. 1. 60.00 (ISBN 0-7100-7374-7); Vol. 2. 60.00 (ISBN 0-7100-7383-6). Routledge & Kegan.
--The Victorian City-Images & Realities, Vol. 2: Shapes on the Ground & a Change of Accent. (Illus.). 1978. pap. 14.95 (ISBN 0-7100-8812-4). Routledge & Kegan.
Dyrek, K., et al, eds. Reactivity of Solids: Proceedings of the 9th International Symposium, Cracow, Sept. 1980, 2 vols. (Materials Science Monographs: No. 10). 1500p. 1983. 189.50 (ISBN 0-444-99707-5). Elsevier.
Dyrenfurth, Michael J. & Householder, Daniel L. Industrial Arts Education: A Review & Synthesis of the Research 1968-1979. 207p. 1979. 12.25 (ISBN 0-318-15494-3, IN183). Natl Ctr Res Voc Ed.
Dyrness, W. A. Christian Art in Asia. 1979. pap. text ed. 12.00x (ISBN 0-391-01157-X). Humanities.
Dyrness, Wayne. Apple Programing Secrets They Didn't Want You to Know. (Illus.). 256p. 1986. 20.95 (ISBN 0-13-039215-4). P-H.
Dyrness, William A. Christian Apologetics in a World Community. LC 82-21383. 180p. 1983. pap. 6.95 (ISBN 0-87784-399-6). Inter-Varsity.
--Let the Earth Rejoice! 192p. (Orig.). 1983. pap. 6.95 (ISBN 0-89107-282-9, Crossway Bks). Good News.
--Themes in Old Testament Theology. LC 79-2380. 1979. pap. 7.95 (ISBN 0-87784-726-6). Inter-Varsity.
Dyroff, Adolf. Die Ethik der Alten Stoa. Vlastos, Gregory, ed. LC 78-19350. (Morals & Law in Ancient Greece Ser.). (Ger. & Gr.). 1979. Repr. of 1897 ed. lib. bdg. 30.50x (ISBN 0-405-11540-7). Ayer Co Pubs.
--Der Peripatos Uber das Greisenalter. 1939. pap. 12.00 (ISBN 0-384-13655-9). Johnson Repr.
Dyrud, Jarl E., jt. ed. see Freedman, Daniel X.
Dyrvik, Stale. Demographic Crises in Norway in the 17th & 18th Centuries. 1977. pap. 8.00x (ISBN 82-00-01627-7, Dist. by Columbia U Pr). Universitet.
Dyrvik, Stale, et al, eds. The Satellite State: Problems in the History of the 17th & 18th Centuries. 1979. pap. 18.00x (ISBN 8-2000-5283-4, Dist. by Columbia U. Pr.). Universitet.
Dys, Pat, jt. auth. see Corbin, Linda.
Dys, Pat, ed. see Corbin, Linda.
Dysard, Dorothy L. I Can, We Can. (CPA Vacation Venture Ser.). (gr. 1-2). 1981. pap. 1.70 student bk. (ISBN 0-664-24339-8); pap. 3.70 leader's guide (ISBN 0-664-24340-1); resource packet 8.35 (ISBN 0-664-24341-X). Westminster.
Dysinger, Wendell S. see Dale, Edgar.
Dysken, jt. ed. see Gibbons.
Dyson. Cell Biology: A Molecular Approach. 2nd ed. 1985. 38.57 (ISBN 0-205-05942-2, 675942). Allyn.
Dyson, A. E. Yeats, Eliot & R. S. Thomas: Riding the Echo. 339p. 1981. text ed. 30.50x (ISBN 0-391-02338-1). Humanities.
Dyson, A. E., jt. auth. see Cox, C. B.
Dyson, A. E., ed. Dickens. LC 72-127564. (Modern Judgement Ser). 1970. pap. text ed. 2.50 (ISBN 0-87695-098-5). Aurora Pubs.
Dyson, Anne, jt. auth. see Genishi, Celia.
Dyson, Anthony. Pictures to Print: The Nineteenth-Century Engraving Trade. (Illus.). 234p. 1985. 28.50 (ISBN 0-317-19287-6); special ed. 115.00 (ISBN 0-317-19288-4). BkPr Ltd.
Dyson, Anthony E. The Crazy Fabric: Essays in Irony. LC 72-10871. (Essay Index Reprint Ser.). 1973. Repr. of 1965 ed. 16.00 (ISBN 0-8369-7214-7). Ayer Co Pubs.
Dyson, Crook. India's Demography: Essays on the Contemporary Population. 211p. 1984. text ed. 16.50x (ISBN 0-391-03108-2). Humanities.
Dyson, E., et al. Yarn Production & Properties. 96p. 1974. 70.00x (ISBN 0-686-63811-5). State Mutual Bk.
Dyson, Freeman. Disturbing the Universe. LC 78-20665. 304p. 1981. pap. 6.68 (ISBN 0-06-090771-1, CN 771, CN). Har-Row.
--Disturbing the Universe: A Life in Science. LC 78-20665. (Sloan Foundation Bk.). 1979. 12.95i (ISBN 0-06-011108-9, HarpT). Har-Row.
--Innenansichten: Erinnerungen in die Zukunft. Zehnder, Jeanette, tr. from Eng. (Science & Society Ser.: No. 38). Orig. Title: Disturbing the Universe. 288p. (Ger.). 1981. 19.95 (ISBN 0-8176-1200-9). Birkhauser.
--Weapons & Hope. LC 82-48675. (Cornelia & Michael Bessie Bk.). 320p. 1984. 17.26 (ISBN 0-06-039031-X). Har-Row.
--Weapons & Hope. LC 83-48343. 341p. 1985. pap. 7.64i (ISBN 0-06-039039-5, CN 1270, CN). Har-Row.
Dyson, Freeman, et al. Values at War: Selected Tanner Lectures on the Nuclear Crisis. 130p. (Orig.). 1983. pap. 5.95 (ISBN 0-87480-226-1). U of Utah Pr.
Dyson, Geoffrey H. The Mechanics of Athletics. 7th rev. ed. LC 77-3430. (Illus.). 264p. 1978. text ed. 34.50x (ISBN 0-8419-0309-3); pap. text ed. 17.50x (ISBN 0-8419-0310-7). Holmes & Meier.
Dyson, George. New Music. (Select Bibliographies Reprint Ser). 1924. 17.00 (ISBN 0-8369-5231-6). Ayer Co Pubs.
--Progress of Music. LC 79-93334. (Essay Index Reprint Ser). 1932. 18.00 (ISBN 0-8369-1287-X). Ayer Co Pubs.
Dyson, Guy. The Kendrick Kindred. 1973. 10.00 (ISBN 0-87511-685-X). Claitors.
Dyson, H. V., ed. Pope: Poetry & Prose with Essays by Johnson, Coleridge, Hazlitt, Etc. 1977. Repr. of 1933 ed. lib. bdg. 20.00 (ISBN 0-8414-1852-7). Folcroft.
Dyson, Henry V. & Butt, John E. Augustans & Romantics, Sixteen Eighty-Nine to Eighteen Thirty. 2nd rev. ed. Repr. of 1950 ed. 39.00x (ISBN 0-403-03061-7). Somerset Pub.
Dyson, Hope & Tennyson, Charles, eds. Dear & Honoured Lady. LC 72-151284. 152p. 1971. 15.00 (ISBN 0-8386-7922-6). Fairleigh Dickinson.
Dyson, J. E. & Williams, D. A. Physics of the Interstellar Medium. LC 80-13713. 194p. 1980. 28.95x (ISBN 0-470-26983-9). Halsted Pr.
Dyson, J. E., ed. Active Galactic Nuclei. LC 84-27277. 350p. 1985. pap. 26.00 (ISBN 0-7190-1097-7, Pub. by Manchester Univ Pr). Longwood Pub Group.
Dyson, James, jt. auth. see Gore, William J.
Dyson, John. The South Seas Dream: An Adventure In Paradise. 256p. 1982. 19.95 (ISBN 0-316-20024-7). Little.
Dyson, Kenneth & Wilks, Stephen, eds. Industrial Crisis: A Comparative Study of the State & Corporate Decline. LC 83-9518. 290p. 1983. 32.50 (ISBN 0-312-51239-2). St Martin.
Dyson, Kenneth H. The State Tradition in Western Europe: A Study of Idea & Institution. 1980. 21.95x (ISBN 0-19-520209-0). Oxford U Pr.
Dyson, Lowell K. Red Harvest: The Communist Party & American Farmers. LC 81-8200. xii, 259p. 1982. 19.95x (ISBN 0-8032-1659-9). U of Nebr Pr.
Dyson, N. A. An Introduction to Nuclear Physics with Applications in Medicine & Biology. (Physics & Medicine in Biology Ser.). 260p. 1981. 59.95x (ISBN 0-470-27277-5). Halsted Pr.
Dyson, Norman Allen. X-rays in Atomic & Nuclear Physics. LC 73-85203. pap. 98.50 (ISBN 0-317-08542-5, 2010051). Bks Demand UMI.
Dyson, R. H., et al. From Athens to Gordion: The Papers of a Memorial Symposium for Rodney S. Young. DeVries, Keith, ed. (University Museum Papers: Vol. I). (Illus.). xix, 168p. (Orig.). 1980. pap. 20.00x (ISBN 0-934718-35-0). Univ Mus of U PA.
Dyson, R. W. A Ninth-Century Political Tract: The De Institutione Regia of Jonas of Orleans. 112p. 1983. 7.00 (ISBN 0-682-40116-1, University). Exposition Pr FL.
Dyson, Robert D. Essentials of Cell Biology. 2nd ed. 1978. text ed. 36.43 (ISBN 0-205-06117-6, 676117). Allyn.
Dyson, Robert H., Jr., ed. see Muscarella, Oscar W.
Dyson, Robert H., Jr., ed. see Winter, Irene J.
Dyson, Roger. The National Health Service: Professionals or Militants? 180p. 1987. 22.50 (ISBN 0-7099-0835-0, Pub. by Croom helm Ltd). Longwood Pub Group.
Dyson, Ronald. Gardening on Chalk & Lime. 256p. 1981. 35.00x (ISBN 0-460-04267-X, Pub. by J M Dent England). State Mutual Bk.
Dyson, Rosamund Shuter see Shuter-Dyson, Rosamund & Gabriel, Clive.
Dyson, S. Cosa: The Utilitarian Pottery. (Memoirs: No. 33). (Illus.). 176p. 1976. 37.00 (ISBN 0-318-12318-5). Am Acad Rome.
Dyson, S. L. The Stories of the Trees. LC 78-175735. (Illus.). 272p. 1974. Repr. of 1890 ed. 40.00x (ISBN 0-8103-3033-4). Gale.
Dyson, Stephen. The Commonware & Brittle Ware: Final Report IV, Part 1, Fascicle 3. LC 43-2669. pap. 15.00 (ISBN 0-685-71742-9). J J Augustin.
Dyson, Stephen L. The Creation of the Roman Frontier. Barb, S., ed. LC 84-42881. 324p. 1985. 35.00x (ISBN 0-691-03577-6). Princeton U Pr.
Dyson, Verne. Anecdotes & Events in Long Island History. LC 70-8296. (Empire State Historical Publications Ser). 1969. 12.50x (ISBN 0-87198-079-7). Friedman.
--Forgotten Tales of Ancient China. 69.95 (ISBN 0-8490-0183-8). Gordon Pr.
--Whitmanland: West Hills Memories of a Poet & His Ancestors. LC 74-3052. 1960. lib. bdg. 15.00 (ISBN 0-8414-3727-0). Folcroft.
Dyson, W. H. Studies in Christian Mysticism. 1977. lib. bdg. 69.95 (ISBN 0-8490-2702-0). Gordon Pr.
Dyson-Hudson, Rada & Little, Michael A. Rethinking Human Adaptation. (Special Study). 200p. 1982. 23.00x (ISBN 0-86531-511-6). Westview.
Dyssegaard, Birgit. The Role of Special Education in an Overall Rehabilitation Program, No. 7. (International Exchange of Information in Rehabilitation Ser.). 87p. 1981. write for info. (ISBN 0-939986-13-2). World Rehab Fund.

Dyte, C. E., jt. auth. see Champ, B. R.

Dywasuk, Colette T., rev. by see Raymond, Louise.

Dzacab, Bolon & Truck, Fred. The Left Ear of the Machine. 25.00 (ISBN 0-938236-00-8). Cookie Pr.

Dzama, Mary Ann & Gilstrap, Robert. Ready to Read: A Parents' Guide. LC 82-24777. (Parent Education Ser.). 154p. 1983. pap. text ed. 8.95x (ISBN 0-471-86637-7, Pub. by Wiley Pr). Wiley.

Dzaman, Fern L. Who's Who in Chiropractic International. 2nd ed. Scheiner, Sidney, et al, eds. LC 80-51366. 1980. 55.00 (ISBN 0-918336-02-3). Chiropractic.

Dzaman, Fern L., et al, eds. Who's Who in Chiropractic, International 1976-78. LC 77-79754. (Illus.). 1977. 49.50 (ISBN 0-918336-01-5). Chiropractic.

D'Zamko, Mary E. & Hedges, William D. Helping Exceptional Students Succeed in the Regular Classroom. 260p. 1985. 18.50 (ISBN 0-13-386046-9, Busn). P-H.

Dzelepy, E. N. The Spanish Plot. 59.95 (ISBN 0-8490-1105-1). Gordon Pr.

Dzeron, Nanoog. Village of Parchanj: First English-Language Edition. 1984p. 1984. 20.00 (ISBN 0-914330-68-3). Panorama West.

Dzhagarov, Georgi. Public Prosecutor. Snow, C. P. & Johnson, Pamela H., eds. Alexieva, Marguerite, tr. LC 71-458336. 86p. 1969. 20.00x (ISBN 0-295-95003-X). U of Wash Pr.

Dzhavad-Zade, M. D. Surgery of Kidney & Ureteral Anomalies. 1980. 12.75 (ISBN 0-8285-1872-6, Pub. by Mir Pubs USSR). Imported Pubns.

Dziak, John, jt. auth. see Rocca, Raymond.

Dziak, John J. Soviet Perceptions of Doctrine & Military Power: The Interaction of Theory & Practice. LC 81-3260. (NSIC Strategy Paper Ser.: No. 36). 80p. 1981. pap. text ed. 5.95x (ISBN 0-8448-1389-3). Crane-Russak Co.

Dziech, Billie W. & Weiner, Linda. The Lecherous Professor: Sexual Harassment on Campus. LC 82-73960. 228p. 1984. 16.95 (ISBN 0-8070-3100-3); pap. 8.95 (ISBN 0-8070-3101-1, BP 690). Beacon Pr.

Dzieduszycka, Teresa, tr. see Mrozek, Slawomir.

Dziedzic, S. Z. & Kearsley, M. W., eds. Glucose Syrups: Science & Technology. (Illus.). 272p. 1985. 52.50 (ISBN 0-85334-299-7, Pub. by Elsevier Applied Sci England). Elsevier.

Dziedzic, Stan. The United States Wrestling Syllabus. LC 81-85635. (Illus.). 208p. 1983. pap. 14.95 (ISBN 0-88011-014-7). Leisure Pr.

Dzielak, Ted & Greiner, Lynn. Injured at Work: A Guide for Washington Workers. LC 84-40664. (Illus.). 152p. (Orig.). 1985. pap. 8.95 (ISBN 0-295-96220-8). U of Wash Pr.

Dziewanowski, M. K. The Communist Party of Poland: An Outline of History. rev. ed. (Russian Research Center Studies Ser.: No. 32). 432p. 1976. 27.50x (ISBN 0-674-15055-4). Harvard U Pr.

--A History of Soviet Russia. 2nd ed. (Illus.). 432p. 1985. pap. text ed. 23.95 (ISBN 0-13-392143-3). P-H.

--Poland in the Twentieth-Century. LC 76-51216. (Illus.). 1977. 27.50x (ISBN 0-231-03577-2); pap. 14.50x (ISBN 0-231-08372-6). Columbia U Pr.

Dziewanowski, Marian K. Communist Party of Poland: An Outline of History. LC 58-7500. (Russian Research Center Studies: No. 32). 1959. 27.50x (ISBN 0-674-15050-3). Harvard U Pr.

Dziewonski, A. & Boschi, E., eds. Physics & the Earth's Interior. (Enrico Fermi Summer School Ser.: No. 78). 720p. 1980. 149.00 (ISBN 0-444-85461-4, North-Holland). Elsevier.

Dziewonski, K. & Bourne, L. S., eds. Urbanization & Settlement Systems: International Perspectives. x ed. (Illus.). 1984. 47.50x (ISBN 0-19-823243-8). Oxford U Pr.

Dzik, Stanley. Aircraft Detail Design Manual. 3rd ed. Rice, Michael S., ed. (Illus.). 110p. 1974. pap. 15.95 (ISBN 0-87994-011-5, Pub. by AvPubns). Aviation.

Dzik, Stanley J. Aircraft Hardware Standards Manual & Engineering Reference. (Illus.). 142p. 1971. pap. 12.95 (ISBN 0-87994-012-3). Aviation.

--Helicopter Design & Data Manual. 2nd rev. ed. (Illus.). 120p. 1974. pap. 9.95 (ISBN 0-87994-010-7, Pub. by AvPubns). Aviation.

Dzinotyiweyi, H. Analogue of the Group Algebra for Topological Semigroups. (Research Notes Ser.: No. 98). 208p. 1984. pap. text ed. 19.95 (ISBN 0-273-08610-3). Pitman Pub MA.

Dzjurawiec, S., jt. auth. see Deregowski, J. B.

Dzrbasjan, M. M., et al. Seventeen Papers on Functions of Complex Variables. LC 51-5559. (Translations Ser.: No. 2, Vol. 32). 1963. 32.00 (ISBN 0-8218-1732-9, TRANS 2-32). Am Math.

Dzulynski, S. & Walton, E. K. Sedimentary Features of Flysch & Greywackes. (Developments in Sedimentology: Vol. 7). 274p. 1965. 81.00 (ISBN 0-444-40185-7). Elsevier.

Dzulynski, Stanislaw & Sanders, John. Current Marks on Firm Mud Bottoms. (Connecticut Academy of Arts & Sciences Transaction: Vol. 42). 96p. 1962. pap. 9.50 (ISBN 0-208-01107-2). Shoe String.

Dzyuba, Ivan. Internationalism or Russification. 263p. 1974. write for info. Ukrainian Pol.

Dzyubenko, G. Land of the Soviets in Verse & Prose, Vol. 1. 398p. 1982. 19.95 (ISBN 0-8285-2519-6, Pub. by Progress Pubs USSR). Imported Pubns.

Dzyubenko, G. & Kondratovich, A., eds. Land of the Soviets in Verse & Prose, Vol. 2. 381p. 1982. 19.95 (ISBN 0-8285-2552-8, Pub. by Progress Pubs USSR). Imported Pubns.

E

E, Gao, ed. see Cao, Xueqin.

E, Jeanne. The Twelve Steps for Smokers. 24p. (Orig.). 1984. pap. 1.10 (ISBN 0-89486-229-4). Hazelden.

E, Liu. Travels of Lao Can. 176p. 1983. pap. 3.95 (ISBN 0-8351-1075-3). China Bks.

E R C Editorial Staff. E R C's President's Guide. 1970. 131.50 (ISBN 0-13-925438-2). P-H.

--Treasurer's Guide. 1976. 131.50 (ISBN 0-13-930503-3). P-H.

E S L A B-E S R I N Symposium, 5th, Noordwijk, The Netherlands, 1971. Infrared Detection Techniques for Space Research: Proceedings. Manno, V. & Ring, J., eds. LC 70-179894. (Astrophysics & Space Library: No. 30). 344p. 1972. lib. bdg. 50.00 (ISBN 90-277-0226-8, Pub. by Reidel Holland). Kluwer Academic.

E. William, JFK School of Government, Harvard University, jt. ed. see Sven B. Lundstedt, Ohio State University.

EA Engineering, Science & Technology, Inc. Staff. Cadmium: Environmental & Community Health Impact. LC 85-70626. (Orig.). 1985. pap. 9.50 (ISBN 0-89364-051-4, 847-86350). Am Petroleum.

EA Engineering, Science & Technology. Inc. Staff. Vanadium: Environmental & Community Health Impact. LC 85-70627. (Orig.). 1985. pap. 10.00 (ISBN 0-89364-052-2, 847-86450). Am Petroleum.

Eacho, E. M., et al. Process Measurement Fundamentals, 3 vols. (Illus.). 1981. Set. 154.00x (ISBN 0-87683-000-9); Vol. 1; 177p. looseleaf 60.00x (ISBN 0-87683-001-7); Vol. 2; 29p. looseleaf 47.00x (ISBN 0-87683-002-5); Vol. 3; 175p. looseleaf lab manuals 47.00x (ISBN 0-317-11887-0); looseleaf lesson plans 1250.00x (ISBN 0-87683-004-1). G P Courseware.

--Pneumatic Measurement & Control Applications, 3 vol. set. (Illus.). 1981. Set. lib. bdg. 154.00x (ISBN 0-87683-010-6); Vol. 1, 400 p. text ed. 60.00x looseleaf (ISBN 0-87683-011-4); Vol. 2, 160p. looseleaf 47.00x (ISBN 0-87683-013-0); Vol. 3, 160p. lab manual solutions looseleaf 47.00x (ISBN 0-317-12060-3); lesson plans, looseleaf 1250.00x (ISBN 0-87683-014-9). G P Courseware.

Eachus, Sara A. The Leedom Family. 1982. 20.00 (ISBN 0-8059-2795-6). Dorrance.

Eacker, Jay N. Problems of Metaphysics & Psychology. LC 82-8053. 260p. 1983. text ed. 22.95x (ISBN 0-88229-685-X); pap. text ed. 11.95x (ISBN 0-88229-814-3). Nelson-Hall.

--Problems of Philosophy & Psychology. LC 75-17548. 216p. 1975. 20.95x (ISBN 0-88229-202-1); pap. 10.95x (ISBN 0-88229-489-X). Nelson-Hall.

Eaddy, P. A. Hull Down, Sea Lore, Sea Legends & the Days of the Sailing Ships. 1977. lib. bdg. 69.95 (ISBN 0-8490-2026-3). Gordon Pr.

Eaddy, Virginia B., jt. auth. see Amacher, Ethel S.

Eade, Alfred T. Expanded Panorama Bible Study Course. (Illus.). 192p. 12.95 (ISBN 0-8007-0086-4). Revell.

--The New Panorama Bible Study Course. Incl. No. 1. A Study of Dispensational Truth. (Illus.). 28p (ISBN 0-8007-0221-2); No. 2. The Study of Angelology. 32p (ISBN 0-8007-0222-0); No. 3. The Second Coming of Christ. 36p (ISBN 0-8007-0223-9); No. 4. The Book of Revelation. (Illus.). 28p (ISBN 0-8007-0434-7). pap. 6.95 ea. Revell.

--Panorama de la Biblia. Orig. Title: New Panorama Bible Study Course. 32p. 1984. pap. 3.75 (ISBN 0-311-03657-0). Casa Bautista.

Eade, Charles, compiled by see Churchill, Winston S.

Eade, D. & Hodgson, J. T., eds. Information Systems in Public Administration: Their Role in Economics & Social Development. 476p. 1981. 59.75 (ISBN 0-444-86275-7, North-Holland). Elsevier.

Eade, Deborah, jt. auth. see Jackson, Tony.

Eade, Gordon E., et al, eds. Designs for Teaching & Learning. LC 72-86268. 188p. 1972. text ed. 28.50x (ISBN 0-8422-5028-X). Irvington.

Eade, J. C. The Forgotten Sky: A Guide to Astrology in English Literature. (Illus.). 244p. 1984. 34.50x (ISBN 0-19-812813-4). Oxford U Pr.

Eade, J. C., jt. auth. see Brissenden, R. F.

Eade, J. C., jt. ed. see Sussex, Roland.

Eaden, J., tr. see Labat, Pere.

Eadeni, June. The Slender Tree, a Life of Alice Meynell. 256p. 1981. 25.00x (ISBN 0-907018-01-7, Pub. by Tab Hse England). State Mutual Bk.

Eades. Damages, Kentucky Law of Eades. 352p. 1985. 59.95 (ISBN 0-317-20123-9). Harrison Co GA.

--Products Liability. (The Law in Kentucky Ser.). incl. latest pocket part supplement 24.95 (ISBN 0-686-90591-1); separate pocket part supplement, 1982 9.45 (ISBN 0-686-90592-X). Harrison Co GA.

--Wrongful Death Actions. (The Law in Kentucky Ser.). incl. latest pocket part supplement 24.95 (ISBN 0-686-90593-8); separate pocket part supplement, 1982 9.45 (ISBN 0-686-90594-6). Harrison Co GA.

Eades, D. Dharawal & Dharga Languages of the New South Wales Coast. (AIAS Research & Regional Studies: No. 8). 1976. pap. text ed. 9.50x (ISBN 0-85575-051-0). Humanities.

Eades, J. S. The Yoruba Today. LC 79-50236. (Changing Cultures Ser.). (Illus.). 1980. 34.50 (ISBN 0-521-22656-2); pap. 11.95 (ISBN 0-521-29602-1). Cambridge U Pr.

Eades, Ronald W. Watson vs. Jones: The Walnut Street Presbyterian Church & the First Amendment. 144p. 1982. 18.50 (ISBN 0-89097-023-8). Archer Edns.

Eadie. Statistical Methods in Experimental Physics. 1984. Repr. 42.50 (ISBN 0-317-11385-2). Elsevier.

Eadie, ed. see Cruden, Alexander.

Eadie, Donald. A User's Guide to Computer Peripherals. (Illus.). 224p. 1982. 27.95 (ISBN 0-13-939660-8). P-H.

Eadie, Douglas C., jt. auth. see Olsen, John B.

Eadie, John. Colossians. 1981. 10.50 (ISBN 0-86524-067-1, 5103). Klock & Klock.

Eadie, John, ed. Early Oriental History: Comprising the Histories of Egypt, Assyria, Persia, Lydia, Phrygia, & Phoenicia. 1852. 20.00 (ISBN 0-8482-0741-6). Norwood Edns.

Eadie, John W. The Breviarium of Festus. (University of London Classical Studies: No. V). 194p. 1967. 65.00 (ISBN 0-485-13705-4, Pub. by Athlone Pr Ltd). Longwood Pub Group.

--Classical Traditions in Early America. LC 76-51864. 265p. (Orig.). 1976. pap. 10.00 (ISBN 0-915932-02-4). Trillium Pr.

Eadie, John W., ed. The Conversion of Constantine. LC 76-25480. (European American Studies). 120p. 1977. pap. text ed. 5.95 (ISBN 0-88275-453-X). Krieger.

Eadie, John W. & Ober, Josiah, eds. The Craft of the Ancient Historian: Essays in Honor of Chester G. Starr. (Orig.). 1985. lib. bdg. 32.50 (ISBN 0-8191-4789-3, Assn Ancient Historians); pap. text ed. 19.75 (ISBN 0-8191-4790-7). U Pr of Amer.

Eadie, John W., jt. ed. see D'Arms, John H.

Eadie, M. & Tyrer, J. H., eds. The Biochemistry of Migraine. 1984. lib. bdg. 57.00 (ISBN 0-85200-731-0, Pub. by MTP Pr England). Kluwer-Academic.

Eadie, M. J. & Tyrer, J. H. Anticonvulsant Therapy. 2nd ed. (Illus.). 1980. text ed. 50.00 (ISBN 0-443-01917-7). Churchill.

Eadie, M. J., jt. auth. see Tyrer, J. H.

Eadie, M. J. & Tyrer, J. H., eds. Biochemical Neurology. LC 82-22859. 278p. 1983. 48.00 (ISBN 0-8451-3009-9). A R Liss.

Eadie, Mervyn, jt. auth. see Sutherland, John M.

Eadie, Mervyn & Tyrer, John, eds. Clinical & Experimental Neurology: Proceedings of the Australian Association of Neurologists, 1983, Vol. 20. 264p. 1984. 67.00 (ISBN 0-683-11202-3). Williams & Wilkins.

Eadie, Mervyn J. & Tyrer, John H. Neurological Clinical Pharmacology. 470p. 1980. text ed. 48.00 (ISBN 0-683-11007-1). Williams & Wilkins.

Eadie, Mervyn J., jt. auth. see Tyrer, John H.

Eadie, Mervyn J., et al, eds. Introduction to Clinical Pharmacology. 142p. 1981. pap. 18.00 (ISBN 0-683-11032-2). Williams & Wilkins.

Eadie, Peter McGregor. The Channel Islands. (Blue Guides Ser.). 24.95 (ISBN 0-393-01534-3); pap. 15.95 (ISBN 0-393-00087-7). Norton.

Eadie, W. T., et al. Statistical Methods in Experimental Physics. LC 75-157034. 296p. 1972. 42.50 (ISBN 0-444-10117-9, North-Holland). Elsevier.

Eadington, William R. Gambling & Society: Interdisciplinary Studies on the Subject of Gambling. (Illus.). 488p. 1976. 54.50x (ISBN 0-398-03459-1). C C Thomas.

Eadington, William R., ed. The Gambling Papers: Proceedings of the Fifth National Conference on Gambling & Risk Taking, 13 Vols. 2000p. 1982. Set. text ed. 380.00 (ISBN 0-942828-17-8). U of Nev Bur Busn.

--Gambling Papers: Proceedings of the Sixth National Conference on Gambling & Risk Taking, 5 vols. 1776p. 1985. text ed. 180.00 (ISBN 0-317-20704-0). U of Nev Bur Busn.

Eadmer. The Life of St. Anselm, Archbishop of Canterbury. Southern, R. W., ed. & tr. from Latin. (Oxford Medieval Texts Ser.). 1972. 31.00x (ISBN 0-19-822225-4). Oxford U Pr.

Eads & Fix, eds. The Reagan Regulatory Strategy: An Assessment. (Changing Domestic Priorities Ser.). 240p. 1984. pap. 12.95x (ISBN 0-87766-346-7); 26.95x (ISBN 0-87766-369-6). Urban Inst.

Eads, George C. The Local Service Airline Experiment. LC 71-141. (Brookings Institution Studies in the Regulations of Economic Activity). pap. 59.30 (ISBN 0-317-20812-8, 2025374). Bks Demand UMI.

Eads, George C. & Fix, Michael. Relief or Reform? Reagan's Regulatory Dilemma. LC 84-5283. (Changing Domestic Priorities Ser.). 283p. 1984. 19.95x (ISBN 0-87766-343-2); pap. 12.95x (ISBN 0-87766-330-0). Urban Inst.

Eads, Sandra, jt. auth. see Post, Beverly.

Eady, Carol M. Her Royal Destiny. 1985. pap. 6.95 (ISBN 0-517-55565-4, Harmony). Crown.

Eagan, Andrea B. Why Am I So Miserable If These Are the Best Years of My Life? (YA) 1979. pap. 2.50 (ISBN 0-380-46136-6, 60134-6, Flare). Avon.

--Why Am I So Miserable If These Are the Best Years of My Life? LC 75-43726. (gr. 8 up). 1976. 11.49i (ISBN 0-397-31655-0). Lipp Jr Bks.

Eagan, Eileen. Class, Culture, & the Classroom: The Student Peace Movement of the 1930s. (American Civilization Ser.). 319p. 1982. 29.95 (ISBN 0-87722-236-3). Temple U Pr.

Eagan, James M. Maximilien Robespierre: Nationalist Dictator. LC 70-127439. (Columbia University Studies in the Social Sciences: No. 437). Repr. of 1938 ed. 14.00 (ISBN 0-404-51437-5). AMS Pr.

--Maximilien Robespierre: Nationalist Dictator. 1972. lib. bdg. 20.00x (ISBN 0-374-92440-6). Octagon.

Eagan, James M., jt. ed. see Langsam, Walter C.

Eagar, Patrick. Test Decade. (Illus.). 224p. 1982. 27.50 (ISBN 0-437-04050-X, Pub. by Worlds Work). David & Charles.

Eage, J. D., et al, eds. John Bardot's Description of the Coasts of North & South Guinea, 1732. 1980. 60.00x (ISBN 0-686-79473-7, Pub. by Hakluyt Soc England). State Mutual Bk.

Eagen, Andrea B. The Newborn Mother: Stages of Her Growth. 192p. 1985. 15.95 (ISBN 0-316-20056-5). Little.

Eagen, Edward P., jt. auth. see Joyce Brothers.

Eager. Marriage of William Bull. 4.95x (ISBN 0-686-14960-2). T E Henderson.

Eager, Alan. A Guide to Irish Bibliographical Material. 2nd ed. 524p. 1981. 75.00x (ISBN 0-85365-931-1, Pub. by Lib Assn England). State Mutual Bk.

Eager, Alan R. A Guide to Irish Bibliographical Material: A Bibliography of Irish Bibliographies and Sources of Information. LC 80-12368. xv, 502p. 1980. lib. bdg. 65.00 (ISBN 0-313-22343-2, EIB/). Greenwood.

Eager, Edward. Half Magic. LC 54-5153. (Illus.). (gr. 4-6). 1954. 9.95 (ISBN 0-15-233078-X, HJ). HarBraceJ.

--Half Magic. LC 84-19816. (Illus.). 228p. (gr. 3-6). 1985. pap. 4.95 (ISBN 0-15-637990-2, VoyB). HarBraceJ.

--Knight's Castle. LC 84-19817. (Illus.). 192p. (gr. 3-6). 1985. pap. 4.95 (ISBN 0-15-647350-X, VoyB). HarBraceJ.

--Magic by the Lake. LC 57-5267. (Illus.). (gr. 3-7). 1957. 7.95 (ISBN 0-15-250441-9, HJ). HarBraceJ.

--Magic or Not? LC 78-71152. (Illus.). 192p. (gr. 3-6). 1985. pap. 4.95 (ISBN 0-15-655121-7, VoyB). HarBraceJ.

--Magic or Not? 1984. 14.00 (ISBN 0-8446-6154-6). Peter Smith.

--Seven-Day Magic. LC 62-17040. (Illus.). (gr. 4-6). 1962. 10.95 (ISBN 0-15-272919-4, HJ). HarBraceJ.

--The Time Garden. LC 85-5505. (Illus.). 188p. (gr. 8-12). 1985. pap. 4.95 (ISBN 0-15-288190-5, VoyB). HarBraceJ.

--The Well-Wishers. LC 85-5247. (Illus.). 191p. (gr. 8-12). 1985. pap. 4.95 (ISBN 0-15-294992-5, VoyB). HarBraceJ.

Eager, Fred. Introducing Italic Handwriting. pap. 1.00 (ISBN 0-910798-06-0). Italimuse.

--Italic Handwriting for Young People. 1978. pap. 6.95 (ISBN 0-02-079960-8, Collier). Macmillan.

--Italic Way to Beautiful Handwriting. 128p. 1974. pap. 6.95 (ISBN 0-02-079990-X, Collier). Macmillan.

--Write Italic. 1965. Bk. 2, 1975 Rev. Ed. pap. 2.95x (ISBN 0-910798-07-9); Bk. 3, 1975, Rev. Ed. pap. 2.95x (ISBN 0-910798-08-7); pap. 0.75x special practice bk. (ISBN 0-910798-05-2). Italimuse.

Eager, George B. How to Succeed in Winning Children to Christ. 190p. 1979. pap. 3.95 (ISBN 0-9603752-0-1). Mailbox.

--Love & Dating. 32p. (Orig.). (gr. 7-12). 1980. pap. 1.00 (ISBN 0-9603752-2-8). Mailbox.

--Teen Talk. 48p. (Orig.). (gr. 7-12). 1981. pap. 1.00 (ISBN 0-9603752-1-X). Mailbox.

--Wake up World! Jesus Is Coming Soon! 40p. (Orig.). (gr. 7-12). 1980. pap. 1.00 (ISBN 0-9603752-3-6). Mailbox.

--Why Wait 'til Marriage? 28p. (Orig.). (gr. 7-12). 1979. pap. 1.00 (ISBN 0-9603752-4-4). Mailbox.

Eager, Irene F. Margaret Anna Cusack: One Woman's Campaign for Women's Rights. (Arlen House Ser.). 256p. pap. 7.95 (ISBN 0-905223-11-X, Dist. by Scribner). M Boyars.

Eager, James L., jt. auth. see Auerbach, Marc.

Eager, Renee. Dining In-Phoenix. (Dining In Ser.). 200p. (Orig.). 1982. pap. 8.95 (ISBN 0-89716-035-5). Peanut Butter.

Eager, Samuel W. Law of Chattel Mortgages & Conditional Sales & Trust Receipts with Forms. xxxii, 1104p. 1941. lib. bdg. 27.50 (ISBN 0-89941-360-9). W S Hein.

Eagers, R. Y. Toxic Properties of Inorganic Flourine Compounds. 1969. 26.00x (ISBN 0-444-20044-4, Pub. by Applied Science). Burgess-Intl Ideas.

--Toxic Properties of Inorganic Fluorine Compounds. 152p. 1969. 22.25 (ISBN 0-444-20044-4, Pub. by Elsevier Applied Sci England). Elsevier.

Eagle, Audrey. Eagle's Trees & Shrubs of New Zealand in Colour. (Illus.). 311p. 1983. Repr. of 1975 ed. 95.00x (ISBN 0-686-84831-4, Pub. by W Collins New Zealand). Intl Spec Bk.

Eagle, Charles T., Jr. & Miniter, John J., eds. Music Psychology Index, Vol. 3. 288p. 1984. 65.00 (ISBN 0-89774-144-7). Oryx Pr.

Eagle, Chester. At the Window. 1985. pap. cancelled (ISBN 0-14-007426-0). Penguin.

Eagle, D. J. & Caverly, D. J. Diagnosis of Herbicide Damage to Crops. (Illus.). 1981. 35.00 (ISBN 0-8206-0294-9). Chem Pub.
Eagle, Dorothy. The Concise Oxford Dictionary of English Literature. 2nd ed. 640p. 1985. pap. 8.95 (ISBN 0-19-881233-7). Oxford U Pr.
Eagle, Dorothy & Carnell, Hilary. The Oxford Literary Guide to the British Isles. LC 76-47430. (Illus.). 1977. 22.50 (ISBN 0-19-869123-8); pap. 9.95 (ISBN 0-19-285098-9, GB617). Oxford U Pr.
Eagle, Dorothy, ed. Concise Oxford Dictionary of English Literature. 2nd, rev. ed. 1970. 35.00 (ISBN 0-19-866108-8). Oxford U Pr.
Eagle, Dorothy & Carnell, Hilary, eds. The Oxford Illustrated Literary Guide to Great Britain & Ireland. (Illus.). 1981. 35.00 (ISBN 0-19-869125-4). Oxford U Pr.
Eagle, Dorothy, jt. ed. see Harvey, Paul.
Eagle, Herb. Russian Formalist Film Theory. (Michigan Slavic Materials Ser.: No. 19). 1981. pap. 10.00 (ISBN 0-930042-42-5). Mich Slavic Pubns.
Eagle, Herbert, ed. see Khinchin, Aleksandr J.
Eagle, John. Becoming a Runner. 1983. 10.00 (ISBN 0-533-05612-8). Vantage.
Eagle, Kelly. Black Streets of Oakland. rev. ed. (Orig.). 1985. pap. 2.50 (ISBN 0-87067-248-7, BH248). Holloway.
Eagle Legal Services. Trust Magic: The Ultimate Tax Shelter. 1985. 19.95. Lifecraft.
Eagle, M. N. The Recent Developments in Psychoanalysis. 1984. 19.95 (ISBN 0-07-018597-2). McGraw.
Eagle, Mary D., ed. The Congress of Women, Held in the Woman's Building, World's Columbian Exposition, Chicago, U. S. A., 1893. LC 74-3944. (Women in America Ser.). (Illus.). 840p. 1974. Repr. of 1894 ed. 59.00x (ISBN 0-405-06090-4). Ayer Co Pubs.
Eagle, Roderick. Shakespeare: New Views for Old. 1977. Repr. of 1930 ed. lib. bdg. 27.00 (ISBN 0-8495-1304-9). Arden Lib.
--Shakespeare-New Views for Old. lib. bdg. 20.00 (ISBN 0-8482-9955-8). Norwood Edns.
Eagle, Solomon. Books in General: Shakespeare, Browning, Swinburne, Blake, Shelley. 273p. 1983. Repr. of 1920 ed. lib. bdg. 25.00 (ISBN 0-89987-223-9). Darby Bks.
Eagle, Steven J. Ohio Mental Health Law. (Baldwin's Ohio Handbook Ser.). 1985. write for info (ISBN 0-8322-0067-0). Banks-Baldwin.
Eaglefield-Hull, A., ed. Dictionary of Modern Music & Musicians. LC 78-139192. (Music Ser). 1971. Repr. of 1924 ed. lib. bdg. 59.50 (ISBN 0-306-70086-7). Da Capo.
Eaglefield-Hull, A., ed. see Beethoven, Ludwig Van.
Eagleman. Meteorology: The Atmosphere in Action. 2nd ed. 416p. 1985. write for info. (ISBN 0-534-03352-0). Wadsworth Pub.
Eagleman, Joe R. Severe & Unusual Weather. 250p. 1982. 34.95 (ISBN 0-442-26195-0). Van Nos Reinhold.
--Severe & Unusual Weather Discussion Guide. 96p. 1982. pap. text ed. 7.95 (ISBN 0-8403-2777-3). Kendall-Hunt.
Eagles. AMB Jos E. Davies: U. S.-U. S. S. R. (Modern American History Ser.: No. III). 1985. text ed. 48.00 (ISBN 0-8240-5655-8). Garland Pub.
Eagles, Charles W. Jonathan Daniels & Race Relations: The Evolution of a Southern Liberal. LC 82-2756. (Twentieth-Century America Ser.). 344p. 1982. text ed. 24.50x (ISBN 0-87049-356-6); pap. text ed. 11.95x (ISBN 0-87049-357-4). U of Tenn Pr.
Eagles, Douglas A. Your Weight. (First Bks). (Illus.). 72p. (gr. 4 up). 1982. PLB 8.90 (ISBN 0-531-04395-9). Watts.
Eagles, Paul. The Planning & Management of Environmentally Sensitive Areas. pap. text ed. 13.95 (ISBN 0-582-30074-6). Longman.
Eagleson, John, ed. Christians & Socialism: Documentation of the Christians for Socialism Movement in Latin America. Drury, John, tr. from Span. LC 74-78452. 256p. (Orig.). 1975. pap. 4.95 (ISBN 0-88344-058-X). Orbis Bks.
Eagleson, John & Scharper, Philip J., eds. Puebla & Beyond. LC 79-24098. 370p. (Orig.). 1979. pap. 9.95 (ISBN 0-88344-399-6). Orbis Bks.
Eagleson, John, jt. ed. see Torres, Sergio.
Eagleson, John, ed. see Torres, Sergio.
Eagleson, John, tr. see Gutierrez, Gustavo.
Eagleson, John, tr. see Miranda, Jose P.
Eagleson, P. S. Land Surface Processes in Atmospheric General Circulation Models. LC 82-9740. 572p. 1983. 62.50 (ISBN 0-521-25222-9). Cambridge U Pr.
Eagleson, Robert D., ed. English in the Eighties. 176p. (Orig.). 1982. pap. text ed. 10.25x (ISBN 0-909955-40-9). Boynton Cook Pubs.
Eaglestone, Arthur A., pseud. Plain Man & the Novel. LC 78-105776. 1970. Repr. of 1940 ed. 19.50x (ISBN 0-8046-0946-2, Pub. by Kennikat). Assoc Faculty Pr.
Eagleton, Alexis C. How to Go into the Art Business & Make a Fortune Out of It. (Illus.). 113p. 1981. 59.75 (ISBN 0-86650-009-X). Gloucester Art.
--Management for Maximal Profits in Art Business. (Illus.). 107p. 1981. 51.75 (ISBN 0-89266-311-1). Am Classical Coll Pr.
Eagleton, C. Responsibility of States in International Law. Repr. of 1928 ed. 23.00 (ISBN 0-527-26050-9). Kraus Repr.
Eagleton, Clyde. Analysis of the Problem of War. LC 72-35. (Select Bibliographies Reprint Ser.). 1972. Repr. of 1937 ed. 12.50 (ISBN 0-8369-9961-4). Ayer Co Pubs.
Eagleton, Ethie. On the Last Frontier. 1973. 5.00 (ISBN 0-87404-027-2). Tex Western.
Eagleton, Mary & Pierce, David. Attitudes to Class in the English Novel: From Walter Scott to David Storey. 1980. 17.95 (ISBN 0-500-51002-4). Thames Hudson.
Eagleton, Terry. Criticism & Ideology: A Study in Marxist Literary Theory. 1978. (Pub by NLB); pap. 6.50 (ISBN 0-8052-7047-7). Schocken.
--The Function of Criticism. 128p. 1984. 20.00 (ISBN 0-8052-7222-4, Pub. by Verso, England); pap. 5.95 (ISBN 0-8052-7223-2). Schocken.
--Literary Theory: An Introduction. 252p. 1983. 29.50x (ISBN 0-8166-1238-2); pap. 9.95 (ISBN 0-8166-1241-2). U of Minn Pr.
--Marxism & Literary Criticism. LC 76-6707. 1976. pap. 3.95 (ISBN 0-520-03243-8, CAL 337). U of Cal Pr.
--The Rape of Clarissa: Writing, Sexuality & Class-Struggle in Richardson. 128p. 1982. 25.00x (ISBN 0-8166-1204-8); pap. 9.95 (ISBN 0-8166-1209-9). U of Minn Pr.
--Walter Benjamin: Or Toward a Revolutionary Criticism. 208p. 1981. 19.50x (ISBN 0-8052-7100-7, Pub. by NLB England); pap. 8.50 (ISBN 0-8052-7099-X). Schocken.
Eagleton, Terry, ed. see Brown, Laura.
Eagleton, Terry, ed. see Kavanagh, James.
Eagleton, Terry, ed. see Smith, Stan.
Eagleton, Thomas F. War & Presidential Power: A Chronicle of Congressional Surrender. 1974. 8.95 (ISBN 0-87140-581-4). Liveright.
Eaglstein, W. H. & Pariser, D. M. Office Techniques for Diagnosing Skin Disease. (Illus.). 1978. 37.95 (ISBN 0-8151-2996-3). Year Bk Med.
Eagly, Robert V., ed. see Christiernin, P. N.
Eagon, Angelo. Catalog of Published Concert Music by American Composers. LC 68-9327. 150p. (Suppl. to 2nd ed.). 1971. 13.00 (ISBN 0-8108-0387-9). Scarecrow.
Eaker, D. Natural Toxins: Proceedings of the 6th International Symposium on Animal, Plant & Microbial Toxins, Uppsala, August, 1979. Wadstrom, T., ed. LC 80-40898. (Illus.). 704p. 1980. 130.00 (ISBN 0-08-024952-3). Pergamon.
Eaker, Helen L., ed. Giovanni Di Conversino Da Ravenna, Dragmalogia De Eligibili Vite Genere. LC 75-39111. 296p. 1980. 28.50 (ISBN 0-8387-1897-3). Bucknell U Pr.
Eaker, Helen L., ed. see Da Ravenna, Giovanni.
Eaker, Helen L., ed. see Di Conversino da Ravenna, Giovanni.
Eaker, J. Gordon. Walter Pater: A Study in Methods & Effects. LC 74-4450. 1933. lib. bdg. 8.50 (ISBN 0-8414-3930-3). Folcroft.
Eaker, Mark R. & Yawitz, Jess B. Macroeconomics. (Illus.). 400p. 1984. 28.95 (ISBN 0-13-542514-X). P-H.
Eakin, B E., jt. auth. see Bloomer, O T.
Eakin, Benjamin. Fairy Tales Mother Never Told You. (Illus.). 104p. (Orig.). 1985. pap. 5.95 (ISBN 0-934411-00-X). Williams Pub Co.
Eakin, David B. & Gerber, Helmut E., eds. George Moore: The Uncollected Short Stories. 1985. 17.50 (ISBN 0-8156-2338-0). Syracuse U Pr.
Eakin, David B., ed. see Moore, George.
Eakin, Ed. Moods of the Prairie. (Illus.). 1985. 4.95 (ISBN 0-89015-001-X). Eakin Pubns.
Eakin, James S., ed. Narrow Gauge Land. 136p. 1983. 24.95 (ISBN 0-912113-03-0); pap. 12.95 (ISBN 0-912113-02-2). Railhead Pubns.
Eakin, Lucille. Nuevo Destino: The Life Story of a Shipibo Bilingual Educator. LC 79-91447. (Museum of Anthropology Ser.: No. 9). (Illus.). 26p. (Orig.). 1980. pap. 2.95x (ISBN 0-88312-159-X); microfiche 1.93x (ISBN 0-88312-246-4). Summer Inst Ling.
Eakin, Mary K., ed. Good Books for Children, Nineteen Fifty to Nineteen Sixty-Five. 3rd ed. LC 66-23687. 1967. 25.00x (ISBN 0-226-17916-8). U of Chicago Pr.
Eakin, Mary M. Scuffy Sandals: A Guide for Church Visitation in the Community. LC 81-15824. 96p. (Orig.). 1982. pap. 5.95 (ISBN 0-8298-0490-0). Pilgrim NY.
Eakin, Patsy. God Said, Part I. 65p. (Orig.). (ps-k). 1981. pap. 2.95 (ISBN 0-931097-06-1). Sentinel Pub.
--God Said, Part II. 89p. (ps-k). 1981. pap. text ed. 2.95 (ISBN 0-931097-11-8). Sentinel Pub.
Eakin, Paul J. Fictions in Autobiography: Studies in the Art of Self-Invention. LC 84-42941. 325p. 1985. text ed. 26.00x (ISBN 0-691-06640-X). Princeton U Pr.
Eakin, Richard M. Great Scientists Speak Again. LC 74-22960. (Illus.). 128p. 1982. 12.95 (ISBN 0-520-04768-0). U of Cal Pr.
--Vertebrate Embryology. 3rd ed. LC 77-88420. (Campus Ser.: No. 208). 1978. pap. 8.50x (ISBN 0-520-03593-3). U of Cal Pr.
Eakin, Sue, ed. see Northup, Solomon.
Eakin, Sue, ed. see Prichard, Walter.
Eakins, Barbara & Eakins, R. Gene. Sex Differences in Human Communication. LC 77-77660. (Illus.). 1978. pap. text ed. 13.50 (ISBN 0-395-25510-4). HM.
Eakins, Pamela S. Mothers in Transition. 182p. 1983. pap. 9.95 (ISBN 0-87073-476-8). Schenkman Bks Inc.
Eakins, R. Gene, jt. auth. see Eakins, Barbara.
Eakins, Rosemary, ed. see Special Libraries Association, Picture Division.
Eakins, William J., jt. auth. see Ryan, Elizabeth B.
Eakle, Arlene, jt. auth. see Cerny, Johni.
Eakle, Arlene H. American Census Schedules. (How-to Ser.). pap. text ed. cancelled (ISBN 0-940764-13-X). Genealog Inst.
--Tax Records: Common Source with Uncommon Value. 1981. pap. text ed. 5.50x (ISBN 0-940764-14-8). Genealog Inst.
Eakle, Arlene H. & Weber, Georgia L. How to Prove Your Family Tree. (How-to Ser). (gr. 8-12). 1978. pap. text ed. 5.50x (ISBN 0-686-10808-6). Genealog Inst.
Eakle, Arlene H. & Cerny, Johni, eds. The Source: A Guidebook of American Genealogy. LC 84-70206. 786p. 1984. 39.95 (ISBN 0-916489-00-0). Ancestry.
Eales, Majorie. An Annotated Guide to Pre-Union Government Publications of the Orange Free State: 1854-1910. 1976. lib. bdg. 23.00 (ISBN 0-8161-7959-X, Hall Reference). G K Hall.
Eales, Mary. Mrs. Mary Eales' Receipts: 1718. (Illus.). 120p. 1985. 15.95x (ISBN 0-317-19752-5, Pub. by Prospect England). U Pr of Va.
Eales, P. G. & De Vos, P. A. A Guide to Bankruptcy. 90.00x (ISBN 0-903486-48-2, Pub. by Prof Bks England). State Mutual Bk.
Eales, Richard. Chess: The History of a Game. LC 84-24685. (Illus.). 240p. 1985. 18.95 (ISBN 0-8160-1195-8). Facts on File.
Ealy, Lawrence O. Republic of Panama in World Affairs, 1903-1950. LC 76-97343. Repr. of 1951 ed. lib. bdg. 15.00x (ISBN 0-8371-2806-4, EARP). Greenwood.
--Yanqui Politics & the Isthmian Canal. LC 74-127385. 1971. 19.95x (ISBN 0-271-01126-2). Pa St U Pr.
Ealy, Steven D. Communication, Speech, & Politics: Habermas & Political Analysis. LC 81-40012. (Illus.). 256p. (Orig.). 1981. lib. bdg. 23.25 (ISBN 0-8191-1728-5); pap. text ed. 12.50 (ISBN 0-8191-1729-3). U Pr of Amer.
Eames, jt. auth. see Morrison.
Eames, A. J. Morphology of the Angiosperms. LC 76-57780. 532p. 1977. Repr. of 1961 ed. 32.50 (ISBN 0-88275-527-7). Krieger.
Eames, Aled. The Twilight of Welsh Sail. (Saint David's Day Bilingual Ser.). (Illus.). 95p. 1984. pap. text ed. 6.75x (ISBN 0-7083-0866-X, Pub. by Univ of Wales Pr England). Humanities.
Eames, Alexandra. Windows & Walls: Designs-Patterns-Projects. LC 80-80753. 160p. 1980. 19.18i (ISBN 0-8487-0507-6). Oxmoor Hse.
Eames, Arthur J. An Introduction to Plant Anatomy. 2nd ed. LC 76-30812. 446p. 1977. Repr. of 1947 ed. 26.50 (ISBN 0-88275-526-9). Krieger.
Eames, Charles & Eames, Ray. A Computer Perspective. Fleck, Glen, ed. LC 72-88399. (Illus.). 1973. 15.00 (ISBN 0-674-15625-0). Harvard U Pr.
Eames, Edwin & Goode, Judith G. Urban Poverty in a Cross-Cultural Context. LC 72-90545. 1973. 17.00 (ISBN 0-02-908720-1). Free Pr.
Eames, Edwin, jt. auth. see Cohen, Eugene N.
Eames, Elizabeth. English Medieval Tiles. (British Museum Ser.). (Illus.). 72p. 1985. pap. 6.95 (ISBN 0-674-25670-0). Harvard U Pr.
Eames, Elizabeth & Blackwell, Kenneth. The Collected Papers of Bertrand Russel: Volume 7 Theory of Knowledge: The 1913 Manuscript. (Collected Papers of Bertrand Russell). (Illus.). 258p. 1984. text ed. 50.00x (ISBN 0-04-920073-9). Allen Unwin.
Eames, Elizabeth R. Bertrand Russell's Theory of Knowledge. LC 77-78529. 1969. 6.00 (ISBN 0-8076-0509-3). Braziller.
Eames, Elizabeth S. Catalogue of Medieval Lead-Glazed Earthenware Tiles in the Department of Medieval & Later Antiquities, British Museum. 794p. 1981. 300.00x (Pub. by Brit Mus Pubns England). State Mutual Bk.
Eames, Emma. Some Memories & Reflections. Farkas, Andrew, ed. LC 76-29934. (Opera Biographies). (Illus.). 1977. Repr. of 1927 ed. lib. bdg. 32.00x (ISBN 0-405-09676-3). Ayer Co Pubs.
Eames, Francis L. New York Stock Exchange. LC 68-28628. Repr. of 1968 ed. lib. bdg. 15.00x (ISBN 0-8371-0066-6, EANY). Greenwood.
Eames, James P. Turbine & Jet-Propelled Aircraft Powerplants. (Illus.). 1954. 5.25 (ISBN 0-910354-06-5). Chartwell.
Eames, John D. The Paramount Story. 1985. 35.00 (ISBN 0-517-55348-1). Crown.
Eames, Marian. Dancing in Prints: A Portfolio Assembled from the Archives of the Dance Collection, 1634-1870. (Illus.). 1964. 25.00 (ISBN 0-87104-060-3). NY Pub Lib.
Eames, Ray, jt. auth. see Eames, Charles.
Eames, S. Morris. Pragmatic Naturalism: An Introduction. LC 76-58441. 256p. 1977. pap. 7.95x (ISBN 0-8093-0803-7). S Ill U Pr.
Eames, Steward, tr. see Piaget, Jean.
Eames, Stewart, tr. see Piaget, Jean.
Eames, Wilberforce. The Bay Psalm Book. 1978. pap. 53.95 (ISBN 0-89102-098-5, Artemis). B Franklin.
--Early New England Catechisms. 1898. 16.00 (ISBN 0-8337-0989-5). B Franklin.
--Early New England Catechisms. LC 68-31081. 1969. Repr. of 1898 ed. 35.00x (ISBN 0-8103-3478-X). Gale.
Eames, Wilberforce, ed. Adventures in Americana: Fourteen Ninety Two to Eighteen Ninety Seven: A Selection of Books from the Library of Herschel V. Jones, 3 Vols. Check-List, 1473-1926. (Rare Books on Americana Ser). (Illus.). 1964. Repr. of 1937 ed. Set. 75.00x (ISBN 0-8154-0123-X). Cooper Sq.
--A List of Editions of the Bay Psalm Book or New England Version of the Psalms, 2 vols. in 1. Incl. Bible. O. T. Psalms. English. Paraphrases. 1912 Bay Psalm Book. facsimile ed. New England Society. 1912. Repr. LC 1-538. 1885. Repr. 23.50 (ISBN 0-8337-0987-9). B Franklin.
Eamill, Hugh M., Jr. The Hidalgo Revolt: Prelude to Mexican Independence. LC 81-4229. (Illus.). xi, 284p. 1981. Repr. of 1966 ed. lib. bdg. 28.75x (ISBN 0-313-22848-5, HAHR). Greenwood.
Eanes, H. Ray. Interpreting Financial Statements of Life & Health Insurance Companies. (FLMI Insurance Education Program Ser.). 1983. pap. text ed. 3.00 (ISBN 0-915322-61-7). LOMA.
Eanses, Michael, jt. auth. see Petsopoulos, Yanni.
Eardley, A. J., et al. Zion: The Story Behind the Scenery. rev. ed. LC 79-51484. (Illus.). 1979. 8.95 (ISBN 0-916122-32-8); pap. 3.75 (ISBN 0-916122-07-7). KC Pubns.
Eardley, Anthony, et al. Le Corbusier's Firminy Church. (Illus.). 120p. 1981. pap. 18.50 (ISBN 0-8478-0380-5). Rizzoli Intl.
Eardley, Kenneth, et al, trs. see Riddell, John.
Eareckson, Joni & Estes, Steve. A Step Further. 2nd ed. (Illus.). 192p. 1980. pap. 5.95 (ISBN 0-310-23971-0). Zondervan.
--A Step Further. 192p. 1982. mass market pb 3.95 (ISBN 0-310-23972-9). Zondervan.
Eareckson, Joni & Musser, Joe. Joni. 1984. pap. 2.95 (ISBN 0-553-22886-2). Bantam.
--Joni. 1976. kivar, large print 7.95 (ISBN 0-310-23967-2); pap. 4.95 (ISBN 0-310-23961-3). Zondervan.
Eareckson, Joni, jt. auth. see Sinclair, Max.
Eargle, D. H., et al. Uranium Geology & Mines, South Texas. (GB 12 Ser.). (Illus.). 59p. 1971. 1.75 (ISBN 0-686-29320-7). Bur Econ Geology.
Eargle, Dolan, Jr. Tickets Please... All About California Railroads. Steinfeld, Naomi, ed. LC 78-75156. (Illus.). 1979. pap. 8.95 (ISBN 0-89395-012-2). Cal Living Bks.
Eargle, John. The Microphone Handbook. 1982. 31.95 (ISBN 0-914130-02-1). Elar Pub Co.
--Sound Recording. 2nd ed. 320p. 1980. 24.95 (ISBN 0-442-22557-1). Van Nos Reinhold.
Earhart, Amelia. The Fun of It. LC 77-16052. (Illus.). 218p. 1977. 12.95 (ISBN 0-915864-56-8); pap. 6.95 (ISBN 0-915864-55-X). Academy Chi Pubs.
--The Fun of It: Random Records of My Own Flying & of Women in Aviation. LC 71-159945. 1975. Repr. of 1932 ed. 40.00x (ISBN 0-8103-4078-X). Gale.
--Twenty Hours Forty Minutes: Our Flight in the Friendship. Gilbert, James, ed. LC 79-7249. (Flight: Its First Seventy-Five Years Ser.). (Illus.). 1979. Repr. of 1928 ed. lib. bdg. 21.00x (ISBN 0-405-12161-X). Ayer Co Pubs.
Earhart, Caroline, jt. auth. see DeJonghe, Marty.
Earhart, E. W., ed. Flat Rolled Products III: Proceedings. LC 62-18702. (Metallurgical Society Conference Ser.: Vol. 13). pap. 42.80 (ISBN 0-317-10398-9, 2000678). Bks Demand UMI.
Earhart, E. W. & Hindson, R. D., eds. Flat Rolled Products II: Semi-Finished & Finished. LC 60-10586. (Metallurgical Society Conference Ser.: Vol. 6). pap. 40.30 (ISBN 0-317-10406-3, 2000669). Bks Demand UMI.
Earhart, H. Byron. Japanese Religion: Unity & Diversity. 3rd ed. 288p. 1982. pap. text ed. write for info. (ISBN 0-534-01028-8). Wadsworth Pub.
--Religions of Japan: Many Traditions Within One Sacred Day. LC 84-47722. (Religious Traditions of the World Ser.: Vol. 1). (Illus.). 160p. 1984. 6.68i (ISBN 0-06-062112-5, HarpR). Har-Row.
Earhart, H. Byron, tr. see Murakami, Shigeyoshi.
Earhart, Lida B. Systematic Study in the Elementary Schools. LC 73-176739. (Columbia University. Teachers College. Contributions to Education: No. 18). Repr. of 1908 ed. 22.50 (ISBN 0-404-55018-5). AMS Pr.
Earhart, Robert L., jt. auth. see Raup, Omer B.
Earickson, Robert. Spatial Behavior of Hospital Patients: A Behavioral Approach to Spatial Interaction in Metropolitan Chicago. LC 79-104877. (Research Papers Ser.: No. 124). 1970. pap. 10.00 (ISBN 0-89065-031-4, 124). U Chicago Dept Geog.
Earith, Emily & Earith, Emily, eds. Meditations for the Divorced. (Gil-gal Meditations Ser.). 80p. (Orig.). 1986. pap. 5.95 (ISBN 0-916895-02-5). Gilgal Pubns.
Earl, D. E. Forest Energy & Economic Development. (Illus.). 1975. 27.50x (ISBN 0-19-854521-5). Oxford U Pr.

Earle, William, compiled by. Obi. facsimile ed. LC 76-38012. (Black Heritage Library Collection). Repr. of 1804 ed. 16.00 (ISBN 0-8369-8980-5). Ayer Co Pubs.

Earle, William, et al, eds. Christianity & Existentialism. (Studies in Phenomenology & Existential Philosophy). 1963. pap. 5.95 (ISBN 0-8101-0084-3). Northwestern U Pr.

Earles, Brent D. The Dating Maze. pap. 3.95 (ISBN 0-8010-3424-8). Baker Bk.

--Proverbs for Graduates. 1984. 5.95 (ISBN 0-8010-3415-9). Baker Bk.

--Psalms for Graduates. 5.95 (ISBN 0-8010-3426-4). Baker Bk.

--The Ten Commandments for Graduates. 112p. 1986. price not set. Baker Bk.

--You're Worth It! But Do You Believe It? 1985. pap. 5.95 (ISBN 0-8010-3427-2). Baker Bk.

Earles, Michael. Manuscripts & Memories: Chapters in Our Literary Tradition. 1973. Repr. of 1935 ed. 15.50 (ISBN 0-8274-1723-3). R West.

Earley, Lawrence E. & Gottschalk, Carl W. Strauss & Welt's Diseases of the Kidney, 2 vols. 3rd ed. 1979. text ed. 50.00 (ISBN 0-316-20314-9). Little.

Earley, Mary D. Stars of the Twenties: 125 Photographs. (Illus.). 1975. 19.95 (ISBN 0-670-66836-2, Studio). Viking.

Earley, Stephen C. An Introduction to American Movies. (Illus., Orig.). (YA) (RL 10). 1978. pap. 4.50 (ISBN 0-451-62351-7, Ment). NAL.

Earll, Robert C. Sublittoral Ecology: The Ecology of the Shallow Sublittoral Benthos. Erwin, David G., ed. (Illus.). 1983. 35.00x (ISBN 0-19-854573-8). Oxford U Pr.

Earlley, Elsie C., jt. auth. see Cook, J. E.

Earl Of Birkenhead. The Hundred Best English Essays. 1929. 15.00 (ISBN 0-8482-7386-9). Norwood Edns.

Earl Of Birkenhead, jt. auth. see Krutch, Joseph W.

Earl of Carnarvon, ed. Letters of Philip Dormer Fourth Earl of Chesterfield to His Godson & Successor. 1977. Repr. of 1890 ed. lib. bdg. 65.00 (ISBN 0-8414-0085-7). Folcroft.

Earl of Cromartie. A Highland History. 1982. 45.00x (ISBN 0-905868-03-X, Pub. by Gavin Pr). State Mutual Bk.

Earl of Harewood, ed. The New Kobbe's Complete Opera Book. rev. ed. LC 76-12106. 663p. 1976. 25.00 (ISBN 0-399-11633-8, Putnam). Putnam Pub Group.

Earl Of Listowell. Critical History of Modern Aesthetics. LC 75-1009. (Studies in Comparative Literature, No. 35). 1974. lib. bdg. 51.95x (ISBN 0-8383-1958-0). Haskell.

Earlougher, R. C., Jr. Advances in Well Test Analysis. 264p. 1977. 22.50 (ISBN 0-317-32908-1); members 7.50 (ISBN 0-317-32909-X). Soc Mining Eng.

Earls, Michael. Manuscripts & Memories: Chapters in Our Literary Tradition. facs. ed. LC 67-26735. (Essay Index Reprint Ser). 1935. 18.00 (ISBN 0-8369-0397-8). Ayer Co Pubs.

--Manuscripts & Memories: Chapters in Our Literary Tradition. 275p. 1982. Repr. of 1935 ed. lib. bdg. 45.00 (ISBN 0-89984-185-6). Century Bookbindery.

Early American Society, ed. Colonial Homes in the Southern States. (Illus.). 4.98 (ISBN 0-517-53272-7). Outlet Bk Co.

--Early Homes of Massachusetts. (Architectural Treasures of Early America Ser.). 1978. 3.98 (ISBN 0-517-53235-2). Crown.

--Early Homes of New England. (Illus.). 3.98 (ISBN 0-517-53274-3). Crown.

--Early Homes of New York & the Mid-Atlantic States. (Illus.). 4.98 (ISBN 0-517-53271-9). Crown.

--Early Homes of Rhode Island. (Illus.). 3.98 (ISBN 0-517-53270-0). Crown.

Early, Charles M., jt. auth. see Hackett, J. Dominick.

Early Childhood Directors Association. Survival Kit for Directors. Baldwin, Sue & Krans, Ellen, eds. (Illus.). 100p. (Orig.). pap. 5.95 (ISBN 0-934140-24-3). Toys 'n Things.

Early, Eileen. Joy in Exile. LC 79-5429. 1980. pap. text ed. 9.25 (ISBN 0-8191-0878-2). U Pr of Amer.

Early, Eleanor. New England Cookbook. (Illus.). 1954. 10.95 (ISBN 0-394-40156-5). Random.

Early, Els, tr. see Mulisch, Harry.

Early, G. Assembly Language: Macro II & PDP II. (Computer Science Ser.). 560p. 1983. 27.95 (ISBN 0-07-018782-7). McGraw.

Early, J., jt. auth. see Kreuzer, R.

Early, Jack. A Creative Kind of Killer. 1984. 12.95 (ISBN 0-531-09835-4). Watts.

--A Creative Kind of Killer. 256p. 1985. pap. 2.95 (ISBN 0-345-31857-9). Ballantine.

--Razzamatazz. 320p. 1985. 15.95 (ISBN 0-531-09796-X). Watts.

Early, James. The Making of Go Down, Moses. LC 72-80404. 148p. 1972. 8.95 (ISBN 0-87074-003-2). SMU Press.

Early, James G., et al, eds. Time-Dependent Failure Mechanisms & Assessment Methodologies. (Illus.). 344p. 1983. 52.50 (ISBN 0-521-25375-6). Cambridge U Pr.

Early, John D. The Demographic Structure & Evolution of a Peasant System: The Guatemalan Population. LC 82-6938. (Illus.). viii, 207p. 1982. 20.00 (ISBN 0-8130-0734-8). U Presses Fla.

Early, Jubal A. War Memoirs. Vandiver, Frank E., ed. LC 60-11858. (Indiana University Civil War Centennial Ser.). (Illus.). 1968. Repr. of 1960 ed. 47.00 (ISBN 0-527-26150-5). Kraus Repr.

Early, Katherine E. For the Benefit & Enjoyment of the People: Cultural Attitudes & the Establishment of Yellowstone National Park. (The Georgetown Monograph in American Studies). 64p. (Orig.). 1984. pap. 3.95 (ISBN 0-87840-415-5). Georgetown U Pr.

Early, Margaret. Holt-Bennett Family History. 1974. 10.00 (ISBN 0-87012-163-4). McClain.

Early, Margaret & Sawyer, Diane J. Reading to Learn in Grades Five to Twelve. 480p. 1984. text ed. 21.95 (ISBN 0-15-575625-7, HC). HarBraceJ.

Early, Paul J., jt. auth. see Sodee, D. Bruce.

Early, Paul J., et al. Textbook of Nuclear Medicine Technology. 3rd ed. LC 78-31659. (Illus.). 692p. 1979. text ed. 37.95 (ISBN 0-8016-1488-0). Mosby.

Early, Richard E. Weavers & War: A True Story. (Illus.). 196p. 1984. 19.95x (ISBN 0-7102-0186-9). Routledge & Kegan.

Early, Richard E., jt. auth. see Plummer, Alfred.

Early, Ruth H. Campbell Chronicles & Family Sketches. LC 77-93960. (Illus.). 554p. 1978. Repr. of 1927 ed. 25.00 (ISBN 0-8063-0798-6). Regional.

Early, Sarah J. Life & Labors of Rev. Jordan W. Early: One of the Pioneers of African Methodism in the West & South. facsimile ed. LC 72-164386. (Black Heritage Library Collection). Repr. of 1894 ed. 16.00 (ISBN 0-8369-8845-0). Ayer Co Pubs.

Early, Stephen T., jt. auth. see Knight, Barbara B.

Early, Stephen T., Jr. Constitutional Courts of the U.S. The Formal & Informal Relationships Between U.S. District Courts, Courts of Appeals & Supreme Court of the U.S. (Quality Paperback Ser.: No. 320). 184p. 1977. pap. 3.95 (ISBN 0-8226-0320-9). Littlefield.

Early, Stephen T., Jr. & Knight, Barbara B. Responsible Government: American & British. LC 80-29601. 336p. 1981. text ed. 24.95x (ISBN 0-88229-658-2); pap. text ed. 12.95x (ISBN 0-88229-776-7). Nelson-Hall.

Earman, John, ed. Testing Scientific Theories. (Minnesota Studies in the Philosophy of Science: Vol. X). (Illus.). 384p. 1984. 39.50x (ISBN 0-8166-1158-0); pap. 16.95x (ISBN 0-8166-1159-9). U of Minn Pr.

Earman, John S., et al, eds. Foundations of Space-Time Theories. LC 77-83503. (Studies in the Philosophy of Science: Vol. 8). (Illus.). 1977. 27.50 (ISBN 0-8166-0807-5). U of Minn Pr.

Earn, Josephine. Looking at Canada. LC 76-8481. (Looking at Other Countries Ser.). (Illus.). 1977. 11.49i (ISBN 0-397-31704-2). Lipp Jr Bks.

Earnest, Adele. The Art of the Decoy: American Bird Carvings. LC 81-51445. (Illus.). 208p. 1982. pap. 14.95 (ISBN 0-916838-58-7); 25.00 (ISBN 0-916838-62-5). Schiffer.

--Folk Art in America. LC 84-51184. (Illus.). 256p. 1984. 35.00 (ISBN 0-88740-020-5). Schiffer.

Earnest, Ernest. The American Eve in Fact & Fiction, 1775-1914. LC 74-19339. 280p. 1974. 18.95x (ISBN 0-252-00448-5). U of Ill Pr.

--Expatriates & Patriots: American Artists, Scholars, & Writers in Europe. LC 68-19469. pap. 80.00 (ISBN 0-317-20097-6, 2023377). Bks Demand UMI.

--The Volunteer Fire Company. LC 78-8785. (Illus.). 224p. 1980. pap. 8.95 (ISBN 0-8128-6094-2). Stein & Day.

Earnest, Ernest P. Foreword to Literature. LC 75-167335. (Essay Index Reprint Ser.). Repr. of 1945 ed. 23.50 (ISBN 0-8369-2767-2). Ayer Co Pubs.

Earnest, Franklin, III. Transitional Man: The Anatomy of a Miracle. LC 81-68047. 76p. 1981. pap. 5.95 (ISBN 0-914480-06-5). Far West Edns.

Earnest, James D. & Tracey, Gerard. John Henry Newman: An Annotated Bibliography of His Tract & Pamphlet Collection. LC 84-48069. (Reference Library of Social Science). 600p. 1984. lib. bdg. 78.00 (ISBN 0-8240-8958-8). Garland pub.

--John Henry Newman: An Annotated Bioliography. LC 84-48069. 256p. 1984. lib. bdg. 40.00 (ISBN 0-8240-8958-8). Garland Pub.

Earnest, Marion R. Criminal Self-Conceptions in the Penal Community of Female Offenders: An Empirical Study. LC 77-90378. 1978. pap. 10.95 perfect bdg. (ISBN 0-88247-511-8). R & E Pubs.

Earnest, Michael P., ed. Neurologic Emergencies. (Illus.). 534p. 1983. text ed. 55.00 (ISBN 0-443-08221-9). Churchill.

Earnest, Virginia. Color Me Successful. (Orig.). 1983. 14.95 (ISBN 0-9610512-1-3); pap. 4.95 (ISBN 0-9610512-0-5). W Stice.

Earney, Fillmore C. Petroleum & Hard Minerals from the Sea. LC 80-17653. (Scripta Series in Geography). 1980. 53.95x (ISBN 0-470-27009-8, Pub. by Halsted Pr). Wiley.

Earnhardt, Ken C. Development Planning & Population Policy in Puerto Rico: From Historical Evolution Towards a Plan for Population Stabilization. LC 77-11187. (Planning Ser: S-5). 1978. 10.00 (ISBN 0-8477-2441-7). U of PR Pr.

Earnhardt, Kent C. Population Research, Policy & Related Studies in Puerto Rico: An Inventory. LC 77-16466. (Planning Ser: S-6). 1984. pap. 8.00 (ISBN 0-8477-2447-6). U of PR Pr.

Earnhart, Hugh G. Student Study Guide for Military History. (Illus.). 122p. (Orig.). 1985. pap. text ed. 9.95x (ISBN 0-8138-1161-9). Iowa St U Pr.

Earnshaw, A., jt. auth. see Greenwood, N. N.

Earnshaw, Brian, jt. auth. see Mowl, Tim.

Earnshaw, George L. Serving Each Other in Love. (Orig.). (YA) 1967. pap. text ed. 2.95 (ISBN 0-8170-0371-1). Judson.

Earnshaw, J. C. & Steer, M. W., eds. The Application of Laser Light Scattering to the Study of Biological Motion. (NATO ASI Series A, Life Sciences: Vol. 59). 675p. 1983. 95.00x (ISBN 0-306-41268-3, Plenum Pr). Plenum Pub.

Earnshaw, Pat. Bobbin & Needle Laces: Identification & Care. 22.95 (ISBN 0-318-00814-9). Robin & Russ.

--A Dictionary of Lace. (Illus.). 240p. 1984. pap. 16.95 (ISBN 0-85263-700-4, Pub. by Shire Pubns England). Seven Hills Bks.

--The Identification of Lace. (Illus.). 160p. pap. 14.95 (ISBN 0-85263-701-2, Pub. by Shire Pubns England). Seven Hills Bks.

Earnshaw, Pat, ed. see Mills, Betty J.

Earp, Frank R. Style of Aeschylus. LC 79-102489. 1970. Repr. of 1948 ed. 9.00x (ISBN 0-8462-1494-6). Russell.

--Way of the Greeks. LC 75-136393. Repr. of 1929 ed. 21.50 (ISBN 0-404-02234-0). AMS Pr.

Earp, Josephine. I Married Wyatt Earp: The Recollections of Josephine Sarah Marcus Earp. Boyer, Glenn G., ed, LC 76-4673. 277p. 1976. pap. 5.95 (ISBN 0-8165-0583-7). U of Ariz Pr.

Earp, Samuel A. & Wildeman, William J. The Blue Water Bait Book: Secrets of Successful Big Game Fishing. LC 74-5273. (A Sports Illustrated Bk). (Illus.). 160p. 1974. 9.95 (ISBN 0-316-20330-0). Little.

Earp, T. W., tr. see Flaubert, Gustave.

Earp, Wyatt S. Wyatt Earp: His Autobiography. Boyer, Glenn G., ed. (Illus., Orig.). 1981. leather 400.00 (ISBN 0-686-36171-7). Y V Bissette.

Earring, Monica F., et al. Prairie Legends. (Indian Culture Ser.). (gr. 6-9). 1978. 1.95 (ISBN 0-89992-069-1). Coun India Ed.

Earthday X Colloquium, University of Denver, April 21-24, 1980. Ecological Consciousness: Essays from the Earthday X Colloquium. Schultz, Robert C. & Hughes, J. Donald, eds. LC 80-6084. 510p. 1981. lib. bdg. 32.00 (ISBN 0-8191-1496-0); pap. text ed. 19.50 (ISBN 0-8191-1497-9). U Pr of Amer.

Earthquake Engineering Research Institute. Eighth World Conference on Earthquake Engineering, Vol. I. 896p. 1984. text ed. 20.00 (ISBN 0-13-246364-4). P-H.

--Eighth World Conference on Earthquake Engineering, Vol. II. 928p. 1984. text ed. 20.00 (ISBN 0-13-246372-5). P-H.

--Eighth World Conference on Earthquake Engineering, Vol. III. 1120p. 1984. text ed. 20.00 (ISBN 0-13-246380-6). P-H.

--Eighth World Conference on Earthquake Engineering, Vol. IV. 928p. 1984. text ed. 20.00 (ISBN 0-13-246398-9). P-H.

--Eighth World Conference on Earthquake Engineering, Vol. V. 1264p. 1984. text ed. 20.00 (ISBN 0-13-246406-3). P-H.

--Eighth World Conference on Earthquake Engineering, Vol. VI. 1024p. 1984. text ed. 20.00 (ISBN 0-13-246414-4). P-H.

--Eighth World Conference on Earthquake Engineering, Vol. VII. 976p. 1984. text ed. 20.00 (ISBN 0-13-246422-5). P-H.

Earthquake Problems Related to the Siting of Critical Facilities, Committee on Seismology. Earthquake Research for the Safer Siting of Critical Facilities. LC 80-82030. 1980. pap. text ed. 5.95 (ISBN 0-309-03082-X). Natl Acad Pr.

Earthy, E. Dora. Valenge Women: The Social & Economic Life of the Valenge Women of Portuguese East Africa. new ed. (Illus.). 251p. 1968. 28.50x (ISBN 0-7146-1660-5, F Cass Co). Biblio Dist.

Eary, David K. The Commerical Guide to Government Packaging, Vol. 1. 226p. 1985. 49.95 (ISBN 0-912702-26-5). Global Eng.

Eary, David K., ed. see Global Engineering Documents.

Eary, Donald F. & Johnson, G. E. Process Engineering: For Manufacturing. (Illus.). 1962. text ed. 32.95 (ISBN 0-13-723122-9). P-H.

Eary, Donald F. & Reed, Edward A. Techniques of Pressworking Sheet Metal: An Engineering Approach to Die Design. 2nd ed. 1974. ref. ed. 39.95 (ISBN 0-13-900696-6). P-H.

Easen, Patrick. Making School-Centred INSET Work. LC 84-23078. 176p. 1985. pap. 13.50 (ISBN 0-7099-1945-X, Pub. by Croom Helm). Longwood Pub Group.

Eash, Dianne, ed. see Wilson, Arthur N.

Eash, Nancy Greene see West, Betty M.

Easlea. Witch Hunting, Magic & the New Philosophy: An Introduction to Debates of the Scientific Revolution, 1450-1750. (Harvester Studies in Philosophy: No. 14). (Illus.). 283p. 1981. 43.00x (ISBN 0-391-01806-X); pap. 17.00x (ISBN 0-391-01808-6). Humanities.

Easley, C. W. Basic Radiation Protection: Principles & Organization. 142p. 1969. 42.95 (ISBN 0-677-02080-5). Gordon.

Easley, Eddie, et al. Contemporary Business: Challenges & Opportunities. (Illus.). 1978. pap. text ed. 21.95 (ISBN 0-8299-0166-3); study guide 9.95 (ISBN 0-8299-0218-X); instrs.' manual avail. (ISBN 0-8299-0476-X); transparency masters avail. (ISBN 0-8299-0477-8). West Pub.

Easley, Grady M. Primer for Small Systems Management. 164p. 1978. text ed. 24.95 (ISBN 0-316-20360-2). Little.

Easley, J. A., jt. ed. see Gallagher, J. M.

Easlick, Kenneth A., et al, eds. Communicating in Dentistry: Sources & Evaluation of Information & Preparation of Manuscripts, Oral Reports, & Proposals for Research. (Illus.). 240p. 1974. spiral 25.50x (ISBN 0-398-02856-7). C C Thomas.

Easman, Chris A., jt. auth. see Easmon, Charles S.

Easmon, C. S. & Jeljaszewicz, J., eds. Medical Microbiology. 1983. Vol. 1. 59.50 (ISBN 0-12-228001-6); Vol. 2. 60.00 (ISBN 0-12-228002-4); Vol. 3. 49.50 (ISBN 0-12-228003-2). Acad Pr.

Easmon, Charles & Gaya, Harold, eds. International Symposium on Infections in the Immunocompromised Host, Second. 1983. 33.00 (ISBN 0-12-228020-2). Acad Pr.

Easmon, Charles S. & Easman, Chris A. Staphylococci & Staphylococcal Infections. 1984. Vol. 1. 65.00 (ISBN 0-12-228101-2); Vol. 2. 70.00 (ISBN 0-12-228102-0). Acad Pr.

Easmon, Charles S. & Jeljaszewicz, Janusz, eds. Medical Microbiology, Vol. 4. 1984. 65.00 (ISBN 0-12-228004-0). Acad Pr.

Eason, David E. Michigan Divorce: Michigan Practice Systems Library Selection. LC 79-92873. loose-leaf 87.50; Suppl. 1984. 24.00; Suppl. 1982. 20.00. Lawyers Co-Op.

Eason, G., et al. Mathematics & Statistics for the Bio-Sciences. LC 79-41815. (Mathematics & Its Applications Ser.). 578p. 1980. pap. 37.95x (ISBN 0-470-27400-X). Halsted Pr.

Eason, Robert L., et al, eds. Adapted Physical Activity: From Theory to Practice (Proceedings of the 3rd International Symposium on Adapted Physical Activities) 358p. 1983. text ed. 22.00x (ISBN 0-931250-40-4, BEA50040). Human Kinetics.

Eason, Thomas F. & Manzler, David L. Why Universal Life. 2nd ed. LC 82-63204. (Illus.). 352p. 1983. pap. 14.95 (ISBN 0-87218-028-X). Natl Underwriter.

Eason, Thomas S. & Webb, Douglas A. Nine Steps to Effective EDP Loss Control. 177p. 1983. 25.00 (ISBN 0-932376-25-8, EY-00006-DP). Digital Pr.

Eason, Tom, jt. auth. see Fitzgerald, Jerry.

Eason, Tom S., et al, eds. Systems Auditability & Control Study, 3 Vols. Russell, Susan H. & Ruder, Brian. Incl. Data Processing Audit Practices Report. pap. text ed. 15.00 (ISBN 0-89413-052-8); Data Processing Control Practices Report. pap. text ed. 15.00 (ISBN 0-89413-051-X); Executive Report. pap. text ed. 15.00 (ISBN 0-89413-050-1). (Illus.). 1977. Set. pap. text ed. 37.50 (ISBN 0-686-86121-3). Inst Inter Aud.

Easop, Harrison, jt. auth. see Mockler, Robert J.

Easson. Bleak House. 1985. lib. bdg. 26.00 (ISBN 0-8240-8989-8). Garland Pub.

Easson, A., ed. see Dickens, Charles.

Easson, A. J. Tax Law & Policy in the EEC. LC 80-41430. (European Practice Ser.). 305p. 1980. lib. bdg. 50.00 (ISBN 0-379-20711-7). Oceana.

Easson, Angus. Elizabeth Gaskell. 1979. 25.00x (ISBN 0-7100-0099-5). Routledge & Kegan.

Easson, Angus, ed. see Gaskell, Elizabeth.

Easson, E. C. & Pointon, R. C., eds. The Radiotherapy of Malignant Disease. (Illus.). 500p. 1985. 69.00 (ISBN 0-387-13104-3). Springer-Verlag.

Easson, Roger R. & Essick, Robert N. William Blake: Book Illustrator, Vol. I. LC 72-82993. 1972. pap. 20.00 (ISBN 0-913130-01-X, American Blake Foundation). St Luke TN.

--William Blake: Book Illustrator, Vol. II. 1979. 125.00 (ISBN 0-913130-07-9, American Blake Foundation); pap. 45.00 (ISBN 0-913130-08-7). St Luke TN.

Easson, Roger R., ed. see Jones, Margaret W.

Easson, Roger R., ed. see Olsen, Sue.

Easson, Roger R., ed. see Osing, Gordan T.

Easson, William M. Dying Child: The Management of the Child or Adolescent Who Is Dying. 2 ed. 126p. 1981. pap. 11.75x (ISBN 0-398-04075-3). C C Thomas.

--Psychiatry Examination Review. 3rd ed. 1983. pap. 12.95 (ISBN 0-668-05485-9). ACC.

--The Severely Disturbed Adolescent: Inpatient, Residential, & Hospital Treatment. LC 69-19764. 249p. 1969. text ed. 25.00 (ISBN 0-8236-6070-2). Intl Univs Pr.

Eassun, Roger R., ed. see Awiaka, Marilou.

East. Home Economics: Past, Present & Future. 1985. 29.95 (ISBN 0-205-06680-1, 236680). Allyn.

East Africa Law Reports. The East Africa Law Reports: 1968-1975, 8 vols. LC 62-51069. Vols. 1968, 1969, & 1970. pap. 160.00 ea. (2051750); Vol. 1971. pap. 154.50 (ISBN 0-317-29964-6); Vol. 1972. pap. 150.00 (ISBN 0-317-29965-4); Vol. 1973. pap. 155.00 (ISBN 0-317-29966-2); Vol. 1974. pap. 152.50 (ISBN 0-317-29967-0); Vol. 1975. pap. 86.30 (ISBN 0-317-29968-9). Bks Demand UMI.

East African Subcommittee for Soil Correlation & Land Evaluation. Report of the Second Meeting of the Eastern African Sub-Committee for Soil Correlation & Land Evaluation: Addis-Ababa, Ethiopia, 25-30 October 1976. (World Soil Resources Reports: No. 47). 131p. 1978. pap. 8.50 (ISBN 92-5-100408-0, F1318, FAO). Unipub.

East, Andy. The Cold War File. LC 83-7584. 376p. 1983. 22.50 (ISBN 0-8108-1641-5). Scarecrow.

East, Anna M. Daniel's Odyssey. 1981. 4.95 (ISBN 0-8062-1834-7). Carlton.

East Asia Medical Studies Center, ed. see Beijing Institute of Traditional Chinese Medicine Staff.

East Asian Studies Program-Ohio State University. Business & Society in Japan: Fundamentals for Businessmen. Richardson, Bradley M., ed. LC 81-2710. 348p. 1981. 34.95x (ISBN 0-03-059321-2). Praeger.

East, Ben. Bears. (Illus.). 1978. 12.95 (ISBN 0-517-53231-X). Crown.

East, Ben & Nentl, Jerolyn. Danger in the Air. Schroeder, Howard, ed. LC 79-53774. (Survival Ser.). (Illus.). 48p. (Orig.). (gr. 3 up). 1979. PLB 7.95 (ISBN 0-89686-047-7); pap. 3.50 o. s. i. (ISBN 0-89686-055-8). Crestwood Hse.

--Desperate Search. Schroeder, Howard, ed. LC 79-5186. (Survival Ser.). (Illus.). 48p. (Orig.). (gr. 3 up). 1979. PLB 7.95 (ISBN 0-89686-043-4). Crestwood Hse.

--Forty Days Lost. Schroeder, Howard, ed. LC 79-5185. (Survival Ser.). (Illus.). 48p. (Orig.). (gr. 3 up). 1979. PLB 7.95 (ISBN 0-89686-042-6). Crestwood Hse.

--Found Alive. Schroeder, Howard, ed. LC 79-53749. (Survival Ser.). (Illus.). 48p. (Orig.). (gr. 3 up). 1979. PLB 7.95 (ISBN 0-89686-044-2). Crestwood Hse.

--Frozen Terror. Schroeder, Howard, ed. LC 79-53747. (Survival Ser.). (Illus.). 48p. (Orig.). (gr. 3 up). 1979. pap. 3.50 (ISBN 0-89686-057-4). Crestwood Hse.

--Mistaken Journey. Schroeder, Howard, ed. LC 79-53775. (Survival Ser.). (Illus.). 48p. (Orig.). (gr. 3 up). 1979. PLB 7.95 (ISBN 0-89686-046-9). Crestwood Hse.

--Trapped in Devil's Hole. Schroeder, Howard, ed. LC 79-53773. (Survival Ser.). 48p. (Orig.). (gr. 3 up). 1979. PLB 7.95 (ISBN 0-89686-048-5). Crestwood Hse.

East, Ben, jt. auth. see Fredrickson, Olive A.

East, Edward M. Mankind at the Crossroads. LC 76-46074. (Anti-Movements in America Ser.). 1977. Repr. of 1926 ed. lib. bdg. 29.00x (ISBN 0-405-09947-9). Ayer Co Pubs.

--Mankind at the Crossroads. 1923. 30.00 (ISBN 0-8482-0743-2). Norwood Edns.

East, Edward M., ed. Biology in Human Affairs. LC 72-313. (Essay Index Reprint Ser.). Repr. of 1931 ed. 23.50 (ISBN 0-8369-2790-7). Ayer Co Pubs.

East, Fred B., jt. ed. see East, Mary Lou.

East, G. C. Chemical Testing & Analysis. 68p. 1971. 70.00x (ISBN 0-686-63752-6). State Mutual Bk.

East, Gordon & Prescott, J. Our Fragmented World: An Introduction to Political Geography. 304p. 1975. pap. 11.95x (ISBN 0-8448-0712-5). Crane-Russak Co.

East, H. Some Statistical Indicators of UK Abstracting & Indexing Services. 1979. 30.00x (ISBN 0-905984-40-4, Pub. by Brit Lib England). State Mutual Bk.

East Harlem Nursing & Health Demonstration & Widdemer, Kenneth. The East Harlem Health Center Demonstration: An Anthology of Pamphlets. Reverby, Susan, ed. LC 83-49134. (The History of American Nursing Ser.). 157p. 1984. Repr. of 1928 ed. lib. bdg. 25.00 (ISBN 0-8240-6513-1). Garland Pub.

East India Company. The Petition & Remonstrance of the Governor & Company, Etc. LC 78-25744. (English Experience Ser.: No. 305). 38p. Repr. of 1628 ed. 8.00 (ISBN 90-221-0305-6). Walter J Johnson.

East India Company & English & Stevens, Henry. Dawn of British Trade to the East Indies. 1886. 29.00 (ISBN 0-8337-3405-9). B Franklin.

East India Company Library. Catalogue of the Library of the Honorable East India Company, 2 Vols. 1969. Set. 43.50 (ISBN 0-8337-0494-X). B Franklin.

East, Lorecia D. My Acadians. (Illus.). 120p. 1981. 7.95 (ISBN 0-89015-273-X). Eakin Pubns.

East, Mary Lou & East, Fred B., eds. Programmers' Handbook of Computer Printer Commands. 1985. pap. 39.95 (ISBN 0-932065-00-7). Cardinal Pt.

East, Maurice A., et al, eds. Why Nations Act: Theoretical Perspectives for Comparative Foreign Policy Studies. Salmore, Stephen A. & Hermann, Charles F. LC 77-22119. (Sage Focus Editions: Vol. 2). 234p. 1978. 24.00 (ISBN 0-8039-0718-4); pap. 12.00 (ISBN 0-8039-0719-2). Sage.

East, N. B., ed. African Theatre: A Checklist of Critical Materials. LC 70-96260. 47p. 1970. pap. text ed. 6.50x (ISBN 0-8419-0025-6, Africana). Holmes & Meier.

East, Reginald. Heal the Sick. LC 77-80678. 160p. (Orig.). 1977. pap. 2.95 (ISBN 0-87123-232-4, 200232). Bethany Hse.

East, Robert. Living above It! 2.00x (ISBN 0-686-29839-X). Cancer Control Soc.

East, Robert A. Business Enterprise in the American Revolutionary Era. LC 78-94923. (Columbia Univ. Studies in the Social Sciences Ser.: No. 439). Repr. of 1938 ed. 17.00 (ISBN 0-404-51439-1). AMS Pr.

--Business Enterprise in the American Revolutionary Era. 1964. 11.25 (ISBN 0-8446-1163-8). Peter Smith.

East, Robert A. see Weaver, Glenn.

East, Robert A. & Judd, Jacob, eds. The Loyalist Americans: A Focus on Greater New York. LC 74-7846. (Illus.). 192p. 1975. 12.00 (ISBN 0-912882-14-X). Sleepy Hollow.

East, Roger, jt. auth. see Day, Alan J.

East, Ronald, ed. The Gallipoli Diary of Sergeant Lawrence of the Australian Engineers. (Illus.). 167p. 24.95 (ISBN 0-522-84232-1, Pub. by Melbourne U Pr Australia). Intl Spec Bk.

East Suffolk (Eng.) Country Library. Gramophone Record Catalogue. LC 77-28824. 1978. Repr. of 1969 ed. lib. bdg. 19.75x (ISBN 0-313-20282-6, ESGR). Greenwood.

East, T. Story of Heart Disease. (Illus.). 148p. 1958. 10.95x (ISBN 0-8464-0886-4). Beekman Pubs.

East, W. Gordon. Geography Behind History. (Illus.). 1967. pap. 6.95x (ISBN 0-393-00419-8, Norton Lib). Norton.

East-West Foundation, jt. auth. see Kushi, Michio.

East West Journal, ed. Natural Childcare: The East West Journal Anthology. 216p. (Orig.). 1985. pap. 10.95 (ISBN 0-936184-01-9). East West Journ.

East West Journal Editors. The Shopper's Guide to Natural & Macrobiotic Foods. 160p. 1985. pap. 9.95 (ISBN 0-89529-233-5). Avery Pub.

--The Whole World Cookbook. (Macrobiotic Home Library). 144p. 1984. pap. 6.95 (ISBN 0-89529-231-9). Avery Pub.

East, William G. The Union of Moldavia & Wallachia, 1859. LC 73-18197. 220p. 1973. Repr. of 1929 ed. lib. bdg. 18.50x (ISBN 0-374-92450-3). Octagon.

East, William N. Medical Aspects of Crime. 1980. lib. bdg. 79.95 (ISBN 0-8490-3160-5). Gordon Pr.

Eastaugh, Steven R. Medical Economics & Health Finance. LC 81-3450. 352p. 1981. 24.95 (ISBN 0-86569-065-0); pap. 15.00 (ISBN 0-86569-066-9). Auburn Hse.

Eastaway, Nigel A., jt. auth. see Gallafent, Richard J.

Eastby, Allen G. The Tenth Men. (Illus.). 384p. 1985. 17.95 (ISBN 0-912526-41-6). Lib Res.

Eastby, John. Functionalism & Interdependence. (The Credibility of Institutions, Policies & Leadership Ser.: Vol. 3). 132p. (Orig.). 1985. lib. bdg. 21.00 (ISBN 0-8191-4418-5, Co-Pub. by White Miller Center); pap. text ed. 8.50 (ISBN 0-8191-4419-3). U Pr of Amer.

Eastcott, H. H. Surgical Procedures: Operations on the Internal Carotid Artery, Vol. 12. (Single Surgical Procedures Ser.). 1984. 25.95 (ISBN 0-87489-520-0). Med Economics.

Eastcott, Michal J. I: The Story of the Self. LC 80-51552. (Illus.). 201p. (Orig.). 1980. pap. 5.50 (ISBN 0-8356-0541-8, Quest). Theos Pub Hse.

Eastcott, R. Sketches of the Origin, Process & Effects of Music. LC 70-159680. (Music Ser). 1971. Repr. of 1793 ed. lib. bdg. 32.50 (ISBN 0-306-70184-7). Da Capo.

Easter, Frances. Bible Studies. (Studies in Luke: No. 1). 1985. pap. 3.50 (ISBN 0-8309-0424-7). Herald Hse.

Easter, K. William, jt. auth. see Howe, Charles W.

Easter Seal Rehabilitation Center of Eastern Fairfield County Staff. Our Special Blend: A Cookbook. Thoman, Louise C., ed. LC 83-73727. (Illus.). 416p. 1984. 13.95 (ISBN 0-9613209-0-7). Easter Rehabilitation Inc.

Easterbrook, David L. African Book Reviews, 1885-1945: An Index to Books Reviewed in Selected English-Language Publications. 1979. lib. bdg. 28.50 (ISBN 0-8161-8003-2, Hall Reference). G K Hall.

Easterbrook, David L. & Lohrentz, Kenneth P. Africana Microfilms at the E. S. Bird Library, Syracuse University: An Annotated Guide. (Foreign & Comparative Studies Program, African Special Publications Ser.: No.7). 72p. 1975. pap. 3.50x (ISBN 0-686-70993-4). Syracuse U Foreign Comp.

Easterbrook, David L., jt. auth. see Myrick, Bismarck.

Easterbrook, Frank H., jt. auth. see Posner, Richard A.

Easterbrook, James. The Determinants of Free Will: A Psychological Analysis of Responsible, Adjustive Behavior. (Personality & Psychopathology Ser.). 1978. 39.50 (ISBN 0-12-227550-0). Acad Pr.

Easterbrook, Micheal. Hawk-Moths of the British Isles. (Shire Natural History Ser.: No. 1). (Orig.). 1985. pap. 3.95 (ISBN 0-85263-743-8, Pub. by Shire Pubns England). Seven Hills Bks.

Easterby, J. H. & Polk, Noel. Guide to the Study & Reading of South Carolina History with a Supplement: A Selected List of Books & Reprints of Books on South Carolina History Published Since 1950. LC 75-11551. 333p. 1975. Repr. of 1950 ed. 16.50 (ISBN 0-87152-210-1). Reprint.

Easterby, James H. & Green, Ruth S., eds. Journal of the Commons House of Assembly: Series One, 9 vols. Incl. November 10, 1736-June 7, 1739. xiv, 764p. 1951 (ISBN 0-87249-900-6); September 12, 1739-March 26, 1741. xiv, 614p. 1952 (ISBN 0-87249-901-4); May 18, 1741-July 10, 1742. xiv, 622p. 1953 (ISBN 0-87249-902-2); September 14, 1742-January 27, 1744. xiv, 608p. 1954 (ISBN 0-87249-903-0); February 20, 1744-May 25, 1745. xiv, 626p. 1955 (ISBN 0-87249-904-9); September 10, 1745-June 17, 1746. xiv, 292p. 1956 (ISBN 0-87249-905-7); September 10, 1746-June 13, 1747. Green, Ruth S., pref. by. xiv, 444p. 1958 (ISBN 0-87249-906-5); January 19, 1748-June 29, 1748. Rogers, George C., Jr., pref. by. xiv, 458p. 1961 (ISBN 0-87249-907-3); March 28, 1749-March 19, 1750. Lee, Charles E. & Rogers, George C., Jr.pref. by. xviii, 550p. 1962 (ISBN 0-87249-908-1). LC 51-62239. (Colonial Records of South Carolina Ser.). 34.95x ea. U of SC Pr.

Easterby, Ronald & Zwaga, Harm, eds. Information Design: The Design & Evaluation of Signs & Printed Material. 656p. 1984. 89.95 (ISBN 0-471-10431-0, Pub. by Wiley-Interscience). Wiley.

Easterby, Ronald, et al, eds. Anthropometry & Biomechanics: Theory & Applications. LC 81-11982. (NATO Conference Series III - Human Factors: Vol. 16). 334p. 1982. 49.50x (ISBN 0-306-40745-0, Plenum Pr). Plenum Pub.

Easterby-Smith, Mark. Evaluating Management Education, Training & Development. 200p. 1985. text ed. price not set (ISBN 0-566-02378-4). Gower Pub Co.

Easterday, Kenneth E. & Henry, Loren L., eds. Activities for Junior High School & Middle School Mathematics: Readings from the Arithmetic Teacher & the Mathematics Teacher. Simpson, F. Morgan. LC 81-14024. (Illus.). 218p. 1981. pap. 8.25 (ISBN 0-87353-188-4). NCTM.

Easterlin, Richard A. Birth & Fortune: The Impact of Numbers on Personal Welfare. LC 79-56369. 205p. 1980. 13.95 (ISBN 0-465-00688-4). Basic.

--Population, Labor Force & Long Swings in Economic Growth: The American Experience. (General Ser: No. 86). (Illus.). 318p. 1968. 19.00 (ISBN 0-87014-474-X, Dist. by Columbia U Pr). Natl Bur Econ Res.

Easterlin, Richard A. & Crimmins, Eileen M. The Fertility Revolution: A Supply-Demand Analysis. LC 85-1163. 208p. 1985. 40.00 (ISBN 0-226-18029-8). U of Chicago Pr.

Easterlin, Richard A. & Ward, David. Immigration. (Dimensions of Ethnicity Ser.). 176p. 1982. pap. text ed. 5.95x (ISBN 0-674-44439-6). Harvard U Pr.

Easterlin, Richard A., ed. Population & Economic Change in Developing Countries. LC 79-12569. (National Bureau of Economic Research Ser.). 581p. 1980. lib. bdg. 52.00x (ISBN 0-226-18026-3). U of Chicago Pr.

Easterling, Cynthia R., et al. Merchandising Mathematics for Retailing. LC 83-19771. (Wiley Retailing-Fashion Merchandising Ser.: No. 1-565). 332p. 1984. pap. text ed. 19.95 (ISBN 0-471-86895-7, Pub. by Wiley). Wiley.

Easterling, Jack & Pasanen, Jack. Confront, Construct, Complete: A Comprehensive Approach to Writing, 2 bks. (gr. 9-12). 1978. pap. text ed. 6.50 ea.; Bk. 1. pap. text ed. (ISBN 0-8104-6031-9); Bk. 2. pap. text ed. (ISBN 0-8104-6032-7); tchr's guide 1.50 (ISBN 0-8104-6029-7). Hayden.

Easterling, Jerry. Country Chaff. 168p. 1983. pap. 5.95 (ISBN 0-8323-0419-0). Binford.

Easterling, K., jt. auth. see Porter, D.

Easterling, K., ed. Mechanisms of Deformation & Fracture: Proceedings of the Interdisciplinary Conference, Held at the University of Lulea-Sweden, 20-22, September 1978. (Strength & Fracture of Materials & Structures). 1979. 105.00 (ISBN 0-08-024258-8). Pergamon.

Easterling, Ken. Introduction to the Physical Metallurgy of Welding. 208p. 1983. text ed. 59.95 (ISBN 0-408-01351-6); pap. text ed. 29.95 (ISBN 0-408-01352-4). Butterworth.

Easterling, P. E. & Knox, B. M., eds. The Cambridge History of Classical Literature: Greek Literature, Vol. I. (Illus.). 800p. 1985. 85.00 (ISBN 0-521-21042-9). Cambridge U Pr.

Easterling, P. E. & Muir, J. V., eds. Greek Religion & Society. (Illus.). 264p. 1985. 39.50 (ISBN 0-521-24552-4); pap. 12.95 (ISBN 0-521-28785-5). Cambridge U Pr.

Easterling, P. E., ed. see Sophocles.

Easterling, Ronald E., intro. by. Reuse of Disposables. (Illus.). 104p. (Orig.). 1983. pap. text ed. 35.00 (ISBN 0-910275-27-0). Assn Adv Med Instrs.

Easterly, Frederick J. The Life of Rt. Rev. Joseph Rosati, D. M., First Bishop of St. Louis, 1789-1843. LC 73-3587. (Catholic University of America. Studies in American Church History: No. 33). Repr. of 1942 ed. 27.00 (ISBN 0-404-57783-0). AMS Pr.

Easterly, Lane, ed. Great Bible Stories for Children. 7.95 (ISBN 0-8407-5351-9). Nelson.

Easterman, Daniel. The Last Assassin. LC 84-18711. 432p. 1985. 16.95 (ISBN 0-385-19794-2). Doubleday.

Eastern Africa Law Reports. The Eastern Africa Law Reports: 1957-1967, 11 vols. LC 62-51069. pap. 160.00 ea. (2051298). Bks Demand UMI.

Eastern Analytical Symposium, 1971. Chemical Analysis of the Environment & Other Modern Techniques. LC 73-82575. (Progress in Analytical Chemistry Ser.: No. 5). pap. 98.50 (ISBN 0-317-27112-1, 2024703). Bks Demand UMI.

Eastern & Western Disciples of Vivekananda. The Life of Swami Vivekananda, 2 Vols. rev. ed. Vol. 1, 1980, 629p. 16.00x (ISBN 0-87481-196-1); Vol. 2. 20.00. Vedanta Pr.

Eastern Kentucky University, Dept. of Geology. Principles of Physical Geology Laboratory Manual. 80p. 1980. pap. text ed. 5.50 (ISBN 0-8403-2285-2). Kendall-Hunt.

Eastgate, Robert J. Master Guide to Creative Financing of Real Estate Investments. LC 82-9313. 243p. 1982. text ed. 89.50 (ISBN 0-87624-366-9). Inst Busn Plan.

Eastham. Biochemical Values in Clinical Medicine. 6th ed. 266p. 1978. pap. 14.00 (ISBN 0-7236-0502-5). PSG Pub Co.

--Clinical Haematology. 5th ed. 336p. 1977. pap. 15.00 (ISBN 0-7236-0456-8). PSG Pub Co.

--Laboratory Guide to Clinical Diagnosis. 5th ed. 380p. 1983. pap. 20.50 (ISBN 0-7236-0653-6). PSG Pub Co.

--Pocket Guide to Differential Diagnosis. 474p. 1980. pap. 17.50 (ISBN 0-7236-0542-4). PSG Pub Co.

--A Pocket Guide to Differential Diagnosis. 2nd ed. 1985. write for info. (ISBN 0-7236-0844-X). PSG Pub Co.

Eastham, Barry C. Chinese Art Ivory. rev. & enl. ed. LC 76-23710. (Illus.). 1976. 19.95 (ISBN 0-89344-003-5). Ars Ceramica.

Eastham, M. S. & Kalf, H. Schrodinger Type Operators with Continuous Spectra. (Research Notes in Mathematics Ser.: No. 65). 208p. 1982. pap. text ed. 28.95 (ISBN 0-273-08526-3). Pitman Pub MA.

Eastham, R. G. Interpretation Klinisch-Chemischer Laborresultate. 2nd ed. Peheim, E., tr. Colombo, J. P., ed. xiv, 258p. 1981. pap. 10.25 (ISBN 3-8055-1879-X). S Karger.

Eastham, Scott. Paradise & Ezra Pound: The Poet As Shaman. 260p. (Orig.). 1983. lib. bdg. 26.75 (ISBN 0-8191-3370-1); pap. text ed. 13.25 (ISBN 0-8191-3371-X). U Pr of Amer.

Eastham, Scott T. Wisdom of the Fool: Stories & Poems. ii, 135p. (Orig.). 1985. pap. 6.95 (ISBN 0-932269-15-X). Wyndham Hall.

Easther, Alfred, compiled by see Lees, Thomas.

Easther, Michael, jt. auth. see Maddock, Shirley.

Easthope, Antony. Poetry As Discourse: New Accents. LC 82-18856. 200p. 1983. 18.95 (ISBN 0-416-32720-6, NO. 2030); pap. 8.95 (ISBN 0-416-32730-3, NO. 2975). Methuen Inc.

Easthope, Gary. Healers & Identity: A Sociological Examination of Alternative Medicine. 152p. 1986. text ed. write for info. (ISBN 0-566-05098-6). Gower Pub Co.

Easthope, Jean, jt. auth. see McCullough, Colleen.

Eastin, J. D., ed. Physiological Aspects of Crop Yield. (Illus.). 1969. 10.00 (ISBN 0-89118-004-4). Am Soc Agron.

Eastin, Roy B., jt. auth. see Schmeckebier, Laurence.

Eastlake, A. The Oneida Community. 69.95 (ISBN 0-8490-0769-0). Gordon Pr.

Eastlake, C. L., tr. see Goethe, Johann V.

Eastlake, Charles. History of the Gothic Revival. LC 71-96937. (Library of Victorian Culture). 1975. pap. text ed. 12.00 (ISBN 0-89257-035-0). Am Life Foun.

--History of the Gothic Revival. 2nd ed. Crools, J. Mordaunt, ed. (Victorian Library). 1978. Repr. of 1872 ed. text ed. 44.75x (ISBN 0-7185-5033-1, Leicester). Humanities.

Eastlake, Charles L. Hints on Household Taste in Furniture, Upholstery & Other Details. LC 73-177519. (Illus.). Repr. of 1872 ed. 22.00 (ISBN 0-405-08480-3). Ayer Co Pubs.

--Methods & Materials of Painting of the Great Schools & Masters, 2 Vols. Orig. Title: Materials for a History of Oil Painting. 1847. pap. 7.50 ea.; Vol. 1. pap. (ISBN 0-486-20718-8); Vol. 2. pap. (ISBN 0-486-20719-6). Dover.

Eastlake, Elizabeth R. Journals & Correspondence of Lady Eastlake, 2 vols. LC 79-37691. (Illus.). Repr. of 1895 ed. Set. 57.50 (ISBN 0-404-56746-0). AMS Pr.

Eastlake, F. Warrington, jt. auth. see Yamada, Yosi-Aki.

Eastlake, William. Bamboo Bed. 336p. 1985. pap. 3.50 (ISBN 0-380-69966-4). Avon.

--The Bronc People. LC 75-7472. (Zia Bks). 254p. 1975. pap. 5.95 (ISBN 0-8263-0379-X). U of NM Pr.

--Go in Beauty. LC 79-56815. (Zia Bks.). 292p. 1980. pap. 6.95 (ISBN 0-8263-0538-5). U of NM Pr.

--Jack Armstrong in Tangier & Other Escapes. LC 84-71147. 1984. 13.00; pap. 6.50 (ISBN 0-917453-02-6); Signed, limited ed. 20.00x (ISBN 0-917453-00-X). Bamberger.

Eastlake, William, ed. Portrait of an Artist with Twenty-Six Horses. (Zia Bks.). 224p. 1980. pap. 6.95 (ISBN 0-8263-0558-X). U of NM Pr.

Eastland, Elizabeth W. Milton's Ethics. LC 76-26903. 1942. lib. bdg. 8.50 (ISBN 0-8414-3939-7). Folcroft.

--Milton's Ethics: A Summary of a Thesis. 55p. 1980. Repr. of 1942 ed. lib. bdg. 10.00 (ISBN 0-8495-1339-1). Arden Lib.

--Milton's Ethics: A Summary of a Thesis. 1978. Repr. of 1942 ed. 10.00 (ISBN 0-8492-4400-5). R West.

Eastland, Jonathan. Creative Techniques in Marine & Seascape Photography. (Illus.). 116p. 1983. 29.95 (ISBN 0-7134-4170-4, Pub. by Batsford England). David & Charles.

Eastlick, John T., jt. auth. see Stueart, Robert D.

Eastman & Head. Broadcast-Cable Programming: Strategies & Practices. 2nd ed. 1984. write for info (ISBN 0-534-03353-9). Wadsworth Pub.

Eastman, A. Theodore. The Baptizing Community: Christian Initiation & the Local Congregation. 144p. (Orig.). 1982. pap. 9.95 (ISBN 0-8164-2419-5, Pub. by Seabury). Winston Pr.

Eastman, Addison. This Is Southeast Asia Today. (Orig.). (YA) (gr. 9 up). 1968. pap. 0.85 (ISBN 0-377-83101-8). Friend Pr.

Eastman, Addison J. A Handful of Pearls: The Epistle of James. LC 78-5797. 106p. 1978. pap. 5.50 (ISBN 0-664-24202-2). Westminster.

Eastman, Albert E., ed. see Hechler, Ken.

Eastman, Ann H. & Parent, Roger, eds. Great Library Promotion Ideas: JCD Library Public Relations Award Winners & Notables 1984. LC 84-24446. 64p. 1985. pap. text ed. 8.95x (ISBN 0-8389-3318-1). ALA.

Eastman, Arthur, et al. The Norton Reader. 6th ed. 1983. pap. 13.95x (ISBN 0-393-95296-7); shorter ed. 11.95x (ISBN 0-393-95299-1); tchr's. guide 3.95x (ISBN 0-393-95303-3). Norton.

Eastman, Arthur, et al, eds. The Norton Reader. 5th ed. 1980. pap. 12.95x (ISBN 0-393-95109-X); pap. text ed. 10.95x shorter ed. o. p. (ISBN 0-393-95113-8); guide to norton reader 3.95x (ISBN 0-393-95116-2). Norton.

Eastman, Arthur M. A Short History of Shakespearean Criticism. LC 85-3201. 442p. 1985. pap. text ed. 16.75 (ISBN 0-8191-4589-0). U Pr of Amer.

Eastman, Arthur M., et al, eds. Norton Anthology of Poetry. 1970. 11.95x (ISBN 0-393-09916-4, NortonC). Norton.

--The Norton Reader. 4th ed. 1280p. 1977. pap. text ed. 10.95x complete ed. (ISBN 0-393-09145-7); pap. text ed. 8.95x shorter ed. (ISBN 0-393-09133-3); students guide 3.95x (ISBN 0-393-09128-7); tchrs'. guide gratis. Norton.

Eastman, Barbara. Ezra Pound's Cantos: The Story of the Text. LC 78-55725. (Ezra Pound Scholarship Ser.). 1979. 15.00x (ISBN 0-915032-02-3). Natl Poet Foun.

Eastman, Byron D. Interpreting Mathematical Economics & Econometrics. LC 84-8303. 130p. 1985. 19.95 (ISBN 0-312-42477-9). St Martin.

Eastman, C. N., ed. Spatial Synthesis in Computer-Aided Building Design. (Illus.). 333p. 1975. 46.25 (ISBN 0-85334-611-9, Pub. by Elsevier Applied Sci England). Elsevier.

Eastman, Carol, jt. ed. see Miller, Jay.

Eastman, Carol, jt. ed. see Schiffman, Harold.

Eastman, Carol M. Aspects of Language & Culture. LC 74-28741. (Publications in Anthropology Ser.). (Illus.). 168p. 1975. pap. text ed. 7.95x (ISBN 0-88316-514-7). Chandler & Sharp.

--Language Planning: An Introduction. Langness, L. L. & Edgerton, Robert B., eds. LC 83-1991. (Publications in Anthropology & Related Fields Ser.). (Illus.). 288p. (Orig.). 1983. pap. text ed. 9.95 (ISBN 0-88316-552-X). Chandler & Sharp.

--Markers in English-Influenced Swahili Conversation: Influenced Swahili Conversation. (Papers in International Studies: Africa Ser.: No. 13). pap. 20.00 (ISBN 0-317-10072-6, 2007417). Bks Demand UMI.

Eastman, Charles A. From the Deep Woods to Civilization: Chapters in the Autobiography of an Indian. LC 77-7226. (Illus.). xxii, 230p. 1977. pap. 6.50 (ISBN 0-8032-5873-9, BB 651, Bison). U of Nebr Pr.

--Indian Boyhood. LC 68-58282. (Illus.). (gr. 3-7). pap. 4.00 (ISBN 0-486-22037-0). Dover.

--Indian Boyhood. (Illus.). 14.00 (ISBN 0-8446-0085-7). Peter Smith.

--Indian Boyhood. 289p. 1975. Repr. of 1902 ed. 16.00 (ISBN 0-87928-066-2). Corner Hse.

--Indian Scout Craft & Lore. 190p. 1974. pap. 4.00 (ISBN 0-486-22995-5). Dover.

--The Indian To-Day. LC 74-7962. Repr. of 1915 ed. 17.50 (ISBN 0-404-11851-8). AMS Pr.

--Red Hunters & the Animal People. LC 74-7964. (Illus.). Repr. of 1904 ed. 21.00 (ISBN 0-404-11852-6). AMS Pr.

--The Soul of the Indian: An Interpretation. LC 79-26355. xvi, 170p. 1980. pap. 4.95 (ISBN 0-8032-6701-0, BB 735, Bison). U of Nebr Pr.

Eastman, Charles W., jt. auth. see Clark, Charles E.

Eastman, Crystal. Crystal Eastman: On Women & Revolution. Cook, Blanche W., ed. 352p. 1978. lib. bdg. 19.95 (ISBN 0-88286-104-2). C H kerr.

--Work Accidents & the Law. LC 70-89757. (American Labor, from Conspiracy to Collective Bargaining Ser., No. 1). 361p. 1969. Repr. of 1910 ed. 25.50 (ISBN 0-405-02118-6). Ayer Co Pubs.

Eastman, Daniel & Juilliard, Ahrgus. Face Fitness: A Man's Guide to Looking His Best. (Illus.). 192p. 1984. 17.95 (ISBN 0-02-534680-6). MacMillan.

Eastman, David. I Can Read About Bees & Wasps. new ed. LC 78-73773. (Illus.). (gr. 2-5). 1979. pap. 1.50 (ISBN 0-89375-203-7). Troll Assocs.

--I Can Read About My Own Body. LC 72-96958. (Illus.). (gr. 2-4). 1973. pap. 1.50 (ISBN 0-89375-057-3). Troll Assocs.

--I Can Read About Prehistoric Animals. new ed. LC 76-54492. (Illus.). (gr. 2-4). 1977. pap. 1.50 (ISBN 0-89375-039-5). Troll Assocs.

--Story of Dinosaurs. LC 81-11363. (Now I Know Ser.). (Illus.). 32p. (gr. k-2). 1982. PLB 9.89 (ISBN 0-89375-648-2); pap. 1.25 (ISBN 0-89375-649-0). Troll Assocs.

--What Is a Fish? LC 81-11373. (Now I Know Ser.). (Illus.). 32p. (gr. k-2). 1982. PLB 9.89 (ISBN 0-89375-660-1); pap. 1.25 (ISBN 0-89375-661-X). Troll Assocs.

Eastman, David, adapted by. Adventure of the Empty House. LC 81-11673. (Illus.). 32p. (gr. 5-9). 1982. PLB 9.79 (ISBN 0-89375-616-4); pap. 2.50; cassettes avail. Troll Assocs.

--Adventure of the Speckled Band. LC 81-11694. (Illus.). 32p. (gr. 5-9). 1982. PLB 9.79 (ISBN 0-89375-618-0, BA413); pap. 2.50 (ISBN 0-317-30901-3, PA721); cassettes avail. Troll Assocs.

--The Final Problem. LC 81-11609. (Illus.). 32p. (gr. 5-9). 1982. PLB 9.79 (ISBN 0-89375-612-1, BF022); pap. 2.50 (ISBN 0-317-30902-1, PF732); cassettes avail. Troll Assocs.

--The Red-Headed League. LC 81-11619. (Illus.). 32p. (gr. 5-9). 1982. PLB 9.79 (ISBN 0-89375-614-8, BR007); pap. 2.50 (ISBN 0-317-30903-X, PR409); cassettes avail. Troll Assocs.

--Sherlock Holmes: The Adventure of the Empty House. LC 81-11673. (Illus.). 32p. (gr. 5-9). 1982. PLB 9.79 (ISBN 0-89375-616-4); pap. 2.50 (ISBN 0-89375-617-2). Troll Assocs.

--Sherlock Holmes: The Adventure of the Speckled Band. LC 81-11694. (Illus.). 32p. (gr. 5-9). 1982. PLB 9.79 (ISBN 0-89375-618-0); pap. 2.50 (ISBN 0-89375-619-9). Troll Assocs.

--Sherlock Holmes: The Final Problem. LC 81-11609. (Illus.). 32p. (gr. 5-9). 1982. PLB 9.79 (ISBN 0-89375-612-1); pap. 2.50 (ISBN 0-89375-613-X). Troll Assocs.

--Sherlock Holmes: The Red-Headed League. LC 81-11619. (Illus.). 32p. (gr. 5-9). 1982. PLB 9.79 (ISBN 0-89375-614-8); pap. 2.50 (ISBN 0-89375-615-6). Troll Assocs.

Eastman, Dick. A Celebration of Praise: Exciting Prospects for Extraordinary Praise. pap. 4.95 (ISBN 0-8010-3420-5). Baker Bk.

--Hour That Changes the World. (Direction Bks.). pap. 2.50 (ISBN 0-8010-3337-3). Baker Bk.

--No Easy Road: Inspirational Thoughts on Prayer. new ed. (Direction Bks.). 1973. pap. 2.50 (ISBN 0-8010-3259-8). Baker Bk.

--The University of the Word. LC 83-17763. 1983. pap. 3.95 (ISBN 0-8307-0903-7, 5018301). Regal.

Eastman, Elaine G. Sister to the Sioux: The Memoirs of Elaine Goodale Eastman, 1885-91. Graber, Kay, ed. LC 77-25018. (Illus.). xvi, 183p. 1985. pap. 5.95 (ISBN 0-8032-6713-4, BB 915, Bison). U Of Nebr Pr.

Eastman, Fred. Christ in the Drama: A Study of the Influence of Christ on the Drama of England & America. facsimile ed. LC 79-167336. (Essay Index Reprints - Shaffer Lectures of Northwestern University, 1946). Repr. of 1947 ed. 15.00 (ISBN 0-8369-2647-1). Ayer Co Pubs.

--Men of Power: Abraham Lincoln, Leo Tolstoy, John Burroughs, Graham Taylor, Vol. 4. facs. ed. LC 74-128236. (Essay Index Reprint Ser). 1939. 18.00 (ISBN 0-8369-1994-7). Ayer Co Pubs.

--Men of Power: Benjamin Franklin, Ralph Waldo Emerson, George Fox, Charles Darwin, Vol. 3. facs. ed. LC 74-128236. (Essay Index Reprint Ser). 1939. 18.00 (ISBN 0-8369-1993-9). Ayer Co Pubs.

--Men of Power: Francis of Assisi, Leonardo Da Vinci, Oliver Cromwell, John Milton, Vol. 2. facs. ed. LC 74-128236. (Essay Index Reprint Ser). 1938. 18.00 (ISBN 0-8369-1992-0). Ayer Co Pubs.

--Men of Power: Nicolai Lenin, Mahatma Gandhi, Edward Livingston Trudeau, Robest Louis Stevenson, Vol. 5. facs. ed. LC 74-128236. (Essay Index Reprint Ser). 1940. 18.00 (ISBN 0-8369-1995-5). Ayer Co Pubs.

--Men of Power: Thomas Jefferson, Charles Dickens, Matthew Arnold, Louis Pasteur, Vol. 1. facs. ed. LC 74-128236. (Essay Index Reprint Ser). 1938. 18.00 (ISBN 0-8369-1991 2). Ayer Co Pubs.

Eastman, H. C. & Stykolt, S. Tariff & Competition in Canada. (Illus.). 1968. 27.50 (ISBN 0-312-78540-2). St Martin.

Eastman, Hope. Lobbying: A Constitutionally Protected Right. LC 77-85166. 35p. 1977. pap. 4.25 (ISBN 0-8447-3267-2). Am Enterprise.

Eastman, Hubbard. Noyesism Unveiled. LC 72-134402. Repr. of 1849 ed. 30.00 (ISBN 0-404-08446-X). AMS Pr.

Eastman, Joel W. Styling vs. Safety: The American Automobile Industry & the Development of Automobile Safety, 1900-1966. 296p. (Orig.). 1984. lib. bdg. 25.00 (ISBN 0-8191-3685-9); pap. text ed. 13.75 (ISBN 0-8191-3686-7). U Pr of Amer.

Eastman, John. Who Lived Where. (Illus.). 320p. 1983. 29.95x (ISBN 0-87196-562-3). Facts on File.

Eastman Kodak. Kodak's Pocket Field Guide to 35mm Photography. 1983. pap. 5.95 (ISBN 0-671-46833-2). S&S.

Eastman Kodak Co. The Reel People Collection (H-50) (Illus.). 125p. 1984. pap. 10.00 (ISBN 0-87985-346-8). Eastman Kodak.

Eastman Kodak Co., ed. Practical Steps to Quality Printing. 24p. 1977. pap. 5.00 (ISBN 0-87985-209-7, Q-72). Eastman Kodak.

Eastman Kodak Co., ed. see Horrell, C. William.

Eastman Kodak Co. Editors. The Joy of Photographing People. LC 83-12215. 240p. 1984. 28.95 (ISBN 0-201-11694-4); pap. 14.95 (ISBN 0-201-11695-2). Addison-Wesley.

Eastman Kodak Company. Analysis, Treatment & Disposal of Ferricyanide in Photographic Effluents. LC 79-57024. 72p. 1980. pap. 5.75 (ISBN 0-87985-244-5, J-54). Eastman Kodak.

--Applied Infrared Photography. LC 81-65754. 84p. 1981. pap. text ed. 6.00 (ISBN 0-87985-288-7, M-28). Eastman Kodak.

--Basic Developing, Printing, Enlarging in Black-&-White. 4th ed. LC 82-82731. (Illus.). 72p. 1977. pap. 3.95 (ISBN 0-87985-182-1, AJ-2). Eastman Kodak.

--Basic Photographic Sensitometry Workbook. (Illus.). 1981. 6.50 (ISBN 0-87985-290-9, NO. Z-22-ED). Eastman Kodak.

--Basic Printing Methods. (Exploring the World of Graphic Communications Ser.). (Illus.). (gr. 7-12). 1976. pap. text ed. 4.95 (ISBN 0-87985-169-4, GA111). Eastman Kodak.

--Cinematographer's Field Guide (H-2) (Illus.). 1982. 8.95 (ISBN 0-87985-310-7). Eastman Kodak.

--Clinical Photography. LC 72-87504. (Illus.). 120p. 1972. pap. 2.95 (ISBN 0-87985-035-3, N-3). Eastman Kodak.

--Conservation of Photographs (F-40) 156p. (Orig.). 1985. pap. 29.95 (ISBN 0-87985-352-2). Eastman Kodak.

--Ergonomic Design For People at Work, Vol. I. (Engineering Ser.). (Illus.). 406p. 1983. 45.00 (ISBN 0-534-97962-9). Lifetime Learn.

--Filters & Lens Attachments for Black-&-White & Color Pictures. 1975. pap. 2.95 (ISBN 0-87985-254-2, AB-1). Eastman Kodak.

--Fire & Arson Photography. 1977. pap. 2.50 (ISBN 0-87985-187-2, M-67). Eastman Kodak.

--Introduction to Color Printer Control for Photofinishers Using Noncomputerized Printers. (Illus.). 1978. pap. 6.50 (ISBN 0-87985-217-8, Z-500). Eastman Kodak.

--Kodak & Eastman Professional Motion Picture Films (H-1) rev. ed. (Illus.). 150p. 1982. pap. write for info. (ISBN 0-87985-296-8). Eastman Kodak.

--Kodak Color Darkroom Dataguide. 7th ed. (Illus.). 34p. 1982. pap. 20.00 spiral bound (ISBN 0-87985-086-8, R-19). Eastman Kodak.

--KODAK Complete Darkroom DATAGUIDE. 5th ed. Orig. Title: QSL Adress Book. 58p. (Orig.). 1984. pap. 19.95 (ISBN 0-87985-355-7). Eastman Kodak.

--Kodak Filters for Scientific & Technical Uses. LC 81-65755. 92p. 1981. pap. 9.95 (ISBN 0-87985-282-8, B-3). Eastman-Kodak.

--Kodak Guide to 35 MM Photography. LC 79-54310. (Illus.). 286p. (Orig.). 1981. text ed. 19.95 (ISBN 0-87985-242-9, AC-95H); pap. 9.95 (ISBN 0-87985-236-4, AC-95S). Eastman Kodak.

--Kodak Master Photoguide. (Illus.). 38p. 1981. spiral bdg. 8.50 (ISBN 0-87985-286-0, AR-21). Eastman Kodak.

--Kodak Microelectronics Seminar - Interface '79, G-102: Proceedings. (Illus.). 180p. 1980. pap. 4.50 (ISBN 0-87985-246-1). Eastman Kodak.

--Kodak Professional Photoguide. (No. R-28). (Illus.). 40p. 1977. 11.50 (ISBN 0-87985-100-7). Eastman Kodak.

--Photolab Design. 52p. 1977. pap. 2.00 (ISBN 0-87985-098-1, K-13). Eastman Kodak.

--Phototypesetting with Kodak Products, 1980. LC 75-36853. (Illus.). 48p. 1982. 8.00 (ISBN 0-87985-168-6, Q-5). Eastman Kodak.

--Physical Properties of Kodak Aerial Films. (Illus.). 32p. 1972. pap. 2.95 (ISBN 0-87985-038-8, M-62). Eastman Kodak.

--Presenting Yourself: S-60. 160p. (Orig.). 1982. pap. text ed. 14.95 (ISBN 0-471-87559-7). Eastman Kodak.

--Processing Chemicals & Formulas. LC 73-82620. (Illus.). 52p. 1977. pap. 1.95 (ISBN 0-87985-069-8, J-1). Eastman Kodak.

--Quality Enlarging with Kodak B-W Papers (G-1) LC 81-68717. (Illus.). 132p. 1982. pap. 10.95 (ISBN 0-87985-279-8). Eastman Kodak.

--The Sourcebook-Kodak Ektagraphic Slide Projectors. 3rd ed. Price, A. L., ed. (Illus.). 100p. 1983. pap. text ed. 8.95 (ISBN 0-87985-295-X, S-74). Eastman Kodak.

--Using Filters. LC 81-67034. (The Kodak Workshop Ser.). (Illus.). 96p. (Orig.). 1981. pap. 8.95 (ISBN 0-87985-277-1, KW-13). Eastman Kodak.

--Using Photography to Preserve Evidence. (Illus.). 48p. 1976. pap. 4.50 (ISBN 0-87985-166-X, M-2). Eastman Kodak.

--Using Process EM-26. (Illus.). 130p. 1981. workbook 45.00 (ISBN 0-87985-289-5, Z-127). Eastman-Kodak.

Eastman Kodak Company, ed. Basic Photography for the Graphic Arts. 4th ed. LC 72-88626. (Illus.). 57p. (Orig., Major revision). 1982. pap. 8.50 (ISBN 0-87985-033-7, Q1). Eastman Kodak.

--Black & White Film & Paper Processing & Process Monitoring. (Illus.). 1984. pap. 6.00 (ISBN 0-318-11894-7, Z-128). Eastman-Kodak.

--Camera-Back Silver Masking with Three-Aim Point Control. (Illus.). 1976. pap. 3.50 (ISBN 0-87985-185-6, Q-7B). Eastman Kodak.

--Copy Preparation & Platemaking Using KODAK PMT Materials. (Illus.). 1980. pap. 4.50 (ISBN 0-87985-261-5, Q-71). Eastman Kodak.

--Filming Sports: The How-to Book for Coaches, Sports Information Directors, Motion Picture - Still Sports Photographers (S-65) (Illus.). 288p. (Orig.). 1981. pap. 19.95 (ISBN 0-87985-268-2). Eastman Kodak.

--Fundamental Techniques of Direct-Screen Color Reproduction. (Illus.). 44p. 1980. pap. 5.50 (ISBN 0-87985-260-7, Q-10). Eastman Kodak.

--A Guide for Processing Black-&-White Motion Picture Films (H-7) LC 79-55036. (Illus.). 1979. pap. 5.95 (ISBN 0-87985-229-1, CAT 143 9892). Eastman Kodak.

--Introduction to Color Photographic Processing. 56p. 1978. pap. 5.75 (ISBN 0-87985-216-X, J-3). Eastman Kodak.

--The Joy of Photography. Bd. with More Joy of Photography. 288p. (Illus.). 312p. 1982. Set. pap. 27.90 (ISBN 0-201-99239-6). Addison-Wesley.

--Joy of Photography: A Guide to the Tools & Techniques of Better Photography. 1981. 24.95 (ISBN 0-201-03916-8); pap. 13.95 o. p. (ISBN 0-201-03915-X). Addison-Wesley.

--Kodak Projection Calculator & Seating Guide. 3rd ed. (Illus.). 1983. pap. 5.95 (ISBN 0-87985-214-3, S-16). Eastman Kodak.

--Kodak Sourcebook: Kodak Ektagraphic Slide Projectors. LC 81-69536. (Illus.). 1984. pap. 11.95 (ISBN 0-87985-335-2, S-74). Eastman-Kodak.

--KW-Eighteen, Lenses for 35mm Cameras. (Kodak Workshop Ser.). (Illus.). 96p. (Orig.). Date not set. pap. 8.95 (ISBN 0-87985-303-4). Eastman Kodak.

--KW-Nineteen, Advanced B-W Photography. (Kodak Workshop Ser.). (Illus.). 96p. (Orig.). Date not set. pap. 8.95 (ISBN 0-87985-304-2). Eastman Kodak.

--KW-Seventeen, Existing-Light Photography. (Kodak Workshop Ser.). 96p. (Orig.). Date not set. pap. 8.95 (ISBN 0-87985-302-6). Eastman Kodak.

--KW Twenty-One, Darkroom Expression. (Kodak Workshop Ser.). (Illus.). 96p. Date not set. pap. 8.95 (ISBN 0-87985-300-X). Eastman Kodak.

--KW-Twenty, the Art of Seeing. (Kodak Workshop Ser.). (Illus.). 96p. (Orig.). Date not set. pap. 8.95 (ISBN 0-87985-305-0). Eastman Kodak.

--KW Twenty-Two, Close-Up Photography. (Kodak Workshop Ser.). (Illus.). 96p. Date not set. pap. 8.95 (ISBN 0-87985-301-8). Eastman Kodak.

--Lithographic Offset Presses: An Illustrated Guide. LC 78-58634. (Illus.). 1978. pap. 5.25 (ISBN 0-87985-219-4, Q-215). Eastman Kodak.

--Medical Infrared Photography. 3rd ed. (Illus.). 76p. (Orig.). 1973. pap. 2.00 (ISBN 0-87985-025-6, N-1). Eastman Kodak.

--More Special Effects for Reproduction. LC 76-52137. (Illus.). 1977. pap. 12.00 (ISBN 0-87985-188-0, Q-171). Eastman Kodak.

--Photofabrication Methods with Kodak Photo Resists. 1983. pap. 3.75 (ISBN 0-87985-013-2, P246). Eastman Kodak.

--Photography Through the Microscope. LC 79-54858. (Illus.). 96p. 1980. pap. 9.95 (ISBN 0-87985-248-8, P-2). Eastman Kodak.

--Planning & Producing Slide Programs. LC 81-67828. (Illus.). 70p. (Orig.). 1984. pap. 12.95 (ISBN 0-87985-291-7, S-30). Eastman-Kodak.

--Proceedings of the Kodak Microelectronics Seminar-Interface '77. 1978. pap. 3.50 (ISBN 0-87985-215-1, G-48). Eastman Kodak.

--Sound: Magnetic Sound Recording for Motion Pictures. LC 77-87984. (Illus.). 1977. pap. text ed. 6.25 (ISBN 0-87985-202-X, S-75). Eastman Kodak.

--Using Kodak Ektachrome R-3 & R-3000 Chemicals. (Illus.). 118p. 1985. wkbk. 60.00 (ISBN 0-87985-361-1). Eastman-Kodak.

Eastman Kodak Company Editors. Kodak Data for Aerial Photagraphy (M-29) 5th ed. LC 75-44815. (Illus.). 136p. 1982. pap. 15.00 (ISBN 0-87985-298-4). Eastman Kodak.

--Kodak Pocket Guide to Nature Photography. 1985. pap. 5.95 (ISBN 0-671-50670-6). S&S.

--Kodak Pocket Guide to Travel Photography. 1985. pap. 5.95. S&S.

Eastman Kodak Company Staff. Creative Darkroom Techniques (AG-18) 3rd & rev. ed. LC 73-87110. (Illus.). 292p. 1983. pap. 15.95 (ISBN 0-87985-309-3). Eastman Kodak.

--Ergonomic Design for People at Work: The Design of Jobs, Vol. II. 1984. 42.00t (ISBN 0-534-03111-0). Lifetime Learn.

--Graphic Design. (Exploring the World of Graphic Communications Ser.). (gr. 7-12). 1976. pap. text ed. 4.95 (ISBN 0-87985-170-8, GA-11-2). Eastman Kodak.

--Kodak Guide to 35mm Photography (AC-95S) LC 83-83259. (Illus.). 286p. 1984. pap. 9.95 (ISBN 0-87985-347-6). Eastman Kodak.

--Printing Color Negatives (E-66) rev. ed. (Illus.). 72p. 1982. pap. 8.95 (ISBN 0-87985-322-0). Eastman Kodak.

Eastman Kodak Company Staff, ed. The Business of Filmmaking. LC 78-55882. (Illus.). 1978. pap. 6.95 (ISBN 0-87985-203-8, H-55). Eastman Kodak.

--Images, Images, Images: The Book of Programmed Multi-Image Production (S-12) 3rd ed. (Illus.). 264p. 1983. pap. 24.95 (ISBN 0-87985-327-1). Eastman Kodak.

Eastman Kodak Company Staff, ed. see Stark, Ron & Solomon, Charles.

Eastman Kodak Editors. Photographing Your Baby: Tips for Taking Better Pictures. LC 84-16788. 1984. 9.95 (ISBN 0-201-11698-7). Addison-Wesley.

Eastman, L. M., ed. see Feller-Roth, Barbara.

Eastman, Lester F., ed. Gallium Arsenide Microwave Bulk & Transit-Time Devices. LC 72-77827. (Modern Frontiers in Applied Science Ser.). (Illus.). 288p. 1972. pap. 13.00x (ISBN 0-89006-014-2). Artech Hse.

Eastman, Lloyd E. Seeds of Destruction: Nationalist China in War & Revolution, 1937-1949. LC 82-42861. 328p. 1984. 32.50x (ISBN 0-8047-1191-7). Stanford U Pr.

--Throne & Mandarins: China's Search for a Policy During the Sino-French Controversy, 1880-1885. LC 67-12098. (Historical Studies: No. 79). 1967. 16.50x (ISBN 0-674-89115-5). Harvard U Pr.

Eastman, Margaret. Seed & Nut Cookery. LC 82-3027. 144p. 1982. Greene.

Eastman, Mary. Aunt Phillis's Cabin: Or, Southern Life As It Really Is. LC 68-57524. (The Muckrakers Ser.). (Illus.). 280p. 1979. lib. bdg. 17.75 (ISBN 0-8398-0450-4). Irvington.

--Dahcotah: Or, Life & Legends of the Sioux Around Fort Snelling. facsimile ed. LC 75-95. (Mid-American Frontier Ser.). (Illus.). 1975. Repr. of 1849 ed. 18.00x (ISBN 0-405-06861-1). Ayer Co Pubs.

--The Romance of Indian Life. LC 77-104445. Repr. of 1852 ed. lib. bdg. 19.00 (ISBN 0-8398-0451-2). Irvington.

Eastman, Mary H. Aunt Phillis's Cabin: Or, Southern Life As It Is. LC 68-58054. (Illus.). Repr. of 1852 ed. 22.50x (ISBN 0-8371-0401-7, EAP&, Pub. by Negro U Pr). Greenwood.

Eastman, Max. Artists in Uniform. 1972. lib. bdg. 20.00x (ISBN 0-374-92453-8). Octagon.

--Enjoyment of Laughter. 401p. 1981. Repr. of 1937 ed. lib. bdg. 25.00 (ISBN 0-89987-207-7). Darby Bks.

--Enjoyment of Poetry. 1951. lib. rep. ed. 30.00x (ISBN 0-684-15162-6, ScribT). Scribner.

--Leon Trotsky: The Portrait of a Youth. LC 73-124774. (BCL Ser. I). Repr. of 1925 ed. 18.00 (ISBN 0-404-02235-9). AMS Pr.

--Marxism Is It Science. 1979. Repr. of 1941 ed. lib. bdg. 25.00 (ISBN 0-8492-4403-X). R West.

--Reflections on the Failure of Socialism. LC 55-7352. 128p. 1981. Devin.

--Reflections on the Failure of Socialism. LC 82-2957. 128p. 1982. Repr. of 1955 ed. lib. bdg. 22.50x (ISBN 0-313-23534-1, EARE). Greenwood.

--The Sense of Humor. 257p. 1983. Repr. of 1922 ed. lib. bdg. 45.00 (ISBN 0-89760-216-1). Telegraph Bks.

--The Young Trotsky. 104p. 1982. pap. 20.00x (ISBN 0-902030-92-2, Pub by New Park Pubns England). State Mutual Bk.

Eastman, Max, tr. see Trotsky, Leon.

Eastman, Max, et al, trs. see Trotsky, Leon.

Eastman, Max F. Art & the Life of Action. facs. ed. LC 75-117785. (Essay Index Reprint Ser). 1934. 19.00 (ISBN 0-8369-1802-9). Ayer Co Pubs.

--Marx, Lenin & the Science of Revolution. LC 73-838. (Russian Studies: Perspectives on the Revolution Ser). 267p. 1973. Repr. of 1926 ed. 21.65 (ISBN 0-88355-034-2). Hyperion Conn.

Eastman, Max. F. Since Lenin Died. LC 73-839. (Russian Studies: Perspectives on the Revolution Ser.). 158p. 1973. Repr. of 1925 ed. 17.60 (ISBN 0-88355-035-0). Hyperion Conn.

Eastman, Moira & Poussard, Wendy. The Christmas Book. LC 80-68368. (Illus.). 40p. 1980. 5.95 (ISBN 0-87793-214-X). Ave Maria.

Eastman, Nicholas J. & Russell, Keith P. Expectant Motherhood. 7th rev. ed. (Illus.). 1983. 7.70i (ISBN 0-316-20396-3). Little.

Eastman, Norris W. & Landrum, Gerald. Underwater Communication: Hand Signals for Scuba Diving. (Illus.). 48p. 1984. pap. 3.95 (ISBN 0-916622-30-4). Princeton Bk Co.

Eastman, P. An End to Pounding: A New Mechanical Flour Milling System in Use in Africa. 64p. (Eng. & Fr.). 1980. pap. 5.00 (ISBN 0-88936-246-7, IDRC152, IDRC). Unipub.

Eastman, P. D. Cat in the Hat Beginner Book Dictionary. LC 64-1157. (Illus.). (gr. k-6). 1964. 5.95 (ISBN 0-394-81009-0); PLB 8.99 (ISBN 0-394-91009-5). Beginner.

--The Cat in the Hat Beginner Book Dictionary. (Illus.). 1984. 8.99 (ISBN 0-394-91009-5). Random.

--Cat in the Hat Beginner Book Dictionary in English & Spanish. LC 66-10688. (Illus., Span. & Eng.). (gr. k-3). 1966. 10.95 (ISBN 0-394-81542-4); PLB 10.99 (ISBN 0-394-91542-9). Beginner.

--Cat in the Hat Beginner Book Dictionary in French & English. LC 65-22650. (Illus., Fr. & Eng.). (gr. 2-3). 1965. 9.95 (ISBN 0-394-81063-5). Beginner.

--Eres Tu Mi Mama? Are You My Mother? LC 67-3636. (Illus., Span. & Eng.). (gr. 1-2). 1967. 5.95 (ISBN 0-394-81596-3). Beginner.

--Flap Your Wings. LC 76-24164. (Picturebacks Ser.). (Illus.). 32p. (ps-3). 1984. pap. 1.50 (ISBN 0-394-83565-4, BYR). Random.

--Flap Your Wings. (Pictureback Book & Cassette Ser.). (Illus.). 32p. (ps-1). 1985. pap. 4.95 incl. cassette (ISBN 0-394-87655-5). Random.

Eastman, P. D., jt. tr. see Rivera, Carlos.

Eastman, Patricia. Sometimes Things Change. LC 83-10090. (Rookie Reader). (Illus.). 32p. (ps-2). 1983. PLB 8.65 (ISBN 0-516-02044-7); pap. 2.50 (ISBN 0-516-42044-5). Childrens.

Eastman, Peggy & Barr, John L. Your Child Is Smarter Than You Think. LC 84-19086. 256p. 1985. 14.95 (ISBN 0-688-02965-5). Morrow.

Eastman, Peter F. Advanced First Aid Afloat. 2nd ed. LC 72-78241. (Illus.). 143p. 1974. pap. 6.00 (ISBN 0-87033-169-8). Cornell Maritime.

--Advanced First Aid for All Outdoors. LC 76-44658. (Illus.). 175p. 1976. pap. 6.00 (ISBN 0-87033-223-6). Cornell Maritime.

Eastman, Philip D. The Alphabet Book. LC 73-16859. (Illus.). 32p. 1974. pap. 1.95 (ISBN 0-394-82818-6, BYR). Random.

--Are You My Mother? LC 60-13495. (Illus.). (gr. 1-2). 1960. 4.95 (ISBN 0-394-80018-4); PLB 5.99 (ISBN 0-394-90018-9). Beginner.

--Best Nest. LC 68-28459. (Illus.). (gr. k-3). 1968. 4.95 (ISBN 0-394-80051-6); PLB 5.99 (ISBN 0-394-90051-0). Beginner.

--Big Dog, Little Dog: A Bedtime Story. (Illus.). (ps-1). 1973. pap. 1.95 (ISBN 0-394-82669-8, BYR). Random.

--The Cat in the Hat Beginner Book Dictionary in French. (ps-2). 1965. 9.95 (ISBN 0-394-81063-5, BYR); PLB 8.99 o. p. (ISBN 0-394-91063-X). Random.

--Flap Your Wings. (Bright Bird Bks). (Illus.). (ps-2). 1969. (BYR). Random.

--Go, Dog, Go. LC 61-7069. (Illus.). (gr. 1-3). 1961. 4.95 (ISBN 0-394-80020-6); PLB 5.99 (ISBN 0-394-90020-0). Beginner.

--Sam & the Firefly. LC 58-11966. (Illus.). (gr. 1-2). 1958. 4.95 (ISBN 0-394-80006-0); PLB 5.99 (ISBN 0-394-90006-5). Beginner.

Eastman, Philip D., jt. auth. see McKie, Roy.

Eastman, R. D. Biochemical Values in Clinical Medicine. 7th ed. (Illus.). 400p. 1985. 15.00 (ISBN 0-7236-0820-2). PSG Pub Co.

Eastman, Richard M. Style: Writing & Reading As the Discovery of Outlook. 3rd ed. 1984. pap. 12.95 (ISBN 0-19-503395-7). Oxford U Pr.

Eastman, Robert E. The Winning Edge in Selling: Successful Techniques that Tip the Balance. 208p. 1983. 16.95 (ISBN 0-13-960989-X, Busn). P-H.

Eastman, Roger, ed. Coming of Age in Philosophy. 567p. 1973. pap. text ed. 18.50 scp (ISBN 0-06-382594-5, HarpC). Har-Row.

--The Ways of Religion. 608p. 1975. pap. text ed. 21.95 scp (ISBN 0-06-382595-3, CP, HarpC). Har-Row.

Eastman School of Music Press. The Future of Musical Education in America: Proceedings of the July 1983 Conference. 1984. 12.50 (ISBN 0-317-30910-2). Music Ed Natl.

Eastman, Sheila & McGee, Timothy J. Barbara Pentland. (Canadian Composers Ser.). 224p. 1983. 27.50x (ISBN 0-8020-5562-1). U of Toronto Pr.

Eastman, Susan Tyler & Klein, Robert. Strategies in Broadcast & Cable Promotion: Commercial Television, Radio, Cable, Pay Television, Public Television. 352p. 1982. pap. text ed. write for info. (ISBN 0-534-01156-X). Wadsworth Pub.

Eastman, Wilbur F. The Canning, Freezing, Curing & Smoking of Meat, Fish, & Game. LC 75-16830. (Illus.). 220p. 1975. o. p. 11.95 (ISBN 0-88266-072-1); pap. 5.95 (ISBN 0-88266-045-4). Garden Way Pub.

Eastman, William R. Limited Edition Photographs: How to Produce & Market Your Own. 2nd ed. LC 80-84694. (Illus.). 73p. (Orig.). 1981. pap. 9.95 (ISBN 0-934420-02-5). Lightbooks.

Eastmann, C. R., ed. see Von Zittel, K. A.

Eastment, Winifred. Down at the Vicarage. 261p. 1967. 24.75x (ISBN 0-905858-08-5, Pub. by Egon England). State Mutual Bk.

Eastom, Thomas A. Working for Life: Careers in Biology. (Illus.). 118p. 1984. 12.95x (ISBN 0-937548-06-5). Plexus Pub.

Easton, A. J., et al. Analysis of Chondritic Material Using Selective Attack by Chlorine. (Illus.). 1981. spiral bdg. 21.50x (ISBN 0-565-00837-4, Pub. by Brit Mus Nat Hist England). Sabbot-Natural Hist Bks.

Easton, Allan. Complex Managerial Decisions Involving Multiple Objectives. LC 79-25513. 446p. 1980. Repr. of 1973 ed. lib. bdg. 26.50 (ISBN 0-89874-079-7). Krieger.

--Decision Making: A Short Course for Professionals. (Professional Development Programs Ser.). 352p. 1976. Set. 64.95x (ISBN 0-471-01700-0). Wiley.

--This Is the Shih Tzu. rev. ed. 1969. 12.95 (ISBN 0-87666-389-7, PS661). TFH Pubns.

Easton, Allen, jt. auth. see Brearley, Joan McD.

Easton, Anthony T. The Home Satellite TV Book: How to Put the World in Your Yard. (Illus.). 224p. 1981. 10.95 (ISBN 0-399-50921-6, Playboy). Putnam Pub Group.

--Satellite TV Handbook. LC 83-60155. 440p. 1983. pap. 16.95 (ISBN 0-672-22055-5). Sams.

--The Under Eight Hundred Dollar Computer Buyer's Guide: Evaluating the New Generation of Small Computers. 1984. pap. 12.95 (ISBN 0-201-04191-X). Addison-Wesley.

Easton, Brian. Social Policy & the Welfare State in New Zealand. 200p. 1980. text ed. 25.00x (ISBN 0-86861-393-2); pap. text ed. 12.50x (ISBN 0-86861-002-X). Allen Unwin.

Easton, Brian & Thomson, Norman. An Introduction to the New Zealand Economy. LC 81-19737. (Illus.). 339p. 1983. text ed. 25.00x (ISBN 0-7022-1920-7); pap. 13.50x (ISBN 0-7022-1940-1). U of Queensland Pr.

Easton, Carol. Straight Ahead: The Story of Stan Kenton. (Quality Paperbacks Ser.). (Illus.). 252p. 1981. pap. 7.95 (ISBN 0-306-80152-3). Da Capo.

Easton, David. A Framework for Political Analysis. LC 78-71147. 1979. pap. 4.50x (ISBN 0-226-18015-8, P834, Phoen). U of Chicago Pr.

--The Political System: An Inquiry into the State of Political Science. 2nd ed. LC 80-39678. 408p. 1981. pap. 12.50x (ISBN 0-226-18017-4). U of Chicago Pr.

--A Systems Analysis of Political Life. LC 78-71148. 1979. pap. 8.95x (ISBN 0-226-18016-6, P833, Phoen). U of Chicago Pr.

Easton, David & Dennis, Jack. Children in the Political System. LC 68-58506. (Midway Reprint Ser.). 1980. pap. text ed. 15.50x (ISBN 0-226-18013-1). U of Chicago Pr.

Easton, David & Hess, Robert. Eight City Study of Child Political Socialization, 1961-1962. 2nd ed. 1975. codebk. write for info. (ISBN 0-89138-022-1). ICPSR.

Easton, Edward. The Miscast Gentleman. 1978. pap. 2.25 (ISBN 0-532-22120-6). Woodhill.

--The Pirate of Hitchfield. 1978. pap. 2.25 (ISBN 0-532-22144-3). Woodhill.

Easton, Edward J. Magnetic Resonance Imaging. LC 85-61596. 175p. Date not set. 49.50 (ISBN 0-943432-54-5). Slack Inc.

Easton, Emily. Roger Williams, Prophet & Pioneer. LC 76-101266. Repr. of 1930 ed. 40.00 (ISBN 0-404-02236-7). AMS Pr.

--Roger Williams, Prophet & Pioneer. LC 71-102235. (Select Bibliographies Reprint Ser). 1930. 32.00 (ISBN 0-8369-5120-4). Ayer Co Pubs.

--Roger Williams: Prophet & Pioneer. LC 78-144994. 399p. 1972. Repr. of 1930 ed. 17.00x (ISBN 0-403-00793-3). Scholarly.

Easton, Freda, jt. auth. see Winters, Wendy G.

Easton, J. W., jt. auth. see McLean, A.

Easton, Loyd D., ed. see Miller, Dickinson S.

Easton, M. Coleman. Masters of Glass. 1985. pap. 2.95 (ISBN 0-445-20064-2, Pub. by Popular Lib). Warner Bks.

Easton, M. G. Illustrated Bible Dictionary. (Baker's Paperback Reference Library). 760p. 1983. pap. 12.95 (ISBN 0-8010-3386-1). Baker Bk.

--The Illustrated Bible Dictionary. 768p. (Orig.). 1983. 12.95 (ISBN 0-89081-384-1). Harvest Hse.

Easton, M. G., tr. see Krummacher, F. W.

Easton, Nina. Reagan's Squeeze on Small Business: How the Adminstration Plan Will Increase Economic Concentration, Vol. 1. Brownstein, Ronald, ed. (Presidential Examiner Ser.: Vol. 1, No. 1). 83p. (Orig.). 1981. pap. text ed. 7.00 (ISBN 0-936486-02-3). Presidential Acct.

--Women Take Charge: Asserting Your Rights in the Marketplace. 202p. 1983. pap. 6.50 (ISBN 0-318-04129-4). Ctr Responsive Law.

Easton, Nina, jt. auth. see Brownstein, Ronald.

Easton, Nina, ed. see Brownstein, Ronald.

Easton, Phoebe J. Marbling: A History & Bibliography. (Illus.). xiii, 190p. 1983. 100.00 (ISBN 0-87093-180-6). Dawsons.

Easton, Richard J. & Graham, George P. Intermediate Algebra. LC 72-4744. (Illus.). 305p. 1973. text ed. 29.50x (ISBN 0-471-22939-3); wkbk. o.p. 13.95x (ISBN 0-471-22943-1). Wiley.

Easton, Robert. China Caravans. LC 81-21742. (Illus.). 156p. 1982. pap. 8.95 (ISBN 0-88496-179-6). Capra Pr.

--Max Brand the Big "Westerner". LC 68-16732. (Illus.). 1970. 19.95 (ISBN 0-8061-0870-3); pap. 11.95 (ISBN 0-8061-1233-6). U of Okla Pr.

--This Promised Land. (The Saga of California Trilogy: Vol. I). 328p. (Orig.). 1982. pap. 9.95 (ISBN 0-88496-183-4). Capra Pr.

Easton, Robert & Brown, MacKenzie. Lord of Beasts: The Saga of Buffalo Jones. LC 61-14501. (Illus.). xvi, 287p. 1970. pap. 5.95 (ISBN 0-8032-5727-9, BB 522, Bison). U of Nebr Pr.

Easton, S., jt. auth. see Lamb, D.

Easton, Stewart. Vigil. 1984. pap. 7.95 (ISBN 0-317-02511-2). Folder Edns.

Easton, Stewart, ed. see Steiner, Rudolf.

Easton, Stewart C. Man & World in the Light of Anthroposophy. LC 74-33879. 1975. pap. 13.50 (ISBN 0-910142-67-X). Anthroposophic.

--Man & World in the Light of Anthroposophy. Rev. ed. 536p. 1982. pap. 11.95 (ISBN 0-88010-006-0). Anthroposophic.

--Man & World in the Light of Anthroposophy. 2nd ed. 543p. 1982. pap. 11.95 (ISBN 0-88010-077-X). Anthroposophic.

--Roger Bacon & His Search for a Universal Science. LC 70-100159. Repr. of 1952 ed. lib. bdg. 15.00x (ISBN 0-8371-3399-8, EARB). Greenwood.

--Rudolf Steiner: Herald of a New Epoch. LC 80-67026. (Illus.). 1980. pap. 10.95 (ISBN 0-910142-93-9). Anthroposophic.

Easton, Stewart C. & Wieruszowski, Helene. The Era of Charlemagne: Frankish State & Society. LC 79-4518. (Anvil Ser.). 192p. 1979. pap. 6.95 (ISBN 0-88275-905-1). Krieger.

Easton, Stewart C., et al, eds. see Steiner, Rudolf.

Easton, Susan M. Humanist Marxism & Wittgensteinian Social Philosophy. LC 83-9391. 148p. 1983. 18.00 (ISBN 0-7190-0935-9, Pub. by Manchester Univ Pr). Longwood Pub Group.

Easton, Thomas A. Careers in Science. LC 83-73707. 1984. 12.25 (ISBN 0-87094-476-2); pap. 9.95 (ISBN 0-87094-546-7). Dow Jones-Irwin.

--How to Write a Readable Business Report. LC 82-73624. 275p. 1983. 14.95 (ISBN 0-87094-393-6). Dow Jones-Irwin.

Easton, Thomas A. & Conant, Ralph W. Cutting Loose: From Employee to Entrepreneur. 220p. 1985. 17.95 (ISBN 0-917253-14-0). Probus Pub Co.

--Using Consultants: A Consumer's Guide for Managers. 192p. 1985. 17.95 (ISBN 0-917253-03-5). Probus Pub Co.

Easton, Tom & Rishcer, Carl. Bioscope. 2nd ed. (Illus.). 640p. 1984. pap. text ed. 19.95 (ISBN 0-675-20137-3); Additional supplements may be obtained from publisher. study guide 9.95 (ISBN 0-675-20233-7). Merrill.

Easton, Tom, et al. Youth League Baseball: Coaching & Playing. (Illus.). 164p. (Orig.). (gr. 2 up). 1984. pap. 6.95 (ISBN 0-87670-082-2, Dist. by Sterling). Athletic Inst.

Eastop, T. D. & McConkey, A. Applied Thermodynamics for Engineering Technologists. 3rd ed. (Illus.). 1978. pap. text ed. 19.95x (ISBN 0-582-44197-8). Longman.

Eastop, Thomas D. & Gasiorek, Janus M. Air Conditioning Through Worked Examples, with Chapters 7 & 8 on Duct Sizing & Fans. LC 73-441904. pap. 91.00 (ISBN 0-317-10833-6). Bks Demand UMI.

Eastop, V. F., jt. auth. see Blackman, R. L.

Eastwick, Ivy O. In & Out the Windows: Happy Poems for Children. LC 73-90841. (Illus.). (ps-3). 1969. 6.95 (ISBN 0-87486-007-5). Plough.

Eastwood, Alice see Fall, Henry C.

Eastwood, Bruce. Directory of Audio-Visual Sources: History of Science, Medicine & Technology. 160p. 1979. 20.00 (ISBN 0-88202-185-0). Watson Pub Intl.

--The Elements of Vision: The Microcosmology of Visual Theory According to Hunayn Ibn Ishaq, Pt. 5. (Transactions Ser: Vol. 72). 1982. 8.00 (ISBN 0-87169-725-4). Am Philos.

Eastwood, D. G., jt. auth. see Harre, R.

Eastwood, David B. Economics of Consumer Behavior: An Introduction to Consumer Economics. 627p. 1985. text ed. 20.01 (098257). Allyn.

Eastwood, DeLyle, ed. New Directions in Molecular Luminescence - STP 822. LC 83-70423. 131p. 1983. pap. text ed. 24.00 (ISBN 0-8031-0212-7, 04-822000-39). ASTM.

Eastwood, Delyle, jt. ed. see Cline Love, L. J.

Eastwood, Dorothy M. The Revival of Pascal: A Study of His Relation to Modern French Thought. LC 37-2631. (Oxford Studies in Modern Languages & Literature). pap. 56.00 (ISBN 0-317-08091-1, 2051242). Bks Demand UMI.

Eastwood, Gerry. Skilled Labor Shortages in the United Kingdom: With Particular Reference to the Engineering Industry. (British-North American Committee Ser.). 52p. 1976. 3.00 (ISBN 0-902594-28-1). Natl Planning.

Eastwood, Gregory L. Core Textbook of Gastroenterology. (Illus.). 416p. 1984. pap. text ed. 24.50 (ISBN 0-397-52102-2, 65-06935, Lippincott Medical). Lippincott.

Eastwood, J. & Wright, W. Aldis. A Glossary of the English Bible Words. 564p. 1981. Repr. of 1866 ed. lib. bdg. 75.00 (ISBN 0-89760-210-2). Telegraph Bks.

Eastwood, J. J. & Smith, F. B. Historical Studies: Selected Articles. 1975. pap. 10.00x (ISBN 0-522-83588-0, Pub. by Melbourne U Pr Australia). Intl Spec Bk.

Eastwood, Mary. Fighting Job Discrimination: Three Federal Approaches. LC 72-188333. (Law & Women Ser.). 1972. pap. 2.00 (ISBN 0-87999-001-5). Today News.

Eastwood, Maud L. Antique Builders Hardware: Knobs & Accessories. (Illus.). 224p. (Orig.). 1982. 19.50 (ISBN 0-9610800-2-7); pap. 17.50 (ISBN 0-9610800-1-9). Ant Doorknob Pub.

Eastwood, Maudie. The Antique Doorknob. (Illus.). 206p. (Orig.). 1976. pap. 8.50 (ISBN 0-9610800-0-0). Ant Doorknob Pub.

Eastwood, Michael R., ed. The Relation Between Physical & Mental Illness: The Physical Status of Psychiatric Patients at a Multiphasic Screening Survey. LC 74-76877. (Clarke Institute of Psychiatry, Monograph Ser.: No. 4). pap. 33.30 (ISBN 0-317-26915-1). Bks Demand UMI.

Eastwood, W. A Book of Science Verse. 279p. 1980. Repr. of 1961 ed. lib. bdg. 30.00 (ISBN 0-89984-177-5). Century Bookbindery.

Easty, David L. & Smolin, Gilbert. External Eye Disease: Vol. 3, BIMR Opthalmology. (International Medical Reviews Ser.). (Illus.). 320p. 1985. text ed. 59.95 (ISBN 0-407-02342-9). Butterworth.

Easu & Rodehaver, Gladys K., eds. Book II of Revelations for the Aquarian Age. 1983. pap. 7.00 (ISBN 0-930208-14-5). Mangan Bks.

Easum, Chester V. Prince Henry of Prussia, Brother of Frederick the Great. LC 75-113061. (Illus.). 403p. Repr. of 1942 ed. lib. bdg. 19.50x (ISBN 0-8371-4697-6, EAPH). Greenwood.

Easum, Dick d' see D'Easum, Dick.

Easwaran, Eknath. The Bhagavad Gita for Daily Living: Chapters 1-6. LC 74-20130. (Commentary, translation & sanskrit text). 1975. 15.00 (ISBN 0-915132-03-6). Nilgiri Pr.

--The Bhagavad Gita for Daily Living: Chapters 7-12. LC 79-1448. 1979. 15.00 (ISBN 0-915132-04-4). Nilgiri Pr.

--The Bhagavad Gita for Daily Living: Chapters 13-18. 512p. 1984. 15.00 (ISBN 0-915132-05-2). Nilgiri Pr.

--The Bhagavad Gita for Daily Living, Vol. 1: The End of Sorrow. LC 79-1448. 1979. pap. 10.00 (ISBN 0-915132-17-6). Nilgiri Pr.

--The Bhagavad Gita for Daily Living, Vol. 2: Like a Thousand Suns. LC 79-1448. 1979. pap. 10.00 (ISBN 0-915132-18-4). Nilgiri Pr.

--The Bhagavad Gita for Daily Living, Vol. 3: To Love Is to Know Me. 512p. 1984. pap. 10.00 (ISBN 0-915132-19-2). Nilgiri Pr.

--Dialogue with Death: The Spiritual Psychology of the Katha Upanishad. LC 80-39764. 288p. (Orig.). 1981. pap. 7.00 (ISBN 0-915132-24-9). Nilgiri Pr.

--Formulas for Transformation: A Mantram Handbook. 264p. 1977. pap. 7.00 (ISBN 0-915132-30-3). Nilgiri Pr.

--Gandhi the Man. 2nd ed. LC 77-25976. (Illus.). 1978. 13.95 (ISBN 0-915132-13-3); pap. 7.95 (ISBN 0-915132-14-1). Nilgiri Pr.

--Gandhi the Man. 192p. 1983. pap. 7.95 (ISBN 0-394-71497-0). Random.

--Instrucciones En la Meditacion. 1980. pap. 1.50 (ISBN 0-915132-23-0). Nilgiri Pr.

--Instructions in Meditation. 1972. pap. 1.50 (ISBN 0-915132-09-5). Nilgiri Pr.

--Love Never Faileth: The Inspiration of St. Francis, St. Augustine, St. Paul & Mother Teresa. (Illus., Orig.). 1985. 12.00 (ISBN 0-915132-31-1); pap. 7.00 (ISBN 0-915132-32-X). Nilgiri Pr.

--A Man to Match His Mountains: Badshah Khan, Nonviolent Soldier of Islam. (Illus.). 1985. 13.95 (ISBN 0-915132-33-8); pap. 7.95 (ISBN 0-915132-34-6). Nilgiri Pr.

--Meditation: An Eight-Point Program. LC 78-10935. 1978. pap. 7.00 (ISBN 0-915132-16-8). Nilgiri Pr.

--The Supreme Ambition: Life's Goal & How to Reach It. LC 81-18991. (Illus.). 176p. 1982. 12.00 (ISBN 0-915132-26-5); pap. 7.00 (ISBN 0-915132-27-3). Nilgiri Pr.

Easwaran, Eknath, ed. God Makes the Rivers to Flow: Passages for Meditation. (Illus.). 96p. 1982. 12.00 (ISBN 0-915132-28-1); pap. 7.00 (ISBN 0-915132-29-X). Nilgiri Pr.

Easwaran, Eknath, tr. from Sanskrit. The Bhagavad Gita. LC 85-10637. 1985. 10.95 (ISBN 0-915132-36-2); pap. 5.95 (ISBN 0-915132-35-4). Nilgiri Pr.

Easy, Ben. The E. M. R. Syndrome: The Married Man's Guide to Extra-Marital Relationships. Slayton, Ben L., ed. 150p. (Orig.). Date not set. pap. price not set. Easy St Pubns.

Easyriders, ed. Best Biker Fiction, No. 3. (Paisano Bks.). 224p. (Orig.). 1984. pap. 2.95 (ISBN 0-440-01832-3). Dell.

Eates, Margot, jt. ed. see Ramsden, E. H.

Eather, Robert. Majestic Lights. (Illus.). 324p. 1980. 49.00 (ISBN 0-87590-215-4). Am Geophysical.

Eathorne, Richard H. The Analysis of Outdoor Recreation Demand: A Review & Annotated Bibliography of the Current State-of-the-Art. (Public Administration Ser.: Bibliography P-563). 93p. 1980. pap. 10.00 (ISBN 0-88066-082-1). Vance Biblios.

Eatock, Marjorie. See No Evil. (Judy Sullivan Romance Ser.). 192p. 1985. 14.95 (ISBN 0-8027-0862-5). Walker & Co.

--Stolen Holiday. (Candlelight Ecstasy Ser.: No. 34). (Orig.). 1982. pap. 1.75 (ISBN 0-440-17742-1). Dell.

Eaton, Allen & Harrison, Shelby H. A Bibliography of Social Surveys. LC 75-17218. (Social Problems & Social Policies Ser.). 1976. Repr. of 1930 ed. 38.50x (ISBN 0-405-07489-1). Ayer Co Pubs.

Eaton, Allen, jt. auth. see Adriani, John.

Eaton, Allen H. Handicrafts of the Southern Highlands. (Illus.). 370p. 1973. pap. 7.95 (ISBN 0-486-22211-X). Dover.

--Handicrafts of the Southern Highlands. (Illus.). 15.25 (ISBN 0-8446-4732-2). Peter Smith.

--Immigrant Gifts to American Life: Some Experiments in Appreciation of the Contributions of Our Foreign Born. LC 73-129395. (American Immigration Collection, Ser. 2). (Illus.). 1970. Repr. of 1932 ed. 15.00 (ISBN 0-405-00576-8). Ayer Co Pubs.

Eaton, Anne T., jt. ed. see Daringer, Helen F.

Eaton, Arthur W. The Famous Mather Byles: Noted Boston Tory Preacher, Poet, & Wit 1707-1788. facsimile ed. LC 74-165626. (Select Bibliographies Reprint Ser). Repr. of 1914 ed. 33.00 (ISBN 0-8369-5933-7). Ayer Co Pubs.

--The Famous Mather Byles, the Noted Boston Tory Preacher, Poet, & Wit. facsimile ed. LC 72-8697. (American Revolutionary Ser.). Repr. of 1914 ed. lib. bdg. 19.00x (ISBN 0-8398-0458-X). Irvington.

Eaton, Arthur W., ed. see Johnston, Elizabeth L.

Eaton, Bili. A Love So Amazing... Memories of Meher Baba. LC 84-23597. 144p. 1984. pap. 8.95 (ISBN 0-913078-55-7). Sheriar Pr.

Eaton, Burnham. High Hearth. 1979. 6.00 (ISBN 0-8233-0302-0). Golden Quill.

Eaton, Charles, intro. by. Karl Knaths: Five Decades of Painting. LC 73-82318. (Illus.). 160p. 1973. pap. 8.00 (ISBN 0-88397-056-2, Pub. by Intl Exhibit Foun). C E Tuttle.

Eaton, Charles E. The Thing King. 104p. 1982. 9.95 (ISBN 0-8453-4743-8). Cornwall Bks.

--The Work of the Wrench. LC 84-45452. 112p. 1985. 13.95 (ISBN 0-317-18787-2). Cornwall Bks.

Eaton, Charlotte. A Last Memory of Robert Louis Stevenson. 62p. 1980. Repr. of 1916 ed. lib. bdg. 10.00 (ISBN 0-8495-1341-3). Arden Lib.

--A Last Memory of Robert Louis Stevenson. LC 77-24071. 1977. lib. bdg. 8.50 (ISBN 0-8414-3988-5). Folcroft.

--Stevenson at Manasquan. LC 76-42995. 1976. lib. bdg. 10.00 (ISBN 0-8414-3919-2). Folcroft.

Eaton, Clement. The Civilization of the Old South: Writings of Clement Eaton. Kirwan, Albert D., ed. LC 68-29638. 328p. 1968. 22.00x (ISBN 0-8131-1162-5). U Pr of Ky.

--The Growth of Southern Civilization, 1790-1860. (New American Nation Ser.). (Illus.). 1961. 17.26xi (ISBN 0-06-011150-X, HarpT). Har-Row.

--Henry Clay & the Art of American Politics. (The Library of American Biography). 209p. 1962. pap. 6.95 (ISBN 0-316-20412-9). Little.

--History of the Southern Confederacy. 1954. pap. text ed. 12.95 (ISBN 0-02-908710-4). Free Pr.

--Jefferson Davis. LC 77-2512. 1979. pap. text ed. 12.95 (ISBN 0-02-908740-6). Free Pr.

--Jefferson Davis: The Sphinx of the Confederacy. LC 77-2512. 1977. 21.95 (ISBN 0-02-908700-7). Free Pr.

--Mind of the Old South. rev. ed. LC 67-11648. (Walter Lynwood Fleming Lectures). (Illus.). x, 348p. 1967. 30.00x (ISBN 0-8071-0443-4); pap. text ed. 8.95x (ISBN 0-8071-0120-6). La State U Pr.

Eaton, Clement, ed. Leaven of Democracy: The Growth of the Democratic Spirit in the Time of Jackson. LC 63-17877. (American Epochs Ser). pap. 4.95 (ISBN 0-8076-0394-5). Braziller.

Eaton, Connie. Circular Stained Glass Pattern Book: 60 Full-Page Designs. (Stained Glass Ser.). 64p. 1985. pap. 3.75 (ISBN 0-486-24836-4). Dover.

--Oval Stained Glass Pattern Book: 60 Full Page Designs. (Stained Glass Ser.). (Illus.). 64p. 1983. pap. 3.50 (ISBN 0-486-24519-5). Dover.

Eaton, David. Historical Atlas of Westmoreland County, Virginia. LC 42-17980. (Illus.). 88p. Repr. of 1942 ed. 25.00 (ISBN 0-685-65066-9). Va Bk.

--A Method to Evaluate the Likelihood of Grain Shortfalls. (Working Paper Ser.: No. 9). 36p. 1978. pap. 2.50 (ISBN 0-318-00182-9). LBJ Sch Pub Aff.

--On Deployment of Health Resources in Rural Valle del Cauca, Colombia. (Working Paper Ser.). 50p. 1979. pap. 2.50 (ISBN 0-318-00173-X). LBJ Sch Pub Aff.

--The Potential for Appropriate Water Resource Technology in Guinea, West Africa. (Working Paper Ser.: No. 19). 52p. 1981. pap. 3.00 (ISBN 0-318-00171-3). LBJ Sch Pub Aff.

--Shale Oil Technology: Status of the Industry. (Working Papers Ser.: No. 7). 39p. 1977. pap. 2.50 (ISBN 0-318-00185-3). LBJ Sch Pub Aff.

Eaton, David & Rohlich, Gerard. The Past & Future of Safe Drinking Water Standards. (Working Paper Ser.: No. 20). 1981. pap. 3.00 (ISBN 0-318-00170-5). LBJ Sch Pub Aff.

Eaton, Evelyn. I Send a Voice. LC 78-7273. (Illus., Orig.). 1978. 10.95 (ISBN 0-8356-0513-2, Quest); pap. 5.50 (ISBN 0-8356-0511-6, Quest). Theos Pub Hse.

--Love Is Recognition. limited ed. LC 78-183569. (Living Poets' Library Ser). pap. 2.50 (ISBN 0-686-01282-8). Dragons Teeth.

--The Shaman & the Medicine Wheel. LC 81-84490. (Illus.). 206p. (Orig.). 1982. 13.95 (ISBN 0-8356-0566-3, Quest); pap. 7.50 (ISBN 0-8356-0561-2, Quest). Theos Pub Hse.

--Snowy Earth Comes Gliding. 1974. pap. 5.50 (ISBN 0-943404-02-9). Bear Tribe.

Eaton, Frank. Pistol Pete - Veteran of the Old West. LC 79-109054. (Illus.). 1979. Repr. of 1952 ed. text ed. 14.95 (ISBN 0-934188-01-7). Evans Pubns.

Eaton, George. Authors' Gold. 1977. Repr. of 1947 ed. 15.00 (ISBN 0-89984-180-5). Century Bookbindery.

Eaton, George T. Photographic Chemistry. rev. ed. 124p. 1984. pap. 7.95 (2067). Morgan.

Eaton, Gerald. Under the Gun. 48p. (Orig.). Date not set. pap. 6.95 (ISBN 0-934553-01-7). Wainwright PA.

Eaton, Gordon, ed. The Role of Heat in the Development of Energy & Mineral Resources in the Northern Basin & Range Province, No. 13. (Special Report Ser.: No.13). 500p. 1983. pap. 30.00 (ISBN 0-934412-13-8). Geothermal.

Eaton, Gordon P., jt. ed. see Smith, Robert B.

Eaton, Horace A. Thomas De Quincey. LC 74-159182. 1971. Repr. of 1936 ed. lib. bdg. 40.00x (ISBN 0-374-92459-7). Octagon.

Eaton, Horance A. Thomas De Quincey: A Biography. 542p. 1983. Repr. of 1936 ed. lib. bdg. 50.00 (ISBN 0-89987-221-2). Darby Bks.

Eaton, Hugh Van see Van Eaton, Hugh.

Eaton, J. & Smithers, j. This Is It: A Manager's Guide to Information Technology. 345p. 1982. text ed. 38.50x (ISBN 0-86003-514-X, Pub. by Philip Allan England); pap. text ed. 19.50x (ISBN 0-86003-614-6). Humanities.

Eaton, J. Robert & Cohen, Edwin. Electric Power Transmission Systems. 2nd ed. (Illus.). 432p. 1983. 29.95 (ISBN 0-13-247304-6). P-H.

Eaton, J. W. The German Influence on Danish Literature. 1973. Repr. of 1929 ed. 30.00 (ISBN 0-8274-1388-2). R West.

Eaton, James D. Real Estate Valuation in Litigation. 489p. 1982. 30.00 (ISBN 0-911780-65-3). Am Inst Real Estate Appraisers.

Eaton, Jan & Mundie, Liz. Cross Stitch & Sampler Book. (Illus.). 176p. 19.95 (ISBN 0-8069-5542-2). Sterling.

Eaton, Jeanette. Leader by Destiny: George Washington, Man & Patriot. (Illus.). 402p. 1984. Repr. of 1938 ed. lib. bdg. 45.00 (ISBN 0-8482-3751-X). Norwood Edns.

--Lone Journey: The Life of Roger Williams. LC 44-8239. (Illus.). 1966. pap. 0.75 (ISBN 0-15-652985-8, VoyB). HarBraceJ.

Eaton, Jeffrey C. The Logic of Theism: An Analysis of the Thought of Austin Farrer. LC 80-67260. 288p. 1980. lib. bdg. 23.25 (ISBN 0-8191-1337-9); pap. text ed. 12.50 (ISBN 0-8191-1338-7). U Pr of Amer.

Eaton, Jeffrey C., ed. For God & Clarity: New Essays in Honor of Austin Farrer. Loades, Ann. (Pittsburgh Theological Monographs New Series: No. 4). 206p. 1983. pap. 15.00 (ISBN 0-915138-52-2). Pickwick.

Eaton, John. Political Economy: A Marxist Textbook. rev. ed. 253p. 1966. pap. 4.25 (ISBN 0-7178-0157-8). Intl Pubs Co.

Eaton, John, jt. auth. see Reid, John.

Eaton, John H. Kingship & the Psalms. LC 76-7105. (Studies in Biblical Theology, Second Ser.: No. 32). 1976. pap. text ed. 14.00x (ISBN 0-8401-3082-1). A R Allenson.

--Life of Andrew Jackson, Major-General in the Service of the United States. LC 77-146393. (First American Frontier Ser). 1971. Repr. of 1824 ed. 26.00 (ISBN 0-405-02846-6). Ayer Co Pubs.

Eaton, John W. & Brewer, George J. Malaria & the Red Cell. LC 84-5747. (Progress in Clinical & Biological Research Ser.: Vol. 155). 186p. 1984. 36.00 (ISBN 0-8451-5005-7). A R Liss.

Eaton, Jonathan. Four Essays in the Theory of Uncertainty & Portfolio Choice. LC 78-75071. (Outstanding Dissertations in Economics Ser.). 1980. lib. bdg. 29.00 (ISBN 0-8240-4145-3). Garland Pub.

Eaton, Jonathan & Gersovitz, Mark. Poor-Country Borrowing in Private Financial Markets & the Repudiation Issue. LC 81-2925. (Princeton Studies in International Finance Ser.: No. 47). 1981. pap. text ed. 4.50x (ISBN 0-88165-218-0). Princeton U Int Finan Econ.

Eaton, Joseph W. Card-Carrying Americans: Privacy, Security & the National I. D. Card Debate. 220p. 1985. 28.50x (ISBN 0-8476-7424-X). Rowman.

Eaton, K. J. & Eaton, K. J., eds. Proceedings of International Conference on Wind Effects on Buildings & Structures: Heathrow Nineteen Seventy-Five. LC 75-2730. 650p. 1976. 125.00 (ISBN 0-521-20801-7). Cambridge U Pr.

Eaton, Katherine. The Theatre of Meyerhold & Brecht. LC 85-9910. (Contributions in Drama & Theatre Studies: No. 19). (Illus.). 160p. 1985. lib. bdg. 27.95 (ISBN 0-313-24590-8, EMB/). Greenwood.

Eaton, Keith, et al. Allergy Therapeutics. (Illus.). 112p. 1982. pap. 13.50 (ISBN 0-7216-0860-4, Pub. by Bailliere-Tindall). Saunders.

Eaton, Laura. The Rushing Tide. (Second Chance at Love Ser.: No. 181). 192p. 1984. pap. 1.95 (ISBN 0-515-07596-5). Jove Pubns.

Eaton, Leonard A. Stirling City. LC 79-165942. (Illus.). 215p. 1971. 13.50x (ISBN 0-85564-051-0, Pub. by U of W Austral Pr). Intl Spec Bk.

Eaton, Manford L. Bio Music. LC 73-87673. (Illus.). 1973. pap. 4.50 (ISBN 0-87110-124-6). Ultramarine Pub.

Eaton, Marcia. Art & Nonart: Reflections on an Orange Crate & a Moose Call. LC 81-65462. (Illus.). 176p. 1983. 35.00 (ISBN 0-8386-3084-7). Fairleigh Dickinson.

Eaton, Margaret E; see Levy, Harold L.

Eaton, Margaret H. & Amey, Vera E. Diary of a Sea Captain's Wife: Tales of Santa Cruz Island. Timbrook, Janice, ed. (Illus.). 272p. 1980. 16.50 (ISBN 0-87461-032-X); pap. 9.50 (ISBN 0-87461-033-8). McNally.

Eaton, Margaret O. The Autobiography of Peggy Eaton. Baxter, Annette K., ed. LC 79-8789. (Signal Lives Ser.). 1980. Repr. of 1932 ed. lib. bdg. 23.00x (ISBN 0-405-12837-1). Ayer Co Pubs.

Eaton, Merrill T., jt. auth. see Kentsmith, David K.

Eaton, Merrill T., et al. Psychiatry. 4th ed. (Medical Outline Ser). 1981. 20.00 (ISBN 0-87488-621-X). Med Exam.

Eaton, Merrill T., Jr., et al. Textbook of Psychiatry. 5th ed. 1985. pap. text ed. write for info. (ISBN 0-87488-838-7). Med Exam.

Eaton, Michael A. Ecclesiastes. Wiseman, D. J., ed. (Tyndale Old Testament Commentary Ser.). 1983. 10.95 (ISBN 0-87784-963-3); pap. 6.95 (ISBN 0-87784-267-1). Inter-Varsity.

Eaton, Morris L. Multivariate Statistics: A Vector Space Approach. LC 83-1215. (Probability & Math Statistics: Applied Probability & Statistic Section Ser.). 512p. 1983. 37.50x (ISBN 0-471-02776-6, 1-345, Pub. by Wiley-Interscience). Wiley.

Eaton, Nancy L., jt. auth. see Boyer, Calvin J.

Eaton, P., ed. see Sorrows, Gene.

Eaton, Peter & Warnick, Marilyn, eds. Marie Stopes: A Preliminary Checklist of Her Writings Together with Some Biographical Notes. 59p. 1977. 14.50x (ISBN 0-85664-397-1, Pub. by Croom Helm Ltd). Longwood Pub Group.

Eaton, Quaintance. The Abaris Companion to Opera. (Illus.). 1980. 35.00 (ISBN 0-913870-71-4). Abaris Bks.

--The Boston Opera Company. (Music Reprint Ser.). 1980. Repr. of 1965 ed. 29.50 (ISBN 0-306-79619-8). Da Capo.

--The Miracle of the Met. (Music Reprint Ser.). (Illus.). xii, 490p. 1982. Repr. of 1968 ed. lib. bdg. 49.50 (ISBN 0-306-76168-8). Da Capo.

--Opera. LC 80-68675. (Illus.). 1980. 35.00 (ISBN 0-913870-71-4). Abaris Bks.

--Opera Caravan. LC 78-9128. (Music Reprint 1978 Ser.). (Illus.). 1978. lib. bdg. 37.50 (ISBN 0-306-77596-4); pap. 6.95 (ISBN 0-306-80089-6). Da Capo.

--Opera Production One: A Handbook. LC 73-20232. (Music Ser.). 266p. 1974. Repr. of 1961 ed. lib. bdg. 29.50 (ISBN 0-306-70635-0). Da Capo.

--Opera Production Two: A Handbook. LC 61-16843. (Illus.). 328p. 1974. 18.95 (ISBN 0-8166-0689-7). U of Minn Pr.

Eaton, Rachel C. John Ross & the Cherokee Indians. LC 76-43694. Repr. of 1921 ed. 24.50 (ISBN 0-404-15526-X). AMS Pr.

Eaton, Randall L. The Cheetah: Nature's Fastest Racer. (Illus.). 144p. (gr. 6 up). 1981. PLB 9.95 (ISBN 0-396-07994-6). Dodd.

--The Cheetah: The Biology, Ecology, & Behavior of an Endangered Species. LC 81-18556. 192p. 1982. Repr. of 1974 ed. lib. bdg. 13.95 (ISBN 0-89874-451-2). Krieger.

Eaton, Richard M. Sufis of Bijapur, Thirteen Hundred to Seventeen Hundred Social Roles of Sufis in Medieaval India. LC 77-71978. (Illus.). 1978. 40.00x (ISBN 0-691-03110-X). Princeton U Pr.

Eaton, Robert C., ed. Neural Mechanisms of Startle Behavior. 398p. 1984. 49.50x (ISBN 0-306-41556-9, Plenum Pr). Plenum Pub.

Eaton, Roy. Trout & Salmon Fishing. LC 80-68897. (Illus.). 192p. 1981. 22.50 (ISBN 0-7153-8117-2). David & Charles.

Eaton, S. Boyd, Jr. & Ferrucci, Joseph T. Radiology of the Pancreas & Duodenum. LC 72-97909. (Monographs in Clinical Radiology: No. 3). (Illus.). 385p. 1973. text ed. 30.00 (ISBN 0-7216-3310-2). Saunders.

Eaton, Samuel D. The Forces of Freedom in Spain 1974-1979. LC 80-8383. (Illus.). 192p. 1981. pap. 11.95 (ISBN 0-8179-7452-0, P-245). Hoover Inst Pr.

Eaton, Seymour. The Roosevelt Bears Go to Washington. (Illus.). 192p. (gr. 6 up). 1981. pap. 4.50 (ISBN 0-486-24163-7). Dover.

--The Roosevelt Bears: Their Travels & Adventures. (Illus.). 192p. 1979. pap. 3.95 (ISBN 0-486-23819-9). Dover.

Eaton, Su, jt. auth. see Bridle, Martin.

Eaton, Theodore H. A Pennsylvanian Dissorophid Amphibian from Kansas. (Occasional Papers: No. 14). 8p. 1973. 1.25 (ISBN 0-317-04787-6). U of KS Mus Nat Hist.

--Study of Organization & Method of the Course of Study in Agriculture in Secondary Schools. LC 78-176740. (Columbia University. Teachers College. Contributions to Education: No. 86). Repr. of 1917 ed. 12.50 (ISBN 0-404-55086-X). AMS Pr.

Eaton, Theodore H., Jr. Teeth of Edestid Sharks. (Museum Ser.: Vol. 12, No. 8). 16p. 1962. 1.25 (ISBN 0-317-04785-X). U of KS Mus Nat Hist.

Eaton, Theodore H., Jr. & Stewart, Peggy Lou. A New Order of Fishlike Amphibia from the Pennsylvanian of Kansas. (Museum Ser.: Vol. 12, No. 4). 24p. 1960. pap. 1.50 (ISBN 0-686-79814-7). U of KS Mus Nat Hist.

Eaton, Thomas R. Shakespeare & the Bible. LC 77-144601. Repr. of 1860 ed. 19.00 (ISBN 0-404-02237-5). AMS Pr.

Eaton, Timothy, ed. see Lattin, Gerald.

Eaton, Tom. Monster Mazes. (Pretzel Ser.). (Illus.). 64p. (Orig.). (gr. 4-6). 1981. pap. 1.25 (ISBN 0-590-32117-X). Scholastic Inc.

--Super Valentines to Cut, Color, & Send. (Illus.). 32p. (Orig.). (gr. 4-6). 1985. pap. 1.95 (ISBN 0-590-31269-3). Scholastic Inc.

Eaton, Trevor. Semantics of Literature. (De Proprietatibus Litterarum Ser. Minor: No. 1). (Orig.). 1966. pap. text ed. 9.50 (ISBN 90-2790-084-1). Mouton.

--Theoretical Semics. (De Proprietatibus Litterarum Ser. Minor: No. 11). 1972. pap. text ed. 13.20x (ISBN 90-2792-116-4). Mouton.

Eaton, Trevor, ed. Essays in Literary Semantics. 120p. (Orig.). 1978. pap. 15.00x (ISBN 3-87276-198-6, Pub. by J Groos W Germany). Benjamins North Am.

Eaton, W. A., jt. ed. see Ho, C.

Eaton, Walter P. The Actor's Heritage. 294p. 1981. Repr. of 1924 ed. lib. bdg. 50.00 (ISBN 0-8495-1358-8). Arden Lib.

--Actor's Heritage. facs. ed. LC 78-128237. (Essay Index Reprint Ser.). 1924. 21.00 (ISBN 0-8369-1827-4). Ayer Co Pubs.

--Bird House Man. LC 72-6078. (Short Story Index Reprint Ser.). Repr. of 1916 ed. 20.50 (ISBN 0-8369-4215-9). Ayer Co Pubs.

--Penguin Persons & Peppermints. LC 72-93335. (Essay Index Reprint Ser). 1922. 19.00 (ISBN 0-8369-1288-8). Ayer Co Pubs.

--Theatre Guild, the First Ten Years. 1971. Repr. of 1929 ed. 25.00x (ISBN 0-403-00922-7). Scholarly.

--Theatre Guild, the First Ten Years, with Articles by the Directors. LC 75-107799. (Select Bibliographies Reprint Ser). 1929. 26.50 (ISBN 0-8369-5180-8). Ayer Co Pubs.

Eaton, Walter R. The Drama in English. 1975. Repr. of 1930 ed. 35.00 (ISBN 0-8274-4117-7). R West.

Eaton, William. The Sociology of Mental Disorders. LC 79-21334. 250p. 1980. 27.50 (ISBN 0-03-046466-8). Praeger.

Eaton, William E. The American Federation of Teachers, 1916-1961: A History of the Movement. LC 75-14248. 253p. 1975. 10.00x (ISBN 0-8093-0708-1). S Ill U Pr.

--The Sociology of Mental Disorders. 2nd ed. 250p. 1985. 31.95t (ISBN 0-03-071024-3); pap. 13.95 (ISBN 0-03-071023-5). Praeger.

Eaton, William E., jt. ed. see Dennis, Lawrence J.

Eaton, William W. & Kessler, Larry G., eds. Epidemiologic Field Methods in Psychiatry: The Nimh Epidemiologic Catchment Area Program. Edited Treatise ed. 1985. 45.00 (ISBN 0-12-228250-7). Acad Pr.

Eaton, Winifred K. Contrasts in the Representation of Death by Sophocles, Webster, & Strindberg. (Salzburg Studies in English Literature, Jacobean Drama Ser.: No. 17). 1975. pap. text ed. 25.50x (ISBN 0-391-01369-6). Humanities.

Eaton-Krauss, M. & Graefe, E. The Small Golden Shrine: Object No. 108 from the Tomb of Tutankhamer. (Illus.). 84p. 1984. text ed. 39.00x (ISBN 0-900416-43-2, Pub. by Aris & Phillip England). Humanities.

Eatwell, David. Steam Locomotives. (Illus.). 64p. 1983. pap. 5.50 (ISBN 0-7134-1835-4, Pub. by Batsford England). David & Charles.

Eatwell, David & Cooper-Smith, John H. Live Steam: Locomotives & Lines Today. (Illus.). 120p. 1980. 19.95 (ISBN 0-7134-2079-0, Pub. by Batsford England). David & Charles.

--Return to Steam: Steam Tours on British Rail from Nineteen Sixty-Nine. 1978. 17.95 (ISBN 0-7134-0864-2, Pub. by Batsford England). David & Charles.

Eatwell, John. Whatever Happened to Britain? 168p. 1982. 39.00x (ISBN 0-563-16545-6, Pub. by BBC Pubns). State Mutual Bk.

--Whatever Happened to Britain? The Economics of Decline. (Illus.). 1984. pap. 7.95 (ISBN 0-19-520443-3, GB 761, GB). Oxford U Pr.

Eatwell, John & Milgate, Murray, eds. Keynes's Economics & the Theory of Value & Distribution. (Illus.). 1983. pap. 9.95x (ISBN 0-19-520442-5). Oxford U Pr.

Eauclaire, Sally. New Color-New Work Eighteen Photographic Essays. LC 84-11131. (Illus.). 276p. 1984. 39.95 (ISBN 0-89659-459-9); pap. 24.95 (ISBN 0-89659-460-2). Abbeville Pr.

--The New Color Photography. LC 80-70940. (Illus.). 1981. 45.00 (ISBN 0-89659-190-5); pap. 24.95 (ISBN 0-89659-196-4). Abbeville Pr.

Eavaldi, Thomas L., jt. auth. see Stern, Louis W.

Eaves & Gallegos. Auditing the Computer Information System. 1986. text ed. price not set (ISBN 0-538-10940-8, J94). SW Pub.

Eaves, B. C. A Course in Triangulations for Solving Equations with Deformations. (Lecture Notes in Economics & Mathematical Systems Ser.: Vol. 234). 302p. 1984. pap. 19.50 (ISBN 0-387-13876-5). Springer-Verlag.

Eaves, B. C., jt. ed. see Dantzig, G. B.

Eaves, B. Curtis, et al, eds. Homotopy Methods & Global Convergence. LC 82-16547. (NATO Conference Series II, Systems Science: Vol. 13). 330p. 1983. 49.50x (ISBN 0-306-41127-X, Plenum Press). Plenum Pub.

Eaves, Derek, jt. auth. see Swinson, R. P.

Eaves, Edgar D. & Carruth, J. H. Introductory Mathematical Analysis. 5th ed. 1978. text ed. 40.03 (ISBN 0-205-05991-0, 5659914); 40.01 (ISBN 0-205-08259-9, 568259); student study guide avail. (ISBN 0-205-05993-7). Allyn.

Eaves, James F. Church Growth Evangelism. LC 82-73614. Date not set. 11.95 (ISBN 0-8054-6240-6). Broadman.

Eaves, L. J., jt. auth. see Eysenck, A J.

Eaves, L. J., jt. auth. see Eysenck, H. J.

Eaves, Lucile. A History of California Labor Legislation. 1910. pap. 40.00 (ISBN 0-384-13760-1). Johnson Repr.

Eaves, Mary L. The Truth Will Make You Free. LC 83-90380. 59p. 1985. 7.95 (ISBN 0-533-05883-X). Vantage.

Eaves, Morris. William Blake's Theory of Art. LC 81-47914. (Illus.). 216p. 1982. cloth 22.00x (ISBN 0-691-03990-9); pap. 10.95x (ISBN 0-691-00340-8). Princeton U Pr.

Eaves, Ronald W. & Medley, Don B. Programming Principles with COBOL II. 1985. text ed. 16.50 wkbk. (ISBN 0-538-10460-0, J46). SW Pub.

Eaves, Ronald W., jt. auth. see Medley, Don B.

Eaves, T. Duncan, ed. see Simms, William G.

Eaves, Thomas F., jt. auth. see Johnson, Paul R.

Eavey, C. B. Chapel Talks. (Pocket Pulpit Library). 120p. 1981. pap. 2.95 (ISBN 0-8010-3365-9). Baker Bk.

--Ninety-Five Brief Talks for Various Occasions. (Pocket Pulpit Library). 104p. 1980. pap. 2.95 (ISBN 0-8010-3255-5). Baker Bk.

Eayrs, James. In Defence of Canada, Vol. II: Appeasement & Rearmament. LC 66-3834. (Studies in the Structure of Power). 1965. 17.50x (ISBN 0-8020-1485-2); pap. 10.00 (ISBN 0-8020-6076-5). U of Toronto Pr.

--In Defence of Canada, Vol. III: Peacemaking & Deterrence. LC 68-3834. (Studies in the Structure of Power). 1977. pap. 10.95 (ISBN 0-8020-6328-4). U of Toronto Pr.

--In Defence of Canada, Vol. IV: Growing up Allied. LC 72-7513. (Studies in the Structure of Power). 1985. 17.50x (ISBN 0-8020-6608-9). U of Toronto Pr.

--In Defence of Canada, Vol. 5: Indochina - Roots of Complicity. (Studies in the Structure of Power Ser.). 432p. 1983. o. p. 45.00x (ISBN 0-8020-2460-2); pap. 17.50 (ISBN 0-8020-6473-6). U of Toronto Pr.

Eban, Abba. Heritage: Civilization & the Jews. (Illus.). 352p. 1984. 32.95 (ISBN 0-671-44103-5). Summit Bks.

--My People. LC 68-27328. (Illus.). 560p. 1984. pap. 14.95 (ISBN 0-394-72759-2). Random.

--My People: The Story of the Jews. LC 68-27328. (Illus.). 1968. 25.00 (ISBN 0-87441-294-3). Behrman.

--The New Diplomacy: International Affairs in the Modern Age. LC 80-6035. 384p. 1983. 19.95 (ISBN 0-394-50283-3). Random.

Ebanoidze, A. Dos Mese en la Aldea o Matrimonio al Estilo de Imeretia. 279p. 1982. 6.95 (ISBN 0-8285-2503-X, Pub. by Raduga Pubs USSR). Imported Pubns.

Ebasco Services Inc. Full Scale Stray Current Test HVDC Power Transmission: The Dallas-Los Angeles. 227p. 1970. pap. 10.00 (ISBN 0-318-12619-2, L19722). Am Gas Assn.

--Preliminary Stray-Current Tests HVDC Power Transmission: The Dallas-Los Angeles. 500p. 1969. 10.00 (ISBN 0-318-12671-0, L19720). Am Gas Assn.

Ebashi, S., ed. Cellular Regulation & Malignant Growth. (Illus.). 540p. 1985. 59.50 (ISBN 0-387-15585-6). Springer Verlag.

Ebashi, S. & Ozawa, E., eds. Muscular Dystrophy: Biomedical Aspects. (Illus.). 302p. 1983. 36.00 (ISBN 0-387-12342-3). Springer-Verlag.

Ebashi, S., et al, eds. Muscle Contraction: Its Regulatory Mechanism. 549p. 1980. 69.50 (ISBN 0-387-10411-9). Springer-Verlag.

Ebashi, Setsuro, ed. Muscular Dystrophy. 518p. 1983. 64.50x (ISBN 0-86008-321-7, Pub. by U of Tokyo Japan). Columbia U Pr.

Ebashi, Setsuro, et al, eds. Calcium Regulation in Biological Systems. 1985. 29.50 (ISBN 0-12-228650-2). Acad Pr.

Ebaugh, Helen R. Out of the Cloister: A Study of Organizational Dilemmas. 177p. 1977. text ed. 12.50x (ISBN 0-292-76007-8). U of Tex Pr.

Ebbatson, Roger. The Evolutionary Self: Hardy, Forster, Lawrence. LC 82-8769. 142p. 1983. text ed. 28.50x (ISBN 0-389-20297-5, 07132). B&N Imports.

--Lawrence & the Nature Tradition: A Theme in English Fiction, 1859-1914. 1980. text ed. 40.50x (ISBN 0-391-01884-1). Humanities.

Ebbe, Shirley, jt. ed. see Baldini, Mario.

Ebbels, D. L. & King, J. E., eds. Plant Health: The Scientific Basis for Administrative Control of Plant Diseases & Pests, Vol. 2. (Organized by the Federation of British Plant Pathologists). 322p. 1979. 69.95x (ISBN 0-470-26954-5). Halsted Pr.

Ebbels, R. N. The Australian Labor Movement: Eighteen Fifty to Nineteen Seven. 19.50x (ISBN 0-392-07633-0, SpS). Sportshelf.

Ebbens, Joan, jt. auth. see Thompson, Linda.

Ebbert, Mary K. By the Way. (Contemporary Poets of Dorrance Ser.). 36p. 1983. 4.95 (ISBN 0-8059-2843-X). Dorrance.

Ebbesen, Ebbe B., jt. ed. see Konecni, Vladimir J.

Ebbeson, Eric, jt. ed. see Crean, David.

Ebbesson, S. O., jt. auth. see Scheich, H.

Ebbesson, Sven, ed. Comparative Neurology of the Telencephalon. LC 79-12145. (Illus.). 528p. 1980. 65.00x (ISBN 0-306-40237-8, Plenum Pr). Plenum Pub.

Ebbighausen, E. B. Astronomy. 5th, rev. ed. 184p. 1985. pap. text ed. 9.95 (ISBN 0-675-20413-5). Merrill.

Ebbin, Steven & Kasper, Raphael. Citizen Groups & the Nuclear Power Controversy: Uses of Scientific & Technological Information. (Environmental Studies). 318p. 1974. pap. 13.50x (ISBN 0-262-55003-2). MIT Pr.

Ebbing, Darell D., jt. auth. see Schenk, George H.

Ebbing, Darrell. General Chemistry. 928p. 1983. text ed. 34.95 (ISBN 0-395-31489-5); instr's. manual 2.00 (ISBN 0-395-31490-9); solns. manual 9.95 (ISBN 0-395-31491-7); study guide 13.95 (ISBN 0-395-31493-3); lab manual 19.95 (ISBN 0-395-31492-5); transparencies 125.00 (ISBN 0-395-34457-3). HM.

Ebbinghaus, H. D., et al. Mathematical Logic. Ferebee, A. S., tr. from Ger. (Undergraduate Texts in Mathematics). (Illus.). 280p. 1984. 28.00 (ISBN 0-387-90895-1). Springer-Verlag.

Ebbinghaus, Hermann. Psychology: An Elementary Text-Book. Meyer, Max, ed. & tr. LC 73-2965. (Classics in Psychology Ser.). Repr. of 1908 ed. 17.00 (ISBN 0-405-05138-7). Ayer Co Pubs.

Ebbitt, David R., jt. auth. see Ebbitt, Wilma R.

Ebbitt, Wilma R. & Ebbitt, David R. Index to English. 7th ed. 1982. pap. 9.75x (ISBN 0-673-15541-2). Scott F.

--Writer's Guide. 7th ed. 1982. pap. 15.15x (ISBN 0-673-15540-4). Scott F.

--Writer's Guide & Index to English. 7th ed. 1982. text ed. 19.50x (ISBN 0-673-15542-0). Scott F.

Ebbot, Elizabeth. Indians in Minnesota. Rosenblatt, Judith, ed. 1985. 25.00 (ISBN 0-8166-1354-0); pap. 12.95 (ISBN 0-8166-1357-5). U of Minn Pr.

Ebbs, John D. The Principle of Poetic Justice Illustrated in Restoration Tragedy. (Salzburg Studies in English Literature, Poetic Drama & Poetic Theory Ser.: No. 4). 211p. 1973. pap. text ed. 25.50x (ISBN 0-391-01370-X). Humanities.

Ebbs, Stephen, jt. auth. see Keogh, Bruce.

Ebbutt, Percy G. Emigrant Life in Kansas. facsimile ed. LC 75-96. (Mid-American Frontier Ser.). (Illus.). 1975. Repr. of 1886 ed. 20.00x (ISBN 0-405-06862-X). Ayer Co Pubs.

EBC, ed. European Brewery Convention: Thesaurus, 2 vols. 2nd ed. 945p. 1983. Set. pap. 120.00 (ISBN 0-904147-39-8). IRL Pr.

Ebdon, David. Statistics in Geography: A Practical Approach. 224p. 1977. 29.95x (ISBN 0-631-16880-X); pap. 12.95x (ISBN 0-631-10131-4). Basil Blackwell.

Ebdon, John. Ebdon's England. (Illus.). 192p. 1985. 14.95 (ISBN 0-7153-8595-X). David & Charles.

--Ebdon's Iliad. (Illus.). 192p. 1983. 17.50 (ISBN 0-434-22196-1, Pub. by W Heinemann Ltd). David & Charles.

--Ebdon's Odyssey. 1979. 14.95 (ISBN 0-432-04020-X, Pub. by W Heinemann Ltd). David & Charles.

Ebdon, L. An Introduction to Atomic Absorption Spectroscopy: A Self Teaching Approach. 1981. pap. text ed. 24.95x (ISBN 0-471-26194-7). Wiley.

Ebdon, L. & Jackson, K. W., eds. Annual Reports on Analytical Atomic Spectroscopy, Vol. 13. 427p. 1985. 99.00 (ISBN 0-85186-687-5, 99610478X, Pub. by Royal Soc Chem UK). Heyden.

Ebe, John A. Point: Instant of Time. (Fundamentals of Mechanics Ser.: Vol. 1). 60p. lib. bdg. write for info. Ebe.

Ebejar, Francis. Leap of Malta Dolphins. (Illus.). 1982. 9.50 (ISBN 0-533-05053-7). Vantage.

Ebel, A. & Simon, P. C., eds. Middle Atmosphere Sciences: A Selection of Papers from the Symposium Organised by the IAMAP & IAGA on the Occasion of the XVIII General Assembly of the IUGG, Hamburg, Federal Republic of Germany, August 1983. 120p. 1985. pap. 33.00 (ISBN 0-08-032592-0). Pergamon.

Ebel, H., et al, eds. Presidential Sports Award Fitness Manual. 2nd ed. DNB Design, tr. (Orig.). 1983. pap. 9.95 (ISBN 0-930447-00-5). FitCom Corp.

Ebel, Hans F., ed. see Dehmlow, Eckehard & Dehmlow, Sigrid.

Ebel, Hans F., ed. see Schmid, Roland & Sapunov, Valentin N.

Ebel, Henry. After Dionysus: An Essay on Where We Are Now. LC 70-156321. 136p. 1972. 15.00 (ISBN 0-8386-7958-7). Fairleigh Dickinson.

Ebel, Holly. Christmas in the Air: A New Fashioned Book for An Old Fashioned Christmas. (Illus.). 96p. (Orig.). 1982. pap. 6.95 (ISBN 0-943786-00-2). HollyDay.

Ebel, Jurgen. Banking in Canada. Blythe, L. N., ed. 80p. (Orig.). 1978. pap. text ed. 19.95x (ISBN 0-7121-0259-0, Pub. by Macdonald & Evans England). Trans-Atlantic.

Ebel, Robert. The Uses of Standardized Testing. LC 77-72595. (Fastback Ser.: No. 93). 49p. 1977. pap. 0.75 (ISBN 0-87367-093-0). Phi Delta Kappa.

Ebel, Robert D. The Michigan Business Activities Tax. LC 71-189476. 1972. 7.00 (ISBN 0-87744-110-3); pap. 3.75 (ISBN 0-87744-142-1). Mich St U Pr.

Ebel, Robert D. & Kamins, Robert M. Who Pays Hawaii's Taxes? A Study of the Incidence of State & Local Taxes in Hawaii for 1970. 135p. 1975. pap. 5.00x (ISBN 0-8248-0403-1). UH Pr.

Ebel, Robert D., ed. Research in Urban Economics: Urban Development & Public Finance, Vol. 4. 1984. 49.50 (ISBN 0-89232-423-6). Jai Pr.

Ebel, Robert L. Essentials of Educational Measurement. 3rd ed. LC 78-13392. 1979. ref. ed. 28.95 (ISBN 0-13-286013-9). P-H.

--Practical Problems in Educational Measurement. (Orig.). 1980. pap. text ed. 11.95 (ISBN 0-669-03164-X). Heath.

Ebel, Robert L. & Frisbie, David A. Essentials of Educational Measurement. 4th ed. (Illus.). 496p. 1986. text ed. 28.95 (ISBN 0-13-286006-6). P-H.

Ebeling, A. & Schweitzer, G. Basic Air Conditioning, 2 Vols. (Illus.). 1971. pap. 8.25 ea.; Vol. 1. (ISBN 0-8104-0791-4); Vol. 2. (ISBN 0-8104-0792-2); transparencies 239.00 (ISBN 0-685-03714-2, A001). Hayden.

Ebeling, Doug. Industrial Innovation in Australia. 45p. (Orig.). 1981. pap. text ed. 18.75x (ISBN 0-85825-161-2, Pub. by Inst Engineering Australia). Brookfield Pub Co.

Ebeling, Erich. Tod und Leben nach den Vorstellungen der Babylonier. LC 78-72732. (Ancient Mesopotamian Texts & Studies). Repr. of 1931 ed. 32.50 (ISBN 0-404-18169-4). AMS Pr.

Ebeling, Gerhard. Luther: An Introduction to His Thought. Wilson, R. A., tr. from Ger. LC 77-99612. 288p. 1970. pap. 6.95 (ISBN 0-8006-1162-4, 1-1162). Fortress.

--The Nature of Faith. Smith, Ronald G., tr. from Ger. LC 62-7194. 192p. 1967. pap. 6.95 (ISBN 0-8006-1914-5, 1-1914). Fortress.

--Truth of the Gospel: An Exposition of Galatians. LC 84-47918. 288p. 1985. 19.95 (ISBN 0-8006-0728-7, 1-728). Fortress.

Ebeling, Gerhard, ed. see Braun, Herbert, et al.

Ebeling, Gerhard, ed. see Kasemann, Ernst, et al.

Ebeling, Gerhard, ed. see Robinson, James M., et al.

Ebeling, Gerhard, et al. The Bible As a Document of the University. Betz, H. D., ed. 1981. pap. 10.00 (ISBN 0-89130-422-3, 00-03-03). Scholars Pr GA.

Ebeling, Nancy B. & Hill, Deborah A., eds. Child Abuse & Neglect: A Guide for Treating the Child & Family. 394p. 1983. text ed. 29.00 (ISBN 0-7236-7040-4). PSG Pub Co.

Ebeling, W., et al, eds. Transport Properties of Dense Plasmas, Vol. 47. (Experientia Supplementa Ser.). 184p. 1984. 29.95 (ISBN 3-7643-1554-7). Birkhauser.

Ebeling, Walter. The Fruited Plain: The Story of American Agriculture. LC 78-62837. 1980. 35.00x (ISBN 0-520-03751-0). U of Cal Pr.

--Urban Entomology. LC 78-72961. 1975. 27.50x (ISBN 0-931876-19-2, 4057). Ag & Nat Res.

Ebelke, John F., jt. auth. see Homberger, Conrad P.

Ebelshauser, Gustav. The Passage: A Tragedy of the First World War. Baumgartner, Richard, ed. (Illus.). 192p. 1984. pap. 10.95 (ISBN 0-9604770-2-0). Griffin Bks.

Eben, Lois E. Getting Kids Started in Arts & Crafts. LC 81-14213. 239p. 1982. 16.95x (ISBN 0-13-354696-9, Parker). P-H.

Ebendorf, Robert, et al. Cutting Edge. Sperath, Albert F., ed. LC 81-620014. (Illus.). 66p. (Orig.). 1981. pap. 5.00 (ISBN 0-939058-01-4). Kentucky Arts.

Ebener, Patricia A., ed. see National Institute of Justice & United States Dept. of Justice.

Ebenfield, jt. auth. see Jussawala.

Ebenstein, Joyce. The Choice. 173p. Date not set. 13.95 (ISBN 0-942070-00-3); pap. 7.95 (ISBN 0-942070-01-1). Bookman Pub.

Ebenstein, Ronnie S., jt. auth. see Arpel, Adrien.

Ebenstein, W. & Fogelman, E. Today's Isms. 8th ed. 1980. 20.95 (ISBN 0-13-924399-2); pap. 16.95 (ISBN 0-13-924381-X). P-H.

Ebenstein, William. Fascism at Work. LC 75-180384. (Studies in Fascism, Ideology & Practice). Repr. of 1934 ed. 29.50 (ISBN 0-404-56120-9). AMS Pr.

--Great Political Thinkers. 4th ed. 1969. text ed. 32.95 (ISBN 0-03-077325-3, HoltC). HR&W.

--The Nazi State. 1973. lib. bdg. 26.00x (ISBN 0-374-92463-5). Octagon.

--Pure Theory of Law. xii, 211p. 1970. Repr. of 1945 ed. text ed. 17.50x (ISBN 0-8377-2100-8). Rothman.

Ebenstein, William & Fogelman, Edwin. Today's Isms: Communism, Facism, Capitalism, Socialism. 9th ed. (Illus.). 272p. 1985. text ed. 22.95 (ISBN 0-13-924481-6); pap. text ed. 17.95 (ISBN 0-13-924473-5). P-H.

Eber, Christine E. Just Momma & Me. LC 75-30308. (Illus.). 39p. (Orig.). (ps-3). 1975. pap. 3.50 (ISBN 0-914996-09-6). Lollipop Power.

Eber, Dorothy, ed. see Pitseolak.

Eber, Dorothy H. Genius at Work: Images of Alexander Graham Bell. (Illus.). 192p. 1982. 16.95 (ISBN 0-670-27389-9, Studio). Viking.

Eber, Irene. Voices from Afar: Modern Chinese Writers on Oppressed Peoples & Their Literature. LC 80-10411. (Michigan Monographs in Chinese Studies: No. 38). 196p. (Orig.). 1980. pap. 6.00 (ISBN 0-89264-038-3). U of Mich Ctr Chinese.

Eber, Irene, ed. see Wilhelm, Richard.

Eber, Jose. Shake Your Head, Darling. LC 82-50639. (Illus.). 208p. (Orig.). 1983. 17.50 (ISBN 0-446-51250-8); pap. 9.95 (ISBN 0-446-37364-8). Warner Bks.

Eber, Victor I. The Pros & Cons in Financial Management for Professionals. LC 71-166924. (Illus.). 12.95 (ISBN 0-686-20664-9). Financial Pr.

--Up Your Equity: Build up Your Personal Net Worth. LC 72-95079. (Illus.). 12.95 (ISBN 0-686-05084-3). Financial Pr.

Eberhard, Arnold. Gemeinsamesleben-Wozu? 44p. (Ger.). 1978. pap. 1.50 (ISBN 3-87630-406-7, Pub. by Prasenz-Verlag, West Germany). Plough.

Eberhard, Carolyn. Biology Laboratory. 328p. 1982. pap. text ed. 17.95x (ISBN 0-03-059963-6). SCP.

Eberhard, Eldon W. The Rumrunners. 1982. 8.50 (ISBN 0-682-49822-X). Exposition Pr FL.

Eberhard, Engelbert. Das Schicksal Als Poetische Idee Bei Homer. 1923. pap. 8.00 (ISBN 0-384-13785-7). Johnson Repr.

Eberhard, Ernest. The New Complete Bull Terrier. 2nd ed. LC 69-19207. (Complete Breed Book Ser.). (Illus.). 256p. 1985. 15.95 (ISBN 0-87605-071-2). Howell Bk.

Eberhard, Johann A. Allgemeine Theorie des Denkens und Empfindens. 1973. Repr. of 1776 ed. 34.00 (ISBN 0-384-13789-X). Johnson Repr.

Eberhard, John P. & Smeallie, Peter H. Guide to the Federal Government for Design & Building Professionals. 96p. 1978. pap. 5.00 (ISBN 0-89062-186-1). Pub Ctr Cult Res.

Eberhard, K. A. Resonances in Heavy Ion Reactions: Bad Honnef, West Germany, 1981 Proceedings. (Lecture Notes in Physics Ser.: Vol. 156). 448p. 1982. 30.00 (ISBN 0-387-11487-4). Springer-Verlag.

Eberhard, Mary J., jt. auth. see Evans, Howard E.

Eberhard, W. Conquerors & Rulers: Social Forces in Medieval China. 2nd rev. ed. 1970. 30.00 (ISBN 0-685-12002-3). Heinman.

Eberhard, William G. Sexual Selection & Animal Genitalia. (Illus.). 288p. 1985. text ed. 25.00x (ISBN 0-674-80283-7). Harvard U Pr.

Eberhard, Wolfram. Cantonese Ballads. (Asian Folklore & Social Life Monograph: No. 30). 1972. 14.00 (ISBN 0-89986-030-3). Oriental Bk Store.

--China's Minorities: Yesterday & Today. 192p. 1982. pap. text ed. write for info (ISBN 0-534-01080-6). Wadsworth Pub.

--Chinese Authors: Fairy Tales & Folk Tales. 1978. Repr. of 1937 ed. lib. bdg. 30.00 (ISBN 0-8492-0763-0). R West.

--Chinese Fables & Parables, No. 15. (Asian Folklore & Social Life Monograph: No. 15). 1972. 17.00 (ISBN 0-89986-018-4). Oriental Bk Store.

--Chinese Fairy Tales & Folk Tales. LC 74-9676. 1937. lib. bdg. 32.50 (ISBN 0-8414-3940-0). Folcroft.

--Chinese Festivals. (Asian Folklore & Social Life Monograph: No. 38). 1972. photocopy 25.00 (ISBN 0-89986-038-9). Oriental Bk Store.

--A History of China. rev., 4th ed. LC 76-7758. 1977. 38.50x (ISBN 0-520-03227-6); pap. 8.95x (ISBN 0-520-03268-3). U of Cal Pr.

--Life & Thought of Ordinary Chinese: Collected Essays. (East Asian Folklore & Social Life Monographs: Vol. 106). 230p. 1982. 22.00 (ISBN 0-89986-337-X). Oriental Bk Store.

--Minstrel Tales from Southeastern Turkey. Dorson, Richard M., ed. LC 80-793. (Folklore of the World Ser.). 1980. Repr. of 1955 ed. lib. bdg. 14.00x (ISBN 0-405-13332-4). Ayer Co Pubs.

--Predigten an Die Taiwanesan. (Asian Folklore & Social Life Monograph: No. 33). (Ger.). 1972. 17.00 (ISBN 0-89986-033-8). Oriental Bk Store.

--Settlement & Social Change in Asia, Vol. 1. pap. 134.00 (ISBN 0-317-11153-1, 2020775). Bks Demand UMI.

--Studies in Hakka Folktales, 2 vols. (Asian Folklore & Social Life Monograph: No. 61). 290p. 1974. photocopy 42.00 (ISBN 0-89986-056-7). Oriental Bk Store.

--Studies in Taiwanese Folktales. Lou Tsu-K'uang, ed. (Asian Folklore & Social Life Monograph: No. 1). 1970. 14.00 (ISBN 0-89986-004-4). Oriental Bk Store.

--Taiwanese Ballads: A Catalogue. (Asian Folklore & Social Life Monograph: No. 22). 1972. 14.00 (ISBN 0-89986-024-9). Oriental Bk Store.

Eberhard, Wolfram, jt. auth. see Boratav, Pertev N.

Eberhard, Wolfram, tr. Folktales of China. LC 65-25440. (Folktales of the World Ser). 1965. 14.00x (ISBN 0-226-18192-8); pap. 9.95x (ISBN 0-226-18193-6, FW2). U of Chicago Pr.

Eberhardt, Isabelle. The Oblivion Seekers & Other Writings. Bowles, Paul, tr. from Fr. LC 75-12962. (Illus.). 88p. (Orig.). 1975. pap. 3.50 (ISBN 0-87286-082-5). City Lights.

Eberhardt, Jo. Good Beginnings with Dairy Goats. 15.00 (ISBN 0-686-26687-0). Dairy Goat.

Eberhardt, Lorraine, jt. auth. see Sanborn, Laura.

Eberhardt, Louise. A Woman's Journey, Vol. I. 1976. pap. 7.00 (ISBN 0-934698-00-7). BDR Learn Prods.

--A Woman's Journey, Vol. II. 1978. pap. 7.00 (ISBN 0-934698-01-5). BDR Learn Prods.

Eberhart, David G. Upa Gurus. 10.00 (ISBN 0-89253-679-9). Ind-US Inc.

Eberhart, Dikkon. On the Verge. LC 79-9810. 224p. 1979. 9.95 (ISBN 0-916144-40-2). Stemmer Hse.

--Paradise. LC 83-4392. 256p. 1983. 14.50 (ISBN 0-916144-52-6). Stemmer Hse.

Eberhart, Elvin T. In the Presence of Humor: A Guide to the Humorous Life. LC 84-62035. 64p. (Orig.). 1985. pap. 9.95. Pilgrim Hse.

Eberhart, George M. Monsters: A Guide to Information on Unaccounted for Creatures, Including Bigfoot, Many Water Monsters, & Other Irregular Animals. LC 82-49029. (Supernatural Studies). 358p. 1983. lib. bdg. 28.00 (ISBN 0-8240-9213-9). Garland Pub.

Eberhart, George M. & Hynek, J. Allen. UFO's & the Extraterrestrial Contact Movement: A Bibliography. LC 84-48874. 600p. 1985. lib. bdg. 50.00 (ISBN 0-8240-8755-0). Garland Pub.

Eberhart, George M., compiled By. A Geo-Bibliography of Anomalies: Primary Access to Observations of UFOs, Ghosts, & Other Mysterious Phenomena. LC 79-6183. xl, 1114p. 1980. lib. bdg. 75.00 (ISBN 0-313-21337-2, EBA/). Greenwood.

Eberhart, John A., jt. auth. see Snook, Helen B.

Eberhart, M. G. Witness at Large. 1982. 15.00x (ISBN 0-7274-0289-7, Pub. by Severn Hse). State Mutual Bk.

Eberhart, Mignon. Another Man's Murder. 160p. 1983. pap. 2.50 (ISBN 0-446-31180-4). Warner Bks.

--The Bayou Road. 14.95 (ISBN 0-88411-297-7, Pub. by Aeonian Pr). Amereon Ltd.

--Family Affair. 240p. 1984. pap. 2.95 (ISBN 0-446-32529-5). Warner Bks.

--Hasty Wedding. (Orig.). 1985. pap. 2.95 (ISBN 0-446-32704-2). Warner Bks.

--Murder in Waiting. 192p. 1983. pap. 2.50 (ISBN 0-446-31242-8). Warner Bks.

--The Patient in Cabin C. 256p. 1985. pap. 2.95 (ISBN 0-446-32505-8). Warner Bks.

--Postmark Murder. 208p. 1983. pap. 2.50 (ISBN 0-446-31181-2). Warner Bks.

--The Promise of Murder. 14.95 (ISBN 0-89190-538-3, Pub. by Am Repr). Amereon Ltd.

--Run Scared. 176p. 1984. pap. 2.50 (ISBN 0-446-31246-0). Warner Bks.

--Speak No Evil. 13.95 (ISBN 0-89190-542-1, Pub. by Am Repr). Amereon Ltd.

--Unidentified Woman. 176p. 1983. pap. 2.50 (ISBN 0-446-31195-2). Warner Bks.

--The Unknown Quantity. 1985. pap. 2.95 (ISBN 0-446-32735-2). Warner Bks.

--Witness at Large. 1983. pap. 2.50 (ISBN 0-446-31205-3). Warner Bks.

--Wolf in Man's Clothing. 224p. 1983. pap. 2.50 (ISBN 0-446-31207-X). Warner Bks.

Eberhart, Mignon G. Alpine Condo Crossfire. LC 84-42527. 224p. 1984. 13.45 (ISBN 0-394-53766-1). Random.

--Alpine Condo Crossfire. 240p. 1985. pap. 2.95 (ISBN 0-446-32855-3). Warner Bks.

--Another Man's Murder. 12.95 (ISBN 0-89190-539-1, Pub. by Am Repr). Amereon Ltd.

--The Cases of Susan Dare. 303p. 1975. Repr. of 1934 ed. lib. bdg. 17.95 (ISBN 0-88411-751-0, Pub. by Aeonian Pr). Amereon Ltd.

--The Chiffon Scarf. 301p. 1975. Repr. of 1939 ed. lib. bdg. 17.95 (ISBN 0-88411-752-9, Pub. by Aeonian Pr). Amereon Ltd.

--Danger in the Dark. 307p. 1975. Repr. of 1936 ed. lib. bdg. 17.95 (ISBN 0-88411-753-7, Pub. by Aeonian Pr). Amereon Ltd.

--The Dark Garden. 312p. 1975. Repr. of 1933 ed. lib. bdg. 17.95 (ISBN 0-88411-754-5, Pub. by Aeonian Pr). Amereon Ltd.

--Fair Warning. 304p. 1975. Repr. of 1936 ed. lib. bdg. 17.95 (ISBN 0-88411-755-3, Pub. by Aeonian Pr). Amereon Ltd.

--Family Fortune. Repr. lib. bdg. 12.95 (ISBN 0-88411-769-3, Pub. by Aeonian Pr). Amereon Ltd.

--From This Dark Stairway. 1976. Repr. of 1931 ed. lib. bdg. 17.95 (ISBN 0-88411-760-X, Pub. by Aeonian Pr). Amereon Ltd.

--The Glass Slipper. 1976. Repr. of 1938 ed. lib. bdg. 16.95 (ISBN 0-88411-756-1, Pub. by Aeonian Pr). Amereon Ltd.

--The Hangman's Whip. 1976. Repr. of 1940 ed. lib. bdg. 16.95 (ISBN 0-88411-757-X, Pub. by Aeonian Pr). Amereon Ltd.

--Hasty Wedding. 1976. Repr. of 1938 ed. lib. bdg. 16.95 (ISBN 0-88411-761-8, 761, Pub. by Aeonian Pr). Amereon Ltd.

--The House on the Roof. 1976. Repr. of 1935 ed. lib. bdg. 16.95 (ISBN 0-88411-762-6, Pub. by Aeonian Pr). Amereon Ltd.

--Hunt with the Hounds. 1983. pap. 2.50 (ISBN 0-446-31199-5). Warner Bks.

--Man Missing. 192p. 1985. pap. 2.95 (ISBN 0-446-32737-9). Warner Bks.

--Murder by an Aristocrat. 1976. Repr. of 1932 ed. lib. bdg. 17.95 (ISBN 0-88411-763-4, Pub. by Aeonian Pr). Amereon Ltd.

--Murder in Waiting. 215p. Repr. of 1973 ed. lib. bdg. 13.95x (ISBN 0-88411-767-7, Pub. by Aeonian Pr). Amereon Ltd.

--The Mystery of Huntings End. 1976. Repr. of 1930 ed. lib. bdg. 18.95x (ISBN 0-88411-764-2, Pub. by Aeonian Pr). Amereon Ltd.

--Next of Kin. 240p. 1984. pap. 2.95 (ISBN 0-446-32501-5). Warner Bks.

--Nine O'Clock Tide. Repr. lib. bdg. 12.95x (ISBN 0-88411-770-7, Pub. by Aeonian Pr). Amereon Ltd.

--The Patient in Cabin C. 231p. 1983. 12.95 (ISBN 0-394-53108-6). Random.

--Patient in Room Eighteen. 1976. Repr. of 1929 ed. lib. bdg. 16.95x (ISBN 0-88411-765-0, Pub. by Aeonian Pr). Amereon Ltd.

--The Pattern. 1976. Repr. of 1937 ed. lib. bdg. 16.95x (ISBN 0-88411-758-8, Pub. by Aeonian Pr). Amereon Ltd.

--Two Little Rich Girls. 223p. Repr. of 1971 ed. lib. bdg. 13.95x (ISBN 0-88411-768-5, Pub. by Aeonian Pr). Amereon Ltd.

--While the Patient Slept. 1976. Repr. of 1930 ed. lib. bdg. 17.95x (ISBN 0-88411-759-6, Pub. by Aeonian Pr). Amereon Ltd.

--The White Cockatoo. 1976. Repr. of 1933 ed. lib. bdg. 17.95x (ISBN 0-88411-766-9, Pub. by Aeonian Pr). Amereon Ltd.

Eberhart, Perry. Treasure Tales of the Rockies. 3rd ed. LC 61-14373. (Illus.). 315p. 1969. 15.95 (ISBN 0-8040-0295-9, 82-72080, Pub by Swallow). Ohio U Pr.

Eberhart, Perry & Schmuck, Philip. Fourteeners: Colorado's Great Mountains. LC 72-75740. (Illus.). 128p. 1970. 15.00 (ISBN 0-8040-0122-7, 82-70761, SB); pap. 8.95 (ISBN 0-8040-0123-5, 82-70779, SB). Ohio U Pr.

Eberhart, Philip. Guide to the Colorado Ghost Towns & Mining Camps. 4th ed. LC 59-11061. (Illus.). 496p. 1969. pap. 13.95 (ISBN 0-8040-0140-5, 82-70860, Pub. by Swallow). Ohio U Pr.

Eberhart, Richard. Collected Poems 1930-1976. 1976. 22.50 (ISBN 0-19-519849-2). Oxford U Pr.

--Fields of Grace. 1972. 12.95 (ISBN 0-19-519710-0). Oxford U Pr.

--Florida Poems. LC 81-8396. (Illus.). 36p. (YA) 1981. 30.00 (ISBN 0-916906-44-2); pap. 15.95 (ISBN 0-916906-45-0). Konglomerati.

--The Long Reach: New & Uncollected Poems 1948-1984. LC 83-23746. 240p. 1984. 17.95 (ISBN 0-8112-0885-0); pap. 8.95 (ISBN 0-8112-0886-9, NDP565). New Directions.

--New Hampshire: Nine Poems. 15p. 1980. pap. 3.00 (ISBN 0-913219-25-8). Pym-Rand Pr.

--Of Poetry & Poets. LC 78-11597. 326p. 1979. 19.95x (ISBN 0-252-00630-5). U of Ill Pr.

--Poem to Poets. (Illus.). 40p. 1975. signed ed. 35.00 (ISBN 0-915778-04-1). Penmaen Pr.

--Quarry: New Poems. 1964. 12.95x (ISBN 0-19-500536-8). Oxford U Pr.

--Selected Poems: Nineteen-Thirty to Nineteen Sixty-Five. LC 65-17453. (Orig.). 1966. pap. 3.95 (ISBN 0-8112-0035-3, NDP198). New Directions.

--Ways of Light. 1980. pap. 15.95x (ISBN 0-19-502737-X). Oxford U Pr.

Eberhart, Richard & Rodman, Selden, eds. War & the Poet. LC 73-19574. 240p. 1974. Repr. of 1945 ed. lib. bdg. 45.00x (ISBN 0-8371-7287-X, EBWP). Greenwood.

Eberhart, Robert C., jt. ed. see Shitzer, Avraham.

Eberhart, Stephen, tr. see Adams, George.

Eberhart, Sylvia, jt. auth. see Cottrell, Leonard S.

Eberle, jt. auth. see Zavada.

Eberle, A. N., et al, eds. Perspectives in Peptide Chemistry. (Illus.). xii, 444p. 1980. 61.75 (ISBN 3-8055-1297-X). S Karger.

Eberle, Bob. Affective Expression Guide. 16p. (Orig.). 1983. pap. 1.50 tchr's guide (ISBN 0-88047-032-1). DOK Pubs.

--Apple Shines. (Illus.). 96p. (gr. 4-8). 1983. wkbk. 7.95 (ISBN 0-86653-130-0, GA 471). Good Apple.

--Chip In. (gr. 3-8). 1981. 7.95 (ISBN 0-86653-050-9, GA 416). Good Apple.

--Imagin-Action. (Illus.). 20p. (Orig.). (gr. 4-12). 1984. 2.95 (ISBN 0-88047-048-8, 8414). DOK Pubs.

--Scamper on. (Illus.). 64p. (Orig.). (gr. k-12). 1984. 5.95 (ISBN 0-88047-047-X, 8413). DOK Pubs.

--Visual Thinking. (Illus.). 64p. (Orig.). 1981. pap. 5.95 (ISBN 0-88047-000-3, 8201). DOK Pubs.

Eberle, Bob & Hall, Rosie. Affective Direction: Planning & Teaching for Thinking & Feeling. (Illus.). 168p. (Orig.). 1978. pap. 9.95 (ISBN 0-914634-58-5). DOK Pubs.

Eberle, Bob & Stanish, Bob. C. P. S. for Kids: A Resource Book for Teaching Creative Problem-Solving to Children. (Illus.). 128p. (Orig.). 1980. tchr's ed 8.95 (ISBN 0-914634-79-8, 8005). DOK Pubs.

Eberle, Bob F. & Hall, Rosie E. Affective Education Guidebook: Classroom Activities in the Realm of Feelings. 176p. (Orig.). 1975. 9.95 (ISBN 0-914634-28-3). DOK Pubs.

Eberle, Gary. Haunted Houses of Grand Rapids, Vol. II. LC 79-55532. (Grand Rapids Haunted Houses Ser.: Vol. II). (Illus.). 84p. Date not set. pap. 3.95 (ISBN 0-935604-01-4). Ivystone.

Eberle, Gerda. Studien und Berufsberatung Aus der Sicht Von Maturanden. (European University Studies: No. 6, Vol. 95). 236p. (Ger.). 1982. 22.10 (ISBN 3-261-05022-5). P Lang Pubs.

Eberle, Irmengarde. Modern Medical Discoveries. 3rd ed. LC 68-17084. (gr. 5-9). 1968. 10.95 (ISBN 0-690-55271-8). Crowell Jr Bks.

--Picture Stories for Children: A Rebus. LC 84-4352. 60p. (ps-3). 1984. 14.95 (ISBN 0-385-29340-2). Delacorte.

--Prairie Dogs in Prairie Dog Town. LC 73-9921. (Illus.). 64p. (gr. 3-6). 1974. Crowell Jr Bks.

Eberle, Jean F. Essentials of Helping Older People. 1982. pap. 5.50 (ISBN 0-932114-02-4). Boars Head.

--The Incredible Owen Girls. (YA) 1977. pap. 4.50 (ISBN 0-932114-00-8). Boars Head.

Eberle, Luke, tr. from Latin. & The Rule of the Master: Regula Magistri. LC 77-3986. (Cistercian Studies Ser: No. 6). 1977. 12.95 (ISBN 0-87907-806-5). Cistercian Pubns.

Eberle, Luke, tr. see Heufelder, Emmanuel.

Eberle, Nancy. Return to Main Street. 1982. 12.95 (ISBN 0-393-01485-1). Norton.

Eberle, R. A. Nominalistic Systems. LC 78-131265. (Synthese Library: No. 30). 217p. 1970. lib. bdg. 29.00 (ISBN 90-277-0161-X, Pub. by Reidel Holland). Kluwer Academic.

Eberle, Robert F. Classroom Cues for Cultivating Multiple Talent. (Illus.). 32p. 1974. tchrs' ed. 3.95 (ISBN 0-914634-19-4). DOK Pubs.

--Scamper: Games for Imagination Development. (Illus.). 64p. (Orig.). 1971. tchrs' ed. 3.50 (ISBN 0-914634-04-6). DOK Pubs.

Eberle, Sarah. What Is Love? (A Happy Day Book). (Illus.). 24p. (Orig.). (gr. k-2). 1980. 1.39 (ISBN 0-87239-410-7, 3642). Standard Pub.

Eberle, Sarah, rev. by see Grogg, Evelyn.

Eberle, Tom. Celebrate! Worship Dramas for the Church Year. 1977. pap. 5.50 (ISBN 0-89536-312-7). CSS of Ohio.

Eberlein, H. D. & Van Dyke Hubbard, Cortlandt. American Georgian Architecture. LC 76-22726. (Architecture & Decorative Arts Ser.). (Illus.). 1976. Repr. of 1952 ed. 32.50 (ISBN 0-306-70796-9). Da Capo.

Eberlein, H. Donaldson, jt. auth. see Richardson, A. E.

Eberlein, Harold D. The Architecture of Colonial America. LC 15-22725. (American Studies). 1968. Repr. of 1915 ed. 33.00 (ISBN 0-384-13795-4). Johnson Repr.

Eberlein, Harold D. & McClure, Abbot. The Practical Book of American Antiques. (Paperback Ser.). (Illus.). 1977. pap. 7.95 (ISBN 0-306-80062-4). Da Capo.

Eberlein, Patrick. Geodesics & Ends in Certain Surfaces Without Conjugate Points. LC 77-28627. (Memoirs Ser.: No. 199). 111p. 1982. pap. 14.00 (ISBN 0-8218-2199-7, MEMO-199). Am Math.

--Surfaces of Nonpositive Curvature. LC 79-15112. (Memoirs: No. 218). 90p. 1979. pap. 10.00 (ISBN 0-8218-2218-7, MEMO-218). Am Math.

Eberling, Ernest J. Congressional Investigations: A Study of the Origin & Development of the Power of Congress to Investigate & Punish for Contempt. 1972. lib. bdg. 29.00x (ISBN 0-374-92465-1). Octagon.

Eberly, Carole. Michigan Cooking...& Other Things. (Illus.). 112p. (Orig.). 1977. pap. 4.95 (ISBN 0-932296-00-9). Eberly Pr.

--More Michigan Cooking...& Other Things, Vol. 2. (Illus.). 112p. (Orig.). 1981. pap. 4.95 (ISBN 0-932296-07-6). Eberly Pr.

--One Hundred & One Apple Recipes. (Illus.). 48p. (Orig.). 1978. pap. 2.50 (ISBN 0-932296-02-5). Eberly Pr.

--One Hundred & One Fruit Recipes. (Illus.). 48p. (Orig.). 1983. pap. 2.50 (ISBN 0-932296-09-2). Eberly Pr.

--One Hundred One Cherry Recipes. (Illus.). 48p. (Orig.). 1984. pap. 2.50 (ISBN 0-932296-11-4). Eberly Pr.

--One Hundred One Vegetable Recipes. (Illus.). 48p. (Orig.). 1981. pap. 2.50 (ISBN 0-932296-08-4). Eberly Pr.

--Our Michigan: Ethnic Tales & Recipes. (Illus.). 192p. (Orig.). 1979. pap. 6.95 (ISBN 0-932296-03-3). Eberly Pr.

--Wild Mushroom Recipes. (Illus.). 64p. (Orig.). 1979. pap. 1.75 (ISBN 0-932296-05-X). Eberly Pr.

Eberly, Carole, ed. Brownie Recipes. (Illus.). 192p. (Orig.). 1983. pap. 5.95 (ISBN 0-932296-10-6). Eberly Pr.

Eberly, David. What Has Been Lost. 1982. pap. 4.95 (ISBN 0-914852-10-8). Good Gay.

Eberly, Donald. How Does My Child's Vision Affect His Reading? (Micromonograph Ser.). 1972. 0.50 (ISBN 0-87207-873-6). Intl Reading.

Eberly, Donald J., jt. ed. see Sherraden, Michael W.

Eberly, Joseph, ed. see International Conference on Multiphoton Processes, 1977, et al.

Eberly, Joyce E., jt. ed. see Masterson, James R.

Eberly, Phillip K. Music in the Air: America's Changing Taste in Popular Music, 1920-1980. (Communication Arts Bks.). (Illus.). 448p. 1982. pap. 22.75x (ISBN 0-8038-4742-4). Hastings.
Eberly, Ralph D. Moonfire. LC 76-24284. 1977. 7.95 (ISBN 0-87212-092-9). Libra.
Eberly, Walter L. Moon Beams & Star Dust. 1966. pap. 2.25x ring bdg. (ISBN 0-87813-204-X). Park View.
Ebers, John. Seven Years of the King's Theatre. LC 79-88490. Repr. of 1828 ed. 24.50 (ISBN 0-405-08481-1, Blom Pubns). Ayer Co Pubs.
Ebershoff-Coles, Susan & Leibenguth, Charla, eds. Motorsports: A Guide to Information Sources. LC 79-13736. (Sports, Games, & Pastimes Information Guide Ser.: Vol. 5). 1979. 60.00x (ISBN 0-8103-1446-0). Gale.
Ebersohn, Wessel. Divide the Night. LC 82-40033. 224p. 1982. pap. 2.95 (ISBN 0-394-70810-5, Vin). Random.
--Store up the Anger. LC 80-2076. 288p. 1981. 12.95 (ISBN 0-385-17406-3). Doubleday.
--Store up the Anger. 208p. 1984. pap. 5.95 (ISBN 0-14-006696-9). Penguin.
Ebersole, Frank. Seasons of the Year: Poems. 64p. 1983. pap. 5.00 (ISBN 0-941452-15-8). Acheron Pr.
Ebersole, Frank B. Language & Perception: Essays in the Philosophy of Language. LC 79-88305. 1979. pap. text ed. 13.75 (ISBN 0-8191-0776-X). U Pr of Amer.
--Meaning & Saying: Essays in the Philosophy of Language. LC 79-88304. 1979. pap. text ed. 12.75 (ISBN 0-8191-0775-1). U Pr of Amer.
--Things We Know: Fourteen Essays on Problems of Knowledge. LC 68-63599. 1968. 7.50 (ISBN 0-87114-016-0). U of Oreg Bks.
Ebersole, Joseph L. & Burke, Barlow. Discovery Problems in Civil Cases. 122p. 1983. text ed. 19.50 (ISBN 0-8290-1491-8). Irvington.
Ebersole, Priscilla & Hess, Patricia. Toward Healthy Aging: Human Needs & Nursing Response. LC 80-26668. (Illus.). 697p. 1981. text ed. 26.95 (ISBN 0-8016-1491-0). Mosby.
Ebersole, Priscilla, jt. auth. see Burnside, Irene.
Ebersole, Robert. Black Pagoda. LC 57-12929. (Illus.). 1957. 8.50 (ISBN 0-8130-0070-X). U Presses Fla.
Eberson, Frederick. Early Medical History of Pinellas Peninsula. LC 78-50560. (Illus.). 1978. 10.00 (ISBN 0-912760-67-2). Valkyrie Pub Hse.
--Early Physicians of the West. LC 79-63659. 1979. 6.95 (ISBN 0-912760-92-3). Valkyrie Pub Hse.
--Profiles: Giants in Medicine. (Illus.). 120p. (Orig.). 1980. pap. 5.95 (ISBN 0-934616-11-6). Valkyrie Pub Hse.
Eberstadt, Fernanda. Low Tide. Gottlieb, Robert, ed. LC 84-48655. 170p. 1985. 13.95 (ISBN 0-394-54429-3). Knopf.
Eberstadt, Isabel. Natural Victims. LC 82-48730. 1983. 15.95 (ISBN 0-394-52951-0). Knopf.
Eberstadt, Nick, ed. Fertility Decline in the Less Developed Countries. LC 80-23528. 382p. 1981. 47.95 (ISBN 0-03-055271-0). Praeger.
Eberstadt And Sons, Edward. Americana Catalog, 4 Vols. 1966. 125.00 (ISBN 0-87266-009-5); deluxe ed. 275.00 (ISBN 0-87266-010-9). Argosy.
Eberstein, Arthur, jt. auth. see Goodgold, Joseph.
Ebert, Alan & Rotchstein, Janice. The Long Way Home. LC 83-26289. 480p. 1984. 16.95 (ISBN 0-517-55365-1). Crown.
--The Long Way Home. 1985. pap. 3.95. Bantam.
--Traditions. 1983. pap. 3.95 (ISBN 0-553-22838-2). Bantam.
Ebert, Barbara. God's World. 1985. pap. 0.98 (ISBN 0-317-30757-6, 2695). Standard Pub.
Ebert, Elizabeth & Simmons, Katherine. The Brush Foundation Study of Child Growth & Development I: Psychometric Tests. (SRCD M Ser.). Repr. of 1943 ed. 11.00 (ISBN 0-527-01527-X, SRCD.M 35). Kraus Repr.
Ebert, Frances H. & Cheatum, Billye A. Basketball. 2nd ed. LC 76-8573. (Illus.). 282p. 1977. pap. text ed. 15.95 (ISBN 0-7216-3306-4). SCP.
Ebert, Friedrich A. General Bibliographical Dictionary, 4 vols. LC 68-19956. 1968. Repr. of 1837 ed. 210.00x (ISBN 0-8103-3304-X). Gale.
Ebert, H., et al, eds. Radiation Protection Optimization-Present Experience & Methods: Proceedings of the European Scientific Seminar, Luxembourg, Oct. 1979. LC 80-41671. (Illus.). 330p. 1981. 55.00 (ISBN 0-08-027291-6). Pergamon.
Ebert, H. G., jt. auth. see Muller, W. A.
Ebert, H. G. & Booz, J., eds. Microdosimetry, 7th Symposium. (Commission of the European Communities Symposium Ser.). 1604p. 1981. 290.50 (ISBN 3-7186-0049-8). Harwood Academic.
Ebert, H. G., jt. ed. see Booz, J.
Ebert, Hilmar, jt. auth. see Dickins, Anthony S.
Ebert, James D. & Sussex, Ian M. Interacting Systems in Development. 2nd ed. LC 78-100552. (Modern Biology Ser.). 338p. 1970. pap. text ed. 18.95x (ISBN 0-03-081306-9, HoltC). HR&W.
Ebert, James D. & Odada, Tokindo S., eds. Mechanisms of Cell Change. LC 78-24040. 358p. 1979. 46.50 (ISBN 0-471-03097-X). Krieger.
Ebert, Jeanne. What Would You Do If...? A Safety Game for You & Your Child. (Illus.). 96p. 1985. pap. 4.95 (ISBN 0-395-37023-X). HM.
Ebert, K. H., ed. Modelling of Chemical Reaction Systems: Proceedings. (Springer Series in Chemical Physics: Vol. 18). (Illus.). 389p. 1981. 39.00 (ISBN 0-387-10983-8). Springer Verlag.
Ebert, Lawrence B., ed. Chemistry of Engine Combustion Deposits. 388p. 1985. 69.50x (ISBN 0-306-41936-X, Plenum Pr). Plenum Pub.
Ebert, M. & Howard, A., eds. Current Topics in Radiation Research, Vol. 11. 1979. 85.00 (ISBN 0-444-85183-6, North Holland). Elsevier.
--Current Topics in Radiation Research, Vol. 13. 1978. 55.50 (ISBN 0-444-85164-X, North-Holland). Elsevier.
Ebert, Paul A. see Zuidema, G. D. & Skinner, D. B.
Ebert, R. J. & Mitchell, T. R. Organizational Decision Processes. LC 74-13324. (Illus.). 320p. 1975. 29.50x (ISBN 0-8448-0619-6); pap. 14.50x (ISBN 0-8448-0620-X). Crane-Russak Co.
Ebert, Robert, ed. Northwest Energy Resource Manual. (Illus.). 96p. 1983. pap. 3.95 (ISBN 0-942886-01-1). Periwinkle Pubns.
--Solar Design: A Handbook for Solar Homebuilders. 1983. pap. write for info. (ISBN 0-942886-02-X). Periwinkle Pubns.
--Solar Home Plan Book. 1983. pap. 3.95 (ISBN 0-942886-03-8). Periwinkle Pubns.
Ebert, Roger. A Kiss Is Still a Kiss: Roger Ebert at the Movies. (Illus.). 264p. 1984. 14.95 (ISBN 0-8362-7957-3). Andrews McMeel Parker.
--Roger Ebert's Movie Home Companion: 400 Films on Cassette, 1980-85. 500p. (Orig.). 1985. pap. 9.95 (ISBN 0-8362-6209-3). Andrews McMeel Parker.
Ebert, Roger see Walsh, Gene.
Ebert, Roger, ed. An Illini Century: One Hundred Years of Campus Life. LC 67-17897. Repr. of 1967 ed. 42.60 (ISBN 0-8357-9681-7, 2019038). Bks Demand UMI.
Ebert, Ronald J., jt. auth. see Adam, Everett E., Jr.
Ebert, Ronald J., jt. auth. see Adam, Everett, Jr.
Ebert, Theodor. Meinung und Wissen in der Philosophie Platons: Untersuchungen Zum Charmides', 'Menon' und 'Staat' x, 234p. (Ger.). 1974. 31.60x (ISBN 3-11-004787-X). De Gruyter.
Ebertin, Elsbeth. Astrology & Romance. Nelson, D. G., tr. from Ger. LC 73-90428. (Illus.). 132p. 1973. Repr. of 1936 ed. 7.95 (ISBN 0-88231-002-X). ASI Pubs Inc.
Ebertin, Reinhold. Annual Diagram as an Aid to Life. 151p. 1973. 8.00 (ISBN 0-86690-085-3, 1086-02). Am Fed Astrologers.
--Applied Cosmobiology. 208p. 1972. 13.50 (ISBN 0-86690-078-0, 1087-01). Am Fed Astrologers.
--Combination of Stellar Influences. 256p. 1972. 13.50 (ISBN 0-86690-087-X, 1089-01). Am Fed Astrologers.
--The Contact Cosmogram. 152p. 1974. 8.00 (ISBN 0-86690-088-8, 1090-02). Am Fed Astrologers.
--Cosmic Marriage. 160p. 1974. 8.00 (ISBN 0-86690-089-6, 1091-01). Am Fed Astrologers.
--Directions, Co-Determinants of Fate. 224p. 1976. 13.50 (ISBN 0-86690-090-X, 1095-02). Am Fed Astrologers.
--Fixed Stars & Their Interpretation. 100p. 1971. 8.00 (ISBN 0-86690-091-8, 1096-01). Am Fed Astrologers.
--Man in Universe. 104p. 1973. 7.00 (ISBN 0-86690-092-6, 1098-02). Am Fed Astrologers.
--Rapid & Reliable Analysis. 68p. 1970. 7.00 (ISBN 0-86690-093-4, 1099-01). Am Fed Astrologers.
--Transits. 136p. 1971. 5.00 (ISBN 0-86690-094-2, 1101-01). Am Fed Astrologers.
--Transits: Forecasting Using the Forty-Five Degree Graphic Ephemeris. Kratzsch, Linda, tr. (Ger.). 1982. pap. text ed. 10.00. ASI Pubs Inc.
Ebertino, Shirley. Computer Assisted Technical Services for a Regional School Library Center. 214p. 1973. 1.00 (ISBN 0-317-36975-X). ALA.
Eberts, C. G., jt. ed. see Eberts, R. E.
Eberts, Marjorie & Gisler, Margaret. Pancakes, Crackers & Pizza: A Book of Shapes. LC 84-7699. (Rookie Readers Ser.). (Illus.). 32p. 1984. lib. bdg. 8.65 (ISBN 0-516-02063-3); pap. 2.50 (ISBN 0-516-42063-1). Childrens.
Eberts, R. E. & Eberts, C. G., eds. Trends in Ergonomics Human Factors II. 652p. 1985. 74.00 (ISBN 0-444-87751-7, North Holland). Elsevier.
Eberts, Randall W., et al. Unions & Public Schools: The Effects of Collective Bargaining on American Education. LC 82-148862. (Politics of Education Ser.). 224p. 1984. 24.00x (ISBN 0-669-06372-X). Lexington Bks.
Eberts, Tony & Grass, Al. Exploring the Outdoors: Southwestern B.C. (Illus.). 208p. 1984. pap. 9.95 (ISBN 0-88839-989-8). Hancock House.
Ebertshauser, Heidi C. Malerei Im 19. Jahrhundert - Munchner Schule. (Illus.). 288p. 1985. 37.50 (ISBN 3-87405-141-2, Pub. by Keyser West Germany). Seven Hills Bks.
Eberwein, Jane D. Dickinson: Strategies of Limitation. LC 84-16335. 320p. 1985. lib. bdg. 25.00x (ISBN 0-87023-473-0). U of Mass Pr.
--Early American Poetry: Bradstreet, Taylor, Dwight, Freneau & Bryant. LC 77-91051. 398p. 1978. pap. 14.50x (ISBN 0-299-07444-7). U of Wis Pr.
Eberwein, Robert T. Film & the Dream Screen: A Sleep & a Forgetting. LC 84-42583. (Illus.). 228p. 1984. text ed. 27.50x (ISBN 0-691-06619-1). Princeton U Pr.
--A Viewer's Guide to Film Theory & Criticism. LC 79-9380. 243p. 1979. 17.00 (ISBN 0-8108-1237-1). Scarecrow.
Ebestin, Reinheld. The Annual Diagram. 160p. 1980. pap. 10.00 (ISBN 0-88231-122-0). ASI Pubs Inc.
Ebey, George W. Adaptability among the Elementary Schools of an American City. LC 71-176741. (Columbia University. Teachers College. Contributions to Education Ser.: No. 817). Repr. of 1940 ed. 22.50 (ISBN 0-404-55817-8). AMS Pr.
Ebeyer, Paul P. Revelations Concerning Napoleon's Escape from St. Helena. 1947. 10.00 (ISBN 0-911116-75-3). Pelican.
Ebihara, May & Gianutsos, Rosamond, eds. Papers in Anthropology & Linguistics. (Annals of the New York Academy of Sciences: Vol. 318). (Orig.). 1978. pap. 21.00x (ISBN 0-89072-077-0). NY Acad Sci.
Ebin, D. G., jt. auth. see Cheeger, J.
Ebin, Lois. Vernacular Poetics in the Middle Ages. LC 83-23606. (Studies in Medieval Culture Ser.: No. 16). xvi, 293p. 1984. 24.95x (ISBN 0-918720-22-2); pap. 14.95x (ISBN 0-918720-19-2). Medieval Inst.
Ebin, Lois A. John Lydgate. (English Author Ser.). 1985. lib. bdg. 19.95 (ISBN 0-8057-6898-X, Twayne). G K Hall.
Ebing, Winifried, jt. auth. see Federal Institute for Biology in Agriculture & Forestry, Institute for Plant Protection Agent Research, Berlin-Dahlem.
Ebinger, Charles, jt. ed. see Alexander, Yonah.
Ebinger, Charles, jt. ed. see Bolet, Adela.
Ebinger, Charles K. The Critical Link: Energy & National Security in the 1980s. LC 81-8065. 304p. 1983. pap. 14.95x (ISBN 0-88410-984-4). Ballinger Pub.
--Foreign Intervention in Civil War: The Politics & Diplomacy of the Angolan Conflict. (Replica Edition Ser.). 340p. 1986. softcover 24.00x (ISBN 0-86531-979-0). Westview.
--Pakistan: Energy Planning in a Strategic Vortex. LC 80-8767. 176p. 1981. 25.00x (ISBN 0-253-37645-9). Ind U Pr.
Ebinger, Charles K. & Morse, Ronald A., eds. U. S.-Japanese Energy Relations: Cooperation & Competition. (Replica Edition Ser.). 275p. 1984. softcover 23.50x (ISBN 0-86531-833-6). Westview.
Ebisch, Walther & Schucking, Levincompiled by. Shakespeare Bibliography. LC 68-20246. 1968. Repr. of 1930 ed. 24.50 (ISBN 0-405-08482-X, Blom Pubns). Ayer Co Pubs.
Eble, Francis X., jt. auth. see Schmeckebier, Laurence F.
Eble, Kenneth. F. Scott Fitzgerald. rev ed. (United States Authors Ser.). 1977. lib. bdg. 13.50 (ISBN 0-8057-7183-2, Twayne). G K Hall.
--William Dean Howells. 2nd ed. (United States Authors Ser.). 1982. lib. bdg. 14.50 (ISBN 0-8057-7372-X, Twayne). G K Hall.
Eble, Kenneth E. The Aims of College Teaching. LC 83-48157. (Higher Education Ser.). 1983. text ed. 16.95x (ISBN 0-87589-575-1). Jossey-Bass.
--The Art of Administration: A Guide for Academic Administrators. LC 78-62572. (Higher Education Ser.). 1978. text ed. 16.95x (ISBN 0-87589-383-X). Jossey-Bass.
--The Craft of Teaching: A Guide to Mastering the Professor's Art. LC 76-11894. (Higher Education Ser.). 1976. 16.95x (ISBN 0-87589-284-1). Jossey-Bass.
--F. Scott Fitzgerald. rev. ed. (United States Authors Ser.: No. 36). 192p. 1984. pap. 5.95 (ISBN 0-8057-7423-8, Twayne). G K Hall.
--Old Clemens & W. D. H. The Story of a Remarkable Friendship. (Southern Literary Studies). 240p. 1985. text ed. 20.00x (ISBN 0-8071-1227-5). La State U Pr.
--Professors as Teachers. LC 78-186579. (Higher Education Ser.). 1972. 18.95x (ISBN 0-87589-118-7). Jossey-Bass.
Eble, Kenneth E. & McKeachie, Wilbert J. Improving Undergraduate Education Through Faculty Development: An Analysis of Effective Programs & Practices. LC 84-43027. (Higher Education Ser.). 1985. text ed. 19.95x (ISBN 0-87589-643-X). Jossey-Bass.
Eble, Kenneth E., ed. Howells: A Century of Criticism. LC 62-13275. 1962. 12.95 (ISBN 0-87074-050-4). SMU Press.
Eblin, Lawrence P. Elements of Chemistry in the Laboratory. 2nd ed. (Illus.). 178p. (Orig.). 1970. spiral bdg. 13.95 (ISBN 0-15-522073-X, HC). HarBraceJ.
Ebling, F. J. & Ewens, W. V., eds. Racial Variations in Man: Proceedings of a Symposium Held at the Royal Geographical Society, London, 1974. LC 75-12803. (Symposia of the Institute of Biology Ser.). 245p. 1976. 53.95x (ISBN 0-470-22955-1). Halsted Pr.
Ebling, F. J. & Henderson, I. W., eds. Biological & Clinical Aspects of Reproduction. (International Congress Ser.: No. 394). 1976. 107.75 (ISBN 90-219-0324-5, Excerpta Medica). Elsevier.
Ebling, Gerhard. Word & Faith. 444p. pap. 15.75 (ISBN 0-317-31483-1, 30-1803-259). Fortress.
Ebling, Ruth, jt. auth. see Reardon, Jean.
Ebner, Hans, Jr. Ten Years of Sad Rain. (Masterworks Ser.: No. 4). (Illus.). 1976. pap. 1.50 (ISBN 0-916982-04-1). Realities.
--Wordmaster. (Masterworks Ser.: No. 10). 1977. pap. 1.50 (ISBN 0-916982-12-2). Realities.
Ebner, James H. God Present As Mystery: A Search for Personal Meaning in Contemporary Theology. LC 76-13750. 1976. pap. 5.95 (ISBN 0-88489-084-8). St Marys.
Ebner, K. E., ed. Subunit Enzymes: Biochemistry & Funtions. (Enzymology Ser.: Vol. 2). 352p. 1975. 59.75 (ISBN 0-8247-6280-0). Dekker.
Ebner, Louise. Exploring Truths Through. pap. 3.95 (ISBN 0-89957-602-8). AMG Pubs.
Ebner, Maria. Connective Tissue Manipulations. LC 84-9636. 230p. 1985. lib. bdg. 17.50 (ISBN 0-89874-763-5). Krieger.
Ebner, Maria, ed. see Heardman, Helen.
Ebneter, Harkus, et al, eds. Dental Atlas. (Illus.). 71p. 1984. pap. text ed. 160.00x (ISBN 0-86715-145-5). Quint Pub Co.
Eboch, Sidney C. Operating Audio-Visual Equipment. 2nd ed. (Illus., Orig.). 1968. pap. text ed. 12.50 scp (ISBN 0-8102-0093-7, HarpC). Har-Row.
Ebon. Revolution. 1968. pap. 1.50 (ISBN 0-88378-002-X). Third World.
Ebon, M. The Andropov File. 304p. 1983. 16.95 (ISBN 0-07-018861-0). McGraw.
Ebon, Martin. Khruschev. (World Leaders: Past & Present Ser.). (Illus.). 112p. 1985. lib. bdg. 15.95x (ISBN 0-87754-562-6). Chelsea Hse.
--Prophecy in Our Time. pap. 2.50 (ISBN 0-87980-125-5). Wilshire.
--Psychic Warfare: Threat or Illusion? 304p. 1983. 15.95 (ISBN 0-07-018860-2). McGraw.
Ebony Editors. Black Revolution: An Ebony Special Issue. LC 72-128545. (Illus.). 1970. 5.95 (ISBN 0-87485-039-8). Johnson Chi.
--Ebony Pictorial History of Black America, 4 vols. 1971 ed. Bennett, Lerone, Jr., ed. Incl. Vol. 1; Vol. 2; Vol. 3; Vol. 4. The 1973 Yearbook. 312p. 10.95 (ISBN 0-87485-059-2). boxed set of 3 vols. 27.95 (ISBN 0-87485-049-5); deluxe slip-case set of 4 vols. 38.90 (ISBN 0-87485-073-8). Johnson Chi.
--Ebony Success Library, Vols. 1-3. Incl. Vol. 1. One Thousand Successful Blacks (ISBN 0-87485-060-6); Vol. 2. Famous Blacks Give Secrets of Success (ISBN 0-87485-061-4); Vol. 3. Career Guide: Opportunities and Resources for You (ISBN 0-87485-062-2). (Illus.). 960p. 1973. Set. 27.95 (ISBN 0-87485-058-4). Johnson Chi.
--Martin Luther King, Jr. (Ebony Picture Biography Ser.). (Illus., Orig.). 1968. pap. 5.00 (ISBN 0-87485-025-8). Johnson Chi.
--White Problem in America. 1966. 3.50 (ISBN 0-87485-020-7). Johnson Chi.
Eboue, Adolphe F. Les Peuples de l'Oubangui-Chari. LC 74-15034. (Illus., Fr.). Repr. of 1933 ed. 14.00 (ISBN 0-404-12039-3). AMS Pr.
Eboussi Boulaga, F. Christianity Without Fetishes: An African Critique & Recapture of Christianity. Barr, Robert R., tr. from Fr. LC 84-5807. 256p. (Orig.). 1984. pap. 11.95 (ISBN 0-88344-432-1). Orbis Bks.
Ebrahim, G. J. Breast Feeding: The Biological Option. LC 78-13096. 1980. text ed. 10.95x (ISBN 0-8052-3701-1). Schocken.
Ebrey, Patricia B. The Aristocratic Families of Early Imperial China. LC 76-40836. (Cambridge Studies in Chinese History, Literature & Institutions). (Illus.). 1978. 37.50 (ISBN 0-521-21484-X). Cambridge U Pr.
Ebrey, Patricia B., ed. Chinese Civilization & Society: A Sourcebook. LC 80-639. 1981. 19.95 (ISBN 0-02-908750-3); pap. text ed. 12.95 (ISBN 0-02-908760-0). Free Pr.
Ebrey, Patricia B., tr. Family & Property in Sung China: Yuan Ts'ai's Precepts for Social Life. LC 84-42580. (Princeton Library of Asian Translations). 328p. 1984. text ed. 37.50x (ISBN 0-691-05426-6). Princeton U Pr.
Ebright, Malcolm. The Tierra Amarilla Grant: A History of Chicanery. LC 80-69638. (Illus.). 80p. (Orig.). 1980. pap. 6.50 (ISBN 0-9605202-0-1). Ctr Land Grant.
Ebrom, Janet D. & Sowa, Richard A. The Sowa Family History: Six Generations of Polish-Texans. LC 80-70502. (Illus.). 220p. 1981. 14.95x (ISBN 0-9605638-0-6); pap. 7.95x (ISBN 0-9605638-1-4). Sowa Bks.
Ebsworth, E. A., ed. Spectroscopic Properties of Inorganic & Organometallic Compounds, Vols. 1-11. Incl. Vol. 1. 1967 Literature. 1968. 32.00 (ISBN 0-85186-003-6); Vol. 2. 1968 Literature. 1969. 36.00 (ISBN 0-85186-013-3); Vol. 3. 1969 Literature. 1970. 37.00 (ISBN 0-85186-023-0); Vol. 4. 1970 Literature. 1971. 41.00 (ISBN 0-85186-033-8); Vol. 5. 1971 Literature. 1972. 43.00 (ISBN 0-85186-043-5); Vol. 6. 1972 Literature. 1973. 47.00 (ISBN 0-85186-053-2); Vol. 7. 1973 Literature. 1974. 61.00 (ISBN 0-85186-063-X); Vol. 8. 1974 Literature. 1975. 65.00 (ISBN 0-85186-073-7); Vol. 9. 1975 Literature. 1976. 72.00 (ISBN 0-85186-083-4); Vol. 10. 1976 Literature. 1977. 82.00 (ISBN 0-685-55715-4, Pub. by Royal Soc Chem London); Vol. 11. 1977 Literature. 1978. 82.00 (ISBN 0-85186-103-2). LC 76-6662. Am Chemical.
Ebsworth, J. W., ed. see Bagford, Ballads.
Ebsworth, J. W., jt. ed. see Chappell, W.
Ebsworth, P., ed. Europe: A Socialist Strategy. 234p. 1979. 35.00x (ISBN 0-686-75517-0, Pub. by Polygon Bks Scotland). State Mutual Bk.

Eburne, Richard. Plain Pathway to Plantations (1624) Wright, Louis B., ed. (Documents Ser.). 1978. 12.00x (ISBN 0-918016-37-1). Folger Bks.

Ebury Press, ed. The British Art & Antiques Yearbook 1981. 772p. 1981. 50.00x (ISBN 0-686-78855-9, Pub. by Ebury Pr England). State Mutual Bk.

--The Connoisseur's Handbook of Antique Collecting. rev. ed. 320p. 1981. 45.00x (ISBN 0-900305-19-3, Pub. by Ebury Pr England). State Mutual Bk.

--Containerisation International Yearbook, 1984. 522p. 1981. 175.00x (ISBN 0-85223-195-4, Pub. by Ebury Pr England). State Mutual Bk.

Eby, Edwin H. Concordance of Walt Whitman's Leaves of Grass & Selected Prose Writings. LC 76-90500. Repr. of 1955 ed. lib. bdg. 55.00x (ISBN 0-8371-2122-1, EBCW). Greenwood.

Eby, Frederick & Arrowood, Charles F. The Development of Modern Education in Theory, Organization, & Practice. 1981. Repr. of 1934 ed. lib. bdg. 45.00 (ISBN 0-89760-207-2). Telegraph Bks.

Eby, Frederick, ed. Early Protestant Educators. LC 76-149656. (BCL Ser. I). Repr. of 1931 ed. 34.50 (ISBN 0-404-02238-3). AMS Pr.

Eby, John W. Hindustan: As Seen by John. (Illus.). 1977. pap. 3.00x (ISBN 0-932218-05-9). Hall Pr.

Eby, Kermit. For Brethren Only. LC 58-14936. pap. 58.50 (ISBN 0-317-28390-1, 2022410). Bks Demand UMI.

Eby, Louise S. Quest for Moral Law. facsimile ed. LC 78-37849. (Essay Index Reprint Ser). Repr. of 1944 ed. 20.00 (ISBN 0-8369-2588-2). Ayer Co Pubs.

Eby, Ray. Bakers Bible Atlas Study Guide. 1977. 4.60 (ISBN 0-686-25535-6); test 1.75 (ISBN 0-686-31725-4); map 1.55 (ISBN 0-686-31726-2). Rod & Staff.

Eby, Richard E. The Amazing Lamb of God: Bedtime Stories to be Read to Children. (Illus.). 128p. 1983. 12.95 (ISBN 0-8007-1336-2). Revell.

--Caught up into Paradise. pap. 2.95 (ISBN 0-8007-8489-8, Spire Bks). Revell.

--Caught up into Paradise. 256p. 1978. 2.95 (ISBN 0-8007-8489-8, Spire Bks). Revell.

--Caught up into Paradise. 256p. 1978. pap. 5.95 (ISBN 0-8007-5066-7, Power Bks). Revell.

--Tell Them I Am Coming. 1980. pap. 5.95 (ISBN 0-8007-5045-4, Power Bks). Revell.

--Tell Them I Am Coming. 160p. 1984. pap. 2.50 (ISBN 0-8007-8496-0, Spire Bks). Revell.

Eby, Ronald K., ed. Durability of Macromolecular Materials. LC 78-31777. (Symposium Ser.: No. 95). 1979. 49.95 (ISBN 0-8412-0485-3). Am Chemical.

Eca de Queiroz. The City & the Mountains. Campbell, Roy, tr. LC 67-17895. Repr. of 1967 ed. 55.30 (ISBN 0-8357-9480-6, 2007857). Bks Demand UMI.

--Letters from England. Stevens, Ann, tr. from Port. LC 70-123109. 192p. 1970. 12.00x (ISBN 0-8214-0080-0, 82-80844). Ohio U Pr.

Eca de Queiroz, Jose M. Dragon's Teeth: A Novel. Serrano, Mary J., tr. from Port. LC 70-98833. 516p. Repr. of 1889 ed. lib. bdg. 24.75x (ISBN 0-8371-3089-1, ECDT). Greenwood.

Eccard, Johann. Neue geistliche und weltliche Lieder zu fuenf und vier Stimmen, 1589. Eitner, Robert, ed. (Publikation aelterer praktischer und theoretischer Musikwerke Ser.: Vol. XXI). (Ger.). 1967. Repr. of 1897 ed. write for info. (ISBN 0-8450-1721-7). Broude.

Eccardt, J. M. Ebenezer Howard. (Clarendon Biography Ser.). (Illus.). 1973. pap. 3.50 (ISBN 0-912728-67-1). Newbury Bks.

Eccles. The Inhibitory Pathways of the Central Nervous System. 140p. 1982. 50.00x (ISBN 0-85323-050-1, Pub. by Liverpool Univ England). State Mutual Bk.

Eccles, jt. auth. see Hellman.

Eccles, Audrey. Obstetrics & Gynaecology in Tudor & Stuart England. LC 81-19374. (Illus.). 160p. 1982. 18.00x (ISBN 0-87338-270-6). Kent St U Pr.

Eccles, David, jt. auth. see Eccles, Sybil.

Eccles, F. Y. Racine in England. LC 74-7036. 1922. lib. bdg. 8.50 (ISBN 0-8414-3936-2). Folcroft.

Eccles, Frances Y. A Century of French Poets. 1973. Repr. of 1909 ed. 30.00 (ISBN 0-8274-1387-4). R West.

Eccles, George S. The Politics of Banking. Hyman, Sidney, ed. 320p. 1982. pap. 13.00 (ISBN 0-87480-209-1). U of Utah Pr.

Eccles, Henry E. Logistics in the National Defense. LC 81-4920. (Illus.). xviii, 347p. 1981. Repr. lib. bdg. 42.50 (ISBN 0-313-22716-0, ECLO). Greenwood.

--Military Concepts & Philosophy. LC 65-14457. pap. 89.80 (ISBN 0-317-08313-9, 2050513). Bks Demand UMI.

Eccles, J. The Human Psyche. (Illus.). 300p. 1980. 29.00 (ISBN 0-387-09954-9). Springer-Verlag.

Eccles, J. C., jt. auth. see Popper, K. R.

Eccles, Sir J. C. & Gibson, W. C. Sherrington: His Life & Thought. LC 78-11359. (Illus.). 1979. 24.00 (ISBN 0-387-09063-0). Springer-Verlag.

Eccles, John & Robinson, Daniel N. The Wonder of Being Human: Our Brain & Our Mind. LC 83-49044. 192p. 1984. 16.95 (ISBN 0-02-908860-7). Free Pr.

--The Wonder of Being Human: Our Brain & Our Mind. LC 84-25562. (New Science Library). 182p. 1985. pap. 8.95 (ISBN 0-87773-312-0). Shambhala Pubns.

Eccles, John, jt. auth. see Popper, Karl.

Eccles, John, ed. Mind & Brain: The Many-Faceted Problems. LC 82-83242. (Illus.). 370p. 1982. 24.95 (ISBN 0-89226-016-5). Paragon Hse.

Eccles, John & Dimitrijevic, M. R., eds. Upper Motor Neurons Functions & Dysfunctions. (Recent Achievements in Restorative Neurology: Vol. 1). (Illus.). xvii, 346p. 1985. 118.75 (ISBN 3-8055-4020-5). S Karger.

Eccles, John C. Facing Reality: Philosophical Adventures by a Brain Scientist. LC 76-121064. (Heidelberg Science Library: Vol. 13). (Illus.). 1970. pap. 15.00 (ISBN 0-387-90014-4). Springer-Verlag.

--The Human Mystery: The Gifford Lectures, University of Edinburgh 1977-78. 272p. (Orig.). 1984. pap. 9.95 (ISBN 0-7102-0198-2). Routledge & Kegan.

--The Physiology of Nerve Cells. LC 68-9181. 288p. 1957. pap. 7.95x (ISBN 0-8018-0182-6). Johns Hopkins.

--Physiology of Synapses. (Illus.). 1964. Repr. 34.00 (ISBN 0-387-03112-X). Springer-Verlag.

--The Understanding of the Brain. 2nd ed. (Illus.). 1976. pap. text ed. 15.95 (ISBN 0-07-018865-3). McGraw.

Eccles, John C., jt. ed. see Karczmar, A. G.

Eccles, John C., ed. see Pontificia Academia Scientiarum, Study Week, 1964.

Eccles, John C., et al. Cerebellum As a Neuronal Machine. (Illus.). 1967. 57.00 (ISBN 0-387-03762-4). Springer-Verlag.

Eccles, Sir John. The Human Mystery. LC 78-12095. (Illus.). 1978. 25.00 (ISBN 0-387-09016-9). Springer-Verlag.

Eccles, M. J., et al. Low Light Level Detectors in Astronomy. LC 82-12881. (Cambridge Astrophysics Ser.). (Illus.). 200p. 1983. 42.50 (ISBN 0-521-24088-3). Cambridge U Pr.

Eccles, M. S., jt. auth. see Tax Institute.

Eccles, Mark. Christopher Marlowe in London. 1967. Repr. lib. bdg. 18.50x (ISBN 0-374-92470-8). Octagon.

--Shakespeare in Warwickshire. (Illus.). 192p. 1961. 15.00x (ISBN 0-299-02330-3); pap. 6.50x (ISBN 0-299-02334-6). U of Wis Pr.

Eccles, Mark, ed. Macro Plays: The Castle of Perseverance, Wisdom, Mankind. (Early English Text Society Ser.). 1969. 17.95x (ISBN 0-19-722265-X). Oxford U Pr.

Eccles, Mark, ed. see Shakespeare, William.

Eccles, Marriner S. Economic Balance & a Balanced Budget. LC 72-2367. (FDR & the Era of the New Deal Ser). 328p. 1973. Repr. of 1940 ed. lib. bdg. 39.50 (ISBN 0-306-70479-X). Da Capo.

Eccles, Robert G. The Transfer Pricing Problem: A Theory for Practice. LC 84-48024. 568p. 1985. 29.00x (ISBN 0-669-09029-8). Lexington Bks.

Eccles, Robert G., jt. auth. see Schlesinger, Leonard.

Eccles, Sybil & Eccles, David. By Safe Hand: Letters of Sybil & David Eccles 1939-42. 384p. 1984. 30.00 (ISBN 0-370-30482-9, Pub. by the Bodley Head). Merrimack Pub Cir.

Eccles, W. J. Canadian Frontier, Fifteen Thirty-Four to Eighteen Twenty-One. rev. ed. LC 70-81783. (Histories of the American Frontier Ser.). (Illus.). 234p. 1983. pap. 10.95x (ISBN 0-8263-0706-X); 19.95x (ISBN 0-8263-0705-1). U of NM Pr.

--France in America. LC 72-79657. (New American Nation Ser.). (Illus.). 1972. 16.95xi (ISBN 0-06-011152-6, HarpT). Har-Row.

Eccles, William. Microprocessor Systems: A 16-Bit Approach. LC 84-9197. 450p. 1985. text ed. 34.95 (ISBN 0-201-11985-4). Addison-Wesley.

Eccles, William J. Canadian Society During the French Regime. LC 68-27288. (E. R. Adair Memorial Lectures Ser.). pap. 44.50 (ISBN 0-317-28412-6, 2022294). Bks Demand UMI.

Eccleshall, Robert. Order & Reason in Politics: Theories of Absolute & Limited Monarchy in Early Modern England. 1978. text ed. 27.50x (ISBN 0-19-713431-9). Oxford U Pr.

Eccleshall, Robert, et al. Political Ideologies: An Introduction. LC 84-6655. 255p. (Orig.). 1984. pap. 9.95 (ISBN 0-09-156131-0, Pub. by Hutchinson Educ). Longwood Pub Group.

Ecclesine, Joseph A. How Not to Make a Million Dollars in Mail Order. LC 81-69201. (Illus.). 60p. 1981. pap. 4.95 (ISBN 0-9606814-0-X). Wry Idea.

Ecclestone, Alan. The Night Sky of the Lord. LC 82-5514. 240p. 1982. 14.95 (ISBN 0-8052-3810-7). Schocken.

--A Staircase for Silence. 158p. 1977. pap. 6.50 (ISBN 0-232-51364-3). Attic Pr.

Ecclestone, Eric. Sir Walter Raleigh. 1941. Repr. 20.00 (ISBN 0-8274-3433-2). R West.

E.C.C.S. European Conference for Construction Steelwork. European Recommendations for Steel Construction. (ECCS Steel Manuals Ser.). 360p. (Orig.). 1981. pap. text ed. 42.00x. Longman.

Echanis, Michael D. Knife Self-Defense for Combat. LC 77-89614. (Ser. 127). 1977. pap. 6.95 (ISBN 0-89750-022-9). Ohara Pubns.

--Stick Fighting for Combat. LC 78-65738. (Ser. 130). (Illus.). 1978. pap. 9.50 (ISBN 0-89750-059-8). Ohara Pubns.

Echaoce, jt. auth. see Bostick.

Echaore & Wentz. Machines. (Science in Action Ser.). (Illus.). 48p. 1984. pap. text ed. 2.85 (ISBN 0-88102-021-4); tchr's guide avail. Janus Bks.

Echaore, Susan. Human Systems. (Science in Action Ser.). (Illus.). 48p. 1984. pap. text ed. 2.85 (ISBN 0-88102-023-0). Janus Bks.

Echaore, Susan D. The Solar System. (Science in Action Ser.). (Illus.). 48p. (gr. 9 up). 1982. pap. text ed. 2.85 (ISBN 0-915510-80-4). Janus Bks.

Echard, William E. Napoleon III & the Concert of Europe. LC 82-12660. 327p. 1983. text ed. 32.50x (ISBN 0-8071-1056-6). La State U Pr.

Echard, William E., ed. Historical Dictionary of the French Second Empire, 1852-1870. LC 84-8958. 928p. 1985. lib. bdg. 87.50 (ISBN 0-313-21136-1, EFE/). Greenwood.

Echau, Robustiano. Sketches of the Island of Negros. Hart, Donn V., tr. LC 78-13403. (Papers in International Series: Southeast Asia Ser.: No. 50). (Illus.). 1978. pap. 10.00x (ISBN 0-89680-070-9, 82-90512, Ohio U Ctr Intl). Ohio U Pr.

--Sketches of the Island of Negros. Hart, Donn V., tr. (Papers in International Studies, Southeast Asia Ser.: No. 50). pap. 45.80 (ISBN 0-317-09574-9, 2007466). Bks Demand UMI.

Echegaray, Hugo. The Practice of Jesus. O'Connell, Matthew J., tr. from Span. LC 83-19341. Orig. Title: La Practica de Jesus. 144p. (Orig.). 1984. pap. 7.95 (ISBN 0-88344-397-X). Orbis Bks.

Echelle, Anthony & Kornfield, Irv, eds. Evolution of Fish Species Flocks. LC 84-51502. 257p. 1984. 28.95 (ISBN 0-89101-058-0); pap. 20.95 (ISBN 0-89101-057-2). U Maine Orono.

Echert, Allan W. The Conquerors, Vol. 3. 928p. 1981. pap. text ed. 4.50 (ISBN 0-553-24647-X). Bantam.

Echeruo, M. J., ed. Igbo Traditional Life, Culture & Literature. Obiechina, E. N. (Africa in Transition Ser.). 1971. 17.50 (ISBN 0-914970-25-9); pap. 10.00 (ISBN 0-914970-27-5). Conch Mag.

Echeruo, Michael. Joyce Cary & the Novel of Africa. LC 72-76609. 200p. 1973. text ed. 19.50x (ISBN 0-8419-0131-7, Africana). Holmes & Meier.

Echeruo, Michael J. Victorian Lagos: Aspects of Nineteenth Century Lagos Life. (Illus.). 1978. text ed. 16.50x (ISBN 0-8419-5031-8). Holmes & Meier.

Echeruo, Michael J. C. Joyce Cary & the Dimensions of Order. 175p. 1979. text ed. 27.50x (ISBN 0-06-491875-0). B&N Imports.

Echevarria, Roberto G., ed. Hispanic Caribbean Literature: Special Issue. 272p. 1980. 11.95. Lat Am Lit Rev Pr.

Echevarria, Roberto G., ed. see Rojo, Antonio B.

Echeverria, Carlos F. Zuniga: An Album of His Sculpture. Zuniga, commentary by. (Illus.). 99.50 (ISBN 0-686-30118-8). Landmark NY.

Echeverria, Durand. The Maupeou Revolution: A Study in the History of Libertarianism, France, 1770-1774. LC 84-21327. 392p. 1985. text ed. 32.50x (ISBN 0-8071-1210-0). La State U Pr.

--Mirage in the West: A History of the French Image of American Society to 1815. 1966. lib. bdg. 24.00x (ISBN 0-374-92489-9). Octagon.

--Mirage in the West: A History of the French Image of American Society to 1815. LC 56-8379. 1957. pap. 10.95 (ISBN 0-691-00560-5). Princeton U Pr.

Echeverria, Edward J. Criticism & Commitment: Major Themes in Contemporary "Post-Critical" Philosophy. (Elementa Ser.: Vol. 20). 273p. 1981. pap. text ed. 28.25x (ISBN 90-6203-753-4, Pub. by Rodopi Holland). Humanities.

Echeverria, Luis, jt. ed. see Nicol, Davidson.

Echewa, T. Obinkaram. The Land's Lord. LC 76-18327. 160p. 1976. 6.50 (ISBN 0-88208-069-5); pap. 3.95 (ISBN 0-88208-070-9). Lawrence Hill.

Echezonam, Osodi E. Anioma's Attainment of Humanity. 104p. 1985. 7.00 (ISBN 0-682-49996-X). Exposition Pr FL.

Echkart, Meister, et al. Treatises & Sermons of Meister Eckhart. Clark, James M. & Skinner, John V., trs. from Ger. & Lat. 267p. 1983. Repr. of 1958 ed. lib. bdg. 21.00 (ISBN 0-88254-869-7). Octagon.

Echlin, Edward P. Deacon in the Church. LC 75-158571. 1971. 4.95 (ISBN 0-8189-0213-2). Alba.

Echlin, Patrick, ed. Analysis of Organic & Biological Surfaces. LC 83-23585. (Chemical Analysis of Monographs on Analytical Chemistry & Its Applications: 1-075). 672p. 1984. text ed. 75.00x (ISBN 0-471-86903-1, Pub. by Wiley Interscience). Wiley.

Echo Books, jt. auth. see Chen, Lydia.

Echols. Meatless Meals. 1983. write for info. (ISBN 0-8120-2163-0); pap. 9.95 (ISBN 0-8120-5523-3). Barron.

Echols, Allan. Saddle Wolves. Bd. with Killers Two. Orig. Title: Keep off My Ranch. 256p. 1973. pap. 0.95 (ISBN 0-532-50410-0, 532-95226-095). Woodhill.

Echols, Allan K. Dead Man's Range. 1979. pap. 1.25 (ISBN 0-8439-0636-7, Leisure Bks). Dorchester Pub Co.

Echols, Barbara E. Vegetarian Delights. LC 80-16610. 13.95 (ISBN 0-8120-5433-4). Barron.

Echols, Barbara E. & Arena, Jay M. The Common-Sense Guide to Good Eating. LC 77-862. 1978. pap. text ed. 6.95 (ISBN 0-8120-0791-3). Barron.

Echols, Eduardus C. Freddus Elephantus et Horatius Porcus Saltans Cincinnatis. 129p. (Lat.). 3.85 (ISBN 0-318-12452-1, 115). Amer Classical.

Echols, Edvardus C. Freddus Elephantus et Horatius Porcus Saltans Cincinnatis. 129p. (Orig., Latin.). (gr. 10-11). 1980. pap. text ed. 4.95x (ISBN 0-88334-139-5). Ind Sch Pr.

Echols, Edward. Voidism. 1981. pap. 3.00 (ISBN 0-682-49813-0). Exposition Pr FL.

Echols, Evaline. Climb up Through Your Valleys. 1980. 6.95 (ISBN 0-87148-174-X); pap. 5.95 (ISBN 0-87148-173-1). Pathway Pr.

Echols, Joan. A New Genus of Pennsylvanian Fish (Grossopterygii, Coelacanthiformes) from Kansas. (Museum Ser.: Vol. 12, No. 10). 27p. 1963. pap. 1.25 (ISBN 0-686-79815-5). U of KS Mus Nat Hist.

Echols, John, jt. ed. see Thung, Yvonne.

Echols, John M. Indonesian Writing in Translation. LC 56-59245. (Cornell University. Modern Indonesia Project. Translation Ser.). pap. 46.00 (ISBN 0-317-10138-2, 2010634). Bks Demand UMI.

--Preliminary Checklist of Indonesian Imprints During the Japanese Period: March 1942 - August 1945. 1963. pap. 1.50 (ISBN 0-87763-025-9). Cornell Mod Indo.

Echols, John M. & Shadily, Hassan. An English-Indonesian Dictionary. LC 72-5638. 660p. (Eng. & Indonesian.). 1975. 49.50x (ISBN 0-8014-0728-1); softcover 29.95x (ISBN 0-8014-9859-7). Cornell U Pr.

--An Indonesian-English Dictionary. 2nd ed. 431p. (Eng. & Indonesian.). 1963. 32.50x (ISBN 0-8014-0112-7). Cornell U Pr.

Echols, John M., ed. Preliminary Checklist of Indonesian Imprints (1945-1949) With Cornell University Holdings. 1965. pap. 3.50 (ISBN 0-87763-021-6). Cornell Mod Indo.

Echols, Margit. The Quilter's Start-to-Finish Workbook. (Illus.). 222p. 1983. pap. 8.17i (ISBN 0-06-463589-9, EH 589). B&N NY.

Echteracht, Arthur C. Middle American Lizards of the Genus Ameiva (Teidae) with Emphasis on Geographic Variation. (Miscellaneous Publications Ser.: No. 55). 86p. 1971. pap. 4.50 (ISBN 0-686-80353-1). U of KS Mus Nat Hist.

Echternacht, G. A Comparative Study of Secondary Schools with Different Score Patterns. 1977. 3.00 (ISBN 0-87447-019-6, 251712). College Bd.

Echternacht, G., jt. auth. see Donlon, T. A.

Echuari, Eustaquio. Vox-Diccionario Basico Latino-Espanol, Espanol-Latino. 8th ed. 830p. (Lat. & Span.). 1978. leatherette 9.95 (ISBN 84-7153-223-9, S-12396). French & Eur.

Eck, Alexandre. Moyen Age Russe. LC 74-149685. Repr. of 1933 ed. 22.00 (ISBN 0-404-02243-X). AMS Pr.

Eck, David J. Gauge-Natural Bundles & Generalized Gauge Theories. LC 81-12834. (Memoirs: No. 247). 50p. 1981. pap. 9.00 (ISBN 0-8218-2247-0). Am Math.

Eck, Diana L. Banaras: City of Light. LC 81-48134. (Illus.). 1982. 25.00 (ISBN 0-394-51971-X). Knopf.

--Banaras: City of Light. LC 82-48566. (Illus.). 446p. 1983. pap. 10.95 (ISBN 0-691-02023-X). Princeton U Pr.

--Darsan: Seeing the Divine Image in India. (Focus on Hinduism & Buddhism Ser.). 64p. 1981. pap. 3.00x. Anima Pubns.

Eck, Ellen, tr. from Eng. Himnos de la Vida Cristiana. 1980. 3.60 (ISBN 0-87509-277-2); pap. 2.25 (ISBN 0-87509-275-6); words & music 4.50. Chr Pubns.

Eck, Jeri, ed. see Yazzie, Alfred W.

Eck, John. Enchiridion of Commonplaces of John Eck. (Twin Brooks Ser.). pap. 9.95 (ISBN 0-8010-3352-7). Baker Bk.

Eck, John E., jt. auth. see Police Executive Research Forum.

Eck, Laurence, jt. auth. see Buzzard, Lynn R.

Eck, Margaret. Lest We Forget. 72p. pap. 0.75 (ISBN 0-686-29125-5); pap. 2.00 3 copies (ISBN 0-686-29126-3). Faith Pub Hse.

Eck, Norman. Contemporary Navajo Affairs. 243p. 1982. 15.00. Navajo Curr.

Eck, Paul & Childers, N. F., eds. Blueberry Culture. 1967. 27.50x (ISBN 0-8135-0535-6). Rutgers U Pr.

Eck, Paul & Childers, Norman F., eds. Blueberry Culture. 1966. 26.00 (ISBN 0-317-03719-6). Horticult Pubns.

Eckankar Studiengruppe Munchen, tr. see Twitchell, Paul.

Eckard, Eugenia. Teenage Patients of Family Planning Clinics: United States, 1978. Cox, Klaudia, ed. (Series Thirteen: No,. 57). 50p. 1981. pap. 1.75 (ISBN 0-686-73365-7). Natl Ctr Health Stats.

--Women Who Use Organized Family Planning Services: United States, 1979. Olmstead, Mary, ed. 55p. 1981. pap. text ed. 1.75 (ISBN 0-8406-0239-1). Natl Ctr Health Stats.

Eckard, Eugenia, jt. auth. see Foster, Jean.

Eckard, Helen M. Statistics of Public Libraries, 1974 (LIBGIS I) (Monograph No. 15). 88p. 1978. pap. 2.50x (ISBN 0-87845-063-7, NCES 77-200). U of Ill Lib Info Sci.

Eckard, Helen M., jt. ed. see Lynch, Mary Jo.

Eckard, Ronald D. & Kearny, Mary Ann. Teaching Conversation Skills in ESL. LC 81-38550. (Language in Education Ser.: No. 38). 55p. 1981. pap. 3.95x (ISBN 0-15-599059-4). Ctr Appl Ling.

Eckardt, A. R., ed. Your People, My People: The Meeting of Jews & Christians. 212p. 7.95 (ISBN 0-686-95188-3). ADL.

Eckardt, A. Roy. Elder & Younger Brothers: The Encounter of Jews & Christians. LC 67-23687. (Illus.). 216p. 1973. pap. 4.95 (ISBN 0-8052-0379-6). Schocken.

Eckardt, A. Roy & Eckardt, Alice L. Long Night's Journey into Day - Life & Faith After the Holocaust. LC 81-14788. 206p. 1982. 16.50 (ISBN 0-8143-1692-1). Wayne St U Pr.

Eckardt, Alice L., jt. auth. see Eckardt, A. Roy.

Eckardt, Wolf Von see Von Eckardt, Wolf.

Eckardt, Wolf von see Von Eckardt, Wolf.

Eckart, J., ed. Kritische Bewertung aktueller Therapiemassnahmen in der Intensivmedizin. (Beitraege zur Intensiv-und Notfallmedizin: Vol. 2). (Illus.). viii, 300p. 1984. pap. 42.75 (ISBN 3-8055-3763-8). S Karger.

--Parenterale Ernaehrung Unter Besonderer Beruecksichtigung der Fettzufuhr, Vol. 13. (Beitraege zu Infusionstherapie und Klinisch Ernaehrung). (Illus.). viii, 192p. 1985. 24.75 (ISBN 3-8055-4164-3). S Karger.

Eckart, L. E., jt. auth. see Weisman, Joel.

Eckart, Richard, ed. see Von Buelow, Hans.

Eckart, Wolfgang. Der Boden Als Anlageobjekt und Produktionsfaktor. (European University Studies: No. 5, Vol 385). 173p. (Ger.). 1982. 21.05 (ISBN 3-8204-7222-3). P Lang Pubs.

Eckartsberg, Rolf Von, jt. ed. see Valle, Ronald S.

Eckblad, Gudrun. Scheme Theory: A Conceptual Framework for Cognitive Motivational Processes. 1981. 35.00 (ISBN 0-12-229550-1). Acad Pr.

Eckblad, James W. Laboratory Manual of Aquatic Biology. 210p. 1978. write for info. wire coil (ISBN 0-697-04627-3). Wm C Brown.

Eckbo, Garrett. Home Landscape: The Art of Home Landscaping. rev. & enl. ed. (Illus.). 1978. 29.50 (ISBN 0-07-018879-3). McGraw.

--Public Landscape: Six Essays on Government & Environmental Design in the San Francisco Bay Area. LC 77-15997. (Illus.). 1978. pap. 7.75x (ISBN 0-87772-249-8). Inst Gov Stud Berk.

--Urban Landscape Design. (Illus.). 1964. 41.50 (ISBN 0-07-018880-7). McGraw.

Eckbo, Paul L. The Future of World Oil. LC 76-16809. 160p. 1976. prof ref 29.95x (ISBN 0-88410-455-9). Ballinger Pub.

Eckbreth, A. C. Spatially Precise Laser Diagnostics for Combustion Temperature & Species. (Energy & Engineering Science Ser.). 1985. 35.00 (ISBN 0-9961006-6-0, Pub. by Abacus England). Heyden.

Ecke, Gustav. Chinese Domestic Furniture. LC 62-21540. (Illus.). 1962. boxed 59.50 (ISBN 0-8048-0098-7). C E Tuttle.

--Chinese Painting in Hawaii: In the Honolulu Academy of Arts & in Private Collections, 3 vols. (Illus.). 425p. 1965. Set. boxed 250.00 (ISBN 0-87022-205-8). UH Pr.

Ecke, Tseng Yu-Ho. Chinese Folk Art. (Illus.). 176p. 1977. pap. text ed. 15.00x (ISBN 0-8248-0572-0). UH Pr.

Ecke, Wolfgan. The Midnight Chess Game. (Illus.). 144p. (gr. 5 up). 1985. 10.95 (ISBN 0-13-582826-0). P-H.

Ecke, Wolfgang. The Bank Holdup. (Illus.). 144p. (gr. 5-9). 1982. 9.95 (ISBN 0-13-056168-1). P-H.

--The Bank Holdup. (Illus.). 144p. (gr. 3-7). 1985. pap. 5.95 (ISBN 0-13-056474-5). P-H.

--The Castle of the Red Gorillas. LC 82-23122. (Illus.). 120p. (gr. 5-9). 1983. PLB 9.95 (ISBN 0-13-120360-6). P-H.

--The Face at the Window. LC 79-15628. (Illus.). (gr. 5-9). 1979. 7.95 (ISBN 0-13-299115-2). P-H.

--The Face at the Window. (Illus.). 128p. (gr. 5-9). 1983. pap. 4.95 (ISBN 0-13-299081-4, Pub. by Treehouse Bks). P-H.

--The Invisible Witness. (Illus.). (gr. 5-9). 1981. 9.95 (ISBN 0-13-505529-6). P-H.

--The Stolen Paintings. (Illus.). (gr. 5-9). 1981. 7.95 (ISBN 0-13-846865-6). P-H.

--The Stolen Paintings. (Illus.). 144p. (gr. 5up). 1985. pap. 5.95 (ISBN 0-13-846916-4). P-H.

Eckel, Denis & Manfred, Hofer. Dictionnaire Allemand-Francais et Francais-Allemand. 1324p. (Fr. & Ger.). 1970. 25.95 (ISBN 0-686-57131-2, M-6184). French & Eur.

Eckel, Edwin B. The Geological Society of America: Life History of a Learned Society. LC 82-15412. (Memoir Ser.: No. 155). (Illus.). 1982. 24.50 (ISBN 0-8137-1155-X). Geol Soc.

Eckel, John C. The First Editions of the Writings of Charles Dickens. LC 72-2098. (Studies in Dickens, No. 52). 1972. Repr. of 1932 ed. lib. bdg. 75.00x (ISBN 0-8383-1488-0). Haskell.

--The First Editions of the Writings of Charles Dickens & Their Values. LC 73-20323. Repr. of 1913 ed. lib. bdg. 35.00 (ISBN 0-8414-3924-9). Folcroft.

Eckel, Peter J. College & University Foodservice Management Standards. (L. J. Minor Foodservice Standards Ser.: Vol. 6). (Illus.). 1985. text ed. 19.50 (ISBN 0-87055-480-8). AVI.

Eckelman, W. C., ed. Receptor Binding Radiotracers, Vol. I. 200p. 1982. 59.00 (ISBN 0-8493-6019-6). CRC Pr.

--Receptor Binding Radiotracers, Vol. II. 248p. 1982. 69.50 (ISBN 0-8493-6020-X). CRC Pr.

--Technetium Ninety-Nine-M: Generators, Chemistry, & Preparation of Radiopharmaceuticals. (Illus.). 168p. 1983. 25.00 (ISBN 0-08-029144-9). Pergamon.

Eckelman, W. C., jt. ed. see Lambrecht, R. M.

Eckelmann, Herman J., Jr., jt. auth. see Newman, Robert C.

Eckelmeyer, Judith A., tr. The Magic Flute: Seventeen Ninety-One Libretto by Emanuel Schikaneder. LC 79-67268. xxix, 65p. 1980. 11.95x (ISBN 0-88946-955-5). E Mellen.

Eckener, Hugo. My Zeppelins. Gilbert, James, ed. Robinson, Douglas, tr. LC 79-7250. (Flight: Its First Seventy-Five Years Ser.). (Illus.). 1979. Repr. of 1958 ed. lib. bdg. 21.00x (ISBN 0-405-12162-8). Ayer Co Pubs.

Eckenfelder see Jenkins, S. H.

Eckenfelder, W. & Santhanam, C., eds. Sludge Treatment. (Pollution, Engineering & Technology Ser.: Vol. 14). 1981. 85.00 (ISBN 0-8247-6977-5). Dekker.

Eckenfelder, W. W. & Englander, A. J. Effluent Variability from Waste Water Treatment Processes & Its Control. 1976. pap. 50.00 (ISBN 0-08-019843-0). Pergamon.

Eckenfelder, W. W. & Ford, D. Water Pollution Control. (Illus.). 17.50 (ISBN 0-8363-0099-8). Jenkins.

Eckenfelder, W. Wesley see Curi, K.

Eckenfelder, Walter W. Principles of Water Quality Management. LC 79-20509. (Illus.). 704p. 1980. 34.95 (ISBN 0-8436-0338-0). Van Nos Reinhold.

Eckenfielder, W. W., jt. ed. see Thackston, Edward L.

Eckenhoff, James E. Controversies in Anesthesiology. (Illus.). 312p. 1979. 33.95 (ISBN 0-7216-3322-6). Saunders.

Eckenhoff, James E., ed. Year Book of Anesthesia, 1981. 1981. 42.95 (ISBN 0-8151-3041-4). Year Bk Med.

Eckenrod, James S. Who Controls the Controllers? A Case Study of Political Behavior. Fraenkel, Jack R., ed. (Crucial Issues in American Government Ser.). (gr. 9-12). 1976. pap. text ed. 7.64 (ISBN 0-205-04908-7, 7649088). Allyn.

Eckenrode, H. J. & Edmunds, Pocahontas W. E. H. Harriman: The Little Giant of Wall Street. Bruchey, Stuart, ed. LC 80-1304. (Railroads Ser.). 1981. Repr. of 1933 ed. lib. bdg. 22.00x (ISBN 0-405-13773-7). Ayer Co Pubs.

Eckenrode, Hamilton J. Jefferson Davis, President of the South. facsimile ed. LC 78-165627. (Select Bibliographies Reprint Ser). Repr. of 1923 ed. 23.50 (ISBN 0-8369-5934-5). Ayer Co Pubs.

--Jefferson Davis: President of the South. 59.95 (ISBN 0-8490-0440-3). Gordon Pr.

--List of the Colonial Soldiers of Virginia. LC 62-51491. 91p. 1984. pap. 5.00 (ISBN 0-8063-0099-X). Genealog Pub.

--The Political History of Virginia During the Reconstruction. LC 78-63902. (Johns Hopkins University. Studies in the Social Sciences. Twenty-Second Ser. 1904: 6-8). Repr. of 1904 ed. 16.50 (ISBN 0-404-61155-9). AMS Pr.

--The Political History of Virginia During the Reconstruction. facsimile ed. LC 76-164387. (Black Heritage Library Collection Ser.). Repr. of 1904 ed. 16.50 (ISBN 0-8369-8846-9). Ayer Co Pubs.

--Revolution in Virginia. 311p. 1964. Repr. of 1916 ed. 18.50 (ISBN 0-208-00525-0, Archon). Shoe String.

--Separation of Church & State in Virginia. LC 75-122164. (Civil Liberties in American History Ser). 1971. Repr. of 1910 ed. lib. bdg. 22.50 (ISBN 0-306-71969-X). Da Capo.

Eckensberger, Lutz H., et al, eds. Cross-Cultural Contributions to Psychology: Selected Papers from the 4th International Conference of the International Association for Cross-Cultural Psychology, Munich, July 28-August 5, 1978. 442p. 1979. pap. text ed. 22.25 (ISBN 90-265-0300-8, Pub. by Swets & Zeitlinger). Hogrefe Intl.

Eckenstein, Lina. Comparative Studies in Nursery Rhymes. LC 68-23469. 1968. Repr. of 1906 ed. 30.00x (ISBN 0-8103-3479-8). Gale.

--Comparative Studies in Nursery Rhymes. 59.95 (ISBN 0-87968-912-9). Gordon Pr.

--A History of the Sinai. LC 78-63461. (The Crusades & Military Orders: Second Ser.). Repr. of 1921 ed. 22.50 (ISBN 0-404-16533-8). AMS Pr.

--A Spell of Words. 59.95 (ISBN 0-8490-1109-4). Gordon Pr.

--Spell of Words: Studies in Language Bearing on Custom. LC 68-23153. 1969. Repr. of 1932 ed. 30.00x (ISBN 0-8103-3892-0). Gale.

--Spell of Words: Studies in Language Bearing on Custom. 1932. 8.25 (ISBN 0-8274-3491-X). R West.

--Woman Under Monasticism. 59.95 (ISBN 0-8490-1318-6). Gordon Pr.

--Woman Under Monasticism: Chapters on Saint-Lore & Convent Life Between A. D. 500 & A. D. 1500. LC 63-11028. 1963. Repr. of 1896 ed. 10.00x (ISBN 0-8462-0363-4). Russell.

Ecker. The Anatomy of the Frog. Haslam, G., tr. from Ger. 1971. 36.80 (ISBN 90-6123-240-6). Lubrecht & Cramer.

Ecker, B. A. Independence Day. 208p. (YA) pap. 2.25 (ISBN 0-380-82990-8, 82990-8, Flare). Avon.

Ecker, Gunter. Theory of Fully Ionized Plasmas. 1972. 76.00 (ISBN 0-12-229750-4). Acad Pr.

Ecker, Richard E. Staying Well. LC 84-4664. 132p. (Orig.). 1984. pap. 4.95 (ISBN 0-87784-967-6). Inter-Varsity.

--The Stress Myth. LC 85-220. 132p. (Orig.). 1985. pap. 4.95 (ISBN 0-87784-330-9). Inter-Varsity.

Ecker, Tom. Track & Field: Technique Through Dynamics. LC 76-3956. (Illus.). 1976. pap. 6.50 (ISBN 0-911520-70-8). Tafnews.

Ecker, Tom & King, Don. Athletic Journal's Encyclopedia of Basketball. LC 82-14373. 214p. 1983. 15.95 (ISBN 0-13-049882-3, Parker). P-H.

Ecker, Tom, et al. Championship Track & Field for Women. (Illus.). 1978. 17.50 (ISBN 0-13-127845-2, Parker). P-H.

Eckerlin, H. & Boyers, A. Energy-Conservation Opportunities in the Small Industrial Plant. Gyftopoulos, Elias P. & Cohen, Karen C., eds. (Industrial Energy-Conservation Manuals Ser.: No. 5). 96p. 1982. loose-leaf 20.00x (ISBN 0-262-05025-0). MIT Pr.

Eckerlin, P. see Hellwege, K. H.

Eckermann, R., ed. see Gmehling, J., et al.

Eckermann, R., ed. see Gmehling, J. & Onken, U.

Eckermann, R., ed. see Knapp, H. & Doring, R.

Eckermann, R., ed. see Sorensen, J. M. & Arlt, W.

Eckermann, Reiner, ed. see Gmehling, J., et al.

Eckermann, Reiner, ed. see Sorenson, J. M. & Arlt, W.

Eckermann, Willigis. Der Physikkommentar Hugolins von Orvieto Oesa: Ein Beitrag zur Erkenntnislehre des spaetmittelalterlichen Augustinismus. (Spaetmittelalter und Reformation, Vol. 5). 160p. 1972. 23.60x (ISBN 3-11-003714-9). De Gruyter.

Eckern, Gilbert & Hardin, Walt. The Ten-Key Touch System on Electronic Calculators: With Business & Industry Applications. (Illus.). 240p. 1983. pap. text ed. 15.95 (ISBN 0-89863-074-6). Star Pub CA.

Eckern, U., et al. Proceedings of the Seventeenth International Conference on Low Temperature Physics, Pts. I & II. Date not set. Set. write for info. (ISBN 0-444-86910-7). Elsevier.

Ecker-Racz, L. Laszlo. It's Your Business: State & Local Finance. 160p. 1976. 2.50 (ISBN 0-318-15804-3). Citizens Forum Gov.

Eckersley, A. P., jt. auth. see Marshall, S. G.

Eckert, Allan. The Frontiersman. 768p. 1980. pap. 4.50 (ISBN 0-553-25036-1). Bantam.

--Whattizit? Nature Pun Quizzes. (Illus.). 48p. (Orig.). 1981. pap. 2.95 (ISBN 0-913428-30-2). Landfall Pr.

--The Wilderness War. LC 78-14862. 1978. 22.00i (ISBN 0-316-20875-2). Little.

Eckert, Allan W. Blue Jacket: War Chief of Shawnees. 177p. (gr. 7 up). 1983. pap. 4.95 (ISBN 0-913428-36-1). Landfall Pr.

--Blue Jacket: War Chief of the Shawnees. LC 69-10656. (Illus.). (gr. 7 up). 1969. 13.45i (ISBN 0-316-20863-9). Little.

--The Conquerors. (The Winning of America Ser.). 1971. 22.00i (ISBN 0-316-20865-5). Little.

--The Dark Green Tunnel. LC 83-12078. (Illus.). 256p. (gr. 7up). 1984. 13.45i (ISBN 0-316-20881-7). Little.

--The Frontiersmen. (The Winning of America Ser.). 1967. 22.00 (ISBN 0-316-20856-6). Little.

--Gateway to Empire. 1982. 22.00i (ISBN 0-316-20861-2). Little.

--Gateway to Empire. 832p. (Orig.). 1984. pap. 4.50 (ISBN 0-553-24118-4). Bantam.

--The Hab Theory. 576p. 1976. 9.95 (ISBN 0-316-20859-0). Little.

--Incident at Hawk's Hill. (Illus.). 173p. (gr. 7 up). 1971. 14.45i (ISBN 0-316-20866-3). Little.

--Johnny Logan: Shawnee Spy. 192p. 1983. 12.45i (ISBN 0-316-20880-9). Little.

--The Scarlet Mansion. 480p. 1985. 19.45i (ISBN 0-316-20883-3). Little.

--The Silent Sky: The Incredible Extinction of the Passenger Pigeon. LC 65-20745. 244p. 1973. pap. 4.95 (ISBN 0-913428-15-9). Landfall Pr.

--Song of the Wild. 252p. 1980. 10.95 (ISBN 0-316-20877-9). Little.

--A Time of Terror: The Great Dayton Flood. LC 65-12444. (Illus.). 341p. 1981. Repr. of 1965 ed. 9.95 (ISBN 0-913428-02-7). Landfall Pr.

--The Wand. (Illus.). 256p. (gr. 3-7). 1985. 13.95 (ISBN 0-316-20882-5). Little.

--Wild Season. LC 67-14449. (Illus.). 256p. 1981. 9.95 (ISBN 0-913428-32-9); pap. 4.95 (ISBN 0-913428-31-0). Landfall Pr.

--Wilderness Empire. LC 69-16974. (The Winning of America Ser.). (Illus.). 1969. 22.00 (ISBN 0-316-20864-7). Little.

Eckert, Allan W., jt. auth. see Karalus, Karl E.

Eckert, Allen. Incident at Hawk's Hill. 192p. (gr. 7 up). 1972. pap. 2.50 (ISBN 0-440-94020-6, LFL). Dell.

Eckert, Allen W. Savage Journey. LC 79-13646. 1979. 10.95 (ISBN 0-316-20876-0). Little.

--Wilderness Empire Seventeen Fifty-Five. 768p. 1980. pap. 4.50 (ISBN 0-553-25208-9). Bantam.

Eckert, Charles. Emergency Room Care. 4th ed. 1981. pap. text ed. 22.95 (ISBN 0-316-20878-7). Little.

Eckert, E. R. & Irvine, T. F., Jr. Heat Transfer Reviews, Nineteen Seventy to Nineteen Seventy-One. 42.00 (ISBN 0-08-021737-0). Pergamon.

Eckert, Ernest R. & Drake, R. M. Analysis of Heat & Mass Transfer. LC 73-159305. (Mechanical Engineering Ser). (Illus.). 832p. 1971. text ed. 54.00 (ISBN 0-07-018925-0). McGraw.

Eckert, Georg, ed. Wilhelm Liebknechts Briefwechsel Mit Karl Marx & Friedrich Engels. (Quellen & Untersuchungen Zur Geschichte der Deutschen & Oesterreichischen Arbeiterbewegung: No. 5). (Illus.). 1963. 51.20x (ISBN 90-2790-154-6). Mouton.

Eckert, H., jt. ed. see Usdin, E.

Eckert, H. U., ed. see Donski, A. V., et al.

Eckert, Helen M., jt. auth. see Espenschade, Anna S.

Eckert, Helen M. & Montoye, Henry J., eds. Exercise & Health. (American Academy of Physical Education Papers: No. 17). 160p. 1984. pap. text ed. 12.00x (ISBN 0-931250-56-0, BECK0056). Human Kinetics.

Eckert, Helen M., jt. ed. see Clarke, David H.

Eckert, J., et al, eds. Echinococcosis-Hydatidosis Surveillance, Prevention & Control: FAO-UNEP-WHO Guidelines. Gemmell, M. & Soulsby, E. (Animal Production & Health Papers: No. 29). 157p. 1982. pap. 11.50 (ISBN 92-5-101205-9, F2343, FAO). Unipub.

Eckert, J. E., jt. auth. see Laidlaw, Harry H., Jr.

Eckert, J. Kevin. The Unseen Elderly. (Illus.). 243p. (Orig.). 1981. 16.00 (ISBN 0-916304-47-7); pap. 6.00 (ISBN 0-916304-45-0). SDSU Press.

Eckert, John E. & Shaw, Frank R. Beekeeping. (Illus.). 1960. 19.95 (ISBN 0-02-534910-4). Macmillan.

Eckert, Lee A., et al. Small Business: An Entrepreneur's Plan. 434p. 1985. pap. text ed. 22.95 (ISBN 0-15-581220-3, HC); instr's manual avail. (ISBN 0-15-581221-1). HarBraceJ.

Eckert, Mark, jt. auth. see Calzonetti, Frank J.

Eckert, Martin D. & Bramesco, Norton J. Radiation: All You Need to Know to Stop Worrying...or Start. LC 80-6137. (Illus.). 256p. (Orig.). 1981. pap. 4.95 (ISBN 0-394-74650-3, V-650, Vin). Random.

Eckert, Robert P. Edward Thomas: A Biography & a Bibliography. LC 78-2619. 1937. 30.00 (ISBN 0-8414-4040-9). Folcroft.

--Edward Thomas: A Biography & a Bibliography. 328p. 1980. Repr. of 1937 ed. lib. bdg. 35.00 (ISBN 0-8482-0718-1). Norwood Edns.

Eckert, Roger. Animal Physiology. LC 77-6648. (Biology Ser.). (Illus.). 558p. 1978. text ed. 30.95 (ISBN 0-7167-0570-2). W H Freeman.

Eckert, Roger & Randall, David. Animal Physiology. 2nd ed. LC 82-18372. (Illus.). 830p. 1983. text ed. 32.95 (ISBN 0-7167-1423-X). W H Freeman.

Eckert, Ross D. The Enclosure of Ocean Resources: Economics & the Law of the Sea. LC 78-70388. (Publications Ser.: No. 210). (Illus.). 1979. 16.95x (ISBN 0-8179-7101-7). Hoover Inst Pr.

Eckert, Sidney W., jt. auth. see Garman, E. Thomas.

Eckert, W. J. Punched Card Methods in Scientific Computation. 1984. 25.00x (ISBN 0-262-05030-7). MIT Pr.

Eckert, William G. Introduction to Forensic Sciences. LC 80-10864. (Illus.). 240p. 1980. pap. text ed. 15.95 (ISBN 0-8016-1489-9). Mosby.

Eckertova, Ludmila. Physics of Thin Films. LC 76-12177. 254p. 1977. 32.50x (ISBN 0-306-30910-6, Plenum Pr). Plenum Pub.

Eckes, Alfred E., Jr. A Search for Solvency: Bretton Woods & the International Monetary System, 1941-1971. LC 75-14433. 369p. 1975. 20.00x (ISBN 0-292-70712-6). U of Tex Pr.

--The United States & the Global Struggle for Minerals. LC 78-11082. 365p. 1979. text ed. 20.00x (ISBN 0-292-78506-2); pap. 9.95x (ISBN 0-292-78511-9). U of Tex Pr.

Eckes, Alfred E., Jr., jt. auth. see Roseboom, Eugene H.

Eckey, Lorelei, et al. One Thousand-One Broadways: Hometown Talent on Stage. 160p. 1982. 12.95 (ISBN 0-8138-1284-4). Iowa St U Pr.

Eckhard, Jacob. Jacob Eckhard's Choirmaster's Book of 1809. Williams, George W., ed. LC 72-149489. (Illus.). xiv, 128p. 1971. 29.95x (ISBN 0-87249-215-X). U of SC Pr.

Eckhardt, August G. Meeting the Educational Needs of the Newly Admitted Lawyer: A Proposal for General Practice Courses. 119p. 1968. pap. 6.75 (ISBN 0-317-32240-0, B205). Am Law Inst.

Eckhardt, August G. & Stumpf, Felix F. A Model for Contiuing Legal Education: Structure, Methods & Curriculum. 399p. 1980. pap. 25.00 (ISBN 0-317-32242-7, B222). Am Law Inst.

Eckhardt, August G., ed. Meeting the Educational Needs of the Newly Admitted Lawyer - A Proposal for General Practice Courses: No. B205. 119p. 1968. pap. 2.31 (ISBN 0-317-30844-0). Am LaW Inst.

Eckhardt, August G. & Stumpf, Felix F., eds. A Model for Continuing Legal Education: Structure, Methods, & Curriculum: No. B222. 399p. 1980. pap. 25.00 (ISBN 0-317-30828-9). Am Law Inst.

Eckhardt, Bob & Black, Charles. The Tides of Power: Conversations on the American Constitution. LC 75-32630. 250p. 1976. 24.50x (ISBN 0-300-01974-2). Yale U Pr.

Eckhardt, C. C., tr. see Schirmacher, Kaethe.

Eckhardt, Carl C., tr. see Schirmacher, K.

Eckhardt, Caroline D., ed. Essays in the Numerical Criticism of Medieval Literature. LC 76-55822. (Illus.). 240p. 1979. 24.50 (ISBN 0-8387-2019-6). Bucknell U Pr.

--The Prophetia Merlini of Geoffrey of Monmouth: A Fifteenth Century English Commentary. 1983. 12.50X (ISBN 0-910956-73-1, SAM-8); pap. 5.00x (ISBN 0-910956-74-X). Medieval Acad.

Eckhardt, Caroline D., et al. The Wiley Reader: Designs for Writing. LC 75-29499. 1976. pap. 15.75x (ISBN 0-673-15668-0). Scott F.

Eckhardt, Celia M. Fanny Wright: Rebel in America. (Illus.). 352p. 1984. 22.50 (ISBN 0-674-29435-1). Harvard U Pr.

Eckhardt, E. Die Dialekt und Auslandertypen des Alteren Englischen Dramas, Part 2: Die Auslandertypen. (Material for the Study of the Old English Drama Ser.: No. 1, Vol. 32). pap. 21.00 (ISBN 0-317-15673-X). Kraus Repr.

Eckhardt, Fred. A Treatise on Lager Beers: How to Make Good Beer at Home. 7th ed. (Illus.). 1983. pap. 2.95 (ISBN 0-9606302-3-6). F Eckhardt Assocs.

Eckhardt, Fred & Takita, Itsuo. The Good Taste of Beer. rev. ed. 1984. pap. 2.75 (ISBN 0-9606302-5-2). F Eckhardt Assocs.

Eckhardt, George H. Electronic Television. LC 74-4674. (Telecommunications Ser). (Illus.). 188p. 1974. Repr. of 1936 ed. 15.00x (ISBN 0-405-06040-8). Ayer Co Pubs.

Eckhardt, Linda W. An American Gumbo. 272p. 1983. 12.95 (ISBN 0-932012-60-4). Texas Month Pr.

--The New West Coast Cuisine. LC 85-9785. (Illus.). 208p. 1985. 16.95 (ISBN 0-87477-358-X); pap. 9.95 (ISBN 0-87477-359-8). J P Tarcher.

--The Only Texas Cookbook. Rodriguez, Barbara, ed. 256p. 1982. 15.95 (ISBN 0-932012-19-1). Texas Month Pr.

Eckhardt, Richard A., et al, eds. The IBM PC Enhancement Handbook for Scientists & Engineers. (The IBM PC Enhancement Handbook: Vol. 1, No. 2). (Illus.). 196p. (Orig.). 1985. pap. 18.95 (ISBN 0-931193-00-1). Cyber Res Inc.

Eckhardt, Robert B. The Study of Human Evolution. (Illus.). 1979. text ed. 39.95 (ISBN 0-07-018902-1). McGraw.

Eckhardt, S. Hungarian-French Concise Dictionary. 1092p. (Hungarian & Fr.). 1973. leatherette 39.95 (ISBN 0-686-92492-4, M-9324). French & Eur.

Eckhardt, S., jt. ed. see Mihich, E.

Eckhardt, S., jt. ed. see Napalkov, N. P.

Eckhardt, William. Compassion Manual. 1979. pap. 4.00 (ISBN 0-318-01700-8). Peace Res Lab.

--Compassion: Toward A Science of Value. 1972. 12.00 (ISBN 0-318-01696-6); pap. 6.00 (ISBN 0-318-01697-4). Peace Res Lab.

--Ideology & Personality in Social Attitudes. 1969. pap. 5.00 (ISBN 0-318-03979-6). Peace Res Lab.

--Pioneers of Peace Research. 1983. 25.00 (ISBN 0-318-01702-4). Peace Res Lab.

Eckhardt, William & Lentz, Theo F. Factors of War-Peace Attitudes. pap. 5.00 (ISBN 0-318-01701-6). Peace Res Lab.

Eckhardt, William & Young, Christopher. Governments Under Fire: Civil Conflict & Imperialism. LC 76-51701. (Comparative Studies Ser.). 379p. 1977. 19.00x (ISBN 0-87536-335-0); pap. 9.50x (ISBN 0-87536-336-9). HRAFP.

--Governments Under Fire: Civil Conflict & Imperialism. 1977. 19.00 (ISBN 0-318-01698-2); pap. 9.50 (ISBN 0-318-01699-0). Peace Res Lab.

Eckhart, J., ed. Sepsis unter besonderer Beruecksichtigung der Ernaehrungsprobleme. (Beitraege zu Infusionstherapie und klinische Ernaehrung: Vol. 10). (Illus.). viii, 208p. 1983. pap. 21.50 (ISBN 3-8055-3677-1). S Karger.

Eckhart, Karl A., ed. see Von Amira, Karl.

Eckhart, Meister. Meister Eckhart: A Modern Translation. pap. 7.95xi (ISBN 0-06-130008-X, TB8, Torch). Har-Row.

--Meister Eckhart: Mystic & Philosopher. Schurmann, Reiner, tr. LC 76-26416. (Studies in Phenomenology & Existential Philosophy Ser.). 320p. 1978. 22.50x (ISBN 0-253-35183-9). Ind U Pr.

Eckhaus, Viktor. Studies in Non-Linear Stability Theory. (Springer Tracts in Natural Philosophy: Vol. 6). (Illus.). 1965. 19.00 (ISBN 0-387-03407-2). Springer-Verlag.

Eckhaus, W. Asymptotic Analysis of Singular Perturbations. (Studies in Mathematics & Its Applications: Vol. 9). 286p. 1979. 59.75 (ISBN 0-444-85306-5, North Holland). Elsevier.

--New Developments in Differential Equations: Proceedings of the Scheveningen Conference, 2nd, the Netherlands, 1975. (North Holland Mathematics Studies: Vol. 21). 348p. 1976. 47.00 (ISBN 0-444-11107-7, North-Holland). Elsevier.

Eckhaus, W. & Van Harten, A. The Inverse Scattering Transformation & the Theory of Solitons: An Introduction. (North Holland Mathematics Studies: Vol. 50). 222p. 1981. 40.50 (ISBN 0-444-86166-1, North-Holland). Elsevier.

Eckhaus, W. & De Jager, E. M., eds. Theory & Applications of Singular Perturbations, Oberwolfach, Germany 1981: Proceedings. (Lecture Note in Mathematics: Vol. 942). 372p. 1982. pap. 21.00 (ISBN 0-387-11584-6). Springer-Verlag.

Eckhaus, Wiktor. Matched Asymptotic Expansions & Singular Perturbations. LC 72-96145. (Mathematics Studies: Vol. 6). 146p. 1973. pap. text ed. 36.25 (ISBN 0-7204-2606-5, North-Holland). Elsevier.

Eckhoff, Lorentz. Shakespeare: Spokesman of the Third Estate. 1978. Repr. of 1954 ed. lib. bdg. 25.00 (ISBN 0-8495-1323-5). Arden Lib.

--Shakespeare: Spokesman of the Third Estate. LC 72-195017. 1954. lib. bdg. 17.50 (ISBN 0-8414-3884-6). Folcroft.

Eckhoff, Lorentz J. Shakespeare: Spokesman of the Third Estate. LC 71-164750. Repr. of 1954 ed. 16.00 (ISBN 0-404-02244-8). AMS Pr.

Eckholm, Erik. Cutting Tobacco's Toll. LC 78-53446. (Worldwatch Papers). 1978. pap. 4.00 (ISBN 0-916468-17-8). Worldwatch Inst.

--Disappearing Species: The Social Challenge. LC 78-66428. (Worldwatch Papers). 1978. pap. 2.00 (ISBN 0-916468-21-6). Worldwatch Inst.

--The Dispossessed of the Earth: Land Reform & Sustainable Development. LC 79-65740. (Worldwatch Papers). 1979. pap. 2.00 (ISBN 0-916468-29-1). Worldwatch Inst.

--Planting for the Future: Forestry for Human Needs. LC 79-62890. (Worldwatch Papers). 1979. pap. 2.00 (ISBN 0-916468-25-9). Worldwatch Inst.

Eckholm, Erik & Brown, Lester R. Spreading Deserts: The Hand of Man. LC 77-81479. (Institute Papers). 1977. pap. 2.00 (ISBN 0-916468-12-7). Worldwatch Inst.

Eckholm, Erik & Newland, Kathleen. Health: The Family Planning Factor. LC 76-52228. (Worldwatch Papers). 1977. pap. 2.00 (ISBN 0-916468-09-7). Worldwatch Inst.

Eckholm, Erik P. Down to Earth: Environment & Human Needs. 220p. 1982. 14.95 (ISBN 0-393-01600-5). Norton.

--Losing Ground: Environmental Stress & World Food Prospects. 223p. 1976. pap. avail.; pap. text ed. 6.95x (ISBN 0-393-09167-8). Norton.

--The Other Energy Crisis: Firewood. (Worldwatch Papers). 1975. pap. 2.00 (ISBN 0-916468-00-3). Worldwatch Inst.

--The Picture of Health: Environmental Sources of Disease. 1977. pap. 5.95 (ISBN 0-393-06440-9). Norton.

Eckholm, Erik P. & Record, Francis. The Two Faces of Malnutrition. LC 76-47787. (Worldwatch Papers). 1976. pap. 2.00 (ISBN 0-916468-08-9). Worldwatch Inst.

Eckholm, Erik P., jt. auth. see Brown, Lester R.

Eckholm, Erik P., ed. Down to Earth: Environment & Human Needs. 256p. 1983. pap. 5.95 (ISBN 0-393-30040-4). Norton.

Eckhouse, Morris. Day-by-Day in Cleveland Browns History. LC 83-80701. (Illus.). 352p. (Orig.). 1984. pap. 14.95 (ISBN 0-88011-189-5). Leisure Pr.

--Day-by-Day in Cleveland Indians History. LC 82-83939. (Illus.). 300p. (Orig.). 1983. pap. 14.95 (ISBN 0-88011-107-0). Leisure Pr.

Eckhouse, Morris & Mastrocola, Carl. This Date in Pittsburgh Pirates History. LC 79-3801. (This Date Ser.). (Illus.). 1980. pap. 9.95 (ISBN 0-8128-6052-7). Stein & Day.

Eckhouse, Richard H., jt. auth. see Levy, Henry M.

Eckhouse, Richard H., jt. auth. see Murdick, Robert G.

Eckhouse, Richard H., Jr. & Morrison, L. Robert. Minicomputer Systems: Organization, Programming & Applications (PDP-11) 2nd ed. (Illus.). 1979. text ed. 37.50 (ISBN 0-13-583914-9). P-H.

Ecklein, Joan. Community Organizers. 2nd ed. LC 83-25899. 271p. (Orig.). 1984. pap. text ed. 15.95 (ISBN 0-471-08922-2). Wiley.

Eckler, A. Ross. Word Recreations: Games & Diversions from Word Ways. LC 79-51884. (Orig.). 1980. pap. 4.95 (ISBN 0-486-23854-7). Dover.

Eckler, A. Ross, ed. Names & Games. (The International Library of Names). 400p. 1985. text ed. 29.50x (ISBN 0-8290-1219-2). Irvington.

Eckler-Scalese, Molly, tr. see O'Hara, William F., Jr.

Eckles, Georgiana. Gold Diggers, Sex Junkies, Needful Lovers. (Cleveland Poets Ser.: No. 30). 20p. (Orig.). 1981. pap. 3.00 (ISBN 0-914946-28-5). Cleveland St Univ Poetry Ctr.

Eckles, Robert B. Purdue Pharmacy: The First Century. LC 78-58099. (Illus.). 114p. 1979. 10.00 (ISBN 0-931682-01-0). Purdue Univ.

Eckles, Robert W. & Carmichael, Ronald L. Supervisory Management. 2nd ed. LC 80-21684. (Management Ser.). 524p. 1981. text ed. 36.00 (ISBN 0-471-05947-1). Wiley.

--Supervisory Management: A Short Course in Supervision. 2nd ed. LC 82-17553. (Professional Development Programs Ser.). 288p. 1983. text ed. 64.95x (ISBN 0-471-87492-2). Wiley.

Eckley, Grace. Children's Lore in "Finnegans Wake". (Irish Studies). (Illus.). 304p. 1985. text ed. 28.00x (ISBN 0-8156-2317-8). Syracuse U Pr.

--Edna O'Brien. (Irish Writers Ser.). 88p. 1974. 4.50 (ISBN 0-8387-7838-0); pap. 1.95 (ISBN 0-8387-7976-X). Bucknell U Pr.

--Finley Peter Dunne. (United States Authors Ser.). 1981. lib. bdg. 12.50 (ISBN 0-8057-7295-2, Twayne). G K Hall.

Eckley, Grace, jt. auth. see Begnal, Michael H.

Eckley, Mary & Norton, Mary J. McCall's Cooking School. 1982. pap. 9.95 (ISBN 0-394-73281-2). Random.

Eckley, Mary, ed. see McCall's Food Staff.

Eckley, Wilton. The American Circus. 1984. lib. bdg. 13.95 (ISBN 0-8057-9017-9, Twayne). G K Hall.

--Herbert Hoover. (United States Authors Ser.). 1980. lib. bdg. 13.50 (ISBN 0-8057-7285-5, Twayne). G K Hall.

Eckman, Fred, et al. Universals of Second Language Acquisition. pap. text ed. 16.95 (ISBN 0-88377-340-6). Newbury Hse.

Eckman, Jean-Pierre, jt. auth. see Collet, Pierre.

Eckman, Lester. The History of the Musar Movement 1840-1945. LC 75-2649. 1975. 8.95 (ISBN 0-88400-041-9). Shengold.

--Revered by All. 2nd ed. LC 73-89418. 1976. 10.00 (ISBN 0-88400-002-8). Shengold.

Eckman, Philip K., ed. Technology & Social Progress. (Science & Technology Ser.: Vol. 18). (Illus.). 1969. 20.00x (ISBN 0-87703-046-4, Pub. by Am Astronaut). Univelt Inc.

Eckmann, B., ed. see Bloom, F.

Eckmann, B., jt. ed. see Dold, A.

Eckmann, B., ed. see Haley, D. K.

Eckmann, B., ed. see Seminar on Triples & Categorical Homology.

Eckmann, B., ed. see Zielke, R.

Eckmann, J. P. & Wittwer, P. Computer Methods & Borel Summability Applied to Feigenbaum's Equation. (Lecture Notes in Physics Ser.: Vol. 227). xiv, 297p. 1985. pap. 16.60 (ISBN 0-387-15215-6). Springer-Verlag.

Eckmann, J. P., et al. A Computer-Assisted Proof of Universality for Area-Preserving Maps. LC 83-22456. (Memoirs: No. 289). 126p. 1984. pap. 12.00 (ISBN 0-8218-2289-6, MEMO-289). Am Math.

Eckmann, Janos. Divan of Gada'i. LC 76-630300. (Uralic & Altaic Ser: Vol. 113). (Illus., Orig.). 1971. pap. text ed. 16.50x (ISBN 0-87750-153-X). Res Ctr Lang Semiotic.

Eckmann, L. Principles of Tetanus. 577p. 1967. 210.00 (ISBN 3-456-00040-5, Pub. by Holdan Bk Ltd UK). State Mutual Bk.

Eckmann, M., jt. auth. see Jeger, M.

Eckoff, William J., ed. see Kant, Immanuel.

Eckols, Steve. DOS-VSE JCL. LC 85-60235. (Illus.). 421p. 1985. pap. 25.00 (ISBN 0-911625-24-0); instr's. guide 45.00 (ISBN 0-911625-26-7). M Murach & Assoc.

--How to Design & Develop Business Systems: A Practical Approach to Analysis, Design & Implementation. LC 83-62380. (Illus.). 279p. (Orig.). 1983. pap. 20.00 (ISBN 0-911625-14-3). M Murach & Assoc.

--How to Design & Develop Business Systems: Case Studies. LC 83-62380. (Illus.). 63p. 1984. pap. 6.00 (ISBN 0-911625-18-6). M Murach & Assoc.

--How to Design & Develop Business Systems: Instructor's Guide. LC 83-62380. (Illus.). 250p. 1984. 3-ring binder 35.00 (ISBN 0-911625-17-8). M Murach & Assoc.

--Report Writer. LC 80-82868. (Illus.). 106p. (Orig.). 1980. pap. 13.50 (ISBN 0-911625-07-0). M Murach & Assoc.

Eckroate, Norma, jt. auth. see Frazier, Anitra.

Eckschlager. Analytical Measurement & Information Advances in the Information Theoretic Approach to Chemical Analyses. 1985. 39.95 (ISBN 0-471-90652-2). Wiley.

Eckschlager, Karel & Stepanek, Vladimir. Information Theory As Applied to Chemical Analysis. LC 79-1405. (A Series of Monographs on Analytical Chemistry & Its Applications: Vol. 53). 1979. 41.50x (ISBN 0-471-04945-X, Pub. by Wiley-Interscience). Wiley.

Eckstein, et al. The Super Scrap Craft Book. 1984. pap. 9.95 (ISBN 0-452-25626-7, Plume). NAL.

Eckstein, A. China's Economic Revolution. LC 76-9176. (Illus.). 1977. 59.50 (ISBN 0-521-21283-9); pap. 15.95 (ISBN 0-521-29189-5). Cambridge U Pr.

Eckstein, Alexander. China's Economic Development: The Interplay of Scarcity & Ideology. LC 74-25951. (Michigan Studies on China Ser.). (Illus.). 1975. pap. 12.50x (ISBN 0-472-08310-4). U of Mich Pr.

Eckstein, Alexander & Dernberger, Robert. Quantitative Measures of China's Economic Output. (Illus.). 1979. text ed. 26.50x (ISBN 0-472-08754-1). U of Mich Pr.

Eckstein, Alexander, ed. Comparison of Economic Systems: Theoretical & Methodological Approaches. LC 79-118085. 1971. pap. 9.25x (ISBN 0-520-02489-3). U of Cal Pr.

Eckstein, Arthur, jt. auth. see Stone, Bernard.

Eckstein, Daniel E., et al. Life Style: What It Is & How to Do It. 2nd ed. 1982. pap. text ed. 4.25 (ISBN 0-8403-2594-0). Kendall-Hunt.

Eckstein, Daniel G., jt. auth. see Baruth, Leroy G.

Eckstein, Eleanor F. Food, People & Nutrition. (Illus.). 1980. text ed. 24.00 (ISBN 0-87055-355-0). AVI.

--Menu Planning. 3rd ed. (Illus.). 1983. text ed. 29.50 (ISBN 0-87055-439-5). AVI.

Eckstein, Everett E. Sunrise on the Mohican. (Illus.). 62p. 1982. 6.00 (ISBN 0-682-49918-8). Exposition Pr FL.

Eckstein, F., jt. ed. see Sundaram, P. V.

Eckstein, Fay, jt. auth. see Eckstein, Warren.

Eckstein, Gustav. Noguchi. 419p. 1984. Repr. of 1931 ed. lib. bdg. 50.00 (ISBN 0-89760-218-8). Telegraph BKS.

Eckstein, H. B., et al. Surgical Pediatric Urology. (Illus.). 533p. 1978. 75.00 (ISBN 0-7216-3325-0). Saunders.

Eckstein, Hans. Der Stuhl: Funktion-Konstruktion-Form, Von der Antike bis zur Gegenwart. (Illus.). 160p. (Ger.). 1980. pap. 15.00 (ISBN 3-87405-103-X, Pub. by Keyser West Germany). Seven Hills Bks.

Eckstein, Harry. Division & Cohesion in Democracy: A Study of Norway. (Center of International Studies). 1966. 31.00 (ISBN 0-691-05611-0); pap. 9.95 (ISBN 0-691-01070-6). Princeton U Pr.

Eckstein, Harry & Gurr, Ted R. Patterns of Authority: A Structural Basis for Political Inquiry. LC 75-19003. pap. 126.50 (ISBN 0-317-09431-9, 2016466). Bks Demand UMI.

Eckstein, Harry, ed. Internal War: Problems & Approaches. LC 80-23162. x, 339p. 1980. Repr. of 1964 ed. lib. bdg. 32.50x (ISBN 0-313-22451-X, ECIW). Greenwood.

Eckstein, Harry H. English Health Service: Its Origins, Structure, & Achievements. LC 58-12966. (Political Studies). (Illus.). Repr. of 1958 ed. 78.80 (ISBN 0-8357-9158-0, 2011603). Bks Demand UMI.

Eckstein, J. & Gleit, J. The Best Joke Book for Kids. (Illus.). 48p. (gr. 7-12). 1977. pap. 2.25 (ISBN 0-380-01734-2, 86629-3, Camelot). Avon.

Eckstein, Jerome. The Deathday of Socrates: Living, Dying & Immortality--the Theater of Ideas in Plato's Phaedo. LC 81-924. 288p. 1981. 18.00 (ISBN 0-914366-19-X). Columbia Pub.

--The Deathday of Socrates: Living, Dying & Immortality-The Theater of Ideas in Plato's "Phaedo". 1981. 17.95 (ISBN 0-914366-19-X); pap. 12.95 (ISBN 0-914366-20-3). Vanguard.

--Platonic Method: An Interpretation of the Dramatic-Philosophic Aspects of the Meno. LC 68-58747. 1968. lib. bdg. 27.50 (ISBN 0-8371-1499-3, ECP/). Greenwood.

Eckstein, Joan. Fun with Making Things: An Activity Book for Kids. 36p. (gr. 3-7). 1979. pap. 1.50 (ISBN 0-380-43315-X, 43315-X, Camelot). Avon.

Eckstein, Joan & Gleit, Joyce. Fun with Growing Things. (Illus.). 1982. pap. 2.95 (ISBN 0-380-00344-9, 23861, Flare). Avon.

Eckstein, Maxwell. Bach, Beethoven, Brahms for Piano. 1935. pap. 7.95 (ISBN 0-8256-2009-0). Music Sales.

--My Favorite Duet Album. 159p. 1948. pap. 7.95 (ISBN 0-8258-0163-X, 03253). Fischer Inc NY.

Eckstein, Maxwell, ed. Junior Let Us Have Music for Piano. (Illus.). 1943. pap. 4.95 (ISBN 0-8258-0192-3, 0-4105). Fischer Inc NY.

--Let Us Have Music for Piano: Seventy-Four Famous Melodies, Vol. 2. (Let Us Have Music Ser.). 111p. pap. 5.95 (ISBN 0-8258-0048-X, 03127). Fischer Inc NY.

--Let Us Have Music for Piano: Seventy-Four Melodies, Vol. 1. (Let Us Have Music Ser.). 112p. pap. 5.95 (ISBN 0-8258-0047-1, 02942). Fischer Inc NY.

--My Favorite Program Album. 158p. 1943. pap. 7.95 (ISBN 0-8258-0161-3, 03198). Fischer Inc NY.

--My Favorite Repertoire Album. pap. 7.95 (ISBN 0-8258-0162-1, 03253). Fischer Inc NY.

--My Favorite Solo Album. 160p. 1944. pap. 7.95 (ISBN 0-8258-0154-0, 03223). Fischer Inc NY.

--Picture Pointers for Piano Technic. 1947. pap. 4.95 (ISBN 0-8258-0175-3, 03451). Fischer Inc NY.

Eckstein, Maxwell, ed. see Schumann, Robert.

Eckstein, O. The Great Recession. (Data Resources Ser.: Vol. 3). 214p. 1978. 40.00 (ISBN 0-444-85204-2, North-Holland). Elsevier.

--Parameters & Policies in the U. S. Economy. (Data Resources Ser.: Vol. 2). 390p. 1976. 63.75 (ISBN 0-7204-9902-X, North-Holland). Elsevier.

Eckstein, O., et al. The DRI Report on U. S. Manufacturing Industries. 208p. 1984. 24.95 (ISBN 0-07-018969-2). McGraw.

Eckstein, Otto. Core Inflation. (Illus.). 128p. 1981. pap. 15.95 (ISBN 0-13-172635-8). P-H.

--Public Finance. 4th ed. (Foundations of Modern Economics Ser.). (Illus.). 1979. text ed. 19.95 (ISBN 0-13-737452-6); pap. text ed. 14.95 (ISBN 0-13-737445-3). P-H.

--Water-Resource Development: The Economics of Project Evaluation. LC 58-7501. (Economic Studies: No. 104). (Illus.). 1958. 20.00x (ISBN 0-674-94785-1). Harvard U Pr.

Eckstein, Otto, jt. auth. see Krutilla, John V.

Eckstein, Otto, ed. Studies in the Economics of Income Maintenance. LC 77-592. (Brookings Institution Studies of Government Finance). 1977. Repr. of 1967 ed. lib. bdg. 22.50x (ISBN 0-8371-9488-1, ECTE). Greenwood.

Eckstein, Peter, jt. auth. see Sichel, Werner.

Eckstein, S. The Poverty of Revolution: The State & the Urban Poor in Mexico. 1977. 35.00 (ISBN 0-691-09367-9). Princeton U Pr.

Eckstein, Shlomo. Land Reform in Latin America: Bolivia, Chile, Mexico, Peru & Venezuela. (Working Paper: No. 275). v, 187p. 1978. 5.00 (ISBN 0-686-36069-9, WP-O275). World Bank.

Eckstein, Stephen D., Jr. A History of Churches of Christ in Texas, 1824-1950. 1963. 6.95 (ISBN 0-88027-098-5); 4.95. Firm Foun Pub.
--The Purpose of Genesis. 1976. pap. 2.75 (ISBN 0-88027-037-3). Firm Foun Pub.
Eckstein, Warren & Eckstein, Fay. Pet Aerobics: How to Solve Your Pets Behavior Problems, Improve Their Health, Lengthen Their Lives & Have Fun Doing It. 1984. 14.95 (ISBN 0-03-063882-8). HR&W.
--Understanding Your Pet: The/Eckstein Method of Pet Therapy & Behavior Training. LC 85-4754. (Illus.). 256p. 1985. 15.95 (ISBN 0-03-000699-6). HR&W.
--Yes, Dog, That's Right! (Illus.). 1980. 2.98 (ISBN 0-931866-03-0). Alpine Pubns.
Eckstorm, Fannie. Penobscot Man. LC 74-128733. (Short Story Index Reprint Ser). 1904. 19.00 (ISBN 0-8369-3624-8). Ayer Co Pubs.
Eckstorm, Fannie H. Indian Place Names of the Penobscot Valley & the Maine Coast. 1974. pap. 5.95 (ISBN 0-89101-028-9). U Maine Orono.
--Indian Place-Names of the Penobscot Valley & the Maine Coast. (The International Library of Names). 1985. Repr. of 1941 ed. text ed. 39.50x (ISBN 0-8290-1236-2). Irvington.
--Old John Neptune & Other Maine Indian Shamans. 209p. 1980. pap. 5.95 (ISBN 0-89101-044-0). U Maine Orono.
Eckstorm, Fanny. Minstrelsy of Maine. LC 79-152248. 1971. Repr. of 1927 ed. 43.00x (ISBN 0-8103-3707-X). Gale.
Eckstrom, Lawrence J. Licensing in Foreign & Domestic Operations, 3 vols. rev. ed. LC 58-13380. 1980. looseleaf in post binders pages 225.00 (ISBN 0-87632-075-2). Boardman.
Eclov, Lee. The Church: Pictures of Christ's Body. (Fisherman Bible Studyguide Ser.). 55p. 1981. saddle stitched 2.95 (ISBN 0-87788-155-3). Shaw Pubs.
ECMT, jt. auth. see OECD.
ECMT, jt. auth. see Organization for Economic Cooperation & Development.
ECMT for OCED. Scope for Railway Transport in Urban Areas: Scope for Railway Transport in Urban Areas. (ECMT Round Table Ser.: No. 47). (Illus.). 375p. (Orig.). 1980. pap. 20.00x (ISBN 92-821-1063-X, 75-80-06-1). OECD.
ECMT Staff, jt. auth. see OECD Staff.
Eco, Umberto. The Name of the Rose. 4th ed. 640p. 1984. pap. 4.95 (ISBN 0-446-32218-0). Warner Bks.
--The Name of the Rose. (General Ser.). 1984. lib. bdg. 16.95 (ISBN 0-8161-3663-7, Large Print Bks). G K Hall.
--Postscript to the Name of the Rose. Weaver, William, tr. from Ital. LC 84-15652. (A Helen & Kurt Wolff Bk.). (Illus.). 96p. 1984. 8.95 (ISBN 0-15-173156-X). HarBraceJ.
--The Role of the Reader: Explorations in the Semiotics of Texts. LC 78-18299. (Advances in Semiotics Ser.). (Illus.). 288p. 1979. 25.00x (ISBN 0-253-11139-0); pap. 10.95x (ISBN 0-253-20318-X). Ind U Pr.
--Semiotics & the Philosophy of Language. LC 82-49016. (Advances in Semiotics Ser.). 320p. 1984. 25.00x (ISBN 0-253-35168-5). Ind U Pr.
--A Theory of Semiotics. LC 74-22833. (Advances in Semiotics Ser.: Midland Bks., No. 217). 368p. 1976. 25.00x (ISBN 0-253-35955-4); pap. 9.95x (ISBN 0-253-20217-5). Ind U Pr.
Eco, Umberto & Sebeok, Thomas A., eds. The Sign of Three: Dupin, Holmes, Pierce. LC 82-49207. (Advances in Semiotics Ser.). (Illus.). 256p. 1984. 22.50x (ISBN 0-253-35235-5). Ind U Pr.
Ecob, E. G., jt. auth. see Davies, Stanley P.
Ecobichon, D. J. & Joy, R. M., eds. Pesticides & Neurological Diseases. 296p. 1982. 76.00 (ISBN 0-8493-5571-0). CRC Pr.
Ecodyne Corporation. Weather Data Handbook. 320p. 1980. 42.50 (ISBN 0-07-018960-9). McGraw.
Ecole Biblique et Archeologique Francaise. Jerusalem. Catalogue de la Bibliotheque de l'ecole Biblique et Archeologique Francaise (Catalog of the Library of the French Biblical & Archaeological School, 13 vols. 1975. lib. bdg. 1405.00 (ISBN 0-8161-1154-5, Hall Library). G K Hall.
Ecole de'Ete De Probabilites De Saint-Flour, 4th, 1974. Proceedings. Fernique, X. M., et al, eds. LC 75-25522. (Lecture Notes in Mathematics: Vol. 480). 293p. 1975. pap. 18.30 (ISBN 0-387-07396-5). Springer-Verlag.
Ecological Analysts. The Sources, Chemistry, Fate & Effects of Chromium in Aquatic Environments. LC 82-71261. (Orig.). 1982. pap. 8.10 (ISBN 0-89364-046-8, 847-89600). Am Petroleum.
Ecological Analysts Inc. & Environmental Affairs Dept., American Petroleum Institute. A Survey of National & State Regulatory Agency Effluent Toxicity Testing & Procedures. LC 83-127589. (Illus.). ix, 52p. 1983. 7.25 (4353). Am Petroleum.
Ecology & Environment, Inc. Toxic Substance Storage Tank Containment. LC 84-22697. (Pollution Technology Review Ser.: No. 116). (Illus.). 274p. 1985. 36.00 (ISBN 0-8155-1018-7). Noyes.
Econometrics Conferences, Ohio State U., 1967 & 1968. Problems & Issues in Current Econometric Practice. Brunner, Karl, ed. 1973. 10.00x (ISBN 0-87776-306-2, AA6). Ohio St U Admin Sci.
Economic & Foreign Affairs Research Association (Tokyo), ed. Statistical Survey of Japan's Economy, 1982. LC 54-43626. (Illus.). 83p. (Orig.). 1982. pap. 20.00x (ISBN 0-8002-3040-X). Intl Pubns Serv.
Economic & Foreign Affairs Research Association (Tokyo), ed. Statistical Survey of Japan's Economy, 1981. LC 54-43626. (Illus.). 83p. (Orig.). 1981. pap. 20.00x (ISBN 0-8002-2963-0). Intl Pubns Serv.
Economic & Social Commission for Asia. Economic & Social Survey of Asia & the Pacific, 1980. 143p. 1983. pap. 11.00 (ISBN 0-686-43279-7, UN81/2F1, UN). Unipub.
Economic & Social Commission for Asia & the Pacific. Quarterly Bulletin of Statistics for Asia & the Pacific, Vols. 2-13. Incl. Vol. 3, Nos. 3 & 4, 2 Pts. No. 3. pap. 5.00 (UN74/2F82); No. 4. pap. 6.00 (UN74/2F92); Vol. 4, Nos. 1-4. 1974, 4 Pts. No. 1, Mar. pap. 6.00 (ISBN 0-686-93535-7, UN75/2F9); No. 2, June. pap. 5.00 (ISBN 0-686-99124-9, UN75/2F10); No. 3. pap. 6.00 (ISBN 0-686-99125-7, UN75/2F11); No. 4, December. pap. 4.00 (ISBN 0-686-99126-5, UN75/2F12); Vol. 5, Nos. 1-4. 1975, 4 Pts. No. 1, March. pap. 6.00 (ISBN 0-686-93539-X, UN76/2F6); No. 2, June. pap. 6.00 (ISBN 0-686-99127-3, UN76/2F7); No. 3, Sept. pap. 6.00 (ISBN 0-686-99128-1, UN76/2F9); No. 4, Dec. pap. 5.00 (ISBN 0-686-99129-X, UN76/2F9); Vol. 6. 1976, 2 Pts. No. 1 & 2 Mar.-Jun. pap. 7.00 (ISBN 0-686-93543-8, UN77/2F5); No. 3: Sept. pap. 6.00 (ISBN 0-686-99130-3, UN77/2F7); Vol. 7. 1977, 4 Pts. Nos. 1 March 1977. pap. 7.00 (ISBN 0-686-93545-4, UN78/2F3); No. 2: June 1977. pap. 5.00 (ISBN 0-686-99131-1, UN78/2F4); No. 3 Sept. 1977. pap. 6.00 (ISBN 0-686-99132-X, UN78/2F5); No. 4 Dec. 1977. pap. 6.00 (ISBN 0-686-99133-8, UN78/2F6); Vol. 8. 1978, 4 Pts. No. 1: March 1976. pap. 6.00 (ISBN 0-686-93549-7, UN78/2F9); No. 2: June 1978. pap. 6.00 (ISBN 0-686-99134-6, UN79/2F5); No. 3. pap. 6.00 (ISBN 0-686-99135-4, UN79/2F6); No. 4. pap. 6.00 (ISBN 0-686-99136-2, UN79/2F7); Vol. 9. 1979, 4 Pts. No. 1: March 1979. pap. 7.00 (ISBN 0-686-93553-5, UN79/2F8); No. 2: June 1979. pap. 6.00 (ISBN 0-686-99137-0, UN79/2F14); No. 3: Sept. 1979. pap. 6.00 (ISBN 0-686-99138-9, UN80/2F5); No. 4: Dec 1979. pap. 6.00 (ISBN 0-686-99139-7, UN80/2F7); Vol. 10, 4 Pts. No. 1: March 1980. pap. 7.00 (UN80/2F14); No. 2: June 1980. pap. 8.00 (UN80/2F16); No. 3: Sept. 1980. pap. 7.00 (UN81/2F2); No. 4: Dec. 1980. pap. 7.00 (UN81/2F4); Vol. 11. 1981, 4 Pts. No. 1: March 1981. pap. 8.00 (UN81/2F9); No. 2: June 1981. pap. 8.00 (UN81/2F13); No. 3: Sept. 1981. pap. 9.00 (UN82/2F2); No. 4: Dec. 1981. pap. 8.00 (UN82/2F4); Vol. 12, Nos. 1-2, 2 Pts. 1982. No. 1. pap. 9.00 (UN84/2F11); No.2. pap. 11.00 (UN83/2F5); No. 3: Sept. 1982. pap. 11.00 (UN83/2F6); No. 4: Dec. 1982. pap. 11.00 (UN83/2F10); Vol. 13, No. 1. March, 1983. (Illus.). 93p. 1983. pap. 11.00 (UN83/2F11). (Asian Economy Ser., UN). Unipub.
Economic & Social Commission for Asia and the Pacific. Small Industry Bulletin for Asia & the Pacific, No. 17. 192p. 1982. pap. 14.00 (ISBN 0-686-86999-0, UN81/2F8, UN). Unipub.
Economic and Social Commission for Asia and the Pacific. Transport & Communication Bulletin for Asia & the Pacific, No. 55. 86p. 1983. pap. text ed. 9.50 (ISBN 0-317-00306-2, UN82/2F12, UN). Unipub.
Economic & Social Committee of the European Communities - General Secretariat, ed. Community Advisory Committees for the Representation of Socio-Economic Interests. 240p. 1980. text ed. 37.95x (ISBN 0-566-00328-7). Gower Pub Co.
Economic & Social Committee of the European Community, General Secretariat. European Interest Groups & Their Relationships with the Economic & Social Committee. 472p. 1980. text ed. 74.50x (ISBN 0-566-00365-1). Gower Pub Co.
Economic Behavior Program Staff. Survey of Consumer Finances. Incl. 1960. 330p. pap. 6.00x (ISBN 0-87944-096-1); 1961. 168p. cloth 10.50x; pap. 6.00x (ISBN 0-87944-097-X); 1965. 284p. pap. 6.00x (ISBN 0-87944-101-1); 1966. 328p. pap. 6.00x (ISBN 0-87944-102-X); 1967. 362p. pap. 6.00x (ISBN 0-87944-103-8); 1968. 304p. cloth 10.50x (ISBN 0-87944-105-4); pap. 6.00x (ISBN 0-87944-104-6); 1969. 341p. pap. 6.00x (ISBN 0-87944-106-2); 1970. 346p. cloth 10.50x (ISBN 0-87944-001-5); pap. 6.00x (ISBN 0-87944-000-7). LC 50-39941. pap. Inst Soc Res.
Economic Commission for Europe. Engineering Equipment & Automation Means for Waste-Water Management in ECE Countries: A Report on Prevailing Practices & Recent Experience in Production & Use of Engineering Equipment & Automation Means for Preventing Water Pollution, Pt. 1. 111p. 1985. pap. 12.50 (UN84/2E13 5071, UN). Unipub.
Economic Commission for Latin America. Development Problems in Latin America: An Analysis by the United Nations Economic Commission for Latin America. (Institute of Latin American Studies-Special Publication). 366p. 1970. 20.00x (ISBN 0-292-70042-3). U of Tex Pr.
Economic Commission for Latin America & the Caribbean. Economic Survey of Latin America & the Caribbean 1982, Vol. II. 186p. 1985. pap. 13.00 (UN84/2G1 5071, UN). Unipub.
Economic Commission for Latin America. Statistical Yearbook for Latin America 1983. 749p. (Eng. & Sp.). 1985. pap. 40.00 (UN84/2G2 5071, UN). Unipub.
Economic Development Foundation. Manual on Plant Layout & Materials Handling. LC 72-186284. 80p. 1971. 7.25 (ISBN 92-833-1011-X, APO45, APO). Unipub.
--Readings on Production Planning & Control. 178p. 1972. 11.75 (ISBN 92-833-1017-9, APO51, APO). Unipub.
Economic Planning Agency-Japan, ed. Economic Survey of Japan, 1979-1980. 29th ed. LC 51-61351. (Illus., Orig.). 1980. pap. 40.00x (ISBN 0-8002-2787-5). Intl Pubns Serv.
Economic Research Centre, et al. Almanac of China's Economy, 1949-1981. Muqiao, Xue, ed. 155.00 (ISBN 0-88410-894-5). Eurasia Pr NY.
Economics & National Security Council. Strategic Minerals: A Resource Crisis. (Illus.). 105p. 1980. pap. text ed. 5.95x (ISBN 0-87855-913-2). Transaction Bks.
Economics & Sociology Department, Iowa State College. Wartime Farm & Food Policy. LC 75-26304. (World Food Supply Ser). (Illus.). 1976. Repr. of 1943 ed. 41.00x (ISBN 0-405-07783-1). Ayer Co Pubs.
Economics Division FAO. Fishing Ports & Markets. 1978. 38.00 (ISBN 0-685-63421-3). State Mutual Bk.
Economics Division, FAO. Fishing Ports & Markets. (Illus.). 416p. 1971. 39.75 (ISBN 0-85238-012-7, FN49, FNB). Unipub.
Economics of Law Practice Section Members & Law Student Division Members. From Law Student to Lawyer: A Career Planning Manual. LC 83-71509. 140p. 1984. pap. 14.95 (ISBN 0-89707-104-2) (ISBN 0-317-16888-6). Amer Bar Assn.
Economist, ed. World Business Cycles. 1st ed. 191p. 1982. 95.00x (ISBN 0-85058-057-9, Pub. by Economist). Gale.
--The World in Figures. (Illus.). 296p. 1985. 69.95 (ISBN 0-528-81049-9). Rand.
Economist, jt. ed. see Africa Magazine.
Economist Editors. Economist, Eighteen Forty-Three to Nineteen Forty-Three: A Centenary Volume. (Essay Index Reprint Ser). Repr. of 1943 ed. 17.75 (ISBN 0-518-10163-0). Ayer Co Pubs.
Economist Staff. Good Book Guide for Business. LC 84-47601. 700p. 1984. 19.23 (ISBN 0-06-181877-1, HarpT). Har-Row.
Economo, Constantin von see Von Economo, Constantin.
Economos, Paul. Seventh Sense. (Illus.). 24p. 1981. pap. 3.00 (ISBN 0-932662-36-6). St Andrews NC.
Economou, E. N. Green's Functions in Quantum Physics. (Springer Series in Solid-State Sciences: Vol. 7). (Illus.). 336p. (Second Corrected & Updated Edition). 1983. 22.00 (ISBN 0-387-12266-4). Springer-Verlag.
Economou, George. Ameriki: Book One, & Selected Earlier Poems. LC 77-3612. 1977. pap. 7.00 (ISBN 0-915342-20-0). SUN.
Economou, George D. The Goddess Natura in Medieval Literature. LC 72-75405. 240p. 1972. 15.00x (ISBN 0-674-35535-0). Harvard U Pr.
Economou, George D., jt. ed. see Ferrante, Joan M.
Economy, J., jt. ed. see Preston, J.
Ecorcheville, Jules, ed. Vingt suites d'orchestre du XVIIe siecle francais, 2 vols. (Illus.). 384p. (Fr.). 1971. Repr. of 1906 ed. 185.00x (ISBN 0-8450-1005-0). Broude.
Ecorcheville, Jules A., ed. Catalogue du Fonds de Musique Ancienne de la Bibliotheque Nationale, 8 vols. in 4. LC 79-166103. (Music Ser). (Illus.). 1973. Repr. of 1914 ed. Set. lib. bdg. 195.00 (ISBN 0-306-70280-0). Da Capo.
Ecotope Group & Solar Horizons, Inc. Common Sense Building & Marketing of Affordable, Energy Efficient Homes. 340p. 1981. ringbinder 39.50 (ISBN 0-934478-34-1). Ecotope.
Ecroyd, Donald & Wagner, Hilda S. Communicate Through Oral Reading. 1979. pap. text ed. 22.95x (ISBN 0-07-018970-6). McGraw.
Ecroyd, Donald H., et al. Voice & Articulation: A Handbook. 1966. pap. 10.80 (ISBN 0-673-05722-4). Scott F.
--Voice & Articulation: Programmed Instruction. 1966. pap. 10.80 (ISBN 0-673-05720-8). Scott F.
Edades, Jean. An Animal ABC. (Illus.). (gr. 3-5). 1979. pap. 2.25x (ISBN 0-686-25221-7, Pub. by New Day Pub). Cellar.
Edades, Jean, jt. auth. see Hashimoto, Yasuko.
Edades, Jean, ed. see Dumia, Mariano A.
Edades, Jean G. Onstage & Offstage. (Illus.). 1983. pap. 9.00 (ISBN 971-10-0051-2, Pub. by New Day Phillippines). Cellar.
Edagawa, Naoyushi, jt. auth. see Friedmann, Lawrence W.
Edari, Ronald S., jt. ed. see Berlowitz, Marvin J.
Edberg, Stephen J. International Halley Watch Amateur Observers' Manual for Scientific Comet Studies. LC 85-20591. (Illus.). 192p. 1983. pap. 9.95 (ISBN 0-89490-102-8). Enslow Pubs.
--International Halley Watch: Amateurs Observers' Manual for Scientific Comet Studies. (Illus.). 192p. 1983. pap. 9.95 (ISBN 0-933346-40-9). Sky Pub.
Edbrooke, jt. auth. see Mather.
Edbury, P., ed. Crusade & Settlement. 368p. 1985. text ed. 41.50x (ISBN 0-906449-78-2, Pub by U of Coll Cardiff UK). Humanities.
Edde, Howard. Environmental Control for Pulp & Paper Mills. LC 83-22011. (Pollution Technology Review Ser.: No. 108). (Illus.). 179p. 1984. 32.00 (ISBN 0-8155-0979-0). Noyes.
Eddelman, Floyd E. American Drama Criticism: Supplement I to the Second Edition. 264p. 1984. 29.50 (ISBN 0-208-01978-2, Archon Bks). Shoe String.
Eddie, G. The Harvesting of Krill. (Southern Ocean Fisheries Survey Programmes: GLO-SO-77-2). 82p. (Eng. & Span., 2nd Printing 1978). 1977. pap. 7.50 (ISBN 92-5-100415-3, F1309, FAO). Unipub.
Eddie, G. C. Road Transport of Fish & Fishery Products. (Fisheries Technical Paper Ser.: No. 232). 54p. (Orig.). 1984. pap. 7.50 (ISBN 92-5-101362-4, F2570, FAO). Unipub.
--Support & Development of the Retail Trade in Perishable Fishery Products. (Fisheries Technical Paper Ser.: No. 235). 53p. (Orig.). 1984. pap. 7.50 (ISBN 92-5-101401-9, F2579, FAO). Unipub.
Eddie, Gordon C. Engineering, Economics & Fisheries Management. 106p. 1983. pap. text ed. 20.50 (ISBN 0-85238-127-1, FN105, FNB). Unipub.
Eddie, T., jt. auth. see Graham, D.
Eddie The Wire. The Complete Guide to Lock Picking. 1981. pap. 9.95 (ISBN 0-686-30630-9). Loompanics.
--How to Bury Your Goods: The Complete Manual of Long-Term Underground Storage. 1981. pap. 4.00 (ISBN 0-686-30627-9). Loompanics.
--How to Make Your Own Professional Lock Tools. 1980. pap. 5.95 (ISBN 0-686-30628-7). Loompanics.
--How to Make Your Own Professional Lock Tools, Vol. 2. 1981. pap. 5.95 (ISBN 0-686-30629-5). Loompanics.
Eddings, Claire N. Secretary's Complete Model Letter Handbook. (Illus.). 1965. 14.95 (ISBN 0-13-797407-8). P-H.
Eddings, David. Castle of Wizardry. (The Belgariad Ser.: Bk. 4). 416p. 1984. pap. 3.50 (ISBN 0-345-30080-7, Del Rey). Ballantine.
--Enchanters' End Game. (The Belgariad Ser.: Bk. 5). 384p. (Orig.). 1984. pap. 3.50 (ISBN 0-345-30078-5, Del Rey). Ballantine.
--Magician's Gambit. (Belgariad Ser.: Bk. 3). 320p. 1984. pap. 2.95 (ISBN 0-345-30077-7, Del Rey). Ballantine.
--Pawn of Prophecy. (The Belgariad Ser.: Bk. 1). 258p. (Orig.). 1984. pap. 2.95 (ISBN 0-345-30997-9, Del Rey). Ballantine.
--Queen of Sorcery. (The Belgariad Ser.: Bk. 2). 327p. (Orig.). 1985. pap. 3.50 (ISBN 0-345-32389-0, Del Rey). Ballantine.
Eddings, Dennis W., ed. The Naiad Voice: Essays on Poe's Satiric Hoaxing. LC 83-3723. 107p. 1983. 18.00x (ISBN 0-8046-9317-X, 5317, Natl U). Assoc Faculty Pr.
Eddington, A. S. The Nature of the Physical World. 361p. 1981. Repr. of 1928 ed. lib. bdg. 30.00 (ISBN 0-89987-209-3). Darby Bks.
Eddington, Arthur S. The Mathematical Theory of Relativity. 3rd ed. LC 74-1458. ix, 270p. 1975. text ed. 13.95 (ISBN 0-8284-0278-7). Chelsea Pub.
--The Nature of the Physical World. LC 77-27200. (Gifford Lectures: 1927). Repr. of 1928 ed. 27.50 (ISBN 0-404-60478-1). AMS Pr.
--Science & the Unseen World. 56p. 1980. Repr. of 1929 ed. lib. bdg. 10.00 (ISBN 0-8495-1426-6). Arden Lib.
--Science & the Unseen World. 1979. Repr. of 1929 ed. lib. bdg. 10.00 (ISBN 0-8414-4004-2). Folcroft.
Eddington, Sir Arthur. The Nature of the Physical World. 1935. 30.00 (ISBN 0-8414-3885-4). Folcroft.
Eddington, Neil A., jt. ed. see Helmer, John.
Eddington, Thomas. Contemporary Art & the Metaphysics of the Art Expression. (An Essential Knowledge Library). (Illus.). 137p. 1983. 59.55 (ISBN 0-86650-051-0). Gloucester Art.
Eddins, John M., jt. auth. see Peters, G. David.
Eddins, Martha, et al. There's More to Musicals Than Music. (Illus.). 72p. 1980. pap. 4.95 (ISBN 0-916642-13-5, 566). Somerset Pr IL.
Eddison, E. R. Mistress of Mistresses. (A Del Rey Bk.). 1978. pap. 2.50 (ISBN 0-345-27220-X). Ballantine.
--The Worm Ouroboros. 192p. pap. 3.95 (ISBN 0-345-30152-8, Del Rey). Ballantine.
Eddison, E. R., tr. Egil's Saga, Skallagrimssonar: Done into English Out of the Icelandic. LC 69-10087. Repr. of 1930 ed. lib. bdg. 22.50x (ISBN 0-8371-0402-5, EGSS). Greenwood.
Eddison, Eric R. Styrbiorn the Strong. Reginald, R. & Melville, Douglas, eds. LC 77-84222. (Lost Race & Adult Fantasy Ser.). 1978. Repr. of 1926 ed. lib. bdg. 24.50x (ISBN 0-405-10975-X). Ayer Co Pubs.
Eddleman, Floyd E., ed. American Drama Criticism: Interpretations, 1890-1977. 2nd ed. (Drama Explication Ser.). 488p. 1979. 32.50 (ISBN 0-208-01713-5). Shoe String.

Eddleman, H. Leo. By Life or By Death: A Practical Commentary on Paul's Letter to the Philippians. 176p. (Orig.). 1981. pap. 3.75 (ISBN 0-682-49700-2, Testament). Exposition Pr FL.

--Hail Mary. rev. ed. 134p. 1983. pap. 4.00 (ISBN 0-682-40143-9). Exposition Pr FL.

--Hail Mary, Are You Heeding the Blessed Virgin? (Orig.). 1982. pap. 4.00 (ISBN 0-682-49899-8). Exposition Pr FL.

--Schools & Churches in American Democracy. 135p. 1983. pap. 5.00 (ISBN 0-682-40144-7). Exposition Pr FL.

Eddleston, Adrian. Immune Reaction in Liver Disease. 95.00x (ISBN 0-272-79509-7, Pub. by Pitman Bks England). State Mutual Bk.

Eddleston, Adrian & Williams, Roger. Immune Reaction in Liver Disease. (Illus.). 1978. 24.95x (ISBN 0-8464-0503-2). Beekman Pubs.

Eddowes, Maurice, jt. auth. see Park, R. D.

Edds, John A. Management Auditing: Concepts & Practice. 432p. 1980. text ed. 19.95 (ISBN 0-8403-2209-7). Kendall-Hunt.

Eddy. Handbook of Organization Management. (Public Administration & Public Policy). 592p. 1983. 99.75 (ISBN 0-8247-1813-5). Dekker.

Eddy, Arthur J. Cubists & Post-Impressionism. LC 77-94575. 1979. Repr. of 1914 ed. lib. bdg. 25.00 (ISBN 0-89341-240-6). Longwood Pub Group.

--Ganton & Co. A Story of Chicago Commercial & Social Life. LC 74-22780. (Labor Movement in Fiction & Non-Fiction). (Illus.). Repr. of 1908 ed. 28.50 (ISBN 0-404-58421-7). AMS Pr.

--Recollections & Impressions of James A. McNeill Whistler. LC 71-176163. (Illus.). Repr. of 1904 ed. 27.50 (ISBN 0-405-08484-6, Blom Pubns). Ayer Co Pubs.

Eddy, B. E. Polyoma Virus. Bd. with Rubella Virus. Norrby, E. (Virology Monographs: Vol. 7). (Illus.). iv, 174p. 1969. 34.00 (ISBN 0-387-80934-1). Springer-Verlag.

Eddy, Cristen C. & Ford, John L. Alcoholism in Women. (Topics in Human Behavior Ser.). 1980. pap. text ed. 9.95 (ISBN 0-8403-2112-0). Kendall-Hunt.

Eddy, D. Screening for Cancer: Theory, Analysis & Design. 1980. 34.95 (ISBN 0-13-796789-6). P-H.

Eddy, Donald D. A Bibliography of John Brown. 210p. 1971. 7.50 (ISBN 0-686-31064-0). Biblio Soc Am.

--A Bibliography of John Brown. LC 72-185918. (Illus.). 210p. 1971. 7.50x (ISBN 0-8139-0937-6, Bibliographical Society of America). U Pr of Va.

Eddy, Donald D., ed. see Johnson, Samuel.

Eddy, Edward D. Colleges for Our Land & Time. LC 73-13456. 328p. 1974. Repr. of 1957 ed. lib. bdg. 17.25x (ISBN 0-8371-7138-5, EDCO). Greenwood.

Eddy, Elizabeth. Litany. (Morning Coffee Chapbook Ser.). (Illus.). 20p. 1984. pap. 6.00 (ISBN 0-915124-97-1). Coffee Hse.

Eddy, Elizabeth M., jt. auth. see Roth, Julius A.

Eddy, Elizabeth M. & Partridge, William L., eds. Applied Anthropology in America. LC 78-6386. 481p. 1978. 39.00x (ISBN 0-231-04466-6); pap. 15.00x (ISBN 0-231-04467-4). Columbia U Pr.

Eddy, Frank W. Archaeology: A Cultural-Evolutionary Approach. (Illus.). 384p. 1984. pap. 22.95 (ISBN 0-13-044057-4). P-H.

--Prehistory in the Navajo Reservoir District, 2 pts. (Illus.). 1966. pap. 7.95 ea. Pt. 1 (ISBN 0-89013-023-X). Pt. 2 (ISBN 0-89013-024-8). Museum NM Pr.

Eddy, Frank W. & Cooley, Maurice E. Cultural & Environmental History of Cienega Valley, Southeastern Arizona. LC 83-17942. (Anthropological Papers: No. 43). 62p. 1983. monograph 7.95x (ISBN 0-8165-0830-5). U of Ariz Pr.

Eddy, Frederick D., ed. The Language Learner. Incl. Definition of Language Competences Through Testing. Brooks, Nelson; Elementary & Junior High School Curricula. Peloro, Filomena C; Modern Foreign Language Learning: Assumptions & Implications. Starr, Wilmarth H; A Six-Year Sequence. Silber, Gordon R; Teaching Aids & Techniques: The Secondary School Language Laboratory. Eddy, Frederick D; The Teaching of Classical & Modern Foreign Languages: Common Areas & Problems. Bree, Josephine P. 70p. 1959. pap. 7.95x (ISBN 0-915432-59-5). NE Conf Teach Foreign.

Eddy, Gary. Waking up, Late. 1977. pap. 2.00 (ISBN 0-918366-04-6). Slow Loris.

Eddy, George, jt. auth. see Olm, Kenneth.

Eddy, George S. Man Discovers God. facs. ed. LC 68-24849. (Essay Index Reprint Ser). 1968. Repr. of 1942 ed. 18.00 (ISBN 0-8369-0401-X). Ayer Co Pubs.

--Pathfinders of the World Missionary Crusade. facs. ed. LC 76-84304. (Essay Index Reprint Ser). 1945. 20.25 (ISBN 0-8369-1127-X). Ayer Co Pubs.

Eddy, George S. & Page, Kirby. Makers of Freedom. facs. ed. LC 79-117786. (Essay Index Reprint Ser). 1926. 21.50 (ISBN 0-8369-1803-7). Ayer Co Pubs.

Eddy, Henry H. & Simonetti, Martha L. Guide to the Published Archives of Pennsylvania. LC 79-623725. 101p. 1976. 3.50 (ISBN 0-911124-09-8). Pa Hist & Mus.

Eddy, James M. & Alles, Wesley F. Death Education. LC 82-2122. (Illus.). 383p. 1982. pap. text ed. 13.95 (ISBN 0-8016-1497-X). Mosby.

Eddy, John. A New Sun: The Solar Results from Skylab. (Illus.). 198p. 1979. 21.00 (ISBN 0-318-13542-6, BO206). Astron Soc Pacific.

--The Teacher & the Drug Scene. (Fastback Ser.: No. 26). (Orig.). 1973. pap. 0.75 (ISBN 0-87367-026-4). Phi Delta Kappa.

Eddy, John, et al, eds. College Student Personnel Development, Administration, & Counseling. 2nd ed. 538p. 1980. lib. bdg. 33.50 (ISBN 0-8191-1230-5); pap. text ed. 21.50 (ISBN 0-8191-1231-3). U Pr of Amer.

Eddy, John P. & Lawson, David M., Jr. Crisis Intervention: A Manual for Education & Action. LC 83-6499. 134p. (Orig.). 1983. pap. text ed. 8.50 (ISBN 0-8191-3231-4). U Pr of Amer.

Eddy, Jonathan & Winship, Peter. Commercial Transactions: Cases, Problems & Materials. LC 84-81934. 1985. text ed. write for info. (ISBN 0-316-20057-3). Little.

Eddy, Junius. The Music Came from Deep Inside: A Story of Artists & Severely Handicapped Children. 1982. 17.95 (ISBN 0-07-018971-X). McGraw.

Eddy, Mary B. Christ & Christmas, Poem. (Illus.). 12.50 (ISBN 0-87952-091-4). First Church.

--Christian Science. pap. 2.00 (ISBN 0-87516-021-2). De Vorss.

--Concordance to Other Writings. 1984. 19.50 (ISBN 0-87952-089-2). First Church.

--Concordance to Science & Health. 1982. 12.50 (ISBN 0-87952-093-0). First Church.

--The First Church of Christ, Scientist, & Miscellany. German Ed. pap. 7.00 (ISBN 0-87952-155-4). First Church.

--The First Church of Christ, Scientist & Miscellany. Date not set. pap. 2.30 (ISBN 0-87952-041-8). First Church.

--Hats Off Andy Capp. (Andy Capp Ser.). (Illus.). 1979. pap. 1.25 (ISBN 0-449-13769-4, GM). Fawcett.

--Manual of the Mother Church, 11 vols. Incl. Vol. 1. Danish. 10.00 (ISBN 0-87952-104-X); Vol. 2. Dutch. 10.00 (ISBN 0-87952-110-4); Vol. 3. French. 10.00 (ISBN 0-87952-118-X); Vol. 4. German. 10.00 (ISBN 0-87952-153-8); Vol. 5. Italian. 7.00 (ISBN 0-87952-181-3); Vol. 6. Norwegian. 10.00 (ISBN 0-87952-196-1); Vol. 7. Portuguese. 7.00 (ISBN 0-87952-206-2); Vol. 8. Spanish. 7.00 (ISBN 0-87952-228-3); Vol. 9. Swedish. 10.00 (ISBN 0-87952-251-8); Vol. 10. Greek. 7.00 (ISBN 0-87952-171-6); Vol. 11. Japanese. 10.00 (ISBN 0-87952-191-0). First Church.

--Manual of the Mother Church, The First Church of Christ, Scientist, in Boston, Massachusetts. standard ed. 7.00 (ISBN 0-87952-061-2); century ed. 7.00 (ISBN 0-87952-063-9); leather 25.00 (ISBN 0-87952-064-7). First Church.

--Miscellaneous Writings, Eighteen Eighty-Three to Eighteen Ninety-Six. Date not set. pap. 4.50 (ISBN 0-87952-229-1). First Church.

--Miscellaneous Writings, Eighteen Eighty-Three to Eighteen Ninety-Six. (Fr.). Date not set. pap. 7.00 (ISBN 0-87952-119-8). First Church.

--Miscellaneous Writings, Eighteen Eighty-Three to Eighteen Ninety-Six. (Ger.). Date not set. pap. 7.00 (ISBN 0-87952-154-6). First Church.

--Miscellaneous Writings, Eighteen Eighty-Three to Eighteen Ninety-Six. Date not set. pap. 2.30 (ISBN 0-87952-040-X). First Church.

--The People's Idea of God, Christian Healings No & Yes. pap. 2.00 (ISBN 0-87952-042-6). First Church.

--Poems. 11.00 (ISBN 0-87952-090-6). First Church.

--Prose Works. new type ed. 30.00 (ISBN 0-87952-074-4); brown new type ed. o.p. 50.00 (ISBN 0-87952-076-0); standard ed. 22.00 (ISBN 0-87952-070-1); new type bonded lea. ed. 47.00 (ISBN 0-87952-075-2). First Church.

--Pulpit & Press. pap. 2.00 (ISBN 0-87952-046-9). First Church.

--Pulpit & Press. 1984. pap. 6.00 (ISBN 0-87952-163-5). First Church.

--Retrospection & Introspection. pap. 2.00 (ISBN 0-87952-044-2). First Church.

--Retrospection & Introspection. French 10.00 (ISBN 0-87952-122-8); German 10.00 (ISBN 0-87952-157-0); Italian 4.00 (ISBN 0-87952-182-1); Portugese 7.00 (ISBN 0-87952-207-0); Spanish 7.00 (ISBN 0-87952-231-3); Swedish 8.00 (ISBN 0-87952-252-6). First Church.

--Rudimental Divine Science & No & Yes. Danish 6.00 (ISBN 0-87952-105-8); German 10.00 (ISBN 0-87952-158-9); Italian 5.00 (ISBN 0-87952-183-X); Portugese 5.00 (ISBN 0-87952-208-9); Swedish 6.00 (ISBN 0-87952-253-4); Spanish 5.00 (ISBN 0-87952-232-1). First Church.

--Rudimental Divine Science: No & Yes. 1976. lib. bdg. 69.95 (ISBN 0-8490-2546-X). Gordon Pr.

--Science & Health with Key to the Scriptures. Date not set. standard ed. 9.00 (ISBN 0-87952-001-9); new type ed. 17.50 (ISBN 0-87952-010-8); new type lea. bdg. 45.00 (ISBN 0-87952-015-9); readers ed. 30.00 (ISBN 0-87952-019-1); lea. bdg. 75.00 (ISBN 0-87952-020-5); Century ed. brown lea. bdg 32.50 (ISBN 0-87952-007-8); pap. 3.50 (ISBN 0-87952-000-0); new type bonded lea. ed. 35.00 (ISBN 0-87952-012-4). First Church.

--Science & Health with Key to the Scriptures. (Polish.). 20.00 (ISBN 0-87952-200-3). First Church.

--Science & Health with Key to the Scriptures. pap. 7.00 Spanish ed. (ISBN 0-87952-225-9); pap. 9.00 German ed. (ISBN 0-87952-150-3); pap. 9.00 French ed. (ISBN 0-87952-116-3). First Church.

--Science & Health with Key to the Scriptures. Indonesian 20.00 (ISBN 0-87952-175-9); Japanese 20.00 (ISBN 0-87952-190-2). First Church.

--Science & Health with Key to the Scriptures. Incl. Vol. 1. Danish Ed. 20.00 (ISBN 0-87952-103-1); Vol. 2. Dutch Ed. 20.00 (ISBN 0-87952-109-0); Vol. 3. French Ed. 20.00 (ISBN 0-87952-117-1); Vol. 4. German Ed. 20.00 (ISBN 0-87952-151-1); Vol. 5. Norwegian Ed. 20.00 (ISBN 0-87952-195-3); Vol. 6. Swedish Ed. 20.00 (ISBN 0-87952-250-X); Vol. 7. Russian Ed. 20.00 (ISBN 0-87952-220-8); Vol. 8. Greek Ed. 15.00 (ISBN 0-87952-170-8); Vol. 9. Italian Ed. 15.00 (ISBN 0-87952-180-5); Vol. 10. Spanish Ed. 15.00 (ISBN 0-87952-226-7). First Church.

--Science & Health with Key to the Scriptures. Date not set. 15.00 (ISBN 0-87952-205-4). First Church.

--Seven Messages to The Mother Church. pap. 2.00 (ISBN 0-87952-045-0). First Church.

--Unity of Good, Rudimental Divine Science. pap. 2.00 (ISBN 0-87952-043-4). First Church.

--Unity of Good, Two Sermons. Danish 8.00 (ISBN 0-87952-106-6); Norwegian 7.00 (ISBN 0-87952-197-X); German 6.00 (ISBN 0-87952-159-7). First Church.

Eddy, Mary B. & Carpenter, Gilbert C., eds. Watches, Prayers, Arguments. 100p. 1985. pap. 12.00 (ISBN 0-930227-01-8). Bookmark CA.

Eddy, Mary Baker. Unity of Good. Indonesian ed. 8.00 (ISBN 0-87952-177-5); French Ed. 5.50 (ISBN 0-87952-123-6). First Church.

Eddy, N. B., et al. Codeine & Its Alternatives for Pain & Cough Relief. (Bulletin of WHO: Vol. 38, No. 5 & Vol. 40, Nos. 1, 3 & 5). 253p. 1968-70. pap. 8.00 (ISBN 92-4-056005-X, 94). World Health.

Eddy, Peter, et al. Chinese Language Study in American Higher Education: State of the Art. (Language in Education Ser.: No. 30). 49p. 1980. pap. text ed. 5.95 (ISBN 0-15-599060-8). Ctr Appl Ling.

Eddy, R. Lee, III. What You Should Know about Marriage, Divorce, Annulment, Separation & Community Property in Louisiana. LC 73-91094. 1974. 6.00 (ISBN 0-682-47861-X); pap. 3.50 (ISBN 0-682-47862-8). Exposition Pr FL.

Eddy, Robert L. Minister's Saturday Night. LC 79-23819. (Orig.). 1980. pap. 6.95 (ISBN 0-8298-0382-3). Pilgrim NY.

Eddy, Ruth & LeBar, John. Learning Tennis Together. LC 81-86512. (Illus.). 160p. 1982. pap. 6.95 (ISBN 0-88011-031-7). Leisure Pr.

Eddy, Samuel & Underhill, James C. How to Know the Freshwater Fishes. 3rd ed. (Pictured Key Nature Ser.). 224p. 1978. text ed. wire coil avail. (ISBN 0-697-04750-4). Wm C Brown.

--Northern Fishes: With Social Reference to the Upper Mississippi Valley. LC 73-83729. pap. 108.50 (ISBN 0-317-27911-4, 2055858). Bks Demand UMI.

Eddy, Samuel, et al. Taxonomic Keys to the Common Animals of the North Central States. 4th. ed. 1982. spiral bdg. 12.95x (ISBN 0-8087-2210-7). Burgess.

Eddy, Samuel K. The King Is Dead: Studies in Near Eastern Resistance to Hellenism, 334-31 B. C. LC 61-10151. pap. 104.50 (ISBN 0-317-08850-5, 2001975). Bks Demand UMI.

--The Minting of Antoniniani A. D. 238-249 & the Smyrna Hoard. (Numismatic Notes & Monographs: 156). (Illus.). 133p. 1967. pap. 12.00 (ISBN 0-89722-056-0). Am Numismatic.

Eddy, W. A., ed. see Swift, Jonathan.

Eddy, W. H. Understanding Marxism: An Approach Through Dialogue. LC 78-10609. 157p. 1979. 19.50x (ISBN 0-8476-6125-3). Rowman.

Eddy, William A. Gulliver's Travels: a Critical Study. 10.75 (ISBN 0-8446-1166-2). Peter Smith.

Eddy, William B. The Manager & the Working Group. LC 84-26283. 192p. 1985. 23.95 (ISBN 0-03-001438-7). Praeger.

--Public Organization Behavior & Development. 1981. text ed. 16.95 (ISBN 0-316-21050-1); pap. text ed. 10.95 (ISBN 0-316-21052-8). Little.

Eddy, William B. & Burke, W. Warner, eds. Behavioral Science & the Manager's Role. 2nd, rev. & enl. ed. LC 79-67692. 375p. 1980. pap. 14.95 (ISBN 0-88390-123-4). Univ Assocs.

Eddy, William B., jt. ed. see Golembiewski, Robert T.

Eddy-Gingrow. Technical Talk. 128p. 1984. pap. text ed. 14.95 (ISBN 0-8403-3316-1). Kendall-Hunt.

Ede, D. A., et al, eds. Vertebrate Limb & Somite Morphogenesis: The Third Symposium of the British Society for Developmental Biology. LC 76-50312. (British Society for Developmental Biology Symposium: No. 3). 1978. 85.00 (ISBN 0-521-21552-8). Cambridge U Pr.

Ede, David, et al. Guide to Islam. 265p. 1983. lib. bdg. 59.50 (ISBN 0-8161-7905-0, Hall Reference). G K Hall.

Ede, Donald A. An Introduction to Developmental Biology. LC 78-16359. (Tertiary Level Biology Ser.). 246p. 1978. 32.95x (ISBN 0-470-26469-1). Halsted Pr.

Ede, Jim. A Way of Life: Kettle's Yard. 1984. 49.50 (ISBN 0-317-14006-X). Cambridge U Pr.

Ede, Mary. Arts & Society in England under William & Mary. (Illus.). 218p. 1979. 23.50x (ISBN 0-8476-6261-6). Rowman.

Ede, Terence, jt. auth. see Fielden, Christopher D.

Edebo, L., et al, eds. Endocytosis & Exocytosis in Host Defence. (Monographs in Allergy: Vol. 17). (Illus.). viii, 272p. 1981. pap. 70.00 (ISBN 3-8055-1865-X). S Karger.

Edeen, Susan & Flatt, Carol. Instant Graphics. LC 84-60319. 1984. pap. 9.95 (ISBN 0-8224-3821-6). Pitman Learning.

Edeiken, Jack. Roentgen Diagnosis of Diseases of the Bone. 3rd ed. (GDR: Section No. 6). (Illus.). 1752p. 1981. 139.00 (ISBN 0-683-02744-1). Williams & Wilkins.

Edeiken, Jack, jt. auth. see Kricun, Morrison E.

Edeine, Bernard. La Sologne: Documents de Litterature Traditionnelle, Vol. 3. (Illus.). 342p. (Fr.). 1975. text ed. 57.60x (ISBN 90-2797-735-6). Mouton.

Edel, Abraham. Analyzing Concepts in Social Science: Science, Ideology & Value, Vol. 1. LC 76-50327. 351p. 1979. 14.95 (ISBN 0-87855-143-3). Transaction Bks.

--Aristotle & His Philosophy. LC 81-7561. xii, 479p. 1982. 26.00x (ISBN 0-8078-1493-8); pap. 12.00x (ISBN 0-8078-4085-8). U of NC Pr.

--Exploring Fact & Value: Science, Ideology, Value. LC 78-62886. 369p. 1980. 16.95 (ISBN 0-87855-229-4). Transaction Bks.

--Interpreting Education, Vol. III. (Science, Ideology, & Values Ser.). 350p. 1985. 24.95 (ISBN 0-88738-059-X). Transaction Bks.

--Science & the Structure of Ethics. LC 61-8082. (Foundations of the Unity of Science Ser: Vol. 2, No. 3). 1961. pap. 2.25x (ISBN 0-226-57593-4, P412, Phoen). U of Chicago Pr.

Edel, Abraham & Edel, May. Anthropology & Ethics: The Quest for Moral Understanding. rev. ed. 280p. 1970. casebound 12.95 (ISBN 0-87855-098-4). Transaction Bks.

Edel, Leon. Bloomsbury: A House of Lions. 1980. pap. 2.75 (ISBN 0-380-50005-1, 50005-1). Avon.

--Bloomsbury: A House of Lions. 1979. 14.37i (ISBN 0-397-01043-5). Har-Row.

--Henry David Thoreau. LC 76-629876. (Pamphlets on American Writers Ser: No. 90). (Orig.). 1970. pap. 1.25x (ISBN 0-8166-0562-9, MPAW90). U of Minn Pr.

--Henry James: A Life. rev. & abr. ed. LC 85-42536. (Illus.). 736p. 1985. 23.99i (ISBN 0-317-19116-0, HarpT). Har-Row.

--Henry James in Westminster Abbey: The Address. (Illus.). 24p. 1976. pap. 7.00 (ISBN 0-932136-02-8). Petronium Pr.

--Henry James: The Conquest of London. 1978. pap. 2.95 (ISBN 0-380-39651-3, 39651-3, Discus). Avon.

--Henry James: The Master. 1978. pap. 2.95 (ISBN 0-380-39685-8, 39685-3, Discus). Avon.

--Henry James: The Master, 1901-1916. LC 76-163225. (Henry James Ser.). (Illus.). 1972. 13.41i (ISBN 0-397-00733-7). Har-Row.

--Henry James: The Middle Years. 1978. pap. 2.95 (ISBN 0-380-39669-6, 39669-6, Discus). Avon.

--Henry James: The Treacherous Years. 1978. pap. 2.95 (ISBN 0-380-39677-7, 39677-7, Discus). Avon.

--Henry James: The Untried Years. 1978. pap. 2.95 (ISBN 0-380-39107-4, 39107-4, Discus). Avon.

--James Joyce: The Last Journey. LC 77-10505. (Studies in Joyce: No. 96). 1977. lib. bdg. 38.95x (ISBN 0-8383-2214-X). Haskell.

--Modern Psychological Novel. 11.25 (ISBN 0-8446-2020-3). Peter Smith.

--The Selected Letters of Henry James. 15.95 (ISBN 0-89190-316-X, Pub. by Am Repr). Amereon Ltd.

--Stuff of Sleep & Dreams: Experiments in Literary Psychology. LC 81-47787. 224p. 1982. 19.23i (ISBN 0-06-014929-9, HarpT). Har-Row.

--Stuff of Sleep & Dreams: Experiments in Literary Psychology. 368p. 1983. pap. 4.95 (ISBN 0-380-63719-7, 63719, Discus). Avon.

--Writing Lives: Principia Biographica. LC 84-5959. 238p. 1984. 15.95 (ISBN 0-393-01882-2). Norton.

Edel, Leon & Laurence, Dan H. A Bibliography of Henry James. 3rd, rev. ed. (Illus.). 1982. 45.00x (ISBN 0-19-818186-8). Oxford U Pr.

Edel, Leon, jt. auth. see Brown, E. K.

Edel, Leon, jt. auth. see James, Henry.

Edel, Leon, ed. The Bodley Head Henry James, 11 vols. Incl. Vol. 1. The Europeans, Washington Square. 392p (ISBN 0-370-00616-X); Vol. 2. The Awkward Age. 430p (ISBN 0-370-00617-8); Vol. 3. The Bostonians. 448p (ISBN 0-370-00625-9); Vol. 4. The Spoils of Poynton. 208p (ISBN 0-370-00626-7); Vol. 5. The Portrait of a Lady. 626p (ISBN 0-370-00640-2); Vol. 6. What Maisie Knew. 284p (ISBN 0-370-00586-4); Vol. 7. The Wings of the Dove. 540p (ISBN 0-370-01423-5); Vol. 8. The Ambassadors. 468p (ISBN 0-370-01432-4); Vol. 9. The Golden Bowl. 604p (ISBN 0-370-01456-1); Vol. 10. The Princess Casamassima. 618p (ISBN 0-370-10237-1); Vol. 11. Daisy Miller, the Turn of the Screw. 198p (ISBN 0-370-10532-X). 1980. 12.95 ea. (Pub. by the Bodley Head); write for info. Merrimack Pub Cir.

--Henry James: Selected Fiction. 1964. pap. 8.50 (ISBN 0-525-47140-5, 0826-240). Dutton.

Edel, Leon, ed. see James, Alice.

Edel, Leon, ed. see James, Henry.

Edel, Leon, ed. see James, Henry & Wells, H. G.

Edel, Leon, ed. see Wilson, Edmund.

Edel, Leon, ed. & intro. by see Wilson, Edmund.

Edel, Leon, ed. see Wilson, Edmund.

Edel, Marjorie. The Place Your Body Is. 98p. 1984. pap. 6.00 (ISBN 0-932136-07-9). Petronium Pr.

Edel, Matthew & Rothenberg, Jerome. Readings in Urban Economics. (Illus.). 544p. 1972. pap. text ed. write for info. (ISBN 0-02-331480-X, 33148). Macmillan.

Edel, Matthew, et al. Shaky Palaces: Home Ownership & Social Mobility in Boston, 1870-1970. 440p. 1984. 40.00x (ISBN 0-231-05626-5, King's Crown Paperbacks); pap. 18.00x (ISBN 0-231-05627-3). Columbia U Pr.

Edel, May, jt. auth. see Edel, Abraham.

Edel, May M. The Chiga of Western Uganda. LC 76-442670. pap. 52.00 (ISBN 0-317-29888-7, 2019413). Bks Demand UMI.

Edel, Richard. Home Workout: Your Complete Guide to Buying & Exercising with Home Fitness Equipment. 1985. pap. 8.95 (ISBN 0-697-00711-1). Wm C Brown.

Edel, Wilbur. A Constitutional Convention: Threat or Challenge? LC 80-27573. 160p. 1981. 29.95x (ISBN 0-03-059073-6). Praeger.

Edelan, Dominic. Isovector Methods for Equations of Balans: With Programs for Computer Assistance in Operator Calculations and an Exposition of Practical Topics of the Exterior Calculus. 536p. 1980. 45.00x (ISBN 90-286-0420-0). Sijthoff & Noordhoff.

Edelberg, Guillermo S. The Procurement of Practices of the Mexican Affiliates of Selected United States Automobile Firms. Bruchey, Stuart & Bruchey, Eleanor, eds. LC 76-5005. (American Business Abroad Ser.). (Illus.). 1976. Repr. of 1976 ed. lib. bdg. 21.00x (ISBN 0-405-09274-1). Ayer Co Pubs.

Edelberg, Harvey, tr. see Shreider, Yu. A.

Edelberg, Lennart. Synopsis of Contents & Index to Sir George Scott Robertson, the Kafirs of the Hindu-Kush. (Illus.). 59p. 1896-1900. Repr. 13.00 (ISBN 0-384-13850-0). Johnson Repr.

Edelbrock, Craig, jt. auth. see Achenbach, Thomas M.

Edelby, Neophytos. Future of Canon Law, Vol. 48. LC 78-100004. (Concilium Ser.). 188p. 6.95 (ISBN 0-8091-0049-5). Paulist Pr.

Edelby, Neophytos & Urresti, Teodoro-J., eds. Religious Freedom. LC 66-29260. (Concilium Ser.: Vol. 18). 191p. 6.95 (ISBN 0-8091-0124-6). Paulist Pr.

Edelby, Neophytos, jt. ed. see Urresti, Teodoro-J.

Edelby, Neophytos, et al, eds. Renewal & Reform of Canon Law. LC 67-30868. (Concilium Ser.: Vol. 28). 191p. 1967. 6.95 (ISBN 0-8091-0125-4). Paulist Pr.

--Sacraments in Theology & Canon Law. LC 68-58308. (Concilium Ser.: Vol. 38). 191p. 1968. 6.95 (ISBN 0-8091-0132-7). Paulist Pr.

Edelen, D. G. Lagrangian Mechanics of Nonconservative Nonholomic Systems. (Mechanics: Dynamical Systems Ser.: No. 2). 314p. 1977. 30.00x (ISBN 90-286-0077-9). Sijthoff & Noordhoff.

Edelen, D. G. & Kydoniefs, A. D. An Introduction to Linear Algebra for Science & Engineering. 2nd ed. (Illus.). 270p. 1976. 25.00 (ISBN 0-444-00195-6). Elsevier.

Edelen, D. G. & Wilson, A. G. Relativity & the Question of Discretization in Astronomy. LC 79-108675. (Springer Tracts in Natural Philosophy: Vol. 20). (Illus.). 1970. 32.00 (ISBN 0-387-05254-2). Springer-Verlag.

Edelen, D. G., jt. auth. see Kadic, A.

Edelen, Dominic G. Applied Exterior Calculus. LC 84-19575. 471p. 1985. pap. text ed. 44.95 (ISBN 0-471-80773-7, Pub. by Wiley-Interscience). Wiley.

Edelen, Ellen A., ed. see Spiegel, Michael S.

Edelestein, Leonard. We Are Accountable. pap. 5.00x (ISBN 0-87574-024-3, 024). Pendle Hill.

Edelfelt, Roy A. & Orvell, Tamar. Teacher Centers: Where, What, Why? LC 78-61321. (Fastback Ser.: No. 117). 1978. pap. 0.75 (ISBN 0-87367-117-1). Phi Delta Kappa.

Edelfelt, Roy A., jt. ed. see Beegle, Charles W.

Edelhart & Lindenmann. Interferon. 1981. 11.95x (ISBN 0-201-03943-5). Cancer Control Soc.

Edelhart, M. & Lindenmann, J. Interferon: The New Hope for Cancer. 224p. 1982. pap. 3.50 (ISBN 0-345-30298-2). Ballantine.

Edelhart, Michael & Garr, Doug. The Complete Computer Compendium. (Illus.). 256p. pap. 12.95 (ISBN 0-201-10437-7). Addison-Wesley.

Edelhart, Michael, jt. auth. see Gluckin, Doreen.

Edelhart, Michael, jt. auth. see Planned Parenthood Federation of America.

Edelhart, Mike. Getting from Twenty to Thirty: Surviving Your First Decade in the Real World. LC 82-21007. 240p. 1983. 10.95 (ISBN 0-87131-381-2); pap. 6.95 (ISBN 0-87131-382-0). M Evans.

--Handbook of Earth Shelter Design. LC 80-2047. (Illus.). 256p. 1982. pap. 11.95 (ISBN 0-385-17308-3, Dolp). Doubleday.

Edelhart, Mike & Davies, Owen. Omni: Online Database Directory. 384p. 1983. 19.95 (ISBN 0-02-535000-5); pap. 10.95 (ISBN 0-02-079910-1). Macmillan.

Edelhart, Mike & Tinen, James. America the Quotable. 640p. 1983. 29.95x (ISBN 0-87196-331-0). Facts on File.

Edelhart, Mike, jt. auth. see Davies, Owens.

Edelheit, Steven. Dark Prophecies: George Orwell & Technology. (George Orwell Ser.). 1979. lib. bdg. 69.95 (ISBN 0-685-96864-2). Revisionist Pr.

Edelhertz, Herbert & Walsh, Marilyn. The White-Collar Challenge to Nuclear Safeguards. LC 77-15816. (Human Affairs Research Center Ser.). (Illus.). 128p. 1978. 20.00 (ISBN 0-669-02058-3). Lexington Bks.

Edelhertz, Herbert & Rogovin, Charles, eds. A National Strategy for Containing White-Collar Crime. LC 79-2373. (Human Affairs Research Center Ser.). 160p. 1980. 20.00x (ISBN 0-669-03166-6). Lexington Bks.

Edelhertz, Herbert, et al. The Containment of Organized Crime. LC 82-48633. (The Battelle Human Affairs Research Center Ser.). 128p. 1984. 21.50x (ISBN 0-669-06364-9). Lexington Bks.

Edelhoch, H., jt. ed. see Chen, R. F.

Edell, Ed. A Special Breed of Man. (Illus.). 233p. 1984. pap. 3.95 (ISBN 0-934588-08-2). Ranger Assocs.

Edell, Ron. How to Save Your Marriage from an Affair. LC 83-3868. 240p. 1983. 14.95 (ISBN 0-672-52764-2). Bobbs.

Edelman, Alice & Stuzin, Roz. How to Survive a Second Marriage. 1980. 11.95 (ISBN 0-8184-0307-1). Lyle Stuart.

Edelman, Bernard. Ownership of the Image. Kingdom, Elizabeth, tr. from Fr. 1979. 22.95x (ISBN 0-7100-0103-7). Routledge & Kegan.

Edelman, Bernard, ed. see New York Vietnam Veterans Memorial Commission.

Edelman, Charles D. & Siegler, Ilene C. Federal Age Discrimination in Employment Law. 364p. 1978. with 1980 suppl 45.00 (ISBN 0-87215-206-5); 1980 suppl 15.00 (ISBN 0-87215-239-1). Michie Co.

Edelman, Chester M., jt. auth. see Gauthier, Bernard.

Edelman, Daniel B., jt. auth. see National Center for State Courts.

Edelman, Elaine. Boom-De-Boom. (Illus.). (ps-2). 1980. 4.95 (ISBN 0-394-84341-X); PLB 5.99 (ISBN 0-394-94341-4). Pantheon.

--I Love My Baby Sister (Most of the Time) LC 83-2563. (Illus.). 32p. (ps-1). 1984. 11.00 (ISBN 0-688-02245-6); lib. bdg. 10.08 (ISBN 0-688-02247-2). Lothrop.

--I Love My Baby Sister: Most of the Time. LC 85-574. (Illus.). 24p. (ps-3). 1985. pap. 3.95 (ISBN 0-14-050547-4, Puffin). Penguin.

Edelman, Gerald M. & Mountcastle, Vernon B. The Mindful Brain: Cortical Organization & the Group-Selective Theory of Higher Brain Function. 128p. 1978. pap. text ed. 8.95x (ISBN 0-262-55007-5). MIT Pr.

Edelman, Gerald M., ed. Cellular Selection & Regulation in the Immune Response. LC 73-93857. (Society of General Physiologists Ser.: Vol. 29). 299p. 1974. 50.50 (ISBN 0-911216-71-5). Raven.

--Molecular Machinery of the Membrane. 75p. 1976. pap. text ed. 8.95x (ISBN 0-262-55006-7). MIT Pr.

Edelman, Gerald M., et al, eds. Dynamic Aspects of Neocortical Function. LC 84-11825. (Neuroscience Institute Monograph). 736p. 1984. 85.00x (ISBN 0-471-80559-9, Pub. by Wiley-Interseince). Wiley.

Edelman, Heinz, illus. Prince Ring: Icelandic Fairy Tale. (Collection of Fairy Tales Ser.). 32p. 1983. 7.95 (ISBN 0-87191-951-6). Creative Ed.

Edelman, I. S., et al, eds. Annual Review of Physiology, Vol. 41. LC 39-15404. (Illus.). 1979. text ed. 20.00 (ISBN 0-8243-0341-5). Annual Reviews.

--Annual Review of Physiology, Vol. 42. LC 39-15404. (Illus.). 1980. text ed. 20.00 (ISBN 0-8243-0342-3). Annual Reviews.

--Annual Review of Physiology, Vol. 44. LC 39-15404. (Illus.). 1982. text ed. 22.00 (ISBN 0-8243-0344-X). Annual Reviews.

--Annual Review of Physiology, Vol. 43. LC 39-15404. (Illus.). 1981. text ed. 20.00 (ISBN 0-8243-0343-1). Annual Reviews.

Edelman, Ian. Discovering Avebury. (Discovering Ser.: No. 280). (Orig.). 1985. pap. 2.50 (ISBN 0-85263-766-7, Pub. by Shire Pubns England). Seven Hills Bks.

Edelman, J. & Chapman, J. M. Basic Biochemistry: A Visual Approach for College & University Students. 1978. pap. text ed. 11.50x (ISBN 0-435-60230-6). Heinemann Ed.

Edelman, Judy. Women on the Job: The Communist View. new ed. 56p. 1973. pap. 0.70 (ISBN 0-87898-101-2). New Outlook.

Edelman, Leonard. Michigan Probate: Michigan Practice Systems Library Selections. LC 79-92366. 87.50; Suppl. 1984. 26.50; Suppl. 1983. 24.00. Lawyers Co-Op.

Edelman, Lily. Israel. 1958. 20.00 (ISBN 0-686-17232-9). Scholars Ref Lib.

--Modern Israel. pap. 2.00 (ISBN 0-87980-101-8). Wilshire.

--Sukkah & the Big Wind. (Holiday Series of Picture Story Books). (Illus.). (gr. k-2). 1956. 5.95 (ISBN 0-8381-0716-8). United Syn Bk.

Edelman, Lily, ed. see Goodman, Lenn E.

Edelman, M. Political Languages: Words That Succeed & Policies That Fail. (Institute for Research on Poverty Monograph). 1977. pap. 5.95 (ISBN 0-12-230662-7). Acad Pr.

Edelman, M., et al, eds. Methods in Chloroplast Molecular Biology. 1152p. 1983. 183.00 (ISBN 0-444-80368-8, I-518-82, Biomedical Pr). Elsevier.

Edelman, Martin. Democratic Theories & the Constitution. LC 83-18143. (Political Theory Ser.). 320p. 1984. 39.50x (ISBN 0-87395-872-1); pap. 16.95x (ISBN 0-87395-873-X). State U NY Pr.

Edelman, Maurice. Disraeli in Love. 416p. 1984. pap. 3.95 (ISBN 0-8128-8040-4). Stein & Day.

--Disraeli Rising. 282p. 1984. pap. 3.95 (ISBN 0-8128-8058-7). Stein & Day.

Edelman, Murray. Politics As Symbolic Action: Mass Arousal & Quiescence. (Institute for Research on Poverty Monograph). 1971. 16.00 (ISBN 0-12-230650-3); pap. 5.95 (ISBN 0-12-230652-X). Acad Pr.

--The Symbolic Uses of Politics: With a New Afterword. LC 84-16195. 232p. 1985. pap. 6.95x (ISBN 0-252-01202-X). U of Ill Pr.

Edelman, Murray J., jt. auth. see Dolbeare, Kenneth M.

Edelman, Richard. Wedding Feast. (Illus.). 1970. pap. 1.50 (ISBN 0-685-04680-X). Oyez.

Edelman, Richard W. The Nine Finger Image. LC 78-71908. 1979. 12.95 (ISBN 0-87929-058-7). Barlenmir.

Edelman, Rita. You Don't Have to Be Chinese to Cook Great Chinese Food. 1975. 4.95 (ISBN 0-913806-57-9). Laddin Pr.

Edelman, Robert. Gentry Politics on the Eve of the Russian Revolution: The Nationalist Party, 1907-1917. 1980. 27.50x (ISBN 0-8135-0885-1). Rutgers U Pr.

Edelman, Rosemary. Fireworks. LC 78-72923. 1979. 9.95 (ISBN 0-87795-213-2). Arbor Hse.

Edelman, Sandra A. Summer People--Winter People. LC 79-17113. (Illus.). 48p. (Orig.). 1979. pap. 2.25 (ISBN 0-913270-44-X). Sunstone Pr.

Edelmann, A., ed. Radioactivity for Pharmaceutical & Allied Research Laboratories. 1960. 52.50 (ISBN 0-12-230850-6). Acad Pr.

Edelmann, Chester., Jr. Pediatric Kidney Disease, 2 Vols. 1978. text ed. 125.00 (ISBN 0-316-21070-6). Little.

Edelmann, Martin & Schmelzer, Menahem, eds. The Damascus Bible, Vol. II. facsimile ed. 230p. 1982. 485.00x (ISBN 0-8018-2903-8). Johns Hopkins.

--The Damascus Bible, Vol. 1, Pt. 1. Orig. Title: Early Hebrew Manuscripts in Facsimile. 250p. 1979. text ed. 528.00x (ISBN 0-8018-1337-9); pap. text ed. 495.00x (ISBN 0-8018-1349-2). Johns Hopkins.

Edelmann, Martin, ed. see Mekhilta, Munich.

Edels, Yvonne. Laryngectomy: Diagnosis to Rehabilitation. 309p. 1983. 30.00 (ISBN 0-89443-814-X). Aspen Systems.

Edelson, Edward. Great Monsters of the Movies. (Illus.). (gr. 4-6). 1974. pap. 1.75 (ISBN 0-671-56108-1). Archway.

--Who Goes There: The Search for Intelligent Life in the Universe. (Illus.). 228p. 1980. pap. 4.95 (ISBN 0-07-018986-2). McGraw.

Edelson, Edward, jt. auth. see Boikess, Robert S.

Edelson, Jacqueline & Lyons, Walter. Institutional Care of the Mentally Impaired Elderly. 288p. 28.50 (ISBN 0-442-25810-0). Van Nos Reinhold.

Edelson, Jane, et al. Readings in Modern Dance, Vol. I. LC 76-359498. (Illus.). v, 82p. (Orig.). 1975. pap. text ed. 9.50x (ISBN 0-932582-13-3). Dance Notation.

Edelson, Marshall. Hypothesis & Evidence in Psychoanalysis. LC 83-9281. 200p. 1984. lib. bdg. 20.00x (ISBN 0-226-18432-3). U of Chicago Pr.

--Hypothesis & Evidence in Psychoanalysis. LC 83-9281. xiv, 180p. 1985. pap. 7.95 (ISBN 0-226-18436-6). U of Chicago Pr.

--Language & Interpretation in Psychoanalysis. LC 84-2547. xvi, 254p. 1984. pap. text ed. 9.00x (ISBN 0-226-18433-1). U of Chicago Pr.

--Sociotherapy & Psychotherapy. LC 73-94997. 1970. 20.00x (ISBN 0-226-18430-7). U of Chicago Pr.

Edelson, Mary B. Seven Cycles: Public Rituals. (Illus.). 64p. (Orig.). 1980. pap. 10.00x (ISBN 0-9604650-0-6). Edelson.

Edelson, Morris, tr. see Brandys, Kazimierz.

Edelson, Morris, tr. see Rius, Jorge.

Edelson, Paul J., et al. Immunological Deficiency Syndromes. LC 73-13446. (Illus.). 220p. 1972. text ed. 24.50x (ISBN 0-8422-7082-5). Irvington.

Edelstein, Alan. An Unacknowledged Harmony: Philo-Semitism & the Survival of European Jewry. LC 81-1563. (Contributions in Ethnic Studies: No. 4). xii, 235p. 1982. lib. bdg. 29.95 (ISBN 0-313-22754-3, EDP/). Greenwood.

Edelstein, Alex S. Comparative Communication Research. (Sage CommTexts Ser.: Vol. 9). 160p. 1982. 17.95 (ISBN 0-8039-1750-3); pap. 9.95 (ISBN 0-8039-1751-1). Sage.

Edelstein, Alex S., et al. Information Societies: Comparing the Japanese & American Experiences. LC 78-71366. 314p. (Orig.). 1979. pap. 15.00x (ISBN 0-295-95667-4, Pub. by Intl Communication Ctr). U of Wash Pr.

Edelstein, Alex S., et al, eds. Information Societies: Comparing the Japanese & American Experiences. LC 78-71366. (Illus.). 1978. pap. 10.95 (ISBN 0-933236-00-X). Intl Comm Ctr.

Edelstein, Andrew J. The Pop Sixties: A Personal & Irreverent Guide. (Illus.). 183p. (Orig.). 1985. pap. 8.95 (ISBN 0-911818-67-7). World Almanac.

Edelstein, Arthur, jt. auth. see Baumbach, Jonathan.

Edelstein, Arthur, ed. Images & Ideas in American Culture: The Functions of Criticism - Essays in Memory of Philip Rahv. LC 78-63584. 232p. 1979. 15.00x (ISBN 0-87451-164-X); pap. 9.00x (ISBN 0-87451-218-2). U Pr of New Eng.

Edelstein, Barbara. The Woman Doctor's Diet for Teenage Girls. 288p. 1985. pap. 2.95 (ISBN 0-345-32091-3). Ballantine.

Edelstein, Barry A. & Couture, Eugene T., eds. Behavioral Assessment & Rehabilitation of the Traumatically Brain Damaged. (Applied Clinical Psychology Ser.). 364p. 1984. 39.50x (ISBN 0-306-41295-0, Plenum Pr). Plenum Pub.

Edelstein, C. D. & Wicks, R. J. An Introduction to Criminal Justice. 1977. text ed. 25.95 (ISBN 0-07-018980-3). McGraw.

Edelstein, David S. Joel Munsell: Printer & Antiquarian. LC 75-164751. (Columbia University. Studies in the Social Sciences: No. 560). Repr. of 1950 ed. 24.50 (ISBN 0-404-51560-6). AMS Pr.

Edelstein, Dov B. Worlds Torn Asunder. 1985. 12.95 (ISBN 0-88125-040-6). Ktav.

Edelstein, Emma J. & Edelstein, Ludwig. Asclepius: A Collection & Interpretation of the Testimonies, 2 vols. in 1. facsimile ed. LC 75-10635. (Ancient Religion & Mythology Ser.). (Eng. & Gr.). 1976. Repr. of 1945 ed. 57.50x (ISBN 0-405-07009-8). Ayer Co Pubs.

Edelstein, J. D. & Warner, M. A Comparative Union Democracy: Organization & Opposition in British & American Unions. LC 75-25204. 378p. 1976. 37.95x (ISBN 0-470-23268-4). Halsted Pr.

Edelstein, J. David & Warner, Malcolm. Comparative Union Democracy: Organization & Opposition in British & American Union. LC 77-80874. 388p. 1979. pap. 14.95x (ISBN 0-87855-623-0). Transaction Bks.

Edelstein, J. M. Wallace Stevens: A Descriptive Bibliography. LC 72-91106. (Pittsburgh Ser. in Bibliography). (Illus.). 1973. 50.00x (ISBN 0-8229-3268-7). U of Pittsburgh Pr.

Edelstein, Joel, jt. auth. see Chilcote, Ronald H.

Edelstein, Joel C., jt. ed. see Chilcote, Ronald H.

Edelstein, L. The Hippocratic Oath. 90p. 1979. 10.00 (ISBN 0-89005-272-7). Ares.

Edelstein, L. & Kidd, I. G., eds. Posidonius: Vol. 1, The Fragments. LC 77-145609. (Classical Texts & Commentaries Ser, No. 13). 352p. 1972. 59.00 (ISBN 0-521-08046-0). Cambridge U Pr.

Edelstein, Linda. Maternal Bereavement: Coping with the Unexpected Death of a Child. LC 83-21124. 186p. 1984. 23.95 (ISBN 0-03-063908-5). Praeger.

Edelstein, Ludwig. Ancient Medicine: Selected Papers of Ludwig Edelstein. Temkin, Owsei & Temkin, C. Lilian, eds. LC 67-12425. pap. 127.50 (ISBN 0-317-28986-1, 2020329). Bks Demand UMI.

--Meaning of Stoicism. LC 66-23463. (Martin Classical Lectures Ser.: No. 21). 1966. 8.95x (ISBN 0-674-55850-2). Harvard U Pr.

Edelstein, Ludwig, jt. auth. see Edelstein, Emma J.

Edelstein, Michael. Overseas Investment in the Age of High Imperialism. LC 82-1329. 480p. 1982. 42.00x (ISBN 0-231-04438-0); pap. 17.00x (ISBN 0-231-04439-9). Columbia U Pr.

Edelstein, N. M., ed. Actinides in Perspective: Proceedings of the Conference Held at Pacific Grove, CA, USA, Sept. 10-15, 1981. (Illus.). 620p. 1982. 83.00 (ISBN 0-08-029193-7). Pergamon.

Edelstein, Sally. This Year's Girl. (Illus.). 64p. 1985. pap. 8.95 (ISBN 0-385-19828-0, Dolp). Doubleday.

Edelstein, Stuart J., jt. auth. see Widom, Joanne M.

Edelstein, Tilden G., jt. ed. see Scheiner, Seth M.

Edelstien, M. Gerald. Trauma, Trance & Transformation: A Clinical Guide to Hypnotherapy. LC 81-10175. 176p. 1981. 20.00 (ISBN 0-87630-278-9). Brunner-Mazel.

Edelston, J., ed. Correspondence of Sir Isaac Newton & Professor Cotes. 323p. 1969. 42.50x (ISBN 0-7146-1597-8, F Cass Co). Biblio Dist.

Edelwich, Jerry & Brodsky, Archie. Burn-Out: Stages of Disillusionment in the Helping Professions. LC 79-27412. 255p. 1980. text ed. 29.95 (ISBN 0-87705-507-6); pap. 16.95 (ISBN 0-89885-035-5). Human Sci Pr.

--Sexual Dilemmas for the Helping Professional. LC 82-9491. 250p. 1982. 20.00 (ISBN 0-87630-314-9). Brunner-Mazel.

Edem, D. A. Introduction to Educational Administration in Nigeria. 233p. 1982. pap. 12.95 (ISBN 0-471-27984-6). Wiley.

Eden, Alvin N. Handbook for New Parents. 224p. 1984. pap. 2.95 (ISBN 0-425-07291-6, Windhover). Berkley Pub.

--Positive Parenting: How to Raise a Healthier & Happier Child (from Birth to Three Years) 1982. pap. 2.95 (ISBN 0-451-11276-8, AE1276, Sig). NAL.

Eden, Anthony. Days for Decision. LC 50-13062. 1969. Repr. of 1950 ed. 15.00 (ISBN 0-527-26300-1). Kraus Repr.

--Foreign Affairs. LC 39-17206. Repr. of 1939 ed. 23.00 (ISBN 0-527-26310-9). Kraus Repr.

--Freedom & Order: Selected Speeches, 1939-1946. Repr. of 1948 ed. 22.00 (ISBN 0-527-26320-6). Kraus Repr.

Eden, C. & Jones, S. Messing about in Problems: A Practical Approach. (Frontiers of Operational Research & Applied Systems Analysis Ser.: Vol. 1). (Illus.). 130p. 1983. 22.00 (ISBN 0-08-029961-X); pap. 10.95 (ISBN 0-08-029960-1). Pergamon.

Eden, C. P., ed. see Taylor, Jeremy.

Eden, D. J. Mental Handicap: An Introduction. (Unwin Education Bks.). 1976. pap. text ed. 7.95x (ISBN 0-04-371042-5). Allen Unwin.

Eden, Dorothy. An Afternoon Walk. 224p. 1979. pap. 2.50 (ISBN 0-449-24020-7, Crest). Fawcett.

--The American Heiress. 1981. pap. 2.95 (ISBN 0-449-24448-2, Crest). Fawcett.

--The American Heiress. 1976. Repr. lib. bdg. 13.95 (ISBN 0-8161-3232-1, Large Print Bks). G K Hall.

--Darkwater. 1978. pap. 2.50 (ISBN 0-449-23544-0, Crest). Fawcett.

--The House on Hay Hill. 224p. 1978. pap. 2.25 (ISBN 0-449-23789-3, Crest). Fawcett.

--An Important Family. LC 81-19026. 320p. 1982. 14.50 (ISBN 0-688-01148-9). Morrow.

--An Important Family. 352p. 1983. pap. 3.50 (ISBN 0-380-63297-7, 63297-7). Avon.

--Lady of Mallow. 1978. pap. 1.95 (ISBN 0-449-23167-4, Crest). Fawcett.

--Melbury Square. 1977. pap. 1.95 (ISBN 0-449-24050-9, Crest). Fawcett.

--The Millionaire's Daughter. 1978. pap. 2.25 (ISBN 0-449-23186-0, Crest). Fawcett.

--Never Call It Loving. 1978. pap. 2.25 (ISBN 0-449-23143-7, Crest). Fawcett.

--Ravenscroft. 1978. pap. 1.95 (ISBN 0-449-23760-5, Crest). Fawcett.

--The Salamanca Drum. 1978. pap. 2.75 (ISBN 0-449-23548-3, Crest). Fawcett.

--Shadow Wife. 1978. pap. 1.95 (ISBN 0-449-23699-4, Crest). Fawcett.

--Siege in the Sun. 1979. pap. 2.25 (ISBN 0-449-23884-9, Crest). Fawcett.

--Sleep in the Woods. 256p. 1981. pap. 2.50 (ISBN 0-449-23706-0, Crest). Fawcett.

--The Sleeping Bride. 192p. (Orig.). 1976. pap. 1.95 (ISBN 0-441-77126-2). Ace Bks.

--Speak to Me of Love. 320p. 1981. pap. 2.95 (ISBN 0-449-23981-0, Crest). Fawcett.

--The Storrington Papers. 1980. pap. 2.50 (ISBN 0-449-24239-0, Crest). Fawcett.

--The Time of the Dragon. 1977. pap. 2.75 (ISBN 0-449-23059-7, Crest). Fawcett.

--The Vines of Yarrabee. 320p. 1980. pap. 1.95 (ISBN 0-449-23184-4, Crest). Fawcett.

--Waiting for Willa. 1977. pap. 1.95 (ISBN 0-449-23187-9, Crest). Fawcett.

--Winterwood. 1980. pap. 1.95 (ISBN 0-449-23185-2, Crest). Fawcett.

Eden, Dorothy, intro. by see Scott, J. T.

Eden, Douglas & Short, Frederick. Political Change in Europe. 1981. 25.00x (ISBN 0-312-62202-3). St Martin.

Eden, Emily. The Semi-Attached Couple & the Semi-Detached House. LC 81-12450. (Virago Modern Classics Ser.). 540p. 1982. pap. 8.95 (ISBN 0-385-27217-0, Virago). Doubleday.

--Up the Country. 1980. Repr. 18.00x (ISBN 0-8364-0660-5, Pub. by Curzon Pr). South Asia Bks.

--Up the Country: Letters from India. (Illus.). 432p. 1983. pap. 9.95 (ISBN 0-86068-440-7, Pub. by Virago Pr). Merrimack Pub Cir.

--Up the Country: Letters Written to Her Sister from the Upper Provinces of India. Thompson, Edward, ed. (Illus.). 432p. 1982. text ed. 27.50x (ISBN 0-7007-0112-5, Pub. by Curzon Pr England). Apt Bks.

Eden, F. M. State of the Poor, 3 vols. new ed. 1966. 225.00x set (ISBN 0-7146-1390-8, F Cass Co). Biblio Dist.

Eden, Frederick M. State of the Poor. Rogers, A. G., ed. LC 68-56502. 1969. Repr. of 1928 ed. 24.50 (ISBN 0-405-08485-4, Blom Pubns). Ayer Co Pubs.

Eden, G., jt. auth. see Eden, R. F.

Eden, Helen. Whistles of Silver, & Other Stories. facsimile ed. LC 72-152939. (Short Story Index Reprint Ser.). (Illus.). Repr. of 1933 ed. 14.50 (ISBN 0-8369-3798-8). Ayer Co Pubs.

Eden, Henry S. & Eden, Murray. Microcomputers in Patient Care. LC 81-1999. (Illus.). 191p. 1981. 28.00 (ISBN 0-8155-0849-2). Noyes.

Eden, Horatia K. Juliana Horatia Ewing & Her Books. LC 71-77001. (Library of Lives & Letters). (Illus.). 1969. Repr. of 1896 ed. 40.00x (ISBN 0-8103-3897-1). Gale.

Eden, Jerome. Orgone Energy: The Answer to Atomic Suicide. LC 72-75477. 1972. 8.95 (ISBN 0-682-47477-0). Exposition Pr FL.

--Planet in Trouble: The UFO Assault on Earth. 1973. 8.50 (ISBN 0-682-47822-9). Exposition Pr FL.

Eden, Lorraine, jt. ed. see Rugman, Alan.

Eden, Lynn. Crisis in Watertown: The Polarization of an American Community. 230p. 1973. pap. 2.95 (ISBN 0-472-06192-5, AA). U of Mich Pr.

Eden, Michael. Rain Forests. (Young Geologist Ser.). (Illus.). 24p. (gr. 1-4). 1982. 5.95 (ISBN 0-370-30369-5, Pub. by the Bodley Head). Merrimack Pub Cir.

--Soils & Plants. (Young Geologist Ser.). (Illus.). 24p. (gr. 1-5). 1984. 6.95 (ISBN 0-370-30599-X, Pub. by the Bodley Head). Merrimack Pub Cir.

--Weather. (Young Geologist Ser.). (Illus.). 24p. (gr. 1-4). 1982. 5.95 (ISBN 0-370-30454-3, Pub. by the Bodley Head). Merrimack Pub Cir.

Eden, Murray, jt. auth. see Eden, Henry S.

Eden, Murray, jt. auth. see Rutstein, David D.

Eden, Murray, jt. ed. see Boretos, John W.

Eden, P., ed. Dictionary of Land Surveyors & Local Cartographers of Great Britain & Ireland. 528p. 1981. 14.00x (ISBN 0-7129-0900-1, Pub. by Dawson). State Mutual Bk.

Eden, P. T., ed. see Seneca.

Eden, R. F. & Eden, G. Impedance Microbiology. 1984. 39.95 (ISBN 0-471-90623-9). Wiley.

Eden, Richard & Landshoff, D. I. The Analytic S-Matrix. LC 66-13387. pap. 73.80 (ISBN 0-317-08713-4, 2022447). Bks Demand UMI.

Eden, Richard, jt. auth. see Bending, Richard.

Eden, Richard J., et al. Energy Economics: Growth, Resources & Policies. LC 80-40858. (Illus.). 1983. pap. 13.95 (ISBN 0-521-28160-1). Cambridge U Pr.

--Energy Economics: Growth, Resources & Policies. LC 80-40858. (Illus.). 445p. 1981. 49.50 (ISBN 0-521-23685-1). Cambridge U Pr.

Eden, Robert. Political Leadership & Nihilism: A Study of Weber & Nietzsche. LC 83-17075. 348p. 1984. 25.00 (ISBN 0-8130-0758-5). U Presses Fla.

Eden, Sydney. The Intelligent Understanding of Stained & Painted Glass. (Illus.). 131p. 1980. 69.85 (ISBN 0-930582-81-0). Gloucester Art.

Edens, Cooper. Caretakers of Wonder. LC 84-144762. (Illus.). 40p. 1981. 12.95 (ISBN 0-914676-78-4, Star & Elephant Bks.); pap. 7.95 (ISBN 0-914676-76-8). Green Tiger Pr.

--If You're Afraid of the Dark, Remember the Night Rainbow. LC 80-105693. (Illus.). 1981. 12.95 (ISBN 0-914676-26-1, Star & Elephant Bks.); pap. 7.95 (ISBN 0-914676-27-X). Green Tiger Pr.

--If You're Afraid of the Dark, Remember the Night Rainbow. 2nd, smaller ed. LC 84-81834. (Illus.). 40p. 1984. 3.95 (ISBN 0-88138-045-8, Star & Elephant Bks.). Green Tiger Pr.

--Inevitable Papers. LC 84-146073. (Illus.). 64p. 1982. pap. 5.95 (ISBN 0-914676-94-6, Star & Elephant Bks.). Green Tiger Pr.

--A Phenomenal Alphabet Book. LC 84-144745. (Illus.). 40p. (Orig.). pap. 7.95 (ISBN 0-914676-91-1, Star & Elephant Bks.). Green Tiger Pr.

--The Starcleaner Reunion. LC 79-122663. (Illus.). 1979. (Star & Elephant Bks.); pap. 8.95 (ISBN 0-914676-77-6). Green Tiger Pr.

--With Secret Friends. LC 84-149490. (Star & Elephant Ser.). (Illus.). 48p. 1981. pap. 8.95 (ISBN 0-914676-57-1). Green Tiger Pr.

Edens, Cooper, et al. Paradise of Ads. (Star & Elephant Ser.). (Illus.). 300p. Date not set. 22.95 (ISBN 0-88138-036-9). Green Tiger Pr.

Edens, David. The Changing Me. (Sexuality in Christian Living Ser.). 48p. (gr. 4-6). 1973. pap. 6.95 (ISBN 0-8054-4411-4). Broadman.

--Estoy Creciendo Estoy Cambiando. Du Plou, Dafne C., tr. (Sexo en la Vida Cristiana Ser). (Illus.). 1983. pap. 1.75 (ISBN 0-311-46252-9). Casa Bautista.

--Marriage: How to Have It the Way You Want It. 170p. 1981. 11.95 (ISBN 0-13-558510-4); pap. 5.95 (ISBN 0-13-558502-3). P-H.

Edens, David G. Oil & Development in the Middle East. LC 79-848. 200p. 1979. 39.95 (ISBN 0-03-049141-X). Praeger.

Edens, W., et al. Teaching Shakespeare. 1977. 21.50x (ISBN 0-691-06339-7). Princeton U Pr.

Eder, Doris L. Three Writers in Exile: Eliot, Pound & Joyce. LC 84-51739. 100p. 1985. 12.50x (ISBN 0-87875-292-7). Whitston Pub.

Eder, Esther. Larchmont Manor: A Tale of Trees & Houses. (Illus.). 1984. pap. 11.95 (ISBN 0-9614252-0-2). Eder Pub.

Eder, F. W., jt. ed. see Martin, H.

Eder, Gernot. Nuclear Forces: Introduction to Theoretical Nuclear Physics. 1968. pap. 12.50x (ISBN 0-262-55004-0). MIT Pr.

Eder, James. Who Shall Succeed? Agricultural Development & Social Inequality on a Philippine Frontier. LC 81-10178. 256p. 1982. 44.50 (ISBN 0-521-24218-5). Cambridge U Pr.

Eder, Josef M. History of Photography. 19.00 (ISBN 0-8446-5687-9). Peter Smith.

--La Photographie Instantanee. Bunnell, Peter C. & Sobieszek, Robert A., eds. LC 76-23056. (Sources of Modern Photography Ser.). (Illus., Fr.). 1979. Repr. of 1888 ed. lib. bdg. 19.00x (ISBN 0-405-09619-4). Ayer Co Pubs.

Eder, Josef-Maria. Geschichte der Photographie, 2 vols. in 1. Bunnell, Peter C. & Sobieszk, Robert A., eds. LC 76-23045. (Sources of Modern Photography Ser.). (Illus., Ger.). 1979. Repr. of 1932 ed. lib. bdg. 48.50x (ISBN 0-405-09607-0). Ayer Co Pubs.

Eder, Joseph M. Ausfuhrliches Handbuch der Photographie: 1891-93, 4 Vols. (Illus.). 476p. Set. pap. 300.00 (ISBN 0-686-82589-6). Saifer.

Eder, Joseph M. & Bunnell, Peter C., eds. Quellenschriften zu den Fruhesten Anfangen der Photographie bis zum XVIII. LC 76-23047. (Sources of Modern Photography Ser.). (Illus., Ger. & Latin.). 1979. Repr. of 1913 ed. lib. bdg. 17.00x (ISBN 0-405-09608-9). Ayer Co Pubs.

Eder, Norman R. National Health Insurance & the Medical Profession in Britain, 1913-1939. Stansky, Peter & Hume, Leslie, eds. LC 81-48358. (Modern British History Ser.). 376p. 1982. lib. bdg. 57.00 (ISBN 0-8240-5154-8). Garland Pub.

Eder, Phanor J. American-Colombian Private International Law. LC 56-8273. 95p. 1956. 15.00 (ISBN 0-379-11405-4). Oceana.

--Colombia. 1976. lib. bdg. 59.95 (ISBN 0-8490-1640-1). Gordon Pr.

--A Comparative Survey of Anglo-American & Latin-American Law. vii, 257p. 1981. Repr. of 1950 ed. lib. bdg. 30.00x (ISBN 0-8377-0541-X). Rothman.

--Law Books in Spanish Translation: A Tentative Bibliography. LC 66-64733. 1966. 10.00 (ISBN 0-8130-0071-8). U Presses Fla.

Edera, Bruno, ed. Full Length Animated Feature Films. (Library of Animation Technology). 1977. 37.50 (ISBN 0-8038-2317-7). Hastings.

Edereain, Forsyth, tr. see Sainte-Beuve, Charles A.

Ederer, Bernard F. Bingo, Gallant Reindeer Dog. 1977. 7.50 (ISBN 0-682-48887-9). Exposition Pr FL.

Edersheim, Alfred. Jesus the Messiah. 1959. pap. 8.95 (ISBN 0-8028-8131-9). Eerdmans.

--Life & Times of Jesus the Messiah. 1972. 19.95 (ISBN 0-8028-8027-4). Eerdmans.

--Old Testament Bible History. 1972. 19.95 (ISBN 0-8028-8028-2). Eerdmans.

--Practical Truths from Elisha. LC 82-18702. 368p. 1983. 11.95 (ISBN 0-8254-2511-5). Kregel.

--Sketch of Jewish Social Life. 1974. pap. 4.95 (ISBN 0-8028-8132-7). Eerdmans.

--Temple, Its Ministry & Services. 1950. 5.95 (ISBN 0-8028-8133-5). Eerdmans.

Edery, David. Mekorot, Israeli Folk Dance Catalogue, 1983. 50p. (Orig.). 1983. pap. 4.50 (ISBN 0-9610756-0-0). D E Pubns.

Edes, Shirley & Philipson, Julia. Peter Christian's Recipes. LC 83-374. (Illus.). vii, 173p. (Orig.). 1983. pap. 9.50 comb bdg. (ISBN 0-936988-09-6). Tompson & Rutter.

Edeskuty, F. J. & Williamson, K. D., Jr., eds. Liquid Cryogens, 2 Vols. 1983. Vol. I, Theory & Equipment, 224p. 66.00 (ISBN 0-8493-5727-6); Vol. II, Properties & Applications, 176p. 55.00 (ISBN 0-8493-5728-4). CRC Pr.

Edeson, W. R. & Pulvenis, J. F. The Legal Regime of Fisheries in the Caribbean Region. LC 83-20155. (Lecture Notes on Coastal & Estuarine Studies: Vol. 7). 204p. 1983. pap. 19.00 (ISBN 0-387-12698-8). Springer-Verlag.

Edet, Edna S., ed. The Griot Sings: Songs from the Black World. 96p. (Orig.). 1978. pap. 5.95 (ISBN 0-89062-064-4, Pub. by Medgar Evers Coll). Pub Ctr Cult Res.

Edey, Harold C. Accounting Queries. LC 82-82487. (Accountancy in Transition Ser.). 296p. 1982. lib. bdg. 44.00 (ISBN 0-8240-5335-4). Garland Pub.

Edey, Maitland A., jt. auth. see Johanson, Donald C.

Edeyrn, Davod A. Dosparth Edeyrn Davod Aur. Williams ab Ithel, John, ed. LC 78-72626. (Celtic Language & Literature: Goidelic & Brythonic). Repr. of 1856 ed. 37.50 (ISBN 0-404-17548-1). AMS Pr.

Edgar, A. H. John Bull & the Papists; or, Passages in the Life of an Anglican Rector, 1846. Wolff, Robert L., ed. (Victorian Fiction Ser.). 1974. lib. bdg. 73.00 (ISBN 0-8240-1527-4). Garland Pub.

Edgar, B. J. Our House: The Birthplace of Pearl S. Buck. (Illus.). 1965p. 2.00 (ISBN 0-87012-010-7). B J Edgar.

Edgar, Betsy. Pocahontas County Cooking Yesterday & Today. 1979. Repr. of 1973 ed. 3.75 (ISBN 0-87012-175-8). McClain.

Edgar, Betsy J. The McNeel Family Record. (Illus.). 1967. 12.50 (ISBN 0-87012-063-8). B J Edgar.

--McNeel Family Record. (Illus.). 1967. 15.00 (ISBN 0-87012-063-8). McClain.

--Our House. (Illus.). 1965. pap. 3.00 (ISBN 0-87012-010-7). McClain.

--Pocahontas County Cooking Yesterday & Today. 1973. 4.00 (ISBN 0-87012-175-8). B J Edgar.

--We Live with the Wheel Chair. (Illus.). 1970. 5.00 (ISBN 0-87012-081-6). B J Edgar.

--We Live with the Wheel Chair. 1970. 5.00 (ISBN 0-87012-081-6). McClain.

Edgar, David. Destiny. 96p. 1978. pap. 6.95 (ISBN 0-413-38910-3, NO.3000). Methuen Inc.

--Mary Barnes. 87p. 1984. pap. 6.95 (ISBN 0-413-54860-0, 4110). Methuen Inc.

--Maydays. 56p. 1984. pap. 4.95 (ISBN 0-413-54180-0, NO. 4161). Methuen Inc.

--Maydays. (Modern Plays Ser.). 148p. (Orig.). 1985. pap. 6.95 (ISBN 0-413-57080-0, 9411). Methuen Inc.

--Wreckers. 1977. pap. 4.95 (ISBN 0-413-38510-8, NO. 2985, Pub. by Eyre Methuen England). Methuen Inc.

Edgar, Donald. The Day of Reckoning. 1984. 30.00x (ISBN 0-906549-35-3, Pub. by J Clare Bks UK); pap. 18.00x (ISBN 0-906549-37-X, Pub. by J Clare Bks UK). State Mutual Bk.

--Express Fifty-Six: A Year in the Life of a Beaverbrook Journalist. 1982. 30.00x (ISBN 0-906549-17-5, Pub. by J Clare Bks England). State Mutual Bk.

--Palace. (Illus.). 200p. 1984. 17.95 (ISBN 0-491-03401-6, Pub. by Salem Hse Ltd). Merrimack Pub Cir.

--The Stalagmen. 1984. 30.00x (ISBN 0-906549-27-2, Pub. by J Clare Bks UK); pap. 18.00x (ISBN 0-906549-29-9, Pub. by J Clare Bks UK). State Mutual Bk.

Edgar, Ellen, jt. auth. see Edgar, James.

Edgar, Eugene B. Mentally Handicapped Children: Education & Training. LC 82-2069. 272p. 1982. pap. text ed. 19.00 (ISBN 0-8391-1735-3, 18198). Pro Ed.

Edgar, Henry see Warren, Josiah.

Edgar, Irving I. Early Jewish Physicians in the State of Michigan. LC 81-82693. (Illus.). 1982. 15.00 (ISBN 0-8022-2394-X). Philos Lib.

--Essays in English Literature & History. (Illus.). 192p. 1972. 8.50 (ISBN 0-8022-2088-6). Philos Lib.

--Meditations in an Anatomy Laboratory & Other Poems. LC 79-87872. 1979. 7.95 (ISBN 0-8022-2353-2). Philos Lib.

--The Origins of the Healing Art. LC 77-82611. (Illus.). 1978. 9.50 (ISBN 0-8022-2214-5). Philos Lib.

--Shakespeare, Medicine & Psychiatry. LC 76-118308. 1970. 9.95 (ISBN 0-8022-2343-5). Philos Lib.

Edgar, J. G. Runnymede & Lincoln Fair: A Story of the Great Charter. 1978. Repr. of 1908 ed. lib. bdg. 10.00 (ISBN 0-8482-0714-9). Norwood Edns.

Edgar, James & Edgar, Ellen. A Chrismon Service. 20p. 1981. pap. text ed. 2.25 (ISBN 0-89536-500-6). CSS of Ohio.

Edgar, Josephine. Margaret Normanby. LC 82-17052. 448p. 1983. 13.95 (ISBN 0-312-51444-1). St Martin.

Edgar, L. Jail Diary of Albie Sachs. Rex Collings Ltd., ed. 25.00x (ISBN 0-86036-092-X, Pub. by R Collings UK). State Mutual Bk.

Edgar, Neal L., ed. AACR2 & Serials: The American View. LC 83-8404. (Cataloging & Classification Quarterly Ser.: Vol. 3, Nos. 2-3). 154p. 1983. text ed. 22.95 (ISBN 0-86656-233-8, B233). Haworth Pr.

Edgar, Neal L. & Ma, Wendy Y., eds. Travel in Asia: A Guide to Information Sources. (Geography & Travel Information Guide Ser.: Vol. 6). 350p. 1982. 60.00x (ISBN 0-8103-1470-3). Gale.

Edgar, P. Study of Shelley. LC 70-116792. (Studies in Shelley, No. 25). 1970. Repr. of 1899 ed. lib. bdg. 39.95x (ISBN 0-8383-1034-6). Haskell.

Edgar, Pamela & Matz, Dale. Adventures of Jason: Mythical Magical Journey into Self-Discovery. LC 85-9695. 64p. (Orig.). (gr. 1-5). 1985. pap. 7.95 (ISBN 0-941992-05-5). Los Arboles Pub.

Edgar, Patricia & Rahim, Syed A. Communication Policy in Developed Countries. 297p. (Orig.). 1984. pap. 17.95x (ISBN 0-7103-0060-3, Kegan Paul). Routledge & Kegan.

Edgar, Pelham. Art of the Novel from 1700 to the Present Time. LC 66-13168. 1965. Repr. of 1933 ed. 16.00x (ISBN 0-8462-0710-9). Russell.

--Study of Shelley. LC 76-26146. 1899. lib. bdg. 20.00 (ISBN 0-8414-3933-8). Folcroft.

Edgar, T. F., ed. Advanced Control & Modeling Techniques. LC 80-20826. (Alchemi Series A: Process Control: Vol 4). 82p. 1984. pap. 30.00 (ISBN 0-8169-0236-4); pap. 15.00 members (ISBN 0-317-17539-4). Am Inst Chem Eng.

--Analysis of Dynamic Systems. (AlChemi Modular Instruction A-Ser.: Vol.1: Vol. 1). 83p. 1980. pap. 30.00 (ISBN 0-8169-0170-8, J-1); pap. 15.00 (ISBN 0-317-03784-6). Am Inst Chem Eng.

--Design of Sampled Data (Computer) Control Systems. (AIChEMI Modular Instruction A-Ser.: Vol. 3). 98p. 1982. pap. 30.00 (ISBN 0-8169-0208-9, J-13); pap. 15.00 members (ISBN 0-317-03786-2). Am Inst Chem Eng.

--Feedback Controller Synthesis. (Alchemi Modular Instruction A-Ser.: Vol. 2). 75p. 1981. pap. 30.00 (ISBN 0-8169-0176-7, J-7); pap. 15.00 (ISBN 0-317-03789-7). Am Inst Chem Eng.

Edgar, Thomas F. Coal Processing & Pollution Control. LC 83-10725. 576p. 1983. 49.95x (ISBN 0-87201-122-4). Gulf Pub.

Edgar, Thomas F. & Seborg, Dale E., eds. Chemical Process Control: Proceedings of the Engineering Foundation Conference, Jan. 18-23, 1981, Sea Island, Ga, Vol. 2. LC 81-71594. 649p. 1982. text ed. 60.00 (ISBN 0-8169-0203-8); text ed. 45.00 (ISBN 0-317-03783-8). Am Inst Chem Eng.

Edidin, Ben M. Jewish Customs & Ceremonies. 178p. 1940. pap. 6.95 (ISBN 0-88482-438-1). Hebrew Pub.

Edie, James E., tr. see Merleau-Ponty, Maurice.

Edie, James M. Speaking & Meaning: The Phenomenology of Language. LC 75-28909. (Studies in Phenomenology & Existential Philosophy). 288p. 1976. 22.50x (ISBN 0-253-35425-0). Ind U Pr.

Edie, James M., ed. see Merleau-Ponty, Maurice.

Edie, James M., et al. Russian Philosophy, 3 vols. LC 64-10928. 1976. Vol. 1. pap. 9.95x (ISBN 0-87049-200-4); Vol. 2. pap. 8.95x (ISBN 0-686-91542-9); Vol. 3. pap. 10.95x (ISBN 0-686-77174-5). U of Tenn Pr.

Edie, James M., et al, eds. Patterns of the Life-World: Essays in Honor of John Wild. (Studies in Phenomenology & Existential Philosophy). 1970. 21.95 (ISBN 0-8101-0311-7). Northwestern U Pr.

Edie, Lionel D. Dollars. 1934. 39.50x (ISBN 0-686-25727-8). Elliots Bks.

--Easy Money: A Study of Low Interest Rates, Their Bearing on the Outlook for the Gold Standard & on the Problem of Curbing a Boom. 1937. 39.50x (ISBN 0-686-51374-6). Elliots Bks.

--Gold Production & Prices Before & After the World War. LC 82-48178. (Gold, Money, Inflation & Deflation Ser.). 136p. 1983. lib. bdg. 22.00 (ISBN 0-8240-5230-7). Garland Pub.

Edie, Lionel D., ed. The Stabilization of Business. LC 73-2503. (Big Business; Economic Power in a Free Society Ser.). Repr. of 1923 ed. 26.00 (ISBN 0-405-05085-2). Ayer Co Pubs.

Ediger, Max. A Vietnamese Pilgrimage. LC 78-53650. (Illus.). 1978. pap. 5.25 (ISBN 0-87303-007-9). Faith & Life.

Ediger, Peter J. The Prophets' Report on Religion in North America. rev. ed. LC 78-150650. 1978. pap. 2.00 (ISBN 0-87303-686-7). Faith & Life.

Edin, Herbert L. & Bourdo, Eric, eds. Illustrated Encyclopedia of Trees, Timbers, & Forests of the World. 1978. 15.95 (ISBN 0-517-53450-9, Harmony). Crown.

Edinberg, Mark A. Mental Health Practice with the Elderly. (Illus.). 432p. 1985. text ed. 26.95 (ISBN 0-13-575994-3). P-H.

Edinborough, Arnold. Canada. (Panorama Bks.). (Illus., Fr.). 1962. 3.95 (ISBN 0-685-11058-3). French & Eur.

Edinburgh, Mark A., jt. auth. see Bradley, Jean C.

Edinburgh National History Society. A Guide to Edinburgh's Countryside. 1983. 30.00x (ISBN 0-904265-82-X, Pub. by Macdonald Pub UK); pap. 20.00x (ISBN 0-904265-83-8). State Mutual Bk.

Edinburgh University. Catalogue of the Graduates. Laing, David, ed. LC 46-164754. (Bannatyne Club, Edinburgh. Publications: No. 106). Repr. of 1858 ed. 24.50 (ISBN 0-404-52861-9). AMS Pr.

--Pharmacological Experiments on Intact Preparations. (Illus.). 1971. 17.25 (ISBN 0-443-00731-4). Churchill.

--Pharmacological Experiments on Isolated Preparations. 2nd ed. (Illus.). 1971. 17.25 (ISBN 0-443-00730-6). Churchill.

Edinburgh University Library. First Supplement to Manuscripts, Edinburgh University Library. (Library Catalogs-Supplements Ser.). lib. bdg. 120.00 (ISBN 0-8161-0319-4, Hall Library). G K Hall.

--Index to Manuscripts, 2 vols. 1964. Set. 175.00 (ISBN 0-8161-0706-8, Hall Library). G K Hall.

Edinger, Claudio. Chelsea Hotel. LC 82-22790. (Illus.). 160p. (Orig.). 1983. pap. 14.95 (ISBN 0-89659-338-X). Abbeville Pr.

Edinger, Claudio, photos by. Venice Beach. LC 85-4015. (Illus.). 156p. 1985. pap. 16.95 (ISBN 0-89659-520-X). Abbeville Pr.

Edinger, Edward. Anatomy of the Psyche: Alchemical Symbolism in Psychotherapy. 250p. 1985. cloth 24.95 (ISBN 0-87548-444-1); pap. 12.95 (ISBN 0-8126-9009-5). Open Court.

Edinger, Edward F. Ego & Archetype. LC 75-188717. (Illus.). 1972. 15.00 (ISBN 0-913430-02-1). C G Jung Foun.

--Ego & Archetype. 1973. pap. 8.95 (ISBN 0-14-021728-2, Pelican). Penguin.

--Melville's Moby Dick: A Jungian Commentary. LC 78-6146. 160p. 1976. pap. 5.95 (ISBN 0-8112-0691-2, NDP460). New Directions.

Edinger, H., jt. ed. see Siegel, Allan.

Edinger, H. G., tr. see Thucydides.

Edinger, James G., jt. auth. see Neiburger, Morris.

Edinger, Lewis J. Kurt Schumacher: A Study in Personality & Political Behavior. (Illus.). 1965. 30.00x (ISBN 0-8047-0247-0). Stanford U Pr.

--Politics in West Germany. 2nd ed. (Ser. in Comparative Politics). 375p. 1977. pap. 10.95 (ISBN 0-316-21081-1). Little.

--West German Politics. (Illus.). 350p. 1985. 30.00x (ISBN 0-231-06090-4); pap. 10.00x (ISBN 0-231-06091-2). Columbia U Pr.

Edinger, Lewis J., jt. auth. see Deutsch, Karl W.

Edinger, Lois V., ed. Education in the Eighties: Curricular Challenges. 192p. 1981. 18.95 (ISBN 0-8106-3170-9); pap. 12.95 (ISBN 0-8106-3169-5). NEA.

Edinger, Lois V., et al, eds. Curricular Challenges. (Education in the Eighties Ser.). 192p. 1981. cloth 18.95 (ISBN 0-8106-3170-9); pap. 12.95 (ISBN 0-8106-3169-5). NEA.

Edinger, William. Samuel Johnson & Poetic Style. LC 77-5137. 1977. 20.00x (ISBN 0-226-18446-3). U of Chicago Pr.

Edington, jt. auth. see Wilson.

Edington, Christopher R. & Ford, Phyllis M. Leadership in Recreation & Leisure Service Organizations. 448p. 1985. 26.95 (ISBN 0-471-86864-7). Wiley.

Edington, David W. Christians & the Third World. 160p. 1982. pap. text ed. 7.95 (ISBN 0-85364-286-9). Attic Pr.

Edington, Everett D., jt. auth. see Donaldson, Kloyd.

Edington, George, jt. auth. see Wilson, Bradford.

Edington, J. M. & Edington, M. A. Ecology & Environmental Planning. 1977. 31.00 (ISBN 0-412-13300-8, NO.6095, Pub. by Chapman & Hall). Methuen Inc.

Edington, J. M. & Hildrew, A. G. Caseless Caddis Larvae of the British Isles. 1981. 25.00x (ISBN 0-686-75591-X, Pub. by Freshwater Bio). State Mutual Bk.

Edington, M. A., jt. auth. see Edington, J. M.

Edington, Robert V., jt. auth. see Foster, Richard H.

Edinin, M. & Johnson, M. H., eds. Immunobiology of Gametes. LC 76-49952. (Clinical & Experimental Immunoreproduction Ser.: No. 4). (Illus.). 1977. 69.50 (ISBN 0-521-21441-6). Cambridge U Pr.

Edis, A. J., et al. Manual of Endocrine Surgery. 2nd ed. (Comprehensive Manuals of Surgical Specialities Ser.). (Illus.). 280p. 1984. 89.00 (ISBN 0-387-90921-4). Springer-Verlag.

Edis, Robert W. Decoration of Town Houses. 2nd ed. (Illus.). 1976. Repr. 17.50x (ISBN 0-85409-909-3). Charles River Bks.

Edison, Thomas A. Diary & Sundry Observations of Thomas Alva Edison. Runes, Dagobert D., ed. LC 68-28588. (Illus.). Repr. of 1968 ed. lib. bdg. 32.50 (ISBN 0-8371-0067-4, EDTE). Greenwood.

Editions Guide Staff. Brittany Travel Guide. (Illus.). 128p. 1985. pap. 4.95 (ISBN 0-02-969410-8). MacMillan.

Editions, Phoebe P. The Flower Garden Planner. 112p. 1985. spiral bdg. 14.95 (ISBN 0-671-50065-1). S&S.

Editions Technip. Drilling Data Handbook. 448p. 1980. 43.00x (ISBN 0-86010-195-9, Pub. by Graham & Trotman England). State Mutual Bk.

Editor, Adam A. Geoelectric & Geothermal Studies. 1976. 55.00 (ISBN 0-9960004-2-9, Pub. by Akademiai Kaido Hungary). Heyden.

Editorial Board. Annual Index to Poetry in Periodicals: 1984. 540p. 1985. 39.99x (ISBN 0-89609-243-7). Granger Bk.

Editorial Board, Granger Book Co. Master Index to Poetry. 2000p. 1985. pap. 199.50x (ISBN 0-317-31559-5). Granger Bk.

--Survey of American Poetry: Civil War & Aftermath (1861-1889), Vol. V. 400p. 1985. lib. bdg. 34.95x (ISBN 0-89609-217-8). Granger Bk.

Editorial Committee Staff & Chun-Ie, Fang. The China Offical Yearbook, 1985-86. 608p. 1985. 85.00 (ISBN 962-7157-01-5). Lincol Enter.

Editors. Discovery Proceedings in Federal Practice. LC 83-9856. 504p. 1984. 70.00 (ISBN 0-07-056739-5, Shepards-McGraw). McGraw.

--Motions in Federal Court: Civil Practice. (Federal Publications). 583p. 1982. write for info. (Pub. By Shepards-McGraw). McGraw.

Editors of Boston Publishing Co. Images of War. Manning, Robert, ed. (The Vietnam Experience Ser.: Vol. 18). (Illus.). 192p. 1986. 16.95 (ISBN 0-939526-18-2). Boston Pub Co.

--North Vietnam. Manning, Robert, ed. (The Vietnam Experience Ser.: Vol. 20). (Illus.). 192p. 1986. 16.95 (ISBN 0-939526-21-2). Boston Pub Co.

--Vietnam Remembered. Manning, Robert, ed. (The Vietnam Experience Ser.: Vol. 19). (Illus.). 192p. 1986. 16.95 (ISBN 0-939526-20-4). Boston Pub Co.

Editors of Fine Woodworking Magazine. Fine Woodworking Techniques, Vo. 7. (Illus.). 240p. 1985. text ed. 17.95 (ISBN 0-918804-42-6, Dist. by W W Norton). Taunton.

Editors of Industrial Design Magazine & Edwards, Sandra. Office Systems Design. (Illus.). 256p. 1985. 47.50 (ISBN 0-86636-009-3). PBC Intl Inc.

Editors of McCall's Neelework & Crafts Staff, ed. McCalls Big Book of Country Needlecrafts. (Illus.). 312p. 1985. pap. 14.95 (ISBN 0-8019-7364-3). Wallace-Homestead.

Editors of PV Magazine. Natural Weight Loss. (Illus.). 176p. not set 14.95 (ISBN 0-87857-529-4). Rodale Pr Inc.

Editors of Sign of the Times Magazine. Sign Design. (Illus.). 256p. 1985. 47.50 (ISBN 0-86636-013-1). PBC Intl Inc.

Editors of the Film World, ed. X-Rated Video Directory. (Orig.). 1985. pap. 4.95 (ISBN 0-87067-925-2, BH929). Holloway.

Edito T. De La Cruz, jt. tr. see Fuentes, Vilma M.

Editura Tehnica. Dictionar Tehnic Poliglot. 1233p. 1984. Repr. of 1967 ed. text ed. 98.50x (ISBN 0-8290-0987-6). Irvington.

Edkins, David. The Prussian Orden Pourle Merite: History of the Blue Max. LC 81-65302. (Illus.). 1981. softcover 10.95 (ISBN 0-939440-05-9). AJAY Ent.

Edkins, Diana. Vanity Fair: Photographs of an Age, 1914-1936. LC 82-7682. (Illus.). 224p. 1982. 40.00 (ISBN 0-517-54625-6, C N Potter). Crown.

Edkins, Diana E., jt. auth. see Newhall, Beaumont.

Edkins, Joseph. The Revenue & Taxation of the Chinese Empire. LC 78-74331. (The Modern Chinese Economy Ser.). 240p. 1980. lib. bdg. 32.00 (ISBN 0-8240-4252-2). Garland Pub.

Edler, Florence. Glossary of Mediaeval Terms of Business, 1200-1600. (Med Acad Amer Pubns). 1934. 32.00 (ISBN 0-527-01690-X). Kraus Repr.

Edler, Friedrich. Dutch Republic & the American Revolution. LC 78-149686. Repr. of 1911 ed. 23.00 (ISBN 0-404-02246-4). AMS Pr.

Edler, Howard, jt. ed. see Lett, J. T.

Edler, Peter. The Dooming Eye. LC 77-92991. (Illus.). 1978. pap. 4.00 (ISBN 0-912292-48-2). The Smith.

Edler, Tim. Crawfish-Man's Fifty Ways to Keep Your Kids from Using Drugs. (Tales from the Atchafalaya Ser.). (Illus.). 52p. (gr. k-8). 1982. 6.00 (ISBN 0-931108-08-X). Little Cajun.

--T-Boy & the Trial for Life: Tim Edler's Tales from the Atchafalaya Ser. (Illus.). 36p. (gr. k-8). 1978. leather 6.00 (ISBN 0-931108-02-0). Little Cajun.

Edler, Tim, tr. see Edler, Timothy J.

Edler, Timothy. The Adventures of Crawfish-Man. (Tim Edler's Tales from the Atchafalaya Ser.). (Illus.). 40p. (gr. k-8). 1979. 6.00x (ISBN 0-931108-04-7). Little Cajun.

--Coocan: Boy of the Swamp. (Tim Edler's Tales from the Atchafclaya Ser.). (Illus.). 40p. (gr. k-8). 1983. leather 6.00 (ISBN 0-931108-09-8). Little Cajun.

--Crawfish-Man Rescues Ron Guidry. (Tim Edler's Tales from the Atchafalaya). (Illus.). (gr. k-8). 1980. lea. 6.00 (ISBN 0-931108-05-5). Little Cajun.

--Crawfish-Man's Night Befo' Christmas. (Illus.). 40p. (gr. k-8). 1984. leather 10.00 (ISBN 0-931108-12-8). Little Cajun.

--Dark Gator. (Tim Edler's New Swamp Wars Ser.). (Illus.). 48p. (gr. k-8). 1980. lea. 6.00 (ISBN 0-931108-06-3). Little Cajun.

--Maurice the Snake & Gaston the Near-Sighted Turtle: Tim Edler's Tales from the Atchafalaya. (Illus.). 36p. (gr. k-8). 1977. lea. 6.00 (ISBN 0-931108-00-4). Little Cajun.

--Rhombus: The Cajun Unicorn. (Tim Edler's Tales from the Atchafalaya Ser.). (Illus.). 40p. (gr. k up). 1984. leather bdg. 10.00 (ISBN 0-931108-10-1). Little Cajun.

--T-Boy in Mossland. (Tim Edler's Tales from the Atchafalaya). (Illus.). 48p. (gr. k-8). 1978. leather 6.00 (ISBN 0-931108-03-9). Little Cajun.

--T-Boy the Little Cajun. (Tim Edler's Tales from the Atchafalaya). (Illus.). 36p. (gr. k-8). 1978. leather 6.00 (ISBN 0-931108-01-2). Little Cajun.

Edler, Timothy J. Santa's Cajun Christmas Adventure. Edler, Tim, tr. (Tim Edler's Tales from the Atchafalaya Ser.). (Illus.). 48p. (gr. k-8). 1981. leather bdg. 6.00 (ISBN 0-931108-07-1). Little Cajun.

Edles, Gary J. & Nelson, Jerome. Federal Regulatory Process: Agency Practices & Procedures. 698p. 1981. 65.00 (ISBN 0-15-100022-0, H39891). HarBraceJ.

Edlich, R. F. & Sipker, D. Current Emergency Therapy, 1984. 1506p. 1984. 95.00 (ISBN 0-8385-1406-5). ACC.

Edlich, Richard F. & Spyker, Daniel, eds. Current Emergency Therapy '85. 1000p. 1985. 85.00 (ISBN 0-89443-574-4). Aspen Systems.

Edlin, Alfred W. Your Borzoi. LC 75-41983. (Your Dog Bk.). 1976. 12.95 (ISBN 0-87714-042-1). Denlingers.

Edlin, Gordon. Genetic Principles: Human & Social Consequences. 464p. 1983. text ed. write for info (ISBN 0-86720-016-2). Jones & Bartlett.

Edlin, Gordon & Golanty, Eric. Health & Wellness. 2nd ed. (Illus.). 667p. 1985. pap. write for info. (ISBN 0-86720-055-3); pap. write for info. student wkbk., 200p (ISBN 0-86720-056-1); instr's. guide avail. (ISBN 0-86720-058-8). Jones & Bartlett.

Edlin, Herbert L. The Tree Key. (Illus.). 280p. 1985. pap. 10.95 (ISBN 0-684-15890-6, ScribT). Scribner.

--What Wood Is That? A Manual of Wood Identification. (Illus.). 1969. 24.95 (ISBN 0-670-75907-4, Studio). Viking.

Edlin, Herbert L. & Huxley, Anthony. Atlas of Plant Life. LC 73-734361. (John Day Bk.). (Illus.). 128p. 1973. 14.37i (ISBN 0-381-98245-9). T Y Crowell.

Edlow, R. B. Galen on Language & Ambiguity "De Captionibus" (On Fallacies) An English Translation of Galen's. (Philosophia Antiqua: No. 31). 1977. pap. text ed. 25.75x (ISBN 90-04-04869-3). Humanities.

Edlund, Ingrid E. The Iron Age & Etruscan Vases in the Olcott Collection at Columbia University New York. LC 79-51542. (Transaction Ser.: Vol. 70, Pt. 1). 1980. pap. 15.00 (ISBN 0-87169-701-7). Am Philos.

Edlund, Mary, jt. auth. see Edlund, Sidney.

Edlund, Sidney & Edlund, Mary. Pick Your Job & Land It. 1973. 5.00 (ISBN 0-686-17213-2). Sandollar Pr.

Edman, David. Once upon an Eternity. 108p. 1984. pap. 6.95 (ISBN 0-89390-052-4). Resource Pubns.

Edman, David, jt. auth. see Paley, Albert.

Edman, Irwin. Adam, the Baby, & the Man from Mars. facs. ed. LC 68-24850. (Essay Index Reprint Ser). 1968. Repr. of 1929 ed. 20.00 (ISBN 0-8369-0404-4). Ayer Co Pubs.

--Arts & the Man. 1960. pap. 5.95 (ISBN 0-393-00104-0, Norton Lib). Norton.

--Contemporary & His Soul. LC 66-25907. Repr. of 1931 ed. 16.50x (ISBN 0-8046-0129-1, Pub. by Kennikat). Assoc Faculty Pr.

--Human Traits & Their Social Significance. 1978. Repr. of 1919 ed. lib. bdg. 30.00 (ISBN 0-8495-1307-3). Arden Lib.

--Philosopher's Quest. LC 72-7973. 275p. 1973. Repr. of 1947 ed. lib. bdg. 18.00x (ISBN 0-8371-6559-8, EDPQ). Greenwood.

Edman, Irwin, ed. see Dewey, John.

Edman, Irwin, ed. see Plato.

Edman, Irwin, ed. & intro. by see Plato.

Edman, Marion. Self-Image of Primary School Teachers: An International Cross-Cultural Study of Twelve Cities. LC 68-19683. 336p. 1968. 16.95x (ISBN 0-8143-1330-2). Wayne St U Pr.

Edman, Marjorie, jt. auth. see Mitchell, H. H.

Edman, Polly, jt. auth. see Jensen, Virginia A.

Edman, V. E. & Laidlaw, R. A. The Fullness of the Spirit. 36p. pap. 0.95 (ISBN 0-87509-083-4). Chr Pubns.

Edman, V. Raymond. The Disciplines of Life. LC 81-84813. 254p. 1982. pap. 3.25 (ISBN 0-89081-276-4). Harvest Hse.

--Finney Lives On. 256p. 1970. pap. 4.95 (ISBN 0-87123-150-6, 210150). Bethany Hse.

--They Found the Secret: Twenty Lives that Reveal a Touch of Eternity. 176p. 1984. pap. 5.95 (ISBN 0-310-24051-4, Clarion Class). Zondervan.

Edmands, Allan, jt. auth. see Edmands, Dodie.

Edmands, Dodie & Edmands, Allan. Child Signs: Understanding Your Child Through Astrology. LC 82-45630. (Illus.). 154p. 1983. pap. 6.95 (ISBN 0-916360-19-9). CRCS Pubns NV.

Edminister, J. Schaum's Outline of Electric Circuits. 2nd ed. (Schaum's Outline Ser.). 304p. 1983. pap. 8.95 (ISBN 0-07-018984-6). McGraw.

Edminister, Joseph. Schaum's Outline of Electromagnetics. (Schaum's Outline Ser). (Illus.). 1979. pap. 8.95 (ISBN 0-07-018990-0). McGraw.

Edminster, Lynn R., jt. auth. see Wallace, Benjamin Bruce.

Edmister, Jane & Foltz, Roger. Ear Training, Vol. 1. Date not set. pap. text ed. 10.95 (ISBN 0-394-32321-1, KnopfC). Knopf.

Edmister, Robert O. Financial Institutions Management. (Financial Ser.). 560p. 1980. text ed. 33.95 (ISBN 0-07-018995-1). McGraw.

Edmister, Wayne C. & Lee, Byung Ik. Applied Hydrocarbon Thermodynamics, Vol. 1. 2nd ed. LC 83-22654. 234p. 1984. 59.95x (ISBN 0-87201-855-5). Gulf Pub.

Edmiston, William F. Diderot & the Family. (Stanford French & Italian Studies: Vol. 39). 160p. 1985. pap. 25.00 (ISBN 0-915838-51-6). Anma Libri.

Edmond, Carolyn E., jt. auth. see Washington, Allyn J.

Edmond, J. B. The Magnificent Charter: The Origin & Role of the Morrill Land-Grant Colleges & Universities. 1978. 12.00 (ISBN 0-682-49079-2, University); pap. 5.50 (ISBN 0-682-49081-4). Exposition Pr FL.

Edmond, J. B., et al. Fundamentals of Horticulture. 4th ed. LC 74-20881. (Illus.). 576p. 1975. text ed. 39.95 (ISBN 0-07-018985-4). McGraw.

Edmond, Lauris. Selected Poems. 128p. (Orig.). Date not set. pap. 13.95x (ISBN 0-19-558126-1). Oxford U Pr.

Edmond, Mary. Hilliard & Oliver: The Lives & Works of Two Great Miniaturists. 238p. 1984. 40.00 (ISBN 0-8390-0333-1). Abner Schram Ltd.

Edmond, Mary, ed. European Parliament Digest 1973, Vol. 1. 350p. 1975. 23.75x (ISBN 0-87471-189-4). Rowman.

Edmond, Shom A. Hors d'Oeuvres: Favorite Recipes from Embassy Kitchens. LC 59-8190. (Illus., Orig.). 1959. pap. 4.25 (ISBN 0-8048-0254-8). C E Tuttle.

Edmond, Wendy & Fleming, Suzie, eds. All Work & No Pay: Women, Housework, & the Wages Due. 128p. 1981. 11.00 (ISBN 0-9502702-3-7); pap. 3.95 (ISBN 0-9502702-2-9). Falling Wall.

Edmonds, A. R. Angular Momentum in Quantum Mechanics. rev. ed. (Investigations in Physics, No. 4). 1968. 22.00x (ISBN 0-691-07912-9). Princeton U Pr.

Edmonds, Alan, jt. auth. see Soyka, Fred.

Edmonds, Ben, jt. auth. see Kooper, Al.

Edmonds, Ben, ed. see Sugerman, Danny.

Edmonds, Cecil J. Kurds, Turks, & Arabs: Politics, Travel, & Research in North-Eastern Iraq, 1919-1925. LC 80-1930. Repr. of 1957 ed. 49.50 (ISBN 0-404-18960-1). AMS Pr.

Edmonds, Charles. A Subaltern's War. 224p. 1984. pap. 7.50 (ISBN 0-907746-38-1, Pub. by A Mott Ltd). Longwood Pub Group.

--T. E. Lawrence. LC 76-52954. (English Biography Ser, No. 31). 1977. lib. bdg. 42.95x (ISBN 0-8383-2177-1). Haskell.

--T. E. Lawrence (of Arabia) 1936. Repr. 20.00 (ISBN 0-8274-3576-2). R West.

Edmonds, Chris w. A Quilt for All Seasons. (Illus.). 40p. 1982. pap. 6.00 (ISBN 0-932946-08-9). Yours Truly.

Edom, Clifton C. Photojournalism: Principles & Practices. 2nd ed. 375p. 1980. text ed. write for info. (ISBN 0-697-04333-9). Wm C Brown.

Edon, Georges. Dictionnaire Francais-Latin. (Fr. & Lat.). 37.50 (ISBN 0-686-57201-7, M-6703). French & Eur.

Edouart, August, jt. auth. see Jackson, F. Nevill.

Edquist, Charles. Capitalism, Socialism & Technology: A Comparative Study of Cuba & Jamaica. 208p. 1985. 26.25x (ISBN 0-86232-393-2, Pub. by Zed Pr England); pap. 10.25 (ISBN 0-86232-394-0, Pub. by Zed Pr England). Biblio Dist.

Edqvist, Lars-Eric & Kindahl, Hans. Prostaglandins in Animal Reproduction, Vol II. (Developments in Animal & Veterinary Sciences Ser.: Vol. 13). 1984. 67.50 (ISBN 0-444-42294-3, I-049-84). Elsevier.

Edralin, Josef S., ed. South Pacific: An Annotated Bibliography on Regional Development. (Country Bibliography Ser.: No. 8). 388p. 1984. pap. 30.00 (CRD174, UNCRD). Unipub.

Edrei, A., et al. Zeros of Sections of Power Series. (Lecture Notes in Mathematics Ser.: Vol. 1002). 115p. 1983. pap. 10.00 (ISBN 0-387-12318-0). Springer Verlag.

Edsall, J. T. & Gutfreund, H. Biothermodynamics: The Study of Biochemical Processes at Equilibrium. LC 82-15971. (Monographs in Molecular Biophysics & Biochemistry Ser.). 248p. 1983. 37.95 (ISBN 0-471-10257-1). Wiley.

Edsall, James. The Golden Age of Single Shot Rifles. 2.75 (ISBN 0-913150-29-0). Pioneer Pr.

--The Revolver Rifles. 2.50 (ISBN 0-913150-30-4). Pioneer Pr.

--The Story of Firearm Ignition. 3.50 (ISBN 0-913150-27-4). Pioneer Pr.

--Volcanic Firearms & Their Successors. 2.50 (ISBN 0-913150-28-2). Pioneer Pr.

Edsall, John T. & Wyman, Jeffries. Biophysical Chemistry, Vol. 1: Thermodynamics, Electrostatics & the Biological Significance of the Properties of Matter. 1958. 72.00 (ISBN 0-12-232201-0). Acad Pr.

Edsall, John T., et al, eds. Advances in Protein Chemistry, Vol. 33. LC 44-8853. (Serial Publication Ser.). 1979. 55.00 (ISBN 0-12-034233-2). Acad Pr.

Edsall, Marian S. Library Promotion Handbook. (Neal-Schuman Professional Bk.). 252p. 1980. lib. bdg. 35.00x (ISBN 0-912700-15-7); pap. 27.50x (ISBN 0-912700-12-2); of 4 cassettes 67.50 set (ISBN 0-89774-123-4). Oryx Pr.

--Practical PR for School Library Media Centers. 165p. 1984. 19.95 (ISBN 0-918212-77-4). Neal-Schuman.

--Roadside Plants & Flowers: A Traveler's Guide to the Midwest & Great Lakes Area. LC 84-40148. (Illus.). 144p. 1985. 17.50 (ISBN 0-299-09700-5); pap. 12.95 (ISBN 0-299-09704-8). U of Wis Pr.

Edsall, Thomas B. The New Politics of Inequality. 288p. 1985. pap. 5.95 (ISBN 0-393-30250-4). Norton.

--The New Politics of Inequality: How Political Power Shapes Economic Policy. 1984. 15.95 (ISBN 0-393-01868-7). Norton.

Edschmid, Kasimir. Lord Byron: The Story of a Passion. 1930. 35.00 (ISBN 0-8274-2984-3). R West.

Edsdom, Nicola. Ali Gator Lives in Florida. (Ali Gator Ser.). (Illus.). 32p. 1985. price not set (ISBN 0-913122-53-X). Mickler Hse.

Edson, Billy D. Lone's Christmas Boots & Other Tales from the Mother Lode. 95p. 1982. pap. 4.50 (ISBN 0-682-49916-1). Exposition Pr FL.

Edson, Charles L. & Jacobs, Barry. The Secondary Mortgage Market Guide. 1985. looseleaf 75.00 (668). Bender.

Edson, Doris, jt. auth. see Barton, Lucy.

Edson, J. T. Beguinage. 176p. 1982. 15.00x (ISBN 0-7278-0530-4, Pub. by Severn Hse). State Mutual Bk.

--Beguinage is Dead. 192p. 1982. 15.00x (ISBN 0-7278-0540-1, Pub. by Severn Hse). State Mutual Bk.

--Cuchilo. 192p. (Orig.). 1983. pap. 2.25 (ISBN 0-425-06284-8). Berkley Pub.

--The Fortune Hunter. 192p. 1984. pap. 2.50 (ISBN 0-425-07658-X). Berkley Pub.

--Gun Wizard. 192p. 1985. pap. 2.50 (ISBN 0-425-08033-1). Berkley Pub.

--Guns in the Night. 192p. 1985. pap. 2.50 (ISBN 0-425-07972-4). Berkley Pub.

--Gunsmoke Thunder. 192p. 1985. pap. 2.50 (ISBN 0-425-07459-5). Berkley Pub.

--The Law of the Gun. 192p. 1984. pap. 2.25 (ISBN 0-425-06840-4). Berkley Pub.

--The Making of a Lawman. (Orig.). 1984. pap. 2.25 (ISBN 0-425-06841-2). Berkley Pub.

--The Man with No Face. 192p. 1983. pap. 2.25 (ISBN 0-425-06337-2). Berkley Pub.

--Old Mocassins on the Trail. 192p. 1985. pap. 2.50 (ISBN 0-425-08278-4). Berkley Pub.

--Ole Devil & the Caplocks. 208p. 1982. 15.00x (ISBN 0-7278-0721-8, Pub. by Severn Hse). State Mutual Bk.

--The Peacemakers. 192p. (Orig.). 1984. pap. 2.50 (ISBN 0-425-07113-8). Berkley Pub.

--The Remittance Kid. 192p. 1982. 15.00x (ISBN 0-7278-0535-5, Pub. by Severn Hse). State Mutual Bk.

--Rio Guns. 192p. 1985. pap. 2.50 (ISBN 0-425-07755-1). Berkley Pub.

--The Rio Hondo War. 192p. 1984. pap. 2.50 (ISBN 0-425-07035-2). Berkley Pub.

--The Rushers. 192p. 1984. pap. 2.50 (ISBN 0-425-07199-5). Berkley Pub.

--Sidewinder. 1981. pap. 1.95 (ISBN 0-425-05070-X). Berkley Pub.

--The Small Texan. 192p. 1985. pap. 2.50 (ISBN 0-425-07594-X). Berkley Pub.

--A Town Called Yellowdog. 192p. 1983. pap. 2.25 (ISBN 0-425-06577-4). Berkley Pub.

--The Town Tamers. 192p. 1985. pap. 2.50 (ISBN 0-425-07682-2). Berkley Pub.

--Trigger Fast. 192p. 1985. pap. 2.50 (ISBN 0-425-08191-5). Berkley Pub.

--The Trouble Busters. 192p. 1984. pap. 2.25 (ISBN 0-425-06849-8). Berkley Pub.

--Waco's Debt. 192p. 1986. 2.50 (ISBN 0-425-08528-7). Berkley Pub.

--The Whip & the Warlance. 192p. 1982. 15.00x (ISBN 0-7278-0525-8, Pub. by Severn Hse). State Mutual Bk.

--White Indians. 192p. 1985. pap. 2.50 (ISBN 0-425-08086-2). Berkley Pub.

--The Wildcats. 192p. 1983. pap. 2.25 (ISBN 0-425-06268-6). Berkley Pub.

--Young Ole Devil. 176p. 1982. 15.00x (ISBN 0-7278-0676-9, Pub. by Severn Hse). State Mutual Bk.

--The Ysabel Kid. 192p. 1985. pap. 2.50 (ISBN 0-425-08393-4). Berkley Pub.

Edson, Jean S. Organ Preludes: An Index to Compositions on Hymn Tunes, Chorales, Plainsong Melodies, Gregorian Tunes & Carols, 2 Vols. LC 73-8960. 1169p. 1970. Set. 55.00 (ISBN 0-8108-0287-2). Scarecrow.

Edson, Laurie. Henri Michaux & the Poetic of Movement. (Stanford French & Italian Studies: Vol. 42). 160p. 1985. pap. 25.00 (ISBN 0-915838-50-8). Anma Libri.

Edson, Merritt, et al, eds. Ship Modeler's Shop Notes. (Illus.). viii, 216p. 1983. pap. 19.95 (ISBN 0-9603456-0-4). Nautical Res.

Edson, Merritt A., Jr., intro. by see Davis, John.

Edson, Milan C. Solaris Farm: A Story of the Twentieth Century. LC 78-154440. (Utopian Literature Ser). (Illus.). 1971. Repr. of 1900 ed. 31.00 (ISBN 0-405-03523-3). Ayer Co Pubs.

Edson, Russell. The Clam Theater. LC 72-11052. (Wesleyan Poetry Program: Vol. 64). 1973. 10.00x (ISBN 0-8195-2064-0). Wesleyan U Pr.

--The Falling Sickness: A Book of Plays. LC 74-23986. 96p. 1975. pap. 3.75 (ISBN 0-8112-0562-2, NDP389). New Directions.

--Gulping's Recital. 96p. 1983. 9.95 (ISBN 0-941062-40-6); pap. 6.95 (ISBN 0-941062-41-4); (signed edition) 30.00 (ISBN 0-941062-42-2). Guignol Bks.

--Ketchup: A Tragi-Comic Opera with Music Composed by Franklin H. Stover. LC 84-72142. 205p. 38.00 (ISBN 0-931553-00-8); complete set of instrumental parts 27.00 (ISBN 0-931553-01-6). Comp Graphics.

--The Reason Why the Closet-Man is Never Sad. LC 76-55942. (Wesleyan Poetry Program: Vol. 84). 1977. 15.00x (ISBN 0-8195-2084-5); pap. 6.95 (ISBN 0-8195-1084-X). Wesleyan U Pr.

--What a Man Can See & Other Fables. LC 60-9954. pap. 6.00 (ISBN 0-912330-13-9, Dist. by Inland Bk). Jargon Soc.

Edson, Steve. How to Develop Your Great Ideas & Become A Success. (Illus.). 120p. (Orig.). 1982. pap. text ed. 10.95 (ISBN 0-9607678-1-9). Technico Bks.

Edstrom, Lois. Object Talks on the Parables of Jesus. (Illus.). 48p. (Orig.). 1984. pap. 2.25 (ISBN 0-87239-721-1, 2857). Standard Pub.

Edstrom, Vivi. Selma Lagerlof. (World Authors Ser.: No. 741). 1984. lib. bdg. 19.95 (ISBN 0-8057-6587-5, Twayne). G K Hall.

Education & Training Comm. Oregon Association of Milk, Food & Environment Sanitarians, Inc. HTST Pasteurizer Operation Manual. (Illus.). 6.50 (ISBN 0-88246-057-9). Oreg St U Bkstrs.

Education Department Staff. Friendship Group Leader's Guide: Year Three. (Orig.). 1984. pap. 10.20 (ISBN 0-933140-95-9). Bd of Pubns CRC.

--Friendship Teacher's Manual: Youth Year Three. 1984. 5.95 (ISBN 0-933140-96-7). Bd of Pubns CRC.

Education Resources Information Center. Current Index to Journals in Education: Semi-Annual Cumulation July-December 1975. LC 75-7532. 1976. 45.00x (ISBN 0-02-468860-6). Macmillan Info.

Educational Challenges Staff. Safe at Home, Safe Alone. 64p. (Orig.). (gr. 3-5). 1985. pap. 5.95 (ISBN 0-917917-01-4). Miles River.

Educational Law Center, Inc. Staff, jt. auth. see Children's Defense Fund Staff.

Educational Management System. McGraw-Hill Interactive Authoring System. 1984. write for info. (ISBN 0-07-019554-4). McGraw.

Educational Materials Sector Committee of the American National Metric Council. Metric Guide for Educational Materials: A Handbook for Teachers, Writers & Publishers. 1977. pap. text ed. 3.00 (ISBN 0-916148-09-2); subscribers 2.00. Am Natl.

Educational Policies Commission. Research Memorandum on Education in the Depression. LC 72-162838. (Studies in the Social Aspects of the Depression). 1971. Repr. of 1937 ed. 17.00 (ISBN 0-405-00841-4). Ayer Co Pubs.

Educational Research & Service Bureau. Teachers: Professionals in Public Service. LC 76-87846. 1969. pap. 0.40x (ISBN 0-8134-1114-9, 1114). Interstate.

Educational Research Associates, ed. Legal Terms for Secretaries. (gr. 11-12). 1974. 3.95 (ISBN 0-89420-096-8, 299900). Natl Book.

Educational Research Council. Agriculture: People & the Land. (Concepts & Inquiry Ser). (gr. 4). 1975. pap. text ed. 12.60 o. p. (ISBN 0-205-04436-0, 8044368); tchrs'. guide 12.60 (ISBN 0-205-04437-9, 8044376). Allyn.

--The American Adventure, 2 vols. (Concepts & Inquiry Ser.). (Orig.). (gr. 8). 1975. Vol. 1. text ed. 22.48 (ISBN 0-205-04623-1, 8046239); o. p. 17.28 (ISBN 0-205-04624-X, 8046247); Vol. 2. text ed. 22.48 (ISBN 0-205-04625-8, 8046255). Allyn.

--Concepts & Inquiry: The Educational Research Council Social Science Program. (gr. k-7). 1971-73. pap. text ed. write for info (ISBN 0-685-03090-3); tchrs. manuals avail. (ISBN 0-685-03091-1). Allyn.

--Early Years: Twenty Thousand B. C. to Seventeen Sixty-Three A. D. (The American Adventure Concepts & Inquiry Ser.). (gr. 8). 1975. pap. text ed. 13.40 (ISBN 0-205-04628-2, 804628X). Allyn.

--Expansion, Conflict, & Reconstruction 1825-1880. (The American Adventure Concepts & Inquiry Ser). (Orig.). (gr. 8). 1975. pap. text ed. 13.40 (ISBN 0-205-04629-0, 8046298). Allyn.

--The Forming of the Republic (1763-1825) (The American Adventure Concept & Inquiry Ser). (gr. 8). 1975. pap. text ed. 13.40 (ISBN 0-205-04630-4, 8046301). Allyn.

--Four World Views. (The Human Adventure, Concepts & Inquiry Ser.). (gr. 5). 1975. pap. text ed. 13.48 (ISBN 0-205-04444-1, 8044449); tchr's guide o. p. 13.48 (ISBN 0-205-04445-X, 8044457). Allyn.

--Greek & Roman Civilization. (The Human Adventure, Concepts & Inquiry Ser.). (gr. 5). 1975. pap. text ed. 13.48 (ISBN 0-205-04446-8, 8044465); tchr's guide 13.48 (ISBN 0-205-04447-6, 8044473). Allyn.

--Into the Twentieth Century (1880-1939) (American Adventure Concepts & Inquiry Ser.). (Orig.). (gr. 8). 1977. pap. 13.40 (ISBN 0-205-04631-2, 804631X). Allyn.

--The Making of Tomorrow (1940-Present) (The American Adventure Concepts & Inquiry Ser.). (gr. 8). 1977. pap. text ed. 13.40 (ISBN 0-205-04627-4, 8046271). Allyn.

--Medieval Civilization. (The Human Adventure, Concepts & Inquiry Ser.). (gr. 5). 1975. pap. text ed. 13.48 (ISBN 0-205-04448-4, 8044481); tchr's. guide 13.48 (ISBN 0-205-04449-2, 804449X). Allyn.

--New World & Eurasian Cultures. (The Human Adventure Concepts and Inquiry Ser). (gr. 6). 1975. pap. text ed. 14.76 (ISBN 0-205-04454-9, 8044546); tchr's guide 11.88 (ISBN 0-205-04455-7, 8044554). Allyn.

Educational Research Council of America. Accountant. Ferris, Theodore N. & Marchak, John P., eds. (Real People at Work Ser.: S). (Illus.). 36p. 1977. 2.70 (ISBN 0-89247-141-7, 9632). Changing Times.

--Actress. rev. ed. Ferris, Theodore N. & Marchak, John P., eds. (Real People at Work Ser: C). (Illus.). 36p. 1977. pap. text ed. 2.70 (ISBN 0-89247-023-2, 9233). Changing Times.

--Advertising Copy Writer. Ferris, Theodore N. & Marchak, John P., eds. (Real People at Work Ser.: Q). (Illus.). 36p. 1977. 2.70 (ISBN 0-89247-122-0, 9613). Changing Times.

--Airplane Machinist. Ferris, Theodore N. & Marchak, John P., eds. (Real People at Work Ser.: R). (Illus.). 36p. 1977. 2.70 (ISBN 0-89247-136-0, 9627). Changing Times.

--Analytical Testing Manager. Ferris, Theodore N. & Marchak, John P., eds. (Real People at Work: Series N). (Illus.). 36p. (Orig.). (gr. 5). 1976. pap. text ed. 2.70 (ISBN 0-89247-094-1, 9522). Changing Times.

--Architect. rev. ed. Ferris, Theodore N., et al, eds. (Real People at Work Ser: K). (Illus.). 36p. 1980. pap. text ed. 2.70 (ISBN 0-89247-083-6, 9433). Changing Times.

--Assistant Bank Manager. rev. ed. Ferris, Theodore N. & Marchak, John P., eds. (Real People at Work Ser: F). (Illus.). 36p. 1976. pap. text ed. 2.70 (ISBN 0-89247-042-9, 9322). Changing Times.

--Astrophysicist. Ferris, Theodore N. & Marchak, John P., eds. (Real People at Work: Series O). (Illus.). 36p. (Orig.). (gr. 5). 1976. pap. text ed. 2.70 (ISBN 0-89247-101-8, 9534). Changing Times.

--Auto Body Repairman. rev. ed. Ferris, Theodore N. & Marchak, John P., eds. (Real People at Work Ser: E). (Illus.). 36p. 1976. pap. text ed. 2.70 (ISBN 0-89247-037-2, 9317). Changing Times.

--Baker. Ferris, Theodore N. & Marchak, John P., eds. (Real People at Work Ser.: Q). (Illus.). 36p. 1977. 2.70 (ISBN 0-89247-124-7, 9615). Changing Times.

--Beautician. rev. ed. Engle, Jacqueline & Marchak, John P., eds. (Real People at Work Ser: C). (Illus.). 36p. 1976. pap. text ed. 2.70 (ISBN 0-89247-025-9, 9235). Changing Times.

--Blacksmith. Ferris, Theodore N. & Marchak, John P., eds. (Real People at Work Ser.: S). (Illus.). 36p. 1977. 2.70 (ISBN 0-89247-146-8, 9637). Changing Times.

--Boat Builders. Ferris, Theodore N. & Marchak, John P., eds. (Real People at Work Ser.: R). (Illus.). 36p. 1977. 2.70 (ISBN 0-89247-135-2, 9626). Changing Times.

--Boot Maker. Ferris, Theodore N., et al, eds. (Real People at Work Ser: I). (Illus.). 36p. 1975. pap. text ed. 2.70 (ISBN 0-89247-060-7, 9410). Changing Times.

--Building Maintenance Worker. rev. ed. Ferris, Theodore N., ed. (Real People at Work Ser: I). (Illus.). 36p. 1980. pap. text ed. 2.70 (ISBN 0-89247-061-5, 9411). Changing Times.

--Cabinetmaker. Ferris, Theodore N. & Marchak, John P., eds. (Real People at Work: Series M). (Illus.). 36p. (Orig.). (gr. 5). 1976. pap. text ed. 2.70 (ISBN 0-89247-090-9, 9511). Changing Times.

--Camera Technician. Ferris, Theodore N. & Marchak, John P., eds. (Real People at Work Ser.: S). (Illus.). 36p. 1977. 2.70 (ISBN 0-89247-142-5, 9633). Changing Times.

--Carpenter. rev. ed. Ferris, Theodore N. & Marchak, John P., eds. (Real People at Work Ser: A). (Illus.). 36p. 1976. pap. text ed. 2.70 (ISBN 0-89247-001-1, 9211). Changing Times.

--Carpet Maker. Ferris, Theodore N. & Marchak, John P., eds. (Real People at Work Ser.: Q). (Illus.). 36p. 1977. 2.70 (ISBN 0-89247-129-8, 9610). Changing Times.

--Cellist. Ferris, Theodore N. & Marchak, John P., eds. (Real People at Work: Series N). (Illus., Orig.). (gr. 5). 1976. pap. text ed. 2.70 (ISBN 0-89247-097-6, 9523). Changing Times.

--Ceramic Worker. rev. ed. Ferris, Theodore N., et al, eds. (Real People at Work Ser: I). (Illus.). 36p. 1980. pap. text ed. 2.70 (ISBN 0-89247-067-4, 9417). Changing Times.

--Chef. rev. ed. Ferris, Theodore N. & Marchak, John P., eds. (Real People at Work Ser: B). (Illus.). 36p. 1976. pap. text ed. 2.70 (ISBN 0-89247-015-1, 9225). Changing Times.

--Chemical Technicians. Ferris, Theodore N. & Marchak, John P., eds. (Real People at Work Ser: F). (Illus.). 36p. 1974. pap. text ed. 2.70 (ISBN 0-89247-049-6, 9329). Changing Times.

--Child-Care Attendants. Ferris, Theodore N. & Marchak, John P., eds. (Real People at Work Ser.: R). (Illus.). 36p. 1977. 2.70 (ISBN 0-89247-134-4, 9625). Changing Times.

--Children's Librarian. Keck, Florence & Marchak, John P., eds. (Real People at Work Ser: A). (Illus.). 36p. 1974. pap. text ed. 2.70 (ISBN 0-89247-003-8, 9213). Changing Times.

--Choices & Decisions: Economics & Society. (Challenges of Our Time Ser.). (Orig.). (gr. 7). 1972. pap. text ed. 14.92 (ISBN 0-205-05035-2, 805035X); tchr's guide o. s. i. 11.88 (ISBN 0-205-05036-0, 8050368). Allyn.

--Citrus Grower. Ferris, Theodore N. & Marchak, John P., eds. (Real People at Work Ser.: B). (Illus.). 36p. 1974. pap. text ed. 2.70 (ISBN 0-89247-014-3, 9224). Changing Times.

--Civil Engineers. Ferris, Theodore N. & Marchak, John P., eds. (Real People at Work: Series N). (Illus.). 36p. (Orig.). (gr. 5). 1976. pap. text ed. 2.70 (ISBN 0-89247-091-7, 9521). Changing Times.

Educational Research Council of America Staff. Coal Miner. rev. ed. Ferris, Theodore N., et al, eds. (Real People at Work Ser.: Vol. I). (Illus.). 36p. 1980. pap. text ed. 2.70 (ISBN 0-89247-064-X, 9414). Changing Times.

--Coast Guard Petty Officer. Ferris, Theodore N. & Marchak, John P., eds. (Real People at Work Ser.: Q). (Illus.). 36p. 1977. 2.70 (ISBN 0-89247-127-1, 9618). Changing Times.

Educational Research Council of America. Commercial Airline Pilot. Ferris, Theodore N. & Marchak, John P., eds. (Real People at Work Ser.: Q). (Illus.). 36p. 1977. pap. 2.70 (ISBN 0-89247-121-2, 9612). Changing Times.

--Computer Operator. rev. ed. Ferris, Theodore N., et al, eds. (Real People at Work Ser: I). (Illus.). 36p. 1980. pap. text ed. 2.70 (ISBN 0-89247-062-3, 9412). Changing Times.

--Congresswoman. Ferris, Theodore N. & Marchak, John P., eds. (Real People at Work: Series M). (Illus.). 36p. (Orig.). (gr. 5). 1976. pap. text ed. 2.70 (ISBN 0-89247-111-5, 9518). Changing Times.

--Contract Cleaner. rev. ed. Ferris, Theodore N., et al, eds. (Real People at Work Ser: J). (Illus.). 36p. 1980. pap. text ed. 2.70 (ISBN 0-89247-071-2, 9421). Changing Times.

--Corporate Lawyer. Ferris, Theodore N. & Marchak, John P., eds. (Real People at Work Ser: I). (Illus.). 36p. 1975. pap. text ed. 2.70 (ISBN 0-89247-068-2, 9418). Changing Times.

--Corrugated Box Worker. Ferris, Theodore N. & Marchak, John P., eds. (Real People at Work Ser.: Q). (Illus.). 36p. 1977. 2.70 (ISBN 0-89247-123-9, 9614). Changing Times.

--Costume Maker. Ferris, Theodore N. & Marchak, John P., eds. (Real People at Work: Series O). (Illus.). 36p. (Orig.). (gr. 5). 1976. pap. text ed. 2.70 (ISBN 0-89247-119-0, 9530). Changing Times.

--Cultures of the World. LC 80-67872. (Concepts & Understanding Ser.). (gr. 4). 1982. 15.96 (ISBN 0-205-06787-5); tchr's ed. 20.80 (ISBN 0-205-06789-1, 8067899); wkbk. 6.12 (ISBN 0-205-06788-3, 806788); tests backline masters 30.40 (ISBN 0-205-07765-X, 8077657). Allyn.

--Dentist. rev. ed. Kunze, Linda J. & Marchak, John P., eds. (Real People at Work Ser: G). (Illus.). 36p. 1976. pap. text ed. 2.70 (ISBN 0-89247-055-0, 9335). Changing Times.

--Dredge Operator. Ferris, Theodore N. & Marchak, John P., eds. (Real People at Work Ser.: Q). (Illus.). 36p. 1977. 2.70 (ISBN 0-89247-125-5, 9616). Changing Times.

--Dressmaker. rev. ed. Ferris, Theodore N. & Marchak, John P., eds. (Real People at Work Ser: C). (Illus.). 36p. 1976. pap. text ed. 2.70 (ISBN 0-89247-020-8, 9230). Changing Times.

--Dry Cleaners. rev. ed. Ferris, Theodore N. & Marchak, John P., eds. (Real People at Work Ser: G). (Illus.). 36p. 1976. pap. text ed. 2.70 (ISBN 0-89247-050-X, 9330). Changing Times.

--Ecologist. rev. ed. Ferris, Theodore N., et al, eds. (Real People at Work Ser: J). (Illus.). 36p. 1980. pap. text ed. 2.70 (ISBN 0-89247-078-X, 9428). Changing Times.

--Economist. Ferris, Theodore N. & Marchak, John P., eds. (Real People at Work: Series M). (Illus.). 36p. (Orig.). (gr. 5). 1976. pap. text ed. 2.70 (ISBN 0-89247-093-3, 9512). Changing Times.

--Electrician. Ferris, Theodore N., et al, eds. (Real People at Work Ser: K). (Illus.). 36p. 1981. pap. text ed. 2.70 (ISBN 0-89247-081-X, 9431). Changing Times.

--Electronic Repairer. Ferris, Theodore N. & Marchak, John P., eds. (Real People at Work Ser.: Q). (Illus.). 36p. 1977. 2.70 (ISBN 0-89247-128-X, 9619). Changing Times.

--Employee Counselor. Ferris, Theodore N. & Marchak, John P., eds. (Real People at Work: Series O). (Illus.). 36p. (Orig.). (gr. 5). 1976. pap. text ed. 2.70 (ISBN 0-89247-104-2, 9535). Changing Times.

--Estimator. rev. ed. Ferris, Theodore N. & Marchak, John P., eds. (Real People at Work Ser: F). (Illus.). 36p. 1976. pap. text ed. 2.70 (ISBN 0-89247-041-0, 9321). Changing Times.

--Executive Housekeeper. rev. ed. Marchak, John P., ed. (Real People at Work Ser: B). (Illus.). 36p. 1976. pap. text ed. 2.70 (ISBN 0-89247-011-9, 9221). Changing Times.

--Fashion Designer. Ferris, Theodore N. & Marchak, John P., eds. (Real People at Work: Series N). (Illus.). 36p. (Orig.). (gr. 5). 1976. pap. text ed. 2.70 (ISBN 0-89247-118-2, 9520). Changing Times.

--FDA Investigator. rev. ed. Kunze, Linda J. & Marchak, John P., eds. (Real People at Work Ser: E). (Illus.). 36p. 1976. pap. text ed. 2.45 (ISBN 0-89247-038-0, 9318). Changing Times.

--Firearms Examiner. Ferris, Theodore N. & Marchak, John P., eds. (Real People at Work Ser.: R). (Illus.). 36p. 1977. 2.70 (ISBN 0-89247-137-9, 9628). Changing Times.

--Firefighters. rev. ed. Muesegaes, Mary & Marchak, John P., eds. (Real People at Work Ser: A). (Illus.). 36p. 1976. pap. text ed. 2.70 (ISBN 0-89247-008-9, 9228). Changing Times.

--Fish Biologist. Kunze, Linda J. & Marchak, John P., eds. (Real People at Work Ser.: G). (Illus.). 36p. 1974. pap. text ed. 2.70 (ISBN 0-89247-056-9, 9336). Changing Times.

--Fisher. rev. ed. Braverman, Jack R. & Marchak, John P., eds. (Real People at Work Ser.: A). (Illus.). 36p. 1977. pap. text ed. 2.70 (ISBN 0-89247-006-2, 9216). Changing Times.

--Florist. rev. ed. Ferris, Theodore N. & Marchak, John P., eds. (Real People at Work Ser: A). 36p. 1976. pap. text ed. 2.70 (ISBN 0-89247-004-6, 9214). Changing Times.

--Food Technologist. Ferris, Theodore N. & Marchak, John P., eds. (Real People at Work: Series M). (Illus.). 36p. (Orig.). (gr. 5). 1976. pap. text ed. 2.70 (ISBN 0-89247-102-6, 9515). Changing Times.

--Forester. rev. ed. Ferris, Theodore N. & Marchak, John P., eds. (Real People at Work Ser: C). (Illus.). 36p. 1976. pap. text ed. 2.70 (ISBN 0-89247-028-3, 9238). Changing Times.

--Furniture Maker. rev. ed. Ferris, Theodore N. & Marchak, John P., eds. (Real People at Work Ser: C). (Illus.). 36p. 1976. pap. text ed. 2.70 (ISBN 0-89247-021-6, 9231). Changing Times.

--Furrier. rev. ed. Ferris, Theodore N. & Marchak, John P., eds. (Real People at Work Ser: E). (Illus.). 36p. 1976. pap. text ed. 2.70 (ISBN 0-89247-030-5, 9310). Changing Times.

--General Store Owner. rev. ed. Ferris, Theodore N. & Marchak, John P., eds. (Real People at Work Ser.: E). (Illus.). 36p. 1976. pap. text ed. 2.70 (ISBN 0-89247-032-1, 9312). Changing Times.

--Graphic Artist. rev. ed. Ferris, Theodore N. & Marchak, John P., eds. (Real People at Work Ser: B). (Illus.). 36p. 1977. pap. text ed. 2.70 (ISBN 0-89247-013-5, 9223). Changing Times.

--The Growth of Civilization. LC 80-67953. (Concepts & Understanding Ser.). (gr. 6). 1982. 18.48 (ISBN 0-205-06795-6); tchr's ed. 23.20 (ISBN 0-205-06797-2, 806797X); tests blackline masters 40.00 (ISBN 0-205-07763-3, 8077673). Allyn.

--Hand Weaver. Ferris, Theodore N. & Marchak, John P., eds. (Real People at Work Ser: A). (Illus.). 36p. 1974. pap. text ed. 2.70 (ISBN 0-89247-000-3, 9210). Changing Times.

--Hardrock Miner. Ferris, Theodore N. & Marchak, John P., eds. (Real People at Work Ser: F). (Illus.). 36p. 1974. pap. text ed. 2.70 (ISBN 0-89247-044-5, 9324). Changing Times.

--Helicopter Pilot. Kunze, Linda J. & Marchak, John P., eds. (Real People at Work Ser: K). (Illus.). 36p. 1976. pap. text ed. 2.70 (ISBN 0-89247-082-8, 9432). Changing Times.

--Home Economist. rev. ed. Ferris, Theodore N. & Marchak, John P., eds. (Real People at Work Ser: J). (Illus.). 36p. 1980. pap. text ed. 2.70 (ISBN 0-89247-073-9, 9423). Changing Times.

--Horticulturist. Ferris, Theodore N. & Marchak, John P., eds. (Real People at Work Ser.: R). (Illus.). 36p. 1977. 2.70 (ISBN 0-89247-133-6, 9624). Changing Times.

--Housing Consultant. Ferris, Theodore N. & Marchak, John P., eds. (Real People at Work Ser.: S). (Illus.). 36p. 1977. 2.70 (ISBN 0-89247-147-6, 9638). Changing Times.

--Industrial Film Maker. rev. ed. Ferris, Theodore N. & Marchak, John P., eds. (Real People at Work Ser: G). (Illus.). 36p. 1976. pap. text ed. 2.70 (ISBN 0-89247-053-4, 9333). Changing Times.

--Industrial Nurse. Ferris, Theodoe N., et al, eds. (Real People at Work Ser: I). (Illus.). 36p. 1975. pap. text ed. 2.70 (ISBN 0-89247-065-8, 9415). Changing Times.

--Instrument Repairer. Ferris, Theodore N. & Marchak, John P., eds. (Real People at Work: Series O). (Illus.). 36p. (Orig.). (gr. 5). 1976. pap. text ed. 2.70 (ISBN 0-89247-110-7, 9537). Changing Times.

--Insulation Knitter. Ferris, Theodore N., et al, eds. (Real People at Work Ser: K). (Illus.). 36p. 1975. pap. text ed. 2.70 (ISBN 0-89247-080-1, 9430). Changing Times.

--Ironworker. Ferris, Theodore N. & Marchak, John P., eds. (Real People at Work: Series O). (Illus.). 36p. (Orig.). (gr. 5). 1976. pap. text ed. 2.70 (ISBN 0-89247-092-5, 9531). Changing Times.

--Judge. rev. ed. Ferris, Theodore N. & Marchak, John P., eds. (Real People at Work Ser.: G). (Illus.). 36p. 1976. pap. text ed. 2.70 (ISBN 0-89247-058-5, 9338). Changing Times.

--Laser Project Engineer. Ferris, Theodore N. & Marchak, John P., eds. (Real People at Work: Series N). (Illus.). 36p. (Orig.). (gr. 5). 1976. pap. text ed. 2.70 (ISBN 0-89247-115-8, 9529). Changing Times.

--Learning about Communities. LC 80-67791. (Concepts & Understanding Ser.). (gr. 2). 1982. 20.00 (ISBN 0-205-07763-3, 8077630); tchr's ed. 17.20 (ISBN 0-205-06781-6, 8067813); dup. masters 5.60 (ISBN 0-205-06780-8, 8067805); blackline masters 20.00 (877633). Allyn.

--Leather Worker. Ferris, Theodore & Marchak, John P., eds. (Real People at Work Ser: B). (Illus.). 36p. 1974. pap. text ed. 2.70 (ISBN 0-89247-010-0, 9220). Changing Times.

--Lock Master. Braverman, Jack R. & Marchak, John P., eds. (Real People at Work Ser: E). (Illus.). 36p. 1974. pap. text ed. 2.70 (ISBN 0-89247-036-4, 9316). Changing Times.

--Luggage Maker. Ferris, Theodore N. & Marchak, John P., eds. (Real People at Work Ser.: R). (Illus.). 36p. 1977. 2.70 (ISBN 0-89247-139-5, 9620). Changing Times.

--Lumber Worker. rev. ed. Ferris, Theodore N. & Marchak, John P., eds. (Real People at Work Ser.: K). (Illus.). 36p. 1980. pap. text ed. 2.70 (ISBN 0-89247-084-4, 9434). Changing Times.

--Machinist. rev. ed. Kunze, Linda J. & Marchak, John P., eds. (Real People at Work Ser.). (Illus.). 36p. 1976. pap. text ed. 2.70 (ISBN 0-89247-057-7, 9337). Changing Times.

--The Making of Our America. LC 80-67910. (Concepts & Understanding Ser.). (gr. 5). 1982. 17.84 (ISBN 0-205-06791-3, 806791); for info dupl. masters 22.00write (ISBN 0-205-06793-X, 806793); write for info. wrkbk dup. masters; blackline mastera 34.00 (ISBN 0-205-07766-8, 807766). Allyn.

--Managing Editor. Ferris, Theodore N. & Marchak, John P., eds. (Real People at Work: Series O). (Illus.). 36p. (Orig.). (gr. 5). 1976. pap. text ed. 2.70 (ISBN 0-89247-098-4, 9533). Changing Times.

--Manufacturing Optician. Ferris, Theodore N. & Marchak, John P., eds. (Real People at Work Ser: B). (Illus.). 36p. 1974. pap. text ed. 2.70 (ISBN 0-89247-019-4, 9229). Changing Times.

--Marine Engineer. Ferris, Theodore N., ed. (Real People at Work Ser: K). (Illus.). 36p. 1975. pap. text ed. 2.70 (ISBN 0-89247-086-0, 9436). Changing Times.

--Market Researcher. Kunze, Linda J. & Marchak, John P., eds. (Real People at Work Ser: J). (Illus.). 36p. 1984. pap. text ed. 2.70 (ISBN 0-89247-072-0, 9422). Changing Times.

--Mechanic-Attendant. rev. ed. Kunze, Linda A. & Marchak, John P., eds. (Real People at Work Ser.: Pt. A). (Illus.). 36p. 1976. pap. text ed. 2.70 (ISBN 0-89247-007-0, 9217). Changing Times.

--Medical Technologist. rev. ed. Kunze, Linda J. & Marchak, John P., eds. (Real People at Work Ser: E). (Illus.). 36p. 1976. pap. text ed. 2.70 (ISBN 0-89247-035-6, 9315). Changing Times.

--Metal Molder. rev. ed. Braverman, Jack R. & Marchak, John P., eds. (Real People at Work Ser: B). (Illus.). 36p. 1976. pap. text ed. 2.70 (ISBN 0-89247-017-8, 9227). Changing Times.

--Metallurgical Technician. rev. ed. Ferris, Theodore N. & Marchak, John P., eds. (Real People at Work Ser: C). 36p. 1976. pap. text ed. 2.70 (ISBN 0-89247-029-1, 9239). Changing Times.

--Meteorologist. rev. ed. Kunze, Linda J. & Marchak, John P., eds. (Real People at Work Ser: G). (Illus.). 36p. 1976. pap. text ed. 2.70 (ISBN 0-89247-054-2, 9334). Changing Times.

--The Metropolitan Community. (Concepts & Understanding Ser.). (gr. 3). 1982. 14.20 (ISBN 0-205-06783-2, 806783X); tchr's ed. 18.64 (ISBN 0-205-06785-9, 8067856); 26.40 (ISBN 0-205-06784-0, 806784); wkbk 5.60 (ISBN 0-205-07764-1). Allyn.

--Nations in Action: International Tensions. (Challenges of Our Time Ser.). (gr. 7). 1972. pap. text ed. 14.92 (ISBN 0-205-05033-6, 8050333); tchrs'. guide o. p. 11.20 (ISBN 0-205-05034-4, 8050341). Allyn.

--Natural Science Chemist. Ferris, Theodore N., et al, eds. (Real People at Work Ser: J). (Illus.). 36p. 1975. pap. text ed. 2.70 (ISBN 0-89247-074-7, 9424). Changing Times.

--Nuclear Plant Designer. Ferris, Theodore N., et al, eds. (Real People at Work Er: J). (Illus.). 36p. 1976. pap. text ed. 2.70 (ISBN 0-89247-079-8, 9429). Changing Times.

--Nuclear Reactor Operator. Ferris, Theodore N. & Marchak, John P., eds. (Real People at Work Ser: G). (Illus.). 36p. 1974. pap. text ed. 2.70 (ISBN 0-89247-059-3, 9339). Changing Times.

--Nursery Worker. Ferris, Theodore N. & Marchak, John P., eds. (Real People at Work: Series M). (Illus.). 36p. (Orig.). (gr. 5). 1976. pap. text ed. 2.70 (ISBN 0-89247-099-2, 9514). Changing Times.

--Oceanographers. Ferris, Theodore N. & Marchak, John P., eds. (Real People at Work: Series M). (Illus.). 36p. (Orig.). (gr. 5). 1976. pap. text ed. 2.70 (ISBN 0-89247-105-0, 9516). Changing Times.

--Office Worker. Ferris, Theodore N., et al, eds. (Real People at Work Ser: G). (Illus.). 36p. 1974. pap. text ed. 2.70 (ISBN 0-89247-052-6, 9332). Changing Times.

--Oil Driller. Ferris, Theodore N. & Marchak, John P., eds. (Real People at Work Ser: C). (Illus.). 36p. 1974. pap. text ed. 2.70 (ISBN 0-89247-024-0, 9234). Changing Times.

--Operating Engineer. Ferris, Theodore N. & Marchak, John P., eds. (Real People at Work Ser.: S). (Illus.). 36p. 1977. 2.70 (ISBN 0-89247-140-9, 9631). Changing Times.

--Our Land & Our People. LC 80-67767. (Concepts & Understanding Ser.). (gr. 1). 1982. 10.92 (ISBN 0-205-06776-X, 806776); tchr's ed. 15.60 (ISBN 0-205-06777-8); dupl. masters 42.00 (ISBN 0-205-06778-6, 8067783). Allyn.

--Paint Chemist. Ferris, Theodore N. & Marchak, John P., eds. (Real People at Work Ser.: S). (Illus.). 36p. 1977. 2.70 (ISBN 0-89247-148-4, 9639). Changing Times.

--Painter Apprentices. Ferris, Theodore N. & Marchak, John P., eds. (Real People at Work Ser.: R). (Illus.). 36p. 1977. 2.70 (ISBN 0-89247-130-1, 9621). Changing Times.

--Paper Makers. rev. ed. Braverman, Jack R. & Marchak, John P., eds. (Real People at Work Ser: E). (Illus.). 36p. 1976. pap. text ed. 2.70 (ISBN 0-89247-034-8, 9314). Changing Times.

--Pest Controller. rev. ed. Kunze, Linda J. & Marchak, John P., eds. (Real People at Work Ser: G). (Illus.). 36p. 1976. pap. text ed. 2.70 (ISBN 0-89247-051-8, 9331). Changing Times.

--Pharmacist. Durkin, James, ed. (Real People at Work Ser: A). (Illus.). 36p. 1974. pap. text ed. 2.70 (ISBN 0-89247-005-4, 9215). Changing Times.

--Photographer. Ferris, Theodore N. & Marchak, John P., eds. (Real People at Work: Series M). (Illus.). 36p. (Orig.). (gr. 5). 1976. pap. text ed. 2.70 (ISBN 0-89247-096-8, 9513). Changing Times.

--Physical Therapists. rev. ed. Ferris, Theodore N., et al, eds. (Real People at Work Ser: K). (Illus.). 1980. pap. text ed. 2.70 (ISBN 0-89247-085-2, 9435). Changing Times.

--Plant Guard. Ferris, Theodore N. & Marchak, John P., eds. (Real People at Work: Series O). (Illus.). 36p. (Orig.). (gr. 5). 1976. pap. text ed. 2.70 (ISBN 0-89247-111-5, 9538). Changing Times.

--Plumber. rev. ed. Ferris, Theodore N. & Marchak, John P., eds. (Real People at Work Ser: E). (Illus.). 36p. 1976. pap. text ed. 2.70 (ISBN 0-89247-031-3, 9311). Changing Times.

--Police Team. rev. ed. Ferris, Theodore N. & Marchak, John P., eds. (Real People at Work Ser: B). (Illus.). 36p. 1976. pap. text ed. 2.70 (ISBN 0-89247-018-6, 9218). Changing Times.

--Power Line Worker. rev. ed. Ferris, Theodore N., et al, eds. (Real People at Work Ser: I). (Illus.). 36p. 1980. pap. text ed. 2.70 (ISBN 0-89247-069-0, 9419). Changing Times.

--Power Plant Worker. Ferris, Theodore H., et al, eds. (Real People at Work Ser. K). (Illus.). 36p. (gr. 3). 1980. pap. text ed. 2.70 (ISBN 0-89247-089-5, 9439). Changing Times.

--Power Transformer Assembler. Ferris, Theodore N., et al, eds. (Real People at Work Ser: J). (Illus.). 36p. 1975. pap. text ed. 2.70 (ISBN 0-89247-077-1, 9427). Changing Times.

--Prejudice & Discrimination. (Challenges of Our Time Ser.). (gr. 7). 1973. pap. text ed. 14.92 (ISBN 0-205-05031-X, 8050317); tchrs'. guide 11.88 (ISBN 0-205-05032-8, 8050325). Allyn.

--Pro Basketball Player. rev. ed. Ferris, Theodore N. & Marchak, John P., eds. (Real People at Work Ser: F). (Illus.). 36p. 1976. pap. text ed. 2.70 (ISBN 0-89247-045-3, 9325). Changing Times.

--Production Planner. Ferris, Theodore N. & Marchak, John P., eds. (Real People at Work Ser.: Q). (Illus.). 36p. 1977. 2.70 (ISBN 0-89247-126-3, 9617). Changing Times.

--Protective Clothing Maker. rev. ed. Ferris, Theodore N., et al, eds. (Real People at Work Ser: J). (Illus.). 36p. 1980. pap. text ed. 2.70 (ISBN 0-89247-070-4, 9420). Changing Times.

--Public Relations Writers. Kunze, Linda J. & Marchak, John P., eds. (Real People at Work Ser: F). (Illus.). 36p. 1974. pap. text ed. 2.70 (ISBN 0-89247-043-7, 9323). Changing Times.

--Quality Control Engineer. rev. ed. Ferris, Theodore N. & Marchak, John P., eds. (Real People at Work Ser: E). (Illus.). 36p. 1976. pap. text ed. 2.70 (ISBN 0-89247-039-9, 9319). Changing Times.

--Real Estate Broker. Ferris, Theodore N. & Marchak, John P., eds. (Real People at Work Ser.: R). (Illus.). 36p. 1977. 2.70 (ISBN 0-89247-131-X, 9622). Changing Times.

--Recreation Leader. Ferris, Theodore N. & Marchak, John P., eds. (Real People at Work Ser.). (Illus.). 36p. 1977. 2.70 (ISBN 0-89247-144-1, 9635). Changing Times.

--Research Scientist. Ferris, Theodore N. & Marchak, John P., eds. (Real People at Work: Series O). (Illus.). 36p. (Orig.). (gr. 5). 1976. pap. text ed. 2.70 (ISBN 0-89247-116-6, 9539). Changing Times.

--Safety Engineer. rev. ed. Ferris, Theodore N. & Marchak, John P., eds. (Real People at Work Ser.: F). (Illus.). 36p. 1976. pap. text ed. 2.70 (ISBN 0-89247-048-8, 9328). Changing Times.

--Sales Representative. Ferris, Theodore N. & Marchak, John P., eds. (Real People at Work: Series O). (Illus.). 36p. (Orig.). (gr. 5). 1976. pap. text ed. 2.70 (ISBN 0-89247-095-X, 9532). Changing Times.

--Seafood Processor. Ferris, Theodore N. & Marchak, John P., eds. (Real People at Work: Series N). (Illus.). 36p. (gr. 5). 1976. pap. text ed. 2.70 (ISBN 0-89247-106-9, 9526). Changing Times.

Educational Research Council of America Staff. Seaman. rev. ed. Braverman, Jack R. & Marchak, John P., eds. (Real People at Work Ser: B). (Illus.). 36p. 1977. pap. text ed. 2.70 (ISBN 0-89247-016-X, 9226). Changing Times.

Educational Research Council of America. Sheetmetal Worker. rev. ed. Eppert, M. R. & Marchak, John P., eds. (Real People at Work Ser: C). (Illus.). 36p. 1976. pap. text ed. 2.70 (ISBN 0-89247-027-5, 9237). Changing Times.

--Shipfitter. Braverman, Jack R. & Marchak, John P., eds. (Real People at Work Ser: C). (Illus.). 36p. 1974. pap. text ed. 2.70 (ISBN 0-89247-026-7, 9236). Changing Times.

--Ship's Engineer. Kunze, Linda J. & Marchak, John P., eds. (Real People at Work Ser: J). (Illus.). 36p. 1975. pap. text ed. 2.70 (ISBN 0-89247-076-3, 9426). Changing Times.

--Shipyard Workers. Ferris, Theodore N. & Marchak, John P., eds. (Real People at Work: Series O). (Illus.). 36p. (Orig.). (gr. 5). 1976. pap. text ed. 2.70 (ISBN 0-89247-107-7, 9536). Changing Times.

--Shoe Repairer. rev. ed. Ferris, Theodore N. & Marchak, John P., eds. (Real People at Work Ser: F). (Illus.). 36p. 1976. pap. text ed. 2.70 (ISBN 0-89247-040-2, 9320). Changing Times.

--Solar Cell Scientist. Ferris, Theodore N. & Marchak, John P., eds. (Real People at Work Ser.: S). (Illus.). 36p. 1977. 2.70 (ISBN 0-89247-143-3, 9634). Changing Times.

--Sound Engineer. Ferris, Theodore N. & Marchak, John P., eds. (Real People at Work Ser.: R). (Illus.). 36p. 1977. 2.70 (ISBN 0-89247-132-8, 9623). Changing Times.

--Space Technologist. Ferris, Theodore N. & Marchak, John P., eds. (Real People at Work Ser.: R). (Illus.). 36p. 1977. 2.70- (ISBN 0-89247-138-7, 9629). Changing Times.

--Special Education Teacher. rev. ed. Kunze, Linda J. & Marchak, John P., eds. (Real People at Work Ser: E). (Illus.). 36p. 1977. pap. text ed. 2.70 (ISBN 0-89247-033-X, 9313). Changing Times.

--Steelworker. Ferris, Theodore N. & Marchak, John P., eds. (Real People at Work: Series M). (Illus.). 36p. (Orig.). (gr. 5). 1976. pap. text ed. 2.70 (ISBN 0-89247-108-5, 9517). Changing Times.

--Supermarket Cashier. rev. ed. McCabe, Bernard & Marchak, John P., eds. (Real People at Work Ser: B). 36p. 1976. pap. text ed. 2.70 (ISBN 0-89247-012-7, 9222). Changing Times.
--Supervisor Trainee. rev. ed. Ferris, Theodore N. & Marchak, John P., eds. (Real People at Work Ser.: A). 36p. 1976. pap. text ed. 2.70 (ISBN 0-89247-002-X, 9212). Changing Times.
--Tailor. Ferris, Theodore N. & Marchak, John P., eds. (Real People at Work Ser.: S). (Illus.). 36p. 1977. 2.70 (ISBN 0-89247-149-2, 9630). Changing Times.
--Technology: Promises & Problems. new ed. (Challenges of Our Time Ser.). (Orig.). (gr. 7). 1972. pap. text ed. 14.92 (ISBN 0-205-05029-8, 8050295); tchrs'. guide 11.88 (ISBN 0-205-05030-1, 8050309). Allyn.
--Telephone Repairman. rev. ed. Spinell, Donald & Marchak, John P., eds. (Real People at Work Ser: A). (Illus.). 36p. 1976. pap. text ed. 2.70 (ISBN 0-89247-009-7, 9219). Changing Times.
--Television News Broadcaster. rev. ed. Ferris, Theodore N., et al, eds. (Real People at Work Ser: I). (Illus.). 36p. 1980. pap. text ed. 2.70 (ISBN 0-89247-063-1, 9413). Changing Times.
--Test Room Engineer. Ferris, Theodore N. & Marchak, John P., eds. (Real People at Work: Series M). (Illus.). 36p. (Orig.). (gr. 5). 1976. pap. text ed. 2.70 (ISBN 0-89247-114-X, 9519). Changing Times.
--Textile Designer. Ferris, Theodore N. & Marchak, John P., eds. (Real People at Work: Series M). (Illus.). 36p. (Orig.). (gr. 5). 1976. pap. text ed. 2.70 (ISBN 0-89247-117-4, 9510). Changing Times.
--Tool & Die Apprentice. Ferris, Theodore N. & Marchak, John P., eds. (Real People at Work: Series N). (Illus.). 36p. (Orig.). (gr. 5). 1976. pap. text ed. 2.70 (ISBN 0-89247-109-3, 9527). Changing Times.
--Tour Director. Ferris, Theodore N. & Marchak, John P., eds. (Real People at Work: Series N). (Illus.). 36p. (Orig.). (gr. 5). 1976. pap. text ed. 2.70 (ISBN 0-89247-103-4, 9525). Changing Times.
--Towboat Pilot. Ferris, Theodore N., et al, eds. (Real People at Work Ser: I). (Illus.). 36p. 1975. pap. text ed. 2.70 (ISBN 0-89247-066-6, 9416). Changing Times.
--Truck Driver. rev. ed. McCabe, Bernard & Marchak, John P., eds. (Real People at Work Ser: C). (Illus.). 36p. 1976. pap. text ed. 2.70 (ISBN 0-89247-022-4, 9232). Changing Times.
--Truck Mechanic. rev. ed. Ferris, Theodore N., et al, eds. (Real People at Work Ser: K). (Illus.). 36p. 1980. pap. text ed. 2.70 (ISBN 0-89247-087-9, 9437). Changing Times.
--Tugboat Pilot. rev. ed. Ferris, Theodore N. & Marchak, John P., eds. (Real People at Work Ser: F). (Illus.). 36p. 1977. pap. text ed. 2.70 (ISBN 0-89247-046-1, 9326). Changing Times.
--Union Representative. Ferris, Theodore N. & Marchak, John P., eds. (Real People at Work Ser. N). (Illus.). 36p. (Orig.). (gr. 5). 1976. pap. text ed. 2.70 (ISBN 0-89247-112-3, 9528). Changing Times.
--Violin Maker. Ferris, Theodore N. & Marchak, John P., eds. (Real People at Work Ser.: Q). (Illus.). 36p. 1977. 2.70 (ISBN 0-89247-120-4, 9611). Changing Times.
--Watch Engineer. Ferris, Theodore N., et al, eds. (Real People at Work Ser: K). (Illus.). 36p. 1975. pap. text ed. 2.70 (ISBN 0-89247-088-7, 9438). Changing Times.
--Water Analyst. Ferris, Theodore N, et al, eds. (Real People at Work Ser: J). (Illus.). 36p. 1975. pap. text ed. 2.70 (ISBN 0-89247-075-5, 9425). Changing Times.
--Welders. rev. ed. Braverman, Jack R. & Marchak, John P., eds. (Real People at Work Ser: F). (Illus.). 36p. 1976. pap. text ed. 2.70 (ISBN 0-89247-047-X, 9327). Changing Times.
--Wheat Farmer. Ferris, Theodore N. & Marchak, John P., eds. (Real People at Work: Series N). (Illus.). 36p. (Orig.). (gr. 5). 1976. pap. text ed. 2.70 (ISBN 0-89247-100-X, 9524). Changing Times.
--Yacht Broker. Ferris, Theodore N. & Marchak, John P., eds. (Real People at Work Ser.: S). (Illus.). 36p. 1977. pap. text ed. 2.70 (ISBN 0-89247-145-X, 9636). Changing Times.

Educational Research Symposium Organized by the Council of Europe & the Research & Development Unit of the Chancellor of the Swedish Universities, Goteborg, Sweden, September 7-12, 1975. Strategies for Research & Development in Higher Education: Proceedings. Entwistle, Noel, ed. 282p. 1976. pap. text ed. 18.50 (ISBN 90-265-0242-7, Pub. by Swets & Zeitlinger Netherlands). Hogrefe Intl.

Educational Resource Information Center. Educational Documents Abstracts, 1977, 2 vols. LC 72-75009. 1978. 75.00 (ISBN 0-02-693190-7). Macmillan Info.

Educational Resources Information Center. Current Index to Journals in Education: Semi-Annual Cumulation. LC 75-7532. 1975. 45.00x (ISBN 0-02-468740-5). Macmillan Info.
--Current Index to Journals in Education: Semi-Annual Cumulation, July-December, 1976. LC 75-7532. 1977. 45.00x (ISBN 0-02-692990-2). Macmillan Info.
--Early Childhood Education: An ERIC Bibliography. 1973. 11.50 (ISBN 0-02-468500-3). Macmillan Info.
--Educational Documents Abstracts, 1978. LC 72-75009. 1979. 90.00 (ISBN 0-02-692870-1). Macmillan Info.
--Educational Documents Index, 1977. LC 71-130348. 1978. 55.00x (ISBN 0-02-693200-8). Macmillan Info.
--Educational Documents Index, 1978. LC 71-130348. 1979. 60.00 (ISBN 0-02-692880-9). Macmillan Info.
--ERIC Education Documents Abstracts, 1976, 2 vols. LC 72-75009. 1977. 75.00 (ISBN 0-02-693080-3). Macmillan Info.
--ERIC Educational Documents Abstracts, 1968. 1969. 60.00 (ISBN 0-02-468670-0). Macmillan Info.
--ERIC Educational Documents Abstracts, 1969. 1970. 60.00 (ISBN 0-02-468680-8). Macmillan Info.
--ERIC Educational Documents Abstracts: 1973. 1974. 60.00 (ISBN 0-02-468810-X). Macmillan Info.
--ERIC Educational Documents Abstracts 1975. LC 72-75009. 1976. 60.00 (ISBN 0-02-693010-2). Macmillan Info.
--ERIC Educational Documents Abstracts, 1970. 1971. 60.00 (ISBN 0-02-468690-5). Macmillan Info.
--ERIC Educational Documents Abstracts, 1971. 1972. 60.00 (ISBN 0-02-468700-6). Macmillan Info.
--ERIC Educational Documents Abstracts, 1972. 1973. 60.00 (ISBN 0-02-468710-3). Macmillan Info.
--ERIC Educational Documents Index: 1970-1971. LC 71-130348. 2000p. 1972. 45.00 (ISBN 0-02-468780-4). Macmillan Info.
--ERIC Educational Documents Index: 1973. 1975. 45.00 (ISBN 0-02-468830-4). Macmillan Info.
--ERIC Educational Documents Index, 1974. 1975. 45.00 (ISBN 0-02-468160-1). Macmillan Info.
--ERIC Educational Documents Index 1975. LC 71-130348. 1976. 45.00 (ISBN 0-02-693000-5). Macmillan Info.
--ERIC Educational Documents Index, 1976. LC 71-130348. 1977. 45.00 (ISBN 0-02-693070-6). Macmillan Info.
--Library & Information Sciences, an ERIC Bibliography. LC 72-82741. 1972. 11.50 (ISBN 0-02-468630-1). Macmillan Info.
--Social Science Skills: Activities for the Secondary Classroom, 7 vols. Incl. American Government Issues. 11.95x (ISBN 0-8077-2649-4); American Lifestyle Issues. 14.95x (ISBN 0-8077-2648-6); Basic Skills. 11.95x (ISBN 0-8077-2650-8); Economic Issues. 11.95 (ISBN 0-8077-2645-1); Energy - Consumer Issues. 15.95x (ISBN 0-8077-2646-X); World Issues. 17.95x (ISBN 0-8077-2643-5); Population Issues. 14.95x (ISBN 0-8077-2644-3). (Orig.). 1981. (ISBN 0-686-77379-9). Tchrs Coll.

Educational Solutions' Staff, jt. auth. see Gattegno, Caleb.

Educational System Staff. Microref for Multiplan. 1984. pap. 14.95 (ISBN 0-8359-4399-2). Reston.

Educational Systems. Microref for Symphony. price not set. P-H.

Educational Systems Corp. Skills in Mathematics, Bks. 1-2. (Cambridge Skill Power Ser.). 192p. Bk. 1. pap. text ed. 7.00 (ISBN 0-8428-2108-2); Bk. 2. pap. text ed. 7.00 (ISBN 0-8428-2110-4); Key Bk. 1. 1.33 (ISBN 0-8428-2109-0). Cambridge Bk.

Educational Systems, Inc. Skills in Reading, 2 bks. (Cambridge Skill Power Ser.). (gr. 9-12). Bk.1 key. pap. text ed. 7.00 (ISBN 0-8428-9004-1); Bk. 2 key. pap. text ed. 7.00 (ISBN 0-8428-9013-0); 1.33 (ISBN 0-8428-9200-1); 1.33 (ISBN 0-8428-9201-X). Cambridge Bk.

Educational Testing Service. First-Year Evaluative Study of the Workshop Center: An Account of the Center's Operations, Clientele & Staffing. 1973. pap. 1.00 (ISBN 0-918374-07-3). Workshop Ctr.

Educational Testing Service & Council on Learning. College Students' Knowledge & Beliefs. LC 80-69767. 200p. (Orig.). 1981. pap. 10.95 (ISBN 0-915390-31-0, Pub. by Change Mag). Transaction Pubs.

Edvardsen, Aril & Harris, Madalene. Dreaming & Achieving the Impossible. 1984. pap. 5.95 (ISBN 0-88419-192-3). Creation Hse.

Edvinsson, Lars, jt. ed. see Owman, Christer.

Edward, Broadhead. George Semmes Simpson, the Wayward Pioneer, 1818-1885. (Illus.). 40p. (Orig.). 1985. pap. 3.50x (ISBN 0-915617-07-2). Pueblo Co Hist Soc.

Edward, Derek, jt. auth. see Tilbury, Fred.

Edward Fifth, King of England. Grants Etc. from the Crown During the Reign of Edward the Fifth. LC 70-164758. (Camden Society Ser: No. 60). Repr. of 1854 ed. 19.00 (ISBN 0-404-50160-5). AMS Pr.

Edward, Gene. A Tale of Three Kings. 120p. 1980. pap. 5.95 (ISBN 0-940232-03-0). Christian Bks.

Edward, Herbert. First Baron Herbert of Cherbury. Wellek, Rene, ed. (British Philosophers & Theologians of the 17th & 18th Centuries Ser.). 51.00 (ISBN 0-317-20380-0). Garland Pub.

Edward, John T., tr. see Schaal, R.

Edward, Joyce, et al. Separation-Individuation Theory & Application. (Clinical Social Work Ser.). 324p. 1981. text ed. 27.50 (ISBN 0-89876-018-6). Gardner Pr.

Edward of Norwich. Master of Game: Oldest English Book on Hunting. Baillie-Grohman, William A. & Baillie-Grohman, F., eds. LC 78-178528. (Illus.). Repr. of 1909 ed. 45.00 (ISBN 0-404-56541-7). AMS Pr.

Edward, Page, Jr. The Mules That Angels Ride. LC 70-188737. 1972. 9.95 (ISBN 0-87955-900-4). O'Hara.

Edward Sixth. Literary Remains of King Edward Sixth, 2 Vols. Nichols, John G., ed. 1964. Repr. of 1857 ed. 52.00 (ISBN 0-8337-2528-9). B Franklin.

Edward, Smith C., jt. ed. see Ramsey, Frederick.

Edward Thompson Company, jt. auth. see West Publishing Company.

Edward, Topol & Neznansky, Fridrikh. Red Square. 336p. 1984. pap. 3.95 (ISBN 0-425-08158-3). Berkley Pub.

Edward, W. Visually & Transfer Skill Mastery, 2 levels. Incl. Level 2. Subtraction & Division (ISBN 0-89039-850-X). pap. 8.50 ea. Ann Arbor FL.

Edwardes, A. Michael. A Season in Hell. LC 72-11088. (Illus.). 326p. 1973. 12.95 (ISBN 0-8008-7015-8). Taplinger.

Edwardes, Marian. Pocket Lexicon & Concordance to the Temple Shakespeare. LC 74-164759. Repr. of 1909 ed. 21.50 (ISBN 0-404-02261-8). AMS Pr.
--Summary of the Literatures of Modern Europe from the Origins to 1400. LC 7-20970. 1968. Repr. of 1907 ed. 48.00 (ISBN 0-527-26400-8). Kraus Repr.

Edwardes, Michael. East-West Passage: The Travel of Ideas, Arts & Inventions Between Asia & the Western World. LC 79-137663. (Illus.). 1971. 8.95 (ISBN 0-8008-2355-9). Taplinger.

Edwardes, Michael, ed. see Russell, William H.

Edwardes, Phil & McConnell, James. Healing for You. 112p. 1985. pap. 6.95 (ISBN 0-7225-0939-1). Thorsons Pubs.

Edwardes, Richard. Damon & Pythias. LC 82-45708. (Malone Society Reprint Ser.: No. 107). Repr. of 1957 ed. 40.00 (ISBN 0-404-63107-X). AMS Pr.

Edwardes, Stephen M. Babur: Diarist & Despot. LC 79-180334. Repr. of 1926 ed. 15.00 (ISBN 0-404-56246-9). AMS Pr.

Edwardes, Stephen M. & Garrett, Herbert L. Mughal Rule in India. LC 75-41084. Repr. of 1930 ed. 27.50 (ISBN 0-404-14537-X). AMS Pr.

Edwardes, Tickmer. The Lore of the Honey-Bee. 1976. lib. bdg. 59.95 (ISBN 0-8490-2184-7). Gordon Pr.

Edwards. Biology. (Easy Way Ser.). (gr. 9-12). 1983. pap. 7.95 (ISBN 0-8120-2625-X). Barron.
--Children & Juveniles. (The Law in North Carolina Ser.). 24.95 (ISBN 0-686-90933-X). Harrison Co GA.
--Georgia Employment Law. 42.95 (ISBN 0-686-90321-8). Harrison Co GA.
--Irish Language: An Annotated Bibliography. 1983. lib. bdg. 43.00 (ISBN 0-8240-9294-5). Garland Pub.
--Linear Regession & Correlation Introduction. 2nd ed. (Illus.). 208p. 1984. text ed. 19.95 (ISBN 0-7167-1593-7); pap. text ed. 11.95 (ISBN 0-7167-1594-5). W H Freeman.
--Lorca: The Theater Beneath the Sand. 20.00 (ISBN 0-317-29145-9). M Boyars.
--North Carolina Probate Handbook. 3rd ed. incl. latest pocket part supplement 54.95 (ISBN 0-686-90929-1); separate pocket part supplement, 1983 10.95. Harrison Co GA.

Edwards & Mellett. Accountancy for Banking Students. 1983. 45.00x (ISBN 0-317-20358-4, Pub. by Inst Bankers UK). State Mutual Bk.

Edwards, et al. The Basic Accounting Cycle. 1975. pap. 9.95 (ISBN 0-256-01707-7). Dow Jones-Irwin.
--The London Bookshop, Vol. 2. 77p. 1981. 60.00x (ISBN 0-686-79276-9, Pub. by Private Libs England). State Mutual Bk.
--Advances in the Management of Cleft Palate. (Illus.). 1981. text ed. 30.00 (ISBN 0-443-01601-1). Churchill.

Edwards, A. Water Gardens, Rock Gardens & Alpine Gardens. 312p. 1986. 13.95 (ISBN 0-686-82963-8); pap. 8.95 (ISBN 0-89496-029-X). Ross Bks.

Edwards, A. & Wohl, G. The Picture Life of Stevie Wonder. 48p. (ps-5). 1977. pap. 1.75 (ISBN 0-380-01907-8, 51656-X, Camelot). Avon.

Edwards, A; see Bleiler, E. F.

Edwards, A. B; see Bleiler, E. F.

Edwards, A. C. A History of Essex. (The Darwen County History Ser.). (Illus.). 128p. 1978. Repr. of 1958 ed. 18.00x (ISBN 0-8476-2311-4). Rowman.

Edwards, A. D. Language in Culture & Class: The Sociology of Language & Education. 1976. pap. text ed. 15.00x (ISBN 0-435-82270-5). Heinemann Ed.

Edwards, A. M., jt. ed. see Newsome, D. H.

Edwards, A. S. MS Pepys Two Thousand Six: Magdalene College, Cambridge, Vol. VI. (Chaucer Facsimile Ser.). 450p. 1985. 144.00 (ISBN 0-937664-69-3). Pilgrim Bks OK.
--Stephen Hawes. (English Authors Ser.). 1983. lib. bdg. 19.95 (ISBN 0-8057-6840-8, Twayne). G K Hall.

Edwards, A. S., ed. The Index of Middle English Prose Handlist I: Manuscripts in the Henry E. Huntington Library at San Marino. 104p. 1985. 30.00 (ISBN 0-85991-164-0, Pub. by Boydell & Brewer). Longwood Pub Group.
--Middle English Prose: A Critical Guide to Major Authors & Genres. 440p. 1984. text ed. 50.00 (ISBN 0-8135-1001-5). Rutgers U Pr.

Edwards, A. S. & Pearsall, Derek, eds. Middle English Prose: Essays on Bibliographical Problems. LC 80-8595. 150p. 1981. lib. bdg. 31.00 (ISBN 0-8240-9453-0). Garland Pub.

Edwards, A. S., ed. see Allen, Rosamund.

Edwards, A. S., ed. see Dahood, Roger.

Edwards, A. S., ed. see Hamel, Mary.

Edwards, A. S., ed. see Reinecke, George F.

Edwards, A. S., ed. see Thomson, David.

Edwards, A. W. Foundations of Mathematical Genetics. LC 76-9168. (Illus.). 1977. 37.50 (ISBN 0-521-21325-8). Cambridge U Pr.
--Likelihood. (Cambridge Sciences Classics). (Illus.). 235p. 1985. pap. 16.95 (ISBN 0-521-31871-8). Cambridge U Pr.

Edwards, Adele. Journals of the Privy Council, 1783-1789. LC 77-144802. (State Records of South Carolina Ser.). xxvi, 276p. 1971. 34.95x (ISBN 0-87249-916-2). U of SC Pr.

Edwards, Adrienne. Honorable Intentions. (To Have & to Hold Ser.: No. 29). 192p. 1984. pap. 1.95 (ISBN 0-515-07831-X). Jove Pubns.

Edwards, Agustin. The Dawn: History of the Birth & Consolidation of the Republic of Chile. 1976. lib. bdg. 59.95 (ISBN 0-8490-1701-7). Gordon Pr.
--My Native Land: Chilean Reminiscence, Folklore, Panorama, Writers. 1976. lib. bdg. 59.95 (ISBN 0-8490-2311-4). Gordon Pr.
--Peoples of Old: Preconquest & Early Colonial Chile. 1976. lib. bdg. 59.95 (ISBN 0-8490-2419-6). Gordon Pr.

Edwards, Alan & Spinks, John. Fighting Men in Miniature. 192p. 1980. 32.95x (ISBN 0-85177-187-4, Pub. by Conway Maritime England). State Mutual Bk.

Edwards, Alfred L., ed. see International Association for the Advancement of Appropriate Technology for Developing Countries, 1979 Symposium.

Edwards, Allen. Flawed Words & Stubborn Sounds: A Conversation with Elliott Carter. LC 77-152660. 1972. 7.95x (ISBN 0-393-02159-9). Norton.

Edwards, Allen D. & Jones, Dorothy, eds. Community & Community Development. (New Babylon Studies in the Social Sciences: No. 23). 1976. text ed. 18.40x (ISBN 90-2797-512-4). Mouton.

Edwards, Allen L. Experimental Design in Psychological Research. 5th ed. 584p. 1984. text ed. 31.50 scp (ISBN 0-06-041873-7, HarpC). Har-Row.
--An Introduction to Linear Regression & Correlation. LC 75-38811. (Illus.). 213p. 1976. pap. text ed. 11.95 (ISBN 0-7167-0561-3). W H Freeman.
--Multiple Regression & the Analysis of Variance & Covariance. LC 79-12873. (Psychology Ser.). (Illus.). 212p. 1979. pap. text ed. 10.95 (ISBN 0-7167-1081-1). W H Freeman.
--Multiple Regression & the Analysis of Variance & Covariance. 2nd ed. LC 84-25915. (Illus.). 221p. 1985. text ed. 19.95 (ISBN 0-7167-1703-4); pap. text ed. 12.95 (ISBN 0-7167-1704-2). W H Freeman.
--The Social Desirability Variable in Personality Assessment & Research. LC 81-20141. vii, 108p. 1982. Repr. lib. bdg. 22.50x (ISBN 0-313-23245-8, EDSD). Greenwood.
--Techniques of Attitude Scale Construction. (Century Psychology Ser.). (Illus.). 1982. text ed. 38.00x (ISBN 0-8290-0067-4); pap. text ed. 19.50x (ISBN 0-8290-0682-6). Irvington.

Edwards, Amelia B. The Phantom Coach. LC 81-19862. (Illus.). 32p. (gr. 5-10). 1982. PLB 9.79 (ISBN 0-89375-634-2); pap. text ed. 2.50 (ISBN 0-89375-635-0). Troll Assocs.
--A Thousand Miles up the Nile. LC 83-4822. (Library of Travel Classics). (Illus.). 528p. (Orig.). 1983. pap. 10.95 (ISBN 0-87477-271-0). J P Tarcher.
--A Thousand Miles up the Nile. 528p. 1983. pap. 11.95 (ISBN 0-7126-0038-8). Hippocrene Bks.
--A Thousand Miles up the Nile. (Travel Classics Ser.). 528p. 1985. lib. bdg. 23.95 (ISBN 0-317-19647-2, Pub. by Century Pubs UK). Hippocrene Bks.

Edwards, Andrea. All Too Soon. 368p. 1985. pap. 3.50 (ISBN 0-380-89512-9). Avon.
--Now Come the Spring. 240p. 1983. pap. 2.95 (ISBN 0-380-83329-8, 83329-8). Avon.
--Power Play. 368p. 1984. pap. 2.95 (ISBN 0-380-87692-2, 87692-2). Avon.

Edwards, Anne. Matriarch: Queen Mary & the House of Windsor. LC 84-60447. (Illus.). 512p. 1984. 18.95 (ISBN 0-688-03511-6). Morrow.
--A Remarkable Woman: A Biography of Katharine Hepburn. LC 85-11523. (Illus.). 472p. 1985. 19.95 (ISBN 0-688-04528-6). Morrow.

--Road to Tara. (General Ser.). 550p. 1983. lib. bdg. 18.95 (ISBN 0-8161-3606-8, Large Print Bks). G K Hall.

--The Road to Tara: The Life of Margaret Mitchell. LC 82-19520. (Illus.). 384p. 1983. 15.95 (ISBN 0-89919-169-X). Ticknor & Fields.

--Road to Tara: The Life of Margaret Mitchell. 1984. pap. 3.95 (ISBN 0-440-17465-1). Dell.

--Sonya: The Life of Countess Tolstoy. 528p. 1983. pap. 8.95 (ISBN 0-88184-050-5). Carroll & Graf.

--Survivors. 1969. pap. 2.25 (ISBN 0-440-18397-9). Dell.

--Vivien Leigh. 1981. pap. 3.95 (ISBN 0-671-44289-9). PB.

Edwards, Anne, et al. Exploring the Purcell Wilderness. LC 78-71661. (Illus.). 112p. 1979. pap. 6.95 (ISBN 0-916890-75-9). Mountaineers.

Edwards, Anthony & Cleverdon, Robert. International Tourism to 1990. (Economist Intelligence Ser.). 296p. 1982. 29.95x (ISBN 0-89011-582-6). Ballinger Pub.

Edwards, Anthony, jt. auth. see Cleverdon, Robert.

Edwards, Anthony S. John Skelton. (The Critical Heritage Ser.). 300p. 1981. 29.95 (ISBN 0-7100-0724-8). Routledge & Kegan.

Edwards, Anthony S., ed. see Cavendish, George.

Edwards, Archie L., Sr. Expository Outlines from Paul's Epistles. (Sermon Outline Ser.). 1978. pap. 2.50 (ISBN 0-8010-3333-0). Baker Bk.

--Outlines on the Gospel of John & First John. (Sermon Outline Ser.). 1978. pap. 1.95 (ISBN 0-8010-3334-9). Baker Bk.

Edwards, Arthur. The Design of Suburbia: A Critical Study in Environmental History. (Illus.). 281p. 1981. 32.50 (ISBN 0-686-72349-X, Pub. by Pembridge England). Shoe String.

Edwards, Arthur C. Beginning String Class Method. 4th. ed. 192p. 1985. write for info. (ISBN 0-697-00295-0). Wm C Brown.

--Persian Caravan. facsimile ed. LC 70-110224. (Short Story Index Reprint Ser.). 1928. 17.00 (ISBN 0-8369-3311-7). Ayer Co Pubs.

--String Ensemble Method: Beginning Class Instruction in Violin, Viola, Cello & Bass. 3rd ed. 185p. 1980. write for info. plastic comb (ISBN 0-697-03514-X). Wm C Brown.

Edwards, Audrey H. Street Trees in Canberra. 72p. (Orig.). 1979. pap. text ed. 5.25 (ISBN 0-7081-0192-5, 1542, Pub. by ANUP Australia). Australia N U P.

Edwards, Averyl. Seventeen Fifty-Two to Eighteen Forty. 1948. 15.00 (ISBN 0-8274-2338-1). R West.

Edwards, B. Quantitative & Accounting Methods. 192p. 1980. pap. text ed. 18.50x (ISBN 0-7121-1704-0). Trans-Atlantic.

Edwards, B., ed. see Gui De Cambrai.

Edwards, B. H., et al. Emerging Technologies for the Control of Hazardous Wastes. LC 83-4022. (Pollution Tech. Rev.: No. 99). (Illus.). 146p. (Orig.). 1983. 24.00 (ISBN 0-8155-0943-X). Noyes.

Edwards, Barba J. & Brilhart, John K. Communications in Nursing Practice. LC 81-1960. (Illus.). 245p. 1981. pap. text ed. 14.95 (ISBN 0-8016-0786-8). Mosby.

Edwards, Barry. The Readable Maths & Statistics Book. (Illus.). 336p. (Orig.). 1980. text ed. 34.95x (ISBN 0-04-310007-4). Allen Unwin.

Edwards, Bateman. Classification of the Manuscripts of Gui De Cambrai's Vengement Alixandre. (Elliott Monographs: Vol. 20). 1926. pap. 15.00 (ISBN 0-527-02623-9). Kraus Repr.

Edwards, Betty. Drawing on the Artist Within. 1985. 16.95 (ISBN 0-671-49386-8). S&S.

--Drawing on the Right Side of the Brain. LC 78-62794. 1979. 15.95 (ISBN 0-87477-087-4); pap. 9.95 (ISBN 0-87477-088-2). J P Tarcher.

Edwards, Betty, jt. auth. see Coleman, Emily.

Edwards, Bill, ed. The Best Show Biz Crosswords Ever. 192p. 1983. 3.98 (ISBN 0-517-40298-X, Bonanza). Outlet Bk Co.

Edwards, Bob. Anybody Who Needs to Be Sure Is in Trouble. LC 82-81009. 72p. 1982. pap. 5.45 (ISBN 0-941780-11-2). Parkhurst Little.

Edwards, Bruce. Kangaroos & Wallabies. (Young Nature Library). (Illus.). 36p. (gr. 6 up). 1974. Repr. of 1972 ed. 2.95 (ISBN 0-88359-002-6). R Curtis Bks.

Edwards, Bruce & Fudge, Edward. A Journey Toward Jesus. 1.50 (ISBN 0-686-12687-4). E Fudge.

Edwards, Bryan. History, Civil & Commercial of the British Colonies in the West Indies, Dublin, 1793-94. LC 78-141085. (Research Library of Colonial Americana). (Illus.). 1972. Repr. of 1794 ed. 79.50 (ISBN 0-405-03282-X). Ayer Co Pubs.

--History, Civil & Commercial, of the British West Indies, 5 Vols. LC 79-164760. Repr. of 1819 ed. Set. 185.00 (ISBN 0-404-02270-7). AMS Pr.

Edwards, C. International Restrictive Business Practices. 1960. text ed. 12.25 (ISBN 0-02-908970-0). Free Pr.

Edwards, C., ed. Gravitational Radiation, Collapsed Objects & Exact Solution: Proceedings. (Lecture Notes in Physics: Vol. 124). (Illus.). 487p. 1980. 35.00 (ISBN 0-387-09992-1). Springer-Verlag.

Edwards, C. A. & Lofty, J. F. Biology of Earthworms. 2nd ed. 1977. 29.95 (ISBN 0-412-14950-8, NO.6096, Pub. by Chapman & Hall). Methuen Inc.

Edwards, C. A. & Lofty, J. R. Biology of Earthworms. (Illus.). pap. 7.95 (ISBN 0-916302-20-2). Bookworm Pub.

Edwards, C. A., ed. Environmental Pollution by Pesticides. LC 72-95067. (Environmental Science Research Ser.: Vol. 3). 552p. 1973. 65.00x (ISBN 0-306-36303-8, Plenum Pr). Plenum Pub.

Edwards, C. H. Readings in Curriculum: A Process Approach. 1977. pap. 7.80x (ISBN 0-87563-068-5). Stipes.

Edwards, C. H. & Penney, David E. Calculus & Analytic Geometry. 1120p. 1982. 36.95 (ISBN 0-13-111609-6). P-H.

Edwards, C. H., Jr. Calculus & the Personal Computer. (Illus.). 192p. 1986. pap. text ed. 12.95 (ISBN 0-13-112319-X). P-H.

--The Historical Development of the Calculus. Rev. ed. (Illus.). 351p. 1979. 33.00 (ISBN 0-387-90436-0). Springer-Verlag.

Edwards, C. H., Jr. & Penney, David E. Calculus & Analytic Geometry. 2nd ed. (Illus.). 1088p. 1986. text ed. 39.95 (ISBN 0-317-29669-8). P-H.

--Calculus & Analytic Geometry, Student Manual. (Illus.). 352p. 1982. pap. 9.95 student manual (ISBN 0-13-111583-9). P-H.

--Elementary Differential Equations with Applications. (Illus.). 608p. 1985. text ed. 29.95 (ISBN 0-13-254129-7). P-H.

Edwards, C. R. & Carey, Robert M. Essential Hypertension As an Endocrine Disease. 320p. 1985. text ed. 89.95 (ISBN 0-407-02274-0). Butterworth.

Edwards, C. W. Overlay Drafting Systems. 192p. 34.95 (ISBN 0-07-019047-X). McGraw.

Edwards, Candy. The Reference Point. LC 82-83712. (Illus.). 80p. (gr. 3-6). 1983. pap. text ed. 5.95 (ISBN 0-86530-042-9, IP 42-9). Incentive Pubns.

Edwards, Carl N. Drug Dependence: Social Regulation & Treatment Alternatives. LC 84-71269. 206p. 1983. 20.00x (ISBN 0-87668-710-9). Aronson.

Edwards, Carol & Carter, Jan. The Data of Day Care, 3 vols. 1984. Set. 50.00x (ISBN 0-317-05755-3, Pub. by Natl. Inst. Social Work). State Mutual Bk.

Edwards, Cassie. Desire's Blossom. 496p. 1985. pap. 3.75 (ISBN 0-8217-1536-4). Zebra.

--Elusive Ecstasy. 480p. 1984. pap. 3.50 (ISBN 0-8217-1408-2). Zebra.

--Eugenia's Embrace. (Orig.). 1982. pap. 3.25 (ISBN 0-89083-952-2). Zebra.

--Forbidden Embrace. 1982. pap. 3.50 (ISBN 0-8217-1105-9). Zebra.

--Forbidden Embrace. 1985. pap. 3.95 (ISBN 0-317-18880-1). Zebra.

--Heart Strings, No. 3. (First Romance Ser.). 192p. (gr. 6-12). 1982. pap. 1.95 (ISBN 0-8439-1153-0, Leisure Bks). Dorchester Pub Co.

--Island Rapture. 336p. (Orig.). 1985. pap. 3.50 (ISBN 0-8439-2209-5, Leisure Bks). Dorchester Pub Co.

--Passion's Web. pap. 3.50 (ISBN 0-8217-1358-2). Zebra.

--Portrait of Desire. 1982. pap. 3.50 (ISBN 0-571-11839-9). Zebra.

--Rapture's Rendezvous. (Orig.). 1982. pap. 3.50 (ISBN 0-8217-1049-4). Zebra.

--Savage Heart. 1985. pap. 3.95 (ISBN 0-8217-1582-8). Zebra.

--Savage Obsession. 1983. pap. 3.50 (ISBN 0-8217-1269-1). Zebra.

--Savage Obsession. 1985. pap. 3.95 (ISBN 0-8217-1639-5). Zebra.

--Secrets of My Heart. 416p. 1983. pap. 3.75 (ISBN 0-8439-2048-3, Leisure Bks). Dorchester Pub Co.

--Secrets of the Heart. 400p. (Orig.). 1982. pap. 3.50 (ISBN 0-8439-1142-5, Leisure Bks). Dorchester Pub Co.

--Silken Rapture. 1983. pap. 3.50 (ISBN 0-8217-1172-5). Zebra.

Edwards, Charleen K., jt. ed. see Martin, John H.

Edwards, Charles. History & Poetry of Finger-Rings. 1977. lib. bdg. 59.95 (ISBN 0-8490-1964-8). Gordon Pr.

Edwards, Charles Beaver. Beyond Plastic Surgery. LC 77-173273. (Illus.). 170p. 1972. text ed. 14.95x (ISBN 0-8143-1462-7). Wayne St U Pr.

Edwards, Charles G. Stress. (Outreach Ser.). 32p. 1982. pap. 0.99 (ISBN 0-8163-0468-8). Pacific Pr Pub Assn.

Edwards, Charles J., jt. auth. see Fenton, Calvin W.

Edwards, Charles L. Bahama Songs & Stories. 1976. lib. bdg. 59.95 (ISBN 0-8490-1471-9). Gordon Pr.

--Bahama Songs & Stories: A Contribution to Folklore. LC 9-46. (American Folkore Society Memoirs Ser.). Repr. of 1895 ed. 27.00 (ISBN 0-527-01055-3). Kraus Repr.

--Understanding Biblical Symbols. 96p. 1981. 6.00 (ISBN 0-682-49704-5). Exposition Pr FL.

Edwards, Charles M., Jr. & Lebowitz, Carl R. Retail Advertising & Sales Promotion. (Illus.). 576p. 1981. text ed. 28.95 (ISBN 0-13-775098-6). P-H.

Edwards, Charles S. The Hell You Say. LC 80-65961. (Illus.). 227p. 1981. 12.95 (ISBN 0-686-32908-2). Old Sparta Pr.

--Hugo Grotius: A Study in Political & Legal Thought. LC 81-4592. 288p. 1982. 22.95 (ISBN 0-88229-624-8). Nelson-Hall.

Edwards, Charlotte. Writing from the Inside Out. 228p. 1984. pap. 9.95 (ISBN 0-89879-130-8). Writers Digest.

Edwards, Chris. Developing Microcomputer-Based Business Systems. (Illus.). 224p. 1983. pap. 19.95 (ISBN 0-13-204545-1). P-H.

--The Fragmented World: Competing Perspectives on Trade, Money & Crisis. (Development & Underdevelopment Ser.). (Orig.). 1985. 35.00 (ISBN 0-416-73390-5, 4029); pap. 14.95 (ISBN 0-416-73400-6, 4023). Methuen Inc.

Edwards, Christine, tr. see Toporkov, V. O.

Edwards, Clark, ed. Government's Role in Solving Societal Problems. 1982. 10.00 (ISBN 0-87771-027-9); pap. 7.00 (ISBN 0-87771-026-0). Grad School.

Edwards, Clark, ed. see Kirk, Russell, et al.

Edwards, Clifford. A Systematic Approach to Instructional Design. pap. text ed. 7.80x (ISBN 0-87563-145-2). Stipes.

Edwards, Clifford H. & Fisher, Robert L. Teaching Elementary School Science: A Competency-Based Approach. 1977. text ed. 29.95 (ISBN 0-275-22510-0). HR&W.

Edwards, Clifford H., et al. Planning, Teaching & Evaluating: A Competency Approach. LC 76-41903. 360p. 1977. 24.95x (ISBN 0-88229-204-8). Nelson-Hall.

Edwards, Clive E. Persistent Pesticides in the Environment. LC 79-141881. (Uniscience Ser). 170p. 1974. 46.00 (ISBN 0-685-38667-8). CRC Pr.

Edwards, Clyde. Orthopedic Shoe Repair Illustrated. (Illus.). 1982. pap. text ed. 4.50 (ISBN 0-931424-10-0). Shoe Serv Inst.

--Problems & Methods in Orthopedic Shoe Repairing. (Illus.). 1981. pap. text ed. 4.50 (ISBN 0-931424-07-0). Shoe Serv Inst.

Edwards, Colin. Delphiniums. (Illus.). 192p. 1981. 22.95x (ISBN 0-460-04423-0, Pub. by J. M. Dent England). Biblio Dist.

Edwards, Conley L., III, compiled by. A Guide to Business Records in the Archives Branch, Virginia State Library. xii, 193p. (Orig.). 1983. pap. 5.00 (ISBN 0-88490-107-6). VA State Lib.

Edwards, Corwin & Bruchey, Stuart. Economic & Political Aspects of International Cartels. Bruchey, Eleanor, ed. LC 76-5006. (American Business Abroad Ser.). 1976. Repr. of 1944 ed. lib. bdg. 17.00x (ISBN 0-405-09275-X). Ayer Co Pubs.

Edwards, Corwin D. Big Business & the Policy of Competition. LC 79-26189. 180p. 1980. Repr. of 1956 ed. lib. bdg. 22.50x (ISBN 0-313-22256-8, EDBB). Greenwood.

--Control of Cartels & Monopolies. LC 67-10657. 388p. 1967. 22.50 (ISBN 0-379-00316-3). Oceana.

--Maintaining Competition: Requisites of a Governmental Policy. LC 71-138224. 337p. 1973. Repr. of 1949 ed. lib. bdg. 21.00x (ISBN 0-8371-5581-9, EDMC). Greenwood.

--Trade Regulation Overseas: The National Laws. LC 64-23357. 768p. 1965. 32.50 (ISBN 0-379-00224-8). Oceana.

Edwards, Cris, et al. Radiation Protection for Dental Radiographers. LC 84-42910. (Illus.). 300p. (Orig.). 1984. pap. 14.95x (ISBN 0-940122-16-2, MAP-12). Multi Media CO.

Edwards, D. A. & Hastings, H. M. Cech & Steenrod Homotopy Theories with Applications to Geometric Topology. (Lecture Notes in Mathematics: Vol. 542). 1976. soft cover 19.00 (ISBN 3-540-07863-0). Springer-Verlag.

Edwards, D. K. Solar Collector Design. rev. ed. LC 78-24684. (Solar Ser.). 68p. (Orig.). 1978. pap. 3.50 (ISBN 0-89168-000-4). L Erlbaum Assocs.

Edwards, D. K., et al. Transfer Processes. 2nd ed. LC 78-7883. (Series in Thermal and Fluids Engineering). (Illus.). 1979. text ed. 48.00 (ISBN 0-07-019041-0). McGraw.

Edwards, D. M., et al. Surveying Fundamentals: A Tutorial Approach. (Illus.). 1977. pap. text ed. 9.90 (ISBN 0-89534-006-2). Am Pub Co WI.

Edwards, D. O., ed. see International Conference on Low Temperature Physics (9th: 1964: Columbus, Ohio).

Edwards, Dale. Founded upon a Rock. 1977. pap. 3.95 (ISBN 0-89265-043-5). Randall Hse.

Edwards, Dan W. Communication Skills for the Helping Professions. 130p. 1983. 19.75x (ISBN 0-398-04766-9). C C Thomas.

Edwards, Dan W. & Letman, Sloan T. Aging & the Urban Environment. 1983. 12.50 (ISBN 0-317-29045-2). Carlinshar.

--Aging in the Urban Community. 120p. 1983. pap. text ed. 12.50 (ISBN 0-934872-05-8). Carlinshar.

--Alcoholism in the Urban Community: A Review of the Literature on Alcohol Abuse & Treatment Strategies, No. 11. LC 82-246065. (Urban Insights Ser.: No. 11). 97p. 1982. pap. 3.95 (ISBN 0-911531-08-4). Loyola U Ctr Urban.

Edwards, Daniel W., jt. auth. see Yarvis, Richard M.

Edwards, David. Basic Remodeling Techniques. Burke, Ken, ed. LC 82-63128. (Illus.). 96p. (Orig.). 1983. pap. 5.95 (ISBN 0-89721-016-6). Ortho.

Edwards, David D. How to Be More Creative. LC 78-71652. (Illus.). 1978. pap. 6.95 (ISBN 0-933264-00-3). Occasional Prods.

Edwards, David G. Existential Psychotherapy: The Process of Caring. (Clinical Social Work Ser.). 205p. 1982. text ed. 18.95 (ISBN 0-89876-007-0). Gardner Pr.

Edwards, David I. Antimicrobial Drug Action. (Illus.). 340p. 1980. pap. text ed. 29.50 (ISBN 0-8391-4118-1). Univ Park.

Edwards, David J. Salmon & Trout Farming in Norway. 1978. 50.00x (ISBN 0-685-63450-7). State Mutual Bk.

--Salmon & Trout Farming in Norway. (Illus.). 208p. 1978. 26.00 (ISBN 0-85238-093-3, FN75, FNB). Unipub.

Edwards, David L. Christian England: From the Eighteenth Century to the First World War, Vol. 3. 1985. pap. 10.95 (ISBN 0-8028-1050-0). Eerdmans.

--Christian England: From the Reformation to the Eighteenth Century, Vol. 2. 1984. pap. 10.95 (ISBN 0-8028-1049-7). Eerdmans.

--Christian England: Its Story to the Reformation, Vol. 1. 351p. 1983. pap. 8.95 (ISBN 0-8028-1048-9). Eerdmans.

--What Anglicans Believe. 128p. 1975. pap. 1.65 (ISBN 0-88028-003-4, 503). Forward Movement.

Edwards, David V. The American Political Experience: An Introduction to Government. 3rd ed. (Illus.). 704p. 1985. text ed. 27.95 (ISBN 0-13-028325-8). P-H.

--The American Political Experience: Learning Guide. 3rd ed. 256p. 1985. text ed. 9.95 (ISBN 0-13-028390-8). P-H.

Edwards, Deborah. Opening Devotions for Womens Groups. 1985. pap. 4.95 (ISBN 0-8010-3428-0). Baker Bk.

Edwards, Deborah C. Wrap It up, I'll Take It. LC 79-55884. (Illus.). 62p. (Orig.). 1980. pap. 3.95 (ISBN 0-9603750-0-7). Teachers Load.

Edwards, Denis. Human Experience of God. 1984. pap. 7.95 (ISBN 0-8091-2559-5). Paulist Pr.

Edwards, Dennis & Pigram, Ron. The Final Link. 144p. 1983. 40.00 (ISBN 0-85936-280-9, Pub. by Baton Pr Ltd UK). State Mutual Bk.

--The Golden Years of the Metropolitan Railway. 144p. 1983. 40.00x (ISBN 0-85936-246-9, Pub. by Baton Pr Ltd UK). State Mutual Bk.

--Metro Memories. 3rd ed. 128p. 1983. 40.00x (ISBN 0-85936-058-X, Pub. by Baton Pr Ltd UK). State Mutual Bk.

--Romance of Metro-Land. 2nd ed. 128p. 1983. 35.00x (ISBN 0-85936-061-X, Pub. by Baton Pr Ltd UK). State Mutual Bk.

Edwards, Don A. Paths to Writing: Developing Prose Power. 1976. text ed. 12.50 (ISBN 0-682-48343-5, University). Exposition Pr FL.

Edwards, Don K. Radiation Heat Transfer Notes. LC 81-4539. (Hemisphere Engineering Paperback Ser.). (Illus.). 370p. (Orig.). 1981. pap. text ed. 24.95 (ISBN 0-89116-231-3). Hemisphere Pub.

Edwards, Donald E. & Kettering, Ronald C. Computer Assisted Practice Set in Financial Accounting: Cook's Solar Energy Systems. LC 82-83660. 96p. 1983. 11.95 (ISBN 0-395-33492-6); instr's manual 2.00 (ISBN 0-395-33493-4). HM.

Edwards, Dorothy. My Naughty Little Sister & Bad Harry's Rabbit. (Illus.). (ps-2). 1981. 8.95x (ISBN 0-13-608935-6). P-H.

--The Witches & the Grinnygog. 176p. (gr. 5-8). 1983. 11.95 (ISBN 0-571-11720-1). Faber & Faber.

Edwards, E. Facsimile of the Manuscript of Diwanizu'l Fakar. 474p. 1977. 55.00x (ISBN 0-686-81307-3, Pub. by Brit Lib England). State Mutual Bk.

Edwards, E., jt. ed. see Ethe, H.

Edwards, E. B. Pattern & Design with Dynamic Symmetry. (Illus.). 11.25 (ISBN 0-8446-2021-1). Peter Smith.

Edwards, E. D. The Dragon Book. 1979. Repr. of 1938 ed. lib. bdg. 30.00 (ISBN 0-8414-4001-8). Folcroft.

Edwards, E. H. Fire & Sword in Shansi: The Story of the Martyrdom of Foreigners & Chinese Christians. LC 74-111738. (American Imperialism: Viewpoints of United States Foreign Policy, 1898-1941). 1970. Repr. of 1903 ed. 21.00 (ISBN 0-405-02014-7). Ayer Co Pubs.

--Saddlery. (Illus.). 9.95 (ISBN 0-85131-151-2, BL2405, Dist. by Miller). J A Allen.

Edwards, E. Hartley. Saddlery. 200p. 1981. 30.00x (ISBN 0-85131-151-2, Pub. by Allen & Co). State Mutual Bk.

Edwards, E. I. Desert Voices. LC 73-3752. (Illus.). 215p. 1973. Repr. of 1958 ed. lib. bdg. 24.75x (ISBN 0-8371-6848-1, EDDV). Greenwood.

--A Sentimental Venture. new ed. LC 76-21423. (Illus.). 71p. 1976. 10.00 (ISBN 0-914224-06-9). Tales Mojave Rd.

Edwards, E. W. Exploring Careers Using Foreign Languages. (Exploring Careers Ser.). 128p. 1982. lib. bdg. 8.97 (ISBN 0-8239-0553-5). Rosen Group.

--Exploring Careers Using Foreign Languages. rev. ed. (Exploring Careers Ser.). 128p. 1985. lib. bdg. 8.97 (ISBN 0-317-19523-9). Rosen Group.

--The Orlando Furioso & Its Predecessor. 1973. Repr. of 1924 ed. 20.00 (ISBN 0-8274-1683-0). R West.

Edwards, Edgar O. & Bell, Philip W. The Theory & Measurement of Business Income. 1961. 24.50x (ISBN 0-520-00376-4). U of Cal Pr.

Edwards, Edgar O., et al. Accounting for Economic Events. LC 79-22971. 1979. text ed. 26.00 (ISBN 0-914348-28-0). Scholars Bk.

Edwards, Edward. Libraries & Founders of Libraries. LC 68-58475. (Bibliography & Reference Ser: No. 260). 1969. Repr. of 1865 ed. 26.00 (ISBN 0-8337-1004-4). B Franklin.

--Lives of the Founders of the British Museum. (Bibliography & Reference Ser.: No. 202). (Illus.). 1969. Repr. of 1870 ed. 32.00 (ISBN 0-8337-1005-2). B Franklin.

Edwards, Edward, ed. Liber Monasterii de Hyda: A Chronicle of the Affairs of England...Hampshire, 455-1203. (Rolls Ser.: No. 45). Repr. of 1866 ed. 44.00 (ISBN 0-317-16692-1). Kraus Repr.

Edwards, Edward A., et al. Operative Anatomy of the Thorax. LC 79-175458. (Illus.). 246p. 1972. text ed. 17.50 (ISBN 0-8121-0371-8). Lea & Febiger.

Edwards, Edward B. Pattern & Design with Dynamic Symmetry. Orig. Title: Dynamarhythmic Design, Ii. pap. 4.00 (ISBN 0-486-21756-6). Dover.

Edwards, Edward O., ed. Employment in Developing Nations: Report on a Ford Foundation Study. LC 74-16724. 1974. 37.00x (ISBN 0-231-03873-9); pap. 16.00x (ISBN 0-231-03874-7). Columbia U Pr.

Edwards, Eleanor M. Music Education for the Deaf. LC 74-76260. 248p. (Orig.). 1974. pap. 6.00 (ISBN 0-914562-00-2). Merriam-Eddy.

Edwards, Eliezer E. Words, Facts & Phrases. 59.95 (ISBN 0-8490-1327-5). Gordon Pr.

--Words, Facts & Phrases: A Dictionary of Curious, Quaint, & Out-of-the-Way Matters. LC 68-21768. 1968. Repr. of 1881 ed. 42.00x (ISBN 0-8103-3087-3). Gale.

Edwards, Elmer E. A Handicappers Guide to Dogtrack Astrology. (Illus.). 104p. 1980. pap. 15.00 (ISBN 0-9604834-0-3). Elmer Edwards.

Edwards, Elwyn & Lees, Frank P. The Human Operator in Process Control. LC 74-19204. (Illus.). 480p. 1974. 44.00x (ISBN 0-85066-069-6). Taylor & Francis.

Edwards, Elwyn H. Buying Horses & Ponies. (Illus.). 176p. 1984. 14.95 (ISBN 0-7207-1537-7, Pub. by Michael Joseph). Merrimack Pub Cir.

--From Paddock to Saddle. (Illus.). 192p. 1985. 16.95 (ISBN 0-7207-1473-7, Pub. by Michael Joseph). Merrimack Pub Cir.

--The Larousse Guide to Horses & Ponies of the World. LC 77-71167. (The Larousse Guide Bks.). (Illus.). 1979. pap. 7.95 (ISBN 0-88332-121-1). Larousse.

Edwards, Elwyn H., ed. A Standard Guide to Horse & Pony Breeds. LC 79-23921. (Illus.). 352p. 1980. 24.95 (ISBN 0-07-019035-6). McGraw.

Edwards, Emily. Painted Walls of Mexico: From Prehistoric Times until Today. (Elma Dill Russell Spencer Foundation Ser.: No. 3). (Illus.). 330p. 1966. 39.95 (ISBN 0-292-73624-X). U of Tex Pr.

Edwards, Eric. Ancestors to Come. LC 75-24938. 1975. 3.00x (ISBN 0-915176-08-4). Pourboire.

--The Edible Crab & Its Fishery in British Waters. (Illus.). 144p. 1979. pap. 13.25 (ISBN 0-85238-100-X, FN78, FNB). Unipub.

Edwards, Ernest P. Appendix for a Field Guide to the Birds of Mexico, 1978. LC 78-185930. 1978. pap. 8.00 (ISBN 0-911882-06-5). E P Edwards.

--A Coded Workbook of Birds of the World: Vol. 1 Non-Passerines. 2nd ed. LC 82-82891. (Illus.). xxi, 134p. 1982. pap. 12.00 plastic comb bdg. (ISBN 0-911882-07-3). E P Edwards.

--Finding Birds in Mexico. 2nd ed. LC 68-58738. (Incl. 1985 Supplement to Finding Birds in Mexico). 1968. 20.00 set (ISBN 0-911882-01-4). E P Edwards.

--Update for Finding Birds in Panama, 1985. (Illus.). 32p. 1985. pap. 3.50 (ISBN 0-911882-09-X). E P Edwards.

Edwards, Ernest P. & Loftin, Horace. Finding Birds in Panama. 2nd ed. LC 73-21847. (Illus., Incl. 1985 Update). 1971. Set. softcover 9.00 (ISBN 0-911882-02-2). E P Edwards.

Edwards, Ernest P., et al. Supplement to Finding Birds in Mexico, 1985. LC 84-81944. (Illus.). 176p. 1985. pap. 12.00 (ISBN 0-911882-08-1). E P Edwards.

Edwards, Ernest W. The Orlando Furioso & Its Predecessor. LC 76-13185. 1976. Repr. of 1924 ed. lib. bdg. 22.50 (ISBN 0-8414-3978-8). Folcroft.

Edwards, Estelle. The Knave of Hearts. (Rapture Romance Ser.: No. 47). 192p. 1984. pap. 1.95 (ISBN 0-451-12632-7, Sig). NAL.

--Moonslide. (Rapture Romance Ser.: No. 21). 1983. pap. 1.95 (ISBN 0-451-12445-6, Sig). NAL.

Edwards, Evangeline D. Chinese Prose Literature of the T'ang Period: A.D. 618-906, 2 vols. LC 70-38067. 1937. Repr. of 1938 ed. Set. 50.00 (ISBN 0-404-56971-4); 25.00 ea. AMS Pr.

--The Dragon Book. 367p. 1980. Repr. of 1938 ed. lib. bdg. 37.50 (ISBN 0-8482-0721-1). Norwood Edns.

Edwards, Evelyn. A Virtuous Woman. 1978. 5.00 (ISBN 0-686-25538-0). Freedom Univ-FSP.

Edwards, Everett E. Bibliography of the History of Agriculture in the United States. LC 76-121222. (Bibliography & Reference Ser.: No. 346). 1970. Repr. of 1930 ed. lib. bdg. 20.50 (ISBN 0-8337-1002-8). B Franklin.

--Bibliography of the History of Agriculture in the U. S. LC 66-27834. 1967. Repr. of 1930 ed. 40.00x (ISBN 0-8103-3102-0). Gale.

Edwards, Everett E., ed. Jefferson & Agriculture: A Sourcebook. LC 75-27636. (World Food Supply Ser). 1976. Repr. of 1943 ed. 14.00x (ISBN 0-405-07778-5). Ayer Co Pubs.

Edwards, F. E. The Eocene Mollusca, 4 Vols. 1848-55. Set. 53.00 (ISBN 0-384-13860-8). Johnson Repr.

Edwards, F. H. Life & Ministry of Jesus. 1982. pap. 14.00 (ISBN 0-686-95353-3). Herald Hse.

Edwards, F. Henry. God Our Help. 1981. pap. 11.00 (ISBN 0-8309-0310-0). Herald Hse.

--History of the Reorganized Church of Jesus Christ of Latter Day Saints Vol. 5: 1890-1902. 1969. 22.50 (ISBN 0-8309-0019-5). Herald Hse.

--The History of the Reorganized Church of Jesus Christ of Latter Day Saints, Vols. 6 & 7. Incl. Vol. 6. 1903-1914. 1970 (ISBN 0-8309-0030-6); Vol. 7. 1915-1925. 1973 (ISBN 0-8309-0075-6). 22.50 ea. Herald Hse.

--History of the Reorganized Church of Jesus Christ of the Latter Day Saints, Vol. 8: 1926-1946. 1976. 22.50 (ISBN 0-8309-0157-4). Herald Hse.

--Meditation & Prayer. LC 79-23708. 1980. pap. 12.00 (ISBN 0-8309-0271-6). Herald Hse.

--A New Commentary on the Doctrine & Covenants. LC 77-7385. 1977. 20.00 (ISBN 0-8309-0187-6). Herald Hse.

--A Students Guide to the Doctrine & Covenants. 1980. pap. 9.00 (ISBN 0-8309-0267-8). Herald Hse.

Edwards, Frances, jt. auth. see Schalliol, Ilyff.

Edwards, Frank. Strange World. 1963. 4.95 (ISBN 0-8184-0087-0). Lyle Stuart.

--Strange World. 208p. 1985. pap. 5.95 (ISBN 0-8065-0978-3). Citadel Pr.

--Strange World of Frank Edwards. Stuart, Rory, ed. 1977. 8.95 (ISBN 0-8184-0252-0). Lyle Stuart.

--Stranger Than Science. 256p. 1983. pap. 4.95 (ISBN 0-8065-0850-7). Citadel Pr.

Edwards, Fred E. The Role of the Faith Mission: A Brazilian Case Study. LC 79-152406. (Illus.). 76p. 1971. pap. 3.45 (ISBN 0-87808-406-1). William Carey Lib.

Edwards, Frederick G. The History of Mendelssohn's Oratorio Elijah. LC 74-24073. Repr. of 1896 ed. 16.00 (ISBN 0-404-12901-3). AMS Pr.

Edwards, G. Memoirs of Libraries. 1976. lib. bdg. 59.95 (ISBN 0-8490-2224-X). Gordon Pr.

--The Treatment of Drinking Problems. 1984. 22.95 (ISBN 0-07-019036-4). McGraw.

Edwards, G. & Busch, C., eds. Drug Problems in Britain: A Review of Ten Years. LC 81-66399. 1981. 48.00 (ISBN 0-12-232780-2). Acad Pr.

Edwards, G., jt. ed. see Edwards, R. A.

Edwards, G. B. The Book of Ebenezer le Page. 416p. (Orig.). 1982. pap. 6.95 (ISBN 0-380-57638-4, 57638-4). Avon.

--The Book of Ebenezer le Page. LC 80-2719. 416p. 1981. 13.95 (ISBN 0-394-51651-6). Knopf.

Edwards, G. C. Public Policy Implementation. (Public Policy Studies: A Multi Volume-Treatise: Vol. 3). 1985. 55.00 (ISBN 0-89232-453-8). Jai Pr.

Edwards, G. E. GDR Society & Social Institutions: Facts & Figures. LC 83-40526. 288p. 1985. 27.50 (ISBN 0-312-31490-6). St Martin.

Edwards, G. F. & Breier, Paul V., eds. Meditative Maxims. 1978. LEB1. pap. 1.00 (ISBN 0-932318-00-2, Little Economy Bks). G F Edwards.

Edwards, G. F., ed. see Coleman, Lucile.

Edwards, G. F., ed. see Mann, Ernest.

Edwards, G. Franklin. The Negro Professional Class. LC 82-11990. 224p. 1982. Repr. of 1959 ed. lib. bdg. 25.00x (ISBN 0-313-22330-0, EDNP). Greenwood.

Edwards, G. Franklin, ed. see Frazier, E. Franklin.

Edwards, G. Roger. Corinthian Hellenistic Pottery. LC 74-10623. (Corinth Ser.: Vol. 7, Pt. 3). (Illus.). 1975. 35.00x (ISBN 0-87661-073-4, NK3840). Am Sch Athens.

Edwards, G. W. Holland of Today. 59.95 (ISBN 0-8490-0367-9). Gordon Pr.

--London. 59.95 (ISBN 0-8490-0552-3). Gordon Pr.

--Paris. 59.95 (ISBN 0-8490-0799-2). Gordon Pr.

--Rome. 59.95 (ISBN 0-8490-0969-3). Gordon Pr.

--Some Old Flemish Towns. 59.95 (ISBN 0-8490-1078-0). Gordon Pr.

--Spain. 59.95 (ISBN 0-8490-1095-0). Gordon Pr.

--Vanished Halls & Cathedrals of France. 69.95 (ISBN 0-8490-1255-4). Gordon Pr.

Edwards, Gabrielle. Coping with Discrimination. 1986. pap. 8.97 (ISBN 0-8239-0659-0). Rosen Group.

--Coping with Venereal Disease. rev. ed. (Coping with Ser.). (Illus.). 1983. lib. bdg. 8.97 (ISBN 0-8239-0512-8). Rosen Group.

--Man & Woman: Inside Homo Sapiens. 8.97 (ISBN 0-8239-0445-8). Rosen Group.

--The Student Biologist Explores Drug Abuse. LC 73-93545. (Student Scientist Ser.). (Illus.). (gr. 7-12). 1975. PLB 8.97 (ISBN 0-8239-0298-6). Rosen Group.

Edwards, Gabrielle & Cimmino, Marion. Barron's How to Prepare for the Advanced Placement Examination - Biology. 2nd ed. Bleifeld, Maurice, ed. (gr. 10-12). 1982. pap. text ed. 7.95 (ISBN 0-8120-2328-5). Barron.

Edwards, Gabrielle I. & Cimmino, Marion. Tecnicas de Laboratorio: Un Texto de Trabajo de Metodos Biomedicos. Casasnovas, Sonia, tr. from Eng. (Span.). (gr. 9-12). 1976. pap. text ed. 6.50 (ISBN 0-8120-0551-1); free tchr's manual with class order 1.25 (ISBN 0-8120-0702-6). Barron.

Edwards, Gabrielle I., ed. Barron's Regents Exams & Answers Biology. rev. ed. LC 58-19074. 300p. (gr. 9-12). 1982. pap. text ed. 4.50 (ISBN 0-8120-3197-0). Barron.

Edwards, Gabrielle J. Coping with Drug Abuse. (Personal Adjustment Ser.). 136p. 1983. lib. bdg. 8.97 (ISBN 0-8239-0612-4). Rosen Group.

Edwards, Gene. The Early Church. 1974. pap. text ed. 4.95 (ISBN 0-940232-02-2). Christian Bks.

--How to Have a Soul Winning Church. 1963. pap. 3.95 (ISBN 0-88243-524-8, 02-0524). Gospel Pub.

--Inward Journey. 250p. 1982. pap. 5.95 (ISBN 0-940232-06-5). Christian Bks.

--Letters to a Devastated Christian. 68p. 1983. pap. 3.95 (ISBN 0-940232-13-8). Christian Bks.

--Our Mission. (Orig.). 1984. pap. 8.95 (ISBN 0-940232-11-1). Christian Bks.

Edwards, Gene, ed. The Divine Romance. 1984. pap. 7.95. Christian Bks.

Edwards, Gene, ed. see Brother Lawrence & Laubach, Frank.

Edwards, Gene, ed. see Fenelon.

Edwards, Gene, ed. see Guyon, Jean.

Edwards, Gene, ed. see Guyon, Jeanne M.

Edwards, Gene, ed. see Molinos, Michael.

Edwards, Geoffrey, jt. ed. see Arbuthnott, Hugh.

Edwards, George. The International Film Poster Book: The Role of the Poster in Cinema Art, Advertising & History. (Illus.). 1985. 24.95 (ISBN 0-318-04521-4, Pub. by Salem Hse Ltd); pap. 14.95 (ISBN 0-318-04522-2, Pub. by Salem Hse Ltd). Merrimack Pub Cir.

Edwards, George, et al, eds. Symposium on Presidential Policy Making. (Orig.). 1984. pap. 8.00 (ISBN 0-918592-71-2). Policy Studies.

Edwards, George C. The Public Presidency: The Pursuit of Popular Support. LC 82-60470. 320p. 1983. text ed. 17.95 (ISBN 0-312-65563-0); pap. text ed. 12.95 (ISBN 0-312-65564-9). St Martin.

Edwards, George C., III. Presidential Influence in Congress. LC 79-21975. (Illus.). 216p. 1980. text ed. 21.95 (ISBN 0-7167-1161-3); pap. text ed. 11.95 (ISBN 0-7167-1162-1). W H Freeman.

Edwards, George C., III & Wayne, Stephen J. Presidential Leadership: Politics & Policy Making. LC 83-61624. 500p. 1985. 39.95 (ISBN 0-312-64037-4); pap. text ed. 16.95 (ISBN 0-312-64038-2). St Martin.

Edwards, George C., III & Wayne, Stephen J., eds. Studying the Presidency. LC 82-17472. 320p. 1983. text ed. 19.95x (ISBN 0-87049-378-7); pap. text ed. 9.95x (ISBN 0-87049-379-5). U of Tenn Pr.

Edwards, George C., III, jt. ed. see Gwyn, William B.

Edwards, George C., III, et al, eds. The Presidency & Public Policy Making. LC 85-40337. (Pitt Series in Policy & Institutional Studies). (Illus.). 1985. lib. bdg. 24.95x (ISBN 0-8229-3522-8); pap. text ed. 9.95x (ISBN 0-8229-5373-0). U of Pittsburgh Pr.

Edwards, George J. Grand Jury. LC 76-156013. Repr. of 1906 ed. 24.50 (ISBN 0-404-09113-X). AMS Pr.

Edwards, George R. Gay-Lesbian Liberation: A Biblical Perspective. 144p. (Orig.). 1984. pap. 9.95 (ISBN 0-8298-0725-X). Pilgrim NY.

Edwards, George T. How Economic Growth & Inflation Happen. LC 82-5882. 225p. 1983. 25.00x (ISBN 0-312-39496-9). St Martin.

--Music & Musicians of Maine. LC 74-135736. Repr. of 1928 ed. 23.00 (ISBN 0-404-07231-3). AMS Pr.

--Music & Musicians of Maine. (Illus.). 542p. 1928. 15.00 (ISBN 0-686-05799-6). O'Brien.

--The Youthful Haunts of Longfellow. 1907. Repr. 25.00 (ISBN 0-8274-3782-X). R West.

Edwards, George T., jt. auth. see Carrington, John C.

Edwards, George W. Break o' Day. facs. ed. LC 74-90580. (Short Story Index Reprint Ser.). 1896. 15.00 (ISBN 0-8369-3063-0). Ayer Co Pubs.

--Evolution of Finance Capitalism. LC 66-22622. Repr. of 1938 ed. 35.00x (ISBN 0-678-00290-8). Kelley.

--Holland of Today. 1909. 20.00 (ISBN 0-8495-1355-3). Arden Lib.

Edwards, George W. & Peterson, Arthur E. New York As an Eighteenth Century Municipality, 2 pts. LC 68-56681. (Columbia University Studies in the Social Sciences: Nos. 177-178). Repr. of 1917 ed. Set. 28.00 (ISBN 0-404-51697-1); 14.00 ea. Pt. 1 Prior To 1731 (ISBN 0-404-51177-5). Pt. 2 1731-1776 (ISBN 0-404-51178-3). AMS Pr.

Edwards, George W., illus. A Book of Old English Love Songs. 1978. Repr. of 1897 ed. lib. bdg. 20.00 (ISBN 0-8495-3820-3). Arden Lib.

Edwards, Gerald D. Reaching Out: The Prevention of Drug Abuse Through Increased Human Intervention. 217p. 1985. pap. 12.00 (ISBN 0-88268-029-3, Pub. by Pulse Bks). Station Hill Pr.

Edwards, Gerald Hamilton see Hamilton-Edwards, Gerald.

Edwards, Gerry & Walker, David. C Three C Four: Mechanisms, Cellular & Environmental Regulation of Photosynthesis. LC 82-49298. 550p. 1983. text ed. 68.00x (ISBN 0-520-05018-5). U of Cal Pr.

Edwards, Gladys B. Anatomy & Conformation of the Horse. LC 73-77060. 224p. 1973. pap. 5.95 (ISBN 0-88376-025-8). Dreenan Pr.

--The New Complete Airedale Terrier. 3rd ed. LC 78-7051. (Complete Breed Book Ser.). (Illus.). 304p. 1978. 15.95 (ISBN 0-87605-005-4). Howell Bk.

Edwards, Gordon. A Climber's Guide to Glacier National Park. LC 76-15238. (Illus.). 155p. 1976. pap. 5.95 (ISBN 0-87842-064-9). Mountain Pr.

--Wild & Old Garden Roses. (Illus.). 162p. 1975. 16.50. Sweetbrier.

Edwards, Goronwy. The Second Century of the English Parliament. 1979. 27.95x (ISBN 0-19-822479-6). Oxford U Pr.

Edwards, Grant, tr. see Baumler, Ernest.

Edwards, Gregory J. The International Film Poster. (Illus.). 224p. 1985. 24.95 (ISBN 0-88162-131-5, Pub. by Salem Hse Ltd); pap. 14.95 (ISBN 0-88162-132-3, Pub. by Salem Hse Ltd). Merrimack Pub Cir.

Edwards, Griffith, jt. auth. see Berridge, Virginia.

Edwards, Griffith & Grant, Marcus, eds. Alcoholism Treatment in Transition. (Illus.). 336p. 1980. pap. 21.50 (ISBN 0-8391-4132-7). Univ Park.

Edwards, Griffith & Littleton, John, eds. Pharmacological Treatments for Alcoholism. LC 83-26488. 400p. 1984. 49.95x (ISBN 0-416-00921-2, 5075). Methuen Inc.

Edwards, Griffith, et al, eds. Drug Use & Misuse: Cultural Perspectives. LC 83-9627. 100p. 1984. 24.95 (ISBN 0-312-21988-1). St Martin.

Edwards, Gus. The Offering: A Play in Two Acts. 1978. pap. 3.35x (ISBN 0-685-60701-1). Dramatists Play.

Edwards, Gwynne. The Discreet Art of Luis Bunuel. (Illus.). 288p. 1985. pap. 12.95 (ISBN 0-7145-2832-3, Dist. by Scribner). M Boyars.

--The Discreet Art of Luis Bunuel: A Reading of His Films. LC 82-71081. (Illus.). 320p. 1983. 30.00 (ISBN 0-7145-2754-8, Dist. by Scribner). M Boyars.

--Dramatists in Perspective: Spanish Theatre in the Twentieth Century. 280p. 1985. 29.95 (ISBN 0-312-21950-4). St Martin.

--Lorca: The Theater Beneath the Sand. 356p. 1982. 20.00 (ISBN 0-7145-2698-3, Dist. by Scribner). M Boyars.

Edwards, H., jt. auth. see Katzeff, I. E.

Edwards, H., jt. auth. see Mitten, C. C.

Edwards, H., ed. Credit Management Handbook. 2nd ed. LC 84-21170. 500p. 1985. text ed. 59.95 (ISBN 0-566-02499-3). Gower Pub Co.

Edwards, H. E., et al, eds. see Association for Radiation Research, Winter Meeting Jan. 3-5, 1979.

Edwards, H. L. Skelton. facs. ed. LC 77-148879. (Select Bibliographies Reprint Ser.). 1949. 19.00 (ISBN 0-8369-5673-7). Ayer Co Pubs.

Edwards, H. R., tr. see Stendhal.

Edwards, H. Sutherland. History of the Opera: From Monteverdi to Donizetti, 2 vols. in 1. LC 77-5587. 1977. Repr. of 1862 ed. lib. bdg. 65.00 (ISBN 0-306-77416-X). Da Capo.

--The Prima Donna: Her History & Surroundings from the 17th to the 19th Century, 2 vols, Vol. 1. LC 77-17875. (Music Reprint Ser.). 1978. Repr. of 1888 ed. Set. lib. bdg. 65.00 (ISBN 0-306-77558-1). Da Capo.

Edwards, Hardy M., jt. auth. see Lassiter, J. W.

Edwards, Harold H. Galois Theory. (Graduate Texts in Mathematics: Vol. 101). (Illus.). 240p. 1984. 22.00 (ISBN 0-387-90980-X). Springer-Verlag.

Edwards, Harold M. Advanced Calculus. LC 79-23792. 524p. 1980. Repr. of 1969 ed. lib. bdg. 27.50 (ISBN 0-89874-047-9). Krieger.

--Fermat's Last Theorem: A Genetic Introduction to Algebraic Number Theory. LC 77-8222. (Graduate Texts in Mathematics Ser.: Vol. 50). 1977. 32.00 (ISBN 0-387-90230-9). Springer-Verlag.

--Riemann's Zeta Function. (Pure & Applied Mathematics: A Series of Monographs & Textbooks, Vol. 59). 1974. 55.00 (ISBN 0-12-232750-0). Acad Pr.

Edwards, Harry. Revolt of the Black Athlete. LC 70-85475. 1970. pap. 14.95 (ISBN 0-02-909030-X). Free Pr.

Edwards, Harry J., Jr. Automatic Controls for Heating & Air Conditioning: Pneumatic-Electric Control Systems. (Illus.). 1980. 27.50 (ISBN 0-07-019046-1). McGraw.

Edwards, Harry S. His Defense & Other Stories. 1972. Repr. of 1899 ed. 18.75 (ISBN 0-8422-8041-3). Irvington.

--Two Runaways & Other Stories. 1972. Repr. of 1889 ed. lib. bdg. 24.00 (ISBN 0-8422-8042-1). Irvington.

Edwards, Harry T. Higher Education & the Unholy Crusade Against Governmental Regulation. LC 80-26334. 62p. (Orig.). 1980. pap. text ed. 2.50x (ISBN 0-934222-04-5). Inst Ed Management.

--Residential Electrical Wiring. (Illus.). 240p. 1982. text ed. 22.95 (ISBN 0-8359-6652-6). Reston.

Edwards, Harry T. & Nordin, Virginia D. An Introduction to the American Legal System: A Supplement to Higher Education & the Law. LC 80-82033. 76p. (Orig.). 1980. pap. text ed. 5.95x (ISBN 0-934222-02-9). Inst Ed Manage.

Edwards, Harry T. & White, James J. Problems, Readings & Materials on the Lawyer as a Negotiator. 484p. 1977. write for info. West Pub.

Edwards, Harry T., et al. Labor Relations Law in the Public Sector. 2nd ed. (Contemporary Legal Education Ser.). 950p. 1979. text ed. 26.00 (ISBN 0-672-83693-9); Statutory Appendix. 5.00 (ISBN 0-672-83969-5); Supplement 1984. 8.00 (ISBN 0-87215-795-4). Michie Co.

Edwards, Maria. Total Youth Ministry: A Handbook for Parishes. LC 76-29885. 1976. pap. 4.50 (ISBN 0-88489-085-6). St Mary's.
Edwards, Marie & Hoover, Eleanor. The Challenge of Being Single. 1975. pap. 3.50 (ISBN 0-451-13431-1, Sig). NAL.
Edwards, Mark. Luther's Last Battles. 250p. 1983. text ed. 28.25x (ISBN 9-004-06892-9, Pub. by E J Brill Holland). Humanities.
Edwards, Mark & Tavard, George. Luther: A Reformer for the Churches. 1983. pap. 4.95 (ISBN 0-8091-2575-7). Paulist Pr.
Edwards, Mark & Tavard, George H. Luther: A Reformer for the Churches; An Ecumenical Study Guide. LC 83-48005. 96p. 1983. pap. 5.50 (ISBN 0-8006-1718-5, 1-1718). Fortress.
Edwards, Mark B. Geological Survey of Norway: No. 394; Bulletin 75. 80p. (Orig.). 1984. pap. 17.00x (ISBN 82-00-31466-9). Universitet.
Edwards, Mark U., Jr. Luther & the False Brethren. LC 75-181. 1975. 20.00x (ISBN 0-8047-0883-5). Stanford U Pr.
--Luther's Last Battles: Politics & Polemics, 1531-46. 272p. 1983. 24.95x (ISBN 0-8014-1564-0). Cornell U Pr.
Edwards, Mark U., Jr., ed. see Moeller, Bernd.
Edwards, Martin. Understanding Dismissal Law. (Waterlow's Business Library). 176p. 1984. pap. 15.60 (ISBN 0-08-039174-5). Pergamon.
Edwards, Mary I., jt. ed. see Duley-Morrow, Margot.
Edwards, Mary L. & Shriberg, Lawrence D. Phonology: Applications in Communicative Disorders. LC 82-25299. (Illus.). 434p. 1983. pap. 25.00 (ISBN 0-933014-80-5). College-Hill.
Edwards, Matilda B. French Men, Women & Books: A Series of Nineteenth-Century Studies. facs. ed. LC 67-26737. (Essay Index Reprint Ser). 1911. 17.00 (ISBN 0-8369-0407-9). Ayer Co Pubs.
--Friendly Faces of Three Nationalities. facs. ed. LC 69-17574. (Essay Index Reprint Ser). 1911. 18.00 (ISBN 0-8369-0072-3). Ayer Co Pubs.
--Six Life Studies of Famous Women. LC 73-39701. (Essay Index Reprint Ser.). Repr. of 1880 ed. 21.50 (ISBN 0-8369-2746-X). Ayer Co Pubs.
Edwards, Michael. Arriving Where We Started: Twenty-Five Years of Voluntary Service Overseas. (Illus.). 208p. (Orig.). 1983. 15.50x (ISBN 0-903031-93-0, Pub. by Intermediate Tech England); pap. 9.75x (ISBN 0-903031-92-2, Pub. by Intermediate Tech England). Intermediate Tech.
--Towards a Christian Poetics. 260p. 13.95x (ISBN 0-8028-3596-1). Eerdmans.
Edwards, Michael, jt. ed. see Usher, Stephen.
Edwards, Michael, tr. see Usher, Stephen & Edwards, Michael.
Edwards, Michael M. Growth of the British Cotton Trade, 1780-1815. LC 67-31864. (Illus.). 1967. 29.50x (ISBN 0-678-06775-9). Kelley.
Edwards, Michelle. Misha the Minstrel. LC 84-62336. (Illus.). 32p. 1985. 8.95 (ISBN 0-930100-19-0). Holy Cow.
Edwards, Milne & Haime, Jules. The Fossil Corals, 5 Pts. 1849-1854. Set. 89.00 (ISBN 0-384-13870-5). Johnson Repr.
Edwards, Mona, jt. auth. see Tate, Sharon.
Edwards, Mona S., jt. auth. see Tate, Sharon L.
Edwards, Myrtle. First Course in Geometry: A Modern Textbook for the High School. 1965. text ed. 7.50 (ISBN 0-682-43014-5, University). Exposition Pr FL.
Edwards, Myrtle S. see Gardner, Virginia.
Edwards, N. How to Make Dolls. pap. 2.00 (ISBN 0-87497-059-8). Assoc Bk.
Edwards, Nancy M. Office Automation: A Glossary & Guide. 275p. 1984. pap. text ed. 59.50 (ISBN 0-471-81859-3). Wiley.
Edwards, Nancy M., ed. Office Automation. 1983. pap. 34.95 (ISBN 0-442-22202-5). Van Nos Reinhold.
Edwards, Nancy M. & Shaw, Carmine, eds. Office Automation: A Glossary & Guide. LC 82-4714. (Information & Communications Management Guides Ser.). 275p. 1982. 59.50 (ISBN 0-86729-012-9, 703-BW). Knowledge Indus.
Edwards, Newton. Courts & the Public Schools. rev. 3rd ed. Garber, Lee O., ed. LC 72-130308. 1971. 28.00x (ISBN 0-226-18606-7). U of Chicago Pr.
Edwards, Newton, jt. auth. see Garber, Lee O.
Edwards, Newton, ed. see Pennsylvania University Bicentennial Conference.
Edwards, Ninian W. History of Illinois, from 1778 to 1833: And Life & Times of Ninian Edwards. facsimile ed. LC 75-97. (Mid-American Frontier Ser.). 1975. Repr. of 1870 ed. 42.00x (ISBN 0-405-06863-8). Ayer Co Pubs.
Edwards, O. Japanese Plays & Playfellows. lib. bdg. 79.95 (ISBN 0-87968-517-4). Krishna Pr.
Edwards, O. C. The Living & Active Word: A Way to Preach from the Bible Today. 166p. 1975. 1.50 (ISBN 0-8164-0265-5, Pub. by Seabury). Winston Pr.
Edwards, O. C., jt. auth. see Bennett, Robert A.
Edwards, O. C., et al. Anglican Theology & Pastoral Care. Griffiss, James, ed. 160p. (Orig.). 1985. pap. 8.95 (ISBN 0-8192-1364-0). Morehouse.
Edwards, O. C., Jr. Elements of Homiletic. LC 84-157333. 110p. (Orig.). 1982. pap. 7.95 (ISBN 0-916134-55-5). Pueblo Pub CO.
--Luke's Story of Jesus. LC 81-43076. 96p. 1981. pap. 4.50 (ISBN 0-8006-1611-1, 1-1611). Fortress.
Edwards, O. C., Jr. & Taylor, Gardner C. Pentecost 3. Achtemeier, Elizabeth, et al, eds. LC 79-7377. (Proclamation 2: Aids for Interpreting the Lessons of the Church Year, Ser. C). 64p. (Orig.). 1980. pap. 3.50 (ISBN 0-8006-4084-5, 1-4084). Fortress.
Edwards, O. C., Jr. & Westerhoff, John H., 3rd, eds. A Faithful Church: Issues in the History of Catechesis. LC 80-81099. 320p. (Orig.). 1981. pap. 14.95 (ISBN 0-8192-1278-4). Morehouse.
Edwards, O. D. & Shepperson, G., eds. Scotland, Europe & the American Revolution. 144p. 1976. 20.00x (ISBN 0-904919-06-4, Pub. by Polygon Bks Scotland). State Mutual Bk.
Edwards, O. E. see International Union of Pure & Applied Chemistry.
Edwards, Oliver. Talking of Books: Conrad, Shakespeare, Bennett. 306p. 1981. Repr. of 1957 ed. lib. bdg. 25.00 (ISBN 0-8495-1357-X). Arden Lib.
Edwards, Owen. Cadillac. LC 85-42867. (Illus.). 144p. 1985. 50.00 (ISBN 0-8478-0608-1). Rizzoli Intl.
--The Quest for Sherlock Holmes. 1981. 40.00x (ISBN 0-906391-15-6, Pub. by Mainstream). State Mutual Bk.
Edwards, Owen, et al. Leslie Gill: A Classical Approach to Photography 1935-1958. LC 83-43049. (Illus.). 63p. 1983. pap. 12.50 (ISBN 0-89494-018-X). New Orleans Mus Art.
--Quintessence: The Quality of Having It. (Illus.). 1983. 12.95 (ISBN 0-517-55090-3). Crown.
Edwards, Owen D. Burke & Hare. 300p. 1980. 35.00x (ISBN 0-686-75516-2, Pub. by Polygon Bks Scotland). State Mutual Bk.
Edwards, Owen D., jt. auth. see Ransom, Bernard.
Edwards, Owen D. & Richardson, Graham, eds. Christmas Observed: A Literary Selection. 211p. 1982. 9.95 (ISBN 0-312-13411-8). St Martin.
Edwards, Owen D., compiled by see Doyle, Arthur Conan.
Edwards, Owen D., jt. ed. see Doyle, David N.
Edwards, Owen D., jt. ed. see Shepperson, George A.
Edwards, P. Food Potential of Aquatic Macrophytes. (Illus.). 51p. 1983. pap. text ed. 7.00 (ISBN 0-89955-382-6, Pub. by ICLARM Philippines). Intl Spec Bk.
Edwards, P., jt. ed. see Muir, Kenneth.
Edwards, P., ed. see Muir, Kenneth.
Edwards, P. D. Anthony Trollope's Son in Australia: The Life & Letters of F.J.A. Trollope (1847-1910) LC 82-4928. 69p. 1983. text ed. 16.50x (ISBN 0-7022-1891-X). U of Queensland Pr.
Edwards, P. D., ed. see Trollope, Anthony.
Edwards, P. G. Australia Through American Eyes: Nineteen Thirty-Five to Nineteen Forty-Five. 1979. 16.95x (ISBN 0-7022-1365-9). U of Queensland Pr.
Edwards, P. I., jt. auth. see Whitehead, P. S.
Edwards, P. J., ed. The Journal of Peter Good: Gardener on the Matthew Flinders Voyage to Terra Australia 1801-1803. 110.00x (ISBN 0-686-78658-0, Pub. by Brit Mus Pubns England). State Mutual Bk.
Edwards, P. K. Strikes in the United States. 1981. 29.95x (ISBN 0-312-76642-4). St Martin.
Edwards, P. K. & Scullion, Hugh. The Social Organization of Industrial Conflict: Control & Resistance in the Workplace. (Warwick Studies in Industrial Relations). 328p. 1984. pap. 11.95x (ISBN 0-631-13586-3). Basil Blackwell.
Edwards, P. M., jt. auth. see Juilland, Alphonse.
Edwards, Page. The Lake: Father & Son. 224p. 1985. 14.95 (ISBN 0-7145-2834-X, Dist. by Scribner). M Boyars.
--Peggy Salte. LC 83-6044. 216p. 1983. 12.95 (ISBN 0-7145-2795-5, Dist. by Scribner). M Boyars.
--Staking Claims. LC 79-66572. 160p. 1982. pap. 7.95 (ISBN 0-7145-2774-2, Dist by Scribner). M Boyars.
Edwards, Page, Jr. The Mules That Angels Ride. 160p. 1979. 11.95 (ISBN 0-7145-0990-6, Dist by Scribner). M Boyars.
--Staking Claims. LC 79-66572. 160p. 1980. 11.95 (ISBN 0-7145-2689-4, Dist by Scribner); pap. 7.95 (ISBN 0-7145-2774-2). M Boyars.
--Touring. 171p. 1979. 11.95 (ISBN 0-7145-2504-9, Dist by Scribner). M Boyars.
Edwards, Pamela. The Terminal Aleph. (Illus.). 80p. 1984. pap. 4.50 (ISBN 0-915572-40-0). Panjandrum.
Edwards, Pamela J., ed. see Hardies, H. Lee.
Edwards, Pamela W., jt. auth. see Gerard, Mireille.
Edwards, Paul. Equiano's Travels. (African Writers Ser.). 1967. pap. text ed. 6.00x (ISBN 0-435-90010-2). Heinemann Ed.
--Heidegger & Death: A Critical Evaluation. (Monist Monographs: No. 1). 72p. 1979. 8.95 (ISBN 0-914417-03-7); pap. 3.95 (ISBN 0-914417-02-9). Hegeler Inst.
Edwards, Paul & Edwards, Sarah. Computer Companion. (The Designer Ser.). three-ring bdg. 39.95 (ISBN 0-88284-338-9). Alfred Pub.
--How to Make Money with Your Personal Computer. (Handy Guide Ser.). 64p. (Orig.). 1984. pap. 3.50 (ISBN 0-88284-264-1). Alfred Pub.
--Working from Home: Everything You Need to Know about Living & Working under the Same Roof. LC 84-23992. (Illus.). 432p. 1985. pap. 11.95 (ISBN 0-87477-240-0). J P Tarcher.
Edwards, Paul, ed. The Encyclopedia of Philosophy, 4 vols. LC 67-10059. 1973. Set. 260.00 (ISBN 0-02-894950-1). Free Pr.
--West African Narrative: An Anthology for Schools. 1965. text ed. 2.75x (ISBN 0-17-511073-5). Humanities.
Edwards, Paul & Pap, Arthur, eds. Modern Introduction to Philosophy. 3rd ed. LC 65-18470. 1973. text ed. 18.95x (ISBN 0-02-909200-0). Free Pr.
Edwards, Paul, jt. tr. see Palsson, Hermann.
Edwards, Paul C., ed. see Wilbur, Ray L.
Edwards, Paul K. Southern Urban Negro As a Consumer. LC 73-89022. (Illus.). Repr. of 1932 ed. 22.50x (ISBN 0-8371-1891-3, EDN&, Pub. by Negro U Pr). Greenwood.
--The Southern Urban Negro As a Consumer. LC 32-6325. (Basic Afro-American Reprint Library). 1970. Repr. of 1932 ed. 17.00 (ISBN 0-384-13875-6). Johnson Repr.
Edwards, Perry. Flowcharting & FORTRAN IV. (Illus.). 132p. 1973. 14.15 (ISBN 0-07-019042-9, G). McGraw.
Edwards, Perry & Broadwell, Bruce. Data Processing: Computers in Action. 2nd ed. 608p. 1982. text ed. write for info (ISBN 0-534-01063-6); write for info. (ISBN 0-534-01064-4). Wadsworth Pub.
--Flowcharting & BASIC. 214p. (Orig.). 1974. pap. text ed. 11.95 (ISBN 0-15-527661-1, HC). HarBraceJ.
Edwards, Peter & Raban, Bridie. Reading Problems: Identification & Treatment. 1978. pap. text ed. 9.00x (ISBN 0-435-10264-8). Heinemann Ed.
Edwards, Peter & Wratten, Stephen D. Ecology of Insect-Plant Interaction. (Studies in Biology: No. 121). 64p. 1980. pap. text ed. 8.95 (ISBN 0-7131-2803-8). E Arnold.
Edwards, Peter D., jt. auth. see Edwards, W. Sterling.
Edwards, Peter G. Prime Ministers & Diplomats: The Making of Australian Foreign Policy 1901-49. 240p. 1983. 45.00x (ISBN 0-19-554389-0). Oxford U Pr.
Edwards, Philip. Shakespeare & the Confines of Art. (Methuen Library Reprint Ser.). 176p. 1981. 27.00x (ISBN 0-416-32200-X, NO. 3581). Methuen Inc.
--Sir Walter Ralegh. LC 76-39784. 1976. Repr. of 1953 ed. lib. bdg. 20.00 (ISBN 0-8414-3969-9). Folcroft.
--Sir Walter Raleigh. 1953. Repr. 25.00 (ISBN 0-8274-3434-0). R West.
--Threshold of a Nation. LC 78-72085. (Illus.). 1980. 34.50 (ISBN 0-521-22463-2). Cambridge U Pr.
--Threshold of a Nation: A Study in English & Irish Drama. LC 78-72085. 264p. 1983. pap. 14.95 (ISBN 0-521-27695-0). Cambridge U Pr.
Edwards, Philip, ed. Hamlet: Prince of Denmark. (The New Cambridge Shakespare Ser.). (Illus.). 250p. 1985. 29.95 (ISBN 0-521-22151-X); pap. 6.95 (ISBN 0-521-29366-9). Cambridge U Pr.
Edwards, Philip, ed. see Kyd, Thomas.
Edwards, Philip, ed. see Massinger, Philip.
Edwards, Philip, ed. see Shakespeare, William.
Edwards, Philip, et al. Shakespeare's Styles. LC 79-51226. 1980. 39.50 (ISBN 0-521-22764-X). Cambridge U Pr.
Edwards, Philip, et al, eds. The Revels History of Drama in English: 1613-1660, Vol. 4. (Illus.). 1982. 55.00x (ISBN 0-416-13050-X, NO. 6423). Methuen Inc.
Edwards, Philip L. Sketch of the Oregon Territory: Or Emigrants Guide. enl. & facsimile ed. 20p. 1979. Repr. of 1842 ed. pap. 3.00 (ISBN 0-87770-047-8). Ye Galleon.
Edwards, Phoebe. Anyone Can Quilt. LC 75-10783. (Orig.). 1975. pap. 2.95 (ISBN 0-87502-039-9). Benjamin Co.
Edwards, R. A Formal Background to Mathematics: Pt. II, A & B. (Universitext). 1170p. 1980. pap. 46.00 (ISBN 0-387-90513-8). Springer-Verlag.
--Fourier Series: A Modern Introduction. LC 79-11932. (Graduate Texts in Mathematics: Pt. 1, Vol. 64). 1979. 24.00 (ISBN 0-387-90412-3). Springer-Verlag.
Edwards, R., ed. A Formal Background to Mathematics Pt. 1, A & B Logic, Sets & Numbers, 2 pts. LC 79-15045. 1979. pap. 39.50 (ISBN 0-387-90431-X). Springer-Verlag.
Edwards, R. A., jt. auth. see McDonald, P.
Edwards, R. A. & Edwards, G., eds. Pedro Calderon de la Barca: Los Cabellos de Absalon. LC 73-4292. 168p. 1973. pap. text ed. 7.00 (ISBN 0-08-017162-1). Pergamon.
Edwards, R. Dudley. Church & State in Tudor Ireland: A History of Penal Laws Against Irish Catholics 1534-1603. LC 76-180608. (Illus.). xliiii, 352p. 1972. Repr. of 1935 ed. 18.00x (ISBN 0-8462-1641-8). Russell.
Edwards, R. E. Fourier Series: A Modern Introduction, Vol. II. rev., 2nd ed. (Graduate Texts in Mathematics Ser.: Vol. 85). 384p. 1982. 44.00 (ISBN 0-387-90651-7). Springer-Verlag.
Edwards, R. E. & Gaudry, G. I. Littlewood-Paley & Multiplier Theory. (Ergebnisse der Mathematik und ihrer Grenzgebiete: Vol. 90). 1977. 37.00 (ISBN 0-387-07726-X). Springer-Verlag.
Edwards, R. E., ed. Integration & Harmonic Analysis on Compact Groups. LC 77-190412. (London Mathematical Society Lecture Notes Ser.: No. 8). 228p. 1972. 24.95 (ISBN 0-521-09717-7). Cambridge U Pr.
Edwards, R. G. Beginnings of Human Life. Head, J. J., ed. LC 79-50741. (Carolina Biology Reader Ser.). (Illus.). 16p. (gr. 10 up). 1981. pap. 1.60 (ISBN 0-89278-217-X, 45-9735). Carolina Biological.
--Conception in the Human Female. LC 80-40423. 1980. 95.00 (ISBN 0-12-232450-1). Acad Pr.
--Test-Tube Babies. Head, J. J., ed. LC 79-50741. (Carolina Biology Readers Ser.). (Illus.). 16p. (gr. 10 up). 1981. pap. 1.60 (ISBN 0-89278-289-7, 45-9689). Carolina Biological.
Edwards, R. G. & Purdy, J. M. Human Conception In Vitro. LC 82-71006. 1982. 49.50 (ISBN 0-12-232740-3). Acad Pr.
Edwards, R. G. & Johnson, M. H., eds. Physiological Effects of Immunity Against Reproductive Hormones. LC 75-12470. (Clinical & Experimental Immunoreproduction Ser.: No. 3). (Illus.). 300p. 1976. 52.50 (ISBN 0-521-20914-5). Cambridge U Pr.
Edwards, R. J., compiled by. Crossword Anagram Dictionary. (Illus.). 1979. 6.95 (ISBN 0-8317-1882-X, Mayflower Bks). Smith Pubs.
Edwards, R. N., jt. ed. see Zipkin, M A.
Edwards, R. T. & Penzler, Otto. Prize Meets Murder. (Whodunit Mystery Ser.: No. 1). 176p. (Orig.). 1984. pap. 2.95 (ISBN 0-671-50988-8). PB.
Edwards, R. W. Sources for Early Modern Irish History, 1534-1641. (Sources of History Ser.). 240p. 1985. 39.50 (ISBN 0-521-25020-X). Cambridge U Pr.
Edwards, R. W. & Brooker, M. P. The Ecology of the Wye. 1982. text ed. 41.50 (ISBN 90-6193-103-7, Pub. by Junk Pubs Netherlands). Kluwer Academic.
Edwards, R. W., jt. ed. see Pascoe, D.
Edwards, R. W., ed. see Zoological Society of London - 29th Symposium.
Edwards, Rachel. The Captain's Lady. 240p. (Orig.). 1980. pap. 1.95 (ISBN 0-89083-640-X). Zebra.
Edwards, Rachelle. Fleet Wedding. (Coventry Romance Ser.: No. 196). 192p. 1982. pap. 1.50 (ISBN 0-449-50299-6, Coventry). Fawcett.
--Fortune's Child, No. 149. 224p. 1981. pap. 1.50 (ISBN 0-449-50222-8, Coventry). Fawcett.
--Lord Heathbury's Revenge. 224p. 1980. pap. 1.75 (ISBN 0-449-50069-1, Coventry). Fawcett.
--The Marriage Bargain. (Coventry Romance Ser.: No. 186). 224p. 1982. pap. 1.50 (ISBN 0-449-50288-0, Coventry). Fawcett.
--The Scoundrel's Daughter. 144p. 1985. pap. 2.25 (ISBN 0-449-20843-5, Crest). Fawcett.
--The Smithfield Bargain. 224p. 1981. pap. 1.95 (ISBN 0-449-50203-1, Crest). Fawcett.
--Wager for Love. 1980. pap. 1.75 (ISBN 0-449-50021-7, Coventry). Fawcett.
Edwards, Ralph. The Dictionary of English Furniture, 3 Vols. (Illus.). 1200p. 1983. 295.00 (ISBN 0-907462-37-5). Antique Collect.
Edwards, Raoul, jt. auth. see Thompson, Thomas.
Edwards, Raoul D., jt. auth. see Thompson, Thomas W.
Edwards, Ray. Choosing & Caring for Garden Shrubs. pap. 4.50 (ISBN 0-7153-7902-X). David & Charles.
--Immunoassay: An Introduction. (Illus.). 192p. 1985. pap. text ed. 23.50x (ISBN 0-433-08165-1, Pub. by W Heinemann Med Bks). Sheridan Med Bks.
--The Nightcrawler Manual. (Illus.). 1981. pap. 5.00 (ISBN 0-914116-20-7). Shields.
Edwards, Raymond. Chess Tactics & Attacking Techniques. (Chess Handbooks: Vol. 5). 1978. pap. 4.95 (ISBN 0-7100-8821-3). Routledge & Kegan.
--Practical Chess Playing. (Routledge Chess Handbooks Ser.). 128p. (Orig.). 1984. pap. 7.95 (ISBN 0-7100-9653-4). Routledge & Kegan.
Edwards, Raymond, jt. auth. see Findley, Robert.
Edwards, Reginald, et al, eds. Relevant Methods in Comparative Education: Report of a Meeting of International Experts. (International Studies in Education: No. 33). (Illus.). 270p. 1973. pap. 13.25 (ISBN 92-820-1003-1, U544, UNESCO). Unipub.
Edwards, Rem B. Pleasures & Pains: A Theory of Qualitative Hedonism. LC 79-4168. 160p. 1979. 19.95x (ISBN 0-8014-1241-2). Cornell U Pr.
--Reason & Religion: An Introduction to the Philosophy of Religion. LC 78-66278. 1979. pap. text ed. 12.25 (ISBN 0-8191-0690-9). U Pr of Amer.
--A Return to Moral & Religious Philosophy in Early America. LC 81-43488. (Illus.). 288p. (Orig.). 1982. PLB 26.00 (ISBN 0-8191-2479-6); pap. text ed. 12.50 (ISBN 0-8191-2480-X). U Pr of Amer.
Edwards, Rem B., ed. Psychiatry & Ethics: Insanity, Rational Autonomy, & Mental Health Care. LC 82-62135. 609p. 1982. 29.95 (ISBN 0-87975-178-9); pap. 15.95 (ISBN 0-87975-179-7). Prometheus Bks.
Edwards, Renee, jt. auth. see Barker, Larry.
Edwards, Rhoda. The Broken Sword. 1978. pap. 2.25 (ISBN 0-532-22132-X). Woodhill.
Edwards, Rice. Topical Reviews in Neurosurgery, Vol. I. 202p. 1982. 32.50 (ISBN 0-7236-0576-9). PSG Pub Co.

Edwards, Richard. The Art of Wen Cheng-ming (Fourteen Seventy to Fifteen Fifty-Nine) pap. 65.50 (ISBN 0-317-29076-2, 2023478). Bks Demand UMI.
--Damon & Pithias. LC 76-136388. (Tudor Facsimile Texts. Old English Plays: No. 45). Repr. of 1908 ed. 49.50 (ISBN 0-404-53345-0). AMS Pr.
--The Field of Stones. (Oriental Studies: No. 5). 1962. 20.00 (ISBN 0-934686-09-2). Freer.
--Li Ti: A Study of the Chinese Painter Li Ti. (Occasional Papers Ser: Vol. 3, No. 3). (Illus.). 1967. pap. 5.00 (ISBN 0-934686-07-6). Freer.
Edwards, Richard & Wild, Robert. The Sentences of Sextus. LC 81-13770. (Society of Biblical Literature Texts & Translations Ser.). 1981. pap. text ed. 12.00 (ISBN 0-89130-528-9, 06-02-22). Scholars Pr GA.
Edwards, Richard, jt. auth. see Bowles, Samuel.
Edwards, Richard, ed. New York's Great Industries. LC 73-2504. (Big Business; Economic Power in a Free Society Ser.). Repr. of 1884 ed. 31.00 (ISBN 0-405-05086-0). Ayer Co Pubs.
Edwards, Richard A. A Concordance to Q. LC 75-6768. (Society of Biblical Literature. Sources for Biblical Study: No. 7). Repr. of 1975 ed. 36.90 (ISBN 0-8357-9568-3, 2017677). Bks Demand UMI.
--Matthew's Story of Jesus. LC 84-48711. 96p. 1985. pap. 4.50 (ISBN 0-8006-1619-7, 1-1619). Fortress.
--Sign of Jonah in the Theology of the Evangelists & Q. LC 74-153931. (Studies in Biblical Theology, 2nd Ser.: No. 18). 1971. pap. text ed. 10.00x (ISBN 0-8401-3068-6). A R Allenson.
Edwards, Richard C. Contested Terrain: The Transformation of the Workplace in America. LC 78-19942. 256p. 1980. pap. 8.95x (ISBN 0-465-01413-5, TB-5051). Basic.
--Labor in Transition. 300p. 1985. 27.50 (ISBN 0-86569-127-4). Auburn Hse.
Edwards, Richard C., et al. The Capitalist System: A Radical Analysis of American Society. 2nd ed. LC 77-1495. (Illus.). 1978. pap. 19.95 ref. ed. (ISBN 0-13-113597-X). P-H.
Edwards, Richard E., tr. see Gutierrez, Carlos M.
Edwards, Richard H. Popular Amusements. LC 75-22812. (America in Two Centuries Ser). 1976. Repr. of 1915 ed. 18.00x (ISBN 0-405-07686-X). Ayer Co Pubs.
Edwards, Richard L., ed. Breaking the Poverty Cycle: Readings on Income Maintenance. LC 72-6358. (Illus.). 111p. 1972. pap. text ed. 4.75x (ISBN 0-8422-0216-1). Irvington.
Edwards, Richard W., Jr. International Monetary Collaboration. 832p. 1985. lib. bdg. 85.00 (ISBN 0-941320-05-7). Transnatl Pubs.
Edwards, Rob, jt. auth. see Durie, Sheila.
Edwards, Robert. Australian Aboriginal Art: The Art of the Alligator Rivers Region Northern Territory. (AIAS New Ser.: No. 15). (Illus.). 1979. text ed. 21.50x (ISBN 0-391-01610-5); pap. text ed. 14.25x (ISBN 0-391-01611-3). Humanities.
--The Montecassino Passion & the Poetics of Medieval Drama. LC 75-22655. 1977. 33.00x (ISBN 0-520-03102-4). U of Cal Pr.
--The Poetry of Guido Guinizelli. 150p. 1985. lib. bdg. 20.00 (ISBN 0-8240-8955-3). Garland Pub.
Edwards, Robert & Steptoe, Patrick. A Matter of Life. LC 80-17293. (Illus.). 208p. 1980. Repr. 9.95 (ISBN 0-688-03698-8). Morrow.
Edwards, Robert, jt. ed. see Gray, Stephen.
Edwards, Robert, ed. see National Seminar on Aboriginal Antiquities in Australia, May 1972.
Edwards, Robert D. & Magee, John. Technical Analysis of Stock Trends. 5th ed. (Illus.). 60.00 (ISBN 0-910944-00-8). Magee.
Edwards, Robert I., tr. see De Rosnay, Joel.
Edwards, Roberta, et al. Stage System for Talented & Gifted Education. (Illus.). 62p. (Orig.). 1984. pap. 3.50x (ISBN 0-9613243-0-9). Trinity County.
Edwards, Rod. The Technique of Jewelry. (Illus.). 1977. 17.50 (ISBN 0-684-15309-2, ScribT). Scribner.
Edwards, Romaine V. Crisis Intervention & How It Works. 88p. 1979. 13.75x (ISBN 0-398-03580-6). C C Thomas.
Edwards, Ronald G. Australian Folk Songs. 1980. Repr. of 1972 ed. lib. bdg. 20.00 (ISBN 0-8492-4407-2). R West.
Edwards, Rosemary. Cut & Color: Animal Patterns. Wallace, Mary H., ed. (Illus.). 48p. (Orig.). 1981. pap. 2.95 (ISBN 0-912315-61-X). Word Aflame.
--Cut & Color: Patterns for Young Children. Wallace, Mary H., ed. (Illus.). 48p. (Orig.). 1980. pap. 2.95 (ISBN 0-912315-59-8). Word Aflame.
Edwards, Rosemary & McNall, Margie W. Craft Book for Children. Wallace, Mary H., ed. (Illus.). 64p. 1983. pap. 3.95 wkbk (ISBN 0-912315-03-2). Word Aflame.
Edwards, Rosemary W. Build Beautiful Bulletin Boards. Wallace, Mary E., ed. (Illus.). 72p. (Orig.). 1981. pap. 3.95 (ISBN 0-912315-60-1). Word Aflame.
Edwards, Ross. Fiddledust. LC 65-25807. 102p. 1965. 4.95 (ISBN 0-8040-0109-X, 82-70670, Pub. by Swallow). Ohio U Pr.
--Microcomputer Art. (Illus.). 240p. 1985. pap. text ed. 19.95 (ISBN 0-13-580218-0). P-H.
Edwards, Roy, tr. see Multatuli.
Edwards, Ruth. Answer Me. (Illus., Orig.). 1983. pap. 7.95 (ISBN 0-89390-041-9). Resource Pubns.
Edwards, Ruth D. An Atlas of Irish History. 2nd ed. (Illus.). 180p. 1981. 21.00x (ISBN 0-416-08110-X, 6497); pap. 10.50 (ISBN 0-416-08120-7, 6496). Methuen Inc.
--Patrick Pearse. 384p. 1980. pap. 7.95 (ISBN 0-571-11351-6). Faber & Faber.
--Patrick Pearse: The Triumph of Failure. LC 78-58294. (Illus.). 1978. 14.95 (ISBN 0-8008-6267-8). Taplinger.
--The Saint Valentine's Day Murders. 192p. 1985. 12.95 (ISBN 0-312-69732-5). St Martin.
Edwards, S., jt. auth. see Edwards, W.
Edwards, S., jt. ed. see Edwards, W.
Edwards, S. A. French Structure in Review. 3rd ed. 1979. pap. text ed. 10.95x (ISBN 0-669-02327-2). Heath.
Edwards, Sally. George Midgett's War. 144p. (gr. 5-7). 1985. 12.95 (ISBN 0-684-18315-3). Scribner.
--Triathlon: A Triple Fitness Sport. 9.95 (ISBN 0-8092-5555-3). Contemp Bks.
--The Triathlon Training & Racing Book. (Illus.). 128p. (Orig.). 1985. pap. 8.95 (ISBN 0-8092-5430-1). Contemp Bks.
--The Woman Runner's Training Diary. (Illus.). 160p. (Orig.). 1984. spiral 7.95 (ISBN 0-8092-5434-4). Contemp Bks.
Edwards, Sam, jt. auth. see Renko, Hal.
Edwards, Sandra, jt. auth. see Editors of Industrial Design Magazine.
Edwards, Sarah, jt. auth. see Edwards, Paul.
Edwards, Sarah A., jt. ed. see Berkey, Robert F.
Edwards, Sebastian. The Order of Liberalization of the External Sector in Developing Countries. (Essays in International Finance Ser.: No. 156). 1984. pap. text ed. 2.50x (ISBN 0-88165-063-3). Princeton U Int Finan Econ.
Edwards, Sherman, jt. auth. see Stone, Peter.
Edwards, Stephen R. Taxonomic Notes on South American Dendrobatid Frogs of the Genus Colostethus. (Occasional Papers: No. 30). 14p. 1974. pap. 1.25 (ISBN 0-686-80354-X). U of KS Mus Nat Hist.
Edwards, Stephen R. & Bell, Bruce M., eds. Pest Control in Museums: A Status Report. (Orig.). 1981. pap. 15.00 (ISBN 0-942924-01-0). Assn Syst Coll.
Edwards, Stewart, ed. The Communards of Paris, Eighteen Seventy-One. LC 72-13387. (Documents of Revolution Ser.). 180p. 1973. pap. 7.95x (ISBN 0-8014-9140-1, CP140). Cornell U Pr.
Edwards, Stewart H. Critics & Composers: Lectures & Radio Talks. 1984. 10.00 (ISBN 0-533-06022-2). Vantage.
Edwards, Sue, et al, eds. see Ticker, E M.
Edwards, Susan. Female Sexuality & the Law. 256p. 1981. 40.00x (ISBN 0-85520-382-X, Pub. by Robertson & Co England). State Mutual Bk.
Edwards, Susan, ed. Gender, Sex & the Law. LC 84-29309. 202p. 1985. 29.00 (ISBN 0-7099-0938-1, Pub. by Croom Helm Ltd). Longwood Pub Group.
Edwards, Susan G., jt. auth. see Murray, Frederick P.
Edwards, Susan S. Women on Trial: A Study of Female Suspects & Defendants in the System of Criminal Justice. LC 83-24840. 288p. 1984. 18.85 (ISBN 0-7190-0995-2, Pub. by Manchester Univ Pr). Longwood Pub Group.
Edwards, T., jt. auth. see Hicks, Tyler G.
Edwards, T. A. The Youth Training Scheme: A New Curriculum, Episode 1. 1984. 25.00x (ISBN 0-905273-96-6, Pub. by Falmer Pr); pap. 16.00x (ISBN 0-905273-95-8). Taylor & Francis.
Edwards, T. A., jt. auth. see Halliwell, J. D.
Edwards, T. C. Foundations for Microstrip Circuit Design. LC 80-41687. 720p. 1981. 37.95x (ISBN 0-471-27994-7, Pub. by Wiley-Interscience). Wiley.
--An Introduction to Microwave Electronics. 150p. 1984. pap. text ed. 14.95 (ISBN 0-7131-3495-X). E Arnold.
Edwards, T. R. Three Russian Writers & the Irrational: Zamyatin, Pil'nyak, & Bulgakov. LC 81-6148. (Cambridge Studies in Russian Literature). 250p. 1982. 44.50 (ISBN 0-521-23670-3). Cambridge U Pr.
Edwards, Ted. Beyond the Last Oasis. (Illus.). 210p. 1985. 19.95 (ISBN 0-88162-125-0, Pub. by Salem Hse Ltd). Merrimack Pub Cir.
Edwards, Ted L., Jr. & Lau, Barbara. Weight Loss to Super Wellness. (Illus.). 176p. (Orig.). 1982. pap. text ed. 8.95 (ISBN 0-938934-07-4). Hills Med.
Edwards, Thomas. Canons of Criticism & Glossary. 7th ed. LC 77-96349. (Eighteenth Century Shakespeare). Repr. of 1765 ed. lib. bdg. 35.00x (ISBN 0-678-05112-7). Kelley.
--Canons of Criticism & Glossary: Being a Supplement to Mr. Warburton's Edition of Shakespeare. 388p. 1970. Repr. of 1765 ed. 30.00x (ISBN 0-7146-2511-6, F Cass Co). Biblio Dist.
--Supplement to Warburton's Edition of Shakespeare. LC 76-164762. Repr. of 1748 ed. 11.50 (ISBN 0-404-02262-6). AMS Pr.
Edwards, Thomas C. A Commentary on the First Epistle to the Corinthians. 1979. 18.00 (ISBN 0-86524-013-2, 4602). Klock & Klock.
--The Epistle to the Hebrews. 394p. 1982. lib. bdg. 13.00 Smythe Sewn (ISBN 0-86524-154-6, 5803). Klock & Klock.
--The Waggamans & Their Allied Families. 1983. 45.00 (ISBN 0-686-89726-9). Reverend Clarke.
Edwards, Tilden. Living Simply Through the Day. 444p. 1985. pap. 9.95 large print ed. (ISBN 0-8027-2492-2). Walker & Co.
--Living Simply Through the Day: Spiritual Survival in a Complex Age. LC 77-14855. 240p. 1978. 10.00 (ISBN 0-8091-0219-6); pap. 6.95 (ISBN 0-8091-2045-3). Paulist Pr.
--Sabbath Time: Understanding & Practice for Contemporary Christians. 144p. 1984. pap. 8.95 (ISBN 0-8164-0526-3, AY7883, Pub. by Seabury). Winston Pr.
--Spiritual Friend: Reclaiming the Gift of Spiritual Direction. LC 79-91408. 272p. 1980. pap. 8.95 (ISBN 0-8091-2288-X). Paulist Pr.
Edwards, Tilden H., ed. Living with Apocalypse: Spiritual Resources for Social Compassion. LC 83-48458. 192p. 1984. 14.37 (ISBN 0-06-062123-0, HarpR). Har-Row.
Edwards, Tilden H., Jr. All God's Children. LC 81-12704. (Journeys in Faith Ser.). 144p. 1982. 9.95 (ISBN 0-687-01016-0). Abingdon.
Edwards, Tony. Hitler & Germany 1919-1939. (History Broadsheets Ser.). 1972. pap. text ed. 7.50x (ISBN 0-435-31175-1). Heinemann Ed.
Edwards, Tony & Furlong, Vivian. The Language of Teaching. 1978. pap. text ed. 10.50x o. p. (ISBN 0-435-80295-X). Heinemann Ed.
Edwards, Tony, jt. auth. see Brown, Colin.
Edwards, Tryon, ed. New Dictionary of Thoughts. rev. ed. 1955. 17.95 (ISBN 0-385-00127-4). Doubleday.
Edwards, U. R., jt. ed. see Austin, C. R.
Edwards, Violet. Group Leader's Guide to Propaganda Analysis. Institute for Propaganda Analysis, ed. (Propaganda Analysis Ser.). 1979. lib. bdg. 69.95 (ISBN 0-8490-3020-X). Gordon Pr.
Edwards, Viv. Language in Multicultural Classrooms. 160p. 1983. pap. 14.95 (ISBN 0-7134-4508-4, Pub. by Batsford England). David & Charles.
Edwards, W. & Edwards, S. Symbol Discrimination & Sequencing. Reusable ed. (Ann Arbor Tracking Program Ser.). 1976. wkbk. 6.50x (ISBN 0-89039-154-8). Ann Arbor FL.
Edwards, W. & Edwards, S., eds. Cursive Tracking: Reusable Edition. (gr. 3). 1972. wkbk. 6.50 (ISBN 0-89039-021-5). Ann Arbor FL.
--Cursive Writing: Words: Reusable Edition, Book 1. (gr. 1-3). 1975. wkbk. 6.50 (ISBN 0-89039-135-1). Ann Arbor FL.
--Cursive Writing: Words: Reusable Edition, Book 2. (gr. 3-6). 1975. wkbk. 6.50 (ISBN 0-89039-136-X). Ann Arbor FL.
--Cursive Writing 2: Reusable Edition. (gr. 1). 1972. wkbk. 6.50 (ISBN 0-89039-051-7). Ann Arbor FL.
--Letter Tracking: Reusable Edition. (Large Type Tracking Ser.). (gr. k-1). 1973. wkbk. 5.00x (ISBN 0-89039-019-3). Ann Arbor FL.
--Letter Tracking: Reusable Edition. (Ann Arbor Tracking Program Ser.). (gr. 3-8). 1975. wkbk. 6.50 (ISBN 0-89039-153-X). Ann Arbor FL.
--Manuscript Tracking: Reusable Edition. (Large Type Tracking Ser.). (gr. k-1). 1975. 5.00x (ISBN 0-89039-017-7). Ann Arbor FL.
Edwards, W. N. The Early History of Palaeontology. (Illus.). 1976. pap. 2.75x (ISBN 0-565-00658-4, Pub. by Brit Mus Nat Hist). Sabbot-Natural Hist Bks.
Edwards, W. Sterling & Edwards, Peter D. Alexis Carrel: Visionary Surgeon. (Illus.). 160p. 1974. 7.25x (ISBN 0-398-03130-4). C C Thomas.
Edwards, Ward & Newman, J. Robert. Multiattribute Evaluation. (Quantitative Applications in the Social Sciences Ser.: Vol. 26). (Illus.). 96p. 1982. pap. 5.00 (ISBN 0-8039-0095-3). Sage.
Edwards, William. Notes on European History, 5 vols. 1979. Repr. of 1927 ed. Set. lib. bdg. 125.00 (ISBN 0-8492-4402-1). R West.
Edwards, William E. Ten Days to a Great New Life. pap. 3.00 (ISBN 0-87980-159-X). Wilshire.
--Thirty Day Action Guide to Big Money Selling. 1972. 49.50 (ISBN 0-13-918698-0). Exec Reports.
Edwards, William J. Twenty-Five Years in the Black Belt. LC 72-111574. Repr. of 1918 ed. cancelled (ISBN 0-8371-4599-6). Greenwood.
Edwards-May, David. Inland Waterways of France. 5th ed. 312p. 1984. 75.00x (ISBN 0-85288-082-0, Pub. by Imray Laurie Norie & Wilson UK). State Mutual Bk.
Edwardson, W. & MacCormack, C. W., eds. Improving Small-Scale Food Industries in Developing Countries. (Illus.). 167p. 1984. pap. 13.00 (ISBN 0-88936-398-6, IDRC-TS48E, IDRC). Unipub.
Edwardss, Marcia & McDonnell, Unity, eds. Symposium Zoological Society London, No. 50. (Serial Publication). 336p. 1982. 49.00 (ISBN 0-12-613350-6). Acad Pr.
Edwing, Don. Mad Variations. 192p. 1984. pap. 1.95 (ISBN 0-446-30339-9). Warner Bks.
Edwing, Don, jt. auth. see DeBartolo, Dick.
Edwinn, Gloria. Just for Starters. LC 80-51771. 272p. 1981. 14.95 (ISBN 0-670-41093-4). Viking.
Edye, Leslie Andrew, jt. ed. see Stace, Helen M.
Edzard, D. O. see Directorate General of Antiguities, Baghdad.
Ee, Patricia M Van see Sellers, John R. & Van Ee, Patricia M.
Ee, T. H., jt. auth. see Wong, Francis.
Ee, Tan S., jt. auth. see Hoffmann, Lutz.
Ee, Tiang Hong. Myths for a Wilderness. (Writing in Asia Ser.). 1976. pap. text ed. 3.50x (ISBN 0-686-60454-7, 00235). Heinemann Ed.
EEC Commission, jt. auth. see Binnie & Parners.
Eecke, Wilfried Ver see Ver Eecke, Wilfried.
Eeden, Frederik Van see Van Eeden, Frederik.
EEE Meter & Service Committee, ed. Handbook for Electricity Metering. 523p. 1982. 25.00 (ISBN 0-931032-11-3). Edison Electric.
Eekelaar, John. Family Law & Social Policy. 2nd ed. (Law in Context Ser.). xviii, 263p. 1984. 31.50x (ISBN 0-297-78274-6, Pub. by Weidenfeld & Nicolson). Rothman.
Eekman, Thomas. Thirty Years of Yugoslav Literature: 1945-1975. (Joint Committee on Eastern Europe Publication Ser.: No. 5). 1978. 15.00 (ISBN 0-930042-21-2). Mich Slavic Pubns.
Eekman, Thomas, jt. auth. see Birnbaum, Henrik.
Eekman, Thomas & Worth, Dean S., eds. Russian Poetics. (UCLA Slavic Studies: Vol. 4). 544p. 1983. 29.95 (ISBN 0-89357-101-6). Slavica.
Eells, Charles P., tr. see Philostratus, Flavius.
Eells, E. S., ed. Fairy Tales from Brazil. LC 17-25892. Repr. of 1917 ed. 20.00 (ISBN 0-527-26500-4). Kraus Repr.
Eells, Ellery T. Rational Decision & Causality. LC 81-18001. (Cambridge Studies in Philosophy). (Illus.). 240p. 1982. 34.50 (ISBN 0-521-24213-4). Cambridge U Pr.
Eells, Elsie. Tales of Enchantment from Spain. LC 78-67706. (The Folktale). (Illus.). Repr. of 1920 ed. 21.50 (ISBN 0-404-16079-4). AMS Pr.
Eells, George. Malice in Wonderland. 360p. 1985. pap. 3.95 (ISBN 0-931773-26-1). Critics Choice Paper.
--Robert Mitchum. 336p. 1985. pap. 3.95 (ISBN 0-515-08213-9). Jove Pubns.
--Robert Mitchum: A Biography. 336p. 1984. 16.95 (ISBN 0-531-09836-2). Watts.
Eells, Hastings. The Attitudes of Martin Bucer Toward the Bigamy of Philip of Hesse. LC 83-45611. Date not set. Repr. of 1924 ed. 32.50 (ISBN 0-404-19829-5). AMS Pr.
Eells, J., ed. Complex Analysis Trieste: Proceedings, 1981. (Lecture Notes in Mathematics Ser.: Vol. 950). 428p. 1982. pap. 23.00 (ISBN 0-387-11596-X). Springer-Verlag.
Eells, James & Lemaire, Luc. Selected Topics in Harmonic Maps. LC 82-25526. (Conference Board of the Mathematical Sciences Ser.: No. 50). 86p. 1983. pap. 17.00 (ISBN 0-8218-5018-0). Am Math.
Eells, James J. Singularities of Smooth Maps. (Notes on Mathematics & Its Applications Ser.). 114p. (Orig.). 1967. 28.95 (ISBN 0-677-01330-2). Gordon.
Eells, John M. LAFCO Spheres of Influence: Effective Planning for the Urban Fringe. (Working Paper: 77-3). 1977. pap. 5.00x (ISBN 0-685-87445-1). Inst Gov Stud Berk.
Eells, John S. Touchstones of Matthew Arnold. LC 76-136388. Repr. of 1955 ed. 22.50 (ISBN 0-404-02263-4). AMS Pr.
Eells, John S., Jr. The Touchstones of Matthew Arnold. 1955. pap. 8.95x (ISBN 0-8084-0302-8). New Coll U Pr.
Eells, M. Justice to the Indian. (Indian Ser.). 11p. pap. 2.95 (ISBN 0-8466-4010-4, I10). Shorey.
--The Stone Age of Oregon. (Shorey Historical Ser.). 16p. pap. 2.95 (ISBN 0-8466-4014-7, I14). Shorey.
--Ten Years of Missionary Work among the Indians at Skokomish. (Illus.). 271p. pap. 19.95 (ISBN 0-8466-0228-8, S228). Shorey.
Eells, Myron. The Indians of Puget Sound: The Notebooks of Myron Eells. Castile, George P., ed. & intro. by. LC 85-40355. (Illus.). 440p. 1985. 40.00 (ISBN 0-295-96262-3); pre-Jan 1986 29.95 (ISBN 0-317-28497-5). U of Wash Pr.
Eells, Richard. Global Corporations: The Emerging System of World Economic Power. rev. ed. LC 75-18008. 1976. pap. text ed. 5.95 (ISBN 0-02-909270-1). Free Pr.
--The Political Crisis of the Enterprise System. LC 79-48016. (Studies of the Modern Corporation Ser.). 1980. 10.00 (ISBN 0-02-909250-7). Free Pr.
Eells, Richard & Nehemkis, Peter. Corporate Intelligence & Espionage: A Blueprint for Executive Decision Making. LC 84-43214. 288p. 1984. 17.95x (ISBN 0-02-909240-X). Free Pr.
Eells, Richard, ed. International Business Philanthropy. LC 79-7338. (Studies of the Modern Corporation Ser.). (Illus.). 1979. 12.95 (ISBN 0-02-909260-4). Free Pr.
Eells, Richard & Walton, Clarence, eds. Man in the City of the Future: A Symposium of Urban Philosophers. LC 68-22641. (Studies of the Modern Corporation Ser.). 1969. 9.95 (ISBN 0-02-909280-9). Macmillan.
Eells, Robert & Nyberg, Bartell. Lonely Walk: The Life of Senator Mark Hatfield. LC 79-50942. 201p. 1979. 7.95 (ISBN 0-915684-49-7). Multnomah.
Eells, Walter C. Communism in Education in Asia, Africa, & the Far Pacific. LC 75-138225. 1971. Repr. of 1954 ed. lib. bdg. 15.00x (ISBN 0-8371-5582-7, EECO). Greenwood.
Eells, Walter C. & Haswell, Harold A. Academic Degrees. LC 70-128397. Repr. of 1960 ed. 35.00x (ISBN 0-8103-3015-6). Gale.
Eells, Walter C., ed. see United States Office of Education, Division of Higher Education.

Een, JoAnn D., et al, eds. Women & Society, Citations 3601 to 6000: An Annotated Bibliography. LC 77-18985. pap. 69.50 (ISBN 0-317-10699-6, 2021890). Bks Demand UMI.

Eeningenburg, Dennis. Workbook on Morality: A Biblical View of Sexuality. 74p. (Orig.). 1981. pap. 3.95 (ISBN 0-8341-0717-1). Beacon Hill.

Eerde, John A. Van see Williamson, Robert C. & Van Eerde, John A.

Eerde, Katherine S. Van see Van Eerde, Katherine S.

Eerde, Katherine Van see Van Eerde, Katherine S.

Eerkes. Classroom Records Software System: Apple Version. 1986. user's manual & software 29.95 (ISBN 0-538-10221-7, J221). SW Pub.

Ees, Erik van see Van Ees, Erik.

Eesa, Naeem M. & Cutkomp, Laurence K. Glossary of Pesticide Toxicology & Related Terms. 80p. (Orig.). 1984. pap. 10.00 (ISBN 0-913702-28-5). Thomson Pub CA.

Eesley, G. L. Coherent Raman Spectroscopy. (Illus.). 150p. 1981. 44.00 (ISBN 0-08-025058-0). Pergamon.

Effects Technology, Inc. Design Manual for Fiber Optic CODEC Link, Vol. V. (User Manual & Handbook Ser.). 150p. 1981. pap. 50.00 (ISBN 0-686-39228-0). Info Gatekeepers.

Effemar. Dice: Craps, How to Play & Win. 12.95x (ISBN 0-685-21931-3). Wehman.

Effendi, Shoghi. The Advent of Divine Justice. rev. ed. LC 84-436. x, 104p. 1984. 15.00 (ISBN 0-87743-195-7); pap. 7.50 (ISBN 0-87743-196-5). Baha'i.

--Call to the Nations: Extracts from the Writings of Shoghi Effendi. LC 79-670140. 1978. 6.95 (ISBN 0-85398-068-3, 108-050); pap. 3.95 o. s. i. (ISBN 0-85398-069-1, 108-051). Baha'i.

--God Passes By. rev. ed. LC 44-51036. 1974. 19.95 (ISBN 0-87743-020-9, 108-010); pap. 13.95 o. s. i. (ISBN 0-87743-034-9, 108-011). Baha'i.

--The Promised Day Is Come. rev. ed. 1980. 14.95 (ISBN 0-87743-132-9, 108-017); pap. 7.95 (ISBN 0-87743-138-8, 108-018). Baha'i.

--Selected Writings of Shoghi Effendi. rev. ed. 1975. pap. 1.95 (ISBN 0-87743-079-9, 308-043). Baha'i.

--The World Order of Baha'u'llah. 2nd rev. ed. LC 56-17685. 1974. 18.95 (ISBN 0-87743-031-4, 108-020); pap. 9.95 (ISBN 0-87743-004-7, 108-021). Baha'i.

Effendi, Shoghi, tr. see Abdu'l-Baha.

Effendi, Shoghi, tr. see Baha'u'llah.

Effert, S. & Meyer-Erkelenz, J. D., eds. Blood Vessels: Eighth Scientific Conference of the Gesellschaft Deutscher Naturforscher & Artze, 20th-21st Oct., 1975 Rottach-Egern. (Illus.). 1976. soft cover 28.40 (ISBN 0-387-07909-2). Springer-Verlag.

Effinger, George A. The Bird of Time. 1986. 12.95 (ISBN 0-385-19232-0). Doubleday.

--The Nick of Time. LC 85-1565. (Science Fiction Ser.). 192p. 1985. 12.95 (ISBN 0-385-19641-5). Doubleday.

Effinger, John R. Woman in All Ages & in All Countries: Women of the Romance Countries. 1981. Repr. of 1907 ed. lib. bdg. 45.00 (ISBN 0-89984-182-1). Century Bookbindery.

Effland, Richard C., jt. ed. see Fielding, Stuart.

Effland, Richard W., et al. Arizona Probate Code Practice Manual. LC 84-133127. 1980. write for info. AZ St Bar.

Effler, Donald B., ed. Blades' Surgical Diseases of the Chest. 4th ed. LC 78-7047. 840p. 1978. 77.95 (ISBN 0-8016-0697-7). Mosby.

Effrat, Andrew. Perspectives on Political Sociology. (Orig.). pap. 9.95 (ISBN 0-8290-1763-1). Irvington.

Effrat, Andrew, ed. Perspectives in Political Sociology. LC 73-4329. 1973. 29.50x (ISBN 0-672-51746-9). Irvington.

Effrat, Marcia P., ed. The Community: Approaches & Applications. LC 73-16604. (Illus.). 1974. pap. text ed. 10.95 (ISBN 0-02-909300-7). Free Pr.

Effron, Benjamin, ed. see Karp, Deborah.

Effron, Joel. Data Communications Techniques & Technologies. (Data Processing Ser.). (Illus.). 228p. 1984. 25.00 (ISBN 0-534-03270-2). Lifetime Learn.

Effron, Joel & Zendex Corporation Staff. Data Communications Techniques & Technology. 225p. 1984. 29.00 (ISBN 0-534-03270-2). Van Nos Reinhold.

Effros, E. G. & Hahn, Frank. Locally Compact Transformation Groups & C-Algebras. LC 52-42839. (Memoirs: No. 75). 93p. 1967. pap. 9.00 (ISBN 0-8218-1275-0, MEMO-75). Am Math.

Effros, E. G., jt. ed. see Araki, H.

Effros, Edward G. Dimensions & C-Algebras. LC 81-1582. (CBMS Regional Conference Series in Mathematics: Vol. 46). 74p. 1981. pap. 9.00 (ISBN 0-8218-1697-7). Am Math.

Effros, R., ed. Emerging Financial Centers. 1150p. 1982. 35.00 (ISBN 0-939934-20-5). Intl Pubns Serv.

Effros, Richard, et al, eds. The Microcirculation: Current Concepts. 1981. 55.00 (ISBN 0-12-232560-5). Acad Pr.

Effros, Robert C., ed. Emerging Financial Centers: Legal & Institutional Framework. xvi, 1150p. 1982. 35.00 (ISBN 0-939934-20-5). Intl Monetary.

--Emerging Financial Centers: Legal & Institutional Framework. LC 82-84226. pap. 160.00 (ISBN 0-317-28833-4, 2020820). Bks Demand UMI.

Efimov, A. V. & Demidovich, B. P. Higher Mathematics-Worked Examples & Problems with Elements of Theory Vol. 1: Linear Analysis & Fundamentals of Analysis. 511p. 1985. 9.95 (ISBN 0-8285-2890-X, Pub. by Mir Pubs USSR). Imported Pubns.

--Higher Mathematics-Worked Examples & Problems with Elements of Theory Vol. 2: Advanced Topics of Mathematical Analysis. 414p. 1985. 9.95 (ISBN 0-8285-2891-8, Pub. by Mir Pubs USSR). Imported Pubns.

Efimov, Dimitri. World War Two & the Destinies of Asian & African Peoples. 150p. 1985. text ed. 15.95x (ISBN 0-86590-733-1, Pub. by Sterling Pubs India). APT Bks.

Efimov, N. V. Higher Geometry. 1980. 11.00 (ISBN 0-8285-1903-X, Pub. by Mir Pubs USSR). Imported Pubns.

Efimov, N. V., et al. Differential Geometry & Calculus of Variations. (Translations Ser.: No. 1 Vol. 6). 1970. Repr. of 1962 ed. 30.00 (ISBN 0-8218-1606-3, TRANS 1-6). Am Math.

Efird, James M. Biblical Books of Wisdom. 96p. 1983. pap. 5.95 (ISBN 0-8170-0999-X). Judson.

--Christ, the Church & the End. (Studies in Colossians & Ephesians Ser.). 112p. 1980. pap. 4.75 (ISBN 0-8170-0862-4). Judson.

--Daniel & Revelation. 1978. pap. 4.95 (ISBN 0-8170-0797-0). Judson.

--How to Interpret the Bible. LC 83-49051. 144p. 1984. pap. 7.95 (ISBN 0-8042-0069-6). John Knox.

--Jeremiah: Prophet under Siege. LC 79-14837. 1979. pap. 4.95 (ISBN 0-8170-0846-2). Judson.

--Marriage & Divorce: What the Bible Says. (Contemporary Christian Concerns Ser.). 96p. (Orig.). 1985. pap. 4.95 (ISBN 0-687-23619-3). Abingdon.

--The New Testament Writings: History, Literature, Interpretation. LC 79-87750. (Biblical Foundation Ser.). 1980. pap. 6.95 (ISBN 0-8042-0246-X). John Knox.

--The Old Testament Prophets Then & Now. 128p. 1982. pap. 6.95 (ISBN 0-8170-0960-4). Judson.

--Old Testament Writings: History, Literature, Interpretation. LC 81-82352. (Biblical Foundations Ser.). (Illus.). 324p. 1982. pap. 11.95 (ISBN 0-8042-0145-5). John Knox.

--These Things Are Written: An Introduction to the Religious Ideas of the Bible. LC 77-15749. (Biblical Foundations Ser.). 1978. pap. 7.95 (ISBN 0-8042-0073-4). John Knox.

Efrat, Elisha. Urbanization in Israel. LC 83-24718. 240p. 1984. 25.00 (ISBN 0-312-83523-X). St Martin.

Efrein, Joel. Cablecasting Production Handbook. LC 74-33617. (Illus.). 210p. 1975. 12.95 (ISBN 0-8306-5768-1, 768). TAB Bks.

--Video Tape Production & Communication Techniques. LC 70-114712. (Illus.). 1970. 12.95 (ISBN 0-8306-0541-X, 541). TAB Bks.

Efrein, Laurie. A Magic Moment: Bach & Beyond. (Illus.). 353p. (Orig.). 1984. pap. 15.00 (ISBN 0-917573-00-5). CAO Times.

Efron, Alexander. Teaching of Physical Sciences in the Secondary Schools of the United States, France & Soviet Russia. LC 75-176742. (Columbia University. Teachers College. Contributions to Education: No. 725). Repr. of 1937 ed. 22.50 (ISBN 0-404-55725-2). AMS Pr.

Efron, Ariadna, jt. auth. see Tsvetaeva, Marina.

Efron, Arthur. Don Quixote & the Dulcineated World. (Paunch Ser.: Nos. 59-60). vii, 204p. 1985. pap. 12.00 (ISBN 0-9602478-6-3). Paunch.

--The Sexual Body: An Interdisciplinary Perspective. LC 82-642121. 314p. 1985. pap. 15.00 (ISBN 0-930195-01-9). Inst Mind Behavior.

Efron, Arthur & Herold, John, eds. Root Metaphor-the Live Thought of Stephen C. Pepper. LC 79-92716. (Paunch Ser.: Nos. 53-54). 224p. 1980. pap. 10.00 (ISBN 0-9602478-4-X). Paunch.

Efron, Arthur, ed. see Boadella, David.

Efron, B. The Jackknife, the Bootstrap & Other Resampling Plans. LC 81-84708. (CBMS-NSF Regional Conference Ser.: No. 38). vii, 92p. 1982. pap. text ed. 14.00 (ISBN 0-89871-179-7). Soc Indus Appl Math.

Efron, Benjamin & Rubin, Alvan D. Coming of Age: Your Bar or Bat Mitzvah. LC 77-78031. (Illus.). 1977. 5.00 (ISBN 0-8074-0084-X, 142530). UAHC.

Efron, D., ed. Psychotomimetic Drugs. 1970. 27.00 (ISBN 0-7204-4063-7, North Holland). Elsevier.

Efron, Daniel, et al, eds. Ethnopharmacologic Search for Psychoactive Drugs. LC 79-3955. 488p. 1979. Repr. of 1967 ed. pap. text ed. 37.50 (ISBN 0-89004-047-8). Raven.

Efron, Daniel H., jt. auth. see Usdin, Earl.

Efron, Daniel H., ed. Psychotomimetic Drugs. LC 73-89388. (Illus.). 365p. 1970. 40.00 (ISBN 0-911216-07-3). Raven.

Efron, Edith. The Apocalyptics: Cancer & the Big Lie - How Environmental Politics Controls What We Know About Cancer. 512p. 1984. 19.95 (ISBN 0-671-41743-6). S&S.

--The News Twisters. 368p. 1973. pap. 1.25 (ISBN 0-532-12133-3). Woodhill.

Efron, Edith & Chambers, Clytia. How CBS Tried to Kill a Book. 240p. 1973. pap. 1.50 (ISBN 0-532-15115-1). Woodhill.

Efron, Marshall & Olsen, Alfa B. Bible Stories You Can't Forget. 96p. (gr. 5 up). 1979. pap. 1.25 (ISBN 0-440-41382-6, YB). Dell.

--Bible Stories You Can't Forget No Matter How Hard You Try. (Illus.). 1976. 9.95 (ISBN 0-525-26500-7, 0966-290). Dutton.

Efron, Marshall, jt. auth. see Olsen, Alfa-Betty.

Efron, Marvin, et al. Project MAVIS Sourcebooks, 6 bks. (Illus.). 212p. (Orig.). 1980. Set. pap. 15.00 (ISBN 0-89994-255-5). Soc Sci Ed.

Efron, V. see Keller, Mark.

Efron, Vera see Keller, Mark.

Efros, A. L. & Pollak, M. Electron-Electron Interactions in Disordered Systems: Modern Problems in Condensed Matter Sciences, Vol. 10. 628p. 1985. 140.75 (ISBN 0-444-86916-6, North Holland). Elsevier.

Efros, A. L., jt. auth. see Shklovskii, B. I.

Efros, Israel I. Ancient Jewish Philosophy. 1976. pap. 5.95x (ISBN 0-8197-0014-2). Bloch.

--Philosophical Terms in the Moreh Nebukim. LC 73-164764. (Columbia University. Oriental Studies: No. 22). Repr. of 1924 ed. 17.00 (ISBN 0-404-50512-0). AMS Pr.

--Problem of Space in Jewish Medieval Philosophy. LC 77-164765. (Columbia University. Oriental Studies: No. 11). Repr. of 1917 ed. 14.75 (ISBN 0-404-50501-5). AMS Pr.

--Problem of Space in Jewish Medieval Philosophy. lib. bdg. 37.50x (ISBN 0-697-00037-0); pap. 7.95x (ISBN 0-89197-904-2). Irvington.

--Studies in Medieval Jewish Philosophy. LC 73-12512. 267p. 1974. 31.50x (ISBN 0-231-03194-7). Columbia U Pr.

Efros, Susan. Moving in. 1981. 5.00 (ISBN 0-686-77709-3). Waterfall Pr.

--Two-Way Streets. 1975. 4.00 (ISBN 0-686-16081-9). Jungle Garden.

--Walking Vanilla. LC 78-66433. 1978. pap. 5.00 (ISBN 0-932278-01-9). Waterfall Pr.

Efros, Susan, ed. This Is Women's Work: An Anthology of Women's Poetry, Prose & Graphics. LC 74-19118. (Illus.). 160p. 1974. pap. 4.95 (ISBN 0-915572-02-8). Panjandrum.

Efstratiou, Nicholas, jt. auth. see Leekley, Dorothy.

Eftekhar, Nas S. Principles of Total Hip Arthroplasty. LC 78-18471. (Illus.). 656p. 1978. text ed. 74.50 (ISBN 0-8016-1496-1). Mosby.

Eftekhar, Nas Ser. Infection in Joint Replacement Surgery: Prevention & Management. (Illus.). 1984. 59.95 (ISBN 0-8016-1505-4). Mosby.

Efthimides, Emil, tr. see Castellano-Giron, Hernan.

Efunde, Agun. Los Secretos De la Santeria. LC 78-60113. (Coleccion Agun Efunde). 1978. pap. 6.95 (ISBN 0-89729-204-9). Ediciones.

Efveraren, C. J. Names of Places in the Transferred Sense in English: Asematological Study. 59.95 (ISBN 0-8490-0703-8). Gordon Pr.

Efvergren, Carl J. Names of Places in a Transferred Sense in English: A Sematological Study. LC 68-17922. 1969. Repr. of 1909 ed. 35.00x (ISBN 0-8103-3233-7). Gale.

Egami, F. & Nakamura, K. Microbial Ribonucleases. LC 68-8784. (Molecular Biology, Bichemistry, & Biophysics Ser.: Vol. 6). 1969. 25.00 (ISBN 0-387-04657-7). Springer-Verlag.

Egami, Namio. The Beginnings of Japanese Art. LC 72-78599. (Heibonsha Survey of Japanese Art Ser.). (Illus.). 176p. 1973. 17.50 (ISBN 0-8348-1006-9). Weatherhill.

Egami, S. Heart of Karate Do. 1976. 15.95x (ISBN 0-685-83542-1). Wehman.

Egami, Shigeru. The Heart of Karate-Do. LC 80-82529. (Illus.). 127p. 1981. 15.50 (ISBN 0-87011-437-9). Kodansha.

Egan. Photometry & Polarization in Remote Sensing. 480p. 1985. 68.00 (ISBN 0-444-00892-6). Elsevier.

Egan, Carol B. Body Buddies. (ps-2). 1982. 5.95 (ISBN 0-86653-060-6, GA 420). Good Apple.

Egan, Clifford L. Neither Peace nor War: Franco-American Relations, 1803 to 1812. LC 82-17272. (Illus.). 288p. 1983. text ed. 30.00x (ISBN 0-8071-1076-0). La State U Pr.

Egan, Clifford L. & Knott, Alexander W., eds. Essays in Twentieth Century American Diplomatic History Dedicated to Professor Daniel M. Smith. LC 81-40030. (Illus.). 238p. (Orig.). 1982. PLB 25.25 (ISBN 0-8191-2125-8); pap. text ed. 12.50 (ISBN 0-8191-2126-6). U Pr of Amer.

Egan, D. F., et al, eds. Developmental Screening 0-5 Years. (Clinics in Developmental Medicine Ser.: Vol. 30). 70p. 1969. text ed. 17.00 (ISBN 0-433-16501-4, Pub. by Spastics Intl England). Lippincott.

Egan, David R. & Egan, Melinda A. Leo Tolstoy: An Annotated Bibliography of English-Language Sources to 1978. LC 79-16536. (The Scarecrow Author Bibliographies Ser.: No. 44). 303p. 1979. 25.00 (ISBN 0-8108-1232-0). Scarecrow.

--V. I. Lenin: An Annotated Bibliography of English-Language Sources to 1980. LC 82-659. 516p. 1982. 37.50 (ISBN 0-8108-1526-5). Scarecrow.

Egan, Desmond. Collected Poems. LC 83-62144. (Irish Art & Poets Ser.). (Illus.). 220p. 1983. 15.00 (ISBN 0-915032-17-1); pap. 8.95 (ISBN 0-915032-18-X). Natl Poet Foun.

Egan, Douglas. Ship Benjamin Sewall. 146p. 1983. 14.50 (ISBN 0-87770-297-7). Ye Galleon.

Egan, E. W., tr. see Cherrier, Francois.

Egan, E. W., tr. see Fronval, George & Dubois, Daniel.

Egan, E. W., tr. see Riviere, Marie-Claude.

Egan, Eileen. Such a Vision of the Street: Mother Teresa; The Spirit & The Work. LC 81-43570. (Illus.). 456p. 1985. 16.95 (ISBN 0-385-17490-X). Doubleday.

Egan, Ferol. The El Dorado Trail: The Story of the Gold Rush Routes Across Mexico. LC 83-16708. xvi, 313p. 1984. pap. 7.95 (ISBN 0-8032-6706-1, BB 863, Bison). U of Nebr Pr.

--Fremont: Explorer for a Restless Nation. (Vintage West Ser.). (Illus.). 582p. 1985. pap. 16.75 (ISBN 0-87417-096-6). U of Nev Pr.

--Sand in a Whirlwind: The Paiute Indian War 1860. (Vintage West Ser.). (Illus.). 316p. 1985. pap. 11.25 (ISBN 0-87417-097-4). U of Nev Pr.

--The Taste of Time. LC 76-48209. 1977. 9.95 (ISBN 0-07-019050-X). McGraw.

Egan, Frank. The Fairy Isle of Coosanure. (Illus.). 96p. (gr. 3-7). 1981. 7.95 (ISBN 0-905473-70-1, Pub. by Wolfhound Pr Ireland). Irish Bks Media.

Egan, Gerard. Change Agent Skills for the Helping & Human Service Professions. LC 84-7804. (Psychology Ser.). 384p. 1985. text ed. 17.00 pub. net (ISBN 0-534-03624-4). Brooks-Cole.

--Exercises in Helping Skills. 2nd ed. 1981. pap. 8.25 pub net (ISBN 0-8185-0480-3). Brooks-Cole.

--Face to Face: The Small Group Experience & Interpersonal Growth. LC 72-90673. (Orig.). 1973. pap. text ed. 9.50 pub net (ISBN 0-8185-0075-1). Brooks-Cole.

--Interpersonal Living: A Skills - Contract Approach to Human Relations Training in Groups. LC 76-6651. 1976. pap. text ed. 12.50 pub net (ISBN 0-8185-0189-8). Brooks-Cole.

--The Skilled Helper: A Model for Systematic Helping & Interpersonal Relating. 2nd ed. LC 74-82756. (Illus.). 1982. text ed. 18.00 pub net (ISBN 0-8185-0479-X); test items avail. (ISBN 0-685-52374-8). Brooks-Cole.

--The Skilled Helper: Model Skills & Methods for Effective Helping. 3rd ed. (Psychology Ser.). 384p. 1985. 25.00 (ISBN 0-534-05904-X). Brooks-Cole.

--You & Me: The Skills of Communicating & Relating to Others. LC 77-6475. (Illus.). 1977. pap. text ed. 11.75 pub net (ISBN 0-8185-0238-X). Brooks-Cole.

Egan, Gerard & Cowan, Michael A. Moving into Adulthood: Themes & Variations in Self--Directed Development for Effective Living. LC 80-15876. 288p. (Orig.). 1980. pap. text ed. 13.00 pub net (ISBN 0-8185-0406-4). Brooks-Cole.

Egan, H. & West, T. S., eds. Harmonization of Collaborative Analytical Studies: International Symposium on Harmonization of Collaborative Analytical Studies, Helsinki Finland, 20-21 September 1981. (IUPAC Symposium Ser.). (Illus.). 260p. 1982. pap. 44.00 (ISBN 0-08-026228-7). Pergamon.

Egan, Harold, jt. auth. see Schuller, Pieter L.

Egan, Harvey D. Christian Mysticism. 300p. (Orig.). 1984. pap. 14.95 (ISBN 0-916134-63-6). Pueblo Pub Co.

--The Spiritual Exercises & the Ignatian Mystical Horizon. LC 76-5742. (Study Aids on Jesuit Topics, Series 4: No. 5). xii, 216p. 1976. smyth sewn 7.00 (ISBN 0-912422-18-1); pap. 6.00 (ISBN 0-912422-14-9). Inst Jesuit.

--What Are They Saying about Mysticism? (WATSA Ser.). 128p. 1982. pap. 3.95 (ISBN 0-8091-2459-9). Paulist Pr.

Egan, Howard T. Gassendi's View of Knowledge: A Study of the Epistemological Basis of His Logic. LC 83-23345. 190p. (Orig.). 1984. lib. bdg. 24.25 (ISBN 0-8191-3737-5); pap. text ed. 13.25 (ISBN 0-8191-3738-3). U Pr of Amer.

Egan, Jack. Your Complete Guide to IRAs & Keoghs: The Simple, Safe Tax Deferred Way to Future Financial Security. LC 81-48152. 224p. 1982. 13.41i (ISBN 0-06-014975-2, HarpT). Har-Row.

Egan, James P. Signal Detection & ROC-Analysis. (Academic Press Ser. in Cognition & Perception). 1975. 49.00 (ISBN 0-12-232850-7). Acad Pr.

Egan, John, et al. Housing & Public Policy: A Role for Mediating Structures. LC 80-20940. 144p. 1981. prof ref 25.00 (ISBN 0-88410-827-9). Ballinger Pub.

Egan, John G., jt. auth. see Prentice, E. Parmalee.

Egan, John P. & Colford, Paul D. Baptism of Resistance-Blood & Celebration: A Road to Wholeness in the Nuclear Age. 1983. pap. 5.95 (ISBN 0-89622-164-4). Twenty-Third.

Egan, John W. Economics of the Pharmaceutical Industry. Higinbotham, Harlow N., et al, eds. LC 82-572. 218p. 1982. 32.95x (ISBN 0-03-061803-7). Praeger.

Egan, Joseph B. Donn Fendler Lost on a Mountain in Maine. LC 77-99178. (Illus.). 1978. 8.95 (ISBN 0-912274-92-1). NH Pub Co.

Egan, Katherine. Beginnings: The Orientation of New Teachers. 20p. 1981. 2.00 (ISBN 0-686-39892-0). Natl Cath Educ.

Egan, Kieran. Education & Psychology: Plato, Piaget & Scientific Psychology. (Orig.). 1983. 16.95x (ISBN 0-8077-2717-2). Tchrs Coll.

--Educational Development. 1979. pap. text ed. 6.95x (ISBN 0-19-502459-1). Oxford U Pr.

--Structural Communication. LC 74-83215. 1976. pap. text ed. 6.95 (ISBN 0-8224-6550-7). Pitman Learning.

Egan, Kieran, jt. auth. see Nyberg, David.

Egan, Lesley. Chain of Violence. LC 84-21158. (Crime Club Ser.). 192p. 1985. 12.95 (ISBN 0-385-19807-8). Doubleday.

--Crime for Christmas. LC 83-11511. (Crime Club Ser.). 192p. 1984. 11.95 (ISBN 0-385-19070-0). Doubleday.

--Little Boy Lost. LC 82-25166. (Crime Club Ser.). (Illus.). 192p. 1983. 11.95 (ISBN 0-385-18840-4). Doubleday.

--Random Death. (Nightingale Ser.). 1982. pap. 9.95 (ISBN 0-8161-3408-1, Large Print Bks). G K Hall.

--Wine of Life. LC 85-10118. (Crime Club Ser.). 192p. 1985. 12.95 (ISBN 0-385-23154-7). Doubleday.

Egan, M. Mark Twain's "Huckleberry Finn". Race, Class & Society. 15.00x (ISBN 0-686-97014-4, Pub. by Scottish Academic Pr Scotland). State Mutual Bk.

Egan, M. David. Concepts in Architectural Acoustics. (Illus.). 192p. 1972. text ed. 46.50 (ISBN 0-07-019053-4). McGraw.

--Concepts in Building Fire Safety. LC 77-12184. 264p. 1978. 42.95x (ISBN 0-471-02229-2, Pub. by Wiley-Interscience). Wiley.

--Concepts in Lighting for Architecture. LC 82-20832. (Illus.). 272p. 1983. 38.00 (ISBN 0-07-019054-2). McGraw.

--Concepts in Thermal Comfort. (Illus.). 224p. 1975. 26.95 (ISBN 0-13-166447-6). P-H.

Egan, M. Winston, jt. auth. see Landau, Elliott D.

Egan, Maurice. Recollections of a Happy Life. 1924. Repr. 20.00 (ISBN 0-8274-3254-2). R West.

Egan, Maurice F. Confessions of a Book-Lover. 1922. 20.00 (ISBN 0-8274-2090-0). R West.

--Ghost in Hamlet. LC 70-144602. Repr. of 1906 ed. 10.00 (ISBN 0-404-02264-2). AMS Pr.

--Ghost in Hamlet. facs. ed. LC 71-152167. (Essay Index Reprint Ser). 1906. 20.00 (ISBN 0-8369-2185-2). Ayer Co Pubs.

--The Ghost in Hamlet & Other Essays in Comparative Literature. 59.95 (ISBN 0-8490-0232-X). Gordon Pr.

--The Life of St. Francis & the Soul of Modern Man. (Illus.). 131p. 1983. 67.45x (ISBN 0-89266-427-4). Am Classical Coll Pr.

Egan, Melinda A., jt. auth. see Egan, David R.

Egan, Michael. Flying, Gray-Haired Yank: The Adventures of a Volunteer in the Civil War. Repr. of 1888 ed. 21.95 (ISBN 0-89201-114-9). Zenger Pub.

--Ibsen. (The Critical Heritage Ser.). 524p. 1985. pap. 15.00 (ISBN 0-7102-0592-9). Routledge & Kegan.

--Mark Twain's Huckleberry Finn: Race, Class & Society. (Text & Context Ser.). 1977. text ed. 9.75x (ISBN 0-391-00930-3); pap. text ed. 5.25x (ISBN 0-85621-061-7). Humanities.

Egan, Michael, jt. auth. see Craig, David.

Egan, Michael, ed. Henry James: The Ibsen Years. 154p. 1972. text ed. 13.00x (ISBN 0-85478-242-7). Humanities.

--Ibsen: The Critical Heritage. (Critical Heritage Ser). 1972. 38.50 (ISBN 0-7100-7255-4). Routledge & Kegan.

Egan, Michael E. & McMillan, Joseph P. Human Function: A Laboratory Manual. (Illus.). 1979. pap. text ed. 18.95 (ISBN 0-7216-3338-2, CBS C). SCP.

Egan, Patricia, tr. see Siochfhradha, Padraig O.

Egan, Patricia B. & Maran, Marie Y. This Way to Wall Street. LC 80-82137. (Illus.). 200p. 1980. pap. 9.95 (ISBN 0-937470-00-3); instructor's manual 5.95 (ISBN 0-937470-01-5). Market Ed.

Egan, Pierce. Life in London; or the Day & Night Scenes of Jerry Hawthorn, Esq. & Corinthian Tom. LC 79-8260. Repr. of 1821 ed. 44.50 (ISBN 0-404-61841-3). AMS Pr.

--The Pilgrims of the Thames in Search of the National! LC 79-8261. Repr. of 1838 ed. 44.50 (ISBN 0-404-61842-1). AMS Pr.

Egan, R. L. Technologist's Guide to Mammography. 120p. 8.75 (ISBN 0-318-12469-6). Am Coll Radiology.

Egan, Robert. Bookstore Book. 1979. pap. 5.95 (ISBN 0-380-46474-8, 46474-8). Avon.

--Drama Within Drama: Shakespeare's Sense of His Art in King Lear, The Winter's Tale, & The Tempest. LC 74-20943. 128p. 1975. 16.00x (ISBN 0-231-03919-0). Columbia U Pr.

--From Here to Fraternity. LC 85-4039. (Illus.). 288p. 1985. pap. 7.95 (ISBN 0-553-34193-6). Bantam.

Egan, Robert L. & McSweeney, Marjorie B. Breast Imaging. (Illus.). 256p. 1984. text ed. 35.00 (ISBN 0-8391-1887-2, 19526). Univ Park.

Egan, Robert S., ed. Topics Aids: Biology: A Catalog in Instructional Media for College Biology. LC 77-13587. 296p. 1978. pap. 5.00x (ISBN 0-89096-042-9). Tex A&M Univ Pr.

Egan, Ronald C. The Literary Works of Ou-Yang Hsiu (1007-72) (Cambridge Studies in Chinese History Literature & Institutions). (Illus.). 320p. 1984. 59.50 (ISBN 0-521-25888-X). Cambridge U Pr.

Egan, Rose F. Genesis of the Theory of Art for Art's Sake: In Germany & in England. LC 74-11067. 1921. lib. bdg. 10.00 (ISBN 0-8414-3948-6). Folcroft.

Egan, Susanna. Patterns of Experience in Autobiography. LC 83-12508. 240p. 1984. 19.95 (ISBN 0-8078-1581-0). U of NC Pr.

Egan, Walter G. & Hilgeman, Theodore W. Optical Properties of Inhomogeneous Materials: Applications to Geology, Astronomy, Chemistry & Engineering. LC 78-20043. 1979. 45.00 (ISBN 0-12-232650-4). Acad Pr.

Egan, William F. Frequency Synthesis by Phase-Lock. LC 80-16917. 279p. 1981. text ed. 42.95x (ISBN 0-471-08202-3, Pub. by Wiley-Interscience). Wiley.

Egar, Margaret, et al. Regeneration in Lower Vertebrates & Invertebrates, 3 vols, Vol. 2. LC 72-8249. 1973. 24.50x (ISBN 0-8422-7051-5). Irvington.

Egay, L. M., jt. ed. see Gomez, Q. J.

Egbert, jt. auth. see Schuurman.

Egbert, Barbara. Action Cheerleading. LC 84-8463. (Illus.). 128p. (gr. 9 up). 1984. 13.95 (ISBN 0-8069-4178-2); lib. bdg. 16.79 (ISBN 0-8069-4179-0); pap. text ed. 8.95 (ISBN 0-8069-7886-4). Sterling.

--Cheerleading & Songleading. LC 80-52322. (Illus.). 128p. (gr. 9 up). 1980. 13.95 (ISBN 0-8069-4626-1); PLB 16.79 (ISBN 0-8069-4627-X); pap. 8.95 (ISBN 0-8069-8950-5). Sterling.

--A Handbook of Physical Conditioning for Pregnant Women. LC 85-3617. (Parks & Recreation Ser.). (Illus.). 44p. (Orig.). 1985. pap. 9.95x (ISBN 0-942280-11-3). Pub Horizons.

Egbert, Donald D. The Beaux-Arts Tradition in French Architecture. Van Zanten, David, ed. LC 79-23798. (Illus.). 220p. 1980. 36.00x (ISBN 0-691-03943-7); pap. 15.50x LPE (ISBN 0-691-10106-X). Princeton U Pr.

Egbert, Donald D. & Persons, S. Socialism & American Life. Incl. Vol. 1. Text (ISBN 0-691-07521-2); Vol. 2. Bibliography. (American Civilization). 1952. 59.00x (ISBN 0-686-86671-1). Princeton U Pr.

Egbert, Donald D. & Persons, Stow, eds. Socialism & American Life: Bibliography - Descriptive & Critical, Vol. 2. LC 52-5828. (Princeton Studies in American Civilization: No. 4). pap. 147.30 (ISBN 0-317-08565-4, 2015480). Bks Demand UMI.

Egbert, Virginia W. The Mediaeval Artist at Work. LC 67-12344. (Illus.). pap. 23.50 (ISBN 0-317-10333-4, 2051010). Bks Demand UMI.

--On the Bridges of Medieval Paris: A Record of Early Fourteenth Century Life. (Illus.). 80p. 1974. text ed. 26.50 (ISBN 0-691-03906-2). Princeton U Pr.

Egbujie, Ihemalol I. The Hermeneutics of the African Traditional Culture: An Interpretative Analysis of African Culture. 175p. (Orig.). 1985. pap. 18.00 (ISBN 0-943324-15-7). Omenana.

Egdahl, R. H. Payer, Provider, Consumer: Industry Confronts Health Care Costs. LC 77-21020. (Springer Series in Industry & Health Care: No. 1). (Illus.). 1977. pap. 19.50 (ISBN 0-387-90295-3). Springer-Verlag.

Egdahl, R. H., ed. Background Papers on Industry's Changing Role in Health Care Delivery. LC 77-13611. (Springer Series on Industry & Health Care: No. 3). 1977. 45.00 (ISBN 0-387-90290-2). Springer-Verlag.

Egdahl, R. H. & Walsh, D. C., eds. Containing Health Benefit Costs: The Self-Insurance Option. (Springer Ser. on Industry & Health Care: Vol. 6). (Illus.). 1979. pap. 18.00 (ISBN 0-387-90385-2). Springer-Verlag.

--Health Services & Health Hazards: The Employee's Need to Know. LC 78-18241. (Springer Ser. on Industry & Health Care: Vol. 4). (Illus.). 1978. pap. 18.00 (ISBN 0-387-90335-6). Springer-Verlag.

--Industry & HMOs: A Natural Alliance. (Springer Ser. on Industry & Health Care: Vol. 5). (Illus.). 1978. pap. 18.00 (ISBN 0-387-90366-6). Springer-Verlag.

Egdahl, R. H., ed. see Wylie, E. J., et al.

Egdahl, Richard H. & Gertman, Paul M. Technology & the Quality of Health Care. LC 78-7307. 336p. 1978. text ed. 42.95 (ISBN 0-89443-025-4). Aspen Systems.

Egdahl, Richard H. & Gertman, Paul M., eds. Quality Assurance in Health Care. LC 76-15770. 372p. 1976. 42.95 (ISBN 0-912862-23-8). Aspen Systems.

--Quality Health Care: The Role of Continuing Medical Education. LC 77-70434. 276p. 1977. 41.95 (ISBN 0-912862-37-8). Aspen Systems.

Egdahl, Richard H. & Mannick, John A., eds. Modern Surgery. LC 76-92016. (Illus.). 1224p. 1970. 95.00 (ISBN 0-8089-0124-9, 791120). Grune.

Egdahl, Richard H. & Walsh, Diana C., eds. Corporate Medical Departments: A Changing Agenda. LC 82-22785. (Industry & Health Care Ser.: Vol. 1). 272p. 1983. prof ref 35.00x (ISBN 0-88410-167-3). Ballinger Pub.

--Industry & Health Care, Vol. 2: Health Cost Management & Medical Practice Patterns. 272p. 1985. professional reference 35.00 (ISBN 0-88410-175-4). Ballinger Pub.

Ege, Arvia M. The Experience of the Christmas Foundation Meeting, 1923. 14p. 1981. pap. 2.50 (ISBN 0-932776-03-5). Adonis Pr.

Ege, Otto F. Pre-Alphabet Days: The History of the Letters of the Alphabet. 1977. lib. bdg. 59.95 (ISBN 0-8490-2464-1). Gordon Pr.

Egeberg, Roger O. General MacArthur & the Man He Called "Doc". (Illus.). 256p. 1983. 12.95 (ISBN 0-88254-854-9). Hippocrene Bks.

Egede, H. P. A Description of Greenland. Repr. of 1818 ed. 30.00 (ISBN 0-527-26550-0). Kraus Repr.

Egede-Nissen, Lars, tr. see Grieg, Nordahl.

Egejuru, Phanuel. Origin & Survival of African Folktales in the New World. 1981. 8.95 (ISBN 0-933184-23-9); pap. 4.95 (ISBN 0-933184-24-7). Flame Intl.

Egejuru, Phanuel A. Black Writers-White Audience: A Critical Approach to African Literature. 1978. 12.50 (ISBN 0-682-48977-8, University). Exposition Pr FL.

--Black Writers, White Audience: A Critical Approach to African Literature. LC 77-94306. (Exposition-University Book Ser.). pap. 63.80 (ISBN 0-317-29168-8, 2055581). Bks Demand UMI.

--Towards African Literary Independence: A Dialogue with Contemporary African Writers. LC 79-6188. (Contributions in Afro-American & African Studies: No. 53). vii, 173p. 1980. lib. bdg. 29.95 (ISBN 0-313-22310-6, EAL/). Greenwood.

Egeland, A., jt. auth. see Brekke, A.

Egeland, Alv, jt. ed. see Anstein Holtet, Jan.

Egeland, Alv, et al, eds. Cosmical Geophysics. (Illus.). 360p. 1973. 33.50x (ISBN 8-200-02256-0, Dist. by Columbia U Pr). Universitet.

Egelkraut, Helmuth L. Jesus' Mission to Jerusalem: Theology, Vol. 80. (European University Studies: Ser. 23). x, 258p. 1976. pap. 28.70 (ISBN 3-261-02133-0). P Lang Pubs.

Egelstaff, P. A. & Poole, M. J. Experimental Neutron Thermalization. LC 79-86201. 1969. 72.00 (ISBN 0-08-006533-3). Pergamon.

Egelston, Roberta R. Career Planning Materials. LC 81-12801. 190p. 1981. 20.00x (ISBN 0-8389-0343-6). ALA.

--Credits & Careers for Adult Learners. LC 84-42834. (Illus.). 160p. 1985. pap. 19.95 (ISBN 0-89950-188-5). McFarland & Co.

Egendorf, Arthur. Healing from the War: Trauma & Transformation after Vietnam. 364p. 1985. 15.95 (ISBN 0-395-37701-3). HM.

Egenter, Nold. Goettersitz aus Schilf und Bambus. (Schweitzer Asiatische Studien: Vol. 4). (Illus.). 152p. 1982. 28.95 (ISBN 3-261-04821-2). P Lang Pubs.

Egenter, Richard. Desecration of Christ. 1967. 4.50 (ISBN 0-8199-0018-4, L38133). Franciscan Herald.

Egenter, Richard & Matussek, Paul. Moral Problems & Mental Health. 1967. 4.95 (ISBN 0-8189-0095-4). Alba.

Egenton, Judy, intro. by. Stubbs: Portraits in Detail. (Illus.). 48p. 1985. pap. 8.95 (ISBN 0-946590-17-6, Pub by Salem Hse Ltd). Merrimack Pub Cir.

Eger, Edith E. Coping & Growth: A Theoretical & Empirical Study for Groups Under Moderate to Severe Stress. (Holocaust Studies Ser.). 1985. text ed. 22.50x (ISBN 0-8290-0292-8). Irvington.

Eger, Edmond I., II, ed. Nitrous Oxide. 416p. 1984. 37.50 (ISBN 0-444-00860-8). Elsevier.

Eger, Ernestina N. A Bibliography of Criticism of Contemporary Chicano Literature. (Chicano Studies Library Publication: No. 5). 295p. (Orig.). 1982. lib. bdg. 25.50x (ISBN 0-918520-03-7); pap. text ed. 16.50x (ISBN 0-918520-02-9). UC Chicano.

Eger, Jeffrey. The Statue in the Harbor: A Story of Two Apprentices. LC 85-61511. (Illus.). 96p. (gr. 4-8). 1985. PLB 7.95 (ISBN 0-382-09145-0); pap. 4.75 (ISBN 0-382-09146-9). Silver.

Eger, Jeffrey, intro. by. The Statue of Liberty Enlightening the World. (Illus.). 66p. 1984. pap. 7.95 (ISBN 0-9608788-5-8). NY Bound.

Egerer, Marlene M. Enrich Your Child's Speech & Language Development. 21p. 1975. pap. text ed. 0.50 (ISBN 0-8134-1726-0, 1726). Interstate.

Egerer, Marlene M. & Frank, Myra G. Holiday Articulation Activities. 1974. text ed. 10.95x (ISBN 0-8134-1630-2). Interstate.

Egermann, Franz. Vom Attischen Menschenbild & Arete und Tragisches Bewusstheit Bei Sophokles und Herodot, 2 vols. in ne. Vlastos, Gregory, ed. LC 78-14613. (Morals & Law in Ancient Greece Ser.). (Ger. & Greek.). 1979. Repr. of 1957 ed. lib. bdg. 21.00x (ISBN 0-405-11588-1). Ayer Co Pubs.

Egermeier, Elsie E. Egermeier's Bible Story Book. 5th ed. LC 68-23397. (Illus.). (gr. k-6). 1969. 14.95 (ISBN 0-87162-006-5, D2005); deluxe ed. 15.95 (ISBN 0-87162-007-3, D2006); pap. 8.95 (ISBN 0-87162-229-7, D2008). Warner Pr.

--Egermeier's Favorite Bible Stories. (gr. k-1). 1965. 7.95 (ISBN 0-87162-014-6, D3695). Warner Pr.

--Egermeier's Picture-Story Life of Jesus. (Illus.). (gr. k-6). 1969. 7.95 (ISBN 0-87162-008-1, D2015). Warner Pr.

--Picture Story Bible ABC Book. rev. ed. (Illus.). (ps-1). 1963. 5.95 (ISBN 0-87162-262-9, D1703). Warner Pr.

Egerod, Soren. Atayal-English Dictionary, 2 vols. (Scandinavian Institute of Asian Studies Monograph: No. 35). 830p. (Atayal & Eng.). 1981. Set. pap. text ed. 41.75x (ISBN 0-7007-0117-6, Pub. by Curzon Pr England); Vol. 1. pap. text ed. (ISBN 0-7007-0118-4); Vol. 2. pap. text ed. (ISBN 0-7007-0119-2). Humanities.

Egert, Eugene. The Holy Spirit in German Literature Until the Twelfth Century. (Studies in German Literature: No. 13). 1973. text ed. 30.00x (ISBN 90-2792-410-4). Mouton.

Egerton, Alix. Milton's Comus: Being the Bridgewater Manuscript. LC 73-14760. 1910. lib. bdg. 20.00 (ISBN 0-8414-3914-1). Folcroft.

Egerton, Clement, tr. from Chinese. The Golden Lotus: A Translation of the Chinese Novel, Chin P'ing Mei, 4 vols. 1572p. 1972. Set. 80.00 (ISBN 0-7100-7349-6); 22.00 ea. Routledge & Kegan.

Egerton, F. C. Salazar. 59.95 (ISBN 0-8490-0988-X). Gordon Pr.

Egerton, F. Clement. Angola in Perspective: Endeavour. LC 73-9706. 288p. 1973. Repr. of 1967 ed. 35.00 (ISBN 0-527-26600-0). Kraus Repr.

Egerton, Francis. Egerton Papers. Collier, J. Payne, ed. LC 74-164767. (Camden Society, London. Publications, First Ser.: No. 12). Repr. of 1840 ed. 51.00 (ISBN 0-404-50112-5). AMS Pr.

Egerton, Frank, ed. see Forbush, Edward H. & Fernald, Charles H.

Egerton, Frank N., ed. American Plant Ecology, Eighteen Ninety-Seven to Nineteen Seventeen: An Original Anthology. LC 77-74202. (History of Ecology Ser.). (Illus.). 1978. lib. bdg. 59.50x (ISBN 0-405-10372-7). Ayer Co Pubs.

--Early Marine Ecology: An Original Anthology. LC 77-74216. (History of Ecology Ser.). 1978. lib. bdg. 37.50x (ISBN 0-405-10386-7). Ayer Co Pubs.

--Ecological Investigations of Stephen Alfred Forbes: An Original Anthology. LC 77-74217. (History of Ecology Ser.). 1978. lib. bdg. 53.00x (ISBN 0-405-10387-5). Ayer Co Pubs.

--Ecological Phytogeography in the Nineteenth Century: An Original Anthology. LC 77-74218. (History of Ecology Ser.). 1978. lib. bdg. 51.00x (ISBN 0-405-10388-3). Ayer Co Pubs.

--Ecological Studies on Insect Parasitism: An Original Anthology. LC 77-73820. (History of Ecology Ser.). 1978. lib. bdg. 24.50x (ISBN 0-405-10389-1). Ayer Co Pubs.

--Natural History, General & Particulor: An Original Anthology, 2 vols. LC 77-74206. (History of Ecology Ser.). (Illus.). 1978. Set. lib. bdg. 99.00x (ISBN 0-405-10376-X). Ayer Co Pubs.

Egerton, Frank N., ed. see Clements, Frederic E.

Egerton, Frank N., ed. see Greene, Edward L.

Egerton, Frank N., ed. see Meyen, Franz J.

Egerton, Frank N., ed. see Van Leeuwenhoek, Antony.

Egerton, Frank N., 3rd, ed. History of American Ecology: An Original Anthology. LC 77-74229. (History of Ecology Ser.). 1978. lib. bdg. 36.50x (ISBN 0-405-10399-9). Ayer Co Pubs.

--History of Ecology Series, 52 bks. 1978. lib. bdg. 1360.00x (ISBN 0-405-10369-7). Ayer Co Pubs.

--Limnology in Wisconsin: An Original Anthology. LC 77-74203. (History of Ecology Ser.). (Illus.). 1978. lib. bdg. 57.50x (ISBN 0-405-10373-5). Ayer Co Pubs.

--Phytopathological Classics of the Eighteenth Century: An Original Anthology. LC 77-74247. (History of Ecology Ser.). (Illus.). 1978. lib. bdg. 47.50x (ISBN 0-405-10416-2). Ayer Co Pubs.

--Phytopathologlical Classics of the Nineteenth Century: An Original Anthology. LC 77-74246. (History of Ecology Ser.). (Illus.). 1978. lib. bdg. 34.50x (ISBN 0-405-10415-4). Ayer Co Pubs.

Egerton, Frank N., 3rd, ed. see Abee, Cleveland.

Egerton, Frank N., 3rd, ed. see Browne, Charles A.

Egerton, Frank N., 3rd, ed. see Chapman, Royal N.

Egerton, Frank N., 3rd, ed. see Conard, Henry S.

Egerton, Frank N., 3rd, ed. see De Reaumur, Rene A. F.

Egerton, Frank N., 3rd, ed. see Derham, William.

Egerton, Frank N., 3rd, ed. see Drude, Oscar.

Egerton, Frank N., 3rd, ed. see Espinas, Alfred V.

Egerton, Frank N., 3rd, ed. see Fernow, Bernhard E., et al.

Egerton, Frank N., 3rd, ed. see Forbes, Edward & Godwin-Austen, Robert.

Egerton, Frank N., 3rd, ed. see Forel, Francois A.

Egerton, Frank N., 3rd, ed. see Henfrey, Arthur.

Egerton, Frank N., 3rd, ed. see Herrick, Francis H.

Egerton, Frank N., 3rd, ed. see Howard, Leland O. & Fiske, William F.

Egerton, Frank N., 3rd, ed. see Johnstone, James.

Egerton, Frank N., 3rd, ed. see Judd, Sylvester D.

Egerton, Frank N., 3rd, ed. see Kofoid, Charles A.

Egerton, Frank N., 3rd, ed. see Linnaeus, Carl.

Egerton, Frank N., 3rd, ed. see Mills, Harlow B., et al.

Egerton, Frank N., 3rd, ed. see Muller, Hermann.

Egerton, Frank N., 3rd, ed. see Murray, John.

Egerton, Frank N., 3rd, ed. see Murray, John & Pullar, Laurence.

Egerton, Frank N., 3rd, ed. see Packard, Alpheus S.

Egerton, Frank N., 3rd, ed. see Pearl, Raymond.

Egerton, Frank N., 3rd, ed. see Pound, Roscoe & Clements, Frederic E.

Egerton, Frank N., 3rd, ed. see Raunkiaer, Christen.

Egerton, Frank N., 3rd, ed. see Ray, John.

Egerton, Frank N., 3rd, ed. see Semper, Karl.

Egerton, Frank N., 3rd, ed. see Shelford, Victor E.

Egerton, Frank N., 3rd, ed. see Von Humboldt, Alexander.

Egerton, Frank N., 3rd, ed. see Warming, Eugenius & Vahl, Martin.

Egerton, Frank N., 3rd, ed. see Watson, Hewett C.

Egerton, Frank N., 3rd, ed. see Whetzel, Herbert H.
Egerton, Frank N., 3rd, ed. see Whittaker, Robert H.
Egerton, Frank, 3rd, ed. see Clements, Frederic E.
Egerton, George. Keynotes. Fletcher, Ian & Stokes, John, eds. LC 76-24384. (Decadent Consciousness Ser.). 1978. lib. bdg. 46.00 (ISBN 0-8240-2758-2). Garland Pub.
Egerton, George, pseud. The Wheel of God. LC 79-8263. Repr. of 1898 ed. 44.50 (ISBN 0-686-63604-X). AMS Pr.
Egerton, George W. Great Britain & the Creation of the League of Nations: Strategy, Politics, & International Organization, 1914-1919. LC 77-17897. xiii, 273p. (Supplementary Volume to The Papers of Woodrow Wilson). 1978. 22.50x (ISBN 0-8078-1320-6). U of NC Pr.
Egerton, Hugh E. Origin & Growth of the English Colonies & Their System of Government. LC 77-89023. Repr. of 1903 ed. cancelled (ISBN 0-8371-1900-6). Greenwood.
--A Short History of British Colonial Policy, 1606-1909. 9th ed. LC 74-15035. Repr. of 1932 ed. 42.50 (ISBN 0-404-12040-7). AMS Pr.
Egerton, Hugh E., ed. see Coke, Daniel P.
Egerton, John. The Bottom Line, about Hemorrhoids, Fissures & Fistulas. Hull, Nancy R., ed. (Illus.). 32p. (Orig.). 1985. pap. text ed. 4.00 (ISBN 0-939838-18-4). Pritchett & Hull.
--Generations: An American Family. LC 82-40465. (Illus.). 272p. 1983. 20.00 (ISBN 0-8131-1482-9). U Pr of Ky.
--Visions of Utopia: Nashoba, Rugby, Ruskin, & the "New Communities" in Tennessee's Past. LC 77-1509. (Tennessee Three Star Bks Ser). (Illus.). 1977. pap. 3.50x (ISBN 0-87049-213-6); 8.50 (ISBN 0-87049-294-2). U of Tenn Pr.
Egerton, John, jt. auth. see Center for Equal Education.
Egerton, Mike. Teaching: The New Challenge-Willingly to School. 127p. 1982. 30.00x (ISBN 0-85225-756-2, Pub. by Careers Con England). State Mutual Bk.
Egerton Philip De, Malpas Grey see Grey De Wilton, Arthur G.
Egerton-Thomas, Christopher. Royal Singles. (Illus.). 176p. (Orig.). 1985. pap. 9.95 (ISBN 0-671-49634-4, Fireside). S&S.
Egetkaroff, M. Terror by Night & Day. (Destiny Ser.). 1980. pap. 4.95 (ISBN 0-686-78675-0). Pacific Pr Pub Assn.
Eggan, Fred. The American Indian: Perspectives for the Study of Social Change. LC 80-67926. (Lewis Henry Morgan Lectures). 192p. 1981. 34.50 (ISBN 0-521-23752-1); pap. 9.95 (ISBN 0-521-28210-1). Cambridge U Pr.
--Essays in Social Anthropology & Ethnology. LC 75-37810. (Univ. of Chicago Studies in Anthropology Ser in Social, Cultural, & Linguistic Anthropology: No. 1). (Illus.). 352p. 1975. pap. 7.00 (ISBN 0-916256-00-6). U Chi Dept Anthro.
--Social Organization of the Western Pueblos. LC 50-9388. (Illus.). 1950. 12.50x (ISBN 0-226-19075-7). U of Chicago Pr.
--Social Organization of the Western Pueblos. LC 50-9388. 1973. pap. 2.95x (ISBN 0-226-19076-5, P557, Phoen). U of Chicago Pr.
Eggan, Fred, et al. Social Anthropology of North American Tribes. enl. ed. LC 55-5123. 574p. 1972. pap. text ed. 3.95 (ISBN 0-226-19074-9, P473, Phoen). U of Chicago Pr.
Eggan, Lawrence C. & Vanden Eynden, Charles. Mathematics: Models & Applications. 1979. text ed. 22.95 (ISBN 0-669-01051-0); instr's manual 1.95 (ISBN 0-669-01052-9). Heath.
Egge, Marion F., jt. auth. see Beidler, Peter G.
Eggebrecht, H., jt. auth. see Gurlitt, W.
Eggebrecht, Hans H., jt. auth. see Dahlhaus, Carl.
Eggebrecht, Lewis C. Interfacing to the IBM Personal Computer. LC 83-61065. 272p. 1983. pap. 15.95 (ISBN 0-672-22027-X, 22027). Sams.
Eggeling, J. & Windisch, E. Catalofue of the Sanskrit Manuscripts in the Library of the India Office: Sanskrit Literature, Vol. 1, Pts. 5-7. 1628p. (Orig.). 1904. pap. 7.50 (ISBN 0-7123-0608-0, Pub by British Lib). Longwood Pub Group.
Eggeling, Julius. The Satapatha Brahmana. (Sacred Bks. of the East: Vols. 12, 26, 41, 43, 44). 5 vols. 90.00 (ISBN 0-686-97483-2); 18.00 ea. Asian Human Pr.
Eggeling, Julius, ed. The Satapatha Brahmana, 5 vols. 1974. lib. bdg. 500.00 (ISBN 0-8490-0994-4). Gordon Pr.
Eggen, Paul, jt. auth. see Kauchak, Donald P.
Eggen, Paul, et al. Strategies for Teachers: Information Processing Models in the Classroom. (Curriculum & Teaching Ser.). (Illus.). 1979. ref. ed. 27.95 (ISBN 0-13-851162-4). P-H.
Eggenberger, David. An Encyclopedia of Battles: Accounts of Over 1,560 Battles from 1479 B. C. to the Present. 544p. 1985. pap. 12.50 (ISBN 0-486-24913-1). Dover.
Eggenschwiler, David. The Christian Humanism of Flannery O'Connor. LC 79-179560. 156p. 1972. 9.95x (ISBN 0-8143-1463-5). Wayne St U Pr.
Eggenstein, Kurt. The Unknown Prophet-Jakob Lorber. 78p. (Orig.). 1979. pap. 3.50 (ISBN 0-912760-99-0). Valkyrie Pub Hse.
Egger, E. L' Hellenisme En France, 2 Vols. 1964. Repr. of 1869 ed. 50.50 (ISBN 0-8337-1022-2). B Franklin.
Egger, Eugrure, jt. auth. see Blanc, Emile.
Egger, Michael L., jt. auth. see Menolascino, Frank J.
Egger, N., jt. ed. see Rhodes, C. K.
Eggerer, H. & Hiber, R., eds. Structural & Functional Aspects of Enzyme Catalysis. (Colloquium Mosbach Ser.: Vol. 32). (Illus.). 280p. 1981. 33.00 (ISBN 0-387-11110-7). Springer-Verlag.
Eggers, John. Will You Help Me Create the Future Today? (a Guide to Making It Happen) (Illus.). 172p. (Orig.). 1981. pap. 10.95 (ISBN 0-914634-84-4). DOK Pubs.
Eggers, Lois A., et al. Sandy. Wheeler, Gerald, ed. (Banner Ser.). 96p. (Orig.). 1985. pap. 5.95 (ISBN 0-8280-0235-5). Review & Herald.
Eggers, Mayer. Ernest Cassirer: An Annotated Bibliography. 1985. lib. bdg. 35.00 (ISBN 0-8240-8992-8). Garland Pub.
Eggers, Ortrud. Occupational Therapy in Treatment of Adult Hemiplegia. 159p. 1984. 28.95 (ISBN 0-89443-823-9). Aspen Systems.
Eggers, Philip. Process & Practice: A Guide to Basic Writing. 1986. pap. 11.95x (ISBN 0-673-15908-6). Scott F.
Eggers, W. J., tr. see Huldermann, Berhnard.
Eggers-Lura, A. Solar Energy for Domestic Heating & Cooling. 1979. 89.00 (ISBN 0-08-022152-1). Pergamon.
--Solar Energy in Developing Countries. 1979. 72.00 (ISBN 0-08-023253-1). Pergamon.
Eggert, Arthur A. Electronics & Instrumentation for the Clinical Laboratory. LC 83-10524. 432p. 1983. 26.95x (ISBN 0-471-86275-4, Pub. by Wiley Med). Wiley.
Eggert, Bernice. It's Not Nice Being a Bitch. 1983. 4.95 (ISBN 0-934860-29-7). Adventure Pubns.
Eggert, Gerald G. Richard Olney: Evolution of a Statesman. LC 73-6878. (Illus.). 432p. 1974. 27.50x (ISBN 0-271-01162-9). Pa St U Pr.
--Steelmasters & Labor Reform, 1886-1923. LC 81-50636. 229p. 1981. 21.95x (ISBN 0-8229-3801-4). U of Pittsburgh Pr.
Eggert, Jim. Invitation to Economics: A Friendly Guide Through the Thickets of "The Dismal Science". (Illus.). 334p. 1984. pap. 9.95 (ISBN 0-86576-046-2); pap. 7.95 student study guide. W Kaufmann.
--Low Cost Earth Shelters. LC 81-18244. 160p. (Orig.). 1982. pap. 7.95 (ISBN 0-8117-2126-4). Stackpole.
Egghe, L. Stopping Time Techniques for Analysts & Probabilists: London Mathematical Society Lecture. 367p. 1985. pap. 29.95 (ISBN 0-521-31715-0). Cambridge U Pr.
Eggink, Harry & Laseau, Paul. Visual Communications Media Handbook. (Illus.). 31p. (Orig.). 1982. pap. 3.00 (ISBN 0-912431-02-4). Ctr Env Des Res.
Egginton, Don A., jt. auth. see Amev, Lloyd R.
Egginton, Joyce. The Poisoning of Michigan. (Illus.). 1980. 13.95 (ISBN 0-393-01347-2). Norton.
Egginton, Mary, et al. The Older Woman's Health Guide. 272p. 1984. 16.95 (ISBN 0-07-042424-1). McGraw.
Eggland, Steven A. Exploring Marketing & Distribution Careers. (gr. 9-12). 1984. text ed. 6.95 (ISBN 0-538-25430-0, Y43). SW Pub.
Eggland, Steven A. & Williams, John W. Human Relations at Work. (gr. 9-12). 1981. text ed. 6.40 wkbk. (ISBN 0-538-07370-5, G37). SW Pub.
Eggland, Steven A., jt. auth. see Williams, John W.
Eggleston. The Hoosier Schoolmaster. (American Classics Ser.). (gr. 9-12). 1977. pap. text ed. 3.99 (ISBN 0-88343-410-5); tchrs'. manual o.p. 1.89 (ISBN 0-88343-411-3); cassettes o.p. 49.00 (ISBN 0-88343-424-5). McDougal-Littell.
--Sensitometry for Photographers. 1985. 69.95 (ISBN 0-240-51144-1). Focal Pr.
Eggleston, Deryck J., jt. auth. see Nally, Fergal F.
Eggleston, Edward. The Beginners of a Nation: A History of the Source & Rise of the Earliest English Settlements in America. LC 2-11842. (American Studies). 1970. Repr. of 1896 ed. 30.00 (ISBN 0-384-13960-4). Johnson Repr.
--The Circuit Rider. Randel, William, ed. (Masterworks of Literature Ser). 1966. 8.95x (ISBN 0-8084-0077-0); pap. 5.95x (ISBN 0-8084-0078-9). New Coll U Pr.
--The Circuit Rider. LC 77-104768. (Novel As American Social History Ser.). 344p. 1970. 28.00x (ISBN 0-8131-1209-5); pap. 9.00x (ISBN 0-8131-0133-6). U Pr of Ky.
--The Circuit Rider: A Tale of the Heroic Age. Repr. of 1878 ed. 10.25 (ISBN 0-8446-1167-0). Peter Smith.
--The Circuit Rider: A Tale of the Heroic Age. 15.95 (ISBN 0-88411-529-1, Pub. by Aeonian Pr). Amereon Ltd.
--Collected Works, 12 vols. Incl. Mister Blake's Walking Stick. 1870. Repr. 18.00 (ISBN 0-686-01753-6); The Book of Queer Stories & Stories Told on a Cellar Door. 1871. Repr. 18.00 (ISBN 0-403-04578-9); The Hoosier School Master. 1871. Repr. 18.00 (ISBN 0-403-03052-8); The End of the World. 1872. Repr. 22.00 (ISBN 0-403-04579-7); The Mystery of Metropolisville. 1873. Repr. 17.00x (ISBN 0-403-02977-5); The Circuit Rider. 1874. Repr. 29.00x (ISBN 0-403-02989-9); The Schoolmaster's Stories for Boys & Girls. 1874. Repr. 39.00 (ISBN 0-403-03052-8); The Hoosier Schoolboy. 1883. Repr. 29.00x (ISBN 0-403-04580-0); Roxy. 1878. Repr. 38.00 (ISBN 0-403-04581-9); The Graysons. 1888. Repr. 23.00x (ISBN 0-403-00207-9); The Faith Doctor. 1891. Repr. 34.00 (ISBN 0-403-04582-7); Duffels. 1893. Repr. 22.00 (ISBN 0-403-03158-3). Set. 450.00 (ISBN 0-403-03456-6). Somerset Pub.
--End of the World: A Love Story. LC 75-94925. (BCL Ser. I). (Illus.). Repr. of 1872 ed. 24.50 (ISBN 0-404-02266-9). AMS Pr.
--The Faith Doctor. LC 68-20011. (Americans in Fiction Ser.). lib. bdg. 16.00 (ISBN 0-8398-0453-9); pap. text ed. 4.95x (ISBN 0-89197-755-4). Irvington.
--The First of the Hoosiers. 1903. lib. bdg. 25.00 (ISBN 0-8414-3889-7). Folcroft.
--Graysons: A Story of Illinois. LC 70-129335. Repr. of 1888 ed. 25.00 (ISBN 0-404-02267-7). AMS Pr.
--The Hoosier School Boy. 13.95 (ISBN 0-89190-418-2, Pub. by Am Repr). Amereon Ltd.
--The Hoosier Schoolmaster. 1899. lib. bdg. 20.00 (ISBN 0-8414-3890-0). Folcroft.
--The Hoosier Schoolmaster. rev. ed. Dixson, Robert J., ed. (American Classics Ser.: Bk. 6). (gr. 9 up). 1974. pap. text ed. 3.80 (ISBN 0-88345-202-2, 18125); cassettes 45.00 (ISBN 0-685-38929-4, 58227). Regents Pub.
--The Hoosier Schoolmaster. LC 83-49054. (Illus.). 240p. 1984. 15.00x (ISBN 0-253-32850-0); pap. 5.95x (ISBN 0-253-20324-4). Ind U Pr.
--The Hoosier Schoolmaster. 14.95 (ISBN 0-89190-419-0, Pub. by Am Repr). Amereon ltd.
--The Mystery of Metropolisville. 320p. 1981. Repr. of 1873 ed. lib. bdg. 45.00 (ISBN 0-89987-210-7). Darby Bks.
--The Mystery of Metropolisville. LC 70-104446. (Illus.). 320p. Repr. of 1873 ed. lib. bdg. 18.50 (ISBN 0-8398-0454-7). Irvington.
--Queer Stories for Boys & Girls. LC 77-89717. (Children's Literature Reprint Ser.). (gr. 4-7). 16.50x (ISBN 0-8486-0214-5). Core Collection.
--Roxy. LC 68-20010. (Americans in Fiction Ser.). (Illus.). lib. bdg. 16.50 (ISBN 0-8398-0455-5); pap. text ed. 4.95x (ISBN 0-89197-926-3). Irvington.
--The Transit of Civilization from England to America in the 17th Century. (Illus.). 344p. 1981. Repr. of 1901 ed. lib. bdg. 50.00 (ISBN 0-89984-183-X). Century Bookbindery.
--Transit of Civilization from England to America in the Seventeenth Century. 10.75 (ISBN 0-8446-2025-4). Peter Smith.
--Ultimate Solution of the American Negro Problem. LC 78-144604. Repr. of 1913 ed. 22.50 (ISBN 0-404-00155-6). AMS Pr.
Eggleston, Edward & Seeyle, Lillie E. Tecumseh & the Shawnee Prophet. 327p. 1981. Repr. of 1878 ed. lib. bdg. 50.00 (ISBN 0-89987-211-5). Darby Bks.
Eggleston, George C. A Carolina Cavalier: A Romance of the American Revolution. 448p. 1983. lib. bdg. 35.00 (ISBN 0-89760-217-X). Telegraph Bks.
--The First of the Hoosiers. LC 72-78694. 1903. Repr. 24.00x (ISBN 0-403-02076-X). Somerset Pub.
--History of the Confederate War. LC 70-100289. Repr. of 1910 ed. 31.00x (ISBN 0-8371-2926-5, EGC&, Pub. by Negro U Pr). Greenwood.
--Man of Honor. facs. ed. (American Fiction Reprint Ser). 1873. 18.00 (ISBN 0-8369-7027-6). Ayer Co Pubs.
--Rebel's Recollections. LC 58-12205. (Indiana University Civil War Centennial Ser.). 1968. Repr. of 1959 ed. 16.00 (ISBN 0-527-26640-X). Kraus Repr.
--Red Eagle & the Wars with the Creek Indians of Alabama. LC 76-43695. Repr. of 1878 ed. 22.50 (ISBN 0-404-15528-6). AMS Pr.
Eggleston, George C., ed. American War Ballads & Lyrics, 2 vols. 250.00 (ISBN 0-87968-612-X). Gordon Pr.
--American War Ballads & Lyrics, Vol. II. LC 77-94084. (Granger Poetry Library). (Illus.). 286p. 1982. Repr. of 1889 ed. 24.75x (ISBN 0-89609-230-5). Granger Bk.
--American War Ballads & Lyrics, Vol.I. LC 77-94084. (Granger Poetry Library). (Illus.). 1978. Repr. of 1889 ed. 24.50x (ISBN 0-89609-083-3). Granger Bk.
Eggleston, George T. Roosevelt, Churchill, & the World War II Opposition. LC 79-1727. (Illus.). 1979. text ed. 12.95 (ISBN 0-8159-5311-9). Devin.
--Virgin Islands. rev. ed. LC 59-14615. 226p. 1973. Repr. of 1959 ed. 14.50 (ISBN 0-88275-087-9). Krieger.
Eggleston, H. G. Convexity. (Cambridge Tracts in Mathematics & Mathematical Physics: No. 47). 1958. 24.95 (ISBN 0-521-07734-6). Cambridge U Pr.
Eggleston, Hazel. Saint Lucia Diary. 1977. pap. 10.00 (ISBN 0-8159-6839-6). Devin.
Eggleston, Jerry, ed. see ASCE Conference, Irrigation & Drainage Division, 1980.
Eggleston, John. The Sociology of the School Curriculum. 1977. pap. 10.95x (ISBN 0-7100-8566-4). Routledge & Kegan.
Eggleston, John, ed. Contemporary Research in the Sociology of Education. 1974. pap. 12.95x (ISBN 0-416-78790-8, NO.2177). Methuen Inc.
--Work Experience in Secondary Schools. (Routledge Education Bks.). 192p. 1983. 21.50x (ISBN 0-7100-9219-9). Routledge & Kegan.
Eggleston, John, ed. see European Research in Curriculum & Evaluation, a Report of the European Contact Workshop Held in Austria in December 1976 by the Committee for the Educational Research of the Council of Europe Council for Cultural Cooperation.
Eggleston, Richard. Evidence, Proof & Probability. 2nd ed. (Law in Context Ser.). xiv, 274p. 1983. 32.50x (ISBN 0-297-78262-2, Pub by Weidenfeld & Nicolson). Rothman.
Eggleston, S. J. Adolescence & Community: The Youth Service in Britain. 1976. 27.50x (ISBN 0-7131-5886-7). Intl Ideas.
Eggleston, Suzie, jt. ed. see Seixas, Frank A.
Eggleston, Suzie, ed. see Seixas, Frank A.
Eggleston, Suzie, jt. ed. see Seixas, Frank A.
Eggleston, Suzie, ed. see Sexias, Frank A.
Eggleston, Wilfrid. The Road to Nationhood: A Chronicle of Dominion-Provincial Relations. LC 70-147218. 337p. 1972. Repr. of 1946 ed. lib. bdg. 17.75x (ISBN 0-8371-5983-0, EGRN). Greenwood.
Eggleston, William, et al, illus. Aperture 96. (Illus.). 80p. 1984. pap. 12.50 (ISBN 0-89381-151-3). Aperture.
Eggleton, Chris, ed. see Pope, J. K.
Eggleton, John E. Discovering the Old Testament. 306p. 1980. Repr. pap. text ed. 7.95 (ISBN 0-933656-07-6). Trinity Pub Hse.
Eggleton, P., et al, eds. Structure & Evolution of Close Binary Systems. LC 76-21688. (Symposium of the International Astronomical Union Ser.: No. 73). 1976. lib. bdg. 55.00 (ISBN 90-277-0682-4, Pub. by Reidel Holland); pap. 45.00 (ISBN 90-277-0683-2). Kluwer Academic.
Eggleton, P. P. & Pringle, J. E., eds. Interacting Binaries. 1985. lib. bdg. 59.00 (ISBN 90-277-1966-7, Pub. by Reidel Holland). Kluwer Academic.
Egglishaw, John J., tr. see Hansen, Martin A.
Eggo, Margaret C. & Burrow, Gerard N., eds. Thyroglobulin: The Prothyroid Hormone. (Progress in Endocrine Research & Therapy Ser.: Vol. 2). 360p. 1985. text ed. 64.50 (ISBN 0-88167-073-1). Raven.
Eggold, Henry J. Preaching Is Dialogue. 144p. 1980. pap. 5.95 (ISBN 0-8010-3358-6). Baker Bk.
Eggspuehler, Jack, intro. by see Taylor, Richard L.
Eggum, Arne. Edvard Munch: Paintings, Sketches & Studies. (Illus.). 306p. 1985. write for info. (ISBN 0-517-55617-0, C N Potter). Crown.
Eggum, Arne, jt. auth. see Elderfield, John.
Eggwertz, S. & Lind, N. C., eds. Probabilistic Methods in the Mechanics of Solids & Structures. (International Union of Theoretical & Applied Mechanics Ser.). (Illus.). xxiv, 610p. 1985. 51.00 (ISBN 0-387-15087-0). Springer-Verlag.
Eghishse. Vasn Vardanay Ew Hayots Paterazmin: On Vardan & the Armenian War. Sanjian, Avedis K., ed. (Classical Armenian Texts). write for info. (ISBN 0-88206-034-1). Caravan Bks.
Egidio, Rhonda K. & Pope, Sharon L. Becoming Assertive: A Trainer's Manual. 62p. 1977. pap. 3.00 (ISBN 0-87013-207-5). Mich St U Pr.
Eginhard & Monk of St. Gall. Early Lives of Charlemagne. Grant, A. J., tr. LC 66-27656. (Medieval Library). Repr. of 1926 ed. 17.50 (ISBN 0-8154-0061-6). Cooper Sq.
Egitkhanoff, Marie A. & Wilson, Ken. Escape. (Daybreak Ser.). 124p. 1982. pap. 4.95 (ISBN 0-8163-0439-4). Pacific Pr Pub Assn.
Eglamour. Sir Eglamour. Cook, Albert S., ed. 1911. 24.50x (ISBN 0-685-69803-3). Elliots Bks.
Eglar, Zekiye S. A Punjabi Village in Pakistan. LC 60-6751. (Illus.). 240p. 1960. 31.00x (ISBN 0-231-02332-4). Columbia U Pr.
Eglash, Albert. Beyond Assertive Discipline: Humanistic Classroom Management. LC 80-50440. (Beyond Assertion Training Ser.: "Dont Step on My Castle!"). (Illus.). 100p. 1981. pap. 20.00 (ISBN 0-935320-18-0). San Luis Quest.
--But Never Shall He Become a Great Leader of His People! The Story of Mtuto Tembo. (Illus.). 100p. (Orig.). 1984. pap. 20.00 (ISBN 0-935320-01-6). San Luis Quest.
--The Case Against Assertion Training. (Beyond Assertion Training Ser.: No. 5). 200p. (Orig.). 1981. pap. 25.00 (ISBN 0-935320-12-1). San Luis Quest.
--Divorce Mediation, the Spirit of Conciliation: Essays for Mediators. LC 81-51419. (Illus.). 150p. 1981. pap. 25.00 (ISBN 0-935320-24-5). San Luis Quest.

--How to Be a Decent Human Being: Cancer, Coronaries & Communication. LC 79-54711. (Beyond-Assertion Training: Humanistic Communication Skills Ser.: No. 1). (Illus., Orig.). 1980. pap. 20.00 (ISBN 0-935320-11-3). San Luis Quest.

--How to Solve Multiple-Choice Math Problems the Easy Right-Brain Way: Exercising Your Commonsense. 100p. (Orig.). 1984. pap. text ed. 20.00 (ISBN 0-935320-50-4). San Luis Quest.

--Humanistic Communication in Love, Sex, & Intimacy. LC 79-54710. (Beyond Assertion Training: Humanistic Communication Skills Ser.: No. 2). (Illus.). 1980. pap. 20.00 (ISBN 0-935320-10-5). San Luis Quest.

--Humanistic Communication Skills: An Alternative to Assertion Training. LC 79-51947. (Beyond Assertion Training Ser.: No. 8). (Illus.). 50p. (Orig.). 1981. pap. 10.00 (ISBN 0-935320-17-2). San Luis Quest.

--Humanistic Communication Skills for Nurses: Sharing, Caring, Trusting. LC 79-54709. (Beyond Assertion Training: Humanistic Communication Skills Ser.: No. 4). (Illus., Orig.). 1980. pap. 20.00 (ISBN 0-935320-09-1). San Luis Quest.

--Long Distance Intimacy: Erotic Gratification & Fulfillment by Telephone-a Tour Guide for Separated Lovers, & Others. (Illus.). 200p. (Orig.). 1982. pap. cancelled (ISBN 0-935320-05-9). San Luis Quest.

--The Mind-Body-Machine Connection: A Psychologist Discusses Biofeedback with Electronic Engineers. 75p. 1981. pap. 15.00 (ISBN 0-935320-23-7). San Luis Quest.

--My Mom's Not Dead: She's in Prison. (Illus.). 60p. (Orig.). 1985. pap. 15.00x (ISBN 0-935320-03-2). San Luis Quest.

--Negotiating Teens from Drugs to Life: A One-Act Play. bilingual ed. Hurst, Michael, tr. (Beyond Assertion Training Ser.: No. 8). (Illus.). 50p. (Orig., Span. & Eng.). 1981. pap. 10.00 (ISBN 0-935320-07-5). San Luis Quest.

--On Being Investigated: The Kafka Experience. 50p. 1984. pap. cancelled (ISBN 0-935320-00-8). San Luis Quest.

--Our Children, Our Selves: Humanistic Communication for Parents. LC 79-54708. (Beyond Assertion Training: Humanistic Communications Skills Ser.: No. 3). (Illus.). 192p. 1980. pap. 20.00 (ISBN 0-935320-08-3). San Luis Quest.

--The Prisoner of Zenda: A Modern Feminist Version of an 1884 Novel. 100p. (Orig.). 1984. pap. 20.00x (ISBN 0-935320-02-4). San Luis Quest.

Egle, K. Entscheidungstheorie. (Interdisciplinary Systems Research Ser.: No. 5). 246p. (Ger.). 1975. pap. 27.95x (ISBN 0-8176-0776-5). Birkhauser.

Egle, Walter P. Economic Stabilization. (University of Cincinnati Ser.). 1952. 22.00x (ISBN 0-691-04123-7). Princeton U Pr.

Egle, William H. Index to Main Families, Persons, Places & Subjects in Egle's Notes & Queries. LC 70-114834. 81p. 1970. 8.50 (ISBN 0-8063-0444-8). Genealog Pub.

--Notes & Queries. Historical, Biographical & Genealogical Relating Chiefly to Interior Pennsylvania, 12 vols. LC 70-114834. 1970. Repr. of 1893 ed. Set. lib. bdg. 175.00 (ISBN 0-8063-0403-0). Genealog Pub.

--Pennsylvania Women in the American Revolution. 1975. Repr. 10.00 (ISBN 0-686-20889-7). Polyanthos.

Egle, William H., jt. auth. see Linn, John B.

Eglesfield, Robert, tr. see Simenon, Georges.

Egleson, Janet F. Design for Writing Workbook. 1970. pap. text ed. write for info. (ISBN 0-02-474140-X, 47414). Macmillan.

Egleston, Melville. The Land System of the New England Colonies. LC 78-63767. (Johns Hopkins University. Studies in the Social Sciences. Fourth Ser. 1886: 11-12). Repr. of 1886 ed. 11.50 (ISBN 0-404-61034-X). AMS Pr.

--The Land System of the New England Colonies. 1973. pap. 9.00 (ISBN 0-384-13963-9). Johnson Repr.

Egleton, Clive. Falcon for the Hawks. LC 83-40573. 192p. 1984. 12.95 (ISBN 0-8027-0781-5). Walker & Co.

--Troika. LC 84-45050. 319p. 1984. 14.95 (ISBN 0-689-11479-6). Atheneum.

Egli, Audrey, jt. auth. see Conway, Tom.

Egli, Glenn. Prayer That Releases Power. LC 81-71753. (Orig.). 1982. pap. 4.95 (ISBN 0-88270-506-7, Pub. by Logos). Bridge Pub.

Egli, H. & Inwood, M. J., eds. The Haemophiliac in the Eighties. (Haemostasis Journal: Vol. 10, Suppl. 1,1981). (Illus.). xii, 310p. 1981. pap. 41.00 (ISBN 3-8055-2885-X). S Karger.

Egli, Jakob. Etymologisch Geographisches Lexikon. (Ger.). 1970. 62.50 (ISBN 3-500-21620-X, M-7371, Pub. by Saendig-Walluf). French & Eur.

Egli, Johann J. Geschichte der Geographischen Namenkunde, 2 vols. 1962. Repr. of 1886 ed. 32.50 (ISBN 0-8337-1025-7). B Franklin.

--Nomina Geographica. 2nd ed. LC 71-173707. (Research & Source Works Ser.: No. 837). 1971. Repr. of 1893 ed. lib. bdg. 57.50 (ISBN 0-8337-1026-5). B Franklin.

Eglin, Peter. Talk & Taxonomy: A Methodological Comparison of Ethnosemantics & Ethnomethodology with Reference to Terms for Canadian Doctors. (Pragmatics & Beyond Ser.: No. 8). x, 125p. 1980. pap. 16.00 (ISBN 90-272-2510-9). Benjamins North Am.

Eglington, G. Environmental Chemistry, Vol. 1. 1975. 30.00 (ISBN 0-85186-755-3, Pub. by Royal Soc Chem London). Am Chemical.

Eglinton, G. & Murphy, Sr. M. T., eds. Organic Geochemistry: Methods & Results. LC 70-107318. (Illus.). 1969. 115.00 (ISBN 0-387-04669-0). Springer-Verlag.

Eglinton, Guy. Reaching for Art. facs. ed. (Essay Index Reprint Ser). 1931. 17.00 (ISBN 0-8369-0408-7). Ayer Co Pubs.

Eglinton, J. Anglo-Irish Essays. 59.95 (ISBN 0-87968-635-9). Gordon Pr.

Eglinton, John. Argle-Irish Essays. 1918. 10.00 (ISBN 0-8274-1346-7). R West.

--Letters from George Moore to Ed Dujardin. LC 72-187174. 1973. lib. bdg. 17.50 (ISBN 0-8414-3892-7). Folcroft.

--Letters to George Moore. LC 77-1316. 1942. lib. bdg. 20.00 (ISBN 0-8414-3980-X). Folcroft.

--Some Essays & Passages. Yeats, W. B., ed. 68p. 1971. Repr. of 1905 ed. 12.50x (ISBN 0-7165-1332-3, BBA 02050, Pub. by Cuala Press Ireland). Biblio Dist.

Eglit, Howard C., jt. auth. see Shepard's & McGraw-Hill.

Eglit, N. Columbus in Numismatics. 1985. pap. 12.00 (ISBN 0-942666-43-7). S J Durst.

Eglitis, Andrejs. Gallows over Europe. Fearnley, Robert & Snitere, Velta, trs. from Latvian. 128p. (Orig.). 1985. pap. 8.95 (ISBN 0-7145-4025-0, +012). Riverrun NY.

Egloff, Brian J. Wreck Bay: An Aboriginal Fishing Community. (AIAS New Ser.: No. 28). 52p. 1981. pap. text ed. 7.50x (ISBN 0-391-02240-7, Pub. by Australian Inst Australia). Humanities.

Egloff, Fred R. El Paso Lawman: G. W. Campbell. LC 82-17169. (The Early West Ser.). (Illus.). 144p. 1982. 12.95 (ISBN 0-932702-22-8); pap. 7.95 (ISBN 0-932702-24-4); leatherbound collectors ed. 75.00 (ISBN 0-932702-23-6). Creative Texas.

Eglsaer, Marie-Therese. Figaro. (Illus.). 80p. 1984. 7.95 (ISBN 0-89962-371-9). Todd & Honeywell.

Egly. Fringe Benefits for Classified Employees in Cities of 100,000 Population or Greater. (Research Bulletin: No. 19). pap. 0.69 (ISBN 0-685-57189-0). Assn Sch Busn.

Egly, T. W., Jr. History of the First New York Regiment 1775-1783. (Illus.). 388p. 1981. 19.95 (ISBN 0-914339-04-4). P E Randall Pub.

Egnatuck, Tony, et al. Middle School: A Position Paper. rev. ed. 12p. 1985. pap. text ed. 2.50 (ISBN 0-918449-04-9). MI Middle Educ.

Egner, Robert E., ed. see Russell, Bertrand.

Egoff, Sheila. Thursday's Child: Trends & Patterns in Contemporary Children's Literature. 340p. 1981. 15.00 (ISBN 0-8389-0327-4). Assn Library Serv.

Egoff, Sheila, et al, eds. Only Connect: Readings on Children's Literature. 2nd ed. (Illus.). 1980. pap. text ed. 10.95x (ISBN 0-19-540309-6). Oxford U Pr.

Egoff, Sheila A. Thursday's Child: Trends & Patterns in Contemporary Children's Literature. LC 81-8066. 340p. 1981. lib. bdg. 15.00x (ISBN 0-8389-0327-4). ALA.

Egoff, Sheila A., ed. One Ocean Touching: Papers from the First Pacific Rim Conference on Children's Literature. LC 78-31308. 260p. 1979. lib. bdg. 16.00 (ISBN 0-8108-1199-5). Scarecrow.

Egolz, W. Chess Combination As a Fine Art: The Work of Kurt Richter. Keres, P., ed. Franklin, Leslie, tr. from Ger. (Illus.). 1977. 15.95x (ISBN 0-8464-0241-6). Beekman Pubs.

Egon Ronay Organisation. Egon Ronay's Guiness Pub Guide 1984: To Food & Accomodation. (Illus.). 348p. 1984. pap. 5.95 (ISBN 0-312-94815-8). St Martin.

--Egon Ronay's Lucas Guide 1984: To Hotels, Restaurants & Inns of Great Britain & Ireland & a Survey of Theatre Buffets & Restaurants. (Illus.). 864p. 1983. pap. 13.95 (ISBN 0-312-94807-7). St Martin.

--Egon Ronay's Lucas Guide 1985. 800p. 1985. pap. 13.95 (ISBN 0-312-94808-5). St Martin.

--Egon Ronay's TWA Guide to 500 Good Restaurants in Major Cities of Europe & the United States: 1984. (Illus.). 416p. pap. 12.95 (ISBN 0-312-94823-9). St Martin.

--Just a Bite: Egon Ronay's Lucas Guide for Gourmets on a Family Budget. (Illus.). 400p. 1984. pap. 5.95 (ISBN 0-312-94833-6). St Martin.

Egone, Egon. Boston Old & New Through Egonegraphs. (Illus.). 96p. 1983. Portfolio Ed. 200.00 (ISBN 0-8283-1891-3). pap. 6.95 (ISBN 0-8283-1893-X). Branden Pub Co.

Egorov, I. Right to Fly. 240p. 1983. pap. 3.95 (ISBN 0-8285-2469-6, Pub. by Progress Pubs USSR). Imported Pubns.

Egorov, Iurii A. The Architectural Planning of St. Petersburg. Dluhosch, Eric, tr. LC 67-24283. pap. 68.80 (ISBN 0-317-09995-7, 2006064). Bks Demand UMI.

Egorov, N., jt. auth. see Kuzin, M.

Egorov, V. G., et al. Eight Papers on Differential Equations. LC 51-5559. (Translations, Ser.: No. 2, Vol. 24). 1963. 26.00 (ISBN 0-8218-1724-8, TRANS 2-24). Am Math.

Egorova, G., tr. see Marfunin, A. S.

Egorychev, G P. Integral Representation & the Computation of Combinatorial Sums. LC 83-22393. (Translations of Mathematical Monographs: No. 59). 286p. 1984. 90.00 (ISBN 0-8218-4512-8). Am Math.

Egoville, Barbara B., jt. auth. see Strong, Jo Ann.

Egrement, Michael. Bride of Frankenstein. 1976. 8.50 (ISBN 0-685-80028-8). Bookfinger.

Egret, Jean. The French Pre-Revolution, 1787-1788. Camp, Wesley D., tr. from Fr. LC 77-78776. (Illus.). 1978. Repr. of 1972 ed. lib. bdg. 27.00x (ISBN 0-226-19142-7). U of Chicago Pr.

Egri, Lajos. Art of Creative Writing. 1968. pap. 2.75 (ISBN 0-8065-0200-2, C263). Citadel Pr.

--Art of Dramatic Writing. 1972. pap. 9.95 (ISBN 0-671-21332-6, Touchstone Bks). S&S.

Egstrom, Glen H. & Schaafsma, Frances. Volleyball. 3rd ed. (Physical Education Ser.). 80p. 1980. pap. text ed. write for info. (ISBN 0-697-07086-7). Wm C Brown.

--Volleyball. (Exploring Sports Ser.). 120p. 1984. pap. 4.95 (ISBN 0-697-00448-1). Wm C Brown.

Eguch, T. & Yamaguchi, Y., eds. Tokyo Topical Symposium on High Energy Physics, 1982: Proceedings of the Symposium Tokyo, Japan, Sept. 7-11, 1982. vi, 392p. 1983. 46.00x (ISBN 9971-950-74-X, Pub. by World Sci Singapore). Taylor & Francis.

Egudu, Romanus. Calabash of Wisdom & Other Igbo Stories. LC 73-85560. 141p. 1973. text ed. 12.95 (ISBN 0-88357-005-X); pap. 4.95 (ISBN 0-88357-004-1). Nok Pubs.

--Four Modern West African Poets. LC 73-85556. 133p. 1977. text ed. 14.95x (ISBN 0-88357-027-0); pap. 5.95 (ISBN 0-88357-028-9). Nok Pubs.

Egudu, Romanus & Nwoga, Donatus. Igbo Traditional Verse. (African Writers Ser.). 1973. pap. text ed. 7.00x (ISBN 0-435-90129-X). Heinemann Ed.

Egudu, Romanus N. Modern African Poetry & the African Predicament. 154p. 1978. text ed. 27.50x (ISBN 0-06-491916-1). B&N Imports.

Egypt, Ophelia S. James Weldon Johnson. LC 73-9521. (Biographies Ser). (Illus.). 40p. (gr. 2-5). 1974. Crowell Jr Bks.

Egyptforce. Street Fighting for Junior Officers. (Interservice Combat in Cities Ser.). (Illus.). 64p. pap. 6.95x (ISBN 0-86695-008-7). Interserv Pub.

Egziabher, Tewolde Berhan Gebre. Participation of a Rural Community in the Identification of Technological Problems in Ethiopia: A Case Study from Welmera Werda: Project on Research & Development Systems in Rural Settings. 61p. 1982. pap. 5.00 (ISBN 92-808-0366-2, TUNU206, UNU). Unipub.

--Technology Generation & the Technological Space: Project on Research and Development Systems in Rural Settings. 31p. 1982. pap. 5.00 (ISBN 92-808-0390-5, TUNU196, UNU). Unipub.

Ehara, N. R., et al, trs. see Nichiren.

Ehde, Martin, Jr. Smoker's Heaven: You Don't Have to Die to Go There. LC 79-57444. (Illus.). 132p. (Orig.). 1980. pap. 4.95 (ISBN 0-936188-01-4). Ehde Pub Co.

Eheart, Brenda K. & Martel, Susan K. The Fourth Trimester. 272p. 1984. pap. 3.50 (ISBN 0-345-31751-3). Ballantine.

Eheart, Brenda K., jt. auth. see Leavitt, Robin L.

Ehle, John. The Changing of the Guard. 1976. pap. 1.75 (ISBN 0-380-00858-0, 31252). Avon.

--Last One Home. LC 84-47567. 320p. 1984. 15.34i (ISBN 0-06-015337-7, HarpT). Har-Row.

--The Winter People. LC 81-47684. 256p. 1982. 13.41i (ISBN 0-06-014930-2, HarpT). Har-Row.

--The Winter People. 1982. pap. 3.95 (ISBN 0-440-39770-7, LE). Dell.

Ehlen-Miller, Margaret, et al. The Gift of Time: Family Activities for Advent, Christmas, Epiphany. (Illus.). 1977. pap. 4.95 (ISBN 0-8192-1224-5). Morehouse.

--A Time of Hope: Family Celebrations & Activities for Lent & Easter. (Illus., Orig.). 1979. pap. 4.95 (ISBN 0-8192-1247-4). Morehouse.

Ehler, Stanley W., jt. auth. see Waldren, Richard P.

Ehlers, A., tr. see D'Espagnat, B.

Ehlers, Anita, tr. see Ferris, Timothy.

Ehlers, Chad, photos by. Sentinels of Solitude: West Coast Lighthouses. LC 81-81324. (Illus.). 88p. (Orig., Text by James Gibbs). 1981. pap. 9.95 (ISBN 0-912856-72-6). Graphic Arts Ctr.

Ehlers, Ekhart. Iran: A Bibliographic Research Survey. 441p. 1980. lib. bdg. 30.00 (ISBN 3-598-21132-5). K G Saur.

Ehlers, Ernest G. & Blatt, Harvey. Petrology: Igneous, Sedimentary, & Metamorphic. LC 81-12517. (Illus.). 732p. 1982. text ed. 37.95 (ISBN 0-7167-1279-2). W H Freeman.

Ehlers, Henry. Crucial Issues in Education. 7th ed. 1981. pap. text ed. 18.95 (ISBN 0-03-058089-7, HoltC). HR&W.

Ehlers, J., ed. Isolated Gravitating Systems in General Relativity. (Enrico Fermi Ser.: Vol. 67). 500p. 1979. 106.50 (ISBN 0-444-85329-4, North Holland). Elsevier.

--Relativity Theory & Astrophysics: Relativity & Cosmology. LC 62-21481. (Lectures in Applied Mathematics Ser.: Vol. 8). 292p. 1979. pap. 25.00 (ISBN 0-8218-1108-8, LAM-8). Am. Math.

--Relativity Theory & Astrophysics: Stellar Structure. LC 62-21481. (Lectures in Applied Mathematics Ser.: Vol. 10). 136p. 1967. 23.00 (ISBN 0-8218-1110-X, LAM-10). Am Math.

Ehlers, J., ed. see Cornell University, Summer Seminar, 1965.

Ehlers, J., et al. Lectures in Statistical Physics. (Lecture Notes in Physics: Vol. 28). (Illus.). vi, 342p. 1974. pap. 17.00 (ISBN 0-387-06711-6). Springer-Verlag.

Ehlers, J., et al, eds. Imaging Processes & Coherence in Physics. (Lecture Notes in Physics Ser.: Vol. 112). 573p. 1980. pap. 39.00 (ISBN 3-540-09727-9). Springer-Verlag.

Ehlers, Jurgen, et al, eds. Texas Symposium on Relativistic Astrophysics, 9th. LC 80-11614. (Annals of the New York Academy of Sciences: Vol. 336). 599p. 1980. 107.00x (ISBN 0-89766-045-5). NY Acad Sci.

Ehlers, Martin. Betrachtungen Uber Die Sittlichkeit der Vergnugens, 2 vols. 1973. Repr. of 1779 ed. Set. 80.00 (ISBN 0-384-13970-1). Johnson Repr.

Ehlers, Robert & Bessel, Richard, eds. Current Soviet Policies: The Documentary Record of the Twenty-Third Congress of the Communist Party of the Soviet Union, Vol. V. 2nd ed. Current Staff of the Soviet Press Staff, tr. from Rus. 175p. (Orig.). 1973. pap. 12.00 (ISBN 0-913601-05-5). Current Digest.

--Current Soviet Policies: The Documentary Record of the Twenty-Fourth Congress of the Communist Party of the Soviet Union, Vol. VI. 2nd ed. Current Digest of the Soviet Press Staff, tr. from Rus. 202p. (Orig.). 1973. pap. 12.00 (ISBN 0-913601-06-3). Current Digest.

Ehlers, Robert, et al, eds. Current Soviet Policies VIII: The Documentary Record of the 26th Congress of the Communist Party of the Soviet Union. Current Digest of the Soviet Press Staff, tr. from Rus. 152p. (Orig.). 1981. pap. 12.00 (ISBN 0-913601-08-X). Current Digest.

Ehlers, Victor M. & Steel, E. W. Municipal & Rural Sanitation. 6th ed. (Sanitary & Water Resources Engineering Ser.). 1965. text ed. 40.95 (ISBN 0-07-019089-5). McGraw.

Ehlers, Walter H. & Krishef, Curtis H. An Introduction to Mental Retardation - A Programmed Text. 2nd ed. (Special Education Ser.). 1977. pap. text ed. 17.95 (ISBN 0-675-08526-8). Merrill.

Ehlers, Walter H., et al. Mental Retardation & Other Developmental Disabilities: A Programmed Introduction. 3rd ed. 520p. 1982. pap. 18.50 add. suppl. may be obtained from Publisher (ISBN 0-675-09816-5). Merrill.

Ehlert, Friedrich W., et al. The Book of Pates & Terrines. LC 83-83312. (Illus.). 192p. 1984. 30.00 (ISBN 0-688-03896-4). Morrow.

Ehlert, Louis. From the Tone World: A Series of Essays. Tretbar, Helen D., tr. from Ger. LC 72-13099. (Essay Index Reprint Ser.). Repr. of 1885 ed. 18.25 (ISBN 0-8369-8156-1). Ayer Co Pubs.

Ehlich, Konrad & Rehbein, Jochen. Augenkommunikation. Methodenreflexion und Beispielanalyse. (Linguistik Aktuell Ser.: No. 2). viii, 150p. 1982. 20.00x (ISBN 9-0272-2722-5). Benjamins North Am.

Ehlich, Konrad, jt. ed. see Coulmas, Florian.

Ehling, William. Fifty Hikes in Central New York: Hikes & Backpacking Trips from the Western Adirondacks to the Finger Lakes. LC 84-70169. (Fifty Hikes Ser.). 208p. (Orig.). 1984. pap. 8.95 (ISBN 0-942440-17-X). Backcountry Pubns.

Ehling, William P. Canoeing Central New York. LC 82-4018. (Canoeing Ser.). (Illus.). 176p. (Orig.). 1982. pap. 8.95 (ISBN 0-942440-01-3). Backcountry Pubns.

--Twenty-Five Ski Tours in Central New York: The Best Cross-Country Skiing Through the Tug Hill Region, the Eastern Ontario Lowlands, & the Appalachian Highlands. LC 80-83578. (Twenty-Five Ski Tours Ser.). (Illus.). 144p. 1980. pap. 5.95 (ISBN 0-89725-019-2). Backcountry Pubns.

Ehlotzky, F. Fundamentals of Laser Interactions. (Lecture Notes in Physics: Vol. 229). ix, 314p. pap. 20.50 (ISBN 0-387-15640-2). Springer Verlag.

Ehly, Stewart W. & Larsen, Stephen C. Peer Tutoring for Individualized Instruction. LC 79-22847. (Illus.). 260p. 1983. Repr. of 1980 ed. text ed. 21.00 (ISBN 0-936104-34-1, 0082). Pro-Ed.

Ehman, Lee & Mehlinger, Howard. Toward Effective Instruction in Secondary Social Studies. LC 82-21894. (Illus.). 476p. 1983. pap. text ed. 19.75 (ISBN 0-8191-2916-X). U Pr of Amer.

Ehmann, James, jt. auth. see Gucwa, David.

Ehmann, Wilhelm. Choral Directing. Wiebe, George D., tr. 1968. 9.95 (ISBN 0-8066-0832-3, 11-9130). Augsburg.

Ehmann, Wilhelm & Haasemann, Frauke. Voice Building for Choirs. rev. ed. Smith, Brenda, tr. from Ger. 141p. Date not set. pap. 8.95 (ISBN 0-937276-02-2). Hinshaw Mus.

Ehmcke, F. H. Graphic Trade Symbols by German Designers. LC 74-75627. (Pictorial Archive Ser.). (Illus.). 64p. 1974. pap. 3.95 (ISBN 0-486-21671-3). Dover.

--Graphic Trade Symbols by German Designers. (Illus.). 7.50 (ISBN 0-8446-5030-7). Peter Smith.

Ehnbom, Daniel J. Indian Miniatures: The Ehrenfeld Collection. (Illus.). 272p. 1985. 50.00 (ISBN 0-933920-08-3, Dist. by Viking Penguin); pap. 25.00 museum distribution only. Hudson Hills.

Ehni. Cervical Arthrosis. 1984. 39.95 (ISBN 0-8151-3047-3). Year Bk Med.

Ehninger, Douglas. Influence, Belief, & Argument: An Introduction to Responsible Persuasion. 192p. 1974. pap. 9.75x (ISBN 0-673-07867-1). Scott F.

Ehninger, Douglas & Brockriede, Wayne. Decision by Debate. 2nd ed. 1978. text ed. 19.50 scp (ISBN 0-06-041867-2, HarpC). Har-Row.

Ehninger, Douglas & Gronbeck, Bruce E. Principles of Speech Communication. 9th ed. 1984. pap. text ed. 15.50x (ISBN 0-673-15877-2). Scott F.

Ehninger, Douglas, ed. see Whately, Richard.

Ehninger, Douglas, et al. Principles & Types of Speech Communication. 9th ed. 1982. 18.60x (ISBN 0-673-15538-2). Scott F.

--Principles & Types of Speech Communication. 10th ed. 1985. 16.95x (ISBN 0-673-18156-1). Scott F.

Ehnmark, Erland. The Idea of God in Homer. 1980. lib. bdg. 59.95 (ISBN 0-8490-3182-6). Gordon Pr.

Ehrard, Jean, jt. auth. see Montesquieu, Charles de.

Ehrardt, Roy. American Railroad Watches: George Townsend 1977, with 1983 Price Guide. 1982. 8.00 (ISBN 0-913902-40-3). Heart Am Pr.

Ehre, Edward, jt. auth. see Marsh, Irving T.

Ehre, Milton. Oblomov & His Creator: The Life & Art of Ivan Goncharov. LC 72-5378. (Studies of the Russian Institute, Columbia University Ser). 375p. 1974. 33.00x (ISBN 0-691-06245-5). Princeton U Pr.

Ehre, Milton, tr. see Gogol, Nikolay.

Ehrebreich, H. Solid State Physics: Advances in Research & Applications, Vol. 37. (Serial Publication Ser.). 1982. 49.50 (ISBN 0-12-607737-1). Acad Pr.

Ehreinberg, Victor. Documents Illustrating the Reigns of Augustus & Tiberius. 2nd ed. Jones, A. H., compiled by. LC 83-45431. Repr. of 1955 ed. 26.50 (ISBN 0-404-20086-9). AMS Pr.

Ehrenberg, A. S. Data Reduction: Analyzing & Interpreting Statistical Data. LC 74-3724. 391p. 1975. 64.95x (ISBN 0-471-23399-4, Pub. by Wiley-Interscience); pap. 24.95x (ISBN 0-471-23398-6). Wiley.

--A Primer in Data Reduction: An Introduction Statistics Textbook. 305p. 1982. 58.95 (ISBN 0-471-10134-6); pap. 21.95 (ISBN 0-471-10135-4). Wiley.

Ehrenberg, C. G. Silvae Mycologicae Berolinensis. 1972. Repr. of 1818 ed. 15.75 (ISBN 90-6123-253-8). Lubrecht & Cramer.

Ehrenberg, Miriam & Ehrenberg, Otto. Optimum Brain Power: A Total Program for Increasing Your Intelligence. (Illus.). 256p. 1985. 15.95 (ISBN 0-396-08391-9). Dodd.

Ehrenberg, Otto, jt. auth. see Ehrenberg, Miriam.

Ehrenberg, Ralph E. Archives & Manuscripts: Maps & Architectural Drawings. LC 82-80609. (Basic Manual Ser.). 64p. 1982. pap. 7.00 (ISBN 0-931828-50-3). Soc Am Archivists.

Ehrenberg, Ralph E., ed. Pattern & Process: Research in Historical Geography. LC 74-23617. (National Archives Conference: Vol. 9). (Illus.). 360p. 1975. 15.00 (ISBN 0-88258-050-7). Howard U Pr.

Ehrenberg, Richard. Capital & Finance in the Age of the Renaissance. LC 63-22259. Repr. of 1928 ed. 35.00x (ISBN 0-678-00015-8). Kelley.

Ehrenberg, Ronald, ed. Research in Labor Economics, Vol. 2. 381p. 1979. 42.50 (ISBN 0-89232-097-4). Jai Pr.

--Research in Labor Economics, Vol. 3. 410p. 1980. lib. bdg. 45.00 (ISBN 0-89232-157-1). Jai Pr.

Ehrenberg, Ronald G. The Regulatory Process & Labor Earnings. LC 79-6953. (Studies in Labor Economics). 1979. 29.50 (ISBN 0-12-233250-4). Acad Pr.

Ehrenberg, Ronald G. & Schumann, Paul L. Longer Hours or More Jobs? An Investigation of Amending Hours Legislation to Create Employment. LC 81-11284. (Cornell Studies in Industrial & Labor Relations: No. 22). 190p. 1982. pap. 12.95 (ISBN 0-87546-091-7). ILR Pr.

Ehrenberg, Ronald G. & Smith, Robert S. Modern Labor Economics. 2nd ed. 1985. text ed. 26.95x (ISBN 0-673-18105-7). Scott F.

Ehrenberg, Ronald G., ed. Research in Labor Economics, Vol. 1. (Orig.). 1977. lib. bdg. 42.50 (ISBN 0-89232-017-6). Jai Pr.

--Research in Labor Economics, Vol. 4. 350p. 1981. 37.50 (ISBN 0-89232-243-8). Jai Pr.

--Research in Labor Economics, Vol. 6. 450p. 1984. 49.50 (ISBN 0-89232-418-X). Jai Pr.

Ehrenberg, Victor. Alexander & the Greeks. Fraenkel Von Velson, Ruth, tr. from Ger. LC 79-4913. 1981. Repr. of 1938 ed. 15.00 (ISBN 0-88355-963-3). Hyperion Conn.

--Aspects of the Ancient World: Essays & Reviews. LC 72-7889. (Greek History Ser.). Repr. of 1946 ed. 20.00 (ISBN 0-405-04785-1). Ayer Co Pubs.

--From Solon to Socrates: Greek History & Civilization During the 6th & 5th Centuries B.C. 2nd ed. (Illus.). 500p. 1973. pap. 14.95x (ISBN 0-416-77760-0, NO. 2179). Methuen Inc.

Ehrenberg, Victor, compiled by. Documents Illustrating the Reigns of Augustus & Tiberius. 2nd ed. 1976. pap. text ed. 10.95x (ISBN 0-19-814819-4). Oxford U Pr.

Ehrenberg, Victor L. Society & Civilization in Greece & Rome. LC 64-19580. (Martin Classical Lectures Ser: No. 18). (Illus.). 1964. 8.95t (ISBN 0-674-81510-6). Harvard U Pr.

Ehrenberg, W. & Gibbons, D. J. Electron Bombardment Induced Conductivity & Its Applications. LC 81-66385. 1981. 96.00 (ISBN 0-12-233350-0). Acad Pr.

Ehrenbourg, Ilya. Out of Chaos. 1972. lib. bdg. 27.50x (ISBN 0-374-92504-6). Octagon.

Ehrenburg, I. Second Day. 366p. 1985. pap. 4.00 (ISBN 0-8285-2793-8, Pub. by Raduga Pubs USSR). Imported Pubns.

Ehrenburg, Iiya & Grossman, Vasily. The Black Book. LC 81-81519. 595p. 1980. 22.95 (ISBN 0-89604-031-3); pap. 12.95 (ISBN 0-89604-032-1). Holocaust Pubns.

Ehrenburg, Ilia G. A Street in Moscow. Volochova, Sonia, tr. LC 75-38496. (Soviet Literature in English Translation Ser.). (Illus.). 284p. 1977. Repr. of 1932 ed. 19.50 (ISBN 0-88355-400-3). Hyperion Conn.

Ehrenburg, Ilya. Actress (with Ivanov's Petya the Cock) Birkett, G. A., ed. LC 66-25017. (Rus.). 1966. 1.75x (ISBN 0-89197-486-5). Irvington.

--Julio Jurenito. Bostok, Anna & Kapp, Yvonne, trs. from Russ. LC 76-9856. 1976. Repr. of 1958 ed. lib. bdg. 24.75x (ISBN 0-8371-8889-X, BOJJ). Greenwood.

--The Life of the Automobile. Neugroschel, Joachim, tr. from Russian. 192p. (Orig.). 1985. pap. 6.75 (ISBN 0-916354-07-5, Pub. by Pluto Pr). Longwood Pub Group.

--Ninth Wave. Shebunina, Tatiana & Castle, Joseph, trs. from Rus. LC 74-10358. 895p. 1974. Repr. of 1955 ed. lib. bdg. 65.00x (ISBN 0-8371-7672-7, EHNW). Greenwood.

Ehrenburg, Ilya, jt. auth. see Simonov, Konstantin.

Ehrendorfer, F., jt. ed. see Nagl, W.

Ehrenfeld, Alfred, tr. see Bettelheim, Charles.

Ehrenfeld, David W. The Arrogance of Humanism. (Galaxy Bks.: No. 637). 1975. pap. 9.95 (ISBN 0-19-502890-2, GB). Oxford U Pr.

Ehrenfeld, John & Bass, Jeffrey. Evaluation of Remedial Action Unit Operations at Hazardous Waste Disposal Sites. LC 84-14834. (Pollution Technology Review Ser.: No. 110). (Illus.). 434p. 1985. 39.00 (ISBN 0-8155-0998-7). Noyes.

Ehrenfield, William, jt. auth. see Wylie, Edwin T.

Ehrenhaft. Ethan Fromm (Wharton) (Book Notes Ser.). (gr. 9-12). 1985. pap. 2.50 (ISBN 0-8120-3513-5). Barron.

--Grapes of Wrath (Steinbeck) (Book Notes Ser.). 1984. pap. 2.50 (ISBN 0-8120-3413-9). Barron.

Ehrenhaft, Peter D. Countertrade & Trading Companies: Trade Trends in the '80s. LC 84-196766. (Illus.). Date not set. 35.00. HarBraceJ.

Ehrenhalt, Alan & Glennon, Michael. Politics in America: Members of Congress in Washington & at Home. LC 81-9848. 1734p. 1983. 29.95 (ISBN 0-87187-259-5). Congr Quarterly.

Ehrenkrantz Group, et al. Solar Energy Performance History Information Series, Three Volume Set (1-3) Vol. 1 Active Solar Energy Systems; Preliminary Design Practice Manual Based on Field Experience, Vol. 2 Solar Domestic Hot Water; A Reference Manual, Vol. 3 Architectural & Engineering Concerns in Solar System Design, Installation, & Operation. 398p. 1982. pap. 69.50x (ISBN 0-89934-158-6, H-017). Solar Energy Info.

Ehrenkranz, Lois B. & Kahn, Gilbert R. Public Relations-Publicity: A Key Link in Communications. (Illus.). 270p. 1983. text ed. 14.50 (ISBN 0-87005-449-X). Fairchild.

Ehrenkreutz, Andrew S., tr. see Reychman, Jan & Zajaczkowski, Ananiasz.

Ehrenpreis, Andreas & Felbinger, Claus. Brotherly Community, the Highest Command of Love: Two Anabaptist Documents of 1650 & 1560. LC 78-21065. 1979. pap. 3.95 (ISBN 0-87486-190-X). Plough.

Ehrenpreis, Anne H., ed. see Bright, Henry A.

Ehrenpreis, Irvin. Acts of Implication: Suggestion & Covert Meaning in the Works of Dryden, Swift, Pope & Austen. (The Beckman Lectures Ser.). 150p. 1981. 33.00x (ISBN 0-520-04047-3). U of Cal Pr.

--Literary Meaning & Augustan Values. LC 73-94275. 120p. 1974. 9.95x (ISBN 0-8139-0564-8). U Pr of Va.

--Swift: The Man, His Works, & the Age, Vol. III: Dean Swift. LC 62-51793. 1066p. 1983. text ed. 35.00x (ISBN 0-674-85835-2). Harvard U Pr.

--The Types Approach to Literature. LC 73-19263. 1945. lib. bdg. 17.50 (ISBN 0-685-44515-1). Folcroft.

Ehrenpreis, Irvin, ed. American Poetry. 244p. 1982. Repr. of 1965 ed. lib. bdg. 35.00 (ISBN 0-89987-035-X). Darby Bks.

--American Poetry. 244p. 1983. Repr. of 1965 ed. lib. bdg. 40.00 (ISBN 0-89987-225-5). Darby Bks.

Ehrenpreis, Leon. Fourier Analysis in Several Complex Variables. (Pure & Applied Mathematics Ser.). 506p. 1970. 64.95x (ISBN 0-471-23400-1, Pub. by Wiley-Interscience). Wiley.

--Fourier Analysis in Several Complex Variables. LC 68-8755. (Pure & Applied Mathematics: Vol. 17). pap. 132.50 (ISBN 0-317-26171-1, 2025185). Bks Demand UMI.

--Theory of Distributions for Locally Compact Spaces. LC 52-42839. (Memoirs: No. 21). 80p. 1982. pap. 14.00 (ISBN 0-8218-1221-1, MEMO-21). Am Math.

Ehrenpreis, S. & Neidel, A, eds. Methods in Narcotics Research. (Modern Pharmacology-Toxicology Ser.: Vol.5). 424p. 1975. 69.75 (ISBN 0-8247-6308-4). Dekker.

Ehrenpreis, S. & Solnitsky, O., eds. Neurosciences Research. Incl. Vol. 1. 1968. 73.50 (ISBN 0-12-512501-1); Vol. 2. 1969. 73.50 (ISBN 0-12-512502-X); Vol. 3. 1970. 73.50 (ISBN 0-12-512503-8); Vol. 4. 1971. 73.50 (ISBN 0-12-512504-6); Vol. 5. 1973. 65.00 (ISBN 0-12-512505-4). Acad Pr.

Ehrenpreis, Seymour & Kopin, Irwin J., eds. Reviews of Neuroscience, Vol. 1. LC 74-80538. 361p. 1974. 50.50 (ISBN 0-911216-84-7). Raven.

--Reviews of Neuroscience, Vol. 3. LC 74-80538. 238p. 1978. 35.50 (ISBN 0-89004-168-7). Raven.

Ehrenpreis, Seymour & Sicuteri, Federigo, eds. Degradation of Endogenous Opioids: Its Relevance in Human Pathology & Therapy. 252p. 1983. text ed. 34.50 (ISBN 0-89004-994-7). Raven.

Ehrenpries, Anne, ed. see Austen, Jane.

Ehrenreich, Barbara. Hearts of Men: American Dreams & the Flight from Commitment. LC 82-45104. 216p. 1983. pap. 6.95 (ISBN 0-385-17615-5, Anch). Doubleday.

Ehrenreich, Barbara & Ehrenreich, John. Long March, Short Spring: The Student Uprising at Home & Abroad. LC 69-19789. 192p. 1969. 5.95 (ISBN 0-85345-086-2); pap. 3.95 (ISBN 0-85345-105-2). Monthly Rev.

Ehrenreich, Barbara & English, Deirdre. Complaints & Disorders: The Sexual Politics of Sickness. (Illus.). 94p. 1974. pap. 3.95 (ISBN 0-912670-20-7). Feminist Pr.

--For Her Own Good: One Hundred Fifty Years of Expert's Advice to Women. LC 77-76234. (Illus.). 1978. pap. 5.95 (ISBN 0-385-12651-4, Anch). Doubleday.

--Witches, Midwives, & Nurses: A History of Women Healers. (Illus.). 48p. 1972. pap. 3.95 (ISBN 0-912670-13-4). Feminist Pr.

Ehrenreich, H., ed. Solid State Physics: Advances in Research & Applications. Incl. Vol. 30. 1975. 74.50 (ISBN 0-12-607730-4); Vol. 31. 1976. 74.50 (ISBN 0-12-607731-2). Acad Pr.

Ehrenreich, H. & Liebert, L., eds. Solid State Physics: Suppl. No. 14 Liquid Crystals. 1978. 59.50 (ISBN 0-12-607774-6). Acad Pr.

Ehrenreich, H., et al, eds. Solid State Physics: Advances in Research & Appliations, Vol. 36. 1981. 49.50 (ISBN 0-12-607736-3). Acad Pr.

Ehrenreich, John, jt. auth. see Ehrenreich, Barbara.

Ehrenreich, John, ed. The Cultural Crisis of Modern Medicine. LC 78-465. 300p. 1979. pap. 7.50 (ISBN 0-85345-515-5); 15.00 (ISBN 0-85345-438-8). Monthly Rev.

Ehrenreich, John H. The Altruistic Imagination: A History of Social Work & Social Policy in the United States. LC 84-45807. (Illus.). 304p. 1985. text ed. 24.50x (ISBN 0-8014-1764-3). Cornell U Pr.

Ehrenreich, Paul. Die Allgemeine Mythologie und Ihre Ethnologischen Grundlagen. Bolle, Kees W., ed. LC 77-79125. (Mythology Ser.). 1978. Repr. of 1915 ed. lib. bdg. 34.50x (ISBN 0-405-10536-3). Ayer Co Pubs.

Ehrens, Susan. Exposed to Light: An Illustrated Biography of Imogen Cunningham. (Illus.). 320p. 1984. cancelled (ISBN 0-295-96080-9). U of Wash Pr.

Ehrensperger, Harold A. & Lehrer, Stanley. Religious Drama: Ends & Means. LC 77-22986. (Illus.). 1977. Repr. of 1962 ed. lib. bdg. 32.50x (ISBN 0-8371-9744-9, EHRD). Greenwood.

Ehrenstein, David. Film: The Front Line, 1984. (Illus.). 183p. (Orig.). 1985. pap. 10.95 (ISBN 0-912869-05-4). Arden Pr.

Ehrenstein, David & Reed, Bill. Rock on Film. (Illus.). 384p. 1981. pap. 9.95 (ISBN 0-933328-12-5). Delilah Bks.

Ehrenstein, G. W. & Erhard, G. Designing with Plastics. 200p. 1984. 35.00 (ISBN 0-02-948770-6). Macmillan.

Ehrenstein, Herbert H., jt. auth. see Barnhouse, Donald G.

Ehrensvard, Gosta C. Man on Another World. LC 65-17287. pap. 47.50 (ISBN 0-317-08495-X, 2020194). Bks Demand UMI.

Ehrenwald, Jan. Anatomy of Genius: Split Brains & Global Minds. 320p. 1984. 26.95 (ISBN 0-89885-148-3). Human Sci Pr.

--The ESP Experience: A Psychiatric Validation. LC 77-75242. 1978. 16.95x (ISBN 0-465-02056-9). Basic.

--New Dimensions of Deep Analysis: A Study of Telepathy in Interpersonal Relationships. LC 75-7377. (Perspectives in Psychical Research Ser.). 1975. Repr. of 1952 ed. 24.50x (ISBN 0-405-07027-6). Ayer Co Pubs.

Ehrenzweig, Albert A. Private International Law: A Comparative Treatise on American International Conflicts Law, Vols. 2 & 3. LC 67-28516. 176p. 1973. 75.00 set (ISBN 0-379-00353-8); 37.50 ea. Oceana.

Ehrenzweig, Albert A., et al. American-Greek Private International Law. LC 56-8413. 111p. 1957. 15.00 (ISBN 0-379-11406-2). Oceana.

--Jurisdiction in a Nutshell. 4th ed. LC 80-312. (Nutshell Ser.). 232p. 1980. pap. 7.95 (ISBN 0-8299-2086-2). West Pub.

Ehrenzweig, Anton. The Hidden Order of Art: A Study in the Psychology of Artistic Imagination. LC 67-20443. (California Library Reprint). 1976. pap. 9.95 (ISBN 0-520-03845-2, CAL 418). U of Cal Pr.

Ehresman & Albaugh. Saturn Return. 104p. 1984. 9.00 (ISBN 0-86690-240-6, 2298-01). Am Fed Astrologers.

Ehresmann, Donald L. Architecture: A Bibliographic Guide to Basic Reference Works, Histories, & Handbooks. LC 83-19600. 338p. 1984. lib. bdg. 55.00 (ISBN 0-87287-394-3). Libs Unl.

--Fine Arts: A Bibliographic Guide to Basic Reference Works, Histories & Handbooks. 2nd ed. LC 79-9051. 1979. lib. bdg. 40.00 (ISBN 0-87287-201-7). Libs Unl.

Ehresmann, Julia M., ed. Pocket Dictionary of Art Terms. LC 74-143464. (Illus.). 1971. pap. 5.70 (ISBN 0-8212-0748-2, 712019). NYGS.

Ehret, Arnold. The Definite Cure of Constipation. 1983. pap. 2.95 (ISBN 0-87904-032-7). Lust.

--Instructions for Fasting & Dieting. 1983. pap. 3.95 (ISBN 0-87904-003-3). Lust.

--Mucusless Diet Healing System. 1976. pap. 3.95 (ISBN 0-87904-004-1). Lust.

--Rational Fasting. 168p. 1971. pap. 2.95 (ISBN 0-87904-005-X). Lust.

--The Story of My Life. 1980. pap. 2.25 (ISBN 0-87904-048-3). Lust.

Ehret, Charles F. & Scanlon, Lynne W. Overcoming Jet Lag. 160p. (Orig.). 1985. pap. 4.95 (ISBN 0-425-05877-8). Berkley Pub.

Ehret, Christopher. Southern Nilotic History: Linguistic Approaches to the Study of the Past. LC 70-116611. Repr. of 1971 ed. 40.70 (ISBN 0-8357-9472-5, 2015430). Bks Demand UMI.

Ehret, Christopher & Posnansky, Merrick. The Archaeological & Linguistic Reconstruction of African History. LC 82-8431. 216p. 1982. 33.00x (ISBN 0-520-04593-9). U of Cal Pr.

Ehret, Walter & Evans, George K. International Book of Christmas Carols. LC 80-13105. (Illus.), 352p. 1980. pap. 14.95 (ISBN 0-8289-0378-6). Greene.

Ehret, Walter, et al. The International Book of Sacred Song. 270p. 1982. pap. 7.95 (ISBN 0-13-471649-3). P-H.

Ehrfeld, W. Elements of Flow & Diffusion Processes in Separation Nozzles. (Springer Tracts in Modern Physics Ser.: Vol. 97). (Illus.). 160p. 1983. 29.00 (ISBN 0-387-11924-8). Springer-Verlag.

Ehrhardt, Alpha L. American Cut Glass Price Guide: Book 1. rev. ed. (Illus.). 1977. plastic ring bdg. 6.95 (ISBN 0-913902-04-7). Heart Am Pr.

Ehrhardt, Anke A., jt. auth. see Money, John.

Ehrhardt, Arnold A. Framework of the New Testament Stories. LC 65-79. 1964. 22.50t (ISBN 0-674-31700-9). Harvard U Pr.

Ehrhardt, Charles W. & Ladd, Mason. Florida Evidence. 2nd ed. LC 84-216066. 1984. write for info. West Pub.

Ehrhardt, Melvin E., jt. auth. see Fish, Raymond M.

Ehrhardt, Roy. American Pocket Watch Identification & Price Guide, Book 2. rev. ed. 1974. plastic ring bdg. 15.00 (ISBN 0-913902-09-8). Heart Am Pr.

--American Pocket Watch Production Totals & Dates, Plus Inventory Pages. 56p. 1979. 3.00 (ISBN 0-913902-30-6). Heart Am Pr.

--Elgin Watch Company Identification & Price Guide with Serial Numbers. rev. ed. (Illus.). 1976. plastic ring bdg, 10.00 (ISBN 0-913902-10-1). Heart Am Pr.

--Hamilton Watch Company Identification & Price Guide, with Serial Numbers. rev. ed. (Illus.). 1981. plastic ring bdg. 10.00 (ISBN 0-913902-12-8). Heart Am Pr.

--The Official Price Guide to Antique Clocks. 3rd ed. LC 82-82663. 549p. 1985. 10.95 (ISBN 0-87637-482-8). Hse of Collectibles.

--Pocket Watch Price Indicator. (Illus.). 1980. plastic ring bdg. 12.00 (ISBN 0-913902-32-2). Heart Am Pr.

--Pocket Watch Price Indicator, 1976. (Illus.). 1975. Repr. plastic ring bdg. 5.00 (ISBN 0-913902-15-2). Heart Am Pr.

--Pocket Watch Price Indicator: 1977. (Illus.). 1976. plastic ring bdg. 7.00 (ISBN 0-913902-21-7). Heart Am Pr.

--Pocket Watch Price Indicator 1978. (Illus.). 1978. plastic ring bdg. 10.00 (ISBN 0-913902-26-8). Heart Am Pr.

--Pocket Watch Price Indicator,1979. (Illus.). 1979. plastic ring bdg. 10.00 (ISBN 0-913902-29-2). Heart Am Pr.

--The Timekeeper. 32p. 1972. pap. 3.00 (ISBN 0-913902-03-9). Heart Am Pr.

--Trademarks. (Illus.). 1976. Repr. plastic ring bdg. 10.00 (ISBN 0-913902-06-3). Heart Am Pr.

--Violin Identification & Price Guide, Bk. 1. (Illus.). 1977. Repr. plastic ring bd. 25.00 (ISBN 0-913902-22-5). Heart Am Pr.
--Violin Identification & Price Guide, Bk. 2. (Illus.). 1978. plastic ring bdg. 25.00 (ISBN 0-913902-24-1). Heart Am Pr.
--Waltham Pocket Watch Identification & Price Guide, with Serial Numbers. (Illus.). 1976. Repr. ring bdg. 10.00 plastic (ISBN 0-913902-17-9). Heart Am Pr.
Ehrhardt, Roy & Ferrell, J. Encyclopedia of Pocket Knives: Book One & Two Price Guide. rev. ed. (Illus.). 1977. plastic ring bdg. 6.95 (ISBN 0-913902-02-0). Heart Am Pr.
Ehrhardt, Roy & Rabeneck, Malvern. Clock Identification & Price Guide, Bk. 1. rev. ed. (Illus.). 1977. Repr. ring bd. 15.00 (ISBN 0-913902-23-3). Heart Am Pr.
Ehrhardt, Roy & Rabeneck, Red. Clock Identification & Price Guide, Bk. 3. 1983. plastic ring bdg. 15.00 (ISBN 0-913902-50-0). Heart Am Pr.
--F. Kroeber Clock Co. Identification & Price Guide. 1983. 8.00 (ISBN 0-913902-49-7). Heart Am Pr.
--Master Index to Thirteen Watch Books. 1980. 4.00 (ISBN 0-686-47738-3). Heart Am Pr.
Ehrhardt, Roy, illus. American Pocket Watches Encyclopedia & Price Guide, Vol. 1. 1982. plastic ring bdg 25.00x (ISBN 0-913902-33-0). Heart Am Pr.
Ehrhardt, Sherry & Planes, Peter. Vintage American & European Wrist Watch Price Guide. 1983. 14.95 (ISBN 0-913902-51-9). Heart Am Pr.
Ehrhardt, Sherry L. & Westbrook, Dorothy F. American Collector Dolls Price Guide Book One: 1891 to 1931. (Illus.). 1975. plastic ring bdg. 8.95 (ISBN 0-913902-14-4). Heart Am Pr.
Ehrhart, E. Polynomes Arithmetiques et Methode des Polyedres en Combinatoire. (International Series of Numerical Mathematics: No. 35). 169p. (Ger.). 1977. pap. 27.95x (ISBN 0-8176-0872-9). Birkhauser.
Ehrhart, W. D. To Those Who Have Gone Home Tired: New & Selected Poems. LC 84-91. 96p. (Orig.). 1984. pap. 6.95 (ISBN 0-938410-22-9). Thunder's Mouth.
--Vietnam-Perkasie: A Combat Marine Memoir. LC 83-9426. 328p. (Orig.). 1983. pap. 13.95x (ISBN 0-89950-076-5). McFarland & Co.
Ehrhart, W. D., jt. auth. see Barry, Jan.
Ehri, Linnea C., et al. Recognition of Words. Murray, Frank B., ed. (Ira Series on the Development of the Reading Process Ser.). 1978. pap. text ed. 3.50 (ISBN 0-87207-523-0). Intl Reading.
Ehrich, Ann M. Early Pottery of the Jebeleh Region. LC 40-5862. (American Philosophical Society, Philadelphia. Memoirs: Vol. 13). pap. 44.30 (ISBN 0-317-08473-9, 2000359). Bks Demand UMI.
Ehrich, Benjamin B. Photographic Guide to the University of California, Berkeley. LC 68-31289. (Illus., Orig.). 1969. pap. 2.95 (ISBN 0-87015-164-9). Pacific Bks.
Ehrich, Benjamin B., jt. auth. see Walczak, Michael.
Ehrich, Gertrude, jt. auth. see Cohen, Leon W.
Ehrich, J. H., jt. auth. see Brodehl, J.
Ehrich, Robert W. & Pleslova-Stikova, Emilie. Homolka: An Eneolithic Site in Bohemia. LC 79-16861. (American School of Prehistoric Research Bulletins: Vol. 24). (Orig.). 1968. pap. 9.25x (ISBN 0-87365-525-7). Peabody Harvard.
Ehrig, H. Universal Theory of Automata. (Illus.). 1976. pap. 18.75x (ISBN 3-519-02054-8). Adlers Foreign Bks.
Ehrig, H. & Mahr, B. Fundamentals of Algebraic Specification I. (EATCS Monographs on Theoretical Computer Science: Vol. 6). 336p. 1985. 29.50 (ISBN 0-387-13718-1). Springer-Verlag.
Ehrig, H., et al, eds. Formal Methods & Software Development. (Lecture Notes in Computer Science Ser.: Vol. 186). xiv, 455p. 1985. pap. 25.10 (ISBN 0-387-15199-0). Springer-Verlag.
--Mathematical Foundations of Software Development. (Lecture Notes in Computer Science: Vol. 185). xiv, 418p. 1985. pap. 22.80 (ISBN 0-387-15198-2). Springer-Verlag.
--Graph-Grammars & Their Application to Computer Science. (Lecture Notes in Computer Science: Vol. 153). 452p. 1983. pap. 26.50 (ISBN 0-387-12310-5). Springer-Verlag.
Ehringer, H. & Hoyaux, G. Energy Conservation in Industry Applications & Techiques. 1983. lib. bdg. 52.00 (ISBN 90-2771-580-7, Pub. by Reidel Holland). Kluwer Academic.
--Energy Conservation in Industry: Combustion Heat & Ranking Cycle Machines. 1983. lib. bdg. 32.50 (ISBN 90-2771-581-5, Pub. by Reidel Holland). Kluwer Academic.
--Energy Conservation in Transport: New Engines & Flywheels. 1983. lib. bdg. 28.00 (ISBN 90-2771-579-3, Pub. by Reidel Holland). Kluwer Academic.
Ehringer, H. & Zito, U., eds. Energy Saving in Buildings: Results of the European Communities Energy R & D & Demonstration Programs (1979-1983) 936p. 1984. 109.00 (ISBN 90-277-1770-2, Pub. by Reidel Holland). Kluwer Academic.
Ehringer, H., jt. ed. see Strub, A. S.
Ehrlich. Shaitan. 3.95 (ISBN 0-317-31823-3). Tor Bks.
Ehrlich, Amy. Annie Finds a Home. LC 81-15910. (Picturebacks Ser.). (Illus.). 32p. (ps-3). 1982. pap. 1.50 (ISBN 0-394-85161-7). Random.
--Bunnies All Day Long. 1985. 7.95 (ISBN 0-318-11859-9). Dial Bks Young.
--Bunnies All Day Long. LC 84-20031. (Illus.). 32p. (ps-2). 1985. 7.95 (ISBN 0-8037-0185-3). Dial Bks Young.
--Bunnies & Their Grandma. 1985. 7.95 (ISBN 0-318-11860-2). Dial Bks Young.
--Bunnies & Their Grandma. LC 84-20030. (Illus.). 32p. (ps-2). 1985. 7.95 (ISBN 0-8037-0186-1). Dial Bks Young.
--The Everyday Train. LC 76-42922. (Illus.). (gr. k-2). 1977. PLB 6.45 (ISBN 0-8037-2192-7). Dial Bks Young.
--Leo, Zack & Emmie. LC 81-2604. (Easy-to-Read Book). (Illus.). 64p. (ps-3). 1981. PLB 8.89 (ISBN 0-8037-4761-6); pap. 2.95 (ISBN 0-8037-4760-8). Dial Bks Young.
--Zeek Silver Moon. LC 70-181787. (Illus.). 32p. (ps-3). 1972. 7.95 (ISBN 0-8037-9825-3); PLB 7.89 (ISBN 0-8037-9826-1). Dial Bks Young.
Ehrlich, Amy, adapted by. The Ewoks & the Lost Children. LC 84-18379. (Illus.). 48p. (ps-2). 1985. PLB 7.99 (ISBN 0-394-97186-8, BYR); pap. 6.95 (ISBN 0-394-87186-3). Random.
--The Random House Book of Fairy Tales. LC 83-13833. (Illus.). 224p. (gr. k-4). 1985. bds. 14.95 (ISBN 0-394-85693-7, BYR); PLB 14.99 (ISBN 0-394-95693-1). Random.
Ehrlich, Amy, ed. see Brown, Dee.
Ehrlich, Ann. The Auxiliary's Role in the Administration of Local Anesthesia. (Illus.). 1983. 2.95 (ISBN 0-940012-02-2). Colwell Syst.
--Business Administration for the Dental Assistant. 2nd ed. LC 75-21039. (Illus.). 1983. 10.95 (ISBN 0-940012-16-2). Colwell Syst.
--Cavity Classification & Related Terminology. (Illus.). 1983. 4.25 (ISBN 0-940012-04-9). Colwell Syst.
--Dental Hand Instruments Identification. (Illus.). 1983. 4.25 (ISBN 0-940012-05-7). Colwell Syst.
--Dental Office Procedures Manual. (Illus.). 164p. 1983. 19.95 (ISBN 0-940012-06-5). Colwell Syst.
--Ethics & Jurisprudence. 1983. 4.25 (ISBN 0-940012-07-3). Colwell Syst.
--Introduction to Dental Charting. (Illus.). 1983. 4.25 (ISBN 0-940012-08-1). Colwell Syst.
--Introduction to Dental Instrument Sterilization & Disinfection. (Illus.). 1983. 3.95 (ISBN 0-940012-09-X). Colwell Syst.
--Introduction to Dental Terminology. (Illus.). 1983. 3.95 (ISBN 0-940012-10-3). Colwell Syst.
--Introduction to the Auxiliary's Role in Oral Surgery. (Illus.). 1983. 4.25 (ISBN 0-940012-11-1). Colwell Syst.
--Managing Insurance Claims in the Dental Office. (Illus.). 1983. 4.95 (ISBN 0-940012-12-X). Colwell Syst.
--Managing Insurance Claims in the Medical Office. (Illus., Orig.). 1983. 5.95 (ISBN 0-940012-13-8). Colwell Syst.
--Medical Office Procedures Manual. (Illus.). 1983. 19.95 (ISBN 0-940012-14-6). Colwell Syst.
--Psychology in the Dental Office. (Illus.). 1983. 4.95 (ISBN 0-940012-15-4). Colwell Syst.
Ehrlich, Ann, jt. auth. see Torres, Hazel O.
Ehrlich, Anne, jt. auth. see Ehrlich, Paul.
Ehrlich, Anne H., jt. auth. see Ehrlich, Paul R.
Ehrlich, Collis. Attack. 160p. (Orig.). 1981. pap. 2.25 (ISBN 0-345-28476-3). Ballantine.
Ehrlich, Cyril. The Piano: A History. (Illus.). 254p. 1976. 21.50x (ISBN 0-87471-895-3). Rowman.
--The Piano: A History. 248p. 1978-1979. 30.00x (ISBN 0-686-79449-4, Pub. by Dent Australia). State Mutual Bk.
Ehrlich, David & Wolf, George. The Bowel Book: A Practical Guide to Good Health. LC 80-54140. 192p. 1981. 12.95x (ISBN 0-8052-3763-1); pap. 6.95 (ISBN 0-8052-0673-6). Schocken.
Ehrlich, David, ed. The Health Care Cost Explosion: Which Way Now? 264p. 1975. pap. 18.25 (ISBN 0-683-02789-1, Pub. by W & W). Krieger.
Ehrlich, E. Japan: A Case of Catching-Up. 1984. 35.50x (ISBN 963-05-3297-2). Humanities.
Ehrlich, Edith, jt. auth. see Heller, Peter.
Ehrlich, Eugen. Fundamental Principles of the Sociology of Law. LC 74-25747. (European Sociology Ser.). 582p. 1975. Repr. 46.50x (ISBN 0-405-06502-7). Ayer Co Pubs.
--Fundamental Principles of the Sociology of the Law. Moll, Walter L., et al, trs. LC 62-10684. (Harvard Studies in Jurisprudence: Vol. 5). xxxvi, 541p. 1979. Repr. of 1936 ed. lib. bdg. 32.50 (ISBN 0-89941-140-1). W S Hein.
Ehrlich, Eugene. Amo, Amas, Amat & More. LC 84-48594. 160p. 1985. 9.57 (ISBN 0-06-181249-8, HarpT). Har-Row.
--How to Study Better & Get Higher Marks. 2nd, rev. ed. LC 76-41684. (Illus.). 1976. 12.45i (ISBN 0-690-01181-4). T Y Crowell.
--Schaum's Outline of Punctuation Capitalization & Spelling. (Schaum's Outline Ser.). 1977. pap. 5.95 (ISBN 0-07-019095-X). McGraw.
--Speak for Success. 288p. 1984. pap. 3.95 (ISBN 0-553-24005-6). Bantam.
Ehrlich, Eugene & Carruth, Gorton. The Oxford Illustrated Literary Guide to the United States. LC 82-8034. (Illus.). 1982. 35.00 (ISBN 0-19-503186-5). Oxford U Pr.
Ehrlich, Eugene & Murphy, Daniel. Basic Grammar for Writing. 128p. 1971. pap. text ed. 4.95 (ISBN 0-07-019103-4). McGraw.
--Basic Vocabulary Builder. (McGraw-Hill Paperbacks). 192p. (Orig.). 1975. pap. 4.95 (ISBN 0-07-019105-0). McGraw.
--Concise Index to English. 1974. pap. 3.95 (ISBN 0-07-019101-8). McGraw.
--English Grammar. (Schaum's Outline Ser.). 224p. 1976. pap. 6.95 (ISBN 0-07-019098-4). McGraw.
--Writing & Researching Term Papers & Reports: A New Guide for Students. (Desk Editions). (gr. 10-12). 1968. pap. 2.95 (ISBN 0-553-22974-5). Bantam.
Ehrlich, Eugene, et al, eds. Oxford American Dictionary. 1980. 16.95 (ISBN 0-19-502795-7). Oxford U Pr.
Ehrlich, Evelyn. Cinema of Paradox: French Filmmaking under the German Occupation. 240p. 1985. 25.00x (ISBN 0-231-05926-4). Columbia U Pr.
Ehrlich, Evelyn & Hochman, Stanley, eds. World Cinema since Nineteen Forty-Five, 2 vols. Date not set. Set. write for info. (ISBN 0-8044-3078-0); Vol. I. write for info. (ISBN 0-8044-3079-9); Vol. II. write for info. (ISBN 0-8044-3081-0). Ungar.
Ehrlich, Everett M. & Scheppach, Raymond C. New Directions in Economic Policy: An Agenda for the 1980's. LC 84-4712. 285p. 1984. 27.95 (ISBN 0-03-063786-4). Praeger.
Ehrlich, Everett M., jt. auth. see Scheppach, Raymond C.
Ehrlich, G. E., ed. Oculocutaneous Manifestations of Rheumatic Diseases. (Rheumatology: Vol. 4). 150p. 1973. 25.75 (ISBN 3-8055-1594-4). S Karger.
Ehrlich, George. Kansas City, Missouri: An Architectural History, 1826-1976. LC 79-64507. (Illus.). 200p. 1979. 19.95 (ISBN 0-913504-52-1). Hist Kansas City.
--Kansas City, Missouri: An Architectural History, 1826-1976. LC 79-64507. 1979. 19.95 (ISBN 0-913504-52-1). Lowell Pr.
Ehrlich, George E. Rehabilitation Management of Rheumatic Conditions. 2nd ed. 400p. 1985. 36.00 (ISBN 0-683-02792-1). Williams & Wilkins.
Ehrlich, Gerd W. Changing Law in a Changing Community: Eleven Lectures to Introduce the Study of Law. LC 83-3523. 112p. (Orig.). 1983. lib. bdg. 22.50 (ISBN 0-8191-3167-9); pap. text ed. 9.25 (ISBN 0-8191-3168-7). U Pr of Amer.
Ehrlich, Gertrude, jt. auth. see Goldhaber, Jacob K.
Ehrlich, Gretel. Solace of Open Spaces. 1985. 14.95 (ISBN 0-670-80678-1). Viking.
--To Touch the Water. Trusky, Tom, ed. LC 80-69276. (Modern & Contemporary Poets of the West Ser.). 60p. (Orig.). 1981. pap. 3.00 (ISBN 0-916272-16-8). Ahsahta Pr.
Ehrlich, Heyward, ed. Light Rays: James Joyce & Modernism. 1984. 15.95 (ISBN 0-88282-302-7). New Horizon NY.
Ehrlich, Heyward, ed. see Fiedler, Leslie, et al.
Ehrlich, Howard J. The Social Psychology of Prejudice: A Systematic Theoretical Review & Propositional Inventory of the American Social Psychological Study of Preujudice. LC 72-10058. pap. 55.50 (ISBN 0-317-10314-8, 2007633). Bks Demand UMI.
Ehrlich, Howard J., jt. auth. see Preiss, Jack J.
Ehrlich, Howard J., jt. ed. see D'Antonio, William V.
Ehrlich, Howard J., ed. see Drucker, Peter F., et al.
Ehrlich, Ida L. Instant Vocabulary. 1983. pap. 3.95 (ISBN 0-671-47722-6). PB.
Ehrlich, Isaac, ed. National Health Policy: What Role for Government. (Publication Ser.: No. 265). (Illus.). 448p. 1982. 27.95 (ISBN 0-8179-7651-5). Hoover Inst Pr.
Ehrlich, J. W., ed. see Blackstone, William.
Ehrlich, J. W., jt. ed. see Ferlinghetti, Lawrence.
Ehrlich, Leonard, et al, eds. Karl Jaspers: Basic Philosophical Writings. LC 82-84812. (Selections Ser.). 600p. 1985. text ed. 55.00x (ISBN 0-8214-0712-0); pap. text ed. 26.95x (ISBN 0-8214-0713-9). Ohio U Pr.
Ehrlich, Leonard H. Karl Jaspers: Philosophy As Faith. LC 73-79505. 292p. 1975. 17.50x (ISBN 0-87023-153-7). U of Mass Pr.
Ehrlich, Madeline. I Made It or The Trials & Tribulations of a Student Nurse: Fifty Years Ago. 1983. 4.95 (ISBN 0-8062-2195-X). Carlton.
Ehrlich, Max. The Big Boys. 288p. 1981. 12.95 (ISBN 0-395-30525-X). HM.
--Shaitan. LC 80-66498. 320p. 1982. 13.95 (ISBN 0-87795-273-6). Arbor Hse.
--Shaitan. (Tor Bks.). 384p. 1983. pap. 3.95 (ISBN 0-523-48075-X, Pinnacle Bks). Tor Bks.
Ehrlich, O. J., jt. auth. see Johnson, A. W.
Ehrlich, Paul & Ehrlich, Anne. Extinction: The Causes & Consequences of the Disappearance of Species. 1981. 16.95 (ISBN 0-394-51312-6). Random.
Ehrlich, Paul & Erlich, Anne H. The End of Affluence. 307p. 1975. lib. bdg. 17.95 (ISBN 0-89190-862-5, Pub. by River City Pr). Amereon Ltd.
Ehrlich, Paul & Harriman, Richard L. How to Be a Survivor. 208p. 1975. lib. bdg. 15.95 (ISBN 0-89190-863-3, Pub. by River City Pr). Amereon Ltd.
Ehrlich, Paul R. The Cold & the Dark: The World after Nuclear War; The Report of the Conference on the Longterm Worldwide Biological Consequences of Nuclear War. (Illus.). 256p. 1984. 12.95 (ISBN 0-393-01870-9). Norton.
--The Population Bomb. rev. ed. 201p. 1975. lib. bdg. 15.95 (ISBN 0-89190-861-7, Pub. by River City Pr). Amereon Ltd.
--Population Bomb. new rev. ed. (Orig.). 1976. pap. 2.50 (ISBN 0-345-28999-4). Ballantine.
Ehrlich, Paul R. & Ehrlich, Anne H. The End of Affluence: A Blueprint for Your Future. 320p. 1974. pap. 2.50 (ISBN 0-345-29049-6). Ballantine.
--Extinction: The Causes & Consequences of the Disappearance of Species. 400p. 1983. pap. 4.50 (ISBN 0-345-28895-5). Ballantine.
Ehrlich, Paul R., jt. auth. see Pirages, Dennis C.
Ehrlich, Paul R., et al. Ecoscience: Population, Resources, Environment. LC 77-6824. (Illus.). 1051p. 1977. pap. text ed. 28.95 (ISBN 0-7167-0029-8). W H Freeman.
--Human Ecology: Problems & Solutions. LC 72-12828. (Illus.). 304p. 1973. pap. 13.95 (ISBN 0-7167-0595-8). W H Freeman.
--The Process of Evolution. 2nd ed. LC 74-3030. (Population Biology Ser.). (Illus.). 416p. 1974. text ed. 40.95 (ISBN 0-07-019133-6). McGraw.
--The Cold & the Dark: The World after Nuclear War. Orr Roberts, Walter, ed. (Illus.). 272p. 1985. pap. 7.95 (ISBN 0-393-30241-5). Norton.
Ehrlich, Reinhart P., ed. Copper Metallurgy. LC 70-633878. pap. 94.80 (ISBN 0-317-10290-7, 2012652). Bks Demand UMI.
Ehrlich, Robert. Norman Mailer: The Radical As Hipster. LC 78-14849. 244p. 1978. lib. bdg. 16.50 (ISBN 0-8108-1160-X). Scarecrow.
--Waging Nuclear Peace: The Technology & Politics of Nuclear Weapons. 1984. lib. bdg. 39.50 (ISBN 0-87395-919-1); pap. 12.95 (ISBN 0-87395-920-5). State U NY Pr.
Ehrlich, Ruth A. & Givens, Ellen M. Patient Care in Radiography. LC 80-39489. (Illus.). 191p. 1981. pap. text ed. 16.95 (ISBN 0-8016-1507-0). Mosby.
Ehrlich, S. Pluralism on & off Course. (Illus.). 276p. 1982. pap. 19.95 (ISBN 0-08-027936-8); 44.00 (ISBN 0-08-028114-1). Pergamon.
Ehrlich, Shelley. How the Rooted Travel. (Juniper Bk.: No. 42). 1983. pap. 4.00 (ISBN 0-686-84327-4, JB41). Juniper Pr WI.
Ehrlich, Stanislaw. Le Pouvoir & les Groupes de Pression: Etude de la Structure Politique du Capitalisme. rev. ed. (Societe, Mouvements Sociaux & Ideologies, Etudes: No. 9). 1971. pap. 14.00x (ISBN 90-2796-903-5). Mouton.
Ehrlich, Stanislaw & Wooton, Graham, eds. Three Faces of Pluralism: Political, Ethnic, & Religious. 232p. 1980. 21.00x (ISBN 0-566-00313-9, 03274-3, Pub. by Gower Pub Co England). Lexington Bks.
Ehrlich, Susanne. Das Kreuzwortratselbuch. (Illus.). 64p. (Ger.). 1983. pap. 3.95 (ISBN 0-8442-2230-5, 2230-5, Passport Bks.). Natl Textbk.
--Das Ratselheft. (Illus.). 72p. (Ger.). 1983. pap. 3.95 (ISBN 0-8442-2227-5, 2227-5, Passport Bks.). Natl Textbk.
Ehrlich, Thomas & Hazard, Geoffrey C., Jr. Going to Law School? Readings on a Legal Career. 252p. 1975. pap. 9.95 (ISBN 0-316-22288-7). Little.
Ehrlich, Vera St. see St. Ehrlich, Vera.
Ehrlich, Virginia. Gifted Children: A Guide for Teachers & Parents. 224p. 1982. 14.95 (ISBN 0-13-356121-6); pap. 6.95 (ISBN 0-13-356113-5). P-H.
Ehrlich, Walter. Presidential Impeachment. LC 73-92315. 1974. pap. text ed. 2.95x (ISBN 0-88273-104-1). Forum Pr IL.
--They Have No Rights. 266p. 1979. pap. 7.95 (ISBN 0-686-95751-2). Jefferson Natl.
--They Have No Rights: Dred Scott's Struggle for Freedom. LC 78-22135. (Contributions in Legal Studies Ser.: No. 9). (Illus.). xvi, 266p. 1979. lib. bdg. 29.95 (ISBN 0-313-20819-0, ETH/). Greenwood.
Ehrlichman, John. The China Card. 1985. 17.95 (ISBN 0-317-20675-3). S&S.
--Witness to Power: The Nixon Years. 1982. pap. 3.95 (ISBN 0-671-45995-3). PB.
Ehrly, A. M., ed. Determination of Tissue Oxygen Pressure in Patients. (Illus.). 112p. 1983. 20.00 (ISBN 0-08-029785-4). Pergamon.
Ehrman, Edith & Morehouse, Ward. Students, Teachers & the Third World in the American College Curriculum. (FAMC Occasional Publication Ser.: No. 19). 80p. (Orig.). 1972. pap. text ed. 3.00x (ISBN 0-936876-10-7). Learn Res Intl Stud.
Ehrman, John. Cabinet Government & War, Eighteen Ninety to Nineteen Forty. x, 137p. 1969. Repr. of 1958 ed. 15.00 (ISBN 0-208-00737-7, Archon). Shoe String.
--The Younger Pitt: The Reluctant Transition. LC 82-42859. (Illus.). 704p. 1983. 39.50x (ISBN 0-8047-1184-4). Stanford U Pr.
--The Younger Pitt: The Years of Acclaim. (Illus.). 726p. 1969. 45.00x (ISBN 0-8047-1186-0). Stanford U Pr.
Ehrman, Kenneth & Flavin, Sean. Taxing California Property. 2nd ed. 1979. with 1984 suppl. 75.00 (ISBN 0-915950-31-6). Bull Pub.

Ehrman, Lee & Parsons, Peter. Behavior Genetics & Evolution. (Illus.). 448p. 1981. text ed. 36.95 (ISBN 0-07-019276-6). McGraw.
Ehrman, Sidney H., ed. see Biron, Armand D.
Ehrmann, Bertha K., ed. see Ehrmann, Max.
Ehrmann, E. L. Readings in Jewish History: From the American Revolution to the Present. 8.95x (ISBN 0-87068-447-7). Ktav.
Ehrmann, Eric, jt. auth. see Miller, Robert L.
Ehrmann, Eric W., jt. auth. see Miller, Robert L.
Ehrmann, Harry W., ed. see International Political Science Association.
Ehrmann, Henry W. Comparative Legal Cultures. 176p. 1976. pap. text ed. 14.95 (ISBN 0-13-153858-6). P-H.
--Organized Business in France. LC 81-4161. (Illus.). xx, 514p. 1981. Repr. of 1957 ed. lib. bdg. 45.00x (ISBN 0-313-23035-8, EHOB). Greenwood.
--Politics in France. 4th ed. (Series in ComparativePolitics). 1976. pap. text ed. 11.95 (ISBN 0-316-22289-5). Little.
--The Teaching of the Social Sciences in the United States. LC 74-3743. 150p. 1975. Repr. of 1954 ed. lib. bdg. 15.00x (ISBN 0-8371-7468-6, EHTS). Greenwood.
Ehrmann, Howard M., ed. see Hallett, Robin.
Ehrmann, Jacques. Un Paradis Desespere: L'Amour, L'Illusion. (Yale Romantic Studies). 1963. pap. 39.50x (ISBN 0-685-69816-5). Elliots Bks.
Ehrmann, Lee & Omenn, Gilbert S., eds. Genetics, Environment & Behavior: Implications for Educational Policy. 1972. 59.50 (ISBN 0-12-233450-7). Acad Pr.
Ehrmann, Max. Desiderata. (Illus.). 1972. 6.95 (ISBN 0-517-53422-3). Crown.
--The Poems of Max Ehrmann. Ehrmann, Bertha K., ed. 1948. 6.50 (ISBN 0-9602450-1-4). R L Bell.
Ehrmann, Michael M. Making Local Rehabilitation Work: Public-Private Relationships. 121p. 1978. 9.00 (ISBN 0-318-14951-6, N599); members 7.00 (ISBN 0-318-14952-4). NAHRO.
Ehrmann, Naftali H. The Rav. Paritzky, Karen, tr. from Ger. (Illus.). 1978. 5.95 (ISBN 0-87306-137-3). Feldheim.
Ehrstein, James R., ed. see Spreading Resistance Symposium.
Ehrstine, John W. The Metaphysics of Byron: A Reading of the Plays. (De Proprietatibus Litterarum Series Practica: No. 120). 145p. (Orig.). 1976. pap. text ed. 18.40x (ISBN 90-2793-483-5). Mouton.
Ehsani, Mehrdad & Kustom, Robert L. Converter Circuits for Superconducting Inductive Energy Storage. LC 85-40055. (TEES Monograph Ser.: No. 4). 286p. 1986. lib. bdg. 42.50x (ISBN 0-89096-257-X). Tex A&M Univ Pr.
Ehterton, Michael, ed. African Plays for Playing, Vol. 2. (African Writers Ser.). 1976. pap. text ed. 5.00x (ISBN 0-435-90179-6). Heinemann Ed.
Ehud, pseud. Shalom Home Study Course in Modern Hebrew. LC 84-90401. 123p. 1984. Repr. of 1978 ed. 19.95 (ISBN 0-9603914-1-X). Kellogg.
Eiben, Christopher J. Fisherman's Journal & Record Book. (Illus.). 172p. 1985. laminated, wire bd. 9.95 (ISBN 0-933509-00-6). Norblo Co.
Eibl-Eibesfeldt, Irenaus. The Biology of Peace & War. (Illus.). 1979. 15.00 (ISBN 0-670-16709-6). Viking.
--Love & Hate: The Natural History of Behavior Patterns. LC 74-10145. (Illus.). xii, 276p. 1974. pap. 7.95 (ISBN 0-8052-0459-8). Schocken.
Eicberg, J. see Bleasdale, John E., et al.
Eich, Dieter & Rincon, Carlos, eds. The Contras: Interviews with Anti-Sandinistas. (Illus.). 128p. (Orig.). 1985. pap. 7.95 (ISBN 0-89935-051-8). Synthesis Pubns.
Eich, Gunter. Selected Poems. Savory, Teo, tr. LC 69-13015. (German Ser: Vol. 3). (Ger. & Eng.). 1975. 15.00 (ISBN 0-87775-020-3); pap. 5.00 (ISBN 0-87775-090-4). Unicorn Pr.
Eich, Gunter see Otten, Anna.
Eich, Gunter, et al. Four German Poets: Gunter Eich, Hilde Domin, Erich Fried, & Gunter Kunert. Stein, Agnes, ed. & tr. from Ger. LC 78-59474. (Contemporary Poets Ser.). 1980. 12.95 (ISBN 0-87376-034-4). Red Dust.
Eichberg, Joseph. Phospholipids in Nervous Tissues. 384p. 1985. 79.50 (ISBN 0-471-86430-7). Wiley.
Eichberger, J., jt. auth. see Siebert, H.
Eichborn & Fuentes. Wirtschaftswoerterbuch Spanisch-Deutsch. (Span. & Ger.). 1974. 120.00 (ISBN 3-430-12390-9, M-7685, Pub. by Econ). French & Eur.
Eichborn, Hermann L. Das Alte Clarinblasen auf Trompeten. LC 78-17261. (Illus.). 50p. (Ger.). 1973. pap. text ed. 6.00 (ISBN 0-914282-09-3). Brass Pr.
--Girolamo Fantini: Ein Virtuos Des Siebzehnten Jahrhunderts und seine Trompeten-Schule. LC 76-40234. (Brass Research Ser: No. 5). (Illus., German.). 1976. pap. text ed. 3.00 (ISBN 0-914282-18-2). Brass Pr.
--The Old Art of Clarino Playing on Trumpets. Simms, Bryan R., tr. from German. (Illus.). 1976. pap. text ed. 6.00 (ISBN 0-685-71407-1, Tromba Pubns). Brass Pr.
Eichborn, R. Kleine Eichborn, Taschenwoerterbuch der Wirtschaftssprache, Vol. 1. (Ger. & Eng., English-German Dictionary of Commercial Terms). 1975. 33.50 (ISBN 3-921392-00-4, M-7495, Pub. by Siebenpunkt Vlg.). French & Eur.
--Kleine Eichborn, Taschenwoerterbuch der Wirtschaftssprache, Vol. 2. (Ger. & Eng., German-English Dictionary of Economic Terms). 1975. 33.50 (ISBN 3-921392-01-2, M-7496, Pub. by Siebenpunkt Vlg.). French & Eur.
--Wirtschafts-Woerterbuch. 4th ed. 2169p. (Ger. & Eng., Dictionary of Economics). write for info (M-7687, Pub. by Econ Vlg.). French & Eur.
Eichborn, R. & Fuentes, A. Wirtschafts-Woerterbuch. 2nd ed. 2174p. (Ger. & Span.). 120.00 (ISBN 3-430-12388-7, M-7686, Pub. by Econ Vlg.). French & Eur.
Eichborn, R. V. Dictionary of Economics, 2 vols. Incl. Vol. 1. English & German. 168.00x (ISBN 3-921392-06-3); plastic bdg. 59.95x (ISBN 3-92139-047-8); Vol. 2. German & English. 168.00x (ISBN 3-921392-07-1); plastic bdg. 59.95x (ISBN 3-92139-055-9). (Eng. & Ger.). 1982. Adlers Foreign Bks.
Eichelberger, Clark M., ed. see Commission To Study The Organization Of Peace.
Eichelberger, Clark M., et al, eds. see Commission To Study The Organization Of Peace.
Eichelberger, Clayton L. Guide to Critical Reviews of United States Fiction, 1870-1910. LC 77-149998. 1971. 22.50 (ISBN 0-8108-0380-1). Scarecrow.
--A Guide to Critical Reviews of U.S. Fiction, 1870-1910, Vol. 2. LC 77-149998. 351p. 1974. 16.50 (ISBN 0-8108-0701-7). Scarecrow.
Eichelberger, James W., jt. ed. see Budde, William L.
Eichelberger, Martin R. Pediatric Trauma Care. 1985. pap. 16.00 (ISBN 0-8391-2006-0, 21067). Univ Park.
Eichelberger, Martin R. & Pratsch, Gerry L. Pediatric Emergencies Manual. (Illus.). 176p. 1984. pap. text ed. 16.00 (ISBN 0-8391-1995-X, 20966). Univ Park.
Eichelberger, Robert L. Our Jungle Road to Tokyo. 1983. Repr. of 1950 ed. 17.95 (ISBN 0-89201-100-9). Zenger Pub.
Eichelberger, Rosa K. Big Fire in Baltimore. LC 78-31311. (Illus.). (gr. 3 up). 1979. 11.95 (ISBN 0-916144-36-4); pap. 7.95 (ISBN 0-916144-37-2). Stemmer Hse.
Eichelman, Burr & Soskis, David A., eds. Terrorism: Interdisciplinary Perspectives. LC 82-24393. (Illus.). 200p. 1983. text ed. 22.50x (ISBN 0-89042-109-9, 42-109-9). Am Psychiatric.
Eichenbaum, J., et al. Seattle. LC 76-4491. (Contemporary Metropolitan Analysis Ser.). (Illus.). 1976. pap. 14.95x prof ref (ISBN 0-88410-437-0). Ballinger Pub.
Eichenbaum, Luise & Orbach, Susie. Understanding Women: A Feminist Psychoanalytic Approach. LC 82-72545. 1983. 15.50 (ISBN 0-465-08864-3). Basic.
--Understanding Women: A Feminist Psychoanalytic Approach. LC 82-72545. 212p. 1984. pap. 7.95 (ISBN 0-465-08865-1, CN-5026). Basic.
--What Do Women Want? LC 82-14150. 288p. 1983. 13.95 (ISBN 0-698-11210-5, Coward). Putnam Pub Group.
--What Do Women Want: Exploring the Myth of Dependency. 224p. 1984. pap. 3.50 (ISBN 0-425-06770-X). Berkley Pub.
Eichenbaum, Sharon & Goldin, Alice. Jewish Awareness Worksheets, 2 vols. pap. 2.95x ea. Vol. 1 (ISBN 0-87441-266-8). Vol. 2 (ISBN 0-87441-270-6). Behrman.
Eichenberg, Fritz. Ape in a Cape: An Alphabet of Odd Animals. LC 52-6908. (Illus.). (ps-3). 12.95 (ISBN 0-15-203722-5, HJ). HarBraceJ.
--Ape in a Cape: An Alphabet of Odd Animals. LC 52-6908. (Illus.). 32p. (ps-3). 1973. pap. 5.95 (ISBN 0-15-607830-9, VoyB). HarBraceJ.
--Art & Faith. (Illus., Orig.). 1952. pap. 2.30x (ISBN 0-87574-068-5). Pendle Hill.
--The Art of the Print: Masterpieces, History, Techniques. LC 74-18024. (Illus.). 608p. 1976. 55.00 (ISBN 0-8109-0103-X). Abrams.
--Dance of Death. LC 82-20780. (Illus.). 136p. 1983. 29.95 (ISBN 0-89659-339-8). Abbeville Pr.
--Dancing in the Moon: Counting Rhymes. LC 55-8674. (Illus.). (gr. k-3). 1956. 12.95 (ISBN 0-15-221443-7, HJ). HarBraceJ.
--Dancing in the Moon: Counting Rhymes. LC 75-8514. (Illus.). 32p. (gr. k-1). 1975. pap. 1.85 (ISBN 0-15-623811-X, VoyB). HarBraceJ.
--Endangered Species & Other Fables with a Twist. LC 79-15247. (Illus.). 128p. 1979. 27.50 (ISBN 0-916144-42-9). Stemmer Hse.
Eichenberg, Fritz, retold by. & illus. Poor Troll: The Story of Ruebezahl & the Princess. LC 82-795. (Illus.). 48p. 1983. 9.95 (ISBN 0-916144-94-1). Stemmer Hse.
Eichenberg, Richard, jt. auth. see Capitanchik, David.
Eichenberger, Shirley. Mother's Day Out: How to Start a Business that Gives Mothers the Day Off. LC 82-42762. 1983. 12.95 (ISBN 0-911391-25-8). Oak Hill KS.
Eichenberger, W., jt. ed. see Siegenthaler, P. A.
Eichengreen, Barry, jt. auth. see Cairncross, Alec.
Eichengreen, Barry, ed. The Gold Standard in Theory & History. 320p. 1985. pap. 11.95 (ISBN 0-317-19342-2, 9614). Methuen Inc.
Eichengreen, Barry J. Sterling & the Tariff, Nineteen Twenty-Nine to Nineteen Twenty-Two. LC 81-6673. (Princeton Studies in International Finance Ser.: No. 48). 1981. pap. text ed. 4.50x (ISBN 0-88165-219-9). Princeton U Int Finan Econ.
Eichenlaub, John E. The Marriage Art. 1979. pap. 1.95 (ISBN 0-440-15422-7). Dell.
--A Minnesota Doctor's Home Remedies for Common & Uncommon Ailments. 3rd ed. LC 80-27588. 271p. 1981. 15.95 (ISBN 0-13-584532-7). P-H.
--A Minnesota Doctor's Home Remedies for Common & Uncommon Ailments. 1976. 12.95 (ISBN 0-13-584557-2, Reward); pap. 3.45 (ISBN 0-13-584490-8). P-H.
--New Approaches to Sex in Marriage. pap. 3.00 (ISBN 0-87980-106-9). Wilshire.
Eichenlaub, Val. Weather & Climate of the Great Lakes Region. LC 78-51526. (Illus.). 1979. text ed. 21.95x (ISBN 0-268-01929-0); pap. text ed. 8.95 (ISBN 0-268-01930-4). U of Notre Dame Pr.
Eichenlaub, Val L., tr. see Theophrastus.
Eichentopf, H. Theodor Storms Erzahlungskunst in Ihrer Entwicklung. 1908. pap. 9.00 (ISBN 0-384-14020-3). Johnson Repr.
Eichenwald, H. & Stoder, J. Practical Pediatric Therapy. 1190p. 1985. text ed. 64.95 (ISBN 0-89573-323-4). VCH Pubs.
Eicher, Carl K. & Staatz, John M. Agricultural Development in the Third World. LC 83-19532. (Studies in Development). 504p. 1984. text ed. 37.50x (ISBN 0-8018-3014-1); pap. text ed. 16.50x (ISBN 0-8018-3015-X). Johns Hopkins.
Eicher, Carl K. & Liedholm, Carl, eds. Growth & Development of the Nigerian Economy. 445p. 1970. text ed. 12.50x (ISBN 0-87013-147-8). Mich St U Pr.
Eicher, David J., ed. Deep-Sky Observing with Small Telescopes. (Illus.). 320p. 1985. pap. 14.95 (ISBN 0-89490-075-7). Enslow Pubs.
Eicher, Don & McAlester, Lee. History of the Earth. (Illus.). 1980. text ed. 34.95 (ISBN 0-13-390047-9). P-H.
Eicher, Don L. Geologic Time. 2nd ed. (Foundations of Earth Sciences Ser.). (Illus.). 160p. 1976. pap. 15.95 (ISBN 0-13-352484-1). P-H.
Eicher, Don L., et al. History of the Earth's Crust. (Illus.). 224p. 1984. 21.95 (ISBN 0-13-389999-3); pap. 16.95 (ISBN --13-389982-9). P-H.
Eicher, George J. The Environmental Control Department in Industry & Government: It's Organization & Operation. 165p. 1982. 28.50x (ISBN 0-9607390-0-9). Words Pr.
Eicher, T., et al. Cyclic Compounds. LC 75-11665. (Topics in Current Chemistry Ser.: Vol. 57). 160p. 1975. 35.00 (ISBN 0-387-07290-X). Springer-Verlag.
Eichert, B. S., et al, eds. Methods of Hydrological Computations for Water Projects: A Contribution to the International Hydrological Programme. (Studies & Reports in Hydrology: No. 38). (Illus.). 122p. 1982. pap. 17.00 (ISBN 92-3-102005-6, U1236, UNESCO). Unipub.
Eichheim, Hubert & Helmling-Mazaud, Brigitte. Mir Faellt auf... Incl. Slides 40S. pns 0.00. 48p. 29.95 (ISBN 3-468-84512-X); Begleitheft,48p. 4.00. Langenscheidt.
Eichholz, Alice & Rose, James M., eds. Free Black Heads of Households in the New York State Federal Census, 1790 to 1830. (Genealogy & Local History Ser.: Vol. 14). 301p. 60.00x (ISBN 0-8103-1468-1). Gale.
Eichholz, Alice, jt. ed. see Rose, James M.
Eichholz, Geoffrey G. Environmental Aspects of Nuclear Power. LC 84-27759. (Illus.). 704p. 1985. 47.50 (ISBN 0-87371-017-7). Lewis Pubs Inc.
Eichholz, Geoffrey G. & Poston, John W. Principles of Nuclear Radiation Detection; & Laboratory Manual. LC 79-88897. (Illus.). 1979. 39.95 (ISBN 0-250-40263-7); lab manual 19.95 (ISBN 0-250-40264-5). Butterworth.
Eichholz, Geoffrey G., ed. Radioisotope Engineering. LC 77-142891. (Illus.). pap. 106.80 (ISBN 0-317-07974-3, 2055012). Bks Demand UMI.
Eichhorn. Evangelizing the American Jew. LC 77-28975. 1978. 12.50 (ISBN 0-8246-0225-0). Jonathan David.
Eichhorn see Steer, Donald R., et al.
Eichhorn, David M. Cain: Son of the Serpent. 160p. 1985. pap. 8.95 (ISBN 0-940646-19-6). Rossel Bks.
--Conversion to Judaism: A History & Analysis. 1966. 20.00x (ISBN 0-87068-019-6). Ktav.
Eichhorn, David M., ed. Joys of Jewish Folklore. LC 80-13936. 534p. 1981. 16.95 (ISBN 0-8246-0254-4). Jonathan David.
Eichhorn, G. L. & Marzilli, L. G., eds. Advances in Inorganic Biochemistry, Vol. 1. 261p. 1979. 39.00 (ISBN 0-444-00323-1, Biomedical Pr). Elsevier.
--Advances in Inorganic Biochemistry, Vol. 6. 392p. 1985. 55.00 (ISBN 0-444-00825-X). Elsevier.
--Metal Ions in Genetic Information Transfer. (Advances in Inorganic Biochemistry Ser.: Vol. 3). 1981. 62.75 (ISBN 0-444-00637-0, Biomedical Pr). Elsevier.
Eichhorn, Heinrich. Astronomy of Star Positions: A Critical Investigation of Star Catalogues, the Methods of Their Construction, & Their Purpose. LC 73-81764. 357p. 1974. 25.00 (ISBN 0-8044-4187-1). Ungar.
Eichhorn, R. M., jt. ed. see Bartnikas, R.
Eichhorn, Susan E., jt. auth. see Evert, Ray F.
Eichhorn, W. & Voeller, J. Theory of the Price Index: Fisher's Test Approach & Generalizations. (Lecture Notes in Economics & Mathematical Systems: Vol. 140). 1976. soft cover 13.00 (ISBN 0-387-08059-7). Springer-Verlag.
Eichhorn, W., et al, eds. see International Seminar, University of Karlsruhe, May-July, 1973.
Eichler, A., ed. see Coleridge, Samuel T.
Eichler, A. W. Bluethendiagramme, 2 vols. (Illus.). 1954. 57.75 (ISBN 3-87429-003-4). Lubrecht & Cramer.
Eichler, Albert. John Hookham Frere, Sein Leben und Sein Werke. 1905. pap. 25.00 (ISBN 0-384-14035-1). Johnson Repr.
Eichler, Barry L. Indenture at Nuzi: The Personal Tidennutu Contracts & Its Mesopotamian Analogues. LC 73-77148. 180p. 1973. 24.50x (ISBN 0-300-01467-8). Yale U Pr.
Eichler, Edward P. & Kaplan, Marshall. The Community Builders. LC 67-13601. (California Studies in Urbanization & Environmental Design). 1967. 26.00x (ISBN 0-520-00380-2). U of Cal Pr.
Eichler, J., et al, eds. Electronic & Atomic Collisions. 900p. 1985. 122.25 (North-Holland); pap. 86.75 (ISBN 0-444-86844-5). Elsevier.
Eichler, Lilian. The Customs of Mankind. 1937. 49.50 (ISBN 0-8482-0740-8). Norwood Edns.
Eichler, M. Einfuehrung in die Theorie der Algebraischen Zahlen und Funktionen. (Mathematische Reihe Ser.: No. 27). 338p. (Ger.). 1963. 67.95x (ISBN 0-8176-0097-3). Birkhauser.
Eichler, Margaret. An Annotated Selected Bibliography of Bibliographies on Women. 1976. pap. 3.50 (ISBN 0-912786-38-8). Know Inc.
Eichler, Margrit & Scott, Hilda, eds. Women in Futures Research. (Women's Studies Quarterly: Vol. 4, No. 1). (Illus.). 124p. 1982. 19.00 (ISBN 0-08-028100-1). Pergamon.
Eichler, Marie H. Developing Basic Writing Skills in English As a Second Language. LC 81-3068. (Pitt Series in English As a Second Language). 174p. (Orig.). 1981. pap. 5.95x (ISBN 0-8229-8211-0). U of Pittsburgh Pr.
Eichler, Martin. Introduction to the Theory of Algebraic Numbers & Functions. (Pure & Applied Mathematics: Vol. 23). 1966. 76.00 (ISBN 0-12-233650-X). Acad Pr.
--Projective Varieties & Modular Forms. LC 78-166998. (Lecture Notes in Mathematics: Vol. 210). 1973. pap. 11.00 (ISBN 0-387-05519-3). Springer-Verlag.
Eichler, Martin & Zagier, Don. The Theory of Jacobi Forms. (Progress in Mathematics Ser.: No. 55). 155p. 1985. text ed. write for info. (ISBN 0-8176-3180-1). Birkhauser.
Eichler, Ned. The Merchant Builders. (Illus.). 296p. 1982. text ed. 32.50x (ISBN 0-262-05026-9). MIT Pr.
Eichler, O., ed. see Lesch, R., et al.
Eichler, O., jt. ed. see Schmier, J.
Eichler, O., jt. ed. see Berde, E.
Eichler, Victor, et al. Regeneration in Lower Vertebrates & Invertebrates, 3 vols, Vol. 3. LC 72-8249. 1972. 24.50x (ISBN 0-8422-7052-3). Irvington.
Eichling, Jeanne. Dogs, 3 Vols. (Illus.). 48p. 1982. Set 60.00 (ISBN 0-686-82187-4). Vol. I (ISBN 0-88014-051-8). Vol. II. Vol. III (ISBN 0-88014-053-4). Mosaic Pr OH.
Eichmann, Adolf. Eichmann Interrogated: Transcripts from the Archives of the Israeli Police. Von Lang, Jochen, ed. Manheim, Ralph, tr. from Ger. 293p. 1983. 16.95 (ISBN 0-374-14666-7). FS&G.
Eichmann, Raymond & DuVal, John. The French Fabliau, B. N. Wilhelm, James & Nelson, Lowry, Jr., eds. LC 83-48234. (Library of Medieval Literature). 150p. 1984. lib. bdg. 36.00 (ISBN 0-8240-9419-0). Garland Pub.
Eichmann, Raymond & Duval, John, eds. The French Fabliau: The M. S. B. N. 837, Vol. 2. Eichmann, Raymond, tr. LC 83-48234. 300p. 1985. lib. bdg. 39.00 (ISBN 0-8240-8907-3). Garland Pub.
Eichmann, Raymond, tr. see Eichmann, Raymond & Duval, John.
Eichner. Atlantean Chronicles. 1972. 9.50 (ISBN 0-686-02510-5). Fantasy Pub Co.
Eichner, A. S. The Megacorp & Oligopoly. LC 75-17115. (Illus.). 450p. 1976. 44.50 (ISBN 0-521-20885-8). Cambridge U Pr.
Eichner, Alfred S. The Emergence of Oligopoly: Sugar Refining As a Case Study. LC 78-16472. (Illus.). 1978. Repr. of 1969 ed. lib. bdg. 28.75x (ISBN 0-313-20598-1, EIEO). Greenwood.
--A Guide to Post-Keynesian Economics. LC 79-1971. 1979. 12.95 (ISBN 0-394-50758-4); pap. 6.95 (ISBN 0-394-73726-1). Pantheon.
--The Megacorp & Oligopoly. LC 79-92295. 378p. 1980. pap. 11.95 (ISBN 0-87332-168-5). M E Sharpe.
--State Development Agencies & Employment Expansion. LC 77-633549. (Policy Papers in Human Resources & Industrial Relations Ser.: No. 18). (Orig.). 1970. pap. 2.50x (ISBN 0-87736-118-5). Nat Gal Can.
--Toward a New Economics: Essays in Post-Keynesian & Institutionalist Theory. LC 84-27724. 208p. 1985. 25.00 (ISBN 0-87332-326-2); pap. 12.95 (ISBN 0-87332-327-0). M E Sharpe.

Eichner, Alfred S. & Brecher, Charles. Controlling Social Expenditures: The Search for Output Measures. LC 78-59180. (Conservation of Human Resources Ser.: No. 8). 224p. 1979. text ed. 23.50x (ISBN 0-916672-83-2). Allanheld.

Eichner, Alfred S., ed. A Guide to Post-Keynesian Economics. LC 79-1971. 216p. 1979. 12.95 (ISBN 0-87332-142-1); pap. 4.95 (ISBN 0-87332-146-4). M E Sharpe.

--Why Economics Is Not Yet a Science. LC 83-12859. 264p. 1983. 25.00 (ISBN 0-87332-249-5); pap. 13.95 (ISBN 0-87332-265-7). M E Sharpe.

Eichner, Donald O. The Inter-American Nuclear Energy Commission: Its Goals & Achievements. Bruchey, Stuart, ed. LC 78-22676. (Energy in the American Economy Ser.). 1979. lib. bdg. 16.00x (ISBN 0-405-11979-8). Ayer Co Pubs.

Eichner, Hans, ed. see Behler, Ernst, et al.

Eichner, Henry M. Atlantean Chronicles. 1971. 9.50 (ISBN 0-87505-267-3). Borden.

Eichner, James. First Book of Local Government. rev ed. (First Books). (gr. 5-9). 1983. PLB 8.90 (ISBN 0-531-04642-7). Watts.

Eichoff, J. Woertatlas der Deutschen Umgangssprachen, Vol. 1. 106p. (Ger.). 1977. 55.00 (ISBN 3-7720-1337-6, M-7689, Pub. by A. Francke). French & Eur.

Eicholz, Robert, et al. Answer Booklet. (Mathematics in Our World Ser.). 1981. Grade 3. pap. text ed. 3.40 (201-15933, Sch Div); Grade 4. pap. text ed. 3.40 (201-15934, Sch Div); Grade 5. pap. text ed. 3.40 (201-15935); Grade 6. pap. text ed. 3.40 (201-15936); Grade 7. pap. text ed. 3.52 (201-15937); Grade 8. pap. text ed. 3.52 (201-15938). Addison-Wesley.

--Extending the Ideas Enrichment Workbook. (Mathematics in Our World Ser.). 1980. pap. text ed. 4.08 (ISBN 0-201-16015-3, Sch Div); pap. text ed. 4.08 (ISBN 0-201-16025-0); Grade 2. tchr's ed. 4.40 (ISBN 0-201-16026-9). Addison-Wesley.

--Extending the Ideas Enrichment Workbook. 2nd ed. (Mathematics in Our World Ser.). 1980. pap. text ed. 5.16 (ISBN 0-201-16035-8); pap. text ed. 5.16 (ISBN 0-201-16045-5); Grade 4. tchr's ed. 5.80 (ISBN 0-201-16046-3). Addison-Wesley.

--Extending the Ideas Enrichment Workbook. 2nd ed. (Mathematics in Our World Ser.). 1980. pap. text ed. 5.16 (ISBN 0-201-16055-2); Grade 5. tchr's ed. 5.80 (ISBN 0-201-16056-0); pap. text ed. 5.16 (ISBN 0-201-16065-X); Grade 6. tchr's ed. 5.80 (201-16066). Addison-Wesley.

--Team Binder: Includes Teacher's Edition & Teacher's Resource Book. (Mathematics in Our World Ser.). 1981. Grade K. pap. text ed. 63.60 (ISBN 0-201-15970-8, Sch Div); Grade 1. pap. text ed. 67.84 (201-15971); Grade 2. pap. text ed. 67.84 (ISBN 0-201-15972-4); Grade 3. pap. text ed. 67.84 (ISBN 0-201-15973-2). Addison-Wesley.

--Team Binder: Includes Teacher's Edition & Teacher's Resource Book. (Mathematics in Our World Ser.). 1981. Grade 4. pap. text ed. 67.84 (ISBN 0-201-15974-0, Sch Div); Grade 5. pap. text ed. 67.84 (ISBN 0-201-15975-9); Grade 6. pap. text ed. 67.84 (ISBN 0-201-15976-7); Grade 7. pap. text ed. 67.84 (ISBN 0-201-15977-5); Grade 8. pap. text ed. 67.84 (ISBN 0-201-15978-3). Addison-Wesley.

Eicholz, Robert E., et al. Mathematics in Our World. Incl. Enrichment Workbook Grade 3. 1979. tchr's ed 5.80 (ISBN 0-201-09836-9); wkbk 5.16 (ISBN 0-201-09835-0); Enrichment Workbook Grade 4. 1979. tchrs' ed. 5.80 (ISBN 0-201-09846-6); wkbk 5.16 (ISBN 0-201-09845-8); Enrichment Workbook Grade 5. 1979. tchrs' ed 5.80 (ISBN 0-201-09856-3); wkbk 5.16 (ISBN 0-201-09855-5); Enrichment Workbook Grade 6. 1979. tchrs' ed 5.80 (ISBN 0-201-09866-0); wkbk 5.16 (ISBN 0-201-09865-2); Enrichment Workbook Grade 7. 1979. tchrs' ed 5.76 (ISBN 0-201-09874-1); wkbk 4.96 (ISBN 0-201-09873-3); Enrichment Workbook Grade 8. 1979. tchrs' ed 5.76 (ISBN 0-201-09884-9); wkbk 4.96 (ISBN 0-201-09883-0). (gr. 3-8, Sch Div). Addison-Wesley.

Eichorn, Dorothy, et al, eds. Present & Past in Middle Life. LC 80-70589. 1982. 42.50 (ISBN 0-12-233680-1). Acad Pr.

Eichorn, G. L. & Marzilli, L. G., eds. Advances in Inorganic Biochemistry, Vol. 4. 322p. 1982. 66.00 (ISBN 0-444-00680-X, Biomedical Pr). Elsevier.

Eichorn, Max. Joys of Jewish Folklore. 440p. 1983. pap. 8.95 (ISBN 0-8246-0301-X). Jonathan David.

Eichrodt, Walther. Ezekiel: A Commentary. LC 71-117646. (Old Testament Library). 608p. 1970. 18.95 (ISBN 0-664-20872-X). Westminster.

--Theology of the Old Testament, 2 Vols. Baker, J., tr. LC 61-11867. (Old Testament Library). 1967. 20.95 ea. Vol. 1, 542p (ISBN 0-664-20352-3). Vol. 2, 574p (ISBN 0-664-20769-3). Westminster.

Eichstaedt, Carl B., jt. auth. see Kalakian, Leonard H.

Eickelman, Christine. Women & Community in Oman. (Illus.). 240p. 1984. 32.50x (ISBN 0-8147-2165-6); pap. 13.50x (ISBN 0-8147-2166-4). NYU Pr.

Eickelman, Dale F. Knowledge & Power in Morocco: The Education of a Twentieth-Century Notable. LC 85-3444. (Princeton Studies on the Near East). (Illus.). 325p. 1985. text ed. 32.50x (ISBN 0-691-09415-2). Princeton U Pr.

--The Middle East: An Anthropological Approach. (Series in Anthropology). (Illus.). 368p. 1983. 20.95 (ISBN 0-13-581603-3). P-H.

--Moroccan Islam: Tradition & Society in a Pilgrimage Center. (Modern Middle East Ser.: No. 1). 323p. 1981. pap. text ed. 12.95x (ISBN 0-292-75062-5). U of Tex Pr.

Eickemeyer, Carl. Over the Great Navajo Trail. LC 74-7965. (Illus.). Repr. of 1900 ed. 21.50 (ISBN 0-404-11853-4). AMS Pr.

Eickenberg, H. U., ed. The Influence of Antibiotics on the Host-Parasite Relationship. (Illus.). 270p. 1982. pap. 27.00 (ISBN 0-387-11680-X). Springer-Verlag.

Eickenden, William E. Professional Guide for Young Engineers. 52p. 1967. 2.00 (ISBN 0-318-12197-2, EC43). Accred Bd Eng & Tech.

Eickhoff, Edith, jt. auth. see Bruce, Isabel.

Eickhoff, Richard P. Local Government: Barrister Handbook. LC 83-105636. vi, 76p. 1982. write for info. Cambridge U Pr.

Eickman, J. L. The Ford Y-Block. (Illus.). 120p. 1984. pap. 12.95 (ISBN 0-87938-185-X). Motorbooks Intl.

Eickmann, Katherine A., tr. see Mori, Hisashi.

Eicoff, Alvin. Or Your Money Back: How to Make a Fortune Merchandise Your Product on Radio, TV, & Cable. LC 82-5020. 192p. 1982. 14.95 (ISBN 0-517-54739-2). Crown.

Eid, Nimr. Legal Aspects of Marketing Behavior in Lebanon & Kuwait. 8.00x (ISBN 0-86685-013-9). Intl Bk Ctr.

Eide, A., et al. Engineering Graphics Fundamentals. 656p. 1985. 34.95 (ISBN 0-07-019126-3). McGraw.

Eide, A. R. & Jenison, R. D. Engineering Fundamentals & Problem Solving. 2nd ed. 416p. 1985. price not set (ISBN 0-07-019318-5). McGraw.

Eide, Arvid R., et al. Engineering Fundamentals & Problem Solving. (Illus.). 1979. text ed. 36.00 (ISBN 0-07-019123-9). McGraw.

Eide, Asbjorn & Thee, Marek, eds. Frontiers of Human Rights Education. 140p. 1984. pap. 15.00x (ISBN 82-00-06776-9). Universitet.

--Problems of Contemporary Militarism. LC 79-3379. 1980. 35.00x (ISBN 0-312-64744-1). St Martin.

Eide, Ashborn, jt. auth. see Kaldor, Mary.

Eide, E. Engineering Production & Cost Function for Tankers. 284p. 1979. 74.50 (ISBN 0-444-41817-2). Elsevier.

Eide, Harald. Alaska Adventures of a Norwegian Cheechako: Greenhorn with a Gold Pan. LC 75-23014. (Illus.). 1975. pap. 5.95 (ISBN 0-88240-063-0). Alaska Northwest.

Eide, Imogenie, jt. auth. see Steffl, Bernita.

Eide, Kjell see Beaug, Mark.

Eide, Lucille. My UFO. LC 81-90261. (Illus.). 81p. (Orig.). 1980. pap. 3.95x (ISBN 0-9610668-1-4). L Eide.

Eidelberg, Lawrence, ed. The Videolog: Programs for General Interest & Entertainment. LC 78-74187. 1979. pap. 20.00 (ISBN 0-917226-08-9, Pub. by Mord Media). Video-Forum.

--The Videolog: Programs for the Health Sciences. LC 78-74188. 1979. pap. 35.00 (ISBN 0-917226-09-7, Pub. by Mord Media). Video-Forum.

Eidelberg, Ludwig. Take off Your Mask. LC 48-4537. pap. 57.80 (ISBN 0-317-10378-4, 2010699). Bks Demand UMI.

Eidelberg, Ludwig, ed. Encyclopedia of Psychoanalysis. LC 67-28974. 1968. 45.00 (ISBN 0-02-909340-6). Free Pr.

Eidelberg, Martin. Watteau's Drawings: Their Use & Significance. LC 76-23616. (Outstanding Dissertations in the Fine Arts - 18th Century). (Illus.). 1977. Repr. of 1965 ed. lib. bdg. 68.00 (ISBN 0-8240-2687-X). Garland Pub.

Eidelberg, Martin, ed. Eva Ziesel: Designer for Industry. (Illus.). 200p. 1984. pap. 24.95 (ISBN 0-226-19473-6, 19473-6, Pub. by Musee des Arts Decortifs de Montreal). U of Chicago Pr.

Eidelberg, Paul. Beyond Detente: Toward an American Foreign Policy. 1977. pap. 9.95 (ISBN 0-89385-008-X). Sugden.

--A Discourse on Statesmanship: The Design & Transformation of the American Polity. LC 74-8913. 480p. 1974. 32.50x (ISBN 0-252-00428-0). U of Ill Pr.

--On the Silence of the Declaration of Independence. LC 76-8759. 148p. 1980. 12.00x (ISBN 0-87023-216-9); pap. text ed. 5.95x (ISBN 0-87023-313-0). U of Mass Pr.

Eidelberg, Shlomo, ed. Jews & the Crusaders: The Hebrew Chronicles of the First & Second Crusades. (Illus.). 200p. 1977. 21.50x (ISBN 0-299-07060-3). U of Wis Pr.

Eidem, Rolf & Viotti, Staffan. Economic Systems: How Resources Are Allocated. LC 78-19199. 111p. 1978. text ed. 26.95x (ISBN 0-470-26364-4). Halsted Pr.

Eidenberg, Eugene & Morey, Roy D. Act of Congress. 1969. 6.50x (ISBN 0-393-05331-8, NortonC); pap. 4.95x (ISBN 0-393-09692-0). Norton.

Eideneier, Hans, ed. Spanos: Eine Byzantinische Satire Als Parodie, Einleitung, Kritischer Text, Kommentar und Glossar. 1977. 84.00x (ISBN 3-11-006606-8). De Gruyter.

Eider, J. R., ed. Attitudinal Judgement. (Series in Social Psychology). (Illus.). 275p. 1984. 29.00 (ISBN 0-387-90911-7). Springer-Verlag.

Eidheim, Harald. Aspects of the Lappish Minority Situation. 86p. 1971. pap. 10.50x (ISBN 8-200-02328-1, Dist. by Columbia U Pr). Universitet.

Eidlin, Fred. Constitutional Democracy: Essays in Comparative Politics. (Replica Edition Ser.). 500p. 1984. softcover 30.00x (ISBN 0-86531-948-0). Westview.

--The Logic of "Normalization". (East European Monograph: No. 74). 278p. 1980. 28.00x (ISBN 0-914710-68-0). East Eur Quarterly.

Eidlin, Fred, tr. see Kaplan, Karel.

Eidlitz, Elizabeth, jt. ed. see Malfetti, James L.

Eidlitz, Leopold. The Nature & Function of Art, More Especially of Architecture. LC 77-4765. (Architecture & Decorative Art Ser.). 1977. Repr. of 1881 ed. lib. bdg. 39.50 (ISBN 0-306-70898-1). Da Capo.

Eidman, Vernon R., jt. auth. see Boehlje, Michael D.

Eidsen, Donald. Some Trust in Chariots. 80p. 1984. text ed. 9.95 (ISBN 0-89390-055-9). Resource Pubns.

Eidsmoe, John. Christian Legal Advisor. 1984. 21.95 (ISBN 0-88062-119-2); pap. 14.95 (ISBN 0-88062-118-4). Mott Media.

--God & Caesar: Christian Faith & Political Action. LC 84-71423. 226p. 1984. 14.95 (ISBN 0-89107-326-4, Crossway Bks); pap. 7.95 (ISBN 0-89107-313-2). Good News.

Eidsvik, Charles V. Cineliteracy: Film Among the Arts. LC 77-94015. (Illus.). 1978. 14.95 (ISBN 0-8180-0708-7). Horizon.

Eidt, Mary B. & Gandy, Joan W., eds. The Complete Guide to Natchez. LC 76-56980. (Illus.). 111p. 1982. pap. text ed. 5.00 (ISBN 0-9609728-0-3). Myrtle Bank.

Eidt, Robert C. Advances in Abandoned Settlement Analysis: Application to Prehistoric Anthrosols in Colombia, South America. LC 84-17502. (Illus.). 159p. 1984. pap. 12.50 (ISBN 0-930450-53-1). U Wis-Mil Ctr Latin Am.

--Pioneer Settlement in Northeast Argentina. LC 71-138058. (Illus.). 294p. 1971. 30.00x (ISBN 0-299-05920-0). U of Wis Pr.

Eiduson, Bernice T. & Beckman, Linda, eds. Science As a Career Choice: Theoretical & Empirical Studies. LC 72-83833. 752p. 1973. 25.00x (ISBN 0-87154-230-7). Russell Sage.

Eie, Minking see Scedrov, Andrej.

Eielberg, Paul. Jerusalem vs. Athens: In Quest of a General Theory of Existence. 412p. (Orig.). 1983. lib. bdg. 31.00 (ISBN 0-8191-3488-0); pap. text ed. 17.50 (ISBN 0-8191-3489-9). U Pr of Amer.

EIFAC. Report on Copper & Freshwater Fish: EIFAC Working Paper on Water Quality Criteria for European Freshwater Fish. (European Inland Fisheries Advisory Commission (EIFAC): Technical Papers: No. 27). 1976. pap. 7.50 (ISBN 0-685-74522-8, F2029, FAO). Unipub.

Eifer, Bert. Developing the Creative Edge in Photography. (Illus.). 220p. (Orig.). 1984. pap. 16.95 (ISBN 0-89879-110-3). Writers Digest.

Eiferman, Lee. Ninety-Five Essential Facts. 16p. (Orig.). 1982. pap. 3.00 (ISBN 0-917061-14-4). Top Stories.

--Real Family Stories: Ninety-Five Essential Facts. 16p. (Orig.). 1982. pap. 3.00 (ISBN 0-917061-14-4). Top Stories.

Eifert, Frank & Stenbock, Evelyn. They Sang with the Spirit. 104p. 1983. pap. 3.95 (ISBN 0-8341-0824-0). Beacon Hill.

Eifert, Harvey C. Answers in the Mail. LC 77-18977. 1978. pap. 4.95x (ISBN 0-915668-29-7). G S E Pubns.

Eifert, Virginia L. Tall Trees & Far Horizons: Adventures & Discoveries of Early Botanists in America. LC 70-39100. (Essay Index Reprint Ser.). (Illus.). Repr. of 1965 ed. 27.50 (ISBN 0-8369-2686-2). Ayer Co Pubs.

Eifert, Virginia S. Birds in Your Backyard. rev. ed. (Popular Science Ser.: Vol. II). (Illus.). 224p. 1967. Ill St Museum.

--Essays on Nature. 274p. 1967. pap. 3.50 (ISBN 0-89792-033-3). Ill St Museum.

--Exploring for Mushrooms. (Story of Illinois Ser.: No. 3). (Illus.). 47p. 1982. pap. 1.00 (ISBN 0-89792-091-0). Ill St Museum.

--Flowers That Bloom in the Spring. rev. ed. (Story of Illinois Ser.: No. 4). (Illus.). 48p. 1970. pap. 1.00 (ISBN 0-89792-045-7). Ill St Museum.

--Invitation to Birds. (Story of Illinois Ser.: No. 5). (Illus.). 64p. 1953. pap. 1.00 (ISBN 0-89792-006-6). Ill St Museum.

--The Story of Illinois: Indian & Pioneer. rev. ed. (Story of Illinois Ser.: No. 1). (Illus.). 24p. 1979. pap. 1.00 (ISBN 0-89792-039-2). Ill St Museum.

Eifert, Virginia S., jt. auth. see Voss, John.

Eifler, Margret E., ed. see Alcover, Madeleine, et al.

Eige, Lillian E. The Kidnapping of Mr. Huey. LC 82-48610. 160p. (gr. 6 up). 1983. 9.57i (ISBN 0-06-021798-7); PLB 9.89g (ISBN 0-06-021799-5). HarpJ.

Eigeldinger, Marc, jt. auth. see Valery, Paul.

Eigen, M. & Schuster, P. The Hypercycle: A Principle of Natural Self-Organization. 1979. 14.00 (ISBN 0-387-09293-5). Springer-Verlag.

Eigen, M., jt. ed. see Balaban, M.

Eigen, Manfred & Winkler, Ruthild. Laws of the Game. LC 81-47550. (Illus.). 368p. 1982. pap. 8.61i (ISBN 0-06-090971-4, CN-971, CN). Har-Row.

--Laws of the Game: How the Principles of Nature Govern Chance. LC 79-3494. (Illus.). 384p. 1981. 19.95 (ISBN 0-394-41806-9). Knopf.

Eigen, Michael. The Psychotic Self & Treatment. 280p. 1985. 25.00 (ISBN 0-87668-896-2). Aronson.

Eigen, Michael, jt. auth. see Coleman, Marie.

Eigenfeld, Neil, jt. auth. see Darlington, C. LeRoy.

Eiger, Marvin & Olds, Sally. The Complete Book of Breastfeeding. 224p. 1973. pap. 3.95 (ISBN 0-553-25444-8). Bantam.

Eiger, Marvin S., jt. auth. see Olds, Sally.

Eigerman, Hyman, ed. see Wordsworth, Dorothy.

Eighme, Lloyd. Insects You Have Seen. LC 79-24141. (Crown Ser.). (gr. 6 up). 1980. pap. 5.95 (ISBN 0-8127-0259-X). Review & Herald.

Eighmey, J., ed. Attitude Research Under the Sun. LC 78-13992. (Proceedings Ser.). 1979. 10.00 (ISBN 0-87757-115-5). Am Mktg.

Eighmey, John, ed. see Attitude Research Conference.

Eighmy, John L. Churches in Cultural Captivity: A History of the Social Attitudes of Southern Baptists. LC 70-111047. 1972. 18.95x (ISBN 0-87049-115-6). U of Tenn Pr.

Eighmy, Judith B., jt. auth. see Will, Connie A.

Eighner, Lars. Bayou Boy & Other Stories. 192p. (Orig.). 1985. pap. 7.95 (ISBN 0-917342-06-2). Gay Sunshine.

Eighth International Biometeorological Congress 9-15 September 1979. Biometeorology Seven: Proceedings, Supplement to Volume 24 of the International Journal of Biometeorology, Pt. 2. Zemel, Z. & Hyslop, N., eds. 1981. pap. text ed. 44.75 (ISBN 90-265-0350-4). Swets North Am.

Eighty-Fifth Symposium of the International Astronomical Union, Victoria, B. C., Canada, August 27-30, 1979. Star Clusters: Proceedings. Hesser, James E., ed. (International Astronomical Union Symposium Ser.: No. 85). 540p. 1980. lib. bdg. 63.00 (ISBN 90-277-1087-2, Pub. by Reidel Holland); pap. 31.50 (ISBN 90-277-1088-0). Kluwer Academic.

Eighty Micro Editors. Eighty Micro's Review Guide. 480p. 1983. softcover 7.95 (ISBN 0-913531-00-6). Green Pub Inc.

Eigler, Friedrich W. & Jakubowski, Hans D. Surgery in Chronic Renal Failure. (Illus.). 256p. 1984. pap. text ed. 43.00 (ISBN 0-317-13126-5). Thieme-Stratton.

Eigler, G. Studien Zur Gliederung der Flechtengattung Lecanora. (Illus.). 10.50 (ISBN 3-7682-0628-9). Lubrecht & Cramer.

Eigner, Edwin M. The Metaphysical Novel in England & America: Dickens, Bulwer, Hawthorne, Melville. LC 76-50246. 1978. 28.50x (ISBN 0-520-03382-5). U of Cal Pr.

Eigner, Edwin M. & Worth, George J. Victorian Criticism of the Novel. (Cambridge English Prose Texts Ser.). 286p. Date not set. price not set. (ISBN 0-521-25515-5); pap. price not set. (ISBN 0-521-27520-2). Cambridge U Pr.

Eigner, Edwin M., ed. Nineteenth Century British Fiction. (An AMS Reprint Ser.). Repr. write for info (ISBN 0-404-61750-6). AMS Pr.

Eigner, Larry. Anything on Its Side. 1974. 16.00 (ISBN 0-685-40881-7); pap. 8.00 (ISBN 0-685-40882-5). Elizabeth Pr.

--Selected Poems. 1972. 6.00 (ISBN 0-685-29871-X); pap. 2.50 (ISBN 0-685-29872-8). Oyez.

--Things Stirring Together or Far Away. 120p. (Orig.). 1974. pap. 5.00 (ISBN 0-87685-187-1). Black Sparrow.

--Time, Details of a Tree. 1979. 12.00 (ISBN 0-686-59677-3); pap. 5.00 (ISBN 0-686-59678-1). Elizabeth Pr.

--Watching How or Why. 1977. bound in boards, slipcased 10.00 (ISBN 0-685-88993-9); in wraps 5.00 (ISBN 0-685-88994-7). Elizabeth Pr.

--Waters; Places; a Time. Grenier, Robert, ed. 166p. (Orig.). 1983. signed ed. 20.00 (ISBN 0-87685-498-6); pap. 7.50 (ISBN 0-87685-497-8). Black Sparrow.

--The World & Its Streets, Places. 180p. (Orig.). 1977. pap. 5.00 (ISBN 0-87685-268-1). Black Sparrow.

Eignmann, Carl H. A Revision of the South American Nematognathi or Catfishes. pap. 55.00 (ISBN 0-384-14040-8). Johnson Repr.

Eigsti, jt. auth. see Clemen.

Eigsti, D. G., jt. auth. see Clemen-Stone, S. A.

Eijndhoven, J. van see Van Eijndhoven, J.

Eijsvoogel, Vincent P., et al, eds. Leukocyte Membrane Determinants Regulating Immune Reactivity. 1976. 70.50 (ISBN 0-12-233750-6). Acad Pr.

Eikeland, Hans M., jt. auth. see Sovik, Nils.

Eikeland, Peter J. Ibsen Studies. LC 76-117595. 1970. (Studies in European Literature, No. 56). 1970. Repr. of 1934 ed. lib. bdg. 39.95x (ISBN 0-8383-1028-1). Haskell.

Eikemeier, H., jt. ed. see Guettinger, W.

Eiken, M. Roentgen Diagnosis of Children. (Illus.). 1979. pap. 19.95 (ISBN 0-8151-3028-7). Year Bk Med.

--Roentgen Diagnosis of the Chest. (Illus.). 84p. 1975. pap. 19.95 (ISBN 0-8151-3026-0). Year Bk Med.

Eikenbary, R. D., jt. ed. see Boethal, D. J.

Eikenberry, Alice. Pueblo: Plays, Players, Playhouses in the Gilded Age, 1865-1900. (Orig.). 1986. pap. write for info. (ISBN 0-915617-08-0). Pueblo Co Hist Soc.

Eiker, Earl E., jt. ed. see Green, Gordon G.

Eiker, Lawrence, tr. Soviet Geography: Accomplishments & Tasks. Harris, Chauncy D., ed. (Illus.). 409p. 7.50 (ISBN 0-318-12735-0). Am Geographical.

Eikhenbaum, B. & Vinogradov, V. Anna Akhmatova: Tri Knigi. 500p. (Rus.). 1985. Repr. of 1923 ed. 35.00 (ISBN 0-88233-914-1). Ardis Pubs.

Eikhenbaum, Boris. Lermontov: An Essay in Literary Historical Evaluation. Parrott, Ray & Weber, Harry, trs. 1981. 20.00 (ISBN 0-686-70084-8); pap. 6.50 (ISBN 0-88233-705-X). Ardis Pubs.

--Russian Prose. Parrott, Ray, tr. from Rus. 250p. 1985. 22.50 (ISBN 0-88233-892-7). Ardis Pubs.

--Tolstoi in the Seventies. Kaspin, A., tr. 1982. 32.50 (ISBN 0-88233-472-7). Ardis Pubs.

--Tolstoi in the Sixties. White, tr. from Rus. 1982. 25.00 (ISBN 0-88233-470-0). Ardis Pubs.

Eikner, Allen V., ed. Religious Perspectives & Problems: An Introduction to the Philosophy of Religion. LC 80-67265. 368p. 1980. lib. bdg. 26.75 (ISBN 0-8191-1215-1); pap. text ed. 15.00 (ISBN 0-8191-1216-X). U Pr of Amer.

Eik-Nes, K. B. & Horning, E. C. Gas Phase Chromatography of Steroids. LC 68-18620. (Monographs on Endocrinology: Vol. 2). (Illus.). 1968. 29.00 (ISBN 0-387-04277-6). Springer-Verlag.

Eik-Nes, Kristen B., ed. The Androgens of the Testis. LC 70-98064. pap. 65.00 (ISBN 0-317-28678-1, 2055037). Bks Demand UMI.

Eikum, A. S. & Seabloom, R. W. Alternative Wastewater Treatment. 1982. 45.00 (ISBN 90-277-1430-4, Pub. by Reidel Holland). Kluwer Academic.

Eiland, Murray L. Chinese & Exotic Rugs. LC 79-11744. (Illus.). 1979. 39.95 (ISBN 0-8212-0745-8, 139092). NYGS.

--Oriental Rugs: A New Comprehensive Guide. (Illus.). 352p. 1982. 50.00 (ISBN 0-8212-1127-7, 651621). NYGS.

Eiland, Murray L., Jr., jt. auth. see Der Manuelian, Lucy.

Eilenberg, Anna. Breaking My Silence. LC 84-72760. (Illus.). 144p. 1984. pap. write for info. Shengold.

--Breaking My Silence. LC 84-72760. (Illus.). 140p. 1985. 11.95 (ISBN 0-88400-112-1). Shengold.

Eilenberg, Howard. What You Should Know about Research Techniques for Retailers. LC 67-28901. (Business Almanac Series No. 14). 1968. 5.95 (ISBN 0-379-11214-0). Oceana.

Eilenberg, S., jt. auth. see Cartan, H.

Eilenberg, Samuel. Automata, Languages, & Machines. (Pure & Applied Mathematics: A Series of Monographs & Textbooks, Vol. 58). Vol. A 1974. 67.50 (ISBN 0-12-234001-9); Vol. B 1976. 60.00 (ISBN 0-12-234002-7). Acad Pr.

Eilenberg, Samuel & Elgot, Calvin. Recursiveness. 1970. 22.50 (ISBN 0-12-234050-7). Acad Pr.

Eilenberg, Samuel & Steenrod, Norman. Foundations of Algebraic Topology. LC 52-5841. (Princeton Mathematical Ser.: Vol. 15). pap. 86.00 (ISBN 0-317-09123-9, 2014638). Bks Demand UMI.

Eilenberger, G. Solitons: Mathematical Methods for Physicists. (Springer Series in Solid-State Sciences: Vol. 19). (Illus.). 192p. 1981. 22.00 (ISBN 0-387-10223-X). Springer-Verlag.

Eiler, Andrew. The Consumer Protection Manual. LC 82-1464. 416p. 1983. 29.95x (ISBN 0-87196-310-8). Facts on File.

Eiler, Lyntha S. & Eiler, Terry, eds. Blue Ridge Harvest: A Region's Folklife in Photographs. LC 80-607940. (Illus.). vi, 116p. 1981. pap. 6.00 (ISBN 0-8444-0341-5). Lib Congress.

Eiler, Terry, jt. ed. see Eiler, Lyntha S.

Eilers, Robert. The Hermes Stone. (Orig.). 1980. pap. 1.95 (ISBN 0-532-23264-X). Woodhill.

Eilers, Robert D. Regulation of Blue Cross & Blue Shield Plans. 1963. 12.00x (ISBN 0-256-00644-X). Irwin.

Eilert, Rick. For Self & Country. 1984. pap. 3.95 (ISBN 0-671-50451-7). PB.

--For Self & Country: For the Wounded in Vietnam the Journey Home Took More Bravery Than Going into Battle, a True Story. LC 83-61854. (Illus.). 320p. 1983. FPT 13.95 (ISBN 0-688-01547-6). Morrow.

Eilhart Von Oberge. Eilhart von Oberge's "Tristrant". Thomas, J. W., ed. & tr. LC 77-10747. viii, 155p. 1978. 13.50x (ISBN 0-8032-0968-1). U of Nebr Pr.

Eilon, S. & King, J. R. Industrial Scheduling Abstracts: 1950-1966. 1967. 11.75 (ISBN 0-934454-50-7). Lubrecht & Cramer.

Eilon, S. & Lampkin, W. Inventory Control Abstracts: 1953-1965. 1968. 14.70 (ISBN 0-934454-53-1). Lubrecht & Cramer.

Eilon, S. & Watson-Gandy. Distribution Management: Mathematical Modelling & Practical Analysis. (Illus.). 240p. 1982. pap. text ed. 29.95x (ISBN 0-85264-191-5). Lubrecht & Cramer.

Eilon, Samuel. The Act of Reckoning. (Statistic Modelling & Decision Science Ser.). 1984. 39.50 (ISBN 0-12-234080-9). Acad Pr.

--Management Control. 2nd ed. 1979. text ed. 22.00 (ISBN 0-08-022482-2); pap. text ed. 10.50 (ISBN 0-08-022481-4). Pergamon.

Eilon, Samuel, et al. Applied Productivity Analysis for Industry. 206p. 1976. pap. text ed. 19.25 (ISBN 0-08-020506-2). Pergamon.

Eilting, Mary. Macmillan Book of Dinosaurs & Other Prehistoric Creatures. LC 84-4372. 80p. (gr. 2-7). 1984. 14.95 (ISBN 0-02-733430-9); pap. 6.95 (ISBN 0-02-043000-0). Macmillan.

EIMAC Division of Varian Laboratory Staff, jt. auth. see Sutherland, Robert I.

Eimas, Peter D. & Miller, Joanne L., eds. Perspectives on the Study of Speech. LC 80-39499. 464p. 1981. text ed. 39.95x (ISBN 0-89859-052-3). L Erlbaum Assocs.

Eimbinder, Jerry, ed. Designing with Linear Integrated Circuits. LC 68-56161. 301p. 1969. 19.75 (ISBN 0-471-23455-9, Pub. by Wiley). Krieger.

Eimeren, W. van see Van Eimeren, W., et al.

Eimerl, Sarel. World of Giotto. LC 67-23024. (Library of Art Ser.). (Illus.). (gr. 7 up). 1967. 19.94 (ISBN 0-8094-0268-8, Pub. by Time-Life). Silver.

Eimermann, Thomas E. Fundamentals of Paralegalism. (Illus.). 420p. 1980. 25.95 (ISBN 0-316-23120-7); instuctor's manual avail. (ISBN 0-316-23121-5). Little.

Eimers, Robert & Aitchison, Robert. Effective Parents - Responsible Children. LC 76-44340. 1977. pap. 5.95 (ISBN 0-07-019108-5). McGraw.

Eimert, Herbert. Das Lexikon der Elektronischen Musik. 426p. (Ger.). 1973. 27.50 (ISBN 3-7649-2083-1, M-7260). French & Eur.

Eimert, Herbert & Stockhausen, Karlheinz, eds. Anton Webern. Black, Leo & Smith, Eric, trs. from Ger. (Die Reihe: No. 2). 1958. pap. 12.00 (ISBN 3-7024-0151-2, 47-26102). Eur-Am Music.

--Electronic Music. (Die Reihe: No. 1). 1958. pap. 14.00 (ISBN 0-900938-10-2, 47-26101). Eur-Am Music.

--Form Space. Cardew, Cornelius, tr. from Ger. (Die Reihe: No. 7). 1965. pap. 14.00 (ISBN 3-7024-0142-3, 47-26107). Eur-Am Music.

--Musical Craftsmanship. Cardew, Cornelius & Black, Leo, trs. from Ger. (Die Reihe: No. 3). 1959. pap. 14.00 (ISBN 0-900938-11-0, 47-26103). Eur-Am Music.

--Reports, Analyses. Black, Leo & Koenig, Ruth, trs. from Ger. (Die Reihe: No. 5). 1961. pap. 14.00 (ISBN 0-900938-13-7, 47-26105). Eur-Am Music.

--Retrospective. Cardew, Cornelius & Koenig, Ruth, trs. (Die Reihe: No. 8). 1978. pap. 6.25 (ISBN 3-7024-0152-0, 50-26108). Eur-Am Music.

--Speech & Music. Shenfield, Margaret & Koenig, Ruth, trs. from Ger. (Die Reihe: No. 6). 1964. pap. 4.75 (ISBN 0-900938-14-5, 50-26106). Eur-Am Music.

--Young Composers. (Die Reihe: No. 4). 1960. pap. 14.00 (ISBN 0-900938-13-7, 47-26104). Eur-Am Music.

Eims, Leroy. Be a Motivational Leader. 144p. 1981. pap. 4.95 (ISBN 0-89693-008-4). Victor Bks.

--Be the Leader You Were Meant to Be. LC 75-5392. 132p. 1975. pap. 4.95 (ISBN 0-88207-723-6). Victor Bks.

--Disciples in Action. LC 81-80284. 320p. (Orig.). 1981. pap. 5.95 (ISBN 0-89109-477-6). NavPress.

--Disciples in Action. 324p. 1981. pap. 6.95 (ISBN 0-88207-343-5). Victor Bks.

--Laboring in the Harvest. 108p. 1985. pap. 4.95 (ISBN 0-89109-530-6). NavPress.

--The Lost Art of Disciple Making. LC 78-17227. 176p. (Orig.). 1978. pap. 5.95 (ISBN 0-89109-472-5, 24729). NavPress.

--The Lost Art of Disciple Making. pap. 5.95 (ISBN 0-310-37281-X). Zondervan.

--Prayer: More Than Words. LC 82-61301. 162p. 1983. pap. 3.95 (ISBN 0-89109-493-8). NavPress.

--What Every Christian Should Know about Growing. LC 75-44842. 168p. 1976. pap. 4.95 (ISBN 0-88207-727-9). Victor Bks.

--Winning Ways. LC 74-77319. 160p. 1974. pap. 4.50 (ISBN 0-88207-707-4). Victor Bks.

--Wisdom from Above. LC 77-92704. 155p. 1978. pap. 4.95 (ISBN 0-88207-761-9). Victor Bks.

Einarsen, Arthur S. Black Brant: Sea Goose of the Pacific Coast. LC 63-10796. (Illus.). 160p. 1965. 11.50x (ISBN 0-295-73730-1). U of Wash Pr.

Einarsson, Magnus. Everyman's Heritage: An Album of Canadian Folk-Life-Notre Patrimoine: Images Du Peuple Canadien. (Illus.). 1978. (Pub. by Natl Mus Canada); pap. 8.95 (ISBN 0-660-00124-1, 56334-0). U of Chicago Pr.

Einarsson, Stefan. A History of Icelandic Literature. LC 57-9519. pap. 105.50 (ISBN 0-317-29923-9, 2021736). Bks Demand UMI.

--History of Icelandic Prose Writers. (Islandica Ser.: Vols. 32 - 33). 1800-1940. 24.00 (ISBN 0-527-00363-8). Kraus Repr.

--Icelandic Grammar, Text & Glossary. 2nd ed. LC 57-9519. 538p. 1949. 29.50x (ISBN 0-8018-0187-7). Johns Hopkins.

Einasto, Jaan & Longair, Malcolm S., eds. The Large Scale Structure of the Universe. 1978. lib. bdg. 58.00 (ISBN 90-277-0895-9, Pub. by Reidel Holland); pap. 37.00 (ISBN 90-277-0896-7, Pub. by Reidel Holland). Kluwer Academic.

Einaudi, Karen, jt. ed. see Fototeca Unione.

Einaudi, Luigi R., ed. Beyond Cuba: Latin America Takes Charge of Its Future. LC 73-8644. 250p. 1973. pap. 14.00x (ISBN 0-8448-0266-2). Crane-Russak Co.

Einaudi, Mario. The Roosevelt Revolution. LC 77-24020. 1977. Repr. of 1960 ed. lib. bdg. 26.75x (ISBN 0-8371-9740-6, EIRR). Greenwood.

Einaudi, Mario & Goguel, Francois. Christian Democracy in Italy & France. LC 69-19224. viii, 229p. 1969. Repr. of 1952 ed. 17.50 (ISBN 0-208-00801-2, Archon). Shoe String.

Einaudi, Mario, et al. Communism in Western Europe. LC 77-143880. ix, 239p. 1971. Repr. of 1951 ed. 18.50 (ISBN 0-208-00411-4, Archon). Shoe String.

Einaudi, Paula F. A Grammar of Biloxi. LC 75-25114. (American Indian Linguistics Ser.). 1976. lib. bdg. 51.00 (ISBN 0-8240-1965-2). Garland Pub.

Einaudi, R., tr. see Nervi, Pier L.

Einberg, Elizabeth. Gainsborough's Giovanna Bacelli. (Illus.). 40p. pap. 3.95 (ISBN 0-905005-60-0, Pub. by Salem Hse Ltd.). Merrimack Pub Cir.

--The Kennedys Abroad: Ann & Peter in Southern Germany. 12.50 (ISBN 0-392-08619-0, SpS). Sportshelf.

Einbinder, Harvey. Myth of the Britannica. LC 63-16997. Repr. of 1964 ed. 20.00 (ISBN 0-384-14050-5). Johnson Repr.

Einbond, Bernard L. The Coming Indoors & Other Poems. LC 78-53258. 1979. boxed 8.50 (ISBN 0-8048-1291-8). C E Tuttle.

Ein-Dor, Phillip & Jones, Carl R. Information Systems Management. 288p. 1985. 35.00; instr's. manual avail. (ISBN 0-444-00409-2). Elsevier.

Ein-Dor, Phillip & Segev, Eli. A Paradigm for Management Information Systems. LC 81-1825. 304p. 1981. 39.95 (ISBN 0-03-058017-X). Praeger.

Einem, Herbert Von. Michelangelo. 2nd ed. 1973. 43.00x (ISBN 0-416-15140-X, NO. 2183). Methuen Inc.

Einem, Herbert Von see Von Einem, Herbert.

Einenkel, E., ed. Catharina, Saint, of Alexandria: The Life of St. Katherine. (EETS, OS Ser.: No. 80). Repr. of 1884 ed. 20.00 (ISBN 0-527-00080-9). Kraus Repr.

Einfeldt, H., jt. auth. see Moeller, J.

Einhard. Life of Charlemagne. 1960. pap. 5.95 (ISBN 0-472-06035-X, 35, AA). U of Mich Pr.

Einhard & Notker. Two Lives of Charlemagne. Thorpe, Lewis, tr. & intro. by. (Classics Ser.). 240p. 1969. pap. 3.95 (ISBN 0-14-044213-8). Penguin.

Einhorn, et al. Effective Employment Interviewing: Unlocking Human Potential. 1982. pap. text ed. 11.90x (ISBN 0-673-15321-5). Scott F.

Einhorn, A. H., ed. Klinische Oekologie in der Paediatrie: Pediatrics & Ecology. (Paediatrische Fortbildungskurse fuer die Praxis: Vol. 38). (Illus.). 201p. 1974. 17.50 (ISBN 3-8055-1653-3). S Karger.

Einhorn, Barbara. Living in Berlin. LC 85-40307. (Illus.). 48p. (gr. 6 up). 1985. PLB 13.00 (ISBN 0-382-09114-0). Silver.

Einhorn, Barbara, tr. see Pashukanis, Evgeny.

Einhorn, Barbara, tr. see Pashukanis, Evgeny B.

Einhorn, Bruce. Mindercise: For a Healthier Way of Living, the Next Step Beyond Diet & Exercise. LC 84-60913. (Illus.). 176p. 1984. 14.95 (ISBN 0-918525-00-4). Noblevision Inc.

Einhorn, David. Minute Manual for DB Master. Pirisino, Jim, ed. 137p. 1983. pap. 12.95 (ISBN 0-913131-02-4). Minuteware.

--Seventh Candle & Other Folk Tales of Eastern Europe. Pashin, Gertrude, tr. LC 68-10968. (gr. 6-8). 1968. 7.95x (ISBN 0-87068-369-1). Ktav.

Einhorn, E. C. Old French: A Concise Handbook. 210p. 1975. 37.50 (ISBN 0-521-20343-0); pap. 14.95 (ISBN 0-521-09838-6). Cambridge U Pr.

Einhorn, Eric & Logue, John. Welfare States in Hard Times: Problems, Policy & Politics in Denmark & Sweden. rev. ed. (Illus.). 72p. 1982. pap. 3.95 (ISBN 0-933522-12-6). Kent Popular.

Einhorn, Eric & Logue, John, eds. Democracy on the Shop Floor? An American Look at Employee Influence in Scandinavia Today. (Illus.). 80p. 1982. pap. text ed. 3.95 (ISBN 0-933522-11-8). Kent Popular.

Einhorn, Franne, jt. auth. see Bin-Nun, Judy.

Einhorn, Henry, jt. auth. see Nutter, G. Warren.

Einhorn, Herbert A. & Robinson, James W. Shareholder Meetings: Dealing with Management & Shareholder Proposals. LC 84-61688. (Corporate Law & Practice Course Handbook Ser.: No. 460). 1984. 40.00. PLI.

Einhorn, Herbert A., jt. auth. see Aranow, Edward R.

Einhorn, Lawrence H., ed. Testicular Tumors: Management & Treatment. LC 79-89999. (Cancer Management Series: Vol. 3). (Illus.). 224p. 1980. 46.00 (ISBN 0-89352-078-0). Masson Pub.

Einhorn, Richard. Epson QX-10: Everything You Need to Know. LC 84-60790. (Illus.). 224p. 1984. pap. 12.95 (ISBN 0-688-02832-2, Quill NY). Morrow.

Einhorn, Robert J. Negotiating from Strength: Leverage in U. S.-Soviet Arms Control Negotiations. LC 85-3409. (The Washington Papers). 1985. 28.95 (ISBN 0-03-005534-2); pap. 9.95 (ISBN 0-03-004769-2). Praeger.

Einhorn, Robert J. & Garrity, Patrick J., eds. Reducing the Risk of Nuclear War. 63p. 1985. 14.95 (ISBN 0-89206-077-8). CSI Studies.

Einsele, G. & Soilacher, A., eds. Cyclic & Event Stratification. (Illus.). 550p. 1982. pap. 32.00 (ISBN 0-387-11373-8). Springer-Verlag.

Einsidler, Bernice, jt. ed. see Hankoff, Leon.

Einsiedel, Albert A., Jr. Improving Project Management: A Self-Instructional Manual. 232p. 1984. 35.00 (ISBN 0-934634-64-5). Intl Human Res.

Einspahr, Bruce, compiled by. Index to the Brown, Driver & Briggs Hebrew Lexicon. LC 76-25479. (Hebrew.). 1976. 25.95 (ISBN 0-8024-4082-7). Moody.

Einspruch, N. VLSI Electronics: Microstructure Science, Vol. 7. 1983. 59.50 (ISBN 0-12-234107-4). Acad Pr.

Einspruch, Norman, ed. VLSI Electronics: Microstructure Science. 1982. Vol. 4. 53.00 (ISBN 0-12-234104-X); Vol. 6. suppl. material 79.00 (ISBN 0-12-234106-6). Acad Pr.

Einspruch, Norman & Huff, Howard, eds. VLSI Electronics: Microstructure Science, Vol. 12. Date not set. 75.00 (ISBN 0-12-234112-0). Acad Pr.

Einspruch, Norman G., ed. Surface & Interface Effects in VLSI, Vol. 10. (VLSI Electronics: Micro Structure Science Ser.). 1985. 65.00 (ISBN 0-12-234110-4). Acad Pr.

--VLSI Electronics: Microstructure Science & Engineering, 2 vols. 1981. 52.00 ea. Vol. 1. Vol. 2 (ISBN 0-12-234102-3). Acad Pr.

--VLSI Electronics: Microstructure Science, Vol. 3. LC 81-2877. 1982. 56.00 (ISBN 0-12-234103-1). Acad Pr.

--VLSI Electronics Microstructure Science, Vol. 5. 1982. 59.00 (ISBN 0-12-234105-8). Acad Pr.

--VLSI Electronics: Microstructure Science, Vol. 9. 1985. 72.00 (ISBN 0-12-234109-0). Acad Pr.

--VLSI Electronics: Microstructure Science Vol. 8: Plasma Processing for VLSI. LC 83-22351. 1984. 69.00 (ISBN 0-12-234108-2). Acad Pr.

--VLSI Handbook. (Handbook Series Candidate). Date not set. 125.00 (ISBN 0-12-234100-7). Acad Pr.

Einspruch, Norman G. & Wisseman, William R., eds. VLSI Electronics, Vol. 11. (Serial Publication Ser.). 1985. 68.50 (ISBN 0-12-234111-2). Acad Pr.

Einstein, A. Italian Madrigal, 3 vols. 1971. Set. 120.00 (ISBN 0-691-09112-9). Princeton U Pr.

Einstein, A. W., Jr., jt. auth. see Einstein, Arthur.

Einstein, Albert. Albert Einstein. Redpath, Ann, ed. (Living Philosophies Ser.). (Illus.). 32p. (gr. 9 up). 1985. lib. bdg. 8.95 (ISBN 0-88682-011-1). Creative Ed.

--Essays in Humanism. 130p. 1983. pap. 4.95 (ISBN 0-8022-2417-2). Philos Lib.

--Essays in Physics. (Philosophical Paperback Ser.). 75p. 1985. pap. 3.95 (ISBN 0-8022-2482-2). Philos Lib.

--Ideas & Opinions. 1954. 4.98 (ISBN 0-517-00393-7). Outlet Bk Co.

--Ideas & Opinions. 368p. pap. 2.25 (ISBN 0-440-34150-7, LE). Dell.

--Ideas & Opinions. 1985. pap. 6.95 (ISBN 0-517-55601-4). Crown.

--Investigations on the Theory of the Brownian Movement. Furth, R., ed. Cowper, A. D., tr. 1926. pap. 3.50 (ISBN 0-486-60304-0). Dover.

--Meaning of Relativity. 5th ed. 1956. 25.00x (ISBN 0-691-08007-0); pap. 6.95 (ISBN 0-691-02352-2). Princeton U Pr.

--Out of My Later Years. 288p. 1973. pap. 6.95 (ISBN 0-8065-0357-2). Citadel Pr.

--Out of My Later Years. LC 70-89016. Repr. of 1950 ed. lib. bdg. 22.50x (ISBN 0-8371-2086-1, EILY). Greenwood.

--Relativity: The Special & General Theory. Lawson, Robert W., tr. 1961. pap. 3.95 (ISBN 0-517-02530-2). Crown.

--Relativity: The Special & General Theory. 13.25 (ISBN 0-8446-1169-7). Peter Smith.

--Sidelights on Relativity. (Popular Science Ser.). 56p. 1983. pap. 2.25 (ISBN 0-486-24511-X). Dover.

--The World As I See It. 1979. pap. 2.95 (ISBN 0-8065-0711-X). Citadel Pr.

Einstein, Albert & Infeld, Leopold. Evolution of Physics. 1967. pap. 9.95 (ISBN 0-671-20156-5, Touchstone Bks). S&S.

Einstein, Albert, et al. The Principle of Relativity. 1924. pap. 3.50 (ISBN 0-486-60081-5). Dover.

--Living Philosophies. LC 75-3009. Repr. of 1931 ed. 27.50 (ISBN 0-404-59128-0). AMS Pr.

Einstein, Alfred. Essays on Music. 1962. pap. 8.95 (ISBN 0-393-00177-6, Norton Lib). Norton.

--Greatness in Music. LC 70-87527. 1972. Repr. of 1941 ed. lib. bdg. 29.50 (ISBN 0-306-71441-8). Da Capo.

--Greatness in Music. LC 76-6984. 1976. pap. 6.95 (ISBN 0-306-80046-2). Da Capo.

--Greatness in Music. LC 75-181148. 287p. 1941. Repr. 29.00 (ISBN 0-403-01549-9). Scholarly.

--Mozart: His Character, His Work. (Orig.). 1945. 39.95x (ISBN 0-19-500538-4). Oxford U Pr.

--Mozart: His Character, His Work. 1965. pap. 10.95 (ISBN 0-19-500732-8, GB). Oxford U Pr.

--Music in the Romantic Era. (Illus.). 1947. 14.95x (ISBN 0-393-09733-1, NortonC). Norton.

--Short History of Music. 1954. pap. 2.95 (ISBN 0-394-70004-X, Vin, V4). Random.

--Shubert: A Musical Portrait. (Music Ser.). ix, 343p. 1981. Repr. of 1951 ed. lib. bdg. 35.00 (ISBN 0-306-76083-5). Da Capo.

Einstein, Alfred, ed. The Golden Age of the Madrigal. Reese, Gustave, tr. LC 74-24074. Repr. of 1942 ed. 24.50 (ISBN 0-404-12902-1). AMS Pr.

Einstein, Arthur & Einstein, A. W., Jr. What You Should Know about Customer Relations. LC 65-22173. (Busiess Almanac Ser.: No. 4). 1966. 5.95 (ISBN 0-379-11204-3). Oceana.

Einstein, C. The Baseball Reader: Favorites from the Fireside Book of Baseball. 384p. 1983. pap. 8.95 (ISBN 0-07-019531-5). McGraw.

--How to Communicate: The Manning, Selvage & Lee Guide to Clear Writing & Speech. 144p. 1985. write for info. (ISBN 0-07-039928-X). McGraw.

Einstein Centennial Celebration, Memphis State University, March 14-16, 1979. After Einstein: Proceedings. Barker, Peter & Shugart, Cecil G., eds. LC 80-27347. (Illus.). 1981. 24.95x (ISBN 0-87870-095-1). Memphis St Univ.

Einstein, Charles. The Baseball Reader. 384p. 1980. 16.30i (ISBN 0-690-01898-3). T Y Crowell.

--How to Coach, Manage & Play Little League Baseball. LC 68-12167. 1969. pap. 5.95 (ISBN 0-671-20291-X, Fireside). S&S.

Einstein, Charles, ed. The Baseball Reader: Favorites from the Fireside Books of Baseball. 1980. 16.30i (ISBN 0-690-01898-3). Har-Row.

Einstein, Elizabeth. The Stepfamily: Living, Loving, & Learning. 210p. 1982. 14.95 (ISBN 0-02-535100-1). Macmillan.

--The Stepfamily: Living, Loving & Learning. LC 84-23635. 214p. 1985. pap. 8.95 (ISBN 0-87773-313-9, 73524-2). Shambhala Pubns.

Einstein, Elizabeth R. Proteins of the Brain & CSF in Health & Disease. (Illus.). 326p. 1982. 37.50x (ISBN 0-398-04657-3). C C Thomas.

Einstein, Gertrude, ed. Learning to Apply New Concepts to Casework Practice. LC 68-59388. 1969. pap. 7.00 (ISBN 0-87304-015-5). Family Serv.

Einstein, Gilles O., jt. auth. see Nocks, Elaine C.

Einstein, Lewis D. Divided Loyalties. LC 78-99690. (Essay Index Reprint Ser). 1933. 27.50 (ISBN 0-8369-1349-3). Ayer Co Pubs.

--Italian Renaissance in England. LC 77-143671. (Research & Source Works Ser.: No. 26). 1971. Repr. of 1903 ed. 26.50 (ISBN 0-8337-1027-3). B Franklin.

Einstein, Paul, jt. auth. see Kuncl, Tom.

Einstein, Rosemarie. Pharmacology: Self Assessment Questions for Students. 168p. 1985. pap. text ed. 19.95 (ISBN 0-409-49054-7). Butterworth.

Einstein, Stanley. Beyond Drugs. LC 73-7940. 1974. pap. text ed. 12.00 (ISBN 0-08-017768-9). Pergamon.

--The Drug User: Personality Issues, Factors, & Theories. 209p. 1983. 75.00x (ISBN 0-306-40913-5, Plenum Pr). Plenum Pub.

Einstein, Stanley, ed. The Community's Response to Drug Use. LC 79-16278. 1980. 53.00 (ISBN 0-08-019597-0). Pergamon.

--Drugs in Relation to the Drug User. 1980. Pergamon.

Einstein, Stanley, jt. ed. see Miller, Louis.

Einstein, Susan, ed. see Selz, Peter.

Einstein, Susan, jt. auth. see Selz, Peter.

Einstein, Xavier. Trivia Mania: History & Geography. 1984. pap. 2.50 (ISBN 0-317-05598-4). Zebra.

--Trivia Mania: Literature. 1984. pap. 2.50 (ISBN 0-317-05597-6). Zebra.

--Trivia Mania: Movies. 1984. pap. 2.50 (ISBN 0-317-05595-X). Zebra.

--Trivia Mania: Science & Nature. 1984. pap. 2.50 (ISBN 0-317-05599-2). Zebra.

--Trivia Mania: Sports. 1984. pap. 2.50 (ISBN 0-317-05600-X). Zebra.

--Trivia Mania: Television. 1984. pap. 2.50 (ISBN 0-317-05596-8). Zebra.

Einzig, Barbara. Color. 1976. pap. 3.00 (ISBN 0-87924-020-2). Membrane Pr.

--Robinson Crusoe: A New Fiction. 62p. (Orig.). 1984. pap. 2.00 (ISBN 0-87924-048-2). Membrane Pr.

Einzig, Hetty, jt. auth. see Cannon, Geoffrey.

Einzig, Paul. Bankers, Statesmen & Economists. facs. ed. LC 67-30185. (Essay Index Reprint Ser). 1935. 18.00 (ISBN 0-8369-0410-9). Ayer Co Pubs.

--Behind the Scenes of International Finance. Wilkins, Mira, ed. LC 78-3912. (International Finance Ser.). 1978. Repr. of 1931 ed. lib. bdg. 17.00x (ISBN 0-405-11216-5). Ayer Co Pubs.

--Case Against Joining the Common Market. 144p. 1971. 27.50 (ISBN 0-312-12320-5). St Martin.

--The Economic Foundation of Fascism. LC 78-63666. (Studies in Fascism: Ideology & Practice). 168p. Repr. of 1934 ed. 24.00 (ISBN 0-404-16929-5). AMS Pr.

--Euro-Bond Market. 1969. 25.00 (ISBN 0-312-26705-3). St Martin.

--Exchange Control. LC 75-41085. Repr. of 1934 ed. 18.00 (ISBN 0-404-14733-X). AMS Pr.

--Foreign Exchange Crises. 2nd ed. LC 68-10638. 1970. 25.00 (ISBN 0-312-29855-2). St Martin.

--History of Foreign Exchange. 2nd ed. LC 74-124951. 1970. 29.95 (ISBN 0-312-37835-1). St Martin.

--Leads & Lags. 1968. 22.50 (ISBN 0-312-47670-1). St Martin.

--Parallel Money Markets: The New Market in London, Vols. 1 & 2. LC 75-143999. 1971. 26.00 ea. Vol. 1 (ISBN 0-312-59605-7). Vol. 2 (ISBN 0-312-59640-5). St Martin.

--Roll-Over Credits: The System of Adaptable Interest Rates. LC 73-87565. 114p. 1974. 22.50 (ISBN 0-312-68950-0). St Martin.

--Textbook of Foreign Exchange. 1966. 22.50 (ISBN 0-312-79380-4). St Martin.

--World Finance, Nineteen Fourteen to Nineteen Thirty-Five. Wilkins, Mira, ed. LC 78-3911. (International Finance Ser.). 1978. Repr. of 1935 ed. lib. bdg. 33.00x (ISBN 0-405-11215-7). Ayer Co Pubs.

Einzig, Paul & Quinn, Brian S. The Euro-Dollar System: Practice & Theory of International Interest Rates. 6th ed. LC 77-78988. 1977. 25.00x (ISBN 0-312-26741-X). St Martin.

Einzig, Richard. Classic Modern Houses in Europe. (Illus.). 176p. 1981. 52.50 (ISBN 0-85139-479-5). Nichols Pub.

Eirich, Frederick R., ed. Rheology: Theory & Applications, 5 vols. 1956-1969. Vol. 1. 1956. 95.00 (ISBN 0-12-234301-8); Vol. 2. 1958. 90.00 (ISBN 0-12-234302-6); Vol. 3. 1959. 90.00 (ISBN 0-12-234303-4); Vol. 4. 1967. 95.00 (ISBN 0-12-234304-2); Vol. 5. 1970. 95.00 (ISBN 0-12-234305-0). Acad Pr.

--Science & Technology of Rubber. 1978. 78.00 (ISBN 0-12-234360-3). Acad Pr.

Eirinberg, Estelle, tr. see Thomas, Edith.

Eis, Arlene L. Legal Looseleafs in Print 1985. 384p. 1985. pap. 50.00 (ISBN 0-939486-07-5). Infosources.

Eis, Arlene L., ed. Legal Newsletters in Print, 1985. 232p. 1985. pap. 50.00 (ISBN 0-939486-06-7). Infosources.

Eis, Carl. The Nineteen Nineteen - Nineteen Thirty Merger Movement in American Industry. LC 77-14773. (Dissertations in American Economic History Ser.). 1978. 19.00 (ISBN 0-405-11032-4). Ayer Co Pubs.

Eis, Ruth. Ornamented Bags for Tallit & Tefllin. Cassuto, Nelda, ed. LC 83-83059. (The Magnes Museum Collection Ser.). 99p. (Orig.). 1984. pap. text ed. 22.50 (ISBN 0-318-01125-5). Magnes Mus.

--Torah Binders of the Judah L. Magnes Museum. LC 79-83877. 80p. 1979. pap. 18.00 (ISBN 0-943376-15-7). Magnes Mus.

Eisberg, John F. Medical Malpractice Litigation: Art & Science. 1982. pap. 32.50 (ISBN 0-86678-015-7). Butterworth MN.

Eisberg, R. & Resnick, R. Quantum Physics: Of Atoms, Molecules, Solids, Nuclei & Particles. 2nd ed. 848p. 1985. 38.50 (ISBN 0-471-87373-X). Wiley.

Eisberg, Robert & Resnick, Robert. Quantum Physics of Atoms, Molecules, Solids, Nuclei & Particles. LC 74-1195. 791p. 1974. text ed. 45.45x (ISBN 0-471-23464-8); avail. solutions (ISBN 0-471-05438-0). Wiley.

Eisberg, Robert M. Applied Mathematical Physics with Programmable Pocket Calculators. (Illus.). 1976. pap. text ed. 18.95 (ISBN 0-07-019109-3). McGraw.

--Fundamentals of Modern Physics. LC 61-6770. (Illus.). 729p. 1961. 45.45x (ISBN 0-471-23463-X). Wiley.

Eisberg, Robert M. & Lerner, Lawrence S. Physics, Foundations & Applications, 2 Vols. 720p. 1981. Vol. 1. text ed. 34.95x (ISBN 0-07-019091-7); Vol. 2. text ed. 34.95x (ISBN 0-07-019092-5). McGraw.

--Physics: Foundations & Applications, Combined Vol. (Illus.). 1552p. 1981. 47.95x (ISBN 0-07-019110-7). McGraw.

EISCAT School. Radar Probing of the Auroral Plasma: Proceedings. Brekke, Asgeir, ed. 1977. pap. 36.00x (ISBN 82-00-02421-0, Dist. by Columbia U Pr). Universitet.

Eisch, J. J., ed. Organometallic Syntheses: Non-Transition Metal Compounds, Vol. 2. LC 80-26998. 1981. 39.50 (ISBN 0-12-234950-4). Acad Pr.

Eischen, Martha. Does Your Small Business Need a Computer? (Illus.). 168p. 1983. 18.95 (ISBN 0-8306-0224-0, 1624). TAB Bks.

Eisdorfer, C. & Friedel. Cognitive & Emotional Disturbance in the Elderly. 1977. 31.50 (ISBN 0-8151-3032-5). Year Bk Med.

Eisdorfer, C. & Fann, W. E., eds. Psychopharmacology & Aging. LC 73-9995. (Advances in Behavioral Biology Ser.: Vol. 6). 253p. 1973. 39.50x (ISBN 0-306-37906-6, Plenum Pr). Plenum Pub.

--Psychopharmacology of Aging. (Illus.). 327p. 1980. text ed. 49.50 (ISBN 0-89335-117-2). SP MED & Sci Bks.

Eisdorfer, C., et al. Models for Clinical Psychopathology. 288p. 1981. text ed. 35.00 (ISBN 0-89335-123-7). SP Med & Sci Bks.

Eisdorfer, Carl. Annual Review of Gerontology & Geriatrics, 1984, Vol. 4. 304p. 1984. 31.95 (ISBN 0-8261-3083-6). Springer Pub.

Eisdorfer, Carl & Cohen, Donna. Mental Health Care of the Aging: A Multidisciplinary Curriculum for Professional Training. 144p. 1982. text ed. 23.95 (ISBN 0-8261-4090-4). Springer Pub.

Eisdorfer, Carl, ed. Annual Review of Gerontology & Geriatrics, Vol. 1. (Illus.). 432p. 1980. text ed. 34.50 (ISBN 0-8261-3080-1). Springer Pub.

--Annual Review of Gerontology & Geriatrics, Vol. 3. 448p. 1982. text ed. 37.95 (ISBN 0-8261-3082-8). Springer Pub.

Eisdorfer, Carl & Fann, William E., eds. Treatment of Psychopathology in the Aging. (Springer Psychiatry Ser.: Vol. 2). 304p. 1982. text ed. 31.95 (ISBN 0-8261-3810-1). Springer Pub.

Eisdorfer, Carl, jt. ed. see Elliott, Glen R.

Eisdorfer, Carl, jt. ed. see Golann, Stuart.

Eisdorfer, Carl, et al. Annual Review of Gerontology & Geriatrics, Vol. 2. 1981. text ed. 34.50 (ISBN 0-8261-3081-X). Springer Pub.

Eisele, Albert. Almost to the Presidency. LC 76-187432. 1972. 20.00 (ISBN 0-87832-005-9). Piper.

Eisele, Carol. Christ in You. (Aglow Bible Study: Bk. 10). 64p. 1977. 2.95 (ISBN 0-930756-22-3, 4220-10). Aglow Pubns.

Eisele, Carolyn & Martin, Richard M., eds. Studies in the Scientific & Mathematical Philosophy of Charles S. Pierce: Essays by Carolyn Eisele. (Studies in Philosophy). 1979. text ed. 38.40x (ISBN 90-279-7808-5). Mouton.

Eisele, Carolyn, ed. see Peirce, Charles S.

Eisele, I., jt. ed. see Becker, J. D.

Eisele, James E., et al. Computer Assisted Planning of Curriculum & Instruction: How to Use Computer Based Resource Units to Individualize Instruction. LC 78-157844. 144p. 1971. pap. 11.95 (ISBN 0-87778-018-8). Educ Tech Pubns.

Eisele, John. Modern Quantum Mechanics with Applications to Elementary Particle Physics: An Introduction to Contemporary Physical Thinking. LC 69-19102. Repr. of 1969 ed. 105.90 (ISBN 0-8357-9936-0, 2051240). Bks Demand UMI.

Eisele, Mark Joseph. The Writings of Paul Rolland: An Annotated Bibliography. 2.50 (ISBN 0-318-18119-3). Am String Tchrs.

Eiselen, Frederick C. Sidon: A Study in Oriental History. LC 70-166011. (Columbia University. Oriental Studies: No. 4). Repr. of 1907 ed. 17.50 (ISBN 0-404-50494-9). AMS Pr.

Eiselen, Frederick Carl, et al, eds. The Abingdon Bible Commentary. 1979. pap. 19.95 (ISBN 0-385-14877-1, Galilee). Doubleday.

Eiselen, Malcolm R. The Rise of Pennsylvania Protectionism. LC 73-18438. (Perspectives in American History Ser.: No. 8). 287p. 1974. Repr. of 1932 ed. lib. bdg. 25.00x (ISBN 0-87991-342-8). Porcupine Pr.

--The Rise of Pennsylvania Protectionsim. (The Neglected American Economists Ser.). 1974. lib. bdg. 61.00 (ISBN 0-8240-1035-3). Garland Pub.

Eiseley, Loren. All the Night Wings. LC 79-51431. 1979. 14.95 (ISBN 0-8129-0838-4, Dist. by Har-Row). Times Bks.

--All the Strange Hours. 1983. 15.50 (ISBN 0-8446-5978-9). Peter Smith.

--All the Strange Hours: The Excavation of a Life. LC 75-22433. 1975. pap. 7.95 (ISBN 0-684-14868-4, SL690, ScribT). Scribner.

--Darwin & the Mysterious Mr. X: New Light on the Evolutionists. LC 80-24833. 1981. pap. 6.95 (ISBN 0-15-623949-3, Harv). HarBraceJ.

--Darwin's Century: Evolution & the Men Who Discovered It. LC 58-6638. 1958. pap. 6.50 (ISBN 0-385-08141-3, Anch). Doubleday.

--Firmament of Time. rev. ed. LC 60-11032. 1960. pap. 5.95 (ISBN 0-689-70068-7, 95). Atheneum.

--Francis Bacon & the Modern Dilemma. facs. ed. LC 71-119955. (Select Bibliographies Reprint Ser). 1962. 17.00 (ISBN 0-8369-5398-3). Ayer Co Pubs.

--The Immense Journey. (YA) 1957. 16.95 (ISBN 0-394-43014-X). Random.

--Immense Journey. 1957. pap. 2.95 (ISBN 0-394-70157-7, Vin). Random.

--The Innocent Assassins. LC 73-5182. 1975. pap. 3.95 (ISBN 0-684-14437-9, ScribT); encore edition 3.95 (ISBN 0-684-14970-2, ScribT). Scribner.

--Invisible Pyramid. LC 71-123826. (Illus.). 1985. pap. 6.95 (ISBN 0-684-12732-6, ScribT). Scribner.

--The Invisible Pyramid. 1983. 14.25 (ISBN 0-8446-5980-0). Peter Smith.

--The Man Who Saw Through Time. LC 72-12150. 128p. 1973. pap. 5.95 (ISBN 0-684-13285-0, SL 429, ScribT). Scribner.

--The Man Who Saw Through Time: Francis Bacon & the Modern Dilemma. 1983. 14.25 (ISBN 0-8446-5979-7). Peter Smith.

--The Night Country. LC 78-162747. (Illus.). 1971. pap. 7.95 (ISBN 0-684-12731-8, ScribT). Scribner.

--Notes of an Alchemist. 1974. pap. 7.95 (ISBN 0-684-13693-7, ScribT). Scribner.

--The Star Thrower. LC 79-10406. 1979. pap. 4.95 (ISBN 0-15-684909-7, Harv). HarBraceJ.

--The Star Thrower. LC 77-87827. 1978. 16.95 (ISBN 0-8129-0746-9). Times Bks.

--The Unexpected Universe. LC 67-20308. 239p. 1972. pap. 4.95 (ISBN 0-15-692850-7, Harv). HarBraceJ.

Eiselt, Horst A. & Von Frajer, Helmut. Operations Research Handbook: Standard Algorithms & Methods with Examples. 1977. 29.60x (ISBN 3-11-007055-3). De Gruyter.

Eiseman, Alvord L. Charles Demuth. (Illus.). 88p. 1982. 25.00 (ISBN 0-8230-1302-2). Watson-Guptill.

Eiseman, Ben. Prognosis of Surgical Disease. LC 79-92615. (Illus.). 534p. 1980. text ed. 51.00 (ISBN 0-7216-3342-0). Saunders.

Eiseman, Ben & Wotkyns, Roger S. Surgical Decision Making. LC 77-84668. (Illus.). 1978. text ed. 40.95 (ISBN 0-7216-3343-9). Saunders.

Eiseman, Ben & Steele, Glen, eds. Follow-Up of the Cancer Patient. LC 81-84767. (Illus.). 232p. 1982. text ed. 40.00 (ISBN 0-86577-021-2). Thieme-Stratton.

Eiseman, Leatrice. Alive with Color: The Total Color System for Women & Men. LC 83-2838. 242p. 1983. 18.95 (ISBN 0-87491-552-X). Acropolis.

Eiseman, Seymour, et al, eds. Drug Abuse: Foundation for a Psychosocial Approach. Hubba, George J. 261p. (Orig.). 1984. pap. text ed. 16.75x (ISBN 0-89503-039-X). Baywood Pub.

Eisemann, Fred, tr. see Chekhov, Anton.

Eisemann, Frederick, tr. see Persky, Serge M.

Eisemann, Frederick, tr. see Schnitzler, Arthur.

Eisemann, Moshe. Yechezkel-Ezekiel, 3 vols. (Art Scroll Tanach Ser.). (Illus.). 832p. 1980. Set. 55.95 (ISBN 0-89906-085-4); Set. pap. 45.95 (ISBN 0-89906-086-2). Mesorah Pubns.

--Yechezkel-Ezekiel, Vol. 2. (Art Scroll Tanach Ser.). 272p. 1980. 17.95 (ISBN 0-89906-077-3); pap. 14.95 (ISBN 0-89906-078-1). Mesorah Pubns.

--Yechezkel-Ezekiel, Vol. 3. (Art Scroll Tanach Ser.). (Illus.). 208p. 1980. 17.95 (ISBN 0-89906-083-8); pap. 14.95 (ISBN 0-89906-084-6). Mesorah Pubns.

Eisemon, Thomas O. The Science Profession in the Third World: Studies from India & Kenya. Altbach, Philip G., ed. LC 82-7662. (Special Studies in Comparative Education). 186p. 1982. 23.95 (ISBN 0-03-062023-6). Praeger.

Eisen, Arlene. Women & Revolution in Viet Nam. (Asia Ser.). (Illus.). 310p. 1984. 29.50x (ISBN 0-86232-175-1, Pub. by Zed Pr England); pap. 10.75 (ISBN 0-86232-176-X, Pub. by Zed Pr England). Biblio Dist.

Eisen, Arnold M. The Chosen People in America: A Study in Jewish Religious Ideology. LC 82-49296. (Modern Jewish Experience Ser.). 288p. 1983. 20.00x (ISBN 0-253-31365-1). Ind U Pr.

Eisen, Carole, jt. auth. see Eisen, Martin.

Eisen, F. H, et al, eds. Ion Beam Processing in Advanced Electronic Materials & Device Technology, Vol. 45. 1985. text ed. 42.00 (ISBN 0-931837-10-3). Materials Res.

Eisen, Fred H. & Chadderton, Lewis T., eds. Ion Implantation. LC 71-153515. (Illus.). 480p. 1971. 132.95 (ISBN 0-677-15000-8). Gordon.

Eisen, G. Enchytroids. Bd. with Tubicolous Annelids. Bush, K. J. (Harriman Alaska Expedition, 1899). (Illus.). 1904. 41.00 (ISBN 0-527-38172-1). Kraus Repr.

Eisen, Gail, jt. auth. see Friedman, Philip.

Eisen, Glen P., jt. auth. see Barlow, C. W.

Eisen, H. N. & Reisfeld, R. A., eds. Contemporary Topics in Molecular Immunology, Vol. 5. (Illus.). 249p. 1976. 35.00x (ISBN 0-306-36105-1, Plenum Pr). Plenum Pub.

Eisen, Harvey, jt. auth. see Agabian, Nina.

Eisen, Herman N. Immunology. 2nd ed. (Illus.). 259p. 1980. pap. text ed. 19.25x (ISBN 0-06-140781-X, 14-07816, Harper Medical). Lippincott.

Eisen, Jeffrey. Powertalk! 192p. pap. 7.95 (ISBN 0-317-01483-8). Cornerstone.

Eisen, Jon & Fine, David. Unknown California. Dorszynski, ed. LC 84-23020. 416p. 1985. pap. 10.95 (ISBN 0-02-048070-9, Collier). Macmillan.

Eisen, Jon, et al. Unknown California. Dorszynski, ed. 416p. 1985. 17.95 (ISBN 0-02-535150-8). Macmillan.

Eisen, M. Elementary Combinatorial Analysis. (Notes on Mathematics & Its Applications Ser.). 248p. 1969. 49.95 (ISBN 0-677-02260-3). Gordon.

--Mathematical Models in Cell Biology & Cancer Chemotherapy. (Lecture Notes in Biomathematics Ser.: Vol. 30). 431p. 1980. pap. 25.00 (ISBN 0-387-09709-0). Springer Verlag.

Eisen, Martin & Eisen, Carole. Finite Mathematics. 1979. text ed. write for info. (ISBN 0-02-472450-5). Macmillan.

Eisen, P. Accounting the Easy Way. (Easy Way Ser.). 320p. 1983. pap. 7.95 (ISBN 0-8120-2623-3). Barron.

Eisen, Peter J. Accounting I. (Business Review Ser.). 288p. 1985. pap. 8.95 (ISBN 0-8120-3574-7). Barron.

Eisen, Sydney & Lightman, Bernard. Victorian Science & Religion: A Bibliography with Emphasis on Evolution, Belief & Unbelief, Comprised of Works Published from Ca. 1900 to 1975. 696p. 1984. lib. bdg. 49.50 (ISBN 0-208-02010-1, Archon Bks). Shoe String.

Eisen, William. Agasha, Master of Wisdom. LC 77-85423. (Illus.). 1977. 10.95 (ISBN 0-87516-241-X). De Vorss.

--The Agashan Discourses. LC 77-85424. (Illus.). 1978. 11.95 (ISBN 0-87516-242-8). De Vorss.

--The English Cabalah, 2 vols, Vol. 1. (Illus.). 608p. 1980. text ed. 16.95 (ISBN 0-87516-390-4). De Vorss.

--The English Cabalah Volume 2: The Mysteries of Phi. LC 79-57053. (Agashan Teachings Ser.). 652p. 1982. 26.95 (ISBN 0-87516-459-5). De Vorss.

--The Essence of the Cabalah. (Illus.). 480p. 1984. 22.95 (ISBN 0-87516-524-9). De Vorss.

Eisenach, Eldon J. Two Worlds of Liberalism: Religion & Politics in Hobbes, Locke, & Mill. LC 80-27255. (Chicago Original Paperback Ser.). 272p. 1981. lib. bdg. 20.00x (ISBN 0-226-19533-3). U of Chicago Pr.
Eisenbach, G. M. & Brod, J., eds. Kidney & Pregnancy. (Contributions to Nephrology: Vol. 25). (Illus.). vi, 170p. 1981. pap. 40.50 (ISBN 3-8055-1798-X). S Karger.
--Vasoactive Renal Hormones. (Contributions to Nephrology: Vol. 12). (Illus.). 1978. pap. 29.00 (ISBN 3-8055-2839-6). S Karger.
Eisenbach, G. M. & Brod, Jan, eds. Non-Vasoactive Renal Hormones. (Contributions to Nephrology: Vol. 13). (Illus.). 1978. pap. 29.00 (ISBN 3-8055-2895-7). S Karger.
Eisenbach, Rina. Calculating & Administering Medications. rev. ed. LC 78-711. (Illus.). 131p. 1978. 7.50x (ISBN 0-8036-3080-8). Davis Co.
Eisenbach, Susan & Sadler, Christopher. Pascal for Programmers. (Illus.). 201p. 1981. pap. 16.00 (ISBN 0-387-10473-9). Springer-Verlag.
Eisenbacher, Mario. Programming Your Timex-Sinclair 1000 in BASIC. (Illus.). 189p. 1983. 17.95 (ISBN 0-13-729871-4); pap. 9.95 (ISBN 0-13-729863-3). P-H.
Eisenbarth, George, jt. ed. see Fellows, Robert.
Eisenbarth, George S., jt. ed. see Haynes, Barton F.
Eisenbeis, Robert A., jt. ed. see Aspinwall, Richard C.
Eisenbeis, Walter. The Key Ideas of Martin Heidegger's Treatise, Being & Time. LC 82-23874. 172p. (Orig.). 1983. lib. bdg. 23.50 (ISBN 0-8191-3009-5); pap. text ed. 11.25 (ISBN 0-8191-3010-9). U Pr of Amer.
--The Key Ideas of Paul Tillich's Systematic Theology. LC 82-21834. 268p. (Orig., Ger. & Eng.). 1983. lib. bdg. 24.75 (ISBN 0-8191-2948-8); pap. text ed. 13.00 (ISBN 0-8191-2949-6). U Pr of Amer.
--A Translation of the Greek Expressions in the Text of "The Gospel of John, A Commentary by Rudolf Bultman". 160p. (Orig.). 1984. lib. bdg. 19.75 (ISBN 0-8191-3884-3); pap. text ed. 11.00 (ISBN 0-8191-3885-1). U Pr of Amer.
Eisenberg. Memoirs of an OB-GYN. 1986. price not set (ISBN 0-87795-779-7). Arbor Hse.
Eisenberg, ed. Radiation Protection: A Systematic Approach to Safety: Proceedings of the 5th Congress of the International Radiation Protection Society, March 1980, Jerusalem, 2 vols. (Illus.). 1055p. 1980. Set. 200.00 (ISBN 0-08-025912-X). Pergamon.
Eisenberg, A. Technical Communication. 1982. 25.00 (ISBN 0-07-019096-8); 22.00 (ISBN 0-07-019097-6). McGraw.
Eisenberg, A. & Globe, Leah A. Secret Weapon & Other Stories of Faith & Valor. (Illus.). (gr. 4-6). 1971. 9.95x (ISBN 0-685-01035-X). Bloch.
Eisenberg, Abne. Communicating Effectively at Work. 201p. (Orig.). 1984. pap. text ed. 9.95x (ISBN 0-88133-032-9). Waveland Pr.
Eisenberg, Abne M. Living Communication. (Illus.). 368p. 1983. pap. text ed. 15.25 (ISBN 0-8191-3492-9). U Pr of Amer.
--Understanding Communication in Business & Professions. (Illus.). 1978. pap. text ed. 13.95 (ISBN 0-02-331850-3, Collier). Macmillan.
Eisenberg, Abne M. & Gamble, Teri K. Painless Public Speaking. (Illus.). 288p. 1982. pap. text ed. write for info. (ISBN 0-02-331830-9). Macmillan.
Eisenberg, Abne M. & Ilardo, Joseph A. Argument: A Guide to Formal & Informal Debate. 2nd ed. (Speech Communication Ser.). (Illus.). 1980. pap. 19.95 (ISBN 0-13-045989-5). P-H.
Eisenberg, Abne M. & Smith, Ralph R., Jr. Nonverbal Communication. 146p. 1971. pap. text ed. 8.95x (ISBN 0-8290-0326-6). Irvington.
Eisenberg, Adi, ed. Ions in Polymers. LC 80-19321. (Advances in Chemistry Ser.: No. 187). 1980. 54.95 (ISBN 0-8412-0482-9). Am Chemical.
Eisenberg, Adi & Yeager, Howard L., eds. Perfluorinated Ionomer Membranes. LC 81-20570. (ACS Symposium Ser.: No. 180). 1982. 54.95 (ISBN 0-8412-0698-8). Am Chemical.
Eisenberg, Anne. Reading Technical Books. LC 78-672. (Illus.). 1978. pap. 14.95 ref. ed. (ISBN 0-13-762138-8). P-H.
Eisenberg, Arlene, jt. auth. see Eisenberg, Howard.
Eisenberg, Arlene, et al. The Special Guest Cookbook: Elegant Menus & Recipes for Those Who Are Allergic to Certain Foods, Bland Dieters, Calorie Counters, Cholesterol Conscious, Diabetic, Hypoglycemic, Kosher, Milk Sensitive, Pritikin Porselytes, Salt-Avoiding, Strictly Vegetarian. LC 81-17106. 400p. 1982. 19.95 (ISBN 0-8253-0090-8). Beaufort Bks NY.
--What to Expect When Your're Expecting. 256p. (Orig.). 1984. pap. 7.95 (ISBN 0-89480-769-2, 769). Workman Pub.
Eisenberg, Azriel. The Book of Books. 163p. 1976. pap. 9.95 (ISBN 0-900689-77-3). Soncino Pr NY.
--The Book of Books: The Story of the Bible Text. 1976. 9.95x (ISBN 0-685-84453-6). Bloch.
--Eyewitnesses to American Jewish History, Pt. 4: The American Jew 1915 to 1969. 1979. 6.00 (ISBN 0-8074-0018-1, 044062). UAHC.
--Fill a Blank Page: A Biography of Solomon Schechter. (Illus.). (gr. 6-11). 3.75 (ISBN 0-8381-0730-3, 10-730). United Syn Bk.
--Jewish Historical Treasures. LC 68-57432. (Illus.). 300p. 1969. 12.50 (ISBN 0-8197-0076-2). Bloch.
--Modern Jewish Life in Literature, 2 Vols. 1952-1968. Vol. 1. 4.50x (ISBN 0-8381-0201-8); Vol. 2. 4.50x (ISBN 0-8381-0207-7). United Syn Bk.
--The Synagogue Through the Ages: An Illustrated History of Judaism's Houses of Worship. LC 73-77284. (Illus.). 1973. 15.00 (ISBN 0-8197-0290-0). Bloch.
--Witness to the Holocaust. LC 80-25961. 649p. 1981. 22.50 (ISBN 0-8298-0432-3); pap. 12.95 (ISBN 0-8298-0614-8). Pilgrim NY.
Eisenberg, Azriel & Arian, Philip. The Story of the Prayer Book. pap. 5.95x. Hartmore.
Eisenberg, Azriel & Globe, Leah A. The Secret Weapon & Other Stories. 200p. 1966. 9.95 (ISBN 0-900689-76-5). Soncino Pr NY.
Eisenberg, Azriel & Robinson, Jessie B. My Jewish Holidays. 208p. (gr. 5-6). 3.95x (ISBN 0-8381-0176-3, 10-176). United Syn Bk.
Eisenberg, Azriel, jt. auth. see Arian, Phillip.
Eisenberg, Azriel, ed. The Lost Generation: Children in the Holocaust. 384p. 1982. 17.95 (ISBN 0-8298-0498-6). Pilgrim NY.
Eisenberg, Azriel & Ain-Globe, Leah, eds. Home at Last. LC 75-4126. 324p. 1976. 7.95 (ISBN 0-8197-0386-9). Bloch.
Eisenberg, Azriel, jt. ed. see Shoshuk, Levi.
Eisenberg, Azriel, et al, eds. Eyewitnesses to American Jewish History: East European Immigration 1881-1920, Pt. 3. (Illus.). 1978. pap. 5.00 (ISBN 0-8074-0017-3, 144061); tchrs'. guide 5.00 (ISBN 0-8074-0021-1, 204063). UAHC.
--Eyewitnesses to American Jewish History: 1492-1793, Pt. 1. 1976. pap. 5.00 (ISBN 0-686-77106-0, 144060); tchrs'. guide 5.00 (ISBN 0-8074-0019-X, 204061). UAHC.
--Eyewitnesses to American Jewish History: The German Immigration 1800-1875, Pt. 2. (Illus.). 1977. pap. 5.00 (ISBN 0-8074-0016-5, 144059); tchrs'. guide 5.00 (ISBN 0-8074-0020-3, 204062). UAHC.
Eisenberg, Barry, tr. see Perez de Ayala, Ramon.
Eisenberg, Ben, jt. auth. see Kess, Sidney.
Eisenberg, Bernard, jt. ed. see Roucek, Joseph S.
Eisenberg, C. G. History of the First Dakota-District of the Evangelical-Lutheran Synod of Iowa & Other States. Richter, Anton H., tr. from Ger. LC 82-17645. 268p. (Orig.). 1983. lib. bdg. 26.25 (ISBN 0-8191-2798-1); pap. text ed. 13.50 (ISBN 0-8191-2799-X). U Pr of Amer.
Eisenberg, Daniel, jt. auth. see Silberman, Howard.
Eisenberg, David & Crothers, Donald M. Physical Chemistry with Applications to the Life Sciences. 1979. 38.95 (ISBN 0-8053-2402-X); instrs'. guide 6.95 (ISBN 0-8053-2403-8). Benjamin-Cummings.
Eisenberg, David & Wright, Thomas L. Encounters With QI: Exploring Chinese Medicine. 1985. 16.95 (ISBN 0-393-02213-7). Norton.
Eisenberg, Diane U. Malcolm Cowley: A Checklist of His Writings, 1916-1973. LC 75-8953. 272p. 1975. 8.95x (ISBN 0-8093-0748-0). S Ill U Pr.
Eisenberg, Evan. The Recording Angel: Aspects of Phonography. 1985. price not set. McGraw.
Eisenberg, Frank, Jr., jt. ed. see Wells, William W.
Eisenberg, Gerson G. Learning Vacations Nineteen Eighty-Two: A Guide to All Season Worldwide Educational Travel. 4th ed. LC 81-21002. 246p. (Orig.). 1982. write for info. (ISBN 0-930080-04-1). Eisenberg Ed.
--Learning Vacations, 1980-81: A Guide to Alumni College Seminars, Museum Trips, Educational Tours, Festivals, & Elderhostels in the United States & Abroad. 3rd ed. LC 80-66452. 340p. (Orig.). 1980. pap. 6.95 (ISBN 0-930080-03-3). Eisenberg Ed.
Eisenberg, H. see International Union of Pure & Applied Chemistry.
Eisenberg, Helen & Eisenberg, Larry. How to Lead Group Singing. LC 78-5428. (Illus.). 62p. 1978. Repr. of 1955 ed. lib. bdg. 22.50x (ISBN 0-313-20431-4, EIHL). Greenwood.
--More Bulletin Boards-ers. 1984. 4.25 (ISBN 0-89536-704-1, 4887). CSS of Ohio.
--Programs & Parties for Christmas. 160p. 1980. pap. 4.50 (ISBN 0-8010-3359-4). Baker Bk.
Eisenberg, Helen, jt. auth. see Eisenberg, Larry.
Eisenberg, Henryk. Biological Macromolecules & Polyelectrolytes in Solution. (Monographs on Physical Biochemistry). (Illus.). 1976. 75.00x (ISBN 0-19-854612-2). Oxford U Pr.
Eisenberg, Howand & Sehnert, Keith W. How to Be Your Own Doctor Sometimes: 10th Anniversary Edition. 1986. pap. 9.95 (ISBN 0-399-51190-3, G&D). Putnam Pub Group.
Eisenberg, Howard & Eisenberg, Arlene. Alive & Well: Decisions in Health. 1979. text ed. 30.95 (ISBN 0-07-019113-1). McGraw.
Eisenberg, Howard, jt. auth. see Kantrowitz, Walter.
Eisenberg, Howard M. & Suddith, Robert L., eds. The Cerebral Microvasculature: Investigation of the Blood-Brain Barrier. LC 80-36736. (Advances in Experimental Medicine & Biology Ser.: Vol. 131). 353p. 1980. 49.50x (ISBN 0-306-40472-9, Plenum Pr). Plenum Pub.
Eisenberg, J. F. & Kleiman, D. G., eds. Advances in the Study of Mammalian Behavior. (American Society of Mammalogists Special Publication Ser.: No.7). 753p. 1983. 45.00 (ISBN 0-943612-06-3). Am Soc Mammalogists.
Eisenberg, J. M. & Greiner, W. Nuclear Theory, Vol. 1: Nuclear Models. 2nd ed. 486p. 1976. pap. 44.75 (ISBN 0-444-10790-8, North-Holland). Elsevier.
--Nuclear Theory, Vol. 2: Excitation Mechanisms of the Nucleus. 2nd ed. LC 78-97200. 422p. 1976. pap. 44.75 (ISBN 0-7204-0158-5, North-Holland). Elsevier.
--Nuclear Theory, Vol. 3: Microscopic Theory of the Nucleus. 2nd ed. 520p. 1976. pap. 49.00 (ISBN 0-7204-0484-3, North-Holland). Elsevier.
Eisenberg, James & Kafka, Francis J. Silk Screen Printing. rev. ed. (Illus.). (gr. 9 up). 1957. pap. 6.00 (ISBN 0-87345-205-4). McKnight.
Eisenberg, Jerome M. Art of the Ancient World: A Guide for the Collector & Investor, Vol. IV. (Illus.). 208p. 1985. 20.00 (ISBN 0-317-29550-0); pap. 15.00 (ISBN 0-317-29551-9). Eisenberg Inc.
--A Collector's Guide to Seashells of the World. Old, William E., Jr., ed. LC 80-14886. (Illus.). 240p. 1980. 24.95 (ISBN 0-07-019140-9). McGraw.
Eisenberg, John F. The Mammalian Radiations: An Analysis of Trends in Evolution, Adaption & Behavior. LC 80-27940. (Illus.). 640p. 1983. pap. 22.00x (ISBN 0-226-19538-4). U of Chicago Pr.
Eisenberg, John F., ed. Vertebrate Ecology in the Northern Neotropics. LC 79-9436. (Symposia of the National Zoological Park Ser.: No. 4). (Illus.). 271p. 1980. text ed. 25.00x (ISBN 0-87474-410-5); pap. text ed. 12.50x (ISBN 0-87474-409-1). Smithsonian.
Eisenberg, John M. & Williams, Snakey V., eds. The Physician's Practice. LC 80-13691. 288p. 1980. 32.50 (ISBN 0-471-05469-0). Krieger.
Eisenberg, Judah M. & Koltun, Daniel S. Theory of Meson Interactions with Nuclei. LC 79-24653. 1980. 68.50x (ISBN 0-471-03915-2, Pub. by Wiley-Interscience). Wiley.
Eisenberg, Larry. Bulletin Board-ers. 1973. 4.25 (ISBN 0-89536-017-9). CSS of Ohio.
--Idea Book for Leaders. 121p. (Orig.). 1974. pap. 4.95 (ISBN 0-89536-106-X). CSS of Ohio.
--Projects & Care Groups. 60p. (Orig.). 1974. pap. 3.75 (ISBN 0-89536-191-4). CSS of Ohio.
--Youth Programs. 188p. (Orig.). 1974. pap. 6.75 (ISBN 0-89536-274-0). CSS of Ohio.
Eisenberg, Larry & Eisenberg, Helen. Fun with Skits, Stunts, & Stories. (Game & Party Books). 64p. 1975. pap. 2.95 (ISBN 0-8010-3367-5). Baker Bk.
Eisenberg, Larry, jt. auth. see Eisenberg, Helen.
Eisenberg, Lee, jt. auth. see Levi, Vicki G.
Eisenberg, Lisa. Break In. LC 83-63331. (South City Cops Ser.). 1984. pap. 4.64 (ISBN 0-8224-6261-3). Pitman Learning.
--Falling Star. LC 79-52653. (Laura Brewster Bks.). 1980. pap. 4.64 (ISBN 0-8224-1081-8). Pitman Learning.
--Fast-Food King. LC 79-52654. (Laura Brewster Bks.). 1980. pap. 4.64 (ISBN 0-8224-1082-6). Pitman Learning.
--Golden Idol. LC 79-52655. (Laura Brewster Bks.). 1980. pap. 4.64 (ISBN 0-8224-1083-4). Pitman Learning.
--Hit Man. LC 83-63332. (South City Cops Ser.). 1984. pap. 4.64 (ISBN 0-8224-6262-1). Pitman Learning.
--House of Laughs. LC 79-52656. (Laura Brewster Bks.). 1980. pap. 4.64 (ISBN 0-8224-1084-2). Pitman Learning.
--Kidnapped. LC 83-63333. (South City Cops Ser.). 1984. pap. 4.64 (ISBN 0-8224-6263-X). Pitman Learning.
--Killer Music. LC 79-52657. (Laura Brewster Bks.). 1980. pap. 4.64 (ISBN 0-8224-1085-0). Pitman Learning.
--Laura Brewster Books, 6 bks. (gr. 6 up). 1980. complete set of 6 bks. & tchrs. guide 25.92 (ISBN 0-8224-1080-X). Pitman Learning.
--Murder Behind the Wheel. LC 83-63330. (South City Cops Ser.). 1984. pap. 4.64 (ISBN 0-8224-6264-8). Pitman Learning.
--On the Run. LC 83-63334. 1984. pap. 4.64 (ISBN 0-8224-6565-5). Pitman Learning.
--The Pay Off Game. LC 83-63335. 1984. pap. 4.64 (ISBN 0-317-07426-1). Pitman Learning.
--Tiger Rose. LC 79-52658. (Laura Brewster Bks.). 1980. pap. 4.64 (ISBN 0-8224-1086-9). Pitman Learning.
Eisenberg, Lisa, jt. auth. see Hall, Katy.
Eisenberg, Lisa, jt. auth. see Kidd, Ronald.
Eisenberg, M. G. & Falconer, J. A. Treatment of the Spinal Cord Injured: An Interdisciplinary Perspective. (Illus.). 152p. 1979. photocopy ed. 19.75x (ISBN 0-398-03833-3). C C Thomas.
Eisenberg, M. Michael. Ulcers. 1978. 8.95 (ISBN 0-394-42753-X). Random.
Eisenberg, Martin A. Introduction to the Mechanics of Solids. LC 78-74682. (Illus.). 1980. text ed. 36.95 (ISBN 0-201-01934-5); solutions manual 3.00 (ISBN 0-201-01935-3). Addison-Wesley.
Eisenberg, Melvin A. Structure of the Corporation: A Legal Analysis. 1977. pap. text ed. 11.95 (ISBN 0-316-22542-8). Little.
Eisenberg, Melvin A. & Cary, William L. Corporations, Cases & Materials: 1984 Supplement. 5th ed. (University Casebook Ser.). 257p. 1984. pap. text ed. 7.50 (ISBN 0-88277-198-1). Foundation Pr.
Eisenberg, Melvin A., jt. auth. see Cary, William.
Eisenberg, Melvin A., jt. auth. see Cary, William L.
Eisenberg, Melvin A., jt. auth. see Fuller, Lon L.
Eisenberg, Mickey, jt. auth. see Copass, Michael K.
Eisenberg, Mickey, jt. auth. see Larson, Eric.
Eisenberg, Mickey & Bergner, Lawrence, eds. CPR-Cardiopulmonary Resuscitation: Evaluating Performance & Potential. (Emergency Health Services Quarterly Ser.: Vol. 1, No. 3). 70p. 1982. pap. text ed. 15.00 (ISBN 0-917724-58-5, B58). Haworth Pr.
Eisenberg, Mickey, et al, eds. Sudden Cardiac Death in the Community. LC 83-21156. 163p. 1984. 27.95 (ISBN 0-03-063843-7). Praeger.
Eisenberg, Mickey S. & Copass, Michael K. Emergency Medical Therapy. 2nd ed. (Saunders Blue Book Ser.). (Illus.). 432p. 1982. pap. 16.95 spiral bound (ISBN 0-7216-3354-4). Saunders.
Eisenberg, Mickey S., et al. Manual of Antimicrobial Therapy & Infectious Diseases. (Illus.). 282p. 1981. 19.00 (ISBN 0-7216-3347-1). Saunders.
Eisenberg, Myron G., et al. Disabled People As Second Class Citizens. (Springer Ser. on Rehabilitation: Vol. 2). 1982. text ed. 26.95 (ISBN 0-8261-3220-0); textbk. quanties 21.95 (ISBN 0-8261-3221-9). Springer Pub.
--Communications in a Health Care Setting. (Illus.). 288p. 1980. 32.75x (ISBN 0-398-03963-1). C C Thomas.
Eisenberg, Myron G., et al, eds. Chronic Illness & Disability Through the Life Span: Effects on Self & Family. (Springer Series in Rehabilitation: Vol. 4). 320p. 1984. text ed. 23.95 (ISBN 0-8261-4180-3). Springer Pub.
Eisenberg, Nancy. Altruistic Emotion, Cognition & Behavior. 272p. Date not set. text ed. 30.00 (ISBN 0-89859-624-6). L Erlbaum Assocs.
Eisenberg, Nancy, ed. The Development of Prosocial Behavior. (Developmental Psychology Ser.). 416p. 1982. 41.50 (ISBN 0-12-234980-6). Acad Pr.
Eisenberg, Nora, jt. auth. see Wiener, Harvey.
Eisenberg, Peter, ed. Maschinelle Sprachanalyse. (Grundlagen der Kommunikation). 1976. pap. text ed. 14.40x (ISBN 3-11-005722-0). De Gruyter.
Eisenberg, Peter L. The Sugar Industry in Pernambuco, 1840-1910: Modernization Without Change. LC 75-117340. 1974. 34.00x (ISBN 0-520-01731-5). U of Cal Pr.
Eisenberg, Phyllis R. Don't Tell Me a Ghost Story. (Illus.). 48p. (ps-3). 1982. 8.95 (ISBN 0-15-224029-2, HJ). HarBraceJ.
--A Mitzvah Is Something Special. LC 77-25664. (Illus.). (gr. k-4). 1978. 10.10i (ISBN 0-06-021807-X); PLB 10.89 (ISBN 0-06-021808-8). HarpJ.
Eisenberg, R. B. Auditory Competence in Early Life: The Roots of Communicative Behavior. (Illus.). 250p. 1975. 24.50 (ISBN 0-8391-0773-0). Univ Park.
Eisenberg, R. L. Diagnostic Imaging in Internal Medicine. 1088p. 1985. 85.00 (ISBN 0-07-019262-6). McGraw.
Eisenberg, Robert S., et al, eds. Membranes, Channels, & Noise. 296p. 1984. 47.50x (ISBN 0-306-41806-1, Plenum Pr). Plenum Pub.
Eisenberg, Ronald L. Atlas of Signs in Radiology. (Illus.). 448p. 1983. text ed. 55.00 (ISBN 0-397-50592-2, 65-07578). Lippincott.
--Critical Diagnostic Pathways in Radiology: An Algorithmic Approach. (Illus.). 488p. 1981. text ed. 57.50 (ISBN 0-397-50525-6, 65-07578, Lippincott Medical). Lippincott.
--Gastrointestinal Radiology: A Pattern Approach. (Illus.). 1056p. 1982. text ed. 99.00 (ISBN 0-397-52113-8, 65-07370, Lippincott Medical). Lippincott.
--Veterans Compensation: An American Scandal. 309p. (Orig.). 1985. 9.95; pap. 5.95 (ISBN 0-930883-01-2). Pierremont Press.
Eisenberg, S., ed. Lipoprotein Metabolism. (Progress in Biochemical Pharmacology: Vol. 15). (Illus.). 1979. 55.00 (ISBN 3-8055-2985-6). S Karger.
Eisenberg, Seymour & Elting. Nine Day Wonder Diet. 1979. pap. 2.25 (ISBN 0-440-16395-1). Dell.
Eisenberg, Sheldon & Patterson, Lewis P. Helping Clients with Special Concerns. LC 81-85322. 1979. pap. 19.95 (ISBN 0-395-30592-6). HM.
Eisenberg, Sheldon, jt. auth. see Patterson, Lewis E.
Eisenberg, Terry., et al. Police-Community Action: A Program for Change in Police-Community Behavior Patterns. LC 72-86839. (Special Studies in U.S. Economic, Social & Political Issues). 1973. 37.00x (ISBN 0-275-28831-5). Irvington.
Eisenberg, Theodore. Civil Rights Legislation. (Contemporary Legal Education Ser.). 960p. 1981. text ed. 25.00 (ISBN 0-672-84378-1); 1983 supplement 7.00 (ISBN 0-87215-580-3). Michie Co.
--Debtor-Creditor Law: Cases & Materials. LC 83-20711. (University Casebook Ser.). 911p. 1983. text ed. write for info. (ISBN 0-88277-159-0); pap. text ed. write for info. tchr's manual 174p (ISBN 0-88277-175-2). Foundation Pr.
Eisenberg, Theodore, et al. Commercial & Debtor-Creditor Law: Selected Statutes. 1435p. 1984. pap. text ed. 30.00 (ISBN 0-88277-188-4). Foundation Pr.
Eisenberger. Materials Science Using Synchrotron Radiation. Date not set. write for info. (ISBN 0-444-00893-4). Elsevier.
Eisenberger, K. The Expert Consumer: A Complete Handbook. 1977. (Spec); pap. 5.95 (ISBN 0-13-295394-3). P-H.
Eisenbichler, Konrad, tr. see Cecchi, Giovan Maria.

Eisenbud, David & Neumann, Walter D. Three-Dimensional Link Theory & Invariants of Plane Curve Singularities. (Annals of Mathematics Studies: No. 110). 185p. 1985. text ed. 37.50x (ISBN 0-691-08380-0); pap. text ed. 13.95x (ISBN 0-691-08381-9). Princeton U Pr.

Eisenbud, Jule. Paranormal Foreknowledge: Problems & Perplexities. LC 81-2941. 312p. 1982. 29.95 (ISBN 0-89885-049-5). Human Sci Pr.

--Parapsychology & the Unconscious. 250p. 1984. 25.00 (ISBN 0-938190-07-5); pap. 12.95 (ISBN 0-938190-08-3). North Atlantic.

--PSI & Psychoanalysis. LC 71-75145. 368p. 1970. 53.50 (ISBN 0-8089-0126-5, 791150). Grune.

Eisenbud, M. & Gleason, G. Electric Power & Thermal Discharges: Thermal Considerations in the Production of Electric Power. 454p. 1969. 85.75 (ISBN 0-677-03290-0). Gordon.

Eisenbud, Merril. Environment, Technology & Health: Human Ecology in Historical Perspective. LC 78-55062. 1978. 32.50x (ISBN 0-8147-2154-0); pap. 17.50x (ISBN 0-8147-2160-5). NYU Pr.

--Environmental Radioactivity. 2nd ed. (Environmental Science: An Interdisciplinary Monograph). 1973. 75.00 (ISBN 0-12-235150-9). Acad Pr.

Eisendrath, Craig R. Unifying Moment: The Psychological Philosophy of William James & Alfred North Whitehead. LC 70-135550. 1971. 20.00t (ISBN 0-674-92100-3). Harvard U Pr.

Eisendrath, Craig R., et al. Out of Discontent: Visions of the Contemporary University. (Illus.). 181p. 1973. 14.50x (ISBN 0-87073-155-6). Schenkman Bks Inc.

Eisendrath, Joseph L., ed. Crash Covers: An Aerophilatelic Adventure. 150p. 15.00 (ISBN 0-318-12358-4); members 12.00 (ISBN 0-318-12359-2). Am Air Mail.

Eisenfeld, J. & Delisi, C., eds. Mathematics & Computers in Biomedical Applications. 390p. 1985. 40.00 (ISBN 0-444-87678-2). Elsevier.

Eisenhardt, Louise, jt. auth. see Cushing, Harvey.

Eisenhart, Connie. Pocketful of Miracles Set I: Filefolder Games, Patterns & Directions. 1984. pap. 6.95 (ISBN 0-318-11994-3) (ISBN 0-318-11995-1). Partner Pr.

Eisenhart, Connie & Bell, Ruth. Pocketful of Miracles Holiday: File Folder Games, Patterns & Directions. 1985. pap. 7.905 (ISBN 0-933212-24-0). Partner Pr.

Eisenhart, L. P. Non-Riemannian Geometry. LC 28-28413. (Colloquium Pbns. Ser.: Vol. 8). 184p. 1981. pap. 29.00 (ISBN 0-8218-1008-1, COLL-8). Am Math.

Eisenhart, Luther P. Riemannian Geometry. rev. ed. 1950. 30.00x (ISBN 0-691-08026-7). Princeton U Pr.

Eisenhauer, Laurel A. & Gerald, Michael C. The Nurse's 1984-85 Guide to Drug Therapy: Drug Profiles for Patient Care. 656p. 1984. 31.95 (ISBN 0-13-627471-4). P-H.

Eisenhauer, Laurel A., jt. auth. see Asperheim, Mary K.

Eisenhower, David. Eisenhower at War: 1943-1945. (Illus.). 1986. 25.00 (ISBN 0-394-41237-0). Random.

Eisenhower, Dwight D. At Ease: Stories I Tell to Friends. 1981. pap. 4.95 (ISBN 0-915992-04-3). Eastern Acorn.

--Crusade in Europe. LC 76-25037. (Politics & Strategy of World War II Ser.). 1977. 45.00 (ISBN 0-306-70768-3); pap. 10.95 (ISBN 0-306-80109-4). Da Capo.

--The Eisenhower Diaries. Ferrell, Robert H., ed. (Illus.). 1981. 19.95 (ISBN 0-393-01432-0). Norton.

--Peace with Justice. LC 61-7096. 273p. 31.00x (ISBN 0-231-02472-X). Columbia U Pr.

--The White House Years. limited ed. Incl. Waging Peace Nineteen Fifty-Six-Nineteen Sixty-One. 50.00 (ISBN 0-385-04992-7). Doubleday.

Eisenhower, John, intro. by see Cohen, Stan.

Eisenhower, Julie, ed. Great Love Stories from the Saturday Evening Post. LC 76-41559. 320p. 1976. 5.95 (ISBN 0-89387-003-X, Co-Pub by Sat Eve Post). Curtis Pub Co.

--Great Westerns from the Saturday Evening Post. LC 76-41560. 320p. 1976. 5.95 (ISBN 0-89387-004-8, Co-Pub by Sat Eve Post). Curtis Pub Co.

--Mystery & Suspense: Great Stories from the Saturday Evening Post. LC 76-41561. 320p. 1976. 5.95 (ISBN 0-89387-005-6, Co-Pub by Sat Eve Post). Curtis Pub Co.

Eisenkramer, Henry E. Classroom Music. LC 78-60416. (Illus.). 1978. pap. 10.95 (ISBN 0-916656-11-X). Mark Foster Mus.

Eisenlohr, L. E. International Narcotics Control. Grob, Gerald N., ed. LC 80-1226. (Addiction in America Ser.). 1981. Repr. of 1934 ed. lib. bdg. 25.00x (ISBN 0-405-13584-X). Ayer Co Pubs.

Eisenman, et al. Five Architects: Eisenman, Graves, Gwathmey Hejduk, Meiser. 2nd ed. 1975. pap. 18.95 (ISBN 0-19-519795-X). Oxford U Pr.

Eisenman, D. A. Intrinsic Measures on Complex Manifolds & Holomorphic Mappings. LC 52-42839. (Memoirs: No. 96). 80p. 1970. pap. 9.00 (ISBN 0-8218-1296-3, MEMO-96). Am Math.

Eisenman, George, ed. Membranes: Lipid Bilayers & Biological Membranes: Dynamic Properties, Vol. 3. 536p. 1975. 95.00 (ISBN 0-8247-6178-2). Dekker.

--Membranes: Macroscopic Systems & Models, Vol. 1. LC 80-1618. pap. 90.00 (ISBN 0-317-28659-5, 2055085). Bks Demand UMI.

--Membranes, Vol. 2: Lipid Bilayers & Antibiotics. 576p. 1973. 95.00 (ISBN 0-8247-6049-2). Dekker.

Eisenman, Patricia & Johnson, Dennis. Coaches' Guide to Nutrition & Weight Control. LC 81-82452. (Illus.). 255p. 1982. pap. text ed. 10.95 (ISBN 0-931250-25-0, BE150025). Human Kinetics.

Eisenman, Peter. House X. LC 80-51622. (Illus.). 168p. 1982. 35.00 (ISBN 0-8478-0355-4); pap. 25.00 (ISBN 0-8478-0346-5). Rizzoli Intl.

--John Hejduk: Seven Houses. (Illus.). 1980. pap. 13.50 (ISBN 0-262-59015-8). MIT Pr.

Eisenman, Peter & Rossi, Aldo. Aldo Rossi in America: 1976-1979. (IAUS Exhibition Catalogs). (Illus.). 1980. pap. 13.50 (ISBN 0-262-59012-3). MIT Pr.

Eisenmann, L. Le Compromis Austro-Hongrois de 1867: Etude Sur le Dualisme. (Central & East European Ser.: Vol. 1). 1904. 35.00 (ISBN 0-87569-018-1). Academic Intl.

Eisenmenger, Erich & Zetner, Karl. Veterinary Dentistry. LC 84-7908. (Illus.). 165p. 1985. text ed. write for info. (ISBN 0-8121-0924-4). Lea & Febiger.

Eisenmenger, Robert W. The Dynamics of Growth in New England's Economy, 1870-1964. LC 66-23926. (New England Research Ser: No. 2). 1967. 16.00x (ISBN 0-8195-8013-9). Wesleyan U Pr.

Eisenmenger, W., et al, eds. Phonon Scattering in Condensed Matter: Proceedings of the Fourth International Conference in Stuttgart, West Germany, August 22-26, 1983. (Springer Series in Solid-State Sciences: Vol. 51). (Illus.). 480p. 1984. 30.00 (ISBN 0-387-12954-5). Springer-Verlag.

Eisenreich, G. & Sube, R. Dictionary of Mathematics, 2 vols. 1460p. (Eng., Fr., Ger. & Rus.). 1982. Set. 168.00 (ISBN 0-444-99706-7). Elsevier.

Eisenreich, G., jt. auth. see Sube, R.

Eisenreich, G., jt. ed. see Sube, R.

Eisenreich, Gunther, jt. auth. see Sube, Ralf.

Eisenreich, S., ed. Physical Behavior of PCBs in the Great Lakes. LC 82-72347. (Illus.). 442p. 1982. 49.95 (ISBN 0-250-40584-9). Butterworth.

Eisenschiml, Otto, ed. see Ripley, Edward H.

Eisenschitz, R. K. Matrix Algebra for Physicists. LC 66-18972. 124p. 1966. 17.50x (ISBN 0-306-30214-4, Plenum Pr). Plenum Pub.

Eisenschmitt, Joachim. Die Szenische Darstellung der Opern G. F. Haendels Auf der Londoner Buhne Seiner Zeit, 2 vols. in 1. LC 80-2275. Repr. of 1940 ed. 29.50 (ISBN 0-404-18843-5). AMS Pr.

Eisenson, John. Voice & Diction: A Program for Improvement. 5th ed. 384p. 1985. pap. text ed. write for info. (ISBN 0-02-331960-7). Macmillan.

Eisenson, Jon. Adult Aphasia. 2nd ed. (Illus.). 336p. 1984. 26.95 (ISBN 0-13-008771-8). P-H.

--Aphasia & Related Disorders in Children. 2nd ed. 294p. 1984. text ed. 28.95 scp (ISBN 0-06-041889-3, HarpC). Har-Row.

Eisenson, Jon & Boase, Paul H. Basic Speech. 3rd ed. (Illus.). 448p. 1975. text ed. 20.95x (ISBN 0-02-331870-8, 33187). Macmillan.

Eisenson, Jon & Ogilvie, Mardel. Communication Disorders in Children. 5th ed. 480p. 1983. text ed. write for info. (ISBN 0-02-332100-8). Macmillan.

--Speech Correction in the Schools. 4th ed. 1977. text ed. write for info. (ISBN 0-02-332070-2, 33207). Macmillan.

Eisenson, Jon, jt. auth. see Pitner, Rudolf.

Eisenstadt, Abraham, ed. see Dubofsky, Melvyn.

Eisenstadt, Abraham, ed. see Horsman, Reginald.

Eisenstadt, Abraham, ed. see Mohl, Raymond A.

Eisenstadt, Abraham S. Charles McLean Andrews: A Study in American Historical Writing. LC 68-54261. (Columbia University Studies in the Social Sciences: No. 588). 16.50 (ISBN 0-404-51588-6). AMS Pr.

Eisenstadt, Abraham S., ed. American History: Recent Interpretations, Vol. II. 2nd ed. Incl. Vol 1. To 1877; Vol 2. Since 1865 (ISBN 0-88295-732-5). LC 69-13256. 1969. pap. text ed. 12.95. Harlan Davidson.

Eisenstadt, Abraham S., et al, eds. Before Watergate. (Brooklyn College Studies on Society in Change: No. 4). 1979. 17.50x (ISBN 0-930888-01-4). Brooklyn Coll Pr.

Eisenstadt, Lemarchand. Political Clientalism, Patronage & Development. (Illus.). 344p. 1981. 27.50 (ISBN 0-8039-9794-9); pap. 12.95 (ISBN 0-8039-9795-7). Sage.

Eisenstadt, Mark & O'Shea, Tim. Artificial Intelligence: Tools, Techniques, & Applications. LC 84-502. 576p. 1984. pap. text ed. 23.95 scp (ISBN 0-06-041894-X, HarpC). Har-Row.

Eisenstadt, Melvin M. Introduction to Mechanical Properties of Materials: An Ecological Approach. 1971. text ed. write for info. (ISBN 0-02-332140-7, 33214). Macmillan.

Eisenstadt, S. N. The Absorption of Immigrants. LC 74-31867. 275p. 1975. Repr. of 1954 ed. lib. bdg. 15.75x (ISBN 0-8371-7947-5, EIAI). Greenwood.

--Revolution & the Transformation of Societies: A Comparative Study of Civilizations. LC 77-5203. 1978. 17.95 (ISBN 0-02-909390-2). Free Pr.

--Tradition, Change, & Modernity. LC 83-11273. 382p. 1983. Repr. of 1973 ed. text ed. 33.50 (ISBN 0-89874-642-6). Krieger.

--The Transformation of Israeli Society. 608p. 1985. 42.50 (ISBN 0-8133-0306-0). Westview.

Eisenstadt, S. N. & Ahimeir, Ora. The Welfare State & Its Aftermath. (Illus.). 340p. 1985. 28.50x (ISBN 0-389-20529-X, 08091). B&N Imports.

Eisenstadt, S. N. & Curelaru, M. The Form of Sociology: Paradigms & Crises. LC 76-7602. 386p. 1976. 44.50 (ISBN 0-471-23472-9, Pub. by Wiley-Interscience). Wiley.

Eisenstadt, S. N. & Roniger, Luis. Patrons, Clients & Friends: Interpersonal Relations & the Structure of Trust in Society. (Themes in the Social Sciences Ser). 352p. 1984. 39.50 (ISBN 0-521-24687-3); pap. 14.95 (ISBN 0-521-28890-8). Cambridge U Pr.

Eisenstadt, S. N. & Graubard, S. R., eds. Intellectuals & Tradition. LC 72-86067. (Van Leer Jerusalem Foundation Ser.). 218p. 1973. text ed. 13.00x (ISBN 0-391-00257-0). Humanities.

Eisenstadt, S. N., jt. ed. see Helle, H. J.

Eisenstadt, S. N., ed. see Weber, Max.

Eisenstadt, S. N., et al, eds. Socialism & Tradition. (Van Leer Jerusalem Foundation Ser.). 262p. 1975. text ed. 13.00x (ISBN 0-391-00375-5). Humanities.

--Orthodoxy, Heterodoxy & Dissent in India. LC 83-26910. (Religion & Society Ser.: No. 23). viii, 179p. 1984. 28.40x (ISBN 3-11-009659-5). Mouton.

Eisenstadt, Samuel N. From Generation to Generation: Age Groups & Social Structure. LC 55-10998. 1964. pap. text ed. 7.95 (ISBN 0-02-909380-5). Free Pr.

Eisenstadt, Samuel N., et al. Analysis of Processes of Role Change. 46p. 1967. pap. 3.95x (ISBN 0-87855-626-5). Transaction Bks.

Eisenstadt, Shmuel. The Prophets-Their Times & Social Ideas: A Marxist Interpretation of Old Testament Radicalism. Rosenfeld, Max, tr. from Yiddish. 1971. Repr. of 1926 ed. 12.00 (ISBN 0-88286-103-4). C H Kerr.

Eisenstadt, Shmuel N. & Rokkan, Stein, eds. Building States & Nations: Models & Data Resources, Vol. 1. LC 73-77873. pap. 99.50 (ISBN 0-317-29692-2, 2021891). Bks Demand UMI.

Eisenstaedt, Alfred. Eisenstaedt on Eisenstaedt. LC 84-20362. (Illus.). 120p. 19.95 (ISBN 0-89659-515-3). Abbeville Pr.

--Eisenstaedt's Guide to Photography. (Handbook Ser.). (Illus.). 176p. 1981. pap. 12.95 (ISBN 0-14-046483-2). Penguin.

--People. (Large Format Ser). (Illus.). 1979. pap. 9.95 (ISBN 0-14-005073-6). Penguin.

--Witness to Our Time. rev. ed. 352p. 1980. 25.00 (ISBN 0-670-77702-1, Studio). Viking.

Eisenstaedt, Alfred, photos by. Eisenstaedt-Aberdeen: Portrait of a City. Vitiello, Gregory, ed. (Illus.). 91p. 1984. 19.95 (ISBN 0-8071-1194-5). La State U Pr.

Eisenstat, Norman C. The Science of Selling Alarm Systems. 180p. 1984. text ed. 19.95 (ISBN 0-409-95118-8). Butterworth.

Eisenstein, Edward M., ed. Aneural Organisms in Neurobiology. LC 74-28345. (Advances in Behavioral Biology Ser.: Vol. 13). 152p. 1975. 29.50x (ISBN 0-306-37913-9, Plenum Pr). Plenum Pub.

Eisenstein, Elizabeth. The Printing Press As an Agent of Change, 2 vols. LC 77-91083. 1979. Vol. 1. 67.50 (ISBN 0-521-21967-1); Vol. 2. 47.50 (ISBN 0-521-21969-8); Set. 99.00 (ISBN 0-521-22044-0). Cambridge U Pr.

--The Printing Press As an Agent of Change, 2 vols. in 1. LC 77-91083. 852p. 1980. pap. 22.95 (ISBN 0-521-29955-1). Cambridge U Pr.

Eisenstein, Elizabeth L. First Professional Revolutionist: Filippo Michele Buonarroti, 1761-1837, a Biographical Essay. LC 59-5357. (Historical Monographs Ser.: No. 38). 1959. 15.00t (ISBN 0-674-30400-4). Harvard U Pr.

--The Printing Revolution in Early Modern Europe. LC 83-10145. 336p. 1984. 34.50 (ISBN 0-521-25858-8); pap. 9.95 (ISBN 0-521-27735-3). Cambridge U Pr.

Eisenstein, Gotthold F. Mathematische Werke, 2 vols. 2nd ed. LC 75-17855. 926p. 1975. write for info. (ISBN 0-8284-0280-9). Chelsea Pub.

Eisenstein, Hester. Contemporary Feminist Thought. (American Women in the Twentieth Century Ser.). 208p. (gr. 10-12). 1983. lib. bdg. 17.95 (ISBN 0-8161-9042-9, Twayne). G K Hall.

--Contemporary Feminist Thought. 224p. 1984. pap. 6.95 (ISBN 0-8161-9048-8). G K Hall.

Eisenstein, Hester & Jardine, Alice. The Future of Difference: The Scholar & the Feminist Conference Series, Vol. 1. 1980. lib. bdg. 27.50 (ISBN 0-8161-9029-1, Univ Bks). G K Hall.

Eisenstein, Hester & Jardine, Alice, eds. The Future of Difference. (The Douglass Ser.). 362p. 1985. pap. text ed. 11.00 (ISBN 0-8135-1112-7). Rutgers U Pr.

Eisenstein, James. Counsel for the United States: U. S. Attorneys in the Political & Legal Systems. LC 77-10562. 1978. 27.50x (ISBN 0-8018-1988-1). Johns Hopkins.

Eisenstein, Miriam. Language Variation & the ESL Curriculum. (Language in Education Ser.: No. 51). 45p. (Orig.). 1983. pap. 6.95 (ISBN 0-87281-320-7). Ctr Appl Ling.

Eisenstein, Phyllis. Born to Exile. 1978. 8.95 (ISBN 0-87054-082-3). Arkham.

--Born to Exile. 1980. pap. 1.95 (ISBN 0-440-10854-3). Dell.

--Shadow of Earth. 1979. pap. 2.25 (ISBN 0-440-18032-5). Dell.

--Sorcerer's Son. 1979. pap. 2.50 (ISBN 0-345-29766-0, Del Rey Bks). Ballantine.

Eisenstein, S. M. Que Viva Mexico! LC 70-169341. (Arno Press Cinema Program). (Illus.). 94p. 1972. Repr. of 1951 ed. 12.00 (ISBN 0-405-03916-6). Ayer Co Pubs.

Eisenstein, Samuel A., ed. Boarding the Ship of Death: D. H. Lawrence's Quester Heroes. (De Proprietatibus Litterarum, Ser. Practica: No. 42). 171p. 1974. pap. text ed. 15.20x (ISBN 90-2792-719-7). Mouton.

Eisenstein, Sarah. Give Us Bread, but Give Us Roses: Working Women's Consciousness in the United States 1890 to the First World War. 220p. (Orig.). 1983. pap. 10.95 (ISBN 0-7100-9479-5). Routledge & Kegan.

Eisenstein, Sergei. The Battleship Potemkin. 1978. pap. 7.95 (ISBN 0-380-30460-0, 30460-0). Avon.

--The Battleship Potemkin. (Lorrimer Classic Screenplay Ser.). (Illus.). o. s. i. 10.95 (ISBN 0-8044-2153-6); pap. 6.95 (ISBN 0-8044-6137-6). Ungar.

--Film Essays with a Lecture. Leyda, Jay, ed. LC 81-47283. (Illus.). 240p. (Orig.). 1981. 25.00 (ISBN 0-691-03970-4); pap. 7.95 (ISBN 0-691-00334-3). Princeton U Pr.

--Film Form. LC 49-8349. 1969. pap. 5.95 (ISBN 0-15-630920-3, Harv). HarBraceJ.

--The Film Sense. LC 47-6064. 1969. pap. 6.95 (ISBN 0-15-630935-1, Harv). HarBraceJ.

--Immoral Memories. Marshall, Herbert, tr. 1984. pap. 13.95 (ISBN 0-395-36569-4). HM.

--Immoral Memories: An Autobiography. Marshall, Herbert, tr. LC 83-8417. 1983. 19.95 (ISBN 0-395-33101-3). HM.

--Ivan the Terrible. (Lorrimer Classic Screenplay Ser.). (Illus.). 12.95 (ISBN 0-8044-2154-4); pap. 8.95 (ISBN 0-8044-6138-4). Ungar.

--Notes of a Film Director. rev. ed. Danko, X., tr. LC 69-19729. (Film Ser). 1970. pap. 7.95 (ISBN 0-486-22392-2). Dover.

--October (Ten Days That Shook the World); Alexander Nevsky; the Battleship Potemkin. (Lorrimer Classic Screenplay Ser.). (Illus.). pap. 11.95 (ISBN 0-8044-6139-2). Ungar.

--On the Composition of the Short Story Scenario. Upchurch, Alan Y., tr. from Rus. (Illus.). 61p. (Orig.). 1984. pap. text ed. 5.95 (ISBN 0-86132-074-3, Pub. by Seagull Bks India). Apt Bks.

Eisenstein, Toby K. & Actor, Paul, eds. Host Defenses to Intracellular Pathogens. (Advances in Experimental Medicine & Biology Ser.: Vol. 162). 530p. 1983. 65.00x (ISBN 0-306-41259-4, Plenum Press). Plenum Pub.

Eisenstein, Zillah R. Feminism & Sexual Equality: Crisis in Liberal America. LC 83-4606. (New Feminist Library). 288p. 1984. 26.00 (ISBN 0-85345-644-5); pap. 10.00 (ISBN 0-85345-645-3). Monthly Rev.

Eisenstein, Zillah R., ed. Capitalist Patriarchy & the Case for Socialist Feminism. LC 77-76162. 394p. 1978. pap. 8.00 (ISBN 0-85345-476-0). Monthly Rev.

Eisenthal, K. B., jt. ed. see Auston, D. H.

Eisenthal, K. B., et al, eds. Picosecond Phenomena III, Garmisch Partenkirchen, FRG, 1982: Proceedings. (Springer Series in Chemical Physics: Vol. 23). (Illus.). 401p. 1982. 33.00 (ISBN 0-387-11912-4). Springer-Verlag.

Eisenthal, Kenneth B., ed. Applications of Picosecond Spectroscopy to Chemistry. 384p. 1984. lib. bdg. 59.00 (ISBN 90-277-1788-5, Pub.by Reidel Academic). Kluwer Academic.

Eisenthal, R., jt. auth. see Wharton, Christopher W.

Eiser, C. The Psychology of Childhood Illness. (Contributions to Psychology & Medicine). (Illus.). 210p. 1985. 27.00 (ISBN 0-387-96096-1). Springer-Verlag.

Eiser, J. R. & Strobe, Wolfgang, eds. Categorization & Social Judgment. (European Monographs in Social Psychology: No. 3). 1973. 36.50 (ISBN 0-12-235350-1). Acad Pr.

Eiser, J. Richard. Social Psychology & Behavioral Medicine. LC 80-42062. 608p. 1982. 52.95x (ISBN 0-471-27994-3, Pub. by Wiley-Interscience). Wiley.

Eiserer, Len. The American Robin: A Backyard Institution. LC 76-25438. (Illus.). 187p. 1976. 23.95 (ISBN 0-88229-228-5). Nelson-Hall.

Eisermann, Moshe. Yechezkel-Ezekiel, Vol. 1. (The Art Scroll Tanach Ser.). 352p. 1977. 17.95 (ISBN 0-89906-075-7); pap. 14.95 (ISBN 0-89906-076-5). Mesorah Pubns.

Eisert, Martin P., jt. auth. see Imundo, Louis V.

Eisert, W. G. & Mendelsohn, M. L., eds. Biological Dosimetry: Cytometric Approaches to Mammalian Systems. (Illus.). 380p. 1984. pap. 26.50 (ISBN 0-387-12790-9). Springer-Verlag.

Eisgruber, Frank, Jr. Gangland's Doom: The Shadow of the Pulps. 64p. 1985. Repr. lib. bdg. 19.95x (ISBN 0-89370-563-2). Borgo Pr.

--Gangland's Doom: The Shadow of the Pulps. (Pulp & Dime Novel Studies: No. 1). (Illus.). 64p. 1985. 19.95x (ISBN 0-930261-71-2); pap. 9.95x (ISBN 0-930261-74-7). Starmont Hse.

Eishenberg, Fritz. Artist on the Witness Stand. LC 84-61828. (Orig.). 1984. pap. 2.30x (ISBN 0-87574-257-2). Pendle Hill.
Eisikovits, Max. Songs of the Martyrs: Hassidic Melodies of Maramures. LC 79-67624. 1980. pap. 7.95 (ISBN 0-87203-089-X). Hermon.
Eisikovits, Zvi & Beker, Jerome, eds. Residential Group Care in Community Context: Insights from the Israeli Experience. LC 85-7682. (Child & Youth Services Ser.: Vol. 7, Nos. 3 & 4). 160p. 1985. text ed. 19.95 (ISBN 0-86656-186-2). Haworth Pr.
Eisiminger, Sterling, jt. auth. see Idol, John L.
Eisinger, Erica M. & McCarty, Mari, eds. Colette: The Woman, the Writer. LC 81-47169. 230p. 1981. 22.50x (ISBN 0-271-00286-7). Pa St U Pr.
Eisinger, Peter K. American Politics: The People & the Policy. 2nd ed. 1982. 16.95 (ISBN 0-316-22564-9); tchr's. manual avail. (ISBN 0-316-22565-7). Little.
--Black Employment in City Government, 1973-1980. LC 83-24847. (Illus.). 58p. (Orig.). 1984. pap. 4.95 (ISBN 0-941410-32-3). Jt Ctr Pol Studies.
--The Politics of Displacement: Racial & Ethnic Transition in Three American Cities. LC 80-12927. (Institute for Research on Poverty Monograph Ser.). 1980. 19.00 (ISBN 0-12-235560-1). Acad Pr.
Eisl, Maria E. Lyrische und Satirische Elemente in Roy Campbell's Dichtung, 2 vols. (Salzburg Studies in England Literature, Poetic Drama & Poetic Theory: No. 46). (Illus.). 1979. Set. pap. text ed. 50.75x (ISBN 0-391-01165-0). Humanities.
Eisler, ed. Trace Metal Concentrations in Marine Organisms. 3500p. 1981. 130.00 (ISBN 0-08-025975-8). Pergamon.
Eisler, B., tr. see Champigneulle, B.
Eisler, Benita. Class Act: America's Last Dirty Secret. 368p. 1983. 18.95 (ISBN 0-531-09802-8). Watts.
Eisler, Benita, ed. The Lowell Offering: Writings by New England Mill Women, 1840-1845. LC 77-24986. 223p. 1980. pap. 5.95i (ISBN 0-06-131996-1, TB1996 TB, CN). Har-Row.
Eisler, Benita, ed. & intro. by. The Lowell Offering: Writings by New England Mill Women (1840-1845) 223p. text ed. 12.50 (ISBN 0-397-01225-X). Brown Bk.
Eisler, Colin. Durer's Animals. 1985. write for info. (ISBN 0-670-28645-1). Viking.
--Master of the Unicorn: The Life & Work of Jean Duvet. LC 77-86223. (Illus.). 1978. 69.50 (ISBN 0-913870-46-3). Abaris Bks.
--Sculptors' Drawings over Six Centuries. (An Agrinde Bk.). (Illus.). 1981. pap. 20.00 (ISBN 0-9601068-7-1). Dodd.
Eisler, Colin & Corbett, Patricia. The Prayer Book of Michelino Da Besozzo. LC 81-68186. (Illus.). 1981. 50.00 (ISBN 0-8076-1016-X). Braziller.
Eisler, Colin, ed. Sculptors' Drawings over Six Centuries. LC 81-65434. (Illus.). 160p. (Orig.). 1981. pap. 20.00. Agrinde Pubns.
Eisler, Hanns. Composing for the Films. 166p. 1981. 39.00x (ISBN 0-234-77148-8, Pub. by Dobson Bks England). State Mutual Bk.
--A Rebel in Music. LC 76-55331. 250p. 1978. pap. 1.95 (ISBN 0-7178-0486-0). Intl Pubs Co.
Eisler, Moritz. Vorlesungen ueber die Juedischen Philosophen des Mittelalters, 3vols in 2. 1965. Repr. of 1884 ed. 39.50 (ISBN 0-8337-4086-5). B Franklin.
Eisler, Paul A. California Uninsured Motorist Law Handbook. 3rd ed. 756p. 1979. 1983 suppl. incl. 75.00 (ISBN 0-911110-27-5). Parker & Son.
Eisler, Paul E. The Metropolitan Opera: The First Twenty-Five Years, 1883-1908. LC 84-6113. (Illus.). 331p. 1984. 29.95 (ISBN 0-88427-046-7, Dist. by Dodd, Mead). North River.
--World Chronology of Music History, 6 vols. plus index. LC 72-4354. (Illus.). 512p. 1972-1980. lib. bdg. 45.00 ea. (ISBN 0-379-16080-3). Oceana.
Eisler, Richard M. & Frederiksen, Lee W. Perfecting Social Skills: A Guide to Interpersonal Behavior Development. LC 80-21209. (Applied Clinical Psycholgy Ser.). 235p. 1981. 22.50x (ISBN 0-306-40592-X, Plenum Pr). Plenum Pub.
Eisler, Robert. Man into Wolf, an Anthropological Interpretation of Sadism, Masochism & Lycanthropy. LC 77-88984. Repr. of 1951 ed. lib. bdg. 18.75x (ISBN 0-8371-2090-X, EIMW). Greenwood.
--Man into Wolf: An Anthropological Interpretation of Sadism, Masochism, & Lycanyhropy. LC 77-2497. 264p. 1978. lib. bdg. 11.95 (ISBN 0-915520-16-8); pap. text ed. 5.95 (ISBN 0-915520-06-0). Ross-Erikson.
Eisler, Rudolf. Philosophen Lexikon. 2nd ed. (Ger.). 1972. 150.00 (ISBN 3-7778-0068-6, M-7583, Pub. by Journalfranz). French & Eur.
Eisman, Greg, jt. auth. see Shaw, Dave.
Eisman, Philip, jt. auth. see Gehlmann, John.
Eisner, Elliot. The Art of Educational Evaluation: A Personal View. (Illus.). 275p. 1984. 33.00x (ISBN 0-905273-62-1, Pub. by Falmer Pr); pap. 19.00x (ISBN 0-905273-61-3, Pub. by Falmer Pr). Taylor & Francis.
Eisner, Elliot, ed. Learning & Teaching the Ways of Knowing: 84th Yearbook, Pt. II. LC 84-62254. (National Society for the Study of Education Ser.). 320p. 1985. lib. bdg. 20.00 (ISBN 0-226-60140-4, Pub. by Natl Soc Stud Educ). U of Chicago Pr.
Eisner, Elliot W. Cognition & Curriculum: A Basis for Deciding What to Teach. LC 81-11804. 96p. 1982. 12.95 (ISBN 0-582-28149-0). Longman.
--Educating Artistic Vision. (Illus.). 352p. 1972. text ed. write for info. (ISBN 0-02-332120-2). Macmillan.
--The Educational Imagination: On the Design & Education of School Programs. 2nd ed. 352p. 1985. text ed. write for info. (ISBN 0-02-332110-5). Macmillan.
--English Primary Schools: Some Observations & Assessments. LC 74-83877. 100p. (Orig.). 1974. pap. text ed. 1.50 (ISBN 0-912674-14-8, 134). Natl Assn Child Ed.
Eisner, Elliot W. & Vallance, Elizabeth. Conflicting Conceptions of Curriculum. LC 73-17616. 1974. 21.00x (ISBN 0-8211-0411-X); text ed. 19.00x 10 or more copies (ISBN 0-685-42630-0). McCutchan.
Eisner, Elliot W., ed. Reading, the Arts & the Creation of Meaning. (Illus.). 1978. 11.95 (ISBN 0-937652-21-0). Natl Art Ed.
Eisner, G. Biomicroscopy of the Peripheral Fundus: An Atlas & Textbook. LC 73-83243. (Illus.). 191p. 1973. text ed. 86.00 (ISBN 0-387-06374-9). Springer-Verlag.
--Eye Surgery: An Introduction to Operative Technique. (Illus.). 1980. 85.00 (ISBN 0-387-09922-0). Springer-Verlag.
Eisner, Gisela. Jamaica, Eighteen Thirty-Nineteen Thirty: A Study in Economic Growth. LC 73-15054. 399p. 1974. Repr. of 1961 ed. lib. bdg. 23.00x (ISBN 0-8371-7157-1, EIJA). Greenwood.
Eisner, Hannah R., jt. auth. see Warmbrod, Catherine P.
Eisner, Harry. Classroom Teachers' Estimation of Intelligence & Industry of High School Students. LC 79-176743. (Columbia University. Teachers College. Contributions to Education: No. 726). Repr. of 1937 ed. 22.50 (ISBN 0-404-55726-0). AMS Pr.
Eisner, J. Michael. William Morris Leiserson: A Biography. (Illus.). 154p. 1967. 19.50x (ISBN 0-299-04360-6). U of Wis Pr.
Eisner, Joel & Krinsky, David. Television Comedy Series: An Episode Guide to 153 TV Sitcoms in Syndication. LC 83-42901. (Illus.). 880p. 1984. lib. bdg. 49.95x (ISBN 0-89950-088-9). McFarland & Co.
Eisner, Lotte. The Haunted Screen: German Cinema & Max Reinhardt. Greaves, Roger, tr. LC 68-8719. Orig. Title: Ecran Demoniaque. 1969. pap. 8.95 (ISBN 0-520-02479-6). U of Cal Pr.
--Murnau. LC 72-82222. 1973. 30.00x (ISBN 0-520-02285-8). U of Cal Pr.
Eisner, Sigmund. Tale of Wonder: A Source Study for the Wife of Bath's Tale. 1957. 15.00 (ISBN 0-8337-1029-X). B Franklin.
--Tale of Wonder, Source Study of the Wife of Bath's Tale. LC 72-192020. 1957. lib. bdg. 17.50 (ISBN 0-8414-3894-3). Folcroft.
--Tristan Legend: A Study in Sources. LC 69-18373. Repr. of 1969 ed. 51.80 (ISBN 0-8357-9474-1, 2015293). Bks Demand UMI.
Eisner, Sigmund, ed. The Kalendarium of Nicholas of Lynn. MacEoin, Gary, tr. from Lat. LC 78-3532. (The Chaucer Library). 260p. 1980. 30.00x (ISBN 0-8203-0449-2). U of Ga Pr.
Eisner, Simon & Gallion, Arthur. The Urban Pattern: City Planning & Design. 5th ed. (Illus.). 512p. 1985. pap. 26.50 (ISBN 0-442-22731-0). Van Nos Reinhold.
Eisner, Simon, jt. auth. see Gallion, Arthur B.
Eisner, U., tr. see Daudel, P.
Eisner, Victor & Callan, Laurence B. Dimensions of School Health. 192p. 1974. 14.75x (ISBN 0-398-02948-2). C C Thomas.
Eisner, Will. Comics & Sequential Art. (Illus.). 154p. 24.95 (ISBN 0-9614728-0-4); pap. 14.95 (ISBN 0-9614728-1-2). Will Eisner Stds.
--A Contract with God. 136p. 1985. signed ed. 25.00 (ISBN 0-87816-017-5); pap. 7.95 (ISBN 0-87816-018-3). Kitchen Sink.
--Signal from Space. Kitchen, Denis, ed. (Illus.). 136p. 1983. pap. 16.95 (ISBN 0-317-00648-7). Kitchen Sink.
--Spirit Color Album. Agger, Jens P., ed. (Spirit Color Album Ser.: Vol. II). (Illus.). 110p. 1983. Repr. 13.95 (ISBN 0-87816-010-8). Kitchen Sink.
--Spirit Color Album. Agger, Jens P., ed. (Spirit Color Album Ser.: Vol. III). (Illus.). 100p. 1983. 13.95 (ISBN 0-87816-011-6). Kitchen Sink.
--Will Eisner Color Treasury. Agger, Jens P., ed. (Illus.). 1982. 13.95 (ISBN 0-87816-006-X). Kitchen Sink.
Eisner, Will & Wood, Wallace. The Outer Space Spirit. Kitchen, Denis, ed. (Illus.). 80p. 1982. pap. 8.95 (ISBN 0-87816-007-8). Kitchen Sink.
Eisold, Kenneth. Loneliness & Communion: A Study of Wordsworth's Thought & Experience. (Salzburg Studies in English Literature, Romantic Reassessment: No. 13). 1973. pap. text ed. 25.50x (ISBN 0-391-01371-8). Humanities.
Eison, Charles L., jt. auth. see Ray, Charles M.
Eison, Irving I. Strategic Marketing in Food Service: Planning for Change. LC 80-16264. 1980. 20.95 (ISBN 0-86730-231-3). Lebhar Friedman.
Eiss, Albert F. Eco-Interaction. 7.95. Beatty.
--Evaluation of Instructional Systems. 152p. 1970. 25.50 (ISBN 0-677-02330-8). Gordon.
--Individualized Learning Program. 1971. 39.95 (ISBN 0-87948-023-8). Beatty.
Eisser, George & Lewy, Julius. Die Altassyrischen Rechtsurkunden von Kueltepe, 2 vols. LC 78-72733. (Ancient Mesopotamian Texts & Studies). Repr. of 1935 ed. 62.50 set (ISBN 0-404-18170-8). AMS Pr.
Eissfeldt, Otto. The Old Testament: An Introduction. LC 65-15399. 1965. 14.95xi (ISBN 0-06-062171-0, RD162, HarpR). Har-Row.
Eissler & Selke, Ruth. Gezeiten. 1976. text ed. 8.00x (ISBN 0-685-52949-5). M S Rosenberg.
Eissler, K. R. Freud As an Expert Witness: The Discussion of War Neuroses Between Freud & Wagner-Jauregg. 490p. 1985. text ed. 40.00 (ISBN 0-8236-2019-0, 02019). Intl Univs Pr.
Eissler, Kurt R. Discourse on Hamlet: A Psychoanalytic Inquiry. LC 73-125475. 656p. (Orig.). 1971. text ed. 40.00 (ISBN 0-8236-1287-2). Intl Univs Pr.
--Leonardo Da Vinci: Psychoanalytic Notes on the Enigma. LC 61-11610. (Illus.). 379p. 1961. text ed. 35.00 (ISBN 0-8236-3000-5). Intl Univs Pr.
--Medical Orthodoxy & the Future of Psychoanalysis. LC 65-18721. 592p. 1965. text ed. 45.00 (ISBN 0-8236-3240-7). Intl Univs Pr.
--The Psychiatrist & the Dying Patient. 1970. pap. text ed. 12.95 (ISBN 0-8236-8265-X, 25720). Intl Univs Pr.
--Victor Tausk's Suicide. LC 82-12725. vi, 322p. 1982. text ed. 32.50 (ISBN 0-8236-6735-9). Intl Univs Pr.
Eissler, Kurt R., ed. Searchlights on Delinquency. 1967. text ed. 40.00 (ISBN 0-8236-6020-6). Intl Univs Pr.
Eissler, Ruch S., et al, eds. Psychoanalytic Assessment: The Diagnostic Profile: an Anthology of the Psychoanalytic Study of the Child. Freud, Anna & Kris, Marianne. LC 75-32280. 373p. 1977. 13.95x (ISBN 0-300-01980-7); pap. 13.95x (ISBN 0-300-01981-5). Yale U Pr.
Eissler, Ruth S. see Solnit, Albert J., et al.
Eissler, Ruth S., ed. The Psychoanalytic Study of the Child, Vol. 26. 1974. 45.00x (ISBN 0-03-001779-3). Yale U Pr.
--The Psychoanalytic Study of the Child, Vol. 27. 1974. 45.00x (ISBN 0-300-01780-4). Yale U Pr.
--The Psychoanalytic Study of the Child: Abstracts & Index, Vols. 1-25. LC 74-79973. 280p. 1975. 45.00x (ISBN 0-300-01778-2). Yale U Pr.
Eissler, Ruth S., et al, eds. The Psychoanalytic Study of the Child, 25 vols. Incl. Vol. 1 (ISBN 0-8236-4520-7); Vol. 2 (ISBN 0-8236-4540-1); Vol. 3-4 (ISBN 0-8236-4560-6); Vol. 5 (ISBN 0-8236-4580-0); Vol. 6 (ISBN 0-8236-4600-9); Vol. 7 (ISBN 0-8236-4620-3); Vol. 8 (ISBN 0-8236-4640-8); Vol. 9 (ISBN 0-8236-4680-7); Vol. 10 (ISBN 0-8236-4700-5); Vol. 11 (ISBN 0-8236-4720-X); Vol. 12 (ISBN 0-8236-4740-4); Vol. 13 (ISBN 0-8236-4760-9); Vol. 14 (ISBN 0-8236-4780-3); Vol. 15 (ISBN 0-8236-4800-1); Vol. 16 (ISBN 0-8236-4820-6); Vol. 17 (ISBN 0-8236-4840-0); Vol. 18 (ISBN 0-8236-4860-5); Vol. 19 (ISBN 0-8236-4880-X); Vol. 20 (ISBN 0-8236-4900-8); Vol. 21 (ISBN 0-8236-4920-2); Vol. 22 (ISBN 0-8236-4940-7); Vol. 23 (ISBN 0-8236-4960-1); Vol. 24 (ISBN 0-8236-4961-X); Vol. 25 (ISBN 0-8236-4962-8). LC 45-11304. 1945. text ed. 30.00 ea. Intl Univs Pr.
--The Psychoanalytic Study of the Child, Vol. 28. 1973. 45.00x (ISBN 0-300-01703-0). Yale U Pr.
--The Psychoanalytic Study of the Child, Vol. 32. LC 45-11304. 1977. 45.00x (ISBN 0-300-02159-3). Yale U Pr.
--Physical Illness & Handicap in Childhood: An Anthology of the Psychoanalytic Study of the Child. Kris, Marianne & Solnit, Albert J. LC 75-34811. 375p. 1977. 44.50x (ISBN 0-300-02005-8); pap. 12.95x (ISBN 0-300-02006-6). Yale U Pr.
--The Psychoanalytic Study of the Child, Vol. 29. LC 45-11304. 500p. 1974. 45.00x (ISBN 0-300-01796-0). Yale U Pr.
--The Psychoanalytic Study of the Child, Vol. 30. LC 75-1934. 800p. 1975. 45.00x (ISBN 0-300-01916-5). Yale U Pr.
--The Psychoanalytic Study of the Child, Vol. 31. LC 45-11304. 1976. 45.00x (ISBN 0-300-02025-2). Yale U Pr.
Eissler, Ruth S., jt. ed. see Solnit, Albert J.
Eissmann, Harold F., et al. Dental Laboratory Procedures: Fixed Partial Dentures, Vol. 2. LC 79-16785. (Illus.). 367p. 1980. text ed. 56.95 (ISBN 0-8016-3517-9). Mosby.
Eissner, W. B., jt. ed. see Burke, P. G.
Eiswirth, Nancy A. & Smith, David E. Cocaine in America. Orig. Title: Current Perspectives on Cocaine. 12p. 1981. pap. 0.60 (ISBN 0-89486-139-5). Hazelden.
Eitan, Israel. Contribution to Biblical Lexicography. (Columbia University. Contributions to Oriental History & Philology: No. 10). Repr. of 1924 ed. 12.50 (ISBN 0-404-50540-6). AMS Pr.
Eitel, Ernes J. Chinese Dictionary: Cantonese Dialect, 3 pts. (Chinese.). 1976. Repr. of 1958 ed. 154.00 (ISBN 0-518-19009-9). Ayer Co Pubs.
Eitel, Jean. The Mandala Tradition in American Quilts. (Illus.). 32p. (Orig.). pap. cancelled (ISBN 0-932946-15-1). Yours Truly.
Eitel, Lorraine, compiled by. The Treasury of Christian Poetry. 189p. 1982. 12.95 (ISBN 0-8007-1291-9). Revell.
Eitel, Wilhelm. Silicate Melt Equilibria. Philips, J. G. & Madgwick, T. G., trs. from Ger. LC 51-62230. pap. 31.50 (ISBN 0-317-11176-0, 2050514). Bks Demand UMI.
--Thermochemical Methods in Silicate Investigation. LC 52-3556. pap. 35.00 (ISBN 0-317-08719-3, 2050515). Bks Demand UMI.
Eitel, Wilhelm, ed. Silicate Science: A Treatise, 5 vols. Incl. Vol. 1. Silicate Structures. 1964 (ISBN 0-12-236301-9); Vol. 2. Glasses, Enamels, Slags. 1964 (ISBN 0-12-236302-7); Vol. 3. Dry Silicate Systems. 1966 (ISBN 0-12-236303-5); Vol. 4. Hydrothermal Silical Systems. 1966 (ISBN 0-12-236304-3); Vol. 5. Ceramics & Hydraulic Binders. 1966 (ISBN 0-12-236305-1). 99.00 ea. Acad Pr.
Eitelberg, Mark, jt. auth. see Binkin, Martin.
Eiteljorg, Harrison. Treasures of American West: Selections from the Collection of Harrison Eiteljorg. (Illus.). 176p. 1982. 45.00 (ISBN 0-9607596-0-3). Eiteljorg Pubns.
Eiteman, David K. & Stonehill, Arthur. Multinational Business Finance. 3rd ed. LC 81-17580. (Business Ser.). (Illus.). 469p. 1982. text ed. 36.95 (ISBN 0-201-03824-2); instr's. manual 9.95 (ISBN 0-201-03835-8). Addison-Wesley.
Eiteman, David K., jt. auth. see Eiteman, Wilford J.
Eiteman, Wilford J. Business Forecasting. 1954. 3.00x (ISBN 0-317-03740-4). Masterco Pr.
--Business Theory for Secretaries 1951. 1968. 5.50x (ISBN 0-912164-04-2). Masterco Pr.
--Essentials of Accounting Theory. LC 61-8425. 1961. 3.50 (ISBN 0-912164-03-4). Masterco Pr.
--Personal Finance & Investment. 1952. 3.25x (ISBN 0-912164-01-8). Masterco Pr.
--Price Determination in Oligopolistic & Monopolistic Situations. LC 60-63554. (Michigan Business Reports Ser.: No. 33). pap. 20.00 (ISBN 0-317-28336-7, 2022095). Bks Demand UMI.
Eiteman, Wilford J. & Eiteman, David K. Leading World Stock Exchanges: Trading Practices & Organization. (Michigan International Business Studies: No. 2). 1964. pap. 3.00 (ISBN 0-87712-116-8). U Mich Busn Div Res.
Eitinger, L. & Schwartz, D., eds. Strangers in the World. 370p. 1981. pap. text ed. 23.50 (ISBN 3-456-80972-7, Pub. by Hans Huber Pubs). J K Burgess.
Eitinger, Leo. Psychological & Medical Effects on Concentration Camps. 122p. 1982. lib. bdg. 15.00 (ISBN 0-8482-0747-5). Norwood Edns.
Eitinger, Leo & Strom, Axel. Mortality & Morbidity After Excessive Stress. 1973. 27.00x (ISBN 8-200-04738-5, Dist. by Columbia U Pr). Universitet.
Eitington, Julius E. The Winning Trainer. LC 83-22595. (Illus.). 400p. (Orig.). 1984. pap. 29.95x (ISBN 0-87201-657-9). Gulf Pub.
Eitner, Lorenz. Neoclassicism & Romanticism: 1750-1850, 2 vols. Incl. Vol. 1. Enlightenment-Revolution. 1970. pap. 18.95 ref. ed. (ISBN 0-13-610907-1); Vol. 2. Restoration-the Twilight of Humanism. (Illus.). 1970. pap. 18.95 ref. ed. (ISBN 0-13-610915-2). pap. P-H.
Eitner, Lorenz E. Gericault: His Life & Work. 360p. 1982. 85.00x (ISBN 0-8014-1468-7). Cornell U Pr.
Eitner, Robert. Das Deutsche Lied Des XV und XVI Jahrhunderts, 2 vols. in 1. LC 71-178529. Repr. of 1876 ed. 42.50 (ISBN 0-404-56542-5). AMS Pr.
Eitner, Robert, ed. Musica Getutscht, 1511. Sebastian Virdung. (Publikation aelterer praktischer und theoretischer Musikwerke Ser: Vol. XI). (Ger.). 1967. Repr. of 1896 ed. 30.00x (ISBN 0-8450-1711-X). Broude.
--Sechzig Chansons zu vier Stimmen aus der ersten Haelfte des 16. Jahrhunderts. (Publikation aelterer praktischer und theoretischer Musikwerke Ser.: Vol. XXIII). (Ger., Fr.). 1967. Repr. of 1899 ed. write for info. (ISBN 0-8450-1723-3). Broude.
Eitner, Robert, ed. see Agricola, Martin.
Eitner, Robert, ed. see Armide & Lully, Jean-Baptiste.
Eitner, Robert, ed. see Depres, Josquin.
Eitner, Robert, ed. see Dressler, Gallus.
Eitner, Robert, ed. see Eccard, Johann.
Eitner, Robert, ed. see Finck, Heinrich & Finck, Hermann.
Eitner, Robert, ed. see Forster, Georg.
Eitner, Robert, ed. see Hassler, Hans Leo.
Eitner, Robert, ed. see Il Giasone & Cavalli, Francesco.
Eitner, Robert, ed. see Leclair, Jean-Marie.
Eitner, Robert, ed. see Oeglin, Erhart.
Eitner, Robert, ed. see Praetorius, Michael.
Eitner, Robert, ed. see Regnart, Jakob.
Eitner, Robert, ed. see Schubiger, P. Anselm.
Eitner, Robert, ed. see Vecchi, Orazio.
Eitner, Robert, ed. see Von Burck, Joachim.
Eitner, Robert, ed. see Walther, Johann.
Eitner, Robert, ed. see Zeuner, Martin.

Eitner, Robert, et al, eds. Einleitung, Biographieen, Melodien, und Gedichte zu Johann Ott's Liedersammlung von 1544. (Publikation aelterer praktischer und theoretischer Musikwerke Ser: Vol. IV). (Ger., Lat.). 1967. Repr. of 1876 ed. 45.00x (ISBN 0-8450-1704-7). Broude.
--Johann Ott's mehrstimmiges deutsches Liederbuch von 1544, 3 vols. in 1. (Publikation aelterer praktischer und theoretischer Musikwerke Ser: Vols. I, II, & III). (Illus., Ger.). 1967. Repr. of 1873 ed. write for info. (ISBN 0-8450-1703-9). Broude.
Eitner, Walter H. Walt Whitman's Western Jaunt. LC 80-29336. (Illus.). 144p. 1981. 17.95x (ISBN 0-7006-0212-7). U Pr of KS.
Eitrem, Samson. Some Notes on the Demonology in the New Testament. 2nd, rev. & enl. ed. LC 79-8098. Repr. of 1966 ed. 16.00 (ISBN 0-404-18409-X). AMS Pr.
Eitzen. Social Problems. 2nd ed. 1983. text ed. 31.43 (ISBN 0-205-07916-4, 817916); instr's manual avail. Allyn.
Eitzen, D. Stanley. In Conflict & Order: Understanding Society. 3rd ed. 520p. 1984. pap. text ed. 20.71 (ISBN 0-205-08273-4, 818273); study guide 7.15 (ISBN 0-205-08275-0, 818275); study guide avail. Allyn.
--Sport in Contemporary Society. 2nd ed. LC 83-61599. 430p. 1984. pap. text ed. 14.95 (ISBN 0-312-75329-2). St Martin.
Eitzen, D. Stanley & Sage, George H. Sociology of American Sport. 2nd ed. 416p. 1982. pap. text ed. write for info. (ISBN 0-697-07182-0); instrs.' manual avail. (ISBN 0-697-07197-9). Wm C Brown.
Eitzen, D. Stanley & Timmer, Doug A. The Sociology of Crime & Criminal Justice. LC 84-13111. 640p. 1985. 26.95 (ISBN 0-471-09758-6). Wiley.
Eitzen, D. Stanley, jt. auth. see Simon, David R.
Eitzen, K. Military Eitzen. (Ger. & Eng.). 1957. pap. 15.95 (ISBN 3-87599-035-8, M-7563, Pub. by Vlg. Offene Worte). French & Eur.
Eitzen, Ruth. Fun to Do All Year Through. 32p. (gr. 3-6). 1982. pap. 2.95 (ISBN 0-8170-0969-8). Judson.
Eizenstat, Stuart E. & Barutio, William H. Andrew Young: The Path to History. 1973. 5.00 (ISBN 0-686-38000-2). Voter Ed Proj.
Eizenstat, Stuart E., et al. Liability of Accountants. 52p. 1972. 8.00 (ISBN 0-318-13940-5, 72-6M); members 5.00 (ISBN 0-318-13941-3). Defense Res.
Ejiogu, C. N., jt. ed. see Ominde, S. H.
Ejiogu, Lem O. Effective Structured Programming. (Illus.). 292p. 1983. 24.95 (ISBN 0-89433-205-8). Petrocelli.
--Software Engineering: Design & Discipline. (Illus.). 300p. 1985. text ed. 32.95 (ISBN 0-89433-276-7). Petrocelli.
--Software Engineering Design & Discipline. (Illus.). 300p. 1985. 32.95 (ISBN 0-89433-276-7). Van Nos Reinhold.
Ejiri, H. & Fukuda, T. Nuclear Spectroscopy & Nuclear Interactions: New Development of Inbeam Spectroscopy & Exotic Nuclear Spectroscopy-Proceedings of the Symposium Held at Osaka, Japan, March 1984. 550p. 1984. 56.00x (ISBN 9971-966-54-9, Pub. by World Sci Singapore). Taylor & Francis.
Ejxenbaum, B. M. O. Henry & the Theory of the Short Story. Titunik, I. R., tr. (Michigan Slavic Contributions: No. 1). 1968. pap. 4.00 (ISBN 0-930042-09-3). Mich Slavic Pubns.
Ek, J. A. Van see Van Ek, J. A.
Ekberg, Carl J. The Failure of Louis XIV's Dutch War. LC 78-21955. xix, 240p. 1979. 22.50x (ISBN 0-8078-1347-8). U of NC Pr.
Ekbote, S. N., jt. auth. see Narlikar, A. V.
Ekdahl, Janis K., ed. American Sculpture: A Guide to Information Sources. LC 74-11544. (Art & Architecture Information Guide Ser.: Vol. 5). 1977. 60.00x (ISBN 0-8103-1271-9). Gale.
Ekechi, F. K. Missionary Enterprise & Rivalry in Igboland, 1857-1914. (Illus.). 296p. 1972. 30.00x (ISBN 0-7146-2778-X, F Cass Co). Biblio Dist.
Ekeh, Peter P. Social Exchange Theory: The Two Traditions. LC 74-79403. 256p. 1974. text ed. 15.00t (ISBN 0-674-81201-8). Harvard U Pr.
Ekeland, I. & Temam, R. Convex Analysis & Variational Problems. (Applied Mathematics & Its Applications Ser.: Vol. 1). 402p. 1976. 72.50 (ISBN 0-444-10898-X, North Holland). Elsevier.
Ekeland, Ivar & Turnbull, Thomas. Infinite-Dimensional Optmization & Convexity. LC 83-50048. (Chicago Lectures in Mathematics). (Illus.). viii, 166p. 1983. lib. bdg. 16.00x (ISBN 0-226-19987-8); pap. text ed. 8.00x (ISBN 0-226-19988-6). U of Chicago Pr.
Ekeland, Ivar, jt. auth. see Aubin, Jean-Pierre.
Ekeland, Norval R. Basic Electronics for Engineering Technology. (Illus.). 736p. 1981. text ed. 31.95 (ISBN 0-13-060467-4). P-H.
Ekeland, Vilhelm. Agenda. Bruce, Lennart, tr. from Swedish. 1976. pap. 3.00 (ISBN 0-685-79188-2, Pub. by Cloud Marauder). Small Pr Dist.
Ekelof, Gunnar. Guide to the Underworld. Lesser, Rika, tr. from Swedish. LC 80-13181. 112p. 1980. 10.00x (ISBN 0-87023-306-8). U of Mass Pr.
--I Do Best Alone at Night. Bly, Robert, tr. 1977. 7.50 (ISBN 0-910350-03-5). Charioteer.
--A Molna Elegy, 2 vols. Rukeyser, Muriel & Sjoberg, Leif, trs. (Illus.). 55p. 1985. boxed set 20.00 (ISBN 0-87775-163-3); pap. 8.00 (ISBN 0-87775-153-6). Unicorn Pr.
--Selected Poems of Gunnar Ekelof. Rukeyser, Muriel & Sjoberg, Leif, trs. from Swedish. LC 66-16109. (Library of Scandinavian Literature). 1971. lib. bdg. 19.50x (ISBN 0-8057-5852-6). Irvington.
Ekelof, Johan, tr. see Nordenskiold, A. E.
Ekelund, jt. auth. see DeLorme.
Ekelund, Robert B. & Herbert, Robert E. History of Economic Theory & Method. 2nd ed. (Illus.). 624p. 1983. text ed. 35.95 (ISBN 0-07-019239-1). McGraw.
Ekelund, Robert B., jt. auth. see Auernheimer, Leonardo.
Ekelund, Robert B., Jr. & Tollison, Robert D. Mercantilism As a Rent-Seeking Society: Economic Regulation in Historical Perspectives. LC 81-40398. (Tex A&M University Economic Ser.: No. 5). 184p. 1982. 19.50x (ISBN 0-89096-120-4). Tex A&M Univ Pr.
Eker, Dorothy. Blossom of His Love. LC 85-50090. 64p. (Orig.). 1985. pap. 4.95 (ISBN 0-938232-57-6). Winston-Derek.
--Land of Upthere. LC 78-56855. 1979. 5.95 (ISBN 0-87212-087-2). Libra.
--Mr. Cinderman Died at Sixty-Eight. LC 79-93041. 1980. 6.95 (ISBN 0-87212-130-5). Libra.
--Reflections of Him. LC 75-393402. 1976. 4.95 (ISBN 0-87212-053-8). Libra.
Eker, Julius, tr. see Sand, George.
Ekerdt, John G., ed. Chemical Engineering Faculties, Nineteen Eighty-Four, Nineteen Eighty-Five, Vol. 10. 254p. 1984. 40.00 (ISBN 0-317-03749-8); pap. 20.00 members (ISBN 0-8169-0321-2). Am Inst Chem Eng.
Ekeren, Glenn Van see Van Ekeren, Glenn.
Ekern, Doris. Suits to Fit Your Man. LC 80-50504. (Illus.). 56p. 1980. pap. 4.00x (ISBN 0-933956-05-3). Sew-Fit.
Ekers, Mitzi A. Arterial Occlusive Disease: Nursing Assessment & Patient Care. (Illus.). 58p. (Orig.). 1984. pap. text ed. 24.95 (ISBN 0-932491-04-9). Res Appl Inc.
Ekert, H., ed. Seminar on Haematology & Oncology. (Journal: Paediatrician: Vol. 9, No. 2). (Illus.). 88p. 1980. softcover 14.25 (ISBN 3-8055-1302-X). S Karger.
Ekert, Henry. Clinical Paediatric Haematology & Oncology. (Illus.). 248p. 1982. text ed. 32.50 (ISBN 0-86793-000-4, B 1510-0). Mosby.
Ekert-Rotholz, Alice. Checkpoint Orinoco. Hutter, Catherine, tr. from Ger. LC 83-14245. 368p. (Eng.). 1983. 15.95 (ISBN 0-88064-012-X). Fromm Intl Pub.
--Rice in Silver Bowls. Hutter, Catherine, tr. from Ger. LC 81-22174. Orig. Title: Reis aus Silberschalen. 432p. 1982. 15.95 (ISBN 0-88064-003-0). Fromm Intl Pub.
--Rice in Silver Bowls. 432p. 1985. pap. 3.95 (ISBN 0-445-20163-0, Pub. by Popular Lib). Warner Bks.
--The Sydney Circle. Hutter, Catherine, tr. from Ger. LC 83-1448. 400p. 1983. 15.95 (ISBN 0-88064-009-X). Fromm Intl Pub.
Ekgren, William. Out of Six Attitudes: A Collection of Poems. 1983. 7.95 (ISBN 0-533-05653-5). Vantage.
Ekholm, Gordon F. see Wauchope, Robert.
Ekiguchi, Kunio. Gift Wrapping: Creative Ideas from Japan. LC 85-40066. (Illus.). 112p. 1985. 14.95 (ISBN 0-87011-723-8). Kodansha.
Ekin, Cemal A., jt. auth. see Mecca, Stephen J.
Ekins, R. P., jt. ed. see Albertini, A.
Ekins, Roy. Worldwide Winemaking Recipes. (Illus.). 114p. Date not set. pap. 3.95 (ISBN 0-900841-53-2, Pub. by Aztex Corp). Argus Bks.
Ekirch, A. Roger. Poor Carolina: Politics & Society in Colonial North Carolina, 1729-1776. LC 80-39889. (Illus.). xix, 305p. 1981. 26.00x (ISBN 0-8078-1475-X). U of NC Pr.
Ekirch, Arthur A. Idea of Progress in America, 1815-1860. 12.00 (ISBN 0-8446-1170-0). Peter Smith.
Ekirch, Arthur A., Jr. Civilian & the Military: A History of the American Anti-Militarist Tradition. LC 72-80273. 1972. pap. 3.00 (ISBN 0-87926-007-6). R Myles.
--Decline of American Liberalism. LC 67-13171. 1967. pap. text ed. 5.95x (ISBN 0-689-70069-5, 111). Atheneum.
--Idea of Progress in America, 1815-1860. (Columbia University Studies in the Social Sciences: No. 511). Repr. of 1944 ed. 17.50 (ISBN 0-404-51511-8). AMS Pr.
--Ideologies & Utopias. 1971. pap. text ed. 7.95x (ISBN 0-8290-0342-8). Irvington.
--Man & Nature in America. LC 63-14925. xvi, 231p. 1973. pap. 4.75 (ISBN 0-8032-5785-6, BB 574, Bison). U of Nebr Pr.
--Progressivism in America: A Study of the Era from Theodore Roosevelt to Woodrow Wilson. 320p. 1974. 4.95 (ISBN 0-531-05564-7). Watts.
Ekirch, Arthur A., Jr., ed. Voices in Dissent. 1964. 6.50 (ISBN 0-685-08137-0); pap. 2.45 (ISBN 0-8065-0023-9, 146). Citadel Pr.
Ekkehardus. Die Chronik Des Ekkehard Von Aura. (Ger). pap. 10.00 (ISBN 0-384-14080-7). Johnson Repr.
Ekken, James A., ed. Trolley Cars Across America. 96p. 1984. 12.95 (ISBN 0-912113-01-4). Railhead Pubns.
Ekken, James S., ed. Stark's Last Interurbans. 80p. 9.95 (ISBN 0-912113-09-X). Railhead Pubns.
Ekker, Neal. Requiem for a River Rat. LC 85-4566. 1985. 15.95 (ISBN 0-934878-58-7). Dembner Bks.
Ekland, Britt. True Britt. 1982. pap. 2.95 (ISBN 0-425-05341-5). Berkley Pub.
--True Britt. (Illus.). 242p. 1981. 9.95 (ISBN 0-13-931089-4). P-H.
Ekland, Britt & Russell, Sue. Sensual Beauty: And How to Achieve It. LC 99-944036. (Illus.). 144p. 1984. pap. 12.95 (ISBN 0-283-99014-7, Pub. by Sidgwick & Jackson). Merrimack Pub Cir.
Ekloef, O., ed. Current Concepts in Pediatric Radiology. (Current Diagnostic Pediatrics: Vol. 1). (Illus.). 1977. 36.00 (ISBN 0-387-08279-4). Springer-Verlag.
Eklund, Bo-Lennart. Modern Greek: Verbal Aspect & Compound Nouns. (Acta Regiae Societatis Scientiarm et Litterarum Gothoburgensis, Humaniora: No. 11). 1976. pap. text ed. 8.50x (ISBN 91-85252-08-5). Humanities.
Eklund, Dara, ed. see Judge, William Q.
Eklund, Emmet E. Peter Fjellstedt: Missionary Mentor to Three Continents. LC 83-71472. (Augustana Historical Society Publication Ser.: No. 30). 197p. 1983. 20.00x (ISBN 0-910184-30-5). Augustana.
Eklund, George. Gone West of Sunrise Highway. 56p. 1983. pap. 4.95 (ISBN 0-941152-03-0). Bearstone Shepherd Pub.
Eklund, Gordon. Devil World. (Star Trek Ser.). (Orig.). 1985. 1.95; pap. 2.95 (ISBN 0-553-24677-1). Bantam.
Eklund, Gordon, jt. auth. see Benford, Gregory.
Eklund, Gordon, jt. auth. see Doc Smith.
Eklund, Ken & Baylon, David. Design Tools for Energy Efficient Homes. 3rd ed. Beckerman, Richard & Stewart, Annie, eds. (Illus.). 126p. 1984. pap. 14.95 (ISBN 0-934478-25-2). Ecotope.
Eklund, Ken, et al. A Solar Water Heater Workshop Manual. Stewart, Annie & Sassaman, Richard, eds. (Illus.). 81p. (Orig.). 1979. pap. 6.00 (ISBN 0-934478-27-9). Ecotope.
Eklund, Sigvard, ed. see International Atomic Energy Agency.
Eklund, Stephen A., jt. auth. see Landis, J. Richard.
Ekman, Joanna, ed. see Pittman, Holly.
Ekman, Joanna, ed. see Wilkinson, Charles K.
Ekman, Karl. Jean Sibelius: His Life & Personality. LC 75-152594. (Illus.). 298p. 1972. Repr. of 1938 ed. lib. bdg. 22.75x (ISBN 0-8371-6027-8, EKJS). Greenwood.
Ekman, Kerstin. The Witches' Circles. Bartlett, June, tr. from Swedish. Orig. Title: Haexringarna. 256p. (Orig.). 1986. pap. 8.95 (ISBN 0-940242-05-2). Fjord Pr.
Ekman, Leonard C. Scenic Geology of the Pacific Northwest. 2nd. ed. LC 61-13278. (Illus.). 1970. 8.95 (ISBN 0-8323-0130-2). Binford.
Ekman, P. & Friesen, W. Unmasking the Face. 1975. 12.95 (ISBN 0-13-938183-X, Spec); pap. 4.25 (ISBN 0-13-938175-9, Spec). P-H.
Ekman, Paul. Darwin & Facial Expression: A Century of Research in Review. 1973. 46.50 (ISBN 0-12-236750-2). Acad Pr.
--The Face of Man: Expressions of Universal Emotions in a New Guinea Village. LC 79-12934. 154p. 1980. lib. bdg. 30.00 (ISBN 0-8240-7130-1). Garland Pub.
--Telling Lies: Clues to Deceit in the Marketplace, Politics & Marriage. 320p. 1985. 17.95 (ISBN 0-393-01931-4). Norton.
Ekman, Paul & Friesen, Wallace v. Unmasking the Face. 2nd ed. (Illus.). xii, 212p. 1984. pap. 8.00 (ISBN 0-89106-024-3, 7281). Consulting Psychol.
Ekman, Paul, ed. Emotion in the Human Face. 2nd ed. LC 81-21621. (Studies in Emotion & Social Interaction: No. 2). (Illus.). 416p. 1983. 42.50 (ISBN 0-521-23992-3); pap. 15.95 (ISBN 0-521-28393-0). Cambridge U Pr.
Ekman, Paul, jt. ed. see Scherer, Klaus R.
Eknoyan. Medical Procedures Manual. 1981. 17.95 (ISBN 0-8151-3053-8). Year Bk Med.
Eknoyan, Garabed & Knochel, James P., eds. The Systemic Consequences of Renal Failure. 1984. 84.50 (ISBN 0-8089-1634-3, 791151). Grune.
Eknoyan, Garabed & Martinex-Maldonado, Manueal, eds. The Physiological Basis of Diuretic Therapy in Clinical Medicine. LC 79-1152. 1985. price not set (ISBN 0-8089-1744-7). Grune.
Ekoko, A. E. British Defence Strategy in Western Africa 1880-1914. 200p. 1985. text ed. 30.00x (ISBN 0-7146-3260-0, BHA-03219, F Cass Co). Biblio Dist.
Ekondy, Akala. Le Congo - Brazzaville: Essai d'analyse et d'explication sociologiquees selon la methode pluraliste. (European University Studies: No. 22, Vol. 73). 532p. (Fr.). 1983. 31.60 (ISBN 3-261-03282-0). P Lang Pubs.
Ekoyan, Garabed, jt. ed. see Suki, Wadi N.
Ekpo, Ekerete. Self Understanding: The Foundation of New Civilization. LC 81-83574. 144p. (Orig.). 1981. pap. 6.50x (ISBN 0-935834-05-2). Rainbow Books.
Ekpo, Monday U., ed. Bureaucratic Corruption in Sub-Saharan Africa: Toward a Search for Causes & Consequences. LC 79-66150. 1979. pap. text ed. 18.50 (ISBN 0-8191-0796-4). U Pr of Amer.
Eksborg, S., et al, eds. Liquid Chromatography in the Biomedical Sciences: Invited Papers from the 15th International Symposium Held in Ronneby, Sweden, 18-21 June 1984. 200p. 1985. pap. 25.00 (ISBN 0-08-032600-5). Pergamon.
Ekstedt, John W. & Griffiths, Curt T. Corrections in Canada: Policy & Practice. LC 84-185777. 407p. Date not set. price not set (ISBN 0-409-83454-8). Butterworth.
Ekstein, Rudolf & Wallerstein, Robert S. The Teaching & Learning of Psychotherapy. rev. ed. LC 70-184442. 277p. 1972. text ed. 30.00 (ISBN 0-8236-6363-9). Intl Univs Pr.
Ekstein, Rudolf, tr. see Schwing, Gertrud.
Ekstein, Rudolph. Children of Time & Space. LC 76-52312. 466p. 1983. 30.00x (ISBN 0-87668-733-8). Aronson.
Eksteins, Modris. The Limits of Reason: The German Democratic Press & the Collapse of Weimar Democracy. (Oxford Historical Monographs). 1975. 45.00x (ISBN 0-19-821862-1). Oxford U Pr.
Eksteins, Modris & Hammerschmidt, Hildegard, eds. Nineteenth-Century Germany: A Symposium. (Illus.). 188p. (Orig., German.). 1983. pap. 17.00x (ISBN 3-87808-179-0, Pub. by G N Verlag Germany). Benjamins North Am.
Ekstrom, Jack, ed. see Way, Walt.
Ekstrom, Jan. Deadly Reunion. Tate, Joan, tr. 256p. 1982. 12.95 (ISBN 0-684-17765-X, ScribT). Scribner.
Ekstrom, K. George Washington Cable. (Essays & Studies on American Language & Literature: Vol. 10). pap. 15.00 (ISBN 0-317-15661-6). Kraus Repr.
Ekstrom, Kjell. George Washington Cable: A Study of His Early Life & Works. LC 68-1601. (American Biography Ser., No. 32). 1969. Repr. of 1950 ed. lib. bdg. 49.95x (ISBN 0-8383-0658-6). Haskell.
Ekstrom, M. P., jt. ed. see Mitra, S. K.
Ekstrom, Margareta. Death's Midwives. Claeson, Eva, tr. 138p. 1985. 17.95 (ISBN 0-86538-046-5); pap. 8.95 (ISBN 0-86538-047-3). Ontario Rev NJ.
Ekstrom, Michael P., ed. Digital Image Processing Techniques. LC 83-22321. (Computer Techniques Ser.). 1984. 49.50 (ISBN 0-12-236760-X). Acad Pr.
Ekstrom, Rosemary, jt. auth. see Reynolds, R.
Ekundare, R. O. Economic History of Nigeria 1860-1960. LC 72-94209. 480p. 1973. text ed. 35.00x (ISBN 0-8419-0135-X, Africana). Holmes & Meier.
Ekvall, Eva M. & Sohl, Christine E. Good Food, Tried & True. (Illus.). 221p. (Orig.). 1983. pap. 7.95 (ISBN 0-9611388-0-7). Gourmet Pubns.
Ekvall, J. C., jt. ed. see Bloom, J. M.
Ekvall, Robert B. Faithful Echo. 1960. pap. 5.95x (ISBN 0-8084-0129-7). New Coll U Pr.
--Fields on the Hoof: Nexus of Tibetan Nomadic Patoralism. (Illus.). 100p. 1983. pap. text ed. 6.95x (ISBN 0-88133-052-3). Waveland Pr.
--The Lama Knows: A Tibetan Legend Is Born. LC 81-4160. (Illus.). 144p. 1981. pap. 5.95 (ISBN 0-88316-541-4). Chandler & Sharp.
--Tibetan Skylines. xii, 240p. 1976. Repr. of 1952 ed. lib. bdg. 17.00x (ISBN 0-374-92522-4). Octagon.
Ekvall, Robert B., tr. see Blo Bzang, Ye Shes.
Ekvall, Shirley, jt. auth. see Palmer, Sushma.
Ekwall. Ekwall Reading Inventory. 1985. 16.07 (ISBN 0-205-06674-7, 236674). Allyn.
Ekwall, E. American & British Pronunciation. Bd. with John Campanius' Lutheran Cathecism in the Delaware Language. Holmer, N., ed. (Essays & Studies on American Language & Literature: Vol. 3). (Essays and Studies on American Language & Literature: Vol. 2). pap. 18.00 (ISBN 0-317-15653-5). Kraus Repr.
Ekwall, Eilbert. Etymological Notes on English Place-Names. (Lund Studies in English: Vol. 27). (Orig.). 1959. pap. 11.00 (ISBN 0-317-15664-0). Kraus Repr.
--Selected Papers by Eilbert Ekwall. (Lund Studies in English: Vol. 33). (Orig.). pap. 22.00 (ISBN 0-317-15668-3). Kraus Repr.
Ekwall, Eilert. American & British Pronunciation. LC 73-4759. 1946. lib. bdg. 12.50 (ISBN 0-8414-1906-X). Folcroft.
--Concise Oxford Dictionary of English Place-Names. 4th ed. 1960. 32.50x (ISBN 0-19-869103-3). Oxford U Pr.
--Shakespeare's Vocabulary: Its Etymological Elements. LC 78-166013. Repr. of 1903 ed. 14.75 (ISBN 0-404-02269-3). AMS Pr.
Ekwall, Eldon E. Locating & Correcting Reading Difficulties. 3rd ed. (Illus.). 192p. 1981. pap. text ed. 11.95 (ISBN 0-675-08062-2). Merrill.
--Locating & Correcting Reading Difficulties. 4th ed. 320p. 1984. pap. 12.95 (ISBN 0-675-20347-3). Merrill.
Ekwall, Eldon E. & Shanker, James L. Diagnosis & Remediation of the Disabled Reader. 2nd ed. 512p. 1976. text ed. 33.93 (ISBN 0-205-07931-8, 237931). Allyn.
--Teaching Reading in the Elementary Schools. 544p. 1985. 22.95 (ISBN 0-675-20121-7); additional supplements avail. Merrill.

Ekwall, Per, et al, eds. Surface Chemistry: Proceedings. 1966. 35.00 (ISBN 0-12-237050-3). Acad Pr.

Ekwensi, Cyprian. Beautiful Feathers. (African Writers Ser.). 1971. pap. text ed. 4.50x (ISBN 0-435-90084-6). Heinemann Ed.

--Burning Grass. (African Writers Ser.). 1962. pap. text ed. 3.50x (ISBN 0-435-90002-1). Heinemann Ed.

--Jagua Nana. (African Writers Ser.). 1975. pap. text ed. 4.50x (ISBN 0-435-90146-X). Heinemann Ed.

--Lokotown & Other Stories. (African Writers Ser.). 1966. pap. text ed. 4.50x (ISBN 0-435-90019-6). Heinemann Ed.

--People of the City. (African Writers Ser.). 1963. pap. text ed. 3.50x (ISBN 0-435-90005-6). Heinemann Ed.

--Restless City & Christmas Gold. (African Writers Ser.). 1975. pap. text ed. 4.50x (ISBN 0-435-90172-9). Heinemann Ed.

--Survive the Peace. (African Writers Ser.). 1976. pap. text ed. 5.50x (ISBN 0-435-90185-0). Heinemann Ed.

Ekwensi, Cyprian O. Drummer Boy. 1960. text ed. 3.95x (ISBN 0-521-04882-6). Cambridge U Pr.

--Passport of Mallam Ilia. 1960. text ed. 3.95x (ISBN 0-521-04883-4). Cambridge U Pr.

--Trouble in Form Six. 1966. text ed. 3.95x (ISBN 0-521-04884-2). Cambridge U Pr.

Ekwuru, E. Songs of Steel. Rex Collings Ltd., ed. 25.00x (ISBN 0-86036-105-5, Pub. by R Collings UK). State Mutual Bk.

El, Amelia Agustini De see De Del Rio, Amelia Agostini.

El Baradei Mohamed, jt. auth. see United Nations Institute for Training & Research.

El Camino Hospital, jt. auth. see Mayers, Marlene.

El Paso Genealogical Society. Births, Deaths, & Marriages in El Paso Newspapers to 1886. 226p. 1982. 22.50 (ISBN 0-89308-171-X). Southern Hist Pr.

Ela, Chipman P. The Banjo Timepiece. 2nd ed. 210p. 1978. pap. 50.00 (ISBN 0-9607464-0-4). C P Ela.

El-Aasser, M. S., ed. Emulsion Polymerisation of Vinyl Acetate. (Illus.). 285p. 1981. 52.00 (ISBN 0-85334-971-1, Pub. by Elsevier Applied Sci England). Elsevier.

El Abiad, A. H., ed. Power Systems Analysis & Planning. LC 82-6228. (Arab School on Science & Technology Ser.). (Illus.). 350p. 1982. text ed. 79.95 (ISBN 0-89116-272-0). Hemisphere Pub.

Elacqua, Ann M., compiled by. Health & Wellness Resource Directory: A Guide to Colorado's Holistic Health Professionals & Services. 150p. (Orig.). 1983. pap. 5.00 (ISBN 0-912539-00-3). Colo Holistic.

Elad, Shlomi & Merari, Ariel, eds. The Soviet Bloc & World Terrorism. 65p. 1984. pap. text ed. 8.00x (ISBN 0-8133-0132-7). Westview.

Elagin, Ivan. V Zale Vselennoi. LC 82-15803. 214p. (Rus.). 1982. pap. 7.50 (ISBN 0-938920-24-3). Hermitage.

Elagin, Ivan, tr. see Benet, Stephen V.

El-Agra, A. M. & Jones, A. J. Theory of Customs Unions. 1981. 30.00 (ISBN 0-312-79737-0). St Martin.

El-Agraa, A. M. The Economics of the European Community. 1980. 39.00 (ISBN 0-312-23285-3). St Martin.

El-Agraa, A. M., ed. The Economics of the European Community. 2nd ed. 352p. 1985. 39.95 (ISBN 0-312-22804-X). St Martin.

El-Agraa, Ali. Trade Theory & Policy: Some Topical Issues. 130p. 1984. 24.50x (ISBN 0-8448-1473-3). Crane-Russak Co.

El-Agraa, Ali M. Britain Within the European Community: The Way Forward. 374p. 1984. 22.50x (ISBN 0-8448-1464-4). Crane Russak Co.

--International Economic Integration. LC 81-21261. 1982. 30.00 (ISBN 0-312-42085-4). St Martin.

--The Theory of International Trade. LC 83-3395. 208p. 1984. 35.00x (ISBN 0-312-79850-4). St Martin.

Elahi, Maudood K., jt. ed. see Kosinski, Leszek.

Elaine. Thank God It's Friday. LC 82-99965. 348p. 1983. 13.95 (ISBN 0-912605-00-6). Connoisseur.

Elam, Daniel. Building Better Babies. LC 80-66070. (Illus.). 168p. (Orig.). 1980. pap. 6.95 (ISBN 0-89087-274-0). Celestial Arts.

Elam, H. & Paley, N. Marketing for the Non-Marketing Executive. 1981. pap. 5.95 (ISBN 0-317-31394-0). AMACOM.

Elam, Houston G. & Paley, Norton. Marketing for the Non-Marketing Executive. (Illus.). 1978. 15.95 (ISBN 0-8144-5465-8). AMACOM.

Elam, J. O., jt. ed. see Safar, P.

Elam, John S. & Cancalon, Paul, eds. Axonal Transport in Neuronal Growth & Regeneration. 300p. 1984. 45.00x (ISBN 0-306-41699-9, Plenum Pr). Plenum Pub.

Elam, Julia C., ed. Blacks on White Campuses: Proceedings of a Special NAFEO Seminar. 114p. (Orig.). 1983. lib. bdg. 16.75 (ISBN 0-8191-3267-5); pap. text ed. 5.25 (ISBN 0-8191-3268-3). U Pr of Amer.

Elam, Keir. Shakespeare's Universe of Discourse: Language-Games in the Comedies. LC 83-18892. (Illus.). 320p. 1984. 49.50 (ISBN 0-521-22592-2); pap. 15.95 (ISBN 0-521-27734-5). Cambridge U Pr.

Elam, Kier. Semiotics of Theatre & Drama. 1980. 21.00 (ISBN 0-416-72050-1, NO. 6391); pap. 9.95 (ISBN 0-416-72060-9, NO. 6392). Methuen Inc.

Elam, Phillip G. Checklist-Guide for Assessing Data Processing Safeguards. LC 82-22320. 64p. 1983. pap. 5.00 (ISBN 0-87576-101-1). Pilot Bks.

Elam, Richard M. Young Visitor to Mars. (Illus.). (gr. 4-7). PLB 6.19 (ISBN 0-8313-0031-0). Lantern.

Elam, Richard M., ed. Teen-Age Suspense Stories. (gr. 6-10). 1963. PLB 6.19 (ISBN 0-8313-0047-7). Lantern.

Elam, Stanely, ed. A Decade of Gallup Polls of Attitudes Toward Education: 1969-1978. 400p. 1978. 5.50 (ISBN 0-87367-767-6); members 4.50 (ISBN 0-317-35552-X). Phi Delta Kappa.

Elam, Stanley, ed. A Decade of Gallup Polls of Attitudes Toward Education: 1969-1978. LC 78-70725. iv, 377p. 1979. pap. 5.50 (ISBN 0-87367-767-6). Phi Delta Kappa.

Elam, Stanley, compiled by. A User's Index to the Phi Delta Kappan, 1970-81. LC 82-61909. 150p. 1982. pap. 7.00 (ISBN 0-87367-785-4). Phi Delta Kappa.

Elam, Stanley M., ed. Cream of the KAPPAN. LC 81-83808. 400p. (Orig.). 1981. 7.50 (ISBN 0-87367-776-5). Phi Delta Kappa.

--Public Schools & the First Amendment: Conference Proceedings. LC 83-60804. 192p. (Orig.). 1983. pap. 5.00 (ISBN 0-87367-787-0). Phi Delta Kappa.

El-Aman, Hasu D. Human Hemorrhoids: Guidebook for Medicine, Reference & Research. LC 83-46101. 150p. 1984. 29.95 (ISBN 0-88164-134-0); pap. 21.95 (ISBN 0-88164-135-9). ABBE Pubs Assn.

Elamatha, K. T. Extravaganza. LC 79-63831. 129p. 1982. 10.00 (ISBN 0-533-04281-X). Vantage.

Eland, J. H. Photoelectron Spectroscopy. LC 73-17763. 1974. 42.95x (ISBN 0-470-23485-7). Halsted Pr.

--Photoelectron Spectroscopy. (Illus.). 272p. 1984. text ed. 49.95 (ISBN 0-408-71057-8). Butterworth.

Elandt-Johnson, Regina C. Probability Models & Statistical Methods in Genetics. LC 75-140177. (A Wiley Publication in Applied Statistics). pap. 153.00 (ISBN 0-317-28077-5, 2055764). Bks Demand UMI.

Elandt-Johnson, Regina C. & Johnson, Norman L. Survival Models & Data Analysis. LC 79-22836. (Wiley Series in Probability & Mathematical Statistics: Applied Probability & Statistics). 457p. 1980. 48.95x (ISBN 0-471-03174-7, Pub. by Wiley-Interscience). Wiley.

Elanore, Mary see Mary Eleanore, Sr.

El-Ansary, Adel I., jt. auth. see Stern, Louis W.

El-Asfouri, Souhail & Johnson, Olin. Computer Organization & Programming: Vax-II. LC 83-3699. (Computer Science Ser.). (Illus.). 544p. 1984. 31.95 (ISBN 0-201-10425-3). Addison-Wesley.

El-Ashry, Mohamed T., ed. Air Photography & Coastal Problems. (Benchmark Papers in Geology: Vol. 38). 1977. 69.50 (ISBN 0-12-786410-5). Acad Pr.

El-Asmar, Fouzi. To Be an Arab in Israel. 248p. 1978. Repr. of 1975 ed. 6.95 (ISBN 0-88728-096-X). Inst Palestine.

--The Wind - Driven Reed & Other Poems. LC 78-13850. (Orig.). 1979. 12.00 (ISBN 0-89410-034-3); pap. 5.00 (ISBN 0-89410-035-1). Three Continents.

Elaster, Kenneth see Born, Warren C.

El Awa, M. S. Punishment in Islamic Law. 162p. Date not set. pap. price not set (ISBN 0-89259-015-7). Am Trust Pubns.

El-Ayouty, Yassin, jt. ed. see Brooks, Hugh C.

El-Ayouty, Yassin, et al, eds. The OAU After Twenty Years: An SAIS Study on Africa. 192p. 1984. 29.95 (ISBN 0-03-062473-8). Praeger.

Elazar, Daniel & Friedman, Murray. Moving up: Ethnic Succession in America, with a Case History from the Philadelphia School System. (Illus.). 64p. 1976. pap. 1.95 (ISBN 0-87495-005-8). Am Jewish Comm.

Elazar, Daniel, ed. Judea, Samaria, & Gaza: Views on the Present & Future. 1982. 16.75 (ISBN 0-8447-3458-6); pap. 9.75 (ISBN 0-8447-3459-4). Am Enterprise.

Elazar, Daniel J. American Federalism: A View From the States. 3rd ed. LC 83-26392. 270p. 1984. pap. 11.95 scp (ISBN 0-06-041884-2, HarpC). Harper-Row.

--The American Partnership: Intergovernmental Co-Operation in the Nineteenth-Century United States. LC 62-17132. pap. cancelled (ISBN 0-317-08709-6, 2020058). Bks Demand UMI.

--Camp David Framework for Peace: A Shift Toward Shared Rule. 1979. 2.25 (ISBN 0-8447-3339-3). Am Enterprise.

--Cities of the Prairie: The Metropolitan Frontier & American Politics. LC 83-27364. (Illus.). 528p. 1984. Repr. of 1970 ed. pap. text ed. 17.75 (ISBN 0-8191-3810-X). U Pr of Amer.

--Community & Polity: The Organizational Dynamics of American Jewry. LC 75-8167. (Illus.). 448p. 1976. pap. 9.95 (ISBN 0-8276-0068-2, 377). Jewish Pubns.

--Jewish Communities in Frontier Societies: Argentina, Australia, & South Africa. 357p. 1983. text ed. 44.50x (ISBN 0-8419-0449-9). Holmes & Meier.

--Kinship & Consent: The Jewish Political Tradition & Its Contemporary Uses. LC 82-21851. 412p. 1983. lib. bdg. 28.00 (ISBN 0-8191-2800-7, Co-pub. by Ctr Jewish Comm Studies); pap. text ed. 14.75 (ISBN 0-8191-2801-5). U Pr of Amer.

--Politics of Belleville: A Profile of the Civil Community. LC 70-182890. 100p. 1971. 19.95 (ISBN 0-87722-013-1). Temple U Pr.

Elazar, Daniel J. & Aviad, Janet. Religion & Politics in Israel: The Interplay of Judaism & Zionism. 32p. 1981. pap. 2.50 (ISBN 0-87495-033-3). Am Jewish Comm.

Elazar, Daniel J. & Cohen, Stuart A. The Jewish Polity: Jewish Political Organization from Biblical Times to the Present. LC 83-48648. (Jewish Political & Social Studies). (Illus.). 1984. 27.50x (ISBN 0-253-33156-0). Ind U Pr.

Elazar, Daniel J. & Friedenreich, Harriet p. The Balkan Jewish Communities: Yugoslavia, Bulguria, Greece, & Turkey. (Illus.). 208p. (Orig.). 1984. lib. bdg. 20.75 (ISBN 0-8191-3473-2, Co-Pub. by Ctr Jewish Comm Studies); pap. text ed. 10.50 (ISBN 0-8191-3474-0). U Pr of Amer.

Elazar, Daniel J. & Kincaid, John. Covenant, Polity, & Constitutionalism. LC 83-23295. 1983. pap. text ed. 11.00 (ISBN 0-8191-3709-X). U Pr of Amer.

Elazar, Daniel J., ed. The Federal Polity. 300p. 1974. pap. text ed. 9.95 (ISBN 0-87855-735-0). Transaction Bks.

--Federalism & Political Integration. 242p. 1985. pap. text ed. 11.50 (ISBN 0-8191-4354-5, Pub by Jerusalem Ctr Public). U Pr of Amer.

--Governing Peoples & Territories. LC 81-20298. (Illus.). 368p. 1982. text ed. 27.50 (ISBN 0-89727-034-7). ISHI PA.

--Republicanism, Representation, & Consent: Views of the Founding Era. LC 79-5466. 137p. (Orig.). 1979. pap. 6.95 (ISBN 0-87855-807-1). Transaction Bks.

--Self Rule-Shared Rule: Federal Solutions to the Middle East Conflict. A Colloquim. 276p. 1985. pap. text ed. 12.25 (ISBN 0-8191-4355-3, Pub. by Jerusalem Ctr Public). U Pr of Amer.

Elazar, Daniel J., ed. see Grodzins, Morton.

Elazar, Daniel J., et al. The Jewish Communities of Scandinavia: Sweden, Denmark, Norway, & Finland. 196p. (Orig.). 1984. lib. bdg. 20.75 (ISBN 0-8191-3471-6, Ctr Jew Com Stud); pap. text ed. 10.25 (ISBN 0-8191-3472-4, Ctr Jew Com Stud). U Pr of Amer.

Elazari-Volkani, Yitzhak. The Communistic Settlements in the Jewish Colonization in Palestine. LC 75-6430. (The Rise of Jewish Nationalism & the Middle East Ser.). 140p. 1975. Repr. of 1927 ed. 16.50 (ISBN 0-88355-317-1). Hyperion Conn.

El Azhary, M. S., ed. The Iran-Iraq War: Historical, Economic & Political Analysis. LC 83-16148. 160p. 1984. 22.50 (ISBN 0-312-43583-5). St Martin.

El Baradei, Mohamed & Franck, Thomas M. The International Law Commission: The Need for a New Direction. (United Nations Policy & Efficacy Studies). 47p. 1981. 5.00 (ISBN 0-686-89886-9, E.81.XV.PE/1). UN.

El Baradei, Mohamed & Gavin, Chloe. Crowded Areas, Crowded Rooms: Institutional Arrangements at UNCLOS III: Some Lessons in Global Negotiations. (United Nations Policy & Efficacy Studies). 27p. 5.00 (ISBN 0-686-89890-7, E.81.XV.PE/3). UN.

Elbashier, A. B. Export Marketing to the Arab World: The Importance of Cultural Differences. 130p. 1982. 90.00x (ISBN 0-86010-392-7, Pub. by Graham & Trotman England). State Mutual Bk.

Elbashir, Ahmed E., ed. The United States, Slavery & the Slave Trade in the Nile Valley. LC 83-14692. 200p. 1983. lib. bdg. 23.25 (ISBN 0-8191-3490-2); pap. text ed. 11.25 (ISBN 0-8191-3491-0). U Pr of Amer.

Elbaum, Henrikh. Analiz Iudeiskikh Glav "Mastera I Margarity" M. Bulgakova. 1981. pap. 8.00 (ISBN 0-88233-713-0). Ardis Pubs.

El-Baz, Edgard & Castel, Boris. Graphical Methods of Spin Algebras in Atomic, Nuclear, & Particle Physics. LC 74-179382. (Theoretical Physics Ser.: Vol. 2). pap. 110.00 (ISBN 0-317-08347-3, 2017694). Bks Demand UMI.

El-Baz, Farouk. Say It in Arabic. pap. 2.50 (ISBN 0-486-22026-5). Dover.

Elbaz, Freema. Teacher Thinking: A Study of Practical Knowledge. LC 82-14418. 224p. 1983. 25.00 (ISBN 0-89397-144-8). Nichols Pub.

Elbaz, Jean S. & Flageul, G. Plastic Surgery of the Abdomen. Keavy, William T., tr. LC 79-84907. (Illus.). 120p. 1979. 38.50x (ISBN 0-89352-036-5). Masson Pub.

Elbe, Guenther Von see Lewis, Bernard & Von Elbe, Guenther.

Elbersen, G. W. Mechanical Replacement Processes in Mobile Soft Calcic Horizons: Their Role in Soil & Landscape Genesis in an Area Near Merida, Spain. (Agricultural Research Reports: No. 919). 220p. 1982. pap. 29.00 (ISBN 90-220-0810-X, PDC254, PUDOC). Unipub.

Elbert, George A., jt. auth. see Elbert, Virginie F.

Elbert, J. L. Duesenberg, the Mightiest American Motor Car. LC 74-26385. (Illus.). 192p. 1951. 21.95 (ISBN 0-911160-49-3). Post-Era.

Elbert, John A. Newman's Concept of Faith. 59.95 (ISBN 0-8490-0729-1). Gordon Pr.

Elbert, Joyce. Crazy Ladies. 1970. pap. 4.50 (ISBN 0-451-13790-6, AE3051, Sig). NAL.

--Red Eye Blues. 1982. pap. 3.95 (ISBN 0-451-13217-3, AE3217, Sig). NAL.

--Return of the Crazy Ladies. 1984. pap. 3.95 (ISBN 0-451-13045-6, Sig). NAL.

--The Three of Us. LC 72-94016. 1973. 7.95 (ISBN 0-87795-052-0). Arbor Hse.

--A Very Cagey Lady. 1980. pap. 2.95 (ISBN 0-451-09936-2, E9936, Sig.). NAL.

Elbert, Lisa. Lead Poisoning in Man. (Illus.). 1978. 20.00 (ISBN 0-916750-31-0). Dayton Labs.

--Mercury Poisoning in Man. (Illus.). 1978. 20.00 (ISBN 0-916750-36-1, CX-10). Dayton Labs.

Elbert, Norbert & Discenza, Richard. Contemporary Supervision. 450p. 1985. text ed. 18.95 (ISBN 0-394-32585-0, RanB). Random.

Elbert, R., et al, eds. Practice in Software Adaption & Maintenance. 1980. 68.00 (ISBN 0-444-85449-5). Elsevier.

Elbert, Samuel H. Dictionary of the Language of Rennell & Bellona: Part One: Rennellese & Bellonese to English. 364p. 1975. 35.00x (ISBN 0-8248-0490-2). UH Pr.

--Spoken Hawaiian. LC 77-98134. (Illus.). 266p. (Orig.). 1970. pap. text ed. 6.00x (ISBN 0-87022-216-3). UH Pr.

Elbert, Samuel H. & Pukui, Mary K. Hawaiian Grammar. LC 78-21692. 210p. 1979. text ed. 15.00x (ISBN 0-8248-0494-5). UH Pr.

Elbert, Samuel H., jt. auth. see Pukui, Mary K.

Elbert, Samuel H., ed. Selections from Fornander's Hawaiian Antiquities & Folk-Lore. (Illus.). 297p. 1959. pap. text ed. 12.00x (ISBN 0-87022-213-9). UH Pr.

Elbert, Samuel H. & Mahoe, Noelani K., eds. Na Mele O Hawaii Nei: One Hundred & One Hawaiian Songs. 110p. (Orig., Hawaiian & Eng, Bi-Lingual Ed). 1970. pap. 4.50 (ISBN 0-87022-219-8). UH Pr.

Elbert, Sarah. A Hunger for Home: Louisa May Alcott & Little Women. 468p. 1984. 24.95 (ISBN 0-87722-317-3). Temple U Pr.

Elbert, Sarah, ed. see Alcott, Louisa May.

Elbert, T., et al, eds. Self-Regulation of the Brain & Behavior. (Illus.). 385p. 1984. 40.00 (ISBN 0-387-12854-9). Springer Verlag.

Elbert, Theodore F. Estimation & Control of Systems. 672p. 1984. 48.50 (ISBN 0-442-22285-8). Van Nos Reinhold.

Elbert, Virginia F., illus. Orchids of the World Coloring Book. (Coloring Bks). 48p. (Orig.). (gr. 4up). 1984. pap. 2.50 (ISBN 0-486-24585-3). Dover.

Elbert, Virginie F. & Elbert, George A. The Miracle Houseplants: African Violets & Other Easy-to-Bloom Plants in the Gesneriad Family. enlg. ed. (Illus.). 1984. 19.95 (ISBN 0-517-55136-5); pap. 11.95 (ISBN 0-517-55137-3). Crown.

Elbin, Paul N. Improvement of College Worship. LC 72-176744. (Columbia University. Teachers College. Contributions to Education: No. 530). Repr. of 1932 ed. 22.50 (ISBN 0-404-55530-6). AMS Pr.

--Making Happiness a Habit. (Festival Ser.). 192p. 1981. pap. 2.75 (ISBN 0-687-23030-6). Abingdon.

Elbing, Alvar. Behavioral Decisions in Organizations. 2nd ed. 1978. text ed. 27.10x (ISBN 0-673-15025-9). Scott F.

Elbl, A., tr. see Pomerantzev, B. I.

Elbogen, I., jt. auth. see Brann, M.

Elborn, Andrew. Bird Adalbert. LC 83-8165. Orig. Title: Der Schone Vogel Adalbert. (Illus.). 28p. (gr. k-3). 1983. 9.95 (ISBN 0-907234-45-3, Pub. by Picture Bk Studio USA). Neugebauer Pr.

--Noah & the Ark & the Animals. LC 84-9438. (Illus.). 28p. (gr. 1 up). 1984. 10.95 (ISBN 0-907234-58-5, Pub. by Picture Bk Studio USA). Neugebauer Pr.

Elborn, Andrew, tr. see Leclerq, Jean Paul.

Elbourne, Edward T. Factory Administration & Accounts. Chandler, Alfred D., ed. LC 79-7543. (History of Management Thought & Practice Ser.). 1980. Repr. of 1919 ed. lib. bdg. 55.50x (ISBN 0-405-12327-2). Ayer Co Pubs.

--Fundamentals of Industrial Administration: An Introduction to Industrial Organization Management & Economics. Chandler, Alfred D., ed. LC 79-7544. (History of Management Thought & Practice Ser.). 1980. Repr. of 1934 ed. lib. bdg. 55.50x (ISBN 0-405-12328-0). Ayer Co Pubs.

Elbourne, Roger. Music & Tradition in Early Industrial Lancashire: Seventeen Eighty to Eighteen Forty. (Folklore Society Mistletoe Ser.). 177p. 1980. 26.00x (ISBN 0-8476-6244-6). Rowman.

--Talking about Dreams: Dream Reports As Personal Narratives. 320p. 1985. text ed. 34.50 (ISBN 0-8290-1582-5). Irvington.

Elbow, Margaret, ed. Patterns in Family Violence. LC 80-52785. (Social Casework Reprint Ser.). pap. 37.00 (ISBN 0-317-28804-0, 2020383). Bks Demand UMI.

Elbow, Peter. Oppositions in Chaucer. LC 75-16216. 180p. 1975. 16.00x (ISBN 0-8195-4087-0). Wesleyan U Pr.

--Writing with Power: Techniques for Mastering the Writing Process. 1981. pap. 7.95 (ISBN 0-19-502913-5, GB 642, GB). Oxford U Pr.
--Writing with Power: Techniques for Mastering the Writing Process. 1981. 25.00x (ISBN 0-19-502912-7). Oxford U Pr.
--Writing Without Teachers. LC 72-96608. 1973. pap. 4.95 (ISBN 0-19-501679-3, GB435, GB). Oxford U Pr.
Elbra, R. A. Database for the Small Computer User. 150p. 1982. pap. 21.00x (ISBN 0-85012-328-3). Intl Pubns Serv.
--Database for the Small Computer User. 150p. 1982. pap. 20.75 (ISBN 0-471-89443-5). Wiley.
Elbra, Tony, jt. auth. see Wood, Michael.
Elbualy, Musallam S. & Schindeler, Joan D. Handbook of Clinical Dermatoglyphs. LC 71-143458. (Illus.). 1971. 7.95x (ISBN 0-87024-191-5). U of Miami Pr.
Elcan, Ruth V. Elements of College Writing. 2nd ed. 1980. pap. text ed. 13.95 (ISBN 0-316-23132-0); instructor's manual avail. (ISBN 0-316-23133-9). Little.
Elcano, Barrett W., jt. auth. see Bullough, Vern L.
Elchaninov, Alexander. The Diary of a Russian Priest. 2nd ed. Ware, Kallistos T., ed. LC 82-16795. 225p. (Orig.). 1982. pap. 7.95 (ISBN 0-88141-000-4). St Vladimirs.
Elcock, E. W. & Michie, D., eds. Machine Intelligence: Machine Representations of Knowledge. (Machine Intelligence Ser.: Vol. 8). 680p. 1977. 114.95x (ISBN 0-470-99059-7). Halsted Pr.
Elcock, Howard. Local Government. 288p. 1982. 25.00x (ISBN 0-416-85750-7, NO. 3682); pap. 12.50x (ISBN 0-416-33170-X, NO. 3683). Methuen Inc.
--Political Behaviour. 1976. pap. 15.95x (ISBN 0-416-81800-5, NO. 2772). Methuen Inc.
Elcock, W. D. The Romance Languages. (Great Language Ser.). 1975. text ed. 46.00x (ISBN 0-571-06152-4). Humanities.
El-Dakhakhni, Wagih M. Strength of Materials. 600p. (Arabic.). 1983. pap. 19.50 (ISBN 0-471-08725-4). Wiley.
Eldarova, I. K., ed. see Lenin, V. I.
Eldefonso, Edward. Law Enforcement & the Youthful Offender: Delinquency & Juvenile Justice. 4th ed. LC 77-13331. 534p. 1983. 29.95 (ISBN 0-471-09628-8); tchrs.' manual 14.00 (ISBN 0-471-87380-2). Wiley.
Eldefonso, Edward & Coffey, Alan R. Criminal Law: History, Philosophy, & Enforcement. (Illus.). 304p. 1980. text ed. 22.80 scp (ISBN 0-06-041879-6, HarpC); instructor's manual avail. (ISBN 0-06-361871-0). Har-Row.
Eldefonso, Edward, et al. Principles of Law Enforcement: An Overview of the Justice System. 3rd ed. LC 80-70901. 383p. 1982. 28.95x (ISBN 0-471-05509-3); tchr's manual (law) avail. (ISBN 0-471-86651-2). Wiley.
Eldefrawi, A. T., jt. ed. see Albuquerque, E. X.
Eldelman, A. I., jt. ed. see Freier, S.
Elder, A., jt. auth. see Vanderberg, Maritz.
Elder, Ann & Kiser, George. Governing American States & Communities: Constraints & Opportunities. 1983. text ed. 22.75x (ISBN 0-673-15358-4). Scott F.
Elder, Arlene A. The Hindered Hand: Cultural Implications of Early African-American Fiction. LC 77-95358. (Contributions in Afro-American & African Studies: No. 39). 1978. lib. bdg. 29.95 (ISBN 0-313-20323-7, EHH/). Greenwood.
Elder, Bruce. Take a Trip to Malaysia. (Take a Trip to Ser.). (Illus.). 32p. (gr. k-3). 1985. PLB 9.40 (ISBN 0-531-04941-8). Watts.
--Take a Trip to Singapore. (Take a Trip to Ser.). (Illus.). 32p. (gr. k-3). 1985. PLB 9.40 (ISBN 0-531-04942-6). Watts.
Elder, C. Appropriating Hegel. (Scots Philosophical Monographs: No. 3). 88p. 1981. text ed. 12.50x (ISBN 0-08-025729-1, Pub. by Aberdeen U Scotland). Humanities.
Elder, Carl A. Youth & Values: Getting Self Together. LC 76-58063. 1978. 5.95 (ISBN 0-8054-5326-1, 4253-26). Broadman.
Elder, Carolyn. Hiking in Muir Inlet. (Illus.). 40p. (Orig.). 1980. pap. 2.00 (ISBN 0-9602876-2-0). Alaska Natural.
Elder, Charles D. & Cobb, Roger W. The Political Uses of Symbols. Rockwood, Irving, ed. LC 82-12722. (Professional Studies in Political Communication). (Illus.). 192p. 1983. text ed. 22.50x (ISBN 0-582-28392-2); pap. text ed. 10.95 (ISBN 0-582-28393-0). Longman.
Elder, Charles D., jt. auth. see Cobb, Roger W.
Elder, Crawford. Appropriating Hegel. Brennan, Andrew & Lyons, William, eds. (Scots Philosophical Monographs: Vol. 3). 116p. 1981. 9.00 (ISBN 0-08-025729-1). Pergamon.
Elder, David A. Kentucky Tort Law: Defamation & the Right of Privacy. 547p. 50.00 (ISBN 0-87215-589-7). Michie Co.
Elder, Dorothy. Revelation: For a New Age. LC 81-65477. 320p. (Orig.). 1981. pap. 11.50 (ISBN 0-87516-446-3). De Vorss.
Elder, E. R., ed. Heaven on Earth: Studies in Medieval Cistercian History, IX. (Cistercian Studies: No. 68). (Orig.). 1982. pap. 7.95 (ISBN 0-87907-868-5). Cistercian Pubns.
--The Roots of the Modern Christian Tradition. 1984. 24.95 (ISBN 0-87907-855-3); pap. 10.00. Cistercian Pubns.
Elder, E. R., ed. see William of St. Thierry.
Elder, E. Rozanne, ed. The Spirituality of Western Christendom. LC 76-22615. (Cistercian Studies Ser.: No. 30). (Illus.). 1976. pap. 6.95 (ISBN 0-87907-987-8). Cistercian Pubns.
--The Way of Love. (Cistercian Fathers Ser.: No. 16). (Illus.). 1977. 7.95 (ISBN 0-87907-616-X); pap. 4.50 (ISBN 0-87907-966-5). Cistercian Pubns.
Elder, E. Rozanne, jt. ed. see Sommerfeldt, John R.
Elder, E. Rozanne, ed. see William of St. Thierry.
Elder, E. Rozanne, et al, eds. Cistercians in the Late Middle Ages: Studies in Medieval Cistercian History. (Cistercian Studies: No. VI). 161p. (Orig.). 1981. pap. 8.95 (ISBN 0-87907-864-2). Cistercian Pubns.
Elder, Eldon. Eldon Elder: Designs for the Theatre. (Illus.). 32p. 1978. pap. text ed. 3.95x (ISBN 0-89676-012-X). Drama Bk.
Elder, Frank. The Book of the Hackle. 1979. 16.95 (ISBN 0-7073-0223-4, Pub. by Scottish Academic Pr Scotland). Columbia U Pr.
Elder, Fred S. Morals & Religion. LC 62-18534. 1963. 5.00 (ISBN 0-8022-0444-9). Philos Lib.
Elder, G. H., Jr., jt. ed. see Dragastin, S. E.
Elder, Gary. Arnulfsaga. (American Dust Ser.: No. 11). 1970. 7.95 (ISBN 0-913218-25-1); pap. 2.95 (ISBN 0-913218-26-X). Dustbooks.
--The Far Side of the Storm: New Ranges of Western Fiction. 4.00 (ISBN 0-88235-025-0). San Marcos.
--Making Touch. (Illus.). 40p. 1981. pap. 3.50 (ISBN 0-914974-28-9). Holmgangers.
--Making Touch. 40p. 1971. pap. 3.00 (ISBN 0-88235-015-3). San Marcos.
Elder, Gary, ed. The Far Side of the Storm: New Ranges of Western Fiction. 216p. 1981. pap. 5.95 (ISBN 0-914974-32-7). Holmgangers.
Elder, Gary, ed. see Tedlock, Ernest.
Elder, Gary, intro. by see Tedlock, Ernest.
Elder, Gladys. The Alienated: Growing Old Today. Bernard, Christine, ed. 144p. 1980. 10.00 (ISBN 0-904613-63-1); pap. 3.45 (ISBN 0-904613-64-X). Writers & Readers.
Elder, Glen H., Jr. Children of the Great Depression: Social Change in the Life Experience. LC 73-87301. (Midway Reprint Ser.). (Illus.). xxiv, 400p. 1984. pap. text ed. 14.00x (ISBN 0-226-20265-8). U of Chicago Pr.
--Family Structure & Socialization. Zuckerman, Harriet & Merton, Robert K., eds. LC 79-8995. (Dissertations on Sociology Ser.). 1980. lib. bdg. 48.50x (ISBN 0-405-12966-1). Ayer Co Pubs.
Elder, Glen H., Jr., ed. Life Course Dynamics: Trajectories & Transitions, 1968-1980. LC 84-21503. (Illus.). 352p. 1985. text ed. 37.50x (ISBN 0-8014-1765-1); pap. text ed. 17.95x (ISBN 0-8014-9323-4). Cornell U Pr.
--Linking Social Structure & Personality. LC 73-94131. (Sage Contemporary Social Science Issues Ser.: No. 12). pap. 40.00 (ISBN 0-317-08978-1, 2021892). Bks Demand UMI.
Elder, H. Y. & Trueman, E. R., eds. Aspects of Animal Movement. LC 79-8520. (Society for Experimental Biology Seminar Ser.: No. 5). (Illus.). 250p. 1980. 54.50 (ISBN 0-521-23086-1); pap. 18.95 (ISBN 0-521-29795-8). Cambridge U Pr.
Elder, H. Y., jt. ed. see Meek, G. A.
Elder, Iva N. Gentle Giants. (Illus.). 160p. 1983. 9.95 (ISBN 0-89015-398-1). Eakin Pubns.
Elder, J. D. Song Games from Trinidad & Tobago. LC 64-25264. (American Folklore Society Bibliographical & Special Ser.: No. 16). 119p. 1965. pap. 3.95x (ISBN 0-292-73508-1). U of Tex Pr.
Elder, Jack S., ed. see Marshall, Fray F.
Elder, James B., jt. ed. see Chantler, Eric N.
Elder, James L., ed. see Stearns, Arthur A.
Elder, Jane, tr. see Seneca, L.
Elder, Jean. Transactional Analysis in Health Care. LC 78-57376. 1978. 14.95 (ISBN 0-201-01512-9, Med-Nurse). Addison-Wesley.
Elder, Jeane. Walnut Creek Learns the Alphabet: From Settlement to Suburbia - a History of Walnut Creek Through the Great Depression. 2nd ed. LC 74-84514. (Illus.). 144p. 1974. pap. 4.95 (ISBN 0-914974-01-7). Holmgangers.
Elder, Jerry O. & Magrab, Phyllis R., eds. Coordinating Services to Handicapped Children: A Handbook for Interagency Collaboration. LC 80-16033. (Illus.). 264p. (Orig.). 1980. pap. text ed. 15.95 (ISBN 0-933716-11-7, 117). P H Brookes.
Elder, Joe. Fifteen Houseplants Even You Can't Kill. 48p. 1984. pap. 3.95 (ISBN 0-425-07369-6). Berkley Pub.
Elder, John. Belief in God in the Twentieth Century. LC 82-81671. 70p. 1982. pap. 3.25 (ISBN 0-9608440-0-7). Nur Pubns.
--The Bowels of the Earth. (Illus.). 1976. 21.95x (ISBN 0-19-854412-X); pap. 8.95x (ISBN 0-19-854413-8). Oxford U Pr.
--The Copie of a Letter Sent into Scotlande, or the Arivall of Prynce of Spaine. LC 72-193. (English Experience Ser.: No. 308). 96p. 1971. Repr. of 1555 ed. 9.50 (ISBN 90-221-0308-0). Walter J Johnson.
--Geothermal Systems. LC 80-49663. 1981. 55.00 (ISBN 0-12-236450-3). Acad Pr.
--A Goodly Heritage - Pioneers for God: Devotional Readings. Armajani, Yahya, tr. from Farsi. LC 83-62806. viii, 141p. (Orig.). 1983. pap. 3.50 (ISBN 0-9608440-1-5). Nur Pubns.
--Imagining the Earth: Poetry & the Vision of Nature. LC 84-23987. 208p. 1985. 17.95x (ISBN 0-252-01177-5). U of Ill Pr.
Elder, Leon. Hot Tubs: How to Build, Maintain & Enjoy Your Own. LC 74-30046. (Illus., Orig.). 1975. pap. 5.95 (ISBN 0-394-72456-9, Vin). Random.
Elder, Leon & Rolens, Lin. Waitress: America's Unsung Heroine. (Illus.). 128p. (Orig.). 1985. pap. 8.95 (ISBN 0-88496-235-0). Capra Pr.
Elder, Lloyd. Blueprints. LC 84-7634. 1984. 6.95 (ISBN 0-8054-6581-2). Broadman.
Elder, Lonne, 3rd. Ceremonies in Dark Old Men. LC 70-87212. 192p. (Orig.). 1969. pap. 6.25 (ISBN 0-374-50792-9). FS&G.
Elder, M. G. & Hendricks, C. H. BIMR Obstetrics & Gynecology Vol. 1: Preterm Labor, Vol. 1. 1981. text ed. 49.95 (ISBN 0-407-02300-3). Butterworth.
Elder, Mark. The Prometheus Operation. LC 80-14577. 312p. 1980. 11.95 (ISBN 0-07-019191-3). McGraw.
Elder, Neil & Thomas, Alastair H. The Consensual Democracies? The Government & Politics of the Scandinavian States. (Illus.). 256p. 1982. 42.95x (ISBN 0-85520-423-0). Basil Blackwell.
--Consensual Democracies? The Government & Politics of the Scandinavian States. (Illus.). 256p. 1984. pap. 11.95x (ISBN 0-85520-716-7). Basil Blackwell.
Elder, Robert B. Rattlesnake Dick: A Novel of Gold Rush Days. LC 82-2496. 1982. pap. 8.95 (ISBN 0-934878-14-5). Dembner Bks.
Elder, Robert E. Foreign Leader Program. LC 74-11986. 115p. 1974. Repr. of 1961 ed. lib. bdg. 15.00x (ISBN 0-8371-7706-5, ELFL). Greenwood.
--Information Machine: The United States Information Agency & American Foreign Policy. LC 68-14105. 1968. 15.95x (ISBN 0-8156-2118-3). Syracuse U Pr.
--The Policy Machine. LC 74-3763. 238p. 1974. Repr. of 1960 ed. lib. bdg. 22.50x (ISBN 0-8371-7462-7, ELPM). Greenwood.
Elder, Rozanne E., ed. The Spirituality of Western Christendom II: The Roots of Modern Christian Spirituality. (Cistercian Studies: Nbr. 55). pap. write for info. (ISBN 0-87907-855-3). Cistercian Pubns.
Elder, Rozanne E., jt. ed. see Sommerfeldt, John R.
Elder, Sam. A Christmas Celebration. LC 84-47709. (Illus.). 1984. 4.81 (ISBN 0-06-015359-8, HarpT). Har-Row.
--A Christmas Treasury. LC 85-42564. (Illus.). 48p. 1985. 48.08i (ISBN 0-06-015455-1, HarpT). Har-Row.
Elder, Shirley, jt. auth. see Ornstein, Norman J.
Elder, Susan B. Vitamin C & Thee. (Illus.). 1978. 20.00 (ISBN 0-916750-74-4). Dayton Labs.
Elder, Will, jt. auth. see Kurtzman, Harvey.
Elder, William. Conversations on the Principal Subjects of Political Economy. (The Neglected American Economists Ser.). 1974. lib. bdg. 61.00 (ISBN 0-8240-1021-3). Garland Pub.
Elder, William V., III & Bartlett, Lu. John Shaw: Cabinetmaker of Annapolis. LC 83-72003. (Illus.). 176p. 1983. pap. 19.50 (ISBN 0-912298-56-1). Baltimore Mus.
Elderen, Bastiaan Van see Van Elderen, Bastiaan.
Elderen, E. Van see Van Elderen, E.
Elderfield, John. The Cut-Outs of Henri Matisse. (Illus.). pap. 14.95 (ISBN 0-8076-0886-6). Braziller.
--Henri Matisse-Cut-Outs. LC 78-56503. 1978. 22.50 (ISBN 0-8076-0885-8); pap. 14.95 (ISBN 0-8076-0886-6). Braziller.
--Kurt Schwitters. LC 85-50284. (Illus.). 1985. 45.00 (ISBN 0-500-23426-4, Dist. by W. W. Norton). Thames Hudson.
--Matisse in the Collection of the Museum of Modern Art. LC 78-56155. (Illus.). 1978. 25.00 (ISBN 0-87070-470-2); pap. 12.50 (ISBN 0-87070-471-0). Museum Mod Art.
--The Modern Drawing: One Hundred Works on Paper from the Collection of the Museum of Modern Art. (Illus.). 216p. 1983. 37.50 (ISBN 0-87070-302-1, 577030). NYGS.
--New Work on Paper One. (Illus.). 56p. 1980. pap. 4.95 (ISBN 0-87070-496-6). Museum Mod Art.
--The Wild Beasts: Fauvism & Its Affinities. (Illus.). 1976. 15.00 (ISBN 0-87070-639-X); pap. 8.95 (ISBN 0-87070-638-1). Museum Mod Art.
Elderfield, John & Eggum, Arne. The Masterworks of Edvard Munch. (Illus.). 1979. pap. 6.95 (ISBN 0-87070-492-3). Museum Mod Art.
Elderfield, John, jt. auth. see Golding, John.
Elders, Fons, ed. Reflexive Water: The Basic Concerns of Mankind. 1977. pap. 5.95x (ISBN 0-285-64749-0, Pub. by Souvenir Pr). Intl Spec Bk.
Elders, L. Aristotle's Theology: A Commentary on the Book of Metaphysics. (Philosophical Texts & Studies). 336p. 1972. text ed. 40.25x (ISBN 90-232-0978-8). Humanities.
Elders of Bible Temple & Iverson, Dick. Principles of Family Life. 2nd ed. (Illus.). 195p. 1981. Bible Temple.
Eldershaw, M. Barnard. Essays in Australian Fiction. LC 70-107697. (Essay Index Reprint Ser.). 1938. 18.00 (ISBN 0-8369-1500-3). Ayer Co Pubs.
--Tomorrow & Tomorrow & Tomorrow. LC 84-7748. 480p. 1984. pap. 9.95 (ISBN 0-385-27980-9, Virago). Doubleday.
Eldersveld, Samuel & Ahmed, Bashiruddin. Citizens & Politics: Mass Political Behavior in India. LC 77-21395. (Illus.). 1978. lib. bdg. 26.00x (ISBN 0-226-20280-1). U of Chicago Pr.
Eldersveld, Samuel J. Democracy in Action: Political Parties. 1952. 3.00 (ISBN 0-686-78143-0). Wahr.
--Political Parties in American Society. LC 81-68790. 1982. 18.95x (ISBN 0-465-05935-X). Basic.
Eldersveld, Samuel J., et al. Elite Images of Dutch Politics: Accommodation & Conflict. 296p. 1981. text ed. 16.50x (ISBN 0-472-10009-2). U of Mich Pr.
Elderton, William & Johnson, Norman L. Systems of Frequency Curves. LC 69-10571. pap. 56.00 (ISBN 0-317-26324-2, 2024451). Bks Demand UMI.
El-Desouti, H. Y. Plastic Technology Dictionary. 331p. (Eng., Fr., Ger. & Arabic.). 1980. 45.00 (ISBN 0-686-92400-2, M-9754). French & Eur.
Eldin, H. K. & Beheshti, H. M. Management Science Applications: Computing & Systems Analysis. 316p. 1981. 31.50 (ISBN 0-444-00422-X, North-Hollland). Elsevier.
Eldin, Peter. The Magic Handbook. (Illus.). 192p. (gr. 3 up). 1985. 9.79 (ISBN 0-671-55040-3); pap. 5.95 (ISBN 0-671-55039-X). Messner.
Eldot, Paula. Governor Alfred E. Smith: The Politician as Reformer. Freidel, Frank, ed. LC 80-8469. (Modern American History Ser.). 420p. 1982. lib. bdg. 61.00 (ISBN 0-8240-4855-5). Garland Pub.
Eldred. Diana Ross. (Rock 'n Pop Stars Ser.). (Illus.). 32p. (gr. 4-12). PLB 7.95 (ISBN 0-317-31158-1). Creative Ed.
--Donny & Marie. (Rock 'n Pop Stars Ser.). (Illus.). 32p. (gr. 4-12). write for info. (ISBN 0-317-31155-7). Creative Ed.
Eldred, Michael, jt. auth. see Roth, Mike.
Eldred, Nelson R. & Crouse, David B. Solving Offset Ink Problems. 96p. 1981. 26.00 (ISBN 0-318-17923-7); members 13.00 (ISBN 0-318-17924-5). Graphic Arts Tech Found.
Eldred, O. John. Women Pastors. 128p. 1981. pap. 4.95 (ISBN 0-8170-0901-9). Judson.
Eldred, Pat & Taylor, Paula. Easy Money-Making Projects. (Creative Games, Projects & Activities Ser.). (Illus.). (gr. 4 up). 1979. pap. 3.95 (ISBN 0-685-99627-1). Creative Ed.
Eldred, Patricia M. Boxing's World Champion: Muhammad Ali. (The Allstars Ser.). (Illus.). (gr. 2-6). 1977. pap. 3.95 (ISBN 0-89812-198-1). Creative Ed.
--Debby Boone. (gr. 4-12). 1979. pap. 3.95 (ISBN 0-87191-096-9). Creative Ed.
--What Do We Do When We're Asleep? (Creative's Questions & Answers Ser.). (Illus.). 32p. (gr. 3-4). 1981. PLB 6.95 (ISBN 0-87191-752-1). Creative Ed.
Eldredge, Charles C. American Imagination & Symbolist Painting. LC 79-55429. (Illus.). 176p. 1980. pap. 8.50 (ISBN 0-913689-16-5). Spencer Muse Art.
Eldredge, David L., jt. auth. see Bates, Donald L.
Eldredge, E. Irving & Vanacore, Connie. New Complete Irish Setter. LC 83-18386. (Illus.). 320p. 1984. 17.95 (ISBN 0-87605-166-2). Howell Bk.
Eldredge, H. J., compiled by. Stage Encyclopedia: A Bibliography of Plays. 1968. Repr. of 1909 ed. 32.00 (ISBN 0-8337-0581-4). B Franklin.
Eldredge, Inman F. & Demmon, Elwood L. Voices from the South: Recollections of Four Foresters. (Illus.). 1977. pap. 4.95 (ISBN 0-89030-032-1). Forest Hist Soc.
Eldredge, L. G., jt. ed. see Devaney, D. M.
Eldredge, N. & Stanley, S. M., eds. Living Fossils. (Casebooks in Earth Sciences). (Illus.). 305p. 1984. 45.00 (ISBN 0-387-90957-5). Springer-Verlag.
Eldredge, Niles. Time Frames: The Re-thinking of Darwinian Evolution & the Theory of Punctuated Equilibria. 1985. 17.95 (ISBN 0-671-49555-0). S&S.
Eldredge, Niles & Cracraft, Joel. Phylogenetic Patterns & the Evolutionary Process. LC 80-375. (Illus.). 1980. 42.00x (ISBN 0-231-03802-X); pap. 15.00. Columbia U Pr.
--Phylogenetic Patterns & the Evolutionary Process: Method & Theory in Comparative Biology. LC 80-375. 349p. 1984. pap. 15.00x (ISBN 0-317-13103-6). Columbia U Pr.
Eldredge, Niles & Tattersall, Ian. The Myths of Human Evolution. LC 81-1118. 192p. 1982. 20.00 (ISBN 0-231-05144-1); pap. 11.95 (ISBN 0-231-05145-X). Columbia U Pr.
Eldredge, Niles, jt. ed. see Cracraft, Joel.
Eldredge, Niles, ed. see Dobzhansky, Theodosius.
Eldredge, Patricia D., jt. auth. see O'Connor, Lisa C.
Eldredge, W. Jay, et al, eds. Current Problems in Congenital Heart Disease. LC 78-15311. 220p. 1979. text ed. 37.00 (ISBN 0-89335-060-5). SP Med & Sci Bks.
Eldredge-Martin, Penni, jt. auth. see Dorn, Lois.

Eldridge. Personal Injury & Property Damage. Incl. Causation & Parties. incl. latest pocket part supplement 24.95; separate pocket part supplement, 1983 15.95 (ISBN 0-686-90542-3); Damages. incl. latest pocket part supplement 24.95 (ISBN 0-686-90543-1); separate pocket part supplement, 1983 13.95 (ISBN 0-686-90544-X); Defenses & Immunities. incl. latest pocket part supplement 24.95 (ISBN 0-686-90545-8); separate pocket part supplement, 1983 17.95 (ISBN 0-686-90546-6); Pleadings & Motions under the CPA. incl. latest pocket part supplement 24.95 (ISBN 0-686-90547-4); separate pocket part supplement, 1982 5.45 (ISBN 0-686-90548-2); Preparation for Trial. incl. latest pocket part supplement 24.95 (ISBN 0-686-90549-0); separate pocket part supplement, 1983 14.95 (ISBN 0-686-90550-4). (Law in Georgia Ser.). One vol. incl. latest pocket part suppl. 24.95; separate pocket part suppl. 1983 13.95. Harrison Co GA.

--Products Liability. (The Law in Georgia Ser.). incl. latest pocket part supplement 24.95 (ISBN 0-686-90560-1); separate pocket part supplement, 1984 17.95 (ISBN 0-686-90561-X). Harrison Co GA.

--Wrongful Death Actions. (The Law in Georgia Ser.). incl. latest pocket part supplement 24.95 (ISBN 0-686-90578-4); separate pocket part supplement, 1984 14.95 (ISBN 0-686-90579-2). Harrison Co GA.

Eldridge, jt. auth. see Cobb.

Eldridge, Albert F., ed. Legislatures in Plural Societies: The Search for Cohesion in National Development. LC 76-28916. xv, 284p. 1977. 18.75 (ISBN 0-8223-0373-6). Duke.

Eldridge, Albert F., Jr. Images of Conflict. LC 77-85994. 1979. text ed. 18.95 (ISBN 0-312-40923-0). St Martin.

Eldridge, Benjamin P. & Watts, William B. Our Rival, the Rascal: A Faithful Portrayal of the Conflict Between the Criminals of This Age & the Defenders of Society, the Police. LC 79-172578. (Criminology, Law Enforcement, & Social Problems Ser.: No. 166). (Illus., With intro. added). 1973. Repr. of 1897 ed. 16.00x (ISBN 0-87585-166-5). Patterson Smith.

Eldridge, Charlotte. The Watcher. (Orig.). 1981. pap. write for info. Shamar Bk.

Eldridge, Colin C., ed. British Imperialism in the Nineteenth Century. LC 84-9984. 288p. 1984. 29.95 (ISBN 0-312-10299-2). St Martin.

Eldridge, David. Flying Dragons, Ancient Reptiles That Ruled the Air. LC 79-87965. (Illus.). 32p. (gr. 3-6). 1980. PLB 9.79 (ISBN 0-89375-241-X); pap. 2.50 (ISBN 0-89375-245-2). Troll Assocs.

--The Giant Dinosaurs, Ancient Reptiles That Ruled the Land. LC 79-87967. (Illus.). 32p. (gr. 3-6). 1980. PLB 9.79 (ISBN 0-89375-242-8); pap. 2.50 (ISBN 0-89375-246-0). Troll Assocs.

--Last of the Dinosaurs, the End of an Age. LC 79-64636. (Illus.). 32p. (gr. 3-6). 1980. PLB 9.79 (ISBN 0-89375-243-6); pap. 2.50 (ISBN 0-89375-247-9). Troll Assocs.

--Sea Monsters, Ancient Reptiles That Ruled the Sea. LC 79-87964. (Illus.). 32p. (gr. 3-6). 1980. PLB 9.79 (ISBN 0-89375-240-1); pap. 2.50 (ISBN 0-89375-244-4). Troll Assocs.

Eldridge, Elleanor. Memoirs of Elleanor Eldridge. facs. ed. (Black Heritage Library Collection). 1843. 14.25 (ISBN 0-8369-8748-9). Ayer Co Pubs.

Eldridge, Francis R. Advertising & Selling Abroad. LC 84-46063. 210p. 1985. lib. bdg. 25.00 (ISBN 0-8240-6757-6). Garland Pub.

Eldridge, Franklin E. Cytogenetics of Livestock. (Illus.). 1985. text ed. 49.50 (ISBN 0-87055-483-2). AVI.

Eldridge, G. C. Victorian Imperialism. (Illus.). 1978. text ed. 20.00x (ISBN 0-391-00823-4); pap. text ed. 10.50x (ISBN 0-391-00824-2). Humanities.

Eldridge, H. J. Properties of Building Materials. (Illus.). pap. 30.30 (ISBN 0-317-08291-4, 2019627). Bks Demand UMI.

Eldridge, Hope T. The Materials of Demography: A Selected & Annotated Bibliography. LC 75-16843. 222p. 1975. Repr. of 1959 ed. lib. bdg. 24.75x (ISBN 0-8371-8166-6, ELMD). Greenwood.

Eldridge, J. E., ed. see Weber, Max.

Eldridge, James, pseud. Twinkle. (Illus.). 64p. (Orig.). 1980. pap. 3.25 (ISBN 0-938900-00-5). Creations Unltd.

Eldridge, John. C. Wright Mills. 128p. 1982. pap. 4.95x (ISBN 0-85312-534-1, NO. 3466). Methuen Inc.

--Recent British Sociology. 276p. 1980. text ed. 30.50x (ISBN 0-333-26639-0, Pub. by Macmillan England). Humanities.

Eldridge, John, ed. C. Wright Mills. (Key Sociologists Ser.). 128p. 1983. pap. 4.95 (ISBN 0-85312-534-1, NO. 3466, Tavistock). Methuen Inc.

Eldridge, Judith. Cabbage or Cauliflower? A Garden Guide for the Identification of Vegetable & Herb Seedlings. LC 83-48520. (Illus.). 144p. 1984. pap. 9.95 (ISBN 0-87923-497-0). Godine.

Eldridge, K. G. An Annotated Bibliography of Genetic Variation in Eucalyptus Camaldulensis. 1975. 30.00x (ISBN 0-85074-023-1, Pub. by For Lib Comm England). State Mutual Bk.

Eldridge, Larry, Jr., jt. auth. see Brock, Ted.

Eldridge, Marian. Walking the Dog & Other Stories. LC 83-12884. 220p. 1985. 10.00 (ISBN 0-7022-1784-0). U of Queensland Pr.

Eldridge, Mary, ed. Growing Old Southern. (Illus.). 120p. 1984. pap. write for info. (ISBN 0-943810-19-1). Inst Southern Studies.

--Wiser, Stronger: Southern Elders. (Southern Exposure Ser.). (Illus.). 152p. 1985. pap. 6.00 (ISBN 0-943810-18-3). Inst Southern Studies.

Eldridge, Niles. The Monkey Business: A Scientist Looks at Creationism. 160p. (Orig.). 1982. pap. 3.95 (ISBN 0-671-53141-7). WSP.

Eldridge, P. Caring for the Disabled Patient. 1978. pap. 13.95 (ISBN 0-87489-141-8). Med Economics.

Eldridge, Paul. Kingdom Without God. 15p. 1951. pap. cancelled (ISBN 0-911826-50-5). Am Atheist.

Eldridge, Paul, jt. auth. see Viereck, George S.

Eldridge, Roger. The Fishers of Darksea. 192p. 1985. 13.95 (ISBN 0-575-03208-1, Pub. by Gollancz England). David & Charles.

Eldridge, Roswell & Fahn, Stanley, eds. Dystonia. LC 75-25112. (Advances in Neurology Ser: Vol. 14). 510p. 1976. 69.50 (ISBN 0-89004-070-2). Raven.

Eldridge, William B. Narcotics & the Law. 2nd ed. LC 67-25528. 1967. 17.50x (ISBN 0-226-20315-8). U of Chicago Pr.

--Narcotics & the Law: A Critique of the American Experiment in Narcotic Drug Control. 2nd ed. x, 246p. (Avail. from th eUniversity of Chicago Press). 1967. 10.00 (ISBN 0-226-20315-8). Am Bar Foun.

Eldrige, Niles, ed. see Mayr, Ernst.

Eleanor Roosevelt Institute Staff. War or Peace in the Twentieth Century. Roff, Sue R., ed. (Illus.). 270p. (gr. 9-12). 1984. binder 49.95 (ISBN 0-89908-502-4). Greenhaven.

Eleazer, et al. Florida Criminal Trial Practice. latest pocket part supplement 55.95_incl. (ISBN 0-686-90166-5); separate pocket part supplement, 1983 (for use in 1984) 17.95. Harrison Co GA.

Eleazer, J. M. Dutch Fork Farm Boy. LC 52-2875. (Illus.). 1968. Repr. 9.95 (ISBN 0-87249-035-1). U of SC Pr.

Electric Company. Tickle Yourself Again with Riddles. LC 78-19699. (Illus.). (gr. k-3). 1979. pap. 1.95 (ISBN 0-394-84152-2, BYR). Random.

--Tickle Yourself with Riddles. LC 77-90197. (ps-4). 1978. pap. 1.95 (ISBN 0-394-83783-5, BYR). Random.

Electric Power Research Institute. Electric Utility Solar Energy Activities. 200p. pap. 18.95x (ISBN 0-930978-21-8, V-019). Solar Energy Info.

Electric Vehicle Council. World Guide to Battery-Powered Road Transportation. 393p. 1980. 50.00 (ISBN 0-317-34116-2, 0479202). Edison Electric.

Electro-Craft Corp. DC Motors, Speed Controls, Servo Systems: An Engineering Handbook. 3rd exp. ed. LC 76-56647. 504p. 1977. text ed. 45.00 (ISBN 0-08-021714-1); pap. text ed. 19.50 (ISBN 0-08-021715-X). Pergamon.

Electron Microscopy Society. Proceedings. Arcenaux, Claude, ed. (Annual). 1967-71 eds. 12.50x,; 1971-74 eds. 15.00x ea. Claitors.

Electronic Design. Four Hundred Ideas for Design, Vol. 3. Grossman, Morris, ed. (Illus.). 1976. 16.60 (ISBN 0-8104-5111-5). Hayden.

Electronic Industries Association, jt. auth. see Zbar, Paul B.

Electronics in the Sawmill Workshop, 1st, Sawmill & Plywood Clinic, Portland, Oregon, March, 1979. Electronics in the Sawmill: Proceedings. LC 79-53861. (A Forest Industries Bk.). (Illus.). 1979. pap. 35.00 (ISBN 0-87930-113-9). Miller Freeman.

Electronics Magazine. Design Techniques for Electronics Engineers. 1978. 42.00 (ISBN 0-07-019158-1). McGraw.

--Large Scale Integration. 1976. 5.00 (ISBN 0-07-019187-5). McGraw.

--Microelectronics Interconnection & Packaging. (Electronics Book Ser.). (Illus.). 1980. 5.00 (ISBN 0-07-019184-0). McGraw.

--Microprocessors. (Illus.). 1975. pap. text ed. 38.00 (ISBN 0-07-019171-9). McGraw.

--New Product Trends in Electronics Number One, No. 1. (Electronic Book Ser.). 1978. 38.00 (ISBN 0-07-019152-2). McGraw.

--Personal Computing: Hardware & Software Basics. 1979. 32.50 (ISBN 0-07-019151-4). McGraw.

Electronics Magazine & Weber, Samuel. Electronic Circuits Notebook: Proven Designs for Systems Applications. 344p. 1981. 37.50 (ISBN 0-07-019244-8). McGraw.

Electronics Magazine Editors. An Age of Innovation: The World of Electronics, 1930-2000. LC 80-14816. (Illus.). 274p. 1981. text ed. write for info. (ISBN 0-07-606688-6). McGraw.

Eleen, Luba. The Illustration of the Pauline Epistles in French & English Bibles of the Twelfth & Thirteenth Century. (Illus.). 1982. 89.00x (ISBN 0-19-817344-X). Oxford U Pr.

Elefteriades. House Officer Guide to ICU Care: The Cardiothoracic Surgical Patient. 176p. 1985. pap. text ed. 18.00 (ISBN 0-8391-2071-0, 21962). Univ Park.

Eleftheriades, Olga. Modern Greek: A Contemporary Grammar. xxvi, 546p. 1985. text ed. 24.95x (ISBN 0-87015-251-3). Pacific Bks.

Eleftheriou, Basil E. The Neurobiology of the Amygdala. LC 77-188921. (Advances in Behavioral Biology Ser.: Vol. 2). 843p. 1972. 75.00x (ISBN 0-306-37902-3, Plenum Pr). Plenum Pub.

Eleftheriou, Basil E., ed. Psychopharmacogenetics. LC 75-23100. 480p. 1975. 45.00x (ISBN 0-306-30881-9, Plenum Pr). Plenum Pub.

Eleftheriou, Basil E. & Scott, J. P., eds. Physiology of Aggression & Defeat. LC 77-164505. 323p. 1971. 39.50x (ISBN 0-306-30547-X, Plenum Pr). Plenum Pub.

Eleftheriou, Basil E. & Sprott, Richard L., eds. Hormonal Correlates of Behavior. Incl. Vol. 1. Lifespan View. 456p. 1975. 45.00x (ISBN 0-306-37504-4); Vol. 2, an Organismic View. 382p. 45.00 (ISBN 0-306-37505-2). LC 75-5938. 1975 (Plenum Pr). Plenum Pub.

Elegant, Robert. Manchu. New ed. 608p. 1982. pap. 3.95 (ISBN 0-449-24445-8, Crest). Fawcett.

--Mandarin. 1984. pap. 4.50 (ISBN 0-671-45175-8). PB.

Elegant, Robert S. China's Red Masters: Political Biographies of the Chinese Communist Leaders. LC 76-136065. (Illus.). 1971. Repr. of 1951 ed. lib. bdg. 15.00x (ISBN 0-8371-5215-1, ELCR). Greenwood.

--Dynasty. 864p. 1982. pap. 3.50 (ISBN 0-449-23655-2, Crest). Fawcett.

Elementary Electronics Editors. The Giant Book of Easy-to-Build Electronic Projects. (Illus.). 352p. (Orig.). 1984. 21.95 (ISBN 0-8306-0199-6, 1599); pap. 15.95 (ISBN 0-8306-0599-1). TAB Bks.

--Second Book of Easy-to-Build Electronic Projects. 192p. (Orig.). 1984. 17.95 (ISBN 0-8306-0679-3, 1679); pap. 13.50 (ISBN 0-8306-1679-9). TAB Bks.

Elementary Science Study. Animals in the Classroom: A Book for Teachers. 1970. 12.32 (ISBN 0-07-017706-6). McGraw.

--The Balance Book: A Guide for Teachers. 2nd ed. 1975. 18.52 (ISBN 0-07-018575-1). McGraw.

--Batteries & Bulbs Two: Student's Book. (gr. 5-9). 1971. text ed. 28.20 (ISBN 0-07-017713-9). McGraw.

--Bones. (gr. 4-6). 1967. picture bk. 8.96 (ISBN 0-07-018496-8). McGraw.

--Brine Shrimp. 1975. tchr's. guide 10.92 (ISBN 0-07-018577-8). McGraw.

--Clay Boats. 2nd ed. 1975. tchr's. guide 8.12 (ISBN 0-07-018579-4). McGraw.

--Crayfish. 2nd ed. 1975. tchr's. guide 14.52 (ISBN 0-07-018580-8). McGraw.

--Drops, Streams, & Containers. 1971. tchr's. guide 20.20 (ISBN 0-07-017692-2). McGraw.

--Earthworms. 1971. tchr's. guide 13.80 (ISBN 0-07-017707-4). McGraw.

--Growing Seeds. 1975. tchr's. guide 12.00 (ISBN 0-07-018521-2). McGraw.

--Heating & Cooling. (gr. 3-8). 1971. tchr's. guide 14.96 (ISBN 0-07-017709-0). McGraw.

--Ice Cubes. 1975. tchr's. guide 17.44 (ISBN 0-07-018522-0). McGraw.

--Kitchen Physics. 2nd ed. 1975. tchr's. guide 17.44 (ISBN 0-07-018523-9). McGraw.

--Life of Beans & Peas. 2nd ed. 1975. 9.16 (ISBN 0-07-018581-6). McGraw.

--Light & Shadows. 2nd ed. 1975. tchr's. guide 11.32 (ISBN 0-07-018582-4). McGraw.

--Mapping. (gr. 3-8). 1971. tchr's guide 19.60 (ISBN 0-07-017718-X). McGraw.

--Match & Measure. (gr. 3-8). 1971. tchr's. guide 19.00 (ISBN 0-07-017721-X). McGraw.

--Microgardening. 2nd ed. 1975. tchr's. guide 8.76 (ISBN 0-07-018583-2). McGraw.

--Mirror Cards. 1975. tchr's guide 14.72 (ISBN 0-07-018524-7). McGraw.

--Mobiles. 2nd ed. 1975. tchr's guide 9.16 (ISBN 0-07-018584-0). McGraw.

--Optics. (gr. 3-8). 1971. tchr's guide 21.48 (ISBN 0-07-017694-9). McGraw.

--Pendulums. 2nd ed. 1975. tchr's guide 12.20 (ISBN 0-07-018585-9). McGraw.

--Pond Water. 2nd ed. 1975. tchr's guide 12.56 (ISBN 0-07-018586-7). McGraw.

--Rocks & Charts. 1975. tchr's guide 8.92 (ISBN 0-07-018527-1). McGraw.

--Sink or Float. (gr. 3-8). 1971. tchr's guide 13.56 (ISBN 0-07-017724-4). McGraw.

--Spinning Tables. 1971. tchr's guide 7.60 (ISBN 0-07-017699-X). McGraw.

--Structures. 1970. tchr's guide 11.76 (ISBN 0-07-017696-5). McGraw.

--Tangrams. 1975. tchr's guide 7.40 (ISBN 0-07-018587-5). McGraw.

--Tracks. 1971. tchr's guide 13.52 (ISBN 0-07-017701-5). McGraw.

--Water Flow. 1971. tchr's guide 14.92 (ISBN 0-07-017733-3). McGraw.

Elementary Science Study Staff. Gases & Airs. 1975. tchr's. guide 17.88 (ISBN 0-07-018519-0). McGraw.

--Geo Blocks. 1975. tchr's guide 8.52 (ISBN 0-07-018520-4). McGraw.

--Starting from Seeds. 1971. tchr's. guide 11.48 (ISBN 0-07-017726-0). McGraw.

--Whistles & Strings. 1971. tchr's. guide 14.80 (ISBN 0-07-017728-7). McGraw.

Elenbass, Virginia. Focus on Neptune. 152p. 1976. 6.00 (ISBN 0-86690-095-0, 1102-01). Am Fed Astrologers.

--Focus on Pluto. 96p. 1974. 4.25 (ISBN 0-86690-096-9, 1103-01). Am Fed Astrologers.

Elenkin, A. A., jt. auth. see Gaidukov, N.

Elerick, Charles, tr. see Elerick, Marisa Luz E.

Elerick, Marisa Luz E. Annotated Bibliography of Technical & Specialized Dictionaries. Elerick, Charles & Teschner, Richard V., trs. from Span. LC 82-50416. 109p. 1982. 20.00 (ISBN 0-87875-234-X). Whitston Pub.

Elert, Werner. Structure of Lutheranism: The Theology & Philosophy of Life of Lutheranism, 16th & 17th Centuries, Vol. 1. Hansen, Walter A., tr. LC 62-19955. 1974. pap. 15.95 (ISBN 0-570-03192-3, 12-2588). Concordia.

Elesh, James, ed. James Ensor: The Complete Graphic Work, 2 vols. LC 79-50679. (Illustrated Bartsch: Vol. 141: Pts. A & B). 1982. Set. 120.00 ea. Abaris Bks.

Elethea, Abba, pseud. The Antioch Suite-Jazz. 36p. 1980. pap. 3.00x (ISBN 0-916418-25-1). Lotus.

Eleutherian Mills-Hagley Foundation. Law, Alcohol, & Order: Perspectives on National Prohibition. Kyvig, David E., ed. LC 84-25225. (Contributions in American History Ser.: No. 110). 256p. 1985. lib. bdg. 35.00 (ISBN 0-313-24755-2, KLA/). Greenwood.

Eleventh Gustave Stern Symposium on Perspectives in Virology, New York, February 1980. Perspectives in Virology, Vol. 11: Proceedings. Pollard, Morris, ed. LC 59-8415. 324p. 1981. 44.00x (ISBN 0-8451-0800-X). A R Liss.

Eleventh Session, New York, 8 March - 30 April 1982. Third United Nations Conference on the Law of the Sea: Official Records: Summary Records of Meetings: Plenary Meetings - 156th to 182nd Meetings, First Committee's 55th & 56th Meetings, and Second Committee's 59th Meeting & Documents, Vol. XVI. 281p. 1985. pap. 27.00 (UN84/5/2, UN). Unipub.

Elevitch, M. D. Americans at Home. LC 75-36319. 128p. (Orig.). 1976. pap. 5.50 (ISBN 0-916452-01-8). First Person.

--Grips or, Efforts to Revive the Host. LC 73-170613. 111p. 1972. 6.95 (ISBN 0-916452-02-6). First Person.

--Grips, or Efforts to Revive the Host. LC 73-170613. 1972. 6.95 (ISBN 0-685-79017-7). Small Pr Dist.

Elevitch, M. D., ed. First Person, Vol. 1. 264p. 1978. pap. 7.50 (ISBN 0-916452-03-4). First Person.

Eley. Die Krise Des Apriori in der Transzendentalen Phanomenologie Edmund Husserls. (Phaenomenologica Ser: No. 10). 1962. lib. bdg. 21.00 (ISBN 90-247-0244-5, Pub. by Martinus Nijhoff Netherlands). Kluwer Academic.

--Metakritik der Formalen Logik. (Phaenomenologica Ser: No. 31). 1969. lib. bdg. 47.50 (ISBN 90-247-0269-0, Pub. by Martinus Nijhoff Netherlands); pap. 36.00 (ISBN 90-247-0268-2). Kluwer Academic.

Eley, D. D., et al. Advances in Catalysis, Vol. 32. (Serial Publication Ser.). 1983. 74.50 (ISBN 0-12-007832-5). Acad Pr.

Eley, D. D., et al, eds. Advances in Catalysis, Vol. 30. 1981. 75.00 (ISBN 0-12-007830-9). Acad Pr.

--Advances in Catalysis, Vol. 31. (Serial Publication Ser.). 1982. 60.00 (ISBN 0-12-007831-7). Acad Pr.

--Advances in Catalysis, Vol. 33. (Serial Publication). Date not set. price not set (ISBN 0-12-007833-3). Acad Pr.

Eley, D. D., et al see Frankenburg, W. G., et al.

Eley, Geoff. Reshaping the German Right: Radial Nationalism & Political Change After Bismarck. LC 79-20711. 1980. text ed. 47.00x (ISBN 0-300-02386-3). Yale U Pr.

Eley, Geoff, jt. auth. see Blackbourn, David.

Eley, Glen D. The Complete Book of Slowpitch Softball. rev. ed. (Illus.). 100p. (Orig.). 1984. pap. 8.95 (ISBN 0-940934-02-7). GDE Pubns OH.

--How to Play & Coach Winning Slo'pitch. rev. ed. (Illus.). 50p. 1984. pap. 5.95 (ISBN 0-940934-01-9). GDE Pubns OH.

--Slowpitch Tips. (Illustrated Instructions Ser.). 1983. pap. 7.95 (ISBN 0-940934-07-8). GDE Pubns OH.

--Umpiring Made Easy: How to Command Respect. (Illus.). 25p. (Orig.). 1983. pap. 3.95 (ISBN 0-940934-03-5). GDE Pubns OH.

Eley, J. T., jt. auth. see Cooper, J. E.

Eley, P. & Worthington, J. Industrial Rehabilitation. (Illus.). 184p. 1984. text ed. 61.95x (ISBN 0-85139-862-6, Pub. by Architectural Pr England). Humanities.

Eley, V., jt. auth. see Hetherington, L.

Elfandsson, Galad. The Black Wolf. 12.00 (ISBN 0-937986-05-4). D M Grant.

Elf-Aquitaine, et al. Exploration for Carbonate Petroleum Reservoirs. LC 81-13144. 213p. 1982. 45.95x (ISBN 0-471-08603-7, Pub. by Wiley-Interscience). Wiley.

El Faruqi, Ismail R., tr. see Ghali, Mirrit B.

El-Fattah, Y. M. & Foulard, C. Learning Systems: Decision, Simulation, & Control. (Lecture Notes in Control & Information Sciences: Vol. 9). (Illus.). 1978. pap. 14.00 (ISBN 0-387-09003-7). Springer-Verlag.

Elfenbein, Eleanor. Grauel. (Illus.). 264p. 1983. 14.50 (ISBN 0-9608896-0-4). Ivory Hse.

Elfenbein, Julien. Business Journalism. 2nd ed. LC 72-91759. Repr. of 1960 ed. lib. bdg. 22.50x (ISBN 0-8371-2433-6, ELBJ). Greenwood.

Elfenbein, Julien, ed. Businesspaper Publishing Practice. Repr. of 1952 ed. lib. bdg. 19.75x (ISBN 0-8371-3090-5, ELBU). Greenwood.

Elfenbein, M. H., jt. auth. see Haimson, B. R.

Elfers, Robert A. A Sojourn in Mosaic. (Orig.). 1979. pap. 2.95 (ISBN 0-377-00089-2). Friend Pr.

Elffers, Joost. Tangram: The Ancient Chinese Shapes Game. Hollingdale, R. J., tr. 1977. pap. 8.95 (ISBN 0-14-004181-8). Penguin.

El-Fikey, Said A. The Tomb of the Vizier Fe-Wer at Saqqara. (Egyptology Today Ser.: No. 4). 55p. 1980. pap. text ed. 29.50x (ISBN 0-85668-158-X, Pub. by Aris & Phillips England). Humanities.

Elflandsson, Galad. The Black Wolf. (Illus.). 176p. 1980. pap. 4.95 (ISBN 0-87818-015-X). Centaur.

Elfman, Blossom. The Return of the Whistler. 192p. 1982. pap. 2.25 (ISBN 0-449-70027-5, Juniper). Fawcett.

--The Sister Act. 1978. 7.95 (ISBN 0-395-26476-6). HM.

--The Strawberry Fields of Heaven. 1982. 2.98 (ISBN 0-517-54830-5). Crown.

Elfner, Lynn E., jt. auth. see King, Charles C.

Elfner, Lynn E., et al. Guide to the Literature of Ohio's Natural Areas. 1973. 1.00 (ISBN 0-86727-067-5). Ohio Bio Survey.

Elfont, Edna. Roar of Thunder, Whisper of Wind: A Portrait of Michigan Waterfalls. McKee, Russell, ed. (Michigan Heritage Bks.: Vol. 5). (Illus.). 128p. 1984. 24.95 (ISBN 0-941912-06-X). TwoPeninsula Pr.

Elfont, Edna A. Roar of Thunder, Whisper of Wind. LC 83-620006. 128p. 1984. 24.95 (ISBN 0-941912-06-X). Mich Nat Res.

Elford, George R. Devil's Guard. 336p. 1985. pap. 3.95 (ISBN 0-440-12014-4). Dell.

Elfrey, Priscilla. The Hidden Agenda: Recognizing What Really Matters at Work. LC 82-8500. (Management Series on Problem Solving, Decision Making & Strategic Thinking). 208p. 1982. 19.95 (ISBN 0-471-86529-X). Wiley.

--Is There Life after College: A Student Career Guide. 256p. 1984. pap. 8.95 (ISBN 0-471-88837-0). Wiley.

Elfring, Gary C. Microcomputer Assembly Language Programming. (Illus.). 224p. 1984. 29.95 (ISBN 0-442-22261-0). Van Nos Reinhold.

Elfvin, Lars-Gosta, ed. Autonomic Ganglia. 527p. 1983. 75.00 (ISBN 0-471-10503-1, Wiley-Interscience). Wiley.

El Gammal, Taher & Allen, Marshall B., Jr. An Atlas of Polytome Pneumography: With Particular Reference to the Midline Ventricles of the Brain. (Illus.). 480p. 1977. phptocopy ed. 57.50x (ISBN 0-398-03531-8). C C Thomas.

Elgar, Edward W. Letters & Other Writings. Young, Percy M., ed. LC 78-66901. (Encore Music Editions Ser.). (Illus.). 1980. Repr. of 1956 ed. 31.50 (ISBN 0-88355-738-X). Hyperion Conn.

Elgar, Frank. Greene-Mercier. Weber, Gudrun, tr. LC 79-670107. (Le Musee de Poche). (Illus.). 1978. pap. 7.50x (ISBN 2-85219-000-1). Intl Bk Co Il.

Elgar, Frank, jt. auth. see Cognia, Raymond.

Elgart, Robert. The BioLab Book: Laboratory Studies in Life. (Illus.). 138p. 1985. 14.95 (ISBN 0-9609098-3-4). Biomat Pub Co.

Elgarten, G. & Posamentier, A. S. Using Computers in Mathematics. 1983. 24.76 (ISBN 0-201-10450-4, Sch Div); 3.88 (ISBN 0-201-10449-0); solutions manual 15.40 (ISBN 0-201-10456-3). Addison-Wesley.

El-Gemayel, Antoine. The Lebanese Legal System. 1985. 125.00 (ISBN 0-935328-28-9). Intl Law Inst.

El-Genk, Mohamed S. & Hoover, Mark D., eds. Space Nuclear Power Systems: The Proceedings on the First Symposium on Space Nuclear Power Systems, 2 Vols. LC 84-16634. 1985. 110.00 (ISBN 0-89464-004-6). Krieger.

Elger, C. E., jt. ed. see Speckmann, E. J.

Elger, Frank, intro. by. Hector Poleo. (Illus.). 1976. pap. 2.00 (ISBN 0-89192-159-1). Interbk Inc.

Elgerd, O. I. Electric Energy Systems Theory: An Introduction. 2nd ed. (Electrical Engineering Ser.). 576p. 1982. 45.00x (ISBN 0-07-019230-8). McGraw.

Elgerd, Olle I. Basic Electric Power Engineering. LC 76-1751. (Electrical Engineering Ser.). 1977. text ed. 36.95 (ISBN 0-201-01717-2); solution Manual 2.50 (ISBN 0-201-01918-3). Addison-Wesley.

Elgers, Pieter T. & Clark, John J. The Lease-Buy Decision: A Simplified Guide to Maximizing Financial & Tax Advantages in the 1980's. LC 80-66131. (Illus.). 1980. 21.95 (ISBN 0-02-909470-4). Free Pr.

Elgers, Pieter T., jt. auth. see Bloom, Robert.

Elgey, Georgette. The Open Window. Underwood, James, tr. from Fr. (Illus.). 212p. 1974. 16.50x (ISBN 0-7130-0122-4, Pub. by Woburn Pr England). Biblio Dist.

Elgin, Catherine Z. With Reference to Reference. LC 82-15488. 208p. 1982. lib. bdg. 27.50 (ISBN 0-915145-52-9); pap. text ed. 12.75 (ISBN 0-915145-53-7). Hackett Pub.

Elgin, Don G. The Comedy of the Fantastic: Ecological Perspectives on the Fantasy Novel. LC 84-10851. (Contributions to the Study of Science Fiction & Fantasy Ser.: No. 15). 204p. 1985. lib. bdg. 29.95 (ISBN 0-313-23283-0, ELC/). Greenwood.

Elgin, Duane. Voluntary Simplicity: Toward a Way of Life That Is Outwardly Simple, Inwardly Rich. LC 81-643. (Illus.). 312p. 1981. 10.95 (ISBN 0-688-00322-2); pap. 5.95 (ISBN 0-686-82943-3). Morrow.

Elgin, James B. Letters & Journals. Walrond, Theodore, ed. LC 6-20542. 1969. Repr. of 1872 ed. 21.00 (ISBN 0-527-26750-3). Kraus Repr.

Elgin, Kathleen & Osterritter, John F. Twenty-Eight Days. LC 73-77779. (Illus.). 64p. (gr. 5 up). 1973. 6.95 (ISBN 0-679-20220-X). McKay.

Elgin, Richard & Knowles, David. Legal Principles of Boundary Location in Arkansas. (Illus.). 323p. 1984. 42.00 (ISBN 0-910845-14-X, 640). Landmark Ent.

Elgin, S. What Is Linguistics? 2nd ed. 1979. pap. 16.95 (ISBN 0-13-952333-2). P-H.

Elgin, Suzette H. And Then There'll Be Fireworks. 192p. 1983. pap. 2.50 (ISBN 0-425-06290-2). Berkley Pub.

--The Gentle Art of Verbal Self-Defense. (Illus.). 272p. 1980. 12.95 (ISBN 0-13-351098-0, Spec); pap. 5.95 (ISBN 0-13-351080-8). P-H.

--More on the Gentle Art of Verbal Self-Defense. 284p. 1983. 12.95 (ISBN 0-13-601138-1); pap. 6.95 (ISBN 0-13-601120-9). P-H.

--Native Tongue. 304p. 1984. pap. 3.50 (ISBN 0-87997-945-3). DAW Bks.

--A Primer of Transformational Grammar: For Rank Beginners. 25p. 1975. pap. 3.00 (ISBN 0-8141-3693-1); pap. 2.00 members. NCTE.

--Star-Anchored, Star-Angered. 160p. 1984. pap. 2.50 (ISBN 0-87997-929-1). DAW Bks.

Elgin, Suzette W. The Grand Jubilee. 240p. 1983. pap. 2.50 (ISBN 0-425-06045-4). Berkley Pub.

Elgin, W. F., ed. Guide to Sound Investment. 4th ed. 1981. 29.00 (ISBN 0-85308-054-2, Pub. by Jordan & Sons England). State Mutual Bk.

Elgood, Chris. Handbook of Management Games. 2nd ed. 146p. 1981. text ed. 44.00x (ISBN 0-566-02229-X). Gower Pub Co.

--Handbook of Management Games. 3rd ed. 352p. 1984. text ed. 46.50x (ISBN 0-566-02442-X). Gower Pub Co.

Elgood, Cyril. Medicine in Persia. LC 75-23665. (Clio Medica: No. 14). (Illus.). Repr. of 1934 ed. 14.50 (ISBN 0-404-58914-6). AMS Pr.

Elgood, Robert. Islamic Arms & Armour. 1979. 175.00 (ISBN 0-85967-470-3). Scolar.

Elgorriaga, Jose A., tr. see Alberti, Rafael.

Elgot, C. C. Selected Papers. (Illus.). 456p. 1982. 39.00 (ISBN 0-387-90698-3). Springer-Verlag.

Elgot, Calvin, jt. auth. see Eilenberg, Samuel.

Elguero, J., et al. The Tautomerism of Heterocycles: Supplement I to Advances in Heteroscyclic Chemistry. (Serial Publication). 1976. 95.00 (ISBN 0-12-020651-X). Acad Pr.

El Guindi, Fadwa, jt. auth. see Callender, Charles.

El Guindy, M. I., ed. Precious Metals 1982: Proceedings of the 6th International Precious Metals Institute Conference, Newport Beach, California, June 7-11, 1982. 600p. 1983. 140.00 (ISBN 0-08-025396-2). Pergamon.

ELH. Critical Essays on Spenser from ELH. LC 76-123199. (English Literary History Ser.). 257p. (Orig.). 1970. pap. 6.95x (ISBN 0-8018-1199-6). Johns Hopkins.

ELH, et al. Critical Essays on Milton from ELH. LC 71-93296. (English Literary Ser.). 290p. 1969. pap. 6.95x (ISBN 0-8018-1094-9). Johns Hopkins.

El-Hadi, Mohamed M. Union List of Arabic Serials in the United States: The Arabic Serials Holdings of Seventeen Libraries. LC 67-157. (University of Illinois Graduate School of Library Science Occasional Papers Ser.: No. 75). pap. 20.00 (ISBN 0-317-29753-8, 2017405). Bks Demand UMI.

El-Hadidi, M. Nabil, jt. auth. see Boulos, Loutfy.

El-Hadidy, B. & Horne, E. E., eds. The Infrastructure of an Information Society: Proceedings of the 1st International Conference in Cairo, Egypt, 13-15 Dec. 1982. 644p. 1984. 69.00 (ISBN 0-444-87549-2, I-303-84, North Holland). Elsevier.

El Hage, S. G., jt. auth. see LeGrand, Y.

El-Hakim, Ali A. The Middle Eastern States & the Law of the Sea. (Illus.). 310p. 1979. 30.00x (ISBN 0-8156-2217-1). Syracuse U Pr.

El Hares, H., jt. auth. see Al Fateh-IFAC Workshop, 1st, Tripoli, Libya, May 1980.

El-Hawary, M. E. Control System Engineering. 1984. text ed. 32.95; solutions manual avail. (ISBN 0-8359-1016-4). Reston.

El-Hawary, M. E. & Christensen, G. S. Optimal Economic Operation of Electric Power Systems. (Mathematics in Science & Engineering Ser.). 1979. 60.00 (ISBN 0-12-236850-9). Acad Pr.

El-Hawary, Mohamed. Electric Power Systems: Design & Analysis. 1982. text ed. 39.95 (ISBN 0-8359-1627-8); instrs'. manual avail. (ISBN 0-8359-1628-6). Reston.

El-Helbawy, Kamal, tr. see Ali-Nadawi, Abul H.

El-Hinnawi, Essam. Environmental Impacts of Production & Use of Energy. (Vol. 1). (Illus.). 1981. 22.50 (ISBN 0-907567-00-2, TYP100, TYP); pap. 17.50 (ISBN 0-907567-15-0, TYP116). Unipub.

El-Hinnawi, Essam & Biswas, Asit K., eds. Renewable Sources of Energy & the Environment. (Natural Resources & the Environment Ser.: Vol. 6). 219p. 1981. 32.50 (ISBN 0-907567-05-3, TYP101, TYP); pap. 17.50 (ISBN 0-907567-10-X, TYP120). Unipub.

El-Hinnawi, Essam E., ed. Nuclear Energy & the Environment. LC 80-40365. (Illus.). 310p. 1980. 62.00 (ISBN 0-08-024472-6). Pergamon.

Elhmann, Paul W., jt. auth. see White, Trentwell M.

El-Hodiri, M., tr. see Makarov, V. L. & Rubinov, A. M.

Elia, Annibale. La Syntaxe du verbe italien: Vol. I, Les constructions a completives des verbes a un complement. (Lingvisticae Investigationes Supplementa: 7). 250p. (Fr.). 1983. text ed. 31.00x (ISBN 90-272-3117-6). Benjamins North Am.

Elia, L. & Fall, J. Word Processimg with SUPERSCRIPSIT & the TRS-80. 1985. 15.64 (ISBN 0-87350-345-7) (ISBN 0-87350-346-5). exercise disk avail. Milady.

Elia, Lewis M. & Fall, Joseph A. Word Processing with Superscripsit & the TRS-80: Models III & 4. Moon, Harry R., ed. (Illus.). 161p. pap. text ed. 10.95 (ISBN 0-87350-345-7); 95.00 (ISBN 0-87350-346-5). Milady.

Elia, P. I Verbi Italiani Ad Uso Degli Stranieri. (It). 6.95 (ISBN 0-685-20240-2). Schoenhof.

Eliach, Yaffa. Hasidic Tales of the Holocaust. 1982. 17.95 (ISBN 0-19-503199-7). Oxford U Pr.

--Hasidic Tales of the Holocaust. 336p. 1983. pap. 4.95 (ISBN 0-380-64725-7, 64725, Discus). Avon.

Eliach, Yaffa & Gurewitsch, Brana. The Liberators: Eyewitness Accounts of the Liberation of Concentration Camps, Liberation Day Vol. I. LC 81-70261. (The Liberators Ser.). (Illus.). 59p. (Orig.). 1981. pap. 8.95 (ISBN 0-9609970-1-6). Ctr For Holo.

Eliade, Mircea. La Colonne Sans Fin. Hetzler, Florence M., tr. (Illus.). 108p. (Orig., Fr.). 1984. lib. bdg. 18.75 (ISBN 0-8191-4162-3); pap. text ed. 9.25 (ISBN 0-8191-4163-1). U Pr of Amer.

--Cosmos & History: The Myth of the Eternal Return. Winks, Robin W., ed. LC 83-49168. (History & Historiography Ser.). 182p. 1985. lib. bdg. 20.00 (ISBN 0-8240-6360-0). Garland Pub.

--The Forbidden Forest. Ricketts, Mac L. & Stevenson, Mary P., trs. from Romanian. LC 76-51618. 1978. text ed. 25.00x (ISBN 0-268-00943-0, 85-09432). U of Notre Dame Pr.

--The Forge & the Crucible: The Origins & Structures of Alchemy. 2nd ed. Corrin, Stephen, tr. LC 78-55040. 1979. pap. 6.95 (ISBN 0-226-20390-5, P780, Phoen). U of Chicago Pr.

--From Primitives to Zen: A Thematic Sourcebook in the History of Religions. LC 66-20775. 1978. 11.49xi (ISBN 0-06-062134-6, RD 249, HarpR). Har-Row.

--A History of Religious Ideas: From the Stone Age to the Eleusinian Mysteries, Vol. 1. Trask, Willard R., tr. from Fr. LC 77-16784. xviii, 490p. 1979. 25.00x (ISBN 0-226-20400-6); pap. 10.95 (ISBN 0-226-20401-4). U of Chicago Pr.

--History of Religious Ideas, Vol. II: From Gautama Buddha to the Triumph of Christianity. Trask, Willard, tr. from Fr. LC 77-16784. 576p. 1982. 25.00x (ISBN 0-226-20402-2). U of Chicago Pr.

--A History of Religious Ideas, Vol. 2: From Gautama Buddha to the Triumph of Christianity. Trask, Willard R., tr. LC 77-16784. vi, 564p. 1984. pap. 14.95 (ISBN 0-226-20403-0). U of Chicago Pr.

--A History of Religious Ideas, Vol. 3: From Muhammad to the Age of Reforms. Hiltebeiten, Alf & Apostolos-Cappadona, Diane, trs. LC 77-16784. 376p. 1985. 27.50 (ISBN 0-226-20404-9). U of Chicago Pr.

--Myth & Reality. pap. 4.33i (ISBN 0-06-090466-6, CN466, CN). Har-Row.

--Myth of the Eternal Return. Trask, Willard R., tr. (Bollingen Ser.: Vol. 46). 1954. 22.50 (ISBN 0-691-09798-4); pap. 7.95 (ISBN 0-691-01777-8). Princeton U Pr.

--Myths, Dreams & Mysteries: The Encounter Between Contemporary Faiths & Archaic Realities. pap. 5.25xi (ISBN 0-06-131943-0, TB 1943, Torch). Har-Row.

--No Souvenirs, Journal, Nineteen Fifty-Seven to Nineteen Sixty-Nine. 1983. 16.00 (ISBN 0-8446-6030-2). Peter Smith.

--No Souvenirs: Journal, 1957-1969. LC 76-9969. 1976. 15.00 (ISBN 0-06-062141-9, HarpR). Har-Row.

--No Souvenirs: Journals, 1957-1969. LC 76-9469. 368p. 1982. pap. 7.64i (ISBN 0-06-062143-5, RD-405, HarpT). Har-Row.

--Occultism, Witchcraft, & Cultural Fashion: Essays in Comparative Religions. LC 75-12230. 1978. pap. 5.95 (ISBN 0-226-20392-1, P755, Phoen). U of Chicago Pr.

--The Old Man & the Bureaucrats. Stevenson, Mary P., tr. 1979. text ed. 10.95x (ISBN 0-268-01497-3). U of Notre Dame Pr.

--Ordeal by Labyrinth: Conservations with Claude-Henri Rocquet. LC 81-21796. (Illus.). x, 226p. 1984. pap. 8.95 (ISBN 0-226-20388-3). U of Chicago Pr.

--Ordeal by Labyrinth: Conversations with Claude-Henri Rocquet. Coltman, Derek, tr. from Fr. LC 81-21796. (Illus.). 1982. 17.50x (ISBN 0-226-20387-5). U of Chicago Pr.

--Patanjali & Yoga. LC 75-10785. (Illus.). 224p. 1975. pap. 5.95 (ISBN 0-8052-0491-1). Schocken.

--Patterns in Comparative Religion. pap. 9.95 (ISBN 0-452-00728-3, Mer). NAL.

--The Quest: History & Meaning in Religion. LC 68-19059. (Midway Reprint Ser.). xii, 180p. 1984. pap. text ed. 7.00x (ISBN 0-226-20386-7). U of Chicago Pr.

--Rites & Symbols of Initiation: The Mysteries of Birth & Rebirth. Orig. Title: Birth & Rebirth. pap. 4.95xi (ISBN 0-06-131236-3, TB1236, Torch). Har-Row.

--Rites & Symbols of Initiation: The Mysteries of Birth & Rebirth. 16.75 (ISBN 0-8446-2027-0). Peter Smith.

--The Sacred & the Profane: The Nature of Religion. Trask, Willard, tr. LC 58-10904. 1968. pap. 4.95 (ISBN 0-15-679201-X, Harv). HarBraceJ.

--The Sacred & the Profane: The Nature of Religion. 1983. 13.50 (ISBN 0-8446-6080-9). Peter Smith.

--Shamanism: Archaic Techniques of Ectasy. Trask, Willard R., tr. (Bollingen Ser.: Vol. 76). 1964. 47.50x (ISBN 0-691-09827-1); pap. 11.95x (ISBN 0-691-01779-4). Princeton U Pr.

--Tales of the Sacred & the Supernatural. LC 81-12924. 108p. 1981. pap. 7.95 (ISBN 0-664-24391-6). Westminster.

--The Two & the One. Cohen, J. M., tr. LC 79-2268. 1979. pap. 7.00 (ISBN 0-226-20389-1, P811). U of Chicago Pr.

--Yoga: Immortality & Freedom. 2nd ed. Trask, Willard R., tr. LC 58-8986. (Bollingen Ser.: Vol. 56). 1970. 42.50x (ISBN 0-691-09848-4); pap. 11.50x (ISBN 0-691-01764-6). Princeton U Pr.

Eliade, Mircea & Kitagawa, Joseph. History of Religions: Essays in Methodology. LC 59-11621. 1959. 12.50x (ISBN 0-226-20394-8). U of Chicago Pr.

Eliade, Mircea & Kitagawa, Joseph, eds. The History of Religions: Essays in Methodology. LC 59-11621. 1973. pap. 3.50 (ISBN 0-226-20395-6, P549, Phoen). U of Chicago Pr.

Eliade, Mircea & Tracy, David, eds. What Is Religion? An Inquiry for Christian Theology, Concilium 136. (New Concilium 1980). 128p. 1980. pap. 5.95 (ISBN 0-8164-2278-8, Pub. by Seabury). Winston Pr.

Eliade, Mircea, jt. ed. see Kitagawa, Joseph M.

Eliades, David K., jt. auth. see Dial, Adolph.

Eliakim, M., ed. International Symposium on Hepatotoxicity. 1974. 39.50 (ISBN 0-12-237850-4). Acad Pr.

Eliakim, M., ed. see Asian-Pacific Congress Of Cardiology.

Eliakim, M., ed. see Asian-Pacific Congress of Cardiology - 4th.

Eliakim, M., et al, eds. Recurrent Polyerositiss: Familial Mediterranean Fever, Periodic Disease. 228p. 1981. 64.25 (ISBN 0-444-80331-9, Biomedical Pr). Elsevier.

Elial, Ernest L. see Geoffroy, Gregory.

Elian, G. The Principle of Sovereignty Over Natural Resources. 250p. 1979. 42.50x (ISBN 90-286-0049-3). Sijthoff & Noordhoff.

Eliard, Michel, ed. see Bourdieu, Pierre & Passeron, J. C.

Elias. Arabic-English Collegiate Dictionary. (Arabic & Eng.). 12.50 (ISBN 0-686-27676-0). Colton Bk.

--Colonic Neoplasms. 1986. price not set. Ishiyaku Euro.

--Elias Arabic-English Modern Dictionary. (Arabic & Eng.). 49.00 (ISBN 0-686-18362-2); pap. 8.50 pocket size (ISBN 0-686-18363-0). Kazi Pubns.

--Elias English-Arabic & Arabic-English Pocket Dictionary. (Arabic & Eng.). pap. text ed. 22.50 (ISBN 0-686-18361-4). Kazi Pubns.

--Elias English-Arabic Modern Dictionary. (Arabic & Eng.). 49.00 (ISBN 0-686-18364-9); pap. 7.50 pocket size (ISBN 0-686-18365-7). Kazi Pubns.

--English-Arabic Collegiate Dictionary. 12.50 (ISBN 0-686-27677-9). Colton Bk.

--Polymerization of Organized Systems. (Midland Macromolecular Monographs). 240p. 1977. 62.50 (ISBN 0-677-15930-7). Gordon.

Elias, ed. English Arabic, Arabic-English Pocket Dictionary. 7.50x (ISBN 0-686-00859-6). Colton Bk.

Elias, A., jt. auth. see Elias, E.

Elias, A. C., Jr. Swift at Moor Park: Problems in Biography & Criticism. LC 81-14830. 280p. 1982. 42.50x (ISBN 0-8122-7822-4). U of Pa Pr.

Elias, A. W., et al, eds. International Bibliography of Citrus Crops: Bibliografia Internacional Das Culturas Citreas. 650p. 1985. 60.00 (ISBN 0-916246-10-8). Biosis Biosciences.

--International Bibliography of Corn: Bibliografia Internacional Do Milho. 1985. Set 3-Parts, 2916p. 250.00 (ISBN 0-916246-06-X); Pt. 1, 976p. 100.00 (ISBN 0-916246-07-8); Pt. 2, 976p. 100.00 (ISBN 0-916246-08-6); Pt. 3. 100.00 (ISBN 0-916246-09-4). Biosis Biosciences.

Elias, Alan N. Gamma-Aminobutyric Acid in the Regulation of Hormone Secretion. (Endocrinology & Metabolism Ser.: Vol. 6). 142p. 1985. 36.50 (ISBN 0-03-069744-1). Praeger.

Elias, Alan N. & Gwinup, Grant. Hirsutism. 156p. 1983. 28.95 (ISBN 0-03-060321-8). Praeger.

Elias, Albert J. The Sonora Mutation. 1978. pap. 1.95 (ISBN 0-380-01963-9, 38463). Avon.

Elias, C. F. Doctor Samuel Johnson as Traveler. LC 76-28301. 1937. lib. bdg. 10.00 (ISBN 0-8414-3909-5). Folcroft.

Elias, Christopher. The Beginner's Investment Handbook: One Hundred & Two Ways to Invest One Thousand or Less...& Make It Pay. 1984. o. p. 15.95 (ISBN 0-87795-519-0); pap. 6.95 (ISBN 0-87795-568-9). Arbor Hse.

Elias, E. Elias Pocket Dictionary: English, Arabic. (Eng. & Arabic.). leatherette 16.95 (ISBN 0-686-92306-5, M-9365). French & Eur.

Elias, E. & Elias, A. English-Arabic; Arabic-English Dictionary. (Eng. & Arabic.). 12.00x (ISBN 0-86685-173-9). Intl Bk Ctr.

Elias, E. A. Arabic-English, English-Arabic Dictionary, 2 vols. rev. & enl. ed. (Arabic & Eng.). Set. 70.00 (ISBN 0-685-55017-6). Heinman.

Elias, E. A. & Elias, E. E. Arabic: Egyptian-Arabic Manual for Self-Study. pap. 7.50 (ISBN 0-685-58558-1). Heinman.

--Arabic: Elias' Practical Grammar & Vocabulary of the Colloquial Arabic. pap. 5.00 (ISBN 0-685-58557-3). Heinman.

Elias, E. A., ed. Arabic-English, English-Arabic Collegiate Dictionary, 2 Vol. (Illus.). Set. 35.00 (ISBN 0-686-46526-1). Heinman.

--Arabic-English, English-Arabic School Dictionary. (Illus., Arabic & Eng.). 20.00 (ISBN 0-686-46527-X). Heinman.

Elias, E. E., jt. auth. see Elias, E. A.

Elias, Edith L. In Georgian Times: Short Character-Studies of the Great Figures of the Period. 1912. Repr. 25.00 (ISBN 0-8274-2561-9). R West.

Elias, Edward. English-Arabic Dictionary, Romanized. (Eng. & Arabic.). 24.50 (ISBN 0-87559-002-0); thumb indexed 29.50 (ISBN 0-87559-003-9). Shalom.

Elias, Elias. Arabic-English Modern Dictionary. (Arabic & Eng.). 1981. 25.00x (ISBN 0-86685-287-5). Intl Bk Ctr.

--Elias' English-Arabic Dictionary. (Eng. & Arabic.). 1979. 25.00x (ISBN 0-86685-288-3). Intl Bk Ctr.

--Elias English-Arabic Practical Dictionary of the Colloquial Arabic of the Middle East. (Arabic & Eng.). 1971. 9.00x (ISBN 0-86685-296-4). Intl Bk Ctr.

Elias, Esther. The Queening of Ceridwen. 1982. 6.95 (ISBN 0-8158-0409-1). Chris Mass.

Elias, Esther H. Profile of Glindy. (Illus.). 128p. 1976. 8.95 (ISBN 0-8158-0337-0). Chris Mass.

Elias, George S. Cafe Au Lait. LC 76-18449. 1976. 7.50 (ISBN 0-87881-050-1); pap. 4.50 (ISBN 0-87881-051-X). Mojave Bks.

Elias, H. & Hyde, D. M. A Guide to Practical Stereology. (Karger Continuing Education Ser.: Vol. 1). (Illus.). x, 306p. 1983. 42.00 (ISBN 3-8055-3466-3). S Karger.

Elias, H., ed. see International Congress for Stereology - 2nd - Chicago - 1967.

Elias, H. G., ed. New Commercial Polymers 1969-1975. 226p. 1977. 32.50 (ISBN 0-677-30950-3). Gordon.

Elias, H-G, ed. Trends in Macromolecular Science. LC 73-86253. (Midland Macromolecular Monographs). 132p. 1973. 25.50 (ISBN 0-677-15860-2). Gordon.

Elias, Hans. Basic Human Anatomy As Seen in the Fetus. LC 68-20944. (Illus.). 176p. 1971. 22.50 (ISBN 0-87527-031-X). Green.

Elias, Hans, et al. Histology & Human Microanatomy. 4th ed. LC 78-9108. 607p. 1978. pap. 36.50 (ISBN 0-471-04929-8, Pub. by Wiley Medical). Wiley.

Elias, Hans-Georg. Macromolecules, 2 vols. Incl. Vol. 1, Structure & Properties. 532p (ISBN 0-306-35111-0); Vol. 2, Synthesis & Materials. 599p. LC 76-46499. 1977. 55.00 ea. (Plenum Pr). Plenum Pub.

Elias, Hans-Georg, ed. Macromolecules, Vol. 2: Synthesis, Materials, & Technology, Vol. 2. 2nd ed. 862p. 1984. 95.00x (ISBN 0-306-41085-0, Plenum Pr). Plenum Pub.

Elias, Hans-Georg & Pethrick, Richard A., eds. Polymer Yearbook. 338p. 1983. 25.00 (ISBN 3-7186-0177-X); pap. 12.00 (ISBN 3-7186-0178-8). Harwood Academic.

Elias, Hans-George. Macromolecules, Vol 1: Structure & Properties. 2nd ed. Stafford, John W., tr. from Ger. 564p. 1984. 65.00x (ISBN 0-306-41077-X, Plenum Pr). Plenum Pub.

Elias, Joel & Robson, John R. The Nutritional Value of Indigenous Wild Plants: An Annotated Bibliography. LC 76-51040. 1978. 18.50x (ISBN 0-87875-112-2). Whitston Pub.

Elias, John L. The Foundations & Practice of Adult Religious Education. LC 81-19327. 312p. 1982. 16.50 (ISBN 0-89874-339-7). Krieger.

--Psychology & Religious Education. 3rd ed. LC 83-7061. 154p. 1984. text ed. 11.50 (ISBN 0-89874-615-9). Krieger.

--Studies in Theology & Education. LC 85-9887. 1985. lib. bdg. price not set (ISBN 0-89874-841-0). Krieger.

Elias, John L. & Merriam, Sharan, eds. Philosophical Foundations of Adult Education. LC 79-21655. 218p. 1980. 14.50 (ISBN 0-88275-971-X). Krieger.

Elias, Joseph. The Haggadah. (The Art Scroll Mesorah Ser.). 224p. 1977. 10.95 (ISBN 0-89906-150-8); pap. 7.95 (ISBN 0-89906-151-6). Mesorah Pubns.

Elias, Judith. Los Angeles: Dream to Reality, 1885-1915. (Santa Susana Press California Masters Ser.: No. 5). (Illus.). 112p. 1983. 70.00 (ISBN 0-937048-33-X). CSUN.

Elias, Jules M. Principles & Techniques in Diagnostic Histopathology: Developments in Immunohistochemistry & Enzyme Histochemistry. LC 82-3411. (Illus.). 342p. 1982. 48.00 (ISBN 0-8155-0903-0). Noyes.

Elias, Julius A. Plato's Defence of Poetry. 256p. 1984. 36.50x (ISBN 0-87395-806-3); pap. 12.95x (ISBN 0-87395-807-1). State U NY Pr.

Elias, Julius A., tr. & intro. by see Schiller, Friedrich.

Elias, M. Elias' Pocket Dictionary Arabic-English. 533p. (Eng. & Arabic.). 1981. 12.95 (ISBN 0-686-91623-9, M-9750). French & Eur.

Elias, M. F. see Storandt, M., et al.

Elias, Merrill F. & Streeten, David H., eds. Hypertension & Cognitive Processes. LC 80-22618. 165p. 1980. pap. text ed. 10.00 (ISBN 0-933786-03-4). Beech Hill.

Elias, Merrill F., jt. ed. see Wood, W. Gibson.

Elias, Merrill F., et al, eds. Special Review of Experimental Aging Research: Progress in Biology. LC 77-23262. 1976. 24.00 (ISBN 0-933786-00-X); professional individual discount 10.00 (ISBN 0-686-67622-X). Beech Hill.

Elias, N. & Whitley, R. Scientific Establishments & Hierarchies. 1982. 42.50 (ISBN 90-277-1322-7, Pub. by Reidel Holland); pap. 19.95 (ISBN 90-277-1323-5). Kluwer Academic.

Elias, Norbert. The History of Manners: The Civilizing Process, Vol. I. Jephcott, Edmund, tr. 1982. pap. 8.95 (ISBN 0-394-71133-5). Pantheon.

--Involvement & Detachment: Contributions to the Sociology of Knowledge. 192p. 1985. 24.95x (ISBN 0-631-12682-1). Basil Blackwell.

--The Loneliness of Dying. 100p. 1985. 12.95 (ISBN 0-631-13902-8). Basil Blackwell.

--Power & Civility: The Civilizing Process, Vol. II. Jephcott, Edmund, tr. LC 82-8157. 376p. 1982. 22.00 (ISBN 0-394-52769-0). Pantheon.

--What Is Sociology? LC 78-2386. 187p. 1978. 21.50x (ISBN 0-231-04550-6); pap. 10.00x (ISBN 0-231-04551-4). Columbia U Pr.

Elias, P. & Sealy, L. S. The British Constitution, Time for Reform? The Rise & Decline of the Doctrine of Fundamental Breach in the English Law of Contact. (Cambridge-Tilburg Law Lectures: No. 4). 76p. pap. 12.00 (ISBN 90-65-4410-85). Kluwer Academic.

--Cambridge-Tilburg Law Lectures Four: The British Constitution - Time or Reform. Date not set. pap. 12.00 (ISBN 90-6544-108-5, Pub. by Kluwer Law Netherlands). Kluwer Academic.

Elias, P., jt. auth. see Csiszar, I.

Elias, P. S. & Cohen, A. J. Radiation Chemistry of Major Food Components. 220p. 1977. 50.75 (ISBN 0-444-41587-4, Biomedical Pr). Elsevier.

Elias, Penelope K., ed. see Rivers, Henry.

Elias, Robert. Victims of the System: Crime Victims & Compensation in American Politics & Criminal Justice. LC 83-383. (Illus.). 352p. 1983. 34.95 (ISBN 0-87855-470-X); pap. 14.95. Transaction Bks.

Elias, Robert H. Entangling Alliances with None: An Essay on the Individual in the American Twenties. 256p. 1973. 8.95x (ISBN 0-393-01097-X). Norton.

Elias, Robert H. & Finch, Eugene D., eds. Letters of Thomas Attwood Digges (1742-1821) LC 81-16450. 666p. 1982. lib. bdg. 34.95x (ISBN 0-87249-412-8). U of SC Pr.

Elias, Stephen. The Dictionary of Intellectual Property Law. 275p. 1985. pap. 19.95 (ISBN 0-917316-98-3). Nolo Pr.

--Legal Research. 1st ed. LC 81-83033. 230p. (Orig.). 1982. pap. 12.95 (ISBN 0-917316-39-8). Nolo Pr.

Elias, Stephen, ed. see Siegel, Warren.

Elias, T. Shrubs for the Landscape. 1986. cancelled (ISBN 0-442-26405-4). Van Nos Reinhold.

Elias, T. O. Groundwork of Nigerian Law. 1976. lib. bdg. 59.95 (ISBN 0-8490-1908-7). Gordon Pr.

--The Modern Law of Treaties. LC 73-94064. 350p. 1974. lib. bdg. 25.00 (ISBN 0-379-00230-2). Oceana.

--New Horizons in International Law. LC 73-94064. 282p. 1979. lib. bdg. 36.00 (ISBN 0-379-20499-1). Oceana.

--Nigerian Land Law & Custom. 1976. lib. bdg. 59.95 (ISBN 0-8490-2346-7). Gordon Pr.

Elias, T. S. & Tillman, R., eds. A Master Plan for the Planning, Planting & Maintenance of Trees on Public Property: A Report to the City of Peekskill, New York. 198p. 1976. pap. 12.00 (ISBN 0-317-35499-X). NY Botanical.

Elias, T. S. & Whittaker, D., eds. A Master Plan for the Planning, Planting & Maintenance of Trees & Other Woody Plants on Public Property in Poughkeepsie, New York. 197p. 1976. pap. 10.00 (ISBN 0-317-35500-7). NY Botanical.

Elias, Thomas. The Complete Trees of North America Field Guide & Natural History. (Outdoor Life-Nature Book). 864p. 1980. 22.95 (ISBN 0-442-23862-2). Van Nos Reinhold.

Elias, Thomas & Dykeman. Field Guide to North American Edible Wild Plants. LC 82-18785. 286p. 1983. 19.95 (ISBN 0-442-22200-9). Van Nos Reinhold.

Elias, Thomas, jt. ed. see Bentley, Barbara.

Elias, Thomas S; see Arroyo, Mary T.

Elias, Thomas S., jt. ed. see Prance, Ghillian T.

Elias, Thomas S., et al. Trees & the Community. 1973. pap. 4.00x (ISBN 0-89327-051-2). NY Botanical.

Elias, William Y. Grapes: Practical Notation for Clusters & Special Effects for Piano & Other Keyboard Instruments. 2nd ed. (Illus.). 132p. (Orig.). 1984. pap. 12.00 (ISBN 0-918728-49-5). Pendragon NY.

Elias, Z. M. Analysis of Axisymmetric Shells by a Mixed Variational Principle. 60p. 1972. pap. text ed. 10.00x (ISBN 0-8156-6037-5, Am U Beirut). Syracuse U Pr.

--Cylindrical Shell Roof Design. 1972. pap. 11.95x (ISBN 0-8156-6036-7, Am U Beirut). Syracuse U Pr.

Eliasberg, W. G. Psychotherapy & Society. 1959. 6.00 (ISBN 0-8022-0446-5). Philos Lib.

Elias De Barjols. Le Troubadour Elias De Barjols. liv, 159p. Repr. of 1906 ed. 21.00 (ISBN 0-384-14110-2). Johnson Repr.

Elias-Olivares, Lucia, ed. Spanish in the U. S. Setting: Beyond the Southwest. LC 83-60507. 268p. 1983. pap. 14.00 (ISBN 0-89763-073-4). Natl Clearinghse Bilingual Ed.

Elias-Olivares, Lucia, jt. ed. see Amastae, Jon.

Eliason, Adolph O. Rise of Commercial Banking Institutions in the United States. LC 75-122227. (Research & Source Ser.: No. 521). 1970. Repr. of 1901 ed. 14.00 (ISBN 0-8337-1030-3). B Franklin.

Eliason, Alan. Business Information Processing. 496p. 1979. text ed. 25.95 (ISBN 0-574-21235-3, 13-4235); instr's guide avail. (ISBN 0-574-21236-1, 13-4236). SRA.

Eliason, Alan & Kitts, Kent D. Business Computer Systems & Applications. 2nd ed. LC 78-18447. 384p. 1979. 16.95 (ISBN 0-574-21215-9, 13-4215); instr's guide 2.25 (ISBN 0-574-21216-7, 13-4216). SRA.

Eliason, Alan L. Mason Oaks: An Online Case Study in Business Systems Design. 128p. 1981. pap. text ed. 9.95 (ISBN 0-574-21310-4, 13-4310); instr's guide avail. (ISBN 0-574-21311-2, 13-4311). SRA.

--Online Business Computer Applications. 496p. 1983. pap. text ed. 16.95 (ISBN 0-574-21405-4, 13-4405); instr's. guide avail. (ISBN 0-574-21406-2, 13-4406). SRA.

--Royal Pines: An On-Line Case Study in Business Systems Design. 144p. (Orig.). 1984. pap. text ed. 9.95 (ISBN 0-574-21700-2, 13-4700); write for info. tchr's ed. (ISBN 0-317-03528-2, 13-4701). SRA.

Eliason, Claudia & Jenkins, Loa T. A Practical Guide to Early Childhood Curriculum. 2nd ed. LC 80-39694. (Illus.). 389p. 1981. pap. text ed. 16.95 (ISBN 0-8016-1511-9). Mosby.

Eliason, Ellen, jt. ed. see Kirk, Dudley.

Eliason, Karine, et al. Make-A-Mix Cookery. LC 78-50687. (Illus.). 1978. pap. 7.95 (ISBN 0-89586-007-4). H P Bks.

--More Make-A-Mix Cookery. LC 80-82533. (Orig.). 1980. pap. 7.95 (ISBN 0-89586-055-4). H P Bks.

Eliason, Norman see Malone, Kemp & Schibsbye, Knud.

Eliason, Norman E. Tarheel Talk: An Historical Study of the English Language in North Carolina to 1860. x, 324p. 1980. Repr. of 1956 ed. lib. bdg. 23.00x (ISBN 0-374-92528-3). Octagon.

Eliason, Peter. The Comeuppance of Dipsey Dolan. (Michael the Archangel Ser.). 162p. (Orig.). (gr. 2-10). 1984. pap. 5.95 (ISBN 0-916777-34-0). W P Allen.

--Only Moments. 287p. (Orig.). 1984. pap. 6.95 (ISBN 0-916777-41-3). W P Allen.

--The Stock Tactics System. 72p. (Orig.). 1984. pap. 17.95 (ISBN 0-916777-99-5). W P Allen.

Eliason, Robert E. Early American Brass Makers. Glover, Stephen L., ed. LC 79-11880. (Brass Research Ser.: No. 10). (Illus.). 1979. pap. text ed. 8.00 (ISBN 0-914282-25-5). Brass Pr.

--Keyed Bugles in the United States. LC 77-39883. (Smithsonian Studies in History & Technology Ser.: No. 19). (Illus.). pap. 20.00 (ISBN 0-317-09454-8, 2004218). Bks Demand UMI.

Eliassen, A., jt. auth. see Roahe, H.

Eliassen, Arnt. Meteorology: An Introductory Course, 2 vols. 1977. Vol. I. pap. 22.00x (ISBN 82-00-02392-3, Dist. by Columbia U Pr); Vol. II. pap. 15.50x (ISBN 82-00-02411-3). Universitet.

Eliasson, Rune, jt. ed. see Von Euler, Ulf S.

Eliastam. Manual of Emergency Medicine. 1983. 24.95 (ISBN 0-8151-3058-9). Year Bk Med.

Eliav, Yaacov. Wanted. Schreiber, Mordecai, tr. LC 84-50676. 272p. 1984. 14.95 (ISBN 0-88400-107-5). Shengold.

Eliav-Feldon, Miriam. Realistic Utopias: The Ideal Imaginary Societies of the Renaissance 1516-1630. (Oxford Historical Monographs). 1982. 41.00x (ISBN 0-19-821889-3). Oxford U Pr.

Elich, Carletta J., jt. auth. see Elich, Joseph.

Elich, Carlotta J. & Elich, Joseph. Trigonometry Using Calculators. LC 79-18934. (Illus.). 1980. text ed. 23.95 (ISBN 0-201-03186-8); instr's. manual 4.00 (ISBN 0-201-03187-6). Addison-Wesley.

Elich, Joseph & Elich, Carletta J. College Algebra with Calculus. (Math-Mallion Ser.). (Illus.). 480p. 1981. text ed. 25.95x (ISBN 0-201-13340-7); instr's. manual 2.50 (ISBN 0-201-13341-5); answer bk. 2.50 (ISBN 0-201-13342-3); student guide 6.95 (ISBN 0-201-13343-1). Addison-Wesley.

--Precalculus with Caculator Applications. (Math-Mallion Ser.). (Illus.). 576p. 1981. text ed. 26.95x (ISBN 0-201-13345-8); instr's. manual 3.00 (ISBN 0-201-13346-6); student solution bk. 6.95 (ISBN 0-201-13348-2); answer bk. 2.50. Addison-Wesley.

Elich, Joseph, jt. auth. see Elich, Carlotta J.

Elich, Joseph, et al. Trigonometry: A Modern Approach. 2nd ed. LC 84-9287. 1985. text ed. 26.95 (ISBN 0-201-10523-3). Addison-Wesley.

Elie, Myrtle R. Trees, Trials & Triumphs of Mundy Township. (Illus.). 106p. 1983. 10.00x (ISBN 0-940404-03-6). Broadblade Pr.

Eliel, E. L. & Allinger, N. L., eds. Topics in Stereochemistry Ser, Vol. 5. 338p. 1970. 28.50 (ISBN 0-471-23750-7, Pub. by Wiley). Krieger.

Eliel, Ernest L. Elements of Stereochemistry. LC 68-57277. pap. 26.00 (ISBN 0-317-28035-X, 2055718). Bks Demand UMI.

Eliel, Ernest L. & Allinger, Norman L., eds. Topics in Stereochemistry. LC 67-13943. 1969. Vol. 4, 280p. 23.50 (ISBN 0-471-23748-5, Pub. by Wiley); Vol. 8, 448pp. 1974. 35.00 (ISBN 0-471-23755-8). Krieger.

--Topics in Stereochemistry, Vol. 10. LC 67-13943. pap. 91.30 (ISBN 0-317-30020-2, 2025020). Bks Demand UMI.

Eliel, Ernest L. & Otsuka, Sei, eds. Asymmetric Reactions & Processes in Chemistry. LC 82-3908. (ACS Symposium Ser.: No. 185). 1982. 39.95 (ISBN 0-8412-0717-8). Am Chemical.

Eliel, Ernest L., et al. Topics in Stereochemistry, Vol. 15. (Topics in Stereo Chemistry Ser.: No. 2-297). 337p. 1984. 97.00 (ISBN 0-471-88564-9, Pub. by Wiley-Interscience). Wiley.

Eliel, Ernest L., et al, eds. Conformational Analysis. LC 81-1083. 1965. 24.95 (ISBN 0-8412-0653-8). Am Chemical.

Eliel, Frank. How to Be a Happy Taxpayer. LC 79-93285. (Illus.). 110p. 1980. pap. 2.95 (ISBN 0-686-27084-3). Plain Talk.

Eliel, Norman L., ed. Topics in Sterochemistry, Vol. 3. LC 67-13943. pap. 97.30 (ISBN 0-317-08878-5, 2055275). Bks Demand UMI.

Elifson, Joan & Gordon, Belita. Strategies for Passing the Georgia Regents' Exam. 3rd ed. 249p. 1985. pap. text ed. 14.95 (ISBN 0-89892-035-3). Contemp Pub Co of Raleigh.

Elifson, Kirk W., et al. Fundamentals of Social Statistics. 416p. 1982. text ed. 22.95 (ISBN 0-394-35023-5, RanC); 6.95 (ISBN 0-394-35025-1). Random.

Elihai, Yohanan. Dictionnaire de l'Arabe Parle Palestinien. 418p. (Fr. & Arabic.). 1974. pap. 22.50 (ISBN 0-686-57132-0, M-6185). French & Eur.

Elijah the Prophet. The Time of the End. 1983. 6.95 (ISBN 0-533-05402-8). Vantage.

Elimelech, Baruch. A Tonal Grammar of Etsako. (Publications in Linguistics Ser.: Vol. 87). 1979. 17.50x (ISBN 0-520-09576-6). U of Cal Pr.

Elimelech, Baruch, ed. see Vass, Winifred K.

Elin-Dor & Jones, C. R. Information Systems Management: Analytical Tools & Techniques. 222p. 1985. 29.95 (ISBN 0-444-00956-6, North-Holland). Elsevier.

Elins, Roberta, jt. auth. see Alexander, Jerome.

Elins, Roberta, jt. auth. see Lerner, Helene.

Elinsky, Peter I. Retirement Magic: Tax Traps & Opportunities. Conti, David J., ed. 80p. 1984. 50.00 (ISBN 0-932648-55-X). Boardroom.

Elinson, H. Down Our Street. 20p. 1975. pap. 1.49 (ISBN 0-8285-1132-2, Pub. by Progress Pubs USSR). Imported Pubns.

Elinson, Jack & Siegmann, Athilia E., eds. Sociomedical Health Indicators. LC 78-74484. 224p. (Orig.). 1979. pap. 11.00x (ISBN 0-89503-013-6). Baywood Pub.

Elinson, Nikolai. En el Patio De Mi Casa. (Illus.). 20p. (Span.). 1975. pap. 1.49 (ISBN 0-8285-1293-0, Pub. by Progress Pubs USSR). Imported Pubns.

Elion & Elion. Electro-Optics Handbook. (Electro-Optics Ser.: Vol. 3). 1979. 65.00 (ISBN 0-8247-6879-5). Dekker.

Elion & Morozov. Optoelectronic Switching Systems in Telecommunications & Computers. (Electro-Optics Ser.). 264p. 1984. 37.50 (ISBN 0-8247-7163-X). Dekker.

Elion, G. & Elion, H. Fiber Optics in Communications Systems. (Electro-Optics Ser.: Vol. 2). 1978. soft cover 65.00 (ISBN 0-8247-7132-X). Dekker.

Elion, H., jt. auth. see Elion, G.

Elion, H. A. & Stewart, D. C., eds. Progress in Nuclear Energy, Series 9. Incl. Vol. 4, Pt. 3; Vol. 6. 1966. 55.00 (ISBN 0-08-011583-7); Vol. 7. 1966; Vol. 9. 55.00 (ISBN 0-08-012716-9); Vol. 10. 55.00 (ISBN 0-08-013394-0); Vol. 11. 55.00 (ISBN 0-08-016920-1); Vol. 12, Pt. 1. 1975. pap. text ed. 6.50 (ISBN 0-08-018967-9). LC 59-8283. write for info. Pergamon.

Eliopolous, Charlotte. Geriatric Nursing. 1980. pap. text ed. 16.25 (ISBN 0-06-318132-0, IntlDept). Har-Row.

--Health Assessment of the Older Adult. 320p. 1983. 14.95 (ISBN 0-201-03345-3, Med-Nurse). Addison-Wesley.

Eliopoulos, Charlotte. Nursing Administration of Long-Term Care. LC 83-8820. 300p. 1983. 34.95 (ISBN 0-89443-878-6). Aspen Systems.

Eliopoulos, Charlotte K. Gerontological Nursing. LC 78-25587. 1979. text ed. 17.25x (ISBN 0-06-043754-5, 64-02283, Lippincott Nursing). Lippincott.

Eliopoulos, Edward, jt. auth. see Greenhalgh, Peter.

Eliopoulos, Nicholas C. Golden Arithmetization. 403p. (Orig.). 1980. pap. text ed. 30.00x (ISBN 0-9605396-0-3). Eliopoulos.

--Oneness of Politics & Religion. 126p. (Orig.). 1970. pap. 3.00x (ISBN 0-9605396-1-1). Eliopoulos.

--Thine Health. Phystiklakis, Nicholas G., ed. (Orig.). 1980. 18.00x (ISBN 0-9605396-2-X). Eliopoulos.

Eliopulos, James. Samuel Beckett's Dramatic Language. LC 74-84241. (De Propietatibus Litterarum, Ser.: No. 100). 131p. 1975. pap. text ed. 15.20x (ISBN 90-2793-232-8). Mouton.

Eliot, Alex. Greece 1985. Eliot, Jane & Fisher, Robert C., eds. (Fisher Annotated Travel Guides Ser.). 272p. 1984. 12.95 (ISBN 0-8116-0060-2, Fisher). NAL.

Eliot, Alexander. Zen Edge. 1979. 3.95 (ISBN 0-8264-0177-5). Continuum.

Eliot, Charles. Charles Eliot, Landscape Architect. facsimile ed. LC 72-190971. (Select Bibliographies Reprint Ser). Repr. of 1902 ed. 66.00 (ISBN 0-8369-5839-X). Ayer Co Pubs.

--East African Protectorate. (Illus.). 334p. 1966. 37.50x (ISBN 0-7146-1661-3, F Cass Co). Biblio Dist.

Eliot, Charles see Brown, Edmund R.

Eliot, Charles W. Conflict Between Individualism & Collectivism in a Democracy, Three Lectures. facs. ed. LC 67-22060. (Essay Index Reprint Ser). 1910. 12.00 (ISBN 0-8369-0411-7). Ayer Co Pubs.

--Durable Satisfaction of Life. LC 71-99691. (Essay Index Reprint Ser.). 1910. 18.00 (ISBN 0-8369-1348-5). Ayer Co Pubs.

--Educational Reform: Essays & Addresses. LC 79-89175. (American Education: Its Men, Institutions & Ideas, Ser. 1). 1969. Repr. of 1898 ed. 16.00 (ISBN 0-405-01413-9). Ayer Co Pubs.

--Four American Leaders. 1978. Repr. of 1906 ed. lib. bdg. 20.00 (ISBN 0-8495-1315-4). Arden Lib.

--Four American Leaders. LC 73-14550. (Franklin, Washington, Channing, Emerson). 1907. lib. bdg. 17.50 (ISBN 0-8414-3916-8). Folcroft.

--Harvard Memories. LC 76-93336. (Essay Index Reprint Ser). 1923. 18.00 (ISBN 0-8369-1289-6). Ayer Co Pubs.

--Harvard Memories. LC 76-93336. (Essay Index Reprint Ser.). (Illus.). 144p. Repr. of 1923 ed. lib. bdg. 15.00 (ISBN 0-8290-0468-8). Irvington.

--Late Harvest: Miscellaneous Papers Written Between Eighty & Ninety. facsimile ed. LC 78-156638. (Essay Index Reprint Ser). Repr. of 1924 ed. 20.00 (ISBN 0-8369-2353-7). Ayer Co Pubs.

--The Religion of the Future. Brown, Edmund R., ed. (International Pocket Library). pap. 3.00 (ISBN 0-8283-1449-7). Branden Pub Co.

--Training for an Effective Life. LC 70-105009. (Essay Index Reprint Ser.). 1915. 13.00 (ISBN 0-8369-1461-9). Ayer Co Pubs.

Eliot, Charles W., ed. Epic & Saga. 438p. Repr. of 1938 ed. lib. bdg. 30.00 (ISBN 0-89984-187-2). Century Bookbindery.

Eliot, Elizabeth. Heiresses & Coronets. (Illus.). 1959. 8.95 (ISBN 0-8392-1061-2). Astor-Honor.

Eliot, Elizabeth A. The Crowned Knot of Fire. LC 79-67045. 1980. 8.95 (ISBN 0-533-04425-1). Vantage.

Eliot, Ellsworth, Jr. Yale in the Civil War. (Illus.). 1932. 75.00x (ISBN 0-685-69817-3). Elliots Bks.

Eliot, George. Adam Bede. (Classics Ser). (gr. 11 up). pap. 1.95 (ISBN 0-8049-0103-1, CL-103). Airmont.

--Adam Bede. 1978. 12.95x (ISBN 0-460-00027-6, Evman); pap. 2.50x (ISBN 0-460-01027-1). Biblio Dist.

--Adam Bede. 466p. 1977. Repr. of 1885 ed. lib. bdg. 17.95x (ISBN 0-89966-265-X). Buccaneer Bks.

--Adam Bede. Paterson, John, ed. LC 68-5227. (gr. 9 up). 1968. pap. 6.50 (ISBN 0-395-05204-1, RivEd). HM.

--Adam Bede. (The Zodiac Press Ser.). 510p. 1979. 15.95 (ISBN 0-7011-1244-1, Pub. by Chatto & Windus). Merrimack Pub Cir.

--Adam Bede. pap. 3.50 (ISBN 0-451-51848-9, CE1848, Sig Classics). NAL.

--Adam Bede. (English Library). 1980. pap. 4.95 (ISBN 0-14-043121-7). Penguin.

--Clerical Life & Sentimental Behaviour. (Illus.). 156p. 1985. Repr. of 1859 ed. 87.50 (ISBN 0-89901-202-7). Found Class Reprints.

--Complete Poems: With Introduction Notice by Matthew Browne. 442p. Repr. of 1984 ed. lib. bdg. 50.00 (ISBN 0-918377-57-9). Russell Pr.

--Daniel Deronda. (The Zodiac Press Ser.). 704p. 1978. 12.95 (ISBN 0-7011-1716-8, Pub. by Chatto & Windus). Merrimack Pub Cir.

--Daniel Deronda. Hardy, Barbara, ed. (English Library). 903p. 1967. pap. 4.95 (ISBN 0-14-043020-2). Penguin.

--Daniel Deronda. 11.50 (ISBN 0-8446-2028-9). Peter Smith.

--Daniel Deronda. Handley, Graham, ed. (The Clarendon Edition of the Novels of George Eliot Ser.). (Illus.). 920p. 1984. 79.00 (ISBN 0-19-812557-7). Oxford U Pr.

--Daniel Derondea. 1979. pap. 3.50 (ISBN 0-451-51204-9, CE1204, Sig Classics). NAL.

--Early Essays. LC 77-6728. 1977. Repr. of 1919 ed. lib. bdg. 10.00 (ISBN 0-8414-3965-6). Folcroft.

--Early Essays. 71p. 1980. Repr. of 1919 ed. lib. bdg. 15.00 (ISBN 0-8492-0787-8). R West.

--Felix Holt, the Radical. 1967. Repr. of 1909 ed. 12.95x (ISBN 0-460-00353-4, Evman). Biblio Dist.

--Felix Holt, the Radical. (Clarendon Edition of the Novels of George Eliot). (Illus.). 1980. 84.00x (ISBN 0-19-812561-5). Oxford U Pr.

--Felix Holt, the Radical. Coveney, Peter, ed. (English Library Ser.). 1973. pap. 5.95 (ISBN 0-14-043084-9). Penguin.

--Felix Holt: The Radical. 1967. pap. text ed. 4.95x (ISBN 0-460-11353-4, Evman). Biblio Dist.

--The George Eliot Letters, Vols. 8 & 9. Haight, Gordon S., ed. LC 52-12063. 1978. 52.00x ea.; Vol. 8. (ISBN 0-300-01968-8); Vol. 9. (ISBN 0-300-02235-2); Set. 104.00x (ISBN 0-300-02251-4). Yale U Pr.

Eliot, George, pseud. George Eliot's Life As Related in Her Letters & Journals, 3 Vols. Cross, J. W., ed. LC 4-17152. 1969. Repr. of 1885 ed. Set. 89.00x (ISBN 0-403-00093-9). Scholarly.

Eliot, George. Middlemarch. Haight, G. S., ed. LC 56-13878. (YA) (gr. 9 up). 1956. pap. 6.50 (ISBN 0-395-05105-3, RivEd). HM.

--Middlemarch. (The Zodiac Press Ser.). 800p. 1979. 15.95 (ISBN 0-7011-1245-X, Pub. by Chatto & Windus). Merrimack Pub Cir.

--Middlemarch. (Orig.). pap. 4.95 (ISBN 0-451-51750-4, CE1750, Sig Classics). NAL.

--Middlemarch. (Norton Critical Editions). 1977. pap. 10.95x (ISBN 0-393-09210-0). Norton.

--Middlemarch. (English Library Ser.). 1965. pap. 4.95 (ISBN 0-14-043002-4). Penguin.

--Middlemarch. Date not set. pap. 10.95 (ISBN 0-394-60507-1, Vin). Random.

--Middlemarch. 816p. (Orig.). 1985. pap. 4.95 (ISBN 0-553-21180-3). Bantam.

--Mill on the Floss. (Classics Ser). (YA) (gr. 10 up). 1964. pap. 2.95 (ISBN 0-8049-0043-4, CL-43). Airmont.

--Mill on the Floss. 1978. 12.95x (ISBN 0-460-00325-9, Evman); pap. 2.95x (ISBN 0-460-11325-9, Evman). Biblio Dist.

--Mill on the Floss. Haight, G. S., ed. LC 62-16032. (YA) (gr. 9 up). 1961. pap. 5.95 (ISBN 0-395-05151-7, RivEd). HM.

--Mill on the Floss. (The Zodiac Press Ser.). 512p. 1978. 12.95 (ISBN 0-7011-1246-8, Pub. by Chatto & Windus). Merrimack Pub Cir.

--Mill on the Floss. pap. 3.95 (ISBN 0-451-51922-1, CE1543, Sig Classics). NAL.

--The Mill on the Floss. (Clarendon Edition of the Novels of George Eliot Ser.). (Illus.). text ed. 64.00x (ISBN 0-19-812560-7). Oxford U Pr.

--The Mill on the Floss. Haight, Gordon S., ed. (World's Classics Ser.). 1982. pap. 3.95 (ISBN 0-19-281567-9). Oxford U Pr.

--Romola. (World's Classics Ser: No. 178). 15.95 (ISBN 0-19-250178-X). Oxford U Pr.

--Romola. Sanders, Andrew, ed. (English Library). 1980. pap. 5.95 (ISBN 0-14-043139-X). Penguin.

--Scenes of Clerical Life. 1976. 12.95x (ISBN 0-460-00468-9, Evman); pap. 2.95x (ISBN 0-460-01468-4, Evman). Biblio Dist.

--Scenes of Clerical Life. Wolff, Robert L., ed. LC 75-491. (Victorian Fiction Ser.). 1975. Repr. of 1858 ed. lib. bdg. 73.00 (ISBN 0-8240-1567-3). Garland Pub.

--Scenes of Clerical Life. Lodge, David, ed. (English Library). (Orig.). 1973. pap. 4.95 (ISBN 0-14-043087-3). Penguin.

--Scenes of Clerical Life. Noble, Thomas A., ed. (Clarendon Edition of the Novels of George Eliot Ser.). 368p. 1985. 44.00 (ISBN 0-19-812559-3). Oxford U Pr.

--Selections from George Eliot's Letters. Haight, Gordon S., ed. LC 84-13222. 585p. 1985. 25.00 (ISBN 0-300-03326-5). Yale U Pr.

--Silas Marner. (Classics Ser). (gr. 9 up). 1964. pap. 1.75 (ISBN 0-8049-0014-0, CL-14). Airmont.

--Silas Marner. (Literature Ser.). (gr. 9-12). 1969. pap. text ed. 4.83 (ISBN 0-87720-715-1). AMSCO Sch.

--Silas Marner. (Bantam Classics Ser.). 192p. (Orig.). (gr. 9-12). 1981. pap. text ed. 1.75 (ISBN 0-553-21048-3). Bantam.

--Silas Marner. Clay, N. L., ed. (Guide Novel Ser.). pap. text ed. 3.95x (ISBN 0-435-16280-2). Heinemann Ed.

--Silas Marner. (The Zodiac Press Ser.). 222p. 1979. 9.95 (ISBN 0-7011-1247-6, Pub. by Chatto & Windus). Merrimack Pub Cir.

--Silas Marner. (YA) (RL 10). pap. 1.95 (ISBN 0-451-51945-0, CE1678, Sig Classics). NAL.

--Silas Marner. (English Library Ser.). 272p. 1968. pap. 2.50 (ISBN 0-14-043030-X). Penguin.

Eliot, George, pseud. Silas Marner. abr. ed. Kramer, Hilton, ed. Bd. with Middlemarch. LC 85-294. (English Classics Ser.). (Illus.). 500p. (YA) (gr. 11-12). Date not set. 18.95 (ISBN 0-317-19756-8, 294); wkbk. avail. McGraw.

Eliot, George. Silas Marner. 13.95 (ISBN 0-88411-275-6, Pub. by Aeonian Pr). Amereon Ltd.

--Silas Marner: The Weaver of Raveloe. 1978. (Evman); pap. 2.95x (ISBN 0-460-01121-9). Biblio Dist.

--Silas Marner (with Reader's Guide) (Amsco Literature Program). (gr. 10-12). 1971. pap. text ed. 5.75 (ISBN 0-87720-814-X); tchr's ed. 3.65 (ISBN 0-87720-914-6). AMSCO Sch.

--The Yale Edition of the George Eliot Letters. Haight, Gordon S., ed. Incl. Vol. 1. 1836-1851. 377p. 1954; Vol. 2. 1852-1858. 513p. 1954. 52.00x (ISBN 0-300-01088-5); Vol. 3. 1859-1861. 475p. 1954. 52.00x (ISBN 0-300-01089-3); Vol. 4. 1862-1868. 502p. 1955; Vol. 5. 1869-1873. 475p. 1955; Vol. 6. 1874-1877. 440p. 1955; Vol. 7. 1878-1880. 535p. 1955. LC 52-12063. 1975. 50.00x ea. Yale U Pr.

Eliot, George & Evans, Marian. Writings of George Eliot with the Life by J. W. Cross, 25 vols. LC 74-114748. (Illus.). Repr. of 1908 ed. Set. 862.50 (ISBN 0-404-02280-4); 34.50 ea. AMS Pr.

Eliot, George see Allen, W. S.

Eliot, George, tr. see De Spinoza, Benedict.

Eliot, George, tr. see Feuerbach, Ludwig.

Eliot, Ida M., jt. auth. see Brackett, Anna C.

Eliot, J. & Moss, B. Nested Transactions: An Approach to Reliable Distributed Computing. (The MIT Press Information Systems Ser. (Research Reports & Notes)). 200p. (Orig.). 1984. 25.00x (ISBN 0-262-13200-1). MIT Pr.

Eliot, J. & Salkind, N. Children's Spatial Development. (Illus.). 312p. 1975. 32.50x (ISBN 0-398-03210-6). C C Thomas.

Eliot, J. N. & Kawazoe, A. Blue Butterflies of the Lycaenopsis-group. (Illus.). 300p. 1983. 56.00x (ISBN 0-565-00860-9, Pub. by Brit Mus Nat Hist England). Sabbot-Natural Hist Bks.

Eliot, J. N., rev. by see Corbet & Pendlebury.

Eliot, James & Kerr, Richard. Rings: Discoveries from Galileo to Voyager. (Illus.). 224p. 1985. 17.50 (ISBN 0-262-05031-5). MIT Pr.

Eliot, Jane, ed. see Eliot, Alex.

Eliot, Jared. Essays Upon Field Husbandry in New England & Other Papers, 1748-1762. Carman, Harry J. & Tugwell, Rexford G., eds. Repr. of 1934 ed. 11.50 (ISBN 0-404-02276-6). AMS Pr.

Eliot, John. A Biographical Dictionary Containing a Brief Account, 2 vols. 290p. Date not set. Repr. Set. lib. bdg. 68.00 (ISBN 0-932051-35-9). Am Repr Serv.

--Christian Commonwealth: Or, the Civil Policy of the Rising Kingdom of Jesus Christ. LC 77-141110. (Research Library of Colonial Americana). 1972. Repr. of 1659 ed. 18.00 (ISBN 0-405-03323-0). Ayer Co Pubs.

--John Eliot's Indian Dialogues: A Study in Cultural Interaction. Bowden, Henry W. & Ronda, James P., eds. LC 80-542. (Contributions in American History: No. 88). (Illus.). 173p. 1980. lib. bdg. 29.95 (ISBN 0-313-21031-4, RID/). Greenwood.

--The Parlement of Pratlers. 1928. 20.00 (ISBN 0-8274-3101-5). R West.

--The Survey, or Topographical Description of France. with a New Mappe. LC 79-84104. (English Experience Ser.: No. 923). (Illus.). 116p. 1979. Repr. of 1592 ed. lib. bdg. 11.50 (ISBN 90-221-0923-2). Walter J Johnson.

Eliot, John & Smith, Ian M. An International Directory of Spatial Tests. 462p. 1983. 198.00x (ISBN 0-7005-0517-2, Pub. by NFER Nelson UK); microfiche 100.00x (ISBN 0-7005-0651-9). Taylor & Francis.

Eliot, Marc. Burt! The Unauthorized Biography. 224p. (Orig.). 1982. pap. 3.95 (ISBN 0-440-00876-X). Dell.

--Televisions: One Season of American Television. LC 82-17015. 208p. 1983. 12.95 (ISBN 0-312-79076-7). St Martin.

Eliot, Philip. Serpent on the Hill. LC 81-69383. 249p. 1982. 12.95 (ISBN 0-941282-00-7). Dallas Pub.

Eliot, Philip, et al. Televising Terrorism: Political Violence in Popular Culture. (Comedia Ser.). 160p. 1984. 15.00 (ISBN 0-906890-38-1, Scribner Book Co); pap. 8.95 (ISBN 0-906890-39-X). M Boyars.

Eliot, R. C., ed. Boiler Fuel Additives for Pollution Reduction & Energy Saving. LC 78-61895. (Energy Tech Rev. 33, Pollution Tech. Rev. 53, Chem Tech. Rev. 120). 1979. 36.00 (ISBN 0-8155-0729-1). Noyes.

--Coal Desulfurization Prior to Combustion. LC 78-56014. (Chemical Technology Review Ser., Pollution Tech. Rev. 45: No. 113). 113p. 1978. 42.00 (ISBN 0-8155-0712-7). Noyes.

Eliot, Robert S. & Breo, Dennis L. Is It Worth Dying For? A Self-Assessment Program to Make Stress Work for You Not Against You. 224p. 1984. 15.95 (ISBN 0-553-05104-0). Bantam.

Eliot, Robert S., et al, eds. Cardiac Emergencies. 2nd ed. LC 82-70437. (Illus.). 550p. 1982. 35.00 (ISBN 0-87993-176-0). Futura Pub.

Eliot, Samuel, ed. Poetry for Children. facsimile ed. LC 76-160905. (Granger Index Reprint Ser.). Repr. of 1879 ed. 21.00 (ISBN 0-8369-6268-0). Ayer Co Pubs.

Eliot, Simon & Stern, Beverly, eds. The Age of Enlightenment: An Anthology of Eighteenth Century Texts, 2 vols. 1980. Vol. 1 354p. 28.50x (ISBN 0-06-491962-5); Vol. 2 264p. 28.50x (ISBN 0-06-491963-3). B&N Imports.

Eliot, T., tr. see Plutarch.

Eliot, T. S. Cats: The Book of the Musical, Based on Old Possum's Book of Practical Cats. LC 82-48026. (Illus.). 1983. pap. 12.95 (ISBN 0-15-615582-6, Harv). HarBraceJ.

--Christianity & Culture. Incl. The Idea of a Christian Society; Notes Towards the Definition of Culture. 202p. 1960. pap. 5.95 (ISBN 0-15-617735-8, HB32, Harv). HarBraceJ.

--The Classics & the Man of Letters. LC 74-2409. (Studies in T. S. Eliot, No. 11). 1974. lib. bdg. 39.95x (ISBN 0-8383-2053-8). Haskell.

--The Cocktail Party. LC 50-14646. 1964. pap. 2.95 (ISBN 0-15-618289-0, Harv). HarBraceJ.

--Collected Poems, 1909-1962. LC 63-21424. 1963. 12.95 (ISBN 0-15-118978-1). HarBraceJ.

--The Complete Poems & Plays, 1909-1950. LC 52-11346. 1952. 18.95 (ISBN 0-15-121185-X). HarBraceJ.

--The Confidential Clerk. LC 54-5253. 1964. pap. 6.95 (ISBN 0-15-622015-6, Harv). HarBraceJ.

--Criticism in America. 1973. lib. bdg. 69.95 (ISBN 0-87968-045-8). Gordon Pr.

--Criticism in America: Its Functions & Status. LC 68-57456. (Studies in T. S. Eliot, No. 11). 1972. Repr. of 1924 ed. lib. bdg. 39.95x (ISBN 0-8383-0541-5). Haskell.

--The Cultivation of Christmas Trees. 1956. 2.00 (ISBN 0-374-13304-2). FS&G.

--Dante. LC 74-2321. (Studies in Dante, No. 9). 1974. lib. bdg. write for info. (ISBN 0-8383-2060-0). Haskell.

--The Elder Statesman. 134p. 1959. 4.95 (ISBN 0-374-14676-4). FS&G.

--Elizabethan Essays. 1973. lib. bdg. 69.95 (ISBN 0-87968-043-1). Gordon Pr.

--Elizabethan Essays. LC 65-15878. (Studies in T. S. Eliot, No. 11). 1969. Repr. of 1934 ed. lib. bdg. 39.95x (ISBN 0-8383-0542-3). Haskell.

--The Family Reunion. LC 39-27242. 1964. pap. 5.95 (ISBN 0-15-630157-1, Harv). HarBraceJ.

--Four Quartets. LC 43-7996. (YA) (gr. 9-12). 1968. pap. 1.95 (ISBN 0-15-633225-6, Harv). HarBraceJ.

--Homage to John Dryden. LC 76-52494. 1974. 15.00 (ISBN 0-8495-1300-6). Arden Lib.

--Homage to John Dryden. 1973. lib. bdg. 59.95 (ISBN 0-87968-042-3). Gordon Pr.

--Homage to John Dryden. (Studies in Dryden, No. 10). 1970. pap. 16.95x (ISBN 0-8383-0024-3). Haskell.

--John Dryden. 1973. lib. bdg. 59.95 (ISBN 0-87968-041-5). Gordon Pr.

--John Dryden. LC 68-913. (Studies in Dryden, No. 10). 1969. Repr. of 1932 ed. lib. bdg. 29.95x (ISBN 0-8383-0692-6). Haskell.

--Murder in the Cathedral. LC 35-1776. 1964. pap. 2.95 (ISBN 0-15-663277-2, Harv). HarBraceJ.

--Old Possum's Book of Practical Cats. LC 39-33125. (Illus.). 1982. 8.95 (ISBN 0-15-168656-4). HarBraceJ.

--Old Possum's Book of Practical Cats. LC 39-33125. 59p. 1968. pap. 1.95 (ISBN 0-15-668570-1, Harv). HarBraceJ.

--Poems Written in Early Youth. LC 67-18781. 1967. pap. 4.95 (ISBN 0-374-50708-2). FS&G.

--Sacred Wood. 7th ed. 171p. 1960. pap. 10.95x (ISBN 0-416-67610-3, NO. 2185). Methuen Inc.

--Selected Essays. LC 32-24259. 1950. 19.95 (ISBN 0-15-180387-0). HarBraceJ.

--Selected Poems. LC 67-23064. (gr. 7-12). 1967. pap. 2.95 (ISBN 0-15-680647-9, Harv). HarBraceJ.

--Selected Prose of T. S. Eliot. Kermode, Frank, ed. 1975. 10.95 (ISBN 0-15-180702-7); pap. 4.95 (ISBN 0-15-680654-1). FS&G.

--Selected Prose of T. S. Eliot. 320p. 1975. 10.95 (ISBN 0-15-180702-7, Co-Pub by FS&G). HarBraceJ.

--Shakespeare & the Stoicism of Seneca. 1979. 28.50 (ISBN 0-685-94345-3). Porter.

--To Criticize the Critic. 189p. 1980. Repr. lib. bdg. 19.50x (ISBN 0-374-92531-3). Octagon.

--Tradition & Experiment in Present Day Literature. lib. bdg. 69.95 (ISBN 0-87968-044-X). Gordon Pr.

--The Use of Poetry & the Use of Criticism Studies in the Relation of Criticism to Poetry in England. 156p. 1985. pap. 3.95 (ISBN 0-571-05871-X). Faber & Faber.

--The Waste Land & Other Poems. LC 56-58835. (Orig.). 1955. pap. 2.95 (ISBN 0-15-694877-X, Harv). HarBraceJ.

--The Waste Land: Facsimile & Transcript. facsimile ed. Eliot, Valerie, ed. LC 73-12627. 149p. 1974. pap. 9.95 (ISBN 0-15-694870-2, Harv). HarBraceJ.

--What Is a Classic? LC 74-4089. (Studies in T. S. Eliot, No. 11). 1974. lib. bdg. 49.95x (ISBN 0-8383-2059-7). Haskell.

Eliot, T. S. & Huxley, Aldous. Three Critical Essays on Modern English Poetry. LC 74-34435. 1973. lib. bdg. 10.00 (ISBN 0-8414-3957-5). Folcroft.

Eliot, T. S., jt. auth. see Dryden, John.

Eliot, T. S., jt. auth. see Gangulee, N.

Eliot, T. S., ed. see Kipling, Rudyard.

Eliot, T. S., ed. see Pound, Ezra.

Eliot, T. S., intro. by see Pound, Ezra L.

Eliot, T. S., tr. see Perse, St. John.

Eliot, T. S., pref. by. The Dark Side of the Moon. LC 74-26099. Repr. of 1947 ed. 19.50 (ISBN 0-404-58526-4). AMS Pr.

Eliot, T. S., et al. Britain at War. LC 70-169301. (The Museum of Modern Art Publications in Reprint). (Illus.). 98p. 1972. Repr. of 1941 ed. 21.00 (ISBN 0-405-01560-7). Ayer Co Pubs.

--Poetry in Prose. LC 78-64019. (Des Imagistes: Literature of the Imagist Movement). Repr. of 1921 ed. 11.00 (ISBN 0-404-17090-0). AMS Pr.

Eliot, T. S., et al, trs. see Perse, Saint-John.

Eliot, Thomas H., jt. auth. see Bragdon, Henry W.

Eliot, Thomas S. The Aims of Poetic Drama. LC 76-47532. 1976. Repr. of 1949 ed. lib. bdg. 10.00 (ISBN 0-8414-3921-4). Folcroft.

--The Literary Criticism of T. S. Eliot: New Essays. Newton-DeMolina, David, ed. 216p. 1977. 36.00 (ISBN 0-485-11167-5, Pub. by Athlone Pr Ltd). Longwood Pub Group.

--Points of View. Hayward, John, ed. LC 78-14116. 1979. Repr. of 1941 ed. 14.50 (ISBN 0-88355-788-6). Hyperion Conn.

Eliot, Valerie, ed. see Eliot, T. S.

Eliot, William G. Story of Archer Alexander: From Slavery to Freedom. LC 72-107506. Repr. of 1885 ed. 15.00x (ISBN 0-8371-3777-2, ELA&, Pub. by Negro U Pr). Greenwood.

Eliott, C. S. & Biedenbach, J. M., eds. Continuing Education Director's Handbook. rev. ed. 448p. 1982. 20.00 (ISBN 0-317-33249-X). Am Soc Ag Eng.

Eliott, P. D. Probabilistic Number Theory Two: Central Limit Theorems. (Grundlehren der Mathematischen Wissenschaften: Vol. 240). 1980. 46.00 (ISBN 0-387-90438-7). Springer-Verlag.

Eliovson, Sima. Garden Beauty of South Africa. (Illus.). 150p. 1982. 21.95 (ISBN 0-86954-075-0, Pub. by Macmillan S Africa). Intl Spec Bk.

--Garden Design for Southern Africa. 238p. 1983. 37.50 (ISBN 0-86954-145-5, Pub. by Macmillan S Africa). Intl Spec Bk.

--Proteas for Pleasure. (Illus.). 228p. 1982. 31.95 (ISBN 0-86954-006-8, Pub. by Macmillan S Africa). Intl Spec Bk.

--Shrubs, Trees & Climbers for Southern Africa. (Illus.). 270p. 1982. 32.50 (ISBN 0-86954-011-4, Pub. by Macmillan S Africa). Intl Spec Bk.

--Wild Flowers of Southern Africa. (Illus.). 310p. 1982. 32.50 (ISBN 0-86954-088-2, Pub. by Macmillan S Africa). Intl Spec Bk.

Elipoulos, Nicholas C. Oneness of Politics & Religion. rev. ed. 169p. 1979. text ed. 6.95 (ISBN 0-9605396-3-8). Eliopoulos.

Elirhart, W. D. The Outer Banks & other Poems. 2nd ed. 52p. 1985. pap. 5.00 (ISBN 0-938566-28-8). Adastra Pr.

Eliseeva, V. I., et al. Emulsion Polymerization & Its Applications in Industry. Teague, Sylvia J., tr. from Rus. LC 81-17477. Orig. Title: Emul'Sionnaya Polimerizatsiya I EE Primenenie V Promyshlenosti. 300p. 1981. 59.50 (ISBN 0-306-10961-1, Consultants). Plenum Pub.

Elisens, Wayne J. Monograph of the Maurandyinae (Scrophulariaceae-Antirrhineae) Anderson, Christiane, ed. LC 85-1266. (Systematic Botany Monographs: Vol. 5). (Illus.). 97p. (Orig.). 1985. pap. 12.00 (ISBN 0-912861-05-3). Am Soc Plant.

Elishakoff, Isaac. Probabilistic Methods in the Theory of Structures. LC 82-13470. 489p. 1983. 52.95x (ISBN 0-471-87572-4, Pub. by Wiley Interscience). Wiley.

Elishe. History of Vardan & the Armenian War. Thomson, Robert W., tr. from Armenian. LC 81-7117. (Harvard Armenian Texts & Studies: 5). (Illus.). 352p. 1982. text ed. 30.00x (ISBN 0-674-40335-5). Harvard U Pr.

Elisofon, Eliot & Fagg, William. The Sculpture of Africa. LC 76-50293. (Illus.). 1978. Repr. of 1958 ed. lib. bdg. 50.00 (ISBN 0-87817-210-6). Hacker.

Elisofon, Eliot, jt. auth. see Robbins, Warren.

Elison, George. Deus Destroyed: The Image of Christianity in Early Modern Japan. LC 72-97833. (East Asian Ser: No. 72). 704p. 1974. 37.50t (ISBN 0-674-19961-8). Harvard U Pr.

Elison, George & Smith, Bardwell L., eds. Warlords, Artists, & Commoners: Japan in the Sixteenth Century. LC 80-24128. (Illus.). 373p. 1981. 20.00x (ISBN 0-8248-0692-1). UH Pr.

Elison, Marilyn. Duffy on the Farm. LC 83-82601. (Big Golden Story Bks.). (Illus.). 24p. (ps-1). 1984. 3.50 (ISBN 0-307-10407-9, 10407, Golden Bks). Western Pub.

Elisseeff, Danielle, jt. auth. see Elisseeff, Vadime.

Elisseeff, Vadime & Elisseeff, Danielle. Art of Japan. (Illus.). 622p. 1985. text ed. 125.00 (ISBN 0-8109-0642-2). Abrams.

Elithorn, A. & Banerji, R., eds. Artificial & Human Intelligence. 350p. 1984. 40.00 (ISBN 0-444-86545-4, North-Holland). Elsevier.

Elizabeth, Charlotte, pseud. Helen Fleetwood. LC 79-8263. Repr. of 1841 ed. 44.50 (ISBN 0-404-61844-8). AMS Pr.

Elizabeth First, Queen Of England. Letters of Queen Elizabeth & James Sixth of Scotland. Bruce, John, ed. LC 75-166015. (Camden Society, London. Publications, First Ser.: No. 46). Repr. of 1849 ed. 24.00 (ISBN 0-404-50146-X). AMS Pr.

--Public Speaking of Queen Elizabeth: Selections from the Official Addresses. Rice, George P., Jr., ed. Repr. of 1951 ed. 11.50 (ISBN 0-404-05288-6). AMS Pr.

Elizabeth, Queen. The True Copie of a Letter from the Queens Maiesty to the Lord Mayor of London. LC 70-25636. (English Experience Ser.: No. 167). 8p. 1969. Repr. of 1586 ed. 7.00 (ISBN 90-221-0167-3). Walter J Johnson.

Elizabeth - Queen Of England. Letters of Queen Elizabeth & King James Sixth of Scotland. 1849. 24.00 (ISBN 0-384-14135-8). Johnson Repr.

Elizabeth I. A Book of Devotions. new ed. 1977. pap. text ed. 4.50x (ISBN 0-901072-57-5). Humanities.

--The Poems of Queen Elizabeth I. Bradner, Leicester, ed. LC 64-17778. 111p. 1964. 10.00x (ISBN 0-87057-082-X). U Pr of New Eng.

Elizakeany, jt. auth. see Annie.

Elizari, M., jt. ed. see Rosenbaum, M.

Elizbieta. Dikou & the Snivelly Snoak. (gr. k-6). 1985. 3.95 (ISBN 0-8120-5622-1). Barron.

--Dikou-Troon Who Walks at Night. (gr. k-6). 1985. 3.95 (ISBN 0-8120-5621-3). Barron.

Elizondo, Salvador. Farabeuf, o la Cronica de un Instante. 183p. (Span.). 1981. pap. 8.00 (ISBN 84-85859-18-9, 2005). Ediciones Norte.

Elizondo, Sergio. Libro Para Batos y Chavalas Chicanas: Spanish - English. LC 76-52262. 1976. pap. 6.00 (ISBN 0-915808-19-6). Editorial Justa.

--Rosa, la Flauta. 1980. pap. 6.00 (ISBN 0-915808-37-4). Editorial Justa.

Elizondo, Virgil & Greinacher, Norbert, eds. Church & Peace. (Concilium 1983: Vol. 164). 128p. (Orig.). 1983. pap. 6.95 (ISBN 0-8164-2444-6, Pub. by Seabury). Winston Pr.

--Religion & Churches in Eastern Europe. (Concilium Ser.: Vol. 154). 128p. (Orig.). 1982. pap. 6.95 (ISBN 0-8164-2385-7, Pub. by Seabury). Winston Pr.

--Tensions Between the Churches of the First World & the Third World, Vol. 144. (Concilium 1981). 128p. (Orig.). 1981. pap. 6.95 (ISBN 0-8164-2311-3, Pub. by Seabury). Winston Pr.

--The Transmission of Faith to the Next Generation. (Concilium Ser.: Vol. 174). 128p. pap. 6.95 (ISBN 0-317-31464-5, 30-30054-1902); pap. 9.05 Canada (ISBN 0-317-31465-3). Fortress.

--Women in a Man's Church, Concilium 134. (New Concilium 1980: Vol. 134). 128p. 1980. pap. 5.95 (ISBN 0-8164-2276-1, Pub. by Seabury). Winston Pr.

Elizondo, Virgil, jt. ed. see Boff, Leonardo.

Elizondo, Virgilio. Galilean Journey: The Mexican-American Promise. LC 82-18852. 144p. (Orig.). 1984. pap. 6.95 (ISBN 0-88344-151-9). Orbis Bks.

Elizondo, Virgilio P. Creemos en Jesucristo. 128p. (Span.). 1982. pap. 2.95 (ISBN 0-89243-153-9). Liguori Pubns.

Elizur, Abraham. Psycho-Organic Syndrome: Its Assessment & Treatment. 54p. 1969. pap. 14.40x (ISBN 0-87424-104-9). Western Psych.

Elizur, Dov. Job Evaluation: A Systematic Approach. 188p. 1980. text ed. 37.25 (ISBN 0-566-02120-X). Gower Pub Co.

Elkan, E., jt. auth. see Reichenbach-Klinke, H.

Elkan, Peter G. The New Model Economy: Economic Inventions for the Rest of the Century. 142p. 1982. 19.25 (ISBN 0-08-028112-5, L115). Pergamon.

Elkana, Y., ed. see Helmholtz, H. von.

Elkana, Y., tr. see Helmholtz, H. von.

Elkana, Yahuda, et al, eds. Debates on the Decline of Science: An Original Anthology. LC 74-25148. (History, Philosophy & Sociology of Science Ser). 1975. Repr. 22.00x (ISBN 0-405-06632-5). Ayer Co Pubs.

Elkana, Yehuda. Discovery of the Conservation of Energy. LC 73-88897. (Monographs in the History of Science). 277p. 1974. text ed. 15.00x (ISBN 0-674-21240-1). Harvard U Pr.

Elkana, Yehuda, ed. The Interaction Between Science & Philosophy: Sambursky Festschrift. 1972. text ed. 18.00x (ISBN 0-391-00255-4). Humanities.

Elkana, Yehuda, jt. ed. see Holton, Gerald.

Elkana, Yehuda, jt. ed. see Mendelsohn, Everett.

Elkana, Yehuda, ed. see Whewell, William.

Elkana, Yehuda, et al, eds. Science, Internationalism & War: An Original Anthology. LC 74-25185. (History, Philosophy & Sociology of Science Ser). 1975. Repr. 16.00x (ISBN 0-405-06633-3). Ayer Co Pubs.

--Toward a Metric of Science: The Advent of Science Indicators. LC 77-24513. (Science, Culture & Society Ser.). 1978. 38.50x (ISBN 0-471-98435-3, Pub. by Wiley-Interscience). Wiley.

Elkana, Yehunda, jt. ed. see Holton, Gerald.

El-Kareh, A. B. & El-Kareh, J. C. Electron Beams, Lenses & Optics, Vols. 1 & 2. 1970. Vol. 1. 76.50 (ISBN 0-12-238001-0); Vol. 2. 76.00 (ISBN 0-12-238002-9). Acad Pr.

El-Kareh, J. C., jt. auth. see El-Kareh, A. B.

Elkayam, Uri & Gleicher, Norbert, eds. Cardiac Problems in Pregnancy: Diagnosis & Management of Maternal & Fetal Disease. LC 82-9938. 638p. 1982. 85.00 (ISBN 0-8451-0216-8). A R Liss.

Elkeles, R. S. & Tavill, A. S. Biochemical Aspects of Human Disease. (Illus.). 729p. 1983. text ed. 95.00 (ISBN 0-632-00012-0, B1521-6). Mosby.

Elkenton, John. The Gene Factory. 240p. (Orig.). 1985. 16.95 (ISBN 0-88184-208-7). Carroll & Graf.

El Khadem, Hassan S., ed. Synthetic Methods for Carbohydrates. LC 76-58888. (ACS Symposium Ser: No. 39). 1977. 29.95 (ISBN 0-8412-0365-2). Am Chemical.

El-khawas, Mohamed. Qaddafi: His Ideology in Theory & Practice. (Illus.). 200p. (Orig.). 1985. 18.95 (ISBN 0-915597-24-1); pap. 9.95 (ISBN 0-915597-23-3). Amana Bks.

El-Khawas, Mohamed A., jt. auth. see Serapiao, Luis B.

El-Khawas, Mohamed A. & Kornegay, Francis A., eds. American-Southern African Relations: Bibliographic Essays. LC 75-25331. (African Bibliographic Ser.: No. 1). 188p. 1975. lib. bdg. 35.00 (ISBN 0-8371-8398-7, EA/A01). Greenwood.

El-Khawas, Mohamed A. see Mohamed A. El-Khawas & Cohen, Barry.

Elkholy, Abdo A. The Arab Moslems in the United States. 1966. 9.95x (ISBN 0-8084-0052-5); pap. 6.95x (ISBN 0-8084-0053-3). New Coll U Pr.

Elkin, Adolphus P. Studies in Australian Totemism. LC 76-44712. Repr. of 1933 ed. 17.00 (ISBN 0-404-15857-9). AMS Pr.

Elkin, Benjamin. Big Jump & Other Stories. LC 58-13127. (Illus.). (gr. 1-2). 1958. PLB 5.99 (ISBN 0-394-90004-9). Beginner.

--King's Wish & Other Stories. LC 60-13491. (Illus.). (gr. 1-2). 1960. Beginner.

--Money. LC 83-7436. (New True Bks.). (Illus.). 48p. (gr. k-4). 1983. PLB 10.60 (ISBN 0-516-01697-0); pap. 3.95 (ISBN 0-516-41697-9). Childrens.

--Six Foolish Fishermen. (Illus.). (gr. k-3). pap. 1.50 (ISBN 0-590-02543-0). Scholastic Inc.

Elkin, Felice. Walter Savage Landor: Studies of Italian Life & Literature. LC 74-8062. 1934. lib. bdg. 10.00 (ISBN 0-8414-3938-9). Folcroft.

Elkin, Frederick. Rebels & Colleagues: Advertising & Social Change in French Canada. (Illus.). 240p. 1973. 17.50x (ISBN 0-7735-0135-5). McGill-Queens U Pr.

Elkin, Frederick & Handel, Gerald. The Child & Society. 4th ed. 312p. 1984. pap. text ed. 10.00 (ISBN 0-394-33276-8, RanC). Random.

Elkin, Ginny, jt. auth. see Yalom, Irvin D.

Elkin, H. V. Cutler: Mustang. (Cutler Ser.). 192p. 1985. pap. 2.25 (ISBN 0-8439-2234-6, Leisure Bks). Dorchester Pub Co.

--Cutler No. 4: Yellowstone. (Orig.). 1980. pap. 1.75 (ISBN 0-505-51512-1, Pub. by Tower Bks). Dorchester Pub Co.

--Cutler: Tiger's Chance. (Cutler Ser.). 224p. 1985. pap. 2.25 (ISBN 0-8439-2307-5, Leisure Bks). Dorchester Pub Co.

--Eagle Man. (Cutler Ser.: No. 1). 1978. pap. 1.50 (ISBN 0-505-51295-5, Pub. by Tower Bks). Dorchester Pub Co.

--Playground. 1979. pap. 2.25 (ISBN 0-505-51423-0, Pub. by Tower Bks). Dorchester Pub Co.

--Tiger's Chance. (Cutler Ser.: No. 6). (Orig.). 1980. pap. 1.95 (ISBN 0-505-51559-8, Pub. by Tower Bks). Dorchester Pub Co.

Elkin, Jack M. Qualified Joint & Survivor Annuities: No. B447. (Requirements for Qualification of Plans). 13p. 1983. pap. 7.50 (ISBN 0-317-31165-4). Am Law Inst.

Elkin, Judith L. Jews of the Latin American Republics. LC 79-17394. xv, 298p. 1980. 25.00 (ISBN 0-8078-1408-3). U of NC Pr.

Elkin, Judith L., ed. see Niehaus, Thomas, et al.

Elkin, Michael. Families Under the Influence: Changing Alcoholic Patterns. LC 83-21933. 224p. 1984. 16.95 (ISBN 0-393-01770-2). Norton.

Elkin, Milton, jt. auth. see Baker, Stephen R.

Elkin, Milton, ed. Radiology of the Urinary System, 2 vols. 1980. Set. text ed. 125.00 (ISBN 0-316-23275-0). Little.

Elkin, P. K., ed. Australian Poems in Perspective: A Collection of Poems & Critical Commentaries. 1978. 22.00x (ISBN 0-7022-1019-6); pap. 12.95x (ISBN 0-7022-1025-0). U of Queensland Pr.

Elkin, Randy D. & Hewitt, Thomas L. Successful Arbitration: Experience in the Preparation & Presentation of Arbitration Cases. (Illus.). 128p. 1980. pap. text ed. 12.95 (ISBN 0-8359-7144-9); instructor's manual (ISBN 0-8359-7145-7). Reston.

Elkin, Randyl D., jt. auth. see Moore, Gary A.

Elkin, Robert, jt. auth. see Cornick, Delroy L.

Elkin, Stanley. A Bad Man. (Obelisk Ser.). 368p. 1984. pap. 10.95 (ISBN 0-525-48132-X, 01063-320). Dutton.

--Criers & Kibitzers, Kibitzers & Criers. 1973. pap. 3.95 (ISBN 0-452-25077-3, Z5077, Plume). NAL.

--The Dick Gibson Show. 400p. 1983. pap. 8.95 (ISBN 0-525-48062-5, 0869-260). Dutton.

--Early Elkin. LC 84-63099. 1985. 15.00 (ISBN 0-917453-04-2); signed ed. 25.00x (ISBN 0-917453-05-0); pap. 7.50 (ISBN 0-917453-03-4). Bamberger.

--The First George Mills. (Limited Edition Ser.). (Illus.). 60p. 1981. signed limited ed. 45.00 (ISBN 0-939722-03-8). Pressworks.

--The Franchiser. LC 79-92109. 360p. 1980. pap. 6.95 (ISBN 0-87923-323-0, Nonpareil Bks). Godine.

--George Mills. (Obelisk Ser.). 516p. 1983. pap. 8.95 (ISBN 0-525-48063-3, 0869-290). Dutton.

--Living End. (Obelisk Ser.). 160p. 1985. pap. 7.95 (ISBN 0-525-48158-3, 0772-230). Dutton.

--Searches & Seizures: Three Novellas. LC 78-58499. 320p. 1978. pap. 6.95 (ISBN 0-87923-253-6, Nonpareil Bks). Godine.

--Stanley Elkin's The Magic Kingdom. LC 84-21109. 1985. 15.95 (ISBN 0-525-24304-6, 01549-460). Dutton.

Elkin, Stanley & Ravenel, Shannon, eds. The Best American Short Stories 1980. 512p. 1981. pap. 6.95 (ISBN 0-14-006033-2). Penguin.

Elkin, Stephen L., jt. ed. see Benjamin, Roger.

Elkin, W. A., jt. auth. see Kisch, C. H.

Elkind, Arnold B., jt. auth. see Cotchett, Joseph W.

Elkind, D. The Child's Reality: Three Developmental Themes. 180p. 1978. 19.95x (ISBN 0-89859-224-0). L Erlbaum Assocs.

Elkind, David. All Grown Up & No Place to Go: Teenagers in Crisis. LC 84-6388. 1984. 17.95 (ISBN 0-201-11378-3, 1726); pap. 8.95 (ISBN 0-201-11379-1, 861). Addison-Wesley.

--The Child & Society. 1979. pap. text ed. 7.95x (ISBN 0-19-502372-2). Oxford U Pr.

--Child Development & Education: A Piagetian Perspective. 1976. pap. text ed. 9.95x (ISBN 0-19-502069-3). Oxford U Pr.

--Children & Adolescents. 3rd ed. 1981. text ed. 21.95x (ISBN 0-19-502820-1); pap. text ed. 8.95x (ISBN 0-19-502821-X). Oxford U Pr.

--The Child's Reality: Three Developmental Themes. LC 78-7351. (John M. MacEachran Memorial Lectures Ser.: Vol. 3). 155p. 1978. 12.95x (ISBN 0-470-26376-8). Halsted Pr.

--The Hurried Child: Growing up Too Fast Too Soon. 224p. 1981. o. p. 11.95 (ISBN 0-201-03966-4); pap. 7.95 (ISBN 0-201-03967-2). Addison-Wesley.

--A Sympathetic Understanding of the Child: Birth to Sixteen. 2nd ed. 1978. text ed. 20.00 (ISBN 0-205-06015-3, 246015). Allyn.

Elkind, David & Weiner, Irving B. Development of the Child. LC 77-14214. 728p. 1978. text ed. 38.00 (ISBN 0-471-23785-X); student study guide 13.95x (ISBN 0-471-03435-5); tchrs. manual avail. (ISBN 0-471-04049-5). Wiley.

Elkind, David & Flavell, John H., eds. Studies in Cognitive Development: Essays in Honor of Jean Piaget. 1969. pap. 11.95x (ISBN 0-19-500878-2). Oxford U Pr.

Elkind, David, ed. see Piaget, Jean.

Elkind, David, jt. auth. see Carnine, Douglas.

Elkind, Henry B., ed. Preventive Management. facs. ed. LC 70-142621. (Essay Index Reprint Ser.). 1931. 18.00 (ISBN 0-8369-2044-9). Ayer Co Pubs.

Elkind, Jerome. Interim Protection. 310p. 1981. lib. bdg. 59.00 (ISBN 90-247-2539-9, Pub. by Martinus Nijhoff Netherlands). Kluwer Academic.

Elkind, Jerome B. Non-Appearance Before the International Court of Justice: Functional & Comparative Analysis. 1984. lib. bdg. 42.00 (ISBN 90-247-2921-1, Pub. by Martinus Nijhoff Netherlands). Kluwer Academic.

Elkind, M. M. & Whitmore, G. G. Radiobiology of Cultured Mammalian Cells. 632p. 1967. 131.95 (ISBN 0-677-10920-2). Gordon.

Elkind, Sue S. No Longer Afraid. 64p. (Orig.). 1985. pap. 5.95 (ISBN 0-931642-16-7). Lintel.

Elkind-Savatsky, Pamela & Kaufman, Judith, eds. Differential Social Impacts of Rural Resource Development. (Social Impact Assessment Ser.). 175p. 1985. pap. text ed. 17.50x (ISBN 0-8133-0077-0). Westview.

Elking, Henry. A View of the Greenland Trade & Whale Fishery, 1722. 1981. 35.00x (ISBN 0-686-98239-8, Pub. by Caedmon of Whitby). State Mutual Bk.

Elkington, Helen. Swimming: A Handbook for Teachers. LC 76-53514. (Illus.). 1978. pap. 10.95x (ISBN 0-521-29027-9). Cambridge U Pr.

Elkington, Helen & Holmgard, Tony. Better Swimming. (Better Bks.). (Illus.). 96p. (gr. 7 up). 17.95x (ISBN 0-7182-0145-0, SpS). Sportshelf.

Elkington, Helen & Holmyard, Tony. Better Swimming for Boys & Girls. 1983. 17.95x (ISBN 0-7182-0145-0). Sportshelf.

Elkington, John. The Ecology of Tomorrow's World: Industry's Environments, Environments's Industry. 311p. 1980. 37.95 (ISBN 0-470-27120-5). Halsted Pr.

--Sun Traps: Energy for a Renewable Future. 408p. 1984. pap. 6.95 (ISBN 0-14-022425-4, Pelican). Penguin.

Elkins, A. C. & Forstner, Lorne, eds. Romantic Movement Bibliography, 1936-1970: A Master Cumulation from ELH, Philological Quarterly & English Language Notes, 7 Vols. LC 77-172773. (Cumulated Bibliography Ser.: No. 3). 1973. Set. 290.00 (ISBN 0-87650-025-4). Pierian.

Elkins, Aaron J. The Dark Place. 192p. 1983. 12.95 (ISBN 0-8027-5565-8). Walker & Co.

--The Dark Place. 204p. (Orig.). 1986. pap. price not set (ISBN 0-445-20041-3, Pub. by Popular Lib). Warner Bks.

--Fellowship of Fear. 256p. 1982. 11.95 (ISBN 0-8027-5478-3). Walker & Co.

Elkins, Aaron J., jt. auth. see James, Roger G.

Elkins, Arthur & Callaghan, Dennis W. Managerial Odyssey: Problems in Business & Its Enviroment. 600p. 1981. text ed. 30.95 (ISBN 0-201-03962-1); instr's. manual 2.50 (ISBN 0-201-03963-X). Addison-Wesley.

Elkins, Carolyn. Community Health Nursing: Skills & Strategies. LC 83-9934. (Illus.). 432p. 1983. text ed. 17.95 (ISBN 0-89303-264-6). Brady Comm.

Elkins, Chris. Heavenly Deception. 1980. pap. 3.95 (ISBN 0-8423-1402-4). Tyndale.

--Heavenly Deception. 1981. pap. 9.95 incl. cassette (ISBN 0-8423-1403-2). Tyndale.

--What Do You Say to a Moonie? 80p. 1981. 2.50 (ISBN 0-8423-7867-7). Tyndale.

Elkins, Darrell T. Aviation Insurance: An Introduction to General Aviation Insurance in the United States. LC 84-80137. 230p. 1984. text ed. 75.00 (ISBN 0-930215-38-9). J A Elkins Brs.

Elkins, David J. Electoral Participation in a South Indian Context. LC 74-27534. 251p. 1975. 18.95 (ISBN 0-89089-015-3). Carolina Acad Pr.

Elkins, David J., jt. auth. see Citrin, Jack.

Elkins, Don, jt. auth. see McCarty, James A.

Elkins, Donald M., jt. auth. see Metcalf, Darrel S.

Elkins, Dov P. Clarifying Jewish Values: Clarification Strategies for Jewish Groups. LC 77-83774. 1977. softbound 10.00 (ISBN 0-918834-02-3). Growth Assoc.
--Experiential Programs for Jewish Groups. LC 78-58512. softcover 10.00 (ISBN 0-918834-05-8). Growth Assoc.
--God's Warriors: Dramatic Adventures of Rabbis in Uniform. LC 74-226. (Illus.). 92p. (gr. 5 up). 1974. 5.95 (ISBN 0-8246-0168-8). Jonathan David.
--Jewish Consciousness Raising: A Handbook of 50 Experiential Exercises for Jewish Groups. LC 77-83775. 1977. softbound 10.00 (ISBN 0-918834-03-1). Growth Assoc.
--Shepherd of Jerusalem. LC 75-39436. (Illus.). (gr. 8-12). 1976. 7.95 (ISBN 0-88400-045-1). Shengold.
--Twelve Pathways to Feeling Better About Yourself. LC 79-88299. 1980. softbound 7.50 (ISBN 0-918834-08-2). Growth Assoc.
Elkins, Dov P., ed. Being Jewish, Being Human: A Gift Book of Poems & Readings. LC 79-88298. Date not set. pap. 16.50 (ISBN 0-918834-07-4). Growth Assoc.
--Glad to Be Me: Building Self-Esteem in Yourself & Others. 1985. pap. write for info. (ISBN 0-13-357319-2). Growth Assoc.
--Loving My Jewishness: Jewish Self Pride & Self-Esteem. LC 78-58511. softbound 10.00 (ISBN 0-918834-04-X). Growth Assoc.
--Rejoice with Jerusalem. 1972. pap. 1.95 (ISBN 0-87677-065-0). Prayer BK.
--Self Concept Sourcebook: Ideas & Activities for Building Self Esteem. LC 79-88300. 1979. softbound 16.00 (ISBN 0-918834-09-0). Growth Assoc.
Elkins, Dov Peretz. Teaching People to Love Themselves: A Leader's Handbook of Theory & Technique for Self-Esteem & Affirmation Training. 2nd rev. ed. LC 78-61670. 1978. softbound 16.00 (ISBN 0-918834-06-6). Growth Assoc.
Elkins, Garland, jt. ed. see Warren, Thomas B.
Elkins, Hervey. Fifteen Years in the Senior Order of Shakers: A Narration of Facts, Concerning That Singular People. LC 72-2984. Repr. of 1853 ed. 16.00 (ISBN 0-404-10746-X). AMS Pr.
Elkins, Jerry W. Ransom from a Poet. LC 81-50913. 116p. 1981. 7.95 (ISBN 0-938232-01-0); pap. 5.95 (ISBN 0-938232-02-9). Winston-Derek.
Elkins, Michael. Forged in Fury. 256p. 1985. Repr. of 1971 ed. 10.95 (ISBN 0-86188-098-6, Pub. by Piatkus Bks). Interbook.
Elkins, Norman. Weather & Bird Behaviour. (Illus.). 320p. 1983. 32.50 (ISBN 0-85661-035-6, Pub. by T & A D Poyser England). Buteo.
Elkins, Patricia. Weekday Early Education: Art Idea Book. LC 77-87252. (Illus.). 1978. spiral bdg 8.50 (ISBN 0-8054-4919-1, 4249-19). Broadman.
Elkins, Phillip W. Church Sponsored Missions. 1974. pap. 3.00 (ISBN 0-88027-003-9). Firm Foun Pub.
Elkins, R., jt. ed. see Albertini, A.
Elkins, Richard E. Major Grammatical Patterns of Western Bukidnon Manobo. (Publications in Linguistics & Related Fields Ser.: No. 26). 76p. 1970. microfiche only 1.93 (ISBN 0-88312-486-6). Summer Inst Ling.
--Manobo-English Dictionary. LC 68-63364. (Oceanic Linguistics Special Publications: No. 3). 376p. (Manobo & Eng.). 1968. pap. text ed. 10.00x (ISBN 0-87022-225-2). UH Pr.
Elkins, Stanley M. Slavery: A Problem in American Institutional & Intellectual Life. 3rd ed. LC 76-615. 1976. 25.00x (ISBN 0-226-20476-6); pap. text ed. 9.50x (ISBN 0-226-20477-4). U of Chicago Pr.
Elkins, Valmai H. The Rights of the Pregnant Parent. rev. ed. 1985. pap. 9.95 (ISBN 0-8052-0795-3). Schocken.
Elkins, W. F. Black Power in the Caribbean. 1976. lib. bdg. 69.95 (ISBN 0-87700-234-7). Revisionist Pr.
--Street Preachers, Faith Healers & Herb Doctors in Jamaica, 1890-1925. (Caribbean Studies Ser). 1976. lib. bdg. 69.95 (ISBN 0-87700-241-X). Revisionist Pr.
Elkins, William R., et al, eds. Literary Reflections. 4th ed. (Illus.). 544p. 1982. pap. 19.95x (ISBN 0-07-019232-4). McGraw.
Elkinton, Amelie, jt. auth. see Woolfenden, John.
Elkinton, Russell J. & Clark, Robert A. The Quaker Heritage in Medicine. (Illus.). 1978. pap. 3.95 (ISBN 0-910286-68-X). Boxwood.
Elkiss, T. H. The Quest for an African Eldorado: Sofala, Southern Zambezia & the Portuguese, 1500-1865. (Illus.). 124p. 1981. write for info. (ISBN 0-918456-41-X). Crossroads MA.
--The Quest for an African Eldorado: Sofala, Southern Zambezia & the Portuguese, 1500-1865. 120p. 1981. 12.00 (ISBN 0-918456-41-X). African Studies Assn.
Elkman, Richard, jt. auth. see National Association of Home Builders.
Elkoff, Marvin. After the Race. 1983. 14.95 (ISBN 0-671-47033-7). S&S.
Elkon, Juliette. Honey Cookbook. 1955. 11.95 (ISBN 0-394-40140-9). Knopf.
Elkon, Juliette & Ross, Elaine. Menus for Entertaining. 1960. 9.95 (ISBN 0-8038-4617-7). Hastings.
Elkonin, D. B., jt. auth. see Zaporozhets, A. V.
El Kordi, Mohamed. Bayeaux Aux XVIIe Siecles: Contribution a L'histoire Urbaine De la France. (Civilisations & Societes: No. 17). (Illus.). 1970. pap. 21.60x (ISBN 0-686-21264-9). Mouton.
Elkouri, Edna A., jt. auth. see Elkouri, Frank.
Elkouri, Frank & Elkouri, Edna A. How Arbitration Works. 3rd ed. LC 72-95857. 845p. 1973. 30.00 (ISBN 0-87179-180-3). BNA.
--How Arbitration Works. 4th ed. 900p. 1985. text ed. 65.00 (ISBN 0-87179-470-5). BNA.
--Legal Status of Federal-Sector Arbitration: Supplement to Third Ed. of How Arbitration Works. 32p. 1980. 5.00 (ISBN 0-87179-331-8). BNA.
Elkow, J. D., jt. auth. see Stack, Herbert.
Elkowitz, Edward B. Geriatric Medicine for the Primary Care Practitioner. 1981. text ed. 26.95 (ISBN 0-8261-3230-8). Springer Pub.
Elkus, Leonore R., ed. see Innes, et al.
Ell, John. Chase a Tall Shadow. (Orig.). 1981. pap. 1.95 (ISBN 0-505-51655-1, Pub. by Tower Bks). Dorchester Pub Co.
--Chase a Tall Shadow. 240p. 1985. pap. 2.25 (ISBN 0-8439-2264-8, Leisure Bks). Dorchester Pub Co.
Ell, P. J. & Walton, S. Radionuclide Ventricular Function Studies: Correlation with ECG, Echo & X-ray Data. 1982. text ed. 99.50 (ISBN 90-247-2639-5, Pub. by Martinus Nijhoff Netherlands). Kluwer Academic.
Ell, P. J. & Williams, E. S. Nuclear Medicine. (Illus.). 296p. 1981. text ed. 39.50 (ISBN 0-632-00682-X, B 1564-X). Mosby.
Ell, P. J. & Holman, B. L., eds. Computed Emission Tomography. (Illus.). 1982. 85.00x (ISBN 0-19-261347-2). Oxford U Pr.
Ell, Peter J., et al. Atlas of Computerized Emission Tomography. (Illus.). 288p. 1980. text ed. 115.00x (ISBN 0-443-02228-3). Churchill.
Ella Blanche. Finding Voice. (Illus.). 101p. 1979. pap. 6.00 (ISBN 0-9601542-3-X). Ivy Hill.
--Homeland. (Illus.). 44p. (Orig.). 1980. softcover 3.00 (ISBN 0-9601542-2-1). Ivy Hill.
--The Other Me. 79p. (Orig.). 1979. pap. 1.50 (ISBN 0-9601542-0-5). Ivy Hill.
--Sidereality. (Illus.). 240p. (Orig.). 1980. pap. 6.00 (ISBN 0-9601542-4-8). Ivy Hill.
Ellacombe, H. T., jt. ed. see Hale, William H.
Ellacombe, Henry. In a Gloucestershire Garden. 194p. 1984. 15.95 (ISBN 0-7126-0027-2, Pub. by Century Pub UK); pap. 11.95. Capability's.
Ellacombe, Henry N. Plant-Lore & Garden-Craft of Shakespeare. 2nd ed. LC 76-166018. Repr. of 1884 ed. 31.00 (ISBN 0-404-02277-4). AMS Pr.
--Shakespeare As an Angler. LC 76-166018. Repr. of 1883 ed. 11.50 (ISBN 0-404-02278-2). AMS Pr.
Ellacuria, Ignacio. Freedom Made Flesh: The Mission of Christ & His Church. Drury, John, tr. from Span. LC 75-29758. Orig. Title: Teolgica Political. 246p. (Orig.). 1976. 8.95x (ISBN 0-88344-140-3). Orbis Bks.
Ellam, J. B. Buddhism & Lamaism. 1984. pap. 5.95 (ISBN 0-916411-79-6, Oriental Classics). Holmes Pub.
Ellam, J. E. The Religion of Tibet: Study of Lamaism. 59.95 (ISBN 0-8490-0940-5). Gordon Pr.
--Swaraj: The Problem of India. xiii, 288p. 1984. Repr. of 1930 ed. text ed. 40.00x (ISBN 0-86590-328-X, Pub by B R Publishing Corp). Apt Bks.
Ellam, Patrick. Yacht Cruising. (Illus.). 1983. 19.50 (ISBN 0-393-03280-9). Norton.
Ellan, S. E. see Ovennell, Marjorie & Ovennell, C. H.
Ellard, G. Ordination Anointings in the Western Church Before 1000 A. D. (Med Acad of Amer Pubns). 1932. 18.00 (ISBN 0-527-01688-8). Kraus Repr.
Ellard, Gerald. Master Alcuin, Liturgist. LC 56-8943. (Jesuit Studies). 1956. 2.95 (ISBN 0-8294-0027-3). Loyola.
Ellard, Palmer T. The Wonder of His Love. 26p. 1985. 5.95 (ISBN 0-533-06379-5). Vantage.
Ellberg, John. Tales of a Rambler. LC 70-110185. (Short Story Index Reprint Ser.: Vol. 1). 1938. 19.00 (ISBN 0-8369-3336-2). Ayer Co Pubs.
Elle Magazine. The Elle Cookbook. (Illus.). 192p. 1984. pap. 12.95 (ISBN 0-7181-2403-0, Pub. by Michael Joseph). Merrimack Pub Cir.
Elle Magazine Staff. The Elle Knitting Book. (Illus.). 128p. 1984. 19.95 (ISBN 0-684-18219-X, ScribT). Scribner.
Ellebaut. Anticlaudien: A Thirteenth Century Adaptation of the Anticlaudianus of Alain De Lille. Creighton, Andrew J., ed. LC 72-94174. (Catholic University of America Studies in Romance Languages & Literatures Ser: No. 27). (Fr). 1969. Repr. of 1944 ed. 24.00 (ISBN 0-404-50327-6). Ams Pr.
Ellebracht, Mary P. Easter Passage: The RCIA Experience. 204p. 1983. pap. 11.95 (ISBN 0-86683-693-4). Winston Pr.
Elledge, Jim. James Dickey: A Bibliography, Nineteen Forty-Seven to Nineteen Seventy-Four. LC 79-10405. (Author Bibliographies Ser.: No. 40). 306p. 1979. 22.50 (ISBN 0-8108-1218-5). Scarecrow.
Elledge, Paul W. & Hoffman, Richard L. Romantic & Victorian: Studies in Memory of William H. Marshall. LC 79-124099. 366p. 1971. 27.50 (ISBN 0-8386-7742-8). Fairleigh Dickinson.
Elledge, Scott. E. B. White: A Biography. LC 83-4032. (Illus.). 348p. 1984. 22.50 (ISBN 0-393-01771-0). Norton.
Elledge, Scott, ed. see Hardy, Thomas.
Elledge, Scott, ed. see Milton, John.
Elledge, W. Paul. Byron & the Dynamics of Metaphor. LC 68-23795. 1968. 9.95x (ISBN 0-8265-1116-3). Vanderbilt U Pr.
Ellefson, Paul V. & Stone, Robert N. U. S. Wood-Based Industry: Industrial Organization & Performance. LC 84-8278. 508p. 1984. 43.95 (ISBN 0-03-063698-1). Praeger.
Ellegard, Alvar. Who Was Junius? LC 78-12218. 1979. Repr. of 1962 ed. lib. bdg. 19.75x (ISBN 0-313-21114-0, ELWJ). Greenwood.
Ellehauge, Martin. English Restoration Drama. LC 74-22294. 1974. Repr. of 1933 ed. lib. bdg. 35.00 (ISBN 0-8414-3931-1). Folcroft.
--English Restoration Drama. 322p. 1980. Repr. of 1933 ed. lib. bdg. 37.50 (ISBN 0-8482-0722-X). Norwood Edns.
--Striking Figures Among Modern English Dramatists. LC 72-195909. 1931. lib. bdg. 18.50 (ISBN 0-8414-3895-1). Folcroft.
Elleman, Barbara. Popular Reading for Children: A Collection of the Booklist Columns. 60p. 1981. pap. 5.00x (ISBN 0-8389-0322-3). ALA.
Elleman, Barbara, ed. Children's Books of International Interest. 3rd ed. LC 84-20336. 102p. 1985. pap. text ed. 7.50x (ISBN 0-8389-3314-9). ALA.
Ellen, Bette. The Adventures of Bernard & Morty. LC 20-888. 80p. (gr. 1 up). 1981. 7.95 (ISBN 0-938066-00-5). Rainville Rose.
Ellen Davis. Physical Therapy in Leprosy for Paramedicals. 235p. 1981. free. Am Leprosy Mission.
Ellen, Roy. Environment, Subsistence & System. LC 81-18035. (Themes in the Social Sciences Ser.). (Illus.). 340p. 1982. 44.50 (ISBN 0-521-24458-7); pap. 14.95 (ISBN 0-521-28703-0). Cambridge U Pr.
Ellen, Roy F. A Guide to the General Conduct of Ethnographic Research. (Research Methods Social Anthropology Ser.: No. 1). 1984. 49.50 (ISBN 0-12-237180-1). Acad Pr.
Ellen, Roy F. & Reason, David, eds. Classifications in Their Social Context. (Language, Thought & Culture Ser.). 1979. 47.00 (ISBN 0-12-237160-7). Acad Pr.
Ellenberg, H., et al, eds. Progress in Botany, Vol. 39. LC 33-15850. (Illus.). 1977. 62.00 (ISBN 0-387-08501-7). Springer-Verlag.
Ellenberg, Jonas H., jt. ed. see Nelson, Karin B.
Ellenberg, Max & Rifkin, Harold. Diabetes Mellitus: Theory & Practice. 3rd ed. 1983. 99.00 (ISBN 0-87488-606-6). Med Exam.
Ellenberger, Carl, Jr. Perimetry: Principles, Technique, & Interpretation. 128p. 1980. text ed. 21.00 (ISBN 0-89004-504-6). Raven.
Ellenberger, D. Fred. History of the Basuto, Ancient & Modern. MacGregor, James C., ed. LC 74-78764. (Illus.). Repr. of 1912 ed. cancelled (ISBN 0-8371-1389-X, Pub. by Negro U Pr). Greenwood.
Ellenberger, Henri F. The Discovery of the Unconscious: The History & Evolution of Dynamic Psychiatry. LC 79-94287. (Illus.). 952p. 1981. pap. 19.95x (ISBN 0-465-01673-1, TB-5091). Basic.
--Discovery of the Unconscious: The History & Evolution of Dynamic Psychiatry. LC 79-94287. (Illus.). 1970. 26.50x (ISBN 0-465-01672-3). Basic.
Ellenberger, J. S. & Mahar, Ellen P., eds. Legislative History of the Securities Act of 1933 & Securities Exchange Act of 1934, 11 vols. 1973. Set. 350.00x (ISBN 0-8377-0802-8); microfilm avail. Rothman.
Ellenberger, W., et al. Atlas of Animal Anatomy for Artists. rev. ed. Brown, Lewis S., ed. Weinbaum, Helen, tr. (Illus.). 192p. (YA) (gr. 9-12). 1956. pap. 6.95 (ISBN 0-486-20082-5). Dover.
--An Atlas of Animal Anatomy for Artists. 2nd rev. & enl. ed. Brown, Lewis S., ed. (Illus.). 16.25 (ISBN 0-8446-2029-7). Peter Smith.
Ellenbogen, Abraham. Letter Perfect: A Business Person's Guide to More Effective Correspondence. (Illus.). 1978. pap. 4.95 (ISBN 0-02-079940-3, Collier). Macmillan.
Ellenbogen, Eileen, tr. see Simenon, Georges.
Ellenbogen, Hellene, tr. see Baumann, Bommi.
Ellenbogen, Leon. Controversies in Nutrition. (Contemporary Issues in Clinical Nutrition Ser.: Vol. 2). (Illus.). 224p. 1981. text ed. 22.00 (ISBN 0-443-08127-1). Churchill.
Ellenbogen, Rudolph, jt. ed. see Lohf, Kenneth A.
Ellenbrook, Edward C. Abstract Society. (Illus.). 64p. (Orig.). 1985. pap. 3.25 (ISBN 0-941634-02-7). In Valley Wichitas.
--Outdoor & Trail Guide to the Wichita Mountains of Southwest Oklahoma. 2nd ed ed. LC 83-140822. (Illus.). 108p. 1984. pap. 6.50 (ISBN 0-941634-01-9). In Valley Wichitas.
Ellenburg, M. Kelly. Effanbee, the Dolls with the Golden Hearts. new ed. 200p. 1973. 14.95 (ISBN 0-913914-10-X). Trojan Pr.
Ellenburg, Stephen. Rousseau's Political Philosophy: An Interpretation from Within. LC 75-30481. 344p. 1976. 29.95x (ISBN 0-8014-0960-8). Cornell U Pr.
Ellenby, Jean. The Medieval Household. (Wingate Ser.). 5.50 (ISBN 0-317-30750-9); pap. 2.50 (ISBN 0-317-30751-7). Cambridge U Pr.
--The Tudor Household. (Wingate Ser.). 5.50 (ISBN 0-317-30754-1); pap. 2.50 (ISBN 0-317-30755-X). Cambridge U Pr.
Ellendorf, F. & Koch, E., eds. Early Pregnancy Factors. (Reproductive & Perinatal Medicine Ser.: No. I). 1985. 35.00 (ISBN 0-916859-07-X). Perinatology.
Ellendorf, F., et al, eds. Physiology & Control of Parturition in Domestic Animals. LC 79-14408. (Developments in Animal & Veterinary Sciences Ser.: Vol. 5). 348p. 1979. 81.00 (ISBN 0-444-41808-3). Elsevier.
Ellens, J. Harold. God's Grace & Human Health. 1982. pap. 8.75 (ISBN 0-687-15326-3). Abingdon.
Ellenshaw, Peter, illus. Peter Ellenshaw: Selected Works, 1929-1983. LC 83-13358. (Contemporary Realists Ser.). (Illus.). 72p. 1983. pap. 11.50x (ISBN 0-913060-21-6). Norton Art.
Ellenson, Ann. Human Relations. 2nd ed. (Illus.). 352p. 1982. text ed. 25.95 (ISBN 0-13-445650-5). P-H.
Ellenthal, Ira. Selling Smart: How the Magazine Pros Sell Advertising. Folio Editors, ed. 1982. 49.95 (ISBN 0-918110-06-8). Folio.
Ellentuck, Albert B. Year End Tax Planning Manual, 1984. 1984. Annual. 56.00 (ISBN 0-88712-213-2). Warren.
Eller, Buddy. U. S. A. & the Olympics: 1984. May, Frank H., ed. (Illus.). 256p. 1983. pap. text ed. 3.95 (ISBN 0-942894-03-0). Strode Comm.
Eller, Buddy & Middleton, Gene. The Amazing Braves: America's Team. (Illus.). 256p. (Orig.). 1982. pap. 3.95 (ISBN 0-942894-00-6). Strode Comm.
Eller, Clyde H., jt. auth. see Swanson, Elizabeth E.
Eller, David, ed. see Tengbom, Mildred.
Eller, Imeldia. We're in the Army Now. 1982. pap. 2.95 (ISBN 0-8423-7862-6). Tyndale.
Eller, John. Rage of Heaven: A Charlie Rope Mystery. 160p. 1982. 10.95 (ISBN 0-312-66246-7). St Martin.
Eller, Meredith F. The Beginnings of the Christian Religion: A Guide to the History & Literature of Judaism & Christianity. 1958. 14.95x (ISBN 0-8084-0392-3); pap. 11.95x (ISBN 0-8084-0393-1). New Coll U Pr.
Eller, Ronald. Miners, Millhands, & Mountaineers: Industrialization of the Appalachian South, 1880-1930. LC 81-16020. (Twentieth Century America Ser.). (Illus.). 298p. 1982. 23.50x (ISBN 0-87049-340-X); pap. 12.50 (ISBN 0-87049-341-8). U of Tenn Pr.
Eller, Scott. Short Season. 144p. (Orig.). (gr. 4-6). 1985. pap. 2.25 (ISBN 0-590-33573-1, Apple Paperbacks). Scholastic Inc.
Eller, Vernard. Cleaning up the Christian Vocabulary. 1976. pap. 2.95 (ISBN 0-87178-153-0). Brethren.
--In Place of Sacraments. 144p. (Orig.). 1972. pap. 2.95 (ISBN 0-8028-1476-X). Brethren.
--The Language of Canaan & the Grammar of Feminism: An Exercise in Wittgensteinian Analysis. 64p. 1982. pap. 2.95 (ISBN 0-8028-1902-8). Eerdmans.
--The Mad Morality. 80p. pap. 3.79 (ISBN 0-687-22899-9). Brethren.
--The Most Revealing Book of the Bible: Making Sense Out of Revelation. 1974. pap. 4.95 (ISBN 0-8028-1572-3). Eerdmans.
--A Pearl of Christian Counsel for the Brokenhearted. LC 82-20028. 152p. (Orig.). 1983. lib. bdg. 21.50 (ISBN 0-8191-2850-3); pap. text ed. 9.25 (ISBN 0-8191-2851-1). U Pr of Amer.
--The Sex Manual for Puritans. 78p. text ed. 3.00 (ISBN 0-687-38309-9). Brethren.
--Towering Babble: God's People Without God's Word. LC 83-4621. (Illus.). 192p. (Orig.). 1983. pap. 7.95 (ISBN 0-87178-855-1). Brethren.
--War & Peace. LC 80-26280. 232p. 1981. pap. 8.95 (ISBN 0-8361-1947-9). Herald Hse.
--War & Peace from Genesis to Revelation. LC 80-26280. (Christian Peace Shelf Ser.). 232p. 1981. pap. 9.95 (ISBN 0-8361-1947-9). Herald Pr.
Eller, Vernard, ed. see Blumhardt, Johann C. & Blumhardt, Christoph F.
Eller, W. Ibsen in Germany. 59.95 (ISBN 0-8490-0381-4). Gordon Pr.
Ellerbach, Richard. Tax Reduction Strategies for Small Business: Planning Techniques for Wealth Accumlation in the Eighties. (Illus.). 145p. 1982. 17.95 (ISBN 0-13-885228-6); pap. 8.95 (ISBN 0-13-885210-3). P-H.
Ellerbe, Suellyn. Fluid & Blood Component Therapy in the Critically Ill & Injured. (Contemporary Issues in Critical Care Nursing: Vol. 1). (Illus.). 224p. 1981. lib. bdg. 20.00 (ISBN 0-443-08129-8). Churchill.
Ellerbusch, Fred, jt. auth. see Cheremisinoff, Paul N.
Ellerby, Leona. King Tut's Game Board. LC 79-91279. (Adult & Young Adult Bks.). (gr. 5 up). 1980. 8.95 (ISBN 0-8225-0765-X). Lerner Pubns.
Ellerman, David P. Economics, Accounting, & Property Theory. LC 82-47648. 224p. 1982. 29.50x (ISBN 0-669-05552-2). Lexington Bks.
Ellershaw, Derek & Schofield, Peter. The Complete Commodore 64 BASIC Course. 256p. 1984. pap. 24.95 (ISBN 0-86161-175-6). Melbourne Hse.
Ellershaw, Henry. Keats Poetry & Prose: With Essays by Charles Lamb, Leigh Hunt, Robert Bridges, & Others. 1922. Repr. 20.00 (ISBN 0-8274-2645-3). R West.

Ellersick, F. W. see Cook, C. E., et al.

Ellerstein, Norman S. Child Abuse & Neglect: A Medical Reference. LC 81-2978. 355p. 1981. 45.00 (ISBN 0-471-05877-7, Pub. by Wiley Med). Wiley.

Ellert & Ellert. German A, 5 bks. (gr. 8-12). 1972. pap. text ed. 7.00 each (ISBN 0-686-57754-X). Learning Line.

--German B, 3 bks. (gr. 8-12). 1972. pap. text ed. 7.00 each (ISBN 0-8449-1423-1). Learning Line.

Ellery, Eloise. Brissot de Warville. 1915. 12.50x (ISBN 0-686-17391-0). R S Barnes.

--Brissot de Warville: A Study in the History of the French Revolution. LC 75-109919. Repr. of 1915 ed. 12.50 (ISBN 0-404-02279-0). AMS Pr.

--Brissot de Warville: A Study in the History of the French Revolution. LC 71-130601. (Research & Source Works: No. 536). 1970. Repr. of 1915 ed. 20.50 (ISBN 0-8337-1032-X). B Franklin.

Ellery Queen. The Chinese Orange Mystery. 300p. 1976. lib. bdg. 16.95x (ISBN 0-89966-153-X). Buccaneer Bks.

--Cop Out. Bd. with Last Woman in His Life. 1982. pap. 2.25 (ISBN 0-451-11562-7, AE1562, Sig). NAL.

--The Dutch Shoe Mystery. 305p. 1976. lib. bdg. 16.75x (ISBN 0-89966-149-1). Buccaneer Bks.

--The Egyptian Cross Mystery. 334p. 1976. lib. bdg. 16.95x (ISBN 0-89966-150-5). Buccaneer Bks.

--The French Powder Mystery. 316p. 1976. lib. bdg. 16.95x (ISBN 0-89966-148-3). Buccaneer Bks.

--The Greek Coffin Mystery. 370p. 1976. lib. bdg. 17.95x (ISBN 0-89966-151-3). Buccaneer Bks.

--The Roman Hat Mystery. 325p. 1976. lib. bdg. 16.95x (ISBN 0-89966-147-5). Buccaneer Bks.

--The Siamese Twin Mystery. 360p. 1980. lib. bdg. 16.95x (ISBN 0-89966-145-9). Buccaneer Bks.

--The Spanish Cape Mystery. 354p. 1976. lib. bdg. 17.95x (ISBN 0-89966-146-7). Buccaneer Bks.

Elles, Gertrude L. & Wood, Ethel M. British Graptolites. 1901-1918. Set. pap. 72.00 (ISBN 0-384-14155-2). Johnson Repr.

Elles, James & Farnell, John. In search of a Common Fisheries Policy. LC 83-16491. 225p. 1984. text ed. 33.95x (ISBN 0-566-00693-6). Gower Pub Co.

Elles, Neil. Community Law Through the Cases. 1973. 18.50 (ISBN 0-685-32576-8). Bender.

Ellesmere, Francis E. Egerton Papers. 1840. 51.00 (ISBN 0-384-14165-X). Johnson Repr.

Ellestad, Myrvin H. Stress Testing: Principles & Practice. 3rd ed. (Illus.). 540p. 1985. text ed. 45.00 (ISBN 0-8036-3112-X). Davis Co.

Ellet, Charles. Mississippi & Ohio Rivers, Containing Plans for the Protection of the Delta from Inundation & Investigations. LC 70-125738. (American Environmental Studies). 1970. Repr. of 1853 ed. 23.50 (ISBN 0-405-02663-3). Ayer Co Pubs.

Ellet, Charles, Jr. Essay on the Laws of Trade. LC 65-26363. Repr. of 1839 ed. 35.00x (ISBN 0-678-00202-9). Kelley.

Ellet, Elizabeth. Women of the American Revolution. LC 68-31269. (American History & Americana Ser., No. 47). 1969. lib. bdg. 99.95x (ISBN 0-8383-0197-5). Haskell.

--The Women of the American Revolution, Vol. I. 348p. 1980. Repr. of 1848 ed. 18.00 (ISBN 0-87928-106-5). Corner Hse.

--The Women of the American Revolution, Vol. II. 312p. 1980. Repr. of 1848 ed. 18.00 (ISBN 0-87928-107-3). Corner Hse.

--The Women of the American Revolution, Vol. III. 396p. 1980. Repr. of 1850 ed. 18.00 (ISBN 0-87928-108-1). Corner Hse.

Ellet, Elizabeth F. The Court Circles of the Republic, or the Beauties & Celebrities of the Nation. facsimile ed. LC 75-1841. (Leisure Class in America Ser.). (Illus.). 1975. Repr. of 1869 ed. 38.50x (ISBN 0-405-06910-3). Ayer Co Pubs.

--The Eminent & Heroic Women of America. LC 74-3945. (Women in America Ser). (Illus.). 884p. 1974. Repr. of 1873 ed. 54.00x (ISBN 0-405-06091-2). Ayer Co Pubs.

--The Pioneer Women of the West. LC 72-13219. (Essay Index Reprint Ser.). Repr. of 1852 ed. 22.50 (ISBN 0-8369-8157-X). Ayer Co Pubs.

--The Pioneer Women of the West. 1979. Repr. of 1879 ed. lib. bdg. 45.00 (ISBN 0-89341-325-9). Longwood Pub Group.

--The Queens of American Society. text ed. 20.00 (ISBN 0-8369-8158-8, 8298). Ayer Co Pubs.

Ellett, Katherine T. Young John Tyler. (Illus.). 1976. 4.75 (ISBN 0-685-65624-1). Dietz.

Elley, Derek. The Epic Film: Myth & History. (Cinema & Society Ser.). (Illus.). 207p. 1984. 26.95 (ISBN 0-7100-9656-9); pap. 12.95 (ISBN 0-7100-9993-2). Routledge & Kegan.

Elley, W. B, et al, eds. The Role of Grammar in a Secondary School Curriculum. 109p. 1979. 7.00 (ISBN 0-317-35311-X, 41943); members 5.00 (ISBN 0-317-35312-8). NCTE.

Ellfeldt, L. This Is Ballroom Dance. (Ballroom Dance Ser.). 1985. lib. bdg. 79.00 (ISBN 0-87700-825-6). Revisionist Pr.

Ellfeldt, Lois. Primer for Choreographers. LC 67-20074. (Illus.). 121p. 1967. pap. 7.95 (ISBN 0-87484-192-5). Mayfield Pub.

Ellfeldt, Lois & Lowman, Charles L. Exercises for the Mature Adult. (Illus.). 120p. 1973. pap. 9.75x spiral (ISBN 0-398-02750-1). C C Thomas.

Ellfort, William, et al, eds. Proceedings: Papers from the 21st Regional Meeting, Vol. I. 1985. pap. 9.00 (ISBN 0-914203-23-1). Chicago Ling.

Elliadi, M. N. Crete, Past & Present. 1977. lib. bdg. 59.95 (ISBN 0-8490-1683-5). Gordon Pr.

Ellickson, Phyllis L., jt. auth. see National Institute of Justice.

Ellickson, Robert C. & Tarlock, A. Dan. Land Use Controls. 1239p. 1981. 31.00 (ISBN 0-316-23299-8). Little.

--Land Use Controls: 1984 Supplement. LC 80-84029. 150p. 1984. pap. 8.50 (ISBN 0-316-23300-5). Little.

Ellicott, Andrew. The Journal of Andrew Ellicott. Cohen, I. Bernard, ed. LC 79-7960. (Three Centuries of Science in America Ser.). (Illus.). 1980. Repr. of 1803 ed. lib. bdg. 39.00x (ISBN 0-405-12541-0). Ayer Co Pubs.

Ellicott, Charles J. Ellicott's Bible Commentary. 1248p. 1981. 49.00x (ISBN 0-7208-0225-3, Pub. by BBC Pubns). State Mutual Bk.

Ellict, George R. Dramatic Providence in Macbeth: A Study of Shakespeare's Tragic Theme of Humanity & Grace, with a Supplementary Essay on King Lear. LC 70-90501. Repr. of 1960 ed. lib. bdg. 27.50x (ISBN 0-8371-3091-3, ELMA). Greenwood.

Elliff, John T. The Reform of the FBI Intelligence Activities. LC 78-70290. 1979. 24.50 (ISBN 0-691-07607-3). Princeton U Pr.

Elliff, Mary. Some Relationships Between Supply & Demand for Newly Trained Teachers: A Survey of the Situation in a Selected Representative State, Missouri. LC 76-176745. (Columbia University. Teachers College. Contributions to Education: No. 654). Repr. of 1935 ed. 22.50 (ISBN 0-404-55654-X). AMS Pr.

Elliff, Thomas D. Praying for Others. LC 79-52341. 1979. pap. 3.50 (ISBN 0-8054-5273-7). Broadman.

Ellig, Bruce R. Executive Compensation - A Total Pay Perspective. 343p. 1981. 32.50 (ISBN 0-07-019144-1). McGraw.

Elliger, K., ed. Twelve Prophets. (Biblia Hebraica Stuttgartensia Ser.). 96p. 1970. pap. 2.50x (ISBN 3-438-05210-5, 61261, Pub. by United Bible). Am Bible.

Elliger, Winfried. Die Darstellung der Landschaft in der griechischen Dichtung: Untersuchungen Zur Antiken Literatur und Geschichte, Vol.15. LC 73-93160. (Ger.). 1975. 82.00 (ISBN 3-11-004794-2). De Gruyter.

Ellik, Ron & Evans, Bill. Universes of E. E. Smith. LC 66-9092. (Illus.). 1966. pap. 5.00 (ISBN 0-911682-03-1). Advent.

Elliman, David, jt. auth. see Challis, James.

Ellin, Atanley. Very Old Money. 320p. 1985. pap. 3.50 (ISBN 0-449-20915-6, Crest). Fawcett.

Ellin, Stanley. The Dark Fantastic. LC 82-60902. 300p. 1983. 13.95 (ISBN 0-89296-059-0); ltd. 50.00 (ISBN 0-89296-060-4). Mysterious Pr.

--The Dark Fantastic. 320p. 1985. pap. 3.50 (ISBN 0-425-08081-1). Berkley Pub.

--Dreadful Summit. (Foul Play Press Ser.). 192p. pap. 4.95 (ISBN 0-914378-66-X). Countryman.

--The Eighth Circle. (Foul Play Press Ser.). 224p. 1981. pap. 4.95 (ISBN 0-914378-67-8). Countryman.

--The Key to Nicholas Street. Barzun, J. & Taylor, W. H., eds. LC 81-47378. (Crime Fiction 1950-1975 Ser.). 191p. 1983. lib. bdg. 18.00 (ISBN 0-8240-4981-0). Garland Pub.

--Mirror Mirror on the Wall. 179p. 1979. lib. bdg. 12.95x (ISBN 0-89966-083-5). Buccaneer Bks.

--The Other Side of the Hall. 13.95 (ISBN 0-317-28208-5, Pub. by Am Repr). Amereon Ltd.

--The Speciality of the House. 268p. Repr. of 1956 ed. lib. bdg. 15.95x (ISBN 0-88411-147-4). Amereon Ltd.

--The Specialty of the House & Other Stories: The Complete Mystery Tales, 1948-1978. LC 79-67149. 557p. 1979. 15.00 (ISBN 0-89296-049-3). Mysterious Pr.

--Very Old Money. 1985. 16.95 (ISBN 0-87795-627-8). Arbor Hse.

Elling, Christian. Rome-the Biography of Its Architecture from Bernini to Thorvaldsen. (Illus.). 1976. Repr. of 1975 ed. 100.00x (ISBN 0-89918-752-8, D-752). Vanous.

Elling, Ray, ed. Traditional & Modern Medical Systems. (Illus.). 100p. 1981. 16.25 (ISBN 0-08-028097-8). Pergamon.

Elling, Ray H. Cross-National Study of Health Systems. LC 79-65229. 253p. 1980. text ed. 15.95 (ISBN 0-87855-270-7). Transaction Bks.

--Socio-Cultural Influences on Health & Health Care. LC 77-85142. (International Health Perspectives Ser.: Vol. 4 of 5). 1977. pap. text ed. 6.00 (ISBN 0-8261-2494-1). Springer Pub.

Elling, Ray H., ed. Cross National Study of Health Systems by Countries & World Region, & Special Problems: A Guide to Information Sources. LC 79-26099. (Health Affairs Information Guide Ser.: Vol. 3). 1980. 60.00x (ISBN 0-8103-1453-3). Gale.

--Cross National Study of Health Systems: Concepts, Methods, & Data Sources: a Guide to Information Sources. LC 79-24028. (Health Affairs Information Guide Ser.: Vol. 2). 1980. 60.00x (ISBN 0-8103-1449-5). Gale.

--National Health Care: Issues & Problems in Socialized Medicine. (Controversy Ser.). 287p. 1971. 11.95x (ISBN 0-88311-204-3). Lieber-Atherton.

Elling, Ray H. & Sokolowska, M., eds. Medical Sociologists at Work. LC 76-6204. 347p. 1977. text ed. 14.95 (ISBN 0-87855-139-5). Transaction Bks.

Ellinger, A. G. & Stewart, T. H. A Post-War History of the Stock Market. 80p. 1984. 15.00 (ISBN 0-85941-153-2, Pub. by Woodhead-Faulkner). Longwood Pub Group.

Ellinger, Charles W. Synopsis of Complete Dentures. LC 74-23703. pap. 91.30 (ISBN 0-317-28606-4, 2055422). Bks Demand UMI.

Ellinger, Esther. Thomas Chatterton the Marvelous Boy. LC 74-13489. 1930. lib. bdg. 15.00 (ISBN 0-8414-3974-5). Folcroft.

Ellinger, Esther P. Southern War Poetry of the Civil War. 1970. Repr. of 1918 ed. 20.50 (ISBN 0-8337-1033-8). B Franklin.

--Thomas Chatterton: The Marvelous Boy. 75p. 1980. Repr. of 1930 ed. lib. bdg. 17.50 (ISBN 0-8492-4408-0). R West.

Ellinger, H. Automotive Systems Fuel Lubrication & Cooling. 1975. pap. 24.95 (ISBN 0-13-055269-0). P-H.

Ellinger, Herb. Automechanics. 3rd ed. (Illus.). 592p. 1983. text ed. 29.95 (ISBN 0-13-054767-0); wkbk. 10.95 (ISBN 0-13-054775-1). P-H.

Ellinger, Herbert. Automotive Electrical Systems 21E. 224p. 1985. pap. text ed. 21.95 (ISBN 0-13-054271-7). P-H.

Ellinger, Herbert E. Automotive Electrical Systems. 1975. 21.95 (ISBN 0-13-054262-8); pap. write for info. P-H.

--Automotive Engines: Theory & Servicing. 432p. 1981. text ed. 24.95 (ISBN 0-13-054999-1); 10.95 (ISBN 0-13-054890-1). P-H.

Ellinger, Herbert E. & Hathaway, Richard B. Automotive Suspension, Steering & Brakes. (Transportation & Technology Ser.). (Illus.). 1980. text ed. 24.95 (ISBN 0-13-054288-1). P-H.

Ellinger, Richard G. Color Structure & Design. 144p. 1980. pap. 9.95 (ISBN 0-442-23941-6). Van Nos Reinhold.

Ellingham, Mark & Fisher, John. Rough Guide to Spain. rev. ed. (The Routledge Rough Guide Ser.). (Illus.). 250p. (Orig.). 1985. pap. 9.95 (ISBN 0-7102-0344-6). Routledge & Kegan.

Ellingham, Mark, et al. Rough Guide to Greece. rev. ed. (Routledge Rough Guides Ser.). 320p. 1984. pap. 7.95 (ISBN 0-7102-0311-X). Routledge & Kegan.

--Rough Guide to Portugal. rev. ed. (Routledge Rough Guides Ser.). 224p. 1984. pap. 7.95 (ISBN 0-7102-0345-4). Routledge & Kegan.

Ellinghausen, Lynn. Kitchen Memories. 7.95 (ISBN 0-918544-71-8). Wimmer Bks.

Ellings, Richard. Embargoes & Sanctions in the Postwar Era: Lessons from American Foreign Policy. (WVSS Ser.). 200p. 1985. pap. 17.95x (ISBN 0-8133-0216-1). Westview.

Ellingsen, Mark. Doctrine & Word. LC 82-21311. 192p. 1983. pap. 9.95 (ISBN 0-8042-0533-7). John Knox.

Ellingson, Careth. Speaking of Children, Their Learning Abilities-Disabilities. LC 73-14256. (Illus.). 300p. 1975. 10.95i (ISBN 0-06-011178-X, HarpT). Har-Row.

Ellingson, Karl. Twenty-Five Hundred Mile Walk: An Oldtimer on the Pacific Crest Trail. (Illus.). 156p. 1982. pap. 4.95 (ISBN 0-931290-69-4). Alchemy Bks.

Ellingson, Marnie. Dolly Blanchard's Fortune. 192p. 1983. 11.95 (ISBN 0-8027-0728-9). Walker & Co.

--The Wicked Marquis. LC 81-71915. 200p. 1982. 11.95 (ISBN 0-8027-0707-6). Walker & Co.

--The Wicked Marquis. 192p. 1983. pap. 2.50 (ISBN 0-380-65821-6, 65821). Avon.

Ellingson, William A., jt. ed. see Cooper, Bernard R.

Ellingston, Jenefer. We Are the Mainstream. McKenna, Constance, ed. (Illus.). 16p. 1981. pap. 1.00 (ISBN 0-915365-02-2). Cath Free Choice.

Ellington, C. D. Complaint Handling for Resident Managers. 70p. 1981. pap. 7.00 (ISBN 0-86718-119-2); pap. 5.00 members. Natl Assn Home.

--Professional Apartmenteering. 348p. 1979. pap. 20.00 (ISBN 0-86718-086-2); pap. 7.50 members. Natl Assn Home.

Ellington, Duke. Great Music of Duke Ellington. pap. 9.95 (ISBN 0-486-20757-9). Dover.

--Music Is My Mistress. LC 75-31665. 1976. pap. 7.95 (ISBN 0-306-80033-0). Da Capo.

Ellington, George. The Women of New York: The Underworld of the Great City. LC 72-2600. (American Women Ser.: Images & Realities). 770p. 1972. Repr. of 1869 ed. 40.00 (ISBN 0-405-04456-9). Ayer Co Pubs.

Ellington, H. I., et al. Games & Simulations in Science Education. 180p. 1981. 27.50x (ISBN 0-89397-093-X). Nichols Pub.

Ellington, Henry. Producing Teaching Materials: A Practical Guide for Teachers & Trainers. 1985. 16.95 (ISBN 0-89397-212-6). Nichols Pub.

Ellington, Henry & Addinall, Eric. Case Studies in Game Design. 200p. 1984. 25.00 (ISBN 0-89397-167-7). Nichols Pub.

Ellington, Henry, jt. auth. see Addinall, Eric.

Ellington, Henry, jt. auth. see Percival, Fred.

Ellington, Henry, et al. A Handbook of Game Design. 150p. 1982. 25.00 (ISBN 0-89397-134-0). Nichols Pub.

Ellington, Howard W., ed. see O'Neil, Barbara T. & Foreman, George C.

Ellington, J. W., ed. see Kant, Immanuel.

Ellington, James W., tr. see Kant, Immanuel.

Ellington, Mark & McVeigh, Shaun. Rough Guide to Morocco. (The Routledge Rough Guides Ser.). 232p. (Orig.). 1985. pap. 9.95 (ISBN 0-7102-0153-2). Routledge & Kegan.

Ellington, Marnie. The Mistress of Langford Court. (Candlelight Regency Ser.: No. 700). (Orig.). pap. 1.75 (ISBN 0-440-15652-1). Dell.

Ellington, Mercer & Dance, Stanley. Duke Ellington in Person. 236p. 1979. pap. 5.95 (ISBN 0-306-80104-3). Da Capo.

Ellington, R. T., ed. Liquid Fuels from Coal. 1977. 42.50 (ISBN 0-12-237250-6). Acad Pr.

Ellington, R. T., jt. auth. see Weil, S. A.

Ellingworth, P. & Nida, E. A. Translator's Handbook on Paul's Letter to the Thessalonians. (Helps for Translators Ser.). 229p. Repr. of 1975 ed. soft cover 3.40x (ISBN 0-8267-0146-9, 08526, Pub. by United Bible). Am Bible.

Ellingworth, Paul & Hatton, Howard. A Translators Handbook on Paul's First Letter to the Corinthians. LC 85-1142. (Helps for Translators Ser.). viii, 352p. 1985. pap. 4.20x (ISBN 0-8267-0140-X). United Bible.

Ellingworth, Paul & Nida, Eugene A. A Translator's Handbook on the Letter to the Hebrews. LC 83-17947. (Helps for Translators Ser.). viii, 364p. 1983. softcover 4.10x (ISBN 0-8267-0150-7, 08782, Pub. by United Bible). Am Bible.

Ellins-Elmakiss, Esther. Catching on to American Idioms. LC 84-50703. (Illus.). 144p. 1984. pap. text ed. 5.95x (ISBN 0-472-08049-0). U of Mich Pr.

Ellinwood, DeWitt C., ed. Ethnicity & the Military in Asia. Enloe, Cynthia. LC 80-20324. 298p. 1980. text ed. 19.95 (ISBN 0-87855-387-8). Transaction Bk.

Ellinwood, Everett M., Jr. & Kilbey, M., eds. Cocaine & Other Stimulants. LC 76-47488. (Advances in Behavioral Biology Ser.: Vol. 21). 731p. 1977. 75.00x (ISBN 0-306-37921-X, Plenum Pr). Plenum Pub.

Ellinwood, L. & Porter, K. Bio-Biographical Index of Musicians in the United States of America since Colonial Times. LC 76-159677. (Music Ser). 1971. Repr. of 1956 ed. lib. bdg. 42.50 (ISBN 0-306-70183-9). Da Capo.

Ellinwood, L., ed. see Landino, Francesco.

Ellinwood, Leonard. History of American Church Music. LC 69-12683. (Music Reprint Ser.). 1970. Repr. of 1953 ed. lib. bdg. 27.50 (ISBN 0-306-71233-4). Da Capo.

Elliot. Kisses. signed edition o.p. 13.95x (ISBN 0-904461-41-6, Pub. by Ceolfrith Pr England). Intl Spec Bk.

Elliot, A. M., tr. see Vidali, Vittorio.

Elliot, Alfred M. Biology of Tetrahymena. LC 73-12911. 508p. 1973. 65.00 (ISBN 0-87933-013-9). Van Nos Reinhold.

Elliot, Alison J. Child Language. LC 80-41240. (Cambridge Textbooks in Linguistics). 180p. 1981. text ed. 37.95 (ISBN 0-521-22518-3); pap. text ed. 10.95 (ISBN 0-521-29556-4). Cambridge U Pr.

Elliot, Alistair. Talking Back. 64p. 1982. 12.50 (ISBN 0-436-14260-0, Pub. by Secker & Warburg UK). David & Charles.

Elliot, Allistair, tr. see Verlaine, Paul.

Elliot, B. J. Bismark: The Kaiser & Germany. (Modern Times Ser.). (Illus.). 164p. (Orig.). (YA) (gr. 9-12). 1972. pap. text ed. 4.25x (ISBN 0-582-20423-2). Longman.

--Western Europe after Hitler. (Modern Times Ser.). (Illus.). 162p. (Orig.). (gr. 9-12). 1968. pap. text ed. 4.75 (ISBN 0-582-20436-4). Longman.

Elliot, Betsy R. How to Help a Missionary. 32p. (Orig.). 1984. pap. 0.75 (ISBN 0-87784-069-5). Inter-Varsity.

Elliot, Bob & Goulding, Ray. From Approximately Coast to Coast...It's the Bob & Ray Show. (General Ser.). 1984. lib. bdg. 14.95 (ISBN 0-8161-3644-0, Large Print Bks). G K Hall.

Elliot, Brian, jt. ed. see Bechofer, Frank.

Elliot, Bruce. Great Secrets of the Master Magicians. (Illus.). 1962. pap. 1.50 (ISBN 0-02-028370-9, Collier). Macmillan.

Elliot, Bruce & Kilderry, Rob. The Art & Science of Tennis. 1983. text ed. 24.95 (ISBN 0-03-062501-7, CBS C). SCP.

Elliot, Carolyn M., jt. ed. see Kelly, Gail P.

Elliot, Charles N. Walt Whitman As Man, Poet, & Friend. LC 73-8682. Repr. of 1915 ed. lib. bdg. 25.00 (ISBN 0-8414-1908-6). Folcroft.

Elliot, Charles W. Winfield Scott: The Soldier & the Man. Kohn, Richard H., ed. LC 78-22379. (American Military Experience Ser.). (Illus.). 1979. Repr. of 1937 ed. lib. bdg. 57.50x (ISBN 0-405-11856-2). Ayer Co Pubs.

Elliot, Cheri, ed. Digest Book of Bowhunting. LC 79-84928. 96p. pap. 3.95 (ISBN 0-695-81317-X). DBI.

Elliot, Colleen M. & Morse, Everett D. Ancestors & Descendants of the Reverend Daniel Morse. (Illus.). 150p. 15.00 (ISBN 0-686-47802-9, BFH 3). Southern Hist Pr.

Elliot, Sumner L. Careful, He Might Hear You. 352p. 1984. pap. 3.95 (ISBN 0-671-50435-5). WSP.
Elliot, T. S. Old Possum's Book of Practical Cats. LC 39-33124. (Illus.). 1982. pap. 4.95 (ISBN --15-668568-X, Harv). HarBraceJ.
--On Poetry & Poets. LC 84-26862. 262p. 1985. pap. 8.95 (ISBN 0-571-08983-6). Faber & Faber.
Elliot, Thomas C. The Earliest Travelers on the Oregon Trail. 1975. pap. 3.00 (ISBN 0-87770-154-7). Ye Galleon.
Elliot, Virgil L. San Francisco Statistical Abstract. 1982 ed. 70p. (Orig.). pap. 9.95 (ISBN 0-9610700-0-5). Statistical Pr.
Elliot, W. Roger & Jones, David L. Encyclopedia of Australian Plants Suitable for Cultivation, Vol. 2. (Illus.). 517p. 59.95 (ISBN 0-85091-143-5). Intl Spec Bk.
Elliot, Wallace W. The History of San Bernardino & San Diego Counties. (Illus.). 204p. 18.00 (ISBN 0-318-17272-0); 3 copies or more 12.60 ea. Riverside Mus.
Elliot, Walter. Coins of Southern India. 159p. 1975. Repr. of 1886 ed. 12.50 (ISBN 0-89684-132-4, Pub. by Cosmo Pubns India). Orient Bk Dist.
Elliot, William I., ed. Wind & Pines. Branner, Noah S., tr. 250p. (Jap.). 75.00 (ISBN 0-918362-00-8). Image Gallery.
Elliot, William Y. & Hall, Hessel D., eds. British Commonwealth at War. facsimile ed. LC 70-134072. (Essay Index Reprint Ser). Repr. of 1943 ed. 27.50 (ISBN 0-8369-2106-2). Ayer Co Pubs.
Elliot-Binns, Christopher. Too Much Tenderness: An Autobiography of Childhood & Youth. 224p. 1983. 17.95 (ISBN 0-7100-9418-3). Routledge & Kegan.
Elliotson, John. John Elliotson on Mesmerism. Kaplan, Fred, ed. (Hypnosis & Altered States of Consciousness Ser.). 1982. Repr. of 1848 ed. lib. bdg. 42.50 (ISBN 0-306-76167-X). Da Capo.
--Numerous Cases of Surgical Operations Without Pain in the Mesmeric State. Bd. with Mesmerism in India; Philosophy of Sleep. (Contributions to the History of Psychology Ser., Vol. X, Pt. A: Orientations). 1978. Repr. of 1843 ed. 30.00 (ISBN 0-89093-159-3). U Pubns Amer.
Elliott. Comparative Economic Systems. 2nd ed. 1984. write for info. (ISBN 0-534-01313-9). Wadsworth Pub.
Elliott, jt. auth. see Stikeman.
Elliott, jt. auth. see Vanagunas.
Elliott, jt. ed. see Judson, Jonn.
Elliott, A. M., tr. see Carrillo, Santiago.
Elliott, Abdulla, tr. see Al-Arif, Ibn.
Elliott, Alan, ed. see Euripides.
Elliott, Alan C. The PC Programming Techniques: Creative BASIC Skills for IBM Personal Computers. (Illus.). 176p. 1984. pap. 14.95 (ISBN 0-89303-755-9). Brady Comm.
Elliott, Alan J. Chinese Spirit-Medium Cults in Singapore. 1981. Repr. of 1955 ed. 15.00 (ISBN 0-89986-347-7). Oriental Bk Store.
Elliott, Albert P. Fatalism in the Works of Thomas Hardy. LC 74-10791. 1972. lib. bdg. 17.50 (ISBN 0-8414-3950-8). Folcroft.
Elliott, Alfred M. & Sloat, Barbara F. Laboratory Guide for Zoology. 6th ed. 1979. pap. text ed. 15.95x (ISBN 0-8087-0522-9). Burgess.
Elliott, Alison G. The Vie de Saint Alexis in the Twelfth & Thirteenth Centuries. LC 83-17389. (Studies in the Romance Languages & Literatures: RLS No. 221). 207p. 1984. pap. 13.00 (ISBN 0-8078-9225-4). U of NC Pr.
Elliott, Andrew, et al. Trio 4. (Trio Poetry Ser.). 72p. (Orig.). 1985. pap. 5.95 (ISBN 0-85640-333-4, Pub. by Blackstaff Pr). Longwood Pub Group.
Elliott, Ann. Christian Folk Art: Crafts & Activities. (Illus.). 1979. pap. 4.95 (ISBN 0-8192-1250-4). Morehouse.
--Eyes to See God. (Illus.). 1977. pap. 6.95 (ISBN 0-8192-1225-3). Morehouse.
Elliott, Arthur E. Paraguay: Its Cultural Heritage, Social Conditions & Educational Problems. LC 70-176746. (Columbia University. Teachers College. Contributions to Education: No. 473). Repr. of 1931 ed. 22.50 (ISBN 0-404-55473-3). AMS Pr.
Elliott, Austin M. SBC's One Hundred & One Laws--& Perhaps More. 109p. 1984. 101.00 (ISBN 0-914285-00-9). Sm Busn Clinic.
Elliott, B. J. Hitler & Germany. (Modern Times Ser.). (Illus.). 176p. (Orig.). (gr. 9-12). 1980. pap. text ed. 4.75 (ISBN 0-582-20425-9). Longman.
Elliott, B. J., jt. auth. see Clarkson, G. P.
Elliott, Blanche B. Jersey: An Isle of Romance. (Illus.). 1979. Repr. of 1923 ed. lib. bdg. 30.00 (ISBN 0-8495-1333-2). Arden Lib.
Elliott, Bob & Goulding, Ray. From Approximately Coast to Coast...It's the Bob & Ray Show. LC 83-45069. (Illus.). 1983. 13.95 (ISBN 0-689-11395-1). Atheneum.
--From Approximately Coast to Coast...It's the Bob & Ray Show. (Nonfiction Ser.). 208p. 1985. pap. 5.95 (ISBN 0-14-007561-5). Penguin.
Elliott, Bob G. & Goulding, Ray. The New! Improved! Bob & Ray Book. (Illus.). 224p. 1985. 14.95 (ISBN 0-399-13085-3). Putnam Pub Group.
Elliott, Brad. Surf's Up! The Beach Boys on Record, 1961-1981. LC 81-80190. (Rock & Roll Reference Ser.: No. 6). 512p. 1981. individuals 24.50 (ISBN 0-87650-118-8); institutions 39.50. Pierian.
Elliott, Brian. Strawberry Shortcake & Baby Needs a Name. (Strawberry Shortcake Ser.). (Illus.). 40p. (ps-3). 1984. cancelled 5.95 (ISBN 0-910313-21-0). Parker Bro.
Elliott, Brian & McCrone, David. The City: Patterns of Domination & Conflict. LC 81-51614. 220p. 1982. 24.00 (ISBN 0-312-13984-5). St Martin.
Elliott, Brian, ed. The Jindyworobaks. (Portable Australian Authors Ser.). 1980. 30.00x (ISBN 0-7022-1296-2); pap. 12.95x (ISBN 0-7022-1297-0). U of Queensland Pr.
Elliott, Brian, tr. see Levy-Bruel, Lucien.
Elliott, Bruce. Village. 592p. 1982. pap. 3.50 (ISBN 0-380-79020-3, 79020-3). Avon.
Elliott, C. M. & Ockendon, J. R. Weak & Variational Methods for Free & Moving Boundary Problems. (Research Notes in Mathematics Ser.: No. 59). 220p. 1982. pap. text ed. 28.50 (ISBN 0-273-08503-4). Pitman Pub MA.
Elliott, Charles. The Bible & Slavery: In Which the Abrahamic & Mosaic Discipline is Considered. 17.25 (ISBN 0-8369-9167-2, 9042). Ayer Co Pubs.
--East Lake Country Club History: Home Course of Bobby Jones. 96p. 1984. 14.95 (ISBN 0-87797-092-0). Cherokee.
--Gone Fishin' 304p. 1985. 14.95 (ISBN 0-89783-036-9). Larlin Corp.
--Gone Huntin' 288p. 1985. 14.95 (ISBN 0-89783-037-7). Larlin Corp.
--Mr. Anonymous: Robert W. Woodruff of Coca-Cola. LC 82-61159. (Illus.). 312p. 1982. 14.95 (ISBN 0-87797-087-4). Cherokee.
--Sinfulness of American Slavery, 2 Vols. Tefft, Benjamin F., ed. LC 68-58055. Repr. of 1850 ed. Set. 33.00x (ISBN 0-8371-0407-6, ELS&). Greenwood.
--Turkey Hunting with Charlie Elliott. LC 82-72985. (Illus.). 288p. 1982. 14.95 (ISBN 0-87797-063-7). Cherokee.
Elliott, Charles, ed. Alexis Lichine's New Encyclopedia of Wines & Spirits. 4th ed. LC 85-40085. 752p. 1985. 40.00 (ISBN 0-394-54672-5). Knopf.
Elliott, Charles, ed. see Amos, William & Amos, Stephen.
Elliott, Charles, ed. see Brown, Lauren.
Elliott, Charles, ed. see Burton, Robert.
Elliott, Charles, ed. see McConnaughey, Bayard & McConnaughey, Evelyn.
Elliott, Charles, ed. see McMahon, James.
Elliott, Charles, ed. see Nathan, Andrew J.
Elliott, Charles, ed. see Niering, William A.
Elliott, Charles, ed. see Rosenfeld, Albert.
Elliott, Charles, ed. see Sutton, Ann & Sutton, Myron.
Elliott, Charles, ed. see Tanizaki, Junichiro.
Elliott, Charles, ed. see Whitney, Stephen.
Elliott, Charles B. Philippines to the End of the Commission Government: A Study in Tropical Democracy. LC 69-10088. 1969. Repr. of 1917 ed. lib. bdg. 24.50x (ISBN 0-8371-0406-8, ELPH). Greenwood.
Elliott, Charles H. Variation in the Achievements of Pupils: A Study of the Achievements of Pupils in the 5th & 7th Grades & in Classes of Different Sizes. LC 73-176747. (Columbia University. Teachers College. Contributions to Education: No. 72). Repr. of 1914 ed. 22.50 (ISBN 0-404-55072-X). AMS Pr.
Elliott, Cheri. Backpacker's Digest. 3rd ed. LC 72-97509. (Illus.). 1981. pap. 9.95 (ISBN 0-910676-21-6, 6536). DBI.
Elliott, Cheri, ed. Archer's Digest. 3rd ed. LC 77-148722. (Illus.). 288p. 1982. pap. 11.95 (ISBN 0-910676-40-2). DBI.
Elliott, Clarence O. A Guide To Data Processing. LC 80-85335. (Irwin Publications for Professional Development Ser.). pap. 52.50 (ISBN 0-317-08333-3, 2021652). Bks Demand UMI.
Elliott, Clark A. Biographical Dictionary of American Science: The Seventeenth Through the Nineteenth Centuries. LC 78-4292. 1979. lib. bdg. 60.50x (ISBN 0-313-20419-5, EAS/). Greenwood.
Elliott, Colleen M., jt. auth. see Alexander, Virginia.
Elliott, Colleen M., ed. The Keowee Courier: 1849-1851; 1857-1861; 1865-1871, Marriage & Death Notices. 210p. 1979. 17.50 (ISBN 0-89308-152-3). Southern Hist Pr.
Elliott, Colleen M. & Moore, John T., eds. Biographical Questionnaires of One Hundred & Fifty Prominent Tennesseans. 400p. 1982. 17.50 (ISBN 0-89308-222-8). Southern Hist Pr.
Elliott, Colleen M., jt. ed. see Moore, John T.
Elliott, Curtis M., jt. auth. see Vaughan, Emmett J.
Elliott, D. Integrated Circuit Mask Technology. 320p. 1984. 35.00 (ISBN 0-07-019261-8). McGraw.
Elliott, D. & Elliott, R. The Control of Technology. (Wykeham Science Ser.: No. 39). 260p. 1976. 8.70x (ISBN 0-8448-1166-1). Crane Russak Co.
Elliott, D. J. Integrated Circuit Fabrication Technology. 1982. 36.50 (ISBN 0-07-019238-3). McGraw.
Elliott, D. Mike, jt. ed. see Wilson, Jan.
Elliott, Dan. The Adventures of Ernie & Bert at the South Pole. LC 84-60187. (Sesame Street Mini-Storybooks). (Illus.). 32p. (ps-3). 1984. pap. 1.25 (ISBN 0-394-86299-6, Pub. by BYR). Random.
--Grover Goes to School. LC 81-15398. (Sesame Street Start-to-Read Bks.). (Illus.). 40p. (gr. 1-3). 1982. PLB 5.99 (ISBN 0-394-95176-X); pap. 3.95 (ISBN 0-394-85176-5). Random.
--Grover Learns to Read. LC 84-27692. (Sesame Street Start-To-Read Books). (Illus.). 40p. (ps-3). 1985. bds. 3.95 (ISBN 0-394-87498-6, BYR); PLB 4.99 (ISBN 0-394-97498-0). Random.
--Oscar's Rotten Birthday. LC 81-2398. (Sesame Street Start-to-Read Bks.). (Illus.). 40p. (gr. k-2). 1981. 3.95 (ISBN 0-394-84848-9); PLB 5.99 (ISBN 0-394-94848-3). Random.
--Two Wheels for Grover. LC 84-4732. (Sesame STreet Start-to-Read Bks.). (Illus.). 40p. (ps-3). 1984. 3.95 (ISBN 0-394-86586-3, Pub. by BYR); lib. bdg. 4.99 GLB (ISBN 0-394-96586-8). Random.
Elliott, Dave, jt. auth. see Wainwright, Hilary.
Elliott, David. Thailand: Origins of Military Rule. 190p. 1978. 20.00x (ISBN 0-905762-10-X, Pub. by Zed Pr England); pap. 7.95x (ISBN 0-905762-11-8, Pub. by Zed Pr England). Biblio Dist.
--Tradition & Renewal: Contemporary Art in the German Democratic Republic. (Illus.). 64p. 1985. pap. 12.50 (ISBN 0-87663-867-1). Universe.
Elliott, David S. Last Raid of the Daltons: Reliable Recital of the Battle with the Bandits at Coffeyville, Kansas. facsimile ed. LC 75-165629. (Select Bibliographies Reprint Ser). Repr. of 1892 ed. 10.00 (ISBN 0-8369-5936-1). Ayer Co Pubs.
Elliott, David W., ed. The Third Indochina Conflict. (Westview Replica Edition Ser.). 250p. 1981. pap. 25.00x (ISBN 0-89158-739-X). Westview.
Elliott, Dietlinde, tr. see Stegemann, Wolfgang.
Elliott, Donald. Alligators & Music. 1984. pap. 12.95 (ISBN 0-87645-093-1, Pub. by Gambit); pap. 8.95 (ISBN 0-87645-118-0, Pub. by Gambit). Harvard Common Pr.
--Frogs & Ballet. LC 78-19566. (Illus.). (gr. 1 up). 1979. smythe sewn 12.95 (ISBN 0-87645-099-0, Pub. by Gambit); pap. 8.95 (ISBN 0-87645-119-9). Harvard Common Pr.
--The St. Louis Fed's Monetarist Model: Whence it Came; How It Thrived, 1970-198 2. Bruchey, Stuart, ed. LC 84-45425. (American Economic History Ser.). 180p. 1985. lib. bdg. 25.00 (ISBN 0-8240-6668-5). Garland Pub.
Elliott, Donald & Arrowood, Clinton. Lambs Tales from Great Operas. LC 80-84719. (Illus.). 96p. 1981. 12.95 (ISBN 0-87645-110-5, Pub. by Gambit); pap. 8.95 (ISBN 0-87645-120-2). Harvard Common Pr.
Elliott, Donald & Arrowood, Clinton L. Alligators & Music. LC 76-1569. (Illus.). (gr. 1 up). 1976. 12.95 (ISBN 0-87645-093-1, H C Press Gambit); pap. 8.95 (ISBN 0-87645-118-0, H C Press Gambit). S&S.
Elliott, Doreen, jt. auth. see Butler, Barbara.
Elliott, Douglas. As You Recover. 32p. 1984. pap. 1.25 (ISBN 0-8010-3414-0). Baker Bk.
--Roots: An Underground Botany. LC 75-46234. (Illus.). 160p. 1976. pap. 7.95 (ISBN 0-85699-132-5). Chatham Pr.
Elliott, Douglas F. & Rao, K. Ramamohan. Fast Transforms: Algorithms, Analyses, Applications. LC 79-8852. (Computer Science & Applied Mathematical Ser.). 1983. 75.00 (ISBN 0-12-237080-5). Acad Pr.
Elliott, Drossoula V. & Elliott, Sloane. We Live in Greece. (Living Here Ser.). (Illus.). 64p. 1984. lib. bdg. 9.90 (ISBN 0-531-03795-9). Watts.
Elliott, E. N., ed. Cotton Is King & Pro-Slavery Arguments. LC 68-55884. Repr. of 1850 ed. 35.00x (ISBN 0-8371-4847-2, ELC/, Pub. by Negro U Pr). Greenwood.
--Cotton Is King, & Pro-Slavery Arguments. (Basic Afro-American Reprint Library). Repr. of 1860 ed. 40.00 (ISBN 0-384-14175-7). Johnson Repr.
Elliott, Ebenezer. The Poetical Works, 2 vols. 836p. Repr. of 1876 ed. 72.00x (ISBN 3-4870-5326-8). Adlers Foreign Bks.
Elliott, Edward C. Charters & Basic Laws of Selected American Universities & Colleges. LC 70-104261. vii, 640p. Repr. of 1934 ed. lib. bdg. 24.00x (ISBN 0-8371-3920-1, ELCL). Greenwood.
--Some Fiscal Aspects of Public Education in American Cities. LC 77-176748. (Columbia University. Teachers College. Contributions to Education: No. 6). Repr. of 1905 ed. 22.50 (ISBN 0-404-55006-1). AMS Pr.
Elliott, Edward C. & Chambers, Merritt M., eds. Charters & Basic Laws of Selected American Universities & Colleges. LC 70-108773. Repr. of 1934 ed. 21.00 (ISBN 0-404-00605-1). AMS Pr.
Elliott, Edwin B. Algebra of Quantics. 2nd ed. LC 63-11320. 11.95 (ISBN 0-8284-0184-5). Chelsea Pub.
Elliott, Elisabeth. Let Me Be a Woman. 1977. pap. 5.95 (ISBN 0-8423-2161-6); pap. 3.95 (ISBN 0-8423-2162-4). Tyndale.
Elliott, Emily. Autumn Rapture. (Candlelight Ecstasy Supreme Ser.: No. 13). (Orig.). 1984. pap. 2.50 (ISBN 0-440-10349-5). Dell.
--The Best Reason of All. (Candlelight Supreme Ser.: No. 88). 1985. pap. 2.75 (ISBN 0-440-10498-X). Dell.
--A Dangerous Attraction. (CandleLight Ecstasy Supreme Ser.: No. 34). (Orig.). 1984. pap. 2.50 (ISBN 0-440-11756-9). Dell.
--Dangerous Interlude. (Candlelight Supreme Ser.: No. 95). (Orig.). 1985. pap. 2.75 (ISBN 0-440-11659-7). Dell.
--Delicate Balance. (Candlelight Ecstasy Ser.: No. 182). 192p. (Orig.). 1983. pap. 1.95 (ISBN 0-440-11817-4). Dell.
--Just His Touch. (Candlelight Ecstasy Supreme Ser.: No. 20). 288p. (Orig.). 1984. pap. 2.50 (ISBN 0-440-14411-6). Dell.
--A Matter of Judgement. (Candlelight Ecstasy Ser.: No. 252). (Orig.). 1984. pap. 1.95 (ISBN 0-440-15529-0). Dell.
--More Than Skin Deep. (Candlelight Ecstasy Ser.: No. 403). (Orig.). 1986. pap. 2.25 (ISBN 0-440-15821-4). Dell.
--Morning's Promise. (Candlelight Ecstasy Ser.: No. 223). 192p. (Orig.). 1984. pap. 1.95 (ISBN 0-440-15829-X). Dell.
--Portrait of My Love. (Candlelight Ecstasy Ser.: No. 140). (Orig.). 1983. pap. 1.95 (ISBN 0-440-16719-1). Dell.
--Stronger Than Passion. (Candlelight Ecstasy Ser.: No. 388). (Orig.). pap. 2.25 (ISBN 0-440-18369-3). Dell.
--Suprise Package. (Candlelight Ecstasy Ser.: No. 343). 1985. pap. 2.25 (ISBN 0-440-18374-X). Dell.
--Tomorrow's Promise. (Candlelight Ecstasy Romance Ser.: No. 303). 192p. (Orig.). 1985. pap. 1.95 (ISBN 0-440-18737-0). Dell.
Elliott, Emory. Power & the Pulpit in Puritan New England. 256p. 1975. 25.50 (ISBN 0-691-07206-X). Princeton U Pr.
--Puritan Influence in American Literature. LC 79-12270. (Illinois Studies in Language & Literature: No. 65). pap. 58.00 (ISBN 0-317-28971-3, 2020232). Bks Demand UMI.
--Revolutionary Writers: Literature & Authority in the New Republic, 1725-1810. 1982. 22.50x (ISBN 0-19-502999-2). Oxford U Pr.
Elliott, Emory, ed. American Colonial Writers Seventeen Thirty-Five to Seventeen Eighty-One. (Dictionary of Literary Biography Ser.: Vol. 31). 300p. 1984. 88.00x (ISBN 0-8103-1709-5). Gale.
Elliott, Francis E., jt. auth. see Fischer, Eric.
Elliott, Frank, ed. see McDonald, Roy.
Elliott, George. The Kissing Man. 144p. 1984. pap. 3.95 (ISBN 0-7736-7069-6). Beaufort Bks NY.
Elliott, George P. From the Berkeley Hills. LC 68-28193. 1969. 12.50 (ISBN 0-89366-093-0). Ultramarine Pub.
--The Mill on the Floss. Byatt, Antonia, intro. by. 1980. pap. 3.95 (ISBN 0-14-043120-9). Penguin.
Elliott, George R. Flaming Minister: A Study of Othello As Tragedy of Love & Hate. LC 74-166020. Repr. of 1953 ed. 19.50 (ISBN 0-404-02306-1). AMS Pr.
--Scourge & Minister: A Study of Hamlet As Tragedy of Revengefulness & Justice. LC 78-166021. Repr. 17.50 (ISBN 0-404-02307-X). AMS Pr.
Elliott, George R., jt. ed. see Roe, Frederick W.
Elliott, Glen R. & Eisdorfer, Carl, eds. Stress & Human Health. (Series in Psychiatry: Vol. 1). 1982. text ed. 34.95 (ISBN 0-8261-4110-2). Springer Pub.
Elliott, H. W., et al, eds. Annual Review of Pharmacology, Vol. 14. LC 61-5649. (Illus.). 1974. text ed. 20.00 (ISBN 0-8243-0414-4). Annual Reviews.
--Annual Review of Pharmacology, Vol. 15. LC 61-5649. (Illus.). 1975. text ed. 20.00 (ISBN 0-8243-0415-2). Annual Reviews.
--Annual Review of Pharmacology & Toxicology, Vol. 16. LC 61-5649. (Illus.). 1976. text ed. 20.00 (ISBN 0-8243-0416-0). Annual Reviews.
--Annual Review of Pharmacology, Vol. 13. LC 61-5649. (Illus.). 1973. text ed. 20.00 (ISBN 0-8243-0413-6). Annual Reviews.
--Annual Review of Pharmacology & Toxicology, Vol. 17. LC 61-5649. (Illus.). 1977. text ed. 20.00 (ISBN 0-8243-0417-9). Annual Reviews.
Elliott, Harley. Animals That Stand in Dreams. 1977. pap. 3.00 (ISBN 0-914610-08-2). Hanging Loose.
--Darkness at Each Elbow. 1981. pap. 4.50 (ISBN 0-914610-21-X). Hanging Loose.
--The Tiger's Spots. LC 76-45383. (Children's Stories Ser.). (Illus.). 64p. 1977. 10.95 (ISBN 0-912278-79-X); pap. 3.95 (ISBN 0-912278-80-3). Crossing Pr.
Elliott, Helen L., ed. see Grizzard, Lewis.
Elliott, Helen L., ed. see Martin, Harold H.
Elliott, Henry W. The Seal Islands of Alaska. (Alaska History Ser: No. 9). (Illus.). 1976. Repr. 16.50x (ISBN 0-919642-72-1). Limestone Pr.
Elliott, Huger. Fashions in Art. facs. ed. LC 75-152168. (Essay Index Reprint Ser). 1937. 21.00 (ISBN 0-8369-2186-0). Ayer Co Pubs.
Elliott, Hugh, jt. auth. see Hancock, James.
Elliott, Inger M. Batik: Fabled Cloth of Java. (Illus.). 240p. 1984. 45.00 (ISBN 0-517-55155-1, C N Potter Bks). Crown.
Elliott, Ingrid G. Hospital Roadmap: A Book to Help Explain the Hospital Experience to Young children. LC 82-80226. (Illus.). 36p. (Orig.). (gr. k-2). 1984. pap. 8.95 (ISBN 0-9608150-0-7). Resources Children.
Elliott, J. Two Nations, Many Cultures: Ethnic Groups in Canada. 1979. 14.50 (ISBN 0-13-935205-8). P-H.
Elliott, J., jt. auth. see Williams, R.

Elliott, J. F. Interception Patrol: An Examination of the Theory of Random Patrol As a Municipal Police Tactic. (Illus.). 88p. 1973. 14.75x (ISBN 0-398-02721-8). C C Thomas.

--The New Police. 88p. 1973. 9.75x (ISBN 0-398-02680-7). C C Thomas.

Elliott, J. F. & Sardino, Thomas J. Crime Control Team: An Experiment in Municipal Police Department Management & Operations. (Illus.). 140p. 1971. 18.75X (ISBN 0-398-00508-7). C C Thomas.

Elliott, J. H. Botany. (Teach Yourself Ser.). 1973. pap. 4.95 (ISBN 0-679-10390-2). McKay.

--Europe Divided: Fifteen Fifty-Nine to Fifteen Ninety-Eight. LC 81-70699. 432p. 1982. pap. 7.95x (ISBN 0-8014-9233-5). Cornell U Pr.

--Imperial Spain 1469-1716. 1977. pap. 10.95 (ISBN 0-452-00782-8, Mer). NAL.

--The Revolt of the Catalans: A Study in the Decline of Spain 1598-1640. LC 83-20929. 641p. 1984. pap. 24.95 (ISBN 0-521-27890-2). Cambridge U Pr.

--Richelieu & Olivares. LC 82-20929. (Cambridge Studies in Early Modern History). 192p. 1984. 29.95 (ISBN 0-521-26205-4); pap. 9.95 (ISBN 0-521-27857-0). Cambridge U Pr.

Elliott, J. H., jt. auth. see Briggs, S. R.

Elliott, J. M. A Key to the Larvae & Adults of British Freshwater Megaloptera & Neuroptera. 1977. 20.00x (ISBN 0-900386-27-4, Pub. by Freshwater Bio). State Mutual Bk.

--Some Methods for the Statistical Analysis of Samples of Benthic Invertebrates. 2nd ed. 1977. 25.00x (ISBN 0-900386-29-0, Pub. by Freshwater Bio). State Mutual Bk.

Elliott, J. M. & Mann, K. H. A Key to the British Freshwater Leeches. 1979. 25.00x (ISBN 0-900386-38-X, Pub. by Freshwater Bio). State Mutual Bk.

Elliott, James P., jt. auth. see Beard, James F.

Elliott, James S. Outlines of Greek & Roman Medicine. LC 77-91526. 1977. Repr. of 1914 ed. lib. bdg. 20.00 (ISBN 0-89341-502-2). Longwood Pub Group.

--Russian for Trade Negotiations with the U.S.S.R. 356p. (Orig.). 1981. pap. text ed. 17.95 (ISBN 0-89357-084-2). Slavica.

Elliott, Janice. Secret Places. 192p. 1981. 9.95 (ISBN 0-312-70871-8). St Martin.

Elliott, Jerry R. The Professional Bartender's Educator. (Illus.). 93p. (Orig.). 1982. pap. 5.95. J R Elliott.

Elliott, Joan. Cats. Duenewald, Doris, ed. (Illus.). 1978. 2.95 (ISBN 0-448-16263-6, G&D). Putnam Pub Group.

--Dogs. LC 78-58087. (Illus.). 1978. PLB 6.09 (ISBN 0-448-13483-7, G&D). Putnam Pub Group.

Elliott, John. Conflict or Co-Operation? The Growth of Industrial Democracy. 306p. 1980. pap. 16.50x (ISBN 0-85038-106-1). Nichols Pub.

--Monarch Notes on Coleridge's the Rime of the Ancient Mariner & Other Poems. (Orig.). pap. 3.50 (ISBN 0-671-00778-5). Monarch Pr.

--Monarch Notes on Wordsworth's Poetry. (Orig.). pap. 2.95 (ISBN 0-671-00729-7). Monarch Pr.

Elliott, John & Pickersgill, Richard. Captain Cook's Second Voyage: The Journals of Lieutenants Elliot & Pickersgill. LC 84-12684. (Illus.). 97p. 1984. 19.75 (ISBN 0-904573-39-7, Pub. by Caliban Bks). Longwood Pub Group.

Elliott, John E. Marx & Engels on Economics, Politics, & Society: Essential Readings with Editorial Commentary. 1981. pap. text ed. 17.95x (ISBN 0-673-16034-3). Scott F.

Elliott, John F., ed. Steelmaking: The Chipman Conference. 1965. 40.00x (ISBN 0-262-05003-X). MIT Pr.

Elliott, John F., jt. ed. see Tien, John K.

Elliott, John H. Old World & the New, Fourteen Ninety-Two to Sixteen Fifty. LC 73-121362. (Studies in Early Modern History). (Illus.). 1970. 24.95 (ISBN 0-521-07937-3); pap. 8.95 (ISBN 0-521-09621-9). Cambridge U Pr.

Elliott, John H. & Martin, R. A. Augsburg Commentary on the New Testament. LC 82-70962. 192p. (Orig.). 1982. 7.95 (ISBN 0-8066-1937-6, 10-9042). Augsburg.

Elliott, John H., jt. auth. see Brown, Jonathan.

Elliott, John R., Jr. & Runnalls, Graham A., eds. The Baptism & Temptation of Christ: The First Day of a Medieval French Passion Play. LC 78-6564. 1978. 24.50x (ISBN 0-300-02199-2). Yale U Pr.

Elliott, John W. Monarch Notes on More's Utopia. (Orig.). pap. 2.95 (ISBN 0-671-00856-0). Monarch Pr.

Elliott, John Y. Our Pastor Has an Outside Job. 1980. pap. 4.50 (ISBN 0-8170-0850-0). Judson.

Elliott, Jolene, ed. see NASAGA Conference, 14th Annual.

Elliott, Katherine, ed. Auxiliaries in Primary Health Care: An Annotated Bibliography. 126p. (Orig.). 1979. pap. 9.75x (ISBN 0-903031-58-2, Pub. by Intermediate Tech England). Intermediate Tech.

Elliott, Katherine, jt. ed. see Skeet, Muriel.

Elliott, L. E. Brazil: Today & Tomorrow. 1976. lib. bdg. 59.95 (ISBN 0-87968-784-3). Gordon Pr.

Elliott, L. E., ed. Chile Today & Tomorrow. 1976. lib. bdg. 59.95 (ISBN 0-8490-1606-1). Gordon Pr.

Elliott, L. F. & Stevenson, F. J., eds. Soils for Management of Organic Wastes & Waste Waters. (Illus.). 1977. 17.50 (ISBN 0-89118-049-4). Am Soc Agron.

Elliott, Larry P. & Schiebler, Gerold L. The X-Ray Diagnosis of Congenital Heart Disease in Infants, Children & Adults: Pathologic, Hemodynamic, & Clinical Correlations As Related to Chest Film. 2nd ed. (Illus.). 424p. 1979. photocopy ed. 45.75x (ISBN 0-398-03857-0). C C Thomas.

Elliott, Lawrence. Little Flower: The Life & Times of Fiorello La Guardia. LC 82-23964. (Illus.). 256p. 1983. 13.95 (ISBN 0-688-02057-7). Morrow.

Elliott, Len, jt. auth. see Dante, Jim.

Elliott, Lloyd H., jt. auth. see Goodpoaster, Andrew J.

Elliott, Lloyd H., ed. see Goodpaster, Andrew J.

Elliott, Malinda, ed. see Knight, Carol B.

Elliott, Marianne. Partners in Revolution: The United Irishmen & France. LC 82-50441. (Illus.). 430p. 1982. 33.00x (ISBN 0-300-02770-2). Yale U Pr.

Elliott, Martha J., jt. auth. see Friendly, Fred W.

Elliott, Martha W. Ethical Issues in Social Work: An Annotated Bibliography. LC 84-4953. 95p. (Orig.). 1984. pap. text ed. 7.00 (ISBN 0-87293-003-3). Coun Soc WK Ed.

Elliott, Martin A., jt. auth. see Lowry, H. H.

Elliott, Martin A., ed. Chemistry of Coal Utilization, Vol. 2. LC 80-13296. 2374p. 1981. 246.50 (ISBN 0-471-07726-7, Pub. by Wiley-Interscience). Wiley.

Elliott, Maud H. This Was My Newport. facsimile ed. LC 75-1842. (Leisure Class in America Ser.). (Illus.). 1975. Repr. of 1944 ed. 20.00x (ISBN 0-405-06911-1). Ayer Co Pubs.

--Uncle Sam Ward & His Circle. facsimile ed. LC 75-1844. (Leisure Class in America Ser.). (Illus.). 1975. Repr. of 1938 ed. 47.50x (ISBN 0-405-06912-X). Ayer Co Pubs.

Elliott, Maude H., jt. auth. see Richards, Laura E.

Elliott, Maurice. The Psychic Life of Jesus. 69.95 (ISBN 0-87968-185-3). Gordon Pr.

--Spiritualism in the Old Testament. 59.95 (ISBN 0-8490-1117-5). Gordon Pr.

Elliott, Michael, jt. auth. see Susskind, Lawrence.

Elliott, Michael, ed. Synthetic Pyrethroids. LC 77-1810. (ACS Symposium Ser.: No. 42). 1977. 29.95 (ISBN 0-8412-0368-7). Am Chemical.

Elliott, Neil. My Years with Capone: Jack Woodford & Al Capone. LC 85-51231. 160p. 1985. pap. 10.95 (ISBN 0-9601574-4-1). Woodford Mem.

Elliott, Norman. How to Be the Lord's Prayer. pap. 2.95 (ISBN 0-910924-26-0). Macalester.

Elliott, Norman W., et al. Typing Power -- Spelling Power, Vol. I. LC 75-8458. 1975. pap. 9.63 scp (ISBN 0-672-96415-5); scp tchr's manual 3.67 (ISBN 0-672-96791-X). Bobbs.

Elliott, Orrin Leslie. Stanford University: The First Twenty-Five Years. Metzger, Walter P., ed. LC 76-55191. (The Academic Profession Ser.). (Illus.). 1977. Repr. of 1937 ed. lib. bdg. 49.50x (ISBN 0-405-10013-2). Ayer Co Pubs.

Elliott, Patrica C. A Practical Guide to the Computer for Tax Practitioners. 1976. pap. 11.50 1983 supplement (ISBN 0-88450-504-9, 1701-B). Lawyers & Judges.

Elliott, Patricia L. see Lind, Carolyn P., pseud.

Elliott, Paul R., jt. auth. see Fox, L. Raymond.

Elliott, Peggy & Mays, Robert E. Early Field Experiences in Teacher Education. LC 79-83630. (Fastback Ser.: No. 125). 1979. pap. 0.75 (ISBN 0-87367-125-2). Phi Delta Kappa.

Elliott, Peggy, jt. auth. see Smith, Carl.

Elliott, Peter. Allied Escort Ships of World War II. (Illus.). 1977. 29.95x (ISBN 0-8464-0126-6). Beekman Pubs.

--Allied Minesweeping in World War II. LC 78-61581. 132p. 1979. 12.95 (ISBN 0-87021-904-9). Naval Inst Pr.

--Allied Minesweeping in World War 2. (Illus.). 132p. 1979. 12.95 (ISBN 0-87021-904-9); bulk rates avail. Naval Inst Pr.

--Questions & Answers on Practical Banking. LC 84-51011. 128p. 1984. pap. 11.95 (ISBN 0-85941-258-X). Woodhead-Faulkner.

Elliott, Peter, jt. auth. see Getzels, Judith N.

Elliott, Philip. The Making of a Television Series: A Case Study in the Sociology of Culture. LC 79-89075. (Communication & Society Ser.: Vol. 2). (Illus.). 180p. 1979. 29.95 (ISBN 0-8039-1355-9); pap. 14.95 (ISBN 0-8039-1356-7). Sage.

Elliott, R., jt. auth. see Elliott, D.

Elliott, R. J., ed. Magnetic Properties of Rare Earth Metals. LC 72-161302. 384p. 1972. 59.50x (ISBN 0-306-30565-8, Plenum Pr). Plenum Pub.

Elliott, R. N. Major Works of R. N. Elliott. Prechter, Robert R., Jr., ed. LC 80-80273. (Illus.). 1984. Repr. of 1938 ed. 34.00 (ISBN 0-932750-01-X). New Classics Lib.

--Nature's Law. (Institute for Economic & Financial Research Ser.). (Illus.). 105p. 1975. 185.85 (ISBN 0-913314-62-5). Am Classical Coll Pr.

--Nature's Law & the Secret of the Universe. (Illus.). 1980. Repr. 137.45 (ISBN 0-89901-008-3). Found Class Reprints.

--The Reconstruction of the Elliott Wave Principle, 2 vols. in one. rev. & enl. ed. (Institute for Economic & Financial Research Ser.). (Illus.). 143p. 1975. Set. 187.50 (ISBN 0-913314-63-3). Am Classical Coll Pr.

Elliott, R. N. & Massey, James G. The Decisive Speculative Significance of the Elliott Wave Theory. (Illus.). 158p. 1980. deluxe ed. 135.50 (ISBN 0-89266-239-5). Am Classical Coll Pr.

Elliott, R. T., tr. see Henry, Victor.

Elliott, R. W. Runes. 1959. pap. 6.50 (ISBN 0-7190-0787-9, Pub. by Manchester Univ Pr). Longwood Pub Group.

Elliott, Rachel P. The New Dogsteps. LC 82-23427. (Illus.). 128p. 1983. pap. 15.95 (ISBN 0-87605-521-8). Howell Bk.

Elliott, Ralph H. Church Growth That Counts. 128p. 1982. pap. 6.95 (ISBN 0-8170-0943-4). Judson.

Elliott, Ralph N. An Elementary Introduction into the Elliott's Wave Theory. (The New Stock Market Reference Library). (Illus.). 129p. 1981. 83.45x (ISBN 0-918968-92-5). Inst Econ Fina.

--The Elliott Wave Principle As a Key to Maximal Stock Market Profits. (Illus.). 167p. 1983. 187.50x (ISBN 0-86654-082-2). Inst Econ Finan.

--The Elliott Wave Principle in Projection Charts, 2 vols. (Illus.). 1985. Set. 227.50 (ISBN 0-86654-161-6). Inst Econ Finan.

--The Elliott Wave Principles As a Key to Maximal Stock Market Profits. (Illus.). 1979. 185.00 (ISBN 0-89266-209-3). Am Classical Coll Pr.

--The Elliott Wave Theory as a Key to Maximal Stock Market Profits, 2 vols. (Illus.). 217p. 1985. Set. 227.50 (ISBN 0-86654-162-4). Inst Econ Finan.

--The Elliott Wave Theory as Outlined in Nature's Law & the Secret of the Universe. (Illus.). 131p. 1983. 187.50 (ISBN 0-89901-114-4). Found Class Reprints.

--The Metaphysical Significance of the Elliott Advancing & Declining Waves, 2 vols. (Illus.). 276p. 1984. Set. 215.25x (ISBN 0-86654-106-3). Inst Econ Finan.

--Nature's Law: The Secret of the Universe, 2 vols. (Illus.). 1985. Set. 247.85 (ISBN 0-86654-172-1). Inst Econ Finan.

--The Ralph Nelson Elliott's Understanding of the Intimate Life of the Stock Market & Its Speculative Expression. Dietrich, Emerson, ed. (Illus.). 187p. 1982. 187.50x (ISBN 0-86654-024-5). Inst Econ Finan.

--The Wave Principle. (Illus.). 1979. deluxe ed. 187.45x (ISBN 0-918968-33-X). Inst Econ Pol.

Elliott, Ralph N. & Flumiani, C. M. The Elliott Wave Theory in Projection Charts. enl. ed. (Illus.). 129p. 1982. 187.50x (ISBN 0-86654-022-9). Inst Econ Finan.

Elliott, Ralph N., jt. auth. see Fibonacci, Leonardo.

Elliott, Ralph N. & Flumiani, C. M., eds. The Reconstruction of the Elliott's Theory of Cycles. (Illus.). 118p. 1982. 98.75x (ISBN 0-86654-033-4). Inst Econ Finan.

Elliott, Ralph W. Runes: An Introduction. LC 80-26090. (Illus.). xvi, 124p. 1981. Repr. of 1959 ed. lib. bdg. 24.75x (ISBN 0-313-22870-1, ELRU). Greenwood.

--Thomas Hardy's English. Crystal, David, ed. (Language Library). 384p. 1984. 34.95x (ISBN 0-631-13659-2). Basil Blackwell.

Elliott, Raymond. Fundamentals of Music. 3rd ed. LC 76-139599. (Illus.). 1971. pap. text ed. 19.95 (ISBN 0-13-341305-5). P-H.

Elliott, Richard. The Sword of Allah. 288p. (Orig.). 1984. pap. 2.95 (ISBN 0-449-12604-8, GM). Fawcett.

Elliott, Richard V. Last of the Steamboats: The Saga of the Wilson Line. LC 70-124312. (Illus.). 217p. 1970. 10.00 (ISBN 0-87033-149-3). Tidewater.

Elliott, Robert C. The Literary Persona. LC 81-19656. (Illus.). 1982. lib. bdg. 20.00x (ISBN 0-226-20502-9). U of Chicago Pr.

--Power of Satire: Magic, Ritual, Art. 1960. pap. 9.95 (ISBN 0-691-01276-8). Princeton U Pr.

--The Shape of Utopia: Studies in a Literary Genre. LC 78-103136. 1970. 15.00x (ISBN 0-226-20500-2). U of Chicago Pr.

Elliott, Robert C., ed. Twentieth Century Interpretations of Moll Flanders. (Twentieth Century Interpretations Ser). 1970. pap. 1.25 (ISBN 0-13-322230-6, Spec). P-H.

Elliott, Robert C., ed. see Bellamy, Edward.

Elliott, Robert H. Public Personnel Administration. LC 84-24892. 1985. pap. text ed. 12.95 (ISBN 0-8359-5998-8); instr's. manual avail. (ISBN 0-8359-5999-6). Reston.

Elliott, Robert J. & Kalton, Nigel J. The Existence of Value in Differential Games. LC 72-4562. (Memoirs: No. 126). 67p. 1972. pap. 9.00 (ISBN 0-8218-1826-0, MEMO-126). Am Math.

Elliott, Robert M. The Most Significant Stock Market Chart Patterns & the Amazing Anticipatory Meaning They Contain. (Illus.). 151p. 1981. 61.25x (ISBN 0-918968-89-5). Inst Econ Finan.

Elliott, Robert N. The New Theory of Cycles As an Explanation for the Direction of the Course of History & the Price Motions of Security & Commodity Values. (Illus.). 1977. 62.95 (ISBN 0-89266-066-X). Am Classical Coll Pr.

Elliott, Roy. Eutectic Solidification Processing. 1983. text ed. 59.95 (ISBN 0-408-10714-6). Butterworth.

Elliott, Russell R. History of Nevada. LC 72-187809. (Illus.). xiv, 479p. 1973. pap. 12.50x (ISBN 0-8032-6710-X, BB 900, Bison). U of Nebr Pr.

--Servant of Power: A Political Biography of Senator William M. Stewart. (History & Political Science Ser.: No. 18). (Illus., Orig.). 1983. pap. 11.25x (ISBN 0-87417-076-1). U of Nev Pr.

Elliott, Ruth. Organization of Professional Training in Physical Education in State Universities. LC 70-176749. (Columbia University. Teachers College. Contributions to Education: No. 268). Repr. of 1927 ed. 22.50 (ISBN 0-404-55268-4). AMS Pr.

Elliott, Ryan. Growing Up Little: Ten Years of Reparenting. 160p. (Orig.). 1985. pap. 6.95 (ISBN 0-9615140-0-0). Phoenix Midwest Pubs.

Elliott, Sarah B. Incident & Other Happenings. LC 79-94717. (Short Story Index Reprint Ser.). 1899. 18.00 (ISBN 0-8369-3096-7). Ayer Co Pubs.

--Some Data & Other Stories of Southern Life. Mackenzie, Clara C., ed. LC 81-9203. (Illus.). 271p. 1981. 12.95 (ISBN 0-933496-01-X). Univ South.

Elliott, Scott F. Evolution & the Rediscovery of Prehistoric Man, 2 vols. (A Great Currents of History Library Bk.). (Illus.). 239p. 1985. Set. 189.75 (ISBN 0-89266-534-3). Am Classical Coll Pr.

Elliott, Sharon. Computers in Action. (Discovering Computers Ser.). (Illus.). 32p. (gr. 6-9). 1985. lib. bdg. 9.40 (ISBN 0-531-03829-7). Watts.

--Living with the Microchip. (Discovering Computers Ser.). (Illus.). 32p. (gr. 6-9). 1985. lib. bdg. 9.40 (ISBN 0-531-03830-0). Watts.

--The Micro. (Discovering Computers Ser.). (Illus.). 32p. (gr. 6-9). 1985. lib. bdg. 9.40 (ISBN 0-531-03827-0). Watts.

--What Are Computers? (Discovering Computers Ser.). (Illus.). 32p. (gr. 6-9). 1885. PLB 9.90 (ISBN 0-531-03828-9). Watts.

Elliott, Shelden D. Opportunities in a Law Career. LC 70-76321. (gr. 8 up). 1969. pap. 1.25 (ISBN 0-8442-6486-5). Natl Textbk.

Elliott, Sloane, jt. auth. see Elliott, Drossoula V.

Elliott, Stephen P., jt. auth. see Facts on File Staff.

Elliott, Sumner L. About Tilly Beamis. 1984. 15.95 (ISBN 0-531-09834-6). Watts.

Elliott, Susan. Becoming Self-Employed: How to Create an Independent Livelihood. (Illus.). 200p. (Orig.). Date not set. pap. 7.95 (ISBN 0-911781-04-8). Live Oak Pubns.

--Ideas That Work. LC 84-21860. 186p. 1985. pap. 9.95 (ISBN 0-911781-02-1). Liberty Pub.

--Ideas That Work: Ten of Today's Most Exciting & Profitable Self-Employment Opportunities. LC 84-21860. (Orig.). 1985. pap. 9.95 (ISBN 0-911781-02-1). Live Oak Pubns.

Elliott, T. C., jt. auth. see Schwieger, R. G.

Elliott, Thomas C. Practical Ideas for the Design, Operation, & Maintenance of Plant Energy Systems. LC 84-7161. (Illus.). 304p. 1984. 29.95 (ISBN 0-07-050583-7). McGraw.

Elliott, Thomas C. & Schwieger, Robert G., eds. The Acid Rain Sourcebook. (Illus.). 296p. 1984. 44.95 (ISBN 0-07-066540-5). McGraw.

Elliott, Thomas C., jt. ed. see O'Keefe, William.

Elliott, Thomas I., tr. see Kawai, Toyoaki.

Elliott, Tom. Clowns, Clients, & Chaos: Starting a Hometown Talent Agency for Fun & Profit. Bancroft, Frances, ed. LC 82-74354. (Illus.). 153p. 1983. pap. 17.95 (ISBN 0-911759-00-X). TEP.

Elliott, Virgil L. San Francisco Statistical Abstract, 1983. 70p. 1983. pap. 11.95 (ISBN 0-9610700-1-3). Statistical Pr.

Elliott, Virgil. L. San Francisco Statistical Abstract, 1984. 74p. 1984. pap. 11.95 (ISBN 0-9610700-2-1). Statistical Pr.

Elliott, W. Rodger & Jones, David L. Encyclopedia of Australian Plants, Vol. 1. (Illus.). 336p. 40.00x (ISBN 0-85091-070-6, Pub. by Lothian). Intl Spec Bk.

Elliott, Walter. The Life of Father Hecker. LC 75-38446. (Religion in America, Ser. 2). 456p. 1972. Repr. of 1891 ed. 28.00 (ISBN 0-405-04065-2). Ayer Co Pubs.

Elliott, Ward E. The Rise of Guardian Democracy: The Supreme Court's Role in Voting Rights Disputes, 1845-1969. LC 73-90611. (Political Studies). 368p. 1974. text ed. 22.50x (ISBN 0-674-77156-7). Harvard U Pr.

Elliott, William. Arabic Etymology of English. 160p. 1983. text ed. 31.00x (ISBN 0-86127-000-2, Pub. by Avebury England). Humanities.

--Carolina Sports by Land & Water: Incidents of Devil-Fishing, Wild-Cat, Deer & Bear Hunting. (Illus.). 292p. 1977. Repr. of 1859 ed. 10.00 (ISBN 0-87921-040-0). Attic Pr.

Elliott, William, tr. see Al-Arif, Ibn.

Elliott, William D. To Middle River: Minnesota North Country New & Selected Poems. LC 84-60990. 70p. (Orig.). 1984. pap. 4.95 (ISBN 0-9613489-1-7). MN North.

Elliott, William I., tr. see Tanikawa, Shuntaro.

Elliott, William T., ed. Elliott's Foe-Ne'tic Spelling Dictionary. 2nd ed. 11.95 (ISBN 0-930364-07-4); pap. 8.95 (ISBN 0-930364-06-6). Seal Pr.

Elliott, William T., tr. see Tanikawa, Shuntaro.

Elliott, William Y., et al. International Control in the Non-Ferrous Metals. Bruchey, Stuart & Bruchey, Eleanor, eds. LC 76-5007. (American Business Abroad Ser.). (Illus.). 1976. Repr. of 1937 ed. 65.00x (ISBN 0-405-09276-8). Ayer Co Pubs.

Elliott-Bateman, Michael, et al. Revolt to Revolution: Studies in the 19th & 20th Century European Experience. (Fourth Dimension of Warfare Ser: Vol. 2). 373p. 1974. 25.00x (ISBN 0-87471-448-6). Rowman.

Elliott-Binns, C. Medicine: The Forgotten Art? 1978. 17.00x (ISBN 0-8464-0625-X). Beekman Pubs.

Elliott-Binns, L. Development of English Theology in the Later Nineteenth Century. LC 72-122411. 1971. Repr. of 1952 ed. 15.00 (ISBN 0-208-01045-9, Archon). Shoe String.

--Innocent Third. xi, 212p. 1968. Repr. of 1931 ed. 16.50 (ISBN 0-208-00393-2, Archon). Shoe String.

Elliott-Binns, Leonard E. From Moses to Elisha: Israel to the End of the Ninth Century B. C. LC 78-10639. (Illus.). 1979. Repr. of 1929 ed. lib. bdg. 27.50x (ISBN 0-313-21015-2, EBFM). Greenwood.

Elliott-Binns, Leonard E., ed. Erasmus the Reformer: A Study in Restatement. LC 83-45655. Date not set. Repr. of 1923 ed. 24.50 (ISBN 0-404-19805-8). AMS Pr.

Ellis, jt. auth. see Guess.

Ellis, jt. auth. see Martin.

Ellis, jt. auth. see Musemeche.

Ellis, ed. see Bradstreet, Anne.

Ellis, A. New Guide to Rational Living. 3.00x (ISBN 0-685-70720-2). Wehman.

Ellis, A., ed. Normality & Pathology in Cognitive Functions. 1982. 43.50 (ISBN 0-12-237480-0). Acad Pr.

Ellis, A. C. Worldmaker. 240p. 1985. pap. 2.95 (ISBN 0-441-91102-1). Ace Bks.

Ellis, A. E. British Freshwater Bivalve Mollusca: Keys & Notes for the Identification of the Species. (A Volume in the Synopses of the British Fauna Ser.). 1978. pap. 12.00 (ISBN 0-12-236950-5). Acad Pr.

--The Rack. 1979. pap. 2.95 (ISBN 0-14-001545-0). Penguin.

Ellis, A. G. Catalogue of Arabic Books in the British Museum, Vol. 1. 501p. 1967. 125.00x (ISBN 0-7141-0603-8, Pub. by Brit Lib England). State Mutual Bk.

--Catalogue of Arabic Books in the British Museum, Vol. 1. 1967. Repr. of 1894 ed. 45.00 (ISBN 0-7141-0603-8, Pub. by British Lib). Longwood Pub Group.

--Catalogue of Arabic Books in the British Museum, Vol. 2. 438p. 1967. 100.00x (ISBN 0-686-81306-5, Pub. by Brit Lib England). State Mutual Bk.

--Catalogue of Arabic Books in the British Museum, Vol. 2. 438p. 1967. Repr. of 1901 ed. 45.00 (ISBN 0-7123-0604-8, Pub. by British Lib). Longwood Pub Group.

Ellis, A. J. Basic Algebra & Geometry for Scientists & Engineers. 187p. 1982. 28.95x (ISBN 0-471-10174-5). Wiley.

--English Dialects; Their Sounds & Homes: Being an Abridgement of the Author's Existing Phonology of English Dialects. (English Dialects Society Publications Ser.: No. 60). pap. 20.00 (ISBN 0-317-15974-7). Kraus Repr.

Ellis, A. J., jt. auth. see Asimow, L.

Ellis, A. J. & Mahon, W. A., eds. Chemistry & Geothermal Systems. 1977. 65.00 (ISBN 0-12-237450-9). Acad Pr.

Ellis, A. R., ed. Under Scott's Command: Lashly's Antarctic Diaries. LC 73-81241. (Illus.). (gr. 10-12). 4.75 (ISBN 0-8008-7936-8). Taplinger.

Ellis, Adrian & Kumar, Krishan. Dilemmas of Liberal Democracies: Studies in Fred Hirsch's Social Limits to Growth. LC 83-13207. (Tavistock Studies in Sociology). 212p. 1984. 27.00x (ISBN 0-422-78460-5, 4002); pap. 12.95x (ISBN 0-422-78470-2, 4001). Methuen Inc.

Ellis, Albert. Anger: How to Live with & Without It. 288p. 1985. pap. 5.95 (ISBN 0-8065-0937-6). Citadel Pr.

--Art & Science of Love. 1960. 7.95 (ISBN 0-8184-0009-9). Lyle Stuart.

--Executive Leadership: A Rational Approach. LC 70-186401. 1978. pap. 5.95 (ISBN 0-917476-11-5). Inst Rational-Emotive.

--A Garland of Rational Songs. 1977. 3.50 (ISBN 0-917476-09-3). Inst Rational-Emotive.

--Growth Through Reason. pap. 4.00 (ISBN 0-87980-264-2). Wilshire.

--How to Live with a Neurotic. pap. 5.00 (ISBN 0-87980-404-1). Wilshire.

--How to Master Your Fear of Flying. LC 77-182928. 1977. pap. 3.95 (ISBN 0-917476-10-7). Inst Rational-Emotive.

--How to Raise an Emotionally Healthy, Happy Child. pap. 5.00 (ISBN 0-87980-208-1). Wilshire.

--Humanistic Psychotherapy: The Rational-Emotive Approach. LC 72-94222. (McGraw-Hill Paperbacks). 288p. 1974. pap. 4.95 (ISBN 0-07-019237-5). McGraw.

--Overcoming Resistance: Rational-Emotive Therapy with Difficult Clients. 240p. 1985. text ed. 21.00 (ISBN 0-8261-4910-3). Springer Pub.

--Reason & Emotion in Psychotherapy. 445p. 1984. pap. 7.95 (ISBN 0-8065-0909-0). Citadel Pr.

--Reason & Emotion in Psychotherapy. 1962. 15.00 (ISBN 0-8184-0122-2). Lyle Stuart.

--Sensuous Person: Critique & Corrections. 1973. 6.00 (ISBN 0-8184-0077-3). Lyle Stuart.

--Sex & the Liberated Man. 384p. 1976. 12.95 (ISBN 0-8184-0222-9). Lyle Stuart.

--Sex Without Guilt. rev. ed. 1966. 4.95 (ISBN 0-8184-0121-4). Lyle Stuart.

--Sex Without Guilt. pap. 5.00 (ISBN 0-87980-145-X). Wilshire.

Ellis, Albert & Abrahms, Eliot R. Brief Psychotherapy in Medical & Health Practice. LC 78-12947. 1978. pap. 16.95 (ISBN 0-8261-2641-3). Springer Pub.

Ellis, Albert & Becker, Irving. Guide to Personal Happiness. 1982. pap. 5.00 (ISBN 0-87980-395-9). Wilshire.

Ellis, Albert & Brancale, Ralph. The Psychology of Sex Offenders. 148p. 1956. 15.50x (ISBN 0-398-04252-7). C C Thomas.

Ellis, Albert & Grieger, Russell. Handbook of Rational-Emotive Therapy. LC 77-21410. 1977. text ed. 29.95 (ISBN 0-8261-2200-0); pap. 19.95 (ISBN 0-8261-2201-9). Springer Pub.

Ellis, Albert & Gullo, John M. Murder & Assassination. 1971. 10.00 (ISBN 0-8184-0057-9). Lyle Stuart.

Ellis, Albert & Harper, Robert. Guide to Successful Marriage. pap. 5.00 (ISBN 0-87980-044-5). Wilshire.

Ellis, Albert & Harper, Robert A. New Guide to Rational Living. pap. 3.00 (ISBN 0-87980-042-9). Wilshire.

Ellis, Albert & Knaus, William. Overcoming Procrastination. 1979. pap. 2.95 (ISBN 0-451-12744-7, AE2744, Sig). NAL.

Ellis, Albert & Knaus, William J. Overcoming Procrastination. LC 76-26333. 1977. pap. 5.95 (ISBN 0-917476-04-2). Inst Rational-Emotive.

Ellis, Albert & Bernard, Michael E., eds. Clinical Applications of Rational-Emotive Therapy. 349p. 1985. 39.50x (ISBN 0-306-41971-8, Plenum Pr). Plenum Pub.

--Rational-Emotive Approaches to the Problems of Childhood. 536p. 1983. 45.00x (ISBN 0-306-41331-0, Plenum Pr). Plenum Pub.

Ellis, Albert C. & Slaten, Jeff. Death Jag. (Orig.). 1980. pap. 1.95 (ISBN 0-532-23312-3). Woodhill.

Ellis, Alec. A History of Children's Reading & Literature. 1968. pap. 10.75 (ISBN 0-08-012586-7). Pergamon.

--How to Find Out About Children's Literature. 3rd ed. 1973. 28.00 (ISBN 0-08-016970-8); pap. text ed. 9.25 (ISBN 0-08-018230-5). Pergamon.

--Library Services for Young People in England & Wales, 1830-1970. 1971. 31.00 (ISBN 0-08-016586-9). Pergamon.

Ellis, Alec C. Educating Our Masters. 160p. 1985. text ed. write for info. (ISBN 0-566-00867-X). Gower Pub Co.

Ellis, Alexander J. Early English Pronunciation, Pt. 1. (EETS, ES Ser.: No. 2). Repr. of 1867 ed. 17.00 (ISBN 0-527-00213-5). Kraus Repr.

--Early English Pronunciation - Existing Dialectal as Compared with West Saxon Pronounciation, Pt. 5. (EETS, ES Ser.: No. 56). Repr. of 1889 ed. 66.00 (ISBN 0-527-00217-8). Kraus Repr.

--Illustrations on Early English Pronounciation of English in the 17th, 18th & 19th Century, Pt. 4. (EETS, ES Ser.: No. 23). Repr. of 1874 ed. 33.00 (ISBN 0-527-00216-X). Kraus Repr.

--Illustrations on Early English Pronunciation of the 14th & 16th Centuries, Pt. 3. (EETS, ES Ser.: No. 14). Repr. of 1871 ed. 28.00 (ISBN 0-527-00215-1). Kraus Repr.

--On Early English Pronounciation of the Thirteenth & Previous Centuries of Anglosaxon, Icelandic, Old Norse & Gothic, Pt. 2. (EETS, ES Ser.: No. 7). Repr. of 1869 ed. 17.00 (ISBN 0-527-00214-3). Kraus Repr.

--On Early English Pronunciation, with Especial Reference to Shakespeare & Chaucer, 5 Vols. LC 68-24964. (Studies in Language, No. 41). 1969. Repr. of 1889 ed. lib. bdg. 159.00x (ISBN 0-8383-0158-4). Haskell.

--On the History of Musical Pitch. LC 77-75197. 1977. Repr. of 1880 ed. lib. bdg. 20.00 (ISBN 0-89341-093-4). Longwood Pub Group.

Ellis, Alexander J. & Mendel, Arthur. Studies in the History of Musical Pitch. (Music Ser.). 238p. 1981. lib. bdg. 27.50 (ISBN 0-306-76020-7). Da Capo.

Ellis, Alfred B. Ewe-Speaking Peoples of the Slave Coast of West Africa. 1964. 16.50x (ISBN 0-910216-01-0). Benin.

--History of the Gold Coast of West Africa. LC 77-75551. (Illus.). Repr. of 1893 ed. cancelled (ISBN 0-8371-1126-9, ELG&, Pub. by Negro U Pr). Greenwood.

--Land of Fetish. LC 79-106871. Repr. of 1883 ed. 22.50x (ISBN 0-8371-3288-6, ELL&, Pub. by Negro U Pr). Greenwood.

--Tshi-Speaking Peoples of the Gold Coast of West Africa. 1964. 16.50x (ISBN 0-910216-02-9). Benin.

--Yoruba-Speaking Peoples of the Slave Coast of West Africa. 1964. 16.50x (ISBN 0-910216-03-7). Benin.

Ellis, Alice T. The Birds of the Air. 156p. 1981. 9.95 (ISBN 0-670-16819-X). Viking.

Ellis, Andrew W. Progress in the Psychology of Language, 2 Vols. 320p. 1985. Vol. I. text ed. 29.95 (ISBN 0-86377-027-4); Vol. II. text ed. 29.95 (ISBN 0-86377-028-2). L Erlbaum Assocs.

--Reading, Writing & Dyslexia: A Cognitive Analysis. 160p. 1984. text ed. 29.95 (ISBN 0-86377-002-9); pap. 14.50 (ISBN 0-86377-003-7). L Erlbaum Assocs.

Ellis, Andrew W. & Young, Andrew W., eds. Human Cognitive Neuropsychology. 256p. Date not set. text ed. 39.95 (ISBN 0-86377-033-9); pap. 14.95 (ISBN 0-86377-034-7). L Erlbaum Assocs.

Ellis, Ann W., ed. Proceedings & Papers of the Georgia Association of Historians, 1984. 145p. (Orig.). 1985. pap. 5.00 (ISBN 0-939346-04-4). GA Assn Hist.

Ellis, Ann W., et al, eds. Proceedings & Papers of the Georgia Association of Historians, 1981. 138p. (Orig.). 1982. pap. 5.00 (ISBN 0-939346-01-X). GA Assn Hist.

--Proceedings & Papers of the Georgia Association of Historians: 1982. 141p. (Orig.). 1983. pap. 5.00 (ISBN 0-939346-02-8). GA Assn Hist.

--Proceedings & Papers of the Georgia Association of Historians, 1983. 130p. (Orig.). 1984. pap. 5.00 (ISBN 0-939346-03-6). GA Assn Hist.

--Proceedings & Papers of the Georgia Association of Historians, 1980. 84p. (Orig.). 1981. pap. 5.00 (ISBN 0-939346-00-1). GA Assn Hist.

Ellis, Anne. The Life of an Ordinary Woman. LC 74-3946. (Women in America Ser). (Illus.). 330p. 1974. Repr. of 1929 ed. 24.00 (ISBN 0-405-06092-0). Ayer Co Pubs.

--The Life of an Ordinary Woman. LC 80-138. (Illus.). xxiv, 301p. 1980. pap. 6.95 (ISBN 0-8032-6704-5, BB 736, Bison). U of Nebr Pr.

--Plain Anne Ellis: More about the Life of an Ordinary Woman. vi, 265p. 1984. 19.95X (ISBN 0-8032-1807-9); pap. 6.95 (ISBN 0-8032-6708-8, BB 817, Bison). U of Nebr Pr.

--Sunshine Preferred: The Philosophy of an Ordinary Woman. LC 84-5141. vi, 249p. 1984. 19.95x (ISBN 0-8032-1810-9); pap. 6.95 (ISBN 0-8032-6709-6, BB 880, Bison). U of Nebr Pr.

Ellis, Anne L. Dabble Duck. LC 83-47692. (Illus.). 32p. (ps-2). 1984. 11.06i (ISBN 0-06-021817-7); PLB 10.89g (ISBN 0-06-021818-5). HarpJ.

Ellis, Annie R., ed. see Burney, Frances.

Ellis, Anthony E. Fish & Shellfish Pathology. Date not set. 69.50 (ISBN 0-12-237490-8). Acad Pr.

Ellis, Archie S. Eloquent Testimony: The Story of the Mental Health Services in Western Australia 1830-1975. (Illus.). xviii, 233p. 1984. 18.00x (ISBN 0-85564-227-0, Pub. by U of W Austral Pr). Intl Spec Bk.

Ellis, Arthur. Stephane Mallarme. LC 77-790. 1977. Repr. of 1927 ed. lib. bdg. 20.00 (ISBN 0-8414-3982-6). Folcroft.

--Stephane Mallarme in English Verse. 1927. Repr. 20.00 (ISBN 0-8274-3886-9). R West.

Ellis, Arthur J. The Divining Rod. LC 77-25879. 1977. lib. bdg. 15.00 (ISBN 0-8414-4103-0). Folcroft.

Ellis, Arthur K. Teaching & Learning Elementary Social Studies. 2nd ed. 1981. text ed. 31.79 (ISBN 0-205-07221-6, 237221). Allyn.

Ellis, Arthur K., et al. Introduction to the Foundations of Education. (Illus.). 384p. 1981. 25.95 (ISBN 0-13-484105-0). P-H.

--Introduction to the Foundations of Education. 2nd ed. (Illus.). 416p. 1986. text ed. 27.95 (ISBN 0-13-484122-0). P-H.

Ellis, Arthur L. The Black Power Brokers. LC 79-65252. 150p. 1980. 13.00 (ISBN 0-86548-009-5). R & E Pubs.

--A Mind on Harlem. LC 78-62232. 1978. soft cover 13.00 (ISBN 0-88247-537-1). R & E Pubs.

Ellis, Audrey. The Pasta Book. (Illus.). 96p. 1985. 8.95 (ISBN 0-86188-456-6, Pub. by Salem Hse Ltd). Merrimack Pub Cir.

--Table Layout & Decoration. (Illus.). 1978. pap. 7.95x (ISBN 0-8464-0907-0). Beekman Pubs.

Ellis, Barbara L. How to Write Themes & Term Papers. 2nd ed. LC 80-27412. 160p. (gr. 10-12). 1981. pap. text ed. 4.95 (ISBN 0-8120-2266-1). Barron.

Ellis, Bettie H. Word Processing: Concepts & Applications. (Illus.). 48p. 1980. 12.16 (ISBN 0-07-019242-1). McGraw.

Ellis, Bret E. Less Than Zero: A Novel. 1985. 15.95 (ISBN 0-671-54329-6). S&S.

Ellis, Brian. Rational Belief Systems. (American Philosophical Quarterly Library of Philosophy). 118p. 1979. 17.50x (ISBN 0-8476-6108-3). Rowman.

Ellis, Brian D. Basic Concepts of Measurement. LC 65-19150. pap. 57.50 (ISBN 0-317-26322-6, 2024450). Bks Demand UMI.

Ellis, Brobury P., ed. & tr. see Beaumarchais, Pierre-Augustin.

Ellis, Bryan, jt. ed. see Douglas, R. W.

Ellis, C. The Christ in Shakespeare's Dramas & Sonnets. 59.95 (ISBN 0-87968-860-2). Gordon Pr.

Ellis, C. Douglas & Schachter, Albert. Ancient Greek: A Structural Programme. (Illus.). 1528p. 1973. wkbk. 27.50x (ISBN 0-7735-0196-7). McGill-Queens U Pr.

Ellis, C. Hamilton. British Trains of Yesteryear. (Illus.). 19.50x (ISBN 0-392-02397-0, SpS). Sportshelf.

--Engines That Passed. LC 72-364512. (Illus.). 1968. lib. bdg. 14.95x (ISBN 0-678-06005-3). Kelley.

--Midland Railway. (Illus.). pap. 8.50x (ISBN 0-392-03937-0, SpS). Sportshelf.

Ellis, Carl, Jr. Beyond Liberation. LC 83-18561. (Illus.). 200p. (Orig.). 1983. pap. 6.95 (ISBN 0-87784-914-5). Inter-Varsity.

Ellis, Carol. Nobody's Perfect. (Turning Points Ser.: No. 11). 1985. pap. 2.50 (ISBN 0-451-13491-5, Sig Vista). NAL.

--See You in September. (Turning Points Ser.: No. 4). (gr. 5-9). 1984. pap. 1.95 (ISBN 0-451-13121-5, Sig Vista). NAL.

--Small Town Summer. (Caprice Romance Ser.: No. 2). 160p. 1984. pap. 1.95 (ISBN 0-441-77161-0, Pub. by Tempo). Ace Bks.

--Summer to Summer. 176p. 1985. pap. 2.25 (ISBN 0-345-31631-2). Ballantine.

--Two by Two Romance, No. 11: Kiss for Good Luck. 176p. (Orig.). 1984. pap. 1.95 (ISBN 0-446-32014-5). Warner Bks.

Ellis, Catherine J. Aboriginal Music: Education for Living: Cross Cultural Experiences from South Australia. LC 83-10630. (The Scholars Library). (Illus.). 236p. 1985. text ed. 37.50x (ISBN 0-7022-1992-4). U of Queensland Pr.

Ellis, Charles & Ellis, Norma. Heirs Together of Life. pap. 5.45 (ISBN 0-85151-311-5). Banner of Truth.

Ellis, Charles, retold by. Shakespeare & the Bible, a Reading from Shakespeare's Merchant of Venice, Shakespeariana Sonnets with Their Scriptural Harmonies. 288p. Repr. of 1982 ed. lib. bdg. 50.00 (ISBN 0-89987-218-2). Darby Bks.

Ellis, Charles D. Investment Policy: How to Win the Losers Game in Investment Management. 200p. 1985. 25.00 (ISBN 0-87094-713-3). Dow Jones-Irwin.

Ellis, Charles G. Early Caucasian Rugs. LC 75-27048. (Illus.). 112p. 1975. pap. 17.50 (ISBN 0-87405-007-3). Textile Mus.

Ellis, Charles G., tr. see Von Bode, Wilhelm & Kuhnel, Ernst.

Ellis, Charles M. Essay on Transcendentalism. LC 70-91761. Repr. of 1954 ed. lib. bdg. 15.00x (ISBN 0-8371-3092-1, ELTR). Greenwood.

Ellis, Chris & Chamberlain, Peter. American Half-Tracks of World War II. (Illus.). 104p. pap. 5.95 (ISBN 0-85242-581-3). Aztex.

Ellis, Chris, jt. auth. see Chamberlain, Peter.

Ellis, Cliff. Zone Press Variations for Winning Basketball. 1975. cancelled (ISBN 0-13-984054-0, Parker). P-H.

Ellis, Conleth. After Doomsday. (Raven Long Poem Ser.). 1981. pap. 4.95 (ISBN 0-317-14954-7); 8.95 (ISBN 0-317-14955-5). Dufour.

Ellis, D. & Pekar, P. Planning Basics for Managers. 1983. pap. 6.95 (ISBN 0-317-31398-3). AMACOM.

Ellis, Daniel. Thrilling Adventures of Daniel Ellis. facsimile ed. LC 76-37303. (Black Heritage Library Collection). Repr. of 1867 ed. 27.00 (ISBN 0-8369-8940-6). Ayer Co Pubs.

Ellis, Darryl J. & Pekar, Peter P. Planning for Non-Planners. 1981. 12.95 (ISBN 0-8144-5593-X). AMACOM.

Ellis, David. Let's Look at Indonesia. pap. 1.50 (ISBN 9971-83-824-9). OMF Bks.

--Wordsworth, Freud & the Spots of Time: Interpretation in 'The Prelude' 200p. 1985. 34.50 (ISBN 0-521-26555-X). Cambridge U Pr.

Ellis, David, jt. auth. see Ellis, Miles.

Ellis, David, tr. see Robert, Guy.

Ellis, David, tr. see Stendhal.

Ellis, David B. Becoming a Master Student. 4th ed. (Illus.). 300p. 1984. pap. 16.95 (ISBN 0-942456-03-3); 30.00 (ISBN 0-942456-00-9). Coll Survival.

--Becoming a Master Student Instuctor's Guide. LC 84-71944. (Illus.). 200p. 1984. 30.00 (ISBN 0-942456-00-9). Coll Survival.

--Survival Tools for Students: Techniques, Skills, Hints, Aids, Resources, Ideas, Procedures, Illustrations, Examples, Instructions, Methods & Suggestions for Success. 3rd ed. LC 81-71530. (Illus.). 226p. 1982. pap. 19.65 (ISBN 0-942456-01-7); pap. text ed. 19.65 (ISBN 0-686-98409-9). Coll Survival.

Ellis, David M. Landlords & Farmers in the Hudson-Mohawk Region, 1790-1850. 1967. lib. bdg. 23.00x (ISBN 0-374-92546-1). Octagon.

--New York: State & City. LC 78-15759. (Illus.). 267p. 1979. 19.50x (ISBN 0-8014-1180-7). Cornell U Pr.

Ellis, David M., et al. History of New York State. rev. ed. (Illus.). 752p. 1967. 32.50 (ISBN 0-8014-0118-6); text ed. 27.50x (ISBN 0-8014-0119-4). Cornell U Pr.

Ellis, Dennis & Nathan, Jay. An Executive's Guide to Time Series Forecasting. LC 84-81422. (Orig.). 1986. pap. text ed. write for info. (ISBN 0-932126-11-1). Graceway.

Ellis, Derek. Animal Behavior & Its Applications. (Illus.). 329p. 1985. 29.95 (ISBN 0-87371-020-7). Lewis Pubs Inc.

--Subordinate Sex. 256p. 1982. 45.00x (ISBN 0-85140-550-9, Pub. by Arlington England). State Mutual Bk.

Ellis, Derek V., ed. Marine Tailings Disposal. LC 82-73416. (Illus.). 368p. 1982. 59.95 (ISBN 0-250-40614-4). Butterworth.

Ellis, Dicki L., et al. Women's Work & Women's Studies 1972. pap. 6.00 (ISBN 0-912786-24-8). Know Inc.

Ellis, Dorsey D. Look unto the Rock: A History of the Presbyterian Church, in West Virginia from 1719 to 1974. LC 82-60889. (Illus.). 372p. (Orig.). 1982. pap. 14.95 (ISBN 0-9609076-0-2). McClain.

Ellis, E. Earle. The World of St. John: The Gospels & the Epistles. 96p. (Orig.). 1984. pap. 4.95 (ISBN 0-8028-0013-0). Eerdmans.

Ellis, Edward. A Chronological History of the Rangeley Lakes Region, Maine. LC 83-80648. (Illus.). 100p. (Orig.). 1983. pap. text ed. 7.50 (ISBN 0-9611126-1-1). E Ellis.

Ellis, Edwin A., ed. see Baums, Roosevelt.

Ellis, Edwin J. Real Blake. LC 75-117994. (Studies in Blake, No. 3). 1970. Repr. of 1906 ed. lib. bdg. 49.95x (ISBN 0-8383-1049-4). Haskell.

Ellis, Edwin J., ed. The Poetical Works of William Blake, Vols. 1 & 2. 1980. Repr. of 1906 ed. lib. bdg. 175.00 set (ISBN 0-8495-1342-1). Arden Lib.

Ellis, Eilish. Emigrants from Ireland, 1847-1852: State-Aided Emigration Schemes from Crown Estates in Ireland. LC 76-39654. 68p. 1983. pap. 5.00 (ISBN 0-8063-0748-X). Genealog Pub.

Ellis, Eleanor A., ed. Northern Cookbook. (Illus.). 358p. 1967. pap. 9.95 (ISBN 0-295-95968-1, Pub. by Hurtig Pubs). U of Wash Pr.

Ellis, Elizabeth A. The Least of My Sisters. LC 79-66928. 229p. 8.95 (ISBN 0-533-04426-X). Vantage.

Ellis, Ella T. Hugo & the Princess Nena. LC 82-16315. 204p. (gr. 5-8). 1983. 10.95 (ISBN 0-689-30953-8). Atheneum.

--Riptide. (Illus.). (gr. 7 up). 1973. pap. 0.95 (ISBN 0-689-70361-9, A-25, Aladdin). Atheneum.

--Roam the Wild Country. LC 67-18990. (Illus.). 224p. (gr. 3-7). 1967. pap. 0.95 (ISBN 0-689-70310-4, A-13, Aladdin). Atheneum.

--Sleepwalker's Moon. LC 79-22665. 252p. (gr. 7 up). 1980. 9.95 (ISBN 0-689-30739-X). Atheneum.

Ellis, Elmo I. Opportunities in Broadcasting. (VGM Career Bks.). (Illus.). 160p. 1983. 7.95 (ISBN 0-8442-6371-0, 6371-0, Passport Bks); pap. 5.95 (ISBN 0-8442-6372-9). Natl Textbk.

Ellis, Eugene, et al, eds. see Farmer, W. D.

Ellis, F. R., ed. Inherited Disease & Anaesthesia. (Monographs in Anaesthesiology: Vol. 9). 464p. 1981. 98.75 (ISBN 0-444-80266-5, Biomedical Pr). Elsevier.

Ellis, F. S. An Alphabetical Table of Contents to Shelley's Poetical Works. LC 74-30275. (Shelley Society Fourth Ser.: No. 6). Repr. of 1888 ed. 20.00 (ISBN 0-404-11517-9). AMS Pr.

Ellis, F. S., ed. see Jacobus De Varagine.

Ellis, F. S., ed. see Lull, Ramon.

Ellis, Florence H. Pueblo Indians, Vol. Two: Archaeologic & Ethnologic Data: Acoma-Laguna Land Claims. (American Indian Ethnohistory Ser: Indians of the Southwest). (Illus.). lib. bdg. 51.00 (ISBN 0-8240-0726-3). Garland Pub.

Ellis, Forrest D., jt. auth. see Helveston, Eugene M.

Ellis, Frances H., ed. see Sachs, Hans.

Ellis, Frank H. Canada's Flying Heritage. 1980. pap. 16.95 (ISBN 0-8020-6417-5). U of Toronto Pr.

Ellis, Frank H., ed. Poems on Affairs of State: Augustan Satirical Verse, 1660-1714, Vol. 6, 1697-1704. (Illus.). 1970. 67.00x (ISBN 0-300-01194-6). Yale U Pr.

--Poems on Affairs of State-Augustan Satirical Verse, 1660-1714, Vol. 7: 1704-1714. LC 63-7938. (Illus.). 760p. 1975. 67.00x (ISBN 0-300-01772-3). Yale U Pr.

--Swift vs. Mainwaring: The Examiner & the Medley. (Illus.). 584p. 1985. 59.00 (ISBN 0-19-812522-4). Oxford U Pr.

--Twentieth Century Interpretations of Robinson Crusoe. (Interpretations Ser). 1969. 9.95 (ISBN 0-13-781997-8, Spec); pap. 1.25 (ISBN 0-13-781989-7). P-H.

Ellis, Franklin. History of Columbia County, New York 1878. (Illus.). 550p. 1985. Repr. of 1878 ed. deluxe ed. write for info. (ISBN 0-932334-57-1). Heart of the Lakes.

Ellis, Frederick S. Lexical Concordance to the Poetical Works of Percy Bysshe Shelley. LC 68-57904. (Bibliography & Reference Ser: No. 237). 1968. Repr. of 1892 ed. 33.50 (ISBN 0-8337-1053-2). B Franklin.

--Lexical Concordance to the Poetical Works of Percy Bysshe Shelley. 1892. 55.00 (ISBN 0-384-14185-4). Johnson Repr.

--St. Tammany Parish: L'autre Cote du lac. LC 80-63. (Illus.). 304p. 1982. 25.00 (ISBN 0-88289-252-5). Pelican.

Ellis, Frederick S., tr. see Lorris, Guillaume de & Clopinel, J.

Ellis, G. F., jt. auth. see Hawking, Steven.

Ellis, G. M., tr. Boso's Life of Alexander III. 122p. 1973. 13.50x (ISBN 0-87471-183-5). Rowman.

Ellis, G. P., jt. auth. see Criddle, W. J.

Ellis, G. P., ed. Chromenes, Chromanones, & Chromones: Chemistry of Heterocyclic Compounds-A Series of Monographs. (Vol. 31). 1196p. 1977. 301.50 (ISBN 0-471-38212-4). Wiley.

Ellis, G. P. & West, G. B., eds. Progress in Medicinal Chemistry, 2 vols. LC 62-2712. Vol. 5. pap. 100.80 (ISBN 0-317-10458-6, 2020709); Vol. 6. pap. 96.00 (ISBN 0-317-10459-4). Bks Demand UMI.

--Progress in Medicinal Chemistry, Vols. 8-15. LC 73-86078. 298p. 1973-78. (Biomedical Pr); Vol. 12. 108.50 (ISBN 0-444-10880-7); Vol. 13. 86.00 (ISBN 0-7204-0650-1); Vol. 14. 75.75 (ISBN 0-7204-0645-5); Vol. 15. 105.50 (ISBN 0-7204-0655-2). Elsevier.

--Progress in Medicinal Chemistry, Vol. 16. LC 62-2712. 292p. 1979. 89.75 (ISBN 0-7204-0667-6, Biomedical Pr). Elsevier.

--Progress in Medicinal Chemistry, Vol. 17. 208p. 1980. 78.25 (ISBN 0-7204-0669-2, Biomedcal Pr). Elsevier.

--Progress in Medicinal Chemistry, Vol. 18. 252p. 1982. 69.00 (ISBN 0-444-80345-9, Biomedical Pr). Elsevier.

--Progress in Medicinal Chemistry, Vol. 19. 1983. 93.75 (ISBN 0-444-80415-3, Biomedical Pr). Elsevier.

--Progress in Medicinal Chemistry, Vol. 20. 368p. 1984. 108.00 (ISBN 0-444-80501-X, Biomedical Pr). Elsevier.

--Progress in Medicinal Chemistry, Vol. 21. 294p. 1985. 83.50 (ISBN 0-444-80603-2). Elsevier.

Ellis, Geoffrey. Napoleon's Continental Blockade: The Case of Alsace. (Oxford Historical Monographs). (Illus.). 1981. 52.00x (ISBN 0-19-821881-8). Oxford U Pr.

Ellis, Geoffrey U. Thackeray. LC 79-160465. (English Literature Ser., No. 33). 1971. Repr. of 1933 ed. lib. bdg. 33.95x (ISBN 0-8383-1300-0). Haskell.

Ellis, George. Specimens of Early English Metrical Romances. Halliwell, J. O., ed. LC 68-55549. (Bohn's Antiquarian Library Ser). Repr. of 1848 ed. 17.50 (ISBN 0-404-50007-2). AMS Pr.

--Specimens of Early English Metrical Romances. 1973. Repr. of 1848 ed. 12.00 (ISBN 0-8274-0587-1). R West.

Ellis, George, jt. auth. see Dewar, David.

Ellis, George, jt. auth. see Neelon, Francis A.

Ellis, George C. Memoir of Sir Benjamin Thompson, Count Rumford, with Notices of His Daughter. LC 72-8777. (American Revolutionary Ser.). 1979. Repr. of 1871 ed. lib. bdg. 38.00x (ISBN 0-8398-0457-1). Irvington.

Ellis, George E. Puritan Age & Rule in the Colony of the Massachusetts Bay, 1629-1685. LC 75-122838. (Research & Source Ser.: No. 522). 1970. Repr. of 1888 ed. lib. bdg. 32.00 (ISBN 0-8337-1054-0). B Franklin.

Ellis, George W. Leopard's Claw. LC 71-144605. Repr. of 1917 ed. 12.50 (ISBN 0-404-00156-4). AMS Pr.

--Negro Culture in West Africa: A Social Study of the Negro Group of Vai-Speaking People, with Its Own Invented Alphabet & Written Language. LC 15-1680. 1971. Repr. of 1914 ed. 25.00 (ISBN 0-384-14190-0). Johnson Repr.

Ellis, George W. & Morris, John E. King Philip's War. LC 76-43697. Repr. of 1906 ed. 28.50 (ISBN 0-404-15529-4). AMS Pr.

Ellis, Glenn. Air Crash Investigation of General Aviation Aircraft. (Illus.). 260p. 1984. 27.95x (ISBN 0-914565-00-1); pap. 17.95 (ISBN 0-914565-01-X). Capstan Pubns.

Ellis, Gwyn P. Medicinal Chemistry Reviews: A Select Bibliography. 170p. 1972. 19.50 (ISBN 0-208-01258-3, Archon). Shoe String.

Ellis, Gwynn P. & Lockhart, Ian M., eds. Chromans & Tocopherols. LC 80-16902. (The Chemistry of Heterocyclic Compounds: Vol. 36). 1981. 198.95 (ISBN 0-471-03038-4, Pub. by Wiley-Interscience). Wiley.

Ellis, H. Early Impressions of Paris. 59.95 (ISBN 0-8490-0072-6). Gordon Pr.

--Nineteenth Century. an Utopian Retrospect. LC 5-3952. Repr. of 1901 ed. 17.00 (ISBN 0-527-26930-1). Kraus Repr.

Ellis, H. B., jt. auth. see Todd, J. P.

Ellis, H. D., jt. auth. see Shepherd, J. W.

Ellis, H. M., et al. Problems in Community Wastes Management. (Public Health Papers Ser: No. 38). 89p. 1969. pap. 2.80 (ISBN 92-4-130038-8, 1352). World Health.

Ellis, Harlan, ed. see Dick-Read, Grantly.

Ellis, Harold. Clinical Anatomy: A Revision & Applied Anatomy for Clinical Students. 7th ed. 502p. 1983. casebound 25.50 (ISBN 0-632-00947-0, B1626-3). Mosby.

--Famous Operations. LC 83-8530. (Illus.). 134p. 1983. 12.95 (ISBN 0-932036-11-2). Harwal Pub Co.

--Varicose Veins. LC 82-3975. (Positive Health Guide Ser.). (Illus.). 112p. 1983. pap. 7.95 (ISBN 0-668-05340-2, 5340). Arco.

Ellis, Harold M. Joseph Dennie & His Circle. LC 73-131489. (BCL Ser. I). Repr. of 1915 ed. 14.50 (ISBN 0-404-02308-8). AMS Pr.

--Joseph Dennie & His Circle: A Study in American Literature from 1792-1812. vii, 285p. pap. 13.00 (ISBN 0-384-14195-1). Johnson Repr.

Ellis, Harry B. The Dilemma of Israel. 1970. pap. 5.25 (ISBN 0-8447-1041-5). Am Enterprise.

Ellis, Harry E. Dr. Pepper: King of Beverages. (Illus.). 268p. 1979. 24.95 (ISBN 0-9607448-0-0). Dr Pepper.

Ellis, Havelock. Affirmations. LC 77-20814. 1977. Repr. of 1915 ed. lib. bdg. 30.00 (ISBN 0-89341-194-9). Longwood Pub Group.

--Art of Life, from the Works of Havelock Ellis. Herbert, Mrs. S., ed. LC 75-105010. (Essay Index Reprint Ser.). 1929. 17.00 (ISBN 0-8369-1462-7). Ayer Co Pubs.

--Chapman. 1979. Repr. of 1934 ed. lib. bdg. 20.00 (ISBN 0-8495-1328-6). Arden Lib.

--Chapman. LC 74-12498. 1934. lib. bdg. 15.00 (ISBN 0-8414-3972-9). Folcroft.

--Chapman. 1934. 20.00 (ISBN 0-8274-2024-2). R West.

--Criminal. LC 70-156014. Repr. of 1890 ed. 12.50 (ISBN 0-404-09114-8). AMS Pr.

--The Criminal. LC 77-88565. 1977. Repr. of 1916 ed. lib. bdg. 25.00 (ISBN 0-89341-462-X). Longwood Pub Group.

--Criminal. 5th, rev. & enl ed. LC 74-172610. (Criminology, Law Enforcement, & Social Problems Ser.: No. 200). (Illus., With intro added 1973). 1973. Repr. of 1914 ed. 15.00x (ISBN 0-87585-200-9). Patterson Smith.

--The Dance of Life. LC 72-9085. 377p. 1973. Repr. of 1923 ed. lib. bdg. 32.50x (ISBN 0-8371-6572-5, ELDL). Greenwood.

--The Dance of Life. 1978. Repr. of 1923 ed. lib. bdg. 20.00 (ISBN 0-8492-0781-9). R West.

--Essays in War-Time. LC 77-90633. (Essay Index Reprint Ser). 1917. 18.00 (ISBN 0-8369-1290-X). Ayer Co Pubs.

--From Rousseau to Proust. facs. ed. LC 68-24851. (Essay Index Reprint Ser). 1968. Repr. of 1935 ed. 18.00 (ISBN 0-8369-0412-5). Ayer Co Pubs.

--The Genius of Europe. LC 74-10374. 1974. Repr. of 1951 ed. lib. bdg. 21.00x (ISBN 0-8371-7680-8, ELGE). Greenwood.

--Man & Woman. LC 73-20621. (Sex, Marriage & Society Ser.). (Illus.). 430p. 1974. Repr. of 1904 ed. 28.00 (ISBN 0-405-05826-8). Ayer Co Pubs.

--Man & Woman. 563p. 1981. Repr. of 1926 ed. lib. bdg. 45.00 (ISBN 0-89760-153-X). Telegraph Bks.

--My Confessional. facs. ed. LC 79-121464. (Essay Index Reprint Ser). 1934. 18.00 (ISBN 0-8369-1918-1). Ayer Co Pubs.

--My Confessional. (Essay Index Reprint Ser.). 245p. 1982. Repr. of 1934 ed. lib. bdg. 15.00 (ISBN 0-8290-0783-0). Irvington.

--My Life: Autobiography of Havelock Ellis. LC 83-45749. Repr. of 1939 ed. 42.50 (ISBN 0-404-20087-7). AMS Pr.

--New Spirit. LC 39-224. 1969. Repr. of 1935 ed. 15.00 (ISBN 0-527-26920-4). Kraus Repr.

--Philosophy of Conflict & Other Essays in War-Time: 2nd Series. LC 70-90634. (Essay Index Reprint Ser.). 1919. 20.00 (ISBN 0-8369-1568-2). Ayer Co Pubs.

--Psychology of Sex. 15.95 (ISBN 0-87523-013-X). Emerson.

--The Psychology of Sex. 2nd ed. LC 78-7414. 1978. pap. 4.95 (ISBN 0-15-674702-2, Harv). HarBraceJ.

--Selected Essays. LC 83-45750. Repr. of 1936 ed. 32.50 (ISBN 0-404-20088-5). Ams Pr.

--Sex & Marriage: Eros in Contemporary Life. LC 77-7264. 1977. Repr. of 1952 ed. lib. bdg. 27.50 (ISBN 0-8371-9667-1, ELSM). Greenwood.

--The Soul of Spain. LC 75-22642. (Illus.). 420p. 1976. Repr. of 1937 ed. lib. bdg. 25.00x (ISBN 0-8371-8373-1, ELSS). Greenwood.

--A Study of British Genius. 1978. Repr. of 1926 ed. lib. bdg. 30.00 (ISBN 0-8495-1319-7). Arden Lib.

--The Task of Social Hygiene. 414p. 1980. Repr. lib. bdg. 25.00 (ISBN 0-8495-1340-5). Arden Lib.

--Thomas Middleton: Best Plays of Old Dramatists, 2 vols. Repr. Set. lib. bdg. 69.00 (ISBN 0-403-00123-4). Scholarly.

--Three Modern Seers. 227p. 1980. Repr. lib. bdg. 35.00 (ISBN 0-8495-1335-9). Arden Lib.

--Three Modern Seers. 59.95 (ISBN 0-8490-1211-2). Gordon Pr.

--Views & Reviews, 2 Vols in 1. facsimile ed. LC 79-111829. (Essay Index Reprint Ser.). 1932. 29.00 (ISBN 0-8369-1606-9). Ayer Co Pubs.

--The World of Dreams. 288p. 1981. Repr. of 1922 ed. lib. bdg. 40.00 (ISBN 0-89987-208-5). Darby Bks.

--The World of Dreams. LC 75-43879. (Illus.). 1976. Repr. of 1922 ed. 40.00x (ISBN 0-8103-3780-0). Gale.

--The Writings of Havelock Ellis, 12 vols. 1975. lib. bdg. 50.00 ea. (ISBN 0-8490-1338-0). Gordon Pr.

Ellis, Havelock & Symonds, John A. Sexual Inversion. LC 75-12312. (Homosexuality: Lesbians & Gay Men in Society, History & Literature Ser.). 1975. Repr. of 1897 ed. 22.00x (ISBN 0-405-07363-1). Ayer Co Pubs.

Ellis, Havelock, ed. see Heine, Heinrich.

Ellis, Havelock, ed. see Talbot, Eugene S.

Ellis, Mrs. Havelock. Personal Impressions of Edward Carpenter. 59.95 (ISBN 0-8490-0817-4). Gordon Pr.

Ellis, Henry. General Introduction to Domesday Book, 2 vols. LC 77-157520. 1060p. 1973. Repr. of 1833 ed. Set. 35.00 (ISBN 0-8063-0482-0). Genealog Pub.

--Journal of the Proceedings of the Late Embassy to China. LC 72-79819. (China Library Ser.). 1972. Repr. of 1817 ed. 40.00 (ISBN 0-8420-1382-2). Scholarly Res Inc.

--Original Letters of Eminent Literary Men. 1973. Repr. of 1843 ed. 75.00 (ISBN 0-8274-1685-7). R West.

--Voyage to Hudson's Bay, by the Dobbs Galley & California, in the Years 1746 & 1747, for Discovering a North West Passage. 1748. 32.00 (ISBN 0-384-14200-1). Johnson Repr.

Ellis, Henry, ed. Chronica Johannis de Oxenedes (to 1292) (Rolls Ser.: No. 13). Repr. of 1859 ed. 44.00 (ISBN 0-317-16660-3). Kraus Repr.

--Original Letters Illustrative of English History, 11 Vols. Repr. of 1846 ed. Set. 302.50 (ISBN 0-404-02310-X); 27.50 ea. AMS Pr.

--Original Letters of Eminent Literary Men of the Sixteenth, Seventeeth, & Eighteenth Centuries. Repr. of 1843 ed. 46.00 (ISBN 0-384-14197-8). Johnson Repr.

--Original Letters of Eminent Literary Men of the 16th, 17th & 18th Centuries. LC 71-166022. (Camden Society, London. Publications, First Ser.: No. 23). Repr. of 1843 ed. 46.00 (ISBN 0-404-50123-0). AMS Pr.

--Pylgrymage of Sir Richard Guylforde to the Holy Land, A. D. 1506. LC 75-166023. (Camden Society, London. Publications, First Ser.: No. 51). Repr. of 1851 ed. 19.00 (ISBN 0-404-50151-6). AMS Pr.

Ellis, Henry, ed. see Brand, John.

Ellis, Henry, ed. see Charles, Nicholas.

Ellis, Henry, ed. see Hall, Edward.

Ellis, Henry, ed. see Holinshed, Raphael.

Ellis, Henry, ed. see Norden, John.

Ellis, Henry, ed. see Smith, Richard.

Ellis, Henry, ed. see Vergilius, Polydorus.

Ellis, Henry, illus. Original Letters of Eminent Literary Men of the 16th, 17th, & 18th Centuries. 460p. 1980. Repr. lib. bdg. 85.00 (ISBN 0-89984-199-6). Century Bookbindery.

Ellis, Henry C. & Hunt, R. Reed. Fundamentals of Human Memory & Cognition. 3rd ed. 288p. 1983. pap. text ed. write for info. (ISBN 0-697-06554-5); instr's. manual avail. (ISBN 0-697-06555-3). Wm C Brown.

Ellis, Herbert A. Shakespeare's Lusty Punning in Love's Labour's Lost. LC 73-86159. (Studies in English Literature Ser.: Vol. 81). 239p. 1974. text ed. 29.50x (ISBN 90-2792-616-6). Mouton.

Ellis, Herbert B., jt. auth. see Todd, James P.

Ellis, Hercules. Romances & Ballads of Ireland. 1980. lib. bdg. 79.95 (ISBN 0-8490-3172-9). Gordon Pr.

Ellis, Hilda R. Road to Hell: A Study of the Conception of the Dead in Old Norse Literature. LC 68-23286. (Illus.). 1968. Repr. of 1943 ed. lib. bdg. 18.75 (ISBN 0-8371-0070-4, ELRH). Greenwood.

Ellis, Howard S. Exchange Control in Central Europe. LC 69-13892. Repr. of 1941 ed. lib. bdg. 17.75x (ISBN 0-8371-4462-0, ELEX). Greenwood.

--Notes on Stagflation. 1978. pap. 2.25 (ISBN 0-8447-3323-7). Am Enterprise.

--Private Enterprise & Socialism in the Middle East. 1970. pap. 5.25 (ISBN 0-8447-1040-7). Am Enterprise.

Ellis, Howard S., ed. The Economy of Brazil. LC 69-16737. 1969. 36.50x (ISBN 0-520-01520-7). U of Cal Pr.

Ellis, Howard S., ed. see Buchanan, Norman S.

Ellis, Iris. S. O. S. Save on Shopping Directory. Jaffe, Marc, ed. LC 81-64190. 768p. 1985. pap. 9.95 (ISBN 0-394-73805-5, Pub. by Villard Bks). Random.

--SOS: Save on Shopping Directory. 9th rev. ed. 1985. pap. 8.95 (ISBN 0-394-72809-2, Pub. by Villard Bks). Random.

Ellis, J. C., jt. auth. see Murray, M. A.

Ellis, J. M. Narration in the German Novelle. LC 78-73602. (Anglica Germanica Ser.: No. 2). 1979. pap. 12.95 (ISBN 0-521-29592-0). Cambridge U Pr.

Ellis, J. P., jt. auth. see Summerhayes, C. P.

Ellis, J. R. Philip Second & Macedonian Imperialism. (Aspects of Greek & Roman Life Ser.). (Illus.). 1977. 19.95 (ISBN 0-500-40028-8). Thames Hudson.

Ellis, J. R., jt. auth. see Milns, R. D.

Ellis, Jack & Helbig, Susan. The Health Care Consultant As a Change Agent. 134p. 1981. 7.00 (ISBN 0-318-12844-6, 1009P); 10.00, with annotated bibliography (ISBN 0-318-12845-4). Am Med Record Assn.

Ellis, Jack, jt. auth. see Harwood, Bruce.

Ellis, Jack, et al. The Film Book Bibliography: 1940-1975. LC 78-4055. 764p. 1979. 37.50 (ISBN 0-8108-1127-8). Scarecrow.

Ellis, Jack C. A History of Film. 2nd ed. (Illus.). 496p. 1985. pap. text ed. 23.95 (ISBN 0-13-389479-7). P-H.

Ellis, Jack D. The Early Life of Georges Clemenceau, 1841-1893. LC 79-19118. 1980. 29.95x (ISBN 0-7006-0196-1). U Pr of KS.

--The French Socialists & the Problem of the Peace 1904-1914. LC 67-14668. 1967. 3.50 (ISBN 0-8294-0028-1). Loyola.

Ellis, James. The Slow-to-Learn. 1973. 6.95x (ISBN 0-85078-072-1); pap. 3.95x (ISBN 0-85078-073-X). Technomic.

Ellis, James, ed. English Drama of the Nineteenth Century: An Index & Finding Guide. 350p. 1985. 175.00x (ISBN 0-918414-15-6). Readex Bks.

Ellis, James, ed. see Gilbert, W. S.

Ellis, James J. Charles Kingsley. 1890. Repr. 25.00 (ISBN 0-8274-3799-4). R West.

Ellis, Jane, ed. see Yakunin, Gleb & Regelson, Lev.

Ellis, Jane, tr. An Early Soviet Saint: The Life of Father Zachariah. 1977. 6.95 (ISBN 0-87243-069-3). Templegate.

Ellis, Janice R. & Hartley, Celia L. Nursing in Today's World: Challenges, Issues & Trends. 2nd ed. (Illus.). 350p. 1984. pap. text ed. 12.50 (ISBN 0-397-54480-4, 64-04214, Lippincott Nursing). Lippincott.

Ellis, Janice R. & Nowlis, Elisabeth A. Nursing: A Human Needs Approach. 3rd ed. 720p. 1985. text ed. 30.50; instr's. manual 2.00; test bank avail. HM.

Ellis, Janice R. & Nowlis, Elizabeth A. Nursing: A Human Needs Approach. 2nd ed. LC 80-82841. (Illus.). 528p. 1981. text ed. 29.95; instr's manual 0.50 (ISBN 0-395-29643-9). HM.

Ellis, Janice R., et al. Modules for Basic Nursing Skills. 3rd ed. LC 83-81801. 1983. Vol. I, 650pps. pap. text ed. 15.50 (ISBN 0-395-34463-8); Vol. II, 650pps. pap. text ed. 15.50 (ISBN 0-395-34464-6); test bank 3.95 (ISBN 0-395-34466-2). HM.

Ellis, Jeffery W. & Beckman, Charles R. A Clinical Manual of Gynecology. (Illus.). 608p. 1983. pap. 17.95 (ISBN 0-8385-1135-X). ACC.

Ellis, Jeffrey. Towards a General Comparative Linguistics. (Janua Linguarum, Ser. Minor: No. 52). (Orig.). 1966. pap. text ed. 16.80x (ISBN 90-2790-584-3). Mouton.

Ellis, Jeffrey W. & Beckman, Charles R. A Clinical Manual of Obstetrics. (Illus.). 800p. 1983. pap. 17.95 (ISBN 0-8385-1140-6). ACC.

Ellis, Jessie C. Index to Illustrations. LC 66-11619. (The Useful Reference Ser. of Library Bks: Vol. 95). 1966. lib. bdg. 13.00x (ISBN 0-87305-095-9). Faxon.

Ellis, Job B. & Everhart, Benjamin M. North American Pyrenomycetes. (Illus.). 1892. 50.00 (ISBN 0-384-14265-6). Johnson Repr.

Ellis, Jody. ABC's of Successful Living. LC 73-84733. 1974. pap. 3.95 (ISBN 0-913270-26-1). Sunstone Pr.

Ellis, Joe. The Church on Purpose: Keys to Effective Church Leadership. LC 82-3175. (Illus.). 112p. (Orig.). 1982. pap. 6.95 (ISBN 0-87239-441-7, 88584). Standard Pub.

Ellis, John. Cassino: The Hollow Victory-The Battle for Rome, January-June 1944. (Illus.). 624p. 1984. 19.95 (ISBN 0-07-019427-0). McGraw.

--A Financial Guide for the Self Employed. 240p. 1974. pap. 4.95 (ISBN 0-8092-8329-8). Contemp Bks.

--The New Financial Guide for the Self-Employed. (Illus.). 256p. 1981. pap. 7.95 (ISBN 0-8092-5899-4). Contemp Bks.

--The Social History of the Machine Gun. LC 74-26204. (Illus.). Repr. of 1975 ed. 46.50 (ISBN 0-8357-9483-0, 2013992). Bks Demand UMI.

--The Social History of the Machine Gun. 17.00 (ISBN 0-405-14209-9). Ayer Co Pubs.

--Visible Fictions. (Illus.). 232p. 1983. pap. 10.95x (ISBN 0-7100-9304-7). Routledge & Kegan.

Ellis, John, jt. auth. see Coward, Rosalind.

Ellis, John & Ferrara, Sergio, eds. Unification of Fundamental Particle Interactions II. 530p. 1983. 79.50x (ISBN 0-306-41166-0, Plenum Pr). Plenum Pub.

Ellis, John A., jt. ed. see Ruck, Hendrick W.

Ellis, John B. Free Love & Its Votaries. LC 77-134430. Repr. of 1870 ed. 35.00 (ISBN 0-404-08474-5). AMS Pr.

Ellis, John H. Medicine in Kentucky. LC 76-51156. (Kentucky Bicentennial Bookshelf Ser.). (Illus.). 112p. 1977. 6.95 (ISBN 0-8131-0232-4). U Pr of Ky.

Ellis, John M. Heinrich Von Kleist: Studies in the Character & Meaning of His Writings. (Studies in the Germanic Languages & Literatures: No. 94). xvii, 194p. 1979. 17.50 (ISBN 0-8078-8094-9). U of NC Pr.

--Kleist's Prinz Friedrich von Homburg: A Critical Study. LC 70-627808. (University of California Publications in Modern Philology Ser.: Vol. 97). pap. 35.00 (ISBN 0-317-08876-9, 2013803). Bks Demand UMI.

--One Fairy Story Too Many: The Brothers Grimm & Their Tales. LC 83-1193. 219p. 1983. 17.50x (ISBN 0-226-20546-0). U of Chicago Pr.

--One Fairy Story Too Many: The Brothers Grimm & Their Tales. LC 83-1193. x, 214p. 1985. pap. text ed. 6.95 (ISBN 0-226-20547-9). U of Chicago Pr.

--The Theory of Literary Criticism: A Logical Analysis. LC 73-83055. (Cal Ser.: No. 355). 1977. pap. 6.95 (ISBN 0-520-03413-9). U of Cal Pr.

Ellis, John O., jt. auth. see Bealer, Alex W.

Ellis, John T. American Catholicism. 2nd ed. Boorstin, Daniel J., ed. LC 69-19274. (Chicago History of American Civilization Ser.). 1969. pap. 4.95 (ISBN 0-226-20556-8, CHAC5). U of Chicago Pr.

--Catholic Bishops: A Memoir. 1983. pap. 6.95 (ISBN 0-89453-463-7). M Glazier.

--Guide to Real Estate License Examination. 3rd ed. (Illus.). 336p. 1983. pap. 21.95 (ISBN 0-13-371088-2). P-H.

Ellis, John T. & Beam, Victoria R. Mastering Real Estate Math in One Day. 1983. pap. 11.95 (ISBN 0-13-559666-1). P-H.

Ellis, John T. & Beck, John A. Guide to the A. S. I. Real Estate License Examinations. LC 84-6913. 1984. 21.95 (ISBN 0-13-368812-7). P-H.

--Guide to the ACT Real Estate License Examinations. LC 83-24202. (Prentice-Hall Series in Real Estate). 1984. pap. text ed. 21.95 (ISBN 0-13-368804-6). P-H.

Ellis, John T. & Trisco, Robert. A Guide to American Catholic History. 2nd, rev. ed. LC 81-17585. 265p. 1982. lib. bdg. 29.85 (ISBN 0-87436-318-7); pap. 19.95 (ISBN 0-87436-315-2). ABC-Clio.

Ellis, John W. Running into Trouble. LC 83-70724. (Illus.). 115p. 1983. pap. 9.95 (ISBN 0-912749-00-8). Brittany Pr.

Ellis, Joseph. The New England Mind in Transition: Samuel Johnson of Connecticut, 1696-1772. LC 73-77149. (Historical Publications, Miscellany Ser.: No. 98). (Illus.). 288p. 1973. 24.50x (ISBN 0-300-01615-8). Yale U Pr.

Ellis, Joseph & Moore, Robert. School for Soldiers: West Point & the Profession of Arms. LC 74-79638. (Illus.). 1974. pap. 5.95 (ISBN 0-19-502022-7, 454, GB). Oxford U Pr.

Ellis, Joseph J. After the Revolution: Profiles of Early American Culture. (Illus.). 272p. 1981. pap. text ed. 5.95x (ISBN 0-393-95200-2). Norton.

Ellis, Josephy & Moore, Robert. School for Soldiers: An Inquiry into West Point. 1974. 19.95x (ISBN 0-19-501843-5). Oxford U Pr.

Ellis, Joyce. The Big Split. rev. ed. 128p. 1983. pap. 3.95 (ISBN 0-8024-0190-2). Moody.

--Plug into a Rainbow. 144p. (Orig.). 1984. pap. 3.95 (ISBN 0-310-47192-3, 12495P, Pub. by Daybreak). Zondervan.

--A Study of the Business Fortunes of William Cotesworth c. 1668-1726. Bruchey, Stuart, ed. LC 80-2805. (Dissertations in European Economic History II). (Illus.). 1981. lib. bdg. 22.00x (ISBN 0-405-13989-6). Ayer Co Pubs.

Ellis, Joyce & Lynn, Claire. Bible Bees. (Illus.). 36p. (gr. k). 1981. 1.25 (ISBN 0-89323-049-9). Bible Memory.

Ellis, Joyce K. Plug into God's Rainbow. LC 84-19213. 1984. pap. 3.95 (ISBN 0-317-14050-7). Zondervan.

Ellis, Joyce K., compiled by. Saved by a Broken Pole & Other Stories. 75p. (Orig.). (gr. 2-6). 1980. pap. 1.75 (ISBN 0-89323-007-3, 096). Bible Memory.

Ellis, Judith M., jt. auth. see Ellis, Peter F.

Ellis, Julia. East Wind. 384p. (Orig.). 1984. pap. 3.95 (ISBN 0-523-42174-5). Pinnacle Bks.

--Glorious Morning. LC 82-72068. 1982. 14.95 (ISBN 0-87795-431-3). Arbor Hse.

Ellis, Julie. Eulalie. 1978. pap. 1.95 (ISBN 0-449-23550-5, Crest). Fawcett.

--Girl in White. pap. 1.75 (ISBN 0-671-80808-7). WSP.

--Glorious Morning. 1984. pap. 3.95 (ISBN 0-8217-1313-2). Zebra.

--The Hampton Women. 384p. 1981. pap. 2.95 (ISBN 0-449-24465-2, Crest). Fawcett.

--Maison Jennie. 293p. 1984. 15.95 (ISBN 0-87795-572-7). Arbor Hse.

--Maison Jennie. 352p. 1985. pap. 3.95 (ISBN 0-523-42357-8). Pinnacle Bks.

--The Only Sin. 1985. 17.95 (ISBN 0-87795-733-9). Arbor Hse.

--The Poles. (Orig.). 1984. pap. 3.95 (ISBN 0-440-06989-0). Dell.

--Rich Is Best. 1985. 16.95 (ISBN 0-87795-629-4). Arbor Hse.

--Savage Oaks. 1979. pap. 2.25 (ISBN 0-449-23996-9, Crest). Fawcett.

Ellis, Keith. Critical Approaches to Ruben Dario. LC 73-93235. (University of Toronto Romance Ser.). 1975. 20.00x (ISBN 0-8020-5309-2). U of Toronto Pr.

--Cuba's Nicholas Guillen: Poetry & Ideology. (University of Toronto Romance Ser.: No. 47). 261p. 1983. 27.50x (ISBN 0-8020-5619-9). U of Toronto Pr.

--Number Power. 1980. pap. 4.95 (ISBN 0-312-57989-6). St Martin.

--Thomas Edison: Genius of Electricity. 99p. 1976. 9.95x (ISBN 0-8448-1010-X). Crane-Russak Co.

Ellis, Keith, tr. see Yanes, Gabriela, et al.

Ellis, L. E. Statistics & Probability (Draft Edition) (School Mathematics Project Further Mathematics Ser). (Illus.). 1971. text ed. 9.95 (ISBN 0-521-08026-6). Cambridge U Pr.

Ellis, Leigh. Green Lady. 208p. 1981. pap. 2.25 (ISBN 0-380-77701-0, 77701). Avon.

--The Quick. 208p. 1982. pap. 2.25 (ISBN 0-380-79640-6, 79640-6). Avon.

--Tessa of Destiny. 1979. pap. 2.50 (ISBN 0-380-75028-7, 75028-7). Avon.

Ellis, Lewis E. Frank B. Kellogg & American Foreign Relations, 1925-1929. LC 74-10636. 303p. 1974. Repr. of 1961 ed. lib. bdg. 22.00 (ISBN 0-8371-7651-4, ELFK). Greenwood.

--Reciprocity, Nineteen Eleven: A Study in Canadian-American Relations. LC 68-57601. (Illus.). 1969. Repr. of 1939 ed. lib. bdg. 15.00 (ISBN 0-8371-0409-2, ELCA). Greenwood.

Ellis, Loudell, jt. auth. see Thacker, Ronald J.

Ellis, Loudell O. Church Treasurer's Handbook. LC 77-10433. 1978. 6.95 (ISBN 0-8170-0762-8); pap. 6.95 (ISBN 0-8170-0780-6). Judson.

Ellis, Loudell O. & Thacker, Ronald J. Intermediate Accounting. 1980. text ed. 37.95 (ISBN 0-07-019252-9). McGraw.

Ellis, Lynn W. The Financial Side of Industrial Research Management. LC 83-19658. 250p. 1984. 41.95x (ISBN 0-471-89056-1, Pub. by Wiley-Interscience). Wiley.

Ellis, M. B. Dematiaceous Hyphomycetes. 608p. 1971. 88.00x (ISBN 0-85198-027-9, Pub. by CAB Bks England). State Mutual Bk.

--More Dematiaceous Hyphomycetes. 507p. 1976. 110.00x (ISBN 0-85198-365-0, Pub. by CAB Bks England). State Mutual Bk.

Ellis, M. Carolyn & Williams, Parham H. Mississippi Evidence. LC 83-208243. xii, 202p. 1983. incl. latest pocket part supplement 45.95 (ISBN 0-317-01697-0); separate Pocket Part Supplement, 1984 10.95. Harrison Co GA.

Ellis, M. J. & Juch, D. The Participation Exemption in the Netherlands. pap. 14.00 (ISBN 90-200-0501-4, Pub. by Kluwer Law Netherlands). Kluwer Academic.

Ellis, Maarten J., et al, eds. see Association Europpeene D'etudes Juridiques et Fiscales.

Ellis, Madeleine B. Rousseau's Socratic Aemilian Myths: A Literary Collation of "Emile" & the "Social Contract". LC 76-28197. 457p. 1977. 15.00x (ISBN 0-8142-0223-3). Ohio St U Pr.

Ellis, Marc. A Year of the Catholic Worker. LC 78-61722. 144p. 1978. pap. 2.45 (ISBN 0-8091-2140-9). Paulist Pr.

Ellis, Marc H. Peter Maurin: Prophet in the Twentieth Century. LC 81-82338. 200p. (Orig.). 1981. pap. 9.95 (ISBN 0-8091-2361-4). Paulist Pr.

Ellis, Margaret H. The Care of Prints & Drawings. Date not set. price not set. AASLH Pr.

Ellis, Maria, ed. Essays on the Ancient Near East in Memory of Jacob Joel Finkelstein. (Connecticut Academy of Arts & Science Memoir: Vol. XIX). (Illus.). xviii, 235p. 1977. 21.50 (ISBN 0-208-01714-3). Shoe String.

Ellis, Maria deJ. Agriculture & the State in Ancient Mesopotamia: An Introduction to Problems of Land Tenure. (Occasional Publications of the Babylonian Fund: Vol. 1). xii, 194p. 1976. 20.00 (ISBN 0-934718-28-8). Univ Mus of U PA.

Ellis, Mark & Ellis, Robert. Atari User's Guide: BASIC & Graphics for the Atari 400, 800, 1200. 288p. 1984. pap. 14.95 (ISBN 0-89303-323-5). Brady Comm.

Ellis, Martin B. & Greguras, Fred M. The Electronic Fund Transfer Act & Federal Board Regulation E: A Compliance Guide for Financial Institutions. (Illus.). 320p. 1982. lib. bdg. 65.00 (ISBN 0-13-251348-X). P-H.

Ellis, Mary. Those Dancing Years. 192p. 1982. 29.00x (ISBN 0-7195-3984-6, Pub. by Murray England). State Mutual Bk.

Ellis, Mel. The Mel Ellis Gift Set No. 1. Incl. Peg Leg Pete. 169p; The Wild Runners. 183p (ISBN 0-910937-13-3); This Mysterious River. 208p (ISBN 0-910937-14-1); Run, Rainey, Run. 152p (ISBN 0-910937-15-X). 1984. pap. 19.95 set (boxed) (ISBN 0-910937-11-7, Pub. by Unicorn-Star). Laranmark.

Ellis, Merle. Cutting up the Kitchen: The Butcher's Guide to Saving Money on Meat & Poultry. LC 75-26502. 216p. 1975. pap. 6.95 (ISBN 0-87701-071-4). Chronicle Bks.

Ellis, Michael D., ed. Dangerous Plants Snakes Anthropods & Marine Life-Toxicity & Treatment. LC 78-50198. 277p. 1978. 18.00 (ISBN 0-914768-32-8). Drug Intl Pubns.

Ellis, Michael J. Why People Play. (Illus.). 192p. 1973. 19.95 (ISBN 0-13-958991-0). P-H.

Ellis, Miles & Ellis, David. Adventure into BBC BASIC. LC 83-16998. 315p. 1984. pap. text ed. 14.95x (ISBN 0-471-90171-7, Pub. by Wiley Pr). Wiley.

Ellis, Mrs. The Mothers of England. 1974. lib. bdg. 59.95 (ISBN 0-685-51355-6). Revisionist Pr.

Ellis, N. R., ed. Aberrant Development in Infancy: Human & Animal Studies. 287p. 1975. 29.95x (ISBN 0-89859-420-0). L Erlbaum Assocs.

Ellis, Nigel, jt. auth. see Bowman, Pat.

Ellis, Norma, jt. auth. see Ellis, Charles.

Ellis, Norman. Employing Staff. 121p. 1984. 10.50 (ISBN 0-7279-0107-9, Pub. by British Med Assoc UK). Taylor & Francis.

Ellis, Norman, ed. International Review of Research in Mental Retardation, Vol. II. 412p. 1982. 41.50 (ISBN 0-12-366211-7). Acad Pr.

--International Review of Research in Mental Retardation, Vol. 10. (Serial Publication Ser.). 1981. 39.50 (ISBN 0-12-366210-9). Acad Pr.

Ellis, Norman E. & Cross, Lee, eds. Planning Programs for Early Education of the Handicapped. (First Chance Ser.). 1976. 9.95 (ISBN 0-8027-9039-9). Walker & Co.

Ellis, Norman R., ed. Aberrant Development in Infancy: Human & Animal Studies. LC 75-9657. 288p. 1975. 18.50 (ISBN 0-470-23859-3, Pub. by Wiley). Krieger.

--Handbook of Mental Deficiency, Psychological Theory & Research. 2nd ed. LC 79-18891. (Illus.). 816p. 1979. text ed. 49.95x (ISBN 0-89859-002-7). L Erlbaum Assocs.

--International Review of Research in Mental Retardation. Incl. Vol. 1. 1966. 65.00 (ISBN 0-12-366201-X); Vol. 2. 1966. 65.00 (ISBN 0-12-366202-8); Vol. 3. 1968. 65.00 (ISBN 0-12-366203-6); Vol. 4. 1970. 65.00 (ISBN 0-12-366204-4); Vol. 5. 1971. 65.00 (ISBN 0-12-366205-2); Vol. 6. 1973. 65.00 (ISBN 0-12-366206-0); Vol. 9. 1978. 55.00 (ISBN 0-12-366209-5). Acad Pr.

--International Review of Research in Mental Retardation, Vol. 12. 1984. 41.00 (ISBN 0-12-366212-5). Acad Pr.

--International Review of Research in Mental Retardation, Vol. 13. (Serial Publication). Date not set. price not set (ISBN 0-12-366213-3). Acad Pr.

Ellis, Oliver C. Shakespeare As a Scientist. LC 76-44822. 1933. lib. bdg. 8.50 (ISBN 0-8414-3951-6). Folcroft.

Ellis, P. B. The Cornish Language & Its Literature. 1974. pap. 14.95 (ISBN 0-7100-9070-6). Routledge & Kegan.

Ellis, P. Berresford. Story of the Cornish Language. pap. 3.95 (ISBN 0-686-25499-6). British Am Bks.

Ellis, P. Berresford, ed. James Connolly: Selected Writings. LC 73-90071. 320p. 1976. pap. 5.95 (ISBN 0-85345-352-7). Monthly Rev.

Ellis, P. Berresford, ed. see Connolly, James.

Ellis, P. E., jt. auth. see Ashall, C.

Ellis, Paul. Aircraft of the Royal Navy. (Illus.). 192p. 1982. 17.95 (ISBN 0-86720-556-3). Jane's Pub Inc.

Ellis, Peter B. Caesar's Invasion of Britain. LC 79-90167. 144p. 1979. 25.00x (ISBN 0-8147-2157-5). NYU Pr.

--Hell or Connaught: The Cromwellian Colonization of Ireland. LC 74-24650. 288p. 1975. 25.00 (ISBN 0-312-36715-5). St Martin.

Ellis, Peter F. The Genius of John: A Composition-Critical Commentary on the Fourth Gospel. (Orig.). 1984. pap. 10.95 (ISBN 0-8146-1328-4). Liturgical Pr.

--Seven Pauline Letters. LC 82-15252. (Orig.). 1982. pap. 8.95 (ISBN 0-8146-1245-8). Liturgical Pr.

Ellis, Peter F. & Ellis, Judith M. John: An Access Guide for Scripture Study. 174p. 1983. pap. 3.95 (ISBN 0-8215-5936-2); leader's guide 2.95 (ISBN 0-8215-5918-4). Sadlier.

Ellis, Philip P. Ocular Therapeutics & Pharmacology. 6th ed. LC 81-9632. (Illus.). 320p. 1981. text ed. 39.95 (ISBN 0-8016-1518-6). Mosby.

Ellis, R. Inborn Errors of Metabolism. 1980. 11.50 (ISBN 0-8151-3104-6). Year Bk Med.

Ellis, R. J., ed. Chloroplast Biogenesis. (Society for Experimental Biology Seminar Ser.: No. 21). 288p. 1985. 70.00 (ISBN 0-521-24816-7). Cambridge U Pr.

Ellis, R. Jeffrey. The Process of Response: An Empirically Derived Approach for Managing in Turbulence. 288p. 1985. 24.95 (ISBN 0-03-063936-0). Praeger.

Ellis, R. L. & Lipetz, M. J. Essentials of Sociology. LC 78-11524. 1979. pap. text ed. 13.95 (ISBN 0-394-33313-6, RanC). Random.

Ellis, R. S. Entropy, Large Deviations, & Statistical Mechanics. (Grundlehren der Mathematischen Wissenschaften, a Series of Comprehensive Studies in Mathematics: Vol. 271). 300p. (Eng.). 1985. 54.00 (ISBN 0-387-96052-X). Springer-Verlag.

Ellis, Ray. Security & Loss Prevention in the Lodging Industry. Roraback, Eileen, ed. 1985. write for info. (ISBN 0-86612-028-9). Educ Inst Am Hotel.

Ellis, Reed. A Journey into Darkness. Jowett, Garth S., ed. LC 79-6673. (Dissertations on Film, 1980). 1980. lib. bdg. 21.00x (ISBN 0-405-12908-4). Ayer Co Pubs.

Ellis, Rennie. We Live in Australia. (Living Here Ser.). (gr. 6-8). 1984. PLB 10.90 (ISBN 0-531-04687-7). Watts.

Ellis, Richard. The Book of Sharks: A Complete Illustrated Natural History of the Sharks of the World. (Illus.). 256p. 1983. pap. 14.95 (ISBN 0-15-613552-3, Harv). HarBraceJ.

--The Book of Whales. LC 80-7640. (Illus.). 1985. pap. 16.95 (ISBN 0-394-73371-1). Knopf.

--Dolphins & Porpoises. LC 82-47823. 1982. 25.00 (ISBN 0-394-51800-4). Knopf.

Ellis, Richard, jt. ed. see Miers, Earl S.

Ellis, Richard E. The Jeffersonian Crisis: Courts & Politics in the Young Republic. 384p. 1974. pap. 6.95 (ISBN 0-393-00729-4). Norton.

--Jeffersonian Crisis: Courts & Politics in the Young Republic. 1971. 19.95x (ISBN 0-19-501390-5). Oxford U Pr.

Ellis, Richard N., ed. New Mexico Historic Documents. LC 75-14656. 140p. 1975. 7.50 (ISBN 0-8263-0385-4); pap. 3.95 (ISBN 0-8263-0386-2). U of NM Pr.

--New Mexico, Past & Present: A Historical Reader. LC 71-153941. 140p. 1971. pap. 8.95 (ISBN 0-8263-0215-7). U of NM Pr.

--Western American Indian: Case Studies in Tribal History. LC 70-181597. xiv, 203p. 1972. 16.95x (ISBN 0-8032-0804-9); pap. 4.95x (ISBN 0-8032-5754-6, BB 548, Bison). U of Nebr Pr.

Ellis, Richard S. Foundation Deposits in Ancient Mesopotamia. LC 78-63541. (Yale Near Eastern Researches Ser.: No. 2). (Illus.). 248p. Repr. of 1968 ed. 27.50 (ISBN 0-404-60262-2). AMS Pr.

Ellis, Robert & Gulick, Denny. Calculus with Analytic Geometry. 2nd ed. (Illus.). 1027p. 1982. text ed. 39.95 (ISBN 0-15-505731-6, HC); solutions manual pt. 1 9.95 (ISBN 0-15-505732-4); solutions manual pt. 2 9.95 (ISBN 0-15-505733-2); solution manuals (all odd numbered exercises) 7.95 (ISBN 0-15-505736-7). HarBraceJ.
--College Algebra. 514p. 1981. text ed. 24.95 (ISBN 0-15-507905-0, HC); answer manual avail. (ISBN 0-15-507906-9). HarBraceJ.
--College Algebra & Trigonometry. 2nd ed. 631p. 1984. text ed. 25.95 (ISBN 0-15-507909-3, HC); answer manual avail. (ISBN 0-15-507910-7). HarBraceJ.
--Fundamentals of College Algebra & Trigonometry. 448p. 1984. text ed. 24.95 (ISBN 0-15-529350-8, HC). HarBraceJ.
Ellis, Robert, jt. auth. see Ellis, Mark.
Ellis, Robert L. Designing Data Networks. (Illus.). 224p. 1986. text ed. 32.95 (ISBN 0-13-201864-0). P-H.
Ellis, Robert S. The Psychology of Individual Differences. 533p. 1980. Repr. of 1930 ed. lib. bdg. 45.00 (ISBN 0-89760-204-8). Telegraph Bks.
Ellis, Roger & Whittington, Dorothy. A Guide to Social Skill Training. 240p. 1981. 32.00x (ISBN 0-7099-0295-6). Brookline Book.
Ellis, Roger & Whittington, Dorothy, eds. New Directions in Social Skill Training. 320p. 1983. 29.95 (ISBN 0-416-00911-5, NO. 5044). Methuen Inc.
Ellis, S. M. George Meredith. LC 75-163502. (Studies in George Meredith, No. 21). 1971. Repr. of 1919 ed. lib. bdg. 59.95x (ISBN 0-8383-1311-6). Haskell.
--George Meredith: His Life & Friends in Relation to His Work. LC 73-11362. 1920. lib. bdg. 17.75 (ISBN 0-8414-1914-0). Folcroft.
--Henry Kingsley, Eighteen Thirty to Eighteen Seventy-Six. 1979. Repr. of 1931 ed. lib. bdg. 30.00 (ISBN 0-8414-4000-X). Folcroft.
--Henry Kingsley Eighteen-Thirty to Eighteen-Seventy Six. 1931. Repr. 20.00 (ISBN 0-8274-2485-X). R West.
--A Mid-Victorian Pepys. 1973. Repr. of 1923 ed. 35.00 (ISBN 0-8274-1442-0). R West.
Ellis, S. M., ed. The Hardman Papers: A Further Selection (1865-1868) from the Letters & Memoirs of Sir Francis Hardman. 357p. 1982. Repr. of 1930 ed. lib. bdg. 45.00 (ISBN 0-89760-213-7). Telegraph Bks.
Ellis, Stanley W. Smogless Days: Adventures in Ten Stanley Steamers. LC 75-170966. (Illus.). 104p. 1971. 14.95 (ISBN 0-8310-7086-2). Howell-North.
Ellis, Stephen. The Rising of the Red Shawls: A Revolt in Madagascar 1895-1899. (African Studies: No. 43). 230p. 1985. 44.50 (ISBN 0-521-26287-9). Cambridge U Pr.
Ellis, Steve. Dante & English Poetry: Shelley to T. S. Eliot. LC 83-23650. 300p. 1983. 39.50 (ISBN 0-521-25126-5). Cambridge U Pr.
Ellis, Steven G. Tudor Ireland: Crown Community & the Conflict of Cultures 1470-1603. 432p. 1985. pap. text ed. 16.95 (ISBN 0-582-49341-2). Longman.
Ellis, Stewart M. Mainly Victorian. LC 75-99692. (Essay Index Reprint Ser.). 1925. 27.50 (ISBN 0-8369-1407-4). Ayer Co Pubs.
--Wilkie Collins, le Fann & Others. 1973. Repr. of 1931 ed. 25.00 (ISBN 0-8274-1416-1). R West.
--Wilkie Collins, le Fanu, & Others. facs. ed. LC 68-29203. (Essay Index Reprint Ser). 1968. Repr. of 1931 ed. 19.00 (ISBN 0-8369-0413-3). Ayer Co Pubs.
Ellis, Susan J. & Noyes, Katherine H. By the People: A History of Americans As Volunteers. LC 78-60156. (Illus.). 308p. 1978. 10.50x (ISBN 0-940576-00-7); pap. 7.25x (ISBN 0-940576-01-5). Energize.
--No Excuses: The Team Approach to Volunteer Management. LC 81-70156. (Volunteer Energy Ser.: No. 2). (Illus.). 70p. 1981. pap. 8.75x (ISBN 0-940576-04-X). Energize.
--Proof Positive: Developing Significant Volunteer Recordkeeping Systems. LC 80-69647. (Volunteer Energy Ser.: No. 1). (Illus.). 50p. 1980. pap. 7.50x (ISBN 0-940576-03-1). Energize.
Ellis, Susan J., ed. Children As Volunteers. LC 83-80067. (Volunteer Energy Ser.: No. 3). (Illus.). 65p. 1983. pap. 8.75x (ISBN 0-940576-05-8). Energize.
Ellis, Sydney. Pharmacology Review. LC 79-13485. (Medical Review Ser.). 1980. pap. 13.00 (ISBN 0-668-04108-0). ACC.
Ellis, T. M. A Structured Approach to FORTRAN 77 Programming. 1982. pap. text ed. 19.95 (ISBN 0-201-13790-9). Addison-Wesley.
Ellis, T. M. & Semenkov, O. I., eds. Advances in CAD-CAM: Proceedings of the 5th International IFIP-IFAC Conference on Programming Research & Operations Logistics in Advanced Manufacturing Technology, PROLOMAT 82, Leningrad, USSR, 16-18 May, 1982. xviii, 720p. 1983. 76.75 (ISBN 0-444-86549-7, I-35-83, North-Holland). Elsevier.
Ellis, T. M., ed. see IFAC-IFIP Symposium, 3rd, MANUFACONT '80, Budapest, Hungary, Oct. 1980.
Ellis, Theodore J. The Potential Role of Oil Shale in the U. S. Energy Mix: Questions of Development & Policy Formulation in an Environment Age. Bruchey, Stuart, ed. LC 78-22677. (Energy in the American Economy Ser.). (Illus.). 1979. lib. bdg. 23.00x (ISBN 0-405-11980-1). Ayer Co Pubs.
Ellis, Vivienne R. Trucanini: Queen or Traitor? rev. ed. (AIAS New Ser.: No. 27). 196p. 1981. text ed. 14.50x (ISBN 0-391-02241-5, Pub. by Australian Inst Australia); pap. text ed. 10.25x (ISBN 0-391-02242-3, Pub. by Australian Inst Australia). Humanities.
Ellis, W. Ashton, ed. see Wagner, Richard.
Ellis, W. Ashton, tr. see Wagner, Richard.
Ellis, Wesley. Lone Star & the Alaskan Guns. (Lone Star Ser.: No. 40). 192p. 1985. pap. 2.50 (ISBN 0-515-08423-9). Jove Pubns.
--Lone Star & the Apache Warrior. (Lone Star Ser.: No. 37). 192p. 1985. pap. 2.50 (ISBN 0-515-08344-5). JOve Pubns.
--Lone Star & the Biggest Gun in the West. (Lone Star Ser.: No. 36). 192p. 1985. pap. 2.50 (ISBN 0-515-08332-1). Jove Pubns.
--Lone Star & the Buffalo Hunters. (Lone Star Ser.: No. 35). 192p. 1985. pap. 2.50 (ISBN 0-515-08233-3). Jove Pubns.
--Lone Star & the California Oil War. (Lone Star Ser.: No. 39). 192p. 1985. pap. 2.50 (ISBN 0-515-08397-6). Jove Pubns.
--Lone Star & the Gold Mine War. (Lone Star Ser.: No. 38). 192p. 1985. pap. 2.50 (ISBN 0-515-08368-2). Jove Pubns.
--Lone Star & the Rio Grande Bandits, No. 34. 192p. 1985. pap. 2.50 (ISBN 0-515-08255-4). Jove Pubns.
Ellis, William. The Journal of William Ellis. LC 78-54936. (Illus.). 1979. 18.50 (ISBN 0-8048-1298-5). C E Tuttle.
--Madagascar Revisited. LC 72-5541. (Black Heritage Library Collection Ser.). 1972. Repr. of 1867 ed. 30.75 (ISBN 0-8369-9139-7). Ayer Co Pubs.
--Polynesian Researches: Hawaii. LC 69-19607. 1969. pap. 6.75 (ISBN 0-8048-0476-1). C E Tuttle.
--Polynesian Researches: Polynesia. LC 69-19601. (Illus.). 1978. pap. 4.50 (ISBN 0-8048-0475-3). C E Tuttle.
--Polynesian Researches: Society Islands. LC 69-345780. (Illus.). 1969. Repr. 4.35 (ISBN 0-8048-0478-8). C E Tuttle.
--Polynesian Researches: Society Islands, Tubuai Islands & New Zealand. LC 69-19605. (Illus.). 1969. Repr. of 1842 ed. 4.35 (ISBN 0-8048-0477-X). C E Tuttle.
Ellis, William & Seidel, Frank. How to Win the Conference. 214p. 1982. 6.95 (ISBN 0-13-439489-5). P-H.
Ellis, William A. Richard Wagner to Mathilde Wesendonck. LC 76-86960. (Reprints Ser). (Illus.). 1970. Repr. of 1905 ed. lib. bdg. 25.00 (ISBN 0-87821-020-2). Milford Hse.
Ellis, William A. & Glasenapp, C. F. Life of Richard Wagner: Being an Authorized English Version of das Leben Richard Wagner, 6 vols. (Music Reprint Ser.). 1977. Repr. of 1902 ed. lib. bdg. 47.50 ea.; Set. lib. bdg. 245.00 (ISBN 0-306-70887-6). Vol. 1 (ISBN 0-306-70881-7). Vol. 2 (ISBN 0-306-70882-5). Vol. 3 (ISBN 0-306-70883-3). Vol. 4 (ISBN 0-306-70884-1). Vol. 5 (ISBN 0-306-70885-X). Vol. 6 (ISBN 0-306-70886-8). Da Capo.
Ellis, William A., ed. & tr. Richard Wagner's Prose Works, 8 vols. Incl. Vol. 1. The Art-Work of the Future (ISBN 0-8450-2101-X); Vol. 3. The Theatre (ISBN 0-8450-2103-6); Vol. 4. Art & Politics (ISBN 0-8450-2104-4); Vol. 5. Actors & Singers (ISBN 0-8450-2105-2); Vol. 6. Religion & Art (ISBN 0-8450-2106-0); Vol. 7. In Paris & Dresden (ISBN 0-8450-2107-9); Vol. 8. Posthumous (ISBN 0-8450-2108-7). (Ger.). 1967. Repr. of 1892 ed. 150.00x set (ISBN 0-8450-2100-1); 22.50x ea. Broude.
Ellis, William Ashton, tr. see Wagner, Richard.
Ellis, William C. A Treatise on the Nature, Symptoms, Causes & Treatment of Insanity: Classics in Psychiatry Ser. LC 75-16700. 1976. Repr. of 1838 ed. 27.50x (ISBN 0-405-07427-1). Ayer Co Pubs.
Ellis, William D. The Bounty Lands. LC 52-5196. (Trilogy Ser.: No. 1). 495p. 1981. pap. 5.95 (ISBN 0-913428-20-5). Landfall Pr.
--The Cuyahoga. LC 66-13558. (Rivers of America Ser). 1975. pap. 4.95 (ISBN 0-913428-17-5). Landfall Pr.
Ellis, William D. & Cunningham, Thomas J., Jr. Clarke of St. Vith: The Sergeants' General. LC 73-94080. (Illus.). 360p. 10.00 (ISBN 0-913228-08-7). Dillon-Liederbach.
Ellis, William D., jt. auth. see Armington, R. Q.
Ellis, William D., jt. ed. see Armington, R. Q.
Ellis, William E. A Man of Books & a Man of the People: E. Y. Mullins & the Crisis Moderate Southern Baptist Leadership. xi, 228p. 1985. text ed. 18.95 (ISBN 0-86554-175-2, MUP-H165). Mercer Univ Pr.
Ellis, William R., Jr., jt. ed. see Orleans, Peter.
Ellis, William T. Billy Sunday. (Golden Oldies Ser.). 1959. pap. 2.95 (ISBN 0-8024-0042-6). Moody.
Ellisen, Stanley A. Divorce & Remarriage in the Church. 1977. pap. 5.95 (ISBN 0-310-35561-3). Zondervan.
--Knowing God's Word. 176p. 1984. pap. 9.95 (ISBN 0-8407-5886-3). Nelson.
Ellisen, Stanley A., ed. see Cheney, Johnston M.
Ellis-Femor, Una, tr. see Ibsen, Henrik.
Ellis-Fermor, U. Some Recent Research in Shakespeare's Imagery. LC 75-2255. (Studies in Shakespeare, No. 24). 1970. Repr. of 1937 ed. lib. bdg. 22.95x (ISBN 0-8383-0343-9). Haskell.
Ellis-Fermor, Una. The Irish Dramatic Movement. 241p. 1977. Repr. of 1939 ed. 23.75x (ISBN 0-8476-6015-X). Rowman.
--Shakespeare the Dramatist. LC 73-2638. 1948. lib. bdg. 9.50 (ISBN 0-8414-1900-0). Folcroft.
--Shakespeare's Drama. Muir, Kenneth, ed. 1980. 26.00x (ISBN 0-416-74090-1, NO. 2044); pap. 10.50x (ISBN 0-416-74100-2, NO. 2043). Methuen Inc.
--Some Recent Research in Shakespeare's Imagery. LC 75-17647. 1937. lib. bdg. 9.50 (ISBN 0-8414-3993-1). Folcroft.
--Study of Shakespeare. LC 76-46453. 1947. lib. bdg. 8.50 (ISBN 0-8414-3949-4). Folcroft.
Ellis-Fermor, Una, tr. see Ibsen, Henrik.
Ellis-Fermor, V. M., ed. see Marlowe, Christopher.
Ellis-Fermour, Una M. The Jacobean Drama: An Interpretation. 4th ed. LC 83-45751. Repr. of 1958 ed. 32.50 (ISBN 0-404-20089-3). AMS Pr.
Ellis-Jones, B., tr. see Walser, Martin.
Ellis-Jones, Barrie. The Cinema. (Heinemann Guided Readers Ser.). (Illus.). 1977. pap. 2.50x (ISBN 0-435-27031-1). Heinemann Ed.
--The Walker After Death. (Heinemann Guided Readers Ser.). 1980. pap. text ed. 2.00x (ISBN 0-435-27058-3). Heinemann Ed.
Ellison. Computer Systems Security. (Infotech Computer State of the Art Reports). 1981. 405.00 (ISBN 0-08-028558-9). Pergamon.
Ellison, A. E., et al, eds. Athletic Training & Sports Medicine. (Illus.). 602p. 1984. 39.00 (ISBN 0-89203-002-X). Amer Acad Ortho Surg.
Ellison, A. J., jt. auth. see Yang, S. J.
Ellison, Al. Ellison's French Menu Reader. (Fr.). 1977. 3.95 (ISBN 0-930580-00-1). Ellison Ent.
--Ellison's Italian Menu Reader. 1977. 3.95 (ISBN 0-930580-02-8). Ellison Ent.
--Ellison's Latin American Menu Reader. (Lat.). 1978. pap. 3.95 (ISBN 0-930580-06-0). Ellison Ent.
--Ellison's Mexican Menu Reader. 1977. pap. 3.95 (ISBN 0-930580-04-4). Ellison Ent.
--Ellison's Swiss Menu Reader. 1978. pap. 3.95 (ISBN 0-930580-05-2). Ellison Ent.
Ellison, Bob A. The Racehorse from Outerspace & Other Tales of the Turf: How to Have Fun & Win at the Races. 84p. (Orig.). 1984. pap. 7.95 (ISBN 0-9613336-0-X). South Bay.
Ellison, Bud. A Friendly Letter to the President. 1985. 5.75 (ISBN 0-8062-2432-0). Carlton.
Ellison, Craig. The Urban Mission: Essays on the Building of a Comprehensive Model for Evangelical Urban Ministry. LC 82-23764. 230p. 1983. pap. text ed. 12.25 (ISBN 0-8191-2968-2). U Pr of Amer.
Ellison, Craig W. Saying Goodbye to Loneliness & Finding Intimacy. LC 82-48927. Orig. Title: Loneliness. 240p. (Orig.). 1983. pap. 7.64i (ISBN 0-06-062242-3, RD/456, HarpR). Har-Row.
Ellison, Craig W., ed. Your Better Self: Christianity, Psychology, & Self-Esteem. LC 82-47742. 224p. (Orig.). 1982. pap. 8.61i (ISBN 0-686-97230-9, RD/408, HarpR). Har-Row.
Ellison, Curtis W. & Metcalf, E. W., Jr. Charles W. Chesnutt: A Reference Guide. (Reference Publications Ser.). 1977. lib. bdg. 20.00 (ISBN 0-8161-7825-9, Hall Reference). G K Hall.
Ellison, Curtis W. & Metcalf, E. W., eds. William Wells Brown & Martin R. Delany: A Reference Guide. 1978. lib. bdg. 30.50 (ISBN 0-8161-8025-3, Hall Reference). G K Hall.
Ellison, D. & Tunnicliffe, W. J. How to Write Simulations Using Microcomputers. 192p. 1984. 19.95 (ISBN 0-07-084722-3). McGraw.
Ellison, D. R., tr. see Abraham, Karl.
Ellison, Darlene. Saying Goodbye. (Illus.). 138p. (Orig.). 1981. pap. 6.95 (ISBN 0-9604344-6-1). Sunrise Pub OR.
Ellison, David L. The Bio-Medical Fix: Human Dimensions of Bio-Medical Technologies. LC 77-91104. 1978. lib. bdg. 27.50 (ISBN 0-313-20038-6, ELB/). Greenwood.
Ellison, David R. The Reading of Proust. LC 83-48057. 232p. 1983. 22.50x (ISBN 0-8018-3048-6). Johns Hopkins.
Ellison, Edward A. Prosperity Restored by the State Rate Tax Plan. LC 85-10104. write for info. (ISBN 0-934005-00-1). Free State Constitution.
Ellison, Emily. First Light: A Novel of a Daughter's Reluctant Understanding of Her Mother's Life. LC 84-27237. 256p. 1985. 14.95 (ISBN 0-688-04949-4). Morrow.
Ellison, Fred P. Brazil's New Novel: Four Northeastern Masters: Jose Lins do Rego, Jorge Amado, Graciliano, Rachel de Queiroz. LC 78-9880. 1979. Repr. of 1954 ed. lib. bdg. 24.75x (ISBN 0-313-21237-6, ELBN). Greenwood.
Ellison, Fred P., tr. see Queiroz, Rachel de.
Ellison, Fred P., et al. Modern Portuguese. LC 70-111970. 1970. text ed. 28.00 (ISBN 0-394-30230-3, KnopfC); tapes 200.00 (ISBN 0-394-30110-2). Knopf.
Ellison, George. Spike's Chess Primer. pap. 5.95 (ISBN 0-946284-20-2, Pub. by Crowood Pr). Longwood Pub Group.
Ellison, Glen R. Cowboys Under the Mogollon Rim. LC 68-9337. (Illus.). 274p. 1968. pap. 9.50 (ISBN 0-8165-0642-6). U of Ariz Pr.
Ellison, Glenn. Run-&-Shoot Football: The New Attack. 194p. 1984. 18.95 (ISBN 0-13-783879-4, Busn). P-H.
Ellison, Glenn R. More Tales from Slim Ellison. LC 80-27498. 195p. 1981. 17.50 (ISBN 0-8165-0715-5); pap. 9.50 (ISBN 0-8165-0681-7). U of Ariz Pr.
Ellison, Gordon N. Thermal Computation for Electrical Equipment. 1984. 34.50 (ISBN 0-442-21923-7). Van Nos Reinhold.
Ellison, H. L. Exodus. LC 81-12917. (Daily Study Bible Old Testament Ser.). 216p. 1982. 12.95 (ISBN 0-664-21803-2); pap. 7.95 (ISBN 0-664-24570-6). Westminster.
--From Babylon to Bethlehem: The People of God from the Exile to the Messiah. 144p. 1984. pap. 5.95 (ISBN 0-8010-3412-4). Baker Bk.
--The Household Church. 120p. 1979. pap. 4.95 (ISBN 0-85364-239-7). Attic Pr.
--The Mystery of Israel: An Exposition of Romans 9-11. 3rd ed. 117p. 1976. pap. 4.95 (ISBN 0-85364-169-2). Attic Pr.
--The Servant of Jehovah. 32p. 1983. pap. 2.50 (ISBN 0-85364-254-0, Pub. by Paternoster UK). Attic Pr.
--Understanding the New Testament: 1 Peter-Revelation. LC 78-9116. 1982. pap. 3.95 (ISBN 0-8054-1341-3). Broadman.
Ellison, H. L., ed. see Howley, G. C. D.
Ellison, Harlan. Alone Against Tomorrow. 312p. 1972. pap. 3.95 (ISBN 0-02-019780-2, Collier). Macmillan.
--Approaching Oblivion. 1985. pap. 7.95 (ISBN 0-312-94018-1). Bluejay Bks.
--The Beast That Shouted Love at the Heart of the World. 256p. 1984. pap. 6.95 (ISBN 0-312-94027-0). Bluejay Bks.
--Deathbird Stories. LC 83-21552. 312p. 1983. pap. 6.95 (ISBN 0-312-94084-X). St Martin.
--An Edge in My Voice. Reynolds, Kay, ed. LC 83-16298. 225p. (Orig.). 1985. 7.95 (ISBN 0-89865-341-X); limited ed. 35.00 (ISBN 0-89865-342-8); pap. 12.95 (ISBN 0-89865-373-8). Donning Co.
--Ellison Wonderland. rev. ed. 192p. 1984. 6.95 (ISBN 0-312-94133-1). Bluejay Bks.
--Gentleman Junkie. (The Ace Ellison Ser.: No. 6). 256p. 1983. pap. 2.50 (ISBN 0-441-27938-4). Ace Bks.
--The Glass Teat. 1983. pap. 2.95 (ISBN 0-441-28988-6, Pub. by Ace Science Fiction). Ace Bks.
--I Have No Mouth & I Must Scream. (Ace Ellison Ser.: Bk. 10). 1983. pap. 3.25 (ISBN 0-441-36395-4, Pub. by Ace Science Fiction). Ace Bks.
--Love Ain't Nothing But Sex Misspelled. 384p. 1983. pap. 2.95 (ISBN 0-441-49547-8). Ace Bks.
--Memos from Purgatory. 208p. 1983. pap. 2.95 (ISBN 0-441-52438-9). Ace Bks.
--No Doors, No Windows. 1983. pap. 2.95 (ISBN 0-441-58328-8, Pub. by Ace Science Fiction). Ace Bks.
--The Other Glass Teat. 400p. 1983. pap. 3.50 (ISBN 0-441-64274-8). Ace Bks.
--Paingod & Other Delusions. 176p. 1983. pap. 2.95 (ISBN 0-441-64576-3, Pub. by Ace Science Fiction). Ace Bks.
--Shatterday. 304p. 1983. pap. 2.95 (ISBN 0-425-07165-0). Berkley Pub.
--Sleepless Nights in the Procrustean Bed: Essays. Clark, Marty, ed. LC 83-27543. (I. O. Evans Studies in the Philosophy & Criticism of Literature: No. 5). 160p. 1984. lib. bdg. 14.95x (ISBN 0-89370-170-X); pap. 7.95x (ISBN 0-89370-270-6); signed, limited 50.00x (ISBN 0-89370-007-X). Borgo Pr.
--Sleepless Nights in the Procrustean Bed: Essays. 176p. 1984. pap. 7.95 (ISBN 0-87877-270-7). Newcastle Pub.
--Spider Kiss. 240p. 1983. pap. 2.95 (ISBN 0-441-77795-3). Ace Bks.
--Stalking the Nightmare. 300p. 1982. 16.00 (ISBN 0-932096-16-6). Phantasia Pr.
--Strange Wine. 1977. pap. 3.50 (ISBN 0-446-30659-2). Warner Bks.
--Web of the City. 224p. 1983. pap. 2.75 (ISBN 0-441-87718-4). Ace Bks.
Ellison, Harlan, ed. Again, Dangerous Visions. 864p. 1983. pap. 10.95 (ISBN 0-425-06182-5). Berkley Pub.
--Dangerous Visions. 576p. 1983. pap. 9.95 (ISBN 0-425-06176-0). Berkley Pub.
--Medea: Harlan's World. 544p. 1985. pap. 10.95 (ISBN 0-553-34170-7). Bantam.
--Medea: Harlan's World. 1985. 20.00 (ISBN 0-932096-36-0). Phantasia Pr.
Ellison, Harold. Portavoces del Eterno. Orig. Title: Old Testament Prophets. 214p. (Span.). 1982. pap. 6.75 (ISBN 0-8254-1201-3). Kregel.
Ellison, Herbert J., jt. auth. see Valenta, Jiri.
Ellison, Herbert J., ed. The Sino-Soviet Conflict: A Global Perspective. LC 81-51279. 432p. 1981. 35.00x (ISBN 0-295-95854-5); pap. 17.95x (ISBN 0-295-95873-1). U of Wash Pr.

--Soviet Policy Toward Western Europe: Implications for the Atlantic Alliance. LC 83-47977. 312p. 30.00x (ISBN 0-295-96035-3); pap. 14.95x (ISBN 0-295-96036-1). U of Wash Pr.

Ellison, Jack S., jt. auth. see Kirk, Robert H.

Ellison, James W. Proud Rachel. LC 75-8880. 256p. 1975. pap. 1.95 (ISBN 0-8128-7000-X). Stein & Day.

--Proud Rachel. 224p. 1984. pap. 3.95 (ISBN 0-8128-8053-6). Stein & Day.

Ellison, Jerome. The Club of Life. LC 80-18444. 1980. pap. 7.95 (ISBN 0-8298-0410-2). Pilgrim NY.

--The Last Third of Life Club. LC 73-13961. 192p. 1973. 5.95 (ISBN 0-8298-0252-5). Pilgrim NY.

--Life's Second Half. 1978. 10.95 (ISBN 0-8159-6116-2). Devin.

--Victory over Age. 1980. pap. 6.95 (ISBN 0-8159-7103-6). Devin.

Ellison, John W. Nelson's Complete Concordance of the Revised Standard Version. 2nd ed. 1136p. 1985. 29.95 (ISBN 0-8407-4954-6). Nelson.

Ellison, John W., ed. Media Librarianship. 300p. 1985. text ed. 35.00 (ISBN 0-918212-81-2). Neal-Schuman.

Ellison, Joseph. California & the Nation, Eighteen Fifty to Eighteen Sixty-Nine. LC 78-87529. (American Scene Ser.). 1969. Repr. of 1927 ed. lib. bdg. 32.50 (ISBN 0-306-71443-4). Da Capo.

Ellison, Joseph W. Opening & Penetration of Foreign Influence in Samoa to 1880. (Studies in History Ser: No. 1). 108p. 1938. pap. 4.95x (ISBN 0-87071-071-0). Oreg St U Pr.

Ellison, Julian, jt. auth. see Swinton, David H.

Ellison, Julie. Emerson's Romantic Style. LC 84-42582. 275p. 1984. text ed. 25.00x (ISBN 0-691-06612-4). Princeton U Pr.

Ellison, Katherine W. & Buckhout, Robert. Psychology & Criminal Justice: Common Grounds. 432p. 1981. text ed. 23.50 scp (ISBN 0-06-041024-8, HarpC). Har-Row.

Ellison, Katherine W. & Genz, John L. Stress & the Police Officer. (Illus.). 224p. 1983. 19.75x (ISBN 0-398-04829-0). C C Thomas.

Ellison, Lee M. The Early Romantic Drama at the English Court. LC 74-23087. 1917. lib. bdg. 15.00 (ISBN 0-8414-1901-9). Folcroft.

Ellison, Lucile W. Butter on Both Sides. LC 79-15808. (Illus.). (gr. 4-6). 1979. 7.95 (ISBN 0-684-16281-4, ScribJ). Scribner.

--A Window to Look Through. 128p. (gr. 4-6). 1982. 9.95 (ISBN 0-684-17438-3, ScribJ). Scribner.

Ellison, Lucille W. The Tie That Binds. (Illus.). 144p. (gr. 4-6). 1981. 9.95 (ISBN 0-684-16875-8, ScribJ). Scribner.

Ellison, Marvin M. The Center Cannot Hold: The Search for a Global Economy of Justice. LC 82-23795. 330p. (Orig.). 1983. lib. bdg. 28.00 (ISBN 0-8191-2963-1); pap. text ed. 15.25 (ISBN 0-8191-2964-X). U Pr of Amer.

Ellison, Mary. Support for Secession: Lancashire & the American Civil War. LC 72-80158. 276p. 1973. 17.00x (ISBN 0-226-20593-2). U of Chicago Pr.

Ellison, Max. The Happenstance. (Illus.). 71p. (YA) 1972. 2.50 (ISBN 0-914402-02-1). Conway Hse.

Ellison, Neil M., jt. ed. see Newell, Guy R.

Ellison, R. Curtis & Restieaux, Norma J. Vectorcardiography in Congenital Heart Disease: A Method for Estimating Severity. LC 75-183449. (Illus.). Repr. of 1972 ed. 55.30 (ISBN 0-8357-9561-6, 2013068). Bks Demand UMI.

Ellison, Ralph. Invisible Man. 1963. 3.95 (ISBN 0-394-60338-9). Modern Lib.

--The Invisible Man. LC 72-10419. (YA) 1972. pap. 3.95 (ISBN 0-394-71715-5, V715, Vin). Random.

--Shadow & Act. pap. 4.95 (ISBN 0-394-71716-3, V-716, Vin). Random.

Ellison, Reuben Y., et al, eds. see Ionesco, Eugene.

Ellison, Rhoda C. Bibb County, Alabama: The First Hundred Years, 1818-1918. LC 83-5875. (Illus.). xiii, 304p. 1984. 29.95 (ISBN 0-8173-0184-4). U of Ala Pr.

Ellison, Robert, jt. auth. see Cordell, A. Robert.

Ellison, Robert S. Independence Rock. 41p. 1984. pap. 3.50 (ISBN 0-87770-136-9). Ye Galleon.

Ellison, S. P., Jr. Annotated Bibliography, & Index, of Conodonts. (Pub. Ser: 6210). (Illus.). 128p. 1962. incl. supplements 2.25 (ISBN 0-318-03316-X). Bur Econ Geology.

--Sulfur in Texas. (Illus.). 48p. 1971. 2.00 (ISBN 0-686-29324-X, HB 2). Bur Econ Geology.

Ellison, Sue, jt. auth. see Ellison, Tom.

Ellison, Thomas. Cotton Trade of Great Britain. 355p. 1968. Repr. of 1886 ed. 30.00x (ISBN 0-7146-1391-6, F Cass Co). Biblio Dist.

--Cotton Trade of Great Britain. LC 68-20034. Repr. of 1886 ed. 35.00x (ISBN 0-678-05044-9). Kelley.

Ellison, Tom & Ellison, Sue. The Whole Work Catalog. (Orig.). Date not set. pap. 9.95 (ISBN 0-911781-05-6). Live Oak Pubns.

Ellison, Virginia H. The Pooh Get-Well Book. 96p. (gr. 1-3). 1975. pap. 1.25 (ISBN 0-440-46971-6, YB). Dell.

--The Pooh Party Book. 160p. (gr. 1-7). 1975. pap. 1.25 (ISBN 0-440-47299-7, YB). Dell.

Ellison, Virginia H. & Milne, A. A. The Pooh Cook Book. 128p. pap. 1.25 (ISBN 0-440-47300-4, YB). Dell.

Ellison, W. James. How to Protect Your Child From Genital Herpes. 6.95 (ISBN 0-317-18913-1). Clay-Jon Pubs.

Ellison, William H. The Federal Indian Policy in California, Eighteen Forty-Six to Eighteen Sixty. LC 73-82393. 1974. Repr. of 1959 ed. soft bdg. 13.00 (ISBN 0-88247-233-X). R & E Pubs.

--A Self-Governing Dominion: California, 1849-1860. (Library Reprint Ser.: Vol. 95). 1978. 30.00x (ISBN 0-520-03713-8). U of Cal Pr.

Ellison, William J. Primer Numbers. 1985. 49.95 (ISBN 0-471-82653-7). Wiley.

Ellisor, Sandra & Morel, Phyllis A., eds. Statistics for Blood Bankers. 179p. 1983. 28.00 (ISBN 0-914404-94-6). Am Assn Blood.

Elliston, Frederick, jt. auth. see Baker, Robert.

Elliston, Frederick, ed. Heidegger's Existential Analytic. 1978. text ed. 28.40x (ISBN 90-279-7514-0). Mouton.

Elliston, Frederick & Feldberg, Michael, eds. Moral Issues in Police Work. LC 84-22259. (Illus.). 316p. 1985. text ed. 27.50x (ISBN 0-8476-7191-7); pap. 13.95x (ISBN 0-8476-7192-5). Rowman & Allanheld.

Elliston, Frederick & McCormick, Peter, eds. Husserl: Expositions & Appraisals. LC 75-19882. 370p. 1976. text ed. 23.95 (ISBN 0-268-01063-3). U of Notre Dame Pr.

--Husserl: Expositions & Appraisals. LC 75-19882. 1978. pap. 10.95x (ISBN 0-268-01064-1). U of Notre Dame Pr.

Elliston, Frederick, et al. Whistleblowing: Managing Dissent in the Workplace. 176p. 1985. 35.95 (ISBN 0-03-070774-9); pap. 14.95 (ISBN 0-03-070776-5). Praeger.

--Whistleblowing Research: Methodological & Moral Issues. LC 84-13294. 192p. 1985. 32.95 (ISBN 0-03-070777-3). Praeger.

Elliston, Frederick A. & Van Schaick, Jane. Legal Ethics: An Annotated Bibliography & Resource Guide. viii, 199p. 1984. text ed. 32.50x (ISBN 0-8377-0545-2). Rothman.

Elliston, Frederick A. & Bowie, Norman E., eds. Ethics, Public Policy & Criminal Justice. LC 82-7974. 512p. 1982. text ed. 30.00 (ISBN 0-89946-138-7). Oelgeschlager.

Elliston, Frederick A., jt. ed. see McCormick, Peter.

Elliston, Frederick A., jt. ed. see Silverman, Hugh J.

Elliston, P., ed. Photography. (Fundamentals of Senior Physics Ser.). 1979. pap. text ed. 7.95x (ISBN 0-85859-187-1, 00500). Heinemann Ed.

Ellito, Charles. Turkey Hunting with Charlie Elliot. 288p. 14.95 (ISBN 0-668-06056-5); pap. 8.95 (ISBN 0-668-06072-7). Arco.

El Liwaru, Maisha Z., jt. auth. see El Liwaru, Saidi J.

El Liwaru, Saidi J. & El Liwaru, Maisha Z. The Muslim Family Reader. Quinlan, Hamid, ed. LC 82-74126. 1984. pap. 4.00 (ISBN 0-89259-028-9). Am Trust Pubns.

Ellman. Collectivisation, Convergence & Capitalism. 1984. 55.00 (ISBN 0-12-237520-3). Acad Pr.

Ellman, Edgar. Recruiting & Selecting Profitable Sales Personnel. 176p. 1981. 3-ring binder 51.95 (ISBN 0-8436-0774-2). Van Nos Reinhold.

Ellman, Edgar S. Put It in Writing: A Complete Guide for Preparing Employee Policy Handbooks. 160p. 1983. comb-bound 59.95 (ISBN 0-8436-0884-6). Van Nos Reinhold.

Ellman, Michael. Planning Problems in the USSR: The Contribution of Mathematical Economics to Their Solution, 1960-1971. LC 73-75861. (Department of Applied Economics Monographs: No. 24). (Illus.). 240p. 1973. Cambridge U Pr.

--Socialist Planning. LC 78-57757. (Modern Cambridge Economics Ser.). 1979. 52.50 (ISBN 0-521-22229-X); pap. 16.95 (ISBN 0-521-29409-6). Cambridge U Pr.

--Soviet Planning Today, Proposals for an Optimally Functioning Economic System. LC 72-145613. (Department of Applied Economics, Occasional Papers: No. 25). (Illus.). 1971. 23.95 (ISBN 0-521-08156-4); pap. 11.95x (ISBN 0-521-09648-0). Cambridge U Pr.

Ellman, Richard. James Joyce. Revised ed. LC 81-22455. (Illus.). 1982. 37.50 (ISBN 0-19-503103-2). Oxford U Pr.

--Ulysses on the Liffey. 1972. 19.95x (ISBN 0-19-519665-1). Oxford U Pr.

Ellman, Richard, jt. auth. see Joyce, Stanislaus.

Ellman, Richard, ed. Edwardians & Late Victorians: Essays of the English Institute. LC 60-13103. 245p. 1960. 22.00x (ISBN 0-231-02418-5). Columbia U Pr.

Ellman, Richard, ed. see Wilde, Oscar.

Ellmann, Mary. Thinking about Women. LC 67-20309. 1970. pap. 4.95 (ISBN 0-15-689900-0, Harv). HarBraceJ.

Ellmann, Richard. The Consciousness of Joyce. 1977. 19.95x (ISBN 0-19-519950-2); pap. 6.95 (ISBN 0-19-502898-8, GB 636). Oxford U Pr.

--Golden Codgers: Biographical Speculations. 1973. 19.95x (ISBN 0-19-211827-7). Oxford U Pr.

--Golden Codgers: Biographical Speculations. LC 73-86067. 1973. pap. 5.95 (ISBN 0-19-519845-X, 465, GB). Oxford U Pr.

--Identity of Yeats. 2nd ed. 1964. 22.50x (ISBN 0-19-501233-X). Oxford U Pr.

--Identity of Yeats. 2nd ed. 1964. pap. 5.95 (ISBN 0-19-500712-3, GB). Oxford U Pr.

--James Joyce. rev. ed. (Illus.). 1982. pap. 14.95 (ISBN 0-19-503381-7, GB149, GB). Oxford U Pr.

--Ulysses on the Liffey. (Illus.). 1972. pap. 7.95 (ISBN 0-19-501663-7, GB). Oxford U Pr.

--Yeats: The Man & the Masks. rev. ed. 1978. (Norton Lib); pap. 6.95 (ISBN 0-393-00859-2). Norton.

Ellmann, Richard, ed. The New Oxford Book of American Verse. LC 75-46354. 1976. 29.95 (ISBN 0-19-502058-8). Oxford U Pr.

Ellmann, Richard & Feidelson, Charles, Jr., eds. The Modern Tradition: Backgrounds of Modern Literature. 1965. text ed. 29.95x (ISBN 0-19-500876-6). Oxford U Pr.

Ellmann, Richard & O'Clair, Robert, eds. Modern Poems: An Introduction to Poetry. 500p. 1976. pap. text ed. 13.95x (ISBN 0-393-09187-2). Norton.

--Norton Anthology of Modern Poetry. 1400p. 1973. 28.95 (ISBN 0-393-09357-3); pap. 21.95x (ISBN 0-393-09348-4). Norton.

Ellmann, Richard see Columbia University. English Institute.

Ellmann, Richard see Joyce, James.

Ellmann, Richard, ed. see Joyce, James.

Ellmann, Richard, intro. by see Joyce, James.

Ellmann, Richard, intro. by see Moscato, Michael & LeBlanc, Leslie.

Ellmann, Richard, ed. see Wilde, Oscar.

Ellmann, Richard, tr. see Michaux, Henri.

Ellner. Pathogenic Microorganisms. Date not set. write for info. (ISBN 0-444-00824-1). Elsevier.

Ellner, Carolyn L. & Barnes, Carol P. Studies in Post-Secondary Teaching: Experimental Results, Theoretical Interpretations, & New Perspectives. LC 82-47853. 240p. 1983. 27.50x (ISBN 0-669-05656-1). Lexington Bks.

Ellner, Joseph, ed. Gipsy Pattern. facsimile ed. LC 75-101807. (Short Story Index Reprint Ser.). 1926. 18.00 (ISBN 0-8369-3195-5). Ayer Co Pubs.

Ellner, Paul D. Current Procedures in Clinical Bacteriology. (Illus.). 240p. 1978. 25.75x (ISBN 0-398-03759-0). C C Thomas.

Ello, Paul, ed. see Dubcek, Alexander.

Elloitt, Charles, ed. The Hachette Guide to French Wines. LC 85-40034. (Illus.). 704p. 1985. 14.95 (ISBN 0-317-19577-8). Knopf.

Ellory, J. C. & Young, T. Red Cell Membranes: A Methodological Approach. (Biological Techniques Ser.). 1982. 55.00 (ISBN 0-12-237140-2). Acad Pr.

Ellory, J. C. & Lew, V. L., eds. Membrane Transport in Red Cells. 1978. 75.00 (ISBN 0-12-237150-X). Acad Pr.

Ellory, J. C., ed. see Royal Society Discussion Meeting, May 12-13 1982.

Ellos, William J. Linguistic Ecumenism: A Barthian Road Back from Babel. LC 83-12484. 116p. (Orig.). 1983. lib. bdg. 21.00 (ISBN 0-8191-3422-8); pap. text ed. 9.25 (ISBN 0-8191-3423-6). U Pr of Amer.

Elloy, J. P. & Piasco, J. M. Classical & Modern Control Through Worked Examples. (International Ser. on Systems & Control: Vol. 3). (Illus.). 200p. 1981. 50.00 (ISBN 0-08-026745-9); pap. 18.75 (ISBN 0-08-026746-7). Pergamon.

El Lozy, Mohamed. Editing in a UNIX Environment: The Vi-Ex Editor. LC 84-22281. 256p. 1985. 19.95 (Busn). P-H.

Ellrich, Robert J. Rousseau & His Reader: The Rhetorical Situation of the Major Works. (Studies in the Romance Languages & Literatures: No. 83). 108p. 1969. pap. 7.00x (ISBN 0-8078-9083-9). U of NC Pr.

Ellrodt, Robert. Neoplatonism in the Poetry of Spenser. 1978. Repr. of 1960 ed. lib. bdg. 35.00 (ISBN 0-8495-1318-9). Arden Lib.

--Neoplatonism in the Poetry of Spenser. LC 75-11942. 1960. lib. bdg. 30.00 (ISBN 0-8414-3991-5). Folcroft.

Ellroy, James. Because the Night. LC 83-63160. 1984. 15.95 (ISBN 0-89296-071-X). Mysterious Pr.

--Blood on the Moon. LC 83-63039. 1984. 14.95 (ISBN 0-89296-069-8). Mysterious Pr.

--Blood on the Moon. 272p. 1985. pap. 3.25 (ISBN 0-380-69851-X). Avon.

--Brown's Requiem. 256p. (Orig.). 1985. pap. 2.95 (ISBN 0-380-78741-5). Avon.

--Brown's Requiem. 256p. 1984. 13.95 (ISBN 0-8052-8185-1, Pub. by Allison & Busby England). Schocken.

--Clandestine. 352p. 1985. pap. 2.95 (ISBN 0-380-81141-3, 60149-4). Avon.

--Clandestine. 342p. 1984. 13.95 (ISBN 0-8052-8197-5, Pub. by Allison & Busby England). Schocken.

Ells, Ernest E. Eells Family History in America: Sixteen Thirty-Three to Nineteen Fifty-Two. 600p. 1985. Repr. of 1969 ed. 25.00x (ISBN 0-932334-72-5). Heart of the Lakes.

Ellsaesser, Lydia Drew. Just Look at All My Families. 209p. pap. 25.00. Southern Hist Pr.

Ellsberg, Edward. Men under the Sea. LC 81-6869. (Illus.). xii, 365p. 1981. Repr. of 1939 ed. lib. bdg. 42.50x (ISBN 0-313-23030-7, ELMU). Greenwood.

--On the Bottom. 1978. Repr. of 1928 ed. lib. bdg. 25.00 (ISBN 0-8492-0780-0). R West.

--Under the Red Sea Sun. LC 73-17860. (Illus.). 500p. 1974. Repr. of 1946 ed. lib. bdg. 24.50x (ISBN 0-8371-7264-0, ELRS). Greenwood.

Ellsberg, Helen. Mines of Julian. (California Mines Ser). 72p. 1972. wrappers 2.95 (ISBN 0-910856-44-3). La Siesta.

Ellsberg, Robert, ed. see Day, Dorothy.

Ellspermann, Gerald L. The Attitude of the Early Christian Latin Writers Toward Pagan Literature & Learning. 295p. 1984. Repr. of 1949 ed. 45.00x (ISBN 0-939738-26-0). Zubal Inc.

Ellsworth, A. Eugene. Aural Harmony. LC 72-138243. 1970. spiral bdg. 19.95 (ISBN 0-910842-00-0, GE9, Pub. by GWM); 34 tapes 134.50 set (ISBN 0-8497-6325-8, GE9T). Kjos.

Ellsworth, Blanche. English Simplified. 4th ed. 32p. 1981. pap. text ed. 4.50 scp (ISBN 0-06-041901-6, HarpC); scp Excer. bk. 6.50 (ISBN 0-06-041902-4). Har-Row.

Ellsworth, Blanche & Higgins, John. English Simplified. 5th ed. 32p. 1985. pap. text ed. 4.50 scpr info. (ISBN 0-06-041903-2, HarpC). Har-Row.

Ellsworth Community College. Behavior Observation & Measurement. Davis, Michael, ed. (RATES Ser.: No. 5). (Illus.). 56p. (Orig.). 1983. pap. 3.00x (ISBN 0-916671-41-0). Material Dev.

--Increasing Existing Behavior. Davis, Michael, ed. (RATES Ser.: No. 6). (Illus.). 72p. (Orig.). 1983. pap. 3.00x (ISBN 0-916671-42-9). Material Dev.

--Instructional Activities Manual. Davis, Michael, ed. (RATES Ser.). (Illus.). 77p. (Orig.). 1983. pap. 3.00x (ISBN 0-916671-46-1). Material Dev.

--Introduction to Systematic Instruction. Davis, Michael, ed. (RATES Ser.: No. 1). (Illus.). 56p. (Orig.). 1983. pap. 3.00x (ISBN 0-916671-40-2). Material Dev.

--Maintaining Behavior. Davis, Michael, ed. (RATES Ser.: No. 8). 60p. (Orig.). 1983. pap. 3.00x (ISBN 0-916671-44-5). Material Dev.

--Reducing & Eliminating Behavior. Davis, Michael, ed. (RATES Ser.: No. 9). (Illus.). 84p. (Orig.). 1983. pap. 3.00x (ISBN 0-916671-45-3). Material Dev.

--Task Analysis. Davis, Michael, ed. (RATES Ser.: No. 2). (Illus.). 56p. (Orig.). 1984. pap. 3.00x (ISBN 0-916671-51-8). Material Dev.

--Teaching New Behavior. Davis, Michael, ed. (RATES Ser.: No. 7). (Illus.). 62p. (Orig.). 1983. pap. 3.00x (ISBN 0-916671-43-7). Material Dev.

Ellsworth, Dee, ed. see Weibel, Kathleen & Heim, Kathleen M.

Ellsworth, Dianne, ed. Union Lists: Issues & Answers. (Current Issues in Serials management Ser.: No. 2). 1982. 24.50 (ISBN 0-87650-141-2). Pierian.

Ellsworth, Donald P. Christian Music in Contemporary Witness: Historical Antecedents & Contemporary Practices. LC 79-52359. 1980. 7.95 (ISBN 0-8010-3338-1). Baker Bk.

Ellsworth, Edward W. Liberators of the Female Mind: The Shirreff Sisters, Educational Reform, & the Women's Movement. LC 78-67910. (Contributions in Women's Studies: No. 7). (Illus.). 1979. lib. bdg. 29.95 (ISBN 0-313-20644-9, ELL). Greenwood.

Ellsworth, Frank L. Law on the Midway: The Founding of the University of Chicago Law School. LC 77-78777. 1977. lib. bdg. 8.95x (ISBN 0-226-20608-4). U of Chicago Pr.

Ellsworth, Gerald C. The Inflexible Pressure of the Elliot Waves upon the Stock Market & Prediction of Major Future Price Movements. (Illus.). 143p. 1983. 91.85x (ISBN 0-86654-064-4). Inst Econ Finan.

Ellsworth, Henry W. Valley of the Upper Wabash, Indiana. facsimile ed. LC 75-98. (Mid-American Frontier Ser.). 1975. Repr. of 1838 ed. 20.00x (ISBN 0-405-06864-6). Ayer Co Pubs.

Ellsworth, Irene B. I Met Angels in the Tangles of Life. LC 84-52166. 118p. (Orig.). 1985. pap. 4.95 (ISBN 0-9614165-0-5). Terhell Bks.

Ellsworth, J. D. Reading Ancient Greek: A Reasonable Approach, 2 Pt. 498p. 1982. 22.50x set (ISBN 0-87291-162-4). Coronado Pr.

Ellsworth, J. W. & Stahnke, A. A. Politics & Political Systems. 1976. text ed. 27.95x (ISBN 0-07-019250-2). McGraw.

Ellsworth, John, Jr. Factory Folkways: Study of Institutional Structure & Change. Stein, Leon, ed. LC 77-70493. (Work Ser.). 1977. Repr. of 1952 ed. lib. bdg. 26.50x (ISBN 0-405-10164-3). Ayer Co Pubs.

Ellsworth, Ken, jt. ed. see Archdeacon, H. C.

Ellsworth, L. E. Charles Lowder & the Ritualist Movement. 234p. 1983. text ed. 38.00x (ISBN 0-232-51535-2, Pub. by D Longman & Todd England). Humanities.

Ellsworth, Leon W., jt. auth. see Burrill, Claude W.

Ellsworth, Liz. Frederick Wiseman: A Guide to References & Resources. 1979. lib. bdg. 29.50 (ISBN 0-8161-8066-0, Hall Reference). G K Hall.

Ellsworth, Lucius F. Craft to National Industry in the Nineteenth Century: A Case Study of the Transformation of the New York State Tanning Industry. new ed. LC 75-2578. (Dissertations in American Economic History). 1975. 31.00x (ISBN 0-405-07259-7). Ayer Co Pubs.

Ellsworth, Lucius F., jt. ed. see Taylor, George R.

Ellsworth, Mary E., tr. see Benitez, Fernando.

Ellsworth, Oliver B., ed. The Berkeley Manuscript. LC 84-7470. (Greek & Latin Music Theory Ser.). (Illus.). x, 317p. 1984. 24.50x (ISBN 0-8032-1808-7). U of Nebr Pr.

Elmes, David G., et al. Methods in Experimental Psychology. 1981. 26.50 (ISBN 0-395-30798-8); instr's manual 1.25 (ISBN 0-395-30799-6). HM.

--Research Methods in Psychology 2. 2nd ed. (Illus.). 1984. 26.95 (ISBN 0-314-85232-8). West Pub.

Elmes, James. Lectures on Architecture. LC 71-174408. Repr. of 1821 ed. 33.00 (ISBN 0-405-08486-2, Blom Pubns). Ayer Co Pubs.

--Memoirs of Sir Christopher Wren. LC 77-94576. 1979. Repr. of 1823 ed. lib. bdg. 60.00 (ISBN 0-89341-241-4). Longwood Pub Group.

--Thomas Clarkson: A Monograph: Being a Contribution Towards the History of the Abolition of the Slave Trade & Slavery. facs. ed. LC 76-89414. (Black Heritage Library Collection Ser). 1854. 16.00 (ISBN 0-8369-8569-9). Ayer Co Pubs.

Elmes, James, jt. auth. see Shepherd, Thomas.

Elmes, James, jt. auth. see Shepherd, Thomas H.

El-Messidi, Kathy G. The Bargain: The Story Behind the Thirty Year Honeymoon of GM & UAW. 141p. 1980. 8.95 (ISBN 0-8290-1578-7). Irvington.

Elmessiri, Abdel, ed. The Palestinian Wedding: A Bilingual Anthology of Contemporary Palestinian Resistance Poetry. Elmessiri, Abdel, tr. from Arabic. (Illus.). 249p. (Arabic, English.). 1982. 20.00 (ISBN 0-89410-095-5); pap. 10.00 (ISBN 0-89410-096-3). Three Continents.

Elmessiri, Abdelwahab M. The Land of Promise: A Critique of Political Zionism. LC 77-83664. 1977. text ed. 11.95x (ISBN 0-930244-02-8); pap. text ed. 7.95x (ISBN 0-930244-01-X). North American Inc.

Elmessiri, Abdelwahab M., jt. auth. see Stevens, Richard P.

Elmhurst, Ernest. The World Hoax: The Jew. 1982. lib. bdg. 69.95 (ISBN 0-87700-328-9). Revisionist Pr.

Elmhurst, Ernest F. The World Hoax. 233p. 1976. pap. 4.50x (ISBN 0-911038-81-7). Noontide.

Elmo, Francis, tr. from Span. I, in Christ Arisen. LC 81-85745. Orig. Title: Yo, en Cristo Resucitado. 100p. 1982. pap. 4.00 (ISBN 0-9607590-0-X). Action Life Pubns.

Elmont, Nancy. The Complete Gas Grill Cookbook. 1982. pap. 4.95 (ISBN 0-916752-52-6). Caroline Hse.

--A Knife for All Seasons. LC 80-70845. (Illus.). 160p. 1981. 11.95 (ISBN 0-916752-48-8). Dorison Hse.

Elmore, D. T. Peptides & Proteins. LC 68-21392. (Cambridge Chemistry Texts Ser). (Illus.). 1968. 32.50 (ISBN 0-521-07107-0); pap. 9.95x (ISBN 0-521-09535-2). Cambridge U Pr.

Elmore, Francis H. Ethnobotany of the Navajo. LC 76-43698. (Univ. of New Mexico Bulletin: Vol. 1, No. 7). Repr. of 1944 ed. 22.50 (ISBN 0-404-15530-8). AMS Pr.

--Shrubs & Trees of the Southwest Uplands. Jackson, Earl, ed. LC 76-14115. (Popular Ser: No. 19). (Illus., Orig.). 1976. pap. 6.00 (ISBN 0-911408-41-X). SW Pks Mnmts.

Elmore, John F., jt. auth. see Weeks, J. Devereux.

Elmore, Patricia. Susannah & the Blue House Mystery. LC 79-20491. (Illus.). 176p. (gr. 4-7). 1980. 10.25 (ISBN 0-525-40525-9, 0996-290). Dutton.

--Susannah & the Blue House Mystery. (Orig.). (gr. 4-6). 1984. pap. 1.95 (ISBN 0-671-43493-4). Archway.

--Susannah & the Poison Green Halloween. LC 82-2493. 128p. (gr. 4-7). 1982. 9.95 (ISBN 0-525-44019-4, 0966-290). Dutton.

Elmore, Paul, jt. auth. see Dean, Michael L.

Elmore, Richard F., jt. auth. see Rand Corporation.

Elmore, Richard F., jt. auth. see Williams, Walter.

Elmore, Richard F., jt. ed. see Williams, Walter.

Elmore, Theo V. Lost Profits. 64p. 1982. 5.00 (ISBN 0-682-49845-9). Exposition Pr FL.

Elmore, Vernon O. Man As God's Creation. 1986. 5.95 (ISBN 0-8054-1636-6). Broadman.

Elmore, William C. & Heald, Mark A. Physics of Waves. LC 68-58209. xiii, 477p. 1983. pap. text ed. 20.00 (ISBN 0-9613127-0-X). Heald Pubns.

--Physics of Waves. 477p. 1985. pap. 9.95 (ISBN 0-486-64926-1). Dover.

El Morya. The Chela & the Path. Prophet, Elizabeth C., ed. LC 76-7634. (Illus.). 142p. (Orig.). 1976. pap. 3.95 (ISBN 0-916766-12-8). Summit Univ.

--Encyclical on World Good Will. 1963. 1.50 (ISBN 0-685-79130-0). Summit Univ.

--Morya. Prophet, Elizabeth C., ed. LC 81-85570. 412p. 1982. pap. 9.95 (ISBN 0-916766-52-7). Summit Univ.

--The Sacred Adventure. LC 81-85464. 148p. 1981. 4.95 (ISBN 0-916766-53-5). Summit Univ.

--A White Paper. 1971. 0.50 (ISBN 0-685-79131-9). Summit Univ.

Elms, Alan C. Personality in Politics. (Illus.). 200p. 1976. pap. text ed. 11.95 (ISBN 0-15-569762-5, HC). HarBraceJ.

Elms, D. An Introduction to Modern Structural Analysis. 230p. 1971. 69.50 (ISBN 0-677-62030-6). Gordon.

Elmslie, Kenwald. Album. (Illus.). pap. 3.50 (ISBN 0-686-09746-7). Kulchur Foun.

Elmslie, Kenward. Communications Equipment. (Burning Deck Poetry Ser.). 1979. pap. 3.00 (ISBN 0-930900-71-5); pap. 20.00 signed handmade (ISBN 0-930900-72-3). Burning Deck.

--Motor Disturbance: "The Frank O'Hara Award Series". (A Full Court Rebound Bk.). 1978. 17.95 (ISBN 0-916190-24-2); pap. 6.00 (ISBN 0-916190-25-0). Full Court NY.

--Moving Right Along. 1980. 10.00 (ISBN 0-915990-21-0); pap. 5.00 (ISBN 0-915990-20-2). Z Pr.

--Tropicalism. LC 75-26459. 80p. (Orig.). 1976. pap. 5.00 (ISBN 0-915990-00-8). Z Pr.

Elmslie, Kenward, ed. see Ashbery, J., et al.

Elmslie, Kenward, ed. see Berkson, Bill.

Elmslie, Kenward, ed. see Burckhardt, Rudy.

Elmslie, Kenward, ed. see Godfrey, John.

Elmslie, Kenward, ed. see Koch, Kenneth, et al.

Elmslie, Kenward, ed. see Padgett, Ron.

Elmslie, Kenward, ed. see Schuyler, James, et al.

Elmslie, Kenward, ed. see Welt, Bernard.

Elmslie, Ronald G. & Ludbrook, J. Introduction to Surgery: One Hundred Topics. 1971. 37.50 (ISBN 0-12-238250-1). Acad Pr.

Elmslie, W. A. Among the Wild Ngoni. 3rd ed. (Illus.). 320p. 1970. Repr. of 1899 ed. 32.50x (ISBN 0-7146-1867-5, BHA-01867, F Cass Co). Biblio Dist.

Elmslie, W. A., ed. The Mishna of Idolatry Aboda Zara. (Texts & Studies Ser.: No. 1, Vol. 8, Pt. 2). pap. 19.00 (ISBN 0-317-15680-2). Kraus Repr.

Elmstrom, George. Advanced Management Strategies for Optometrists. LC 81-84306. 1982. 67.00 (ISBN 0-87873-030-3). Prof Press.

--Holistic Considerations for the Advancing Optometrist. LC 81-84401. 1982. pap. 13.00 (ISBN 0-87873-029-X). Prof Press.

Elmwood Publishing Company. Psalms of Reflection: A Selection of Psalm Verses for Those Who Mourn. 1979. pap. 1.25 (ISBN 0-931396-00-X). Elmwood Pub Co.

El-Nahal, Galal H. The Judicial Administration of Ottoman Egypt in the Seventeenth Century. LC 79-52488. (Studies in Middle Eastern History: No. 4). 1979. 20.00x (ISBN 0-88297-024-0). Bibliotheca.

El-Najjar, Mahmoud Y. & McWilliams, K. Richard. Forensic Anthropology: The Structure, Morphology, & Variation of Human Bone & Dentition. (Illus.). 208p. 1978. photocopy ed. 21.75x (ISBN 0-398-03648-9). C C Thomas.

El-Namaki, M. S. Problems of Management in a Developing Environment: The Case of Tanzania (State Enterprises Between 1967 & 1975) 270p. 1979. 42.75 (ISBN 0-444-85303-0, North Holland). Elsevier.

Elnett, Elaine. Historic Origin & Social Development of Family Life in Russia. LC 72-153317. Repr. of 1926 ed. 16.00 (ISBN 0-404-02322-3). AMS Pr.

Elo, Arpad E. The Rating of Chess Players Past & Present. LC 78-24077. 1979. 12.95 (ISBN 0-668-04721-6). Arco.

Elodi, P., ed. Proteinase Action. (Symposia Biologica Hungary Ser.: Vol. 25). 500p. 1984. 55.00 (ISBN 0-9910002-7-7, Pub. by Akademiai Kaido Hungary). Heyden.

Elon, Amos. Herzl. (Illus.). 496p. 1985. pap. 12.95 (ISBN 0-8052-0790-2). Schocken.

--Israelis: Founders & Sons. 340p. 1983. pap. 6.95 (ISBN 0-14-022476-9, Pelican). Penguin.

--Understanding Israel: A Social Studies Approach. Sugarman, Morris J., ed. LC 76-18282. (Illus.). 256p. (gr. 9 up). 1976. pap. text ed. 6.95x (ISBN 0-87441-234-X). Behrman.

Elon, Amos, et al. The Israelis: Photographs of a Day in May. (Illus.). 256p. 1985. 35.00 (ISBN 0-8109-0806-9). Abrams.

Elon, Florence. Self-Made. 84p. 1984. 12.95 (ISBN 0-436-14612-6, Pub. by Secker & Warburg UK). David & Charles.

Elon, Menachem, ed. The Principles of Jewish Law. 866p. 1975. 50.00 (ISBN 0-87855-188-3). Transaction Bks.

Elonka, S. M. Standard Basic Math & Applied Plant Calculations. 1977. text ed. 28.50 (ISBN 0-07-019297-9). McGraw.

Elonka, S. M. & Kohan, A. L. Standard Heating & Power Boiler Plant Questions & Answers. 2nd ed. 672p. 1984. 44.50 (ISBN 0-07-019277-4). McGraw.

Elonka, Stephen M. Marmaduke Surfaceblow's Salty Technical Romances. LC 79-14107. 320p. 1979. 20.50 (ISBN 0-88275-967-1). Krieger.

--Standard Plant Operators Manual. 3rd ed. LC 79-22089. (Illus.). 416p. 1980. 36.50 (ISBN 0-07-019298-7). McGraw.

Elonka, Stephen M. & Higgins, Alex. Standard Boiler Room Questions & Answers. 3rd ed. (Illus.). 384p. 1982. 32.95 (ISBN 0-07-019301-0). McGraw.

Elonka, Stephen M. & Minich, Quaid W. Standard Refrigeration & Air Conditioning Questions & Answers. 3rd ed. (Illus.). 416p. 1983. 36.95 (ISBN 0-07-019317-7). McGraw.

Elonka, Stephen M. & Parsons, Alonzo R. Standard Instrumentation Questions & Answers for Production-Processes Control, 2 vols. in 1. Incl. Vol. 1. Measuring Systems; Vol. 2. Control Systems. LC 79-1385. 1979. Repr. of 1962 ed. lib. bdg. 32.50 (ISBN 0-88275-896-9). Krieger.

Elonka, Stephen M. & Robinson, Joseph R. Standard Plant Operator's Questions & Answers, 2 vols. 2nd ed. 1981. Set. 49.50 (ISBN 0-07-079191-0); Vol. 1. 27.00 (ISBN 0-07-019315-0); Vol. 2. 27.00 (ISBN 0-07-019316-9). McGraw.

Elonka, Stephen M., jt. auth. see Higgins, Alex.

Elonka, Stephen M., jt. auth. see Moore, Arthur H.

Elorza. Matematicas para Ciencias del Comportamiento. 300p. (Span.). 1984. pap. text ed. write for info. (ISBN 0-06-310700-7, Pub. by HarLA Mexico). Har-Row.

Elot, Maryse. From Zero to Eternity. 1985. 6.95 (ISBN 0-533-06558-5). Vantage.

Elovitz, Mark H. A Century of Jewish Life in Dixie: The Birmingham Experience. LC 73-22716. (Judaic Studies: No. 5). 256p. 1974. 18.75 (ISBN 0-8173-6901-5). U of Ala Pr.

Elpern, Barry S., jt. auth. see Tobias, Jerry V.

Elphick, R. & Giliomee, H., eds. The Shaping of South African Society. 1980. 30.00x (ISBN 0-582-64644-8); pap. text ed. 12.95x (ISBN 0-582-64687-1). Longman.

Elphick, Richard. Kraal & Castle: Khoikhoi & the Founding of White South Africa. LC 76-49723. (Historical Publications, Miscellany: No. 116). (Illus.). 1977. 31.00x (ISBN 0-300-02012-0). Yale U Pr.

El piner, Isaak E Imovich. Ultrasound: Physical, Chemical, & Biological Effects (Authorized Translation From the Russian) by F. L. Sinclair. LC 64-7760. pap. 95.30 (ISBN 0-317-08454-2, 2003361). Bks Demand UMI.

Elqin, M. Thackeray. 59.95 (ISBN 0-8490-1187-6). Gordon Pr.

El-Rayyes, Riad. Guerrillas for Palestine. LC 76-15869. 1976. 25.00 (ISBN 0-312-35280-8). St Martin.

Elrick, George. The Science Fiction Handbook: For Readers & Writers. LC 78-59828. (Illus.). 1978. pap. 8.95 (ISBN 0-914090-52-6). Chicago Review.

Elrick, Harold, et al. Living Longer & Better: Guide to Optimal Health. LC 78-366. (Illus.). 300p. 1978. pap. 5.95 (ISBN 0-89037-125-3). Anderson World.

Elrington, C. R., ed. see Ussher, James.

Elrington, C. R., jt. ed. see Wilkes, J. J.

Elrington, G. A., ed. see Gilson, Etienne H.

Elrod, Bruce C. Your Hit Parade. 3rd ed. (Illus.). 390p. lib. bdg. 15.95 (ISBN 0-9614805-2-1). B C Elrod.

Elrod, J. W. Being & Existence in Kierkegaard's Pseudonymous Works. 1975. 29.00x (ISBN 0-691-07204-3). Princeton U Pr.

Elrod, James L., Jr. & Wilkinson, James A. Hospital Project Financing & Refinancing under Prospective Payment. 164p. (Orig.). 1985. 19.95 (ISBN 0-939450-57-7, 061160). Am Hospital.

Elrod, John W. Kierkegaard & Christendom. LC 80-8547. 384p. 1981. 29.00 (ISBN 0-691-07261-2). Princeton U Pr.

Elrod, Linda H. Kansas Family Law Handbook. 1983. 155.00 (ISBN 0-318-04146-4). KS Bar CLE.

Elrod, Mavis. American Colonial Life. (Social Studies). 24p. (gr. 5-9). 1979. wkbk. 5.00 (ISBN 0-8209-0248-9, SS-15). ESP.

Elrod, Mavis S. Energy & Man. (Science Ser.). 24p. (gr. 5-9). 1976. wkbk. 5.00 (ISBN 0-8209-0148-2, S-10). ESP.

Elrod, Ron E. Engineering Handbook for Advertising Structures. 750p. 1985. pap. write for info. (ISBN 0-911380-67-1). Signs of Times.

Els, Betty V. The Bombers Moon. LC 85-47591. 129p. (gr. 4 up). 1984. 11.95 (ISBN 0-374-30864-0). FS&G.

Els, Theo van see Van Els, Theo, et al.

El Saadawi, N. The Hidden Face of Eve: Women in the Arab World. 1981. 30.00x (ISBN 0-686-31985-0, Pub. by Turoe Pr). State Mutual Bk.

El Saadawi, Nawal. The Hidden Face of Eve: Women in the Arab World. Hetata, Sherif, tr. from Egyptian. LC 81-68358. 212p. 1982. pap. 9.95 (ISBN 0-8070-6701-6, BP 627). Beacon Pr.

El Saffar, Ruth. Beyond Fiction: The Recovery of the Feminine in the Novels of Cervantes. LC 83-1067. 240p. 1984. lib. bdg. 19.00 (ISBN 0-520-04866-0). U of Cal Pr.

Elsas, Christoph. Neuplatonische und gnostische Weltablehnung in der Schule Plotins. (Religionsgeschichtliche Versuche und Vorarbeiten Ser., Vol. 34). 1975. 45.60 (ISBN 3-11-003941-9). De Gruyter.

Elsasser, Albert B., jt. auth. see Heizer, Robert.

Elsasser, Albert B., jt. auth. see Heizer, Robert F.

Elsasser, Albert B., ed. see Brown, Vinson.

Elsasser, Nan, et al. Las Mujeres: Conversations from a Hispanic Community. 162p. pap. 8.95 (ISBN 0-912670-60-6); Teaching guide, 45p. 4.00 (ISBN 0-912670-74-6). Feminist Pr.

--Las Mujeres: Conversations from a Hispanic Community. (Women's Lives - Women's Work Ser.). (Illus.). 162p. (gr. 11 up). 1981. o. p. 14.95 (ISBN 0-912670-84-3); pap. 8.95 (ISBN 0-912670-70-3); teaching guide 4.00 (ISBN 0-912670-80-0). Feminist Pr.

Elsasser, Walt er M. Atom & Organism: A New Approach to Theoretical Biology. LC 66-21832. pap. 38.30 (ISBN 0-317-27619-0, 2014639). Bks Demand UMI.

Elsasser, Walter M. Memoirs of a Physicist in the Atomic Age. (Illus.). 1978. 20.00 (ISBN 0-88202-178-8). Watson Pub Intl.

Elsayed, E. A. & Boucher, T. O. Analysis & Control of Production Systems. (Illus.). 304p. 1985. text ed. 34.95 (ISBN 0-13-032897-9). P-H.

Elsberg, John. Home Style Cooking on Third Avenue. LC 81-51819. 126p. 1982. 8.95 (ISBN 0-917976-14-2). White Ewe.

--The Price of Reindeer. (WEP Poetry Ser.: No. 2). 1979. pap. 2.00 (ISBN 0-917976-05-3). White Ewe.

Elsberg, Ted. Career Exploration: You & Your Future. LC 75-10352. (Illus.). 1975. 6.95 (ISBN 0-87005-145-8); wkbk. 3.50 (ISBN 0-87005-152-0). Fairchild.

Elsbree, Langdon. The Rituals of Life: Patterns in Narratives. (Series in Modern Literary Criticism). 1982. 15.00x (ISBN 0-8046-9295-5, Pub. by Kennikat). Assoc Faculty Pr.

Elsbree, Langdon, et al. The Heath Handbook of Composition. 10th ed. 560p. 1981. text ed. 12.95 (ISBN 0-669-03352-9); pap. text ed. 9.95 (ISBN 0-669-03353-7); instr's guide with tests 1.95 (ISBN 0-669-03356-1); wkbk. 6.95 (ISBN 0-669-03456-8); answer key to wkbk. 1.95 (ISBN 0-669-04701-5); diagnostic achievement tests 1.95 (ISBN 0-669-03355-3); student wkbk. for handbk. 6.95 (ISBN 0-669-05530-1); answer key for student wkbk. 1.95 (ISBN 0-669-05529-8). Heath.

--Heath's Brief Handbook of Usage. 9th ed. 1977. pap. text ed. 8.95x (ISBN 0-669-00588-6). Heath.

--Heath's College Handbook of Composition. text ed. 9.95x (ISBN 0-669-99960-1); pap. text ed. 7.95x (ISBN 0-669-00562-2); instructor's manual free (ISBN 0-669-00570-3); wkbk. 4.50x (ISBN 0-669-99978-4). Heath.

Elsbree, Oliver W. The Rise of the Missionary Spirit in America 1790-1815. LC 79-13028. (Perspectives in American History Ser.: No. 55). 1980. Repr. of 1928 ed. 19.50x (ISBN 0-87991-376-2). Porcupine Pr.

Elsbree, Willard S. American Teacher: Evolution of a Profession in a Democracy. LC 74-104262. Repr. of 1939 ed. lib. bdg. 35.00x (ISBN 0-8371-3921-X, ELAT). Greenwood.

--Teacher Turnover in the Cities & Villages of New York State. LC 75-176750. (Columbia University. Teachers College. Contributions to Education: No. 300). Repr. of 1928 ed. 22.50 (ISBN 0-404-55300-1). AMS Pr.

Elsby, F. H. Marketing & the Sales Manager. 1969. pap. 13.25 (ISBN 0-08-006536-8). Pergamon.

Elsby, W. L. The Engineer & Construction Control. 96p. 1981. pap. 11.75x (ISBN 0-7277-0117-7). Am Soc Civil Eng.

Elschner, J. Singular Ordinary Differential Operators & Pseudodifferential Equations. (Lecture Notes in Mathematics: Vol. 1128). 200p. 1985. pap. 14.40 (ISBN 0-387-15194-X). Springer-Verlag.

Elsdale, Henry. Studies in the Idylls. LC 70-148774. Repr. of 1878 ed. 17.00 (ISBN 0-404-08748-5). AMS Pr.

Elsdon, Ronald. Bent World. LC 81-8261. 200p. (Orig.). 1981. pap. 4.95 (ISBN 0-87784-834-3). Inter-Varsity.

Elsdon-Dew, R. W. & Jackson, J. M., eds. Aminoglutethimide: An Alternative Therapy for Breast Carcinoma. (Royal Society of Medicine Ser.: No. 53). 56p. 1983. pap. 9.50 (ISBN 0-8089-1549-5, 791157). Grune.

Elsdon-Dew, R. W., et al, eds. The Cardiovascular, Metabolic & Psychological Interface. (Royal Society of Medicine International Congress & Symposium Ser.: No. 14). 86p. 1979. pap. 16.00 (ISBN 0-8089-1219-4, 791155). Grune.

--Topics in Cardiovascular Medicine. (Royal Society of Medicine International Congress & Symposium Ser.: No. 34). 56p. 1981. pap. 14.50 (ISBN 0-8089-1318-2, 791156). Grune.

Elsdon-Dew, Robin W. & Birdwood, George F., eds. Transdermal Nitrates in Ischaemic Heart Disease, No. 59. (Royal Society of Medicine Ser.). 56p. 1983. 9.50 (ISBN 0-8089-1574-6, 791158). Grune.

Else, Gerald F., tr. see Aristotle.

Else, John F., jt. auth. see Hamilton, Nina.

Elsea, A. R., jt. auth. see Fletcher, E. E.

Elsea, A. R., et al. Evaluation of the Influence of Absorbed & Absorbed Hydrogen on the Mechanical Properties & Fracture Behavior of Materials to Be Used in a Hydrogen-Gas Transmission System. 185p. 1974. pap. 10.00 (ISBN 0-318-12610-9, L21177). Am Gas Assn.

Elsea, Janet G. The Four-Minute Sell. 1984. 12.95 (ISBN 0-671-49194-6). S&S.

Elsebai, Ismail, ed. Bladder Cancer. 1983. Vol. I, 216p. 68.00 (ISBN 0-8493-5733-0); Vol. II, 224p. 68.00 (ISBN 0-8493-5734-9). CRC Pr.

Elsen, Albert. Modern European Sculpture 1918-1945: Unknown Beings & Other Realities. 1979. pap. 10.95 (ISBN 0-8076-0921-8). Braziller.

Elsen, Albert & Atelier, Johnson. Casting: A Survey of Cast Metal Sculpture in the 80's. (Illus.). 28p. (Orig.). 1982. 6.00x (ISBN 0-686-45741-2). Fuller Golden Gal.

Elsen, Albert E. The Gates of Hell by Auguste Rodin. LC 84-51717. (Illus.). 272p. 1985. 39.50x (ISBN 0-8047-1273-5); pap. 16.95 (ISBN 0-8047-1281-6, SP 174). Stanford U Pr.

--In Rodin's Studio: A Photographic Record of Sculpture in the Making. (Illus.). 192p. 1980. 35.00x (ISBN 0-8014-1329-X). Cornell U Pr.

--Origins of Modern Sculpture: Pioneers & Premises. LC 73-90927. (Illus.). 192p. 1974. pap. 10.95 (ISBN 0-8076-0737-1). Braziller.

--The Partial Figure in Modern Sculpture, from Rodin to 1969. LC 73-106903. (Illus.). 1969. pap. 10.00 (ISBN 0-912298-03-0); pap. 8.00 (ISBN 0-912298-04-9). Baltimore Mus.

--Paul Jenkins. LC 75-101622. (Contemporary Artists Ser.). (Illus.). 288p. 1973. 65.00 (ISBN 0-8109-0215-X). Abrams.
--Purposes of Art. 4th ed. LC 80-26290. 451p. 1981. pap. text ed. 26.95 (ISBN 0-03-049766-3, HoltC). HR&W.
Elsen, Albert E., ed. Rodin Rediscovered. (Illus.). 375p. 1981. 42.50 (ISBN 0-89468-000-5, 753521). NYGS.
--Rodin Rediscovered. LC 81-9576. (Illus.). pap. 5.00 (ISBN 0-686-81955-1). Natl Gallery Art.
Elser, Smoke & Brown, Bill. Packin' in on Mules & Horses. (Illus.). 228p. 1980. pap. 9.95 (ISBN 0-87842-127-0). Mountain Pr.
Elseth, G. D. & Baugardner, D. Genetics. (Illus.). 720p. 1984. 34.95 (ISBN 0-201-03953-2); solutions manual 4.95 (ISBN 0-201-03482-4). Addison-Wesley.
Elsevier Science Publishing Co. Agriculture Catalog, 1984. 1984. write for info. Elsevier.
Elsevier Science Publishing Company, ed. Engineering & Technology Catalog, 1984. Date not set. write for info. Elsevier.
Elsey, George M. Roosevelt & China. 180p. 1979. 22.50 (ISBN 0-89453-121-2). M Glazier.
El'sgol'c, L. E. Qualitative Methods in Mathematical Analysis. LC 64-16170. (Translations of Mathematical Monographs: Vol. 12). 250p. 1980. pap. 36.00 (ISBN 0-8218-1562-8, MMONO-12). Am Math.
Elsgolts, L. Differential Equations & the Calculus of Variations. Yankovsky, George, tr. from Rus. (Illus.). 440p. 1970. 17.95x (ISBN 0-8464-0335-8). Beekman Pubs.
El'Sgol'Ts, L. E. Differential Equations. (Russian Monographs). (Illus.). 372p. 1961. 98.25 (ISBN 0-677-20060-9). Gordon.
Elsgolts, L. E. & Norkin, S. B. Introduction to the Theory & Application of Differential Equations with Deviating Arguments. 1973. 61.50 (ISBN 0-12-237750-8). Acad Pr.
El-Shaarawi, A. H., ed. Time Series Methods in Hydrosciences: Proceedings of the International Conference, Burlington, Ontario, Canada, October 6-8, 1981. (Developments in Water Science Ser.: No. 17). 614p. 1982. 85.00 (ISBN 0-444-42102-5). Elsevier.
El-Shafie, Mahmoud A., jt. ed. see Dorner, Peter.
El-Shakhs, Salah S., jt. auth. see Lutz, Jesse G.
El-Shakhs, Salah S., jt. ed. see Obudho, R. A.
El-Shamy, Hasan M., ed. Folktales of Egypt. LC 79-9316. (Folktales of the World Ser.). 1980. pap. 9.95x (ISBN 0-226-20625-4). U of Chicago Pr.
El-Sharif, Nabil, jt. auth. see Samet, Philip.
El Shater, Safaa. The Novels of Mary Shelley. (Salzburg Studies in English Literature: Romantic Reassessment Ser.: No. 59). (Orig.). 1977. pap. text ed. 25.50x (ISBN 0-391-01372-6). Humanities.
El Shazly, E. M., compiled by. Geology of Uranium & Thorium: 1961-1966, Vol. 2. Incl. Geology of Uranium & Thorium. Shazly, E. M. El, compiled by. (Bibliographical Ser.: No. 31). 134p. 1962. pap. write for info. (ISBN 92-0-044062-2, ISP21/4, IAEA). (Bibliographical Ser.: No. 31). 102p. 1968. pap. write for info. (ISBN 92-0-044168-8, ISP2131, IAEA). Unipub.
El Shazly, Saad. The Crossing of the Suez. Benson, Susan, ed. (Illus.). 333p. 1980. 20.00 (ISBN 0-9604562-0-1, 80-67107). Am Mideast.
El-Sherbini, A A. Food Security Issues in the Arab Near East: A Report of the United Nations Economic Commission for Western Asia. LC 79-40254. (Illus.). 1979. 46.00 (ISBN 0-08-023447-X). Pergamon.
El-Shobokshy, Mohammad S., jt. auth. see Hesketh, Howard E.
Elshout, A. J., jt. ed. see Beilke, S.
Elshtain, Jean B. Public Man, Private Woman: Women in Social & Poltical Thought. LC 81-47122. 376p. 1981. 32.50 (ISBN 0-691-07632-4); pap. 9.55 (ISBN 0-691-02206-2). Princeton U Pr.
Elshtain, Jean B., ed. The Family in Political Thought. LC 81-11435. 368p. 1982. lib. bdg. 24.00x (ISBN 0-87023-341-6); pap. text ed. 11.95x (ISBN 0-87023-342-4). U of Mass Pr.
Elskamp, Karen K. & Munzert, Alfred W. Test Your Sex Appeal. LC 80-85277. (Test Yourself Ser.). 64p. 1981. pap. 3.95 (ISBN 0-671-42627-3). Monarch Pr.
Elskamp, Karen K., ed. see Munzert, Alfred W.
Elskus, Albinas. Art of Painting on Glass. (Illus.). 152p. 1982. (ScribT); pap. 12.95 (ISBN 0-684-17643-2). Scribner.
Elsman, Max. How to Get Your First Job: A Field Guide for Beginners. 1985. pap. 4.95 (ISBN 0-517-55739-8). Crown.
Elsman, Max & National Institute for Work & Learning. Industry-Education-Labor Collaboration: An Action Guide for Collaborative Councils. 100p. 1981. 5.00 (ISBN 0-318-15742-X). Natl Inst Work.
Elsmere, Jane S. Justice Samuel Chase. LC 80-82875. (Illus.). 369p. 1981. 14.95x (ISBN 0-937174-00-9). Janevar Pub.
Elsner, Charlotte, tr. see Park, Robert E.
Elsner, Don Von see Von Elsner, Don.
Elsner, E. Spanish Sunshine. 1976. lib. bdg. 59.95 (ISBN 0-8490-2653-9). Gordon Pr.
Elsner, Henry, Jr., ed. see Park, Robert E.
Elsner, Robert & Gooden, Brett. Diving & Asphyxia: A Comparative Study of Animals & Man. LC 82-21998. (Physiological Society Monograph: No. 40). 175p. 1983. 54.50 (ISBN 0-521-25068-4). Cambridge U Pr.
Elsom, John. Erotic Theatre. LC 73-15277. (Illus.). 288p. 1974. 10.00 (ISBN 0-8008-2465-2). Taplinger.
--Post-War British Theatre. rev. ed. (Illus.). 1979. pap. 9.50 (ISBN 0-7100-0168-1). Routledge & Kegan.
Elsom, John, ed. Postwar British Theatre Criticism. 224p. 1980. 25.00x (ISBN 0-7100-0535-0). Routledge & Kegan.
Elsom, John R. Lightning Over the Treasury Building: An Expose of Our Banking & Currency Monstrosity. 1979. lib. bdg. 59.95 (ISBN 0-8490-2960-0). Gordon Pr.
Elson, Arthur. Modern Composers of Europe. LC 77-90802. 1978. Repr. of 1904 ed. lib. bdg. 35.00 (ISBN 0-89341-419-0). Longwood Pub Group.
--Woman's Work in Music. LC 76-22330. (Illus.). 1976. Repr. of 1904 ed. lib. bdg. 30.00 (ISBN 0-89341-013-6). Longwood Pub Group.
--Woman's Work in Music. LC 75-33688. Repr. of 1931 ed. cancelled (ISBN 0-89201-009-6). Zenger Pub.
Elson, Benjamin F. & Pickett, Velma B. Beginning Morphology & Syntax. rev. ed. LC 82-63016. 200p. 1983. text ed. 11.00 (ISBN 0-88312-925-6); microfiche (3) 3.80 (ISBN 0-88312-538-2). Summer Inst Ling.
Elson, C. M., tr. see Rozanov, Y. A.
Elson, Charles. Wieland & Shaftesbury. LC 79-166024. (Columbia University. Germanic Studies, Old Ser.: No. 16). Repr. of 1913 ed. 22.50 (ISBN 0-404-50416-7). AMS Pr.
Elson, Diane. A Christmas Book. (Illus.). 104p. (gr. 6 up). 1983. 12.95 (ISBN 0-437-37703-2, Pub. by Worlds Work). David & Charles.
--A Country Book. (Illus.). 104p. (gr. 6 up). 1983. 12.95 (ISBN 0-437-37704-0, Pub. by Worlds Work). David & Charles.
Elson, Diane, ed. Cats! Cats! (Illus.). 112p. (gr. 1-5). 1985. 10.95 (ISBN 0-437-37706-7, Pub. by Worlds Work). David & Charles.
--Value: The Representation of Labour in Capitalism. 1980. text ed. 31.75x (ISBN 0-906336-07-4); pap. text ed. 13.50x (ISBN 0-906336-08-2). Humanities.
Elson, Elliot, et al, eds. Cell Membranes: Methods & Review, Vol. 1. 211p. 1983. 29.50x (ISBN 0-306-41298-5, Plenum Pr). Plenum Pub.
--Cell Membranes: Methods & Review, Vol. 2. 390p. 1984. 52.50x (ISBN 0-306-41761-8, Plenum Pr). Plenum Pub.
Elson, Henry W. & Brady, Matthew B. The Civil War Through the Camera. 27.50 (ISBN 0-405-12294-2). Ayer Co Pubs.
Elson, Howard. Barry. (Illus.). 128p. 1984. 18.95 (ISBN 0-86276-134-4); pap. 10.95 (ISBN 0-86276-133-6). Proteus Pub NY.
--Early Rockers. (Illus.). 128p. (Orig.). 1983. 14.95 (ISBN 0-86276-087-9); pap. 9.95 (ISBN 0-86276-086-0). Proteus Pub NY.
--James Last. (Illus.). 64p. 1983. 15.95 (ISBN 0-86276-174-3); pap. 9.95 (ISBN 0-86276-120-4). Proteus Pub NY.
Elson, Howard & Brunton, John. Whatever Happened to...? The Great Pop & Rock Music Nostalgia Book. (Illus.). 160p. 1981. pap. 8.95 (ISBN 0-906071-40-2). Proteus Pub NY.
Elson, Laurence G., Sr. Thor's Castle. 1984. 13.95 (ISBN 0-533-05784-1). Vantage.
Elson, Lawrence. It's Your Body. (Illus.). 576p. 1973. text ed. 40.95 (ISBN 0-07-019299-5). McGraw.
Elson, Lawrence, jt. auth. see Kapit, Wynn.
Elson, Lawrence M. The Zoology Coloring Book. (Illus.). 240p. 1982. pap. 8.61i (ISBN 0-06-460301-6, CO301). B&N NY.
Elson, Louis. Curiosities of Music. 59.95 (ISBN 0-87968-978-1). Gordon Pr.
--History of American Music. 59.95 (ISBN 0-8490-0316-4). Gordon Pr.
--The National Music of America. 59.95 (ISBN 0-8490-0712-7). Gordon Pr.
--Woman in Music. 69.95 (ISBN 0-87968-459-3). Gordon Pr.
Elson, Louis C. Curiosities of Music. LC 77-90801. 1978. Repr. of 1908 ed. lib. bdg. 35.00 (ISBN 0-89341-418-2). Longwood Pub Group.
--Elson's Music Dictionary. LC 70-173097. xii, 306p. 1972. Repr. of 1905 ed. 43.00x (ISBN 0-8103-3268-X). Gale.
--European Reminiscences Musical & Otherwise. LC 72-125046. (Music Ser.). (Illus.). 301p. 1972. Repr. of 1896 ed. lib. bdg. 32.50 (ISBN 0-306-70011-5). Da Capo.
--Great Composers & Their Work. facsimile ed. LC 71-37472. (Essay Index Reprint Ser). Repr. of 1898 ed. 19.50 (ISBN 0-8369-2545-9). Ayer Co Pubs.
--Great Composers & Their Work. LC 77-90806. 1978. Repr. of 1898 ed. lib. bdg. 30.00 (ISBN 0-89341-423-9). Longwood Pub Group.
--History of American Music. (Illus.). 1971. Repr. 29.00 (ISBN 0-8337-1055-9). B Franklin.
--The National Music of America & Its Sources. LC 70-159950. (Illus.). 1975. Repr. of 1911 ed. 43.00x (ISBN 0-8103-4039-9). Gale.
--Shakespeare in Music. LC 76-155627. Repr. of 1901 ed. 12.50 (ISBN 0-404-02323-1). AMS Pr.
--Shakespeare in Music: A Collation of the Chief Musical Allusions in the Plays of Shakespeare, with an Attempt at Their Explanation & Derivation, Together with Much of the Original Music. LC 78-113646. (Select Bibliographies Reprint Ser). 1900. 26.00 (ISBN 0-8369-5257-X). Ayer Co Pubs.
Elson, Mark. Concepts of Programming Languages. LC 72-94972. (Illus.). 333p. 1973. text ed. 26.95 (ISBN 0-574-17922-4, 13-0922); instr's guide avail. (ISBN 0-574-17923-2, 13-0923). SRA.
--Data Structures. LC 75-1451. 306p. 1975. text ed. 27.95 (ISBN 0-574-18020-6, 13-4020). SRA.
Elson, Reginald, jt. auth. see Hardy, Alan G.
Elson, Robert. Prelude to War. (World War II Ser.). (Illus.). 1976. 14.95 (ISBN 0-8094-2450-9). Time-Life.
Elson, Robert E. Javanese Peasants & the Colonial Sugar Industry: Impact & Change in an East Java Residency, 1830-1940. 312p. 1985. pap. 19.95x (ISBN 0-19-582619-1). Oxford U Pr.
Elson, Ruth M. Guardians of Tradition: American Schoolbooks of the Nineteenth Century. LC 64-17219. (Illus.). xvi, 424p. 1972. pap. 6.95x (ISBN 0-8032-5755-4, BB 553, Bison). U of Nebr Pr.
Elson, Ruth Miller. Myths & Mores in American Best Sellers, 1865-1965. Burke, Robert E. & Freidel, Frank, eds. (Modern American History Ser.). Date not set. 40.00 (ISBN 0-8240-5667-1). Garland Pub.
Elspass, Margy L. North Light Dictionary of Art Terms. LC 84-22713. (Illus.). 312p. 1984. pap. 10.95 (ISBN 0-89134-096-3, North Light). Writers Digest.
Elspeth. Bedroom in a Country Cottage. 1973. pap. 2.50 (ISBN 0-87588-079-7). Hobby Hse.
--Country Store. 1975. pap. 2.50 (ISBN 0-87588-105-X). Hobby Hse.
--New England Sitting Room. 1974. 2.50 (ISBN 0-87588-094-0). Hobby Hse.
--Strawberry Sweetshop. 1973. pap. 0.75 (ISBN 0-87588-103-3). Hobby Hse.
--Victorian Christmas: 1876. 1974. pap. 2.50 (ISBN 0-87588-106-8). Hobby Hse.
Elst, E. Vander, ed. Societe International De Chirurgie Orthopedique et de Traumatology: Fifty Years of Achievement. (Illus.). 1979. 18.90 (ISBN 0-387-08968-3). Springer-Verlag.
Elst, Philip Van Der see Van Der Elst, Philip.
Elstein, Arthur S., et al. Medical Problem Solving. LC 77-21505. 1978. 25.00x (ISBN 0-674-56125-2). Harvard U Pr.
Elstein, Max & Sparks, Richard. Intrauterine Contraception, Vol. 1. Briggs, Michael, ed. (Annual Research Reviews Ser.). 1978. 12.00 (ISBN 0-88831-021-8). Eden Pr.
Elstein, Max, jt. ed. see Parke, Dennis V.
Elster, E., ed. Beitraege Zur Deutschen Literaturwissenschaft, Nos. 1-40 In 14 Vols. 1907-1931. Set. 525.00 (ISBN 0-384-03788-7). Johnson Repr.
Elster, Ernst. Prinzipien Der Literaturwissenschaft: Einfuhrung Von Herman Salinger und Alois Arnoldner, 2 Vols. in 1. 1972. 72.00 (ISBN 0-384-14280-X). Johnson Repr.
Elster, Jon. Explaining Technical Change: A Case Study in the Philosophy of Science. LC 82-9702. (Studies in Rationality & Social Change). (Illus.). 304p. 1983. 39.50 (ISBN 0-521-24920-1); pap. 12.95 (ISBN 0-521-27072-3). Cambridge U Pr.
--Logic & Society: Contradictions & Possible Worlds. LC 77-9550. pap. 60.80 (ISBN 0-317-29028-2, 2020429). Bks Demand UMI.
--Making Sense of Marx. (Studies in Marxism & Social Theory). (Illus.). 608p. 1985. 49.50 (ISBN 0-521-22896-4); pap. 15.95 (ISBN 0-521-29705-2). Cambridge U Pr.
--Sour Grapes. (Studies in the Subversion of Rationality). 220p. Date not set. pap. price not set. (ISBN 0-521-31368-6). Cambridge U Pr.
--Sour Grapes: Studies in the Subversion of Rationality. LC 82-22034. 220p. 1983. 32.50 (ISBN 0-521-25230-X). Cambridge U Pr.
--Ulysses & the Sirens. LC 78-15444. 1979. 34.50 (ISBN 0-521-22388-1). Cambridge U Pr.
--Ulysses & the Sirens: Studies in Rationality & Irrationality. 330p. 1985. pap. 11.95 (ISBN 0-521-26984-9). Cambridge U Pr.
Elster, Jon, ed. The Multiple Self. (Studies in Rationality & Social Change). 240p. Date not set. price not set (ISBN 0-521-26033-7). Cambridge U Pr.
Elster, Jon & Hylland, Aanund, eds. The Foundations of Social Choice Theory. (Studies in Rationality & Social Change). 240p. Date not set. price not set (ISBN 0-521-25735-2). Cambridge U Pr.
Elster, Robert, ed. Economics Information Resources Directory, 3 pts. 800p. Set. pap. text ed. cancelled (ISBN 0-8103-1689-7). Gale.
Elstob, Eric. Sweden: A Political & Cultural History. (Illus.). 209p. 1979. 18.50x (ISBN 0-8476-6220-9). Rowman.
Elston, Andrew S., ed. see Waianae Coast Culture & Art Project.
Elston, Angela M. What Are Feathers after All but Glory. (Cleveland Poets Ser.: No. 25). 35p. (Orig.). 1980. pap. 2.50 (ISBN 0-914946-22-6). Cleveland St Univ Poetry Ctr.
Elston, Lee. Square Pegs & Round Holes: How to Match the Personality to the Job. LC 84-73007. 72p. (Orig.). 1984. pap. 8.95 (ISBN 0-9614220-0-9). First Step Ent.
Elston, W. E., jt. ed. see Chapin, C. E.
Elstun, Esther N. Richard Beer-Hofmann: His Life & Work. LC 82-14990. (Penn State Studies in German Literature). 225p. 1983. 24.95x (ISBN 0-271-00335-9). Pa St U Pr.
El-Swaffy, S. A. & Moldenhauer, W. C., eds. Soil Erosion & Conservation. 806p. 35.00 (ISBN 0-935734-11-2). Soil Conservation.
El-Swaify, S. A., jt. ed. see Kussow, W.
Elswit, Sharon. Animal Homes. LC 83-80882. (Golden ThinkAbout Bks.). (Illus.). 48p. (gr. 1-4). 1984. 4.95 (ISBN 0-307-12506-8, 12506, Golden Bks). Western Pub.
Elsworth, J. D. Andrey Bely: A Critical Study of the Novels. LC 83-1793. (Cambridge Studies in Russian Literature). 220p. 1984. 39.50 (ISBN 0-521-24724-1). Cambridge U Pr.
Elsworth, John V. The Johnson Organs: The Story of One of Our Famous American Organ Builders. Paterson, Donald R., ed. LC 82-73770. 160p. (Orig.). 1984. pap. 15.95 (ISBN 0-9610092-0-9). Boston Organ Club.
Elsworth, Steve. Acid Rain: In the UK & Europe. 54p. (Orig.). 1984. pap. 5.95 (ISBN 0-86104-791-5, Pub. by Pluto Pr). Longwood Pub Group.
Elterman, Brad. Shoot the Stars: How to Become a Celebrity Photographer. LC 85-71055. (Illus.). (gr. 10 up). 1985. pap. 12.95 (ISBN 0-933781-00-8). Cal Features.
Eltherington, L. G., jt. auth. see Barnes, C. D.
Elting, jt. auth. see Eisenberg, Seymour.
Elting, Irving. Dutch Village Communities on the Hudson River. LC 78-63758. (Johns Hopkins University. Studies in the Social Sciences. Fourth Ser. 1886: 1). Repr. of 1886 ed. 11.50 (ISBN 0-404-61026-9). AMS Pr.
--Dutch Village Communities on the Hudson River. pap. 9.00 (ISBN 0-384-14288-5). Johnson Repr.
Elting, John R. American Army Life. (Illus.). 352p. 1982. 35.00 (ISBN 0-684-17500-2, ScribT). Scribner.
--The Battle of Bunker's Hill. LC 75-3540. (Revolutionary War Bicentennial Ser.). (Illus.). 1975. lib. bdg. 16.95 (ISBN 0-912480-11-4). Freneau.
--Battles for Scandinavia. LC 81-5698. (World War II Ser). 22.60 (ISBN 0-8094-3396-6, Pub. by Time-Life). Silver.
--Battles for Scandinavia. Time Life Bks Editors, ed. (World War II Ser.). (Illus.). 208p. 1981. 14.95 (ISBN 0-8094-3395-8). Time-Life.
--The Battles of Saratoga. LC 77-89325. (Revolutionary War Bicentennial Ser.). (Illus.). 1977. lib. bdg. 16.95 (ISBN 0-912480-13-0). Freneau.
--The Superstrategists: Great Captains, Theorists, & Fighting Men Who Have Shaped the History of Warfare. 320p. 1985. 19.95 (ISBN 0-684-18353-6, ScribT). Scribner.
Elting, John R., jt. auth. see Esposito, Vincent J.
Elting, John R., ed. Military Uniforms in America: The Era of the American Revolution, 1755-1795, Vol. 1. LC 74-21513. (Military Uniforms in America Ser.). (Illus.). 154p. 1976. 25.00 (ISBN 0-89141-025-2). Presidio Pr.
Elting, John R. & McAfee, Michael J., eds. Military Uniforms in America: Long Endure, The Civil War Period, 1852-1867, Vol. III. (Military Uniforms in America Ser.). (Illus.). 160p. 1982. cloth 35.00 (ISBN 0-89141-143-7). Presidio Pr.
Elting, John R., et al. A Dictionary of Soldier Talk. LC 82-42642. 383p. 1984. 35.00 (ISBN 0-684-17862-1, ScribT). Scribner.
Elting, Mary. The Answer Book about Animals. (The Answer Bks.). (Illus.). (gr. 3-7). 1984. pap. 2.95 (ISBN 0-448-13801-8, G&D). Putnam Pub Group.
--The Answer Book about Computers. (The Answer Bks.). (Illus.). (gr. 3-7). 1984. pap. 2.95 (ISBN 0-448-13803-4, G&D). Putnam Pub Group.
--The Answer Book about Robots & Other Inventions. (The Answer Bks.). (Illus.). 80p. (gr. 3-7). 1984. pap. 2.95 (ISBN 0-448-13802-6, G&D). Putnam Pub Group.
--The Answer Book about You. (The Answer Bks.). (gr. 3-7). 1984. pap. 2.95 (ISBN 0-448-13800-X, G&D). Putnam Pub Group.
--The Hopi Way. LC 72-88692. (Two Worlds Bks.). (Illus.). 64p. (gr. 4 up). 1969. 3.95 (ISBN 0-87131-097-X). M Evans.
Elting, Mary & Folsom, Michael. The Mysterious Grain: Science in Search of the Origin of Corn. LC 67-10832. (Illus.). 128p. (gr. 7 up). 1967. 4.50 (ISBN 0-87131-076-7). M Evans.
--Q Is for Duck. (Illus.). 64p. (ps-3). 1980. 11.95 (ISBN 0-395-29437-1, Clarion); pap. 3.95 (ISBN 0-395-30062-2). HM.
Elting, Mary & Goodman, Ann. Dinosaur Mysteries. (Illus.). 64p. (gr. 1-7). 1980. 4.95 (ISBN 0-448-47487-5, G&D). Putnam Pub Group.
Elting, Mary & McKown, Robin. A Mongo Homecoming. LC 73-88695. (Two Worlds Bks). (Illus.). 64p. (gr. 4-6). 1969. 3.95 (ISBN 0-87131-099-6). M Evans.
Elting, Mary & Wyler, Rose. The Answer Book about You. (Illus.). 1980. 6.95 (ISBN 0-448-16566-X, G&D). Putnam Pub Group.

--A New Answer Book. LC 77-71531. (Illus.). (gr. 3-8). 1977. 6.95 (ISBN 0-448-12899-3, G&D); PLB 6.99 (ISBN 0-448-13418-7). Putnam Pub Group.

Eltis, David & Walvin, James. The Abolition of the Atlantic Slave Trade: Origins & Effects in Europe, Africa, & the Americas. LC 80-52290. 328p. 1981. 25.00x (ISBN 0-299-08490-6). U of Wis Pr.

Eltis, W. A. & Sinclair, P. J., eds. The Money Supply & the Exchange Rate. (Illus., Orig.). 1981. pap. text ed. 19.95x (ISBN 0-19-877168-1). Oxford U Pr.

Eltis, Walter, jt. auth. see Bacon, Robert.

Eltis, Walter, ed. The Classical Theory of Economic Growth. LC 83-16154. 382p. 1984. 29.95 (ISBN 0-312-14264-1). St Martin.

El Tom, M. E., ed. Developing Mathematics in Third World Countries. (North Holland Mathematics Studies: Vol. 33). 208p. 1979. 47.00 (ISBN 0-444-85260-3, North Holland). Elsevier.

Elton & Gruber, eds. Portfolio Theory, Vol. 11. (TIMS Studies in the Management Sciences). 264p. 29.25 (ISBN 0-318-14462-X). Inst Mgmt Sci.

Elton, Arthur, ed. see Klingender, Francis D.

Elton, C. J., et al, eds. Evaluating New Telecommunications Services. LC 78-4684. (NATO Conference Series II, Systems Science: Science Vol. 6). 798p. 1978. 105.00x (ISBN 0-306-40004-9, Plenum Pr). Plenum Pub.

Elton, C. S. Animal Ecology. 1966. pap. 7.95x (ISBN 0-412-20080-5, NO.6098, Pub. by Chapman & Hall). Methuen Inc.

--The Ecology of Animals. 3rd ed. 1977. pap. 6.95 (ISBN 0-412-20390-1, NO. 6099, Pub. by Chapman & Hall). Methuen Inc.

--The Ecology of Invasions by Animals & Plants. 1977. 11.95 (ISBN 0-412-21460-1, NO.6100, Pub. by Chapman & Hall). Methuen Inc.

--The Pattern of Animal Communities. 1966. pap. 19.95 (ISBN 0-412-21880-1, NO. 6579, Pub. by Chapman & Hall). Methuen Inc.

Elton, Charles. Voles, Mice & Lemmings. 1971. Repr. of 1942 ed. 33.10 (ISBN 3-7682-0275-5). Lubrecht & Cramer.

Elton, Charles & Elton, Mary. The Great Book Collectors. 1977. lib. bdg. 59.95 (ISBN 0-8490-1898-6). Gordon Pr.

Elton, Charles I. The Career of Columbus. 1976. lib. bdg. 59.95 (ISBN 0-8490-1573-1). Gordon Pr.

--The Career of Columbus. 307p. 1983. Repr. of 1892 ed. lib. bdg. 65.00 (ISBN 0-89984-188-0). Century Bookbindery.

--William Shakespeare: His Family & Friends. Thompson, A. Hamilton, ed. LC 72-166025. Repr. of 1904 ed. 34.50 (ISBN 0-404-02324-X). AMS Pr.

Elton, Charles I. & Elton, Mary A. The Great Book Collectors. 15.00 (ISBN 0-8369-6972-3, 7853). Ayer Co Pubs.

Elton, Diana, et al. Psychological Control of Pain. 354p. 1983. 45.00 (ISBN 0-8089-1611-4). Acad Pr.

Elton, E. J. & Gruber, M. J., eds. Portfolio Theory: Twenty Five Years after. (TIMS Studies in the Management Sciences: Vol. 11). 256p. 1979. 32.50 (ISBN 0-444-85279-4, North Holland). Elsevier.

Elton, Edwin J. & Gruber, Martin J. Modern Portfolio Theory & Investment Analysis. 2nd ed. LC 83-21595. 636p. 1984. text ed. 35.95 (ISBN 0-471-87482-5); write for info. (ISBN 0-471-80446-0). Wiley.

Elton, G., ed. Annual Bibliography of British & Irish History: Publications of 1979. 1981. text ed. 30.50x (ISBN 0-391-01774-8). Humanities.

--Annual Bibliography of British & Irish History: Publications of 1977. 1978. text ed. 23.00x (ISBN 0-391-00881-1). Humanities.

--Annual Bibliography of British & Irish History, 1978. 1979. text ed. 27.25x (ISBN 0-391-01054-9). Humanities.

--Annual Bibliography of British & Irish History 1976. 1977. text ed. 29.00x (ISBN 0-391-00753-X). Humanities.

--Annual Bibliography of British & Irish History 1981. 196p. 1982. text ed. 38.00x (ISBN 0-391-02728-X, Pub. by Harvester England). Humanities.

--Royal Historical Society: Annual Bibliography of British & Irish History 1982, Vol. 8. 203p. 1983. text ed. 38.00x (ISBN 0-391-02942-8, Harvester Pr). Humanities.

Elton, G. R. England under the Tudors. 2nd ed. (Illus.). 1974. pap. 17.95x (ISBN 0-416-70690-8, NO.2189). Methuen Inc.

--F. W. Maitland. LC 85-40439. 128p. 1985. 15.00x (ISBN 0-300-03528-4). Yale U Pr.

--Policy & Police: The Enforcement of the Reformation in the Age of Thomas Cromwell. 458p. Date not set. pap. price not set. (ISBN 0-521-31309-0). Cambridge U Pr.

--Political History: Principles & Practice. Winks, Robin W., ed. LC 83-49167. (History & Historiography Ser.). 180p. 1985. lib. bdg. 20.00 (ISBN 0-8240-6361-9). Garland Pub.

--Reform & Reformation: England, 1509-1558. LC 77-6464. (Harvard Paperback Ser.: No. 146, The New History of England). 1979. 25.00x (ISBN 0-674-75245-7); pap. 8.95x (ISBN 0-674-75248-1). Harvard U Pr.

Elton, G. R., jt. auth. see Fogel, Robert W.

Elton, G. R., ed. Annual Bibliography of British & Irish History, 1980. 209p. 1981. text ed. 38.00x (ISBN 0-391-02383-7, Pub. by Harvester England). Humanities.

Elton, G. R., ed. see Hughes, Kathleen.

Elton, G. R., ed. see Jack, R. Ian.

Elton, Gelffrey R. Renaissance & Reformation, Thirteen Hundred to Sixteen Forty-Eight. 3rd ed. (Ideas & Institutions in Western Civilization: Vol. 3). 1976. pap. text ed. write for info. (ISBN 0-02-332840-1). Macmillan.

Elton, Geoffrey R. Essays on Tudor & Stuart Politics & Government: Papers & Reviews 1973-1981, Vol. 3. LC 73-79305. 512p. 1982. 54.50 (ISBN 0-521-24893-0). Cambridge U Pr.

--Reform & Renewal, Thomas Cromwell & the Common Weal. (Wiles Lectures, 1972). 230p. 1973. pap. 11.95 (ISBN 0-521-09809-2). Cambridge U Pr.

--The Tudor Constitution: Documents & Commentary. 2nd ed. LC 81-15216. 522p. 1982. 69.50 (ISBN 0-521-24506-0); pap. 19.95 (ISBN 0-521-28757-X). Cambridge U Pr.

Elton, Geoffrey R., ed. Annual Bibliography of British & Irish History, 1975. 1976. text ed. 31.75x (ISBN 0-391-00619-3). Humanities.

--The Royal Historical Society Annual Bibliography of British & Irish History Publications of 1984. 192p. 1985. 25.00 (ISBN 0-312-69474-1). St Martin.

--The Royal Historical Society Annual Bibliography of British & Irish History: Publications of 1983. LC 81-641280. 208p. 1984. 29.95 (ISBN 0-312-69472-5). St Martin.

Elton, Gerald. The Art & Science of Physiognomy, 2 vols. (A Human Development Library Bk.). (Illus.). 237p. 1985. Set. 167.75 (ISBN 0-89920-096-6). Am Inst Psych.

Elton, Godfrey E. Revolutionary Idea in France, 1789-1871. 2nd ed. LC 74-147116. Repr. of 1931 ed. 17.50 (ISBN 0-404-02325-8). AMS Pr.

Elton, J. F. Travels & Researches among the Lakes & Mountains of Eastern & Central Africa. new ed. Cotterill, H. B., ed. (Illus.). 417p. 1968. 45.00x (ISBN 0-7146-1806-3, F Cass Co). Biblio Dist.

Elton, John, jt. auth. see Bennett, Richard.

Elton, Mary, jt. auth. see Elton, Charles.

Elton, Mary A., jt. auth. see Elton, Charles I.

Elton, O. Dickens & Thackeray. LC 77-98682. (Studies in Fiction, No. 34). 1970. Repr. of 1924 ed. lib. bdg. 29.95x (ISBN 0-8383-0973-9). Haskell.

Elton, Oliver. The Augustan Ages. 427p. 1980. Repr. of 1899 ed. lib. bdg. 45.00 (ISBN 0-8495-1346-4). Arden Lib.

--The Augustan Ages. LC 74-3085. 1899. lib. bdg. 42.50 (ISBN 0-8414-3928-1). Folcroft.

--The Brownings. LC 71-169189. (Studies in Browning, No. 4). 1972. Repr. of 1924 ed. lib. bdg. 32.95x (ISBN 0-8383-1331-0). Haskell.

--The Brownings. 1973. Repr. of 1924 ed. 18.45 (ISBN 0-8274-1689-X). R West.

--Dickens & Thackeray. LC 72-193731. 1924. lib. bdg. 10.00 (ISBN 0-8414-3898-6). Folcroft.

--Dickens & Thackeray. 1978. 16.50 (ISBN 0-685-89409-6). Porter.

--The English Muse. 1973. lib. bdg. 5.00 (ISBN 0-8414-3899-4). Folcroft.

--The English Muse: A Sketch. 1977. lib. bdg. 50.00 (ISBN 0-8495-1302-2). Arden Lib.

--Essays & Addresses. 1978. Repr. of 1939 ed. lib. bdg. 25.00 (ISBN 0-8495-1310-3). Arden Lib.

--Essays & Addresses. facs. ed. LC 67-86746. (Essay Index Reprint Ser). 1939. 19.00 (ISBN 0-8369-1179-2). Ayer Co Pubs.

--Essays & Addresses. LC 72-193944. 1939. lib. bdg. 25.00 (ISBN 0-8414-3996-6). Folcroft.

--Introduction to Michael Drayton. (Research & Source Ser.: No. 150). 1970. Repr. of 1895 ed. lib. bdg. 26.00 (ISBN 0-8337-4804-1). B Franklin.

--Introduction to Michael Drayton. LC 74-10782. 1895. lib. bdg. 15.00 (ISBN 0-8414-3952-4). Folcroft.

--Literary Fame: A Renaissance Study. LC 74-12470. lib. bdg. 8.50 (ISBN 0-8414-3970-2). Folcroft.

--Milton Il Penseroso. LC 73-13546. Repr. of 1891 ed. lib. bdg. 8.00 (ISBN 0-8414-3906-0). Folcroft.

--Modern Studies. facs. ed. LC 67-26739. (Essay Index Reprint Ser). 1907. 20.00 (ISBN 0-8369-0414-1). Ayer Co Pubs.

--Modern Studies. LC 72-194354. 1907. lib. bdg. 12.50 (ISBN 0-8414-3997-4). Folcroft.

--Modern Studies. 1980. Repr. of 1907 ed. lib. bdg. 30.00 (ISBN 0-8492-0799-1). R West.

--Nature of Literary Criticism. LC 74-12462. 1935. lib. bdg. 8.50 (ISBN 0-8414-3968-0). Folcroft.

--Poetic Romancers After Eighteen Fifty. LC 74-12473. 1914. lib. bdg. 8.50 (ISBN 0-8414-3966-4). Folcroft.

--Sheaf of Papers. LC 72-194754. 1923. lib. bdg. 20.00 (ISBN 0-8414-3917-6). Folcroft.

--Shelley. 1978. Repr. of 1924 ed. lib. bdg. 10.00 (ISBN 0-8495-1314-6). Arden Lib.

--Shelley. LC 76-17044. 1924. lib. bdg. 8.50 (ISBN 0-8414-3975-3). Folcroft.

--Sir Walter Scott. LC 72-193214. 1924. lib. bdg. 9.50 (ISBN 0-8414-3998-2). Folcroft.

--A Survey of English Literature: Eighteen Thirty to Eighteen Eighty, 2 vols. (Vol. I 434 pp., Vol. II 432 pp.). 1980. Repr. of 1932 ed. Set. lib. bdg. 100.00 (ISBN 0-8492-0786-X). R West.

--A Survey of English Literature: Seventeen Eighty to Eighteen Thirty, 2 vols. (Vol. I 456 pp., Vol. II 475 pp.). 1980. Repr. of 1912 ed. Set. lib. bdg. 100.00 (ISBN 0-8492-0785-1). R West.

--A Survey of English Literature: Seventeen Thirty to Seventeen Eighty, 2 vols. 1980. Set. lib. bdg. 100.00 (ISBN 0-8492-0784-3). R West.

--A Survey of English Literature, 1730-1780, 2 vols. LC 77-3043. 1977. 97.50 (ISBN 0-8414-3961-3). Folcroft.

--A Survey of English Literature, 1780-1830, 2 vols. LC 77-5511. 1977. Repr. of 1912 ed. Set. 97.50 (ISBN 0-8414-3963-X). Folcroft.

--A Survey of English Literature, 1830-1880, 2 vols. LC 75-41086. (BCL Ser. II). Repr. of 1932 ed. Set. 75.00 (ISBN 0-404-14900-6). AMS Pr.

--A Survey of English Literature: 1830-1880, 2 vols. LC 77-7594. 1977. Repr. of 1932 ed. lib. bdg. 97.50 (ISBN 0-8414-3967-2). Folcroft.

--Tennyson. LC 74-8903. 1901. lib. bdg. 9.00 (ISBN 0-8414-3942-7). Folcroft.

--Tennyson & Arnold. 1978. 16.50 (ISBN 0-685-89416-9). Porter.

--Tennyson & Matthew Arnold. LC 73-909. 1972. lib. bdg. 9.50 (ISBN 0-8414-1609-5). Folcroft.

--Tennyson & Matthew Arnold. LC 75-163127. (Studies in Comparative Literature, No. 35). 1971. Repr. of 1924 ed. lib. bdg. 48.95x (ISBN 0-8383-1305-1). Haskell.

--Tennyson & Matthew Arnold. 96p. 1980. Repr. of 1924 ed. lib. bdg. 12.50 (ISBN 0-8492-4411-0). R West.

--Wordsworth. LC 74-12494. 1924. lib. bdg. 8.50 (ISBN 0-8414-3962-1). Folcroft.

--Wordsworth. 96p. 1980. Repr. of 1924 ed. 15.00 (ISBN 0-8492-0788-6). R West.

Elton, Oliver, compiled by. Verse from Pushkin & Others. LC 72-114517. 1971. Repr. of 1935 ed. lib. bdg. 22.50 (ISBN 0-8371-4822-7, EVLP). Greenwood.

Elton, Oliver, tr. Saxo: The First Nine Book of the Danish History of Saxo-Grammaticus. (Folk-Lore Society, London, Monographs: Vol. 33). pap. 47.00 (ISBN 0-317-15651-9). Kraus Repr.

Elton, Oliver, et al. George Saintsbury, the Memorial Volume: A New Collection of His Essays and Paper. 1978. Repr. of 1945 ed. lib. bdg. 25.00 (ISBN 0-8495-4829-2). Arden Lib.

Elton, Sam. New Model of Solar System. LC 66-18990. 1967. 5.00 (ISBN 0-8022-0450-3). Philos Lib.

Elton, W. R. Shakespeare's World: Renaissance Intellectual Contexts: a Selective Annotated Guide, 1966-1971. LC 76-52681. (Reference Library of the Humanities Ser.: Vol. 83). 476p. 1980. lib. bdg. 73.00 (ISBN 0-8240-9890-0). Garland Pub.

El Torky, Mohamed A., jt. auth. see Correa, Hector.

Eltringham, D. P. Imports & Exports. flexi-cover 2.40 (ISBN 0-08-018124-4). Pergamon.

Eltringham, R., et al. Post-Anasthetic Recovery. Durkin, M. & Andrewes, S., eds. (Illus.). 130p. 1983. pap. 17.00 (ISBN 0-387-12631-7). Springer-Verlag.

Eltringham, S. K. The Ecology & Conservation of Large African Mammals. (Illus.). 304p. 1980. text ed. 49.95 (ISBN 0-8391-1493-1). Univ Park.

--Elephants. (Blandford Mammal Ser.). (Illus.). 264p. 1982. 19.95 (ISBN 0-7137-1041-1, Pub. by Blandford Pr England). Sterling.

--Wildlife Resources & Economic Development. 325p. 1984. 39.95 (ISBN 0-471-90213-6). Wiley.

Eltzbacher. Anarchism. 272p. 1970. 18.50 (ISBN 0-912378-01-8). Chips.

Eltzbacher, Paul. Anarchism: Exponents of the Anarchist Philosophy. Martin, James J., ed. Byington, Steven T., tr. LC 72-8550. (Essay Index Reprint Ser.). 1972. Repr. of 1960 ed. 21.00 (ISBN 0-8369-7311-9). Ayer Co Pubs.

Eluard, Paul. Anthologie des Ecrits sur l'Art. (Illus.). 328p. 1972. 80.00 (ISBN 0-686-55964-9). French & Eur.

--Au Rendez-Vous Allemand. 80p. 1976. 5.95 (ISBN 0-686-55965-7). French & Eur.

--Capitale de la Douleur. Bd. with L' Amour la Poesies. (Coll. Soleil). 12.50 (ISBN 0-685-36045-8). French & Eur.

--Capitale de la Douleur: Avec: L'Amour la Poesie. new ed. 256p. 1970. 4.50 (ISBN 0-686-55966-5). French & Eur.

--Corps Memorable. 43.75 (ISBN 0-685-34113-5). French & Eur.

--Derniers Poemes d'Amour. pap. 8.50 (ISBN 0-685-34114-3). French & Eur.

--Derniers Poemes d'Amour. 193p. 1963. 4.95 (ISBN 0-686-55967-3). French & Eur.

--Donner a Voir. 216p. 1978. 3.95 (ISBN 0-686-55968-1). French & Eur.

--Le Dur Desir de Durer. (Illus.). 120p. 1968. 25.00 (ISBN 0-686-55969-X). French & Eur.

--Grain-d'Aile. (Illus.). 36p. 1977. 12.95 (ISBN 0-686-55970-3). French & Eur.

--La Jarre Peut-Elle etre plus belle que l'Eau. 320p. 1951. 5.95 (ISBN 0-686-55972-X). French & Eur.

--Last Love Poems of Paul Eluard. Kallet, Marilyn, tr. LC 79-23216. xx, 100p. 1980. 13.95x (ISBN 0-8071-0681-X). La State U Pr.

--Une Lecon de Morale. 184p. 1949. 4.95 (ISBN 0-686-55973-8). French & Eur.

--Lettres a Joe Bousquet. 140p. 1973. 8.95 (ISBN 0-686-55974-6). French & Eur.

--Le Livre Ouvert (1938-1944) 240p. 1947. 6.95 (ISBN 0-686-55975-4). French & Eur.

--Une Longue Reflexion Amoureuse. (Illus.). 9.95 (ISBN 0-686-55976-2). French & Eur.

--Oeuvres Completes, 2 tomes. Dumas & Scheler, eds. (Bibl. de la Pleiade). 1968. Set. lea. 84.45 (ISBN 0-685-11447-3). French & Eur.

--Poemes Politiques. 60p. 1948. 2.50 (ISBN 0-686-55977-0). French & Eur.

--Poemes pour Tous. 2nd ed. 246p. 1953. 12.50 (ISBN 0-686-55978-9). French & Eur.

--Poesie Ininterrompue. 160p. 1969. 3.95 (ISBN 0-686-55979-7). French & Eur.

--Poesies, 1913-1926. 224p. 1970. 4.95 (ISBN 0-686-55980-0). French & Eur.

--Selected Poems. price not set. Riverrun NY.

--Les Sentiers et les Routes de la Poesie. 176p. 1954. & eur 5.951500french (ISBN 0-686-55981-9). French & Eur.

--A Toute Epreuve. (Illus.). 104p. 1984. Additional 32 page booklet included. 75.00 (ISBN 0-8076-1102-6). Braziller.

--Uninterrupted Poetry: Selected Writings of Paul Eluard. Alexander, Lloyd, tr. from Fr. LC 77-22122. 1977. Repr. of 1975 ed. lib. bdg. 24.75 (ISBN 0-8371-9779-1, ELSW). Greenwood.

--La Vie Immediate. 256p. 1967. 4.95 (ISBN 0-686-55982-7). French & Eur.

Eluard, Paul & Breton, Andre. L' Immaculee Conception. 96p. 1961. 4.95 (ISBN 0-686-55971-1). French & Eur.

Eluard, Paul see Apollinaire, Guillaume & Guillaume, Paul.

Eluard, Paul, jt. auth. see Char, Rene.

Elusorr, Suzanne, jt. auth. see Cameron, Charles.

Elv, James W. The Crisis of Conservative Virginia: The Byrd Organization & the Politics of Massive Resistance. LC 75-43742. (Twentieth-Century America Ser.). pap. 58.50 (ISBN 0-317-28041-4, 2025560). Bks Demand UMI.

Elvander, Nile, jt. ed. see Heidenheimer, Arnold J.

Elvander, Patrick E. & Wells, Elizabeth F. The Taxonomy of Saxifraga (Saxifragaceae) Section Boraphila Subsection Integrifoliae in Western North America: A Revision of The Genus Heuchera (Saxifrageae) in Eastern North America. Anderson, Christiane, ed. LC 84-393. (Systematic Botany Monographs Ser.). (Illus.). 121p. (Orig.). 1984. pap. 16.00 (ISBN 0-912861-03-7). Am Soc Plant.

Elvee, Richard Q., ed. Mind in Nature: New Concepts of Mind in Science & Philosophy; The Nobel Conference XVII. LC 82-48155. 176p. (Orig.). 1983. pap. 7.64i (ISBN 0-06-250285-9, CN4046, HarpR). Har-Row.

Elvenstar, Diane. Children: To Have or Have Not: A Guide to Making & Living with Your Decision. 240p. 1982. 13.95 (ISBN 0-936602-39-2); pap. 9.95 (ISBN 0-936602-40-6). Kampmann.

Elvenstar, Diane C. First Comes Love: Deciding Whether or Not to Get Married. LC 83-3870. 256p. 1983. 14.95 (ISBN 0-672-52775-8). Bobbs.

Elver, Erin, jt. auth. see Fleetwood, Jucker.

Elvers, Lita M., jt. ed. see Brown, James K.

Elverson, Virginia T., ed. Houston Fine Arts Cookbook. (Illus.). 272p. 1983. 19.95 (ISBN 0-292-73024-1). U of Tex Pr.

Elves, Michael W. The Lymphocytes. 604p. 1972. 40.00x (ISBN 0-686-80812-6, Pub. by Lloyd-Luke England). State Mutual Bk.

Elvey, Linda B. Where Do I Go from Here. 1983. 6.00 (ISBN 0-8062-2194-1). Carlton.

Elvin, Charles N. Handbook of Mottoes: Borne by the Nobility, Gentry, Cities, Public Cos., Etc. LC 70-151294. 294p. 1971. Repr. of 1860 ed. suppl. with index 15.00 (ISBN 0-8063-0481-2). Genealog Pub.

Elvin, Lionel. Introduction to the Study of Literature. LC 74-11343. 1949. lib. bdg. 15.00 (ISBN 0-8414-3958-3). Folcroft.

--The Place of Commonsense in Educational Thought. (Unwin Educational Books). 1977. text ed. 22.50x (ISBN 0-04-370078-0). Allen Unwin.

Elvin, Lionel, ed. The Educational Systems in the European Community: A Guide. 288p. 1981. 20.00x (ISBN 0-85633-223-2, Pub. by NFER Nelson UK). Taylor & Francis.

Elvin, Malcolm, ed. see Powys, John C.

Elvin, Margo, jt. auth. see McLean, Gary N.

Elvin, Mark. Pattern of the Chinese Past: A Social & Economic Interpretation. LC 72-78869. 346p. 1973. 27.50x (ISBN 0-8047-0826-6); pap. 8.95x (ISBN 0-8047-0876-2). Stanford U Pr.

Elvin, Mark, jt. auth. see Blunden, Caroline.

Elvin, Mark, ed. Transport in Transition: The Evolution of Traditional Shipping in China. Watson, Andrew, tr. from Japanese. (Michigan Abstracts of Chinese & Japanese Works on Chinese History: No. 3). 93p. 1972. pap. 5.00 (ISBN 0-89264-903-8). U of Mich Ctr Chinese.

Elvin, Mark & Skinner, G. William, eds. The Chinese City Between Two Worlds. LC 73-89858. (Studies in Chinese Society). (Illus.). 480p. 1974. 32.50x (ISBN 0-8047-0853-3). Stanford U Pr.

Elvin, Mark, ed. see Whelan, T. S.
Elvin, Mark, tr. see Hoshi Ayao.
Elvin, Mark, tr. see Yoshinobu, Shiba.
Elving, Bruce F., illus. Atlas & Station Directory. 9th ed. LC 84-81432. (Illus.). 144p. 1984. pap. 7.50 (ISBN 0-917170-05-9). F M Atlas.
Elving, P., jt. auth. see Kolthoff, I.
Elving, P. J. see Barth, Howard G., et al.
Elving, P. J., jt. auth. see Kolthoff, I. M.
Elving, P. J., jt. auth. see Kolthoff, P. J.
Elving, Philip J., jt. auth. see Kolthoff, I. M.
Elving, Phillip J. see Kolthoff, I. M. & Elving, P. J.
Elvin-Lewis, P., jt. auth. see Lewis, Walter H.
El-Wakil, M. M. Nuclear Energy Conversion. rev. ed. LC 78-6169. 682p. 1982. 38.00 (ISBN 0-89448-015-4). Am Nuclear Soc.
--Nuclear Heat Transport. rev. ed. LC 78-61691. 514p. 1981. 32.00 (ISBN 0-317-02612-7). Am Nuclear Soc.
--Powerplant Technology. 1984. 48.00 (ISBN 0-07-019288-X). McGraw.
Elwang, William W. The Negroes of Columbia, Missouri: A Concrete Study of the Race Problem. LC 73-99374. (Illus.). 84p. 1972. Repr. of 1904 ed. lib. bdg. 10.00 (ISBN 0-8411-0045-4). Metro Bks.
Elward, James & Van Slyke, Helen. Ask for Nothing More. LC 83-48344. 256p. 1984. 14.37 (ISBN 0-06-015137-4, HarpT). Har-Row.
--Ask for Nothing More. 1985. pap. 3.95 (ISBN 0-8217-1643-3). Zebra.
Elward, James, jt. auth. see Van Slyke, Helen.
Elward, Margaret & Whiteway, Catherine E. Encyclopedia of Guinea Pigs. (Illus.). 224p. 1980. 12.95 (ISBN 0-87666-916-X, H-975). TFH Pubns.
Elwart, Joan P., jt. auth. see Pitrone, Jean M.
Elwell. Phonics Workbooks. Incl. Bk. A. (gr. 1). pap. text ed. 3.60 (ISBN 0-87895-106-7). 4.40 (ISBN 0-87895-109-1); transparencies 16.96 (ISBN 0-686-67233-X); ans. key 0.50 (ISBN 0-685-93115-3); Bk. B. (gr. 2). pap. text ed. 3.52 (ISBN 0-87895-203-9). 4.48 (ISBN 0-87895-206-3); transparencies 16.29 (ISBN 0-685-58352-X); ans. key 0.50 (ISBN 0-685-58353-8); Bk. C. (gr. 3). pap. text ed. 3.44 (ISBN 0-87895-303-5). transparencies 15.95 (ISBN 0-685-58355-4); ans. key 0.50 (ISBN 0-685-58356-2). (MCP Basic Phonics Program Ser.). 1976. pap. Modern Curr.
--Two-Color New Phonics Workbooks. Incl. Bk. A. (gr. 1). pap. text ed. 3.96 (ISBN 0-87895-136-9); tchr's ed. 2.00 (ISBN 0-87895-135-0); Bk. B. (gr. 2). pap. text ed. 3.88 (ISBN 0-87895-223-3); teacher's ed 2.00 (ISBN 0-87895-228-4); Bk. C. (gr. 3). pap. text ed. 3.80 (ISBN 0-87895-320-5); teacher's ed 2.00 (ISBN 0-87895-322-1). (MCP Basic Program Ser.). 1976. pap. Modern Curr.
Elwell, Clarence E. Influence of the Enlightenment on the Catholic Theory of Religious Education in France, 1750-1850. LC 66-27064. 1967. Repr. of 1944 ed. 10.00x (ISBN 0-8462-0980-2). Russell.
Elwell, D. & Pointon, A. J. Physics for Engineers & Scientists. 2nd ed. LC 77-16193. 356p. 1979. pap. 28.95x (ISBN 0-470-26872-7). Halsted Pr.
Elwell, D. & Scheel, H. J. Crystal Growth from High Temperature Solutions. 1975. 98.50 (ISBN 0-12-237550-5). Acad Pr.
Elwell, Dennis. Man-Made Gemstones. LC 78-41291. 191p. 1979. 74.95x (ISBN 0-470-26606-6). Halsted Pr.
Elwell, Edward H. Portland & Vicinity. (Illus.). 138p. 1975. pap. 4.95 (ISBN 0-9600612-3-1). Greater Portland.
Elwell, Ellen S. & Levenson, Edward R., eds. Jewish Women's Studies Guide (College Level) 112p. (Orig.). 1982. pap. 6.95 (ISBN 0-9602036-5-6). Biblio NY.
Elwell, Peter. The King of the Pipers. LC 83-22176. (Illus.). 32p. (gr. 1-5). 1984. SBE 10.95 (ISBN 0-02-733460-0). Macmillan.
Elwell, W. T. & Gidley, J. A. Atomic Absorption Spectrophotometry. 2nd ed. 1966. 21.00 (ISBN 0-08-012063-6). Pergamon.
Elwell, Walter, intro. by see Bagster, Samuel.
Elwell, Walter A. Evangelical Dictionary of Theology. LC 84-71575. 1984. 29.95 (ISBN 0-8010-3413-2). Baker Bk.
Elwell, Walter A., ed. The Shaw Pocket Bible Handbook. 400p. 1984. 9.95 (ISBN 0-87788-683-0). Shaw Pubs.
Elwell-Sutton, C. Learn the Persian Language. 14.50 (ISBN 0-87559-120-5). Shalom.
Elwell-Sutton, L. P. Colloquial Persian. (Trubner's Colloquial Manuals Ser.). 1975. pap. 7.95 (ISBN 0-7100-8083-2). Routledge & Kegan.
--Modern Iran. 1976. lib. bdg. 59.95 (ISBN 0-8490-2267-3). Gordon Pr.
Elwell-Sutton, L. P., ed. Bibliographical Guide to Iran: The Middle East Library Committee Guide. LC 82-22748. 488p. 1983. text ed. 35.00x (ISBN 0-389-20339-4). B&N Imports.
Elwell-Sutton, L. P., tr. see Dashti, Ali.
Elwell-Sutton, Laurence. Persian Oil: A Study in Power Politics. LC 73-13325. 343p. 1975. Repr. of 1955 ed. lib. bdg. 21.50x (ISBN 0-8371-7122-9, ELPO). Greenwood.
Elwell-Sutton, Laurence P. Persian Oil: A Study in Power Politics. LC 75-6469. (History & Politics of Oil Ser). 343p. 1976. Repr. of 1955 ed. 19.50 (ISBN 0-88355-288-4). Hyperion Conn.
Elwell-Sutton, Lawrence P. Elementary Persian Grammar. pap. 22.95 (ISBN 0-521-09206-X). Cambridge U Pr.
--The Persian Metres. 200p. 1976. 52.50 (ISBN 0-521-21089-5). Cambridge U Pr.
Elwenspoek, Curt. Jew Suss Oppenheimer, the Great Financier, Gallant & Adventurer of the 18th Century: A Study Based on Various Documents, Private Papers & Traditions. Cattle, Edward, tr. 1980. lib. bdg. 64.95 (ISBN 0-8490-3190-7). Gordon Pr.
Elwes, tr. see Spinoza, Benedict D.
Elwes, Alfred, tr. see Capello, Hermenegildo C. & Ivens, Roberto.
Elwes, Alfred, tr. see Serpa Pinto, Alexandre A.
Elwes, R. H., tr. see Spinoza, Benedict.
Elwess, Brewster. The Most Beautiful Jewish Woman in the History of Mankind. (Illus.). 1978. deluxe ed. 62.50 (ISBN 0-930582-17-9). Gloucester Art.
Elwin, Malcolm. De Quincey. LC 72-160754. 1971. Repr. of 1935 ed. 19.50x (ISBN 0-8046-1571-3, Pub. by Kennikat). Assoc Faculty Pr.
--Landor: A Replevin. 502p. 1983. Repr. of 1958 ed. lib. bdg. 45.00 (ISBN 0-8495-1430-4). Arden Lib.
--The Life of Llewelyn Powys. 1946. Repr. 30.00 (ISBN 0-8274-2892-8). R West.
--The Life of Llewelyn Powys. 300p. 30.00x (ISBN 0-905459-69-5, Pub. by Redcliffe Pr Ltd). State Mutual Bk.
--Lord Byron's Wife. 556p. Repr. of 1962 ed. lib. bdg. 50.00 (ISBN 0-89984-192-9). Century Bookbindery.
--Old Gods Falling. facs. ed. LC 73-142622. (Essay Index Reprint Ser). 1939. 21.00 (ISBN 0-8369-2045-7). Ayer Co Pubs.
--Old Gods Falling. 1973. Repr. of 1939 ed. 30.00 (ISBN 0-8274-1283-5). R West.
--The Playgoer's Handbook to Restoration Drama. LC 74-22296. 1974. Repr. of 1928 ed. lib. bdg. 20.00 (ISBN 0-8414-3923-0). Folcroft.
--The Pleasure Ground: A Miscellany of English Writing. 1947. 25.00 (ISBN 0-89984-037-X). Century Bookbindery.
--Savage Landor. 498p. 1983. Repr. of 1941 ed. lib. bdg. 40.00 (ISBN 0-8495-1359-6). Arden Lib.
--Victorian Wallflowers. LC 78-58256. (Essay Index in Reprint Ser.). (Illus.). 1978. 27.25x (ISBN 0-8486-3018-1). Core Collection.
Elwin, Malcolm, ed. see Powys, John C.
Elwin, Malcom. The Playgoer's Handbook to Restoration Drama. 1978. Repr. of 1928 ed. lib. bdg. 30.00 (ISBN 0-8495-1312-X). Arden Lib.
Elwin, Verrier. The Baiga. LC 78-20885. Repr. of 1939 ed. 37.50 (ISBN 0-404-15919-2). AMS Pr.
--Folk-Tales of Mahakoshal. Dorson, Richard M., ed. LC 80-745. (Folklore of the World Ser.). 1980. Repr. of 1944 ed. lib. bdg. 57.50x (ISBN 0-405-13311-1). Ayer Co Pubs.
--Tribal Myths of Orissa. Dorson, Richard M., ed. LC 80-746. (Folklore of the World Ser.). 1980. Repr. of 1954 ed. lib. bdg. 74.50x (ISBN 0-405-13312-X). Ayer Co Pubs.
Elwin, Warwick, ed. Some Eighteenth Century Men of Letters, Vols. I & II. 1040p. 1980. Repr. of 1902 ed. Set. lib. bdg. 100.00 (ISBN 0-89987-203-4). Darby Bks.
Elwin, Whitwell. Some Eighteenth Century Men of Letters, 2 Vols. LC 75-113333. (Illus.). 1970. Repr. of 1902 ed. Set. 75.00x (ISBN 0-8046-0950-0, Pub. by kennikat). Assoc Faculty Pr.
--Some Eighteenth Century Men of Letters, 2 vols. 1973. Repr. of 1902 ed. 44.50 set (ISBN 0-8274-0598-7). R West.
Elwitt, Sanford. The Making of the Third Republic: Class & Politics in France, 1868-1884. LC 73-90866. xx, 330p. 1975. 27.50x (ISBN 0-8071-0077-3). La State U Pr.
Elwood. Invitation to Japanese Civilization. write for info. Watts.
Elwood, Ann & Raht, John. Walking Out. Becker, Mark, ed. 176p. (gr. 7 up). 1979. pap. 1.50 (ISBN 0-448-17080-9, Pub. by Tempo). Ace Bks.
Elwood, Ann & Wood, Linda. Windows in Space. 1981. 10.95 (ISBN 0-8027-6431-2); lib. bdg. 11.85 (ISBN 0-8027-6432-0). Walker & Co.
Elwood, Ann, jt. auth. see Darragh, Ida.
Elwood, Ann, jt. auth. see Madigan, Carol.
Elwood, Ann, et al. Macmillan Illustrated Almanac for Kids. LC 81-82099. (Illus.). 400p. (gr. 4 up). 1981. 12.95 (ISBN 0-02-535420-5); pap. 7.95x (ISBN 0-02-043040-X). Macmillan.
--Macmillan Illustrated Almanac for Kids. (Illus.). 446p. (gr. 5-9). 1984. pap. 7.95 (ISBN 0-02-043040-X). Macmillan.
Elwood, Annel K. Memoirs of the Literary Ladies of England from the Commencement of the Last Century, 2 vols. LC 72-37692. Repr. of 1843 ed. Set. 65.00 (ISBN 0-404-56749-5). AMS Pr.
Elwood, Douglas. Faith Encounters Ideology: Christian Discernment & Social Change. xvi, 318p. (Orig.). 1985. pap. 16.00 (ISBN 971-10-0201-9, Pub. by New Day Philippines). Cellar.
Elwood, Douglas J. & Magdamo, Patricia L. Christ in the Philippine Context. 1971. wrps. 6.00 (ISBN 0-686-18694-X). Cellar.
Elwood, Douglas J. see Nakpil, Emerito.
Elwood, Douglas J., ed. Asian Christian Theology: Emerging Themes. rev. ed. LC 80-21228. 342p. 1980. pap. 14.95 (ISBN 0-664-24354-1). Westminster.
--The Humanities in Christian Higher Education in Asia: Ethical & Religious Perspectives. 1978. pap. 6.50x (ISBN 0-686-23913-X, Pub. by New Day Pub). Cellar.
Elwood, Douglas J., jt. ed. see Nacpil, Emerito.
Elwood, J. Harold, jt. auth. see Elwood, J. Mark.
Elwood, J. Mark & Elwood, J. Harold. Epidemiology of Anencephalus & Spina Bifida. (Illus.). 1980. text ed. 75.00x (ISBN 0-19-261220-4). Oxford U Pr.
Elwood, J. Murray. Growing Together in Marriage. LC 76-51468. 176p. 1977. pap. 2.95 (ISBN 0-87793-128-3). Ave Maria.
--Kindly Light: The Spiritual Vision of John Henry Newman. LC 79-52444. 128p. (Orig.). 1979. pap. 2.95 (ISBN 0-87793-185-2). Ave Maria.
Elwood, John W. Elwood's Stories of the Old Ringgold Cavalry, 1847-1865. (Illus.). 326p. 1985. Repr. of 1914 ed. perfect bdg. 16.20 (ISBN 0-318-03862-5). Closson Pr.
Elwood, Maren. Characters Make Your Story. 1973. text ed. 11.95 (ISBN 0-87116-019-6). Writer.
Elwood, Muriel. The Bigamous Dutchess. 320p. 1975. pap. 1.50 (ISBN 0-685-50968-0). Woodhill.
--Deeper the Heritage. 1976. pap. 1.75 (ISBN 0-532-17137-3). Woodhill.
--Towards the Sunset. 1976. pap. 1.75 (ISBN 0-532-17143-8). Woodhill.
--Web of Destiny. 1976. pap. 1.75 (ISBN 0-532-17147-0). Woodhill.
Elwood, R. W., ed. Parental Behaviour of Rodents. LC 82-8625. 296p. 1983. text ed. 53.95x (ISBN 0-471-10252-0, Pub. by Wiley-Interscience). Wiley.
Elwood, Ralph C., ed. Russian & Eastern European History: Selected Papers from the Second World Congress for Soviet & East European Studies. 306p. 1984. pap. 18.00 (ISBN 0-933884-28-1). Berkeley Slavic.
Elwood, Ralph C. see McNeal, Robert H.
Elwood, Robert, ed. Discovering the Other: Humanities East & West. LC 82-50983. (Interplay Ser.: Vol. 4). (Illus.). 197p. 1984. text ed. 25.50x (ISBN 0-317-13510-4); pap. text ed. 17.50x (ISBN 0-89003-151-7). Undena Pubns.
Elwood, Roger. Historias Extranas de Brujeria. Lockward, George, tr. from Eng. 112p. (Span.). 1974. pap. 1.60 (ISBN 0-89922-028-2). Edit Caribe.
--Salvation Behind Bars. 1977. pap. 1.50 (ISBN 0-505-51142-8, Pub. by Tower Bks). Dorchester Pub Co.
Elwood, Roger, jt. auth. see Ghidalia, Vic.
Elwood, Roger, ed. Future Quest. (Orig.). 1973. pap. 0.95 (ISBN 0-380-01204-9, 16808). Avon.
--Night of the Sphinx & Other Stories. LC 73-21482. (Science Fiction Bks). Orig. Title: When the Cold Came & Other Stories. (Illus.). (gr. 4-8). 1974. PLB 3.95g (ISBN 0-8225-0954-7). Lerner Pubns.
--Tomorrow, New Worlds of Science Fiction. LC 75-17783. 228p. (gr. 7 up). 1975. 5.95 (ISBN 0-87131-185-2). M Evans.
Elwood, Roger, ed. see Holly, J. Hunter, et al.
Elwood, Roger, ed. see Zebrowski, George, et al.
Elwood, Sean, ed. The Nineteen Eighty-Four Show. (Illus.). 160p. 1984. pap. 14.95 (ISBN 0-930794-99-0). Station Hill Pr.
Elwood, Sean H., ed. Nineteen Eighty Four: A Preview. (Illus.). 168p. (Orig.). 1983. pap. write for info. (ISBN 0-914661-00-0). Feldman Fine Arts.
Elwood, Willis J. & Tuxford, A. Felicite, eds. Some Manchester Doctors... A Biographical Collection. LC 84-20093. 250p. 1985. 24.50 (ISBN 0-7190-1754-8, Pub. by Manchester Univ Pr). Longwood Pub Group.
Elwork, Amiram & Sales, Bruce D. Making Jury Instructions Understandable. 431p. 1982. 35.00 (ISBN 0-87215-450-5). Michie Co.
Elworthy, F. T. The Evil Eye: An Account of an Ancient & Widespread Superstition. 75.00 (ISBN 0-87968-421-6). Gordon Pr.
Elworthy, Frederic T. An Outline of the Grammar of the Dialect of West Somerset... (English Dialect Society Publications Ser.: No. 19). pap. 12.00 (ISBN 0-317-15737-X). Kraus Repr.
--The West Somerset Word-Book: East Devon. (English Dialect Society Publications Ser.: No. 50). pap. 86.00 (ISBN 0-317-15936-4). Kraus Repr.
Elworthy, Frederick. The Evil Eye. (Illus.). 472p. 1982. 22.50 (ISBN 0-8126-0257-9). Citadel Pr.
Elworthy, Frederick T. The Dialect of West Somerset. (English Dialect Society (Series D) Publications: No. 7). pap. 16.00 (ISBN 0-317-15485-0). Kraus Repr.
Elworthy, K. D. Stochastic Differential Equations on Manifolds. LC 82-4426. (London Mathematical Society Lecture Note Ser.: No. 70). 326p. 1982. pap. 32.50 (ISBN 0-521-28767-7). Cambridge U Pr.
Ely, Alex. A Destiny at Dawn. Orig. Title: Erich's Sunrise. 161p. 1981. 7.50 (ISBN 0-682-49709-6). Exposition Pr FL.
Ely, Barbara R. The Gypsum Throne. (Shield Romance Ser.). 1984. pap. 6.95 (ISBN 0-932906-11-7). Pan-Am Publishing Co.
Ely, Ben-Ezra S. There She Blows: A Narrative of a Whaling Voyage, in the Indian & South Atlantic Oceans. Dahl, Curtis, ed. LC 76-142726. (American Maritime Library: Vol. 3). (Illus.). 208p. 1971. 10.00 (ISBN 0-8195-4032-3); ltd. ed. 15.00 (ISBN 0-8195-4033-1). Mystic Seaport.
Ely, C. A. Shallow-Water Asteroidea & Ophiuroidea of Hawaii. (BMB Ser.). Repr. of 1942 ed. 12.00 (ISBN 0-527-02284-5). Kraus Repr.
Ely, Carolanne. Love Wounds & Multiple Fractures: Poems. 1975. pap. 3.00 (ISBN 0-915342-02-2). SUN.
Ely, Donald P., jt. auth. see Gerlach, Vernon S.
Ely, Evelyn & Hughes, Phyllis. Ojos de Dios. (Illus.). 1972. pap. 2.25 (ISBN 0-89013-056-6). Museum NM Pr.
Ely, James W., Jr., jt. ed. see Bodenhamer, David J.
Ely, John. Stimulation Treatment Handbook. 272p. 1985. 40.00 (ISBN 0-87814-284-3). PennWell Bks.
Ely, John H. Democracy & Distrust: A Theory of Judicial Review. LC 79-19859. (Harvard Paperbacks Ser.). 280p. 1981. 17.50x (ISBN 0-674-19636-8); pap. 7.95 (ISBN 0-674-19637-6). Harvard U Pr.
Ely, Laurence. The Teenager in the Space Age. LC 72-97463. (Personal Guidance, Social Adjustment Ser.). (gr. 7-12). 1973. lib. bdg. 8.97 (ISBN 0-8239-0276-5). Rosen Group.
Ely, Northcutt, ed. see Federal Oil Conservation Board.
Ely, P. Bring the Lab Back to Life. (Language Teaching Methodology Ser.). 128p. 1984. pap. 5.50 (ISBN 0-08-031087-7); cassette 10.60 (ISBN 0-08-031097-4); kit 16.10 (ISBN 0-08-031098-2). Pergamon.
Ely, R. Unto God & Caesar: Religious Issues in the Emerging Commonwealth 1891-1906. 1976. 22.00x (ISBN 0-522-84093-0, Pub. by Melbourne U Pr). Intl Spec Bk.
Ely, R. T. Introduction to Political Economy. rev ed. 1901. 23.00 (ISBN 0-527-27000-8). Kraus Repr.
Ely, R. V., ed. Microfocal Radiography. LC 80-40653. 1981. 69.50 (ISBN 0-12-238140-8). Acad Pr.
Ely, Richard. Accuracy in Rhythm. 46p. 1981. pap. 9.95 (ISBN 0-938170-03-1). Wimbledon Music.
Ely, Richard T. French & German Socialism in Modern Times. LC 72-5551. (Select Bibliographies Reprint Ser.). 1972. Repr. of 1883 ed. 19.00 (ISBN 0-8369-6904-9). Ayer Co Pubs.
--Ground Under Our Feet: An Autobiography. Metzger, Walter P., ed. LC 76-55184. (The Academic Profession Ser.). (Illus.). 1977. Repr. of 1938 ed. lib. bdg. 26.50x (ISBN 0-405-10011-6). Ayer Co Pubs.
--Hard Times: An Introduction to Political Economy. 1889. 20.00 (ISBN 0-686-17727-4). Quest Edns.
--Hard Times: The Way in & the Way Out. 1931. 15.00 (ISBN 0-686-17726-6). Quest Edns.
--Labor Movement in America. LC 74-89731. (American Labor, from Conspiracy to Collective Bargaining, Ser. 1). 399p. 1969. Repr. of 1890 ed. 19.00 (ISBN 0-405-02119-4). Ayer Co Pubs.
--Monopolies & Trust. LC 73-2505. (Big Business; Economic Power in a Free Society Ser.). Repr. of 1912 ed. 18.00 (ISBN 0-405-05087-9). Ayer Co Pubs.
--The Past & Present of Political Economy. 1973. pap. 9.00 (ISBN 0-384-14290-7). Johnson Repr.
--The Past & the Present of Political Economy. LC 78-63743. (Johns Hopkins University. Studies in the Social Sciences. Second Ser. 1884: 3). Repr. of 1884 ed. 11.50 (ISBN 0-404-61013-7). AMS Pr.
--Recent American Socialism. LC 76-42810. Repr. of 1885 ed. 11.50 (ISBN 0-404-60063-8). AMS Pr.
--Recent American Socialism. 1973. pap. 9.00 (ISBN 0-384-14291-5). Johnson Repr.
--Socialism. 1894. 20.00 (ISBN 0-686-17728-2). Quest Edns.
Ely, Richard T., et al, eds. Foundations of National Prosperity: Studies in the Conservation of Permanent National Resources. LC 19-1787. 1971. Repr. of 1918 ed. 30.00 (ISBN 0-384-16495-1, D055). Johnson Repr.
Ely, Robert. Fire Officer's Guide: Fire Apparatus Maintenance. Lyons, Paul R., ed. LC 75-15054. (Fire Officer's Guide Ser.). (Illus.). 392p. 1975. 10.50 (ISBN 0-87765-039-X). Natl Fire Prot.
Ely, Silas J., jt. auth. see Betts, Richard M.
Ely, Vivian & Barnes, Michael. Starting Your Own Marketing Business. 2nd ed. Dorr, Eugene, ed. (Occupational Manuals & Projects Marketing Ser.). (Illus.). (gr. 11-12). 1978. pap. text ed. 8.68 (ISBN 0-07-019307-X). McGraw.
Elyaderani, Morteza, et al. Invasive Uroradiology: A Manual of Diagnostic & Therapeutic Techniques. (Illus.). 224p. 1984. 40.00 (ISBN 0-669-07537-X, Collamore). Heath.
Elyanov, A. Economic Growth & the Market in the Developing Countries. 277p. 1982. 7.45 (ISBN 0-8285-2456-4, Pub. by Progress Pubs USSR). Imported Pubns.
Elyot, Kevin. Coming Clean. LC 83-25377. 124p. (Orig.). 1984. pap. 8.50 (ISBN 0-571-13228-6). Faber & Faber.
Elyot, Thomas. The Boke Named the Governor, 2 Vols. Croft, Herbert S., ed. 1967. 55.50 (ISBN 0-8337-1058-3). B Franklin.
--The Book Named the Governor. 1975. Repr. of 1962 ed. 12.95x (ISBN 0-460-00227-9, Evman). Biblio Dist.
--Castel of Helthe. LC 37-11679. Repr. of 1541 ed. 35.00x (ISBN 0-8201-1176-7). Schol Facsimiles.
--Four Political Treatises: 1533-1541. LC 67-10273. 1967. 55.00x (ISBN 0-8201-1015-9). Schol Facsimiles.

Elyot, Sir Thomas. Of the Knowledge Which Maketh a Wise Man. Howard, Edwin J., ed. (Illus.). 1946. limited to 200 copies 17.50x (ISBN 0-686-17396-1). R S Barnes.
--Sir Thomas Elyot's The Defence of Good Women. Howard, Edwin J., ed. 1940. limited to 500 copies 10.00x (ISBN 0-686-17401-1). R S Barnes.
Elytis, Odysseus. The Axion Esti. Keeley, Edmund & Savidis, George, trs. from Gr. LC 79-49274. (Pitt Poetry Ser.). 1979. pap. 5.95 (ISBN 0-8229-5318-8). U of Pittsburgh Pr.
--Odysseus Elytis: Selected Poems. Keeley, Edmund & Sherrard, Philip, trs. from Greek. LC 81-65282. 96p. 1981. 12.95 (ISBN 0-670-29246-X). Viking.
--The Sovereign Sun: Selected Poems. Friar, Kimon, tr. from Greek. LC 74-77777. 200p. 1974. 19.95 (ISBN 0-87722-019-0). Temple U Pr.
--Sovereign Sun: Selected Poems. Friar, Kimon, tr. from Gr. 200p. 1979. pap. 9.95 (ISBN 0-87722-113-8). Temple U Pr.
--Sporades. McKinsey, Martin, tr. from Greek. 80p. 1983. 35.00 (ISBN 0-915192-10-1); pap. 12.00 (ISBN 0-915192-09-8). Pomegranate.
El-Zaim, Issam. Changing Patterns in World Economy & the Transition to a New International Economic Order: With Special Reference to the Arab World: Project on Socio-Cultural Development Alternatives in a Changing World: Sub-project on the Transformation of the World. 16p. 1982. pap. 5.00 (ISBN 92-808-0315-8, TUNU202, UNU). Unipub.
Elzas, Barnett A. The Jews of South Carolina, from the Earliest Times to the Present Day. LC 77-187364. (Illus.). 352p. 1972. Repr. of 1905 ed. 23.50 (ISBN 0-87152-092-3). Reprint.
Elze, Karl. Essays on Shakespeare. Schmitz, L. Dora, tr. LC 74-113365. 1970. Repr. of 1874 ed. 25.00x (ISBN 0-8046-1015-0, Pub. by Kennikat). Assoc Faculty Pr.
--Essays on Shakespeare. 1973. Repr. of 1874 ed. 11.95 (ISBN 0-8274-1688-1). R West.
--A Letter to C. M. Ingleby...Containing Notes & Conjectural Emendations on Shakespeare's Cymbaline. LC 76-166026. Repr. of 1885 ed. 11.50 (ISBN 0-404-02326-6). AMS Pr.
--Notes on Elizabethan Dramatists with Conjectural Emendations of the Text. LC 70-166027. Repr. of 1880 ed. 15.00 (ISBN 0-404-02327-4). AMS Pr.
--William Shakespeare: A Literary Biography. LC 73-166028. Repr. of 1888 ed. 37.50 (ISBN 0-404-02328-2). AMS Pr.
--William Shakespeare: A Literary Biography. Schmitz, L. Dora, tr. 587p. 1982. Repr. of 1888 ed. lib. bdg. 50.00 (ISBN 0-89760-214-5). Telegraph Bks.
Elze, Reinhard. Pabst-Kaiser-Konige: Und Die Mittelalterliche Herrschaftssymbolik. 302p. 1982. 70.00x (ISBN 0-86078-098-8, Pub. by Variorum). State Mutual Bk.
--Papste-Kaiser-Konige end die mittelater-liche Heerschaftssymbolik. 302p. 1982. 75.00x (ISBN 0-86078-098-8, Pub. by Variorum England). State Mutual Bk.
El Zeini, Hanny, jt. auth. see Sety, Omm.
Elzerman, A. W. Your Future in Salesmanship & Sales Management. LC 72-95054. (Careers in Depth Ser.). (gr. 7-12). 1973. PLB 8.97 (ISBN 0-8239-0273-0). Rosen Group.
Elzey, Freeman F. Elementary Statistical Techniques. LC 84-12722. (Statistics Ser.). 225p. 1985. text ed. 15.00 pub net (ISBN 0-534-04668-1). Brooks-Cole.
--A First Reader in Statistics. 2nd ed. LC 74-83225. 1974. pap. text ed. 6.50 pub net (ISBN 0-8185-0140-5). Brooks-Cole.
--An Introduction to Statistical Methods in the Behavioral Sciences. LC 76-9924. (Brooks-Cole Series in Statistics). 1976. pap. text ed. 11.25 pub net (ISBN 0-8185-0194-4). Brooks-Cole.
--Introductory Statistics: A Microcomputer Approach. LC 84-12722. (Statistics Ser.). 260p. 1984. pap. text ed. 24.00 pub net (ISBN 0-534-03280-X). Brooks-Cole.
--A Programmed Introduction to Statistics. 2nd ed. LC 79-161489. 385p. (Orig.). 1971. pap. text ed. 13.75 pub net (ISBN 0-8185-0018-2). instructor's manual avail. (ISBN 0-685-23471-1). Brooks-Cole.
--Statistics: A Microcomputer Approach with Utility Supporting Software. 256p. 1984. pap. write for info. Wadsworth Pub.
Elzinga, Kenneth G. & Breit, William. The Antitrust Penalties: A Study in Law & Economics. LC 75-43316. 1976. 18.50x (ISBN 0-300-01999-8). Yale U Pr.
Elzinga, Kenneth G., jt. auth. see Breit, William.
Elzinga, Kenneth G., ed. Economics: A Reader. 3rd ed. 1978. pap. text ed. 13.50 scp (ISBN 0-06-041912-1, HarpC). Har-Row.
Elzinga, Kenneth G., jt. ed. see Briet, William.
Elzinga, Kenneth G., ed. see Hemenway, David.
Elzinga, Marshall, ed. Methods in Protein Sequence Analysis. LC 82-80733. (Experimental Biology & Medicine). 640p. 1982. 69.50 (ISBN 0-89603-038-5). Humana.
Elzinga, Richard J. Fundamentals of Entomology. 2nd ed. (Illus.). 464p. 1981. text ed. 31.95 (ISBN 0-13-338194-3). P-H.
Emad, Parvis. Heidegger & the Phenomenology of Values. LC 81-53002. 179p. 1981. 18.95 (ISBN 0-941318-00-1). Torey Pr.
Emal, Janet & Kern, Barbara. Kids Cook Microwave. 1983. pap. 4.95 (ISBN 0-89586-271-9). H P Bks.
Emami, Mary L. & Coulson, Suzzanne. Color Me Natural with Wholesome Homemade Food Coloring. LC 78-71614. (Illus.). 117p. 1979. spiral bdg. 5.95 (ISBN 0-9602316-0-9). Emami-Coalson.
Emami, Mary Lou & Coulson, Suzanne. Color Me Natural with Wholesome, Homemade Food Coloring. (Illus.). 117p. (Orig.). 1978. pap. 5.95 (ISBN 0-686-74777-1). Emami-Coulson.
Emans, S. Jean & Goldstein, Donald P. Pediatric & Adolescent Gynecology. 2nd ed. (Little, Brown Clinical Pediatrics Ser.). 1982. text ed. 32.50 (ISBN 0-316-23402-8). Little.
Emanual, N., ed. Problems in Chemical Kinetics. 223p. 1981. pap. 7.00 (ISBN 0-8285-2076-3, Pub. by Mir Pubs USSR). Imported Pubns.
Emanuel, David & Emanuel, Elizabeth. Style for All Seasons. (Illus.). 1983. 25.00 (ISBN 0-907516-13-0, Pub by Pavilion Michael Joseph). Merrimack Pub Cir.
Emanuel, Edward F. Action & Idea: The Roots of Entertainment. 120p. 1982. pap. text ed. 9.95 (ISBN 0-8403-2845-1). Kendall-Hunt.
Emanuel, Elizabeth, jt. auth. see Emanuel, David.
Emanuel, H. D. The Latin Texts of the Welsh. (History & Law Ser.: No. 22). 565p. 1967. text ed. 32.00x (ISBN 0-7083-0112-6, Pub. by Univ of Wales Pr England). Humanities.
Emanuel, James A. Black Man Abroad: The Toulouse Poems. LC 77-95004. 76p. 1978. perfect bdg. 3.50x (ISBN 0-916418-16-2). Lotus.
--The Broken Bowl: New & Uncollected Poems. LC 82-83858. 72p. 1983. pap. 4.50x perf. bnd. (ISBN 0-916418-42-1). Lotus.
--A Chisel in the Dark: Poems Selected & New. LC 79-89034. 73p. 1980. pap. 4.00x perf. bound (ISBN 0-916418-22-7). Lotus.
--Langston Hughes. (United States Authors Ser.). 1967. lib. bdg. 13.50 (ISBN 0-8057-0388-8, Twayne). G K Hall.
--A Poet's Mind: L6. McConochie, Jean, ed. (Regents Readers Ser.). pap. text ed. 2.75 (ISBN 0-88345-497-1, 20975). Regents Pub.
Emanuel, James A. & Gross, Theodore L., eds. Dark Symphony: Negro Literature in America. LC 68-54984. 1968. 19.50 (ISBN 0-02-909550-6); pap. text ed. 17.95 (ISBN 0-02-909540-9). Free Pr.
Emanuel, Lynn. Hotel Fiesta: Poems. LC 84-2447. (Contemporary Poetry Ser.). 42p. 1984. 10.95x (ISBN 0-8203-0727-0); pap. 6.95 (ISBN 0-8203-0728-9). U of Ga Pr.
--Oblique Light. LC 79-11007. 32p. 1979. pap. 4.00 (ISBN 0-918366-13-5). Slow Loris.
Emanuel, Sr. M. Dic Mihi Latine. 50p. (Eng. & Lat.). 1.50 (ISBN 0-318-12449-1, B2). Amer Classical.
Emanuel, Muriel, ed. Contemporary Architects. (Illus.). 933p. 1980. 70.00x (ISBN 0-312-16635-4). St Martin.
Emanuel, Muriel, et al, eds. Contemporary Artists. 2nd ed. LC 82-25048. (Illus.). 1000p. 1983. 70.00x (ISBN 0-312-16643-5). St Martin.
Emanuel, Myron, et al. Corporate Economic Education Programs. LC 79-117. 1979. 8.00 (ISBN 0-910586-29-2). Finan Exec.
Emanuel, N. M. Kinetics of Experimental Tumour Processes. (Illus.). 350p. 1982. 77.00 (ISBN 0-08-024909-4). Pergamon.
Emanuel, N. M., et al. Liquid-Phase Oxidation of Hydrocarbons. LC 66-12888. 350p. 1967. 39.50x (ISBN 0-306-30292-6, Plenum Pr). Plenum Pub.
--Oxidation of Organic Compounds: Solvent Effects in Radical Reactions. 350p. 1984. 95.00 (ISBN 0-08-022067-3). Pergamon.
Emanuel, Nikolai, et al. Liquid-phase Oxidation of Hydrocarbons. LC 66-12888. pap. 91.00 (ISBN 0-317-27888-6, 2055792). Bks Demand UMI.
Emanuel, Pericles & Leff, Edward. Introduction to Feedback Control Systems. (Electrical Engineering). (Illus.). 1979. text ed. 42.00 (ISBN 0-07-019310-X). McGraw.
Emanuel, Pericles J. Motors, Generators, Transformers & Energy. (Illus.). 560p. 1985. text ed. 32.95 (ISBN 0-13-604026-8). P-H.
Emanuel, Steven & Knowles, Steven. Contracts: Emanuel Law Outlines. 2nd ed. 436p. 1984. pap. 12.95 (ISBN 0-317-31517-X). Nolo Pr.
Emanuel, W. V. Wild Asses: A Journey Through Persia. LC 76-180336. Repr. of 1939 ed. 27.50 (ISBN 0-404-56248-5). AMS Pr.
Emanuels, George. John Muir Inventor. (Illus.). 1985. 16.50 (ISBN 0-914330-73-X). Panorama West.
--John Muir Inventor. LC 85-60102. (Illus.). 1985. 16.50 (ISBN 0-914330-74-8). Diablo Bks.
--Walnut Creek. LC 84-70073. (Illus.). 1984. 20.00 (ISBN 0-9607520-2-1). Diablo Bks.
--Ygnacio Valley Eighteen Thirty-Four to Nineteen Seventy. (Illus.). 1985. 20.00. Diablo Bks.
Emanuelson & Rosenlight. Handbook of Critical Care Nursing. (Red Book Ser.). 1986. price not set (ISBN 0-471-80418-5). Wiley.
Emanuelson, Kathy L & Desmore, Mary J. Acute Respiratory Care. LC 81-50072. (Series in Critical Care Nursing). (Illus.). 216p. (Orig.). 1981. pap. text ed. 15.95 (ISBN 0-471-88804-4). Wiley.
Emanuelson, Margaret. Lost Yesterdays. LC 83-61128. 1983. pap. text ed. 5.00 (ISBN 0-932050-22-0). New Puritan.
Eman-Wheeless, Virginia, ed. see Conference on Communication, Language & Sex, 1st Annual.
Emark, Donald R., jt. ed. see Erickson, Joan G.
E Maung. Burmese Buddhist Law. LC 77-87483. Repr. of 1937 ed. 25.00 (ISBN 0-404-16812-4). AMS Pr.
Embar, Chellam. Getting a Job in Hard Times. 96p. 1983. pap. 10.00 (ISBN 0-88075-001-4). Concepts Unlmted.
--People, People, Everywhere! 60p. (Orig.). 1983. pap. 6.99 (ISBN 0-88075-002-2). Concepts Unlmted.
Embden, Ludwig Von see Heine, Heinrich.
Embden, Ludwig Von see Von Embden, Ludwig.
Ember, Carol R. & Ember, Melvin. Anthropology. 4th ed. (Illus.). 624p. 1985. text ed. 27.95 (ISBN 0-13-037045-2). P-H.
--Cultural Anthropology. 3rd ed. (Illus.). 416p. 1981. 23.95 (ISBN 0-13-195230-7); wkbk. 11.95 (ISBN 0-13-195263-3). P-H.
--Cultural Anthropology. 4th ed. (Illus.). 432p. 1985. pap. text ed. 23.95 (ISBN 0-13-195421-0). P-H.
Ember, Carol R., jt. auth. see Ember, Melvin.
Ember, Ildiko. Music in Painting. (Illus.). 82p. 16.00 (ISBN 0-317-20005-4). Newbury Bks.
Ember, Melvin & Ember, Carol R. Marriage, Family & Kinship: Comparative Studies of Social Organization. LC 82-83702. (Comparative Studies Ser.). 409p. 1983. 30.00 (ISBN 0-87536-113-7); pap. 15.00 (ISBN 0-87536-114-5). HRAFP.
Ember, Melvin, jt. auth. see Ember, Carol R.
Emberley, Barbara. Drummer Hoff. (Illus.). (ps-1). 1967. PLB 9.95x (ISBN 0-13-220822-9, Pub. by Treehouse); pap. 4.95 (ISBN 0-13-220855-5). P-H.
--Story of Paul Bunyan. (Illus.). (ps-3). 1963. pap. 3.95 (ISBN 0-13-850784-8). P-H.
Emberley, Ed. A Birthday Wish. (Illus.). (gr. k-3). 1977. 8.70i (ISBN 0-316-23409-5). Little.
--A Circle Drawing Book. 1984. 13.45 (ISBN 0-316-23425-7); pap. 5.95 (ISBN 0-316-23426-5). Little.
--Drawing Book of Animals. (Illus.). 32p. (gr. 1-3). 1970. 7.95 (ISBN 0-316-23597-0). Little.
--Ed Emberley's A. B. C. (Illus.). 56p. (gr. k-2). 1978. 10.45i (ISBN 0-316-23408-7). Little.
--Ed Emberley's Big Green Drawing Book. LC 79-16247. (Illus.). (gr. k up). 1979. 12.45i (ISBN 0-316-23595-4); pap. 6.70i (ISBN 0-316-23596-2). Little.
--Ed Emberley's Big Orange Drawing Book. (Illus.). 96p. 1980. 9.95 (ISBN 0-316-23418-4); pap. 6.70i (ISBN 0-316-23419-2). Little.
--Ed Emberley's Big Purple Drawing Book. (Illus.). (gr. 1 up). 1981. 10.45i (ISBN 0-316-23422-2); pap. 5.70i (ISBN 0-316-23423-0). Little.
--Ed Emberley's Crazy Mixed-up Face Game. (Illus.). 32p. (gr. 1 up). 1981. 9.70i (ISBN 0-316-23420-6); pap. 4.95 (ISBN 0-316-23421-4). Little.
--Ed Emberley's Drawing Book: Make a World. LC 70-154962. (gr. 2 up). 1972. 9.70i (ISBN 0-316-23598-9). Little.
--Ed Emberley's Drawing Book of Faces. (Illus.). 32p. (gr. k-3). 1975. 9.70i (ISBN 0-316-23609-8). Little.
--Ed Emberley's Great Thumbprint Drawing Book. (Illus.). (gr. 1 up). 1977. 7.25i (ISBN 0-316-23613-6). Little.
--Green Says Go. LC 68-21165. (Illus.). (ps-3). 1968. 13.45i (ISBN 0-316-23599-7). Little.
--Klippity Klop. (Illus.). 32p. (gr. k-3). 1974. 5.95 (ISBN 0-316-23607-1). Little.
--The Wing on a Flea: A Book About Shapes. (Illus.). (ps up). 1961. 11.45 (ISBN 0-316-23600-4). Little.
--The Wizard of Oz. (Illus.). 32p. (gr. 1-3). 1975. 6.95 (ISBN 0-316-23610-1). Little.
Emberley, Ed E. Ed Emberley Little Drawing Book of Birds. (gr. 1 up). 1973. pap. 1.00 (ISBN 0-316-23602-0). Little.
--Ed Emberley Little Drawing Book of Farms. (gr. 1 up). 1973. pap. 1.00 (ISBN 0-316-23603-9). Little.
--Ed Emberley Little Drawing Book of Trains. (gr. 1 up). 1973. pap. 1.00 (ISBN 0-316-23604-7). Little.
--Ed Emberley Little Drawing Book of Weirdoes. (gr. 1 up). 1973. pap. 1.00 (ISBN 0-316-23605-5). Little.
--Ed Emberley Little Drawing Books. (gr. 1 up). 1978. 4.00 (ISBN 0-316-23614-4). Little.
Emberley, Michael. Dinosaurs! A Drawing Book. (Illus.). 48p. (gr. 3 up). 1980. 10.45i (ISBN 0-316-23417-6). Little.
--Dinosaurs! A Drawing Book. (Reading Rainbow Ser.). (Illus.). 48p. (gr. 3 up). 1985. pap. 4.95 (ISBN 0-316-23631-4). Little.
--More Dinosaurs! And Other Prehistoric Beasts. LC 83-9822. (Illus.). 64p. (gr. 3 up). 1983. PLB 9.70i (ISBN 0-316-23424-9). Little.
--The Sports Equipment Book. (Illus.). 32p. (gr. 3 up). 1982. 12.45i (ISBN 0-316-23405-2). Little.
Emberley, Rebecca. Drawing with Numbers & Letters. (gr. 6 up). 1981. 7.95 (ISBN 0-316-23406-0). Little.
Emberlin, Diane D. Contributions of Women: Science. LC 76-30621. (Contributions of Women Ser.). (Illus.). (gr. 6 up). 1977. PLB 8.95 (ISBN 0-87518-136-8). Dillon.
Emberlin, J. C. Introduction to Ecology. (Illus.). 304p. 1983. pap. text ed. 14.95x (ISBN 0-7121-0965-X). Intl Ideas.
Emberson, Frances G. Mark Twain's Vocabulary. 1978. Repr. of 1935 ed. lib. bdg. 10.00 (ISBN 0-8495-1316-2). Arden Lib.
--Mark Twain's Vocabulary. 53p. 1980. Repr. of 1935 ed. lib. bdg. 12.50 (ISBN 0-89987-206-9). Darby Bks.
--Mark Twain's Vocabulary. LC 73-16345. 1935. lib. bdg. 16.50 (ISBN 0-8414-3922-2). Folcroft.
Emberton, Jane. Pods: Wildflowers & Weeds in Their Final Beauty. 1984. 19.00 (ISBN 0-8446-6117-1). Peter Smith.
Embertson, Jane. Pods: Wildflowers & Weeds in Their Final Beauty. (Illus.). 1979. pap. 14.95 (ISBN 0-684-15543-5, ScribT). Scribner.
Embery, Joan & Lucaire, Ed. Joan Embery's Collection of Amazing Animal Facts. LC 82-12864. (Illus.). 224p. (gr. 7 up). 1983. 14.95 (ISBN 0-385-28486-1). Delacorte.
--Joan Embery's Collection of Amazing Animal Facts. 1984. pap. 3.50 (ISBN 0-440-14232-6). Dell.
Embery, Joan & Vavra, Robert. On Horses. (Illus.). 128p. 1984. 24.95 (ISBN 0-688-04070-5). Morrow.
Emblen, D. L. & Solkov, Arnold. Before & After. 560p. 1986. pap. text ed. 12.95 (ISBN 0-394-33963-0, RanC). Random.
Emblen, D. L., jt. auth. see Hall, Donald.
Embleton, C. & King, C. A. Glacial & Periglacial Morphology, 2 vols. 2nd ed. Incl. Vol. 1. Glacial Geomorphology. LC 75-14188; Vol. 2. Periglacial Geomorphology. LC 75-14187. 1975. pap. Halsted Pr.
Embleton, Clifford, ed. The Geomorphology of Europe. 465p. 1984. 79.95 (ISBN 0-471-80070-8, Pub. by Wiley-Interscience). Wiley.
Embleton, Clifford & Thornes, John, eds. Process in Geomorphology. LC 79-18747. 436p. 1979. pap. 32.95x (ISBN 0-470-26808-5). Halsted Pr.
Embleton, Clifford, et al, eds. Geomorphology: Present Problems & Future Prospects. (Illus.). 1978. text ed. 32.50x (ISBN 0-19-874078-6). Oxford U Pr.
Emblidge, David, ed. The Third Berkshire Anthology: A Collection of Literature & Art. (Illus.). 208p. (Orig.). 1982. pap. 7.50 (ISBN 0-9609540-0-7). Berkshire Writ.
Emblod, Mary. Outrageous Fortune. 1981. pap. 2.25 (ISBN 0-380-78493-9, 78493-9, Flare). Avon.
Embo Workshop on Patelets: Cellular Response Mechanisms & Their Biological Significance. Platelets, Cellular Response Mechanisms & Their Biological Significance: Proceedings. Rotman, A. & Meyer, F. A., eds. LC 80-41257. (A Wiley-Interscience Publication). pap. 87.30 (ISBN 0-317-27728-6, 2052095). Bks Demand UMI.
Embree, A. T., ed. see Ikram, S. M.
Embree, Ainslie, ed. Alberuni's India. abr. ed. Sachau, Edward C., tr. 1971. pap. 2.75x (ISBN 0-393-00568-2, Norton Lib). Norton.
Embree, Ainslie T. Charles Grant & British Rule in India. LC 77-166029. (Columbia University Studies in the Social Sciences: No. 606). 10.00 (ISBN 0-404-51606-8). AMS Pr.
--India's Search for National Unity. 1981. Repr. 12.50x (ISBN 0-8364-0691-5, Pub. by Chanakya India). South Asia Bks.
Embree, Ainslie T., ed. The Hindu Tradition. 448p. 1972. pap. 4.95 (ISBN 0-394-71702-3, V696, Vin). Random.
--Pakistan's Western Borderlands. LC 76-43386. 158p. 1977. 14.75 (ISBN 0-89089-074-9). Carolina Acad Pr.
Embree, Ainslie T., jt. ed. see De Bary, William T.
Embree, Edwin R. Brown Americans. LC 78-122075. Repr. of 1945 ed. 25.00x (ISBN 0-678-03153-3). Kelley.
--Indians of the Americas. 1970. pap. 2.95 (ISBN 0-02-031990-8, Collier). Macmillan.
Embree, Edwin R., jt. auth. see Johnson, Charles S.
Embree, Esther. Now Rings the Bell. (Illus.). 1978. pap. 2.95 (ISBN 0-89367-023-5). Light & Life.
Embree, Glenn, jt. auth. see Miller, Ray.
Embree, Harland D. Organic Chemistry: Brief Course. 1983. text ed. 26.05x (ISBN 0-673-15435-1); study guide 10.95 (ISBN 0-673-15853-5). Scott F.
Embree, John F. Acculturation among the Japanese of Kona, Hawaii. LC 43-1209. (American Anthropological Association Memoirs Ser.). 18.00 (ISBN 0-527-00558-4). Kraus Repr.
--The Japanese Nation, a Social Survey. LC 75-8766. (Illus.). 308p. 1975. Repr. of 1945 ed. lib. bdg. 20.00x (ISBN 0-8371-8117-8, EMJN). Greenwood.
--Suye Mura: A Japanese Village. LC 40-1477. (Illus.). 1939. 15.00x (ISBN 0-226-20631-9). U of Chicago Pr.
--Suye Mura: A Japanese Village. LC 40-1477. (Illus.). 1964. pap. 3.25 (ISBN 0-226-20632-7, P173, Phoen). U of Chicago Pr.
Embree, John F., compiled by. Japanese Peasant Songs. LC 44-2122. (AFS M Ser.). Repr. of 1943 ed. 15.00 (ISBN 0-527-01090-1). Kraus Repr.
Embree, Lester, ed. Essays in Memory of Aron Gurwitsch. LC 84-17413. (Current Continental Research Ser.: 007). (Illus.). 584p. (Orig.). 1985. lib. bdg. 33.50 (ISBN 0-8191-4308-1, Pub by Ctr Adv Res); pap. text ed. 23.75 (ISBN 0-8191-4309-X). U Pr of Amer.
Embree, Lester, ed. see Gurwitsch, Aron.
Embree, Lester, tr. see Ricoeur, Paul.

Embree, Lester E., ed. Life-World & Consciousness: Essays for Aron Gurwitsch. LC 71-162930. (Northwestern University Studies in Phenomenology & Existential Philosophy Ser.). pap. 160.00 (ISBN 0-317-09049-6, 2010161). Bks Demand UMI.

Embree, Lester E., tr. see Bachelard, Suzanne.

Embree, T., ed. see De Bary, William T.

Embretson, Susan. Test Design: Contributions from Psychology & Psychometrics. 1985. 39.50 (ISBN 0-12-238180-7). Acad Pr.

Embrey, Peter G. & Fuller, John P. A Manual of New Mineral Names, 1892-1978. 1980. 55.00x (ISBN 0-19-858501-2). Oxford U Pr.

Embry, Bob. Tole'n. rev. ed. (Illus.). 84p. 1982. pap. 7.95 (ISBN 0-917119-10-X, 45-1028). Priscillas Pubns.

Embry, Jessie L., ed. see Shipps, Jan, et al.

Embry, Joan. My Wild World. 1981. pap. 3.50 (ISBN 0-440-15941-5). Dell.

Embry, Lynn. Motivation Marvels. (gr. k-6). 1981. 6.95 (ISBN 0-916456-99-4, GA 242). Good Apple.

--Rx for the Classroom Blahs. (Illus.). 64p. (gr. 4-8). 1983. wkbk. 5.95 (ISBN 0-86653-104-1, GA 462). Good Apple.

--Super Sheets III. (gr. 3-6). 1982. 5.95 (ISBN 0-86653-055-X, GA 408). Good Apple.

--Super Sheets IV. (gr. 3-8). 1982. 5.95 (ISBN 0-86653-075-4, GA 409). Good Apple.

--Super Sheets One. (gr. 3-6). 1980. 5.95 (ISBN 0-916456-65-X, GA 180). Good Apple.

--Super Sheets Two. (gr. 3-6). 1980. 5.95 (ISBN 0-916456-66-8, GA 181). Good Apple.

Embry, Margaret. Blue-Nosed Witch. (Illus.). 48p. (gr. 3-6). 1956. 6.95 (ISBN 0-8234-0011-5). Holiday.

--The Blue-Nosed Witch. (Illus.). (gr. 2-5). 1983. pap. 1.95 (ISBN 0-553-15198-3). Bantam.

Embry, Mike. Basketball in the Blue Grass State: The Championship Teams. LC 82-83924. (Illus.). 192p. (Orig.). 1983. pap. 10.95 (ISBN 0-88011-120-8). Leisure Pr.

--March Madness: The Kentucky High School Basketball Tournament. (Illus.). 312p. 1985. 14.95 (ISBN 0-89651-452-8); pap. 9.95 (ISBN 0-89651-453-6). Icarus.

Embry, P. G., jt. auth. see Hey, M. H.

Embse, Thomas J. Van Der see Murray, John V. & Van Der Embse, Thomas J.

Embury, David A. Fine Art of Mixing Drinks. rev. ed. LC 58-5572. (Illus.). 1948. pap. 4.95 (ISBN 0-385-09683-6, Dolp). Doubleday.

Emch, G. G. Mathematical & Conceptual Foundations of Twentieth Century Physics. (Mathematical Studies: Vol. 100). 1985. 55.00 (ISBN 0-444-87585-9, North-Holland). Elsevier.

EMCT Staff. Competitive Position & Future of Inland Waterway Transport. (ECMT Roundtable 49). (Illus.). 95p. (Orig.). 1981. pap. text ed. 7.50 (ISBN 92-821-1065-6, 75-81-01-1). OECD.

Emde, Fritz, jt. auth. see Jahnke, Eugene.

Emde, Robert N., ed. Rene Spitz: Dialogues from Infancy. LC 83-26461. 495p. 1984. text ed. 40.00 (ISBN 0-8236-5787-6). Intl Univs Pr.

Emde, Robert N. & Harmon, Robert J., eds. Continuities & Discontinuities in Development. (Topics in Developmental Psychobiology Ser.). 438p. 1984. 39.50x (ISBN 0-306-41563-1, Plenum Pr). Plenum Pub.

--The Development of Attachment & Affiliative Systems. LC 82-3818. (Topics in Developmental Psychobiology Ser.). 331p. 1982. text ed. 22.50 (ISBN 0-306-40849-X, Plenum Pr). Plenum Pub.

Emde, Robert N., et al. Emotion Expression in Infancy: A Biobehavioral Study. LC 76-4609. (Psychological Issues Monograph: No. 37). 210p. 1976. text ed. 20.00 (ISBN 0-8236-1651-7); pap. text ed. 18.50 (ISBN 0-8236-1650-9). Intl Univs Pr.

Emde, W. von der see Von Der Emde, W. & Tench, H. B.

Emden, Cecil S. Pepys Himself. LC 80-17177. xi, 146p. 1980. Repr. of 1963 ed. lib. bdg. 22.50x (ISBN 0-313-22607-5, EMPH). Greenwood.

Emden, P. H. Randlords. 59.95 (ISBN 0-8490-0927-8). Gordon Pr.

Emden, Paul H. Money Powers of Europe. LC 82-48302. (The World Economy Ser.). 428p. 1983. lib. bdg. 50.00 (ISBN 0-8240-5357-5). Garland Pub.

--Regency Pageant. 295p. 1980. Repr. of 1936 ed. lib. bdg. 35.00 (ISBN 0-89987-204-2). Darby Bks.

Emecheta, Buchi. The Bride Price: Young Ibo Girl's Love; Conflict of Family & Tradition. LC 75-46608. 175p. 1976. 6.95 (ISBN 0-8076-0818-1); pap. 4.95 (ISBN 0-8076-0951-X). Braziller.

--Destination Biafra. 272p. 1982. 14.95 (ISBN 0-8052-8119-3, Pub. by Allison & Busby England). Schocken.

--Double Yoke. LC 83-7048. 163p. 1983. 12.95 (ISBN 0-8076-1078-X). Braziller.

--Double Yoke. 163p. 1985. pap. 5.95 (ISBN 0-8076-1128-X). Braziller.

--In the Ditch. 128p. 1980. pap. 4.95 (ISBN 0-8052-8010-3, Pub. by Allison & Busby England). Schocken.

--The Joys of Motherhood. LC 78-24640. 1979. 8.95 (ISBN 0-8076-0914-5); pap. 4.95 (ISBN 0-8076-0950-1). Braziller.

--The Moonlight Bride. LC 82-17816. 77p. (gr. 6-10). 1983. 7.95 (ISBN 0-8076-1062-3); pap. 4.95 (ISBN 0-8076-1063-1). Braziller.

--Nowhere to Play. LC 80-40596. 72p. (gr. 4-8). 1981. 6.95 (ISBN 0-8052-8058-8, Pub. by Allison & Busby England). Schocken.

--The Rape of Shavi. 178p. 1985. 12.95 (ISBN 0-8076-1117-4); pap. 6.95 (ISBN 0-8076-1118-2). Braziller.

--Second-Class Citizen. LC 75-10909. 175p. 1975. 6.95 (ISBN 0-8076-0801-7). Braziller.

--Second-Class Citizen. LC 82-24355. 175p. 1983. pap. 4.95 (ISBN 0-8076-1066-6). Braziller.

--The Slave Girl. LC 77-77559. 1977. 7.95 (ISBN 0-8076-0872-6); pap. 4.95 (ISBN 0-8076-0952-8). Braziller.

--The Wrestling Match. LC 82-17750. 74p. (gr. 6-10). 1983. 7.95 (ISBN 0-8076-1060-7); pap. 4.95 (ISBN 0-8076-1061-5). Braziller.

Emejuaiwe, S. D., ed. see International Conference GIAM, 6th.

Emel, Tey. The Brass Ass. 1985. 14.95 (ISBN 0-87949-260-0). Ashley Bks.

Emeleus, H. J. Chemistry of Fluorine & Its Compounds. (Current Chemical Concepts Monograph). 1969. 44.50 (ISBN 0-12-238150-5). Acad Pr.

Emeleus, H. J., ed. Advances in Inorganic Chemistry & Radiochemistry, Vol. 27. Sharpe, A. G. (Serial Publication ser.). 1983. 58.00 (ISBN 0-12-023627-3). Acad Pr.

Emeleus, H. J. & Sharp, A. G., eds. Advances in Inorganic Chemistry & Radiochemistry. Incl. Vol. 17. 1975. 85.00 (ISBN 0-12-023617-6); Vol. 18. 1976. 85.00 (ISBN 0-12-023618-4); Vol. 19. 1976. 85.00 (ISBN 0-12-023619-2). (Serial Publication). Acad Pr.

Emeleus, H. J. & Sharpe, A. G., eds. Advances in Inorganic Chemistry & Radiochemistry. Incl. Vol. 1. 1959. 85.00 (ISBN 0-12-023601-X); Vol. 2. 1960. 85.00 (ISBN 0-12-023602-8); Vol. 3. 1961. 85.00 (ISBN 0-12-023603-6); Vol. 4. 1962. 85.00 (ISBN 0-12-023604-4); Vol. 5. 1963. 85.00 (ISBN 0-12-023605-2); Vol. 6. 1964. 85.00 (ISBN 0-12-023606-0); Vol. 7. 1965. 85.00 (ISBN 0-12-023607-9); Vol. 8. 1966. 85.00 (ISBN 0-12-023608-7); Vol. 9. 1966. 85.00 (ISBN 0-12-023609-5); Vol. 10. 1968. 85.00 (ISBN 0-12-023610-9); Vol. 11. 1968. 85.00 (ISBN 0-12-023611-7); Vol. 12. 1970. 85.00 (ISBN 0-12-023612-5); Vol. 13. 1970. 85.00 (ISBN 0-12-023613-3); Vol. 14. 1972. 85.00 (ISBN 0-12-023614-1); Vol. 15. 1972. 85.00 (ISBN 0-12-023615-X); Vol. 16. 1974. 85.00 (ISBN 0-12-023616-8); Vol. 20. 1977. 85.00 (ISBN 0-12-023620-6); Vol. 21. 1978. 75.00 (ISBN 0-12-023621-4); Vol. 22. 1979. 80.00 (ISBN 0-12-023622-2). Acad Pr.

--Advances in Inorganic Chemistry & Radiochemistry, Vol. 23. 1980. 80.00 (ISBN 0-12-023623-0). Acad Pr.

--Advances in Inorganic Chemistry & Radiochemistry, Vol. 24. (Serial Publication Ser.). 1981. 70.00 (ISBN 0-12-023624-9). Acad Pr.

--Advances in Inorganic Chemistry & Radiochemistry, Vol. 25. 340p. 1982. 70.00 (ISBN 0-12-023625-7). Acad Pr.

--Advances in Inorganic Chemistry & Radiochemistry, Vol. 28. 1984. 58.00 (ISBN 0-12-023628-1). Acad Pr.

--Advances in Inorganic Chemistry & Radiochemistry, Vol. 29. (Serial Publication). Date not set. price not set (ISBN 0-12-023629-X). Acad Pr.

Emeleus, H. J., jt. ed. see Sharpe, A. G.

Emelity, L. A. Operation & Control of Ion-Exchange Processes for Treatment of Radioactive Wastes. (Technical Reports Ser.: No. 78). (Illus.). 145p. 1967. pap. 10.00 (ISBN 92-0-125067-3, IDC78, IAEA). Unipub.

Emeljanow, Victor, ed. Chekhov: The Critical Heritage. (The Critical Heritage Ser.). 496p. 1981. 50.00x (ISBN 0-7100-0374-9). Routledge & Kegan.

Emellos, Ruth P., jt. auth. see Van Arsdale, May B.

Emelus, K. G. & Woolsey, G. A., eds. Discharges in Electronegative Gases. 162p. 1970. cancelled (ISBN 0-85066-035-1). Taylor & Francis.

Emel'yanova, V. S. & Evstyukhin, A. I., eds. High Purity Metals & Alloys: Fabrication, Properties, & Testing. LC 67-19386. 175p. 1967. 35.00x (ISBN 0-306-10793-7, Consultants). Plenum Pub.

Emeneau, M. B., jt. ed. see Burrow, T.

Emeneau, M. B., tr. see Kalidasa.

Emeneau, M. B., tr. see Vetalapanchavimsati.

Emeneau, Murray B. Brahui & Dravidian Comparative Grammar. LC 62-63439. (University of California Publications in Linguistics Ser.: Vol. 27). pap. 25.80 (ISBN 0-317-10121-8, 2011685). Bks Demand UMI.

--Kota Texts, 2 vols. in 1. LC 78-67707. (The Folktale). 31.50 (ISBN 0-404-16084-0). AMS Pr.

--Language & Linguistic Area: Essays by Murray B. Emeneau. Dil, Anwar S., ed. LC 79-66058. (Language Science & National Development Ser.). xvi, 372p. 1980. 27.50x (ISBN 0-8047-1047-3). Stanford U Pr.

--Ritual Structure & Language Structure of the Todas. LC 74-84603. (Transactions Ser.: Vol. 64, Pt. 6). 1974. 10.00. Am Philos.

--The Strangling Figs in Sanskrit Literature. LC 49-2733. (University of California Publications in Classical Philology: Vol. 13, No. 10). pap. 20.00 (ISBN 0-317-09833-0, 2021166). Bks Demand UMI.

--Today Grammar & Texts. LC 82-72155. (Memoirs Ser.: Vol. 155). 1984. 35.00 (ISBN 0-87169-155-8); pap. 29.00. Am Philos.

Emeneau, Murray B. & Burrow, T. Dravidian Borrowings from Indo-Aryan. LC 62-63438. (University of California Publications in Linguistics: Vol. 26). pap. 32.80 (ISBN 0-317-10183-8, 2011684). Bks Demand UMI.

Emeneau, Murray B., compiled by. Union List of Printed Indic Texts & Translations in American Libraries. (Amer Oriental Ser.). 1935. 37.00 (ISBN 0-527-02681-6). Kraus Repr.

Emenegger, Robert. UFO's Past, Present & Future. 1980. pap. 2.75 (ISBN 0-345-29047-X). Ballantine.

Emener, William G. Rehabilitation, Administration, & Supervision. LC 81-11576. (Illus.). 416p. (Orig.). 1981. pap. 19.00 (ISBN 0-8391-1688-8). Pro Ed.

--Rehabilitation Counselor Preparation & Development: Selected Critical Issues. 434p. 1985. 39.50x (ISBN 0-398-05173-9). C C Thomas.

Emener, William G., et al. Critical Issues in Rehabilitation Counseling. (Illus.). 224p. 1984. 29.50x (ISBN 0-398-04882-7). C C Thomas.

Emenheiser, Daniel A. Professional Discotheque Management. LC 80-20910. 248p. 1980. 22.95 (ISBN 0-8436-0768-8). Van Nos Reinhold.

Emenhiser, Jedon A., ed. Rocky Mountain Urban Politics. 166p. (Orig.). 1971. pap. 6.95 (ISBN 0-87421-041-0). Utah St U Pr.

Emergency Program Branches of the I. W. W. Industrial Unionist, Vols. 1-2. Repr. lib. bdg. 155.00x (ISBN 0-8371-9165-3, IN00). Greenwood.

Emerich, A. D., ed. Community Industries of the Shakers: A New Look. Benning, A. H. (Illus.). 48p. 1983. pap. 8.00 (ISBN 0-89062-154-3). Shaker Her Soc.

Emerick, Lon. ALD: A New Test for Aphasia. 27.00 (ISBN 0-686-69371-X). Northern Mich.

--Parent Interview: Guidelines for Student & Practicing Speech Clinicians. LC 77-76575. 1969. pap. 1.50x (ISBN 0-8134-1090-8, 1090). Interstate.

Emerick, Lon, jt. auth. see Van Riper, Charles.

Emerick, Lon L. A Casebook of Diagnosis & Evaluation in Speech Pathology. (Illus.). 224p. 1981. pap. text ed. 20.95 (ISBN 0-13-117358-8). P-H.

--Speaking for Ourselves. 86p. 1984. pap. text ed. 6.75x (ISBN 0-8134-2313-9, 2319). Interstate.

--Therapy for Young Stutterers. LC 71-100553. 1970. pap. 1.95x (ISBN 0-8134-1128-9, 1128). Interstate.

--With Slow & Halting Tongue. 1983. pap. 0.50 (ISBN 0-8134-2311-2). Interstate.

--A Workbook in Clinical Audiometry. (Illus.). 152p. 1971. spiral 14.50x (ISBN 0-398-02159-7). C C Thomas.

Emerick, Lon L. & Hatten, John T. Diagnosis & Evaluation in Speech Pathology. 2nd ed. (Illus.). 1979. ref. ed. 27.95 (ISBN 0-13-208512-7). P-H.

Emerick, Lon L. & Haynes, William O. Diagnosis & Evaluation in Speech Pathology. 3rd ed. (Illus.). 368p. 1986. text ed. 28.95 (ISBN 0-13-208646-8). P-H.

Emerick, Lon L. & Jupin, Lawrence. That's Easy For You to Say: An Assault on Stuttering. LC 85-417. 264p. 1985. pap. 8.95 (ISBN 0-932620-43-4). Betterway Pubns.

Emerick, Robert H. Troubleshooters Handbook for Mechanical Systems. LC 68-28413. (Illus.). 1969. 49.50 (ISBN 0-07-019314-2). McGraw.

Emerik, John C., jt. auth. see Mutel, Cornelia F.

Emerine, Richard, et al. A Planning Study for Investigation of Corporate Structures in the Telecommunications Common Carrier Industry. 1973. pap. 18.00x (ISBN 0-89011-462-5, TEC-101). Abt Bks.

Emerine, Steve, ed. see Sheaffer, Jack.

Emeritus, jt. auth. see Verkade, Pieter E.

Emerson & Imbode. Aquatic Dynamics. (Environmental Science & Technology Ser.). 1986. price not set (ISBN 0-471-81272-2). Wiley.

Emerson & Johnson, G. M., eds. The Journals & Miscellaneous Notebooks of Ralph Waldo Emerson: 1866-1882, Vol. 16. (Illus.). 624p. 1982. text ed. 45.00x (ISBN 0-674-48479-7). Harvard U Pr.

Emerson, A. R. Handmade Jewelry. (Illus.). 83p. 1977. pap. 5.50 (ISBN 0-85219-011-5, Pub. by Batsford England). David & Charles.

Emerson, Ann-Jannette. James & Mary Veatch Ellis: Their Sons & Other Descendants. LC 85-80122. (Illus.). 512p. Date not set. price not set (ISBN 0-9614755-0-1). R C Emerson.

Emerson, B. K., et al. Geology & Paleontology. (Harriman Alaska Expedition, 1899 Ser.). Repr. of 1904 ed. 41.00 (ISBN 0-527-38164-0). Kraus Repr.

Emerson, Bill & Tamagni, Judy. Ain't Possible. 1983. 8.95 (ISBN 0-533-04829-X). Vantage.

Emerson, C. & Warr, P. G. Economic Evaluation of Mineral Processing Projects. (Development Studies Centre: Occ. pap. 32). 29p. 1983. pap. text ed. 5.95 (ISBN 0-909150-91-5, Pub. by ANUP Australia). Australia N U P.

Emerson, Carl, tr. see Bakhtin, Mikhail.

Emerson, Caryl, ed. see Bakhtin, Mikhail.

Emerson, Caryl, tr. see Bakhtin, M. M.

Emerson, Charles L. & Emerson, Elma H. Hatful of Stars. 244p. 1985. 16.95 (ISBN 0-8059-2941-X). Dorrance.

Emerson, Connie. How to Make Money Writing Fillers. 266p. (Orig.). 1985. pap. 8.95 (ISBN 0-89879-196-0, 1389). Writers Digest.

--Write on Target. LC 81-11668. 1981. 12.95 (ISBN 0-89879-062-X). Writers Digest.

Emerson, Donald E. Richard Hildreth. LC 78-64201. (Johns Hopkins University. Studies in the Social Sciences. Sixty-Fourth Ser. 1946: 2). Repr. of 1946 ed. 18.50 (ISBN 0-404-61307-1). AMS Pr.

Emerson, Dorothy. Among the Mescalero Apaches: The Story of Father Albert Braun, O. F. M. LC 73-76302. 224p. 1973. pap. 8.50 (ISBN 0-8165-0714-7). U of Ariz Pr.

Emerson, E. W. Life & Letters of Charles Russell Lowell. 499p. 1980. Repr. of 1907 ed. lib. bdg. 20.00 (ISBN 0-89984-176-7). Century Bookbindery.

Emerson, Earl W. Poverty Bay. 256p. 1985. pap. 2.95 (ISBN 0-380-89647-8). Avon.

--The Rainy City. (Thomas Black Ser. No. 1). 240p. 1985. pap. 2.95 (ISBN 0-380-89517-X). Avon.

Emerson, Earle W. Fill the World with Phantoms. (Orig.). 1979. pap. 1.75 (ISBN 0-532-17215-9). Woodhill.

Emerson, Edward W. Charles Eliot Norton: Two Addresses. 1973. Repr. of 1912 ed. 15.00 (ISBN 0-8274-1441-2). R West.

--Early Years of the Saturday Club, 1855-1870. facs. ed. LC 67-23211. (Essay Index Reprint Ser). 1918. 24.50 (ISBN 0-8369-0415-X). Ayer Co Pubs.

--Emerson in Concord. LC 79-78149. (Library of Lives & Letters). (Illus.). 1970. Repr. of 1889 ed. 40.00x (ISBN 0-8103-3601-4). Gale.

--Emerson in Concord: A Memoir. 1889. lib. bdg. 8.25 (ISBN 0-8414-3999-0). Folcroft.

--Henry Thoreau As Remembered by a Young Friend. LC 68-19227. (Illus.). 1968. Repr. of 1917 ed. 3.00 (ISBN 0-912130-00-8). Thoreau Found.

--Life & Letters of Charles Russell Lowell. LC 71-137909. (American History & Culture in the Nineteenth Century Ser). 1971. Repr. of 1907 ed. 36.50x (ISBN 0-8046-1477-6, Pub. by Kennikat). Assoc Faculty Pr.

--Life & Letters of Charles Russell Lowell. 1973. Repr. of 1907 ed. 15.00 (ISBN 0-8274-1585-0). R West.

Emerson, Edward W., ed. Correspondence Between John Sterling & Ralph Waldo Emerson with a Sketch of Sterling's Life. LC 70-122649. 1971. Repr. of 1897 ed. 15.00x (ISBN 0-8046-1297-8, Pub. by Kennikat). Assoc Faculty Pr.

Emerson, Edward W., ed. see Emerson, Ralph Waldo.

Emerson, Edwin. A History of the Nineteenth Century Year by Year, 3 vols. 1980. lib. bdg. 495.00 (ISBN 0-8490-3206-7). Gordon Pr.

--A History of the 19th Century Year by Year, 3 vols. 1977. lib. bdg. 300.00 (ISBN 0-8490-2009-3). Gordon Pr.

Emerson, Ellen. Indian Myths. 59.95 (ISBN 0-8490-0400-4). Gordon Pr.

Emerson, Ellen R. Masks, Heads, & Faces with Some Considerations Respecting the Rise & Development of Art. (Illus.). 1979. Repr. of 1891 ed. lib. bdg. 45.00 (ISBN 0-8495-1324-3). Arden Lib.

Emerson, Ellen T. The Life of Jackson Emerson. Hall, G. K., ed. LC 80-14908. (Twayne's American Literary Manuscript Ser.). (Illus.). 269p. 1981. 26.00 (ISBN 0-8057-9651-7, Twayne). G K Hall.

Emerson, Elma H., jt. auth. see Emerson, Charles L.

Emerson, Everett. The Authentic Mark Twain: A Literary Biography of Samuel L. Clemens. LC 83-10626. 330p. 1984. 29.95x (ISBN 0-8122-7897-6). U of Pa Pr.

--The Authentic Mark Twain: A Literary Biography of Samuel L. Clemens. LC 83-10626. (Illus.). 360p. 1985. pap. text ed. 14.95 (ISBN 0-8122-1214-2). U of Pa Pr.

--Puritanism in America. (World Leaders Ser.). 1977. lib. bdg. 12.50 (ISBN 0-8057-7692-3, Twayne). G K Hall.

Emerson, Everett, ed. American Literature, Seventeen Sixty-Four to Seventeen Eighty-Nine: The Revolutionary Years. 320p. 1977. 29.50x (ISBN 0-299-07270-3). U of Wis Pr.

Emerson, Everett & Bernhard, Winfred E., eds. Letters from New England: The Massachusetts Bay Colony, 1629-1638. LC 75-32484. (The Commonwealth Ser.: Vol. 2). 286p. 1976. 17.50x (ISBN 0-87023-209-6). U of Mass Pr.

Emerson, Everett H. John Cotton. (Twayne's United States Authors Ser). 1965. pap. 5.95x (ISBN 0-8084-0180-7, T80, Twayne). New Coll U Pr.

Emerson, Everett H., ed. Major Writers of Early American Literature: Introductions to Nine Major Writers. LC 72-1378. 310p. 1972. 25.00x (ISBN 0-299-06190-6); pap. 9.95t (ISBN 0-299-06194-9). U of Wis Pr.

Emerson, Frank C., ed. Economics of Environmental Problems. (Michigan Business Papers: No. 58). 114p. 1973. pap. 5.00 (ISBN 0-87712-108-7). U Mich Busn Div Res.

Emerson, Geraldine M., ed. Aging. (Benchmark Papers in Human Physiology: Vol. 11). 1977. 56.00 (ISBN 0-12-786420-2). Acad Pr.

Emerson, Gloria. Some American Men. 1985. 17.95 (ISBN 0-671-24588-0). S&S.

--Winners & Losers. 432p. 1985. pap. 7.95 (ISBN 0-14-008216-6). Penguin.

Emerson, Harrington. Efficiency As a Basis for Operation & Wages. Chandler, Alfred D., ed. LC 79-7545. (History of Management Thought & Practice Ser.). 1980. Repr. of 1909 ed. lib. bdg. 16.00x (ISBN 0-405-12329-9). Ayer Co Pubs.

--Efficiency As a Basis for Operation & Wages. 4th ed. LC 75-16248. (Management History Ser.: No. 63). 266p. Repr. of 1914 ed. 17.50 (ISBN 0-87960-069-1). Hive Pub.

--Twelve Principles of Efficiency. 5th ed. LC 76-5897. (Management History Ser.: No. 32). 441p. Repr. of 1919 ed. 23.75 (ISBN 0-87960-042-X). Hive Pub.

Emerson, Haven. A Monograph on the Epidemic of Poliomyelitis (Infantile Paralysis) in New York City in 1946. Rosenkrantz, Barbara G., ed. LC 76-25662. (Public Health in America Ser.). (Illus.). 1977. Repr. of 1917 ed. lib. bdg. 37.50x (ISBN 0-405-09817-0). Ayer Co Pubs.

Emerson, Haven & Luginbuhl, Martha. Local Health Units for the Nation. Rosenkrantz, Barbara G., ed. LC 76-25661. (Public Health in America Ser.). (Illus.). 1977. Repr. of 1945 ed. lib. bdg. 29.00x (ISBN 0-405-09816-2). Ayer Co Pubs.

Emerson, Haven & Grob, Gerald N., eds. Alcohol & Man: The Effects of Alcohol on Man in Health & Disease. LC 80-1227. (Addiction in America Ser.). 1981. Repr. of 1932 ed. lib. bdg. 38.00x (ISBN 0-405-13585-8). Ayer Co Pubs.

Emerson, Hough. The Covered Wagon. 19.95 (ISBN 0-89190-617-7, Pub. by Am Repr). Amereon Ltd.

Emerson, James C., ed. The Life of Christ in the Conception & Expression of Chinese & Oriental Artists. (The Great Art Masters of the World Ser.). (Illus.). 117p. 1983. 61.75 (ISBN 0-86650-054-5). Gloucester Art.

Emerson, Janet. Only You. (Turning Points Ser.: No. 12). 1985. pap. 2.50 (ISBN 0-451-13534-2, Sig Vista). NAL.

Emerson, Jill. Week As Andrea Benstock. LC 74-18161. 1975. 7.95 (ISBN 0-87795-100-4). Arbor Hse.

Emerson, Julie. The Collectors: Early European Ceramics & Silver. LC 82-60159. (Illus.). 94p. (Orig.). 1982. pap. 15.95 (ISBN 0-932216-08-0). Seattle Art.

Emerson, Katherine, ed. Symposium on Measurement of Reference. 66p. 1974. 4.00 (ISBN 0-317-34820-5). Library Admin.

Emerson, Kathy L. The Mystery of Hilliard's Castle. (gr. 6-9). 1985. pap. 6.95 (ISBN 0-89272-213-4). Down East.

--Wives & Daughters: The Women of Sixteenth Century England. LC 82-50408. 1984. 30.00 (ISBN 0-87875-246-3). Whitston Pub.

Emerson, Larry & Oleksy, Walter. Builder's & Contractor's Guide to New Methods & Materials in Home Construction. LC 82-23098. 283p. 1983. 45.00 (ISBN 0-13-086033-6). P-H.

Emerson, Lloyd & Paquette, Laurence. Fundamental Mathematics for the Management & Social Sciences. alt. ed. 688p. 1981. text ed. 30.31 (ISBN 0-205-07166-X, 567166-3); tchrs. ed. o. p. avail. Allyn.

Emerson, Mark. Two by Two Romance, No. 14: Looking at You. (Romance Ser.). (Illus.). 160p. 1984. pap. 2.25 (ISBN 0-446-32170-2). Warner Bks.

Emerson, Michael, ed. Europe's Stagflation: Causes & Cures. 1984. 16.95x (ISBN 0-19-828487-X). Oxford U Pr.

Emerson, Nathaniel B. Pele & Hiiaka: A Myth from Hawaii. LC 75-35190. Repr. of 1915 ed. 22.50 (ISBN 0-404-14218-4). AMS Pr.

--Pele & Hiiaka: A Myth from Hawaii. LC 77-83040. (Illus.). 1978. 15.00 (ISBN 0-8048-1251-9). C E Tuttle.

--Unwritten Literature of Hawaii: The Sacred Songs of the Hula. LC 65-12971. (Illus.). 1965. pap. 5.50 (ISBN 0-8048-1067-2). C E Tuttle.

--Unwritten Literature of Hawaii; the Sacred Songs of the Hula. Repr. of 1909 ed. 39.00x (ISBN 0-403-03720-4). Scholarly.

Emerson, O. B. Billy Budd Notes. Bd. with Typee Notes. (Orig.). 1968. pap. 3.25 (ISBN 0-8220-0238-8). Cliffs.

--Faulkner's Early Literary Reputation in America. Litz, Walton, ed. LC 83-18321. (Studies in Modern Literature: No. 30). 430p. 1984. 49.95 (ISBN 0-8357-1467-5). UMI Res Pr.

Emerson, O. B. & Michael, Marion C., eds. Southern Literary Culture: A Bibliography of Masters' & Doctors' Theses. LC 78-10771. 400p. 1979. 25.00 (ISBN 0-8173-9514-8). U of Ala Pr.

Emerson, O. F. A Brief History of the English Language. 1925. 30.00 (ISBN 0-8274-1977-5). R West.

--The History of the English Language. 1895. 30.00 (ISBN 0-8274-2505-8). R West.

Emerson, Oliver F. Chaucer - Essays & Studies: A Selection from the Writings of Oliver Farrar Emerson, 1860-1927. 1929. 16.00 (ISBN 0-8274-2049-8). R West.

--Chaucer Essays & Studies. LC 76-40304. 1929. lib. bdg. 45.00 (ISBN 0-8414-3984-2). Folcroft.

--Chaucer; Essays & Studies. 455p. 1980. Repr. of 1929 ed. lib. bdg. 45.00 (ISBN 0-8482-0719-X). Norwood Edns.

--Chaucer: Essays & Studies-a Selection from the Writings of Oliver Farrar Emerson, 1860-1927. LC 78-114907. (Select Bibliographies Reprint Ser). 1929. 27.50 (ISBN 0-8369-5311-8). Ayer Co Pubs.

--History of the English Language. LC 70-145520. 1971. Repr. of 1909 ed. 45.00x (ISBN 0-8103-3666-9). Gale.

--John Dryden & a British Academy. LC 74-13154. 1921. lib. bdg. 5.00 (ISBN 0-8414-3964-8). Folcroft.

--A Middle English Reader. LC 75-41087. Repr. of 1905 ed. 34.50 (ISBN 0-404-14784-4). AMS Pr.

--A Middle English Reader. 1977. Repr. of 1932 ed. lib. bdg. 40.00 (ISBN 0-8492-0724-X). R West.

--An Outline History of the English Language. 1973. lib. bdg. 15.00 (ISBN 0-8414-3973-7). Folcroft.

Emerson, Oliver F., ed. A Middle English Reader: Edited, with Grammatical Introduction, Notes & Glossary. 478p. 1981. Repr. of 1978 ed. lib. bdg. 50.00 (ISBN 0-89987-212-3). Darby Bks.

Emerson, Peter, ed. Thoracic Medicine. 1981. text ed. 99.95 (ISBN 0-407-00210-3). Butterworth.

Emerson, Peter H. Naturalistic Photography for Students of the Art. LC 72-9195. (The Literature of Photography Ser.). Repr. of 1889 ed. 21.00 (ISBN 0-405-04905-6). Ayer Co Pubs.

--Naturalistic Photography for Students of the Art. 3rd ed. Incl. The Death of Naturalistic Photography. LC 72-9197. (The Literature of Photography Ser.). 20.00 (ISBN 0-405-04906-4); pap. 4.95 (ISBN 0-685-32644-6). Ayer Co Pubs.

Emerson, Peter M., jt. ed. see Johnston, George M.

Emerson, R. W. Napoleon: The Man of the World. Davidson, F., ed. 1947. pap. 6.00 (ISBN 0-527-27150-0). Kraus Repr.

Emerson, R. W., tr. see Dante Alighieri.

Emerson, Ralph W. Emerson's Essays. LC 17-32304. 438p. 1981. pap. 5.72i (ISBN 0-06-090906-4, CN906, CN). Har-Row.

Emerson, Ralph Waldo. Collected Works of Ralph Waldo Emerson: Nature, Addresses, & Lectures, Vol. 1. Ferguson, Alfred E., et al, eds. 1979. 22.50x (ISBN 0-674-13970-4); pap. 8.95x (ISBN 0-674-60476-8). Harvard U Pr.

--The Collected Works of Ralph Waldo Emerson. Slater, Joseph, ed. (First Series: Vol. 2). 1979. 27.50x (ISBN 0-674-13980-1, Belknap Pr). Harvard U Pr.

--Complete Works, 12 Vols. Emerson, Edward W., ed. LC 79-15830. Repr. of 1904 ed. Set. 348.00 (ISBN 0-404-05480-3); 29.00 ea. AMS Pr.

--The Correspondence of Thomas Carlyle & Ralph Waldo Emerson, 2 vols. Repr. of 1883 ed. 50.00 (ISBN 0-8274-3836-2). R West.

--Early Lectures of Ralph Waldo Emerson, Vols. 1 & 3. Incl. Vol. 1. Whicher, Stephen E., ed. (Illus.). 1964. 27.50x (ISBN 0-674-22150-8); Vol. 3. 1838-1842. Spiller, Robert E. & Williams, Wallace E., eds. 1972. 32.50x (ISBN 0-674-22152-4). LC 59-5160 (Belknap Pr). Harvard U Pr.

--Emerson-Clough Letters. LC 77-7319. 1977. lib. bdg. 15.00 (ISBN 0-8414-5820-0). Folcroft.

--Emerson Year Book. LC 77-7292. 1977. lib. bdg. 17.50 (ISBN 0-8414-1729-6). Folcroft.

--Emerson's Literary Criticism. Carlson, Eric W., ed. LC 75-38053. (Regents Critics Ser.). l, 251p. 1979. 21.50x (ISBN 0-8032-1403-0). U of Nebr Pr.

--English Traits. Jones, Howard M., ed. LC 66-23464. (The John Harvard Library). 1966. 16.50x (ISBN 0-674-25725-1). Harvard U Pr.

--Essays. 378p. 1980. 12.95x (ISBN 0-460-00012-8, Evman); pap. 4.95x (ISBN 0-460-01012-3, Evman). Biblio Dist.

--Essays. Ferguson, Alfred R. & Carr, Jean F., eds. (Second Ser.: Vol. III). (Illus.). 320p. 1983. text ed. 25.00x (ISBN 0-674-13990-9, Belknap Pr). Harvard U Pr.

--Essays & Essays. LC 79-100634. (Merrill Standard Ser). 1975. pap. 4.00 (ISBN 0-675-09388-0). Brown Bk.

--Essays & Lectures. Porte, Joel, ed. LC 83-5447. 1344p. 1983. 27.50 (ISBN 0-940450-15-1, Pub. by Library of America). Literary Classics.

--Essays: First & Second Series. (Riverside Library). 16.95 (ISBN 0-395-08125-4). HM.

--Essays of Emerson. Spiller, Robert E., ed. 416p. pap. 3.95 (ISBN 0-671-44148-5). WSP.

--Five Essays on Man & Nature. Spiller, Robert E., ed. LC 54-9979. (Crofts Classics Ser). 128p. 1954. pap. 3.75x (ISBN 0-88295-034-7). Harlan Davidson.

--In Praise of Books. 116p. 1981. Repr. of 1901 ed. lib. bdg. 30.00 (ISBN 0-8495-1427-4). Arden Lib.

--Journals & Miscellaneous Notebooks of Ralph Waldo Emerson, 16 Vols. Incl. Vol. 1. 1819-1822. Gilman, W. H., et al, eds. 1960. 30.00x (ISBN 0-674-48450-9); Vol. 2. 1822-1826. Gilman, W. H., et al, eds. 1961. 30.00x (ISBN 0-674-48451-7); Vol. 4. 1832-1834. Ferguson, Alfred R., ed. 1964; Vol. 5. 1835-1838. Sealts, M. M., Jr., ed. 1965. 30.00x (ISBN 0-674-48454-1); Vol. 6. 1824-1838. Orth, Ralph W., ed. 1966. 30.00x (ISBN 0-674-48456-8); Vol. 7. 1838-1842. Plumstead, A. W. & Hayford, Harrison, eds. 1969. 30.00x (ISBN 0-674-48457-6); Vol. 8. 1841-1843. Gilman, W. H. & Parsons, J. E., eds. 1970. 32.50x (ISBN 0-674-48470-3); Vol. 9. 1843-1847. Orth, Ralph H. & Ferguson, Alfred R., eds. 1971. 30.00x (ISBN 0-674-48471-1); Vol. 10. 1847-1848. Sealts, Merton M., Jr., ed. 1973. 32.50x (ISBN 0-674-48473-8); Vol. 11. 1848-1851. Gilman, William H. & Plumstead, A. W., eds. 1975. text ed. 35.00x (ISBN 0-674-48474-6); Vol. 12. 1835-1862. Allardt, Linda, ed. 1976. 37.50x (ISBN 0-674-48475-4); Vol. 13. 525p. 1977. text ed. 35.00 (ISBN 0-674-48476-2); Vol. 14. 523p. 1978. text ed. 37.50x (ISBN 0-674-48477-0); Vol. 15. 1860-1866. 608p. 1982. text ed. 40.00x (ISBN 0-674-48478-9). LC 60-11554. (Illus., Belknap Pr). Harvard U Pr.

--Letters from Ralph Waldo Emerson to a Friend, 1838-1853. Norton, Charles E., ed. LC 78-122651. 1971. Repr. of 1899 ed. 16.50x (ISBN 0-8046-1299-4, Pub. by Kennikat). Assoc Faculty Pr.

--Letters of Ralph Waldo Emerson, 6 Vols. Rusk, R. L., ed. LC 39-12289. 1939. Set. 220.00x (ISBN 0-231-00724-8). Columbia U Pr.

--Light of Emerson. 337p. 1980. Repr. of 1930 ed. lib. bdg. 37.50 (ISBN 0-8482-0737-8). Norwood Edns.

--On Love & Friendship. 4.95 (ISBN 0-88088-141-0). Peter Pauper.

--On Man & God. 1961. 4.95 (ISBN 0-88088-145-3). Peter Pauper.

--Parnassus. 2nd ed. 1972. Repr. of 1875 ed. lib. bdg. 14.00 (ISBN 0-8422-8043-X). Irvington.

--Parnassus. 1973. Repr. of 1874 ed. 35.00 (ISBN 0-8274-0590-1). R West.

--The Portable Emerson. Bode, Carl & Cowley, Malcolm, eds. 664p. 1981. pap. 6.95 (ISBN 0-14-015094-3). Penguin.

--Representative Men. Simon, Myron, ed. LC 79-92838. (The Mind of Man Ser.). (Illus.). 224p. 1980. text ed. 30.00 (ISBN 0-934710-02-3). J Simon.

--Select Writings of Ralph Waldo Emerson. 351p. 1980. Repr. lib. bdg. 15.00 (ISBN 0-89760-124-6). Telegraph Bks.

--Selected Essays. Ziff, Larzer, ed. (Penguin American Library). 360p. 1982. pap. 3.95 (ISBN 0-14-039013-8). Penguin.

--Selected Prose & Poetry. 2nd ed. Cook, Reginald L., ed. LC 69-277140. (Rinehart Editions). 1969. pap. text ed. 12.95 (ISBN 0-03-077140-4, HoltC). HR&W.

--Selected Writings. 1981. pap. 3.95x (ISBN 0-394-32981-3, T14, Mod LibC). Modern Lib.

--The Selected Writings. McQuade, Donald, ed. LC 80-27210. (Modern Library College Editions). 911p. 1981. pap. text ed. 3.95 (ISBN 0-394-32662-8, RanC). Random.

--Selected Writings of Ralph Waldo Emerson. Gilman, William H., ed. (Orig.). pap. 3.95 (ISBN 0-451-51832-2, CE1832, Sig Classics). NAL.

--The Selected Writings of Ralph Waldo Emerson. Atkinson, Brooks, ed. LC 83-42942. 1940. 9.95 (ISBN 0-394-60418-0). Modern Lib.

--Selections from Ralph Waldo Emerson. Whicher, Stephen, ed. LC 61-16166. (YA) (gr. 9 up). 1960. pap. 5.95 (ISBN 0-395-05112-6, RivEd). HM.

--Self-Reliance. 1967. 4.95 (ISBN 0-88088-149-6). Peter Pauper.

--Self Reliance. 2nd ed. Dekovic, Gene, ed. LC 75-12544. (Illus.). 96p. 1983. 12.00 (ISBN 0-937088-07-2); pap. 8.00 (ISBN 0-937088-08-0). Illum Pr.

--Uncollected Lectures. Ghodes, Clarence, ed. LC 74-13155. 1973. lib. bdg. 17.50 (ISBN 0-8414-3977-X). Folcroft.

--The Works of Ralph Waldo Emerson, 5 vols. Set. 85.00 (ISBN 0-8274-3763-3). R West.

Emerson, Ralph Waldo & Carlyle, Thomas. The Correspondence of Emerson & Carlyle. Slater, Joseph, ed. LC 63-17539. pap. 158.00 (ISBN 0-8357-9063-0, 2017253). Bks Demand UMI.

Emerson, Ralph Waldo, jt. auth. see Carlyle, Thomas.

Emerson, Ralph Waldo, ed. Parnassus. facsimile ed. LC 73-116400. (Granger Index Reprint Ser). 1874. 25.50 (ISBN 0-8369-6141-2). Ayer Co Pubs.

Emerson, Ralph Waldo, ed. see Very, Jones.

Emerson, Ralph Waldo, et al, eds. see Ossoli, Margaret F.

Emerson, Robert & Grumbach, Jane, eds. Monologues: Men. LC 76-1027. 56p. 1976. pap. 3.95x (ISBN 0-910482-78-0). Drama Bk.

--Monologues: Women. LC 76-1965. 56p. 1976. pap. 3.95x (ISBN 0-910482-79-9). Drama Bk.

Emerson, Robert, jt. ed. see Grumbach, Jane.

Emerson, Robert D., ed. Seasonal Agricultural Labor Markets in the United States. (Illus.). 564p. 1984. pap. text ed. 28.40x (ISBN 0-8138-1638-6). Iowa St U Pr.

Emerson, Robert L. Allegheny Passage: An Illustrated History of Blair County. (Illus.). 136p. 1984. 22.95 (ISBN 0-89781-098-8). Windsor Pubns Inc.

--Fast Food: The Endless Shakeout. LC 79-17145. 1979. 21.95 (ISBN 0-86730-235-6). Lebhar Friedman.

Emerson, Robert M. Contemporary Field Research: A Collection of Readings. 1983. 13.95 (ISBN 0-316-23630-6). Little.

--Judging Delinquents: Context & Process in Juvenile Court. LC 70-75047. 307p. 1969. 24.95x (ISBN 0-202-23001-5). Aldine Pub.

Emerson, Rupert. Political Modernization: The Single Party System. (Monograph Series in World Affairs: Vol. 1, 1963-64 Ser., Bk. 1). (Orig.). 1963. 3.95 (ISBN 0-87940-000-5). Monograph Series.

--Self-Determination Revisited in the Era of Decolonization. (Occasional Papers in International Affairs: No. 9). 70p. 1984. pap. text ed. 6.25 (ISBN 0-8191-4050-3). U Pr of Amer.

--State & Sovereignty in Modern Germany. LC 79-1626. 1981. Repr. of 1928 ed. 22.50 (ISBN 0-88355-931-5). Hyperion Conn.

Emerson, Rupert & Kilson, Martin, eds. The Political Awakening of Africa. LC 81-4166. (The Global History Ser.: No. S-124). x, 175p. 1981. Repr. of 1965 ed. lib. bdg. 19.75x (ISBN 0-313-23013-7, EMPA). Greenwood.

Emerson, Rupert, et al. Government & Nationalism in Southeast Asia. LC 75-30120. (Institute of Pacific Relations). Repr. of 1942 ed. 24.50 (ISBN 0-404-59519-7). AMS Pr.

Emerson, S. U., et al. Current Topics in Microbiology & Immunology, Vol. 73. LC 15-12910. 1976. 49.00 (ISBN 0-387-07593-3). Springer-Verlag.

Emerson, Sally. Listeners. 174p. 1984. 14.95 (ISBN 0-7181-2134-1, Pub. by Michael Joseph). Merrimack Pub Cir.

Emerson, Sandra L. & Darnovsky, Marcy. Database for the IBM PC. LC 84-9377. 1438p. 1984. pap. 14.95 (ISBN 0-201-10483-0). Addison-Wesley.

Emerson, Stephen. Neighbors. 100p. (Orig.). 1982. pap. 6.00 (ISBN 0-939180-19-7). Tombouctou.

--The Wife. 96p. 1985. 6.00 (ISBN 0-942986-02-4). Longriver Bks.

Emerson, Steven. The American House of Saud: The Secret Petrodollar Connection. 1985. 18.95 (ISBN 0-531-09778-1). Watts.

Emerson, Terrance R. Coin Investor's Handbook: A Numismatic Primer & Resource Guide to the Commercial Coin Market. 288p. 1985. 21.95 (ISBN 0-13-140419-9); pap. 14.95 (ISBN 0-13-140401-6). P-H.

Emerson, Thomas E. Mississippian Stone Images in Illinois: Circular Number Six. (Illus.). 50p. (Orig.). 1982. pap. write for info. (ISBN 0-942704-00-2). U IL-Archaeological.

Emerson, Thomas E. & Jackson, Douglas K. The BBB Motor Site. LC 83-18196. (American Bottom Archaeology: Selected Fai-270 Site Reports Ser.: Vol. 6). (Illus.). 454p. 1984. pap. 13.95 (ISBN 0-252-01068-X). U of Ill Pr.

Emerson, Thomas E., jt. auth. see Fortier, Andrew C.

Emerson, Thomas E., et al. The Florence Street Site. (American Bottom Archaeology: Selected FAI-270 Site Reports Ser.: Vol. 2). (Illus.). 366p. 1983. pap. 12.95x (ISBN 0-252-01064-7). U of Ill Pr.

Emerson, Thomas I. System of Freedom of Expression. LC 75-102331. 1971. pap. 7.95 (ISBN 0-394-71143-2, V143, Vin). Random.

Emerson, Tom. Hangar Flying: The Story of One Man's Fascination with Airplanes. LC 84-50972. (Gem Books - Historical). (Illus.). 340p. (Orig.). pap. cancelled (ISBN 0-317-05981-5). U Pr of Idaho.

Emerson, Vivian J. The Measurement of Breath Alcohol. 70p. 1981. 30.00x (ISBN 0-9502425-7-8, Pub. by Scottish Academic Pr Scotland). Columbia U Pr.

Emerson, W. A., jt. auth. see Irwin, James B., Jr.

Emerson, W. K., jt. auth. see Jacobson, M. K.

Emerson, W. W., et al, eds. Modification of Soil Structure. 438p. 1978. 101.95 (ISBN 0-471-99530-4, Pub. by Wiley-Interscience). Wiley.

Emerson, William A., ed. see Aston, Athina.

Emerson, William A., Jr., jt. auth. see Irwin, James B.

Emerson, William K. Chevrons: Illustrated History & Catalog of U. S. Army Insignia. LC 82-600002. (Illus.). 298p. 1983. text ed. 49.50 (ISBN 0-87474-412-1). Smithsonian.

Emerson, William K. & Jacobson, Morris K. American Museum of Natural History Guide to Shells. 1976. 8.95 (ISBN 0-394-73048-8). Knopf.

Emerson, William M. Tennessee Supplement for Modern Real Estate Practice. 130p. (Orig.). 1981. pap. 8.95 (ISBN 0-88462-338-6, 1510-46, Real Estate Ed). Longman USA.

Emerson, William S. Guide to the Chemical Industry: Technology, R & D, Marketing, & Employment. LC 83-7035. 336p. 1983. 37.50 (ISBN 0-471-89040-5, Pub. by Wiley-Interscience). Wiley.

Emerson, Willis G. Smoky God. (Illus.). 1908. pap. 4.95 (ISBN 0-910122-20-2). Amherst Pr.

Emerson-Tennent, J. The Story of the Guns. 386p. 1984. Repr. of 1864 ed. 32.00x (ISBN 0-85546-167-5, Pub. by Richmond Pub England). State Mutual Bk.

Emert, Joyce R. Louis Martin: Father of a Saint. LC 83-2728. 208p. (Orig.). 1983. pap. 9.95 (ISBN 0-8189-0446-1). Alba.

Emert, Phyllis R. Illustrated Track & Field Dictionary for Young People. (Illus.). (gr. 4 up). 1981. pap. 2.50 (ISBN 0-13-451310-X). P-H.

--The Pretzel Book. LC 84-167042. (Illus.). 160p. 1984. pap. 4.95 (ISBN 0-912661-01-1). Woodsong Graph.

Emerton, E. Erasmus of Rotterdam. 59.95 (ISBN 0-8490-0122-6). Gordon Pr.

Emerton, E., tr. see Gregory Seventh, Pope.

Emerton, Ephraim. Desiderius Erasmus of Rotterdam. 1900. 35.00 (ISBN 0-8274-2167-2). R West.

--Humanism & Tyranny: Studies in the Italian Trecento. 12.00 (ISBN 0-8446-5871-5). Peter Smith.

--An Introduction to the Study of the Middle Ages: 375-814. 1979. Repr. of 1895 ed. lib. bdg. 30.00 (ISBN 0-8495-1325-1). Arden Lib.

--An Introduction to the Study of the Middle Ages (375-814) 1978. Repr. of 1900 ed. lib. bdg. 35.00 (ISBN 0-8482-0713-0). Norwood Edns.

--An Introduction to the Study of the Middle Ages. 17.50 (ISBN 0-686-17010-5). Quality Lib.

--Learning & Living: Academic Essays. facs. ed. LC 67-30209. (Essay Index Reprint Ser). 1921. 18.00 (ISBN 0-8369-0416-8). Ayer Co Pubs.

--Mediaeval Europe Eight Fourteen to Thirteen Hundred. 1978. Repr. of 1894 ed. lib. bdg. 35.00 (ISBN 0-8482-0712-2). Norwood Edns.

--Medieval Europe: Eight Fourteen to Thirteen Hundred. 1979. Repr. of 1895 ed. lib. bdg. 35.00 (ISBN 0-8492-0782-7). R West.

--Medieval Europe, Eight Fourteen to Thirteen Hundred: An Introduction to the Study of the Middle Ages, 2 vols. Set. 250.00 (ISBN 0-8490-0599-X). Gordon Pr.

Emerton, Ephraim, ed. see Boniface, Saint.

Emerton, Ephraim, ed. see Gregory Seventh, Pope.

Emerton, J. A., ed. Prophecy: Essays Presented to Georg Fohrer on His Sixty-Fifth Birthday. (Beihefte zur Zeitschrift fur Die Alttestamentliche Wissenschaft: No. 155). 240p. 1980. text ed. 36.80x (ISBN 3-11-007761-2). De Gruyter.

Emerton, J. A. & Reif, Stefan C., eds. Interpreting the Hebrew Bible. LC 81-21668. (University of Cambridge Oriental Publication Ser.: No. 32). 1982. 49.50 (ISBN 0-521-24424-2). Cambridge U Pr.

Emerton, James H. Common Spiders of the United States. 1902. pap. 4.50 (ISBN 0-486-20223-2). Dover.

--Common Spiders of the United States. 14.50 (ISBN 0-8446-2032-7). Peter Smith.

Emerton, M. D. Principles & Practice of Nursing. 2nd ed. (Nursing Ser.). (Illus.). 411p. (Orig.). 1980. pap. text ed. 15.75x (ISBN 0-7022-1522-8). U of Queensland Pr.

Emerton, Norma E. The Scientific Reinterpretation of Form. LC 84-45139. (Cornell History of Science Ser.). 318p. 1984. 29.95x (ISBN 0-8014-1583-7). Cornell U Pr.

Emerton, Wolseley P. An Abridgment of Adam Smith's Inquiry into the Nature & Causes of the Wealth of Nations. 406p. Repr. of 1881 ed. lib. bdg. 65.00 (ISBN 0-89987-217-4). Darby Bks.

Emery. Intermediate Microeconomics. (College Outline Ser.). 1984. pap. text ed. 8.95 (ISBN 0-15-600027-X, BFP). HarBraceJ.

--Principles of Economics: Microeconomics. (College Outline Ser.). 1984. pap. text ed. 9.95 (ISBN 0-15-600053-9, BFP). HarBraceJ.

--Registers for Detection & Prevention of Genetic Disease. 1979. 29.50 (ISBN 0-8151-3114-3). Year Bk Med.

Emery, jt. auth. see King.

Emery, et al. English Fundamentals: Form B. 8th ed. 333p. 1986. pap. price not set (ISBN 0-02-333120-8). Macmillan.

Emery, Alan E. Antenatal Diagnosis of Genetic Disease. LC 73-595585. (Illus.). 1973. 9.00x (ISBN 0-443-00986-4). Churchill.

--Elements of Medical Genetics. 6th ed. (Illus.). 1983. pap. text ed. 14.75 (ISBN 0-443-02724-2). Churchill.

--Recombinant DNA Technology. LC 84-11830. (Medical Publications Ser.). 1985. pap. 17.95 (ISBN 0-471-90363-9). Wiley.

Emery, Alan E. & Pullen, Ian, eds. Psychological Aspects of Genetic Counselling. 1984. 36.00 (ISBN 0-12-238220-X); pap. 16.00 (ISBN 0-12-238222-6). Acad Pr.

Emery, Anne. First Love, True Love. LC 56-5376. 192p. (gr. 7-10). 1956. 8.95 (ISBN 0-664-32140-2). Westminster.

--Stepfamily. LC 79-26908. 140p. 1980. 9.50 (ISBN 0-664-32660-9). Westminster.

Emery, C. F. Horny. LC 68-17304. (Illus.). (gr. 2 up). 1967. PLB 9.26 (ISBN 0-87783-017-7). Oddo.

Emery, Carla. The Old Fashioned Recipe Book: The Encyclopedia of Country Living. 1977. pap. 14.95 (ISBN 0-553-34080-8). Bantam.

Emery, Clark. World of Dylan Thomas. LC 61-21742. 1962. pap. 19.95x (ISBN 0-87024-308-X). U of Miami Pr.

Emery, Clark M., jt. ed. see Matthews, Arthur D.

Emery, D. W., jt. auth. see Pence, R. W.

Emery, David, jt. auth. see Seaton, Paul.

Emery, David, ed. Who's Who in International Golf. (Who's Who in Sports Ser.). (Illus.). 128p. 12.95 (ISBN 0-87196-790-1). Facts on File.

--Who's Who in International Showjumping & Equestrianism. (Who's Who in Sports Ser.). (Illus.). 128p. 1983. 12.95 (ISBN 0-87196-791-X). Facts on File.

--Who's Who in International Tennis. (Who's Who in Sports Ser.). (Illus.). 128p. 1983. 12.95 (ISBN 0-87196-789-8). Facts on File.

--Who's Who in the Nineteen Eighty-Four Olympics. pap. 9.95 (ISBN 0-318-01943-4, Pub. by Michael Joseph). Merrimack Pub Cir.

--Who's Who in the Olympics 1984. (Illus.). 192p. (Orig.). 1984. pap. 9.95 (ISBN 0-7207-1519-9). Merrimack Pub Cir.

Emery, Donald W. Sentence Analysis. LC 61-15386. 1961. pap. text ed. 14.95 (ISBN 0-03-010770-9, HoltC). HR&W.

--Variant Spellings in Modern American Dictionaries. rev. ed. LC 73-83843. 130p. (Orig.). 1973. pap. 5.70 (ISBN 0-8141-5630-4). NCTE.

Emery, Donald W. & Kierzek, John M. English Fundamentals: Form A. 8th. ed. 310p. 1985. text ed. write for info. (ISBN 0-02-333080-5). Macmillan.

Emery, Donald W., et al. English Fundamentals: Form B. 7th ed. 1981. pap. text ed. write for info. (ISBN 0-02-333560-2). Macmillan.

--English Fundamentals: Form C. 7th ed. 1982. text ed. write for info. (ISBN 0-02-333610-2). Macmillan.

Emery, Edwin. History of the American Newspaper Publishers Association. LC 78-110269. Repr. of 1950 ed. lib. bdg. 18.75x (ISBN 0-8371-4495-7, EMAN). Greenwood.

Emery, Edwin & Emery, Michael. The Press & America: An Interpretive History of the Mass Media. 5th ed. (Illus.). 624p. 1984. text ed. 30.95 (ISBN 0-13-697988-2). P-H.

Emery, Emma Wilson. Aunt Puss & Others: Old Days in the Piney Woods, Vol. 3. (Texas Folklore Society Paisano Books Ser.). 1969. 10.00 (ISBN 0-88426-022-4). Encino Pr.

Emery, F. E. & Trist, E. L. Towards a Social Ecology: Contextual Appreciation of the Future in the Present. LC 70-178778. 256p. 1973. 25.00x (ISBN 0-306-30563-1, Plenum Pr). Plenum Pub.

Emery, Fred. Colonel Bogey's Coloring Book for Golfers. (Illus.). 52p. (Orig.). 1981. 80.00 (ISBN 0-932746-02-0). Today News.

--Futures We Are in. (Studies in the Quality of Working Life: No. 5). 1977. lib. bdg. 21.95 (ISBN 90-207-0662-4, Pub. by Martinus Nijhoff Netherlands). Kluwer Academic.

Emery, Fred & Emery, Merrelyn. A Choice of Futures. (Studies in the Quality of Working Life: No. 4). 1976. lib. bdg. 23.00 (ISBN 90-207-0635-7, Pub. by Martinus Nijhoff Netherlands). Kluwer Academic.

Emery, Fred & Thorsrud, Elnar. Democracy at Work. (Studies in the Quality of Working Life: No. 2). 1976. lib. bdg. 23.00 (ISBN 90-207-0633-0, Pub. by Martinus Nijhoff Netherlands). Kluwer Academic.

Emery, Fred, jt. auth. see Ackoff, Russell.

Emery, Frederic B. Violin Concerto. LC 75-93979. (Music Reprints Ser.). 1969. Repr. of 1928 ed. lib. bdg. 59.50 (ISBN 0-306-71822-7). Da Capo.

--The Violinist's Encyclopedic Dictionary. LC 77-75206. 1979. Repr. of 1928 ed. lib. bdg. 35.00 (ISBN 0-89341-105-1). Longwood Pub Group.

Emery, Frederick E. & Trist, E. L. Towards a Social Ecology. LC 74-26842. 256p. 1975. pap. 5.95x (ISBN 0-306-20015-5, Rosetta). Plenum Pub.

Emery, Gary. A New Beginning: How You Can Change Your Life Through Cognitive Therapy. 1984. pap. 6.95 (ISBN 0-671-50771-0, Touchstone Bks). S&S.

--Own Your Own Life: How the New Cognitive Therapy Can Make You Feel Wonderful. 1982. 15.95 (ISBN 0-453-00428-8, H428, Sig); pap. 4.50 (ISBN 0-451-13967-4). NAL.

Emery, Gary, jt. auth. see Beck, Aaron T.

Emery, Gary, et al, eds. New Directions in Cognitive Therapy. LC 81-1264. 295p. 1981. 20.00 (ISBN 0-89862-606-4, 2606). Guilford Pr.

Emery, Glenice M. Come, Search with Me. LC 84-90035. 92p. 1984. 7.95 (ISBN 0-533-06123-7). Vantage.

Emery, Glyn. Elements of Computer Science. (Illus.). 1977. pap. text ed. 14.00x (ISBN 0-8464-0366-8). Beekman Pubs.

Emery, Helen F. The Puritan Village Evolves: A History of Wayland, Massachusetts. LC 81-5185. (Illus.). 384p. 1981. 15.00x (ISBN 0-914016-78-4). Phoenix Pub.

Emery, Henry C. Politician, Party & People. 1913. 29.50x (ISBN 0-685-89771-0). Elliots Bks.

--Speculation on the Stock & Produce Exchanges of the United States. LC 70-76663. (Columbia University, Studies in the Social Sciences Ser.: No. 18). Repr. of 1896 ed. 12.50 (ISBN 0-404-51018-3). AMS Pr.

Emery, Irene. Primary Structure of Fabrics. LC 80-52671. (Illus.). 400p. 1980. 35.00 (ISBN 0-87405-016-2). Textile Mus.

Emery, James C. see Bernard, Dan, et al.

Emery, James J. & Oppenheimer, Michael C. The U. S. Export-Import Bank: Policy Dilemmas & Choices. (Illus.). 175p. 1983. pap. 19.00x (ISBN 0-86531-807-7). Westview.

Emery, James J., et al. Technology Trade with the Middle East: Policy Issues & Economic Trends. (Special Studies in International Economics & Business). 350p. 1985. pap. 26.50x (ISBN 0-8133-7043-4). Westview.

Emery, Jared M. & Little, James H. Phacoemulsification & Aspiration of Cataracts: Surgical Techniques, Complications & Results. LC 79-13047. 326p. 1979. text ed. 54.50 (ISBN 0-8016-3028-2). Mosby.

Emery, Jared M. & McIntyre. Extracapsular Cataract Surgery. LC 81-12470. (Illus.). 1983. 124.95 (ISBN 0-8016-1552-6). Mosby.

Emery, Jared M. & Jacobson, Adrienne C., eds. Current Concepts in Cataract Surgery. 8th biennial ed. (Illus.). 432p. 1984. pap. 75.00 (ISBN 0-8385-1404-9). ACC.

--Current Concepts in Cataract Surgery: Selected Proceedings of the Seventh Bienniel Cataract Surgical Congress. (Illus.). 353p. 1982. 75.00 (ISBN 0-8385-1405-7). ACC.

Emery, John. European Spoons Before Seventeen Hundred. 214p. 1982. 60.00x (ISBN 0-85976-012-X, Pub. by Donald Pubs Scotland). State Mutual Bk.

--Summer Ends Now. 164p. 1980. 14.95x (ISBN 0-7022-1467-1); pap. 7.95 (ISBN 0-7022-1468-X). U of Queensland Pr.

Emery, John J., ed. Properties of Flexible Pavement Materials - STP 807. LC 82-83521. 178p. 1983. text ed. 25.00 (ISBN 0-8031-0257-7, 04-807000-08). ASTM.

Emery, Joy S. Stage Costume Techniques. (Theatre & Drama Ser.). (Illus.). 368p. 1981. 30.95 (ISBN 0-13-840330-9). P-H.

Emery, K. O. & Skinner, Brian J. Mineral Deposits of the Deep-Ocean Floor. LC 78-59181. 72p. 1978. pap. 4.95x (ISBN 0-8448-1363-X). Crane-Russak Co.

Emery, K. O. & Uchupi, Elazer. The Geology of the Atlantic Ocean. 1985. 98.00 (ISBN 0-387-96032-5). Springer-Verlag.

--Geology of the Atlantic Ocean. (Illus.). xx, 1050p. 1985. 126.50 (ISBN 0-387-96033-3); chart set 45.00. Springer-Verlag.

Emery, Ken. HP-41 M-Code for Beginners. Jarett, Keith, ed. LC 85-61881. 200p. 1985. pap. text ed. 18.95 (ISBN 0-9612174-7-2). Synthetix.

Emery, Laura. George Eliot's Creative Conflict: The Other Side of Silence. LC 75-3768. 1976. 27.50x (ISBN 0-520-02979-8). U of Cal Pr.

Emery, Lee. Aquaculture Audio-Visual Films Catalog. 12p. 1982. pap. 4.00x (ISBN 0-913235-17-2). Am Fisheries Soc.

Emery, Leslie. Horseshoeing Theory & Hoof Care. 2nd ed. (Illus.). 280p. 1986. text ed. price not set. Lea & Febiger.

Emery, Lucilius A. Concerning Justice. 1914. 39.50x (ISBN 0-685-69818-1). Elliots Bks.

Emery, Lynne F. Black Dance in the United States: From 1619 to 1970. LC 79-7761. (Dance Ser.). 1980. Repr. of 1972 ed. lib. bdg. 34.00x (ISBN 0-8369-9290-3). Ayer Co Pubs.

Emery, Marc. Furniture by Architects: Five Hundred International Masterpieces of Twentieth-Century Design & Where to Buy Them. LC 83-2581. (Illus.). 264p. 1983. 49.50 (ISBN 0-8109-0930-8). Abrams.

Emery, Maurice W. How to Buy Graphics & or Printing Guide. (Illus., Orig.). pap. text ed. 5.50 (ISBN 0-912359-00-5). M & M Grap.

Emery, Merrelyn, jt. auth. see Emery, Fred.

Emery, Michael. America's Leading Daily Newspapers. 36p. (Orig.). 1983. pap. 6.00x (ISBN 0-89730-114-5). R J Berg & Co.

Emery, Michael & Smythe, Ted C. Readings in Mass Communication: Concept & Issues in the Mass Media. 5th ed. 576p. 1982. pap. text ed. write for info. (ISBN 0-697-04215-4). Wm C Brown.

Emery, Michael, jt. auth. see Emery, Edwin.

Emery, Richard W. Heresy & Inquisition in Narbonne. LC 75-166031. (Columbia University Studies in the Social Sciences: No. 480). 17.50 (ISBN 0-404-51480-4). AMS Pr.

Emery, Robert, et al. Alternate Test Manual to Accompany Gerald C. Davison, John M. Neale Abnormal Psychology. 2nd ed. LC 77-13940. pap. 26.30 (ISBN 0-317-07794-5, 2016477). Bks Demand UMI.

Emery, Robert E. The Japanese Money Market. LC 83-48452. 160p. 1984. 20.50x (ISBN 0-669-07208-7). Lexington Bks.

Emery, Sarah & Cloud, Josie, eds. I Remember: A Collection of the Writings of Denton Senior Citizens. LC 81-66721. (Illus.). xii, 123p. (Orig.). 1981. pap. 6.00 (ISBN 0-9606146-0-5). Denton Senior Ctr.

Emery, Sarah & Cloud, Josie H., eds. Strength to Climb: A Collection of the Writing of Twelve Senior Citizens. LC 84-70421. x, 277p. 1984. pap. 10.00 (ISBN 0-9606146-1-3). Denton Senior Ctr.

Emery, Sarah A. Reminiscences of a Newburyport Nonagenarian. LC 78-5010. (Illus.). 1978. Repr. of 1879 ed. 27.50 (ISBN 0-917890-09-4). Heritage Bk.

Emery, Sarah E. Seven Financial Conspiracies Which Have Enslaved the American People. LC 75-112. (The Radical Tradition in America Ser). 112p. 1975. Repr. of 1891 ed. 14.95 (ISBN 0-88355-216-7). Hyperion Conn.

Emery, Sherman R. Styled for Living. 1983. 40.00 (ISBN 0-943370-00-0). Van Nos Reinhold.

Emery, Sherman R. & Cohen, Edie L. Dining by Design. (Illus.). 224p. 1984. text ed. 45.00 (ISBN 0-943370-05-1). Inter Design.

Emery, Sherman R., ed. Styled for Living. LC 83-50429. (Illus.). 240p. 1983. 40.00 (ISBN 0-943370-00-0). Inter Design.

Emery, Sherman R., jt. ed. see Cohen, Edie L.

Emery, Stephen A., tr. see Dessoir, Max.

Emery, Stephen A., tr. see Dilthey, Wilhelm.

Emery, Stewart. Actualizations: You Don't Have to Rehearse to Be Yourself. LC 77-76276. 1978. pap. 7.95 (ISBN 0-385-13122-4, Dolp). Doubleday.

--Actualizations: You Don't Have to Rehearse to Be Yourself. Rogin, Neal, ed. 237p. 1980. pap. 6.95 (ISBN 0-8290-0965-5). Irvington.

--Actualizations: You Don't Have to Rehearse to Be Yourself. Rogin, Neal, ed. 237p. 1980. Repr. of 1978 ed. 16.95 (ISBN 0-8290-0222-7). Irvington.

--The Owner's Manual for Your Life. 224p. 1984. pap. 3.50 (ISBN 0-671-46424-8). PB.

Emery, Stewart & Rogin, Neal. The Owner's Manual for Your Life: The Book You Should Have Gotten at Birth & Didn't. LC 79-6862. 216p. 1982. 12.95 (ISBN 0-385-15510-7). Doubleday.

Emery, W. B., et al. The Fortress of Buhen. 1979. 250.00x (ISBN 0-85698-063-3, Pub. by Egypt Exploration). State Mutual Bk.

Emery, W. J., jt. ed. see Pickard, G. L.

Emery, Walter. Commodity Year Book, 1985. 44.95 (ISBN 0-910418-17-9). Commodity Res.

Emery, Walter, ed. Commodity Year Book 1982. 385p. 1982. 32.95 (ISBN 0-910418-14-4). Commodity Res.

Emery, William. Culinary Design & Decoration. 135p. 1980. 26.95 (ISBN 0-8436-2187-7). Van Nos Reinhold.

Emery, William H. The Flavor of Spain. 352p. 1983. 16.95 (ISBN 0-8436-2254-7). Van Nos Reinhold.

Emery, William T., tr. see Dilthey, Wilhelm.

Emes, John H. & Nowak, Thomas J. Introduction to Pathophysiology: Basic Principles of the Disease Process. (Illus.). 480p. 1983. text ed. 25.00 (ISBN 0-8391-1775-2, 16594). Univ Park.

Emett, Charlie & Hutton, Mick. Walking Though Northern England. (Illus.). 192p. 1982. 14.95 (ISBN 0-7153-8285-3). David & Charles.

Emett, Rowland. Alarms & Excursions & Other Transports. (Illus.). 1979. 16.95 (ISBN 0-7195-3428-3). Transatlantic.

Emezi, Cletus E. Administration for Development in Africa. LC 79-1938. (Contemporary African Politics Ser.). 1979. 10.00 (ISBN 0-914970-15-1); pap. 5.00 (ISBN 0-914970-16-X). Conch Mag.

Emhardt, William C. Eastern Church in the Western World. LC 74-131039. Repr. of 1928 ed. 15.75 (ISBN 0-404-02329-0). AMS Pr.

Emhardt, William C. & Lamsa, G. M. Oldest Christian People. LC 71-126651. Repr. of 1926 ed. 14.50 (ISBN 0-404-02339-8). AMS Pr.

Emig, C. C. British & Other Phoronids: Keys & Notes for the Identification of the Species. (Synopses of the British Fauna Ser.). 1979. pap. 12.00 (ISBN 0-12-238750-3). Acad Pr.

Emig, Jane, ed. see Domjan, Evelyn A.

Emig, Jane, ed. see Domjan, Joseph & Domjan, Evelyn A.

Emig, Janet. The Composing Processes of Twelfth Graders. LC 77-163358. (Research Report Ser.: No. 13). (Illus.). 151p. (Orig.). 1971. pap. 5.74 (ISBN 0-8141-0803-2). NCTE.

--The Web of Meaning: Essays on Writing, Teaching, Learning, & Thinking. Goswami, Dixie & Butler, Maureen, eds. 192p. (Orig.). 1983. pap. text ed. 9.75x (ISBN 0-86709-047-2). Boynton Cook Pubs.

Emig, P., tr. see Nevanlinna, F. & Nevanlinna, R.

Emig, P., tr. see Nevanlinna, R.

Emil, Jane. All about Rivers. LC 83-4868. (Question & Answer Bk.). (Illus.). 32p. (gr. 3-6). 1984. lib. bdg. 9.59 (ISBN 0-89375-979-1); pap. text ed. 1.95 (ISBN 0-89375-980-5). Troll Assocs.

Emiliani, Cesare. The Sea: The Oceanic Lithosphere. LC 62-18366. (Ideas & Observations on Progress in the Study of the Seas Ser.: Vol. 7). 1738p. 1981. 213.95x (ISBN 0-471-02870-3, Pub. by Wiley-Interscience). Wiley.

Emilio, Louis F. History of the Fifty-Fourth Regiment of Massachusetts Volunteer Infantry, 1863 - 1865. (Basic Afro-American Reprint Library). 1969. Repr. of 1891 ed. 25.00 (ISBN 0-384-14330-X). Johnson Repr.

Emilio, Luis F. History of the Fifty-Fourth Regiment of Massachusetts Volunteer Infantry, 1863-1865. LC 69-18538. (American Negro: His History & Literature Ser., No. 2). 1969. Repr. of 1894 ed. 19.00 (ISBN 0-405-01861-4). Ayer Co Pubs.

Emily, compiled by see Wine Advisory Board.

Emin, Ahmed. Development of Modern Turkey As Measured by Means of Its Press. LC 72-76713. (Columbia University. Studies in the Social Sciences: No. 142). Repr. of 1914 ed. 16.50 (ISBN 0-404-51142-2). AMS Pr.

--Turkey in the World War. (Economic & Social History of the World War, Turkish Ser.). 1930. 75.00x (ISBN 0-317-27631-X). Elliots Bks.

Emin, G. Seven Songs about Armenia. 232p. 1981. 6.95 (ISBN 0-8285-2343-6, Pub. by Progress Pubs USSR). Imported Pubns.

--Songs of Armenia. 206p. 1979. 4.95 (ISBN 0-8285-1641-3, Pub. by Progress Pubs USSR). Imported Pubns.

Eminescu, Mihail. Poems. 69.95 (ISBN 0-87968-466-6). Gordon Pr.

Emiohe, Matthew O. Search for Love. 224p. 1983. 11.00 (ISBN 0-682-49954-4). Exposition Pr FL.

Emiot, Israel. The Birobidzhan Affair: A Yiddish Writer in Siberia. Rosenfeld, Max, tr. from Yiddish. LC 81-2511. 220p. 1981. 13.95 (ISBN 0-8276-0191-3, 477). Jewish Pubns.

Emissora Nacional de Radiodifusao. Portuguese: A Conversational Course. 1980. pap. text ed. 5.95 (ISBN 0-940630-09-5, T7089). Playette Corp.

Emken, Edward A., et al. Geometrical & Positional Fatty Acid Isomers. 344p. 25.00 (ISBN 0-318-12895-0); members 17.00 (ISBN 0-318-12896-9). Am Oil Chemists.

Emlen, J. Merritt. Ecology: An Evolutionary Approach. LC 71-172805. 1973. text ed. 26.95 (ISBN 0-201-01894-2). Addison-Wesley.

Emlen, John T. Land Bird Communities of Grand Bahama Island: The Structure & Dynamics of an Avifauna. 129p. 1977. 9.00 (ISBN 0-943610-24-9). Am Ornithologists.

--Land Bird Communities of Grand Bahama Island: The Structure & Dynamics of an Avifauna. xi, 129p. 1977. 9.00 (ISBN 0-318-12918-3); members 8.00 (ISBN 0-318-12919-1). Am Ornithologists.

Emler, N., tr. see Doise, W. & Mugny, G.

Emlet. Challenges & Prospects for Advanced Medical Systems. 1979. 33.50 (ISBN 0-8151-3117-8). Year Bk Med.

Emley, Alban M. Song of a Soul. 96p. 1973. pap. 4.95 (ISBN 0-911336-76-1). Sci of Mind.

Emling, John F. Value Perspectives Today: Toward an Integration with Jean Paiget's New Discipline in Relation to Modern Educational Leaders. LC 75-39114. 393p. 1978. 28.50 (ISBN 0-8386-1905-3). Fairleigh Dickinson.

Emlyn-Jones, C. J. The Ionians & Hellenism: A Study of the Cultural Achievement of the Early Greek Inhabitants of Asia Minor. (States & Cities of Ancient Greece Ser.). (Illus.). 256p. 1980. 30.00x (ISBN 0-7100-0470-2). Routledge & Kegan.

Emmanuel, Arghiri. Appropriate of Underdeveloped Technology. (Wiley-IRM Series on Multinationals). 186p. 1982. 29.95x (ISBN 0-471-10467-1, Pub. by Wiley-Interscience). Wiley.

--Profit & Crises. LC 83-40186. 432p. 1984. 29.95 (ISBN 0-312-64790-5). St Martin.

--Unequal Exchange: A Study of the Imperialism of Trade. Pearce, Brian, tr. from Fr. LC 78-158920. (Illus.). 1972. pap. 6.95 (ISBN 0-85345-188-5). Monthly Rev.

Emmanuel, E. Stephen, jt. auth. see Freudberg, Frank.

Emmanuel, Harry. Diamonds & Precious Stones. 1977. 79.95 (ISBN 0-8490-1716-5). Gordon Pr.

Emmanuel, Sr. M. Via Latina. 50p. (Lat. & Eng.). 1.50 (ISBN 0-318-12465-3). Amer Classical.

Emmanuel, W. D. Cameras: The Facts, a Collector's Guide, 1957-1964. Matheson, Andrew, ed. LC 80-41969. (Illus.). 528p. 1981. 54.95 (ISBN 0-240-51062-3). Focal Pr.

Emme, E. M., ed. Two Hundred Years of Flight in America: A Bicentennial Survey. 326p. 35.00 (ISBN 0-317-26100-2, Pub. by Am Astro Soc); pap. 25.00 (ISBN 0-317-26101-0). Univelt Inc.

Emme, Eugene M., ed. Science Fiction & Space Futures: Past & Present. (AAS History Ser.: Vol. 5). (Illus.). 278p. 1982. lib. bdg. 35.00x (ISBN 0-87703-172-X, Pub. by Am Astronaut); pap. text ed. 25.00x (ISBN 0-87703-173-8). Univelt Inc.

--Twenty-Five Years of the American Astronautical Society, Historical Reflections & Projections, 1954-1979. (AAS History Ser.: Vol. 2). (Illus.). 248p. 1980. lib. bdg. 25.00x (ISBN 0-87703-117-7); pap. 15.00x (ISBN 0-87703-118-5). Univelt Inc.

--Two Hundred Years of Flight in America. (AAS History Ser.: Vol. 1). (Illus.). 1979. softcover 25.00x (Pub. by Am Astronaut); text ed. 35.00x. Univelt Inc.

--Two Hundred Years of Flight in America. 2nd ed. (AAS History Ser.: Vol. 1). (Illus.). 1977. lib. bdg. 35.00x (ISBN 0-87703-091-X); soft cover 25.00x (ISBN 0-87703-101-0). Univelt Inc.

Emme, Eugene M., ed. see Bland, William M., Jr.

Emmel, Hildegard. History of the German Novel. Summerfield, Ellen, tr. LC 84-151640. 398p. 1985. 38.00 (ISBN 0-8143-1770-7). Wayne St U Pr.

Emmel, John F., jt. auth. see Emmel, Thomas C.

Emmel, Thomas C. An Introduction to Ecology & Population Biology. (Illus.). 224p. 1973. pap. 6.95x (ISBN 0-393-09371-9). Norton.

Emmel, Thomas C. & Emmel, John F. The Butterflies of Southern California. (Science Ser.: No. 26). (Illus.). 148p. 1973. 7.00 (ISBN 0-938644-06-8); 4.00 (ISBN 0-938644-05-X). Nat Hist Mus.

Emmel, Victor E. & Cowdry, E. V. Laboratory Technique in Biology & Medicine. 4th ed. LC 64-13546. 1970. Repr. of 1964 ed. 24.00 (ISBN 0-88275-016-X). Krieger.

Emmelkamp, Paul M., jt. ed. see Foa, Edna B.

Emmelkamp, Paul M. G. Phobic & Obsessive-Compulsive Disorders: Theory, Research, & Practice. (Plenum Behavior Therapy Ser.). (Illus.). 368p. 1982. 27.50 (ISBN 0-306-41044-3, Plenum Pr). Plenum Pub.

Emmen, A. H., ed. Supercomputer Applications: Proceedings of the Supercomputer Applications Symposium Amsterdam, the Netherlands, Nov. 7-9, 1984. 262p. 1985. 44.50 (ISBN 0-444-87752-5, North Holland). Elsevier.

Emmens, C. W. Guppy Handbook. (Illus.). pap. 6.95 (ISBN 0-87666-084-7, PS-668). TFH Pubns.

Emmens, C. W. & Axelrod, Herbert. Fancy Guppies for the Advanced Hobbyist. 1968. pap. 4.95 (ISBN 0-87666-086-3, M526). TFH Pubns.

Emmens, Carol A. Album of the Sixties. LC 80-21295. (Picture Albums Ser.). (Illus.). (gr. 5 up). 1981. 9.60 (ISBN 0-531-04199-9). Watts.

--Famous People on Film. LC 77-3449. 365p. 1977. 22.50 (ISBN 0-8108-1051-4). Scarecrow.

--Short Stories on Film. LC 78-13488. 1978. lib. bdg. 25.00 (ISBN 0-87287-146-0). Libs Unl.

--Stunt Work & Stunt People. (Triumph Bks). (Illus.). 96p. 1982. lib. bdg. 8.90 (ISBN 0-531-04411-4). Watts.

Emmens, Carol A., ed. Children's Media Market Place. 2nd ed. LC 82-82058. 353p. 1982. pap. 29.95 (ISBN 0-918212-33-2). Neal-Schuman.

--Non-Theatrical Film Distributors: Sales Service Policies. 72p. 1974. 5.00 (ISBN 0-317-34120-0); members 2.50 (ISBN 0-317-34121-9); bulk rates avail. EFLA.

Emmens, Carol A. & Maglione, Harry, eds. An Audio-Visual Guide to American Holidays. LC 78-6230. 284p. 1978. lib. bdg. 18.00 (ISBN 0-8108-1140-5). Scarecrow.

Emmens, Cliff W. The Marine Aquarium in Theory & Practice. (Illus.). 208p. 1975. 19.95 (ISBN 0-87666-446-X, PS-735). TFH Pubns.

Emmens, Clifford W. How to Keep & Breed Tropical Fish. (Illus.). 256p. 1983. 9.95 (ISBN 0-87666-499-0, H-910). TFH Pubns.

Emmens, Clifford W. & Axelrod, Herbert. Catfishes for the Advanced Hobbyist. 9.95 (ISBN 0-87666-018-9, PS-650). TFH Pubns.

Emmer, Edmund T., et al. Classroom Management for Secondary Teachers. Worsham, Murray E., ed. (Illus.). 160p. 1984. text ed. 16.95 (ISBN 0-13-136150-3); pap. text ed. 12.95 (ISBN 0-317-01505-2). P-H.

Emmer, P. C. & Wesseling, H. L., eds. Reappraisals in Overseas History: Essays on Post-War Historiography About European Expansion. (Comparative Studies in Overseas History: No. 2). 248p. 1979. lib. bdg. 36.00 (ISBN 90-6021-444-7, Pub. by Leiden Univ Holland); pap. 20.00 (ISBN 90-6021-447-1, Pub. by Leiden Univ Holand). Kluwer Academic.

Emmerich, Andre. Art Before Columbus. (Illus.). 1983. pap. 8.95 (ISBN 0-671-47073-6, Touchstone Bks). S&S.

--Sweat of the Sun & Tears of the Moon: Gold & Silver in Pre-Columbian Art. LC 77-72685. (Illus.). 1977. Repr. of 1965 ed. 35.00 (ISBN 0-87817-208-4). Hacker.

Emmerich, Anne C. Dolorous Passion of Our Lord Jesus Christ. 1980. lib. bdg. 64.95 (ISBN 0-8490-3100-1). Gordon Pr.

--The Dolorous Passion of Our Lord Jesus Christ. LC 83-70406. 382p. 1983. pap. 10.00 (ISBN 0-89555-210-8). TAN Bks Pubs.

--Life of Jesus Christ & Biblical Revelations, 4 vols. Schmoeger, C. E., ed. LC 79-90066. 1979. Set. pap. 30.00 (ISBN 0-89555-127-6); Vol. 1. (ISBN 0-89555-123-3); Vol. 2. pap. (ISBN 0-89555-124-1); Vol. 3. (ISBN 0-89555-125-X); Vol. 4. (ISBN 0-89555-126-8). TAN Bks Pubs.

--The Life of the Blessed Virgin Mary. Palairet, Michael, tr. from Ger. 1970. pap. 10.00 (ISBN 0-89555-048-2). TAN Bks Pubs.

Emmerich, Claude L., jt. auth. see Siff, Elliott J.

Emmerich, Herbert. Federal Organization & Administrative Management. LC 75-135704. 314p. 1971. 18.00 (ISBN 0-8173-4813-1). U of Ala Pr.

Emmerich, Janet. Anthony Trollope: His Perception of Character & the Traumatic Experience. LC 79-3734. 1980. text ed. 15.75 (ISBN 0-8191-0918-5); pap. text ed. 7.50 (ISBN 0-8191-0919-3). U Pr of Amer.

Emmerich, Oliver. Two Faces of Janus: The Saga of Deep South Change. LC 72-94351. 176p. 1973. 1.00 (ISBN 0-87805-017-5). U Pr of Miss.

Emmerich, Werner, et al. Energy Does Matter. (Illus.). 1963. 7.95 (ISBN 0-8027-0096-9). Walker & Co.

Emmerichs, Jack. How to Build a Program. (Illus.). 352p. (Orig.). 1983. pap. 19.95 (ISBN 0-88056-068-1). Dilithium Pr.

--How to Build a Program. (Illus.). 400p. 1983. 21.95 (ISBN 0-8306-0622-X, 1622). TAB Bks.

--The Programmer's Toolbox. LC 84-3196. 418p. 1984. pap. 19.95 (ISBN 0-88056-303-6); incl. disk 39.95 (ISBN 0-88056-229-3). Dilithium Pr.

Emmerick, A. C. Life of the Blessed Virgin Mary. (Roman Catholic Ser.). 1979. lib. bdg. 69.95 (ISBN 0-8490-2959-7). Gordon Pr.

Emmerick, R. E. The Sutra of Golden Light: A Mahayana Text. 1980. write for info. Dharma Pub.

Emmerling, F. A., jt. ed. see Axelrad, E. L.

Emmerling, Mary & Trask, Richard. Collecting American Country: A Style & Source Book. LC 83-2207. (Illus.). 276p. 1983. 35.00 (ISBN 0-517-54957-3, C N Potter Bks). Crown.

Emmerling, Mary E. American Country: A Style & Source Book. 1980. 30.00 (ISBN 0-517-53846-6, C N Potter Bks). Crown.

Emmerling, Trudy, et al. A Gifted Program That Works. 163p. 1982. pap. text ed. 15.95 (ISBN 0-87804-769-7). Mafex.

Emmers, Amy P. After the Lesson Plan: Realities of High School Teaching. LC 81-156. 1981. pap. 11.50x (ISBN 0-8077-2605-2). Tchrs Coll.

Emmers, Carol A. Album of Television. LC 79-22778. (gr. 5 up). 1980. PLB 9.60 (ISBN 0-531-01503-3, A15). Watts.

Emmers, Raimond. Pain: A Spike-Interval Coded Message in the Brain. 144p. 1981. text ed. 36.00 (ISBN 0-89004-650-6). Raven.

Emmers, Raimond & Akert, Konrad. Stereotaxic Atlas of the Brain of the Squirrel Monkey. (Illus.). 120p. 1963. 100.00x (ISBN 0-299-02690-6). U of Wis Pr.

Emmers, Raimond & Tasker, Ronald R. The Human Somesthetic Thalamus: With Maps for Physiological Target Localization During Stereotactic Neurosurgery. LC 74-80534. 112p. 1975. 91.00 (ISBN 0-911216-72-3). Raven.

Emmerson, A. M. The Microbiology & Treatment of Life-Threatening Infections. (Antimicrobial Chemotherapy Research Studies). 189p. 1982. 44.95x (ISBN 0-471-90049-4, Pub. by Res Stud Pr). Wiley.

Emmerson, B. T. Hyperuricaemia & Gout in Clinical Practice. 159p. 1983. pap. 19.00 (ISBN 0-683-10006-8). Williams & Wilkins.

Emmerson, Donald K. Indonesia's Elite: Political Culture & Cultural Politics. LC 75-36525. 304p. 1976. 34.95x (ISBN 0-8014-0917-9). Cornell U Pr.

--Rethinking Artisanal Fisheries Development: Western Concepts, Asian Experiences. (Working Paper: No. 423). x, 97p. 1980. 5.00 (ISBN 0-686-36074-5, WP-0423). World Bank.

Emmerson, George S. SS Great Eastern: The Greatest Iron Ship. LC 80-69345. (Illus.). 216p. 1981. 18.95 (ISBN 0-7153-8054-0). David & Charles.

Emmerson, Grace I. Hosea: An Israelite Prophet in Judean Perspective. (JSOT Supplement Ser.: No. 28). 224p. 1984. text ed. 28.50x (ISBN 0-905774-68-X, Pub. by JSOT Pr England); pap. text ed. 11.95x (ISBN 0-905774-69-8, Pub. by JSOT Pr England). Eisenbrauns.

Emmerson, Joan S., compiled by. Catalogue of the Pybus Collection of Medical Books, Letters & Engravings from the 15th-20th Centuries Held in the University Library, Newcastle upon Tyne. (Illus.). 280p. 1982. 60.00 (ISBN 0-7190-1295-3, Pub. by Manchester Univ Pr). Longwood Pub Group.

Emmerson, John K. A View from Yenan. LC 79-1019. 15p. (Orig.). 1979. pap. 1.50 (ISBN 0-934742-02-2, Inst Study Diplomacy). Geo U Sch For Serv.

Emmerson, Richard K. Antichrist in the Middle Ages: A Study of Medieval Apocalypticism, Art, & Literature. LC 79-3874. (Illus.). 320p. 1981. 35.00x (ISBN 0-295-95716-6). U of Wash Pr.

Emmerson, Walter L. Reformation & the Advent Movement. 224p. pap. 9.95 (ISBN 0-8280-0168-5). Review & Herald.

Emmert, Kirk R., ed. Winston Churchill on Empire. 325p. lib. bdg. 24.95 (ISBN 0-89089-167-2). Carolina Acad Pr.

Emmert, Philip & Donaghy, William C. Human Communication: Elements & Contexts. 419p. 1951. text ed. 19.95 (ISBN 0-394-34972-5, RanC). Random.

Emmert, Philip & Lukasko-Emmert, Victoria J. Interpersonal Communication. 3rd ed. 352p. 1984. pap. text ed. write for info (ISBN 0-697-04225-1); instrs.' manual avail. (ISBN 0-697-04226-X). Wm C Brown.

Emmerton, Anton. Blood Red Sky. 1985. pap. 3.50 (ISBN 0-8217-1586-0). Zebra.

Emmerton, Bill & Sehested, Ove H. Running for Your Life. 1979. pap. 1.25 (ISBN 0-8439-0627-8, Leisure Bks). Dorchester Pub Co.

Emmery, Lena, jt. auth. see Taylor, Sally.

Emmet, Boris. California & Hawaiian Sugar Refining Corporation of San Francisco, California. LC 76-126654. Repr. of 1928 ed. 23.00 (ISBN 0-404-02353-3). AMS Pr.

Emmet, Boris & Jeuck, John E. Catalogues & Counters: A History of Sears, Roebuck & Company. LC 50-7387. 1950. 45.00x (ISBN 0-226-20710-2). U of Chicago Pr.

Emmet, D., ed. see Stocks, John L.

Emmet, Dorothy. The Effectiveness of Causes. (SUNY Series in Philosophy). 152p. lib. bdg. 34.50x (ISBN 0-87395-940-X); pap. text ed. 14.95x (ISBN 0-87395-941-8). State U NY Pr.

--Function, Purpose & Powers: Some Concepts in the Study of Individuals & Societies. LC 70-180877. 300p. 1972. 29.95 (ISBN 0-87722-007-7). Temple U Pr.

Emmet, Dorothy, jt. auth. see MacIntyre, Alasdair.

Emmet, Dorothy M. Whitehead's Philosophy of Organism. LC 81-4141. (Illus.). xiii, 291p. 1981. Repr. of 1966 ed. lib. bdg. 29.50x (ISBN 0-313-23070-6, EMWP). Greenwood.

Emmet, E. R. Handbook of Logic: The Use of Reason. 1966. 5.75 (ISBN 0-8022-0455-4). Philos Lib.

--Mind Tickling Brain Teasers. 251p. 1982. pap. 4.95 (ISBN 0-13-583435-X). P-H.

Emmet, Eric R. Brain Puzzler's Delight. LC 68-31403. (Illus.). 1978. 12.95 (ISBN 0-89490-166-4). Enslow Pubs.

--Handbook of Logic. (Quality Paperback Ser.: No. 178). 236p. 1974. pap. 4.95 (ISBN 0-8226-0178-8). Littlefield.

--Learning to Think. 172p. 1981. Repr. 11.95 (ISBN 0-87523-195-0); tchr's. guide, 80p. 12.95x (ISBN 0-89490-206-7). Enslow Pubs.

--Mind Tickling Brain Teasers. LC 77-90769. (Illus.). 1980. 12.95 (ISBN 0-87523-192-6). Enslow Pubs.

--Puzzles for Pleasure. LC 71-189618. (Illus.). 310p. 1972. 13.95 (ISBN 0-87523-178-0). Enslow Pubs.

Emmet, Maitland, jt. ed. see Heath, John.

Emmet, Robert. Speech From the Dock. McEneaney, Kevin T., ed. (Irish Historical Pamphlet Ser.: No. 1). 10p. (Orig.). 1982. pap. 3.00 (ISBN 0-939254-03-4). At-Swim.

Emmett, jt. ed. see Croke.

Emmett, A. J. & O'Rourke, M. G., eds. Malignant Skin Tumours. (Illus.). 1982. 87.00 (ISBN 0-443-02268-2). Churchill.

Emmett, Carolyn C., jt. auth. see Sage, Howard.

Emmett, Chris. Shanghai Pierce: A Fair Likeness. (Illus.). 326p. 1953. 9.95 (ISBN 0-8061-1151-8). U of Okla Pr.

Emmett, J. C., ed. Second SCI-RSC: Medical Chemistry Symposium. 332p. 1984. 43.00 (ISBN 0-85186-935-1, Pub. by Royal Soc Chem UK). Heyden.

Emmett, J. T. Six Essays. 270p. 1972. Repr. of 1891 ed. 32.00 (ISBN 0-384-14335-0). Johnson Repr.

Emmett, Kathleen & Machamer, Peter. Perception: An Annotated Bibliography of Philosophical & Related Writings. LC 75-24086. (Reference Library of the Humanities: Vol. 39). 400p. 1975. lib. bdg. 26.00 (ISBN 0-8240-9966-4). Garland Pub.

Emmett, Steven W., ed. Theory & Treatment of Anorexia Nervosa & Bulimia: Biomedical, Sociocultural, & Psychological Perspectives. 352p. 1985. 30.00 (ISBN 0-87630-384-X). Brunner-Mazel.

Emmett, Williams, ed. see Williams, Emmett.

Emmichoven, F. W. The Anthroposophical Understanding of the Soul. Schwarzkopf, Friedemann, tr. from Ger. 170p. (Orig.). 1983. pap. 8.95 (ISBN 0-88010-019-2). Anthroposophic.

Emming, S. G., ed. see ESRO Summer School in Space Physics, 3rd, Albach, Austria, July 19-August 13, 1965.

Emminghaus, Hermann. Die Psychischen Storungen Des Kindesalters. LC 75-16701. (Classics in Psychiatry Ser.). (Illus., Ger.). 1976. Repr. of 1887 ed. 23.50x (ISBN 0-405-07428-X). Ayer Co Pubs.

Emmison, F. G. Archives & Local History. 2nd ed. (Illus.). 111p. 1974. bds. 15.00x (ISBN 0-8476-1283-X). Rowman.

--Essex Wills (England, Vol. 2. LC 82-80974. 292p. 1984. lib. bdg. 17.95 (ISBN 0-88082-005-5). New Eng Hist.

--Introduction to Archives. new ed. 51p. 1978. pap. 4.50x (ISBN 0-8476-6153-9). Rowman.

--Wills of the County of Essex, England, 1558-1565, Vol. 1. LC 82-80974. (Illus.). 397p. lib. bdg. 43.75 (ISBN 0-915156-51-2). Natl Genealogical.

Emmitt, Robert. Actaeon Homeward. 212p. 1980. pap. 4.50 (ISBN 0-8040-9010-6). Stonehenge.

--The Legend of Ogden Jenks. 203p. 1980. pap. 5.95 (ISBN 0-8263-0559-8). U of NM Pr.

Emmons, Andrea L. Letters I Wish I'd Mailed to the Man Who Divorced Me to Marry a Waitress. 1978. pap. 1.50 (ISBN 0-8439-0537-9, Leisure Bks). Dorchester Pub Co.

Emmons, Arthur B., 3rd, jt. auth. see Burdsall, Richard L.

Emmons, Charles F. Chinese Ghosts & ESP: A Study of Paranormal Beliefs & Experiences. LC 81-18236. 307p. 1982. 19.00 (ISBN 0-8108-1492-7). Scarecrow.

Emmons, Chester W., et al. Medical Mycology. 3rd ed. LC 76-15676. (Illus.). 592p. 1977. text ed. 19.50 (ISBN 0-8121-0566-4). Lea & Febiger.

Emmons, David. Leaving Word. Gale, Vi, ed. LC 78-54881. (Prescott First Bk.). (Illus.). 1978. ltd. ed. 20.00 (ISBN 0-915986-11-6); pap. 5.00 (ISBN 0-915986-12-4). Prescott St Pr.

Emmons, David M. Garden in the Grasslands: Boomer Literature of the Central Great Plains. LC 70-125100. (Illus.). xiv, 220p. 1971. 18.50x (ISBN 0-8032-0753-0). U of Nebr Pr.

Emmons, Ebenezer. American Geology: Statement of the Principles of the Science, with Full Illustrations of the Characteristic American Fossils, 2 vols. in one. LC 73-17818. (Natural Sciences in America Ser.). (Illus.). 544p. 1974. Repr. 37.50x (ISBN 0-405-05734-2). Ayer Co Pubs.

Emmons, Frances C. Poems from the Heart. iv, 50p. 1984. pap. 5.95 (ISBN 0-932269-08-7). Wyndham Hall.

Emmons, Frederick E. American Passenger Ships: The Ocean Lines & Liners, 1875-1983. LC 83-50652. (Illus.). 192p. 1985. 38.50 (ISBN 0-87413-248-7). U Delaware Pr.

--City School Attendance Service. LC 79-176751. (Columbia University. Teachers College. Contributions to Education Ser.: No. 200). Repr. of 1926 ed. 22.50 (ISBN 0-404-55200-5). AMS Pr.

Emmons, Frederick E. & Huntington, T. W., Jr., eds. Traveler's Book of Verse. LC 77-108582. (Granger Index Reprint Ser). 1928. 23.50 (ISBN 0-8369-6110-2). Ayer Co Pubs.
Emmons, H. H. Light of Emerson: A Complete Digest with Key-Word Concordance. The Cream of All He Wrote. 1979. Repr. of 1930 ed. lib. bdg. 30.00 (ISBN 0-8414-4039-5). Folcroft.
Emmons, Howard W., ed. Fundamentals of Gas Dynamics. LC 57-6331. (High Speed Aerodynamics & Jet Propulsion Ser.: Vol. 3). pap. 160.00 (ISBN 0-317-09255-3, 2000878). Bks Demand UMI.
Emmons, M. L., jt. auth. see Alberti, R. E.
Emmons, Michael & Richardson, David. The Assertive Christian. Frost, Miriam, ed. 144p. (Orig.). 1981. pap. 6.95 (ISBN 0-86683-755-8). Winston Pr.
Emmons, Michael L. The Inner Source: A Guide to Meditative Therapy. LC 78-466. 1978. pap. 3.95 (ISBN 0-915166-48-8). Impact Pubs Cal.
Emmons, Michael L., jt. auth. see Alberti, Robert E.
Emmons, Robert D. Turfgrass Science & Management. (Illus.). 384p. 1984. text ed. 23.00; instr's guide 2.85. Delmar.
Emmons, Shirlee & Sonntag, Stanley. The Art of the Song Recital. LC 78-66978. 1979. pap. text ed. 17.95 (ISBN 0-02-870530-0). Schirmer Bks.
Emmons, Terence. The Russian Landed Gentry & the Peasant Emancipation of 1861. LC 68-29654. pap. 124.00 (ISBN 0-317-20620-6, 2024574). Bks Demand UMI.
Emmons, Terence & Vucinich, Wayne S., eds. The Zemstvo in Russia: An Experiment in Local Self-Government. LC 81-3897. 464p. 1982. 49.50 (ISBN 0-521-23416-6). Cambridge U Pr.
Emmons, Terrence. The Formation of Political Parties & the First National Elections in Russia. (Illus.). 576p. 1983. text ed. 45.00x (ISBN 0-674-30935-9). Harvard U Pr.
Emmons, Tim & England, S. Anne. Selling Survival: How to Play the Sales Game & Win Through Success. LC 83-62307. 100p. (Orig.). 1984. pap. text ed. 9.95 (ISBN 0-88247-708-0). R & E Pubs.
Emmons, Vicki. Simply Seafood. (Illus.). 224p. (Orig.). 1983. pap. 4.95 (ISBN 0-89933-043-6). DeLorme Pub.
Emmons, Viva. Roots of Peace. LC 73-78911. (Orig.). 1969. pap. 1.75 (ISBN 0-8356-0505-1, Quest). Theos Pub Hse.
Emmons, W. H. Mines of Tuscarora, Cortez & Other Northern Nevada Districts. 220p. 14.95 (ISBN 0-913814-64-4). Nevada Pubns.
Emmons, William H. Gold Deposits of the World: With a Section on Prospecting. LC 74-350. (Vol. 13). (Illus.). 562p. 1974. Repr. of 1937 ed. gold 43.00x (ISBN 0-405-05912-4). Ayer Co Pubs.
Emmott, William, jt. auth. see Pennant-Rea, Rupert.
Emms, David & MacDowell, Robert, eds. P. G. Wodehouse at Dulwich. (Wodehouse Monographs: No. 5). 44p. (Orig.). Date not set. pap. 16.50 (ISBN 0-87008-104-7). Heineman.
Emolumento, V. Dizionario Commerciale Francese-Italiano. 533p. (Fr. & Ital.). 1978. pap. 37.50 (ISBN 88-7075-024-8, M-9281). French & Eur.
Emond. Color Atlas of Infectious Diseases. 1984. pap. 35.00 (ISBN 0-8151-3121-6). Year Bk Med.
Emond, R. T. Color Atlas of Infectious Diseases. (Year Book Color Atlas Ser). (Illus.). 384p. 1974. 47.95 (ISBN 0-8151-3118-6). Year Bk Med.
Emonds, Gerhardt. Guidelines for National Implementation of the Convention on International Trade in Endangered Species of Wild Fauna & Flora. (Environmental Policy & Law Papers: No. 17). 148p. 1981. pap. 12.50 (ISBN 0-686-97536-7, IUCN104, IUCN). Unipub.
Emony, Elliot & Quartermain, Peter, eds. American Writers of the Early Republic. (Dictionary of Literary Biography Ser.: Vol. 37). 600p. 1985. 88.00x (ISBN 0-8103-1715-X). Gale.
Emory, jt. auth. see Lewis.
Emory, C. William. Business Research Methods. rev. ed. 1980. 27.95x (ISBN 0-256-02260-7). Irwin.
Emory, C. William, jt. auth. see Niland, Powell.
Emory, Frank. Hidden Opportunities: The High School Graduate's Guide. LC 85-90768. 96p. (Orig.). 1985. pap. 12.00 (ISBN 0-934681-00-7). Emory Pub Co.
Emory, K. P. Archaeology of Mangareva & Neighboring Atolls. (BMB Ser.). Repr. of 1939 ed. 14.00 (ISBN 0-527-02271-3). Kraus Repr.
--Archaeology of Nihoa & Necker Islands. (BMB Ser.). Repr. of 1928 ed. 21.00 (ISBN 0-527-02159-8). Kraus Repr.
--Archaeology of the Pacific Equatorial Islands. (BMB Ser.). pap. 10.00 (ISBN 0-527-02229-2). Kraus Repr.
--Island of Lanai: A Survey of Nat Culture. (BMB Ser.). Repr. of 1924 ed. 32.00 (ISBN 0-527-02115-6). Kraus Repr.
--Stone Remains in the Society Islands. (BMB Ser.). Repr. of 1933 ed. 25.00 (ISBN 0-527-02222-5). Kraus Repr.
--Tuamatuan Stone Structures. (BMB Ser.). Repr. of 1934 ed. 15.00 (ISBN 0-527-02224-1). Kraus Repr.
--Tuamotuan Religious Structures & Ceremonies. (BMB Ser.). Repr. of 1947 ed. 14.00 (ISBN 0-527-02299-3). Kraus Repr.
Emory, Kenneth P. Material Culture of the Tuamotu Archipelago. (Pacific Anthropological Records: No. 22). 253p. 1975. 16.50 (ISBN 0-910240-53-1). Bishop Mus.
Emory, Meade, jt. auth. see Bittker, Boris I.
Emory, Stephen, et al, eds. see Wilson, Mary Jane.
Emory Univ. School of Law & American Law Inst., American Bar Assoc. Committee on Continuing Professional Education. Estate Planning for Interests in a Closely Held Business: ALI-ABA Course of Study Materials. LC 83-185619. 1982. write for info. Am Law Inst.
Emory University Law & Economics Center, jt. auth. see Federal Reserve Bank of Atlanta.
Emotions Anonymous International. Emotions Anonymous. LC 79-103619. 251p. 1982. Repr. of 1978 ed. post paid 6.75 (ISBN 0-9607356-0-7, RA790.A1E5633). Emotions Anony Intl.
Empedocles. The Fragments of Empedocles. Leonard, William E., tr. from Gr. & intro. by. LC 73-85282. 100p. 1973. 12.00 (ISBN 0-87548-300-3); pap. 4.95 (ISBN 0-87548-301-1). Open Court.
Emperaire, J. C. & Audebert, A., eds. Homologous Artificial Insemination. (Clinics in Andrology Ser.: Vol. 1). (Illus.). x, 234p. 1980. lib. bdg. 47.00 (ISBN 90-247-2269-1). Kluwer Academic.
Empereur, James L. Prophetic Anointing: God's Call to the Sick, the Elderly, & the Dying. (Message of the Sacraments Ser.: Vol. 7). 1982. text ed. 15.95 (ISBN 0-89453-397-5); pap. 10.95 (ISBN 0-89453-233-2). M Glazier.
Emperor, J. B. The Catullian Influence in English Lyric Poetry, Circa 1600-1650. LC 78-159183. 133p. 1973. Repr. of 1928 ed. lib. bdg. 14.50x (ISBN 0-374-92589-5). Octagon.
Emperor Maurice. Maurice's Strategikon. Dennis, George T., ed. & tr. from Lat. LC 83-10590. (The Middle Ages Ser.). 208p. 1984. 25.00x (ISBN 0-8122-7899-2). U of Pa Pr.
Empey, Arthur G. Tales from a Dugout. LC 79-101808. (Short Story Index Reprint Ser.). 1918. 18.00 (ISBN 0-8369-3196-3). Ayer Co Pubs.
Empey, D. W., jt. auth. see Hughes, D. T.
Empey, LaMar T. American Delinquency: Its Meaning & Construction. 1982. 28.00x (ISBN 0-256-02677-7). Dorsey.
--The Future of Childhood & Juvenile Justice. LC 79-15129. xi, 422p. 1979. 20.00x (ISBN 0-8139-0832-9). U Pr of Va.
Emphraim Karo, Joseph ben see Karo, Joseph Ben Ephraim.
Empie, Paul C. Lutherans & Catholics in Dialogue: Personal Notes for a Study. LC 80-69754. (Orig.). 1981. pap. 4.50 (ISBN 0-8006-1449-6, 1-1449). Fortress.
Empie, Paul C., et al, eds. Lutherans & Catholics in Dialogue I-III. LC 74-83330. 1974. pap. 6.95 (ISBN 0-8066-1451-X, 10-4190). Augsburg.
--Papal Primacy & the Universal Church. LC 74-83329. 1974. pap. 6.50 (ISBN 0-8066-1450-1, 10-4870). Augsburg.
--Teaching Authority & Infallibility in the Church, No. 6. LC 79-54109. (Lutherans & Catholics in Dialogue). 352p. (Orig.). 1979. pap. 6.95 (ISBN 0-8066-1733-0, 10-6222). Augsburg.
Employee Benefit Research Institute Staff, jt. auth. see Andrews, Emily S.
Employee Benefit Research Institute. Analysis of Alternative Vesting Requirements for Private Pensions. 35p. (Orig.). 1980. stapled cover 10.00 (ISBN 0-86643-011-3). Employee Benefit.
--The Application of Modeling Techniques to Retirement Income Policy Issues. Salisbury, Dallas L., ed. 69p. (Orig.). 1980. pap. 10.00 (ISBN 0-86643-010-5). Employee Benefit.
--Arranging the Pieces: The Retirement Income Puzzle. Salisbury, Dallas L., ed. LC 80-25427. 52p. (Orig.). 1980. pap. 10.00 (ISBN 0-86643-009-1). Employee Benefit.
--A Bibliography of Research: Health Care Programs. LC 81-12521. 584p. 1981. loose-leaf 25.00 (ISBN 0-86643-021-0). Employee Benefit.
--A Bibliography of Research: Retirement Income & Capital Accumulation Programs. LC 81-12484. 403p. 1981. loose-leaf 25.00 (ISBN 0-86643-022-9). Employee Benefit.
Employee Benefit Research Institute Staff & Chollet, Deborah J. Employer-Provided Health Benefits: Coverage, Provisions & Policy Issues. LC 84-3977. (Orig.). 1984. pap. 15.00 (ISBN 0-86643-033-4). Employee Benefit.
Employee Benefit Research Institute, et al. Fundamentals of Employee Benefit Programs. LC 83-16590. 1983. pap. 15.00 (ISBN 0-86643-035-0). Employee Benefit.
Employee Benefit Research Institute Staff. Fundamentals of Employee Benefit Programs. 2nd ed. LC 85-6764. 1985. 28.00 (ISBN 0-86643-042-3); pap. 15.00 (ISBN 0-86643-041-5). Employee Benefit.
Employee Benefit Research Institute. Pension Plan Termination Insurance: Does the Foreign Experience Have Relevance for the United States? Tolo, Kenneth W., ed. LC 79-90574. 160p. (Orig.). 1979. pap. 25.00 (ISBN 0-86643-000-8). Employee Benefit.
--Retirement Income Opportunities in an Aging America: Income Levels & Adequacy, Vol. 2. LC 81-5494. 121p. (Orig.). 1982. pap. 15.00 (ISBN 0-86643-014-8). Employee Benefit.
--Retirement Income Policy: Considerations for Effective Decision Making. LC 80-81075. 77p. (Orig.). 1980. pap. 10.00 stapled cover (ISBN 0-86643-007-5). Employee Benefit.
--Retirement Income Programs: Directions for Future Research. 52p. (Orig.). 1980. pap. 10.00 stapled cover (ISBN 0-86643-006-7). Employee Benefit.
--Should Pension Assets Be Managed for Social-Political Purposes? Salisbury, Dallas L., ed. LC 80-65232. 381p. (Orig.). 1980. pap. 10.00 (ISBN 0-86643-001-6). Employee Benefit.
Employee Relocation Council, ed. E-R-C Directory, 1985. 21st ed. 1985. pap. 20.00 (ISBN 0-912614-11-0). Employee.
--A Guide to Employee Relocation & Relocation Policy Development. 3rd ed. 1985. 20.00 (ISBN 0-912614-10-2). Employee.
Employment & Training Administration, U. S. Dept. of Labor. A Guide to Job Analysis. (Illus.). 488p. (Orig.). 1982. pap. 12.00x (ISBN 0-916671-04-6). Material Dev.
Empson, Ralph H. The Cult of the Peacock Angel: A Short Account of the Yezidi Tribes of Kurdistan. LC 77-87646. Repr. of 1928 ed. 21.00 (ISBN 0-404-16416-1). AMS Pr.
Empson, William. Collected Poems. LC 49-7861. 1961. pap. 4.95 (ISBN 0-15-618839-2, Harv). HarBraceJ.
--English Pastoral Poetry. facsimile ed. LC 74-177956. (Essay Index Reprint Ser.). Repr. of 1938 ed. 19.50 (ISBN 0-8369-2546-7). Ayer Co Pubs.
--Milton's God. LC 80-40109. 320p. 1981. pap. 16.95 (ISBN 0-521-29910-1). Cambridge U Pr.
--Milton's God. LC 78-14409. 1978. Repr. of 1961 ed. lib. bdg. 27.50x (ISBN 0-313-21021-7, EMMG). Greenwood.
--Seven Types of Ambiguity. 1947. pap. 6.95 (ISBN 0-8112-0037-X, NDP204). New Directions.
--Some Versions of Pastoral. LC 52-1182. 1960. pap. 5.95 (ISBN 0-8112-0038-8, NDP92). New Directions.
--Structure of Complex Words. 3rd. ed. 450p. 1979. Repr. of 1951 ed. 22.50x (ISBN 0-8476-6207-1). Rowman.
--Using Biography. 280p. 1985. 17.50 (ISBN 0-674-93160-2). Harvard U Pr.
Emrich, Duncan. American Folk Poetry: An Anthology. LC 74-3499. (Illus.). 864p. 1974. 29.45i (ISBN 0-316-23722-1). Little.
--Folklore of the American Land. pap. 8.95 (ISBN 0-316-23721-3). Little.
--Riddles & Jokes & Foolish Facts. (gr. 4-6). 1976. pap. 1.50 (ISBN 0-590-04281-5). Scholastic Inc.
Emrich, H. M., ed. The Role of Endorphins & Neuropsychiatry. (Modern Problems in Pharmacopsychiatry: Vol. 17). (Illus.). viii, 292p. 1981. 56.75 (ISBN 3-8055-2918-X). S Karger.
Emrich, H. M. & Aldenhoff, J. B., eds. Basic Mechanisms in the Action of Lithium: Proceedings of a Symposium at Schloss Ringberg, Bavaria, Germany, October 4-6, 1981. (International Congress Ser.: No. 572). 272p. 1982. 74.50 (ISBN 0-444-90249-X, Excerpta Medica). Elsevier.
Emrich, H. M., et al. Anticonvulsants in Affective Disorders. (International Congress Ser.: Vol. 626). 1984. 48.00 (ISBN 0-444-90375-5, I-209-84). Elsevier.
Emrich, Walter. Handbook of Charcoal Making. 1985. lib. bdg. 39.50 (ISBN 0-318-04127-8, Pub. by Reidel Holland). Kluwer Academic.
Emrich, Wilhelm. Franz Kafka. Buehne, Sheema Z., tr. xviii, 562p. 1985. pap. 18.95 (ISBN 0-317-30233-7). Ungar.
--Franz Kafka: A Critical Study of His Writings. Buehne, Sheema Z., tr. LC 68-12121. 1968. 30.00 (ISBN 0-8044-2168-4); pap. 15.95 (ISBN 0-8044-6136-8). Ungar.
--Franz Kafka: A Critical Study of His Writings. price not set. Ungar.
Emrick, Roy, jt. ed. see Tomizuka, Carl.
Emrys, Barbara. Wild Women Don't Get the Blues. 52p. 1977. 4.00 (ISBN 0-934816-00-X). Metis Pr Inc.
Emsheimer, Ernst, jt. auth. see Haslund-Christensen, Henning.
Emshock. Teardrops & Silicon. Erickson, Steve, et al, eds. (Illus.). 1978. pap. 1.67 (ISBN 0-686-08740-2); pap. 1.95 (ISBN 0-686-08741-0). FAS Pubs.
--Teardrops & Silicon. (Illus.). 1978. saddle-stitch 2.97 (ISBN 0-9603504-0-3). Vongrutnorv Og.
Emshoff, James R. Managerial Breakthroughs: Action Techniques for Strategic Change. (Illus.). 1980. 15.95 (ISBN 0-8144-5612-X). AMACOM.
Emshoff, James R. & Sisson, Roger L. Design & Use of Computer Simulation Models. (Illus.). 1970. write for info. (ISBN 0-02-333720-6, 33372). Macmillan.
Emsley & Miyazawa, T. NMR Analyses of Molecular Conformations & Conformational Equilibria with the Lanthanide Probe Method, Vol. 14, No. 2. (Illus.). 45p. 1981. pap. 25.00 (ISBN 0-08-027104-9). Pergamon.
Emsley, Clive. British Society & the French Wars, Seventeen Ninety-Three to Eighteen Fifteen. (Illus.). 216p. 1979. 19.50x (ISBN 0-8476-6115-6). Rowman.
--Policing & Its Context, 1750-1870. LC 82-24111. 200p. 1984. 20.00x (ISBN 0-8052-3891-3). Schocken.
Emsley, Clive, ed. Conflict & Stability in Europe. 384p. 1979. 35.00 (ISBN 0-7099-0154-2, Pub. by Croom Helm Ltd); pap. 9.00 (ISBN 0-7099-0155-0). Longwood Pub Group.
Emsley, Clive & Walvin, James, eds. Artisans, Peasants & Proletarians. 224p. 1985. 19.95 (ISBN 0-7099-3635-4, Pub. by Croom Helm Ltd). Longwood Pub Group.
Emsley, H. H. Opthalmic Lenses. (Illus.). 340p. 1984. pap. 25.00x (ISBN 0-87556-375-9). Saifer.
Emsley, J. W. & Feeney, J., eds. Progress in Nuclear Magnetic Resonance Spectroscopy, Vol. 14. 370p. 1982. 125.00 (ISBN 0-08-029698-X). Pergamon.
Emsley, J. W. & Sutcliffe, L. H., eds. Progress in NMR Spectroscopy: Vol. 11 Complete. LC 66-17931. 282p. 1978. 96.00 (ISBN 0-08-020325-6). Pergamon.
--Progress in Nuclear Magnetic Resonance Spectroscopy, Vols. 1-10. Incl. Vol. 1. 1962. 76.00 (ISBN 0-08-011322-2); Vol. 2. 1963; Vol. 3. 1965; Vol. 4. 1966. 76.00 (ISBN 0-08-012717-7); Vol. 5. 1970. 76.00 (ISBN 0-08-012834-3); Vol. 6. 1971; Vol. 7. 1971; Vol. 8, 3 pts. 1972. Vol. 8, Complete. 76.00 (ISBN 0-08-017018-8); Pts. 1-3. pap. 15.50 ea.; Pt. 1. pap. -1971 (ISBN 0-08-016662-8); Pt. 2. pap. -1971 (ISBN 0-08-016757-8); Pt. 3. pap. -1972 (ISBN 0-08-016857-4); Vol. 9, 3 pts. Vol. 9, Complete. 76.00 (ISBN 0-08-017704-2); Pts. 1-3. pap. 13.75 ea.; Vol. 10. Pt. 1, 1975. pap. 8.00 (ISBN 0-08-017703-4); Pt. 2, 1976. pap. 14.00 (ISBN 0-08-019463-X); Pts. 3 & 4, 1977. 75.00 (ISBN 0-08-019464-8); One Vol. Ed. 76.00 (ISBN 0-08-019466-4). write for info. Pergamon.
Emsley, J. W., et al. High Resolution Nuclear Magnetic Resonance Spectroscopy. 1966. 54.00 (ISBN 0-08-011824-0). Pergamon.
Emsley, J. W., et al, eds. Progress in Nuclear Magnetic Resonance Spectroscopy, Vol. 15. (Illus.). 430p. 1984. 120.00 (ISBN 0-08-031510-0). Pergamon.
Emsley, James W. Nuclear Magnetic Resonance of Liquid Crystals. 1984. lib. bdg. 76.00 (ISBN 90-277-1878-4, Pub. by Reidel Holland). Kluwer Academic.
Emsley, John & Hall, Dennis. Chemistry of Phosphorous. 1976. text ed. 44.00 (ISBN 0-06-318042-1, IntlDept). Har-Row.
Emsley, K., jt. auth. see Fraser, C. M.
Emsley, Zubin W., jt. ed. see Bauman, Edward J.
Emslow, P. H., Jr., jt. ed. see Parkhill, D. F.
Emson, P. C., ed. Chemical Neuroanatomy. (Illus.). 575p. 1983. text ed. 91.00 (ISBN 0-89004-608-5). Raven.
Emswiler, James P. & Moore, Joseph. Handbook for Peer Ministry. LC 81-84351. 128p. (Orig.). 1982. pap. 4.95 (ISBN 0-8091-2427-0). Paulist Pr.
Emswiler, Sharon & Neufer, Thomas. Women & Worship. rev., expanded ed. LC 83-48459. 144p. 1984. pap. 6.95i (ISBN 0-06-066101-1, RD 507, HarpR). Har-Row.
Emswiler, Thomas N. Money for Your Campus Ministry, Church, or Other Non-Profit Organization: How to Get It. LC 81-52373. (Illus.). 152p. 1981. pap. 7.95 (ISBN 0-9606652-0-X). Wesley Found.
Emswiler, Tom N. The Click in the Clock: Meditations for Junior Highs. LC 81-11875. 128p. (Orig.). (gr. 7-9). 1981. pap. 5.95 (ISBN 0-8298-0470-6). Pilgrim NY.
Emswiler, Tom N., jt. auth. see Neufer, Sharon.
Emswiler, Tom N., et al. A Complete Guide to Making the Most of Video in Religious Settings: How to Produce, Find, Use & Distribute Video in the Church & Synagogue. LC 85-50019. 128p. (Orig.). 1985. pap. 9.95 (ISBN 0-9606652-1-8). Wesley Found.
Emurian, Ernest K. Famous Stories of Inspiring Hymns. (Interlude Books). 186p. 1975. pap. 4.95 (ISBN 0-8010-3317-9). Baker Bk.
--Forty Stories of Famous Gospel Songs. (Interlude Bks). 1972. pap. 4.50 (ISBN 0-8010-3267-9). Baker Bk.
--Living Stories of Famous Hymns. (Interlude Bks). 1971. pap. 3.95 (ISBN 0-8010-3260-1). Baker Bk.
--Stories of Christmas Carols. (Paperback Program Ser). 1969. pap. 4.50 (ISBN 0-8010-3265-2). Baker Bk.
Emy, H. V. Liberals, Radicals & Social Politics, 1892-1914. LC 72-85435. 320p. 1973. 44.50 (ISBN 0-521-08740-6). Cambridge U Pr.
Enamorado, Cuesta J. Porto Rico, Past & Present: The Island after Thirty Years of American Rule. LC 74-14231. (The Puerto Rican Experience Ser). (Illus.). 180p. 1975. Repr. 12.00x (ISBN 0-405-06220-6). Ayer Co Pubs.
Enarson, Elaine P. Woods-Working Women: Sexual Integration in the U. S. Forest Service. LC 83-6725. 182p. 1984. text ed. 18.95x (ISBN 0-8173-0188-7). U of Ala Pr.
Enarson, Harold L. A Trip to the People's Republic of China: The Great Adventure. 63p. (Orig.). 1975. pap. 2.50x (ISBN 0-8142-0261-6). Ohio St U Pr.
Enayat, Hamid. Modern Islamic Political Thought. (Modern Middle East Ser.: No. 8). 220p. 1982. text ed. 20.00x (ISBN 0-292-75069-2); pap. text ed. 9.95 (ISBN 0-292-75070-6). U of Tex Pr.
Enby, Gunnel. Let There Be Love: Sex & the Handicapped. LC 74-21696. 84p. 1975. 7.50 (ISBN 0-8008-4652-4). Taplinger.

Encarnacao, J. & Schlechtendahl, E. G. Computer Aided Design: Fundamentals & System Architectures. (Symbolic Computation Ser.). (Illus.). 350p. 1983. 32.00 (ISBN 0-387-11526-9). Springer-Verlag.

Encarnacao, J., ed. File Structures & Data Bases for CAD: Proceedings of the IFIP-WG 5-2 Working Conference, Seeheim, Federal Republic of Germany, September 14-16, 1981. 372p. 1982. 47.00 (ISBN 0-444-86462-8, North Holland). Elsevier.

Encarnacao, J., et al, eds. CAD-CAM As a Basis for Development of Technology in Developing Nations: Proceedings of th IFIP WG 5.2 Working Conference, Sao Paulo, Brazil, October 1981. 437p. 1982. 76.75 (ISBN 0-444-86320-6). Elsevier.

Encarnacao, Jose L., ed. Eurographics 81: Proceedings of the International Conference & Exhibition, Technische Hochschule Darmstadt, BRD, 9-11 Sept., 1981. xii, 336p. 1982. 42.75 (ISBN 0-444-86284-6, North-Holland). Elsevier.

Encarnacion, Jesus F. Souvenir: Nurses & Nursing on Postage Stamps. 48p. 1984. 6.95 (ISBN 0-533-05865-1). Vantage.

Encausse, Gerard, jt. auth. see Anderson, L. H.

Encausse, Helene C. d' see D'Encausse, Helene C.

Encel, S. Cabinet Government in Australia. rev. 2nd ed. (Illus.). viii, 255p. 1974. pap. 16.50x (ISBN 0-522-84063-9, Pub. by Melbourne U Pr). Intl Spec Bk.

Encel, Sol, jt. ed. see Bell, Colin.

Encel, Sol, ed. see Martin, Jean.

Encel, Solomon, et al, eds. The Art of Anticipation: Values & Methods in Forecasting. LC 75-34506. 1976. 12.50x (ISBN 0-87663-719-5, Pica). Universe.

Ench, J. R. Not of This Generation. 1983. 10.95 (ISBN 0-533-05565-2). Vantage.

Enchi, Fumiko. Masks. Carpenter, Juliet W., tr. from Japanese. LC 82-48726. 1983. 11.95 (ISBN 0-394-50945-5). Knopf.

--Masks. LC 83-48033. (The Library of Contemporary World Literature). 160p. 1983. pap. 5.95 (ISBN 0-394-72218-3, Vin). Random.

--The Waiting Years. LC 72-15864. 203p. 1971. 12.95x (ISBN 0-87011-159-0). Kodansha.

--The Waiting Years. Bester, John, tr. from Jap. LC 72-15864. 203p. 1980. pap. 5.25 (ISBN 0-87011-424-7). Kodansha.

Encinas, Lydia. Raggedy Ann & Andy's Sewing Book. LC 76-11629. (Illus.). 1977. 7.95 (ISBN 0-672-52242-X). Bobbs.

Encinosa, Enrique, jt. auth. see Kaplan, Hank.

Encisco, Jorge. Design Motifs of Ancient Mexico. (Illus.). 1947. pap. 3.50 (ISBN 0-486-20084-1). Dover.

--Design Motifs of Ancient Mexico. (Illus.). 11.75 (ISBN 0-8446-0613-8). Peter Smith.

--Designs from Pre-Columbian Mexico. (Illus.). 14.50 (ISBN 0-8446-0088-1). Peter Smith.

Enciso, Jorge. Designs from Pre-Columbian Mexico. 1971. pap. 3.00 (ISBN 0-486-22794-4). Dover.

Enck, John J. Wallace Stevens: Images & Judgments. LC 64-11169. (Crosscurrents-Modern Critiques Ser.). 271p. 1964. 7.95 (ISBN 0-8093-0120-2). S Ill U Pr.

Encke, F., ed. see Zander, Robert.

Encyclopedie Mensuelle d'Outre-mer. Tunisia Fifty-Four: Seventy-Two Years of Franco-Tunisian Collaboration. LC 76-97378. (Fr). Repr. of 1954 ed. cancelled (ISBN 0-8371-2442-5). Greenwood.

Enczi, Endre. Uristen Az Abece Minden Betuje. LC 68-8924. (Hungarian.). 1968. pap. 6.00 (ISBN 0-911050-31-0). Occidental.

End, Wolfgang, et al. Software Development: Manual for the Planning, Realization & Installation of D P Systems. 345p. 1983. 53.95x (ISBN 0-471-26238-2, Pub. by Wiley Heyden). Wiley.

Endacott, G. B. Government & People in Hong Kong, Eighteen Forty-One to Nineteen Sixty-Two: A Constitutional History. LC 82-6127. (Illus.). xiv, 263p. 1982. Repr. of 1964 ed. lib. bdg. 35.00x (ISBN 0-313-23595-3, ENGP). Greenwood.

Endacott, G. B. & Hinton, A. Fragrant Harbour: A Short History of Hong Kong. LC 76-57678. 1977. Repr. of 1962 ed. lib. bdg. 18.50x (ISBN 0-8371-9456-3, ENFH). Greenwood.

Endacott, G. W. Woodworking & Furniture Making. (Drake Home Craftman Ser.). (Illus.). 1976. pap. 5.95 (ISBN 0-8069-8804-5). Sterling.

Endacott, George B. Hong Kong Eclipse. Birch, Alan, ed. (Illus.). 1978. text ed. 32.50x (ISBN 0-19-580374-4). Oxford U Pr.

Ende, Franz. The Great Book of Games. 144p. 9.95 (ISBN 3-88963-182-7). Blue Cat.

--Great Book of Games, Vol. 1. 144p. 9.95 (ISBN 3-88963-182-7). Elcomp.

Ende, Michael. Momo. LC 84-10157. (Illus.). 240p. 1985. 14.95 (ISBN 0-385-19093-X). Doubleday.

--The Neverending Story. (General Ser.). 1984. lib. bdg. 16.95 (ISBN 0-8161-3707-2, Large Print Bks). G K Hall.

--The Neverending Story: Movie Edition. Manheim, Ralph, tr. 368p. 1984. pap. 6.95 (ISBN 0-14-007431-7). Penguin.

--The Neverending Story: Official Tie-In Edition. Manheim, Ralph, tr. from German. 352p. 1984. pap. 6.95 (ISBN 0-14-007619-0). Penguin.

Ende, Michael & Manheim, Ralph. The Neverending Story. Manheim, Ralph, tr. from Ger. LC 82-45197. (Illus.). 432p. 1983. 15.95 (ISBN 0-385-17622-8). Doubleday.

Ende, Richard C. von see Von Ende, Richard C.

Ende, Rudolf Vom see Vom Ende, Rudolf.

Ende, Stuart A. Keats & the Sublime. LC 76-8420. 1976. 22.00x (ISBN 0-300-02010-4). Yale U Pr.

Endean, R., jt. auth. see Seventh International Symposium on Animal, Plant, & Microbial Toxins, Brisbane, Australia, 11-16 July, 1982.

Endean, R., jt. ed. see Jones, O. A.

Endean, Robert. Australia's Great Barrier Reef. LC 82-2063. (Illus.). 348p. 1983. text ed. 29.95x (ISBN 0-7022-1678-X). U of Queensland Pr.

Endell, Fritz A. Old Tavern Signs: An Excursion into the History of Hospitality. LC 68-26572. (Illus.). 1968. Repr. of 1916 ed. 40.00x (ISBN 0-8103-3505-0). Gale.

Endelman, Gary E. Solidarity Forever: Rose Schneiderman & the Women's Trade Union League. 32.00 (ISBN 0-405-14079-7). Ayer Co Pubs.

Endelman, Judith E. The Jewish Community of Indianapolis, 1849 to the Present. LC 83-49513. (The Modern Jewish Experience Ser.). (Illus.). 320p. 1984. 17.50x (ISBN 0-253-33150-1). Ind U Pr.

Endelman, Judith E., jt. auth. see Rudolph, L. C.

Endelman, Todd M. The Jews of Georgian England, 1714-1830: Tradition & Change in a Liberal Society. LC 78-78390. (Illus.). 370p. 1979. 14.50 (ISBN 0-8276-0119-0, 437). Jewish Pubns.

Endemann, Carl T. La Dorada: The Romance of San Francisco. LC 78-56990. (Illus.). 40p. (Orig.). 6.50 (ISBN 0-686-74116-1); pap. 3.75 (ISBN 0-931926-02-5). Gondwana Bks.

--Forks in the Road. 48p. 7.50 (ISBN 0-931926-05-X); pap. 3.75 (ISBN 0-931926-04-1). Gondwana Bks.

--The Ring of Alta Napa. 35p. pap. 1.75 (ISBN 0-931926-01-7). Gondwana Bks.

--Voyage into the Past: Continuous Life in Thirty Five Centuries. LC 81-81554. 1981. 9.95 (ISBN 0-931926-10-6). Gondwana Bks.

--Voyage into the Past: Continuous Life Through 35 Centuries. LC 81-81554. (Illus.). 1981. 9.95 (ISBN 0-931926-10-6). Alta Napa.

--Voyage to Gondwana: The Third "Lost Continent". LC 78-5699. (Illus., Orig.). 1979. pap. 9.95 (ISBN 0-931926-06-8). Alta Napa.

Endemann, Carl T., jt. ed. see Dow, Michael.

Ender, K. L., jt. auth. see Newton, F. B.

Ender, Richard & Kim, John, eds. Symposium on Energy Policy. (Orig.). 1984. pap. 8.00 (ISBN 0-918592-77-1). Policy Studies.

Ender, Steven C., jt. ed. see Winston, Roger B., Jr.

Enderb, Judith. Meet Super Duper Rick Martin. 1985. pap. 2.50 (ISBN 0-451-13868-6, Sig Vista). NAL.

Enderby, Nigel, jt. auth. see Hawkins, Hedley.

Enderby, Pamela M. Frenchay Dysarthria Assessment. LC 82-19826. (Illus.). 60p. 1983. test manual & scoring forms 19.50 (ISBN 0-933014-82-1). College-Hill.

--Frenchay Dysarthria Assessment. 60p. 1983. 8.50 (ISBN 0-933014-83-X). College-Hill.

Enderes, Bruno, et al. Verkehswesen Im Kriege: Die Osterreichischen Eisenbahnen; Militarische Verkehrs Probleme Osterreich-Ungarns. (Wirtschafts-Und Sozialgeschichte des Weltkrieges (Osterreichische Und Ungarische Serie)). (Ger.). 1931. 75.00x (ISBN 0-317-27634-4). Elliots Bks.

Enderle, G. Computer Graphics Programming. (Symbolic Computation Ser.). 450p. 1984. 39.00 (ISBN 0-387-11525-0). Springer-Verlag.

Enderle, Judith. Kisses for Sale. 176p. (Orig.). (gr. 7 up). 1985. pap. 2.25 (ISBN 0-590-33262-7, Wildfire). Scholastic Inc.

--Programmed For Love. 176p. pap. 1.95 (ISBN 0-441-68250-2). Ace Bks.

--Ready, Set, Love. (Caprice Ser.: No. 64). 144p. 1985. pap. 2.25 (ISBN 0-441-70834-X, Pub. by Tempo). Ace Bks.

--Secrets. (First Love Ser.). 154p. (YA) 1984. pap. 1.95 (ISBN 0-671-53415-7). PB.

--Sing a Song of Love. 160p. 1984. pap. 1.95 (ISBN 0-441-76726-5). Ace Bks.

--Someone for Sara. (Caprice Romance Ser.: No. 10). 192p. 1984. pap. 1.95 (ISBN 0-441-77461-X, Pub. by Tempo). Ace Bks.

--S.W.A.K. Sealed with a Kiss. (Caprice Romance Ser.). 202p. (gr. 6 up). 1983. pap. 1.95 (ISBN 0-441-79115-8, Pub. by Tempo). Ace Bks.

--T.L.C. Tender Loving Care. (Caprice Romance Ser.: No. 51). 144p. 1985. pap. 2.25 (ISBN 0-441-80050-5). Ace Bks.

--When Wishes Come True. (Caprice Ser.: No. 30). 160p. 1985. pap. 1.95 (ISBN 0-441-88258-7). Ace Bks.

--Will I See You Next Summer? (Caprice Romance Ser.: No. 45). 160p. 1984. pap. 1.95 (ISBN 0-441-88987-5). Ace Bks.

Enderle, Judith, jt. auth. see Tessler, Stephanie G.

Enderle, Judith, ed. see Tessler, Stephanie G.

Enderle, Judith A. Good Junk. 32p. (ps-3). 1982. 5.95 (ISBN 0-525-66720-2). Dandelion Pr.

--Let's Be Friends Again. LC 78-73536. (Illus.). (gr. k-3). Date not set. price not set (ISBN 0-89799-156-7); pap. price not set (ISBN 0-89799-074-9). Dandelion Pr.

Enderle, Judith J. Sixteen Sure Ways to Succeed With Sean. (Magic Moments Ser.: No. 6). 1984. pap. 1.95 (ISBN 0-451-13258-0, Sig Vista). NAL.

Enderlein, Fritz. Commercial, Business & Trade Laws: German Democratic Republic, Release 1. 1984. looseleaf 125.00 (ISBN 0-379-22502-6). Oceana.

Enders, Bernd. Mastering BASIC on the TRS-80 Model 100. 19.95 (ISBN 0-452-25575-9, Plume). NAL.

Enders, Pat. Pioneer Woman. 1979. 6.25 (ISBN 0-941490-13-0). Solo Pr.

Enders, Thomas O. & Mattione, Richard P. Latin America: The Crisis of Debt & Growth. LC 83-73219. 90p. 1984. pap. 6.95 (ISBN 0-8157-2387-3). Brookings.

Endersby, Frank. The Boy & the Horse. (Illus.). 16p. 1980. 5.50 (ISBN 0-85953-098-1, Pub. by Child's Play England). Playspaces.

--Holidays. (Choices Ser.). (Illus.). 12p. (ps). 1984. 3.50 (ISBN 0-85953-189-9, Child's Play England). Playspaces.

--Jasmine & The Cat. (Tantrums Ser.). (Illus.). 12p. (ps). 1984. 3.50 (ISBN 0-85953-183-X, Child's Play England). Playspaces.

--Jasmine & The Flowers. (Tantrums Ser.). 12p. (ps). 1984. 3.50 (ISBN 0-85953-184-8, Child's Play England). Playspaces.

--Jasmine's Bath Time. (Tantrums Ser.). 12p. (ps). 1984. 3.50 (ISBN 0-85953-185-6, Child's Play England). Playspaces.

--Jasmine's Bed Time. (Tantrums Ser.). 12p. (ps). 1984. 3.50 (ISBN 0-85953-186-4, Child's Play England). Playspaces.

--The Pet Shop. (Choices Ser.). (ps). 1984. 3.50 (ISBN 0-317-07210-2, Child's Play England). Playspaces.

--Pocket Money. (Choices Ser.). (ps). 1984. 3.50 (ISBN 0-85953-190-2, Child's Play England). Playspaces.

Endersby, Frank, ed. Wall Paper. (Choices Ser.). 12p. (ps). Date not set. 3.50 (ISBN 0-85953-188-0, Child's Play England). Playspaces.

Enderson, Mary B. Cake Calendar. LC 80-66709. (Illus.). 144p. 1981. 21.95x (ISBN 0-686-81446-0). Continental CA.

Enderton, Herbert B. A Mathematical Introduction to Logic. 1972. 19.25i (ISBN 0-12-238450-4). Acad Pr.

Enderwick, Peter. Multinational Business & Labour. LC 84-17771. 224p. 1985. 27.50 (ISBN 0-312-55252-1). St Martin.

Enderwick, Peter, jt. auth. see Buckley, Peter J.

Endicott, Bradford M., jt. auth. see Schmid, Michael.

Endicott, J. G., jt. auth. see West, M. P.

Endicott, John E. & Heaton, William P. The Politics of East Asia: China, Japan, Korea. LC 77-1346. 1978. pap. text ed. 25.00x (ISBN 0-89158-128-6). Westview.

Endicott, John E., et al, eds. American Defense Policy. 4th ed. LC 77-23161. pap. 160.00 (ISBN 0-317-08186-1, 2017569). Bks Demand UMI.

Endicott, John F., jt. ed. see Rorabacher, David B.

Endicott, K. M. An Analysis of Malay Magic. 1970. pap. 13.50x (ISBN 0-19-582513-6). Oxford U Pr.

Endicott, Katherine. Seasonal Expectations: An Essential Guide to Gardening, Foods, Festivals, & Outings in the Greater San Francisco Bay Area. (Illus.). 208p. (Orig.). 1984. pap. 8.95 (ISBN 0-917747-00-3). Belles Lettres.

Endicott, Kirk. Batek Negrito Religion: The World-View & Rituals of a Hunting & Gathering People of Peninsular Malaysia. (Illus.). 1979. 39.00x (ISBN 0-19-823197-0). Oxford U Pr.

Endicott, Lane D. Beyond the Rainbow Mists: A Journey That Takes You Out of This World. 1984. 6.50 (ISBN 0-8062-1614-X). Carlton.

Endicott, M. L. Vagabond Globetrotting: State of the Art. LC 84-80473. 142p. (Orig.). 1984. pap. 8.95 (ISBN 0-916649-00-8). Enchiridion.

Endicott, Stephen. James G. Endicott: Rebel Out of China. 1980. 20.00 (ISBN 0-8020-2377-0); pap. 9.95 (ISBN 0-8020-6409-4). U of Toronto Pr.

Endicott, William C., jt. auth. see Whitehill, Walter M.

Endleman, Robert. Psyche & Society: Explorations in Psychoanalytic Sociology. 448p. 1981. 35.00x (ISBN 0-231-04992-7). Columbia U Pr.

Endler, John A. Geographic Variation, Speciation, & Clines. LC 76-45896. (Monographs in Population Biology: No. 10). (Illus.). 1977. 28.50 (ISBN 0-691-08187-5); pap. 12.50 (ISBN 0-691-08192-1). Princeton U Pr.

--Natural Selection in the Wild. LC 85-42683. (Monographs in Population Biology: No. 21). (Illus.). 240p. 1986. 40.00 (ISBN 0-691-08386-X); pap. 13.95 (ISBN 0-691-08387-8). Princeton U Pr.

Endler, Norman S. Holiday of Darkness: A Psychologist's Personal Journey Out of His Depression. LC 81-16179. 169p. 1982. 18.50 (ISBN 0-471-86250-9, Pub. by Wiley-Interscience). Wiley.

Endler, Norman S. & Hunt, Joseph M. Personality & the Behavioral Disorders, 2 vols. 2nd ed. LC 83-23443. (Personality Processes Ser.). 1288p. 1984. Set. 80.00x (ISBN 0-471-86567-2, 1-341, Pub. by Wiley Interscience). Wiley.

Endler, Norman S., jt. auth. see Magnusson, David.

Endler, O. Valuation Theory. LC 72-92285. (Universitext). xii, 243p. 1972. pap. 18.50 (ISBN 0-387-06070-7). Springer-Verlag.

Endlicher, S., jt. auth. see Poeppig, E.

Endo, H., et al, eds. Chemistry & Biological Actions of 4-Nitroquinoline 1-Oxide. LC 6-129622. (Recent Results in Cancer Research: Vol. 34). (Illus.). 1971. 26.00 (ISBN 0-387-05230-5). Springer-Verlag.

Endo, Mitsuko, jt. auth. see Ortiz, Elisabeth L.

Endo, Russell, jt. ed. see Munoz, Faye U.

Endo, Russell, et al, eds. Asian-Americans: Social & Psychological Perspectives, Vol. II. LC 72-84064. 1980. pap. 7.95x (ISBN 0-8314-0058-7). Sci & Behavior.

Endo, Shusako. Wonderful Fool. Mathy, Francis, tr. from Japanese. LC 83-47553. 224p. 1983. 13.41 (ISBN 0-06-859853-X, HarpT). Har-Row.

Endo, Shusaku. Golden Country. Mathy, Francis, tr. LC 70-123898. 1970. 5.25 (ISBN 0-8048-0213-0). C E Tuttle.

--A Life of Jesus. Schuchert, Richard, tr. from Japanese. LC 78-61721. 192p. 1979. pap. 3.95 (ISBN 0-8091-2319-3). Paulist Pr.

--The Samurai. Gessel, Van C., tr. from Japanese. LC 82-57851. 272p. 1982. 12.45i (ISBN 0-06-859852-1, HarpT). Har-Row.

--The Samurai. LC 84-40225. 272p. 1984. pap. 7.95 (ISBN 0-394-72726-6, Vin). Random.

--The Sea & Poison. Gallagher, Michael, tr. from Japanese. LC 80-16867. 176p. 1985. pap. 5.95 (ISBN 0-8008-7022-0). Taplinger.

--The Sea & Poison: A Novel. Gallagher, Michael, tr. from Japanese. LC 80-16867. Orig. Title: Umi to Dokuyaku. 167p. 1980. 8.95 (ISBN 0-8008-7021-2). Taplinger.

--Silence. Johnston, William, tr. from Japanese. LC 78-27168. 1980. pap. 5.95 (ISBN 0-8008-7186-3). Taplinger.

--Silence. Johnston, William, tr. from Jap. LC 78-27168. 1979. 9.95 (ISBN 0-8008-7183-9). Taplinger.

--Stained Glass Elegies: Stories. Gessel, Van C., tr. 166p. 1985. 13.95 (ISBN 0-396-08643-8). Dodd.

--Volcano. Schuchert, Richard A., tr. from Japanese. LC 79-23678. 175p. 1980. 8.95 (ISBN 0-8008-8032-3). Taplinger.

--Volcano. Schuchert, Richard A., tr. from Japanese. LC 79-23678. 176p. 1985. pap. 5.95 (ISBN 0-8008-8033-1). Taplinger.

--When I Whistle. Gessel, Van C., tr. from Japanese. LC 79-13183. Orig. Title: Kuchibue wo Fuku Toki. 273p. 1980. pap. 5.95 (ISBN 0-8008-8244-X). Taplinger.

Endo, T., jt. ed. see Thomae, H.

Endore, S. Guy, tr. see Ewers, Hanns H.

Endrei, Walter. L' Evolution Des Techniques Du Filage & Du Tissage Du Moyen Age a la Revolution Industrielle. (Industrie & Artisanat: No. 4). 1968. pap. 14.00x (ISBN 90-2796-135-2). Mouton.

Endrenyi, J. Reliability Modeling in Electric Power Systems. LC 78-6222. 1978. 79.95x (ISBN 0-471-99664-5, Pub. by Wiley-Interscience). Wiley.

Endrenyi, Laszlo, ed. Kinetic Data Analysis: Design & Analysis of Enzyme & Pharmacokinetic Experiments. LC 81-120. 438p. 1981. 69.50x (ISBN 0-306-40724-8, Plenum Pr). Plenum Pub.

Endres, Clifford W. Joannes Secundus: The Latin Love Elegy in the Renaissance. 239p. 1981. 25.00 (ISBN 0-208-01832-8, Archon). Shoe String.

Endres, Dieter. Die Besteuerung Gesellschaftsrechtlicher Vermogensubertragungen. (European University Studies: No. 5, Vol. 382). xiv, 340p. (Ger.). 1982. 37.90 (ISBN 3-8204-7205-3). P Lang Pubs.

Endres, H., et al see Von Wiesner, J. & Von Regel, C.

Endres, Jeannette & Rockwell, Robert E. Food, Nutrition, & the Young Child. LC 80-10848. (Illus.). 312p. 1980. pap. text ed. 14.95 (ISBN 0-8016-4139-X). Mosby.

Endres, Jo Ellen, et al. Road to New Horizons: Adjustment Training. 130p. (Orig.). 1971. pap. 4.75x (ISBN 0-916671-29-1). Material Dev.

Endres, Joseph G. Opportunities in Food Science & Technology. (gr. 8 up). 1969. pap. 1.25 (ISBN 0-8442-6480-6). Natl Textbk.

Endres, Michael E. The Morality of Capital Punishment: Equal Justice under the Law. 176p. (Orig.). 1985. pap. 5.95 (ISBN 0-89622-224-1). Twenty Third.

Endress, Gerhard. An Introduction to Islamic History. 220p. 1985. 18.50x (ISBN 0-85224-496-7, Pub. by Edinburgh U Pr Scotland). Columbia U Pr.

Endreweit, Marie, jt. auth. see Brenner, Barbara.

Endroczi, E., ed. Cellular & Molecular Bases of Neuroendocrine Processes. 1976. 41.50 (ISBN 0-9960007-1-2, Pub. by Akademiai Kaido Hungary). Heyden.

Endroczi, E. & De Wied, D., eds. Integrative Neurohumoral Mechanisms. (Developments in Neuroscience Ser.: Vol. 16). 560p. 1983. 40.00 (ISBN 0-444-80487-0, I-093-83, Biomedical Pr). Elsevier.

Endroczi, E., et al, eds. Neuropeptides & Psychosomatic Processes. 1984. 79.00 (ISBN 0-9910000-6-4, Pub. by Akademiai Kaido Hungary). Heyden.

--Neuropeptides, Neurotransmitters & Regulation of Endocrine Processes: Proceedings of the International Conference on Intergrative Neurohumoral Mechanisms. 1984. 56.00 (ISBN 0-9910000-5-6, Pub. by Akademiai Kaido Hungary). Heyden.

--Neuropeptides, Neurotransmitters, & Regulation of Endocrine: Processes-Neuropeptides & Psychosomatic, 2 Vols. 1984. 113.00 (ISBN 0-9910000-7-2, Pub. by Akademiai Kaido Hungary). Heyden.

Endrodi, S. The Dynastinae of the World. (Entomologica Ser.). 1985. lib. bdg. 153.50 (ISBN 90-6193-138-X, Pub. by Junk Pub Netherlands). Kluwer-Academic.

Endruweit, Herausgegeben G., et al, eds. Handbuch der Arbeitsbeziehungen: Deutschland-Oesterreich-Schweiz. xiv, 522p. (Ger.). 1985. 79.20x (ISBN 3-11-009533-5). De Gruyter.

Ends, Earl J. & Page, Curtis W. Organizational Team Building. (Illus.). 218p. 1984. pap. text ed. 10.25 (ISBN 0-8191-3754-5). U Pr of Amer.

Endsley, Richard & Bradbard, Marilyn. Quality Day Care: A Handbook of Choices for Parents & Caregivers. (Illus.). 256p. 1981. (Spectrum); pap. 5.95 (ISBN 0-13-745422-8). P-H.

Endsley, William R. Peer Tutorial Instruction. Langdon, Danny G., ed. LC 79-23110. (Instructional Design Library). 104p. 1980. 19.95 (ISBN 0-87778-148-6). Educ Tech Pubns.

Endzelins, J. Comparative Phonology & Morphology of the Baltic Languages. Schmalsteig, William R. & Jegers, Benjamin, trs. from Lith. LC 71-144010. (Slavistic Printings & Reprintings Ser.: No. 85). 357p. 1971. text ed. 54.00x (ISBN 90-2791-915-1). Mouton.

Eneberg, Kaa, tr. see Bjorkegren, Hans.

Enehjelm, Curt A. Australian Finches. Friese, U. Erich, tr. from Ger. Orig. Title: Australische Prachtfinken. (Illus.). 1979. 4.95 (ISBN 0-87666-987-9, KW-027). TFH Pubns.

Enehjelm, Curt Af see Af Enehjelm, Curt.

Enekwe, Ossie. Broken Pots. 1977. staple bdg. 3.00 (ISBN 0-912678-31-3). Greenfld Rev Pr.

Enelow, Allen J. Elements of Psychotherapy. 1977. text ed. 19.95x (ISBN 0-19-502205-X). Oxford U Pr.

Enelow, Allen J. & Swisher, Scott N. Interviewing & Patient Care. 2nd ed. 1979. text ed. 20.95x (ISBN 0-19-502545-8); pap. text ed. 9.95x (ISBN 0-19-502546-6). Oxford U Pr.

Enelow, H. G., ed. see Kohler, Kaufmann.

Enelow, James M. & Hinich, Melvin J. The Spatial Theory of Voting: An Introduction. LC 83-7758. 334p. 1984. 39.50 (ISBN 0-521-25507-4); pap. 12.95 (ISBN 0-521-27515-6). Cambridge U Pr.

Enemark, Donald C. Feasibility Study & Design of an Antenna Pointing System with an in-Loop, Time Shared Digital Computer. LC 76-135076. 241p. 1970. 19.00 (ISBN 0-403-04499-5). Scholarly.

Energy Commission of the European Communities. Energy Conservation in Industry, 3 vols. Bd. with Combustion & Heat Recovery. 47.00; Engines & Batteries. 27.00; Applications & Technologies. 38.00. 1984. Set. 105.00 (ISBN 3-18-419095-1, 990700062, Pub. by VDI Verlag Gmbh Dusseldorf). Heyden.

Energy Engineering Board, Assembly of Engineering, National Research Council. Criteria for Energy Storage R&D. LC 76-47080. 1976. pap. 7.75 (ISBN 0-309-02530-3). Natl Acad Pr.

Energy, Environment, & Resource Center, the University of Tennessee see Bohm, Robert A., et al.

Energy, Environment, & Resources Center,the University of Tennessee see Bohm, Robert A., et al.

Energy Impact Associates, Inc. Social Impact Assessment, Monitoring, & Management by the Electric Energy Industry: State-of-the-Practice (AIF-NESP-012) (National Environmental Studies Project: NESP Reports). 150p. 1977. 45.00 (ISBN 0-318-13592-2); to NESP sponsors 15.00 (ISBN 0-318-13593-0). Atomic Indus Forum.

Energy Information Administration. Annual Energy Outlook, 1983 with Projections to 1995. Date not set. write for info. (ISBN 0-444-99584-6). Elsevier.

--Solar Collector Manufacturing Activity. Bereny, J. A., ed. 46p. 1980. pap. 9.95x (ISBN 0-930978-12-9, H-024). Solar Energy Info.

Energy Policy Project Staff. A Time to Choose: America's Energy Future. LC 74-14787. (Ford's Foundation's Energy Policy Project Ser.). 528p. 1974. 25.00 (ISBN 0-88410-023-5); pap. 12.95 prof ref (ISBN 0-88410-024-3). Ballinger Pub.

Energy Resources Center. Illustrated Guide to Home Retrofitting for Energy Savings. Knight, et al, eds. LC 80-23568. (Illus.). 384p. 1981. 19.95 (ISBN 0-07-019490-4). McGraw.

Energy Task Force. The College & University Energy Management Workbook. 21.50 (ISBN 0-913359-22-X); members 15.00. Assn Phys Plant Admin.

--Controlling Energy Through Microprocessor Utilization. 77p. 21.00 (ISBN 0-913359-13-0). Assn Phys Plant Admin.

--Financing Campus Energy Conservation Projects: A Series, 8 papers. 50p. 27.00 (ISBN 0-317-07495-4); members 15.00. Assn Phys Plant Admin.

Energy Technology Conference (1977: Houston, TX) Dynamic Analysis of Pressure Vessel & Piping Components: Presented at the Energy Technology Conference, Houston, Texas, September 18-23, 1977. Sundararajan, C., ed. LC 77-82209. (Illus.). pap. 28.30 (ISBN 0-317-09157-3, 2017309). Bks Demand UMI.

Energyworks Inc., jt. auth. see Berkeley Planning Associates Inc.

Energyworks, Inc. Staff. Energy-Efficient Products & Systems: A Comparative Catalog for Architects & Engineers. 860p. 1983. incl. three 6 month updates 135.00 (ISBN 0-471-87336-5, Pub. by Wiley-Interscience); pap. Jan. 1983 update (ISBN 0-471-88223-2); pap. 1.00 2nd supplement (ISBN 0-471-87887-1); pap. Jan. 1984 update (ISBN 0-471-80697-8). Wiley.

Enerson, Laura. Our Library Lives in a Bus. LC 77-71462. (gr. 3-5). 1977. 3.50 (ISBN 0-930480-01-5). R H Barnes.

Enfantin, Barthelemy P. Economie Politique et Politique. 2nd ed. LC 71-135178. 1971. Repr. of 1832 ed. 20.50 (ISBN 0-8337-1061-3). B Franklin.

--Life Eternal: Past--Present--Future. Rothwell, Fred, tr. from Fr. 138p. 7.95 (ISBN 0-912050-62-4). Open Court.

Enfield, Gertrude D. Verse Choir Technique. 1973. text ed. 2.25 (ISBN 0-686-09412-3). Expression.

Eng, C., jt. auth. see Buchanan, C. R.

Eng, E., tr. see Tellenbach, Hubertus.

Eng, J. Van Der see Van Der Eng, J., et al.

Eng, Jan Van Der see Van Der Eng, Jan & Meijer, Jan M.

Eng, Jan Van Der & Meijer, Jan M., eds. The Brothers Karamazov by F. M. Dostoevski. 1971. text ed. 16.80x (ISBN 90-2791-758-2). Mouton.

Eng, Paul. Spear Hand. LC 84-71241. (Praying Mantis Kung-Fu Ser.: Vol. 1). (Illus.). 176p. 1985. 19.95 (ISBN 0-918869-01-3); pap. 10.95 (ISBN 0-918869-00-5). Carroll St Pr.

Eng, Steve, jt. auth. see Yeatman, Ted.

Eng, Steve, ed. see Coleman, Lucile.

Eng, Steve, ed. see Counselman, Mary E.

Enga, John. Aircraft Inspection & Maintenance Records. (Aviation Technician Training Course Ser.). 92p. (Orig.). 1979. pap. text ed. 5.95 (ISBN 0-89100-094-1, EA-IAR). Aviation Maintenance.

Engar, Keith. Merlin's Tale of Arthur's Magic Sword. (Orig.). 1982. playscript 3.00 (ISBN 0-87602-228-X). Anchorage.

Engard, Rodcey G. & Cabat, Erni. Arizona Wildflowers, Bk. 1. LC 84-72111. (Illus.). 1984. write for info. (ISBN 0-913521-02-7). Cabat Studio Pubns.

Engard, Rodney G., jt. auth. see Cabat, Erni.

Engberg, Holger L. Mixed Banking & Economic Growth in Germany, 1850-1931. Bruchey, Stuart, ed. LC 80-2806. (Dissertations in European Economic History II). (Illus.). 1981. lib. bdg. 26.50x (ISBN 0-405-13990-X). Ayer Co Pubs.

Engberg, Robert. John Muir Summering in the Sierra. LC 83-16918. (Illus.). 176p. 1984. 21.50x (ISBN 0-299-09620-3); pap. 12.95x (ISBN 0-299-09624-6). U of Wis Pr.

Engberg, Robert, ed. John Muir to Yosemite & Beyond: Writings from the Years 1863-1875. Wesling, Donald. (Illus.). 194p. 1980. 21.50x (ISBN 0-299-08270-9); pap. 7.95 (ISBN 0-299-08274-1). U of Wis Pr.

Engberg, Susan. Pastorale. LC 82-4730. (Illinois Short Fiction Ser.). 168p. 1982. 11.95x (ISBN 0-252-00993-2); pap. 5.95 (ISBN 0-252-00994-0). U of Ill Pr.

--Stay Be the River. 1985. 15.95 (ISBN 0-670-80620-X). Viking.

Engberg-Pedersen, Troels. Aristotle's Theory of Moral Insight. 1983. 42.00x (ISBN 0-19-824667-6); pap. 11.95x (ISBN 0-19-824797-4). Oxford U Pr.

Engdahl, David E. Constitutional Power: Federal & State. (Nutshell Ser.). 411p. 1974. pap. 7.95 (ISBN 0-317-00012-8). West Pub.

Engdahl, Sylvia. Doors of the Universe. LC 80-18804. 276p. (gr. 7 up). 1981. PLB 12.95 (ISBN 0-689-30807-8, Argo). Atheneum.

Engdahl, Sylvia L. Enchantress from the Stars. (Illus.). (gr. 6 up). pap. 0.95 (ISBN 0-689-70309-0, A-12, Aladdin). Atheneum.

--Far Side of Evil. LC 77-134808. (Illus.). (gr. 7-9). 1971. PLB 6.50 (ISBN 0-689-20649-6). Atheneum.

--The Far Side of Evil. (Illus.). 304p. 1971. pap. 0.95 (ISBN 0-689-70357-0, A-28, Aladdin). Atheneum.

--Our World Is Earth. LC 79-11788. (Illus.). (ps-4). 1979. 9.95 (ISBN 0-689-30678-4). Atheneum.

--This Star Shall Abide. 256p. (gr. 5-9). 1979. pap. 2.50 (ISBN 0-689-70458-5, A-87, Aladdin). Atheneum.

Enge, Harald A. Introduction to Nuclear Physics. 1966. 36.95 (ISBN 0-201-01870-5). Addison-Wesley.

Engebrecht, Pat. The Promise of Moonstone. 192p. 1984. pap. 2.25 (ISBN 0-449-70093-3, Juniper). Fawcett.

Engebretson, David. The Stephen King Concordance. (Studies in Literary Criticism: No. 13). (Illus., Orig.). 1985. 17.95x (ISBN 0-930261-09-7); pap. 9.95x (ISBN 0-930261-08-9). Starmont Hse.

Engebretson, David, jt. auth. see Collings, Michael R.

Engebretson, Doug. Empty Saddles, Forgotten Names. 205p. 1982. pap. 7.95 (ISBN 0-87970-156-0). North Plains.

Engel. Brothels of Nevada. 3rd, rev. ed. 256p. 1980. pap. 2.95 (ISBN 0-87067-803-5, BH803). Holloway.

Engel, jt. auth. see Baker.

Engel, A. & Banker, B. Q. Myology. 1104p. 1985. price not set (ISBN 0-07-079570-3). McGraw.

Engel, A. J. From Clergyman to Don. 1984. pap. 16.95 (ISBN 0-19-820070-6). Oxford U Pr.

--From Clergyman to Don: The Rise of the Academic Profession in Nineteenth-Century Oxford. 1983. 49.50x (ISBN 0-19-822606-3). Oxford U Pr.

Engel, A. von see Von Engel, A.

Engel, Alfred J., jt. ed. see Mahalingam, R.

Engel, Allison & Engel, Margaret. Food Finds: America's Best Local Foods & the People Who Produce Them. LC 83-48345. (Illus.). 224p. (Orig.). 1984. pap. 12.45i (ISBN 0-06-091114-X, CN 1114, CN). Har-Row.

Engel, Arnold, jt. auth. see Roberts, Jean.

Engel, Arnold, et al. Plan & Operation of the Hanes I Augmentation Survey of Adults 25-74 Years: United States 1974-1975. Stevenson, Taloria, ed. (Series 1: No. 14). 1978. pap. text ed. 1.75 (ISBN 0-8406-0124-7). Natl Ctr Health Stats.

Engel, Arthur. Perspectives in Health Planning. (Heath Clark Lectures, 1967). 88p. 1968. 28.50 (ISBN 0-485-26320-3, Pub. by Athlone Pr Ltd). Longwood Pub Group.

Engel, Barbara A. Mothers & Daughters: Women of the Intelligentsia in Nineteenth Century Russia. LC 82-14611. (Illus.). 224p. 1983. 32.50 (ISBN 0-521-25125-7). Cambridge U Pr.

--Mothers & Daughters: Women of the Intelligentsia in Nineteenth Century Russia. 230p. 1985. pap. 9.95 (ISBN 0-521-31301-5). Cambridge U Pr.

Engel, Bernard. Alaskan Crude. 1981. pap. 2.25 (ISBN 0-8439-0827-0). Dorchester Pub Co.

Engel, Bernard F. Marianne Moore. (Twayne's United States Authors Ser.). 1964. pap. 5.95x (ISBN 0-8084-0210-2, T54, Twayne). New Coll U Pr.

Engel, Bernard F. & Julius, Patricia W., eds. A New Voice for a New People: Midwestern Poetry 1800-1910. 148p. (Orig.). 1985. lib. bdg. 20.50 (ISBN 0-8191-4451-7); pap. text ed. 8.75 (ISBN 0-8191-4452-5). U Pr of Amer.

Engel, Bernard T., et al. Hemodynamics & Aging. 166p. 1977. text ed. 29.50x (ISBN 0-8422-7252-6). Irvington.

Engel, Beth B. Big Words. (Illus.). 160p. (gr. 5-9). 1982. 11.50 (ISBN 0-525-66779-2, 01117-330). Lodestar Bks.

Engel, Bonnie J., jt. auth. see Smith, Pamela K.

Engel, C. W., jt. auth. see Engel Enterprises.

Engel, Carl. Alla Breve. facs. ed. LC 71-128238. (Essay Index Reprint Ser). 1921. 20.00 (ISBN 0-8369-1919-X). Ayer Co Pubs.

--Discords Mingled: Essays on Music. facs. ed. LC 67-28752. (Essay Index Reprint Ser). 1931. 16.00 (ISBN 0-8369-0417-6). Ayer Co Pubs.

--An Introduction to the Study of National Music: Comprising Researches into Popular Songs, Traditions & Customs. LC 74-24075. Repr. of 1866 ed. 29.50 (ISBN 0-404-12904-8). AMS Pr.

--The Literature of National Music. LC 74-24076. Repr. of 1879 ed. 11.00 (ISBN 0-404-12905-6). AMS Pr.

--The Literature of National Music. LC 77-75201. 1977. Repr. of 1879 ed. lib. bdg. 12.50 (ISBN 0-89341-103-5). Longwood Pub Group.

--Music of the Most Ancient Nations, Particularly of the Assyrians, Egyptians, & Hebrews, with Special Reference to Recent Discoveries in Western Asia & in Egypt. LC 73-114875. (Select Bibliographies Reprint Ser). 1909. 26.50 (ISBN 0-8369-5279-0). Ayer Co Pubs.

--Musical Instruments. LC 77-75199. 1977. Repr. of 1875 ed. lib. bdg. 17.50 (ISBN 0-89341-095-0). Longwood Pub Group.

--Musical Myths & Facts, 2 vols. in 1. LC 76-25760. 1976. Repr. of 1876 ed. lib. bdg. 50.00 (ISBN 0-89341-026-8). Longwood Pub Group.

--Researches into the Early History of the Violin Family. LC 77-75189. 1977. Repr. of 1883 ed. lib. bdg. 20.00 (ISBN 0-89341-094-2). Longwood Pub Group.

Engel, Carl & Howard, John T., eds. Music from the Days of George Washington. (Music Reprint Ser.). 103p. 1983. Repr. of 1931 ed. lib. bdg. 27.50 (ISBN 0-306-76086-X). Da Capo.

Engel, Carl & Strunk, W. Oliver, eds. Music from the Days of George Washington. LC 73-36418. Repr. of 1931 ed. 19.50 (ISBN 0-404-07230-5). AMS Pr.

Engel, Dave, ed. see Truchinski, L. E.

Engel, David, et al. The McGraw-Hill Guide to World Literature, Volume 1: Homer to Cervantes. 336p. 1985. pap. 9.95 (ISBN 0-07-019525-0). McGraw.

--The McGraw-Hill Guide to World Literature, Volume 2: Moliere to Beckett. (McGraw-Hill Paperbacks Ser.). 336p. 1985. pap. 9.95 (ISBN 0-07-019526-9). McGraw.

Engel, David D. The Multiple Stochastic Integral. (Memoirs of the American Mathematical Society: Vol. 265). 83p. 1982. pap. 9.00 (ISBN 0-8218-2265-9, MEMO-265). Am Math.

Engel, David H. Japanese Gardens for Today: A Practical Handbook. LC 59-8191. (Illus.). 1959. 45.00 (ISBN 0-8048-0301-3). C E Tuttle.

Engel, David M. Code & Custom in a Thai Provincial Court: The Interaction of Formal & Informal Systems of Justice. LC 78-50936. (Association for Asian Studies Monograph: No. 34). 230p. 1978. pap. 4.95x (ISBN 0-8165-0622-1). U of Ariz Pr.

--Law & Kingship in Thailand During the Reign of King Chulalongkorn. LC 74-20343. (Michigan Papers on South & Southeast Asia: No. 9). x, 131p. (Orig.). 1975. pap. 6.50x (ISBN 0-89148-009-9). Ctr S&SE Asian.

Engel, E. A History of English Literature. 1902. Repr. 25.00 (ISBN 0-8274-2508-2). R West.

Engel, Elliot & King, Margaret F. The Victorian Novel Before Victoria: Britsh Fiction During the Reign of William IV (1830-1837) LC 83-26978. 176p. 1984. 22.50 (ISBN 0-312-84331-3). St Martin.

Engel Enterprises & Engel, C. W. Stimulating Simulations. 2nd ed. 112p. 1979. pap. 7.50 ea. (ISBN 0-8104-5170-0). Atari Version (ISBN 0-8104-5197-2, 5197). Microsoft Version (5170). VIC Version (5173). Apple Version (6317). Commodore 64 Version (5201). TI-99-4A Version (6404). Hayden.

Engel, Eva L., ed. German Narrative Prose, Vol. 1. 15.95 (ISBN 0-85496-021-X). Dufour.

Engel, F., jt. auth. see Marx, K.

Engel, F., ed. Chilca. (Prehistoric Andean Ecology, Man, Settlement & the Environment Ser.: Vol. 4). 186p. 1984. pap. text ed. 45.50x (ISBN 0-391-02773-5). Humanities.

Engel, Frederic, ed. Stone Typology. (Prehistoric Andean Ecology-Man, Settlement & Environment in the Andes Ser.: Vol. 3). 185p. 1983. pap. text ed. 45.50x (ISBN 0-391-02395-0). Humanities.

Engel, Frederic A., ed. The Deep South, Vol. 2. (Prehistoric Andean Ecology Ser.). 155p. 1981. pap. text ed. 45.50x (ISBN 0-391-02311-X). Humanities.

Engel, Frederic-Andre, ed. Paloma. (Prehistoric Andean Ecologys Ser.: Vol. 1). 1980. text ed. 45.50x (ISBN 0-391-01873-6). Humanities.

Engel, Friederich & Stackel, Paul. Urkunden Zur Geschichte Der Nichteuklidischen Geometrie, 2 Vols. (Ger). Repr. of 1913 ed. Set. 95.00 (ISBN 0-384-63370-6). Johnson Repr.

Engel, George. Fainting: Physiological & Psychological Considerations. 2nd ed. (Illus.). 208p. 1962. 18.00x (ISBN 0-398-00510-9). C C Thomas.

Engel, George L. Psychological Development in Health & Disease. LC 62-13582. Repr. of 1962 ed. 89.20 (ISBN 0-8357-9556-X, 2013069). Bks Demand UMI.

Engel, George L. & Morgan, W. L., Jr. Interviewing the Patient. LC 73-81834. 1973. pap. 9.50 (ISBN 0-7216-3393-5). Saunders.

Engel, George L., jt. auth. see Morgan, William L.

Engel, H. J. & Lichtlen, P., eds. Nitrates III-Cardiovascular Effects: Proceedings. (Illus.). 705p. 1981. 34.50 (ISBN 0-387-10761-4). Springer-Verlag.

Engel, Heinrich. Japanese House: A Tradition for Contemporary Architecture. LC 63-20587. (Illus.). 1964. 65.00 (ISBN 0-8048-0304-8). C E Tuttle.

--Measure & Construction of the Japanese House. LC 84-51859. (Illus.). 152p. 1985. pap. 15.00 (ISBN 0-8048-1492-9). C E Tuttle.

Engel, Herbert. Handbook of Creative Learning Exercises. LC 73-75394. (Building Blocks of Human Potential Ser.). 276p. 1973. 17.95x (ISBN 0-87201-162-3). Gulf Pub.

Engel, Herbert M. How to Delegate: A Guide to Getting Things Done. LC 83-1675. 254p. 1983. 15.95x (ISBN 0-87201-170-4). Gulf Pub.

Engel, Howard. Murder on Location. 222p. 1985. 12.95 (ISBN 0-312-55314-5). St Martin.

--Murder Sees the Light: A Benny Cooperman Mystery. 256p. 1985. 13.95 (ISBN 0-312-55324-2). St Martin.

--The Ransom Game. LC 84-13281. 218p. 1984. 11.95 (ISBN 0-312-66383-8). St Martin.

--The Ransom Game. (Crime Monthly Ser.). 224p. 1985. pap. 3.50 (ISBN 0-14-007741-3). Penguin.

--Suicide Murders. 200p. 1984. 11.95 (ISBN 0-312-77527-X). St Martin.

--The Suicide Murders. (Crime Ser.). 224p. 1985. pap. 3.50 (ISBN 0-14-007740-5). Penguin.

Engel, Irving. Structural Principles. (Illus.). 384p. 1984. text ed. 29.95 (ISBN 0-13-854019-5). P-H.

Engel, J. & Kessler, I., eds. The War Injuries of the Upper Extremity. (Progress in Surgery: Vol. 16). (Illus.). 1979. pap. 41.75 (ISBN 3-8055-2900-7). S Karger.

Engel, J. M., et al, eds. Thermologic Methods. (Applied Thermology Ser.). 350p. 1985. lib. bdg. 39.50 (ISBN 0-89573-410-9). VCH Pubs.

Engel, J. Ronald. Sacred Sands: The Struggle for Community in the Indiana Dunes. (Illus.). 288p. 1982. 26.95x (ISBN 0-8195-5073-6). Wesleyan U Pr.

--Sacred Sands: The Struggle for Community in the Indiana Dunes. (Illus.). xxii, 354p. 1985. pap. 12.95 (ISBN 0-8195-6129-0). Wesleyan U Pr.

Engel, Jack. Advertising: The Process & Practice. (Marketing Ser.). (Illus.). 1980. text ed. 34.95x (ISBN 0-07-019511-0). McGraw.

Engel, James F. Contemporary Christian Communications: Its Theory & Practice. LC 79-432. 1979. 16.95 (ISBN 0-8407-5152-4). Nelson.

Engel, James F. & Blackwell, Roger D. Consumer Behavior. 4th ed. 700p. 1982. text ed. 35.95x (ISBN 0-03-059242-9); instr's. manual 20.00 (ISBN 0-03-059243-7). Dryden Pr.

Engel, James F. & Norton, Wilbert H. What's Gone Wrong with the Harvest? 192p. 1975. pap. 6.95 kivar (ISBN 0-310-24161-8). Zondervan.

Engel, James F., et al. Promotional Strategy. 5th ed. 1983. 29.95x (ISBN 0-256-02846-X). Irwin.

Engel, James P. & Talarzyk, W. Wayne. Cases in Promotional Strategy. 1984. 12.95x (ISBN 0-256-03100-2). Irwin.

Engel, Joel. Handwriting Analysis Self-Taught. (Illus.). 1980. 10.95 (ISBN 0-525-66687-7, 01063-320); pap. 7.95 (ISBN 0-525-66697-4, 0772-270). Lodestar Bks.

Engel, Johann J. Schriften, 12 vols. 4323p. 1801-06. Repr. 495.00 (ISBN 0-384-14361-X). Johnson Repr.

Engel, L. A. Gas Mixing & Distribution in the Lung. (Lung Biology in Health & Disease Ser.). 440p. 1985. 75.00 (ISBN 0-8247-7284-9). Dekker.

Engel, L. K. Fred Astaire Dance Book. (Ballroom Dance Ser.). 1985. lib. bdg. 70.00 (ISBN 0-87700-795-0). Revisionist Pr.

Engel, Lehman. The American Musical Theater. rev. ed. 240p. 1975. pap. 5.95 (ISBN 0-02-012280-2, Collier). Macmillan.

--Getting the Show On. 1983. 14.95 (ISBN 0-02-870680-3). Schirmer Bks.

--Getting the Show On. (A Schirmer Book). 1983. 14.95 (ISBN 0-02-870680-3). Macmillan.

--The Making of a Musical. 176p. 1986. pap. 6.95 (ISBN 0-87910-049-4). Limelight Edns.

--The Musical Theater Workshop. (Sound Seminars Ser.). 2 bks., 24 tapes, listening guide 370.00x (ISBN 0-88432-066-9, 11500). J Norton Pubs.

--Words with Music. 300p. 1980. pap. 6.95 (ISBN 0-02-870370-7). Macmillan.

--Words with Music: The Broadway Musical Libretto. LC 80-15412. 1981. pap. 9.95 (ISBN 0-02-870370-7). Schirmer Bks.

Engel, Leonard, ed. Junior Pictorial Encyclopedia of Science. (Illus.). 11.25 (ISBN 0-8446-0089-X). Peter Smith.

Engel, Lorenz. Among the Plains Indians. LC 74-102895. (Nature & Man Ser.). (Illus.). (gr. 5-12). 1970. PLB 9.95 (ISBN 0-8225-0564-9). Lerner Pubns.

Engel, Lothar, et al. An Atlas of Polymer Damage. (Illus.). 1981. reference 50.00 (ISBN 0-13-050013-5). P-H.

Engel, Louis. From Handel to Halle. LC 72-8544. (Essay Index Reprint Ser.). 1972. Repr. of 1890 ed. 23.50 (ISBN 0-8369-7312-7). Ayer Co Pubs.

Engel, Louis & Boyd, Brendan. How to Buy Stocks. 7th ed. pap. 4.50 (ISBN 0-553-24654-2). Bantam.

Engel, Louis, jt. auth. see Boyd, Brendan.

Engel, Madeline H., jt. auth. see Tomasi, Silvano M.

Engel, Margaret, jt. auth. see Engel, Allison.

Engel, Marian. Monodromos. LC 73-85572. (Anansi Fiction Ser.: No. 27). 250p. 1973. 4.95 (ISBN 0-88784-427-8, Pub. by Hse Anansi Pr Canada). U of Toronto Pr.

Engel, Marty. End Times Dictionary. (Illus.). 144p. (Orig.). 1982. pap. 3.95 (ISBN 0-943878-00-4). Charismatic.

Engel, Mary. Psychopathology in Childhood: Social, Diagnostic, & Therapeutic Aspects. 183p. 1972. pap. text ed. 10.95 (ISBN 0-15-573028-2, HC). HarBraceJ.

Engel, Michael. State & Local Politics: Fundamentals & Perspectives. LC 84-51678. 352p. 1985. text ed. 24.95 (ISBN 0-312-75615-1); instr's. manual avail. St Martin.

Engel, Monroe. Fish. LC 84-2721. (Phoenix Fiction Ser.). vi, 218p. 1985. pap. 6.95 (ISBN 0-226-20835-4). U of Chicago Pr.

Engel, Monroe, ed. Uses of Literature. LC 73-82627. (English Studies: No. 4). 256p. 1973. pap. 5.95x (ISBN 0-674-93155-6). Harvard U Pr.

Engel, P., jt. ed. see Hossfeld, D. K.

Engel, Paul, jt. auth. see Childs, Marquis.

Engel, Paul C. Enzyme Kinetics: The Steady-State Approach. 2nd ed. LC 81-16864. (Outline Studies in Biology). 96p. 1982. pap. 7.50x (ISBN 0-412-23970-1, NO. 6628, Pub. by Chapman & Hall England). Methuen Inc.

Engel, Peter. A Controlling Interest. 336p. 1983. pap. 3.50 (ISBN 0-441-11726-0). Ace Bks.

--Tender Offers. 384p. 1983. 14.95 (ISBN 0-312-79093-7). St Martin.

Engel, Peter A. Impact Wear of Materials. (Tribology Ser.: Vol. 2). 340p. 1976. 76.75 (ISBN 0-444-41533-5). Elsevier.

Engel, Robert E., jt. auth. see Kraus, John.

Engel, Rudolf C. Abnormal Electroencephalograms in the Neonatal Period. (Illus.). 144p. 1975. 19.50x (ISBN 0-398-03318-8). C C Thomas.

Engel, S. Analyzing Informal Fallacies. 1980. pap. 14.95 (ISBN 0-13-032854-5). P-H.

Engel, S. Morris. The Language Trap: Or How to Defend Yourself Against the Tyranny of Words. 224p. 1984. 16.95 (ISBN 0-13-523044-6); pap. 6.95 (ISBN 0-13-523036-5). P-H.

--The Study of Philosophy. LC 80-27458. 1981. text ed. 26.95 (ISBN 0-03-047511-2, HoltC). HR&W.

--With Good Reason: An Introduction to Informal Fallacies. 2nd ed. LC 81-51843. 223p. 1982. pap. text ed. 10.95 (ISBN 0-312-88517-2). St Martin.

Engel, S. Morris, tr. see Ansky, S.

Engel, Salo & Metall, R. A., eds. Law, State & International Legal Order: Essays in Honor of Hans Kelsen. LC 64-16881. 1964. 21.00x (ISBN 0-87049-052-4). U of Tenn Pr.

Engel, Sue. Nobody Ever Asked... 1984. 12.95 (ISBN 0-533-06012-5). Vantage.

Engel, Wilson F., ed. see Shirley, James.

Engeland, T., et al. Microscopic Theories for Collective Phenomena in Atomic Nuclei: Proceedings of the Nordic Winter School on Nuclear Physics Hemsdal, Norway, April 10-21, 1983. (International Review of Nuclear Physics Ser.: Vol. 1). 1984. 55.00x (ISBN 9971-950-90-1, Pub. by World Sci Singapore); pap. 26.00x (ISBN 9971-950-91-X, Pub. by World Sci Singapore). Taylor & Francis.

Engelbarts, Rudolf. Books in Stir: A Bibliographic Essay About Prison Libraries & About Books Written by Prisoners & Prison Employees. LC 70-180625. 168p. 1972. 11.00 (ISBN 0-8108-0450-6). Scarecrow.

--Librarian Authors: A Biobibliography. LC 80-28035. 282p. 1981. lib. bdg. 21.95x (ISBN 0-89950-007-2). McFarland & Co.

Engelberg, Edward. The Unknown Distance: From Consciousness to Conscience, Goethe to Camus. LC 74-188974. 383p. 1972. 20.00x (ISBN 0-674-92965-9). Harvard U Pr.

Engelberg, Marvin W. Audiological Evaluation for Exaggerated Hearing Level. (Illus.). 132p. 1970. 14.50x (ISBN 0-398-00513-3). C C Thomas.

Engelberger, J. Robotics in Practice. 1983. pap. 24.95 (ISBN 0-317-31400-9). AMACOM.

Engelberger, Joseph F. Robotics in Practice: Management & Applications of Robotics In Industry. LC 80-66866. (Illus.). 1981. 44.95 (ISBN 0-8144-5645-6); pap. 24.95 (ISBN 0-8144-7587-6). AMACOM.

Engelbert, Ernest A., ed. Competition for California Water: Alternative Resolutions. Scheuring, Ann F. 224p. 1982. 28.50 (ISBN 0-520-04822-9, CAL 602); pap. 8.95 (ISBN 0-520-04823-7). U of Cal Pr.

--Water Scarcity: Impacts on Western Agriculture. LC 84-48702. (Illus.). 550p. 1985. 42.50 (ISBN 0-520-05300-1, CAL720); pap. 12.95 (ISBN 0-520-05313-3). U of Cal Pr.

Engelbourg, Saul. International Business Machines: A Business History. LC 75-41753. (Companies & Men: Business Enterprises in America). (Illus.). 1976. 38.50x (ISBN 0-405-08070-0). Ayer Co Pubs.

--Power & Morality: American Business Ethics, 1840-1914. LC 79-8288. (Contributions in Economics & Economic History Ser.: No. 28). 1980. lib. bdg. 27.50 (ISBN 0-313-20871-9, ENP/). Greenwood.

Engelbrecht, A., ed. see Claudianus Mamertus.

Engelbrecht, A., ed. see Faustus, Saint.

Engelbrecht, A., ed. see Rufinius, Tyrannius.

Engelbrecht, C. A., ed. Quantum Optics-Cathedral Peak, South Africa 1981: Proceedings. (Lecture Notes in Physics: Vol. 155). 329p. 1982. pap. 22.00 (ISBN 0-387-11498-X). Springer-Verlag.

Engelbrecht, Helmuth C. Johann Gottlieb Fichte: A Study of His Political Writings with Special Reference to His Nationalism. LC 68-54262. (Columbia University Studies in the Social Sciences: No. 383). 1971. Repr. of 1926 ed. 14.50 (ISBN 0-404-51383-2). AMS Pr.

Engelbrecht, J. Nonlinear Wave Processes of Deformation in Solids. (Monographs & Studies in Mathematics: No. 16). 240p. 1983. text ed. 59.95 (ISBN 0-273-08574-3). Pitman Pub MA.

Engelbrecht, Ted D., et al. Federal Taxation of Estates, Gifts, & Trusts. (Illus.). 528p. 1981. 38.95 (ISBN 0-13-313858-5). P-H.

Engelbrecht-Wiggans, Richard & Shuvik, Martin. Auctions, Bidding, & Contracting: Uses & Theory. (Studies in Game Theory & Mathematical Economics). 1983. 35.00x (ISBN 0-8147-7827-5). NYU Pr.

Engelbrekston, Sune. Stars, Planets & Galaxies. (Knowledge Through Color Ser.: No. 54). 160p. 1975. pap. 3.95 (ISBN 0-553-23528-1). Bantam.

Engelder, Theodore, et al, trs. see Pieper, Francis.

Engeldinger, Eugene A., jt. auth. see Fairbanks, Carol.

Engelen, G. B. & Van Lissa, R. V. Aqua-Vu Three: Hydrological Surveys in the Algarve, Portugal, Part I. (Communications of the Institute of Earth Sciences, Ser A: No. 3). 1979. pap. text ed. Cancelled (ISBN 90-6203-009-2). Humanities.

Engeler, E., ed. Logic of Programs Workshop Zuerich, 1979: Proceedings. (Lecture Notes in Computer Science Ser.: Vol. 125). 245p. 1981. pap. 16.00 (ISBN 0-387-11160-3). Springer-Verlag.

Engeler, E., ed. see Symposium on Semantics of Algorithmic Languages.

Engelfriet, C. P., et al, eds. Immunoheamatology. (Research Monographs in Immunology: Vol. 5). 400p. 1984. 96.50 (ISBN 0-444-80541-9, I-272-84). Elsevier.

Engelfriet, J. Simple Program Schemes & Formal Languages. (Lecture Notes in Computer Science Ser.: Vol. 20). vii, 254p. 1974. pap. 18.00 (ISBN 0-387-06953-4). Springer-Verlag.

Engelhardt, Fred. Forecasting School Population. LC 72-176752. (Columbia University. Teachers College. Contributions to Education Ser.: No. 171). Repr. of 1925 ed. 22.50 (ISBN 0-404-55171-8). AMS Pr.

Engelhardt, H. High Performance Liquid Chromatography. Gutnikov, G., tr. from Ger. LC 78-22002. (Chemical Laboratory Practice Ser.). (Illus.). 1978. 34.00 (ISBN 0-387-09005-3). Springer-Verlag.

Engelhardt, H. T., ed. see Trans-Disciplinary Symposium on Philosophy & Medicine, 1st Galveston, May 9-11, 1974.

Engelhardt, H. Tristam. The Foundations of Bioethics. 416p. 1985. 24.95 (ISBN 0-19-503608-5). Oxford U Pr.

Engelhardt, H. Tristram & Spicker, Stuart F., eds. Mental Health: Philosophical Perspectives. LC 77-24974. (Philosophy & Medicine Ser.: No. 4). 1977. lib. bdg. 29.00 (ISBN 90-277-0828-2, Pub. by Reidel Holland). Kluwer Academic.

Engelhardt, H. Tristram, jt. auth. see Bondesor, William B.

Engelhardt, H. Tristram, Jr., jt. auth. see Spicker, Stuart F.

Engelhardt, H. Tristram, Jr. & Callahan, Daniel, eds. Morals, Science & Sociality. LC 78-14481. (The Foundations of Ethics & Its Relationships to Sciences: Vol. III). 1978. pap. 7.95 (ISBN 0-916558-03-7). Hastings Ctr Inst Soc.

Engelhardt, H. Tristram, Jr., jt. ed. see Callahan, Daniel.

Engelhardt, James F. Let Freedom Ring. (Children's Theatre Playscript Ser.). 1975. pap. 2.25x (ISBN 0-88020-035-9). Coach Hse.

Engelhardt, Jon M., et al. Helping Children Understand & Use Numerals. 1984. pap. text ed. 21.43 (ISBN 0-205-08091-X, 238091). Allyn.

Engelhardt, Nickolaus L. School Building Program for Cities. LC 76-176753. (Columbia Univ. Teachers College Contribs. Ser.: No. 96). Repr. of 1918 ed. 22.50 (ISBN 0-404-55096-7). AMS Pr.

Engelhardt, Tristram H., Jr. & Caplan, Arthur, eds. Scientific Controversies: Case Studies in the Resolution & Closure of Disputes in Sciences & Technology. 704p. Date not set. price not set. (ISBN 0-521-25565-1). Cambridge U Pr.

Engelhardt, Tristram, Jr., tr. see Schutz, Alfred & Luckmann, Thomas.

Engelhardt, Wolf V. The Origin of Sediments & Sedimentary Rocks. Johns, William D., tr. from Ger. (Sedimentarey Petrology Ser.: Pt. 3). (Illus.). 359p. 1977. lib. bdg. 46.10 (ISBN 3-5106-5077-8). Lubrecht & Cramer.

Engelhardt, Zephyrin. Missions & Missionaries of California, 4 Vols. (Illus.). lib. bdg. 185.00 (ISBN 0-87821-019-9). Milford Hse.

Engelhart, Margaret, jt. auth. see Kurelek, William.

Engeli, M., et al. Refined Iterative Methods for Computation of the Solution & the Eigenvalues of Self-Adjoint Boundary Value Problems. (MIM Ser.: No. 8). (Illus.). 108p. 1959. pap. 20.95x (ISBN 0-8176-0098-1). Birkhauser.

Engel-Janosi, Friedrich. Four Studies in French Romantic Historical Writing. LC 78-64220. (Johns Hopkins University. Studies in the Social Sciences.: No. 71 1953: 2). Repr. of 1955 ed. 17.50 (ISBN 0-404-61324-1). AMS Pr.

--The Growth of German Historicism. LC 78-64195. (Johns Hopkins University. Studies in the Social Sciences. Sixty-Second Ser. 1944: 2). Repr. of 1944 ed. 15.00 (ISBN 0-404-61301-2). AMS Pr.

Engelkamp, J. & Zimmer, H. D. Dynamic Aspects of Language Processing: Focus & Presupposition. (Springer Series in Language & Communication: Vol. 16). (Illus.). 145p. 1983. 25.00 (ISBN 0-387-12433-0). Springer-Verlag.

Engelken, David. Beyond Undiscovered Denver Dining. (Illus.). 78p. 1983. pap. 3.95 (ISBN 0-9610064-1-2). Undiscovered.

Engelken, David, et al. Undiscovered Denver Dining. 2nd ed. (Illus.). 84p. 1983. pap. 3.95 (ISBN 0-9610064-0-4). Undiscovered.

Engelken, Ralph & Engelken, Rita. The Art of Natural Farming & Gardening. 1981. 9.95 (ISBN 0-942066-00-6). Barrington IA.

Engelken, Rita, jt. auth. see Engelken, Ralph.

Engelkes, James R. & Vandergoot, David. Introduction to Counseling. 1982. 27.95 (ISBN 0-395-30800-3). HM.

Engelking, R. Dimension Theory. (Mathematical Library Ser.: Vol. 19). 314p. 1979. 64.00 (ISBN 0-444-85176-3, North Holland). Elsevier.

Engell, James. The Creative Imagination: Enlightenment to Romanticism. LC 80-20265. 435p. 1981. text ed. 17.00x (ISBN 0-674-17572-7). Harvard U Pr.

Engell, James, ed. Johnson & His Age. (Harvard English Studies: No. 12). (Illus.). 500p. 1984. text ed. 25.00x (ISBN 0-674-48075-9); pap. text ed. 8.95x (ISBN 0-674-48076-7). Harvard U Pr.

Engell, James, ed. see Coleridge, Samuel Taylor.

Engelman, Donald M., ed. Annual Review of Biophysics & Biophysical Chemistry, Vol. 14. LC 79-188446. (Illus.). 478p. 1985. text ed. 47.00 (ISBN 0-8243-1814-5). Annual Reviews.

Engelman, Edmund. Bergasse Nineteen: Sigmund Freud's Home & Offices, Vienna 1938. LC 80-23056. pap. 38.30 (ISBN 0-317-26501-6, 2024040). Bks Demand UMI.

Engelman, Richard M. & Levitsky, Sidney, eds. A Textbook of Clinical Cardioplegia. LC 81-69558. (Illus.). 512p. 1982. 59.50 (ISBN 0-87993-167-1). Futura Pub.

Engelman, Uriah Z. The Rise of the Jew in the Western World. LC 73-2194. (The Jewish People; History, Religion, Literature Ser.). Repr. of 1944 ed. 22.00 (ISBN 0-405-05260-X). Ayer Co Pubs.

Engelmann. Static & Rotating Electromagnetic Devices. (Electrical Engineering & Electronics Series). 760p. 1982. 59.75 (ISBN 0-8247-1697-3). Dekker.

Engelmann, Arthur, et al. History of Continental Civil Procedure. (Continental Legal History Ser.: Vol. 7). lxiii, 948p. 1969. Repr. of 1927 ed. 37.50x (ISBN 0-8377-2101-6). Rothman.

Engelmann, Barbara A. & Engelmann, Michael A. Cutting Your Taxes: A Guide for Minnesotans. Reutiman, Sherry, ed. LC 84-90308. 145p. (Orig.). 1984. pap. 6.95 (ISBN 0-916407-00-4). Finan Guide Bks.

Engelmann, Bernt. Germany Without Jews. 400p. 1984. pap. 4.95 (ISBN 0-553-24445-0). Bantam.

Engelmann, C., et al. Modern Methods for the Determination of Non-Metals in Non-Ferrous Metals: Applications to Particular Systems of Metallurgical Importance. (Illus.). xiii, 410p. 1985. 76.00x (ISBN 3-11-010342-7). De Gruyter.

Engelmann, George J. Labor among Primitive Peoples, Showing the Development of the Obstetric Science of Today. LC 75-23705. (Illus.). Repr. of 1882 ed. 20.00 (ISBN 0-404-13257-X). AMS Pr.

Engelmann, Larry. Intemperance: The Lost War Against Liquor. LC 79-7103. (Illus.). 1979. 12.95 (ISBN 0-02-909520-4). Free Pr.

Engelmann, Michael A., jt. auth. see Engelmann, Barbara A.

Engelmann, Paul, jt. auth. see Wittgenstein, Ludwig.

Engelmann, R. J. & Slinn, W. G., eds. Precipitation Scavenging (1970) Proceedings. LC 70-609397. (AEC Symposium Ser.). 508p. 1970. pap. 20.75 (CONF-700601); microfiche 4.50 (ISBN 0-87079-308-X, CONF-700601). DOE.

Engelmann, Rudolf J. & Sehmel, George A., eds. Atmosphere-Surface Exchange of Particulate & Gaseous Pollutants (1974) Proceedings. LC 75-38716. (ERDA Symposium Ser.). 1000p. 1976. pap. 33.00 (ISBN 0-87079-138-9, CONF-740921); microfiche 4.50 (ISBN 0-87079-139-7, CONF-740921). DOE.

Engelmann, Ruth. Leaf House: Days of Remembering. LC 80-8201. 256p. 1982. 13.41i (ISBN 0-06-011282-4, HarpT). Har-Row.

Engelmann, Seigfried & Engelmann, Therese. Give Your Child a Superior Mind. 320p. 1981. 6.95 (ISBN 0-346-12532-4). Cornerstone.

Engelmann, Siegfried. Direct Instruction. Longdom, Danny G., ed. LC 79-24814. (Instructional Design Library). 128p. 1980. 19.95 (ISBN 0-87778-142-7). Educ Tech Pubns.

--Preventing Failure in the Primary Grades. 1969. text ed. 20.95 (ISBN 0-574-50050-2, 5-0050); pap. text ed. 15.95 (ISBN 0-574-50051-0, 5-0051). SRA.

--Teach Your Child to Read in 100 Easy Lessons. Haddox, Phyllis & Bruner, Elaine, eds. (Illus.). 416p. 1983. 14.95 (ISBN 0-346-12557-X). Cornerstone.

Engelmann, Siegfried & Carnine, Douglas. Theory of Instruction: Principles & Applications. (Illus.). 385p. 1982. text ed. 29.50x (ISBN 0-8290-0977-9). Irvington.

Engelmann, Siegfried & Colvin, Goeffrey. Generalized Compliance Training. LC 83-9745. (Illus.). 256p. (Orig.). 1983. pap. text ed. 19.00 (ISBN 0-936104-31-7, 0375). Pro Ed.

Engelmann, Th. W. Th. W. Engelmanm: Some Papers & His Bibliography. 264p. 1984. pap. text ed. 32.75x (ISBN 90-6203-656-2, Pub. by Radopi Holland). Humanities.

Engelmann, Therese, jt. auth. see Engelmann, Seigfried.

Engelmayer, Sheldon & Waxman, Robert. Lord's Justice: One Judge's War Against the Infamous Dalkon Shield. LC 85-6114. 312p. 1985. 17.95 (ISBN 0-385-23051-6, Anchor Pr). Doubleday.

Engelmayer, Sheldon D. & Wagman, Robert J. Lord's Justice. LC 85-6114. write for info. Amer Bar Assn.

Engelmeier, Darlette, ed. see Engelmeier, Philip A.

Engelmeier, Philip A. Auctioneering. Paulaha, Richard & Engelmeier, Darlette, eds. Orig. Title: Be a Journeyman Auctioneer. (Illus.). 48p. (Orig.). 1980. pap. 10.00 (ISBN 0-686-70078-3). Engelmeier.

Engeln, Oscar D. Von & Urquhart, Jane M. Story Key to Geographic Names. LC 72-113299. 1970. Repr. of 1924 ed. 24.50x (ISBN 0-8046-1330-3, Pub. by Kennikat). Assoc Faculty Pr.

Engeln, Oscar Dedrich Von & Urquhart, Jane M. The Story Key to Geographic Names. LC 74-13855. 279p. 1976. Repr. of 1924 ed. 43.00x (ISBN 0-8103-4062-3). Gale.

Engels, Donald W. Alexander the Great & the Logistics of the Macedonian Army. LC 76-52025. 1978. 30.00x (ISBN 0-520-03433-3); pap. 5.95 (ISBN 0-520-04272-7, CAL 472). U of Cal Pr.

Engels, F. Cartas Sobre el Materialismo Historico. 35p. 1980. pap. 0.80 (ISBN 0-8285-2184-0, Pub. by Progress Pubs USSR). Imported Pubns.

--La Guerra Campesina en Alemania. 215p. (Span.). 1981. 3.00 (ISBN 0-8285-2155-7, Pub. by Progress Pubs USSR). Imported Pubns.
--Origen de la Familia, la Propiedad Privada y el Estado. 214p. 1981. 3.95 (ISBN 0-8285-1353-8, Pub. by Progress Pubs USSR). Imported Pubns.
Engels, F., jt. auth. see Marx, K.
Engels, Frederick. Anti-Duhring. 1976. 4.95 (ISBN 0-8351-0473-7); pap. 3.25 (ISBN 0-8351-0010-3). China Bks.
--Anti-Duhring: Herr Eugen Duhring's Revolution in Science. 402p. 1984. 29.95x (ISBN 0-88286-082-8). C H Kerr.
--Condition of the Working Class in England. 351p. 1973. 14.95x (ISBN 0-8464-1082-6). Beekman Pubs.
--Dialectics of Nature. 399p. 1940. 7.50 (ISBN 0-7178-0049-0); pap. 3.50 (ISBN 0-7178-0048-2). Intl Pubs Co.
--Engels on Capital. new ed. LC 73-94192. 144p. 1974. pap. 1.75 (ISBN 0-7178-0409-7). Intl Pubs Co.
--Germany: Revolution & Counter-Revolution. rev. ed. LC 69-20353. 160p. (Orig.). 1969. pap. 1.95 (ISBN 0-7178-0077-6, NW). Intl Pubs Co.
--Ludwig Feuerbach. 1976. 4.95 (ISBN 0-8351-0141-X). China Bks.
--Ludwig Feuerbach, & the Outcome of Classical German Philosophy. 95p. 1941. pap. 1.25 (ISBN 0-7178-0120-9). Intl Pubs Co.
--Origin of the Family, Private Property, & the State. 2nd ed. Leacock, Eleanor B., ed. LC 79-184309. 274p. 1972. 10.00 (ISBN 0-7178-0338-4); pap. 3.95 (ISBN 0-7178-0359-7). Intl Pubs Co.
--The Peasant War in Germany. LC 66-21949. (Illus.). 191p. 1966. pap. 1.95 (ISBN 0-7178-0152-7). Intl Pubs Co.
--Role of Force in History: A Study of Bismark's Policy of Blood & Iron. Wargermann, Ernst, ed. 108p. 1968. 11.95x (ISBN 0-8464-1128-8). Beekman Pubs.
--Socialism: From Utopia to Science. 5th ed. Aveling, Edward, tr. 1974. pap. text ed. 0.75 (ISBN 0-935534-27-X). NY Labor News.
--Socialism, Utopian & Scientific. Aveling, Edward, tr. from Ger. 135p. lib. bdg. 12.95; pap. 2.25 (ISBN 0-88286-031-3). C H Kerr.
--Socialism: Utopian & Scientific. 1975. pap. 1.95 (ISBN 0-8351-0357-9). China Bks.
--Socialism: Utopian & Scientific. 96p. 1935. pap. 1.50 (ISBN 0-7178-0191-8). Intl Pubs Co.
--Socialism: Utopian & Scientific. LC 72-92659. 64p. 1972. pap. 1.25 (ISBN 0-87348-264-6). Path Pr NY.
--Socialism: Utopian & Scientific-With an Essay on "The Mark". Aveling, Edward, tr. from Ger. LC 77-4356. 1977. Repr. of 1935 ed. lib. bdg. 15.00x (ISBN 0-8371-9622-1, ENSO). Greenwood.
Engels, Frederick & Marx, Karl. Germany-Revolution & Counterrevolution. 155p. 1969. 11.95x (ISBN 0-8464-1100-8). Beekman Pubs.
Engels, Frederick, jt. auth. see Marx, Karl.
Engels, Frederick, ed. see Marx, Karl.
Engels, Frederick, jt. auth. see Marx, Karl.
Engels, Friederich, jt. auth. see Marx, Karl.
Engels, Friedrich. Anti-Duhring. 502p. 1975. 5.95 (ISBN 0-8285-0011-8, Pub. by Progress Pubs USSR). Imported Pubns.
--The Bakuninists at Work. 26p. 1971. pap. 0.75 (ISBN 0-8285-0013-4; Pub. by Progress Pubs USSR). Imported Pubns.
--The Condition of the Working Class in England. 351p. 1973. 3.45 (ISBN 0-8285-0020-7, Pub. by Progress Pubs USSR). Imported Pubns.
--The Condition of the Working Class in England. Henderson, W. O. & Chaloner, W. H., trs. (Illus.). 1958. 27.50x (ISBN 0-8047-0633-6); pap. 8.95x (ISBN 0-8047-0634-4). Stanford U Pr.
--Contribucion al Problema de la Vivienda. 125p. (Span.). 1978. pap. 1.45 (ISBN 0-8285-1668-5, Pub. by Progress Pubs USSR). Imported Pubns.
--Del Socialismo Utopico al Socialismo Cientifico. 88p. (Span.). 1979. pap. 1.95 (ISBN 0-8285-1342-2, Pub. by Progress Pubs USSR). Imported Pubns.
--Engels as Military Critic: Articles Reprinted from the "Volunteer Journal" & the "Manchester Guardian" of the 1860's. LC 75-26213. 1976. Repr. of 1959 ed. lib. bdg. 24.75x (ISBN 0-8371-8407-X, ENMC). Greenwood.
--The German Revolutions. LC 67-15314. 256p. 1967. pap. 2.95x (ISBN 0-226-20869-9, P256, Phoen). U of Chicago Pr.
--The German Revolutions: The Peasant War in Germany. L., intro. by. Incl. Germany: Revolution & Counter-Revolution. LC 67-15314. 1967. 17.50x (ISBN 0-226-20868-0). U of Chicago Pr.
--The Housing Question. 109p. 1979. pap. 1.95 (ISBN 0-8285-0029-0, Pub. by Progress Pubs USSR). Imported Pubns.
--Letters of the Young Engels. 279p. 1976. 3.45 (ISBN 0-8285-0031-2, Pub. by Progress Pubs USSR). Imported Pubns.
--Ludwig Feuerbach & the End of Classical German Philosophy. 61p. 1969. pap. 0.75 (ISBN 0-8285-0032-0, Pub. by Progress Pubs USSR). Imported Pubns.
--Ludwig Feuerbach & the Outcome of Classical German Philosophy. LC 76-42701. 104p. Repr. of 1934 ed. 18.00 (ISBN 0-404-15369-0). AMS Pr.
--Ludwig Feuerbach y el Fin De la Filosofia Clasica Alemana. 67p. (Span.). 1978. pap. 1.45 (ISBN 0-8285-1672-3, Pub. by Progress Pubs USSR). Imported Pubns.
--On Historical Materialism. LC 76-42699. (BCL Ser.: II). Repr. of 1940 ed. 11.50 (ISBN 0-404-15370-4). AMS Pr.
--Origin of the Family: Private Property & the State. LC 72-85711. 1972. pap. 3.45 (ISBN 0-87348-261-1). Path Pr NY.
--El Papel Del Trabajo en la Transformacion del Mono en Hombre. 18p. (Span.). 1977. pap. 0.75 (ISBN 0-8285-1354-6, Pub. by Progress Pubs USSR). Imported Pubns.
--The Part Played by Labour in the Transition from Ape to Man. 16p. 1972. pap. 0.75 (ISBN 0-8285-0044-4, Pub. by Progress Pubs USSR). Imported Pubns.
--The Peasant Question in France & Germany. 27p. 1976. pap. 0.75 (ISBN 0-8285-0045-2, Pub. by Progress Pubs USSR). Imported Pubns.
--The Peasant War in Germany. 208p. 1974. 3.95 (ISBN 0-8285-0046-0, Pub. by Progress Pubs USSR). Imported Pubns.
--El Problema Campesino en Francia y en Alemania. 29p. (Span.). 1979. pap. 1.95 (ISBN 0-8285-1673-1, Pub. by Progress Pubs USSR). Imported Pubns.
--The Wages System. 56p. 1977. pap. 0.95 (ISBN 0-8285-0061-4, Pub. by Progress Pubs USSR). Imported Pubns.
Engels, Friedrich & Marx, Karl. Basic Writings on Politics & Philosophy. LC 59-12053. pap. 7.50 (ISBN 0-385-09420-5, Anch). Doubleday.
Engels, Friedrich, jt. auth. see Marx, Karl.
Engels, Friedrich, ed. see Marx, Karl.
Engels, Friedrich, tr. & intro. by see Marx, Karl.
Engels, Friedrich, jt. auth. see Marx, Karl.
Engels, H. Numerical Quadrature & Cubature. LC 79-41235. (Computational Mathematics and Application Ser.). 1980. 74.00 (ISBN 0-12-238850-X). Acad Pr.
Engels, John. Blood Mountain. LC 76-26854. (Pitt Poetry Ser.). 1977. 12.95x (ISBN 0-8229-3338-1); ltd. ed. o.p. 20.00x (ISBN 0-8229-3289-X); pap. 5.95 (ISBN 0-8229-5277-7). U of Pittsburgh Pr.
--The Seasons in Vermont. (Illus.). 28p. 1982. pap. 5.00 (ISBN 0-918092-36-1); signed cloth 25.00 (ISBN 0-918092-35-3). Tamarack Edns.
--Vivaldi in Early Fall. LC 80-24571. (Contemporary Poetry Ser.). 112p. 1981. 9.95x (ISBN 0-8203-0543-X); pap. 5.95 (ISBN 0-8203-0552-9). U of Ga Pr.
--Weather-Fear: New & Selected Poems, 1958-1982. LC 82-13591. (Contemporary Poetry Ser.). 144p. 1983. 12.50x (ISBN 0-8203-0654-1); pap. 6.95 (ISBN 0-8203-0655-X). U of Ga Pr.
Engels, Vincent. Adirondack Fishing in the Nineteen Thirties: A Lost Paradise. (Illus.). 1978. 8.95 (ISBN 0-8156-0144-1). Syracuse U Pr.
Engels, W. Advances in Invertebrate Reproduction. 1984. 92.50 (ISBN 0-444-80568-0, I-183-84). Elsevier.
Engels, W. & Pohl, H., eds. German Yearbook on Business History, 1982. (Illus.). 186p. 1982. 15.20 (ISBN 0-387-11892-6). Springer-Verlag.
--German Yearbook on Business History, 1983. Martin, E., tr. from Ger. 160p. 1984. 17.70 (ISBN 0-387-13061-6). Springer Verlag.
--German Yearbook on Business History, 1984. 170p. 1985. 16.00 (ISBN 0-387-15491-4). Springer-Verlag.
Engels, Wolfram. The Optimal Monetary Unit. 136p. 1982. text ed. 18.50x (ISBN 3-593-32843-7). Irvington.
Engelsfeld. Croatian Thru Conversation. 4th ed. 1982. 12.50 (ISBN 0-317-19019-9, Y785). Vanous.
Engelsfeld, M. Croatian Through Conversation. 4th, rev. ed. 1982. pap. text ed. 12.50 (ISBN 0-686-46528-8). Heinman.
--Croatian Through Conversation & Phrase Book for Tourists. 4th ed. 250p. 1982. pap. 12.50 (ISBN 0-89918-785-4, Y785). Vanous.
Engelsman, Coert. Heavy Construction Cost File, 1985: Unit Prices. 256p. 1985. pap. 39.95 (ISBN 0-442-26703-7). Van Nos Reinhold.
--Watch It, Mr. Contractor. 1986. cancelled (ISBN 0-442-22314-5). Van Nos Reinhold.
Engelsman, Joan C. The Feminine Dimension of the Divine. LC 79-13884. 204p. 1979. pap. 9.95 (ISBN 0-664-24268-5). Westminster.
Engelsman, S. B., ed. Families of Curves & the Origins of Partial Differentiation. (North-Holland Mathematics Studies: No. 93). 238p. 1984. 29.00 (ISBN 0-444-86897-6, I-126-84). Elsevier.
Engelsohn, Harold S. Programming Programmable Calculators. (Computer Programming Ser.). 1978. pap. 12.95 (ISBN 0-8104-5105-0). Hayden.
--Trigonometry: A Complete & Concrete Approach. (Illus.). 1981. text ed. 28.95 (ISBN 0-07-019419-X). McGraw.
Engelsohn, Harold S. & Feit, Joseph. Basic Mathematics: Arithmetic & Algebra. LC 79-21287. 532p. 1980. pap. 34.00 (ISBN 0-471-24145-8). Wiley.
Engel'son, Ja. L., et al. Seven Papers on Analysis. LC 51-5559. (Translations Ser.: No. 2, Vol. 60). 1967. 36.00 (ISBN 0-8218-1760-4, TRANS 2-60). Am Math.
Engelson, JoyceS., ed. see Shealy, C. Norman.
Engelson, Morris. Modern Spectrum Analyzer Theory & Application. 275p. 1984. text ed. 55.00 (ISBN 0-89006-150-5). Artech Hse.
Engelson, Morris & Telewski, Fred. Spectrum Analyzer Theory & Applications. LC 73-81244. (Modern Frontiers in Applied Science Ser.). pap. 71.80 (ISBN 0-317-30035-0, 2025050). Bks Demand UMI.
Engelstad, Orvis P., ed. Nutrient Mobility in Soils: Accumulation & Losses. (Illus.). 1970. pap. 3.00 (ISBN 0-89118-759-6). Soil Sci Soc Am.
Engelstein, Joel M., ed. Cataract Surgery: Current Options & Problems. 592p. 1983. 79.50 (ISBN 0-8089-1617-3, 791159). Grune.
Engelstein, Laura. Moscow, 1905: Working-Class Organization & Political Conflict. LC 81-50786. 320p. 1982. 32.50x (ISBN 0-8047-1118-6). Stanford U Pr.
Engelzakis, Benedict. New & Old in God's Revelation. (Studies in Relations Between Spirit & Tradition in the Bible). 128p. 1982. text ed. 12.95 (ISBN 0-913836-89-3). St Vladimirs.
Engeman, Richard H. The Jacksonville Story. (Illus.). 1980. 10.00x (ISBN 0-943388-01-5); pap. 2.95 (ISBN 0-943388-02-3). South Oregon.
--Preliminary Guide to Local History Materials: Jacksonville Museum Library. (Illus.). 86p. 1978. 5.00x (ISBN 0-943388-00-7). South Oregon.
Engeman, Thomas S., jt. auth. see Benson, George C.
Engemann, Joseph G. & Hegner, Robert W. Invertebrate Zoology. 3rd ed. 1981. text ed. write for info. (ISBN 0-02-333780-X). Macmillan.
Engen. Rhode Island Test of Language Structure. (Illus.). 112p. 1983. pap. text ed. 49.95 (ISBN 0-8391-1790-6, 18406). Univ Park.
Engen, Gavin. Kit Cars. LC 77-6203. (Superwheels & Thrill Sports Bks.). (Illus.). (gr. 3-9). 1977. PLB 8.95 (ISBN 0-8225-0417-0). Lerner Pubns.
Engen, John Van see Van Engen, John.
Engen, Orrin A. Writer of the Plains: The Biography of B. M. Bower. new ed. (Illus.). 56p. (Orig.). 1973. 6.00 (ISBN 0-686-05538-1); text ed. 3.60 (ISBN 0-686-05539-X). Pontine Pr.
Engen, Rodney. Kate Greenaway: A Biography. LC 80-14850. (Illus.). 240p. 1981. 29.95 (ISBN 0-8052-3775-5). Schocken.
--Laurence Housman. (The Artist & the Critic Ser.). (Illus.). 168p. cancelled (ISBN 0-904995-04-6). Parkwest Pubns.
--Randolph Caldecott. 1981. 27.00x (ISBN 0-905368-02-9, Pub. by Jupiter England). State Mutual Bk.
--Richard Doyle. (The Artist & the Critic Ser.). (Illus.). 216p. cancelled (ISBN 0-904995-05-4). Parkwest Pubns.
Engen, Rodney K. Dictionary of Nineteenth Century British Wood Engravers. 320p. 1985. lib. bdg. 65.00 (ISBN 0-85964-139-2). Chadwyck-Healey.
Engen, S. Stochastic Abundance Models: With Emphasis on Biological Communities & Species Diversity. 126p. 1978. 18.95x (ISBN 0-412-15240-1, NO.6102, Pub. by Chapman & Hall England). Methuen Inc.
Engen, Sadie O. God Set the Sails. (Trailblazer Ser.). 1982. pap. 5.95 (ISBN 0-8163-0455-6). Pacific Pr Pub Assn.
--John Tay: Messenger to Pitcairn. (Trailblazer Ser.). 1981. pap. 5.95 (ISBN 0-8163-0405-X). Pacific Pr Pub Assn.
Engen, Sadie O., et al. Living & Learning. 1980. 7.95 (ISBN 0-8280-0051-4, 12510-4). Review & Herald.
Engen, Trygg. The Perception of Odors. (Series in Cognition & Perception). 1982. 30.00 (ISBN 0-12-239350-3). Acad Pr.
Enger, Clifford. Lightning Strikes Twice. 1984. 11.95 (ISBN 0-934860-35-1). Adventure Pubns.
Enger, Eldon D., et al. Environmental Science: The Study of Interrelationships. 544p. 1982. pap. text ed. write for info. (ISBN 0-697-04729-6); instr's manual avail. (ISBN 0-697-04745-8); transparencies avail. (ISBN 0-697-04749-0). Wm C Brown.
--Concepts in Biology. 3rd ed. 512p. 1982. pap. text ed. write for info. (ISBN 0-697-04712-1); instrs.' manual avail. (ISBN 0-697-04715-6); lab manual o.p. avail. (ISBN 0-697-04714-8). Wm C Brown.
--Concepts in Biology. 4th ed. 560p. 1985. pap. text ed. write for info. (ISBN 0-697-05023-8); lab manual avail. (ISBN 0-697-04799-7); instr's. manual avail. (ISBN 0-697-05101-3); transparencies avail. (ISBN 0-697-05102-1). Wm C Brown.
--Environmental Science: The Study of Interrelationships. 2nd ed. 568p. 1986. pap. text ed. price not set (ISBN 0-697-00643-X); price not set instr's. manual (ISBN 0-697-00642-5); price not set transparencies (ISBN 0-697-00641-7). Wm C Brown.
--Essentials of Allied Health Science. 320p. 1978. pap. text ed. write for info. (ISBN 0-697-04547-1). Wm C Brown.
Enger, Norman. Management Standards for Developing Information Systems. 1980. pap. 5.95 (ISBN 0-8144-7527-2). AMACOM.
Enger, Norman & Bassler, Richard. Computer Systems & Public Administrators. 1976. pap. 12.50 (ISBN 0-916580-01-6). College Readings.
Enger, Norman L. Documentation Standards for Computer Systems. 2nd ed. LC 79-5289. (Illus.). 1980. text ed. 25.00 (ISBN 0-89321-119-2). Tech Pr Inc.
--Management Standards for Developing Information Systems. LC 76-41827. pap. 59.80 (ISBN 0-317-20774-1, 2023906). Bks Demand UMI.
Enger, Norman L. & Howerton, Paul W. Computer Security: A Management Audit Approach. LC 80-65874. pap. 68.00 (ISBN 0-317-27070-2, 2023536). Bks Demand UMI.
Enger, Ralph. The History of the Norwegian Club of San Francisco. 1970. pap. 11.00 (ISBN 0-88247-102-3). R & E Pubs.
Enger, Ronald L. Do It Yourself (At Home) Sewing Machine Care & Repair. (Illus.). 33p. 1978. pap. 3.95 (ISBN 0-685-59470-X). R L Enger.
Engerbretson. A Programmed Instruction Manual of the Human Muscle System. 176p. 1985. pap. text ed. 12.95 (ISBN 0-8403-3535-0). Kendall-Hunt.
Engerman, Jeanne, jt. auth. see Frederick, Richard.
Engerman, Stanley, jt. auth. see Fogel, Robert W.
Engerman, Stanley L. & Genovese, Eugene D. Race & Slavery in the Western Hemisphere. LC 74-2965. (Quantitative Studies in History Ser). 472p. 1974. 44.00 (ISBN 0-691-04625-5). Princeton U Pr.
Engerman, Stanley L., jt. auth. see Fogel, Robert W.
Engeroff, K. & Lovelace-Kaeufer, C. English-German Dictionary of Idioms. (Eng. & Ger.). 22.75x (ISBN 3-1900-6217-X). Adlers Foreign Bks.
Enggass, Catherine, tr. see Forssman, Erik.
Enggass, Catherine, tr. see Malvasia, Carlo C.
Enggass, Catherine, tr. see Manetti, Antonio.
Enggass, Catherine, tr. see Puppi, Lionello.
Enggass, Catherine, tr. see Ridolfi, Carlo.
Enggass, Robert. Early Eighteenth-Century Sculpture in Rome: An Illustrated Catalogue Raisonne, 2 vols. LC 75-16353. 480p. 1976. 87.50x (ISBN 0-271-01200-5). Pa St U Pr.
Enggass, Robert & Brown, Jonathan. Italy & Spain: 1600-1750. (Sources & Documents in the History of Art Ser). 1970. pap. 17.95 ref. ed. (ISBN 0-13-508101-7). P-H.
Enggass, Robert, tr. see Malvasia, Carlo C.
Enggass, Robert, tr. see Ridolfi, Carlo.
Engh, Charles A. & Bobyn, J. D. Biological Fixation in Total Hip Arthroplasty. LC 84-51922. 1985. 95.00 (ISBN 0-943432-36-7). Slack Inc.
Engh, Rohn. Sell & Re-Sell Your Photos. LC 81-1877. (Illus.). 323p. 1981. 14.95 (ISBN 0-89879-046-8). Writers Digest.
--A Very Simple Garden Book: Vegetables. LC 75-42507. (Illus.). 160p. 1977. 6.95 (ISBN 0-8397-8580-1). Eriksson.
Engholm, Eva. Bird Infirmary. LC 72-6617. (Illus.). 1973. 6.95 (ISBN 0-8008-0742-1). Taplinger.
Engineer, Asghar A. The Origin & Development of Islam. 248p. 1980. 18.95x (ISBN 0-940500-33-7). Asia Bk Corp.
--The Origin & Development of Islam: An Essay on Its Socio-Economic Growth. 248p. 1980. text ed. 18.95 (ISBN 0-86131-174-4, Pub. by Orient Longman Ltd India). Apt Bks.
Engineer, Asghar A., ed. Communal Riots in Post-Independence India. 288p. 1984. text ed. 30.00 (ISBN 0-86131-494-8, Pub. by Sangam Bks India). Apt Bks.
Engineer, Asghar Ali. The Bohras. 1980. text ed. 22.50x (ISBN 0-7069-0836-8, Pub. by Vikas India). Advent NY.
Engineering & Mining Journal Editors, compiled by. E-MJ Operating Handbook of Mineral Processing, Vol. II. 2nd ed. 500p. 1980. 29.50 (ISBN 0-07-019527-7). McGraw.
Engineering Concepts Curriculum Project - State University of New York. Man & His Technology. (Illus.). 256p. 1973. text ed. 25.00 (ISBN 0-07-019510-2). McGraw.
Engineering Corporation. Engineering & Application Manual for AEC Companies: Size Reduction Division. 100p. 1982. 80.00 (ISBN 0-910447-01-2). Application Eng Corp.
Engineering Economics Committee. Engineering Economics Bibliography. Miles, H. V., ed. 98p. 1969. 8.95 (ISBN 0-317-36002-7, 01-01-R015). TAPPI.
Engineering Equipment Users Association. Guide to the Preparation of Engineering Specifications. (Orig.). 1981. pap. 10.95x (ISBN 0-85072-116-4, Pub. by Design Council England). Intl Spec Bk.
Engineering Equipment Users Association Staff. Systematic Fault Diagnosis. (Illus.). 168p. 1982. text ed. 38.00x (ISBN 0-7114-5739-5). Longman.
Engineering Foundation Conference, Jan. 1978. Evaluation & Prediction of Subsidence. American Society of Civil Engineers, compiled By. 600p. 1979. pap. 36.00x (ISBN 0-87262-137-5). Am Soc Civil Eng.
Engineering Foundation Conference, Mar. 1974. Foundations for Dams. 480p. 1974. pap. 27.50x (ISBN 0-87262-100-6). Am Soc Civil Eng.
Engineering Foundation Conference, Nov. 1974. The Constructed Environment with Man as the Measure. 322p. pap. 22.00x (ISBN 0-87262-157-X). Am Soc Civil Eng.
Engineering Foundation Conference, Nov. 1976. Evaluation of Dam Safety. American Society of Civil Engineers, compiled By. 529p. 1977. pap. 16.00x (ISBN 0-87262-088-3). Am Soc Civil Eng.

Engineering Foundation Conference on Modeling of Casting & Welding Processes II, New Hampshire, July 31 - August 5, 1983. Grain Refinement in Castings & Welds. David, S. A. & Abbaschian, G. J., eds. (Proceedings). 458p. 45.00 (ISBN 0-89520-477-0, 247); members 30.00 (ISBN 0-317-37161-4); student members 15.00 (ISBN 0-317-37162-2). Metal Soc.

Engineering Foundation Conference on Use of Shotcrete for Underground Structural Support. Use of Shotcrete for Underground Structural Support: Proceedings of the Engineering Foundation Conference, Berwick Academy, South Berwick, Maine, July 16-20, 1973 - with the Cooperation of ASCE & ACI. (American Concrete Institute Ser.: SP-45). (Illus.). pap. 118.80 (ISBN 0-317-10278-8, 2019550). Bks Demand UMI.

Engineering Foundation Conference, 1979. Improved Hydrologic Forecastings: Why & How. 458p. 1980. pap. 32.50x (ISBN 0-87262-203-7). Am Soc Civil Eng.

Engineering Index, Inc. Engineering Index Thesaurus. LC 72-78325. 1972. 19.50 (ISBN 0-02-468550-X). Macmillan Info.

Engineering Industry Training Board, London, ed. Static Electrical Equipment Winding & Building, 2 vols. (Engineering Craftsmen: No. G1). (Illus.). 1968. Set. spiral bdg. 69.95x (ISBN 0-89563-022-2). Vol. 2 (ISBN 0-85083-128-8). Intl Ideas.

Engineering Industry Training Board, ed. Training for Capstan, Turret, & Sequence Controlled Lathe Setters & Operators, 21 vols. (Illus.). 1973. Set. 89.95x (ISBN 0-89563-023-0). Intl Ideas.

--Training for Drilling Machine Operators, 17 vols. (Illus.). 1978. Set. 69.95x (ISBN 0-89563-024-9). Intl Ideas.

--Training for Fixed Headstock Single Spindle Automatic Lathe Setters & Operators, 30 vols. (Illus.). 1978. folder 89.95x (ISBN 0-85083-425-2). Intl Ideas.

--Training for Industrial Site Radiography, 14 vols. Incl. Vol. 1. Introduction to Radiography; Vol. 2. Ionizing Radiations; Vol. 4. Image Formation; Vol. 5. Safety; Vol. 6. X-Ray Equipment; Vol. 7. Gamma-Ray Equipment; Vol. 8. Exposure; Vol. 9. Operations; Vol. 10. Pipe-Crawler Equipment. 69.95. (Illus.). 1977. Set. 42.50x (ISBN 0-89563-025-7). Intl Ideas.

--Training for Manual Metal-Arc Welders, 14 vols. Incl. Vol. 1. Metal-Arc Welding; Vol. 2. Welding Electrodes; Vol. 3. Joints & Weld Symbols; Vol. 4. Limiting Distortion; Vol. 5. Basic Welding; Vol. 6. Plate Surfaces; Vol. 7. Fillet Joints; Vol. 8. Single Vee Butt Joints; Vol. 9. Pipe Welding; Vol. 10. Fault Diagnosis; Vol. 11. Branch Connections. 69.95. (Illus.). 1974. Set. 43.95x (ISBN 0-89563-026-5). Intl Ideas.

--Training for Milling Machine Operators & Setters, 22 vols. (Illus.). 1977. Set. 69.95x (ISBN 0-89563-027-3). Intl Ideas.

--Training for Multi-Spindle Automatic Lathe Setters & Operators, 31 vols. (Illus.). 1979. Set. folder 89.95x (ISBN 0-85083-463-5). Intl Ideas.

--Training for Operators of Numerically Controlled Machines. Incl. Vol. 1. Introduction to NC Machine Tool; Vol. 2. Rotating Tool; Vol. 3. Rotating Work; Vol. 4. Milling Cutters; Vol. 5. Tape NC Machines; Vol. 6. Automatic Tool & Work Exchanging; Vol. 7. X, Y, & Z Axes; Vol. 8. Positioning of the Tool & Workpiece; Vol. 9. Emergency Stop & Switching Operations; Vol. 10. Operation. 79.95. 1973. Set. 62.50x (ISBN 0-89563-028-1). Intl Ideas.

Engineering Industry Training Board. Training for Pipe Fitters, 23 vols. 1976. 75.00x (ISBN 0-89563-031-1). Intl Ideas.

Engineering Industry Training Board, ed. Training for Power Press Setters & Operators, 17 vols. (Illus.). 1973. Set. folder 67.50x (ISBN 0-89563-048-6). Intl Ideas.

--Training for Riggers-Erectors, 15 vols. (Illus.). 1976. Set. 67.50x (ISBN 0-89563-030-3). Intl Ideas.

--Training for Sliding Headstock Single Spindle Automatic Lathe (Swiss Auto) Setters & Operators, 26 vols. (Illus.). 1978. Set. folder 79.95x (ISBN 0-85083-426-0). Intl Ideas.

Engineering Management Conference, Melbourne, Australia, March 1979. Engineering Management Update. 78p. (Orig.). 1979. pap. text ed. 24.00x (ISBN 0-85825-105-1, Pub. by Inst Engineering Australia). Brookfield Pub Co.

Engineering Manpower Commission. Demand for Engineers, 1981. (Illus.). 1982. 75.00x (ISBN 0-87615-112-8, 231-82). AAES.

--Demand for Engineers, 1982. 1983. pap. 100.00x (ISBN 0-87615-113-6, 231-83). AAES.

--Engineering & Technology Degrees, 1983, 3 parts. (Illus.). 1984. pap. 200.00 (ISBN 0-87615-034-2, 201-83 (A, B, C)); pap. 75.00 part I: by Schools (ISBN 0-87615-044-X); pap. 100.00 part II: by Minorities (ISBN 0-87615-054-7); pap. 75.00 part III: by Curriculum (ISBN 0-87615-064-4). AAES.

--Engineering & Technology Enrollments, Fall 1983, 2 pts. 1984. pap. 101.00x part I: Engineering Enrollments (ISBN 0-87615-085-7, 207-84 (A,B)); pap. 101.00x part II: Technology Enrollments (ISBN 0-87615-095-4); pap. 202.00 (ISBN 0-87615-075-X). AAES.

--Engineers' Salaries: Special Industry Report, 1982. (Illus.). 1982. pap. 225.00x (ISBN 0-87615-123-3, 301-82). AAES.

--Engineers' Salaries: Special Industry Report, 1983. (Illus.). 250p. pap. 226.00x (ISBN 0-87615-124-1, 301-83). AAES.

--Professional Income of Engineers, 1983. Incl. Professional Income of Engineers: 1984. Engineering Manpower Commission Staff. Sheridan, P. J., ed. (Illus.). 120p. (Orig.). 1984. pap. 75.00. (Illus.). 1983. 75.00x (ISBN 0-87615-135-7, 302-83). AAES.

Engineering Manpower Commission Staff see Engineering Manpower Commission.

Engineering Manpower Commission Staff. Engineering & Technology Degrees, 1984, Pt. I. Sheridan, P. J., ed. 50p. (Orig.). 1985. pap. 75.00 (ISBN 0-87615-045-8). AAES.

--Engineering & Technology Degrees, 1984, Pt. II. Sheridan, Patrick J., ed. 144p. (Orig.). 1985. pap. 100.00 (ISBN 0-87615-055-5). AAES.

--Engineering & Technology Degrees 1984, Pt. III. Sheridan, Patrick J., ed. 86p. (Orig.). 1985. pap. 75.00 (ISBN 0-87615-065-2). AAES.

--Engineering & Technology Enrollments Fall 1984: Pt. I, Engineering Enrollments. Heydt, Carolyn, ed. 410p. 1984. pap. 100.00 (ISBN 0-87615-086-5). AAES.

--Engineering & Technology Enrollments, Fall 1984: Pt. II-Technology Enrollments. Heydt, Carolyn, ed. 300p. 1985. pap. 100.00 (ISBN 0-87615-096-2). AAES.

--Engineers' Salaries: Special Industry Report 1984. Sheridan, P. J., ed. (Illus.). 250p. (Orig.). 1984. 225.00 (ISBN 0-87615-125-X). AAES.

--Professional Income of Engineers 1984. Sheridan, P. J., ed. (Illus.). 120p. (Orig.). 1984. pap. 75.00 (ISBN 0-317-18024-X). AAES.

--Salaries of Engineers in Education 1984. Sheridan, P. J., ed. (Illus.). 75p. (Orig.). 1984. pap. 55.00 (ISBN 0-87615-155-1). AAES.

Engineering Research Associates, Inc. High Speed Computing Devices. (The Charles Babbage Institute Reprint Series for the History of Computing: Vol. 4). (Illus.). 1983. Repr. of 1950 ed. 38.00x (ISBN 0-938228-02-1). Tomash Pubs.

Engineering Research Associates Staff. High-Speed Computing Devices. (Illus.). 451p. 1984. 38.00 (ISBN 0-262-05028-5). MIT Pr.

--High-Speed Computing Devices, Vol. IV. (Charles Babbage Institute Reprint for the History of Computing Ser.). (Illus.). 451p. 1984. Repr. of 1950 ed. text ed. 38.00x (ISBN 0-262-05028-5). MIT Pr.

Engineering Societies Library Staff. Classed Subject Catalog of the Engineering Societies Library, New York City, 1st Supplement. 1965. 110.00 (ISBN 0-8161-0700-9, Hall Library). G K Hall.

--Classed Subject Catalog of the Engineering Societies Library, New York City, 2nd Supplement. 1966. 110.00 (ISBN 0-8161-0752-1, Hall Library). G K Hall.

--Classed Subject Catalog of the Engineering Societies Library, New York City, 3rd Supplement. 1967. 110.00 (ISBN 0-8161-0756-4, Hall Library). G K Hall.

--Classed Subject Catalog of the Engineering Societies Library, New York City, 4th Supplement, 1968 & 5th Supplement, 1969. Fourth Suppl. 110.00 (ISBN 0-8161-0817-X, Hall Library); Fifth Suppl. 110.00 (ISBN 0-8161-0836-6). G K Hall.

--Classed Subject Catalog of the Engineering Societies Library, New York City, 8th Supplement. 1972. lib. bdg. 110.00 (ISBN 0-8161-0982-6, Hall Library). G K Hall.

--Classed Subject Catalog of the Engineering Societies Library, New York City, 9th Supplement. 1973. lib. bdg. 110.00 (ISBN 0-8161-1050-6, Hall Library). G K Hall.

--Classed Subject Catalog of the Engineering Societies Library, New York City, 10th Supplement. 1974. 110.00 (ISBN 0-8161-1123-5, Hall Library). G K Hall.

--Classed Subject Catalog of the Engineering Societies Library, New York City, 6th Supplement. 1970. 110.00 (ISBN 0-8161-0883-8, Hall Library). G K Hall.

--Classed Subject Catalog of the Engineering Societies Library, New York City, 7th Supplement. 1971. lib. bdg. 110.00 (ISBN 0-8161-0913-3, Hall Library). G K Hall.

--Classed Subject Catalog of the Engineering Societies Library, New York City, 12 vols. 1185.00, incl. index (ISBN 0-8161-0653-3, Hall Library); index alone 100.00 (ISBN 0-8161-0237-6). G K Hall.

Engineering Society of Detroit. ESD Refresher Course Manual for the Professional Engineering Examination: Part I, Fundamentals of Engineering. 160p. 1981. wc & shrink wrapped 24.00 (ISBN 0-8403-2549-5). Kendall-Hunt.

Engineering Staff of Archive. Streaming. (Illus.). 196p. (Orig.). pap. 14.95 (ISBN 0-9608810-0-X). Archive Corp.

Engineering Staff of Texas Instruments Inc. T T L Data Book for Design Engineers: 1981 Supplement. 2nd. rev. ed. LC 81-50954. 380p. pap. 8.75 (ISBN 0-89512-108-5, LCC 5772). Tex Instr Inc.

Engineers Joint Council Editors. Thesaurus of Engineering & Scientific Terms. rev. ed. LC 68-6569. 1969. flexible cover 125.00x (ISBN 0-87615-163-2). AAES.

Engisch, Hillary & Smalley, Parke. Skiing Freestyle: Official Training Guide of the U. S. Freestyle Ski Team. (Illus.). 192p. 1985. pap. 14.95 (ISBN 0-317-19585-9). Taylor Pub.

England, jt. ed. see Vanselow.

England, A. Scripted Drama. 260p. 1981. 42.50 (ISBN 0-521-23235-X). Cambridge U Pr.

England, A. B. Byron's "Don Juan" & Eighteenth-Century Literature: A Study of Some Rhetorical Continuities & Discontinuities. LC 73-16943. 197p. 1975. 19.50 (ISBN 0-8387-1417-X). Bucknell U Pr.

--Energy & Order in the Poetry of Swift. LC 78-75200. 1980. 24.50 (ISBN 0-8387-2367-5). Bucknell U Pr.

England, Alan, jt. auth. see Sherry, Sylvia.

England, Barbara R. Glossarized Charts of Noam Chomsky's Grammar. LC 78-56641. (Illus.). 1978. pap. text ed. 6.75x (ISBN 0-916062-03-1). Physsardt.

England, Clark M., jt. auth. see Garrison, Ronald B.

England, David, ed. see IFSTA Committee.

England, David A. Television & Children. LC 83-83089. (Fastback Ser.: No. 207). 50p. (Orig.). 1984. pap. 0.75 (ISBN 0-87367-207-0). Phi Delta Kappa.

England, David A. & Flatley, Joannis K. Homework & Why. LC 84-62988. (Fastback Ser.: No. 218). 50p. (Orig.). 1985. pap. 0.75 (ISBN 0-87367-218-6). Phi Delta Kappa.

England, Diane L., ed. see McGill, Ormond.

England, Doris, et al, eds. Development of Competencies in Associate Degree Nursing: A Nursing Perspective. 14p. 1978. 4.50 (ISBN 0-88737-325-9, 23-1713). Natl League Nurse.

England, E. B., intro. by. & notes see Plato.

England, Ernest J., jt. auth. see Pearman, John W.

England, Eugene. Dialogues with Myself: Personal Essays on Mormon Experience. 205p. (Orig.). 1984. pap. 7.50 (ISBN 0-941214-21-4, Orion). Signature Bks.

England, Flora D. Alabama Notes, Vol. 3-4, 2 vols. in 1. LC 76-39656. 282p. 1978. 15.00 (ISBN 0-8063-0816-8). Genealog Pub.

England, George, et al, eds. Functioning of Complex Organizations. Negandhi, Anant & Wilpert, Bernard. LC 80-21966. 368p. 1981. text ed. 35.00 (ISBN 0-89946-067-4). Oelgeschlager.

England, George A. The Air Trust. LC 75-28854. (Classics of Science Fiction Ser.). (Illus.). 333p. 1976. 15.40 (ISBN 0-88355-368-6); pap. 10.00 (ISBN 0-88355-453-4). Hyperion-Conn.

--Darkness & Dawn. LC 75-13253. (Classics of Science Fiction Ser.). (Illus.). 690p. 1973. 16.50 (ISBN 0-88355-108-X); pap. 5.95 (ISBN 0-88355-137-3). Hyperion Conn.

--Elixir of Hate. 1976. lib. bdg. 12.95x (ISBN 0-89968-176-X). Lightyear.

--Flying Legion. 1976. lib. bdg. 12.95 (ISBN 0-89968-177-8). Lightyear.

--The Golden Blight. LC 74-15968. (Science Fiction Ser.). (Illus.). 352p. 1975. Repr. of 1916 ed. 25.50x (ISBN 0-405-06288-5). Ayer Co Pubs.

England, George W., et al. The Manager & the Man: A Cross-Cultural Study of Personal Values. LC 74-11582. 97p. 1974. 9.50x (ISBN 0-87338-161-0, Pub. by Comp. Adm. Research Inst.). Kent St U Pr.

--Organizational Functioning in Cross-Cultural Perspective. LC 78-31169. 325p. 1979. 17.50x (ISBN 0-87338-225-0). Kent St U Pr.

England, J. M. Medical Research: A Statistical & Epidemiological Approach. (Illus.). 128p. 1975. pap. text ed. 10.00 (ISBN 0-443-01139-7). Churchill.

England, J. M., jt. auth. see Assendelft, Van.

England, J. Merton & Reither, Joseph. Women Pilots with the AAF, Nineteen Forty-One - Nineteen Forty-Four. (USAF Historical Studies: No. 55). 122p. 1946. pap. text ed. 17.00x (ISBN 0-89126-138-9). MA-AH Pub.

England, John. Letters of the Late Bishop England to the Hon. John Forsyth, on the Subject of Domestic Slavery. LC 74-97400. Repr. of 1844 ed. 15.00x (ISBN 0-8371-2648-7, LEE&, Pub. by Negro U Pr). Greenwood.

England, John & Rear, John. Industrial Relations & Law in Hong Kong. (East Asian Social Science Monographs). (Illus.). 1981. 49.95x (ISBN 0-19-580479-1). Oxford U Pr.

England, John C., ed. Living Theology in Asia. LC 82-2288. 256p. (Orig.). 1982. pap. 9.95 (ISBN 0-88344-298-1). Orbis Bks.

England, Kathy. What Is Faith? (Illus.). 27p. 1981. pap. 3.95 (ISBN 0-87747-876-7). Deseret Bk.

England, Marjorie A. A Color Atlas of Life Before Birth: Normal Fetal Development. (Illus.). 224p. 1983. 49.95 (ISBN 0-8151-3119-4). Year Bk Med.

England, Mark, jt. auth. see Lawrence, David.

England, Martha W. Garrick & Stratford. LC 62-17403. (Illus.). 72p. (Orig.). 1962. pap. 8.00 (ISBN 0-87104-084-0). NY Pub Lib.

--Garrick's Jubilee. LC 64-17109. 283p. 1964. 6.25 (ISBN 0-8142-0046-X). Ohio St U Pr.

England, Martha W. & Sparrow, John. Hymns Unbidden: Donne, Herbert, Blake, Emily Dickinson & the Hymnographers. LC 66-28617. (Illus.). 153p. 1966. 15.00 (ISBN 0-87104-092-1). NY Pub Lib.

England, Nora C. A Gammar of Mam, a Mayan Language. (Texas Linguistics Ser.). 367p. 1983. text ed. 25.00x (ISBN 0-292-72726-7). U of Tex Pr.

England, Nora C., ed. Papers in Mayan Linguistics. (Miscellaneous Publications in Anthropology No. 6; Studies in Mayan Linguistics: No. 2). v, 310p. 1978. pap. 15.00 (ISBN 0-913134-87-2). Mus Anthro Mo.

England, Paul. Favorite Operas by German & Russian Composers. 8.25 (ISBN 0-8446-4733-0). Peter Smith.

England, Paul, tr. see Von Riesemann, Oskar.

England, Paula & Farkas, George. Households, Employment & Gender: The Demographic Transformation of the Post-War United States. (Social Institutions & Social Change Ser.). (Orig.). 1986. lib. bdg. price not set (ISBN 0-202-30322-5); pap. text ed. price not set (ISBN 0-202-30323-3). Aldine Pub.

England, Richard. Schoonerman. (Illus.). 304p. 1982. 17.95 (ISBN 0-370-30377-6, Pub. by the Bodley Head). Merrimack Pub Cir.

England, Robert E., jt. auth. see Brudney, Jeffrey L.

England, Robert E., jt. auth. see Pelissero, John P.

England, Roger, compiled by. How to Make Basic Hospital Equipment. (Illus.). 86p. (Orig.). 1979. pap. 7.75x (ISBN 0-903031-60-4, Pub. by Intermediate Tech England). Intermediate Tech.

England, S. Anne, jt. auth. see Emmons, Tim.

England, Wendy. In the Shadow of the Cat. 1980. pap. 2.25 (ISBN 0-8439-0803-3). Dorchester Pub Co.

England, William L., jt. ed. see Roberts, Stephen D.

Englander, A. Arthur & Petzold, Paul. Filming for Television. (Library of Film & Television Practice). 1976. 21.50 (ISBN 0-8038-2320-7). Hastings.

Englander, A. J., jt. auth. see Eckenfelder, W. W.

Englander, David. Landlord & Tenant in Urban Britain: 1838-1918. 1983. 45.00x (ISBN 0-19-822680-2); pap. 16.95x (ISBN 0-19-820070-6). Oxford U Pr.

Englander, David, jt. auth. see Gaskill, Arthur L.

Englander, Joe. They Ride the Rodeo: The Men & Women of the American Amateur Rodeo Circuit. (Illus.). 1979. pap. write for info. (Collier). Macmillan.

Englander, Lois, et al. The Jewish Holiday Do-Book. new ed. 1977. 9.95x (ISBN 0-685-76976-3). Bloch.

Englander, Nancy, jt. auth. see Nickse, Ruth S.

Englander, Roger. Opera! What's All the Screaming About? LC 82-23742. (Illus.). 192p. (gr. 6 up). 1983. 12.95 (ISBN 0-8027-6491-6). Walker & Co.

Englander, W., jt. auth. see Saxon, J.

Engle, Earl T. & Pincus, Gregory, eds. Hormones & the Aging Process. 1956. 55.00 (ISBN 0-12-239050-4). Acad Pr.

Engle, Eloise. The Finns in America. LC 77-73740. (In America Bks). (Illus.). (gr. 5 up). 1977. PLB 7.95 (ISBN 0-8225-0229-1). Lerner Pubns.

--National Governments Around the World. LC 72-179013. (Around the World Ser.). (Illus.). (gr. 5 up). 1973. 10.50 (ISBN 0-8303-0117-8). Fleet.

Engle, Eloise & Lott, Arnold. Man in Flight: Biomedical Achievements in Aerospace. LC 79-63780. (A Supplement to the American Astronautical Society History Ser.). (Illus.). 414p. 1979. 20.00x (ISBN 0-915268-24-8). Univelt Inc.

Engle, Eloise & Paananen, Lauri. The Winter War: The Russo-Finnish Conflict, 1939-1940. (A Westview Encore Edition Ser.). 176p. 1985. Repr. of 1973 ed. softcover 18.00x (ISBN 0-8133-0149-1). Westview.

Engle, Eloise K., jt. auth. see Ransom, M. A.

Engle, Gary D. This Grotesque Essence: Plays from the American Minstrel Stage. LC 77-16617. xxix, 200p. 1978. 20.00x (ISBN 0-8071-0370-5). La State U Pr.

Engle, Hualing N., jt. ed. see Engle, Paul.

Engle, Jacqueline, ed. see Educational Research Council of America.

Engle, Joanna. Cap'n Kid Goes to the South Pole. LC 82-61013. (Sea World Mini-Storybooks). (Illus.). 32p. (gr. 1-6). 1983. pap. 1.25 saddlestitched (ISBN 0-394-85643-0). Random.

Engle, Jon. Servants of God: The Lives of the 10 Gurus of the Sikhs. LC 79-63457. (Illus.). 192p. 1980. pap. 6.00 (ISBN 0-89142-035-5). Sant Bani Ash.

Engle, Madeleine L. The Twenty-Four Days Before Christmas: An Austin Family Story. (Illus.). 48p. 1984. 7.95 (ISBN 0-87788-843-4). Shaw Pubs.

Engle, Margarita. Smoketree. 20p. 1983. 7.00 (ISBN 0-913719-64-1); pap. 2.00 (ISBN 0-913719-63-3). High-Coo Pr.

Engle, Mary A. & Perloff, Joseph K. Congenital Heart Disease after Surgery: Benefits, Residua & Sequelae. (Illus.). 438p. 1983. text ed. 40.00 (ISBN 0-914316-37-0). Yorke Med.

Engle, Mary A., ed. Pediatric Cardiovascular Disease. LC 80-15616. (Cardiovascular Clinics Ser.: Vol. 11, No. 2). (Illus.). 475p. 1980. text ed. 48.00x (ISBN 0-8036-3204-5). Davis Co.

Engle, Patricia L. The Use of Vernacular Languages in Education: Language Medium in Early School Years for Minority Language Groups. (Bilingual Ed. Ser.: No. 3). 33p. 1975. pap. 4.95x (ISBN 0-15-599062-4). Ctr Appl Ling.

Engle, Paul. American Song, a Book of Poems. LC 76-11505. (BCL Ser.: II). Repr. of 1934 ed. 16.50 (ISBN 0-404-15285-6). AMS Pr.

--The Governor Drove Us up the Wall: A Guide to Nehemiah. 1985. pap. text ed. 4.95 (ISBN 0-934688-11-7); pap. text ed. 3.95 leader's guide (ISBN 0-934688-13-3). Great Comm Pubns.

--Worn Earth. LC 72-144738. (Yale Ser. of Younger Poets: No. 31). Repr. of 1932 ed. 18.00 (ISBN 0-404-53831-2). AMS Pr.

Engle, Paul & Zielinski, John M. Portrait of Iowa. (Illus.). 176p. 1985. pap. 9.95 (ISBN 0-317-29256-0, 99060). Wallace-Homestead.

Engle, Paul & Engle, Hualing N., eds. Writing from the World. (International Bks.). 272p. pap. 4.50 (ISBN 0-317-04117-7). U of Iowa Pr.

Engle, Paul E. Discovering the Fullness of Worship. (Illus.). 129p. (Orig.). 1978. pap. 4.95 (ISBN 0-934688-01-X). Great Comm Pubns.

--Worship Planbook. (Orig.). 1981. pap. 3.95 (ISBN 0-934688-03-6). Great Comm Pubns.

Engle, R. W. Shallow-Water Crabs. LC 82-9706. (Synopses of the British Fauna Ser.: No. 25). (Illus.). 220p. 1983. 42.50 (ISBN 0-521-24963-5). Cambridge U Pr.

Engle, Tom, jt. auth. see Shugart, Cooksey.

Englebardt, Leland S. Living Together: What's the Law? 1981. Outlet 1.00 (ISBN 0-517-54072-X, Michelman Books). Crown.

--You Have a Right: A Guide for Minors. LC 79-4678. (gr. 6 up). 1979. 11.25 (ISBN 0-688-41893-7); PLB 11.88 (ISBN 0-688-51893-1). Lothrop.

Englebardt, Stanley L. Kids & Alcohol, the Deadliest Drug. LC 75-20327. 64p. (gr. 5 up). 1975. PLB 10.88 (ISBN 0-688-51717-X). Lothrop.

--Miracle Chip: The Microelectronic Revolution. LC 79-2422. (Illus.). (gr. 5 up). 1979. 11.25 (ISBN 0-688-41908-9); PLB 11.88 (ISBN 0-688-51908-3). Lothrop.

Englebert, Omer. Hero of Molokai. (Illus.). 1977. 4.00 (ISBN 0-8198-0057-0); pap. 3.00 (ISBN 0-8198-0058-9). Dghtrs St Paul.

--The Last of the Conquistadors, Junipero Serra, 1713-1784. Woods, Katherine, tr. LC 74-5924. (Illus.). 368p. 1974. Repr. of 1956 ed. lib. bdg. 21.25x (ISBN 0-8371-7523-2, ENJS). Greenwood.

--Saint Francis of Assisi: A Biography. abr. ed. 1979. pap. 3.95 (ISBN 0-89283-071-9). Servant.

Englebert, Victor. The Goats of Agadez. LC 72-76363. (Illus.). 48p. (gr. k-4). 1973. 5.50 (ISBN 0-15-231118-1, HJ). HarBraceJ.

Englebretsen, G. Logical Negation. 72p. 1981. pap. text ed. 6.25x (ISBN 90-232-1814-0, Pub. by Van Gorcum Holland). Humanities.

--Three Logicians. 120p. 1981. pap. text ed. 10.25x (ISBN 90-232-1815-9, Pub. by Van Gorcum Holland). Humanities.

Engledow, Frank & Amey, Leonard, eds. Britain's Future in Farming. 180p. 1980. 47.00x (ISBN 0-900394-21-8, Pub. by Geographical Pubns). State Mutual Bk.

Englefield, Dermot & Drewry, Gavin, eds. Information Sources in Politics & Political Science: A Survey Worldwide. LC 84-2819. (Guides to Information Sources Ser.). 528p. 1984. text ed. 69.95 (ISBN 0-408-11470-3). Butterworth.

Englefield, Ronald. The Mind at Work & Play. Wells, G. A. & Oppenheimer, David, eds. LC 84-42851. 158p. 1985. 24.95 (ISBN 0-87975-254-8). Prometheus Bks.

Englehardt, H. Tristam, jt. ed. see Spicker, Stuart F.

Englehardt, H. Tristram, jt. auth. see Brody, Baruch A.

Englehardt, H. Tristram, Jr., et al, eds. Clinical Judgment: A Critical Appraisal. (Philosophy & Medicine Ser.). 1979. 29.50 (ISBN 90-277-0952-1, Pub. by Reidel Holland). Kluwer Academic.

Englehardt, Zelma. Beyond the Bayous: Poetry. 1962. 3.50. Claitors.

Englehart, Steve & Rogers, Marshall. I Am Coyote. Mullaney, Dean, ed. (Orig.). 1985. pap. 7.95 (ISBN 0-913035-00-9). Eclipse Bks.

Englekirk, John E. Edgar Allan Poe in Hispanic Literature. 504p. 3.90 (ISBN 0-318-14258-9). Hispanic Inst.

--La Narrativa Uruguaya: Estudio Critico-Bibliografico. Ramos, Margaret M., ed. LC 68-2896. 338p. 1983. Repr. of 1967 ed. lib. bdg. 19.95x (ISBN 0-89370-792-9). Borgo Pr.

Englekirk, John E., et al. Outline History of Spanish American Literature. 4th ed. 1981. pap. text ed. 12.95x (ISBN 0-89197-326-5). Irvington.

Englekirk, John E., et al, eds. Anthology of Spanish-American Literature, 2 vols. 2nd ed. (Span.). 1968. Vol. 1. pap. text ed. 19.95 (ISBN 0-13-038786-X); Vol. 2. pap. text ed. 19.95 (ISBN 0-13-038794-0). P-H.

Englekirk, Robert & Hart, Gary. Earthquake Design of Concrete & Masonry Buildings: Response Spectrual Analysis & General Earthquake Modeling Considerations, Vol. I. (Illus.). 160p. 1982. 30.00 (ISBN 0-13-223065-8). P-H.

Englekirk, Robert E. & Hart, Gary C. Earthquake Design of Concrete Masonry Buildings: Strength Design of One to Four Buildings. (Illus.). 224p. 1984. text ed. 33.95 (ISBN 0-13-223156-5). P-H.

Engleman, Earl W. Pocketful of Smiles. (Illus.). 1979. pap. 4.50 (ISBN 0-933992-03-3). Coffee Break.

Engleman, Finis E. Pleasure Was Mine, Pt. 2. 1980. 8.95x (ISBN 0-8134-2062-8, 2062). Interstate.

--Pleasure Was Mine: Seventy Years in Education. LC 71-143328. x, 210p. 1971. text ed. 5.95x (ISBN 0-8134-1230-7, 1230). Interstate.

Engleman, S. R., jt. auth. see Thomson, A. W.

Englemann, Jeanne M. Cocaine: Beyond the Looking Glass Discussion Guide. 32p. (Orig.). 1984. pap. 6.95 (ISBN 0-89486-227-8). Hazelden.

--Falling Back: The Dry Drunk Syndrome Discussion Guide. 24p. (Orig.). 1984. pap. 6.95 (ISBN 0-89486-226-X). Hazelden.

Englent, D., et al. An Approach to Problem Solving in Genetics. 1984. pap. text ed. 7.40x (ISBN 0-87563-107-X). Stipes.

Engler & Boquist. Cases in Managerial Finance. 1982. 26.95 (ISBN 0-256-02784-6). Business Pubns.

Engler, A. Hochgebirgsflora Des Tropischen Afrikas. (Akad. D. Wissenschaften, Berlin Ser.). 461p. (Ger.). 1975. pap. text ed. 70.40x (ISBN 3-87429-088-3). Lubrecht & Cramer.

--Syllabus der Pflanzenfalien: Kapitael V, 2 - Bryophytina, Laubmoose. 13th Ed. ed. Gerloff, J., et al, eds. (Illus.). 109p. (Ger.). 1983. pap. 18.04x (ISBN 3-443-02001-1). Lubrecht & Cramer.

--Syllabus der Pflanzenfamilien, 2 vols. 12th ed. Incl. Vol. 1. Allgemeiner Teil: Bakterien Bis Gymnospermen. 1954. 30.34 (ISBN 3-4433-9015-3); Vol. 2. Angiospermen Vebersicht Ueber Die Florengebiete der Erde. 1964. 55.00 (ISBN 3-4433-9016-1). (Illus.). Lubrecht & Cramer.

--Versuch einer Entwicklungsgeschichte der Pflanzenwelt Insbesondere der Florengebiete Seit der Tertiaerperiode. 1971. 63.00 (ISBN 3-7682-0749-8). Lubrecht & Cramer.

Engler, A. & Drude, O., eds. Vegetation der Erde. Repr. of 1976 ed. of 13 vols. 700.00 set (ISBN 3-7682-0984-9). Lubrecht & Cramer.

Engler, Barbara O. Personality Theories: An Introduction. LC 78-69596. (Illus.). 1979. text ed. 25.50 (ISBN 0-395-26772-2); instr's. manual 1.00 (ISBN 0-395-26773-0). HM.

--Personality Theories: An Introduction. 2nd ed. LC 84-80709. 560p. 1985. text ed. 24.95 (ISBN 0-395-34237-6); instr's. manual 2.00 (ISBN 0-395-34238-4). HM.

Engler, Calvin, jt. auth. see Bernstein, Leopold A.

Engler, George. Hibachi Cookery in the American Manner. (Eng. & Japanese.). pap. 9.50 (ISBN 0-8048-0245-9). C E Tuttle.

Engler, Kay. The Structure of Realism: The Novelas Contemporaneas de Benito Perez Galdos. (Studies in the Romance Languages & Literatures Ser: No. 184). 193p. 1977. 14.50x (ISBN 0-8078-9184-3). U of NC Pr.

Engler, Larry & Fijan, Carol. Making Puppets Come Alive: A Method of Learning & Teaching Hand Puppetry. LC 72-6623. (Illus.). 192p. 1980. pap. 9.95 (ISBN 0-8008-5073-4). Taplinger.

Engler, Richard E., Jr. The Challenge of Diversity. LC 72-167337. (Essay Index Reprint Ser.). Repr. of 1964 ed. 21.50 (ISBN 0-8369-2687-0). Ayer Co Pubs.

Engler, Robert. The Brotherhood of Oil: Energy Policy & the Public Interest. LC 76-56189. 1985. price not set (ISBN 0-226-20948-2); pap. 11.95 (ISBN 0-226-20949-0). U of Chicago Pr.

--Politics of Oil: A Study of Private Power & Democratic Directions. 2nd ed. LC 61-17192. 1976. pap. 5.95 (ISBN 0-226-20947-4, P284, Phoen). U of Chicago Pr.

Engler, Winfried. Lexikon der Franzoesischen Literatur. (Ger.). 1974. 27.50 (ISBN 3-520-38801-4, M-7259). French & Eur.

Englert, Marianne, jt. ed. see Bohrmann, Hans.

Englert, Sebastian. Diccionario Rapanui-Espanol, Redactado en la Isla de Pascua. LC 75-35191. (Span. & Rapanui.). Repr. of 1938 ed. 15.00 (ISBN 0-404-14219-2). AMS Pr.

Engles, Friedrich, jt. auth. see Marx, Karl.

Englesher, Charles J. Interfacing & Digital Experiments with Your APPLE. (Illus.). 320p. (Orig.). 1984. 21.95 (ISBN 0-8306-0717-X, 1717); pap. 15.50 (ISBN 0-8306-1717-5). TAB Bks.

Englesman, Coert. Engelsman's Maintenance Manual for Condominiums: Cooperatives & Rental Apartment Complexes. 200p. 1984. pap. 34.95 (ISBN 0-442-22251-3). Van Nos Reinhold.

Eng-Liedmeier, Jeanne Van Der see Van Der Eng-Liedmeier, Jeanne.

Englisch, Lothar. The Advanced Machine Language Book for the Commodore 64. 210p. (Orig.). 1984. pap. text ed. 14.95 (ISBN 0-916439-06-2). Abacus Soft.

Englisch, Lothar & Walkowiak, Jorg. Presenting the Atari ST. 1985. write for info. Abacus Soft.

English. Basic Guide to Dog Training & Obedience. 1979. 4.95 (ISBN 0-399-50804-X, Perigee). Putnam Pub Group.

English, A. Armed Forces of Latin America: Their Histories, Development, Present Strength & Military Potential. (Illus.). 480p. 1985. 50.00 (ISBN 0-7106-0321-5). Jane's Pub Inc.

--On Infantry. 288p. 1984. 14.95 (ISBN 0-03-001409-3). Praeger.

English Association, ed. The Modern Muse; Poems of To-Day: British & American. LC 34-27210. (Granger Poetry Library). 1976. Repr. of 1934 ed. 18.75x (ISBN 0-89609-029-9). Granger Bk.

--Poems of To-Day: First & Second Series. LC 77-88079. (Granger Poetry Library). 1976. Repr. of 1915 ed. 27.50x (ISBN 0-89609-036-1). Granger Bk.

English, B. Strict Settlement: A Guide for Historians. Saville, J., ed. (Occasional Papers in Economic & Social History). 144p. 1983. pap. text ed. 13.00x (ISBN 0-85958-439-9, Pub. by U of Hull of UK). Humanities.

English, Barbara. The Lord of Holderness, Ten Eighty-Six to Twelve Sixty: A Study in Feudal Society. (Illus.). 1979. 52.00x (ISBN 0-19-713437-8). Oxford U Pr.

English Benedictine Congregation Members & Rees, Daniel. Consider Your Call. (Cistercian Studies Ser.: No. 20). 447p. 1980. 17.95 (ISBN 0-87907-820-0). Cistercian Pubns.

English, Betty L. Behind the Headlines at a Big City Paper. LC 84-23401. (Illus.). 160p. (gr. 6 up). 1985. 13.00 (ISBN 0-688-03936-7). Lothrop.

--You Can't Be Timid with a Trumpet: Notes from the Orchestra. LC 80-13348. (Illus.). 64p. (gr. 5 up). 1980. 11.25 (ISBN 0-688-41963-1); PLB 11.88 (ISBN 0-688-51963-6). Lothrop.

English, Bill. The Cultivator. LC 84-82617. 235p. (Orig.). 1985. pap. 6.95 (ISBN 0-934558-14-0). Entwhistle Bks.

English, Brad. Total Telemarking. LC 83-83417. (Illus., Orig.). 1984. pap. 15.95 (ISBN 0-915789-00-0). East River Pub CO.

English, Burt H. Liberacion Nacional in Costa Rica: The Development of a Political Party in a Transitional Society. LC 73-107880. (University of Florida Latin American Monographs: No. 8). (Illus.). 1971. 10.00 (ISBN 0-8130-0296-6). U Presses Fla.

English, Burton C., et al, eds. Future Agricultural Technology & Resource Conservation. 336p. 1984. text ed. 26.65 (ISBN 0-8138-0771-9). Iowa St U Pr.

English, Colin C. The National Trust Book of Sorbets, Flummeries & Fools. (Illus.). 96p. 1985. 9.95 (ISBN 0-7153-8609-3). David & Charles.

English, D. Anthony, ed. see Thune, Ensaf & Prigozy, Ruth.

English, Darrel S., et al. Genetic & Reproductive Engineering. LC 73-22048. 1974. 29.75x (ISBN 0-8422-5157-X); pap. text ed. 9.50x (ISBN 0-8422-0383-4). Irvington.

English, David. The Legend: The Illustrated Story of the Bee Gees. 144p. (Orig.). 1984. pap. 9.95 (ISBN 0-7043-2393-1, Pub. by Quartet Bks). Merrimack Pub Cir.

English, Deirdre, jt. auth. see Ehrenreich, Barbara.

English, Donald E. Political Uses of Photography in the Third French Republic, 1871-1914. Kirkpatrick, Diane, ed. LC 83-24239. (Studies in Photography: No. 3). 278p. 1984. 39.95 (ISBN 0-8357-1473-X). UMI Res Pr.

English, Dori, jt. auth. see Wiggins, James D.

English Dramatists. Plays from Moliere. 320p. 1980. Repr. of 1883 ed. lib. bdg. 32.50 (ISBN 0-89760-548-9). Telegraph Bks.

English, E. Schuyler. A Companion to the New Scofield Reference Bible. 1972. 6.95 (ISBN 0-19-526872-5). Oxford U Pr.

--Ordained of the Lord: H. A. Ironside. LC 76-13873. (Illus.). 1976. pap. 4.95 (ISBN 0-87213-143-2). Loizeaux.

--Re-Thinking the Rapture. 1954. pap. 2.25 (ISBN 0-87213-144-0). Loizeaux.

--Things Surely to Be Believed. 1970. Repr. of 1946 ed. 4.95 (ISBN 0-87213-146-7). Loizeaux.

English, Earl & Hach, Clarence. Scholastic Journalism. 7th ed. 332p. 1984. text ed. 15.95 (ISBN 0-8138-1400-6); pap. text ed. 12.95 (ISBN 0-8138-1390-5). Iowa St U Pr.

English, Fenwick W. & Kaufman, Roger A. Needs Assessment: A Focus for Curriculum Development. LC 75-16109. 69p. 1975. pap. text ed. 4.00 (ISBN 0-87120-069-4, 611-75048). Assn Supervision.

English, Fenwick W. & Steffy, Betty E. Educational Consulting: A Guidebook for Practitioners. LC 83-20536. 1984. 28.95 (ISBN 0-87778-189-3). Educ Tech Pubns.

English, Fenwick W., jt. auth. see Kaufman, Roger.

English, Fenwick W., jt. auth. see Steeves, Frank L.

English, Fenwick W. & Davis, O. L., Jr., eds. Fundamental Curriculum Decisions: ASCD 1983 Yearbook. LC 82-74237. 175p. (Orig.). 1983. pap. text ed. 10.00 (ISBN 0-87120-117-8, 610-83290). Assn Supervision.

English, Frank P. & Keats, Warren A. Reconstructive & Plastic Surgery of the Eyelids. (Illus.). 112p. 1975. photocopy ed. 16.75x (ISBN 0-398-03386-2). C C Thomas.

English, Gerald, ed. see Loose Leaf Reference Services.

English, H. E. & Scott, Anthony, eds. Renewable Resources in the Pacific: Proceedings of the Twelfth Pacific Trade & Development Conference, Held in Vancouver, Canada, September 7-11, 1981. 293p. 1982. pap. 20.00 (ISBN 0-88936-312-9, IDRC181, IDRC). Unipub.

English, H. Edward, jt. auth. see Masson, Francis.

English, J. & McLaughlin, K. Kitchener: An Illustrated History. 230p. 1983. text ed. 23.50x (ISBN 0-88920-137-4, Pub. by Wilfrid Laurier U Pr); pap. text ed. 14.50x (ISBN 0-88920-141-2). Humanities.

English, J. M. Cost Effectiveness: Economic Evaluation of Engineered Systems. LC 68-28500. Repr. of 1968 ed. 59.90 (ISBN 0-8357-9868-2, 2013052). Bks Demand UMI.

English, J. Morley. Project Evaluation. 350p. 1984. pap. text ed. 29.95. Macmillan.

English, James, Jr., et al. Principles of Organic Chemistry. 4th ed. 1971. text ed. 37.95 (ISBN 0-07-019520-X). McGraw.

English, Jane. Sex Equality. LC 76-53000. (Illus.). 256p. 1977. pap. text ed. 19.95 (ISBN 0-13-807586-7). P-H.

English, Jane, jt. auth. see Bolinger, Judith.

English, Jane, tr. see Chuang Tsu.

English, Jane, tr. see Lao Tsu.

English, Jane B. Different Doorway: Adventures of a Caesarean Born. LC 85-80840. (Illus.). 152p. 1985. 14.95 (ISBN 0-934747-38-5); pap. 7.95 (ISBN 0-934747-39-3). Earth Heart.

English, John. Choosing Life: The Significance of Personal History in Decision Making. LC 78-58315. 240p. 1978. pap. 6.95 (ISBN 0-8091-2113-1). Paulist Pr.

--The Decline of Politics: The Conservatives & the Party System 1901-1920. (Canadian Government Ser.). 1977. 27.50x (ISBN 0-8020-5386-6). U of Toronto Pr.

--Social Services in Scotland. 200p. 1980. pap. 12.50x (ISBN 0-7073-0264-1, Pub. by Scottish Academic Pr Scotland). Columbia U Pr.

English, John, ed. The Future of Council Housing. (Illus.). 208p. 1982. 28.50 (ISBN 0-7099-0900-4, Pub. by Croom Helm Ltd). Longwood Pub Group.

English, John A. A Perspective on Infantry. LC 81-5230. 368p. 1981. 24.95 (ISBN 0-03-059699-8). Praeger.

English, John A. & Addicott, James, eds. The Mechanized Battlefield: A Tactical Analysis. (Illus.). 202p. 1984. pap. 30.00 (ISBN 0-08-025405-5). Pergamon.

English, John W. Criticizing the Critics. (Humanistic Studies in the Communication Arts). 1979. 14.95 (ISBN 0-8038-1270-1); pap. text ed. 7.95 (ISBN 0-8038-1272-8). Hastings.

English, L. & Szczepanowski, N. The Anatomy of the Fifteen Forty-One Disk Drive. Dykema, G., tr. from German. 320p. 1984. pap. 19.95 (ISBN 0-916439-01-1). Abacus Soft.

English Language Institute. English Conversation Practices. (Intensive Course in English Ser.). 1968. pap. 4.95x (ISBN 0-472-08306-6). U of Mich Pr.

--English Pattern Practices: Establishing the Patterns As Habits. rev. 3rd ed. (Intensive Course in English Ser.). (Illus., Orig.). (gr. 9 up). 1958. pap. 6.95x (ISBN 0-472-08302-3). U of Mich Pr.

--English Pronunciation: Exercises in Sound Segments, Intonation & Rhythm. rev. 2nd ed. (Intensive Course in English Ser). (Orig.). (gr. 9 up). 1958. pap. 5.95x (ISBN 0-472-08303-1). U of Mich Pr.

--Vocabulary in Context. (Intensive Course in English Ser.). 1964. pap. 5.95x (ISBN 0-472-08305-8). U of Mich Pr.

English Language Institute & Krohn, Robert. English Sentence Structure. rev. 4th ed. (Intensive Course in English Ser.). 1971. pap. 6.95x (ISBN 0-472-08307-4). U of Mich Pr.

English Language Services. Agriculture, 3 vols. (Special English Ser.). pap. write for info.; Vol. 1. pap. (ISBN 0-02-973620-X); Vol. 2. pap. (ISBN 0-02-973630-7); Vol. 3. pap. (ISBN 0-02-973640-4, 97205); write for info. set of 3 tapes for vols. 1 & 2; write for info. set of 4 tapes for vol. 3 (ISBN 0-685-14591-3). Macmillan.

--Audio-Lingual English Series, 6 Workbks. 1967. Bk. 1. pap. 4.95 (ISBN 0-02-972060-5); Bk. 2. pap. 4.95 (ISBN 0-02-972070-2); Bk. 3. pap. 4.95 (ISBN 0-02-972080-X); Bk. 4. pap. 4.95 (ISBN 0-02-972090-7); Bk. 5. pap. 4.95 (ISBN 0-02-972100-8); Bk. 6. pap. 4.95 (ISBN 0-02-972110-5); teachers' guide 3.60 (ISBN 0-02-972130-X); tapes avail. (ISBN 0-685-14671-5). Macmillan.

--Aviation, 2 Vols. (Special English Ser.). pap. write for info.; Vol. 1. pap. (ISBN 0-02-973700-1); Vol. 2. pap. (ISBN 0-02-973710-9); write for info. sets of 4 tapes for ea. vol. Macmillan.

--Aviation Maintenance. (Special English Ser.). pap. 7.48 (ISBN 0-02-973720-6); of 4 tapes 116.00 set (ISBN 0-02-982180-0, 98218). Macmillan.

--Banking. (Special English Ser.). pap. 7.48 (ISBN 0-02-973650-1); tapes 93.70 (ISBN 0-02-982250-5). Macmillan.

--Black Tulip. (English Readers Ser). pap. 5.20 (ISBN 0-02-971420-6). Macmillan.

--Cowboys in Alaska, & Other Stories. (English Readers Ser). pap. 5.20 (ISBN 0-02-971370-6). Macmillan.

--Drills & Exercises in English Pronunciation Series, 3 bks. Incl. Consonants & Vowels. pap. text ed. (ISBN 0-02-971850-3); 24 tapes 145.00 (ISBN 0-685-22926-2, 98300); Stress & Intonation, Part I. pap. text ed. (ISBN 0-02-971860-0); 14 tapes 85.00 (ISBN 0-685-22928-9, 98360); Stress & Intonation, Part 2. pap. text ed. (ISBN 0-02-971870-8); 16 tapes 95.00 (ISBN 0-685-22930-0, 98361). (gr. 7-12). 1967. pap. text ed. 3.60 ea. Macmillan.

--Engineering, 2 Vols. (Special English Ser.). pap. write for info.; Vol. 1. pap. (ISBN 0-02-973660-9); Vol. 2. pap. (ISBN 0-02-973690-0); write for info. sets of 4 tapes for vol. 1 (ISBN 0-685-15066-6); write for info. sets of 3 tapes for vol. 2 (ISBN 0-685-15067-4). Macmillan.

--English Grammar Exercises, 3 Bks. 1965. pap. write for info.; Bk. 1. pap. (ISBN 0-02-971800-7); Bk. 2. pap. (ISBN 0-02-971810-4). Bk. 3. Macmillan.

--English Nine Hundred Series, 6 Bks. pap. write for info. (97114-97119); write for info. tchr's manual (ISBN 0-685-15077-1, 97120); write for info. wkbks. (97121-97126); write for info. ea. 3 sets of 10 tapes for ea. bk; write for info. complete tape set (ISBN 0-685-15080-1). Macmillan.

--English Pronunciation: A Manual for Teachers. 1968. pap. 6.00 (ISBN 0-02-971880-5). Macmillan.

--English This Way, 12 bks. 1963-65. Bks. 1-6. pap. write for info.; Bks. 7-12. pap. write for info.; Bks. 1-6. write for info. tchr's manual & key (ISBN 0-685-27109-9, 97106); Bks. 7-12. write for info. tchr's manual key (ISBN 0-02-971060-X, 97113); tapes avail. (ISBN 0-02-971130-4). Macmillan.

--Four Short Mysteries. (Collier-Macmillan English Readers Ser.). pap. 5.20 (ISBN 0-02-971470-2). Macmillan.

--International Trade. (Special English Ser.). pap. 7.48 (ISBN 0-02-973730-3); of 3 tapes 93.70 set (ISBN 0-02-983350-7). Macmillan.

--Island of Truth, & Other Stories. (Collier-Macmillan English Readers Ser.). pap. 5.20 (ISBN 0-02-971380-3). Macmillan.

--Key to English Adjectives, 2 Bks. (Key to English Ser.). pap. 5.00 ea. Bk. 1. Bk. 2. Macmillan.

--Key to English Figurative Expressions. (Key to English Ser.). pap. 5.00 (ISBN 0-02-971740-X). Macmillan.

--Key to English Letter Writing. (Key to English Ser.). pap. 5.00 (ISBN 0-02-971790-6). Macmillan.

--Key to English Nouns. (Key to English Ser.). pap. 5.00 (ISBN 0-02-971760-4). Macmillan.

--Key to English Prepositions, 2 Bks. (Key to English Ser.). pap. write for info. Bk. 1. Bk. 2. Macmillan.

--Key to English Two-Word Verbs. (Key to English Ser.). pap. 4.12 (ISBN 0-02-971720-5). Macmillan.

--Key to English Verbs. (Key to English Ser.). pap. 5.00 (ISBN 0-02-971730-2). Macmillan.

--Key to English Vocabulary. (Key to English Ser). pap. 5.00 (ISBN 0-02-971750-7). Macmillan.

--Love Letter. (Collier-Macmillan English Readers Ser). pap. 3.48 (ISBN 0-02-971500-8). Macmillan.

--Medicine, 3 Vols. (Special English Ser). pap. write for info. Vol. 1. Vol. 2. Vol. 3. write for info. ea. sets of 4 tapes for vols. 1 & 2; write for info. set of 5 tapes for vol. 3 (ISBN 0-686-57561-X). Macmillan.

--Murder Now & Then. (Collier-Macmillan English Readers). pap. 3.48 (ISBN 0-02-971320-X). Macmillan.

--People Speak, & Other Stories. (Collier-Macmillan English Readers). pap. 5.20 (ISBN 0-02-971350-1). Macmillan.

--Practical English Grammar. 1968. pap. 6.92 (ISBN 0-02-971830-9); wkbk. 6.92 (ISBN 0-02-971840-6, 97184). Macmillan.

--Readings & Conversations: About the United States, Its People, Its History & Its Customs, 2 vols. rev. ed. 1976. text ed. 4.50 ea.; Vol. 1. (ISBN 0-87789-195-8); Vol. 2. (ISBN 0-87789-196-6); Set. cassette tapes 95.00 (ISBN 0-87789-201-6). Cassettes 1. Cassettes 2 (ISBN 0-87789-202-4). Eng Language.

--Scenes of America. (Collier-Macmillan English Readers). pap. 3.64 (ISBN 0-02-971430-3). Macmillan.

--Silver Elephant, & Other Stories. (Collier-Macmillan English Readers). pap. 5.20 (ISBN 0-02-971360-9). Macmillan.

--They Came to America. (Collier-Macmillan English Readers). pap. 3.64 (ISBN 0-02-971290-4). Macmillan.

--Vanishing Lady, & Other Stories. (English Readers Ser.). pap. 3.64 (ISBN 0-02-971310-2). Macmillan.

English Language Services, ed. see Keller, Helen.

English Language Teaching Documents, ed. Projects in Materials Design. (English Language Teaching Documents Ser.). 260p. 1983. pap. 10.00 (ISBN 0-08-030307-2). Pergamon.

English, Mary S. Aunt Mary's Wonderland: Short Stories for Children. (ps-2). 1984. 7.50 (ISBN 0-682-40228-1). Exposition Pr FL.

--One-Way Street. 339p. 1983. pap. 4.95 (ISBN 0-682-49998-6). Exposition Pr FL.

English, Maurice. Midnight in the Century. LC 64-20847. 69p. 1964. 5.00 (ISBN 0-8040-0204-5, 82-71363, Pub. by Swallow). Ohio U Pr.

English, Maurice, intro. by see Sullivan, Louis H.

English, Morley J., ed. Economics of Engineering & Social Systems. LC 73-37644. 332p. 1972. 24.95 (ISBN 0-471-24180-6, Pub. by Wiley). Krieger.

English, O. Spurgeon & Pearson, Gerald H. J. Emotional Problems of Living. 3rd ed. 640p. 1963. 10.95x (ISBN 0-393-01078-3). Norton.

English, Oliver S. & Finch, Stuart M. Introduction to Psychiatry. 3rd ed. 1964. 16.95x (ISBN 0-393-09738-2, NortonC). Norton.

English, Oliver S. & Pearson, G. H. Common Neuroses of Children & Adults. 1937. 6.95x (ISBN 0-393-01005-8, NortonC). Norton.

English, P., ed. Datacommunications, 3 vols, No. 8. (Computer State of the Art Report: Series 11). 500p. 1983. Set. 500.00 (ISBN 0-08-028579-1). Pergamon.

English, P. R., et al. The Sow: Improving Her Efficiency. 2nd ed. (Illus.). 352p. 1982. Repr. of 1977 ed. 22.95 (ISBN 0-85236-127-0, Pub. by Farming Pr UK). Diamond Farm Bk.

English, Paul W. World Regional Geography: A Question of Place. 2nd ed. LC 84-3497. 583p. 1984. text ed. 30.95x (ISBN 0-471-09295-9). Wiley.

English, Peter C. Shock, Physiological Surgery & George Washington Crile: Medical Innovation in the Progressive Era. LC 79-8579. (Contributions in Medical History: No. 5). xi, 271p. 1980. lib. bdg. 35.00 (ISBN 0-313-21490-5, EMI/). Greenwood.

English, R. William & Oberle, Judson B., eds. Rehabilitation Counselor Supervision: A National Perspective. 1980. 3.00 (ISBN 0-686-36377-9, 70517W34); members 2.50 (ISBN 0-686-37296-4). Am Assn Coun Dev.

English, Raymond, jt. auth. see Norman, Edward R.

English, Raymond, jt. auth. see Lefever, Ernest W.

English, Richard A., jt. ed. see Hasenfeld, Yeheskel.

English, Robert. Federal Government Subcontract Forms, 2 vols. LC 82-17817. 1983. 265.00 (ISBN 0-317-12009-3). Callaghan.

English, Robert J. Business Contract Forms. LC 83-23312. (Business Practice Library Ser.: 1-692). 536p. 1984. 75.00x (ISBN 0-471-80162-3, Pub. by Wiley Law Pubns). Wiley.

English, Sandal. Fruits of the Desert. 181p. (Orig.). 1981. pap. 7.95 (ISBN 0-9607758-0-3). Ariz Daily Star.

English, Sarah J. Vin Vignettes: Stories of Famous French Wines. 104p. 1984. 12.95 (ISBN 0-89015-452-X); slipcase 16.95 (ISBN 0-89015-481-3). Eakin Pubns.

English Speaking Union. Laugh Before Breakfast. (Illus.). 1985. cancelled (ISBN 0-87482-128-2). Wake-Brook.

English-Speaking Union of the United States & the International Peace Academy Seminar. Peacekeeping: Helped or Hindered by the Media? (IPA Report Ser.: No. 15). 32p. 1982. pap. 5.50 (ISBN 0-937722-02-2). Intl Peace.

English, Suzanne. Goodbye, Mr. Valentine. LC 76-4230. 1977. 5.95 (ISBN 0-87212-066-X). Libra.

English, T. Saunders, ed. Ocean Resources & Public Policy. LC 77-103298. (Public Policy Issues in Resource Management Ser.: No. 5). (Illus.). 192p. 1973. text ed. 25.00x (ISBN 0-295-95260-1). U of Wash Pr.

English, Thomas E. Commercial Loan Manual: An Analysis of Oklahoma's Version of the UCC. 235p. (Orig.). 1984. pap. 30.00 (ISBN 0-916737-00-4). Okla Bankers.

English, W. E. & Lien, David A. Complete Guide for Easy Car Care. (Illus.). 384p. 1975. 22.95 (ISBN 0-13-160226-8). P-H.

English, William F. Anatomy & Allied Sciences for Lawyers. 464p. 1941. lib. bdg. 25.00 (ISBN 0-89941-370-6). W S Hein.

English, William H. Conquest of the Country Northwest of the River Ohio, 1778-1783, 2 vols. in 1. Bd. with Life of General George Rogers Clark. LC 70-146394. (First American Frontier Ser.). (Illus.). 1194p. 1971. Repr. of 1896 ed. 71.50 (ISBN 0-405-02847-4). Ayer Co Pubs.

Englman, R. The Jahn-Teller Effect in Molecules & Crystals. LC 77-37113. (Wiley Monographs in Chemical Physics). (Illus.). pap. 92.50 (ISBN 0-317-09429-7, 2019668). Bks Demand UMI.

Englom, V. On the Origin & Early Development of the Auxiliary Do. (Lund Studies in English: Vol. 6). pap. 18.00 (ISBN 0-317-15663-2). Kraus Repr.

Englund, Harold M., jt. ed. see Calvert, Seymour.

Englund, Harold M., ed. see International Clean Air Congress, 2nd.

Englund, Kenneth J., et al. Proposed Pennsylvanian System Stratotype. West Virginia & Virginia. LC 78-74893. (AGI Selected Guidebook Ser.: No. 1). 1979. pap. 20.00 (ISBN 0-913312-08-8). Am Geol.

Englund, Sergia, tr. see Balthasar, Hans Urs Von.

Englund, Sergia, tr. see Muggeridge, Malcolm, et al.

Englund, Sr. Sergia, tr. see Lubac, Henri De.

Englund, Steven. Grace of Monaco: An Interpretive Biography. LC 83-20742. (Illus.). 336p. 1984. 17.95 (ISBN 0-385-18812-9). Doubleday.

Englund, Steven, jt. auth. see Ceplair, Larry.

Englund, Steven, jt. auth. see Ford, Edward E.

Englund, Violet V. The Strand. LC 77-76176. (Illus.). 1977. pap. 6.95 (ISBN 0-9601258-0-9). Golden Owl Pub.

Engman, E. T., jt. ed. see Carter, W. D.

Engman, John. Alcatraz. (Burning Deck Poetry Ser.). 24p. (Orig.). 1980. pap. 10.00 (ISBN 0-930900-84-7). Burning Deck.

--Keeping Still, Mountain. LC 83-81250. (Orig.). 1984. pap. 4.00 (ISBN 0-913123-00-5). Galileo.

Engman, Suzy, jt. auth. see Grossman, Cheryl S.

Engnell, Ivan. Rigid Scrutiny: Critical Essays on the Old Testament. Willis, John T., tr. LC 70-76166. 1969. 15.00x (ISBN 0-8265-1133-3). Vanderbilt U Pr.

--A Rigid Scrutiny: Critical Essays on the Old Testament. Willis, John T., ed. (Vanderbilt University Press Bks.). 303p. 1969. 15.00x (ISBN 0-8265-1133-3). U of Ill Pr.

Engquist, B. & Smedsaas, T., eds. PDE Software-Modules, Interfaces & Systems: Proceedings of the IFIP TC 2 Working Conference Held in Soderkoping, Sweden, 22-26 August 1983. 454p. 1984. 50.00 (ISBN 0-444-87620-0, North-Holland). Elsevier.

Engram, Eleanor. Science, Myth, Reality: The Black Family in One-Half Century of Research. LC 81-1262. (Contributions in Afro-American & African Studies: No. 64). (Illus.). xviii, 216p. 1982. lib. bdg. 29.95 (ISBN 0-313-22835-3, ESM/). Greenwood.

Engrand, Bernard. L' Industrie Photographique en France. Bunnell, Peter C. & Sobieszek, Robert A., eds. LC 78-67656. (Sources of Modern Photography Ser.). (Fr.). 1979. Repr. of 1934 ed. lib. bdg. 17.00x (ISBN 0-405-09897-9). Ayer Co Pubs.

Engrav, Loren H., jt. auth. see Heimbach, David M.

Engs, Robert F. Freedom's First Generation: Black Hampton, Virginia, 1861-1890. LC 79-5046. (Illus.). 1980. 10.95x (ISBN 0-8122-7768-6). U of Pa Pr.

Engs, Ruth & Wantz, Molly. Teaching Health Education in the Elementary School. LC 77-79371. (Illus.). 1978. text ed. 27.95 (ISBN 0-395-25483-3); instr's manual 1.00 (ISBN 0-395-25484-1). HM.

Engs, Ruth C., et al. Health Games Students Play: Creative Strategies for Health Education. 1976. perfect binding 10.95 (ISBN 0-8403-1238-5). Kendall-Hunt.

Engsberg, Cornelius, jt. auth. see Snyder, Mary Lucia.

Engster, Hermann. Poesie einer Achsenzeit. (European University Studies: No. 1, Vol. 667). 384p. (Ger.). 1983. 44.20 (ISBN 3-8204-7703-9). P Lang Pubs.

Engstorm, Paul F., et al. Advances in Cancer Control: Epidemiology & Research. LC 84-7894. (Progress In Clinical & Biological Research Ser.: Vol. 156). 482p. 1984. 58.00 (ISBN 0-8451-5006-5). A R Liss.

Engstrand, Iris H. Serra's San Diego: Father Junipero Serra & California's Beginnings. (Illus.). 6p. 1982. 2.95 (ISBN 0-918740-02-9). San Diego Hist.

Engstrand, Iris W. Spanish Scientists in the New World: The Eighteenth-Century Expeditions. LC 80-50863. (Illus.). 234p. 1981. 27.50x (ISBN 0-295-95764-6). U of Wash Pr.

Engstroem, E. Swedish-English, English-Swedish Technical Dictionary, 2 vols. rev. enl ed. (Swedish & Eng.). Set. 125.00 (ISBN 0-685-42614-9). Heinman.

Engstrom, jt. auth. see Hay.

Engstrom, Alfred G. Darkness & Light: Lectures on Baudelaire, Flaubert Nerval, Huysmans, Racine, & "Time & Its Images in Literature". LC 75-20433. (Romance Monographs: No. 16). 1975. 15.00x (ISBN 84-399-4488-8). Romance.

Engstrom, Arne, jt. auth. see Finean, J. B.

Engstrom, Barbie. Egypt & a Nile Cruise. (Engstrom's Travel Experience Guides Ser.). (Illus.). 394p. (Orig.). 1984. 15.95 (ISBN 0-916588-05-X). Kurios Pr.

--Engstrom's Guide to India, Nepal & Sri Lanka. rev. ed. (Engstrom's Travel Experience Guides Ser.). (Illus.). 228p. Date not set. pap. 14.50. Kurios Pr.

--Engstrom's Guide to Paris with Twelve Walking Tours. (Engstrom's Travel Experience Guides Ser.). (Illus.). 250p. (Orig.). Date not set. pap. 14.95 (ISBN 0-916588-10-6). Kurios Pr.

--Engstrom's Guide to Safaris in Kenya & Tanzania. (Engstrom's Travel Experience Guides Ser.). (Illus.). 250p. (Orig.). Date not set. pap. 14.50 (ISBN 0-916588-07-6). Kurios Pr.

--Faith to Know. LC 77-94207. (Christian Guidebook Ser.). (Illus., Orig.). Date not set. pap. 10.50 (ISBN 0-932210-01-5). Kurios Found.

--Faith to See: Reflections & Photographs. LC 74-25540. (Illus.). 64p. 1979. pap. 3.00 (ISBN 0-932210-00-7). Kurios Found.

--India Nepal & Sri Lanka. (Engstrom's Travel Exprience Guide Ser.). (Illus.). 228p. (Orig.). 1981. pap. 14.50 (ISBN 0-916588-06-8). Kurios Pr.

--A Kurios Foundation's Guide to Dealing with Abusive People. (A Kurios Foundation Guide Ser.). (Illus.). 250p. (Orig.). Date not set. pap. 9.95 (ISBN 0-932210-02-3). Kurios Found.

Engstrom, Elizabeth. When Darkness Loves Us. LC 84-16519. 256p. 1985. 14.95 (ISBN 0-688-04175-2). Morrow.

--When Darkness Loves Us. 256p. 1986. pap. 3.50 (ISBN 0-8125-8226-8, Dist. by Warner Pub Services & St. Martin). Tor Bks.

Engstrom, Georgianna, ed. Play: The Child Strives Toward Self-Realization. LC 76-177237. (Illus.). 72p. (Orig.). 1971. pap. text ed. 3.50 (ISBN 0-912674-30-X, NAEYC 129). Natl Assn Child Ed.

--The Significance of the Young Child's Motor Development. LC 70-177238. 55p. (Orig.). 1971. pap. text ed. 3.00 (ISBN 0-912674-32-6, NAEYC #128). Natl Assn Child Ed.

Engstrom, J. Eric. The Medallic Portraits of Sir Winston Churchill. 1977. 12.00 (ISBN 0-685-51522-2, Pub by Spink & Son England). S J Durst.

Engstrom, Karen M. Consent Manual: Policies, Laws, Procedures. LC 80-14269. 100p. 1981. pap. 10.00 (ISBN 0-87125-062-4). Cath Health.

--Healthcare Consent Manual: Policies, Laws, Procedures, 2nd ed. LC 82-22199. 115p. 1985. pap. 13.50 (ISBN 0-87125-078-0). Cath Health.

Engstrom, Paul F., et al. Advances in Cancer Control: Research & Development. LC 83-894. (Progress in Clinical & Biological Research Ser.: Vol. 120). 544p. 1983. 62.00 (ISBN 0-8451-0120-X). A R Liss.

Engstrom, Robert E. & Putman, Marc. Planning & Design of Townhouses & Condominiums. LC 79-64813. (Illus.). 246p. 1979. pap. 37.00 (ISBN 0-87420-587-5, P20); pap. 27.75 members. Urban Land.

Engstrom, Ted. Your Gift of Administration. LC 83-8327. 192p. 1983. 9.95 (ISBN 0-8407-5297-0). Nelson.

Engstrom, Ted W. For the Workaholic I Love. Juroe, David J., ed. 192p. 1984. 10.95 (ISBN 0-8007-1220-X). Revell.

--Un Lider No Nace, Se Hace. 256p. 1980. 3.95 (ISBN 0-88113-330-2). Edit Betania.

--The Making of a Christian Leader. 1976. pap. 6.95 (ISBN 0-310-24221-5). Zondervan.

--Motivation to Last a Lifetime. 96p. 1983. gift ed. 8.95 (ISBN 0-310-24250-9); pap. 3.95 (ISBN 0-310-24251-7). Zondervan.

--The Pursuit of Excellence. 128p. (Orig.). 1982. gift ed. 8.95 (ISBN 0-310-24240-1); pap. 3.95 (ISBN 0-310-24241-X). Zondervan.

Engstrom, Ted W. & Larson, Robert C. The Fine Art of Friendship. 176p. 1985. 9.95 (ISBN 0-8407-5419-1). Nelson.

Engstrom, Ted W. & MacKenzie, Alex. Managing Your Time. LC 67-17239. (Orig.). (YA) 1968. pap. 3.50 (ISBN 0-310-24262-2). Zondervan.

Engstrom, Ted W., jt. auth. see Dayton, Edward R.

Engstrom, Victoria. The Forges of Chiltonville. (Pilgrim Society Notes Ser.: No. 26). 1.00 (ISBN 0-940628-16-3). Pilgrim Hall.

Engstrom, Victoria B. Eel River Valley. (Pilgrim Society Notes Ser.: No. 23). 1.00 (ISBN 0-940628-15-5). Pilgrim Hall.

Enguang, Wang, jt. ed. see Renyong, Wu.

Enguidanos, Miguel. La Poesia De Luis Pales Matos. 2nd ed. LC 76-8010. (Coleccion Uprex Serie Estudios Literarios: No. 47). 109p. (Span.). 1976. pap. 1.85 (ISBN 0-8477-0047-X). U of PR Pr.

Engvick, William, ed. Lullabies & Night Songs. LC 65-22880. (Illus.). (ps-3). 1965. 24.95 (ISBN 0-06-021820-7). HarpJ.

Engwall, Lars. Newspapers As Organizations. 288p. 1979. text ed. 43.50x (ISBN 0-566-00262-0). Gower Pub Co.

Engwall, Lars & Johanson, Jan, eds. Some Aspects of Control in International Business. 122p. 1980. pap. 12.00 (ISBN 0-317-07415-6). Transnatl Pubs.

Enholm, Eric. Basic Story Structure: The Structural Method for English Composition. 3rd ed. 1968. 8.50 (ISBN 0-685-06810-2); pap. 7.00 (ISBN 0-685-06811-0). Bayside.

Enis & Cox. Marketing Classics: A Selection of Influential Articles. 5th ed. 1985. 22.86 (ISBN 0-205-08341-2, 138341). Allyn.

Enis, Ben. Marketing Principles. 3rd ed. 1980. 28.20x (ISBN 0-673-16110-2). study guide 10.95 (ISBN 0-673-16111-0). Scott F.

--Personal Selling: Foundations, Process, & Management. LC 78-12171. (Illus.). 1979. text ed. 27.10x (ISBN 0-673-16132-3). Scott F.

Enis, Ben E., jt. auth. see Murphy, Patrick E.

Enis, Ben M., jt. auth. see Chonko, Lawrence B.

Enis, Ben M. & Roering, Kenneth J., eds. Review of Marketing 1981. (Illus.). 271p. (Orig.). 1981. pap. text ed. 21.00 (ISBN 0-87757-150-3). Am Mktg.

Enk, Jean & Hendricks, Meg. Shortcuts for Teachers: Strategies for Reducing Classroom Workload. LC 81-81392. 1981. pap. 6.95 (ISBN 0-8224-6373-3). Pitman Learning.

Enk, P. J. Ad Propertii Carmina Commentarius Criticus, Zutpen. Commager, Steele, ed. LC 77-70813. (Latin Poetry Ser.). 1978. Repr. of 1911 ed. lib. bdg. 58.00 (ISBN 0-8240-2954-2). Garland Pub.

Enker, Warren E. Carcinoma of the Colon & Rectum. (Illus.). 1978. 47.75 (ISBN 0-8151-3120-8). Year Bk Med.

Enking, Ragna, tr. see Codino, Fausto.

Enkvist, Nils E. Caricatures of Americans on the English Stage Prior to 1870. LC 68-26273. 1968. Repr. of 1951 ed. 22.50x (ISBN 0-8046-0134-8, Pub. by Kennikat). Assoc Faculty Pr.

--Linguistic Stylistics. (Janua Linguarum Ser. Critica: No. 5: No. 5). 1973. pap. text ed. 12.80x (ISBN 90-2792-382-5). Mouton.

En-Lai, Chou. In Quest: Poems of Chou En-Lai. 2nd ed. Lin, Nancy T., tr. from Chinese. LC 79-84647. 51p. 1979. pap. 2.95 (ISBN 0-917056-41-8, Pub. by Joint Pub Co China). Cheng & Tsui.

Enlander, Derek. Computers in Medicine: An Introduction. 120p. 1984. 15.00. Med Software.

--Microcomputer Programs in Medicine, Vol. I. (Illus.). 116p. 1983. 80.00 (ISBN 0-88672-000-1). Med Software.
--Microcomputer Programs in Medicine, Vol. II. 105p. 1984. 80.00. Med Software.
Enlander, Derek, jt. auth. see Wolf, Paul.
Enlander, Derek, ed. Computers in Laboratory Medicine. 1975. 39.50 (ISBN 0-12-239950-1). Acad Pr.
Enlart, Camille. Les Monuments des Croises dans le Royaume de Jerusalem, 4 vols. LC 78-63336. (The Crusades & Military Orders: Second Ser.). Repr. of 1927 ed. Set. 495.00 (ISBN 0-404-17050-1). AMS Pr.
Enloe, Cynthia. Does Khaki Become You? The Militarization of Women's Lives. 224p. 1983. 20.00 (ISBN 0-89608-184-2); pap. 8.00 (ISBN 0-89608-183-4). South End Pr.
--Ethnic Conflict & Political Development: An Analytic Study. (Ser. in Comparative Politics). 282p. 1973. pap. text ed. 10.95 (ISBN 0-316-24020-6). Little.
--Ethnic Soldiers: State Security in Divided Societies. LC 79-5418. 288p. 1980. 23.00x (ISBN 0-8203-0507-3). U of Ga Pr.
--Police, Military, & Ethnicity. LC 79-64569. 179p. 1980. text ed. 14.95 (ISBN 0-87855-302-9). Transaction Bks.
Enloe, Cynthia see Ellinwood, DeWitt C.
Enlow, D. K., compiled by. We Drive an Eighteen Wheeler. LC 81-67320. 136p. (Orig.). 1981. pap. 2.95 (ISBN 0-87509-305-1). Chr Pubns.
Enlow, David, compiled by. We Drive an Eighteen Wheeler. 136p. 1981. pap. 2.49 (ISBN 0-318-17251-8). Transport Chr.
Enlow, David, ed. see Meloon, Walter.
Enlow, David R. Church Usher: Servant of God. LC 80-66769. 64p. (Orig.). 1980. pap. 1.95 (ISBN 0-87509-284-5). Chr Pubns.
Enlow, David R., jt. auth. see Parker, Paul E.
Enlow, Donald H. A Handbook of Facial Growth. 2nd ed. LC 75-293. (Illus.). 423p. 1982. 34.95 (ISBN 0-7216-3386-2). Saunders.
Enlow, Harold L. Carving Figure Caricatures in the Ozark Style. LC 74-17879. (Illus.). 48p. 1975. pap. 2.50 (ISBN 0-486-23151-8). Dover.
--Carving Figure Caricatures in the Ozark Style. (Illus.). 11.25 (ISBN 0-8446-5183-4). Peter Smith.
--How to Carve Folk Figures & a Cigar-Store Indian. LC 78-64855. (Illus.). 1979. pap. 2.95 (ISBN 0-486-23748-6). Dover.
Enlow, Jack. Glosario de Nombres Biblicos. 96p. 1981. pap. 2.25 (ISBN 0-311-03655-4). Casa Bautista.
Enlow, Margie, ed. see Rizer, Arden, Jr.
Enna, S. J. & Yamamura, H. D., eds. Neurotransmitter Receptors, 2 pts. (Receptors & Recognition Ser. B: Vols. 9 & 10). 1980. Set. 90.00x (ISBN 0-686-80428-7, NO. 2178, Pub. by Chapman & Hall); Pt. 1: Amino Acids, Peptides & Benzodiazepines. 49.95x (ISBN 0-412-16250-4, NO. 6399); Pt. 2: Biogenic Amines. 49.95x (ISBN 0-412-23130-1, 2157). Methuen Inc.
Enna, S. J., jt. ed. see Coyle, Joseph T.
Enna, S. J., et al, eds. Antidepressants: Neurochemical, Behavioral, & Clinical Perspectives. (Central Nervous System Pharmacology Ser.). 275p. 1981. Set. 46.00 (ISBN 0-89004-534-8). Raven.
--Brain Neurotransmitters & Receptors in Aging & Age-Related Disorders. (Aging Ser.: Vol. 17). 292p. 1981. text ed. 46.00 (ISBN 0-89004-643-3). Raven.
Ennals, R. Artificial Intelligence: Applications to Logical Reasoning & Historical Research. (Cognitive Sciences Ser.). 1985. 29.95 (ISBN 0-470-20181-9). Halsted Pr.
Ennals, Richard. Beginning Micro-PROLOG. (Hands On! Computer Bks.). 212p. (Orig.). 1984. pap. 15.34 (ISBN 0-06-669000-5). Har-Row.
Enneking, John J. see Curtis, Tony.
Enneking, William F. Musculoskeletal Tumor Surgery, 2 vol. (Illus.). 1585p. 1983. Set. text ed. 250.00 (ISBN 0-443-08092-5). Churchill.
Ennemoser, Joseph. The History of Magic. large type ed. (Illus.). pap. 8.50 (ISBN 0-910122-45-8). Amherst Pr.
Ennes, James M., Jr. Assault on the Liberty: The True Story of the Israeli Attack on an American Intelligence Ship. LC 79-4793. 1980. 13.95 (ISBN 0-394-50512-3). Random.
Ennes, W. B., Jr., ed. Introduction to Crop Protection. (Foundation for Modern Crop Service Ser.: Vol. 2). (Illus.). 1979. 20.00 (ISBN 0-89118-033-8). Am Soc Agron.
Ennew, Judith. The Western Isles Today. LC 79-13643. (Changing Cultures Ser.). (Illus.). 1980. 34.50 (ISBN 0-521-22590-6); pap. 10.95 (ISBN 0-521-29572-6). Cambridge U Pr.
Ennico, Clifford R., ed. see Bonner, Tricia K., et al.
Ennico, Clifford R., jt. auth. see Merritt, Raymond W.
Ennis, Daniel & Mullen, Kenneth. The Operating Characteristic Curves Manual: Infinite Lot Size, Single Sampling Plans. 1980. lib. bdg. 26.00 (ISBN 0-8161-2208-3, Hall Medical). G K Hall.
Ennis, Edith E., et al. The Transcription Specialist: A Text-Workbook. 315p. 1981. pap. text ed. 18.95 spiralbnd. (ISBN 0-15-592348-X, HC); instr's. manual avail. (ISBN 0-15-592349-8); tape program 225.00 (ISBN 0-15-592350-1); key to tape program avail. (ISBN 0-15-592351-X); trainee materials 9.95 (ISBN 0-15-592352-8). HarBraceJ.
Ennis, Frank, ed. Human Immunity to Viruses. LC 83-12299. 1983. 45.00 (ISBN 0-12-239980-3). Acad Pr.
Ennis, Joseph T. & Dowsett, David J. Vascular Radionuclide Imaging: A Clinical Atlas. LC 82-17594. 239p. 1982. 100.00 (ISBN 0-471-25670-6, Pub. by Wiley Med). Wiley.
Ennis, Lambert. Thackeray: The Sentimental Cynic. (Nortwestern University. Humanities Ser.: No. 25). Repr. of 1950 ed. 28.00 (ISBN 0-404-50725-5). AMS Pr.
Ennis, Mary Gratia. The Vocabulary of the Institutiones of Cassiodorus with Special Advertence to the Technical Terminology & Its Sources, No. 9. (Studies in Medieval & Renaissance Latin). 186p. 1983. Repr. of 1939 ed. 38.00x (ISBN 0-939738-24-4). Zubal Inc.
Ennis, Philip H. & Winger, Howard W., eds. Seven Questions About the Profession of Librarianship: Proceedings of the 26th Annual Conference of the Graduate Library School. LC 62-994. (University of Chicago Studies in Library Science). 1962. 7.50x (ISBN 0-226-21027-8). U of Chicago Pr.
Ennis, Seamus, tr. see Sayers, Peig.
Ennis, Stephanie. Counseling Techniques in Astrology. 98p. 1982. 7.00 (ISBN 0-86690-026-8, 2584-01). Am Fed Astrologers.
--Decanates & Dwads. 72p. 1983. 7.00 (ISBN 0-86690-239-2, 2568-01). Am Fed Astrologers.
Enniss, Stephen C., jt. ed. see Mason, Robert M.
Ennius, Quintus. The Tragedies of Ennius: The Fragments. Jocelyn, H. D., ed. LC 67-11525. (Cambridge Classical Texts & Commentaries Ser.: No. 10). pap. 120.30 (ISBN 0-317-29380-X, 2024481). Bks Demand UMI.
Ennodius, Magnus F. Opera Omnia. (Corpus Scriptorum Ecclesiasticorum Latinorum Ser.: Vol. 6). 1882. pap. 60.00 (ISBN 0-384-14370-9). Johnson Repr.
Enns, H. & Haering, R. R., eds. Modern Solid State Physics, Vol. 2: Phonons & Their Interactions. (Simon Fraser Summer School Lectures Ser., 1968). 208p. 1969. 57.75 (ISBN 0-677-13220-4). Gordon.
Enns, Herman. This We Believe, Leader's Guide. LC 78-130643. 1970. pap. 1.75 (ISBN 0-87303-846-0). Faith & Life.
Enns, Paul P. Joshua: Bible Study Commentary. (Bible Study Commentary). 160p. (Orig.). 1981. pap. 4.95 (ISBN 0-310-44041-6). Zondervan.
--Judges: A Bible Study Commentary. (Bible Study Commentary Ser.). 160p. (Orig.). 1982. pap. 5.95 (ISBN 0-310-44051-3). Zondervan.
--Ruth: A Bible Study Commentary. 96p. (Orig.). 1982. pap. 3.95 (ISBN 0-310-44061-0). Zondervan.
Enns, Richard H., et al, eds. Nonlinear Phenomena in Physics & Biology. LC 81-15882. (NATO ASI Series B, Physics: Vol. 75). 620p. 1981. text ed. 89.50x (ISBN 0-306-40880-5, Plenum Pr). Plenum Pub.
Eno, David. The Vegetarian Barbecue. (Illus.). 112p. (Orig.). 1985. pap. 4.95 (ISBN 0-7225-0792-5). Thorsons Pubs.
Eno, Robert B. Teaching Authority in the Early Church. (Message of the Fathers of the Church Ser.: Vol. 14). 1984. 15.00 (ISBN 0-89453-354-1); pap. 7.95 (ISBN 0-89453-325-8). M Glazier.
Enoch & Trethowan. Uncommon Psychiatric Syndromes. 2nd ed. 208p. 1979. 26.00 (ISBN 0-7236-0517-3). PSG Pub Co.
Enoch, J. M. & Tobey, F. L., eds. Vertebrate Photoreceptor Optics. (Springer Series in Optical Sciences: Vol. 23). (Illus.). 520p. 1981. 49.50 (ISBN 0-387-10515-8). Springer-Verlag.
Enoch, J. M., jt. ed. see Dawson, W. W.
Enoch, Jay M., et al. Quantitative Layer-by-Layer Perimetry: An Extented Analysis. (Current Ophthalmology Monographs). (Illus.). 256p. 1980. 39.00 (ISBN 0-8089-1282-8, 791165). Grune.
Enoch Pratt Free Library. Eastern Shore of Maryland: An Annotated Bibliography. Pritchett, Morgan H., ed. LC 80-50399. (Illus.). 233p. 1980. 29.95 (ISBN 0-937692-00-X). Queen Anne Pr.
Enoch, Yvonne. Group Piano-Teaching. 1974. 8.75x (ISBN 0-19-318423-0). Oxford U Pr.
--Let's Play. 1977. pap. text ed. 3.80 (ISBN 0-87563-138-X). Stipes.
Enoch, Yvonne & Lyke, James. Creative Piano Teaching. 1977. pap. text ed. 8.80x (ISBN 0-87563-142-8). Stipes.
Enochs, James. Restoration of Confidence: Common Sense & Common Purpose. LC 81-83975. 48p. 1981. 2.00 (ISBN 0-87367-777-3). Phi Delta Kappa.
Enochs, James C. The Restoration of Standards: The Modesto Plan. LC 79-89539. (Fastback Ser.: No. 129). (Orig.). 1979. pap. 0.75 (ISBN 0-87367-129-5). Phi Delta Kappa.
Enochson, L., jt. auth. see Otnes, R. K.
Enochson, Loren, jt. auth. see Otnes, Robert K.
Enock, C. Mexico. 1976. lib. bdg. 59.95 (ISBN 0-8490-2243-6). Gordon Pr.
Enock, C. R. The Tropics: Their Resources, People & Future. 1976. lib. bdg. 59.95 (ISBN 0-8490-2770-5). Gordon Pr.
Enock, C. Reginald. Mexico: Its Ancient & Modern Civilization. 1976. lib. bdg. 59.95 (ISBN 0-8490-0629-5). Gordon Pr.
--The Secret of the Pacific: Origins of the Toltecs, Aztecs, Mayas, & Incas. 1977. lib. bdg. 59.95 (ISBN 0-8490-2584-2). Gordon Pr.
Enockson, Paul G. A Guide for Selecting Computers & Software for Small Businesses. 1983. 21.95 (ISBN 0-8359-2642-7); pap. text ed. 14.95 (ISBN 0-8359-2641-9). Reston.
Enoeda, K. Karate Defence & Attack. 1984. 22.00x (ISBN 0-901764-04-3, Pub. by P H Crompton Ltd UK). State Mutual Bk.
Enoeda, K. & Mack, C. Shotokan Karate Free Fighting Techniques. 1984. 27.00x (ISBN 0-317-14249-6, Pub. by P H Crompton Ltd UK). State Mutual Bk.
Enoeda, Keinsuke. Shotokan: Advanced Kata, 3 vols. LC 83-70077. (Illus.). 132p. (Orig.). 1983. pap. 13.95 ea. Vol. 1 (ISBN 0-946062-03-X). Vol. 2 (ISBN 0-946062-04-8). Unique Pubns.
Enos, Chris. Gar-baj. LC 81-70289. (Illus.). 54p. (Orig.). 1982. pap. 5.00 (ISBN 0-89822-025-4). Visual Studies.
Enos, J. L., jt. auth. see Park, W. H.
Enos, Paul & Perkins, R. D. Quaternary Sedimentation in South Florida. LC 76-44123. (Memoir: No. 147). (Illus.). 1977. 34.00 (ISBN 0-8137-1147-9). Geol Soc.
Enquist, L. W., jt. ed. see Denniston, K. J.
Enquist, Olov. The Night of the Tribades. 1978. pap. 3.35x (ISBN 0-685-08728-X). Dramatists Play.
Enquist, Per Olov. The Night of the Tribades: A Play from 1889. Shideler, Ross, tr. from Swedish. 81p. 1977. 9.95 (ISBN 0-8090-7365-X). Hill & Wang.
Enrick, N. L. Manufacturing Analysis for Productivity & Quality-Cost Enhancement. 2nd ed. 158p. 1983. 23.00 (ISBN 0-686-48156-9, 1204). T-C Pubns CA.
Enrick, Norbert L. Experimentation & Statistical Validation. LC 81-20928. 1983. lib. bdg. 15.95 (ISBN 0-89874-445-8). Krieger.
--Handbook of Effective Graphic & Tabular Communication. LC 79-4483. 224p. 1980. 13.75 (ISBN 0-88275-914-0). Krieger.
--Industrial Engineering Manual: For the Textile Industry. 2nd ed. LC 77-15461. 360p. 1978. lib. bdg. 23.65 (ISBN 0-88275-631-1). Krieger.
--Management Control Manual for the Textile Industry. 2nd rev. ed. LC 79-13206. 250p. 1980. lib. bdg. 23.65 (ISBN 0-88275-994-9). Krieger.
--Management Handbook of Decision-Oriented Statistics. LC 79-13534. 356p. 1980. lib. bdg. 15.40 (ISBN 0-88275-984-1). Krieger.
--Management Planning: A Systems Approach. LC 67-27823. 240p. 1967. 27.50 (ISBN 0-686-74219-2). Krieger.
--Market & Sales Forecasting: A Quantitative Approach. rev. ed. LC 78-9090. 208p. 1979. 13.75 (ISBN 0-88275-690-7). Krieger.
--Time Study Manual for the Textile Industry. 2nd ed. LC 81-17159. 1982. lib. bdg. 23.65 (ISBN 0-89874-044-4). Krieger.
Enrick, Norbert L., jt. auth. see Myers, Buddy L.
Enright, D. J. Academic Year. (Twentieth-Century Classics). 264p. 1985. pap. 5.95 (ISBN 0-19-281876-7). Oxford U Pr.
--The Apothecary's Shop. LC 75-15663. 236p. 1975. Repr. of 1957 ed. lib. bdg. 24.75x (ISBN 0-8371-8222-0, ENAS). Greenwood.
--Collected Poems. 1981. 27.50x (ISBN 0-19-211941-9). Oxford U Pr.
--Instant Chronicles: A Life. 64p. 1985. pap. 6.95 (ISBN 0-19-211971-0). Oxford U Pr.
--Literature for Man's Sake. LC 72-192045. 1955. lib. bdg. 15.00 (ISBN 0-8414-3971-0). Folcroft.
--Mania for Sentences. LC 84-48300. 220p. 1985. 15.95 (ISBN 0-87923-549-7). Godine.
--Robert Graves & the Decline of Modernism. LC 74-12209. 1960. lib. bdg. 8.50 (ISBN 0-8414-3960-5). Folcroft.
--The Terrible Shears. LC 74-5966. (Wesleyan Poetry Program Ser.: Vol. 73). 72p. 1974. 15.00x (ISBN 0-8195-2073-X); pap. 6.95 (ISBN 0-8195-1073-4). Wesleyan U Pr.
--The Typewriter Revolution & Other Poems. LC 73-158612. 143p. 1971. 15.95 (ISBN 0-912050-07-1, Library Pr). Open Court.
Enright, D. J., ed. Fair of Speech: The Uses of Euphemism. 208p. 1985. 15.95 (ISBN 0-19-212236-3). Oxford U Pr.
--The Oxford Book of Death. 1983. 19.95 (ISBN 0-19-214129-5). Oxford U Pr.
Enright, D. J., ed. see Johnson, Samuel.
Enright, D. J., jt. ed. see Ninomiya, Takamichi.
Enright, Dennis J. Commentary on Goethe's Faust. 158p. 1980. Repr. of 1949 ed. lib. bdg. 20.00 (ISBN 0-8414-1916-7). Folcroft.
Enright, Elizabeth. Gone-Away Lake. LC 57-5172. (Illus.). (gr. 4-6). 1966. pap. 4.95 (ISBN 0-15-636460-3, VoyB). HarBraceJ.
--Return to Gone-Away. LC 61-6113. (Illus.). 191p. (gr. 3-7). 1973. pap. 1.15 (ISBN 0-15-676900-X, AVB74, VoyB). HarBraceJ.
--The Riddle of the Fly & Other Stories. facsimile ed. LC 70-121538. (Short Story Index Reprint Ser.). Repr. of 1959 ed. 17.00 (ISBN 0-8369-3494-6). Ayer Co Pubs.
--Thimble Summer. 144p. (gr. 2-6). 1976. pap. 2.25 (ISBN 0-440-48681-5, YB). Dell.
--Thimble Summer. LC 38-27586. (Illus.). 124p. (gr. 4-6). 1938. reinforced bdg. 11.95 (ISBN 0-03-015686-6). HR&W.
Enright, J. T. The Timing of Sleep & Wakefulness. (Studies of Brain Function: Vol. 3). (Illus.). 1980. pap. 31.00 (ISBN 0-387-09667-1). Springer-Verlag.
Enright, Jim, jt. ed. see Tanner, Chuck.
Enright, T. J. Lectures on Representations of Complex Semi-Simple Lie Groups. (Tata Institute Lectures on Mathematics Ser.). 91p. 1981. pap. 10.50 (ISBN 0-387-10829-7). Springer-Verlag.
Enright, Thomas E., et al. Compute's Guide to Telecomputing on the Apple. Compute Editors, ed. (Orig.). 1985. pap. 9.95 (ISBN 0-942386-98-1). Compute Pubns.
Enright, Tim, tr. see O'Guiheen, Michael.
Enright-Clark Shoukri, D., ed. Liber Apologeticus de Omni Statu Humanae Naturae: A Defence of Human Nature in Every State, a Moral Play by Thomas Chaundler. (Publications to the Modern Humanities Research Association: Vol. 5). (Illus.). x, 208p. 1974. avail. Modern Humanities Res.
Enrique, Mig A. House of Images. 205p. (Orig.). 1984. pap. 7.50x (ISBN 971-10-0107-1, Pub. by New Day Philippines). Cellar.
Enriquez & Bautista. English-Tagalog-Visayan Pocket Dictionary. (Eng. & Tagalog.). 4.00x (ISBN 0-686-05265-X). Colton Bk.
Enriquez & Guzman. English-Tagalog, Tagalog-English Pocket Dictionary. (Eng. & Tagalog.). 3.50x (ISBN 0-686-00861-8). Colton Bk.
Enriquez & Quimba. English-Tagalog-Ilocano Pocket Dictionary. (Eng. & Tagalog.). 4.00x (ISBN 0-686-05264-1). Colton Bk.
Enriquez, Antonio. Dance a White Horse to Sleep: And Other Stories. (Asian & Pacific Writings Ser). 1977. 16.95x (ISBN 0-7022-1471-X); pap. 8.50x (ISBN 0-7022-1472-8). U of Queensland Pr.
Enriquez, Antonio R. Surveyors of the Liguasan Marsh. (Asian & Pacific Writing Ser.). 131p. 1981. text ed. 18.00 (ISBN 0-7022-1532-5); pap. 9.75 (ISBN 0-7022-1533-3). U of Queensland Pr.
Enriquez, Collin M. A Burmese Arcady. LC 77-87075. Repr. of 1923 ed. 25.50 (ISBN 0-404-16814-0). AMS Pr.
--A Burmeses Loneliness: A Tale of Travel in Burma, the Southern Shan States & Keng Tung. LC 77-87076. Repr. of 1918 ed. 26.00 (ISBN 0-404-16815-9). AMS Pr.
--Races of Burma. 2nd ed. LC 77-87013. (Illus.). 152p. Repr. of 1933 ed. 29.50 (ISBN 0-404-16816-7). AMS Pr.
Enriquez, Edmund C. The Golden Gospel. (Illus.). 96p. (gr. 6-12). 1981. pap. 5.95 (ISBN 0-88290-198-2). Horizon Utah.
Enriquez, Evangelina, jt. auth. see Mirande, Alfredo.
Enriquez, Helen, jt. auth. see Fried, Elliot.
Enriquez, Martha, jt. auth. see Auvenshine, Martha.
Enriquez, Mig A. Three Phillipines Epic Plays: Lam-ang, Labaw Donggon & Bantugan. 198p. 1983. (Pub. by New Day Phillipines); pap. 10.00 (ISBN 0-686-39823-8). Cellar.
Enriquez De Guzman, Alonso. Life & Acts of Don Alonzo Enriquez De Guzman, a Knight of Seville of the Order of Santiago Ad. 1518-1543. Markham, Clements R., tr. & intro. by. LC 77-126272. (Hakluyt Society First Ser.: No. 29). 1970. Repr. of 1862 ed. lib. bdg. 29.50 (ISBN 0-8337-2228-X). B Franklin.
Enrody, Ladislaus. Hope Unlimited. 1962. 2.50 (ISBN 0-8198-0060-0); pap. 1.50 (ISBN 0-8198-0061-9). Dghtrs St Paul.
Enroth, Ronald, et al. A Guide to Cults & New Religions. LC 83-44. 200p. (Orig.). 1983. pap. 5.95 (ISBN 0-87784-837-8). Inter-Varsity.
Enroth, Ronald M. & Melton, Gordon J. Why Cults Succeed Where the Church Fails. 128p. 1985. 6.95 (ISBN 0-87178-932-9). Brethren.
Enroth, Ronald M., et al. The Story of the Jesus People: A Factual Survey. (Illus.). 256p. 1972. pap. 5.95 (ISBN 0-85364-131-5). Attic Pr.
Ensanian, Berj N. How to Master School with Superthinking - the Handbook of Successful Learning. 2nd ed. LC 78-60104. (Illus.). 1978. pap. 4.95 (ISBN 0-932032-01-X). Found Pub.
Enscoe, Gerald. Eros & the Romantics. LC 67-30548. (Studies in English Literature: Vol. 45). 1967. text ed. 18.40x (ISBN 90-2790-282-8). Mouton.
Enscoe, Gerald, jt. ed. see Gleckner, Robert.
Enser, A. G. Filmed Books & Plays: A List of Books & Plays from Which Films Have Been Made, 1928-1983. LC 84-21789. (A Grafton Bk.). 640p. 1985. 44.00x (ISBN 0-669-09735-7). Lexington Bks.
--Filmed Books & Plays Nineteen Twenty-Eight to Nineteen Seventy-Four. 552p. 1975. 26.50x (ISBN 0-233-96676-5, 05784-3, Pub. by Gower Pub Co England). Lexington Bks.
--Filmed Books & Plays: 1928-1974. rev. ed. 1975. 59.50 (ISBN 0-12-785201-8). Acad Pr.
--A Subject Bibliography of the First World War: Books in English 1914-1978. 488p. 1979. 39.00x (ISBN 0-233-96742-7, 05782-7, Pub. by Gower Pub Co England). Lexington Bks.

--A Subject Bibliography of the Second World War: Books in English 1975-1983. LC 84-13619. 225p. 1985. text ed. 35.50 for info. (ISBN 0-566-03514-6). Gower Pub Co.

Enser, A. G. S., ed. A Subject Bibliography of the Second World War: Books in English 1939-1974. (Grafton Bks.). 567p. 1977. 39.00 (ISBN 0-317-06888-1, 05783-5). Lexington Bks.

Ensign, Forest C. Compulsory School Attendance & Child Labor. LC 72-89176. (American Education: Its Men, Institutions & Ideas Ser). 1969. Repr. of 1921 ed. 20.00 (ISBN 0-405-01414-7). Ayer Co Pubs.

Ensign, Grayson H. & Howe, Edward. Bothered? Bewildered? Bewitched? Your Guide to Practical Supernatural Healing. LC 84-60177. 320p. 1984. pap. 9.95 kivar (ISBN 0-9613185-0-3). Recovery Pubns.

Ensign, Lynn N. & Knapton, Robyn E. The Complete Dictionary of Television & Film. LC 83-42634. 256p. 1985. 35.00 (ISBN 0-8128-2922-0). Stein & Day.

Ensign, Marie & Adler, Laurie N. Strategic Planning: Contemporary Viewpoints. (The Dynamic Organization Ser.). 231p. 1985. lib. bdg. 37.50 (ISBN 0-87436-448-5). ABC-Clio.

Ensign, Marie S. & Adler, Laurie N., eds. The Employee: Contemporary Viewpoints. (Human Resource Management Ser.). 247p. 1985. 37.50. ABC-Clio.

Ensign, Ruth S. Make That Story Live! (Orig.). (gr. 7-9). 1965. pap. 2.25 (ISBN 0-8042-9317-1). John Knox.

Ensinger, Earl W. Problems in Artistic Woodturning. LC 78-60054. (Illus.). 1978. pap. 8.95 (ISBN 0-918036-07-0). Woodcraft Supply.

Enskat, Rainer. Kants Theorie Des Geometrischen Gegenstandes. (Quellen & Studien Zur Philosophie: Vol. 13). 1978. 45.20x (ISBN 3-11-007644-6). De Gruyter.

Ensko, Stephen G. American Silversmiths & Their Marks: The Definitive Edition, 1948. 2nd ed. (Illus.). 287p. 1983. pap. 6.00 (ISBN 0-486-24428-8). Dover.

Ensko, Stephen G. & Wenham, Edward. English Silver 1675-1825. rev. ed. (Illus.). 144p. 1980. 24.95x (ISBN 0-938186-00-0). Arcadia Pr.

Enslein, K., ed. Data Acquisition & Processing in Biology & Medicine: Proceedings. Incl. Vol. 3. Rochester Conference, 1963 (ISBN 0-08-010904-7); Vol. 4. Rochester Conference, 1964; Vol. 5. Rochester Conference, 1966 (ISBN 0-08-012671-5). Vols. 3 & 5. 40.00 ea. Pergamon.

Enslein, Kurt, et al, eds. Statistical Methods for Digital Computers. LC 60-6509. (Mathematical Methods for Digital Computers Ser.: Vol. 3). 454p. 1977. 59.95 (ISBN 0-471-70690-6, Pub. by Wiley-Interscience). Wiley.

Ensley, Francis G. Leader's Guide for Use with Persons Can Change, by Francis Gerald Ensley. LC 69-101739. pap. 20.00 (ISBN 0-317-10063-7, 2001430). Bks Demand UMI.

Ensley, Helen. Poe's Rhymes. 1981. pap. 2.50 (ISBN 0-910556-17-2). Enoch Pratt.

Enslin. Forms, Pt. 4: The Fusion. 1973. 25.00 (ISBN 0-685-36868-8). Elizabeth Pr.

--Views. 1973. 16.00 (ISBN 0-685-36866-1); pap. 8.00 (ISBN 0-685-36867-X). Elizabeth Pr.

Enslin, Theodore. Agreement, & Back. 1969. 5.00 (ISBN 0-685-00999-8). Elizabeth Pr.

--Axes LII. 1981. pap. 1.75 (ISBN 0-686-35947-X). Ziesing Bros.

--Circles. 3.00 (ISBN 0-686-15295-6). Great Raven Pr.

--Etudes. 1972. 16.00 (ISBN 0-685-27711-9); pap. 8.00 (ISBN 0-685-27712-7). Elizabeth Pr.

--The Fifth Direction. (Orig.). 1980. pap. 6.00 (ISBN 0-915316-80-3). Pentagram.

--Forms-Coda. 1974. 25.00 (ISBN 0-685-46791-0). Elizabeth Pr.

--Forms, Pt. 2: The Tessaract. 1971. 15.00 (ISBN 0-685-01002-3). Elizabeth Pr.

--Forms, Pt. 3: The Experiences. 1972. 20.00 (ISBN 0-685-27710-0). Elizabeth Pr.

--In Duo Concertante. (Orig.). 1981. pap. 9.00 ltd. signed (ISBN 0-915316-93-5). Pentagram.

--A Man in Stir. (Illus., Orig.). 1983. pap. 10.00 ltd. signed (ISBN 0-937596-06-X). Pentagram.

--Markings. 62p. (Orig.). 1981. pap. 3.00 (ISBN 0-87924-042-3). Membrane Pr.

--May Fault. 24p. 1979. pap. 4.00 (ISBN 0-686-30871-9). Great Raven Pr.

--The Mornings. 1974. signed 15.00 (ISBN 0-686-20330-5, Pub. by Shaman Drum Pr); pap. 3.50 (ISBN 0-686-20331-3). Small Pr Dist.

--Music for Several Occasions. 69p. (Orig.). 1985. pap. 4.00 (ISBN 0-87924-056-3). Membrane Pr.

--Opus O. 68p. (Orig.). 1981. pap. 3.00 (ISBN 0-87924-039-3). Membrane Pr.

--Papers. 1976. 16.00 (ISBN 0-685-79199-8). Elizabeth Pr.

--Place Where I Am Standing. 1964. pap. 3.00 (ISBN 0-685-00997-1). Elizabeth Pr.

--Ranger, Vol. I. 2nd rev. ed. 432p. 1980. 30.00 (ISBN 0-913028-79-7); pap. 12.95 (ISBN 0-913028-78-9). North Atlantic.

--Ranger, Vol. 1. 432p. 1978. 30.00 (ISBN 0-913028-58-4); pap. 8.95 (ISBN 0-913028-51-7). North Atlantic.

--Ranger Volume II. 256p. (Orig.). 1980. 30.00 (ISBN 0-913028-75-4); pap. 9.95 (ISBN 0-913028-74-6). North Atlantic.

--Sitio. LC 73-86250. 50p. 1974. pap. 2.00 (ISBN 0-914102-02-8). Bluefish.

--Synthesis. 400p. 1975. pap. 6.00 (ISBN 0-913028-36-3). North Atlantic.

--To Come Home (To) 3.00 (ISBN 0-318-11913-7). Great Raven Pr.

--To Come to Have Become. 1966. pap. 8.00 (ISBN 0-685-00998-X). Elizabeth Pr.

--Two Geese. 1980. pap. 4.00 (ISBN 0-915316-86-2). Pentagram.

--With Light Reflected. (Orig.). 1973. 7.50 (ISBN 0-912090-39-1); pap. 2.45 (ISBN 0-912090-38-3). Sumac Mich.

Enslin, Theodore, ed. F. P. 1982. pap. 1.95 (ISBN 0-917488-12-1). Ziesing Bros.

Enslin, Theodore, et al. Knee Deep in the Atlantic. 1981. pap. 18.50 (ISBN 0-915316-89-7). Pentagram.

Ensminger, A. H. & Ensminger, M. E. Foods & Nutrition Encyclopedia, 2 vols. (Illus.). 2432p. 1983. Set. 99.00x (ISBN 0-941218-05-8). Pegus Pr.

Ensminger, Dale. Ultrasonics: The Low & High-Intensity Applications. LC 72-90963. (Illus.). pap. 146.80 (ISBN 0-317-07982-4, 2055005). Bks Demand UMI.

Ensminger, Douglas & Bomani, Paul. Conquest of World Hunger & Poverty. (Illus.). 140p. 1980. text ed. 8.50x (ISBN 0-8138-1140-6). Iowa St U Pr.

Ensminger, E. M. & Parker, Richard. Swine Science. 5th ed. LC 82-84359. (Illus.). (gr. 9-12). 1984. 38.00 (ISBN 0-8134-2289-2); text ed. 28.50x. Interstate.

Ensminger, J., ed. see Leakey, L. S., et al.

Ensminger, M. E. Beef Cattle Science. 5th ed. LC 74-29763. (Illus.). 1556p. 1976. 39.95 (ISBN 0-8134-1752-X, 1752); text ed. 29.95x. Interstate.

--The Complete Book of Dogs. LC 74-13. (Illus.). 960p. 1977. 25.00 (ISBN 0-498-01457-6). A S Barnes.

--The Complete Encyclopedia of Horses. LC 74-9282. (Illus.). 720p. 1977. 29.50 (ISBN 0-498-01508-4). A S Barnes.

--Dairy Cattle Science. 2nd ed. LC 78-78193. (Illus.). 630p. 1980. 35.95 (ISBN 0-8134-2079-2, 2079); text ed. 26.95x. Interstate.

--Horses & Horsemanship. 5th ed. LC 76-45238. (Illus.). 537p. 1977. 26.50 (ISBN 0-8134-1888-7); text ed. 19.95x. Interstate.

--Horses & Tack. 1977. 22.95 (ISBN 0-395-24766-7). HM.

--Poultry Science. 2nd ed. (Illus.). (gr. 9-12). 1980. 31.95 (ISBN 0-8134-2087-3, 2087); text ed. 23.95x. Interstate.

Ensminger, M. E. & Olentine, C. G., Jr. Feeds & Nutrition. (Illus.). 1978. Complete, 1417 Pgs. 49.50 (ISBN 0-941218-01-5); Abridged, 824 Pgs. 35.50 (ISBN 0-941218-02-3). Ensminger.

Ensminger, M. E., ed. Animal Science. 8th ed. LC 83-80064. (Illus.). 1047p. 1983. 39.95 (ISBN 0-8134-2294-9, 2294); text ed. 29.95x. Interstate.

Ensminger, M. E., jt. auth. see Ensminger, A. H.

Ensminger, M. Eugene. Sheep & Wool Science. 4th ed. LC 73-79612. (gr. 9-12). 1970. text ed. 27.35 (ISBN 0-8134-1113-0); text ed. 20.50x. Interstate.

Ensminger, R. M. Stockman's Handbook. 6th ed. 1983. 39.95 (ISBN 0-8134-2295-7, 2295); text ed. 29.95x. Interstate.

Ensor, Allison. Mark Twain & the Bible. LC 76-80092. pap. 35.00 (ISBN 0-317-27668-9, 2019517). Bks Demand UMI.

Ensor, Allison E., ed. see Clemens, Samuel L.

Ensor, D. M. The Comparative Endocrinology of Prolactin. 1978. 53.00 (ISBN 0-412-12720-2, NO.6103, Pub. by Chapman & Hall). Methuen Inc.

Ensor, David. With Lord Roberts Through the Kyber Pass. (Illus.). (gr. 7 up). 13.75x (ISBN 0-392-05610-0). Sportshelf.

Ensor, George. Inquiry Concerning the Population of Nations. LC 67-16339. Repr. of 1818 ed. 39.50x (ISBN 0-678-00209-6). Kelley.

Ensor, H. Blaine see Oakley, Carey.

Ensor, James. The Prints of James Ensor. LC 76-184012. 1972. Repr. of 1952 ed. lib. bdg. 29.50 (ISBN 0-306-70439-0). Da Capo.

Ensor, Laura, tr. see Loti, Pierre.

Ensor, Phyllis A. & Means, Richard K. Instructor's Resource & Method Handbook in Health Education. 2nd, rev. ed. 1979. pap. text ed. 27.95 (ISBN 0-205-06750-6). Allyn.

Ensor, Phyllis G., et al. Personal Health: Confronting Your Health Behavior. 1977. pap. text ed. 28.00 (ISBN 0-205-05737-3, 6257372); instr's manual avail. (ISBN 0-205-05738-1, 6257380). Allyn.

--Personal Health. 2nd ed. 500p. 1984. pap. text ed. 18.95x (ISBN 0-471-80370-7). Wiley.

--Personal Health. 2nd ed. 600p. 1985. pap. text ed. write for info. (ISBN 0-02-333800-8). Macmillan.

Ensor, Richard & Antl, Moris. The Management of Foreign Exchange Risk. 265p. 1982. 88.00x (ISBN 0-8002-3416-2). Intl Pubns Serv.

Ensor, Robert C. England, Eighteen Seventy to Nineteen Fourteen. (Oxford History of England Ser.). 1936. 34.95x (ISBN 0-19-821705-6). Oxford U Pr.

Ensor, Wendy-Ann. Heroes & Heroines in Music. (Illus.). 1981. pap. 5.00x (ISBN 0-19-321105-X); cassette 18.00x. Oxford U Pr.

--More Heroes & Heroines in Music. (Illus.). 1982. pap. 5.00x (ISBN 0-19-321106-8); cassette 18.00 (ISBN 0-19-321107-6). Oxford U Pr.

Ensrud, Barbara. The Pocket Guide to Cheese. 144p. 1981. pap. 4.95 (ISBN 0-399-50518-0, Perigee). Putnam Pub Group.

--The Pocket Guide to Wine: A Discriminating Guide to Good Wine. (Illus.). 144p. (Orig.). 1985. pap. 7.95 (ISBN 0-399-51145-8, Perigee). Putnam Pub Group.

--Wine with Food: A Guide to Entertaining Through the Seasons. (Illus.). 224p. 1984. 16.95 (ISBN 0-312-92026-1). Congdon & Weed.

Enstron, Federich, et al, eds. Boston's Best Guide. Cable, Harold & Nunez, B. Albert, trs. Date not set. pap. 2.57 (ISBN 0-686-32590-7). M Kennedy.

Enswiler, James P. The Religious Education Handbook: A Practical Parish Guide. LC 79-26008. 108p. (Orig.). 1980. pap. 4.95 (ISBN 0-8189-0398-8). Alba.

Enteen, George M. The Soviet Scholar-Bureaucrat: M. N. Pokrovskii & the Society of Marxist Historians. LC 78-50002. 1978. 28.75x (ISBN 0-271-00548-3). Pa St U Pr.

Enteen, George M., et al. Soviet Historians & the Study of Russian Imperialism. LC 78-27563. (Penn State Studies: No. 45). 1979. pap. text ed. 4.95x (ISBN 0-271-00211-5). Pa St U Pr.

Entelek Inc. Theory of Income Determination. 1963. pap. text ed. 3.95x (ISBN 0-02-333670-6, 33367). Macmillan.

Entelis, John P. Algeria. (Westview Profiles-Nations of the Contemporary Middle East). 130p. 1985. 24.00x (ISBN 0-86531-470-5). Westview.

--Comparative Politics of North Africa: Algeria, Morocco, & Tunisia. (Illus.). 240p. 1980. pap. 8.95x (ISBN 0-8156-2214-7). Syracuse U Pr.

Entenza, John. The Work of Jan De Swart. (Illus.). 34p. 1961. 1.00 (ISBN 0-686-91823-1). Galleries Coll.

Enterkin, Hugh & Reynolds, Gerald. Estimating for Builders & Surveyors. 2nd ed. 1978. 27.50x (ISBN 0-434-90542-9). Intl Ideas.

Enterline, H. T. & Thompson, J. J. Pathology of the Esophagus. (Illus.). 225p. 1984. 45.00 (ISBN 0-387-90896-X). Springer-Verlag.

Enterline, James Robert. Viking America: The Norse Crossings & Their Legacy. LC 76-175370. (Illus.). xix, 217p. 1972. 9.95 (ISBN 0-385-02585-8). J R Enterline.

Enters, Angna. First Person Plural. (Ser. in Dance). (Illus.). 1978. Repr. of 1937 ed. lib. bdg. 25.00 (ISBN 0-306-77594-8). Da Capo.

--On Mime. LC 65-21130. 1965. pap. 8.95 (ISBN 0-8195-6056-1). Wesleyan U Pr.

Enthoven, A. J. Accounting Education in Economic Development Management. 1981. 42.75 (ISBN 0-444-86195-5). Elsevier.

Enthoven, Alain C. & Freeman, A. Myrick, 3rd, eds. Pollution, Resources & the Environment. new ed. (Illus.). 1973. pap. 7.95x (ISBN 0-393-09933-4). Norton.

Enthoven, Jacqueline. Stitches of Creative Embroidery. (Illus.). 1964. pap. 14.95 (ISBN 0-442-22318-8). Van Nos Reinhold.

Entin, Elliot E., jt. auth. see Raynor, Joel O.

Entine, Alan D. & Mueller, Jean E. Perspectives on Mid-Life. (Technical Bibliographies on Aging Ser. 2). 1977. 4.00x (ISBN 0-88474-076-5, 05755-X). Lexington Bks.

Enting, Brian. Neath the Mantle of Rangi. (Illus.). 148p. 1980. 22.50 (ISBN 0-85467-036-X, Pub. by Viking Sevenseas). Intl Spec Bk.

Entmacher, Paul S. & Lew, Edward A. Underwriting the Physical Risk. (FLMI Insurance Education Program Ser.). 1971. pap. 5.00 (ISBN 0-915322-22-6). LOMA.

Entman, Robert M., jt. auth. see Paletz, David L.

Entner, Marvin L. Russo-Persian Commercial Relations, 1828-1914. LC 65-64001. (University of Florida Social Sciences Monographs: No. 28). (Illus.). 1965. pap. 3.50 (ISBN 0-8130-0073-4). U Presses Fla.

Entrekin, Charles. All Pieces of a Legacy. 54p. (Orig.). 1975. pap. 3.00 (ISBN 0-917658-03-5). BPW & P.

--Casting for the Cutthroat & Other Poems. 48p. (Orig.). 1980. pap. 3.95 (ISBN 0-917658-13-2). BPW & P.

Entrekin, Dee. Make Your Own Silk Flowers. LC 74-31705. (Illus.). 80p. 1981. pap. 7.95 (ISBN 0-8069-8994-7). Sterling.

Entrekin, Nina, jt. auth. see Applegate, Minerva.

Entrevernes Group. Signs & Parables: Semiotics & Gospel Texts. Phillips, Gary, tr. from Fr. LC 78-12840. (Pittsburgh Theological Monographs: No. 23). Orig. Title: Signes et Paraboles. 1978. pap. 15.50 (ISBN 0-915138-35-2). Pickwick.

Entrikin, John B., jt. auth. see Cheronis, Nicholas.

Entrikin, John B., jt. auth. see Cheronis, Nicholas D.

Entwhistle, Noel & Ramsden, Paul. Understanding Student Learning. 272p. 1983. 27.50 (ISBN 0-89397-171-5). Nichols Pub.

Entwisle, Doris B. & Doering, Susan G. The First Birth: A Family Turning Point. LC 80-22741. (Illus.). 352p. 1981. text ed. 32.50x (ISBN 0-8018-2408-7). Johns Hopkins.

Entwisle, Doris R. Word Associations of Young Children. (Illus.). 613p. 1966. 40.00x (ISBN 0-8018-0189-3). Johns Hopkins.

Entwisle, Doris R. & Hayduk, Leslie A. Early Schooling: Cognitive & Affective Outcomes. LC 82-82. 240p. 1982. text ed. 30.00x (ISBN 0-8018-2761-2). Johns Hopkins.

--Too Great Expectations: The Academic Outlook of Young Children. LC 77-23344. (Illus.). 240p. 1978. text ed. 28.00x (ISBN 0-8018-1986-5). Johns Hopkins.

Entwisle, Doris R., jt. auth. see Huggins, William H.

Entwisle, Frank. Abroad in England. (Illus.). 1983. 15.00 (ISBN 0-393-01755-9). Norton.

Entwisle, W. F. Bantams. (Illus.). 144p. 1981. 16.50 (ISBN 0-86230-034-7). Saiga.

Entwistle, A. W., ed. Studies in Culture, Linguistics, & Speechology. 1985. 22.50x (ISBN 0-8364-1257-5, Pub. by Swati Pub). South Asia Bks.

Entwistle, Beverly M., jt. auth. see Lange, Brian M.

Entwistle, Harold. Antonio Gramsci: Conservative Schooling for Radical Politics. (Routledge Education Bks.). 1979. pap. 9.50x (ISBN 0-7100-0334-X). Routledge & Kegan.

Entwistle, Noel. New Directions in Educational Psychology One: Teaching & Learning. (New Directions in Education Ser.). (Illus.). 300p. 1984. 36.00x (ISBN 0-905273-72-9, Pub. by Falmer Pr); pap. 20.00x (ISBN 0-905273-71-0, Pub. by Falmer Pr). Taylor & Francis.

--Styles of Learning & Teaching: An Integrative Outline of Educational Psychology for Students, Teachers, & Lecturers. LC 80-41172. 293p. 1981. 59.95x (ISBN 0-471-27901-3, Pub. by Wiley-Interscience); pap. 26.95x (ISBN 0-471-10013-7). Wiley.

Entwistle, Noel, ed. see Educational Research Symposium Organized by the Council of Europe & the Research & Development Unit of the Chancellor of the Swedish Universities, Goteborg, Sweden, September 7-12, 1975.

Entwistle, P. F., jt. auth. see Adams, P. H.

Entwistle, W. J. The Spanish Language, Together with Portuguese, Catalan & Basque. 1975. lib. bdg. 69.95 (ISBN 0-8490-1102-7). Gordon Pr.

Entwistle, W. J. & Morison, W. A. Russian & the Slavonic Languages. (The Great Languages Ser). (Illus.). 407p. 1974. text ed. 25.50x (ISBN 0-571-06109-5). Humanities.

--Russian & the Slavonic Languages. 407p. 1982. Repr. of 1949 ed. lib. bdg. 65.00 (ISBN 0-8495-1429-0). Arden Lib.

Entwistle, William J. The Arthurian Legend in the Literatures of the Spanish Peninsula. LC 26-5215. 1975. Repr. of 1925 ed. 21.00 (ISBN 0-527-27350-3). Kraus Repr.

Entwistle, William J. & Gillett, Eric. The Literature of England: Five Hundred to Nineteen Forty-Two A.D. 1977. Repr. of 1943 ed. lib. bdg. 20.00 (ISBN 0-8414-3995-8). Folcroft.

Entwistle, William S. The Arthurian Legend in the Literatures of the Spanish Peninsula. LC 75-6563. 278p. 1975. Repr. of 1925 ed. 12.50x (ISBN 0-87753-059-9). Phaeton.

Entz, Angeline J. Elijah: Brave Prophet. (BibLearn Ser.). (gr. 1-6). 1978. 5.95 (ISBN 0-8054-4244-8, 4242-44). Broadman.

Entzminger, Robert L. Divine Word: Milton & the Redemption of Language. (Duquesne Studies; Language & Literature Ser.: Vol. 6). 240p. 1985. text ed. 20.00x (ISBN 0-8207-0172-6). Duquesne.

Enueart, Jamrs L. Edward Weston's California Landscapes. (Illus.). 144p. 1984. slipcased 100.00 (ISBN 0-8212-1576-0, 258652). NYGS.

Enuma Elish. Le Poeme Babylonien de la Creation. LC 78-72734. (Ancient Mesopotamian Texts & Studies). Repr. of 1935 ed. 24.50 (ISBN 0-404-18173-2). AMS Pr.

--The Seven Tablets of Creation, 2 vols. LC 73-18850. (Luzac's Semitic Text & Translation Ser.: Nos. 12 & 13). (Illus.). Repr. of 1902 ed. Set. 45.00 (ISBN 0-404-11344-3). AMS Pr.

Enviromental Design Press. Evergreen Form Studies. 1983. 25.95 (ISBN 0-442-22337-4). Van Nos Reinhold.

--How to Make Cities Liveable: Design Guidelines for Urban Homesteading. Robinette, Gary O., ed. 149p. 1984. 27.50 (ISBN 0-442-22203-3). Van Nos Reinhold.

--Landscaping to Save Energy. 1986. price not set (ISBN 0-442-22210-6). Van Nos Reinhold.

Environment Resources Ltd. Cleaning & Conditioning Agents: Their Impact on the Environment in the EEC. 138p. 1978. 33.00x (ISBN 0-86010-108-8, Pub. by Graham & Trotman England). State Mutual Bk.

Environment Training Programme, Dakar, jt. auth. see United Nations Environment Programme, Nairobi.

Environmental Affairs Dept., American Petroleum Institute, jt. auth. see Ecological Analysts Inc.

Environmental Communications. Big Art: Megamurals & Supergraphics. Teacher, Stuart, et al, eds. LC 77-14043. (Illus.). 1977. lib. bdg. 19.80 (ISBN 0-89471-007-9); pap. 7.95 (ISBN 0-89471-006-0). Running Pr.

--Musical Houses: Homes & Secret Retreats of Music Stars. LC 80-22152. (Illus., Orig.). 1980. lib. bdg. 19.80 (ISBN 0-89471-112-1); pap. 7.95 (ISBN 0-89471-138-5). Running Pr.

Environmental Defense Fund & Boyle, Robert H. Malignant Neglect. LC 78-20373. 1979. 10.00 (ISBN 0-394-41070-X). Knopf.

Environmental Design Press. Trees of the West. 20.50 (ISBN 0-442-22207-6). Van Nos Reinhold.
--Water Conservation in Landscape Design & Management. 1984. 27.50 (ISBN 0-442-22204-1). Van Nos Reinhold.
Environmental Engineering Conference, Canberra Australia, 1979. The Status of the National Environment. 110p. (Orig.). 1979. pap. text ed. 24.00x (ISBN 0-85825-115-9, Pub. by Inst Engineering Australia). Brookfield Pub Co.
Environmental Impact Analysis Research Council at the Chicago National Convention, Oct. 1978. Appropriate Technology in Water Supply & Waste Disposal. American Society of Civil Engineers, ed. 280p. 1979. pap. 17.00x (ISBN 0-87262-148-0). Am Soc Civil Eng.
Environmental Law Institute. Legal Barriers to Solar Heating & Cooling of Buildings. 368p. 1980. 50.00x (ISBN 0-89499-006-3). Bks Business.
Environmental Law Institute & American Law Institute-American Bar Association Committee on Continuing Professional Education. Hazardous Wastes, Superfund, & Toxic Substances: ALI-ABA Course of Study Material. LC 84-103431. (Illus.). 594p. Date not set. price not set. Am Law Inst.
Environmental Law Institute, jt. auth. see ALI-ABA Committee on Continuing Professional Education.
Environmental Protection Agency. Toxic Substances Control Act Inspection Manual, Pt. 1, Vols. I & II. 341p. 1982. pap. 49.00 (ISBN 0-86587-056-X). Gov Insts.
Environmental Research & Technology, Inc. Atmospheric Dispersion Modeling for Emergency Preparedness. (National Environmental Studies Project: NESP Reports). 60p. 1981. 45.00 (ISBN 0-318-13561-2, AIF-NESP-022); NESP sponsors 15.00 (ISBN 0-318-13562-0). Atomic Indus Forum.
Environmental Resources Ltd. The Economics of Recycling. 167p. 1978. 19.00x (ISBN 0-86010-123-1, Pub. by Graham & Trotman England). State Mutual Bk.
--Environmental Impact of Energy Strategies within the EEC. flexi-cover 32.00 (ISBN 0-08-025681-3). Pergamon.
--Product Planning: The Relationship Between Product Characteristics & Environmental Impact. 312p. 1978. 26.00x (ISBN 0-86010-126-6, Pub. by Graham & Trotman England). State Mutual Bk.
Environmental Resources Ltd., ed. The Law & Practice Relating to Pollution Control in the Member States of the European Communities, 10 vols. 1982. Set. 850.00 (ISBN 0-686-82384-2, Pub. by Graham & Trotman England); 90.00x ea. State Mutual Bk.
Environmental Resources Ltd, ed. see Commission of the European Communities.
Environmental Resources Ltd., produced by. Acid Rain: A Review of the Phenomenon in the EEC & Europe. 159p. 1983. 23.00 (ISBN 0-89059-031-1, GT100, GP). Unipub.
Environmental Science Deptartment of the Massachusetts Audubon Society. The Home Tune-Up Manual. (Illus.). 156p. (Orig.). 1985. pap. 9.95 (ISBN 0-931790-62-X). Brick Hse Pub.
Environmental Studies Board. An Assessment of Mercury in the Environment. 1978. pap. 9.50 (ISBN 0-309-02736-5). Natl Acad Pr.
--Chloroform, Carbon Tetrachloride & Other Halomethanes: An Enviromental Assessment. 304p. 1978. pap. 10.25 (ISBN 0-309-02763-2). Natl Acad Pr.
--The International Mussel Watch. vi, 248p. 1980. pap. text ed. 12.95 (ISBN 0-309-03040-4). Natl Acad Pr.
--Kepone, Mirex, Hexachlorocyclopentadiene. 1978. pap. 7.25 (ISBN 0-309-02766-7). Natl Acad Pr.
--Long-Range Environmental Outlook. x, 198p. 1980. pap. text ed. 11.95 (ISBN 0-309-03038-2). Natl Acad Pr.
--OCS Oil & Gas: An Assessment. 1978. pap. 8.75 (ISBN 0-309-02739-X). Natl Acad Pr.
--Polychlorinated Biphenyls. 1979. pap. 8.75 (ISBN 0-309-02885-X). Natl Acad Pr.
Environmental Studies Board Commission on Natural Resources, National Research Council. Decision Making for Regulating Chemicals in the Environment. 288p. 1975. pap. 14.25 (ISBN 0-309-02401-3). Natl Acad Pr.
Environmental Studies Board, National Research Council. Causes & Effects of Stratospheric Ozone Reduction: An Update. 339p. 1982. pap. text ed. 13.95 (ISBN 0-309-03248-2). Natl Acad Pr.
--Contemporary Pest Control Practices & Prospects: Report of the Executive Committee. LC 75-43468. (Pest Control Ser.: An Assessment of Present & Alternative Technologies, Vol. 1). 506p. 1976. pap. 13.25 (ISBN 0-309-02410-2). Natl Acad Pr.
--On Prevention of Significant Deterioration of Air Quality. 141p. 1981. pap. text ed. 7.95 (ISBN 0-309-03137-0). Natl Acad Pr.
Environmental Studies Board, Natl Research Council. Corn-Soybeans Pest Control. (Pest Control Ser.: An Assessment of Present & Alternative Technologies, Vol. 2). 169p. 1976. pap. 6.95 (ISBN 0-309-02411-0). Natl Acad Pr.
--Cotton Pest Control. LC 75-37180. (Pest Control Ser.: An Assessment of Present & Alternative Technologies, Vol. 3). 139p. 1976. pap. 6.50 (ISBN 0-309-02412-9). Natl Acad Pr.
--Pest Control: An Assesssment of Present & Alternative Technologies, Vols. 1-3 &5. 1976. pap. 27.00 set (ISBN 0-309-02409-9). Natl Acad Pr.
--Pest Control & Public Health. LC 75-45777. (Pest Control Ser.: Vol.5). 282p. 1976. pap. 9.50 (ISBN 0-309-02414-5). Natl Acad Pr.
Environmental Systems Corporation Staff. Environmental Effects of Cooling Towers: AIF-NESP-026. (National Environmental Studies Project: NESP Reports). 1983. 50.00 (ISBN 0-318-02234-6). Atomic Indus Forum.
Envirosphere Company Staff. NEPA Decision Criteria for Operating License Reviews: AIF-NESP-024. (National Environmental Studies Project: NESP Reports). 1981. 45.00 (ISBN 0-318-02232-X). Atomic Indus Forum.
Enyart, David K. Applying for Your Church. LC 84-71852. 72p. (Orig.). pap. 2.95 (ISBN 0-89900-192-0). College Pr Pub.
Enyart, Ruby M. Before Their Eyes. 60p. 1956. pap. 1.00 (ISBN 0-88243-475-6, 02-0475). Gospel Pub.
Enyeart, James L. Jerry N. Uelsmann: Twenty-Five Years, A Retrospective. LC 82-12736. 231p. 1982. 39.95 (ISBN 0-8212-1519-1, 477400). NYGS.
Enyedi & Meszaros, eds. Development of Settlement Systems. (Studies in Geography in Hungary: Vol. 15). 1980. 29.00 (ISBN 0-9960014-5-X, Pub. by Akademiai Kaido Hungary). Heyden.
Enyedi, Gyorgy & Volgyes, Ivan, eds. The Effect of Modern Agriculture on Rural Developement. LC 80-25232. (Pergamon Policy Studies on International Developement Comparative Rural Transformations Ser.). (Illus.). 256p. 1982. 36.00 (ISBN 0-08-027179-0). Pergamon.
Enyingi, Peter, et al. Cataloging Legal Literature: A Manual on AACR2 & Library of Congress Subject Headings for Legal Material with Illustrations. LC 84-6313. (AALL Publ. Ser.: No. 22). 1984. looseleaf 65.00x (ISBN 0-8377-0120-1). Rothman.
Enz, C. P. & Mehra, J., eds. Physical Reality & Mathematical Description: Dedicated to Josef Maria Jauch on the Occasion of His Sixtieth Birthday. LC 74-81937. xxiii, 552p. 1974. lib. bdg. 66.00 (ISBN 90-277-0513-5, Pub. by Reidel Holland). Kluwer Academic.
Enz, C. P., ed. see International Conference, Geneva, 1979.
Enz, C. P., ed. see Pauli, Wolfgang.
Enz, Jacob. The Christian & Warfare. 104p. 1972. pap. 2.95 (ISBN 0-8361-1684-4). Herald Hse.
Enz, Jacob J. The Christian & Warfare: The Old Testament, War & the Christian. (Christian Peace Shelf Ser.). 104p. 1972. pap. 2.95 (ISBN 0-8361-1684-4). Herald Pr.
Enzel, Hajnalka V., ed. see Enzel, Robert G.
Enzel, Robert G. The White Book of Ski Areas. Enzel, Hajnalka V., ed. (Illus.). 348p. 1982. write for info. Inter-Ski.
Enzel, Robert G., ed. The White Book of Ski Areas. 9th ed. 416p. 1984. write for info. (ISBN 0-931636-09-4). Inter-Ski.
--The White Book of Ski Areas, 1984-85. 9th ed. write for info. (ISBN 0-931636-05-1). Inter-Ski.
Enzensberger, Hans M. Critical Essays. Grimm, Reinhold, ed. LC 81-19612. (German Library: Vol. 98). 320p. 1982. 19.50x (ISBN 0-8264-0258-5); pap. 8.95 (ISBN 0-8264-0268-2). Continuum.
Enzer, Selwyn. Some Societal Impacts of Alternative Energy Policies. 52p. 1975. 6.00 (ISBN 0-318-14423-9, WP21). Inst Future.
Enzer, Selwyn, et al. Neither Feast nor Famine. LC 78-3128. (Illus.). 1978. 21.50x (ISBN 0-669-02317-5). Lexington Bks.
En-Zhi, Mu, et al. Correlation of the Chinese Silurian. Berry, W. B., ed. (Special Paper Ser.: No. 202). (Illus.). 1985. write for info. (ISBN 0-8137-2202-0). Geol Soc.
Enzi, G., et al, eds. Obesity: Pathogenesis & Treatment. (Serono Symposia Ser.: Vol. 28). 1981. 55.00 (ISBN 0-12-240150-6). Acad Pr.
Enzinga, Netfa, et al. I Was Kidnapped by Idi Amin. (Orig.). 1979. pap. 1.95 (ISBN 0-87067-662-8, BH662). Holloway.
Enzinger, Franz M. & Weiss, Sharon W. Soft Tissue Tumors. LC 82-3402. (Illus.). 840p. 1983. text ed. 110.95 (ISBN 0-8016-1499-6). Mosby.
Enzler, Clarence. In the Presence of God. pap. 4.95 (ISBN 0-87193-055-2). Dimension Bks.
--My Other Self. pap. 5.95 (ISBN 0-87193-056-0). Dimension Bks.
Enzler, Clarence J. Let Us Be What We Are. 5.95 (ISBN 0-87193-136-2). Dimension Bks.
--Mi Otro Yo. 1984. pap. 7.95 (ISBN 0-87193-213-X). Dimension BKs.
Enzmann, Dieter R. Imaging of Infections & Inflammations of the Central Nervous System: Computed Tomography, Ultrasound, & Nuclear Magnetic Resonance. (Illus.). 360p. 1984. text ed. 67.00 (ISBN 0-89004-981-5). Raven.
Eoff, S. H., ed. see Rodriruez, Mario B., et al.
Eoff, Sherman, et al. Zalacain el Aventurero. Babcock, U. C. & Ramirez-Araujo, Alejandro, eds. LC 49-8551. (Graded Spanish Readers: Bk. 4). (Span). 1954. pap. text ed. 6.50 (ISBN 0-395-04127-9). HM.
Eoff, Sherman H. & Ramirez, Noemi. Composicion-Conversacion. LC 68-24611. pap. 60.80 (ISBN 0-8357-9860-7, 2012579). Bks Demand UMI.
Eogan, George. Excavations at Knowth. (Royal Irish Academy Monograph in Archeology). (Illus.). 358p. 1985. 42.00 (ISBN 0-901714-34-8, Pub. by Salem Acad). Merrimack Pub Cir.
Eois, Rachel Du see DuBois, Rachel.
Eorsi, G. Comparative Civil (Private) Law: Law Types, Law Groups, the Roads of Legal Development. Pulay, Gabor, et al, trs. from Hungarian. 651p. 1979. 53.00 (ISBN 0-9960016-5-4, Pub. by Akademiai Kaido Hungary). Heyden.
EORTC, see European Organization for Research & Treatment of Cancer.
Eoyang, Eugene C., ed. see Ai Qing.
Eoyang, Thomas T. An Economic Study of the Radio Industry in the United States of America. LC 74-4675. (Telecommunications Ser). 228p. 1974. Repr. of 1936 ed. 15.00x (ISBN 0-405-06041-6). Ayer Co Pubs.
EP Books, ed. Folk Lore & Legends of England. 1972. Repr. of 1890 ed. 14.95x (ISBN 0-8464-0418-4). Beekman Pubs.
EPA & State Laboratories, compiled by. EPA Manual of Chemical Methods for Pesticides and Devices. (Illus.). 1363p. (Incl. 3 supplements & binder). 1983. in U.S. 68.50 (ISBN 0-935584-23-4); outside U.S. 71.50 (ISBN 0-318-17091-4). Assoc Official.
Epachin, Betty C., jt. auth. see Paul, James L.
Epanchin, Betty C. & Paul, James L. Casebook for Educating the Emotionally Disturbed. 288p. 1982. pap. text ed. 12.95 (ISBN 0-675-20018-0). Merrill.
Epand, Len, jt. auth. see Rogers, Kenny.
Epaulic. Freedom Through Knowledge. 1981. 5.50 (ISBN 0-8062-1602-6). Carlton.
Epenshade, Edward, Jr. & Morrison, Joel L., eds. Rand McNally Goode's World Atlas. 17th ed. (Illus.). 384p. 1985. text ed. 19.95 (ISBN 0-528-63005-9); pap. text ed. 13.28 (ISBN 0-528-63006-7). Rand.
Epes, Mary, et al. The Comp-Lab Exercises. 2nd ed. (Illus.). 384p. 1986. pap. text ed. 16.95 (ISBN 0-13-154048-3). P-H.
--The Comp-Lab Exercises: Self-Teaching Exercises for Basic Writing. 1980. pap. text ed. 16.95 (ISBN 0-13-153601-X). P-H.
Eph'al, Israel. The Ancient Arabs: Nomads on the Borders of the Fertile Cresent 9th-5th Centuries B.C. 265p. 1982. text ed. 35.50x (ISBN 9-65223-400-1, Pub. by E J Brill Holland). Humanities.
Ephraem, Saint Repentance. pap. 1.95 (ISBN 0-686-18718-0). Eastern Orthodox.
Ephraim, Asher. Relative Productivity, Factor Intensity & Technology in the Manufacturing Sectors of the U.S. & the U.K. During the Nineteenth Century. Bruchey, Stuart, ed. LC 76-39822. (Nineteen Seventy-Seven Dissertations Ser.). (Illus.). 1977. lib. bdg. 21.00x (ISBN 0-405-09902-9). Ayer Co Pubs.
Ephremides, A., ed. Random Processes: Multiplicity & Canonical Decompositions, Pt. 1. LC 75-1287. (Benchmark Papers in Electrical Engineering & Computer Science: No. 11). 352p. 1973. 57.50 (ISBN 0-87933-022-8). Van Nos Reinhold.
Ephron, Amy. Cool Shades. 93p. (Orig.). 1984. pap. 2.95 (ISBN 0-440-11434-9). Dell.
Ephron, B. K. Emotional Difficulties in Reading: A Psychological Approach to Study Problems. LC 79-138226. 289p. 1972. Repr. of 1953 ed. lib. bdg. 18.75x (ISBN 0-8371-5583-5, EPED). Greenwood.
Ephron, Delia. How to Eat Like a Child. pap. 5.95 (ISBN 0-345-29654-0). Ballantine.
--How to Eat Like a Child: & Other Lessons in Not Being a Grownup. (Illus.). 1978. 7.95 (ISBN 0-670-38331-7). Viking.
--Santa & Alex. (Illus.). 1983. pap. 5.70i (ISBN 0-316-24301-9). Little.
--Teenage Romance: Or, How to Die of Embarrassment. LC 81-411. (Illus.). 144p. 1981. 10.95 (ISBN 0-670-69503-3). Viking.
--Teenage Romance: Or, How to Die of Embarrassment. 1982. pap. 5.95 (ISBN 0-345-30457-8). Ballantine.
Ephron, Delia, jt. auth. see Bodger, Lorraine.
Ephron, Nora. Crazy Salad Plus Nine. (Orig.). 1984. pap. 3.95 (ISBN 0-671-50715-X). PB.
--Heartburn. LC 82-48999. 1983. 11.95 (ISBN 0-394-53180-9). Knopf.
--Heartburn. (General Ser.). 267p. 1983. lib. bdg. 13.95 (ISBN 0-8161-3616-5, Large Print Bks). G K Hall.
--Heartburn. 224p. 1984. pap. 3.50 (ISBN 0-671-49678-6). PB.
Ephrussi, Boris. Hybridization of Somatic Cells. LC 79-39783. (Illus.). 192p. 1972. 22.00 (ISBN 0-691-08114-X); pap. 8.50 (ISBN 0-691-08117-4). Princeton U Pr.
Epictetus. Discourses, 2 Vols. (Loeb Classical Library: No. 131, 218). 12.50x ea. Vol. 1 (ISBN 0-674-99145-1). Vol. 2 (ISBN 0-674-99240-7). Harvard U Pr.
--Enchiridion. Higginson, T. W., tr. 1955. pap. 3.56 scp (ISBN 0-672-60170-2, LLA8). Bobbs.
--Handbook of Epictetus. White, Nicholas P., tr. from Greek. LC 83-267. (HPC Classic Ser.). Orig. Title: Encheiridion. 36p. 1983. pap. text ed. 2.75 (ISBN 0-915145-69-3). Hackett Pub.
--The Manuell of Epictetus. Sanford, J., tr. LC 77-6877. (English Experience Ser.: No. 869). 1977. Repr. of 1567 ed. lib. bdg. 7.00 (ISBN 90-221-0869-4). Walter J Johnson.
--The Most Meaningful Writings by Epictetus. Roswell, Steve C., tr. (The Most Meaningful Classics in World Culture Ser.). (Illus.). 1979. 49.75 (ISBN 0-89266-183-6). Am Classical Coll Pr.
Epictis, N. B., et al. Unified Valence Bond Theory of Electronic Structure. (Lecture Notes in Chemistry: Vol. 29). 303p. 1982. pap. 23.40 (ISBN 0-387-11491-2). Springer-Verlag.
Epicurus. Epicurea. Usener, H., ed. (Classical Studies Ser.). (Lat.). Repr. of 1887 ed. lib. bdg. 49.00x (ISBN 0-697-00059-1). Irvington.
--Epicurus, the Extant Remains, with Short Critical Apparatus. Bailey, Cyril, tr. LC 78-14117. (Illus.). 1980. Repr. of 1926 ed. 32.50 (ISBN 0-88355-789-4). Hyperion Conn.
--Epicurus's Morals. Digby, John, tr. LC 74-158299. Repr. of 1712 ed. 28.00 (ISBN 0-404-54114-3). AMS Pr.
--Letters, Principal Doctrines & Vatican Sayings. Geer, Russell, tr. LC 61-18059. (Orig.). 1964. pap. 5.99 scp (ISBN 0-672-60353-5, LLA141). Bobbs.
--The Philosophy of Epicurus: Letters, Doctrines, and Parallel Passages from Lucretius. Strodach, George K., ed. LC 63-2787. pap. 68.00 (ISBN 0-317-08924-2, 2006366). Bks Demand UMI.
EPIE Institute. The Educational Software Selector. 2nd ed. 800p. 1985. 59.95x (ISBN 0-8077-2779-2). Tchrs Coll.
Epifanov, G. Solid State Physics. 333p. 1979. 8.95 (ISBN 0-8285-1521-2, Pub. by Mir Pubs USSR). Imported Pubns.
Epigraphic Survey. Reliefs & Inscriptions at Karnak, IV: The Battle Reliefs of King Sety I. LC 84-61870. (Oriental Institute Publications Ser.: No. 107). 1985. write for info. portfolio (ISBN 0-918986-42-7). Oriental Inst.
--The Temple of Khonsu, Vol. 1: Scenes of King Herihor in the Court with Translations of Texts. LC 78-59119. (Oriental Institute Publications: No. 100). (Illus.). 1979. 90.00x (ISBN 0-918986-20-6). Oriental Inst.
--The Temple of Khonsu: Vol. 2, Scenes & Inscriptions in the Court & the First Hypostyle Hall. LC 80-82999. (Oriental Institute Publications Ser.: Vol. 103). 1981. pap. 95.00x incl. 96 plates in portfolio (ISBN 0-918986-29-X). Oriental Inst.
--The Tomb of Kheruef: Theban Tomb No. 192. LC 79-88739. (Oriental Institute Publications Ser.: Vol. 102). (Illus.). 1980. 90.00x (ISBN 0-918986-23-0). Oriental Inst.
Epilepsy International Symposium, 10th. Advances in Epileptology: Proceedings. Wada, Juhn A. & Penry, J. Kiffin, eds. 594p. 1980. text ed. 94.50 (ISBN 0-89004-511-9). Raven.
Epilepsy International Symposium, 11th., et al. Advances in Epileptology: Proceedings. Canger, Raffaele, ed. 510p. 1980. text ed. 80.50 (ISBN 0-89004-510-0). Raven.
Epilepsy International Symposium, 12th. Copenhagen, Denmark, et al. Advances in Epileptology: Proceedings. Dam, Mogens, et al, eds. 724p. 1981. 97.50 (ISBN 0-89004-611-5). Raven.
Epilepsy International Symposium, 13th., et al. Advances in Epileptology: Proceedings. Akimoto, Haruo, et al, eds. 560p. 1982. text ed. 108.00 (ISBN 0-89004-798-7). Raven.
Epinal. Antique French Jumping Jacks. pap. 2.50 (ISBN 0-486-23712-5). Dover.
--Antique Paper Dolls: The Edwardian Era. LC 75-2935. (Illus.). 1975. pap. 3.50 (ISBN 0-486-23175-5). Dover.
Epiotis, N. D. Theory of Organic Reactions. LC 77-17405. (Reactivity & Structure Ser.: Vol. 5). (Illus.). 1978. 63.00 (ISBN 0-387-08551-3). Springer-Verlag.
--Unified Valence Bond Theory of Electronic Structure-Applications. (Lecture Notes in Chemistry: Vol. 34). 585p. 1983. pap. 41.40 (ISBN 0-387-12000-9). Springer-Verlag.
Epiotis, N. D., et al. Structural Theory of Organic Chemistry. LC 76-57966. (Topics in Current Chemistry: Vol. 70). 1977. 59.00 (ISBN 0-387-08099-6). Springer-Verlag.
Episcopal Church. Prayer Book Guide to Christian Education. 224p. 1983. pap. 9.95 (ISBN 0-8164-2422-5, Pub. by Seabury). Winston Pr.
Episcopal Church Center. The Work You Give Us to Do: A Mission Study. 179p. (Orig.). 1982. pap. 4.95 (ISBN 0-8164-7116-9, Pub. by Seabury); study guide 1.25 (ISBN 0-8164-7117-7). Winston Pr.
Episcopal Churchwomen of All Saints. La Bonne Cuisine: Cooking New Orleans Style. (Illus.). pap. 9.95 (ISBN 0-9606880-0-5). ECS Inc.
Episcopal Day School Mothers' Club. Southern Secrets. (Illus.). 256p. (YA) 1979. pap. 7.95 (ISBN 0-918544-30-0). Wimmer Bks.
Epker, Bruce N. & Wolford, Larry M. Dentofacial Deformities: Surgical-Orthodontic Correction. LC 80-12405. (Illus.). 490p. 1980. text ed. 79.95 (ISBN 0-8016-1606-9). Mosby.
Epley, Boyd. Dynamic Strength Training for the Athletes. (Micropower Ser.). 160p. 1985. deluxe ed. 17.95 incl. diskette (ISBN 0-697-00593-3); pap. 8.95 (ISBN 0-697-00591-7). Wm C Brown.
--When, How & Why to Begin Lifting Weights...the Nebraska Way. 82p. (Orig.). 1983. pap. text ed. 4.95 (ISBN 0-317-06999-3). Body Enterprises.

Epley, Donald R. Arkansas Supplement for Modern Real Estate Practice. 3rd ed. LC 84-15900. 156p. (Orig.). 1984. pap. text ed. 9.95 (ISBN 0-88462-485-4, 1510-37, Real Estate Ed). Longman USA.
Epley, Donald R. & Boykin, James H. Basic Income Property Appraisal. LC 81-14929. (Finance Ser.). (Illus.). 450p. 1982. text ed. 36.95 (ISBN 0-201-03206-6). Addison-Wesley.
Epley, Donald R. & Millar, James A. Basic Real Estate Finance & Investment. 2nd ed. LC 83-12455. 619p. 1984. text ed. 35.50 (ISBN 0-471-87498-1). Wiley.
Epley, Donald R. & Rabianski, Joseph. Principles of Real Estate Decisions. LC 80-21354. 1981. text ed. 33.95 (ISBN 0-201-03188-4); instrs' manual 9.95 (ISBN 0-201-03189-2). Addison-Wesley.
Epley, Thelma M. Models for Thinking: Activities to Enhance Modes of Thought. 75p. 5.25 (ISBN 0-318-02192-7). NSLTIGT.
--Models for Thinking: Activities to Enhance Modes of Thought. 75p. 1982. 5.25 (ISBN 0-318-16014-5, 34). NSLTIGT.
Epling, P. J., jt. auth. see Kirk, Jerome.
Epling, Phillip K. Law of Pine Mountain. 1981. 9.95 (ISBN 0-87012-395-5). McClain.
Epp, C. D., jt. auth. see Bernard, C. H.
Epp, David. Labor Law. new & rev. ed. LC 76-26109. (Legal Almanac Ser.: No. 7). 120p. 1976. lib. bdg. 5.95 (ISBN 0-379-11102-0). Oceana.
Epp, Donald J. & Malone, John W., Jr. Introduction to Agricultural Economics. 1981. text ed. write for info. (ISBN 0-02-333940-3). Macmillan.
Epp, Eldon J. & Gordon, Fee D., eds. New Testament Textual Criticism: Its Significance for Exegesis. (Illus.). 94.00x (ISBN 0-19-826175-6). Oxford U Pr.
Epp, Frank H. The Israelis. LC 80-52. 208p. 1979. 13.95 (ISBN 0-8361-1924-X). Herald Pr.
--Mennonites in Canada, Vol. 1. 1983. 14.95 (ISBN 0-318-01066-6). Mennonite Pub.
--Mennonites in Canada, Nineteen Twenty to Nineteen Forty, Vol. II. LC 82-81339. 640p. 1982. text ed. 21.95x (ISBN 0-8361-1255-5). Herald Pr.
--The Palestinians. LC 76-12976. (Illus.). 240p. 1976. 10.00 (ISBN 0-8361-1338-1). Herald Pr.
--The Palestinians. LC 76-12976. 240p. 1976. 10.00 (ISBN 0-8361-1338-1). Herald Hse.
Epp, Margaret. The Earth is Round. pap. 4.00. Herald Hse.
--Eight, Tulpengasse: A Church Blossom's in Vienna. 276p. 1978. pap. 4.95. Herald Hse.
--A Fountain Sealed. 240p. 1982. pap. 5.95. Herald Hse.
--Sarah & the Darnley Boys. 120p. (gr. 6-12). 1981. pap. 2.95 (ISBN 0-88207-490-3). Victor Bks.
--Sarah & the Lost Friendship. LC 78-65203. (Illus.). 131p. (gr. 2-4). 1979. pap. 2.95 (ISBN 0-88207-483-0). Victor Bks.
--Sarah & the Magic Twenty-Fifth. LC 76-50172. 131p. (gr. 3-7). 1977. pap. 2.95 (ISBN 0-88207-477-6). Victor Bks.
Epp, Michael, tr. see Krussman, Gerd.
Epp, Michael, tr. see Krussmann, Gerd.
Epp, Michael E., tr. see Krussmann, Gerd.
Epp, Robert. Kinoshita Yuji. (World Authors Ser.). 1982. lib. bdg. 19.95 (ISBN 0-8057-6505-0, Twayne). G K Hall.
Eppard, Philip, jt. auth. see Monteiro, George.
Eppel, Emanuel M. & Eppel, M. Adolescents & Morality: A Study of Some Moral Values & Dilemmas of Working Adolescents in the Context of a Changing Climate of Opinion. (International Library of Sociology & Social Reconstruction Ser.). (Illus.). 1966. text ed. 9.00x (ISBN 0-7100-3455-5). Humanities.
Eppel, M., jt. auth. see Eppel, Emanuel M.
Eppen, et al. M.B.A. Degree. LC 79-55484. 1979. pap. 5.95 (ISBN 0-914090-81-X). Chicago Review.
Eppen, Gary D. & Gould, F. J. Introductory Management Science. (Illus.). 736p. 1984. text ed. 31.95 (ISBN 0-13-501973-7). P-H.
--Quantitative Concepts for Management: Decision-Making Without Algorithms. 2nd ed. (Illus.). 768p. 1985. text ed. 31.95 (ISBN 0-13-746637-4). P-H.
Eppen, Gary D., ed. Energy: The Policy Issues. LC 75-14800. xiv, 122p. 1975. 15.00x (ISBN 0-226-21175-4); pap. 2.95x (ISBN 0-226-21176-2). U of Chicago Pr.
Eppenbach, Sarah. Alaska's Southeast: Touring the Inside Passage. 2nd, rev. ed. (Illus.). 315p. 1985. pap. 11.95 (ISBN 0-914718-97-5). Pacific Search.
Eppenberger, H. M. & Perriard, J., eds. Developmental Processes in Normal & Diseased Muscle. (Experimental Biology & Medicine Ser.: Vol. 9). (Illus.). x, 294p. 1984. 81.00 (ISBN 3-8055-3765-4). S Karger.
Eppenstein, Simon, et al. Festschrift zum siebzigsten Geburtstage David Hoffman's. (Vol. 2). 23.00 (ISBN 0-405-12249-7). Ayer Co Pubs.
--Festschriftum, 3 vols. Katz, Steven, ed. LC 79-7161. (Jewish Philosophy, Mysticism & History of Ideas Ser.). 1980. Repr. of 1914 ed. Set. lib. bdg. 69.00x (ISBN 0-405-12247-0); lib. bdg. 23.00x ea. Vol. 1 (ISBN 0-405-12248-9). Vol. 2 (ISBN 0-405-12249-7). Vol. 3 (ISBN 0-405-12304-3). Ayer Co Pubs.
Epperly, Robert W. & Cohen, Arthur M. Interactive Career Development: Integrating Employer & Employee Goals. 112p. 1984. 29.95 (ISBN 0-03-001677-0). Praeger.
Epperson, A. Ralph. The Unseen Hand: An Introduction to the Conspiratorial View of History. (Illus.). 474p. (Orig.). 1985. pap. 12.95 (ISBN 0-9614135-0-6). Publius Pr.
Epperson, Arlin, et al. Leisure Counseling: An Aspect of Leisure Education. (Illus.). 392p. 1977. 30.75x (ISBN 0-398-03619-5). C C Thomas.
Epperson, Arlin F. Private & Commercial Recreation: A Text & Reference. LC 76-56453. 385p. 1977. text ed. 34.45 (ISBN 0-471-24335-3). Wiley.
Epperson, Eleanor & Epperson, John. Timberjack & the Chief, Bk. 1. (Illus.). 148p. (gr. 6-8). 1985. 12.95 (ISBN 0-9614114-0-6). Pillar Point Pr.
Epperson, Gordon. The Art of Cello Teaching. 6.95 (ISBN 0-318-18105-3). Am String Tchrs.
Epperson, James, ed. see Shakespeare, William.
Epperson, John, jt. auth. see Epperson, Eleanor.
Eppert, F., et al. German As It Is Spoken Deutsch wie man es Spricht. Learner's Grammar I. 65p. (Orig.). 1979. pap. 6.00x (ISBN 3-87276-327-X, Pub. by J Groos W Germany); 6.00x (ISBN 3-87276-326-1, Pub. by J Groos W Germany); 16 cassettes 207.00 (ISBN 0-686-88569-4). Benjamins North Am.
--German As It Is Spoken Deutsch wie man es Spricht. Learner's Grammar II. 88p. (Orig.). 1981. pap. 7.00x (ISBN 3-87276-331-8, Pub. by J Groos W Germany); wkbk 10.00 (ISBN 3-87276-330-X, Pub. by J Groos W Germany); 15 cassettes 194.00 (ISBN 0-686-88571-6). Benjamins North Am.
--German As It Is Spoken Deutsch wie man es Spricht, Models & Patterns I. 130p. (Orig.). 1979. pap. 8.00x (ISBN 3-87276-325-3, Pub. by J Groos W Germany). Benjamins North Am.
--German As It Is Spoken Deutsch wie man es spricht. Models & Patterns II. 120p. (Orig.). 1981. pap. 9.00x (ISBN 3-87276-329-6, Pub. by J Groos W Germany). Benjamins North Am.
--German As It Is Spoken Deutsch wie man es spricht. Models & Patterns III. 152p. (Orig.). 1981. pap. 10.00x (ISBN 3-87276-333-4, Pub. by J Groos W Germany). Benjamins North Am.
Eppert, M. R., ed. see Educational Research Council of America.
Eppes, Bill G. & Whiteman, Daniel E. Cost Accounting for the Construction Firm. LC 83-21752. (Construction Management & Engineering Ser.: 1102). 174p. 1984. 32.95x (ISBN 0-471-88537-1, Pub. by Wiley-Interscience). Wiley.
Eppes, Susan B. Through Some Eventful Years. Cushman, Joseph D., Jr., ed. LC 68-21660. (Floridiana Facsimile & Reprint Ser). 1968. Repr. of 1926 ed. 12.75 (ISBN 0-8130-0074-2). U Presses Fla.
Eppinger, Hans & Hess, Leo. Vagotonia: A Clinical Study in Vegetative Neurology. Kraus, Walter G. & Jelliffe, Smith E., trs. (Nervous & Mental Disease Monographs: No. 20). 1915. 19.00 (ISBN 0-384-14525-6). Johnson Repr.
Eppink, Norman R. One Hundred & One Prints: The History & Techniques of Printmaking. (Illus.). 272p. 1972. 32.50 (ISBN 0-8061-0915-7); pap. 14.95 (ISBN 0-8061-1181-X). U of Okla Pr.
Epple, A. see Pang, P. K.
Epple, Anne O. Amphibians of New England. LC 82-73602. (Illus.). 1983. pap. 7.95 (ISBN 0-89272-159-6). Down East.
--Something from Nothing Crafts. (Creative Craft Ser.). (Illus.). 192p. 1976. pap. 6.95 (ISBN 0-8019-6370-2). Chilton.
Epple, August & Stetson, Milton. Avian Endocrinology. 1980. 55.00 (ISBN 0-12-240250-2). Acad Pr.
Epple, Dennis. Petroleum Discoveries & Government Policy: An Econometric Study of Supply. LC 75-25626. 160p. 1975. prof ref 25.00 (ISBN 0-88410-420-6). Ballinger Pub.
Eppler, Elizabeth E., ed. International Bibliography of Jewish Affairs 1966-1967: A Select List of Books & Articles Published in the Diaspora. LC 74-84654. 365p. 1976. 35.00x (ISBN 0-8419-0177-5). Holmes & Meier.
--International Bibliography on Jewish Affairs: A Selected Annotated List of Books & Articles Published in the Diaspora, 1976-1977. 450p. 1982. 38.00x (ISBN 0-86531-164-1). Westview.
Eppler, R., ed. Laminar Turbulent Transitions. (International Union of Theoretical & Applied Mechanics). (Illus.). 432p. 1980. 43.70 (ISBN 0-387-10142-X). Springer-Verlag.
Epprecht, Russell. Further. (New York Quartet Ser.: Vol. I). 215p. (Orig.). 1983. pap. 8.95 (ISBN 0-912195-10-X). Domesday Bks.
--Step on It. (New York Quartet Ser.: Vol. III). 200p. (Orig.). Date not set. pap. 8.95 (ISBN 0-912195-12-6). Domesday Bks.
--Yardstick. (New York Quarter Ser.: Vol. II). 208p. (Orig.). 1984. pap. 8.95 (ISBN 0-912195-11-8). Domesday Bks.
Eppright, Ercel S., et al. Teaching Nutrition. 2nd ed. LC 63-24032. pap. 89.30 (ISBN 0-317-28207-7, 2022764). Bks Demand UMI.
Epps, Anna C. & Pisano, Joseph C. Med Rep at Tulane: A Longitudinal Study Health Professions Education of Minorities & the Disadvantaged. 125p. 1985. 12.00 (ISBN 0-87993-233-3). Futura Pub.
Epps, Charles H., ed. Complications in Orthopedic Surgery, 2 vols. LC 78-17997. 1978. Set. 112.00x (ISBN 0-397-50382-2, 65-01308, Lippincott Medical). Lippincott.
Epps, Charles H., Jr. Complications in Orthopedic Surgery. (Illus.). 1200p. 1985. text ed. price not set (ISBN 0-397-50638-4, Lippincott Medical). Lippincott.
Epps, Edgar, jt. auth. see Gurin, Patricia.
Epps, Edgar G. Cultural Pluralism. LC 73-17617. 1974. 21.00x (ISBN 0-8211-0412-8); text ed. 19.00x 10 or more copies. McCutchan.
Epps, Garrett. The Floating Island: A Tale of Washington. 1985. 14.95 (ISBN 0-395-37702-1). HM.
Epps, Louvella, jt. auth. see Harris, Teresa.
Epps, Preston H., tr. see Aristotle.
Eppsteiner & Maloney, eds. The Path of Compassion, Writings on Buddhism & Social Action. 1985. 9.95 (ISBN 0-934834-52-0). White Pine.
Epstein & Troy. Barron's Guide to Law Schools. 5th ed. LC 80-11446. 1982. pap. 6.95 (ISBN 0-8120-2436-2). Barron.
Epstein see Steer, Donald R., et al.
Epstein, A., jt. auth. see Weikart, D. P.
Epstein, A. L. Ethos & Identity. 1978. pap. 7.50 (ISBN 0-422-76370-5, NO. 3706, Pub. by Tavistock England). Methuen Inc.
--The Experience of Shame in Melanesia: An Essay in the Anthropology of Affect. (Occasional Papers Ser.: No. 40). 58p. 1984. pap. text ed. 8.25x (Pub. by Royal Anthro Inst England). Humanities.
--Urbanization & Kinship: The Domestic Domain on the Copperbelt of Zambia, 1950-6. LC 81-67899. (Studies in Anthropology). 1982. 44.00 (ISBN 0-12-240520-X). Acad Pr.
Epstein, A. L., ed. The Craft of Social Anthropology. 1979. 28.00 (ISBN 0-08-023693-6). Pergamon.
--The Craft of Social Anthropology. 2nd ed. 420p. 1978. 24.95 (ISBN 0-87855-280-4). Transaction Bks.
Epstein, A. S. & Weikart, D. P. The Longitudinal Follow-Up of the Ypsilanti-Carnegie Infant Education Project. 80p. 1980. pap. 10.00 (ISBN 0-931114-06-3, 26). High-Scope.
Epstein, Abraham. The Challenge of the Aged. LC 75-17219. (Social Problems & Social Policy Ser.). 1976. Repr. of 1928 ed. 32.00x (ISBN 0-405-07490-5). Ayer Co Pubs.
--Facing Old Age: A Study of Old Age Dependency in the United States & Old Age Pensions. LC 79-169381. (Family in America Ser.). 374p. 1972. Repr. of 1922 ed. 22.00 (ISBN 0-405-03858-5). Ayer Co Pubs.
--Insecurity: A Challenge to America. 2nd ed. LC 68-16353. 1968. Repr. of 1938 ed. 24.00x (ISBN 0-87586-005-2). Agathon.
--Negro Migrant in Pittsburgh: A Study in Social Economics. LC 79-92231. (American Negro: His History & Literature, Ser. No. 3). 1970. Repr. of 1918 ed. 12.00 (ISBN 0-405-01924-6). Ayer Co Pubs.
Epstein, Abraham & White, Morris. Shorthand, Typewriting & Secretarial Training. 1958. pap. 3.95 (ISBN 0-399-50814-7, G&D). Putnam Pub Group.
Epstein, Alan. Psychodynamics of Inconjunctions. LC 83-5908. (Illus.). 224p. 1984. pap. 8.95 (ISBN 0-87728-555-1). Weiser.
Epstein, Alan, jt. ed. see Sprague, James.
Epstein, Alan N., jt. ed. see Sprague, James M.
Epstein, Ann S. & Weikart, David P. The Ypsilanti-Carnegie Infant Education Project: Longitudinal Follow-up. LC 80-10939. (Monographs of the High-Scope Educational Research Foundation: No. 6). 65p. (Orig.). 1980. pap. 10.00 (ISBN 0-931114-06-3). High-Scope.
Epstein, Ann W., jt. auth. see Kazhdan, A. P.
Epstein, Arthur J., jt. ed. see Miller, Joel S.
Epstein, Arthur W. Anatomist's Dream of Love. 1966. 3.95 (ISBN 0-87212-005-8). Libra.
Epstein, Barbara A., ed. see Association of Mental Health Librarians.
Epstein, Barbara L. The Politics of Domesticity: Women, Evangelism, & Temperance in Nineteenth-Century America. LC 80-16671. 188p. 1981. 19.50x (ISBN 0-8195-5050-7). Wesleyan U Pr.
Epstein, Benjamin, jt. ed. see De Oliveira, J. Tiago.
Epstein, Benjamin R., jt. auth. see Forster, Arnold.
Epstein, Bernard. Partial Differential Equations: An Introduction. LC 75-11905. 284p. 1975. Repr. of 1962 ed. 16.50 (ISBN 0-88275-330-4). Krieger.
Epstein, Bertram. Immediate & Retention Effects of Interpolated Rest Periods on Learning Performance. LC 70-176754. (Columbia University. Teachers College. Contributions to Education: No. 949). Repr. of 1949 ed. 22.50 (ISBN 0-404-55949-2). AMS Pr.
Epstein, Beryl. Fashion Is Our Business. facs. ed. LC 72-117787. (Essay Index Reprint Ser). 1945. 18.00 (ISBN 0-8369-1920-3). Ayer Co Pubs.
Epstein, Beryl & Epstein, Samuel. Dr. Beaumont & the Man with the Hole in His Stomach. LC 77-8236. (Science Discovery Bk. Ser.). (Illus.). (gr. 3-5). 1978. PLB 6.99 (ISBN 0-698-30680-5, Coward). Putnam Pub Group.
Epstein, Beryl, jt. auth. see Epstein, Sam.
Epstein, Beryl, jt. auth. see Epstein, Samuel.
Epstein, Brian. A Cellarful of Noise. (Rock & Roll Remembrances Ser.: No. 4). 168p. 1984. individuals 16.50; institutions 19.50. Pierian.
Epstein, Cathleen, tr. see Wandruszka, Adam.
Epstein, Charles J., ed. Risk, Communication, & Decision Making in Genetic Counseling. LC 79-5120. (Alan R. Liss Ser.: Vol. 15, No. 5c). 1979. 43.00 (ISBN 0-8451-1030-6). March of Dimes.
Epstein, Charles J., et al, eds. see Birth Defects Conference, 1978, San Francisco.
Epstein, Charles M. & Andriola, Mary R. Introduction to EEG & Evoked Potentials. (Illus.). 240p. 1983. text ed. 23.75 (ISBN 0-397-50598-1, 65-07636, Lippincott Medical). Lippincott.
Epstein, Charlotte. An Introduction to the Human Services: Developing Knowledge, Skills, & Sensitivity. (Illus.). 368p. 1981. text ed. 27.95 (ISBN 0-13-484501-3). P-H.
--The Nurse Leader: Philosophy & Practice. 304p. 1982. text ed. 21.95 (ISBN 0-8359-5027-1); pap. text ed. 16.95 (ISBN 0-8359-5026-3). Reston.
--Special Children in Regular Classrooms. 1983. text ed. 18.95 (ISBN 0-8359-7044-2). Reston.
Epstein, Cynthia F. Woman's Place: Options & Limits in Professional Careers. LC 75-98139. 1970. 22.00x (ISBN 0-520-01581-9); pap. 3.95 (ISBN 0-520-01870-2, CAL227). U of Cal Pr.
--Women in Law. LC 80-68954. 382p. 1981. 18.50 (ISBN 0-465-09205-5). Basic.
--Women in Law. LC 82-45611. 456p. 1983. pap. 10.95 (ISBN 0-385-18431-X, Anch). Doubleday.
Epstein, Cynthia F. & Coser, Rose L., eds. Access to Power: Cross-National Studies of Women & Elites. (Illus.). 269p. 1980. text ed. 12.50x (ISBN 0-04-301118-7). Allen Unwin.
Epstein, D. B. Cohomology Operations: Lectures by N. E. Steenrod. (Annals of Mathematics Studies: No. 50). 1962. 11.50x (ISBN 0-691-07924-2). Princeton U Pr.
Epstein, Daniel M. The Book of Fortune. LC 81-18907. 64p. 1982. 14.95 (ISBN 0-87951-146-X); deluxe ed. 50.00 (ISBN 0-87951-151-6); pap. 6.95 (ISBN 0-87951-152-4). Overlook Pr.
--The Follies. LC 76-8059. 60p. 1977. 14.95 (ISBN 0-87951-048-X); pap. 8.95 (ISBN 0-87951-075-7). Overlook Pr.
--No Vacancies in Hell. 1973. 4.95 (ISBN 0-87140-574-1); pap. 2.50 (ISBN 0-87140-286-6). Liveright.
--Young Men's Gold. LC 77-20739. 72p. 1978. 14.95 (ISBN 0-87951-071-4); pap. 8.95 (ISBN 0-87951-076-5). Overlook Pr.
Epstein, Daniel M., jt. auth. see Bergman, David.
Epstein, David. Beyond Orpheus: Studies in Musical Structure. 1979. 32.50x (ISBN 0-262-05016-1). MIT Pr.
Epstein, David & Epstein, Shelia. The Art of Engagement: How to Build a Strong Foundation of Communication for Marriage. (Illus.). 306p. 1983. 19.95 (ISBN 0-914615-00-9). I N Inst.
Epstein, David F. The Political Theory of "The Federalist". LC 83-17858. 208p. 1984. lib. bdg. 22.00x (ISBN 0-226-21299-8). U of Chicago Pr.
Epstein, David G. Brasilia, Plan & Reality: A Study of Planned & Spontaneous Urban Settlement. LC 72-186103. 1973. 33.00x (ISBN 0-520-02203-3). U of Cal Pr.
--Debtor-Creditor Law in a Nutshell. 2nd ed. LC 79-25091. (Nutshell Ser.). 324p. 1980. pap. text ed. 8.95 (ISBN 0-8299-2072-2). West Pub.
Epstein, David G. & Landers, Jonathan M. Debtors & Creditors Cases & Materials. 2nd ed. LC 82-7088. (American Casebook Ser.). 725p. 1982. 21.95 (ISBN 0-314-66044-5); 1983 teacher's manual avail. (ISBN 0-314-73913-0). West Pub.
Epstein, David G. & Martin, James A. Basic Uniform Commercial Code Teaching Materials. 2d ed. LC 83-1153. (American Casebook Ser.). 667p. 1983. text ed. 21.95 (ISBN 0-314-71764-1). West Pub.
Epstein, David G. & Nickles, Steve H. Consumer Law in a Nutshell. 2nd ed. LC 80-27848. (Nutshell Ser.). 418p. 1981. pap. text ed. 8.95 (ISBN 0-8299-2130-3). West Pub.
Epstein, David G. & Sheinfeld, Myron M. Business Reorganization Under the Bankruptcy Code Materials. LC 79-28176. (American Casebook Ser.). 216p. 1980. pap. 9.95 (ISBN 0-8299-2070-6). West Pub.
Epstein, David J., et al. Unclaimed Property Law & Reporting Forms, 4 vols. 1984. looseleaf 350.00 (ISBN 0-317-09673-7, 136). Bender.
Epstein, David L., ed. Chandler's & Grant's Glaucoma. 3rd ed. LC 84-26115. (Illus.). 531p. 1985. text ed. write for info. (ISBN 0-8121-0972-4). Lea & Febiger.
Epstein, Dena J. Music Publishing in Chicago Before 1871: The Firm of Root & Cady, 1858-1871. (Detroit Studies in Music Bibliography Ser.: No. 14). 1969. pap. 2.00 (ISBN 0-911772-36-7). Info Coord.
--Sinful Tunes & Spirituals: Black Folk Music to the Civil War. LC 77-6315. (Music in American Life Ser.). (Illus.). 1981. pap. 9.95x (ISBN 0-252-00875-8). U of Ill Pr.
Epstein, Donna J. Writing for the Women's Market. 160p. (Orig.). pap. cancelled (ISBN 0-89471-285-3); lib. bdg. cancelled (ISBN 0-89471-286-1). Running Pr.

Epstein, E. Common Skin Disorders: A Physician's Illustrated Manual with Patient Instruction Sheets. (Illus.). 1983. pap. 27.95 (ISBN 0-87489-308-9). Med Economics.

Epstein, Earl B. No More Mr. Nice Guy: Business Karate for Getting to the Top & Staying There. LC 78-65295. 1979. 9.95 (ISBN 0-87863-173-9). Farnswth Pub.

Epstein, Ed & Morella, Joe. Judy: The Films of Judy Garland. 1970. pap. 8.95 (ISBN 0-8065-0206-1, 0206-1). Citadel Pr.

Epstein, Edmund L. Language & Style. (New Accents Ser.). 1978. pap. 9.95x (ISBN 0-416-83280-6, NO. 2193). Methuen Inc.

--The Ordeal of Stephen Dedalus: The Conflict of the Generations in James Joyce's "A Portrait of the Artist As a Young Man". LC 73-7714. (Arcturus Books Paperbacks). 231p. 1973. pap. 2.65 (ISBN 0-8093-0649-2). S Ill U Pr.

Epstein, Edmund L., ed. see Joyce, James.

Epstein, Edward. Exploring Careers in Podiatry. (Careers in Depth Ser.). 140p. (YA) 1983. lib. bdg. 8.97 (ISBN 0-8239-0551-9). Rosen Group.

Epstein, Edward & Votaw, Dow. Rationality, Legitimacy, Responsibility: Search for New Directions in Business & Society. LC 78-18302. 1978. pap. 19.50x (ISBN 0-673-16135-8). Scott F.

Epstein, Edward J. Between Fact & Fiction: The Problem of Journalism. (Orig.). (YA) 1975. pap. 4.95 (ISBN 0-394-71396-6, Vin). Random.

--News from Nowhere: Television & the News. 1974. pap. 4.95 (ISBN 0-394-71998-0, V-988, Vin). Random.

Epstein, Edward Z. Notorious Divorces. 307p. 1977. 8.95 (ISBN 0-8184-0224-5). Lyle Stuart.

Epstein, Edward Z. & Morella, Joseph. Lucy. LC 72-86171. 1973. 7.95 (ISBN 0-8184-0150-8). Lyle Stuart.

Epstein, Edward Z., jt. auth. see Morella, Joe.

Epstein, Edward Z., et al. Films of World War Two. (Illus.). 256p. 1975. pap. 6.95 (ISBN 0-8065-0482-X). Citadel Pr.

Epstein, Ellen R., jt. auth. see Lewit, Jane.

Epstein, Elliot M., et al, eds. Guide to Law Schools. 6th ed. 1984. pap. 8.95 (ISBN 0-8120-2772-8). Barron.

--Guide to the Most Prestigious Colleges. 3rd ed. 1984. pap. 7.95 (ISBN 0-8120-2828-7). Barron.

--Index of College Majors. 13th ed. 256p. (gr. 10-12). 1982. 17.95 (ISBN 0-8120-5450-4); pap. 9.95 (ISBN 0-8120-2460-5). Barron.

--Profiles of American Colleges. 14th ed. 1984. Vol. I, Descriptions of the Colleges. pap. 12.95 (ISBN 0-8120-2791-4); Vol. II, Index of College Majors. pap. 10.95 (ISBN 0-8120-2792-2); (Cloth Vol. I) 28.95; (Cloth Vol. II) 19.95. Barron.

--Profiles of American Colleges: The Northeast. 6th ed. 1984. pap. 7.95 (ISBN 0-8120-2795-7). Barron.

Epstein, Elliott M., et al. Barron's Guide to Law Schools. 6th ed. LC 84-9316. 1984. 8.95 (ISBN 0-8120-2772-8). Barron.

Epstein, Ervin. Controversies in Dermatology. (Illus.). 512p. 1984. 55.00 (ISBN 0-7216-3398-6). Saunders.

Epstein, Ervin & Epstein, Ervin, Jr. Skin Surgery, 2 vols. 5th ed. (Illus.). 1276p. 1982. Set. 215.00x (ISBN 0-398-04540-2). C C Thomas.

Epstein, Ervin & Epstein, Ervin, Jr., eds. Techniques in Skin Surgery. LC 79-11457. (Illus.). 203p. 1979. text ed. 18.00 (ISBN 0-8121-0677-6). Lea & Febiger.

Epstein, Erwin, Sr. Regional Dermatology: A System of Diagnosis for Nondermatologists. 2nd ed. 464p. 1984. 59.50 (ISBN 0-8089-1674-2, 791167); pap. 19.50 (ISBN 0-8089-1695-5, 791166). Grune.

Epstein, Eugene & Freund, William C. People & Productivity: The New York Stock Exchange Guide to Financial Incentives & the Quality of Work Life. LC 84-71126. 132p. 1984. 19.95 (ISBN 0-87094-510-6). Dow Jones-Irwin.

Epstein, G. & Schwartz, S., eds. Mold Design & Moldmaking for Plastics Products. 300p. 1985. 45.00 (ISBN 0-938648-21-7). T-C Pubns CA.

Epstein, George. Adhesives & Adhesive Bonding: Theoretical & Practical Aspects. 121p. 1984. 55.00 (ISBN 0-938648-16-0). T-C Pubns Ca.

Epstein, George, jt. ed. see Dunn, J. Michael.

Epstein, George, et al, eds. Kevlar Composites. LC 80-53544. (Illus.). 122p. 1980. 34.00 (ISBN 0-938648-02-0). T-C Pubns CA.

Epstein, Gerald. Waking Dream Therapy: Dream Process as Imagination. LC 80-25925. 237p. 1981. 24.95 (ISBN 0-89885-018-5). Human Sci Pr.

Epstein, Gerald, ed. Studies in Non-Deterministic Psychology. LC 80-13820. (New Directions in Psychotheraphy Ser.: Vol. V). 294p. (Series editor Paul T. Olsen). 1980. 29.95 (ISBN 0-87705-654-4). Human Sci Pr.

Epstein, Gloria J. Help Yourself to Chronic Pain Relief: The Patient's Point of View. LC 81-80224. 104p. (Orig.). 1981. pap. 4.95 (ISBN 0-9605792-0-6). Manchester Group.

Epstein, H. Domestic Animals of China. LC 73-152339. (Illus.). 166p. 1971. 39.50x (ISBN 0-8419-0073-6). Holmes & Meier.

--Domestic Animals of China. 164p. 1969. cloth 45.00x (ISBN 0-686-45812-5, Pub. by CAB Bks England). State Mutual Bk.

--Domestic Animals of Nepal. LC 75-6685. (Illus.). 160p. 1977. 39.50x (ISBN 0-8419-0202-X). Holmes & Meier.

--Origin of the Domestic Animals of Africa, 2 Vols. LC 76-136941. (Illus.). 1971. Set. 125.00x (Africana). Vol. 1 575p (ISBN 0-8419-0066-3). Vol. 2 720p (ISBN 0-8419-0067-1). Holmes & Meier.

Epstein, Hans, tr. see Wandruszka, Adam.

Epstein, Helen. Children of the Holocaust. 1980. pap. 3.95 (ISBN 0-553-22500-6). Bantam.

--The Companies She Keeps: Tina Packer Builds a Theater. LC 85-6485. (Illus.). 128p. (Orig.). 1985. pap. 8.95 (ISBN 0-9614696-0-9). Plunkett Lake Pr.

Epstein, Henry F. & Wolf, Stewart, eds. Genetic Analysis of the Chromosome: Studies of Duchenne Muscular Dystrophy & Related Disorders. (Advances in Experimental Medicine & Biology: Vol. 154). 344p. 1982. 37.50x (ISBN 0-306-41129-6, Plenum Pr). Plenum Pub.

Epstein, Henry F., jt. ed. see Pearson, Mark L.

Epstein, Herman. Traumatic Dislocation of the Hip. LC 79-9482. 336p. (Orig.). 43.00 (ISBN 0-683-02906-1). Krieger.

Epstein, Herman T. Strategy for Education. LC 71-124614. 1970. 14.95x (ISBN 0-19-501261-5). Oxford U Pr.

Epstein, Howard M. & Kanner, Gerald B., eds. News Dictionary: Vol. 5, 1968. annual LC 65-17649. (Illus.). 1969. 14.95 (ISBN 0-87196-087-7). Facts on File.

Epstein, I., ed. Tractate Baba Kamma. 1977. 22.95 (ISBN 0-900689-59-5). Soncino Pr NY.

--Tractate Baba Kamma. 1964. student's ed. 15.00 (ISBN 0-900689-67-6). Soncino Pr NY.

--Tractate Berakoth. 1960. 22.95 (ISBN 0-900689-56-0). Soncino Pr NY.

--Tractate Erubin. 1983. 22.95 (ISBN 0-900689-80-3). Soncino Pr NY.

--Tractate Gitten. 1973. 22.95 (ISBN 0-900689-58-7). Soncino Pr NY.

--Tractate Hullin. 1980. 22.95 (ISBN 0-900689-17-X). Soncino Pr NY.

--Tractate Kethuboth. 1971. 22.95 (ISBN 0-900689-06-4). Soncino Pr NY.

--Tractate Pesachim. 1983. 22.95 (ISBN 0-900689-81-1). Soncino Pr NY.

--Tractate Sanhadrin. 1969. 22.95 (ISBN 0-900689-04-8). Soncino Pr NY.

--Tractate Shabbath, 2 vols. 1972. Set. 45.95 (ISBN 0-900689-62-5). Soncino Pr NY.

--Tractate Yoma. 1974. 22.95 (ISBN 0-900689-63-3). Soncino Pr NY.

--Tractates Baba Bathra, 2 Vols. 1976. Set. write for info. (ISBN 0-900689-64-1). Soncino Pr NY.

Epstein, Ira. The Proficient Reader. LC 84-87971. 384p. 1985. pap. text ed. write for info. (ISBN 0-395-35020-4); instr's manual avail. (ISBN 0-395-35021-2). HM.

Epstein, Irwin & Tripodi, Tony. Research Techniques for Program Planning, Monitoring & Evaluation. LC 76-51825. 178p. 1977. 21.50x (ISBN 0-231-03944-1). Columbia U Pr.

Epstein, Irwin, jt. ed. see Tripodi, Tony.

Epstein, Isadore. The Faith of Judaism. 418p. 1954. pap. 8.75 (ISBN 0-900689-13-7). Soncino Pr NY.

--Step by Step in the Jewish Religion. 143p. 1958. pap. 4.95 (ISBN 0-900689-12-9). Soncino Pr NY.

Epstein, Isidore. Faith of Judaism. pap. 8.75x (ISBN 0-900689-13-7). Bloch.

--Judaism. (Orig.). 1959. pap. 4.95 (ISBN 0-14-020440-7, Pelican). Penguin.

--Step by Step in the Jewish Religion. PLB 4.95x. Bloch.

Epstein, Israel. Notes on Labor Problems in Nationalist China. LC 78-74341. (The Modern Chinese Economy Ser.). 159p. 1980. lib. bdg. 20.00 (ISBN 0-8240-4281-6). Garland Pub.

--Tibet Transformed. (Illus.). 566p. (Orig.). 1983. pap. 9.95 (ISBN 0-8351-1087-7). China Bks.

Epstein, Israel, et al. The Chinese Communists. Gelder, George S., ed. LC 74-10101. (China Studies from Confucius to Mao Ser). (Illus.). xlii, 290p. 1975. Repr. of 1946 ed. 25.85 (ISBN 0-88355-166-7). Hyperion Conn.

Epstein, Ita. Ba'sha'ar: Yahadus & Middos Text & Workbook. (Illus.). text ed. 4.00 (ISBN 0-914131-02-8, A10). Torah Umesorah.

Epstein, Jacob. Epstein: An Autobiography. facsimile ed. LC 74-27978. (Modern Jewish Experience Ser.). (Illus.). 1975. Repr. of 1955 ed. 34.50x (ISBN 0-405-06707-0). Ayer Co Pubs.

--Let There Be Sculpture. LC 78-64021. (Des Imagistes: Literature of the Imagist Movement). Repr. of 1940 ed. 31.00 (ISBN 0-404-17094-3). AMS Pr.

Epstein, Jacob & Haskell, Arnold L. The Sculptor Speaks: A Series of Conversations on Art. LC 73-172922. (Illus.). Repr. of 1932 ed. 22.00 (ISBN 0-405-08487-0). Ayer Co Pubs.

Epstein, James. The Lion of Freedom: Feargus O'Connor & the Chartist Movement, 1832-1842. (Illus.). 327p. 1982. 33.00 (ISBN 0-85664-922-8, Pub. by Croom Helm Ltd). Longwood Pub Group.

Epstein, James & Thompson, Dorothy, eds. The Chartist Experience-Studies in Working-Class Radicalism & Culture 1830 to 1860. 416p. 1982. text ed. 28.50x (ISBN 0-333-32971-6, 41403, Pub. by Macmillan England); pap. text ed. 13.00x (ISBN 0-333-32972-4, 41424). Humanities.

Epstein, Jane & Magnus, Laury. Common Ground: A Reader. 1982. pap. text ed. 14.70x (ISBN 0-673-15505-6). Scott F.

Epstein, Jason & Barlow, Elizabeth. East Hampton: A History & Guide. (Illus.). Date not set. pap. 8.95 (ISBN 0-394-72736-3). Random.

--The Hudson River Valley: A History & Guide. (Illus.). 1985. pap. write for info. Random.

Epstein, Jerome & Gaines, John. Clinical Respiratory Care of the Adult Patient. LC 82-22628. (Illus.). 448p. 1983. pap. text ed. 19.95 (ISBN 0-89303-209-3). Brady Comm.

Epstein, Jolie. Curious George Joins the Show. (Curious George Activity Bks.). 24p. (gr. k-3). pap. 1.50 (ISBN 0-590-33810-2). Scholastic Inc.

--The Kindles Find a Home. (The Kindles Ser.). 32p. (Orig.). (gr. k-3). 1985. pap. 1.95 (ISBN 0-590-33802-1). Scholastic Inc.

Epstein, Joseph. Ambition: Secret Passion. 1982. pap. 4.95 (ISBN 0-14-005986-5). Penguin.

--Familiar Territory: Observations on American Life. 1979. 17.50x (ISBN 0-19-502604-7). Oxford U Pr.

--The Middle of My Tether: Familiar Essays. LC 83-42650. 1983. 14.95 (ISBN 0-393-01772-9). Norton.

--A Natural History of Snobbery. Date not set. price not set (ISBN 0-670-50472-6). Viking.

--Plausible Prejudices: Essays on American Writing. 1985. 17.95 (ISBN 0-393-01918-7). Norton.

Epstein, Joseph, ed. Masters: Portraits of Great Teachers. LC 80-68180. 224p. 1981. 14.95 (ISBN 0-465-04420-4). Basic.

Epstein, Joshua M. Measuring Military Power: The Soviet Air Threat to Europe. LC 83-43070. (Illus.). 312p. 1984. 22.50x (ISBN 0-691-07671-5). Princeton U Pr.

--Measuring Military Power: The Soviet Air Threat to Europe. (Illus.). 304p. 1984. 40.00 (ISBN 0-85066-279-6). Taylor & Francis.

Epstein, Joyce L., ed. The Quality of School Life. LC 80-5350. 320p. 1981. 31.50x (ISBN 0-669-03869-5). Lexington Bks.

Epstein, Joyce L. & Karweit, Nancy L., eds. Friends in School: Patterns of Selection & Influence in Secondary Schools. LC 82-22822. 1983. 32.50 (ISBN 0-12-240540-4). Acad Pr.

Epstein, Judy. Keeping Score. LC 75-324266. 33p. 1975. 2.00 (ISBN 0-87886-067-3). Ithaca Hse.

Epstein, Julius, ed. see Schubert, Franz.

Epstein, June. No Music by Request: A Portrait of the Gorman Family. (Illus.). 216p. 20.95x (ISBN 0-00-216438-8, Pub. by W Collins Australia). Intl Spec Bk.

Epstein, Klaus. The Genesis of German Conservatism. 747p. 1975. 50.00 (ISBN 0-691-05121-6); pap. 22.00x LPE (ISBN 0-691-10030-6). Princeton U Pr.

Epstein, Klaus, jt. auth. see Fay, Sidney B.

Epstein, Laura. Helping People: The Task-Centered Approach. LC 79-21084. (Illus.). 266p. 1980. pap. text ed. 14.95 (ISBN 0-8016-1509-7). Mosby.

--How to Provide Social Services with Task Centred Methods, Vol. 1. 1982. 25.00x (ISBN 0-317-05786-3, Pub. by Natl Inst Social Work). State Mutual Bk.

Epstein, Laura, jt. auth. see Reid, William J.

Epstein, Laurence, jt. auth. see Feiner, Arthur.

Epstein, Laurence, jt. auth. see Loney, Glenn.

Epstein, Laurily K., ed. Women & the News. (Illus.). 1978. 13.95 (ISBN 0-8038-8087-1). Hastings.

Epstein, Lawrence. Exploring Careers in Computer Sales. 1986. pap. 8.97 (ISBN 0-8239-0667-1). Rosen Group.

--Theater Market Place. 600p. 1982. pap. 29.95x (ISBN 0-87196-545-3). Facts on File.

Epstein, Lawrence J. Samuel Goldwyn. (Filmmakers Ser.). 1981. lib. bdg. 15.95 (ISBN 0-8057-9282-1, Twayne). G K Hall.

--Zion's Call: Christian Contributions to the Origins & Development of Israel. LC 84-15184. 176p. (Orig.). 1984. lib. bdg. 21.75 (ISBN 0-8191-4185-2); pap. text ed. 11.25 (ISBN 0-8191-4186-0). U Pr of Amer.

Epstein, Lee. Conservatives in Court. LC 84-15287. 216p. 1985. text ed. 17.95x (ISBN 0-87049-449-X). U of Tenn Pr.

Epstein, Leon D. Governing the University: The Campus & the Public Interest. LC 73-20967. (Jossey-Bass Series in Higher Education). pap. 67.30 (ISBN 0-317-30471-2, 2023876). Bks Demand UMI.

--Politics in Wisconsin. 233p. 1958. 20.00x (ISBN 0-299-01730-3). U of Wis Pr.

Epstein, Leonard H., jt. auth. see Blanchard, Edward B.

Epstein, Leslie. Goldkorn Tales. 252p. 1985. 16.95 (ISBN 0-525-24286-4, 01646-490). Dutton.

--King of the Jews. 1980. pap. 2.50 (ISBN 0-380-48074-3, 48074-3). Avon.

--Regina. 288p. 1982. 13.95 (ISBN 0-698-11203-2, Coward). Putnam Pub Group.

--Regina. 256p. 1984. pap. 3.95 (ISBN 0-380-65540-3, 65540, Bard). Avon.

Epstein, Lewis C. Relativity Visualized. LC 82-84280. (Illus.). 200p. 1985. pap. 12.95 (ISBN 0-935218-05-X). Insight Pr CA.

--Thinking Physics. (Illus.). 562p. 1985. pap. 14.95 (ISBN 0-935218-06-8). Insight Pr Ca.

--Thinking Physics Is Gedanken Physics. 2nd, enl. ed. (Illus.). 600p. 1983. 14.95x (ISBN 0-935218-04-1). Insight Pr CA.

Epstein, Lewis C. & Hewitt, P. Thinking Physics, Pt. II. (Illus.). 253p. 1981. pap. 6.95x (ISBN 0-935218-01-7). Insight Pr CA.

Epstein, Louis M. The Jewish Marriage Contract: A Study in the Status of the Woman in Jewish Law. LC 73-2195. (The Jewish People; History, Religion, Literature Ser.). Repr. of 1927 ed. 33.00 (ISBN 0-405-05261-8). Ayer Co Pubs.

--Marriage Laws in the Bible & the Talmud. 1942. 25.00 (ISBN 0-384-14535-3). Johnson Repr.

--Sex Laws & Customs in Judaism. rev. ed. LC 67-22751. 1968. 11.95x (ISBN 0-87068-041-2). Ktav.

Epstein, M. A., jt. auth. see Richter, G. W.

Epstein, M. A. & Achong, B. G., eds. The Epstein-Barr Virus. (Illus.). 1979. 77.00 (ISBN 0-387-09272-2). Springer-Verlag.

Epstein, M. A., jt. ed. see Richter, G. W.

Epstein, M. E., ed. Kidney in Liver Disease. 612p. 1982. 82.00 (ISBN 0-444-00655-9, Biomedical Pr). Elsevier.

Epstein, Marc J. Corporate Social Performance: The Measurement of Product & Service Contributions. 133p. pap. 15.95 (ISBN 0-86641-050-3, 7792). Natl Assn Accts.

--The Effect of Scientific Management on the Development of the Standard Cost System. new ed. Brief, Richard P., ed. LC 77-87298. (Development of Contemporary Accounting Thought Ser). 1978. lib. bdg. 22.00x (ISBN 0-405-10937-7). Ayer Co Pubs.

Epstein, Marc J., jt. auth. see Book, Stephen A.

Epstein, Mary Anne, ed. Nucleation, Growth, & Impurity Effects in Crystallization Process Engineering. LC 82-11460. (AICHE Symposium: Vol. 78). 90p. 1982. pap. 22.00 (ISBN 0-8169-0226-7, S-215); pap. 12.00 members (ISBN 0-686-47547-X). Am Inst Chem Eng.

Epstein, Mary F., jt. auth. see Diamond, Seymour.

Epstein, Max C. Gleanings from My Years. (Illus.). 124p. (Orig.). 1983. 5.25 (ISBN 0-9612046-0-5); pap. 3.50 (ISBN 0-9612046-1-3). Epstein M C.

Epstein, Melech. Jewish Labor in the U. S. A., 1882-1952. rev. ed. 1969. 50.00x (ISBN 0-87068-042-0). Ktav.

Epstein, Michael, jt. auth. see Cullinhan, Douglas.

Epstein, Michael A. Modern Intellectual Property. 650p. 1984. 75.00 (ISBN 0-15-003467-9, Law & Business). HarBraceJ.

Epstein, Morris. All about Jewish Holidays & Customs. rev. ed. (gr. 5-6). 1969. pap. 6.95x (ISBN 0-87068-500-7). Ktav.

--My Holiday Story Book. rev. ed. (gr. 4-5). 1958. pap. 4.50x (ISBN 0-87068-368-3). Ktav.

--A Picture Parade of Jewish History. 1977. pap. 3.95 (ISBN 0-8197-0024-X). Bloch.

Epstein, Mortimer. Early History of the Levant Company. LC 68-24162. 1968. Repr. of 1908 ed. 27.50x (ISBN 0-678-00416-1). Kelley.

--English Levant Company, Its Foundation & Its History to Sixteen Hundred Forty. LC 68-58996. (Research & Source Ser.: No. 193). 1969. Repr. of 1908 ed. 20.50 (ISBN 0-8337-1065-6). B Franklin.

Epstein, Murray & Oster, James R. Hypertension: A Practical Approach. (Illus.). 208p. 1984. 35.00 (ISBN 0-7216-3397-8). Saunders.

Epstein, N., jt. auth. see Mathur, K. B.

Epstein, Natalie, jt. auth. see Oppenheimer, Lillian.

Epstein, Nathan B., jt. auth. see Westley, William A.

Epstein, Noel, et al. Language, Ethnicity & the Schools: Policy Alternatives for Bilingual-Bicultural Education. (Policy Paper: No. 4). ix, 104p. 1977. 4.00 (ISBN 0-318-14398-4). Inst Educ Lead.

Epstein, Paul D. Using Performance Measurement in Local Government: A Guide to Improving Decisions, Performance & Accountability. (Council on Municipal Performance Ser.). (Illus.). 256p. 1984. 34.50 (ISBN 0-442-21603-3). Van Nos Reinhold.

Epstein, Perle. Pilgrimage: Adventures of a Wandering Jew. 1979. 12.95 (ISBN 0-395-27620-9). HM.

Epstein, R. B., et al, trs. see Hua, Tripitaka Master.

Epstein, R. L. Degrees of Unsolvability: Structure & Theory. (Lecture Notes in Mathematics: Vol. 759). 240p. 1980. pap. 20.00 (ISBN 0-387-09710-4). Springer-Verlag.

Epstein, Ralph C. The Automobile Industry: Its Economic & Commercial Development. LC 72-5045. (Technology & Society Ser.). (Illus.). 429p. 1972. Repr. of 1928 ed. 26.50 (ISBN 0-405-04697-9). Ayer Co Pubs.

--GATX: A History of the General American Transportation Corporation, 1898-1948. Bruchey, Stuart, ed. LC 80-1305. (Railroads Ser.). (Illus.). 1981. Repr. of 1948 ed. lib. bdg. 20.00x (ISBN 0-405-13774-5). Ayer Co Pubs.

Epstein, Rhoda & Conley, Virginia. Developing a Master's Program in Nursing. 37p. 1978. 4.95 (ISBN 0-88737-194-9, 15-1747). Natl League Nurse.

Epstein, Richard & Gregory, Charles O. Cases & Materials on Torts. 4th ed. LC 83-81566. 1456p. 1984. text ed. 34.00i (ISBN 0-316-24571-2). Little.

Epstein, Richard A. Medical Malpractice: The Case for Contract. 63p. (Reprinted from 1976 ABF Res. J., No. 1). 1976. 2.50 (ISBN 0-317-33344-5). Am Bar Foun.

--Modern Products Liability Law. LC 80-11486. (Quorum Ser.). ix, 210p. 1980. lib. bdg. 35.00 (ISBN 0-89930-002-2, EPL/, Quorum). Greenwood.
--Takings: Private Property & the Power of Eminent Domain. 384p. 1985. text ed. 25.00x (ISBN 0-674-86728-9). Harvard U Pr.
--The Theory of Gambling & Statistical Logic. rev. ed. 1977. 49.50 (ISBN 0-12-240760-1). Acad Pr.
--A Theory of Strict Liability: Toward a Reformulation of Tort Law. (The Cato Papers Ser.: No. 8). 141p. 1979. pap. 4.00x (ISBN 0-932790-08-9). Cato Inst.
Epstein, Richard A. & Paul, Jeffrey, eds. Labor Law & the Employment Market: Foundations & Applications. 237p. 1985. pap. 9.95 (ISBN 0-88738-623-7). Transaction Bks.
Epstein, Richard L. Initial Segments of Degrees Below O. LC 80-28538. (MEMO Ser.: No. 241). 102p. 1981. pap. 9.00 (ISBN 0-8218-2241-1). Am Math.
--Minimal Degrees of Unsolvability & the Full Approximation Construction. LC 75-20308. (Memoirs: No. 162). 136p. 1975. pap. 13.00 (ISBN 0-8218-1862-7, MEMO-162). Am Math.
Epstein, Rita, ed. see Baglini, Norman A.
Epstein, Rita, ed. see Lalley, Edward P.
Epstein, Robert, ed. see Skinner, B. F.
Epstein, Robert, ed. see Thoreau, Henry D.
Epstein, Robert A. International Harms. 52p. (Reprinted from Journal of Legal Studies 391 (1975)). 1975. 2.00 (ISBN 0-317-33338-0). Am Bar Foun.
Epstein, Robert M. Prince Eugene at War: Eighteen Hundred Nine. LC 84-81744. (Napoleon's Commanders Ser.). (Illus.). 160p. 1984. 24.95 (ISBN 0-913037-05-2). Empire Games Pr.
Epstein, Robert S. Query Processing Techniques for Distributed, Relational Data Base Systems. Stone, Harold, ed. LC 82-6949. (Computer Science: Distributed Database Systems Ser.: No. 13). 106p. 1982. 34.95 (ISBN 0-8357-1341-5). UMI Res Pr.
Epstein, Ronald B., tr. see Hua, Tripitaka Master.
Epstein, Roslyn. American Indian Needlepoint Designs for Pillows, Belts, Handbags & Other Projects. (Illus.). 48p. (Orig.). 1973. pap. 1.95 (ISBN 0-486-22973-4). Dover.
Epstein, S., ed. see Stout, R. D. & Doty, W. D.
Epstein, S. E., jt. ed. see Kaltenbach, M.
Epstein, Sabin, jt. auth. see Harrop, John.
Epstein, Sam & Epstein, Beryl. Charles De Gaulle: Defender of France. LC 72-6254. (Century Biographies Ser.). (Illus.). (gr. 4-8). 1973. PLB 4.47 (ISBN 0-8116-4756-0). Garrard.
--The First Book of Electricity. LC 76-41317. (First Bks.). (Illus.). 72p. (gr. 4-6). 1977. PLB 8.90 (ISBN 0-531-00522-4). Watts.
--Game of Baseball. LC 65-10098. (Sports Library Ser). (Illus.). (gr. 3-6). 1965. PLB 7.12 (ISBN 0-8116-6651-4). Garrard.
--Harriet Tubman: Guide to Freedom. LC 68-22638. (Americans All Ser.). (Illus.). (gr. 3-6). 1968. PLB 7.98 (ISBN 0-8116-4550-9). Garrard.
--Henry Aaron: Home-Run King. LC 75-9966. (Sports Library). (Illus.). 96p. (gr. 3-6). 1975. PLB 7.98 (ISBN 0-8116-6674-3). Garrard.
--Jackie Robinson: Baseball's Gallant Fighter. LC 74-4499. (Sports Library). (Illus.). 96p. (gr. 3-6). 1974. PLB 7.98 (ISBN 0-8116-6668-9). Garrard.
--Mexico. rev. ed. (First Bk.). (Illus.). 72p. (gr. 4 up). 1983. PLB 8.90 (ISBN 0-531-04530-7). Watts.
--She Never Looked Back: Margaret Mead in Samoa. LC 78-31821. (Science Discovery Ser.). (Illus.). (gr. 3-7). 1980. PLB 6.99 (ISBN 0-698-30715-1, Coward). Putnam Pub Group.
--Washington, D. C. LC 30-25022. (First Books About Washington Ser.). (gr. 4 up). 1981. PLB 8.90 (ISBN 0-531-04253-7). Watts.
--Willie Mays: Baseball Superstar. LC 74-20954. (Sports Library). (Illus.). 96p. (gr. 2-6). 1975. PLB 7.98 (ISBN 0-8116-6671-9). Garrard.
--A Year of Japanese Festivals. LC 73-22045. (Around the World Holidays Ser.). (Illus.). 96p. (gr. 4-7). 1974. PLB 7.98 (ISBN 0-8116-4954-7). Garrard.
Epstein, Sam, et al. What's for Lunch? The Eating Habits of Seashore Creatures. LC 85-4964. (Illus.). 48p. (gr. 1-4). 1985. PLB 10.95 (ISBN 0-02-733500-3). Macmillan.
Epstein, Samuel. Change for a Penny. 16.95 (ISBN 0-8488-0078-8, Pub. by Amereon Hse). Amereon Ltd.
--JacKnife for a Penny. 16.95 (ISBN 0-8488-0077-X, Pub. by Amereon Hse). Amereon Ltd.
--Mister Peale's Mammoth. 9.95 (ISBN 0-8488-0079-6, Pub. by Amereon Hse). Amereon Ltd.
Epstein, Samuel & Epstein, Beryl. Spring Holidays. LC 64-12340. (Holiday Bks.). (gr. 2-5). 1964. PLB 8.37 (ISBN 0-8116-6553-4). Garrard.
--Tunnels. (Illus.). 128p. (gr. 5 up). 1985. 13.95 (ISBN 0-316-24573-9). Little.
Epstein, Samuel, jt. auth. see Epstein, Beryl.
Epstein, Samuel, jt. auth. see Williams, Beryl.
Epstein, Samuel & Lederberg, Joshua, eds. Drugs of Abuse: Their Genetic & Other Chronic Nonpsychiatric Hazards. 1971. 30.00x (ISBN 0-262-05009-9). MIT Pr.
Epstein, Samuel S. The Politics of Cancer. LC 78-985. 600p. 1978. 12.50 (ISBN 0-87156-193-X). Sierra.
Epstein, Samuel S. & Grundy, Richard D., eds. Consumer Health & Product Hazards: Cosmetics & Drugs, Pesticides, Food Additives Vol. 2 of the Legislation of Product Safety, Vol. 2. 1974. 30.00x (ISBN 0-262-05015-3). MIT Pr.
--Consumer Health & Product Hazards: Chemicals, Electronic Products, Radiation Vol. 1 of the Legislation of Product Safety. 1974. 30.00x (ISBN 0-262-05013-7). MIT Pr.
Epstein, Samuel S., et al. Hazardous Waste in America: Our Number One Environmental Crisis. LC 82-3304. (The Sierra Club Paperback Library). 640p. 1983. 27.50 (ISBN 0-87156-294-4); pap. 12.95 (ISBN 0-87156-807-1). Sierra.
Epstein, Sarah G. The Prints of Edvard Munch: Mirror of His Life. Van Nimmen, Jane, ed. LC 82-62882. (Illus.). 210p. (Orig.). 1983. pap. 12.95 (ISBN 0-942946-02-2). Ober Coll Allen.
Epstein, Saul T. The Variation Method in Quantum Chemistry. 1974. 77.00 (ISBN 0-12-240550-1). Acad Pr.
Epstein, Scarlett. Capitalism, Primitive & Modern: Some Aspects of Tolai Economic Growth. x, 200p. 1969. 7.50 (ISBN 0-87013-133-8). Mich St U Pr.
Epstein, Scarlett, ed. see Institute of Cultural Affairs International Editors.
Epstein, Seymore. Caught in That Music. 1980. pap. 1.50 (ISBN 0-380-00077-6, 20305). Avon.
Epstein, Seymour. The Dream Museum. 1973. pap. 1.25 (ISBN 0-380-01150-6, 15222). Avon.
Epstein, Shelia, jt. auth. see Epstein, David.
Epstein, Sherrie S. Penny the Medicine Maker: The Story of Penicillin. LC 60-14006. (Medical Bks for Children). (Illus.). (gr. k-5). 1960. PLB 3.95 (ISBN 0-8225-0006-X). Lerner Pubns.
Epstein, Simon. Antisemitism in France. LC 85-10644. 240p. 1985. 15.95 (ISBN 0-915765-13-6); pap. 7.95 (ISBN 0-915765-14-4). Natl Pr Inc.
Epstein, Steven. Wills & Wealth in Medieval Genoa, 1150-1250. (Harvard Historical Studies: No. 103). (Illus.). 288p. 1985. text ed. 22.50x (ISBN 0-674-95356-8). Harvard U Pr.
Epstein, T. Scarlett. Urban Food Marketing & Third World Rural Development: The Structure of Producer-Seller Markets. (Illus.). 272p. 28.50 (ISBN 0-7099-0911-X, Pub. by Croom Helm Ltd). Longwood Pub Group.
Epstein, T. Scarlett & Watts, Rosemary A., eds. The Endless Day: Some Case Material on Asian Rural Women. LC 81-15394. (Women in Development Ser.: Vol. 3). (Illus.). 181p. 1981. 35.00 (ISBN 0-08-028106-0). Pergamon.
Epstein, Vivian S. The ABC's of What a Girl Can Be. (Illus.). 32p. (ps-3). 1980. pap. 4.95 (ISBN 0-9601002-2-9). V S Epstein.
--History of Colorado for Children. (Illus.). 32p. (ps-4). 1977. pap. 4.95 (ISBN 0-9601002-1-0). V S Epstein.
--History of Women for Children. 32p. (ps-5). 1984. 4.95 (ISBN 0-9601002-3-7). V S Epstein.
Epstein, William. John Cleland: Images of a Life. LC 74-9798. 1974. 26.00x (ISBN 0-231-03725-2). Columbia U Pr.
--The Last Chance: Nuclear Proliferation & Arms Control. LC 75-22765. 1976. 17.95 (ISBN 0-02-909660-X). Free Pr.
--The Prevention of Nuclear War: A United Nations Perspective. LC 84-2248. 1984. 25.00 (ISBN 0-89946-184-0). Oelgeschlager.
Epstein, William & Feld, Bernard, eds. New Directions in Disarmament. LC 81-4494. 240p. 1981. 41.95 (ISBN 0-03-059366-2); pap. 7.95 O.P. (ISBN 0-03-060089-8). Praeger.
Epstein, William & Webster, Lucy, eds. We Can Avert a Nuclear War. LC 82-7974. 192p. 1983. 25.00 (ISBN 0-89946-202-2); pap. 12.50 (ISBN 0-89946-204-9). Oelgeschlager.
Epstein, Y. M., jt. ed. see Baum, A.
Epstein, Yechiel M. Aruch Hashulchan, 8 Vols. (Heb.). deluxe ed. 50.00 (ISBN 0-87559-097-7). Shalom.
Epstin, Vivian S. The ABCs of What a Girl Can Be. write for info. V S Epstein.
Epting, Franz & Landfield, Alvin W., eds. Anticipating Personal Construct Psychology. LC 84-22171. (Illus.). xii, 322p. 1985. 25.00x (ISBN 0-8032-2862-7). U of Nebr Pr.
Epting, Franz R. Personal Construct Counseling & Psychotherapy. LC 83-19773. (Wiley Series on Methods in Psychotherapy). 224p. 1984. 29.95x (ISBN 0-471-90169-5, 1420, Pub. by Wiley-Interscience). Wiley.
Epting, Franz R. & Neimeyer, Robert A., eds. Personal Meanings of Death. LC 83-8529. (Death Education, Aging & Health Care Ser.). (Illus.). 246p. 1983. text ed. 34.50 (ISBN 0-89116-363-8). Hemisphere Pub.
Epton, Roger, ed. Chromatography of Synthetic & Biological Polymers: Column Packings, GPC, GF & Gradient Elution, Vol. 1. LC 77-30672. 368p. 1978. 68.95x (ISBN 0-470-99379-0). Halsted Pr.
--Chromatography of Synthetic & Biological Polymers: Hydrophobic, Ion-Exchange & Affinity Methods, Vol. 2. LC 77-40142. 353p. 1978. 79.95 (ISBN 0-470-26366-0). Halsted Pr.
Epton, S. R., et al, eds. Managing Interdisciplinary Research. 245p. 1985. 29.95 (ISBN 0-471-90317-5, Pub. by Wiley-Interscience). Wiley.
Equal Rights Amendment Project, compiled by. The Equal Rights Amendment: A Bibliographic Study. Miller, Anita & Greenberg, Hazel, eds. LC 76-24999. xxvii, 367p. 1976. lib. bdg. 45.00 (ISBN 0-8371-9058-4, ERA/). Greenwood.
Equiano, Olaudah. Life of Olaudah Equiano, Or, Gustavus Vassa, the African. LC 76-88409. Repr. of 1837 ed. 19.75x (ISBN 0-8371-1839-5, EOE&, Pub. by Negro U Pr). Greenwood.
Equilbecq, F. V. Essai sur la Litterature Merveilleuse des Noirs. LC 78-20149. (Collection de contes et de chansons populaires: Vol. 41). Repr. of 1913 ed. 21.50 (ISBN 0-404-60391-2). AMS Pr.
--Essai sur la Litterature Merveilleuse des Noirs, 2 vols. LC 78-20150. (Collection de contes et de chansons populaires: Vols. 42-43). Repr. of 1916 ed. Set. 43.00 (ISBN 0-404-60441-2). AMS Pr.
Equipe Ecologie et Anthropologie Des Societes Pastorales, ed. Pastoral Production & Society. LC 78-19139. (Illus.). 1979. 54.50 (ISBN 0-521-22253-2); pap. 18.95x (ISBN 0-521-29416-9). Cambridge U Pr.
Equipo, Nauta. Enciclopedia de la Vida Sexual. (Span.). 175.00 (ISBN 0-686-92275-1, S-33939). French & Eur.
Equipo Reactor de Ceac. Diccionario de la Construccion. 650p. (Span.). 1978. pap. 26.50 (ISBN 84-329-2608-6, S-50225). French & Eur.
--Diccionario de la Decoracion. 792p. (Span., Fr., Eng., Ger. & Ital.). 1973. 44.25 (ISBN 84-329-5010-6, S-12256). French & Eur.
--Manual del Automovil en 5 Idiomas: Diccionario Idiomatico del Automovil. 240p. (Span., Fr., Eng., It. & Ger.). 1974. 8.50 (ISBN 84-329-1403-7, S-50224). French & Eur.
Equipo Reactor de CEAC, ed. Diccionario del Automovil. 916p. (Span.). 1978. 37.50 (ISBN 84-329-1010-4, S-14232). French & Eur.
Equity Publishing Corporation, jt. auth. see Puerto Rico.
ERA. The Engineering of Microprocessor Systems: Guidelines on System Development. LC 79-40952. 1979. 25.00 (ISBN 0-08-025435-7); pap. 8.00 (ISBN 0-08-025434-9). Pergamon.
Erades, Lambertus & T. M. C. Asser Institute. Essays on International & Comparative Law in Honour of Judge Erades. LC 83-6316. 1983. 95.00 (ISBN 9-02-472838-X, Pub. by Martinus Nijhoff Netherlands). Kluwer Academic.
Erades, P. A. Points of Modern English Syntax. Robat, N. J., ed. (Contributions to English Studies). 260p. 1975. pap. text ed. 17.75 (ISBN 90-265-0184-6, Pub. by Swets Pub Serv Holland). Swets North Am.
Eranko, Olavi, et al, eds. Histochemistry & Cell Biology of Autonomic Neurons: Sif Cells, & Paraneurons. (Advances in Biochemical Psychopharmacology Ser.: Vol. 25). (Illus.). 410p. 1980. text ed. 64.50 (ISBN 0-89004-495-3). Raven.
Erasmus. Adages (One to Five Hundred) Phillips, Margaret M. & Mynors, R. A., trs. (Collected Works of Erasmus: Vol. 31). 1982. 65.00x (ISBN 0-8020-2373-8). U of Toronto Pr.
--Christian Humanism & the Reformation: Selected Writings with the Life of Erasmus by Beatus Rhenanus. Olin, John C., ed. 11.25 (ISBN 0-8446-2035-1). Peter Smith.
--Enchiridion Militis Christiani. O'Donnell, Anne M., ed. (Early English Text Society Ser.). (Illus.). 1981. text ed. 42.00x (ISBN 0-19-722284-6). Oxford U Pr.
--Enchiridion of Erasmus. Himelick, Raymond, tr. 12.00 (ISBN 0-8446-0614-6). Peter Smith.
--Erasmi Opera Omnia, Vol. 7. Waszink, J., ed. 1977. 121.50 (ISBN 0-7204-6157-X, North-Holland). Elsevier.
--Inquistio De Fide: A Colloquy by Desiderius Erasmus Roterodamus, 1524. 2nd ed. Thompson, Craig, ed. xiii, 137p. 1975. Repr. of 1950 ed. 16.50 (ISBN 0-685-51693-8, Archon). Shoe String.
--Literary & Educational Writings, Antibarbari, De Copia, De Rationae Studii, Parabolae. Thompson, Craig R., ed. LC 78-6904. (Collected Works of Erasmus: Vols. 23 & 24). 1978. 95.00x (ISBN 0-8020-5395-5). U of Toronto Pr.
--The Praise of Folly. Dean, Leonard F., ed. 268p. 1983. pap. 4.45 (ISBN 0-87532-105-4). Hendricks House.
--Praise of Folly. Radice, Betty, tr. (Classics Ser.). 252p. 1971. pap. 4.95 (ISBN 0-14-044240-5). Penguin.
--Selections from Erasmus,...Principally from his Epistles. Allen, P. S., ed. (College Classical Ser.). 610p. 1982. 22.50 (ISBN 0-89241-361-1); pap. 11.50 (ISBN 0-89241-116-3). Caratzas.
Erasmus, et al. German Humanism & Reformation: Selected Writings. Becker, Reinhard P., ed. LC 82-7278. (The German Library: Vol. 6). 299p. 1982. 24.50x (ISBN 0-8264-0251-8); pap. 8.95 (ISBN 0-8264-0261-5). Continuum.
Erasmus, Charles J. In Search of the Common Good: Utopian Experiments Past and Future. LC 76-50461. 1977. 22.95 (ISBN 0-02-909630-8). Free Pr.
--In Search of the Common Good: Utopian Experiments Past & Future. 420p. 1985. pap. 12.95x (ISBN 0-02-909640-5). Free Pr.
Erasmus, Desiderius. Anti-Polemus. 59.95 (ISBN 0-87968-648-0). Gordon Pr.
--Apophthegmes, That Is to Saie, Prompte Saiynges. Udall, Nicholas, tr. from Lat. LC 76-6160. (English Experience Ser.: No. 99). 1969. Repr. of 1542 ed. 83.00 (ISBN 90-221-0099-5). Walter J Johnson.
--A Booke Called in Latyn Enchiridian & in Englysshe the Manuell of the Christen Knyght. LC 70-25758. (English Experience Ser.: No. 156). 340p. 1969. Repr. of 1533 ed. 28.00 (ISBN 90-221-0156-8). Walter J Johnson.
--The Censure & Judgement of Erasmus: Whyther Dyuorsemente Stondeth with the Lawe of God. Lesse, N., tr. LC 76-38177. (English Experience Ser.: No. 452). 160p. 1972. Repr. of 1550 ed. 15.00 (ISBN 90-221-0452-4). Walter J Johnson.
--Ciceronianus: Or, A Dialogue on the Best Style of Speaking. Scott, Izora, tr. LC 73-176755. (Columbia University. Teachers College. Contributions to Education: No. 21). Repr. of 1908 ed. 22.50 (ISBN 0-404-55021-5). AMS Pr.
--Collected Works of Erasmus: Literary & Educational Writings, 2 vols. Sowards, J. Kelley, ed. (Collected Works of Erasmus: Nos. 25 & 26). 800p. Date not set. Set. 75.00x (ISBN 0-8020-5521-4). U of Toronto Pr.
--Colloquies of Erasmus. Thompson, Craig R., tr. LC 64-22246. 1965. 45.00x (ISBN 0-226-21481-8). U of Chicago Pr.
--Comparation of a Virgin & a Martyr, 1537. Paynell, Thomas, tr. from Latin. LC 70-101148. 1970. Repr. of 1537 ed. 25.00x (ISBN 0-8201-1072-8). Schol Facsimiles.
--The Complaint of Peace. Paynell, T., tr. 86p. 1974. 10.95 (ISBN 0-87548-276-7); pap. 4.95 (ISBN 0-87548-195-7). Open Court.
--The Complaint of Peace. Hirten, William J., ed. Paynell, Thomas, tr. LC 46-5043. 180p. 1976. Repr. lib. bdg. 30.00x (ISBN 0-8201-1211-9). Schol Facsimiles.
--The Complaint of Peace. LC 73-6126. (English Experience Ser.: No. 592). 96p. 1973. Repr. of 1559 ed. 7.00 (ISBN 90-221-0592-X). Walter J Johnson.
--De Contemptu Mundi. Paynell, Thomas, tr. LC 67-18715. 1967. 30.00x (ISBN 0-8201-1016-7). Schol Facsimiles.
--The Correspondence of Erasmus, Letters, 1501-1514, Vol. 2. Corrigan, Beatrice, ed. LC 72-47422. (Collected Works of Erasmus: Vol. 2). (Illus.). 1975. 75.00x (ISBN 0-8020-1983-8). U of Toronto Pr.
--Correspondence of Erasmus, Vol. 3: Letters 298-445 (1514-1516) Mynors. Mynors, R. A. & Thomson, D. F., trs. LC 72-97422. (Collected Works of Erasmus: Vol. 3). (Illus.). 1976. 75.00x (ISBN 0-8020-2202-2). U of Toronto Pr.
--The Correspondence of Erasmus, Vol. 4: Letters 446-593. Mynors, R. A. & Thomson, D. F., trs. LC 72-97422. (Collected Works of Erasmus: Vol. 4). 1977. 75.00x (ISBN 0-8020-5366-1). U of Toronto Pr.
--The Correspondence of Erasmus, Vol. 5: Letters 594-841 (July 1517 - April 1518) Mynors, R. A. & Thomson, D. F., trs. LC 78-6904. (Collected Works of Erasmus: Vol. 5). 1979. 75.00x (ISBN 0-8020-5429-3). U of Toronto Pr.
--The Correspondence of Erasmus, Vol. 6: Letters 842-992 (May 1518 - June 1519) Mynors, R. A. & Thomson, D. F., trs. (Collected Works of Erasmus: Vol. 6). 1981. 75.00x (ISBN 0-8020-5500-1). U of Toronto Pr.
--The Critical Writing by Desiderius Erasmus on the Spiritual Conditions of His Times & the Psychological Impulses Motivating the Actions of Men. (Illus.). 123p. 1984. 89.45 (ISBN 0-89920-106-7). Am Inst Psych.
--Education of a Christian Prince. Born, Lester K., tr. 1965. lib. bdg. 27.50x (ISBN 0-374-92603-4). Octagon.
--Erasmus on His Times: A Shortened Version of the Adages of Erasmus. Phillips, Margaret M., ed. 1967. pap. 8.95 (ISBN 0-521-09413-5). Cambridge U Pr.
--Essential Erasmus. Dolan, John P., tr. (Orig.). 1964. pap. 3.95 (ISBN 0-452-00673-2, Mer). NAL.
--An Exhortation to the Diligent Studye of Scripture. Roy, W., tr. LC 72-5983. (English Experience Ser.: No. 510). 156p. 1973. Repr. of 1529 ed. 11.50 (ISBN 90-221-0510-5). Walter J Johnson.
--The First Tome or Volume of the Paraphrase of Erasmus Upon the Newe Testamente. LC 75-23361. 1350p. 1975. Repr. of 1548 ed. lib. bdg. 100.00x (ISBN 0-8201-1159-7). Schol Facsimiles.
--The Historical Significance of Desiderius Erasmus in the Light of the Protestant Revolution & the Catholic Church As Revealed by His Most Famous Pronouncements, 2 vols. (Illus.). 396p. 1985. Set. 207.50 (ISBN 0-89266-523-8). Am Classical Coll Pr.
--A Lytle Treatise of the Maner & Forme of Confession. LC 79-39487. (English Experience Ser.: No. 553). (Illus.). 232p. 1973. Repr. of 1535 ed. 16.00 (ISBN 90-221-0553-9). Walter J Johnson.
--One Dialogue or Colloquy Entitled Diversoria. LC 71-26509. (English Experience Ser.: No. 244). 20p. 1970. Repr. of 1566 ed. 7.00 (ISBN 90-221-0244-0). Walter J Johnson.

Erdman, Walter. Die Ehe Im Alten Griechenland. Vlastos, Gregory, ed. LC 78-19349. (Morals & Law in Ancient Greece Ser.). (Ger. & Gr.). 1979. Repr. of 1934 ed. lib. bdg. 30.50x (ISBN 0-405-11541-5). Ayer Co Pubs.

Erdmann, A., ed. Lydgate's "Siege of Thebes", Part 1: The Text. (EETS ES Ser.: Vol. 108). Repr. of 1911 ed. 40.00 (ISBN 0-317-15616-0). Kraus Repr.

Erdmann, Axel, ed. see Lydgate, John.

Erdmann, Carl. The Origin of the Idea of Crusade. Baldwin, Marshall W. & Goffart, Walter, trs. from Ger. 1977. 52.50 (ISBN 0-691-05251-4). Princeton U Pr.

Erdmenger, Jurgen. The European Community Transport Policy: Towards a Common Transport Policy. 120p. 1984. text ed. 32.95x (ISBN 0-566-00656-1). Gower Pub Co.

Erdnase, Samuel R. Expert at the Card Table. 1946. pap. 3.00 (ISBN 0-685-19474-4). Powner.

Erdoes, E. G., ed. Bradykinin, Kallidin & Kallikrein. (Handbook of Experimental Pharmacology: Vol. 25). (Illus.). 1970. 162.30 (ISBN 0-387-04847-2). Springer-Verlag.

--Bradykinin, Kallidin, & Kallikrein-Supplement. (Handbook of Experimental Pharmacology: Vol. 25, Suppl.). (Illus.). 1979. 212.40 (ISBN 0-387-09356-7). Springer-Verlag.

Erdoes, Paul, ed. Studies in Pure Mathematics: To the Memory of Paul Turan. 400p. 1983. 78.00 (ISBN 0-8176-1288-2). Birkhauser.

Erdoes, Richard. A. D. One Thousand: Living on the Brink of Apocalypse: A History of the Tenth Century for Those Who Hope to See the Year 2000. LC 85-42773. (Illus.). 320p. 1985. 19.95 (ISBN 0-06-250295-6, HarpR). Har-Row.

--Native Americans: The Pueblos. LC 83-9250. (Illus.). 96p. (gr. 5 up). 1983. 16.95 (ISBN 0-8069-2744-5); PLB 19.99 (ISBN 0-8069-2745-3). Sterling.

--Native Americans: The Sioux. LC 81-85036. (Illus.). 96p. (gr. 6-9). 1982. 16.95 (ISBN 0-8069-2742-9); lib. bdg. 19.99 (ISBN 0-8069-2743-7). Sterling.

--Saloons of the Old West. LC 79-2220. (Illus.). 1979. 13.95 (ISBN 0-394-49824-0). Knopf.

--Saloons of the Old West. LC 84-22537. (Illus.). 288p. 1985. pap. 12.50 (ISBN 0-935704-25-6). Howe Brothers.

Erdoes, Richard, jt. auth. see John Lame Deer.

Erdoes, Richard, illus. The Richard Erdoes Illustrated Treasury of Classic Unlaundered Limericks. LC 84-11014. (Illus.). 160p. 1984. pap. 6.95 (ISBN 0-917439-01-5). Balsam Pr.

Erdogan, F. & Ezzat, H. Fracture of Pipelines & Cylinders Containing a Circumferential Crack. 1983. bulletin no. 288 14.00 (ISBN 0-318-01893-4). Welding Res Coun.

Erdos, P., et al, eds. Combinatorial Theory & its Applications. (Colloquia Mathematica Societatis Janos Bolyai: Vol. 4). 1202p. 1970. 127.50 (ISBN 0-7204-2038-5, North Holland). Elsevier.

--Combinational Set Theory: Partition Relations for Cardinals. (Studies in Logic & the Foundations of Mathematics: Vol. 106). 348p. 1984. 52.00 (ISBN 0-444-86157-2, North Holland). Elsevier.

Erdos, Paul & Robinson, John M. The Physics of Actinide Compounds. (Physics of Solids & Liquids). 225p. 1983. 39.50x (ISBN 0-306-41150-4, Plenum Press). Plenum Pub.

Erdos, Paul L. Professional Mail Surveys. Rev. ed. LC 82-10024. 296p. 1983. lib. bdg. 29.50 (ISBN 0-89874-530-6). Krieger.

Erdos, Renee F. Teaching by Correspondence. (Illus.). 1967. 7.50 (ISBN 92-3-100658-4, U657, UNESCO). Unipub.

Erdos, Richard. One Thousand Remarkable Facts About Booze. 192p. 1981. pap. 5.95 (ISBN 0-8317-0958-8, Rutledge Pr). Smith Pubs.

Erdozain, Placido. Archbishop Romero: Martyr of Salvador. McFadden, John & Warner, Ruth, trs. from Sp. LC 81-2007. Orig. Title: Monsenor Romero: Martis de la Iglesia Popular. (Illus.). 128p. (Orig.). 1981. pap. 4.95 (ISBN 0-88344-019-9). Orbis Bks.

Erdrich, Louise. Jacklight: Poems. 48p. 1984. pap. 6.95 (ISBN 0-03-068682-2, Owl Bks.). HR&W.

--Love Medicine. 256p. 1984. pap. 13.95 (ISBN 0-03-070611-4, Owl Bks). HR&W.

--Love Medicine. LC 85-7517. 288p. 1985. pap. 5.95 (ISBN 0-553-34249-5). Bantam.

Erdsneker, Barbara. Mathematics Simplified & Self-Taught. 6th ed. LC 81-14912. 192p. 1982. pap. 6.95 (ISBN 0-668-05357-7, 5357). Arco.

--Office Guide to Business Mathematics. LC 83-15900. 224p. 1984. 4.95 (ISBN 0-668-05801-3). Arco.

Erdsneker, Barbara & Haller, Margaret. Civil Service Arithmetic & Vocabulary. LC 81-7988. 256p. 1981. pap. 8.00 (ISBN 0-668-04872-7). Arco.

Erdsneker, Barbara & Saunders, Brigitte. Mathematics Workbook for the ACT. LC 82-4097. 304p. 1982. pap. 6.95 (ISBN 0-668-05443-3, 5443). Arco.

Erdt, Terrence. Jonathan Edwards: Art & the Sense of the Heart. LC 80-5380. (New England Writers Ser.). 144p. 1980. lib. bdg. 13.50x (ISBN 0-87023-304-1). U of Mass Pr.

Erdtman, G. Handbook of Palynology: Morphology, Taxonomy, Ecology. (Illus.). 1968. 36.95x (ISBN 0-02-844250-4). Hafner.

--Pollen & Spore Morphology & Plant Taxonomy. (Introduction to Polynology Ser.: Vol. 2). 1972. Repr. of 1957 ed. 17.95x (ISBN 0-02-844310-1). Hafner.

--World Pollen Flora, 4 vols. Incl. Vol. 1. Coriariaceae. 1970. pap.; Vol. 2. Gyrostemonaceae. Prijanto, B. 1970. pap.; Vol. 3. Batidacene. Prijanto, B. 1970. pap.; Vol. 4. Globularioceae. Praglowski, J. & Gyllander, K. 1971. pap.. (Illus.). Set. pap. 39.95x (ISBN 0-02-844210-5). Hafner.

Erdtmann, Gerhard. Neutron Activation Tables. (Topical Presentations in Nuclear Chemistry Ser.: Vol. 6). (Illus.). 146p. 1976. 57.50x (ISBN 3-527-25693-8). VCH Pubs.

Erdtmann, Gerhard & Soyka, W. The Gamma-Rays of the Radionuclides: Tables for Applied Gamma Ray Spectrometry. (Topical Presentations in Nuclear Chemistry Ser.: Vol. 7). 862p. 1979. 175.00x (ISBN 0-89573-022-7). VCH Pubs.

Erdtmann, Greta. The Path to Math. (The Gentle Revolution Ser.). (Illus.). 60p. (ps). 1981. 7.95 (ISBN 0-936676-11-6). Better Baby.

Erdy, Miklos. The Sumerian, Ural-Altaic, Magyar Relationship: A History of Research, Pt. 1, the 19th Century. LC 72-112303. (Studia Sumiro-Hungarica: Vol. 3). (Illus.). 530p. (Bilingual text). 1974. 18.00 (ISBN 0-914246-53-4). Gilgamesh Pub.

Erdy, Miklos, ed. Studia Sumiro-Hungarica, 3 vols. 1968-1974. Set. 44.00 (ISBN 0-914246-50-X). Gilgamesh Pub.

Erdy, Miklos, jt. ed. see Feher, Matyas.

Erecinska, Maria & Wilson, David F., eds. Inhibitors of Mitochondrial Function. (International Encyclopedia of Pharmacology & Therapeutics Ser.: Section 107). (Illus.). 324p. 1981. 88.00 (ISBN 0-08-027380-7). Pergamon.

Eremenko, Valentin A., et al. Liquid-Phase Sintering. LC 78-107537. 75p. 1970. 25.00x (ISBN 0-306-10839-9, Consultants). Plenum Pub.

Eremin, I. I., et al. Twelve Papers on Real & Complex Function Theory. LC 51-5559. (Translations Ser.: No. 2, Vol. 88). 1970. 37.00 (ISBN 0-8218-1788-4, TRANS 2-88). Am Math.

Eren, Nuri. Turkey, NATO & Europe: A Deteriorating Relationship? (The Atlantic Papers: No. 34). 54p. 1977. pap. 4.75x (ISBN 0-86598-061-6, Pub. by Atlantic Inst France). Allanheld.

Erenberg, Lewis A. Steppin' Out: New York Nightlife & the Transformation of American Culture, 1890-1930. LC 80-930. (Contributions in American Studies Ser.: No. 50). (Illus.). xix, 291p. 1981. lib. bdg. 29.95 (ISBN 0-313-21342-9, EUN/). Greenwood.

--Steppin' Out: New York Nightlife & the Transformation of American Culture, 1890-1930. LC 84-2770. (Illus.). xx, 292p. 1984. pap. 9.95 (ISBN 0-226-21515-6). U of Chicago Pr.

Erenius, Gillis. Criminal Negligence & Individuality. (Institutet for Rattsvetenskaplig Forskning: No. 85). 282p. 1976. pap. text ed. 20.00x (ISBN 91-1-767071-3, Pub. by P. A. Norstedt & Soners, Stockholm). Rothman.

Erens, Pamela. A Fight for Freedom. (Illus.). (gr. 6-12). 1977. pap. 2.95 (ISBN 0-915288-32-X). Shameless Hussy.

Erens, Patricia. The Jew in American Cinema. LC 83-48106. (Jewish Literature & Culture Ser.). (Illus.). 512p. 1985. 27.50x (ISBN 0-253-14500-7). Ind U Pr.

--Masterpieces: Famous Chicagoans & Their Paintings. LC 79-88242. (Illus.). 150p. (Orig.). 1979. pap. 5.95 (ISBN 0-9603920-0-9). P Erens.

Erens, Patricia, ed. Sexual Stratagems: The World of Women in Film. LC 76-20310. (Illus.). 1979. 15.00 (ISBN 0-8180-0706-0); pap. 8.95 (ISBN 0-8180-0707-9). Horizon.

Erenwein, Leslie. Mystery Raider. 1975. pap. 0.95 (ISBN 0-685-54124-X, LB297NK, Leisure Bks). Dorchester Pub Co.

--Rio Renegade. 1975. pap. 0.95 (ISBN 0-685-54125-8, LB296NK, Leisure Bks). Dorchester Pub Co.

Eres, Beth K. Legal & Legislative Information Processing. LC 79-7063. (Illus.). xvi, 299p. 1980. lib. bdg. 35.00 (ISBN 0-313-21343-7, ERL/). Greenwood.

Eresian, W. J., et al. Mathematics & Physical Science, 2 vols. Incl. Vol. 1-Mathematics. Eresian, W. J., et al. (Illus.). 370p. 1979. text ed. 60.00x looseleaf (ISBN 0-87683-026-2); lesson plans 250.00x (ISBN 0-87683-029-7); Vol. 2-Physical Science. Eresian, W. J., et al. 318p. text ed. 60.00x looseleaf (ISBN 0-87683-027-0); lesson plan 250.00x (ISBN 0-317-11852-8). (Illus.). 688p. 1979. Set. 120.00x (ISBN 0-87683-025-4); write for info. lesson plans (ISBN 0-87683-028-9). G P Courseware.

Erevan University Press. A Polyglot Dictionary of Plant Names. 180p. 1981. pap. 40.00x (ISBN 0-686-82330-3, Pub. by Collets). State Mutual Bk.

Erf, Robert K. Speckle Metrology. (Quantum Electronics Ser.). 1978. 62.50 (ISBN 0-12-241360-1). Acad Pr.

Erf, Robert K., ed. Holographic Nondestructive Testing. 1974. 76.00 (ISBN 0-12-241350-4). Acad Pr.

Erf, Stephen & Badel, Julie. Hospital Restructuring: Employment Law Pitfalls. LC 84-62732. (Illus.). 140p. (Orig.). 1985. pap. 16.95 (ISBN 0-931028-64-7). Pluribus Pr.

Erfft, Shirley. Little Things Mean a Lot. 1982. 5.95 (ISBN 0-8062-1897-5). Carlton.

Erfurt, John C. A Compendium of Information Relevant to Manpower Agencies. 1973. pap. 7.00x (ISBN 0-87736-330-7). U of Mich Inst Labor.

Erfurt, John C. & Foote, Andrea. Blood Pressure Control Programs in Industrial Settings. 83p. 1979. pap. 7.00 (ISBN 0-87736-334-X). U of Mich Inst Labor.

Erfurt, John C., jt. auth. see Ferman, Louis A.

Erfurt, John C., jt. auth. see Foote, Andrea.

Erfurt, John C., jt. auth. see Foote, Andrea E.

Erfurt, John C., jt. auth. see Foote, Andrea.

Erfurth, Waldemar. Last Finnish War. 1979. 22.00 (ISBN 0-89093-205-0). U Pubns Amer.

Ergang, Robert & Rohr, Donald G. Europe from the Renaissance to Waterloo. 3rd ed. 1967. pap. text ed. 22.95 (ISBN 0-669-04354-0). Heath.

--Europe Since Waterloo. 3rd ed. 1967. text ed. 23.95 (ISBN 0-669-05205-1). Heath.

Ergang, Robert R. Herder & the Foundations of German Nationalism. 1967. lib. bdg. 24.00x (ISBN 0-374-92622-0). Octagon.

--The Myth of the All-Destructive Fury of the Thirty Years' War. 1956. stiff, printed wrappers 7.50x (ISBN 0-686-17408-9). R S Barnes.

Ergas, H. & Okayama, J. Changing Market Structures in Telecommunications: An OECD Report. 1984. 67.50 (ISBN 0-444-86855-0, I-001-84). Elsevier.

Ergonomics Society, UK. Proceedings of the Ergonomics Society's Conference, 1983. Coombes, Karenna, ed. LC 83-6165. 214p. 1982. pap. 47.50x (ISBN 90-313-0500-6). Taylor & Francis.

Ergood, Bruce & Kuhre, Bruce E., eds. Appalachia: Social Context, Past & Present. 2nd ed. 1982. pap. text ed. 21.95 (ISBN 0-8403-2805-2). Kendall-Hunt.

Erguvanli, Eser E. The Function of Word Order in Turkish Grammar. LC 83-18129. (Linguistics Ser.: Vol. 106). 192p. 1984. lib. bdg. 15.00x (ISBN 0-520-09955-9). U of Cal Pr.

Erhard, G., jt. auth. see Ehrenstein, G. W.

Erhard, Ludwig. Germany's Comeback in the World Market. Johnston, W. H., tr. LC 76-15289. (Illus.). 1976. Repr. of 1954 ed. lib. bdg. 18.50x (ISBN 0-8371-8948-9, ERGC). Greenwood.

--Prosperity Through Competition. Roberts, Edith T. & Wood, John B., trs. LC 75-27681. 260p. 1976. Repr. of 1958 ed. lib. bdg. 17.50x (ISBN 0-8371-8457-6, ERPC). Greenwood.

Erhard, Thomas. Nine Hundred American Plays: A Synopsis History of American Theatre. (YA) 1978. PLB 15.00 (ISBN 0-8239-0406-7). Rosen Group.

Erhardt, Carl L. & Berlin, Joyce E. Mortality & Morbidity in the United States. LC 74-83140. (Vital & Health Statistics Monographs, American Public Health Association). 224p. 1974. text ed. 20.00t (ISBN 0-674-58740-5). Harvard U Pr.

Erhardt, Myra, jt. auth. see Charrow, Veda.

Erhardt, Rhoda P. Developmental Hand Dysfunction. (Illus.). 152p. 1982. pap. text ed. 24.50 (ISBN 0-943596-01-7, RAMSCO 00400). Ramsco Pub.

Erhardt, Roy. The Official Price Guide to Antique Clocks. 4th ed. 1985. 11.95 (ISBN 0-87637-241-8). Hse of Collectibles.

--Pocket Watch Price Guide, Book 3: Foreign and American. (Illus.). 1976. plastic ring bdg. 10.00 (ISBN 0-913902-16-0). Heart Am Pr.

--Set of Price Guides to Townsend Books. 1982. 9.00 (ISBN 0-913902-47-0). Heart Am Pr.

Erhardt, Roy & Rabeneck, Malvern. Clock Identification & Price Guide, Bk. 2. 1979. plastic ring bdg. 15.00 (ISBN 0-913902-27-6). Heart Am Pr.

Erhardt, Tell & Badalamenti, Rosalyn T. Chef Tell's Quick Cuisine: Gourmet Cooking, Simple, Fast, Delicious. LC 81-19870. (Illus.). 288p. (Orig.). 1982. 14.95 (ISBN 0-446-51240-0). Warner Bks.

Erhardt, Tell & Kranzdorf, Hermie. Chef Tell Tells All: A Gourmet Guide from the Market to the Table. LC 79-52440. (Illus.). 272p. 1979. pap. 9.95 (ISBN 0-916838-48-X). Schiffer.

--Chef Tell Tells All: A Gourmet Guide from the Market to the Table. LC 79-52440. (Illus.). 272p. 1979. 14.95 (ISBN 0-916838-27-7). Schiffer.

Erhart, Katherine P. The Development of the Facing Head Motif on Greek Coins & Its Relation to Classical Art. Freedberg, Sydney J., ed. LC 78-74366. (Outstanding Disserations in the Fine Arts Ser.). (Illus.). 1979. lib. bdg. 61.00 (ISBN 0-8240-3954-8). Garland Pub.

Erh-Soon Tay, Alice, jt. tr. see Kamenka, Eugene.

ERIC & Adult Education Association of the U. S. A. Register of Research: Investigation in Adult Education. 1968 2.30 (ISBN 0-88379-012-2); 1970 6.90 (ISBN 0-88379-013-0); 8.00 (ISBN 0-88379-030-0). A A A C E.

ERIC (Educational Information Center) Current Index to Journals in Education: Semi-Annual Cumulation, January-June, 1977. LC 75-7532. 1977. 45.00x (ISBN 0-02-693050-1). Macmillan Info.

ERIC (Educational Resources Information Center) Current Index to Journals in Education: Semi-Annual Cumulation, July-December, 1977. LC 75-7532. 1978. 45.00x (ISBN 0-02-693060-9). Macmillan Info.

--Current Index to Journals in Education: Semi-Annual Cumulation, January-June, 1978. LC 75-7532. 1978. 45.00x (ISBN 0-02-693120-6). Macmillan Info.

ERIC-RCS. Especially for Teachers: ERIC Documents on the Teaching of Writing 1966-1981. 175p. 1982. 9.75 (ISBN 0-8141-1582-9). NCTE.

Ericcson, Samuel, jt. auth. see Buzzard, Lynn.

Erichsen, Ann. Anorexia Nervosa: The Broken Circle. Dally, Peter, pref. by. 150p. (Orig.). 1985. pap. 8.95 (ISBN 0-571-13537-4). Faber & Faber.

Erichsen, Heino, jt. auth. see Erichsen, Jean.

Erichsen, Heino R., jt. auth. see Nelson-Erichsen, Jean.

Erichsen, Jean & Erichsen, Heino. The Adoption Kit: U. S. Adoptions. 2nd ed. (How to Adopt: No. 3). 40p. (Orig.). 1982. pap. 6.95 (ISBN 0-935366-22-9). Los Ninos.

Erichsen, Jean N. Copito: The Christmas Chihuahua. (Illus.). 80p. 12.95x (ISBN 0-943864-08-9); pap. 2.95x (ISBN 0-943864-07-0). MD Bks.

Erichsen, N., jt. auth. see Ross, J. A.

Erichsson, Iwan. Register over Dast Magazin, Vol. I-XV, 1968-1982. LC 85-11366. 146p. 1985. Repr. lib. bdg. 19.95x (ISBN 0-89370-875-5). Borgo Pr.

Erick, Meriam. Pregnancy & Nutrition: The Complete Guide & Calendar for D.I.E.T., 1986-1987. rev., 2nd ed. (Illus.). 156p. (Orig.). 1985. pap. 11.95 (ISBN 0-9613063-1-9). Grinnen-Barrett Pub Co.

Erick, Miriam. Pregnancy & Nutrition: The Complete Guide & Calendar for D.I.E.T. During Pregnancy, 1986. (Illus.). 120p. (Orig.). 1985. pap. 7.95t (ISBN 0-9613063-2-7). Grinnen-Barrett Pub Co.

--Pregnancy & Nutrition: The Complete Guide Calendar for D.I.E.T. During Pregnancy 1985-1986. (Illus.). 148p. (Orig.). 1984. 12.95 (ISBN 0-9613063-0-0). Grinnen-Barrett Pub Co.

--Pregnancy & Nutrition: The Complete Guide for D.I.E.T. During Pregnancy & After. (Illus.). 64p. (Orig.). 1985. pap. 4.95 (ISBN 0-9613063-3-5). Grinnen-Barrett Pub Co.

Erickison, Joan G. Speech Reading an Aid to Communication. LC 77-93152. 1978. pap. text ed. 3.25x (ISBN 0-8134-2013-X, 2013). Interstate.

Ericksen, Aase. Playground Design: Outdoor Environments for Learning & Development. (Illus.). 164p. 1985. 40.00 (ISBN 0-442-22257-2). Van Nos Reinhold.

Ericksen, D., tr. see Vinogradov, V. V.

Ericksen, Donald H. Oscar Wilde. (English Authors Ser.). 1977. lib. bdg. 12.50 (ISBN 0-8057-6680-4, Twayne). G K Hall.

Ericksen, E. Gordon. The Territorial Experience: Human Ecology As Symbolic Interaction. LC 80-14861. (Illus.). 224p. 1980. text ed. 20.00x (ISBN 0-292-78038-9). U of Tex Pr.

Ericksen, Ephraim E. The Psychological & Ethical Aspects of Mormon Group Life. 101p. 1974. Repr. of 1922 ed. 9.95 (ISBN 0-87480-090-0). U of Utah Pr.

Ericksen, Gregory K., jt. auth. see Jenkins, Michael D.

Ericksen, Robert P. Theologians under Hitler: Gerhard Kittel, Paul Althaus, & Emanuel Hirsch. LC 84-40731. (Illus.). 256p. 1985. 20.00x (ISBN 0-300-02926-8). Yale U Pr.

Ericksen, Stanford C. The Essence of Good Teaching: Helping Students Learn & Remember What They Learn. LC 84-47983. (Higher Education Ser.). 1984. 18.95x (ISBN 0-87589-615-4). Jossey-Bass.

Ericksenn, Lief. The Long Lens Book: All about Zoom Tele & Supertele Lenses & Pro Techniques of Using Them. (Illus.). 144p. 1983. 24.95 (ISBN 0-8174-4241-3, Amphoto); pap. 16.95 (ISBN 0-8174-4240-5). Watson-Guptill.

Ericksenn, Lief & Sincebaugh, Els. Adventures in Close-Up Photography: Rediscovering Familiar Environments Through Details. 144p. 1983. 24.50 (ISBN 0-8174-3501-8, Amphoto). Watson-Guptill.

Ericsko, Mae. Quiz for Christian Wives. 32p. 1976. pap. 0.95 (ISBN 0-930756-20-7, 541003). Aglow Pubns.

Erickson, jt. auth. see Statham.

Erickson, A. J., Jr., ed. Applied Mining Geology. LC 84-81473. (Illus.). 222p. 1984. pap. 35.00 (ISBN 0-89520-431-2, 431-2). Soc Mining Eng.

Erickson, Arvel B. The Public Career of Sir James Graham. LC 74-382. 433p. 1974. Repr. of 1952 ed. lib. bdg. 20.00x (ISBN 0-8371-7383-3, ERJG). Greenwood.

Erickson, Arvel B., jt. auth. see Jones, Wilbur D.

Erickson, C. L. The Perils of Probation. (Illus.). 238p. 1980. spiral bdg. 16.75x (ISBN 0-398-04013-3). C C Thomas.

Erickson, C. T. Luftwaffe. pap. 3.00x (ISBN 0-392-07325-0, SpS). Sportshelf.

Erickson, Carlton K., jt. ed. see Goodwin, Donald W.

Erickson, Carlton W. Administering Instructional Media Programs. LC 68-12281. (Illus.). 1968. text ed. write for info. (ISBN 0-02-333980-2, 33398). Macmillan.

Erickson, Carolly. Bloody Mary. 560p. 1985. pap. 9.95 (ISBN 0-312-08508-7). St Martin.

--Civilization & Society in the West. 1978. pap. 17.95x (ISBN 0-673-15123-9). Scott F.

--The First Elizabeth. 464p. 1983. 19.95 (ISBN 0-671-41746-0). Summit Bks.

--The First Elizabeth. 464p. 1984. pap. 9.95 (ISBN 0-671-50393-6). Summit Bks.

--Great Harry: The Extravagant Life of Henry VIII. 448p. 1984. pap. 9.95 (ISBN 0-671-50392-8). Summit Bks.

--The Medieval Vision: Essays in History & Perception. LC 75-10179. 1976. text ed. 19.95x (ISBN 0-19-501964-4); pap. text ed. 8.95x (ISBN 0-19-501963-6). Oxford U Pr.

--Mistress Anne: The Exceptional Life of Anne Boleyn. 464p. 1984. 19.95 (ISBN 0-671-41747-9). Summit Bks.

Erickson, Charlotte. The Freezer Cookbook. (Illus.). 456p. 1981. pap. 8.95 (ISBN 0-8092-5888-9). Contemp Bks.

--Invisible Immigrants: The Adaptation of English & Scottish Immigrants in 19th Century America. LC 75-161437. (Illus.). 519p. 1972. 19.95x (ISBN 0-87024-213-X). U of Miami Pr.

Erickson, Charlotte, ed. Emigration from Europe 1815-1914: Select Documents. (Documents in Economic History Ser.). 1976. text ed. 17.50x (ISBN 0-7136-1616-4). Humanities.

Erickson, Clint, jt. ed. see Teague, Robert.

Erickson, D. H. Armstrong's Fight for FM Broadcasting: One Man Vs. Big Business & Bureaucracy. LC 73-40. 248p. 1973. 16.75 (ISBN 0-8173-4818-2). U of Ala Pr.

Erickson, David L. Colorado Corporate Forms. LC 83-24042. 471p. 1984. 62.50. Callaghan.

Erickson, David M. Uranium Development in Less Developed Countries: A Handbook of Concerns. (Lincoln Institute Monograph: No. 81-4). 83p. 1981. pap. text ed. 14.00 (ISBN 0-686-30624-4). Lincoln Inst Land.

Erickson, David R. & Pryde, Everett H. Handbook of Soy Oil Processing & Utilization. 598p. 7.00 (ISBN 0-318-12897-7). Am Oil Chemists.

Erickson, Donald A., ed. Educational Organization & Administration. LC 76-18037. (Readings in Educational Research Ser.). 1977. 32.50x (ISBN 0-8211-0415-2); text ed. 29.50x 10 or more copies. McCutchan.

Erickson, Donald A. & Reller, Theodore L., eds. The Principal in Metropolitan Schools. LC 78-62641. (Contemporary Educational Issues Ser.). 347p. 1978. 24.00x (ISBN 0-8211-0417-9); text ed. 21.50x ten or more copies. McCutchan.

Erickson, Dorie A. Start Your Own Private School-Legally, 2 vols. Incl. Canyon Christian Academy: An Alternate Education K-12. LC 80-51386. (Illus.). 55p. (Orig.). pap. free (ISBN 0-937242-01-2). LC 80-51385. 65p. (Orig.). 1980. pap. 11.95x set (ISBN 0-937242-00-4). Scandia Pubs.

Erickson, Duane E., et al. Microcomputers on the Farm: Getting Started. 56p. (Orig.). 1985. pap. 9.95 (ISBN 0-8138-1156-2). Iowa St U Pr.

Erickson, E. Walfred. Swedish-American Periodicals. Scott, Franklyn D., ed. LC 78-15206. (Scandinavians in America Ser.). 1979. lib. bdg. 16.00x (ISBN 0-405-11635-7). Ayer Co Pubs.

Erickson, Edgar L. One Hundred Years of British Colonial Policy. LC 58-4393. (Augustana College Library Occasional Papers: No. 2). 19p. 1958. pap. 0.50 (ISBN 0-910182-23-X). Augustana Coll.

Erickson, Edsel, jt. auth. see Erickson, Ruth.

Erickson, Edsel L., et al. Child Abuse & Neglect: A Guidebook for Educators & Community Leaders. 2nd ed. 264p. 1984. pap. text ed. 14.95x (ISBN 0-918452-62-7); case 19.95 (ISBN 0-918452-75-9). Learning Pubns.

Erickson, Edward W. Economic Incentives, Industrial Structure & the Supply of Crude Oil Discoveries in the U. S., 1946-58-59. Bruchey, Stuart, ed. LC 78-22678. (Energy in the American Economy Ser.). (Illus.). 1979. lib. bdg. 14.00x (ISBN 0-405-11981-X). Ayer Co Pubs.

Erickson, Edward W. & Waverman, Leonard, eds. The Energy Question: An International Failure of Policy. LC 73-91565. Vol. 1, The World. pap. 99.00 (ISBN 0-317-11031-4, 2014203); Vol. 2, North America. pap. 103.50 (ISBN 0-317-11032-2). Bks Demand UMI.

Erickson, Eric H., Jr., et al. A Scanning Electron Microscope of the Honey Bee. 280p. 1985. text ed. 35.00x (ISBN 0-317-19356-2). Iowa St U Pr.

Erickson, Erling A. Banking in Frontier Iowa, Eighteen Hundred Thirty-Six to Eighteen Hundred Sixty-Five. LC 75-146931. (Illus.). 1971. 8.50 (ISBN 0-8138-0160-5). Iowa St U Pr.

Erickson, Florence H. Play Interviews for Four Year Old Hospitilized Children. (SRCD M). 1958. pap. 14.00 (ISBN 0-527-01575-X). Kraus Repr.

Erickson, Frances G., jt. auth. see Cornell, Dale D.

Erickson, Frederick & Schultz, Jeffrey J. The Counselor As Gatekeeper: Social Interaction in Interviews. LC 81-19043. (Language, Thought & Culture Ser.). 1981. 34.00 (ISBN 0-12-240580-3). Acad Pr.

Erickson, Fritz & Vonk, John A. Student Guide for Learning BASIC, for Classroom or Independent Study, Vol. II: TRS 80 Models III & IV. LC 83-82120. 136p. (Orig.). 1983. pap. text ed. 9.95 (ISBN 0-918452-54-6). Learning Pubns.

Erickson, Fritz J., jt. auth. see Vonk, John A.

Erickson, Garth & Klaus, Victor. Wills Probate Procedure for Manitoba & Saskatchewan. 2nd ed. 81p. 1981. 4.95 (ISBN 0-88908-503-X). Self Counsel Pr.

Erickson, Gerald & Schwartz, Harold L., eds. Social Class in the Contemporary United States: Papers from Second Midwest Marxist Scholars Conference. LC 77-92856. (Studies in Marxism: Vol. 2). 101p. 1977. 7.95x (ISBN 0-930656-04-0); pap. 2.50 (ISBN 0-930656-02-4). MEP Pubns.

Erickson, Gerald D. & Hogan, Terrence P. Family Therapy: An Introduction to Theory & Technique. 2nd ed. LC 80-28686. 448p. (Orig.). 1981. pap. text ed. 13.75 pub net (ISBN 0-8185-0437-4). Brooks-Cole.

Erickson, Gregg K., jt. auth. see Tussing, Arlon R.

Erickson, Gregory. Wall Street's Reference Guide. 1985. text ed. 24.95 (ISBN 0-8359-8535-0); pap. 17.95 (ISBN 0-8359-8534-2). Reston.

Erickson, Gustav. Balanced Distribution. LC 64-13322. 1964. 5.00 (ISBN 0-8022-0457-0). Philos Lib.

Erickson, Helen. Young Person's Guide to the Opera. (Masterworks of the Opera Ser.). 160p. (gr. 6 up). PLB 15.96 (ISBN 0-382-06444-5). Silver.

Erickson, Helen & Tomlin, Evelyn. Modeling & Role Modeling: A Theory & Paradigm for Nursing. (Illus.). 240p. 1983. text ed. 22.95 (ISBN 0-13-586198-5); pap. 19.95 (ISBN 0-13-586180-2). P-H.

Erickson, I. A Love Story for Anne Frank. 1982. 10.00 (ISBN 0-533-04905-9). Vantage.

Erickson, J. Gunnar & Hearn, Edward R. Musician's Guide to Copyright. rev. ed. 160p. 14.95 (ISBN 0-684-17900-8, ScribT). Scribner.

Erickson, J. Irving. Sing It Again! 1985. 12.95 (ISBN 0-910452-58-X). Covenant.

--Twice-Born Hymns. 1976. pap. 8.95 (ISBN 0-910452-30-X). Covenant.

Erickson, J. L., ed. Orienting Polymers: Proceedings of a Workshop Held at the IMA, University of Minnesota, Minneapolis, March 21-26, 1983. (Lecture Notes in Mathematics Ser.: Vol. 1063). vii, 166p. 1984. pap. 12.00 (ISBN 0-387-13340-2). Springer-Verlag.

Erickson, J. Wayne. The Mountain's Hostage. 290p. 1980. 12.50 (ISBN 0-682-49654-5, Banner). Exposition Pr FL.

Erickson, James C., III, jt. auth. see Tarrow, Arthur B.

Erickson, Janet D. & Sproul, Adelaide. Print Making Without a Press. LC 65-19672. pap. 30.80 (ISBN 0-317-10485-3, 2007245). Bks Demand UMI.

Erickson, Jeffrey & Richards, Susan. Hey, Let's Play with the Apple IIe! (Learn Together Ser.). 128p. (gr. 4-6). 1984. pap. 19.95 incl. disk (ISBN 0-88693-071-5). Banbury Bks.

--Hey, Let's Play with the PCjr! (Learn Together Ser.). 128p. (gr. 4-6). 1984. pap. 19.95 (ISBN 0-88693-072-3). Banbury Bks.

Erickson, Joan G. & Emark, Donald R., eds. Communication Assessment of the Bilingual - Bicultural Child. LC 80-21398. (Illus.). 392p. 1981. pap. 16.00 (ISBN 0-8391-1599-7). Pro Ed.

Erickson, Joan G., jt. ed. see Omark, Donald R.

Erickson, John. Dada: Performance, Poetry & Art. (World Authors Ser.: No. 703). 171p. 1984. lib. bdg. 18.95 (ISBN 0-8057-6550-6, Twayne). G K Hall.

--The Road to Berlin: Continuing the History of Stalin's War with Germany. (Illus.). 700p. 1983. 42.50x (ISBN 0-89158-795-0). Westview.

--The Road to Stalingrad. 604p. 1983. 40.00x (ISBN 0-86531-744-5). Westview.

--The Soviet High Command. LC 84-51550. (Illus.). 905p. 1984. pap. 60.00x (ISBN 0-86531-743-7). Westview.

Erickson, John & Feuchtwanger, E. J. Soviet Military Power & Performance. ix, 219p. 1979. 25.00 (ISBN 0-208-01779-8, Archon). Shoe String.

Erickson, John, jt. ed. see Drillock, David.

Erickson, John D. Nommo: African Fiction in French. (Francophone Studies: Black Africa). 285p. 1979. 15.95 (ISBN 0-917786-08-4). Summa Pubns.

Erickson, John R. Ace Reid: Cowpoke. (Illus.). 190p. 1984. 15.95 (ISBN 0-916941-00-0). Maverick Bks.

--Alkali County Tales. (Illus.). 100p. (Orig.). (gr. 3up). 1984. 9.95 (ISBN 0-916941-06-X); pap. 5.95 (ISBN 0-9608612-8-9). Maverick Bks.

--Cowboys Are Partly Human. 110p. (Orig.). (gr. 3 up). 1983. 9.95 (ISBN 0-9608612-6-2); pap. 5.95 (ISBN 0-9608612-4-6). Maverick Bks.

--The Devil in Texas & Other Cowboy Tales. LC 82-90172. (Illus.). 96p. 1982. pap. 5.95 (ISBN 0-9608612-0-3). Maverick Bks.

--Essays on Writing & Publishing. 45p. (Orig.). 1985. pap. 5.00 (ISBN 0-916941-13-2). Maverick Bks.

--The Further Adventures of Hank the Cowdog. (Hank the Cowdog Ser.: 2nd.). 93p. (Orig.). (gr. 3). 1983. 9.95 (ISBN 0-9608612-7-0); pap. 5.95 (ISBN 0-9608612-5-4). Maverick Bks.

--Hank the Cowdog. (Illus.). 105p. (Orig.). 1983. 9.95 (ISBN 0-916941-05-1); pap. 5.95 (ISBN 0-9608612-2-X). Maverick Bks.

--Hank the Cowdog: Faded Love. (Hank the Cowdog Ser.). (gr. 3 up). 1985. talking bk. 13.95 (ISBN 0-916941-12-4). Maverick Bks.

--Hank the Cowdog: It's a Dog's Life. (Hank the Cowdog Ser.). (Illus.). 100p. (Orig.). (gr. 3). 9.95 (ISBN 0-916941-04-3); pap. 5.95 (ISBN 0-9608612-9-7). Maverick Bks.

--Hank the Cowdog: Murder in the Middle Pasture. (Hank the Cowdog Ser.). 91p. (Orig.). (gr. 3 up). 1985. pap. 5.95 (ISBN 0-916941-07-8). Maverick Bks.

--The Hunter. LC 83-45007. (Double D Western Ser.). 192p. 1984. 11.95 (ISBN 0-385-18897-8). Doubleday.

--The Modern Cowboy. LC 80-28751. (Illus.). xii, 247p. 1980. pap. 6.95 (ISBN 0-8032-6707-X, BB 864, Bison). U of Nebr Pr.

--Panhandle Cowboy. LC 79-24929. (Illus.). xiv, 213p. 1980. pap. 5.95 (ISBN 0-8032-6702-9, BB 777, Bison). U of Nebr Pr.

--Through Time & the Valley. (Illus.). 260p. 1983. pap. 7.95 (ISBN 0-9608612-1-1). Maverick Bks.

Erickson, Jon, tr. see Luthi, Max.

Erickson, Jon J. & Rollo, F. David, eds. Digital Nuclear Medicine. (Illus.). 274p. 1982. pap. text ed. 22.25 (ISBN 0-397-50532-9, 65-06786, Lippincott Medical). Lippincott.

Erickson, Jon L., jt. ed. see Scott, Charles T.

Erickson, Jon T. & Cain, H. Thomas. Navajo Textiles from the Read Mullan Collection. (Illus.). 80p. 1981. pap. 12.95 (ISBN 0-295-95858-8). U of Wash Pr.

Erickson, Jonathan. C-64 Telecommunications. 180p. 1984. pap. 16.95 (ISBN 0-07-881149-X, 149-X). Osborne-McGraw.

Erickson, Jonathan & Baran, Nicholas. Using R: Base: Base 4000. 256p. (Orig.). 1985. pap. 18.95 (ISBN 0-07-881171-6, 171-6). Osborne McGraw.

Erickson, Jonathan & Cramer, William D. The Apple Graphics & Sound Book. 256p. (Orig.). 1985. pap. cancelled (ISBN 0-88134-167-3, 167-3). Osborne McGraw.

--The IBM PCjr Image Maker: Graphics on the IBM PCjr. 200p. (Orig.). 1984. pap. 15.95 (ISBN 0-07-881138-4, 138-4). Osborne-McGraw.

--MacTelecommunications. 180p. (Orig.). 1984. pap. 17.95 (ISBN 0-07-881155-4, 155-4). Osborne-McGraw.

Erickson, Jonathan & Sayre, Robert. The Model 100 Book: A Guide to Portable Computing. 380p. (Orig.). 1984. pap. 17.95 (ISBN 0-88134-124-X, 124-X). Osborne-McGraw.

Erickson, Joyce. In Straw & Story: Christmas Resources for Home & Church. rev. ed. (Illus.). 192p. 1983. pap. 10.95 (ISBN 0-87178-417-3). Brethren.

Erickson, Judith B. Directory of Youth Organizations. LC 83-11499. 86p. (Orig.). 1983. pap. text ed. 9.95 (ISBN 0-938510-04-5). Boys Town Ctr.

Erickson, K. Please, Lord, Untie My Tongue. LC 12-2816. 1983. pap. 2.50 (ISBN 0-570-03881-2). Concordia.

Erickson, Karen. I Can Do Something When There's Nothing to Do. (I Can Do It Ser.). (Illus.). 32p. (ps). 1985. pap. 4.95 (ISBN 0-590-33496-4). Scholastic Inc.

--I Can Get Organized. (I Can Do It Ser.). (Illus.). 32p. (ps). 1985. 4.95 (ISBN 0-590-33493-X). Scholastic Inc.

--I Can Settle Down. (I Can Do It Ser.). (Illus.). 32p. 1985. 4.95 (ISBN 0-590-33494-8). Scholastic Inc.

--I Can Share. (I Can Do It Ser.). (Illus.). 32p. 1985. 4.95 (ISBN 0-590-33495-6). Scholastic Inc.

Erickson, Karly, jt. auth. see Flack, Dora.

Erickson, Keith, jt. auth. see Cheatham, T. Richard.

Erickson, Keith V., ed. Plato: True & Sophistic Rhetoric. (Orig.). 1980. pap. text ed. 69.00x (ISBN 90-6203-489-6). Humanities.

Erickson, Kenneth. The Power of Praise. 1984. pap. 4.95 (ISBN 0-570-03925-8, 12-2859). Concordia.

Erickson, Kenneth A. Christian Time Management. 128p. (Orig.). 1985. pap. 4.95 (ISBN 0-570-03972-X, 12-3007). Concordia.

Erickson, Kenneth A. & Smith, Albert W. Atlas of Colorado. 88p. 1985. 29.50 (ISBN 0-87081-142-8); pap. 12.50 (ISBN 0-87081-143-6). Colo Assoc.

Erickson, Kenneth P. The Brazilian Corporative State & Working-Class Politics. 1978. 33.00x (ISBN 0-520-03162-8). U of Cal Pr.

Erickson, Lawrence, jt. auth. see Otto, Wayne.

Erickson, Lawrence G., jt. ed. see Hatcher, Thomas C.

Erickson, Lawrence W. Microcomputer Activities for Office Procedures. (gr. 9-12). 1984. pap. 4.80 (ISBN 0-538-11220-4, K22). SW Pub.

Erickson, Lee. Robert Browning: His Poetry & His Audiences. LC 83-45934. 304p. 1984. 25.00x (ISBN 0-8014-1618-3). Cornell U Pr.

Erickson, Leo G., jt. auth. see Cox, Eli P.

Erickson, Lois J., tr. Songs from the Land of Dawn. facs. ed. LC 68-58828. (Granger Index Reprint Ser). 1949. 14.00 (ISBN 0-8369-6014-9). Ayer Co Pubs.

Erickson, Lonni R. Creation vs. Evolution: A Comparison. 30p. write for info. Scandia Pubs.

--The Teaching of Evolution in Public Schools: A Comparison of Evolution & Special Creation. (Illus.). 40p. (Orig.). 1980. pap. 3.95 (ISBN 0-937242-03-9). Scandia Pubs.

Erickson, Lynn. Dawnfire. (Tapestry Romance Ser.). 320p. (Orig.). 1984. pap. 3.50 (ISBN 0-671-46969-X). PB.

--Some Distant Shore. 1985. pap. 3.50 (ISBN 0-671-50162-3). PB.

Erickson, Maria. Hospital Volunteers Handbook. 35p. (Orig.). 1980. Pkg. of 4. pap. 9.95 (ISBN 0-918452-23-6). Learning Pubns.

Erickson, Marilyn T. Child Psychopathology: Behavior Disorders & Developmental Disabilities. 2nd ed. (Illus.). 368p. 1982. reference 28.95 (ISBN 0-13-131094-1). P-H.

Erickson, Marilyn T., jt. auth. see Gabel, Stewart.

Erickson, Marilyn T., et al. Readings in Behavior Modification. LC 73-8528. 1973. 29.75x (ISBN 0-8422-5106-5); pap. 14.95x (ISBN 0-8422-0312-5). Irvington.

--Readings in Behavior Modification Research with Children. LC 73-8536. 1973. pap. text ed. 18.95x (ISBN 0-8422-0313-3). Irvington.

Erickson, Mary. Don't Cry for Anna. (Jesus, the Wonder Worker Ser.). 48p. (gr. 3-6). 1985. pap. 3.95 (ISBN 0-89191-683-0, 56838, Chariot Bks). Cook.

--Survival at Sea. (Jesus the Wonder Worker Ser.). 48p. (gr. 3-6). 1985. pap. 3.95 (ISBN 0-89191-695-4, 56952, Chariot Bks). Cook.

Erickson, Melvin & Long, Katherine. Clinton: A Pictorial History. (Illus.). 200p. 1983. 22.95x (ISBN 0-940286-01-7). Quest Pub IL.

Erickson, Millard J. Christian Theology, Vol. 1. 432p. 1983. 19.95 (ISBN 0-8010-3391-8). Baker Bk.

--Christian Theology, Vol. 2. 432p. 1984. 17.95 (ISBN 0-8010-3419-1). Baker Bk.

--Christian Theology, Vol. 3. 1985. 19.95 (ISBN 0-8010-3425-6). Baker Bk.

--Contemporary Options in Eschatology: A Study of the Millennium. LC 77-89406. 1977. 9.95 (ISBN 0-8010-3262-8). Baker Bk.

Erickson, Millard J., ed. New Life: Readings in Christian Theology. LC 79-53903. 1979. pap. 12.95 (ISBN 0-8010-3340-3). Baker Bk.

--Readings In Christian Theology. 1973. pap. 12.95 (ISBN 0-8010-3305-5). Baker Bk.

Erickson, Milton H. The Essential Erickson: Selected Papers on Hypnosis & Psychotherapy. Rossi, Ernest L., ed. 550p. Date not set. text ed. price not setx (ISBN 0-8290-1081-5). Irvington.

--Healing in Hypnosis. Rossi, Ernest L., et al, eds. LC 82-6632. (The Seminars, Workshops, & Lectures of Milton H. Erickson: Vol. 1). (Illus.). 300p. 1983. text ed. 39.50x incl. audio cassette (ISBN 0-8290-0739-3). Irvington.

--Hypnotic Alteration of Sensory, Perceptual & Psychophysiological Processes. Rossi, Ernest L., ed. (The Collected Papers of Milton H. Erickson on Hypnosis: Vol. II). 368p. 1980. pap. 17.50x (ISBN 0-8290-1207-9). Irvington.

--Hypnotic Alteration of Sensory, Perceptual & Psychophysiological Processes. Rossi, Ernest L., ed. (The Collected Papers of Milton H. Erickson on Hypnosis: Vol. II). 368p. 1980. text ed. 29.95x (ISBN 0-8290-0543-9). Irvington.

--The Hypnotic Investigation of Psychodynamic Processes. Rossi, Enerst L., ed. (The Collected Papers of Milton H. Erickson on Hypnosis: Vol. III). 368p. 1980. pap. 17.50x (ISBN 0-8290-1208-7). Irvington.

--The Hypnotic Investigation of Psychodynamic Processes. Rossi, Ernest L., ed. (The Collected Papers of Milton H. Erickson on Hypnosis: Vol. III). 368p. 1980. text ed. 29.95x (ISBN 0-8290-0544-7). Irvington.

--Innovative Hypnotherapy. Rossi, Ernest L., ed. (The Collected Papers of Milton H. Erickson on Hypnosis: Vol. IV). 570p. 1980. pap. 19.95x (ISBN 0-8290-1209-5). Irvington.

--Innovative Hypnotherapy. Rossi, Ernest L., ed. (The Collected Papers of Milton H. Erickson on Hypnosis: Vol. IV). 570p. 1980. text ed. 37.50x (ISBN 0-8290-0545-5). Irvington.

--The Nature of Hypnosis & Suggestion. Rossi, Enerst L., ed. (The Collected Papers of Milton H. Erickson on Hypnosis: Vol. I). 570p. 1980. pap. 19.95 (ISBN 0-8290-1206-0). Irvington.

--The Nature of Hypnosis & Suggestion. Rossi, Ernest L., ed. (The Collected Papers of Milton H. Erickson on Hypnosis: Vol. I). 570p. 1980. text ed. 37.50x (ISBN 0-8290-0542-0). Irvington.

--The Wisdom of Milton H. Erickson. Havens, Ronald A., ed. 350p. 1985. text ed. 39.50x (ISBN 0-8290-0963-9). Irvington.

Erickson, Milton H. & Rossi, Ernest L. Experiencing Hypnosis: Theraputic Approaches to Altered States. LC 80-26957. 300p. 1981. text ed. 39.50x incl. two audio cassettes (ISBN 0-8290-0246-4). Irvington.

--Hypnotherapy: An Exploratory Casebook. LC 78-23839. 512p. (Orig.). 1980. text ed. 39.50x incl. audio cassette (ISBN 0-8290-0347-9). Irvington.

Erickson, Milton H., jt. auth. see Cooper, Linn F.

Erickson, Milton H. & Rossi, Ernest, eds. Hypnotic Investigation of Psychodynamic Processes. LC 79-15939. (Collected Papers of Milton H. Erickson on Hypnosis: Vol. 3). 367p. 1980. 29.95x (ISBN 0-470-26723-2). Halsted Pr.

Erickson, Milton H., et al. Life Reframing in Hypnosis: The Seminars, Workshops & Lectures of Milton H. Erickson, Vol. II. Rossi, Ernest L. & Ryan, Margaret O., eds. 330p. 1985. text ed. 39.50 (ISBN 0-8290-1581-7). Irvington.

--Hypnotic Realities: The Induction of Clinical Hypnosis & Forms of Indirect Suggestion. LC 76-20636. 1976. incl. audio cassette 27.95x (ISBN 0-8290-0112-3). Irvington.

Erickson, Myron L., et al. Antitrust & Trade Regulation: Cases & Materials. LC 76-8108. 430p. 1982. pap. 25.45 (ISBN 0-471-87014-5, Pub. by Grid). Wiley.

Erickson, Nancy S. Women & the Supreme Court: Anatomy is Destiny. 74p. 2.00 (ISBN 0-318-13444-6). Assn Libertarian Fem.

Erickson, Neil L., II & Noble, Virginia B. The Whole, New & Vital Permanent Weight Loss Program. LC 84-72981. (Illus.). 117p. 1985. pap. 5.95 (ISBN 0-931979-20-X). Algonquin Enter.

Erickson, P. C. Stand Tall. (Illus., Orig.). 1978. pap. 2.95 (ISBN 0-89036-111-8). Hawkes Pub Inc.

Erickson, Paul A. Environmental Impact Assessment: Principles & Applications. 1979. 49.50 (ISBN 0-12-241550-7). Acad Pr.

Erickson, Paul D. Reagan Speaks: The Making of an American Myth. 192p. 1985. text ed. 16.95 (ISBN 0-8147-2167-2). NYU Pr.

Erickson, Paul R. Growing Pains. LC 85-50086. (Illus.). 74p. (gr. 7-10). 1985. 0.95 (ISBN 0-938232-61-4). Winston-Derek.

Erickson, Peter. Patriarchal Structures in Shakespeare's Drama. LC 84-601. 225p. 1985. 24.50x (ISBN 0-520-04806-7). U of Cal Pr.

Erickson, Peter & Kahn, Coppelia, eds. Shakespeare's "Rough Magic". LC 83-40112. (Illus.). 320p. 1985. 37.50 (ISBN 0-87413-247-9). U Delaware Pr.

Erickson, Phoebe. Black Penny. (Illus.). (gr. 3-6). 1982. pap. 5.50 (ISBN 0-317-13562-7). P Erickson.

--Who's in the Mirror? (gr. 1-3). Repr. of 1965 ed. PLB 4.95 (ISBN 0-317-13837-5). P Erickson.

Erickson, Rica. The Dempsters. LC 79-670115. 1979. 22.50x (ISBN 0-85564-126-6, Pub. by U of W Austral Pr). Intl Spec Bk.

--Plants of Prey. 1977. 15.00 (ISBN 0-85564-099-5, Pub. by U of W Austral Pr). Intl Spec Bk.

--Triggerplants. (Illus.). 229p. 1982. 22.95 (ISBN 0-85564-100-2, Pub. by U of W Austral Pr). Intl Spec Bk.

Erickson, Richard C. Inpatient Small Group Psychotherapy: A Pragmatic Approach. 246p. 1984. 24.75x (ISBN 0-398-04945-9). C C Thomas.

Erickson, Richard J. International Law & the Revolutionary State: A Case Study of the Soviet Union & Customary International Law. LC 72-8649. 268p. 1972. lib. bdg. 20.00 (ISBN 0-379-00169-1). Oceana.

Erickson, Robert. Sound Structure in Music. LC 72-9352. (Illus.). 1975. 30.00x (ISBN 0-520-02376-5). U of Cal Pr.

--The Structure of Music: a Listener's Guide: A Study of Music in Terms of Melody & Counterpoint. LC 75-31361. 1977. Repr. of 1955 ed. lib. bdg. 22.50x (ISBN 0-8371-8519-X, ERSM). Greenwood.

Erickson, Robert A., ed. see Arbuthmot, John.

Erickson, Roger. Maggie & David. 224p. 1981. pap. 2.50 (ISBN 0-449-14431-3). Fawcett.

Erickson, Ronald E., jt. auth. see Szymanski, Herman A.

Erickson, Rosemary, et al. Paroled but Not Free. LC 73-4039. 129p. 1973. text ed. 19.95 (ISBN 0-87705-095-3); pap. text ed. 9.95 (ISBN 0-87705-109-7). Human Sci Pr.

Erickson, Russell. A Toad for Tuesday. LC 73-19900. (Illus.). 64p. (gr. k-4). 1974. PLB 10.88 (ISBN 0-688-51569-X). Lothrop.

Erickson, Russell E. Warton & Morton. LC 76-9017. (Illus.). 64p. (gr. k-4). 1976. PLB 10.88 (ISBN 0-688-51771-4). Lothrop.

--Warton & the Castaways. LC 79-21963. (Illus.). 112p. (gr. k-3). 1982. 11.75 (ISBN 0-688-41939-9); PLB 11.88 (ISBN 0-688-51939-3). Lothrop.

--Warton & the King of the Skies. 96p. (gr. k-6). 1981. pap. 1.50 (ISBN 0-440-49406-0, YB). Dell.

--Warton & the King of the Skies. LC 78-4919. (Illus.). (gr. k-4). 1978. 10.00 (ISBN 0-688-41852-X); PLB 10.88 (ISBN 0-688-51852-4). Lothrop.

--Warton & the Traders. LC 78-25689. (Warton & Morton Ser.). (Illus.). (gr. k-3). 1979. 10.00 (ISBN 0-688-41886-4); PLB 10.88 (ISBN 0-688-51886-9). Lothrop.

--Warton's Christmas Eve Adventure. LC 77-4847. (Illus.). (gr. k-4). 1977. PLB 11.88 (ISBN 0-688-51822-2). Lothrop.

Erickson, Ruth & Erickson, Edsel. Children with Reading Problems: A Guidebook for Parents. 2nd ed. LC 76-58796. 206p. 1979. lib. bdg. 9.95x (ISBN 0-918452-11-2); pap. 6.45 (ISBN 0-918452-12-0). Learning Pubns.

Erickson, Stephen A. Human Presence: At the Boundaries of Meaning. LC 83-24944. 150p. 1984. 12.95X (ISBN 0-86554-094-2, MUP/H86). Mercer Univ Pr.

--Language & Being: An Analytic Phenomenology. LC 74-99823. pap. 43.30 (ISBN 0-317-08818-1, 2016780). Bks Demand UMI.

Erickson, Steve. Days Between Stations: A Novel. 1985. 15.95 (ISBN 0-671-53275-8, Poseidon). S&S.

--Management Tools for Everyone. 1986. pap. 12.95. Petrocelli.

Erickson, Steve, et al, eds. see Emshock.

Erickson, Steve M. Management Tools for Everyone. (Illus.). 160p. 1981. 17.50 (ISBN 0-89433-131-0). Petrocelli.

Erickson, V. L. & Julien, H. L., eds. Gas Turbine Heat Transfer: 1978. 1978. 18.00 (ISBN 0-685-66801-0, H00125). ASME.

Erickson, W. Bruce, jt. auth. see Rudelius, William.

Erickson, Wayne R. & Pate, Charles E. The Broomhandle Pistol, Eighteen Ninety-Six to Nineteen Thirty-Six. 300p. 1985. 49.95x (ISBN 0-9614095-0-9). E & P Enter.

Ericksson, C. Maillard Reactions in Food: Proceedings of the International Symposium, Uddevalla, Sweden, September 1979. (Progress in Food & Nutrition Science Ser.: Vol. 5). (Illus.). 500p. 1982. 155.00 (ISBN 0-08-025496-9). Pergamon.

Erickstad, H. G. The Prophecies of Nostradamus in Historical Sequence from A.D. 1550-2005. LC 80-53660. 218p. 1982. 10.00 (ISBN 0-533-04862-1). Vantage.

Ericson. Klader: Creating Fantastic Clothes. 1984. pap. 17.95 (ISBN 0-937274-13-5). Dodd.

Ericson, Carolyn. Citizens & Foreigners of the Nacogdoches District, 1809-1836, Vol. II. LC 82-106713. 49p. (Orig.). 1985. pap. 7.50 (ISBN 0-911317-37-6). Ericson Bks.

--Nacogdoches Headrights. 1977. 20.00 (ISBN 0-686-20420-4). Polyanthos.

Ericson, Carolyn & Ingmire, Frances, eds. First Settlers of the Louisiana Territory, 2 Vols. Incl. Vol. II. 243p. pap. 19.50 (ISBN 0-911317-13-9). LC 82-84532. 1983. Set. pap. 30.00 (ISBN 0-911317-14-7). Ericson Bks.

--First Settlers of the Louisiana Territory: Orleans Territory Grants from American State Papers, Class VIII, Public Lands, Vol. 1. LC 82-84532. 235p. (Orig.). pap. 19.50 (ISBN 0-911317-09-0). Ericson Bks.

--First Settlers of the Mississippi Territory. LC 82-83848. 110p. (Orig.). Set. pap. 19.50 (ISBN 0-911317-07-4). Ericson Bks.

--First Settlers of the Missouri Territory, 2 vols. Incl. Vol. I. 182p. pap. 15.00 (ISBN 0-911317-10-4); Vol. II. 185p. pap. 15.00 (ISBN 0-911317-11-2). LC 82-84533. 182p. 1983. Set. pap. 25.00 (ISBN 0-911317-12-0). Ericson Bks.

Ericson, Carolyn, ed. see Harris, Ollie K. & Slover, Elizabeth.

Ericson, Carolyn, ed. see National Archives-War Department, 1912.

Ericson, Carolyn, ed. see Toole, Blanche.

Ericson, Carolyn, ed. see White, Gifford.

Ericson, Carolyn R., ed. First Settlers of the Republic of Texas, Vol. 1. 278p. 1982. pap. 19.95 (ISBN 0-911317-00-7). Ericson Bks.

--First Settlers of the Republic of Texas, Vol. 2. 273p. 1982. pap. 19.95 (ISBN 0-911317-01-5). Ericson Bks.

Ericson, E. E., jt. auth. see Andrews, Robert.

Ericson, Edward E., abridged by see Solzhenitsyn, Alexsandr I., Jr.

Ericson, Edward E., Jr. Radicals in the University. LC 75-27011. (Publications Ser.: No. 144). 1975. 12.95 (ISBN 0-8179-6441-X). Hoover Inst Pr.

--Solzhenitsyn: The Moral Vision. 1982. pap. 6.95 (ISBN 0-8028-1718-1, 1718-1). Eerdmans.

Ericson, Edward E., Jr., ed. see Solzhenitsyn, Alexsandr I.

Ericson, Edward L. American Freedom & the Radical Right. LC 81-71132. 128p. 1982. 9.95 (ISBN 0-8044-5355-1); pap. 4.95 (ISBN 0-8044-6141-4). Ungar.

--The Free Mind Through the Ages. 180p. 1985. 14.95 (ISBN 0-8044-5358-6); pap. 7.95 (ISBN 0-8044-6149-X). Ungar.

Ericson, Georgia. Aunt Hank's Rock House Kitchen: A Cookbook with a Story. 1977. 15.00x (ISBN 0-686-31816-1). Crosby County.

Ericson, J. E. see Earle, Timothy.

Ericson, Jack T. Genealogy & Local History: Title List. (Pts. 2 & 3). 85p. 1981. write for info. Microfilming Corp.

Ericson, Jack T., ed. The Americans for Democratic Action Papers, 1932-1965: A Guide to the Microform Edition. 121p. 1979. 25.00 (ISBN 0-667-00540-4). Microfilming Corp.

--Earl Browder Papers, 1891-1975: A Guide to the Microfilm Edition. LC 76-47562. 60p. 1976. pap. 50.00 (ISBN 0-88455-997-1). Microfilming Corp.

--Folk Art in America. (Illus.). 1979. pap. 7.95 (ISBN 0-8317-3412-4, Mayflower Bks). Smith Pubs.

--Genealogy & Local History: Guide to Part I. 173p. 1981. reference 50.00 (ISBN 0-667-00649-4). Microfilming Corp.

--Indian Rights Association Papers: A Guide to the Microfilm Edition, 1864-1973. 233p. 1975. pap. 50.00 (ISBN 0-88455-947-5). Microfilming Corp.

--Missionary Society of Connecticut Papers, 1759-1948: A Guide to the Microform Edition. 49p. 1976. pap. 15.00 (ISBN 0-667-00289-8). Microfilming Corp.

--Shaker Collection of the Western Reserve Historical Society. 77p. 1977. pap. 7.50 (ISBN 0-667-00522-6). Microfilming Corp.

--Students for a Democratic Society Papers, Nineteen Fifty-Eight to Nineteen Seventy: A Guide to the Microfilm Edition of the Original Records in the State Historical Society of Wisconsin. 82p. 1977. 17.50 (ISBN 0-667-00542-0). Microfilming Corp.

Ericson, Jack T. & Haggerty, Donald, eds. Robert R. Livingstone Papers, Sixteen Fifty-Eight to Eighteen Eighty-Eight: A Guide to the Microfiche Edition. 53p. 1980. pap. text ed. 30.00 (ISBN 0-667-00632-X). Microfilming Corp.

Ericson, Joe, ed. see Devereaux, Linda E.

Ericson, Joe E. Banks & Bankers in Early Texas: Eighteen Thirty-Five to Eighteen Seventy-Five. 1976. 15.00 (ISBN 0-686-20853-6). Polyanthos.

--Judges of the Republic of Texas, Eighteen Thirty-Six through Eighteen Forty-Six. (Illus.). 350p. 1980. 20.00 (ISBN 0-911317-04-X). Ericson Bks.

Ericson, Jon. Motion by Motion: A Commentary on Parlimentary Procedure. 130p. 1983. pap. text ed. 9.95x (ISBN 0-8290-1272-9). Irvington.

Ericson, Jonathan & Earle, Timothy, eds. Contexts for Prehistoric Exchange. (Studies in Archaelogy Ser.). 1982. 36.00 (ISBN 0-12-241580-9). Acad Pr.

Ericson, Jonathon E. & Purdy, Barbara A., eds. Prehistoric Quarries & Lithic Production. LC 83-18822. (New Directions in Archaeology Ser.). (Illus.). 170p. 1984. 39.50 (ISBN 0-521-25622-4). Cambridge U Pr.

Ericson, Jonathon E., et al, eds. Peopling of the New World. LC 81-22800. (Anthropological Papers: No. 23). (Illus.). 364p. 1982. 19.95 (ISBN 0-87919-095-7). Ballena Pr.

Ericson, Kay. The Solar Jobs Book. LC 80-17886. 220p. 1980. pap. 9.95 (ISBN 0-931790-12-3). Brick Hse Pub.

Ericson, Lennart, ed. see Ericson, Lois.

Ericson, Lois. Fabrics Reconstructed: A Collection of Surface Changes. Ericson, Lennart, ed. (Illus.). 175p. 1985. pap. 13.95 wkbk. (ISBN 0-911985-03-4). Eric's Pr.

Ericson, Lois & Frode, Diane E. Design & Sew It Yourself: A Workbook for Creative Clothing. rev. ed. (Illus.). 120p. 1983. pap. 14.95 (ISBN 0-911985-00-X). Eric's Pr.

Ericson, Maria, jt. auth. see Johnston, George.

Ericson, Mary J. Backyard Birddom. LC 66-19146. (Illus.). 1974. 2.95 (ISBN 0-87208-079-X); pap. 2.00 (ISBN 0-87208-010-2). Island Pr.

Ericson, Michael, ed. Scanner Master Metro D. C. - Baltimore Guide. (Scanner Master Frequency Guides Ser.: No. 6). (Illus.). 128p. 1984. 12.95 (ISBN 0-939430-05-3). Scanner Master.

Ericson, Nina. Klader: Creating Fantastic Clothes. (Illus.). 176p. 1984. pap. 17.95 (ISBN 0-937274-13-5, Dist. by Dodd, Mead). Lark Bks.

Ericson, Norman R., jt. auth. see Perry, Lloyd M.

Ericson, R. Cancer Treatment: What You Can Do. 3.95 (ISBN 0-9601644-1-3). Cancer Control Soc.

Ericson, R. F., ed. Improving the Human Condition, Quality & Stability in Social Systems: Proceedings, Silver Anniversary International Meeting, London, England, August 20-24, 1979. LC 79-66355. 1979. 89.00 (ISBN 0-387-90442-5). Springer-Verlag.

Ericson, Richard V. Reproducing Order: A Study of Police Patrol Work. (Canadian Studies in Criminology). 256p. 1982. 30.00x (ISBN 0-8020-5569-9); pap. 13.95 (ISBN 0-8020-6475-2). U of Toronto Pr.

Ericson, Richard V. & Baranek, Patricia M. The Ordering of Justice: A Study of Accused Persons as Defendants in the Criminal Process. (Canadian Studies in Criminology). 288p. 1982. 30.00x (ISBN 0-8020-2451-3); pap. 13.95 (ISBN 0-8020-6463-9). U of Toronto Pr.

Ericson, T. E., ed. Interaction of High-Energy Particles with Nuclei. (Italian Physical Society: Course 38). 1967. 70.00 (ISBN 0-12-368838-8). Acad Pr.

Ericson, Virginia, jt. auth. see Townsend, Sallie.

Ericsson, Henry. Sixty Years a Builder: The Autobiography of Henry Ericsson. LC 72-5046. (Technology & Society Ser.). (Illus.). 388p. 1972. Repr. of 1942 ed. 23.00 (ISBN 0-405-04698-7). Ayer Co Pubs.

Ericsson, K. Anders & Simon, Herbert A. Protocol Analysis: Verbal Reports as Data. 264p. 1984. 30.00x (ISBN 0-262-05029-3). MIT Pr.

--Protocol Analysis: Verbal Reports As Data. 440p. 1985. pap. text ed. 13.50x (ISBN 0-262-55012-1, Pub. by Bradford). MIT Pr.

Ericsson, Lars O. Justice in the Distribution of Economic Resources. (Stockholm Studies in Philosophy Ser.: No.6). (Illus.). 1976. pap. text ed. 21.00x (ISBN 91-22-00066-6). Humanities.

Ericsson, Mary K. A Ragusan Bride: Dubrovnik to San Francisco. LC 80-51686. 141p. 1981. perfect bound 10.00 (ISBN 0-918660-16-5). Ragusan Pr.

Ericsson, Ronald J., jt. auth. see Glass, Robert H.

Ericsson, T., ed. Computers in Materials Technology: Proceedings of the Conference Held in Linkoping, June 1980. 200p. 1981. 39.00 (ISBN 0-08-027570-2). Pergamon.

Ericsson, Y., ed. Progress in Caries Prevention: European Organization for Caries Research (ORCA) - 25th Anniversary. (Caries Research: Vol. 12, Suppl. 1). (Illus.). 1978. pap. 13.25 (ISBN 3-8055-2920-1). S Karger.

Ericsson, Y., jt. ed. see Gron, P.

Erie Society for Genealogical Research, Inc, ed. Erie County, Pennsylvania Naturalizations 1825-1906. LC 83-80629. 1983. 25.00 (ISBN 0-318-00767-3). Walsworth's.

Eriksen, Charles W. Behavior & Awareness: A Symposium of Research & Interpretation. LC 62-15952. pap. 41.50 (ISBN 0-317-20098-4, 2023378). Bks Demand UMI.

Eriksen, James A. Mother Raccoon & Family. (Illus.). 20p. 1978. pap. 2.95 (ISBN 0-915288-37-0). Shameless Hussy.

Eriksen, Peter, et al. Funen - the Heart of Denmark. Caie, Graham D. & Caie, Ann, trs. from Danish. (Denmark in Print & Pictures). (Illus.). 161p. 1980. 12.95 (ISBN 87-7429-032-0, Pub. by Det Danske Selskab Denmark). Nordic Bks.

Eriksen, Ronald G. How to Get I. D. in Canada. 2nd ed. LC 84-81635. (Illus.). 1984. pap. 7.95 (ISBN 0-915179-13-X). Loompanics.

Eriksen, Ronald G., II. Getaway: Driving Techniques for Evasion & Escape. 3nd ed. (Illus.). 1983. pap. 5.95 (ISBN 0-317-03304-2). Loompanics.

--How to Find Missing Persons: A Handbook for Investigators. rev. ed. 98p. 1984. pap. 9.95 (ISBN 0-915179-04-0). Loompanics.

Erikson, A. & Nylander, E., eds. Erik Benzelius' Letters to His Learned Friends. (Acta- Regiae Societatis Scientiarum et Litterarum Gothoburgensis HumaniorSer.: No. 22). 200p. 1983. pap. text ed. 23.50x (ISBN 91-85252-32-8, Pub. by Acta Universitas Sweden). Humanities.

Erikson, Erik H. Childhood & Society. 1964. (NortonC); pap. 3.95x (ISBN 0-393-09622-X). Norton.

--Dimensions of a New Identity. 1979. pap. 3.95 (ISBN 0-393-00923-8). Norton.

--Dimensions of a New Identity: Jefferson Lectures 1973. LC 73-22289. 125p. 1974. 10.95 (ISBN 0-393-05515-9). Norton.

--Gandhi's Truth: On the Origins of Militant Nonviolence. 1970. (Norton Lib); pap. 4.95 (ISBN 0-393-00741-3). Norton.

--Identity & the Life Cycle. LC 79-9750. 1980. 14.95x (ISBN 0-393-01246-8); pap. 4.95 (ISBN 0-393-00949-1). Norton.

--Identity & the Life Cycle: Selected Papers. (Psychological Issues Monograph: No. 1, Vol. 1, No. 1). 171p. (Orig.). 1967. 17.50 (ISBN 0-8236-2460-9). Intl Univs Pr.

--Identity: Youth & Crisis. 1968. pap. 5.95x (ISBN 0-393-09786-2). Norton.

--Insight & Responsibility. 1964. 14.95x (ISBN 0-393-01023-6, NortonC); pap. 7.95x (ISBN 0-393-09451-0). Norton.

--The Life Cycle Completed: A Review. 1982. 11.95 (ISBN 0-393-01622-6). Norton.

--The Life Cycle Completed: A Review. 1985. pap. 4.95 (ISBN 0-393-30229-6). Norton.

--Life History & the Historical Moment. 1975 14.95x, (ISBN 0-393-01103-8, N860). Norton.

--Young Man Luther. 1962. pap. 5.95 (ISBN 0-393-00170-9). Norton.

Erikson, Erik H. & Newton, Huey P. In Search of Common Ground. Erikson, Kai T., ed. 160p. 1973. 12.95 (ISBN 0-393-05483-7). Norton.

Erikson, Erik H., ed. Adulthood. 1978. pap. 9.95x (ISBN 0-393-09086-8). Norton.

Erikson, Erik H., jt. ed. see Smelser, Neil J.

Erikson, George, ed. see Baskower, Pat & Williams, Joanne.

Erikson, George, ed. see Grey, Zane.

Erikson, Jeffrey & Richards, Susan. Hey, Let's Play with the 64! (Learn Together Ser.). 128p. (gr. 4-6). 1984. pap. 19.95 (ISBN 0-88693-070-7). Banbury Bks.

Erikson, Joan M. Saint Francis & His Four Ladies. LC 71-127178. (Illus.). 1970. 6.95 (ISBN 0-393-05427-6). Norton.

--Universal Bead. LC 68-20819. (Illus.). 1969. 13.95 (ISBN 0-393-04233-2). Norton.

Erikson, Joan M., et al. Activity, Recovery, Growth: The Communal Role of Planned Activities. (Illus.). 1976. 10.95 (ISBN 0-393-01126-7, Norton Lib); pap. 4.95 (ISBN 0-393-00886-X). U of NC Pr.

Erikson, Kai T. Everything in Its Path. 1978. pap. 8.95 (ISBN 0-671-24067-6, Touchstone Bks). S&S.

--Wayward Puritans: A Study in the Sociology of Deviance. LC 66-16140. (Deviance & Criminology Ser.). 228p. 1968. pap. text ed. 14.95x (ISBN 0-471-24427-9). Wiley.

Erikson, Kai T., ed. see Erikson, Erik H. & Newton, Huey P.

Erikson, Kate, jt. auth. see Best, Joan.

Erikson, L. G., ed. An Analysing Account of the Conference on the African Refugee Problem. 234p. 1981. 25.00 (ISBN 0-317-07357-5). Transnatl Pubs.

Erikson, Lynn. A Woman of San Francisco. (A Woman's Destiny Ser.: No. 1). (Orig.). 1982. pap. 2.95 (ISBN 0-440-09845-9). Dell.

Erikson, Milton H. My Voice Will Go with You: The Teaching Tales of Milton H. Erikson, M. D. 1982. 18.95 (ISBN 0-393-01583-1). Norton.

Erikson, Paul. Beautiful Sinners. LC 82-81998. 384p. 1982. pap. 3.50 (ISBN 0-86721-185-7). Jove Pubns.

--The Dynast. 1982. pap. 2.95 (ISBN 0-425-05304-0). Berkley Pub.

Erikson, Robert S., et al. American Public Opinion: Its Origins, Content, & Impact. 2nd ed. LC 79-17806. 337p. 1980. pap. text ed. 15.00 (ISBN 0-471-03139-9). Wiley.

Eriksson. The Reformers: An Historical Survey of Pioneer Experiments in the Treatment of Criminals. 1976. 27.50 (ISBN 0-444-99030-5, ERE/, Pub. by Elsevier). Greenwood.

Eriksson & Furberg, eds. Swimming Medicine IV. (International Series on Sport Sciences). 1978. 39.50 (ISBN 0-8391-1214-9). Univ Park.

Eriksson, A., jt. auth. see Astroms, P.

Eriksson, A. W., et al, eds. Population Structure & Genetic Disorders: Proceedings of the 7th Sigfred Juselius Foundation Symposia. LC 80-40143. 1981. 132.00 (ISBN 0-12-241450-0). Acad Pr.

Eriksson, C. J., jt. ed. see Lindros, K. O.

Eriksson, Ejnar. Illustrated Handbook in Local Anaesthesia. 2nd ed. LC 79-65870. (Illus.). 159p. 1980. text ed. 45.00 (ISBN 0-7216-3399-4). Saunders.

Eriksson, Erik. Principles & Applications of Hydrochemistry. 200p. 1985. 37.00 (ISBN 0-412-25040-3, 9671). Methuen Inc.

Eriksson, Eva. Hocus Pocus. (Victor & Rosalie Bks.). (Illus.). 32p. (ps-3). 1985. PLB 7.95 (ISBN 0-87614-235-8). Carolrhoda Bks.

--Jealousy. (Victor & Rosalie Bks.). (Illus.). 32p. (ps-3). 1985. PLB 7.95 (ISBN 0-87614-237-4). Carolrhoda Bks.

--One Short Week. LC 84-17644. (Victor & Rosalie Bks.). (Illus.). 32p. (ps-3). 1985. PLB 7.95 (ISBN 0-87614-234-X). Carolrhoda Bks.

--The Tooth Trip. (Victor & Rosalie Bks.). (Illus.). 32p. (ps-3). 1985. PLB 7.95 (ISBN 0-87614-236-6). Carolrhoda Bks.

Eriksson, H. & Gustafsson, J. A. Steroid Hormone Receptors: Structure & Function. 1984. 96.25 (ISBN 0-444-80559-1, I-070-84). Elsevier.

Eriksson, K., jt. auth. see Forsander, O.

Eriksson, K., ed. see International Conference Held in Helsinki, June 4-8, 1979, et al.

Eriksson, L. G., ed. Analysing Account of Conference on the African Refugee Problem. Melander, G., et al. 233p. 1982. text ed. 32.50x (ISBN 0-8419-9741-1). Holmes & Meier.

Eriksson, Paul S. The Bird Finder's Three Year Notebook, 1985. rev. ed. LC 75-19198. (Illus.). 384p. 1984. plastic comb 12.95 (ISBN 0-8397-1029-1). Eriksson.

Eriksson, Paul S., jt. ed. see Krutch, Joseph W.

Erin, Jon, jt. auth. see Lanciano, Claude.

Eringen, A. C., ed. Recent Advances in Engineering Science, 5 Vols. (Orig.). 1967-69. Vol. 1, 878p. 166.50 (ISBN 0-677-10790-0); Vol. 2, 456p. 119.25 (ISBN 0-677-10800-1); Vol. 3, 568p. 131.95 (ISBN 0-677-11880-5); Vol. 4, 362p. 93.75 (ISBN 0-677-13100-3); Vol. 5, 862p., 2 pt. set. 198.75 (ISBN 0-677-13780-X). Gordon.

Eringen, A. Cemal. Mechanics of Continua. 2nd ed. LC 78-2334. 608p. 1980. lib. bdg. 42.50 (ISBN 0-88275-663-X). Krieger.

Eringen, A. Cemal & Suhubi, Erdogan S. Elastodynamics. 1974. Vol. 1. 1974. 78.00 (ISBN 0-12-240601-X); Vol. 2. 1975. 119.50 (ISBN 0-12-240602-8). Acad Pr.

Eringen, A. Cemal, ed. Continuum Physics, 4 vols. 1971. Vol. 1. 1971. 89.00 (ISBN 0-12-240801-2); Vol. 2. 1975. 94.50 (ISBN 0-12-240802-0); Vol. 3. 1976. 74.50 (ISBN 0-12-240803-9); Vol. 4. 1976. 77.50 (ISBN 0-12-240804-7). Acad Pr.

Eringer, Robert. Strike for Freedom! The Story of Lech Walesa & Polish Solidarity. LC 82-12978. 320p. 1982. 11.95 (ISBN 0-396-08065-0). Dodd.

Erisman, A. M., et al, eds. Electric Power Problems: The Mathematical Challenge. LC 80-54282. xix, 531p. 1981. text ed. 41.00 (ISBN 0-89871-173-8). Soc Indus-Appl Math.

Erisman, Fred. Frederic Remington. LC 75-7009. (Western Writers Ser.: No. 16). (Illus., Orig.). 1975. pap. text ed. 2.00x (ISBN 0-88430-015-3). Boise St Univ.

Erisman, Fred & Etulain, Richard W., eds. Fifty Western Writers: A Bio-Bibliographical Sourcebook. LC 81-13462. xiv, 562p. 1982. lib. bdg. 45.00 (ISBN 0-313-22167-7, EWW/). Greenwood.

Erisman, H. Michael. Cuba's International Relations: The Anatomy of a Nationalistic Foreign Policy. (Westview Special Study on Latin America & the Caribbean). 220p. 1985. 34.00x (ISBN 0-8133-0042-8); pap. text ed. 13.95x (ISBN 0-8133-0043-6). Westview.

Erisman, H. Michael, ed. The Caribbean Challenge: U. S. Policy in a Volatile Region. LC 83-10515. (Latin American & the Caribbean Special Studies). 195p. 1983. lib. bdg. 24.00x (ISBN 0-86531-527-2); pap. text ed. 10.95x (ISBN 0-86531-528-0). Westview.

Erisman, Michael & Martz, John D. Colossus Challenged: The Struggle for Caribbean Influence. LC 82-60034. (WVSS on Latin America & the Caribbean). 262p. 1982. 19.50x (ISBN 0-86531-362-8). Westview.

Er-Jin, Chen. China: Crossroads Socialism. Munro, Robin, tr. from Chinese. 192p. 1983. 25.50 (ISBN 0-8052-7158-9, Pub. by NLB England); pap. 10.95 (ISBN 0-8052-7180-5). Schocken.

Erk, Rien Van see Van Erk, Rien.

Erkkila, Barbara H. Hammers on Stone: The History of Cape Ann Granite. LC 80-54367. (Illus.). 208p. 1981. 18.95 (ISBN 0-931474-19-1). TBW Bks.

Erkkila, Betsy. Walt Whitman Among the French: Poet & Myth. LC 79-3204. 1980. 26.00x (ISBN 0-691-06426-1). Princeton U Pr.

Erlande, Albert. The Life of John Keats. 1929. lib. bdg. 45.00 (ISBN 0-8414-3990-7). Folcroft.

Erlander, S. Optimal Spatial Interaction & the Gravity Model. (Lecture Notes in Economics & Mathematical Systems Ser.: Vol. 173). (Illus.). 107p. 1980. pap. 15.00 (ISBN 0-387-09729-5). Springer-Verlag.

Erlandsen, Stanley L. & Meyer, Ernest A., eds. Giardia & Giardiasis: Biology, Pathogenesis & Epidemiology. 435p. 1984. 65.00x (ISBN 0-306-41539-9, Plenum Pr). Plenum Pub.

Erlandson. Diagnostic Transmission Electron Miscroscopy of Human Tumors: The Interpretation of Submicroscopic Structures in Neoplastic Cells. LC 81-11717. (Masson Monographs in Diagnostic Pathology: Vol. 3). (Illus.). 208p. 1981. 49.50x (ISBN 0-89352-138-8). Masson Pub.

Erlandson, Becker. Church Fellowship. 1980. 0.80 (ISBN 0-8100-0113-6, 15N0373). Northwest Pub.

Erlanger, B. F., jt. ed. see Montagnoli, G.

Erlanger, Ellen. Jane Fonda: More Than a Movie Star. LC 83-27542. (The Achievers Ser.). (Illus.). (gr. 4-9). 1984. PLB 6.95 (ISBN 0-8225-0485-5). Lerner Pubns.

Erlanger, George C. International Monetary Chaos & a Positive Plan for the Monetary Reconstruction of the World. (Illus.). 141p. 1985. 117.45 (ISBN 0-86654-167-5). Inst Econ Finan.

Erlanger, Phillipe. Margaret of Anjou: Queen of England. Hyams, Edward, tr. LC 79-161438. (Illus.). 251p. 1970. 9.95x (ISBN 0-87024-214-8). U of Miami Pr.

Erlen, Jonathon. The History of the Health Care Sciences, 1700 to the Present: An Annotated Bibliography. Multhauf, Robert & Wells, Ellen, eds. LC 82-49187. (Bibliographies of the History of Science & Technology Ser.). 1000p. 1984. lib. bdg. 100.00 (ISBN 0-8240-9166-3). Garland Pub.

Erlenmeyer-Kimling, L., et al, eds. Life Span Research on the Prediction of Psychopathology. 336p. 1985. text ed. 36.00 (ISBN 0-89859-587-8). L Erlbaum Assocs.

Erler, Bob & Souter, John C. Catch Me Killer. 1981. 3.50 (ISBN 0-8423-0214-X). Tyndale.

Erler, Fritz. Democracy in Germany. LC 65-16683. (Center for International Affairs Ser). 1965. 8.95x (ISBN 0-674-19700-3). Harvard U Pr.

Erlewine, Michael. Astrophysical Directions. 140p. 1977. 12.00 (ISBN 0-86690-097-7, 1104-03). Am Fed Astrologers.

--Manual of Computer Programming for Astrologers. 224p. 1980. 13.95 (ISBN 0-86690-099-3, 1184-03). Am Fed Astrologers.

Erley, Duncan & Mosena, David. Energy-Conserving Development Regulations: Current Practice. (PAS Reports: No. 7352). 58p. 1980. 12.00 (ISBN 0-318-12968-X); members 6.00 (ISBN 0-318-12969-8). Am Plan Assn.

Erlich. Geomicrobiology. 1981. 39.75 (ISBN 0-8247-1183-1). Dekker.

Erlich, et al. Business Administration for the Medical Assistant. 2nd ed. LC 81-67045. (Illus.). 1983. 10.95 (ISBN 0-940012-01-4). Colwell Syst.

Erlich, Ann. The Role of Computers in Dental Practice Management. LC 81-67044. (Illus.). 8.95 (ISBN 0-940012-00-6). Colwell Syst.

--Role of Computers in Medical Practice Management. LC 81-69069. (Illus.). 8.95 (ISBN 0-940012-18-9). Colwell Syst.

Erlich, Anne H., jt. auth. see Ehrlich, Paul.

Erlich, Avi. Hamlet's Absent Father. LC 77-9420. 1977. text ed. 32.00 (ISBN 0-691-06340-0). Princeton U Pr.

Erlich, Gloria C. Family Themes & Hawthorne's Fiction: The Tenacious Web. 190p. 1984. text ed. 22.50 (ISBN 0-8135-1028-7). Rutgers U Pr.

Erlich, Haggai. Ethiopia & the Challenge of Inpendence. 270p. 1986. lib. bdg. 30.00x (ISBN 0-931477-48-4). Lynne Rienner.

--The Struggle Over Eritrea, 1962-1978: War & Revolution in the Horn of Africa. (Publication Ser.: No. 260). 176p. 1982. pap. 10.95 (ISBN 0-8179-7602-7). Hoover Inst Pr.

Erlich, Henry, et al. Molecular Biology of Rifomycin. 182p. 1973. text ed. 28.50x (ISBN 0-8422-7089-2). Irvington.

Erlich, Lillian. Money Isn't Important: The Life of Maurice Gusman. LC 76-14508. (Illus.). 176p. 1976. 9.95 (ISBN 0-912458-76-3). E A Seemann.

Erlich, Melville, ed. Lubricating Grease Guide. LC 84-61641. (Illus.). 140p. (Orig.). 1984. pap. 10.00 (ISBN 0-9613935-0-5). Natl Lubrica Grease.

Erlich, Richard D. & Dunn, Thomas P., eds. Clockwork Worlds: Mechanized Environments in SF. LC 82-1718. (Contributions to the Study of Science Fiction & Fantasy Ser.: No. 7). xii, 369p. 1983. lib. bdg. 35.00 (ISBN 0-313-23026-9, DCW/). Greenwood.

Erlich, Richard D., jt. ed. see Dunn, Thomas P.

Erlich, Sara R. The Times of the Acacias on the Way to Schechinah. 1983. 7.95 (ISBN 0-533-05611-X). Vantage.

Erlich, Victor. Russian Formalism: History-Doctrine. 2nd ed. (Slavistic Printings & Reprintings Ser: No. 4). 1965. text ed. 23.60x (ISBN 90-2790-450-2). Mouton.

--Russian Formalism: History-Doctrine. 3rd ed. 1981. pap. 10.95x (ISBN 0-300-02635-8, Y-397). Yale U Pr.

Erlich, Victor, et al, eds. For Wiktor Weintraub: Essays in Polish Literature, Language, and History Presented on the Occassion of His 65th Birthday. new ed. (Slavistic Printings & Reprintings Ser: No. 312). 621p. 1975. text ed. 86.00x (ISBN 90-2793-346-4). Mouton.

Erlich, Y. H., et al, eds. Modulators, Mediators, & Specifiers in Brain Function. LC 79-14523. (Advances in Experimental Medicine & Biology Ser.: Vol. 116). 343p. 1979. 49.50x (ISBN 0-306-40173-8, Plenum Pr). Plenum Pub.

Erlingsson, Thorsteinn. Ruins of the Saga Time. LC 76-43951. (Viking Society for Northern Research, Extra Ser.: No. 2). (Illus.). 120p. Repr. of 1899 ed. 30.00 (ISBN 0-404-60022-0). AMS Pr.

Erlitz, Jon. Turning Back the Clock in Federal Housing Policy: The Impact on Poor Families of the Recommendations of the Presidential Commission on Housing. 1982. pap. 1.50 (ISBN 0-318-00896-3). Comm Serv Soc NY.

Ermakov, jt. auth. see Schepin.

Ermakov, I. D. Etiudy Po Psikhologii Tvorchestva Pushkina. (Rus.). 1981. 15.00 (ISBN 0-88233-500-6); pap. 5.00 (ISBN 0-88233-501-4). Ardis Pubs.

Erman. Chemistry of the Monoterpenes: An Encyclopedia Handbook, Pt. A. (Studies in Organic Chemistry). 720p. 1985. 145.00 (ISBN 0-8247-1573-X). Dekker.

--Chemistry of the Monoterpenes: An Encyclopedia Handbook, Pt. B. (Studies in Oraganic Chemistry). 624p. 1985. 145.00 (ISBN 0-8247-7312-8). Dekker.

Erman, Adolf. A Handbook of Egyptian Religions. LC 76-27517. (Illus.). 1976. Repr. of 1907 ed. lib. bdg. 30.00 (ISBN 0-89341-032-2). Longwood Pub Group.

--Life in Ancient Egypt. Tirard, H. M., tr. (Illus.). pap. 7.95 (ISBN 0-486-22632-8). Dover.

Erman, Adolf, ed. Ancient Egyptians: A Source Book of Their Writings. 13.25 (ISBN 0-8446-2036-X). Peter Smith.

Erman, Adolph. Life in Ancient Egypt. LC 68-56523. (Illus.). Repr. of 1894 ed. 25.00 (ISBN 0-405-08488-9, Blom Pubns). Ayer Co Pubs.

--Life in Ancient Egypt. 16.75 (ISBN 0-8446-0090-3). Peter Smith.

--Literature of the Ancient Egyptians. LC 68-56522. Repr. of 1927 ed. 20.00 (ISBN 0-405-08489-7, Blom Pubns). Ayer Co Pubs.

--Travels in Siberia: Including Excursions Northwards, Down the Obi, to the Polar Circle, & Southwards, to the Chinese Frontier. LC 70-115535. (Russia Observed, Ser., No. 1). 1970. Repr. of 1848 ed. 51.00 (ISBN 0-405-03025-8). Ayer Co Pubs.

Ermann, M. David & Lundman, Richard J. Corporate Deviance. LC 81-6849. 198p. 1982. pap. text ed. 16.95 (ISBN 0-03-044386-5). HR&W.

Ermann, M. David & Lundman, Richard J., eds. Corporate & Governmental Deviance: Problems of Organizational Behavior in Contemporary Society. 2nd ed. 1982. pap. text ed. 8.95x (ISBN 0-19-503036-2). Oxford U Pr.

Ermans, A. M. & Mbulamonko, N. M. The Role of Cassava in the Etiology of Endemic Goitre & Cretinism. 182p. 1980. pap. 13.00 (ISBN 0-88936-220-3, IDRC136, IDRC). Unipub.

Ermarth, Elizabeth. Realism & Consensus in the English Novel. LC 82-61360. 304p. 1983. 26.50x (ISBN 0-691-06560-8). Princeton U Pr.

Ermarth, Elizabeth D. George Eliot, No. 414. (Twayne English Author Ser.). 180p. (Orig.). 1985. lib. bdg. 14.95 (ISBN 0-8057-6910-2, Twayne). G K Hall.

Ermarth, Michael. Wilhelm Dilthey: The Critique of Historical Reason. 11.00x (ISBN 0-226-21743-4). U of Chicago Pr.

Ermentrout, Robert A. Forgotten Men: The Civilian Conservation Corps. 112p. 1982. 6.50 (ISBN 0-682-49805-X). Exposition Pr FL.

Ermisch, John. The Political Economy of Demographic Change. (Policy Studies Institute Ser.). xiv, 317p. 1983. text ed. 60.00x (ISBN 0-435-83230-1). Gower Pub Co.

Ermler, W. C. see Mulliken, Robert S.

Ermler, W. C., jt. ed. see Mulliken, Robert.

Ermolaev, Herman. Mikhail Sholokhov & His Art. LC 81-47123. (Illus.). 460p. 1982. 32.00 (ISBN 0-691-07634-0). Princeton U Pr.

--Soviet Literary Theories 1917-1934: The Genesis of Socialist Realism. 1977. Repr. of 1963 ed. lib. bdg. 20.00x (ISBN 0-374-92625-5). Octagon.

Ermoyan, Arpi, ed. The Society of Illustrators Twenty Seventh Annual Exhibition of American Illustration. (Illus.). 440p. 1986. 49.95 (ISBN 0-942604-09-1). Madison Square.

Ern, Melissa, ed. Programmed Instruction: Leukemia. (Illus.). 72p. 1984. pap. text ed. 7.50 (ISBN 0-89352-221-X). Masson Pub.

Ernenwein, Leslie. Ambush at Jubilo Junction. 1976. pap. 0.95 (ISBN 0-685-69142-X, LB361, Leisure Bks). Dorchester Pub Co.

--Give a Man a Gun. 1975. pap. 0.95 (ISBN 0-685-52175-3, LB239NK, Leisure Bks). Dorchester Pub Co.

--Gun Hawk. 1979. pap. 1.50 (ISBN 0-8439-0621-9, Leisure Bks). Dorchester Pub Co.

--Rebel Yell. 1979. pap. 1.25 (ISBN 0-505-51358-7, Pub. by Tower Bks). Dorchester Pub Co.

--Renegade Ramrod. 1976. pap. 0.95 (ISBN 0-685-64016-7, LB345, Leisure Bks). Dorchester Pub Co.

--Trigger Justice. 1977. pap. 1.25 (ISBN 0-8439-0447-X, Leisure Bks). Dorchester Pub Co.

--The Way They Died. 1978. pap. 1.50 (ISBN 0-505-51275-0, Pub. by Tower Bks). Dorchester Pub Co.

Ernest. Year Book of Ophthalmology, 1984. 1984. 44.95 (ISBN 0-8151-3138-0). Year Bk Med.

Ernest & Whinney, eds. The Taxation Aspects of Acquisitions & Mergers of Corporations. 192p. 1980. pap. 34.00 (ISBN 90-2000-629-0, Pub. by Kluwer Law Netherlands). Kluwer Academic.

Ernest, et al. Effective Marketing for Motor Carriers: Planning for Improved Profitability. 173p. 1984. text ed. 50.00 (ISBN 0-88711-071-1). Am Trucking Assns.

Ernest, Charlotte, jt. auth. see Ernest, John.

Ernest, J. T., ed. Year Book of Ophthalmology, 1982. (Illus.). 385p. 1982. 44.95 (ISBN 0-8151-3136-4). Year Bk Med.

--Year Book of Ophthalmology, 1983. 1983. 44.95 (ISBN 0-8151-3137-2). Year Bk Med.

Ernest, John. Charting the Operator Terrain. LC 76-3583. (Memoirs: No. 171). 207p. 1976. pap. 16.00 (ISBN 0-8218-1871-6, MEMO-171). Am Math.

Ernest, John & Ashmun, Richard. Selling Principles & Practices. 5th ed. LC 79-17748. (Illus.). 1980. text ed. 17.28 (ISBN 0-07-019620-6). McGraw.

Ernest, John & Ernest, Charlotte. Basic Business Mathematics. 1977. text ed. write for info. (ISBN 0-02-472610-9). Macmillan.

Ernest, John, jt. auth. see Haas, Kenneth B.

Ernest, Maurice. Everyday Chronic Maladies. 1974. lib. bdg. 69.95 (ISBN 0-685-51368-8). Revisionist Pr.

Ernest, P. Edward, ed. Family Album of Favorite Poems. (Illus.). (gr. 7-9). 1959. 12.95 (ISBN 0-399-12932-4, G&D). Putnam Pub Group.

Ernest, Verleigh. Typing. college ed. LC 72-142516. 1971. pap. 15.12 scp (ISBN 0-672-96002-8); tchrs' manual o.p. 7.95 (ISBN 0-672-96003-6); wkbk. o.p. 11.50 (ISBN 0-672-96004-4). Bobbs.

Ernest Wittenberg Associates. The Ernest Wittenberg Guide to Winning in Washington. 240p. 1986. 29.95 (ISBN 0-88730-029-4); pap. 12.95x (ISBN 0-88730-030-8). Ballinger Pub.

Ernesti, J. H. Enzyklopaedisches Handbuch Elner Allgemeineu Geschichte der Philosophie und Ihrer Literatur. (Ger.). 86.00 (ISBN 3-87784-016-7, M-7083). French & Eur.

Ernest-Moriarty, Sandra B. The ABC'S of Typography: A Practical Guide to the Art & Science of Typography. rev. ed. LC 77-80333. 188p. 1984. text ed. 12.50 (ISBN 0-317-14819-2); pap. text ed. 8.95 (ISBN 0-317-14820-6). Art Dir.

Ernestus, Horst & Plassman, Engelbert. Libraries in the Federal Republic of Germany. 2nd ed. Andrews, John S., tr. from Ger. (Illus.). xiv, 288p. pap. text ed. 25.00x (2341-H). ALA.

Erney, Richard A. The Public Life of Henry Dearborn. Kohn, Richard H., ed. LC 78-22419. (American Military of Experience Ser.). 1979. lib. bdg. 27.50x (ISBN 0-405-11893-7). Ayer Co Pubs.

Erney, Tom, jt. auth. see Myrick, Robert D.

Ernle, Rowland E. Light Reading of Our Ancestors. facs. ed. LC 73-124234. (Select Bibliographies Reprint Ser). 1927. 17.00 (ISBN 0-8369-5422-X). Ayer Co Pubs.

Erno, N. & Janos, K. Magyor-Angol Muszaki Szotar: Hungarian-English Technical Dictionary. 752p. (Hungarian & Eng.). 1957. 95.00 (ISBN 963-05-0607-6, M-9359). French & Eur.

Ernotte, Andre & Tiber, Elliott. High Street. 1977. pap. 1.50 (ISBN 0-380-00927-7, 31898). Avon.

Ernst. Aged Patient: Source Book Allied Health Professional. 1982. 32.95 (ISBN 0-8151-3133-X). Year Bk Med.

Ernst & Whinney, eds. The Fourth Directive. 1979. lib. bdg. 60.00 (ISBN 0-903393-46-8). Kluwer Academic.

Ernst, Alice H. Trouping in the Oregon Country. LC 74-15552. (Illus.). 197p. 1974. Repr. of 1961 ed. lib. bdg. 24.75x (ISBN 0-8371-7821-5, EROC). Greenwood.

Ernst & Whinney & Cleveland Consulting Associates. Transportation Accounting & Control: Guidelines for Distribution Management. 1983. non-members 50.00 (ISBN 0-86641-092-9); members 25.00. Natl Coun Phys Dist.

--Warehouse Accounting & Control: Guidelines for Distribution & Financial Managers. 1985. 50:00 (ISBN 0-318-03941-9); members 25.00 (ISBN 0-318-03942-7). Natl Coun Phys Dist.

Ernst & Whinney, jt. auth. see Cox, David B.

Ernst, Barbara, jt. auth. see Blake, Jim.

Ernst, Bernard, jt. auth. see Waite, Malden D.

Ernst, Bernard M. & Carrington, Hereward. Houdini & Conan Doyle: The Story of a Strange Friendship. LC 72-174861. Repr. of 1933 ed. 16.00 (ISBN 0-405-08490-0, Blom Pubns). Ayer Co Pubs.

Ernst, Bruno. The Magic Mirror of M. C. Escher. (Illus.). 1977. pap. 10.95 (ISBN 0-345-24243-2). Ballantine.

Ernst, C. & Angst, J. Birth Order: Its Influence on Personality. (Illus.). 340p. 1983. 32.00 (ISBN 0-387-11248-0). Springer-Verlag.

Ernst, Carl H. & Barbour, Roger W. Turtles of the United States. LC 72-81315. (Illus.). 384p. 1972. 45.00x (ISBN 0-8131-1272-9). U Pr of KY.

Ernst, Carl W. Postal Service in Boston, 1639-1893. 1975. 3.00 (ISBN 0-89073-004-0). Boston Public Lib.

--Words of Ecstasy in Sufism. (SUNY Series in Islam). 230p. 1985. lib. bdg. 34.50x (ISBN 0-87395-917-5); pap. text ed. 12.95x (ISBN 0-87395-918-3). State U NY Pr.

Ernst, David. The Evolution of Electronic Music. LC 76-41624. (Illus.). 1977. pap. text ed. 14.95 (ISBN 0-02-870880-6). Schirmer Bks.

Ernst, Dieter, ed. The New International Divison of Labour, Technology & Underdevelopment: Consequences for the Third World. 646p. 1982. text ed. 48.50x (ISBN 3-593-32644-2). Irvington.
Ernst, E., et al. A Bibliography of Termite Literature: 1966-1978. 1985. write for info. (ISBN 0-471-90466-X). Wiley.
Ernst, Earle. The Kabuki Theatre. (Illus.). 323p. 1974. pap. text ed. 5.95x (ISBN 0-8248-0319-1, Eastwest Ctr). UH Pr.
Ernst, Earle, jt. auth. see Haar, Francis.
Ernst, Earle, ed. Three Japanese Plays from the Traditional Theatre. LC 75-31473. (Illus.). 200p. 1976. Repr. of 1959 ed. lib. bdg. 22.50x (ISBN 0-8371-8532-7, ERTJ). Greenwood.
Ernst, Edgar. Fahrplanerstellung und Umlaufdisposition Im Containerschiffsverkehr. (European University Studies Ser.: No. 5, Vol. 377). 136p. (Ger.). 1982. 16.30 (ISBN 3-8204-5822-0). P Lang Pubs.
Ernst, Eldon. Moment of Truth for Protestant America: Interchurch Campaigns Following World War I. LC 74-16567. (American Academy of Religion. Dissertation Ser.). 1974. pap. 9.95 (ISBN 0-88420-120-1, 010103). Scholars Pr GA.
Ernst, Ervin. International Commodity Agreements. 1982. lib. bdg. 29.00 (ISBN 90-247-2648-4, Pub. by Martinus Nijhoff Netherlands). Kluwer Academic.
Ernst, F., ed. see Simenon, Georges.
Ernst, Franklin H., Jr. Alienation & Invalidation. 1981. pap. 7.50x (ISBN 0-916944-28-X). Addresso'set.
--Bad Guys & Psychological Racketeers. 1982. pap. 17.00x (ISBN 0-916944-25-5). Addresso'set.
--Defining Games, Game Moves & Payoff in Transactional Analysis: Psychological Rackets. 1981. pap. 7.50x (ISBN 0-916944-30-1). Addresso'set.
--The Game Diagram. 1972. pap. 4.95x (ISBN 0-916944-19-0). Addresso'set.
--Get-on-with, Getting Well & Get Winners. 3rd ed. 1974. softbound 3.95x (ISBN 0-916944-00-X). Addresso'set.
--Leaving Your Mark. 2nd ed. 1973. softbound 4.95x (ISBN 0-916944-05-0). Addresso'set.
--The Moves of the Games People Play. 1981. pap. 9.50 (ISBN 0-916944-32-8). Addresso'set.
--Outline of the Activity of Listening. 3rd ed. 1973. softbound 3.95x (ISBN 0-916944-09-3). Addresso'set.
--Psychological Rackets & the Racket Diagram. 1981. pap. 9.50 (ISBN 0-916944-34-4). Addresso'set.
--Transactional Analysis in Psychobiology: From Prince to Frog to Principle. 1981. pap. 9.50 (ISBN 0-916944-36-0). Addresso'set.
--Who's Listening - Handbook of the Listening Activity. LC 73-84380. 1973. 15.95x (ISBN 0-916944-15-8). Addresso'set.
Ernst, Frederic. New French Self-Taught. 390p. (Fr.). 1982. pap. text ed. 4.76i (ISBN 0-06-463614-3, EH 614). B&N NY.
Ernst, Frederic & Bashour, Dora. New French Self-Taught. 1982. pap. 4.76i (ISBN 0-06-463614-3, EH-614). Har-Row.
Ernst, George. New England Miniature: A History of York, Maine. LC 61-14421. 1961. 10.00 (ISBN 0-87027-063-X). Cumberland Pr.
Ernst, George A., tr. see Gaboriau, Emile.
Ernst, George C., et al. Principles of Structural Equilibrium: A Study of Equilibrium Conditions by Graphic, Force-Moment & Virtual Displacement. LC 62-7876. pap. 42.50 (ISBN 0-317-10687-2, 2001977). Bks Demand UMI.
Ernst, George W. & Newell, Allen. G. P. S. A Case Study in Generality & Problem Solving. (ACM Monograph Ser). 1969. 70.00 (ISBN 0-12-241050-5). Acad Pr.
Ernst, George W., jt. auth. see Pao, Yoh-Han.
Ernst, I. & Ernst von Morgenstern, F. Woerterbuch der Chemie, Vol. 1. 891p. (Eng. & Ger., English-German Dictionary of Chemistry). 36.00 (ISBN 3-87097-011-1, M-7037). French & Eur.
--Woerterbuch der Chemie, Vol. 2. 892p. (Eng. & Ger., English-German Dictionary of Chemistry). 44.00 (ISBN 3-87097-012-X, M-7036). French & Eur.
Ernst, J. Escape King: The Story of Harry Houdini. (Illus.). (gr. 3-7). 1975. pap. 1.50 (ISBN 0-13-283424-3). P-H.
Ernst, James E. Roger Williams: New England Firebrand. LC 76-90097. (BCL Ser.: I). Repr. of 1932 ed. 24.50 (ISBN 0-404-02355-X). AMS Pr.
Ernst, Jimmy. A Not-So-Still Life: A Child of Europe's Pre-World War II Art World & His Remarkable Homecoming to America. 1983. 14.95 (ISBN 0-312-57955-1, Pub. by Marek). St Martin.
--A Not-So-Still Life: A Child of Europe's Pre-World War II Art World & His Remarkable Homecoming to America. (Illus.). 288p. 1985. pap. 8.95 (ISBN 0-312-57956-X, Pub. by Marek). St Martin.
Ernst, John. Jesse James. LC 76-10206. (Illus.). (gr. 4-7). 1976. PLB 9.95 (ISBN 0-13-509695-2); pap. 1.95 (ISBN 0-13-509661-8). P-H.
--Sadhana in Our Daily Lives: A Handbook for the Awakening of the Spiritual Self. LC 81-51360. 320p. (Orig.). 1981. pap. 9.95 (ISBN 0-9606482-0-8). Valley Lights.
Ernst, John F., jt. auth. see Porter, Stuart R.
Ernst, John F., ed. see Porter, Stuart R.
Ernst, Joseph W. With Compass & Chain. Bruchey, Stuart, ed. LC 78-56727. (Management of Public Lands in the U. S. Ser.). 1979. lib. bdg. 28.50x (ISBN 0-405-11331-5). Ayer Co Pubs.
Ernst, Kathryn. Charlie's Pets. LC 77-15656. (Illus.). (gr. k-3). 1978. PLB 4.95 reinforced (ISBN 0-517-52999-8). Crown.
--ESP McGee & The Mysterious Magician. 96p. (gr. 2-6). 1983. pap. 2.25 (ISBN 0-380-84079-0, 84079-9, Camelot). Avon.
Ernst, Kathryn F. Danny & His Thumb. (Illus.). (ps-3). 1973. (Pub. by Treehouse); pap. 3.95 (ISBN 0-13-196808-4). P-H.
Ernst, Ken. Games Students Play: And What to Do About Them. LC 72-86578. (Illus.). 128p. 1972. pap. 5.95 (ISBN 0-912310-16-2). Celestial Arts.
Ernst, Klaus. Tradition & Progress in the African Village: Non-Capitalist Reform of Rural Communities in Mali - The Sociological Problems. LC 74-22292. 350p. 1977. 32.50x (ISBN 0-312-81235-3). St Martin.
Ernst, Lisa C. The Prize Pig Surprise. LC 83-26760. (Illus.). 32p. (ps-2). 1984. 10.25 (ISBN 0-688-03797-6); lib. bdg. 9.55 (ISBN 0-688-03798-4). Lothrop.
--Sam Johnson & the Blue Ribbon Quilt. LC 82-9980. (Illus.). 32p. (gr. k-3). 1983. 11.75 (ISBN 0-688-01516-6); lib. bdg. 11.88 (ISBN 0-688-01517-4). Lothrop.
Ernst, M. & Steigert, W. Programming with Assembler Language ASS 300. 316p. 1980. 41.95 (ISBN 0-471-25671-4, Wiley Heyden). Wiley.
Ernst, M. L. The First Freedom. LC 73-166324. (Civil Liberties in American History Ser.). 316p. 1971. Repr. of 1946 ed. lib. bdg. 39.50 (ISBN 0-306-70242-8). Da Capo.
Ernst, M. L. & Lindey, A. The Censor Marches on. LC 73-164512. (Civil Liberties in American History Ser.). 346p. 1971. Repr. of 1940 ed. lib. bdg. 39.50 (ISBN 0-306-70295-9). Da Capo.
Ernst, M. L. & Seagle, W. To the Pure: A Study of Obscenity & the Censor. LC 28-30424. 1928. 21.00 (ISBN 0-527-27650-2). Kraus Repr.
Ernst, Mark R. & Kronser, Christopher F. The Denver Pneus: Federal Office Facility. (Illus.). iii, 33p. 1978. 4.00 (ISBN 0-938744-09-7, R78-1). U of Wis Ctr Arch-Urban.
Ernst, Mary O. A Guide Through the Dissertation Process. LC 81-22301. 56p. 1982. pap. 9.95x (ISBN 0-88946-626-2). E Mellen.
Ernst, Max. Beyond Painting: And Other Writings by the Artist & His Friends. LC 83-45752. Repr. of 1948 ed. 57.50 (ISBN 0-404-20090-7). AMS Pr.
--The Hundred Headless Woman. bi-lingual ed. Tanning, Dorothea, tr. from Fr. LC 81-67737. Orig. Title: La Femme 100 Tetes. (Illus.). 325p. 1981. 30.00 (ISBN 0-8076-1023-2); pap. 14.95 (ISBN 0-8076-1024-0). Braziller.
--A Little Girl Dreams of Taking the Veil. Tanning, Dorothea, tr. from Fr. LC 82-9700. Orig. Title: Reve d'une petite fille qui voulut entrer au Carmel. (Illus.). 176p. (Bilingual ed.). 1982. 30.00 (ISBN 0-8076-1051-8); pap. 14.95 (ISBN 0-8076-1052-6). Braziller.
--Une Semaine De Bonte: A Surrealistic Novel in Collage. 2nd ed. LC 75-17362. (Illus.). 224p. 1976. pap. 6.95 (ISBN 0-486-23252-2). Dover.
--Une Semaine De Bonte: A Surrealistic Novel in Collage. 15.50 (ISBN 0-8446-5454-X). Peter Smith.
Ernst, Morris & Lorentz, Pare. Censored: The Private Life of the Movies. LC 72-160230. (Moving Pictures Ser). xvi, 199p. 1971. Repr. of 1930 ed. lib. bdg. 13.95x (ISBN 0-89198-031-8). Ozer.
Ernst, Morris & Loth, David. People Know Best. 1949. 4.50 (ISBN 0-8183-0225-9). Pub Aff Pr.
Ernst, Morris L. & Schwartz, Alan U. Censorship. 1964. 6.95 (ISBN 0-685-14842-4). Macmillan.
--Privacy: The Right to Be Let Alone. LC 77-10983. (Milestones of Law Ser.). 1977. Repr. of 1962 ed. lib. bdg. 22.50x (ISBN 0-8371-9805-4, ERPR). Greenwood.
Ernst, Nora S. & West, Helen L. Nursing Home Staff Development: A Guide for Inservice Programs. 144p. 1983. text ed. 15.95 (ISBN 0-8261-3860-8). Springer Pub.
Ernst, R. Dictionary of Chemical Terms, 2 vols. Vol. 1, Ger-Eng. 33.70x (ISBN 3-8709-7011-1); Vol. 2, Eng-Ger. 41.20x (ISBN 3-8709-7012-X). Adlers Foreign Bks.
--German-English, English-German Dictionary of Industrial Technics, 2 vols. 4th, rev., enl. ed. (Ger. & Eng.). Set. 150.00 (ISBN 0-686-77968-1). German-english (ISBN 3-87097-096-0). English-german (ISBN 3-87097-068-5). Heinman.
--Woerterbuch der Industriellen Technik, Vol. 1. (Ger. & Eng., Dictionary of Industrial Engineering). 1974. 80.00 (ISBN 3-87097-060-X, M-7001). French & Eur.
--Woerterbuch der Industriellen Technik, Vol. 2. (Eng. & Ger., Dictionary of Industrial Engineering). 1975. 80.00 (ISBN 3-87097-068-5, M-7000). French & Eur.
--Woerterbuch der Industriellen Technik, Vol. 3. (Ger. & Fr.). 1965. 64.00 (ISBN 3-87097-005-7, M-6999). French & Eur.
--Woerterbuch der Industriellen Technik, Vol. 4. (Fr. & Ger.). 1968. 56.00 (ISBN 3-87097-006-5, M-6998). French & Eur.
--Woerterbuch der Industriellen Technik, Vol. 5. 2nd ed. (Ger. & Span.). 1973. 56.00 (ISBN 3-87097-069-3, M-6997). French & Eur.
--Woerterbuch der Industriellen Technik, Vol. 7. (Port. & Ger.). 1963. 48.00 (ISBN 3-87097-009-X, M-6995). French & Eur.
--Woerterbuch der Industriellen Technik, Vol. 8. (Port. & Ger.). 1967. 48.00 (ISBN 3-87097-010-3, M-6994). French & Eur.
Ernst, R. D., et al. Complex Chemistry. (Structure & Bonding Ser.: Vol. 57). (Illus.). 210p. 1984. 45.00 (ISBN 0-387-13411-5). Springer-Verlag.
Ernst, Richard. Dictionary of Chemistry, Vol. 1. (Eng. & Ger.). 1961. 36.00 (ISBN 3-87097-011-1, M-7124). French & Eur.
--Dictionary of Chemistry, Vol. 2. (Eng. & Ger.). 1963. 44.00 (ISBN 3-87097-012-X, M-7123). French & Eur.
--Dictionary of Engineering & Technology: English-German, Vol. II. 5th ed. 1000p. 1985. 69.00 (ISBN 0-19-520485-9). Oxford U Pr.
--Dictionary of Engineering & Technology: With Extensive Treatment of the Most Modern Techniques & Processes, Vol. 2, English-German. 4th, rev. & enl. ed. (Eng. & Ger.). 1975. text ed. 69.00x (ISBN 0-19-520109-4). Oxford U Pr.
Ernst, Richard, compiled by. Comprehensive Dictionary of Engineering & Technology, 2 vols. 1085p. 1985. Vol. 1, French & English. 100.00 (ISBN 0-521-30377-X); Vol. 2, English & French. 110.00 (ISBN 0-521-30378-8). Cambridge U Pr.
Ernst, Richard, ed. Dictionary of Engineering & Technology, Vol. 1. 4th ed. 1980. 69.00x (ISBN 0-19-520269-4). Oxford U Pr.
Ernst, Richard L. & Yett, Donald E. Physician Location & Specialty Choice. LC 85-5469. 550p. 1985. text ed. price not set (ISBN 0-910701-03-2, 00655). Health Admin Pr.
Ernst, Robert. Immigrant Life in New York City, Eighteen Twenty-Five to Eighteen Sixty-Three. LC 79-11450. 1979. Repr. of 1949 ed. lib. bdg. 23.00x (ISBN 0-374-92624-7). Octagon.
--Rufus King: American Federalist. LC 68-15747. (Institute of Early American History & Culture Ser.). xiii, 446p. 1968. 30.00 (ISBN 0-8078-1070-3). U of NC Pr.
Ernst, Roy, jt. auth. see Hunsberger, Donald.
Ernst, Sandra B. The ABC's of Typography. LC 77-80333. (Illus.). 1978. 12.50 (ISBN 0-910158-09-6); pap. 8.95 (ISBN 0-685-86896-6). Art Dir.
Ernst, Sheila & Goodison, Lucy. In Our Own Hands. LC 81-9013. (Illus.). 336p. 1981. 12.95 (ISBN 0-87477-199-4); pap. 7.95 (ISBN 0-87477-190-0). J P Tarcher.
Ernst, W. Lord Chesterfield. 45.00 (ISBN 0-8274-2987-8). R West.
--Lord Chesterfield, 2 Vols. 354p. 1982. Repr. Set. lib. bdg. 85.00 (ISBN 0-89987-216-6). Darby Bks.
--Memoirs of the Life of Philip Dormer Fourth Earl of Chesterfield. 1973. Repr. of 1893 ed. 50.00 (ISBN 0-8274-1386-6). R West.
--Memoirs of the Life of Philip Dormer, Fourth Earl of Chesterfield: With Numerous Letters Now First Published from the Newcastle Papers, 2 vols. 354p. 1981. Repr. of 1893 ed. Set. lib. bdg. 100.00 (ISBN 0-89760-220-X). Telegraph Bks.
Ernst, W., ed. Memoirs of the Life of Philip Dormer Fourth Earl of Chesterfield: Numerous Letters Now First Published from the Newcastle Papers. 1978. Repr. of 1893 ed. lib. bdg. 50.00 (ISBN 0-8495-1306-5). Arden Lib.
Ernst, W. G. Earth Materials. (gr. 10 up). 1969. pap. text ed. 15.95 (ISBN 0-13-222604-9). P-H.
--Petrologic Phase Equilibria. LC 76-3699. (Illus.). 333p. 1976. 41.95 (ISBN 0-7167-0279-7). W H Freeman.
Ernst, W. G., ed. The Environment of the Deep Sea, Vol. 2. (Illus.). 384p. 1982. 45.95 (ISBN 0-13-282822-7). P-H.
--The Geotectonic Development of California, Vol. 1. (Illus.). 720p. 1981. text ed. 45.95 (ISBN 0-13-353938-5). P-H.
--Metamorphism & Plate Tectonic Regimes. LC 74-23374. (Benchmark Papers in Geology Ser: No. 17). 448p. 1975. 76.00 (ISBN 0-12-786447-4). Acad Pr.
--Subduction Zone Metamorphism. LC 74-25224. (Benchmark Papers in Geology Ser: No. 19). 1975. 72.00 (ISBN 0-12-786448-2). Acad Pr.
Ernst, W. G., jt. ed. see Perrine, Richard L.
Ernst, Wallace G. & Seki, Y. Comparative Study of Low-Grade Metamorphism in the California Coast Ranges & the Outer Metamorphic Belt of Japan. LC 74-98022. (Geological Society of America Ser.: No. 127). pap. 84.50 (ISBN 0-317-28383-9, 2025464). Bks Demand UMI.
Ernst-Browning, W., ed. see Chesterfield, Lord.
Ernst von Morgenstern, F., jt. auth. see Ernst, I.
Ero, J. & Szucs, J., eds. Nuclear Structure Study with Neutrons. LC 73-17651. 496p. 1974. 75.00x (ISBN 0-306-30770-7, Plenum Pr). Plenum Pub.
Erodes, Richard & Ortiz, Alfonso. American Indian Myth & Legends. LC 84-42669. (Illus.). 504p. 1984. 19.45 (ISBN 0-394-50796-7). Pantheon.
Eroes, Maria Von see Mussner, Franz.
Erofeev, Benedict. Moscow Circles. Dorell, J. R., tr. (Russian.). 1982. 12.95 (ISBN 0-906495-26-1). Writers & Readers.
--Moscow Circles. 192p. 1984. pap. 5.95 (ISBN 0-906495-74-1). Writers & Readers.
Erofeev, Venedikt. Moscow to the End of the Line. Tjalsma, William, tr. from Rus. LC 79-5169. 1980. 8.95 (ISBN 0-8008-5374-1). Taplinger.
Eron, Carol. The Fast Track to the Top Jobs in New Medical Careers. LC 83-27314. (Fast Track Guides). 128p. 1984. pap. 6.95 (ISBN 0-399-50982-8, G&D). Putnam Pub Group.
Eron, Carol, jt. auth. see Horn, Carole.
Eron, Judy & Morgan, Geoffrey. Charlie Rich. (Rock 'n Pop Stars Ser.). (Illus.). (gr. 4-12). 1975. pap. 3.95 (ISBN 0-89812-116-7). Creative Ed.
Eron, Leonard D. & Callahan, Robert, eds. Relation of Theory to Practice in Psychotherapy. LC 69-13705. 1969. 37.50x (ISBN 0-202-26017-8). Irvington.
Erondelle, Pierre E., tr. see Lescarbot, Marc.
Eros, J. S., ed. see Mannheim, Karl.
Erpenbach, William, jt. auth. see Heddesheimer, Janet.
Errante, Guido. Sulla Lirica Romanza Delle Origini. 441p. (It.). 1943. pap. 8.50x (ISBN 0-913298-44-1). S F Vanni.
Errecart, Felipa M. Hang Tough! Basque Cooking, Life & Ways. (Illus.). 240p. (Orig.). 1986. pap. 9.95 (ISBN 0-89407-063-0). Strawberry Hill.
Errera, Alberto. Storia dell'Economia Politica Nei Secoli Dix-Septieme e Dix-Huitieme Negli Stati della Repubblica Veneta, Corredata Da Documenti Inediti: Economica Politicanes Secoli 17e Negli Stati Del la Republica Veneta Corredate Da Documen; Inediti, 2 vols. 1965. 35.50 (ISBN 0-8337-1066-4). B Franklin.
Errichetti, Linda. Dancin' Skates. 1984. 8.95 (ISBN 0-533-05994-1). Vantage.
Errico, Rocco A. The Ancient Aramaic Prayer of Jesus. (Illus.). 82p. 1978. pap. 4.95 (ISBN 0-911336-69-9). Sci of Mind.
--Let There Be Light: The Seven Keys. 180p. (Orig.). 1985. pap. 7.95 (ISBN 0-87516-555-9). De Vorss.
Erridge. Self Assessment Questions & Answers for Dental Assistants. 128p. 1979. pap. 11.50 (ISBN 0-7236-0524-6). PSG Pub Co.
Errington, Frederick K. Karavar: Masks & Power in a Melanesian Ritual. Turner, Victor, ed. 1974. text ed. 27.00x (ISBN 0-8290-0339-8). Irvington.
--Manners & Meaning in West Sumatra: The Social Context of Consciousness. LC 83-21893. (Illus.). 240p. 1984. 21.00x (ISBN 0-300-03159-9). Yale U Pr.
Errington, J. Joseph. Language & Social Change in Java: Linguistic Reflexes of Modernization in Traditional Royal Polity. LC 84-19033. (Monographs in International Studies, Southeast Asia: No. 65). xiv, 198p. 1985. pap. text ed. 12.00x (ISBN 0-89680-120-9, 82-90660, Ohio U Ctr Intl). Ohio U Pr.
Errington, Lindsay. Social & Religious Themes in English Art, 1840-1860. LC 83-48701. (Theses from the Courtauld Institute of Art Ser.). (Illus.). 584p. 1984. lib. bdg. 70.00 (ISBN 0-8240-5977-8). Garland Pub.
Errington, Paul L. Muskrats & Marsh Management. LC 77-14177. (Illus.). x, 183p. 1978. pap. 4.50 (ISBN 0-8032-5892-5, BB 664, Bison). U of Nebr Pr.
--Of Men & Marshes. fasc. ed. (Illus.). 1957. pap. 9.45x (ISBN 0-8138-2350-1). Iowa St U Pr.
--Of Predation & Life. facsimile ed. (Illus.). 1967. pap. 12.75x (ISBN 0-8138-2325-0). Iowa St U Pr.
--The Red Gods Call. (Illus.). 172p. 1973. 9.50 (ISBN 0-8138-1340-9). Iowa St U Pr.
Errington, R. M. The Dawn of Empire: Rome's Rise to World Power. LC 75-176296. (Illus.). 330p. 1972. pap. 6.95x 452p., 1973 (ISBN 0-8014-9128-2, CP128). Cornell U Pr.
Errolle, Ralph, jt. auth. see Coffin, Berton.
Erschen, Olivia. Cakes & Pastries. Lammers, Susan, ed. LC 85-70884. (California Culinary Academy Ser.). (Illus.). 128p. (Orig.). 1985. pap. 7.95 (ISBN 0-89721-059-X). Ortho.
Ersek, Robert A. Pain Control with Transcutaneous Electrical Neuro Stimulation (Tens) LC 78-50175. 280p. 1981. 23.75 (ISBN 0-87527-168-5). Green.
Erseus, C., jt. ed. see Bonomi, G.
Ersevim, Ismail. Prophet Eshref & Other Short Stories: A Panorama of Psychic Adventures. 96p. 1983. 6.50 (ISBN 0-682-49974-9). Exposition Pr FL.
Ershkowitz, Herbert. The Origin of the Whig & Democratic Parties, New Jersey Politics, 1820-1837. LC 82-17652. (Illus.). 300p. (Orig.). 1983. lib. bdg. 26.00 (ISBN 0-8191-2769-8); pap. text ed. 13.00 (ISBN 0-8191-2770-1). U Pr of Amer.
Ershler, A. B., jt. ed. see Frumkin, A. N.
Ershov, A. & Koster, C. H., eds. Methods of Algorithmic Language Implementation. (Lecture Notes in Computer Science: Vol. 47). 1977. pap. 21.00 (ISBN 0-387-08065-1). Springer-Verlag.
Ershov, A., ed. see International Symposium on Theoretical Programming.
Ershov, A. P. & Knuth, D. E., eds. Algorithms in Modern Mathematics & Computer Science: Proceedings. (Lecture Notes in Computer Science Ser.: Vol. 122). 487p. 1981. pap. 26.50 (ISBN 0-387-11157-3). Springer-Verlag.
Ershov, B. A., jt. auth. see Ionin, B. I.
Ershov, V. V. & Nikiforov, G. A. Quinonediazides. (Studies in Organic Chemistry: Vol. 7). 302p. 1981. 74.50 (ISBN 0-444-42008-8). Elsevier.

Ershov, Yu. L. & Palyutin, E. A. Mathematical Logic. 303p. 1984. 7.95 (ISBN 0-8285-2879-9, Pub. by Mir Pubs USSR). Imported Pubns.

Erskine, A., jt. auth. see Stuart, J.

Erskine, Albert, jt. ed. see Warren, Robert Penn.

Erskine, Beatrice S. Palestine of the Arabs. LC 75-6431. (The Rise of Jewish Nationalism & the Middle East Ser). 255p. 1975. Repr. of 1935 ed. 25.00 (ISBN 0-88355-318-X). Hyperion Conn.

Erskine, Caldwell. God's Little Acre. 11.95 (ISBN 0-88411-456-2, Pub. by Aeonian Pr). Amereon Ltd.

Erskine, Charles. Twenty Years Before the Mast. LC 82-2271. (Illus.). 328p. 1985. pap. 4.95 (ISBN 0-87474-415-6, ERTYP). Smithsonian.

Erskine, Irene. Laboratory Guide for Anatomy & Physiology. 176p. 1980. pap. text ed. 9.95 (ISBN 0-8403-2350-6). Kendall-Hunt.

Erskine, J., ed. see Hearn, Lafcadio.

Erskine, Jim. Bedtime Story. LC 81-3163. 32p. (ps-1). 1982. PLB 8.95 (ISBN 0-517-54540-3). Crown.

--Bert & Susie's Messy Tale. LC 78-24564. (Illus.). (ps-1). 1979. PLB 5.95 (ISBN 0-517-53475-4). Crown.

--Fold a Banana: And One Hundred Forty Six Other Things to Do When You're Bored. (Illus.). 1978. pap. 1.98 (ISBN 0-517-53503-3, C N Potter Bks). Crown.

Erskine, Jim & Boldman, Craig. Scrambled Chickens & Seventy Four Other Eccentric How-To's. LC 81-6904. (Illus., Orig.). 1982. pap. 4.95 (ISBN 0-03-059908-3, Owl Bks). HR&W.

Erskine, Jim & Cooper, Bobbi G. The Ultimate Fat Book. (Illus.). 1982. pap. 3.95 (ISBN 0-03-062086-4, Owl Bks). HR&W.

Erskine, Jim & Moran, George. Hug a Teddy. 1980. 1.98 (ISBN 0-517-54215-3, C N Potter Bks). Crown.

Erskine, John. Complete Life. facs. ed. LC 74-134073. (Essay Index Reprint Ser). 1943. 21.50 (ISBN 0-8369-2153-4). Ayer Co Pubs.

--The Delight of Great Books. 1973. 25.00 (ISBN 0-8274-0412-3). R West.

--Elizabethan Lyric. LC 67-21712. 1967. Repr. of 1903 ed. 10.00x (ISBN 0-87752-031-3). Gordian.

--Galahad: Enough of His Life to Explain His Reputation. 340p. 1983. Repr. of 1926 ed. lib. bdg. 25.00 (ISBN 0-8495-1432-0). Arden Lib.

--George Edward Woodberry. LC 73-16658. 1930. lib. bdg. 6.50 (ISBN 0-8414-3918-4). Folcroft.

--An Institute of the Law of Scotland in the Order of Sir George Mackenzie's Institutions of That Law, 2 vols. in 1. LC 78-67527. (Scottish Enlightenment Ser.). Repr. of 1773 ed. 155.00 (ISBN 0-404-17470-1). AMS Pr.

--Kinds of Poetry & Other Essays. LC 66-259410. 1966. Repr. of 1920 ed. 21.00x (ISBN 0-8046-0136-4, Pub. by Kennikat). Assoc Faculty Pr.

--Leading American Novelists. facs. ed. LC 67-22091. (Essay Index Reprint Ser). 1910. 18.00 (ISBN 0-8369-0419-2). Ayer Co Pubs.

--The Literary Discipline. 231p. 1980. Repr. of 1927 ed. lib. bdg. 25.00 (ISBN 0-8495-1345-6). Arden Lib.

--Literary Discipline. LC 74-90635. (Essay Index Reprint Ser). 1923. 18.00 (ISBN 0-8369-1257-8). Ayer Co Pubs.

--Literary Discipline. 1973. lib. bdg. 11.95 (ISBN 0-8414-4009-3). Folcroft.

--The Literary Discipline. LC 23-8332. Repr. of 1924 ed. 14.00 (ISBN 0-384-14600-7). Johnson Repr.

--Moral Obligation to Be Intelligent & Other Essays. LC 70-93337. (Essay Index Reprint Ser). 1921. 17.00 (ISBN 0-8369-1291-8). Ayer Co Pubs.

--My Life in Music. LC 73-8158. (Illus.). 283p. 1973. Repr. of 1950 ed. lib. bdg. 15.75x (ISBN 0-8371-6950-X, ERLM). Greenwood.

--Sincerity: A Story of Our Time. 356p. 1983. Repr. of 1929 ed. lib. bdg. 20.00 (ISBN 0-8495-1431-2). Arden Lib.

Erskine, John, et al. Early Histories of the New York Philharmonic, 3 vols. in one. Incl. The Philharmonic Society of New York, a Memorial; The Philharmonic Society of New York & Its Seventy-Fifth Anniversary, a Retrospect; The Philharmonic Society of New York, Its First Hundred Years. (Music Reprint Ser., 1978). (Illus.). 1979. Repr. of 1943 ed. lib. bdg. 49.50 (ISBN 0-306-77537-9). Da Capo.

Erskine, John T. Millionaire for God (C. T. Studd) 1968. pap. 2.50 (ISBN 0-87508-611-X). Chr Lit.

Erskine, Kathryn A. What You Always Wanted to Know about Operating a Small Business but Didn't Know Who to Ask. (Illus.). 69p. (Orig.). 1980. pap. 9.95 (ISBN 0-9605058-0-6). Erskine.

Erskine, Noel L. Decolonizing Theology: A Caribbean Perspective. LC 80-21784. 144p. (Orig.). 1981. pap. 6.95 (ISBN 0-88344-087-3). Orbis Bks.

Erskine, Robert. Graphic Work of Merlyn Evans. (Orig.). pap. 3.95 (ISBN 0-901486-55-8, Pub. by Victoria & Albert Mus UK). Faber & Faber.

Erskine, Stuart R. King Edward the Seventh & Some Other Figures. facs. ed. LC 67-22092. (Essay Index Reprint Ser.). 1936. 18.00 (ISBN 0-8369-1331-0). Ayer Co Pubs.

Erskine, William. A History of India under the Two First Sovereigns of the House of Taimur, Baber & Humayun, 2 vols. 1212p. 1972. Repr. of 1854 ed. 75.00 set (ISBN 0-7165-2118-0, BBA 03538, Pub. by Irish Academic Pr). Biblio Dist.

Erskine, William, jt. ed. see Witcombe, John R.

Erskine-Hill, Howard. The Augustan Idea in English Literature. 400p. 1983. text ed. 64.50 (ISBN 0-7131-6373-9). E Arnold.

Erskine-Hill, Howard & Smith, Anne, eds. The Art of Alexander Pope. LC 78-62593. (Critical Studies Ser.). 235p. 1979. text ed. 28.50x (ISBN 0-685-62564-8). B&N Imports.

Erskine-Hill, Howard & Storey, Graham, eds. Revolutionary Prose of the English Civil War. LC 82-12904. (Cambridge English Prose Texts). (Illus.). 280p. 1983. 42.50 (ISBN 0-521-24404-8); pap. 14.95 (ISBN 0-521-28670-0). Cambridge U Pr.

Erskine Lindrop, Audrey. Nicola. 1982. 15.00x (ISBN 0-85617-327-4, Pub. by Severn Hse). State Mutual Bk.

Erslev, Allan, frwd. by see Reizenstein, Peter.

Erslev, Allan J. & Gabuzda, Thomas G. Pathophysiology of Blood. 2nd ed. LC 78-24813. (Illus.). 1979. pap. text ed. 16.95 (ISBN 0-7216-3403-6). Saunders.

Ersov, N. N. & Komarov, A. N., eds. Projet de Lexique Minier Russe-Francais. 183p. (Fr. & Rus.). 1972. pap. 22.50 (ISBN 0-686-56769-2, M-6468). French & Eur.

Erspamer, V., ed. Five-Hydroxytryptamine & Related Indolealkylamines. (Handbook of Experimental Pharmacology: Vol. 19). (Illus.). 1966. 106.00 (ISBN 0-387-03536-2). Springer-Verlag.

Erst, Stephen J. Receiving Systems Design. 300p. 1984. text ed. 61.00 (ISBN 0-89006-135-1). Artech Hse.

Erstling, Jay A. The Right to Organize. vi, 82p. 1977. 14.25 (ISBN 92-2-101790-7, ILO65, ILO). Unipub.

Ertavy-Barath, Joseph M., ed. see Domokos, Varga.

Erte. Designs by Erte: Fashion Drawings & Illustrations from "Harper's Bazaar". LC 76-24054. (Illus.). 1976. pap. 6.95 (ISBN 0-486-23397-9). Dover.

--Designs by Erte: Fashion Drawings & Illustrations from Harper's Bazaar. Blum, S., ed. (Illus.). 18.00 (ISBN 0-8446-5571-6). Peter Smith.

--Erte at Ninety: The Complete Graphics. (Illus.). 224p. 1982. 75.00 (ISBN 0-525-93258-5). Dutton.

--Erte's Costumes & Sets for "Der Rosenkavalier" in Full Color. (Illus.). 48p. 1980. pap. 6.95 (ISBN 0-486-23998-5). Dover.

--Erte's Costumes & Sets for "Der Rosenkavalier" in Full Color: Nineteen Eighty Glyndebourne Festival Production. 15.25 (ISBN 0-8446-5756-5). Peter Smith.

--Erte's Fashion Designs: Haper's Bazaar, 1918-1932. (Illus.). 1982. 18.00 (ISBN 0-8446-5884-7). Peter Smith.

--Erte's Fashion Designs: Two Hundred & Eighteen Designs from Harper's Bazaar, 1918-1932. (Illus.). 88p. 1981. 6.50 (ISBN 0-486-24203-X). Dover.

--Erte's Fashion Paper Dolls of the Twenties. LC 77-70855. (Illus.). 1978. pap. 3.50 (ISBN 0-486-23627-7). Dover.

--Erte's Theatrical Costumes in Full-Color. (Illus.). 1979. pap. 6.00 (ISBN 0-486-23813-X). Dover.

--Erte's Theatrical Costumes in Full Color. 16.50 (ISBN 0-8446-5757-3). Peter Smith.

--Graphics in Full Color: Five Complete Suites: the Seasons, the Alphabet, the Numerals, the Aces & the Precious Stones. LC 77-91513. (Illus.). 1978. pap. 6.95 (ISBN 0-486-23580-7). Dover.

Erte, illus. New Erte Graphics in Full Color. (Fine Arts Ser.). (Illus.). 48p. 1984. pap. 6.95 (ISBN 0-486-24645-0). Dover.

Erte & Tierney, Tom, illus. More Erte Fashion Paper Dolls in Full Color. (Paper Dolls Ser.). 32p. 1984. pap. 3.50 (ISBN 0-486-24630-2). Dover.

Ertekin, Turqay, jt. auth. see Donohue, David A.

Ertel, James. Compton Yearbook, 1983. 510p. (YA) 1983. write for info. Ency Brit Inc.

Ertel, James, ed. Britannica Book of the Year, 1982. 768p. 1982. write for info. Ency Brit Inc.

--Britannica Book of the Year, 1983. (Illus.). 768p. (YA) 1983. write for info. Ency Brit Inc.

--Compton Yearbook, 1982. 512p. 1982. write for info. Ency Brit Inc.

Ertel, Kenneth & Walsh, Lawrence. Wholesaling & Physical Distribution. Dorr, Eugene L., ed. (Occupational Manuals & Projects in Marketing Ser.). 1978. pap. text ed. 8.68 (ISBN 0-07-019627-3). McGraw.

Ertl, G. & Kuppers, J. Low Energy Electrons & Surface Chemistry. LC 74-82758. (Monographs in Modern Chemistry: Vol. 4). (Illus.). 261p. 1974. 57.70x (ISBN 3-527-25562-1). VCH Pubs.

Ertl, G., jt. ed. see Rhodin, T. N.

Ertl, John, jt. auth. see Konrad, Patricia.

Eruch, et al. Tales from the New Life with Meher Baba. 191p. 1976. 8.95 (ISBN 0-940700-10-7); pap. 4.95 (ISBN 0-940700-09-3). Meher Baba Info.

Erugin, Nikolai P. Linear Systems of Ordinary Differential Equations. (Mathematics in Science & Engineering: Vol. 28). 1966. 71.00 (ISBN 0-12-241856-6). Acad Pr.

Erulkar, Mary, pseud. Mandala Two to the Fifth Power. (Writers Workshop Redbird Ser.). 48p. 1975. 12.00 (ISBN 0-88253-574-9); pap. text ed. 4.80 (ISBN 0-88253-573-0). Ind-US Inc.

Erva, Judith P. Van see Van Erva, Judith P.

Erven, Bernard L., jt. auth. see Foster, D. Lynn.

Erven, J. & Falkowski, B. J. Low Order Cohomology & Applications. (Lecture Notes in Mathematics Ser.: Vol. 877). 126p. 1981. pap. 12.00 (ISBN 0-387-10864-5). Springer-Verlag.

Erven, Lawrence. Techniques of Fire Hydraulics. (Fire Science Ser). 1972. text ed. write for info. (ISBN 0-02-473000-9, 47300). Macmillan.

Erven, Lawrence W. Handbook of Emergency Care & Rescue. rev. ed. 1976. text ed. write for info. (ISBN 0-02-472630-3). Macmillan.

Ervin. Memory Bank for Critical Care: EKG's & Cardiac Drugs. 2nd ed. (Illus.). 220p. 10.95 (ISBN 0-683-09530-7). Williams & Wilkins.

Ervin, Gary W. Memory Bank for Critical Care: EKG's & Cardiac Drugs. 2nd ed. pap. 10.95 (ISBN 0-935236-22-8). Nurseco.

Ervin, Gary W. & Long, Sylvia. Memory Bank for Hemodynamic Monitoring. (Memory Bank Ser.). (Illus.). 1984. pap. 10.95 (ISBN 0-935236-20-1). Nurseco.

--Memory Bank for Hemodynamic Monitoring: The Pulmonary Artery Catheter. 1984. 10.95 (ISBN 0-683-09532-3). Williams & Wilkins.

Ervin, Jane. How to Help Your Preschooler Become a Good Reader. 1983. 35.95scp (ISBN 0-205-07835-4, 237835). Allyn.

--How to Improve your Child's Reading over the Summer. 1983. 35.95scp (ISBN 0-205-07836-2, 237836). Allyn.

--Phonics Manual & Lesson Plans, Level D. (gr. 4). 1977. 2.00 (ISBN 0-87895-445-7). Modern Curr.

--Phonics Workbook, Level D. (MCP Basic Phonics Program). (gr. 4). 1977. 3.40 (ISBN 0-87895-441-4). Modern Curr.

--Reading with Your Child: A Number One Priority. 1983. 35.95scp (ISBN 0-205-07554-1, 237554). Allyn.

--Short Guide to the New Grammar. LC 68-28174. (Aegeus Series in English & Comparative Literature). 1968. text ed. 5.95 (ISBN 0-87252-008-0). Tinnon-Brown.

--Two-Color New Phonics Workbook, Level D. (gr. 4). 1977. 3.76 (ISBN 0-87895-442-2). Modern Curr.

Ervin, Jean, ed. The Minnesota Experience: An Anthology. 1979. 17.95x (ISBN 0-914828-04-5); pap. 9.75 (ISBN 0-914828-05-3). Adams Minn.

Ervin, M. C., ed. In-situ Testing for Geotechnical Investigation: Proceedings of an Extension Course on In-situ Testing for Geotechnical Investigations, Sydney, May-June 1983. 140p. 1983. lib. bdg. 26.00 (ISBN 90-6191-506-6, Pub. by Balkema RSA). IPS.

Ervin, Paula. Women Exploited: The True Stories of the Other Victims of Abortion. 200p. (Orig.). 1985. pap. 6.95 (ISBN 0-87973-847-2, 847). Our Sunday Visitor.

Ervin, Sam J. Preserving the Constitution: The Autobiography of Senator Sam Ervin. 450p. 1984. 19.95 (ISBN 0-87215-781-4). Michie Co.

Ervin, Sam J., Jr. Humor of a Country Lawyer. LC 83-7045. (Illus.). xii, 212p. 1983. 12.95 (ISBN 0-8078-1566-7). U of NC Pr.

--The Whole Truth: The Watergate Conspiracy by Sam Ervin. 1981. 16.95 (ISBN 0-394-48029-5). Random.

Ervin, Sam J., Jr. & Clark, Ramsey. Role of the Supreme Court: Policymaker or Adjudicator. 85p. 1970. 11.25 (ISBN 0-8447-2018-6). Am Enterprise.

Ervin, Sam J., Jr., jt. auth. see Harvard Civil Rights-Civil Liberties Law Review.

Ervin, Sara S. South Carolinians in the Revolution. LC 65-24109. (Illus.). 217p. 1981. Repr. of 1949 ed. 15.00 (ISBN 0-8063-0104-X). Genealog Pub.

Ervin, Spencer. Henry Ford vs. Truman H. Newberry: The Famous Senate Election Contest. LC 73-19143. (Politics & People Ser.). 634p. 1974. Repr. 42.00x (ISBN 0-405-05867-5). Ayer Co Pubs.

Ervin, Thomas. Real Estate Revolution! Who Will Survive. 1980. 12.95 (ISBN 0-88462-387-4, 1983-01, Real Estate Ed). Longman USA.

Ervin, Thomas & Hart, Don. The Homeowner's Almanac. LC 80-66065. (Illus.). 128p. (Orig.). 1980. pap. write for info. (ISBN 0-936682-00-0). Conquest Corp MI.

Ervin, Viola G. One Way to Tell It. (Illus.). 1982. 16.95 (ISBN 0-916624-33-1). Troy State Univ.

Ervin, William R. Let Us Alone. (Illus.). 128p. pap. text ed. 12.95 (ISBN 0-915447-00-2). Ervin Pub Co.

Ervin, Wilma. On the Edge: The East Village. LC 85-40273. (Illus.). 84p. (Orig.). 1985. pap. 9.95 (ISBN 0-8129-1287-X). Times Bks.

Ervine, John G. Bernard Shaw: His Life, Work & Friends. LC 83-45753. Repr. of 1956 ed. 57.50 (ISBN 0-404-20091-5). AMS Pr.

--Mrs. Martin's Man. LC 83-45754. Repr. of 1915 ed. 29.50 (ISBN 0-404-20092-3). AMS Pr.

--Oscar Wilde: A Present Time Appraisal. LC 83-45755. Repr. of 1952 ed. 32.50 (ISBN 0-404-20093-1). AMS Pr.

Ervine, St. John, ed. see Royal Society of Literature, United Kingdom.

Ervine, St. John G. Mountain & Other Stories. facsimile ed. LC 72-101809. (Short Story Index Reprint Ser.). 1928. 17.00 (ISBN 0-8369-3197-1). Ayer Co Pubs.

Ervin-Tripp, S. & Mitchell-Kernan, C., eds. Child Discourse. 1977. 20.00 (ISBN 0-12-241950-2). Acad Pr.

Ervin-Tripp, Susan M. Language Acquisition & Communicative Choice: Essays by Susan M. Ervin-Tripp. Dil, Anwar S., ed. LC 72-97206. (Language Science & National Development Ser). xvi, 384p. 1973. 27.50x (ISBN 0-8047-0831-2). Stanford U Pr.

--Language Development. (Master Lectures on Developmental Psychology: Manuscript No. 1336). 7.50 (ISBN 0-912704-24-1). Am Psychol.

Erway, E. A. Listening: A Programmed Approach. 2nd ed. 1979. pap. 20.95 (ISBN 0-07-019660-5). McGraw.

Erwin, Alan R. The Power Exchange. 256p. 1984. pap. 2.95 (ISBN 0-441-67574-3). Ace Bks.

Erwin, Bette J. & Dinwiddie, Elza. Test Without Trauma: How to Overcome Test Anxiety & Score Higher on Every Test. LC 82-82312. 192p. (Orig.). 1983. pap. 7.95 (ISBN 0-448-16607-0, G&D). Putnam Pub Group.

Erwin, C., jt. auth. see Paustian, Paul W.

Erwin, D. C., et al, eds. Phytophthora: It's Biology, Taxonomy, Ecology & Pathology. 392p. 1983. text ed. 76.00 (ISBN 0-89054-050-0). Am Phytopathol Soc.

Erwin, David G., ed. see Earll, Robert C.

Erwin, E. Behavior Therapy: Scientific, Philosophical & Moral Foundations. 1978. 39.50 (ISBN 0-521-22293-1); pap. 12.95 (ISBN 0-521-29439-8). Cambridge U Pr.

Erwin, Edward. Behavior Therapy: Philosophical & Empirical Foundations. write for info. (ISBN 0-12-242150-7). Acad Pr.

--The Concept of Meaninglessness. LC 75-101456. pap. 43.80 (ISBN 0-317-08076-8, 2020330). Bks Demand UMI.

Erwin, Frank, ed. see Ad Hoc Group on Uniform Selection Guidelines, et al.

Erwin, Gayle D. The Jesus Style. 211p. 1985. 9.95 (ISBN 0-8499-0509-5, 0509-5). Word Bks.

Erwin, Joe & Dukelow, Richard W. Comparative Primate Biology, Vol. 3: Reproduction & Development. 430p. 1985. write for info. (ISBN 0-8451-4003-5). A R Liss.

Erwin, Joe & Mitchell, G. Comparative Primate Biology, Vol. 2A: Behavior & Ecology, Vol. 2A. (CPB Ser.). 596p. 1985. write for info. (ISBN 0-8451-4001-9). A R Liss.

Erwin, Joe & Swindler, Daris R. Comparative Primate Biology, Vol. 1: Systematics, Evolution & Anatomy. 754p. 1985. write for info. (ISBN 0-8451-4000-0). A R Liss.

Erwin, John S. Like Some Green Laurel: Letters of Margaret Johnson Erwin, 1821-1863. LC 80-23545. (Illus.). xxiv, 154p. 1981. 17.50x (ISBN 0-8071-0761-1). La State U Pr.

Erwin, John W. Lyric Apocalypse: Reconstruction in Ancient & Modern Poetry. LC 83-20823. (Scholars Press Studies in the Humanities). 229p. 1984. 24.75 (ISBN 0-89130-666-8, 00 01 03); pap. 16.50 (ISBN 0-89130-672-2). Scholars Pr GA.

Erwin, Joseph, et al. Captivity & Behavior: Primates in Breeding Colonies, Laboratories, & Zoos. (Primate Behavior & Development Ser.). 1979. 39.95 (ISBN 0-442-22329-3). Van Nos Reinhold.

Erwin, Joseph A., ed. Lipids & Biomembranes of Eukaryotic Microorganisms. (Cell Biology Ser.). 1973. 77.50 (ISBN 0-12-242050-0). Acad Pr.

Erwin, Mabel D., et al. Clothing for Moderns. 6th ed. (Illus.). 1979. text ed. write for info. (ISBN 0-02-334220-X). Macmillan.

Erwin, Marvin M. The Fisherman's March. LC 83-90466. (Illus.). 292p. 1984. 14.95 (ISBN 0-914598-23-6). Erwin Marvin M.

--The Fisherman's March: An Autobiography. LC 83-90466. (Illus.). 292p. 1984. 14.95 (ISBN 0-914598-23-6). Erwin Marvin M.

Erwin, T. L., et al, eds. Carabid Beetles. 1979. lib. bdg. 118.50 (ISBN 90-6193-596-2, Pub. by Junk Pubs Netherlands). Kluwer Academic.

Erxleben, A. W. Depositional Systems in the Canyon Group (Pennsylvanian System), North-Central Texas. (Report of Investigations Ser.: RI 82). (Illus.). 76p. 1980. Repr. of 1975 ed. 4.00 (ISBN 0-318-03216-3). Bur Econ Geology.

Erythraspis, J. I., tr. see D'Avennes, P.

Esar, Evan. The Comic Encyclopedia. LC 77-82939. 1978. 12.50 (ISBN 0-385-06205-2). Doubleday.

--Esar's Comic Dictionary. 4th rev. & enl. ed. LC 82-45244. 672p. 1983. 19.95 (ISBN 0-385-15891-2). Doubleday.

--Twenty Thousand Quips & Quotes. LC 68-18096. 1968. 15.95 (ISBN 0-385-00047-2). Doubleday.

Esarde, Edward E. Persian Cats. Rugenstein, Ed, ed. (Illus.). 96p. 1983. 4.95 (ISBN 0-87666-859-7, KW-061). TFH Pubns.

Esarey, Gary. Pronunciation Exercises for Advanced Learners of English As a Second Language. (Pittsburgh Ser. in English As a Second Language). (Orig.). 1977. pap. text ed. 5.95x (ISBN 0-8229-8207-2). U of Pittsburgh Pr.

Esarey, Gary, jt. auth. see Bruder, Mary N.

Esarey, Logan, ed. see Harrison, William H.

Esau, Helmut, et al. Language & Communication. 1980. pap. 8.75 (ISBN 0-917496-15-9). Hornbeam Pr.

Esau, K. The Phloem. (Encyclopedia of Plant Anatomy: Vol. 2). (Illus.). 505p. 1969. lib. bdg. 75.20X (ISBN 3-443-14002-5). Lubrecht & Cramer.

Esau, Katherine. Anatomy of Seed Plants. 2nd ed. LC 76-41191. 550p. 1977. text ed. 39.45 (ISBN 0-471-24520-8). Wiley.

--Viruses in Plant Hosts: Form, Distribution & Pathologic Effects. LC 68-9831. (John Charles Walker Lecture Ser.: 1968). pap. 58.80 (ISBN 0-317-09037-2, 2015359). Bks Demand UMI.

--Viruses in Plant Hosts: Form, Distribution, & Pathologic Effects. LC 68-9831. (The John Charles Walker Lectures Ser.: 1968). pap. 58.80 (ISBN 0-317-27779-0, 2015359). Bks Demand UMI.

Esau, M. Spirit of the Great Western. 128p. 30.00x (ISBN 0-86093-110-2, Pub. by ORPC Ltd UK). State Mutual Bk.

Esau, P. see Mrak, E. M. & Stewart, G. F.

Esbensen, Barbara. Swing Around the Sun. LC 65-19583. (General Juvenile Bks). (Illus.). (gr. 5-11). 1965. PLB 3.95 (ISBN 0-8225-0253-4). Lerner Pubns.

Esbensen, Barbara J. Cold Stars & Fireflies: Poems of the Four Seasons. LC 83-45051. (Illus.). 80p. (gr. 3-7). 1984. 10.53i (ISBN 0-690-04362-7); PLB 10.89g (ISBN 0-690-04363-5). Crowell Jr Bks.

Esbensen, Thorwald. Student Contracts. Langdon, Danny G., ed. LC 77-25411. (Instructional Design Library). (Illus.). 100p. 1978. 19.95 (ISBN 0-87778-121-4). Educ Tech Pubns.

Esbensen, Thorwald & Richards, Philip. Family Designed Learning. LC 74-83216. 1976. pap. 5.95 (ISBN 0-8224-2825-3). Pitman Learning.

Esberey, Joy E. Knight of the Holy Spirit: A Study of William Lyon Mackenzie King. 336p. 1980. 25.00 (ISBN 0-8020-5502-8). U of Toronto Pr.

Esbitt, Milton. International Capital Flows & Domestic Economic Fluctuation: The United States During the 1830's. LC 77-14779. (Dissertations in American Economic History Ser.). 1978. 37.50 (ISBN 0-405-11033-2). Ayer Co Pubs.

Esbjornson, Robert, ed. The Manipulation of Life: Nobel Conference XIX. LC 84-47723. (Nobel Lecture Ser.). 160p. (Orig.). 1984. pap. 7.64 (ISBN 0-06-250296-4). Har-Row.

Escabi, Elsa, jt. auth. see Escabi, Pedro.

Escabi, Pedro & Escabi, Elsa. La Decima. LC 76-7976. (Estudio Etnografico De la Cultura Popular De Puerto Rico: Pt. 2). (Illus.). 480p. (Orig., Span.). 1976. pap. text ed. 11.25 (ISBN 0-8477-2502-2). U of PR Pr.

Escabi, Rodolfo S. Tecnologia Farmaceutica Industrial. LC 76-46412. (Orig., Span.). 1977. pap. 10.00 (ISBN 0-8477-2321-6). U of PR Pr.

Escalada, F. N. Aeronautical Law. 881p. 1979. 37.50x (ISBN 90-286-0098-1). Sijthoff & Noordhoff.

Escalante, Bernardino de. Discourse of the Navigation Which the Portugales Doe Make to the Realmes & Provinces of the East Partes of the Worlde. Frampton, John, tr. from Port. LC 76-6127. (English Experience Ser.: No. 593). 46p. 1973. Repr. of 1579 ed. 9.50 (ISBN 90-221-0593-8). Walter J Johnson.

Escalante, E., ed. Underground Corrosion - STP 741. 210p. 1981. 26.00 (ISBN 0-8031-0703-X, 04-741000-27). ASTM.

Escalona, S. M. Life Laughter. 136p. 1982. 8.50 (ISBN 0-8059-2815-4). Dorrance.

Escalona, Sibylle K. Application of the Level of Aspiration Experiment to the Study of Personality. LC 77-176756. (Columbia University. Teachers College. Contributions to Education: No. 937). Repr. of 1948 ed. 22.50 (ISBN 0-404-55937-9). AMS Pr.

Escalona, Sybelle K. & Leitch, Mary. Early Phases of Personality Development: A Non-Normative Study of Infant Behavior. (SRCD M). 1952. pap. 15.00 (ISBN 0-527-01554-7). Kraus Repr.

Escamilla, Hugo. Sinfonia Sexual. (Pimienta Collection Ser). (Span.). 1977. pap. 1.00 (ISBN 0-88473-259-2). Fiesta Pub.

Escamilla, Roberto. Prisoners de la Esperanza. 1983. pap. 4.50 (ISBN 0-8358-0438-0). Upper Room.

--Prisoners of Hope. 1982. 4.50 (ISBN 0-8358-0437-2). Upper Room.

Escande, Xavier-Yves. French Key Words: The Basic Two Thousand Word Vocabulary Arranged by Frequency in a Hundred Units with Comprehensive French & English Indexes. (Oleander Language & Literature Ser.: Vol. 14). 144p. (Orig.). 1983. 17.50 (ISBN 0-906672-23-6); pap. text ed. 5.95 (ISBN 0-906672-24-4). Oleander Pr.

Escandell, Noemi. Cuadros. SLUSA, ed. LC 81-85665. (Illus.). 56p. (Span.). 1982. pap. 5.00x (ISBN 0-9606758-0-9). SLUSA.

Escandon, R. Como Llegar a Ser Vencedor. 128p. (Span.). 1982. pap. 3.95 (ISBN 0-311-46092-5, Edit Mundo). Casa Bautista.

Escandon, Ralph. Bilingual Vocabulary for the Medical Profession. (Span. & Eng.). 1982. text ed. 9.30 (ISBN 0-538-22690-0, V69). SW Pub.

Escarpenter & Fargas, Claudio. The Economics of International Ocean Transport: The Cuban Case Before 1958. Lerdau, Enrique & Lerdau, Federico, trs. from Span. LC 65-16361. pap. 51.80 (ISBN 0-317-26018-9, 2023712). Bks Demand UMI.

Escarpenter, Claudio. Economics of International Ocean Transport: The Cuban Case Before 1958. 208p. 1965. 17.50x (ISBN 0-299-03590-5). U of Wis Pr.

Escarpit, Denise, ed. see International Research Society on Children's Literature.

Escarpit, Robert. Open Letter to God. Bernstein, Joseph M., tr. (Open Letter Ser). (Orig.). 1968. pap. 2.25 (ISBN 0-685-11971-8, 12). Heineman.

--Sociology of Literature. Pick, E., tr. 104p. 1971. 27.50x (ISBN 0-7146-2729-1, F Cass Co). Biblio Dist.

Escarpit, Robert & Bouazis, Charles, eds. Systemes Partiels De Communication: Publications De la Maison Des Sciences De L'homme De Bordeaux - Travaux & Recherches De L'institut De Litterature & De Technique Artistiques De Masse. 1972. pap. 10.40x (ISBN 90-2797-039-4). Mouton.

Escarpit, Robert, jt. ed. see Barker, Ronald.

Esch, Dortha & Lepley, Marvin. Evaluation of Joint Motion: Methods of Measurement & Recording. LC 73-93576. (Illus.). 50p. 1974. 5.75x (ISBN 0-8166-0714-1). U of Minn Pr.

--Musculoskeletal Function: An Anatomy & Kinesiology Laboratory Manual. LC 73-93577. (Illus.). 112p. 1974. text ed. 7.50x (ISBN 0-8166-0716-8). U of Minn Pr.

Esch, Gerald W. & McFarlane, Robert W., eds. Thermal Ecology II: Proceedings. LC 76-28206. (ERDA Symposium Ser.). 414p. 1976. pap. 18.25 (ISBN 0-87079-223-7, CONF-750425); microfiche 4.50 (ISBN 0-87079-224-5, CONF-750425). DOE.

Esch, Gerald W. & Nikol, Brent B., eds. Regulation of Parasite Populations. 1977. 39.50 (ISBN 0-12-241750-X). Acad Pr.

Esch, P. van Der. Prelude to War: The International Repercussion of the Spanish Civil War. 1976. lib. bdg. 59.95 (ISBN 0-8490-2469-2). Gordon Pr.

Esch, Robert & Walker, Roberta. Art of Styling Paragraphs. (gr. 9-12). Date not set. pap. text ed. 2.75 (ISBN 0-8120-2360-9). Barron.

Eschbach, A., tr. see Hoffbauer, Johannes C.

Eschbach, Achim, ed. Zeichen ueber Zeichen ueber Zeichen: 15 Studien Ueber Charles W. Morris. (Illus.). 324p. (Orig., Ger. & Eng.). 1981. pap. 41.00x (ISBN 3-87808-558-3). Benjamins North Am.

Eschbach, Achim & Trabant, Juergen, eds. History of Semiotics. (Foundations of Semiotics Ser.: 7). 386p. 1983. 50.00x (ISBN 90-272-3277-6). Benjamins North Am.

Esche, Sharon, jt. auth. see Booth, Charles.

Esche, Sharon, jt. auth. see Licari, Louis.

Eschelbach, Claire J. & Shober, Joyce L. Aldous Huxley: A Bibliography, Nineteen Sixteen to Nineteen Fifty-Nine. 1979. Repr. 16.00x (ISBN 0-374-92626-3). Octagon.

Eschenauer, H. & Olhoff, N., eds. Optimization Methods in Structure Design. 460p. 1983. text ed. 24.95 (ISBN 3-411-01654-X, Pub. by Bibliographisches Institut). Birkhauser.

Eschenauer, Jorg. Das Recht auf Arbeit in Ethisch-Politischer Perspektive. (European University Studies: No. 31, Vol. 48). 326p. (Ger.). 1983. 37.35 (ISBN 3-8204-7853-1). P Lang Pubs.

Eschenbach, Vilfred. The Wall Street Maximal Physical Fitness Handbook. (Illus.). 109p. 1983. 55.85x (ISBN 0-86654-065-2). Inst Econ Finan.

Eschenbach, Wolfram. Parzival. Hatto, A. T., tr. (Classics Ser.). 432p. 1980. pap. 5.95 (ISBN 0-14-044361-4). Penguin.

Eschenbach, Wolfram Von. Parzival. 1961. pap. 5.95 (ISBN 0-394-70188-7, V-188, Vin). Random.

Eschenbach, Wolfram Von see Von Eschenbach, Wolfram.

Eschenfelder, A. H. Magnetic Bubble Technology. (Springer Series in Solid State Sciences: Vol. 14). (Illus.). 360p. 1980. 49.80 (ISBN 0-387-09822-4). Springer-Verlag.

--Magnetic Bubble Theory. 2nd corrected & updated ed. (Springer Series in Solid-State Sciences: Vol. 14). (Illus.). 364p. 1981. pap. 38.00 (ISBN 0-387-10790-8). Springer-Verlag.

Eschenroeder, Alan, jt. ed. see Swann, Robert L.

Escher, M. C. & Locher, J. C. World of M. C. Escher. pap. 9.95 (ISBN 0-451-79961-5, G9961, Abrams Art Bks). NAL.

Escher, M. C. & Locher, J. L. The Infinite World of M. C. Escher. (Illus.). 152p. 1985. text ed. 14.98 (ISBN 0-8109-8059-2). Abrams.

Escherich, Peter. Social Biology of the Bushy-Tailed Woodrat, Neotoma Cinerea. (U.C. Publications in Zoology Ser.: Vol. 110). 1981. pap. 14.00x (ISBN 0-520-09595-2). U of Cal Pr.

Escherich, Peter C. & McManus, Roger E., eds. Sources of Federal Funding for Biological Research. 1983. pap. 15.00 (ISBN 0-942924-04-5). Assn Syst Coll.

Eschholz, Paul & Rosa, Alfred, eds. Language Awareness. 3rd ed. LC 81-51837. 332p. 1982. pap. text ed. 11.95 (ISBN 0-312-46693-5); Instr's. manual avail. St Martin.

--Subject & Strategy: A Rhetoric Reader. 3rd ed. LC 84-51145. 550p. 1985. pap. text ed. 11.95 (ISBN 0-312-77469-9); instrs. manual avail. St Martin.

Eschholz, Paul, jt. ed. see Rosa, Alfred.

Eschholz, Paul A., ed. Critics on Willian Dean Howells. LC 74-11430. (Readings in Literary Criticism Ser: No. 23). 128p. 1975. 5.95x (ISBN 0-87024-271-7). U of Miami Pr.

Eschholz, Paul A., jt. ed. see Rosa, Alfred F.

Eschleman, Marian M. Introductory Nutrition & Diet Therapy. (Illus.). 368p. 1983. pap. text ed. 16.00 (ISBN 0-397-54241-0, 64-01970, Lippincott Nursing). Lippincott.

Eschman, Donald F., jt. auth. see Dorr, John A., Jr.

Eschman, Karl. Changing Forms in Modern Music. 2nd ed. LC 67-26898. (Illus.). 213p. 1967. 5.00 (ISBN 0-911318-01-1). E C Schirmer.

Eschmann, et al. Ball & Roller Bearings. LC 84-13120. (BRO Handbook Methods in the Neuroscience Ser.). 488p. 1985. 34.95x (ISBN 0-471-26283-8). Wiley.

Eschmeyer, William N. & Herald, Earl S. Field Guide to the Pacific Coast Fishes of North America. 1983. 19.95 (ISBN 0-395-26873-7); pap. 11.95 (ISBN 0-395-33188-9). HM.

Eschner, Arthur R. & Black, Peter E., eds. Readings in Forest Hydrology. (Illus.). 293p. 1975. text ed. 27.50x (ISBN 0-8422-5228-2). Irvington.

Escholier, Raymond. Victor Hugo. Galantiere, Lewis, tr. 1973. Repr. of 1930 ed. 25.00 (ISBN 0-8274-0413-1). R West.

Escholz, Paul & Rosa, Alfred. Outlooks & Insights: A Reader for Writers. LC 82-60463. 600p. 1983. pap. text ed. 13.95 (ISBN 0-312-59164-0); instr's. manual avail. St Martin.

Eschwege, E., ed. Advances in Diabetes Epidemiology: Proceedings of the International Symposium on the Advances in Diabetes Epidemiology, Abbaye de Fontevraud, France, 3-7 May 1982. (INSERM Symposium Ser.: No. 22). 408p. 1983. 81.00 (ISBN 0-444-80453-6, Biomedical Pr). Elsevier.

Esco Foundation For Palestine Inc. Palestine: A Study of Jewish, Arab, & British Policies, 2 Vols. LC 47-2569. Repr. of 1947 ed. Set. 144.00 (ISBN 0-527-27750-9). Kraus Repr.

Escobal, Patricio P. Las Sacas. (Span.). 1974. pap. 5.00 (ISBN 0-317-02310-1). Edit Mensaje.

Escobal, Pedro R. Methods of Orbit Determination. LC 75-11889. 500p. 1976. Repr. of 1965 ed. 35.00 (ISBN 0-88275-319-3). Krieger.

Escobar, Alice. Art Lessons from Around the World. LC 82-7952. 224p. 1982. pap. 14.50 (ISBN 0-13-047399-5, Busn). P-H.

--One Hundred Sixty-Seven New Art Lessons for a Single Class Period. (Illus.). 1978. 15.50x (ISBN 0-13-634873-4, Parker). P-H.

Escobar, Javier I., jt. ed. see Becerra, Rosina M.

Escobar, M. R. & Friedman, H., eds. Macrophages & Lymphocytes: Nature, Functions, & Interaction, Pt. A. LC 79-9566. (Advances in Experimental Medicine & Biology Ser.: Vol. 121A). 660p. 1980. 75.00x (ISBN 0-306-40285-8, Plenum Pr). Plenum Pub.

--Macrophages & Lymphocytes: Nature, Functions & Interaction, Pt. B. (Advances in Experimental Medicine & Biology Ser.: Vol. 121B). 625p. 1980. 75.00x (ISBN 0-306-40286-6, Plenum Pr). Plenum Pub.

Escobar, Samuel. Irrupcion Juvenil. LC 77-17648. 96p. (Orig., Span.). 1978. pap. 2.50 (ISBN 0-89922-106-8). Edit Caribe.

Escobar, Samuel & Driver, John. Christian Mission & Social Justice. LC 78-6035. (Mennonite Missionary Study Ser.: No. 5). 112p. 1978. pap. 3.95 (ISBN 0-8361-1855-3). Herald Pr.

Escobar, Thyrza. Essentials of Natal Interpretation. 200p. 1982. 10.00 (ISBN 0-86690-100-0, 1107-01). Am Fed Astrologers.

--Side Lights of Astrology. pap. 4.00 (ISBN 0-912368-04-7). Golden Seal.

--The Star Wheel Technique. pap. 12.00 (ISBN 0-912368-04-7). Golden Seal.

Escobedo, Theresa H., ed. Early Childhood Bilingual Education: A Hispanic Perspective. LC 82-25624. (Bilingual Education Ser.). 1983. pap. text ed. 19.95x (ISBN 0-8077-2721-0). Tchrs Coll.

Escoffey, Raymond, jt. auth. see Thomas, Merlin.

Escoffier, A. Escoffier Cook Book. (International Cook Book Ser). Orig. Title: Guide Culinaire. 1941. 9.95 (ISBN 0-517-50662-9). Crown.

Escoffier, Cracknell H. Le Guide Culinaire. 1979. 39.95 (ISBN 0-317-12941-4). Van Nos Reinhold.

Escoffier, Francis & Higginbotham, Jay, eds. A Voyage to Dauphin Island in 1720: The Journal of Bertet De la Clue. Escoffier, Francis & Higginbotham, Jay, trs. LC 73-91909. (Illus., Fr.). 1974. 7.95 (ISBN 0-914334-02-6). Museum Mobile.

Escoffier, Francis, tr. see Escoffier, Francis & Higginbotham, Jay.

Escogida, Obra, et al. Ana Maria Matute. (gr. 11-12). 1982. pap. 8.95x (ISBN 0-88334-162-X). Ind Sch Pr.

Escot, Pozzi, jt. auth. see Cogan, Robert.

Escott, Colin & Hawkins, Martin. Sun Records. (Illus.). 1980. pap. 8.95 (ISBN 0-8256-3161-0). Music Sales.

Escott, J. Newspaper Boy. (Guided Readers Ser.). (gr. 10-12). 1980. pap. text ed. 2.00x (ISBN 0-435-27068-0). Heinemann Ed.

Escott, Paul D. After Secession: Jefferson Davis & the Failure of Confederate Nationalism. LC 78-5726. xvi, 296p. 1978. 25.00x (ISBN 0-8071-0369-1). La State U Pr.

--Slavery Remembered: A Record of Twentieth Century Slave Narratives. LC 78-12198. xv, 221p. 1979. 17.50 (ISBN 0-8078-1340-0); pap. 7.00x (ISBN 0-8078-1343-5). U of NC Pr.

Escott, T. H. Anthony Trollope. His Public Services, Private Friends & Literary Originals. LC 67-27595. 1967. Repr. of 1903 ed. 22.50x (ISBN 0-8046-0137-2, Pub by Kennikat). Assoc Faculty Pr.

--Club Makers & Club Members. 1973. Repr. of 1914 ed. 40.00 (ISBN 0-8274-0544-8). R West.

--Edward Bulwer. LC 75-113309. 1970. Repr. of 1910 ed. 25.50x (ISBN 0-8046-1016-9, Pub. by Kennikat). Assoc Faculty Pr.

--Edward Bulwer: First Baron Lytton of Knebworth: A Social, Personal, & Political Monograph. 1977. Repr. of 1910 ed. lib. bdg. 30.00 (ISBN 0-8495-1305-7). Arden Lib.

--Platform, Press, Politics & Play: Being Pen & Ink Sketches of Contemporary Celebrities from the Tone to the Thames, Via Avon & Isis. 396p. 1984. Repr. lib. bdg. 50.00 (ISBN 0-8482-3750-1). Norwood Edns.

--Platform, Press, Politics & Plays: Being Pen & Ink Sketches of Contemporary Celeberties. (Victorian Age Ser). 45.00 (ISBN 0-8482-0745-9). Norwood Edns.

--Politics & Letters. 1973. Repr. of 1886 ed. 35.00 (ISBN 0-8274-1682-2). R West.

Escott, Thomas H. Great Victorians: Memories & Personalities. 1916. lib. bdg. 40.00 (ISBN 0-8414-3943-5). Folcroft.

--Masters of English Journalism. LC 74-2282. 1974. Repr. of 1911 ed. lib. bdg. 40.00 (ISBN 0-8414-3937-0). Folcroft.

--Masters of English Journalism: A Study of Personal Forces. LC 74-98834. Repr. of 1911 ed. lib. bdg. 22.50x (ISBN 0-8371-3020-4, ESME). Greenwood.

--Social Transformations of the Victorian Age. LC 73-12848. 1897. lib. bdg. 45.00 (ISBN 0-8414-3908-7). Folcroft.

Escott-Stump, Sylvia. Nutrition & Diagnosis-Related Care. LC 84-17145. (Illus.). 344p. 1985. pap. 23.50 (ISBN 0-8121-0950-3). Lea & Febiger.

Escoubes, M., ed. see Conference on Vacuum Microbalance Techniques (12th: 1974: Lyon, France).

Escoula, Yvonne. Six Blue Horses. LC 70-103044. (gr. 5-9). 1970. 10.95 (ISBN 0-87599-162-9). S G Phillips.

Escourolle, Raymond & Poirier, Jacques. Manual of Basic Neuropathology. 2nd ed. Rubinstein, Lucien J., tr. LC 77-80748. (Illus.). 1978. pap. text ed. 15.95 (ISBN 0-7216-3406-0). Saunders.

Escreet, P. K. Introduction to the Anglo-American Cataloguing Rules. 384p. 1971. 18.00x (ISBN 0-233-96033-3, 05787-8, Pub. by Gower Pub Co England). Lexington Bks.

Escribano, jt. auth. see Sanchez, F.

Escribano, Jose. Por Aqui. tchrs. guide & cassettes 74.00 (ISBN 0-686-82067-3); student textbook 7.95 (ISBN 0-88436-911-0, 70277). EMC.

Escritt, Leonard B. Sewerage & Sewage Treatment: International Practice. LC 83-1300. 450p. 1984. 58.95x (ISBN 0-471-10339-X, Pub. by Wiley-Interscience). Wiley.

Escriva, Josemaria. The Way of the Cross. (Illus.). 123p. 1983. 10.95 (ISBN 0-906138-05-1); pap. 6.95 (ISBN 0-906138-06-X); pocket size 3.95 (ISBN 0-906138-07-8). Scepter Pubs.

Escriva de Balaguer, Josemaria. Christ Is Passing by. LC 74-78783. 276p. (Foreign language editions avail). 1977. pap. 6.95 (ISBN 0-933932-04-9). Scepter Pubs.

--Friends of God. 301p. 1981. 14.50 (ISBN 0-906138-03-5); deluxe ed. 24.00 (ISBN 0-906138-04-3); pap. 8.95 (ISBN 0-906138-02-7). Scepter Pubs.

--Holy Rosary. (Illus.). 49p. 1979. 5.95 (ISBN 0-933932-45-6); pap. 2.95 (ISBN 0-933932-44-8). Scepter Pubs.

--The Way. (Foreign language editions avail.). 1965. 8.95 (ISBN 0-933932-00-6). Scepter Pubs.

--The Way. Orig. Title: Camino. 1985. pap. 3.95 (ISBN 0-933932-49-9). Scepter Pubs.

Escudero, J., jt. auth. see Garcia, R. V.

Escudero, Jose, jt. auth. see Garcia, Rolando V.

Escudero, Jose A. De see Carroll, H. Bailey & Haggard, J. Villasana.

Escuela De Economia Domestica. Tabla de Composicion de Alimentos de Uso Corriente en Puerto Rico. pap. 1.85 (ISBN 0-8477-2305-4). U of PR Pr.

Esdaile, Arundell. Age of Elizabeth Fifteen Forty-Seven to Sixteen Three. LC 72-190600. 1931. lib. bdg. 8.50 (ISBN 0-8414-1112-3). Folcroft.

--Bibliography & Various Readings, George Meredith. LC 72-4494. (Studies in George Meredith, No. 21). 1972. Repr. of 1911 ed. lib. bdg. 56.95x (ISBN 0-8383-1511-9). Haskell.

--Bibliography of the Writings in Prose & Verse of George Meredith. LC 74-23912. 1907. lib. bdg. 16.50 (ISBN 0-8414-3945-1). Folcroft.

--The British Museum Library: A Short History & Survey. LC 78-31145. (Library Association Ser.). 1979. Repr. of 1948 ed. lib. bdg. 37.50x (ISBN 0-313-20940-5, ESBM). Greenwood.

--List of English Tales & Prose Romances Printed Before 1740. LC 74-13114. 1912. lib. bdg. 20.00 (ISBN 0-8414-3979-6). Folcroft.

Esdaile, Arundell J. The Age of Elizabeth. LC 74-22280. 1974. Repr. of 1931 ed. lib. bdg. 8.50 (ISBN 0-8414-3935-4). Folcroft.

--Mariage En Droit Canonique, 2 Vols. (Fr). 1969. Repr. of 1891 ed. Set. 47.00 (ISBN 0-8337-1072-9). B Franklin.

Esmiol, Barbara & Dodd, Sandra. If You Love Me-Show Me How: The Life Study Method for Giving & Getting Sexual Pleasure. 192p. 1984. pap. 6.95 (ISBN 0-13-450396-1). P-H.

Esmond, Truman H., Jr. Budgeting Procedures for Hospitals: 1982 Edition. LC 82-13852. 208p. 1982. 38.75 (ISBN 0-939450-14-3, 061140). AHPI.

Esnault. Dictionnaire des Argots Francais. (Fr.). 16.50 (ISBN 0-685-36663-4). French & Eur.

Espada-Matta, Alberto. Church & State in the Social Context of Latin America. 1985. 7.95 (ISBN 0-533-06592-5). Vantage.

Espadas, Orlando T., ed. Casos y Ejercicios Sobre Proyectos Agricolas. 480p. 1975. pap. 5.00 (ISBN 0-686-39631-6). World Bank.

Espejel, Carlos. Mexican Folk Ceramics. (Illus.). 220p. 1982. 35.00 (ISBN 84-7031-222-7, Pub. by Editorial Blume Spain). Intl Spec Bk.

--Mexican Folk Crafts. (Illus.). 237p. 1982. 35.00 (ISBN 84-7031-058-5, Pub. by Editorial Blume Spain). Intl Spec Bk.

--Mexican Toys. Humphries, B., tr. from Span. (Illus.). 120p. cancelled (ISBN 0-87905-404-2, Pub. by Mexican Min Ed Mexico). Gibbs M Smith.

Espeland, Pamela. The Story of Arachne. LC 80-66796. (Myths for Modern Children Ser.). (Illus.). 32p. (gr. 1-4). 1980. PLB 5.95g (ISBN 0-87614-130-0). Carolrhoda Bks.

--The Story of Baucis & Philemon. LC 80-27674. (A Myth for Modern Children Ser.). (Illus.). 32p. (gr. 1-4). 1981. PLB 5.95g (ISBN 0-87614-140-8). Carolrhoda Bks.

--The Story of Cadmus. LC 80-66795. (Myths for Modern Children Ser.). (Illus.). 32p. (gr. 1-4). 1980. PLB 5.95g (ISBN 0-87614-128-9). Carolrhoda Bks.

--The Story of King Midas. LC 80-66794. (Myths for Modern Children Ser.). (Illus.). 32p. (gr. 1-4). 1980. PLB 5.95g (ISBN 0-87614-129-7). Carolrhoda Bks.

--The Story of Pygmalion. LC 80-15792. (Myths for Modern Children Ser.). (Illus.). 32p. (gr. 1-4). 1981. PLB 6.95g (ISBN 0-87614-127-0, AACR1). Carolrhoda Bks.

--Theseus & the Road to Athens. LC 80-27713. (Myths for Modern Children Ser.). (Illus.). 32p. (gr. 1-4). 1981. PLB 6.95g (ISBN 0-87614-141-6). Carolrhoda Bks.

--Why Do We Eat? (Creative's Questions & Answers Library). (Illus.). 32p. (gr. 3-4). 1981. PLB 6.95 (ISBN 0-87191-747-5). Creative Ed.

Espeland, Pamela & Waniek, Marilyn. The Cat Walked Through the Casserole: And Other Poems for Children. LC 84-11381. (Illus.). 40p. (gr. k-4). 1984. PLB 9.95 (ISBN 0-87614-268-4). Carolrhoda Bks.

Espenak, Liljan. Dance Therapy: Theory & Application. (Illus.). 210p. 1981. 19.75x (ISBN 0-398-04110-5). C C Thomas.

Espenschade, Anna. Motor Performance in Adolescence. (SRCD: Vol. 5, No. 1). 1940. 11.00 (ISBN 0-527-01513-X). Kraus Repr.

Espenschade, Anna S. & Eckert, Helen M. Motor Development. 2nd ed. (Special Education Ser.). 368p. 1980. pap. text ed. 16.95 (ISBN 0-675-08142-4). Merrill.

Espenshade, Abraham H. Pennsylvania Place Names. LC 68-30591. 1969. Repr. of 1925 ed. 34.00x (ISBN 0-8103-3234-5). Gale.

--Pennsylvania Place Names. LC 71-112824. (Pennsylvania State College History & Political Science Ser: No. 1). (Illus.). 375p. 1970. Repr. of 1925 ed. 20.00 (ISBN 0-8063-0416-2). Genealog Pub.

Espenshade, Edward B. & Morrison, Joel L., eds. The World Book Atlas. LC 84-61526. (Illus.). 448p. (gr. 8-12). 1985. lib. bdg. write for info. (ISBN 0-7166-3173-3). World Bk.

Espenshade, Edward B., Jr., ed. Goode's World Atlas. 16th ed. Morrison, Joel. LC 73-21108. 384p. 1978. text ed. 19.95 (ISBN 0-528-83125-9); pap. text ed. 15.95 (ISBN 0-528-63007-5). Rand.

Espenshade, Thomas J. The Cost of Children in Urban United States. LC 76-4798. (Population Monograph Ser.: No. 14). 1976. Repr. of 1973 ed. lib. bdg. 22.50 (ISBN 0-8371-8835-0, ESCC). Greenwood.

--Investing in Children: New Estimates of Parental Expenditure. LC 84-5098. 124p. (Orig.). 1984. pap. 12.95x (ISBN 0-87766-332-7). Urban Inst.

Espenshade, Thomas J. & Serow, William J., eds. The Economic Consequences of Slowing Population Growth. (Studies in Population Ser.). 1978. 38.50 (ISBN 0-12-242450-6). Acad Pr.

Espenson, James H. Chemical Kinetics & Reaction Mechanisms. (Advanced Chemistry Ser.). (Illus.). 240p. 1981. text ed. 36.95 (ISBN 0-07-019667-2). McGraw.

Esper, E. J. Icones Fucorum Cum Characteribus Systematicis Synonymis Auctorum & Descriptionibus Novarum Specierum. 1966. Repr. of 1797 ed. 84.00 (ISBN 3-7682-0262-3). Lubrecht & Cramer.

Esper, Erwin A. Technique for the Experimental Investigation of Associative Interference in Artificial Linguistics. (LM). 1925. pap. 16.00 (ISBN 0-527-00805-2). Kraus Repr.

Esper, George & Associated Press. The Eyewitness History of the Vietnam War: 1961-1975. 224p. 1983. pap. 9.95 (ISBN 0-345-30865-4). Ballantine.

Esper, Thomas, tr. see Von Staden, Heinrich.

Esperabe De Artega, Enrique. Diccionario Enciclopedico y Critico De los Hombres De Espana. 530p. (Espn.). 1956. pap. 6.95 (ISBN 84-290-0972-8, S-50137). French & Eur.

Esperance, Francis A., jt. ed. see Friedman, Eli A.

Esperet, Eric. Langage et Origine Sociale des Eleves: Exploration. 2nd ed. 281p. (Fr.). 1982. 22.10 (ISBN 3-261-04754-2). P Lang Pubs.

Esperti, Robert A. & Peterson, Renno L. The Handbook of Estate Planning. LC 85-47. 304p. 1985. 32.50 (ISBN 0-07-019672-9). McGraw.

--Incorporating Your Talents: A Guide to the One-Person Corporation, or How to Lead a Sheltered Life. LC 82-14860. 243p. 1984. 19.95 (ISBN 0-07-019669-9). McGraw.

Espey, John. Empty Box Haiku. 24p. (Orig.). 1980. s & l wrappers 20.00 (ISBN 0-936576-02-2). Symposium Pr.

Espey, John J. Ezra Pound's Mauberley: A Study in Composition. 1974. pap. 2.25 (ISBN 0-520-02618-7). U of Cal Pr.

Espina, Noni. Repertoire for the Solo Voice: A Fully Annotated Guide to Works for the Solo Voice Published in Modern Editions and Covering Material from the 13th Century to the Present, Vols. 1&2. LC 76-30441. 1341p. 1977. 70.00 (ISBN 0-8108-0943-5). Scarecrow.

--Vocal Solos for Christian Churches: A Descriptive Reference of Solo Music for the Church Year. 3rd ed. LC 84-51398. 256p. 25.00 (ISBN 0-8108-1730-6). Scarecrow.

Espinas, Alfred V. Des Societies Animals: Animal Societies. Egerton, Frank N., 3rd, ed. LC 77-74219. (History of Ecology Ser.). 1978. Repr. of 1878 ed. lib. bdg. 34.00 (ISBN 0-405-10390-5). Ayer Co Pubs.

Espinasse, Francis. Life of Ernest Renan. 1895. Repr. 20.00 (ISBN 0-8274-2925-8). R West.

--Literary Recollections & Sketches. 1893. Repr. 40.00 (ISBN 0-8274-2957-6). R West.

Espinel, Vincente. The History of the Life of the Squire Marcos de Obregon, 2 vols. in 1. Langton, Algernon, tr. LC 80-2578. Repr. of 1816 ed. 76.50 (ISBN 0-404-19110-X). AMS Pr.

Espinos, Gilberto, ed. see Alcala, Gaspar.

Espinosa, A. M. Spanish for Doctors & Nurses. 1978. 15.50 (ISBN 0-8151-3147-X). Year Bk Med.

Espinosa, Ann L., tr. see Otero, George G. & Smith, Gary R.

Espinosa, Ann L., tr. see Switzer, Kenneth A. & Redden, Charlotte A.

Espinosa, Aurelio M. The Folklore of Spain in the American Southwest: Traditional Spanish Folk Literature in Northern New Mexico & Southern Colorado. Espinosa, J. Manuel, ed. & intro. by. LC 85-40473. (Illus.). 336p. 1985. 24.95 (ISBN 0-8061-1942-X). U of Okla Pr.

Espinosa, Aurelio M. & Wonder, John P. Gramatica Analitica. 400p. 1975. text ed. 22.95 (ISBN 0-669-82941-2). Heath.

Espinosa, Aurelio M., ed. Cuentos populares espanoles, 3 pts. in 1 vol. LC 74-166039. Repr. of 1926 ed. 48.50 (ISBN 0-404-51805-2). AMS Pr.

Espinosa, Aurelio M., frwd. by. Hispanic Influences in the United States. (Illus.). 64p. (Orig.). 1975. pap. 2.95 (ISBN 0-913456-47-0, Pub. by Spanish Inst). Interbk Inc.

Espinosa, Aurelio M., ed. see Mason, J. Alden.

Espinosa, Aurelio M., Jr., jt. auth. see Turk, Laurel H.

Espinosa, Carmen G. Shawls, Crinolines & Filigree: Dress & Adornment of the Women of New Mexico. LC 72-138042. (Illus.). 80p. 1970. 8.00 (ISBN 0-87404-026-4). Tex Western.

Espinosa, G., et al, eds. Solid State Nuclear Track Detectors: Proceedings of the 12th International Conference, Mexico, 4-10 September 1983. LC 84-201795. 651p. 1984. 110.00 (ISBN 0-08-031420-1). Pergamon.

Espinosa, Ismael E., tr. see Otero, George G. & Smith, Gary R.

Espinosa, J. C. Birth Control: Why Are They Lying to Women? 1979. 6.95 (ISBN 0-533-03922-3). Vantage.

Espinosa, J. Manuel, ed. & intro. by see Espinosa, Aurelio M.

Espinosa, Jose L. Practica Mercantil y Documentacion. (Span.). 1982. text ed. 4.25 (ISBN 0-538-22240-9, V24). SW Pub.

Espinosa, Jose M. Spanish Folk-Tales from New Mexico. LC 38-9815. (AFS M). Repr. of 1937 ed. 21.00 (ISBN 0-527-01082-0). Kraus Repr.

Espinosa, Juan & Zimbalist, Andrew. Economic Democracy: Worker's Participation in Chilean Industry, 1970-1973. LC 81-14941. (Studies in Social Discontinuity). (Updated Student Edition). 1981. pap. 11.00 (ISBN 0-12-242751-3). Acad Pr.

Espinosa, Juan E. & Zimbalist, Andrew, eds. Economic Democracy. 1978. 35.00 (ISBN 0-12-242750-5). Acad Pr.

Espinosa, Maria. Longing. 336p. (Orig.). 1985. pap. 9.95 (ISBN 0-933529-01-5). Cayuse Pr.

Espinosa, Mayra C., tr. see LaBrucherie, Roger A.

Espinosa, Williams & Janka, Les. Defense or Aggression? U. S. Arms Export Control Laws & the Israeli Invasion of Lebanon. (Illus.). 1982. pap. 1.00x (ISBN 0-318-01024-0). Am Educ Trust.

Espinosa y Tello, Jose. Spanish Voyage to Vancouver & the North-West Coast of America. Jane, Cecil, tr. LC 70-136389. (Illus.). Repr. of 1930 ed. 10.00 (ISBN 0-404-02356-8). AMS Pr.

Espinoza, A. M., jt. auth. see Radin, Paul.

Espinoza, Alurista D., tr. see Espinoza, Herberto.

Espinoza, Herberto. Viendo Morir a Teresa y Otros Relatos. Espinoza, Alurista D., tr. LC 83-60436. (Illus.). 112p. (Orig., Eng. & Span.). 1983. pap. 5.00x (ISBN 0-939558-04-1). Maize Pr.

Espinoza, Luis R. & Osterland, C. Kirk, eds. Circulating Immune Complexes. LC 82-83042. (Illus.). 317p. 1983. 37.50 (ISBN 0-87993-188-4). Futura Pub.

Espinoza, Max. Fronteras. 224p. (Orig.). 1980. pap. 2.25 (ISBN 0-87067-007-7, BH007). Holloway.

Espirit, Julie Du St. see Du St. Espirit, Sr. Julie.

Espiritu, Augusto C. & Green, Reginald H. The International Context of Rural Poverty in the Third World: Issues for Research & Action by Grassroots Organizations & Legal Activists. 100p. (Orig.). 1985. pap. 8.00x (ISBN 0-936876-40-9). Learn Res Intl Stud.

Espiritu, Percy. Let's Speak Ilokano. 320p. 1984. pap. text ed. 15.00x (ISBN 0-8248-0822-3). UH Pr.

Espiritu, Socorro C. A Study of the Treatment of the Philippines in Selected Social Studies Textbooks Published in the U. S. for Use in Elementary & Secondary Schools. LC 74-76469. 1974. Repr. of 1954 ed. soft bdg. 12.00 (ISBN 0-88247-234-8). R & E Pubs.

Esplen, Mike see Milne, John.

Esposito, Anthony. Fluid Power with Applications. (Illus.). 1980. text ed. 28.95 (ISBN 0-13-322701-4). P-H.

Esposito, Barbara, et al. Prison Slavery. Bardsley, Kathryn, ed. (Illus., Orig.). 1982. pap. 12.95 (ISBN 0-910007-00-4). Comm Abol Prison.

Esposito, F. Paul & Witten, Louis, eds. Asymptotic Structure of Space-Time. LC 77-487. 442p. 1977. 69.50x (ISBN 0-306-31022-8, Plenum Pr). Plenum Pub.

Esposito, John C. Cornerstone Contract Kit: How to Buy & Sell a Used Car. 1981. pap. 3.95 (ISBN 0-346-12540-5). Cornerstone.

--Vanishing Air. 328p. 1970. pap. 0.95 (ISBN 0-686-36549-6). Ctr Responsive Law.

Esposito, John L. Islam & Politics. LC 84-16135. (Contemporary Issues in the Middle East Ser.). 288p. 1984. 28.00x (ISBN 0-8156-2322-4); pap. 12.95x (ISBN 0-8156-2323-2). Syracuse U Pr.

--Women in Muslim Family Law. LC 81-18273. (Contemporary Issues in the Middle East Ser.). 172p. 1982. pap. text ed. 10.95X (ISBN 0-8156-2278-3). Syracuse U Pr.

Esposito, John L., ed. Islam & Development: Religion & Sociopolitical Change. LC 80-25119. (Contemporary Issues in the Middle East Ser.). 292p. 1980. pap. text ed. 9.95x (ISBN 0-8156-2230-9). Syracuse U Pr.

--Voices of Resurgent Islam. 1983. 22.95x (ISBN 0-19-503339-6); pap. 11.95x (ISBN 0-19-503340-X). Oxford U Pr.

Esposito, John L., jt. ed. see Donohue, John J.

Esposito, Joseph L. Evolutionary Metaphysics: The Development of Peirce's Theory of Catagories. LC 80-15736. (Illus.). x, 252p. 1980. 21.95x (ISBN 0-8214-0551-9, 82-83442). Ohio U Pr.

--Schelling's Idealism & Philosophy of Nature. 294p. 1978. 24.50 (ISBN 0-8387-1904-X). Bucknell U Pr.

--The Transcendence of History: Essays on the Evolution of Historical Consciousness. LC 84-5217. viii, 200p. 1984. text ed. 24.95x (ISBN 0-8214-0779-1). Ohio U Pr.

Esposito, Michael S., ed. Yeast Molecular Biology-Recombinant DNA: Recent Advances. LC 84-4096. (Illus.). 349p. 1984. 35.00 (ISBN 0-8155-0987-1). Noyes.

Esposito, Phil, et al. We Can Teach You to Play Hockey. 1977. 2.95 (ISBN 0-346-12303-8). Cornerstone.

Esposito, R., ed. see Doll, John P. & Orazem, Frank.

Esposito, Tony, jt. ed. see King, Jean C.

Esposito, Vincent J. & Elting, John R. Military History & Atlas of the Napoleonic Wars. LC 77-14708. Repr. of 1968 ed. 74.50 (ISBN 0-404-16950-3). AMS Pr.

Espy, Hilda C. & Creamer, Lex. Another World: Central America. (Illus.). 1970. 14.95 (ISBN 0-670-12939-9). Viking.

Espy, Richard. The Politics of the Olympic Games. LC 78-62861. 1979. 12.95 (ISBN 0-520-03777-4); pap. 6.95 (ISBN 0-520-04395-2, CAL 493). U of Cal Pr.

Espy, Rosalie & Martin, Clyde I. Fun with Dusty. (Illus.). (gr. k-1). 1958. text ed. 4.00 (ISBN 0-87443-031-3). Benson.

Espy, Willard. Have a Word on Me: A Celebration of Language. 1984. pap. 6.95 (ISBN 0-671-50772-9, Touchstone Bks). S&S.

Espy, Willard R. An Almanac of Words at Play. (Illus.). 352p. 1975. 12.95 (ISBN 0-517-52090-7, C N Potter Bks); pap. 7.95 (ISBN 0-517-52463-5, C N Potter). Crown.

--The Garden of Eloquence: A Rhetorical Bestiary. LC 83-47530. (Illus.). 224p. 1983. 16.30 (ISBN 0-06-181256-0, HarpT). Har-Row.

--The Garden of Eloquence: A Rhetorical Bestiary. (Obelisk Ser.). (Illus.). 224p. 1985. pap. 9.95 (ISBN 0-525-48196-6, 0966-290). Dutton.

--The Life & Works of Mr. Anonymous. 1979. pap. 2.75 (ISBN 0-380-45047-X, 45047-X). Avon.

--Oysterville: Roads to Grandpa's Village. (Illus.). 288p. 1977. 12.95 (ISBN 0-517-52196-2, C N Potter Bks); pap. 9.95 (ISBN 0-517-54913-1). Crown.

--Word Puzzles. LC 83-14354. 192p. (Orig.). 1983. pap. 7.95 (ISBN 0-934878-31-5). Dembner Bks.

Espy, William R. A Children's Almanac of Words at Play. LC 82-7593. (Illus.). (gr. 3-9). 1983. 15.95 (ISBN 0-517-54660-4, C N Potter); pap. 8.95 (ISBN 0-517-54666-3). Crown.

Esquemeling, John. The Buccaneers of America. 480p. 1976. Repr. of 1684 ed. 17.95 (ISBN 0-87928-071-9). Corner Hse.

Esquenazi-Mayo, Roberto & Meyer, Michael C., eds. Latin American Scholarship Since World War II: Trends in History, Political Science, Literature, Geography, & Economics. LC 73-125101. xii, 335p. 1971. 25.50x (ISBN 0-8032-0783-2). U of Nebr Pr.

Esquerre, Paul-Joseph. The Applied Theory of Accounts. Brief, Richard P., ed. LC 77-87269. (Development of Contemporary Accounting Thought Ser.). 1978. Repr. of 1914 ed. lib. bdg. 40.00x (ISBN 0-405-10898-2). Ayer Co Pubs.

Esquilo. Tragedias. pap. 1.95 (ISBN 0-685-11603-4). French & Eur.

Esquire, D. J. Secrets of Angling. 62p. 1970. boxed 6.75 (ISBN 0-88395-001-4). Freshet Pr.

Esquire Editors. Fifty Who Made the Difference. LC 84-40176. 565p. 1984. 19.45 (ISBN 0-394-53912-5, Pub. by Villard Bks). Random.

Esquire Editors, jt. auth. see Laskin, David.

Esquire Editors, jt. auth. see Pesmen, Curtis.

Esquire Magazine. First Sports Reader. facs. ed. Graffis, H. B., ed. LC 78-134074. (Essay Index Reprint Ser). 1945. 20.00 (ISBN 0-8369-2188-7). Ayer Co Pubs.

Esquire Magazine Editors. Man at His Best: The Esquire Guide to Style. (Illus.). 1985. 24.95 (ISBN 0-201-11989-7). Addison-Wesley.

Esquire Magazine Editors & Crocker, Deborah. Esquire Ultimate Fitness. LC 84-21695. (Illus.). 240p. 1985. 19.95 (ISBN 0-201-11990-0). Addison-Wesley.

Esquirol, E. D. The Basic Problems of Insanity. (Illus.). 114p. 1982. 69.85 (ISBN 0-89920-034-6). Am Inst Psych.

Esquirol, Etienne. Des Maladies Mentales: Considerees Sous les Rapports Medical Hygienique et Medico-Legal, 3 vols. in 2. LC 75-16703. (Classics in Psychiatry). (Illus., Fr.). 1976. Repr. of 1838 ed. Set. 122.00x (ISBN 0-405-07464-6); 60.50x ea. Vol. 1 (ISBN 0-405-07465-4). Vols. 2-3 (ISBN 0-405-07466-2). Ayer Co Pubs.

Esquivel, Julia. Threatened with Resurrection: Amenazado de Resurreccion. 128p. (Eng. & Span.). 1982. pap. 4.95 (ISBN 0-87178-844-6). Brethren.

ESRIN-ESLAB Symposium, 2nd Frascati, Italy 23-27, September, 1968. Low-Frequency Waves & Irregularities in the Ionosphere: Proceedings. D'Angelo, N., ed. (Astrophysics & Space Science Library: No.14). 218p. 1969. lib. bdg. 37.00 (ISBN 90-277-0114-8, Pub. by Reidel Holland). Kluwer Academic.

ESRIN-ESLAB Symposium, 4th, Frascati, Italy, July 6-10, 1970. Mesospheric Models & Related Experiments: Proceedings. Fiocco, G., ed. LC 70-154737. (Astrophysics & Space Science Library: No.25). 298p. 1971. lib. bdg. 42.00 (ISBN 90-277-0200-4, Pub. by Reidel Holland). Kluwer Academic.

ESRO Summer School in Space Physics, 3rd, Albach, Austria, July 19-August 13, 1965. Electromagnetic Radiation in Space: Proceedings. Emming, S. G., ed. (Astrophysics & Space Science Library: No. 9). 307p. 1968. 37.00 (ISBN 90-277-0116-4, Pub. by Reidel Holland). Kluwer Academic.

Ess, Barbara & Branca, Glenn, eds. Just Another Asshole. 192p. (Orig.). 1983. pap. 4.95 (ISBN 0-913803-93-6). Just Another.

Ess, Donald H. Van see Van Ess, Donald H.

Ess, Dorothy Van see Van Ess, Dorothy.

Ess, Josef Von. Zwischen Hadit und Theologie: Studien Zum Entstehen Praedestinatianischer Ueberlieferung. LC 73-91809. (Studien Zur Sprache, Geschichte und Kultur Des Islamischen Orients, N.F. Vol. 7). (Ger.). 1974. 53.20x (ISBN 3-11-004290-8). De Gruyter.

Ess, Warren A. van see Van Ess, Warren A.

Essa, Eva. A Practical Guide to Solving Preschool Behavior Problems. LC 82-70426. (Illus.). 288p. (Orig.). 1983. pap. text ed. 11.80 (ISBN 0-8273-2082-5). Delmar.

Essad, Bey. Blood & Oil in the Orient. Talmey, Elsa, tr. LC 72-1046. Repr. of 1932 ed. 12.50 (ISBN 0-404-00796-1). AMS Pr.

Essary, Loris, jt. auth. see Clark, Carl D.

Esse, Jay. Randy's New Year & Random Rhymes. 82p. 1983. 5.95 (ISBN 0-533-05699-3). Vantage.

Essel, I. K., jt. auth. see Konig, W.

Essen, Juliet & Wedge, Peter. Continuities in Childhood Disadvantage, No. 6. (DHSS Studies in Deprivation & Disadvantage). 200p. 1982. text ed. 27.00x (ISBN 0-435-82283-7). Gower Pub Co.

Essen, M. R. The Cosine Pi Lambda Theorem. LC 75-17547. (Lecture Notes in Mathematics Ser.: Vol. 467). 112p. (Orig.). 1975. pap. 13.00 (ISBN 0-387-07176-8). Springer-Verlag.

Essenmacher, Gerald. Color Vision in Man. (Illus.). 1978. 20.00 (ISBN 0-916750-17-5). Dayton Labs.

--CPR Cardio-Pulmonary Resuscitation. (Illus.). 1978. 20.00 (ISBN 0-916750-19-1). Dayton Labs.

--Sickle Cell Anemia. (Illus.). 1978. 20.00 (ISBN 0-916750-51-5). Dayton Labs.

--Ski Injury Biomechanics. (Illus.). 1978. 20.00 (ISBN 0-916750-52-3). Dayton Labs.

Essenmacher, Gerald L. Back Problems in Teens. 1978. 20.00 (ISBN 0-916750-07-8, CX-5). Dayton Labs.

Essenwanger, O. M. Applied Statistics in Atmospheric Science, Part A: Frequency Distribution & Curve-Fitting. (Developments in Atmospheric Science Ser.: Vol. 4A). 412p. 1976. 93.75 (ISBN 0-444-41327-8). Elsevier.

Esser, A. H., ed. Behavior & Environment: The Use of Space by Animals & Men. LC 73-142038. 430p. 1971. 35.00x (ISBN 0-306-30521-6, Plenum Pr). Plenum Pub.

Esser, A. H. & Greenbie, B. B., eds. Design for Communality & Privacy. LC 78-7055. 352p. 1978. 37.50x (ISBN 0-306-40010-3, Plenum Pr). Plenum Pub.

Esser, Cajetan. Origins of the Order of Friars Minor. (Orig.). 1970. 12.50 (ISBN 0-8199-0414-7). Franciscan Herald.

Esser, Helen M. Flexibility & Health Through Yoga. (Illus.). 1978. pap. text ed. 10.95 (ISBN 0-8403-2236-4). Kendall-Hunt.

Esser, Josef. Why Am I...? A New Thought on Genetics. 122p. 1980. 8.95 (ISBN 0-8059-2716-6). Dorrance.

Esser, Juergen & Huebler, Axel, eds. Forms & Functions: Papers in General, English, & Applied Linguistics Presented to Vilem Fried on the Occasion of His 65th. Birthday. (Tuebinger Beitraege zur Linguistik: No. 149). 284p. 1981. 47.00x (ISBN 3-87808-149-9). Benjamins North Am.

Esser, K., ed. see International Congress of Botany, Edinburgh, 1964.

Esser, Karl. Cryptogams: Cyanobacteria, Algae, Fungi, Lichens, Textbook & Practical Guide. Hackston, Michael G. & Webster, John, trs. LC 80-41070. 624p. 1982. text ed. 85.00 (ISBN 0-521-23621-5). Cambridge U Pr.

Esser, Karl & Kuenen, Rudolf. Genetics of Fungi. Steiner, Erich, tr. 1968. 62.60 (ISBN 0-387-03784-5). Springer-Verlag.

Esser, Kevin. Streetboy Dreams. LC 83-42922. 178p. (Orig.). 1983. pap. 7.95 (ISBN 0-933322-11-9). Sea Horse.

Esser, P. D. & Johnston, R. E., eds. Technology of Nuclear Magnetic Resonance. 272p. 1984. pap. 29.00 (ISBN 0-317-17712-5). Soc Nuclear Med.

Esser, Peter, et al, eds. Digital Imaging: Clinical Advances in Nuclear Medicine. LC 82-16941. (Illus.). 304p. 1983. 37.50 (ISBN 0-932004-13-X). Soc Nuclear Med.

Esser, Peter D., ed. Emission Computed Tomography: Current Trends. LC 83-6853. (Illus.). 320p. (Orig.). 1983. pap. text ed. 29.50 (ISBN 0-932004-16-4). Soc Nuclear Med.

Esser, Peter D., et al. Functional Mapping of Organ Systems & Other Computer Topics. LC 81-51827. (Illus.). 272p. 1981. 30.50 (ISBN 0-932004-09-1). Soc Nuclear Med.

Esser, Thomas J. Effective Report Writing in Vocational Evaluation & Work Adjustment Programs. (Illus.). 118p. (Orig.). 1974. pap. 8.00x (ISBN 0-916671-22-4). Material Dev.

--Gathering Information for Evaluation Planning. 60p. (Orig.). 1980. pap. 4.75x (ISBN 0-916671-11-9). Material Dev.

Esser, William L. Dictionary of Natural Foods. LC 83-72140. (Illus.). 1983. pap. 4.95 (ISBN 0-914532-30-8). Natural Hygiene.

Essers, J. A., ed. Computational Methods for Turbulent, Transonic, & Viscous Flows. LC 83-187. (A Von Karman Institute Bk.). 360p. 1983. text ed. 49.95 (ISBN 0-89116-273-9). Hemisphere Pub.

Essert, Charles E. Secret Splendor. 147p. 1973. 6.00 (ISBN 0-8022-2107-6). Philos Lib.

Essertier, Daniel. Psychologie & Sociologie. LC 68-56802. (Fr). 1968. Repr. of 1927 ed. 22.50 (ISBN 0-8337-1073-7). B Franklin.

Essery, Bob & Jenkinson, David. An Illustrated History of L. M. S. Locomotives: General Review & Locomotive Liveries, Vol. 1. 248p. 70.00x (ISBN 0-86093-087-4, Pub. by ORPC Ltd UK). State Mutual Bk.

Essery, R. J. An Illustrated History of L. M. S. Wagons, Vol. 1. 188p. 49.00x (ISBN 0-86093-127-7, Pub. by ORPC Ltd UK). State Mutual Bk.

--An Illustrated History of L. M. S. Wagons, Vol. 2. 188p. 50.00x (ISBN 0-86093-255-9, Pub. by ORPC Ltd UK). State Mutual Bk.

--An Illustrated History of Midland Wagons, Vol. 1. 176p. 35.00x (ISBN 0-86093-040-8, Pub. by ORPC Ltd UK). State Mutual Bk.

--An Illustrated History of Midlands Wagons, Vol. 2. 176p. 35.00x (ISBN 0-86093-041-6, Pub. by ORPC Ltd UK). State Mutual Bk.

Essery, R. J., et al. British Goods Wagon. LC 73-95620. (Illus.). 1970. lib. bdg. 17.95x (ISBN 0-678-05664-1). Kelley.

Essex, Arthur C. Essex Papers. Airy, O., ed. Repr. of 1890 ed. 27.00 (ISBN 0-384-14670-8). Johnson Repr.

Essex, Don L. Bonding Versus Pay-As-You-Go in the Financing of School Buildings. LC 70-176757. (Columbia University. Teachers College. Contributions to Education: No. 496). Repr. of 1931 ed. 22.50 (ISBN 0-404-55496-2). AMS Pr.

Essex Institute. Essex Institute Historical Collections, Vols. 1-20. Set. 595.00; Set. pap. 475.00. Johnson Repr.

Essex, Marianna. Torrent of Love. (Rapture Romance Ser.: No. 41). 192p. (Orig.). 1983. pap. 1.95 (ISBN 0-451-12607-6, Sig). NAL.

Essex, Myron, et al, eds. Viruses in Naturally Occurring Cancers. LC 80-67166. (Cold Spring Harbor Conferences on Cell Proliferation Ser.: Vol. 7). (Illus.). 1284p. 1980. 2 bk. set 158.50x (ISBN 0-87969-131-X). Cold Spring Harbor.

Essex-Cater. Manual of Public Health & Community Medicine. 3rd ed. 740p. 1979. 79.00 (ISBN 0-7236-0477-0). PSG Pub Co.

Essick, Edward. Essentials of Computer Data Processing. abr. ed. 448p. 1984. pap. text ed. 21.95 (ISBN 0-574-21440-2, 13-4440); write for info. tchr's ed. (ISBN 0-574-21441-0, 13-4441); study guide 8.95 (ISBN 0-574-21442-9, 13-4442). SRA.

--RPG-II Programming. 354p. 1981. pap. text ed. 20.95 (ISBN 0-574-21315-5, 13-4315); instr's. guide avail. (ISBN 0-574-21316-3, 13-4316). SRA.

Essick, Edward, jt. auth. see Dock, V. Thomas.

Essick, Edward L. RPG for System 360 & System 370. (Orig.). 1973. pap. text ed. 20.95 scp (ISBN 0-06-382625-9, HarpC). Har-Row.

Essick, Robert & Paley, Morton D. Robert Blair's "The Grave". 1982. 90.00 (ISBN 0-85967-529-7). Scolar.

Essick, Robert, ed. The Visionary Hand: Essays for the Study of William Blake's Art & Aesthetics. LC 72-96392. (Illus.). 600p. 1973. 18.50 (ISBN 0-912158-22-0); pap. 12.50 (ISBN 0-912158-41-7). Hennessey.

Essick, Robert N. The Separate Plates of William Blake: A Catalogue. LC 82-7588. (Illus.). 344p. 1983. 80.00x (ISBN 0-691-04011-7). Princeton U Pr.

--William Blake: Printmaker. LC 79-3205. (Illus.). 1980. 65.00x (ISBN 0-691-03954-2). Princeton U Pr.

--The Works of William Blake in the Hunington Collections: A Complete Catalogue. LC 85-10689. (Illus.). 224p. 1985. 20.00 (ISBN 0-87328-084-9). Huntington Lib.

Essick, Robert N., jt. auth. see Easson, Roger R.

Essick, Robert N. & Pearce, Donald, eds. Blake in His Time. LC 77-15759. (Illus.). pap. cancelled (ISBN 0-317-10420-9, 2055494). Bks Demand UMI.

Essien-Udom, E. U. & Garvey, Amy, eds. More Philosophy & Opinions of Marcus Garvey: Previously Published Papers, Vol. 3. (Illus.). 248p. 1977. 27.50x (ISBN 0-7146-1751-2, F Cass Co); pap. 9.95x (ISBN 0-7146-4027-1, Pub. by Cass Co). Biblio Dist.

Essig, Alvin, jt. auth. see Caplan, S. Roy.

Essig, D. James. The Bonds of Wickedness: American Evangelicals Against Slavery, 1770-1808. 224p. 1982. 29.95 (ISBN 0-87722-282-7). Temple U Pr.

Essig, Sheila, jt. auth. see Walker, Jacquelyn S.

Esslemont, J. E. Baha'u'llah & the New Era: An Introduction to the Baha'i Faith. 5th rev. ed. LC 80-24305. 1980. pap. 3.50 (ISBN 0-87743-160-4, 231-005). Baha'i.

--Baha'u'llah & the New Era: An Introduction to the Baha'i Faith. 4th rev. ed. LC 79-21937. 1980. 16.95 (ISBN 0-87743-136-1, 231-004). Baha'i.

Esslemont, Peter. Brithers A' A Minut a Day with Burns. 1973. Repr. of 1939 ed. 10.00 (ISBN 0-8274-1687-3). R West.

Esslemont, R. J., et al. Fertility Management in Cattle. (Illus.). 256p. 1985. 24.00x (ISBN 0-00-383032-2, Pub. by Collins England). Sheridan.

Esslen, E. The Acute Facial Palsies. (Schriftenreihe Neurologie Ser.: No. 18). 1977. 31.00 (ISBN 0-387-08018-X). Springer-Verlag.

Esslen, Rainer. Back to Nature in Canoes: A Guide to American Waters. LC 75-39780. (Illus.). 1976. pap. 6.95 (ISBN 0-914366-04-1). Columbia Pub.

--Back to Nature in Canoes: A Guide to American Waters. (Illus.). 346p. 1985. pap. 6.95 (ISBN 0-914366-04-1). Vanguard.

Esslin, Martin. The Age of Television. LC 81-12552. (Illus.). 144p. 1981. pap. 10.95 (ISBN 0-7167-1338-1). W H Freeman.

--An Anatomy of Drama. (Drama Bk.). 125p. 1977. 7.50 (ISBN 0-8090-2632-5); pap. 4.95 (ISBN 0-8090-0550-6). Hill & Wang.

--Antonin Artaud. (Modern Masters Ser.). 1977. pap. 4.95 (ISBN 0-14-004368-3). Penguin.

--Bertolt Brecht. LC 74-76246. (Columbia Essays on Modern Writers Ser.: No. 42). 48p. 1969. pap. 2.50 (ISBN 0-231-02962-4, MW42). Columbia U Pr.

--Brecht: A Choice of Evils- A Critical Study of the Man, His Work, & His Opinions. 4th ed. (Illus.). 315p. 1984. pap. 9.95 (ISBN 0-413-54750-7, NO. 4102). Methuen Inc.

--Mediations: Essays on Brecht, Beckett & the Media. LC 81-48547. 256p. 1982. pap. 9.95 (ISBN 0-394-17970-6, E805, Ever). Grove.

--Mediations: Essays on Brecht, Beckett & the Media. LC 80-16076. 240p. 1980. 22.50x (ISBN 0-8071-0771-9). La State U Pr.

--Pinter: The Playwright. 4th ed. (Illus.). 288p. 1984. pap. 9.95 (ISBN 0-413-51550-8, 4145). Methuen Inc.

--The Theatre of the Absurd. rev. ed. LC 72-94410. 448p. 1973. Repr. of 1961 ed. 27.95 (ISBN 0-87951-005-6). Overlook Pr.

--Theatre of the Absurd. 3rd ed. 424p. 1983. pap. 5.95 (ISBN 0-14-020929-8, Pelican). Penguin.

Esslin, Martin, ed. Illustrated Encyclopedia of World Theater. (Illus.). 320p. 1981. pap. 12.95 (ISBN 0-500-27207-7). Thames Hudson.

--Samuel Beckett: A Collection of Critical Essays. 1965. text ed. 12.95 (ISBN 0-13-072991-4, Spec). P-H.

Esslinger, Dean R. Friends for Two Hundred Years: A History of Baltimore's Oldest School. LC 83-80846. (Illus.). 258p. 1983. 15.00 (ISBN 0-9610826-0-7). Friends Sch Balt.

--Immigrants & the City: Ethnicity & Mobility in a 19th Century Midwestern City. 1975. 15.95x (ISBN 0-8046-9108-8, Pub. by Kennikat). Assoc Faculty Pr.

Esslinger, William. Politics & Science. 1955. 5.00 (ISBN 0-8022-0458-9). Philos Lib.

Essman, W. & Valzelli, L., eds. Current Developments in Psychopharmacology, Vol. VI. LC 75-642512. (Illus.). 339p. 1981. text ed. 60.00 (ISBN 0-89335-090-7). SP Med & Sci Bks.

Essman, W. B. & Valzelli, L., eds. Neuropharmacology: Clinical Applications. (Illus.). 500p. 1982. text ed. 55.00 (ISBN 0-89335-154-7). SP Med & Sci Bks.

Essman, W. B., jt. ed. see Abrams, R.

Essman, Walter B., ed. Hormonal Actions in Non-Endocrine Systems. 213p. 1983. text ed. 38.50 (ISBN 0-89335-170-9). SP Med & Sci Bks.

--Neurotransmitters, Receptors, & Drug Action. LC 79-23862. (Illus.). 220p. 1980. text ed. 35.00 (ISBN 0-89335-108-3). SP Med & Sci Bks.

--Perspectives in Clinical Endocrinology. (Illus.). 390p. 1980. text ed. 45.00 (ISBN 0-89335-077-X). SP Med & Sci Bks.

--Regulatory Processes in Clinical Endocrinology. 300p. 1982. text ed. 30.00 (ISBN 0-89335-171-7). SP Med & Sci Bks.

Essner, Adam, ed. see Sallustius.

Essner, Warren, jt. auth. see Brady, James.

Essoe, Gabe. Films of Clark Gable. (Illus.). 1970. 12.00 (ISBN 0-8065-0011-5); pap. 7.95 (ISBN 0-8065-0273-8). Citadel Pr.

--Tarzan of the Movies. (Illus.). 224p. 1972. pap. 7.95 (ISBN 0-8065-0295-9). Citadel Pr.

Essrig, Harry. Judaism. (gr. 11 up). 1984. Barron.

Essrig, Harry & Segal, Abraham. Israel Today. rev. ed. LC 77-7536. (Illus.). (YA) (gr. 8-10). 1977. text ed. 8.50 (ISBN 0-8074-0007-6, 142601); tchr's guide o.p. 5.00 (ISBN 0-686-83000-8, 202601). UAHC.

Estabrook, G. F., ed. Proceedings of the Eighth International Conference on Numerical Taxonomy. LC 75-31878. (Illus.). 429p. 1976. 38.95 (ISBN 0-7167-0555-9). W H Freeman.

Estabrook, Leigh, jt. auth. see Heim, Kathleen.

Estabrook, R., et al, eds. Microsomes & Drug Oxidations. LC 73-6403. 486p. 1973. 30.00 (ISBN 0-683-02918-5, Pub. by W & W). Krieger.

Estabrook, Ronald, jt. ed. see Horecker, Bernard.

Estabrook, Ronald W. see Colowick, Sidney P. & Kaplan, Nathan O.

Estabrook, Ronald W., jt. ed. see Srere, Paul A.

Estabrook, Todd. Fully Fit in Sixty Minutes a Week: The Complete Shape-Up Program for Men. (Illus.). 64p. 1983. pap. 2.95 (ISBN 0-943392-06-3). Tribeca Comm.

Estabrooks, George H. Hypnotism. rev. ed. 1959. pap. 6.50 (ISBN 0-525-47038-7, 0631-190). Dutton.

Estades, Rosa. Patrones de Participacion Politica de los Puertorriquenos en la Ciudad de Nueva York. Gardenas-Ruiz, Manuel, tr. LC 77-12112. 1978. pap. 5.00 (ISBN 0-8477-2446-8). U of PR Pr.

--Patterns of Political Participation of Puerto Ricans in New York. LC 77-11625. 1978. pap. 5.00 (ISBN 0-8477-2445-X). U of PR Pr.

Estades De Camara, Maria E., tr. see Beirne, Charles J.

Estafanous, Fawzy G., ed. Opioids in Anesthesia. (Illus.). 352p. 1984. text ed. 34.95 (ISBN 0-409-95183-8). Butterworth.

Estafen, Bernard D. The Comparative Management of Firms in Chile. LC 78-633856. (International Business Research Institute Ser: No. 4). 217p. 1972. 6.95 (ISBN 0-87925-001-1). Ind U Busn Res.

--The Systems Transfer Characteristics of Firms in Spain: A Comparative Management Study of American & Spanish Business Organizations. (International Business Research Institute Ser: No. 5). 160p. 1973. 5.00 (ISBN 0-87925-005-4). Ind U Busn Res.

Estall, R. C. & Buchanan, R. Olgilvie. Industrial Activity & Economic Geography: A Study of the Forces Behind the Geographical Location of Productive Activity in Manufacturing Industry. 3rd rev. ed. 1973. (Hutchinson U Lib); pap. text ed. 13.75x (ISBN 0-09-117311-6, Hutchinson U Lib). Humanities.

Estaver, Marguerite. A Symphony of Leaves. LC 73-77467. 58p. 1973. 4.00 (ISBN 0-8233-0192-3). Golden Quill.

Estaver, Paul. Salisbury Beach, 1954. (Series Eight). 1983. pap. 4.00 (ISBN 0-931846-24-2). Wash Writers Pub.

Esteban, Claude. Transparent God. Cloutier, David, tr. from Fr. LC 80-84603. (Modern Poets in Translation Ser.: Vol. II). ix, 107p. (Orig.). 1983. text ed. 17.00x (ISBN 0-916426-07-6); pap. 6.95 (ISBN 0-916426-08-4). KOSMOS.

--White Road. Cloutier, David, tr. LC 78-64433. 1979. 7.50 (ISBN 0-910350-04-3). Charioteer.

Esteban, Manuel A. Georges Feydeau. (World Authors Ser.: No. 704). 171p. 1983. lib. bdg. 20.95 (ISBN 0-8057-6551-4, Twayne). G K Hall.

Estella, Mary. Natural Foods Cookbook. (Illus.). 160p. (Orig.). 1985. pap. 10.95 (ISBN 0-87040-583-7). Japan Pubns USA.

Estelman, Loren D. The Glass Highway. 224p. (Orig.). 1984. pap. 2.95 (ISBN 0-523-42263-6). Pinnacle Bks.

Estep, Gerald A. Social Placement of the Portuguese in Hawaii As Indicated by Factors in Assimilation: Thesis. LC 73-78062. 1974. Repr. of 1941 ed. soft bdg. 10.00 (ISBN 0-88247-271-2). R & E Pubs.

Estep, H. C. How Wooden Ships Are Built. (Illus.). 1983. 22.50 (ISBN 0-393-03288-4). Norton.

Estep, Samuel D., jt. auth. see Stason, Edwin B.

Estep, William R. The Anabaptist Story. 1975. pap. 6.95 (ISBN 0-8028-1594-4). Eerdmans.

--Renaissance & Reformation. 320p. (Orig.). pap. text ed. 19.95 (ISBN 0-8028-0050-5). Eerdmans.

Ester, P. Consumer Behavior & Energy Conservation. 1985. lib. bdg. 37.90 (ISBN 90-247-3134-8, Pub. by Martinus Nijhoff Netherlands). Kluwer Academic.

Ester, P., et al, eds. Consumer Behavior & Energy Policy. 440p. 1984. 57.75 (ISBN 0-444-86849-6). Elsevier.

Esterer, Arnulf K. Towards a Unified Faith. LC 62-20870. 1963. 5.00 (ISBN 0-8022-0459-7). Philos Lib.

Estergreen, N. Morgan. Kit Carson: A Portrait in Courage. 320p. 1980. pap. 9.95 (ISBN 0-8061-1601-3). U of Okla Pr.

Esterik, Penny Van see Van Esterik, Penny.

Esterly, Nancy B., jt. auth. see Solomon, Lawrence M.

Esterman, Ben. The Eye Book: A Specialist's Guide to Your Eyes & Their Care. LC 77-11660. (Illus.). 1977. 10.95 (ISBN 0-915556-04-9); pap. 5.95 (ISBN 0-915556-03-0). Great Ocean.

Esterman, L., jt. ed. see Bates, D. R.

Estermann, Alfred, compiled by. Registerband (to Complete Collection of Zeitschriften Des Jungen Deutschland) 200p. Repr. of 1972 ed. 24.00 (ISBN 0-384-50046-3). Johnson Repr.

Estermann, Barbara. John Clare: An Annotated Primary & Secondary Bibliography. LC 84-48861. (Reference Library of the Humanities). 300p. 1985. lib. bdg. 40.00 (ISBN 0-8240-8754-2). Garland Pub.

Estermann, Carlos. The Ethnography of Southwestern Angola, Vol. 1: The Non-Bantu Peoples, The Ambo Ethnic Group. Gibson, Gordon, ed. LC 75-8794. (Illus.). 228p. 1976. text ed. 44.50x (ISBN 0-8419-0204-6, Africana). Holmes & Meier.

--Ethnography of Southwestern Angola, Vol. 2: The Hero People. LC 75-8794. (Illus.). 1981. text ed. 29.50x (ISBN 0-8419-0206-2, Africana). Holmes & Meier.

--The Ethnography of Southwestern Angola, Vol. 2: The Nyaneka-Nkumbi People. Gibson, Gordon D., ed. LC 75-8794. (Illus.). 249p. 1978. text ed. 44.50x (ISBN 0-8419-0205-4, Africana). Holmes & Meier.

Estermann, Immanuel, ed. Recent Research in Molecular Beams: A Collection of Papers Dedicated to Otto Stern on the Occasion of His 70th Birthday. 1959. 44.00 (ISBN 0-12-243250-9). Acad Pr.

Estermann, Immanuel see Marton, L.

Esterson, A., jt. auth. see Laing, R. D.

Estes & Vaughan. Reading & Learning in the Content Classroom: Diagnostic & Instructional Strategies. abr. ed. 1985. 20.71 (ISBN 0-205-05986-4, 235986). Allyn.

Estes, Bill & Geraghty, John. RX for RV Performance & Mileage: How to Diagnose Your RVs Mechanical Problems & Make Your Engine More Powerful. 360p. 1983. 14.95 (ISBN 0-934798-06-0). TL Enterprises.

Estes, Carmen A., jt. auth. see Gunter, Laurie M.

Estes, Carol & Sessions, Keith W., eds. Controlled Wildlife: Vol. 1, Federal Permit Procedures. 304p. 1984. pap. 55.00 (ISBN 0-942924-05-3). Assn Syst Coll.

--Controlled Wildlife: Vol. 2, Federally Controlled Species. 1983. pap. 55.00 (ISBN 0-942924-06-1). Assn Syst Coll.

Estes, Carrol L., et al. Political Economy, Health & Aging. (Gerontology Ser.). 1984. text ed. 16.95 (ISBN 0-316-25062-7); pap. text ed. 9.95 (ISBN 0-316-25061-9). Little.

Estes, Carroll L. The Aging Enterprise: A Critical Examination of Social Policies & Services for the Aged. LC 79-83571. (Social & Behavioral Science Ser.). 1979. 19.95x (ISBN 0-87589-410-0). Jossey-Bass.

--Fiscal Austerity & Aging: Shifting Government Responsibility for the Elderly. LC 83-3440. (Sage Library of Social Research: Vol. 152). 1983. 28.00 (ISBN 0-8039-2073-3); pap. 14.00 (ISBN 0-8039-2074-1). Sage.

Estes, Carroll L., jt. ed. see Minkler, Meredith.

Estes, D. Timothy. A Humanizing Ministry. LC 84-15669. 160p. 1984. pap. 7.95 (ISBN 0-8361-3365-X). Herald Pr.

Estes, Eleanor. The Coat-Hanger Christmas Tree. LC 73-75433. (Illus.). 96p. (gr. 4-7). 1973. pap. 1.95 (ISBN 0-689-70449-6, A-79, Aladdin). Atheneum.

--Ginger Pye. LC 51-10446. (Illus.). (gr. 3-7). 10.95 (ISBN 0-15-230930-6, HJ). HarBraceJ.

--Ginger Pye. LC 51-10446. (Illus.). (gr. 4-8). 1972. pap. 4.95 (ISBN 0-15-634750-4, VoyB). HarBraceJ.

--Hundred Dresses. LC 44-8963. (Illus.). (gr. k-3). 10.95 (ISBN 0-15-237374-8, HJ). HarBraceJ.

--The Hundred Dresses. LC 73-12940. (Illus.). 80p. (gr. k-3). 1974. pap. 4.95 (ISBN 0-15-642350-2, VoyB). HarBraceJ.

--Middle Moffat. LC 42-36272. (Illus.). (gr. 3-7). 12.95 (ISBN 0-15-253663-9, HJ). HarBraceJ.

--The Middle Moffat. LC 79-11970. (Illus.). (gr. 4-7). 1979. pap. 2.95 (ISBN 0-15-659536-2, VoyB). HarBraceJ.

--The Moffat Museum. LC 83-8427. (Illus.). 262p. (gr. 3-7). 1983. 10.95 (ISBN 0-15-255086-0, HJ). HarBraceJ.

--Moffats. LC 41-51893. (gr. 4-6). 1968. 10.95 (ISBN 0-15-255095-X, HJ). HarBraceJ.

--Moffats. LC 41-51893. (Illus.). (gr. 4-6). 1968. pap. 5.95 (ISBN 0-15-661850-8, VoyB). HarBraceJ.

--Pinky Pye. LC 58-5708. (Illus.). (gr. 4-6). 1958. 10.95 (ISBN 0-15-262076-1, HJ). HarBraceJ.

--Pinky Pye. LC 75-31581. (Illus.). 192p. (gr. 4-6). 1976. pap. 1.75 (ISBN 0-15-671840-5, VoyB). HarBraceJ.

--Rufus M. LC 43-51239. (Illus.). (gr. 3-7). 8.95 (ISBN 0-15-269415-3, HJ). HarBraceJ.

--Witch Family. LC 60-11250. (Illus.). (gr. 3-7). 1960. 11.95 (ISBN 0-15-298571-9, HJ). HarBraceJ.

--Witch Family. LC 60-11250. (Illus.). (gr. 4-6). 1965. pap. 2.95 (ISBN 0-15-697645-5, VoyB). HarBraceJ.

Estes, George. The Rawhide Railroad. (Shorey Historical Ser.). (Illus.). 56p. pap. 3.95 (ISBN 0-8466-0266-0, S266). Shorey.

Estes, Gerald M., jt. ed. see Cooper, Stuart L.

Estes, Glenn E., jt. ed. see Hannigan, Jane A.

Estes, Helen E. Anagraphs: A Slew of Sight Puzzles. LC 80-54813. 1981. pap. 2.95 (ISBN 0-8027-7178-5). Walker & Co.

Estes, Hiawatha T. Distinctive Homes. (Illus.). 1983. 2.00x (ISBN 0-911008-24-1). H Estes.

--Hallmark Homes. (Illus.). 1983. 2.00x (ISBN 0-911008-26-8). H Estes.

--Homes by Hiawatha. (Illus.). 1983. 2.00x (ISBN 0-911008-27-6). H Estes.

--Prize Homes. (Illus.). 1983. 2.00x (ISBN 0-911008-28-4). H Estes.

--Ranch & Modern Homes. (Illus.). 1983. 3.00x (ISBN 0-911008-25-X). H Estes.

--Town & Country Homes. (Illus.). 1983. 2.00x (ISBN 0-911008-29-2). H Estes.

Estes, J. Worth. Hall Jackson & the Purple Foxglove: Medical Practice & Research in Revolutionary America, 1760-1820. LC 79-63083. (Illus.). 309p. 1979. 25.00x (ISBN 0-87451-173-9). U Pr of New Eng.

Estes, J. Worth see Hawes, Lloyd E.

Estes, Jack C. Compound Interest & Annuity Tables. 240p. (Orig.). 1976. pap. 5.95 (ISBN 0-07-019683-4). McGraw.

--Handbook of Interest & Annuity Tables. 1976. 44.95 (ISBN 0-07-019681-8). McGraw.

--Interest Amortization Tables. (McGraw-Hill Paperbacks). 224p. (Orig.). 1976. pap. 5.95 (ISBN 0-07-019680-X). McGraw.

Estes, Jack C. & Kokus, J. Real Estate License Preparation Course for the Uniform Examinations: For Salesmen & Brokers. (Illus.). 224p. 1976. 29.95 (ISBN 0-07-019670-2). McGraw.

Estes, James M. Christian Magistrate & State Church: The Reforming Career of Johannes Brenz. 208p. 1982. 30.00x (ISBN 0-8020-5589-3). U of Toronto Pr.

Estes, James R., et al. Grasses & Grasslands: Systematics & Ecology. LC 81-40294. (Illus.). 400p. 1982. 27.50x (ISBN 0-8061-1776-1); pap. 13.50x (ISBN 0-8061-1778-8). U of Okla Pr.

Estes, John E. & Senger, Leslie W. Remote Sensing: Techniques for Environmental Analysis. LC 73-8601. 340p. 1975. 33.45x (ISBN 0-471-24595-X). Wiley.

Estes, M. Tit for Tat. facsimile ed. LC 72-38649. (Black Heritage Library Collections). Repr. of 1856 ed. 22.50 (ISBN 0-8369-9007-2). Ayer Co Pubs.

Estes, Nada J. & Heinemann, M. Edith. Alcoholism: Development, Consequences & Interventions. 2nd ed. LC 81-14036. (Illus.). 385p. 1982. pap. text ed. 16.95 (ISBN 0-8016-1500-3). Mosby.

Estes, Nada J., et al. Nursing Diagnosis of the Alcoholic Person. LC 80-11057. (Illus.). 250p. 1980. pap. text ed. 14.95 (ISBN 0-8016-1558-5). Mosby.

Estes, Nyle. The Mark of Death Claw. 253p. 1983. 11.95x (ISBN 0-938936-15-8); pap. 3.95x (ISBN 0-938936-14-X). Daring Bks.

Estes, R. Gymnophions, Caudata. (Encyclopedia of Paleoherpetology: Pt. 2). (Illus.). 115p. 1976. pap. text ed. 59.35 (ISBN 3-437-30339-2). Lubrecht & Cramer.

--Sauria terrestria, Amphisbaenia. (Encyclopedia of Paleoherpetology Ser.: Pt. 10A). (Illus.). 249p. 1983. lib. bdg. 100.80 (ISBN 0-318-04101-4). Lubrecht & Cramer.

Estes, Ralph. The Auditor's Report & Investor Behavior. LC 82-47774. (Illus.). 144p. 1982. 20.00x (ISBN 0-669-05584-0). Lexington Bks.

--Corporate Social Accounting. LC 75-42445. 176p. 1976. 23.50 (ISBN 0-471-24592-5). Krieger.

--Dictionary of Accounting. 2nd ed. 160p. 1985. text ed. 18.50 (ISBN 0-262-05032-3); pap. 5.95 (ISBN 0-262-55011-3). MIT Pr.

Estes, Ralph W. A Dictionary of Accounting. 176p. 1981. text ed. 18.50x (ISBN 0-262-05024-2); pap. 5.95 (ISBN 0-262-55009-1). MIT Pr.

Estes, Richard J. The Social Progress of Nations. 224p. 1984. 24.95 (ISBN 0-03-059582-7). Praeger.

Estes, Rose. The Case of the Dancing Dinosaur. LC 83-63444. (Find Your Fate Mystery Ser.: No. 2). (Illus.). 128p. (gr. 4-7). 1985. PLB 4.99 (ISBN 0-394-96431-4, BYR); pap. 1.95 (ISBN 0-394-86431-X, BYR). Random.

--Children of the Dragon. LC 84-22318. (Illus.). 224p. (gr. 4-9). 1985. PLB 5.99 (ISBN 0-394-96433-0, BYR); pap. 2.95 (ISBN 0-394-86433-6). Random.

--Circus of Fear. LC 83-50050. (Dungeons & Dragons Endless Quest Book Ser.). 160p. (gr. 5up). 1983. pap. 2.00 (ISBN 0-394-72102-0). Random.

--Indiana Jones & the Lost Treasure of Sheba. (Find Your Fate Adventure Ser.). (Illus.). 115p. (Orig.). 1984. pap. 1.95 (ISBN 0-345-31664-9). Ballantine.

--The Trail of Death. LC 85-60429. (Find Your Fate Ser.). (Illus.). 128p. (gr. 4-7). 1985. pap. 2.95 (ISBN 0-394-86432-8, BYR). Random.

Estes, Ross & Duncan, Robert J. Tioga, I Remember Things. 1978. 9.95 (ISBN 0-89015-178-4). Eakin Pubns.

Estes, Steve, jt. auth. see Eareckson, Joni.

Estes, W. K., ed. Handbook of Learning & Cognitive Processes: Conditioning & Behavior Theory, 5 vols, Vol. 2. Incl. Vol. 3. Approaches to Human Learning & Motivation. 373p. 1976. (ISBN 0-89859-455-3); Vol. 4. Attention & Memory. 436p. 1976. (ISBN 0-89859-146-5); Vol. 5. Human Information Processing. 384p. 1978. (ISBN 0-89859-457-X); Vol. 6. Linguistic Functions in Cognitive Theory. 320p. 1978.. (ISBN 0-89859-458-8). 303p. 1975. 29.95 ea. L Erlbaum Assocs.

--Handbook of Learning & Cognitive Processes, 6 vols. Incl. Vol. 1. Introduction to Concepts & Issues. LC 75-20113. 303p. 1975; Vol. 2. Conditioning & Behavior Therapy. Estes, W. K. LC 75-20113. 373p. 1975. 18.50x (ISBN 0-470-24586-7); Vol. 3. Approaches to Human Learning & Motivation. LC 76-15010. 373p. 1976. 18.50x (ISBN 0-470-15121-8); Vol. 4. Attention & Memory. LC 76-26002. 1976; Vol. 5. Human Information Processing. LC 78-3847. 337p. 1978. 26.50x (ISBN 0-470-26310-5); Vol. 6. Linguistic Functions in Cognitive Theory. 1978. 18.00x (ISBN 0-470-26311-3). Halsted Pr.

Estes, William K. Learning Theory & Mental Development. 1970. 38.50 (ISBN 0-12-243550-8). Acad Pr.

Estes, William K., ed. Handbook of Learning & Cognitive Processes: Introduction to Concepts & Issues, Vol. 1. 303p. 1975. text ed. 29.95x (ISBN 0-89859-145-7). L Erlbaum Assocs.

--Models of Learning, Memory & Choice: Selected Papers. LC 82-9823. 410p. 1982. 33.95 (ISBN 0-03-059266-6). Praeger.

Estes, William K., jt. ed. see Bush, Robert R.

Estes, Winston. Another Part of the House. 1978. pap. 1.75 (ISBN 0-380-01959-0, 38406). Avon.

Estes, Winston M. Andy Jessup. 1977. pap. 1.75 (ISBN 0-380-01852-7, 36491). Avon.

--Another Part of the House. LC 70-91674. 1970. 9.57i (ISBN 0-397-00632-2). Har-Row.

--Homefront. pap. 1.95 (ISBN 0-380-01768-7, 35014). Avon.

--A Simple Act of Kindness. 1977. pap. 1.75 (ISBN 0-380-01807-1, 35634). Avon.

--A Streetful of People. 1978. pap. 1.75 (ISBN 0-380-01917-5, 37614). Avon.

Estess, Sybil P., jt. auth. see Schwartz, Lloyd.

Estess, Ted L. Elie Wiesel. LC 80-5337. (Literature and Life Ser.). 142p. 1980. 13.95 (ISBN 0-8044-2184-6). Ungar.

Esteva, Gustavo. The Struggle for Rural Mexico. Orig. Title: La Batalla En el Mexico Rural. (Illus.). 320p. 1983. text ed. 27.95 (ISBN 0-89789-025-6). Bergin & Garvey.

Esteves, Roberto, jt. ed. see Burk, Leslie Chamberlin.

Estevez, Jaime, jt. ed. see Lozoya, Jorge.

Estevez, O., ed. see International Cancer Congress, 12th, Buenos Aires, 5-11 October 1978.

Estey, Dale. A Lost Tale. 1980. 9.95 (ISBN 0-312-49885-3). St Martin.

--A Lost Tale. 224p. 1984. pap. 2.75 (ISBN 0-425-07133-2). Berkley Pub.

Estey, Emily. Where Did Yesterday Go. 1983. 7.95 (ISBN 0-932052-33-9). North Country.

Estey, Marten. The Unions: Structure, Development, & Management. 3rd ed. 153p. 1981. pap. text ed. 8.95 (ISBN 0-15-592952-6, HC). HarBraceJ.

Estey, Marten S., ed. Labor Relations Policy in an Expanding Economy: American Academy of Political & Social Science. LC 74-10648. 152p. 1974. Repr. of 1961 ed. lib. bdg. 15.00x (ISBN 0-8371-7645-X, ESLR). Greenwood.

Esthus, Raymond A. From Enmity to Alliance: U. S.-Australian Relations, 1931-41. LC 64-20486. 192p. 1964. 16.50x (ISBN 0-295-73792-1). U of Wash Pr.

--Theodore Roosevelt & the International Rivalries. LC 71-102172. (American Diplomatic History Ser.). 165p. 1982. 16.95x (ISBN 0-941690-04-0); pap. 9.95x (ISBN 0-941690-05-9); pap. text ed. 7.45x. Regina Bks.

Esti, B. Hungary Liberation: Selected Documents. (Illus.). 1975. 6.50x (ISBN 0-89918-358-1, H-358). Vanous.

Estienne, Henri. Frankfort Book Fair. Thompson, James W., tr. (Bibliography & Reference Ser.: No. 145). (Lat & Eng). 1968. Repr. of 1911 ed. 29.00 (ISBN 0-8337-3519-5). B Franklin.

Estienne, Robert. Dictionariolum Puerorum Tribus Linguis: Lat., Ang. & Gall. Conscriptum. LC 72-194. (English Experience Ser.: No. 351). 616p. (Lat., Eng. & Fr.). 1971. Repr. of 1552 ed. 76.00 (ISBN 90-221-0351-X). Walter J Johnson.

Estigarribia, Jose F. Epic of the Chaco: Marshal Estigarribia's Memoirs of the Chaco War, 1932-1935. Ynsfran, Pablo M., ed. LC 69-19008. Repr. of 1950 ed. lib. bdg. 32.00x (ISBN 0-8371-1020-3, TLEC). Greenwood.

Estill, A. D. The Sources of Synge. 1978. 16.50 (ISBN 0-685-89414-2). Porter.

Estill, Adelaide. Sources of Synge. LC 74-10977. 1939. lib. bdg. 12.50 (ISBN 0-8414-3954-0). Folcroft.

Estivals, Robert. La Statistique Bibliographie De la France Sous la Monarchie Au XVIIIE Siecle. (Livre & Societes: No. 2). 1965. pap. 34.40x (ISBN 90-2796-138-7). Mouton.

Estlake, Allan. The Oneida Community: A Record of an Attempt to Carry Out the Principles of Christian Unselfishnes & Scientific Race-Improvement. LC 72-4179. Repr. of 1900 ed. 11.50 (ISBN 0-404-10758-3). AMS Pr.

Estleman, Loren. The Midnight Man. (The Amos Walker Ser.). 256p. 1984. pap. 2.95 (ISBN 0-523-42186-9). Pinnacle Bks.

--The Stranglers. 176p. 1986. pap. 2.50 (ISBN 0-449-12848-2, GM). Fawcett.

--The Wister Trace. (Frontier Library). 1986. pap. 11.95 (ISBN 0-915463-32-6, Dist. by Kampmann). Jameson Bks.

Estleman, Loren D. Aces & Eights. 208p. 1982. pap. 2.25 (ISBN 0-523-41842-6). Pinnacle Bks.

--Angel Eyes. 256p. 1984. pap. 2.75 (ISBN 0-523-42185-0). Pinnacle Bks.

--Dr. Jekyll & Mr. Holmes. 256p. 1980. pap. 2.95 (ISBN 0-14-005665-3). Penguin.

--Every Brilliant Eye. 1985. price not set. HM.

--The Glass Highway. (Amos Walker Mystery Ser.). 179p. 1983. 13.95 (ISBN 0-395-34636-3). HM.

--Gun Man. LC 85-10248. (Double D Western Ser.). 192p. 1985. 12.95 (ISBN 0-385-23067-2). Doubleday.

--Kill Zone. LC 83-63041. 224p. 1984. 14.95 (ISBN 0-89296-065-5). Mysterious Pr.

--The Midnight Man. 230p. 1982. 12.95 (ISBN 0-395-32204-9). HM.

--Mister St. John. LC 82-45869. (Double D Western Ser.). 192p. 1983. 11.95 (ISBN 0-385-18713-0). Doubleday.

--Mister St. John. 224p. (Orig.). 1985. pap. 2.50 (ISBN 0-449-12717-6, GM). Fawcett.

--Motor City Blue. 1980. 9.95 (ISBN 0-395-29447-9). HM.

--Roses Are Dead. price not set. Mysterious Pr.

--Roses are Dead. 237p. 1985. 15.95 (ISBN 0-89296-136-8, Pub. by Hill & Wang). FS&G.

--Stranglers. LC 84-10242. (Double D Western Ser.). 192p. 1984. 11.95 (ISBN 0-385-19326-2). Doubleday.

--Sugartown. LC 84-12910. 220p. 1984. 13.95 (ISBN 0-395-36449-3). HM.

--This Old Bill. LC 83-20766. (Double D Western Ser.). 216p. 1984. 11.95 (ISBN 0-385-19165-0). Doubleday.

--This Old Bill. 288p. 1985. pap. 2.95 (ISBN 0-523-42575-9). Pinnacle Bks.

Estleman, Loren D., ed. see Watson, John H.

Estner, Lois J., jt. auth. see Cohen, Nancy W.

Estner, Lois J., jt. auth. see Cohen, Nancy Wainer.

Estoppel. Symphony Applications: A Manager's Toolkit. 1985. pap. 19.95 (ISBN 0-471-82430-5). Wiley.

Estrada, Alvaro. Maria Sabina: Her Life & Chants. Rothenberg, Jerome, ed. Munn, Henry, tr. from Span. LC 80-20866. (New Wilderness Ser.). 242p. 1981. 16.95 (ISBN 0-915520-33-8); pap. 8.95 (ISBN 0-915520-32-X). Ross-Erikson.

Estrada, Billie. How to Play Hopscotch: A Game Created by Children. (Illus.). 48p. (Orig.). (gr. k-6). 1974. pap. 5.95 (ISBN 0-9690490-0-5). B Estrada.

Estrada, Francisco. A Way to Transfiguration: Mi Primera Transfiguracion. 1985. 10.00 (ISBN 0-533-06623-9). Vantage.

Estrada, Francisco Lopez see Lopez Estrada, Francisco & Keller, John E.

Estrada, Jose R. Dias Sin Gloria. 64p. (Span.). 1980. pap. 1.95 (ISBN 0-311-08213-0, Edit Mundo). Casa Bautista.

Estrada, Leobardo. Grandes Hombres de la Biblia. 235p. 1975. pap. 5.25 (ISBN 0-311-04656-8). Casa Bautista.

Estrada, Norhma Gomez see Holton, James S. & Gomez-Estrada, Norhma.

Estrada, Rita. With Time & Tenderness. (Candlelight Ecstasy Ser.: No. 133). (Orig.). 1983. pap. 1.95 (ISBN 0-440-19587-X). Dell.

Estrada, Sergio & Gitler, Carlos, eds. Perspectives in Membrane Biology. 1974. 65.50 (ISBN 0-12-243650-4). Acad Pr.

Estragon, Vladimir. Waiting for Dessert. LC 81-15929. (Illus.). 224p. 1982. 13.95 (ISBN 0-670-74864-1). Viking.

Estreicher, Donna G., jt. auth. see Arnold, L. Eugene.

Estreicher, Karol J. Bibliografia Polska, 39 Vols. 1870. Set. 1800.00 (ISBN 0-384-14680-5); Set. pap. 1600.00 (ISBN 0-384-14681-3). Johnson Repr.

Estrella, Gregorio & Shell, Olive, eds. Cuentos del Hombre Cacataibo (Cashibo) II. (Comunidades y Cultura Peruanas: No. 11). 90p. 1977. pap. 4.25 (ISBN 0-88312-340-1); microfiche 1.93x (ISBN 0-88312-745-8). Summer Inst Ling.

Estrella, Luisa. Entibiame la Cama. (Pimienta Collection Ser.). (Sp.). 1977. pap. 1.00 (ISBN 0-88473-255-X). Fiesta Pub.

Estrella, Manuel M., Jr. & Forst, Martin L. The Family Guide to Crime Prevention. LC 81-2490. 253p. 1982. 12.95 (ISBN 0-8253-0036-3). Beaufort Bks NY.

--The Family Guide to Crime Prevention. 256p. 1983. pap. 3.50 (ISBN 0-523-42099-4). Pinnacle Bks.

Estrello, Francisco E. Senderos de Comunion. 1.75 (ISBN 0-8358-0416-X). Upper Room.

Estrello, Francisco E., tr. see White, D. M.

Estrin, jt. auth. see Botvinnik.

Estrin, Allen. The Hollywood Professionals, Vol. 6: Capra, Cukor, Brown. LC 72-1786. (Illus.). 1979. 12.00 (ISBN 0-498-02237-4). A S Barnes.

Estrin, Herman A. Technical & Professional Writing. 1976. pap. text ed. write for info. (ISBN 0-686-23137-6). Preston.

Estrin, J., tr. see Chaichian, M. & Nelipa, N. F.

Estrin, Jack C. American History Made Simple. rev. ed. (Made Simple Ser.). pap. 4.95 (ISBN 0-385-01214-4). Doubleday.

--World History Made Simple. rev. ed. (Made Simple Ser.). pap. 4.95 (ISBN 0-385-01220-9). Doubleday.

Estrin, Mark. Lillian Hellman: A Reference Guide. 1980. lib. bdg. 27.50 (ISBN 0-8161-7907-7, Hall Reference). G K Hall.

Estrin, Michael. Treasury of Hobbies & Crafts. pap. 2.00 (ISBN 0-87497-086-5). Assoc Bk.

Estrin, Norman. The Cosmetic Industry: Scientific & Regulatory Foundations. Jungermann, Eric, ed. (Cosmetic Science & Technology Ser.: Vol. 2). (Illus.). 720p. 1984. 95.00 (ISBN 0-8247-7105-2). Dekker.

Estrin, Saul. Self Management: Economic Theory & Yugoslav Practice. LC 83-5239. (Soviet & East European Studies). 257p. 1984. 49.50 (ISBN 0-521-24497-8). Cambridge U Pr.

Estrin, Saul & Holmes, Peter. French Planning in Theory & Practice. 224p. 1982. text ed. 29.50x (ISBN 0-04-339028-5). Allen Unwin.

Estrin, Y. & Panov, V. N. Comprehensive Chess Openings, 3 vols. Incl. Open Games, Vol. 1. 22.00 (ISBN 0-08-023103-9); pap. 12.95 (ISBN 0-08-023102-0); Semi-Open Games, Vol. 2. 18.75 (ISBN 0-08-024110-7); pap. 10.95 (ISBN 0-08-024109-3); Closed Games, Vol. 3. 22.00 (ISBN 0-08-024112-3); pap. 12.95 (ISBN 0-08-024111-5). (Illus.). 1980. 59.00 (ISBN 0-08-024114-X). pap. 33.00 (ISBN 0-08-024113-1). Pergamon.

Estrin, Y. B. & Glaskov, I. B. Play the King's Gambit: King's Gambit Accepted, Vol. 1. Neat, K. P., tr. (Illus.). 200p. 1982. 22.00 (ISBN 0-08-026873-0); pap. 13.95 (ISBN 0-08-026872-2). Pergamon.

--Play the King's Gambit: King's Gambit Declined, Vol. 2. Neat, K. P., tr. (Pergamon's Chess Openings Ser.). (Illus.). 130p. 1982. 20.00 (ISBN 0-08-026875-7); pap. 11.95 (ISBN 0-08-026874-9). Pergamon.

Estrin, Yakov. Gambits. Marfia, Jim, tr. from Russian. (Illus.). 91p. (Orig.). 1983. pap. 5.00 (ISBN 0-931462-20-7). Chess Ent Inc.

--Three Double King Pawn Openings. Marfia, Jim, tr. from Russian. (Illus.). 86p. (Orig.). 1982. pap. 5.00 (ISBN 0-931462-19-3). Chess Ent Inc.

--Wilkes-Barre Variation, Two Knights Defense. (Illus.). 114p. 1978. pap. 4.00 (ISBN 0-931462-00-2). Chess Ent Inc.

Estroff, Sue E. Making It Crazy: An Ethnography of Psychiatric Clients in an American Community. LC 79-64660. 338p. 1981. 22.50 (ISBN 0-520-03963-7). U of Cal Pr.

Estudio, Guias de, jt. auth. see Bridges, Julian C.

Estudio, Guias de, jt. auth. see Price, J. M.

Estudios, Guias de, jt. auth. see Allen, Carlos.

Estudios, Guias de, jt. auth. see Crane, James.

Estupinian, Rafael. A Toston. 1973. 5.50x (ISBN 0-916304-09-4). SDSU Press.

Estvan, Bela. War Pictures from the South. LC 74-179516. (Select Bibliographies Reprint Ser). Repr. of 1863 ed. 22.00 (ISBN 0-8369-6645-7). Ayer Co Pubs.

E. S. Van, Der Straeten see Van Der Straeten, E. S.

Esveldt-Dawson, Karen & Kazdin, Alan E. How to Use Self Control. 26p. 1982. 5.00 (ISBN 0-89079-067-1). Pro Ed.

Esveldt-Dawson, Karen, jt. auth. see Kazdin, Alan E.

Eswaran, K. S. Mathematical Formulae & Tables. 84p. 1981. 30.00x (ISBN 0-86125-149-0, Pub. by Orient Longman India). State Mutual Bk.

Esway, Judy. Prayers of a Working Mother. (Getting Book Line Ser.). 32p. (Orig.). 1985. pap. 1.50 (ISBN 0-89622-269-1). Twenty-Third.

Eszenyi, Sandor, et al, trs. see Portisch, Lajos & Sarkozy, Balazs.

Eszterhas, Istvan. Szamuzott a Szabadsag Igajaban. 1978. perfect bdg. 10.00 (ISBN 0-912404-10-8). Alpha Pubns.

ET D Staff. Color TV Trouble Factbook: Problems & Solutions. 3rd ed. LC 76-21178. 1976. pap. 14.95 (ISBN 0-8306-1119-3). TAB Bks.

ETA Offshore Seminars, Inc. Technology of Offshore Drilling, Completion & Production. LC 75-21903. 426p. 1976. 51.95x (ISBN 0-87814-066-2). Pennwell Bks.

Etcheberry, O. A. American-Chilean Private International Law. LC 60-16610. (Bilateral Studies in Private International Law: No. 10). 96p. 1960. 15.00 (ISBN 0-379-11410-0). Oceana.

Etchecopar, R. D. Titmice of the World. 1981. 750.00x (ISBN 0-686-78892-3, Pub. by Wheldon & Wesley England). State Mutual Bk.

Etchemendy, Nancy. Stranger From the Stars. (Illus.). 154p. (Orig.). (gr. 3-6). pap. 2.25 (ISBN 0-380-83568-1, 83568-1, Camelot). Avon.

--The Watchers of Space. (Illus.). 124p. (Orig.). (gr. 3-7). 1980. pap. 1.75 (ISBN 0-380-75374-X, 78220-0, Camelot). Avon.

Etcheson, Craig. The Rise & Demise of Democratic Kampuchea. (Illus.). 300p. 1984. 29.50 (ISBN 0-86531-650-3). Westview.

Etcheverry, G. P., ed. Nevada Government Today. 36p. write for info. NV League Cities.

Etchison, Birdie, jt. auth. see Nason, Diane.

Etchison, Birdie L. Don't Drop the Sugar Bowl in the Sink! LC 84-80057. 144p. 1984. pap. 4.50 (ISBN 0-88243-485-3, 02-0485). Gospel Pub.

--Me & Greenley. LC 81-6487. (Illus.). 112p. (gr. 4-10). 1981. pap. 3.95 (ISBN 0-8361-1966-5). Herald Pr.

--Strawberry Mountain. LC 81-7093. (Illus.). 136p. (Orig.). (gr. 3-8). 1982. pap. 3.95 (ISBN 0-8361-1981-9). Herald Pr.

Etchison, Dennis. The Dark Country. (Illus.). 232p. 1983. 15.00 (ISBN 0-910489-00-9). Scream Pr.

--The Dark Country. 224p. 1984. pap. 2.95 (ISBN 0-425-07136-7). Berkley Pub.

--Red Dreams. (Illus.). 240p. 1985. lib. bdg. 15.00 (ISBN 0-910489-04-1). Scream Pr.

Etemad, Hamid, jt. auth. see Sethi, S. Prakash.

Eterovich, Adam S. Croatian & Dalmatian Coats of Arms. LC 77-95024. (Illus.). 260p. 1978. pap. 8.00 softcover (ISBN 0-918660-06-8). Ragusan Pr.

--Croatian Pioneers in America, 1685-1900. LC 78-1109. 1979. perfect 10.00 (ISBN 0-918660-10-6). Ragusan Pr.

--Dalmatians from Croatia & Montenegrin Serbs in the West & South, 1800-1900. LC 74-155333. 1971. softcover 8.00 (ISBN 0-88247-103-1). Ragusan Pr.

--A Guide & Bibliography to Research on Yugoslavsa in the United States & Canada. LC 75-10423. 200p. 1978. soft cover 8.00 (ISBN 0-918660-07-6). Ragusan Pr.

--A Guide & Bibliography to Research on Yugoslavs in the United States & Canada. LC 75-10423. 1975. softcover 8.00 (ISBN 0-88247-341-7). Ragusan Pr.

--Orthodox Church Directory of the United States. 1968. softcover 5.00 (ISBN 0-88247-126-0). Ragusan Pr.

--Yugoslav Survey of California, Nevada, Arizona & the South, 1830-1900. LC 70-155332. 1971. softcover 8.00 (ISBN 0-88247-104-X). Ragusan Pr.

--Yugoslavs in Nevada: Eighteen Fifty-Nine to Nineteen Hundred. LC 72-85223. 1972. softcover 8.00 (ISBN 0-88247-189-9). Ragusan Pr.

Eterovich, Francis H. Aristotle's Nicomachean Ethics: Commentary & Analysis. LC 80-5202. 331p. 1980. text ed. 25.25 (ISBN 0-8191-1056-6); pap. text ed. 14.00 (ISBN 0-8191-1057-4). U Pr of Amer.

Eterovich, Francis H., ed. Who's Who of Americans & Canadians of Croation Descent. LC 80-52911. 394p. (Orig.). 1981. perfect bound 20.00 (ISBN 0-918660-17-3). Ragusan Pr.

Eterovich, Francis H. & Spalatin, Christopher, eds. Croatia: Land, People & Culture, 2 vols. LC 65-2286. (Illus.). Vol. 1. 1964 27.50 (ISBN 0-8020-3122-6); Vol. 2. 1970 35.00 (ISBN 0-8020-3226-5). U of Toronto Pr.

Etgen, William M. & Reaves, Paul M. Dairy Cattle Feeding & Management. 6th ed. LC 63-20646. 638p. 1978. text ed. 44.95 (ISBN 0-471-71199-3). Wiley.

Etgen, William M., jt. auth. see Trimberger, George W.

Eth, Spencer & Pynoos, Robert S. Post-Traumatic Stress Disorder in Children. (Progress in Psychiatry Ser.). 100p. 1985. text ed. 15.95X (ISBN 0-88048-067-X, 48-067-X). Am Psychiatric.

Ethall, Jeffrey L., jt. auth. see Loomis, Vincent V.

Ethe, H. & Edwards, E., eds. Catalogue of the Persian Manuscripts in the India Office Library. rev. ed. 759p. (Orig.). 1980. pap. 35.00 (ISBN 0-903359-25-1, Pub. by British Lib). Longwood Pub Group.

Ethe, Jane. Easy-to-Make Felt Bean Bag Toys. (Illus., Orig.). 1981. pap. 2.50 (ISBN 0-486-23884-9). Dover.

Ethe, Jane & Kirshon, Josephine. Easy & Attractive Gifts You Can Sew: Step-by-Step Instructions for 20 Presents. (Illus.). 48p. 1978. pap. 3.95 (ISBN 0-486-23638-2). Dover.

Ethell, Jeff & Christy, Joe. B-52 Strato Fortress at War. 1981. encore ed. 5.50 (ISBN 0-684-16980-0, ScribT). Scribner.

Ethell, Jeff, jt. auth. see Ohlrich, Walter.

Ethell, Jeffrey & Price, Alfred. Air War South Atlantic. LC 83-26731. (Illus.). 260p. 1984. 17.95 (ISBN 0-02-536300-X). Macmillan.

Ethell, Jeffrey L. Moving Up to Twin-Engine Airplanes. (Illus.). 1979. 8.95 (ISBN 0-8306-9790-X); pap. 4.95 (ISBN 0-8306-2270-5, 2270). TAB Bks.

--P-38 Lightning. (World War II Combat Aircraft Ser.). (Illus.). 1984. 6.98 (ISBN 0-517-55247-7). Crown.

--Warbirds Illustrated: American Warplanes from WW II-Korea, No. 1. (No. 15). (Illus.). 64p. 1983. pap. 10.95 (Arms & Armour Pr). Sterling.

--Warbirds Illustrated: American Warplanes from WW II-Korea, No. 2, No. 16. (Illus.). 64p. 1983. pap. 10.95 (ISBN 0-85368-577-0, Arms & Armour Pr). Sterling.

Ethell, Jeffrey L., jt. auth. see Fry, Garry L.

Etheredge, jt. auth. see Huskey.

Etheredge, E. E. Management Techniques in Surgery: Bedside Care of the Surgical Patient. Date not set. 22.95 (ISBN 0-471-87914-2). Wiley.

Etheredge, Lloyd S. Can Governments Learn? American Foreign Policy & Central American Revolutions. 200p. 1985. 32.50 (ISBN 0-08-027218-5); pap. 13.95 (ISBN 0-08-032401-0). Pergamon.

--A World of Men: The Private Sources of American Foreign Policy. 1978. text ed. 19.95x (ISBN 0-262-05019-6). MIT Pr.

Etheredge, Randall & Etheridge, Warren. The Football Quiz Book. 124p. 1980. pap. 3.50 (ISBN 0-8015-2720-1, Hawthorn). Dutton.

Etherege, George. Dramatic Works of Sir George Etherege, 2 Vols. Brett-Smith, H. F., ed. LC 76-145003. 1971. Repr. of 1927 ed. Set. 39.00 (ISBN 0-403-00956-1). Scholarly.

--The Man of Mode. Barnard, John, ed. (New Mermaids Ser.). 1979. pap. 7.95x (ISBN 0-393-90041-X). Norton.

--The Man of Mode. Carnochan, W. B., ed. LC 66-17766. (Regents Restoration Drama Ser). xxii, 158p. 1966. 15.50x (ISBN 0-8032-0357-8); pap. 4.50x (ISBN 0-8032-5356-7, BB 256, Bison). U of Nebr Pr.

--The Plays of Sir George Etherege. Cordner, Michael, ed. LC 82-1180. (Plays by Renaissance & Restoration Dramatists Ser.). (Illus.). 384p. 1982. 42.50 (ISBN 0-521-24654-7); pap. 15.95 (ISBN 0-521-28879-7). Cambridge U Pr.

--She Would If She Could. Taylor, Charlene M., ed. LC 76-128913. (Regents Restoration Drama Ser). xxx, 132p. 1971. pap. 3.95x (ISBN 0-8032-6700-2, BB 281, Bison). U of Nebr Pr.

Etherege, George see Harris, Brice.

Etherege, George see Wilson, John H.

Etherege, Sir George. Letters of Sir George Etherege. Bracher, Frederick, ed. LC 70-187870. 1974. 38.50x (ISBN 0-520-02218-1). U of Cal Pr.

Etheridge, David E. Mozart's Clarinet Concerto: The Clarinetists' View. LC 82-20420. 144p. 1983. 19.95 (ISBN 0-88289-372-6). Pelican.

Etheridge, Elizabeth W. The Butterfly Caste: A Social History of Pellagra in the South. LC 70-176431. (Contributions in American History Ser.: No. 17). 278p. 1972. lib. bdg. 29.95 (ISBN 0-8371-6276-9, EHP/). Greenwood.

Etheridge, Eugene W. The Man from Oz: A Paraphrase Drama of the Book of Job in Blank Verse. LC 72-79811. 94p. 1972. 5.50 (ISBN 0-8233-0178-8). Golden Quill.

Etheridge, J. W. Targums of Onkelos & Jonathan Ben Uzziel on the Pentateuch with the Fragments of the Jerusalem Targum from the Chaldee. 1969. Repr. of 1865 ed. 59.50x (ISBN 0-87068-045-5). Ktav.

Etheridge, Sanford G., tr. see Sextus Empiricus.

Etheridge, Truman H. Rightly Dividing. 1955. 6.00 (ISBN 0-88027-017-9). Firm Foun Pub.

Etheridge, Warren, jt. auth. see Etheredge, Randall.

Etherington, Charles L. Protestant Worship Music: Its History & Practice. LC 77-15990. (Illus.). 1978. Repr. of 1962 ed. lib. bdg. 35.00x (ISBN 0-313-20024-6, ETPW). Greenwood.

Etherington, Dan M. Multi-Period Budgeting & the Economic Assessment of Perennial Corporation Intercropping Systems. (Development Studies Centre - Occasional Paper: No. 26). 47p. (Orig.). 1982. pap. text ed. 2.00 (ISBN 0-909150-51-6, 1106, Pub. by ANUP Australia). Australia N U P.

Etherington, Don, jt. auth. see Brown, Margaret R.

Etherington, Don, jt. auth. see Roberts, Matt.

Etherington, J. W. Another Life. LC 83-90938. 315p. 1985. 14.95 (ISBN 0-533-05946-1). Vantage.

Etherington, John R. Environment & Plant Ecology. 2nd ed. LC 81-16167. 487p. 1982. 69.95x (ISBN 0-471-10136-2, Pub. by Wiley-Interscience); pap. 29.95x (ISBN 0-471-10146-X, Pub. by Wiley-Interscience). Wiley.

--Wetland Ecology. (Studies in Biology: No. 154). 64p. 1983. pap. text ed. 8.95 (ISBN 0-7131-2865-8). E Arnold.

Etherington, Norman. Preachers, Peasants & Politics in Southeast Africa 1835-1880: African Christian Communities Natal, Pondoland & Zululand. (Royal Historical Society-Studies in History: Vol. 12). 230p. 1978. text ed. 35.50x (ISBN 0-901050-48-2, Pub. by Swiftbks England). Humanities.

--Rider Haggard. (English Authors Ser.: No. 383). 1984. lib. bdg. 15.95 (ISBN 0-8057-6869-6, Twayne). G K Hall.

--Theories of Imperialism: War, Conquest & Capital. LC 83-21381. 304p. 1984. 28.50x (ISBN 0-389-20444-7, 08006). B&N Imports.

Etherington-Smith, Meredith. Patou. (Illus.). 144p. 1984. 19.95 (ISBN 0-312-59817-3, Pub. by Marek); pap. 11.95 (ISBN 0-312-59816-5, Pub. by Marek). St Martin.

Etherton, Michael. The Development of African Drama. 368p. (Orig.). 1983. text ed. 27.50x (ISBN 0-8419-0812-5, Africana); pap. text ed. 13.50x (ISBN 0-8419-0813-3). Holmes & Meier.

--Development of African Drama. 370p. 1982. cased 50.00x (ISBN 0-686-44681-X, Pub. by Hutchinson); pap. 39.00x. State Mutual Bk.

Etherton, Percy T. Crisis in China. LC 78-111739. (American Imperialism: Viewpoints of United States Foreign Policy, 1898-1941). 1970. Repr. of 1927 ed. 18.00 (ISBN 0-405-02015-5). Ayer Co Pubs.

Etherton, Percy T. & Tiltman, H. Hessell. Pacific: A Forecast. LC 74-111754. (American Imperialism: Viewpoints of United States Foreign Policy, 1898-1941). 1970. Repr. of 1928 ed. 20.00 (ISBN 0-405-02016-3). Ayer Co Pubs.

Ethics, Humanisms & Medicine Conference, University of Michigan, Ann Arbor, MI. 1981 & Basson, Marc D. Troubling Problems in Medical Ethics: The Third Volume in a Series on Ethics, Humanism & Medicine, Proceedings. LC 81-20723. (Progress in Clinical & Biological Research: Vol. 76). 306p. 1981. 28.00 (ISBN 0-8451-0076-9). A R Liss.

Ethier, S. N. & Kurtz, T. G. Markov Processes: Characterization & Convergence. (Probability & Mathematical Statistics Ser.). 1985. 49.95 (ISBN 0-471-08186-8). Wiley.

Ethier, Wilfred. Modern International Economics. 1984. 20.95x (ISBN 0-393-95250-9); instr's. manual avail. (ISBN 0-393-95427-7); study guide 8.95x (ISBN 0-393-95424-2). Norton.

Ethington, Evelyn C. Creative Wheat Cookery: Three Hundred Easy Tips, Tasty Recipes & Low Cost Ideas for Using Wheat & Gluten in the Home. LC 75-5321. (Illus.). 1975. pap. 5.95 (ISBN 0-88290-046-3). Horizon Utah.

Ethophilus. Die Obsiegende Tugend. 250p. Repr. of 1743 ed. 27.00 (ISBN 0-384-14770-4). Johnson Repr.

Ethridge, E. C., jt. auth. see Hench, L. L.

Ethridge, James. Directory of Directories, 1983. 1003p. 145.00x (ISBN 0-8103-0273-X). Gale.

Ethridge, James M., ed. Directory of Information Service. 3rd ed. LC 77-641771. 1985. pap. text ed. 110.00x (ISBN 0-8103-0271-3). Gale.

Ethridge, Kenneth E. Toothpick. LC 85-42883. 128p. 1985. 10.95 (ISBN 0-8234-0585-0). Holiday.

Ethridge, Marcus E., jt. auth. see Bingham, Richard D.

Ethridge, Willie S. Side by Each. LC 73-83034. 192p. 1973. 8.95 (ISBN 0-8149-0733-4). Vanguard.

--You Can't Hardly Get There from Here. LC 65-28523. 1965. 7.95 (ISBN 0-8149-0089-5). Vanguard.

Ethyl Corporation. Food for America's Future. LC 72-14156. (Essay Index Reprint Ser.). Repr. of 1960 ed. 15.25 (ISBN 0-518-10009-X). Ayer Co Pubs.

Etiemble. L' Art d'ecrire. 16.50 (ISBN 0-685-36551-4). French & Eur.

Etienne, Gilbert. Bangladesh: Development in Perspective. 1979. 12.00x (ISBN 0-8364-0497-1, Macmillan India). South Asia Bks.

--India's Changing Rural Scene: 1963-1979. 1982. 18.95x (ISBN 0-19-561429-1). Oxford U Pr.

Etienne, Mona & Leacock, Eleanor, eds. Women & Colonization: Anthropological Perspectives. (Illus.). 352p. 1980. 29.95x (ISBN 0-686-75098-5); pap. 12.95 (ISBN 0-686-75099-3). Bergin & Garvey.

--Women & Colonization: Anthropological Perspectives. LC 79-15318. 352p. 1980. 16.95 (ISBN 0-03-052586-1); pap. 16.95 (ISBN 0-03-052581-0). Praeger.

Etienne-Nugue, Jocelyn. Crafts & Arts of Living in the Cameroon. Gavronsky, Serge, tr. LC 81-1112. (Illus.). 160p. 1982. 22.50 (ISBN 0-8071-1032-9). La State U Pr.

Etier, A. Faborn & Etier, Betty A. Individualized Typing. 176p. (Orig.). 1983. pap. text ed. 15.67 scp (ISBN 0-672-97934-9); scp instr's. guide 3.67 (ISBN 0-672-97935-7); scp tapes 393.25 (ISBN 0-672-97939-X). Bobbs.

Etier, Betty A., jt. auth. see Etier, A. Faborn.

Etier, Betty A., et al. Individualized Typing Simulations & Working Papers. (gr. 11-12). 1984. pap. text ed. 18.08 scp (ISBN 0-317-00346-1); scp instr's guide 3.67 (ISBN 0-672-98354-0). Bobbs.

Etier, Faborn, jt. auth. see Rowe, John L.

Etkin, Bernard. Dynamics of Atmospheric Flight. LC 73-165946. (Illus.). 579p. 1972. text ed. 49.00x (ISBN 0-471-24620-4). Wiley.

--Dynamics of Flight Stability & Control. 2nd ed. LC 81-13058. 370p. 1982. text ed. 43.45 (ISBN 0-471-08936-2). Wiley.

Etkin, William. Social Behavior from Fish to Man. abr. ed. LC 67-28654. 1967. pap. 2.45x (ISBN 0-226-22037-0, P533, Phoen). U of Chicago Pr.

Etkin, William, ed. Social Behavior & Organization Among Vertebrates. LC 64-13974. (Illus.). 1964. 15.00x (ISBN 0-226-22036-2). U of Chicago Pr.

Etkind, Mark, ed. Boris Kustodiev: Paintings, Graphic Works, Book Illustrations, Theatrical Designs. LC 81-20685. (Illus.). 280p. 1984. 49.50 (ISBN 0-8109-1200-7). Abrams.

Etlin, Richard A. The Architecture of Death: The Transformation of the Cemetery in Eighteenth-Century Paris. (Illus.). 442p. 1983. 37.50 (ISBN 0-262-05027-7). MIT Pr.

Etling, Arlen W. Characteristics of Facilitators: The Ecuador Project & Beyond. 283p. (Orig.). 1975. pap. 6.00 (ISBN 0-932288-32-4). Ctr Intl Ed U of MA.

--Collaboration for Materials Development. 49p. (Orig.). 1977. pap. 4.00 (ISBN 0-932288-41-3). Ctr Intl Ed U of MA.

Etling, Harold H. Emmanuel, God with Us: Studies in Matthew. pap. 4.95 (ISBN 0-88469-107-1). BMH Bks.

--Our Heritage: Brethren Beliefs & Practices. pap. 4.95 (ISBN 0-88469-022-9). BMH Bks.

Etmekjian, James, ed. Anthology of Western Armenian Literature. LC 80-10608. 500p. 1980. 30.00x (ISBN 0-88206-026-0). Caravan Bks.

--A Graded West Armenian Reader: Selections from Armenian Literature. (Illus.). 187p. (Armenian.). 1963. 6.95 (ISBN 0-318-15082-4). Natl Assn Arm.

Etnier, David A., jt. auth. see Williams, James D.

Etnier, Elizabeth L., jt. ed. see Travis, Curtis C.

Eto, H. & Matsui, K., eds. R&D Management Systems in Japanese Industry. 332p. 1984. 54.00 (ISBN 0-444-86808-9, North Holland). Elsevier.

Eto, Morifusa. Organophosphorus Pesticides: Organic & Biological Chemistry. LC 73-90239. (Uniscience Ser.). 375p. 1974. 74.00 (ISBN 0-8493-5021-2). CRC Pr.

Eton, William. A Survey of the Turkish Empire. LC 73-6278. (The Middle East Ser.). Repr. of 1798 ed. 37.50 (ISBN 0-405-05334-7). Ayer Co Pubs.

Etons, Ursula. Angel Dusted: A Family's Nightmare. 1981. pap. 4.95 (ISBN 0-686-96782-8). Macmillan.

Ets, Marie H. Elephant in a Well. LC 74-83935. (Illus.). 32p. (gr. k-3). 1972. PLB 11.50 (ISBN 0-670-29169-2). Viking.

--Gilberto & the Wind. LC 63-8527. (gr. k-3). 1978. pap. 3.95 (ISBN 0-14-050276-9, Puffin). Penguin.

--Gilberto & the Wind. (Illus.). (ps-1). 1963. PLB 9.95 (ISBN 0-670-34025-1). Viking.

--In the Forest. (Picture Puffins Ser). (Illus.). (ps-2). 1976. pap. 3.95 (ISBN 0-14-050180-0, Puffin). Penguin.

--In the Forest. (Illus.). (ps-1). 1944. PLB 10.95 (ISBN 0-670-39687-7). Viking.

--Just Me. (Viking Seafarer Ser). (Illus.). (gr. k-2). 1978. pap. 3.95 (ISBN 0-14-050325-0, Puffin). Penguin.

--Just Me. (Illus.). (ps-2). 1965. 10.50 (ISBN 0-670-41109-4). Viking.

--Just Me. (Illus.). (gr. k-3). 1985. bk. & cassette 19.95 (ISBN 0-941078-75-2); pap. 12.95 bk. & cassette (ISBN 0-941078-73-6); cassette, 4 paperbacks & guide 27.95 (ISBN 0-941078-74-4). Live Oak Media.

--Play with Me. (Picture Puffin Ser.). 1976. pap. 3.95 (ISBN 0-14-050178-9, Puffin). Penguin.

--Play with Me. (Illus.). (ps-1). 1955. PLB 13.95 (ISBN 0-670-55977-6). Viking.

Ets, Marie H. & Labastida, Aurora. Nine Days to Christmas. (Illus.). (ps-2). 1959. PLB 13.95 (ISBN 0-670-51350-4). Viking.

Etsell, Karen & Brennan, Elaine. How to Open a Country Inn. rev. enl. ed. LC 81-67696. (Illus.). 220p. 1983. pap. 8.95 (ISBN 0-912944-79-X). Berkshire Traveller.

Ets-Hokin, Judith. The San Francisco Dinner Party Cookbook. rev. ed. LC 81-68589. 256p. 1982. pap. 9.95 (ISBN 0-89087-338-0). Celestial Arts.

Ettaba, Saheb. ANSCR. LC 78-86907. 1969. 12.95 (ISBN 0-87272-005-5). Brodart.

Ettari, Francesco. Giardeno of Marino Jonata Agnonese. LC 79-166032. (Columbia University. Studies in Romance Philology & Literature: No. 38). Repr. of 1924 ed. 15.00 (ISBN 0-404-50638-0). AMS Pr.
Etteldorf, Raymond. The End & the Beginning. 1979. pap. text ed. 5.75x (ISBN 0-86140-012-7). Humanities.
Ettema, James S. Working Together: A Study of Cooperation among Producers, Educators, & Researchers to Create Educational Television. 220p. (Orig.). 1980. pap. 14.00x (ISBN 0-87944-251-4). Inst Soc Res.
Ettema, James S. & Whitney, D. Charles, eds. Individuals in Mass Media Organizations: Creativity & Constraint. (Sage Annual Reviews of Communication Research Ser.: Vol. 10). (Illus.). 300p. 1982. 25.00 (ISBN 0-8039-1766-X); pap. 12.50 (ISBN 0-8039-1767-8). Sage.
Ettema, James S., jt. auth. see Johnston, Jerome.
Etten, Mary J., jt. auth. see Saxon, Sue V.
Ettensohn, F. R. & Dever, G. R., eds. Carboniferous Geology from the Appalachian Basin to the Illinois Basin Through Eastern Ohio & Kentucky. 293p. avail. Am Geol.
Ettenson, Herb, ed. The Puzzle Lover's Daily Crossword, No. 4. 128p. 1982. pap. 1.75 (ISBN 0-425-05543-4). Berkley Pub.
Ettenson, Herbert. Daily Crosswords, No. 2. 1982. pap. 1.75 (ISBN 0-441-13536-6). Ace Bks.
--Daily Crosswords, No. 3. 1982. pap. 1.75 (ISBN 0-441-13542-0). Ace Bks.
Etter, D. M. Problem Solving Software Supplement to "Problem Solving with Structured FORTRAN 77". 1984. pap. 10.00 (ISBN 0-8053-2526-3). Benjamin Cummings.
--Problem Solving with Structured FORTRAN 77. 1984. 24.95 (ISBN 0-8053-2522-0); instr's. manual 5.95 (ISBN 0-8053-2523-9); software supplement package 50.00 (ISBN 0-8053-2524-7). Benjamin-Cummings.
--Structured FORTRAN 77 for Engineers & Scientists. 1982. 22.95 (ISBN 0-8053-2520-4); instr's guide 5.95 (ISBN 0-8053-2521-2); software supplement package 50.00 (ISBN 0-8053-2517-4); application software supplement 12.00 (ISBN 0-8053-2518-2). Benjamin-Cummings.
--WATFIV: Structured Programming & Problem Solving. 1984. pap. 22.95 (ISBN 0-8053-2502-6); instr's. guide 15.95 (ISBN 0-8053-2503-4). Benjamin Cummings.
Etter, Dave. Alliance, Illinois. 240p. 1983. 14.95 (ISBN 0-933180-43-8). Spoon Riv Poetry.
--Alliance, Illinois. 240p. 1984. pap. 8.95 (ISBN 0-933180-65-9). Spoon Riv Poetry.
--Boondocks. (Crow King Editions Ser.). 64p. (Orig.). 1982. pap. 3.00 (ISBN 0-930600-15-0). Uzzano Pr.
--Bright Mississippi. (WNJ Ser.: No. 3). 1975. 10.00 (ISBN 0-686-61895-5); pap. 6.00 (ISBN 0-686-61896-3). Juniper Pr WI.
--Cornfields. LC 80-52084. 80p. 1980. pap. 3.95 (ISBN 0-933180-18-7). Spoon Riv Poetry.
--Home State. 112p. 1985. pap. 4.95 (ISBN 0-933180-64-0). Spoon Riv Poetry.
--West of Chicago. 81p. (Orig.). 1982. 4.50 (ISBN 0-933180-27-6). Spoon Riv Poetry.
Etter, Don. Curtis Park. LC 78-73982. 1980. 17.50 (ISBN 0-87081-077-4). Colo Assoc.
Etter, Don D. Auraria: Where Denver Began. LC 72-85656. (Illus.). 100p. 1980. pap. 8.95 (ISBN 0-87081-093-6). Colo Assoc.
Etter, Don D., jt. auth. see West, William A.
Etter, Les. Basketball Superstars: Three Great Pros. LC 73-9659. (Sports Ser.). (Illus.). 96p. (gr. 3-6). 1974. PLB 7.12 (ISBN 0-8116-6667-0). Garrard.
--Big Down Gamble. LC 58-23789. (Illus.). (gr. 6-9). 1968. 6.95g (ISBN 0-8038-0680-9); PLB 7.95 (ISBN 0-8038-0681-7). Hastings.
--Cool Man on the Court. LC 76-85230. (Illus.). (gr. 6-9). 1969. 7.95g (ISBN 0-8038-1245-0). Hastings.
--Fast Break Forward. LC 72-79494. (Illus.). (gr. 6-9). 1969. PLB 6.95 (ISBN 0-8038-2265-0). Hastings.
--The Game of Hockey. LC 77-4720. (Sports Ser.). (Illus.). (gr. 3-6). 1977. PLB 7.98 (ISBN 0-8116-6682-4). Garrard.
--Get Those Rebounds! (gr. 4 up). 1978. 6.95 (ISBN 0-8038-2685-0). Hastings.
--Hockey's Masked Men: Three Great Goalies. LC 75-28413. (Sports Library). (Illus.). 80p. (gr. 3-6). 1976. lib. bdg. 7.98 (ISBN 0-8116-6676-X). Garrard.
--Soccer Goalie. LC 69-14456. (Illus.). (gr. 6-9). 1969. PLB 6.95 (ISBN 0-8038-6686-0). Hastings.
--Vince Lombardi: Football Legend. LC 74-18076. (Sports Library). (Illus.). 96p. (gr. 3-6). 1975. PLB 7.98 (ISBN 0-8116-6670-0). Garrard.
Etter, Les, jt. auth. see Durant, John.
Etter, Lewis, ed. see Whitley, Joseph E. & Whitley, Nancy O.
Etter, Lewis E. Atlas of Roentgen Anatomy of the Skull. rev. ed. (Illus.). 232p. 1970. photocopy ed. 27.50x (ISBN 0-398-00525-7). C C Thomas.
--Glossary of Words & Phrases Used in Radiology, Nuclear Medicine & Ultrasound. 2nd ed. 384p. 1970. 33.50x (ISBN 0-398-00526-5). C C Thomas.
--Roentgenography & Roentgenology of the Temporal Bone, Middle Ear, & Mastoid Process. 2nd ed. (Illus.). 240p. 1972. 21.75x (ISBN 0-398-02473-1). C C Thomas.
Etter, Mildred F. Exercise for the Prone Patient. LC 68-10537. (Illus.). 172p. (Orig.). 1968. pap. 5.95x (ISBN 0-8143-1337-X, Savoyard). Wayne St U Pr.
Etter, Robert A. Homes, Buy Right-Sell Right or How to Avoid the Ripoff When Buying or Selling Your Home. 1976. pap. 4.95 (ISBN 0-930628-00-4). Patchwork Pubns.
Etter, Roberta & Schneider, Stuart. Halley's Comet: Memories of 1910. 96p. 1985. 19.95 (ISBN 0-89659-588-9). Abbeville Pr.
Etterich, Otto, jt. ed. see Plockinger, Erwin.
Etter-Lewis, Gwendolyn E., jt. auth. see Crauder, Renee C.
Etterlin, Ferdinand M. Tanks of th e World, 1982-1983: Flottentaschenbuch. Simpkin, Richard, tr. from Ger. (Tanks of the World Flottentaschenbuch Ser.). (Illus.). 827p. 1983. 64.95x (ISBN 0-933852-34-7). Nautical & Aviation.
Ettesvold, Paul M. La Belle Epoque Exhibition Checklist. Horbar, Any, ed. 24p. (Orig.). 1983. pap. 2.95 (ISBN 0-87099-342-9). Metro Mus Art.
--The Eighteenth Century Woman. Cone, Poly, et al, eds. (Illus., Orig.). 1982. pap. 2.95 (ISBN 0-87099-296-1). Metro Mus Art.
Ettin, Andrew V. Literature & the Pastoral. LC 83-26052. 212p. 1984. 22.50x (ISBN 0-300-03160-2). Yale U Pr.
Ettinger, Amos A. James Edward Oglethorpe, Imperial Idealist. (Illus.). xi, 348p. 1968. Repr. of 1936 ed. 24.00 (ISBN 0-208-00664-8, Archon). Shoe String.
--Oglethorpe: A Brief Biography. Spalding, Phinizy, ed. LC 84-8403. xxix, 81p. 1984. 7.95x (ISBN 0-86554-110-8, MUP/H104). Mercer Univ Pr.
Ettinger, Andrew, ed. see Freedman, Melvin H. & Silver, Samuel M.
Ettinger, Blanche & Perfetto, Edda. Machine Transcription: Language Skills for Information Processing. 256p. 1984. pap. text ed. 16.95 (ISBN 0-574-20720-1, 13-3720); avail.tchr's ed. (ISBN 0-574-20721-X, 13-3721); wkbk. 9.95t (ISBN 0-574-20722-8, 13-3722); audio tape cassettes set of 12 60 min. tapes 150.00t (ISBN 0-574-20724-4, 13-3724). SRA.
Ettinger, Blanche & Popham, Estelle. Opportunities in Office Occupations. LC 76-1406. (VGM Career Bks.). (Illus.). (gr. 8 up). 1976. PLB 7.95 (ISBN 0-8442-6500-4, 6500-4); pap. 5.95 (ISBN 0-8442-6501-2, 6501-2). Natl Textbk.
Ettinger, Blanche & Popham, Estelle L. Opportunities in Secretarial Careers. (VGM Career Bks.). (Illus.). 160p. 1983. 7.95 (ISBN 0-8442-6260-9, 6260-9, Passport Bks.); pap. 5.95 (ISBN 0-8442-6261-7, 6261-7). Natl Textbk.
Ettinger, David. Hebrew-English Pictorial Dictionary. (Hebrew & Eng.). 27.50 (ISBN 0-87559-018-7). Shalom.
Ettinger, Elzbieta, ed. see Luxemburg, Rosa.
Ettinger, L. J. The Rockhound & Prospector's Bible: A Reference & Study Guide to Rocks, Minerals, Gemstones & Prospecting. (Illus.). 140p. 1985. pap. price not set (ISBN 0-9614840-0-4). Ettinger.
Ettinger, Mary L. Dispensary. 1983. 5.95 (ISBN 0-8062-2158-5). Carlton.
Ettinger, R. C. Man into Superman: The Startling Potential of Human Evolution... & How to Be a Part of It. 1974. pap. 1.50 (ISBN 0-380-00047-4, 19588). Avon.
Ettinger, Richard P. & Golieb, D. E. Credits & Collections. 5th ed. 1962. text ed. 28.95 (ISBN 0-13-192641-1). P-H.
Ettinger, Stephen J. & Suter, Peter F. Canine Cardiology. LC 77-97547. (Illus.). 1970. 42.00 (ISBN 0-7216-3437-0). Saunders.
Ettinger, Stephen J., ed. Textbook of Veterinary Internal Medicine: Diseases of the Dog & Cat. 2nd ed. LC 81-406909. (Illus.). 2258p. 1983. Set. 120.00 (ISBN 0-7216-3427-3); Vol. 1. 67.00 (ISBN 0-7216-3423-0); Vol. 2. 67.00 (ISBN 0-7216-3426-5). Saunders.
Ettinghausen, Richard. Ancient Glass in the Freer Gallery of Art. (Illus.). 1962. pap. 3.00x (ISBN 0-934686-14-9). Freer.
--Selected & Annotated Bibliography of Books & Periodicals in Western Languages Dealing with the Near & Middle East, with Special Emphasis on Medieval & Modern Times. LC 70-180337. Repr. of 1954 ed. 24.50 (ISBN 0-404-56249-3). AMS Pr.
Ettinghausen, Richard & Yarshater, Ehsan, eds. Highlights of Persian Art. LC 79-4746. (Persian Art Ser.: Vol. 1). (Illus.). 390p. 1982. 65.00 (ISBN 0-8390-0282-3). Abner Schram Ltd.
--Highlights of Persian Art. LC 79-4746. (Persian Art Ser.). 1983. 50.00x (ISBN 0-89158-295-9). Caravan Bks.
Ettinghausen, Richard, et al. Prayer Rugs. LC 74-15703. (Illus.). 139p. 1974. pap. 18.50 (ISBN 0-87405-004-9). Textile Mus.
Ettisch, Ernst. The Hebrew Vowels & Consonants as Symbols of Ancient Astronomic Concepts. Zohn, Harry, tr. from Ger. (Illus.). 1986. 19.50 (ISBN 0-8283-1883-2). Branden Pub Co.
Ettkin, Lawrence P. & Cudd, Kermit G. International Directory of Business & Economics Periodicals. 1980. 28.00 (ISBN 0-89683-015-2). New London Pr.
Ettl, H. Die Gattung Chloromonas Gobi Emend Wille. 1970. pap. 42.00 (ISBN 3-7682-5434-8). Lubrecht & Cramer.
--Die Gattungen Carteria und Provasoliella. (Nova Hedwigia: Suppl. 60). 1979. lib. bdg. 35.00x (ISBN 3-7682-5460-7). Lubrecht & Cramer.
Ettl, H., ed. see Pascher, A.
Ettl, H., et al, eds. see Pascher, A.
Ettles, C. M., jt. auth. see Cameron, A.
Ettlin, W. A. & Solberg, G. Microsoft BASIC Made Easy. 275p. 1983. pap. 17.95. McGraw.
Ettlin, Walter & Solberg, Gregory. The MBASIC Handbook. (Illus.). 457p. (Orig.). 1983. pap. 17.95 (ISBN 0-07-881102-3, 102-3). Osborne-McGraw.
Ettlin, Walter A. Multiplan Made Easy. 14.95 (ISBN 0-07-881135-X, 135-X). Osborne-McGraw.
--Multiplan Made Easy: Macintosh Edition. LC 84-22757. 200p. 1984. pap. 15.95 (ISBN 0-07-881153-8, 153-8). Osborne-McGraw.
--WordStar Made Easy. 2nd ed. 132p. (Orig.). 1982. pap. 12.95 (ISBN 0-07-931090-7, 90-7). Osborne-McGraw.
Ettlin, Walter A. & Solberg, Gregory. The Microsoft BASIC Book! Macintosh Edition. 464p. (Orig.). 1985. pap. 18.95 (ISBN 0-07-881169-4, 169-4). Osborne McGraw.
Ettling, John. The Germ of Laziness: Rockefeller Philanthropy & Public Health in the New South. LC 81-4174. (Illus.). 272p. 1981. text ed. 18.50x (ISBN 0-674-34990-3). Harvard U Pr.
Ettlinger, Catherine, jt. auth. see Jacobson, Carlotta K.
Ettlinger, Helen, jt. auth. see Ettlinger, L. D.
Ettlinger, John R. & Spirt, Diana. Choosing Books for Young People. LC 82-11659. 238p. 1982. lib. bdg. 25.00x (ISBN 0-8389-0366-5). ALA.
Ettlinger, L. D. & Ettlinger, Helen. Botticelli. (The World of Art Ser.). (Illus.). 216p. 1985. pap. 9.95 (ISBN 0-500-20153-6). Thames Hudson.
Ettlinger, Leopold D. Antonio & Piero Pollaiuolo. 1978. 95.00x (ISBN 0-7148-1768-6, Pub. by Phaidon Pr). State Mutual Bk.
Ettore Majorana Course on Subnuclear Physics, Eleventh, Held at Erice, Italy, July 1973 see Zichichi, A.
Ettorre, E. M. Lesbians, Women & Society. 1980. pap. 8.95 (ISBN 0-7100-0330-7). Routledge & Kegan.
Ettre, L. S. Open Tubular Columns in Gas Chromatography. LC 65-13583. 164p. 1965. 25.00x (ISBN 0-306-30188-1, Plenum Pr). Plenum Pub.
Ettre, L. S. & Zlatkis, A. Seventy-Five Years of Chromatography: A Historical Dialogue. (Journal of Chromatography Ser.: Vol. 17). 502p. 1979. 64.00 (ISBN 0-444-41754-0). Elsevier.
Etualin, Richard W., ed. Western Films: A Brief History. (Illus.). 96p. 1983. pap. text ed. 9.95x (ISBN 0-89745-048-5). Sunflower U Pr.
Etue, E. & Chalmers, P. D. Take Charge of Your Health: A Personal Health Record & Reference. (Illus.). 128p. (Orig.). 1985. pap. 6.95 spiral bdg. (ISBN 0-920197-12-4, Pub. by Summerhill CN). Sterling.
Etulain, Richard. Owen Wister. LC 73-8336. (Western Writers Ser: No. 7). 1973. pap. 2.00x (ISBN 0-88430-006-4). Boise St Univ.
Etulain, Richard W. A Bibliographical Guide to the Study of Western American Literature. LC 82-8579. xviii, 317p. 1982. 24.50x (ISBN 0-8032-1801-X). U of Nebr Pr.
Etulain, Richard W., jt. auth. see Paul, Rodman W.
Etulain, Richard W., jt. auth. see Stegner, Wallace.
Etulain, Richard W., ed. The American Literary West. 79p. 1980. pap. text ed. 9.95x (ISBN 0-89745-006-X). Sunflower U Pr.
--Jack London on the Road: The Tramp Diary & Other Hobo Writings. LC 78-17039. 209p. 1979. pap. 7.95 (ISBN 0-87421-098-4). Utah St U Pr.
Etulain, Richard W., jt. ed. see Erisman, Fred.
Etulain, Righard W., jt. ed. see Douglass, William A.
E-tu Zen Sun, tr. see Shih Min-hsiung.
Etzel, B. C. & LeBlanc, J. M., eds. New Developments in Behavioral Research: Theory, Method, & Application: In Honor of Sidney W. Bijou. 656p. 1977. 39.95x (ISBN 0-89859-356-5). L Erlbaum Assocs.
Etzel, Joan & Mason, Michael. Psycho Business Skills: How to Survive & Thrive in the Corporate Arena. 110p. 1983. 13.95 (ISBN 0-13-732644-0); pap. 6.95 (ISBN 0-13-732636-X). P-H.
Etzel, Mary E., jt. auth. see Ammon, Jeanne E.
Etzel, Michael J. & Woodside, Arch G. Cases in Retailing Strategy. 304p. 1984. pap. write for info. (ISBN 0-02-334370-2). Macmillan.
Etzell, Paul S., jt. auth. see Everson, Lloyd K.
Etzenhouser, R. From Palmyra, New York, Eighteen Thirty to Independence, Missouri, Eighteen Ninety-Four. LC 73-134393. Repr. of 1894 ed. 29.50 (ISBN 0-404-08435-4). AMS Pr.
Etzioni, A. An Immodest Agenda: Rebuilding America Before the 21st Century. (New Press Ser.). 464p. 1982. 26.95 (ISBN 0-07-019723-7). McGraw.
--An Immodest Agenda: Rebuilding America Before the 21st Century. 432p. 1984. pap. 9.95 (ISBN 0-07-019724-5). McGraw.
--Modern Organizations. 1964. pap. 14.95 (ISBN 0-13-596049-5). P-H.
Etzioni, Amitai. Active Society. LC 61-14107. 1971. pap. text ed. 16.95 (ISBN 0-02-909580-8). Free Pr.
--Capital Corruption: An Assault on American Democracy. 1984. 16.95 (ISBN 0-15-115469-4). HarBraceJ.
--Comparative Analysis of Complex Organizations. rev. ed. LC 74-21488. 1975. pap. text ed. 16.95 (ISBN 0-02-909620-0). Free Pr.
--Demonstration Democracy. 122p. 1970. 26.95 (ISBN 0-677-02610-2). Gordon.
--The Organizational Structure of the Kibbutz. Zuckerman, Harriet & Merton, Robert K., eds. LC 79-8996. (Dissertations on Sociology Ser.). 1980. lib. bdg. 25.50x (ISBN 0-405-12967-X). Ayer Co Pubs.
--Political Unification: A Comparitive Study of Leaders & Forces. LC 74-12176. 366p. 1974. Repr. of 1965 ed. 16.50 (ISBN 0-88275-196-4). Krieger.
--The Semi-Professions & Their Organization: Teachers, Nurses, Social Workers. LC 69-10481. pap. 87.50 (ISBN 0-317-29974-3, 2051760). Bks Demand UMI.
--Social Problems. (Foundations of Modern Sociology Ser.). 192p. 1976. pap. text ed. 14.95 (ISBN 0-13-817403-2). P-H.
Etzioni, Amitai & Lehman, Edward. A Sociological Reader in Complex Organizations. 3rd ed. LC 79-27722. 559p. 1980. text ed. 29.95 (ISBN 0-03-047461-2, HoltC). HR&W.
Etzioni, Amitai & Remp, Richard. Technological Shortcuts to Social Change. LC 72-83834. 236p. 1973. 10.95x (ISBN 0-87154-236-6). Russell Sage.
Etzioni-Halevy, Eva. Bureaucracy & Democracy: A Political Dilemma. 240p. 1983. 29.95x (ISBN 0-7100-9573-2). Routledge & Kegan.
--Bureaucracy & Democracy: A Political Dilemma. 240p. 1985. pap. 9.95x (ISBN 0-7102-0053-6). Routledge & Kegan.
--The Knowledge Elite & the Failure of Prophecy. (Controversies in Sociology Ser.: No. 18). 120p. 1985. text ed. 19.50x (ISBN 0-04-301192-6); pap. text ed. 9.50x (ISBN 0-04-301193-4). Allen Unwin.
--Political Manipulation & Administrative Power: A Comparative Study. (International Library of Sociology). 1980. 26.95x (ISBN 0-7100-0352-8). Routledge & Kegan.
--Social Change: Modernization & Post-Modernization. 280p. 1981. 30.00x (ISBN 0-7100-0767-1); pap. 11.95x (ISBN 0-7100-0768-X). Routledge & Kegan.
Etzioni-Halevy, Eva & Shapira, Rina. Political Culture in Israel: Cleavage & Integration among Israeli Jews. LC 76-24350. (Special Studies). 1977. text ed. 39.95 (ISBN 0-275-23790-7). Praeger.
Etzkorn, Gerard J., jt. ed. see Kelley, Francis E.
Etzkorn, Girard J., ed. Guillelmi de Ockham: Scriptum in Librum Primum Sententiarum, Ordinatio, Opera Theologica, Vol. 3, Distinctiones 4-18. 1977. 46.00 (ISBN 0-686-27929-8). Franciscan Inst.
Etzkorn, Girard J. & Kelley, Francis E., eds. Guillelmi de Ockham: Scriptum in Librum Primum Sententiarum, Ordinatio, Opera Theologica, Vol. 4, Distinctiones 19-48. 1979. 48.00 (ISBN 0-686-27932-8). Franciscan Inst.
Etzkorn, K. Peter. Georg Simmel: The Conflict in Modern Culture & Other Essays. LC 67-25064. 1968. text ed. 11.25x (ISBN 0-8077-1296-5). Tchrs Coll.
--Music & Society: The Later Writings of Paul Honigsheim. LC 78-21234. 350p. 1979. Repr. of 1973 ed. 21.50 (ISBN 0-88275-831-4). Krieger.
Etzkowitz, Henry. Is America Possible? Social Problems from Conservative, Liberal, & Socialist Perspectives. 2nd ed. 400p. 1980. pap. text ed. 20.95 (ISBN 0-8299-0329-1). West Pub.
Etzkowitz, Henry & Schwab, Peter. Is America Necessary? Conservative, Liberal & Socialist Perspectives of U.S. Political Institutions. LC 75-45037. (Illus.). 650p. 1976. pap. text ed. 20.95 (ISBN 0-8299-0090-X). West Pub.
Etzler, John A. Collected Works of John Adolphus Etzler. LC 77-7124. 1977. Repr. 60.00x (ISBN 0-8201-1290-9). Schol Facsimiles.
Etzler, Marilynn E., jt. auth. see Goldstein, Irwin J.
Etzoini, Amatai, jt. auth. see Gross, Edward.
Etzold, Thomas & Gaddis, John L. Containment: Documents on American Policy & Strategy 1945-1950. LC 77-20024. 449p. 1978. 39.00x (ISBN 0-231-04398-8); pap. 17.00x (ISBN 0-231-04399-6). Columbia U Pr.
Etzold, Thomas H., jt. auth. see Ullman, Harlan K.
Etzold, Thomas H., tr. & intro. by. Aspects of Sino-American Relations since 1784. LC 77-15586. 173p. 1985. pap. text ed. 5.95x (ISBN 0-531-05399-7). Wiener Pub Inc.
Eu, B. C. Semiclassical Theories of Molecular Scattering. (Springer Series in Chemical Physics: Vol. 26). (Illus.). 240p. 1984. 32.00 (ISBN 0-387-12410-1). Springer-Verlag.
Eu, March K. Sons of Chong. McFadden, S. Michele, ed. (Illus.). (gr. 3 up). 1978. pap. 6.95 (ISBN 0-89262-022-6). Career Pub.
Eubank, Judith. Land & Leasing. Leecraft, Jodie, ed. (Illus.). 287p. (Orig.). 1984. pap. text ed. 12.00 (ISBN 0-88698-094-1, 1.00110). PETEX.
Eubank, Keith. Munich. LC 83-22552. (Illus.). xiv, 322p. 1984. Repr. of 1963 ed. lib. bdg. 45.00x (ISBN 0-313-24286-0, EUMU). Greenwood.
--Origins of World War Two. LC 73-77338. (Europe Since 1500 Ser.). 1969. pap. 7.95x (ISBN 0-88295-733-3). Harlan Davidson.

--Paul Cambon: Master Diplomat. LC 78-6089. (Illus.). 1978. Repr. of 1960 ed. lib. bdg. 19.75x (ISBN 0-313-20502-7, EUPC). Greenwood.
--Summit at Teheran. LC 84-25538. (Illus.). 528p. 1985. 21.95 (ISBN 0-688-04336-4). Morrow.
--Summit Conferences, 1919-1960. (Illus.). 1966. 16.50x (ISBN 0-8061-0716-2). U of Okla Pr.
--Summitt at Tehran. 1985. 21.95 (ISBN 0-317-26492-3). Morrow.
Eubank, Keith, ed. The Road to World War II: A Documentary History. LC 74-179768. 1973. pap. 12.95x (ISBN 0-88295-734-1). Harlan Davidson.
Eubank, Nancy. The Lindberghs: Three Generations. LC 75-12517. (Minnesota Historic Sites Pamphlet Ser.: No. 12). (Illus.). 1975. pap. 1.50 (ISBN 0-87351-094-1). Minn Hist.
--A Living Past: Fifteen Historic Places in Minnesota. rev. ed. (Minnesota Historic Sites Pamphlet Ser.: No. 7). (Illus.). 32p. 1978. pap. 2.75 (ISBN 0-87351-077-1). Minn Hist.
--The Russians in America. LC 72-3598. (In America Bks.). (Illus.). 96p. (gr. 5-11). 1979. PLB 7.95 (ISBN 0-8225-0226-7). Lerner Pubns.
Eubank, W. Keith. World War Two: Roots & Causes. (Problems in European Civilization Ser.). 216p. 1975. pap. text ed. 5.95x (ISBN 0-669-93096-2). Heath.
Eubanks, Cecil L. Karl Marx & Friedrich Engels, an Analytical Bibliography. LC 75-24779. (Reference Library of Social Science: Vol. 23). 1978. lib. bdg. 29.00 (ISBN 0-8240-9957-5). Garland Pub.
--Karl Marx & Friedrich Engels: An Analytical Bibliography. rev. ed. LC 81-43337. (Reference Library of Social Science). 325p. 1983. lib. bdg. 50.00 (ISBN 0-8240-9293-7). Garland Pub.
Eubanks, David, jt. auth. see Wasserberger, Jonathan.
Eubanks, David H., ed. see Cohen, Eddi.
Eubanks, I. Dwaine & Derner, Otis C. Chemistry in Civilization. LC 74-80913. pap. 68.10 (ISBN 0-317-08908-0, 2055101). Bks Demand UMI.
Eubanks, Lon. University of Illinois Football: The Fighting Illini. LC 76-7853. (College Sports Ser.). 1976. 9.95 (ISBN 0-87397-065-9). Strode.
Eubanks, S. Thomas, jt. auth. see Speriglio, Milo A.
Eucharius Roesslin. On Minerals & Mineral Products. (Ars Medica: Section 1V, Vol. 1). 1978. 112.00x (ISBN 3-11-006907-5). De Gruyter.
Eucherius, Saint Formulae Spiritalis Intellegentiae. Wotke, C., ed. Repr. of 1894 ed. unbound 50.00 (ISBN 0-384-14795-X). Johnson Repr.
Eucken, Christoph. Isokrates: Seine Positionen in der Auseinandersetzung mit den zeitgenoessischen Philosophen. 304p. 1983. 55.20 (ISBN 3-11-008646-8). De Gruyter.
Euclid. Elements. Todhunter, Isaac, ed. 1967. Repr. of 1933 ed. 12.95x (ISBN 0-460-00891-9, Evman). Biblio Dist.
--The Elements, 3 vols. Heath, Thomas L., ed. 1926. Vol. 1. pap. 7.50 (ISBN 0-486-60088-2); Vol. 2. pap. 7.50 (ISBN 0-486-60089-0); Vol. 3. pap. 7.50 (ISBN 0-486-60090-4). Dover.
Euclides, Valeria P., tr. see Conrad, Joseph H., et al.
Eudaly, Maria S. De. El Cuidado de Dios. Villasenor, Emma Z., tr. (gr. 1-3). 1983. pap. 0.95 (ISBN 0-311-38555-9). Casa Bautista.
Eudin, Xenia J. & North, Robert C. Soviet Russia & the East, 1920-1927: A Documentary Survey. 1957. 35.00x (ISBN 0-8047-0477-5). Stanford U Pr.
Eudin, Xenia J. & Slusser, Robert M. Soviet Foreign Policy, Nineteen Twenty-Eight to Nineteen Thirty-Four: Documents & Materials, 2 Vols. LC 66-25465. 1967. Vol. 1. 29.75x (ISBN 0-271-73114-1); Vol. 2. 29.75x (ISBN 0-271-73129-X). Pa St U Pr.
Eudin, Xenia J., jt. auth. see North, Robert C.
Eudin, Xenia J., et al. Soviet Russia & the West, 1920-1927: A Documentary Survey. 1957. 35.00x (ISBN 0-8047-0478-3). Stanford U Pr.
Eugene, P. M. I Am a Daughter of the Church. Clare, M. V., Sr., tr. 667p. 1982. pap. 15.00 (ISBN 0-87061-050-3). Chr Classics.
--I Want to See God. Clare, M. V., Sr., tr. 549p. 1982. pap. 15.00 (ISBN 0-87061-051-1). Chr Classics.
Eugene, Toni. Koalas & Kangaroos: Strange Animals of Australia. Crump, Donald J., ed. LC 81-607859. (Books for Young Explorers Ser.: Set 8). 32p. (ps-3). 1981. 12.20 (ISBN 0-87044-403-4). Natl Geog.
Eugene, Toni see National Geographic Society.
Eugenics Society Annual Symposium, 11th, London, 1973. Equalities & Inequalities in Education: Proceedings. Cox, Peter R., et al, eds. 1976. 33.00 (ISBN 0-12-194240-6). Acad Pr.
Eugenie & Penick, Ib. The Good Morning Book. (Golden Touch & Feel Bks.). (Illus.). 20p. (gr. k). 1983. 4.95 (ISBN 0-307-12154-2, 12154, Golden Bks). Western Pub.
Eugenie & Penick, Ib, illus. The Good Night Book. (Golden Touch & Feel Bks.). (Illus.). 20p. (gr. k). 1983. comb binding 4.95 (ISBN 0-307-12155-0, 12155, Golden Bks). Western Pub.
Eugippius. Excerpta Ex Operibus S. Augustini, Pts. 1 & 2. Bd. with Vita Sancti Severini. Repr. of 1886 ed. (Corpus Scriptorum Ecclesiasticorum Latinorum Ser: Vol. 9). (Lat.). Repr. of 1885 ed. 90.00 (ISBN 0-384-14805-0). Johnson Repr.
--Leben Des Heiligen Severin. 3rd ed. Rodenbery, C., tr. (Ger.). Repr. of 1912 ed. 12.00 (ISBN 0-384-14820-4). Johnson Repr.
--Life of Saint Severin & Other Minor Works. LC 65-12908. (Fathers of the Church Ser: Vol. 55). 132p. 1965. 14.95x (ISBN 0-8132-0055-5). Cath U Pr.
Eugster, Carla. Somebody's Brother. 1983. pap. 6.00 (ISBN 0-686-89395-6). Samisdat.
Eugster, Ernest. Television Programming Across National Boundaries: The EBU & OIRT Experience. LC 83-71835. (Illus.). 250p. 1983. 55.00 (ISBN 0-89006-128-9). Artech Hse.
Euh, Yoon-dae. Commerical Banks & the Creditworthiness of Less Developed Countries. Dufey, Gunter, ed. LC 79-22721. (Research for Business Decisions: No. 11). 116p. 1980. 34.95 (ISBN 0-8357-1050-5). UMI Res Pr.
Eulalie, illus. Mother Goose Rhymes. (Illus.). 48p. (ps-3). 1978. 4.95 (ISBN 0-448-40114-2, G&D). Putnam Pub Group.
Eulau, Heinz. Technology & Civility: The Skill Revolution in Politics. LC 76-48483. (Publications Ser.: No. 167). 1977. pap. 5.95x (ISBN 0-8179-6672-2). Hoover Inst Pr.
Eulau, Heinz & Prewitt, Kenneth. Labyrinths of Democracy: Adaptations, Linkages, Representation, & Policies in Urban Politics. LC 72-77129. 1973. 49.50x (ISBN 0-672-51155-X); pap. text ed. 16.95x (ISBN 0-89197-821-6). Irvington.
Eulau, Heinz & Sprague, John D. Lawyers in Politics: A Study in Professional Convergence. LC 84-577. xii, 164p. 1984. Repr. of 1964 ed. lib. bdg. 25.00x (ISBN 0-313-24422-7, EULP). Greenwood.
Eulau, Heinz & Wahlke, John C. The Politics of Representation: Continuities in Theory & Research. LC 78-17128. pap. 78.00 (ISBN 0-317-29687-6, 2021894). Bks Demand UMI.
Eulau, Heinz, jt. auth. see Wahlke, John.
Eulau, Heinz & Czudnowski, M. Moshe, eds. Elite Recruitment in Democratic Politics: Comparative Studies Across the Nations. LC 76-2698. 299p. 1976. 21.95x (ISBN 0-470-15056-4). Halsted Pr.
Eulau, Heinz & Lewis-Beck, Michael S., eds. Economic Conditions & Electoral Outcomes: The United States & Western Europe. 256p. (Orig.). 1985. 24.00x (ISBN 0-87586-071-0); pap. 15.00x (ISBN 0-87586-072-9). Agathon.
Eulberg, Mary T. Fair are Fowl. 16p. 1980. 7.00 (ISBN 0-913719-44-7); pap. 2.00 (ISBN 0-913719-43-9). High-Coo Pr.
Eulenberg, Milton D., et al. Intermediate Algebra: A College Approach. LC 74-180243. Repr. of 1972 ed. 97.00 (ISBN 0-8357-9913-1, 2055123). Bks Demand UMI.
--Introductory Algebra. 3rd ed. LC 74-24338. 374p. lib. bdg. 28.95 (ISBN 0-471-24686-7). Krieger.
Eulenberger, Peter. Anwendung des Simulationsmodells BAYMO 70 auf die Stadtentwicklungsplanung, Vol. 2. (Interdisciplinary Systems Research Ser.: No. 44). 94p. (Ger.). 1980. pap. 18.95x (ISBN 0-8176-0969-5). Birkhauser.
Eulenberger, Peter, jt. auth. see Schuclein, Werner.
Eulenburg, Milton D., et al. Introductory Algebra. 3rd ed. LC 74-24338. 360p. 1975. text ed. 31.45x (ISBN 0-471-24686-7); avail. answers (ISBN 0-471-24687-5). Wiley.
Eulenspiegel, Till. Here Beginneth a Merye Jest of a Man That Was Called Howleglas. LC 76-37137. (English Experience Ser.: No. 311). 96p. 1971. Repr. of 1528 ed. 21.00 (ISBN 90-221-0311-0). Walter J Johnson.
Euler, C. Von see Von Euler, C. & Lagercrantz, H.
Euler, Curt Von see Von Euler, Curt & Ottoson, David.
Euler, Harrison L. County Unification in Kansas. LC 74-176758. (Columbia University. Teachers College. Contributions to Education: No. 645). Repr. of 1935 ed. 22.50 (ISBN 0-404-55645-0). AMS Pr.
Euler, L. Elements of Algebra. ix, 596p. 1984. Repr. of 1840 ed. 28.00 (ISBN 0-387-96014-7). Springer-Verlag.
Euler, Leonhard. Letters of Euler on Different Subjects in Natural Philosophy, 2 vols. in one. LC 74-26260. (History, Philosophy & Sociology of Science Ser). 1975. Repr. 59.00x (ISBN 0-405-06588-4). Ayer Co Pubs.
--Opera Omnia. Swiss Society of Natural Sciences Euler-Committee, ed. (Secundia Ser.: Vol. 17). 312p. 1983. text ed. 85.00 (ISBN 3-7643-1447-8). Birkhauser.
Euler, Manfred. Physikunterricht: Anspruch und Realitaet, Vol. 5. (Didaktik und Naturewissenshaft). 254p. (Ger.). 1982. 30.55 (ISBN 3-8204-7103-0). P Lang Pubs.
Euler, Robert & Tikalsky, Frank, eds. The Grand Canyon: Up Close & Personal. 1980. pap. 7.25 (ISBN 0-916552-10-1). Acoma Bks.
Euler, Robert C. Southern Paiute Ethnohistory. (Glen Canyon Ser: No. 28). Repr. of 1966 ed. 24.00 (ISBN 0-404-60678-4). AMS Pr.
Euler, Robert C., jt. auth. see Smithson, Carma L.
Euler, Robert C., ed. The Archaeology, Geology, & Paleobiology of Stanton's Cave, Grand Canyon NP, AZ. 141p. 11.00 (ISBN 0-938216-21-X). GCNHA.
Euler, Robert C., jt. ed. see Gumerman, George J.
Euler, Ulf S. Von see Von Euler, Ulf S. & Eliasson, Rune.
Euler, Von see Von Euler.
Eulo, Elena Y. Ice Orchids. 336p. 1984. pap. 3.50 (ISBN 0-425-06322-4). Berkley Pub.
Eulo, Ken. Bloodstone. 1982. pap. 3.50 (ISBN 0-671-46091-9). PB.
--The Brownstone. (Orig.). 1982. pap. 3.50 (ISBN 0-671-46090-0). PB.
--The Deathstone. (Orig.). 1982. pap. 3.50 (ISBN 0-671-45285-1). PB.
--The Ghost of Veronica Gray. 1985. pap. 3.95 (ISBN 0-671-54303-2). PB.
--Nocturnal. 336p. (Orig.). 1983. pap. 3.50 (ISBN 0-671-43065-3). PB.
Eunapius see Philostratus.
Eunson, Dale. The Day They Gave Babies Away. LC 72-84484. (Illus.). 64p. 1970. 6.95 (ISBN 0-374-31760-7). FS&G.
Eurich, Alvin C., ed. Major Transitions in the Human Life Cycle. LC 81-47067. 544p. 1981. 28.50x (ISBN 0-669-04559-4). Lexington Bks.
Eurich, Nell. Science in Utopia: A Mighty Design. LC 67-14339. pap. 65.40 (ISBN 0-317-09457-2, 2017014). Bks Demand UMI.
Eurich, Nell P. Corporate Classrooms: The Learning Business. LC 85-3845. 163p. 1985. pap. text ed. cancelled (ISBN 0-931050-25-1). Carnegie Found.
--Systems of Higher Education in Twelve Countries: A Comparative View. LC 81-1245. 172p. 1981. 30.95 (ISBN 0-03-059391-3). Praeger.
Euripides. Alcestis. Murray, Gilbert, tr. 1915. pap. text ed. 3.95x (ISBN 0-04-882025-3). Allen Unwin.
--Alcestis. Arrowsmith, William, tr. (Greek Tragedy in New Translations Ser). 1974. 19.95x (ISBN 0-19-501861-3). Oxford U Pr.
--Alcestis. Dale, A. M., ed. (Plays of Euripides Ser.). 1954. pap. 10.95x (ISBN 0-19-872097-1). Oxford U Pr.
--Alcestis & Other Plays. rev. ed. Vellacott, Philip, tr. (Classics Ser.). 1953. pap. 2.95 (ISBN 0-14-044031-3). Penguin.
--Andromache. Stevens, P. T., ed. (Plays of Euripides Ser.). 1971. 15.95x (ISBN 0-19-814183-1); pap. 11.95x (ISBN 0-19-872118-8). Oxford U Pr.
--The Bacchae. Cacoyannis, Michael, tr. (Orig.). 1982. pap. 1.95 (ISBN 0-451-62058-5, MJ2058, Ment). NAL.
--Bacchae. 2nd ed. Dodds, E. R., ed. (Plays of Euripides Ser.). 1960. 15.95x (ISBN 0-19-814120-3). Oxford U Pr.
--Bacchae & Other Plays. rev. ed. Vellacott, Philip, tr. Incl. The Women of Troy; Helen; Ion. (Classics Ser.). (Orig.). 1954. pap. 3.50 (ISBN 0-14-044044-5). Penguin.
--The Bacchae of Euripides: A New Translation with a Critical Essay. Sutherland, Donald, tr. LC 68-11566. x, 142p. 1968. pap. 3.50x (ISBN 0-8032-5194-7, BB 377, Bison). U of Nebr Pr.
--The Bakkhai by Euripides. Bagg, Robert, tr. from Greek. LC 77-90732. 96p. 1978. 10.00x (ISBN 0-87023-190-1); pap. 5.95x (ISBN 0-87023-191-X). U of Mass Pr.
--The Children of Herakles. Arrowsmith, William, ed. Taylor, Henry & Brooks, Robert, trs. (The Greek Tragedy in New Translation Ser.). 1981. 19.95x (ISBN 0-19-502914-3). Oxford U Pr.
--Cyclops. Simmonds, D. M. & Timberlake, R. R., eds. text ed. 6.95 (ISBN 0-521-04946-6). Cambridge U Pr.
--Electra. Denniston, J. D., ed. 1973. pap. 14.95x (ISBN 0-19-872094-7). Oxford U Pr.
--Euripides: Four Tragedies, Vol. II. Grene, David & Lattimore, Richmond, eds. Incl. Cyclops & Heracles. Arrowsmith, William, tr; Iphigenia in Tauris. Bynner, Witter, tr; Helen. Lattimore, Richmond, tr. LC 56-6639. 264p. 1956. pap. 6.00x (ISBN 0-226-30781-6, P309, Phoen). U of Chicago Pr.
--Euripides: Four Tragedies, No. 1. Grene, David & Lattimore, Richmond, eds. Incl. Alcestis. Lattimore, Richmond, tr; Medea. Warner, Rex, tr; Heracleidae. Gladstone, Ralph, tr; Hippolytus. Grene, David, tr. LC 55-5787. 221p. 1955. pap. 6.00x (ISBN 0-226-30780-8, P308, Phoen). U of Chicago Pr.
--Euripides: Four Tragedies, No. 3. Grene, David & Lattimore, Richmond, eds. Incl. Hecuba. Arrowsmith, William, tr; Andromache. Nims, John F., tr; The Trojan Women. Lattimore, Richmond, tr; Ion. Willetts, Ronald F., tr. LC 55-5787. 255p. 1958. pap. 6.00x (ISBN 0-226-30782-4, P310, Phoen). U of Chicago Pr.
--Euripides: Four Tragedies, No. 4. Grene, David & Lattimore, Richmond, eds. Incl. Rhesus. Lattimore, Richmond, tr; The Suppliant Women. Jones, Frank, tr; Orestes. Arrowsmith, William, tr; Iphigenia in Aulis. Walker, Charles R., tr. LC 55-5787. 308p. 1968. pap. 6.00x (ISBN 0-226-30783-2, P311, Phoen). U of Chicago Pr.
--Euripides: Three Tragedies, No. 5. Grene, David & Lattimore, Richard, eds. Incl. Electra. Vermeule, Emily T., tr; The Phoenician Women. Wyckoff, Elizabeth, tr; The Bacchae. Arrowsmith, William, tr. LC 55-5787. 228p. 1959. pap. 6.00x (ISBN 0-226-30784-0, P312, Phoen). U of Chicago Pr.
--Fabulae, 3 vols. Murray, Gilbert, ed. Incl. Vol. 1. Cyclops, Alcestis, Medea, Heraclidae, Hippolytus, Andromacha, Hecuba. 1901; Vol. 2. Supplices, Hercules, Ion, Troiades, Electra, Iphigenia Taurica. 1981; Vol. 3. Helena, Phoenissae, Orestes, Bacchae, Iphigenia Aulidensis, Rhesus. 2nd ed. 1913. 19.95x (ISBN 0-19-814524-1). (Oxford Classical Texts Ser.). Oxford U Pr.
--Helen. Arrowsmith, William, ed. Michie, James & Leach, Colin, trs. (The Greek Tragedy in New Translation Ser.). 1981. 19.95x (ISBN 0-19-502870-8). Oxford U Pr.
--Helen, the Trojan Women, the Baccae. Curry, Neil, tr. (Translations from Greek & Roman Author Ser.). 160p. 1981. pap. 7.95 (ISBN 0-521-28047-8). Cambridge U Pr.
--Heracles: With Introduction & Commentary. Bond, Godfrey W., ed. 1981. 62.00x (ISBN 0-19-814012-6). Oxford U Pr.
--Hippolytos. Barrett, W. S., ed. 1964. 33.50x (ISBN 0-19-814167-X). Oxford U Pr.
--Hippolytus. Bagg, Robert, tr. (Greek Tragedy in New Translation Ser). 1973. 19.95x (ISBN 0-19-501740-4). Oxford U Pr.
--Hippolytus: Freely Adapted from the Hippolytus of Euripides. LC 63-11979. pap. 26.80 (ISBN 0-317-28640-4, 2055364). Bks Demand UMI.
--Hippolytus in Drama & Myth. Sutherland, Donald, tr. LC 60-13112. vi, 124p. 1960. pap. 4.50x (ISBN 0-8032-5195-5, BB 103, Bison). U of Nebr Pr.
--Ion. Murray, Gilbert, tr. 1954. pap. text ed. 3.95x (ISBN 0-04-882034-2). Allen Unwin.
--Iphigeneia at Aulis. Merwin, W. S. & Dimock, George E., Jr., trs. from Greek. (Greek Tragedy in New Translations Ser.). 1978. 19.95x (ISBN 0-19-502272-6). Oxford U Pr.
--The Iphigeneia at Aulis of Euripides. Connor, W. R., ed. LC 78-18572. (Greek Texts & Commentaries Ser.). (Illus.). 1979. Repr. of 1891 ed. lib. bdg. 17.00x (ISBN 0-405-11416-8). Ayer Co Pubs.
--Iphigeneia in Tauris. Lattimore, Richmond, tr. (Greek Tragedy in New Translations Ser.). 1973. 19.95x (ISBN 0-19-501736-6). Oxford U Pr.
--Iphigenia at Aulis. Lumley, Jane, tr. from Greek. LC 82-45748. (Malone Society Reprint Ser.: No. 14). Repr. of 1909 ed. 40.00 (ISBN 0-404-63014-6). AMS Pr.
--Iphigenia in Tauris. Murray, Gilbert, tr. 1910. pap. text ed. 3.95x (ISBN 0-04-882036-9). Allen Unwin.
--Iphigenia in Tauris. Platnauer, M., ed. 186p. Repr. of 1984 ed. 13.00x (ISBN 0-86516-060-0). Bolchazy Carducci.
--Medea. Elliott, Alan, ed. 1969. pap. 8.95x (ISBN 0-19-912006-4). Oxford U Pr.
--Medea. Page, Denys, ed. (Plays of Euripides Ser.). 1938. pap. text ed. 10.95x (ISBN 0-19-872092-0). Oxford U Pr.
--Medea & Hippolytus. Waterlow, Sydney, tr. (Temple Greek & Latin Classics: No. 5). Repr. of 1906 ed. 18.50 (ISBN 0-404-07905-9). AMS Pr.
--Medea & Other Plays. Vellacott, Philip, tr. Incl. Hecabe; Electra; Heracles. (Classics Ser.). (Orig.). 1963. pap. 2.95 (ISBN 0-14-044129-8). Penguin.
--Orestes & Other Plays. Vellacott, Philip, tr. (Penguin Classics). 448p. 1972. pap. 4.95 (ISBN 0-14-044259-6). Penguin.
--The Phoenician Women. Arrowsmith, William, ed. Burian, Peter & Swann, Brian, trs. (The Greek Tragedy in New Translation Ser.). 1981. 19.95x (ISBN 0-19-502923-2). Oxford U Pr.
--The Phoenissae of Euripides. Connor, W. R., ed. LC 78-18595. (Greek Texts & Commentaries Ser.). 1979. Repr. of 1911 ed. lib. bdg. 19.00x (ISBN 0-405-11436-2). Ayer Co Pubs.
--Rhesos. Braun, Richard E., tr. from Greek. (Greek Tragedy in New Translations). 1978. 19.95x (ISBN 0-19-502049-9). Oxford U Pr.
--The Rhesus. Murray, Gilbert, tr. 1913. pap. text ed. 3.95x (ISBN 0-04-882040-7). Allen Unwin.
--Ten Plays of Euripides. Hadas, Moses & McLean, John H., trs. from Gr. Incl. Alcestis; Andromache; Bacchants; Electra; Hippolytus; Ion; Iphigenia among the Taurians; Iphigenia at Aulis; Medea; Trojan Women. (Bantam Classics Ser.). (Orig., Incl. introduction to each play & glossary). (gr. 11-12). 1981. pap. 2.95 (ISBN 0-553-21160-9). Bantam.
--Three Plays of Euripides. Roche, Paul, tr. from Greek. & intro. by. Incl. Alcestis; Medea; The Bacchae. 126p. 1974. pap. 3.95x (ISBN 0-393-09312-3). Norton.
--The Tragedies of Euripides in English Verse, 3 vols. Way, Arthur S., ed. 54.00 (ISBN 0-8369-6973-1, 7854). Ayer Co Pubs.
--Tragoediae, 3 vols. 1389p. 1985. 45.00 (ISBN 0-89005-415-0). Ares.
--The Trojan Women. Sartre, Jean-Paul, adapted by. pap. 1.65 (ISBN 0-394-71074-6, V-74, Vin). Random.
--Trojan Women. Barlow, S., ed. 24.50x (ISBN 0-86516-094-5); pap. 12.00x (ISBN 0-86516-069-4). Bolchazy Carducci.
--Works, Vol. 1. Incl. Rhesus; Hecuba; Daughters of Troy; Helen; Iphigenia at Aulis. (Loeb Classical Library: No. 9). 12.50x (ISBN 0-674-99010-2). Harvard U Pr.

--Works, Vol. 2. Incl. Orestes; Iphigeneia in Taurica; Andromache; Cyclops; Electra. (Loeb Classical Library: No. 10). 12.50x (ISBN 0-674-99011-0). Harvard U Pr.
--Works, Vol. 3. Incl. Madness of Hercules; Children of Hercules; Phoenician Maidens; Suppliants; Bacchanals. (Loeb Classical Library: No. 11). 12.50x (ISBN 0-674-99012-9). Harvard U Pr.
--Works, Vol. 4. Incl. Hippolytus; Medea; Alcestis; Ion. (Loeb Classical Library: No. 12). 12.50x (ISBN 0-674-99013-7). Harvard U Pr.
Euripides see Fitts, Dudley.
Euripides see Hadas, Moses.
Euripides see Lind, Levi R.
Euripides see Oates, Whitney J. & O'Neill, Eugene, Jr.
Euripides see Robinson, Charles A., Jr.
Euro-Data Analysts. Profits & Markets in the Global Paper, Paperboard, & Packaging Industries. (Illus.). 180p. 1983. pap. 595.00 (ISBN 0-87930-152-X, 541). Miller Freeman.
Euro Food Chem. Recent Developments in Food Analysis: Proceedings Euro Food Chem, I. Baltes, W., et al, eds. (Illus.). 500p. (Orig.). 1982. pap. 61.30x (ISBN 3-527-25942-2). VCH Pubs.
Eurocean. Petroleum & the Marine Environment. 750p. 1980. 55.00x (ISBN 0-86010-215-7, Pub. by Graham & Trotman England). State Mutual Bk.
Eurochem, 1980. Opportunities & Constraints: Proceedings. 436p. 1981. 90.00x (ISBN 0-85295-123-X, Pub. by Inst Chem Eng England). State Mutual Bk.
Eurodata Analysts. The Pulp, Paper & Paperboard Industry: Profits, Future Development & Investment Risk, Long & Short Term-A Global Scenario. (Illus.). 150p. 1982. pap. 495.00 (ISBN 0-87930-141-4, 526). Miller Freeman.
Euromech 38 Colloquium, Louvain-la-Neuve, Belgium, 3-5 September, 1973. Gyrodynamics: Proceedings. Willems, P. Y., ed. (Illus.). 300p. 1974. 28.40 (ISBN 0-387-06776-0). Springer-Verlag.
Euromoney, ed. Country Risk. 1981. 125.00x (ISBN 0-686-79173-8, Pub. by Euromoney England). State Mutual Bk.
--Currency Risk & the Corporation. 1985. 100.00x (ISBN 0-686-79175-4, Pub. by Euromoney England). State Mutual Bk.
--The Directory of Euromarket Borrowers. 1985. 150.00 (ISBN 0-686-79167-3, Pub. by Euromoney England). State Mutual Bk.
--The Eurodollar Bond Market. 1981. 100.00x (ISBN 0-686-79172-X, Pub. by Euromoney England). State Mutual Bk.
--Floating Rate Notes. 1981. 124.00x (ISBN 0-686-79171-1, Pub. by Euromoney England). State Mutual Bk.
--International Financial Law. 1981. 135.00x (ISBN 0-686-79177-0, Pub. by Euromoney England). State Mutual Bk.
--Investing in the U. S. 1981. 150.00x (ISBN 0-686-79169-X, Pub. by Euromoney England). State Mutual Bk.
--The Management of Foreign Exchange Risk. 1985. 140.00x (ISBN 0-686-79174-6, Pub. by Euromoney England). State Mutual Bk.
--Management Principles for Finance in the Multinational. 1981. 125.00x (ISBN 0-686-79176-2, Pub. by Euromoney England). State Mutual Bk.
--Project Financing. 1985. 150.00x (ISBN 0-686-79170-3, Pub. by Euromoney England). State Mutual Bk.
--Trade Financing. 1985. 100.00x (ISBN 0-686-79057-X, Pub. by Euromoney England). State Mutual Bk.
Euromoney Staff, ed. International Capital Markets. 1985. 125.00x (ISBN 0-686-79168-1, Pub. by Euromoney England). State Mutual Bk.
Euromonitor. World Energy: The Facts & the Future. 352p. 22.50x (ISBN 0-87196-564-X). Facts on File.
Euromonitor Publications Ltd., ed. The Book of Forecasts. 1985. 250.00x (ISBN 0-903706-57-1, Pub. by Euromonitor). State Mutual Bk.
European Anatomical Congress, 4th. Abstracts. (Acta Anatomica: Vol. 99, No. 3). 1977. 38.75 (ISBN 3-8055-2776-4). S Karger.
European Association for Legal & Fiscal Studies. Branches & Subsidiaries in the European Common Market, Legal & Tax Aspects. 2nd ed. 322p. 1976. text ed. 27.50x (ISBN 0-903393-21-2). Rothman.
European Astronomical Meeting, 1st, Athens, 1972. Galaxies & Relativistic Astrophysics: Proceedings, Vol. 3. Hadjidemetriou, J. & Barbanis, B., eds. LC 73-10665. (Illus.). 240p. 1974. 77.90 (ISBN 0-387-06416-8). Springer-Verlag.
--Solar Activity & Related Interplanetary & Terrestrial Phenomenon: Proceedings, Vol. 1. Xanthakis, J., ed. (Illus.). 200p. 1973. 58.50 (ISBN 0-387-06314-5). Springer-Verlag.
--Stars & the Milky Way System: Proceedings, Vol. 2. Mavridis, L. N., ed. LC 73-9108. (Illus.). 300p. 1974. 85.00 (ISBN 0-387-06383-8). Springer-Verlag.
European Automated Manufacturing Conference, 2nd, Birmingham, UK, May 1983. Automated Manufacturing, 1983: Proceedings. Rooks, B., ed. iv, 452p. 1983. 81.00 (ISBN 0-444-86687-6, 1-277-83, North-Holland). Elsevier.
European Brewery Convention. Elsevier's Dictionary of Brewing. 264p. 1983. 83.00 (ISBN 0-444-42131-9). Elsevier.
European Brewery Convention, ed. European Brewery Convention: Proceedings of the International Congress, 18th, Copenhagen, 1981. 740p. 80.00 (ISBN 0-904147-30-4). IRL Pr.
--European Brewery Convention: Proceedings of the International Congress, 19th, London, 1983. (Illus.). 728p. 1983. 90.00 (ISBN 0-904147-50-9). IRL Pr.
--European Brewery Convention: Proceedings of the International Congress, 17th, West Berlin, 1979. 874p. 1979. 70.00 (ISBN 9-070143-09-7). IRL Pr.
--European Brewery Convention: Proceedings of the International Congress, 16th, Amsterdam, 1977. 831p. 1977. 70.00 (ISBN 9-070143-03-8). IRL Pr.
European Centre for Higher Education. International Directory of Higher Education Research Institutions, Vol. 33. (IBEDATA Ser.). 139p. 1981. pap. 11.50 (ISBN 92-3-001928-3, U1190, UNESCO). Unipub.
European Chemoreception Research Organisation, Symposium, Netherlands, 1979. Preference Behaviour & Chemoreception: Proceedings. Kroeze, J. H., ed. 326p. 1979. 33.00 (ISBN 0-904147-12-6). IRL Pr.
European Chemoreception Research Organisation, 2nd Interdisciplinary Symposium, Switzerland, 1975. Structure-Activity Relationships in Chemoreception: Proceedings. Benz, G., ed. 197p. 20.00 (ISBN 0-904147-03-7). IRL Pr.
European Colloquium, 3rd, Aug. 1-6, 1971. Current Problems in Electrophotography: Proceedings. Berg, W. F. & Hauffe, K., eds. 1972. 66.00 (ISBN 3-11-003699-1). De Gruyter.
European Commission on Agriculture Working Party on Water Resources & Irrigation, Tel Aviv, Israel, 1970. Drainage Materials: European Commission on Agriculture: Working Party on Water Resources & Irrigation, Tel Aviv, Israel, 1970. (Irrigation & Drainage Papers: No. 9). 126p. (Eng., Fr. & Span., 4th Printing 1976). 1972. pap. 9.00 (ISBN 0-686-93183-1, F978, FAO). Unipub.
European Committee of Associations of Gear & Transmission Element Manufacturers (EUROTRANS), ed. Glossary of Transmission Elements: Gears. (Illus., In 8 languages). 1976. lib. bdg. 30.00x (ISBN 3-7830-0104-8). Marlin.
European Committee on Crime Problems & Brydensholt, Hans H. Prison Management: Study. LC 84-163253. write for info. Amer Bar Assn.
European Computing Congress. Eurocomp Seventy-Eight: Proceedings. Online Conferences Ltd., ed. 1978. text ed. 119.00x (ISBN 0-903796-23-6, Pub. by Online Conferences England). Brookfield Pub Co.
European Conference of Ministers of Transport. European Rules Concerning Road Traffic, Signs & Signals: Proceedings. 177p. 1974. 4.00x (ISBN 92-82-11020-6). OECD.
--Infrastructural Capacity Problems Raised by International Transit. (ECMT Roundtables Ser.). (Illus.). 135p. (Orig.). 1980. pap. text ed. 4.50x (ISBN 92-821-1059-1, 7580021). OECD.
European Conference of Ministers of Transport, 46th Round Table. Tariff Policies for Urban Transport. 107p. (Fr. & Eng.). 1980. 4.50x (ISBN 9-2821-1060-5). OECD.
European Conference of Ministers of Transport. Trends in Transport Investment & Expediture in 1979: Statistical Report on Road Accidents in 1980, Vol. II. 108p. (Orig.). 1982. pap. 10.00x (ISBN 92-821-1076-1). OECD.
European Conference on Electronic Design Automation, Brighton, UK, Sept. 1981. Electronic Design Automation. (IEE Conference Publication: No. 200). 290p. 1981. 98.00 (ISBN 0-85296-243-6). Inst Elect Eng.
European Conference on Microcirculation, 7th, Aberdeen, 1972, Pt. II. Clinical Aspects of Microcirculation: Proceedings. (Bibliotheca Anatomica: No. 12). (Illus.). 563p. 1973. 121.75 (ISBN 3-8055-1572-3). S Karger.
European Conference on Microcirculation, 7th, Aberdeen, Aug.-Sept. 1972, Part I. Methodology in Microcirculation: Proceedings. Lewis, D. H. & Ditzel, J., eds. (Bibliotheca Anatomica: No. 11). 1973. 121.75 (ISBN 3-8055-1571-5). S Karger.
European Conference on Microcirculation, 8th, le Touquet 1974. Recent Advances in Critical Microcirculatory Research. Lewis, D. H., ed. (Bibliotheca Anatomica: No. 13). (Illus.). 380p. 1975. 60.00 (ISBN 3-8055-2277-0). S Karger.
European Conference on Mixing & Centrifugal Separation, 1st. Proceedings. 1975. text ed. 49.00x (ISBN 0-900983-39-6, Dist. by Air Science Co.). BHRA Fluid.
European Conference on Mixing, 3rd. Proceedings, 2 vols. Stephens, H. S. & Stapleton, C. A., eds. (European Conferences on Mixing Ser.). 500p. 1979. Set. PLB 65.00x (ISBN 0-906085-31-4, Dist. by Air Science Co.). BHRA Fluid.
European Conference on Optical Fibre Communication, 1st, London, 1975. Optical Fibre Communication: September 16-18, 1975. (Institution of Electrical Engineers Conference Publication Ser.: No. 132). pap. 56.00 (ISBN 0-317-10151-X, 2012127). Bks Demand UMI.
European Conference on Psychosomatic Research, 12th, Bodo, July 1978. Proceedings. Freyberger, H., ed. (Psychotherapy & Psychosomatics: Vol. 32, No. 1-4). (Illus.). 55.50 (ISBN 3-8055-3044-7). S Karger.
European Conference on Psychosomatic Research, 9th, Vienna, April 1972. Topics of Psychosomatic Research: Proceedings. Freyberger, H., ed. (Psychotherapy & Psychosomatic: Vol. 22, Nos. 2-6). 305p. 1973. Repr. 38.50 (ISBN 3-8055-1616-9). S Karger.
European Conference on Psychosomatic Research, 11th, Heidelberg, September 14-17, 1976. Toward a Theory of Psychosomatic Disorders: Proceedings. Brautigam, Walter & Von Rad, Michael, eds. (Psychotherapy & Psychosomatics: Vol. 28, Nos. 1-4). 1977. 41.75 (ISBN 3-8055-2747-0). S Karger.
European Congress of Sleep Research, 1st Basel, Oct. 1972. Sleep: Physiology, Biochemistry, Psychology, Pharmacology, Clinical Implications. Koella, W. P., et al, eds. (Illus.). 1973. 77.50 (ISBN 3-8055-1604-5). S Karger.
European Congress on Ballistocardiography & Cardiovascular Dynamics, 8th, Ljubliana, 1971. Proceedings, 2 pts. Juznic, G., ed. Incl. Pt. 1. Hemodynamic Stress & Relief of the Heart. 1973; Pt. 2. Biomedical Science & Cardiovascular Dynamics. 1971. (Bibliotheca Cardiologica: Nos. 30 & 31). Pt. 1. 35.75 (ISBN 3-8055-1374-7); Pt. 2. 49.00 (ISBN 3-8055-1375-5). S Karger.
European Congress on Electron Microscopy, 5th. Image Processing & Computer-Aided Design in Electronics: Proceedings. Hawkes, P. W., ed. 1973. 75.50 (ISBN 0-12-333365-2). Acad Pr.
European Congress on Molecular Spectroscopy 8th 1965 Denmark. Molecular Spectroscopy. pap. 81.80 (ISBN 0-317-12977-5, 2020713). Bks Demand UMI.
European Congress on Sleep Research, 5th, Amsterdam, September 1980. Sleep Nineteen Eighty. Koella, W. P., ed. (Illus.). xiv, 466p. 1981. 105.75 (ISBN 3-8055-2045-X). S Karger.
European Congress on Sleep Research, 4th, Tirgu-Mures, September 1978. Sleep Nineteen Seventy-Eight. Popoviciu, L., et al, eds. 1980. 118.00 (ISBN 3-8055-0778-X). S Karger.
European Congress on Sleep Research, 2nd, Rome, April 8-11, 1974. Sleep Nineteen Seventy-Four: Instinct, Neurophysiology, Endocrinology, Episodes, Dreams, Epilepsy & Intracranialpathology. Koella, W. P., et al, eds. 400p. 1975. 80.50 (ISBN 3-8055-2069-7). S Karger.
European Congress on Sleep Research, 3rd, Montpellier, Sept. 1976. Sleep Nineteen Seventy-Six: Memory, Environment, Epilepsy, Sleep Staging: Proceedings. Koella, W. P. & Levin, P., eds. 1977. 78.75 (ISBN 3-8055-2663-6). S Karger.
European Congress on Thermography, 1st, Amsterdam, Jun 1974. Thermography. Aarts, N. J., ed. (Bibliotheca Radiologica: Vol. 6). (Illus.). xiv, 262p. 1975. pap. 41.75 (ISBN 3-8055-2134-0). S Karger.
European Convention of Constructional Steelwork. European Recommendations for the Fire Safety of Steel Structures. 106p. 1983. 70.25 (ISBN 0-444-42120-3). Elsevier.
European Dialysis & Transplant Assoc., 1974, Tel Aviv. Dialysis, Transplantation & Nephrology: Proceedings, Vol. 11. Moorhead, John, ed. (Illus.). 600p. 1975. 45.00x (ISBN 0-8464-0326-9). Beekman Pubs.
European Dialysis & Transplant Assoc. Dialysis, Transplantation & Nephrology: Proceedings, Vol. 12. Moorhead, J. F., ed. (Illus.). 1976. text ed. 49.00x (ISBN 0-8464-0327-7). Beekman Pubs.
European Dialysis & Transplant Association Staff. Proceedings of the European Dialysis & Transplant Association- European Renal Association, Vol. 20. Davison, A. M. & Guillou, P. J., eds. 850p. 1984. text ed. 75.00 (ISBN 0-272-79769-3, Pub. by Pitman Books Ltd UK). Urban & S.
European Directories, ed. The Dictionary of Toiletry & Cosmetic Manufacturers in Western Europe. 1985. 129.00x (ISBN 0-686-78875-3, Pub. by European Directories England). State Mutual Bk.
--The Directory of Pollution Control Equipment Manufacturers in Western Europe. 1985. 100.00x (ISBN 0-686-78879-6, Pub. by European Directories England). State Mutual Bk.
--Directory of Pump, Valve & Compressor Manufacturers in Western Europe. 1985. 100.00x (ISBN 0-686-78876-1, Pub. by European Directories England). State Mutual Bk.
European Federation of Chemical Engineering. Particle Technology: Proceedings of the European Federation of Chemical Engineering, European Symposium, Amsterdam, Holland, June 3-5, 1980, Vols. A & B. Schonert, K., et al, eds. (E FCE Publication Ser.: No. 7). 1232p. 1980. text ed. 85.00x (ISBN 3-921567-27-0, Pub. by Dechema Germany). Scholium Intl.
European Federation of Chemical Engineering, 2nd Intl. Conference on Phase Equilibria & Fluid Properties in the Chemical Industry, Berlin, 1980. Phase Equilibria & Fluid Properties in the Chemical Industry: Proceedings, Pts. 1 & 2. (EFCE Publication Ser.: No. 11). 1012p. 1980. text ed. 92.50x (ISBN 3-921567-35-1, Pub. by Dechema Germany). Scholium Intl.
European Foundation for Management Development, jt. ed. see American Assembly of Collegiate Schools of Business.
European Geophysical Symposium, August 1980, Budapest. Geomagnetic Pulsations. Orr, D., ed. 100p. 1983. pap. 27.50 (ISBN 0-08-026508-1). Pergamon.
European Heating & Ventilating Associations, ed. The International Dictionary of Heating, Ventilating, & Air Conditioning. LC 79-41714. 416p. 1982. 79.95x (ISBN 0-419-11650-8, NO. 6553, E&FN Spon England). Methuen Inc.
European Immunology Meeting, 4th, Budapest, Hungary, April 12-14, 1978. Immunology, 1978. Gergely, J., et al, eds. 1978. 48.50 (ISBN 0-9960012-7-1). Heyden.
European Institute for Transuranium Elements. Fission Gas Behaviour in Nuclear Fuels: Joint Research Centre Workshop, Germany, October 1978, Proceedings. Ronchi, C., et al, eds. (European Applied Research Reports Special Topics Ser.). 350p. 1979. pap. text ed. 115.50 (ISBN 3-7186-0010-2). Harwood Academic.
European Institute of Social Security. EISS Yearbook, Nineteen Seventy-Eight to Nineteen Eighty: Social Security Reforms in Europe, Pt. II. 288p. 1982. pap. 29.00 cancelled (ISBN 90-3120-135-9, Pub. by Kluwer Law Netherlands). Kluwer Academic.
--EISS Yearbook, Nineteen Seventy-Eight to Nineteen Eighty: The Retirement Age in Europe, Pt. I. 224p. 1982. pap. 24.00 cancelled (ISBN 90-3120-134-0, Pub. by Kluwer Law Netherlands). Kluwer Academic.
--Yearbook of the European Institute of Social Security 1974-1977, 2 pts. 1979. Pt. 1. pap. 27.00 (ISBN 9-0312-0079-4, Pub. by Kluwer Law Netherlands); Pt. 2. pap. 37.50 (ISBN 9-0312-0080-8). Kluwer Academic.
European Marine Biology Symposium Staff. Fourth European Marine Biology Symposium. Crisp, D. J., ed. LC 71-173829. pap. 152.50 (ISBN 0-317-28414-2, 2022442). Bks Demand UMI.
European Meeting of the Institute of Management Sciences & of the Econometric Institute, Warsaw, 1966. Pseudo-Boolean Methods for Bivalent Programming. Ivanescu, P. L. & Rudeanu, S., eds. (Lecture Notes in Mathematics: Vol. 23). 1966. pap. 10.70 (ISBN 0-387-03606-7). Springer-Verlag.
European Meeting on Cybernetics & Systems Research, Linz, Austria, Mar. 1978. General Systems Methodology, Organization & Management, Cognition & Learning: Symposia. Pichler, Franz R. & Hanika, Francis de P., eds. LC 75-6641. (Progress in Cybernetics & Systems Research: Vol. 7). (Illus.). 393p. 1980. text ed. 110.00 (ISBN 0-89116-195-3). Hemisphere Pub.
European Meeting on Cybernetics & Systems Research, 5th, Vienna, Austria, April 1980. Progress in Cybernetics & Systems Research, Vol. 9. Trappl, Robert, et al, eds. LC 75-6641. (Illus.). 532p. 1982. text ed. 110.00 (ISBN 0-89116-238-0). Hemisphere Pub.
--Progress in Cybernetics & Systems Research: Proceedings, Vol. 11. Trappl, Robert, et al, eds. LC 75-6641. (Illus.). 601p. 1982. text ed. 110.00 (ISBN 0-89116-240-2). Hemisphere Pub.
European Meeting on Cybernetics & Systems Research, Linz, Austria, Mar. 1978. Progress in Cybernetics & Systems Research: Symposia, Vol. 6. Pichler, Franz R. & Trappl, Robert, eds. LC 75-6641. (Progress in Cybernetics & Systems Research: Vol. 6). (Illus.). 398p. 1982. text ed. 110.00 (ISBN 0-89116-194-5). Hemisphere Pub.
European Meeting on Cybernetics & Systems Research, 5th, Vienna, Austria, April 1980. Structure & Dynamics of Socioeconomic Systems, Cybernetics in Organization & Management, Engineering Systems Methodology, Systems Research on Science & Technology: Proceedings. Trappl, Robert, et al, eds. LC 75-6641. (Progress in Cybernetics & Systems Research: Vol. 10). (Illus.). 562p. 1982. text ed. 110.00 (ISBN 0-89116-239-9). Hemisphere Pub.
European Nutrition Conference, 2nd, Munich, 1976. Abstracts. Zoellner, N., et al, eds. (Nutrition & Metabolism: Vol. 20, No. 3). 1976. 15.75 (ISBN 3-8055-2441-2). S Karger.
--Proceedings. Incl. Vol. 21, Nos. 1-3. Main Papers. 38.50 (ISBN 3-8055-2704-7); Vol. 21, No. 4. Round Table on Comparison of Dietary Recommendation in Different European Countries. 6.50 (ISBN 3-8055-2705-5); Vol. 21, Suppl. 1. Short Communications. 38.50 (ISBN 3-8055-2636-9). (Nutrition & Metabolism: Vol. 21, Nos. 1-4 & Suppl. 1). 1977. complete 54.50 (ISBN 3-8055-2681-4). S Karger.
European Organization for Caries Research, Board, ed. Reports of ORCA on Water Fluoridation. (Caries Research: Vol. 8, Suppl. 1). 36p. 1974. 7.25 (ISBN 3-8055-1707-6). S Karger.
European Organization for Research & Treatment of Cancer (E.O.R.T.C.) International Antimicrobial Therapy Project Group, Lausanne, 1978. Therapy & Prevention of Infections in Cancer Patients: Proceedings. Glauser, M. & Klastersky, J., eds. (Illus.). 1979. pap. 25.00 (ISBN 0-08-024434-3). Pergamon.

European Organization for Research & Treatment of Cancer. Treatment of Neoplastic Lesions of the Nervous System: Proceedings of a Symposium Sponsored by the European Organization for Research & Treatment of Cancer (EORTC), Brussels, April, 1980. Hildebrand, J. & Gangji, D., eds. (Illus.). 178p. 1982. 55.00 (ISBN 0-08-027989-9). Pergamon.

European Organization for Research on Treatment of Cancer, Plenary Session, Paris, 1969. Advances in the Treatment of Acute (Blastic) Leukemias: Proceedings. Mathe, G., ed. LC 71-117717. (Recent Results in Cancer Research: Vol. 30). (Illus.). xi, 177p. 1970. 29.00 (ISBN 0-387-04995-9). Springer-Verlag.

--Aseptic Environments & Cancer Treatment: Proceedings. Mathe, G., ed. (Recent Results in Cancer Research: Vol. 29). (Illus.). vii, 52p. 1970. 20.00 (ISBN 0-387-04994-0). Springer-Verlag.

European Pacemaker Colloquium, Brussels, 2nd, April, 1977. To Pace or Not to Pace, Controversial Subjects on Cardiac Pacing: Proceedings. Thalen, Hilbert J. & Harthorne, Warren, eds. 1978. lib. bdg. 68.40 (ISBN 90-247-2070-2, Pub. by Reidel Holland). Kluwer Academic.

European Peptide Symposium, 9th, France, 1968. Peptides: Proceedings. Bricas, E., ed. 1968. 24.50 (ISBN 0-444-10156-X, North-Holland). Elsevier.

European Petroleum Technical Organizations. European Model Code of Safe Practice in the Storage & Handling of Petroleum Products: Oil Spills at Sea & on Shore. (Illus.). 97p. 1974. 15.00 (ISBN 0-85334-456-6, Pub. by Elsevier Applied Sci England). Elsevier.

--European Model Code of Safe Practice in the Storage & Handling of Petroleum Products: Prevention of Ground & Surface Water Pollution by Oil from Storage Tanks & During the Transport of Oil. 24p. 1974. 13.00 (ISBN 0-85334-457-4, Pub. by Elsevier Applied Sci England). Elsevier.

--European Model Code of Safe Practice in the Storage & Handling of Petroleum Products: Operations, Pt. 1. 83p. 1973. 13.00 (ISBN 0-85334-465-5, Pub. by Elsevier Applied Sci England). Elsevier.

European Production Study Group Meeting, Loughborough Univ., 1981. Employment Consequences of Technological Change: Proceedings. Bosworth, Derek L., ed. 236p. 1984. text ed. 34.50x (ISBN 0-8419-5086-5). Holmes & Meier.

European Research Association. Die Deutsche Universitat im Schnittpunkt Amerikanischer & Sozialistischer Organisationsprinzipien. (Monographien). 320p. 1982. 24.50 (ISBN 0-931922-01-1). Eurolingua.

--Hamburger for America & the World. (Transworld Identity Ser.: Vol. 3). 133p. 1984. 12.00 (ISBN 0-931922-15-1). Eurolingua.

European Research Association & Jutila, Sakari. Finlandization for Finland & the World. (Monographien). 83p. 1983. 12.00 (ISBN 0-931922-07-0). Eurolingua.

European Research in Curriculum & Evaluation, a Report of the European Contact Workshop Held in Austria in December 1976 by the Committee for the Educational Research of the Council of Europe Council for Cultural Cooperation. Experimental Education for Pupils Aged Ten to Fourteen. Eggleston, John, ed. 218p. 1977. pap. text ed. 16.25 (ISBN 0-686-27810-0, Pub. by Swets & Zeitlinger). Hogrefe Intl.

European Science Foundation Staff, et al. Medical Responsibility in Western Europe: Research Study of the European Science Foundation. LC 85-2837. 1985. pap. 69.50 (ISBN 0-387-15365-9). Springer-Verlag.

European Security Study. Strengthening Conventional Deterrence in Europe: Proposals for the 1980s. LC 83-42831. 260p. 1983. 9.95 (ISBN 0-312-76600-9); 35.00. St Martin.

European Seminar on Computerized Axial Tomography in Clinical Practice, 1st. Proceedings. Moseley, I. F. & DuBoulay, G. H., eds. LC 77-1618. 1977. pap. 49.00 (ISBN 0-387-08116-X). Springer-Verlag.

European Society for Comparative Physiology & Biochemistry, 1st Conference, Liege, Belgium, 1979. Animals & Environment Fitness; Physiological & Biochemical Aspects of Adaptations & Ecology: Proceedings, 2 vols. Gilles, R., ed. (Illus.). 638p. 1980. Vol. 1. 125.00 (ISBN 0-08-024938-8); Vol. 2. 54.00 (ISBN 0-08-024939-6). Pergamon.

European Society for Stereotactic & Functional Neurosurgery, 5th Meeting, Zurich, July, 1981, jt. auth. see World Society for Stereotactic & Functional Neurosurgery, 8th Meeting, Zurich, July 1981.

European Society for Surgical Research, 13th, Helsinki, May 1978. Abstracts. Lempinen, M., et al, eds. (European Surgical Research: Vol. 10). 1978. pap. 16.75 (ISBN 3-8055-2922-8). S Karger.

European Society for Surgical Research, 10th, Paris, 1975. Abstracts. Cachera, J. P., ed. (European Surgical Research: Vol. 8, Suppl. 2). 1976. 19.25 (ISBN 3-8055-2397-1). S Karger.

European Society for Surgical Research, 12th, Congress, Warsaw 1977. Abstracts. Olszewski, W. L., ed. (European Surgical Research: Vol. 9, Suppl. 1). 1977. 15.75 (ISBN 3-8055-2746-2). S Karger.

European Symposium of the Working Party on Routine Computer Programs in Chemical Engineering, 5th, 1972. Decision, Design & the Computer: Proceedings, No. 35. 270p. 1981. 72.00x (ISBN 0-85295-076-4, Pub. by Inst Chem Eng England). State Mutual Bk.

European Symposium on Calcified Tissues - 8th, Jerusalem, 1971 & Menczel. Calcified Tissue. 1971. 49.00 (ISBN 0-12-490650-8). Acad Pr.

European Symposium on Calcified Tissues, 10th, Hamburg, 1973. Calcium Metabolism, Bone & Metabolic Bone Diseases: Proceedings. Kuhlencordt, F. & Kruse, H. P., eds. (Illus.). xx, 381p. 1975. 42.00 (ISBN 0-387-06990-9). Springer-Verlag.

European Symposium on Marine Biology, 12th. Physiology & Behaviour of Marine Organisms: Proceedings. McLusky, D. S. & Berry, A. J., eds. LC 77-30559. 1978. text ed. 72.00 (ISBN 0-08-021548-3). Pergamon.

European Symposium on Medical Enzymology - 1st - Milan - 1960. Proceedings. Dioguardi, Nicola, ed. 1962. 73.50 (ISBN 0-12-216950-6). Acad Pr.

European Symposium on Thermal Analysis & Dollimore. Thermal Analysis: Proceedings. 1981. 61.95 (ISBN 0-471-25664-1, Wiley Heyden). Wiley.

European Symposium, 3rd, Zurich. Vitamin B-Twelve: Proceedings. Zayalak, B. J. & Friedrich, W., eds. 1979. 88.00x (ISBN 3-11-007668-3). De Gruyter.

European Syndicate of Soccer Experts. Soccer: Techniques & Tactics. Cross, Jeff, ed. Gill, Wendy, tr. from Ger. Orig. Title: Fussball Perfekt. (Illus.). 1978. pap. 5.95 (ISBN 0-89149-028-0). Jolex.

European Tax Consultants Congress, Strasbourg, October 1978. Fiscalite En Europe: Proceedings. Confederation Fiscale Europeenne, ed. 242p. 1980. pap. 29.00 (ISBN 9-0200-0578-2, Pub. by Kluwer Law Netherlands). Kluwer Academic.

Europhysics Study Conference, Plitvice Lakes, Yugoslavia, 1972. Intermediate Processes in Nuclear Reactions: Proceedings. Cindro, N., et al, eds. (Lecture Notes in Physics: Vol. 22). (Illus.). 349p. 1973. pap. 18.30 (ISBN 0-387-06526-1). Springer-Verlag.

Europool. Secondary Materials in Domestic Refuse As Energy Sources. 80p. 1977. 16.50x (ISBN 0-86010-064-2, Pub. by Graham & Trotman England). State Mutual Bk.

Europool Limited. The Disposal & Recycling of Scrap Metal from Cars & Large Household Apparatus. 164p. 1978. 90.00x (ISBN 0-86010-154-1, Pub. by Graham & Trotman England). State Mutual Bk.

Europort Conference, 1973. Wear, Lubrication & Repair: Proceedings. 40p. 1973. limp bdg. 9.00 (ISBN 0-900976-36-5, Pub. by Inst Marine Eng). Intl Spec Bk.

Euro-Training, tr. see Didactic Systems Staff.

Eusden, John. Zen & Christian: The Journey Between. 224p. 1981. 10.95 (ISBN 0-8245-0099-7). Crossroad NY.

Eusden, John, jt. auth. see Westerhoff, John H.

Eusden, John D., ed. & tr. see Ames, William.

Eusebeius. The History of the Church: From Christ to Constantine. Williamson, G. A., tr. from Latin. LC 75-22726. Orig. Title: Historia Ecclesiastica. 432p. 1975. pap. 9.95 (ISBN 0-8066-1509-5, 10-3045). Augsburg.

Eusebio, Thomas C. Guide to Health Insurance. 1981. 15.00 (ISBN 0-686-31056-X, 29122). Rough Notes.

Eusebius. The History of the Church from Christ to Constantine. Williamson, G. A., tr. (Classics Ser.). 1981. pap. 5.95 (ISBN 0-14-044138-7). Penguin.

--History of the Church (From Christ to Constantine) Williamson, G. A., tr. 1985. Repr. of 1965 ed. 16.95 (ISBN 0-317-19661-8, Pub. by Dorset Pr). Hippocrene Bks.

--The Proof of the Gospel, 2 vols. in one. Ferrar, W. J., ed. (Twin Brooks Ser.). 568p. 1981. pap. 12.95 (ISBN 0-8010-3366-7). Baker Bk.

Eusebius Pamphili. Ecclesiastical History, 2 Vols. (Loeb Classical Library: No. 153, 265). 12.50x ea. Vol. 1 (ISBN 0-674-99169-9). Vol. 2 (ISBN 0-674-99293-8). Harvard U Pr.

--Ecclesiastical History, Bks. 6-10. (Fathers of the Church Ser: Vol. 29). 325p. 1955. 17.95x (ISBN 0-8132-0029-6). Cath U Pr.

--Ecclesiastical History: Books 1-5. LC 65-27501. (Fathers of the Church Ser: Vol. 19). 347p. 1953. 18.95x (ISBN 0-8132-0019-9). Cath U Pr.

Eush, Dianne, ed. see International Gemological Symposium.

Euske, Kenneth J. Management Control: Planning, Control, Measurement & Evaluation. LC 82-12236. (Paperback Series in Accounting). (Illus.). 128p. 1983. pap. 9.95 (ISBN 0-201-10494-6). Addison-Wesley.

Eustace, C. J. Infinity of Questions: Studies in the Art of Religion & the Religion of Art in the Lives of Helen Foley, Katherine Mansfield, et al. 170p. 1946. 10.00 (ISBN 0-87556-595-6). Saifer.

Eustace, Cecil J. Infinity of Questions. facs. ed. LC 70-84356. (Essay Index Reprint Ser). 1946. 16.50 (ISBN 0-8369-1080-X). Ayer Co Pubs.

Eustace, Herbert W. Christian Science, Its "Clear, Correct Teaching" & Complete Writings. 1037p. 1978. 16.00 (ISBN 0-9611156-0-2). Eustace CSB.

--Letter Excerpts, Statements on Christian Science. 36p. 1976. pap. 3.00 (ISBN 0-9611156-1-0). Eustace CSB.

Eustace, Katherine, jt. auth. see Greenacre, Francis.

Eustace, Timothy, ed. Statesmen & Politicians of the Stuart Age. LC 84-18223. 224p. 1985. 27.50 (ISBN 0-312-75729-8). St Martin.

Eustace Anthony, Evans see Anthony, Evans E.

Eustachio, Romano. Musica Duorum, Vol. 6. (Monuments of Renaissance Music Ser.). 1975. 100.00x (ISBN 0-226-22646-8). U of Chicago Pr.

Eustice, James. Tax Reform Act of 1984: A Selective Analysis. 1984. 27.50 (ISBN 0-317-17511-4). Warren.

Eustice, James, jt. auth. see Bittker, Boris.

Eustice, James S. & Ferguson, M. Carr. Federal Income Tax Legislation of 1962-1964 in Perspective. 185p. 1965. pap. 9.00 (ISBN 0-317-30773-8, B294). Am Law Inst.

Eustice, James S. & Kuntz, Joel D. Federal Income Taxation of S Corporations: Cumulative Supplementation. rev. ed. 1985. 96.00 (ISBN 0-88262-802-X). Warren.

Eustice, James S., jt. auth. see Bittker, Boris I.

Eustis, Alvin. Moliere As Ironic Contemplator. LC 72-94465. (De Proprietatibus Litterarum, Ser. Practica: No. 40). 231p. 1974. pap. text ed. 26.00x (ISBN 90-2792-507-0). Mouton.

Eustis, Alvin, tr. see Chevalier, Francois.

Eustis, Helen. The Horizontal Man. LC 75-44970. (Crime Fiction Ser). 1976. Repr. of 1946 ed. lib. bdg. 21.00 (ISBN 0-8240-2365-X). Garland Pub.

--Horizontal Man. (Crime Ser.). 1982. pap. 3.95 (ISBN 0-14-000718-0). Penguin.

--The Redheaded Woman. LC 84-145828. (Illus.). 36p. (Orig.). (gr. 7 up). 1983. pap. 6.95 (ISBN 0-88138-013-X, Star & Elephant Bks.). Green Tiger Pr.

Eustis, Morton. Players at Work. LC 79-84511. (Illus.). 1937. 18.00 (ISBN 0-405-08491-9, Blom Pubns). Ayer Co Pubs.

--Players at Work: Acting According to the Actors. facs. ed. LC 67-23216. (Essay Index Reprint Ser). 1937. 18.00 (ISBN 0-8369-0432-X). Ayer Co Pubs.

Eustis, Nancy & Greenberg, Jay. Long-Term Care for Older Persons: A Policy Perspective. LC 83-7080. (Social Gerontology Ser.). 250p. 1983. pap. text ed. 9.25 pub net (ISBN 0-534-02910-8). Brooks-Cole.

Eustis, O. B. Notes from the North Country. 248p. 1983. pap. 8.95 (ISBN 0-472-06346-4). U of Mich Pr.

Eutheo, jt. auth. see Salvianus.

Euw, Eric Von see Graham, Ian & Von Euw, Eric.

Euw, Eric Von see Von Euw, Eric.

Euw, Eric von see Von Euw, Eric & Graham, Ian.

Euwe, M. Strategy & Tactics in Chess. 1973. pap. 4.95 (ISBN 0-679-14035-2). McKay.

Euwe, Machgielis. Meet the Masters. LC 78-90636. (Essay Index Reprint Ser). 1940. 20.00 (ISBN 0-8369-1258-6). Ayer Co Pubs.

Euwe, Max & Blaine, M. The Logical Approach to Chess. (Chess Ser.). (Illus.). 224p. 1982. pap. 4.50 (ISBN 0-486-24353-2). Dover.

Euwe, Max & Hopper, David. A Guide to Chess Endings. 256p. 1976. pap. 3.95 (ISBN 0-486-23332-4). Dover.

Euwe, Max & Meiden, Walter. Chess Master vs. Chess Amateur. rev. ed. LC 73-84051. 315p. 1971. 11.95 (ISBN 0-679-13251-1); pap. 6.95 (ISBN 0-679-14040-9). McKay.

Evalds, Victoria K., compiled by. National Union List of African Development Plans, Censuses & Statistical Abstracts. 180p. 1985. lib. bdg. 30.00 (ISBN 3-598-10576-2). K G Saur.

Evaluation Consultants Inc. Realval: Apple II Plus Version. 1984. 250.00 ea. (ISBN 0-07-021110-8). Apple II plus. TRS-80 Model III (ISBN 0-07-021112-4). McGraw.

Evan, Frederica. Computer Publishers & Publications: An International Directory & Yearbook, 1985. 2nd. ed. 500p. 1985. 95.00 (ISBN 0-88709-009-5); pap. 90.00 (ISBN 0-88709-008-7). Comm Trends Inc.

Evan, Frederica, ed. Computer Publishers & Publications: An International Directory & Yearbook. 1984 ed. 400p. 1983. pap. 85.00x (ISBN 0-88709-000-1). Comm Trends Inc.

--Computer Publishers & Publications: Supplement, 1984. 85p. 1984. pap. 35.00x (ISBN 0-88709-005-2). Comm Trends Inc.

Evan, John. Mobile Home Buyer's Bible. LC 79-51492. 1979. pap. 14.95 (ISBN 0-9602644-0-X). Concours Pub.

Evan, William M. Knowledge & Power in a Global Society. LC 81-8728. (Focus Editions Ser.). (Illus.). 320p. 28.00 (ISBN 0-8039-1659-0); pap. 14.00 (ISBN 0-8039-1660-4). Sage.

--Organization Theory: Structures, Systems, & Environments. LC 76-22742. 312p. 1976. 37.50x (ISBN 0-471-01512-1). Wiley.

Evan, William M., ed. Interorganizational Relations. LC 77-25062. 1978. pap. 13.95x (ISBN 0-8122-7745-7). U of Pa Pr.

--Law & Sociology: Exploratory Essays. LC 78-23950. xii, 235p. 1979. Repr. of 1962 ed. lib. bdg. 24.75x (ISBN 0-313-20729-1, EVLS). Greenwood.

--The Sociology of Law: A Social-Structural Perspective. LC 78-24669. (Illus.). 1980. text ed. 21.95 (ISBN 0-02-909760-6). Free Pr.

Evanczuk, Stephen. Microprocessor Systems: Software, Hardware, & Architecture. LC 83-19969. 389p. 1983. 39.50 (ISBN 0-07-019756-3). McGraw.

Evang, Karl. Health Services in Norway. 1976. pap. 17.00x (ISBN 8-200-02373-7, Dist. by Columbia U Pr). Universitet.

Evangelakis, Miltiades G. A Manual for Residential & Day Treatment of Children. (Illus.). 392p. 1974. 39.75x (ISBN 0-398-03118-5). C C Thomas.

Evangelical Alliance of Great Britain. The UK Christian Handbook. 430p. 1983. 15.00 (ISBN 0-317-17790-7). MARC.

Evangelical Sisterhood of Mary, tr. see Schlink, Basilea.

Evangelical Teacher Training Association. More Training When Meeting. 32p. 1982. pap. 2.95 (ISBN 0-317-02858-8); leader's planbook 3.95 (ISBN 0-910566-36-4). Evang Tchr.

--Training When Meeting. 32p. 1981. pap. text ed. 2.95 (ISBN 0-910566-33-X); planbook 3.95 (ISBN 0-910566-34-8). Evang Tchr.

--Video Seminar Planbook for Dynamic Bible Teaching. 64p. 1983. pap. 4.95 (ISBN 0-910566-60-7). Evang Tchr.

Evangeline. Travels with Angie. 1981. 6.75 (ISBN 0-8062-1838-X). Carlton.

Evangelism Commission. Who Are the Saints? 1.25 (ISBN 0-8309-0190-6). Herald Hse.

Evangelista, Susan. Carlos Bulosan & His Poetry: A Biography & Anthology. LC 84-40710. 192p. 1985. pap. text ed. 20.00x (ISBN 0-295-96232-1). U of Wash Pr.

Evangelou, Phylo. Livestock Development in Kenya's Maasailand: Pastoralists Transition to a Market Economy. (A Westview Replica Ser.). 315p. 1984. pap. 26.50x (ISBN 0-86531-881-6). Westview.

Evangelou, Phylo, jt. ed. see Simpson, James R.

Evanier, David. The One-Star Jew: Short Stories by David Evanier. LC 82-73714. 240p. (Orig.). 1983. pap. 15.00 (ISBN 0-86547-098-7). N Point Pr.

Evanoff, Philip C. & Gerlach, Werner, eds. Surface Strength Terminology. (Illus.). 65p. 1983. pap. 39.95 non-members (ISBN 0-89852-411-3); pap. 26.77 members. TAPPI.

Evanoff, Viad. Fresh-Water Fisherman's Bible. rev. ed. LC 79-7684. (Outdoor Bible Ser.). (Illus.). 1980. pap. 5.95 (ISBN 0-385-14405-9). Doubleday.

Evanoff, Vlad. A Complete Guide to Fishing. rev. ed. LC 80-2251. (Illus.). 1981. 11.89 (ISBN 0-690-04090-3); PLB 10.89 (ISBN 0-690-04091-1). Crowell Jr Bks.

--Complete Guide to Fishing. pap. 2.00 (ISBN 0-87980-250-2). Wilshire.

--Fishing Rigs for Fresh & Salt Water. (Illus.). 182p. 9.95 (ISBN 0-06-011257-3). Brown Bk.

--One Thousand & One Fishing Tips & Tricks. 1978. pap. 3.95 (ISBN 0-346-12336-4). Cornerstone.

--One Thousand & One Fishing Tips & Tricks. (Illus.). 1966. 10.95i (ISBN 0-06-070738-0, HarpT). Har-Row.

Evanovich, Peter & Kerner, Martin. Precalculus: A Functional Approach to Algebra & Trigonometry. 1981. text ed. 28.00x (ISBN 0-8162-2715-2); study guide & instr's manual avail. Holden-Day.

Evans. The Ancient Welsh Bards. 211p. 1980. Repr. of 1764 ed. lib. bdg. 40.00 (ISBN 0-8495-1336-7). Arden Lib.

--Bold Commitment. 1983. 4.95 (ISBN 0-88207-284-6). Victor Bks.

--Emergency Medicine. 1981. text ed. 49.95 (ISBN 0-407-00172-7). Butterworth.

--Evaluation of Medical Images. (Medical Physics Handbook Ser.: No. 10). 1981. 28.00 (ISBN 0-9960021-6-2, Pub. by Inst Physics England). Heyden.

--Opening & Closing Arguments. (The Law in Georgia Ser.). incl. latest pocket part supplement 24.95 (ISBN 0-686-90538-5); separate pocket part supplement, 1984 18.95 (ISBN 0-686-90539-3). Harrison Co GA.

--Sagomi Gambit. 3.95 (ISBN 0-317-31808-X). Tor Bks.

--Solitary Man. 3.95 (ISBN 0-317-31809-8). Tor Bks.

--Takeover. 3.50 (ISBN 0-317-31811-X). Tor Bks.

Evans & Matthews. Systematics & Nesting Behavior of Australian Bembix Sand Wasps -(Hymenoptera, Sphecidae) (Memoirs Ser: No. 20). (Illus.). 1973. 35.00x (ISBN 0-686-17148-9). Am Entom Inst.

Evans, et al, eds. see Hansen, Joseph.

Evans, A. Introduction to Ore Geology. (Geoscience Texts Ser.: Vol. 2). 1980. 54.00 (ISBN 0-444-19473-8); pap. 24.50 (ISBN 0-444-19472-X). Elsevier.

Evans, A., jt. auth. see D'Angio, G.

Evans, A. A., ed. Victorian Poetry. 1979. Repr. of 1958 ed. lib. bdg. 20.00 (ISBN 0-8482-0716-5). Norwood Edns.

Evans, A. G., ed. Fracture in Ceramic Materials: Toughening Mechanisms, Machining Damage, Shock. LC 84-14763. (Illus.). 420p. 1985. 42.00 (ISBN 0-8155-1005-5). Noyes.

Evans, A. G., jt. ed. see Bradt, R. C.

Evans, A. H., jt. auth. see Wilson, B. Scott.

Evans, A. J. Reading & Thinking. 1979. Bk. 1. pap. text ed. 3.75x (ISBN 0-8077-2563-3); Bk. 2. pap. text ed. 3.75x (ISBN 0-8077-2564-1); pap. text ed. 1.50x manual (ISBN 0-8077-2565-X). Tchrs Coll.

Evans, A. J. & Palmer, Marilyn. More Writing about Pictures: Using Pictures to Develop Language & Writing Skills. (gr. 1-3). 1982. Bk. 1: Familiar Places. pap. 3.95x (ISBN 0-8077-6037-4); Bk. 2: Action & Activity. pap. 3.95x (ISBN 0-8077-6038-2); Bk. 3: Supplement-Fables. pap. 3.95x (ISBN 0-8077-6039-0); tchr's. manual 2.95x (ISBN 0-8077-6040-4). Tchrs Coll.

--Writing about Pictures: Using Pictures to Develop Language & Writing Skills, 6 bks. (gr. 1-3). 1982. Bk. 1: Completing Sentences. pap. text ed. 3.75x (ISBN 0-8077-5994-5); Bk. 2: Writing Sentences. pap. text ed. 3.75x (ISBN 0-8077-6031-5); Bk. 3: Getting At The Story. pap. text ed. 3.75x (ISBN 0-8077-6032-3); Bk. 4: Linking Story Ideas. pap. text ed. 3.75x (ISBN 0-8077-6033-1); Bk. 5: Writing Your Story, I. pap. text ed. 3.75x (ISBN 0-8077-6034-X); Bk. 6: Writing Your Story, II. pap. text ed. 3.75x (ISBN 0-8077-6035-8); tchrs. manual 2.95x (ISBN 0-8077-6036-6). Tchrs Coll.

Evans, A. J., et al. Education & Training of Users of Scientific & Technical Information: UNISIST Guide for Teachers. (Illus.). 143p. (2nd Printing 1982). 1977. pap. 10.50 (ISBN 92-3-101452-8, U746, UNESCO). Unipub.

Evans, A. M., ed. Metallization Associated with Acid Magmatism. LC 76-366369. (International Geological Correlation Programme Ser.: Vol. 6). 385p. 1982. 58.95x (ISBN 0-471-09995-3, Pub. by Wiley-Interscience). Wiley.

Evans, A. R., ed. see Markley, Rayner W.

Evans, A. R., ed. see Sheeler, W. D., et al.

Evans, A. R., ed. see Sheeler, W. D. & Bayley, S. C.

Evans, A. W. Carlyle. (Masters of Literature). 1909. 25.00 (ISBN 0-8274-2004-8). R West.

Evans, A. W., tr. see France, Anatole.

Evans, A. W., tr. see Lemaitre, Jules.

Evans, Alan. Dauntless. 1985. 14.95 (ISBN 0-8027-0864-1). Walker & Co.

--Urban Economics. 208p. 1985. 45.00x (ISBN 0-631-14194-4); pap. 14.95x (ISBN 0-631-14195-2). Basil Blackwell.

Evans, Alan & Eversley, David, eds. The Inner City: Employment & Industry. (Centre for Environmental Studies Ser.). 1980. text ed. 80.00x (ISBN 0-435-84355-9). Gower Pub Co.

Evans, Alan, jt. ed. see Wingo, Lowdon.

Evans, Alan L. Personality Characteristics & Disciplinary Attitudes of Child-Abusing Mothers. LC 80-69240. 145p. 1981. perfect bdg. 11.95 (ISBN 0-86548-033-8). R & E Pubs.

Evans, Alan W., jt. auth. see Wingo, Lowdon.

Evans, Alexander W. Supplementary Report on the Cladoniae of Connecticut. (Connecticut Academy of Arts & Sciences Transaction: Vol. 35). 626p. 1944. pap. 16.00 (ISBN 0-208-00890-X). Shoe String.

Evans, Alfred J. Shakespeare's Magic Circle. facs. ed. LC 72-128884. (Select Bibliographies Reprint Ser.). 1956. 15.00 (ISBN 0-8369-5504-8). Ayer Co Pubs.

Evans, Alfred S., ed. Viral Infections of Humans. LC 76-9650. 616p. 1976. 39.50x (ISBN 0-306-30880-0, Plenum Pr); pap. 15.00x (ISBN 0-306-31137-2). Plenum Pub.

--Viral Infections of Humans: Epidemiology & Control. 2nd ed. LC 82-3684. 775p. 1982. 49.50 (ISBN 0-306-40676-4, Plenum Med Bk). Plenum Pub.

--Viral Infections of Humans: Epidemiology & Control. 2nd ed. 757p. 1984. pap. 24.50x (ISBN 0-306-41635-2, Plenum Med Bk). Plenum Pub.

Evans, Alfred S. & Feldman, Harry A., eds. Bacterial Infections in Humans: Epidemiology & Control. 744p. 1984. pap. 27.50x (ISBN 0-306-41705-7, Plenum Med Bk). Plenum Pub.

--Bacterial Infections of Humans: Epidemiology & Control. 744p. 1982. 59.50x (ISBN 0-306-40967-4, Plenum Pr). Plenum Pub.

Evans, Alice F. & Evans, Robert A. Introduction to Christianity: A Case Method Approach. pap. 3.99 (ISBN 0-8042-1314-3). John Knox.

Evans, Alice F., jt. auth. see Evans, Robert A.

Evans, Allan, ed. see Balducci Pegolotti, F.

Evans, Allan R. Energy & Environment. 265p. 1980. pap. text ed. 8.95x (ISBN 0-933694-15-6). COMPress.

Evans, Alona E. & Murphy, John F., eds. Legal Aspects of International Terrorism. new ed. LC 78-404. 736p. 1978. 40.00x (ISBN 0-669-02185-7). Lexington Bks.

Evans, Alvis J., et al. Basic Electronics Technology. Luecke, Gerald & Krone, Kenneth M., eds. (Electronic Technology Ser.). (Illus.). 464p. 1985. text ed. 19.95 (ISBN 0-89512-179-4, LCB8601). Tex Instr Inc.

Evans & Leedham, ed. Aspects of Educational Technology, Vol. IX. 308p. 1975. 35.00 (ISBN 0-85038-291-2). Nichols Pub.

Evans, Ann. How to Form a Buying Club. 2nd ed. 51p. 1978. 2.50 (ISBN 0-318-15073-5). NASCO.

Evans, Anthony, jt. ed. see Pask, Joseph.

Evans, Anthony E. & Muramatsu, Mitsuo, eds. Radiotracer Techniques & Applications, Vols. 1 & 2. 1977. Vol. 1. 115.00 (ISBN 0-8247-6496-X); Vol. 2. 89.75 (ISBN 0-8247-6497-8). Dekker.

Evans, Archibald A. Hours of Work in Industrialised Countries. xiv, 164p. 1978. 11.40 (ISBN 92-2-101296-4). Intl Labour Office.

--Hours of Work in Industrialized Countries. xiv, 164p. (2nd Impression). 1978. pap. 11.50 (ISBN 92-2-101296-4, ILO132, ILO). Unipub.

Evans, Arthur. The Palace of Minos, 4 Vols. in 7. LC 63-18048. 1921. 750.00x (ISBN 0-8196-0129-2). Vol. 1 (ISBN 0-8196-0130-6). Vol. 2, Pt. 1 (ISBN 0-8196-0131-4). Vol. 2, Pt. 2 (ISBN 0-8196-0141-1). Vol. 3 (ISBN 0-8196-0132-2). Vol. 4, Pt. 1 (ISBN 0-8196-0133-0). Vol. 4, Pt. 2 (ISBN 0-8196-0134-9). Index (ISBN 0-8196-0135-7). Biblo.

--Witchcraft: The Gay Counterculture. 1977. pap. 5.95 (ISBN 0-915480-01-8). Fag Rag.

Evans, Arthur B. Jean Cocteau & His Films of Orphic Identity. (Illus.). 174p. 1975. 22.50 (ISBN 0-87982-011-X). Art Alliance.

Evans, Arthur B. & Evans, Sebastian. Leicestershire Words, Phrases & Proverbs. (English Dialect Society Publications Ser.: No. 31). pap. 33.00. Kraus Repr.

Evans, Arthur J. Through Bosnia & the Herzegovina on Foot During the Insurrection August & September 1875. LC 73-135804. (Eastern Europe Collection Ser). 1970. Repr. of 1877 ed. 31.00 (ISBN 0-405-02746-X). Ayer Co Pubs.

Evans, Arthur J. & Andrew, Murray. Anthropology & the Classics: Six Lectures Delivered Before the University of Oxford. Marett, R. R., ed. 1978. pap. 20.00 (ISBN 0-8495-3719-3). Arden Lib.

Evans, Arthur N. The Automobile. (Cambridge Topic Bks.). (Illus.). 52p. (gr. 5 up). 1985. PLB 7.95 (ISBN 0-8225-1232-7). Lerner Pubns.

--The Motor Car. LC 82-9713. (Cambridge Introduction to the History of Mankind Topic Bk.). (Illus.). 48p. 1983. pap. 4.50 (ISBN 0-521-28416-3). Cambridge U pr.

Evans, Arthur R., Jr. The Literary Art of Eugene Fromentin: A Study in Style & Motif. 166p. 1964. 16.00x (ISBN 0-8018-0191-5). Johns Hopkins.

Evans, Arthur R., Jr., ed. On Four Modern Humanists: Hofmannsthal, Gundolf, Curtius, Kantorowicz. LC 76-90945. (Princeton Essays Literature). 1970. 25.00x (ISBN 0-691-06174-2). Princeton U Pr.

Evans, Audrey, et al. Advances in Neuroblastoma Research. LC 84-27758. (PCBR Ser.: Vol. 175). 632p. 1985. 78.00 (ISBN 0-8451-5025-1). A R Liss.

Evans, Audrey E. Modern Concepts in Brain Tumor Therapy: Laboratory & Clinical Investigation. (Illus.). 220p, 1979. text ed. 61.50 (ISBN 0-7194-0020-1, Pub. by Castle Hse England). J K Burgess.

Evans, Audrey E., ed. Advances in Neuroblastoma Research. (Progress in Cancer Research & Therapy Ser.: Vol. 12). 360p. 1980. 54.50 (ISBN 0-89004-459-7, 516). Raven.

--Modern Concepts in Brain Tumor Therapy: Laboratory & Clinical Investigations. (Illus.). 1979. 79.95x (ISBN 0-7194-0020-1). Intl Ideas.

Evans, Augusta. St. Elmo. 440p. 1980. Repr. of 1896 ed. lib. bdg. 19.95 (ISBN 0-89968-210-3). Lightyear.

--St. Elmo. 415p. 1984. Repr. lib. bdg. 19.95x (ISBN 0-89966-487-3). Buccaneer Bks.

Evans, Augusta J. St. Elmo: A Novel. LC 74-15736. (Popular Culture in America Ser.). 576p. 1975. Repr. 38.00x (ISBN 0-405-06371-7). Ayer Co Pubs.

Evans, Austin P. Episode in the Struggle for Religious Freedom. LC 74-130618. Repr. of 1924 ed. 19.00 (ISBN 0-404-02357-6). AMS Pr.

Evans, Austin P., ed. see Scott, Ernest F.

Evans, B. The Early English Baptists, 2 vols. (Illus.). 1977. Repr. of 1862 ed. Vol. 1, 298 pp. 9.50 (ISBN 0-87921-041-9); Vol. 2, 362 pp. 9.50 (ISBN 0-87921-045-1). Attic Pr.

Evans, B., jt. auth. see Knapton, J.

Evans, B. I. Keats. LC 74-6371. (Studies in Keats, No. 19). 1974. lib. bdg. 39.95x (ISBN 0-8383-1858-4). Haskell.

--William Morris & His Poetry. LC 74-23889. 1925. lib. bdg. 17.50 (ISBN 0-8414-3947-8). Folcroft.

Evans, B. Ifor. Literature & Science. LC 74-23911. 1954. lib. bdg. 17.50 (ISBN 0-8414-3941-9). Folcroft.

--Tradition & Romanticism: Studies in English Poetry from Chaucer to W. B. Yeats. x, 213p. 1973. Repr. of 1940 ed. 17.50 (ISBN 0-208-00577-3, Archon). Shoe String.

Evans, B. Ifor & Greg, W. W., eds. Jack Juggler. LC 82-45686. (Malone Society Reprint Ser.: No. 83). Repr. of 1936 ed. 40.00 (ISBN 0-404-63083-9). AMS Pr.

Evans, Barbara. Freedom to Choose: The Life & Work of Dr. Helena Wright, Pioneer of Contraception. 288p. 1985. 19.95 (ISBN 0-370-30504-3, Pub. by the Bodley Head). Merrimack Pub Cir.

Evans, Barbara L., jt. ed. see Evans, Gareth.

Evans, Barbara L., jt. ed. see Evans, Gareth L.

Evans, Barrie, pseud. O.R. (Orig.). 1982. pap. 3.95 (ISBN 0-440-17623-9). Dell.

Evans, Barrie, et al, eds. Changing Design. 379p. 1982. 51.95 (ISBN 0-471-28045-3). Wiley.

Evans, Barry. Housing Rehabilitation Handbook. (Illus.). 1980. 49.50 (ISBN 0-85139-293-8, Pub. by Architectural Pr). Nichols Pub.

Evans, Benjamin. Daylight in Architecture. LC 80-26066. (Illus.). 204p. 1982. 42.50x (ISBN 0-07-019768-7). McGraw.

--Keats: A Critical Biographical Study. LC 77-131699. 1971. Repr. of 1934 ed. 9.00x (ISBN 0-403-00586-8). Scholarly.

Evans, Benjamin I. English Literature Between the Wars. LC 74-22489. 1974. Repr. of 1948 ed. lib. bdg. 17.50 (ISBN 0-8414-3925-7). Folcroft.

--English Poetry in the Later Nineteenth-Century. 2nd ed. LC 79-3330. Repr. of 1966 ed. 39.50 (ISBN 0-404-18399-9). AMS Pr.

--Keats. LC 74-16285. 1974. Repr. of 1934 ed. lib. bdg. 15.00 (ISBN 0-8414-3987-7). Folcroft.

--A Short History of English Drama. LC 77-27446. 1978. Repr. of 1950 ed. lib. bdg. 19.75x (ISBN 0-8371-9072-X, EVED). Greenwood.

--William Morris & His Poetry. LC 74-120987. (Poetry & Life Ser.). Repr. of 1925 ed. 7.25 (ISBN 0-404-52512-1). AMS Pr.

Evans, Bergen. The Psychiatry of Robert Burton. LC 72-4487. 1972. Repr. of 1944 ed. lib. bdg. 17.00x (ISBN 0-374-92638-7). Octagon.

--The Word-A-Day Vocabulary Builder. 1982. pap. 1.95 (ISBN 0-345-30610-4). Ballantine.

Evans, Bergen, ed. Fifty Essays. LC 72-5798. (Essay Index Reprint Ser.). 1972. Repr. of 1936 ed. 22.00 (ISBN 0-8369-2988-8). Ayer Co Pubs.

Evans, Bertrand. Shakespeare's Tragic Practice. 1979. 34.50x (ISBN 0-19-812094-X). Oxford U Pr.

Evans, Bertrand & Lynch, James J. Dialogues on the Teaching of Literature. 11.95x (ISBN 0-8084-0397-4); pap. 8.95x (ISBN 0-8084-0398-2). New Coll U Pr.

Evans, Bertrand, ed. The College Shakespeare: Fifteen Plays & the Sonnets. 736p. 1973. pap. text ed. write for info. (ISBN 0-02-334440-7, 33444). Macmillan.

Evans, Bill, jt. auth. see Ellik, Ron.

Evans, Blakemore G., ed. Shakespeare Prompt-Books of the Seventeenth Century. Vol. III The Comedy of Errors, A Midsummer Night's Dream. boxed 25.00 (ISBN 0-317-01375-0); Vol. V Smock Alley Macbeth. boxed 25.00 (ISBN 0-317-01376-9). U Pr of Va.

Evans, Brian & Waites, Bernard. IQ & Mental Testing: An Unnatural Science & Its Social History. (Critical Social Studies). 228p. 1981. text ed. 30.00x (ISBN 0-391-01911-2, Pub. by Macmillan England); pap. text ed. 12.00 (ISBN 0-333-25649-2). Humanities.

Evans, Bruce D. C-Bundles & Compact Transformation Groups. LC 82-11544. (Memoirs of the American Mathematical Society Ser.: No. 269). 63p. 1982. pap. 9.00 (ISBN 0-8218-2269-1, MEMO/269). Am Math.

Evans, C. New Waite's Compendium of Natal Astrology. 1971. pap. 8.95 (ISBN 0-87728-125-4). Weiser.

Evans, C. J. & Karpel, S. Organotin Compounds in Modern Technology. (Journal of Organometallic Chemistry Library: Vol. 16). 280p. 1985. 72.25 (ISBN 0-444-42422-9). Elsevier.

Evans, C. O. Subject of Consciousness. (Muirhead Library of Philosophy). 1970. text ed. 18.00x (ISBN 0-391-00037-3). Humanities.

Evans, C. S. Cinderella. (Illus.). 1982. 10.95 (ISBN 0-434-95862-X, Pub. by W Heinemann Ltd). David & Charles.

--Preserving the Person: A Look at the Human Sciences. 178p. 1982. pap. 5.95 (ISBN 0-8010-3385-3). Baker Bk.

--Sleeping Beauty. (Illus.). 1982. 10.95 (ISBN 0-434-95860-3, Pub. by W Heinemann). David & Charles.

Evans, C. Stephen. Existentialism: The Philosophy of Despair & the Quest for Hope. LC 83-11198. (Orig.). 1984. 6.95 (ISBN 0-310-43741-5, 11198P, Pub. by Academie Bks). Zondervan.

--Kierkegaard's Fragments & Postscripts. 304p. 1983. text ed. 18.45x (ISBN 0-391-02737-9). Humanities.

--Philosophy of Religion. LC 84-25198. (Contours of Christian Philosophy Ser.). 180p. (Orig.). 1985. pap. 6.95 (ISBN 0-87784-343-0). Inter-Varsity.

Evans, C. Stephen, ed. see Holmes, Arthur F.

Evans, C. Stephen, ed. see Wolfe, David L.

Evans, C. W. Powdered & Particulate Rubber Technology. (Illus.). 107p. 1978. 24.00 (ISBN 0-85334-773-5, Pub. by Elsevier Applied Sci England). Elsevier.

--Practical Rubber Compounding & Processing. (Illus.). 205p. 1981. 37.00 (ISBN 0-85334-901-0, Pub. by Elsevier Applied Sci England). Elsevier.

Evans, C. W., ed. Developments in Rubber & Rubber Composites, Vol. 1. (Illus.). 184p. 1980. 33.50 (ISBN 0-85334-892-8, Pub. by Elsevier Applied Sci England). Elsevier.

--Developments in Rubber & Rubber Composites, Vol. 2. (Illus.). 183p. 1983. 44.50 (ISBN 0-85334-173-7, I-460-82, Pub. by Elsevier Applied Sci England). Elsevier.

Evans, Caradoc. Fury Never Leaves Us: A Miscellany of Caradoc Evans. Harris, John, intro. by. LC 85-71577. (Miscellany Ser.: Vol. 4). (Illus.). 220p. 1985. pap. 10.95 (ISBN 0-907476-38-4, Pub. by Poetry Wales Pr UK). Dufour.

--My Neighbors: Stories of the Welsh People. LC 73-121539. (Short Story Index Reprint Ser). 1920. 17.00 (ISBN 0-8369-3495-4). Ayer Co Pubs.

Evans, Carl D., et al, eds. Scripture in Context: Essays on the Comparative Method. LC 80-10211. (Pittsburgh Theological Monograph Ser.: No. 34). 1980. pap. 17.00 (ISBN 0-915138-43-3). Pickwick.

Evans, Carl M. Atari BASIC: Faster & Better. 300p. 19.95 (ISBN 0-936200-29-4). Blue Cat.

Evans, Carl M., ed. see Rosenfelder, Lewis.

Evans, Carl M., ed. see Verheiden, Eric.

Evans, Carol, jt. ed. see Johnson, Walter.

Evans, Cerinda W. Collis Potter Huntington, 2 vols. (Mariners Museum). (Illus.). 775p. 1954. Set. 12.50x (ISBN 0-8139-0376-9). U Pr of Va.

Evans, Charles. American Bibliography, 14 vols. Incl. Vols 1-12. 180.00 (ISBN 0-8446-1173-5); Vol. 13. 1799-1800. 30.00 (ISBN 0-8446-1174-3); Vol. 14. Index to Vols. 1-13. Bristol, R. P., compiled by. 30.00 (ISBN 0-8446-1175-1). Peter Smith.

Evans, Charles & Pinhorn, Malcolm. Blackmansbury: Summaries of Principal Contents in Volumes 1-9 with Index to Volumes 7-9. 69.00x (ISBN 0-901262-12-9, Pub. by Pinhorns UK). State Mutual Bk.

Evans, Charles H. Electronic Amplifiers: Theory, Design, & Use. LC 76-3950. 1979. pap. text ed. 26.00 (ISBN 0-8273-1626-7); instr's. manual 6.15 (ISBN 0-8273-1627-5). Delmar.

Evans, Charles H., ed. Exports, Domestic & Foreign from the American Colonies to Great Britain, from 1697 to 1789. LC 75-22813. (America in Two Centuries Ser). 1976. Repr. of 1884 ed. 20.00x (ISBN 0-405-07683-5). Ayer Co Pubs.

Evans, Charles M. New Plants from Old: Pruning & Propagating for the Indoor Gardener. 1976. pap. 3.95 (ISBN 0-394-73116-6). Random.

Evans, Charles W., Jr. Babylon: The Oldest & Most Corrupt Harlot. 1984. 12.95 (ISBN 0-533-05914-3). Vantage.

Evans, Christina L. Memory Bank for Medications. Neal, Margo C., ed. (Orig.). 1985. pap. 15.95 (ISBN 0-935236-26-0). Nurseco.

Evans, Christina L. & Lewis, Sharon K. Nursing Administration of Psychiatric Mental Care. 1985. write for info. (ISBN 0-87189-099-2). Aspen Systems.

Evans, Christine. Looking Inland. 56p. 1983. pap. 8.25 (ISBN 0-907476-24-4). Dufour.

Evans, Christopher. Capella's Golden Eye. 256p. 1982. pap. 2.50 (ISBN 0-441-09115-6, Pub. by Ace Science Fiction). Ace Bks.

--Landscapes of the Night. 1985. pap. 5.95 (ISBN 0-671-55190-6). WSP.

--Landscapes of the Night: How & Why We Dream. Evans, Peter, ed. 256p. 1984. 16.95 (ISBN 0-670-41777-7). Viking.

--The Making of the Micro: A History of the Computer. 120p. 1981. pap. 14.95 (ISBN 0-442-22240-8). Van Nos Reinhold.

--The Micro Millenium. 320p. 1981. pap. 3.95 (ISBN 0-671-46212-1). WSP.

--The Micro Millenium. 256p. 1980. 10.95 (ISBN 0-686-98078-6). Telecom Lib.

--The Micro Millennium. 1980. 10.95 (ISBN 0-670-47400-2). Viking.

Evans, Christopher, intro. by. Understanding Yourself. 1980. pap. 4.95 (ISBN 0-451-13453-2, Sig). NAL.

Evans, Christopher, tr. see Falassi, Alessandro & Catoni, Guiliano.

Evans, Chuck. Jewelry: Contemporary Design & Techniques. LC 82-74005. (Illus.). 296p. 1983. 24.95 (ISBN 0-87192-141-3, 141-3). Davis Mass.

--Jewelry: Contemporary Designs & Techniques. (Illus.). 296p. 1983. 24.95 (ISBN 0-87192-141-3, Pub. by Davis Mass). Sterling.

Evans, Claire. Apollo's Dream. (Second Chance at Love Ser.: No. 64). 192p. 1982. pap. 1.75 (ISBN 0-515-06675-3). Jove Pubns.

--Come Winter's End. (Second Chance at Love Ser.: No. 115). 192p. 1983. pap. 1.95 (ISBN 0-515-07203-6). Jove Pubns.

Evans, Clifford, jt. auth. see Rye, Owen S.

Evans, Clifford, jt. ed. see Meggers, Betty.

Evans, Coleen. Living True. 132p. 1985. pap. 4.50 (ISBN 0-89693-321-0). Victor Bks.

Evans, Colin W. Hose Technology. 2nd ed. (Illus.). 226p. 1979. 40.75 (ISBN 0-85334-830-8, Pub. by Elsevier Applied Sci England). Elsevier.

Evans, Colleen. The Vine Life. 144p. 1983. pap. 4.95 (ISBN 0-310-60301-3, PUb by Chosen Bks). Zondervan.

--Vine Life. 144p. 1980. lib. bdg. 6.95 (ISBN 0-310-60300-5, Pub by Chosen Bks). Zondervan.

Evans, Colleen T. A Deeper Joy. 160p. 1982. 10.95 (ISBN 0-8007-1306-0). Revell.

--Give Us This Day Our Daily Bread: Asking for & Sharing Life's Necessities. 160p. 1982. pap. 3.50 (ISBN 0-687-14743-3). Abingdon.

--Love Is an Everyday Thing. rev. ed. 128p. 1984. pap. 4.95 (ISBN 0-8007-5157-4, Power Bks). Revell.

--A New Joy. (Orig.). 1975. pap. 1.50 (ISBN 0-89129-015-X). Jove Pubns.

--Start Loving, Keep Loving. LC 84-28722. 120p. 1985. pap. 5.95 (ISBN 0-385-19754-3, Galilee). Doubleday.

Evans, Craig. On Foot Through Europe: A Trail Guide to Austria, Switzerland & Liechtenstein. LC 82-600. (Illus.). 228p. (Orig.). 1982. pap. 9.25 (ISBN 0-688-01159-4, Quill NY). Morrow.

--On Foot Through Europe: A Trail Guide to Europe's Long-Distance Footpaths. LC 82-593. (Illus.). 240p. (Orig.). 1982. pap. 7.25 (ISBN 0-688-01156-X, Quill NY). Morrow.
--On Foot Through Europe: A Trail Guide to France & the Benelux Nations. LC 82-599. (Illus.). 396p. (Orig.). 1982. pap. 10.50 (ISBN 0-688-01171-3, Quill NY). Morrow.
--On Foot Through Europe: A Trail Guide to Scandinavia. LC 82-601. (Illus.). 420p. 1982. pap. 12.50 (ISBN 0-688-01191-8, Quill NY). Morrow.
--On Foot Through Europe: A Trail Guide to Spain & Portugal. Whitney, Stephen, ed. (Illus.). 368p. 1980. lib. bdg. 10.95 (ISBN 0-933710-15-1); pap. 5.95 (ISBN 0-933710-14-3). Foot Trails.
--On Foot Through Europe: A Trail Guide to Spain & Portugal. LC 82-603. (Illus.). 192p. (Orig.). 1982. pap. 9.25 (ISBN 0-688-01195-0, Quill NY). Morrow.
--On Foot Through Europe: A Trail Guide to Spain & Portugal. 1982. 9.25 (ISBN 0-688-01195-0). Morrow.
--On Foot Through Europe: A Trail Guide to the British Isles. LC 82-604. (Illus.). 372p. (Orig.). 1982. pap. 10.50 (ISBN 0-688-01164-0, Quill NY). Morrow.
--On Foot Through Europe: A Trail Guide to West Germany. LC 82-602. (Illus.). 192p. 1982. pap. 9.25 (ISBN 0-688-01197-7, Quill NY). Morrow.
--On Foot Through Europe: A Trail Guide to West Germany. 1982. 9.25 (ISBN 0-688-01197-7). Morrow.
Evans, D. & Body, R. Freedom & Stability in the World Economy. 128p. 1976. 15.00 (ISBN 0-85664-119-7, Pub. by Croom Helm Ltd). Longwood Pub Group.
Evans, D., jt. auth. see Wright, G. G.
Evans, D. A., jt. ed. see Lumsden, W. H.
Evans, D. A., jt. ed. see Lumsden, W. H. R.
Evans, D. Delta. The Ancient Bards of Britain. 1973. Repr. of 1906 ed. 35.00 (ISBN 0-8274-0542-1). R West.
Evans, D. Ellis. The Labyrinth of Continental Celtic. 1981. 15.50x (ISBN 0-85672-210-3, Pub. by Brit Acad England). State Mutual Bk.
Evans, D. J., ed. Parallel Processing Systems: An Advanced Course. LC 81-38445. (Illus.). 350p. 1982. 44.50 (ISBN 0-521-24366-1). Cambridge U Pr.
--Software for Numerical Mathematics. 1974. 73.00 (ISBN 0-12-243750-0). Acad Pr.
--Sparsity & Its Applications. 352p. 1985. 39.50 (ISBN 0-521-26272-0). Cambridge U Pr.
Evans, D. J., ed. see International Symposium on Hydrometallurgy.
Evans, D. J., et al, eds. International Laterite Symposium. LC 78-73974. (Illus.). 1979. text ed. 33.00x (ISBN 0-89520-255-7). Soc Mining Eng.
Evans, D. M. Special Tests & Their Meanings. 12th rev. ed. (Illus.). 272p. 1981. pap. 7.95 (ISBN 0-571-18034-5). Faber & Faber.
Evans, D. Moirer. History of the Commercial Crises 1857-58 & the Stock Exchange Panic of 1859. LC 71-77750. (Research & Source Works, Ser.: No. 356). 1969. Repr. of 1859 ed. 22.50 (ISBN 0-8337-1082-6). B Franklin.
Evans, D. Morier. The Commercial Crisis Eighteen Forty-Seven to Eighteen Forty-Eight. 2nd ed. LC 68-20037. 1969. Repr. of 1849 ed. 29.50x (ISBN 0-678-00515-X). Kelley.
--Facts, Failures, & Frauds Revelations, Financial, Mercantile, Criminal. LC 68-24163. Repr. of 1859 ed. 45.00x (ISBN 0-678-00394-7). Kelley.
--History of the Commercial Crisis 1857-1858. LC 74-84577. Repr. of 1859 ed. 37.50x (ISBN 0-678-00517-6). Kelley.
--Speculative Notes & Notes on Speculation, Ideal & Real. 1968. Repr. of 1864 ed. 16.00 (ISBN 0-8337-1089-3). B Franklin.
--Speculative Notes & Notes on Speculation: Ideal & Real. LC 73-85788. Repr. of 1864 ed. 35.00x (ISBN 0-678-00560-5). Kelley.
Evans, D. Morier, ed. Commercial Crisis Eighteen Forty-Seven to Eighteen Forty-Eight. 1970. Repr. of 1848 ed. 19.00 (ISBN 0-8337-1081-8). B Franklin.
Evans, D. P. Backache. (Illus.). 280p. 1982. text ed. 26.00 (ISBN 0-8391-1739-6). Univ Park.
Evans, D. S. Astronomy. (Teach Yourself Ser.). 1975. pap. 6.95 (ISBN 0-679-10416-X). McKay.
Evans, D. S., jt. auth. see Jacobson, D. M.
Evans, D. S., ed. Breaking up Bell: Essays on Industrial Organization & Regulation. 298p. 1983. 26.50 (ISBN 0-444-00734-2, North-Holland). Elsevier.
Evans, D. S., ed. see I.A.U. Symposium, No. 4, Uppsala, Sweden, August 10-14, 1970.
Evans, D. Simon, ed. see Doble, G. H.
Evans, Daryl. Explorations in Time, Nos. 911-912. 1975. 10.00 (ISBN 0-686-20375-5). CPL Biblios.
Evans, Daryl P. The Lives of Mentally Retarded People. 300p. 1982. lib. bdg. 32.00x (ISBN 0-86531-270-2); pap. text ed. 13.50x (ISBN 0-86531-271-0). Westview.
Evans, David. As Mad As a Hatter. 224p. 1982. text ed. 17.25x (ISBN 0-904387-90-9, Pub. by Alan Sutton England). Humanities.
--A Bibliography of Stained Glass. 214p. 1982. text ed. 60.00 (ISBN 0-85991-087-3, BAB-04836, Pub. by Boydell & Brewer). Longwood Pub Group.
--Big Road Blues: Tradition & Creativity in the Folk Blues. LC 77-76177. (Illus.). 368p. 1981. 32.50 (ISBN 0-520-03484-8). U of Cal Pr.
--The Ingenious Mr. Pedersen. 132p. 1979. Repr. of 1978 ed. text ed. 10.75x (ISBN 0-904387-29-1, Pub. by Alan Sutton England). Humanities.
--The Planning of Nonformal Education. (Fundamentals of Educational Planning: No. 30). 102p. 1981. pap. 6.00 (ISBN 92-803-1082-8, U1152, UNESCO). Unipub.
--Tommy Johnson. (The Paul Oliver Blues Ser.). pap. 2.95 (ISBN 0-913714-46-1). Legacy Bks.
Evans, David & Hoxeng, James, eds. The Eucador Project. Clason, Carla & Massee, Robin, trs. from Eng. & Fr. (Technical Notes Ser.: No.1). 23p. (Orig.). 1972. pap. 1.00 (ISBN 0-932288-03-0). Eng. Fr (ISBN 0-932288-05-7). Span (ISBN 0-932288-04-9). Ctr Intl Ed U of MA.
Evans, David, ed. see Batten, Adrian.
Evans, David, jt. ed. see Hartwig, Gunther.
Evans, David, tr. see Karolak, Tadeusz.
Evans, David A. Real & False Alarms. LC 84-73284. 64p. 1985. pap. 5.25 (ISBN 0-933532-45-8). BkMk.
--What the Tallgrass Says? 120p. pap. 6.95 (ISBN 0-931170-17-6). Ctr Western Studies.
Evans, David A. & Hankamer, Jorge, eds. Situations & Speech Acts: Toward a Formal Semantics of Discourse. (Outstanding Dissertations in Linguistics Ser.). 225p. 1985. 35.00 (ISBN 0-8240-5446-6). Garland Pub.
Evans, David A., et al, eds. Handbook of Plant Cell Culture, Vol. 2. LC 82-73774. 550p. 1983. 49.50 (ISBN 0-02-949780-9). Macmillan.
Evans, David A., jt. ed. see Sharp, William R.
Evans, David E. Dursley & Cam. 125p. 1981. text ed. 8.75x (ISBN 0-904387-88-7, Pub. by Alan Sutton England). Humanities.
Evans, David G. Practitioners Guide to Alcoholism & the Law. 93p. 1983. 7.95 (ISBN 0-89486-177-8). Hazelden.
Evans, David J. Geographical Perspectives in Juvenile Delinquency. 144p. 1980. text ed. 34.50x (ISBN 0-566-00351-1). Gower Pub Co.
Evans, David J., ed. Preconditioning Methods: Analysis & Application. (Topics in Computer Mathematics Ser.: Vol. 1). 568p. 1983. 74.50 (ISBN 0-677-16320-7). Gordon.
Evans, David L., jt. auth. see Counter, S. Allen.
Evans, David M. The Pastor in a Teaching Church. 96p. 1983. pap. 5.95 (ISBN 0-317-00688-6). Judson.
--Shaping the Church's Ministry with Youth. (Orig.). pap. 3.95 (ISBN 0-8170-0342-8). Judson.
Evans, David O. Social Romanticism in France, Eighteen Thirty to Eighteen Forty-Eight. LC 77-96180. 1969. Repr. of 1951 ed. lib. bdg. 15.00x (ISBN 0-374-92641-7, Dist. by NYGS). Octagon.
Evans, David P., et al, eds. Handbook of Plant Cell Culture, Vol. 1: Techniques for Propagation & Breeding. LC 82-73774. 1983. 53.00 (ISBN 0-02-949230-0). Macmillan.
Evans, David R. Technology in Nonformal Education. (Issue Paper Ser.: No. 2). 36p. (Orig.). 1977. pap. 3.00 (ISBN 0-932288-38-3). Ctr Intl Ed U of MA.
Evans, David R. & Hearn, Margaret T. Essential Interviewing: A Programmed Approach to Effective Communication. 2nd ed. LC 83-7767. (Psychology (Counseling) Ser.). 290p. 1983. pap. text ed. 13.50 pub net (ISBN 0-534-02964-7). Brooks-Cole.
Evans, David R., ed. see Bass, William M.
Evans, David S., intro. by. Eleventh Texas Symposium on Relativistic Astrophysics. (Annals of the New York Academy of Sciences: Vol. 422). 396p. 79.00x (ISBN 0-89766-234-2); pap. 79.00x (ISBN 0-89766-235-0). NY Acad Sci.
Evans, David S., et al, eds. Herschel at the Cape: Diaries & Correspondence of Sir John Herschel, 1834-1838. (History of Science Ser.: No. 1). (Illus.). 436p. 1969. 24.50x (ISBN 0-292-78387-6). U of Tex Pr.
Evans, Deane, jt. auth. see Levy, Emanuel.
Evans, Derek & Fulwiler, David. Who's Nobody in America. LC 81-47457. 132p. (Orig.). 1981. pap. 4.95 (ISBN 0-03-059327-1). HR&W.
Evans, Don. Trials & Tribulations of Staggerlee Booker T. Brown: A Play in Two Acts. 1985. pap. 3.35x (ISBN 0-317-18648-5). Dramatists Play.
Evans, Don A. Texas Business Law. LC 80-17836. 885p. 1980. 19.95x (ISBN 0-88289-251-7); Workbook 1982. pap. 12.95x (ISBN 0-88289-305-X). Pelican.
Evans, Donald. Faith, Authenticity, & Morality. 1980. 30.00x (ISBN 0-8020-5424-2). U of Toronto Pr.
--Struggle & Fulfillment: The Inner Dynamics of Religion & Morality. LC 80-8050. 256p. 1981. pap. 8.95 (ISBN 0-8006-1426-7, 1-1426). Fortress.
Evans, Donald D. & Adler, Laurie N., eds. Appropriate Technology for Development: A Discussion with Case Histories. (Special Studies in Social, Political, & Economic Development). 1979. softcover 35.00x (ISBN 0-89158-567-2). Westview.
Evans, Dorinda. Mather Brown: Early American Artist in England. LC 82-169. (Illus.). 1982. 32.50 (ISBN 0-8195-5069-8). Wesleyan U Pr.
Evans, Doris. Saguaro. LC 80-50647. (Popular Ser.: No. 28). (Illus.). 1980. pap. 4.95 (ISBN 0-911408-55-X). SW Pks Mnmts.
Evans, Dorothy & Claiborn, William, eds. Mental Health Issues & the Urban Poor. LC 73-19708. 1974. pap. text ed. 10.75 (ISBN 0-08-017830-8). Pergamon.
Evans, Douglas. Western Energy Policy. LC 78-23315. 1979. 25.00x (ISBN 0-312-86392-6). St Martin.
Evans, Douglas B. Auto Tour Guide to the Lake Mead National Recreation Area. LC 76-160215. (Illus.). 40p. (Orig.). 1971. pap. 0.50 (ISBN 0-911408-22-3). SW Pks Mnmts.
Evans, Douglas K. Sabre Jets over Korea: A Firsthand Account. (Illus.). 272p. (Orig.). 1984. pap. 15.50 (ISBN 0-8306-2352-3, 2352). TAB Bks.
Evans, E., jt. auth. see Reimer, B., Jr.
Evans, E. A. Tritium & Its Compounds. 441p. 1966. 26.00 (ISBN 0-442-02339-1, Pub. by Van Nos Reinhold). Krieger.
Evans, E. D. A History of Wales Sixteen Sixty to Eighteen Fifteen. (Welsh History Text Bks.: Vol. 2). 267p. 1979. text ed. 11.00x (ISBN 0-7083-0624-1, Pub. by Univ of Wales Pr England). Humanities.
Evans, E. E. Irish Heritage. (Illus.). 1950. 15.00 (ISBN 0-85221-009-4). Dufour.
--The Personality of Ireland: Habitat Heritage & History. LC 72-83667. (Wiles Lectures, 1971). (Illus.). 176p. 1973. 22.95 (ISBN 0-521-08684-1). Cambridge U Pr.
--Personality of Ireland: Habitat, Heritage & History. Rev. & enlarged ed. 130p. 1981. pap. text ed. 8.00x (ISBN 0-85640-238-9, Pub. by Blackstaff Pr Ireland). Humanities.
Evans, E. Estyn. Irish Folkways. (Illus.). 1966. pap. 10.95 (ISBN 0-7100-2888-1). Routledge & Kegan.
Evans, E. Estyn & Turner, Brian S. Ireland's Eye: The Photographs of Robert John Welch. (Illus.). 196p. 1977. 19.95 (ISBN 0-85640-127-7, Pub. by Blackstaff Pr). Longwood Pub Group.
Evans, E. Everett. Alien Minds. 1976. Repr. of 1955 ed. lib. bdg. 14.95 (ISBN 0-88411-981-5, Pub. by Aeonian Pr). Amereon Ltd.
--Man of Many Minds. 1976. Repr. of 1953 ed. lib. bdg. 13.95 (ISBN 0-88411-982-3, Pub. by Aeonian Pr). Amereon Ltd.
Evans, E. F. & Wilson, J. P., eds. Psychophysics & Physiology of Hearing. 1978. 66.00 (ISBN 0-12-244050-1). Acad Pr.
Evans, E. G. & Griffiths, P. Syzygies. (London Mathematical Society Lecture Note Ser.: No. 106). 160p. Date not set. pap. price not set. (ISBN 0-521-31411-9). Cambridge U Pr.
Evans, E. J. The Great Reform Act of 1832. (Lancaster Pamphlet Ser.). 60p. 1983. pap. 3.95 (ISBN 0-416-34450-X, NO. 3849). Methuen Inc.
Evans, E. P. Animal Symbolism in Ecclesiastical Architecture. 59.95 (ISBN 0-87968-638-3). Gordon Pr.
Evans, Edmund. My Diary. (Illus.). 129p. 1979. 6.95 (ISBN 0-374-35106-6). FS&G.
--Reminiscences of Edmund Evans. McLean, Ruari, ed. 1967. 10.40x (ISBN 0-19-818126-4). Oxford U Pr.
Evans, Edna. Tales from the Grand Canyon: Some True, Some Tall. LC 84-62643. (Illus.). 100p. 1985. pap. 7.95 (ISBN 0-87358-375-2). Northland.
Evans, Edward, jt. auth. see Reimer, Bennett.
Evans, Edward G. Developing Library Collections. LC 78-27303. (Library Science Text). 340p. 1979. lib. bdg. 28.00 (ISBN 0-87287-145-2); 20.00 (ISBN 0-87287-247-5). Libs Unl.
Evans, Edward W. Walter Savage Landor: A Critical Study. LC 74-22322. 1974. Repr. of 1907 ed. lib. bdg. 8.50 (ISBN 0-8414-3929-X). Folcroft.
Evans, Edward W., Jr. Walter Savage Landor: A Critical Study. LC 74-103186. 1970. Repr. of 1892 ed. 19.50x (ISBN 0-8046-0823-7, Pub. by Kennikat). Assoc Faculty Pr.
Evans, Edwin. Handbook to the Chamber & Orchestral Music of Johannes Brahms, 2 vols. LC 76-129468. (Research & Source Works: No. 55). 1970. Repr. of 1912 ed. 34.50 (ISBN 0-8337-1088-5). B Franklin.
--Handbook to the Pianoforte Works of Johannes Brahms. LC 71-19766. 327p. 1936. Repr. 19.50 (ISBN 0-8337-1088-5). B Franklin.
--Handbook to the Vocal Works of Brahms. LC 70-129468. 599p. 1912. Repr. 30.50 (ISBN 0-8337-1088-5). B Franklin.
--Historical, Descriptive & Analitical Account of the Entire Works of Brahms, 4 vols. 1984. Repr. of 1912 ed. lib. bdg. 90.00 set (ISBN 0-317-01744-6). Longwood Pub Group.
--Technics of the Organ. LC 78-13905. 1978. Repr. of 1938 ed. lib. bdg. 15.00 (ISBN 0-89341-437-9). Longwood Pub Group.
Evans, Edwin, tr. see Berlioz, Hector.
Evans, Edwin, tr. see Jean-Aubry, Georges.
Evans, Edwin, Sr. Handbook to the Chamber & Orchestral Music of Johannes Brahms. (First Series). 1976. lib. bdg. 32.00x (ISBN 0-403-03802-2). Scholarly.
--Handbook to the Chamber Music of Johannes Brahms. (Second Series). 1976. lib. bdg. 39.00x (ISBN 0-403-03596-1). Scholarly.
--Handbook to the Piano Forte Works of Johannes Brahms. 1976. 17.00x (ISBN 0-403-03800-6). Scholarly.
Evans, Eli. The Provincials. LC 73-80747. 1976. pap. 7.95 (ISBN 0-689-70532-8, 221). Atheneum.
Evans, Elizabeth. Eudora Welty. LC 81-2812. (Literature &00927003x.). 185p. 1981. 13.95 (ISBN 0-8044-2187-0). Ungar.
--Ring Lardner. LC 79-4829. (Literature and Life Ser.). 160p. 1980. 13.95 (ISBN 0-8044-2185-4). Ungar.
--Thomas Wolfe. LC 82-40275. 190p. 1984. 13.95 (ISBN 0-8044-2188-9). Ungar.
Evans, Elizabeth E. The Abuse of Maternity. LC 73-20623. (Sex, Marriage & Society Ser.). 134p. 1974. Repr. of 1875 ed. 17.00x (ISBN 0-405-05798-9). Ayer Co Pubs.
Evans, Elizabeth M. see Lefebvre, Georges.
Evans, Ellen. Convention Girls. 224p. 1983. pap. 2.50 (ISBN 0-8439-2021-1, Leisure Bks). Dorchester Pub Co.
Evans, Ellen L. The German Center Party, 1870-1933: A Study in Political Catholicism. LC 80-27668. 448p. 1981. 35.00x (ISBN 0-8093-0997-1). S Ill U Pr.
Evans, Ellis D. Contemporary Influences in Early Childhood Education. 2nd ed. LC 74-16007. 1975. text ed. 22.95 (ISBN 0-03-089584-7, HoltC). HR&W.
Evans, Ellis D. & McCandless, Boyd R. Children & Youth. 2nd ed. LC 77-26045. 1978. 21.95 (ISBN 0-03-019316-8, HoltC); study 7.95 (ISBN 0-03-042991-9); instr. manual 25.00 (ISBN 0-03-039326-4). HR&W.
Evans, Elwood. Puget Sound. facs. ed. (Shorey Historical Ser.). 16p. pap. 1.95 (ISBN 0-8466-0051-X, S51). Shorey.
--Washington Territory. facs. ed. 51p. pap. 4.95 (ISBN 0-8466-0129-X, S129). Shorey.
Evans, Emyr E. Irish Heritage: The Landscape, the People & Their Work. LC 83-45756. Repr. of 1942 ed. 36.50 (ISBN 0-404-20094-X). AMS Pr.
Evans, Eric J. The Forging of the Modern State. 480p. 1983. 33.00 (ISBN 0-582-48969-5); pap. text ed. 14.95 (ISBN 0-582-48970-9). Longman.
Evans, Eric W. & Creigh, S. W., eds. Industrial Conflict in Britain. 292p. 1977. 29.50x (ISBN 0-7146-3023-3, F Cass Co). Biblio Dist.
Evans, Ernest. Calling a Truce to Terror: The American Response to International Terrorism. LC 78-22722. (Contributions in Political Science Ser: No. 29). (Illus.). 1979. lib. bdg. 27.50 (ISBN 0-313-21140-X, EIT/). Greenwood.
Evans, Eugene D. Golgotha. 160p. 1982. 8.00 (ISBN 0-682-49856-4, Banner). Exposition Pr FL.
Evans, Evan, pseud. Border Bandit. 245p. 1976. Repr. of 1947 ed. lib. bdg. 13.95 (ISBN 0-89190-201-5, Pub. by River City Pr). Amereon Ltd.
--Gunman's Legacy. 257p. 1976. Repr. of 1949 ed. lib. bdg. 16.95 (ISBN 0-89190-202-3, Pub. by River City Pr). Amereon Ltd.
--Montana Rides. 300p. 1976. Repr. of 1933 ed. lib. bdg. 13.95 (ISBN 0-89190-203-1, Pub. by River City Pr). Amereon Ltd.
Evans, Evan. Montana Rides Again. 256p. 1982. pap. 2.25 (ISBN 0-441-53616-6, Pub. by Charter Bks). Ace Bks.
Evans, Evan, pseud. Montana Rides Again. 253p. 1976. Repr. of 1934 ed. lib. bdg. 15.95x (ISBN 0-89190-204-X, Pub. by River City Pr). Amereon Ltd.
--Outlaw Valley. 253p. 1976. Repr. of 1953 ed. lib. bdg. 15.95 (ISBN 0-89190-205-8, Pub. by River City Pr). Amereon Ltd.
--Outlaws Code. 210p. 1976. Repr. of 1954 ed. lib. bdg. 13.95x (ISBN 0-89190-206-6, Pub. by River City Pr). Amereon Ltd.
--Rescue of Broken Arrow. 249p. 1976. Repr. of 1948 ed. lib. bdg. 13.95x (ISBN 0-89190-207-4, Pub. by River City Pr). Amereon Ltd.
--Sawdust & Sixguns. 246p. 1976. Repr. of 1950 ed. lib. bdg. 15.95x (ISBN 0-89190-208-2, Pub. by River City Pr). Amereon Ltd.
Evans, Evan. Sixgun Legacy. 256p. 1983. pap. 2.25 (ISBN 0-441-76858-X). Ace Bks.
Evans, Evan, pseud. Smuggler's Trail. 241p. 1976. Repr. of 1950 ed. lib. bdg. 13.95 (ISBN 0-89190-209-0, Pub. by River City Pr). Amereon Ltd.
--The Song of the Whip. 261p. 1975. Repr. of 1936 ed. lib. bdg. 13.95 (ISBN 0-89190-210-4, Pub. by River City Pr). Amereon Ltd.
--Strange Courage. 213p. 1975. Repr. of 1952 ed. lib. bdg. 13.95 (ISBN 0-89190-211-2, Pub. by River City Pr). Amereon Ltd.
Evans, Evan. Strange Courage. 1982. pap. 2.25 (ISBN 0-441-78856-4). Ace Bks.
Evans, Evelyn J. A Tropical Library Service: The Story of Ghana's Libraries. 256p. 1964. 15.00 (ISBN 0-233-95719-7, 05788-6, Pub. by Gower Pub Co England). Lexington Bks.
Evans, F. C. A First Geography of the West Indies. (gr. 5 up). 1974. 8.95x (ISBN 0-521-20112-8). Cambridge U Pr.
--A First Geography of Trinidad & Tobago. 2nd ed. LC 67-21957. (Illus.). text ed. 6.95x (ISBN 0-521-20180-2). Cambridge U Pr.
Evans, F. C. & Young, N. The Bahamas. LC 76-16133. (Illus.). 1977. 6.95x (ISBN 0-521-21292-8). Cambridge U Pr.
Evans, F. Gaynor. Atlas of Human Anatomy. 204p. 1957. 7.50x (ISBN 0-87471-222-X). Rowman.
--Atlas of Human Anatomy Simplified. (Quality Paperback Ser.: No. 60). 204p. (Orig.). 1975. pap. 1.95 (ISBN 0-8226-0060-9). Littlefield.

--Biomechanical Studies of the Musculo-Skeletal System. 232p. 1961. 23.50x (ISBN 0-398-04102-4). C C Thomas.

Evans, F. J., jt. ed. see Kihlstrom, J. F.

Evans, F. J., jt. ed. see Van Dixhoorn, J. J.

Evans, Faith, ed. see Marx, Jenny, et al.

Evans, Fanny-Maude. Changing Memories into Memoirs: A Guide to Writing Your Life Story. LC 83-48787. 160p. 1984. 13.41 (ISBN 0-06-015293-1, HarpT); pap. 4.76 (ISBN 0-06-463599-6). Har-Row.

Evans, Frances G., ed. Studies on the Anatomy & Function of Bone & Joints. (Illus.). 1966. 36.00 (ISBN 0-387-03677-6). Springer-Verlag.

Evans, Frank B. Pennsylvania Politics, 1872-1877: A Study in Political Leadership. LC 67-66003. 360p. 1966. 7.95 (ISBN 0-911124-22-5). Pa Hist & Mus.

Evans, Frank B., compiled by. The History of Archives Administration: A Select Bibliography. (Documentation, Libraries & Archives: Bibliographies & Reference Works: No. 6). 255p. 1979. 17.50 (ISBN 92-3-101646-6, U982, UNESCO). Unipub.

--Modern Archives & Manuscripts: A Select Bibliography. LC 75-23058. 209p. 1975. pap. 11.00 (ISBN 0-931828-03-1). Soc Am Archivists.

Evans, Frank B. & Pinkett, Harold T., eds. Research in the Administration of Public Policy. LC 74-7381. (National Archives Conference Ser.: Vol. 7). 1975. 10.45x (ISBN 0-88258-040-X). Howard U Pr.

Evans, Frank B., et al. A Basic Glossary for Archivists, Manuscript Curators, & Records Managers. 19p. 1974. pap. 2.00 (ISBN 0-931828-02-3). Soc Am Archivists.

Evans, Frank L., ed. Maintenance Supervisor's Handbook. LC 62-21195. pap. 94.30 (ISBN 0-317-10662-7, 2051984). Bks Demand UMI.

Evans, Frank L., Jr. Equipment Design Handbook for Refineries & Chemical Plants, 2 Vols. 2nd ed. LC 79-50245. Vol. 1, 196p. 1979 37.95x (ISBN 0-87201-254-9); Vol. 2, 370p. 1980 41.95x (ISBN 0-87201-255-7). Gulf Pub.

Evans, Frederick J., jt. ed. see Kihlstrom, John F.

Evans, Frederick W. Autobiography of a Shaker, & Revelation of the Apocalypse. enl. ed. LC 72-2986. Repr. of 1888 ed. 10.00 (ISBN 0-404-10748-6). AMS Pr.

--Autobiography of a Shaker & Revelation of the Apocalypse. LC 79-187481. (The American Utopian Adventure Ser.). xvi, 271p. Repr. of 1888 ed. lib. bdg. 25.00x (ISBN 0-87991-002-X). Porcupine Pr.

--Shaker Communism: Or, Tests of Divine Inspiration. LC 72-2987. Repr. of 1871 ed. 14.50 (ISBN 0-404-10749-4). AMS Pr.

--Shaker Music: Inspirational Hymns & Melodies Illustrative of the Resurection, Life & Testimony of the Shakers. LC 72-2988. Repr. of 1875 ed. 27.50 (ISBN 0-404-10750-8). AMS Pr.

--Shakers: Compendium of the Origin, History, Principles, Rules & Regulations, Government & Doctrines of the United Society of Believers in Christ's Second Appearing. 4th ed. LC 72-2985. (Communal Societies in America). Repr. of 1867 ed. 14.00 (ISBN 0-404-10747-8). AMS Pr.

Evans, Freeman. Covered Wagons. 1984. pap. 3.50 (ISBN 0-345-30484-5). Ballantine.

Evans, G., ed. see Shakespeare, William.

Evans, G. B., ed. Shakespeare: Aspects of Influence. (Harvard English Studies: No. 7). 1976. 15.00x (ISBN 0-674-80330-2, EVSA); pap. 5.95x (ISBN 0-674-80331-0, EVSX). Harvard U Pr.

Evans, G. Blakemore, ed. Shakespearean Prompt-Books of the Seventeenth Century. Incl. Vol. 3, Pt. 1. The Comedy of Errors; Vol. 3, Pt. 2. A Midsummer Night's Dream; Vol. 4. Hamlet; Vol. 5, Pt. 1 & 2. Smock Alley Macbeth. LC 60-2680. pap. 25.00x boxed set vol. 3 pt. 1 & 2 (ISBN 0-8139-0216-9); Vol. 5. pap. 25.00x boxed set pt. 1 & 2 (ISBN 0-8139-0301-7). U Pr of Va.

--Shakespearean Prompt-Books of the Seventeenth Century: The Smock Alley Othello, Vol. VI, Part I & II. LC 60-2680. 1981. 25.00x (ISBN 0-8139-0831-0). U Pr of Va.

Evans, G. Blakemore, ed. see Shakespeare, William, et al.

Evans, G. Blakemore, et al, eds. see Shakespeare, William.

Evans, G. C. Functionals & Their Applications: Selected Topics Including Integral Equations. LC 19-12273. (Colloquium Publications: No. 5(1)). 136p. 1918. 24.30 (ISBN 0-317-32966-9, OP-13791); pap. 19.30 (ISBN 0-317-32967-7). Am Math.

--The Logarithmic Potential, Discontinuous Dirichlet & Neumann Problems. LC 28-28410. (Colloguium Publications: No. 6). 150p. 1927. 25.60 (ISBN 0-317-32976-6, OP-13792); pap. 20.60 (ISBN 0-317-32977-4). Am Math.

Evans, G. C., et al, eds. Light As an Ecological Factor II: The 16th Symposium of the British Ecological Society, March 26-28, 1974. LC 76-921. (British Ecological Society Symposia Ser.). 616p. 1976. 73.95x (ISBN 0-470-15043-2). Halsted Pr.

Evans, G. Clifford. The Quantitative Analysis of Plant Growth. LC 77-183156. (Studies in Ecology: Vol. 1). 1973. 40.00x (ISBN 0-520-02204-1). U of Cal Pr.

Evans, G. E. Management Techniques for Librarians. (Library & Information Science Ser.). 276p. 1976. 17.00 (ISBN 0-12-243850-7). Acad Pr.

Evans, G. Edward. Management Techniques for Librarians. 2nd ed. (Library & Informaion Science Ser.). 1983. 23.00 (ISBN 0-12-243856-6). Acad Pr.

Evans, G. Edward & Abbey, Karin. Bibliography of Language Arts Materials for Native North Americans, 1975-76. 153p. 1979. pap. 5.00 (ISBN 0-935626-14-X). U Cal AISC.

Evans, G. Edward & Clark, Jeffrey. North American Indian Language Materials. 154p. 1980. pap. 5.00 (ISBN 0-935626-15-8). U Cal AISC.

Evans, G. Edward, jt. auth. see Bloomberg, Marty.

Evans, G. Edward, et al. Bibliography of Language Arts Materials for Native North Americans, 1965-74. 283p. 1977. pap. 5.00 (ISBN 0-935626-13-1). U Cal AISC.

Evans, G. Nesta. Religion & Politics in Mid-Eighteenth Century Anglesey. 251p. 1953. text ed. 17.25x (ISBN 0-7083-0071-5, Pub. by Univ of Wales Pr England). Humanities.

Evans, G. Owen, et al. The Terrestrial Acari of the British Isles-an Introduction to Their Morphology, Biology & Classification, Vol. 1: Introduction & Biology. (Illus.). 219p. 1961. Repr. of 1968 ed. 14.00x (ISBN 0-565-00696-7, Pub. by Brit Mus Nat Hist England). Sabbot-Natural Hist Bks.

Evans, G. R. Alan of Lille: The Frontiers of Theology in the Twelfth Century. LC 83-1834. 240p. 1983. 52.50 (ISBN 0-521-24618-0). Cambridge U Pr.

--Augustine on Evil. LC 81-21793. 220p. 1983. 32.50 (ISBN 0-521-24526-5). Cambridge U Pr.

--The Language & Logic of the Bible: The Earlier Middle Ages. 224p. 1984. 34.50 (ISBN 0-521-26371-9). Cambridge U Pr.

--The Mind of St. Bernard of Clairvaux. 1983. text ed. 35.00x (ISBN 0-19-826667-7). Oxford U Pr.

Evans, G. R. & Singer, C. C. The Church & the Sword. 2nd ed. LC 82-50234. 1983. pap. text ed. 5.00 (ISBN 0-932050-20-4). New Puritan.

Evans, G. Rosemary. Anselm & a New Generation. 1980. 32.50x (ISBN 0-19-826651-0). Oxford U Pr.

--Anselm & Talking About God. 1978. 29.95x (ISBN 0-19-826647-2). Oxford U Pr.

--Old Arts & New Theology: The Beginnings of Theology As an Academic Discipline. 1980. text ed. 34.95x (ISBN 0-19-826653-7). Oxford U Pr.

Evans, G. Russell. Consent to Disaster: Congress, the Constitution & the Panama Canal Swindle. (Constitutional Bookshelf Ser.). 350p. 1984. 16.50 (ISBN 0-930095-00-6). Signal Bks.

Evans, Gail G., jt. auth. see Bayles, Mary Ann.

Evans, Gareth. Collected Papers. 280p. 1984. 24.95 (ISBN 0-19-824737-0). Oxford U Pr.

--The Varieties of Reference. McDowell, John, ed. (Illus.). 1982. 34.95x (ISBN 0-19-824685-4); pap. 10.95x (ISBN 0-19-824686-2). Oxford U Pr.

Evans, Gareth & Evans, Barbara L., eds. Plays in Review: 1956-1980. 256p. 1985. 17.95 (ISBN 0-416-01171-3, 9684). Methuen Inc.

Evans, Gareth L. The Language of Modern Drama. (Rowman & Littlefield University Library). 252p. 1977. 17.50x (ISBN 0-87471-990-9). Rowman.

--The Upstart Crow: An Introduction to Shakespeare's Plays. Evans, Barbara L., ed. 414p. 1982. text ed. 24.95x (ISBN 0-460-10256-7, BKA 04802, Pub. by J M Dent England); pap. text ed. 11.95x (ISBN 0-460-11256-2, 04803, Pub. by J M Dent England). Biblio Dist.

Evans, Garth & McDowell, John, eds. Truth & Meaning: Essays in Semantics. 1976. 54.00x (ISBN 0-19-824517-3). Oxford U Pr.

Evans, Gary. Environmental Stress. LC 82-1336. (Illus.). 400p. 1983. 42.50 (ISBN 0-521-24636-9); pap. 14.95 (ISBN 0-521-31859-9). Cambridge U Pr.

Evans, Gary R., jt. auth. see Sherman, Howard J.

Evans, Gary T. & Hayes, Richard E. Equipping God's People. (Church's Teaching Ser.: Introductory). 80p. 1979. pap. 1.25 (ISBN 0-86683-896-1, Pub. by Seabury). Winston Pr.

Evans, Gayna. Toyah. (Illus.). 32p. 1984. pap. 3.95 (ISBN 0-86276-102-6). Proteus Pub NY.

Evans, George, jt. auth. see MacLeish, Charles.

Evans, George, ed. The Letters of Charles Olson & Cid Corman, Vol. 1. LC 85-61154. 272p. (Orig.). 1985. 25.00 (ISBN 0-915032-13-9); pap. 12.95 (ISBN 0-915032-14-7). Natl Poet Foun.

Evans, George B., ed. see Buckingham, Nash.

Evans, George E. Ask the Fellows Who Cut the Hay. (Illus.). 262p. (Orig.). 1965. pap. 6.95 (ISBN 0-571-06353-5). Faber & Faber.

--The Strength of the Hills: An Autobiography. LC 83-20651. (Illus.). 172p. 1985. pap. 8.95 (ISBN 0-571-13550-1). Faber & Faber.

Evans, George G. History of the United States Mint & Coinage. LC 77-77253. (Illus.). 1977. Repr. of 1892 ed. lib. bdg. 15.00 (ISBN 0-915262-11-8). S J Durst.

Evans, George H., Jr. British Corporation Finance, 1775-1850. LC 78-64292. (Johns Hopkins University. Studies in the Social Sciences. Extra Volumes.: 23). 216p. 1983. Repr. of 1936 ed. 24.50 (ISBN 0-404-61392-6). AMS Pr.

Evans, George K., jt. auth. see Ehret, Walter.

Evans, Geraint. A Knight at the Opera. (Illus.). 256p. 1984. 19.95 (ISBN 0-7181-2322-0, Pub. by Michael Joseph). Merrimack Pub Cir.

Evans, Geraint N. Uncommon Obdurate: The Several Public Careers of J. F. W. Des Barres. LC 72-84547. (Illus.). 1969. 10.00 (ISBN 0-87577-000-2); pap. 12.50. Peabody Mus Salem.

Evans, Geraldine. First-Line Supervision in the Public Schools. LC 68-21547. 18p. 1968. pap. text ed. 1.25x (ISBN 0-8134-1025-8, 1025). Interstate.

Evans, Geraldine & Maas, John M. Job Satisfaction & Teacher Militancy: Some Teacher Attitudes. LC 70-79298. (Illus.). 68p. 1969. pap. text ed. 2.00x (ISBN 0-8134-1105-X, 1105). Interstate.

Evans, Gillian. Learning in Medieval Times. Reeves, Marjorie, ed. (Then & There Ser.). (Illus.). 112p. (Orig.). (gr. 7-12). 1974. pap. text ed. 3.95 (ISBN 0-582-20535-2). Longman.

Evans, Gillian, ed. St. Anselm, Archbishop of Canterbury: A Concordance to the Works of St. Anselm, 4 vols. LC 82-48973. (Orig.). 1985. Set. lib. bdg. 400.00 (ISBN 0-527-03661-7). Kraus Intl.

Evans, Gillian R., tr. see Alan Of Lille.

Evans, Glen, intro. by. Texas in Bloom: Photographs from Texas Highways Magazine. (The Louise Lindsey Merrick Texas Environment Ser.: No. 7). (Illus.). 148p. 1984. 24.95 (ISBN 0-89096-180-8). Tex A&M Univ Pr.

Evans, Glen, ed. see American Society of Journalists & Authors.

Evans, Gloria. The Wall. LC 77-75466. (Illus.). 1977. 4.95 (ISBN 0-8499-2804-4). Word Bks.

Evans, Grant. The Yellow Rainmakers: Are Chemical Weapons Being Used in Southeast Asia? 160p. 1983. 24.00 (ISBN 0-8052-7164-3, Pub. by NLB England); pap. 7.50 (ISBN 0-8052-7165-1). Schocken.

Evans, Grant & Rowley, Kelvin. Red Brotherhood at War. 296p. 1984. 27.50 (ISBN 0-8052-7213-5, Pub. by Verso England); pap. 9.95 (ISBN 0-8052-7214-3). Schocken.

Evans, Griffith C. Logarithmic Potential, 2 vols. in 1. 2nd ed. Incl. Fundamental Existence Theorems. Bliss, Gilbert A. Repr. of 1927 ed. 19.50 (ISBN 0-8284-0305-8). Chelsea Pub.

Evans, Gwynne B., jt. ed. see Williams, George W.

Evans, H. C. Pod Rot of Cacao Caused by Moniliophthora (Monilia) Roreri. 44p. 1981. 39.00x (ISBN 0-85198-484-3, Pub. by CAB Bks England). State Mutual Bk.

Evans, H. E. Mechanisms of Creep Fracture. 328p. 1984. 57.00 (ISBN 0-85334-193-1, Pub. by Elsevier Applied Sci England). Elsevier.

Evans, H. H., ed. see Society of American Foresters.

Evans, H. J. & Lloyd, D. Mutagen-Induced Chromosome Damage in Man. LC 78-60354. 1979. 42.00x (ISBN 0-300-02315-4). Yale U Pr.

Evans, H. J., jt. auth. see Buckton, K. E.

Evans, H. J., et al, eds. Human Radiation Cytogenetics. 1967. 17.00 (ISBN 0-444-10188-8, North-Holland). Elsevier.

--Edinburgh Conference, 1979: International Workshop on Human Gene Mapping, 5th, July 1979. (Human Gene Mapping: No. 5). (Illus.). vi, 236p. 1980. pap. 27.75 (ISBN 3-8055-0649-X). S Karger.

Evans, H. Meurig & Thomas, W. O. Welsh-English, English-Welsh Dictionary. (Welsh & Eng.). 35.00 (ISBN 0-87557-091-7, 091-7). Saphrograph.

Evans, H. Sherwood, ed. see Thurman, Thomas D.

Evans, Harold. Front Page History: Events of Our Century That Shook the World. (Illus.). 192p. 1984. 17.95 (ISBN 0-88162-051-3, Pub. by Salem Hse Ltd). Merrimack Pub Cir.

--Good Times, Bad Times. LC 83-48833. 1984. 17.95 (ISBN 0-689-11465-6). Atheneum.

Evans, Harold & World Press Photo Foundation, eds. Eyewitness: Twenty-Five Years Through World Press Photos. LC 81-9452. (Illus.). 192p. 1981. 19.95 (ISBN 0-688-00654-X). Morrow.

Evans, Harold, ed. see Searle, Ronald.

Evans, Harold, jt. auth. see Jackman, Brian.

Evans, Harry B. Publica Carmina: Ovid's Books from Exile. LC 82-10899. xii, 202p. 1983. 23.50x (ISBN 0-8032-1806-0). U of Nebr Pr.

Evans, Helen F. Abstracts of the Probate Records of Strafford County, N.H. 1771-1799. 2nd ed. xv, 237p. 1983. 35.00 (ISBN 0-917890-37-X). Heritage Bk.

Evans, Helen M. & Dumesil, Carla D. Invitation to Design. 2nd ed. 1982. text ed. write for info. (ISBN 0-02-334540-3). Macmillan.

Evans, Henri, tr. see Hountondji, Paulin J.

Evans, Henry. History of Conjuring & Magic. 59.95 (ISBN 0-8490-0322-9). Gordon Pr.

--The Napoleon Myth. 59.95 (ISBN 0-8490-0704-6). Gordon Pr.

Evans, Henry C., Jr. Chile & Its Relations with the United States. Repr. of 1927 ed. 22.00 (ISBN 0-384-14883-2). Johnson Repr.

Evans, Herbert A. English Masques. LC 72-10413. 1897. lib. bdg. 30.00 (ISBN 0-8414-0712-6). Folcroft.

--English Masques. 245p. 1983. Repr. of 1906 ed. lib. bdg. 27.50 (ISBN 0-8495-1360-X). Arden Lib.

Evans, Herbert A, ed. English Masques. facsimile ed. LC 71-169757. (Select Bibliographies Reprint Ser.). Repr. of 1897 ed. 20.00 (ISBN 0-8369-5977-9). Ayer Co Pubs.

Evans, Herndon J. The Newspaper Press in Kentucky. LC 76-24340. (Kentucky Bicentennial Bookshelf Ser.). (Illus.). 138p. 1976. 6.95 (ISBN 0-8131-0221-9). U Pr of Ky.

Evans, Hilary. The Art of Picture Research: A Guide to Current Practice, Procedure, Techniques & Resources. (Illus.). 23.50 (ISBN 0-7153-7763-9). David & Charles.

--Evidence for UFOs. (Illus.). 160p. (Orig.). 1984. pap. 5.95 (ISBN 0-85030-350-8, Pub. by Aquarian Pr England). Sterling.

--Harlots, Whores & Hookers: A History of Prostitution. LC 78-70399. (Illus.). 1979. 12.95 (ISBN 0-8008-2119-X). Taplinger.

--Picture Librarianship. (Outlines of Modern Librarianship Ser.). 136p. 1980. text ed. 12.00 (ISBN 0-85157-294-4, Pub. by Bingley England). Shoe String.

--Visions, Apparitions, Alien Visitors: A Comparative Study of the Entity Enigma. (Illus.). 320p. 1984. 14.95 (ISBN 0-85030-414-8, Pub. by Aquarian Pr England). Sterling.

Evans, Hilary & Evans, Mary. The Life & Art of George Cruikshank. LC 77-19166. (Illus.). 1978. 35.00 (ISBN 0-87599-227-7). S G Phillips.

--The Party That Lasted One Hundred Days: The Late Victorian Season; a Social Study. (Illus.). 1976. text ed. 16.00x (ISBN 0-356-08363-2). Humanities.

Evans, Hiram W. The Rising Storm: An Analysis of the Growing Conflict Over the Political Dilemma of Roman Catholics in America. Grob, Gerald, ed. LC 76-46075. (Anti-Movements in America). 1977. lib. bdg. 27.50x (ISBN 0-405-09948-7). Ayer Co Pubs.

Evans, Howard. Comparative Ethology & Evolution of the Sand Wasps. LC 66-18245. 1966. 32.50x (ISBN 0-674-15201-8). Harvard U Pr.

--Sir Randal Cremer: His Life & Work. LC 74-147455. (Garland Library of War & Peace: Peace Leaders: Biographies & Memoirs). xviii, 356p. 1973. Repr. of 1909 ed. lib. bdg. 42.00 (ISBN 0-8240-0250-4). Garland Pub.

--Sir Randal Cremer: His Life & Writings. 1976. lib. bdg. 59.95 (ISBN 0-8490-2609-1). Gordon Pr.

Evans, Howard, jt. auth. see Thody, Philip.

Evans, Howard E. The Bethylidae of America North of Mexico: Memoir Twenty-Seven. (Illus.). 332p. 1978. 28.00 (ISBN 0-686-40425-4). Am Entom Inst.

--Life on a Little-Known Planet. LC 84-86. (Illus.). 1984. pap. 9.95 (ISBN 0-226-22258-6). U of Chicago Pr.

--The Pleasures of Entomology: Portraits of Insects & the People Who Study Them. LC 84-600318. (Smithsonian Nature Bks.). (Illus.). 238p. 1985. pap. 14.95 (ISBN 0-87474-421-0, EVPEP). Smithsonian.

--Wasp Farm. LC 77-90903. (Illus.). 208p. (Orig.). 1985. pap. text ed. 9.95x (ISBN 0-8014-9315-3). Cornell U Pr.

Evans, Howard E. & Christensen, George C. Miller's Anatomy of the Dog. 2nd ed. (Illus.). 1181p. 1979. 47.50 (ISBN 0-7216-3438-9). Saunders.

Evans, Howard E. & De Lahunta, Alexander. Miller's Guide to the Dissection of the Dog. 2nd ed. (Illus.). 318p. 1980. 19.50 (ISBN 0-7216-3444-3). Saunders.

Evans, Howard E. & Eberhard, Mary J. The Wasps. LC 71-124448. (Ann Arbor Science Library Ser.). 272p. 1970. 7.95 (ISBN 0-472-00118-3). U of Mich Pr.

Evans, Howard E., jt. auth. see Evans, Mary A.

Evans, Howard E., et al. Insect Biology: A Textbook of Entomology. (Illus.). 1984. 32.95 (ISBN 0-201-11981-1). Addison-Wesley.

Evans, Howard Ensign & Evans, Mary A. Australia: A Natural History. LC 83-10471. (Illus.). 208p. 1983. 39.95 (ISBN 0-87474-418-0); pap. 19.95 (ISBN 0-87474-417-2). Smithsonian.

Evans, Hubert, tr. see Petrushevsky, I. P.

Evans, Hugh. The Gorse Glen. Humphreys, E. Morgan, tr. from Welsh. LC 77-87691. Repr. of 1948 ed. 19.50 (ISBN 0-404-16483-8). AMS Pr.

Evans, Humphrey Ap see Ap Evans, Humphrey.

Evans, Hywell. Governmental Regulation of Industrial Relations: A Comparative Study of United States & British Experience. 128p. 1961. pap. 2.50 (ISBN 0-87546-016-X). ILR Pr.

Evans, I. L., tr. see Parvan, Vasile.

Evans, I. O. Jules Verne, & His Work. 1976. Repr. of 1965 ed. lib. bdg. 13.95 (ISBN 0-88411-906-8, Pub. by Aeonian Pr). Amereon Ltd.

--Jules Verne & His Work. 188p. 1980. Repr. of 1965 ed. lib. bdg. 35.00 (ISBN 0-89760-224-2). Telegraph Bks.

Evans, Ian M. & Meyer, Luanna H. An Educative Approach to Behavior Problems: A Practical Decision Model for Interventions with Severely Handicapped Learners. LC 84-19980. (Illus.). 224p. (Orig.). 1985. pap. text ed. 18.95 (ISBN 0-933716-44-3, 443). P H Brookes.

Evans, Ianto. Lorena Stoves. 2nd ed. 1981. pap. 4.00 (ISBN 0-917704-14-2). Appropriate Techn Proj.

Evans, Ifor. Biology. (Science World Ser.). (Illus.). 40p. 1984. lib. bdg. 9.90 (ISBN 0-531-04743-1). Watts.

Evans, Ifor & Lawrence, H. Christopher Saxton, Mapmaker. (Illus.). 185p. 40.00 (ISBN 0-87556-675-8). Saifer.

Evans, Ifor L. British in Tropical Africa, an Historical Outline. LC 74-94476. (Illus.). Repr. of 1929 ed. cancelled (ISBN 0-8371-2351-8, EVT&, Pub. by Negro U Pr). Greenwood.

Evans, Ifor M. & Lawrence, Heather. Christopher Saxton: Elizabethan Map-Maker, Vol. 6. (Cartographica Ser.). xvi, 186p. 1979. 45.00x (ISBN 0-901869-06-6, Pub. by Holland Pr England). W G Arader.

Evans, Irene & Paradise, Paul. All about Canaries. rev ed. (Illus.). 96p. 1976. 4.95 (ISBN 0-87666-753-1, PS-315). TFH Pubns.

Evans, Ivor, pref. by see Brewer, E. Cobham.

Evans, Ivor H. Among Primitive Peoples in Borneo. LC 76-44714. Repr. of 1922 ed. 32.50 (ISBN 0-404-15920-6). AMS Pr.

--Papers on the Ethnology & Archaeology of the Malay Peninsula. LC 76-44715. Repr. of 1927 ed. 27.50 (ISBN 0-404-15921-4). AMS Pr.

--The Religion of the Tempusak Dusuns of North Borneo. LC 77-86972. Repr. of 1953 ed. 40.00 (ISBN 0-404-16707-1). AMS Pr.

--Studies in Religion, Folklore & Custom in British North Borneo & the Malay Peninsula. (Illus.). 299p. 1970. Repr. of 1923 ed. 37.50x (ISBN 0-7146-2007-6, F Cass Co). Biblio Dist.

Evans, Ivor H., ed. Brewer's Dictionary of Phrase & Fable. 1248p. 1982. 60.00x (ISBN 0-304-30706-8, Pub. by Cassell England). State Mutual Bk.

Evans, J. Adolescent & Pre-Adolescent Psychiatry. LC 81-71578. 448p. 1983. 47.00 (ISBN 0-8089-1473-1, 791168). Grune.

Evans, J. & Ilfeld, E. Good Beginnings: Parenting in the Early Years. 200p. 1982. pap. 12.95 (ISBN 0-931114-15-2, 28). High-Scope.

Evans, J. A. Herodotus. (World Authors Ser.). 1982. lib. bdg. 16.95 (ISBN 0-8057-6488-7, Twayne). G K Hall.

Evans, J. Claude, Jr., tr. see Waldenfels, Bernhard, et al.

Evans, J. D. Aristotle's Concept of Dialectic. LC 76-22982. 1977. 29.95 (ISBN 0-521-21425-4). Cambridge U Pr.

--The Prehistoric Antiquities of the Maltese Islands. (Illus.). 340p. 1971. 150.00 (ISBN 0-485-11093-8, Pub. by Athlone Pr Ltd). Longwood Pub Group.

Evans, J. G., jt. auth. see Exton-Smith, A. N.

Evans, J. G., jt. ed. see Limbrey, Susan.

Evans, J. G., ed. see Taliesin The Bard.

Evans, J. G., et al, eds. The Effect of Man on the Landscape: The Highland Zone. (CBA Research Report Ser.: No. 11). 129p. 1975. pap. text ed. 23.00x (ISBN 0-900312-27-0, Pub. by Coun Brit Archaeology). Humanities.

Evans, J. Grimley, jt. auth. see Caird, F. I.

Evans, J. Grimley & Caird, F. I., eds. Advanced Geriatric Medicine Four. (Advanced Geriatric Medicine Ser.). 224p. 1984. text ed. 39.50 (ISBN 0-272-79767-7, Pitman Med UK). Urban & S.

Evans, J. Grimley, jt. ed. see Caird, F. I.

Evans, J. H., III & Lewis, B. L. A Framework for Evaluating Internal Audit Risk. Holman, Richard, ed. (Reseach Report Ser.: No. 25). (Illus.). 48p. 1982. pap. text ed. 13.50 (ISBN 0-89413-094-3). Inst Inter Aud.

Evans, J. Harvey. Ship Structural Design Concepts: Second Cycle. LC 82-34536. (Illus.). 525p. 1983. text ed. 45.00 (ISBN 0-87033-303-8). Cornell Maritime.

Evans, J. Harvey, ed. Ship Structural Design Concepts. (Illus.). 837p. 1975. 45.00x (ISBN 0-87033-209-0). Cornell Maritime.

Evans, J. L. Knowledge & Infallibility. 1979. 22.50 (ISBN 0-312-45906-8). St Martin.

Evans, J. M., ed. see Milton, John.

Evans, J. Martin. America: The View from Europe. 1979. pap. 3.95 (ISBN 0-393-00955-6). Norton.

--Housing, Climate & Comfort. 186p. 1980. 53.95x (ISBN 0-470-26884-0). Halsted Pr.

Evans, J. P., jt. auth. see Welles, E. R.

Evans, J. P., jt. auth. see Welles, E. R., 3rd.

Evans, J. Robert. Blowing the Whistle on Intercollegiate Sports. LC 74-78842. 168p. 1974. 17.95x (ISBN 0-911012-94-X). Nelson-Hall.

--Personal Productivity Through Creative Living. 192p. 1981. pap. text ed. 7.95 (ISBN 0-8403-2561-4). Kendall-Hunt.

Evans, J. Warren. Horses: A Guide to Selection, Care, & Enjoyment. LC 80-29070. (Illus.). 683p. 1981. text ed. 29.95 (ISBN 0-7167-1253-9). W H Freeman.

Evans, J. Warren, et al. The Horse. LC 76-22686. (Animal Science Ser.). (Illus.). 766p. 1977. 34.95 (ISBN 0-7167-0491-9). W H Freeman.

Evans, Jack. Stegel Movement Activities. new ed. Alexander, Frank, ed. (Illus.). 1978. 4.95 (ISBN 0-915256-05-3). Front Row.

--Techniques of One Design Racing. LC 75-18555. (Illus.). 96p. 1975. pap. 5.95 (ISBN 0-87799-043-3). Aztex.

Evans, Jack M., jt. auth. see Cain, Sandra E.

Evans, Jack M., jt. auth. see Cain, Sandra G.

Evans, Jacob, jt. auth. see Lyon, Fern.

Evans, Jacque, jt. auth. see Leptich, Anne.

Evans, James. Guide to the Amerikansky Russky Viestnik, Vol. 1: 1894-1914. LC 79-55333. 522p. 1979. pap. 12.50x (ISBN 0-917242-05-X). Carpatho-Rusyn Res Ctr.

Evans, James C. Tom Jones Notes. (Orig.). 1972. pap. 2.95 (ISBN 0-8220-1293-6). Cliffs.

Evans, James E. & Wall, John E. A Guide to Prose Fiction in the Tatler & the Spectator. LC 76-24751. (Reference Library of the Humanities Ser.: Vol. 71). 1977. lib. bdg. 61.00 (ISBN 0-8240-9926-5). Garland Pub.

Evans, James R. America's Choice. LC 80-71089. 150p. (Orig.). 1981. lib. bdg. 11.95 (ISBN 0-933028-17-2). Fisher Inst.

Evans, James R., jt. auth. see Sobotowicz, William S.

Evans, James R., et al. Applied Production & Operations Management. (Illus.). 650p. 1984. text ed. 30.95 (ISBN 0-314-77992-2); instrs.' manual & test bank avail. (ISBN 0-314-77994-9); transparency masters avail. (ISBN 0-314-80574-5). West Pub.

Evans, James S. An Uncommon Gift. LC 82-25930. 180p. 1983. 10.95 (ISBN 0-664-27009-3, A Bridgebooks Publication). Westminster.

Evans, Jane. Twelve Doors to the Soul. LC 78-64907. (Illus., Orig.). 1979. pap. 5.75 (ISBN 0-8356-0521-3, Quest). Theos Pub Hse.

Evans, Janet. Natural Science Picture Sourcebook. (Illus.). 192p. 1984. pap. 14.95 (ISBN 0-442-22170-3). Van Nos Reinhold.

Evans, Janet M., ed. American Biographical Institute Research Association Annual Membership Roster: Vol. 2. (Illus., Orig.). 1983. write for info. (ISBN 0-934544-14-X). Am Biog Inst.

Evans, Jay. The Kayaking Book. LC 73-82750. (Illus.). 224p. 1983. pap. 9.95 (ISBN 0-8289-0501-0). Greene.

Evans, Jean. Make Ready the Way: An Advent-Christmas Journal Book. 64p. (Orig.). 1981. pap. text ed. 4.95 (ISBN 0-89390-030-3). Resource Pubns.

--Three Men: An Experiment in the Biography of Emotion. LC 77-13599. 1977. Repr. of 1954 ed. lib. bdg. 27.50x (ISBN 0-8371-9858-5, EVTM). Greenwood.

Evans, Jean, jt. auth. see Hornsby, June.

Evans, Jeff, jt. ed. see Miles, Irvine.

Evans, Jeremy. The Complete Guide to Windsurfing. 1983. 15.95 (ISBN 0-87196-137-7). Facts on File.

--The Complete Guide to Windsurfing. Clark, Philip, ed. (Illus.). 192p. 1984. pap. 9.95 (ISBN 0-87196-248-9). Facts on File.

Evans, Jewell. Love & Other Madness. LC 77-90575. 1977. 5.95 (ISBN 0-87208-130-3); pap. 2.95 (ISBN 0-87208-109-5). Island Pr.

Evans, Jimmy, jt. auth. see Bell, Peter.

Evans, Joan. The Endless Web: John Dickinson & Co. Ltd., Eighteen Hundred & Four to Nineteen Fifty-Four. LC 78-2673. (Illus.). xvi, 273p. 1978. Repr. of 1955 ed. lib. bdg. 26.75x (ISBN 0-313-20361-X, EVEW). Greenwood.

--English Art Thirteen Hundred Seven to Fourteen Sixty-One. LC 79-91817. (Illus.). 272p. 1980. Repr. of 1949 ed. lib. bdg. 40.00 (ISBN 0-87817-261-0). Hacker.

--John Ruskin. LC 70-117998. (English Biography Ser., No. 31). 1970. Repr. of 1952 ed. lib. bdg. 49.95x (ISBN 0-8383-1053-2). Haskell.

--Magical Jewels of the Middle Ages & the Renaissance. 15.50 (ISBN 0-8446-5572-4). Peter Smith.

--Magical Jewels of the Middle Ages & the Renaissance Particularly in England. LC 75-26288. (Illus.). 288p. 1976. pap. 5.95 (ISBN 0-486-23367-7). Dover.

--Monastic Architecture in France from the Renaissance to the Revolution. LC 79-91816. (Illus.). 822p. 1980. Repr. of 1964 ed. lib. bdg. 75.00 (ISBN 0-87817-260-2). Hacker.

--Monastic Architecture in France: From the Renaissance to the Revolution. LC 64-2430. (Illus.). pap. 160.00 (ISBN 0-317-10560-4, 2050739). Bks Demand UMI.

--Monastic Iconography in France from the Renaissance to the Revolution. LC 67-12317. (Illus.). 1969. 80.00 (ISBN 0-521-06960-2). Cambridge U Pr.

--Pattern. 1976. Vol. 1. pap. 9.95 (ISBN 0-306-80040-3); Vol. 2. pap. 9.95 (ISBN 0-306-80041-1). Da Capo.

--Pattern: A Study of Ornament in Western Europe from 1180 to 1900, 2 vols. LC 73-90614. (Illus.). 1975. Repr. of 1931 ed. lib. bdg. 75.00 (ISBN 0-87817-151-7). Hacker.

--Romanesque Architecture of the Order of Cluny. LC 75-136385. (Illus.). Repr. of 1938 ed. 46.00 (ISBN 0-404-02358-4). AMS Pr.

--Taste & Temperament: A Brief Study of Psychological Types in Their Relation to the Visual Arts. LC 78-13857. (Illus.). 1980. Repr. of 1939 ed. 19.50 (ISBN 0-88355-790-8). Hyperion Conn.

--Time & Chance: The Story of Arthur Evans & His Forbears. LC 70-114519. (Illus.). 410p. 1974. Repr. of 1943 ed. lib. bdg. 22.75x (ISBN 0-8371-4737-9, EVTC). Greenwood.

Evans, Joan, ed. The Lamp of Beauty: Writings on Art by John Ruskin. (Landmarks in Art History Ser.). 344p. 1980. pap. 14.95 (ISBN 0-8014-9197-5). Cornell U Pr.

Evans, Joan & Serjeantson, Mary, eds. English Mediaeval Palidaries. (EETS OS Ser.: Vol. 190). Repr. of 1932 ed. 20.00 (ISBN 0-317-15614-4). Kraus Repr.

Evans, Joan, tr. see Diaz De Gamez.

Evans, Job M. The Evans Guide for Counseling Dog Owners. LC 84-1092. (Illus.). 160p. 1985. 12.95 (ISBN 0-87605-660-5). Howell Bk.

Evans, Joe L. & Waldorf, Lawrence, eds. Individual Onsite Wastewater Systems, Vol. 8: Proceedings of the Eighth National Conference, 1981. LC 76-50983. (Illus.). 325p. 1982. 35.00 (ISBN 0-940006-01-4). Natl Sanit Foun.

Evans, Joe L., jt. ed. see McClelland, Nina I.

Evans, Joel, jt. auth. see Berman, Barry.

Evans, Joel R. & Berman, Barry. Marketing. 656p. 1982. text ed. write for info. (ISBN 0-02-334500-4). Macmillan.

--Marketing. 816p. 1985. text ed. write for info. (ISBN 0-02-334700-7). Macmillan.

Evans, Joel R., jt. auth. see Berman, Barry.

Evans, Joel R., ed. Consumerism in the United States: An Inter-Industry Analysis. LC 79-25341. 470p. 1980. 48.95x (ISBN 0-03-056846-3). Praeger.

Evans, John, pseud. Halo for Satan. LC 84-60847. (Quill Mysterious Classic Ser.). 256p. 1984. pap. 3.50 (ISBN 0-688-03920-0, Quill NY). Morrow.

--Halo in Blood. LC 84-60848. (Quill Mysterious Classic Ser.). 256p. 1984. pap. 3.50 (ISBN 0-688-03921-9, Quill NY). Morrow.

Evans, John. Photographic Lighting in Practice. (Illus.). 160p. 1984. 22.50 (ISBN 0-7153-8406-6). David & Charles.

Evans, John, jt. auth. see Wiswell, Glenn.

Evans, John, ed. see White, Eric W.

Evans, John, et al, eds. Human Gene Mapping Five. (March of Dimes Ser.: Vol. 15, No. 11). 1979. 30.00 (ISBN 3-8055-0649-X). March of Dimes.

Evans, John A. & Bosniak, Morton. The Kidney. (Atlas of Tumor Radiology Ser.). (Illus.). 1971. 58.50 (ISBN 0-8151-3164-X). Year Bk Med.

Evans, John C. The Environment of Early Man in the British Isles. LC 74-29803. 256p. 1975. 36.50x (ISBN 0-520-02973-9). U of Cal Pr.

--Shorthand. 1963. pap. 4.76i (ISBN 0-06-463225-3, EH 225, EH). B&N NY.

Evans, John C., jt. auth. see Berman, Louis.

Evans, John C., ed. Trends & Development in Papermaking. (Pulp & Paper Focus Bk.). (Illus.). 168p. (Orig.). 1985. pap. 39.50 (ISBN 0-87930-161-9). Miller Freeman.

Evans, John G. An Introduction to Environmental Archaeology. LC 77-90903. (Illus.). 144p. 1978. 27.50x (ISBN 0-8014-1172-6); pap. 9.95x (ISBN 0-8014-9170-3). Cornell U Pr.

Evans, John G., ed. The Black Book of Carmarthen. LC 78-72688. (Series of Old Welsh Texts: Vol. 5). Repr. of 1906 ed. 36.00 (ISBN 0-404-60585-0). AMS Pr.

--Facsimile & Text of the Book of Aneirin, 2 vols. LC 78-72771. (Series of Old Welsh Texts: Vol. 8). Repr. of 1922 ed. Set. 62.50 (ISBN 0-404-60588-5). AMS Pr.

--Facsimile of the Black Book of Carmarthen. LC 78-72661. (Series of Old Welsh Texts: Vol. 3). Repr. of 1908 ed. 27.50 (ISBN 0-404-60583-4). AMS Pr.

--Facsimile of the Chirk Codex of the Welsh Laws. LC 78-72669. (Series of Old Welsh Texts: Vol. 6). Repr. of 1909 ed. 42.50 (ISBN 0-404-60586-9). AMS Pr.

--Kymdeithas Amlyn Ac Amic. LC 78-72675. (Series of Old Welsh Texts: Vol. 10). Repr. of 1909 ed. 14.50 (ISBN 0-404-60593-1). AMS Pr.

--Poetry by Medieval Welsh Bards. LC 78-72677. (Series of Old Welsh Texts: Vol. 11B). Repr. of 1926 ed. 64.50 (ISBN 0-404-60595-8). AMS Pr.

--The Poetry in the Red Book of Hergest. LC 78-72676. (Series of Old Welsh Texts: Vol. 11A). Repr. of 1911 ed. 32.50 (ISBN 0-404-60594-X). AMS Pr.

--The White Book Mabinogion. LC 78-72670. (Series of Old Welsh Texts: Vol. 7). Repr. of 1907 ed. 52.50 (ISBN 0-404-60587-7). AMS Pr.

Evans, John G. & Rhys, J., eds. The Text of the Book of Llan Dav. LC 78-72667. (Series of Old Welsh Texts: Vol. 4). Repr. of 1893 ed. 62.50 (ISBN 0-404-60584-2). AMS Pr.

Evans, John G., jt. ed. see Rhys, John.

Evans, John H. The Poems of George Crabbe: A Literary & Historical Study. 20.25 (ISBN 0-8369-7108-6, 7942). Ayer Co Pubs.

Evans, John L. The Kievan Russian Principality, 860-1240. LC 80-70109. (Illus.). 139p. (Orig.). 1981. pap. 12.00x (ISBN 0-86733-012-0). Assoc Faculty Pr.

--Russia & the Khanates of Central Asia to 1865. LC 81-68026. 148p. (Orig.). 1982. pap. text ed. 11.50x (ISBN 0-86733-014-7). Assoc Faculty Pr.

Evans, John M. An Introduction to Clinical Scotometry. 1938. 75.00x (ISBN 0-685-89759-1). Elliots Bks.

Evans, John P. & Mannion, John B. A Breach of Fate. (Orig.). 1980. pap. 2.25 (ISBN 0-449-14325-2, GM). Fawcett.

Evans, John S. Management of Human Capacity. 1978. 99.00x (ISBN 0-905440-34-X, Pub. by MCB Pubns). State Mutual Bk.

Evans, John T. Seventeenth-Century Norwich: Politics, Religion, & Government 1620-1690. (Illus.). 1979. 49.00x (ISBN 0-19-822476-1). Oxford U Pr.

Evans, John W. Kennedy Round in American Trade Policy: The Twilight of the GATT? LC 77-139725. (Center for International Affairs Ser). 1971. 25.00x (ISBN 0-674-50275-2). Harvard U Pr.

Evans, John Whitney. The Newman Movement. 264p. 1980. 16.95 (ISBN 0-268-01453-1). U of Notre Dame Pr.

Evans, Jon. Cosmetic Tests on Living Animals: The Truth about the Beauty Business. free. Beauty Without Cruelty.

Evans, Jonathan. Kremlin Correction. 352p. (Orig.). 1984. pap. 3.95 (ISBN 0-8125-0282-5). Tor Bks.

--Misfire. 512p. 1982. pap. 3.50 (ISBN 0-523-48032-6). Pinnacle Bks.

--The Sagomi Gambit. 416p. (Orig.). 1983. pap. 3.95 (ISBN 0-523-48064-4, Pinnacle Bks). Tor Bks.

--The Solitary Man. 448p. (Orig.). 1983. pap. 3.95 (ISBN 0-8125-0279-5, Pinnacle Bks). Tor Bks.

--Takeover. 416p. 1982. pap. 3.50 (ISBN 0-523-48044-X). Pinnacle Bks.

Evans, Jonathan, ed. Thinking & Reasoning: Psychological Approaches. (International Library of Psychology). 300p. 1983. 21.95x (ISBN 0-7100-9460-4). Routledge & Kegan.

Evans, Jonathan S. The Psychology of Deductive Reasoning. (International Library of Psychology). 190p. 1982. 29.95x (ISBN 0-7100-0923-2). Routledge & Kegan.

Evans, Joseph C., Jr. The Metaphysics of Transcedental Subjectivity: Descates, Kant & W. Sellars. (Bochumer Studien Zur Philisophie Band 5). 138p. 1984. 26.00x (ISBN 90-6032-256-8, Pub. by B R Gruener Netherlands). Benjamins North Am.

Evans, Joseph R. & Wetz, Jon H. Atlas of Operative Dentistry. (Illus.). 188p. 1985. pap. text ed. 38.00x (ISBN 0-86715-168-4). Quint Pub CO.

Evans, Joseph W., tr. see Maritain, Jacques.

Evans, Joyce. Practical Problems in Mathematics for Cosmetology. LC 81-71649. (Illus.). 128p. 1983. pap. text ed. 7.40 (ISBN 0-8273-1380-2); instr's. guide 3.30 (ISBN 0-8273-1381-0). Delmar.

Evans, Judith & Ilfeld, Ellen. Good Beginnings: Parenting in the Early Years. LC 82-885. (Illus.). 177p. (Orig.). 1982. pap. 12.95 (ISBN 0-931114-15-2). High-Scope.

Evans, Judith L. Children in Africa: A Review of Psychological Research. LC 71-113095. 1970. pap. 6.50x (ISBN 0-8077-1297-3). Tchrs Coll.

Evans, Julian. Plantation Forestry in the Tropics. (Illus.). 1982. pap. 19.95x (ISBN 0-19-859489-5). Oxford U Pr.

Evans, Julian, ed. Foreign Exchange: New Travel Stories. 256p. 1985. 18.95 (ISBN 0-241-11488-8, Pub. by Hamish Hamilton England). David & Charles.

--London Tales. 240p. 1984. 16.95 (ISBN 0-241-11123-4, Pub by Hamish Hamilton). David & Charles.

Evans, June B. Ancestors Coloring Book. LC 84-71724. (Illus.). 32p. (Orig.). (gr. 1-12). 1984. pap. 6.00 (ISBN 0-9611114-2-9). Bryn Ffyliaid.

--Anthony Evans of Colonial Southside Virginia: Lines of Banks, Blackwell, Bugg, Burnett, Davis, Evans, Fox, Ingram, Mathews, Smith, Walker, & a Sourcebook for Related Materials. LC 83-70347. (Illus.). 182p. 1983. 22.50 (ISBN 0-9611114-0-2). Bryn FFyliaid.

--Men of Matadequin, Three Hundred Years from New Kent County, Virginia: Sourcebook for Related Lines, Banks, Blackwell, Burnett, Durvin, Gaulding, Goodman, Lipscomb, McGhee, Parsley, Slaughter, Weisiger, Wood, Zall. LC 84-70618. (Illus.). 198p. 1984. 23.25 (ISBN 0-9611114-1-0). Bryn Ffyliaid.

Evans, K. M. Planning Small-Scale Research. 88p. 1978. 5.00x (ISBN 0-85633-149-X, Pub. by NFER Nelson UK). Taylor & Francis.

--Planning Small Scale Research. 3rd ed. 80p. 1985. 8.00 (ISBN 0-7005-0677-2). Taylor & Francis.

Evans, K. T. & Knight, B. Forensic Radiology. (Illus.). 160p. 1981. text ed. 34.25 (ISBN 0-632-00587-4, B 1614-X). Mosby.

Evans, Karen, ed. Santa Fe-the City in Photographs. (Illus.). 80p. (Orig.). 1984. pap. 14.95 (ISBN 0-916795-01-2). Gannon.

Evans, Katherine. Boy Who Cried Wolf. LC 60-8429. (Illus.). (gr. k-2). 1960. PLB 9.50 (ISBN 0-8075-0863-2). A Whitman.

Evans, Kathleen A., jt. auth. see Krush, Anne J.

Evans, Ken. The Young Cyclist's Handbook. LC 83-15708. (Illus.). 160p. (gr. 7 up). 1984. 9.95 (ISBN 0-668-06047-6). Arco.

Evans, Ken, jt. auth. see Westell, Frank.

Evans, L. The Chess Beat. (Pergamon Chess Ser.). 96p. 1982. 19.95 (ISBN 0-08-026926-5, P115); pap. 11.95 (ISBN 0-08-026925-7). Pergamon.

--Convergent Strabismus. 1982. 72.00 (ISBN 90-619-3806-6, Pub. by Junk Pubs Netherlands). Kluwer Academic.

Evans, L. H. The United States & UNESCO. LC 75-37631. 224p. 1971. 12.00 (ISBN 0-379-00130-6). Oceana.

Evans, L. H., ed. Decade of Development: Problems & Issues. LC 66-30300. 183p. 1966. 11.00 (ISBN 0-379-00333-3). Oceana.

Evans, L. K. Pioneer History of Greene County, Pennsylvania. 1969. Repr. of 1941 ed. 10.00 (ISBN 0-87012-043-3). McClain.

Evans, L. T., ed. Crop Physiology. LC 73-91816. (Illus.). 384p. 1975. 57.50 (ISBN 0-521-20422-4); pap. 20.95x (ISBN 0-521-29390-1). Cambridge U Pr.

Evans, L. T. & Peacock, W. J., eds. Wheat Science-Today & Tomorrow. LC 80-41871. (Illus.). 300p. 1981. 47.50 (ISBN 0-521-23793-9). Cambridge U Pr.

Evans, Lansing B., jt. auth. see Freedman, M. David.

Evans, Larry. Chess Catechism. LC 78-101872. 1973. pap. 6.95 (ISBN 0-671-21531-0, Fireside). S&S.

--Chess in Ten Easy Lessons. pap. 5.00 (ISBN 0-87980-015-1). Wilshire.

--Gnomes Games. (Illus.). 64p. 1980. pap. 4.50 (ISBN 0-8431-4045-3). Troubador Pr.

--How to Draw Prehistoric Monsters. LC 78-26225. (Illus., Orig.). 1978. pap. 3.95 (ISBN 0-8431-1721-4, 97-3). Troubador Pr.

--How to Draw Robots & Spaceships. (Illus., Orig.). 1982. pap. 4.50 (ISBN 0-8431-4004-6). Troubador Pr.

--Illustration Guide for Architects, Designers & Students. 304p. 1982. pap. 19.95 (ISBN 0-442-22199-1). Van Nos Reinhold.

--Illustration Guide for Architects, Designers & Students, Vol. 2. (Illus.). 304p. 1986. pap. cancelled (ISBN 0-442-22198-3). Van Nos Reinhold.

--In Visibles. (Illus.). 1977. pap. 2.95 (ISBN 0-8431-1746-X, 84-1). Troubador Pr.

--Invisibles Two. (Illus.). 40p. (Orig.). 1981. pap. 2.95 (ISBN 0-8431-1711-7). Troubador Pr.

--New Ideas in Chess. 1978. pap. 2.95 (ISBN 0-346-12325-9). Cornerstone.

--Space Warp (Warrior Robot Patrol) (Illus.). 32p. (Orig.). 1978. pap. 3.50 (ISBN 0-8431-4098-4, 98-1). Troubador Pr.

--Three-D Maze Art. LC 80-16987. (Illus.). (gr. 1-12). 1979. pap. 4.95 (ISBN 0-8431-4012-7). Troubador Pr.

--Three-D Mazes, Vol. 1. (Illus.). 40p. 1976. pap. 2.95 (ISBN 0-8431-1744-3). Troubador Pr.

--Three-D Mazes, Vol. 2. (Illus.). 40p. 1977. pap. 2.95 (ISBN 0-8431-4079-8). Troubador Pr.

--Three-D Monster Mazes. (Illus.). 40p. 1976. pap. 2.95 (ISBN 0-8431-1745-1). Troubador Pr.

--Three-D Optical Illusions. 32p. 1977. pap. 4.95 (ISBN 0-8431-1739-7). Troubador Pr.

Evans, Larry, jt. auth. see Gorey, Edward.

Evans, Larry, et al, eds. Drug Use in Psychiatry. 174p. 1983. text ed. 28.00 (ISBN 0-683-10013-0). Williams & Wilkins.

--Depression: Diagnosis & Management. 150p. 1985. pap. 25.00 (ISBN 0-683-12101-4). Williams & Wilkins.

Evans, Lary, jt. auth. see Smith, Donald N.

Evans, Laura & Belknap, Buzz. Desolation River Guide: Green River Wilderness. LC 74-80877. (Illus.). 56p. 1974. waterproof 10.95 (ISBN 0-916370-06-2); pap. 6.95 (ISBN 0-916370-05-4). Westwater.

--Dinosaur River Guide: Flaming Gorge, Dinosaur National Monument. LC 73-79803. (Illus.). 64p. 1973. waterproof 10.95 (ISBN 0-916370-04-6); pap. 6.95 (ISBN 0-916370-03-8). Westwater.

Evans, Laurence. United States Policy & the Partition of Turkey: 1914-1924. LC 78-64242. (Johns Hopkins University. Studies in the Social Sciences. Eighty-Second Ser. 1964: 2). Repr. of 1965 ed. 32.00 (ISBN 0-404-61347-0). AMS Pr.

--United States Policy & the Partition of Turkey 1914-1924. (Studies in Historical & Political Science: Eighty-Second Series (1964)). 448p. 1965. 36.00x (ISBN 0-8018-0192-3). Johns Hopkins.

Evans, Laurence, ed. see Wilmington, Martin W.

Evans, Laurie A., jt. ed. see Close, Arthur C.

Evans, Laurie A., jt. ed. see Colgate, Craig.

Evans, Laurie A., jt. ed. see Colgate, Craig, Jr.

Evans, Lawrence, ed. see Pater, Walter.

Evans, Lawton B. A History of Georgia for Use in Schools. LC 70-187381. (Illus.). 426p. 1972. Repr. of 1908 ed. 25.00 (ISBN 0-87152-076-1). Reprint.

Evans, Lee S. Chemical & Process Plant: A Guide to the Selection of Engineering Materials. 2nd ed. LC 80-20355. 190p. 1980. 44.95x (ISBN 0-470-27064-0). Halsted Pr.

Evans, Leonard A., ed. see Kaplan, Barbara J.

Evans, Les & Myers, Allen. Watergate & the Myth of American Democracy. LC 73-93712. 224p. 1974. pap. 4.95 (ISBN 0-87348-362-6). Path Pr NY.

Evans, Les, ed. Disaster in Chile: Allende's Strategy & Why It Failed. LC 73-93631. (Illus.). 1974. pap. 6.95 (ISBN 0-87348-357-X). Path Pr NY.

--James P. Cannon As We Knew Him. LC 76-25382. (Illus.). 1976. 23.00 (ISBN 0-87348-474-6); pap. text ed. 6.95 (ISBN 0-87348-500-9). Path Pr NY.

Evans, Les, ed. see Cannon, James P.

Evans, Leslie, ed. China after Mao. LC 78-59264. (Illus.). 1978. lib. bdg. 20.00 (ISBN 0-913460-61-3); pap. 5.95 (ISBN 0-913460-64-8). Monad Pr.

Evans, Leslie, ed. see P'eng Shu-Tse.

Evans, Lester C. Paradise Island. (Illus.). 1967. pap. 4.95 (ISBN 0-910122-12-1). Amherst Pr.

Evans, Linda. Linda Evans Beauty & Exercise Book: Inner & Outer Beauty. Derek, Sean C., ed. (Illus.). 192p. 1983. pap. 9.95 (ISBN 0-671-46498-1, Wallaby); pap. 89.50 10-copy counter display (ISBN 0-671-93149-0). PB.

Evans, Lionel. Total Communication: Structure & Strategy. LC 81-85672. (Illus.). xiv, 162p. 1982. 12.95 (ISBN 0-913580-75-9). Gallaudet Coll.

--Total Communication: Structure & Strategy. 1983. 10.95 (ISBN 0-317-05939-4). Gallaudet Coll.

Evans, Louis H. Your Thrilling Future. 1982. pap. 4.95 (ISBN 0-8423-8573-8). Tyndale.

Evans, Louis H., Jr. Covenant to Care. 120p. 1982. pap. 3.95 (ISBN 0-88207-355-9). Victor Bks.

Evans, Lucille, jt. auth. see Strauser, Kitty.

Evans, Luther H. The Virgin Islands from Naval Base to New Deal. LC 74-3728. (Illus.). 365p. 1975. Repr. of 1945 ed. lib. bdg. 21.00x (ISBN 0-8371-7457-0, EVVI). Greenwood.

Evans, M. Blakemore, tr. see Bahlsen, Leopold.

Evans, M. Blakemore, et al. Shorter College German. 3rd ed. LC 56-5843. (Illus.). 1956. text ed. 12.95x (ISBN 0-89197-403-2); pap. text ed. 7.95x (ISBN 0-89197-404-0). Irvington.

Evans, M. E. The Life of Beetles. LC 74-18499. (Illus.). 1975. 22.95x (ISBN 0-02-844330-6). Hafner.

Evans, M. J., tr. see Loserth, Johann.

Evans, M. S., jt. auth. see Wood, J. M.

Evans, M. W., ed. Dynamical Processes in Condensed Matter. (Advances in Chemical Physics Ser.). 1985. 95.00 (ISBN 0-471-80778-8). Wiley.

Evans, M. W., et al, eds. Memory Function Approaches to Stochastic Problems in Condensed Matter. (Advances in Chemical Physics Ser.: Pt. 1). 640p. 1985. 85.00 (ISBN 0-471-80482-7). Wiley.

Evans, Malcolm, ed. see Hill, Don.

Evans, Mansel, ed. see Maarek, Gerard.

Evans, Marchsll C., jt. auth. see Chamblee, Ronald F.

Evans, Margaret. The Aquarium Opens at Ten. (Illus., Orig.). (gr. 8-12). Date not set. pap. text ed. price not set (ISBN 0-88839-996-0). Hancock House.

Evans, Margaret, ed. Discretion & Control. LC 78-19864. (Sage Research Progress Ser. in Criminology: Vol. 9). 160p. 1978. 20.00 (ISBN 0-8039-1128-9); pap. 9.95 (ISBN 0-8039-1129-7). Sage.

Evans, Margaret R. Sacred Cantatas: An Annotated Bibliography, 1960-1979. LC 81-20825. 206p. 1982. lib. bdg. 29.95x (ISBN 0-89950-044-7). McFarland & Co.

Evans, Margiad. Autobiography. 1984. 11.95. Riverrun NY.

--Country Dance. 1980. 11.50 (ISBN 0-7145-3593-1); pap. 4.95 (ISBN 0-7145-3728-4). Riverrun NY.

--Ray of Darkness. 1980. 11.50 (ISBN 0-7145-3727-6); pap. 4.95 (ISBN 0-7145-3607-5). Riverrun NY.

Evans, Mari. I Look at Me. 1974. pap. 1.95 (ISBN 0-685-41469-8). Third World.

--Nightstar Nineteen Seventy-Three to Nineteen Eighty. Keys, Romey T., ed. LC 79-54308. (Special Publications Ser.). (Illus.). 78p. (Orig.). 1981. pap. 5.25x (ISBN 0-934934-07-X). Ctr Afro-Am Stud.

Evans, Mari, ed. Black Women Writers, Nineteen Fifty to Nineteen Eighty: A Critical Evaluation. LC 81-43914. 576p. 1984. 22.95 (ISBN 0-385-17124-2, Anchor Pr); pap. 12.95 (ISBN 0-385-17125-0, Anchor Pr). Doubleday.

Evans, Marian, jt. auth. see Eliot, George.

Evans, Marian, tr. see Strauss, David F.

Evans, Marie & Iacobelli, Claire. Read English, Bk. 6. (Speak English Ser.). (Illus.). 80p. (Orig.). 1983. pap. text ed. 4.95 (ISBN 0-88499-680-8). Inst Mod Lang.

Evans, Marie, tr. see Roche, Daniel.

Evans, Marilyn & Hansen, Beverly. A Clinical Guide to Pediatric Nursing. 2nd ed. 384p. (Orig.). 1984. pap. 23.95 (ISBN 0-8385-1129-5). ACC.

Evans, Mariwyn. Opportunities in Real Estate. (VGM Career Bks.). (Illus.). 160p. 1983. 7.95 (ISBN 0-8442-6289-7, 6289-7, Passport Bks.); pap. 5.95 (ISBN 0-8442-6290-0, 6290-0). Natl Textbk.

Evans, Mark. Pepito: The Little Dancing Dog. LC 78-65354. (Illus.). (gr. k-4). 1979. 6.95 (ISBN 0-87592-063-2). Scroll Pr.

--Soundtrack: The Music of the Movies. (Paperback Ser.). 1979. pap. 6.95 (ISBN 0-306-80099-3). Da Capo.

Evans, Mark, jt. auth. see Stack, Robert.

Evans, Martha M., ed. Dyslexia: An Annotated Bibliography. LC 81-20319. (Contemporary Problems of Childhood Ser.: No. 5.). (Illus.). xxvi, 644p. 1982. lib. bdg. 49.95 (ISBN 0-313-21344-5, EVD/). Greenwood.

Evans, Martha N., tr. see Felman, Shoshana.

Evans, Martin. Caribou Canadian Switcher. 80p. 1977. pap. 7.95 (ISBN 0-85242-500-7). Aztex.

--Evening Star. 222p. 1978. pap. 11.95 (ISBN 0-85242-634-8). Aztex.

--Introducing Model Steam Locomotive Construction. 82p. 1981. 20.00x (ISBN 0-907266-05-3, Pub. by Dickson England). State Mutual Bk.

--Introducing Model Steam Locomotive Construction. (Illus.). 96p. (Orig.). 1983. pap. 9.95 (ISBN 0-317-14339-5, Pub by ARGUS). Aztex.

--L.B.S.C.'s Shop, Shed & Road. 192p. 1977. pap. 8.50 (ISBN 0-85242-708-5). Aztex.

--Model Locomotive Boilers. (Illus.). 144p. 1977. pap. 8.95 (ISBN 0-85242-483-3). Aztex.

--Model Locomotive Valve Gears. (Illus.). 102p. 1985. pap. 8.95 (ISBN 0-85242-162-1, Pub. by Argus). Aztex.

--The Model Steam Locomotive. (Illus.). 208p. (Orig.). 1983. pap. 19.95 (ISBN 0-85242-817-0, Pub. by Argus). Aztex.

Evans, Martin, jt. auth. see Greenly, H.

Evans, Martin J., jt. auth. see Piercy, Nigel.

Evans, Mary. Garden Books, Old & New. LC 71-162512. 1971. Repr. of 1926 ed. 35.00x (ISBN 0-8103-3743-6). Gale.

--How to Make Historic American Costumes. LC 78-159952. (Illus.). xii, 178p. 1976. Repr. of 1942 ed. 46.00x (ISBN 0-8103-4141-7). Gale.

--Lucien Goldmann. (Marxist Theory & Contemporary Capitalism Ser.: No. 34). 190p. 1981. text ed. 28.00x (ISBN 0-391-02373-X, Pub. by Harvester England). Humanities.

--Simone de Beauvoir: A Feminist Mandarin. 192p. 1985. pap. 8.95 (ISBN 0-422-79510-0, Pub. by Tavistock England). Methuen Inc.

--Woman in the Bible. 1982p. (Orig.). pap. text ed. 9.95 (ISBN 0-85364-337-7). Attic Pr.

Evans, Mary & Morgan, David. Work on Women: A Guide to Literature. viii, 84p. 1979. 10.95x (ISBN 0-422-77130-9, NO. 2852, Pub. by Tavistock England); pap. 6.95x (ISBN 0-422-77140-6, NO. 2853). Methuen Inc.

Evans, Mary, jt. auth. see Evans, Hilary.

Evans, Mary & Ungerson, Clare, eds. Sexual Divisions: Patterns & Processes. 224p. 1983. pap. 12.50 (ISBN 0-422-78440-0, NO. 3835, Pub. by Tavistock). Methuen Inc.

Evans, Mary A. & Evans, Howard E. William Morton Wheeler, Biologist. LC 76-129117. (Illus.). 1970. 25.00x (ISBN 0-674-95330-4). Harvard U Pr.

Evans, Mary A., jt. auth. see Evans, Howard Ensign.

Evans, Mary A., jt. auth. see Evans, Tom.

Evans, Mary Anne see Eliot, George.

Evans, Mary C. A Decade of Dreams. (Illus.). 160p. 1982. 12.95 (ISBN 0-87833-325-8); pap. 7.95 (ISBN 0-686-46034-0). Taylor Pub.

Evans, Mary J. Woman in the Bible. LC 84-4641. 160p. 1984. pap. 5.95 (ISBN 0-87784-978-1). Inter-Varsity.

Evans, Mary J. & Anderson, Deborah. Tales from Hans Christian Andersen. 1983. pap. 3.00 (ISBN 0-87602-257-3). Anchorage.

Evans, Mary J., jt. auth. see Davis, Jed H.

Evans, Mary S., tr. see Arbeau, T.

Evans, Mary S., tr. see Arbeau, Thoinot.

Evans, Mary S., tr. see Blasis, Carlo.

Evans, Maryanne see Eliot, George, pseud.

Evans, Maurice. G. K. Chesterton. LC 72-3187. (English Literature Ser., No. 33). 1972. Repr. of 1939 ed. lib. bdg. 39.95x (ISBN 0-8383-1504-6). Haskell.

--Spenser's Anatomy of Heroism: A Commentary on the Faerie Quenne. LC 74-96087. 1970. 47.50 (ISBN 0-521-07662-5). Cambridge U Pr.

Evans, Maurice, ed. see Bell, Quentin.

Evans, Maurice, ed. see Chapman, George, et al.

Evans, Maurice, ed. see Sidney, Philip.

Evans, Maurice S. Black & White in Southeast Africa: A Study in Sociology. LC 78-78765. (Illus.). Repr. of 1911 ed. cancelled (ISBN 0-8371-1390-3, EVB&, Pub. by Negro U Pr). Greenwood.

Evans, Max. The Great Wedding. LC 83-12014. 110p. 1983. pap. 5.95 (ISBN 0-8263-0701-9). U of NM Pr.

--The Hi Lo Country. (Zia Bks). 176p. 1983. pap. 4.95 (ISBN 0-8263-0697-7). U of NM Pr.

--The Mountain of Gold. (Zia Bks.). 96p. 1983. pap. 4.95 (ISBN 0-8263-0696-9). U of NM Pr.

--My Pardner. LC 75-187421. (Illus.). 104p. (gr. 5-9). 1972. 3.95 (ISBN 0-395-13725-X). HM.

--My Pardner. (Illus.). 100p. (gr. 7-12). 1984. pap. 5.95 (ISBN 0-8263-0699-3). U of NM Pr.

--The Rounders. 2nd ed. LC 83-10224. 180p. 1983. pap. 6.95 (ISBN 0-8263-0695-0). U of NM Pr.

--Shadow of Thunder. LC 69-20469. 78p. 1969. 6.50 (ISBN 0-8040-0274-6, 82-71934, Pub. by Swallow). Ohio U Pr.

--Xavier's Folly & Other Stories. LC 83-25907. 120p. 1984. pap. 5.95 (ISBN 0-8263-0700-0). U of NM Pr.

Evans, May G. Music & Edgar Allan Poe: A Bibliographical Study. LC 68-54418. (Illus.). 1968. Repr. of 1939 ed. lib. bdg. 15.00x (ISBN 0-8371-0410-6, EVMP). Greenwood.

Evans, Medford S. Revolt on the Campus. LC 78-23371. 1979. Repr. of 1961 ed. lib. bdg. 22.50x (ISBN 0-313-21160-4, EVRC). Greenwood.

Evans, Merv. New Directions for Black America. LC 83-72221. 1984. 14.95 (ISBN 0-914391-03-8); lib. bdg. 12.95 (ISBN 0-914391-01-1); pap. 9.95 (ISBN 0-914391-02-X). Comm People.

Evans, Mervin. Index to Political Contributors to the Los Angeles City Council. 62p. 1985. pap. text ed. 35.00 (ISBN 0-914391-06-2); DOS or CPM Computer. disk 35.00 (ISBN 0-914391-07-0). Comm People.

Evans, Michael & Jack, Ian. Sources of English Legal & Constitutional History. LC 84-185118. 413p. Date not set. price not set (ISBN 0-409-49382-1). Butterworth.

Evans, Michael K. Macroeconomic Activity: Theory, Forecasting, & Control. LC 69-11111. (Illus.). 1969. text ed. 37.00 scp (ISBN 0-06-041918-0, HarpC). Har-Row.

--The Truth about Supply-Side Economics. LC 82-72392. 230p. 1983. 17.95 (ISBN 0-465-08778-7). Basic.

Evans, Michael W. Productive Software Test Management. LC 84-3585. 218p. 1984. 32.95x (ISBN 0-471-88311-5, Pub. by Wiley-Interscience). Wiley.

Evans, Michael W., et al. Principles of Productive Software Management. 240p. 1983. 34.95x (ISBN 0-471-89796-5, Pub. by Wiley-Interscience). Wiley.

Evans, Michele. Fearless Cooking Against the Clock. 384p. 1983. pap. 3.95 (ISBN 0-671-47641-6). PB.

--Fearless Cooking for Company: Michele Evans' Most Requested Recipes. LC 83-40088. 323p. 1984. 17.95 (ISBN 0-8129-1100-8). Times Bks.

--Fearless Cooking for One. 320p. (Orig.). 1983. pap. 4.95 (ISBN 0-671-49294-2). PB.

Evans, Mike. The Art of the Beatles. LC 84-62001. (Illus.). 144p. 1985. price not set (ISBN 0-688-04777-7, Pub. by Beech Tree Bks). Morrow.

Evans, Monica A., jt. ed. see Batts, H. Lewis.

Evans, Morgan O. Theories & Criticisms of Sir Henry Maine. viii, 93p. 1981. Repr. of 1896 ed. lib. bdg. 18.50x (ISBN 0-8377-0540-1). Rothman.

Evans, Myfanwy, ed. Axis: A Quarterly Review of Contemporary Abstract Painting & Sculpture, No. 1-8. LC 68-9236. (Contemporary Art Ser.). (Illus.). 1968. Repr. of 1937 ed. 33.00 (ISBN 0-405-00715-9). Ayer Co Pubs.

--Painter's Object. LC 73-109022. (Contemporary Art Ser). (Illus.). 1971. Repr. of 1937 ed. 16.00 (ISBN 0-405-00742-6). Ayer Co Pubs.

Evans, Myron, jt. auth. see Coffey, William.

Evans, Myron W., et al. Molecular Dynamics & Theory of Broad Band Spectroscopy. LC 81-11592. 866p. 1982. 132.50 (ISBN 0-471-05977-3, Pub. by Wiley-Interscience). Wiley.

Evans, N. Dean, jt. auth. see Neagley, Ross L.

Evans, N. L. & Hope, C. W. Nuclear Power: Futures, Costs & Benefits. LC 84-1806. 200p. 1984. 29.95 (ISBN 0-521-26191-0). Cambridge U Pr.

Evans, Nancy, jt. auth. see Appelbaum, Judith.

Evans, Nancy, jt. auth. see Banks, Ann.

Evans, Nancy J., ed. Facilitating the Development of Women Students. LC 84-82378. (Student Services Ser.: No. 29). (Orig.). 1985. pap. text ed. 9.95x (ISBN 0-87589-767-3). Jossey-Bass.

Evans, Nesta. East Anglian Linen Industry: Rural Industry & the Local Economy 1500-1850. (Pasold Studies in Textile History: Vol. 5). 192p. 1985. 35.50 (ISBN 0-566-00847-5). Gower Pub Co.

Evans, Nigel. The Architect & the Computer, a Guide Through the Jungle. (Illus.). 40p. 1982. pap. 6.00 (ISBN 0-900630-77-9, Pub. by RIBA). Intl Spec Bk.

Evans, Norma P. Monroe County, (West) Virginia Marriages: A Composite List of Marriage Bonds, Parental Permits, & Returns from 1799-1850. LC 84-73368. (Orig.). 1985. pap. 15.00x (ISBN 0-937418-12-9). N P Evans.

--So You Want to Write Your Family History. LC 83-82903. (Illus.). 47p. (Orig.). 1983. pap. text ed. 6.50x (ISBN 0-937418-09-9). N P Evans.

--Wyoming County, (West) Virginia Death Records: 1853-1890. LC 84-72968. (Illus.). iv, 67p. (Orig.). 1984. pap. text ed. 15.00x (ISBN 0-937418-11-0). N P Evans.

Evans, Norma P., ed. Federal Census, Wyoming County, Virginia (Now West Virginia) 1860. LC 81-66325. 60p. (Orig.). 1981. pap. 15.00x (ISBN 0-937418-04-8). N P Evans.

--First Families of McDowell County, (West) Virginia. LC 81-70681. (Illus.). 62p. (Orig.). 1981. pap. 12.50x (ISBN 0-937418-05-6). N P Evans.

Evans, Norma P., compiled by. Grandpa with a Stick: Joseph Theolin Landry - His Ancestors & Descendants. LC 80-67365. (Illus.). 100p. (Orig.). 1980. pap. 17.50x (ISBN 0-937418-02-1). N P Evans.

Evans, Norma P., ed. Marriage Records, Wyoming County, West Virginia 1854-1880. LC 79-56632. (Illus.). 1980. pap. 12.50x (ISBN 0-937418-01-3). N P Evans.

Evans, Norma P., compiled by. A Register of the Marriages Celebrated in Greenbrier County (West) Virginia from 1781-1849. LC 82-82599. 84p. 1983. pap. 15.00x (ISBN 0-937418-07-2). N P Evans.

Evans, Norman. Beginning Teaching in Professional Partnership. LC 78-13675. 102p. 1978. pap. text ed. 6.50x (ISBN 0-8419-6215-4). Holmes & Meier.

--The Knowledge Revolution: Making the Link Between Learning & Work. 192p. 1981. 25.00x (Pub. by Marston Bk Serv). State Mutual Bk.

--Learning, Teaching, & Work. 176p. 1981. 50.00x (ISBN 0-86216-055-3, Pub. by McIntyre England). State Mutual Bk.

--Post-Education Society: Recognising Adults As Learners. LC 84-12750. 160p. 1984. 26.00 (ISBN 0-7099-0919-5, Pub. by Croom Helm Ltd); pap. 11.95 (ISBN 0-7099-0948-9). Longwood Pub Group.

--The Preliminary Evaluation of the In-Service B.Ed. Degree. 21.00x (ISBN 0-85633-221-6, Pub. by NFER Nelson UK). Taylor & Francis.

Evans, Olive. Secrets of the Forest. (gr. 3-12). 1985. pap. text ed. 5.00 (ISBN 0-88734-502-6). Players Pr.

Evans, Oliver. Anais Nin. LC 67-11703. (Crosscurrents-Modern Critiques Ser.). 239p. 1968. 7.95 (ISBN 0-8093-0285-3). S Ill U Pr.

--The Young Mill-Wright & Miller's Guide. LC 72-5047. (Technology & Society Ser.). (Illus.). 438p. 1972. Repr. of 1850 ed. 32.00 (ISBN 0-405-04699-5). Ayer Co Pubs.

Evans, Oliver H. George Henry Boker. (United States Authors Ser.: No. 476). 1984. lib. bdg. 18.50 (ISBN 0-8057-7417-3, Twayne). G K Hall.

Evans, P. H. Rhys see Rhys Evans, P. H., et al.

Evans, P. L., jt. auth. see Long, W. E.

Evans, P. R. & Goss-Custard, J. D., eds. Coastal Waders & Wildfowl in Winter. LC 83-17149. 300p. 1984. 54.50 (ISBN 0-521-25928-2). Cambridge U Pr.

Evans, Patricia R. see Blandford, Linda A.

Evans, Paul. Art Pottery of the U.S. LC 74-19578. (Illus.). 358p. 1974. pap. 14.95 (ISBN 0-684-14029-2). Everybodys Pr.

--The Early Trope Repertory of Saint Martial de Limoges. LC 66-11971. (Princeton Studies in Music Ser.: No. 2). pap. 75.50 (ISBN 0-317-09859-4, 2055287). Bks Demand UMI.

Evans, Paul, jt. auth. see Wilson, Jim.

Evans, Paul D. Holland Land Company. LC 68-35709. Repr. of 1924 ed. 37.50x (ISBN 0-678-01065-X). Kelley.

Evans, Paul F. City Life: A Perspective from Baltimore, 1968-1978. LC 79-54852. (Illus.). 1981. 20.00 (ISBN 0-935132-01-5); pap. 15.00 (ISBN 0-935132-00-7). C H Fairfax.

Evans, Peter. Cystitis. 1979. 10.95x (ISBN 0-8464-0053-7). Beekman Pubs.

--Dependent Development: The Alliance of Multinational, State, & Local Capital in Brazil. LC 78-70291. 1979. 38.00 (ISBN 0-691-07606-5); pap. 9.95 (ISBN 0-691-02185-6). Princeton U Pr.

--The Englishman's Daughter. LC 82-16532. 256p. 1983. 13.95 (ISBN 0-394-53036-5). Random.

--The Music of Benjamin Britten. 1979. 29.50x (ISBN 0-8166-0836-9). U of Minn Pr.

--Titles. 1978. 10.00 (ISBN 0-345-27719-8). Ballantine.

--Your World Two Thousand: Technology 2000. Date not set. price not set. Facts on File.

Evans, Peter, jt. auth. see Babbington, Bruce.

Evans, Peter, jt. auth. see Barnard, Christiaan.

Evans, Peter, ed. see Evans, Christopher.

Evans, Peter, et al, eds. Bringing the State Back In. (Illus.). 384p. Date not set. price not set (ISBN 0-521-30786-4); pap. price not set (ISBN 0-521-31313-9). Cambridge U Pr.

Evans, Phil. Motivation. (Essential Psychology Ser.). 1975. pap. 4.50x (ISBN 0-416-83160-5, NO. 2777). Methuen Inc.

Evans, Phil, jt. auth. see Clarke, Nita.

Evans, Phil, jt. auth. see Pollock, Eileen.

Evans, Phil, et al. America's Four-Hundredth Anniversary Handbook. Storie, Beth P. & Rogers, H. B., eds. LC 83-51607. (Illus.). 64p. (Orig.). (gr. 8). 1984. pap. 4.95 (ISBN 0-912367-05-9). Storie McOwen.

Evans, Philip R., jt. auth. see Sudhalter, Richard M.

Evans, R., jt. auth. see Kong, F.

Evans, R., ed. Physical Testing of Plastics - STP 736. 125p. 1981. 15.00 (ISBN 0-8031-0768-4, 04-736000-19). ASTM.

Evans, R. C. Forty Years in the Mormon Church: Why I Left It. 1976. Repr. of 1920 ed. 6.95 (ISBN 0-89315-054-1). Lambert Bk.

Evans, R. D., jt. auth. see Wagner, C. F.

Evans, R. E. The American War of Independence. LC 76-22413. (Cambridge Topic Bks). (Illus.). (gr. 5-10). 1977. PLB 7.95 (ISBN 0-8225-1201-7). Lerner Pubns.

--The War of American Independence. (Cambridge Introduction to the History of Mankind Ser.). (Illus.). 48p. (gr. 6-9). 1976. pap. 4.50 (ISBN 0-521-20903-X). Cambridge U Pr.

Evans, R. G. & Williamson, M. F. Extending Canadian Health Insurance: Options for Pharmacare & Denticare. (Ontario Economic Council Research Studies). 1978. pap. 14.00 (ISBN 0-8020-3353-9). U of Toronto Pr.

Evans, R. J. The Making of the Hapsburg Monarchy: Fifteen Fifty to Seventeen Hundred. 1979. 36.95x (ISBN 0-19-822560-1); pap. 16.95x (ISBN 0-19-873085-3). Oxford U Pr.

--Rudolf II & His World: A Study in Intellectual History 1576-1612. (Illus.). 1984. 18.95x (ISBN 0-19-821961-X). Oxford U Pr.

Evans, R. W. & Wilshire, B. Creep of Metals & Alloys. 314p. 1985. text ed. 56.00x (ISBN 0-904357-59-7, Metals Soc). Brookfield Pub Co.

Evans, Rand B., ed. see Watson, Robert.

Evans, Ray. Drawing & Painting Architecture: An Anatomy of Drawing & Painting Buildings. 160p. 1983. 18.95 (ISBN 0-442-22197-5); pap. 12.95 (ISBN 0-442-22196-7). Van Nos Reinhold.

Evans, Raymond E. Math Mastery: A Worktext. 299p. (gr. 6). 1984. pap. 7.50 (ISBN 0-937820-50-4); Answer Key. 2.25 (ISBN 0-937820-51-2). Westsea Pub.

Evans, Richard. McEnroe: A Rage for Perfection. (Illus.). 182p. 1985. pap. 4.95 (ISBN 0-450-05586-8, Pub. by Sidgwick & Jackson). Merrimack Pub Cir.

--The Making of Social Psychology: Discussions with Creative Contributors. 1980. pap. text ed. 13.95 (ISBN 0-89876-077-1). Gardner Pr.

--Music Administration: An Annotated Bibliography. 20p. (Orig.). 1981. pap. text ed. 10.00 (ISBN 0-911009-01-9). Prestige Pubns.

--Nasty: Ilie Nastase vs. Tennis. rev. ed. LC 80-51609. (Illus.). 272p. (Orig.). 1980. pap. 8.95 (ISBN 0-8128-6065-9). Stein & Day.

Evans, Richard, jt. auth. see Pray, Lawrence M.

Evans, Richard, ed. Tales from the Tennis Court: An Anthology of Tennis Writings. (Illus.). 224p. 1984. 14.95 (ISBN 0-283-99005-8, Pub. by Sidgwick & Jackson). Merrimack Pub Cir.

Evans, Richard I. Carl Rogers: The Man & His Ideas. 192p. 1975. pap. 3.95 (ISBN 0-525-47396-3). Dutton.

--Dialogue with B.F. Skinner. LC 81-15377. 156p. 1981. 27.95x (ISBN 0-03-059922-9). Praeger.

--Dialogue with C. G. Jung. LC 81-15371. 256p. 1981. 34.95x (ISBN 0-03-059927-X). Praeger.

--Dialogue with Carl Rogers. LC 81-15373. 286p. 1981. 35.95x (ISBN 0-03-059929-6). Praeger.

--Dialogue with Erich Fromm. LC 81-15376. 160p. 1981. 27.95x (ISBN 0-03-059924-5). Praeger.

--Dialogue with Erik Erikson: And Reactions from Ernest Jones. LC 81-15379. 188p. 1981. 31.95x (ISBN 0-03-059923-7). Praeger.

--Dialogue with Gordon Allport. LC 81-15378. 186p. 1981. 31.95x (ISBN 0-03-059926-1). Praeger.

--Dialogue with Jean Piaget. LC 81-15374. 254p. 1981. 35.95x (ISBN 0-03-059931-8). Praeger.

--Dialogue with R.D. Laing. LC 81-15372. 250p. 1981. 35.95x (ISBN 0-03-059928-8). Praeger.

--Psychology & Arthur Miller. 156p. 1981. 29.95 (ISBN 0-03-059932-6). HR&W.

Evans, Richard I., ed. The Making of Social Psychology: Discussions with Creative Contributors. LC 79-16034. 350p. 1980. pap. 12.95x (ISBN 0-470-26812-3). Halsted Pr.

Evans, Richard J. Collecting & Restoring Old Steam Engines. (Modern Automotive Ser.). 1980. 12.95 (ISBN 0-8306-9718-7); pap. 7.95 (ISBN 0-8306-2061-3, 2061). TAB Bks.

--Collecting & Restoring Old Steam Engines. 192p. 10.00 (ISBN 0-318-14846-3, S133). Midwest Old Settlers.

--The Feminist Movement in Germany, Eighteen Ninety-Four to Nineteen Thirty-Three. LC 75-31571. (Sage Studies in 20th Century History: Vol. 6). pap. 81.50 (ISBN 0-317-08765-7, 2021895). Bks Demand UMI.

--The Feminists: Women's Emancipation Movements in Europe, America & Australasia 1840-1920. LC 77-77490. 1977. pap. text ed. 14.95x (ISBN 0-06-492044-5). B&N Imports.

Evans, Richard J., ed. The German Working Class, Eighteen Eighty-Eight to Nineteen Thirty-Three: The Politics of Everyday Life. LC 81-12724. (Illus.). 260p. 1982. 28.50x (ISBN 0-389-20118-9). B&N Imports.

--Society & Politics in Wilhelmine Germany. LC 77-14746. 305p. 1978. text ed. 24.50x (ISBN 0-06-492036-4). B&N Imports.

Evans, Richard J. & Lee, W. R., eds. The German Family: Essays on the Social History of the Family in Nineteenth & Twentieth Century Germany. 1981. 28.50x (ISBN 0-389-20101-4). B&N Imports.

Evans, Richard J. & Lee, W. Robert, eds. The German Peasantry. 224p. 1985. 27.50 (ISBN 0-312-32597-5). St Martin.

Evans, Robert, tr. see Polisensky, J. V.

Evans, Robert A. & Evans, Alice F. Human Rights: A Dialogue Between the First & Third Worlds. LC 82-18780. 272p. (Orig.). 1983. pap. 9.95 (ISBN 0-88344-194-2). Orbis Bks.

Evans, Robert A., jt. auth. see Evans, Alice F.

Evans, Robert A. & Parker, Thomas D., eds. Christian Theology: A Case Method Approach. LC 76-9963. 1976. pap. 9.95xi (ISBN 0-06-062252-0, HarpR, RD 176, HarpR). Har-Row.

Evans, Robert A., et al. Casebook for Christian Living: Value Formation for Families & Congregations. pap. 6.25 (ISBN 0-8042-2032-8). John Knox.

Evans, Robert C. Introduction to Crystal Chemistry. 2nd ed. (Illus.). 1964. pap. text ed. 29.95 (ISBN 0-521-09367-8). Cambridge U Pr.

Evans, Robert C., jt. auth. see Garraway, Michael O.

Evans, Robert F. Four Letters of Pelagius: On the Grounds for Authenticity of 4 of the 20 Works Ascribed by De Plinval to Pelagius. LC 68-11594. 1968. text ed. 12.00x (ISBN 0-685-00379-5). A R Allenson.

--Soldiers of Rome: Praetorians & Legionnaires. (Illus.). 160p. 1985. 14.95 (ISBN 0-932020-36-4). Seven Locks Pr.

Evans, Robert G., jt. auth. see Humphrey, Clifford C.

Evans, Robert H. Coexistence: Communism & Its Practice in Bologna, 1945-1965. 1967. 21.95 (ISBN 0-268-00051-4). U of Notre Dame Pr.

--Life & Politics in a Venetian Community. LC 76-21256. (International Studies). 1977. text ed. 19.95x (ISBN 0-268-01256-3); pap. 6.95 (ISBN 0-268-01257-1). U of Notre Dame Pr.

Evans, Robert J. Paintings by G. P. A. Healy. (Handbook of Collections Ser.: No. 2). (Illus.). 26p. 1974. pap. 0.75 (ISBN 0-89792-056-2). Ill St Museum.

Evans, Robert L. The Fall & Rise of Man, If... LC 72-97467. 259p. 1973. 6.95 (ISBN 0-9606698-0-9); pap. 3.95 (ISBN 0-9606698-1-7). R L Evans.

Evans, Robert L. & Randall, LaVeta, eds. Cimarron Family Legends, Vol. 1. (Illus.). 1978. 35.00 (ISBN 0-934188-02-5). Evans Pubns.

--Cimarron Family Legends, Vol. 2. LC 80-67133. (Illus.). 1979. text ed. 35.00x (ISBN 0-934188-03-3). Evans Pubns.

Evans, Robert L., ed. see Colgan, Helen H., et al.

Evans, Robert O. Milton's Elisions. LC 66-63842. (University of Florida Humanities Monographs: No. 21). 1966. pap. 3.50 (ISBN 0-8130-0076-9). U Presses Fla.

--The Osier Cage: Rhetorical Devices in Romeo & Juliet. LC 66-16233. 120p. 1966. 10.00x (ISBN 0-8131-1123-4). U Pr of Ky.

Evans, Robert O., ed. Graham Greene: Some Critical Considerations. LC 63-22005. 304p. 1963. pap. 8.00x (ISBN 0-8131-0114-X). U Pr of Ky.

Evans, Robert O., jt. ed. see Biles, Jack I.

Evans, Robert O., ed. see Borges, Jorge L.

Evans, Robert O., tr. see Borges, Jorge L.

Evans, Robin. The Fabrication of Virtue: English Prison Architecture, 1750-1840. LC 81-18105. (Illus.). 380p. 1982. 77.50 (ISBN 0-521-23955-9). Cambridge U Pr.

Evans, Robley D. The Atomic Nucleus. LC 82-20946. 1982. Repr. of 1955 ed. 62.00 (ISBN 0-89874-414-8). Krieger.

Evans, Roger. How to Play Guitar. 1980. 10.95 (ISBN 0-312-39608-2); pap. 5.95 (ISBN 0-312-39609-0). St Martin.

--How to Play Piano. (Illus.). 112p. 1981. 11.95 (ISBN 0-312-39600-7); pap. 5.95 (ISBN 0-312-39601-5). St Martin.

--How to Read Music. 1979. 10.95 (ISBN 0-517-53897-0). Crown.

Evans, Roger, jt. auth. see Durston, Pat.

Evans, Rose. Friends of All Creatures. LC 84-90073. (Illus.). 128p. 12.95 (ISBN 0-917507-00-2); pap. 7.95 (ISBN 0-917507-01-0). Sea Fog Pr.

Evans, Rupert & Herr, Edward. Foundations of Vocational Education. 3rd ed. Taylor, Robert E., ed. (Merrill Series in Career Programs). 1978. text ed. 24.95 (ISBN 0-675-08442-3). Merrill.

Evans, Rupert, et al. Education for Employment: The Background & Potential of the 1968 Vocational Education Amendments. LC 70-627280. (Policy Papers in Human Resources & Industrial Relations Ser.: No. 14). 120p. (Orig.). 1969. pap. 2.50x (ISBN 0-87736-114-2). U of Mich Inst Labor.

Evans, Ruth & Battis, Emma. Childhood Rhythms. 1954. 4.50 (ISBN 0-910354-01-4). Chartwell.

Evans, S. The Slow Rapprochement: Britain & Turkey in the Age of Kemal Ataturk, 1919-38. 123p. 1982. pap. text ed. 9.25x (ISBN 0-906719-04-6, Pub. by Eothen Pr England). Humanities.

Evans, Sabastian, tr. High History of the Holy Graal. (Illus.). 395p. 1969. 16.95 (ISBN 0-227-67727-7). Attic Pr.

Evans, Sara. Personal Politics: The Roots of Women's Liberation in the Civil Rights Movement & the New Left. LC 79-22485. 1980. pap. 3.95 (ISBN 0-394-74228-1, Vin). Random.

Evans, Sebastian. Brother Fabian's Manuscripts. LC 82-49105. (Degeneration & Regeneration Ser.). 274p. 1984. lib. bdg. 35.00 (ISBN 0-8240-5568-3). Garland Pub.

Evans, Sebastian, jt. auth. see Evans, Arthur B.

Evans, Sebastian, tr. see Geoffrey of Monmouth.

Evans, Sharon & Denney, M. Ray. Reading Achievement Program for the Moderately & Severely Retarded. LC 74-81202. xviii, 30p. 1974. pap. text ed. 2.50 (ISBN 0-8134-1665-5, 1665). Interstate.

Evans, Shirlee. Tree Tall & the Whiteskins. 112p. (gr. 9 up). 1985. pap. 3.95 (ISBN 0-8361-3402-8). Herald Pr.

Evans, Stanley G., ed. Return to Reality: Some Essays on Contemporary Christianity. 1954. 39.50x (ISBN 0-317-07644-2). Elliots Bks.

Evans, Stephens. Subjectivity & Religious Belief. LC 82-40062. 238p. 1982. pap. text ed. 12.25 (ISBN 0-8191-2665-9). U Pr of Amer.

Evans, Susan & Brown, Kirsten. Fashionsmarts. LC 80-82156. 256p. (Orig.). 1980. pap. 2.50 (ISBN 0-87216-723-2). Jove Pubns.

Evans, Susan H., jt. auth. see Clarke, Peter.

Evans, Susan H. & Clarke, Peter, eds. The Computer Culture. LC 84-52255. (ITT Key Issues Lecture Ser.). 112p. (Orig.). 1984. pap. write for info. (ISBN 0-932431-01-1). White River.

Evans, T. F., ed. Shaw: The Critical Heritage. (Critical Heritage Ser.). 1976. 36.00x (ISBN 0-7100-8280-0). Routledge & Kegan.

--Shaw: The Critical Heritage. (The Critical Heritage Ser.). 1984. pap. 15.00 (ISBN 0-7102-0396-9). Routledge & Kegan.

Evans, T. J. Bituminous Coal in Texas. (Illus.). 65p. 1974. Repr. 3.50 (ISBN 0-686-29325-8, HB 4). Bur Econ Geology.

Evans, T. Lodwig. The People of Pembrokeshire: Being the Prize Essay of Haverfordwest Eisteddfod. 1909. 20.00 (ISBN 0-8482-0744-0). Norwood Edns.

Evans, Tabor. Longarm & the Cowboy's Revenge. (Longarm Ser.: No. 79). 192p. 1985. pap. 2.50 (ISBN 0-515-08232-5). Jove Pubns.

--Longarm & the Frontier Duchess. (Longarm Ser.: No. 81). 192p. 1985. pap. 2.50 (ISBN 0-515-08343-7). Jove Pubns.

--Longarm & the Lone Star Legend. (Giant Longarm Saga). 1985. pap. 2.95 (ISBN 0-515-07386-5). Jove Pubns.

--Longarm & the Lone Star Rescue. 288p. 1985. pap. 3.50 (ISBN 0-515-08250-3). Jove Pubns.

--Longarm & the Lone Star Vengeance. (Giant Longarm Saga). 320p. 1985. pap. 2.95 (ISBN 0-515-07085-8). Jove Pubns.

--Longarm & the Stagecoach Bandits. (Longarm Ser.: No. 84). 192p. 1985. pap. 2.50 (ISBN 0-515-08422-0). Jove Pubns.

--Longarm & the Tenderfoot. (Longarm Ser.: No. 83). 192p. 1985. pap. 2.50 (ISBN 0-515-08396-8). Jove Pubns.

--Longarm in the Bitteroots. (Longarm Ser.: No. 82). 192p. 1985. pap. 2.50 (ISBN 0-515-08367-4). Jove Pubns.

--Longarm on the Santa Cruz, No. 78. 192p. 1985. pap. 2.50 (ISBN 0-515-08254-6). Jove Pubns.

Evans, Taliesin. Hydraulic Mining in California in Eighteen Eighty-Three. Jones, William R., ed. (Illus.). 1981. pap. 1.00 (ISBN 0-89646-052-5). Outbooks.

Evans, Ted R. Applications of Lasers to Chemical Problems. LC 82-1904. (Techniques of Chemistry Ser.: Vol. 10). 291p. 1982. text ed. 63.50x (ISBN 0-471-04949-2, Pub. by Wiley-Interscience). Wiley.

Evans, Teresa B., jt. ed. see Dillow, Rex O.

Evans, Thomas G. & Taylor, Martin E. International Accounting & Reporting. 400p. 1985. text ed. write for info. (ISBN 0-02-334550-0). Macmillan.

Evans, Thomas G., jt. auth. see Granof, Michael H.

Evans, Thomas G. & Wright, Toblas A., eds. Baptisms from Sixteen Thirty-Nine to Eighteen Hundred in the Reformed Dutch Church, New York, 2 Vols. 1298p. 1968. Repr. of 1902 ed. 75.00 (ISBN 0-8398-0152-1). Parnassus Imprints.

Evans, Thomas G., et al. The Impact of Statement of Financial Accounting Standards No. 8 on the Foreign Exchange Risk Management Practices of American Multinationals: An Economic Impact Study. LC 78-74442. (The Financial Accounting Standards Board Research Report). 184p. (Orig.). 1978. pap. 6.00 (ISBN 0-910065-06-3). Finan Acct.

Evans, Thomas W. The Memoirs of Henrich Heine. 1973. Repr. of 1884 ed. 30.00 (ISBN 0-8274-0414-X). R West.

Evans, Tom & Evans, Mary A. Guitars: Music, History, Construction & Players from the Renaissance to Rock. (Illus.). 479p. 1978. 29.95 (ISBN 0-87196-321-3); pap. 14.95x (ISBN 0-87196-636-0). Facts on File.

Evans, Tony & Green, Cadida L. English Cottages. 160p. 1984. pap. 12.95 (ISBN 0-14-007339-6). Penguin.

Evans, Tony & Green, Candida L. English Cottages. (Illus.). 160p. 1983. 25.00 (ISBN 0-670-29670-8, Studio). Viking.

Evans, Tricia. Drama in English Teaching. LC 84-12753. 192p. 1984. 26.00 (ISBN 0-7099-0923-3, Pub. by Croom Helm Ltd). Longwood Pub Group.

--Teaching English. (Illus.). 212p. 1982. pap. 11.95 (ISBN 0-7099-0902-0, Pub. by Croom Helm Ltd). Longwood Pub Group.

Evans, U. R. An Introduction to Metallic Corrosion. 300p. 1981. 45.00x (ISBN 0-7131-2758-9, Pub. by E Arnold England). State Mutual Bk.

Evans, Ulick R. The Corrosion & Oxidation of Metals. 1094p. 1971. Repr. 110.00x (ISBN 0-8448-1067-3). Crane-Russak Co.

--The Corrosion & Oxidation of Metals: Supplementary Volume, No. One. 488p. 1968. 59.50x (ISBN 0-8448-1066-5). Crane-Russak Co.

--The Corrosion & Oxidation of Metals: Supplementary Volume, No. Two. 432p. 1976. 97.50x (ISBN 0-8448-1065-7). Crane-Russak Co.

Evans, Virden, et al. Physical Education Activities: For Lifetime Sports Participation. 2nd ed. 153p. (Orig.). 1981. pap. text ed. 8.95x (ISBN 0-89459-094-4). Hunter Textbks.

Evans, Virginia M. Bee in the Wind. 1965. 3.00 (ISBN 0-8233-0022-6). Golden Quill.

--Eyes of the Tiger. 1970. 4.00 (ISBN 0-8233-0139-7). Golden Quill.

Evans, W., jt. auth. see Lindsey, Ben B.

Evans, W. Bryce. Improving Your Speech: "Here's How". 1976. perfect bdg. 9.95 (ISBN 0-8403-1404-3). Kendall Hunt.

Evans, W. C., jt. auth. see Trease, G. E.

Evans, W. E. The Chemistry of Death. 120p. 1963. 15.75x (ISBN 0-398-00530-3). C C Thomas.

Evans, W. E., et al, eds. Applied Pharmacokinetics: Principles of Therapeutic Drug Monitoring. 2nd ed. 900p. 1986. price not set. (ISBN 0-915486-07-5). Applied Therapeutics.

Evans, W. Glyn. Beloved Adversary. Link, Julie A., ed. 96p. 1985. pap. 4.95 (ISBN 0-310-29371-5, Pub. by Daybreak). Zondervan.

--Daily with the King. LC 79-21970. 1979. pap. 5.95 (ISBN 0-8024-1739-6). Moody.

Evans, W. H. Preparation & Characterisation of Mammalian Plasma Membranes. (Techniques in Biochemistry & Molecular Biology Ser.: Vol. 7, Pt. 1). 1978. pap. 28.00 (ISBN 0-7204-4222-2, 7:1). Elsevier.

Evans, W. H., jt. auth. see Hook, J. N.

Evans, W. McKee. Ballots & Fence Rails: Reconstruction on the Lower Cape Fear. (Illus.). 328p. 1974. pap. 7.95 (ISBN 0-393-00711-1, Norton Lib). Norton.

--To Die Game: The Story of the Lowry Band, Indian Guerrillas of Reconstruction. LC 77-142335. xiv, 282p. 1971. 25.00x (ISBN 0-8071-0816-2); pap. 7.95 (ISBN 0-8071-0379-9). La State U Pr.

Evans, Wainwright, jt. auth. see Lindsey, Ben B.

Evans, Walker. Walker Evans at Work. LC 79-1661. 256p. 1982. 18.22i (ISBN 0-06-011104-6, HarpT). Har-Row.

--Walker Evans At Work. LC 79-1661. (Illus.). 240p. 1985. pap. 15.34i (ISBN 0-06-091248-0, CN 1248, CN). Har-Row.

--Walker Evans First & Last. LC 77-11824. (Illus.). 208p. 1985. pap. 15.34i (ISBN 0-06-091115-8, CN 1115, CN). Har-Row.

--Walker Evans: Photographs for the Farm Security Admininistration, 1935-1938. LC 74-149598. (Photography Ser.). 1974. Repr. of 1970 ed. lib. bdg. 32.50 (ISBN 0-306-70099-9). Da Capo.

--Walker Evans: Photographs for the Farm Security Administration, 1935-1938. LC 74-23992. (Illus.). 1975. pap. 12.95 (ISBN 0-306-80008-X). Da Capo.

Evans, Walker, jt. auth. see Agee, James.

Evans, Walker, photos by. Walker Evans: First & Last. LC 77-11824. (Illus.). 1978. 33.60i (ISBN 0-06-011261-1, HarpT). Har-Row.

Evans, Walter B., Jr. & Skardon, Mary A. Cedar Bog. (Annual Monograph Ser.). Orig. Title: Journal-Walter B. Evans. (Illus.). 54p. 1974. pap. 3.00 (ISBN 0-686-28231-0). Clark County Hist Soc.

Evans, Warren D., jt. auth. see Owens, Thomas R.

Evans, Wayne O. & Cole, Johnathan O. Your Medicine Chest: A Consumer's Guide to the Effects of Prescription & Non Prescription Drugs. LC 78-7497. 1978. pap. 5.95 (ISBN 0-316-25823-7). Little.

Evans, Wayne O. & Kline, Nathan S., eds. Psychotropic Drugs in the Year 2000: Use by Normal Humans. 192p. 1971. 19.50x (ISBN 0-398-02191-0). C C Thomas.

Evans, Webster. Rubs of the Green: Golf's Triumphs & Tragedies. (Illus.). 1970. 8.95 (ISBN 0-7207-0251-8). Transatlantic.

Evans, Wilbur & Little, Bill. Texas Longhorn Baseball: Kings of the Diamond. LC 82-50032. (College Sports Series: Baseball). 490p. 1983. 17.95 (ISBN 0-87397-234-1). Strode.

Evans, Wilbur & McElroy, H. B. The Twelfth Man: A Story of Texas A & M Football. LC 74-81347. (College Sports Ser.). 1982. 10.95 (ISBN 0-87397-217-1). Strode.

Evans, Wilbur, jt. auth. see Stowers, Carlton.

Evans, Willa M. Ben Jonson & Elizabethan Music. 2nd ed. LC 65-18503. (Music Ser). 1965. Repr. of 1929 ed. 19.50 (ISBN 0-306-70907-4). Da Capo.

--Henry Lawes, Musician & Friend of Poets. (MLA RFS). 1941. 22.00 (ISBN 0-527-27900-5). Kraus Repr.

Evans, William. Las Grandes Doctrinas de la Biblia. Orig. Title: Great Doctrines of the Bible. (Span.). pap. 3.95 (ISBN 0-8254-1222-6). Kregel.

--The Great Doctrines of the Bible. rev. ed. 350p. 1974. enlarged edition 10.95 (ISBN 0-8024-3301-4). Moody.

--How to Prepare Sermons. 1964. 9.95 (ISBN 0-8024-3725-7). Moody.

--Journey to Harley Street. 15.00 (ISBN 0-392-16316-0, SpS). Sportshelf.

Evans, William A. Management Ethics: An Intercultural Perspective. (Dimensions in International Business Ser.). 256p. 1981. lib. bdg. 15.00 (ISBN 0-89838-055-3). Kluwer-Nijhoff.

--The Mayaad. 363p. 1983. 17.95 (ISBN 0-87141-066-4). Manyland.

Evans, William A. & Sklar, Elizabeth S., eds. Detroit to Fort Sackville, 1778-1779: The Journal of Normand MacLeod. LC 77-13078. (Illus.). 181p. 1978. text ed. 16.00x (ISBN 0-8143-1589-5). Wayne St U Pr.

Evans, William E., et al, eds. Applied Pharmacokinetics: Principles of Therapeutic Drug Monitoring. LC 80-53408. (Illus.). 1980. 34.00x (ISBN 0-915486-03-2). Applied Therapeutics.

Evans, William H. & Jacobs, Paul H. Illinois Tests in the Teaching of English. write for info. S Ill U Pr.

Evans, William M. Ballots & Fence Rails: Reconstruction on the Lower Cape Fear. xiii, 314p. 1967. 25.00x (ISBN 0-8078-1029-0). U of NC Pr.

Evans, William R. Robert Frost & Sidney Cox: Forty Years of Friendship. LC 80-54464. 315p. 1981. 25.00x (ISBN 0-87451-195-X). U Pr of New Eng.

Evansen, Virginia, jt. auth. see Wolfers, Elsie E.

Evansen, Virginia B., jt. auth. see Wolfers, Elsie E.

Evanson, John M., jt. auth. see Woolley, David E.

Evanson, Roy. Illustrating Your Newsletter. (Illus.). 1982. pap. 3.95 (ISBN 0-916068-19-6). Groupwork Today.

--Illustrating Your Newsletters, No. II. (Illus.). 12p. (Orig.). 1984. clipart 3.95 (ISBN 0-916068-21-8, 30). Groupwork Today.

--Promoting Fund Raising. (Clipping Art Ser.). (Illus.). 1975. 3.95 (ISBN 0-916068-01-3). Groupwork Today.

Evans-Pritchard, E. E. Anthropology & History: A Lecture. 22p. 1971. pap. 2.95 (ISBN 0-7190-0254-0, Pub. by Manchester Univ Pr). Longwood Pub Group.

Evans-Pritchard, E. E., et al, eds. Essays Presented to C. G. Seligman. LC 70-106834. (Illus.). Repr. of 1934 ed. 23.75x (ISBN 0-8371-3456-0, ETS&, Pub. by Negro U Pr). Greenwood.

Evans-Pritchard, Edward. A History of Anthropological Thought. Singer, Andre, ed. LC 80-68955. 256p. 1981. 16.50x (ISBN 0-465-02998-1). Basic.

Evans-Pritchard, Edward E. The Azande: History & Political Institutions. 1971. 39.95x (ISBN 0-19-823170-9). Oxford U Pr.

--Kinship & Marriage among the Nuer. (Illus.). 1951. 32.50x (ISBN 0-19-823104-0). Oxford U Pr.

--Nuer: A Description of the Modes of Livelihood & Political Institutions of a Nilotic People. (Illus.). 1940. pap. 8.95x (ISBN 0-19-500322-5). Oxford U Pr.

--Nuer Religion. (Illus.). 1956. 8.95x (ISBN 0-19-874003-4). Oxford U Pr.

--The Political System of the Anuak of the Anglo-Egyptian Sudan. LC 74-15036. (London School of Economics & Political Science Monographs on Social Anthropology: No. 4). Repr. of 1940 ed. 19.50 (ISBN 0-404-12041-5). AMS Pr.

--Theories of Primitive Religion. 1965. pap. 8.95x (ISBN 0-19-823131-8). Oxford U Pr.

Evans-Pritchard, Edward E., ed. Zande Trickster. (Oxford Library of African Literature). 1967. 17.95x (ISBN 0-19-815123-3). Oxford U Pr.

Evanston Conference, Oct. 11-15, 1975. Brauer Groups: Proceedings. Zelinsky, D., ed. (Lecture Notes in Mathematics: Vol. 549). 1976. soft cover 13.00 (ISBN 0-387-07989-0). Springer-Verlag.

Evans-Wentz, W. Y. Cuchama & Sacred Mountains. Waters, Frank & Adams, Charles L., eds. LC 81-8749. (Illus.). xxxii, 196p. 1982. 22.95 (ISBN 0-8040-0411-0, 82-75554, Pub. by Swallow). Ohio U Pr.

Evans-Wentz, W. Y., ed. Tibetan Book of the Dead. 3rd ed. 1957. 24.95x (ISBN 0-19-501435-9). Oxford U Pr.

--Tibetan Book of the Dead. (Illus.). 1960. pap. 6.95 (ISBN 0-19-500223-7, GB). Oxford U Pr.

--Tibetan Book of the Great Liberation. 1954. 22.95x (ISBN 0-19-501437-5). Oxford U Pr.

--Tibetan Book of the Great Liberation. (Illus.). 1968. pap. 9.95 (ISBN 0-19-500293-8, GB). Oxford U Pr.

--Tibetan Yoga & Secret Doctrines. 2nd ed. 1958. 24.95x (ISBN 0-19-501438-3). Oxford U Pr.

--Tibetan Yoga & Secret Doctrines. (Illus.). 1967. pap. 10.95 (ISBN 0-19-500278-4, GB). Oxford U Pr.

--Tibet's Great Yogi, Milarepa. 2nd ed. (Illus.). 1969. pap. 8.95 (ISBN 0-19-500301-2, 294, GB). Oxford U Pr.

Evan-Wanowski, R. Resonance Oscillations in Mechanical Systems. 1976. 68.00 (ISBN 0-444-41474-6). Elsevier.

Evaristi, Marcella. Commedia. 39p. 1983. pap. 5.95 (ISBN 0-907540-34-1, NO.3986). Methuen Inc.

Evarts, et al. Winning Through Accomodation: The Mediator's Handbook. 192p. 1983. pap. text ed. 14.95 (ISBN 0-8403-3116-9). Kendall-Hunt.

Evarts, C. M. see Hip Society.

Evarts, C. McCollister, ed. Surgery of the Musculoskeletal System, 4 Vols. (Illus.). 1983. text ed. 250.00 (ISBN 0-443-08078-X). Churchill.

Evarts, Edward V., et al. Neurophysiological Approaches to Higher Brain Functions. LC 83-25922. (Neuroscience Institute Monograph Ser.: 1-693). 198p. 1984. 39.95 (ISBN 0-471-80557-2, Pub. by Wiley-Interscience). Wiley.

Evarts, Hal. Jay-Jay & the Peking Monster. 1984. 15.25 (ISBN 0-8446-6166-X). Peter Smith.

Evarts, Hal G. Bigfoot. 190p. (gr. k-3). pap. 2.95 (ISBN 0-689-70487-9, A-114, Aladdin). Atheneum.

--Bigfoot. LC 73-1329. 192p. (gr. 7-12). 1973. o. p. 7.95 (ISBN 0-684-13388-1, ScribJ); pap. 2.95 (ISBN 0-689-70487-9). Scribner.

--The Purple Eagle Mystery. LC 75-27704. (Encore Edition Ser.). 218p. (gr. 7-10). 1976. 1.79 (ISBN 0-684-14531-6, ScribJ). Scribner.

Evarts, Prescott, Jr. How to Prepare for the American College Test: ACT. (Orig.). 1979. pap. 5.95 (ISBN 0-07-019767-9). McGraw.

Evarts, Susan. The Art & Craft of Greeting Cards. LC 74-16740. 1982. pap. 13.95 (ISBN 0-89134-048-3). North Light Pub.

Evatt, B. L., et al, eds. Megakaryocyte Biology & Precursors: In Vitro Cloning & Cellular Properties. 350p. 1981. 93.00 (ISBN 0-444-00585-4, Biomedical Pr). Elsevier.

Evatt, Cris & Feld, Bruce. The Givers & the Takers. (Illus.). 256p. 1983. 12.95 (ISBN 0-02-536690-4). Macmillan.

Evatt, Crislynne. How to Organize Your Closet... & Your Life! 1981. pap. 2.95 (ISBN 0-345-29800-4). Ballantine.

Evatt, Herbert V. King & His Dominion Governors. 2nd ed. 324p. 1967. Repr. of 1936 ed. 30.00x (ISBN 0-7146-1471-8, BHA-01471, F Cass Co). Biblio Dist.

--Rum Rebellion: A Study of the Overthrow of Governor Bligh by John Macarthur & the New South Wales Corps, Including the John Murtagh Macrossan Memorial Lectures Delivered at the University of Queensland, June, 1937. 17.00 (ISBN 0-8369-7109-4, 7943). Ayer Co Pubs.

--The Task of Nations. LC 79-152595. 279p. 1972. Repr. of 1949 ed. lib. bdg. 15.00x (ISBN 0-8371-6028-6, EVTN). Greenwood.

Evdokimov, F. E. Fundamentals of Electricity. Roberts, George, tr. from Russian. 518p. 1971. 17.00x (ISBN 0-8464-0436-2). Beekman Pubs.

--Fundamentals of Electricity. 518p. 1977. 7.95 (ISBN 0-8285-0780-5, Pub. by Mir Pubs USSR). Imported Pubns.

Eve, M. & Musson, D., eds. Socialist Register: Nineteen Eighty-Two. (Socialist Register Ser.: 1982). 314p. 1982. text ed. 16.75x (ISBN 0-85036-292-X, Pub. by Merlin England). Humanities.

Eve, Martin & Musson, David. Socialist Register: Nineteen Eighty-Two. 1982. 6.50 (ISBN 0-85345-624-0). Monthly Rev.

Evelan, R. R. How to Read the Bible: A Step by Step Manual. 1984. 4.75 (ISBN 0-89536-700-9, 4883). CSS of Ohio.

--How to Read the Bible: Leader's Guide. 1984. 1.95 (ISBN 0-89536-716-5, 4891). CSS of Ohio.

Eveland, H. E. & Tennissen, A. C. Physical Geology Laboratory Manual. 4th ed. 96p. 1979. pap. text ed. 8.95 (ISBN 0-8403-2565-7, 40256502). Kendall-Hunt.

Eveland, Wilbur C. Ropes of Sand: America's Failure in the Middle East. 1980. 14.95 (ISBN 0-393-01336-7). Norton.

Eve le Gallienne, tr. see Ibsen, Henrik.

Evelegh, Robin. Peace Keeping in a Democratic Society: The Lessons of Northern Ireland. 1978. 21.50x (ISBN 0-7735-0502-4). McGill-Queens U Pr.

Eveleigh, David. Firegrates & Kitchen Ranges. (Shire Album Ser.: No. 99). (Illus.). 32p. 1985. pap. 3.50 (ISBN 0-85263-629-6, Pub. by Shire Pubns England). Seven Hills Bks.

Eveleigh, David J. Candle Lighting. 06/1985 ed. (Shire Album Ser.: No. 132). (Illus.). 32p. (Orig.). pap. 3.50 (ISBN 0-85263-726-8, Pub. by Shire Pubns England). Seven Hills Bks.

Eveleigh, Virgil. Introduction to Control Systems Design. (Electrical & Electronic Engineering Ser.). 1971. text ed. 48.00 (ISBN 0-07-019773-3). McGraw.

Eveleth, P. B. & Tanner, J. M. World-Wide Variation in Human Growth. LC 75-10042. (International Biological Programme Ser.: No. 8). (Illus.). 544p. 1977. 99.00 (ISBN 0-521-20806-8). Cambridge U Pr.

Eveleth, Phyllis, tr. see Ianni, Octavio.

Eveling, Stanley. The Buglar Boy & His Swish Friend. 30p. 1983. pap. 5.95 (ISBN 0-907540-41-4, NO. 4048, Pub. by Salamander Press). Methuen Inc.

Evely, Louis. Faith of a Modern Man. 1.95 (ISBN 0-317-06468-1). Dimension Bks.

--That Man Is You. Bonin, Edmond, tr. LC 63-23494. 297p. 1964. pap. 3.95 (ISBN 0-8091-1697-9). Paulist Pr.

--We Dare to Say Our Father. 120p. 1975. pap. 1.45 (ISBN 0-385-06274-5, Im). Doubleday.

Evelyn, John. Acetaria: A Discourse of Sallets. facs. ed. 244p. 1983. 27.50x (ISBN 0-907325-12-2, Pub. by Prospect England). U Pr of Va.

--Devotionaries Book. LC 73-3159. 1936. lib. bdg. 17.50 (ISBN 0-8414-1903-5). Folcroft.

--Diary of John Evelyn, 2 vols. in 1. Bray, William, ed. 1973. Repr. of 1952 ed. 9.95x (ISBN 0-460-00220-1, Evman). Biblio Dist.

--The Diary of John Evelyn, 2 vols. Bray, William, ed. 1907. 40.00 set (ISBN 0-8274-2175-3). R West.

--The Diary of John Evelyn. Bowle, John, ed. 1983. 37.50x (ISBN 0-19-251011-8). Oxford U Pr.

--Life of Mrs. Godolphin: Now First Published & Edited by Samuel Lord Bishop of Oxford, Chancellor of the Most Noble Order of the Garter. LC 72-5552. (Select Bibliographies Reprint Ser.). 1972. Repr. of 1847 ed. 21.00 (ISBN 0-8369-6905-7). Ayer Co Pubs.

Evelyn, John & Currie, Kit. Acetaria: A Discourse of Sallets. rev. ed. LC 85-12630. (Illus.). 148p. 1985. Repr. of 1699 ed. deluxe ed. 180.00 ltd. ed. (ISBN 0-933841-01-9). Still Point TX.

Evelyn-Marie. Daniel Scott & the Monster. (Illus.). 32p. (gr. k-3). 1985. 7.95 (ISBN 0-9614746-1-0); PLB 9.95 (ISBN 0-9614746-2-9); bk. & cassette 11.95 (ISBN 0-9614746-0-2). Berry Bks.

Evelyn Marie. Pick Your Own Strawberries. (Illus.). 32p. (gr. k-3). 1983. 4.95 (ISBN 0-8062-1892-4). Carlton.

Even, S. & Kariv, O., eds. Automata, Languages, & Programming. (Lecture Notes in Computer Sciences Ser.: Vol. 115). 552p. 1981. pap. 29.00 (ISBN 0-387-10843-2). Springer-Verlag.

Even, Shimon. Graph Algorithms. LC 79-17150. 249p. 1979. 34.95 (ISBN 0-914894-21-8). Computer Sci.

Evenari, M., et al. Hot Deserts & Arid Shrublands, Vols. 12A & B. (Ecosystems of the World Ser.). Date not set. Set. price not set (ISBN 0-444-42297-8). Vol. 12A (ISBN 0-444-42282-X). Vol. 12B (ISBN 0-444-42296-X). Elsevier.

Evenari, Michael, et al. Negev: The Challenge of a Desert. LC 75-119073. (Illus.). 1971. 18.50x (ISBN 0-674-60670-1). Harvard U Pr.

--The Negev: The Challenge of a Desert. 2nd ed. (Illus.). 464p. 1982. text ed. 35.00x (ISBN 0-674-60672-8). Harvard U Pr.

Evenden, B. S. & Stone, D. R. Seismic Prospecting Instruments: Instrument Performance & Testing, Vol. 2. 2ND, enl. ed. (Geo-Exploration Monographs: No. 3). (Illus.). 158p. 1984. text ed. 23.80x (ISBN 3-443-13014-3). Lubrecht & Cramer.

--Seismic Prospecting Instruments: Vol. 2: Instrument Performance & Testing. (Geoexploration Monographs: Ser. 1, No. 3). (Illus.). 195p. 1971. lib. bdg. 23.00x (ISBN 3-4431-3004-6). Lubrecht & Cramer.

Evenhouse, Bill. Reasons One, Sects & Cults with Non-Christian Roots. 120p. (Orig.). 1981. pap. text ed. 3.90 (ISBN 0-933140-23-1); tchr's manual, 61 pgs. 3.90 (ISBN 0-933140-24-X). Bd of Pubns CRC.

Evenhuis, Francis D. Massinger's Imagery. (Salzburg Studies in English Literature, Jacobean Drama Studies: No. 14). 176p. 1973. pap. text ed. 25.50x (ISBN 0-391-01373-4). Humanities.

Evenhuis, M. L., jt. auth. see Hall, J. C.

Evenhuis, N. L. An Indexed Bibliography of Bombyliidae: Insecta Diptera. (Theses Zoologicae Ser.: No. 4). (Illus.). 494p. 1985. lib. bdg. 56.00 (ISBN 3-7682-1379-X). Lubrecht & Cramer.

Evenhuis, N. L., jt. auth. see Hall, Jack C.

Evenhuis, Neal L., jt. auth. see Hall, Jack C.

Evennett, H. Outram. Spirit of the Counter-Reformation. LC 68-11282. 1970. pap. 4.95x (ISBN 0-268-00425-0). U of Notre Dame Pr.

Evennett, Henry O. The Cardinal of Lorraine & the Council of Trent: A Study in the Counter-Reformation. LC 83-45592. Date not set. Repr. of 1940 ed. 57.50 (ISBN 0-404-19885-6). AMS Pr.

Evens, Lori. Autumn Kisses. 1984. 8.95 (ISBN 0-8034-8412-7, Avalon). Bouregy.

Evens, P., jt. auth. see Barnard, C.

Evensen, Gregory L. Security in America. LC 80-52172. 155p. 1980. 12.50 (ISBN 0-89697-041-8). Intl Univ Pr.

Evensen, Jane B., ed. see Gold, Joseph.

Evensen, Ken L. Healing Love: The Inner Power of All Things. 9.95 (ISBN 0-533-04807-9). Vantage.

Evensen, Ronald C., ed. see Holcombe, Robert A.

Even-Shoshan, Abraham, ed. The Complete Hebrew Dictionary in Seven Volumes. (Illus.). 3236p. (Eng. & Hebrew.). text ed. 140.00 (ISBN 965-17-0083-1). K Sefer.

--The Complete Hebrew Dictionary in Three Volumes. (Illus.). 1664p. (Eng. & Hebrew.). text ed. 80.00 (ISBN 965-17-0084-X). K Sefer.

--Condensed Hebrew Dictionary. (Illus.). 824p. (Hebrew.). 1982. text ed. 35.00 (ISBN 965-17-0103-X). K Sefer.

--The Dictionary for School. (Illus.). 728p. (Hebrew.). 1982. text ed. 10.00 (ISBN 965-17-0082-3). K Sefer.

--The New Biblical Concordance in Three Volumes. (Illus.). 2384p. (Hebrew.). 1982. text ed. 79.00 (ISBN 965-17-0147-1). K Sefer.

--The New Biblical Concordance in Two Volumes. (Illus.). 1304p. (Hebrew.). 1981. text ed. 54.00 (ISBN 965-17-0148-X). K Sefer.

--A New Concordance of the Bible. 1288p. 1982. text ed. 39.00 (ISBN 965-17-0098-X). Ridgefield Pub.

--A New Concordance of the Old Testament: Using the Hebrew & Aramaic Text. 1328p. 43.00 (ISBN 0-8010-3417-5). Baker Bk.

--The Student's Dictionary. (Illus.). 592p. (Hebrew.). 1982. text ed. 12.00 (ISBN 965-17-0105-6). K Sefer.

Evenson. Paris: A Century of Change, Eighteen Seventy-Eight to Nineteen Seventy-Eight. LC 78-10257. 1979. pap. 16.95x (ISBN 0-300-02667-6). Yale U Pr.

Evenson, Dean & Shamberg, Michael, eds. Radical Software & the Realistic Hope Foundations, Vol. 1, No. 5. 120p. 1972. pap. 17.50 (ISBN 0-677-10975-X). Gordon.

Evenson, Edward B., et al, eds. Tills & Related Deposits: Proceedings of the INQUA Symposia on the Genesis & Lithology of Quaternary Deposits, USA 1981, Argentina 1982. 1983. lib. bdg. 45.00 (ISBN 90-6191-511-2, Pub. by Balkema RSA). IPS.

Evenson, Flavis, ed. see Music Education National Conference.

Evenson, Gregory L. Security in America. 155p. 1984. 17.95 (ISBN 0-318-03777-7). Intl Univ Pr.

Evenson, Norma. Le Corbusier: The Machine & the Grand Design. LC 60-6079. (Planning & Cities Ser). (Illus., Orig.). 1969. 7.95 (ISBN 0-8076-0514-X); pap. 5.95 O.P. (ISBN 0-8076-0518-2). Braziller.

--Two Brazilian Capitals: Architecture & Urbanism in Rio de Janeiro & Brasilia. LC 72-91293. (Illus.). 416p. 1973. 45.00x (ISBN 0-300-01540-2). Yale U Pr.

Evenson, Robert E. & Kislev, Yoav. Agricultural Research & Productivity. LC 74-15210. (Illus.). 224p. 1975. 24.50x (ISBN 0-300-01815-0). Yale U Pr.

Evenson, Vera S., jt. auth. see Smith, Alexander H.

Everaerd, W., et al, eds. Development in Adolescence. 1983. lib. bdg. 43.50 (ISBN 0-89838-581-4, Pub. by Martinus Nijhoff Netherlands). Kluwer Academic.

Everaerts, F. M., ed. see Deyl, Z., et al.

Everaerts, F. M., et al. Isotachophoresis: Theory, Instrumentation & Applications. (Journal of Chromatography Library: Vol. 6). 418p. 1976. 91.50 (ISBN 0-444-41430-4). Elsevier.

Everaerts, F. M., et al, eds. Analytical Isotachophoresis. (Analytical Chemistry Symposia Ser.: Vol. 6). 234p. 1981. 59.75 (ISBN 0-444-41957-8). Elsevier.
Everall, Ronald J. The New, Fully Illustrated Book in Vibrant Colours of the Most Dramatic Birds in the Universe. (Illus.). 116p. 1982. 69.75 (ISBN 0-89266-321-9). Am Classical Coll Pr.
Everand, Peggie. Involuntary Strangers. 1981. 29.00x (ISBN 0-906549-10-8, Pub. by J Clare Bks England). State Mutual Bk.
Everard & Tanner, J. L. Reinforced Concrete Design. (Schaum Outline Ser.). 1966. text ed. 9.95 (ISBN 0-07-019770-9). McGraw.
Everard, jt. auth. see Polunin, O.
Everard, John, tr. from Arabic. The Divine Pymander of Hermes Mercurius Trismegistus. LC 73-84044. (Secret Doctrine Reference Ser.). 140p. 1985. Repr. of 1884 ed. 10.00 (ISBN 0-913510-07-6). Wizards.
Everard, Kenneth, jt. auth. see McCullough, Robert J.
Everdale, Carl P. The Contributions of Lenin & Mao Tse-Tung to the Communist Theories Advanced by Marx & Engel, 2 vols. (Illus.). 277p. 1982. Set. 187.45x (ISBN 0-930008-98-7). Inst Econ Pol.
--The Contributions of Lenin & Mao-Tse-Tung to the Communist Theories Advanced by Marx & Engels, 2 vols. (Illus.). 317p. 1985. Set. 227.45 (ISBN 0-86722-111-9). Inst Econ Pol.
Everdell, M. H. Statistical Mechanics & Its Chemical Applications. 1975. 55.00 (ISBN 0-12-244450-7). Acad Pr.
Everdell, Romeyn. Master Production Scheduling Training Aid. 29p. 1973. 19.50 (ISBN 0-935406-11-5). Am Prod & Inventory.
Everdell, Romeyn, jt. auth. see Rath & Strong, Inc.
Everdell, William R. The End of Kings: A History of Republics & Republicans. 19.95 (ISBN 0-02-909930-7). Free Pr.
Everden, Margery. The Dream Keeper. LC 84-88. (Illus.). 160p. (gr. 6 up). 1985. 10.25 (ISBN 0-688-04638-X). Lothrop.
Everden, Sue, jt. auth. see Shrader, Robert D.
Everding, H. Edward, Jr. & Wilbanks, Dana M. Decision Making & the Bible. LC 75-11656. 160p. 1975. pap. 5.95 (ISBN 0-8170-0668-0). Judson.
Evered, H., jt. auth. see Wallnig, G.
Evered, H., jt. auth. see Wallnig, Gunter.
Evered, Harry, jt. auth. see Wallnig, Gunter.
Evered, James F. A Motivational Approach to Selling. 224p. 1982. 15.95 (ISBN 0-8144-5738-X). AMACOM.
--Shirt-Sleeves Management. 160p. 1981. 14.95 (ISBN 0-8144-5636-7). AMACOM.
--Shirt-Sleeves Management. LC 80-67962. pap. 47.00 (ISBN 0-317-10215-X, 2022625). Bks Demand UMI.
--Shirt-Sleeves Management. LC 80-67962. 192p. 1981. pap. 14.95 (ISBN 0-8144-7626-0); pap. 7.95 pap. AMACOM.
Evered, Roger. Futures Planning in Management. (CPL Bibliographies Ser.: No. 5). 52p. 1979. 7.00 (ISBN 0-86602-005-5). Coun Plan Librarians.
--Futures Planning in Management: Bibliography & Information Sources. (CPL Bibliographies: No. 5). 52p. 1979. pap. 7.00 (ISBN 0-86602-005-5). CPL Biblios.
Everest, A. S., jt. auth. see Barlow, B. V.
Everest, A. S., jt. auth. see Tayler, R. J.
Everest, Allan S. Morgenthau, The New Deal & Silver. LC 72-2368. (FDR & the Era of the New Deal Ser.). 209p. 1973. Repr. of 1950 ed. lib. bdg. 32.50 (ISBN 0-306-70469-2). Da Capo.
--Moses Hazen & the Canadian Refugees in the American Revolution. LC 76-54260. 1976. 12.95 (ISBN 0-8156-0129-8). Syracuse U Pr.
--Rum Across the Border: The Prohibition Era in Northern New York. (York State Bks). (Illus.). 1978. 12.95 (ISBN 0-8156-0152-2). Syracuse U Pr.
--The War of Eighteen Twelve in the Champlain Valley. (A New York State Study). (Illus.). 264p. 1981. 19.95x (ISBN 0-8156-2240-6). Syracuse U Pr.
Everest, Alton. Handbook of Multichannel Recording. LC 75-20842. 322p. 1975. o.p 13.95 (ISBN 0-8306-5781-9); pap. 9.95 (ISBN 0-8306-4781-3, 781). TAB Bks.
Everest, F. A. How to Build a Small Budget Recording Studio from Scratch: With 12 Tested Designs. LC 79-14398. (Illus.). 1979. pap. 11.95 (ISBN 0-8306-1166-5, 1166). TAB Bks.
Everest, F. Alton. Acoustic Techniques for Home & Studio. 2nd ed. (Illus.). 352p. 1984. 19.95 (ISBN 0-8306-0696-3, 1696); pap. 15.50 (ISBN 0-8306-1696-9). TAB Bks.
--Critical Listening. (Illus.). 106p. (Orig.). 1982. pap. text ed. 129.95 (ISBN 0-9608352-0-2); 10 narrations on 5 cassettes incl. F A Everest.
--The Master Handbook of Acoustics. (Illus.). 352p. 1983. 18.95 (ISBN 0-8306-0008-6); pap. 13.50 (ISBN 0-8306-1296-3, 1296). TAB Bks.
Everest, Frank K., Jr. The Fastest Man Alive. Gilbert, James, ed. LC 79-7251. (Flight: Its First Seventy-Five Years Ser.). (Illus.). 1979. Repr. of 1958 ed. lib. bdg. 23.00x (ISBN 0-405-12163-6). Ayer Co Pubs.
Everest, G. Database Management. 1986. write for info. (ISBN 0-07-019781-4). McGraw.
Everest, Gordon, jt. auth. see Davis, Gordon B.
Everest, Harvey W. Divine Demonstration. 8.75 (ISBN 0-89225-078-X). Gospel Advocate.
Everest, Kelvin. Coleridge's Secret Ministry: The Context of the Conversation Poems 1795-1798. 324p. 1979. text ed. 27.50x (ISBN 0-06-492043-7). B&N Imports.
Everest, Kelvin, ed. Shelley Revalued: Essays from the Gregynog Conference. LC 83-3735. 248p. 1983. text ed. 28.50x (ISBN 0-389-20390-4). B&N Imports.
Everest, Larry. Bhopal: The Anatomy of a Massacre. 1985. price not set (ISBN 0-916650-26-X); pap. price not set (ISBN 0-916650-25-1). Banner Pr NY.
Everett, Alan. Finishes. (Mitchell's Building Ser.). (Illus.). 200p. 1971. pap. 14.95 (ISBN 0-7134-3335-3, Pub. by Batsford, Pub. by Batsford England). David & Charles.
Everett, Alexander. America; Or, a General Survey of the Political Situation of the Several Powers of the Western Continent. Hudson, Michael, ed. (The Neglected American Economists Ser.). 1974. lib. bdg. 61.00 (ISBN 0-8240-1002-7). Garland Pub.
--Journal of the Proceedings of the Friends of Domestic Industry: In General Convention Met at the City of New York, October 26, 1831. Hudson, Michael, ed. Bd. with British Opinions on the Protecting System. (The Neglected American Economists Ser.). 1975. lib. bdg. 61.00 (ISBN 0-8240-1003-5). Garland Pub.
Everett, Alexander H. America: Or, a General Survey of the Political Situation of the Several Powers of the Western Continent. LC 70-117505. Repr. of 1827 ed. lib. bdg. 35.00x (ISBN 0-678-00651-2). Kelley.
--New Ideas on Population. 2nd ed. LC 65-26364. Repr. of 1826 ed. 25.00x (ISBN 0-678-00276-2). Kelley.
Everett, B. Auden. (Writers & Critics Ser.). 117p. 1980. 22.50 (ISBN 0-912378-04-2). Chips.
Everett, B., ed. All's Well That Ends Well. 1981. 3.75 (ISBN 0-14-070720-4). Penguin.
Everett, B., ed. see Shakespeare, William.
Everett, B. S. An Introduction to Latent Variable Models. LC 84-12677. (Monographs on Statistics & Applied Probability). 150p. 1984. text ed. 20.00 (ISBN 0-412-25310-0, 9196, Pub. by Chapman & Hall England). Methuen Inc.
Everett, Betty S. I Want to Be Like You, Lord: Bible Devotion for Girls. (Young Readers Ser.). 112p. (Orig.). 1984. pap. 3.75 (ISBN 0-8066-2112-5, 10-3196). Augsburg.
--Who Am I, Lord? LC 82-72645. (Young Readers Ser.). 112p. (Orig.). (gr. 3-6). 1983. pap. 3.75 (ISBN 0-8066-1951-1, 10-7072). Augsburg.
Everett, Boyd N., Jr. The Organization of an Alaskan Expedition. LC 84-80852. 112p. (Orig.). 1984. pap. 9.95 (ISBN 0-918803-00-4). Gorak Bks.
Everett, Brenda H., tr. see De Felice, Renzo.
Everett, C. & Koop, Elizabeth. Sometimes Mountains Move. 1983. pap. 2.50 (ISBN 0-8423-6062-X). Tyndale.
Everett, Charles. Fresh Water Fishes. (Illus.). 45p. pap. 1.00 (ISBN 0-8323-0126-4). Binford.
Everett, Charles C. Theism & the Christian Faith. Hale, Edward, ed. LC 75-3139. Repr. of 1909 ed. 34.00 (ISBN 0-404-59148-5). AMS Pr.
Everett, Craig A. Divorce Mediation: Perspectives on the Field. LC 85-8428. (Journal of Divorce Ser.: Vol. 8, 314). 29.95 (ISBN 0-86656-457-8). Haworth Pr.
Everett, D. H. Colloid Science, Vols. 1-2. LC 72-95096. Vol. 1 1970-71 Literature. 1973 36.00 (ISBN 0-85186-508-9, Pub. by Royal Soc Chem London); Vol. 2 1972-74 Literature. 1976 47.00. Am Chemical.
Everett, David. Rustler's Blood. 1979. pap. 1.75 (ISBN 0-8439-0702-9, Leisure Bks). Dorchester Pub Co.
--Works of David Everett. LC 82-3390. 1983. 60.00x (ISBN 0-8201-1378-6). Schol Facsimiles.
Everett, Donald E. San Antonio Legacy. LC 79-66067. (Illus.). 121p. 1979. 10.00 (ISBN 0-911536-83-3). Trinity U Pr.
--San Antonio: The Flavor of Its Past, 1845-1898. LC 74-27616. (Illus.). 162p. 1983. Repr. of 1975 ed. pap. 16.00 (ISBN 0-939980-00-2). Trinity U Pr.
--Trinity University: A Record of One Hundred Years. LC 68-24632. (Illus.). 1968. 5.00 (ISBN 0-911536-21-3). Trinity U Pr.
Everett, Dorothy. Essays on Middle English Literature. Kean, Patricia, ed. LC 77-17994. 1978. Repr. of 1959 ed. lib. bdg. 24.75x (ISBN 0-313-20117-X, EVEM). Greenwood.
Everett, Edward. Orations & Speeches, on Various Occasions. LC 72-4963. (The Romantic Tradition in American Literature Ser.). 642p. 1972. Repr. of 1836 ed. 43.00 (ISBN 0-405-04634-0). Ayer Co Pubs.
Everett, Edward D. Cow Country. LC 82-11803. (Western Frontier Library). 258p. 1982. Repr. of 1942 ed. lib. bdg. 28.50x (ISBN 0-313-23656-9, DACC). Greenwood.
Everett, Frank E. Brierfield: Plantation Home of Jefferson Davis. LC 72-156351. 168p. 1979. Repr. of 1971 ed. text ed. 3.95 (ISBN 0-87805-002-7). U Pr of Miss.
Everett, George A., Jr. A Select Bibliography of Gunter Grass from 1956 to 1973, Including the Works, Editions, Translations & Critical Literature. LC 74-1420. 1974. 15.00 (ISBN 0-89102-041-1). B Franklin.
Everett, Graham. Strange Coast. (Illus., Orig.). 1979. pap. 5.00 (ISBN 0-918092-15-9). Tamarack Edns.
Everett, Graham, jt. ed. see Clemente, Vince.
Everett, Henry L. The People's Program, the Twentieth Century Is Theirs: A Romance of the Expectations of the Present Generation. LC 76-42806. Repr. of 1892 ed. 17.50 (ISBN 0-404-60064-6). AMS Pr.
Everett, J. L., jt. auth. see Fenner, T. W.
Everett, J. Rutherford. Religion in Economics: A Study of John B. Clark, Richard T. Ely & Simon N. Patten. 1982. Repr. of 1946 ed. lib. bdg. 17.50x (ISBN 0-87991-866-7). Porcupine Pr.
Everett, Jana M. Women & Social Change in India. 1979. 19.95 (ISBN 0-312-88731-0). St Martin.
--Women & Social Change in India. 228p. 1979. 35.00x (ISBN 0-686-78823-0, Pub. by Bks India England). State Mutual Bk.
Everett, John P. Fundamental Skills of Algebra. LC 78-176759. (Columbia University. Teachers College. Contributions to Education: No. 324). Repr. of 1928 ed. 22.50 (ISBN 0-404-55324-9). AMS Pr.
Everett, John R. Religion in Human Experience: A Comparative Study. 1977. lib. bdg. 59.95 (ISBN 0-8490-2509-5). Gordon Pr.
Everett, L. G., et al. Vadose Zone Monitoring for Hazardous Waste Sites. LC 84-16509. (Pollution Technology Review Ser.: No. 112). (Illus.). 358p. 1985. 36.00 (ISBN 0-8155-1000-4). Noyes.
Everett, Lorne G. Groundwater Monitoring. LC 80-82885. (Illus.). 480p. 1980. 150.00x (ISBN 0-931690-14-5). Genium Pub.
Everett, Mark R. Medical Education in Oklahoma: The University of Oklahoma School of Medicine & Medical Center, 1900-1931. LC 70-177333. (Illus.). 300p. 1972. 24.50x (ISBN 0-8061-0988-2); pap. 12.95x (ISBN 0-8061-1237-9). U of Okla Pr.
Everett, Mark R. & Allen, Alice. Medical Education in Oklahoma: The University of Oklahoma School of Medicine & Medical Center, 1932-1964, Vol. 2. 1980. 29.50x (ISBN 0-8061-1541-6). U of Okla Pr.
Everett, Michael. The Golden Eagle. 60p. 1981. 10.00x (ISBN 0-85158-119-6, Pub. by Blackwood & Sons England). State Mutual Bk.
Everett, Michael, jt. auth. see Hammand, Nicholas.
Everett, Michael W., jt. ed. see Waddell, Jack O.
Everett, Millard, jt. auth. see Densford, Katherine.
Everett, N. B. Functional Neuroanatomy. 6th ed. LC 70-135680. (Illus.). 357p. 1971. text ed. 14.50 (ISBN 0-8121-0324-6). Lea & Febiger.
Everett, Percival. Walk Me to the Distance. LC 84-8845. 240p. 1985. 14.95 (ISBN 0-89919-321-8). Ticknor & Fields.
Everett, Percival L. Suder. 170p. 1983. 13.50 (ISBN 0-670-68110-5). Viking.
Everett, Robinson O. Military Justice in the Armed Forces of the United States. LC 75-42097. 338p. 1976. Repr. of 1956 ed. lib. bdg. 19.50x (ISBN 0-8371-8642-0, EVMJ). Greenwood.
Everett, Robinson O. & Leach, Richard H. Urban Problems & Prospects. LC 65-28034. (Library of Law & Contemporary Problems). 240p. 1965. 10.00 (ISBN 0-379-11506-9). Oceana.
Everett, Robinson O., ed. Anti-Poverty Programs. LC 66-29880. (Library of Law & Contemporary Problems). 254p. 1966. 10.00 (ISBN 0-379-11507-7). Oceana.
Everett, Robinson O. & Johnston, John D., Jr., eds. Housing. LC 68-54245. (Library of Law & Contemporary Problems Ser.: No. 9). 376p. 1968. Repr. of 1967 ed. 20.00 (ISBN 0-379-11509-3). Oceana.
Everett, Robinson O., jt. ed. see Baade, Hans W.
Everett, Samuel, jt. ed. see Arndt, Christian O.
Everett, T. H. The New York Botanical Garden Illustrated Encyclopedia of Horticulture, 10 vols. 1980. Set. lib. bdg. 600.00 (ISBN 0-8240-7222-7). Garland Pub.
Everett, Thomas H. The New York Botanical Garden Illustrated Encyclopedia of Horticulture, Vols. 7-10. LC 80-65941. 1468p. 1982. 240.00 (ISBN 0-686-82042-8). Garland Pub.
Everett, W. N., ed. Ordinary & Partial Differential Equations. (Lecture Notes in Mathematics Ser.: Vol. 827). (Illus.). 271p. 1980. pap. 20.00 (ISBN 0-387-10252-3). Springer-Verlag.
Everett, Wade. The Big Drive. 128p. 1981. pap. 1.75 (ISBN 0-345-29142-5). Ballantine.
--Fort Starke. 160p. (Orig.). 1980. pap. 1.75 (ISBN 0-345-28851-3). Ballantine.
--Shotgun Marshal. 1981. pap. 1.75 (ISBN 0-345-29434-3). Ballantine.
--The Warrior. 160p. 1981. pap. 1.75 (ISBN 0-345-29432-7). Ballantine.
Everett, Walter K. Faulkner's Art & Characters. LC 68-31478. (Orig.). (gr. 9 up). 1969. pap. text ed. 4.50 (ISBN 0-8120-0392-6). Barron.
Everett, William B. & Coombs, Gary B. Mule Car & Trolley: The Story of the Santa Barbara Street Railway. LC 84-61366. (Illus.). viii, 128p. 1984. 18.50x (ISBN 0-911773-04-5). Inst Am Res.
Everett, William J. Blessed Be the Bond: Christian Perspectives on Marriage & Family. LC 84-48712. 144p. 1985. pap. 6.95 (ISBN 0-8006-1831-9, 1-1831). Fortress.
Everett, William W. & Bachmeyer, T. J. Disciplines in Transformation: A Guide to Theology & the Behavioral Sciences. LC 78-68570. 1979. pap. text ed. 11.50 (ISBN 0-8191-0692-5). U Pr of Amer.
Everett-Heath, John. Soviet Helicopters: Design, Development & Tactics. 1983. 24.95 (ISBN 0-86720-662-4). Jane's Pub Inc.
Evergreen Productions, ed. see Bathersfield, Arnold.
Everhard, Jim. Cute & Other Poems. 80p. (Orig.). 1982. limited signed, & specialy bound 35.00x (ISBN 0-917342-92-5); pap. 4.95 (ISBN 0-917342-93-3). Gay Sunshine.
Everhard, Kenneth & Burrow, James L. Business Principles & Management. (gr. 9-12). 1984. text ed. 11.30 (ISBN 0-538-07290-3, G29). SW Pub.
Everhart, Benjamin M., jt. auth. see Ellis, Job B.
Everhart, Gail & Everhart, Jim. Thirty-Nine & Holding. (Illus.). 48p. (Orig.). 1983. pap. 2.95 (ISBN 0-8220-1469-6). Cliffs.
Everhart, Jim. Forty Is...!? (Orig.). 1969. pap. 2.95 (ISBN 0-8220-1468-8). Cliffs.
--Illustrated Texas Dictionary of the English Language, 5 Vols. pap. 2.95 ea.; Vol. 1. (ISBN 0-8220-1477-7); Vol. 2. (ISBN 0-8220-1478-5); Vol. 3. (ISBN 0-8220-1479-3); Vol. 4. (ISBN 0-8220-1480-7); Vol. 5. (ISBN 0-8220-1487-4). Cliffs.
Everhart, Jim, jt. auth. see Everhart, Gail.
Everhart, John L., ed. Engineering Properties of Nickel & Nickel Alloys. LC 74-141242. 229p. 1971. 39.50x (ISBN 0-306-30513-5, Plenum Pr). Plenum Pub.
Everhart, Marion E. Everhart on Easements. LC 80-53457. (Illus.). 420p. 1981. 46.50 (ISBN 0-935988-19-X). Todd Pub.
Everhart, Robert B. Reading, Writing & Resistance: Adolescence & Labor in a Junior High School. (Critical Social Thought Ser.). 288p. 1983. 21.95x (ISBN 0-7100-9450-7). Routledge & Kegan.
Everhart, Robert B., ed. The Public School Monopoly: A Critical Analysis of Education & the State in American Society. LC 81-20635. (Illus.). 608p. 1982. pap. 14.95 (ISBN 0-88410-388-9). PIPPR.
Everhart, Ronald. A Louisiana Heron-Snowy Egert Nesting Area. (Illus.). 112p. 1984. 25.00x (ISBN 0-915261-00-6). World Nature.
Everhart, Ronald E. Glen Canyon-Lake Powell: The Story Behind the Scenery. 48p. 1983. 8.95 (ISBN 0-916122-86-7); pap. 3.75 (ISBN 0-916122-85-9). KC Pubns.
Everhart, Thomas E., jt. auth. see Angelakos, Diogenes J.
Everhart, W. Harry & Youngs, William D. Principles of Fishery Science. 2nd ed. (Illus.). 343p. 1981. 22.50x (ISBN 0-8014-1334-6). Cornell U Pr.
Everhart, William. The National Park Service. LC 82-10884. (Westview Library of Federal Departments, Agencies, & Systems). (Illus.). 198p. 1982. lib. bdg. 25.00x (ISBN 0-86531-130-7); pap. text ed. 11.50x (ISBN 0-86531-498-5). Westview.
Everiss, S. F. Animal Management, 3 Vols. 1982. 125.00x set (ISBN 0-86082-195-1, Pub. by Natl Ext England). State Mutual Bk.
Everist, Burton. The Christian Family Craftbook. LC 78-62064. 1978. pap. 5.95 (ISBN 0-8192-1239-3). Morehouse.
Everist, Norma J. Education Ministry in the Congregation: Eight Ways We Learn from One Another. LC 83-70515. 240p. (Orig.). 1983. pap. 10.95 (ISBN 0-8066-2021-8, 10-2006). Augsburg.
Everitt, A. Abstract Expressionism. LC 77-80188. (Modern Movements in Art Ser.). 1978. pap. 2.50 (ISBN 0-8120-0880-4). Barron.
Everitt, Alan. Landscape & Community in England. 375p. 1985. 35.00 (ISBN 0-907628-42-7). Hambledon Press.
Everitt, Alastair, ed. Wuthering Heights: An Anthology of Criticism. 208p. 1967. 25.00x (ISBN 0-7146-1046-1, F Cass Co). Biblio Dist.
Everitt, Arthur V. & Burgess, John A. Hypothalamus, Pituitary & Aging. (Illus.). 808p. 1976. 67.50x (ISBN 0-398-03346-3). C C Thomas.
Everitt, B. S. The Analysis of Contingency Tables. 1977. 12.95 (ISBN 0-412-14970-2, NO.6105, Pub. by Chapman & Hall). Methuen Inc.
--Graphical Techniques for Multivariate Data. 146p. 1978. 29.00 (ISBN 0-444-19461-4). Elsevier.
Everitt, B. S. & Dunn, G. Advanced Methods of Data Exploration & Modelling. LC 83-292. xix, 253p. 1983. text ed. 20.00x (ISBN 0-435-82294-2). Heinemann Ed.
Everitt, B. S. & Hand, D. J. Finite Mixture Distributions. (Monographs in Applied Probability & Statistics). 143p. 1981. 22.00 (ISBN 0-412-22420-8, NO. 2234, Pub. by Chapman & Hall). Methuen Inc.
Everitt, B. S., jt. auth. see Dunn, G.
Everitt, Brian. Cluster Analysis. viii, 136p. 1980. pap. text ed. 16.00x (ISBN 0-435-82296-9). Heinemann Ed.
Everitt, C. W., et al see Brush, Stephen G.
Everitt, Charles P. Adventures of a Treasure Hunter: A Rare Bookman in Search of American History. 296p. 1986. pap. write for info. (ISBN 0-916638-12-X). Meyerbooks.

Everitt, David. Indian Territory. 208p. (Orig.). 1982. pap. 2.25 (ISBN 0-8439-1041-0, Leisure Bks). Dorchester Pub Co.
--Rustler's Blood. 208p. 1985. pap. 2.25 (ISBN 0-8439-2254-0, Leisure Bks). Dorchester Pub Co.
Everitt, David, jt. auth. see Schechter, Harold.
Everitt, Elizabeth, jt. ed. see Joy, J. L.
Everitt, Graham. English Caricaturists & Graphic Humourists of the Nineteenth Century: How They Illustrated & Interpreted Their Times. fascimile ed. LC 77-37523. (Essay Index Reprint Ser). Repr. of 1885 ed. 19.00 (ISBN 0-8369-2547-5). Ayer Co Pubs.
Everitt, James A. The Third Power: Farmers to the Front (Fourth Edition) facsimile ed. LC 74-30630. (American Farmers & the Rise of Agribusiness Ser.). (Illus.). 1975. Repr. of 1907 ed. 29.00x (ISBN 0-405-06799-2). Ayer Co Pubs.
Everitt, N., ed. see Akheizer, N. I.
Everitt, N., ed. see Akheizer, N. I. & Glazman, I. M.
Everitt, W. N. & Lewis, R. T., eds. Ordinary Differential Equations & Operators. (Lecture Notes in Mathematics: Vol. 1032). 521p. 1983. pap. 25.00 (ISBN 0-387-12702-X). Springer-Verlag.
Everitt, W. N. & Sleeman, B. D., eds. Ordinary & Partial Differential Equations: Proceedings. (Lecture Notes in Mathematics Ser.: Vol. 846). 384p. 1981. pap. 24.00 (ISBN 0-387-10569-7). Springer-Verlag.
Everitt, W. N., ed. see Conference on the Theory of Ordinary & Partial Differential Equations, Dundee, Scotland, 1972.
Everitt, W. N., ed. see Fourth Conference Held at Dundee, Scotland, Mar 30-Apr 2, 1976.
Everitt, W. N., ed. see Naimark, M. A.
Everitt, W. N., ed. see Symposium, Dundee, 1974.
Everling, W. Exercises in Computer Systems Analysis. (Lecture Notes in Computer Science: Vol. 35). viii, 184p. 1975. pap. 15.00 (ISBN 0-387-07401-5). Springer-Verlag.
Everly, George & Girdano, Daniel. The Stress Mess Solution. LC 79-14652. 174p. 1980. pap. 8.95 (ISBN 0-13-852616-8). P-H.
Everly, George S. & Robert H. L. Feldman & Associates. Occupational Health Promotion: Health Behavior in the Workplace. 325p. 1985. text ed. 28.95x (ISBN 0-471-89533-4). Wiley.
Everly, George S., jt. auth. see Girdano, Daniel A.
Everly, George S., Jr. & Rosenfeld, Robert. The Nature & Treatment of the Stress Response: A Practical Guide for Clinicians. 215p. 1981. 19.95x (ISBN 0-306-40677-2, Plenum Pr). Plenum Pub.
Everly, George S., Jr., jt. auth. see Girdano, Daniel A.
Everly, George S., Jr., ed. see Millon, Theodore.
Everman, Eric. Dialogue with the Unconscious. (Illus.). 1982. 6.95 (ISBN 0-533-05247-5). Vantage.
Everman, W. D. Orion. LC 75-322771. (Ithaca House Fiction Ser.). 94p. 1975. 4.50 (ISBN 0-87886-055-X). Ithaca Hse.
Everman, Welch D. Jerzy Kosinski: The Literature of Violation. LC 84-356. (Milford Series: Popular Writers of Today: Vol. 47). 160p. (Orig.). 1986. lib. bdg. 15.95x (ISBN 0-89370-176-9); pap. text ed. 7.95x (ISBN 0-89370-276-5). Borgo Pr.
Evermann, Barton W., jt. auth. see Jordan, David S.
Evernden, Margery. Davy Crockett & His Coonskin Cap. (Children's Theatre Playscript Ser.). 1956. pap. 2.25x (ISBN 0-88020-025-1). Coach Hse.
--The Frog Princess & the Witch. (Children's Theatre Playscript Ser.). 1963. pap. 2.25x (ISBN 0-88020-028-6). Coach Hse.
--King Arthur's Sword. (Children's Theatre Playscript Ser.). 1959. pap. 2.25x (ISBN 0-88020-034-0). Coach Hse.
--The King of the Golden River. (Children's Theatre Playscript Ser.). 1955. pap. 2.25x (ISBN 0-88020-033-2). Coach Hse.
--The Kite Song. LC 84-4367. 192p. (gr. 6-9). 1984. 10.25 (ISBN 0-688-01200-0). Lothrop.
--Rumpelstiltskin. (Children's Theatre Playscript Ser.). 1955. pap. 2.25x (ISBN 0-88020-051-0). Coach Hse.
--The Secret of Han Ho. (Children's Theatre Playscript Ser.). 1956. pap. 2.00x (ISBN 0-88020-052-9). Coach Hse.
Evernden, Neil. The Natural Alien: Humankind & Environment. 176p. 1985. 19.95 (ISBN 0-8020-2552-8). U of Toronto Pr.
Everngam, Gary G., jt. auth. see Bregman, Douglas M.
Everote, Warren P. Agricultural Science to Serve Youth: Outcomes of a Course in Experimental Science for Secondary-School Students. LC 72-176760. (Columbia University. Teachers College. Contributions to Education: No. 901). Repr. of 1943 ed. 22.50 (ISBN 0-404-55901-8). AMS Pr.
Everroad, Edward & Michalegko, Dianne. Flashbacks: An Introduction to Cinema. (Illus.). 360p. 1983. write for info. (ISBN 0-911629-00-9). Prinroad Pubs.
Everroad, Jim. Five-Minute Total Shape-Up Program. 1980. 1.95 (ISBN 0-8431-0156-3). Price Stern.
--How to Flatten Your Stomach. (Illus.). 1978. pap. 1.95 (ISBN 0-8431-0461-9). Price Stern.
--How to Flatten Your Stomach, Bk. 2. 32p. 1983. pap. 1.95 (ISBN 0-8431-0914-9). Price Stern.
Everroad, Jim & Moscow, Lonna. How to Trim Your Hips & Shape Your Thighs. (Illus., Orig.). 1979. pap. 1.95 (ISBN 0-8431-0668-9). Price Stern.
Evers & Haegerstam. Handbook of Dental Local Anesthesia. 208p. 1982. 99.00 (ISBN 0-907789-00-5, Pub. by Schultz Med Info England). State Mutual Bk.
Evers, Alf. The Catskills: From Wilderness to Woodstock. LC 82-6495. 848p. 1984. 32.50 (ISBN 0-87951-162-1). Overlook Pr.
Evers, Christopher. The Old House Doctor. LC 83-43153. (Illus.). 192p. 1985. 17.95 (ISBN 0-87951-090-0). Overlook Pr.
Evers, Dora, jt. auth. see Feingold, S. Norman.
Evers, H. D. Monks, Priests & Peasants: A Study of Buddhism & Social Structure in Central Ceylon. (Monographs & Theoretical Studies in Sociology & Anthropology in Honour of Nels Anderson: Vol. 1). (Illus.). 1973. text ed. 31.50x (ISBN 90-04-03461-7). Humanities.
Evers, Hans-Dieter, ed. The Sociology of Southeast Asia: Readings on Social Change & Development. (Illus.). 1980. 45.00x (ISBN 0-19-580408-2). Oxford U Pr.
Evers, Helen, jt. ed. see Isaacs, Bernard.
Evers, J., jt. auth. see Evers, P.
Evers, Larry, ed. The South Corner of Time: Hopi, Navaio, Papago, Yaqui Tribal Literature. LC 76-617570. (Sun Tracks Ser.: No. 6). 240p. 1981. pap. 17.50 (ISBN 0-8165-0731-7). U of Ariz Pr.
Evers, Ona C. Everybody's Dowser Book. LC 77-76983. (Illus.). 1977. pap. 3.95 (ISBN 0-918900-01-8). Onaway.
Evers, P. & Evers, J. Sixty Recipes-M.S.-Metabolic Diseases. 1.00 (ISBN 0-943080-02-9). Cancer Control Soc.
Evers, Robert A., jt. auth. see Winterringer, Glen S.
Eversaul, George A. Clinical Nutrition. Date not set. 85.00 (ISBN 0-9601978-2-6, 0-9601-7826). G A Eversaul.
--Dental Kinesiology. LC 78-66982. 1978. 57.50x (ISBN 0-9601978-1-8). G A Eversaul.
Everse, Johannes, et al, eds. The Pyridine Nucleotide Coenzymes. 416p. 1982. 60.00 (ISBN 0-12-244750-6). Acad Pr.
Eversen, H., et al, eds. Compendium of Case Law Relating to the European Communities, 1976. Sperl, H. & Usher, J. A. 562p. 1978. 76.50 (ISBN 0-444-85206-9, North Holland). Elsevier.
Eversen, H. J., et al, eds. Compendium of Case Law Relating to the European Communities, 1973. LC 74-23454. 304p. 1975. 85.00 (ISBN 0-444-10794-0, North-Holland). Elsevier.
--Compendium of Case Law Relating to the European Communities, 1974. 348p. 1976. 76.75 (ISBN 0-444-11047-X, North-Holland). Elsevier.
Eversley, David. Social Theories of Fertility & the Malthusian Debate. LC 74-9219. 313p. 1975. Repr. of 1959 ed. lib. bdg. 18.25x (ISBN 0-8371-7628-X, EVST). Greenwood.
Eversley, David & Kollmann, Wolfgang. Population Change & Social Planning. 600p. 1982. text ed. 98.50 (ISBN 0-7131-6345-3). E Arnold.
Eversley, David, jt. ed. see Donnison, David V.
Eversley, David, jt. ed. see Evans, Alan.
Eversley, David E., et al. Population Growth & Planning Policy: Housing & Employment Location in the West Midlands. (Illus.). 88p. 1965. 24.00x (ISBN 0-7146-1583-8, F Cass Co). Biblio Dist.
Eversley, G. Shaw-Lefevre. Peel & O'Connell. LC 71-102610. (Irish Culture & History Ser). 1970. Repr. of 1887 ed. 28.50x (ISBN 0-8046-0787-7, Pub. by Kennikat). Assoc Faculty Pr.
Eversley, George J. Gladstone & Ireland: The Irish Policy of Parliament from 1850-1894. LC 74-114520. 1971. Repr. of 1912 ed. lib. bdg. 22.50x (ISBN 0-8371-4795-6, EVGI). Greenwood.
Eversole, James, jt. auth. see Sacher, Jack.
Eversole, Lewis R. Clinical Outline of Oral Pathology: Diagnosis & Treatment. 2nd ed. LC 84-7870. (Illus.). 434p. 1984. text ed. 39.50 (ISBN 0-8121-0929-5). Lea & Febiger.
Everson, David H. Public Opinion & Interest Groups in American Politics. 224p. 1982. text ed. 9.95 (ISBN 0-531-05642-2). Watts.
Everson, David H., jt. ed. see David, Paul T.
Everson, George. The Story of Television: The Life of Philo T. Farnsworth. LC 74-4677. (Illus.). 270p. 1974. Repr. of 1949 ed. 18.00x (ISBN 0-405-06042-4). Ayer Co Pubs.
Everson, H. J., et al, eds. Compendium of Case Law Relating to the European Communities, 1975. Sperl, H. & Usher, J. 432p. 1977. 89.50 (ISBN 0-7204-0579-3, North-Holland). Elsevier.
Everson, I. The Living Resources of the Southern Ocean. (Southern Ocean Fisheries Survey Programmes: No. 77-1). 160p. (Eng. & Span.). 1977. pap. 10.50 (ISBN 92-5-100428-5, F1321, FAO). Unipub.
Everson, Ida G. George Henry Calvert: American Literary Pioneer. 1973. lib. bdg. 20.50x (ISBN 0-374-92644-1). Octagon.
Everson, Lloyd K. & Etzell, Paul S. Hematologic Diseases: Focus on Clinical Diagnosis. 1983. 30.00 (ISBN 0-87488-837-9). Med Exam.
Everson, Tilden C., et al. Spontaneous Regression of Cancer: A Study & Abstract of Reports in the World Medical Literature & of Personal Communications Concerning Spontaneous Regression of Malignant Disease. LC 66-10199. (Illus.). pap. 142.00 (ISBN 0-317-07796-1, 2051567). Bks Demand UMI.
Everson, William. American Bard: The Preface to the First Edition of Leaves of Grass Arranged in Verse. LC 81-68382. 48p. 1982. 12.95 (ISBN 0-670-11706-4). Viking.
--American Silent Film. LC 77-25188. (Illus.). 1978. 29.95x (ISBN 0-19-502348-X). Oxford U Pr.
--American Silent Film. (Illus.). 1978. pap. 9.95 (ISBN 0-19-503208-X, GB 708, GB). Oxford U Pr.
--Archetype West. 1977. 8.95 (ISBN 0-685-79488-1); pap. 3.95 (ISBN 0-685-79489-X). Oyez.
--Birth of a Poet. Bartlett, Lee, ed. 202p. (Orig.). 1982. 14.00 (ISBN 0-87685-538-9); pap. 10.00 (ISBN 0-87685-537-0); signed ed. 25.00 (ISBN 0-87685-539-7). Black Sparrow.
--Earth Poetry. 1971. pap. 3.50 folio (ISBN 0-685-29873-6, Pub. by Oyez). Small Pr Dist.
--Earth Poetry. 10.95 (ISBN 0-685-50211-2, Pub by Oyez); pap. 4.95 (ISBN 0-685-50212-0). Oyez.
--Films of Laurel & Hardy. 1983. 12.00 (ISBN 0-685-08133-8); pap. 9.95 (ISBN 0-8065-0146-4). Citadel Pr.
--Man-Fate: The Swan Song of Brother Antoninus. LC 73-89480. 96p. 1974. 6.95 (ISBN 0-8112-0520-7); pap. 2.75 (ISBN 0-8112-0521-5, NDP369). New Directions.
--The Masks of Drought. 110p. 1980. 10.00 (ISBN 0-87685-435-8); pap. 4.00 (ISBN 0-87685-434-X). Black Sparrow.
--Renegade Christmas. 30p. 1984. deluxe ed. 150.00 (ISBN 0-935716-29-7). Lord John.
--The Residual Years. rev. ed. LC 68-25585. 1968. 3.95 (ISBN 0-8112-0273-9). New Directions.
--River Root: A Suzygy for the Bicentennial of These States. 1976. signed ltd. ed. 50.00 (ISBN 0-685-79268-4); pap. 2.50 (ISBN 0-685-79269-2). Oyez.
--Tendril in the Mesh. (Western Bks.). 1974. pap. 150.00x (ISBN 0-9600372-3-3). Cayucos.
--The Veritable Years: 1949-1966. 350p. 1978. pap. 8.50 (ISBN 0-87685-378-5). Black Sparrow.
Everson, William, ed. see Jeffers, Robinson.
Everson, William K. Bad Guys: A Pictorial History of the Movie Villain. (Photos). 1968. pap. 8.95 (ISBN 0-8065-0198-7, C264). Citadel Pr.
--Classics of the Horror Film. (Illus.). 256p. 1974. 14.00 (ISBN 0-8065-0437-4). Citadel Pr.
--Classics of the Horror Film. (Illus.). 256p. 1984. pap. 9.95. Citadel Pr.
--The Detective in Film. (Illus.). 256p. 1972. 9.95 (ISBN 0-8065-0298-3); pap. 7.95 (ISBN 0-8065-0448-X). Citadel Pr.
--Love in the Film. (Illus.). 256p. 1981. pap. 7.95 (ISBN 0-8065-0778-0). Citadel Pr.
--Love in the Film: Seventy Years of Romantic Classics. (Illus.). 1979. 14.95 (ISBN 0-8065-0644-X). Citadel Pr.
--Pictorial History of the Western Film. (Illus.). 1971. 10.00 (ISBN 0-685-00330-2); pap. 9.95 (ISBN 0-8065-0257-6). Citadel Pr.
Everstine, Diana S. & Everstine, Louis. People in Crisis: Strategic Therapeutic Interventions. LC 82-23969. 256p. 1983. 25.00 (ISBN 0-87630-286-X). Brunner-Mazel.
Everstine, Louis, jt. auth. see Everstine, Diana S.
Evert, Carl F., Jr., jt. auth. see Bennet, William S.
Evert, Judi. Introduction to Hospitality: Recreation Careers. (gr. 7-10). 1975. pap. text ed. 7.33 activity ed. (ISBN 0-87345-185-6). McKnight.
Evert, Ray, et al. Laboratory Topics in Biology. 1979. text ed. 13.95x (ISBN 0-87901-103-3). Worth.
Evert, Ray F. & Eichhorn, Susan E. Laboratory Topics in Botany. 3rd ed. (Illus.). vii, 196p. 1981. lab manual 13.95x (ISBN 0-87901-142-4). Worth.
Evert-Lloyd, Chris & Amdur, Neil. Chrissie, My Own Story. (Illus.). 240p. 1984. pap. 7.95 (ISBN 0-671-50847-4, Fireside). S&S.
Everton, Ann R. Price Discrimination. 1976. 90.00x (ISBN 0-905440-18-8, Pub. by MCB Pubns). State Mutual Bk.
Everton, C. Better Billiards & Snooker. (Illus.). 96p. 1980. 9.95 (ISBN 0-7182-1441-2, Pub. by Kaye & Ward). David & Charles.
Everton, Clive. Better Billiards & Snooker. rev. ed. (Better Sport Bk.). (Illus.). 90p. text ed. 17.95x (ISBN 0-7182-1441-2, SpS). Sportshelf.
Everton, Ian. Alienation. 210p. (Orig.). 1982. pap. 7.50 (ISBN 0-907040-10-1, Pub. by GMP England). Alyson Pubns.
--Alienation: A Novel on British Gay Movement. 216p. (Orig.). 1982. pap. 7.50 (ISBN 0-907040-10-1). Gay Mens Pr.
Everton, Macduff. El Circo Magico Modelo: Finding the Magic Circus. LC 79-88199. (Illus.). (gr. k-4). 1979. PLB 7.95g (ISBN 0-87614-106-8). Carolrhoda Bks.
Everts, Katherine J. Vocal Expression. 330p. 1979. Repr. lib. bdg. 20.00 (ISBN 0-89987-201-8). Darby Bks.
Evertson, Carolyn M., et al. Classroom Management for Elementary Teachers. (Illus.). 176p. 1984. 16.95 (ISBN 0-13-136135-X); pap. 12.95 (ISBN 0-13-136127-9). P-H.
Evertts, E. L., et al. The Holt Basic Reading System, Grade 2, Levels 9 & 10. Incl. Level 9. People Need People. text ed. 11.72 (ISBN 0-03-070895-8); tchrs' annotated ed. 6.12 (ISBN 0-03-084338-3); Level 10. The Way of the World. text ed. 11.72 (ISBN 0-03-080073-0); tchrs' annotated ed. 6.04 (ISBN 0-03-080077-3). 1973 (HoltE). HR&W.
--The Holt Basic Reading System, Grade 3, Levels 11 & 12. Incl. Level 11. Never Give up! text ed. 12.52 (ISBN 0-03-070900-8); tchrs' annotated ed. 6.12 (ISBN 0-03-084342-1); Level 12. Special Happenings. text ed. 12.52 (ISBN 0-03-080079-X); tchrs' annotated ed. 6.12 (ISBN 0-03-080083-8). 1973 (HoltE). HR&W.
Evert van, de Vliert see Allen, Vernon L. & Van de Vliert, Evert.
Everwine, Peter. Collecting the Animals. LC 72-94240. 1970. pap. 3.95 (ISBN 0-689-10542-8). Atheneum.
--Keeping the Night. LC 77-5194. 1977. pap. 3.95 (ISBN 0-689-10833-8). Atheneum.
--Keeping the Night. 1978. signed ed. 25.00x (ISBN 0-686-16132-7). Penumbra Press.
Every, Dale Van see Van Every, Dale.
Every, Dale van see Van Every, Dale.
Every, Dale Van see Van Every, Dale.
Every, Edward Van see Van Every, Edward.
Every, George. Byzantine Patriarchate, Four Hundred Fifty-One to Twelve Hundred Four. 2nd rev. ed. LC 78-63340. (The Crusades & Military Orders: Second Ser.). Repr. of 1962 ed. 21.50 (ISBN 0-404-17015-3). AMS Pr.
Every, George, et al, eds. Time of the Spirit. LC 84-10696. 256p. (Orig.). 1984. pap. text ed. 9.95 (ISBN 0-88141-035-7). St Vladimirs.
Every Frost, Joan van see Van Every Frost, Joan.
Eves, C. Washington. The West Indies. 1976. lib. bdg. 59.95 (ISBN 0-8490-2815-9). Gordon Pr.
Eves, Charles K. Matthew Prior: Poet & Diplomatist. LC 73-1151. 1973. Repr. of 1939 ed. lib. bdg. 26.00x (ISBN 0-374-92646-8). Octagon.
Eves, Edward. Land-Rover Restoration & Maintenance Manual. (Illus.). 208p. 1986. 18.95 (ISBN 0-7153-8429-5). David & Charles.
Eves, Howard. Elementary Matrix Theory. 1980. pap. 6.50 (ISBN 0-486-63946-0). Dover.
--Great Moments in Mathematics, 2 Vols. (Dolciani Mathematical Expositions Ser.: Vols. 5 & 7). 1983. pap. 15.00 Before 1650 (Vol. 1, 284p) (ISBN 0-88385-310-8); pap. 15.00 After 1650 (Vol. 2, 273p) (ISBN 0-88385-311-6); pap. 22.00 2 Vol. Set (ISBN 0-88385-312-4). Math Assn.
--Great Moments in Mathematics After 1650. LC 81-86186. (Dolciani Mathematical Expositions Ser.: Vol. 7). 259p. 1982. 27.00 (ISBN 0-88385-307-8). Math Assn.
--Great Moments in Mathematics Before 1650. LC 80-81046. (Dolciani Mathematical Exposition Ser.: No. 5). 1981. cloth 25.00 (ISBN 0-88385-305-1). Math Assn.
--An Introduction to the History of Mathematics. 5th ed. 1983. text ed. 39.95 (ISBN 0-03-062064-3, CBS C). SCP.
--Survey of Geometry. rev. ed. 1972. text ed. 42.14 (ISBN 0-205-03226-5, 5632269). Allyn.
Eves, Howard W. In Mathematical Circles, 2 Vols. 1969. Set. write for info. (ISBN 0-685-19591-0, PWS0671, Prindle); write for info. PWS Pubs.
--Mathematical Circles Adieu. 1977. write for info. (ISBN 0-87150-240-2, PWS 1941, Prindle). PWS Pubs.
--Mathematical Circles Revisited. (Illus.). 1971. text ed. write for info. (ISBN 0-87150-121-X, PWS0951, Prindle); text ed. write for info. (ISBN 0-685-04722-9). PWS Pubs.
--Mathematical Circles Squared. 186p. 1972. text ed. write for info. (ISBN 0-87150-154-6, PWS 1201, Prindle). PWS Pubs.
Eveson, J. W., jt. auth. see Lucas, R. D.
Evett, Arthur. Understanding the Space-Time Concepts of Special Relativity. 162p. 1982. 21.95x (ISBN 0-470-27333-X). Halsted Pr.
Evett, David. Strange Loops. (Cleveland Poets Ser.: No. 38). 63p. (Orig.). 1985. pap. 5.00 (ISBN 0-914946-47-1). Cleveland St Univ Poetry Ctr.
Evett, Elisa. The Critical Reception of Japanese Art in Late Nineteenth Century Europe. Foster, Stephen C., ed. LC 82-13702. (Studies in the Fine Arts: The Avant Garde: No. 36). 182p. 1982. 39.95 (ISBN 0-8357-1368-7). UMI Res Pr.
Evett, Jack & Pinckney, Richard P. FORTRAN Programming with Applications to Engineering: An Introductory FORTRAN Manual. LC 80-22695. 208p. 1981. pap. 10.95x (ISBN 0-910554-32-3). Engineering.
Evett, Jack, jt. auth. see Liu, Cheng.
Evett, Jack B. Surveying. LC 78-8332. 273p. 1979. text ed. 34.00x (ISBN 0-471-03132-1); tchrs' manual avail. (ISBN 0-471-04076-2). Wiley.
Evett, Jack B., tr. see Liu, Cheng.
Evett, Marianne B., ed. see Porter, Henry.
Evetts, Echo. China Mending: A Guide to Repairing & Restoration. (Illus.). 152p. 1978. 15.95 (ISBN 0-571-10822-9). Faber & Faber.
--China Mending: A Guide to Repairing & Restoration. rev. ed. LC 83-5519. (Illus.). 155p. 1983. pap. 7.95 (ISBN 0-571-13058-5). Faber & Faber.
Evey, Ethel L. Stowaway to Texas. 201p. (gr. 4-7). pap. 5.95 (ISBN 0-89896-101-7). Larksdale.
--Stowaway to Texas. Darst, Shelia S., ed. 201p. (Orig.). (gr. 4-7). 1982. 8.95 (ISBN 0-89896-102-5). Larksdale.
Evgrafov, M. A. Analytic Functions. 1978. pap. text ed. 7.50 (ISBN 0-486-63648-8). Dover.

--Asymptotic Estimates & Entire Functions. (Russian Tracts on the Physical Sciences Ser.). (Illus.). 192p. 1962. 49.95 (ISBN 0-677-20070-6). Gordon.

Evinger, William R., jt. auth. see D'Aleo, Richard J.

Evirviades, Marios L., jt. ed. see Kitromilides, Paschalis M.

Evison, Evera I., ed. Angles, Saxons, & Jutes: Essays Presented to J. N. L. Myres. (Illus.). 1981. 63.00x (ISBN 0-19-813402-9). Oxford U Pr.

Evison, Lilian, jt. ed. see James, A.

Evitt, William R. Sporopollenin Dinoflagellate Cysts: Their Morphology & Interpretation. LC 84-72457. (Illus.). 349p. 1985. 30.00 (ISBN 0-317-19725-8). Am Assn Strat.

Evitts, William J. Captive Bodies, Free Spirits: The Story of Southern Slavery. (Illus.). 160p. (gr. 5-9). 1985. 9.79 (ISBN 0-671-54094-7). Messner.

--A Matter of Allegiances: Maryland from 1850 T0 1861. LC 73-19336. (Studies in Historical & Political Science, 92nd Ser). (Illus.). 224p. 1974. 20.00x (ISBN 0-8018-1520-7). Johns Hopkins.

Evjen, Hal, ed. Mnemai: Classical Studies in Memory of Karl K. Hulley. LC 84-5362. (Scholars Press Homage Ser.). 1984. 26.95 (ISBN 0-89130-743-5, 00 16 05). Scholars Pr GA.

Evjen, John O. Scandinavian Immigrants in New York, 1630-1674. LC 76-39383. (Illus.). xxiv, 438p. 1972. Repr. of 1916 ed. 22.50 (ISBN 0-8063-0501-0). Genealog Pub.

Evler, R. C. & Gummerman, G. S., eds. Investigations of the Southwestern Anthropological Research Group: An Experiment in Archaeological Cooperation. (MNA Bulletin Ser.: No. 50). 1978. pap. 5.95 (ISBN 0-89734-018-3). Mus Northern Ariz.

Evliya, Efendi. Narrative of Travels in Europe, Asia & Africa in the 17th Century, 2 Vols. in 3. (Oriental Translation Fund Ser: No. 32). Repr. of 1834 ed. Set. 55.00 (ISBN 0-384-14895-6). Johnson Repr.

Evola, Julius. Metaphysics of Sex. Ormrod, J. A., tr. from Ital. LC 82-11909. (Illus.). 384p. 1983. pap. 9.95 (ISBN 0-89281-025-4). Inner Tradit.

--Metaphysics of Sex. 1982. 34.00x (ISBN 0-85692-053-3, Pub. by E-W Pubns England). State Mutual Bk.

Evola, Niccolo D. Origini e dottrina del fascismo. LC 79-180385. Repr. of 1935 ed. 20.00 (ISBN 0-404-56121-7). AMS Pr.

Evolutionary Biology Staff. Evolutionary Biology, Vol. 6, 1972. Vol. 1. pap. 113.80 (ISBN 0-317-26223-8); Vol. 6. pap. 81.50. Bks Demand UMI.

Evors, E. M. The Thoreau Calender. LC 73-563. 1973. lib. bdg. 15.00 (ISBN 0-8414-1503-X). Folcroft.

Evory, Ann, ed. Contemporary Authors New Revision Series, 13 vols. Incl. Vol. 1. 1980 (ISBN 0-8103-1930-6); Vol. 2. 1980 (ISBN 0-8103-1931-4); Vol. 3. 1981 (ISBN 0-8103-1932-2); Vol. 4. 1981 (ISBN 0-8103-1933-0); Vol. 5. 1982 (ISBN 0-8103-1934-9); Vol. 6. 1982 (ISBN 0-8103-1935-7); Vol. 7. 570p. 1982 (ISBN 0-8103-1936-5); Vol. 8. 600p. 1983 (ISBN 0-8103-1937-3); Vol. 9. 600p. 1983 (ISBN 0-8103-1938-1); Vol. 10. 600p. 1983 (ISBN 0-8103-1939-X); Vol. 11. 600p. 1984 (ISBN 0-8103-1940-3); Vol. 12. 600p. 1984 (ISBN 0-8103-1941-1); Vol. 13. 600p. 1984 (ISBN 0-8103-1942-X). LC 81-640179. 85.00x ea. Gale.

Evory, Ann, jt. ed. see Gareffa, Peter.

Evory, Ann, jt. ed. see Locher, Frances C.

Evoy, John J. The Rejected: Psychological Consequences of Parental Rejection. LC 81-47172. 272p. 1982. 24.95x (ISBN 0-271-00285-9). Pa St U Pr.

Evrard, jt. auth. see Nichols.

Evrard, Franklin H. Successful Parole. 140p. 1971. 14.00x (ISBN 0-398-00532-X). C C Thomas.

Evrard, Gwen. Homespun Crafts From Scraps. LC 82-18832. (Illus.). 168p. (Orig.). 1983. pap. 17.95 (ISBN 0-8329-0253-5). New Century.

Evrard-Blanquart, L. D. La Photographie. Bunnell, Peter C. & Sobieszk, Robert A., eds. LC 76-23042. (Sources of Modern Photography Ser.). 1979. Repr. of 1870 ed. lib. bdg. 14.00x (ISBN 0-405-09604-6). Ayer Co Pubs.

Evreino, Nikolai. Theatre in Life. LC 76-149211. 1927. 24.50 (ISBN 0-405-08492-7, Blom Pubns). Ayer Co Pubs.

Evreinov, Nikolai. Samoe Glavnoe. (Rus.). 1980. 13.00 (ISBN 0-88233-700-9); pap. 4.50 (ISBN 0-88233-701-7). Ardis Pubs.

Evrie, John H. Van see Van Evrie, John H.

Evslin, Bernard. Hercules. LC 83-23834. (Illus.). 160p. (gr. 5up). 1984. 9.75 (ISBN 0-688-02748-2). Morrow.

--Jason & the Argonauts. (Illus.). 176p. (gr. 5 up). 1986. 13.50 (ISBN 0-688-06245-8). Morrow.

Evslin, Bernard, et al. The Greek Gods. (Illus.). 120p. (gr. 7 up). 1984. pap. 2.25 (ISBN 0-590-33456-5, Point). Scholastic Inc.

--Heroes & Monsters of Greek Myth. (Illus.). 112p. (gr. 7 up). 1984. pap. 2.25 (ISBN 0-590-33457-3, Point). Scholastic Inc.

Evstigneev, J. V., jt. auth. see Arkin, V. I.

Evstyukhin, A. I., jt. ed. see Emel'yanova, V. S.

Evual, Thomas, jt. auth. see Cheffers, John T.

Evyatar, A. & Rosenbloom, P. Motivated Mathematics. LC 80-40491. (Illus.). 250p. 1981. 27.95 (ISBN 0-521-23308-9). Cambridge U Pr.

E.W. Beth Memorial Colloquium, Paris, 1964. Logic & Foundations of Science: Proceedings. Destouches, J. L., ed. 137p. 1967. lib. bdg. 21.00 (ISBN 90-277-0076-1, Pub. by Reidel Holland). Kluwer Academic.

EW Engineering Staff, ed. see Van Brunt, Leroy B.

Ewald. Diary of the American War. LC 79-623. 1979. 36.00x (ISBN 0-300-02153-4). Yale U Pr.

Ewald, Alex C. The Tatler. 478p. 1981. Repr. lib. bdg. 35.00 (ISBN 0-89760-206-4). Telegraph Bks.

Ewald, Alexander C. The Right Hon. Benjamin Disraeli, Earl of Beaconsfield, K. G. & His Times, 5. 150.00 (ISBN 0-8274-3283-6). R West.

--The Rt. Hon. Benjamin Disraeli, Earl of Beaconsfield, K. G. & His Times, 2 vols. 1979. Repr. of 1884 ed. Set. lib. bdg. 85.00 (ISBN 0-89987-200-X). Darby Bks.

Ewald, Carl. The Spider: And Other Stories by Carl Ewald. Le Gallienne, Eva, tr. from Danish. LC 79-8043. (Illus.). 96p. 1980. Crowell Jr Bks.

Ewald, Dan, jt. auth. see Anderson, Sparky.

Ewald, Ellen B. Recipes for a Small Planet. (Illus., Orig.). 1975. pap. 2.50 (ISBN 0-345-27430-X). Ballantine.

Ewald, Ellen B., jt. auth. see Lappe, Frances M.

Ewald, Hans. Acupressure Techniques: For the Self Treatment of Minor Ailments. 96p. (Orig.). 1984. pap. 4.95 (ISBN 0-7225-1114-0). Thorsons Pubs.

Ewald, Helen R. Writing As Process: Invention & Convention. 1983. 14.95 (ISBN 0-675-20014-8). Additional supplements may be obtained from publisher. Merrill.

Ewald, Robert B., ed. see Sherman, Anthony C.

Ewald, Wendy. Portraits & Dreams. (Illus.). 123p. 1985. 15.95 (ISBN 0-86316-087-5); pap. 8.95 (ISBN 0-86316-088-3). Writers & Readers.

Ewald, Wendy, ed. Appalachia: A Self-Portrait. LC 79-52385. 1979. pap. 8.95 (ISBN 0-917788-20-6). Gnomon Pr.

Ewald, William & Mandelker, Daniel. Street Graphics. 175p. 1977. Repr. 15.00 (ISBN 0-318-14686-X); 10.50 (ISBN 0-318-14687-8). Landscape Architecture.

Ewald, William B., Jr. Eisenhower the President: Crucial Days, 1951-1960. LC 80-22929. 420p. 1981. 12.95 (ISBN 0-13-246868-9). P-H.

--Rogues, Royalty & Reporters: The Age of Queen Anne Through Its Newspapers. LC 78-17410. 1978. Repr. of 1956 ed. lib. bdg. 22.75x (ISBN 0-313-20506-X, EWRR). Greenwood.

--Who Killed Joe McCarthy? 1984. 17.95 (ISBN 0-671-44946-X). S&S.

Ewald, William P. & Young, W. Arthur. Practical Optics. Roberts, Richard H., ed. (Illus.). 280p. 1983. pap. text ed. 45.00 (ISBN 0-911705-00-7). Image Makers.

Ewald, William R. One Hundred Short Films about the Human Environment. LC 82-1617. 157p. 1982. lib. bdg. 16.25 (ISBN 0-87436-338-1); pap. 6.75 (ISBN 0-87436-341-1). ABC-Clio.

Ewald, William R., ed. Environment & Policy: The Next Fifty Years. LC 68-27344. pap. 89.90 (ISBN 0-317-07768-6, 2017618). Bks Demand UMI.

Ewald, William R., Jr., ed. Environment for Man: The Next Fifty Years. LC 67-14215. (Midland Bks.: No. 102). (Illus.). Repr. of 1967 ed. 60.50 (ISBN 0-8357-9207-2, 2017619). Bks Demand UMI.

Ewalds, H. L. & Wanhill, R. J. Fracture Mechanics. 304p. 1984. pap. text ed. 24.50 (ISBN 0-7131-3515-8). E Arnold.

Ewalt, Norma. Decadent Dinners & Lascivious Lunches. 2nd ed. 240p. (Orig.). 1985. pap. 11.95 (ISBN 0-939650-43-6). Jende-Hagan Bk.

--Really Rotten Recipes. LC 84-72432. (Illus.). 48p. 1984. pap. 3.95 (ISBN 0-9609318-1-3). Clear Creek.

Ewalt, Norma & Huth, Tom. Decadent Dinners & Lascivious Lunches. LC 82-71880. (Illus.). 320p. 1982. 10.95 (ISBN 0-9609318-0-5). Clear Creek.

Ewalt, Patricia L., ed. Toward a Definition of Clinical Social Work. LC 80-81821. 104p. 1980. pap. 7.95x (ISBN 0-87101-086-0). Natl Assn Soc Wkrs.

Ewan, Christine & White, Ruth. Teaching Nursing: A Self-Instructional Handbook. LC 84-16980. 250p. (Orig.). 1984. pap. 15.00 (ISBN 0-7099-0936-5, Pub. by Croom Helm Ltd). Longwood Pub Group.

Ewan, Christine E., jt. ed. see Cox, Kenneth R.

Ewan, Dale & Heaton, Leroy. Physics for Technical Education. (Illus.). 720p. 1981. text ed. 29.95 (ISBN 0-13-674127-4). P-H.

Ewan, J. Introduction to the Reprint of Pursh's Flora Americae Septentrionalis. 118p. 1980. pap. text ed. 8.75 (ISBN 3-7682-1272-6). Lubrecht & Cramer.

Ewan, J. & Ewan, N. D. Biographical Dictionary of Rocky Mountain Naturalists. 1982. 42.00 (ISBN 90-313-0415-8, Pub. by Junk Pubs Netherlands). Kluwer Academic.

Ewan, Joseph. William Bartram: Botanical & Zoological Drawings, 1756-88. LC 68-8640. (Memoirs Ser.: Vol. 74). (Illus.). 1968. 50.00 (ISBN 0-87169-074-8). Am Philos.

Ewan, Joseph, ed. Short History of Botany in the United States. 174p. 1969. lib. bdg. 8.50 (ISBN 0-02-844360-8). Lubrecht & Cramert.

Ewan, N. D., jt. auth. see Ewan, J.

Ewans, Michael. Janacek's Tragic Operas. LC 77-93894. 288p. 1978. 22.50x (ISBN 0-253-37504-5). Ind U Pr.

--Wagner & Aeschylus: The "Ring" & The "Oresteia". LC 82-12762. 272p. 1983. 32.50 (ISBN 0-521-25073-0). Cambridge U Pr.

Ewans, Michael C. Haytor Granite Tramway & Stover Canal. LC 66-80. (Illus.). 1964. 9.95x (ISBN 0-678-05665-X). Kelley.

Eward, Ronald S. The Competition & Deregulation of International Telecommunications. 1985. text ed. 50.00 (ISBN 0-89006-158-0). Artech Hse.

--The Competition for Markets in International Telecommunications. 150p. 1984. text ed. 55.00 (ISBN 0-89006-149-1). Artech Hse.

Ewars, John, jt. auth. see Wildschut, William.

Ewart, Charles. The Healing Needles. LC 73-83953. 176p. 1973. pap. 1.25 (ISBN 0-87983-065-4). Keats.

Ewart, Ernest A. Rolling Road. facsimile ed. LC 73-110186. (Short Story Index Reprint Ser.). 1926. 18.00 (ISBN 0-8369-3337-0). Ayer Co Pubs.

Ewart, Frank J. The Phenomenon of Pentecost. 208p. (Orig.). 1947. pap. 4.95 (ISBN 0-912315-32-6). Word Aflame.

Ewart, Frank J., ed. Jesus: The Man & Mystery. 160p. 1973. Repr. of 1941 ed. 3.95 (ISBN 0-912315-47-4). Word Aflame.

Ewart, Gavin. The Gavin Ewart Show. 1971. 7.00 (ISBN 0-685-27780-1, Pub. by Trigram Pr); signed 15.00 (ISBN 0-685-27781-X); pap. 4.00 (ISBN 0-685-27782-8). Small Pr Dist.

Ewart, Gavin, ed. Penguin Book of Light Verse. 1982. pap. 6.95 (ISBN 0-14-042270-6). Penguin.

Ewart, John S. Roots & Causes of the War, Nineteen Fourteen-Nineteen Eighteen, 2 vols. 200.00 (ISBN 0-8490-0972-3). Gordon Pr.

Ewart, Neil. Everyday Phrases: Their Origins & Meanings. 162p. 1985. 9.95 (ISBN 0-7137-1354-2, Pub by Blanford). Sterling.

Ewart, Neil & O'Connell, Nina. The Lore of Flowers. 192p. 1983. 19.95 (ISBN 0-7137-1176-0, Pub. by Blandford Pr England). Sterling.

Ewart, Neil, ed. The Writer & the Reader: A Book of Literary Quotations. 160p. 1985. 12.95 (ISBN 0-7137-1403-4, Pub by Blandford). Sterling.

Ewart, Park J., et al. Applied Managerial Statistics. (Illus.). 688p. 1982. 30.95 (ISBN 0-13-041335-6). P-H.

--Probability for Statistical Decision Making. (Illus.). 400p. 1974. ref. ed. 28.95 (ISBN 0-13-711614-4). P-H.

Ewart, W., jt. auth. see Norris, G.

Ewban, Kay, et al. BBC Micro Gamemaster. (Illus.). 159p. (Orig.). 1984. pap. 11.95 (ISBN 0-246-12581-0, Pub. by Granada England). Sheridan.

Ewbank, Henry L., jt. auth. see Auer, J. Jeffery.

Ewbank, Inga-Stina. A Midsummer Night's Dream. 1985. lib. bdg. 27.00 (ISBN 0-8240-9027-6). Garland Pub.

Ewbank, Kay & James, Mike. The Spectrum Gamesmaster. (Illus.). 160p. (Orig.). 1984. pap. 13.95 (ISBN 0-246-12515-2, Pub. by Granada England). Sheridan.

Ewbank, Kay, et al. Electron Gamemaster. (Illus.). 162p. (Orig.). 1984. pap. 11.95 (ISBN 0-246-12514-4, Pub. by Granada England). Sheridan.

Ewbank, Thomas. A Descriptive & Historical Account of Hydraulic & Other Machines for Raising Water, Ancient & Modern. LC 72-5048. (Technology & Society Ser.). 598p. 1972. Repr. of 1842 ed. 33.00 (ISBN 0-405-04700-2). Ayer Co Pubs.

Ewbank, Weeb, jt. auth. see Broeg, R.

Ewbank, William W. The Poems of Cicero. Commager, Steele, ed. LC 77-70814. (Latin Poetry Ser.). 1978. lib. bdg. 34.00 (ISBN 0-8240-2955-0). Garland Pub.

Ewe, K., jt. auth. see Otto, P.

Ewedemi, Soga, jt. auth. see Nelli, Humbert O.

Ewegen, Robert, jt. auth. see Johnson, Byron.

Ewegen, Robert, jt. auth. see Johnson, Byron L.

Ewell, Barbara C. Kate Chopin. (Literature & Life Ser.). 180p. 1985. 13.95 (ISBN 0-8044-2190-0). Ungar.

Ewell, George W. Radar Transmitters: Systems, Modulators & Devices. (Illus.). 300p. 1982. 32.50 (ISBN 0-07-019843-8). McGraw.

Ewell, Judith. Indictment of a Dictator: The Extradition & Trial of Marcos Perez Jimenez. LC 81-40475. 216p. 1981. 20.50x (ISBN 0-89096-109-3). Tex A&M Univ Pr.

--Venezuela: A Century of Change. LC 83-40093. 272p. 1984. 22.50x (ISBN 0-8047-1213-1). Stanford U Pr.

Ewell, Marshall D. A Manual of Medical Jurisprudence for the Use of Students at Law & of Medicine. viii, 409p. 1981. Repr. of 1887 ed. lib. bdg. 30.00x (ISBN 0-8377-0542-8). Rothman.

Ewell, Peter T. & Poleman, Thomas T. Uxpanapa: Agricultural Development in the Mexican Tropics. LC 80-12208. (Pergamon Policy Studies). 220p. 1980. 30.00 (ISBN 0-08-025967-7). Pergamon.

Ewen & Nelson. Elementary Technical Mathematics. 3rd ed. 546p. write for info. (ISBN 0-534-02861-6). Watts.

Ewen, Alfred. Bell's Miniature Series of Great Writers: Shakespeare. 128p. 1980. Repr. of 1904 ed. lib. bdg. 20.00 (ISBN 0-89984-178-3). Century Bookbindery.

--Shakespeare. 1904. lib. bdg. 20.00 (ISBN 0-8482-9953-1). Norwood Edns.

--Shakespeare. 126p. Date not set. Repr. of 1904 ed. lib. bdg. 20.00 (ISBN 0-8495-1433-9). Arden Lib.

Ewen, C. L'Estrange. Lotteries & Sweepstakes. LC 72-80143. (Illus.). 1973. Repr. of 1932 ed. lib. bdg. 24.50 (ISBN 0-405-08493-5). Ayer Co Pubs.

Ewen, Cecil. A Guide to the Origin of British Surnames. 59.95 (ISBN 0-8490-0273-7). Gordon Pr.

--A History of Surnames of the British Isles. 59.95 (ISBN 0-8490-0349-0). Gordon Pr.

Ewen, Cecil H. Guide to the Origin of British Surnames. LC 68-30596. 1969. Repr. of 1938 ed. 34.00x (ISBN 0-8103-3123-3). Gale.

--History of Surnames of the British Isles: A Concise Account of Their Origin, Evolution, Etymology & Legal Status. LC 68-30597. 1968. Repr. of 1931 ed. 43.00x (ISBN 0-8103-3124-1). Gale.

--Witchcraft & Demonianism. LC 79-8631. (Illus.). Repr. of 1933 ed. 48.50 (ISBN 0-404-18410-3). AMS Pr.

Ewen, Dale & Akers, Lynn R. Trigonometry with Applications. (Illus.). 384p. 1984. 24.95 (ISBN 0-201-11312-0); instr's manual 2.00 (ISBN 0-201-11314-7). Addison-Wesley.

Ewen, Dale & Schurter, Neil. Physics for Career Education. 2nd ed. (Illus.). 448p. 1982. 27.95 (ISBN 0-13-672329-2). P-H.

Ewen, Dale & Topper, Michael A. Mathematics for Technical Education. 2nd ed. (Illus.). 496p. 1983. text ed. 27.95 (ISBN 0-13-565168-9). P-H.

--Technical Calculus. (Illus.). 1977. 29.95 (ISBN 0-13-898122-1). P-H.

--Technical Calculus. 2nd ed. (Illus.). 656p. 1986. text ed. 29.95 (ISBN 0-13-898164-7). P-H.

Ewen, David. All the Years of American Popular Music. LC 77-6733. 1977. 24.95 (ISBN 0-13-022442-1). P-H.

--The Book of European Light Opera. LC 77-1795. 1977. Repr. of 1962 ed. lib. bdg. 34.50x (ISBN 0-8371-9520-9, EWBE). Greenwood.

--Composers of Tomorrow's Music: A Non-Technical Introduction to the Musical Avant-Garde Movement. LC 79-18514. (Illus.). 1980. Repr. of 1971 ed. lib. bdg. 24.75x (ISBN 0-313-22107-3, EWCT). Greenwood.

--Composers of Yesterday: A Biographical & Critical Guide. LC 73-181150. 488p. 1937. Repr. 59.00 (ISBN 0-403-01551-0). Scholarly.

--Dictators of the Baton. LC 77-92507. (Essay Index in Reprint Ser.). (Illus.). 1978. Repr. 28.50x (ISBN 0-8486-3002-5). Core Collection.

--George Gershwin: His Journey to Greatness. LC 77-6821. (Illus.). 1977. Repr. of 1970 ed. lib. bdg. 25.00x (ISBN 0-8371-9663-9, EWGG). Greenwood.

--Man with the Baton. facs. ed. LC 68-57316. (Essay Index Reprint Ser). 1936. 19.50 (ISBN 0-8369-0433-8). Ayer Co Pubs.

--Men of Popular Music. LC 72-6818. (Essay Index Reprint Ser). 1972. Repr. of 1944 ed. 21.00 (ISBN 0-8369-7263-5). Ayer Co Pubs.

--Men of Popular Music. (Essay Index Reprint Ser.). 215p. 1982. Repr. of 1944 ed. lib. bdg. 18.00 (ISBN 0-8290-0811-X). Irvington.

--Pioneers in Music. LC 72-6816. (Essay Index Reprint Ser). 1972. Repr. of 1940 ed. 27.50 (ISBN 0-8369-7262-7). Ayer Co Pubs.

--Twentieth Century Composers. facs. ed. LC 68-16930. (Essay Index Reprint Ser). 1937. 22.00 (ISBN 0-8369-0434-6). Ayer Co Pubs.

--World of Twentieth Century Music. LC 68-11358. 1968. 19.95 (ISBN 0-13-968776-9). P-H.

Ewen, David, jt. auth. see Cross, Milton.

Ewen, David, ed. American Popular Songs from the Revolutionary War to the Present. 1966. 19.95 (ISBN 0-394-41705-4). Random.

Ewen, David, compiled by. Composers since Nineteen Hundred. LC 72-102368. (Illus.). 639p. 1969. 28.00 (ISBN 0-8242-0400-X). Wilson.

Ewen, David, ed. From Bach to Stravinsky: The History of Music by Its Foremost Critics. LC 79-124770. Repr. of 1933 ed. 12.50 (ISBN 0-404-02359-2). AMS Pr.

--From Bach to Stravinsky: The History of Music by Its Foremost Critics. LC 68-54419. (Illus.). 1968. Repr. of 1933 ed. lib. bdg. 16.25x (ISBN 0-8371-0411-4, EWBS). Greenwood.

Ewen, David, compiled by. Great Composers: Thirteen Hundred-Nineteen Hundred. LC 65-24585. (Illus.). 429p. 1983. 23.00 (ISBN 0-8242-0018-7). Wilson.

Ewen, David, ed. Musicians Since Nineteen Hundred. LC 78-12727. 970p. 1978. 50.00 (ISBN 0-8242-0565-0). Wilson.

Ewen, David, compiled by. Popular American Composers. LC 62-9024. (Illus.). 217p. 1962. 12.00 (ISBN 0-8242-0040-3). Wilson.

--Popular American Composers: First Supplement. LC 62-9024. (Illus.). 121p. 1972. 9.00 (ISBN 0-8242-0436-0). Wilson.

Ewen, David, ed. Songs of America: A Cavalcade of Popular Songs with Commentaries. LC 77-26155. (Illus.). 1978. Repr. of 1947 ed. lib. bdg. 29.75 (ISBN 0-313-20166-8, EWSA). Greenwood.

Ewen, Doris & Ewen, Mary. An ABC of Children's Names. LC 84-144939. (Illus.). 30p. (ps-4). 1983. 7.95 (ISBN 0-914676-41-5, Star & Elephant Bks.). Green Tiger Pr.

Ewen, Elizabeth. Immigrant Women in the Land of Dollars: Life & Culture on the Lower East Side. 320p. 1985. 26.00 (ISBN 0-85345-681-X); pap. 11.00 (ISBN 0-85345-682-8). Monthly Rev.

Ewen, Elizabeth, jt. auth. see Ewen, Stuart.

Ewen, Frederic. Bertolt Brecht: His Life, His Art, & His Times. 1969. pap. 5.95 (ISBN 0-8065-0194-4). Citadel Pr.

--Bibliography of Eighteenth Century English Literature. LC 68-25310. (Reference Ser., No. 44). 1969. Repr. of 1935 ed. lib. bdg. 40.95x (ISBN 0-8383-0937-2). Haskell.

--Heinrich Heine Self-Portrait & Other Prose Writings. Ewen, Frederic, tr. 550p. 1974. pap. 5.95 (ISBN 0-8065-0452-8). Citadel Pr.

--Heroic Imagination. 768p. 1984. 24.95 (ISBN 0-8065-0895-7). Citadel Pr.

--Prestige of Schiller in England, 1788-1859. Repr. of 1932 ed. 22.50 (ISBN 0-404-02364-9). AMS Pr.

Ewen, Frederic, ed. The Poetry of Heinrich Heine. 320p. 1983. pap. 5.95 (ISBN 0-8065-0076-X). Citadel Pr.

Ewen, Lynda A. Which Side Are You On? The Brookside Mine Strike in Harlan County, Kentucky, 1973-74. (Illus.). 139p. (Orig.). 1979. pap. 5.95 (ISBN 0-917702-09-3). Vanguard Bks.

Ewen, Lynda Ann. Corporate Power & Urban Crisis in Detroit. LC 77-71981. 1978. 35.00 (ISBN 0-691-09373-3). Princeton U Pr.

Ewen, Mary, jt. auth. see Ewen, Doris.

Ewen, R. Opening Leads. LC 73-83447. 1969. pap. 4.95 (ISBN 0-13-637363-1). P-H.

Ewen, Robert. Defensive Bidding Quiz Book. 105p. (Orig.). 1980. pap. 5.95 (ISBN 0-87643-039-6). M Lisa Precision.

--Defensive Bidding Quiz Book. 105p. 1980. 5.95 (ISBN 0-87643-039-6). Barclay Bridge.

--An Introduction to Theories of Personality. 2nd ed. 1985. text ed. 22.25i (ISBN 0-12-245156-2); instr's manual 5.00i (ISBN 0-12-245157-0). Acad Pr.

Ewen, Robert B., ed. see Wei, C. C.

Ewen, Sol J. & Glickstein, Cyrus. Ultrasonic Therapy in Periodontics. (Illus.). 144p. 1968. photocopy ed. 15.50x (ISBN 0-398-00535-4). C C Thomas.

Ewen, Stuart. Captains of Consciousness. LC 75-34432. 1976. pap. 5.95 (ISBN 0-07-019846-2). McGraw.

Ewen, Stuart & Ewen, Elizabeth. Channels of Desire: Mass Images & the Shaping of American Consciousness. 320p. 1982. 12.95 (ISBN 0-07-019850-0); pap. 7.95 (ISBN 0-07-019848-9). McGraw.

Ewens, Jim & Herrington, Pat. The Hospice Handbook. LC 82-73364. (Illus.). 242p. (Orig.). 1982. pap. 8.95 (ISBN 0-939680-10-6). Bear & Co.

Ewens, W. J. Mathematical Population Genetics. LC 79-18938. (Biomathematics Ser.: Vol. 9). (Illus.). 1979. 38.00 (ISBN 0-387-09577-2). Springer-Verlag.

Ewens, W. V., jt. ed. see Ebling, F. J.

Ewens, William L. Becoming Free: The Struggle for Human Development. LC 84-13872. 328p. 1984. 30.00 (ISBN 0-8420-2208-2); pap. text ed. 9.95 (ISBN 0-8420-2233-3). Scholarly Res Inc.

Ewenstein, Neal, jt. auth. see Wade, Alex.

Ewer, Bernard C. Applied Psychology. Repr. of 1923 ed. 20.00 (ISBN 0-89987-051-1). Darby Bks.

Ewer, J. R. & Latorre, G. A Course in Basic Scientific English. (English As a Second Language Bk.). 199p. 1969. pap. text ed. 6.95x (ISBN 0-582-52009-6); teacher's bk. 3.95x (ISBN 0-582-52059-2). Longman.

Ewer, Mary A., tr. see Arsen'ev, Nicolai S.

Ewer, Michael S., jt. auth. see Ali, M. Khalil.

Ewer, R. F. Ethology of Mammals. LC 68-21946. 416p. 1969. 37.50x (ISBN 0-306-30382-5, Plenum Pr). Plenum Pub.

Ewer, T. K. Practical Animal Husbandry. (Illus.). 272p. 1982. text ed. 26.00 (ISBN 0-7236-0635-8). PSG Pub Co.

Ewerbeck, H. Differential Diagnosis in Pediatrics. 470p. 1980. spiral bdg. 25.00 (ISBN 0-387-90474-3). Springer-Verlag.

Ewers, Carolyn. Long Journey: A Biography of Sidney Poitier. (Illus.). 1981. pap. 1.95 (ISBN 0-451-09732-7, Sig). NAL.

Ewers, Hanns H. Alraune. Reginald, R. & Menville, Douglas, eds. Endore, S. Guy, tr. LC 75-46269. (Supernatural & Occult Fiction Ser.). 1976. lib. bdg. 25.50x (ISBN 0-405-08130-8). Ayer Co Pubs.

--Edgar Allan Poe. 55p. 1980. Repr. of 1917 ed. lib. bdg. 10.00 (ISBN 0-8495-1347-2). Arden Lib.

--Edgar Allan Poe. LC 72-13659. 1973. Repr. of 1917 ed. lib. bdg. 12.50 (ISBN 0-8414-1225-1). Folcroft.

Ewers, John C. Blackfeet: Raiders on the Northwestern Plains. LC 58-7778. (Civilization of the American Indian Ser.: No. 49). (Illus.). 1976. Repr. of 1958 ed. 22.95 (ISBN 0-8061-0405-8). U of Okla Pr.

--The Blackfeet: Raiders on the Northwestern Plains. LC 58-7778. (The Civilization of the American Indian Ser.: Vol. 49). (Illus.). 377p. 1983. pap. 12.95 (ISBN 0-8061-1836-9). U of Okla Pr.

--Blackfeet: Their History. (Illus.). 96p. Date not set. pap. 6.95 (ISBN 0-88839-170-6). Hancock House.

--The Horse in Blackfoot Indian Culture. LC 55-60591. (Classics in Smithsonian Anthropology Ser.: No. 3). (Illus.). 374p. 1980. pap. text ed. 15.00x (ISBN 0-87474-419-9). Smithsonian.

--The Horse in Blackfoot Indian Culture with Comparative Material from Other Western Tribes. Repr. of 1955 ed. 59.00x (ISBN 0-403-03606-2). Scholarly.

--Indian Life on the Upper Missouri. (Civilization of the American Indian Ser.: No. 89). (Illus.). 1968. 15.95 (ISBN 0-8061-0777-4). U of Okla Pr.

--Plains Indian Painting: A Description of Aboriginal American Art. LC 76-43701. Repr. of 1939 ed. 24.50 (ISBN 0-404-15533-2). AMS Pr.

Ewers, John C., ed. Indian Art in Pipestone: George Catlin's Portfolio in the British Museum. LC 78-2974. (Illus.). 80p. 1979. 15.00x (ISBN 0-87474-420-2). Smithsonian.

Ewers, John C., ed. see Denig, Edwin T.

Ewers, John C., ed. see Wildschut, William.

Ewers, John C., et al. Early White Influence upon Plains Indian Painting. (Shorey Indian Ser.). (Illus.). 25p. Repr. of 1957 ed. pap. 3.95 (ISBN 0-8466-4031-7, I31). Shorey.

--Views of a Vanishing Frontier. (Illus.). 150p. (Orig.). 1984. 29.95 (ISBN 0-936364-12-2); pap. 14.95 (ISBN 0-936364-13-0). Joslyn Art.

--Views of a Vanishing Frontier. LC 83-25558. (Illus.). 103p. 1984. 29.95 (ISBN 0-936364-12-2). U of Nebr Pr.

Ewert, Alan. Outdoor Adventure & Self Concept: A Research Analysis. 42p. 1983. pap. 5.00 (ISBN 0-943272-17-3). Inst Recreation Res.

Ewert, Alfred. The French Language. 2nd ed. (Great Language Ser.). 1943. text ed. 12.00x (ISBN 0-571-07019-1). Humanities.

Ewert, Charles. Canaan. 272p. 1984. pap. 3.75 (ISBN 0-380-88039-3). Avon.

--No Man's Brother. 320p. (Orig.). 1984. pap. 3.95 (ISBN 0-380-86215-8, 86215). Avon.

Ewert, Christian. Islamische Funde in Balaguer und die Aljaferia in Zaragoza. (Madrider Forschungen, Vol. 7). (Illus.). 281p. 1971. 96.00 (ISBN 3-11-003613-4). De Gruyter.

--Spanisch-Islamische Systeme Sich Kreuzender Boegen. (Madrider Forschungen Ser: Vol. 12, Pt. 1). 1978. 180.00x (ISBN 3-11-006967-9). De Gruyter.

Ewert, David. And Then Comes the End. LC 79-28410. 216p. 1980. pap. 6.95 (ISBN 0-8361-1921-5). Herald Pr.

--Called to Teach. 242p. 1980. pap. 5.95 (ISBN 0-317-31428-9). Herald Pr.

--The Holy Spirit in the New Testament. LC 82-95089. 336p. 1983. pap. 11.95 (ISBN 0-8361-3309-9). Herald Hse.

Ewert, F. K. Rock Grouting. (Illus.). 420p. 1985. 65.00 (ISBN 0-387-15252-0). Springer-Verlag.

Ewert, J. P. Neuroethology. (Illus.). 1980. pap. 27.50 (ISBN 0-387-09790-2). Springer-Verlag.

Ewert, Jorg-Peter, et al, eds. Advances in Vertebrate Neuroethology. (NATO ASI Series No. A, Life Sciences: Vol. 56). 1256p. 1983. 150.00x (ISBN 0-306-41197-0, Plenum Pr). Plenum Pub.

Ewett, David. And Then Comes the End. LC 79-28416. 216p. 1980. pap. 6.95. Herald Hse.

Ewin, R. E. Cooperation & Human Values: A Study of Moral Reasoning. 1981. 22.50 (ISBN 0-312-16956-6). St Martin.

Ewin, Wilson. You Can Lead Roman Catholics to Christ. 171p. pap. 4.00. Bible Baptist.

Ewing, A. C. The Fundamental Questions of Philosophy. 260p. 1985. pap. 8.95x (ISBN 0-7100-0586-5). Routledge & Kegan.

--Hearing Aids, Lip Reading & Clear Speech. 128p. 1967. text ed. 10.95 (ISBN 0-7190-0315-6, Pub. by Manchester Univ Pr). Longwood Pub Group.

--Value & Reality: Philosophical Case for Theism. (Muirhead Library of Philosophy). 1973. text ed. 29.00x (ISBN 0-391-00285-6). Humanities.

Ewing, A. F. Industrie en Afrique. Calvet, Francoise, tr. from Eng. (Recherches Africaines: No. 8). 1970. pap. 14.40x (ISBN 90-2796-443-2). Mouton.

Ewing, A. W., jt. auth. see Ewing, I. R.

Ewing, Agnew R. Gardening from Ignorance to Bliss. 96p. 1984. 11.95 (ISBN 0-533-05783-3). Vantage.

Ewing, Alfred C. The Definition of Good. LC 78-59021. 1979. Repr. of 1947 ed. 20.25 (ISBN 0-88355-695-2). Hyperion Conn.

--Ethics. 1965. pap. text ed. 9.95 (ISBN 0-02-910030-5). Free Pr.

--Morality of Punishment. LC 70-108233. (Criminology, Law Enforcement, & Social Problems Ser.: No. 116). (With new intro. added). 1970. Repr. of 1929 ed. 20.00x (ISBN 0-87585-116-9). Patterson Smith.

--Short Commentary on Kant's Critique of Pure Reason. 2nd ed. LC 39-13499. 1967. pap. 9.00x (ISBN 0-226-22778-2, P265, Phoen). U of Chicago Pr.

Ewing, C. S., jt. auth. see Penn, Audrey.

Ewing, C. W., jt. auth. see Vassos, B. H.

Ewing, Channing L., et al. Impact Injury of the Head & Spine. (Illus.). 678p. 1983. 88.50x (ISBN 0-398-04702-2). C C Thomas.

Ewing, Charles. Yesterday's Washington, D. C. LC 76-10376. (Historic Cities Ser: No. 24). (Illus.). 160p. 1976. 9.95 (ISBN 0-912458-68-2). E A Seemann.

Ewing, Charles P. Crisis Intervention As Psychotherapy. 1978. pap. 9.95x (ISBN 0-19-502271-8). Oxford U Pr.

Ewing, Charles P., ed. Psychology, Psychiatry & the Law: A Clinical & Forensic Handbook. LC 85-60449. 576p. 1985. text ed. 39.95 (ISBN 0-943158-11-7). Pro Resource.

Ewing, Cortez A. Congressional Elections, Eighteen Ninety-Six to Nineteen Forty-Four. LC 84-19825. xiii, 110p. 1984. Repr. of 1947 ed. lib. bdg. 25.00x (ISBN 0-313-24681-5, EWCE). Greenwood.

--Presidential Elections from Abraham Lincoln to Franklin D. Roosevelt. LC 70-142857. (Illus.). 226p. 1972. Repr. of 1940 ed. lib. bdg. 22.50x (ISBN 0-8371-5956-3, EWPE). Greenwood.

--Primary Elections in the South: A Study in Uniparty Politics. LC 80-12616. (Illus.). xii, 112p. 1980. Repr. of 1953 ed. lib. bdg. 19.75x (ISBN 0-313-22452-8, EWPR). Greenwood.

Ewing, Cortez A. & Dangerfield, Royden J. Documentary Source Book in American Government & Politics. LC 73-19144. (Politics & People Ser.). 844p. 1974. Repr. 57.50x (ISBN 0-405-05868-3). Ayer Co Pubs.

Ewing, David. Using 1-2-3 Workbook & Disk. (One-Two-Three Ser.). 250p. 1984. 29.95 (ISBN 0-88022-075-9, 142). Que Corp.

Ewing, David & LeBlond, Geoffrey. Using Symphony. LC 84-60645. (Symphony Ser.). 700p. 1984. pap. 19.95 (ISBN 0-88022-124-0, 141). Que Corp.

Ewing, David P. One-Two-Three Macro Library. LC 84-62755. (One-Two-Three Ser.). 250p. 1985. pap. 19.95 (ISBN 0-88022-147-X, 174); IBM Format. disk 79.90 (245). Que Corp.

Ewing, David W. Do it My Way or You're Fired! Employee Rights & the Changing Role of Management Prerogatives. (Wiley Management Series on Problem Solving, Decision Making & Strategic Thinking: I-578). 387p. 1983. 19.50 (ISBN 0-471-86843-4, Pub. by Wiley-Interscience). Wiley.

--Freedom Inside the Organization: Bringing Civil Liberties to the Workplace. 1978. pap. 4.95 (ISBN 0-07-019847-0). McGraw.

--Writing for Results in Business, Government, the Sciences & the Professions. 2nd ed. LC 79-11756. 448p. 1979. 32.50 (ISBN 0-471-05036-9). Wiley.

--Writing for Results: In Business, Government, the Sciences & the Professions. 2nd ed. 464p. 1985. pap. 14.95 (ISBN 0-471-82590-5). Wiley.

Ewing, David W., ed. Science Policy & Business: The Changing Relations of Europe & the United States. LC 72-86387. 140p. 1973. 8.95x (ISBN 0-674-79460-5, Pub. by Harvard Busn. School). Harvard U Pr.

--Technological Change & Management. LC 78-125645. 1970. 10.00x (ISBN 0-674-87230-4, Pub. by Harvard Busn. School). Harvard U Pr.

Ewing, Elizabeth. Fur in Dress. (Illus.). 192p. 1981. 32.00 (ISBN 0-7134-1741-2, Pub. by Batsford England). David & Charles.

--Women in Uniform Through the Centuries. (Illus.). 160p. 1975. 19.50x (ISBN 0-87471-690-X). Rowman.

Ewing, Fayette C. Hamlet: An Analytic & Psychologic Study. 1978. Repr. of 1934 ed. lib. bdg. 10.00 (ISBN 0-8495-1311-1). Arden Lib.

--Hamlet: An Analytic & Psychologic Study. LC 72-6574. Repr. of 1934 ed. lib. bdg. 8.50 (ISBN 0-8414-0129-2). Folcroft.

Ewing, G. Instrumental Methods of Chemical Analysis. 5th ed. LC 84-12209. 608p. 1984. 42.00 (ISBN 0-07-019857-8). McGraw.

Ewing, Galen & Ashworth, Harry A., eds. The Laboratory Recorder. LC 74-22364. 129p. 1974. 35.00x (ISBN 0-306-35301-6, Plenum Pr). Plenum Pub.

Ewing, Galen W. Analytical Instrumentation: A Laboratory Guide for Chemical Analysis. LC 66-5557. (Illus.). pap. 42.80 (ISBN 0-317-09110-7, 2019392). Bks Demand UMI.

Ewing, Galen W., jt. auth. see Vassos, Basil H.

Ewing, Galen W., ed. Environmental Analysis. 1977. 55.00 (ISBN 0-12-245250-X). Acad Pr.

Ewing, Galen W., jt. ed. see Simmons, Ivor L.

Ewing, George M. Calculus of Variations with Applications. (Mathematics Ser.). 352p. 1985. pap. 8.50 (ISBN 0-486-64856-7). Dover.

--Living on a Shoestring: A Scrounge Manual for the Hobbyist. (Illus.). 1983. pap. 7.97 (ISBN 0-88006-059-X, BK7393). Green Pub Inc.

Ewing, George W. The Well-Tempered Lyre: Songs & Verse of the Temperance Movement. LC 77-8523. (Bicentennial Series in American Studies: No. 5). 1977. 16.95 (ISBN 0-87074-000-8). SMU Press.

Ewing, Gerald W., jt. auth. see Silber, Kenneth H.

Ewing, H. E; see Miller, G. S., Jr.

Ewing, H. Griffin. Innovative Corporate & Executive Strategy: Understanding & Meeting Financial Challenges. LC 80-25687. (Illus.). 256p. 1981. 23.95x (ISBN 0-88229-545-4). Nelson-Hall.

Ewing, Henry E. Manual of External Parasites. (Illus.). 226p. 1929. photocopy ed. 22.50x (ISBN 0-398-04253-5). C C Thomas.

Ewing, I. R. & Ewing, A. W. The Handicap of Deafness. 323p. 1980. Repr. lib. bdg. 45.00 (ISBN 0-89984-175-9). Century Bookbindery.

Ewing, J. Franklin. Hyperbrachycephaly As Influenced by Cultural Conditioning. (Harvard University Peabody Museum of Archaeology & Ethnology Papers). pap. 16.00 (ISBN 0-527-01257-2). Kraus Repr.

Ewing, James M., jt. auth. see Young, James B.

Ewing, John & Kosniowski, Czes. Puzzle It Out: Cubes, Groups & Puzzles. 64p. 1982. pap. 4.95 (ISBN 0-521-28924-6). Cambridge U Pr.

Ewing, John A. Drinking: Alcohol in American Society - Issues & Current Research. Rouse, Beatrice A., ed. 443p. 1978. 19.95 (ISBN 0-318-15319-X); pap. 8.95 (ISBN 0-318-15320-3). Natl Coun Alcoholism.

Ewing, John A. & Rouse, Beatrice A., eds. Drinking: Alcohol in American Society - Issues & Current Research. LC 76-47522. 456p. 1978. 26.95x (ISBN 0-88229-129-7); pap. text ed. 13.95x (ISBN 0-88229-569-1). Nelson-Hall.

Ewing, John I. & Rabinowitz, Philip D. Ocean Margin Drilling Program Atlases, Vol. 4. (Regional Atlas Ser.). 1984. write for info. (ISBN 0-86720-254-8, Marine Sci Intl). Jones & Bartlett.

Ewing, John S. & Norton, N. P. Broadlooms & Businessmen: A History of the Bigelow-Sanford Carpet Company. LC 54-12236. (Studies in Business History: No. 17). (Illus.). 1955. 30.00x (ISBN 0-674-08350-4). Harvard U Pr.

Ewing, Joseph E. Fixed Partial Prosthesis. 2nd, rev. ed. LC 59-14308. pap. 72.00 (ISBN 0-317-28605-6, 2055423). Bks Demand UMI.

Ewing, Kathleen M. A. Aubrey Bodine, Baltimore Pictorialist, 1906-1970. LC 85-45042. (Illus.). 104p. 1985. 29.95 (ISBN 0-8018-3151-2). Johns Hopkins.

Ewing, Kathryn. A Private Matter. LC 74-23673. (gr. 4-8). 1975. 7.95 (ISBN 0-15-263576-9, HJ). HarBraceJ.

--Things Won't Be the Same. LC 80-7982. (gr. 4-6). 1980. 8.95 (ISBN 0-15-285663-3, HJ). HarBraceJ.

Ewing, Kenneth D. Trade Unions, the Labor Party, & the Law. 249p. 1983. 34.00x (ISBN 0-686-83097-0, Pub. by Edinburgh U Pr Scotland). Columbia U Pr.

Ewing, Kristine L. Care & Maintenance of Paper Machine Clothing. LC 76-53915. (Bibliographic Ser.: No. 274). 1977. pap. 12.00 (ISBN 0-87010-048-3). Inst Paper Chem.

--Mill Maintenance I: General Mill Maintenance, Fires & Explosions. LC 78-387. (Bibliographic Ser.: No. 280). 1978. pap. 30.00 (ISBN 0-87010-030-0). Inst Paper Chem.

--Mill Maintenance II: Large Machinery. LC 78-387. (Bibliographic Ser.: No. 281). 1978. pap. 13.00 (ISBN 0-87010-031-9). Inst Paper Chem.

--Mill Maintenance III: Instruments & Small Equipment. LC 78-387. (Bibliographic Ser.: No. 282). 1978. pap. 13.00 (ISBN 0-87010-032-7). Inst Paper Chem.

Ewing, Lucie L. George Frederick Watts, Sandro Botticelli, Matthew Arnold. LC 73-8983. Repr. of 1904 ed. lib. bdg. 15.00 (ISBN 0-8414-1910-8). Folcroft.

Ewing, Lucy E. George Frederick Watts, Sandro Botticelli, Matthew Arnold. 64p. 1980. Repr. of 1904 ed. lib. bdg. 15.00 (ISBN 0-8495-1344-8). Arden Lib.

Ewing, Majl, jt. ed. see MacIntyre, C. F.

Ewing, Margaret K., tr. see Cendrars, Blaise.

Ewing, Neil. Games, Stunts, & Exercises: A Physical Education Handbook for Elementary School Teachers. 1964. pap. 3.95 (ISBN 0-8224-3275-7). Pitman Learning.

Ewing, R. E., ed. The Mathematics of Reservoir Simulation. LC 83-51501. (Frontiers in Applied Mathematics: No. 1). (Illus.). xii, 186p. 1984. text ed. 24.50 (ISBN 0-89871-192-4). Soc Indus-Appl Math.

Ewing, Russ, jt. auth. see Cahill, Tim.

Ewing, Russell C., ed. Six Faces of Mexico: History, People, Geography, Government, Economy, Literature & Art. LC 66-18533. pap. 80.00 (ISBN 0-317-28563-7, 2055251). Bks Demand UMI.

Ewing, S. A Guide to over One Thousand Things You Can Get for Free. 32p. 1984. pap. 5.95 (ISBN 0-934650-07-1). Sunnyside.

Ewing, S. B. Burtonian Melancholy in the Plays of John Ford. LC 77-96156. 1969. Repr. of 1940 ed. lib. bdg. 15.00x (ISBN 0-374-92660-3). Octagon.

Ewing, Steve. American Cruisers of WW II. LC 84-61620. (A Pictorial Encylopedia Ser.). (Illus.). 152p. (Orig.). 1984. pap. 9.95 (ISBN 0-933126-51-4). Pictorial Hist.

--U. S. S. Enterprise (CV-Six), the Most Decorated Ship of World War II: A Pictorial History. LC 82-61737. (Illus.). 132p. 1982. 7.95 (ISBN 0-933126-24-7). Pictorial Hist.

Ewing, Steven. The "Lady Lex" & the "Blue Ghost". A Pictorial History of the U.S.S. Lexingtons CU-2 & CU-16. LC 83-61338. (Illus.). 48p. 1983. pap. 5.95 (ISBN 0-933126-35-2). Pictorial Hist.

Ewing, T. E., jt. auth. see Morton, R. A.

Ewing, Thomas E. Between the Hammer & the Anvil? Chinese & Russian Policies in Outer Mongolia, 1911-1921. LC 80-52924. (Indiana University Uralic & Altaic Ser.: Vol. 138). 300p. 1980. 20.00 (ISBN 0-933070-06-3). Ind U Res Inst.

Ewing, Upton C. The Essene Christ. LC 61-10608. (Illus.). 1977. pap. 9.95 (ISBN 0-8022-0461-9). Philos Lib.

--The Essene Christ. 438p. pap. 12.95 (ISBN 0-317-07627-2). Edenite.

--The Prophet of the Dead Sea Scrolls. LC 62-21558. 1977. pap. 4.95 (ISBN 0-8022-0462-7). Philos Lib.

--Prophet of the Dead Sea Scrolls. 148p. pap. 6.95 (ISBN 0-317-07628-0). Edenite.

Ewing, W. H. Identification of Enterobacteriacea. Date not set. write for info. (ISBN 0-444-00841-1). Elsevier.

Ewing, William A., intro. by. Horst. (Illus.). 24p. (Orig.). 1984. pap. 15.00 (ISBN 0-933642-08-3). Intl Ctr Photo.

Ewins, D. J. Modal Testing: Theory & Practice. (Mechanical Engineering Research Studies Ser.: No. 1-535). 150p. 1984. text ed. 31.95x (ISBN 0-471-90472-4, Pub. by Wiley). Wiley.

Ewins, D. J. & Srinivasan, A. V., eds. Vibrations of Bladed Disk Assemblies. 1983. pap. text ed. 34.00 (ISBN 0-317-02660-7, G00235). ASME.

Ewles, L. & Simnett, I. Promoting Health: A Practical Guide to Health Education. Date not set. price not set (ISBN 0-471-90514-3). Wiley.

Ewlyn-Jones, Lord, intro. by see Rose, Andrew.

Ewton, Ralph W. & Ornstein, Jacob, eds. Studies in Language & Linguistics 1972-73. LC 79-97794. viii, 252p. 1972. pap. text ed. 5.00 (ISBN 0-87404-018-3). Tex Western.

Ewton, Ralph W., Jr. The Literary Theories of August Wilhelm Schlegel. (De Propietatibus Litterarum, Ser. Practica: No. 47). 120p. (Orig.). 1972. pap. text ed. 8.80x (ISBN 0-686-22543-0). Mouton.

Ewton, Ralph W., Jr. & Ornstein, Jacob. Studies in Language & Linguistics, 1969-70. pap. 5.00 (ISBN 0-87404-019-1). Tex Western.

Ewusie, J. Yanney. Elements of Tropical Ecology. (Orig.). 1980. pap. text ed. 16.50x (ISBN 0-435-93700-6). Heinemann Ed.

Ewy, D. & Ewy, R. Preparation for Breast Feeding. 1983. pap. 2.95 (ISBN 0-451-12485-5, Sig). NAL.

Ewy, Donna. Preparation for Parenthood: How to Create a Nurturing Family. 1985. 6.95 (ISBN 0-452-25691-7, Plume). NAL.

Ewy, Donna & Ewy, Rodger. Death of a Dream: Miscarriage, Stillbirth & Newborn Loss. (Illus.). 176p. 1984. pap. 10.95 (ISBN 0-525-48080-3, 01063-320). Dutton.

--Preparation for Breast Feeding. rev. ed. LC 83-45162. (Illus.). 192p. 1985. pap. 6.95 (ISBN 0-385-18948-6). Doubleday.

--Preparation for Childbirth. 224p. 1974. pap. 2.95 (ISBN 0-451-11921-5, AE1921, Sig). NAL.

--Preparation for Childbirth. 3rd, rev. ed. LC 81-15879. (Illus.). 180p. 1982. pap. 7.95 (ISBN 0-87108-602-6). Pruett.

Ewy, Donna & Ewy, Roger. The Cycle of Life: Guide to a Healthy Pregnancy. (Illus.). 196p. 1982. pap. 7.25 (ISBN 0-525-93182-1, 0704-210). Dutton.

--The Cycle of Life: Guide to Family-Centered Childbirth. (Illus.). 196p. 1982. pap. 7.25 (ISBN 0-525-93183-X, 0704-210). Dutton.

--The Cycle of Life: Guide to Parenting You & Your Newborn. (Illus.). 196p. 1982. pap. 7.25 (ISBN 0-525-93184-8, 0704-210). Dutton.

--Teen Pregnancy: The Challenges We Faced, the Choices We Made. 1985. pap. 3.95 (ISBN 0-451-13915-1, Sig). NAL.

Ewy, Donna, jt. auth. see Ewy, Roger.

Ewy, Gordon A. & Bressler, Rubin, eds. Cardiovascular Drugs & the Management of Heart Disease. 768p. 1982. text ed. 82.50 (ISBN 0-89004-568-2). Raven.

--Current Cardiovascular Drug Therapy. 346p. 1984. pap. text ed. 19.50 (ISBN 0-88167-012-X). Raven.

Ewy, R., jt. auth. see Ewy, D.

Ewy, Rodger, jt. auth. see Ewy, Donna.

Ewy, Roger & Ewy, Donna. Teen Pregnancy. (Illus., Orig.). 1984. pap. 14.95 (ISBN 0-87108-652-2). Pruett.

Ewy, Roger, jt. auth. see Ewy, Donna.

Exander, Max. Mansex: Short Stories. (Illus.). 192p. (Orig.). 1985. pap. 8.95 (ISBN 0-917342-05-4). Gay Sunshine.

Excoffier, Jean-Louis, jt. auth. see Colin, Henri.

Execicom Systems Corporation. IFPS-Personal User's Manual: Release 1.0. LC 83-82445. 550p. 1984. 3 ring binder 30.00 (ISBN 0-911941-01-0). Execucom Sys Corp.

Execucom Staff. Impressionist User's Manual. 550p. 1985. with computer system 995.00 (ISBN 0-911941-03-7). Execucom Sys Corp.

Execucom Systems Corp. IFPS User's Manual: Release 9.0. LC 83-99. 550p. 1983. pap. 30.00 (ISBN 0-911941-00-2). Execucom Sys Corp.

Executive Enterprises Inc. Employee Termination Handbook: Legal and Psychological Guidelines for Employers. 189p. 1982. 16.95 (ISBN 0-13-274548-8); pap. 7.95 (ISBN 0-13-274530-5). P-H.

Executive Health Examiners. Coping with Executive Stress. (Executive Health Examiners Ser.). (Illus.). 288p. 1983. 15.95 (ISBN 0-07-019862-4). McGraw.

--Executive Fitness. (Executive Health Examiners Ser.). (Illus.). 192p. 1982. 15.95 (ISBN 0-07-019863-2). McGraw.

--Executive Nutrition & Diet. (Executive Health Examiners Ser.). (Illus.). 288p. 1982. 15.95 (ISBN 0-07-019861-6). McGraw.

--Stress Management for the Executive. 352p. 1985. pap. 7.95 (ISBN 0-425-08396-9). Berkley Pub.

Executive Intelligence Review, ed. LaRouche: Will this Man Become President? (Illus.). 264p. 1983. pap. 4.95 (ISBN 0-933488-28-9). New Benjamin.

Executive Report Corporation Editorial Staff. Executive's Credit & Collection Guide. 1970. 119.50 (ISBN 0-13-293977-0). P-H.

Executive Reports Corporation. Family Tax Guide. LC 85-12877. Date not set. 44.95 (ISBN 0-13-302878-X). Exec Reports.

Executive Reports Corporation & Frank, Harvey. The ERC Closely-Held Corporation Guide. 2nd ed. LC 83-16455. 1984. 110.50 (ISBN 0-13-283631-9). P-H.

Executive Reports Corporation Editorial Staff. The ERC Tax Shelter Desk Manual. 1976. 89.50 (ISBN 0-13-885244-8). Exec Reports.

--ERC's President's Guide. 1970. 97.50 (ISBN 0-13-697581-X). Exec Reports.

--Executive's Credit & Collections Guide. 1970. 89.50 (ISBN 0-13-293977-0). Exec Reports.

--Executive's Desk Manual for Profitable Employee Handling. 1972. 89.50 (ISBN 0-13-294579-7). Exec Reports.

--Executive's Tax Desk Manual. 1971. 89.50 (ISBN 0-13-294561-4). Exec Reports.

--Miracle Secretary's Guide. 1979. 49.50 (ISBN 0-13-585562-4). Exec Reports.

--Professional's Tax Desk Manual. 1971. 89.50 (ISBN 0-13-725432-6). Exec Reports.

--Tax Shelter Opportunities in Real Estate. 1978. 89.50 (ISBN 0-13-885269-3). Exec Reports.

--Tax Sheltered Opportunities for the Owner of a Closely-Held Business. 1981. 119.50 (ISBN 0-13-886507-8). Exec Reports.

--Tax Shelters in Executive Compensation. 1979. 89.50 (ISBN 0-13-886721-6). Exec Reports.

--The Treasurer's Guide. 1976. 97.50 (ISBN 0-13-930503-3). Exec Reports.

Executive Reports Corporation Staff. Travel & Entertainment Deduction Guide: With Answers to Vital Questions on How to Nail Down Big Cash Savings under the All-New T&E Setup. LC 85-1619. 1985. 35.00 (ISBN 0-13-930090-2). Exec Reports.

Executype, ed. see Skinner, Steve.

Exeler, Adolf & Mette, Norbert, eds. A People's Theology. 192p. pap. 9.95 cancelled (ISBN 0-8245-0477-1). Crossroad NY.

Exell, Joseph S. Practical Truths from Jonah. LC 82-18671. 240p. 1983. 8.95 (ISBN 0-8254-2525-5). Kregel.

Exell, T. S., jt. auth. see Spence, H. D.

Exit Photography Group, ed. Survival Programs: In Britain's Inner Cities. (Illus.). 216p. 1982. pap. 17.00 (ISBN 0-335-10111-9, Pub. by Open Univ Pr). Taylor & Francis.

Exler, F. J. The Form of the Ancient Greek Letter of the Epistolary Papyri. 1976. 10.00 (ISBN 0-89005-120-8). Ares.

Exler, Samuel. Ambition, Fertility, Loneliness. 72p. (Orig.). 1982. pap. 5.95 (ISBN 0-931642-11-6). Lintel.

Exley, C. L. A History of the Torksey & Mansfield China Factories. (Illus.). 1970. 15.00 (ISBN 0-685-53311-5). ARS Ceramica.

Exley, Frederick. A Fan's Notes. 1980. pap. 2.95 (ISBN 0-671-41187-X). PB.

--A Fan's Notes. 368p. 1977. pap. 2.95 (ISBN 0-671-41187-X). WSP.

--A Fan's Notes. (Vintage Contemporaries Ser.). 1985. pap. 5.95 (ISBN 0-394-72915-3, Vin). Random.

Exley, Helen. What It's Like to Be Me. 2nd ed. (Illus.). 127p. 1984. pap. 10.95 (ISBN 0-377-00144-9). Friend Pr.

Exley, Helen, jt. auth. see Exley, Richard.

Exley, Jo E. Texas Tears & Texas Sunshine: Voices of Frontier Women. LC 84-40140. (Centennial Series of the Association of Former Students: No. 17). (Illus.). 264p. 1985. 14.95 (ISBN 0-89096-215-4). Tex A&M Univ Pr.

Exley, Richard & Exley, Helen. A Child's View of Christmas. (Illus.). 64p. (gr. 3-8). 1981. 7.50 (ISBN 0-8298-0463-3). Pilgrim NY.

Exley, Richard D. The Other God: Seeing God As He Really Is. LC 79-51902. 1979. pap. 3.95 (ISBN 0-88270-359-5, Pub. by Logos). Bridge Pub.

Exline, Christopher H., et al. The City: Patterns & Processes in the Urban Ecosystem. (Illus.). 300p. (Orig.). 1981. lib. bdg. 34.00x (ISBN 0-89158-904-X); pap. 15.00 (ISBN 0-89158-905-8). Westview.

Exlog. Field Geologist's Training Guide. (The Exlog Series of Petroleum Geology & Engineering Handbooks). (Illus.). 298p. 1985. text ed. 34.00 (ISBN 0-317-14155-4). Intl Human Res.

--Mud Logging: Principles & Interpretations. (The Exlog Series of Petroleum Geology & Engineering Handbooks). (Illus.). 98p. 1985. text ed. 26.00 (ISBN 0-88746-044-5). Intl Human Res.

--Theory & Applications of Drilling Fluid Hydraulics. (The Exlog Series of Petroleum Geology & Engineering Handbooks). (Illus.). 208p. 1985. text ed. 27.00 (ISBN 0-88746-045-3). Intl Human Res.

EXLOG Staff. Coring Operations: Procedures for Sampling & Analysis of Bottomhole & Sidewall Cores. Whittaker, Alun, ed. (The EXLOG Series of Petroleum Geology & Engineering Handbooks). (Illus.). 191p. 1985. text ed. 29.00 (ISBN 0-88746-053-4). Intl Human Res.

--Formation Evaluation: Geological Procedures. Whittaker, Alun, ed. (The EXLOG Series of Petroleum Geology & Engineering Handbooks). (Illus.). 175p. 1985. text ed. 29.00 (ISBN 0-88746-054-2). Intl Human Res.

--Theory & Evaluation of Formation Pressures: A Pressure Detection Reference Handbook. Whittaker, Alun, ed. (EXLOG Series of Petroleum Geology & Engineering Handbooks). (Illus.). 225p. 1985. text ed. 32.00 (ISBN 0-88746-052-6). Intl Human Res.

Exman, Eugene. Brothers Harper. LC 65-14651. (Illus.). 1965. 15.34 (ISBN 0-06-011200-X, HarpT). Har-Row.

--House of Harper. LC 67-22498. 1967. 15.34 (ISBN 0-06-011201-8, HarpT). Har-Row.

Exner, Franz. Krieg Und Kriminalitat in Osterreich: Mit Einem Beitrag Uber die Krimalitat der Militarpersonen. (Wirtschafts-Und Sozialgeschichte des Weltkrieges (Osterreichische Und Ungarische Serie)). (Ger.). 1927. 75.00x (ISBN 0-317-27498-8). Elliots Bks.

Exner, J. E. & Weiner, I. B. The Rorschach, a Comprehensive System: Assessment of Children & Adoloscents. LC 74-8888. (Personality Processes Ser.: Vol. 1). 449p. 1982. 57.50 (ISBN 0-471-09364-5). Wiley.

Exner, John E. The Rorschach: A Comprehensive System. (Personality Processes Ser.: Current Research & Advanced Interpretation: Vol. 2). 448p. 1978. 57.50 (ISBN 0-471-04166-1, Pub. by Wiley-Interscience). Wiley.

Exner, John E., Jr. A Workbook in the Rorschach Technique Emphasizing the Beck & Klopper Systems. (Illus.). 124p. 1967. photocopy ed. 15.75x (ISBN 0-398-00536-2). C C Thomas.

Exner, John F. The Rorschach Systems. LC 68-31431. 392p. 1969. 45.00 (ISBN 0-8089-0128-1, 791180). Grune.

Exner, Jurgen H., ed. Detoxication of Hazardous Waste. LC 82-70696. (Illus.). 362p. 1982. 39.95 (ISBN 0-250-40521-0). Butterworth.

Exner, Richard, tr. see Fuchs, G. B.

Exner, Richard, tr. see Piontek, Heinz.

Expansion Joint Manufacturers Association. Standards of the Expansion Joint Manufacturers Association. 152p. 1980. 40.00 (ISBN 0-318-16766-2). Tubular Exch.

Experience & the Future Discussion Group, compiled by. Poland Today: The State of the Republic. Vale, Michel, et al, trs. from Polish. LC 81-8782. 256p. 1981. 20.00 (ISBN 0-87332-201-0); pap. 7.95 (ISBN 0-87332-205-3). M E Sharpe.

Experiential Education Advisory Panel. Experiential Education Policy Guidelines. Miguel, Richard J., ed. 54p. 1979. 4.50 (ISBN 0-318-15471-4, RD 160). Natl Ctr Res Voc Ed.

Experimental Technology Incentives Program. Toward Competitive Provision of Public Record Message Services. 1981. 75.00 (ISBN 0-686-37963-2). Info Gatekeepers.

Expert Committee on the Public Health Aspects of Housing, 1st, Geneva, 1961. Report. (Technical Report Ser: No. 225). 60p. (Eng, Fr, Span.). 1961. pap. 1.20 (ISBN 92-4-120225-4). World Health.

Expert Consultation on Fishing for Squid & Other Cephalopods. Contributed Papers: Supplement One. (Fisheries Reports: No. 170, Suppl. 1). (Illus.). 1976. pap. 17.00 (ISBN 92-5-100034-4, F818, FAO). Unipub.

Expert, Henry, ed. Maitres Musiciens de la Renaissance Francaise, 23 vols. Incl. Vol. 1. Premier Fascicule des Melanges. De Lassus, Orlando (ISBN 0-8450-1201-0); Vol. 2. Premier Fascicule des 150 Psaumes. Goudimel, Claude (ISBN 0-8450-1202-9); Vol. 3. Musique, Premier Fascicule. Costeley, Guillaume (ISBN 0-8450-1203-7); Vol. 4. Deuxieme Fascicule des 150 Psaumes. Goudimel, Claude (ISBN 0-8450-1204-5); Vol. 5. Trente et une Chansons Musicales: Claude de Sermisy, Clement Janequin et al (ISBN 0-8450-1205-3); Vol. 6. Troisieme Fascicule des 150 Psaumes. Goudimel, Claude (ISBN 0-8450-1206-1); Vol. 7. Chansons Attaingnant. Janequin, Clement (ISBN 0-8450-1207-X); Vol. 8. Missa "de Beata Virgine", Missa "Ave Maria". Brumel, Antoine & De la Rue, Pierre. (ISBN 0-8450-1208-8); Vol. 9. Missa "Alma Redemptoris - Missa "Mente Tota". Mouton, J. & Fevin, A. de. (ISBN 0-8450-1209-6); Vol. 10. Chansonnettes Mesurees de Ian-Antoine de Baif. Mauduit, Jacques (ISBN 0-8450-1210-X); Vol. 11. Dodecacorde, Premier Fascicule. LeJeune, Claude (ISBN 0-8450-1211-8); Vol. 12. Le Printemps, Premier Fascicule. LeJeune, Claude (ISBN 0-8450-1212-6); Vol. 13. Le Printemps, Deuxieme Fascicule. LeJeune, Claude (ISBN 0-8450-1213-4); Vol. 14. Le Printemps, Troisieme Fascicule. LeJeune, Claude (ISBN 0-8450-1214-2); Vol. 15. Poesies de P. de Ronsard et Autres Poetes. Regnard, Francois (ISBN 0-8450-1215-0); Vol. 16. Melanges Premier Fascicule. LeJeune, Claude (ISBN 0-8450-1216-9); Vol. 17. Melanges, Premier Fascicule. Du Caurroy, Eustache (ISBN 0-8450-1217-7); Vol. 18. Musique, Deuxieme Fascicule. Costeley, Guillaume (ISBN 0-8450-1218-5); Vol. 19. Musique, Troiseme Fascicule. Costeley, Guillaume (ISBN 0-8450-1219-3); Vol. 20. Pseaumes en Vers Mezurez, Premier Fascicule. LeJeune, Claude (ISBN 0-8450-1220-7); Vol. 21. Pseaumes en vers Mezurez. LeJeune, Claude (ISBN 0-8450-1221-5); Vol. 22. Pseaumes en vers Mezurez, Troisieme Fascicule. LeJeune, Claude (ISBN 0-8450-1222-3); Vol. 23. Danceries, Premier Volume. Gervaise, Claude & Du Terte, Estienne. (ISBN 0-8450-1223-1). (Illus., Repr. of 1894-1908 ed). 1964. pap. 525.00x set (ISBN 0-8450-1200-2); pap. 25.00x ea. Broude.

--Monuments de la musique francaise au temps de la Renaissance, 10 vols. Incl. Vol. I. Octonaires de la vanite et inconstance du monde (I-VIII) LeJeune, Claude (ISBN 0-8450-1231-2); Vol. II. Messes a quatre voix. Certon, Pierre (ISBN 0-8450-1232-0); Vol. III. Airs de plusiers musiciens reduits a quatre parties. Le Blanc, Didier (ISBN 0-8450-1233-9); Vol. IV. Premier Livre Des Amours De Pierre De Ronsard, (I-XIX) De Bertrand, Anthoine (ISBN 0-8450-1234-7); Vol. V. Premier livre des Amours de Pierre de Ronsard, (XX-XXXV) De Bertrand, Anthoine (ISBN 0-8450-1235-5); Vol. VI. Second livre des Amours de Pierre de Ronsard (ISBN 0-8450-1236-3); Vol. VII. Troisieme livre de chansons. De Bertrand, Anthoine (ISBN 0-8450-1237-1); Vol. VIII. Octonaires de la vanite et inconstance du monde, (IX-XII; Pseaumes des Meslanges de 1612; Dialoque e a sept parties. LeJeune, Claude (ISBN 0-8450-1238-X); Vol. IX. Messes a quatre voix. Goudimel, Claude (ISBN 0-8450-1239-8); Vol. X. Premier livre des Octonaires de la vanite du Monde. De l'Estocart, Paschal (ISBN 0-8450-1240-1). (Illus.). 1952. pap. 275.00x set (ISBN 0-8450-1230-4); pap. 35.00x ea. Broude.

Expert, Henry, ed. see De Ronsard, Pierre, et al.

Expert, Henry, ed. see Janequin, Clement, et al.

Expert Systems. Financial Wizard for the Macintosh. 1985. 49.95 (ISBN 0-8104-7560-X). Hayden.

--Framework: On-the-Job Applications. 200p. 19.95 (ISBN 0-317-12834-5). P-H.

Expert Systems Staff. Framework: On-the-Job Application. 265p. 1985. pap. 29.95 incl. disk (ISBN 0-912677-50-3). Ashton-Tate Bks.

--Framework: On-the-Job Applications. Ashton-Tate, ed. (Framework Books). 300p. 1984. pap. 19.95 incl. disk (ISBN 0-912677-22-8). Ashton-Tate Bks.

Expertise International, Ltd. Distributed Processing, 2 vols. Incl. Vol. 1. Management Report. pap. 18.00 (ISBN 0-89435-025-0); Vol. 2. Technical Report. 505p. pap. 35.00 (ISBN 0-89435-026-9). (Illus.). 1978. pap. QED Info Sci.

Explosive Volcanism, Geophysics Research Board, National Research Council. Explosive Volcanism: Inception, Evolution, & Hazards. 1983. text ed. 24.50 (ISBN 0-309-03393-4). Natl Acad Pr.

Express Publishing Co. Favorite Recipes from Famous New Orleans. rev. ed. (Travel Ser.: No. L-23). (Illus.). 64p. 1981. pap. text ed. write for info. (ISBN 0-938440-12-8). Colourpicture.

Extein, Irl L., ed. Medical Mimics of Psychiatric Disorders. (Progress in Psychiatry Ser.). 128p. 1985. text ed. 15.95x (ISBN 0-88048-092-0, 48-092-0). Am Psychiatric.

Exter, Patricia D. The Lunchbox Book. LC 85-7891. (Illus.). 160p. (Orig.). (YA) 1985. 14.95 (ISBN 0-935526-11-0); pap. 6.95 (ISBN 0-935526-12-9). McBooks Pr.

Exton, H. Q Hypergeometric Functions & Applications. (Mathematics & its Applications). 355p. 1983. 53.95x (ISBN 0-470-27453-0). Halsted Pr.

Exton, Harold. Handbook of Hypergeometric Integrals: Theory, Applications, Tables, Computer Programs. LC 78-40120. (Mathematics & Its Applications Ser.). 316p. 1978. 79.95x (ISBN 0-470-26342-3). Halsted Pr.

--Multiple Hypergeometric Functions & Applications. LC 76-20720. (Mathematics & It's Applications Ser.). 312p. 1977. 56.95x (ISBN 0-470-15190-0). Halsted Pr.

Exton, Peter & Kleitz, Dorsey. Milestones into Headstones: Mini Biographies of 50 Fascinating Americans Buried in Washington, DC. (Orig.). 1985. pap. 9.95 (ISBN 0-914440-84-5). EPM Pubns.

Exton, William, Jr. Selling Leverage: How to Motivate People to Buy. LC 83-22948. (Illus.). 1984. 18.95 (ISBN 0-13-805433-9, Busn); pap. 7.95 (ISBN 0-13-805425-8). P-H.

Exton-Smith & Caird. Metabolic & Nutritional Disorders in the Elderly. 238p. 1980. 26.00 (ISBN 0-7236-0537-8). PSG Pub Co.

Exton-Smith, A. N. Geriatrics. (Illus.). 352p. 1979. text ed. 30.00 (ISBN 0-8391-1456-7). Univ Park.

Exton-Smith, A. N. & Evans, J. G. Care of the Elderly: Meeting the Challenge of Dependency. 324p. 1977. 43.50 (ISBN 0-8089-1055-8, 791190). Grune.

Exton-Smith, A. N., jt. ed. see Barbagallo-Sangiorgi, G.

Extraordinary General Assembly,Poland,1973, jt. auth. see General Assembly 15th,Sydney,1973.

Exum, William H. Paradoxes of Protest: Black Student Activism in a White University. 336p. 1985. 34.95 (ISBN 0-87722-377-7). Temple U Pr.

Exupery, Antoine de Saint see De Saint Exupery, Antoine.

Exupery, Antoine de Saint see Saint-Exupery, Saint Antoine De.

Ey, Henri. Consciousness: A Phenomenological Study of Being Conscious & Becoming Conscious. Flodstrom, John H., tr. LC 76-26429. (Studies in Phenomenology & Existential Philosophy Ser.). (Illus.). 448p. 1978. 29.50x (ISBN 0-253-31408-9). Ind U Pr.

Eybers, G. W., ed. Select Constitutional Documents Illustrating South Africa History, 1795-1910. LC 71-78766. Repr. of 1918 ed. 27.00x (ISBN 0-8371-1391-1, EYD&). Greenwood.

Eyck, Erich. Bismarck & the German Empire. 1964. pap. 7.95 (ISBN 0-393-00235-7, N235, Norton Lib). Norton.

--History of the Weimar Republic. LC 62-17219. 1970. Vol. 1. pap. text ed. 3.25x (ISBN 0-689-70218-3, 152A); Vol. 2. pap. text ed. 3.95x (ISBN 0-689-70219-1, 152B). Atheneum.

--A History of the Weimar Republic, 2 vols. Hanson, Harlan P. & Waite, Robert G. L., trs. Incl. Vol. 1. From the Collapse of the Empire to Hindenburg's Election. 373p. 1962; Vol. 2. From the Locarno Conference to Hitler's Seizure of Power. 535p. 1963. 30.00x (ISBN 0-674-40351-7). LC 62-17219. Harvard U Pr.

--Pitt Versus Fox: Father & Son, 1735-1806. LC 72-13742. viii, 396p. 1972. Repr. lib. bdg. 27.50x (ISBN 0-374-92673-5). Octagon.

Eyck, Erich & Miall, Bernard, trs. Gladstone. 505p. 1966. 30.00x (ISBN 0-7146-1472-6, F Cass Co). Biblio Dist.

Eyck, Frank, ed. see Hertz, Frederick.

Eyde, Albert C. & Zeller, Beatriz P. Spanish for Business: Intermediate Level. 162p. (Orig.). 1984. pap. 110.00x incl. 6, 1 hour audio cassettes (ISBN 0-88432-129-0, S24300). J Norton Pubs.

Eyde, Donna R. & Rich, Jay. Psychological Distress in Aging: A Family Management Model. LC 82-164440. 254p. 1982. 30.50 (ISBN 0-89443-667-8). Aspen Systems.

Eyde, Lorraine Dittrich. Work Values & Background Factors As Predictors of Women's Desire to Work. 1962. pap. 2.00x (ISBN 0-87776-108-6, R108). Ohio St U Admin Sci.

Eye, Alexander von see Nesselroade, John R. & Von Eye, Alexander.

Eye, Eugene. I Quit: Subliminal Audio Conditioning Helps You Stop Smoking. LC 81-81352. 35p. (Orig.). 1981. wkbk. & 2 tape cassette album 49.50 (ISBN 0-939968-00-2). Pub Mgmt Assoc.

Eyer, Dianne W., jt. auth. see Gonzalez-Mena, Janet.

Eyer, Mary S. He Restoreth My Soul. LC 82-1363. 98p. 1982. 6.95 (ISBN 0-87747-908-9). Deseret Bk.

Eyer, Richard C. Devotions of Hope. 1984. 2.00 (ISBN 0-89536-653-3, 0418). CSS of Ohio.

Eyerly, Jeanenette. Bonnie Jo, Go Home. LC 72-1863. (gr. 7 up). 1972. 12.45i (ISBN 0-397-31390-X). Lipp Jr Bks.

--Goodbye to Budapest. LC 74-4347. (gr. 5 up). 1974. 11.06i (ISBN 0-397-31496-5). Lipp Jr Bks.

Eyerly, Jeannette. Angel Baker, Thief. LC 84-47634. 224p. (YA) (gr. 7 up). 1984. 12.02i (ISBN 0-397-32096-5); PLB 11.89g (ISBN 0-397-32097-3). Lipp Jr Bks.

--Escape from Nowhere. LC 69-11995. (gr. 7 up). 1969. 13.41i (ISBN 0-397-31070-6). Lipp Jr Bks.

--Girl Like Me. LC 66-10022. (gr. 7 up). 1966. 13.41i (ISBN 0-397-30869-8). Lipp Jr Bks.

--He's My Baby Now. (gr. 7-10). 1978. pap. 1.95 (ISBN 0-686-85648-1). Archway.

--He's My Baby Now. (gr. 6 up). 1985. pap. 2.25 (ISBN 0-671-55269-4). PB.

--If I Loved You Wednesday. (gr. 7-10). 1982. pap. 1.95 (ISBN 0-671-43491-8). Archway.

--If I Loved You Wednesday. LC 80-7772. 128p. (gr. 7up). 1980. 11.49i (ISBN 0-397-31913-4); PLB 11.89 (ISBN 0-397-31914-2). Lipp Jr Bks.

--More Than a Summer's Love. 176p. (gr. 12 up). 1983. pap. text ed. 2.25 (ISBN 0-671-45660-1). Archway.

--The Phaedra Complex. (gr. 7-9). 1979. pap. 1.75 (ISBN 0-671-43214-1). Archway.

--Radigan Cares. (gr. 7-9). 1978. pap. 1.50 (ISBN 0-671-29914-X). Archway.

--Radigan Cares. LC 71-11722. (gr. 7-9). 1970. PLB 9.89 (ISBN 0-397-31152-4). Lipp Jr Bks.

--See Dave Run. (gr. 7-9). 1979. pap. 1.75 (ISBN 0-671-56031-X). Archway.

--See Dave Run. LC 78-8139. (gr. 6-12). 1978. 10.10i (ISBN 0-397-31819-7). Lipp Jr Bks.

--The Seeing Summer. LC 81-47440. (Illus.). 128p. (gr. 4-6). 1981. 11.06i (ISBN 0-397-31965-7); PLB 10.89g (ISBN 0-397-31966-5). Lipp Jr Bks.

--The Seeing Summer. 128p. (gr. 3-6). 1984. pap. 1.95 (ISBN 0-671-45661-X). Archway.

--Seth & Me & Rebel Make Three. LC 82-48463. 128p. (YA) (gr. 7 up). 1983. 10.10i (ISBN 0-397-32042-6); PLB 9.89g (ISBN 0-397-32043-4). Lipp Jr Bks.

Eyerman, Ron. False Consciousness & Ideology in Marxism. 319p. 1981. text ed. 38.50x (ISBN 0-391-02313-6, Pub. by Almquist & Wiksell Sweden). Humanities.

Eyers, A. S. Practical Woodwork for Laboratory Technicians. LC 79-117463. 1970. 14.50 (ISBN 0-08-015962-1). Pergamon.

Eyes, David & Lichty, Ron. Programming the 65816. (Illus.). 288p. 1985. pap. 22.95 (ISBN 0-89303-789-3). Brady Comm.

Eyestone, R. Public Policy Formation. (Public Policy Studies: A Multi-Volume Treatise: Vol. 2). 1985. 55.00 (ISBN 0-89232-372-8). Jai Pr.

Eyestone, Robert. From Social Issues to Public Policy. LC 78-13334. (Viewpoints on American Politics Ser.). pap. 51.50 (ISBN 0-317-27942-4, 2055980). Bks Demand UMI.

--The Threads of Public Policy: A Study in Political Leadership. 216p. pap. text ed. 7.95x (ISBN 0-8290-0325-8). Irvington.

Eyges, Leonard. The Classical Electromagnetic Field. (Illus.). 432p. 1980. pap. text ed. 8.95 (ISBN 0-486-63947-9). Dover.

Eyjolfs, Stella. America. 1984. 5.95 (ISBN 0-533-06015-X). Vantage.

Eyken, Willem van der see Van der Eyken, Willem.

Eykhoff, P. System Identification Parameter & State Estimation. LC 73-2781. 555p. 1974. 124.95x (ISBN 0-471-24980-7, Pub. by Wiley-Interscience). Wiley.

Eykhoff, P., ed. Trends & Progress in System Identification. LC 80-41994. (IFAC Ser. for Graduate, Research Workers & Practicing Engineers: Vol. 1). (Illus.). 410p. 1981. 77.00 (ISBN 0-08-025683-X). Pergamon.

Eykhoff, P., ed. see Pugachev.

Eyler, Ellen C. Early English Gardens & Garden Books. LC 63-15259. (Folger Guides to the Age of Shakespeare). 1963. pap. 3.95 (ISBN 0-918016-30-4). Folger Bks.

Eyler, John M. Victorian Social Medicine: The Ideas & Methods of William Farr. 1979. 25.00x (ISBN 0-8018-2246-7). Johns Hopkins.

Eyler, Roberta, jt. auth. see Kitazawa, Harriet.

Eyles, Allen. James Stewart. LC 84-40252. (Illus.). 288p. 1984. 17.95 (ISBN 0-8128-2980-8). Stein & Day.

--John Wayne. LC 79-911. (Illus.). 333p. 1982. pap. 14.95 (ISBN 0-498-02590-X). A S Barnes.

Eyles, Allen, ed. Inside the Hollywood Reporter. 1984. pap. cancelled (ISBN 0-671-50856-3). S&S.

Eyles, Allen, et al, eds. The House of Horror: The Complete Story of Hammer Films. (Illus.). 144p. 1984. pap. 8.95 (ISBN 0-8044-6152-X). Ungar.

Eyles, Desmond. The Doulton Burslem Wares. 200p. 1981. 80.00x (ISBN 0-09-138260-2, Pub. by Barrie & Jenkins England). State Mutual Bk.

--Doulton Burslem Wares. (Illus.). 191p. 1980. 62.50 (ISBN 0-09-138260-2, Pub. by Barrie & Jenkins England). Seven Hills Bks.

--The Doulton Lambeth Wares. (Illus.). 179p. 1975. 52.50x (ISBN 0-8476-1337-2). Rowman.

--The Doulton Lambeth Wares. (Illus.). 179p. 1975. 62.50 (ISBN 0-09-124240-1, Pub. by Barrie & Jenkins England). Seven Hills Bks.

Eyles, John, jt. auth. see Jones, Emrys.

Eyles, Johy & Woods, Kevin J. The Social Geography of Medicine & Health. LC 83-2921. 275p. 1983. 32.50x (ISBN 0-312-73292-9). St Martin.

Eyles, N., ed. Glacial Geology: An Introduction for Engineers & Earth Scientists. LC 83-17418. (Illus.). 431p. 1983. 60.00 (ISBN 0-08-030264-5); pap. 17.95 (ISBN 0-08-030263-7). Pergamon.

Eyles, Wilfred C. Book of Opals. LC 64-14193. (Illus.). 1964. 20.00 (ISBN 0-8048-0068-5). C E Tuttle.

Eylmann, Erhard. Die Eingeborenen der Kolonie Suedaustralien. (Illus.). Repr. of 1908 ed. 47.00 (ISBN 0-384-14987-1). Johnson Repr.

Eylon, D., jt. ed. see Froes, F. H.

Eylon, Daniel, ed. Titanium for Energy & Industrial Applications. (Illus.). 403p. 36.00 (ISBN 0-89520-386-3); members 24.00 (ISBN 0-317-36266-6); student members 12.00 (ISBN 0-317-36267-4). ASM.

Eyman, Joy S. How to Convict a Rapist. LC 79-3824. 186p. 1982. pap. 10.95 (ISBN 0-8128-6147-7). Stein & Day.

--How to Convict a Rapist. LC 79-3824. 228p. 1980. 9.95 (ISBN 0-8128-2712-0). Stein & Day.

--Prisons for Women: A Practical Guide to Administration Problems. 200p. 1971. 14.50x (ISBN 0-398-00537-0). C C Thomas.

Eyman, Scott, jt. auth. see Giannetti, Louis.

Eyman, William, jt. auth. see Gerald, Mark.

Eymerich, Nicolau. Le Manuel Des Inquisiteurs (Avignon, 1376) Avec les Commentaires De Francisco Pena, Docteur En Droit Canon & En Droit Civil (Rome, 1578. (Le Savoir Historique: No. 8). 1973. pap. 11.20 (ISBN 90-2797-250-8). Mouton.

Eynden, Charles Vanden see Eggan, Lawrence C. & Vanden Eynden, Charles.

Eynern, Gert V. Woerterbuch zur Politischen Oekonomie. 2nd ed. (Ger.). 1977. pap. 19.95 (ISBN 3-531-21148-X, M-6902). French & Eur.

Eynon, Dana. Adventures Through the Bible. rev. ed. LC 79-1031. 176p. (gr. 3-6). 1980. pap. 7.95 tchr's book (ISBN 0-87239-378-X, 3234). Standard Pub.

--My New Life with Christ: Baptismal Certificate. (Certificate Booklets Ser.). (Illus.). 16p. (gr. 3-9). 1982. pap. 0.95 self-cover (ISBN 0-87239-529-4, 1177). Standard Pub.

--Through the Bible in a Year: Pupil Workbook. 64p. (gr. 3-7). 1975. wkbk. 1.95 (ISBN 0-87239-011-X, 3239). Standard Pub.

--Through the Bible in a Year: Teacher. LC 74-27239. 176p. 1975. tchr's manual 7.95 (ISBN 0-87239-028-4, 3237). Standard Pub.

Eyo, Ekpo, jt. auth. see Willet, Frank.

Eyraud, C., ed. see Conference on Vacuum Microbalance Techniques (12th: 1974: Lyon, France).

Eyre, A. G see Allen, W. S.

Eyre, A. G., ed. Longman Simplified English Series, 27 bks. Incl. The Adventures of Huckleberry Finn. Twain, Mark (ISBN 0-582-52840-2); The Adventures of Tom Sawyer. Twain, Mark (ISBN 0-582-52816-X); Best Stories of Thomas Hardy. Hardy, Thomas; Call for the Dead. Le Carre, John; Castle of Danger. Stewart, Mary (ISBN 0-582-52688-4); The Coral Island. Ballantyne, R. M; Far from the Madding Crowd. Hardy, Thomas (ISBN 0-582-52597-7); Hound of the Baskervilles. Doyle, Arthur Conan (ISBN 0-582-52910-7); Jane Eyre. Bronte, Charlotte; Journey to the Center of the Earth. Verne, Jules; Kidnapped. Stevenson, Robert Louis (ISBN 0-582-52914-X); Moby Dick. Melville, Herman; Pride & Prejudice. Austen, Jane (ISBN 0-582-52913-1); The Prisoner of Zenda. Hope, Anthony (ISBN 0-582-52841-0); Round the World in Eighty Days. Verne, Jules (ISBN 0-582-52806-2); Sherlock Holmes Short Stories. Doyle, Arthur Conan (ISBN 0-582-52911-5); Spinechillers (ISBN 0-582-52672-8); The Strange Case of Dr. Jekyll & Mr. Hyde. Stevenson, Robert Louis (ISBN 0-582-52547-0); A Summer Romance & Other Short Stories. Cave, Hugh (ISBN 0-582-52647-7); A Tale of Two Cities. Dickens, Charles (ISBN 0-582-52821-6); Tales of Mystery & Imagination. Poe, Edgar Allan (ISBN 0-582-52817-8); Tales from Shakespeare. Lamb, Charles & Lamb, Mary. (ISBN 0-582-52851-8); The Thirty-Nine Steps. Buchan, John (ISBN 0-582-52798-8); Three Men in a Boat. Jerome, Jerome K; The Three Musketeers. Dumas, Alexandre (ISBN 0-582-52827-5); Vanity Fair. Thackeray, W. M; Wuthering Heights. Bronte, Emily (ISBN 0-582-52318-4). (English As a Second Language Bks.). (Suitable for intermediate secondary school & adult students). 1956-81. pap. 2.45x ea. Longman.

Eyre, A. G., ed. see Cave, Hugh.

Eyre, A. G., ed. see Dickens, Charles.

Eyre, A. G., ed. see Doyle, Arthur Conan.

Eyre, A. G., ed. see Galsworthy, John, et al.

Eyre, A. G., ed. see Twain, Mark.

Eyre, Anthony, tr. see Benvenuti, Stefano & Rizzoni, Gianni.

Eyre, Dorothy. Rainbow Brite Saves Spring. (Golden Melody Bks.). 32p. (ps-2). 1985. write for info. (ISBN 0-307-12278-6, 12278, Pub. by Golden Bks). Western Pub.

Eyre, Edward. Edward Eyre's Autobiographical Narrative 1832-1839. Waterhouse, Jill, ed. LC 83-62657. (Illus.). 230p. 1985. 19.75 (ISBN 0-904573-32-X, Pub. by Caliban Bks). Longwood Pub Group.

Eyre, F. H. F. H. Eyre: Autobiography of a Forester. LC 82-61073. 98p. (Orig.). 1982. pap. 3.00 (ISBN 0-939970-15-5, SAF 82-04). Soc Am Foresters.

Eyre, Linda & Eyre, Richard. Teaching Children Joy. (Illus.). 194p. 1980. 9.95 (ISBN 0-87747-816-3). Deseret Bk.

--Teaching Children Responsibility. LC 82-12842. (Illus.). 247p. 1982. 9.95 (ISBN 0-87747-918-6). Deseret Bk.

Eyre, Linda, jt. auth. see Eyre, Richard.

Eyre, Richard & Eyre, Linda. Teaching Children Joy. Knowles, Eleanor, ed. 180p. pap. 8.95 (ISBN 0-317-14407-3). Deseret Bk.

--Teaching Children Responsibility. Knowles, Eleanor, ed. LC 82-12842. 180p. pap. 8.95 (ISBN 0-87747-891-0). Deseret Bk.

Eyre, Richard, jt. auth. see Eyre, Linda.

Eyre, S. R. The Real Wealth of Nations. LC 77-93019. 1978. 27.50x (ISBN 0-312-66525-3). St Martin.

Eyre, S. R., ed. World Vegetation Types. LC 78-147779. 264p. 1971. 39.00x (ISBN 0-231-03503-9). Columbia U Pr.

Eyres, D. J. Ship Construction. 2nd ed. (Illus.). 340p. 1978. pap. 22.50x (ISBN 0-434-90556-9). Sheridan.

Eyres, David J. Fishing Boat Designs: Small Steel Fishing Boats, Vol. 4. (Fisheries Technical Papers: No. 239). (Illus.). 52p. 1985. pap. 7.50 (ISBN 92-5-102108-2, F2660, FAO). Unipub.

Eyres, Lawrence. The Elders of the Church. 1975. pap. 2.25 (ISBN 0-87552-258-0). Presby & Reformed.

Eyre-Todd, George, ed. Scottish Poetry of the Eighteenth Century. LC 74-98755. Repr. of 1896 ed. lib. bdg. 27.50x (ISBN 0-8371-3096-4, EYEC). Greenwood.

--Scottish Poetry of the Seventeenth Century: Robert Aytoun, David Murray, Robert Ker, William Alexander, William Drummond, Marquis of Montrose, The Samples of Beltress. 296p. 1983. Repr. of 1895 ed. lib. bdg. 45.00 (ISBN 0-89987-220-4). Darby Bks.

Eyrich, Howard A. Three to Get Ready: A Christian Premarital Counselor's Manual. 1978. pap. 3.95 (ISBN 0-87552-259-9). Presby & Refomed.

Eyring, H., et al. Basic Chemical Kinetics. LC 79-26280. 493p. 1980. 54.50x (ISBN 0-471-05496-8, Pub. by Wiley-Interscience). Wiley.

Eyring, H., et al, eds. Physical Chemistry: An Advanced Treatise in Eleven Volumes. Incl. Vol. 1. Thermodynamics. Jost, W., ed. 1971. 95.00 (ISBN 0-12-245601-7); Vol. 2, Statistical Mechanics. Eyring, H., ed. 1967. 87.00, by subscription 70.50 (ISBN 0-12-245602-5); Vol. 3. Electronic Structure of Atoms & Molecules. Henderson, D., ed. 1969. 95.00 (ISBN 0-12-245603-3); Vol. 4. Molecular Properties. Henderson, D., ed. 1970. 99.50 (ISBN 0-12-245604-1); Vol. 5. Valency. Eyring, H., ed. 1970. 99.50 (ISBN 0-12-245605-X); Vol. 6A. General Introduction & Gas Reactions. Jost, W., ed. 1974. Pt. A. 95.00 (ISBN 0-12-245606-8); Pt. B, 1975. 95.00 (ISBN 0-12-245656-4); Vol. 7. Reactions in Condensed Phases. Eyring, H., ed. 1975. 95.00 (ISBN 0-12-245607-6); Vol. 8. Liquid State. Henderson, D., ed. Pt. A, 1971. 70.00 (ISBN 0-12-245608-4); Pt. B. 87.00 (ISBN 0-12-245658-0); Vol. 9. Electrochemistry. Eyring, H., ed. 1970. Pt. A. 87.00 (ISBN 0-12-245609-2); Pt. B. 87.00 (ISBN 0-12-245659-9). Pt. B; Vol. 10. Solid State Chemistry. Jost, W., ed. 1970. 95.00 (ISBN 0-12-245610-6); Vol. 11 Pt. A. Mathematical Applications. Henderson, D., ed. 1975. 95.00 (ISBN 0-12-245611-4); Pt. B. 101.50 (ISBN 0-12-245661-0). Acad Pr.

Eyring, Henry. Reflections of a Scientist. LC 83-7109. (Illus.). 101p. 1983. 6.95 (ISBN 0-87747-944-5). Deseret Bk.

Eyring, Henry & Henderson, Douglas, eds. Theoretical Chemistry: Advances & Perspectives, Vol. 4: Periodiocities in Chemistry & Biology. 1978. 72.00 (ISBN 0-12-681904-1). Acad Pr.

--Theoretical Chemistry: Advances in Perspectives, Vol. 2. 1976. 72.00 (ISBN 0-12-681902-5). Acad Pr.

Eyring, Henry, jt. ed. see Henderson, Douglas.

Eyring, Henry, et al. Statistical Mechanics & Dynamics. 2nd ed. LC 78-1073. 785p. 1982. 39.95 (ISBN 0-471-37042-8, Pub. by Wiley-Interscience). Wiley.

Eyring, Henry, et al, eds. Annual Review of Physical Chemistry, Vol. 23. LC 51-1658. (Illus.). 1972. text ed. 20.00 (ISBN 0-8243-1023-3). Annual Reviews.

--Annual Review of Physical Chemistry, Vol. 24. LC 51-1658. (Illus.). 1973. text ed. 20.00 (ISBN 0-8243-1024-1). Annual Reviews.

--Annual Review of Physical Chemistry, Vol. 26. LC 51-1658. (Illus.). 1975. text ed. 20.00 (ISBN 0-8243-1026-8). Annual Reviews.

--Annual Review of Physical Chemistry, Vol. 25. LC 51-1658. (Illus.). 1974. text ed. 20.00 (ISBN 0-8243-1025-X). Annual Reviews.

Eyring, L. Progress in the Science & Technology of the Rare Earths. write for info. Pergamon.

Eyring, L., ed. Rare Earth Research, Vol. 3. (Rare Earth Research Ser.). 770p. 1965. 180.50 (ISBN 0-677-10130-9). Gordon.

Eyring, L., jt. ed. see Gschneider, K. A.

Eyring, L., jt. ed. see Gschneidner, K. A.

Eyring, L., jt. ed. see Gschneidner, K. A., Jr.

Eyring, LeRoy, ed. Advances in High Temperature Chemistry. Vol. 1. 1967. 85.00 (ISBN 0-12-021501-2); Vol. 2. 1969. 85.00 (ISBN 0-12-021502-0); Vol. 3.1971. 85.00 (ISBN 0-12-021503-9); Vol. 4.1972. 85.00 (ISBN 0-12-021504-7). Acad Pr.

Eys, Jan van see Van Eys, Jan.

Eys, Jan Van see Van Eys, Jan.

Eys, Jan Van see Van Eys, Jan & Sullivan, Margaret P.

Eysenbach, Mary L. American Manufactured Exports, 1879-1914: A Study of Growth & Comparative Advantage. Bruchey, Stuart & Bruchey, Eleanor, eds. LC 76-5010. (American Business Abroad Ser.). (Illus.). 1976. 29.00x (ISBN 0-405-09278-4). Ayer Co Pubs.

Eysenck, A J. & Eaves, L. J. The Causes & Effects of Smoking. 116p. 1980. 49.00x (ISBN 0-85117-186-9, Pub. by Smith England). State Mutual Bk.

Eysenck, H. Intelligence Controversy: H. J. Eysenck vs Leon Kamin. LC 80-28571. 192p. 1981. 17.95 (ISBN 0-471-08884-6, Pub. by Wiley-Interscience). Wiley.

Eysenck, H. J. Biological Basis of Personality. (Illus.). 420p. 1977. 43.50x (ISBN 0-398-00538-9). C C Thomas.

--Check Your Own IQ. (Illus., Orig.). 1962. pap. 2.95 (ISBN 0-14-020656-6, Pelican). Penguin.

--Handbook of Abnormal Psychology. 928p. 1973. 175.00x (ISBN 0-272-76056-0, Pub. by Pitman Bks England). State Mutual Bk.

--The Inequality of Man. 1975. 10.95 (ISBN 0-912736-16-X). EDITS Pubs.

--The Psychology of Sex. (Illus.). 208p. 1979. 17.50 (ISBN 0-460-04332-3, Pub. by J M Dent England). Biblio Dist.

--Sex & Personality. 262p. 1976. text ed. 17.50x (ISBN 0-292-77529-6). U of Tex Pr.

Eysenck, H. J. & Eaves, L. J. The Causes & Effects of Smoking. LC 79-48085. (Illus.). 400p. 1981. 39.95 (ISBN 0-8039-1454-7). Sage.

Eysenck, H. J. & Eysenck, Sybil B. G. Personality Structure & Measurement. LC 68-15875. 1968. text ed. 11.95 (ISBN 0-912736-08-9). EDITS Pubs.

Eysenck, H. J. & Frith, C. D. Reminiscence, Motivation, & Personality: A Case Study in Experimental Psychology. LC 76-40136. (Illus.). 451p. 1977. 42.50x (ISBN 0-306-30924-6, Plenum Pr). Plenum Pub.

Eysenck, H. J. & Fulker, D. W. The Structure & Measurement of Intelligence. (Illus.). 1979. 25.00 (ISBN 0-387-09028-2). Springer-Verlag.

Eysenck, H. J. & Nias, D. K. Astrology: Science or Superstition? (Illus.). 288p. 1982. 12.95 (ISBN 0-312-05806-3). St Martin.

Eysenck, H. J. & Rachman, S. Causes & Cures of Neurosis. LC 64-21700. 1964. text ed. 11.95 (ISBN 0-912736-03-8). EDITS Pubs.

Eysenck, H. J. & Sargent, Carl. Know Your Own PSI-Q. 192p. 1984. pap. 8.95 (ISBN 0-911818-45-6). World Almanac.

Eysenck, H. J., ed. Encyclopedia of Psychology. 2nd ed. 1979. 39.50x (ISBN 0-8264-0097-3). Continuum.

--Handbook of Abnormal Psychology. 2nd ed. LC 72-97452. 1973. text ed. 42.00 (ISBN 0-912736-13-5). EDITS Pubs.

--A Model for Intelligence. (Illus.). 269p. 1982. 37.00 (ISBN 0-387-11676-1). Springer-Verlag.

--A Model for Personality. (Illus.). 281p. 1981. 32.00 (ISBN 0-387-10318-X). Springer-Verlag.

Eysenck, H. J. & Rachman, S., eds. Advances in Behaviour Research & Therapy, Vol. 1, Pt. 1. 1977. pap. 21.00 (ISBN 0-08-022257-9). Pergamon.

--Covert Conditioning: A Review & Evaluation. (Advances in Behaviour Research & Therapy Ser.: Vol. 2, No. 2). 1979. pap. 21.00 (ISBN 0-08-024271-5). Pergamon.

Eysenck, H. J. & Wilson, G. D., eds. The Psychological Basis of Ideology. 1978. 34.50 (ISBN 0-8391-1221-1). Univ Park.

Eysenck, Hans & Eysenck, Sybil. Psychoticism As a Dimension of Personality. LC 76-28570. 232p. 1976. 22.50x (ISBN 0-8448-1016-9). Crane-Russak Co.

Eysenck, Hans J. Know Your Own I.Q. (Orig.). 1962. pap. 2.95 (ISBN 0-14-020516-0, Pelican). Penguin.

--Personality, Genetics, & Behavior: Selected Papers. Speilberger, Charles D., ed. LC 81-15765. (Centennial Psychology Ser.). 352p. 1982. 37.95 (ISBN 0-03-059009-4). Praeger.

--The Scientific Study of Personality. LC 81-20077. xiii, 320p. 1982. Repr. of 1952 ed. lib. bdg. 37.50x (ISBN 0-313-23241-5, EYSS). Greenwood.

Eysenck, Hans J. & Eysenck, Michael W. Personality & Individual Differences: A Natural Science Approach. (Perspectives on Individual Differences Ser.). 410p. 1985. 29.50x (ISBN 0-306-41844-4, Plenum Pr). Plenum Pub.

Eysenck, Hans J. & Sargent, Carl. Know Your Own PSI-Q. 192p. 1984. 8.95 (ISBN 0-345-31305-4). Ballantine.

Eysenck, Hans J. & Wilson, Glenn. Know Your Own Personality. (Pelican Ser.). 208p. 1976. pap. 3.95 (ISBN 0-14-021962-5, Pelican). Penguin.

Eysenck, Hans J. & Wilson, Glenn D. The Experimental Studies of Freudian Theories. 1973. 39.95x (ISBN 0-416-78010-5, NO. 2196). Methuen Inc.

Eysenck, M. W. A Handbook of Cognitive Psychology. 432p. 1984. text ed. 39.95 (ISBN 0-86377-016-9); pap. text ed. 19.95 (ISBN 0-86377-017-7). L Erlbaum Assocs.

Eysenck, Michael. Attention & Arousal: Cognition & Performance. (Illus.). 209p. 1982. 34.50 (ISBN 0-387-11238-3). Springer-Verlag.

Eysenck, Michael W. Human Memory: Theory, Research & Individual Differences, Vol. 22. 1977. text ed. 21.00 (ISBN 0-08-020405-8). Pergamon.

Eysenck, Michael W., jt. auth. see Eysenck, Hans J.

Eysenck, Sybil, jt. auth. see Eysenck, Hans.

Eysenck, Sybil B. G., jt. auth. see Eysenck, H. J.

Eyseneck, Hans J. & Kelly, Betty N. I Do: How to Choose Your Mate & Have a Happy Marriage. (Illus.). 224p. (Orig.). 1985. pap. 8.95 (ISBN 0-911818-84-7). World Almanac.

Eysings, Roorda Van see Van Eysings, Roorda & Smilde, K. W.

Eysman, Harvey A. Courier's Fist. LC 80-27338. 256p. 1981. 12.95 (ISBN 0-8253-0034-7). Beaufort Bks NY.

Eyster, James J. The Negotiation & Administration of Hotel Management Contracts. 2nd, rev. ed. (Illus.). 209p. 1980. text ed. 22.95 (ISBN 0-937056-04-9). Cornell U Sch Hotel.

Eytan, Rachel. The Fifth Heaven. Simpson, Philip, tr. from Hebrew. 445p. 1985. 15.95 (ISBN 0-8276-0248-0). Jewish Pubns.

Eyton, Audrey. The F-Plan Diet. LC 82-17969. 256p. 1983. 12.95 (ISBN 0-517-54934-4). Crown.

--The F-Plan Diet. 256p. (Orig.). 1984. pap. 3.95 (ISBN 0-553-23951-1). Bantam.

--The F-Plus Diet. 288p. 1985. 13.95 (ISBN 0-517-55738-X). Crown.

Eyton, Audrey, jt. auth. see Carper, Jean.

Eyton, John S. Dancing Fakir & Other Stories. LC 77-101810. (Short Story Index Reprint Ser.). 1922. 14.50 (ISBN 0-8369-3198-X). Ayer Co Pubs.

Eyzaguirre, C. Physiology of the Nervous System. 1985. 17.50 (ISBN 0-8151-3184-4). Year Bk Med.

Eyzaguirre, Carlos & Fidone, Salvatore J. Physiology of the Nervous System. 2nd ed. (Illus.). 430p. 1975. 20.95 (ISBN 0-8151-3182-8); pap. 19.95 (ISBN 0-8151-3183-6). Year Bk Med.

Eze, Osita C. Human Rights in Africa: Some Selected Problems. LC 82-16809. 310p. 1985. 22.50x (ISBN 0-312-39962-6). St Martin.

Ezekiel, H. Second India Studies: Overview. 1978. 4.50x (ISBN 0-8364-0251-0). South Asia Bks.

Ezekiel, Hannan. The Economic Times' Statistical Survey of the Indian Economy. (Illus.). 230p. 1984. text ed. 40.00 (ISBN 0-7069-2498-3, Pub. by Vikas India). Advent NY.

Ezekiel, Hannan & Pavaskar, Madhoo. Second India Studies: Services. 1976. 4.50x (ISBN 0-333-90155-X). South Asia Bks.

Ezekiel, Hannan, ed. Corporate Sector in India. 176p. 1984. text ed. 35.00x (ISBN 0-7069-2497-5, Pub. by Vikas India). Advent NY.

Ezekiel, Jonathan, jt. auth. see Blum, Richard H.

Ezekiel, Mordecai. Twenty-Five Hundred Dollars a Year: From Scarcity to Abundance. LC 72-2369. (FDR & the Era of the New Deal Ser). 348p. 1973. Repr. of 1936 ed. lib. bdg. 39.50 (ISBN 0-306-70468-4). Da Capo.

Ezekiel, Mordecai & Fox, Karl A. Methods of Correlation & Regression Analysis: Linear & Curvilinear. 3rd ed. LC 59-11993. (Illus.). 548p. 1959. 55.95 (ISBN 0-471-25014-7, Pub. by Wiley-Interscience). Wiley.

Ezekiel, Mordecai, jt. auth. see Blau, Gerda.

Ezekiel, Nissim. Three Plays. (Writers Workshop Bluebird Ser.). 95p. 1975. pap. text ed. 4.00 (ISBN 0-88253-659-1). Ind-US Inc.

Ezekiel, Raphael S. Voices from the Corner: Poverty & Racism in the Inner City. 232p. 1984. 24.95 (ISBN 0-87722-358-0). Temple U Pr.

Ezekiel, S. & Arditty, H. J., eds. Fiber-Optic Rotation Sensors, Cambridge, MA: Proceedings, 1981. (Springer Ser. in Optical Sciences: Vol. 32). (Illus.). 440p. 1982. 37.00 (ISBN 0-387-11791-1). Springer-Verlag.

Ezekiel, Tish O. Floaters. LC 83-45498. 256p. 1984. 14.95 (ISBN 0-689-11446-X). Atheneum.

Ezell, Edward C. The Great Rifle Controversy: Search for the Ultimate Infantry Weapon from World War II Through Vietnam & Beyond. 352p. 1984. 29.95 (ISBN 0-8117-0709-1). Stackpole.

--Handguns of the World. LC 81-8575. (Illus.). 704p. 1981. 39.95 (ISBN 0-8117-0816-0). Stackpole.

--Small Arms Today: Latest Reports on the World's Weapons & Ammunition. 256p. (Orig.). 1984. pap. 16.95 (ISBN 0-8117-2197-3). Stackpole.

Ezell, Gene, jt. auth. see Anspaugh, David.

Ezell, Greta, jt. auth. see Ezell, Paul.

Ezell, John S. Innovations in Energy: The Story of Kerr-McGee. LC 79-4737. (Illus.). 1979. 24.95 (ISBN 0-8061-1585-8). U of Okla Pr.

--The South Since Eighteen Sixty-Five. 2nd ed. LC 74-15132. 1978. 17.95x (ISBN 0-8061-1480-0). U of Okla Pr.

Ezell, John S., ed. see Miranda, Francisco De.

Ezell, Lee & Gilbert, Lela. The Cinderella Syndrome: Discovering God's Plan When Your Dreams Don't Come True. 176p. (Orig.). 1985. pap. 4.95 (ISBN 0-89081-475-9). Harvest Hse.

Ezell, Macel D. Unequivocal Americanism: Right-Wing Novels in the Cold War Era. LC 77-3725. 160p. 1977. 16.00 (ISBN 0-8108-1033-6). Scarecrow.

Ezell, Mancil. Making Nonprojected Visuals & Displays. new ed. LC 74-21565. 64p. 1975. pap. 3.95 (ISBN 0-8054-3419-4). Broadman.

Ezell, Paul & Ezell, Greta. The Aguiar Collection in the Arizona Pioneers' Historical Society. 1964. pap. 3.60 (ISBN 0-916304-00-0). SDSU Press.

Ezell-Kalish, Susan, et al, eds. Proposal Writer's Swipe File. LC 81-50258. 162p. 1981. pap. 16.95 (ISBN 0-914756-45-1). Taft Group.

Ezenwe, Uka. ECOWAS & the Economic Integration of West Africa. LC 83-40187. 200p. 1984. 27.50 (ISBN 0-312-23687-5). St Martin.

Ezeokoli, Victoria, ed. African Theater: A Nigerian Prototype. LC 79-5150. cancelled (ISBN 0-88357-087-4); pap. text ed. cancelled (ISBN 0-88357-088-2). NOK Pubs.

Ezer, Mitchel. Uniform Commercial Code Bibliography. 539p. 1972. Incl. 1978 suppl. 35.00 (ISBN 0-317-30896-3, B396); Suppl. 1978 only. pap. 15.00 (ISBN 0-317-30897-1, B398); Study outline. pap. 2.48 (ISBN 0-317-30898-X, B390). Am Law Inst.

Ezera, R. Swing. 318p. 1985. pap. 4.00 (ISBN 0-8285-2965-5, Pub. by Raduga Pubs USSR). Imported Pubns.

Ezergailis, Andrew. The Nineteen Seventeen Revolution in Latvia. (East European Monographs: No. 8). 281p. 1974. 25.00x (ISBN 0-914710-01-X). East Eur Quarterly.

Ezergailis, Inta. Women Writers: The Divided Self. (Studien zur Germanistik, Anglistik und Komparatistik: Vol. 109). 120p. 1982. 15.00x (ISBN 3-416-01674-2, Pub. by Bouvier Verlag W Germany). Benjamins North Am.

Ezergalis, Inta. Women Writers-The Divided Self: Analyses of Novels by Christa Wolf, Ingeborg Bachmann, Doris Lessing, & Others. 1982. 36.00x (ISBN 3-416-01674-2, Pub. by Bouvier Verlag Ger). State Mutual BK.

Ezersky, Bella. Mastera: The Artists. LC 81-20204. (Illus.). 120p. (Rus.). 1982. pap. 8.00 (ISBN 0-938920-10-3). Hermitage.

Ezorsky, Gertrude, ed. Philosophical Perspectives on Punishment. LC 72-37999. 1972. 44.50x (ISBN 0-87395-212-X); pap. 11.95x (ISBN 0-87395-213-8). State U NY Pr.

Ezpinoza, Alurista H. & Gutierrez-Revueltas, Pablo, eds. Literatura Fronteriza. LC 82-62213. 176p. 1983. pap. 8.00 (ISBN 0-939558-03-3). Maize Pr.

Ezra, A. A. Principles & Practice of Explosive Metalworking. 270p. 1981. 75.00x (ISBN 0-901994-05-7, Pub. by Portcullio Pr). State Mutual Bk.

Ezra, G. S. Symmetry Properties of Molecules. (Lecture Notes in Chemistry Ser.: Vol. 28). 202p. 1982. pap. 17.70 (ISBN 0-387-11184-0). Springer-Verlag.

Ezra, Kate, tr. see Zahan, Dominique.

Ezra, Nehemeah. Beacon Small-Group Bible Studies, First & Second Timothy, Titus: Being Christian in Today's World. 1983. pap. 2.50 (ISBN 0-8341-0622-1). Beacon Hill.

Ezrachi, Y., jt. auth. see Tal, E.

Ezrahi, Sidra D. By Words Alone: The Holocaust in Literature. LC 79-56908. 1980. 19.00x (ISBN 0-226-23335-9). U of Chicago Pr.

--By Words Alone: The Holocaust in Literature. LC 79-56908. xiv, 262p. 1982. pap. 7.50x (ISBN 0-226-23336-7). U of Chicago Pr.

Ezzat, H., jt. auth. see Erdogan, F.

Ezzati, Trena M. Ambulatory Care Utilization Patterns of Children & Young Adults: National Ambulatory Medican Care Survey United States, January-December 1975. Stevenson, Taloria, ed. (Ser. 13: No. 39). 1978. pap. text ed. 1.75 (ISBN 0-8406-0134-4). Natl Ctr Health Stats.

Ezzell, Ben & Ezzell, Mary. The Delian Book of the Dead. 80p. 1985. pap. 8.50 (ISBN 0-940918-09-9). Dragon Tree.

Ezzell, Ben & Ezzell, Mary, eds. Amazon Mutual Wants You, Vol. 1. LC 82-1. (Illus.). 32p. 1982. pap. 6.00 (ISBN 0-940918-11-0). Dragon Tree.

--Amazon Mutual Wants You, Vol. 2. (Illus.). 32p. 1982. pap. 7.50 (ISBN 0-940918-13-7, 82-003). Dragon Tree.

Ezzell, Ben R. & Ezzell, Mary M., eds. The Handbook of Traps & Tricks. 2nd ed. (Illus.). 104p. (Orig.). 1981. pap. 9.95 (ISBN 0-940918-01-3, 81-002). Dragon Tree.

Ezzell, Ben R., et al, eds. Dragon Tree Spell Book. (Illus.). 80p. (Orig.). 1981. pap. text ed. 8.50 (ISBN 0-940918-02-1, 81-003). Dragon Tree.

Ezzell, Marilyn. The Clue in Witchcrest Well. (Susan Sand Mystery Ser.). (Orig.). (gr. 3-9). 1982. pap. 1.95 (ISBN 0-523-41742-X). Pinnacle Bks.

--The Mystery of Hollowhearth House. (Susan Sand Mystery Ser.: No. 1). (Orig.). (gr. 3-9). 1982. pap. 1.95 (ISBN 0-523-41701-2). Pinnacle Bks.

--The Password to Diamonddwarf Dale. (Susan Sand Ser.: No. 6). 192p. (Orig.). 1983. pap. 1.95 (ISBN 0-523-41963-5). Pinnacle Bks.

--The Phantom of Featherford Falls. (Susan Sand Mystery: No. 5). 192p. (gr. 5-7). 1983. pap. 1.95 (ISBN 0-523-41744-6). Pinnacle Bks.

--The Search for the Snowship Songs. (Susan Sand Ser.: No. 7). 192p. (Orig.). 1984. pap. 2.25 (ISBN 0-523-41964-3). Pinnacle Bks.

--The Secret of Clovercrest Castle. (Susan Sand Mystery Ser.: No. 2). (Orig.). (gr. 3-9). 1982. pap. 1.95 (ISBN 0-523-41741-1). Pinnacle Bks.

--Susan Sand No. 4: The Riddle of Raggedrock Ridge. 192p. (Orig.). 1982. pap. 1.95 (ISBN 0-523-41743-8). Pinnacle Bks.

Ezzell, Mary. Book of Plots, No. 1. 32p. Date not set. pap. 7.50 (ISBN 0-940918-15-3, 82-005). Dragon Tree.

--Desert Plots. (AMLA Ser.: No. 2). 32p. Date not set. pap. 7.50 (ISBN 0-940918-12-9, 82-003). Dragon Tree.

Ezzell, Mary, jt. auth. see Ezzell, Ben.

Ezzell, Mary, jt. ed. see Ezzell, Ben.

Ezzell, Mary, et al, eds. Book of Artifacts. (Illus.). 32p. 1982. pap. 8.50 (ISBN 0-940918-17-X, 82-002). Dragon Tree.

Ezzell, Mary M., jt. ed. see Ezzell, Ben R.

Ezzo, Elsie B. Bought for a Dollar & Other Exciting Stories of China. 96p. 1969. pap. 1.25 (ISBN 0-88243-505-1, 02-0505). Gospel Pub.

F

F. A. The Legal Regime of Foreign Private Investment in the Sudan & Saudi Arabia: A Case Study of Developing Countries. LC 83-7611. (Cambridge Studies in International & Comparative Law). 1984. 79.50 (ISBN 0-521-25286-5). Cambridge U Pr.

F A O see Food & Agriculture Organization.

F & S Press Book, jt. auth. see Siafaca, Katie.

F & S Press Book, jt. ed. see Gingerich, Duane.

F & S Press Book, ed. see Turk, Michael H.

F & S Press Research Staff, ed. Occupational Medicine: Surveillance, Diagnosis & Treatment. Turk, Michael H. (Health Care Economics & Technology Ser.). 238p. 1982. 34.95 (ISBN 0-86621-005-9). F&S Pr.

F., G. B. A. A Discovery of the Great Subtiltie & Wonderful Wisdom of the Italians. LC 74-80221. (English Experience Ser.: No. 656). 1974. Repr. of 1591 ed. 10.50 (ISBN 90-221-0656-X). Walter J Johnson.

F. Lewis, Publications LTD, ed. The F. S. Mackenna Collection of English Porcelain, 3 vols. 508p. 1981. Set. 150.00x (ISBN 0-686-79197-5, Pub. by Lewis Pubs). Vol. 1, Chelsea (ISBN 0-85317-009-6). Vol. 2, Worcester (ISBN 0-85317-014-2). Vol. 3, Plymouth & Bristol (ISBN 0-85317-015-0). State Mutual Bk.

F., T. The Copie of a Letter Sent from Sea by a Gentleman. LC 72-5984. (English Experience Ser.: No. 511). 1973. Repr. of 1589 ed. 6.00 (ISBN 90-221-0511-3). Walter J Johnson.

F. W. Faxon Co. Cumulated Dramatic Index. 1909-1949, 2 vols. 1965. lib. bdg. 615.00 (ISBN 0-8161-0402-6, Hall Library). G K Hall.

--Cumulated Magazine Subject Index. 1907-1949, 2 Vols. 1964. Set. 615.00 (ISBN 0-8161-0401-8, Hall Library). G K Hall.

Fa, John E., ed. The Barbary Macaque: A Case Study in Conservation. LC 84-11618. 388p. 1984. 49.50x (ISBN 0-306-41733-2, Plenum Pr). Plenum Pub.

F.A.A. How to Become a Pilot: The Step by Step Guide to Flying. LC 74-8723. (Illus.). pap. 8.95 (ISBN 0-8069-8386-8). Sterling.

FAA Department of Transportation. Airman's Information Manual & ATC Procedures, 1984. Rev. ed. (Illus.). 260p. 1984. pap. 9.95. Astro Pubs.

--Aviation Instructor's Handbook (AC 60.14) (Illus.). 124p. (Orig.). 1977. pap. text ed. 6.00 (ISBN 0-941272-02-8). Astro Pubs.

FAA, Department of Transportation. Fundamentals of Instructing Flight & Ground Instructors. (Illus.). 112p. 1979. pap. text ed. 8.95 (ISBN 0-941272-12-5, AP 490). Astro Pubs.

FAA, Dept. of Transportation. Aviation Weather Services. (Illus.). 132p. 1981. pap. text ed. 6.00 (ISBN 0-941272-09-5, AC 0045B). Astro Pubs.

FAA Dept. of Transportation. Fundamentals of Instructing & Ground Instructor Basic-Advanced Question Book (with answers) rev. ed. (Illus.). 104p. (Orig.). 1984. pap. text ed. 4.25 (ISBN 0-941272-22-2). Astro Pubs.

--IFR Pilot Exam-O-Gram (AP 105) (Illus.). 100p. 1985. pap. text ed. 5.50 (ISBN 0-941272-08-7). Astro Pubs.

--Instrument Flying Handbook (AC 61-27C) (Illus.). 268p. (Orig.). 1980. pap. text ed. 8.50 (ISBN 0-941272-20-6). Astro Pubs.

--Instrument Rating Question Book (with Answers) 260p. 1985. pap. text ed. 6.50 (ISBN 0-941272-24-9). Astro Pubs.

--Pilot's Federal Aviation Regulations. Composite ed. 264p. 1985. pap. text ed. 8.95. Astro Pubs.

--Private Pilot Airplane Written Test Guide (With Answers) (Illus.). 156p. 1979. pap. text ed. 5.95 (ISBN 0-941272-13-3). Astro Pubs.

--Private Pilot Question Book (with Answers) (Illus.). 160p. 1984. pap. text ed. 5.00 (ISBN 0-317-18182-3). Astro Pubs.

--VFR Pilot Exam-O-Grams (AP 104) (Illus.). 124p. (Orig.). 1985. pap. text ed. 5.95 (ISBN 0-941272-07-9). Astro Pubs.

Faaland, Just. Population & the World Economy in the 21st Century. LC 82-10579. 272p. 1982. 35.00 (ISBN 0-312-63123-5). St Martin.

Faaland, Just, ed. Aid & Influence: The Case of Bangladesh. LC 80-13481. 1980. 27.50 (ISBN 0-312-01492-9). St Martin.

Faas, Ekbert. Ted Hughes: The Unaccommodated Universe (with Selected Critical Writings by Ted Hughes & Two Interviews) 250p. 1980. 14.00 (ISBN 0-87685-460-9); pap. 7.50 (ISBN 0-87685-459-5); signed ed. 30.00 (ISBN 0-87685-461-7). Black Sparrow.

--Towards a New American Poetics: Essays & Interviews: Olson, Duncan, Snyder, Creeley, Bly, Ginsberg. 300p. 1979. 14.00 (ISBN 0-87685-389-0); pap. 7.50 (ISBN 0-87685-388-2). Black Sparrow.
--Tragedy & After: Euripides, Shakespeare, & Goethe. 256p. 1984. 25.00x (ISBN 0-7735-0416-8). McGill-Queens U Pr.
--Young Robert Duncan: Portrait of the Poet as Homosexual in Society. 400p. (Orig.). 1983. 20.00 (ISBN 0-87685-489-7); pap. 12.50 (ISBN 0-87685-488-9). Black Sparrow.
Faas, Larry A. Children with Learning Problems: A Handbook for Teachers. LC 79-89741. (Illus.). 1980. text ed. 25.95 (ISBN 0-395-28352-3); instr's. manual 1.00 (ISBN 0-395-28353-1). HM.
--Emotionally Disturbed Child: A Book of Readings. (Illus.). 400p. 1975. 22.75x (ISBN 0-398-00539-7). C C Thomas.
--Learning Disabilities: A Competency-Based Approach. 2nd ed. (Illus.). 480p. 1981. pap. text ed. 26.95 (ISBN 0-395-29699-4); instr's. manual 1.00 (ISBN 0-395-29700-1). HM.
Faas, Larry A., ed. Learning Disabilities: A Book of Readings. (Illus.). 272p. 1972. 13.75x (ISBN 0-398-02276-3). C C Thomas.
Faase, Thomas P. Making the Jesuits More Modern. LC 81-40388. (Illus.). 478p. (Orig.). 1981. lib. bdg. 30.00 (ISBN 0-8191-1761-7); pap. text ed. 18.50 (ISBN 0-8191-1762-5). U Pr of Amer.
Faatz, Anita J. The Nature of Choice & Other Selected Writings. LC 83-72424. (Studies in Modern Society: No. 18). 1984. 34.50 (ISBN 0-404-16043-3). AMS Pr.
Fabb, John. Flying & Ballooning from Old Photographs. LC 79-56467. (Illus.). 120p. 1980. 19.95 (ISBN 0-7134-2015-4, Pub. by Batsford England). David & Charles.
--Victorian & Edwardian Army from Old Photographs. 1975. 19.95 (ISBN 0-7134-2973-9, Pub. by Batsford England). David & Charles.
Fabb, W. E. & Fry, J. Principles of Practice Management. 1984. lib. bdg. 40.00 (ISBN 0-85200-859-7, Pub. by MTP Pr England). Kluwer Academic.
Fabb, W. E. & Heffernan, M. W. Focus on Learning in Family Practice. 253p. 1976. 15.00 (ISBN 0-318-17262-3). Soc Tchrs Fam Med.
Fabb, W. E. & Marshall, J. R. The Assessment of Clinical Competence in General Family Practice. 202p. 1983. text ed. write for info. (Pub. by MTP Pr England). Kluwer Academic.
--The Nature of General Family Practice. 600p. 1983. 36.00x (ISBN 0-942068-09-2). Bogden & Son.
Fabb, W. E. & Marshall, J. R., eds. The Nature of General Family Practice. 1983. lib. bdg. 36.00 (ISBN 0-85200-489-3, Pub. by MTP Pr England). Kluwer Academic.
Fabbri, Andrea G. Image Processing of Geological Data. 272p. 1984. 32.50 (ISBN 0-442-22536-9). Van Nos Reinhold.
Fabbri, Helen. Dear Pete: The Life of Pete Rose. Names, Larry D., ed. (Illus.). 320p. 1985. 24.95 (ISBN 0-910937-36-2); leather 125.00 (ISBN 0-910937-37-0). Laranmark.
Fabbri Magazine Editors, ed. Great Sweaters to Knit. (Illus.). 80p. 1983. pap. 9.95 (ISBN 0-684-17973-3, ScribT). Scribner.
Fabbri, Toni & Thorne, Gregory W. Mac Graphics. LC 84-16440. (Illus.). 224p. (Orig.). 1984. 21.95 (ISBN 0-8306-0861-3, 1861); pap. 14.95 (ISBN 0-8306-1861-9). TAB Bks.
Fabbri, Tony. Animation, Games, & Graphics for the Timex 1000. (Personal Computing Ser.). (Illus.). 240p. 1984. text ed. 13.95 (ISBN 0-13-037318-4). P-H.
--Animation, Games, & Sound for the Apple II-IIe. (P-H Personal Computing Ser.). (Illus.). 144p. 1984. pap. text ed. 17.95 incl. cassette (ISBN 0-13-037284-6); incl. disk 31.95 (ISBN 0-13-037276-5). P-H.
--Animation, Games & Sound for the IBM Personal Computer. (Illus.). 224p. 1983. pap. text ed. 19.50 (ISBN 0-13-037689-2). P-H.
--Animation, Games & Sound for the TI 99-4A. (Prentice-Hall Personal Computing Ser.). (Illus.). 224p. 1985. pap. text ed. 17.95 (ISBN 0-13-037227-7). P-H.
--Animation, Games, & Sound for the VIC-20. (Personal Computing Ser.). (Illus.). 224p. 1984. pap. 15.95 (ISBN 0-13-037342-7); incl. disk 29.95 (ISBN 0-13-037334-6). P-H.
--Animation, Games, & Sounds for the Commodore 64. (Prentice-Hall Personal Computing Ser.). (Illus.). 224p. 1984. pap. text ed. 16.95 (ISBN 0-13-037375-3). P-H.
--Using & Programming the Apple IIc: Including Ready-to-Run Programs. (Illus.). 256p. 1985. 19.95 (ISBN 0-8306-0981-4, 1981); pap. 14.95 (ISBN 0-8306-1981-X). TAB Bks.
Fabbricante, Thomas & Sultan, William J. Practical Meat Cutting & Merchandising, Vol. 1: Beef. 2nd ed. (Illus.). 1978. pap. text ed. 16.50 (ISBN 0-87055-273-2). AVI.
--Practical Meat Cutting & Merchandising, Vol. 2: Pork, Lamb & Veal. (Illus.). 1975. pap. text ed. 16.50 (ISBN 0-87055-177-9). AVI.
Fabbrini, A. & Steinberger, E., eds. Recent Progress in Andrology. (Proceedings of the Serono Symposia: Vol. 14). 1979. 60.00 (ISBN 0-12-247350-7). Acad Pr.
Fabbro, Mario D. How to Make Children's Furniture & Play Equipment. 2nd ed. LC 83-15856. (Illus.). 208p. (Orig.). 1984. pap. 8.95 (ISBN 0-668-05925-7). Arco.
Fabel, Arthur. Cosmic Genesis. (Tielhard Studies). 1981. 2.00 (ISBN 0-89012-028-5). Anima Pubns.
Fabel, Robin F. Bombast & Broadsides: The Lives of George Johnstone. (Illus.). 1984. write for info. (ISBN 0-916624-36-6). Troy State Univ.
Fabelinskii, I. L. Molecular Scattering of Light. LC 67-10534. 622p. 1968. 69.50x (ISBN 0-306-30308-6, Plenum Pr). Plenum Pub.
Fabell, Walter. Nature's Clues. (Illus.). (gr. 4-6). 1964. PLB 6.95 (ISBN 0-8038-4992-3). Hastings.
Fabella, Virginia, ed. Asia's Struggle for Full Humanity: Towards a Relevant Theology. LC 80-14923. 229p. (Orig.). 1980. pap. 8.95 (ISBN 0-88344-015-6). Orbis Bks.
Fabella, Virginia & Torres, Sergio, eds. Doing Theology in a Divided World. LC 84-14712. 224p. (Orig.). 1985. pap. 11.95 (ISBN 0-88344-197-7). Orbis Bks.
--Irruption of the Third World: Challenge to Theology. LC 82-18851. 304p. (Orig.). 1983. pap. 10.95 (ISBN 0-88344-216-7). Orbis Bks.
Fabella, Virginia, jt. ed. see Torres, Sergio.
Fabens, Joseph W. In the Tropics. text ed. 16.75 (ISBN 0-8369-9226-1, 9080). Ayer Co Pubs.
Faber, A. D. Cigar Label Art. (Illus.). 1949. lib. bdg. 10.00 (ISBN 0-87282-126-9). CHB-ALF.
--Smokers, Segars & Stickers. (Illus.). 1949. lib. bdg. 10.00. CHB-ALF.
Faber, Adele & Mazlish, Elaine. How to Talk So Kids Will Listen & Listen So Kids Will Talk. 256p. 1982. pap. 4.95 (ISBN 0-380-57000-9, 60203-2). Avon.
--Liberated Parents-Liberated Children. 1975. pap. 3.50 (ISBN 0-380-00466-6, 65649). Avon.
Faber, Alyce E. Read-O-Mat: Syllabus. 1976. pap. text ed. 5.85 (ISBN 0-89420-006-2, 114008); cassette recordings 35.85 (ISBN 0-89420-179-4, 114000). Natl Book.
Faber, Bernard E. A Teacher's Treasury of Quotations. LC 84-43218. 400p. 1985. lib. bdg. 39.95 (ISBN 0-89950-150-8). McFarland & Co.
Faber, Carl A. On Listening. LC 80-4512. 1976. 5.95 (ISBN 0-918026-02-4). Perseus Pr.
--Poems. LC 59-4760. 1974. 4.95 (ISBN 0-918026-01-6). Perseus Pr.
Faber, Charles F. Baseball Ratings: The All-Time Best Players at Each Position Ranked by the Faber System. LC 84-43206. 128p. 1985. pap. 13.95 (ISBN 0-89950-158-3). McFarland & Co.
Faber, Donald & Korn, Henri, eds. Neurobiology of the Mauthner Cell. LC 78-66351. 302p. 1978. 45.50 (ISBN 0-89004-233-0). Raven.
Faber, Doris. Eleanor Roosevelt: First Lady of the World. LC 84-20861. (Women of Our Time Ser.). (Illus.). 64p. (gr. 2-6). 1985. 9.95 (ISBN 0-670-80551-3). Viking.
--Harry Truman. LC 72-2076. (Illus.). 96p. (gr. 3 up). 1973. 9.89 (ISBN 0-200-71906-8, B32230, AbS-J). Har-Row.
--The Life of Lorena Hickok: E. R.'s Friend. LC 79-91302. (Illus.). 382p. 1980. 12.95 (ISBN 0-688-03631-7). Morrow.
--Love & Rivalry: Three Exceptional Pairs of Sisters. LC 83-6566. (Illus.). 204p. (gr. 7 up). 1983. 13.95 (ISBN 0-670-44221-6, Viking Kestrel). Viking.
--Margaret Thatcher: Britain's Iron Lady. LC 85-40442. (Women of Our Time Ser.). (Illus.). 64p. (gr. 2-6). 1985. 9.95 (ISBN 0-670-80785-0). Viking.
--The Perfect Life: The Shakers in America. LC 73-90968. (Illus.). 224p. (gr. 7 up). 1974. 10.95 (ISBN 0-374-35819-2). FS&G.
Faber, Federick W. Bethlehem. LC 78-66306. 1978. pap. 10.00 (ISBN 0-89555-080-6). TAN Bks Pubs.
Faber, Frederick. Self-Deceit. 1983. pap. 5.00x (ISBN 0-87574-050-2, 050). Pendle Hill.
Faber, Frederick W. The Blessed Sacrament. LC 78-66302. 1978. pap. 11.00 (ISBN 0-89555-077-6). TAN Bks Pubs.
--The Creator & Creature. LC 78-66301. 1978. pap. 9.50 (ISBN 0-89555-076-8). TAN Bks Pubs.
--The Foot of the Cross: The Sorrows of Mary. LC 78-66303. 1978. pap. 10.00 (ISBN 0-89555-078-4). TAN Bks Pubs.
--Precious Blood. LC 78-66300. 1979. pap. 7.50 (ISBN 0-89555-075-X). TAN Bks Pubs.
--Spiritual Conferences. LC 78-66304. 1978. pap. 9.00 (ISBN 0-89555-079-2). TAN Bks Pubs.
Faber, Fredrick W. Hymns. 1977. Repr. of 1881 ed. 20.00 (ISBN 0-8274-4295-5). R West.
Faber, Gail & Lasagna, Michele. Whispers from the First Californians. 2nd ed. (California History Ser.). (Illus.). 1981. permabound student's ed. 13.95 (ISBN 0-936480-02-5); pap. text ed. 9.95 student's ed., 223p. (ISBN 0-936480-00-9); Tchr's ed., 240p. 3-ring binder 19.95 (ISBN 0-936480-01-7). Magpie Pubns.
Faber, Geoffrey. Oxford Apostles. 467p. 1974. 7.95 (ISBN 0-571-10495-9). Faber & Faber.
--Oxford Apostles: A Character Study of the Oxford Movement. 1979. Repr. of 1933 ed. lib. bdg. 35.00 (ISBN 0-8482-3953-9). Norwood Edns.
Faber, Geoffrey C. Oxford Apostles: A Character Study of the Oxford Movement. LC 75-30022. Repr. of 1933 ed. 34.50 (ISBN 0-404-14027-0). AMS Pr.
Faber, George S. The Origin of Pagan Idolatry. Feldman, Burton & Richardson, Robert D., eds. LC 78-60891. (Myth & Romanticism Ser.). 1984. lib. bdg. 240.00 (ISBN 0-8240-3559-3). Garland Pub.
Faber, Gladys. Spring Harvest. 15.95 (ISBN 0-89190-599-5, Pub. by Am Repr). Amereon Ltd.
Faber, Heije. Pastoral Care in the Modern Hospital. De Waal, Hugo, tr. LC 70-168632. 160p. 1972. 10.95 (ISBN 0-664-20922-X). Westminster.
--Psychology of Religion. LC 75-43721. 348p. 1976. 13.95 (ISBN 0-664-20748-0). Westminster.
--Striking Sails: A Pastoral View of Growing Older in Our Society. Mitchell, Kenneth R., tr. 160p. 1984. pap. 10.95 (ISBN 0-687-39941-6). Abingdon.
Faber, Inez M. Out Here on Soap Creek. 180p. 1982. 12.95 (ISBN 0-8138-1286-0). Iowa St U Pr.
Faber, J., jt. ed. see Chandebois, Rosine.
Faber, J. Job & Thornburg, Kent L. Placental Physiology: Structure & Function of Fetomaternal Exchange. (Illus.). 208p. 1983. text ed. 40.50 (ISBN 0-89004-978-5). Raven.
Faber, John. Great News Photos & the Stories Behind Them. 1978. pap. 6.00 (ISBN 0-486-23667-6). Dover.
--Great News Photos & the Stories Behind Them. rev. 2nd ed. 14.75 (ISBN 0-8446-5758-1). Peter Smith.
Faber, John, Jr., ed. see AIP Conference Proceedings No. 89, Argonne National Laboratory, 1981.
Faber, Knud H. Nosography. 2nd rev ed. LC 75-23706. (Illus.). 1976. Repr. of 1930 ed. 22.00 (ISBN 0-404-13258-8). AMS Pr.
Faber, M. Introduction to Modern Austrian Capital Theory. (Lecture Notes in Economics & Mathematical Systems: Vol. 167). 1979. pap. 17.00 (ISBN 0-387-09121-1). Springer-Verlag.
Faber, M. D. Culture & Consciousness: The Social Meaning of Altered Awareness. LC 80-36683. 296p. 1981. text ed. 29.95x (ISBN 0-87705-505-X); professional 29.95 (ISBN 0-686-96741-0). Human Sci Pr.
Faber, Marilyn M. & Reinhardt, Adina M. Promoting Health Through Risk Reduction. 1982. text ed. write for info. (ISBN 0-02-334850-X). Macmillan.
Faber, Marion, tr. see Hildesheimer, Wolfgang.
Faber, Marion, tr. see Nietzsche, Friedrich.
Faber, Marion, et al, trs. see Reich, Wilhelm.
Faber, Melvin D., ed. Design Within: Psychoanalytic Approaches to Shakespeare. LC 84-45232. 553p. 1970. 30.00x (ISBN 0-87668-707-9). Aronson.
Faber, Peter. A Christmas Book. Tate, tr. 24p. 1980. 8.50 (ISBN 0-7207-1118-5, Pub. by Michael Joseph). Merrimack Pub Cir.
Faber, Peter L. & Holbrook, Martin E. Subchapter S Manual: A Special Tax Break for Small Business Corporation. LC 83-128142. 250p. 1983. pap. 24.95x (85912-4). P-H.
Faber, Phyllis M. Common Wetland Plants of Coastal California. (Illus.). 120p. 1982. 12.00 (ISBN 0-9607890-0-6). Pickleweed.
Faber, R. B. Essentials of Solid State Electronics. 735p. 1985. 32.95 (ISBN 0-471-86575-3); lab guide avail. (ISBN 0-471-81492-X). Wiley.
Faber, Richard. The Brave Courtier: Sir William Temple. 176p. 1983. 32.00 (ISBN 0-571-11982-4). Faber & Faber.
--High Road to England. LC 85-4466. 224p. 1985. 29.95 (ISBN 0-571-13509-9). Faber & Faber.
Faber, Rodney B. Applied Electricity & Electronics for Technology. 2nd ed. LC 77-15037. (Electronics Technology Ser.). 477p. 1982. text ed. 29.95 (ISBN 0-471-05792-4); avail. solutions (ISBN 0-471-86322-X). Wiley.
Faber, Samuel J. & Faber, Stuart J. Attorneys Medical Handbook. 256p. (Orig.). 1981. pap. text ed. 32.50 (ISBN 0-89074-085-2). Lega Bks.
Faber, Stuart J. Business Transaction Forms. 2nd, rev. ed. 300p. 1983. pap. text ed. 38.50 (ISBN 0-89074-094-1). Lega Bks.
--California Discovery Handbook. 3rd ed. 319p. (Orig.). 1983. pap. text ed. 34.50 (ISBN 0-89074-082-8). Lega Bks.
--California Sentencing Handbook. 1978. pap. 26.50 (ISBN 0-89074-054-2). Lega Bks.
--Consumers: A Self-Defense Manual. new ed. 84p. (Orig.). 1974. pap. 1.95 (ISBN 0-89074-005-4). Good Life.
--Debtor-Creditor Litigation Handbook. 2nd & rev. ed. 400p. 1983. pap. text ed. 36.50 (ISBN 0-89074-081-X). Lega Bks.
--Faber's Evidence Courtroom Book. (Orig.). 1979. pap. 44.50 (ISBN 0-89074-071-2). Good Life.
--Faber's Evidence Courtroom Book. 359p. 1979. pap. text ed. 44.50 (ISBN 0-89074-071-2). Lega Bks.
--Handbook of Civil Procedure, 2 Vols. 4rd rev. ed. 1982. pap. 51.50 (ISBN 0-89074-070-4). Good Life.
--Handbook of Civil Procedure, 2 Vols. 4th, rev. ed. 793p. 1982. pap. text ed. 51.50 (ISBN 0-89074-070-4). Lega Bks.
--Handbook of Commercial Law. 1979. pap. 31.50 (ISBN 0-89074-061-5). Lega Bks.
--Handbook of Construction Law. 2nd ed. 399p. 1984. pap. text ed. 34.50 (ISBN 0-89074-078-X). Lega Bks.
--Handbook of Consumer Law. 3rd, Rev. ed. 1984. pap. 35.50 (ISBN 0-89074-060-7). Lega Bks.
--Handbook of Criminal Law. 360p. (Orig.). 1981. pap. text ed. 35.50 (ISBN 0-89074-088-7). Lega Bks.
--Handbook of Criminal Procedure, 2 vols. 4th, rev. ed. 439p. 1985. pap. text ed. 51.50 (ISBN 0-89074-076-3). Lega Bks.
--Handbook of Family Law. 4th, Rev. ed. 484p. 1982. pap. text ed. 41.50 (ISBN 0-686-34400-6). Lega Bks.
--Handbook of Guardianships & Conservatorships. 4th & rev. ed. 457p. 1984. pap. text ed. 36.50 (ISBN 0-686-37115-1). Lega Bks.
--Handbook of Landlord-Tenant Law. 2nd ed. 286p. 1982. pap. 35.50 (ISBN 0-89074-095-X). Lega Bks.
--Handbook of Legal Tips for Building Contractors. rev. ed. 60p. (Orig.). 1976. pap. 6.95 (ISBN 0-89074-004-6). Good Life.
--Handbook of Litigation Forms, 2 Vols. 2nd ed. 604p. 1983. pap. text ed. 51.50 (ISBN 0-89074-052-6). Lega Bks.
--Handbook of Real Estate Law, 2 vols. 3rd ed. 650p. 1985. Set. pap. text ed. 51.50 (ISBN 0-89074-083-6). Lega Bks.
--How to Avoid & Beat Traffic Tickets. 56p. (Orig.). 1974. pap. 4.95 (ISBN 0-89074-002-X). Good Life.
--How to Get Rid of Your Wife: And No Court Will Ever Convict You. 200p. 1974. 7.95 (ISBN 0-685-50674-6). Good Life.
--How to Outsmart Your Landlord (If You're a Tenant) or How to Outsmart Your Tenant (If You're a Landlord) rev. ed. 176p. 1982. pap. 6.95 (ISBN 0-89074-057-7). Good Life.
--If the Cops Come, Eat This Book. rev. ed. 100p. 1975. pap. 3.95 (ISBN 0-89074-014-3). Good Life.
--Landlord-Tenant Problems: Texas Edition. 1978. pap. 7.95 (ISBN 0-89074-059-3). Lega Bks.
--Legal Practice Handbook. 556p. (Orig.). 1981. pap. text ed. 47.50 (ISBN 0-89074-087-9). Lega Bks.
--Let's Explore Central America. 100p. 1975. pap. 1.95 (ISBN 0-89074-013-5). Good Life.
--Nonprofit Corporation Law Handbook. 2nd, Rev. ed. 295p. 1984. pap. text ed. 36.50 (ISBN 0-89074-093-3). Lega Bks.
--Real Estate Liens Encumbrances & Secured Transactions. 2nd ed. 1979. pap. 27.50 (ISBN 0-89074-065-8). Lega Bks.
--Why Not Go to West Africa. new ed. 79p. (Orig.). 1974. pap. 1.95 (ISBN 0-89074-006-2). Good Life.
Faber, Stuart J. & Levison, Teddi. The Upside-Downs of Jealousy, Possessiveness & Insecurity. 100p. 1975. pap. text ed. 4.95 (ISBN 0-89074-012-7). Good Life.
Faber, Stuart J. & Lovett, Steven R. Arbitration Handbook. 2nd rev. ed. 1982. pap. 31.50 (ISBN 0-89074-072-0). Good Life.
Faber, Stuart J & Lovett, Steven R. Arbitration Handbook. 2nd, rev. ed. 272p. 1982. pap. text ed. 31.50 (ISBN 0-89074-072-0). Lega Bks.
Faber, Stuart J. & Niles, Edward I. Handbook of Corporation Law, 2 vols. 3rd, Rev. ed. 707p. 1983. pap. text ed. 49.50 (ISBN 0-89074-084-4). Lega Bks.
Faber, Stuart J., jt. auth. see Faber, Samuel J.
Faber, Stuart J., et al. Angel Dust: What Everyone Should Know about PCP. 1982. pap. 7.95 (ISBN 0-89074-066-6). Lega Bks.
Faber, Tobias. Danish Architecture, History of. Stevenson, Frederic R., tr. from Danish. (Denmark in Print & Pictures Ser.). (Illus.). 316p. 1978. 15.95 (ISBN 87-7429-033-9, Pub. by Det Danske Selskab Denmark). Nordic Bks.
Fabera, J., ed. Equadiff IV: Proceedings, Prague, August 22 - 26, 1977. LC 79-11103. (Lecture Notes in Mathematics: Vol. 703). 1979. pap. 26.00 (ISBN 0-387-09116-5). Springer-Verlag.
Fabes, jt. auth. see Douglis.
Fabes, G. D. H. Lawrence: His First Editions. 59.95 (ISBN 0-87968-989-7). Gordon Pr.
Fabes, Gilbert H. D. H. Lawrence: His First Editions. 1978. Repr. of 1933 ed. lib. bdg. 15.00 (ISBN 0-8495-1626-9). Arden Lib.
--D. H. Lawrence: His First Editions. 104p. 1980. Repr. of 1933 ed. lib. bdg. 15.00 (ISBN 0-89987-275-1). Darby Bks.
--D. H. Lawrence-His First Editions: Points & Values. LC 76-49819. 1933. lib. bdg. 25.00 (ISBN 0-8414-4157-X). Folcroft.
--The First Editions of A. E. Coppard, A. P. Herbert & Charles Morgan. 1972. Repr. of 1932 ed. lib. bdg. 25.00 (ISBN 0-685-28111-6). Folcroft.
--The First Editions of Ralph Hale Mottram. 1979. Repr. of 1934 ed. lib. bdg. 25.00 (ISBN 0-8414-4313-0). Folcroft.
--The First Editions of Ralph Hale Mottram. 1934. Repr. 22.50 (ISBN 0-8274-2348-9). R West.
--John Galsworthy: His First Editions. 1978. Repr. of 1932 ed. lib. bdg. 15.00 (ISBN 0-8495-1614-5). Arden Lib.
--John Galsworthy: His First Editions. LC 73-10489. 1973. Repr. of 1932 ed. lib. bdg. 17.50 (ISBN 0-8414-1972-8). Folcroft.
--Modern First Editions: Points & Values: First Series. LC 74-11169. lib. bdg. 25.00 (ISBN 0-8414-4230-4). Folcroft.

--Modern First Editions: Points & Values, Second Series. 1931. lib. bdg. 25.00 (ISBN 0-8414-4218-5). Folcroft.

--Modern First Editions: Points & Values Third Series. lib. bdg. 25.00 (ISBN 0-8414-4232-0). Folcroft.

Fabian, D. J. & Watson, L. M., eds. Band Structure Spectroscopy of Metals & Alloys. 1973. 119.50 (ISBN 0-12-247440-6). Acad Pr.

Fabian, Derek J., ed. Soft X-Ray Band Spectra & the Electronic Structures of Metals & Materials. 1969. 65.00 (ISBN 0-12-247450-3). Acad Pr.

Fabian, Derek J., et al, eds. Inner-Shell & X-Ray Physics of Atoms & Solids. LC 81-11945. (Physics of Atoms & Molecules Ser.). 976p. 1981. 125.00x (ISBN 0-306-40819-8, Plenum Pr). Plenum Pub.

Fabian, Erica, jt. auth. see Wanderer, Zev.

Fabian, Erika, jt. auth. see Moldavy, Albert.

Fabian, Erika, jt. auth. see Moldvay, Albert.

Fabian, Gerald. Odissea Finita. 1969. signed ed. 5.00 (ISBN 0-686-28710-X); pap. 2.00 (ISBN 0-686-28711-8). Man-Root.

Fabian, J. & Hartmann, H. Light Absorption of Organic Colorants: Theoretical Treatment & Empirical Rules. (Reactivity & Structure Ser.: Vol. 12). (Illus.). 280p. 1980. 86.00 (ISBN 0-387-09914-X). Springer-Verlag.

Fabian, Johannes. Jamaa: A Charismatic Movement in Katanga. 1971. 16.95 (ISBN 0-8101-0339-7). Northwestern U Pr.

--Time & the Other. 224p. 1983. 31.50x (ISBN 0-231-05590-0); pap. 15.00 (ISBN 0-231-05591-9). Columbia U Pr.

Fabian, John. Fishing for Beginners. Cornacchia, Pete, ed. LC 72-94249. (Illus.). 144p. (gr. 7 up). 1973. pap. 2.95 (ISBN 0-689-70468-2, A-97, Aladdin). Atheneum.

Fabian, Josephine. The Jackson Hole Story, 1833. 192p. pap. 6.95 (ISBN 0-914740-13-X). Western Epics.

Fabian, Larry L. & Schiff, Ze'ev, eds. Israelis Speak: About Themselves & the Palestinians. LC 75-51150. 1977. text ed. 10.00 (ISBN 0-87003-007-8); pap. text ed. 5.00 (ISBN 0-87003-008-6). Carnegie Endow.

Fabian, M. E. Semiconductor Laser Diodes: A User's Handbook. 1981. 140.00x (ISBN 0-686-71789-9, Pub. by Electrochemical Scotland). State Mutual Bk.

Fabian, Margaret W. My Friend Luke, the Stenciller. LC 83-50689. (Illus.). 35p. (gr. 3-4). 1985. pap. 7.95 over boards (ISBN 0-931474-25-6). TBW Bks.

Fabian, Marsha, jt. auth. see Hoover, Mary.

Fabian, Miriam, jt. ed. see Cashdollar, Pat.

Fabian, Monroe. Mr. Sully Portrait Painter: The Works of Thomas Sully, 1783-1872. LC 83-600010. (Illus.). 128p. 1983. 35.00x (ISBN 0-87474-426-1). Smithsonian.

Fabian, P., tr. see Breuer, Georg.

Fabian, R. Gerry. Doubleheader. 12p. 1983. pap. 1.00 (ISBN 0-686-46878-3). Samisdat.

--A Fallen Woman. 12p. 1981. pap. 1.00 (ISBN 0-686-33136-2). Samisdat.

Fabian, Rainer & Adam, Hans C. Masterpieces of Early Travel Photography: In Search of a New World. LC 83-12495. Orig. Title: Fruehe Reise Mit der Kamera. (Illus.). 360p. 1983. 50.00 (ISBN 0-86565-034-9). Vendome.

Fabian Society - London. Where Stands Democracy? facs. ed. LC 76-117788. (Essay Index Reprint Ser). 1940. 14.00 (ISBN 0-8369-1651-4). Ayer Co Pubs.

Fabian Society - London - International Research Section. Hitler's Route to Baghdad. facs. ed. LC 70-142624. (Essay Index Reprint Ser). 1939. 20.00 (ISBN 0-8369-2046-5). Ayer Co Pubs.

Fabian, Vaclav & Hannan, James. Introduction to Probability & Mathematical Statistics. LC 84-12998. (Wiley Series in Probability & Mathematical Statistics: 1-345). 448p. 1985. text ed. 42.95 (ISBN 0-471-25023-6, Pub. by Wiley Interscience). Wiley.

Fabian, William M. Fiction Finder Manual. (gr. 4-12). 1984. 6.95 (ISBN 0-916625-08-7); Grades 7-12. study sheets kit 9.95 (ISBN 0-916625-10-9). Computer Assis.

Fabilli, Mary. Animal Kingdom. 1975. pap. 2.50 (ISBN 0-685-56096-1). Oyez.

--Aurora Bligh & Early Poems. 5.00 (ISBN 0-685-04661-3); pap. 2.50 (ISBN 0-685-04662-1). Oyez.

Fabiny, T. Martin Luther's Last Will & Testament: A Facsimile of the Original Document, with an Account of Its Origins, Composition & Subsequent History. 51p. 1984. text ed. 25.50x (ISBN 0-904720-15-2, Pub. by Ussher Pr Dublin). Humanities.

Fabio, Anthony di see Di Fabio, Anthony.

Fabiola, Cabeza de Baca see Cabeza de Baca, Fabiola.

Fabisch, Judith. A Window's Guide to Living Alone. 128p. 1983. pap. 4.95 (ISBN 0-310-43481-5). Zondervan.

Fabisch, Victoria. The A's & B's: Your Guide to Academic Scholarships, 1986-1987. 8th ed. LC 78-52571. 80p. 1985. pap. 4.00 (ISBN 0-917760-61-1). Octameron Assocs.

Fabish, Susan. On-The-Job Technical Writing. (Illus.). 1984. 44.50 (ISBN 0-916780-25-2). CES.

Fabisoff, Sylvia G. & Tripp, Wendell, eds. A Bibliography of Newspapers in Fourteen New York Counties. 14.00 (ISBN 0-917334-02-7). Fenimore Bk.

Fable, Edmund, Jr. The True Life of Billy the Kid. LC 80-18408. 78p. (Orig.). 1980. Repr. of 1881 ed. collector's edition 95.00 (ISBN 0-932702-11-2). Creative Texas.

Fabos, Julius G. Planning the Total Landscape: A Guide to Intelligent Land Use. (Illus.). 1979. lib. bdg. 23.50x (ISBN 0-89158-172-3). Westview.

Fabos, Julius Gy. Land Use Planning: From Global to Local Challenge. 300p. 1985. 39.95 (ISBN 0-412-25200-7, 5068, Pub. by Chapman & Hall England); pap. 18.95 (ISBN 0-412-25210-4, 5069). Methuen Inc.

Fabozzi, Frank & Masonson, Leslie N., eds. Corporate Cash Management: Techniques & Analysis. LC 84-71295. 385p. 1984. 47.50 (ISBN 0-87094-477-0). Dow Jones-Irwin.

Fabozzi, Frank J. Equipment Leasing: A Comprehensive Guide for Executives. LC 87-67118. 250p. 1981. 40.00 (ISBN 0-87094-264-6). Dow Jones-Irwin.

--Winning the Interest Rate Game: A Guide to Debt Options. 324p. 1984. 30.00 (ISBN 0-917253-01-9). Probus Pub Co.

Fabozzi, Frank J. & Feldman, Stephen. Smart Money: An Investment Game Plan for Those Who Made It & Want to Keep It. 200p. 1985. 18.95 (ISBN 0-917253-16-7). Probus Pub Co.

Fabozzi, Frank J. & Greenfield, Harry I. The Handbook of Economic & Financial Measures. LC 83-73708. 225p. 1984. 50.00 (ISBN 0-87094-466-5). Dow Jones-Irwin.

Fabozzi, Frank J. & Zarb, Frank G. The Handbook of Financial Markets: Securities, Options and Futures. LC 80-70448. 825p. 1981. 50.00 (ISBN 0-87094-216-6). Dow Jones-Irwin.

Fabozzi, Frank J., jt. auth. see Fong, H. Gifford.

Fabozzi, Frank J., ed. Floating Rate Instruments: Characteristics, Valuation & Portfolio Strategies. 250p. 1985. 40.00 (ISBN 0-917253-15-9). Probus Pub Co.

--The Handbook of Mortgage-Backed Securities. 648p. 1985. 45.00 (ISBN 0-917253-04-3). Probus Pub Co.

--Readings in Investment Management. 1983. pap. 13.95x (ISBN 0-256-02934-2). Irwin.

Fabozzi, Frank J. & Feldstein, Sylvan G., eds. The Municipal Bond Handbook, Vol. I. LC 83-70058. 304p. 1983. 50.00 (ISBN 0-87094-307-3). Dow Jones-Irwin.

Fabozzi, Frank J. & Kipnis, Gregory, eds. Stock Index Futures. LC 83-70863. 225p. 1984. 37.50 (ISBN 0-87094-424-X). Dow Jones-Irwin.

Fabozzi, Frank J. & Pollack, Irving M., eds. The Handbook of Fixed Income Securities. LC 82-71874. 850p. 1983. 50.00 (ISBN 0-87094-306-5). Dow Jones-Irwin.

Fabozzi, Frank J., jt. ed. see Chrystie, Thomas L.

Fabozzi, Frank J, jt. ed. see Nevitt, Peter K.

Fabozzi, Frank J., jt. ed. see Feldstein, Sylvan G.

Fabra Poch, Pompeu. Diccionario General de la Lengua Catalana. 9th ed. 1778p. (Catalan.). 1978. 52.50 (ISBN 84-350-0120-2, S-50080). French & Eur.

Fabre, Genevieve. Drumbeats, Masks, & Metaphor: Contemporary Afro-American Theatre. Dixon, Melvin, tr. from Fr. (Illus.). 320p. 1983. text ed. 20.00x (ISBN 0-674-21678-4). Harvard U Pr.

Fabre, Genevieve E., et al, eds. Afro-American Poetry & Drama, Seventeen Sixty to Nineteen Seventy-Five: A Guide to Information Sources. LC 74-11518. (American Literature, English Literature, & World Literatures in English Information Guide Ser.: Vol. 17). 1979. 60.00x (ISBN 0-8103-1208-5). Gale.

Fabre, Gladys C. & Rose, Barbara. Leger & the Modern Spirit: An Avant-Garde Alternative to Non-Objective Art. (Illus.). 560p. (Orig.). 1983. pap. 35.00 (ISBN 0-295-96072-8). U of Wash Pr.

Fabre, J., ed. Afrique de l'Ouest West Africa: Introduction Geologique et Termes Stratigraphiques-Geological Introduction & Stratigraphic Terms. LC 83-13418. (Lexique Stratigraphique International: Nouvelle Series No. 1). (Illus.). 426p. 1983. 65.00 (ISBN 0-08-030267-X); pap. 22.00 (ISBN 0-08-030277-7). Pergamon.

Fabre, J., jt. ed. see McMichael, A.

Fabre, J. Henri. The Hunting Wasps. 1930. 20.00 (ISBN 0-8482-3987-3). Norwood Edns.

--The Life of the Spider. 1912. 30.00 (ISBN 0-8482-3989-X). Norwood Edns.

Fabre, Jean H. Social Life in the Insect World. facsimile ed. Miall, Bernard, tr. LC 78-179517. (Select Bibliographies Reprint Ser). Repr. of 1912 ed. 23.50 (ISBN 0-8369-6646-5). Ayer Co Pubs.

Fabre, Josep P. Picasso. 1985. 14.95 (ISBN 0-8478-0652-9). Rizzoli Intl.

--Picasso. LC 85-42962. (Illus.). 128p. 1985. 14.95 (ISBN 0-8478-0652-9). Rizzoli Intl.

Fabre, Josep Palau i see Fabre, Josep P.

Fabre, Michel. The Unfinished Quest of Richard Wright. Barzun, Isabel, tr. from Fr. (Illus.). 1973. 15.00 (ISBN 0-688-02857-8). Morrow.

--The Unfinished Quest of Richard Wright. Barzun, Isabel, tr. from Fr. LC 73-4227. 1979. pap. 7.95 (ISBN 0-688-07857-5). Morrow.

--The World of Richard Wright. LC 85-6230. (Center for the Study of Southern Culture Ser.). 1985. 25.00x (ISBN 0-87805-258-5). U Pr of Miss.

Fabre, Michel & Davis, Charles T. Richard Wright: A Primary Bibliography. 1982. lib. bdg. 39.00 (ISBN 0-8161-8410-0, Hall Reference). G K Hall.

Fabre, Michel, ed. see Wright, Richard.

Fabreau, Donald F. & Gillespie, Joseph E. Modern Police Administration. (P-H Series in Criminal Justice). (Illus.). 1978. ref. 27.95 (ISBN 0-13-597229-9). P-H.

Fabrega, Horacio, Jr. Disease & Social Behavior: An Elementary Exposition. 1974. pap. 13.95x (ISBN 0-262-56020-8). MIT Pr.

Fabrega, Horacio, Jr. & Silver, Daniel B. Illness & Shamanistic Curing in Zinacantan: An Ethnomedical Analysis. LC 73-80621. 304p. 1973. 22.50x (ISBN 0-8047-0844-4). Stanford U Pr.

Fabretti, Raffaelo. Aqueducts of Ancient Rome. (Printed Sources of Western Art Ser.). (Illus.). 216p. (Latin.). 1981. pap. 35.00 slipcase (ISBN 0-915346-51-6). A Wofsy Fine Arts.

Fabri, Charles. Discovering Indian Sculpture. (Illus.). 84p. 1970. 10.00 (ISBN 0-88253-798-9); pap. 5.00 (ISBN 0-88253-037-2). Ind-US Inc.

Fabri, Felix. The Wanderings of Felix Fabri: Circa 1480-1483 A.D, 2 Vols. Stewart, Aubrey, tr. LC 74-141802. Set. 98.00 (ISBN 0-404-09140-7); Vol. 9-10 (Vol. 2, Pts. 1-2) 49.00 (ISBN 0-686-81995-0); 32.50 (ISBN 0-686-81996-9). AMS Pr.

Fabri, Janet. Automatic Storage Optimization. Stone, Harold, ed. LC 82-6995. (Computer Science: Systems Programming Ser.: No. 9). 306p. 1982. 49.95 (ISBN 0-8357-1346-6). UMI Res Pr.

Fabri, Ralph. Color: A Complete Guide for Artists. (Illus.). 176p. 1967. 23.95 (ISBN 0-8230-0700-6). Watson-Guptill.

Fabricant, Carole. Swift's Landscape. LC 82-165. 336p. 1982. text ed. 28.50x (ISBN 0-8018-2721-3). Johns Hopkins.

Fabricant, Michael. Deinstitutionalizing Delinquent Youth. 222p. 1980. pap. text ed. 9.95 (ISBN 0-87073-892-5). Schenkman bks Inc.

--Juvenile Injustice: Dilemmas of the Family Court System. LC 82-235008. 198p. (Orig.). 1981. pap. 8.00 (ISBN 0-88156-003-0). Comm Serv Soc NY.

--Juveniles in the Family Courts. LC 82-47927. 176p. 1982. 24.50x (ISBN 0-669-05706-1). Lexington Bks.

Fabricant, Neil & Hallman, Robert M. Toward a Rational Power Policy: Energy, Politics & Pollution. LC 70-163462. 8.95 (ISBN 0-8076-0623-5). Braziller.

Fabricant, S. The Trend of Government Activity in the United States Since 1900. LC 52-7402. (National Bureau of Economic Research. General Ser.). 22.00 (ISBN 0-527-03017-1). Kraus Repr.

Fabricant, Solomon. The Economic Growth of the United States. (Canada-U.S. Prospects Series: No. 5). 88p. 1979. 5.00 (ISBN 0-88806-060-2). Inst C D Howe.

--The Economic Growth of the United States: Perspective & Prospective. (Canadian-U. S. Prospect Ser.). 96p. 1979. 5.00 (ISBN 0-88806-060-2). Natl Planning.

--Employment in Manufacturing, 1899-1939: An Analysis of Its Relation to the Volume of Production. LC 75-19711. (National Bureau of Economic Research Ser.). (Illus.). 1975. Repr. 29.00x (ISBN 0-405-07591-X). Ayer Co Pubs.

--Measuring Productivity: Trends & Comparisons from the 1st International Productivity Symposium. 250p. 1984. pap. 46.50 (ISBN 0-89059-034-6, UPB133, UPB). Unipub.

--The Output of Manufacturing Industries, 1899-1937. LC 75-19712. (National Bureau of Economic Research Ser.). (Illus.). 1975. Repr. 52.00x (ISBN 0-405-07592-8). Ayer Co Pubs.

--Studies in Social & Private Accounting. LC 82-82488. (Accountancy in Transition Ser.). 300p. 1982. lib. bdg. 44.00 (ISBN 0-8240-5337-0). Garland Pub.

Fabricius, Cajus. Galen's Exzerpte aus Aelteren Pharmakologen. (Ars Medica: Abt. 2, Griechisch-Lateinische Medizin Vol. 2). x, 266p. 1972. 46.80x (ISBN 3-11-001802-0). De Gruyter.

Fabricius, J. C. Systema Antialorum, Secundum Ordines, Genera, Species. 1970. Repr. of 1805 ed. 26.75 (ISBN 90-6123-060-8). Lubrecht & Cramer.

Fabricius, Klaus, jt. ed. see Saunders, Red.

Fabrick, Martin N. & O'Rourke, Joseph J. Environmental Planning for Design & Construction. LC 81-23070. (Construction Management & Engineering Ser.). 304p. 1982. 48.50x (ISBN 0-471-05848-3, Pub. by Wiley-Interscience). Wiley.

Fabricus, Sara see Sandel, Cora, pseud.

Fabrikant, Benjamin, et al. To Enjoy Is to Live: Psychotherapy Explained. LC 76-40141. 278p. 1977. 20.95x (ISBN 0-88229-148-3). Nelson-Hall.

Fabris, N. Immunology & Ageing. 1982. lib. bdg. 37.50 (ISBN 90-247-2640-9, Pub. by Martinus Nijhoff Netherlands). Kluwer Academic.

Fabritsky, B. & Shmeliov, I. Treasures of Medieval Russia. 336p. 1974. 40.00x (ISBN 0-317-14303-4, Pub. by Collet's). State Mutual Bk.

Fabrizio, R., et al. The Rhetoric of No. 2nd ed. LC 73-16247. 1974. pap. text ed. 14.95 (ISBN 0-03-089234-1, HoltC); instr's manual 19.95 (ISBN 0-03-089405-0). HR&W.

Fabrizius, Peter. Lacht am Besten. Bell, Clair H., ed. LC 57-5200. (Illus., Ger.). 1957. text ed. 14.00x (ISBN 0-89197-262-5). Irvington.

--Wer Zuletzt Lacht. Bell, Clair H., ed. LC 52-7510. (Illus., Ger.). 1963. pap. text ed. 9.95x (ISBN 0-89197-468-7). Irvington.

Fabro, Cornelio. God in Exile: Modern Atheism. Gibson, Arthur, tr. LC 68-20846. 1272p. 1968. slipcase 35.00 (ISBN 0-8091-0053-3). Paulist Pr.

Fabroni, Al G. Miracle of Natural Self-Cure. 1981. 6.00 (ISBN 0-8062-1581-X). Carlton.

Fabry, Anne de see De Fabry, Anne & Hilgar, Marie-France.

Fabry, Joseph. Swing Shift: Building the Liberty Ships. LC 81-14449. (Illus.). 224p. (Orig.). 1982. pap. 7.95 (ISBN 0-89407-049-5). Strawberry Hil.

Fabry, Joseph, tr. see Nestroy, Johann.

Fabry, Joseph, et al, trs. see Kraus, Karl.

Fabry, Joseph B. The Pursuit of Meaning. rev. ed. LC 68-12839. 185p. 1968. pap. 5.95 (ISBN 0-06-250302-2). Inst Logo.

Fabry, Joseph B., et al, eds. Logotherapy in Action. LC 79-51917. 379p. 1979. 19.95 (ISBN 0-317-06212-3). Inst Logo.

Fabrycky, W., jt. auth. see Blanchard, B.

Fabrycky, W. J. & Thuesen, G. J. Engineering Economy. 5th ed. (Illus.). 1977. text ed. 34.95. P-H.

Fabrycky, Walter J. & Thuesen, G. J. Economic Decision Analysis. 2nd ed. 1980. text ed. 31.95 (ISBN 0-13-223248-0). P-H.

Fabrycky, Walter J. & Torgerson, Paul. Applied Operations Research & Management Science. (Illus.). 576p. 1984. 34.95 (ISBN 0-13-041459-X). P-H.

Fabrycky, Wolter J. & Thuesen, Gerald J. Engineering Economy. 6th ed. (Illus.). 624p. 1984. text ed. 37.95 (ISBN 0-13-277723-1). P-H.

Fabryova, Jana, tr. see Novotny, Frantisek.

Fabun, Don. Communications: The Transfer of Meaning. 1968. pap. write for info. (ISBN 0-02-477490-1, 47749). Macmillan.

--Corporation As a Creative Environment. 1972. pap. text ed. write for info. (ISBN 0-02-475240-1, 47524). Macmillan.

--Dimensions of Change. 1971. text ed. write for info, (ISBN 0-02-475500-1, 47550). Macmillan.

Fabunmi, L. A. The Sudan in Anglo-Egyptian Relations. LC 73-15242. (Illus.). 466p. 1974. Repr. of 1960 ed. lib. bdg. 20.75x (ISBN 0-8371-7165-2, FASU). Greenwood.

Fabyanic, Thomas A. Strategic Air Attack in the United States Air Force: A Case Study. 216p. 1977. pap. text ed. 22.00x (ISBN 0-89126-029-3). MA-AH Pub.

Facaros, Dana. Greek Island Hopping. 2nd ed. (Handbooks for the Independent Traveler Ser.). (Illus.). 352p. 1982. pap. 12.95 (ISBN 0-7221-3460-6, Pub. by Sphere Bks). Hippocrene Bks.

Facaros, Dana & Pauls, Michael. Florida. 120p. (Orig.). 1985. pap. 5.95 (ISBN 0-87052-138-1). Hippocrene Bks.

--Mediterranean Island Hopping: The Italian Islands, Corsica & Malta. (Travel Ser.). (Illus.). 500p. 1981. pap. 12.95 (ISBN 0-88254-589-2, Regnery-Gateway). Hippocrene Bks.

--Mediterranean Island Hopping: The Spanish Islands. 2nd ed. (Handbooks for the Independent Traveller Ser.). (Illus.). 304p. 1982. pap. 12.95 (ISBN 0-88254-588-4, Regnery-Gateway). Hippocrene Bks.

--New York & the Mid-Atlantic States. (Handbooks for the Independent Traveller Ser.). (Illus.). 257p. (Orig.). 1982. pap. 12.95 (ISBN 0-89526-856-6, Pub. by Regnery-Gateway). Hippocrene Bks.

--Old South: A Traveler's Guide to Virginia, North Carolina & South Carolina. 170p. (Orig.). 1985. pap. 8.95 (ISBN 0-87052-066-0). Hippocrene Bks.

Facchetti, S. Mass Spectrometry of Large Molecules. 1985. 85.25 (ISBN 0-444-42456-3). Elsevier.

Facchetti, S., ed. Analytical Techniques for Heavy Metals in Biological Fluids: Lectures of a Course Held at the Joint Research Centre, Ispar, Italy, 22-26 June, 1981. 287p. 1983. 83.00 (ISBN 0-444-42212-9, I-183-83). Elsevier.

--Applications of Mass Spectrometry to Trace Analysis: Lectures, Ispra, Italy, 1980. 322p. 1982. 78.75 (ISBN 0-444-42042-8). Elsevier.

Faccin, Dominic. Spiritual Exercises According to Saint Bonaventure. Colligan, Owen A., tr. (Spirit & Life Ser). 1955. 3.00 (ISBN 0-686-11568-6). Franciscan Inst.

Faccini, J. M., jt. auth. see Greaves, P.

Facey, A. B. Fortunate Life. 1985. 30.00 (ISBN 0-670-80307-3). Viking.

Facey, Paul W. The Legion of Decency: A Sociological Analysis of the Emergence & Development of a Social Pressure Group. LC 73-21596. (Dissertations on Film). 1974. 16.00 (ISBN 0-405-04871-8). Ayer Co Pubs.

Facey, Philip A., tr. see Bataille, Georges.

Facey, Philip A., tr. see Memmi, Albert.

Fachgruppe Presse-Rundfunk-und Archivare, ed. Dokumentation in Presse und Rundfunk. (Presse, Rundfunk und Filmarchive-Mediendokumentation: Vol. 6). 251p. 1984. pap. 20.00 (ISBN 3-598-20336-5). K G Saur.

Fachinger, B., jt. auth. see Hundsalz, A.

Fachmann, W., jt. auth. see Souci, S. W.

Fachredaktion. Woerterbuch Medizinischer Fachausdruecke. 2nd ed. (Ger.). 1973. 25.00 (ISBN 3-13-437802-7, M-6913). French & Eur.

Facione, Peter A. & Scherer, Donald. Logic & Logical Thinking: A Modular Approach. LC 77-24173. 1984. Repr. of 1978 ed. text ed. 24.95x (ISBN 0-918024-33-1). Ox Bow.

Facione, Peter A., et al. Values & Society: An Introduction to Ethics & Social Philosophy. 1978. pap. text ed. 20.95 (ISBN 0-13-940338-8). P-H.

Fackelman, G. E. & Nunamaker, D. M. A Manual of Internal Fixation in the Horse. (Illus.). 110p. 1982. 54.00 (ISBN 0-387-10096-2). Springer-Verlag.

Fackenheim, Emil L. Encounters Between Judaism & Modern Philosophy: A Preface to Future Jewish Thought. LC 80-16437. 288p. 1980. pap. 7.95 (ISBN 0-8052-0656-6). Schocken.

--God's Presence in History. 1972. pap. 6.95xi (ISBN 0-06-131690-3, TB1690, Torch). Har-Row.

--The Jewish Return into History: Reflections in the Age of Auschwitz & a New Jerusalem. LC 77-87861. 312p. 1980. pap. 6.95 (ISBN 0-8052-0649-3). Schocken.

--The Jewish Return into History: Reflections in the Age of Auschwitz & a New Jerusalem. LC 77-87861. 1978. 14.95 (ISBN 0-8052-3677-5). Schocken.

--Metaphysics & Historicity. (Aquinas Lecture). 1961. 7.95 (ISBN 0-87462-126-7). Marquette.

Fackenheim, Emil. L. Quest for Past & Future: Essays in Jewish Theology. LC 83-12692. 336p. 1983. Repr. of 1968 ed. lib. bdg. 39.75x (ISBN 0-313-22738-1, FAQP). Greenwood.

Fackenheim, Emil L. The Religious Dimension in Hegel's Thought. LC 81-21914. xiv, 274p. 1982. pap. 10.00x (ISBN 0-226-23350-2). U of Chicago Pr.

--The Religious Dimension in Hegel's Thought. 1984. 16.25 (ISBN 0-8446-5997-5). Peter Smith.

Fackenhein, Emil L. To Mend the World: Foundations of Future Jewish Thought. LC 81-16614. 352p. (Orig.). 1982. 22.50x (ISBN 0-8052-3795-X); pap. 12.95 (ISBN 0-8052-0699-X). Schocken.

Fackenthal, Frank D. Greater Power, & Other Addresses. facs. ed. LC 68-55845. (Essay Index Reprint Ser). 1949. 14.00 (ISBN 0-8369-0436-2). Ayer Co Pubs.

Fackerall, Virginia, ed. see Haroldsen, Mark O.

Facklam, Howard & Facklam, Margery. From Cell to Clone: The Story of Genetic Engineering. LC 79-87515. (gr. 7 up). 1979. 9.95 (ISBN 0-15-230262-X, HJ). HarBraceJ.

Facklam, Howard, jt. auth. see Facklam, Margery.

Facklam, Margery. Wild Animals, Gentle Women. LC 77-88961. (Illus.). (gr. 7 up). 1978. 5.95 (ISBN 0-15-296987-X, HJ). HarBraceJ.

Facklam, Margery & Facklam, Howard. The Brain: Magnificent Mind Machine. LC 81-47529. (Illus.). 1982. 12.95 (ISBN 0-15-211388-6, HJ). HarBraceJ.

Facklam, Margery, jt. auth. see Facklam, Howard.

Facklam, R., et al, eds. Recent Developments in Laboratory Identification Techniques. (International Congress Ser.: Vol. 519). 210p. 1980. 42.25 (ISBN 0-444-90152-3, Excerpta Medica). Elsevier.

Fackler, Eli. Seven Rivers. (Orig.). 1982. pap. 1.95 (ISBN 0-440-17986-6). Dell.

Fackler, Elizabeth. Arson. 192p. 1984. 12.95 (ISBN 0-396-08285-8). Dodd.

--Arson. 224p. 1985. pap. 2.95 (ISBN 0-931773-31-8). Critics Choice Paper.

Fackler, Herbert V. That Tragic Queen: The Deidre Legend in Anglo-Irish Literature. (Salzburg Studies in English Literature, Poetic Drama & Poetic Theory Ser.: No. 39). 1978. pap. text ed. 25.50x (ISBN 0-391-01374-2). Humanities.

Fackler, J. P., Jr., ed. Symmetry in Chemical Theory: Application of Group Theoretical Techniques to the Solution of Chemical Problems. LC 73-12620. (Benchmark Papers in Inorganic Chemistry: Vol. 4). 508p. 1974. 56.00 (ISBN 0-87933-018-X). Van Nos Reinhold.

Fackler, John P., ed. Inorganic Syntheses, Vol. 21. LC 39-23015. (Inorganic Synthesis Ser.). 215p. 1982. 40.50x (ISBN 0-471-86520-6, Pub. by Wiley-Interscience). Wiley.

Fackler, Mark. Ride the Hot Wind. LC 77-78850. 1978. pap. 2.95 (ISBN 0-88419-126-5). Creation Hse.

Fackler, Mark, jt. auth. see Katterjohn, Arthur.

Fackre, Gabriel. The Christian Story. rev. ed. 304p. 1985. pap. 12.95 (ISBN 0-8028-1989-3). Eerdmans.

Fackre, Gabriel, jt. auth. see Charter, Jan.

Facktor, Ron, ed. Lafile. 2000p. 1984. 39.95 (ISBN 0-911241-03-5). Am Soc Landscape.

Facos, James. Silver Wood. 1977. pap. 1.75 (ISBN 0-686-38383-4). Eldridge Pub.

Factor, Regis, jt. auth. see Turner, Stephen.

Facts on File. Disarmament & Nuclear Tests, 1960-63. Sobel, Lester A., ed. LC 64-56719. (Interim History Ser.). pap. 31.00 (ISBN 0-317-20497-1, 2022916). Bks Demand UMI.

Facts on File Digest Staff. Yearbook, 1979. 1980. lib. bdg. 65.00 (ISBN 0-87196-038-9). Facts on File.

Facts on File Staff & Elliott, Stephen P. Reference Guide to the Supreme Court. LC 83-16440. 1985. write for info. (ISBN 0-8160-0018-2). Facts on File.

Factus, ed. Uniforms, Badges & Intelligence Data, etc. of the German Force. (War Documents Ser.: No. 24). (Illus.). 64p. 1983. pap. 5.95 (ISBN 0-86663-993-4). Ide Hse.

Faculty of Comparative Literature, Livingston College. A Syllabus of Comparative Literature. 2nd ed. McCormick, John O., ed. LC 72-8502. 233p. 1972. 13.00 (ISBN 0-8108-0555-3). Scarecrow.

Fadal, Richard G. & Nalebuff, Donald J., eds. The Practical Application of Total & Specific IGE Measurement in Allergic Disorders. 304p. cancelled (ISBN 0-8151-3204-2). Year Bk Med.

Fadala, Sam. Black Powder Handgun. LC 81-65102. 288p. (Orig.). 1981. pap. 11.95 (ISBN 0-910676-22-4, 9266). DBI.

--The Complete Black Powder Handbook. LC 79-54268. (Illus.). 288p. 1979. pap. 11.95 (ISBN 0-695-81311-0). DBI.

--The Complete Shooter. LC 84-71763. (Illus.). 448p. (Orig.). 1984. pap. 17.95 (ISBN 0-910676-65-8). DBI.

--Gun Digest Black Powder Loading Manual. LC 82-72296. (Illus.). 224p. (Orig.). 1982. pap. 11.95 (ISBN 0-910676-50-X). DBI.

--Sam Fadala's Muzzleloading Notebook. 256p. 1985. 17.95 (ISBN 0-8329-0406-6, Pub. by Winchester Pr). New Century.

--Successful Deer Hunting. LC 83-72342. 288p. 1983. pap. 11.95 (ISBN 0-910676-64-X). DBI.

Fadanelli, R. Dizionario Italiano-Russo, Russo-Italiane. 286p. (Ital. & Rus.). leatherette 5.95 (ISBN 0-686-92582-3). French & Eur.

Faddeev, D. K. & Sominskii, I. S. Problems in Higher Algebra. Brenner, Joel L., tr. LC 65-18946. 498p. 1965. pap. 10.95 (ISBN 0-7167-0426-9). W H Freeman.

Faddeev, D. K., jt. auth. see Delone, B. N.

Faddeev, D. K., ed. see Steklov Institute of Mathematics, Academy of Science, U. S. S. R., No. 80.

Faddeev, D. K., et al. Five Papers on Logic, Algebra, & Number Theory. LC 51-5559. (Translations Ser.: No. 2, Vol. 3). 1956. 24.00 (ISBN 0-8218-1703-5, TRANS 2-3). Am Math.

Faddeev, L. D. & Slavnov, A. A. Gauge Fields: Introduction to Quantum Theory. 1981. 51.95 (ISBN 0-8053-9016-2). Benjamin-Cummings.

Faddeev, L. D. & Mal'Cev, A. A., eds. Topology: General & Algebraic Topology & Applications, Proceedings of the International Topological Conference Held in Leningrad, August 23-27, 1982. (Lecture Notes in Mathematics Ser.: Vol. 1060). vi, 389p. 1984. 21.00 (ISBN 0-387-13337-2). Springer-Verlag.

Faddeev, L. D., et al, eds. see Vinogradov, I. M.

Faddeeva, V. N. Computational Methods of Linear Algebra. 1959. pap. 7.50 (ISBN 0-486-60424-1). Dover.

Faddeeva, V. N., ed. Automatic Programming & Numerical Methods of Analysis. LC 76-37618. (Seminars in Mathematics Ser.: Vol. 18). 1972. 25.00x (ISBN 0-306-18818-X, Consultants). Plenum Pub.

Faddeeva, V. N., ed. see Steklov Institute of Mathematics, Academy of Sciences, U S S R, No. 96.

Fadden, John see Kahionhes, pseud.

Fadeev, Aleksandr A. Leningrad in the Days of the Blockade. Charques, R. D., tr. from Rus. LC 77-156189. 1971. Repr. of 1946 ed. lib. bdg. 22.50x (ISBN 0-8371-6137-1, FALE). Greenwood.

Fadeeva, V. N., ed. see Steklov Institute of Mathematics, Academy of Sciences, USSR, No. 84.

Fadel, Ann Allen, jt. auth. see Jones, Rae Donna.

Fadell, E. & Fournier, G., eds. Fixed Point Theory: Proceedings. (Lecture Notes in Mathematics Ser.: Vol. 886). 511p. 1981. pap. 29.00 (ISBN 0-387-11152-2). Springer-Verlag.

Fadely, Jack L. & Hosler, Virginia. Confrontation in Adolescence. LC 78-6709. (Illus.). 148p. 1979. pap. text ed. 12.95 (ISBN 0-8016-1553-4). Mosby.

Fadely, Jack L. & Hosler, Virginia N. Case Studies in Left & Right Hemispheric Functioning. (Illus.). 182p. 1983. 19.50x (ISBN 0-398-04792-8). C C Thomas.

--Developmental Psychometrics: A Resource Book for Mental Health Workers & Educators. (Illus.). 168p. 1980. 19.75x (ISBN 0-398-04056-7). C C Thomas.

--Understanding the Alpha Child at Home & School: Left & Right Hemispheric Function in Relation to Personality & Learning. (Illus.). 256p. 1979. photocopy ed. 25.75x (ISBN 0-398-03862-7). C C Thomas.

Fadely, Jack L., jt. auth. see Hosler, Virginia N.

Faden, Arnold M. Economics of Space & Time: The Measure Theoretic Foundations of Social Science. 1977. 23.50x (ISBN 0-8138-0500-7). Iowa St U Pr.

Faden, B., ed. see Tolstoi, L. N.

Faden, B. R., ed. Computer Programs Directory 1971. 1972. 25.00 (ISBN 0-02-468930-0). Macmillan Info.

Faden, Ruth, jt. ed. see Beauchamp, Tom L.

Fader, Bruce. Industrial Noise Control. LC 81-2158. 251p. 1981. 35.95x (ISBN 0-471-06007-0, Pub. by Wiley-Interscience). Wiley.

Fader, Daniel. The New Hooked on Books. 1981. pap. 2.75 (ISBN 0-425-05473-X). Berkley Pub.

Fader, Herbert L., ed. see Kaung, Stephen.

Fader, Herbert L., ed. see Nee, Watchman.

Fader, Herbert L., ed. see Watchman, Nee.

Fader, Herbert L., et al, eds. see Nee, Watchman.

Fader, Shirley S. From Kitchen to Career: How Any Woman Can Skip Low-Level Jobs & Start in the Middle or at the Top. 1977. 9.95 (ISBN 0-8128-2350-8). Stein & Day.

--Princess Who Grew Down. (Illus.). (gr. k-2). 1968. PLB 6.98 (ISBN 0-87460-122-3). Lion Bks.

--Successfully Ever After: A Young Woman's Guide to Career Happiness. (McGraw-Hill Paperback Ser.). 300p. 1982. 15.95 (ISBN 0-07-019890-X); pap. 6.95 (ISBN 0-07-019889-6). McGraw.

Faderman, Lillian. Scotch Verdict: Dame Gordon vs. Pirie & Woods. LC 83-7989. (Illus.). 388p. 1983. 17.50 (ISBN 0-688-01559-X). Morrow.

--Scotch Verdict: Dame Gordon vs. Pirie & Woods. LC 83-8620. (Illus.). 388p. 1983. pap. 8.70 (ISBN 0-688-02054-2, Quill NY). Morrow.

--Surpassing the Love of Men: Love Between Women from the Renaissance to the Present. Guarnaschelli, Maria, ed. LC 80-24482. (Illus.). 488p. 1981. 18.95 (ISBN 0-688-03733-X); pap. 10.95 (ISBN 0-688-00396-6, Quill). Morrow.

Fadia, Babu L. State Politics in India, 2 vols. 1125p. 1984. Set. text ed. 55.50x (ISBN 0-391-02827-8, Pub. by Radiant Pub India); Vol. 1. text ed. write for info. (ISBN 0-391-03204-6); Vol. 2. text ed. write for info. (ISBN 0-391-03206-2). Humanities.

Fadia, Babulal. Pressure Groups in Indian Politics. (Illus.). 295p. 1980. text ed. 23.00x (ISBN 0-391-01795-0). Humanities.

Fadieev, Aleksandr A. The Nineteen. Charques, R. D., tr. from Rus. LC 72-90293. (Soviet Literature in English Translation Ser). 293p. 1973. Repr. of 1929 ed. 19.50 (ISBN 0-88355-003-2). Hyperion Conn.

Fadiman, Clifton. The Lifetime Reading Plan. new, rev. ed. LC 77-14289. 1978. 15.34 (ISBN 0-690-01499-6). T Y Crowell.

--Wally the Wordworm. LC 83-9181. (Illus.). (gr. 3 up). 1984. 10.95 (ISBN 0-88045-038-X); pap. text ed. 8.95 cassette. Stemmer Hse.

Fadiman, Clifton & Howard, James. Empty Pages: A Search for Writing Competence in School & Society. LC 79-52662. 1979. text ed. 8.95 (ISBN 0-8224-2700-1); pap. 6.95 (ISBN 0-8224-2701-X). Pitman Learning.

Fadiman, Clifton, ed. Clifton Fadiman's Fireside Reader. 18.95 (ISBN 0-88411-546-1, Pub. by Aeonian Pr). Amereon Ltd.

--The World Treasury of Children's Literature, 2 vols. (Illus.). (ps-3). in slipcase 40.00 (ISBN 0-316-27302-3). Little.

Fadiman, Clifton, pref. by see International Paper Co.

Fadiman, James & Frager, Robert. Teorias Da Personalidad. (Span.). 1979. pap. text ed. 14.30 (ISBN 0-06-313100-5, Pub. by HarLA Mexico). Har-Row.

Fadiman, James, jt. auth. see Frager, Robert.

Fadiman, James, jt. auth. see Hendricks, C. Gaylord.

Fadiman, Jeffrey A. The Moment of Conquest: Meru, Kenya, 1907. LC 79-10870. (Papers in International Studies: Africa Ser.: No. 36). 1979. pap. 5.50x (ISBN 0-89680-081-4, 82-91874, Ohio U Ctr Intl). Ohio U Pr.

--An Oral History of Tribal Warfare: The Meru of Mt. Kenya. LC 81-16940. xiii, 185p. 1982. text ed. 20.95x (ISBN 0-8214-0632-9, 82-84051); pap. 10.00x (ISBN 0-8214-0633-7, 82-84069). Ohio U Pr.

Fadiman, Regina K. Faulkner's Intruder in the Dust: Novel into Film. LC 77-8417. (Illus.). 1978. 21.95x (ISBN 0-87049-214-4). U of Tenn Pr.

--Faulkner's Light in August: A Description & Interpretation of the Revisions. LC 74-8242. pap. 61.80 (ISBN 0-317-29700-7, 2022060). Bks Demand UMI.

Fadiman, William. Hollywood Now. 1972. 6.95 (ISBN 0-87140-556-3). Liveright.

Fadner, Donald E. The Responsible God: A Study of the Christian Philosophy of H. Richard Niebuhr. LC 75-29373. (American Academy of Religion. Dissertation Ser.). 1975. pap. 10.25 (ISBN 0-89130-041-4, 010113). Scholars Pr GA.

Fadness, Arley. Blueprint for Lent. 1983. 10.00 (ISBN 0-89536-603-7). CSS of Ohio.

--Karizma: The Women of the Bible. 1979. 7.25 (ISBN 0-317-04058-8). CSS of Ohio.

Fadok, George T. Effective Design of Codasyl Data Base. 400p. 1984. pap. text ed. 29.95. Macmillan.

Faegri, K. & Van Der Pijl, L. The Principles of Pollination Ecology. 2nd ed. 304p. 1972. 21.50 (ISBN 0-08-023160-8). Pergamon.

Faelten, Sharon. Ten Ways to Live Longer. Prevention Magazine, ed. (Prevention Health Classics Ser.). 1982. pap. 3.95 (ISBN 0-87857-380-1, 05-0775-1). Rodale Pr Inc.

Faelten, Sharon & Prevention Magazine Editors. The Allergy Self-Help Book: A Complete Guide to Detection & Natural Treatment of Allergies. 384p. 1983. 19.95 (ISBN 0-87857-458-1). Rodale Pr Inc.

Faelten, Sharon, ed. see Jones, Marjorie H.

Faenson, L. Italian Cassoni from the Art Collections of Soviet Museums. 266p. 1983. 50.00 (ISBN 0-8285-2636-2, Pub. by Aurora Pubs USSR). Imported Pubns.

Faerber, W. Catholic Catechism. LC 78-68498. 122p. 1978. pap. 3.00 (ISBN 0-89555-086-5, 307). TAN Bks Pubs.

Faere, R. Laws of Diminishing Returns. (Lecture Notes in Economics & Mathematical Systems Ser.: Vol. 176). (Illus.). 97p. 1980. pap. 15.00 (ISBN 0-387-09744-9). Springer-Verlag.

Faessler, A., ed. Progress in Particle & Nuclear Physics, Vol. 13: Nuclear & Subnuclear Degrees of Freedom & Lepton Nucleus Scattering. (Illus.). 540p. 1985. 102.00 (ISBN 0-08-031743-X). Pergamon.

Fafowora, Oladapo O. Pressure Groups & Foreign Policy. 1985. 12.95 (ISBN 0-533-06103-2). Vantage.

Fafunwa, A. Babs & Aisiku, J U., eds. Education in Africa: A Comparative Study. 1982. pap. text ed. 12.50x (ISBN 0-04-370113-2). Allen Unwin.

Fagan, B. M., jt. auth. see Oliver, Roland.

Fagan, Brian. The Aztecs. (Illus.). 322p. 1984. pap. 14.95 (ISBN 0-7167-1585-6). W H Freeman.

--California Coastal Passages. Young, Noel, ed. LC 80-25968. (Illus.). 168p. (Orig.). 1981. pap. 16.95 (ISBN 0-88496-161-3, Co-Pub by ChartGuide). Capra Pr.

--California Coastal Passages. LC 80-25968. (Illus.). 159p. 1981. pap. 16.95 (ISBN 0-938206-03-6). ChartGuide Ltd.

Fagan, Brian M. Anchoring: A Primer on Seamanship. (Illus.). 112p. 1986. pap. 10.95 (ISBN 0-87742-200-1). Intl Marine.

--Archaeology: A Brief Introduction. 2nd ed. 1982. pap. text ed. 7.95 (ISBN 0-316-25991-8). Little.

--Bareboating. LC 84-47754. (Illus.). 288p. 1985. 34.95 (ISBN 0-87742-173-0). Intl Marine.

--Clash of Cultures. (Illus.). 318p. text ed. 28.95 (ISBN 0-7167-1634-8); pap. 15.95 (ISBN 0-7167-1622-4). W H Freeman.

--Cruising Guide to Californa's Channel Islands. LC 83-14606. (Illus.). 288p. (Orig.). 1983. pap. 19.95 (ISBN 0-930030-32-X). Western Marine Ent.

--Cruising Guide to the Channel Islands. LC 79-35. 288p. 1979. pap. 19.95 (ISBN 0-88496-093-5). Capra Pr.

--In the Beginning: An Introduction to Archaeology. 5th ed. LC 84-7887. 1984. text ed. 23.95 (ISBN 0-316-25988-8). Little.

--People of the Earth: An Introduction to World Prehistory. Fourth ed. 1982. pap. 16.95 (ISBN 0-316-27319-8). Little.

--Prehistoric Times. LC 82-24235. (Scientific American Readers Ser.). (Illus.). 320p. 1983. text ed. 29.95 (ISBN 0-7167-1490-6); pap. text ed. 14.95 (ISBN 0-7167-1491-4). W H Freeman.

--World Prehistory: A Brief Introduction. 1979. pap. text ed. 9.95 (ISBN 0-316-26000-2). Little.

Fagan, Brian M., intro. by. Civilization: Readings from Scientific American. LC 78-15780. (Illus.). 158p. 1979. text ed. 21.95 (ISBN 0-7167-1024-2); pap. text ed. 11.95 (ISBN 0-7167-1023-4). W H Freeman.

Fagan, Cyril. The Solunars Handbook. 132p. 1976. pap. 6.95 (ISBN 0-940058-03-0). Clancy Pubns.

Fagan, Gus, ed. & tr. see Rakovsky, Christian.

Fagan, Harry. Empowerment: Skills for Parish Social Action. LC 79-52106. 64p. 1979. pap. 3.95 (ISBN 0-8091-2210-3). Paulist Pr.

Fagan, Joen & Shepherd, Irma L., eds. Gestalt Therapy Now: Theory, Techniques, Applications. 1971. pap. 7.21i (ISBN 0-06-090237-X, CN237, CN). Har-Row.

Fagan, John M. Beautiful North Carolina. 2nd ed. LC 79-18081. (Illus.). 72p. 1984. 12.95 (ISBN 0-89802-075-1); pap. 7.95 (ISBN 0-89802-074-3). Beautiful Am.

Fagan, Kathy. Raft. 64p. 1985. 13.50 (ISBN 0-525-24326-7, 01311-390); pap. 7.50 (ISBN 0-525-48164-8, 0728-220). Dutton.

Fagan, Kevin. Basic Drabble. 128p. 1983. pap. 1.95 (ISBN 0-449-12536-X, GM). Fawcett.

--Drabble. 132p. (Orig.). 1981. pap. 3.95 (ISBN 0-449-90052-5, Columbine). Fawcett.

--Drabble...In the Fast Lane. (Orig.). 1985. pap. 4.95 (ISBN 0-449-90135-1, Columbine). Fawcett.

Fagan, L. Map of Cheshire County, New Hampshire, 1858. 1981 ed. (Illus.). 36p. 1981. Repr. of 1858 ed. boxed unbound sheets 27.95 (ISBN 0-911653-00-7). Old Maps.

Fagan, Louis A. The Life & Correspondence of Sir Anthony Panizzi, 2 Vols. LC 70-130597. 1970. Repr. Set. 44.50 (ISBN 0-8337-1095-8). B Franklin.

Fagan, Michael. Beautiful Delaware. Shangle, Robert D., ed. LC 80-21494. (Illus.). 72p. 1980. 12.95 (ISBN 0-89802-207-X); pap. 7.95 (ISBN 0-89802-208-8). Beautiful Am.

Fagan, Myron C. Documentations of Reds & Fellow Travelers in Hollywood. 100p. pap. 6.00 (ISBN 0-89562-097-9). Sons Lib.

Fagan, Pete & Schaffer, Mark. The Office Humor Book. 64p. 1985. 3.95 (ISBN 0-517-55567-0). Crown.

Fagan, Stuart I. Central American Economic Integration: The Politics of Unequal Benefits. LC 74-633252. (Research Ser.: No. 15). 1970. pap. 2.00x (ISBN 0-87725-115-0). U of Cal Intl St.

Fagan, Ted & Moran, William, eds. The Encyclopedic Discography of Victor Recordings: Pre-Matrix Series. The Consolidated Talking Machine Company, Eldridge R. Johnson, & the Victor Talking Machine Company, 12 January 1900 to 23 April 1903; with a special appendix, The Victor Talking Machine Company, by B. L. Aldridge. LC 82-9343. (Illus.). lxix, 393p. 1983. lib. bdg. 49.95 (ISBN 0-313-23003-X, FPM/). Greenwood.

Fagan, Tom, ed. see Dickens, Charles.

Fagan, William T., et al. Measures for Research & Evaluation in the English Language Arts. LC 74-31744. 235p. 1975. pap. 9.25 (ISBN 0-8141-3099-2). NCTE.

Fagan, William T., et al, eds. Measures for Research & Evaluation in the English Language Arts, Vol. 2. 245p. 1985. pap. text ed. 16.75 (ISBN 0-8141-3101-8). NCTE.

Fagarasanu, I. Surgery of the Liver & Intrahepatic Bile Ducts. Heimlich, Henry, ed. LC 77-86984. (Illus.). 490p. 1972. 32.50 (ISBN 0-87527-007-7). Green.

Fagard, P. Guideline for Dairy Accounting. (Animal Production & Health Papers: No. 21). 39p. 1980. pap. 7.50 (ISBN 92-5-100998-8, F2127, FAO). Unipub.

Fage, J. D. An Atlas of African History. 2nd. rev. ed. LC 78-16131. (Illus.). 1978. text ed. 37.50x (ISBN 0-8419-0429-4, Africana); pap. text ed. 19.50x (ISBN 0-8419-0430-8). Holmes & Meier.

--Ghana: A Historical Perspective. LC 83-1543. xiii, 122p. 1983. Repr. of 1959 ed. lib. bdg. 23.75x (ISBN 0-313-23884-7, FAGH). Greenwood.

--A History of Africa. LC 78-54921. 1979. text ed. 24.95 (ISBN 0-394-47490-2, KnopfC). Knopf.

--History of West Africa. 4th ed. LC 71-85742. (Illus.). 1969. 34.50 (ISBN 0-521-07406-1); pap. 11.95x (ISBN 0-521-09579-4). Cambridge U Pr.

Fage, J. D. & Oliver, Roland A. Papers in African Prehistory. LC 74-77286. (Illus.). 1970. 44.50 (ISBN 0-521-07470-3); pap. 14.95 (ISBN 0-521-09566-2). Cambridge U Pr.

Fage, J. D., jt. ed. see Oliver, Roland.

Fage, John. Supreme Court Practice & Procedure. 1980. 30.00x (ISBN 0-686-97116-7, Pub. by Fourmat England). State Mutual Bk.

Fagen, Patricia W. Exiles & Citizens: Spanish Republicans in Mexico. LC 72-3781. (Latin American Monographs: No. 29). 262p. 1973. 15.95x (ISBN 0-292-72002-5). U of Tex Pr.

Fagen, Richard R. The Transformation of Political Culture in Cuba. LC 77-83117. (Illus.). xii, 270p. 1969. 20.00x (ISBN 0-8047-0702-2); pap. 7.95x (ISBN 0-8047-0814-2). Stanford U Pr.

Fagen, Richard R. & Tuohy, William S. Politics & Privilege in a Mexican City. xiv, 210p. 1972. 17.50x (ISBN 0-8047-0809-6); pap. 2.95 O.P. (ISBN 0-8047-0879-7, SP135). Stanford U Pr.

Fagen, Richard R., ed. Capitalism & the State in U. S. Latin American Relations. LC 78-65394. 1979. 30.00x (ISBN 0-8047-1020-1); pap. 7.95x (ISBN 0-8047-1040-6). Stanford U Pr.

Fagen, Richard R. & Pellicer, Olga, eds. The Future of Central America: Policy Choices for the U. S. & Mexico. LC 82-62447. 248p. 1983. cloth 20.00x (ISBN 0-8047-1177-1); pap. 11.95x (ISBN 0-8047-1190-9). Stanford U Pr.

Fagen, Richard R., jt. ed. see Cotler, Julio.

Fagen, Richard R., et al. Cubans in Exile: Disaffection & the Revolution. LC 68-26777. 1968. 13.50x (ISBN 0-8047-0673-5). Stanford U Pr.

Fagen, Robert M. Animal Play Behavior. (Illus.). 1981. text ed. 35.00x (ISBN 0-19-502760-4); pap. text ed. 18.95x (ISBN 0-19-502761-2). Oxford U Pr.

Fagen, Stanly, et al. Teaching Children Self-Control: Preventing Emotional & Learning Problems in the Elementary School. (Special Education Ser.). 288p. 1975. pap. text ed. 16.95 (ISBN 0-675-08783-X). Merrill.

Fagence, Michael. Citizen Participation in Planning. 1977. text ed. 31.00 (ISBN 0-08-020397-3); pap. text ed. 16.00 (ISBN 0-08-020398-1). Pergamon.

Fager, Charles. Selma, Nineteen Sixty-Five: The March That Changed the South. LC 85-35221. (Illus.). 271p. 1985. pap. 10.95 (ISBN 0-8070-0405-7, BP 695). Beacon Pr.

Fager, Charles E. White Reflections on Black Power. LC 67-13982. pap. 29.50 (ISBN 0-317-10004-1, 2012961). Bks Demand UMI.

Fagerbaugh, Shizuko & Strauss, Anselm. Politics of Pain Management: Staff-Patient Interaction. LC 77-75114. 1977. pap. text ed. 19.95 (ISBN 0-201-06909-1, Med-Nurse). Addison-Wesley.

Fagerberg, Holsten. A New Look at the Lutheran Confession. Lund, Gene J., tr. 336p. 1981. 14.95 (ISBN 0-570-03223-7, 15-2121). Concordia.

Fagerlind, I. & Saha, L. Education & National Development: A Comparative Perspective. (Illus.). 200p. 1983. 32.00 (ISBN 0-08-028915-0); pap. 13.00 (ISBN 0-08-030202-5). Pergamon.

Fagerstrom, Grethe & Hansson, Gunilla. Our New Baby: A Picture Story of Parents & Children. (Barron's Educational Ser.). (Illus.). (gr. k-6). 1982. text ed. 8.95 (ISBN 0-8120-5458-X). Barron.

Fagerstrom, Stan. Catch More Crappie. (Illus.). 1977. pap. 5.95 (ISBN 0-916682-06-4). Outdoor Empire.

Fagerstrom, William H. Mathematical Facts & Processes Prerequisite to the Study of Calculus. LC 76-176761. (Columbia University. Teachers College. Contributions to Education Ser.: No. 572). Repr. of 1933 ed. 22.50 (ISBN 0-404-55572-1). AMS Pr.

Fages, Jean B. & Pagano, Christian. The Super Eight Book. rev. ed. 364p. (Fr.). 1971. pap. 19.95 (ISBN 0-686-57183-5, M-6251). French & Eur.

Fages, Jean-Baptiste. Diccionario de los Medios de Comunicacion: Tecnica, Semiologia, Linguistica. 288p. (Span.). 1978. pap. 18.95 (ISBN 84-7366-022-6, S-50121). French & Eur.

Fages, Jean Baptiste & Pagano, Christian. Dictionnaire des Media. 364p. (Fr.). 1971. pap. 22.50 (ISBN 0-686-56848-6, M-6626). French & Eur.

Faget, M. A., jt. auth. see Bond, A. C.

Fagg. Fabulous Beasts. (Mysteries Ser.). (Illus.). 24p. (gr. 4-7). pap. 3.95 (ISBN 0-317-31295-2). Creative Ed.

--Lost Cities. (Mysteries Ser.). (Illus.). 24p. (gr. 4-7). pap. 3.95 (ISBN 0-317-31297-9). Creative Ed.

Fagg, C. D. How They Built Long Ago. Sington, Adrian, ed. (Illus.). 80p. (gr. 5 up). 1981. lib. bdg. 9.90 (ISBN 0-531-09184-8). Watts.

Fagg, Christopher. Ancient Greece. LC 78-68532. (Modern Knowledge Library). (Illus.). (gr. 5 up). 1979. PLB 9.90 s&l (ISBN 0-531-09124-4, Warwick Press). Watts.

Fagg, John E. Latin America: A General History. 3rd ed. (Illus.). 1977. text ed. write for info. (ISBN 0-02-334770-8, 33478). Macmillan.

--Pan Americanism: Its Meaning & History. LC 81-17176. (Anvil Ser.). 218p. 1982. pap. text ed. 6.50 (ISBN 0-89874-258-7). Krieger.

Fagg, Lawrence W. Two Faces of Time. LC 85-40412. (Illus.). 210p. (Orig.). 1985. pap. 7.75 (ISBN 0-8356-0599-X, Quest). Theos Pub Hse.

Fagg, Murray, jt. auth. see Wrigley, John W.

Fagg, William, jt. auth. see Elisofon, Eliot.

Fagg, William, 3rd. Yoruba: Sculpture of West Africa. Pemberton, John, ed. LC 81-48113. (Illus.). 208p. 1982. 40.00 (ISBN 0-394-52358-X); pap. 19.95 (ISBN 0-394-71039-8). Knopf.

Faggett, H. L. & Ford, Nick A., eds. Baltimore Afro-American: Best Short Stories by Afro-American Writers 1925-50. LC 50-12374. 1950. 22.00 (ISBN 0-527-04930-1). Kraus Repr.

Fagin, Gerald M., jt. auth. see Burns, J. Patout.

Fagin, Gerald M., ed. Vatican II: Open Questions & New Horizons. (Theology & Life Ser.: Vol. 8). pap. 6.95 (ISBN 0-89453-366-5). M Glazier.

Fagin, Henry, jt. ed. see Schnore, Leo F.

Fagin, Larry. I'll Be Seeing You. LC 77-28219. 1978. 17.95 (ISBN 0-916190-10-2); pap. 6.00 (ISBN 0-916190-11-0). Full Court NY.

--Rhymes of a Jerk. 7.00 (ISBN 0-686-09760-2); pap. 3.50 (ISBN 0-686-09761-0). Kulchur Foun.

Fagin, N. Bryllion. Phenomenon of Sherwood Anderson: A Study in American Life & Letters. 156p. 1980. Repr. of 1927 ed. lib. bdg. 18.00 (ISBN 0-8495-1726-5). Arden Lib.

--The Phenomenon of Sherwood Anderson: A Study in American Life & Letters. LC 73-11374. 1973. lib. bdg. 17.50 (ISBN 0-8414-1977-9). Folcroft.

Fagiolo, Maurizio. Bernini. (Illus.). 80p. (Orig.). 1981. pap. 12.50 (ISBN 0-935748-42-3). Scala Books.

Fagles, Robert. I, Vincent: Poems from the Pictures of Van Gogh. LC 77-85537. (Princeton Essays on the Arts). (Illus.). 1978. 19.50 (ISBN 0-691-06353-2); pap. 7.95x (ISBN 0-691-01344-6). Princeton U Pr.

Fagles, Robert, tr. see Aeschylus.

Fagles, Robert, tr. see Bacchylides.

Fagles, Robert, tr. see Sophocles.

Faglia, G., et al. Pituitary Microadenomas. LC 79-41478. (Serono Symposia: No. 29). 1980. 79.50 (ISBN 0-12-248150-X). Acad Pr.

Fagnan, E. Additions Aux Dictionnaires Arabes (Arabic-French) 194p. (Arabic & Fr.). 1969. 20.00x (ISBN 0-86685-107-0). Intl Bk Ctr.

Fagniez, Gustave C. Etudes sur l'Industrie et la Classe Industrielle a Paris aux 13e et au 14e Siecle. LC 73-126393. (Research & Source Works: No. 566). (Fr). 1970. Repr. of 1877 ed. 32.50 (ISBN 0-8337-1096-6). B Franklin.

Fagnon, Michael, tr. from Ger. S.S. Werwolf Combat Instruction Manual. LC 82-6286. (Illus.). 200p. 1982. 16.95 (ISBN 0-87364-248-1). Paladin Pr.

Fago, John C., ed. see Hope-Hawkins, Anthony.

Fago, John C., ed. see London, Jack.

Fago, John N. Vincent Lombardi-Pele. (Pendulum Illustrated Biography Ser.). (Illus.). (gr. 4-12). 1979. text ed. 5.00 (ISBN 0-88301-370-3); pap. text ed. 1.95 (ISBN 0-88301-358-4); wkbk. 1.25 (ISBN 0-88301-382-7). Pendulum Pr.

Fago, John N. & Farr, Naunerle C. Jim Thorpe - Althea Gibson. (Pendulum Illustrated Biography Ser.). (Illus.). (gr. 4-12). 1979. text ed. 5.00 (ISBN 0-88301-372-X); pap. text ed. 1.95 (ISBN 0-88301-360-6); wkbk. 1.25 (ISBN 0-88301-384-3). Pendulum Pr.

Fago, John N. & Toan, Debbie. Houdini - Walt Disney. (Pendulum Illustrated Biography Ser.). (Illus.). (gr. 4-12). 1979. text ed. 5.00 (ISBN 0-88301-362-2); pap. text ed. 1.95 (ISBN 0-88301-350-9); wkbk 1.25 (ISBN 0-88301-374-6). Pendulum Pr.

Fago, John N., jt. auth. see Farr, Naunerle C.

Fago, John N., ed. see Dana, Richard H.

Fago, John N., ed. see Defoe, Daniel.

Fago, John N., ed. see Doyle, Arthur Conan.

Fago, John N., ed. see Kipling, Rudyard.

Fago, John N., ed. see Porter, William S.

Fago, John N., ed. see Swift, Jonathan.

Fago, John N., ed. see Twain, Mark.

Fago, John N., ed. see Wells, H. G.

Fagrell, B., jt. ed. see Messmer, K.

Faguet, E. Balzac. LC 73-21621. (Studies in French Literature, No. 45). 1974. lib. bdg. 36.95x (ISBN 0-8383-1778-2). Haskell.

--On Reading Nietzsche. 75.00 (ISBN 0-87968-278-7). Gordon Pr.

Faguet, Emile. Balzac. 1973. Repr. of 1914 ed. 25.00 (ISBN 0-8274-0710-6). R West.

--Drame Ancien, Drame Moderne. LC 74-168695. (Research & Source Works Ser: No. 8). 280p. (Theater & Drama; No. 25). 1972. Repr. of 1924 ed. lib. bdg. 20.50 (ISBN 0-8337-4093-8). B Franklin.

--Flaubert. Devonshire, R. L., tr. from Fr. 238p. 1981. Repr. of 1914 ed. lib. bdg. 45.00 (ISBN 0-89987-264-6). Darby Bks.

--Initiation into Literature. Home Gordon, Bart, tr. 220p. (Fr.). 1980. Repr. of 1913 ed. lib. bdg. 25.00 (ISBN 0-89987-253-0). Darby Bks.

--Initiation into Literature. 1913. Repr. 25.00 (ISBN 0-8274-2572-4). R West.

--A Literary History of France. 1907. Repr. 40.00 (ISBN 0-8274-2955-X). R West.

--Politicians & Moralists of the Nineteenth Century. facs. ed. LC 75-128239. (Essay Index Reprint Ser.). 1928. 19.00 (ISBN 0-8369-1828-2). Ayer Co Pubs.

Faguet, Robert A., jt. ed. see Friedmann, Claude T.

Fagunwa, D. O. Forest of a Thousand Daemons: A Hunter's Sage. Soyinka, Wole, tr. 1983. 12.95 (ISBN 0-394-53411-5). Random.

Fahamed, Omer S. Mental Health Services: Medical Analysis Index with Reference Bibliography. LC 85-47850. 150p. 1985. 29.95 (ISBN 0-88164-374-2); pap. 21.95 (ISBN 0-88164-375-0). ABBE Pubs Assn.

Faheem, Ahmed D., jt. auth. see Favazza, Armando R.

Faherty, Patrick J. The Fastest Truck in Vietnam. LC 83-62163. 156p. (Orig.). 1983. pap. 4.95 (ISBN 0-914705-00-8). Pull-Pr.

Faherty, Robert, ed. see Marquis, Thomas B.

Faherty, Ruth. Westies: From Head to Tail. (Illus.). 232p. 1981. 19.95 (ISBN 0-931866-08-1). Alpine Pubns.

Faherty, William B. Deep Roots & Golden Wings. LC 82-62229. 192p. 1983. 25.00 (ISBN 0-933150-82-2). River City MO.

--Dream by the River. rev. ed. (Illus.). 1981. Repr. of 1973 ed. 4.95 (ISBN 0-933150-21-0). River City MO.

Fahey, Brain W. & Sultan, Jan H. The Balance of Power: The Rolfing Process. (The Health Reference Ser.). (Illus.). 224p. 1985. 18.00 (ISBN 0-943920-52-3); pap. 10.00 (ISBN 0-943920-53-1). Metamorphous Pr.

Fahey, Charles J. & Wakin, Edward. The Catholic Guide to the Mature Years. LC 84-60747. 144p. 1984. pap. 6.95 (ISBN 0-87973-603-8, 603). Our Sunday Visitor.

Fahey, Dennis. The Rulers of Russia: Jewish Bolshevism & Jewish Influence in the Soviet Government. 1980. lib. bdg. 59.95 (ISBN 0-8490-3098-6). Gordon Pr.

Fahey, Edmund B. Rum Road to Spokane: A Story of Prohibition. (Illus.). 150p. 1975. 6.95 (ISBN 0-686-15663-3). U of MT Pubns Hist.

Fahey, Frank & Fahey, Maria. Chapters from the American Experience, Vol. 2. (American History Ser.). (Illus.). 1971. pap. text ed. 18.95 (ISBN 0-13-128124-0). P-H.

Fahey, Frank & Fahey, Marie, eds. Chapters from the American Experience, Vol. 1. (American History Ser.). (Illus.). 1971. pap. text ed. 18.95 (ISBN 0-13-128108-9). P-H.

Fahey, Frank J., jt. auth. see Vrga, Djuro J.

Fahey, James C. Ships & Aircraft of the U. S. Fleet: 1950, 1958, & 1965 Editions, 3 vols. LC 76-15840. (Illus.). 192p. 1980. soft bdg. slipcased 18.95 (ISBN 0-87021-647-3). Naval Inst Pr.

--Ships & Aircraft of the U. S. Fleet: 1950, '58, & '65 Editions, 3 Vols. (Illus.). 192p. 1980. Set. 18.95 (ISBN 0-87021-647-3); bulk rates avail. Naval Inst Pr.

Fahey, James C., ed. The Ships & Aircraft of the U. S. Fleet: 1939, '41, '42 & '45 Editions, 4 Vols. (Illus.). 208p. 1976. Set. incl. slipcase 18.95 (ISBN 0-87021-171-4); bulk rates avail. Naval Inst Pr.

Fahey, James J. Pacific War Diary, 1942-1945. LC 73-21341. (Illus.). 404p. 1974. Repr. of 1963 ed. lib. bdg. 31.25x (ISBN 0-8371-6176-2, FAWD). Greenwood.

Fahey, James T. Pacific War Diary: 1942-1945. (World-at-War Ser.). 1982. pap. 2.50 (ISBN 0-89083-673-6). Zebra.

Fahey, John. Charley Patton. (The Paul Oliver Blues Ser.). pap. 2.95 (ISBN 0-913714-29-1). Legacy Bks.

--The Days of the Hercules. LC 78-63289. (Illus.). 324p. 1978. 10.95 (ISBN 0-89301-057-X). U Pr of Idaho.

Fahey, Kathleen. National Parks in Urban Areas: An Annotated Bibliography. (CPL Bibliographies Ser.: No. 90). 67p. 1982. 10.00 (ISBN 0-86602-090-X). Coun Plan Librarians.

Fahey, Liam. Energy Management in Industrial Firms. LC 79-7939. (Outstanding Dissertations in Economics Ser.). 350p. 1984. lib. bdg. 36.00 (ISBN 0-8240-4187-9). Garland Pub.

Fahey, Maria, jt. auth. see Fahey, Frank.

Fahey, Marie, jt. ed. see Fahey, Frank.

Fahey, Michael A. & Meyendorff, John. Trinitarian Theology: East & West St. Thomas Aquinas-St. Gregory Palamas. LC 77-28080. (Patriarch Athenagoras Memorial Lectures). 43p. 1977. pap. 2.45 (ISBN 0-916586-18-9). Holy Cross Orthodox.

Fahey, Robert J., et al. Computers, Science & Management Dynamics. LC 72-102175. 1969. 12.00 (ISBN 0-910586-38-1). Finan Exec.

Fahey, Thomas D., jt. auth. see Brooks, George A.

Fahey, William A., jt. auth. see Richardson, Ben.

Fahidy, T. Z. Principles of Electrochemical Reactor Analysis. (Chemical Engineering Monographs: Vol. 18). 1985. 68.75 (ISBN 0-444-42451-2). Elsevier.

Fahie, J. J. Galileo: His Life & Work. (Illus.). Repr. of 1903 ed. lib. bdg. 47.00x (ISBN 0-697-00003-6). Irvington.

--History of Wireless Telegraphy, 1838-99. LC 77-161144. (History of Broadcasting: Radio to Television Ser). 1971. Repr. of 1901 ed. 30.00 (ISBN 0-405-03565-9). Ayer Co Pubs.

Fahien, Ray. Fundamentals of Transport Phenomena. (Chemical Engineering Ser.). (Illus.). 640p. 1983. 42.00 (ISBN 0-07-019891-8). McGraw.

Fahim, Hussein M. Dams, People & Development: The Aswan High Dam Case. LC 80-23929. (Pergamon Policy Studies on International Development). 208p. 1981. 21.00 (ISBN 0-08-026307-0). Pergamon.

--Egyptian Nubians: Resettlement & Years of Coping. LC 82-24723. xiv, 197p. 1983. 19.95 (ISBN 0-87480-215-6). U of Utah Pr.

Fahim, Hussein M., ed. Indigenous Anthropology in Non-Western Countries. LC 80-68077. 293p. 1982. lib. bdg. 24.75 (ISBN 0-89089-197-4); pap. text ed. 12.95 (ISBN 0-89089-198-2). Carolina Acad Pr.

Fahimuddin, M. Domestic Water Buffalo. 392p. 1981. 30.00x (ISBN 0-686-72948-X, Pub. by Oxford & IBH India). State Mutual Bk.

Fahl, Kathryn A., compiled by. Forest History Museums of the World. (Guides to Forest & Conservation History of North America Ser.: No. 6). (Illus.). 83p. 1983. pap. text ed. 9.00x (ISBN 0-8223-0265-9). Forest Hist Soc.

Fahl, Kathryn A., ed. Forest History Museums of the World: Guides to Forest Conservation History of North America, No 6. (Illus.). viii, 75p. (Orig.). 1983. pap. 7.50 (ISBN 0-89030-043-7). Forest Hist Soc.

Fahl, Ronald J. North American Forest & Conservation History: A Bibliography. 408p. 1977. 20.00 (ISBN 0-317-34156-1). Forest Hist Soc.

Fahlander, Inger, jt. auth. see MacDermot, Niall.

Fahlbeck, Reinhold. Labour Law In Sweden: A Brief Outline. 66p. 1981. pap. 11.00 (ISBN 0-317-07419-9). Transnatl Pubs.

Fahlberg, W. J. & Groschal, D., eds. Occurrence Diagnoses & Sources of Hospital-Associated Diseases. (Hospital Associated Disease Ser.: Vol. 1). 1978. 35.00 (ISBN 0-8247-6724-1). Dekker.

Fahlman, Betsy. Pennsylvania Modern: Charles Demuth of Lancaster. LC 83-8116. (Illus.). 74p. 1983. 11.95 (ISBN 0-87633-054-5). Phila Mus Art.

Fahlman, Scott E. NETL: A System for Representing & Using Real-World Knowledge. (Artificial Intelligence Ser.). (Illus.). 278p. 1979. text ed. 27.50x (ISBN 0-262-06069-8). MIT Pr.

Fahm, Lattee A. The Waste of Nations: The Economic Utilization of Human Waste in Agriculture. LC 79-88260. (LandMark Studies). (Illus.). 188p. 1980. text ed. 28.50x (ISBN 0-916672-28-X). Allanheld.

Fahmy, Hoda, jt. auth. see Lynch, Patricia D.

Fahmy, Ismail. Negotiating for Peace in the Middle East: An Arab View. LC 82-49057. 336p. 1983. 30.00x (ISBN 0-8018-3016-8). Johns Hopkins.

Fahn, A. Plant Anatomy. 3rd ed. LC 81-13813. (Illus.). 528p. 1982. 66.00 (ISBN 0-08-028030-7); pap. 29.50 (ISBN 0-08-028029-3). Pergamon.

--Secretory Tissues in Plants. 1979. 53.00 (ISBN 0-12-247650-6). Acad Pr.

Fahn, Abraham. Plant Anatomy. 2nd ed. LC 73-5808. 616p. 1974. pap. text ed. 29.50 (ISBN 0-08-028029-3). Pergamon.

Fahn, Stanley, jt. ed. see Eldridge, Roswell.

Fahn, Stanley, et al, eds. Experimental Therapeutics of Movement Disorders. (Advances in Neurology Ser.: Vol. 37). 340p. 1983. text ed. 54.50 (ISBN 0-89004-695-6). Raven.

--Cerebral Hypoxia & Its Consequences. LC 78-57236. (Advances in Neurology Ser.: Vol. 26). 366p. 1979. text ed. 52.50 (ISBN 0-89004-296-9). Raven.

--Myoclonus. (Advances in Neurology Ser.: Vol. 43). (Illus.). 768p. 1985. text ed. 125.00 (ISBN 0-88167-122-3). Raven.

Fahner. Sales Manager's Model Letter Desk Book. 1977. 32.95 (ISBN 0-13-787663-7, Parker). P-H.

Fahner, Hal. Successful Sales Management: A New Strategy for Modern Sales Managers. LC 82-24085. 264p. 1983. 50.00 (ISBN 0-13-870402-3). P-H.

Fahnestock, Jeanne & Secor, Marie. A Reader in Argument. 448p. 1985. pap. text ed. 12.95 (ISBN 0-394-33155-9, RanC). Random.

--A Rhetoric for Argument. 1986. pap. text ed. 12.95 (ISBN 0-394-34757-9, RanC). Random.

Fahnestock, Jeanne, jt. auth. see Secor, Marie.

Fahnestock, Lee, tr. from Fr. The Making of the Pre by Francis Ponge. LC 77-25156. (Illus.). 240p. 1982. pap. 14.95 (ISBN 0-8262-0381-7). U of Mo Pr.

Fahnestock, Lee, tr. see Ponge, Francis.

Fahnestock, Murray. Know Your Model A Ford: The Gem from the River Rouge. LC 75-41921. (Illus.). 1958. 11.95 (ISBN 0-911160-30-2). Post-Era.

--Model T Ford Owner. LC 83-61109. (Illus.). 528p. 1983. 21.95 (ISBN 0-911160-23-X). Post-Era.

Fahnestock, Murray, ed. The Model T Speed Secrets, Fast Ford Handbook. (Illus.). 192p. 1968. pap. 10.00 (ISBN 0-911160-17-5). Post-Era.

--Those Wonderful Unauthorized Accessories for Model A Ford. LC 73-164930. (Illus.). 256p. 1971. pap. 12.95 (ISBN 0-911160-27-2). Post-Era.

Fahrenbruch, Alan & Bube, Richard. Fundamentals of Solar Cells. LC 82-13919. 1983. 68.00 (ISBN 0-12-247680-8). Acad Pr.

Fahrion, Muriel, illus. Strawberry Shortcake's Make-&-Do Book. (Strawberry Shortcake Bks.). (Illus.). 64p. (ps-3). 1980. pap. 2.95 (ISBN 0-394-84573-0). Random.

Fahrmann, Willi. The Long Journey of Lukas B. Bell, Anthea, tr. from Ger. LC 84-6100. Orig. Title: Der Lange Weg des Lukas B. 288p. (gr. 7 up). 1985. 12.95 (ISBN 0-02-734330-8). Bradbury Pr.

Fahrner, R. Hoelderlins Begegnung Mit Goethe und Schiller. pap. 9.00 (ISBN 0-384-15080-2). Johnson Repr.

--Wortsinn und Wortschoepfung Bei Meister Eckehart. pap. 9.00 (ISBN 0-384-15090-X). Johnson Repr.

Fahrner, Rudiger. Hooked on Skiing. (Hooked on... Sports Ser.). (Illus.). 102p. (Orig.). 1980. pap. 5.95 (ISBN 0-938864-01-7). Ipswich Pr.

Fahrney, Ralph R. Horace Greeley & the Tribune in the Civil War. LC 77-135663. (American Scene Ser). 1970. Repr. of 1936 ed. lib. bdg. 29.50 (ISBN 0-306-71120-6). Da Capo.

Fahs, Charles B. Government in Japan: Recent Trends in Its Scope & Operation. LC 75-30105. (Institute of Pacific Relations Ser.). Repr. of 1940 ed. 16.00 (ISBN 0-404-59520-0). AMS Pr.

Fahs, Lois S. Swing Your Partner: Old Time Dances of New Brunswick & Nova Scotia. 1939. pap. 9.95x (ISBN 0-931814-01-4). Comm Stud.

Fahs, Mary E., jt. auth. see Lief, Nina R.

Fahs, Mary Ellen, jt. auth. see Lief, Nina R.

Fahs, Ned C., jt. ed. see Hamilton, D. Lee.

Fahs, Sophia L. Uganda's White Man of Work. 185p. 5.80 (ISBN 0-686-05597-7). Rod & Staff.

Fahs, Sophia L. & Cobb, Alice. Old Tales for a New Day: Early Answers to Life's Eternal Questions. LC 80-84076. (Library of Liberal Religion). (gr. 3-9). 1980. 11.95 (ISBN 0-87975-138-X); tchr's manual 9.95 (ISBN 0-87975-131-2). Prometheus Bks.

Fa-Hsien. Travels of Fah-Hian & Sung-Yun, Buddhist Pilgrims from China to India. Beal, Samuel, tr. LC 67-66343. Repr. of 1869 ed. 25.00x (ISBN 0-678-07259-0). Kelley.

Fa-hsien, Fl. The Travels of Fa-hsien, 399 to 144 A.D. Or Record of the Buddhistic Kingdoms. Giles, M. A. & Giles, H. A., trs. from Fr. LC 81-13362. xx, 96p. 1982. Repr. of 1956 ed. lib. bdg. 19.75x (ISBN 0-313-23240-7, FATR). Greenwood.

Fahy, B., tr. see Habig, Marion A.

Fahy, Carole. Cooking with Beer. 1978. pap. 3.00 (ISBN 0-486-23661-7). Dover.

--Cooking with Beer. 10.75 (ISBN 0-8446-5683-6). Peter Smith.

Fahy, Christopher. Greengroundtown. Hunting, Constance, ed. 1978. pap. 3.50 (ISBN 0-913006-13-0). Puckerbrush.

--Nightflyer. 288p. 1982. pap. 2.95 (ISBN 0-515-06217-0). Jove Pubns.

Fahy, Everett. Metropolitan Flowers. Allison, Ellyn, ed. (Illus.). 112p. (Orig.). 1983. 29.50 (ISBN 0-8109-1317-8). Abrams.

--Some Followers of Domenico Ghirlandajo. LC 75-23790. (Outstanding Dissertations in the Fine Arts - 15th Century). (Illus.). 1976. lib. bdg. 50.00 (ISBN 0-8240-1986-5). Garland Pub.

Fahy, Frank J. Sound & Structural Vibration: Radiation, Transmission & Response. 1985. 60.00 (ISBN 0-12-247670-0). Acad Pr.

Fahy, Peter C., jt. ed. see Persley, Garrielle J.

Faibisoff, Sylvia G., jt. ed. see Bonn, George S.

Faid, Mary. No Stars So Bright. DeRoin, Gene, ed. (Aston Hall Presents Ser.). (Orig.). 1979. pap. 1.50 (ISBN 0-89936-007-6). Aston Hall.

Faid, Robert W. Lydia: Seller of Purple. 345p. 1984. pap. 4.95 (ISBN 0-88270-569-5). Bridge Pub.

--A Scientific Approach to Christianity. LC 82-72003. 1982. pap. 4.95 (ISBN 0-88270-535-0, Pub. by Logos). Bridge Pub.

Faider, Paul. Repertoire Des Index et Lexiques D'Auteurs Latins. LC 77-150150. (Fr). 1971. Repr. of 1926 ed. lib. bdg. 16.50 (ISBN 0-8337-1097-4). B Franklin.

Faigley, Lester & Witte, Stephen P. Evaluating College Writing Programs. 136p. 1984. 8.50 (ISBN 0-317-37085-5). NCTE.

Faigley, Lester, jt. auth. see Witte, Stephen R.

Faigley, Lester, et al. Assessing Writers' Knowledge & Processes of Composing. Farr, Marcia, ed. (Writing Research Ser.). 288p. 1985. text ed. 32.50 (ISBN 0-89391-226-3); pap. 17.95 (ISBN 0-89391-320-0). Ablex Pub.

Failing, George E. Did Christ Die for All? 1980. 1.25 (ISBN 0-937296-02-3, 222-B). Presence Inc.

--Presence. 32p. 1977. pap. 1.00 (ISBN 0-937296-04-X, 221-A). Presence Inc.

--Secure & Rejoicing. 1980. 0.95 (ISBN 0-937296-03-1, 223-A). Presence Inc.

Failing, Patricia. Best-Loved Art from American Museums. (Illus.). 1983. 19.95 (ISBN 0-517-55168-3, C N Potter Bks). Crown.

Fails Management Institute. Financial Management for Contractors. Jackson, Ira J., 3rd & Gilliam, Marita H., eds. (Illus.). 236p. 1981. 36.50 (ISBN 0-07-019887-X). McGraw.

Faiman, Michael, jt. ed. see Nievergelt, Jurg.

Fain, B. Theory of Rate Processes in Condensed Media. (Lecture Notes in Chemistry Ser.: Vol. 20). (Illus.). 166p. 1980. 21.00 (ISBN 0-387-10249-3). Springer Verlag.

Fain, Haskell. Between Philosophy & History: The Resurrection of Speculative Philosophy of History Within the Analytic Tradition. LC 70-90946. 1970. 31.00x (ISBN 0-691-07158-6). Princeton U Pr.

Fain, James W. Rodeos. LC 82-23460. (New True Bks.). (Illus.). 48p. (gr. k-4). 1983. PLB 10.60 (ISBN 0-516-01685-7); pap. 3.95 (ISBN 0-516-41685-5). Childrens.

Fain, Jeff. The Burning. 288p. 1984. pap. 2.95 (ISBN 0-8439-2160-9, Leisure Bks). Dorchester Pub Co.

Fain, Stephen M., et al. Teaching in America. 1979. pap. text ed. 14.70x (ISBN 0-673-15056-9). Scott F.

Faine, Jules. Dictionnaire Francais-Creole. 480p. (Fr. Creole.). 1975. pap. 39.95 (ISBN 0-686-57291-2, M-4608). French & Eur.

Fainlight, Ruth. Cages. 1966. 11.00 (ISBN 0-8023-1129-6). Dufour.

--To See the Matter Clearly & Other Poems. 1969. 11.00 (ISBN 0-8023-1181-4). Dufour.

Fainsod, Merle. How Russia Is Ruled. rev. ed. LC 63-11418. (Russian Research Center Studies: No. 11). 1963. 30.00x (ISBN 0-674-41000-9). Harvard U Pr.

--International Socialism & the World War. 1966. lib. bdg. 20.00x (ISBN 0-374-92679-4). Octagon.

Fainsod, Merle, jt. auth. see Hough, Jerry F.

Fainsod, Merle, et al. Government & the American Economy. 3rd ed. 1959. 13.95x (ISBN 0-393-09553-3, NortonC). Norton.

Fainstein, Norman I. & Fainstein, Susan S. Restructuring the City: The Political Economy of Urban Redevelopment. LC 82-17191. (Illus.). 352p. 1983. text ed. 27.50x (ISBN 0-582-28292-6); 15.95x (ISBN 0-582-28293-4). Longman.

--Urban Policy Under Capitalism. (Urban Affairs Annual Reviews Ser.: Vol. 22). (Illus.). 320p. 1982. 28.00 (ISBN 0-8039-1797-X); pap. 14.00 (ISBN 0-8039-1798-8). Sage.

Fainstein, Susan S., jt. auth. see Fainstein, Norman I.

Fainstein, Victor, jt. ed. see Bodey, Gerald P.

Faiola, Theodora & Pullen, Jo A. McGraw-Hill Guide to Clothing. MacGowan, Sandra, ed. (Illus.). 384p. 1981. text ed. 21.32 (ISBN 0-07-019855-1). McGraw.

Fair, A. A. The Bigger They Come. Penzler, Otto, ed. LC 84-60104. (Quill Mysterious Classics Ser.). 246p. 1984. pap. 3.95 (ISBN 0-688-03137-4). Morrow.

Fair, A. A. see also Gardner, Erle S.

Fair, Charles M. The Dying Self. LC 77-82538. 1969. 17.50x (ISBN 0-8195-4004-8). Wesleyan U Pr.

--Physical Foundations of the Psyche. LC 63-8861. 1963. 20.00x (ISBN 0-8195-3037-9). Wesleyan U Pr.

Fair, D. E. & De Juvigny, F. Leonard. Bank Management in a Changing Domestic & International Environment. 1982. lib. bdg. 57.00 (ISBN 90-247-2606-9, Pub. by Martinus Nijhoff Netherlands). Kluwer Academic.

Fair, D. E., ed. Government Policies & the Working of Financial Systems in Industrialized Countries. 1985. lib. bdg. 50.50 (ISBN 90-247-3076-7, Pub. by Martinus Nijhoff Netherlands). Kluwer Academic.

Fair, Donald E., ed. International Lending in a Fragile World Economy. 150p. 1984. lib. bdg. 74.00 (ISBN 0-686-40722-9, Pub. by Martinus Nijhoff Netherlands). Kluwer Academic.

Fair, Erik. Right Stuff for New Hang Glider Pilots. (Illus.). 170p. 1985. pap. 7.95 (ISBN 0-913581-00-3). Publitec.

Fair, Gordon M. & Okun, Daniel A. Water & Wastewater Engineering, 2 vols. LC 66-16139. Vol. 1, Water Supply & Wastewater Removal. pap. 128.00 (ISBN 0-317-11201-5, 2055401); Vol. 2, Water Purification & Wastewater Treatment & Disposal. pap. 160.00 (ISBN 0-317-11202-3). Bks Demand UMI.

Fair, Gordon M., et al. Water & Wastewater Engineering: Water Supply & Wastewater Removal, Vol. 1. LC 66-16139. 489p. 1966. 53.45x (ISBN 0-471-25130-5). Wiley.

Fair, H. D. & Walker, R. F. Energetic Materials. Incl. Vol. 1. Physics & Chemistry of the Inorganic Azides. 503p. 69.50x (ISBN 0-306-37076-X); Vol. 2. Technology of the Inorganic Azides. 296p. 65.00x (ISBN 0-306-37077-8). LC 76-30808. (Illus.). 1977 (Plenum Pr). Plenum Pub.

Fair, Harold L. Class Devotions: Nineteen Eighty-Five to Nineteen Eighty-Six. 10th ed. 128p. (Orig.). 1985. pap. 5.95 (ISBN 0-687-08625-6). Abingdon.

--Class Devotions, Ninteen Eighty-Four to Ninteen Eighty-Five. 128p. (Orig.). 1984. pap. 5.95 (ISBN 0-687-08624-8). Abingdon.

Fair, James R., Jr. The North Arkansas Line: The Story of the Missour & North Arkansas Railroad. LC 78-9627. 320p. 1982. Repr. of 1969 ed. 15.00 (ISBN 0-8310-7077-3). Howell-North.

Fair, Jeff, ed. see Klein, Thomas J.

Fair, John. Dorset Birds. 1982. 37.00x (ISBN 0-905868-12-9, Pub. by Gavin Pr). State Mutual Bk.

Fair, Judy, ed. Microforms Management in Special Libraries: A Reader. LC 78-13494. (Meckler Publishing's Series in Library Micrographics Management: No. 5). 1979. 21.95x (ISBN 0-913672-15-7). Microform Rev.

Fair, Marvin L. Port Administration in the United States. LC 54-8653. (Illus.). Repr. of 1954 ed. 44.30 (ISBN 0-8357-9074-6, 2015259). Bks Demand UMI.

Fair, Marvin L. & Guandolo, John. Transportation Regulation. 9th ed. 496p. 1983. text ed. write for info. (ISBN 0-697-08515-5). Wm C Brown.

Fair, Marvin L. & Williams, Ernest W., Jr. Transportation & Logistics. rev. ed. 1981. 28.50 (ISBN 0-256-02308-5). Business Pubns.

Fair, Michael L., ed. Master Handbook of One Thousand & One More Practical Electronic Circuits. (Illus.). 1979. pap. 19.95 (ISBN 0-8306-7804-2, 804). TAB Bks.

Fair, Phillip, jt. auth. see Rabold, Ted.

Fair, R. B., et al, eds. Impurity Diffusion & Gettering in Silicon, Vol. 36. LC 85-7226. 1985. text ed. 36.00 (ISBN 0-931837-01-4). Materials Res.

Fair, Ray C. Specification, Estimation, & Analysis of Macroeconomic Models. (Illus.). 384p. 1984. text ed. 35.00x (ISBN 0-674-83180-2). Harvard U Pr.

Fair, Ronald. Rufus. 2nd ed. LC 79-88743. 58p. 1980. pap. 4.00x perf. bound (ISBN 0-916418-21-9). Lotus.

Fair, Ronald L. Many Thousand Gone: An American Fable. 114p. 1973. Repr. of 1965 ed. 7.95x (ISBN 0-911860-42-8). Chatham Bkseller.

--World of Nothing. LC 71-105237. 1970. 15.00 (ISBN 0-89366-096-5). Ultramarine Pub.

--World of Nothing: Two Novellas. 133p. 1970. 5.95x (ISBN 0-911860-44-4). Chatham Bkseller.

Fair, Susan, et al. The Guide to Consciousness Lowering: (Or How to Avoid Enlightenment) (Illus.). 72p. (Orig.). Date not set. pap. 5.95 (ISBN 0-9613443-0-X). These Jokes.

Fair, Sylvia. The Bedspread. LC 81-11152. (Illus.). 32p. (gr. k-3). 1982. 12.25 (ISBN 0-688-00877-1). Morrow.

Fairall, P. A., jt. auth. see O'Connor, D.

Fairbairn, A. N., ed. The Leicestershire Plan. (Organization in Schools Ser.). 1980. text ed. 30.00x (ISBN 0-435-80298-4). Heinemann Ed.

Fairbairn, Ann. Five Smooth Stones. 944p. 1975. pap. 4.95 (ISBN 0-553-25203-8). Bantam.

--Five Smooth Stones. 1966. 10.95 (ISBN 0-517-50687-4). Crown.

Fairbairn, J. W., ed. see Anthraquinone Symposium, Buergenstock-Luzern, September, 1978.

Fairbairn, J. W., ed. see Symposium, Bissone (Lugano) Switzerland, Sept. 1975.

Fairbairn, James. Fairbairn's Crests of the Families of Great Britain & Ireland. LC 68-25887. (Illus.). 800p. 1968. 32.50 (ISBN 0-8048-0177-0). C E Tuttle.

Fairbairn, Kay, jt. auth. see Alexander, Sharon K.

Fairbairn, Lynda, compiled by. Paint & Painting Catalogue. (Illus.). 118p. 1985. pap. 8.95 (ISBN 0-905005-68-6, Pub. by Salem Hse Ltd). Merrimack Pub Cir.

Fairbairn, Patrick. The Pastoral Epistles. 1980. 17.25 (ISBN 0-86524-053-1, 7107). Klock & Klock.

Fairbairn, T'eo L. & Tisdell, Clem. Economic Growth Among Small Pacific Countries: Can It Be Sustained? (Working Papers Ser.: No. 83-5). 23p. 1983. pap. text ed. 6.00 (CRD160, UNCRD). Unipub.

Fairbairn, W. E. Get Tough. (Illus.). 120p. 1974. Repr. 14.95 (ISBN 0-87364-002-0). Paladin Pr.

Fairbairn, W. Ronald. Psychoanalytic Studies of the Personality. 1966. Repr. of 1952 ed. 25.00x (ISBN 0-7100-1361-2). Routledge & Kegan.

Fairbairn, William E. Scientific Self-Defence. (Illus.). 175p. pap. 17.95x (ISBN 0-86695-003-6). Interserv Pub.

Fairbairns, Zoe. Benefits. 224p. 1983. pap. 2.95 (ISBN 0-380-63164-4, 63164-4, Bard). Avon.

--Here Today. 256p. 1984. pap. 3.95 (ISBN 0-380-89497-1). Avon.

--Stand We At Last. 624p. 1984. pap. 3.95 (ISBN 0-380-65565-9, 65565). Avon.

Fairbairns, Zoe & Cameron, James. Peace Moves: Nuclear Protest in the 1980's. (Illus.). 96p. (Orig.). 1984. pap. 8.95 (ISBN 0-7011-2828-3, Pub. by Chatto & Windus-Hogarth Pr). Merrimack Pub Cir.

Fairbairns, Zoe, et al. Tales I Tell My Mother. LC 80-50993. 161p. 1980. 12.50 (ISBN 0-89608-112-5); pap. 7.50 (ISBN 0-89608-111-7). South End Pr.

Fairbank & Reischaue. Harvard-Yenching Library Set, Vols. 1-72. lib. bdg. 208.33 ea. Garland Pub.

Fairbank & Schultheis. Applied Business Math. 1980. text ed. 12.55 (ISBN 0-538-13450-X, M45). SW Pub.

Fairbank, Alfred. A Book of Scripts. 2nd ed. (Illus.). 48p. 1977. pap. 6.50 (ISBN 0-571-11080-0). Faber & Faber.

--A Handwriting Manual. (Illus.). 144p. 1976. pap. 5.95 (ISBN 0-8230-2186-6); sheet stock avail. Watson-Guptill.

Fairbank, Ben, jt. auth. see Foster, Nancy H.

Fairbank, Calvin. Reverend Calvin Fairbank During Slavery Times. LC 70-97450. Repr. of 1890 ed. 17.50x (ISBN 0-8371-2690-8, FAF&). Greenwood.

Fairbank, John K. China Talks & the United States & China. 606p. 66.95, cassette included (ISBN 0-317-35807-3, T602). Soc Intercult Ed Train & Res.

--China: The People's Middle Kingdom & the U. S. A. LC 67-17307. 1967. 10.00x (ISBN 0-674-11651-8, Belknap Pr). Harvard U Pr.

--Chinabound: A Fifty Year Memoir. LC 81-47656. (Illus.). 481p. 1983. pap. 9.62i (ISBN 0-06-039028-X, CN1041, CN). Har-Row.

--Chinese-American Interactions: A Historical Summary. LC 74-22192. (Brown & Haley Lectures Ser.: Yr. 1974). pap. 24.00 (ISBN 0-317-29961-1, 2051726). Bks Demand UMI.

--Trade & Diplomacy on the China Coast: The Opening of the Treaty Ports, 1842-1854, 2 Vols. in 1. LC 65-100264. (Historical Studies: No. 62-63). 1954. Set. 20.00x (ISBN 0-674-89835-4). Harvard U Pr.

--Trade & Diplomacy on the China Coast: The Opening of the Treaty Ports 1842-1854. LC 69-10365. (Illus.). 1953. pap. 10.95 (ISBN 0-8047-0648-4, SP94). Stanford U Pr.

--The United States & China. 4th ed. LC 78-13667. (Illus.). 1979. 20.00x (ISBN 0-674-92435-5); pap. 8.95 (ISBN 0-674-92436-3). Harvard U Pr.

--The United States & China. 4th, enlarged ed. (Illus.). 656p. 1983. text ed. 20.00x (ISBN 0-674-92437-1); pap. 7.95 (ISBN 0-674-92438-X). Harvard U Pr.

Fairbank, John K. & Kwang-Ching, Lui. Cambridge History of China: Late Ch'ing, Vol. 11:1800-1911, Part 2. LC 76-29852. (Cambridge History of China). (Illus.). 1980. 100.00 (ISBN 0-521-22029-7). Cambridge U Pr.

Fairbank, John K. & Reischauer, Edwin O. China: Tradition & Transformation. LC 77-77980. (Illus.). 1978. text ed. 22.95 (ISBN 0-395-25813-8). HM.

Fairbank, John K. & Teng Ssu-Yu. Ch'ing Administration: Three Studies. LC 60-7991. (Harvard-Yenching Institute Studies: No. 19). 1960. pap. 5.00x (ISBN 0-674-12700-5). Harvard U Pr.

Fairbank, John K. see Kierman, Frank A., Jr.

Fairbank, John K., ed. The Cambridge History of China: Late Ch'ing, 1800-1911, Vol. 10: 1800-1911, Part 1. LC 76-29852. (Cambridge History of China). 100.00 (ISBN 0-521-21447-5). Cambridge U Pr.

--The Cambridge History of China: Vol. 12: Republican China 1912-1949, Pt. 1. LC 76-29852. (Illus.). 1002p. 1983. 100.00 (ISBN 0-521-23541-3). Cambridge U Pr.

--Chinese Thought & Institutions. LC 57-5272. 1957. 30.00x (ISBN 0-226-23402-9). U of Chicago Pr.

--Chinese Thought & Institutions. LC 57-5272. 1967. pap. 4.50x (ISBN 0-226-23403-7, P270, Phoen). U of Chicago Pr.

--Chinese World Order: Traditional China's Foreign Relations. LC 68-14255. (East Asian Ser: No. 32). (Illus.). 1968. pap. 8.95x (ISBN 0-674-12601-7). Harvard U Pr.

--The Missionary Enterprise in China & America. LC 74-82191. (Studies in American-East Asian Relations: No. 6). 442p. 1974. text ed. 25.00x (ISBN 0-674-57655-1). Harvard U Pr.

Fairbank, John K., jt. ed. see Barnett, Suzanne W.

Fairbank, John K., jt. ed. see Bowie, Robert R.

Fairbank, John K., et al. Japanese Studies of Modern China: A Bibliographical Guide to Historical & Social Science Research on the 19th & 20th Centuries. (Harvard-Yenching Institute Studies: No. 26). 1970. pap. 8.00x (ISBN 0-674-47249-7). Harvard U Pr.

--Our China Prospects. LC 77-79208. (Memoirs Ser.: Vol. 121). 1977. pap. 5.00 (ISBN 0-87169-121-3). Am Philos.

--East Asia: Tradition & Transformation. 2nd ed. LC 77-77994. (Illus.). 1978. text ed. 30.95 (ISBN 0-395-25812-X). HM.

Fairbank, John King. Chinabound: A Fifty Year Memoir. LC 81-47656. 480p. 1982. 19.23i (ISBN 0-06-039005-0, HarpT). Har-Row.

Fairbank, Roswell E. & Schutheis, Robert. Mathematics for the Consumer. (gr. 9-12). 1980. text ed. 9.80 (ISBN 0-538-13150-0, M15). SW Pub.

Fairbank, Roswell E., et al. Applied Business Mathematics. 12th ed. (gr. 9-12). 1985. 12.95 (ISBN 0-317-18598-5, M46). SW Pub.

Fairbank, T. J., jt. auth. see Wynne-Davies, Ruth.

Fairbank, Thomas J., tr. see Soeur, Robert.

Fairbank, Wilma. Adventures in Retrieval: Han Murals & Shang Bronze Molds. LC 79-173410. (Harvard-Yenching Institute Studies: No. 28). 187p. 1972. pap. 8.50x (ISBN 0-674-00575-9). Harvard U Pr.

Fairbank, Wilma, compiled by see Ssu-ch'eng, Liang.

Fairbanks & Schultheis. Consumer Math. (gr. 9-12). 1983. text ed. 10.60 (ISBN 0-538-13160-8, M16). SW Pub.

Fairbanks, Arthur. Athenian Lekythoi with Outline Drawing in Glaze Varnish on a White Ground, 2 vols. in 1, Vol. 6. Bd. with Vol. 7. Athenian Lekythoi with Outline Drawing in Matt Color on a White Ground. Repr. of 1914 ed. (Michigan University Studies Humanistic Ser). (Illus.). Repr. of 1907 ed. 74.00 (ISBN 0-384-38806-X). Johnson Repr.

--Greek Art. LC 63-10265. (Our Debt to Greece & Rome Ser.). (Illus.). Repr. of 1930 ed. 17.50 (ISBN 0-8154-0062-4). Cooper Sq.

--Introduction to Sociology. 1896. 15.00 (ISBN 0-686-17696-0). Quality Lib.

Fairbanks, Carol. More Women in Literature: Criticism of the Seventies. LC 78-26405. 465p. 1979. 22.50 (ISBN 0-8108-1193-6). Scarecrow.

Fairbanks, Carol & Engeldinger, Eugene A. Black American Fiction: A Bibliography. LC 78-1351. 359p. 1978. 22.50 (ISBN 0-8108-1120-0). Scarecrow.

Fairbanks, Carol & Sundberg, Sara B. Farm Women on the Prairie Frontier: A Sourcebook for Canada & the United States. LC 83-4498. (Illus.). 251p. 1983. lib. bdg. 17.50 (ISBN 0-8108-1625-3). Scarecrow.

Fairbanks, Charles H. Florida Anthropology. pap. 7.00 (ISBN 0-685-02245-5). Johnson Repr.

Fairbanks, Charles H., jt. auth. see Milanich, Jerald T.

Fairbanks, G. H., et al. Spoken Sinhalese, Bk. I & Cassettes I. (Spoken Language Ser.). 1980. Set. 125.00x (ISBN 0-87950-444-7). Spoken Lang Serv.

--Spoken Sinhalese, Bk. II & Cassettes II. (Spoken Language Ser.). 1980. Set. 105.00x (ISBN 0-87950-445-5). Spoken Lang Serv.

--Spoken Sinhalese, Bks. I, II & Cassettes I, II. (Spoken Language Ser.). 1980. 220.00x (ISBN 0-87950-446-3). Spoken Lang Serv.

--Spoken Sinhalese. (Spoken Languages Ser.). (Prog. Bk.). 1979. Bk. I, Lessons 1-24, 415 p. pap. 12.00x (ISBN 0-87950-440-4); Bk. II Lessons 25-36, 260 p. pap. 12.00x (ISBN 0-87950-442-0); cassettes I for bk. I (21 dual track) 120.00x (ISBN 0-87950-441-2); cassettes II for bk. II (13 dual track) 100.00x (ISBN 0-87950-443-9). Spoken Lang Serv.

Fairbanks, George R. History & Antiquities of the City of St. Augustine, Florida: Founded A. D. 1565. Gannon, Michael V., ed. LC 75-15750. (Floridiana Facsimile& Reprint Ser.). 1975. Repr. of 1858 ed. 8.50 (ISBN 0-8130-0403-9). U Presses Fla.

Fairbanks, Gordon H. & Misra, Bal G. Spoken & Written Hindi. 504p. 1966. 29.50x (ISBN 0-8014-0123-2). Cornell U Pr.

Fairbanks, Gordon H. & Stevick, Earl W. Spoken East Armenian. LC 75-15932. (Spoken Language Ser). 428p. (Prog. Bk.). 1975. pap. 12.00x (ISBN 0-87950-420-X). cassettes, six dual track 60.00x (ISBN 0-87950-421-8); course bk. with cassettes 65.00x (ISBN 0-87950-422-6). Spoken Lang Serv.

Fairbanks, Gordon H., et al. Russian Readings in Popular Science. LC 63-8805. (gr. 9 up). 1963. 25.00x (ISBN 0-231-02566-1). Columbia U Pr.

Fairbanks, Grant. Voice & Articulation Drillbook. 2nd ed. (gr. 12). 1960. text ed. 17.50 scp (ISBN 0-06-041990-3, HarpC). Har-Row.

Fairbanks, Henry G. Louise Imogen Guiney: Laureate of the Lost. LC 73-176128. 1972. 12.95x (ISBN 0-87343-039-5). Magi Bks.

Fairbanks, Jo Ann A. Illustrated Soccer Rules. (Illus.). 128p. (Orig.). 1983. pap. 4.95 (ISBN 0-8092-5520-0). Contemp Bks.

Fairbanks, John A. Illustrated Soccer Rules. 128p. 4.95 (ISBN 0-8092-5520-0). Contemp Bks.

Fairbanks, Jonathan & Bates, Elizabeth B. American Furniture Sixteen Twenty to the Present. (Illus.). 576p. 1981. 50.00 (ISBN 0-399-90096-9, Marek). Putnam Pub Group.

Fairbanks, Jonathan L. & Moffett, Kenworth W. Directions in Contemporary American Ceramics. Purvis, Cynthia M., ed. LC 84-60500. (Illus.). 87p. (Orig.). 1984. pap. 9.95 (ISBN 0-87846-240-6). Mus Fine Arts Boston.

Fairbanks, L. A., jt. ed. see McGuire, M. T.

Fairbanks, Lebron. Beacon Small-Group Bible Studies, Acts, Pt. II: The Continuing Mission of the Church. Wolf, Earl C., ed. 96p. (Orig.). 1984. pap. 2.50 (ISBN 0-8341-0947-6). Beacon Hill.

--Beacon Small-Group Bible Studies, Philippians, Colossians, Experiencing His Peace. 72p. 1982. pap. 2.50 (ISBN 0-8341-0778-3). Beacon Hill.

Fairbanks, Robert P., jt. auth. see Fisher, Glenn W.

Fairbanks, Virgil F., et al. Clinical Disorders of Iron Metabolism. 2nd ed. LC 75-139797. (Illus.). 486p. 1971. 99.50 (ISBN 0-8089-0677-1, 791210). Grune.

Fairbansk, Arthur. Introduction to Sociology. 1896. 15.00 (ISBN 0-8482-3988-1). Norwood Edns.

Fairbridge, Maurice H. Studies in Biblical & Semitic Symbolism. 1977. lib. bdg. 59.95 (ISBN 0-8490-2700-4). Gordon Pr.

Fairbridge, R. Encyclopedia of World Regional Geology, Pt. 3. 1986. price not set (ISBN 0-87933-266-2). Van Nos Reinhold.

Fairbridge, R., ed. Encyclopedia of Atmospheric Sciences & Astrogeology. (Encyclopedia of Earth Sciences Ser: Vol. II). 1967. 91.50 (ISBN 0-12-786458-X). Acad Pr.

Fairbridge, R. W., ed. The Encyclopedia of Geochemistry & Environmental Sciences. LC 75-152326. (Encyclopedia of Earth Sciences Ser.: Vol. IVA). 1321p. 1972. 98.00 (ISBN 0-87933-180-1). Van Nos Reinhold.

--The Encyclopedia of Geomorphology. LC 68-58342. (Encyclopedia of Earth Sciences Ser.: Vol. III). 1295p. 1968. 98.00 (ISBN 0-87933-179-8). Van Nos Reinhold.

Fairbridge, R. W. & Bourgeois, J., eds. The Encyclopedia of Sedimentology. LC 78-18259. (Encyclopedia of Earth Sciences Ser.: Vol. VI). 901p. 1978. 98.00 (ISBN 0-87933-152-6). Van Nos Reinhold.

Fairbridge, R. W. & Finkl, C. W., Jr., eds. The Encyclopedia of Soil Science: Part 1, Physics, Chemistry, Biology, Fertility, & Technology. LC 78-31233. (Encyclopedia of Earth Sciences Ser.: Vol. XII). 700p. 1979. 81.00 (ISBN 0-87933-176-3). Van Nos Reinhold.

Fairbridge, Rhodes W., jt. auth. see Michel, Jean-Pierre.

Fairbridge, Rhodes W., jt. auth. see Richards, Horace G.

Fairbridge, Rhodes W., ed. Encyclopedia of World Regional Geology: Part I: Western Hemisphere Including Australia & Antarctica, Pt. 1. LC 75-1406. (Encyclopedia of Earth Sciences Ser: Vol. 8A). 1975. 76.00 (ISBN 0-12-786461-X). Acad Pr.

Fairbridge, Rhodes W., ed. see Nilsen, Tor H.

Fairbrook, Paul. College & University Food Service Manual. LC 79-50956. (Illus.). 1979. pap. 17.50x (ISBN 0-9602456-0-X). Colman Pubs.

--Public Relations & Merchandising: A Handbook for College & University Food Services. LC 84-71563. (Illus.). 1984. pap. 22.00x (ISBN 0-9602456-1-8). Colman Pubs.

Fairbrothers, D. E., jt. ed. see Jensen, U.

Fairburn, Eleanor. The White Seahorse. 288p. 1985. pap. 6.95 (ISBN 0-86327-075-1, Pub. by Wolfhound Pr Ireland). Irish Bks Media.

Fairchild, jt. auth. see Beauregard.

Fairchild, Arthur H. The Making of Poetry: A Critical Study of Its Nature & Value. 1912. Repr. 15.00 (ISBN 0-8274-2664-X). R West.

--Shakespeare & the Arts of Design: Architecture, Sculpture & Painting. LC 70-174863. Repr. of 1937 ed. 17.00 (ISBN 0-405-08494-3, Blom Pubns). Ayer Co Pubs.

--Shakespeare & the Tragic Theme. 1978. Repr. of 1944 ed. lib. bdg. 25.00 (ISBN 0-8495-1617-X). Arden Lib.

--Shakespeare & the Tragic Theme. 145p. 1980. Repr. of 1944 ed. lib. bdg. 25.00 (ISBN 0-89987-258-1). Darby Bks.

--Shakespeare & the Tragic Theme. LC 73-11385. 1944. lib. bdg. 17.50 (ISBN 0-8414-1974-4). Folcroft.

--Studies in Honor of A. H. R. Fairchild. Prouty, Charles T., ed. 1946. Repr. 25.00 (ISBN 0-8274-3536-3). R West.

Fairchild, B. H., Jr. Such Holy Song: Music As Idea, Form, & Image in the Poetry of William Blake. LC 79-92809. 120p. 1980. 15.00x (ISBN 0-87338-238-2). Kent St U Pr.

Fairchild, Betty & Hayward, Nancy. Now That You Know: What Every Parent Should Know About Homosexuality. LC 78-22251. 228p. 1981. pap. 6.95 (ISBN 0-15-667702-4, Harv). HarBraceJ.

Fairchild, Betty J., jt. auth. see Croke, Katherine B.

Fairchild Book Division Research Staff. Fairchild's Financial Manual of Retail Stores: 1980. (Illus.). 324p. 1980. pap. text ed. 50.00 (ISBN 0-87005-362-0). Fairchild.

--Fairchild's Textile & Apparel Financial Directory: 1980. 260p. 1980. text ed. 45.00 (ISBN 0-87005-361-2). Fairchild.

--SN Distribution Study Grocery Store Sales, 1980. 1980. pap. text ed. 27.50 (ISBN 0-87005-313-2). Fairchild.

--SN Distribution Study of Grocery Store Sales, 1981. 250p. 1981. pap. 30.00 (ISBN 0-87005-370-1). Fairchild.

Fairchild Book Research Dept. Electronic News Financial Fact Book & Directory, 1985. 24th ed. 520p. 1985. pap. 125.00 (ISBN 0-87005-502-X). Fairchild.

Fairchild Book Research Division. Electronic News Financial Fact Book & Directory. 23rd ed. 500p. 1984. pap. 125.00 (ISBN 0-87005-469-4). Fairchild.

--Fairchild Textile & Apparel Directory. 210p. 1983. pap. 50.00 (ISBN 0-87005-442-2). Fairchild.

--Fairchild's Financial Manual of Retail Stores. 54th ed. 300p. 1981. pap. 50.00 (ISBN 0-87005-385-X). Fairchild.

--Fairchild's Financial Manual of Retail Stores. 270p. 1982. pap. 60.00 (ISBN 0-87005-416-3). Fairchild.

--Fairchild's Financial Manual of Retail Stores. 270p. 1983. pap. 60.00 (ISBN 0-87005-443-0). Fairchild.

--Fairchild's Financial Manual of Retail Stores, 1984. 57th ed. 255p. 1984. pap. 60.00 (ISBN 0-87005-471-6). Fairchild.

--Fairchild's Financial Manual of Retail Stores. 58th ed. 230p. 1985. pap. 60.00 (ISBN 0-87005-504-6). Fairchild.

--Fairchild's Textile & Apparel Financial Directory. 8th ed. 230p. 1981. pap. 45.00 (ISBN 0-87005-384-1). Fairchild.

--Fairchild's Textile & Apparel Financial Directory. 187p. 1982. pap. 50.00 (ISBN 0-87005-415-5). Fairchild.

--Fairchild's Textile & Apparel Financial Directory. 12th ed. 160p. 1985. pap. 50.00 (ISBN 0-87005-503-8). Fairchild.

--Fairchild's Textile & Apparel Financial Directory, 1984. 11th ed. 190p. 1984. pap. 50.00 (ISBN 0-87005-470-8). Fairchild.

Fairchild Book Special Projects Division. Supermarket News Distribution Study of Grocery Store Sales, 1982. (Illus.). 290p. 1982. pap. 30.00 (ISBN 0-87005-409-0). Fairchild.

Fairchild Camera & Instrument Co. Semiconductor & Integrated Circuit Fabrication Techniques. 1979. 24.95 (ISBN 0-87909-668-3). Reston.

Fairchild, Daniel, et al. Everything You Always Wanted to Know About Drinking Problems: & Then a Few Things You Didn't Want to Know. Fairchild, Thomas N., ed. (Illus., Orig.). 1978. pap. text ed. 6.50x (ISBN 0-932194-04-4). Health Comm.

Fairchild, David. Logic: A First Course. 201p. 1977. pap. text ed. 11.25 (ISBN 0-8191-0117-6). U Pr of Amer.

Fairchild, Edwardj. Agricultural Chemical & Pesticides: Handbook of the Toxic Effects. (Illus.). 230p. 1978. text ed. 60.00 (ISBN 0-7194-0002-3, Pub. by Castle Hse England). J K Burgess.

Fairchild, Effie L. & Neal, Larry L., eds. Common-Unity in the Community: A Forward-Looking Program of Recreation & Leisure Service for the Handicapped. 114p. 1975. pap. 4.50 (ISBN 0-943272-10-6). Inst Recreation Res.

Fairchild, Erika & Webb, Vincent J. The Politics of Crime & Criminal Justice. LC 84-27590. 1985. 22.00 (ISBN 0-8039-2423-2); pap. 10.95 (ISBN 0-8039-2424-0). Sage.

Fairchild, G. B. Notes on Neotropical Tabanidae XIX: The Tabanus Lineola Complex. 1983. 7.50 (ISBN 0-318-02797-6). Entomol Soc.

Fairchild, Henry P. Dictionary of Sociology & Related Sciences. LC 76-110377. Repr. of 1955 ed. lib. bdg. 35.00x (ISBN 0-8371-4581-3, FADS). Greenwood.

--Dictionary of Sociology & Related Sciences. (Quality Paperback Ser.: No. 120). 342p. 1977. pap. 4.95 (ISBN 0-8226-0120-6). Littlefield.

--The Melting-Pot Mistake. Grob, Gerald, ed. LC 76-46076. (Anti-Movements in America). 1977. Repr. of 1926 ed. lib. bdg. 21.00x (ISBN 0-405-09949-5). Ayer Co Pubs.

--Versus: Reflections of a Sociologist. LC 74-86015. 1969. Repr. of 1950 ed. 21.00x (ISBN 0-8046-0557-2, Pub by Kennikat). Assoc Faculty Pr.

Fairchild, Hoxie N. Religious Trends in English Poetry, 6 vols. Incl. Vol. 1. Protestantism & the Cult of Sentiment: 1700-1740 (ISBN 0-231-08821-3); Vol. 2. Religious Sentimentalism in the Age of Johnson: 1740-1780. 1942 (ISBN 0-231-08822-1); Vol. 3. Romantic Faith: 1780-1830. 1949 (ISBN 0-231-08823-X); Vol. 4. Christianity & Romanticism in the Victorian Era: 1830-1880. 1957 (ISBN 0-231-08824-8); Vol. 5. Gods of a Changing Poetry: 1880-1920. 1962 (ISBN 0-231-08825-6); Vol. 6. Valley of Dry Bones: 1920-1965. 1968 (ISBN 0-231-08826-4). LC 39-12839. 42.00x ea. Columbia U Pr.

Fairchild, James H. Oberlin: The Colony & the College. Dayton, Donald W., ed. (The Higher Christian Life Ser.). 377p. 1985. 45.00 (ISBN 0-8240-6416-X). Garland Pub.

Fairchild, Johnson E., ed. Basic Beliefs: The Religious Philosophies of Mankind. 9.50x (ISBN 0-911378-03-0). Sheridan.

--Personal Problems & Psychological Frontiers. 8.50x (ISBN 0-911378-18-9). Sheridan.

--Women, Society & Sex. 255p. 1952. 8.50x (ISBN 0-911378-28-6). Sheridan.

Fairchild Market Research Div. Dresses: Women's, Misses' & Juniors' (Fairchild Fact Files Ser.). 55p. 1984. pap. 15.00 (ISBN 0-87005-487-2). Fairchild.

Fairchild Market Research Division. Consumer Market Development, 1983. (Fact File Ser.). (Illus.). 50p. 1984. pap. text ed. 15.00 (ISBN 0-87005-466-X). Fairchild.

--Consumer Market Developments. (Fact File Ser.). (Illus.). 100p. 1980. pap. 15.00 (ISBN 0-87005-350-7). Fairchild.

--Consumer Market Developments. (Fairchild Fact Files Ser.). (Illus.). 59p. 1982. pap. 15.00 (ISBN 0-87005-427-9). Fairchild.

--Consumer Market Developments. (Fairchild Fact File Ser.). (Illus.). 55p. 1985. pap. 15.00 (ISBN 0-87005-490-2). Fairchild.

--Consumer Market Developments-1981. (Fairchild Fact Files). (Illus.). 70p. 1981. pap. 15.00 (ISBN 0-87005-397-3). Fairchild.

--The Customer Speaks. (Fairchild Fact File Ser.). 1979. pap. 20.00 (ISBN 0-87005-317-5). Fairchild.

--The Customer Speaks: Nineteen Eighty. (Fact File Ser.). (Illus.). 76p. 1980. pap. 15.00 (ISBN 0-87005-345-0). Fairchild.

--Department Store Sales. (Fairchild Fact File Ser.). (Illus.). 55p. 1985. pap. 15.00 (ISBN 0-87005-489-9). Fairchild.

--Department Store Sales - 1981. (Fairchild Fact Files Ser.). (Illus.). 55p. 1982. pap. text ed. 15.00 (ISBN 0-87005-398-1). Fairchild.

--Department Store Sales, 1983. (Fairchild Fact File Ser.). (Illus.). 50p. 1983. pap. text ed. 15.00 (ISBN 0-87005-465-1). Fairchild.

--Dresses: Women's, Misses', Juniors' (Fairchild Fact Files Ser.). (Illus.). 51p. 1983. pap. text ed. 15.00 (ISBN 0-87005-428-7). Fairchild.

--Fashion Accessories (Men's & Women's) (Fairchild Fact Files Ser.). (Illus.). 60p. 1981. pap. text ed. 15.00 (ISBN 0-87005-388-4). Fairchild.

--Fashion Accessories (Men's & Women's) (Fact File Ser.). (Illus.). 55p. 1983. pap. text ed. 15.00 (ISBN 0-87005-456-2). Fairchild.

--Fashion Accessories: Men's & Women's. (Fairchild Fact Files Ser.). (Illus.). 55p. 1985. pap. 15.00 (ISBN 0-87005-521-6). Fairchild.

--Footwear (Men's, Women's. Boys' & Girls') Fact File 1985. 8th ed. (Fairchild Fact Files Ser.). (Illus.). 50p. 1985. pap. 15.00 (ISBN 0-87005-524-0). Fairchild.

--Footwear-1982. (Fairchild Facts Files Ser.). (Illus.). 73p. 1982. pap. 15.00 (ISBN 0-87005-422-8). Fairchild.

--Home Electronics. (Fairchild Fact File Ser.). 1979. pap. 15.00 (ISBN 0-87005-320-5). Fairchild.

--Home Textiles. (Fairchild Fact File Ser.). (Illus.). 51p. 1982. pap. text ed. 15.00 (ISBN 0-87005-425-2). Fairchild.

--Home Textiles. (Fact File Ser.). (Illus.). 55p. 1984. pap. 15.00 (ISBN 0-87005-486-4). Fairchild.

--Hosiery-Legwear-Bodywear (Men's, Women's, Children's) (Fairchild Fact Files Ser.). (Illus.). 51p. 1982. pap. 15.00 (ISBN 0-87005-420-1). Fairchild.

--Hosiery-Legwear: (Men's, Women's, Children's) (Fact File Ser.). (Illus.). 55p. 1984. pap. 15.00 (ISBN 0-87005-481-3). Fairchild.

--Household Furniture & Bedding. (Fairchild Fact Files Ser.). (Illus.). 51p. 1982. pap. 15.00 (ISBN 0-87005-417-1). Fairchild.

--Infants', Toddlers', Boys' & Girls' Wear. (Fairchild Fact Files Ser.). (Illus.). 55p. 1985. pap. 15.00 (ISBN 0-87005-522-4). Fairchild.

--Infants' Toddlers' Girls' & Boys' (Fact File Ser.). (Illus.). 1983. pap. text ed. 15.00 (ISBN 0-87005-457-0). Fairchild.

--Major Appliances & Electric Housewares. (Fairchilds Fact Files Ser.). (Illus.). 50p. 1983. pap. text ed. 15.00 (ISBN 0-87005-464-3). Fairchild.

--Major Appliances & Electrical Housewares. (Fairchild Fact Files Ser.). (Illus.). 64p. 1981. pap. text ed. 15.00 (ISBN 0-87005-396-5). Fairchild.

--Major Appliances & Electrical Housewares. (Fairchild Fact Files Ser.). (Illus.). 55p. 1985. pap. 15.00 (ISBN 0-87005-528-3). Fairchild.

--Market Pacesetters (Young Adults) (Fairchild Fact Files Ser.). (Illus.). 1981. pap. text ed. 15.00 (ISBN 0-87005-390-6). Fairchild.

--Men's Furnishings & Work Wear. (Fairchild Fact Files Ser.). (Illus.). 56p. 1981. pap. text ed. 15.00 (ISBN 0-87005-455-4). Fairchild.

--Men's Furnishings & Work Wear. (Fairchild Fact Files Ser.). 55p. 1985. pap. 15.00 (ISBN 0-87005-526-7). Fairchild.

--Men's Sportswear, Casual Wear, Jeans. (Fairchild Fact File Ser.). (Illus.). 54p. 1982. pap. 15.00 (ISBN 0-87005-423-6). Fairchild.

--Men's Sportswear, Casual Wear, Jeans. (Fact File Ser.). (Illus.). 55p. 1984. pap. 15.00 (ISBN 0-87005-484-8). Fairchild.

--Men's Tailored Clothing & Rainwear. (Fairchild Fact Files Ser.). (Illus.). 55p. 1985. pap. 15.00 (ISBN 0-87005-527-5). Fairchild.

--Men's Tailored Clothing: Separates & Rainwear. (Fact File Ser.). (Illus.). 52p. 1983. pap. text ed. 15.00 (ISBN 0-87005-461-9). Fairchild.

--Men's, Women's & Children's Footwear - 1981. (Fairchild Fact Files Ser.). (Illus.). 73p. 1981. pap. text ed. 15.00 (ISBN 0-87005-392-2). Fairchild.

--Personal Electronics. special ed. (Fact File Ser.). (Illus.). 50p. 1983. pap. text ed. 15.00 (ISBN 0-87005-458-9). Fairchild.

--Retailing-Merchandising Trends. (Fairchild Fact File Ser.). (Illus.). 55p. 1984. pap. 15.00 (ISBN 0-87005-488-0). Fairchild.

--Soft Surface Floor Coverings. (Fairchild Fact Files Ser.). (Illus.). 51p. 1982. pap. 15.00 (ISBN 0-87005-421-X). Fairchild.

--The Sports-Leisure Market (Special) (Fact Files Ser.). (Illus.). 65p. 1982. pap. 15.00 (ISBN 0-87005-418-X). Fairchild.

--The Textile-Apparel Industries. (Fairchild Fact Files Ser.). (Illus.). 64p. 1981. pap. text ed. 15.00 (ISBN 0-87005-395-7). Fairchild.

--The Textile-Apparel Industries. (Fairchild Fact Files Ser.). (Illus.). 55p. 1985. pap. 15.00 (ISBN 0-87005-531-3). Fairchild.

Fairchild Market Research Division, ed. The Textile-Apparel Industry. (Fairchild Fact File Ser.). (Illus.). 50p. 1983. pap. 15.00 (ISBN 0-87005-463-5). Fairchild.

Fairchild Market Research Division. Toiletries, Beauty Aids, Cosmetics, Fragrances. (Fairchild Fact Files Ser). 51p. 1982. pap. 15.00 (ISBN 0-87005-419-8). Fairchild.
--Toiletries, Beauty Aids, Cosmetics, Fragrances. (Fact File Ser.). (Illus.). 55p. 1984. pap. 15.00 (ISBN 0-87005-480-5). Fairchild.
--Women's Coats, Suits, Rainwear & Furs. (Fairchild Fact File Ser.). (Illus.). 1981. pap. 15.00 (ISBN 0-87005-391-4). Fairchild.
--Women's Coats, Suits, Rainwear & Furs. (Fairchild Fact Files Ser.). (Illus.). 55p. 1985. pap. 15.00 (ISBN 0-87005-523-2). Fairchild.
--Women's Coats, Suits, Rainwear, Furs. (Fact File Ser.). (Illus.). 50p. 1983. pap. text ed. 15.00 (ISBN 0-87005-459-7). Fairchild.
--Women's Inner Fashions: Nightwear, Daywear, & Loungewear. (Fact File Ser.). (Illus.). 50p. 1983. pap. text ed. 15.00 (ISBN 0-87005-462-7). Fairchild.
--Women's Inner Fashions: Nightwear, Daywear, & Loungewear. (Fairchild Fact Files Ser.). (Illus.). 55p. 1985. pap. 15.00 (ISBN 0-87005-520-8). Fairchild.
--Women's, Misses' & Juniors' Sportswear, Casualwear, Separates, Jeans. (Fairchild Fact File Ser.). (Illus.). 1982. pap. 15.00 (ISBN 0-87005-424-4). Fairchild.
Fairchild Market Research Division Editors, ed. Department Store Sales, 1982. (Fairchild Fact Files Ser.). (Illus.). 55p. 1982. pap. text ed. 15.00 (ISBN 0-87005-426-0). Fairchild.
Fairchild Market Research Division Staff. Department Store Sales. 2nd. ed. (Fairchild Fact Files). (Illus.). 55p. 1986. pap. 15.00 (ISBN 0-87005-529-1). Fairchild.
--Footwear (Men's, Women's, Boys', Girls') (Fact File Ser.). (Illus.). 55p. 1984. pap. 15.00 (ISBN 0-87005-483-X). Fairchild.
--Furniture & Bedding: Mattresses, Dual-Purpose Sleep Furniture, Etc. (Fact File Ser.). (Illus.). 55p. 1984. pap. 15.00 (ISBN 0-87005-479-1). Fairchild.
--Sports-Fitness: Leisure Markets. special ed. (Fact File Ser.). (Illus.). 55p. 1984. pap. 15.00 (ISBN 0-87005-482-1). Fairchild.
--Sportswear, Casual Wear, Separates, Jeans (Women's, Misses, Junior's) (Factfile Ser.). (Illus.). 55p. 1984. pap. 15.00 (ISBN 0-87005-485-6). Fairchild.
Fairchild Market Reserch Div. A Statistical Analysis of Retailing. (Fact Files Ser.). (Illus.). 55p. 1985. pap. 15.00 (ISBN 0-87005-525-9). Fairchild.
Fairchild, Morgan. Morgan Fairchild's Super Looks. (Orig.). 1984. pap. 17.95 (ISBN 0-671-50961-6, Wallaby). PB.
--Super Looks. pap. 11.95 (ISBN 0-671-50033-3). S&S.
Fairchild Research Division. Women's Inner Fashions: Nightwear, Daywear, & Loungewear. (Illus.). 1981. pap. 12.50 (ISBN 0-87005-394-9). Fairchild.
Fairchild Research Staff. Fairchild's Market Directory of Women's & Children's Apparel. 2nd ed. 96p. 1979. pap. 9.50 (ISBN 0-87005-311-6). Fairchild.
Fairchild, Roy. Finding Hope Again: A Guide to Counseling Depression. LC 79-2988. 160p. 1985. pap. 6.68 (ISBN 0-06-062326-8, HarpR). Har-Row.
Fairchild, Roy W. Finding Hope Again: A Pastor's Guide to Counseling Depressed Persons. LC 79-2988. 160p. 1980. 9.95i (ISBN 0-06-062325-X, HarpR). Har-Row.
Fairchild Special Projects Division. SN Distribution Study of Grocery Store Sales, 1984. 330p. 1984. pap. 40.00 (ISBN 0-87005-472-4). Fairchild.
Fairchild Special Projects Division Staff. SN Distribution Study of Grocery Store Sales. 310p. 1985. pap. 40.00 (ISBN 0-87005-501-1). Fairchild.
Fairchild, Thomas N., ed. see Fairchild, Daniel, et al.
Fairchild, Tony. The America's Cup Challenge: There is No Second. LC 99-943285. (Illus.). 233p. 1983. 19.95 (ISBN 0-333-32527-3, Pub. by Nautical Bks England). Sheridan.
Fairchild, W. W., et al. Eocene & Oligocene Forminifera from the Santa Cruz Mountains, California. LC 72-627811. (University of California Publications in Geological Sciences: Vol. 81). pap. 41.00 (ISBN 0-317-19892-0, 2014894). Bks Demand UMI.
Fairchilds, Cissie. Domestic Enemies: Servants & Their Masters in Old Regime France. LC 83-48059. 344p. 1984. 32.50x (ISBN 0-8018-2978-X). Johns Hopkins.
Fairchilds, Cissie C. Poverty & Charity in Aix-en-Provence, 1640-1789. LC 75-36930. (Studies in Historical & Political Science Ninety-Fourth Ser.: No. 1 (1976)). (Illus.). 216p. 1976. 20.00x (ISBN 0-8018-1677-7). Johns Hopkins.
Faircloth, Charlotte P. Limitations on Benefits & Contributions on Behalf of Individual Plan Participants: No. B356. (Requirements for Qualification of Plans). 17p. 1978. pap. 4.50 (ISBN 0-317-31164-6). Am Law Inst.
Faircloth, Cyril E. Escape from the City of Gold. 1981. 15.00x (ISBN 0-7223-1380-2, Pub. by Stockwell Bk). State Mutual Bk.
Faircloth, Dorothy. Fire & Water - A Night at the Bar. 56p. 1983. 5.50 (ISBN 0-682-49989-7). Exposition Pr FL.
--God's Love in Bloom. 1982. 5.95 (ISBN 0-533-05432-X). Vantage.
Faircloth, Marjorie A., jt. auth. see Faircloth, Samuel R.
Faircloth, Mary E., et al. Mosby's Review of Practical Nursing. 8th ed. LC 81-14105. (Illus.). 352p. 1982. pap. text ed. 14.95 (ISBN 0-8016-3538-1). Mosby.
Faircloth, Rudy & Carter, W. Horace. Ernie Pyle, Typewriter Soldier. (Illus.). 84p. 1982. 3.20 (ISBN 0-937866-04-0). Atlantic Pub Co.
Faircloth, Samuel R. & Faircloth, Marjorie A. Phonetic Science: A Program of Instruction. (Illus.). 144p. 1973. pap. text ed. 16.95. P-H.
Faircloth, Terence A. & Sennholz, Robert F. Tax Treatment of Commodity Futures & Futures Options. 28p. (Orig.). 1984. pap. 2.95 (ISBN 0-915513-10-2). Ctr Futures Ed.
Fairclough, A. Cornwall's Railways: A Pictorial Survey. 96p. 1981. 35.00x (ISBN 0-686-97152-3, Pub. by D B Barton England). State Mutual Bk.
Fairclough, Chris. Take a Trip to England. (Take a Trip Ser.). (Illus.). 32p. (gr. 1-3). 1982. PLB 8.40 (ISBN 0-531-04416-5). Watts.
--Take a Trip to Holland. (Take a Trip Ser.). (Illus.). 32p. 1982. PLB 8.40 (ISBN 0-531-04417-3). Watts.
--Take a Trip to Italy. (Take a Trip to Ser.). (Illus.). 32p. (gr. 1-3). 1981. lib. bdg. 8.40 (ISBN 0-531-04319-3). Watts.
--Take a Trip to West Germany. (Take a Trip to Ser.). (Illus.). 32p. (gr. 1-3). 1981. lib. bdg. 8.40 (ISBN 0-531-04320-7). Watts.
Fairclough, Chris, jt. auth. see Keeler, Stephan.
Fairclough, G. Thomas, ed. see Fitzpatrick, Lilian L.
Fairclough, Henry R. Classics & Our Twentieth-Century Poets. LC 75-168001. (Stanford University. Stanford Studies in Language & Literature: Vol. 2, Pt. 2). Repr. of 1927 ed. 18.00 (ISBN 0-404-51804-4). AMS Pr.
--Love of Nature Among the Greeks & Romans. LC 63-10298. (Our Debt to Greece & Rome Ser). (Illus.). Repr. of 1930 ed. 17.50 (ISBN 0-8154-0063-2). Cooper Sq.
Fairclough, Oliver & Leary, Emmeline. Textiles by William Morris & Co. (Illus., Orig.). 1981. pap. 20.00 (ISBN 0-686-79147-9). Eastview.
Fairclough, Peter, ed. Three Gothic Novels. Incl. Castle of Otronto. Walpole, Horace; Vathek. Bockford, William; Frankenstein. Shelley, Mary W. (English Library Ser.). (Orig.). 1968. pap. 3.95 (ISBN 0-14-043036-9). Penguin.
Fairclough, Tom, tr. see Hutchins, Edward H.
Fairer, David. Pope's Imagination. LC 84-832. 208p. 1984. 31.50 (ISBN 0-7190-1080-2, Pub. by Manchester Univ Pr). Longwood Pub Group.
Faires, Barbara, jt. auth. see Faires, Douglas.
Faires, Douglas & Faires, Barbara. Calculus & Analytic Geometry. 1026p. 1983. text ed. write for info. (ISBN 0-87150-323-9, 33L 2571, Prindle). PWS Pubs.
Faires, J. Douglas, jt. auth. see Burden, Richard L.
Faires, R. A. & Boswell, G. G. Radioisotope Lab Techniques. 4th ed. LC 80-41045. 272p. 1980. text ed. 49.95 (ISBN 0-408-70940-5). Butterworth.
Faires, Virgil M. Design of Machine Elements. 4th ed. 1965. text ed. write for info. (ISBN 0-02-335950-1, 33595). Macmillan.
Faires, Virgil M. & Keown, Robert M. Mechanism. 5th ed. LC 80-13135. 346p. 1980. Repr. of 1960 ed. lib. bdg. 21.50 (ISBN 0-89874-182-3). Krieger.
Faires, Virgil M. & Simmang, Clifford M. Problems on Thermodynamics. 6th ed. 1978. pap. write for info. (ISBN 0-02-335230-2, 33523). Macmillan.
--Thermodynamics. 6th ed. (Illus.). 1978. text ed. write for info. (ISBN 0-02-335530-1, 33553). Macmillan.
Faires, Virgil M. & Wingren, Roy M. Problems on the Design of Machine Elements. 4th ed. 1965. text ed. 8.95x (ISBN 0-02-335960-9, 33596). Macmillan.
Fairfax, Ann. Penelope. 176p. (Orig.). 1982. pap. 1.95 (ISBN 0-515-05400-3). Jove Pubns.
Fairfax, Bryan. Walking London's Waterways. (Illus.). 192p. 1985. 14.95 (ISBN 0-7153-8584-4). David & Charles.
Fairfax, Edward, tr. Tasso's Jerusalem Delivered. LC 62-7386. (Centaur Classics Ser.). 566p. 1962. 19.95x (ISBN 0-8093-0063-X). S Ill U Pr.
Fairfax, Gwen. Lover in Disguise. (Candlelight Ecstasy Ser.: No. 213). 192p. (Orig.). 1984. pap. 1.95 (ISBN 0-440-15086-8). Dell.
Fairfax, John & Moat, John. The Way to Write. 96p. 1981. 9.95 (ISBN 0-312-85832-9); pap. 3.95 (ISBN 0-312-85833-7). St Martin.
Fairfax, Kate. Sweet Fire. 272p. pap. 2.95 (ISBN 0-441-79119-0); pap. text ed. 3.25 (ISBN 0-441-79120-4). Ace Bks.
Fairfax, Lucy. Hebridean Childhood. 128p. 1981. 40.00x (ISBN 0-904002-56-X, Pub. by R Drew Pub Scotland). State Mutual Bk.
Fairfax, Lynn. Aphrodite's Legend. (Second Chance at Love: No. 28). 192p. (Orig.). 1982. pap. 1.75 (ISBN 0-515-06335-5). Jove Pubns.
--Guarded Moments. (Second Chance at Love Ser.: No. 96). 192p. 1983. pap. 1.75 (ISBN 0-515-06860-8). Jove Pubns.
--Heartland. (Second Chance at Love Ser.: No. 37). 192p. (Orig.). 1982. pap. 1.75 (ISBN 0-515-06282-0). Jove Pubns.
Fairfax, Sally K., jt. auth. see Dana, Samuel T.
Fairfax-Blakeborough, Noel, ed. Jack Fairfax-Blakeborough: Memoirs. 1978. 11.95 (ISBN 0-85131-269-1, NL51, Dist. by Miller). J A Allen.
Fairfax-Lucy, Alice, jt. auth. see Lucy, Mary E.
Fairfax-Lucy, Alice, ed. see Lucy, Mary E.
Fairfield, Darrell. Amber's Delight. (Amber Ser.: No. 3). (Orig.). 1982. pap. 2.25 (ISBN 0-440-10040-2). Dell.
--Amber's Fancy. (Amber Ser.: No. 2). (Orig.). 1982. pap. 2.25 (ISBN 0-440-10043-7). Dell.
--Amber's Passion. (Orig.). 1982. pap. 2.25 (ISBN 0-440-10193-X). Dell.
--Amber's Pleasure. 160p. 1982. pap. 2.25 (ISBN 0-440-10195-6). Dell.
--Amber's Thrill. (Orig.). 1982. pap. 2.25 (ISBN 0-440-10208-1). Dell.
Fairfield, Francis G. & Croly, Jane. The Clubs of New York: Sorosis, 2 vols. in 1. facsimile ed. LC 75-1845. (Leisure Class in America Ser.). 1975. Repr. of 1873 ed. 25.50x (ISBN 0-405-06944-8). Ayer Co Pubs.
Fairfield, Gail. Choice Centered Tarot. 3rd ed. 160p. (Orig.). 1981. pap. 7.95 (ISBN 0-9609650-2-5). Choices.
--Choice Centered Tarot. 150p. 1985. pap. 7.95 (ISBN 0-87877-084-4). Newcastle Pub.
--Choice Centered Tarot. 150p. 1985. Repr. lib. bdg. 17.95x (ISBN 0-89370-684-1). Borgo Pr.
Fairfield, James G. All That We Are We Give. LC 77-14510. 192p. 1977. pap. 4.95 (ISBN 0-8361-1839-1). Herald Pr.
Fairfield, James G. T. When You Don't Agree. LC 77-3133. 240p. 1977. pap. text ed. 4.95 (ISBN 0-8361-1819-7). Herald Pr.
Fairfield, John H. Known Violin Makers. 1983. Repr. text ed. 22.00x (ISBN 0-918624-00-2). Virtuoso.
--Known Violin Makers. LC 76-166227. 198p. 1982. Repr. of 1942 ed. lib. bdg. 29.00x (ISBN 0-403-01552-9). Scholarly.
Fairfield, Leslie P. John Bale: Mythmaker for the English Reformation. LC 75-19953. 250p. 1976. 9.75 (ISBN 0-911198-42-3). Purdue U Pr.
Fairfield, R. P., ed. Federalist Papers: From the Original Text of Hamilton, Madison, Jay. 15.75 (ISBN 0-8446-2041-6). Peter Smith.
Fairfield, Roy P. Person-Centered Graduate Education. LC 77-77206. 270p. 1977. 19.95 (ISBN 0-87975-069-3). Prometheus Bks.
Fairfield, Roy P., ed. The Federalist Papers. 2nd ed. LC 80-8862. 368p. 1981. pap. text ed. 6.95x (ISBN 0-8018-2607-1). Johns Hopkins.
--Humanistic Frontiers in American Education. LC 79-166138. 334p. 1971. 14.95 (ISBN 0-87975-054-5). Prometheus Bks.
Fairfield, Sheila, jt. auth. see Paxton, John.
Fairgrieve. London in Your Pocket. (City in Your Pocket Ser.). 1984. pap. 2.95 (ISBN 0-8120-2973-9). Barron.
Fairhall, David & Peyton, Mike. Pass Your Yachtmaster's. 144p. 1982. 35.00x (ISBN 0-333-31957-5, Pub. by Nautical England). State Mutual Bk.
Fairholt, F. W. The Art, Architecture, Heraldry & Archeology Dictionary Profusely Illustrated, 3 vols. (Illus.). 430p. 1985. Repr. Set. 385.85 (ISBN 0-89901-214-0). Found Class Reprints.
Fairholt, Frederick W. Costume in England, 2 vols. 4th ed. LC 68-21769. 1968. Repr. of 1885 ed. 48.00x (ISBN 0-8103-3506-9). Gale.
--A Dictionary of Terms in Art. 59.95 (ISBN 0-8490-0047-5). Gordon Pr.
Fairholt, Frederick W., ed. Dictionary of Terms in Art. LC 68-30630. (Illus.). 1969. Repr. of 1854 ed. 37.00x (ISBN 0-8103-3071-7). Gale.
--Lord Mayors Pageants: Being Collections Towards a History of These Annual Celebrations, Pts. 1 & 2. Repr. of 1843 ed. 32.00 (ISBN 0-384-15105-1). Johnson Repr.
Fairholt, Fredrick W. A Glossary of Costume in England, Vol. 11. (Illus.). 1976. Repr. write for info. (ISBN 0-7158-1142-8). Charles River Bks.
Fairhurst, Alan & Aoothill, Eric. The Blandford Guide to Trees of the British Countryside. (Illus.). 144p. 1981. 24.95 (ISBN 0-7137-0938-3, Pub. by Blandford Pr England). Sterling.
Fairhurst, Alan, jt. auth. see Soothill, Eric.
Fairhurst, Charles, ed. see Symposium on Rock Mechanics(16th, 1975, University of Minnesota).
Fairhurst, Richard E. The Fairhurst Essays: A Public Look at a Private Memoir. (Illus.). 404p. 1981. 14.95 (ISBN 0-935284-20-6). Patrice Pr.
Fairky, Irene R. E. E. Cummings & Ungrammar. LC 75-12072. 1977. 10.00 (ISBN 0-88370-004-2). Watermill Pubs.
Fairleigh, Runa. An Old-Fashioned Mystery. Morse, L. A., ed. 256p. 1984. pap. 2.95 (ISBN 0-380-69286-4, 69286-4). Avon.
Fairless, Caroline. Hambone. (Illus.). 48p. 1980. 8.95 (ISBN 0-912766-97-2). Tundra Bks.
Fairley, Barker. Barker Fairley Selected Essays on German Literature. Symington, Rodney, ed. LC 83-49517. (Canadian Studies in German Language & Literature: Vol. 29). 378p. (Orig.). 1984. pap. text ed. 35.80 (ISBN 0-8204-0107-2). P Lang Pubs.
--Charles M. Doughty. 1927. 30.00 (ISBN 0-8274-2037-4). R West.
--Heinrich Heine: An Interpretation. LC 77-709. 1977. Repr. of 1954 ed. lib. bdg. 24.75x (ISBN 0-8371-9338-9, FAHH). Greenwood.
Fairley, Barker see Willoughby, L. A.
Fairley, Barker, tr. see Goethe, Johann W.
Fairley, G. Hamilton, et al. Leukemia & Lymphoma. LC 74-26642. 238p. 1974. Repr. 49.50 (ISBN 0-8089-0858-8, 791220). Grune.
Fairley, James. An Irish Beast Book. 2nd, rev. ed. (Illus.). 334p. 1984. pap. 8.95 (ISBN 0-85640-314-8, Pub. by Blackstaff Pr). Longwood Pub Group.
--Irish Whales & Whaling. (Illus.). 244p. 1981. 8.95 (ISBN 0-85640-232-X, Pub. by Blackstaff Pr). Longwood Pub Group.
Fairley, John. Great Racehorses in Art. LC 84-10403. (Illus.). 224p. 1984. 65.00 (ISBN 0-8131-1516-7). U Pr of KY.
Fairley, John & Welfare, Simon. Arthur C. Clarke's World of Strange Powers. (Illus.). 248p. 1985. 19.95 (ISBN 0-399-13066-7). Putnam Pub Group.
Fairley, Lincoln. Facing Mechanization: The West Coast Longshore Plan. (Monograph & Research Ser.: No. 23). 447p. 1979. 10.50 (ISBN 0-89215-101-3). U Cal LA Indus Rel.
Fairley, M. C. Safety, Health & Welfare in the Printing Industry. 1969. pap. 5.75 (ISBN 0-08-013033-X). Pergamon.
Fairley, Michael. With Friends Like That. LC 80-22068. 1985. 15.95 (ISBN 0-87949-194-9). Ashley Bks.
Fairley, R. E., jt. auth. see Riddle, W. E.
Fairley, William, tr. see Seignobos, Charles.
Fairley, William B. & Mosteller, Frederick. Statistics & Public Policy. LC 76-10415. (Behavioral Science-Quantitative Methods Ser.). 1977. text ed. 30.95 (ISBN 0-201-02185-4, Sch Div). Addison-Wesley.
Fairlie, Alison. Imagination & Language. LC 80-40307. (Illus.). 400p. 1981. 75.00 (ISBN 0-521-23291-0); pap. 19.95 (ISBN 0-521-26921-0). Cambridge U Pr.
--Leconte De Lisle's Poems on the Barbarian Races. Repr. of 1947 ed. 40.00 (ISBN 0-686-19853-0). Ridgeway Bks.
Fairlie, Henry. The Seven Deadly Sins Today. LC 79-893. (Illus.). 1979. pap. 5.95 (ISBN 0-268-01698-4, 85-16981). U of Notre Dame Pr.
Fairlie, John A. Centralization of Administration in New York State. LC 77-77990. (Columbia University, Studies in the Social Sciences Ser.: Vol. 25). Repr. of 1898 ed. 18.00 (ISBN 0-404-51025-6). AMS Pr.
Fairlie, John A., ed. see Garner, James W.
Fairlie, Robert. Railways or No Railways. 147p. 1984. 14.95 (ISBN 0-912113-07-3). Railhead Pubns.
Fairman, Charles. History of the Supreme Court of the United States, Vol. VII: Reconstruction & Reunion 1864-1888, Pt. 2. 800p. 1986. 75.00x (ISBN 0-02-536910-5). Macmillan.
--History of the Supreme Court, Vol. 5: Reconstruction & Reunion, 1864-1888. 1971. 60.00 (ISBN 0-02-541390-2). Macmillan.
--Mr. Justice Miller & the Supreme Court, 1862-1890. LC 66-24688. (Illus.). 1966. Repr. of 1939 ed. 12.50x (ISBN 0-8462-0801-6). Russell.
Fairman, Charles & Morrison, Stanley. Fourteenth Amendment & the Bill of Rights: The Incorporation Theory. LC 71-25622. (American Constitutional & Legal History Ser). 1970. Repr. of 1949 ed. lib. bdg. 35.00 (ISBN 0-306-70029-8). Da Capo.
Fairman, Joan. A Penny Saved. (Illus.). (gr. 1-4). 1971. PLB 6.19 (ISBN 0-8313-0036-1). Lantern.
Fairman, Marion, ed. see Solon, Gidada.
Fairman, Marion A. Biblical Patterns in Modern Literature. LC 72-85235. 128p. 1972. 3.95 (ISBN 0-913228-04-4). Dillon-Liederbach.
Fairman, Paula. Forbidden Destiny. 512p. 1981. pap. 2.95 (ISBN 0-523-41795-0). Pinnacle Bks.
--The Fury & the Passion. (Orig.). 1981. pap. 2.95 (ISBN 0-523-41798-5). Pinnacle Bks.
--Jasmine Passion. 288p. (Orig.). 1981. pap. 2.95 (ISBN 0-523-41783-7). Pinnacle Bks.
--Passion's Promise. 352p. 1983. pap. 3.25 (ISBN 0-523-41750-0). Pinnacle Bks.
--Ports of Passion. (Orig.). 1980. pap. 2.50 (ISBN 0-523-40697-5). Pinnacle Bks.
--Range of Passion. (Orig.). 1984. pap. 2.95 (ISBN 0-523-41996-1). Pinnacle Bks.
--River of Passion. 352p. (Orig.). 1983. pap. 3.50 (ISBN 0-523-41995-3). Pinnacle Bks.
--Southern Rose. 384p. (Orig.). 1981. pap. 2.95 (ISBN 0-523-41800-0). Pinnacle Bks.
--Storm of Desire. 1981. pap. 2.95 (ISBN 0-523-41797-7). Pinnacle Bks.
--The Tender & the Savage. 384p. (Orig.). 1980. pap. 2.75 (ISBN 0-523-41006-9). Pinnacle Bks.
--Wild Hearts. (Orig.). 1984. pap. 2.95 (ISBN 0-523-41997-X). Pinnacle Bks.
--Wildest Passion. 304p. (Orig.). 1982. pap. 3.25 (ISBN 0-523-42034-X). Pinnacle Bks.
Fairmont Press. Economic Thickness for Industrial Insulation. (Illus.). 191p. 1983. text ed. 24.00 (ISBN 0-915586-72-X). Fairmont Pr.
--Process Energy Conservation Manual. 154p. 1984. text ed. 30.00 (ISBN 0-915586-73-8). Fairmont Pr.
Fairmount Press, Inc., jt. auth. see Thumann, Albert.
Fairpo, C. G., jt. auth. see Fairpo, J. E.
Fairpo, J. E. & Fairpo, C. G. Dictionary for Dental Students. write for info. Heinman.
Fairs, Nabih A., tr. see Al-Hamdani & Al-Hasan Ibn Ahmad.

Fairservis, Walter A., Jr. Asia. (Illus.). 256p. 1981. 50.00 (ISBN 0-8109-0695-3). Abrams.
--The Roots of Ancient India: The Archaeology of Early Indian Civilization. 2nd. rev ed. LC 74-33510. xxxiv, 480p. 1975. pap. 7.95x (ISBN 0-226-23429-0, P636, Phoen). U of Chicago Pr.

Fairweather, A. M., ed. Aquinas on Nature & Grace. LC 54-10259. (Library of Christian Classics). 382p. 1978. pap. 10.95 softcover (ISBN 0-664-24155-7). Westminster.

Fairweather, Alan M. The Word As Truth: A Critical Examination of the Christian Doctrine of Revelation in the Writings of Thomas Aquinas & Karl Barth. LC 78-26040. 1979. Repr. of 1944 ed. lib. bdg. 18.75x (ISBN 0-313-20808-5, FAWT). Greenwood.

Fairweather, Brenda C., et al. Communication Systems for Severely Handicapped Persons. (Illus.). 112p. 1983. 15.75x (ISBN 0-398-04809-6). C C Thomas.

Fairweather, D. V., jt. auth. see Liu, D. T.

Fairweather, Eileen, et al. Only the Rivers Run Free: Northern Ireland -- The Women's War. 352p. (Orig.). 1984. pap. 8.95 (ISBN 0-86104-668-4, Pub. by Pluto Pr). Longwood Pub Group.

Fairweather, Eugene R., et al, eds. A Scholastic Miscellany: Anselm to Ockham. LC 56-5104. (Library of Christian Classics). 454p. 1982. pap. 11.95 (ISBN 0-664-24418-1). Westminster.

Fairweather, G. W. & Davidson, W. S. An Introduction to Community Experimentation. 288p. 1985. 34.95 (ISBN 0-07-019904-3). McGraw.

Fairweather, George W. & Tornatzky, Louis G. Experimental Methods for Social Policy Research. LC 76-25590. 1977. pap. text ed. 14.75 (ISBN 0-08-021236-0). Pergamon.

Fairweather, George W., et al. Creating Change in Mental Health Organizations. 200p. 1974. pap. text ed. 11.75 (ISBN 0-08-017832-4). Pergamon.

Fairweather, Graeme. Finite Element Galerkin Methods for Differential Equations. (Lecture Notes in Pure & Applied Mathematics Ser.: Vol. 34). 1978. 45.00 (ISBN 0-8247-6673-3). Dekker.

Fairweather, Janet. Seneca the Elder. (Cambridge Classical Studies). 384p. 1981. 52.50 (ISBN 0-521-23101-9). Cambridge U Pr.

Fairweather, L., ed. see Dickens, P. & McConville, S.

Fairweather, Nancy. Render unto Caesar. 1978. pap. 1.95 (ISBN 0-8439-0515-8, Leisure Bks). Dorchester Pub Co.
--Shadows on the Moon. 1978. pap. 1.50 (ISBN 0-505-51234-3, Pub. by Tower Bks). Dorchester Pub Co.

Fairweather, Owen. Practice & Procedure in Labor Arbitration. 2nd ed. 808p. 1983. 42.50 (ISBN 0-87179-365-2). BNA.

Fairweather, Paul D. & Johnson, Donovan. Symbolic Regression Psychology. 231p. 1982. text ed. 18.50x (ISBN 0-8290-0420-3). Irvington.

Fairweather, Sally H. Picasso's Concrete Sculptures. LC 82-3024. (Illus.). 160p. 1982. 35.00 (ISBN 0-933920-28-8). Hudson Hills.

Fairweather, William. Among the Mystics. facs. ed. LC 68-20298. (Essay Index Reprint Ser.). 1936. 14.00 (ISBN 0-8369-0437-0). Ayer Co Pubs.
--Background of the Epistles. 1977. 16.50 (ISBN 0-86524-118-X, 8002). Klock & Klock.
--Background of the Gospels. 1977. 17.00 (ISBN 0-86524-117-1, 8001). Klock & Klock.
--Jesus & the Greeks. 1977. lib. bdg. 59.95 (ISBN 0-8490-2096-4). Gordon Pr.

Faison, Eleanora. Becoming. LC 76-19386. (Illus.). 32p. (ps-3). 1976. pap. 4.50 (ISBN 0-9607432-0-0). E Patterson Pr.

Faison, S. L. Art Museums of New England: Connecticut & Rhode Island, Vol. 1. 160p. 1982. pap. 8.95 (ISBN 0-87923-373-7). Godine.

Faison, S. Lane, Jr. The Art Museums of New England. LC 80-83952. (Guide Ser.: No. 3). (Illus.). 548p. 1982. 35.00 (ISBN 0-87923-372-9). Godine.
--Art Museums of New England: Massachusetts, Vol. 2. 256p. 1982. pap. 9.95 (ISBN 0-87923-432-6). Godine.
--Art Museums of New England: New Hampshire, Vermont, & Maine, Vol. 3. 128p. 1982. pap. 8.95 (ISBN 0-87923-433-4). Godine.

Faiss, Fritz W. Concerning the Way of Color: An Artist's Approach. 2nd ed. LC 76-23022. (Illus.). 120p. 1977. Wkbk. Incl. pap. text ed. 15.00x (ISBN 0-916678-02-4). Green Hut.
--Hackney Jade & the War Horse. LC 76-15322. (Illus.). 64p. 1977. ltd. ed. signed 18.50x (ISBN 0-916678-00-8); hand-colored, signed ltd. ed. 200.00x (ISBN 0-916678-01-6). Green Hut.
--Modern Art & Man's Search for the Self. (Illus.). 30p. 1974. pap. 9.00x ltd. ed. signed (ISBN 0-916678-12-1); pap. 75.00x hand-colored, signed ltd. ed. (ISBN 0-916678-13-X). Green Hut.
--Out of Loneliness. (Illus.). 71p. 1972. pap. 10.00x ltd. ed. (ISBN 0-916678-06-7). Green Hut.

Faiss, Fritz W., ed. Lenticle: Two Radio Interviews with Fritz Faiss. (Illus.). 63p. 1972. pap. 15.00x ltd ed., signed (ISBN 0-916678-08-3); pap. 9.00x single interview, ltd. ed., signed (ISBN 0-916678-09-1). Green Hut.

Faissner, Helmut, et al, eds. Proceedings of the International Neutrino Conference, Aachen 1976. 1977. 84.00 (ISBN 0-9940011-5-0, Pub. by Vieweg & Sohn Germany). Heyden.

Fait, Hollis F. Experience in Movement. 3rd ed. (Illus.). Repr. of 1976 ed. text ed. cancelled (ISBN 0-8290-0631-1). Irvington.

Fait, Hollis F. & Dunn, John M. Special Physical Education. 5th ed. 1984. text ed. 28.95 (ISBN 0-03-058546-5, CBS C). SCP.

Fait, Hollis F., jt. auth. see Shivers, Jay S.

Faith America Foundation. A Citizen's Guide to Winning Elections. LC 82-70508. (Illus.). 104p. (Orig.). 1982. pap. 6.95 (ISBN 0-942770-00-5). FaithAmerica.

Faith, Barbara. Kill Me Gently, Darling. 1978. pap. 1.95 (ISBN 0-532-19208-7). Woodhill.

Faith, C. Algebra I: Rings, Modules, & Categories. LC 72-96724. (Die Grundlehren der Mathematischen Wissenschaften: Vol. 190). (Illus.). xxiii, 565p. 1973. 54.00 (ISBN 0-387-05551-7). Springer-Verlag.

Faith, C. & Wiegand, S., eds. Module Theory: Proceedings, Seattle, August 15-18, 1977. LC 79-4636. (Lecture Notes in Mathematics: Vol. 700). 1979. pap. 17.00 (ISBN 0-387-09107-6). Springer-Verlag.

Faith, Carl. Injective Modules & Injective Quotient Rings. (Lecture Notes in Pure & Applied Mathematics Ser.: Vol. 72). (Illus.). 120p. 1982. 25.00 (ISBN 0-8247-1632-9). Dekker.

Faith, Carl & Page, Stanley. FPF Ring Theory: Faithful Modules & Generators of Mod-R. LC 83-24067. (London Mathematical Society Lecture Note Ser.: No. 88). 176p. 1984. pap. text ed. 19.95 (ISBN 0-521-27738-8). Cambridge U Pr.

Faith, Karlene. Soledad Prison: University of the Poor. LC 74-84559. 1975. pap. 5.95 (ISBN 0-8314-0038-2). Sci & Behavior.

Faith, Nicholas. Safety in Numbers: The Mysterious World of Swiss Banking. LC 82-70121. 384p. 1982. 15.95 (ISBN 0-670-61463-7). Viking.
--Sold: The Rise & Fall of the House of Sotheby. 320p. 1985. 17.95 (ISBN 0-02-536970-9). Macmillan.

Faithorn, Peri E., jt. auth. see Bellak, Leopold.

Faivre, Milton I. How to Raise Rabbits for Fun & Profit. LC 73-81277. 244p. 1973. 21.95x (ISBN 0-911012-47-8); pap. 11.95 (ISBN 0-88229-493-8). Nelson-Hall.

Faizi, A. Q. Milly: A Tribute to Amelia E. Collins. 52p. pap. 2.50 (ISBN 0-85398-074-8). G Ronald Pub.
--The Prince of Martyrs: A Brief Account of Imam Husayn. 74p. 1977. pap. 2.75 (ISBN 0-85398-073-X, 339-003). G Ronald Pub.
--Stories from The Delight of Hearts: The Memoirs of Haji Mirza Haydar-'Ali. LC 79-91219. (Illus.). 176p. 1980. 11.95 (ISBN 0-933770-11-1). Kalimat.

Faizi, Gloria. The Baha'i Faith: An Introduction. rev. ed. LC 72-84825. 1972. pap. 1.95 (ISBN 0-87743-051-9, 231-059). Baha'i.

Faizullaev, Dzharulla. Laminar Motion of Multiphase Media in Conduits. LC 69-12511. pap. 37.50 (ISBN 0-317-08405-4, 2020680). Bks Demand UMI.

Fajardo, Juan C. Cucalambe Decimas Cubanas: Seleccion de Rumores del Hormigo. LC 84-80491. (Coleccion Clasicos Cubanos Ser.). 160p. (Orig., Span.). 1984. pap. 6.95 (ISBN 0-89729-351-7). Ediciones.

Fajardo, Luis F. Pathology of Radiation Injury. LC 82-15373. (Masson Monographs in Diagnostic Pathology: Vol. 6). (Illus.). 300p. 1982. 69.50 (ISBN 0-89352-182-5). Masson Pub.

Fajardo, Raoul J. The Sound of the Flute: The Cuban Impact. (Illus.). 216p. (Orig.). 1981. pap. 5.00 (ISBN 0-940774-00-3). Lit Renewal.

Fajardo, Roque. Helping your Alcoholic Before He or She Hits Bottom. 182p. 1976. 7.95 (ISBN 0-318-15330-0). Natl Coun Alcoholism.

Fajardo, Salvador J. & Wilcox, John, eds. At Home & Beyond: New Essays on Spanish Poets of the Twenties. LC 82-60341. 150p. (Orig.). 1983. pap. 20.00 (ISBN 0-89295-022-6). Society Sp & Sp-Am.

Fajn, Max. Le Journal Des Hommes Libres De Tous les Pays 1792-1800. (New Babylon Studies in the Social Sciences: No. 20). (Illus.). 194p. (Orig.). 1976. pap. text ed. 20.80 (ISBN 90-2797-541-8). Mouton.

Fajon, Robert, ed. see Destouches, Andre C.

Fak, V., ed. Security: IFIP-SEC '83. 290p. 1984. 39.00 (ISBN 0-444-86669-8, North-Holland). Elsevier.

Fakes, Dennis. Points with Punch. 1982. pap. 5.00 (ISBN 0-89536-534-0). CSS of Ohio.

Fakes, Dennis R. Points with Punch, Vol. 2. 1983. 5.00 (ISBN 0-89536-596-0). CSS of Ohio.

Fakhouri, Hani. Kafr El-Elow: An Egyptian Village in Transition. 134p. 1984. pap. text ed. 6.95x (ISBN 0-88133-039-6). Waveland Pr.

Fakhry, Ahmed. The Pyramids. 2nd ed. LC 61-8645. 272p. 1974. pap. 9.95 (ISBN 0-226-23473-8, P571, Phoen). U of Chicago Pr.

Fakhry, Majid. A History of Islamic Philosophy. 2nd ed. 450p. 1983. 28.00x (ISBN 0-231-05532-3). Columbia U Pr.

Fakhry, Tamir. The Gospel Unified. 1984. 11.00 (ISBN 0-533-05126-6). Vantage.

Fakinos, Aris. The Marked Men. LC 73-137868. 288p. 1971. 6.95 (ISBN 0-87140-516-4); pap. 2.45 (ISBN 0-87140-263-7). Liveright.

Fakkema, Robert, jt. auth. see Bannerman, Glenn.

Faktor, M. M. & Garrett, I. Growth of Crystals from the Vapour. 1974. 35.00x (ISBN 0-412-11320-1, NO. 6106, Pub. by Chapman & Hall). Methuen Inc.

Falace, Donald A., jt. auth. see Little, James W.

Falaise, Maxime De La see De La Falaise, Maxime.

Falassi, Alessandro. Folklore by the Fireside: Text & Context of the Tuscan "Veglia". LC 79-11903. (Illus.). 399p. 1980. 20.00x (ISBN 0-292-72430-6). U of Tex Pr.
--Italian Folklore: An Annotated Bibliography. LC 83-48281. (Reference Library of the Humanities, Folklore Bibliographies Ser.). 425p. 1985. lib. bdg. 60.00 (ISBN 0-8240-9041-1). Garland Pub.

Falassi, Alessandro & Catoni, Guiliano. Palio: History Rites & Images of Siena's Festival. Evans, Christopher & Borgese, Elizabeth, trs. (Illus.). 369p. 1983. 65.00x (ISBN 0-8103-1643-9, Pub. by Electra Editrice). Gale.

Falassi, Alessandro, jt. auth. see Dundes, Alan.

Falb, Lewis W. Jean Anouilh. LC 72-79928. (Literature and Life Ser.). (Illus.). 176p. 1977. 13.95 (ISBN 0-8044-2189-7). Ungar.

Falb, P., jt. auth. see Athans, Michael.

Falbe, J. Carbon Monoxide in Organic Synthesis. Adams, C. R., tr. LC 77-108917. (Illus.). 1970. 44.00 (ISBN 0-387-04814-6). Springer-Verlag.

Falbe, J., ed. New Syntheses with Carbon Monoxide. (Reactivity & Structure Ser.: Vol. 11). (Illus.). 450p. 1980. 145.00 (ISBN 0-387-09674-4). Springer-Verlag.

Falbe, Jurgen, ed. Chemical Feedstocks from Coal. LC 81-3022. 647p. 1982. 115.95 (ISBN 0-471-05291-4, Pub. by Wiley-Interscience). Wiley.

Falberg, Howard. What You Should Know about Personnel Management. LC 68-23567. (Business Almanac Ser: No. 12). 89p. 1968. 5.95 (ISBN 0-379-11212-4). Oceana.

Falbo, Toni, ed. The Single-Child Family. LC 83-1612. 304p. 1984. 27.50 (ISBN 0-89862-630-7). Guilford Pr.

Falcain, Eileen O. Children of the Salmon. 350p. 1984. 16.95 (ISBN 0-907085-76-8, Pub. by Ward River Pr Ireland); pap. 8.95 (ISBN 0-907085-75-X, Pub. by Ward River Pr Ireland). Irish Bks Media.

Falcao De Freitas, A., ed. see World Congress on Ballistocardiography & Cardiovascular Dynamics, 2nd, Oporto, 1969.

Falcetta, Joseph J., jt. ed. see Kaufman, Herman S.

Falcione, Raymond. Guide to Better Communication in Government Service. (PROCOM Ser.). 1984. pap. 9.95 (ISBN 0-673-15565-X). Scott F.

Falcione, Raymond L. & Greenbaum, Howard H. Organizational Communication: Abstracts, Analysis, & Overview, Vol. 5. (Illus.). 288p. 1980. 36.00 (ISBN 0-8039-1384-2); pap. 17.95 (ISBN 0-8039-1385-0). Sage.

Falcione, Raymond L., jt. auth. see Greenbaum, Howard H.

Falcione, Raymond L., jt. auth. see Hellweg, Susan A.

Falck, Robert. Notre Dame Conductus: A Study of the Repertory. (Wissenschaftliche Abhandlungen - Musicological Studies Ser.: No. 33). 300p. 1981. lib. bdg. 75.00 (ISBN 0-912024-35-6). Inst Mediaeval Mus.

Falck, Robert & Rice, Timothy, eds. Cross-Cultural Perspectives on Music. 288p. 1982. 30.00x (ISBN 0-8020-5510-9). U of Toronto Pr.

Falcke, F. K. & Lorentz, G., eds. Handbook of Acid-Proof Construction. 448p. 1985. text ed. 97.80 (ISBN 0-89573-370-6). VCH Pubs.

Falck-Ytter, Harald. Aurora: The Northern Lights in Mythology, History & Science. Alexander, Robin, tr. (Illus.). 192p. 1985. 30.00 (ISBN 0-88010-123-7). Anthroposophic.

Falco, Giorgio. The Holy Roman Republic: A Historic Profile of the Middle Ages. Kent, K. V., tr. from Italian. LC 80-19696. Orig. Title: La Santa Romana Republica. 336p. 1980. Repr. of 1965 ed. lib. bdg. 42.50x (ISBN 0-313-22395-5, FAHR). Greenwood.

Falco, Maria J. Bigotry: Ethnic, Machine, & Sexual Politics in a Senatorial Election. LC 79-7468. (Contributions in Political Science Ser.: No. 34). 1980. lib. bdg. 29.95 (ISBN 0-313-20726-7, FBI/). Greenwood.
--Truth & Meaning in Political Science: An Introduction to Political Inquiry. 2nd ed. LC 82-25095. 160p. 1983. pap. text ed. 11.00 (ISBN 0-8191-3048-6). U Pr of Amer.

Falco, Maria J., ed. Through the Looking Glass: Epistemology & the Conduct of Inquiry, an Anthology. LC 79-66471. 1979. pap. text ed. 17.75 (ISBN 0-8191-0841-3). U Pr of Amer.

Falcoff, Mark. Small Countries, Large Issues: Studies in U. S. Latin American Asymmetries. 1984. 14.95 (ISBN 0-8447-3562-0); pap. 5.95 (ISBN 0-8447-3563-9). Am Enterprise.

Falcoff, Mark & Dolkart, Ronald, eds. Prologue to Peron: Argentina in Depression & War, 1930-1943. LC 74-22961. 250p. 1976. 28.50x (ISBN 0-520-02874-0). U of Cal Pr.

Falcoff, Mark & Pike, Fredrick B., eds. The Spanish Civil War, Nineteen Thirty-Six to Nineteen Thirty-Nine: American Hemispheric Perspectives. LC 81-14644. xxiv, 357p. 1982. 25.95x (ISBN 0-8032-1961-X). U of Nebr Pr.

Falcoff, Mark & Royal, Robert, eds. Crisis & Opportunity: U. S. Policy in Central America & the Caribbean. LC 84-1660. 503p. 1984. 19.00 (ISBN 0-89633-081-8); pap. 12.00 (ISBN 0-89633-082-6). Ethics & Public Policy.

Falcoff, Mark, et al. The Crisis in Latin America: Strategic, Economic & Political Dimensions. Wiarda, Howard J., ed. LC 84-295. (AEI Studies: No. 397). 1984. pap. 2.95 (ISBN 0-8447-3543-4). Am Enterprise.

Falcon, C., et al. Diccionario de la Mitologia Clasica. 633p. (Span.). 1980. pap. 25.00 (ISBN 84-206-1961-2, S-32723). French & Eur.

Falcon, Guillermo N., jt. auth. see Bonner, Thomas, Jr.

Falcon, Hal. How to Analyze Handwriting. 160p. 1964. pap. 1.95 (ISBN 0-346-12161-2). Cornerstone.

Falcon, Luis N. & De Crespo, Patria C. Los Maestros De Instuccion Publica De Puerto Rico: Perfiles Sociologicos y Profesionales. pap. 3.75 (ISBN 0-8477-2711-4). U of PR Pr.

Falcon, Luis Nieves. La Opinion Publica y las Aspiraciones De los Puertorriquenos. 5.00 (ISBN 0-8477-2479-4); pap. 3.75 (ISBN 0-8477-2486-7). U of PR Pr.

Falcon, Rafael. La Emigracion Puertorriquena a Nueva York en los Cuentos de Jose Luis Gonzalez, Pedro Juan Soto y Jose Luis Vivas Maldonado. LC 83-50875. (Serie de Estudios y Ensayos). 175p. (Orig., Span.). 1984. pap. 14.95 (ISBN 0-918454-40-9). Senda Nueva.
--La Iglesia Menonita Hispana en Norte America: 1932-1982. LC 85-61020. 208p. (Span.). 1985. 14.95 (ISBN 0-8361-1272-5). Herald Pr.

Falcon, Walter P., jt. auth. see Stern, Joseph J.

Falcon, Walter P. & Papanek, Gustav F., eds. Development Policy Two: The Pakistan Experience. LC 70-160113. (Center for International Affairs Ser). (Illus.). xvi, 267p. 1971. 17.50x (ISBN 0-674-20270-8). Harvard U Pr.

Falcon, Walter P., et al. The Cassava Economy of Java. LC 82-42912. (Illus.). xxii, 212p. 1984. 38.50x (ISBN 0-8047-1194-1). Stanford U Pr.

Falcon, William D., jt. auth. see Cannavale, Frank J.

Falconbridge, Alexander. Account of the Slave Trade on the Coast of Africa. LC 77-168002. Repr. of 1788 ed. 14.50 (ISBN 0-404-00255-2). AMS Pr.

Falconbridge, Anna M. Narrative of Two Voyages to the River Sierra Leone During the Years 1791-1793. Repr. of 1967 ed. 29.50x (ISBN 0-7146-1146-8, F Cass Co). Biblio Dist.

Falcone, David J. & Henderson-James, Douglas, eds. The Rise & Fall of Procompetitive Approaches to Health Services Financing in the United States. (Duke Policy Studies). 400p. text ed. cancelled (ISBN 0-8223-0580-1). Duke.

Falcone, Guiseppe, et al. Bacterial & Viral Inhibition & Modulation of Host Defences: FEMS Symposia, Pisa, 1982. 1984. 27.00 (ISBN 0-12-247980-7). Acad Pr.

Falcone, J. D. How to Design, Build, Remodel, & Maintain Your Home. 2nd ed. 1984. 32.95 (ISBN 0-471-81843-7). Halsted Pr.

Falcone, James S., Jr., ed. Soluble Silicates. LC 82-115114. (ACS Symposium Ser.: No. 194). 1982. 39.95 (ISBN 0-8412-0730-5). Am Chemical.

Falcone, Joseph D. How to Design, Build, Remodel & Maintain Your Home. 1980. pap. write for info. (Fireside). S&S.

Falconer, C. M. The Writings of Andrew Lang. LC 73-13899. 1894. lib. bdg. 8.50 (ISBN 0-8414-4156-1). Folcroft.

Falconer, D. S. Introduction to Quantitative Genetics. 2nd ed. (Illus.). 1981. pap. text ed. 26.95x (ISBN 0-582-44195-1). Longman.
--Problems on Quantitative Genetics. LC 82-4965. 128p. 1983. pap. 7.95x (ISBN 0-582-44679-1). Longman.

Falconer, Ian R., ed. Lactation. LC 70-159524. (Illus.). 443p. 1971. 32.50x (ISBN 0-271-01140-8). Pa St U Pr.

Falconer, J. A., jt. auth. see Eisenberg, M. G.

Falconer, John I., jt. auth. see Bidwell, Percy.

Falconer, Keith. Guide to England's Industrial Heritage. LC 80-8027. (Illus.). 270p. 1980. text ed. 35.00x (ISBN 0-8419-0646-7). Holmes & Meier.

Falconer, Lee. Gazeteer of the Hyborian World of Conan. LC 80-19671. 160p. 1980. Repr. of 1977 ed. lib. bdg. 14.95x (ISBN 0-89370-031-2). Borgo Pr.

Falconer, Lee N. & May, Julian, eds. A Gazeteer of the Hyborian World of Conan. LC 77-79065. 1977. 14.95x (ISBN 0-916732-19-3); pap. text ed. 4.95x (ISBN 0-916732-01-0). Starmont Hse.

Falconer, P. & Drury, J. Building & Planning for Industrial Storage & Distribution. (Illus.). 320p. 1975. text ed. 103.95x (ISBN 0-85139-274-1, Pub. by Architectural Pr England). Humanities.

Falconer, Peter. Commodore 64 Sound & Graphics. (Illus.). 156p. (Orig.). (gr. 6up). pap. 12.95 (ISBN 0-86161-144-6). Melbourne Hse.

Falconer, R. H. The Kilt Beneath My Cassock. 1978. 15.00x (ISBN 0-905312-02-3, Pub. by Scottish Academic Pr Scotland); pap. 7.50x (ISBN 0-905312-07-4). Columbia U Pr.

Falconer, Thomas. Chevrolet Corvette. (AutoHistory Ser.). (Illus.). 136p. 1983. 14.95 (ISBN 0-85045-500-6, Pub. by Osprey England). Motorbooks Intl.

Falconer, William. Universal Dictionary of the Marine. LC 72-87321. (Illus.). Repr. of 1780 ed. lib. bdg. 50.00x (ISBN 0-678-05655-2). Kelley.

Falconi, Gonazalo, jt. auth. see Daines, David R.

Falconieri, John V., ed. see Lopez-Rubio, Jose.

Faldi, Italo. Pittori Viterbesi Di Cinque Secoli. LC 77-106770. (Illus., It.). 1970. 87.50x (ISBN 0-271-00119-4). Pa St U Pr.

Fale, Thomas. Horologographia: The Art of Dialling. LC 79-171755. (English Experience Ser.: No. 328). 1971. Repr. of 1593 ed. 21.00 (ISBN 90-221-0328-5). Walter J Johnson.

Falen, James E. Isaac Babel, Russian Master of the Short Story. LC 74-1169. 284p. 1974. 19.95x (ISBN 0-87049-156-3). U of Tenn Pr.

Faler, Kate. This Is the Abyssinian Cat. (Illus.). 192p. 1983. 14.95 (ISBN 0-87666-866-X, PS-783). TFH Pubns.

Faler, Paul G. Mechanics & Manufacturers in the Early Industrial Revolution: Lynn, Massachusetts 1780-1860. LC 80-21619. (American Social History Ser.). 310p. 1981. 39.50x (ISBN 0-87395-504-8); pap. 10.95x (ISBN 0-87395-505-6). State U NY Pr.

Fales, D. A., Jr., jt. auth. see Cummings, A. L.

Fales, Dan. Single-Propeller Boating. (Illus.). 126p. (Orig.). 1985. pap. 9.95 (ISBN 0-8306-1770-1, 1770). TAB Bks.

Fales, Dean A., Jr., ed. Essex Institute Historical Collections Index: 1908 to 1931. 1966. 30.00 (ISBN 0-88389-055-0). Essex Inst.

Fales, E. D., Jr. The Book of Expert Driving. LC 79-83943. (Illus.). 1979. pap. 5.95 (ISBN 0-8015-0808-8, Hawthorn). Dutton.

Fales, Harold A. & Kenny, Frederic. Inorganic Quantitative Analysis. (Illus.). 1955. 37.50x (ISBN 0-89197-501-2). Irvington.

Fales, James, et al. Manufacturing: A Basic Text for Industrial Arts. (Illus.). 1980. 17.96 (ISBN 0-87345-586-X, B82088); instr's guide 5.68 (ISBN 0-87345-587-8); activities 6.00 (ISBN 0-87345-588-6). McKnight.

Fales, John T. Functional Housekeeping in Hotels & Motels. LC 72-142508. 1971. text ed. 21.17 scp (ISBN 0-672-96080-X); scp tchr's manual 7.33 (ISBN 0-672-96082-6); wkbk. o.p. 7.95 (ISBN 0-672-96081-8). Bobbs.

Fales, Martha G. Joseph Richardson & Family: Philadelphia Silversmiths. LC 74-5911. (Illus.). 340p. 1974. 24.50x (ISBN 0-8195-4076-5). Wesleyan U Pr.

--Silver at the Essex Institute. LC 83-80762. (E. I. Museum Booklet Ser.). (Illus.). 64p. (Orig.). 1983. pap. 4.95 (ISBN 0-88389-086-0). Essex Inst.

Faletto, Enzo, jt. auth. see Cardoso, Fernando E.

Falewski de Leon, George, ed. see Symposium on Muscular Dystrophy, Jerusalem 1976.

Faley, Ronald J. The Cup of Grief. LC 77-6839. 1977. pap. 4.95 (ISBN 0-8189-0352-X). Alba.

Falger, P., jt. ed. see Appels, A.

Falicov, L. M., et al, eds. Valence Fluctuations in Solids: Proceedings of the International Conference at Santa Barbara, California, Jan. 27-30, 1981. 466p. 1981. 74.50 (ISBN 0-444-86204-8, North-Holland). Elsevier.

Falik, Marilyn. Ideology & Abortion Policy Politics. 240p. 1983. 39.95 (ISBN 0-03-062813-X). Praeger.

Falk. Regulating Politics & World Order. 1973. text ed. 12.95 (ISBN 0-317-06260-3). W H Freeman.

Falk, Bernard. Rachel the Immortal. LC 70-91900. 1935. 22.00 (ISBN 0-405-08495-1, Blom Pubns). Ayer Co Pubs.

--Thomas Rowlandson: His Life & Art, a Documentary Record. LC 83-45757. (Illus.). Repr. of 1949 ed. 62.50 (ISBN 0-404-20095-8). AMS Pr.

Falk, Bonnie H. Forget-Me-Not. LC 84-90501. (Illus.). 192p. 1984. pap. 7.95 (ISBN 0-9614108-0-9). Falk.

Falk, Byron A. & Falk, Valerie R. Personal Name Index to the New York Times Index, 1851-1974, 22 vols. Incl. Vol. 1. 351p. 1976. lib. bdg. 28.00 (ISBN 0-89902-101-8); Vol. 2. 602p. 1977. lib. bdg. 45.00 (ISBN 0-89902-102-6); Vol. 3. 569p. 1977. lib. bdg. 43.50 (ISBN 0-89902-103-4); Vol. 4. 494p. 1977. lib. bdg. 39.00 (ISBN 0-89902-104-2); Vol. 5. 436p. 1977. lib. bdg. 36.50 (ISBN 0-89902-105-0); Vol. 6. 639p. 1978. lib. bdg. 51.00 (ISBN 0-89902-106-9); Vol. 7. 769p. 1978. lib. bdg. 60.00 (ISBN 0-89902-107-7); Vol. 8. 674p. 1978. lib. bdg. 55.50 (ISBN 0-89902-108-5); Vol. 9. 455p. 1978. lib. bdg. 42.00 (ISBN 0-89902-109-3); Vol. 10. 492p. 1979. lib. bdg. 45.00 (ISBN 0-89902-110-7); Vol. 11. 838p. 1979. lib. bdg. 73.25 (ISBN 0-89902-111-5); Vol. 12. 648p. 1979. lib. bdg. 58.00 (ISBN 0-89902-112-3); Vol. 13. 600p. 1980. lib. bdg. 54.50 (ISBN 0-89902-113-1); Vol. 14. 600p. 1980. lib. bdg. 54.50 (ISBN 0-89902-114-X); Vol. 15. 417p. 1980. lib. bdg. 40.25 (ISBN 0-89902-115-8); Vol. 16. 624p. 1980. lib. bdg. 60.50 (ISBN 0-89902-124-7); Vol. 17. 659p. 1981. lib. bdg. 64.00 (ISBN 0-89902-117-4); Vol. 18. 600p. 1981. lib. bdg. 64.00 (ISBN 0-89902-119-0); Vol. 19. 636p. 1981. lib. bdg. 64.00 (ISBN 0-89902-119-0); Vol. 20. 669p. 1982. lib. bdg. 65.00 (ISBN 0-89902-120-4); Vol. 21. 421p. 1982. lib. bdg. 61.00 (ISBN 0-89902-121-2); Vol. 22. 446p. 1983. lib. bdg. 62.00 (ISBN 0-89902-122-0). LC 76-12217. Vols. 1-22. lib. bdg. 899.00 (ISBN 0-89902-100-X). Roxbury Data.

--Personal Name Index to the New York Times Index, 1975-1979 Supplement: Vol. 25, N-Z. 434p. 1985. lib. bdg. 51.00 (ISBN 0-89902-125-5). Roxbury Data.

--Personal Name Index to the New York Times Index 1975-1979 Supplement, Vol. 23, A-F. 411p. 1984. lib. bdg. 48.00 (ISBN 0-89902-123-9). Roxbury Data.

--Personal Name Index to The New York Times Index, 1975-1979 Supplement, Vol. 24, G-M. 412p. 1984. lib. bdg. 49.50 (ISBN 0-89902-124-7). Roxbury Data.

Falk, Candace. Love, Anarchy & Emma Goldman. LC 83-18405. 500p. 1984. 25.00 (ISBN 0-03-043626-5). HR&W.

Falk, Cathy. Action Rhymes: Bible Learning Through Movement. 48p. 1985. pap. 2.50 (ISBN 0-87239-920-6, 3202). Standard Pub.

--God's Care. (Bible Activities for Little People Ser.: Bk. 1). 24p. (Orig.). (ps-k). 1983. pap. 1.25 (ISBN 0-87239-676-2, 2451). Standard Pub.

--God's Friends. (Bible Activities for Little People Ser.: BK. 2). 24p. (Orig.). (ps-k). 1983. pap. 1.25 (ISBN 0-87239-677-0, 2452). Standard Pub.

--God's Son. (Bible Activities for Little People Ser.: Bk. 3). 24p. (Orig.). (ps-k). 1983. pap. 1.25 (ISBN 0-87239-678-9, 2453). Standard Pub.

--We Love God. (Bible Lessons for Little People Ser.: Bk. 2). 144p. (Orig.). (ps-k). 1983. pap. 7.95 (ISBN 0-87239-613-4, 3360). Standard Pub.

--We Please God. (Bible Activities Ser.: Bk. 4). 24p. (Orig.). (ps-k). 1983. pap. 1.25 (ISBN 0-87239-679-7, 2454). Standard Pub.

--Year-Round Preschool Activity Patterns. 48p. (Orig.). (ps-k). 1983. pap. 4.50 (ISBN 0-87239-680-0, 2141). Standard Pub.

Falk, Dean, jt. ed. see Armstrong, Este.

Falk, Doris. Biology Teaching Methods. LC 79-19132. 302p. (Prog. Bk.). 1980. Repr. of 1971 ed. lib. bdg. 18.50 (ISBN 0-89874-038-X). Krieger.

Falk, Doris V. Eugene O'Neill & the Tragic Tension. 2nd ed. 236p. 1982. Repr. of 1958 ed. 12.00x (ISBN 0-87752-222-7). Gordian.

--Eugene O'Neill & the Tragic Tension: An Interpretive Study of the Plays. 1974. pap. 10.00x (ISBN 0-8135-0791-X). Rutgers U Pr.

--Lillian Hellman. LC 78-4299. (Literature & Life Ser.). 189p. 1978. 13.95 (ISBN 0-8044-2194-3); pap. 6.95 (ISBN 0-8044-6144-9). Ungar.

Falk, Edwin A. Fighting Bob Evans. LC 75-103651. (Select Bibliographies Reprint Ser). 1931. 33.00 (ISBN 0-8369-5151-4). Ayer Co Pubs.

--From Perry to Pearl Harbor: The Struggle for Supremacy in the Pacific. LC 73-21285. (Illus.). 362p. 1974. Repr. of 1943 ed. lib. bdg. 22.50 (ISBN 0-8371-6161-4, FAPP). Greenwood.

Falk, Esther, tr. see Segal, Yocheved.

Falk, Eugene H. The Poetics of Roman Ingarden. LC 79-29655. xxi, 213p. 1981. 20.00x (ISBN 0-8078-1436-9); pap. 11.00x o. p. (ISBN 0-8078-4068-8). U of NC Pr.

--Renunciation As a Tragic Focus: A Study of Five Plays. LC 72-78701. (American Guidebook Ser.). 1954. Repr. 29.00x (ISBN 0-403-04236-4). Somerset Pub.

--Types of Thematic Structure. LC 67-16775. 1967. 15.00x (ISBN 0-226-23609-9). U of Chicago Pr.

Falk, Gerhard, jt. auth. see Falk, Ursula A.

Falk, Gina S., jt. auth. see Falk, Steven.

Falk, H., ed. CCNY Physics Symposium: In Celebration of Melvin Lax's Sixtieth Birthday. 364p. (Orig.). 1983. pap. text ed. write for info. (ISBN 0-9611452-0-X). City Coll Physics.

Falk, H. S. & Torp, Alf. Norwegisch-Daenisches Etymologisches Woerterbuch, Vol. 1. 2nd ed. (Norwegian & Danish.). 1960. 55.00 (ISBN 3-533-00505-4, M-7570, Pub. by Carl Winter). French & Eur.

--Norwegisch-Daenisches Etymologisches Woerterbuch, Vol. 2. 2nd ed. (Norwegian & Danish.). 1960. 55.00 (ISBN 3-533-00506-2, M-7571, Pub. by Carl Winter). French & Eur.

--Norwegisch Daenisches Etymologisches Woerterbuch: Mit Literatur-Nachweisen Strittiger Etymologien Sowie Deutschem und Altnordischen Woerterverzeichnis, 2 Vols. 2nd ed. 1722p. (Norwegian & Danish.). 1960. Set. 80.00x (ISBN 8-200-00085-0, Dist. by Columbia U Pr). Universitet.

Falk, Hans L., ed. see American Physiological Society.

Falk, Harvey. Jesus the Pharisee: New Look at the Jewishness of Jesus. (Orig.). 1985. pap. 8.95 (ISBN 0-8091-2677-X). Paulist Pr.

Falk, Herbert A. Corporal Punishment: A Social Interpretation of Its Theory & Practice in the Schools of the United States. LC 70-176762. (Columbia University. Teachers College. Contributions to Education: No. 835). Repr. of 1941 ed. 22.50 (ISBN 0-404-55835-6, CE835). AMS Pr.

Falk, Hjalmar, jt. auth. see Shetelig, Hakon.

Falk, Howard. Handbook Computer Application for Small or Medium Business. LC 83-70782. 384p. 1983. 19.95 (ISBN 0-8019-7393-7). Chilton.

--Microcomputer Communications in Business. LC 84-45161. 400p. (Orig.). 1984. pap. 18.95 (ISBN 0-8019-7512-3). Chilton.

Falk, I. S., et al. The Costs of Medical Care: A Summary of Investigations on the Economic Aspects of the Prevention & Care of Illness, No. 27. LC 71-180568. (Medicine & Society in America Ser). 652p. 1972. Repr. of 1933 ed. 34.00 (ISBN 0-405-03950-6). Ayer Co Pubs.

Falk, Irving, jt. auth. see Gordon, George N.

Falk, Irving A., jt. auth. see Gordon, George N.

Falk, Isidore S., et al. The Incidence of Illness & the Receipt & Costs of Medical Care Among Representative Families: Experiences in Twelve Consecutive Months During 1928-1931. LC 75-17220. (Social Problems & Social Policy Ser.). (Illus.). 1976. Repr. of 1933 ed. 25.50x (ISBN 0-405-07491-3). Ayer Co Pubs.

Falk, Isidore Sydney. Security Against Sickness: A Study of Health Insurance. LC 79-38822. (FDR & the Era of the New Deal Ser). 424p. 1972. Repr. of 1936 ed. lib. bdg. 49.50 (ISBN 0-306-70447-1). Da Capo.

Falk, J. A., et al, eds. Cardiovascular Disease: Rheumatic Fever, Heart Transplantation & Immunological Aspects. 1977. text ed. 34.00x (ISBN 0-8422-7280-1). Irvington.

Falk, J. E. & Fiacco, A. V. Mathematical Programming with Parameters & Multi-Level Constraints. 100p. 1981. pap. 42.00 (ISBN 0-08-023621-9). Pergamon.

Falk, Jim. Global Fission: The Battle over Nuclear Power. (Illus.). 1982. pap. 12.95 (ISBN 0-19-554316-5). Oxford U Pr.

Falk, John R. The Complete Guide to Bird Dog Training. LC 82-62601. 1976. 16.95 (ISBN 0-8329-2161-0, Pub. by Winchester Pr). New Century.

--The Practical Hunter's Dog Book. LC 84-2419. (Illus.). 1984. pap. 11.95 (ISBN 0-8329-0317-5, Pub. by Winchester Pr). New Century.

Falk, Julia S. Language & Linguistics: Bases for a Curriculum. (Language in Education Ser.: No. 10). 27p. 1978. pap. 3.95x (ISBN 0-15-599063-2). Ctr Appl Ling.

--Linguistics & Language: A Survey of Basic Concepts & Implications. 2nd ed. LC 77-22927. 1978. pap. text ed. 25.00x (ISBN 0-673-15670-2). Scott F.

Falk, Kathryn. How to Write a Romance & Get it Published. 560p. 1984. pap. 4.95 (ISBN 0-451-12903-2, Sig). NAL.

--How to Write a Romance & Get it Published: With Intimate Advice form the World's Most Popular Romance Writers. 380p. 1983. 5.98 (ISBN 0-517-54944-1). Crown.

--Love's Leading Ladies. (Illus.). 364p. (Orig.). 1982. pap. 6.95 (ISBN 0-523-41525-7). Pinnacle Bks.

Falk, Lawrence C., ed. see Puckett, Dale & Dibble, Peter.

Falk, Lee. The Assassins: No. 14. (Phantom Ser.). 1975. pap. 0.95 (ISBN 0-380-00298-1, 23283). Avon.

--The Curse of the Two-Headed Bull. 1975. pap. 0.95 (ISBN 0-380-00381-3, 24729). Avon.

--Goggle-Eyed Pirates. 1974. pap. 0.95 (ISBN 0-380-01223-5, 18184). Avon.

--The Golden Circle. (The Phantom Ser., No. 5). 1973. pap. 0.75 (ISBN 0-380-01225-1, 14894). Avon.

--The Hydra Monster. 1973. pap. 0.75 (ISBN 0-380-01275-8, 17061). Avon.

--The Island of Dogs. (Phantom Ser.: No. 13). (Orig.). 1975. pap. 0.95 (ISBN 0-380-00243-4, 23085). Avon.

--Killer's Town. (Phantom Ser.: No. 9). 1973. pap. 0.95 (ISBN 0-380-01312-6, 17731). Avon.

--Mandrake the Magician in Hollywood. Brown, Leonard, ed. LC 76-159555. (Illus.). 1977. pap. 5.95 (ISBN 0-87897-009-6). Nostalgia Pr.

--The Phantom. Brown, Leonard, ed. (Illus.). 1977. pap. 5.95 (ISBN 0-87897-010-X). Nostalgia Pr.

Falk, Marcia. Love Lyrics from the Bible: A Translation & Literary Study of the Song of Songs. (Bible & Literature Ser.: No. 4). 1981. text ed. 19.95x (ISBN 0-907459-06-4, Pub. by Almond Pr England); pap. text ed. 9.95 (ISBN 0-907459-07-2, Pub. by Almond Pr England). Eisenbrauns.

Falk, Marvin W. Alaskan Maps: A Cartobibliography of Alaska to 1900. LC 82-49265. 275p. 1983. lib. bdg. 68.00 (ISBN 0-8240-9132-9). Garland Pub.

Falk, Mervyn L., jt. auth. see Wicka, Donna K.

Falk, Mervyn L., ed. Cleft Palate Team Addresses the Speech Clinician. 248p. 1971. 22.50x (ISBN 0-398-00542-7). C C Thomas.

Falk, Murray H. Tax Court Declaratory Judgement Proceedings: No. B375. (Procedural Law Affecting Qualified Plans Ser.). 13p. 1978. pap. 4.50 (ISBN 0-317-31255-3). Am Law Inst.

Falk, Nancy A. & Gross, Rita M., eds. Unspoken Worlds. LC 79-2989. (Women's Religious Lives Ser.). 304p. (Orig.). 1980. pap. text ed. 5.95x (ISBN 0-06-063492-8, RD 308, HarpR). Har-Row.

Falk, Pamela. Petroleum & Mexico's Future. (A Westview Special Study on Latin America & the Caribbean). 1985. 15.00 (ISBN 0-86531-629-5). Westview.

Falk, Pamela S. Cuban Foreign Policy: Caribbean Tempest. LC 81-47890. 1985. x (ISBN 0-669-05127-6). Lexington Bks.

Falk, Peter A. Law, Morality, & War in the Contemporary World. LC 84-19288. viii, 120p. 1984. Repr. of 1963 ed. lib. bdg. 29.75x (ISBN 0-313-24682-3, FALM). Greenwood.

Falk, Peter H. The Photographic Art Market. (Illus.). 117p. 1981. pap. text ed. 29.95 (ISBN 0-940926-00-8). Photo Arts Ctr.

Falk, Peter H., ed. The Photograph Collector's Resource Directory. 1985. pap. 19.95 (ISBN 0-913069-05-1). Photo Arts Ctr.

--The Photographer's Complete Guide to Exhibition & Sales Spaces. 1985. pap. 19.95 (ISBN 0-913069-06-X). Photo Arts Ctr.

--Who Was Who in American Art. LC 85-50119. (Illus.). 744p. 1985. lib. bdg. 115.00x (ISBN 0-932087-00-0). Sound View Pr.

Falk, Peter H. & Persky, Robert S., eds. The Photograph Collectors' Resource Directory. 200p. 1983. pap. 19.95 (ISBN 0-913069-00-0). Photo Arts Ctr.

Falk, Quentin. Travels in Greeneland: The Cinema of Graham Greene. (Illus.). 230p. 1985. 22.95 (ISBN 0-7043-2425-3, Pub. by Quartet Bks). Merrimack Pub Cir.

Falk, R. A. Aftermath of Sabbatino. LC 65-19486. (Hammarskjold Forum Ser.: No. 7). 240p. 1965. 12.50 (ISBN 0-379-11807-6). Oceana.

Falk, Richard. The End of World Order: Essays on Normative International Relations. 358p. 1983. text ed. 45.00x (ISBN 0-8419-0739-0); pap. text ed. 19.50x (ISBN 0-8419-0894-X). Holmes & Meier.

Falk, Richard & Kim, Samuel. An Approach to World Order Studies & the World System. 32p. 1982. pap. 2.00. World Policy.

Falk, Richard, jt. auth. see Lifton, Robert J.

Falk, Richard, ed. The Question of Intervention. 200p. Date not set. 18.50x (ISBN 0-8419-0641-6). Holmes & Meier.

Falk, Richard & Kim, Samuel, eds. Toward a Just World Order. (Studies on a Just World Order Series: Vol. I). 652p. 1982. pap. 16.50 (ISBN 0-317-36518-5, Pub. by Westview Pr.). World Policy.

Falk, Richard, et al, eds. The United Nations & a Just World Order, Vol. III. (Studies on a Just World Order). 500p. 37.50x (ISBN 0-86531-240-0); pap. 15.00x (ISBN 0-86531-250-8). Westview.

Falk, Richard A. Future Worlds. LC 75-43478. (Headline Ser.: 229). (Illus.). 1976. pap. 3.00 (ISBN 0-87124-034-3). Foreign Policy.

--A Global Approach to National Policy. LC 75-2817. 384p. 1975. text ed. 22.50t (ISBN 0-674-35445-1). Harvard U Pr.

--Human Rights & State Sovereignty. LC 80-22620. 180p. 1981. text ed. 32.50x (ISBN 0-8419-0619-X); pap. text ed. 15.75x (ISBN 0-8419-0620-3). Holmes & Meier.

--The Role of Domestic Courts in International Legal Order, Vol. 3. (Procedural Aspects of International Law Ser.). 1964. 20.00x (ISBN 0-8139-0836-1). U Pr of Va.

--A Study of Future Worlds. LC 74-10139. (Preferred Worlds for the 1990's Ser.). (Illus.). 1975. pap. text ed. 16.95 (ISBN 0-02-910080-1). Free Pr.

--The Vietnam War & International Law, 4 vols. Incl. Vol. 1. 1967. 57.50x (ISBN 0-691-09211-7); pap. 17.50x (ISBN 0-691-02751-X); Vol. 2. 1969. 45.00x (ISBN 0-691-09214-1); pap. 12.50 (ISBN 0-691-02752-8); Vol. 3. The Widening Context. 1972. 62.50x (ISBN 0-691-09224-9); pap. 13.95x (ISBN 0-691-02753-6); Vol. 4. The Concluding Phase. 1976. 67.50x (ISBN 0-691-09230-3); pap. 19.50xLPE (ISBN 0-691-10041-1). LC 67-31295. pap. Princeton U Pr.

--A World Order Perspective on Authoritarian Tendencies. (Working Policy Papers). (Illus.). 67p. (Orig.). 1980. pap. text ed. 2.00. World Policy.

--A World Order Perspective on Authoritarian Tendencies. 67p. 1980. pap. 2.00x. Transaction Bks.

Falk, Richard A. & Kim, Samuel S., eds. The War System: An Interdisciplinary Approach. LC 79-19566. (Westview Special Studies in Peace, Conflict, & Conflict Resolution). 660p. 1980. pap. text ed. 18.00x (ISBN 0-86531-042-4). Westview.

Falk, Richard A. & Mendlovitz, Saul H., eds. Disarmament & Economic Development, 4 vols. (The Strategy of World Order). 672p. 1966. Set. pap. 6.00 (ISBN 0-317-34491-9). World Policy.

--International Law. (The Strategy of World Order). 382p. 1966. 6.00 (ISBN 0-317-34492-7). World Policy.

--The Strategy of World Order, 3 vols. Incl. Vol. 1. Toward a Theory of War Prevention. Lasswell, Harold D., frwd. by.; Vol. 2. International Law. Friedmann, Wolfgang, frwd. by. pap. 6.00 (ISBN 0-911646-02-7); Vol. 3. The United Nations. Schacter, Oscar, frwd. by. pap. 7.00 (ISBN 0-911646-03-5); Vol. 4. Disarmament & Economic Development. Singer, David, frwd. by. pap. 6.00 (ISBN 0-911646-04-3); pap. 15.00 set (ISBN 0-686-86126-4). 1966. pap. 15.00 set (ISBN 0-911646-00-0). World Policy.

--The United Nations. (The Strategy of World Order). 848p. 1966. pap. 7.00 (ISBN 0-317-34493-5). World Policy.

Falk, Richard A., jt. ed. see Black, C. E.

Falk, Richard A., ed. see Wright, Quincy.

Falk, Richard A., et al. Toward a Just World Order, Vol. I. LC 81-23744. (Studies on a Just World Order). 652p. (Orig.). 1982. lib. bdg. 38.00x (ISBN 0-86531-242-7); pap. text ed. 16.50x (ISBN 0-86531-251-6). Westview.

--International Law: A Contemporary Perspective. LC 85-3318. (Studies on a Just World Order: Vol. 2). 500p. 1985. 50.00x (ISBN 0-86531-241-9); pap. text ed. 21.00x (ISBN 0-86531-252-4). Westview.

Falk, Richard J. & Barnet, Richard J., eds. Security in Disarmament. (Center of International Studies). 1965. 45.00x (ISBN 0-691-07520-4); pap. 13.50x (ISBN 0-691-02158-9, 80). Princeton U Pr.

Falk, Robert, jt. auth. see Radin, Sheldon.

Falk, Robert, ed. Literature & Ideas in America: Essays in Memory of Harry Hayden Clark. LC 74-27708. xi, 243p. 1975. 15.00x (ISBN 0-8214-0180-7, 82-81784). Ohio U Pr.

Falk, Robert P., ed. American Literature in Parody: A Collection of Parody, Satire, & Literary Burlesque of American Writers Past & Present. LC 77-22745. 1977. Repr. of 1955 ed. lib. bdg. 27.50x (ISBN 0-8371-9741-4, FAAL). Greenwood.

Falk, S. J. Qajar Paintings: Persian Oil Paintings of the 18th & 19th Centuries. (Illus.). 112p. 1974. 62.50x (ISBN 0-571-10128-3, Pub. by Sotheby Pubns England). Biblio Dist.

Falk, S. Uno & Salkind, Alvin J. Alkaline Storage Batteries. LC 77-82980. (Electrochemical Society Ser.). 1969. 91.95x (ISBN 0-471-25362-6, Pub. by Wiley-Interscience). Wiley.

Falk, Signi L. Archibald MacLeish. (Twayne's United States Authors Ser). 1965. pap. 5.95x (ISBN 0-8084-0054-1, T93, Twayne). New Coll U Pr.

--Tennessee Williams. 2nd ed. (United States Authors Ser.). 1978. lib. bdg. 13.50 (ISBN 0-8057-7202-2, Twayne). G K Hall.

--Tennessee Williams. (United States Authors Ser.). 1985. pap. 6.95 (ISBN 0-8057-7445-9, Twayne). G K Hall.

Falk, Stanley L. Bataan: The March of Death. 256p. 1985. pap. 3.50 (ISBN 0-515-08297-X). Jove Pubns.

--Batan: The March of Death. LC 82-80840. (Blockbusting War Bks.). 264p. 1984. pap. 2.95 (ISBN 0-515-07299-0). Jove Pubns.

Falk, Stephen. Fundamentals of Sailboat Racing: A Complete Guide to Getting the Most from Your Boat & from Yourself. 160p. 1983. Repr. of 1973 ed. 6.95 (ISBN 0-312-31151-6). St Martin.

Falk, Steven & Falk, Gina S. Menu for Murder. (Illus.). 98p. Date not set. Repr. of 1984 ed. loose leaf 24.95 (ISBN 0-9615049-0-0). Schuchman.

Falk, Toby & Archer, Mildred. Indian Miniatures in the India Office Library. (Illus.). 560p. 1981. 145.00x (ISBN 0-85667-100-2, Pub. by Sotheby Pubns England). Biblio Dist.

Falk, Toby, ed. Treasures of Islam. LC 85-50362. (Illus.). 400p. 1985. 45.95 (ISBN 0-85667-196-7, Pub. by P Wilson Pubs). Sotheby Pubns.

Falk, Ursula A. & Falk, Gerhard. The Nursing Home Dilemma. LC 75-36565. 1976. softbound 9.95 (ISBN 0-88247-399-9). R & E Pubs.

Falk, Valerie R., jt. auth. see Falk, Byron A.

Falk, Walter. Handbuch der Literarwissenschaftlichen Komponentenanalyse: Theorie, Operationen, Praxis einer Methode der Neuen Epochenforschung. (Beitraege z. neven Epochenforschung Ser.: Vol. 3). 227p. (Ger.). 1983. 29.45 (ISBN 3-8204-7524-9). P Lang Pubs.

Falkberget, Johan. Fourth Night Watch. Popperwell, Ronald G., tr. from Norwegian. LC 68-9016. (Nordic Translation Ser.). Orig. Title: Den Fjerde Nattevakt. 338p. 1968. 15.00x (ISBN 0-299-05094-7); pap. 6.00x (ISBN 0-685-20707-2). U of Wis Pr.

Falke, Horst, ed. The Continental Permian in West, Central, & South Europe. (Nato Mathematical & Physical Sciences Ser.: No. 22). 1976. lib. bdg. 53.00 (ISBN 90-277-0664-6, Pub. by Reidel Holland). Kluwer Academic.

Falke, Konrad, jt. auth. see Zapol, Warren.

Falkehag, Ingemar, jt. ed. see Inglett, George.

Falken, Linda C. Ella in the Castle. (Golden Magical Places Ser.). (Illus.). 16p. (ps-k). 1984. 6.95 (ISBN 0-307-17100-0, 17100, Golden Bks). Western Pub.

Falkenberg, Aslaug, jt. auth. see Falkenberg, Johannes.

Falkenberg, Johannes & Falkenberg, Aslaug. The Affinal Relationship System of the Australian Aborigines in the Port Keats District. 224p. 1981. 23.00x (ISBN 0-686-69760-X, Dist. by Columbia U Pr). Universitet.

Falkenberg, P. Die Rhodomelaceen Des Golfes Von Neapel und der Angrenzenden Meenesabschnitte. (Fauna & Flor d. Golfes v. Neapel). (Illus., Ger.). 1979. Repr. of 1901 ed. lib. bdg. 113.75x (ISBN 3-87429-143-X). Lubrecht & Cramer.

Falkenberg, P. R. Fifteen Days to Study Power. 2nd ed. (Illus.). 378p. (Orig.). 1985. pap. 12.95 (ISBN 0-939800-01-2). Greencrest.

Falkenberg, Philippe R. Fifteen Days to Study Power. LC 81-81330. (Illus.). 378p. (Orig.). (gr. 10-12). 1981. pap. 12.95 (ISBN 0-939800-00-4). Greencrest.

Falkenhayn, Erich Von. The German General Staff & Its Decisions, 1914-16. facsimile ed. LC 71-179518. (Select Bibliographies Reprint Ser). Repr. of 1920 ed. 28.00 (ISBN 0-8369-6647-3). Ayer Co Pubs.

Falkenheim, Jacqueline V. Roger Fry & the Beginnings of Formalist Art Criticism. Kuspit, Donald B., ed. LC 80-23577. (Studies in the Fine Arts: Criticism: No. 8). 170p. 1980. 39.95 (ISBN 0-8357-1086-6). UMI Res Pr.

Falkenmark, Malin, ed. Rural Water Supply & Health: The Need for a New Strategy. (Scandinavian Institute of African Studies). (Illus.). 118p. 1983. text ed. 17.50x (ISBN 0-8419-9763-2, Africana). Holmes & Meier.

Falkenstein, Adam. Die Haupttypen der Sumerischen Beschwoerung Literarisch Untersucht. (Ger). pap. 10.00 (ISBN 0-384-15125-6). Johnson Repr.

--Literarische Keilschrifttexte aus Uruk. LC 78-72735. (Ancient Mesopotamian Texts & Studies). Repr. of 1931 ed. 27.50 (ISBN 0-404-18174-0). AMS Pr.

Falkenstein, Chris, jt. auth. see Reid, Don.

Falkenstein, H. P. Formability of Aluminium Sheet Alloys. 1984. 33.00 (ISBN 0-9911000-5-0, Pub. by Aluminium W Germany). Heyden.

Falkenstern, Ferdinand. A Twentieth Century Commentary on Plato's Political Philosophy. (Illus.). 129p. 1981. 69.85 (ISBN 0-89266-319-7). Am Classical Coll Pr.

Falkman, Kai. Robot & Meaning. 194p. 1984. 16.95 (ISBN 0-85974-105-2, Pub. by Salem Hse Ltd); pap. 8.95 (ISBN 0-85974-109-5). Merrimack Pub Cir.

Falkmer, S., et al. Evolution & Tumour Pathology of the Neuroendocrine System. (Fernstorm Foundation Ser.: Vol. 4). 1984. 140.75 (ISBN 0-444-80560-5). Elsevier.

Falkner, Ann. Without Our Past: A Handbook for the Preservation of Canada's Architectural Heritage. (Illus.). 1976. 20.00x (ISBN 0-8020-2239-1); pap. 8.95 (ISBN 0-8020-6298-9). U of Toronto Pr.

Falkner, David, jt. auth. see Oh, Sadaharu.

Falkner, F. Prevention of Perinatal Mortality & Morbidity. (Child Health & Development: Vol. 3). (Illus.). vi, 182p. 1984. 31.50 (ISBN 3-8055-3854-5). S Karger.

Falkner, F., ed. Fundamentals of Mortality Risks During the Perinatal Period & Infancy. (Monographs in Paediatrics: Vol. 9). (Illus.). 190p. 1977. 36.25 (ISBN 3-8055-2651-2). S Karger.

--Prevention of Infant Mortality & Morbidity. (Child Health & Development: Vol. 4). (Illus.). viii, 176p. 1985. 38.00 (ISBN 3-8055-3989-4). S Karger.

Falkner, F. & Tanner, J. M., eds. Human Growth, Vol. 1: Principles & Prenatal Growth. LC 78-1440. (Illus.). 654p. 1978. 45.00x (ISBN 0-306-34461-0, Plenum Pr). Plenum Pub.

--Human Growth, Vol. 2: Postnatal Growth. LC 78-1440. (Illus.). 652p. 1978. 45.00x (ISBN 0-306-34462-9, Plenum Pr). Plenum Pub.

--Human Growth, Vol. 3: Neurobiology & Nutrition. 624p. 1979. 45.00x (ISBN 0-306-34463-7, Plenum Pr). Plenum Pub.

Falkner, F., et al, eds. see Delange, F.

Falkner, Frank, jt. ed. see Gracey, Michael.

Falkner, Frank, jt. ed. see Roche, Alex F.

Falkner, J. Meade. The Lost Stradivaruis. (Detective Ser.). 93p. 1982. pap. 3.00 (ISBN 0-486-24334-6). Dover.

--Moonfleet. (Illus.). 256p. 1984. pap. 7.95 (ISBN 0-946159-16-5, Pub. by Salem Hse Ltd). Merrimack Pub Cir.

Falkner, J. Meade see Bleiler, E. F.

Falkner, Murry C. Falkners of Mississippi: A Memoir. LC 67-24417. (Illus.). xxvi, 206p. 1967. 22.50x (ISBN 0-8071-0446-9). La State U Pr.

Falkner, Thomas. A Description of Patagonia & the Adjoining Parts of South America. LC 75-41088. Repr. of 1935 ed. 21.50 (ISBN 0-404-14747-X). AMS Pr.

Falkoff, Bernard. Can I Play with the Computer, Too? Computing for Preschoolers. (Learn Together Ser.). 128p. 1984. pap. 19.95 ea. Commodore 64 version (ISBN 0-88693-073-1). Apple IIe version. pap. 19.95 (ISBN 0-88693-074-X). PCjr version (ISBN 0-88693-075-8). Banbury Bks.

Falkow, S. Infectious Multiple Drug Resistance. (Advanced Biochemistry Ser.). 300p. 1975. 26.50x (ISBN 0-85086-049-0, NO. 2944, Pub. by Pion England). Methuen Inc.

Falkowski, B. J., jt. auth. see Erven, J.

Falkowski, Lawrence, jt. auth. see Hopple, Gerald W.

Falkowski, Lawrence S., ed. Psychological Models in International Politics. (Special Studies in International Relations). 1979. lib. bdg. 33.00x (ISBN 0-89158-377-7); pap. text ed. 13.50x (ISBN 0-86531-043-2). Westview.

Falkowski, Paul G., ed. Primary Productivity in the Sea. LC 80-24664. (Environmental Science Research Ser.: Vol. 19). 542p. 1980. 67.50 (ISBN 0-306-40623-3, Plenum Pr). Plenum Pub.

Falkson, Barry. Fatal Friend. LC 84-22796. 288p. 1985. 14.95 (ISBN 0-688-04182-5). Morrow.

Falkus, Christopher. The Life & Times of Charles II. (Kings & Queens of England Ser.). (Illus.). 224p. 1973. text ed. 17.50x (ISBN 0-297-99427-1, GWN 04700, Pub. by Weidenfeld & Nicolson England). Biblio Dist.

Falkus, Hugh. Master of Cape Horn: W. A. Nelson 1839-1929. (Illus.). 1982. 27.50 (ISBN 0-575-03089-5, Pub. by Gollancz England). David & Charles.

Falkus, Hugh & Kerr, Joan. From Sydney Cove to Duntroon: An Australian Family Album. (Illus.). 128p. 1982. 24.95 (ISBN 0-575-03039-9, Pub. by Gollancz England). David & Charles.

Falkus, M. E. The Industrialization of Russia Seventeen Hundred to Nineteen Fourteen. (Studies in Economic & Social History). 64p. (Orig.). 1972. pap. text ed. 6.25x (ISBN 0-333-11649-6). Humanities.

Falkus, Malcolm. A History of North Thames Gas. 128p. 1985. 20.00 (ISBN 0-85941-266-0, Pub. by Woodhead-Faulkner). Longwood Pub Group.

Fall, Bernard. Hell in a Very Small Place: The Siege of Dien Bien Phu. (Quality Paperbacks Ser.). (Illus.). 535p. 1985. pap. 11.95 (ISBN 0-306-80231-7). Da Capo.

Fall, Bernard B. Last Reflections on a War. Fall, Dorothy, ed. LC 67-28638. 288p. 1972. pap. 3.95 (ISBN 0-8052-0329-X). Schocken.

--Street Without Joy. 4th ed. LC 64-23038. (Illus.). 408p. 1972. pap. 4.95 (ISBN 0-8052-0330-3). Schocken.

--The Two Vietnams: A Political & Military Analysis. (A Encore Ser.). 498p. 1985. pap. 42.50x (ISBN 0-8133-0092-4). Westview.

--The Viet-Minh Regime. LC 75-11493. 196p. 1975. Repr. of 1956 ed. lib. bdg. 22.50x (ISBN 0-8371-8197-6, FAVM). Greenwood.

Fall, Bernard B., ed. Ho Chi Minh on Revolution: Selected Writings, 1920-66. (A Westview Encore Edition-Softcover Ser.). 389p. 1985. pap. 36.00x (ISBN 0-8133-0093-2). Westview.

Fall, Dorothy, ed. see Fall, Bernard B.

Fall, Henry C. List of the Coleoptera of Southern California, 2 vols. in 1 Bd. with A Handbook of the Trees of California. Eastwood, Alice. 86p. Repr. of 1905 ed. 282p. Repr. of 1901 ed. 46.00 (ISBN 0-384-15128-0). Johnson Repr.

Fall, J., jt. auth. see Elia, L.

Fall, Joseph A., jt. auth. see Elia, Lewis M.

Fall, Malick. The Wound. Wake, Clive, tr. (African Writers Ser.). 1973. pap. text ed. 5.00x (ISBN 0-435-90144-3). Heinemann Ed.

Fall, S. M. & Lynden-Bell, D., eds. The Structure & Evolution of Normal Galaxies. LC 80-42026. (Illus.). 280p. 1981. 39.50 (ISBN 0-521-23907-9). Cambridge U Pr.

Fall Symposium on Business Graphics. Business Graphics, 1976: Advance Printing of Papers Summaries. Hou, Shou L., ed. LC 76-46764. pap. 28.00 (ISBN 0-317-30051-2, 2025039). Bks Demand UMI.

Fall, Thomas. Jim Thorpe. LC 72-94793. (Crocodile Paperback Ser.). (Illus.). (gr. 2-5). 1970. pap. 2.95 (ISBN 0-690-46219-0); lib. bdg. 10.89 (ISBN 0-690-46218-2). Crowell Jr Bks.

Falla & Sibson. A New Guide to the Birds of New Zealand. 39.95 (ISBN 0-00-219622-0, Collins Pub England). Greene.

Falla, Jack. The Echoes Ring Again: History of Boston College Sports. LC 82-20929. (Illus.). 224p. 25.00 (ISBN 0-8289-0486-3). Greene.

Falla, Manuel De see De Falla, Manuel.

Falla, N A., jt. auth. see Morton, J.

Falla, P. S., ed. The Oxford English-Russian Dictionary. 1070p. 1984. 60.00 (ISBN 0-19-864117-6). Oxford U pr.

Falla, P. S., tr. see Hildebrand, Klaus.

Falla, P. S., tr. see Kolakowski, Leszek.

Falla, P. S., tr. see Mommsen, Wolfgang J.

Falla, R. A. & Sibson, R. B. The New Guide to the Birds of New Zealand. (Illus.). 247p. 1983. 17.95 (ISBN 0-00-216928-2, Pub. by W Collins New Zealand). Intl Spec Bk.

Falla, Terry, ed. Be Our Freedom, Lord: Responsive Prayers & Readings for Contemporary Worship. 376p. (Orig.). 1985. pap. 11.95 (ISBN 0-8028-0014-9). Eerdmans.

Fallaci, Oriana. Interview with History. 1977. pap. 7.95 (ISBN 0-395-25223-7). HM.

--Letter to a Child Never Born. 1982. pap. 2.95 (ISBN 0-671-45162-6). WSP.

--A Man. 1981. pap. 3.95 (ISBN 0-671-43487-X). PB.

Fallada, Hans. Little Man, What Now? Sutton, Eric, tr. 384p. 1983. pap. 8.95 (ISBN 0-89733-086-2). Academy Chi Pubs.

Fallah, Skaidrite M. Evoked Biological Responses of Plants - Annotated Bibliography. 60p. 1974. pap. 3.95 (ISBN 0-917200-03-9). ESPress.

--Psychoenergetics: Annotated Bibliography. 90p. 1974. pap. 5.50 (ISBN 0-917200-08-X). ESPress.

Fallaize, E. N. The Origins of Civilization. 1928. 10.00 (ISBN 0-8482-3994-6). Norwood Edns.

Fallani, Giovanni, et al. Francesco Petrarca, Citizen of the World. Bernardo, Aldo S., ed. LC 79-13968. 1980. pap. 39.50 (ISBN 0-87395-392-4). State U NY Pr.

FallCreek, Stephanie & Mettler, Molly. A Healthy Old Age: A Sourcebook for Health Promotion with Older Adults. rev ed. LC 83-18414. (Journal of Gerontological Social Work Ser.: Vol. 6, Nos. 2 & 3). 313p. 1984. text ed. 24.95 (ISBN 0-86656-247-8, B247). Haworth Pr.

Fallding, H. & Miles, C. Drinking, Community & Civilization: The Account of a New Jersey Interview Study. LC 73-620137. (Rutgers Center of Alcohol Studies: Monograph No. 9). 1974. 4.00 (ISBN 0-911290-41-9). Rutgers Ctr Alcohol.

Fallding, Harold. The Sociological Task. LC 68-24428. 1968. 29.50x (ISBN 0-89197-416-4). Irvington.

Fallen, Nancy & McGovern, Jill. Young Children with Special Needs. (Special Education Ser.). 1978. text ed. 22.95 (ISBN 0-675-08382-6). Merrill.

Fallen, Nancy H. & Umansky, Warren. Young Children with Special Needs. 2nd ed. 544p. 1984. 26.95 (ISBN 0-675-20400-3); additional supplements avail. Merrill.

Fallen-Bailey, Darrel G. & Byer, Trevor A. Energy Options & Policy Issues in Developing Countries. (Working Paper: No.350). vi, 107p. 1979. 5.00 (ISBN 0-686-36157-1, WP-0350). World Bank.

Fallenbuchl, Z. East-West Technology Transfer: Study of Poland, 1971-1980. 199p. (Orig.). 1983. pap. text ed. 22.00x (ISBN 92-64-12484-5). OECD.

Fallenbuchl, Zbigniew M. & McMillan, Charles H., eds. Partners in East-West Economic Relations: The Determinants of Choice. (Pergamon Policy Studies). (Illus.). 1980. 56.00 (ISBN 0-08-022497-0). Pergamon.

Faller, Kathleen C. Social Work with Abused & Neglected Children: A Manual of Interdisciplinary Practice. 256p. 1981. text ed. 19.95 (ISBN 0-02-910280-4). Free Pr.

Fallers, Lloyd A. Bantu Bureaucracy: A Century of Political Evolution Among the Basoga of Uganda. LC 65-10270. 1965. 12.50x (ISBN 0-226-23678-1). U of Chicago Pr.

--Bantu Bureaucracy: A Century of Political Evolution Among the Basoga of Uganda. LC 65-10270. 1965. pap. 2.25x (ISBN 0-226-23680-3, P197, Phoen). U of Chicago Pr.

--Inequality: Social Stratification Reconsidered. LC 73-78665. xi, 330p. 1974. pap. 3.95x (ISBN 0-226-23684-6, P578, Phoen). U of Chicago Pr.

Falletta, Nicholas. The Paradoxicon: A Collection of Contradictory Challenges, Problematical Puzzles, & Impossible Illustrations. LC 81-43736. (Illus.). 256p. 1983. 14.95 (ISBN 0-385-17932-4). Doubleday.

Falley, Margaret D. Irish & Scotch-Irish Ancestral Research: A Guide to the Genealogical Records, Methods & Sources in Ireland, 2 vols. LC 80-83867. 1167p. 1984. Repr. of 1962 ed. Set. 60.00 (ISBN 0-8063-0916-4). Genealog Pub.

Fallick, J. L., jt. auth. see Elliot, R. F.

Fallick, J. L. & Elliot, R. F., eds. Incomes Policies, Inflation & Relative Pay. (Illus.). 304p. 1981. text ed. 29.95x (ISBN 0-04-331077-X); pap. text ed. 12.50x (ISBN 0-04-331078-8). Allen Unwin.

Fallier, Jeanne H. Handling Public Relations: A Publicity Handbook for Non-Profit Groups. (Illus.). 55p. (Orig.). 1985. pap. price not set (ISBN 0-9611554-3-4). Rugging Rm.

--Jeanne H. Fallier Traditional Rug Hooking Manual. LC 1-187000352. (Illus.). 42p. 1983. pap. 7.95 (ISBN 0-9611554-0-X). Rugging Rm.

--Littler Critters. LC 52-561. (Illus.). 58p. (Orig.). 1984. pap. 8.95 (ISBN 0-9611554-2-6). Rugging Rm.

Fallik, Fred & Brown, Bruce L. Statistics for Behavioral Sciences. LC 82-73400. 572p. 1983. pap. 25.00x (ISBN 0-256-02405-7). Dorsey.

Fallis, A. M., ed. Ecology & Physiology of Parasites: A Symposium Held at University of Toronto, 1970. LC 70-151365. pap. 67.00 (ISBN 0-317-26914-3, 2023613). Bks Demand UMI.

Fallis, George. Housing Programs & Income Distribution in Canada. (Ontario Economic Council Research Studies). 184p. 1980. pap. 10.00. U of Toronto Pr.

Fallis, Richard. Irish Renaissance. LC 81-21198. 319p. 1977. 22.00x (ISBN 0-8156-2186-8); pap. 9.95x (ISBN 0-8156-2187-6). Syracuse U Pr.

Fallis, William J. Points for Emphasis Nineteen Eighty-Five to Eighty-Six. 1985. pap. 3.75 large type (ISBN 0-8054-1494-0); pap. 2.95 (ISBN 0-8054-1495-9). Broadman.

Fallodon, Grey. Fallodon Papers. 1926. lib. bdg. 12.50 (ISBN 0-8414-9133-X). Folcroft.

Fallon, Berlie J. Two Hundred Tips to Students on How to Study. 2nd ed. 48p. 1982. pap. 1.50 (ISBN 0-8134-2213-2). Interstate.

Fallon, Berlie J., jt. auth. see Bell, Camille G.

Fallon, Berlie J., compiled by. Forty Innovative Programs in Early Childhood Education. LC 72-95010. 1973. pap. 6.75 (ISBN 0-8224-3075-4). Pitman Learning.

Fallon, Beth C. Training Leaders for Family Life Education. LC 82-10200. (Workshop Models for Family Life Education Ser.). 124p. 1982. plastic comb 14.95 (ISBN 0-87304-188-7). Family Serv.

Fallon, Brian, ed. see Fallon, Padraic.

Fallon, Carlos. Value Analysis. Orig. Title: Value Analysis to Improve Productivity. 277p. 1980. 15.00 (ISBN 0-318-16550-3, B1020). Soc Am Value E.

--Value Analysis, Vol. 1. rev., 2nd ed. LC 80-16194. (Illus.). 277p. 1980. pap. 12.50 (ISBN 0-937144-01-0). Triangle Pr.

Fallon, Carol. The Art of the Indian Basket in North America. LC 75-21766. (Illus.). 56p. 1975. pap. 2.50 (ISBN 0-913689-17-3). Spencer Muse Art.

Fallon, D. J. Art of Ballroom Dancing. (Ballroom Dance Ser.). 1985. lib. bdg. 64.00 (ISBN 0-87700-766-7). Revisionist Pr.

Fallon, Daniel. The German University: A Heroic Ideal in Conflict with the Modern World. LC 80-66184. 120p. 1980. 12.50x (ISBN 0-87081-088-X). Colo Assoc.

Fallon, E. B. The Appraiser's Handbook: A Unique Guide to Appraising Land, Buildings & Machinery with Specialized Information for Industrial Engineers. LC 74-21441. 1975. 40.00 (ISBN 0-682-48191-2, Banner). Exposition Pr FL.

--The Appraiser's Handbook: A Unique Guide to Appraising Land, Buildings, & Machinery, with Specialized Information for Industrial Engineers. LC 74-21441. pap. 116.30 (ISBN 0-317-29161-0, 2055587). Bks Demand UMI.

Fallon, Eileen. Words of Love: A Complete Guide to Romance Fiction. LC 82-49132. (Reference Library of the Humanities: Vol. 382). 386p. 1983. lib. bdg. 22.00 (ISBN 0-8240-9204-X). Garland Pub.

Fallon, Eldon E. Trial Handbook for Louisiana Lawyers. LC 81-81708. 69.50; Suppl. 1984. 19.00; Suppl. 1983. 17.00. Lawyers Co-Op.

Fallon, Francis T. Second Corinthians. (New Testament Message Ser.: Vol. 11). 12.95 (ISBN 0-89453-199-9); pap. 6.95 (ISBN 0-89453-134-4). M Glazier.

Fallon, Ivan & Srodes, James. Dream Maker: The Rise & Fall of John Z. De Lorean. LC 83-9497. 288p. 1983. 16.95 (ISBN 0-399-12821-2, Putnam). Putnam Pub Group.

Fallon, John F. & Caplan, Arnold I., eds. Limb Development & Regeneration, Pt. A. LC 82-20391. (Progress in Clinical & Biological Research Ser.: Vol. 110A). 672p. 1982. 68.00 (ISBN 0-8451-0170-6). A R Liss.

Fallon, John F., ed. see Sawyer, Roger H.

Fallon, Michael. The Winston Commentary on the Gospels. 470p. 1982. pap. 12.95 (ISBN 0-86683-680-2). Winston Pr.

Fallon, Michael & Saunders, Jim. Muscle Building for Beginners. LC 64-10506. (Illus., Orig.). 1967. pap. 1.95 (ISBN 0-668-01131-9, 1130). Arco.

Fallon, N. Middle East Oil Money & Its Future Expenditure. 239p. 1976. 19.00x (ISBN 0-86010-024-3, Pub. by Graham & Trotman England). State Mutual Bk.

--Winning Business in Saudi Arabia. 61p. 1976. 65.00x (ISBN 0-86010-043-X, Pub. by Graham & Trotman England). State Mutual Bk.

Fallon, Niall. The Armada in Ireland. LC 77-95546. (Illus.). 1979. 18.50x (ISBN 0-8195-5028-0). Wesleyan U Pr.

--The Armada in Ireland. 256p. 1981. 40.00x (ISBN 0-540-07151-X, Pub. by Stanford Maritime England). State Mutual Bk.

--The Armada in Ireland. 256p. 1982. 40.00x (Pub. by Stanford Maritime England). State Mutual Bk.

Fallon, Norman. Shortwave Listener's Handbook. rev., 2nd ed. (Illus., Orig.). 1976. pap. 6.50 (ISBN 0-8104-5044-5). Hayden.

Fallon, Padraic. Poems & Versions. Fallon, Brian, ed. 112p. pap. 7.50 (ISBN 0-85635-431-7). Carcanet.

Fallon, Patricia, jt. auth. see Rozendal, Nancy.

Fallon, Peter & Golden, Sean. Soft Day: A Miscellany of Contemporary Irish Writing. 224p. 1982. 50.00x (ISBN 0-905473-21-3, Pub. by Wolfhound Pr Ireland). State Mutual Bk.

Fallon, Peter, ed. see Behan, Brendan.

Fallon, Peter, ed. see Boyle, Patrick.

Fallon, Peter, jt. ed. see Carpenter, Andrew.

Fallon, Peter, jt. ed. see Golden, Sean.

Fallon, Peter, ed. see O'Kelly, Seamus.

Fallon, Peter, tr. see Siochfhradha, Padraig O.

Fallon, Peter, et al, eds. see Friel, Brian.

Fallon, Robert T. Captain or Colonel: The Soldier in Milton's Life & Art. LC 84-2308. (Illus.). 304p. 1984. 29.00 (ISBN 0-8262-0447-3). U of Mo Pr.

Fallon, T. H., Jr., ed. The Experts Crossword Puzzle Book, No. 15. LC 74-5609. (Illus.). 80p. 1974. pap. 2.50 (ISBN 0-385-00843-0). Doubleday.

--The Experts' Crossword Puzzle Book, No. 16. (Illus.). 80p. 1975. pap. 2.95 (ISBN 0-385-09000-5). Doubleday.

--Experts' Crossword Puzzle Book, No. 17. LC 76-22894. (Illus.). pap. 2.95 (ISBN 0-385-11560-1). Doubleday.

--The Experts' Crossword Puzzle Book, No. 18. (Illus.). 80p. 1977. pap. 2.95 (ISBN 0-385-11561-X). Doubleday.

--The Experts' Crossword Puzzle Book, No. 19. 1978. pap. 2.95 (ISBN 0-385-12973-4). Doubleday.

--The Experts' Crossword Puzzle Book, No. 20. 1979. pap. 2.95 (ISBN 0-385-12974-2). Doubleday.

Fallon, Thomas, et al. Red Dust Three: New Writing. LC 72-12794. 1979. 8.95 (ISBN 0-87376-026-3). Red Dust.

Fallon, William K. AMA Management Handbook. 2nd ed. LC 82-11530. 1568p. 1983. 69.95 (ISBN 0-8144-0100-7). AMACOM.

Fallon, William K., ed. Effective Communication on the Job. 3rd ed. 320p. 1981. 17.95 (ISBN 0-8144-5698-7). AMACOM.

--Leadership on the Job: Guides to Good Supervision. 320p. 1982. 17.95 (ISBN 0-8144-5727-4). AMACOM.

Falloon, Ian R., et al. Family Management of Schizophrenia: A Study of Clinical, Social, Family & Economic Benefits. LC 84-21295. (Series in Contemporary Medicine & Public Health). 1985. text ed. 26.50x (ISBN 0-8018-2429-X). Johns Hopkins.

--Family Care of Schizophrenia. LC 82-11742. (Family Therapy Ser.). 480p. 1984. 35.00 (ISBN 0-89862-049-X, 2049). Guilford Pr.

Fallowell, Duncan & Ashley, April. April Ashley's Odyssey. (Illus.). 287p. 1983. 15.95 (ISBN 0-224-01849-3, Pub. by Jonathan Cape). Merrimack Pub Cir.

Fallows, David. Dufay. 288p. 1982. 35.00x (ISBN 0-460-04446-X, Pub. by Dent Australia). State Mutual Bk.

--Dufay. (The Master Musicians Ser.). (Illus.). 334p. 1982. text ed. 19.95x (ISBN 0-460-03180-5, BKA 04754, Pub. by J. M. Dent England). Biblio Dist.

Fallows, Deborah. A Mother's Work. 250p. 1985. 16.95 (ISBN 0-395-36218-0). HM.

Fallows, James. National Defense. 1981. 12.95 (ISBN 0-394-51824-1). Random.

--National Defense. LC 81-52873. (Illus.). 224p. 1982. pap. 4.95 (ISBN 0-394-75306-2, Vin). Random.

Fallows, James M. The Water Lords: The Report on Industry & Environmental Crisis in Savannah, Georgia. LC 70-149318. (Ralph Nader Study Group Reports Ser.). 1971. 12.95 (ISBN 0-670-75160-X, Grossman). Viking.

Fallows, Marjorie R. Irish Americans: Identity & Assimilation. (Ethnic Groups in American Life Ser.). 1979. ref. ed. o.p. 13.95 (ISBN 0-13-506261-6); pap. text ed. 14.95 (ISBN 0-13-506253-5). P-H.

Fallows-Hammond, Patricia. Three Hundred Years at the Keyboard: A Piano Sourcebook from Bach to the Moderns. LC 83-23056. 312p. 1984. 15.95 (ISBN 0-89496-043-1). Ross Bks.

Falls, jt. auth. see Payne.

Falls, C. B. ABC Book. (ps). 1957. 8.95a (ISBN 0-385-07663-0); PLB (ISBN 0-385-07698-3); pap. 1.95 (ISBN 0-385-08097-2, Zephyr). Doubleday.

Falls, Caroline E., jt. auth. see Wiedenbach, Ernestine.

Falls, Cyril. The Critic's Armoury. 1973. lib. bdg. 25.00 (ISBN 0-8414-4015-8). Folcroft.

--Rudyard Kipling: A Critical Study. LC 72-13996. 1915. lib. bdg. 20.00 (ISBN 0-8414-1312-6). Folcroft.

Falls, Cyril B. Armageddon, Nineteen Hundred Eighteen. 14.95 (ISBN 0-405-13280-8). Ayer Co Pubs.

--Rudyard Kipling: A Critical Study. 208p. 1980. Repr. of 1915 ed. lib. bdg. 20.00 (ISBN 0-8495-1710-9). Arden Lib.

Falls, Gregory A. The Forgotten Door. (Orig.). 1985. pap. 3.00 (ISBN 0-87602-242-5). Anchorage.

--The Pushcart War. (Orig.). 1985. pap. 3.00 (ISBN 0-87602-248-4). Anchorage.

Falls, Harold & Baylor, Ann. Essentials of Fitness. 1980. pap. 18.95 (ISBN 0-03-056777-7, CBS C). SCP.

Falls, Harold B., ed. Exercise Physiology. 1968. 66.00 (ISBN 0-12-248050-3). Acad Pr.

Falls, William R. Investigations in the College Physical Sciences. 1977. pap. text ed. 10.95 (ISBN 0-8403-1752-2). Kendall-Hunt.

Falls, William R., jt. auth. see Payne, Charles A.

Fallside, F., ed. Control System Design by Pole-Zero Assignment. 1978. 44.00 (ISBN 0-12-248250-6). Acad Pr.

Fallside, Frank & Woods, William A., eds. Computer Speech Processing. (International Book Ser.). (Illus.). 496p. 1985. text ed. 39.95 (ISBN 0-13-163841-6). P-H.

Falmagne. Elements of Psychophysical Theory. 1985. 59.00 (ISBN 0-19-503493-7, 72-10-006). Oxford U Pr.

Falmagne, R. J., ed. Reasoning: Representation & Process in Children & Adults. 288p. 1975. 29.95x (ISBN 0-89859-230-5). L Erlbaum Assocs.

Falmagne, Rachel J., ed. Reasoning: Representation & Process in Children & Adults. 275p. 1975. 18.00x (ISBN 0-470-25369-X). Halsted Pr.

Falnes, Oscar J. National Romanticism in Norway. LC 68-54263. (Columbia University. Studies in the Social Sciences: No. 386). Repr. of 1933 ed. 21.50 (ISBN 0-404-51386-7). AMS Pr.

--Norway & the Nobel Peace Prize. LC 72-168003. Repr. of 1938 ed. 14.50 (ISBN 0-404-02365-7). AMS Pr.

Falola, Eto I. Family Planning for Developing Countries. (Illus.). 160p. 1982. 8.50 (ISBN 0-682-49759-2). Exposition Pr FL.

Falola, Toyin & Ihonvbere, Julius. The Rise & Fall of Nigeria's Second Republic: 1979-1984. (Illus.). 302p. 1985. 30.95x (ISBN 0-86232-379-7, Pub. by Zed Pr England); pap. 12.25 (ISBN 0-86232-380-0, Pub. by Zed Pr England). Biblio Dist.

Falola, Toyin, jt. ed. see Olanrewaju, S. A.

Fals-Borda, Orlando. Peasant Society in the Colombian Andes: A Sociological Study of Saucio. LC 76-40222. (Illus.). 1976. Repr. of 1962 ed. lib. bdg. 22.50x (ISBN 0-8371-9283-8, FBPS). Greenwood.

--Subversion & Social Change in Colombia. Quayle, Jacqueline, tr. from Spanish. LC 69-19458. 238p. 1969. 29.00x (ISBN 0-231-03148-3). Columbia U Pr.

Falson, Walter P., jt. auth. see Timmer, C. Peter.

Falstein, L. D. Basic Mathematics for College Students (You Can Count on Yourself) 1982. pap. text ed. 26.95 (ISBN 0-201-13361-X); test bklt 4.00 (ISBN 0-201-13362-8). Addison-Wesley.

Falstein, Louis. Laughter on a Weekday. 1965. 8.95 (ISBN 0-8392-1147-3). Astor-Honor.

Falster, P. & Rolstadas, A., eds. Production Management Systems: Proceedings of the IFIP TC 5 International Workshop on Automation of Production Planning & Control, Trondheim, Norway, Sept. 1980. viii, 222p. 1981. 38.50 (ISBN 0-444-86176-9, North-Holland). Elsevier.

Falterman, Wesley E. My Dream. 48p. (gr. 4 up). 1985. 5.95 (ISBN 0-8059-2991-6). Dorrance.

Faltings, G. & Wustholz, G. Rational Points, Vol. 6. (Aspects of Mathematics Ser.). 1984. write for info. (ISBN 0-9904001-5-8, Pub. by Vieweg & Sohn Germany). Heyden.

Faltz, Leonard M. Reflexivization: A Study in Universal Syntax. Hankamer, Jorge, ed. (Outstanding Dissertations in Linguistics Ser.). 300p. 1985. 35.00 (ISBN 0-8240-5480-6). Garland Pub.

Faltz, Leonard M., jt. auth. see Keenan, Edward L.

Faludi, Andreas. Planning Theory. LC 73-11236. 312p. 1973. 30.00 (ISBN 0-08-017741-7); pap. 14.00 (ISBN 0-08-017756-5). Pergamon.

Faludi, Andreas, ed. Essays on Planning Theory & Education, Vol. 20. LC 77-30343. 1978. 11.75 (ISBN 0-08-021223-9). Pergamon.

--A Reader in Planning Theory. LC 72-11536. 416p. 1973. text ed. 32.00 (ISBN 0-08-017066-8); pap. text ed. 11.75 (ISBN 0-08-017067-6). Pergamon.

Faludy, George. Selected Poems of George Faludy. Skelton, Robin, ed. & tr. from Hungarian. 224p. 1985. text ed. 18.95 (ISBN 0-8203-0809-9); pap. 9.95 (ISBN 0-8203-0839-0). U of Ga Pr.

Falusi, A. O. & Williams, L. B. Nigeria Fertilizer Sector Present Situation & Future Prospects. (Technical Bulletin Ser.: T-18). (Illus.). 96p. (Orig.). 1981. pap. 4.00 (ISBN 0-88090-017-2). Intl Fertilizer.

Falvey, Jack. After College: The Business of Getting Jobs. Williamson, Susan, ed. (Orig.). 1985. pap. 9.95 (ISBN 0-913589-17-9). Williamson Pub Co.

Falvey, Mary A. Community-Based Curriculum: Instructional Strategies for Students with Severe Handicaps. 260p. (Orig.). 1985. pap. text ed. 19.95 (ISBN 0-933716-49-4, 494). P H Brookes.

Falvo, Donna R. Effective in Patient Education: A Guide to Increased Compliance. 244p. 1984. 26.75 (ISBN 0-89443-561-2). Aspen Systems.

Falwell, Jerry. Champions for God. 132p. 1985. pap. 4.95 (ISBN 0-89693-534-5). Victor Bks.

--Fasting. 1981. pap. 2.50 (ISBN 0-8423-0849-0). Tyndale.

--When It Hurts Too Much to Cry. 160p. 1984. 9.95 (ISBN 0-8423-7993-2). Tyndale.

--Wisdom for Living. 156p. 1984. pap. 4.95 (ISBN 0-89693-370-9). Victor Bks.

Falwell, Jerry, jt. auth. see Towns, Elmer.

Falwell, Jerry & Hindson, Edward E., eds. The Liberty Bible Commentary. LC 83-7280. (Illus.). 2736p. 1983. 29.95 (ISBN 0-8407-5295-4). Nelson.

Falzon, Grazio, tr. Only the Birds Protest: Poems from the Maltese of Mario Azzopardi. (Poetry Chapbook Ser.). 1979. 3.00 (ISBN 0-932191-02-9). Mr Cogito Pr.

Falzone, Mary G. Elder Tastes. 1983. 5.95 (ISBN 0-533-05094-4). Vantage.

Fama, Eugene F. Foundations of Finance: Portfolio Decisions & Securities Prices. LC 75-36771. (Illus.). 1976. text ed. 21.95x (ISBN 0-465-02499-8). Basic.

Fama, Eugene F. & Miller, Merton H. Theory of Finance. 346p. 1972. 30.95x (ISBN 0-03-086732-0). Dryden Pr.

Famera, Karen, jt. ed. see Zaimont, Judith L.

Famie, John J. A History of Electric Telegraphy to the Year 1837. LC 74-4678. (Telecommunications Ser.). (Illus.). 566p. 1974. Repr. of 1884 ed. 38.50x (ISBN 0-405-06044-0). Ayer Co Pubs.

Family Circle. Family Circle Recipes America Loves Best. LC 81-84898. (Illus.). 384p. 1982. 15.95 (ISBN 0-8129-1008-7). Times Bks.

Family Circle Editors. All-Time Baking Favorites. 9.98 (ISBN 0-405-11406-0). Ayer Co Pubs.

--Carefree Summer Meals: Great Summer Cookbook. 9.98 (ISBN 0-405-12050-8). Ayer Co Pubs.

--Classic One-Dish Meals. 9.98 (ISBN 0-405-11409-5). Ayer Co Pubs.

--Creative Chicken Cookbook. 9.95 (ISBN 0-405-11397-8). Ayer Co Pubs.

--Creative Crafts. 9.95 (ISBN 0-405-11408-7). Ayer Co Pubs.

--Delicious Deserts: More Than Three Hundred Recipes for Cookies, Cakes, Pies, Puddings, Ice Cream, & Other Irresistible Sweets. LC 84-40097. (Illus.). 288p. (Orig.). 1984. pap. 6.95 (ISBN 0-8129-6341-5). Times Bks.

--Do-It Yourself Decorating. 9.98 (ISBN 0-405-11396-X). Ayer Co Pubs.

--Family Circle Decorative Crafts for Your Home. 9.98 (ISBN 0-405-12055-9). Ayer Co Pubs.

--Family Circle Gifts for All Seasons. 9.98 (ISBN 0-405-12053-2). Ayer Co Pubs.

--Favorite Cheese Recipes: Family Circle Guide to Cheese-Cookery. 9.98 (ISBN 0-405-12051-6). Ayer Co Pubs.

--Great Meals on a Tight Budget: More Than 250 Recipes & Dozens of Tips to Save You Money. LC 84-40098. (Illus.). 314p. (Orig.). 1984. pap. 6.95 (ISBN 0-8129-6340-7). Times Bks.

--Needlecrafts. 9.98 (ISBN 0-405-12056-7). Ayer Co Pubs.

--Simply Delicious Meals. 9.98 (ISBN 0-405-11956-9). Ayer Co Pubs.

Family Circle Editors & Walsh, Marie T. The Natural Way to Beauty. 9.98 (ISBN 0-405-12054-0). Ayer Co Pubs.

Family Circle Editors, ed. Family Circle Favorite Recipes Cookbook. (Illus.). 1977. 10.95 (ISBN 0-918668-03-4). Paramount.

Family Circle Food Staff & Fletcher, Anne M. Great Ground-Beef Recipes. LC 73-11785. (Family Circle Books). (Illus.). 168p. 1976. 9.98x (ISBN 0-405-09842-1). Ayer Co Pubs.

Family Circle Food Staff, jt. auth. see Milo, Mary.

Family Circle Staff, ed. Great Meals in One Dish. LC 85-40275. (Illus.). 336p. (Orig.). 1986. pap. 6.95 (ISBN 0-8129-1270-5). Times Bks.

--Perfect Poultry: More than 200 Recipes & Dozens of Tips for Making Delicious Meals with Chicken & Turkey. LC 85-40274. (Illus.). 288p. (Orig.). 1986. pap. 6.95 (ISBN 0-8129-1210-1). Times Bks.

Family, F. & Landau, D. P. Kinetics of Aggregation & Gelation. xxi, 272p. 1985. 44.50 (ISBN 0-444-86912-3). Elsevier.

Family Handyman Magazine. Family Handyman Answer Book Number 2. 1983. pap. 12.95 (ISBN 0-8359-1839-4). Reston.

Family Handyman Magazine Editors. The Furniture Maker's Handbook. (Illus.). 282p. 1981. pap. 15.95 (ISBN 0-684-17313-1, ScribT). Scribner.

Family Handyman Magazine Staff. America's Handyman Book. rev. ed. (Illus.). 1983. 16.95 (ISBN 0-684-16296-2). Scribner.

Family Handyman Staff. The Early American Furniture-Making Handbook. LC 72-38945. (Illus.). 160p. 1972. 14.95 (ISBN 0-684-12869-1, ScribT); pap. 9.95 (ISBN 0-684-15060-3). Scribner.

Family Law Reporter Editorial Staff. Desk Guide to the Uniform Marriage & Divorce Act. Rev. ed. 106p. 1982. pap. text ed. 10.00 (ISBN 0-87179-378-4). BNA.

Family Law Sect. Fathers, Husbands & Lovers: Legal Rights & Responsibilities. 318p. 1979. pap. 15.00 (ISBN 0-686-47924-6, 5130014). Amer Bar Assn.

Family Law Symposium & Maine State Bar Association Continuing Legal Education Staff. Family Law Symposium: Child Custody & Visitation: An Agonizing Decision (Portland, Maine, May 6 & 7, 1983) LC 83-167303. (Illus.). 232p. 1983. 20.00 (ISBN 0-318-03587-1). Maine St Bar.

Family Service Association of America. Detailed Instructions for a Time Analysis, Vol. 3. (Time & Cost Analysis Ser.). 54p. 1968. pap. 8.50 (ISBN 0-87304-075-9). Family Serv.

--Dimensions of Alcoholism Treatment. 63p. 1978. 3.25 (ISBN 0-318-15315-7). Natl Coun Alcoholism.

--A New Perspective on Social Work. LC 73-81140. 40p. 1973. pap. 2.00 (ISBN 0-87304-106-2). Family Serv.

--Preparing for Time Analysis, Vol. 1. (Time & Cost Analysis Ser.). 1968. pap. 4.00 (ISBN 0-87304-073-2). Family Serv.

Family Service Association of America, Research Dept. & Frankiel, Ruth V. A Review of Research on Parent Influences on Child Personality. LC 59-1935. pap. 20.00 (ISBN 0-317-10343-1, 2050172). Bks Demand UMI.

Family Service Association of America. Selecting Services, Service Elements & Activities, Vol. 2. (Time & Cost Analysis Ser.). 38p. 1968. pap. 6.50 (ISBN 0-87304-074-0). Family Serv.

--The Significance of the Father: Four Papers from the FSAA Biennial Meeting, Washington, D.C., April, 1959. pap. 20.00 (ISBN 0-317-10308-3, 2007668). Bks Demand UMI.

--Social Work Assistants in Family Service Agencies. 1969. pap. 1.50 (ISBN 0-87304-039-2). Family Serv.

--Who Spoke for the Poor? 1880-1914. 36p. 1968. pap. 3.00 (ISBN 0-87304-049-X). Family Serv.

Family-University of Wisconsin. Family: Changing Faces of American Families. 174p. 1985. pap. 15.95 (ISBN 0-8403-3553-9). Kendall Hunt.

Family Welfare Association. Guide to the Social Services (U.K.) 1982. 70th ed. LC 55-33805. 326p. (Orig.). 1982. pap. 16.50x (ISBN 0-900954-15-9). Intl Pubns Serv.

Family Works Staff. Building Outdoor Structures. LC 83-45384. 160p. (Orig.). 1984. pap. 10.95 (ISBN 0-8019-7503-4). Chilton.

Family Workshop Inc. Building Outdoor Furniture. LC 83-45383. 160p. (Orig.). 1984. pap. 10.95 (ISBN 0-8019-7502-6). Chilton.

--Focus on Photography. LC 83-45387. 160p. (Orig.). 1984. pap. 12.95 (ISBN 0-8019-7499-2). Chilton.

--The Great Mechanical Wooden Toy Box. 156p. (Orig.). 1984. pap. 10.95 (ISBN 0-8019-7508-5). Chilton.

Family Workshop, Inc. Staff. Celebrations of Christmas. LC 85-47331. 248p. 1985. pap. 19.95 (ISBN 0-8019-7448-8). Chilton.

--Focus on Photography, Bk. 2. LC 83-45387. 168p. 1984. pap. 12.95 (ISBN 0-8019-7501-8). Chilton.

Famine Inquiry Commission of India. Report on Bengal. LC 75-26302. (World Food Supply Ser). 1976. Repr. of 1945 ed. 20.00x (ISBN 0-405-07781-5). Ayer Co Pubs.

Famous Artists School. How to Draw & Paint Landscapes. (Illus.). 96p. 1983. pap. 7.64 (ISBN 0-06-464070-1, BN 4070). B&N NY.

--How to Draw & Paint Portraits. (Illus.). 96p. 1983. pap. 7.64i (ISBN 0-06-464071-X, BN 4071). B&N NY.

--How to Draw & Paint the Human Figure. Munce, Howard & Cortina, F. A., eds. (Illus.). 96p. 1983. pap. 7.64i (ISBN 0-06-464069-8, BN 4069). B&N NY.

--How to Draw Animals. 96p. 1983. pap. 7.64i (ISBN 0-06-464068-X, BN 4068). B&N NY.

Famularo. Joe Famularo's Vegetable Cookbook. 1985. 14.95 (ISBN 0-8120-5609-4). Barron.

Famularo, J. J. Handbook of Human Resources Administration. 1986. write for info. (ISBN 0-07-019914-0). McGraw.

Famularo, Joe & Imperiale, Louise. Joy of Pasta. 1983. 14.95 (ISBN 0-8120-5510-1). Barron.

Famularo, Joseph. Handbook of Personnel Forms, Records & Reports. LC 81-19303. 640p. 1982. 79.95 (ISBN 0-07-019913-2). McGraw.

Famularo, Joseph J. Handbook of Modern Personnel Administration. (Illus.). 1280p. 1972. 73.50 (ISBN 0-07-019912-4). McGraw.

--Organization Planning Manual. rev. ed. (Illus.). 1979. 55.00 (ISBN 0-8144-5538-7). AMACOM.

Famularo, Loe & Imperiale, Louise. Vegetables: The New Main Course Cookbook. (Illus.). 1985. 15.95. Barron.

Fan, Ch'Eng-ta. The Five Seasons of a Golden Year: A Chinese Pastoral. dual language ed. Bullett, Gerald W., tr. LC 81-670010. (Renditions Ser.). 180p. (Chinese.). 1981. 14.50x (ISBN 0-295-95834-0, Pub. by Chinese Univ Hong Kong). U of Wash Pr.

Fan, J. C. & Johnson, N. M. Energy Beam-Solid Interactions & Transient Thermal Processing: Proceedings of the 6th Symposium on Energy Beam Solid Interactions & Transient Thermal Processing, Boston, MA, 1983. (Materials Research Society Symposia Ser.: Vol. 23). 788p. 1984. 95.00 (ISBN 0-444-00903-5, North Holland). Elsevier.

Fan, Kok Sim. Women in Southeast Asia: A Bibliography. 1982. lib. bdg. 57.50 (ISBN 0-8161-8407-0, Hall Reference). G K Hall.

Fan, L. T., jt. auth. see Wen, C. Y.

Fan, Liang-Shing, jt. auth. see Carbaugh, Robert J.

Fan, Shi, ed. Stamps of China Nineteen Seventy-Eight to Nineteen Eighty-One. 148p. (Orig.). 1983. pap. 24.95 (ISBN 0-8351-0995-X). China Bks.

Fan, Tsen-Chung. Dr. Johnson & Chinese Culture. LC 73-15538. 1945. lib. bdg. 17.50 (ISBN 0-8414-4158-8). Folcroft.

Fan, Ts'Un-Chung. Dr. Johnson & Chinese Culture. 50p. 1980. Repr. of 1945 ed. lib. bdg. 10.00 (ISBN 0-8495-1714-1). Arden Lib.

Fanaroff, Avroy A. & Martin, Richard J. Behrman's Neonatal-Perinatal Medicine: Diseases of the Fetus & Infant. 3rd ed. LC 82-6371. (Illus.). 1190p. 1983. text ed. 74.95 (ISBN 0-8016-0580-6). Mosby.

Fanaroff, Avroy A., jt. auth. see Klaus, Marshall H.

Fanatan, Mircea. Driving: Self Defense. (Illus.). 96p. (Orig.). 1984. pap. 7.50 (ISBN 0-89962-358-1). Todd & Honeywell.

Fanburg. Sacoidosis & Other Granulatons Diseases of the Lung. (Lung & Biology in Health & Disease Ser.: Vol. 19). 544p. 1983. 69.75 (ISBN 0-8247-1866-6). Dekker.

Fancais, W. The Nilgiris. (Madras District Gazetteers). 394p. 1984. Repr. of 1910 ed. text ed. 75.00x (ISBN 0-86590-377-8, Pub. by B R Pub Corp Delhi). Apt Bks.

Fance, W. J. The Students' Technology of Breadmaking & Flour Confectionery. rev. ed. (Illus.). 464p. 1983. pap. 22.00 (ISBN 0-7100-9046-3). Routledge & Kegan.

Fance, W. J., ed. The New International Confectioner. 3rd rev. ed. (Illus.). 908p. 1981. 110.00 (ISBN 0-685-90333-8, Virtue & Co.). Van Nos Reinhold.

Fancey, Dyane. A Religion of Skin, Vol. 9. Lott, Clarinda H., ed. (New Poets Ser.). (Illus.). 50p. 1981. pap. 2.95 (ISBN 0-932616-07-0). New Poets.

Fancher, Betsy. Lost Legacy of Georgia's Golden Isles. LC 78-12511. (Illus.). 224p. 1979. Repr. of 1971 ed. 14.95 (ISBN 0-89783-000-8). Larlin Corp.

Fancher, C., jt. auth. see Nanassy, L.

Fancher, Carlton M. Personal Ecology. 2nd ed. 264p. 1981. pap. text ed. 16.95 (ISBN 0-8403-2352-2). Kendall-Hunt.

Fancher, Gordon & Myers, Gerald, eds. Philosophical Essays on Dance: With Responses from Choreographers, Critics & Dancers. LC 81-67061. 178p. (Orig.). 1981. pap. 8.95x (ISBN 0-87127-126-5). Dance Horiz.

Fancher, Hampton & Peoples, David. The Illustrated Blade Runner. (Illus.). 96p. 1982. pap. 6.95 (ISBN 0-943128-01-3). Blue Dolphin.

Fancher, Paul S. Research in Support of Motor Truck Brake System Design & Development. (Illus.). 141p. 1980. 12.00 (ISBN 0-938654-27-6, BRAKE). Indus Dev Inst Sci.

Fancher, Raymond E. The Intelligence Men: Makers of the I.Q. Controversy. (Illus.). 1985. 17.95 (ISBN 0-393-01982-9). Norton.

--Pioneers In Psychology. (Illus.). 1979. pap. text ed. 9.95x (ISBN 0-393-09082-5). Norton.

--Pioneers in Psychology. 1979. instrs' manual avail. (ISBN 0-393-95076-X). Norton.

--Psychoanalytic Psychology: The Development of Freud's Thought. LC 73-1273. (Illus.). 1973. pap. 6.95x (ISBN 0-393-09356-5). Norton.

Fancher, Terry. Racquetball One, Two, Three. (Illus.). 128p. (Orig.). 1984. pap. text ed. 6.95 (ISBN 0-87670-062-8, Dist. by Sterling). Athletic Inst.

Fancher, Terry & Shay, Arthur. Forty Common Errors in Racquetball & How to Correct Them. LC 77-23707. 1978. pap. 6.95 (ISBN 0-8092-7703-4). Contemp Bks.

Fanck, A., jt. auth. see Schneider, H.

Fandel, jt. auth. see British Horse Society & Pony Club.

Fandel, G. & Spronk, J., eds. Multiple Criteria Decision Methods & Applications. (Illus.). xiv, 404p. 1985. 42.00 (ISBN 0-387-15596-1). Springer-Verlag.

Fandel, John. Bach & a Catbird. LC 78-61306. pap. 4.50 (ISBN 0-87957-006-7). Roth Pub.

--Body of Earth. LC 79-181993. pap. 2.50 (ISBN 0-87957-000-8). Roth Pub.

--The Deserted Greenhouse. pap. 3.50 (ISBN 0-87957-004-0). Roth Pub.

--God's Breath in Man. LC 77-76604. 1977. pap. 1.50 (ISBN 0-87957-005-9). Roth Pub.

--A Morning Answer. 1984. pap. 3.35 (ISBN 0-88028-041-7). Forward Movement.

Fanderlik, I. Optical Properties of Glass. (Glass Science & Technology Ser.: Vol. 5). 1983. 81.00 (ISBN 0-444-99652-4, I-384-83). Elsevier.

Fan Dianian, jt. auth. see Xu Liangying.

Fandozzi, Phillip R. Nihilism & Technology: A Heideggerian Investigation. LC 82-17337. 158p. (Orig.). 1983. lib. bdg. 22.00 (ISBN 0-8191-2825-2); pap. text ed. 9.75 (ISBN 0-8191-2826-0). U Pr of Amer.

Fandrich, B., ed. see Van Dine, D.

Fane, Julian. Gentleman's Gentleman. 148p. 1981. 17.50 (ISBN 0-241-10434-3, Pub. by Hamish Hamilton England). David & Charles.

--Revolution Island. 352p. 1980. 17.95 (ISBN 0-241-10319-3, Pub. by Hamish Hamilton England). David & Charles.

Fane, Mildmay. Raguaillo D'Oceano & Candy Restored: From the London & Huntingdon Mss. 1640, 1641. Leech, Clifford, ed. (Mat. for the Study of the Old English Drama Ser. 2: Vol.l 15). pap. 21.00 (ISBN 0-317-16143-1). Kraus Repr.

Fane, Pamela La see La Fane, Pamela.

Fane, X., jt. auth. see Baker, K.

Fanelli, Giovanni. Brunelleschi. (Illus.). 80p. (Orig.). 1980. pap. 12.50 (ISBN 0-935748-01-6). Scala Books.

Fanelli, Giovanni, ed. Florence Lost, 2 vols. (Illus.). 292p. Set. 300.00 (ISBN 0-8478-5405-1). Rizzoli Intl.

Fanelli, Jenny, ed. see Tanaka, Shelley.

Fanelli, Maresa. Aujourd'hui. 2nd ed. 1980. text ed. 21.95 (ISBN 0-669-02503-8); wkbk. 8.95 (ISBN 0-669-02504-6); tapes-reels 75.00 (ISBN 0-669-02506-2); cassettes 35.00 (ISBN 0-669-02507-0); demo tape 1.95 (ISBN 0-669-02508-9); tapescript 1.95 (ISBN 0-669-02505-4). Heath.

--Histoires et Idees. 1978. pap. text ed. 10.95x (ISBN 0-669-01532-6). Heath.

Fanelli, Maresa & Guggenheim, Michel. Aujourd 'hui. (Illus.). 544p. text ed. 14.95x (ISBN 0-669-93104-7); student wkbk. 4.95x (ISBN 0-669-00010-8); reels 55.00 (ISBN 0-669-00011-6); cassettes 55.00 (ISBN 0-686-57777-9). Heath.

Faner, Robert D. Walt Whitman & Opera. (Arcturus Books Paperbacks). 261p. 1972. pap. 2.55 (ISBN 0-8093-0572-0). S Ill U Pr.

--Walt Whitman & Opera. 261p. 1972. Repr. of 1951 ed. lib. bdg. 7.00x (ISBN 0-8093-0592-5). S Ill U Pr.

Fanfani, Amintore. Catholicism, Protestantism & Capitalism. LC 78-38251. (The Evolution of Capitalism Ser.). 234p. 1972. Repr. of 1935 ed. 23.50 (ISBN 0-405-04119-5). Ayer Co Pubs.

--Catholicism, Protestantism, & Capitalism. LC 84-40363. 272p. 1984. pap. text ed. 8.95 (ISBN 0-268-00752-7, 85-07527). U of Notre Dame Pr.

Fanfare House, Inc. Arcade Games for the Commodore 64. 1985. FPT 32.95 (ISBN 0-03-001049-7). CBS Ed.

Fang, Achilles, tr. see Ssu-Ma Kuang.

Fang, C. S. CHEMCALC (TM) 2: Gas & Liquid Flow Calculations. LC 85-836. (CHEMCALC (TM) Software for Chemical Engineers Ser.). 1985. 3-ring binder with Floppy Disk 265.00x (ISBN 0-87201-086-4). Gulf Pub.

--CHEMCALC (TM) 3: Convective Heat Transfer. LC 85-837. (CHEMCALC (TM) Software for Chemical Engineers Ser.). 1985. 3-ring binder with Floppy Disk 265.00x (ISBN 0-87201-087-2). Gulf Pub.

Fang, Carl, tr. see Foster, Harry.

Fang, Carl, tr. see Kaung, Stephen.

Fang, Carl, tr. see Morgan, G. Campbell.

Fang, Chaoying, jt. ed. see Goodrich, L. Carrington.

Fang, F. Y., jt. ed. see Winterkorn, Hans F.

Fang, Fu-An. Chinese Labour: An Economic & Statistical Survey of the Labour Conditions & Labour Movements in China. LC 78-22780. (The Modern Chinese Economy Ser.: Vol. 34). 185p. 1980. lib. bdg. 24.00 (ISBN 0-8240-4282-4). Garland Pub.

Fang, Hsien-T'Ing. The Triumph of the Factory System in England. LC 78-15111. (Perspectives in European History Ser.: No. 17). (Illus.). 310p. 1979. Repr. of 1930 ed. lib. bdg. 27.50x (ISBN 0-87991-624-9). Porcupine Pr.

Fang, Ilse M., ed. Chinesische Anthologie: Ubersetzungen Aus Dem Wen Hsuan, 2 Vols. Von Zach, Erwin, tr. LC 58-6581. (Harvard-Yenching Institute Studies: No. 18). 1958. Set. pap. 30.00x (ISBN 0-674-12650-5). Harvard U Pr.

Fang, Irving, jt. auth. see Feltgen, Dennis.

Fang, Irving E. Television News, Radio News. 4th, rev. ed. LC 84-61461. (Illus.). 440p. 1985. text ed. 25.95 (ISBN 0-9604212-3-8). Rada Pr.

--Those Radio Commentators. (Illus.). 1977. 14.95x (ISBN 0-8138-1500-2); 2 records incl. Iowa St U Pr.

Fang, Joong. Numbers Racket: The Aftermath of New Math. LC 68-8247. 1968. 19.50 (ISBN 0-8046-0138-0, Pub. by Kennikat). Assoc Faculty Pr.

Fang, Josephine R. & Songe, Alice H. International Guide to Library, Archival, & Information Science Associations. 2nd ed. 448p. 1980. 32.50 (ISBN 0-8352-1285-8). Bowker.

Fang, Josephine Riss & Nauta, Paul, eds. International Guide to Library & Information Science Education: A Reference Source for Educational Programs in the Information Fields World-Wide. (IFLA Publication Ser.: Vol. 32). 536p. 1985. lib. bdg. 46.00 (ISBN 3-598-20396-9). K G Saur.

Fang, L. S. Manual of Clinical Nephrology. 231p. 1983. 16.95 (ISBN 0-07-019901-9). McGraw-Pretest.

Fang, L. Z. & Ruffini, R. Cosmology of the Early Universe. (Advanced Series in Astrophysics: Vol. 1). 350p. 37.00x (ISBN 9971-950-92-8, Pub. by World Sci Singapore); pap. 21.00x (ISBN 9971-950-93-6, Pub. by World Sci Singapore). Taylor & Francis.

Fang, L. Z. & Ruffini, J., eds. Basic Concepts in Relativistic Astrophysics. 1983. 33.00x (ISBN 9971-950-66-9, Pub. by World Sci Singapore). Taylor & Francis.

Fangel, Ester, et al. Danish Pulled Thread Embroidery. LC 76-49327. Orig. Title: Danish Embroidery. (Illus.). 1977. pap. 3.50 (ISBN 0-486-23474-6). Dover.

Fangel, Esther, et al. Danish Pulled Thread Embroidery: With English & Danish Text. 12.75 (ISBN 0-8446-5573-2). Peter Smith.

Fanger, Donald. The Creation of Nikolai Gogol. LC 79-14135. 1979. 20.00x (ISBN 0-674-17565-4). Harvard U Pr.

--The Creation of Nikolai Gogol. 320p. 1982. pap. 7.95 (ISBN 0-674-17564-6, Belknap Pr). Harvard U Pr.

--Dostoevsky & Romantic Realism: A Study of Dostoevsky in Relation to Balzac, Dickens, Gogol. LC 65-13841. 1968. pap. 7.00x (ISBN 0-226-23747-8). U of Chicago Pr.

Fanger, P. O. Thermal Comfort: Analysis & Applications in Environmental Engineering. LC 81-20935. 244p. 1982. Repr. of 1970 ed. 24.50 (ISBN 0-89874-446-6). Krieger.

Fang-Kuei, Li see Li, Fang-Kuei.

Fangmeier, Jurgen, ed. see Barth, Carl.

Fang Yu-Wang, Fred. Character Text for Chinese Dialogues. 5.25 (ISBN 0-88710-007-4). Far Eastern Pubns.

Fang-Yu Wang, Fred. Chinese Dialogues. 8.95 (ISBN 0-88710-014-7); tapes avail. (ISBN 0-88710-015-5). Far Eastern Pubns.

Fanin, Ferne, ed. Cumulative Index to Nursing & Allied Health Literature, Vol. 24. LC 78-643434. 1979. 80.00 (ISBN 0-910478-15-5). Glendale Advent Med.

Faniran. Humid Tropical Geomorphology. LC 82-14896. 1984. text ed. 35.00 o. p. (ISBN 0-582-64346-5); pap. text ed. 17.95 (ISBN 0-582-64351-1). Longman.

Faniran, A. Man's Physical Environment. (Orig.). 1980. pap. text ed. 22.50x (ISBN 0-435-95042-8). Heinemann Ed.

Faniran, A. & Areola, A. The Essentials of Soil Study. LC 79-670194. 1977. 14.50x (ISBN 0-435-95311-7). Heinemann Ed.

Faniran, A., jt. auth. see Ajaegbu, H. I.

Fankhauser, Jerry. The Power of Affirmations. 56p. 1983. pap. 6.00 (ISBN 0-942494-40-7). Coleman Pub.

Fankhauser, Jerry & Paulson, Sig. From a Chicken to an Eagle. 62p. 1982. pap. 5.00 (ISBN 0-942494-04-0). Coleman Pub.

Fann, K. T. Wittgenstein's Conception of Philosophy. LC 65-24178. 1969. 15.95x (ISBN 0-520-01615-7); pap. 7.95x (ISBN 0-520-01837-0, CAMPUS 171). U of Cal Pr.

Fann, K. T., ed. Ludwig Wittgenstein: The Man & His Philosophy. rev. ed. 1978. text ed. 16.50x (ISBN 0-391-00897-8); pap. text ed. 9.45x (ISBN 0-391-00865-X). Humanities.

--Symposium on J. L. Austin. (International Library of Philosophy & Scientific Method). (Illus.). 1979. Repr. of 1969 ed. text ed. 32.50x (ISBN 0-391-00981-8). Humanities.

Fann, W. E., jt. ed. see Eisdorfer, C.

Fann, W. E., et al, eds. Phenomenology & Treatment of Psychophysiological Disorders. (Illus.). 335p. 1982. text ed. 35.00 (ISBN 0-89335-151-2). SP Med & Sci Bks.

Fann, William, et al, eds. Phenomenology & Treatment of Psychosexual Disorders. 192p. 1983. text ed. 25.00 (ISBN 0-89335-184-9). SP Med & Sci Bks.

--Tardive Dyskinesia. LC 79-4468. (Illus.). 505p. 1980. text ed. 65.00 (ISBN 0-89335-076-1). SP Med & Sci Bks.

Fann, William E. & Maddox, George L. Drug Issues in Geropsychiatry. LC 74-1491. 122p. 1974. pap. 9.50 (ISBN 0-683-03002-7). Krieger.

Fann, William E., jt. ed. see Eisdorfer, Carl.

Fann, William E., et al, eds. Phenomenology & Treatment of Alcoholism. new ed. LC 79-23224. (Illus.). 350p. 1980. text ed. 35.00 (ISBN 0-89335-097-4). SP Med & Sci Bks.

--Phenomenology & Treatment of Anxiety. new ed. LC 78-32092. (Illus.). 455p. 1979. 35.00 (ISBN 0-89335-070-2). SP Med & Sci Bks.

Fannin, Alice, et al. Woman: An Affirmation. 1979. pap. text ed. 12.95 (ISBN 0-669-01991-7); instr's manual 1.95 (ISBN 0-669-01992-5). Heath.

Fannin, Angela. Porch Chatter: A Texas Gallery. (Illus.). 104p. 1984. 17.95 (ISBN 0-89015-456-2). Eakin Pubns.

Fannin, Angela, jt. auth. see Fannin, Jerry W.

Fannin, Angela F. Johnnies, Biffies, Outhouses, Etc. (Illus.). 104p. 1980. 6.95 (ISBN 0-89015-259-4). Eakin Pubns.

Fannin County Historical Commission. Tempting Traditions. Jones, Barbara C., ed. 280p. (Orig.). 1982. pap. 11.95 (ISBN 0-9609602-0-1). Fannin County.

Fannin, Jerry W. & Fannin, Angela. The Armadillo Handbook. 1982. 4.95 (ISBN 0-89015-325-6). Eakin Pubns.

Fanning, Anthony E. Planets, Stars & Galaxies. (Illus.). 1966. pap. 3.75 (ISBN 0-486-21680-2). Dover.

--Planets, Stars & Galaxies: Descriptive Astronomy for Beginners. (Illus.). 12.75 (ISBN 0-8446-2042-4). Peter Smith.

Fanning, Charles. Finley Peter Dunne & Mr. Dooley: The Chicago Years. LC 77-75483. (Illus.). 304p. 1978. 28.00x (ISBN 0-8131-1365-2). U Pr of Ky.

Fanning, Charles, ed. Mr. Dooley & the Chicago Irish: An Anthology. LC 76-6339. (Irish Americans Ser). 1976. 37.50 (ISBN 0-405-09334-9). Ayer Co Pubs.

Fanning, David. Marketing Company Shares. 288p. 1982. text ed. 42.00x (ISBN 0-566-02174-9). Gower Pub Co.

--Pension Funds: Issues in Accounting & Finance. 54p. 1981. 110.00x (ISBN 0-86176-052-2, Pub. by MCB Pubns). State Mutual Bk.

Fanning, David & Pendelbury, Maurice. Company Accounts: A Guide. (Illus.). 224p. 1984. text ed. 29.00x (ISBN 0-04-332092-9); pap. text ed. 12.95x (ISBN 0-04-332093-7). Allen Unwin.

Fanning, David, ed. Handbook of Management Accounting. 496p. (Orig.). 1983. text ed. 54.00x (ISBN 0-566-02236-2). Gower Pub Co.

Fanning, Edmund. Voyages Around the World. (Illus.). 499p. 1970. Repr. of 1833 ed. 35.00 (ISBN 0-8398-0551-9). Parnassus Imprints.

--Voyages to the South Seas & to the Northwest Coast of America. enl. ed. 1970. Repr. of 1838 ed. 16.95 (ISBN 0-87770-012-5). Ye Galleon.

--Voyages to the South Seas, Indian & Pacific Oceans, China Sea, North - West Coast, Feejee Islands, South Shetlands. (Illus.). 324p. 1970. Repr. of 1838 ed. 30.00 (ISBN 0-8398-0552-7). Parnassus Imprints.

Fanning, John & Sullivan, George. Work When You Want to Work. 1985. pap. 3.50 (ISBN 0-671-52561-1). PB.

Fanning, John W. A Common Sense Approach to Community Living Arrangements for the Mentally Retarded. (Illus.). 112p. 1975. 15.75x (ISBN 0-398-03300-5). C C Thomas.

Fanning, Kent A. & Manheim, Frank T. The Dynamic Environment of the Ocean Floor. LC 78-24651. 512p. 1981. 46.00x (ISBN 0-669-02809-6). Lexington Bks.

Fanning, Marilyn. The Not-So-Golden Years. 156p. 1984. pap. 4.95 (ISBN 0-88207-611-6). Victor Bks.

Fanning, Martha, jt. auth. see Cooper, Mildred.

Fanning, Melody S., jt. auth. see Dunton, Sabina M.

Fanning, Nathaniel. Fanning's Narrative: Being the Memoirs of Nathaniel Fanning, an Officer of the Revolutionary Navy 1778-1783. Barnes, John S., ed. LC 67-29043. (Eyewitness Accounts of the American Revolution Ser., No. 1). 1968. Repr. of 1912 ed. 15.00 (ISBN 0-405-01105-9). Ayer Co Pubs.

Fanning, Odom. Opportunities in Environmental Careers. LC 74-25902. (VGM Career Bks.). (Illus.). 1975. 7.95 (ISBN 0-8442-6381-8, 6381-8); pap. text ed. 5.95 (ISBN 0-8442-6382-6, 6382-6). Natl Textbk.

Fanning, Robbie. One Hundred Butterflies. LC 79-14776. 190p. (gr. 3-6). 1979. 8.95 (ISBN 0-664-32654-4). Westminster.

--Open Chain's Selected Annotated Bibliography of Self-Publishing. (Illus.). 1978. 2.00 (ISBN 0-932086-00-4). Fibar Designs.

--Open Chain's Selected Annotated Bibliography of Self-Study in the Needlearts. (Illus.). 1978. 2.00 (ISBN 0-932086-01-2). Fibar Designs.

Fanning, Robbie & Fanning, Tony. The Complete Book of Machine Quilting. (Illus.). 224p. pap. 14.95 (ISBN 0-8019-6803-8). Chilton.

Fanning, Robbie, jt. auth. see Fanning, Tony.

Fanning, Ronan. Independent Ireland. (Helicon History of Ireland Ser.: Vol. 9). 230p. (Orig.). 1983. 22.95 (ISBN 0-318-03201-5, Pub. by Educ Co Ireland); pap. 9.95 (ISBN 0-318-03202-3, Pub. by Educ Co Ireland). Irish Bk Ctr.

Fanning, Tom, ed. see Masalski, William J.

Fanning, Tom, ed. see Mulcahy, Michael E.

Fanning, Tony & Fanning, Robbie. Get It All Done & Still Be Human. LC 78-14633. 1979. 8.95 (ISBN 0-8019-6767-8). Chilton.

Fanning, Tony, jt. auth. see Fanning, Robbie.

Fanny, Aunt. Junior Jewish Cook Book. (Illus.). (gr. 5-6). 1956. pap. 4.95x (ISBN 0-87068-361-6). Ktav.

Fano, L., jt. auth. see Fano, U.

Fano, U. & Fano, L. Physics of Atoms & Molecules: An Introduction to the Structure of Matter. LC 76-184808. 456p. 1973. text ed. 35.00x (ISBN 0-226-23782-6). U of Chicago Pr.

Fanon, Frantz. Black Skin, White Masks. Markmann, Charles L., tr. 1967. pap. 6.95 (ISBN 0-394-17990-0, E817, Ever). Grove.

--Les Damnes de la Terre. (Petite Coll. Maspero). pap. 5.50 (ISBN 0-685-33977-7). French & Eur.

--A Dying Colonialism. Chevalier, Haakon, tr. 1967. pap. 9.95 (ISBN 0-394-17262-0, E430, Ever). Grove.

--Peau Noire, Masques Blancs. (Coll. La Condition Humaine). 8.95 (ISBN 0-685-35936-0). French & Eur.

--Peau noire, masques blancs. (Coll. Points). pap. 4.95 (ISBN 0-685-35937-9). French & Eur.

--Pour la Revolution Africaine. (Petite Coll. Maspero). pap. 4.50 (ISBN 0-685-35634-5). French & Eur.

--Sociologie d'une Revolution. (Petite Coll. Maspero). pap. 3.95 (ISBN 0-685-35635-3). French & Eur.

--Toward the African Revolution. Chevalier, Haakon, tr. 1968. pap. 2.25 (ISBN 0-394-17149-7, B219, BC). Grove.

--Wretched of the Earth. Farrington, Constance, tr. 1965. pap. 3.95 (ISBN 0-394-17327-9, B342, BC). Grove.

Fanqin, Yu, tr. see Lanyun, Liu.

Fanselow, John F. Breaking Rules: Alternatives for Language Teachers. (English As a Second Language Bk.). 1985. pap. text ed. 17.95x (ISBN 0-582-79733-0). Longman.

Fanselow, John F. & Light, Richard Li, eds. Bilingual, ESOL & Foreign Language Teacher Preparation: Models, Practices, Issues. 263p. 1978. 9.00 (ISBN 0-318-16633-X). Tchrs Eng Spkrs.

Fanshawe, Elizabeth. Rachel. 28p. (ps-2). 1983. bds. 3.95 (ISBN 0-370-10783-7, Pub by the Bodley Head). Merrimack Pub Cir.

Fanshawe, Richard, tr. see Guarini, Battista.

Fanshel, David. On the Road to Permanency: An Expanded Data Base for Service to Children in Foster Care. (Orig.). 1982. pap. text ed. 18.95 (ISBN 0-87868-141-8, AM-34). Child Welfare.

--Toward More Understanding of Foster Parents. LC 74-28598. 1975. soft bdg. 14.00 (ISBN 0-88247-319-0). R & E Pubs.

Fanshel, David & Moss, Freda. Playback: A Marriage in Jeopardy Examined. LC 72-170925. 1972. 25.00x (ISBN 0-231-03573-X); pap. 14.00x (ISBN 0-231-03574-8); 6 cassettes o.p. 100.00 (ISBN 0-685-00288-8). Columbia U Pr.

Fanshel, David & Shinn, Eugene. Children in Foster Care: A Longitudinal Investigation. LC 77-2872. (Social Work & Social Issues Ser.). 520p. 1978. 42.50x (ISBN 0-231-03576-4). Columbia U Pr.

Fanshel, David, jt. auth. see Jaffee, Benson.

Fanshel, David, ed. Future of Social Work Research. LC 79-92733. 198p. 1980. pap. 12.95 (ISBN 0-87101-084-4). Natl Assn Soc Wkrs.

Fanshell, D., jt. auth. see Labov, W.

Fansler, Dean S. Chaucer & the Roman De la Rose. 1914. 11.25 (ISBN 0-8446-1176-X). Peter Smith.

--Filipino Popular Tales, with Comparative Notes. LC 22-1008. (AFS M). Repr. of 1921 ed. 37.00 (ISBN 0-527-01064-2). Kraus Repr.

Fansler, Harriott E. Evolution of Technic in Elizabethan Tragedy. LC 68-59214. 1968. Repr. of 1914 ed. 10.00x (ISBN 0-87753-014-9). Phaeton.

Fansler, Homer F. History of Tucker County. 1977. Repr. of 1962 ed. 25.00 (ISBN 0-87012-056-5). McClain.

Fant, Ake & Klingborg, Arne. Rudolf Steiner's Sculpture in Dornach. Westerberg, Erik, tr. (Illus.). 85p. (Ger.). 1975. 20.95 (ISBN 0-85440-301-9, Pub. by Steinerbooks). Anthroposophic.

Fant, Clyde. Preaching for Today. 1977. pap. 7.64i (ISBN 0-06-062332-2, RD-204, HarpR). Har-Row.

Fant, Clyde, compiled by. The Best of Open Windows. LC 81-67201. 1981. 7.95 (ISBN 0-8054-5290-7). Broadman.

Fant, Clyde E., Jr., jt. ed. see Pinson, William M., Jr.

Fant, David J., Jr. A. W. Tozer: A Twentieth Century Prophet. LC 64-21945. (Illus.). 180p. 1964. pap. 3.95 (ISBN 0-87509-048-6). Chr Pubns.

Fant, G. & Tatham, M. A. Auditory Analysis & Perception of Speech. 1976. 89.50 (ISBN 0-12-248550-5). Acad. Pr.

Fant, G. & Scully, C., eds. The Larynx & Language. (Phonetica: Vol. 34, No. 4). (Illus.). 1977. 10.25 (ISBN 3-8055-2809-4). S Karger.

Fant, Gunnar. Acoustic Theory of Speech Production. rev. ed. (DACSR Ser.: No. 2). 1970. text ed. 41.00x (ISBN 90-2791-600-4). Mouton.

--Speech Sounds & Features. (Current Studies in Linguistics Ser.: No. 4). 224p. 1974. 30.00x (ISBN 0-262-06051-5). MIT Pr.

Fant, Jesse E., et al. Report Four-Metes & Bounds Descriptions. rev. ed. (Illus.). 161p. (Orig.). 1980. 22.10 (ISBN 0-87518-207-0). Fant-Freeman-Madson.

Fant, Lou. The American Sign Language Book. 9.95. Contemp Bks.

--The American Sign Language Phrase Book. 256p. (Orig.). 1983. pap. 9.95 (ISBN 0-8092-5507-3). Contemp Bks.

Fant, Louie J., Jr. Ameslan-an Introduction to American Sign Language. LC 72-90793. 10.95 (ISBN 0-917002-37-7). Joyce Media.

--Intermediate Sign Language. LC 78-61003. (Illus.). 225p. (gr. 7 up). 1980. text ed. 24.95 (ISBN 0-917002-54-7). Joyce Media.

--Noah. new ed. (Illus.). 14p. 1973. pap. text ed. 5.00 (ISBN 0-917002-70-9). Joyce Media.

--Say It with Hands. (Illus.). 1964. 7.50 (ISBN 0-913072-02-8). Natl Assn Deaf.

--Sign Language: Fourth Most Used Language in the U. S. A. LC 77-93544. (Illus.). 1977. pap. 19.95 (ISBN 0-917002-13-X, 159). Joyce Media.

Fant, Louie, Jr., ed. Noah-in Sign Language. pap. 5.00 (ISBN 0-917002-10-5). Joyce Media.

Fant, Maureen B., jt. ed. see Lefkowitz, Mary R.

Fanta. Christopher G. Marlowe's Agonists: An Approach to the Ambiguity of His Plays. LC 74-143220. (LeBaron Russell Briggs Prize Honors Essays in English Ser: 1970). 1970. pap. 2.50x (ISBN 0-674-55060-9). Harvard U Pr.

Fanta, D. Hormonal Therapy of Acne. (Illus.). viii, 91p. 1980. pap. 20.10 (ISBN 0-387-81586-4). Springer-Verlag.

Fantachi, Roberto, jt. ed. see Flohn, Hermann.

Fantapie, Alain, tr. see Fisher, David & Bragonier, Reginald, Jr.

Fante, John. Ask the Dust. 165p. 1982. 14.00 (ISBN 0-87685-444-7); pap. 6.00 (ISBN 0-87685-443-9). Black Sparrow.

--Dreams from Bunker Hill. 151p. (Orig.). 1982. 14.00 (ISBN 0-87685-529-X); pap. 6.50 (ISBN 0-87685-528-1). Black Sparrow.

--Nineteen Thirty-Three Was a Bad Year. 160p. (Orig.). 1985. 14.00 (ISBN 0-87685-656-3); deluxe ed. 25.00 (ISBN 0-87685-657-1); pap. 8.50 (ISBN 0-87685-655-5). Black Sparrow.

--The Road to Los Angeles. 167p. (Orig.). 1985. 17.50 (ISBN 0-87685-650-4); deluxe ed. 25.00 (ISBN 0-87685-651-2); pap. 10.00 (ISBN 0-87685-649-0). Black Sparrow.

--Wait Until Spring, Bandini. 270p. (Orig.). 1983. 17.50 (ISBN 0-87685-555-9); signed ed. o.p. 25.00 (ISBN 0-87685-556-7); pap. 8.50 (ISBN 0-87685-554-0). Black Sparrow.

--The Wine of Youth: Selected Stories of John Fante. 269p. (Orig.). 1985. 20.00 (ISBN 0-87685-583-4); pap. 10.00 (ISBN 0-87685-582-6). Black Sparrow.

Fantel, Hans. Better Listening. 192p. 1983. pap. 6.95 (ISBN 0-684-17892-3, ScribT). Scribner.

Fantel, Hans, tr. see Lowith, Karl.

Fantham, Elaine. Comparative Studies in Republican Latin Imagery. LC 77-185710. (Phoenix Supplementary Volumes Ser.). 224p. 1972. 22.50x (ISBN 0-8020-5262-2). U of Toronto Pr.

--Seneca's Troades: A Literary Introduction with Text, Translation, & Commentary. LC 82-47592. (Illus.). 465p. 1982. 45.00x (ISBN 0-691-03561-X). Princeton U Pr.

Fanthorpe, Lionel, jt. auth. see Fanthorpe, Patricia.

Fanthorpe, Patricia & Fanthorpe, Lionel. The Black Lion. LC 80-19214. 160p. 1980. lib. bdg. 14.95x (ISBN 0-89370-094-0). Borgo Pr.

--The Holy Grail Revealed: The Real Secret of Rennes-le-Chateau. LC 82-4303. 128p. 1982. Repr. lib. bdg. 15.95x (ISBN 0-89370-660-4). Borgo Pr.

Fanthorpe, U. A., et al. The Crystal Zoo. 48p. (gr. 5-9). 1985. 9.95 (ISBN 0-19-276054-8, Pub. by Oxford U Pr Childrens). Merrimack Pub Cir.

Fanti, R., et al, eds. VLBI & Compact Radio Sources. 1984. lib. bdg. 54.00 (ISBN 90-277-1739-7, Pub. by Reidel Holland); pap. 24.50 (ISBN 90-277-1740-0). Kluwer Academic.

Fanti, Silvio. Against Marriage. LC 77-9218. 1978. 7.95 (ISBN 0-8022-2215-3). Philos Lib.

Fantin, Mario. Mani Rimdu-Nepal: The Buddhist Dance Drama of Tengpoche (1976) (Illus.). 1978. 40.00 (ISBN 0-685-87094-4). Heinman.

Fantini, Beatriz C. de see Moran, Patrick R.

Fantini, Girolamo. Modo per imparare a Sonare di Tromba. Tarr, Edward H., tr. LC 75-17501. (Brass Research Ser.: No. 7). (Illus.). 1978. Repr. of 1638 ed. 25.00 (ISBN 0-914282-10-7). Brass Pr.

Fantini, Mario & Weinstein, Gerald. Toward a Contact Curriculum. 55p. 0.95 (ISBN 0-686-74916-2). ADL.

Fantini, Mario D. & Sinclair, Robert L., eds. Education in School & Nonschool Settings: 84th Yearbook, Pt. I. LC 84-62253. (National Society for the Study of Education Ser.). 320p. 1985. lib. bdg. 20.00x (ISBN 0-226-60139-0, Pub. by Natl Soc Stud Educ). U of Chicago Pr.

Fantino, Edmund & Logan, Cheryl A. The Experimental Analysis of Behavior: A Biological Perspective. LC 78-31685. (Psychology Ser.). (Illus.). 559p. 1979. text ed. 25.95 (ISBN 0-7167-1036-6). W H Freeman.

Fantino, Edmund J. & Reynolds, George S. Introduction to Contemporary Psychology. LC 74-23201. (Illus.). 610p. 1975. text ed. 25.95 (ISBN 0-7167-0761-6); test items avail. W H Freeman.

Fantom, I., ed. see Wind Energy Systems, 2nd International Symposium.

Fantoni, Barrn. Colemanballs Two. (Illus.). 96p. 1984. pap. 3.95 (ISBN 0-233-97700-7, Pub. by Private Eye UK). David & Charles.

Fantoni, Barry. Mike Dime. 208p. 1981. 9.95 (ISBN 0-531-09948-2). Watts.

Fantoni, Barry, ed. Colemanballs. (Illus.). 96p. 1982. pap. 3.95 (ISBN 0-233-97490-3, Pub. by Private Eye UK). David & Charles.

Fanu, J. S. Le see Le Fanu, J. S.

Fanu, J. Sheridan Le see Le Fanu, J. Sheridan.

Fanu, Joseph Le see Le Fanu, Joseph S.

Fanu, Joseph S. Le see Le Fanu, Joseph S.

Fanu, Richard le see Newman, Sasha M., et al.

Fanu, Thomas P. le see Le Fanu, Thomas P.

Fanu, Thomas P. le see Peet, Henry.

Fanu, William Le see Le Fanu, William.

Fanu, William R. Le see Le Fanu, William R.

FAO. Advances in Aquaculture. 1978. 150.00 (ISBN 0-685-63391-8). State Mutual Bk.

--European Inland Water Fish. 1978. 35.00 (ISBN 0-685-63401-9). State Mutual Bk.

FAO & IAEA. Laboratory Training Manual on Radioimmunoassay in Animal Reproduction. (Technical Report Ser.: No. 233). 269p. (Orig.). 1984. pap. text ed. 45.00 (ISBN 92-0-115084-9, IDC233, IAEA). Unipub.

FAO & ILO. Chainsaws in Tropical Forests. (Training Ser.: No. 2). 96p. 1980. pap. 10.25 (ISBN 92-5-100932-5, F2116, FAO). Unipub.

FAO Conference, 11th Session, Rome, 1961. Report on the 11th Session of the FAO Conference: Romans, Italy, 1961. 1962. pap. 4.50 (ISBN 0-685-36331-7, F358, FAO). Unipub.

FAO Conference, 12th Session, Rome, 1963. Report of the Twelfth Session of the FAO: Rome, Italy, 1963. 1964. pap. 4.50 (ISBN 0-685-36332-5, F366, FAO). Unipub.

FAO Executive Director. Report on the World Food Program. 1965. pap. 4.50 (ISBN 0-685-36329-5, F397, FAO). Unipub.

FAO Fisheries Department. FAO Fisheries Department List of Publications & Documents: 1948-1978. 3rd, Rev. ed. (Fisheries Reports: No. 100). 241p. 1979. pap. 7.50 (ISBN 0-686-93225-0, F2053, FAO). Unipub.

FAO Fisheries Technology Service & Hamabe, Mototsugu, eds. Squid Jigging from Small Boats. 84p. 1982. 42.95x (ISBN 0-85238-122-0, Pub. by Fishing News England). State Mutual Bk.

FAO-IAEA-WHO Expert Committee. Geneva, 1969. Wholesomeness of Irradiated Food with Special Reference to Wheat, Potatoes & Onions: Report. (Technical Report Ser.: No. 451). (Also avail. in French & Spanish). 1970. pap. 2.00 (ISBN 92-4-120451-6). World Health.

FAO In-Service Consultation on Middle-Level Training in Agricultural Marketing in African & Near East Countries, Nairobi, Kenya, 1974. Training in Agricultural & Food Marketing at Middle Level: Report. (Development Documents: No. 12). 99p. 1974. pap. 7.50 (ISBN 0-686-92717-6, F1228, FAO). Unipub.

FAO Nutrition Meetings. Specifications for the Identity & Purity of Some Food Additives: Including Food Colors, Flavour Enhancers, Thickening Agents, & Others. (Nutrition Meetings Reports: No. 54b). 216p. 1976. pap. 22.00 (ISBN 0-685-66331-0, F1181, FAO). Unipub.

FAO Regional Population Workshop for Latin America, Santiago, Chile, 1974. Summary Report. (Illus.). 40p. 1976. pap. 7.50 (ISBN 0-685-66343-4, F1214, FAO). Unipub.

FAO-WHO Ad Hoc Expert Committee. Rome, 1971. Energy & Protein Requirements: Report. (Technical Report Ser.: No. 522). (Also avail. in French). 1973. pap. 3.20 (ISBN 92-4-120522-9). World Health.

FAO-WHO Esperts on Pesticide Residues. Geneva, 1975. Pesticide Residues in Food: Report. (Technical Report Ser.: No. 592). (Also avail. in French & Spanish). 1976. pap. 2.40 (ISBN 92-4-120592-X). World Health.

FAO-WHO Expert Committee on Food Additives. Rome, 1974, 18th. Evaluation of Certain Food Additives: Report. (Technical Report Ser.: No. 557). (Also avail. in French & Spanish). 1974. pap. 2.00 (ISBN 92-4-120557-1). World Health.

FAO-WHO Expert Committee on Food Additives. Geneva, 1972, 16th. Evaluation of Certain Food Additives & the Contaminants Mercury, Lead, & Cadmium: Report. (Technical Report Ser.: No. 505). (Also avail. in French & Spanish). 1972. pap. 1.60 (ISBN 92-4-120505-9). World Health.

FAO-WHO Expert Committee on Food Additives. Geneva, 1975, 19th. Evaluation of Certain Food Additives; Some Food Colours, Thickening Agents, Smoke Condensates & Certain Other Substances: Report. (Technical Report Ser.: No. 576). (Also avail. in French & Spanish). 1975. pap. 2.00 (ISBN 92-4-120576-8). World Health.

FAO-WHO Expert Committee on Food Additives. Rome, 1971, 15th. Evaluation of Food Additives. Some Enzymes, Modified Starches & Certain Other Substances; Toxicological Evaluations & Specifications & a Review of the Technological Efficacy of Some Antioxidants: Report. (Technical Report Ser.: No. 488). (Also avail. in French, Russian & Spanish). 1972. pap. 1.60 (ISBN 92-4-120488-5). World Health.

FAO-WHO Expert Committee on Food Additives. Geneva, 1970, 14th. Evaluation of Food Additives: Specifications for the Identity & Purity of Food Additives & Their Toxocological Evaluation: Some Extraction Solvents & Certain Other Substances & a Review of the Technological Efficacy of Some Antimicrobial Agent: Report. (Technical Report Ser.: No. 462). (Also avail. in French, Russian & Spanish). 1971. pap. 2.00 (ISBN 92-4-120462-1). World Health.

FAO-WHO Expert Committee on Food Additives. Rome, 1973, 17th. Toxicological Evaluation of Certain Food Additives with a Review of General Principles & of Specifications: Report. (Technical Report Ser.: No. 539). (Also avail. in French & Spanish). 1974. pap. 2.00 (ISBN 92-4-120539-3). World Health.

FAO-WHO Expert Committee on Nutrition, Rome, 1974, 9th. Food & Nutrition Strategies in National Development: Report. (Technical Report Ser.: No. 584). (Also avail. in French & Spanish). 1976. pap. 2.80 (ISBN 92-4-120584-9). World Health.

FAO-WHO Expert Committee on Veterinary Public Health. Geneva, 1974. Veterinary Contribution to Public Health Practice: Report. (Technical Report Ser.: No. 573). (Also avail. in French & Spanish). 1975. pap. 3.20 (ISBN 92-4-120573-3). World Health.

FAO-WHO Experts on Pesticide Residues. Evaluation of Some Pesticide Residues in Food: Monographs. Incl. 1971. (No. 1). 1972. pap. 6.00 (ISBN 92-4-166501-7, 688); 1972. (No. 2). 1973. pap. 10.00 (ISBN 92-4-166502-5); 1973. (No. 3). 1974. pap. 8.40 (ISBN 92-4-166503-3); 1974. (No. 4). 1975. pap. 19.20 (ISBN 92-4-166504-1). (Pesticide Residues Ser.). (Also avail. in French). pap. World Health.

FAO-WHO Experts on Pesticide Residues. Geneva, 1968. Pesticide Residues in Food: Report. (Technical Report Ser.: No. 417). (Also avail. in French & Spanish). 1969. pap. 2.00 (ISBN 92-4-120417-6). World Health.

FAO-WHO Experts on Pesticide Residues. Rome, 1969. Pesticide Residues in Food: Report. (Technical Report Ser.: No. 458). (Also avail. in French, Russian & Spanish). 1970. pap. 2.00 (ISBN 92-4-120458-3). World Health.

FAO-WHO Experts on Pesticide Residues. Rome, 1970. Pesticide Residues in Food: Report. (Technical Report Ser.: No. 474). (Also avail. in French & Spanish). 1971. pap. 2.00 (ISBN 92-4-120474-5). World Health.

FAO-WHO Experts on Pesticide Residues. Geneva, 1971. Pesticide Residues in Food: Report. (Technical Report Ser.: No. 502). (Also avail. in French, Russian & Spanish). 1972. pap. 1.60 (ISBN 92-4-120502-4). World Health.

FAO-WHO Experts on Pesticide Residues. Rome, 1972. Pesticide Residues in Food: Report. (Technical Report Ser.: No. 525). (Also avail. in french & spanish). 1973. pap. 1.60 (ISBN 92-4-120525-3). World Health.

FAO-WHO Experts on Pesticide Residues. Geneva, 1973. Pesticide Residues in Food: Report. (Technical Report Ser.: No. 545). (Also avail. in French, Russian & Spanish). 1974. pap. 2.40 (ISBN 92-4-120545-8). World Health.

FAO-WHO Experts on Pesticide Residues. Rome, 1975. Pesticide Residues in Food: Report. (Technical Report Ser.: No. 574). (Also avail. in French & Spanish). 1975. pap. 2.40 (ISBN 92-4-120574-1). World Health.

FAO-WHO Joint Committee Expert Committee on Nutrition, 8th. Proceedings. (Technical Report Ser: No. 477). 80p. 1971. pap. 2.00 (ISBN 92-4-120477-X, 413). World Health.

FAO-WHO Joint Expert Committee, Geneva, 1968. African Trypanosomiasis: A Report. (Technical Report Ser: No. 434). 79p. 1969. pap. 2.00 (ISBN 92-4-120434-6, 1541). World Health.

FAO-WHO Joint Expert Committee on Food Additives, Geneva, 1975. Evaluation of Certain Food Additives: 19th Report of the Joint FAO-WHO Expert Committee on Food Additives, Geneva, 1975. (Nutrition Meetings Reports: No. 55). 23p. 1975. pap. 4.75 (ISBN 92-5-101811-1, F129, FAO). Unipub.

FAO - WHO Joint Expert Committee on Food Additives. Evaluation of Mercury, Lead, Cadmium & Food Additives Amaranth, Diethylpyrocarbonate, & Octyl Gallate. (WHO Food Additives Ser: No. 4). 84p. 1972. pap. 2.40 (ISBN 92-4-166004-X). World Health.

FAO-WHO Joint Expert Committee on Food Additives, 1st Session, Rome, 1956. General Principles Governing the Use of Food Additives: Report. (Nutrition Meetings Reports: No. 15). 22p. 1957. pap. 4.50 (ISBN 92-5-101824-3, F376, FAO). Unipub.

FAO - WHO Joint Expert Committee on Food Additives. Review of the Technological Efficiency of Some Antioxidants & Synergists. (WHO Food Additives Ser: No. 3). 144p. 1972. pap. 3.20 (ISBN 92-4-166003-1). World Health.

--Specifications for the Identity & Purity of Some Enzymes & Certain Other Substances. (WHO Food Additives Ser: Vol. 2). 174p. 1972. pap. 3.60 (ISBN 92-4-166002-3). World Health.

--Toxicological Evaluation of Some Enzymes, Modified Starches & Certain Other Substances. (WHO Food Additives Ser: Vol. 1). 109p. 1972. pap. 2.40 (ISBN 92-4-166001-5). World Health.

FAO-WHO Joint Expert Committee on Milk Hygeine, 3rd, Geneva, 1969. Report. (Technical Report Ser: No. 453). 82p. 1970. pap. 2.00 (ISBN 92-4-120453-2, 1144). World Health.

FAO-WHO Joint Expert Committee on Milk Hygiene 1st, Geneva, 1956. Report. (Technical Report Ser: No. 124). 54p. (Eng. & Span.). 1957. pap. 1.20 (ISBN 92-4-120124-X). World Health.

FAO-WHO Joint Expert Committee on Zoonoses, 3rd, Geneva, 1966. Report. (Technical Report Ser: No. 378). 127p. (Eng, Fr, Rus, & Span.). 1968. pap. 2.80 (ISBN 92-4-120378-1). World Health.

FAO-WHO Meeting. Geneva, 1974. Use of Mercury & Alternative Compounds As Seed Dressings: Report. (Technical Report Ser.: No. 555). (Also avail. in French & Spanish). 1974. pap. 2.00 (ISBN 92-4-120555-5). World Health.

FAO-WHO Meeting on Insect Viruses. Geneva, 1972. Use of Viruses for the Control of Insect Pests & Disease Vectors: Report. (Technical Report Ser.: No. 531). (Also avail. in French & Spanish). 1973. pap. 1.60 (ISBN 92-4-120531-8). World Health.

Faolain, Sean O. The Short Story. 269p. 1983. pap. 6.95 (ISBN 0-85342-302-4, Pub. by Mercier Pr Ireland). Irish Bks Media.

Faolain, Turlough. Blood on the Harp: Irish Rebel History in Ballad. LC 83-61046. 510p. 1983. 28.50 (ISBN 0-87875-275-7); pap. 15.00 (ISBN 0-87875-276-5). Whitston Pub.

Faqih, I. Glimpses of Islamic History. 16.50 (ISBN 0-686-63900-6). Kazi Pubns.

Faquet, E. Flaubert. lib. bdg. 59.95 (ISBN 0-8490-0179-9). Gordon Pr.

Far Eastern Economic Review, ed. Asia Yearbook, 1981. (Illus.). 284p. (Orig.). 1980. pap. 14.95x (ISBN 962-7010-10-3). Intl Pubns Serv.

--Asia Yearbook, 1982. (Illus.). 280p. (Orig.). 1981. pap. 14.50x (ISBN 962-7010-11-1). Intl Pubns Serv.

--Asia Yearbook, 1983. LC 74-641208. (Illus.). 296p. 1983. pap. 17.50 (ISBN 962-7010-14-6). Intl Pubns Serv.

Far Eastern Economic Review Limited Staff, compiled by. All Asia Guide. 13th ed. LC 75-320378. (Illus.). 704p. (Orig.). 1985. pap. 11.95 (ISBN 0-8048-1478-3, Pub. by Far Eastern Economic Review Hong Kong). C E Tuttle.

Far West Editions. The Birthday Book. 46p. 1982. text ed. 10.00 (ISBN 0-686-47071-0). Far West Edns.

--Material for Thought, No.7. LC 77-89507. 76p. 1977. pap. 2.50 (ISBN 0-914480-03-0). Far West Edns.

--Material for Thought, No. 8. LC 79-56899. 88p. 1979. pap. 2.95 (ISBN 0-914480-05-7). Far West Edns.

--Material for Thought, No. 9. LC 81-68048. 94p. 1981. pap. 3.95 (ISBN 0-914480-07-3). Far West Edns.

--Material for Thought, Vol.74 & 76, Nos. 7 & 8. Bound Vol. pap. 7.95 (ISBN 0-686-47075-3). Far West Edns.

--Material For Thought: Spring 1976. LC 73-94407. 1976. pap. 2.95 (ISBN 0-914480-02-2). Far West Edns.

--Material for Thought: 1970. 31p. 1970. pap. 0.50 (ISBN 0-686-47079-6). Far West Edns.

--Material for Thought: 1971. 47p. 1971. pap. 0.50 (ISBN 0-686-47081-8). Far West Edns.

--Material for Thought: 1972. 63p. 1972. pap. 0.50 (ISBN 0-686-47082-6). Far West Edns.

--Material for Thought: 1974. LC 73-94407. 114p. 1974. pap. 2.00 (ISBN 0-914480-01-4). Far West Edns.

--Material for Thought: 1983. LC 73-94407. 96p. 1983. pap. 4.95 (ISBN 0-317-17277-8). Far West Edns.

--Speaking of My Life. 149p. 1979. pap. 4.95 (ISBN 0-686-47084-2). Far West Edns.

Fara, Patricia. Computers: How They Work & What They Do. (Illus.). 48p. 1983. 9.95 (ISBN 0-7207-1343-9, Pub. by Michael Joseph). Merrimack Pub Cir.

Farabee, W. C. Indian Tribes of Eastern Peru. (HU PMP). 1922. 22.00 (ISBN 0-527-01216-5). Kraus Repr.

--Inheritance of Digital Malformation in Man. (Harvard University Peabody Museum of Archaeology & Ethnology Papers Ser). pap. 10.00 (ISBN 0-527-01194-0). Kraus Repr.

Farace, Richard V., et al. Communicating...& Organizing. 204p. 1976. text ed. 22.95 (ISBN 0-394-34968-7, RanC). Random.

Faraci, Piero. Expenditures, Staff, & Salaries of Planning Agencies. (PAS Reports: No. 245). 55p. 1969. 6.00 (ISBN 0-318-12986-8). Am Plan Assn.

Faraday. Faraday's Chemical History of a Candle: Six Illustrated Lectures with Notes & Experiments. (Science Alive Ser.). (Illus.). 150p. 1980. cancelled 10.00x (ISBN 0-914090-86-0); pap. 6.95x (ISBN 0-914090-87-9). Chicago Review.

Faraday, Ann. The Dream Game. 1976. pap. 4.33i (ISBN 0-06-080371-1, P371, PL). Har-Row.

--Dream Power. 320p. 1984. pap. 3.50 (ISBN 0-425-07443-9). Berkley Pub.

Faraday, Lucy W. Edda I: The Divine Mythology of the North, 2: The Heroic Mythology of the North, 2 Vols. in 1. (Popular Studies in Mythology, Romance & Folklore: Nos. 12 & 13). Repr. of 1902 ed. 11.00 (ISBN 0-404-53512-7). AMS Pr.

Faraday, M. & Porter, G. Chemical Manipulation. (Royal Institution Library of Science). (Illus.). 656p. 1974. 24.00 (ISBN 0-85334-596-1, Pub. by Elsevier Applied Sci England). Elsevier.

Faraday, Winifred, tr. The Druidic Triads, or the Wisdom of the Cymry. 1984. pap. 4.95 (ISBN 0-916411-85-0, Pub. by Sure Fire). Holmes Pub.

Farag, Fahmy. The Opposing Virtues: Two Essays. (New Yeats Papers: No. 15). 1978. pap. text ed. 9.75x (ISBN 0-85105-323-8, Dolmen Pr). Humanities.

Farag, Ihab H. & Melsheimer, Stephen S., eds. Fundamentals & Applications of Solar Energy, Pt. II. LC 80-16305. (AIChE Symposium Ser.: Vol. 77). 96p. 1981. pap. 32.00 (ISBN 0-8169-0218-6, S-210); pap. 17.00 members (ISBN 0-686-47540-2). Am Inst Chem Eng.

Farag, M. M. Materials & Process Selection in Engineering. (Illus.). 320p. 1979. 63.00 (ISBN 0-85334-824-3, Pub. by Elsevier Applied Sci England). Elsevier.

--Materials & Process Selection in Engineering. (Illus.). 320p. 1979. 64.00 (ISBN 0-686-48182-8, 0704). T-C Pubns CA.

Farag, Mahmoud, ed. Aluminium Industry in Egypt: Proceedings. 352p. pap. 24.00 (ISBN 0-9911001-5-8, Pub. by Aluminium W Germany). Heyden.

Faraggi, H. & Ricci, R. A. Nuclear Spectroscopy & Nuclear Reactions with Heavy Ions. (Enrico Fermi Summer School of Physics: No. 62). 596p. 1976. 123.50 (ISBN 0-7204-0450-9, North-Holland). Elsevier.

Faragher, John M. Women & Men on the Overland Trail. LC 78-10290. (Yale Historical Publications, Miscellany Ser.: No. 121). 304p. 1979. 31.00x (ISBN 0-300-02267-0); pap. 8.95x (ISBN 0-300-02605-6). Yale U Pr.

Farago. Handbook of Dimensional Measurement. (Illus.). 400p. 39.95 (ISBN 0-318-13215-X, P61). Am Soc QC.

Farago, Francis T. Abrasive Methods Engineering, Vol. 1. LC 76-14970. (Illus.). 366p. 1976. 45.00 (ISBN 0-8311-1112-7). Indus Pr.

--Abrasive Methods Engineering, Vol. 2. LC 76-14970. (Illus.). 508p. 1980. 55.00 (ISBN 0-8311-1134-8). Indus Pr.

--Handbook of Dimensional Measurement. 2nd ed. (Illus.). 524p. 1982. 45.00 (ISBN 0-8311-1136-4). Indus Pr.

Farago, Ladislas. Aftermath. 1975. pap. 1.95 (ISBN 0-380-00407-0, 25387). Avon.

--The Last Days of Patton. 352p. 1981. 12.95 (ISBN 0-07-019940-X). McGraw.

--Patton: Ordeal & Triumph. (Illus.). 1964. 25.00 (ISBN 0-8392-1084-1). Astor-Honor.

--Tenth Fleet. 1962. 19.95 (ISBN 0-8392-1112-0). Astor-Honor.

--War of Wits: The Anatomy of Espionage & Intelligence. LC 75-31362. (Illus.). 379p. 1976. Repr. of 1954 ed. lib. bdg. 32.50x (ISBN 0-8371-8518-1, FAWW). Greenwood.

Farago, Ladislas & Sinclair, Andrew. Royal Web: The Story of Princess Victoria & Frederick of Prussia. (Illus.). 384p. 1982. 12.95 (ISBN 0-07-019941-8). McGraw.

Farago, Ladislas, ed. German Psychological Warfare. LC 72-4666. (International Propaganda & Communications Ser.). 302p. 1972. Repr. of 1942 ed. 24.50 (ISBN 0-405-04747-9). Ayer Co Pubs.

Farah, Badie, jt. auth. see Sharifi, Mohsen.

Farah, C. & Lobban, R. Three Studies on National Integration in the Arab World. (Information Papers: No. 12). 34p. (Orig.). 1974. pap. text ed. 2.75 (ISBN 0-937694-28-2). Assn Arab-Amer U Grads.

Farah, Caesar E. The Dhayl in Medieval Arabic Historiography. (American Oriental Society Essays: 6). 1967. pap. 3.00 (ISBN 0-940490-96-X). Am Orient Soc.

--Islam: Beliefs & Observances. rev. ed. LC 72-135505. (Orig.). (YA) 1970. pap. 6.50 (ISBN 0-8120-0277-6). Barron.

Farah, Charles, Jr. From the Pinnacle of the Temple. LC 79-89218. 1979. (Pub. by Logos); pap. 4.95 (ISBN 0-88270-462-1). Bridge Pub.

Farah, Cynthia & Nickerson, Marina. Country Music: A Look at the Men Who've Made It. LC 81-70858. 88p. pap. 8.95 (ISBN 0-9607514-0-8). C M Pub.

Farah, Madelain. Lebanese Cuisine. 1979. 8.00 (ISBN 0-89955-011-8, Pub. by Madelain Farah); pap. 6.50 (ISBN 0-89955-202-1, Pub. by Madelain Farah). Intl Spec Bk.

--Lebanese Cuisine. 6th, rev. ed. 1982. spiral binding 8.50 (ISBN 0-9603050-1-7); pap. 6.95 (ISBN 0-9603050-2-5). Lebanese Cuisine.

--Marriage & Sexuality in Islam: A Translation of al-Ghazali's Book on the Etiquette of Marriage from the Ihya' 192p. 1984. 20.00x (ISBN 0-87480-231-8). U of Utah Pr.

Farah, Madelain & Habib, Leila. Pocket Bread Potpourri: Meals in Minutes. 112p. 1984. spiral bdg. 8.95 (ISBN 0-9603050-3-3). Lebanese Cuisine.

Farah, Mark G., jt. auth. see Mikesell, Raymond F.

Farah, Nuruddin. From a Crooked Rib. (African Writers Ser.). 1970. pap. text ed. 4.50x (ISBN 0-435-90080-3). Heinemann Ed.

--A Naked Needle. (African Writers Ser.). 1976. pap. text ed. 6.00x (ISBN 0-435-90184-2). Heinemann Ed.

--Sardines. 256p. 1982. 13.95 (ISBN 0-8052-8126-6, Pub. by Allison & Busby England). Schocken.

--Sweet & Sour Milk. (African Writers Ser.: No. 226). 237p. (Orig.). 1980. pap. text ed. 6.00x (ISBN 0-435-90226-1). Heinemann Ed.

Farah, Nuruddin see Nuruddin, Farah.

Farah, T. T., ed. Crisis in Lebanon. LC 84-40572. 240p. cancelled (ISBN 0-312-17391-1). St Martin.

Farah, Tawfic E., ed. Political Behavior in the Arab States. 240p. 1983. lib. bdg. 24.50x (ISBN 0-86531-524-8); pap. text ed. 11.50x (ISBN 0-86531-525-6). Westview.

Farah, Victor W., jt. auth. see Horn, Frederick F.

Faral, Edmond. Jongleurs En France Au Moyen Age. LC 79-140971. (Research & Source Works Ser.: No. 606). 1971. Repr. of 1910 ed. 23.50 (ISBN 0-8337-1099-0). B Franklin.

--Mimes Francais Du XIIIe Siecle: Contribution a L'histoire Du Theatre Comique Au Moyen Age. LC 77-178533. Repr. of 1910 ed. 20.00 (ISBN 0-404-56599-9). AMS Pr.

--Recherches Sur les Sources Latines Des Contes et Romans Courtois Du Moyen Age. LC 72-178580. Repr. of 1913 ed. 35.00 (ISBN 0-404-56600-6). AMS Pr.

Faral, Edmond, ed. La Legende Arthurienne, 3 vols. Incl. Tome I: Des Origines a Geoffroy de Monmouth; Tome II: Geoffroy de Monmouth; Tome III: Documents. LC 75-178511. (Fr.). Repr. of 1929 ed. 35.00 ea. Vol. 1 (ISBN 0-404-56516-6). Vol. 2 (ISBN 0-404-56517-4). Vol. 3 (ISBN 0-404-56518-2). Set. 105.00 (ISBN 0-404-56515-8). AMS Pr.

Faramazian, R. Desarme y La Economia. 208p. (Span.). 1982. 4.95 (ISBN 0-8285-2499-8, Pub. by Progress Pubs USSR). Imported Pubns.

Faramazyan, R. U. S. A. Militarism & Economy. 271p. 1974. 4.45 (ISBN 0-8285-0387-7, Pub. by Progress Pubs USSR). Imported Pubns.

Faramazyan, R. A. U. S. A. Militarism & the Economy - A Soviet View. 271p. 1975. 12.95x (ISBN 0-8464-0941-0). Beekman Pubs.

Faramund, L. E. Von. Die Glueckseligste Insul Auf der Ganzen Welt. 260p. Repr. of 1728 ed. 30.00 (ISBN 0-384-15133-7). Johnson Repr.

Faraone, Joseph J. & Stewart, Jane L. Paraclete Power: A Study Guide for the Acts of the Apostles. LC 77-16475. 1978. pap. 3.50 (ISBN 0-8189-0361-9). Alba.

Fararo, Thomas J. Mathematical Ideas & Sociological Theory. 175p. 1984. text ed. 24.50 (ISBN 0-677-16635-4). Gordon.

--Mathematical Sociology: An Introduction to Fundamentals. LC 78-2379. 830p. 1978. Repr. of 1973 ed. lib. bdg. 41.50 (ISBN 0-88275-664-8). Krieger.

Farau, Alfred. I Long for a New Humanity. Solann, Evelyn, tr. from Ger. Orig. Title: Wo ist die Jugend, die ich rufe? 87p. 1981. pap. 4.95 (ISBN 0-9607886-0-3). Echo Stage Co.

Faraud, Henri J. Dix-Huit Ans Chez Les Sauvages: Voyages Et Missions De Monseigneur Henry Faraud. Repr. of 1866 ed. 28.00 (ISBN 0-384-15135-3). Johnson Repr.

--Dix-Huit Ans Chez les Sauvages: Voyages et Missions De Mgr. Henry Faraud Paris-Bruxelles 1866. (Canadiana Avant 1867: No.12). 1966. 26.00x (ISBN 90-2796-329-0). Mouton.

Farb, Nathan. The Adirondacks. (Illus.). 184p. 35.00 (ISBN 0-8478-0583-2); pap. 19.95 (ISBN 0-8478-0584-0). Rizzoli Intl.

Farb, Peter. Word Play. 432p. 1975. pap. 5.95 (ISBN 0-553-24908-8). Bantam.

--Word Play. 1973. 16.95 (ISBN 0-394-48675-7). Knopf.

Farb, Peter & Armelagos, George. Consuming Passions: The Anthropology of Eating. 1983. pap. 4.95 (ISBN 0-671-43420-9). WSP.

Farb, Peter, jt. auth. see Hay, John.

Farb, Robert L. Administration of Justice Memoranda: Juvenile Interrogation Warnings Required for 16 & 17 Year-Olds, No. 83-06. LC 84-621362. 1983. 2.00. U of NC Inst Gov.

Farb, Robert L., jt. ed. see Brannon, Joan G.

Farb, Roderick. Shipwrecks: Diving the Graveyard of the Atlantic. Williams, Barbara E., ed. (Illus., Orig.). 1985. pap. 12.95 (ISBN 0-89732-034-4). Menasha Ridge.

Farb, Stanley N. Otolaryngology. 5th ed. (Medical Exam Review Bks.: Vol. 16). 1983. pap. text ed. 25.00 (ISBN 0-87488-116-1). Med Exam.

--Otorhinolaryngology. 3rd ed. (Medical Outline Ser.). pap. text ed. 25.00 (ISBN 0-87488-661-9). Med Exam.

Farber & Fisher. Toxic Injury of the Liver, Pt. A. (Liver: Normal Function & Disease Ser.: Vol. 2). 1979. 75.00 (ISBN 0-8247-6838-8). Dekker.

--Toxic Injury of the Liver, Pt. B. (Liver: Normal Function & Disease: Vol. 2). 1979. 65.00 (ISBN 0-8247-6839-6). Dekker.

Farber, jt. auth. see Knoepfel.

Farber, Ann, et al. A Brief Course in Arithmetic. 213p. 1985. pap. text ed. 21.95 (ISBN 0-912675-08-X); manual avail. (ISBN 0-912675-10-1). Ardsley.

Farber, Anne & Rogler, LLoyd H. Unitas: Hispanic & Black Children in a Healing Community. 144p. 1982. pap. 8.95 (ISBN 0-87073-506-3). Schenkman Bks Inc.

Farber, B. Conceptions of Kinship. 29.95 (ISBN 0-444-99076-3, FCN/, Pub. by Elsevier). Greenwood.

--Effects of a Severely Mentally Retarded Child on Family Integration. (SRCD M). 1959. pap. 16.00 (ISBN 0-527-01578-4). Kraus Repr.

--Family Organization and Crisis: Maintenance of Integration in Families with a Severely Mentally Retarded Child. (SRCD M). 1960. pap. 15.00 (ISBN 0-527-01583-0). Kraus Repr.

Farber, Barry A., ed. Stress & Burnout in the Human Service Professions. (Pergamon General Psychology Ser.). (Illus.). 272p. 1983. 25.00 (ISBN 0-08-028801-4). Pergamon.

Farber, Carol R., jt. auth. see Levy, Wilbert J.

Farber, Daniel A., jt. auth. see Findley, Roger W.

Farber, David J., jt. auth. see Uhlig, Ronald P.

Farber, Donald C. Producing Theatre: A Comprehensive Legal & Business Guide. LC 81-1025. 384p. 1981. 17.95x (ISBN 0-89676-051-0). Drama Bk.

Farber, Donald C. & Baumgarten, Paul. Producing, Financing, & Distributing Film. LC 72-87054. 224p. 1973. pap. 15.95x (ISBN 0-89676-075-8). Drama Bk.

Farber, E., ed. The Pathology of Transcription & Translation. (Biochemistry of Disease Ser: Vol. 2). 192p. 1972. 37.50 (ISBN 0-8247-1180-7). Dekker.

Farber, Eugene, et al, eds. Psoriasis: Proceedings of the Third International Symposium. 560p. 1982. 54.50 (ISBN 0-8089-1472-3, 791225). Grune.

Farber, Eugene M., ed. see International Symposium on Psoriasis-Stanford University, 1971.

Farber, Evan, intro. by. Combined Retrospective Index to Book Reviews in Humanities Journals 1802-1974, 10 Vols. 1983. 1250.00 (ISBN 0-89235-061-X). Res Pubns Conn.

Farber, Evan I. Classified List of Periodicals for the College Library. 5th rev. ed. LC 72-76264. (The Useful Reference Ser. of Library Bks: Vol. 99). 1972. lib. bdg. 15.00x (ISBN 0-87305-099-1). Faxon.

--Combined Retrospective Index to Book Reviews in Scholarly Journals, 1886-1974, 15 vols. LC 79-89137. 1979. lib. bdg. 1650.00 (ISBN 0-8408-0172-6). Res Pubns Conn.

Farber, Evan I. & Walling, Ruth. The Academic Library: Essays in Honor of Guy R. Lyle. LC 74-2098. 183p. 1974. 15.00 (ISBN 0-8108-0712-2). Scarecrow.

Farber, Jason E. & Barger, Geoffrey R. Bulls, Bears & Dogs. LC 84-70878. 160p. 1984. 13.95 (ISBN 0-918301-00-9); pap. 7.95 (ISBN 0-918301-25-4). Albright.

Farber, Jerry. Field Guide to the Aesthetic Experience. LC 82-83129. 284p. (Orig.). 1982. pap. 5.95x (ISBN 0-943292-15-8). Foreworks.

Farber, Joan, jt. auth. see Farber, Rose.

Farber, Joseph & Hope, Henry. Palladio's Architecture & Its Influences: A Photographic Guide. (Illus.). 1980. pap. 6.95 (ISBN 0-486-23922-5). Dover.

Farber, Joseph C. & Reed, Henry H. Palladio's Architecture & Its Influence: A Photographic Guide. 17.00 (ISBN 0-8446-5759-X). Peter Smith.

Farber, Lawrence. Estate Planning Strategies for Physicians. 200p. 1985. pap. 18.95 (ISBN 0-87489-256-2). Med Economics.
--Tax Strategy for Physicians. 3rd ed. 300p. 1985. 24.95 (ISBN 0-87489-387-9). Med Economics.
Farber, Lawrence, ed. Medical Economics Encyclopedia of Practice & Financial Management. 1984. 69.95 (ISBN 0-87489-343-7). Med Economics.
--Personal Money Management For Physicians. 3rd ed. 264p. 1981. casebound 24.95 (ISBN 0-87489-253-8). Med Economics.
Farber, Marjorie. Excerpts from...The Romantic Method. Rasch, Alexis & Royse, David, eds. (Orig.). 1983. pap. 2.00 (ISBN 0-916965-01-5). Beaux-Arts Pr.
--The Human Organism: Half Animal, Half Machine. 56p. (Orig.). 1983. pap. 3.95 (ISBN 0-916965-00-7). Beaux Arts.
Farber, Marvin. Naturalism & Subjectivism. LC 59-11896. 1959. pap. 19.95x (ISBN 0-87395-036-4). State U NY Pr.
--The Search for an Alternative: Philosophical Perspectives of Subjectivism & Marxism. LC 83-23448. 238p. 1984. 25.00 (ISBN 0-8122-7921-2). U of Pa Pr.
Farber, Marvin, ed. Philosophic Thought in France & the United States: Essays Representing Major Trends in Contemporary French & American Philosophy. pap. 160.00 (ISBN 0-317-09067-4, 2010107). Bks Demand UMI.
--Philosophical Essays in Memory of Edmund Husserl. LC 68-19270. Repr. of 1968 ed. lib. bdg. 18.25x (ISBN 0-8371-0071-2, FAPE). Greenwood.
Farber, Maurice L. Theory of Suicide. Kastenbaum, Robert, ed. LC 76-19568. (Death & Dying Ser.). 1977. Repr. of 1968 ed. lib. bdg. 17.00x (ISBN 0-405-09564-3). Ayer Co Pubs.
Farber, Norma. All Those Mothers at the Manger. LC 85-42610. (Illus.). 32p. (ps-1). 1985. 11.06i (ISBN 0-06-021869-X); PLB 10.89g (ISBN 0-06-021870-3). HArpJ.
--How Does It Feel to Be Old? 3rd ed. LC 79-11516. (Illus.). 36p. 1981. pap. 4.95 (ISBN 0-916870-42-1). Creative Arts Bk.
--How Does It Feel to Be Old? LC 79-11516. (Illus.). (ps-3). 1979. 9.95 (ISBN 0-525-32414-3, Unicorn Bk.). Dutton.
--How the Hibernators Came to Bethlehem. LC 80-7685. (Illus.). 32p. (gr. k-3). 1980. PLB 7.85 (ISBN 0-8027-6353-7). Walker & Co.
--How the Left-Behind Beasts Built Ararat. LC 77-14650. (Illus.). (gr. 1-3). 1978. 7.50 (ISBN 0-8027-6313-8); PLB 7.45 (ISBN 0-8027-6314-6). Walker & Co.
--How to Ride a Tiger. LC 83-4289. (Illus.). 32p. (gr. k-3). 1983. PLB 9.95 (ISBN 0-395-34553-7). HM.
--Mercy Short: A Winter Journal, North Boston, 1692-1693. 160p. (YA) 1982. 11.95 (ISBN 0-525-44014-3, 01160-350, Unicorn Bk). Dutton.
--Never Say Ugh! to a Bug. LC 78-13948. (Illus.). 32p. (gr. k-3). 1979. PLB 11.88 (ISBN 0-688-84140-6). Greenwillow.
--Shekhina: Forty Poems. 96p. 1984. 15.95 (ISBN 0-9610662-1-0); pap. 9.95 (ISBN 0-9610662-2-9). Capstone Edns.
Farber, Norma & Lobel, Arnold. As I Was Crossing Boston Common. (Illus.). 32p. 1982. pap. 3.95 (ISBN 0-916870-43-X). Creative Arts Bks.
Farber, Norma, tr. see Salinas, Pedro.
Farber, Paul L. The Emergence of Onithology As a Scientific Discipline: Seventeen Sixty to Eighteen Fifty. 1982. 39.50 (ISBN 90-277-1410-X, Pub. by Reidel Holland). Kluwer Academic.
Farber, Paul L., jt. ed. see Osler, Margaret J.
Farber, Robert. Farber: Nudes. (Illus.). 156p. 1983. 27.50 (ISBN 0-8174-3851-3, Amphoto). Watson-Guptill.
--The Fashion Photographer. (Illus.). 192p. 1981. 24.95 (ISBN 0-8174-3850-5, Amphoto). Watson-Guptill.
--The Fashion Photographer. (Illus.). 192p. 1984. pap. 14.95 (ISBN 0-8174-3852-1, Amphoto). Watson-Guptill.
--Professional Fashion Photography. (Illus.). 1978. 24.95 (ISBN 0-8174-2440-7, Amphoto). Watson-Guptill.
--Professional Fashion Photography: New, Updated Edition of an AMPHOTO Bestseller. Rev. ed. 1983. pap. 14.95 (ISBN 0-8174-5549-3, Amphoto). Watson-Guptill.
Farber, Rose. More Masks to Color, Cut Out & Wear. (Coloring Experiences Ser.). 48p. (Orig.). 1983. pap. 2.95 (ISBN 0-8431-0484-8). Price Stern.
Farber, Rose & Farber, Joan. Masks to Color, Cut-Out & Wear. 1972. pap. 2.50 (ISBN 0-8431-0197-0). Price Stern.
Farber, Samuel. Revolution & Reaction in Cuba, 1933-1960: A Political Sociology from Machado to Castro. LC 76-7190. 1976. 22.00x (ISBN 0-8195-4099-4). Wesleyan U Pr.
Farber, Seymour M. & Wilson, Roger H. The Air We Breathe: A Study of Man & His Environment. (Illus.). 432p. 1961. 35.50x (ISBN 0-398-00544-3). C C Thomas.
Farber, Shereen D. Neurorehabilitation: A Multisensory Approach. (Illus.). 282p. 1982. 19.50 (ISBN 0-7216-3571-7). Saunders.
Farber, Stephen. Movie Rating Game. 1972. pap. 8.00 (ISBN 0-8183-0182-1). Pub Aff Pr.
Farber, Stephen & Green, Marc. Hollywood Dynasties. LC 83-46126. (Illus.). 368p. 1984. 16.95 (ISBN 0-88715-000-4). Delilah Bks.
--Hollywood Dynasties. 416p. 1985. pap. 3.95 (ISBN 0-449-20799-4, Crest). Fawcett.
Farber, Susan L. Identical Twins Reared Apart. LC 79-3085. 1980. text ed. 26.50x (ISBN 0-465-03228-1). Basic.
Farber, Thomas. Curves of Pursuit. 192p. 1984. 14.95 (ISBN 0-399-12870-0, Putnam). Putnam Pub Group.
--Curves of Pursuit. 192p. 1985. pap. 3.50 (ISBN 0-380-69838-2, Bard). Avon.
--Hazards to the Human Heart. LC 84-45100. 144p. 1984. pap. 6.95 (ISBN 0-916870-70-7, A Donald S. Ellis Book). Creative Arts Bk.
--Who Wrote the Book of Love? LC 84-45096. 127p. 1984. pap. 6.95 (ISBN 0-916870-69-3, A Donald S. Ellis Book). Creative Arts Bk.
Farber, W. M., ed. see Murtha, Alan.
Farber, W. O. Constitutional Revision Comment in Gubernatorial Messages & Party Platforms. 1969. write for info. U of SD Gov Res Bur.
--Constitutional Revision in South Dakota: Ballot Issues in 1972. 1972. write for info. U of SD Gov Res Bur.
--Improving County Government: Reorganizaton & Consolidation. 1963. write for info. U of SD Gov Res Bur.
Farber, W. O. & Cape, William H. A Report on County Consolidation in South Dakota with Special Reference to Buffalo & Jerauld Counties. 1968. write for info. U of SD Gov Res Bur.
Farber, William. Business Letters Simplified & Self-Taught. LC 82-3890. 160p. 1982. 11.95 (ISBN 0-668-05554-5); pap. 5.95 (ISBN 0-668-05394-1). Arco.
Farber, William, jt. auth. see Clem, Alan L.
Farber, William O. Revenue Sharing: Trick or Treat? 1973. write for info. U of SD Gov Res Bur.
Farberman, Harvey. Foundations of Interpretive Sociology: Original Essays in Symbolic Interaction. Denzin, Norman K., ed. (Studies in Symbolic Interaction: Suppl. 1). 1985. 49.50 (ISBN 0-89232-550-X). Jai Pr.
Farberman, Harvey A., jt. ed. see Stone, Gregory P.
Farberow, Norman L., jt. auth. see Reynolds, David K.
Farberow, Norman L., ed. The Many Faces of Suicide: Indirect Self-Destructive Behavior. LC 79-18797. (Illus.). 1979. 29.95 (ISBN 0-07-019944-2). McGraw.
Farberow, Norman L., jt. ed. see Shneidman, Edwin S.
Farbman, Evelyn. Signals: A Grammar & Guide for Writers. LC 84-81970. 384p. 1984. pap. text ed. write for info. (ISBN 0-395-36989-4). HM.
Farbregd, T., et al. Finnish-Norwegian-Finnish Dictionary (Suomi-Noria-Suomi) 636p. (Finnish & Norwegian.). 1981. pap. 18.95 (ISBN 951-0-10498-1, M-9644). French & Eur.
Farbstein, Abraham, tr. see Baumer, Franz.
Farbstein, Jay & Kafrowitz, Min. People in Places: Experiencing, Using & Changing. LC 78-5044. (Illus.). 1978. (Spec); pap. 4.95 (ISBN 0-13-656777-0, Spec). P-H.
Farca, E., et al, trs. see Sadoveanu, Mihail.
Fardan, Dorothy B. Understanding Self & Society. LC 80-81696. 220p. 1981. 13.95 (ISBN 0-8022-2370-2). Philos Lib.
Fardelmann, Charlotte. Islands Down East: A Visitor's Guide. (Illus.). 128p. (Orig.). 1984. pap. 8.95t (ISBN 0-89272-189-8). Down East.
Fardjadi, Homa, tr. see Shariati, Ali.
Fardjam, Faridah. Crystal Flower & the Sun. LC 71-128814. (Illus.). (gr. k-5). 1972. PLB 4.95g (ISBN 0-87614-017-7). Carolrhoda Bks.
Fardjam, Faridah & Azaad, Meyer. Uncle New Year. LC 77-128810. (Illus.). (gr. k-5). 1972. PLB 4.95g (ISBN 0-87614-014-2). Carolrhoda Bks.
Fardo, Stephen W. & Patrick, Dale R. Electrical Power Systems Technology. (Illus.). 256p. 1985. text ed. 29.95 (ISBN 0-13-247404-2). P-H.
--Rotating Electrical Machinery & Power Systems. (Illus.). 304p. 1985. text ed. 29.95 (ISBN 0-13-783309-1). P-H.
Fardo, Stephen W. & Prewitt, Roger W. Basic Electricity: A Lab Text. 2nd ed. (Illus.). 222p. 1983. pap. 14.95x (ISBN 0-89917-384-5). Tichenor Pub.
Fardo, Stephen W., jt. auth. see Patrick, Dale.
Fardo, Stephen W., jt. auth. see Patrick, Dale R.
Fardo, Stephen W., jt. auth. see Prewitt, Roger W.
Fardon, David. Free Yourself from Neck Pain & Headache. 190p. 1983. 13.95 (ISBN 0-13-330720-4); pap. 6.95 (ISBN 0-13-330712-3). P-H.
Fardon, David F. Free Yourself from Back Pain. (Illus.). 252p. 1984. 16.95 (ISBN 0-13-330655-0); pap. 7.95 (ISBN 0-13-330648-8). P-H.
--Osteoporosis: Your Head Start to the Prevention of Fractures. 288p. 1985. 15.95 (ISBN 0-02-537120-7). Macmillan.
Fardon, G. R. San Francisco in the 1850's. (Illus.). 11.25 (ISBN 0-8446-5574-0). Peter Smith.
--San Francisco in the 1850's: 32 Photographic Views by G. R. Fardon. (Illus.). 1977. pap. 3.00 (ISBN 0-486-23459-2). Dover.
Fardwell, Francis V. Landscape in the Works of Marcel Proust. LC 76-168004. (Catholic University of America. Studies in Romance Languages & Literatures: No. 35). Repr. of 1948 ed. 29.00 (ISBN 0-404-50335-7). AMS Pr.
Fardy, Paul S., et al. Cardiac Rehabilitation: Implications for the Nurse & Other Health Professionals. LC 80-16296. (Illus.). 283p. 1980. pap. text ed. 19.95 (ISBN 0-8016-1610-7). Mosby.
Fare, Rolf, et al. The Measurement of Efficiency of Production. 1985. lib. bdg. 32.00 (ISBN 0-89838-155-X). Kluwer Academic.
Fareed, George C., et al. Molecular Biology of Polyomaviruses & Herpesviruses. LC 82-23750. 247p. 1983. 52.95 (ISBN 0-471-05058-X, Pub. by Wiley Interscience). Wiley.
Fareed, Jawed, ed. Perspectives in Hemostasis: Proceedings of a Symposium Held at Loyola University, Maywood, Ill., U. S. A. 11 May 1979. (Illus.). 400p. 1981. 55.00 (ISBN 0-08-025092-0). Pergamon.
Farelane, Alexan. The Quest of Aah. 616p. 1981. 30.00x (ISBN 0-9507559-0-7, Pub. by Lashbrook & Knight). State Mutual Bk.
Farella, John R. The Main Stalk: A Synthesis of Navajo Philosophy. LC 84-8803. 221p. 1984. 19.95x (ISBN 0-8165-0859-3). U of Ariz Pr.
Farentinos, Robert C., jt. auth. see Radcliffe, James C.
Farer, Tom J. The Future of the Inter-American System. LC 78-31153. (Special Studies). 315p. 1979. 39.95 (ISBN 0-03-047391-8). Praeger.
--Toward a Humanitarian Diplomacy: A Primer for Policy. LC 79-3514. 1981. 25.00x (ISBN 0-8147-2565-1). NYU Pr.
--The United States & the Inter-American System: Are There Functions for the Forms, No. 17. (Studies in Transnational Legal Policy). 77p. 3.50 (ISBN 0-318-13190-0). Am Soc Intl Law.
--War Clouds on the Horn of Africa: The Widening Storm. 2nd, rev. ed. LC 78-75279. 1979. text ed. 10.00 (ISBN 0-87003-014-0); pap. 5.00 (ISBN 0-87003-013-2). Carnegie Endow.
Fares, Lawrence T., tr. see Geagea, Nilo.
Farewell, Christopher. An East-India Collation. LC 72-171756. (No. 380). 102p. 1971. Repr. of 1633 ed. 9.50 (ISBN 90-221-0380-3). Walter J Johnson.
Farewell, V., jt. ed. see Matthews, D. E.
Farfan, H. F. Mechanical Disorders of the Low Back. LC 73-3348. pap. 64.50 (ISBN 0-317-07820-8, 2055424). Bks Demand UMI.
Fargas, Claudio, jt. auth. see Escarpenter.
Farge, John La see La Farge, John.
Farge, Mabel La see Adams, Henry.
Farge, Oliver La see La Farge, Oliver.
Farge, Oliver La see La Farge, Oliver & Morgan, Arthur N.
Farge, Sheila La see Haugen, Tormod.
Farge, Y. & Fontana, M. P. Electronic & Vibrational Properties of Point Defects in Ionic Crystals. (Defects in Crystalline Solids Ser.: Vol. 11). 271p. 1979. 68.00 (ISBN 0-444-85272-7, North Holland). Elsevier.
Fargeau. Balzac et la Recherche de l'Absolu. 32.95 (ISBN 0-685-34095-3). French & Eur.
Farges, Albert M. By the End of the Century, Who Will Be Number One? (Illus.). 1980. deluxe ed. 75.15x (ISBN 0-930008-55-3). Inst Econ Pol.
Fargher, Douglas C. Fargher's English Manx Dictionary. 1979. text ed. 68.25x (ISBN 0-904980-23-5). Humanities.
Fargo, Gail B. Talks to Truth Searchers. LC 74-75082. 64p. 1974. 4.75 (ISBN 0-8022-2138-6). Philos Lib.
Farguhar, Ellen E., et al. Curriculum Materials 1974: Annual. new ed. 40p. 1974. pap. text ed. 2.00 (ISBN 0-87120-010-4, 611-74014). Assn Supervision.
Farguharson, J. B. & Holt, S. C. Europe from Below: An Assessment of Franco-German Popular Contacts. LC 75-591. 224p. 1975. 22.50 (ISBN 0-312-26915-3). St Martin.
Farhady, Hossein, jt. auth. see Hatch, Evelyn.
Farhang, Mansour. U. S. Imperialism: The Spanish American War to the Iranian Revolution. LC 81-50136. 250p. 1981. 20.00 (ISBN 0-89608-095-1); pap. 7.00 (ISBN 0-89608-094-3). South End Pr.
Farhar-Pilgrim, Barbara & Unseld, Charles T. America's Solar Potential: A National Consumer Study. Shama, Avraham, ed. LC 82-5231. (Studies in Energy Conservation & Solar Energy). 464p. 1982. 41.95x (ISBN 0-03-061696-4). Praeger.
Farhi, David. The Limits to Dissent: Facing the Dilemmas Posed by Terrorism. 4.00 (ISBN 0-686-26003-1). Aspen Inst Human.
Farhi, E. & Jackiw, R., eds. Dynamical Gauge Symmetry Breaking. vi, 404p. 1982. 42.00x (ISBN 9971-950-24-3, Pub. by World Sci Singapore); pap. 21.00x (ISBN 9971-950-25-1, Pub. by World Sci Singapore). Taylor & Francis.
Farhi, Moris. The Last of Days. 1984. pap. 3.95 (ISBN 0-8217-1485-6). Zebra.
Faria, A. J., jt. auth. see Webster, J.
Faria, A. J., et al. Compete: A Dynamic Marketing Simulation. 3rd ed. 1984. 15.95 (ISBN 0-256-03060-X). Business Pubns.
Faria, Anthony, jt. auth. see Johnson, H. Webster.
Faria, Gussie De see De Favia, Gussie.
Faria, Irvin & Peek, Ronald W. Gymnastics: Floor Exercise. LC 79-109498. (Sports Techniques Ser). 1972. 3.95 (ISBN 0-87670-008-3); pap. 1.95 (ISBN 0-87670-056-3). Athletic Inst.
--Gymnastics: Horizontal Bar. LC 79-109498. (Sports Techniques Ser). 1972. 3.95 (ISBN 0-87670-009-1); pap. 1.95 (ISBN 0-87670-055-5). Athletic Inst.
Faria, Irvin E. Cycling Physiology for the Serious Cyclist. (Illus.). 160p. 1978. 16.75x (ISBN 0-398-03683-7). C C Thomas.
Faria, L., jt. ed. see Sih, G. C.
Faribault, G., jt. auth. see McDonald, B. R.
Faribault, G. B. Catalogue d'ourvages sur l'histoire de l'amerique, et en Particulier sur Celle du Canada, da la Louisiane, de L'acadie et Autres Lieux. (Canadiana Avant 1867: No. 13). 1966. 14.80x (ISBN 90-2796-330-4). Mouton.
Faribault, George B., ed. Catalogue d'Ouvrages sur l'Histoire de l'Amerique. 1966. Repr. of 1837 ed. 18.00 (ISBN 0-384-15145-0). Johnson Repr.
Faricy, John H., jt. auth. see Thompson, Ralph B.
Faricy, Robert. The End of the Religious Life. 96p. 1983. pap. 6.95 (ISBN 0-86683-690-X). Winston Pr.
--Praying for Inner Healing. LC 79-92857. 94p. (Orig.). 1979. pap. 3.50 (ISBN 0-8091-2250-2). Paulist Pr.
--Seeking Jesus in Contemplation & Discernment. (Ways of Prayer Ser.: Vol. 7). 4.95 (ISBN 0-89453-367-3). M Glazier.
Faricy, Robert, jt. auth. see Rooney, Lucy.
Faricy, Robert S. The Spirituality of Teilhard de Chardin. 128p. (Orig.). 1981. pap. 5.95 (ISBN 0-86683-608-X). Winston Pr.
Faricy, Robert S. J. Praying. 120p. 1980. pap. 3.50 (ISBN 0-03-056661-4). Winston Pr.
Faricy, William H., jt. auth. see Dressel, Paul L.
Farid, A. H. Prayers of Muhammad. 1969. 10.25x (ISBN 0-87902-050-4). Orientalia.
Farid, Abdel M., ed. Oil & Security in the Arabian Gulf. 1981. 22.50x (ISBN 0-312-58284-6). St Martin.
--The Red Sea: Prospects for Stability. LC 84-40040. 192p. 1984. 25.00 (ISBN 0-312-66716-7). St Martin.
Farid, Anne. A Vocabulary Workbook: Prefixes, Roots & Suffixes for ESL Students. 240p. 1985. pap. text ed. 9.95 (ISBN 0-13-942913-1). P-H.
Farid, Nadir R., ed. HLA in Endocrine & Metabolic Disorders. LC 80-70600. 1981. 55.00 (ISBN 0-12-247780-4). Acad Pr.
Farid ud-Din Attar. The Conference of the Birds. Afkham Darbandi & Davis, Dick, trs. (Classics Ser.). 240p. 1984. pap. 5.95 (ISBN 0-14-044434-3). Penguin.
Fariello, Ruggero G., et al, eds. Neurotransmitters, Seizures, & Epilepsy II. 392p. 1984. text ed. 63.50 (ISBN 0-88167-057-X). Raven.
Faries, Clyde J., ed. Concepts & Projects in Public Speaking. 136p. 1984. pap. text ed. 13.95 (ISBN 0-8403-3370-6, 40337001). Kendall-Hunt.
Faries, David. Advice from the Soccer Pros. LC 79-64730. (Illus.). 176p. 1980. pap. 5.95 (ISBN 0-89037-219-5). Anderson World.
Farina, A. M. Developmental Games & Rhythms for Children. (Illus.). 816p. 1981. 48.75x (ISBN 0-398-04022-2). C C Thomas.
Farina, Giulio, ed. see Pareto, Vilfredo.
Farina, John. An American Experience of God: The Spirituality of Isaac Hecker. LC 81-80875. 240p. 1981. 11.95 (ISBN 0-8091-0321-4). Paulist Pr.
--Hecker Studies: Essays on the Thought of Isaac Hecker. LC 83-60654. 196p. (Orig.). 1983. pap. 6.95 (ISBN 0-8091-2555-2). Paulist Pr.
Farina, Mario V. Flowcharting. 1970. pap. 14.95 ref. ed. (ISBN 0-13-322750-2). P-H.
--FORTRAN IV Self-Taught. 1966. pap. 18.95 (ISBN 0-13-329722-5). P-H.
--Programming in BASIC: The Time-Sharing Language. (Orig.). 1968. pap. 18.95 ref. ed. (ISBN 0-13-730424-2). P-H.
Farina, Richard. Been Down So Long It Looks Like up to Me. 1983. pap. 5.95 (ISBN 0-14-006536-9). Penguin.
--Been Down So Long It Looks Like up to Me. 1983. 14.75 (ISBN 0-670-15476-8). Viking.
Farinas, Maurice E. see O'Neal, William B.
Farinella, Savatore F., ed. Night Blooming: A Remembrance of Allyn Amunson. 1976. pap. 2.00 (ISBN 0-915480-05-0). Good Gay.
Farington, Joseph. The Diary of Farington, Joseph, R. A, 7 vols. Garlick, Kenneth, et al, eds. Incl. Vols. 1 & 2. Set. text ed. 100.00x (ISBN 0-300-02314-6); text ed. 50.00x ea. Vol. 1 (ISBN 0-300-02294-8). Vol. 2 (ISBN 0-300-02295-6); Vols. 3 & 4. Set. text ed. 100.00x (ISBN 0-300-02371-5); text ed. 50.00x ea. Vol. 3 (ISBN 0-300-02369-3). Vol. 4 (ISBN 0-300-02370-7); Vols. 5 & 6. Set. text ed. 100.00x (ISBN 0-300-02418-5); text ed. 50.00x ea. Vol. 5 (ISBN 0-300-02416-9). Vol. 6 (ISBN 0-300-02417-7). Vol. 9. pap. text ed. 50.00 (ISBN 0-300-02890-3); Vol. 10. pap. text ed. 50.00 (ISBN 0-300-02857-1). LC 78-7056. (Studies in British Art Ser.). 1979. Yale U Pr.
--The Diary of Joseph Farington, Vols. XIII & XIV. Cave, Kathryn, ed. LC 78-7056. (Studies in British Art). 1984. Vol. 13, 320 pgs. Vol. 14, 384 pgs. text ed. 100.00x set (ISBN 0-300-03183-1). Yale U Pr.

--The Diary of Joseph Farington, Vols. XV & XVI. Cave, Kathryn, ed. LC 78-7056. (Studies in British Art). 1985. Vol. XV, 320 p.; Vol. XVI, 328 p. text ed. 100.00 set (ISBN 0-300-03270-6). Yale U Pr.
--The Diary of Joseph Farington, Vols. 11 & 12. Cave, Kathryn, ed. LC 78-7056. (Studies in British Art Ser.). 1000p. 1983. Set. text ed. 100.00x (ISBN 0-300-03124-6). Yale U Pr.
--The Diary of Joseph Farington: January 1808 Through December 1810, Vols. 9 & 10. Cave, Kathryn, ed. LC 78-7056. (Studies in British Art). 1000p. 1982. Set. text ed. 100.00x (ISBN 0-300-02859-8). Yale U Pr.
--The Diary of Joseph Farington, R. A. Volumes 7 & 8: January 1805 Through December 1807. LC 78-7056. (Published for the Paul Mellon Center for Studies in British Art Ser.). 360p. 1982. text ed. 100.00x (ISBN 0-300-02768-0, Set); Vol. 7. text ed. 50.00x each (ISBN 0-300-02783-4); Vol. 8. text ed. 50.00x (ISBN 0-300-02784-2). Yale U Pr.
Fariq, K. A. A History of Arabic Literature: Umayyad Period. 1978. 15.00x (ISBN 0-7069-0661-6, Pub. by Vikas India). Advent NY.
Fariq, Khurshid A. Tarikh Al-Ridda: Gleaned from al-Iktifa of al-Balansi with Notes & An Introduction. 183p. (Arabic.). 1981. text ed. 20.00x (ISBN 0-7069-1334-5, Pub. by Vikas India). Advent NY.
Faris. My Bible Story Reader, 5 vols. pap. 2.95 ea. Schmul Pub Co.
Faris, Alexander. Jacques Offenbach. 1981. 25.00 (ISBN 0-684-16797-2, ScribT). Scribner.
Faris, E. McGruder. Accounting & Law in a Nutshell. LC 83-23509. (Nutshell Ser.). 377p. 1984. pap. text ed. 8.95 (ISBN 0-314-79453-0). West Pub.
Faris, Ellsworth. The Nature of Human Nature. (Reprints in Sociology Ser). 1971. lib. bdg. 26.00x (ISBN 0-697-00217-9); pap. text ed. 6.95x (ISBN 0-89197-864-X). Irvington.
--The Nature of Human Nature. abr. ed. (Midway Reprint Ser.). 1977. pap. text ed. 10.00x (ISBN 0-226-23815-6). U of Chicago Pr.
--Nature of Human Nature & Other Essays in Social Psychology. facs. ed. LC 69-17575. (Essay Index Reprint Ser). 1937. 19.00 (ISBN 0-8369-0073-1). Ayer Co Pubs.
Faris, Ellsworth, et al, eds. Intelligent Philanthropy. LC 69-16231. (Criminology, Law Enforcement, & Social Problems Ser.: No. 82). 1969. Repr. of 1930 ed. 15.00x (ISBN 0-87585-082-0). Patterson Smith.
Faris, F. McGruder. Accounting for Lawyers. 4th ed. 600p. 1982. 30.00 (ISBN 0-87215-410-6). Michie Co.
Faris, Irwin. The Management of the Diabetic Foot. LC 82-4127. (Illus.). 131p. 1983. pap. 21.00 (ISBN 0-443-02315-8). Churchill.
Faris, John T. Men Who Conquered. facs. ed. LC 68-55846. (Essay Index Reprint Ser). 1922. 14.00 (ISBN 0-8369-0438-9). Ayer Co Pubs.
--Old Trails & Roads in Penn's Land. LC 75-83485. (Keystone State Historical Publications Ser: No. 8). (Illus.). 1969. Repr. of 1927 ed. 19.50x (ISBN 0-87198-508-X). Friedman.
--Romance of Forgotten Men. facs. ed. LC 68-58787. (Essay Index Reprint Ser). 1928. 23.75 (ISBN 0-8369-1033-8). Ayer Co Pubs.
Faris, N. A. The Book of Knowledge. 14.95 (ISBN 0-686-18617-6). Kazi Pubns.
--Foundation of Articles of Faith. 7.50 (ISBN 0-686-18607-9). Kazi Pubns.
--The Mysteries of Almsgiving. pap. 4.50 (ISBN 0-686-18616-8). Kazi Pubns.
--The Mysteries of Fasting. pap. 3.75 (ISBN 0-686-18615-X). Kazi Pubns.
--The Mysteries of Purity. pap. 4.75 (ISBN 0-686-18614-1). Kazi Pubns.
Faris, Nabih A., ed. The Arab Heritage. LC 79-2856. 279p. 1981. Repr. of 1944 ed. 30.00 (ISBN 0-8305-0030-8). Hyperion Conn.
--The Arab Heritage. LC 84-27929. (Illus.). xii, 279p. 1985. Repr. of 1944 ed. lib. bdg. 55.00x (ISBN 0-313-23371-3, FAAH). Greenwood.
Faris, Nabik A., tr. see Al-Ghazzali.
Faris, Paul. Ozark Log Cabin Folks: The Way They Were. LC 82-82816. (Illus.). 143p. 1983. pap. 14.95 (ISBN 0-914546-43-0). Rose Pub.
Faris, Robert E. Chicago Sociology, Nineteen Twenty-Nineteen Thirty-Two. LC 76-122368. (Midway Reprints Ser.; Heritage of Sociology Ser.). 1979. pap. text ed. 6.00x (ISBN 0-226-23819-9). U of Chicago Pr.
Faris, Robert E. & Dunham, H. Warren. Mental Disorders in Urban Areas. LC 65-16168. 1965. pap. 2.45x (ISBN 0-226-23816-4, P183, Phoen). U of Chicago Pr.
Faris, W. G. Self-Adjoint Operators. (Lecture Notes in Mathematics Ser.: Vol. 433). vii, 115p. 1975. pap. 13.00 (ISBN 0-387-07030-3). Springer-Verlag.
Faris, Wendy B. Carlos Fuentes. LC 82-40281. (Literature & Life Ser.). 259p. 1983. 16.50 (ISBN 0-8044-2193-5); pap. 6.95 (ISBN 0-8044-6143-0). Ungar.
Farish, Donald. Introduction to Biology: A Human Perspective. 550p. 1984. text ed. write for info (ISBN 0-87150-787-0, 4561, Pub. by Willard Grant Pr). PWS Pubs.
Farish, Hunter D. Circuit Rider Dismounts, a Social History of Southern Methodism 1865-1900. LC 77-87534. (American Scene Ser). 1969. Repr. of 1938 ed. 45.00 (ISBN 0-306-71450-7). Da Capo.
Farish, Kay, jt. auth. see Hutchison, Becky.
Farish, Margaret K., ed. Orchestral Music in Print. LC 79-24460. (Music in Print Ser.: Vol. 5). 1016p. 1979. lib. bdg. 135.00 (ISBN 0-88478-010-4). Musicdata.
--Orchestral Music in Print: Educational Section. LC 78-11929. (Music in Print Ser.). 78p. 1978. pap. 10.00 (ISBN 0-88478-009-0). Musicdata.
Farish, Margaret K, ed. Orchestral Music in Print: 1983 Supplement. LC 83-13336. (Music in Print Ser.). 237p. 1983. lib. bdg. 75.00 (ISBN 0-88478-014-7). Musicdata.
Farish, Margaret K., ed. String Music in Print. 2nd ed. LC 80-18425. (Music in Print Ser.: Vol. 6). 464p. 1980. Repr. lib. bdg. 85.00 (ISBN 0-88478-011-2). Musicdata.
--String Music in Print: Supplement, 1984. LC 84-3478. 1984. lib. bdg. 75.00 (ISBN 0-88478-016-3). Musicdata.
Farish, Philip, ed. The Recruiters Handbook. 30.00 (ISBN 0-318-01037-2). Enterprise IL.
Farish, Starr. Voice of Silence. 5th ed. (Illus.). 119p. 1983. pap. 6.95 (ISBN 0-9605492-2-6). Touch Heart.
Farish, Starr, ed. see Gittner, Louis.
Faristzaddi, Millard. Itations of Jamaica & I Rastafari. LC 82-82460. (Illus.). 192p. (Orig.). 1982. 9.95 (ISBN 0-394-62435-1, E836, Ever). Grove.
Farjam, Farideh. The Crystal Flower & the Sun. new & rev. ed. Jabbari, Ahmad, ed. & tr. from Persian. LC 83-60453. (Illus.). 24p. (Orig.). (gr. k up). 1983. pap. 4.95 (ISBN 0-939214-16-4). Mazda Pubs.
Farjam, Farideh & Azaad, Meyer. Uncle Noruz (Uncle New Year) Jabbari, Ahmad, ed. & tr. from Persian. LC 83-60450. (Illus.). 24p. (Orig.). (gr. k up). 1983. pap. 4.95 (ISBN 0-939214-14-8). Mazda Pubs.
Farjenel, Fernand. Through the Chinese Revolution. LC 72-79820. (China Library Ser.). 1972. Repr. of 1916 ed. 29.00 (ISBN 0-8420-1381-4). Scholarly Res Inc.
Farjeon, Benjamin L. Devlin the Barber. LC 75-32743. (Literature of Mystery & Detection). 1976. Repr. of 1888 ed. 16.00x (ISBN 0-405-07869-2). Ayer Co Pubs.
Farjeon, Eleanor. Faithful Jenny Dove, & Other Stories. LC 78-128734. (Short Story Index Reprint Ser.). 1925. 17.00 (ISBN 0-8369-3625-6). Ayer Co Pubs.
--The Glass Slipper. (gr. 5 up). 1979. pap. 1.50 (ISBN 0-448-17104-X, Pub. by Tempo). Ace Bks.
--The Glass Slipper. 159p. 1981. Repr. PLB 10.95x (ISBN 0-89966-360-5). Buccaneer Bks.
--The Glass Slipper. 108p. 1981. Repr. PLB 10.95x (ISBN 0-89967-034-2). Harmony Raine.
--Little Bookroom. LC 83-49007. (Illus.). 320p. (gr. 3 up). 1984. pap. 5.95 (ISBN 0-87923-522-5). Godine.
--Nursery Rhymes of London Town. 2nd ed. (Illus.). 122p. 1977. pap. 4.50 (ISBN 0-7156-0736-7, Pub. by Duckworth England). Biblio Dist.
Farjeon, Eleanor & Farjeon, Herbert. Kings & Queens. (Illus.). 64p. 1985. 8.95x (ISBN 0-460-06127-5, Pub. by J M Dent England). Biblio Dist.
Farjeon, Herbert, jt. auth. see Farjeon, Eleanor.
Farjoun, Emmanuel & Machover, Moshe. The Laws of Chaos. 192p. Date not set. 24.00 (ISBN 0-8052-7160-0, Pub. by NLB England); pap. 14.95 (ISBN 0-8052-7161-9). Schocken.
Farkas. Qualitative Theory of Differential Equations, 2 vols. (Colloquia Mathematica Ser.: Vol. 30). 1090p. 1982. Set. 159.75 (ISBN 0-444-86173-4, North-Holland). Elsevier.
--Sociology of Science & Research. 1980. 51.00 (ISBN 0-9960016-7-0, Pub. by Akademiai Kaido Hungary). Heyden.
Farkas, Adalbert, jt. ed. see Cusumano, James A.
Farkas, Andre. Romantic at Heart & Other Faults. 1980. pap. 3.00 (ISBN 0-916696-11-1). Cross Country.
Farkas, Andrew. Opera & Concert Singers: An Annotated International Bibliography of Books & Pamphlets. LC 83-49310. (Reference Library of the Humanities). 300p. 1984. lib. bdg. 50.00 (ISBN 0-8240-9001-2). Garland Pub.
Farkas, Andrew, jt. auth. see Biancolli, Louis.
Farkas, Andrew, ed. Opera Biographies, 42 vols. (Opera Biographies). 1977. Repr. lib. bdg. 1154.00 (ISBN 0-405-09666-6). Ayer Co Pubs.
--Titta Ruffo: An Anthology. LC 83-10681. (Contributions to the Study of Music & Dance Ser.: No. 4; Opera Biographies). (Illus.). xii, 289p. 1984. lib. bdg. 35.00 (ISBN 0-313-23783-2, FRU/). Greenwood.
Farkas, Andrew, ed. see Albani, Emma.
Farkas, Andrew, ed. see Bispham, David.
Farkas, Andrew, ed. see Callas, Evangelia & Blochman, Lawrence G.
Farkas, Andrew, ed. see Calve, Emma.
Farkas, Andrew, ed. see Corsi, Mario.
Farkas, Andrew, ed. see Cushing, Mary W.
Farkas, Andrew, ed. see Eames, Emma.
Farkas, Andrew, ed. see Gaisberg, Frederick W.
Farkas, Andrew, ed. see Gigli, Beniamino.
Farkas, Andrew, ed. see Hauk, Minnie.
Farkas, Andrew, ed. see Henschel, Horst & Friedrich, Ehrhard.
Farkas, Andrew, ed. see Hernandez-Girbal, F.
Farkas, Andrew, ed. see Heylbut, Rose & Gerber, Aime.
Farkas, Andrew, ed. see Jeritza, Maria.
Farkas, Andrew, ed. see Klein, Herman.
Farkas, Andrew, ed. see Lawton, Mary.
Farkas, Andrew, ed. see Lehman, Lilli.
Farkas, Andrew, ed. see Litvinne, Felia.
Farkas, Andrew, ed. see Marchesi, Blanche.
Farkas, Andrew, ed. see Martens, Frederick H.
Farkas, Andrew, ed. see Maude, Jenny M.
Farkas, Andrew, ed. see Maurel, Victor.
Farkas, Andrew, ed. see Mingotti, Antonio.
Farkas, Andrew, ed. see Moore, Edward C.
Farkas, Andrew, ed. see Moore, Grace.
Farkas, Andrew, ed. see Moses, Montrose J.
Farkas, Andrew, ed. see Palmegiani, Francesco.
Farkas, Andrew, ed. see Pearse, Cecilia M. & Hird, Frank.
Farkas, Andrew, ed. see Pinza, Ezio & Magidoff, Robert.
Farkas, Andrew, ed. see Rogers, Francis.
Farkas, Andrew, ed. see Rosenthal, Harold D.
Farkas, Andrew, ed. see Ruffo, Titta.
Farkas, Andrew, ed. see Slezak, Leo.
Farkas, Andrew, ed. see Stagno Bellincioni, Bianca & Bellincioni, Gemma.
Farkas, Andrew, ed. see Tetrazzini, Luisa.
Farkas, Andrew, ed. see Teyte, Maggie.
Farkas, Andrew, ed. see Tibbett, Lawrence.
Farkas, Andrew, ed. see Traubel, Helen & Hubler, Richard G.
Farkas, Andrew, ed. see Van Vechten, Carl.
Farkas, Andrew, ed. see Wagner, Charles L.
Farkas, Daniel. Data Communications: Terms, Concepts & Definitions. 120p. 1983. 3 ring binder 39.95 (ISBN 0-935506-13-6). Carnegie Pr.
Farkas, Daniel J. Micro UNIX: A Guide to UNIX in the Microcomputer Environment. (Illus.). 320p. (Orig.). pap. cancelled (ISBN 0-916688-81-X, 81-X). Creative Comp.
Farkas, Donka, et al, eds. Proceedings: Papers from the Parasession on the Lexicon. LC 78-56478. 364p. 1978. pap. 8.00 (ISBN 0-914203-10-X). Chicago Ling.
Farkas, Donka F. Intensional Descriptions & the Romance Subjunctive Mood. Hankamer, Jorge, ed. (Outstanding Dissertations in Linguistics Ser.). 160p. 1985. 25.00 (ISBN 0-8240-5426-1). Garland Pub.
Farkas, Emil & Corcoran, John. Martial Arts: Traditions, History, People. LC 82-11940. (Illus.). 437p. 1983. 14.98 (ISBN 0-8317-5805-8). Smith Pubs.
--The Overlook Marital Arts Dictionary. LC 81-47415. (Illus.). 320p. 1985. pap. 9.95 (ISBN 0-87951-996-7). Overlook Pr.
--The Overlook Martial Arts Dictionary. LC 81-47415. (Illus.). 320p. 1983. 16.95 (ISBN 0-87951-133-8). Overlook Pr.
Farkas, Emil, ed. see Urquidez, Benny.
Farkas, F. Chris, jt. ed. see Gardener, Russell M.
Farkas, G. L., jt. ed. see Dudits, D.
Farkas, George, jt. auth. see England, Paula.
Farkas, H. M. & Kra, I. Riemann Surfaces. (Graduate Texts in Mathematics). (Illus.). 350p. 1980. pap. 35.00 (ISBN 0-387-90465-4). Springer-Verlag.
Farkas, H. M., jt. ed. see Chavel, I.
Farkas, I. Introduction to Linear Algebra. 1975. 23.75 (ISBN 0-9960018-3-2, Pub by. A Hilger England). Heyden.
Farkas, J. Optimum Design of Metal Structures. 222p. 1984. 54.95x (ISBN 0-470-27482-4). Halsted Pr.
Farkas, Karl. Zurueck ins Morgen. 1946. 3.00 (ISBN 0-685-57211-0). M S Rosenberg.
Farkas, L., et al, eds. Flavonoids & Bioflavonoids, 1981. (Studies in Organic Chemistry: Vol. 11). 534p. 1982. 95.75 (ISBN 0-444-99694-X). Elsevier.
Farkas, L. G. Anthropometry of the Head & Face in Medicine. 294p. 1981. 75.00 (ISBN 0-444-00557-9, Biomedical Pr). Elsevier.
Farkas, M., ed. Differential Equations. (Colloquia Mathematica Societatis Janos Bolyai: Vol. 15). 418p. 1977. 85.00 (ISBN 0-7204-0496-7, North-Holland). Elsevier.
Farkas, Mary, ed. see Sasaki, Sokei-an.
Farkas, Paul, jt. auth. see Knapp, Albert.
Farkas, Philip. Art of French Horn Playing. (Illus.). 1956. pap. 12.95 (ISBN 0-87487-021-6). Birch Tree Gr.
Farkas, Susan, ed. see Journalism Reseach Fellows of 1982.
Farkas, Susan C., ed. see Journalism Research Fellows.
Farkas, Tiber. Introduction to Criminal Justice. 1977. pap. text ed. 16.25 (ISBN 0-8191-0184-2). U Pr of Amer.
Farkasfalvy, Denis, jt. auth. see Farmer, William R.
Farks, G. L., ed. see International Protoplast Symposium, 5th, July 1979, Szeged, Hungary.
Farland, Grace. Official Price Guide to Antiques & Other Collectibles. (Illus.). 448p. 10.75 (ISBN 0-318-14883-8). Midwest Old Settlers.
Farland, Kathryn. Miss Monica Marries. 192p. 1984. 12.95 (ISBN 0-8027-0801-3). Walker & Co.
Farleigh, John. Engraving on Wood. (Illus.). 50p. 1954. 6.50 (ISBN 0-85219-596-6, Pub. by Batsford England). David & Charles.
Farley. Radio Man: Miles Cabot on Venus. 5.00 (ISBN 0-686-00476-0); pap. 2.00 (ISBN 0-686-00477-9). Fantasy Pub Co.
Farley, Alan E., tr. see Alexandroff, Paul.
Farley, Alice R., jt. auth. see Farley, Eugene J.
Farley, Belmont M. What to Tell the People about the Public Schools: A Study of the Content of the Public School Publicity Program. LC 73-176763. (Columbia University. Teachers College. Contributions to Education: No. 355). Repr. of 1929 ed. 22.50 (ISBN 0-404-55355-9). AMS Pr.
Farley, Benjamin W., ed. see Calvin, John.
Farley, Benjamin W., tr. see Calvin, John.
Farley, Carol. Korea: A Land Divided. LC 83-7789. (Discovering Our Heritage Ser.). (Illus.). 143p. (gr. 5 up). 1984. PLB 10.95 (ISBN 0-87518-244-5). Dillon.
--Loosen Your Ears. LC 76-25206. (Illus.). 224p. (gr. 3-7). 1977. 7.95 (ISBN 0-689-30553-2). Atheneum.
--Mystery in the Ravine. (Illus.). 132p. 1983. pap. 1.95 (ISBN 0-380-00745-2, 60558-9, Camelot). Avon.
--Mystery of the Fiery Message. (Illus.). 108p. 1983. pap. 1.95 (ISBN 0-380-81927-9, 81927-9, Camelot). Avon.
--Mystery of the Fog Man. (Illus.). 112p. 1974. pap. 1.95 (ISBN 0-380-00102-0, 61663-7, Camelot). Avon.
Farley, Edward. Ecclesial Man: A Social Phenomenology of Faith & Reality. LC 73-88359. 304p. 1975. 11.50 (ISBN 0-8006-0272-2, 1-272). Fortress.
--Ecclesial Reflection: An Anatomy of Theological Method. LC 81-43088. 1982. 29.95 (ISBN 0-8006-0670-1). Fortress.
--Theologia: The Fragmentation & Unity of Theological Education. LC 82-48621. 224p. 1983. pap. 14.95 (ISBN 0-8006-1705-3). Fortress.
Farley, Eugene J. Barron's How to Prepare for the High School Equivalency Examination-the Social Studies Test. LC 80-15825. 1980. pap. text ed. 6.95 (ISBN 0-8120-2056-1). Barron.
--Barron's How to Prepare for the High School Equivalency Examination: The Reading Skills Test. LC 79-28101. 1980. pap. text ed. 5.95 (ISBN 0-8120-2057-X). Barron.
--Barron's Preview Examination to Prepare for the High School Equivalency Tests. 2nd, rev. ed. 1979. pap. text ed. 25.00 (ISBN 0-8120-0992-4). Barron.
Farley, Eugene J. & Farley, Alice R. Barron's Getting Ready for the High School Equivalency Examination: Beginning Preparation in Reading & English. LC 72-81811. 1973. pap. text ed. 5.95 (ISBN 0-8120-0442-6). Barron.
--Barron's How to Prepare for the High School Equivalency Examination (GED) The Science Test. (gr. 11-12). 1982. pap. text ed. 6.95 (ISBN 0-8120-2055-3). Barron.
--Developing Reading Skills for the High School Equivalency Examination (Ged) in Social Studies, Science, & Literature: In 26 Lessons. LC 72-84413. 1972. pap. text ed. 6.95 (ISBN 0-8120-0487-6). Barron.
Farley, Frank. Scandinavian Influences in the English-Romantic Movement. lib. bdg. 59.95 (ISBN 0-8490-0997-9). Gordon Pr.
Farley, Frank & Gordon, Neal J., eds. Psychology & Education: The State of the Union. LC 80-82902. (National Society for the Study of Education Series on Contemporary Educational Issues). 400p. 1981. 25.50x (ISBN 0-8211-0506-X); text ed. 22.75x 10 or more copies. McCutchan.
Farley, Frank E., jt. auth. see Kittredge, George L.
Farley, G. M. Zane Grey, a Documented Portrait: The Man, the Bibliography, the Filmography. 1985. 24.00 (ISBN 0-916620-78-6). Portals Pr.
Farley, G. M. & Pelton, Robert W. Satan Unmasked: Principles & Practice of Christian Exorcism. LC 78-70632. (Illus.). 1979. 7.50 (ISBN 0-916620-24-7). Portals Pr.
Farley, Gordon K., et al. Handbook of Child & Adolescent Psychiatric Emergencies. 1979. pap. 15.95 (ISBN 0-87488-656-2). Med Exam.
--Handbook of Child & Adolescent Psychiatric Emergencies & Crises. 2nd ed. 1985. pap. text ed. price not set (ISBN 0-87488-616-3). Med Exam.
Farley, James A. Behind the Ballots: A Personal History of a Politician. LC 72-2370. (FDR & the Era of the New Deal Ser). (Illus.). 402p. 1973. Repr. of 1938 ed. lib. bdg. 45.00 (ISBN 0-306-70475-7). Da Capo.
--Behind the Ballots: The Personal History of a Politician. LC 78-114521. (Illus.). 392p. 1972. Repr. of 1938 ed. lib. bdg. 19.00x (ISBN 0-8371-4738-7, FABB). Greenwood.
--Jim Farley's Story: The Roosevelt Years. LC 84-10729. (Illus.). x, 388p. 1984. Repr. of 1948 ed. lib. bdg. 45.00x (ISBN 0-313-24566-5, FAJF). Greenwood.
--Jim Farley's Story: The Roosevelt Years. LC 83-45758. Repr. of 1948 ed. 40.00 (ISBN 0-404-20096-6). AMS Pr.
Farley, James H., tr. see Simon, Marcel.
Farley, Jennie. Academic Women & Employment Discrimination: A Critical Annotated Bibliography. LC 82-3570. (ILR Bibliography Ser.: No. 16). 112p. 1982. pap. 8.95 (ISBN 0-87546-092-5). ILR Pr.
--Affirmative Action & the Woman Worker: Guidelines for Personnel Management. LC 78-11719. 1979. 15.95 (ISBN 0-8144-5498-4). AMACOM.

--Affirmative Action & the Woman Worker: Guidelines for Personnel Management. LC 78-11719. pap. 59.30 (ISBN 0-317-26010-3, 2023886). Bks Demand UMI.

Farley, Jennie, ed. Sex Discrimination in Higher Education: Strategies for Equality. LC 81-9604. 168p. 1981. pap. 7.50 (ISBN 0-87546-089-5). ILR Pr.

--The Woman in Management: Career & Family Issues. LC 83-2338. 112p. (Orig.). 1983. pap. 8.95 (ISBN 0-87546-100-X). ILR Pr.

--Women Workers in Fifteen Countries: Essays in Honor of Alice Hanson Cook. LC 85-2375. (Cornell International Industrial & Labor Relations Reports Ser.: No. 11). 1985. 24.00 (ISBN 0-87546-113-1); pap. 9.95 (ISBN 0-87546-114-X). ILR Pr.

Farley, Joanne. Vocational Education Outcomes: A Thesaurus of Outcome Questions. 60p. 1979. 4.50 (ISBN 0-318-15594-X, RD 170). Natl Ctr Res Voc Ed.

Farley, John. Gametes & Spores: Ideas about Sexual Reproduction, 1750-1914. LC 82-87. (Illus.). 312p. 1982. text ed. 27.50x (ISBN 0-8018-2738-8). Johns Hopkins.

--The Spontaneous Generation Controversy from Descartes to Oparin. LC 76-47379. 1977. text ed. 22.50x (ISBN 0-8018-1902-4). Johns Hopkins.

Farley, John E. Majority-Minority Relations. (Illus.). 384p. 1982. 27.95 (ISBN 0-13-545574-X). P-H.

Farley, John J. You Can't Take It with You. Reed, R., ed. LC 81-83622. 1982. pap. 6.95 (ISBN 0-88247-616-5). R & E Pubs.

Farley, John U. & Brandes, Ove, eds. Advances in International Marketing, Vol. 1. 1984. 40.00 (ISBN 0-89232-275-6). Jai Pr.

Farley, Joseph, jt. ed. see Alkon, Daniel L.

Farley, Josh, ed. see Kahn, Terry.

Farley, Lauren, jt. auth. see Farley, Michael.

Farley, Lawrence T. Change Processes in International Organizations. 224p. 1982. pap. 9.95 (ISBN 0-87073-036-3). Schenkman Bks Inc.

Farley, Lin. Sexual Shakedown. 1980. pap. 2.50 (ISBN 0-446-91251-4). Warner Bks.

Farley, M. Foster. Indian Summer: An Account of a Visit to India. 211p. 1977. pap. text ed. 11.75 (ISBN 0-8191-0051-X). U Pr of Amer.

Farley, Margaret A. Personal Commitments: Making, Keeping, Breaking. 175p. 1985. 12.95 (ISBN 0-86683-476-1, AY8640). Winston Pr.

Farley, Michael. Scuba Equipment Care & Maintenance. (Illus.). 176p. 1980. pap. text ed. 9.95 (ISBN 0-932248-01-2). Marcor Pub.

Farley, Michael & Farley, Lauren. Baja California Diver's Guide. (Illus.). 224p. (Orig.). 1984. pap. 12.95x (ISBN 0-932248-05-5). Marcor Pub.

--California Seafood Cuisine. 280p. (Orig.). 1984. write for info. (ISBN 0-932248-04-7); pap. write for info. Marcor Pub.

Farley, Miriam S. American Far Eastern Policy & the Sino-Japanese War. LC 75-30122. (Institute of Pacific Relations Ser.). Repr. of 1938 ed. 11.50 (ISBN 0-404-59521-9). AMS Pr.

--The Problem of Japanese Trade Expansion in the Post-War Situation. LC 75-30106. (Institute of Pacific Relations Ser.). Repr. of 1940 ed. 11.50 (ISBN 0-404-59523-5). AMS Pr.

Farley, Nicholas. Handbook of Garden Equipment. 288p. 1980. 39.00x (ISBN 0-460-04381-1, Pub. by J M Dent England). State Mutual Bk.

Farley, O. William. Rural Social Work Practice. 256p. 1982. text ed. 22.95 (ISBN 0-02-910480-7). Free Pr.

Farley, Patrick, et al. Mastering BASIC: A Beginner's Guide. 1979. pap. text ed. 6.50 (ISBN 0-89669-039-3). Collegium Bk Pubs.

Farley, Philip J., et al. Arms Across the Sea. LC 77-91804. 1978. 22.95 (ISBN 0-8157-2746-1); pap. 8.95 (ISBN 0-8157-2745-3). Brookings.

Farley, Ralph M. The Radio Beasts. 1976. lib. bdg. 10.95x (ISBN 0-89968-030-5). Lightyear.

Farley, Reuben W., et al. Trigonometry: A Unitized Approach. (Illus.). 1975. pap. text ed. 28.95 (ISBN 0-13-930909-8). P-H.

Farley, Reynolds. Blacks & Whites: Narrowing the Gap? LC 84-638. (Social Trends in the United States Ser.). (Illus.). 304p. 1984. text ed. 19.50x (ISBN 0-674-07631-1). Harvard U Pr.

Farley, S. Brent. Spiritually Yours. LC 81-82054. 160p. 1982. 6.95 (ISBN 0-88290-192-3, 1068). Horizon Utah.

Farley, Venner. Second Level Nursing: Study Modules. LC 80-70482. (Associate Degree Nursing Ser.). (Illus.). 272p. (Orig.). 1981. pap. text ed. 12.40 (ISBN 0-8273-1876-6); tchr's. ed. 6.05 (ISBN 0-8273-1877-4). Delmar.

Farley, Venner M. First Level Nursing-Study Modules. (Nursing-Registered Ser.). 1981. pap. 12.40 (ISBN 0-8273-1873-1); 6.05 (ISBN 0-8273-1875-8). Delmar.

Farley, Walter. The Black Stallion. LC 41-21882. (Illus.). 192p. (gr. 5-9). 1982. gift edition 8.95 (ISBN 0-394-85114-5). Random.

--Black Stallion. LC 41-21882. (Illus.). (gr. 3-7). 1944. (BYR); PLB 8.99 (ISBN 0-394-90601-2). Random.

--Black Stallion & Flame. (Illus.). (gr. 5 up). 1960. (BYR); PLB 8.99 (ISBN 0-394-90615-2). Random.

--Black Stallion & Satan. (Illus.). (gr. 4-6). 1949. (BYR); PLB 8.99 (ISBN 0-394-90605-5). Random.

--The Black Stallion & the Girl. (gr. 4 up). 1971. (BYR); PLB 8.99 (ISBN 0-394-92145-3). Random.

--Black Stallion Challenged. (Illus.). (gr. 5-9). 1964. (BYR); PLB 8.99 (ISBN 0-394-90617-9). Random.

--The Black Stallion: Comic Book Album. LC 83-60188. (Black Stallion Comic Bks.). (Illus.). 48p. (gr. 3-7). 1983. pap. 2.95 (ISBN 0-394-86025-X). Random.

--The Black Stallion Legend. LC 83-1870. (Black Stallion Bks.). (Illus.). 224p. (gr. 5-9). 1983. 8.95 (ISBN 0-394-86026-8); PLB 9.99 (ISBN 0-394-96026-2). Random.

--The Black Stallion Legend. LC 83-1870. (Black Stallion Bks.: No. 20). (Illus.). 192p. 1985. pap. 2.95 (ISBN 0-394-87500-1, BYR). Random.

--The Black Stallion Mystery. (gr. 4-6). 1957. (BYR); PLB 8.99 (ISBN 0-394-90613-6). Random.

--The Black Stallion Picture Book. LC 78-20653. (Illus.). (gr. 1-6). 1979. 5.95 (ISBN 0-394-84174-3, BYR); PLB 6.99 (ISBN 0-394-94174-8). Random.

--The Black Stallion Returns. LC 45-8763. (Black Stallion Ser.). (Illus.). 208p. (gr. 5 up). 1982. 9.95 (ISBN 0-394-85509-4). Random.

--The Black Stallion Returns: A Comic Book Album. LC 83-62721. (The Black Stallion Comic Bks.). (Illus.). (gr. 3-7). 1984. pap. 3.95 (ISBN 0-394-86341-0, BYR). Random.

--The Black Stallion Returns: Movie Storybooks. Spinner, Stephanie, ed. LC 82-3861. (Illus.). 64p. (gr. 2-7). 1982. 5.95 (ISBN 0-394-85412-8); PLB 6.99 (ISBN 0-394-95412-2). Random.

--The Black Stallion Revolts. LC 49-6117. (gr. 4-9). 1977. (BYR); pap. 2.95 (ISBN 0-394-83613-8). Random.

--Black Stallion's Courage. (Illus.). (gr. 4-6). 1956. (BYR); pap. 1.95 (ISBN 0-394-83918-8). Random.

--Black Stallion's Filly. (Illus.). (gr. 4-6). 1952. 3.95 (ISBN 0-394-90608-X, BYR); PLB 8.99; pap. 1.95 (ISBN 0-394-83916-1). Random.

--Black Stallion's Ghost. (Illus.). (gr. 5-9). 1969. 3.95 (ISBN 0-394-90618-7, BYR); PLB 7.99; pap. 1.95 (ISBN 0-394-83919-6). Random.

--Black Stallion's Sulky Colt. (Illus.). (gr. 4-6). 1954. (BYR); PLB 8.99 (ISBN 0-394-90610-1); pap. 2.95 (ISBN 0-394-83917-X). Random.

--Blood Bay Colt. (Illus.). (gr. 4-6). 1950. (BYR); pap. 2.95 (ISBN 0-394-83915-3). Random.

--The Great Dane Thor. 192p. (gr. 4-7). pap. 1.97 (ISBN 0-440-93095-2, LFL). Dell.

--The Horse-Tamer. LC 58-9030. (Black Stallion Bks.). 160p. 1980. (BYR); pap. 1.95 (ISBN 0-394-84374-6). Random.

--Island Stallion. (Illus.). (gr. 5-6). 1948. (BYR); pap. 2.95 (ISBN 0-394-84376-2). Random.

--Island Stallion Races. (Illus.). (gr. 4-6). 1965. (BYR). Random.

--Island Stallion's Fury. (Illus.). (gr. 5-6). 1951. (BYR). Random.

--Little Black, a Pony. LC 61-7789. (Illus.). (gr. 1-2). 1961. PLB 5.99 (ISBN 0-394-90021-9). Beginner.

--Little Black Goes to the Circus. LC 63-13866. (Illus.). (gr. k-3). 1963. PLB 5.99 (ISBN 0-394-90033-2). Beginner.

--Little Black Pony Races. (Illus.). (ps-1). 1968. (BYR). Random.

--Man O' War. (Illus.). (gr. 4-6). 1962. 4.95 (ISBN 0-394-90616-0, BYR). Random.

--Man O' War. LC 62-9000. (Black Stallion Bks.). (Illus.). 352p. (gr. 5-9). 1983. pap. 2.95 (ISBN 0-394-86015-2). Random.

--Son of the Black Stallion. (Illus.). (gr. 4-6). 1947. (BYR); PLB 7.99 (ISBN 0-394-90603-9); pap. 2.95 (ISBN 0-394-83612-X). Random.

--Walter Farley's Black Stallion Books, 4 bks. Incl. The Black Stallion. LC 41-21882; The Black Stallion Returns. LC 45-8763; The Black Stallion & Satan. LC 49-6117; The Black Stallion Mystery. LC 57-7527. (gr. 4-9). 1979. Boxed Set. pap. 7.80 (ISBN 0-394-84176-X, BYR). Random.

Farley-Hills, David. The Benevolence of Laughter: Comic Poetry of the Commonwealth & Restoration. 212p. 1974. 16.50x (ISBN 0-87471-502-4). Rowman.

--The Comic in Renaissance Comedy. 200p. 1981. 28.50x (ISBN 0-389-20013-1, 06787). B&N Imports.

--Rochester. (The Critical Heritage Ser.). 288p. 1985. pap. 15.00 (ISBN 0-7102-0594-5). Routledge & Kegan.

--Rochester's Poetry. 230p. 1978. 21.50x (ISBN 0-8476-6078-8). Rowman.

Farley-Hills, David, ed. Rochester: The Critical Heritage. 1978. 34.00x (ISBN 0-7100-7157-4). Routledge & Kegan.

Farlie, Barbara & Abell, Vivian. Flower Craft. LC 78-55664. (Illus.). 1978. 14.95 (ISBN 0-685-53358-1); pap. 10.95 (ISBN 0-672-52150-4). Bobbs.

Farlie, Barbara L. & Clarke, Charlotte L. All about Doll Houses. LC 75-513. (Illus.). 272p. 1975. 16.95 (ISBN 0-672-51976-3). Bobbs.

--All about Doll Houses. LC 75-513. (Illus.). 1977. pap. 10.95 (ISBN 0-672-52367-1). Bobbs.

Farlie, Barbara L., jt. auth. see Abell, Vivian.

Farlie, Dennis J., jt. auth. see Budge, Ian.

Farlow. Self-Organizing Methods in Modeling: GMDH Type Algorithms. (Statistics - Textbooks & Monographs). 344p. 1984. 55.00 (ISBN 0-8247-7161-3). Dekker.

Farlow, George. How to Successfully Sell Information by Mail. 120p. 1982. pap. 10.00 (ISBN 0-936300-05-1). Pr Arden Park.

Farlow, Helen. Publicizing & Promoting Programs. 1979. 24.95x (ISBN 0-07-019947-7). McGraw.

Farlow, Robert L., jt. auth. see Clark, Cal.

Farlow, S. J. Partial Differential Equations for Scientists & Engineers. 300p. (Japanese.). 1983. pap. 29.95 (ISBN 0-471-88698-X). Wiley.

Farlow, Stanley J. Partial Differential Equations for Scientists & Engineers. LC 81-12993. 402p. 1982. text ed. 38.00x (ISBN 0-471-08639-8); solutions manual avail. (ISBN 0-471-09582-6). Wiley.

Farlow, Susan. Made in America: A Guide to Tours of Workshops, Farms, Mines & Industries. northeast ed. (Orig.). 1979. pap. 7.95 (ISBN 0-8038-0477-6). Hastings.

Farlow, W. C. The Marine Algae of New England & Adjacent Coast. (Illus.). 1969. Repr. of 1881 ed. 35.00 (ISBN 3-7682-0582-7). Lubrecht & Cramer.

Farlow, W. G. Mushroom Hunters Guide & Common Poisonous Plants. LC 82-72605. (Illus.). 60p. (Orig.). 1982. pap. 4.95 (ISBN 0-89708-084-X). And Bks.

--Some Edible & Poisonous Fungi. facs. ed. (Shorey Lost Arts Ser.). 20p. pap. 0.95 (ISBN 0-8466-6001-6, U1). Shorey.

Farls, D., jt. auth. see Stokes, Roberta.

Farm & Land Institute. Tax Planning for Real Estate Transactions. 356p. 22.50 (ISBN 0-318-15196-0, 14-1001). Natl Assoc Realtors.

Farm Foundation & Resources for the Future, Inc. Land Economics Research: Papers Presented at a Symposium Held at Lincoln, Nebraska, June 16-23, 1961. Ackerman, Joseph, et al, eds. LC 77-86388. (Resources for the Future, Inc. Publications). 296p. Repr. of 1962 ed. 55.00 (ISBN 0-404-60327-0). AMS Pr.

Farm Journal. Farm Journal's Choice Chocolate Recipes. 1982. pap. 2.50 (ISBN 0-345-30184-6). Ballantine.

--Farm Journal's Complete Cake Decorating Book. LC 82-45540. (Illus.). 160p. 1983. 15.95 (ISBN 0-385-18376-3). Doubleday.

Farm Journal, ed. Farm Journal's Homemade Breads. rev., enl. & updated ed. LC 84-45565. (Illus.). 352p. 1985. 16.95 (ISBN 0-385-19906-6). Doubleday.

Farm Journal, et al. Let's Make a Patchwork Quilt: Using a Variety of Sampler Blocks. LC 80-500. (Illus.). 128p. 1980. 15.95 (ISBN 0-385-15734-7, Anchor Pr). Doubleday.

Farm Journal Editors. Farm Journal's Complete Pie Book. 1981. pap. 2.50 (ISBN 0-345-29782-2). Ballantine.

--Farm Journal's Cookbook. 1981. pap. 2.95 (ISBN 0-345-29781-4). Ballantine.

--Farm Journal's Country-Style Microwave Cookbook. 224p. (Orig.). 1984. pap. 2.95 (ISBN 0-345-31360-7). Ballantine.

--Homemade Cookies. 1981. pap. 2.50 (ISBN 0-345-29783-0). Ballantine.

Farm Journal Editors & Manning, Elise W. Farm Journal's Best Ever Recipes. (Illus.). 1977. 19.95 (ISBN 0-385-12966-1). Doubleday.

--Farm Journal's Choice Chocolate Recipes. (Illus.). 1979. 12.95 (ISBN 0-385-14777-5). Doubleday.

--Farm Journal's Complete Home Baking Book. (Illus.). 1979. 15.95 (ISBN 0-385-14915-8). Doubleday.

Farm Journal Editors & Nichols, Nell B. Farm Journal's Country Cookbook. rev. & enl. ed. LC 73-175372. (Illus.). 480p. 1972. 15.95 (ISBN 0-385-03036-3). Doubleday.

--Homemade Candy. LC 79-121953. (Illus.). 1972. 9.95 (ISBN 0-385-01893-2). Doubleday.

Farm Journal Editors, et al. Farm Journal's Freezing & Canning Cookbook. rev. ed. LC 77-81787. (Illus.). 1978. 14.95 (ISBN 0-385-13444-4). Doubleday.

Farm Journal Food Editors. Farm Journal's Best Ever Vegetable Recipes. LC 82-46053. (Illus.). 288p. 1984. 14.95 (ISBN 0-385-18849-8). Doubleday.

--Farm Journal's Country-Style Microwave Cookbook. LC 80-19928. 128p. (Orig.). 1980. pap. 3.95x (ISBN 0-89795-012-7). Farm Journal.

--Farm Journal's Everyday Favorite Recipes. LC 80-19769. 128p. (Orig.). 1980. pap. 3.95x (ISBN 0-89795-011-9). Farm Journal.

Farm Journal Staff & WArd, Patricia A. Farm Journal's Best-Ever Cookies. LC 80-948. (Illus.). 1980. 14.95 (ISBN 0-385-17146-3). Doubleday.

--Farm Journal's Best Ever Pies. LC 81-43122. (Illus.). 228p. 1981. 17.95 (ISBN 0-385-17729-1). Doubleday.

Farm Journal's Food Editors. Chicken Twice a Week. LC 76-12306. 128p. (Orig.). 1976. pap. 3.95 (ISBN 0-89795-019-4). Farm Journal.

--Farm Journal's Country-Style Microwave Cookbook 2. LC 82-12025. 128p. (Orig.). 1982. pap. 3.95 (ISBN 0-89795-014-3). Farm Journal.

--Farm Journal's Ground Beef Roundup. LC 82-12107. 128p. (Orig.). 1982. pap. 3.95 (ISBN 0-686-84082-8). Farm Journal.

--Farm Journal's Molded Salads & Desserts. LC 76-10410. 128p. (Orig.). 1976. pap. 3.95 (ISBN 0-89795-017-8). Farm Journal.

--Farm Journal's Picnic & Barbecue Cookbook. Ward, Patricia, ed. (Illus.). 168p. 1982. 13.95 (ISBN 0-89795-013-5). Farm Journal.

Farma, William J. Prose, Poetry & Drama for Oral Interpretation. 1930. Repr. 25.00 (ISBN 0-8274-3215-1). R West.

Farma, William J., ed. Prose, Poetry & Drama for Oral Interpretation, First Ser. facs. ed. LC 73-139759. (Granger Index Reprint Ser). 1930. 27.00 (ISBN 0-8369-6213-3). Ayer Co Pubs.

--Prose, Poetry & Drama for Oral Interpretation, Second Ser. facsimile ed. LC 73-139759. (Granger Index Reprint Ser). 1936. 27.00 (ISBN 0-8369-6223-0). Ayer Co Pubs.

Farmakides, Anne. Advanced Modern Greek. LC 82-48914. (Yale Linguistic Ser.). 400p. 1983. pap. text ed. 22.50x (ISBN 0-300-03023-1). Yale U Pr.

--A Manual of Modern Greek, Vol. I. LC 82-48915. (Yale Linguistic Ser.). 304p. 1983. pap. text ed. 14.95x (ISBN 0-300-03019-3). Yale U Pr.

--A Manual of Modern Greek, Vol. II. LC 82-48916. (Yale Linguistic Ser.). 304p. 1983. pap. text ed. 14.95x (ISBN 0-300-03020-7). Yale U Pr.

--Modern Greek Reader, No. I. LC 82-48913. (Yale Linguistic Ser.). 278p. 1983. pap. text ed. 14.95x (ISBN 0-300-03021-5). Yale U Pr.

--Modern Greek Reader, No. II. LC 82-48913. (Yale Linguistic Ser.). 260p. 1983. pap. text ed. 14.95 (ISBN 0-300-03022-3). Yale U Pr.

Farmakides, Anne, ed. Manual of Modern Greek, No. I. rev. ed. 96p. 1983. 7.95x (ISBN 0-317-01511-7); self study course, with cassettes 160.45, (ISBN 0-88432-120-7, SGR101). J Norton Pubs.

Farmakides, Anne, et al, eds. The Teaching of Modern Greek in the English Speaking World. (The Modern Greek Language Ser.: No. 1). 140p. (Orig.). 1984. pap. text ed. 10.00 (ISBN 0-917653-01-7). Hellenic Coll Pr.

Farman, Dorothy J. Auden in Love. 1985. pap. 7.95 (ISBN 0-452-00772-0, Mer). NAL.

Farman, Edgar. The Bulldog: A Monograph. 304p. 1985. 45.00 (ISBN 0-947647-12-0, Pub. by Fanciers Supplies). Longwood Pub Group.

Farmar, Edward J. Modernizing Control Systems: New Management Patterns for the Retrofit Project. LC 83-18399. (ISA Monograph Ser.: No. 8). 192p. 1984. text ed. 24.95x (ISBN 0-87664-467-1). Instru Soc.

Farmazyan, R. Disarmament & the Economy. 172p. 1981. 5.80 (ISBN 0-8285-2098-4, Pub. by Progress Pubs USSR). Imported Pubns.

Farmer. Father to the Stars. 2.75 (ISBN 0-317-31847-0). Tor Bks.

--Jesus on Mars. 1.95 (ISBN 0-317-31856-X). Tor Bks.

--Other Log of Phileas Fogg. 2.50 (ISBN 0-317-31877-2). Tor Bks.

--Tits & Clits, No. 6. (Women's Humor Ser.). (Illus.). 1980. 1.50 (ISBN 0-918440-07-6). Nanny Goat.

Farmer & Anderson. Business Transcription. 192p. 1973. text ed. 11.20x (ISBN 0-7715-0740-2). Forkner.

Farmer & Chevli. Tits & Clits, No. 5. (Women's Humor Ser.). (Illus.). 1979. 1.25 (ISBN 0-918440-06-8). Nanny Goat.

Farmer & Lyvely. Tits & Clits, No. 2. (Women's Humor Ser.). (Illus.). 1976. 1.25 (ISBN 0-918440-03-3). Nanny Goat.

Farmer, jt. auth. see Chevli.

Farmer, jt. auth. see Lyvely.

Farmer, A. S. Synopsis of Biological Data on the Norway Lobster: Nephrops Norvegicus (Linnaeus, 1758) (Fisheries Synopses: No. 112). (Illus.). 97p. 1975. pap. 7.50 (ISBN 92-5-101906-1, F845, FAO). Unipub.

Farmer, Albert J. Walter Pater As a Critic of English Literature. LC 73-9788. 1931. lib. bdg. 15.00 (ISBN 0-8414-1970-1). Folcroft.

Farmer, Ann D. Jessamyn West. LC 82-71033. (Western Writers Ser.: No. 53). (Illus., Orig.). 1982. pap. 2.00x (ISBN 0-88430-027-7). Boise St Univ.

Farmer, Ann K. Modularity in Syntax: A Study in Japanese & English. (Current Studies in Linguistics). 224p. 1984. text ed. 30.00x (ISBN 0-262-06087-6). MIT Pr.

Farmer, B. H. An Introduction to South Asia. 253p. 1984. pap. 10.95x (ISBN 0-416-72610-0, NO. 4026). Methuen Inc.

Farmer, Bertram H. Pioneer Peasant Colonization in Ceylon. LC 76-8924. (Illus.). 1976. Repr. of 1957 ed. lib. bdg. 31.50x (ISBN 0-8371-8888-1, FAPI). Greenwood.

Farmer, Beverly. Alone: A Novel. 1985. pap. 4.95 (ISBN 0-14-007799-5). Penguin.

--Milk: Stories. 192p. 1985. pap. 5.95 (ISBN 0-14-007184-9). Penguin.

Farmer, Charles & Farmer, Kathy, eds. Digest Book of Outdoor Cooking. LC 79-50067. 96p. pap. 3.95 (ISBN 0-695-81285-8). DBI.

Farmer, Charles J. Backpack Fishing. LC 73-20839. (Illus.). 224p. 1976. pap. 6.95 (ISBN 0-89149-018-3). Jolex.

--Digest Book of Canoeing. LC 79-50060. 96p. pap. 3.95 (ISBN 0-695-81287-4). DBI.

--Digest Book of Canoes, Kayaks, & Rafts. LC 76-50749. (Illus.). 192p. 1977. pap. 5.95 (ISBN 0-695-80719-6). DBI.

Farmer, D., jt. auth. see Dard, R.

Farmer, D., et al, eds. Cellular Automata: Proceedings of the Internat. Workshop on Cellular Automata, Los Alamos, NM,March 7-11, 1983. 248p. 1984. 30.00 (ISBN 0-444-86850-X, I-199-84). Elsevier.

Farmer, D. H., jt. tr. see Webb, J. F.
Farmer, David. Flannery O'Connor: A Descriptive Bibliography. LC 80-8480. 152p. 1981. lib. bdg. 24.00 (ISBN 0-8240-9493-X). Garland Pub.
--Procurement & Materials Management. 1981. 90.00x (ISBN 0-86176-093-X, Pub. by MCB Pubns). State Mutual Bk.
--Purchasing Management Handbook. LC 84-18659. 712p. 1985. text ed. 65.95 (ISBN 0-566-02471-3). Gower Pub Co.
Farmer, David, jt. auth. see Baily, Peter.
Farmer, David, compiled by. Ezra Pound: An Exhibition. (Illus.). 1967. pap. 5.00 (ISBN 0-87959-006-8). U of Tex H Ransom Ctr.
--Siegfried Sassoon: A Memorial Exhibition. LC 77-628295. (Illus.). 1969. pap. 5.00 (ISBN 0-87959-007-6). U of Tex H Ransom Ctr.
Farmer, David & Taylor, Bernard, eds. Corporate Planning & Procurement. LC 74-19369. 272p. 1975. 21.50 (ISBN 0-470-25499-8). Krieger.
Farmer, David, jt. ed. see Bowden, Edwin T.
Farmer, David H. Saint Hugh of Lincoln. (Cistercian Studies: No. 87). xi, 114p. 1985. pap. 8.00 (ISBN 0-87907-887-1). Cistercian Pubns.
Farmer, David H., ed. The Oxford Dictionary of Saints. 1978. pap. 8.95 (ISBN 0-19-283036-8). Oxford U Pr.
Farmer, David H. & Taylor, Bernard, eds. Corporate Planning & Procurement. 352p. (Orig.). 1982. Repr. of 1975 ed. 24.95 (ISBN 0-434-91910-1, Pub. by W Heinemann Ltd). David & Charles.
Farmer, David J. Crime Control: The Use & Misuse of Police Resources. (Criminal Justice & Public Safety Ser.). 252p. 1984. 25.00x (ISBN 0-306-41688-3, Plenum Pr). Plenum Pub.
Farmer, Edward L. Early Ming Government: The Evolution of Dual Capitals. (East Asian Monographs: No. 65). 425p. 1976. text ed. 22.50x (ISBN 0-674-22175-3). Harvard U Pr.
Farmer, Ernest. Pupil Transportation: The Essential of Program Service. LC 74-22528. x, 230p. 1975. pap. text ed. 4.95 (ISBN 0-8134-1688-4, 1688). Interstate.
Farmer, Evan R., jt. auth. see Provost, Thomas T.
Farmer, Evelyn. Second Math Helper. (Classroom Pairing: Math Tutorial Program Ser.). 64p. (gr. k-1). 1975. 2.95 (ISBN 0-87594-141-9). Book-Lab.
Farmer, F. M. Original Boston Cooking School Cookbook. pap. 6.95 (ISBN 0-452-25314-4, Z5314, Plume). NAL.
Farmer, Fannie. The Boston Cooking School Cook Book. 75.00 (ISBN 0-87968-092-X). Gordon Pr.
Farmer, Fannie M. The Original Boston Cooking-School Cookbook 1896. 624p. 1984. pap. 4.95 (ISBN 0-451-12892-3, Sig). NAL.
Farmer, Frances. Will There Really Be a Morning? 1982. pap. 3.95 (ISBN 0-440-19292-7). Dell.
Farmer, Frances, ed. Wilson Reader. (Docket Ser.: Vol. 4). 286p. (Orig.). 1956. pap. 2.50 (ISBN 0-379-11304-X). Oceana.
Farmer, G. M., et al. Keyboarding: An Introductory Course. 96p. 1985. 7.25 (ISBN 0-7715-0926-X). Forkner.
Farmer, Gale E., jt. auth. see Brady, Stephen W.
Farmer, George L. Education: The Dilemma of the Spanish-Surname American. LC 70-543. 55p. 1982. lib. bdg. 39.95x (ISBN 0-89370-712-0). Borgo Pr.
--A Panorama of the Afro-American. 58p. 1983. Repr. of 1971 ed. lib. bdg. 39.95x (ISBN 0-89370-780-5). Borgo Pr.
Farmer, George T., Jr., jt. auth. see Fichter, Lynn S.
Farmer, Geraldine M. & Brown, Muriel J. Machine Transcription: A Brief Course. LC 81-65398. (Illus.). 72p. (gr. 10-12). 1981. pap. text ed. 3.53x (ISBN 0-912036-48-6); tchr's resource manual 4.42x (ISBN 0-912036-49-4); instructional narrative 18 cassettes 250.00x (ISBN 0-912036-50-8). Forkner.
Farmer, Helen S. Counseling Programs & Service for Women in Nontraditional Occupations. 56p. 1978. 4.50 (ISBN 0-318-15436-6, IN133). Natl Ctr Res Voc Ed.
Farmer, Helen S. & Backer, Thomas E. New Career Options for Women: A Three-Part Series for Counselors, Counselor Trainers & Women Thinking About Careers, 3 pts. 1977. Set. 39.95 (ISBN 0-87705-266-2); Pt. 1, 349 p. 29.95 (ISBN 0-87705-297-2); Pt. 2, 60p. 7.95 (ISBN 0-87705-272-7); Pt. 3, 144pp. 19.95 (ISBN 0-87705-273-5). Human Sci Pr.
Farmer, Henry G. Historical Facts for the Arabian Musical Influence. LC 75-173164. 27.50 (ISBN 0-405-08496-X, Blom Pubns). Ayer Co Pubs.
--History of Music in Scotland. LC 70-100613. (Music Ser). (Illus.). 1970. Repr. of 1947 ed. lib. bdg. 39.50 (ISBN 0-306-71865-0). Da Capo.
--Rise & Development of Military Music. LC 79-107801. (Select Bibliographies Reprint Ser). 1912. 16.00 (ISBN 0-8369-5204-9). Ayer Co Pubs.
--Studies in Oriental Musical Instruments: First & Second Ser, 2 vols. in 1. LC 77-75185. 1977. Repr. of 1939 ed. lib. bdg. 30.00 (ISBN 0-89341-056-X). Longwood Pub Group.
Farmer, Henry G. & Smith, Herbert. New Mozartiana. LC 74-24077. (Illus.). Repr. of 1935 ed. 19.50 (ISBN 0-404-12906-4). AMS Pr.
Farmer, Henry G., ed. see Chelebi, Ewliya.
Farmer, Henry G., ed. & tr. see Salvador-Daniel, Francesco.
Farmer, Herbert H. Revelation & Religion: Studies in the Theological Interpretation of Religious Types. LC 77-27177. (Gifford Lectures: 1950). (Illus.). 256p. Repr. of 1954 ed. 31.00 (ISBN 0-404-60505-2). AMS Pr.
Farmer, I. W. Engineering Behavior of Rocks. LC 82-20853. 213p. 1983. 43.00 (ISBN 0-412-25280-5, NO. 6842, Pub. by Chapman & Hall); pap. 21.00 (ISBN 0-412-13980-4, NO. 6781). Methuen Inc.
--Strata Mechanics: Proceedings of the Symposium, Newcastle Upon Tyne, April 5-7, 1982. (Developments in Geotechnical Engineering Ser.: Vol. 32). 290p. 1982. 85.00 (ISBN 0-444-42086-X). Elsevier.
Farmer, Ian, jt. auth. see Attwell, Peter.
Farmer, Ian. W. Coal Mine Structures. 364p. 1985. 59.95 (ISBN 0-412-25030-6, NO. 9133, Pub. by Chapman & Hall England). Methuen Inc.
Farmer, J. A. Tribunals & Government. (Law in Context Ser.). xiii, 250p. 1974. text ed. 14.95x (ISBN 0-297-76837-9, Pub. by Weidenfeld & Nicholson England). Rothman.
Farmer, J. B., tr. see De Vries, H.
Farmer, James. Lay Bare the Heart: An Autobiography of the Civil Rights Movement. 362p. 1985. 16.95 (ISBN 0-87795-624-3). Arbor Hse.
Farmer, James, jt. auth. see Lippert, Frederick G., III.
Farmer, James H. Broken Wings: Hollywood's Air Crashes. LC 84-60464. (Illus.). 120p. (Orig.). 1984. pap. 9.95 (ISBN 0-933126-46-8). Pictorial Hist.
--Celluloid Wings. (Illus.). 384p. 1984. pap. 15.95 (ISBN 0-8306-2374-4, 2374). TAB Bks.
Farmer, James O., Jr. The Metaphysical Confederacy: James Henley Thornwell & the Synthesis of Southern Values. (Illus.). 320p. 1986. 25.95x (ISBN 0-86554-182-5, MUP/H171). Mercer Univ Pr.
Farmer, John. A Genealogical Register of the First Settlers of New England. lib. bdg. 59.95 (ISBN 0-8490-0214-1). Gordon Pr.
--A Genealogical Register of the First Settlers of New-England: 1620-1675. LC 64-19761. 355p. 1983. Repr. of 1829 ed. 17.50 (ISBN 0-8063-0108-2). Genealog Pub.
--An Historical Sketch of the Town of Amherst. LC 72-91706. 64p. 1972. Repr. of 1837 ed. 10.00 (ISBN 0-912274-26-3). NH Pub Co.
Farmer, John David. Ensor: Major Pioneer of Modern Art. LC 76-16639. (Illus.). 128p. 1977. 17.50 (ISBN 0-8076-0840-8); pap. 9.95 (ISBN 0-8076-0836-X). Braziller.
Farmer, John N. Lecture Outline & Guide for Introductory Zoology. 128p. 1984. pap. text ed. 9.95 (ISBN 0-8403-3440-0). Kendall-Hunt.
Farmer, John S. Merry Songs & Ballads & Musa Pedestris: Musa Pedestris, 6 vols. Repr. of 1896 ed. Set. 85.00 (ISBN 0-8154-0066-7). Cooper Sq.
--Merry Songs & Ballads Prior to the Year A. D. 1800, 5 Vols. 1964. Repr. of 1895 ed. 85.00 (ISBN 0-8154-0064-0). Cooper Sq.
--Musa Pedestris: Three Centuries of Canting Songs & Slang Rhymes, 1536-1896. LC 66-2866. 1964. Repr. of 1896 ed. 20.00 (ISBN 0-8154-0065-9). Cooper Sq.
--Public School Word-Book. LC 68-17988. 1968. Repr. of 1900 ed. 35.00x (ISBN 0-8103-3280-9). Gale.
--The Public School Word-Book. 1900. 30.00 (ISBN 0-8274-3224-0). R West.
Farmer, John S. & Henley, W. E. Slang & Its Analogues, Past & Present, 7 Vols. in 3. LC 5-16232. 1890-1904. Set. 130.00 (ISBN 0-527-28300-2). Kraus Repr.
Farmer, John S., ed. The Maid's Metamorphosis Sixteen Hundred. 1979. Repr. lib. bdg. 20.00 (ISBN 0-89987-017-1). Darby Bks.
--Tudor Facsimile Texts, 149 titles in 146 vols. Repr. of 1914 ed. Set. 7227.00 (ISBN 0-404-53300-0); 49.50 ea. AMS Pr.
Farmer, Kathy, jt. ed. see Farmer, Charles.
Farmer, Kenneth C. Ukrainian Nationalism in the Post-Stalin Era: Myth, Symbols & Ideology in Soviet Nationalities Policy. (Studies in Contemporary History: Vol. 4). 253p. 1980. lib. bdg. 36.50 (ISBN 90-247-2401-5, Pub. by Martinus Nijhoff). Kluwer Academic.
Farmer Magazine. Country Kitchen Cookbook: Eighteen Ninety-Four to Nineteen Seventy-Nine. (Illus.). 1979. pap. 5.95 (ISBN 0-8015-1786-9, Hawthorn). Dutton.
Farmer, Mary A. Be An Angel. (Illus.). 10p. 1981. pap. 4.00 (ISBN 0-943574-07-2). That Patchwork.
--Special Santas. (Illus.). 18p. 1981. pap. 4.00 (ISBN 0-943574-08-0). That Patchwork.
Farmer, Mary Ann. Pilots, Partners & Pals. (Illus.). 12p. 1982. pap. 4.00 (ISBN 0-943574-16-1). That Patchwork.
Farmer, MaryAnn. Warmest Witches To You. (Illus.). 12p. 1982. pap. 4.00 (ISBN 0-943574-18-8). That Patchwork.
Farmer, Norman K., Jr. Poets & the Visual Arts in Renaissance England. LC 83-14771. (Illus.). 138p. 1984. text ed. 25.00x (ISBN 0-292-78711-1). U of Tex Pr.
Farmer, P., jt. auth. see Gomersall, A.
Farmer, P. B. & Walker, J. M. The Molecular Basis of Cancer. 352p. 1985. pap. 29.95 (ISBN 0-471-82755-X). Wiley.
Farmer, Paul. France Reviews: Its Revolutionary Origins. 1963. lib. bdg. 16.50x (ISBN 0-374-92698-0). Octagon.
--Vichy: Political Dilemma. 1977. Repr. of 1955 ed. lib. bdg. 29.00x (ISBN 0-374-92700-6). Octagon.
Farmer, Paul W., jt. auth. see Catanese, Anthony J.
Farmer, Penelope. August the Fourth. LC 75-2713. (Illus.). (gr. 3-6). 1976. 5.95 (ISBN 0-87466-070-X, Pub. by Parnassus); PLB 4.77 (ISBN 0-87466-071-8). HM.
--Beginnings: Creation Myths of the World. LC 78-23279. (Illus.). 160p. 1979. 9.95 (ISBN 0-689-50101-3, McElderry Bk). Atheneum.
Farmer, Penelope, tr. see Oz, Amos.
Farmer, Penny. Energy Conservation in Buildings 1973-1983: A Bibliography of European & American Literature on Government, Commercial & Domestic Buildings. 107p. (Orig.). 1983. pap. text ed. 39.50 (ISBN 0-946655-00-6). Scholium Intl.
Farmer, Penny, jt. ed. see Gomersall, Alan.
Farmer, Philip J. A Barnstormer in Oz. 1982. pap. 5.95 trade (ISBN 0-425-05641-4). Berkley Pub.
--A Barnstormer in Oz. 304p. 1983. pap. 2.95 mass (ISBN 0-425-06274-0). Berkley Pub.
--Behind the Walls of Terra. 224p. 1984. pap. 2.75 (ISBN 0-425-07558-3). Berkley Pub.
--The Book of Philip Jose Farmer. (Orig.). 1982. pap. 2.50 (ISBN 0-425-05298-2). Berkley Pub.
--The Cache. rev. ed. 288p. 1981. pap. 2.75 (ISBN 0-523-48534-4). Pinnacle Bks.
--Cache. pap. 2.75 (ISBN 0-317-31828-4). Tor Bks.
--The Classic Philip Jose Farmer, 1964-1973, No. 2. LC 84-7081. (Classics of Modern Science Fiction Ser.). 1984. 8.95 (ISBN 0-517-55545-X). Crown.
--The Dark Design. LC 77-5138. (Riverworld Ser.). (YA) 1984. pap. 2.95 (ISBN 0-425-07284-3). Berkley Pub.
--Dark Is the Sun. 1981. 9.95 (ISBN 0-345-27684-1, Del Rey). Ballantine.
--Dark Is the Sun. 384p. 1980. pap. 2.50 (ISBN 0-345-29680-X, Del Rey). Ballantine.
--Dayworld. 336p. 1985. 16.95 (ISBN 0-399-12967-7, Putnam). Putnam Pub Group.
--The Fabulous Riverboat. 416p. 1985. pap. 2.95 (ISBN 0-425-07756-X). Berkley Pub.
--Father to the Stars. 320p. (Orig.). 1981. pap. 2.75 (ISBN 0-523-48504-2). Pinnacle Bks.
--Flight to Opar. 224p. 1976. pap. 2.95 (ISBN 0-87997-875-9). DAW Bks.
--The Gates of Creation. 224p. 1981. pap. 2.75 (ISBN 0-441-27390-4). Ace Bks.
--The Gates of Creation. (World of Tiers Ser.: No. 2). 192p. 1984. pap. 2.75 (ISBN 0-425-07193-6). Berkley Pub.
--Gods of Riverworld. 336p. 1983. 14.95 (ISBN 0-399-12843-3, Putnam). Putnam Pub Group.
--Gods of Riverworld. 336p. 1985. pap. 3.50 (ISBN 0-425-07448-X). Berkley Pub.
--The Grand Adventure. 320p. 1984. pap. 7.95 (ISBN 0-425-07211-8). Berkley Pub.
--The Green Odyssey. 224p. 1983. pap. 2.50 (ISBN 0-425-06159-0). Berkley Pub.
--Hadon of Ancient Opar. (Science Fiction Ser.). 1981. pap. 2.95 (ISBN 0-87997-873-2, UE1873). DAW Bks.
--Image of the Beast. 336p. 1985. pap. 3.50 (ISBN 0-425-07708-X). Berkley Pub.
--Inside, Outside. (Science Fiction Rediscovery Ser.). 1975. pap. 1.95 (ISBN 0-380-00260-4, 22830). Avon.
--Inside Outside. 1980. lib. bdg. 12.50 (ISBN 0-8398-2622-2, Gregg). G K Hall.
--Jesus on Mars. 1979. pap. 1.95 (ISBN 0-523-40184-1). Pinnacle Bks.
--Lavalite World. (World of Tiers Ser.). 288p. 1982. pap. 2.75 (ISBN 0-441-47422-5). Ace Bks.
--The Lavalite World. (World of Tiers Ser.: No. 5). 1983. 18.00 (ISBN 0-932096-21-2). Phantasia Pr.
--Lord of the Trees. Bd. with The Mad Goblin. 1980. pap. 2.50 (ISBN 0-441-49252-5). Ace Bks.
--The Lovers. 1981. 8.95 (ISBN 0-345-28032-6, Del Rey). Ballantine.
--The Magic Labyrinth. 416p. 1984. pap. 2.95 (ISBN 0-425-07687-3). Berkley Pub.
--The Maker of Universes. (World of Tiers Ser.: No. 1). 256p. 1984. pap. 2.75 (ISBN 0-425-07378-5). Ace Bks.
--The Maker of Universes. rev. ed. (The World of Tiers Ser.). 224p. 1980. Repr. of 1962 ed. 15.00 (ISBN 0-932096-07-7). Phantasia Pr.
--Night of Light. 1983. pap. 2.50 (ISBN 0-425-06291-0, Medallion). Berkley Pub.
--Night of Light. Del Rey, Lester, ed. LC 75-404. (Library of Science Fiction). 1975. lib. bdg. 21.00 (ISBN 0-8240-1409-X). Garland Pub.
--The Other Log of Phileas Fogg. 288p. (Orig.). 1982. pap. 2.50 (ISBN 0-523-48508-5). Pinnacle Bks.
--Philip Jose Farmer: The Complete Riverworld Novels, 5 bks. Incl. To Your Scattered Bodies Go; The Fabulous Riverboat; The Dark Design; Riverworld; The Magic Labyrinth. 1982. Boxed Set. pap. 13.25 (ISBN 0-425-05835-2). Berkley Pub.
--A Private Cosmos. 288p. 1981. pap. 2.50 (ISBN 0-441-67954-4). Ace Bks.
--A Private Cosmos. (World of Tiers Ser.: No. 3). 288p. 1984. pap. 2.75 (ISBN 0-425-07299-1). Berkley Pub.
--River of Eternity. 1983. 17.00 (ISBN 0-932096-28-X). Phantasia Pr.
--Riverworld & Other Stories. 272p. 1984. pap. 2.75 (ISBN 0-425-06487-5). Berkley Pub.
--Riverworld & Other Stories. 1981. lib. bdg. 16.95 (ISBN 0-8398-2618-4, Gregg). G K Hall.
--Stations of the Nightmare. 288p. (Orig.). 1982. pap. 2.75 (ISBN 0-523-48522-0). Pinnacle Bks.
--Strange Relations. 1978. pap. 1.75 (ISBN 0-380-00095-4, 41418). Avon.
--Times Last Gift. (Del Rey Bks). 1977. pap. 1.50 (ISBN 0-345-25843-6). Ballantine.
--Time's Last Gift. 256p. 1985. pap. 2.95 (ISBN 0-8125-3764-5). Tor Bks.
--To Your Scattered Bodies Go. 1980. lib. bdg. 13.50 (ISBN 0-8398-2620-6, Gregg). G K Hall.
--Traitor to the Living. 288p. (Orig.). 1985. pap. 2.95 (ISBN 0-8125-3766-1). Tor Bks.
--Two Hawks from Earth. 320p. 1985. pap. 2.95 (ISBN 0-425-08092-7). Berkley Pub.
--The Unreasoning Mask. 272p. 1983. pap. 2.95 (ISBN 0-425-06590-1). Berkley Pub.
--The Wind Whales of Ishmael. 160p. 1981. pap. 1.95 (ISBN 0-441-89240-X). Ace Bks.
Farmer, Philip J. & Rosny, J. H. Ironcastle. 176p. 1976. pap. 1.95 (ISBN 0-87997-545-8). DAW Bks.
Farmer, Philip J. see Trout, Kilgore, pseud.
Farmer, Philip Jose. Lavalite World. (World of Tiers Ser.: No. 5). 288p. 1985. pap. 2.75 (ISBN 0-425-07515-X). Berkley Pub.
Farmer, Philip Jose, intro. by see Upfield, Arthur W.
Farmer, Phillip J. Riverworld War. 112p. 1980. 6.95 (ISBN 0-933180-13-6). Ellis Pr.
Farmer, R. D., jt. auth. see Miller, D. L.
Farmer, Richard. Essay on the Learning of Shakespeare. LC 73-168006. Repr. of 1789 ed. 10.00 (ISBN 0-404-02366-5). AMS Pr.
--Junkman's Guide. LC 73-80843. 178p. pap. 3.95 (ISBN 0-8128-2469-5). Stein & Day.
Farmer, Richard & Kowalewski, Victor. Law Enforcement & Community Relations. 160p. 1976. 17.95 (ISBN 0-87909-434-6). Reston.
Farmer, Richard, ed. see Abdallah, Wagdy M.
Farmer, Richard, ed. see Bhat, Rajendra R.
Farmer, Richard, ed. see Choi, Frederick D. & Mueller, Gerhard G.
Farmer, Richard, ed. see Frieder, Larry A.
Farmer, Richard, ed. see Garland, John.
Farmer, Richard, ed. see Greene, William N.
Farmer, Richard, ed. see Hawes, Jon M.
Farmer, Richard, ed. see McConnell, Donald K., Jr.
Farmer, Richard, ed. see Morano, Roy W.
Farmer, Richard, ed. see Ramsower, Reagan M.
Farmer, Richard D. T. & Hirsch, Steven R., eds. The Suicide Syndrome. 256p. 1980. 29.95 (ISBN 0-85664-868-X, Pub. by Croom Helm Ltd). Longwood Pub Group.
Farmer, Richard E., jt. auth. see Monahan, Lynn H.
Farmer, Richard G., et al, eds. Clinical Gastroenterology. (Illus.). 608p. 1983. text ed. 67.00 (ISBN 0-89004-780-4). Raven.
Farmer, Richard N. Business: A Novel Approach. 378p. 1983. pap. 12.95. Cedarwood Pr.
--Business: A Novel Approach. 372p. 1984. pap. 8.95 (ISBN 0-89815-128-7). Ten Speed Pr.
--Incidents in International Business. 3rd ed. 5.95 (ISBN 0-318-00091-1). Cedarwood Pr.
--Incidents in International Business. 4th ed. 4.95 (ISBN 0-930417-01-1). Cedarwood Pr.
--Islandia Revisited. 1984. 10.00. Cedarwood Pr.
Farmer, Richard N. & Hogue, W. Dickerson. Corporate Social Responsibility. 2nd ed. LC 84-40848. 224p. 1985. pap. 14.95x (ISBN 0-669-10293-8). Lexington Bks.
Farmer, Richard N. & Lombardi, John V. Readings in International Business. 3rd ed. 1984. 9.95 (ISBN 0-318-00092-X). Cedarwood Pr.
Farmer, Richard N. & Richman, Barry M. International Business. 3rd ed. 13.95 (ISBN 0-318-00090-3). Cedarwood Pr.
--International Business. 4th ed. 1984. 12.95 (ISBN 0-930417-00-3). Cedarwood Pr.
Farmer, Richard N., jt. auth. see Richman, Barry M.
Farmer, Richard N., ed. Advances in International Comparative Management, Vol. 1. 1983. 40.00 (ISBN 0-89232-251-9). Jai Pr.
Farmer, Richard N., ed. see Bartlett, Roger W.
Farmer, Richard N., ed. see Bindon, Kathleen R.
Farmer, Richard N., ed. see Chan, T. S.
Farmer, Richard N., ed. see Dawley, Donald L.
Farmer, Richard N., ed. see Harlan, Kenneth M.
Farmer, Richard N., ed. see Hearth, Douglas.
Farmer, Richard N., ed. see Joo, Jalaleddin Soroosh.
Farmer, Richard N., ed. see Larkins, Ernest R.
Farmer, Richard N., ed. see McKnight, Reed H.
Farmer, Richard N., ed. see Magann, Julia H.
Farmer, Richard N., ed. see St. Pierre, Kent E.
Farmer, Robert A. One Thousand Ideas for English Term Papers. LC 67-11921. (One Thousand Ideas for Term Papers Ser). 156p. 1967. pap. 1.95 (ISBN 0-668-01548-9). Arco.
--What You Should Know about Contracts. 1979. pap. 3.95 (ISBN 0-346-12345-3). Cornerstone.
Farmer, Silas. History of Detroit & Wayne County & Early Michigan: A Chronological Cyclopedia of the Past & Present. LC 68-26178. 1969. Repr. of 1890 ed. 70.00x (ISBN 0-8103-3326-0). Gale.
Farmer, Silas, jt. auth. see Hall, Theodore P.

Farmer, Thomas W. Pediatric Neurology. 3rd ed. (Illus.). 768p. 1982. text ed. 75.00 (ISBN 0-06-140802-6, 14-08020, Harper Medical). Lippincott.
Farmer, Val. Making the Good Life Better. Benedict, Ruth, ed. LC 85-60850. 64p. 1985. pap. 5.95 (ISBN 0-89821-049-6). Reiman Assocs.
Farmer, W. D. Homes for Pleasant Living. 37th ed. (Illus.). 88p. (Orig.). 1981. pap. 4.00 (ISBN 0-931518-14-8). W D Farmer.
--Homes for Pleasant Living. 36th ed. (Illus.). 72p. (Orig.). 1980. pap. 3.50 (ISBN 0-931518-13-X). W D Farmer.
--Homes for Pleasant Living. 39th ed. (Illus.). 80p. (Orig.). 1982. pap. 4.50 (ISBN 0-931518-16-4). W D Farmer.
--Homes for Pleasant Living. 40th ed. (Illus.). 72p. (Orig.). 1983. pap. 4.50 (ISBN 0-931518-17-2). W D Farmer.
--Homes for Pleasant Living. 42nd. ed. (Illus.). 80p. 1984. pap. 5.00 (ISBN 0-931518-19-9). W D Farmer.
--Homes for Pleasant Living: Country & Victorian Style Homes. 38th. ed. (Illus.). 113p. (Orig.). 1982. pap. 5.00 (ISBN 0-931518-15-6). W D Farmer.
--Homes For Pleasant Living: Duplex Homes. 43rd ed. Ellis, Eugene, et al, eds. (Illus., Orig.). 1984. pap. 3.50 (ISBN 0-931518-18-0). W D Farmer.
--Small Homes for Pleasant Living. 35th ed. (Illus.). 40p. (Orig.). 1980. pap. 2.50 (ISBN 0-931518-12-1). W D Farmer.
--Vacation Retirement Homes. 33rd ed. (Illus.). 72p. (Orig.). 1979. pap. 3.50 (ISBN 0-931518-10-5). W D Farmer.
Farmer, W. Paul, jt. auth. see Witlzing, Lawrence P.
Farmer, Walter A. & Farrell, Margaret A. Systematic Instruction in Science for the Middle & High School Years. LC 79-4252. (Illus.). 1980. pap. text ed. 17.30 (ISBN 0-201-02435-7, Sch Div). Addison-Wesley.
Farmer, Walter A., jt. auth. see Farrell, Margaret A.
Farmer, Walter A., jt. auth. see Sipe, H. Craig.
Farmer, Wesley M. Sea-Slug Gastropods. (Illus.). 177p. (Orig.). 1980. pap. 9.57 (ISBN 0-937772-00-3). Farmer Ent.
Farmer, William R. Jesus & the Gospel. LC 81-43078. 1982. 22.95 (ISBN 0-8006-0666-3). Fortress.
--The Synoptic Problem: A Critical Analysis. LC 76-13764. 320p. 1981. 18.95x (ISBN 0-915948-02-8). Mercer Univ Pr.
Farmer, William R. & Farkasfalvy, Denis. The Formation of the New Testament Canon: An Ecumenical Approach. LC 82-62417. (Theological Inquiries Ser.). 1983. pap. 7.95 (ISBN 0-8091-2495-5). Paulist Pr.
Farmer, William R., ed. New Synoptic Studies: The Cambridge Gospel Conference & Beyond. LC 83-13396. 533p. 1983. 32.95x (ISBN 0-86554-087-X, MUP/H76). Mercer Univ Pr.
--Synopticon. 1969. 80.00 (ISBN 0-521-07464-9). Cambridge U Pr.
Farmer, William R. & Moule, C. F., eds. Christian History & Interpretation: Studies Presented to John Knox. LC 67-15306. pap. 116.00 (ISBN 0-317-08479-8, 2022449). Bks Demand UMI.
Farmers Weekly, ed. Farm Workshop & Maintenance. (Illus.). 192p. 1972. text ed. 15.95x (ISBN 0-8464-0404-4). Beekman Pubs.
Farmstead Magazine Editors. The Homesteader's Manual. (Illus.). 336p. (Orig.). 1983. o.p 19.95 (ISBN 0-8306-0629-7, 1629); pap. 13.50 (ISBN 0-8306-1629-2). TAB Bks.
Farnagle, A. E. The Not So Goody Gum Drop Shop: A Play in One Act. 32p. (Orig.). (gr. 3-8). 1984. pap. 3.50 (ISBN 0-916565-06-8). Whitehall Pr.
Farnagle, A. E. & Smith, W. Hovey. Farnagle's Fables for Children & Adults. (Illus.). 64p. (Orig.). (gr. 1-5). 1984. pap. 4.25 (ISBN 0-916565-04-1). Whitehall Pr.
Farnam, Anne. Textiles & Embroidery at the Essex Institute. LC 83-80761. (E. I. Museum Booklet Ser.). (Illus.). 64p. Date not set. pap. 4.95 (ISBN 0-88389-087-9). Essex Inst.
Farnam, Anne, ed. see Guren, Pamela, et al.
Farnam, Anne, ed. see Norton, Bettina A.
Farnam, Anne, ed. see Payson, Huldah S.
Farnam, Anne, et al. Furniture of the Essex Institute. LC 80-66232. (E. I. Museum Booklet Ser.). (Illus.). 64p. (Orig.). 1980. 4.95 (ISBN 0-88389-102-6). Essex Inst.
Farnam, Henry W. Chapters in the History of Social Legislation in the United States to 1860. LC 73-111778. Repr. of 1938 ed. 22.50 (ISBN 0-404-00157-2). AMS Pr.
--Shakespeare's Economics. LC 76-28220. 1931. lib. bdg. 17.50 (ISBN 0-8414-4203-7). Folcroft.
Farnan, Dorothy J. Auden in Love. (Illus.). 269p. 1984. 17.95 (ISBN 0-671-50418-5). S&S.
Farnan, Nancy J., jt. auth. see Goldman, Elizabeth.
Farndale, W. A., jt. ed. see Leicester, J. H.
Farnell, Ida. Spanish Prose - Poetry, Old - New. facsimile ed. LC 70-165630. (Select Bibliographies Reprint Ser). Repr. of 1920 ed. 17.00 (ISBN 0-8369-5937-X). Ayer Co Pubs.
Farnell, John, jt. auth. see Elles, James.
Farnell, L. R. The Higher Aspects of Greek Religion. 1977. 10.00 (ISBN 0-89005-206-9). Ares.
--Outline History of Greek Religion. 160p. 1974. 10.00 (ISBN 0-89005-025-2). Ares.
Farnell, Lewis R. The Attributes of God. LC 77-27205. (Gifford Lectures Ser.: 1924-25). 296p. Repr. of 1925 ed. 34.50 (ISBN 0-404-60475-7). AMS Pr.
--The Cults of the Greek States, 5 vols. Incl. Vol. 1. Cronos, Zeus, Hera, Athena. 50.00 (ISBN 0-89241-029-9); Vol. 2. Artemis, Aphrodite. 50.00 (ISBN 0-89241-030-2); Vol. 3. Cults of the Mother of the Gods, Raeh, Cybele. 50.00 (ISBN 0-89241-031-0); Vol. 4. Poseidon, Apollo. 60.00 (ISBN 0-89241-032-9); Vol. 5. Hermes, Dionysos, Hestia Hephaistos, Ares, the Minor Cults. 60.00 (ISBN 0-89241-033-7). (Illus.). 1977. Repr. 250.00x set (ISBN 0-89241-049-3). Caratzas.
--Greece & Babylon: A Comparative Sketch of Mesopatamian, Anatolian, & Hellenic Religions. 1977. lib. bdg. 59.95 (ISBN 0-8490-1906-0). Gordon Pr.
--The Higher Aspects of Greek Religion. LC 77-27158. (Hibbert Lectures Ser.: 1911). Repr. of 1912 ed. 16.00 (ISBN 0-404-60413-7). AMS Pr.
Farnell, Richard. Local Planning in Four English Cities. 132p. 1983. text ed. 32.00x (ISBN 0-566-00616-2). Gower Pub Co.
Farnell, Sarah K. Legal Constraints on Methane Gas Development. LC 82-622283. 1982. write for info. U Al Law.
Farnell, Stewart. The Political Ideas of The Divine Comedy: An Introduction. 152p. (Orig.). 1985. lib. bdg. 20.50 (ISBN 0-8191-4528-9); pap. text ed. 8.75 (ISBN 0-8191-4529-7). U Pr of Amer.
Farner, D. S., jt. ed. see Assenmacherm, I.
Farner, D. S., ed. see Leuthold, W.
Farner, Donald, et al, eds. Avian Biology, Vol. 6. LC 79-178216. 1982. 65.00 (ISBN 0-12-249406-7). Acad Pr.
Farner, Donald S. & King, James R. Avian Biology, 5 vols. Vol. 1, 1971. 89.50 (ISBN 0-12-249401-6); Vol. 2, 1972. 89.50 (ISBN 0-12-249402-4); Vol. 3, 1973. 79.50 (ISBN 0-12-249403-2); Vol. 4, 1974. 69.50 (ISBN 0-12-249404-0); Vol. 5, 1975. 94.50. Acad Pr.
Farner, Donald S. & Lederis, Karl, eds. Neurosecretion: Molecules, Cells, Systems. LC 81-21016. 558p. 1982. 69.50 (ISBN 0-306-40760-4, Plenum Pr). Plenum Pub.
Farner, Donald S., et al, eds. Avian Biology, Vol. 7. 1983. 69.50 (ISBN 0-12-249407-5). Acad Pr.
--Avian Biology, Vol. 8. Date not set. 49.50 (ISBN 0-12-249408-3). Acad Pr.
Farner, Oskar. Zwingli the Reformer: His Life & Work. (Illus.). 135p. 1968. Repr. of 1952 ed. 12.50 (ISBN 0-208-00694-X, Archon). Shoe String.
Farnes, Norma, ed. see Milligan, Spike.
Farnes, Patricia, ed. Haemic Cells In Vitro. (In Vitro Journal Back Volumes: Vol. 4). 182p. 1969. 15.00 (ISBN 0-317-36062-0). Tissue Culture Assn.
Farness, Jay, jt. auth. see Jones, Peder.
Farneti, Paolo. The Italian Party System: Nineteen Forty-Six to Nineteen Seventy-Nine. Finer, S. E. & Mastropaolo, A., eds. 240p. 1985. 27.50 (ISBN 0-312-43923-7). St Martin.
Farnette, Cherrie. Newspaper Know-How. (Choose-a-Card Ser.). (Illus.). 32p. (gr. 2-6). 1981. pap. text ed. 5.95 (ISBN 0-86530-011-9, IP-119). Incentive Pubns.
--The Study Skills Shop. (Choose-a-Card Ser.). (Illus.). 32p. (gr. 2-6). 1980. pap. text ed. 5.95 (ISBN 0-913916-69-2, IP 69-2). Incentive Pubns.
Farnette, Cherrie, et al. People Need Each Other. LC 78-70902. (Kids & Careers Ser.). (Illus.). 112p. (gr. 2-6). 1979. pap. text ed. 5.95 (ISBN 0-913916-63-3, IP633). Incentive Pubns.
--At Least a Thousand Things to Do. LC 77-83655. (Kids & Careers Ser.). (Illus.). 104p. (gr. 2-6). 1977. pap. text ed. 5.95 (ISBN 0-913916-53-6, IP 53-6). Incentive Pubns.
--Cents-Abilities. LC 78-70903. (Kids & Careers Ser.). (Illus.). 64p. (gr. 2-6). 1979. pap. text ed. 5.95 (ISBN 0-913916-64-1, IP 641). Incentive Pubns.
--I've Got Me & I'm Glad. LC 77-83654. (Kids & Careers Ser.). (Illus.). 104p. (gr. 2-6). 1977. pap. text ed. 5.95 (ISBN 0-913916-52-8, IP 52-8). Incentive Pubns.
--Kids' Stuff: Reading & Writing Readiness. LC 75-5347. (The Kids' Stuff Ser). (Illus.). 332p. (ps-2). 1975. 10.95 (ISBN 0-913916-13-7, IP 13-7). Incentive Pubns.
--Special Kids' Stuff. LC 76-505. (Illus.). 300p. (gr. 4-8). 1976. 10.95 (ISBN 0-913916-20-X, IP 20-X); avail. four dup master sets o.s.i. 5.95 ea. Incentive Pubns.
Farnfield, Carolyn A. A Guide to Sources of Information in the Textile Industry. 130p. 1974. 40.00x (ISBN 0-686-63767-4). State Mutual Bk.
Farnfield, Carolyn A. & Perry, D. R. Identification of Textile Materials. 262p. 1975. 99.00x (ISBN 0-686-63769-0). State Mutual Bk.
Farnham, Albert B. Home Taxidermy for Pleasure & Profit. (Illus.). 246p. pap. 3.50 (ISBN 0-936622-12-1). A R Harding Pub.
Farnham, Albert S. Home Manufacture of Furs & Skins. (Illus.). 283p. pap. 3.50 (ISBN 0-936622-10-5). A R Harding Pub.
--Home Tanning & Leather Making Guide. (Illus.). 176p. pap. 3.50 (ISBN 0-936622-11-3). A R Harding Pub.
Farnham, Arthur L. & Farnham, Lorraine J. Teddy's Birthday Party. 1984. 5.95 (ISBN 0-533-05944-5). Vantage.
--Teddy's Trip to Africa. 1982. 5.95 (ISBN 0-533-05288-2). Vantage.
Farnham, C. Evangeline. American Travelers in Spain. LC 77-168007. (Columbia University. Studies in Romance Philology & Literature: No. 29). Repr. of 1921 ed. 15.00 (ISBN 0-404-50629-1). AMS Pr.
Farnham, C. H. Life of Francis Parkman. LC 68-24975. (American Biography Ser., No. 32). 1969. Repr. of 1901 ed. lib. bdg. 54.95x (ISBN 0-8383-0938-0). Haskell.
Farnham, Charles H. Life of Francis Parkman. LC 71-108480. 1970. Repr. of 1901 ed. 15.00x (ISBN 0-403-00208-7). Scholarly.
--A Life of Francis Parkman. 394p. 1983. Repr. of 1905 ed. lib. bdg. 65.00 (ISBN 0-89760-239-0). Telegraph Bks.
Farnham, Dwight T. Scientific Industrial Efficiency. LC 73-9692. (Management History Ser.: No. 36). (Illus.). 101p. 1973. Repr. of 1917 ed. 18.50 (ISBN 0-87960-039-X). Hive Pub.
Farnham, Eliza W. Life in Prairie Land. LC 72-2601. (American Women Ser: Images & Realities). 412p. 1972. Repr. of 1846 ed. 22.00 (ISBN 0-405-04457-7). Ayer Co Pubs.
Farnham, Elizabeth M. Schools & Universities. 1969. pap. text ed. 4.95 (ISBN 0-88499-051-6). Inst Mod Lang.
Farnham, Emily. Charles Demuth: Behind a Laughing Mask. LC 70-108804. (Illus.). Repr. of 1971 ed. 72.50 (ISBN 0-8357-9721-X, 2016212). Bks Demand UMI.
Farnham, Fern. Madame Dacier, Scholar & Humanist. LC 73-93075. softcover 7.95 (ISBN 0-912216-12-3). Angel Pr.
Farnham, Henry W. Shakespeare's Economics. 1931. 16.50x (ISBN 0-686-51309-6). Elliots Bks.
Farnham, Lorraine J., jt. auth. see Farnham, Arthur L.
Farnham, Marynia F., jt. auth. see Lundberg, Ferdinand.
Farnham, Moulton M. Sailing for Beginners. rev. ed. (Illus.). 257p. 1981. 15.95 (ISBN 0-02-537140-1). Macmillan.
Farnham, Rebecca & Link, Irene. Effects of the Works Program on Rural Relief. LC 73-165682. (Research Monograph Ser.: Vol. 13). 1971. Repr. of 1938 ed. lib. bdg. 19.50 (ISBN 0-306-70345-9). Da Capo.
Farnham, Stanley E. Guide to Thermoformed Plastic Packaging: Sales Builder-Cost Cutter. LC 72-156481. 472p. 1972. 21.95 (ISBN 0-8436-1206-1). Van Nos Reinhold.
Farnham, Thomas J. History of the Oregon Territory. 107p. 1982. 9.95 (ISBN 0-87770-246-2). Ye Galleon.
--Travels in the Great Western Prairies, 2 vols. in 1. LC 68-16231. (The American Scene Ser.). 612p. 1973. Repr. of 1843 ed. lib. bdg. 75.00 (ISBN 0-306-71012-9). Da Capo.
--Weston: The Forging of a Connecticut Town. LC 79-14521. (Illus.). 1979. 13.50x (ISBN 0-914016-59-8). Phoenix Pub.
Farnham, Willard, ed. see Shakespeare, William.
Farnham, Willard E., ed. see Shakespeare, William.
Farnham-Diggory, Sylvia. Learning Disabilities: A Psychological Perspective. LC 78-5514. (Developing Child Ser.). 1978. 8.95x (ISBN 0-674-51921-3); pap. 3.95 (ISBN 0-674-51922-1). Harvard U Pr.
Farnham-Diggory, Sylvia, ed. Information Processing in Children. 1972. 39.50 (ISBN 0-12-249550-0). Acad Pr.
Farni, D. A. The Manchester Ship Canal & the Rise of the Port of Manchester. 128p. 1980. 17.95 (ISBN 0-7190-0795-X, Pub. by Manchester Univ Pr). Longwood Pub Group.
Farnie, D. A. The English Cotton Industry & the World Market 1815-1896. (Illus.). 1979. 52.00x (ISBN 0-19-822478-8). Oxford U Pr.
Farnol, Jeffery. Shadow, & Other Stories. LC 75-122696. (Short Story Index Reprint Ser). 1929. 17.00 (ISBN 0-8369-3529-2). Ayer Co Pubs.
Farnol, Jeffrey. The Amateur Gentleman. 1975. lib. bdg. 24.30x (ISBN 0-89966-086-X). Buccaneer Bks.
--The Broad Highway. (Barbara Cartland's Library of Love: Vol. 16). 213p. 1980. 12.95x (ISBN 0-7156-1476-2, BPA-03487, Pub. by Duckworth England). Biblio Dist.
--The Broad Highway. 1975. lib. bdg. 21.05x (ISBN 0-89966-085-1). Buccaneer Bks.
--The Definite Object. 1975. lib. bdg. 16.70x (ISBN 0-89966-087-8). Buccaneer Bks.
--The Money Moon. 1975. lib. bdg. 15.30x (ISBN 0-89966-090-8). Buccaneer Bks.
Farnsworth, Allan. Contracts. LC 81-84829. 1982. text ed. 28.50 (ISBN 0-316-27461-5). Little.
Farnsworth, B. A. & Young, Larry C. Nautical Rules of the Road: The International & Unified Inland Rules. 2nd ed. LC 83-10047. 212p. 1984. 13.50 (ISBN 0-87033-308-9). Cornell Maritime.
Farnsworth, Beatrice. Aleksandra Kollontai: Socialism, Feminism, & the Bolshevik Revolution. LC 79-67775. (Illus.). xvi, 432p. 1980. 35.00x (ISBN 0-8047-1073-2). Stanford U Pr.
Farnsworth, David & McKenney, James. U. S. - Panama Relations, 1903-1978: A Study in Linkage Politics. (Replica Edition Ser.). 314p. 1983. pap. 27.00x (ISBN 0-86531-969-3). Westview.
Farnsworth, E. Allan. An Introduction to the Legal System of the United States. 2nd ed. LC 83-15405. 192p. 1983. lib. bdg. 17.50 (ISBN 0-379-20720-6); 12.50 (ISBN 0-379-20716-8). Oceana.
Farnsworth, E. Allan & Honnold, John. Cases & Materials on Commercial Law. 4th ed. LC 84-28603. (University Casebook Ser.). 1168p. 1984. text ed. write for info. (ISBN 0-88277-226-0). Foundation Pr.
Farnsworth, E. Allan & Honnold, John O. The Law of Sales & Sales Financing, Cases & Materials on, 4th Ed., & Cases & Materials on Commercial Law, 3rd Ed. 1982 Supplement. (University Casebook Ser.). 58p. 1982. pap. text ed. write for info. (ISBN 0-88277-098-5). Foundation Pr.
Farnsworth, E. Allan & Young, William F., Jr. Contracts, Cases & Materials on. 3rd ed. LC 80-15040. (University Casebook Ser.). 1192p. 1980. text ed. 24.50 (ISBN 0-88277-009-8). Foundation Pr.
Farnsworth, E. Allen & Honnold, John. Cases & Materials, Commercial Law. (University Casebook Ser.). 107p. 1985. pap. text ed. write for info. (ISBN 0-88277-267-8). Foundation Pr.
Farnsworth, James. Last Rider from Lonesome Canyon. 1978. pap. 1.25 (ISBN 0-532-12587-8). Woodhill.
--Six Gun Showdown. 1978. pap. 1.25 (ISBN 0-532-12582-7). Woodhill.
Farnsworth, Kenneth B. An Archaeological Survey of the Macoupin Valley. (Reports of Investigations: No. 26). (Illus.). 54p. 1979. pap. 3.00 (ISBN 0-89792-050-3). Ill St Museum.
Farnsworth, Kenneth B. & Koski, Ann L. Massey & Archie: A Study of Two Hopwellian Homesteads in the Western Illinois Uplands. LC 85-13281. (Kampsville Archeological Center Research Ser.: No. 3). (Illus.). 280p. (Orig.). 1985. pap. 9.95 (ISBN 0-942118-20-0). Ctr Amer Arche.
Farnsworth, Kenneth C. Journey to Healing. Lambert, Herbert, ed. (Orig.). 1985. pap. 8.95 (ISBN 0-8272-1706-4). CBP.
Farnsworth, Kirk E. Integrating Psychology & Theology: Elbows Together but Hearts Apart. LC 81-40100. 94p. 1982. lib. bdg. 21.00 (ISBN 0-8191-1851-6); pap. text ed. 8.00 (ISBN 0-8191-1852-4). U Pr of Amer.
Farnsworth, Kirk E. & Lawhead, Wendell H. Life Planning. 96p. (Orig.). 1981. pap. 7.95 (ISBN 0-87784-840-8). Inter-Varsity.
Farnsworth, Marjorie. The Young Woman's Guide to an Academic Career. LC 73-80357. 128p. (gr. 9 up). 1974. lib. bdg. 8.97 (ISBN 0-8239-0286-2). Rosen Group.
Farnsworth, Mona. Footsteps That Follow. 1976. pap. 1.25 (ISBN 0-532-12380-8). Woodhill.
--The Menace of Marble Hill. 1977. pap. 1.25 (ISBN 0-532-12507-X). Woodhill.
Farnsworth, N. R., jt. auth. see Taylor, W. I.
Farnsworth, Norman, jt. ed. see Taylor, William I.
Farnsworth, Philo T. Adaptation Processes in Public School Systems As Illustrated by a Study of Five Selected Innovations in Educational Service in New York, Connecticut & Massachusetts. LC 77-176764. (Columbia University. Teachers College. Contributions to Education: No. 801). Repr. of 1940 ed. 22.50 (ISBN 0-404-55801-1). AMS Pr.
Farnsworth, Robert. Three or Four Hills & A Cloud: Wesleyan Poetry, Vol. 106. LC 82-4932. 64p. 1982. 15.00x (ISBN 0-8195-2108-6); pap. 6.95 (ISBN 0-8195-1108-0). Wesleyan U Pr.
Farnsworth, Robert M. Melvin B. Tolson, 1898-1966: Plain Talk & Poetic Prophecy. (Illus.). 480p. 1984. text ed. 38.00x (ISBN 0-8262-0433-3). U of Mo Pr.
Farnsworth, Robert M., jt. ed. see Ray, David.
Farnsworth, Robert M., ed. see Tolson, Melvin B.
Farnsworth, T. Managing for Success: The Farnsworth Formula. 192p. 1982. 19.95 (ISBN 0-07-084547-6). McGraw.
Farnsworth, William O. Uncle & Nephew in the Old French Chansons De Geste. LC 70-168008. (Columbia University. Studies in Romance Philology & Literature: No. 14). Repr. of 1913 ed. 22.00 (ISBN 0-404-50614-3). AMS Pr.
Farnum, Dorothy, jt. auth. see Rawlinson, Arthur.
Farnum, Hy. Jackie, with Love: We, the People of Camelot. LC 74-82899. 92p. 1975. 6.95 (ISBN 0-915790-01-7); padded cover 2.95 (ISBN 0-915790-02-5); pap. 1.50 (ISBN 0-915790-03-3). Farnum Films.
Farnworth, A. J. & Delmenico, J. Permanent Setting of Wool. 52p. 1971. 39.00x (ISBN 0-900541-18-0, Pub. by Meadowfield Pr England). State Mutual Bk.
Farnworth, E. Allan. Cases & Materials on Commercial Paper. 3rd ed. LC 84-7997. (University Casebook Ser.). 491p. 1984. text ed. 19.50 (ISBN 0-88277-178-7). Foundation Pr.
Farnworth, E. G. & Golley, F. B., eds. Fragile Ecosystems: Evaluation of Research & Applications in the Neotropics. LC 74-8290. (Illus.). 280p. 1974. pap. 20.00 (ISBN 0-387-06695-0). Springer-Verlag.

Farnworth, Warren. Approaches to Collage. LC 75-42539. (Illus.). (YA) (gr. 4 up). 1976. 9.95 (ISBN 0-8008-0280-2). Taplinger.
--Clay in the Primary School. 1973. 15.95 (ISBN 0-7134-2323-4, Pub. by Batsford England). David & Charles.
--Pin & Thread Art. LC 74-29203. (Illus.). 96p. 1975. 8.95 (ISBN 0-8008-6452-2). Taplinger.
Farny, Henry, ed. see Hughes, Jon C.
Farny, Michael. New England Over the Handlebars: A Cyclist's Guide. (Illus., Orig.). 1975. pap. 9.70i (ISBN 0-316-27465-8). Little.
Faro, Sebastian. Diagnosis & Management of Pelvic Infections in Primary Care Medicine. 300p. 1985. 39.50 (ISBN 0-683-03040-X). Williams & Wilkins.
Farook, Omar. Quranic Arabic. pap. 3.95 (ISBN 0-686-18328-2). Kazi Pubns.
Farook, Omar & Rauf, A. Quran for Children. pap. 5.95 (ISBN 0-686-63912-X). Kazi Pubns.
Farooq, Ghazi M. & Simmons, George B., eds. Fertility in Developing Countries: An Economic Perspective on Research & Policy Issues. LC 83-40609. 300p. 1985. 30.00 (ISBN 0-312-28752-6). St Martin.
Faroqhi, Suraiya. Towns & Towns of Ottoman Anatolia: Trade, Crafts & Food Production in an Urban Setting 1520-1650. LC 83-7198. (Cambridge Studies in Islamic Civilization). (Illus.). 424p. 1984. 59.50 (ISBN 0-521-25447-7). Cambridge U Pr.
Farouk, Brimah K. Georgia State Senate District Thirty-Five Democratic Primaries of 1982. 1982. 1.00 (ISBN 0-686-38025-8). Voter Ed Proj.
Farouk, Brimah K. & Hudlin, Richard A. Population Trends in Majority Black Counties in Eleven Southern States: 1900 to 1980. 1981. 1.00 (ISBN 0-686-38018-5). Voter Ed Proj.
Farouk, Brimah K., jt. auth. see Hudlin, Richard A.
Farouka, Saleh & Grabner, John R., Jr. Creative Selling & the Systems Concept: The Motor Carrier Selection Process, 2 vols. (Illus.). 1970. Vol. 1. pap. text ed. 15.00 (ISBN 0-88711-040-1); Vol. 2. pap. text ed. 15.00 (ISBN 0-88711-041-X). Am Trucking Assns.
Farquhar & Shapiro. Strategic Business Planning in Canada. 104p. 1983. 125.00 (ISBN 0-317-36608-4, CS-75); members 25.00 (ISBN 0-317-36609-2). Conference Bd.
Farquhar, A., jt. auth. see Sloan, A.
Farquhar, Francis P. History of the Sierra Nevada. LC 65-24178. 1965. pap. 7.95 (ISBN 0-520-01551-7, CAL75). U of Cal Pr.
Farquhar, Francis P., ed. see Brewer, William H.
Farquhar, George. The Beaux' Stratagem. Fifer, Charles N., ed. LC 77-89834. (Regents Restoration Drama Ser.). xxxvi, 145p. 1977. 15.50x (ISBN 0-8032-0384-5); pap. 3.95x (ISBN 0-8032-5384-2, BB 279, Bison). U of Nebr Pr.
--The Beaux' Strategem. Cordner, Michael, ed. (New Mermaids Ser.). pap. 2.95x (ISBN 0-393-90007-X). Norton.
--Complete Works, 2 Vols. Stonehill, Charles, ed. LC 67-28475. 1967. Repr. of 1930 ed. Set. 50.00x (ISBN 0-87752-032-1). Gordian.
--The Recruiting Officer. (Hereford Classics). 1969. pap. text ed. 4.00x (ISBN 0-435-22291-0). Heinemann Ed.
--The Recruiting Officer. Ross, John, ed. (New Mermaids Ser.). 1977. pap. 4.95x (ISBN 0-393-90039-8). Norton.
--The Recruiting Officer. Shugrue, Michael, ed. LC 65-15341. (Regents Restoration Drama Ser.). xxii, 137p. 1965. 13.50x (ISBN 0-8032-0358-6); pap. 3.25x (ISBN 0-8032-5357-5, BB 253, Bison). U of Nebr Pr.
--The Recruiting Officer. Dixon, Peter, ed. & pref. by. LC 85-3124. (The Revels Plays Ser.). (Illus.). 307p. 1985. 35.00 (ISBN 0-7190-1534-0, Pub. by Manchester Univ Pr). Longwood Pub Group.
Farquhar, George see Harris, Brice.
Farquhar, George see Wilson, John H.
Farquhar, Ian E., jt. ed. see Armitage, Jonathan G.
Farquhar, J. N. An Outline of Religious Literature of India. 1984. Repr. 30.00 (ISBN 0-89684-287-8). Orient Bk Dist.
Farquhar, J. W. Diabetes in Your Teens. LC 81-67474. (Churchill Livingstone Patient Handbook Ser.: No. 10). (Illus.). 156p. 1982. pap. text ed. 4.95 (ISBN 0-443-02220-8). Churchill.
Farquhar, James D. Creation & Imitation. LC 76-29199. 1976. 27.50 (ISBN 0-917736-02-8). Nova-NYIT U Pr.
Farquhar, James W. The Diabetic Child. (Patient Handbook Ser.). (Illus.). 96p. 1981. pap. 3.50 (ISBN 0-443-02193-7). Churchill.
Farquhar, John W. The American Way of Life Need Not Be Hazardous to Your Health. (Illus.). 208p. 1979. pap. 6.95 (ISBN 0-393-00963-7). Norton.
Farquhar, John W., intro. by see Ryder, Beverly A.
Farquhar, Judith & Gajdusek, D. Carleton, eds. Kuru: Early Letters & Field Notes from the Collection of D. Carleton Gajdusek. 366p. 1981. text ed. 58.00 (ISBN 0-89004-359-0). Raven.
Farquhar, Judith, jt. ed. see Murata, Alice K.
Farquhar, Marilyn G., jt. ed. see Tixier-Vidal, A.
Farquhar, Oswald C., ed. Geotechnology in Massachusetts. LC 82-70207. (Illus.). 626p. 1982. text ed. 25.00 (ISBN 0-9604712-0-0). Univ Mass Grad.
Farquhar, R. M., jt. auth. see York, D.
Farquhar, R. M., jt. ed. see Hamilton, E. I.
Farquhar, Roger B. Old Homes & History of Montgomery County, Maryland. (Illus.). 1981. 35.00 (ISBN 0-910086-06-0). Am Hist Res.
Farquharson, Arthur. Marcus Aurelius, His Life & His World. Rees, D. A., ed. & pref. by. LC 75-11854. (Illus.). 154p. 1975. Repr. of 1951 ed. lib. bdg. 15.00x (ISBN 0-8371-8139-9, FAMAU). Greenwood.
Farquharson, John, jt. auth. see Hiden, John.
Farquharson, John E. The Plough & the Swastika: The NSDAP & Agriculture in Germany 1928-45. LC 74-31570. (Sage Studies in 20th Century History Ser.: Vol. 5). pap. 80.00 (ISBN 0-317-29682-5, 2021897). Bks Demand UMI.
--The Western Allies & the Politics of Food: Agrarian Management in Postwar Germany. LC 85-3977. (Illus.). 288p. 1985. 31.95 (ISBN 0-907582-24-9, Pub. by Berg Pubs). Longwood Pub Group.
Farquharson, Robin. Theory of Voting. LC 70-81417. 1969. 18.50x (ISBN 0-300-01121-0). Yale U Pr.
Farr, Barbara. Super Soy! Delicious Protein Without Meat. LC 76-2982. (Illus.). 1976. 6.95 (ISBN 0-87983-134-0); pap. 3.95 (ISBN 0-87983-102-2). Keats.
Farr, Charlie M. Better Food by Farr. 1985. 12.95 (ISBN 0-317-28879-2). Vantage.
Farr, Cheryl A., ed. Shaping the Local Economy: Current Perspectives on Economic Development. LC 84-6693. (Practical Management Ser.). (Illus.). 183p. (Orig.). 1984. pap. text ed. 19.95 (ISBN 0-87326-034-1). Intl City Mgt.
Farr, Chester N. Random Thoughts on Dickens. LC 77-21125. 1977. Repr. of 1931 ed. lib. bdg. 6.00 (ISBN 0-8414-4351-3). Folcroft.
Farr, D. F., jt. auth. see Miller, O. K., Jr.
Farr, Dennis. English Art: 1870-1940. (Oxford History of English Art Ser.). (Illus.). 1979. pap. 22.95 (ISBN 0-19-281855-4); 54.00x (ISBN 0-19-817208-7). Oxford U Pr.
Farr, Diana. Five at Ten: Prime Ministers' Consorts Since 1957. (Illus.). 192p. 1985. 18.95 (ISBN 0-233-97733-3, Pub. by A Deutsch England). David & Charles.
Farr, Donald. Mustang Boss 302. 1983. 12.95 (ISBN 0-941596-03-6). Mustang Pubns.
--Mustang How To. 1983. pap. 6.95 (ISBN 0-941596-04-4). Mustang Pubns.
Farr, Donald, jt. auth. see Dobbs, Larry.
Farr, Dorothy M. John Ford & the Caroline Theatre. 184p. 1979. text ed. 28.50x (ISBN 0-06-492065-8). B&N Imports.
Farr, Edward, ed. Select Poetry, Chiefly Devotional, of the Reign of Queen Elizabeth, 2 Vols. 1845. Vol. 1. 41.00 (ISBN 0-384-15165-5); Vol. 2. 41.00 (ISBN 0-384-15166-3). Johnson Repr.
Farr, Elizabeth. Genesis for Young Seekers. (FGC). 108p. (gr. 8-12). 1958. text ed. 0.75 (ISBN 0-318-14146-9). Friends Genl Conf.
Farr, Finis. Margaret Mitchell of Atlanta. 1976. pap. 1.75 (ISBN 0-380-00810-6, 20594). Avon.
Farr, Florence. The Music of Speech. LC 78-64022. (Des Imagistes). Repr. of 1909 ed. 11.00 (ISBN 0-404-17095-1). AMS Pr.
Farr, Gerald G. Biology Illustrated. (Illus.). 117p. 1979. pap. text ed. 5.95x (ISBN 0-89641-054-4). American Pr.
--Botany Illustrated. (Illus.). 52p. 1979. pap. text ed. 3.95x (ISBN 0-89641-055-2). American Pr.
--Zoology Illustrated. (Illus.). 65p. 1979. pap. text ed. 3.95x (ISBN 0-89641-056-0). American Pr.
Farr, Grahame. Royal Deeside Line. LC 68-23820. (Illus.). 1968. 17.95x (ISBN 0-678-05596-3). Kelley.
--West Country Passenger Steamers. LC 67-103343. (Illus.). 1967. 24.95x (ISBN 0-678-05656-0). Kelley.
Farr, James see Ball, Terence.
Farr, James A. & Wright, Jackson. Estate Planner's Handbook, 1982: Supplement. LC 79-88997. 1982. 17.50 (ISBN 0-316-27475-5). Little.
Farr, James F. Loring's A Trustee's Handbook. 6th ed. 1962. 20.00 (ISBN 0-316-27471-2). Little.
Farr, James F. & Jackson, Wright, Jr. An Estate Planner's Handbook. 4th ed. 1979. 55.00 (ISBN 0-316-27474-7). Little.
Farr, James F. & Wright, Jackson W. An Estate Planner's Handbook. 4th ed. 528p. 1979. incl. 1985 suppl. 55.00 (ISBN 0-316-27476-3). Little.
--An Estate Planners Handbook: 1984 Supplement. 1984. pap. write for info. Little.
--Supplement to An Estate Planner's Handbook, 1985. 1985. pap. write for info. Little.
Farr, James F., jt. auth. see Landy, Frank J.
Farr, James R., jt. auth. see Jawad, Maan H.
Farr, Judith. The Life & Art of Elinor Wylie. LC 83-7987. (Illus.). 256p. 1983. text ed. 22.50x (ISBN 0-8071-1107-4). La State U Pr.
Farr, Kenneth H. Personalism & Party Politics: Institutionalization of the Popular Democratic Party of Puerto Rico. LC 73-75406. 143p. (Orig.). 1973. 4.95 (ISBN 0-913480-12-6); pap. 2.95 (ISBN 0-913480-13-4). Inter Am U Pr.
Farr, Kenneth R. Personalismo y Politica De Partidos: La Institucionalizacion Del Partido Popular Democratico De Puerto Rico. Benitez, Jesus, tr. from Eng. LC 73-75406. 268p. 1975. 4.95 (ISBN 0-913480-25-8); pap. 2.95 (ISBN 0-913480-26-6). Inter Am U Pr.
Farr, M. L. How to Know the True Slime Molds. (Picture Key Nature Ser.). 200p. 1981. write for info. wire coil (ISBN 0-697-04779-2). Wm C Brown.
Farr, Marcia, ed. Advances in Writing Research, Vol. 1. (Writing Research Ser.). 372p. 1985. text ed. 39.50 (ISBN 0-89391-179-8). Ablex Pub.
Farr, Marcia, ed. see Applebee, Arthur.
Farr, Marcia, ed. see Faigley, Lester, et al.
Farr, Marcia, ed. see Freedman, Sarah W.
Farr, Marcia, ed. see Teale, William & Sulzby, Elizabeth.
Farr, Marie L. Myxomycetes. LC 76-19370. (Flora Neotropica Monograph: No. 16). 1976. pap. 22.50x (ISBN 0-89327-003-2). NY Botanical.
Farr, Martyn. The Great Caving Adventure. (Illus.). 236p. 12.95 (ISBN 0-946609-10-1, P110). Haynes Pubns.
Farr, Michael. The Work Book. 1982. 10.00 (ISBN 0-686-36295-0); instr's. guide 5.28 (ISBN 0-686-37286-7). McKnight.
Farr, Naunerle. America Becomes a World Power, 1890-1920. Calhoun, D'Ann & Bloch, Lawrence W., eds. (Basic Illustrated History of America Ser.). (Illus.). (gr. 4-12). 1977. text ed. 5.00 (ISBN 0-88301-256-1); pap. text ed. 1.95 (ISBN 0-88301-199-9); student book 1.25 (ISBN 0-88301-236-7). Pendulum Pr.
--America Today, 1945-1981. Calhoun, D'Ann & Bloch, Leonard W., eds. (Basic Illustrated History of America). (Illus.). (gr. 4-12). 1977. text ed. 5.00 (ISBN 0-88301-259-6). Pendulum Pr.
--America Today: 1945-1981. Calhoun, D'Ann & Bloch, Lawrence W., eds. (Basic Illustrated History of America Ser.). (Illus.). (gr. 4-12). 1976. pap. text ed. 1.95 (ISBN 0-88301-234-0); 1.25 wkbk (ISBN 0-88301-246-4). Pendulum Pr.
--Americans Move Westward: Eighteen Hundred to Eighteen Fifty. Calhoun, D'Ann & Bloch, Lawrence W., eds. (Basic Illustrated History of America Ser.). (Illus.). (gr. 4-12). 1976. pap. text ed. 1.95 (ISBN 0-88301-227-8). Pendulum Pr.
--Americans Move Westward, Eighteen Hundred to Eighteen Fifty. Calhoun, D'Ann & Bloch, Lawrence W., eds. (Basic Illustrated History of America). (Illus.). (gr. 4-12). 1977. text ed. 5.00 (ISBN 0-88301-252-9); wkbk. 1.25 (ISBN 0-88301-239-1). Pendulum Pr.
--Before the Civil War, Eighteen Thirty to Eighteen Sixty. Calhoun, D'Ann & Bloch, Lawrence W., eds. (Basic Illustrated History of America Ser.). (Illus.). (gr. 4-12). 1977. text ed. 5.00 (ISBN 0-88301-253-7). Pendulum Pr.
--Civil War, Eighteen Fifty to Eighteen Seventy-Six. Calhoun, D'Ann & Bloch, Lawrence W., eds. (Basic Illustrated History of America). (Illus.). (gr. 4-12). 1977. text ed. 5.00 (ISBN 0-88301-254-5). Pendulum Pr.
--The Fight for Freedom. Calhoun, D'Ann & Bloch, Lawrence W., eds. (Basic Illustrated History of America). (Illus.). (gr. 4-12). 1977. text ed. 5.00 (ISBN 0-88301-249-9). Pendulum Pr.
--The Industrial Era, 1865-1915. Calohoun, D'Ann & Bloch, Lawrence W., eds. (Basic Illustrated History of America). (Illus.). (gr. 4-12). 1977. text ed. 5.00 (ISBN 0-88301-255-3). Pendulum Pr.
--Madame Curie - Albert Einstein. (Pendulum Illustrated Biography Ser.). (Illus.). (gr. 4-12). 1979. text ed. 5.00 (ISBN 0-88301-368-1); pap. text ed. 1.95 (ISBN 0-88301-356-8); wkbk. 1.25 (ISBN 0-88301-380-0). Pendulum Pr.
--The New World, 1500-1750. Calhoun, D'Ann & Bloch, Lawrence W., eds. (Basic Illustrated History of America). (Illus.). (gr. 4-12). 1977. text ed. 5.00 (ISBN 0-88301-248-0). Pendulum Pr.
--Problems of the New Nation: 1800-1830. Calhoun, D'Ann & Bloch, Lawrence W., eds. (Basic Illustrated History of America). (Illus.). (gr. 4-12). 1977. text ed. 5.00 (ISBN 0-88301-251-0). Pendulum Pr.
--The Roaring Twenties & the Great Depression, 1920-1940. Calhoun, D'Ann & Bloch, Lawrence W., eds. (Basic Illustrated History of America). (Illus.). (gr. 4-12). 1977. text ed. 5.00 (ISBN 0-88301-257-X). Pendulum Pr.
--The United States Emerges, 1783-1800. Calhoun, D'Ann & Bloch, Lawrence W., eds. (Basic Illustrated History of America). (Illus.). (gr. 4-12). 1977. text ed. 5.00 (ISBN 0-88301-250-2). Pendulum Pr.
--World War II, Nineteen Forty to Nineteen Forty-Five. Calhoun, D'Ann & Bloch, Lawrence W., eds. (Basic Illustrated History of America). (gr. 4-12). 1977. text ed. 5.00 (ISBN 0-88301-258-8). Pendulum Pr.
Farr, Naunerle & Dostert, Dennis. Before the Civil War: Eighteen Thirty to Eighteen Sixty. Bloch, Lawrence W., ed. (Basic Illustrated History of America Ser.). (Illus.). (gr. 4-12). 1976. pap. text ed. 1.95 (ISBN 0-88301-226-X); student activity bk. 1.25 (ISBN 0-88301-238-3). Pendulum Pr.
--The Civil War: Eighteen Fifty to Eighteen Seventy-Six. Bloch, Lawrence W., ed. (Basic Illustrated History of America Ser.). (Illus., Orig.). (gr. 4-12). 1976. pap. text ed. 1.95 (ISBN 0-88301-228-6); 1.25 (ISBN 0-88301-240-5). Pendulum Pr.
--The Fight for Freedom: 1750-1783. Bloch, Lawrence W., ed. (Basic Illustrated History of America Ser.). (Illus., Orig.). (gr. 4-12). 1976. 1.95 (ISBN 0-88301-229-4); pap. 1.25 (ISBN 0-88301-241-3). Pendulum Pr.
--The Industrial Era: 1865-1915. Bloch, Lawrence W., ed. (Basic Illustrated History of America Ser.). (Illus., Orig.). (gr. 4-12). 1976. pap. text ed. 1.95 (ISBN 0-88301-225-1); 1.25 (ISBN 0-88301-237-5). Pendulum Pr.
--The New World: Fifteen Hundred to Seventeen Fifty. Bloch, Lawrence W., ed. (Basic Illustrated History of America Ser.). (Illus., Orig.). (gr. 4-12). 1976. pap. text ed. 1.95 (ISBN 0-88301-230-8); 1.25 (ISBN 0-88301-242-1). Pendulum Pr.
--Problems of the New Nation: 1800-1830. Bloch, Lawrence W., ed. (Basic Illustrated History of America Ser.). (Illus., Orig.). (gr. 4-12). 1976. pap. text ed. 1.95 (ISBN 0-88301-231-6); 1.25 (ISBN 0-88301-243-X). Pendulum Pr.
--The Roaring Twenties & the Great Depression: 1920-1940. Bloch, Lawrence W., ed. (Basic Illustrated History of America Ser.). (Illus., Orig.). (gr. 4-12). 1976. pap. text ed. 1.95 (ISBN 0-88301-232-4); 1.25 (ISBN 0-88301-244-8). Pendulum Pr.
--The United States Emerges: 1783-1800. Bloch, Lawrence W., ed. (Basic Illustrated History of America Ser.). (Illus., Orig.). (gr. 4-12). 1976. pap. text ed. 1.95 (ISBN 0-88301-233-2). Pendulum Pr.
--World War II: Nineteen Forty to Nineteen Forty-Five. Bloch, Lawrence W., ed. (Basic Illustrated History of America Ser.). (Illus., Orig.). (gr. 4-12). 1976. pap. text ed. 1.95 (ISBN 0-88301-235-9); 1.25 (ISBN 0-88301-247-2). Pendulum Pr.
Farr, Naunerle, ed. see Bronte, Charlotte.
Farr, Naunerle, ed. see Bronte, Emily.
Farr, Naunerle, ed. see Clemens, Samuel.
Farr, Naunerle, ed. see Cooper, James F.
Farr, Naunerle, ed. see Dickens, Charles.
Farr, Naunerle, ed. see Dumas, Alexandre.
Farr, Naunerle, ed. see Hawthorne, Nathaniel.
Farr, Naunerle, ed. see London, Jack.
Farr, Naunerle, ed. see Orczy, Baroness.
Farr, Naunerle, ed. see Poe, Edgar Allan.
Farr, Naunerle, ed. see Scott, Walter.
Farr, Naunerle, ed. see Sewell, Anna.
Farr, Naunerle, ed. see Stoker, Bram.
Farr, Naunerle, ed. see Verne, Jules.
Farr, Naunerle, ed. see Wallace, Lew.
Farr, Naunerle, ed. see Wells, H. G.
Farr, Naunerle, ed. see Wyss, Johann.
Farr, Naunerle C. Abraham Lincoln-Franklin D. Roosevelt. (Pendulum Illustrated Biography Ser.). (Illus.). (gr. 4-12). 1979. text ed. 5.00 (ISBN 0-88301-366-5); pap. text ed. 1.95 (ISBN 0-88301-354-1); wkbk. 1.25 (ISBN 0-88301-378-9). Pendulum Pr.
--Babe Ruth-Jackie Robinson. (Pendulum Illustrated Biography Ser.). (Illus.). (gr. 4-12). 1979. text ed. 5.00 (ISBN 0-88301-371-1); pap. text ed. 1.95 (ISBN 0-88301-359-2); wkbk 1.25 (ISBN 0-88301-383-5). Pendulum Pr.
--Davy Crockett-Daniel Boone. (Pendulum Illustrated Biography Ser.). (Illus.). (gr. 4-12). 1979. text ed. 5.00 (ISBN 0-88301-363-0); pap. text ed. 1.95 (ISBN 0-88301-351-7); wkbk. 1.25 (ISBN 0-88301-375-4). Pendulum Pr.
--George Washington-Thomas Jefferson. (Pendulum Illustrated Biography Ser.). (Illus.). (gr. 4-12). 1979. text ed. 5.00 (ISBN 0-88301-367-3); pap. text ed. 1.95 (ISBN 0-88301-355-X); wkbk. 1.25 (ISBN 0-88301-379-7). Pendulum Pr.
--Thomas Edison - Alexander Graham Bell. (Pendulum Illustrated Biography Ser.). (Illus.). (gr. 4-12). 1979. text ed. 5.00 (ISBN 0-88301-369-X); pap. text ed. 1.95 (ISBN 0-88301-357-6); wkbk. 1.25 (ISBN 0-88301-381-9). Pendulum Pr.
Farr, Naunerle C. & Fago, John N. Amelia Earhart - Charles Lindbergh. (Pendulum Illustrated Biography Ser.). (Illus.). (gr. 4-12). 1979. text ed. 5.00 (ISBN 0-88301-361-4); pap. text ed. 1.95 (ISBN 0-88301-349-5); wkbk. 1.25 (ISBN 0-88301-373-8). Pendulum Pr.
Farr, Naunerle C., jt. auth. see Fago, John N.
Farr, Robert M. & Moscovici, Serge, eds. Social Representations. LC 83-18823. (European Studies in Social Psychology). 450p. 1984. 69.50 (ISBN 0-521-24800-0). Cambridge U Pr.
Farr, Roger. Reading: What Can Be Measured? (IRA-Elva Knight Research Fund Monograph). 1970. 4.95 (ISBN 0-87207-803-5). Intl Reading.
Farr, Roger & Roser, Nancy. Teaching a Child to Read. 514p. 1979. text ed. 21.95 (ISBN 0-15-586650-8, HC). HarBraceJ.
Farr, Roger, et al, eds. Improving Reading Research. LC 76-795. 120p. 1976. pap. text ed. 5.00 (ISBN 0-87207-484-6). Intl Reading.
Farr, Sidney S. Appalachian Women: An Annotated Bibliography. LC 80-5174. 208p. 1981. 20.00x (ISBN 0-8131-1431-4). U Pr of Ky.
--More Than Moonshine: Appalachian Recipes & Recollections. LC 82-13524. 176p. 1983. 14.95 (ISBN 0-8229-3475-2); pap. 6.95 (ISBN 0-8229-5347-1). U of Pittsburgh Pr.
Farr, Walter G., Jr., et al. Decentralizing City Government: A Practical Study of a Radical Proposal for New York City. LC 72-83567. (Special Studies in U.S. Economic, Social, & Political Issues). 1972. 26.00x (ISBN 0-275-06330-5). Irvington.

Farr, William. Vital Statistics: A Memorial Volume of Selections from the Reports & Writings of William Farr. Humphreys, Noel A. & Sanitary Institute of Great Britain, eds. LC 75-38128. (Demography Ser.). (Illus.). 1976. Repr. of 1885 ed. 42.00x (ISBN 0-405-18600-2). Ayer Co Pubs.
Farr, William & Toole, K. Ross. Montana: Images of the Past. LC 78-7408. (Illus.). 1978. 35.00 (ISBN 0-87108-514-3). Pruett.
--Montana: Images of the Past. (Illus.). 1984. pap. 14.95 (ISBN 0-87108-666-2). Pruett.
Farr, William E. The Reservation Blackfeet, 1885-1945: A Photographic History of Cultural Survival. LC 83-47975. 232p. 1985. 24.95 (ISBN 0-295-96040-X). U of Wash Pr.
Farraday, Chelsea. Disco. 1978. pap. 1.95 (ISBN 0-8439-0599-9, Leisure Bks). Dorchester Pub Co.
--Intimate Strangers. 1979. pap. 1.95 (ISBN 0-8439-0608-1, Leisure Bks). Dorchester Pub Co.
--A Legend in Her Own Time. 1979. pap. 1.95 (ISBN 0-8439-0690-1, Leisure Bks). Dorchester Pub Co.
--Vital Parts. 1979. pap. 2.25 (ISBN 0-505-51444-3, Pub. by Tower Bks). Dorchester Pub Co.
Farraday, R. V. & Charlton, F. G. Hydraulic Factors in Bridge Design. 110p. 1983. 29.75x (ISBN 0-946466-00-9). Am Soc Civil Eng.
Farragut, Jones J. Forty Fathoms Down (The Silent Service No. 2) (Orig.). 1981. pap. 2.75 (ISBN 0-440-12655-X). Dell.
Farrall, Arthur W. Engineering for Dairy & Food Products. 2nd ed. LC 79-1171. (Illus.). 1980. lib. bdg. 36.00 (ISBN 0-88275-859-4). Krieger.
--Food Engineering System: Vol. 2, Utilities. (Illus.). 1979. text ed. 29.50 soft cover (ISBN 0-87055-283-X, 274). AVI.
Farrall, Arthur W. & Basselman, James A. Dictionary of Agricultural & Food Engineering. LC 78-71856. 450p. 1979. 24.35 (ISBN 0-8134-2023-7, 2023); text ed. 18.25x. Interstate.
Farrall, Lyndsay A. The Origins & Growth of the English Eugenics Movement. Rosenberg, Charles, ed. (The History of Hereditarian Thought Ser.). 342p. 1985. Repr. of 1970 ed. lib. bdg. 41.00 (ISBN 0-8240-5810-0). Garland Pub.
Farran, Christopher. Infant Colic: What It Is & What You Can Do About It. 106p. 1982. 10.95 (ISBN 0-684-17779-X, ScribT). Scribner.
--Infant Colic: What It Is & What You Can Do About It. 144p. 1984. pap. 5.95 (ISBN 0-684-18153-3, ScribT). Scribner.
Farrand, John, ed. The Audubon Society Master Guide to Birding, 3 Vols. (Illus.). 1984. Boxed set. 42.00 (ISBN 0-394-54121-9). Knopf.
Farrand, John, Jr., ed. The Audubon Society Encyclopedia of Animal Life. LC 82-81466. (Illus.). 600p. 1982. 19.95 (ISBN 0-517-54657-4, Pub. by Potter). Crown.
--The Audubon Society Master Guide to Birding, 3 vols. Incl. Vol. 1. Loons-Sandpipers. 447p. 13.95 (ISBN 0-394-53382-8); Vol. 2. Gulls-Dippers. 398p. 13.95 (ISBN 0-394-53384-4); Vol. 3. Old-World Warblers-Sparrows. 399p. 13.95 (ISBN 0-394-53383-6). LC 83-47945. (Illus.). 1983. 3 vol. set 42.00 (ISBN 0-394-54121-9). Knopf.
Farrand, John, Jr., ed. see Audubon Society.
Farrand, Livingston. Basis of American History: 1500-1900. 1978. Repr. of 1904 ed. lib. bdg. 40.00 (ISBN 0-8495-1612-9). Arden Lib.
--Basis of American History 1500-1900. 1904. lib. bdg. 30.00 (ISBN 0-8482-9993-0). Norwood Edns.
--Basketry Designs of the Salish Indians. LC 73-3514. (Jesup North Pacific Expedition. Publications: Vol. 1). Repr. of 1900 ed. 15.00 (ISBN 0-404-58116-1). AMS Pr.
--Traditions of the Chilcotin Indians. LC 73-3516. (Jesup North Pacific Expedition. Publications: Vol. 2, Pt. 1). Repr. of 1900 ed. 17.50 (ISBN 0-404-58102-1). AMS Pr.
--Traditions of the Quinault Indians - Extracts. facs. ed. 54p. pap. 4.95 (ISBN 0-8466-0004-8, S4). Shorey.
Farrand, Livingston & Kahnweiler, W. S. Traditions of the Quinault Indians. LC 73-3518. (Jesup North Pacific Expedition. Publications: Vol. 2, Pt. 3). Repr. of 1902 ed. 17.50 (ISBN 0-404-58119-6). AMS Pr.
Farrand, Max. The Constitution. lib. bdg. 59.95 (ISBN 0-87968-935-8). Gordon Pr.
--The Development of the United States. 1918. 40.00 (ISBN 0-8482-3976-8). Norwood Edns.
--Fathers of the Constitution. 1921. 8.50x (ISBN 0-686-83547-6). Elliots Bks.
--The Framing of the Constitution of the United States. 1913. 45.00 (ISBN 0-8482-3983-0). Norwood Edns.
--Framing of the Constitution of the United States. 1913. 30.00 (ISBN 0-300-00445-1); pap. 8.95x 1962 (ISBN 0-300-00079-0, Y53). Yale U Pr.
--The Records of the Federal Convention of 1787, 4 vols. rev. ed. Incl. Vol. 1. (Illus.). xxv, 606p. 1967. 40.00x (ISBN 0-300-00447-8); Vol. 2. (Illus.). 667p. 1967. 40.00x (ISBN 0-300-00448-6); Vol. 3. 630p. 1967. 47.00x (ISBN 0-300-00449-4); Vol. 4. xii, 230p. 1967. 26.00 (ISBN 0-300-00450-8). pap. Yale U Pr.
Farrand, Max see Johnson, Allen & Nevins, Allan.
Farrand, Max, ed. see Dwight, Margaret V.
Farrand, Max, tr. see Jellinek, Georg.
Farrand, William R., et al. An Archaeological Investigation on the Loboi Plain, Baringo District, Kenya. (Technical Reports: No. 4). (Illus.). 1976. pap. 3.50x (ISBN 0-932206-13-1). U Mich Mus Anthro.
Farrands, Barry J. Everything You Always Wanted to Know About Solar Energy: But Didn't Know Who to Ask. Sinclair, Dale, ed. LC 80-81372. (Illus.). 425p. (Orig.). 1980. pap. 39.95x (ISBN 0-936982-00-4). Promise Corp.
Farrant, Don W. Haunted Houses of Grand Rapids, Vol. I. LC 79-55532. (Grand Rapids Haunted Houses Ser.: Vol. I). (Illus.). 72p. Date not set. pap. 3.95 (ISBN 0-935604-00-6). Ivystone.
--Real Ghosts Don't Wear Sheets. (Illus.). 80p. (Orig.). pap. 7.00 (ISBN 0-935604-02-2). Ivystone.
Farrant, P., jt. auth. see Meire, H. B.
Farrant, Sarah. The Tavern Wench. 224p. 1980. pap. 1.95 (ISBN 0-345-28604-9). Ballantine.
Farrant, Smith J., jt. auth. see Ashwood, M. J.
Farrar & Maleska. Crossword Puzzle Book, No. 122. pap. 3.95 (ISBN 0-686-60946-8, Fireside). S&S.
Farrar, Austin. Rebirth of Images: The Making of Saint John's Apocalypse. 13.25 (ISBN 0-8446-0617-0). Peter Smith.
Farrar, Becky. Centennial Clairette Eighteen Eighty to Nineteen Eighty. 333p. 1980. 20.00 (ISBN 0-9609406-0-X). Greens Creek.
Farrar, C. L. & Leeming, D. W. Military Ballistics: A Basic Manual. 225p. 1983. 27.00 (ISBN 0-08-028342-X); pap. 12.50 (ISBN 0-08-028343-8). Pergamon.
Farrar, Clarence E., jt. ed. see Mowree, Paul S.
Farrar, Clarence E., jt. ed. see Mowrer, Paul S.
Farrar, Dean. Ruskin As a Religious Teacher. 1978. Repr. of 1904 ed. lib. bdg. 10.00 (ISBN 0-8495-1616-1). Arden Lib.
--Ruskin As a Religious Teacher. LC 73-2834. 1973. lib. bdg. 8.50 (ISBN 0-8414-1957-4). Folcroft.
Farrar, Donald R., jt. auth. see Vander Linden, Peter J.
Farrar, Eleanor, jt. auth. see Powell, Arthur G.
Farrar, Eliza W. The Young Lady's Friend, by a Lady. LC 74-3947. (Women in America Ser). 452p. 1974. Repr. of 1836 ed. 32.00x (ISBN 0-405-06093-9). Ayer Co Pubs.
Farrar, Elizabeth R. Recollections of Seventy Years. Baxter, Annette K., ed. LC 79-8791. (Signal Lives Ser.). 1980. Repr. of 1866 ed. lib. bdg. 30.00x (ISBN 0-405-12838-X). Ayer Co Pubs.
Farrar, Emmie F. Old Virginia Houses: The Moback Bay Country & Along the James. 1981. 12.98 (ISBN 0-517-01013-5). Crown.
Farrar, Estelle S. H. P. Sinclaire, Jr., Glassmaker, Vol. 1: The Years Before 1920. (Illus.). viii, 152p. 1974. pap. 10.00 (ISBN 0-686-09327-5). Corning.
--H. P. Sinclaire, Jr., Glassmaker, Vol. 2: The Manufacturing Years. (Illus.). viii, 119p. 1975. pap. 10.00 (ISBN 0-686-10549-4). Corning.
Farrar, Estelle S. & Spillman, Jane S. The Complete Cut & Engraved Glass of Corning. (Illus.). 1978. 14.95 (ISBN 0-517-53432-0). Crown.
Farrar, Estelle S., jt. auth. see Spillman, Jane S.
Farrar, F. W. The First Book of Kings. 1981. 19.00 (ISBN 0-86524-035-3, 1101). Klock & Klock.
--The Life & Work of St. Paul. 1980. 2 vol. set 43.95 (ISBN 0-86524-055-8, 8402). Klock & Klock.
--The Second Book of Kings. 1981. 19.00 (ISBN 0-86524-036-1, 1201). Klock & Klock.
Farrar, Frederic W. Life of Christ. 1980. 15.00 (ISBN 0-911376-01-1). Fountain Publications Oregon.
--Life of Christ. 1982. lib. bdg. 24.95 (ISBN 0-86524-089-2, 9508). Klock & Klock.
Farrar, Frederick W. Agrippina: Empress of Depravity. (Golden Age of Rome Ser.). 1978. pap. 2.50 (ISBN 0-89083-354-0). Zebra.
--Great Books. LC 72-6859. (Essay Index Reprint Ser.). Repr. of 1898 ed. 20.00 (ISBN 0-8369-7261-9). Ayer Co Pubs.
--Great Books. 1898. Repr. 15.00 (ISBN 0-8274-2440-X). R West.
--Men I Have Known. 1897. Repr. 17.50 (ISBN 0-8274-2722-0). R West.
Farrar, G. E., Jr., jt. auth. see Dean, W. B.
Farrar, Geraldine. Such Sweet Compulsion: The Autobiography of Geraldine Farrar. LC 72-107802. (Select Bibliographies Reprint Ser). 1938. 25.50 (ISBN 0-8369-5205-7). Ayer Co Pubs.
--Such Sweet Compulsion, the Autobiography of Geraldine Farrar. LC 70-100656. (Music Ser). 1970. Repr. of 1938 ed. lib. bdg. 32.50 (ISBN 0-306-71863-4). Da Capo.
Farrar, Glennys & Henyey, Frank, eds. Problems in Unification & Supergravity: Conference Proceedings, La Jolla Institute, 1983. LC 84-71246. (AIP Conference Proceedings Ser.: No. 116). 185p. 1984. lib. bdg. 35.50 (ISBN 0-88318-315-3). Am Inst Physics.
Farrar, Helen G. How Evil the Word. 1974. pap. 0.95 (ISBN 0-380-00155-1, 21329). Avon.
Farrar, Janet & Farrar, Stuart. A Witches Bible, 2 vols. (Illus., Orig.). 1984. Vol. I - The Sabbats. pap. 10.95 (ISBN 0-939708-06-X); Vol. II - The Rituals. pap. 10.95 (ISBN 0-939708-07-8); pap. 21.90 boxed set (ISBN 0-939708-08-6). Magickal Childe.
--A Witches Bible. 1984. boxed set 21.90 (ISBN 0-939708-08-6). Magickal Childe.
Farrar, Janet, jt. auth. see Farrar, Stewart.
Farrar, John C. Forgotten Shrines. LC 74-144709. (Yale Series of Younger Poets: No. 2). Repr. of 1919 ed. 18.00 (ISBN 0-404-53802-9). AMS Pr.
--Literary Spotlight. 1924. Repr. 13.50 (ISBN 0-8482-3990-3). Norwood Edns.
Farrar, John C., ed. Literary Spotlight. facs. ed. LC 70-117789. (Essay Index Reprint Ser). 1924. 21.50 (ISBN 0-8369-1874-6). Ayer Co Pubs.
Farrar, Kenneth G. Hurry Gringo. Ashton, Sylvia, ed. LC 78-31374. 1985. 14.95 (ISBN 0-87949-143-4). Ashley Bks.
Farrar, L. L., Jr. Arrogance & Anxiety: The Ambivalence of German Power, 1848-1914. LC 81-10374. (Iowa Studies in History: Vol. 1). 231p. 1981. text ed. 18.00 (ISBN 0-87745-112-5). U of Iowa Pr.
Farrar, Margaret. Crosswords from the Times (Daily) 96p. 1982. pap. 5.95 (ISBN 0-671-45874-4, Fireside). S&S.
--Crosswords from the Times (Daliy, No 42. 96p. 1982. pap. 5.95 (ISBN 0-671-44772-6, Fireside). S&S.
--The Funk & Wagnall's-Los Angeles Crossword Treasury, 3 vols. (Funk & W Bk.). 1978. pap. 3.95i ea.; Vol. 1. (ISBN 0-308-10311-4); Vol. 2. (ISBN 0-308-10312-2). T Y Crowell.
--Margaret Farrar's Super Crossword Book. 256p. 1982. pap. 7.95 (ISBN 0-671-45690-3, Fireside). S&S.
--S&S Crosswords from the Times, No. 38. 1980. 3.95 (ISBN 0-686-62843-8, 25503, Fireside). S&S.
Farrar, Margaret & Maleska, Eugene. Crossword Puzzle Book, No 129. 64p. 1982. pap. 5.95 (ISBN 0-671-44393-3, Fireside). S&S.
Farrar, Margaret & Maleska, Eugene T. The Simon & Schuster Crossword Puzzle Treasury, No. 27. 1985. pap. 6.95 (ISBN 0-671-55753-X). S&S.
--Simon & Schuster's Crossword Puzzle Book Series 133. 1984. pap. 5.95 (ISBN 0-671-50202-6, Fireside Bks). S&S.
Farrar, Margaret, jt. auth. see Maleska, Eugene T.
Farrar, Margaret, ed. Margaret Farrar's Super Crossword Book, No. 2. 256p. 1983. 7.95 (ISBN 0-671-49436-8, Fireside). S&S.
--The Simon & Schuster Crossword Puzzle Treasury, No. 25. 1984. pap. 5.95 (ISBN 0-671-47949-0, Fireside). S&S.
--Simon & Schuster Crossword Treasury, No. 26. 64p. 1985. pap. 6.95 (ISBN 0-671-54195-1, Fireside). S&S.
--Simon & Schuster Crosswords from the Times, Series 38. (Orig.). 1980. pap. 5.95 (ISBN 0-671-25503-7, Fireside). S&S.
--Simon & Schuster's Large-Type Crosswords, No. 6. 96p. (Orig.). pap. 4.95 (ISBN 0-671-43644-9, Fireside). S&S.
--Simon & Schuster's Super Crossword Book No. 3. 1985. pap. 7.95 (ISBN 0-671-55754-8). S&S.
Farrar, Margaret & Maleska, Eugene T., eds. Simon & Schuster Crossword Puzzle Book. (Series: No. 132). 64p. 1983. spiral bound 5.95 (ISBN 0-671-44396-8, Fireside). S&S.
--Simon & Schuster's Crossword Puzzle Book. 64p. 1984. spiral bd. 5.75 (ISBN 0-671-50202-6, Fireside). S&S.
--Simon & Schuster's Crossword Puzzle Book, No. 134. 1984. 5.95 (ISBN 0-671-50204-2, Fireside). S&S.
--Simon & Schuster's Crossword Puzzle Book, No. 135. 64p. 1985. pap. 5.95 (ISBN 0-671-54192-7, Fireside). S&S.
Farrar, Margaret P. Simon & Schuster Crosswords from the Times, Series 37: A Daily Collection. 1979. 5.95 (ISBN 0-671-25082-5, Fireside). S&S.
--Simon & Schuster Large Type Crosswords, No. 4. 1979. pap. 5.95 (ISBN 0-671-24792-1, Fireside). S&S.
Farrar, Margaret P. & Maleska, Eugene T. Crossword Puzzle Book, No. 118. 1979. pap. 5.95 (ISBN 0-671-24097-8, Fireside). S&S.
--Simon & Schuster Crossword Puzzle Book, No. 119. 1979. pap. 4.95 (ISBN 0-671-24098-6, Fireside). S&S.
--Simon & Schuster Crossword Puzzle Book, No. 120. 1979. 5.95 (ISBN 0-671-24099-4, Fireside). S&S.
--Simon & Schuster Crossword Puzzle Book, No. 121. 1980. 4.95 (ISBN 0-671-24100-1, Fireside). S&S.
Farrar, Margaret P., ed. Crossword Puzzle Book, No. 100. 1970. 5.95 (ISBN 0-671-20743-1, Fireside). S&S.
--Crossword Puzzle Book, No. 110. 1975. spiral bdg. 4.95 (ISBN 0-671-22171-X, Fireside). S&S.
--Crossword Puzzle Book, No. 112. 5.95 (ISBN 0-671-22430-1, Fireside). S&S.
--Crossword Puzzle Book, No. 113. 1977. pap. 5.95 (ISBN 0-671-22760-2, Fireside). S&S.
--Crossword Puzzle Book, No. 116. Maleska, Eugene T. 1978. spiral bound 4.95 (ISBN 0-671-24095-1, Fireside). S&S.
--Crossword Treasury, Nos. 1-16. Incl. No. 1. pap. 3.95 (ISBN 0-671-21927-8); No. 2. pap. 5.95 (ISBN 0-671-21928-6); No. 3. pap. 5.95 (ISBN 0-671-21929-4); No. 4. pap. 5.95 (ISBN 0-671-21931-6); No. 5. pap. 5.95 (ISBN 0-671-21932-4); No. 6. pap. 3.95 (ISBN 0-671-10393-8); No. 7. pap. 3.95 (ISBN 0-671-21933-2); No. 8. pap. 3.95 (ISBN 0-671-21934-0); No. 9. pap. 5.95 (ISBN 0-671-21935-9); No. 10. pap. 5.95 (ISBN 0-671-21936-7); No. 11. pap. 3.95 (ISBN 0-671-21937-5); No. 12. pap. 4.95 (ISBN 0-671-21938-3); No. 13. pap. 4.95 (ISBN 0-671-21939-1); No. 14. pap. 3.95 (ISBN 0-671-21940-5); No. 15. pap. 4.95 (ISBN 0-671-10726-7); No. 16. pap. 5.95 (ISBN 0-671-10819-0). pap. (Fireside). S&S.
--Crossword Treasury, No. 17. (Orig.). 1975. pap. 5.95 (ISBN 0-671-22128-0, Fireside). S&S.
--Crossword Treasury, No. 19. 1978. pap. 4.95 (ISBN 0-671-24132-X, Fireside). S&S.
--Crossword Treasury, No. 20. 1978. pap. 5.95 (ISBN 0-671-24411-6, Fireside). S&S.
--Crosswords from the Times, No. 25. 1972. 4.95 (ISBN 0-671-21353-9, Fireside). S&S.
--Crosswords from the Times, No. 26. 1973. spiral bdg. 5.95 (ISBN 0-671-21515-9, Fireside). S&S.
--Crosswords from the Times, No. 27. 1973. 5.95 (ISBN 0-671-21619-8, Fireside). S&S.
--Crosswords from the Times, No. 28. 1974. spiral bdg. 5.95 (ISBN 0-671-21847-6, Fireside). S&S.
--Crosswords from the Times, No. 29 (Daily) 1975. spiral bdg. 5.95 (ISBN 0-671-22094-2, Fireside). S&S.
--Crosswords from the Times, No. 30 (Sunday) (Orig.). 1976. pap. 5.95 (ISBN 0-671-22267-8, Fireside). S&S.
--Crosswords from the Times, No. 31. 1977. spiral bdg. 4.95 (ISBN 0-671-22396-8, Fireside). S&S.
--Crosswords from the Times, No. 32. 1977. spiral 4.95 (ISBN 0-671-22761-0, Fireside). S&S.
--Crosswords from the Times, No. 33. 1978. spiral bdg. 4.95 (ISBN 0-671-24117-6, Fireside). S&S.
--Large Type Crosswords, No. 3. 1978. 3.95 (ISBN 0-671-24135-4, Fireside). S&S.
--Simon & Schuster Crossword from the Times, Series 36: A Daily Collection. 1979. pap. 3.95 (ISBN 0-671-24795-6, Fireside). S&S.
--Simon & Schuster Crosswords from the Times, Series 34. 1979. spiral 3.95 (ISBN 0-686-67343-3, Fireside). S&S.
--Simon & Schuster Crosswords from the Times, Series 35: A Sunday Collection. 1979. pap. 3.95 (ISBN 0-671-24778-6, Fireside). S&S.
Farrar, Margaret P. & Maleska, Eugene T., eds. Crossword Puzzle Book, No. 115. 1978. spiral bdg. 4.95 (ISBN 0-671-24094-3, Fireside). S&S.
--Crossword Puzzle Book, No. 117. 1978. spiral 4.95 (ISBN 0-671-24096-X, Fireside). S&S.
Farrar, R. A. Survey by Prismatic Compass. 16p. 1980. pap. text ed. 4.00x (ISBN 0-900312-96-3, Pub. by Coun Brit Archaeology). Humanities.
Farrar, Ronald T. College 101. 187p. (Orig.). 1984. pap. 6.95 (ISBN 0-87866-269-3). Petersons Guides.
--Reluctant Servant: The Story of Charles G. Ross. LC 68-20094. 265p. 1969. 21.00x (ISBN 0-8262-0072-9). U of Mo Pr.
Farrar, Rowena R. Grace Moore & Her Many Worlds. LC 81-67955. (Illus.). 312p. 1982. 17.95 (ISBN 0-8453-4723-3). Cornwall Bks.
Farrar, Stewart. What Witches Do. 2nd ed. (Illus.). 208p. 1983. pap. 8.95 (ISBN 0-919345-17-4). Phoenix Pub WA.
Farrar, Stewart & Farrar, Janet. Eight Sabbats for Witches. (Illus.). 192p. 1983. Repr. of 1981 ed. 13.95 (ISBN 0-919345-25-5). Phoenix Pub WA.
Farrar, Stuart, jt. auth. see Farrar, Janet.
Farrar, Susan C. Samantha on Stage. LC 78-64958. (Illus.). (gr. 4-7). 1979. 7.95 (ISBN 0-8037-7574-1); PLB 7.45 (ISBN 0-8037-7577-6). Dial Bks Young.
Farrar, Victor J. Purchase of Alaska. 1971. Repr. of 1935 ed. 39.00x (ISBN 0-403-00590-6). Scholarly.
Farrar, W. E. & Lambert, H. P. Infectious Diseases. (Pocket Picture Guides to Clinical Medicine Ser.). 100p. 1984. text ed. 11.95 (ISBN 0-683-03041-8). Williams & Wilkins.
Farrar, W. E., jt. auth. see Lambert, H. P.
Farrar, W. Edmund, jt. auth. see Lambert, Harold P.
Farrara, Frank, jt. auth. see Lyttle, Richard B.
Farre, Henry. Sky Fighters of France: Aerial Warfare, Nineteen Fourteen to Nineteen Eighteen. Gilbert, James, ed. Rush, Catharine, tr. LC 79-7252. (Flight: Its First Seventy-Five Years Ser.). (Illus.). 1979. Repr. of 1919 ed. lib. bdg. 19.00x (ISBN 0-405-12164-4). Ayer Co Pubs.
Farrell. Ohio Municipal Code, Nineteen Sixty-Two to Nineteen Eighty-One, 3 vols. 11th ed. 2368p. 155.00; suppl. incl. Anderson Pub Co.
Farrell, A. S. Mono & Disaccharides in Water. 1986. 100.00x (ISBN 0-08-023919-6). Pergamon.
Farrell, Anthony J., et al. The Seven Sages of Rome & the Book of Sinbad: An Analytical Bibliography. LC 82-49137. (Reference Library of the Humanities). 175p. 1984. lib. bdg. 39.00 (ISBN 0-8240-9196-5). Garland Pub.
Farrell, B. A. The Standing of Psychoanalysis. (Oxford Paperback University Ser.). 1981. text ed. 18.95x (ISBN 0-19-219133-0); pap. 9.95x (ISBN 0-686-86550-2). Oxford U Pr.
Farrell, B. A. see Smith, B. Babington.

Farrell, Brian. Sean Lemass. (Gill's Irish Lives Ser.). 1983. 15.95 (ISBN 0-7171-1074-5, Pub by Gill & Macmillan Ireland); pap. 6.95 (ISBN 0-7171-1010-9). Irish Bk Ctr.

Farrell, Brian, ed. Communications & Community in Ireland. (The Thomas Davis Lecture Ser.). 133p. (Orig.). 1984. pap. 6.95 (ISBN 0-85342-727-5, Pub. by Mercier Pr Ireland). Irish Bks Media.

Farrell, Bryan H. Hawaii, the Legend That Sells. LC 81-16177. (Illus.). 418p. 1982. text ed. 20.00x (ISBN 0-8248-0766-9). UH Pr.

Farrell, C. How to Operate a Successful Dance Studio. (Ballroom Dance Ser.). 1985. lib. bdg. 79.00 (ISBN 0-87700-763-2). Revisionist Pr.

Farrell, C. Frederick, Jr. & Farrell, Edith R. Marguerite Youncenar in Counterpoint. 126p. (Orig.). 1984. lib. bdg. 20.50 (ISBN 0-8191-3607-7); pap. text ed. 8.75 (ISBN 0-8191-3608-5). U Pr of Amer.

Farrell, C. Frederick, Jr. & Farrell, Edith R., trs. from Fr. Louise Labe's Complete Works. LC 85-51268. iv, 134p. 1985. 18.50 (ISBN 0-87875-319-2). Whitston Pub.

Farrell, Catharine H. Word Weaving: A Storytelling Guide. (Illus.). 60p. 1983. pap. 6.00 (ISBN 0-936434-12-0). SF Stud Ctr.

Farrell, Catharine H. & Nessel, Denise D. Effects of Storytelling: An Ancient Art for Modern Classrooms. 36p. (Orig.). 1982. write for info. (ISBN 0-936434-04-X). Zellerbach F F.

Farrell, Catherine & Nessel, Denise. Word Weaving: A Teaching Sourcebook. 120p. 1984. lab manual 10.00 (ISBN 0-936434-15-5). Zellerbach f f.

Farrell, Catherine E., jt. auth. see Butler, Francis J.

Farrell, Catherine H. Word Weaving: A Storytelling Guide. (Illus.). 80p. 1983. pap. text ed. write for info. (ISBN 0-936434-12-0). Zellerbach F F.

Farrell, Catherine H. & Nessel, Denise. Word Weaving: A Teaching Sourcebook. 144p. 1984. pap. write for info. (ISBN 0-936434-15-5). SF Stud Ctr.

Farrell, Christine, jt. auth. see Webb, Adrian.

Farrell, Christopher & Artz, Thomas. The Sacraments Today: Their Meaning & Celebration. LC 78-69750. 1978. pap. 2.95 (ISBN 0-89243-087-7). Liguori Pubns.

Farrell, Cliff. Comanch-Ride the Wild Trail. 1982. pap. 2.50 (ISBN 0-451-11565-1, AE1565, Sig). NAL.

--Cross Fire the Renegade. 1983. pap. 2.95 (ISBN 0-451-12389-1, Sig). NAL.

Farrell, Clive, jt. auth. see Rothschild, Miriam.

Farrell, Dianne & Hayes, Ruth M., eds. What Is a City: Young People Reply. (Illus.). 1969. 1.00 (ISBN 0-89073-017-2). Boston Public Lib.

Farrell, Don A. Guam: 1898-1918. 2nd ed. Koontz, Phyllis, ed. (The Pictorial History of Guam Ser.). (Illus.). 210p. 1985. 15.95 (ISBN 0-930839-01-3). Micronesian.

--Liberation Nineteen Forty Four: The Pictorial History of Guam. Koontz, Phyllis, ed. (Illus.). (gr. 8-12). 1984. Repr. 15.95 (ISBN 0-930839-00-5). Micronesian.

Farrell, Edith R., jt. auth. see Farrell, C. Frederick, Jr.

Farrell, Edith R., tr. see Bachelard, Gaston.

Farrell, Edith R., jt. tr. see Farrell, C. Frederick, Jr.

Farrell, Edward. Can You Drink This Cup? pap. 4.95 (ISBN 0-87193-179-6). Dimension Bks.

--Celtic Meditations. 3.95 (ISBN 0-87193-033-1). Dimension Bks.

--The Father Is Very Fond of Me. 6.95 (ISBN 0-87193-029-3). Dimension Bks.

--Prayer Is a Hunger. 4.95 (ISBN 0-87193-031-5). Dimension Bks.

--Surprised by the Spirit. 4.95 (ISBN 0-87193-030-7). Dimension Bks.

Farrell, Eileen. To Be or Not to Be. 164p. 1964. 5.95 (ISBN 0-933932-26-X); pap. 2.50 (ISBN 0-933932-27-8). Scepter Pubs.

Farrell, Gabriel. Story of Blindness. LC 56-7212. 1956. 16.50x (ISBN 0-674-83940-4). Harvard U Pr.

Farrell, George E. Actinomycosis of the Thorax. (Illus.). 144p. 1981. 22.50 (ISBN 0-87527-205-3). Green.

Farrell, Gerald J., jt. auth. see Kosicki, George W.

Farrell, Gordon H., jt. auth. see Briscall, C. M.

Farrell, H. Clyde & Kens, Paul. Buying, Renting & Borrowing in Texas: The Rules of the Game. LC 80-52895. (Illus.). 278p. 1980. 10.95 (ISBN 0-937606-00-6); pap. 6.95 (ISBN 0-937606-01-4). Tex Consumer.

Farrell, J. G. The Siege of Krishnapur. 344p. 1985. pap. 4.95 (ISBN 0-88184-195-1). Carroll & Graf.

--Singapore Grip. 455p. 1985. pap. 5.95 (ISBN 0-88184-124-2). Carroll & Graf.

--Troubles. 411p. 1975. pap. 4.95 (ISBN 0-14-003973-2, Pub. by Penguin England). Irish Bk Ctr.

Farrell, J. J. Zachary Taylor, 1784-1850 & Millard Fillmore, 1800-1874: Chronology, Documents, Bibliographical Aids. LC 78-116061. (Presidential Chronology Ser). 1971. 8.00 (ISBN 0-379-12078-X). Oceana.

Farrell, J. J., ed. James K. Polk, 1795-1849: Chronology, Documents, Bibliographical Aids. LC 75-102942. (Presidential Chronology Ser.). 92p. 1970. 8.00 (ISBN 0-379-12069-0). Oceana.

Farrell, Jack, jt. auth. see Grossman, William.

Farrell, James J. Inventing the American Way of Death, 1830-1920. (American Civilization Ser.). 287p. 1980. 29.95 (ISBN 0-87722-180-4). Temple U Pr.

Farrell, James L. Guide to Portfolio Management. (McGraw-Hill Guide Series in Finance). (Illus.). 368p. 1983. text ed. 24.95 (ISBN 0-07-019970-1). McGraw.

Farrell, James L., ed. Integrated Aircraft Navigation. 1976. 59.00 (ISBN 0-12-249750-3). Acad Pr.

Farrell, James T. Collected Poems. LC 65-16314. 1965. 7.95 (ISBN 0-8303-0042-2). Fleet.

--Eight Short, Short Stories & Sketches. LC 81-10855. 1981. 10.00 (ISBN 0-933292-08-2); pap. 3.50 (ISBN 0-933292-07-4). Arts End.

--Father & Son. LC 76-6340. (Irish Americans Ser). 1976. Repr. of 1940 ed. 38.50 (ISBN 0-405-09335-7). Ayer Co Pubs.

--French Girls Are Vicious & Other Stories. LC 55-7890. 1955. 11.95 (ISBN 0-8149-0095-X). Vanguard.

--Judgement Day. 464p. 1973. pap. 1.25 (ISBN 0-380-01311-8, 14282). Avon.

--New Year's Eve - 1929. LC 67-30058. 144p. 4.50 (ISBN 0-912292-02-4). The Smith.

--Reflections at Fifty. LC 54-11517. 1954. 10.00 (ISBN 0-8149-0096-8). Vanguard.

--Sam Holman. LC 83-60204. 246p. 1983. 17.95 (ISBN 0-87975-202-5). Prometheus Bks.

--Studs Lonigan. 1976. pap. 3.95 (ISBN 0-380-00934-X, 59758-6, Bard). Avon.

--Studs Lonigan. Bd. with Young Lonigan; The Young Manhood of Studs Lonigan; Judgment Day. 1110p. Date not set. 19.50 (ISBN 0-8149-0791-1). Vanguard.

--What Time Collects. 432p. 1974. pap. 1.50 (ISBN 0-532-15124-0). Woodhill.

--When Time Was Born. LC 66-16296. 1966. 3.50 (ISBN 0-912292-04-0); signed ltd. ed. 25.00 (ISBN 0-912292-05-9). The Smith.

Farrell, James T., ed. see Mencken, Henry L.

Farrell, James T., et al. The Smith-Fourteen. Boxer, Ray & Smith, Harry, eds. LC 64-9367. 350p. (Orig.). 1972. 6.50 (ISBN 0-912292-23-7); pap. 3.50 (ISBN 0-685-24695-7). The Smith.

Farrell, Jane. Illustrated Guide to Orthopedic Nursing. 2nd ed. (Illus.). 400p. 1982. pap. text ed. 15.75 (ISBN 0-397-54274-7, 64-01988, Lippincott Nursing). Lippincott.

Farrell, John C. & Smith, Asa P., eds. Image & Reality in World Politics. LC 68-18994. 140p. (Orig.). 1968. pap. 10.00 (ISBN 0-231-08588-5). Columbia U Pr.

--Theory & Reality in International Relations. LC 68-18993. 108p. 1967. pap. 9.50x (ISBN 0-231-08587-7). Columbia U Pr.

Farrell, John J. The Immigrant & the School in New York City: A Program for Citizenship. Cordasco, Francesco, ed. LC 80-845. (American Ethnic Groups Ser.). 1981. lib. bdg. 21.00x (ISBN 0-405-13417-7). Ayer Co Pubs.

Farrell, John P. Revolution As Tragedy: The Dilemma of the Moderate from Scott to Arnold. LC 79-26000. (Illus.). 304p. 1980. 24.95x (ISBN 0-8014-1278-1). Cornell U Pr.

Farrell, Joseph E. One Day at a Time. (Orig.). 1976. pap. 1.50 (ISBN 0-89243-056-7, 29085). Liguori Pubns.

Farrell, Joseph P., jt. auth. see Schiefelbein, Ernesto.

Farrell, Kate, jt. auth. see Koch, Kenneth.

Farrell, Kathleen L. & Ferrara, John A. Shoplifting: The Antishoplifting Guidebook. LC 85-3613. 176p. 1985. 31.95 (ISBN 0-03-003094-3). Praeger.

Farrell, Kathy & Sweeney, Mary. What Can We Do Today, Mommy. (Illus.). 127p. (Orig.). 1980. 6.95 (ISBN 0-9604118-0-1). Growing Together.

Farrell, Kenneth T. Spices, Condiments & Seasonings. (Illus.). 1985. 55.00 (ISBN 0-87055-464-6). AVI.

Farrell, Kirby. Shakespeare's Creation: The Language of Magic & Play. LC 75-8447. 254p. 1976. 15.00x (ISBN 0-87023-184-7). U of Mass Pr.

Farrell, Lee, ed. see Leahy, Barbara H.

Farrell, Lois, jt. auth. see Blanchard, J. Richard.

Farrell, M. J., pseud. Devoted Ladies. 1985. pap. 6.95 (ISBN 0-14-016101-5, Pub. by Virago Mod Classics). Penguin.

Farrell, M. J. Fuller Employment. (Institute of Economic Affairs, Hobart Papers Ser.: No. 34). 1967. pap. 2.50 technical (ISBN 0-255-69529-2). Transatlantic.

Farrell, M. J., pseud. The Rising Tide. 1985. pap. 6.95 (ISBN 0-317-18964-6, Pub. by Virago Mod Classics). Penguin.

Farrell, Margaret, jt. auth. see Kanai, Shozo.

Farrell, Margaret A. & Farmer, Walter A. Systematic Instruction in Mathematics for the Middle & High School Years. LC 79-4250. (Illus.). 1980. pap. text ed. 17.30 (ISBN 0-201-02436-5, Sch Div). Addison-Wesley.

Farrell, Margaret A., jt. auth. see Farmer, Walter A.

Farrell, Maureen & Cohen, I. Bernard, eds. William Whiston. LC 80-2088. (Development of Science Ser.). (Illus.). 1981. lib. bdg. 32.00x (ISBN 0-405-13854-7). Ayer Co Pubs.

Farrell, Michael. Arming the Protestants: The Formation of the Ulster Special Constabulary & the Royal Ulster Constabulary, 1920-1927. 384p. (Orig.). 1983. pap. 11.95 (ISBN 0-86104-705-2). Pluto Pr.

--Northern Ireland: Orange State. 2nd ed. 406p. 1980. pap. 11.95 (ISBN 0-86104-300-6). Pluto Pr.

Farrell, Michael & Greer, Gaylon E. Tax Shelters: Illusions, Delusions & Economic Reality. (American Association of Individual Investors Library of Financial Planning). 256p. 1985. 29.95 (ISBN 0-930369-04-1). Invest Info.

Farrell, Michael D., jt. auth. see Greer, Gaylon E.

Farrell, Michael P. & Rosenberg, Stanley. Men at Midlife. LC 81-3624. 242p. 1981. o. p. 22.95 (ISBN 0-86569-073-1); pap. 15.00 (ISBN 0-86569-062-6). Auburn Hse.

Farrell, Michael R. Who Made All Our Streetcars Go? LC 73-85194. (Illus.). 320p. 1973. 16.00 (ISBN 0-9601320-1-5). Baltimore NRHS.

Farrell, Pat. Time for Me. (Everyday Ser.). (Illus.). 26p. (Orig.). 1983. pap. 3.00 (ISBN 0-915517-01-9). Everyday Ser.

Farrell, Patricia & Lundegren, Herberta M. The Process of Recreation Programming: Theory & Technique. 2nd ed. LC 82-17626. 296p. 1983. text ed. 27.45 (ISBN 0-471-86181-2). Wiley.

Farrell, Paul V., jt. auth. see Heinritz, Stuart F.

Farrell, Paul V., ed. see National Association of Purchasing Management.

Farrell, Peter. EDY: It's Impact on Staff Training in Mental Handicap. LC 85-315. 256p. 1985. 25.00 (ISBN 0-7190-1753-X, Pub. by Manchester Univ Pr). Longwood Pub Group.

Farrell, Philip, ed. Lung Development: Biological & Clinical Perspectives, 2 vols. LC 82-1616. 1982. Vol. 1: Biochemistry & Physiology. 55.00 (ISBN 0-12-249701-5); Vol. 2: Neonatal Respiratory Distress. 44.00 (ISBN 0-12-249702-3). Acad Pr.

Farrell, R. A. & Swigert, V. Deviance & Social Control. LC 81-5791. 1982. pap. text ed. 11.00 (ISBN 0-394-33309-8, RanC). Random.

Farrell, R. B. Dictionary of German Synonyms. 3rd ed. LC 75-36175. (Ger.). 1977. 59.50 (ISBN 0-521-21189-1); pap. 16.95 (ISBN 0-521-29068-6). Cambridge U Pr.

Farrell, R. H. Multivariate Calculation. (Springer Series in Statistics). 430p. 1985. 42.00 (ISBN 0-387-96049-X). Springer-Verlag.

--Techniques of Multivariate Calculation. (Lecture Notes in Mathematics: Vol. 520). 1976. pap. 20.00 (ISBN 0-387-07695-6). Springer-Verlag.

Farrell, Robert, jt. ed. see Dewhirst, Martin.

Farrell, Robert A. & Swigert, Victoria L., eds. Social Deviance. 2nd ed. LC 78-6566. 1978. pap. text ed. 12.80 (ISBN 0-397-47385-0, HarpC). Har-Row.

Farrell, Robert T., jt. auth. see Hill, Thomas D.

Farrell, Robert T., jt. ed. see Salu, Mary.

Farrell, Ronda P., jt. auth. see Westrich, Julia C.

Farrell, Steven G. Wonder Voyages upon Unmoving Clouds. LC 84-90410. 64p. 1984. 6.50 (ISBN 0-8233-0391-8). Golden Quill.

Farrell, Susan C. Directory of Contemporary American Musical Instrument Makers. LC 80-24924. (Illus.). 232p. 1981. text ed. 24.00x (ISBN 0-8262-0322-1). U of Mo Pr.

Farrell, Thomas J. Developing Writing Skills. 1983. pap. 12.95 (ISBN 0-89702-037-5). PAR Inc.

Farrell, Thomas J. & Burns, Robert E. Public Speaking Plus. 304p. pap. text ed. 13.15 (ISBN 0-89702-045-6). PAR Inc.

Farrell, Tom. Nantucket 1970. LC 82-90113. 233p. (Orig.). 1982. pap. 3.95 (ISBN 0-943306-00-0). Pier Pr.

Farrell, Wes, jt. auth. see Cole, Gerald.

Farrell, William R. The U. S. Government Response to Terrorism, 1972-1980: In Search of an Effective Strategy. LC 82-50665. (National & International Terrorism Ser.). 142p. 1982. lib. bdg. 23.50x (ISBN 0-86531-402-0). Westview.

Farrelly, D. J. Goethe & Inner Harmony: A Study of "Schoene Seele" in the Apprenticeship of William Meister. 220p. 1973. 10.00x (ISBN 0-7165-2157-1, Pub. by Irish Academic Pr Ireland). Biblio Dist.

Farrelly, David. The Book of Bamboo. LC 84-5366. (Illus.). 320p. (Orig.). 1984. 25.00 (ISBN 0-87156-824-1); pap. 14.95 (ISBN 0-87156-825-X). Sierra.

Farrelly, Frank & Brandsma, Jeff. Provocative Therapy. LC 74-78101. 1974. Repr. 10.95x (ISBN 0-916990-03-6). Meta Pubns.

Farrelly, John. God's Work in a Changing World. 346p. (Orig.). 1985. lib. bdg. 25.50 (ISBN 0-8191-4523-8); pap. text ed. 14.25 (ISBN 0-8191-4524-6). U Pr of Amer.

Farrelly, M. J. Settlement After the War in South Africa. LC 78-118468. 1971. Repr. of 1900 ed. 25.50x (ISBN 0-8046-1217-X, Pub. by Kennikat). Assoc Faculty Pr.

Farrelly, M. Natalena. Thomas Francis Meehan 1854-1942: A Memoir. LC 44-8793. (Monograph: No. 20). (Illus.). 1944. 10.00x (ISBN 0-930060-02-4). US Cath Hist.

Farren, George. Essays on the Varieties in Mania, Exhibited by the Characters of Hamlet, Ophelia, Lear, & Edgar. LC 74-168009. Repr. of 1833 ed. 14.00 (ISBN 0-404-02367-3). AMS Pr.

Farren, Mark, ed. Infant Mortality & Health in Latin America: An Annotated Bibliography from the 1979-82 Literature. 172p. (Eng., Fr., Span. & Portuguese.). 1985. pap. 13.00 (ISBN 0-88936-419-2, IDRC226, IDRC). Unipub.

Farren, Mick. Black Leather Jacket. 96p. 1985. 19.95 (ISBN 0-89659-591-9). Abbeville Pr.

--Protectorate. 240p. 1985. pap. 2.75 (ISBN 0-441-68680-X). Ace Bks.

Farren, Mick & Marchbank, Pearce. Elvis Presley. 1978. pap. 4.95 (ISBN 0-8256-3921-2, Omnibus). Music Sales.

Farren, Mick, jt. auth. see Dalton, David.

Farren, Mike, compiled by. Elvis Presley in His Own Words. (Illus.). 128p. 1981. pap. 5.95 (ISBN 0-8256-3921-2, Quick Fox). Putnam Pub Group.

Farren, Pat, ed. What Will It Take to Prevent Nuclear War? 256p. 1983. 13.95 (ISBN 0-87073-984-0); pap. 6.95 (ISBN 0-87073-985-9). Schenkman Bks Inc.

Farrenc, Aristide & Farrenc, Louise, eds. Le Tresor des pianistes, 23 vols. LC 77-8873. (Music Reprint Ser.). (Illus.). 1978. Repr. of 1872 ed. lib. bdg. 47.50 ea.; lib. bdg. 950.00 set (ISBN 0-306-77380-5). Da Capo.

Farrenc, Louise. Trio in E Minor for Piano, Flute & Cello: Opus 45. (Women Composers Ser.: No. 3). 86p. 1979. Repr. of 1862 ed. 24.50 (ISBN 0-306-79553-1). Da Capo.

Farrenc, Louise, jt. ed. see Farrenc, Aristide.

Farrer, Anne & Tregear, Mary. Ling Suhua. 24p. 1983. 20.00x (ISBN 0-317-20330-4, Pub. by Ashmolean Mus UK). State Mutual Bk.

Farrer, Austin. Finite & Infinite: A Philosophical Essay. 312p. (Orig.). 1979. pap. 8.95 (ISBN 0-8164-2001-7, Pub. by Seabury). Winston Pr.

Farrer, Austin M. The Freedom of the Will. LC 81-20229. (The Gifford Lectures). 330p. 1982. Repr. of 1960 ed. lib. bdg. 29.50x (ISBN 0-313-23295-4, FAFW). Greenwood.

Farrer, Donald, jt. auth. see Cross, Jean.

Farrer, H. Gynaecological Care. 166p. 1979. 40.00x (ISBN 0-85896-624-7, Pub. by Pitman Bks England). State Mutual Bk.

Farrer, J. A. Military Manners & Customs: The Laws & Observations of Warfare in Ancient & Modern Times. lib. bdg. 59.95 (ISBN 0-8490-0636-8). Gordon Pr.

Farrer, James A. Books Condemned to Be Burnt. LC 72-7292. 1972. Repr. of 1892 ed. lib. bdg. 16.50 (ISBN 0-8414-0283-3). Folcroft.

--Literary Forgeries. 1973. lib. bdg. 9.00 (ISBN 0-8414-4017-4). Folcroft.

--Literary Forgeries. LC 68-23156. 1969. Repr. of 1907 ed. 30.00x (ISBN 0-8103-3305-8). Gale.

--Military Manners & Customs. LC 68-21771. 1968. Repr. of 1885 ed. 30.00x (ISBN 0-8103-3510-7). Gale.

Farrer, K. T. Fancy Eating That! A Closer Look at Food Additives & Contaminants. (Illus.). 194p. (Orig.). 1984. pap. 11.25x (ISBN 0-522-84243-7, Pub. by Melbourne U Pr Australia). Intl Spec Bk.

Farrer, Reginald. Alpines & Bog Plants. LC 75-42433. 1976. Repr. of 1908 ed. 12.50 (ISBN 0-913728-10-1). Theophrastus.

--English Rock Garden, Two Vols. LC 75-23059. (Illus.). 1976. Repr. of 1919 ed. 35.00 (ISBN 0-913728-06-3). Theophrastus.

--In a Yorkshire Garden. LC 73-87457. (Illus.). 1973. Repr. of 1909 ed. 12.50 (ISBN 0-685-61147-7). Theophrastus.

--My Rock Garden. LC 72-161605. (Illus.). 1971. Repr. of 1907 ed. 8.50 (ISBN 0-913728-04-7). Theophrastus.

--On the Eaves of the World, 2 vols. LC 75-46508. (Illus.). 1977. Repr. of 1917 ed. write for info (ISBN 0-685-78306-5). Theophrastus.

--The Rainbow Bridge. LC 76-47496. (Illus.). 1976. Repr. of 1921 ed. 15.00 (ISBN 0-913728-15-2). Theophrastus.

Farrer, Reginald J. On the Eaves of the World, 2 Vols. LC 79-136386. (BCL Ser.: I). Repr. of 1917 ed. Set. 57.50 (ISBN 0-404-02368-1). AMS Pr.

Farrer, Thomas H. Studies in Currency Eighteen Ninety-Eight. LC 67-19961. Repr. of 1898 ed. 37.50x (ISBN 0-678-00397-1). Kelley.

Farrer-Baynes, William, jt. auth. see Knehr, Adolph.

Farrer-Brown, Geoffrey. Color Atlas of Cardiac Pathology. (Illus.). 1977. 55.00 (ISBN 0-8151-3209-3). Year Bk Med.

Farrie, Hugh. Highways & Byways in Literature. 337p. 1980. Repr. of 1910 ed. lib. bdg. 25.00 (ISBN 0-89987-252-2). Darby Bks.

--Highways & Byways in Literature (Swift, Dr. Johnson, Edward Young, Bunyan) 1910. lib. bdg. 25.00 (ISBN 0-8414-9113-5). Folcroft.

Farrier, Denis. Country Vet. LC 72-6615. 1973. 6.95 (ISBN 0-8008-1950-0). Taplinger.

Farringdon, M. G. Word Processing. 250p. Date not set. price not set (ISBN 0-521-25337-3); pap. 14.95 (ISBN 0-521-27321-8). Cambridge U Pr.

Farrington. Aggression & Dangerousness. LC 84-13112. (Current Research in Forensic Psychiatry & Psychology Ser.: Vol. 3). 1985. 46.95 (ISBN 0-471-90556-9). Wiley.

Farrington, Ann. Until We Meet Again. 1977. pap. 1.50 (ISBN 0-532-15288-3). Woodhill.

Farrington, B. Samuel Butler & the Odyssey. LC 73-3148. 1973. lib. bdg. 12.50 (ISBN 0-8414-1960-4). Folcroft.

--Samuel Butler & the Odyssey. LC 73-21626. (English Literature Ser., No. 33). 1974. lib. bdg. 46.95x (ISBN 0-8383-1777-4). Haskell.

Farrington, B., jt. auth. see Barker, D. E.

Farrington, B., tr. see Schapera, Isaac.

Farrington, Benjamin. Francis Bacon. LC 72-8974. (English Biography Ser., No. 31). 1973. Repr. of 1951 ed. lib. bdg. 49.95x (ISBN 0-8383-1685-9). Haskell.

--Francis Bacon, Philosopher of Industrial Science. 1979. Repr. of 1949 ed. lib. bdg. 18.00x (ISBN 0-374-92706-5). Octagon.

--Hand & Foot in Ancient Greece. 119p. 1980. Repr. of 1947 ed. lib. bdg. 18.50 (ISBN 0-8492-4615-6). R West.

--Head & Hand in Ancient Greece. LC 77-656. 1977. Repr. of 1947 ed. lib. bdg. 20.00 (ISBN 0-8414-4161-8). Folcroft.

--Philosophy of Francis Bacon. LC 65-4151. 1967. pap. 1.95x (ISBN 0-226-23885-7, P249, Phoen). U of Chicago Pr.

--Samuel Butler & the Odyssey. 1979. Repr. of 1929 ed. lib. bdg. 12.50 (ISBN 0-8495-1633-1). Arden Lib.

--What Darwin Really Said. LC 82-5557. (What They Really Said Ser.). 124p. (gr. 10-12). 1982. pap. 4.95 (ISBN 0-8052-0720-1). Schocken.

Farrington, Conor. Aaron Thy Brother. (The Irish Play Ser.). Date not set. pap. 1.95x (ISBN 0-912262-38-9). Proscenium.

Farrington, Constance, tr. see Fanon, Frantz.

Farrington, D. P., jt. auth. see West, D. J.

Farrington, David P., jt. auth. see Gunn, John.

Farrington, David P. & Tarling, Roger, eds. Prediction in Criminology. (SUNY Series on Critical Issues in Criminal Justice). 282p. 1985. lib. bdg. 39.50 (ISBN 0-88706-004-8); pap. text ed. 14.95 (ISBN 0-88706-003-X). State U NY Pr.

Farrington, David P., et al, eds. Psychology, Law & Legal Processes. (Oxford Sociolegal Studies). 1979. text ed. 28.00x (ISBN 0-391-01026-3). Humanities.

Farrington, Davis D. The Essay. 1924. 20.00 (ISBN 0-8482-3979-2). Norwood Edns.

Farrington, E. A. A Clinical Materia Medica. 1979. 40.00x (ISBN 0-686-78829-X, Pub. by Bks India England). State Mutual Bk.

Farrington, Frederic E. Public Primary School System in France, with Special Reference to the Training of Teachers. LC 70-176765. (Columbia University. Teachers College. Contributions to Education: No. 7). Repr. of 1906 ed. 22.50 (ISBN 0-404-55007-X). AMS Pr.

Farrington, Jane. Wyndham Lewis. 128p. 1980. 35.00x (ISBN 0-85331-434-9, Pub. by Lund Humphries England). State Mutual Bk.

Farrington, S. Kip. Fishing with Hemingway & Glassel. 10.95 (ISBN 0-911660-23-2). Yankee Peddler.

--Tony the Tuna. 1976. 6.95 (ISBN 0-911660-25-9). Yankee Peddler.

Farrington, S. Kip, Jr. Labrador Retriever: Friend & Worker. (Illus.). 176p. 1976. 13.95 (ISBN 0-8038-4295-3). Hastings.

Farrington, William. Prehistoric & Historic Pottery of the Southwest: A Bibliography. 1975. pap. 2.25 (ISBN 0-913270-45-8). Sunstone Pr.

Farrington, William, et al. Working with Plant Supplies & Services. (Illus.). 144p. 1980. pap. text ed. 10.24 (ISBN 0-07-019965-5). McGraw.

Farrior, J. S., jt. ed. see Roberson, R. E.

Farris, Beverly W. Mizz-O the Monkey Could Not Find His Toothpaste. 1985. 4.95 (ISBN 0-533-06371-X). Vantage.

Farris, Charlotte J., jt. auth. see Smith, Amanda J.

Farris, Christine. Mining the Beaches for Watches & Small Change. LC 81-4385. (Illus.). 48p. (YA) 1981. 30.00 (ISBN 0-916906-32-9); pap. 15.95 (ISBN 0-916906-33-7). Konglomerati.

Farris, Donald E., jt. auth. see Simpson, James R.

Farris, Edmond J. Art Students' Anatomy. 2nd ed. (Illus.). 159p. 1953. pap. 3.95 (ISBN 0-486-20744-7). Dover.

--Art Students' Anatomy. LC 62-8634. 1961. lib. bdg. 10.50x (ISBN 0-88307-088-X). Gannon.

Farris, Edmond J., ed. Care & Breeding of Laboratory Animals. LC 50-10593. Repr. of 1950 ed. 132.50 (ISBN 0-8357-9852-6, 2011871). Bks Demand UMI.

Farris, Edmond J. & Griffith, John Q., Jr., eds. Rat in Laboratory Investigation. 2nd ed. (Illus.). 1963. Repr. of 1949 ed. 50.00h (ISBN 0-02-844550-3). Hafner.

Farris, Frances B. From Rattlesnakes to Road Agents: Rough Times on the Frio. Sonnichsen, C. L., ed. LC 84-2500. (Chisholm Trail Ser.: No. 3). (Illus.). 160p. 1985. 14.95 (ISBN 0-912646-94-2); pap. 7.95 (ISBN 0-87565-005-8). Tex Christian.

Farris, John. All Heads Turn When the Hunt Goes By. 320p. 1986. pap. 3.50 (ISBN 0-8125-8264-0, Dist. by Warner Pub Services & St. Martin). Tor Bks.

--The Captors. 320p. 1985. pap. 3.50 (ISBN 0-8125-8260-8, Dist. by Pinnacle Bks, Warner Pub Services & St. Martin). Tor Bks.

--Catacombs. 1982. pap. 3.50 (ISBN 0-440-11580-9). Dell.

--The Fury. 352p. 1985. pap. 3.50 (ISBN 0-8125-8262-4, Dist. by Warner Pub Services & St. Martin). Tor Bks.

--Harrison High. 1982. pap. 3.95 (ISBN 0-440-13448-X). Dell.

--The Minotaur. 384p. 1985. pap. 3.95 (ISBN 0-8125-8258-6). Tor Bks.

--Sharp Practice. 1982. pap. 2.95 (ISBN 0-440-17760-X). Dell.

--Son of the Endless Night. 509p. 1985. 16.95 (ISBN 0-312-74468-4). St Martin.

--The Uninvited. 272p. 1983. pap. 3.50 (ISBN 0-440-19712-0). Dell.

Farris, Kenna E. The World's Strangest Secret: Judgement Day 20th Century Style. 24.95 (ISBN 0-318-03803-X). Port Love Intl.

Farris, Martin T. & Sampson, Roy J. Public Utilities: Regulation, Management & Ownership. (Illus.). 368p. 1984. Repr. text ed. 25.95x (ISBN 0-88133-034-5). Waveland Pr.

Farris, Martin T., jt. auth. see Bess, H. David.

Farris, Martin T., jt. auth. see Sampson, Roy.

Farris, Miriam, jt. auth. see Allott, Kenneth.

Farris, Paul & Quelch, John. Advertising & Promotion Management: A Managers Guide to Theory & Practice. LC 81-70915. 312p. 1983. pap. 19.95 (ISBN 0-8019-7369-4). Chilton.

Farris, Paul, jt. auth. see Albion, Mark S.

Farris, Paul, ed. Future Frontiers in Agricultural Marketing Research. 342p. 1983. text ed. 25.50x (ISBN 0-8138-0560-0). Iowa St U Pr.

Farris, Paul W., jt. auth. see Quelch, John A.

Farris, William W. Population, Disease & Land in Early Japan, 645-900. (Harvard-Yenching Institute Monograph Ser.: No. 24). (Illus.). 400p. 1984. text ed. 20.00x (ISBN 0-674-69031-1). Harvard U Pr.

Farrish, Raymond O. & Hsiao, James C. China's Modern Economy. 256p. 1985. 29.95x (ISBN 0-03-063762-7); pap. text ed. 12.95tx (ISBN 0-03-063763-5). Praeger.

Farrison, William E. William Wells Brown: Author & Reformer. LC 69-19275. (Negro American Biographies & Autobiographies Ser.). 1969. 25.00x (ISBN 0-226-23897-0). U of Chicago Pr.

Farriss, Nancy M. Maya Society Under Colonial Rule: The Collective Enterprise of Survival. LC 83-43071. (Illus.). 584p. 1984. 60.00x (ISBN 0-691-07668-5); pap. 19.50x (ISBN 0-691-10158-2). Princeton U Pr.

Farrokhaad, F. Rebirth. Martin, D., tr. LC 83-51701. 133p. 1984. pap. 12.95x (ISBN 0-89003-136-3). Undena Pubns.

Farrokhzaad, Foroogh. A Rebirth: Poems. Martin, David C., tr. (Illus.). 172p. Date not set. pap. 9.95 (ISBN 0-939214-30-X). Mazda Pubs.

Farrokhzad, Forugh. Another Birth. Javadi, Hasan & Sallee, Susan, trs. from Farsi. 144p. (Orig.). 1981. pap. 10.00 (ISBN 0-89410-361-X). Three Continents.

Farrow & Hill. Montessori on a Limited Budget. Rev. ed. LC 74-29539. (Illus.). 300p. 1984. Repr. of 1972 ed. 19.50x (ISBN 0-916011-00-3); Tchrs. Ed. tchr's ed. avail. (ISBN 0-916011-00-3). Ed Sys Pub.

Farrow, Daena. Using Applied Psychology in Personnel Management. 1982. wkbk 8.95 (ISBN 0-8359-8131-2). Reston.

Farrow, Dana. Staffing. pap. text ed. 16.95 (ISBN 0-8359-7083-3); instr's manual avail. (ISBN 0-8359-7100-7). Reston.

Farrow, Elvira & Hill, Carol. Montessori on a Limited Budget: A Manual for the Amateur Craftsman. LC 74-29539. (Illus.). 291p. 1975. pap. 19.50 (ISBN 0-915676-01-X). Ed Sys Pub.

Farrow, H. F. Computerisation Guidelines. 100p. 1979. pap. 24.05 (ISBN 0-471-89437-0). Wiley.

Farrow, H. T. Computerisation Guidelines. 1979. pap. 21.00x (ISBN 0-85012-205-8). Intl Pubns Serv.

Farrow, Hazel. Painting Warps. 1980. 4.50 (ISBN 0-686-27269-2). Robin & Russ.

Farrow, John. Damien the Leper. 1954. pap. 3.95 (ISBN 0-385-02918-7, D3, Im). Doubleday.

Farrow, M. A., ed. Index to Wills Proved in the Consistory Court of Norwich: 1370-1550. (Brit. Record Soc. Index Lib. Ser.: Vol. 69-70). Repr. of 1945 ed. 85.00 (ISBN 0-317-16119-9). Kraus Repr.

Farrow, M. A. & Millican, Percy, eds. Index of Wills Proved in the Consistory Court of Norwich: 1550-1603. (Brit. Record Soc. Index Lib. Ser.: Vol. 73-75). Repr. of 1950 ed. 79.00 (ISBN 0-317-16130-X). Kraus Repr.

Farrow, Nigel, jt. ed. see Lock, Dennis.

Farrow, Percy E. God's Eternal Design. 1980. pap. 12.00 (ISBN 0-8309-0272-4). Herald Hse.

Farrow, Peter. What Use Are Moose? LC 83-4883. pap. 2.50 (ISBN 0-89621-078-2). Thorndike Pr.

--The Yankee Trivia Book. (Illus.). 128p. (Orig.). 1985. pap. 5.95 (ISBN 0-89769-073-3). L Tapley.

Farrow, Peter & Lampert, Diane. Twyllyp. (Illus.). (gr. 3-7). 1963. 7.95 (ISBN 0-8392-3040-0). Astor-Honor.

Farrow, Stephen S. Faith, Fancies & Fetish or Yoruba Paganism. LC 76-98718. (Illus.). Repr. of 1926 ed. 17.50x (ISBN 0-8371-2759-9, FFF&, Pub. by Negro U Pr). Greenwood.

Farrow, W. M. How I Became a Crack Shot with Hints to Beginners. Wolfe, Dave, ed. (Illus.). 204p. Repr. 16.50 (ISBN 0-935632-02-6); write for info. (ISBN 0-935632-03-4). Wolfe Pub Co.

Farrugia & Gammons. Carrying British Mails. 6.50. StanGib.

Farrugia, Jean Y. Letter Box, History of the Post Office Pillar & Wall Boxes. 32.50x (ISBN 0-87556-086-5). Saifer.

Farrukhzad, Furugh. Bride of Acacias. Kessler, Jascha, tr. LC 82-1156. 1983. 25.00x (ISBN 0-88206-050-3). Caravan Bks.

Farschman, Marc W. Setting the Captives Free! A Practical Guide to Breaking the Power of Satan Over Your Life. LC 85-61138. 146p. (Orig.). 1985. pap. 4.95 (ISBN 0-934285-00-4). New Life Faith.

Farson, Daniel. A Traveller to Turkey. 224p. 1985. 19.95 (ISBN 0-7102-0281-4). Routledge & Kegan.

Farson, Dave, jt. auth. see Cinnamon, Kenneth.

Farson, Negley. Going Fishing. (Illus.). 1984. 15.50f (ISBN 0-393-01750-8). Norton.

--Sailing Across Europe. (Century Travellers Ser.). 288p. 1985. pap. 9.95 (ISBN 0-7126-0802-8, Pub. by Century Pubs UK). Hippocrene Bks.

--The Way of a Transgressor. 447p. 1984. pap. 9.95 (ISBN 0-88184-089-0). Carroll & Graf.

Farson, Richard E., ed. Science & Human Affairs. LC 64-18925. (Orig.). 1965. pap. 4.95x (ISBN 0-8314-0006-4). Sci & Behavior.

Farson, Robert. The Cape Cod Canal. 1977. pap. 9.95 (ISBN 0-8195-6050-2). Wesleyan U Pr.

Farsoun, Samih, jt. ed. see Hagopian, Elaine.

Farsoun, Samih K., ed. Arab Society: Continuity & Change. 160p. 1985. 24.50 (ISBN 0-7099-1082-7, Pub. by Croom Helm Ltd). Longwood Pub Group.

Farstad, Arthur L. & Hodges, Zane C., eds. The Greek New Testament According to the Majority Text. 78p. 1982. 13.95 (ISBN 0-8407-4963-5). Nelson.

Farstrup, Alan E., jt. auth. see Bristow, Page S.

Farthing, Alison. The Mystical Beast. (Illus.). (gr. 2-5). 1978. 6.95 (ISBN 0-8038-4707-6). Hastings.

Farthing, Bill. Odiyan Country Cookbook. (Illus.). 1977. pap. 6.50 (ISBN 0-913546-19-4). Dharma Pub.

Farthing, Geoffrey. Exploring the Great Beyond. LC 77-17692. (Orig.). 1978. pap. 4.25 (ISBN 0-8356-0508-6, Quest). Theos Pub Hse.

Farudi, Daryush, jt. auth. see Robinson, Ruth.

Farukhi, N M., ed. Heat Transfer: Niagara Falls 1984, No. 236. LC 84-14588. (AICHE Symposium Ser.: Vol. 80). 469p. 1984. pap. 80.00 (ISBN 0-8169-0325-5). Am Inst Chem Eng.

Farukhi, Nayeem M., ed. Heat Transfer: Seattle Nineteen Eighty-Three. LC 83-11194. (AIChE Symposium: Vol. 79). 438p. 1983. pap. 60.00 (ISBN 0-8169-0250-X); pap. 30.00 members (ISBN 0-317-03733-1). Am Inst Chem Eng.

Faruqee, F., jt. auth. see Amin, R.

Faruqee, Rashid. Analyzing the Impact of Health Services: Project Experiences from India, Ghana, & Thailand. (Working Paper: No. 546). 44p. 1982. pap. 3.00 (ISBN 0-8213-0117-9). World Bank.

--Integrating Family Planning with Health Services: Does it Help? LC 82-8405. (World Bank Staff Working Papers: No. 515). (Orig.). 1982. pap. 3.00 (ISBN 0-8213-0003-2). World Bank.

--Kenya: Population & Development. xii, 213p. 1980. pap. 15.00 (ISBN 0-686-36110-5, RC-8010). World Bank.

Faruqee, Rashid & Johnson, Ethna. Health, Nutrition, & Family Planning in India: A Survey of Experiments & Special Projects. (Working Paper: No. 507). xi, 97p. 1982. pap. 5.00 (ISBN 0-686-39757-6, WP-0507). World Bank.

Faruqi, Harith. Law Dictionary (Arabic-English) 288p. 1972. 30.00x (ISBN 0-86685-085-6). Intl Bk Ctr.

--Law Dictionary (English-Arabic) rev. ed. 1972. 35.00x (ISBN 0-86685-065-1). Intl Bk Ctr.

Faruqi, I. Azad. The Tarjuman Al-Qura'n: A Critical Analysis of Maulana Abul Kalam Azad's Approach to the Understanding of the Qura'n. 128p. 1983. text ed. 15.95x (ISBN 0-7069-1342-6, Pub. by Vikas India). Advent NY.

Faruqi, Lois I. Al see Al Faruqi, Lois I.

Faruqi, R. I., tr. see Haykal, M. H.

Faruqi, Shakil, jt. auth. see Dubey, Vinod.

Faruque, Omar. Graphic Communication As a Design Tool. (Illus.). 224p. 1984. 29.95 (ISBN 0-442-22633-0). Van Nos Reinhold.

Farvar, Taghi. International Development & the Human Environment. new ed. 1973. pap. 14.95 (ISBN 0-02-468980-7). Macmillan Info.

Farvour, James. Commodore 64 Arcade Game Design. (Illus.). 200p. (Orig.). Date not set. pap. 16.95 (ISBN 0-912003-45-6). Bk Co.

--Microsoft BASIC Decoded & Other Mysteries. (TRS-80 Information Ser.: Vol. II). (Illus.). 312p. (Orig.). 1981. pap. 29.95 (ISBN 0-936200-01-4). Blue Cat.

Farvour, James L. Commodore 64 Library: Character Graphics. Trapp, Charles & Wiener, Paul, eds. (Commodore Library). (Illus.). 96p. 1984. pap. text ed. 9.95 (ISBN 0-936200-56-1). Blue Cat.

--TRS-DOS 2.3 Decoded & Other Mysteries. (TRS-80 Information Ser.: Vol. 6). (Illus.). 298p. (Orig.). 1982. pap. 29.95 (ISBN 0-936200-07-3). Blue Cat.

Farwell, Beatrice. The Cult of Images: Baudelaire & the 19th-Century Media Explosion. LC 77-620058. (Illus.). 150p. (Orig.). 1977. pap. 15.00 (ISBN 0-295-96183-X, Pub. by Univ. Art Museum, UC Santa Barbara). U of Wash Pr.

--French Popular Lithographic Imagery, 1815-1870: Genre: Urban & Military, Vol. 3. (Chicago Visual Library: No. 44). (Illus.). 219p. 1983. text ed. 55.00 incl. fiche (ISBN 0-226-69014-8, CVL 44). U of Chicago Pr.

--French Popular Lithographic Imagery, 1815-1870: Lithographs & Literature, Vol. 1. LC 81-10334. (Illus.). 100p. 1982. text-fiche 55.00 (ISBN 0-226-69011-3); text ed. 55.00 vol. 2, Portraits & Types, 1982 (ISBN 0-226-69012-1). U of Chicago Pr.

--Manet & the Nude, A Study in Iconography in the Second Empire. LC 79-57509. (Outstanding Dissertations in the Fine Arts Ser.: No. 5). 290p. 1982. lib. bdg. 61.00 (ISBN 0-8240-3929-7). Garland Pub.

Farwell, Brice, ed. Guide to the Music of Arthur Farwell & to the Microfilm Collection of His Work. LC 72-569. (Illus.). 1972. pap. 10.00x (ISBN 0-9600484-0-5). B Farwell.

Farwell, Byron. Burton: A Biography of Sir Richard Francis Burton. LC 75-5778. 431p. 1975. Repr. of 1963 ed. lib. bdg. 21.25x (ISBN 0-8371-8056-2, FABU). Greenwood.

--Eminent Victorian Soldiers: Seekers of Glory. (Illus.). 1985. 17.95 (ISBN 0-393-01884-9). Norton.

--The Gurkhas. LC 83-42661. (Illus.). 320p. 1984. 17.95 (ISBN 0-393-01773-7). Norton.

--The Man Who Presumed: A Biography of Henry M. Stanley. LC 73-15205. (Illus.). 334p. 1974. Repr. of 1957 ed. lib. bdg. 19.25x (ISBN 0-8371-7160-1, FAMW). Greenwood.

--Queen Victoria's Little Wars. (Illus.). 1985. 6.95 (ISBN 0-393-30235-0). Norton.

Farwell, Georgie, jt. auth. see Farwell, William.

Farwell, Hermon W. The Majority Rules: A Manual of Procedure for MOST Groups. LC 80-65783. 120p. (Orig.). 1980. pap. 5.95 (ISBN 0-9604216-0-2). High Pubs.

Farwell, Robert F., jt. auth. see Schmitt, Neil M.

Farwell, Ted, jt. auth. see Goeldner, C. R.

Farwell, William. Easy Does It Furniture Restoration: The Vermont Way. LC 70-113905. (Illus.). 1962. pap. 2.50 (ISBN 0-8048-0156-8). C E Tuttle.

Farwell, William & Farwell, Georgie. What Is It Worth? Advice on Buying & Selling Antiques. LC 73-75282. 1973. pap. 3.25 (ISBN 0-8048-0980-1). C E Tuttle.

Farzan, Sattar, et al. A Concise Handbook of Respiratory Diseases. 2nd ed. text ed. 25.95 (ISBN 0-8359-0999-9). Reston.

Farzin, Yeganeh. The Effect of Discount Rate & Substitute Technology on Depletion of Exhaustible Resources. LC 82-8612. (World Bank Staff Working Papers: No. 516). (Orig.). 1982. pap. 5.00 (ISBN 0-8213-0004-0). World Bank.

Fasal, Paul, jt. auth. see Arnold, Harry L., Jr.

Fasana, Fortunato, ed. Hydrocele in the Temperate & Tropical Countries, 2 Vols. 1983. Vol. I. 55.00 (ISBN 0-8493-6076-5); Vol. II. 55.00 (ISBN 0-8493-6077-3). CRC Pr.

Fasana, Paul, jt. auth. see Malinconico, S. Michael.

Fasanella, R. M., ed. Eye Surgery: Innovations & Trends, Pitfalls, Complications. (Illus.). 352p. 1977. photocopy ed. 38.50x (ISBN 0-398-03621-7). C C Thomas.

Fasano, A. & Primcerio, M., eds. Free Boundary Problems: Theory & Applications, Vol. 1. (Research Notes in Mathematics Ser.: No. 78). 272p. 1983. pap. text ed. 28.50 (ISBN 0-273-08589-1). Pitman Pub MA.

--Free Boundary Problems: Theory & Applications, Vol. 2. (Research Notes in Mathematics: No. 79). 448p. 1983. pap. text ed. 28.50 (ISBN 0-273-08590-5). Pitman Pub MA.

Fascell, Dante B., ed. International News: Freedom Under Attack. LC 78-66210. (Illus.). 320p. 1979. 25.00 (ISBN 0-8039-1229-3). Sage.

Fasching, Darrell J. The Thought of Jacques Ellul: A Systematic Exposition. LC 81-22529. (Toronto Studies in Theology: Vol. 7). 272p. 1982. 49.95x (ISBN 0-88946-961-X). E Mellen.

Fasching, Darrell J., ed. The Jewish People in Christian Preaching. LC 84-16607. (Symposium Ser.: Vol. 10). 125p. 1984. 19.95x (ISBN 0-88946-702-1). E Mellen.

Fase, M. M., jt. auth. see Boeschoten, W. C.

Faseb, Philip L. & Katz, Dorothy D., eds. Human Health & Disease. LC 76-53166. (Biological Handbks: Vol. 2). (Illus.). 1977. 60.00 (ISBN 0-08-030072-3). Pergamon.

Fasel, George. Edmund Burke. (English Authors Ser.: No. 286). 169p. 1983. lib. bdg. 13.50 (ISBN 0-8057-6861-0, Twayne). G K Hall.

Fasel, Ida. The Meanings of Cleave. 1978. 4.50 (ISBN 0-89015-220-9). Eakin Pubns.

Fasenmyer, et al. Your Education: Supplemental & Summer Study Workbooks. (gr. k-6). 1970. pap. text ed. 5.50 ea. Beatty.

Fasham, M. J., ed. Flows of Energy & Materials in Marine Ecosystems: Theory & Practice. (NATO Conference Ser. IV: Marine Sciences: Vol. 13). 744p. 1984. 110.00x (ISBN 0-306-41519-4, Plenum Pr). Plenum Pub.

Fashion Group Inc. Your Future in the Beauty Business. Rev. ed. Le Vathes, Christine, ed. LC 68-31559. (Careers in Depth Ser). (Illus.). (gr. 9 up). 1979. PLB 8.97 (ISBN 0-8239-0482-2). Rosen Group.

Fashion Group Inc., Members and Friends. The Last Word: Exploring Careers in Contemporary Communication. Ovesy, Regina, ed. 128p. (gr. 7-12). 1983. lib. bdg. 8.97 (ISBN 0-8239-0526-8). Rosen Group.

Fashion Group Members see LeVathes, Christine.

Fashoyin, Tayo. Industrial Relations in Nigeria: Development & Practice. (Illus.). 208p. 1981. pap. text ed. 9.95x (ISBN 0-582-64250-7). Longman.

Fasi, M. El see International Scientific Committee for the Drafting of a General History of Africa.

Fasken, W. H. Israel's Racial Origin & Migrations. 1984. lib. bdg. 79.95 (ISBN 0-87700-564-8). Revisionist Pr.

Faslund, Elysabeth N. This Is My Apple, Go Get Your Own. (Herland Ser.: No. 4). 30p. 1983. pap. 3.50 (ISBN 0-934996-23-7). Am Stud Pr.

Fasman, et al. Equal Employment Audit Handbook. 1983. pap. text ed. 95.00 (ISBN 0-88057-003-2). Exec Ent Inc.

Fasman, Gerald D. Handbook of Biochemistry & Molecular Biology, CRC: Proteins Section, 3 vols. 3rd ed. LC 75-29514. (Handbook Ser.). 1976. Vol. 1, 427 Pgs. 66.00 (ISBN 0-87819-504-1); Vol. 2, 790p. 86.50 (ISBN 0-87819-505-X); Vol. 3, 633p. 76.50 (ISBN 0-87819-510-6). CRC Pr.

Fasman, Gerald D., ed. Handbook of Biochemistry & Molecular Biology, CRC: Lipids, Carbohydrates, & Steroids Section, Vol. 1. 3rd ed. LC 75-29514. (Handbook Ser.). 570p. 1976. 76.50 (ISBN 0-87819-508-4). CRC Pr.

Fasman, Gerald D, ed. Handbook of Biochemistry & Molecular Biology, CRC: Nucleic Acids Section, 2 vols. 3rd ed. LC 75-29514. (Handbook Ser.). 1976. Vol. 1. 76.50 (ISBN 0-87819-506-8); Vol. 2, 923p. 86.50 (ISBN 0-87819-507-6). CRC Pr.

Fasman, Gerald D., ed. Handbook of Biochemistry & Molecular Biology, CRC: Physical & Chemical Data Section, 2 vols. 3rd ed. Incl. Pt. 1. Physical & Chemical Data. LC 75-29514. (Handbook Ser.). 1976. Vol. 1, 576 Pgs. 76.50 (ISBN 0-87819-509-2); Vol. 2, 456 Pgs. 66.00 (ISBN 0-8493-0516-0). CRC Pr.

Fasnacht, H. D., et al. How to Use Business Machines. 3rd ed. 1969. text ed. 8.60 (ISBN 0-07-019972-8). McGraw.

Fasol, Al. A Guide to Self-Improvement in Sermon Delivery. 128p. 1983. pap. 5.95 (ISBN 0-8010-3507-4). Baker Bk.

Fasol, Al, compiled by. Selected Readings in Preaching. 1980. pap. 3.95 (ISBN 0-8010-3490-6). Baker Bk.

Fasold, Ralph. The Sociolinguistics of Society. 352p. 1984. 45.00x (ISBN 0-631-13385-2); pap. 14.95x (ISBN 0-631-13462-X). Basil Blackwell.

--Tense Marking in Black English: A Linguistic & Social Analysis. (Urban Language Ser.). 1972. pap. 12.95x (ISBN 0-15-599064-0). Ctr Appl Ling.

Fasold, Ralph & Shuy, Roger, eds. Analyzing Variation in Language. LC 75-15973. 327p. 1975. pap. 7.95 (ISBN 0-87840-207-1). Georgetown U Pr.

Fasold, Ralph W. Variation in the Form & Use of Language: A Sociolinguistics Reader. LC 83-20620. 424p. (Orig.). 1984. pap. 11.95 (ISBN 0-87840-214-4). Georgetown U Pr.

Fasold, Ralph W., jt. auth. see Walfman, Walt.

Fasold, Ralph W. & Shuy, Roger W., eds. Teaching Standard English in the Inner City. LC 72-120748. (Urban Language Ser). 140p. 1970. pap. 8.00 (ISBN 0-15-599065-9). Ctr Appl Ling.

Fasolo, Ugo. Titian. (Illus.). 95p. (Orig.). 1980. pap. 12.50 (ISBN 0-935748-09-1). Scala Books.

Fass, Arnold L. & Newman, Claire M. Unified Mathematics: Content, Methods, Materials for Elementary School Teachers. 448p. 1975. text ed. 16.95x (ISBN 0-669-89359-5). Heath.

Fass, Barbara. La Belle Dame Sans Merci & the Aesthetics of Romanticism. LC 73-8365. 304p. 1974. text ed. 15.95x (ISBN 0-8143-1509-7). Wayne St U Pr.

Fass, Bernie & Caggiano, Rosemary. Children Are People. 48p. (gr. 2-10). 1977. pap. 7.95 (ISBN 0-86704-003-3). Clarus Music.

--The Four Seasons. 48p. (gr. k-6). 1976. pap. 7.95 (ISBN 0-86704-001-7). Clarus Music.

--Happy Birthday Party Time. 48p. (gr. k-6). 1976. pap. 7.95 (ISBN 0-86704-002-5). Clarus Music.

--The Power Is You. 48p. (gr. 2-12). 1979. pap. 7.95 (ISBN 0-86704-005-X). Clarus Music.

--The Weather Company. 48p. (gr. k-8). 1978. pap. 7.95 (ISBN 0-86704-004-1). Clarus Music.

Fass, Bernie & Wolfson, Mack. The Halloween Machine. (gr. k-9). 1984. pap. 15.95, 48 pgs. (ISBN 0-86704-009-2); pap. 2.50 student's ed., 32 pgs. (ISBN 0-86704-010-6). Clarus Music.

Fass, Bernie, et al. Old MacDonald Had a Farm. 32p. (gr. k-4). 1981. pap. 7.95 (ISBN 0-86704-007-6). Clarus Music.

Fass, David E. The Shofar That Lost Its Voice. (Illus.). 48p. 1982. 6.95 (ISBN 0-8074-0168-4, 103500). UAHC.

Fass, Marion F. & Vahldieck, Linda M. Teaching Patient Education Skills: A Curriculum for Residents. 200p. 1983. 15.50 (ISBN 0-318-17256-9); members 10.50 (ISBN 0-318-17257-7). Soc Tchrs Fam Med.

Fass, Paula S. The Damned & the Beautiful: American Youth in the 1920s. LC 76-42644. 1977. 35.00x (ISBN 0-19-502148-7). Oxford U Pr.

--The Damned & the Beautiful: American Youth in the 1920's. LC 76-42644. 1977. pap. 9.95 (ISBN 0-19-502492-3, GB567, GB). Oxford U Pr.

Fass, Peter J., jt. auth. see Haft, Robert J.

Fass, Peter M. & Wittner, Derek A. Blue Sky Practice. (Securities Law Ser.). 1984. pap. text ed. 65.00 (ISBN 0-87632-453-7). Boardman.

Fass, Peter M., jt. auth. see Haft, Robert J.

Fassam, Meg, jt. auth. see Madge, Nicola.

Fassbender, A. G., et al. Energy Efficient Industrial Technology in Europe & Japan. LC 83-13065. (Energy Technology Review No. 85). (Illus.). 416p. 1984. 45.00 (ISBN 0-8155-0958-8). Noyes.

Fassbender, H. G. Pathology of Rheumatic Diseases. Loewi, G., tr. from Ger. (Illus.). 360p. 1975. 61.00 (ISBN 0-387-07289-6). Springer-Verlag.

Fassbender, H. G., et al. Articular Cartilage & Osteoarthrosis. (Illus.). 64p. 1983. pap. text ed. 15.00 (ISBN 3-456-81251-5, Pub. by Hans Huber Switzerland). J K Burgess.

Fassbender, William. You & Your Health. 3rd ed. LC 83-21866. 446p. (Orig.). 1984. pap. text ed. 20.45 (ISBN 0-471-89882-1). Wiley.

Fassbinder, Rainer W. Querelle: The Film Book. LC 83-80816. (Illus.). 180p. 1983. pap. 16.95 (ISBN 0-394-62477-7, E861, Ever). Grove.

--Rainer Werner Fassbinder Plays. Calandra, Denis, ed. (Orig.). 1985. 21.95 (ISBN 0-933826-79-6); pap. 8.95 (ISBN 0-933826-82-6). Performing Arts.

Fasse, Ferdinand. Geschichte als Problem von Literatur, Vol. 9. (Arbeiten zur Esthetick, Didaktik, Literatur und Sprachwissenshaft). 289p. (Ger.). 1983. 34.20 (ISBN 3-8204-7422-6). P Lang Pubs.

Fassett, Kaffe. Glorious Knits: Thirty Designs for Sweaters, Dresses. Vests & Shawls. (Illus.). 1985. 19.95 (ISBN 0-517-55843-2, C N Potter Bks). Crown.

Fassett, Norman C. Manual of Aquatic Plants. rev. ed. (Illus.). 416p. 1957. 17.50x (ISBN 0-299-01450-9). U of Wis Pr.

--Spring Flora of Wisconsin. 4th ed. LC 74-27307. (Illus.). 430p. 1976. 17.50x (ISBN 0-299-06750-5); pap. 9.50x (ISBN 0-299-06754-8). U of Wis Pr.

Fassi, Carlo. Figure Skating with Carlo Fassi. 1981. (ScribT); pap. 11.95 (ISBN 0-684-17644-0). Scribner.

Fassiotto, Marie-Jose. Madame de Lambert (1647-1733) ou le Feminisme Moral. LC 84-47692. (American University Studies II (Romance Languages & Literature): Vol. 7). 150p. (Orig.). 1984. text ed. 20.30 (ISBN 0-8204-0131-5). P Lang Pubs.

Fassler, Barbara E., jt. auth. see Walvoord.

Fassler, D. & Lay, N. Encounter with a New World: A Reading-Writing Text for Speakers of English As a Second Language. 1979. pap. 13.50 (ISBN 0-13-274910-6). P-H.

Fassler, Joan. All Alone with Daddy: A Young Girl Plays the Role of Mother. LC 76-80120. (Illus.). 32p. (ps-3). 1975. 10.95 (ISBN 0-87705-009-0). Human Sci Pr.

--The Boy with a Problem: Johnny Learns to Share His Troubles. LC 78-147125. (Illus.). 32p. (ps-3). 1971. 10.95 (ISBN 0-87705-054-6). Human Sci Pr.

--Don't Worry Dear. LC 74-147124. (Illus.). 32p. (ps-3). 1971. 10.95 (ISBN 0-87705-055-4). Human Sci Pr.

--Helping Children Cope. LC 77-6943. 1978. 14.95 (ISBN 0-02-693500-7). Free Pr.

--Howie Helps Himself. LC 74-12284. (Concept Bks). (Illus.). 32p. (gr. k-2). 1975. PLB 10.75 (ISBN 0-8075-3422-6). A Whitman.

--The Man of the House. LC 73-80122. (Illus.). 32p. (ps-3). 1975. 10.95 (ISBN 0-87705-010-4). Human Sci Pr.

--My Grandpa Died Today. LC 71-147126. (Illus.). 32p. (ps-3). 1983. 11.95 (ISBN 0-87705-053-8); pap. 4.95 (ISBN 0-89885-174-2). Human Sci Pr.

--One Little Girl. LC 76-80120. (Illus.). 32p. (ps-3). 1969. 10.95 (ISBN 0-87705-008-2). Human Sci Pr.

Fassman, Paula & Tavares, Suzanne. Gallery. (Illus.). 1982. pap. 7.50x (ISBN 0-19-503132-6). Oxford U Pr.

Fassnacht, C. Theory & Practice of Observing Behavior. (Behavioural Development Monographs). 1982. 36.00 (ISBN 0-12-249780-5). Acad Pr.

Fassnacht, Karl. Unternehmungsplanung und Mitbestimmung Nach Dem Betriebsverfassungsgesetz. (European University Studies: No. 5, Vol. 381). 248p. (Ger.). 1982. 28.40 (ISBN 3-8204-5846-8). P Lang Pubs.

Fassnacht, Philip R., et al. The Atari 400 & 800 Microcomputers. (Nanos Reference Cards Ser.). (Illus.). 22p. (Orig.). 1983. pap. 5.95 (ISBN 0-915069-19-9). Nanos Sys.

--The IBM PC Microcomputer. (Nanos Reference Cards Ser.). 24p. (Orig.). 1984. 5.95 (ISBN 0-915069-24-5). Nanos Sys.

--Reference Card for the IBM PCjr Microcomputer. 24p. (Orig.). 1984. 5.95 (ISBN 0-915069-26-1). Nanos Sys.

--The TRS-80 & TDP-100 Color BASIC & Extended System. rev. ed. (Nanos Reference Cards Ser.). (Illus.). 16p. 1982. 4.95 (ISBN 0-915069-08-3). Nanos Sys.

Fast, Aganetha. The Power of Christ's Love in China. LC 71-188251. 134p. 1972. pap. 2.00 (ISBN 0-87303-667-0). Faith & Life.

Fast, Barbara, jt. auth. see Fast, Julius.

Fast, Barry, ed. The Catfish Cookbook. rev. ed. LC 82-11253. 128p. (Orig.). 1983. pap. 6.95 (ISBN 0-914788-76-0). East Woods.

Fast, Bette, jt. auth. see Fast, Howard.

Fast, C. R., jt. auth. see Howard, G. C.

Fast, Franziska, jt. ed. see Nusberg, Charlotte.

Fast, Gerhard. Cuentos Folkloricos de los Achual. (Comunidades y Culturas Peruanas: No. 3). 242p. 1976. 7.25x (ISBN 0-88312-746-6); microfiche (3) 3.80 (ISBN 0-88312-540-4). Summer Inst Ling.

Fast, Gerhard & Larson, Mildred. Introduccion al Idioma Aguarana. (Documento Trabajo Ser.: No. 3). 111p. 1974. 5.25xop (ISBN 0-88312-775-X); microfiche only (2) 2.86 (ISBN 0-88312-395-9). Summer Inst Ling.

Fast, Gertrud. Orchideenkultur: Botanische Grundlagen Pflanzenbeschreibungen. 2ND ed. (Illus.). 1981. 38.95 (ISBN 3-8001-6133-8). Lubrecht & Cramer.

Fast, H. A. Jesus & Human Conflict. LC 58-10315. 215p. 1959. 6.95 (ISBN 0-8361-1382-9). Herald Hse.

Fast, Heinhold. Quellen zur Geschichte der Taufer in der Schweiz, Vol. 2: Ostschweiz. (Ger.). 1974. 59.00x (ISBN 0-8361-1197-4). Herald Pr.

Fast, Henry A. Jesus & Human Conflict. LC 58-10315. 215p. 1959. 6.95 (ISBN 0-8361-1382-9). Herald Pr.

Fast, Howard. April Morning. (gr. 6 up). 1962. pap. 2.95 (ISBN 0-553-24161-3). Bantam.

--April Morning. (YA) 1961. 8.95 (ISBN 0-517-50681-5). Crown.

--Citizen Tom Paine. 2nd ed. LC 82-84625. 352p. 1983. pap. 6.95 (ISBN 0-394-62464-5, E854, Ever). Grove.

--The Crossing. LC 84-60569. (Illus.). 213p. Date not set. pap. 7.95 (ISBN 0-911020-10-1). NJ Hist Soc.

--The Establishment. 1980. pap. 4.50 (ISBN 0-440-12393-3). Dell.

--Establishment. 1979. 11.95 (ISBN 0-395-28160-1). HM.

--Freedom Road. (Literature Ser). (gr. 10-12). 1970. pap. text ed. 5.33 (ISBN 0-87720-752-6). AMSCO Sch.

--The Hessian. 288p. (gr. 9 up). 1980. pap. 2.25 (ISBN 0-440-13536-2). Dell.

--The Immigrants. 1978. pap. 4.50 (ISBN 0-440-14175-3). Dell.

--The Immigrants. 1977. 12.95 (ISBN 0-395-25699-2). HM.

--The Immigrant's Daughter. 336p. 1985. 17.95 (ISBN 0-395-39381-7). HM.

--The Jews: Story of a People. 384p. 1978. pap. 3.95 (ISBN 0-440-34444-1). Dell.

--The Legacy. 1981. lib. bdg. 17.95 (ISBN 0-8161-3292-5, Large Print Bks). G K Hall.

--The Legacy. 359p. 1981. 14.95 (ISBN 0-395-31260-4). HM.

--The Legacy. 1982. pap. 3.95 (ISBN 0-440-14719-0). Dell.

--The Magic Door. (Illus.). 80p. (gr. 3-7). 1980. pap. 1.95 (ISBN 0-380-51193-2, 51193-2, Camelot). Avon.

--Max. 400p. 1982. 15.95 (ISBN 0-395-32506-4). HM.

--Max. (General Ser.). 1983. lib. bdg. 18.95 (ISBN 0-8161-3495-2, Large Print Bks). G K Hall.

--Max. 1983. pap. 3.95 (ISBN 0-440-16106-1). Dell.

--My Glorious Brothers. new ed. LC 77-11154. (Illus.). 1977. pap. 6.95 (ISBN 0-88482-758-5). Hebrew Pub.

--The Outsider. 311p. 1984. 15.95 (ISBN 0-395-36101-X). HM.

--The Outsider. 1984. lib. bdg. 17.95 (ISBN 0-8161-3760-9, Large Print Bks). G K Hall.

--The Outsider. 1985. pap. 3.95 (ISBN 0-440-16778-7). Dell.

--The Passion of Sacco & Vanzetti, a New England Legend. LC 72-138227. 254p. 1972. Repr. of 1953 ed. lib. bdg. 24.75x (ISBN 0-8371-5584-3, FASV). Greenwood.

--The Proud & the Free. Date not set. pap. price not set. HM.

--Second Generation. 1979. pap. 4.50 (ISBN 0-440-17915-7). Dell.

--The Second Generation. 1978. 10.95 (ISBN 0-395-26683-1). HM.

--Spartacus. 1980. pap. 3.95 (ISBN 0-440-17649-2). Dell.

--Spartacus. 1982. Repr. lib. bdg. 17.95x (ISBN 0-89966-433-4). Buccaneer Bks.

--Spartacus. (General Ser.). 1984. lib. bdg. 15.95 (ISBN 0-8161-3670-X, Large Print Bks). G K Hall.

--Time & the Riddle. 15.00 (ISBN 0-517-53769-9, Pub. by Ward Ritchie). Crown.

--Time & the Riddle: Thirty-One Zen Stories. (Orig.). 1981. pap. 6.95 (ISBN 0-395-29180-1). HM.

Fast, Howard & Fast, Bette. The Picture Book History of the Jews. 60p. 1942. 5.95 (ISBN 0-88482-771-2). Hebrew Pub.

Fast, Irene. Gender Identity: A Differentiation Model. 192p. 1984. text ed. 29.95; pap. 19.95 (ISBN 0-88163-031-4). Analytic Pr.

Fast, Irene, ed. Event Theory: A Piaget-Freud Integration. 325p. 1985. text ed. 22.50 (ISBN 0-89859-618-1). L Erlbaum Assocs.

Fast, J. D. Entropy. 2nd ed. 332p. 1970. 93.75x (ISBN 0-677-61260-5). Gordon.

Fast, Johan D. Interaction of Metals & Gases, Vol. 1. Thermodynamics & Phase Relations. 1965. 64.00 (ISBN 0-12-249801-1). Acad Pr.

Fast, Jonathan. The Beast. 1982. pap. 2.95 (ISBN 0-345-29896-9). Ballantine.

--Golden Fire: A Novel of Ancient India. 1985. 18.95 (ISBN 0-87795-764-9). Arbor Hse.

Fast, Julius. The Body Book. (Orig.). 1981. pap. 2.25 (ISBN 0-505-51678-0, Pub. by Tower Bks). Dorchester Pub Co.

--Body Language. LC 72-106592. (Illus.). 192p. 1970. 9.95 (ISBN 0-87131-039-2). M Evans.

--Body Language. 1982. pap. 2.95 (ISBN 0-671-46267-9). PB.

--The Body Language of Sex, Power & Aggression. 1984. pap. 2.95 (ISBN 0-515-07899-9). Jove Pubns.

--The Body Language of Sex, Power, & Aggression. LC 76-47665. 192p. 1977. 7.95 (ISBN 0-87131-222-0). M Evans.

--Body Politics. (Orig.). 1980. pap. 2.25 (ISBN 0-505-51513-X, Pub. by Tower Bks). Dorchester Pub Co.

--The Pleasure Book. LC 75-15815. (Illus.). 1977. pap. 5.95 (ISBN 0-8128-2169-6). Stein & Day.

--Psyching up. LC 76-46584. 1978. 8.95 (ISBN 0-8128-2154-8). Stein & Day.

Fast, Julius & Bernstein, Meredith. Sexual Chemistry. 1984. pap. 3.50 (ISBN 0-671-49934-3). PB.

--Sexual Chemistry: What it Is, How to Use it. LC 83-16389. 216p. 1983. 12.95 (ISBN 0-87131-417-7). M Evans.

Fast, Julius & Fast, Barbara. Talking Between Lines. 1980. pap. 2.50 (ISBN 0-671-83244-1). PB.

Fast, Julius & Wells, Hal. Bisexual Living. LC 74-30475. 240p. 1975. 6.95 (ISBN 0-87131-172-0). M Evans.

Fast, Julius, jt. auth. see Henreid, Paul.

Fast, Norman D. The Rise & Fall of Corporate New Venture Divisions. Dufey, Gunter, ed. LC 78-27096. (Research for Business Decisions Ser.: No. 3). 228p. 1978. 39.95 (ISBN 0-8357-0950-7). UMI Res Pr.

Fast, R. W., ed. Advances in Cryogenic Engineering, Vol. 27. LC 57-35598. 1252p. 1982. 105.00x (ISBN 0-306-41103-2, Plenum Pr). Plenum Pub.

--Advances in Cryogenic Engineering, Vol. 29. 1072p. 1984. 95.00x (ISBN 0-306-41703-0, Plenum Pr). Plenum Pub.

Fasteau, Marc. The Male Machine. 1976. pap. 8.95 (ISBN 0-385-28623-6, Delta). Dell.

Fastenrath, Fritz, ed. Railroad Track; Theory & Practice: Material Properties, Cross Sections, Welding & Treatment. Grant, Walter, tr. from Ger. LC 80-5340. (Illus.). 1980. 85.00 (ISBN 0-8044-4231-2). Ungar.

Fastlicht, S. Tooth Mutilations & Dentistry in Pre-Columbian Mexico. LC 74-25143. 1976. text ed. cancelled (ISBN 0-88474-020-X). U of S Cal Pr.

Fastlicht, Samuel. Tooth Mutilations & Dentistry in Pre-Columbian Mexico. (Illus.). 152p. 1976. 58.00 (ISBN 0-931386-79-9). Quint Pub Co.

Fastnedge, R. Shearer Furniture Designs. 1966. 8.95 (ISBN 0-685-52092-7). Transatlantic.

Fastnedge, Ralph. Sheraton Furniture. (Illus.). 224p. 1983. 49.50 (ISBN 0-907462-47-2). Antique Collect.

--Sheraton Furniture. (Illus.). 224p. 1985. 49.50 (ISBN 0-907462-47-2). Apollo.

Fasulis, Mary. How to Know & Choose Your Men Through Palmistry. 128p. (Orig.). 1984. pap. 5.95 (ISBN 0-446-38113-6). Warner Bks.

Fasulo, Amerigo. The Angry People. 1984. 11.95 (ISBN 0-533-05961-5). Vantage.

Fasulo, Linda. Representing America: Experience of U. S. Diplomats at the UN. LC 84-3477. 352p. 1984. 29.95 (ISBN 0-03-070414-6). Praeger.

Fate, Terry, jt. auth. see Charlotte-Georgi.

Fatehally, Laeeq, ed. Women in the Third World. 155p. 1980. pap. 7.95x (ISBN 0-86590-016-7, Jaico Books India). Apt Bks.

Fatemi, Faramarz S., jt. auth. see Fatemi, Nasrollah S.

Fatemi, Nasrollah S. While the United States Slept. LC 81-65538. 480p. 1981. 25.00 (ISBN 0-8453-4721-7). Cornwall Bks.

Fatemi, Nasrollah S. & Fatemi, Faramarz S. Love, Beauty, & Harmony in Sufism. 12.95 (ISBN 0-8453-2248-6). Cornwall Bks.

Fatemi, Nasrollah S. & Williams, Gail W. Multinational Corporations. rev. 2nd ed. cloth 12.00 (ISBN 0-8453-1879-9). Cornwall Bks.

Fatemi, Nasrollah S., ed. Problems of Balance of Payment & Trade. LC 74-4971. 261p. 1975. 18.50 (ISBN 0-8386-1587-2). Fairleigh Dickinson.

Fates, Gil. What's My Line? 1980. pap. 3.95 (ISBN 0-346-12396-8). Cornerstone.

Fath, Creekmore, ed. The Lithographs of Thomas Hart Benton. new ed. LC 78-70912. (Illus.). 245p. 1979. 29.95 (ISBN 0-292-74621-0). U of Tex Pr.

Fath, Gerald. Health Care Ministries. 2nd ed. LC 80-12620. 1980. pap. 8.50 (ISBN 0-87125-061-6). Cath Health.

Fath, Irene, jt. auth. see Maas, Wolfgang.

Father of Candor. An Enquiry into the Doctrine, Lately Propagated, Concerning Libels, Warrants, & the Seizure of Papers. facsimile ed. LC 76-121100. (Civil Liberties in American History Ser.). 136p. 1970. Repr. of 1764 ed. 22.50 (ISBN 0-306-71970-3). Da Capo.

Father Sheedy. Questions Catholics Ask. LC 78-58466. 1978. pap. 4.95 (ISBN 0-87973-738-7). Our Sunday Visitor.

Father Andrew. The Life & Letters of Father Andrew. LC 82-80473. (Treasures from the Spiritual Classics Ser.). 64p. 1982. pap. 2.95 (ISBN 0-8192-1310-1). Morehouse.

Fatheringham, R. see Wiin-Nielsen, A.

Fathi, jt. auth. see Ontario Centre for Microelectronics.

Fathman, Ann K. SLOTE (Second Language Oral Test of English) (Illus.). 144p. 1983. 15.95 (ISBN 0-88084-124-9). Alemany Pr.

Fathman, Ann K. & Quinn, Mary E. Science Discoveries for Language Learning: Ideas for Physical Science. (The Teacher IDEA Ser.). 64p. (Orig.). 1983. pap. text ed. write for info. (ISBN 0-88499-628-X). Inst Mod Lang.

Fathman, C. Garrison, ed. Isolation, Characterization & Utilization of T Lymphocyte Clones. 1982. 65.00 (ISBN 0-12-249920-4). Acad Pr.

Fathman, Doris, jt. auth. see Fathman, George.

Fathman, George & Fathman, Doris. Live Foods: One Hundred Ninety-Two Recipes. 2.75x (ISBN 0-686-29918-3). Cancer Control Soc.

Fathy, Hassan. Architecture for the Poor. LC 72-95133. 1973. 25.00x (ISBN 0-226-23915-2). U of Chicago Pr.

--Architecture for the Poor. LC 72-95133. (Illus.). xviii, 234p. 1973. pap. 11.95 (ISBN 0-226-23916-0, P660, Phoen). U of Chicago Pr.

Fatio. The Happy Lioness. 113p. 1980. PLB 9.95 (ISBN 0-07-020069-6). McGraw.

Fatio, Louise. Happy Lion. (Illus.). (gr. k-3). 1964. PLB 10.95 (ISBN 0-07-020044-0). McGraw.

--Happy Lion & the Bear. (gr. k-3). 1964. PLB 8.95 (ISBN 0-07-020060-2). McGraw.

Fatjo, Thomas I., Jr. & Miller, Keith. With No Fear of Failure. 240p. 1984. pap. 2.95 (ISBN 0-425-07274-6). Berkley Pub.

Fatooh, Audrey A., et al. Style & Sense: Court Reporting, Transcribing, Legal. LC 84-28744. 192p. 1986. spiral wire 15.95 (ISBN 0-88280-109-0). ETC Pubns.

Fator, Sue. The Adventures of Timoteo. pap. 1.25 (ISBN 0-89985-992-5). Christ Nations.

Fatout, Paul. Indiana Canals. LC 85-3721. (Illus.). 225p. 1985. pap. 11.00 (ISBN 0-911198-78-4). Purdue U Pr.

--Mark Twain on the Lecture Circuit. (Illus.). 1960. 11.25 (ISBN 0-8446-1177-8). Peter Smith.

--Mark Twain on the Lecture Circuit. 1969. 2.89. S Ill U Pr.

--Meadow Lake: Gold Town. LC 69-15995. (Illus.). xiv, 178p. 1974. pap. 3.95 (ISBN 0-8032-5788-0, BB 576, Bison). U of Nebr Pr.

Fatout, Paul, ed. Mark Twain Speaking. LC 76-15986. (Illus.). 672p. 1976. 35.00 (ISBN 0-87745-056-0). U of Iowa Pr.

--Mark Twain Speaks for Himself. LC 77-81462. (Illus.). 256p. 1978. 11.00 (ISBN 0-911198-49-0). Purdue U Pr.

Fatrell, Jon, jt. auth. see Gill, Chris.

Fatt, Amelia. Conservative Chic. LC 82-40368. (Illus.). 172p. 1983. 19.95 (ISBN 0-8129-1041-9); pap. 10.95 (ISBN 0-8129-6328-8). Times Bks.

Fatt, Helene, jt. auth. see Griffin, John R.

Fatt, Irving. Polarographic Oxygen Sensor: Its Theory of Operation & Its Application in Biology, Medicine & Technology. LC 82-6581. 290p. (Orig.). 1982. Repr. of 1976 ed. 59.95 (ISBN 0-89874-511-X). Krieger.

Fattah, Michel. Christiana. LC 80-53458. 1982. 12.95 (ISBN 0-9605662-0-1). Roundtable Pub.

--Eternal Fire. LC 83-63202. 512p. 1985. 16.95 (ISBN 0-915677-04-0). Roundtable Pub.

Fatteh, Adbullah. Medicolegal Investigation of Gunshot Wounds. LC 76-6957. (Illus.). 1976. 27.25 (ISBN 0-397-50356-3, 65-01399, Lippincott Medical). Lippincott.

Fattorini, H. O. Encyclopedia of Mathematics & Its Applications: The Cauchy Problem, Vol. 18. 1984. 69.50 (ISBN 0-317-14396-4, 30238-2). Cambridge U Pr.

--Second Order Linear Differential Equations in Banach Spaces. (Mathematical Studies: Vol. 108). 1985. 40.75 (ISBN 0-444-87698-7, North-Holland). Elsevier.

Fattoross, Camille, jt. auth. see Scarpato, Nonna Maria.

Fattorusso, J., ed. Wonders of Italy. 16th rev. ed. 1974. 60.00 (ISBN 0-685-12054-6). Heinman.

Fattorusso, V., jt. auth. see Ritter, O.

Fau, Margaret E., compiled by. Gabriel Garcia Marquez: An Annotated Bibliography, 1947-1979. LC 80-784. x, 198p. 1980. lib. bdg. 39.95 (ISBN 0-313-22224-X, FGM/). Greenwood.

Faubion, Nina L. Some Edible Mushrooms & How to Cook Them. 2nd ed. LC 62-15309. (Illus.). 1972. 8.95 (ISBN 0-8323-0119-1). Binford.

Faubus, Orval E. Down from the Hills. (Illus.). 528p. 1980. text ed. 25.00 (ISBN 0-686-29007-0). Faubus.

Fauchald, Kristian. The Polychaete Worms, Definitions & Keys to the Orders, Families & Genera. (Science Ser.: No. 28). (Illus.). 188p. 1977. 6.00 (ISBN 0-938644-08-4). Nat Hist Mus.

Fauchard, Pierre. Surgeon Dentist or Treatise of the Teeth, 2 vols. in 1. Lindsay, Lilian, tr. LC 68-54853. (Illus.). lib. bdg. 25.00 (ISBN 0-87821-007-4). Milford Hse.

Faucher, Elizabeth. Charles in Charge. 128p. (Orig.). (gr. 7 up). 1984. pap. 2.25 (ISBN 0-590-33550-2, Point). Scholastic Inc.

Faucher, L. Manchester in 1844: It's Present Condition & Future Prospects. Culverwell, J. P., ed. 152p. 1969. 24.00x (ISBN 0-7146-1392-4, Pub by F Cass Co). Biblio Dist.

Faucher, Real. Fires & Crucifixions. 16p. 1979. pap. 1.00 (ISBN 0-686-28227-2). Samisdat.

Faucheux, Claude. Psychologie Sociale Theorique et Experimentale. (Recueil De Textes Choisis et Presentes Textes De Sciences Sociales: No. 8). 1971. pap. 14.00x (ISBN 90-2796-920-5). Mouton.

Fauci, jt. auth. see Lichtenstein.

Fauci, Anthony S., jt. auth. see Cupps, Thomas R.

Fauci, Anthony S., jt. auth. see Lichtenstein, Lawrence M.

Fauci, Anthony S. & Ballieux, Rudy, eds. Antibody Production in Man: In Vitro Synthesis & Clinical Implications. LC 79-928. 1979. 39.50 (ISBN 0-12-249950-6). Acad Pr.

--Human B-Lymphocyte Function: Activation & Immunoregulation. 352p. 1982. text ed. 71.50 (ISBN 0-89004-620-4). Raven.

Fauci, Anthony S., jt. ed. see Gallin, John I.

Faucon, Bernard. Summer Camp. (Illus.). 100p. 1982. 22.50 (ISBN 0-937950-00-9). Xavier-Moreau.

Fauconnier, Gilles. Mental Spaces: Aspects of Meaning Construction in Natural Language. (Illus.). 184p. 1985. text ed. 25.00x (ISBN 0-262-06094-9, Pub. by Bradford). MIT Pr.

--Theoretical Implications of Some Global Phenomena in Syntax. Hankamer, Jorge, ed. LC 78-66574. (Outstanding Dissertations in Linguistics Ser.). 1985. 40.00 (ISBN 0-8240-9687-8). Garland Pub.

Fauconnier, Guido, jt. auth. see Ceuleman, Mieke.

Faude, Wilson, jt. auth. see Friedland, Joan.

Faude, Wilson H. Renaissance of Mark Twain's House. 1977. lib. bdg. 20.00x (ISBN 0-89244-074-0, Pub. by Queens Hse). Amereon Ltd.

Faudel-Phillips, H. Breaking & Schooling. pap. 3.95 (ISBN 0-85131-185-7, BL6785, Dist. by Miller). J A Allen.

--Breaking & Schooling Horses. 7.50x (ISBN 0-87556-237-X). Saifer.

--The Driving Book. pap. 3.95 (ISBN 0-85131-032-X, BL2338, Dist. by Miller). J A Allen.

Faugeras, O. D. Fundamentals in Computer Vision. LC 82-14624. 500p. 1983. 42.50 (ISBN 0-521-25099-4). Cambridge U Pr.

Faugere, Marie-Claude, jt. auth. see Malluche, H. H.

Faughn, Jerry S., jt. auth. see Kuhn, Karl F.

Faugno, Emily. Astro-Power at the Racetrack. 270p. 1984. 17.95 (ISBN 0-86690-277-5, 2460-01). Am Fed Astrologers.

Faugsted, George E., Jr. The Chilenos in the California Gold Rush. LC 73-76008. pap. 10.00 (ISBN 0-88247-210-0). R & E Pubs.

Faukland, Elizabeth. The Tragedy of Miriam: The Faire Queene of Iewry. LC 82-45773. (Malone Society Reprint Ser.: No. 42). Repr. of 1613 ed. 40.00 (ISBN 0-404-63042-1). AMS Pr.

Faul, Carol, jt. auth. see Faul, Henry.

Faul, Henry & Faul, Carol. It Began with a Stone: A History of Geology from the Stone Age to the Age of Plate Tectonics. LC 83-3683. 1983. 230p. 38.95x (ISBN 0-471-89735-3, Pub. by Wiley-Interscience); pap. 19.95x 264p. (ISBN 0-471-89605-5). Wiley.

Faul, Roberta, ed. Learning About the Built Environment. 75p. pap. 3.00 (ISBN 0-318-02810-7, Pub. by Natl Endow Arts). Pub Ctr Cult Res.

--Open Space. (National Endowment for the Arts Design Arts Program Selected Grants Ser.). 64p. 1980. pap. 3.00x (ISBN 0-89062-176-4). Partners Livable.

--Places for the Arts. (National Endowment for the Arts Design Arts Program Selected Grants Ser.). 69p. 1981. pap. 3.00x (ISBN 0-89062-175-6). Partners Livable.

Faulconer, Anne M. The Virginia House: A Home for Three Hundred Years. LC 83-51774. (Illus.). 176p. 1984. 25.00 (ISBN 0-88740-004-3). Schiffer.

Faulconer, James E., jt. auth. see Packard, Dennis J.

Faulder, Carolyn. Breast Cancer: A Guide to Its Early Detection & Treatment. 186p. 1983. pap. 5.95 (ISBN 0-86068-287-0, Pub. by Virago Pr). Merrimack Pub Cir.

Faulder, Carolyn, jt. auth. see Brown, Paul.

Faules, Don F. & Alexander, Dennis C. Communication & Social Behavior: A Symbolic Interaction Perspective. LC 76-46610. (Speech Communication Ser.). (Illus.). 1978. pap. text ed. 15.95 (ISBN 0-201-01982-5); instr's manual o.p. 3.00. Addison-Wesley.

Faules, Don F. & Rieke, Richard D. Directing Forensics. 2nd ed. 1978. pap. text ed. 16.95x (ISBN 0-89582-007-2). Morton Pub.

Faulett, C. Robert. A Practice Pamphlet on Workers Compensation. (Practice Pamphlet Ser.: No. 1). 55p. (Orig.). 1982. pap. 12.00 (ISBN 0-318-02454-3). SC Bar CLE.

Faulhaber. Judaism, Christianity & Germany. Smith, George D., tr. from Ger. 116p. 1981. Repr. of 1934 ed. lib. bdg. 30.00 (ISBN 0-89987-263-8). Darby Bks.

Faulhaber, Charles B. The Medieval Manuscripts, 2 vols. 1983. Set. 75.00 (ISBN 0-87535-133-6). Hispanic Soc.

Faulhaber, Charles B., et al. Bibliography of Old Spanish Texts. 3rd ed. (Bibliographical Ser.: No. 4). 380p. 1984. 30.00x (ISBN 0-942260-35-X). Hispanic Seminary.

Faulhaber, Clare W., tr. see Peyret, Raymond.

Faulhaber, Gerald, jt. auth. see Baughcum, Allan.

Faulhaber, Martha & Underhill, Janet. Music: Invent Your Own. LC 74-13315. (Music Involvement Ser). (Illus.). 48p. (gr. 3 up). 1974. PLB 10.25 (ISBN 0-8075-5355-7). A Whitman.

Faulk, Ed. Computer in Your Pocket. 160p. 1983. pap. 14.95 (ISBN 0-88190-070-2, BO070). Datamost.

--How to Write a TRS-80 Program. (How to Write Ser.). (Illus.). 224p. 1982. pap. 14.95 (ISBN 0-88190-033-8, BO033). Datamost.

--How to Write an IBM PC Program. (How to Write Ser.). (Illus.). 1982. pap. 14.95 (ISBN 0-88190-028-1, BO028). Datamost.

Faulk, Ed, ed. How to Write a Program II. (How to Write Ser.). (Illus.). 200p. 1983. pap. 14.95 (ISBN 0-88190-007-9, BO007). Datamost.

--How to Write an Apple Program. (How to Write Ser.). (Illus.). 224p. 1982. pap. 14.95 (ISBN 0-88190-027-3, BO027). Datamost.

Faulk, Henry. Group Captives: The Re-Education of German Prisoners of War in Britain, 1945-1948. 1977. text ed. 20.00x (ISBN 0-391-00725-4). Humanities.

Faulk, Mrs. Hugh L. & Jones, Billy W. The History of Twiggs County, Georgia. (Illus.). 1970. Repr. of 1960 ed. 17.50 (ISBN 0-89308-009-8). Southern Hist Pr.

Faulk, John H. Fear on Trial. rev. ed. 295p. 1983. pap. 7.95 (ISBN 0-292-72442-X). U of Tex Pr.

--The Uncensored John Henry Faulk. 224p. 1985. 16.95x (ISBN 0-87719-013-5). Texas Month Pr.

Faulk, Odie B. Arizona: A Short History. LC 75-108808. (Illus.). 1970. pap. 7.95 (ISBN 0-8061-1222-0). U of Okla Pr.

--Geronimo Campaign. LC 72-83042. (Illus.). 1969. 22.50x (ISBN 0-19-500544-9). Oxford U Pr.

Faulk, Odie B. & Jones, Billy M. Miracle of the Wilderness: The Continuing American Revolution. LC 76-57766. 1977. pap. text ed. 5.95 (ISBN 0-89097-010-6); 8.95 (ISBN 0-89097-015-7). Archer Edns.

Faulk, Odie B. & Von Kuehneli, Erik M. Great Issues 75: A Forum on Important Questions Facing the American Public, Vol. 7. LC 76-26349. (Illus.). 1976. 8.95 (ISBN 0-916624-03-X). Troy State Univ.

Faulk, Odie B., jt. auth. see Carroll, John A.

Faulk, Odie B., jt. auth. see Stout, Joseph A.

Faulk, Odie B. & Stout, Joseph A., Jr., eds. The Mexican War: Changing Interpretations. LC 72-94389. 243p. 1973. 12.95x (ISBN 0-8040-0642-3, 82-73484, SB); pap. 5.95 (ISBN 0-8040-0643-1, 82-73492, SB). Ohio U Pr.

Faulk, Terry R. Simple Methods of Mining Gold. 2nd ed. (Wild & Woolly West Ser. No. 10). (Illus., Orig.). 1981. 8.00 (ISBN 0-910584-97-4); pap. 1.50 (ISBN 0-910584-98-2). Filter.

Faulkenberry, Luces M. An Introduction to Operational Amplifiers: With Linera IC Applications. 2nd ed. LC 81-13043. (Electronic Technology Ser.). 560p. 1982. text ed. 31.95x (ISBN 0-471-05790-8); solutions manual 5.00 (ISBN 0-471-86319-X). Wiley.

Faulkenheim, Victor C., ed. Citizens & Groups in Chinese Politics. (Michigan Monographs in Chinese Studies: No. 56). 200p. (Orig.). 1985. text ed. 15.00 (ISBN 0-89264-065-0); pap. text ed. 10.00 (ISBN 0-89264-066-9). U of Mich Ctr Chinese.

Faulkenstein, Dezmon A. Faulkenstein's Theories Are Loose on the Earth. 1982. 7.95 (ISBN 0-533-04690-4). Vantage.

Faulker, William. Light in August: Typescript. (Faulkner Manuscripts Ser.). 100.00 (ISBN 0-8240-6814-9). Garland Pub.

Faulkes, Anthony, ed. Snorri Sturluson - Edda: Prologue & Gylfaginning. (Illus.). 1982. 29.95x (ISBN 0-19-811175-4). Oxford U Pr.

Faulkner. American Economic History. 1924. 20.00 (ISBN 0-686-17729-0). Quest Edns.

--As I Lay Dying. (Book Notes). 1985. pap. 2.50 (ISBN 0-8120-3502-X). Barron.

--Oeuvres Romanesques: Sartoris, Le Bruit et le Fureur, Sanctuaire, Tandis que J'Agonise, Vol. 1. 1760p. 52.50 (ISBN 0-686-56509-6). French & Eur.

Faulkner, Audrey, et al. When I Was Comin' up: An Oral History of Aged Blacks. 221p. 1982. 19.50 (ISBN 0-208-01952-9, Archon). Shoe String.

Faulkner, Barry. Sketches from an Artist's Life. 1973. 15.00 (ISBN 0-87233-023-0). Bauhan.

Faulkner, Brooks R. Burnout in Ministry. LC 81-67752. 1981. pap. 5.95 (ISBN 0-8054-2414-8). Broadman.

Faulkner, Charles H. Old Stone Fort: Exploring an Archaeological Mystery. LC 68-17145. (Illus.). 1968. pap. 4.95 (ISBN 0-87049-086-9). U of Tenn Pr.

Faulkner, Charles H. & McCollough, C. R., eds. Fifth Report of the Normandy Archaeological Project. (Orig.). 1978. pap. text ed. 23.95 (ISBN 0-87049-286-1, Pub. by U of TN Dept. of Anthropology). U of Tenn Pr.

--Fourth Report of the Normandy Archaeological Project. (Orig.). 1977. pap. text ed. 14.95 (ISBN 0-87049-247-0, Pub. by U of TN Dept. of Anthropology). U of Tenn Pr.

Faulkner, Christopher. Jean Renoir: A Guide to References & Resources. 1979. lib. bdg. 47.00 (ISBN 0-8161-7912-3, Hall Reference). G K Hall.

Faulkner, Chuck. Seven Hundred & Fifty Helpful Household Hints. Friedman, Robert S., ed. LC 82-19820. 160p. (Orig.). 1983. pap. 6.95 (ISBN 0-89865-262-6). Donning Co.

Faulkner, Claude W. Byron's Political Verse Satire. LC 73-7625. 1947. lib. bdg. 8.50 (ISBN 0-8414-1966-3). Folcroft.

--Writing Good Sentences. 3rd ed. 320p. 1981. pap. text ed. 16.95 (ISBN 0-02-336470-X, Pub. by Scribner). Macmillan.

Faulkner, Claude W., jt. auth. see Jones, Alexander E.

Faulkner, D., et al, eds. Integrity of Offshore Structures. (Illus.). 662p. 1981. 87.00 (ISBN 0-85334-989-4, Pub. by Elsevier Applied Sci England). Elsevier.

Faulkner, D. J. & Fenical, W. H., eds. Marine Natural Products Chemistry. LC 76-58470. (NATO Conference Ser. IV, Marine Sciences: Vol. 1). 433p. 1977. 55.00x (ISBN 0-306-32921-2, Plenum Pr). Plenum Pub.

Faulkner, D. W. At Dunkard Creek. (Hollow Spring Poetry Ser.). 60p. (Orig.). 1983. pap. 6.95 (ISBN 0-686-39715-0). Hollow Spring Pr.

Faulkner, Donald W., ed. see Cowley, Malcolm.

Faulkner, Edward A., Jr. Guide to Efficient Burner Operation: Gas, Oil, & Dual-Fuel. 32.00 (ISBN 0-915586-35-5). Fairmont Pr.

Faulkner, Edward H. Plowman's Folly. 154p. 1943. 10.95 (ISBN 0-8061-0124-5); pap. 5.95 (ISBN 0-8061-1169-0). U of Okla Pr.

--Uneasy Money. 114p. 1946. 9.95x (ISBN 0-8061-0149-0). U of Okla Pr.

Faulkner, Edwin J. & Weymuller, Frederick. Ed Faulkner's Tennis: How to Play It, How to Teach It. (Illus.). 1970. pap. 12.95 (ISBN 0-385-27039-9, Dial). Doubleday.

Faulkner, Edwin J., ed. Man's Quest for Security. facs. ed. LC 74-117790. (Essay Index Reprint Ser). 1966. 18.00 (ISBN 0-8369-1921-1). Ayer Co Pubs.

Faulkner, Elizabeth, jt. auth. see Martin, Fran.

Faulkner, Florence. A Challenge for Two. 1982. 8.95 (ISBN 0-686-84158-1, Avalon). Bouregy.

--House of Hostile Women. (YA) 1978. 8.95 (ISBN 0-685-05589-2, Avalon). Bouregy.

--Magic Legacy. 1984. 8.95 (ISBN 0-8034-8443-7, Avalon). Bouregy.

--Season of Deception. (YA) 1981. 8.95 (ISBN 0-686-84675-3, Avalon). Bouregy.

Faulkner, G. L., jt. auth. see Roseneau, J. C.

Faulkner, Hal, jt. auth. see Perry, Cheryl.

Faulkner, Harold U. Chartism & the Churches. LC 79-76712. (Columbia University. Studies in the Social Sciences: No. 173). Repr. of 1916 ed. 12.50 (ISBN 0-404-51173-2). AMS Pr.

--Chartism & the Churches: A Study in Democracy. 152p. 1970. Repr. of 1916 ed. 32.50x (ISBN 0-7146-1308-8, F Cass Co). Biblio Dist.

--The Decline of Laissez Faire 1897-1917. LC 76-48800. (The Economic History of the United States Ser.). 464p. 1977. pap. 12.95 (ISBN 0-87332-102-2). M E Sharpe.

--Politics, Reform & Expansion: 1890-1900. (New American Nation Ser.). 1959. 17.26xi (ISBN 0-06-011210-7, HarpT). Har-Row.

Faulkner, Harold U see Johnson, Allen & Nevins, Allan.

Faulkner, J. Meade. Moonfleet. (Illus.). 256p. 1983. pap. 2.25 (ISBN 0-441-54208-5, Pub. by Tempo). Ace Bks.

Faulkner, John. Cabin Road. LC 79-86496. xxvi, 198p. 1969. pap. 5.95x (ISBN 0-8071-0144-3). La State U Pr.

--Men Working. 1975. Repr. of 1941 ed. 13.95 (ISBN 0-916242-05-6). Yoknapatawpha.

Faulkner, John A. Cyprian: The Churchman. 1977. lib. bdg. 59.95 (ISBN 0-8490-1698-3). Gordon Pr.

Faulkner, John R. Octonion Planes Defined by Quadratic Jordan Algebras. LC 52-42839. (Memoirs: No. 104). 71p. 1970. pap. text ed. 9.00 (ISBN 0-8218-1804-X, MEMO-104). Am Math.

Faulkner, Joseph. Religion's Influence in Contemporary Society: Readings in the Sociology of Religion. LC 72-76586. 608p. 1972. text ed. 15.95 (ISBN 0-675-09105-5). Merrill.

Faulkner, Joseph E., jt. auth. see Bord, Richard J.

Faulkner, Judith R., ed. see MUMPS Users' Group Meeting.

Faulkner, Kenneth K., jt. auth. see Lachman, Ernest.

Faulkner, Larry R., jt. auth. see Bard, Allen J.

Faulkner, Lynn L., ed. Handbook of Industrial Noise Control. LC 75-41315. (Illus.). 608p. 1976. 47.50 (ISBN 0-8311-1110-0). Indus Pr.

Faulkner, Margaret. I Skate! LC 79-15932. (Illus.). (gr. 3-7). 1979. 8.95g (ISBN 0-316-26002-9). Little.

Faulkner, Margherita. Acappella. 32p. 1983. 20.00 (ISBN 0-913719-70-6); pap. 5.00 (ISBN 0-913719-69-2). High-Coo Pr.

--Timepeace. (W. N. J. Ser.: No. 16). 1981. signed ed. o.p. 20.00 (ISBN 0-686-79774-4); 10.00 (ISBN 0-686-79775-2); pap. 6.00 (ISBN 0-686-79776-0). Juniper Pr WI.

Faulkner, Paul, jt. auth. see Brecheen, Carl.

Faulkner, Peter. Against the Age: An Introduction to William Morris. (Illus.). 192p. 1980. text ed. 28.50x (ISBN 0-04-809012-3). Allen Unwin.

--Angus Wilson: Mimic & Moralist. 240p. 1980. 16.95 (ISBN 0-670-12692-6). Viking.

--Modernism. (The Critical Idiom Ser.). 1977. pap. 5.50x (ISBN 0-416-83710-7, NO. 2779). Methuen Inc.

Faulkner, Peter, ed. William Morris: The Critical Heritage. (The Critical Heritage Ser.). 480p. 1973. 38.50x (ISBN 0-7100-7520-0). Routledge & Kegan.

--William Morris: The Critical Heritage. (The Critical Heritage Ser.). 1984. pap. 15.00 (ISBN 0-7102-0393-4). Routledge & Kegan.

Faulkner, Peter, ed. see Bage, Robert.

Faulkner, Peter T., ed. Silent Bomb: A Guide to the Nuclear Energy Controversy. (Illus.). 1977. 12.50 (ISBN 0-394-41323-7). Random.

--The Silent Bomb: A Guide to the Nuclear Energy Controversy. (Illus.). 1977. pap. 3.95 (ISBN 0-394-72270-1, Vin). Random.

Faulkner, Quentin. J. S. Bach's Keyboard Technique: A Historical Introduction. (Illus.). 80p. (Orig.). 1984. pap. 8.50 (ISBN 0-570-01326-7, 99-1250). Concordia.

Faulkner, R. F. & Impey, O. R. Shino & Oribe Kiln Sites. 96p. 1981. 40.00x (ISBN 0-900090-84-7, Pub. by Ashmolean Mus UK). State Mutual Bk.

Faulkner, R. J. & Impey, O. R. Shino & Oribe Kiln Sites. (Illus.). 96p. (Orig.). 1981. pap. 15.50 (ISBN 0-903697-11-4, Pub. by R G Sawers UK). C E Tuttle.

Faulkner, R. O. The Ancient Egyptian Coffin Texts: Spells 1-354, Vol. I. 285p. 1978. Repr. of 1973 ed. text ed. 36.50x (ISBN 0-85668-005-2, Pub. by Aris & Phillips England). Humanities.

--The Ancient Egyptian Coffin Texts: Spells 355-787, Vol. II. 308p. 1977. text ed. 36.50x (ISBN 0-85668-051-6, Pub. by Aris & Phillips England). Humanities.

--The Ancient Egyptian Coffin Texts: Spells 788-1185 & Index, Vol. III. 204p. 1978. text ed. 36.50x (ISBN 0-85668-104-0, Pub. by Aris & Phillips England). Humanities.

--The Ancient Egyptian Pyramid Texts. (Egyptology Ser.). 344p. (Orig.). 1985. pap. 26.00 (ISBN 0-86516-124-0). Bolchazy-Carducci.

Faulkner, R. O., et al, trs. see Simpson, William K.

Faulkner, Ray & Faulkner, Sarah. Inside Today's Home. 4th ed. LC 74-11832. (Illus.). 1975. text ed. 31.95 (ISBN 0-03-089480-8, HoltC). HR&W.

Faulkner, Ray, et al. Art Today: An Introduction to the Visual Arts. 5th ed. LC 69-19919. (Illus.). 1974. pap. text ed. 26.95 (ISBN 0-03-089627-4, HoltC). HR&W.

Faulkner, Raymond. A Concise Dictionary of Middle Egyptian. 327p. (Egyptian & Eng.). 1976. Repr. of 1972 ed. text ed. 21.50x (ISBN 0-900416-32-7, Pub. by Aris & Phillips England). Humanities.

Faulkner, Robert K. The Jurisprudence of John Marshall. LC 80-14281. xii, 307p. 1980. Repr. of 1968 ed. lib. bdg. 32.50x (ISBN 0-313-22508-7, FAJU). Greenwood.

--Richard Hooker & the Politics of a Christian England. LC 79-65776. 195p. 1981. 28.50x (ISBN 0-520-03993-9). U of Cal Pr.

Faulkner, Robert R. Hollywood Studio Musicians: Their Work & Careers in the Recording Industry. LC 85-3166. (Illus.). 228p. 1985. pap. text ed. 11.75 (ISBN 0-8191-4587-4). U Pr of Amer.

--Music on Demand: Composers & Careers in the Hollywood Film Industry. LC 82-2676. (Illus.). 281p. 1982. 24.95 (ISBN 0-87855-403-3). Transaction Bks.

Faulkner, Sarah, jt. auth. see Faulkner, Ray.

Faulkner, Theodore A. & Aiken, W. Corporal Punishment in Schools. 350p. (Supplemented annually). 20.00 (ISBN 0-87526-172-8). Gould.

Faulkner, Thomas C. & Blair, Rhonda L., eds. Selected Letters & Journals of George Crabbe. (Illus.). 500p. 1985. 69.00 (ISBN 0-19-812570-4). Oxford U Pr.

Faulkner, Trader. Peter Finch: A Biography. LC 79-2400. (Illus.). 1980. 12.95 (ISBN 0-8008-6281-3). Taplinger.

Faulkner, Trevor. The Thames & Hudson Manual of Direct Metal Sculpture. (Illus.). 1978. 18.95 (ISBN 0-500-67015-3). Thames Hudson.

--The Thames & Hudson Manual of Direct Metal Sculpture. (Illus.). 1980. pap. 10.95 (ISBN 0-500-68015-9). Thames Hudson.

Faulkner, Virginia, ed. Roundup: A Nebraska Reader. LC 57-8597. (Illus.). xvi, 491p. 1975. pap. 6.95 (ISBN 0-8032-5807-0, BB 593, Bison). U of Nebr Pr.

Faulkner, Virginia & Luebke, Frederick C., eds. Vision & Refuge: Essays on the Literature of the Great Plains. LC 81-10418. xiv, 146p. 1982. 13.95x (ISBN 0-8032-1960-1). U of Nebr Pr.

Faulkner, Virginia, ed. see Cather, Willa.

Faulkner, Virginia, jt. ed. see Slote, Bernice.

Faulkner, Whitney. The American Dream, Bk. 1: Emily's Destiny. pap. 3.50 (ISBN 0-8217-1203-9). Zebra.

--The American Dream Book: Jane's Promise, Vol. 2. 1983. pap. 3.50 (ISBN 0-8217-1280-2). Zebra.

--The American Dream, No. 3: Kathryn's Quest. 1984. pap. 3.50 (ISBN 0-8217-1388-4). Zebra.

--Emily's Destiny. (The American Dream: Bk. 1). (Orig.). 1983. pap. 3.50 (ISBN 0-8217-1203-9). Zebra.

--Kathryn's Quest. (The American Dream Ser.: No. 3). 464p. 1984. pap. 3.50 (ISBN 0-8217-1388-4). Zebra.

Faulkner, Wiliam. The Reivers: Typescript Draft. Blotner, et al, eds. (William Faulkner Manuscripts Ser.). 200.00 (ISBN 0-8240-6834-3). Garland Pub.

Faulkner, Willard R. & King, John W., eds. Handbook of Clinical Laboratory Data, CRC. 2nd ed. LC 68-54212. (Handbook Ser.). 1968. 28.00 (ISBN 0-87819-722-2). CRC Pr.

Faulkner, Willard R. & Meites, Samuel, eds. Selected Methods for the Small Clinical Chemistry Laboratory. LC 80-66258. (Selected Methods of Clinical Chemistry Ser.: Vol. 9). 414p. 1982. AACC member 30.00 (ISBN 0-915274-13-2); non-member 40.00. Am Assn Clinical Chem.

Faulkner, William. Absalom, Absalom. (Modern Library College Editions Ser.). 1966. pap. 3.25x (ISBN 0-394-30978-2, T78, RanC). Random.

--Absalom, Absalom. 1966. 17.95 (ISBN 0-394-41400-4). Random.

--Absalom, Absalom! LC 72-398. (Illus.). 1972. pap. 3.95 (ISBN 0-394-71780-5, V780, Vin). Random.

--Absalom, Absalom (Nineteen Thirty-Six) (William Faulkner Manuscripts Ser.). 1985. text ed. 100.00 (ISBN 0-8240-6817-3). Garland Pub.

--As I Lay Dying. 1964. 13.95 (ISBN 0-394-41581-7). Random.

--As I Lay Dying. (YA) 1964. pap. 2.95 (ISBN 0-394-70254-9, Vin). Random.

--As I Lay Dying. Blotner, Josef, et al, eds. (William Faulkner Manuscripts Ser.). 1985. text ed. 100.00 (ISBN 0-8240-6809-2). Garland Pub.

--Collected Stories. (YA) 1956. 22.95 (ISBN 0-394-41967-7). Random.

--Collected Stories of William Faulkner. (YA) 1977. pap. 8.95 (ISBN 0-394-72257-4, Vin). Random.

--Fable. 1954. 15.95 (ISBN 0-394-42400-X). Random.

--A Fable. LC 77-3039. 1978. pap. 3.95 (ISBN 0-394-72413-5, Vin). Random.

--Father Abraham. LC 83-42304. 80p. 1984. 16.45 (ISBN 0-394-53722-X). Random.

--Father Abraham, Nineteen Twenty-Six. Blotner, J., et al, eds. (William Faulkner Manuscripts Ser.). 100.00 (ISBN 0-8240-6801-7). Garland Pub.

--Faulkner: A Comprehensive Guide to the Brodsky Collection, Vol. 3: The De Gaulle Story by William Faulkner. Brodsky, Louis D. & Hamblin, Robert W., eds. LC 82-6966. (Center for the Study of Southern Culture Ser.). (Illus.). 1985. 35.00x (ISBN 0-87805-228-3); pap. 14.95 (ISBN 0-87805-254-2). U Pr of Miss.

--Faulkner: A Comprehensive Guide to the Brodsky Collection, Vol. 4. Brodsky, Louis D. & Hamblin, Robert W., eds. (Center for the Study of Southern Culture Ser.). (Illus.). 1985. 35.00 (ISBN 0-87805-253-4). U Pr of Miss.

--The Faulkner Reader. LC 59-5911. 1959. 8.95 (ISBN 0-394-60399-0). Modern Lib.

--Flags in the Dust. Day, Douglas, ed. 1973. 13.95 (ISBN 0-394-46591-1). Random.

--Flags in the Dust. Day, Douglas, ed. LC 74-3315. (YA) 1974. pap. 3.95 (ISBN 0-394-71239-0, V-239, Vin). Random.

--Flags in the Dust: Manuscripts. Blotner, J., et al, eds. (William Faulkner Manuscripts Ser.). 100.00 (ISBN 0-8240-6807-6). Garland Pub.

--Flags in the Dust: Typescript. Blotner, J., et al, eds. (William Faulkner Manuscrips Ser.). 100.00 (ISBN 0-8240-6808-4). Garland Pub.

--Go Down, Moses. 1942. 17.95 (ISBN 0-394-42646-0). Random.

--Go Down, Moses. LC 72-8062. 416p. (YA) 1973. pap. 2.95 (ISBN 0-394-71884-4, Vin). Random.

--Hamlet. 1940. 16.95 (ISBN 0-394-42759-9). Random.

--Hamlet. (YA) 1956. pap. 4.95 (ISBN 0-394-70139-9, V139, Vin). Random.

--Helen: A Courtship (ISBN 0-916242-11-0). limited edition, deluxe box & binding 155.00 (ISBN 0-686-63443-8). Yoknapatawpha.

--Helen: Courtship & Mississippi Poems. LC 81-50422. 168p. 1981. 12.95 (ISBN 0-916242-12-9). Yoknapatawpha.

--Intruder in the Dust. (Modern Library College Editions Ser.). 1967. pap. 4.95 (ISBN 0-394-71792-9, T88, RanC). Random.

--Intruder in the Dust. 1948. 13.95 (ISBN 0-394-43074-3). Random.

--Jealousy & Episode. LC 77-903. 1977. lib. bdg. 16.00 (ISBN 0-8414-4173-1). Folcroft.

--Knight's Gambit. Blotner, Joseph, ed. 256p. (YA) 1978. pap. 2.95 (ISBN 0-394-72729-0, Vin). Random.

--Knight's Gambit (1949) Blotner, J., et al, eds. (William Faulkner Manuscripts Ser.). 100.00 (ISBN 0-8240-6824-6). Garland Pub.

--Light in August. (Modern Library College Editions Ser.). 1965. pap. 3.50 (ISBN 0-394-30968-5, T68, RanC). Random.

--Light in August. 1967. 16.95 (ISBN 0-394-43335-1). Random.

--Light in August. 512p. (YA) 1972. pap. 4.95 (ISBN 0-394-71189-0, V189, Vin). Random.

--Light in August: Manuscript. (Faulkner Manuscripts Ser.). 100.00 (ISBN 0-8240-6813-0). Garland Pub.

--The Mansion. 1959. pap. 5.95 (ISBN 0-394-70282-4). Random.

--The Mansion: Typescript Draft, 2 vols. Blotner, et al, eds. (William Faulkner Manuscripts Ser.). Set. 200.00 (ISBN 0-8240-6832-7). Garland Pub.

--The Mansion: Typescript Setting Copy, 2 vols. Blotner, et al, eds. (William Faulkner Manuscripts Ser.). Set. 200.00 (ISBN 0-317-20406-8). Garland Pub.

--Marble Faun, & a Green Bough. reissue ed. 1965. 10.95 (ISBN 0-394-40385-1). Random.

--The Marionettes. Polk, Noel, ed. LC 77-8994. (Bibliographical Society of the University of Va.). (Illus.). xxxii, 106p. 1978. 12.95x (ISBN 0-8139-0734-9). U Pr of Va.

--Marionettes. LC 75-27485. (Illus.). 1979. boxed ltd ed 125.00 (ISBN 0-916242-01-3). Yoknapatawpha.

--Mayday. LC 76-22410. (Illus.). 1980. text ed. 8.95 (ISBN 0-268-01339-X). U of Notre Dame Pr.

--Mirrors of Chartres Street. 93p. 1980. Repr. of 1953 ed. lib. bdg. 17.50 (ISBN 0-8492-4628-8). R West.

--Mosquitoes. 1955. 6.95 (ISBN 0-87140-936-4). Liveright.

--Mosquitoes. 1985. pap. cancelled (ISBN 0-87140-133-9). Norton.

--Mosquitoes. 352p. 1984. pap. write for info. (ISBN 0-87140-133-9). Liveright.

--Mosquitoes. 1985. pap. 4.95 (ISBN 0-671-55731-9). WSP.

--New Orleans Sketches. Collier, Carvel, ed. LC 68-14495. 1968. 13.95 (ISBN 0-394-43818-3). Random.

--Novels Nineteen Thirty to Nineteen Thirty-Five: As I Lay Dying, Light in August, Pylon. Blotner, Joseph & Polk, Noel, eds. LC 84-23424. 1985. 27.50 (ISBN 0-940450-26-7). Library of America.

--Portable Faulkner. rev. ed. Cowley, Malcolm, ed. (Viking Portable Library: No. 18). (gr. 10 up). 1977. pap. 7.95 (ISBN 0-14-015018-8). Penguin.

--Pylon. reissue ed. 1965. 13.95 (ISBN 0-394-44156-7). Random.

--Pylon (1935) Blotner, et al, eds. (William Faulkner Mnauscripts Ser.). 100.00 (ISBN 0-8240-6816-5). Garland Pub.

--Reivers. 1962. 17.95 (ISBN 0-394-44229-6). Random.

--Reivers. 1962. pap. 3.95 (ISBN 0-394-70339-1, V339, Vin). Random.

--The Reivers: Typescript Setting Copy. Blotner, et al, eds. (William Faulkner Manuscripts Ser.). 200.00 (ISBN 0-8240-6835-1). Garland Pub.

--Requiem for a Nun. 1951. 13.95 (ISBN 0-394-44274-1). Random.

--Requiem for a Nun. LC 74-17145. 1975. pap. 3.95 (ISBN 0-394-71412-1, Vin). Random.

--Requiem for a Nun: Pleliminary Material, 2 vols. Blotner, et al, eds. (William Faulkner Manuscripts Ser.). 200.00 (ISBN 0-8240-6825-4). Garland Pub.

--Requiem for a Nun: Revised Galley Proofs. Blotner, et al, eds. (William Faulkner Manuscripts Ser.). 100.00 (ISBN 0-8240-6827-0). Garland Pub.

--Requiem for a Nun: Typescript. Blotner, et al, eds. (William Faulkner Manuscripts Ser.). 100.00 (ISBN 0-8240-6826-2). Garland Pub.

--Sanctuary. 1962. pap. 4.95 (ISBN 0-394-70381-2). Random.

--Sanctuary. Blotner, et al, eds. (William Faulkner Manuscripts Ser.). Date not set. manuscript 100.00 (ISBN 0-8240-6810-6). Garland Pub.

--Sanctuary: The Original Text. Polk, Noel, ed. 296p. 1981. 14.95 (ISBN 0-394-51278-2). Random.

--Santuary: Carbon Typescript. Blotner, et al, eds. (William Faulkner Manscripts Ser.). 100.00 (ISBN 0-8240-6811-4). Garland Pub.

--Sartoris. 1966. 15.95 (ISBN 0-394-44375-6). Random.

--Sartoris. 1983. pap. 3.50 (ISBN 0-452-00646-5, Mer). NAL.

--Selected Short Stories of William Faulkner. LC 62-9690. 1962. 5.95 (ISBN 0-394-60456-3). Modern Lib.

--Short Stories. Blotner, et al, eds. (William Faulkner Manuscripts). 100.00 (ISBN 0-8240-6836-X). Garland Pub.

--Soldeir's Pay: Carbon Typescript. Blotner, ed. (William Faulkner Manuscripts Ser.). 100.00 (ISBN 0-8240-6803-3). Garland Pub.

--Soldiers' Pay. new ed. LC 79-114374. 1954. 9.95 (ISBN 0-87140-935-6); pap. 6.95 (ISBN 0-87140-207-6). Liveright.

--Soldiers' Pay. 320p. pap. cancelled (ISBN 0-87140-207-6). Liveright.

--Soldiers' Pay. 1985. pap. 4.95 (ISBN 0-671-55730-0). WSP.

--Soldier's Pay: Typescript. Blotner, ed. (William Faulkner Manuscripts Ser.). 100.00 (ISBN 0-8240-6802-5). Garland Pub.

--Sound & the Fury. (Modern Library Editions). 1967. pap. 2.95x (ISBN 0-394-30994-4, T94, RanC). Random.

--Sound & the Fury. new, corrected ed. Polk, Noel, ed. LC 84-42626. 384p. 1966. 17.95 (ISBN 0-394-53241-4). Random.

--Sound & the Fury. 1954. pap. 3.95 (ISBN 0-394-70005-8, V5, Vin). Random.

--The Sound & the Fury: Carbon Typescript. Polk, Noel, ed. (William Faulkner Manuscripts Ser.). 100.00 (ISBN 0-317-20510-2). Garland Pub.

--The Sound & the Fury: Manuscript. Polk, Noel, ed. (William Faulkner Manuscripts Ser.). 100.00 (ISBN 0-8240-6805-X). Garland Pub.

--These Thirteen. Polk, Noel, ed. (William Faulkner Manuscripts Ser.). Date not set. 100.00 (ISBN 0-8240-6812-2). Garland Pub.

--Three Famous Short Novels. Incl. Spotted Horses; Old Man; Bear. 1958. pap. 3.95 (ISBN 0-394-70149-6, V-149, Vin). Random.

--Town. 1957. 13.95 (ISBN 0-394-42452-2). Random.

--Town. 1961. pap. 4.95 (ISBN 0-394-70184-4, V184, Vin). Random.

--The Town: Preliminary Materials. Millgate, Michael, ed. (William Faulkner Manuscripts Ser.). 100.00 (ISBN 0-8240-6831-9). Garland Pub.

--The Town: Typescript. Millgate, Michael, ed. (William Faulkner Manuscripts Ser.). Date not set. 100.00 (ISBN 0-8240-6830-0). Garland Pub.

--Uncollected Stories of William Faulkner. Blottner, Joseph, ed. LC 80-6120. 732p. 1981. 17.95 (ISBN 0-394-40044-5, V-656, Vin); pap. 7.95 (ISBN 0-394-74656-2). Random.

--Unvanquished. 1965. pap. 4.95 (ISBN 0-394-70351-0, V351, Vin). Random.

--Vision in Spring. Sensibar, Judith L., intro. by. (Illus.). 134p. 1984. 14.95 (ISBN 0-292-78712-X). U of Tex Pr.

--Wild Palms. 1964. pap. 8.95 (ISBN 0-394-60513-6, V262, Vin). Random.

--The Wild Palms. Botner, J., et al, eds. (William Faulkner Manuscripts). 100.00 (ISBN 0-8240-6819-X). Garland Pub.

--The Wild Palms (1939) William Faulkner Manuscripts. Blotner, J., et al, eds. 100.00 (ISBN 0-317-26448-6). Garland Pub.

--Wishing Tree. (Illus.). (gr. 4 up). 1967. 8.95 (ISBN 0-394-45222-4). Random.

Faulkner, William, jt. auth. see Foote, Horton.

Faulkner, William, jt. auth. see Sayre, Joel.

Faulkner, William F. Mosquitoes: Nineteen Twenty-Seven. Blotner, J., et al, eds. (William Faulkner Manuscripts Ser.). Date not set. 100.00 (ISBN 0-8240-6804-1). Garland Pub.

Faull, Sandra, jt. ed. see Lester, Daniel.

Faullkner, Edward A. Guide to Efficient Boiler Operation: Gas, Oil, Dual Fuel. 1981. text ed. 32.00 (ISBN 0-915586-35-5). Fairmont Pr.

Faulstich, H. & Kommerell, B. Amanita Toxins & Poisoning: International Amanita Symposium, Heidelberg 1978. (Illus.). 246p. 1980. pap. text ed. 32.50x. Lubrecht & Cramer.

Fauman, Beverly J. & Fauman, Michael. Emergency Psychiatry for the House Officer. (HO). (Illus.). 184p. 1981. soft cover 10.95 (ISBN 0-683-03046-9). Williams & Wilkins.

Fauman, Michael, jt. auth. see Fauman, Beverly J.

Faunce, Hilda. Desert Wife. LC 80-22163. (Illus.). xiv, 305p. 1981. 23.50x (ISBN 0-8032-1957-1); pap. 6.95 (ISBN 0-8032-6853-X, BB 761, Bison). U of Nebr Pr.

Faunce, Patricia S. Women & Ambition: A Bibliography. LC 79-18347. 724p. 1980. lib. bdg. 37.50 (ISBN 0-8108-1242-8). Scarecrow.

Faunce, William. Problems of an Industrial Society. 2nd ed. Munson, Eric M., ed. 256p. 1981. pap. text ed. 18.95 (ISBN 0-07-020105-6). McGraw.

Faunce-Brown, Daphne. Snuffles' House. LC 82-12116. (Stories to Learn by Ser.). (Illus.). 32p. (gr. k-3). 1983. PLB 11.25 (ISBN 0-516-08943-9); pap. 2.95 (ISBN 0-516-48943-7). Childrens.

Fauntleroy, Fran. Houston Epicure: 1983-84. (Epicure Ser.). 150p. 1983. pap. 5.95 (ISBN 0-89716-126-2). Peanut Butter.

Faupel, Charles E. The Ecology of Disaster: An Application of a Conceptual Model. 245p. 1985. text ed. 24.50x (ISBN 0-8290-1350-4); pap. text ed. 14.95x (ISBN 0-8290-1532-9). Irvington.

Faupel, Charles E., et al. Disaster Beliefs & Emergency Planning. 259p. 1985. pap. text ed. 12.95x (ISBN 0-8290-1530-2). Irvington.

--Disaster Beliefs & Emergency Planning. 259p. 1985. text ed. 24.50x (ISBN 0-8290-1361-X). Irvington.

Faupel, David W. The American Pentecostal Movement: A Bibliographic Essay. LC 76-361994. (Occasional Bibliographic Papers of the B. L. Fisher Library: No. 2). 56p. 1972. 3.00 (ISBN 0-914368-01-X). Asbury Theological.

Faupel, David W., ed. see Godbey, W. B.

Faupel, Joseph F. & Fisher, Franklin E. Engineering Design: A Synthesis of Stress Analysis & Materials Engineering. 2nd ed. LC 80-16727. 1056p. 1981. 58.95x (ISBN 0-471-03381-2, Pub. by Wiley-Interscience). Wiley.

Fauquier, Francis. An Essay on the Ways & Means for Raising Money for the Support of the Present War, Without Increasing Public Debts. (History of English Economic Thought Ser). 1970. Repr. of 1756 ed. 15.00 (ISBN 0-384-15185-X). Johnson Repr.

Faur, Jose. Golden Doves with Silver Dots: Semiotics & Textuality in Rabbinic Tradition. LC 84-47967. (Jewish Literature & Culture Ser.). 352p. 1985. 27.50 (ISBN 0-253-32600-1). Ind U Pr.

Faure, Edgar, et al. Learning to Be: The World of Education Today & Tomorrow. Herrera, Felipe & Kaddoura, Abdul-Razzak. LC 72-89288. 313p. (Orig., 7th Imprint 1982). 1972. pap. 20.25 (ISBN 92-3-101017-4, U349, UNESCO). Unipub.

Faure, Elie. The Soul of Japan. lib. bdg. 59.95 (ISBN 0-8490-1089-6). Gordon Pr.

Faure, G. & Powell, J. L. Strontium Isotope Geology. LC 72-75720. (Minerals, Rocks & Inorganic Materials Ser.: Vol. 5). (Illus.). 200p. 1972. 22.00 (ISBN 0-387-05784-6). Springer-Verlag.

Faure, Gabriel. A Fully Illustrated Pictorial Review of the Italian Lakes. (Illus.). 177p. 1985. 97.45 (ISBN 0-86650-142-8). Gloucester Art.

--Gabriel Faure: His Life Through Letters. Nectoux, Jean-Michael, ed. Underwood, J. A., tr. LC 83-6010. (Illus.). 416p. 1984. 40.00 (ISBN 0-7145-2768-8, Dist. by Scribner). M Boyars.

Faure, Gunter. Principles of Isotope Geology. LC 77-4479. (Intermediate Geology Ser.). 464p. 1977. text ed. 48.50 (ISBN 0-471-25665-X). Wiley.

Faure, Jean. Bed of Roses. (Second Chance at Love Ser.: No. 240). 192p. 1985. pap. 1.95 (ISBN 0-425-07767-5). Berkley Pub.

Faure, R., jt. auth. see Kaufmann, Arnold.

Faure, Sebastian. Does God Exist? lib. bdg. 59.95 (ISBN 0-8490-0054-8). Gordon Pr.

Fauriel, C. C. History of Provencal Poetry. LC 68-753. (Studies in French Literature, No. 45). 1969. Repr. of 1860 ed. lib. bdg. 59.95x (ISBN 0-8383-0546-6). Haskell.

Fauriol, Georges A. Foreign Policy Behavior of Caribbean States: Guyana, Haiti & Jamaica. LC 83-21709. (Illus.). 356p. (Orig.). 1984. lib. bdg. 25.00 (ISBN 0-8191-3671-9); pap. text ed. 13.00 (ISBN 0-8191-3672-7). U Pr of Amer.

Fauriol, Georges A., jt. auth. see Moorer, Thomas H.

Faurisson, Robert. Faurisson on the Holocaust. (Illus.). 200p. (Orig.). pap. cancelled (ISBN 0-939484-09-9). Inst Hist Rev.

--The Holocaust Debate: Revisionist Historians Versus Six Million Jews. 1980. lib. bdg. 59.95 (ISBN 0-686-62797-0). Revisionist Pr.

--Is the Diary of Anne Frank Genuine? 64p. 1985. 5.00 (ISBN 0-939484-19-6). Inst Hist Rev.

Faurot, Albert. Arranging Tropical Flowers. (Illus.). 1979. pap. 8.75x (ISBN 0-686-25215-2, Pub. by New Day Pub). Cellar.

--Culture Currents of World Art. 1974. 8.00x (ISBN 0-686-18696-6). Cellar.

Faurot, Albert, jt. auth. see Vista, Isabel D.

Faurot, Albert, ed. Prayers of Great Men Selected & Interpreted. 1976. wrps. 3.25x (ISBN 0-686-09434-4). Cellar.

Faurot, Jeannette L., ed. Chinese Fiction from Taiwan: Critical Perspectives. LC 80-7490. (Studies in Chinese Literature & Society). 288p. 1980. 20.00x (ISBN 0-253-12409-3). Ind U Pr.

Faurote, Fay L., jt. auth. see Arnold, Horace L.

Faurre, Pierre & Depeyrot, Michel. Elements of System Theory. LC 76-3056. 1976. 47.00 (ISBN 0-7204-0440-1, North-Holland). Elsevier.

Fausboll, A., tr. see Raunkiaer, Christen.

Fausboll, Anne I., tr. see Soderhjelm, H.

Fausboll, V. Catalogue of the Mandalay Manuscripts in the India Office Library. 52p. (Orig.). 1897. pap. 2.25 (ISBN 0-86013-066-5, Pub. by British Lib). Longwood Pub Group.

Fausboll, V., jt. auth. see Muller, F. Max.

Fausboll, V., ed. Buddhist Birth Stories; or Jataka Tales, Vol. 1. Davids, Rhys T., tr. LC 78-72443. Repr. of 1880 ed. 42.50 (ISBN 0-404-17309-8). AMS Pr.

Fausel, Donald F., ed. The Social Work General Practitioner. 1973. 38.50x (ISBN 0-8422-5117-0). Irvington.

Fauset, A. H. Folklore from Nova Scotia. LC 32-8895. (American Folklore Society Memoirs). Repr. of 1931 ed. 21.00 (ISBN 0-527-01076-6). Kraus Repr.

Fauset, Arthur H. Black Gods of the Metropolis, Negro Religious Cults of the Urban North. LC 73-120251. 1970. Repr. lib. bdg. 16.00x (ISBN 0-374-92714-6). Octagon.

--Black Gods of the Metropolis: Negro Religious Cults of the Urban North. LC 75-133446. 1971. pap. 8.95x (ISBN 0-8122-1001-8, Pa Paperbks). U of Pa Pr.

Fauset, Jessie. Plum Bun: A Novel Without a Moral. 400p. 1985. 15.95 (ISBN 0-86358-057-2, Pandora Pr); pap. 8.95 (ISBN 0-86358-044-0, Pandora Pr). Routledge & Kegan.

Fauset, Jessie R. Chinaberry Tree. LC 70-95405. Repr. of 1931 ed. 17.00 (ISBN 0-404-00256-0). AMS Pr.

--Chinaberry Tree: A Novel of American Life. LC 74-89033. Repr. of 1931 ed. 27.50x (ISBN 0-8371-1919-7, FAC&, Pub. by Negro U Pr). Greenwood.

--The Chinaberry Tree: A Novel of American Life. 19.95 (ISBN 0-405-18503-0). Ayer Co Pubs.

--Comedy, American Style. LC 76-95401. Repr. of 1933 ed. 12.00 (ISBN 0-404-00257-9). AMS Pr.

--Comedy, American Style. LC 79-90131. Repr. of 1933 ed. cancelled (ISBN 0-8371-1992-8, FAA&, Pub. by Negro U Pr). Greenwood.

--There Is Confusion. LC 73-18575. Repr. of 1924 ed. 23.50 (ISBN 0-404-11386-9). AMS Pr.

Fausett, H. I. Keats, a Study in Development. 123p. 1966. Repr. of 1922 ed. 13.50 (ISBN 0-208-00188-3, Archon). Shoe String.

Fausold, Martin L. Gifford Pinchot, Bull Moose Progressive. LC 73-7672. (Illus.). 270p. 1973. Repr. of 1961 ed. lib. bdg. 15.50x (ISBN 0-8371-6943-7, FAGP). Greenwood.

--James W. Wadsworth, Jr. The Gentleman from New York. LC 75-6111. (Illus.). 460p. 1975. 20.00x (ISBN 0-8156-2171-X). Syracuse U Pr.

--The Presidency of Herbert C. Hoover. (American Presidency Ser.). 272p. 1985. 22.50x (ISBN 0-7006-0259-3). U Pr of KS.

Fausold, Martin L. & Mazuzan, George T., eds. The Hoover Presidency: A Reappraisal. LC 74-13876. (Illus.). 1974. 32.50x (ISBN 0-87395-280-4). State U NY Pr.

Fauss, O. F. What God Hath Wrought: The Complete Works of O. F. Fauss. Wallace, Mary H., ed. (Illus.). 300p. (Orig.). 1985. pap. 6.95 (ISBN 0-912315-84-9). Word Aflame.

Fausset, A. R. Fausset's Bible Dictionary. (Illus.). 1970. 9.95 (ISBN 0-310-24311-4). Zondervan.

Fausset, H. L'Anson. The Flame & the Light: Vedanta & Buddhism. 59.95 (ISBN 0-8490-0173-0). Gordon Pr.

Fausset, High I. Studies in Idealism. 278p. 1982. Repr. of 1923 ed. lib. bdg. 30.00 (ISBN 0-89760-230-7). Telegraph Bks.

Fausset, Hugh. The Flame & the Light. LC 76-2081. 232p. 1976. pap. 3.75 (ISBN 0-8356-0478-0, Quest). Theos Pub Hse.

Fausset, Hugh A. Flame & the Light: Meanings in Vedanta & Buddhism. LC 69-10089. Repr. of 1969 ed. lib. bdg. 15.00x (ISBN 0-8371-0996-5, FAVB). Greenwood.

Fausset, Hugh I. Samuel Taylor Coleridge. (Illus.). 1971. Repr. of 1926 ed. 39.00x (ISBN 0-403-00792-5). Scholarly.

--Walt Whitman: Poet of Democracy. LC 67-28777. (Illus.). 1969. Repr. of 1942 ed. 9.00x (ISBN 0-8462-1307-9). Russell.

Fausset, Hugh I'Anson. Tennyson: A Modern Portrait. 309p. 1982. Repr. of 1923 ed. lib. bdg. 30.00 (ISBN 0-89760-235-8). Telegraph Bks.

Fausset, Hugh L. Poets & Pundits: Essays & Addresses. LC 67-25261. Repr. of 1947 ed. 24.75x (ISBN 0-8046-0139-9, Pub. by Kennikat). Assoc Faculty Pr.

--Studies in Idealism. LC 65-18603. Repr. of 1923 ed. 21.00x (ISBN 0-8046-0140-2, Pub. by Kennikat). Assoc Faculty Pr.

Faust, A. B. Guide to the Materials for American History in Swiss & Austrian Archives. 1916. 24.00 (ISBN 0-527-00695-5). Kraus Repr.

Faust, A. B., ed. see Adams, John Q.

Faust, A. B., ed. see Wieland, Christopher M.

Faust, Albert. The German Element in the U. S, 2 vols. LC 78-145009. 1927. Repr. 49.00x (ISBN 0-403-00959-6). Scholarly.

Faust, Albert B. German Element in the United States, 2 Vols. LC 69-18773. (American Immigration Collection Ser., No. 1). (Illus.). 1969. Repr. of 1927 ed. Set. 50.50 (ISBN 0-405-00580-6); Vol. 1. 25.50 (ISBN 0-405-00520-2); Vol. 2. 25.50 (ISBN 0-405-00521-0). Ayer Co Pubs.

Faust, Aly. Chemistry of Natural Waters. LC 80-70322. 400p. 1981. text ed. 49.95 (ISBN 0-250-40387-0). Butterworth.

Faust, Augustus F. Brazil: Education in an Expanding Economy. LC 77-2635. (U. S. Department of Health, Education, & Welfare, Bulletin 1959: No. 13). 1977. Repr. of 1959 ed. lib. bdg. 15.00x (ISBN 0-8371-9558-6, FABR). Greenwood.

Faust, Bernhard C. Catechism of Health. Basse, J. H., tr. from Ger. LC 74-180574. (Medicine & Society in America Ser). 116p. 1972. Repr. of 1794 ed. 14.00 (ISBN 0-405-03951-4). Ayer Co Pubs.

Faust, Bertha. Hawthorne's Contemporaneous Reputation. 1967. lib. bdg. 14.00x (ISBN 0-374-92717-0). Octagon.

Faust, Candy, jt. auth. see Faust, David.

Faust, Charles L., ed. Fundamentals of Electrochemical Machining. LC 72-150646. pap. 92.80 (ISBN 0-317-08009-1, 2051971). Bks Demand UMI.

Faust, Clarence H. & Johnson, Thomas H. Jonathan Edwards. 1981. Repr. of 1935 ed. lib. bdg. 40.00 (ISBN 0-89760-234-X). Telegraph Bks.

Faust, Clarence H. & Feingold, Jessica, eds. Approaches to Education for Character: Strategies for Change in Higher Education. LC 70-83386. 451p. 1969. 33.00x (ISBN 0-231-03262-5). Columbia U Pr.

Faust, Cosette & Thompson, Stith. Old English Poems. LC 74-8993. 1918. lib. bdg. 25.00 (ISBN 0-8414-4193-6). Folcroft.

Faust, David. The Limits of Scientific Reasoning. LC 84-5172. 220p. 1984. 25.00x (ISBN 0-8166-1356-7); pap. 12.95 (ISBN 0-8166-1359-1). U of Minn Pr.

Faust, David & Faust, Candy. Puppet Plays with a Point. rev. ed. 160p. 1979. pap. 7.95 (ISBN 0-87239-248-1, 3364). Standard Pub.

Faust, David, jt. auth. see Arbuthnot, Jack.

Faust, David E. Contracts from Larsa Dated in the Reign of Rim-Sin. LC 78-63537. (Yale Oriental Series: Babylonian Texts: No. 8). (Illus.). 120p. Repr. of 1941 ed. 42.50 (ISBN 0-404-60258-4). AMS Pr.

Faust, Drew G. The Ideology of Slavery: Proslavery Thought in the Antebellum South, 1830-1860. LC 81-3755. (Library of Southern Civilization). 412p. 1981. text ed. 35.00x (ISBN 0-8071-0855-3); pap. text ed. 8.95x (ISBN 0-8071-0892-8). La State U Pr.

--James Henry Hammond & the Old South: A Design for Mastery. LC 82-8939. (Southern Biography Ser.). (Illus.). 407p. 1982. text ed. 30.00x (ISBN 0-8071-1048-5); pap. 8.95x (ISBN 0-8071-1248-8). La State U Pr.

--A Sacred Circle: The Dilemma of the Intellectual in the Old South, 1840-1860. LC 77-4547. 208p. 1978. text ed. 18.50x (ISBN 0-8018-1967-9). Johns Hopkins.

Faust, Ernest C. Life History Studies on Montana Trematodes. (Illus.). 1918. 12.00 (ISBN 0-384-15190-6). Johnson Repr.

Faust, Frederic L. & Brantingham, Paul J. Juvenile Justice Philosophy: Readings, Cases & Comments. 2nd ed. (Criminal Justice Ser.). 1978. pap. text ed. 23.95 (ISBN 0-8299-0179-5). West Pub.

Faust, Frederick see Brand, Max.

Faust, Gerald W., jt. auth. see Anderson, Richard C.

Faust, Harriet. Enough of Christmas. (Orig.). 1980. pap. 2.50 (ISBN 0-937172-08-1). JLJ Pubs.

Faust, Henri. Half-Light & Overtones. LC 71-144735. (Yale Series of Younger Poets: No. 28). Repr. of 1929 ed. 18.00 (ISBN 0-404-53828-2). AMS Pr.

Faust, Irvin. Foreign Devils. LC 72-97685. 1973. 7.95 (ISBN 0-87795-056-3). Arbor Hse.

--Newsreel. 288p. 1982. pap. 2.75 (ISBN 0-523-41555-9). Pinnacle Bks.

--Willy Remembers. LC 79-157508. 1971. 6.95 (ISBN 0-87795-017-2). Arbor Hse.

--The Year of the Hot Jock & Other Stories. 228p. 1985. 14.95 (ISBN 0-525-24343-7, 01549-460). Dutton.

Faust, Irwin. Willy Remembers. 1983. 15.95 (ISBN 0-87795-017-2); pap. 7.95 (ISBN 0-87795-265-5). Arbor Hse.

Faust, Joan L. The New York Times Book of Annuals & Perennials. (Illus.). 1980. 16.95 (ISBN 0-8129-0857-0). Times Bks.

--The New York Times Book of Flower Gardening. LC 79-51449. (Illus.). 288p. 1982. pap. 9.95 (ISBN 0-8129-6317-2). Times Bks.

--The New York Times Book of House Plants. LC 72-91701. (Illus.). 288p. 1983. pap. 9.95 (ISBN 0-8129-6320-2). Times Bks.

--The New York Times Book of House Plants. (Illus.). 1973. 16.95 (ISBN 0-8129-0309-9). Times Bks.

--The New York Times Book of Vegetable Gardening. LC 74-80483. (Illus.). 288p. 1982. Repr. of 1974 ed. pap. 9.95 (ISBN 0-8129-6273-7). Times Bks.

--The New York Times Book of Vegetable Gardening. LC 74-80483. (Illus.). 1975. 16.95 (ISBN 0-8129-0501-6). Times Bks.

Faust, Joan L., ed. The New York Times Garden Book. 1977. pap. 5.95 (ISBN 0-685-75024-8, 345-25682-4-495). Ballantine.

Faust, John W., Jr., ed. see Conference on Silicon Carbide, 3rd, 1973.

Faust, Karl I. Campaigning in the Philippines. LC 72-111740. (American Imperialism: Viewpoints of United States Foreign Policy, 1898-1941). 1970. Repr. of 1899 ed. 23.00 (ISBN 0-405-02017-1). Ayer Co Pubs.

Faust, Langdon L., ed. American Women Writers: A Critical Reference Guide from Colonial Times to the Present, Vol. 1, A-L. Abr. ed. LC 82-40286. 445p. 1983. pap. 14.95 (ISBN 0-8044-6164-3). Ungar.

--American Women Writers: A Critical Reference Guide from Colonial Times to the Present, Vol. 2, M-Z. Abr. ed. LC 82-40286. 445p. 1983. pap. 14.95 (ISBN 0-8044-6165-1). Ungar.

Faust, Langdon L., jt. ed. see Mainiero, Lina.

Faust, Martin L. Constitution Making in Missouri: The Convention of 1943-1944. 186p. 1971. 1.00 (ISBN 0-318-15793-4). Citizens Forum Gov.

Faust, Naomi F. All Beautiful Things. 2nd ed. LC 82-83853. 104p. 1983. pap. 5.00 perf. bnd. (ISBN 0-916418-49-9). Lotus.

Faust, Norma. Lecciones para el Aprendizaje del Idioma Shipibo-Conibo. (Documento del Trabajo (Peru) Ser.: No. 1). 160p. 1973. pap. 6.00x (ISBN 0-88312-783-0); microfiche (2) 2.86x (ISBN 0-88312-353-3). Summer Inst Ling.

Faust, Norma W. Gramatica Cocama: Lecciones para el Aprendizaje del Idioma Cocama. (Peruvian Linguistic Ser.: No. 6). 173p. 1972. pap. 3.00x (ISBN 0-88312-766-0); microfiche (2) 2.86 (ISBN 0-88312-388-6). Summer Inst Ling.

Faust, Paula, ed. An Introduction to Fund Raising: The Newcomers' Guide to Development. 92p. 1983. 14.50 (ISBN 0-89964-214-4). Coun Adv & Supp Ed.

Faust, Ron. Death Fires. 1980. pap. 1.95 (ISBN 0-449-14376-7, GM). Fawcett.

--Nowhere to Run. 192p. 1981. pap. 2.25 (ISBN 0-449-14439-9, GM). Fawcett.

--Snowkill. 208p. 1981. pap. 2.25 (ISBN 0-686-97418-2, Leisure Bks). Dorchester Pub Co.

Faust, Samuel D. & Aly, Osman M. Chemistry of Water Treatment. LC 82-72854. 1983. text ed. 49.95 (ISBN 0-250-40388-9). Butterworth.

Faust, Samuel D. & Hunter, Joseph V., eds. Organic Compounds in Aquatic Environment. LC 72-172938. (Illus.). pap. 160.00 (ISBN 0-317-07861-5, 2055013). Bks Demand UMI.

Faust, V., ed. see Ladewig, D. & Hobi, V.

Faust, Verne. Five Ways of Parenting: One That Works! LC 79-65211. 1980. 26.95 (ISBN 0-934162-01-8). Thomas Paine Pr.

--I Know More About You Than You Ever Dreamed Possible. LC 79-88004. 1980. 19.95 (ISBN 0-934162-00-X). Thomas Paine Pr.

--Self Esteem in the Classroom. LC 79-65212. 1980. 26.95 (ISBN 0-934162-02-6). Thomas Paine Pr.

Fausten, Dietrich K. The Consistency of British Balance of Payments Policies. 210p. 1975. text ed. 37.50x (ISBN 0-8419-5008-3). Holmes & Meier.

Fauster, Carl U. Libbey Glass, Since 1818. (Illus.). 450p. 30.00 (ISBN 0-686-25838-X). Ant & Hist Glass.

Fauster, Carl U., ed. Libbey Glass, since Eighteen Eighteen: Pictorial History & Collectors Guide. 1979. 30.00 (ISBN 0-686-25838-X). Len Beach Pr.

Fausto, Nelson, et al. Liver Regeneration, No. 2. LC 72-13504. (Illus.). 220p. 1973. text ed. 24.00x (ISBN 0-8422-7080-9). Irvington.

Faustos of Buzand. Buzandaran Patmutiwn: The Epic Histories. Garsoian, Nina G., ed. LC 83-14297. (Classical Armenian Texts). 1984. 50.00x (ISBN 0-88206-033-3). Caravan Bks.

Faustus, Johann. The Historie of Damnable Live & Deserved Death of Doctor John Faustus. Gent, P. F., tr. LC 74-26934. (English Experience Ser.: No. 173). 80p. 1969. Repr. of 1592 ed. 14.00 (ISBN 90-221-0173-8). Walter J Johnson.

Faustus, Saint Praeter Sermones Pseudo-Eusebianos Opera. Engelbrecht, A., ed. (Corpus Scriptorum Ecclesiasticorum Latinorum Ser: Vol. 21). 1891. unbound 50.00 (ISBN 0-384-15200-7). Johnson Repr.

Fauth, Roy D. Prayers for All Reasons. 1980. 3.50 (ISBN 0-89536-448-4). CSS of Ohio.

Fautsko, Timothy, jt. auth. see Jorgensen, James.

Fauve-Chamoux, A., jt. auth. see Dupaquier, Jacques.

Fauvel. Le Roman de Fauvel. 1914-19. 34.00 (ISBN 0-384-15220-1); pap. 28.00 (ISBN 0-384-15210-4). Johnson Repr.

Fauvel, John, jt. auth. see Chant, Colin.

Fauver, L. B. Double Eagle & Eagle Gold: American Counters, Pt. I. (Illus.). 100p. 1983. 9.95 (ISBN 0-9607162-1-1). Oak Grove Pubns.

--Exonumia Symbolism & Classification: A Catalogue of Kettle Pieces & an Examination of the Symbolism & Classification of Kettle Pieces & of American Exonumia of the Hard Times, Compromise, & Civil War Periods. (Illus.). 368p. 1982. 60.00 (ISBN 0-9607162-0-3). Oak Grove Pubns.

--Half Eagle Gold: American Counters Part II. (Illus.). 102p. 1985. 9.95 (ISBN 0-9607162-3-8). Oak Grove Pubns.

Fauver, William. The Memory Dynamics System for Memory & Learning Improvement: Summary of the Theory & Methods. 31p. 1982. pap. 4.95 (ISBN 0-939036-02-9). Knowledge Bank.

Fauver, William & Birch, Robert L. Memory Dynamics: A Complete Memory System. 1981. 59.95 (ISBN 0-939036-01-0); spiral binding 44.95 (ISBN 0-939036-00-2). Knowledge Bank.

Faux, David D., jt. auth. see Adams, J. Michael.

Faux, I. D. & Pratt, M. J. Computational Geometry for Designing & Manufacture. LC 78-40637. 329p. 1979. pap. 29.95x (ISBN 0-470-27069-1). Halsted Pr.

Faux, Ian, jt. auth. see Heath, Leslie G.

Faux, Jeff, jt. auth. see Alperovitz, Gar.

Faux, Marian. Clear & Simple Guide to Resume Writing. (Clear & Simple Ser.). 144p. (Orig.). 1982. pap. 6.95 (ISBN 0-671-44678-9). Monarch Pr.

--The Complete Resume Guide. LC 79-12208. (Orig.). 1979. pap. 6.95 (ISBN 0-671-18393-1). Monarch Pr.

--Entering the Job Market: The College Graduate's Guide to Job Hunting. 160p. 1984. pap. 7.95 (ISBN 0-671-50413-4). Monarch Pr.

--The Executive Interview: How to Get One, How to Get Through One, How to Come Out a Winner. 176p. 1985. 15.95 (ISBN 0-312-27428-9). St Martin.

--Resumes for Professional Nurses. (Job Finders Ser.). 144p. (Orig.). 1982. pap. 6.95 (ISBN 0-671-43452-7). Monarch Pr.

--Resumes for Sales & Marketing. (Job Finders Ser.). 144p. (Orig.). 1982. pap. 6.95 (ISBN 0-671-43451-9). Monarch Pr.

--Successful Free-Lancing: The Complete Guide to Establishing & Running Any Kind of Free-Lance Business. LC 82-5595. 256p. 1982. 11.95 (ISBN 0-312-77478-8). St Martin.

Faux, Marian, jt. auth. see Stewart, Marjabelle.

Faux, Marion. Childless by Choice: Choosing Childlessness in the Eighties. LC 83-2038. 216p. 1984. 13.95 (ISBN 0-385-15845-9, Anchor Pr). Doubleday.

--Successful Free-Lancing: The Complete Guide to Establishing & Running Any Kind of Freelance Business. 256p. 1983. pap. 5.95 (ISBN 0-312-77479-6). St Martin.

Faux, William. Memorable Days in America. LC 71-95144. Repr. of 1823 ed. 33.50 (ISBN 0-404-02371-1). AMS Pr.

Fava, Claudio G. & Vigano, Aldo. The Films of Frederico Fellini. (Illus.). 256p. 1985. pap. 9.95 (ISBN 0-8065-0928-7). Citadel Pr.

Fava, R. A., jt. ed. see Marton, L.

Fava, S. F., jt. auth. see Gist, N. P.

Favago, Zadislas. The Last Days of Patton. 1983. pap. 3.95 (ISBN 0-425-06750-5). Berkley Pub.

Favaro, P. J. An Educator's Guide to Microcomputers & Learning. (Illus.). 192p. 1985. 19.95 (ISBN 0-13-240839-2); pap. 14.95 (ISBN 0-13-240821-X). P-H.

Favaro, Peter J. Puzzles, Pirates & Princesses. (Illus.). 200p. (Orig.). (gr. 6-12). Date not set. pap. 9.95 (ISBN 0-88190-399-X, BO399). Datamost.

Favata, Raymond. The Romper Room Song Book of Musical Adventures: Alphabetcha! LC 83-23185. (Illus.). 64p. (ps-2). 1984. 5.95 (ISBN 0-89845-055-1, CB0551). Caedmon.

Favazza, Armando R. & Faheem, Ahmed D. Themes In Cultural Psychiatry: An Annoted Bibliography 1975-1980. LC 82-2738. 208p. 1982. 30.00 (ISBN 0-8262-0377-9). U of MO Pr.

Favazza, Armando R. & Oman, Mary. Anthropological & Cross-Cultural Themes in Mental Health: An Annotated Bibliography, 1925-1974. LC 76-48620. (Univ of Missouri Studies: Vol. 65). 392p. 1977. 30.00x (ISBN 0-8262-0215-2). U of Mo Pr.

Favazza, Auggie & Buckley, Steve. Mariner Mania. McNabb, David, ed. (Illus.). 140p. 1983. pap. 8.95 (ISBN 0-930096-49-5). G Gannett.

Favela, Ramon. Diego Rivera: The Cubist Years. LC 84-60891. (Illus.). 176p. (Orig.). 1984. pap. text ed. 30.00x (ISBN 0-910407-11-8). Phoenix Art.

Favell, Judith E. The Power of Positive Reinforcement: A Handbook of Behavior Modification. (Illus.). 288p. 1977. 20.75 (ISBN 0-398-03620-9). C C Thomas.

Favell, Judith E. & Greene, James W. How to Treat Self-Injurious Behavior. 46p. 1981. 6.00 (ISBN 0-89079-055-8). Pro Ed.

Faver, Catherine A. Women in Transition: Career, Family, & Life Satisfaction in Three Cohorts. 192p. 1984. 27.95 (ISBN 0-03-072026-5). Praeger.

Favero, Giampaolo Bordignon see Bordignon Favero, Giampaolo.

Faversham, Julie O., jt. auth. see Royle, Edwin M.

Faverty, Frederic E. Matthew Arnold the Ethnologist. LC 68-54264. (Northwestern University. Humanities Ser.: No. 27). Repr. of 1951 ed. 25.00 (ISBN 0-404-50727-1). AMS Pr.

Faverty, Frederic E., ed. Victorian Poets: A Guide to Research. 2nd ed. LC 68-15636. 1968. 27.50x (ISBN 0-674-93660-4). Harvard U Pr.

Favez, Gerard, et al, eds. The Cells of the Alveolar Unit. (Current Problems in Clinical Biochemistry Ser.: Vol. 13). (Illus.). 225p. 1983. pap. text ed. 28.00 (ISBN 3-456-81304-X, Pub. by Hans Huber Switzerland). J K Burgess.

Favile, Curtis. Stanzas for an Evening Out: Poems 1968-1977. 1977. 7.50 (ISBN 0-685-04175-1); sewn in wrappers 4.00 (ISBN 0-685-04176-X). L Pubns.

Favill, John. Outline of the Spinal Nerves. (Illus.). 212p. 1946. 24.75x (ISBN 0-398-05133-X). C C Thomas.

Faville, Mary, ed. see De Ford, Tamara.

Favish, Melody. Christmas in Scandinavia. (Illus.). 160p. 1982. write for info. Trollpost.

Favors, Jean. Time Trap. (Micro Adventure Ser.: No. 4). 128p. (Orig.). (gr. 4-7). 1984. pap. 1.95 (ISBN 0-590-33168-X). Scholastic Inc.

Favors, Jean M. The Big Freeze. (Micro Adventure Ser.: No. 8). 128p. (Orig.). (gr. 6 up). 1985. pap. 1.95 (ISBN 0-590-33383-6). Scholastic Inc.

--James Bond in Programmed for Danger. 128p. 1985. pap. 1.95 (ISBN 0-345-32456-0). Ballantine.

Favour, Alpheus H. Old Bill Williams: Mountain Man. LC 62-10767. 234p. 1962. pap. 6.95 (ISBN 0-8061-1698-6). U of Okla Pr.

Favour, John. Antiquitie Triumphing over Noveltie. LC 76-171757. (English Experience Ser.: No. 325). 602p. 1971. Repr. of 1619 ed. 72.00 (ISBN 90-221-0325-0). Walter J Johnson.

Favre, A. & Hasselmann, K., eds. Turbulent Fluxes Through the Sea Surface, Wave Dynamics, & Prediction, Vol. 1. (NATO Conference Series V, Air-Sea Interactions: Vol. 1). 691p. 1978. 89.50x (ISBN 0-306-40005-7, Plenum Pr). Plenum Pub.

Favre, David S. Wildlife: Cases, Law & Policy. LC 82-71698. 277p. (Orig.). 1983. 17.50 (ISBN 0-86733-023-6, #5023). Assoc Faculty Pr.

Favre, David S. & Loring, Murray, eds. Animal Law. LC 82-23130. xii, 253p. 1983. lib. bdg. 35.00 (ISBN 0-89930-021-9, LAL/, Quorum). Greenwood.

Favre, Georges. La Musique francaise de piano avant 1830. LC 76-43917. (Music & Theatre in France in the 17th & 18th Centuries). Repr. of 1953 ed. 22.50 (ISBN 0-404-60158-8). AMS Pr.

Favre, Henri. Larousse des poissons d'aquarium. Rousselet-Blanc, Pierre, ed. (Larousse des animaux familiers). (Illus.). 120p. (Fr.). 1975. 19.25x (ISBN 2-03-014854-7). Larousse.

Favre, Jean-Paul & November, Andre. Color & Communication. 1979. 72.50 (ISBN 0-8038-1273-6). Hastings.

Favre, Jules. Government of the National Defence from the Thirtieth of June to the Thirty-First of October, 1870. Clark, H., tr. Repr. of 1873 ed. 26.00 (ISBN 0-404-07125-2). AMS Pr.

Favret-Saada, Jeanne. Deadly Words. Cullen, Catherine, tr. from Fr. LC 79-41607. (Illus.). 1981. 57.50 (ISBN 0-521-22317-2); pap. text ed. 15.95 (ISBN 0-521-29787-7). Cambridge U Pr.

Favretti, Joy, jt. auth. see Favretti, Rudy.

Favretti, Joy P., jt. auth. see Favretti, Rudy J.

Favretti, Rudy & Favretti, Joy. For Every House a Garden: A Guide for Reproducing Period Gardens (1700-1900) LC 76-51128. (Illus.). 1977. pap. 4.95 (ISBN 0-87106-080-9). Globe Pequot.

Favretti, Rudy J. & Favretti, Joy P. Landscapes & Gardens for Historic Buildings: A Handbook for Reproducing & Creating Authentic Landscape Settings. LC 78-17200. (Illus.). 202p. 1979. pap. 13.00 (ISBN 0-910050-34-1). AASLH Pr.

Faw, Chalmer, ed. Lardin Gabas: A Land, a People, a Church. new ed. (Illus.). 128p. 1973. 2.50 (ISBN 0-87178-511-0). Brethren.

Faw, Marc. A Verdi Discography. 264p. 1983. 21.95 (ISBN 0-937664-63-4). Pilgrim Bks OK.

Faw, Terry. Schaum's Outline of Child Psychology. (Illus., Orig.). 1979. pap. 6.95 (ISBN 0-07-020110-2). McGraw.

Fawaz, Leila T. Merchants & Migrants in Nineteenth Century Beirut. (Harvard Middle Eastern Studies: No. 18). (Illus.). 240p. 1983. text ed. 20.00x (ISBN 0-674-56925-3). Harvard U Pr.

Fawcet, F. J. Peterborough Symposium on Cardiology. 1975. pap. text ed. 30.00x. State Mutual Bk.

Fawcett & Downs. The Relationship of Theory & Research. 1985. pap. write for info. (ISBN 0-8385-8365-2). ACC.

Fawcett, Anthony. John Lennon: One Day at a Time: A Personal Biography of the Seventies. rev. ed. LC 80-8060. (Illus.). 192p. 1981. pap. 8.95 (ISBN 0-394-17754-1, E772, Ever). Grove.

Fawcett, Benjamin. A Compassionate Address to the Christian Negroes in Virginia. LC 72-168011. Repr. of 1756 ed. 11.50 (ISBN 0-404-00258-7). AMS Pr.

Fawcett, Bill. Quest for the Unicorn's Horn. (Swordquest Ser.). 160p. 1985. pap. 2.95 (ISBN 0-441-69715-1). Ace Bks.

Fawcett, Bradly K. The Z8000 Microprocessor: A Design Handbook. (Illus.). 323p. 1982. text ed. 29.95 (ISBN 0-13-983742-6); pap. text ed. 23.95 (ISBN 0-13-983734-5). P-H.

Fawcett, Carolyn, tr. see Chiara, M. L.

Fawcett, Charles & Burn, Richard, eds. The Travels of the Abbe Carre in India & the Near East: 1672 to 1674, 3 vols. in 1. (Hakluyt Society Works Ser.: No. 2, Vols. 95-97). (Illus.). Repr. of 1947 ed. 123.00 (ISBN 0-317-15815-5). Kraus Repr.

Fawcett, Cheryl. Know & Grow, Vol. 1. LC 82-21567. 1983. pap. 4.95 (ISBN 0-87227-086-6). Reg Baptist.

--Know & Grow, Vol. 2. LC 82-21567. 1983. pap. 4.95 (ISBN 0-87227-090-4). Reg Baptist.

Fawcett, Chris. The New Japanese House: Ritual & Anti-Ritual Patterns of Dwelling. LC 80-8224. (Icon Editions Ser.). (Illus.). 192p. 1981. 25.00i (ISBN 0-06-433010-9, HarpT). Har-Row.

Fawcett, Clara H. On Making, Mending & Dressing Dolls. 170p. 1975. pap. 6.95 (ISBN 0-87588-105-X). Hobby Hse.

Fawcett, David M. & Callander, Lee A. Native American Painting: Selections from the Museum of the American Indian. 96p. 1982. pap. 15.95x (ISBN 0-934490-40-6). Mus Am Ind.

Fawcett, Don. The Cell. 2nd ed. (Illus.). 928p. 1981. text ed. 40.00 (ISBN 0-7216-3584-9). Saunders.

Fawcett, Don W. & Newburne, James W. Workshop on Cellular & Molecular Toxicology. LC 79-26853. 300p. Repr. of 1980 ed. 22.00 (ISBN 0-683-06996-9). Krieger.

Fawcett, Don W., jt. auth. see Bloom, William.

Fawcett, Don W. & Bedford, Michael J., eds. Spermatozoon: Maturation, Motility, Surface Properties & Comparative Aspects. LC 79-9196. (Illus.). 464p. 1979. text ed. 60.00 (ISBN 0-8067-0601-5). Urban & S.

Fawcett, E. Douglas. Hartmann the Anarchist: The Doom of the Great City. LC 74-15970. (Science Fiction Ser). (Illus.). 222p. 1975. Repr. of 1893 ed. 20.00x (ISBN 0-405-06290-7). Ayer Co Pubs.

Fawcett, Edgar. The Buntling Ball: A Graeco-American Play & Social Satire. facsimile ed. LC 75-908. (Leisure Class in America Ser.). 1975. Repr. of 1885 ed. 14.00x (ISBN 0-405-06940-5). Ayer Co Pubs.

--Hopeless Case. facs. ed. LC 76-85683. (American Fiction Reprint Ser). 1880. 17.00 (ISBN 0-8369-7012-8). Ayer Co Pubs.

--Social Silhouettes: Being the Impressions of Mr. Mark Manhattan. fascimile ed. LC 75-1846. (Leisure Class in America Ser.). 1975. Repr. of 1885 ed. 22.00x (ISBN 0-405-06913-8). Ayer Co Pubs.

Fawcett, Edmund & Thomas, Tony. The American Condition. LC 81-48033. 448p. 1982. 18.22i (ISBN 0-06-038030-6, HarpT). Har-Row.

Fawcett, F. J., ed. Cardiology: Peterborough Symposium. 1975. pap. 11.95x (ISBN 0-8464-1081-8). Beekman Pubs.

Fawcett, Henry. The Economic Position of the British Labourer. LC 83-48478. (The World of Labour-English Workers' 1850-1890 Ser.). 256p. 1984. lib. bdg. 30.00 (ISBN 0-8240-5706-6). Garland Pub.

--Pauperism: Its Causes & Remedies. LC 74-1334. Repr. of 1871 ed. lib. bdg. 27.50x (ISBN 0-678-01067-6). Kelley.

Fawcett, Howard. Hazardous & Toxic Materials: Safe Handling & Disposal. LC 84-5148. 296p. 1984. text ed. 35.00x (ISBN 0-471-80483-5, Pub. by Wiley Interscience). Wiley.

Fawcett, Howard H., ed. Safety & Accident Prevention in Chemical Operations. 2nd ed. Wood, William S. LC 82-2623. 910p. 1982. 91.00 (ISBN 0-471-02435-X, Pub. by Wiley-Interscience). Wiley.

Fawcett, J. E. Outer Space: New Challenges in Law & Policy. (Illus.). 1984. 24.95x (ISBN 0-19-825398-2). Oxford U Pr.

Fawcett, J. E. & Parry, Audrey. Law & International Resource Conflicts. 1981. 59.00x (ISBN 0-19-825359-1). Oxford U Pr.

Fawcett, J. R. Hydraulic Circuits & Control Systems. 240p. 1982. 110.00x (ISBN 0-85461-078-2, Pub. by Trade & Tech). State Mutual Bk.

--Hydraulic Servo-Mechanisms & Their Applications. 130p. 1979. 65.00x (ISBN 0-85461-026-X, Pub. by Trade & Tech). State Mutual Bk.

--Pneumatic Circuits & Low Cost Automation. 150p. 1969. 25.00x (ISBN 0-85461-029-4, Pub. by Trade & Tech England). Brookfield Pub Co.

--Pneumatic Circuits & Low Cost Automation. 150p. 1982. 70.00x (Trade & Tech). State Mutual Bk.

Fawcett, Jacqueline. Analysis & Evaluation of Conceptual Models of Nursing. LC 83-5340. 307p. 1983. 19.95x (ISBN 0-8036-3409-9). Davis Co.

Fawcett, James. International Economic Conflicts: Their Prevention & Resolution. LC 77-374401. 1977. 20.00x (ISBN 0-905118-06-5). Intl Pubns Serv.

--Law & Power in International Relations. 144p. 1982. 23.95 (ISBN 0-571-10537-8). Faber & Faber.

Fawcett, James T. Psychology & Population: Behavioral Research Issues in Fertility & Family Planning. LC 70-137425. 149p. (Orig.). 1970. pap. text ed. 3.95 (ISBN 0-87834-001-7). Population Coun.

Fawcett, James T. see Arnold, Fred, et al.

Fawcett, James T., jt. auth. see Bulatao, Rodolfo A.

Fawcett, James T., jt. ed. see Chen, Peter S.

Fawcett, James T., et al, eds. Women in the Cities of Asia: Migration & Urban Adaptation. 365p. 1984. pap. 23.50x (ISBN 0-86531-814-X). Westview.

Fawcett, Jane, ed. Seven Victorian Architects. LC 76-42090. (Illus.). 1977. 19.75x (ISBN 0-271-00500-9). Pa St U Pr.

Fawcett, John. Christ Precious to Those That Believe. 1979. 10.00 (ISBN 0-86524-026-4, 8901). Klock & Klock.

Fawcett, Kenneth, et al, eds. HLA Techniques for Blood Bankers. (Illus.). 175p. 1984. text ed. 30.00 (ISBN 0-915355-00-0). Am Assn Blood.

Fawcett, Lawrence & Greenwood, Barry J. Clear Intent: The Government Cover-Up of the UFO Experience. 272p. 1984. 15.95 (ISBN 0-13-136656-4); pap. 8.95 (ISBN 0-13-136649-1). P-H.

Fawcett, L'Estrange. Film Facts & Forecasts. lib. bdg. 59.95 (ISBN 0-8490-1830-7). Gordon Pr.

Fawcett, Marion, jt. auth. see Crowther, S. J.

Fawcett, Millicent. What I Remember. LC 74-33939. (Pioneers of the Woman's Movement Ser.). (Illus.). 272p. 1975. Repr. of 1925 ed. 19.50 (ISBN 0-88355-261-2). Hyperion-Conn.

Fawcett, Mrs. H. Some Eminent Women of Our Times. 1889. Repr. 20.00 (ISBN 0-8274-3454-5). R West.

Fawcett, Richard G. & National Federation of State High School Associations. Debating United States Welfare Reform: A Preliminary Analysis. LC 83-174249. (National Federation Pubns. Ser.). 118p. 1984. 4.95. Natl Fed High Schl Assns.

Fawcett, Robin P. Cognitive Linguistics & Social Interaction. Towards an Integrated Model of a Systemic Functional Grammar & the other Components of a Communicating Mind. (Exeter Linguistic Studies Ser.: No. 3). xiv, 290p. (Orig.). 1980. pap. 17.00x (ISBN 3-87276-228-1, Pub. by J Groos W Germany). Benjamins North Am.

Fawcett, Robin P., et al, eds. The Semiotics of Culture & Language Vol. 1: Language as Social Semiotic. LC 83-242230. (Open Linguistics Ser.). 166p. 1984. 25.00 (ISBN 0-86187-295-9). F Pinter Pubs.

--The Semiotics of Culture & Language Vol. 2: Language & Other Semiotic Systems of Culture. LC 83-242230. (Open Linguistics Ser.). 179p. 1984. 25.00 (ISBN 0-86187-469-2, Pub. by Frances Pinter). Longwood Pub Group.

Fawcett, Sarah, ed. see Clement, Olivier.

Fawcett, Stephen B., jt. auth. see Borck, Leslie E.

Fawcett, Stephen B., jt. auth. see Mathews, R. Mark.

Fawcett, Susan & Sandberg, Alvin. Evergreen: A Guide to Writing. 2nd ed. 400p. 1983. pap. text ed. 15.95 (ISBN 0-395-34107-8); instr's manual 1.00 (ISBN 0-395-34108-6); instr's support package 1.50 (ISBN 0-395-35615-6). HM.

--Grassroots: The Writer's Handbook. 2d ed. 288p. 1982. pap. text ed. 15.95 (ISBN 0-395-32572-2); instr's. annotated ed. 16.95 (ISBN 0-395-32573-0); test package 2.25 (ISBN 0-395-33177-3). HM.

--Grassroots: The Writer's Workbook, Form B. LC 80-68139. 272p. 1981. pap. text ed. 15.95 (ISBN 0-395-29726-5); instr's. manual 0.50 (ISBN 0-395-29727-3). HM.

Fawcette, Bill. Quest for the Dragon's Eye. (Swordquest Ser.). 160p. 1985. pap. 2.95 (ISBN 0-441-69709-7). Ace Bks.

Fawkes, Charles, ed. see Donne, John.

Fawkes, Richard. Dion Boucicault. 21.95 (ISBN 0-7043-2221-8, Pub. by Quartet England). Charles River Bks.

--Dion Boucicault: A Biography. (Illus.). 280p. 1983. 21.95 (ISBN 0-7043-2221-8, Pub. by Quartet Bks); pap. 11.95 (ISBN 0-7043-3406-2). Merrimack Pub Cir.

Fawkes, Richard, jt. auth. see Langdon, Michael.

Fawkes, Sandy. Killing Time: Journey into Nightmare. LC 78-27405. (Illus.). 1979. 8.95 (ISBN 0-8008-4463-7). Taplinger.

Fawkes, Wally. The World of Trog. (Illus.). 96p. 1977. bds. 8.75x (ISBN 0-8476-3128-1). Rowman.

Fawkner, H. W. Timescapes of John Fowles. LC 82-48606. 180p. 1983. 19.50 (ISBN 0-8386-3175-4). Fairleigh Dickinson.

Fawssett, John. North Aegean Islands. (Greek Island Ser.). 160p. (Orig.). 1984. pap. 9.95 (ISBN 0-903909-29-4, Pub. by Roger Lascelles England). Bradt Ent.

Fawtier, Robert. Capetian Kings of France: Monarchy & Nation, 987-1328. (Illus.). 1969. pap. 14.95 (ISBN 0-312-11900-3). St Martin.

Fawzy, F., jt. ed. see Gaind, T.

Fax, Elton. Hashar. 1980. 5.95 (ISBN 0-8285-1845-9, Pub. by Progress Pubs USSR). Imported Pubns.

Faxn. Jean-Louis Forain. 1982. lib. bdg. 91.00 (ISBN 0-8240-9343-7). Garland Pub.

Faxon, Alicia. Jean-Louis Forain: Artist, Realist, Humanist. LC 82-82986. (Illus.). 56p. 1982. pap. 6.00 (ISBN 0-88397-042-2, Pub. by Intl Exhibit Foun). C E Tuttle.

Faxon, Alicia, jt. auth. see Brayer, Yves.

Faxon, Alicia C. Jean-Louis Forain: A Catalogue Raisonne of the Prints. (Art & Architecture Ser.). 500p. 1982. lib. bdg. 83.00 (ISBN 0-8240-9343-7). Garland Pub.

--Women & Jesus. LC 72-11868. 1973. 4.95 (ISBN 0-8298-0244-4). Pilgrim NY.

Faxon, F. W. Literary Annuals & Gift Books. 224p. 1981. 60.00x (ISBN 0-686-79272-6, Pub. by Private Libs England). State Mutual Bk.

Faxon, Nathaniel W. Massachusetts General Hospital, 1935-1955. LC 59-12968. (Illus.). 1959. 30.00x (ISBN 0-674-55150-8). Harvard U Pr.

Fax Stangways, A. H. Cecil Sharp. (Music Reprint Ser.). 1980. Repr. of 1933 ed. lib. bdg. 25.00 (ISBN 0-306-76019-3). Da Capo.

Fay. Beaumarchais ou La Fredaine de Figaro. 16.95 (ISBN 0-685-34032-5). French & Eur.

--Heidegger: The Critique of Logic. 1977. pap. 26.00 (ISBN 90-247-1931-3, Pub. by Martinus Nijhoff Netherlands). Kluwer Academic.

Fay, et al, eds. Hearing & Sound Communication in Fishes: Proceedings in Life Sciences Ser. (Illus.). 704p. 1981. 59.00 (ISBN 0-387-90590-1). Springer-Verlag.

Fay, Allen, jt. auth. see Lazarus, Arnold.

Fay, Amy. Music Study in Germany. (Music Reprint Ser.: 1979). 1979. Repr. of 1880 ed. lib. bdg. 39.50 (ISBN 0-306-79541-8). Da Capo.

Fay, Ann, ed. see Anderson, Leone C.

Fay, Ann, ed. see Aylesworth, Jim.

Fay, Ann, ed. see Bernstein, Joanne, et al.

Fay, Ann, ed. see Bernstein, Joanne & Cohen, Paul.

Fay, Ann, ed. see Bernstein, Joanne E. & Cohen, Paul.

Fay, Ann, ed. see Broekel, Ray & White, Laurence B., Jr.

Fay, Ann, ed. see Bunting, Eve.

Fay, Ann, ed. see Christian, Mary B.

Fay, Ann, ed. see Cohen, Peter Z.

Fay, Ann, ed. see Collins, Pat L.

Fay, Ann, ed. see Corey, Dorothy.

Fay, Ann, ed. see DeBruyn, Monica.

Fay, Ann, ed. see Delton, Judy.

Fay, Ann, ed. see Green, Phyllis.

Fay, Ann, ed. see Heide, Florence P. & Heide, Roxanne.

Fay, Ann, ed. see Kline, Suzy W.

Fay, Ann, ed. see Lapp, Eleanor.

Fay, Ann, ed. see Miescke, Lori.

Fay, Ann, ed. see Mueller, Virginia.

Fay, Ann, ed. see Nixon, Joan L.

Fay, Ann, ed. see Osborn, Lois.

Fay, Ann, ed. see Pape, Donna L.

Fay, Ann, ed. see Smith, Carole.

Fay, Ann, ed. see Stanek, Muriel.

Fay, Ann, ed. see Velde, Vivian V.

Fay, Ann, ed. see Vigna, Judith.

Fay, Anne, ed. see Broekel, Ray & White, Laurence B., Jr.

Fay, Anne, ed. see Latta, Richard.

Fay, Bernard. American Experiment. 1969. Repr. of 1929 ed. 24.50x (ISBN 0-8046-0142-9, Pub. by Kennikat). Assoc Faculty Pr.

--Bibliographie Critique des Ouvrages Francais Relatifs Aux Etats-Unis 1770-1800. LC 68-56725. 1968. 15.00 (ISBN 0-8337-1102-4). B Franklin.

--Franklin: The Apostle of Modern Times. 1929. 30.00 (ISBN 0-8274-2370-5). R West.

--Revolutionary Spirit in France & America. Guthrie, Ramon, tr. LC 66-26824. Repr. of 1927 ed. 28.50 (ISBN 0-8154-0067-5). Cooper Sq.

--Roosevelt & His America. 59.95 (ISBN 0-8490-0970-7). Gordon Pr.

--Two Franklins. LC 70-93277. Repr. of 1933 ed. 18.50 (ISBN 0-404-02372-X). AMS Pr.

Fay, Brian. Social Theory & Political Practice. (Controversies in Sociology). 1975. pap. text ed. 8.95x (ISBN 0-04-300048-7). Allen Unwin.

Fay, C. E. see Marton, L.

Fay, Charles & Wallace, Marc J., Jr. Research Based Decisions. Donnelly, Paul S., ed. 1985. text ed. 21.95 (ISBN 0-394-32869-8, RanC); price not set tchr's. ed. Random.

Fay, Charles H., jt. auth. see Wallace, Marc J., Jr.

Fay, Charles R. Imperial Economy & Its Place in the Formation of Economic Doctrine. LC 74-29638. 151p. 1975. Repr. of 1934 ed. lib. bdg. 22.50x (ISBN 0-8371-8007-4, FAIE). Greenwood.
--World of Adam Smith. 1960. 15.00x (ISBN 0-678-08053-4). Kelley.
Fay, Clifford T., Jr., jt. auth. see Tarr, Stanley B.
Fay, Clifford T., Jr., et al. Managerial Accounting for the Hospitality Service Industries. 2nd ed. 616p. 1976. text ed. write for info (ISBN 0-697-08406-X); instrs.' manual avail. (ISBN 0-697-08415-9). Wm C Brown.
--Basic Financial Accounting for the Hospitality Industry. rev. ed. Berman, Susan, ed. 1982. 26.95 (ISBN 0-86612-010-6). Educ Inst Am Hotel.
Fay, Dick, jt. auth. see Bowen, Rich.
Fay, E. G. Ruben Dario in New York. 59.95 (ISBN 0-8490-0977-4). Gordon Pr.
Fay, Edward A. Concordance of the Divina Commedia. LC 68-26352. (Studies in Italian Literature, No. 46). 1969. Repr. of 1888 ed. lib. bdg. 79.95x (ISBN 0-8383-0183-5). Haskell.
Fay, Eliot G. Lorenzo in Search of the Sun: D. H. Lawrence in Italy, Mexico & the American Southwest. LC 76-168012. Repr. of 1953 ed. 11.50 (ISBN 0-404-02373-8). AMS Pr.
Fay, F. H., et al, eds. A Field Manual of Procedures for Postmortem Examination of Alaskan Marine Mammals. (IMS Report Ser.: No. R79-1). write for info. (ISBN 0-914500-09-0). U of AK Inst Marine.
Fay, Francesca C. & Smith, Kathy S. Childbearing after Thirty-Five: The Risks & the Rewards. 192p. 1985. 17.95 (ISBN 0-917439-08-2); pap. 9.95 (ISBN 0-917439-05-8). Balsam Pr.
Fay, H. C., ed. & intro. by see Plautus.
Fay, Irene. Daybook from a Kitchen Drawer. LC 85-13490. (Illus.). 1985. 16.95 (ISBN 0-915361-25-6). Adama Pubs Inc.
Fay, James, et al. CA Almanac: 1986-1987. (Illus.). 696p. 1985. pap. 12.95 (ISBN 0-89141-244-1). Presidio Pr.
Fay, James, et al, eds. The California Almanac 1984-1985. (Illus.). 696p. (Orig.). 1985. pap. 12.95 (ISBN 0-89141-153-4). Presidio Pr.
Fay, Jennifer, jt. auth. see Adams, Caren.
Fay, Jessica B. & Oliver, Merle J. We Love to Cook (If It's Easy) LC 75-2850. (Illus.). 123p. 1975. pap. 3.95 (ISBN 0-88435-003-7). Chateau Pub.
Fay, John. Approaches to Criminal Justice Training. 264p. (Orig.). 1979. pap. 12.00x (ISBN 0-89854-051-8). U. of GA Inst Govt.
--The Helicopter: History, Piloting & How It Flies. LC 76-54073. (Illus.). 1977. 15.95 (ISBN 0-7153-7249-1). David & Charles.
Fay, Judith, jt. auth. see Davidson, Audrey.
Fay, Leo, compiled by. Organization & Administration of School Reading Programs. (Reading Research Profiles Bibliography Ser.). 1975. 2.00 (ISBN 0-87207-821-3). Intl Reading.
--Reading in the Content Fields. rev. ed. (Annotated Bibliographies Ser.). 1975. 1.25 (ISBN 0-87207-302-5). Intl Reading.
Fay, Loren V., jt. auth. see Clint, Florence.
Fay, Marie. Children's Dreams. 1982. pap. 1.50 (ISBN 0-939878-06-2). Dreams Unltd.
Fay, Marion, jt. auth. see Winnett, Tom.
Fay, Martha. A Mortal Condition. 352p. 1984. pap. 3.95 (ISBN 0-425-07196-0). Berkley Pub.
--A Mortal Condition: Eight Stories of Survival, Hope & Loss. 352p. 1983. 16.95 (ISBN 0-698-11251-2, Coward). Putnam Pub Group.
Fay, Mary S. War of Eighteen-Twelve Veterans in Texas. McFarland, Mae W., ed. LC 79-53367. 1979. 27.50 (ISBN 0-686-27003-7). Polyanthos.
Fay, Peter. The Blue-Greens. (Studies in Biology: No. 160). 80p. 1984. pap. text ed. 8.95 (ISBN 0-7131-2878-X). E Arnold.
Fay, Peter W. The Opium War, 1840-1842. (Illus.). 432p. 1976. pap. 8.95x (ISBN 0-393-00823-1). Norton.
--The Opium War, 1840-1842. LC 74-30200. (Illus.). xxi, 406p. 1975. 29.50 (ISBN 0-8078-1243-9). U of NC Pr.
Fay, R. R., jt. ed. see Popper, A. N.
Fay, Rimmon C. Southern California's Deteriorating Marine Environment: An Evaluation of the Health of the Benthic Marine Biota of Ventura, Los Angeles & Orange Counties. LC 72-83453. (Environmental Studies Ser: No. 2). (Illus.). 76p. 1972. pap. 4.50x (ISBN 0-912102-06-3). Cal Inst Public.
Fay, Sir Sam. The War Office at War. 1976. Repr. 15.00x (ISBN 0-85409-883-6). Charles River Bks.
Fay, Sidney B. & Epstein, Klaus. Rise of Brandenburg-Prussia to 1786. LC 81-8334. 156p. 1981. pap. text ed. 5.50 (ISBN 0-89874-377-X). Krieger.
Fay, Sidney B., tr. see Fueter, Eduard.
Fay, Stephan. Beyond Greed. (Illus.). 304p. 1983. pap. 6.95 (ISBN 0-14-006688-8). Penguin.
Fay, Stephen. The Ring: Anatomy of an Opera. (Illus.). 218p. 1985. 25.00 (ISBN 0-89341-532-4). Longwood Pub Group.
Fay, Theodore S. Norman Leslie: A Tale of Present Times, 2 vols. LC 78-64072. Repr. of 1835 ed. 75.00 set (ISBN 0-404-17250-4). AMS Pr.
--Norman Leslie: A Tale of Present Times. 1972. Repr. of 1835 ed. lib. bdg. 32.00 (ISBN 0-8422-8044-8). Irvington.
Fay, W. Emerging Language in Autistic Children. (Illus.). 232p. 1980. text ed. 19.95 (ISBN 0-8391-1586-5). Univ Park.
Fay, Warren H. Temporal Sequence in the Perception of Speech. (Janua Linguarum, Ser. Minor: No. 45). (Orig.). 1966. pap. text ed. 13.60x (ISBN 90-2790-579-7). Mouton.
Fayad, Marwan & Motamen, Homa. Economics of the Petrochemical Industry. 180p. 1985. 27.50x (ISBN 0-312-23444-9). St Martin.
Faye, C. U. see De Ricci, S. & Wilson, W. J.
Faye, Eleanor E. Clinical Low Vision. 1976. pap. 19.95 (ISBN 0-316-27620-0). Little.
--Clinical Low Vision. 2nd ed. 505p. 1984. pap. text ed. 28.50 (ISBN 0-316-27621-9). Little.
--The Low Vision Patient. LC 76-117150. 256p. 1970. 43.50 (ISBN 0-8089-0654-2, 791230). Grune.
Faye, Eleanor E. & Hood, Clare M. Low Vision: A Symposium Marking the 20th Anniversary of the Lighthouse Low Vision Service. (Illus.). 320p. 1975. photocopy ed. 39.50x (ISBN 0-398-03372-2). C C Thomas.
Faye, Eugene De. Gnostiques et Gnosticisme: Etude Critique Des Documents Du Gnosticisme Chretien Aux Deuxieme et Troisieme Siecles. LC 77-84699. Repr. of 1913 ed. 34.00 (ISBN 0-404-16106-5). AMS Pr.
Faye, Sondra. Play Infinity. LC 82-62908. 75p. 1983. 3.95 (ISBN 0-938232-27-4). Winston-Derek.
Fayed, A. A. Flora of Egypt. Hadidi, Nabil M., ed. (Taeckholmia Additional Ser.: No. 1: 93-97 (1980) Family 162. Globulariaceae). (Illus.). 5p. 1981. 6.75x (ISBN 0-686-34408-1). Lubrecht & Cramer.
Fayed, M. E. & Otten, Lambert, eds. Handbook of Powder Science & Technology. (Illus.). 656p. 1984. 79.50 (ISBN 0-442-22610-1). Van Nos Reinhold.
Fayemi, A. Olusegun. Pathology Speciality Board Review. 5th ed. 1983. pap. text ed. 28.50 (ISBN 0-87488-305-9). Med Exam.
Fayemi, A. Olusegun, jt. auth. see Ali, Majid.
Fayemi, A. Olusegun, et al. Medical Examination Review: Pathology. 8th ed. 1984. pap. text ed. write for info. (ISBN 0-87488-267-2). Med Exam.
Fayen, E. G., jt. auth. see Lancaster, F. W.
Fayen, Emily G. The Online Catalog: Improving Public Access to Library Materials. LC 83-12009. (Professional Librarian Ser.). 148p. 1983. professional o.s.i. 34.50 (ISBN 0-86729-054-4); pap. 27.50 professional (ISBN 0-86729-053-6, 235-BW). Knowledge Indus.
Fayers, F. J. Enhanced Oil Recovery. (Developments in Petroleum Science Ser.: Vol. 13). 596p. 1981. 78.75 (ISBN 0-444-42033-9). Elsevier.
Fayers, Heather. Small Claims Court Guide for British Columbia. 6th ed. 136p. 1981. 5.95 (ISBN 0-88908-131-X). Self Counsel Pr.
Fayerweather, John. Facts & Fallacies of International Business. LC 84-690. vii, 184p. 1984. Repr. of 1962 ed. lib. bdg. 29.75x (ISBN 0-313-24218-6, FAFF). Greenwood.
--Host National Attitudes Toward Multinational Corporations. LC 81-13875. 366p. 1982. 44.95 (ISBN 0-03-059776-5). Praeger.
--International Business Strategy & Administration. 2nd ed. LC 82-1784. 568p. 1982. text ed. 27.50x (ISBN 0-88410-889-9). Ballinger Pub.
Fayerweather Street School. The Kids' Book of Divorce. Rofes, Eric, ed. LC 80-28831. 112p. 1981. 9.95 (ISBN 0-86616-003-5). Greene.
Fayerweather Street School Staff. The Kids' Book about Death & Dying. Rofes, Eric, ed. 132p. (gr. 5 up). 1985. 13.95 (ISBN 0-316-75390-4). Little.
Fayette, Marie-Madeleine De La see De La Fayette, Marie-Madeleine.
Fay-Halle, Antoinette & Mundt, Barbara. Porcelain of the Nineteenth Century. LC 82-50108. (Illus.). 296p. 1982. 85.00 (ISBN 0-8478-0437-2). Rizzoli Intl.
Fayle, C. Ernest. The War & the Shipping Industry. (Economic & Social History of the World War, British Ser.). 1927. 75.00x (ISBN 0-317-27655-7). Elliots Bks.
Fayod, V. Prodrome D'Une Histoire Naturelle Des Agaricinees. 1968. Repr. of 1889 ed. 14.00 (ISBN 90-6123-064-0). Lubrecht & Cramer.
Fayolle, G., jt. ed. see Baccelli, F.
Fayre, Jillian. Whispers of the Heart. 192p. 1981. pap. 2.95 (ISBN 0-671-43867-0, Wallaby). S&S.
Fazelas, Gy I & Kosa, F. Forensic Fetal Osteology. 1979. 41.50 (ISBN 0-9960011-9-0, Pub. by Akademiai Kaido Hungary). Heyden.
Fazey, C. The Aetiology of Psychoactive Substance Use: A Report & Critically Annotated Bibliography on Research into the Aetiology of Alcohol, Nicotine, Opiate & Other Psychoactive Substance Use. 226p. (With the Financial Support of the United Nations Fund for Drug Abruse Control). 1977. pap. 18.00 (ISBN 92-3-101508-7, U776, UNESCO). Unipub.
Fazia, Alba Della see Anouilh, Jean.
Fazio, Anthony F. A Concurrent Validation Study of the NCHS' General Well-Being Schedule. Stevenson, Taloria, ed. (Series 2: No. 73). 1977. pap. 1.95 (ISBN 0-8406-0105-0). Natl Ctr Health Stats.
Fazio, Antoinette & Ritota, Michael C. Johnny Goes to the Doctor. (Illus.). 41p. (gr. k-1). 1982. 5.95 (ISBN 0-8059-2846-4). Dorrance.
Fazio, G. G., ed. Infrared & Submillimeter Astronomy. (Astrophysics & Space Science Library: No. 63). 1977. lib. bdg. 34.00 (ISBN 90-277-0791-X, Pub. by Reidel Holland). Kluwer Academic.
Fazio, G. G., et al, eds. Astronomy from Space: Proceedings of the Topical Meeting of the COSPAR Interdisciplinary Scientific Commission E (Meetings E3, E4, & E5) of the COSPAR 25th Plenary Meeting held in Graz, Austria, 25 June - 7 July 1984. (Illus.). 220p. 1985. pap. 49.50 (ISBN 0-08-033192-0, PUb by PPL). Pergamon.
Fazio, James R. The Woodland Steward: A Practical Guide to the Management of Small Private Forests. (Illus.). 220p. (Orig.). Date not set. pap. 14.95 (ISBN 0-9615031-0-6). Woodland ID.
Fazio, James R. & Gilbert, Douglas. Public Relations & Communication for Natural Resource Managers. 400p. 1981. text ed. 24.95 (ISBN 0-8403-2439-1). Kendall-Hunt.
Fazio, Michael, jt. ed. see Craycroft, Robert.
Fazio, Michael W. & Prenshaw, Peggy W., eds. Order & Image in the American Small Town. LC 80-24300. (Southern Quarterly Ser.). 1981. 12.50x (ISBN 0-87805-130-9). U Pr of Miss.
Fazl-i-Ali. Dictionary of Persian & English Languages. 668p. (Persian & Eng.). 1979. Repr. of 1885 ed. 39.00x (ISBN 0-89684-266-5, Pub. by Cosmo Pubns India). Orient Bk Dist.
Fazzalare, Graciela L. Woodcarving Simplified. LC 83-70780. (Illus.). 208p. 1983. 16.95; pap. 10.95 (ISBN 0-8019-7149-7). Chilton.
Fazzini, Eugene, et al. A Manual for Surgical Pathologists. (Illus.). 112p. 1972. photocopy ed. 13.75x (ISBN 0-398-02277-1). C C Thomas.
Fazzini, Eugene P. Interpretation of Lung Biopsies. (Biopsy Interpretation Ser.). Date not set. write for info. (ISBN 0-89004-332-9, 469). Raven.
Fazzini, Richard A. Art from the Age of Akhenaten. LC 73-87455. (Illus.). 1974. pap. 0.75 (ISBN 0-87273-000-X). Bklyn Mus.
--Images for Eternity. LC 75-13976. (Illus.). 1975. pap. 12.00 (ISBN 0-913696-27-7). Bklyn Mus.
Fazzolare, R. A. & Smith, C. B. Changing Energy Use, Vol. 1. 165.00 (ISBN 0-08-025559-0). Pergamon.
--Changing Energy Use Futures, Vol. 2. 165.00 (ISBN 0-08-025560-4). Pergamon.
--Changing Energy Use Futures, Vol. 3. 165.00 (ISBN 0-08-025561-2). Pergamon.
--Changing Energy Use Futures, Vol. 4. 165.00 (ISBN 0-08-025562-0). Pergamon.
Fazzolare, Rocco A. & Smith, Craig B. Changing Energy Use Futures: Second International Conference on Energy Use Management, October 1979, L. A., Ca, 4 vols. (Illus.). 1979. 525.00 (ISBN 0-08-025099-8). Pergamon.
Fazzolari, R., jt. auth. see Third International Conference on Energy Use Management (ICEUM), Berlin, 26-30 October, 1981.
Fazzone, Roger A. Working with Troubled Children & Youth. 1979. pap. text ed. 5.95 (ISBN 0-89669-024-5). Collegium Bk Pubs.
Fe, Lu. God Bless Our HUD Home: Downtowner Congregate Housing. 1983. 7.95 (ISBN 0-533-05597-0). Vantage.
Fea, Allan. Secret Chambers & Hiding-Places. rev. ed. 3rd ed. LC 79-155739. 1971. Repr. of 1901 ed. 45.00x (ISBN 0-8103-3385-6). Gale.
Fea, Valerie. Multi-Media Librarian. 127p. 1982. 30.00x (ISBN 0-85225-754-6, Pub. by Careers Con England). State Mutual Bk.
Feachem, R. G., jt. auth. see Cairncross, S.
Feachem, Richard, jt. ed. see Bayliss-Smith, Timothy.
Feachem, Richard, et al. Water, Health & Development: An Interdisciplinary Evaluation. 286p. 1981. 35.00x (ISBN 0-905402-06-5, Pub. by Tri-Med England). State Mutual Bk.
Feachem, Richard, et al, eds. Water, Wastes & Health in Hot Climates. LC 76-18946. 399p. 1977. 63.95x (ISBN 0-471-99410-3, Pub. by Wiley-Interscience). Wiley.
Feachem, Richard G. & Bradley, David J. Appropriate Technology for Water Supply & Sanitation: Health Aspects of Excreta & Sullage Management - A State-of-the-Art Review, Vol. 3. 303p. 1980. pap. 15.00 (ISBN 0-686-39785-1, WS-8005). World Bank.
Feachem, Richard G., et al. Sanitation & Disease: Health Aspects of Excreta & Wastewater. 501p. 1983. 74.95x (ISBN 0-471-90094-X, Pub. by Wiley-Interscience). Wiley.
Fead, Lou. Easy Diver. (Illus., Orig.). pap. 4.95 (ISBN 0-918888-02-6). Deepstar Pubns.
Fead, Lou, ed. see International Conference on Underwater Education, 10th, Anaheim, California, November 9-13, 1978.
Fead, Lou, ed. see International Conference on Underwater Education, 9th, Miami Beach, Fla., Sep. 29 - Oct. 2, 1977.
Feagans, Lynne & Garvey, Catherine. The Origins & Growth of Communication. LC 83-10041. 432p. 1984. 39.50 (ISBN 0-89391-164-X). Ablex Pub.
Feagans, Lynne, ed. The Language of Children Reared in Poverty: Implications for Evaluation & Interventions. LC 81-14939. (Educational Psychology Ser.). 1981. 34.00 (ISBN 0-12-249980-8). Acad Pr.
Feagans, Lynne, jt. ed. see McKinney, James D.
Feagans, Raymond J. The Railroad That Ran by the Tide. (Illus.). 146p. 1981. Repr. of 1972 ed. 15.00 (ISBN 0-8310-7094-3). Howell-North.
Feagin, Clairece, jt. auth. see Feagin, Joseph.
Feagin, Crawford. Variation & Change in Alabama English: A Sociolinguistic Study of the White Community. 395p. 1979. pap. text ed. 10.95 (ISBN 0-87840-210-1). Georgetown U Pr.
Feagin, Joe. The Urban Real Estate Game: Playing Monopoly With Real Money. 252p. 1983. 14.95 (ISBN 0-13-937797-2); pap. 7.95 (ISBN 0-13-937789-1). P-H.
Feagin, Joe R. Ghetto Social Structure: A Survey of Black Bostonians. LC 74-21138. 1975. soft bdg. 11.00 (ISBN 0-88247-308-5). R & E Pubs.
--Racial & Ethnic Relations. 2nd ed. (Illus.). 400p. 1984. text ed. 27.95 (ISBN 0-13-750125-0). P-H.
--Social Problems: A Critical Power - Conflict Perspective. (Illus.). 432p. (Orig.). 1982. pap. 22.95 (ISBN 0-13-817338-9). P-H.
--Social Problems: A Critical Power Conflict Perspective. 2nd ed. (Illus.). 448p. 1986. text ed. 22.95 (ISBN 0-13-817362-1). P H.
Feagin, Joe R., jt. ed. see Stephan, Walter G.
Feagin, Joseph & Feagin, Clairece. Discrimination American Style: Institutional Racism & Sexism. LC 78-6197. 1978. (Spec); pap. 4.95 (ISBN 0-13-215889-2). P-H.
Feagin, Susan, jt. auth. see Kirsch, Elisabeth.
Feagins, Mary E. Tending the Light. 1984. pap. 5.00x (ISBN 0-87574-255-6, 255). Pendle Hill.
Fear, Daniel E., ed. Surviving the Unexpected: A Curriculum Guide for Wilderness Survival & Survival from Natural & Man Made Disasters. rev., 3rd ed. (Illus.). 91p. 1974. spiral bdg. 5.00 (ISBN 0-913724-00-9). Survival Ed Assoc.
Fear, David E. Technical Communication. 2nd ed. 1981. pap. text ed. 17.35x (ISBN 0-673-15401-7). Scott F.
--Technical Writing. 2nd ed. 1978. pap. text ed. 10.00 (ISBN 0-394-32100-6, RanC). Random.
Fear, David E. & Schiffhorst, Gerald J. Short English Handbook. 2nd ed. 1982. pap. 10.30 (ISBN 0-673-15545-5). Scott F.
--Short English Workbook. 2nd ed. 1982. pap. 9.95 (ISBN 0-673-15534-X). Scott F.
Fear, Eugene H. Surviving the Unexpected Wilderness Emergency: A Text for Body Management Under Stress. rev., 6th ed. LC 73-78035. (Illus.). 1979. pap. 5.00 (ISBN 0-913724-02-5). Survival Ed Assoc.
--Teaching with Survival Graphics: Illustrated Visuals on Survival Philosophy, No. 1. rev. ed. (A B C Ser.). 1979. pap. 3.00 (ISBN 0-913724-08-4). Survival Ed Assoc.
Fear, Gene. Defensive Living Preview Book: Illustrated Graphics for Teaching Response to Modern Emergencies. 1978. pap. 2.00 (ISBN 0-913724-18-1). Survival Ed Assoc.
--Fundamentals of Outdoor Enjoyment: Text or Teaching Guide for Coping with Outdoor Environments, All Seasons. (Illus.). 1976. pap. 5.00 (ISBN 0-913724-09-2). Survival Ed Assoc.
--Teaching with Survival Graphics No. 2. (D.E.F. Ser). (Illus.). 1975. pap. 3.00 (ISBN 0-913724-12-2). Survival Ed Assoc.
--Teaching with Survival Graphics No. 3. (G.I.J. Ser). (Illus.). 1975. pap. 3.00 (ISBN 0-913724-13-0). Survival Ed Assoc.
Fear, Gene, jt. auth. see LaValla, Rick.
Fear, Leona K. New Ventures-Free Methodist Missions Nineteen Sixty to Nineteen Seventy-Nine. (Orig.). 1979. pap. 1.50 (ISBN 0-89367-036-7). Light & Life.
Fear, R. A. The Evaluation Interview. 3rd ed. 32.50 (ISBN 0-07-020218-4). McGraw.
Fear, Richard A. & Ross, James F. Jobs, Dollars & EEO: How to Hire More Productive Entry-Level Workers. LC 82-274. (Illus.). 240p. 1983. 22.95 (ISBN 0-07-020199-4). McGraw.
Feare, C. J. The Starling. (Shire Natural History Ser.: No. 7). (Orig.). 1985. pap. 3.95 (ISBN 0-85263-764-0, Pub. by Shire Pubns England). Seven Hills Bks.
Feare, Christopher. The Starling. (Illus.). 1984. 27.95x (ISBN 0-19-217705-2). Oxford U Pr.
Feare, Ronald E. Practice with Idioms. 1980. pap. text ed. 7.95x (ISBN 0-19-502782-5). Oxford U Pr.
Fearey, Robert A. The Occupation of Japan, Second Phase, Nineteen Forty-Eight to Nineteen Fifty. LC 72-176133. 239p. 1972. Repr. of 1950 ed. lib. bdg. 17.75x (ISBN 0-8371-6271-8, FEOJ). Greenwood.
Fearheiley, Don. The Gift of Hope. 1979. saddle-wire 2.50 (ISBN 0-8054-9732-3). Broadman.
--Star Too Far. (Orig.). 1957. pap. 1.75 (ISBN 0-8054-9701-3). Broadman.
Fearing, Bertie B. & Allen, Jo. Teaching Technical Writing in the Secondary School. (Theory & Research into Practice Ser.). 56p. (Orig.). 1984. pap. 6.00 (ISBN 0-8141-5295-3). NCTE.
Fearing, Ginny, ed. see Walline, Margaret W.
Fearing, Jerry. The Story of Minnesota. (Illus.). 75p. (gr. 4-6). 1977. pap. 3.50 (ISBN 0-87351-053-4). Minn Hist.
Fearing, Kelly, et al. Art & the Creative Teacher. (Illus.). 1971. tchr's bk. 20.00. Benson.

--The Creative Eye, 2 Vols. (Illus.). (gr. 7-8). 1979. Vol. 1. text ed. 21.32 gr. 7 (ISBN 0-87443-009-7); Vol. 2. text ed. 21.32 gr. 8 (ISBN 0-87443-010-0); tchr's manual for both vols. 4.00 (ISBN 0-87443-011-9). Benson.

--Helping Children See Art & Make Art, 2 levels. (Illus.). 1982. Primary Level. text ed. 32.00 (ISBN 0-87443-062-3); Intermediate Level. text ed. 44.00 (ISBN 0-87443-063-1). Benson.

Fearing, Kenneth. The Big Clock. LC 75-444971. (Crime Fiction Ser). 1976. Repr. of 1946 ed. lib. bdg. 21.00 (ISBN 0-8240-2366-8). Garland Pub.

--Collected Poems of Kenneth Fearing. LC 75-41089. Repr. of 1940 ed. 19.00 (ISBN 0-404-14661-9). AMS Pr.

--New & Selected Poems. LC 83-12960. xxiv, 143p. 1983. Repr. of 1956 ed. lib. bdg. 27.50x (ISBN 0-313-24175-9, FENE). Greenwood.

Fearn, Jacqueline. Discovering Heraldry. (Discovering Ser.: No. 250). (Illus., Orig.). 1983. pap. 4.50 (ISBN 0-85263-476-5, Pub. by Shire Pubns Eng). Seven Hills Bks.

--Domestic Bygones. 2.95 (ISBN 0-913714-08-9). Legacy Bks.

--Thatch & Thatching. (Shire Album Ser.: No. 16). (Illus.). 32p. 1985. pap. 3.50 (ISBN 0-85263-337-8, Pub. by Shire Pubns England). Seven Hills Bks.

Fearn, John R. From Afar. LC 84-11160. 28p. 1984. Repr. of 1982 ed. lib. bdg. 12.95x (ISBN 0-89370-797-X). Borgo Pr.

--Survivor of Mars. 40p. 1983. Repr. of 1982 ed. lib. bdg. 12.95x (ISBN 0-89370-796-1). Borgo Pr.

--Tales of Wonder. 40p. 1983. Repr. lib. bdg. 12.95x (ISBN 0-89370-799-6). Borgo Pr.

--Worlds Within. LC 84-11035. 32p. 1984. Repr. of 1982 ed. lib. bdg. 12.95x (ISBN 0-89370-798-8). Borgo Pr.

Fearn, Leif. Development Writing. 174p. 1980. pap. text ed. 9.85 (ISBN 0-940444-05-4). Kabyn.

--Developmental Writing & the Writing Kabyn. 70p. (gr. 2-9). 1981. 1.00 (ISBN 0-940444-07-0). Kabyn.

--The Fear. 178p. (gr. 2 up). 1983. 8.50 (ISBN 0-940444-20-8). Kabyn.

--The First First I Think. 91p. (gr. 1-3). 1981. 6.50 (ISBN 0-940444-14-3). Kabyn.

--First I Think: Then I Write My Think. 160p. (gr. 3-12). 1981. 6.50 (ISBN 0-940444-13-5). Kabyn.

--Geocabulary Cards. (gr. 3-9). 1978. card pack 8.40 (ISBN 0-940444-06-2). Kabyn.

--Reading in the Mind. 41p. (gr. 1-7). 1984. 25.00 (ISBN 0-940444-22-4). Kabyn.

--Teaching for Thinking. 193p. (Orig.). 1980. pap. text ed. 8.70 (ISBN 0-940444-04-6). Kabyn.

--Writing a Story: A Writer's Self-Report. 59p. 1983. 4.50 (ISBN 0-940444-21-6). Kabyn.

Fearn, Leif & Garner, Irene A. The Alpha Cards. 54p. (gr. 2-9). 1982. card pack 14.00 (ISBN 0-940444-12-7). Kabyn.

--Maneras de Divertirme con Mi Mente. (Illus.). 182p. (gr. 3-9). 1982. 6.50 (ISBN 0-940444-16-X). Kabyn.

Fearn, Leif & Goldman, Elizabeth. Writing Kabyn: Assessment & Editing. 96p. (gr. 2-9). 1981. classroom kit 25.00 (ISBN 0-940444-11-9). Kabyn.

--Writing Kabyn: Products. 148p. (gr. 2-9). 1982. classroom kit 45.00 (ISBN 0-940444-09-7). Kabyn.

--Writing Kabyn: Sentences-Paragraphs. 125p. (gr. 2-9). 1982. classroom kit 60.00 (ISBN 0-940444-08-9). Kabyn.

--Writing Kabyn: Technology. 76p. (gr. 2-9). 1981. classroom Kit 40.00 (ISBN 0-940444-10-0). Kabyn.

Fearn, Leif & Goliaz-Benson, Ursula. Forty-Two Ways to Have Fun with My Mind. 58p. (ps-6). 1976. 4.50 (ISBN 0-940444-00-3). Kabyn.

Fearn, Leif & Golisz-Benson, Ursula. Fifty-Two Ways to Have Fun with My Mind. (Illus.). 62p. (gr. 1-3). 1975. 4.50 (ISBN 0-940444-01-1). Kabyn.

--Seventy-Two Ways to Have Fun with My Mind. (Illus.). 80p. (Orig.). 1976. 4.50 (ISBN 0-940444-03-8). Kabyn.

--Sixty-Two Ways to Have Fun with My Mind. (Illus.). 72p. (Orig.). (gr. 3-6). 1982. 4.50 (ISBN 0-940444-02-X). Kabyn.

Fearn, Leif, et al. Human Development Program Supplementary Idea Guide. rev. ed. 1975. 8.95 (ISBN 0-86584-008-3). Palomares & Assoc.

Fearn, Robert M. Labor Economics: The Emerging Synthesis. 1981. text ed. 21.95 (ISBN 0-316-27636-7). Little.

Fearne, Charles. An Essay on the Learning of Contingent Remainders & Executory Devises, 2 vols. 10th ed. Butler, Charles & Smith, Josiah W., eds. 1980. Repr. of 1844 ed. Set. lib. bdg. 95.00x (ISBN 0-8377-0539-8). Rothman.

Fearnley, Robert, tr. see Eglitis, Andrejs.

Fearns, Peter. Business Studies: An Integrated Approach. 1981. 20.00x (ISBN 0-340-25570-6, Pub. by Hodder & Stoughton England). State Mutual Bk.

Fearnside, Philip M. Human Carrying Capacity of the Brazillian Rainforest. 352p. 1985. 35.00x (ISBN 0-231-06104-8). Columbia U Pr.

Fearnside, W. Ward. About Thinking. 1980. pap. text ed. 18.95 (ISBN 0-13-000844-3). P-H.

Fearon, George, jt. auth. see Brown, Ivor.

Fearon, George, jt. auth. see Brown, Ivor J.

Fearon, Harold E. Fundamentals of Production-Operations Management. 2nd ed. (Illus.). 1982. pap. text ed. 13.95 (ISBN 0-314-69647-4); tchrs.' manual avail. (ISBN 0-314-71089-2). West Pub.

Fearon, Henry B. Sketches of America. LC 68-56487. 1969. Repr. of 1818 ed. 31.00 (ISBN 0-405-08497-8, Blom Pubns). Ayer Co Pubs.

--Sketches of America. 2nd ed. LC 70-100124. Repr. of 1818 ed. 35.00x (ISBN 0-678-00584-2). Kelley.

Fearon, Mary & Hirstein, Sandra. Celebrating Our Sacraments. 1985. Boxed Set. 79.95 (ISBN 0-697-02066-5); Program Director's Guide. 4.50 (ISBN 0-697-02058-4). Wm C Brown.

Fearon, Mary & Hirstein, Sandra J. Celebrating the Gift of Forgiveness. 64p. 1982. pap. 2.95 (ISBN 0-697-01792-3); program manual 6.95 (ISBN 0-697-01793-1). Wm C Brown.

--Celebrating the Gift of Jesus. 64p. 1982. pap. 2.95 (ISBN 0-697-01794-X); program manual 6.95 (ISBN 0-697-01795-8). Wm C Brown.

--The Eucharist Makes Us One. 1983. box set 79.95 (ISBN 0-697-01843-1); program dir. guide 4.50 (ISBN 0-697-01844-X); write for info. student leaflets; tchr's manual, pre-school to junior levels 3.25 (ISBN 0-697-01845-8); attendance certificates 6.95 (ISBN 0-697-01973-X). Wm C Brown.

--Thy Kingdom Come. 1984. boxed set 79.95 (ISBN 0-697-01962-4); program dir. guide 4.50 (ISBN 0-697-01963-2); write for info. students leaflets; write for info. tchrs' guide preschool to junior levels; attendance cert. 6.95 (ISBN 0-697-01973-X). Wm C Brown.

Fearon, Mary & Tully, Mary J. Wonder-Filled. 1983. pap. 3.10 (ISBN 0-697-01853-9); tchr's. manual 6.00 (ISBN 0-697-01854-7); parent book 3.50 (ISBN 0-697-01855-5). Wm C Brown.

Fearon, Mary, jt. auth. see Tully, Mary Jo.

Fearon, P. The Origins & Nature of the Great Slump, 1929-1932. LC 79-636. (Studies in Economic & Social History). 1979. pap. text ed. 6.00x (ISBN 0-391-00982-6). Humanities.

Fearon, Peter, jt. auth. see Aldcroft, Derek.

Fearon, Peter, jt. ed. see Aldcroft, Derek H.

Fears, Ann, et al. Women in Texas. 1982. 16.95 (ISBN 0-89015-305-1). Eakin Pubns.

Fears, J. R. Princeps A Diis Electus: The Divine Election of the Emperor as a Political Concept at Rome. (Papers & Monographs: No. 26). (Illus.). 351p. 1977. 24.50 (ISBN 0-318-12329-0). Am Acad Rome.

Fears, J. Wayne. Backcountry Cooking. LC 79-4900. (Illus.). 160p. 1980. 11.95 (ISBN 0-914788-19-1); pap. 7.95 (ISBN 0-914788-20-5). East Woods.

--Cooking the Wild Harvest. LC 84-9142. (Illus.). 190p. (Orig.). 1984. pap. 12.95 (ISBN 0-934802-14-9). ICS Bks.

--Successful Turkey Hunting. Helgeland, Glenn, ed. LC 82-74192. (On Target Ser.). (Illus.). 92p. (Orig.). 1984. pap. 4.95 (ISBN 0-913305-01-4). Target Comm.

--Trout Fishing the Southern Appalachians. LC 79-1277. (Illus.). 192p. 1979. pap. 7.95 (ISBN 0-914788-10-8). East Woods.

Fears, Jerry. Boom, Cash, & Balderdash: A Different Look at Fairbanks During Pipeline Construction. LC 77-87430. (Illus.). 1978. 8.95 (ISBN 0-918270-02-2). That New Pub.

Fearson, Daniel. Spink's Catalogue of British Commemorative Medals. 1985. 22.95 (ISBN 0-03-004214-3, Pub. by Webb & Bower). HR&W.

Feasley, Charles E. Serving Learners at a Distance: A Guide to Program Practices. Fife, Jonathan D., ed. & frwd. by. LC 84-160901. (ASHE-ERIC Higher Education Research Report Ser.: No. 5, 1983). 69p. (Orig.). 1983. pap. 7.50 (ISBN 0-913317-04-7). Assn Study Higher Educ.

Feast, W. J., jt. ed. see Clark, David T.

Feaster, Thelma & Marshall, Bonnie C. Catalog of Resource Organizations for Improving Reading, Writing, & Oral Communication Skills. 66p. 1980. 5.10 (ISBN 0-318-15420-X, IN217). Natl Ctr Res Voc Ed.

Feastr, Thelma J., et al. Databases & Clearinghouses: Information Resources for Education. 156p. 1979. 9.75 (ISBN 0-318-15440-4, IN 167). Natl Ctr Res Voc Ed.

Feather, A. G. Stanley's Story, or Through the Wilds of Africa. LC 74-99411. (African History Ser). (Illus.). 533p. 1969. Repr. of 1890 ed. lib. bdg. 29.00 (ISBN 0-8411-0084-5). Metro Bks.

Feather, C. J., tr. see Alekhine, A.

Feather, Frank, ed. Through the Eighties: Thinking Globally, Acting Locally. 1980. 12.50 (ISBN 0-930242-11-4). World Future.

Feather, John P. The Provincial Book Trade in Eighteenth Century England. (Cambridge Studies in Publishing & Printing History). 206p. Date not set. price not set. (ISBN 0-521-30334-6). Cambridge U Pr.

Feather, Leonard. The Encyclopedia of Jazz. Orig. Title: New Edition of the Encyclopedia of Jazz. 1960. 25.00 (ISBN 0-8180-1203-X). Horizon.

--Encyclopedia of Jazz. (Quality Paperbacks Ser.). (Illus.). 527p. 1984. pap. 15.95 (ISBN 0-306-80214-7). Da Capo.

--Encyclopedia of Jazz in the Sixties. 1967. 25.00 (ISBN 0-8180-1205-6). Horizon.

--The Encyclopedic Yearbook of Jazz. (Roots of Jazz Ser.). 190p. 1985. Repr. of 1956 ed. lib. bdg. 29.50 (ISBN 0-306-76289-7). Da Capo.

--From Satchmo to Miles. (Roots of Jazz Ser.). (Illus.). 258p. 1984. Repr. of 1972 ed. 25.00 (ISBN 0-306-76230-7). Da Capo.

--Inside Jazz. LC 77-23411. (Roots of Jazz Ser.). (Illus.). 1977. lib. bdg. 22.50 (ISBN 0-306-77437-2); pap. 5.95 (ISBN 0-306-80076-4). Da Capo.

--The New Yearbook of Jazz. (Roots of Jazz Ser.). 188p. 1985. Repr. of 1958 ed. lib. bdg. 29.50 (ISBN 0-306-76288-9). Da Capo.

--The Passion for Jazz. LC 80-15133. (Illus.). 1980. 9.95 (ISBN 0-8180-1221-8). Horizon.

Feather, Leonard & Gitler, Ira. The Encyclopedia of Jazz in the Seventies. LC 76-21196. (Illus.). 1976. 25.00 (ISBN 0-8180-1215-3). Horizon.

Feather, Leonard & Tracy, Jack. Laughter from the Hip, the Lighter Side of Jazz. (Paperbacks Ser.). 1979. pap. 5.95 (ISBN 0-306-80092-6). Da Capo.

Feather, Leonard G., tr. see Goffin, Robert.

Feather, Milton S., jt. ed. see Waller, George R.

Feather, N. T., jt. ed. see Atkinson, J. W.

Feather, Noel & Helgeland, Glenn. Battling Bucks. 1985. 12.95 (ISBN 0-913305-06-5). Target Comm.

Feather, Norman T. Values in Education & Society. LC 75-2812. (Illus.). 1975. 14.95 (ISBN 0-02-910200-6). Free Pr.

Feather, Norman T., ed. Expectations & Actions: Expectancy-Value Methods in Psychology. 448p. 1982. text ed. 39.95x (ISBN 0-89859-080-9). L Erlbaum Assocs.

Featherman, Buzz. The Fun & Fantasy Book. LC 80-54612. (Illus.). 144p. (Orig.). 1981. pap. text ed. 5.95 (ISBN 0-932238-04-1, Pub. by Avant Bks.). Slawson Comm.

Featherman, David L. & Hauser, Robert M. Opportunity & Change. (Studies in Population Ser.). 1978. 30.00 (ISBN 0-12-250350-3). Acad Pr.

Featherston, Phyllis & Ostler, Barbara. The Bed & Breakfast Guide for the United States & Canada. 382p. (Orig.). 1985. avail. (ISBN 0-9611298-1-6). Natl Bed.

Featherstone,. Better Military Modelling. (Illus.). 96p. 1980. 9.95 (ISBN 0-7182-1447-1, Pub. by Kaye & Ward). David & Charles.

Featherstone, David. Doris Ulmann: American Portraits. LC 84-15208. (Illus.). 224p. 1985. 60.00 (ISBN 0-8263-0783-3); pap. 29.95 (ISBN 0-8263-0804-X). U of NM Pr.

--Postures, the Studio Photographs of Marsha Burns. Alinder, James, ed. LC 81-71995. (Untitled Ser.: No. 28). (Illus.). 56p. (Orig.). 1982. pap. 15.00 (ISBN 0-933286-25-2). Friends Photography.

Featherstone, David, ed. & intro. by. Observations: Essays on Documentary Photography. (Untitled Ser.: No. 35). (Illus.). 130p. (Orig.). 1984. pap. 12.00 (ISBN 0-933286-39-2, 84-80869). Friends Photography.

Featherstone, David, ed. see Shaw, Susan.

Featherstone, Donald. Weapons & Equipment of the Victorian Soldier. (Illus.). 1978. 19.95 (ISBN 0-7137-0847-6, Pub. by Blandford Pr England). Sterling.

Featherstone, Donald & Robinson, Keith. Battles with Model Tanks. (Illus.). 160p. 1979. 12.95 (ISBN 0-88254-541-8, Pub. by Macdonald & Jane's England). Hippocrene Bks.

Featherstone, Helen. A Difference in the Family: Living with a Disabled Child. 288p. 1981. pap. 6.95 (ISBN 0-14-005941-5). Penguin.

Featherstone, Jeffrey, jt. auth. see Sevcenko, Ihor.

Featherstone, Joseph. Schools Where Children Learn. LC 75-148664. 1971. pap. 2.95 (ISBN 0-87140-251-3). Liveright.

--What Schools Can Do. 1976. 8.95 (ISBN 0-87140-619-5). Liveright.

Featherstone, Mike, jt. auth. see Hepworth, Mike.

Featherstone, R. E. & Nalluri, C. Civil Engineering Hydraulics: Essential Theory with Worked Examples. (Illus.). 384p. 1982. text ed. 23.50x (ISBN 0-246-11483-5). Sheridan.

Featherstone, R. E. & James, A., eds. Urban Drainage Systems. 229p. 1982. text ed. 76.95 (ISBN 0-273-08596-4). Pitman Pub MA.

Featherstone, Robert M. & Simon, Alexander. A Pharmacologic Approach to the Study of the Mind. (Illus.). 428p. 1959. 34.75 (ISBN 0-398-04254-3). C C Thomas.

Featherstone, Vaughn J. Charity Never Faileth. LC 80-10528. 121p. 1980. 6.95 (ISBN 0-87747-806-6). Deseret Bk.

--The Disciple of Christ. Knowles, Eleanor, ed. LC 84-71706. 100p. 6.95 (ISBN 0-317-14403-0). Deseret Bk.

--Purity of Heart. LC 82-72728. 103p. 1982. 6.95 (ISBN 0-87747-914-3). Deseret Bk.

Featherstone, William B. Curriculum of the Special Class: Its Underlying Principles. LC 74-176766. (Columbia University. Teachers College. Contributions to Education: No. 544). Repr. of 1932 ed. 22.50 (ISBN 0-404-55544-6, CE544). AMS Pr.

Featherstonhaugh, George W. A Canoe Voyage up the Minnay Sotor, 2 Vols. LC 71-111618. 788p. 1970. Repr. of 1847 ed. 20.00 (ISBN 0-87351-057-7). Minn Hist.

--Excursion Through the Slave States from Washington on the Potomac, to the Frontier of Mexico. LC 68-55885. Repr. of 1844 ed. 17.50x (ISBN 0-8371-0413-0, FEE&, Pub. by Negro U Pr). Greenwood.

Feaurdent, F., jt. auth. see DeRouge, J.

Feaver, Douglas A. & Gallagher, Edward J. Humanistic Perspectives on the City: A Selected Bibliography, Humanities Perspectives on Technology Program, No.934. 1975. 6.50 (ISBN 0-686-20379-8). CPL Biblios.

Feaver, William. Masters of Caricature: From Hogarth & Gillray to Carfe & Levine. LC 80-47020. (Illus.). 224p. 1981. 25.00 (ISBN 0-394-50904-8). Knopf.

Feazel, Charles E., ed. see Membrane Processes for Industry, Symposium, May 19-20,1966.

Febles, Jorge. Cuentos Olvidados De Alfonso Hernandez Cata. LC 81-52007. (Senda Antologica). 250p. (Orig., Span.). 1981. pap. 10.95 (ISBN 0-918454-27-1). Senda Nueva.

FEBS Lecture Course held at the University of Konstanz. Mobility & Recognition in Cell Biology: Proceedings. Sund, Horst & Veeger, Ces, eds. xii, 586p. 1983. 76.00 (ISBN 3-11-009536-X). De Gruyter.

FEBS Meeting, Amsterdam, August, 1972, Eighth. Mitochondria & Membranes: Proceedings, Vol. 28. 1973. 30.00 (ISBN 0-444-10423-2, North-Holland). Elsevier.

FEBS Symposium on DNA, Liblice, 24-29 September, 1979. DNA: Recombination, Interactions & Repair. Zadrazil, S. & Sponar, J., eds. (Vol. 63). (Illus.). 600p. 1980. 110.00 (ISBN 0-08-025494-2). Pergamon.

Febure. Amour Sacre, Amour Profane; Autour de l'Heptameron. (Coll. Idees). pap. 4.50 (ISBN 0-685-34188-7). French & Eur.

Febvre, Lucien. Life in Renaissance France. Rothstein, Marian, tr. from Fr. LC 77-7454. 1979. 10.00x (ISBN 0-674-53175-2); pap. 4.95x (ISBN 0-674-53180-9). Harvard U Pr.

--The Problem of Unbelief in the Sixteenth Century: The Religion of Rabelais. Gottlieb, Beatrice, tr. from Fr. (Illus.). 528p. 1982. text ed. 35.00x (ISBN 0-674-70825-3). Harvard U Pr.

--The Problem of Unbelief in the Sixteenth Century: The Religion of Rabelais. Gottlieb, Beatrice, tr. 552p. 1985. pap. 9.95x (ISBN 0-674-70826-1). Harvard U Pr.

Febvre, Lucien & Bataillon, Lionel. Geographical Introduction to History. Mountford, E. G. & Paxton, J. H., trs. LC 72-11735. Orig. Title: The Earth & Human Evolution. (Illus.). 388p. 1975. Repr. of 1925 ed. lib. bdg. 22.50x (ISBN 0-8371-6710-8, FEGI). Greenwood.

Febvre, Lucien & Martin, Henri-Jean. The Coming of the Book: The Impact of Printing 1450-1800. 1976. 30.00 (ISBN 0-8052-7026-4, Pub. by NLB). Schocken.

Febvre, Lucien P. Martin Luther: A Destiny. Tapley, Roberts, tr. LC 83-45640. Date not set. Repr. of 1929 ed. 37.50 (ISBN 0-404-19850-3). AMS Pr.

Fecel, D. Craig. How to Profit from the Psycle. 310p. 1983. 16.95 (ISBN 0-943940-08-7). Rich & Snyder.

Fecher, Charles A. Mencken: A Study of His Thought. LC 77-21154. 1978. 15.00 (ISBN 0-394-41354-7). Knopf.

--Philosophy of Jacques Maritain. LC 70-90705. Repr. of 1953 ed. lib. bdg. 16.00x (ISBN 0-8371-2287-2, FEJM). Greenwood.

Fecher, Constance. The Link Boys. LC 75-149219. (Illus.). 192p. (gr. 4 up). 1971. 4.50 (ISBN 0-374-34497-3). FS&G.

Fecher, Roger J., ed. Applying Corporate Management Strategies. LC 84-82371. (Higher Education Ser.: No. 50). (Orig.). 1985. pap. text ed. 9.95x (ISBN 0-87589-748-7). Jossey-Bass.

Fecher, Vincent J. Religion & Aging: An Annotated Bibliography. LC 82-81019. 119p. 1982. 16.00 (ISBN 0-911536-96-5); pap. 9.00 (ISBN 0-911536-97-3). Trinity U Pr.

Fechner, Amrei. I Am a Little Pony. (Little Animal Stories Ser.). 24p. Date not set. 5.95 (ISBN 0-8120-5667-1). Barron.

Fechner, Amrei & Spanner, Helmut. I Am a Little Dog. (Little Animal Stories Ser.). (Illus.). 24p. (ps). 1983. 5.95 (ISBN 0-8120-5514-4). Barron.

--I Am a Little Dog. (Little Animal Stories Ser.). (ps). 1984. 1.25 (ISBN 0-8120-5588-8). Barron.

--I Am a Little Elephant. (Little Animal Stories Ser.). (Illus.). 24p. 1984. 5.95 (ISBN 0-8120-5515-2). Barron.

--I Am a Little Elephant. (Little Animal Stories Ser.). (ps). 1984. 1.25 (ISBN 0-8120-5586-1). Barron.

--I Am a Little Lion. (Little Animal Stories Ser.). (Illus.). 24p. (ps). 1984. 5.95 (ISBN 0-8120-5516-0). Barron.

--I Am a Little Lion. (Little Animal Stories Ser.). (ps). 1984. 1.25 (ISBN 0-8120-5585-3). Barron.

Fechner, Amrei, jt. auth. see Spanner, Helmut.

Fechner, Gustav T. The Little Book of Life After Death. Kastenbaum, Robert, ed. LC 76-19570. (Death & Dying Ser.). 1977. Repr. of 1904 ed. lib. bdg. 15.00x (ISBN 0-405-09565-1). Ayer Co Pubs.

Fechner, Paul & Alpar, John J. Intraocular Lenses. (Illus.). 304p. 1985. text ed. 48.00 (ISBN 0-86577-123-5). Thieme-Stratton.

Fechner, Robert E., jt. auth. see Mills, Stacey E.

Fecht, Gerald. The Complete Parent's Guide to Soccer. (Illus.). 1979. pap. 9.95 (ISBN 0-673-16184-6). Scott F.

Fechter, S. A., jt. auth. see Lavine, R. Z.

Fechtner, Leopold. Five Thousand One & Two Liners for Any & Every Occasion. 1982. pap. 4.95 (ISBN 0-13-321547-4, Reward). P-H.

--Galaxy of Funny Gags, Puns, Quips & Putdowns. 1982. pap. 4.95 (ISBN 0-13-345959-4, Reward). P-H.

Feck, Luke. Yesterday's Cincinnati. LC 75-14411. (Illus.). 1977. pap. 5.95 (ISBN 0-912458-91-7). E A Seemann.

Feczko, Kathy. The Great Bunny Race. LC 84-8634. (Giant First-Start Readers Ser.). (Illus.). 32p. (gr. k-12). 1985. PLB 9.89 (ISBN 0-8167-0357-4); pap. text ed. 2.50 (ISBN 0-8167-0437-6). Troll Assocs.

--Halloween Party. LC 84-8635. (Giant First Start Reader Ser.). (Illus.). 32p. (gr. k-2). 1985. PLB 9.89 (ISBN 0-8167-0354-X); pap. text ed. 2.50 (ISBN 0-8167-0434-1). Troll Assocs.

--Three Little Chicks. LC 84-8629. (Giant First Start Reader Ser.). (Illus.). 32p. (gr. k-2). 1985. PLB 9.89 (ISBN 0-8167-0355-8); pap. text ed. 2.50 (ISBN 0-8167-0435-X). Troll Assocs.

--Umbrella Parade. LC 84-8650. (Giant First Start Reader Ser.). (Illus.). 32p. (gr. k-2). 1985. PLB 9.89 (ISBN 0-8167-0356-6); pap. text ed. 2.50 (ISBN 0-8167-0436-8). Troll Assocs.

Feda, J. Mechanics of Particulate Materials: The Principles. (Development in Geotechnical Materials Ser.: Vol. 30). 440p. 1982. 78.75 (ISBN 0-444-99713-X). Elsevier.

--Stress in Subsoil & Methods of Final Settlement Calculation. (Developments in Geotechnical Materials Ser.: Vol. 18). 216p. 1978. 53.25 (ISBN 0-444-99800-4). Elsevier.

Fedapt. Box Office Guidelines. rev. ed. 72p. 1978. pap. text ed. 7.50x (ISBN 0-9602942-0-1). Drama Bk.

--Subscription Guidelines. rev. 2nd ed. (Illus.). 68p. 1977. pap. text ed. 7.50x (ISBN 0-9602942-1-X). Drama Bk.

Fedden, Henry R. Suicide: A Social & Historical Study. LC 72-80703. (Illus.). Repr. of 1938 ed. 27.00 (ISBN 0-405-08498-6, Blom Pubns). Ayer Co Pubs.

Fedden, Katharine. Manor Life in Old France: From the Journal of the Sire De Gouberville for the Years 1549-1562. LC 70-168013. Repr. of 1933 ed. 21.00 (ISBN 0-404-02374-6). AMS Pr.

Fedden, Katharine W. The Basque Country. 1974. lib. bdg. 59.95 (ISBN 0-87700-297-5). Revisionist Pr.

Fedden, Robin. Phoenix Land. LC 66-20190. (Illus.). 1966. 6.50 (ISBN 0-8076-0380-5). Braziller.

Fedden, Robin & Kenworthy-Browne, John. The Country House Guide to England Scotland & Wales. (Illus.). 1979. 24.95 (ISBN 0-393-01259-X). Norton.

Fedden, Robin, et al. Personal Landscape: An Anthology of Exile. 1977. Repr. of 1945 ed. 25.00 (ISBN 0-89984-180-5). Century Bookbindery.

Fedders, Andrew & Salvadori, Cynthia. Peoples & Cultures of Kenya. 164p. 1980. 30.00x (ISBN 0-686-79161-4, Pub. by Collins England). State Mutual Bk.

Feddes, R. A., et al. Simulation of Field Water Use & Crop Yield. LC 78-10697. (Simulation Monographs Ser.). 188p. 1979. pap. 34.95x (ISBN 0-470-26463-2). Halsted Pr.

Fedeli, P. Catullus' Carmen, Sixty One. rev. ed. (London Studies in Classical Philology: No. 9). 200p. 1983. text ed. 37.50x (ISBN 90-70265-62-1, Pub. by Gieben Holland). Humanities.

Feder & Burrell. Impact of Seafood Cannery Waste on the Benthic Biota & Adjacent Waters at Dutch Harbor Alaska. (IMS Report Ser.: No. R82-1). 225p. 21.00. U of AK Inst Marine.

Feder & Paul. Distribution & Abundance of Some Epibenthic Invertebrates of Cook Inlet, Alaska. (IMS Report Ser.: No. R80-3). 167p. 12.00 (ISBN 0-914500-11-2). U of AK Inst Marine.

Feder, et al. Insuring the Nation's Health: Market Competition, Catastrophic & Comprehensive Approaches. 227p. 1981. pap. 10.95x (ISBN 0-87766-298-3, 32400). Urban Inst.

--The Infaunal Invertebrates of the Southeastern Bering Sea. (IMS Report Ser.: No. R78-6). 346p. 22.85 (ISBN 0-914500-13-9). U of AK Inst Marine.

Feder, A., ed. see Hilarius, Saint.

Feder, Bernard & Feder, Elaine. The Expressive Arts Therapies. (Illus.). 224p. 1980. 14.95 (ISBN 0-13-298059-2, Spec); pap. 6.95 (ISBN 0-13-298042-8). P-H.

Feder, Elaine, jt. auth. see Feder, Bernard.

Feder, Georg, jt. auth. see Larsen, Jens P.

Feder, Gergson & Just, Richard. Adoption of Agricultural Innovations in Developing Countries: A Survey. (Working Paper: No. 444). 67p. 1981. 3.00 (ISBN 0-686-36056-7, WP-0444). World Bank.

Feder, Gershon. On Exports & Economic Growth. (Working Paper: No. 508). 24p. 1982. pap. 3.00 (ISBN 0-686-39765-7, WP-0508). World Bank.

Feder, Happy Jack. Clown Skits for Everyone. LC 84-3109. (Illus.). 160p. 1984. 12.95 (ISBN 0-668-05997-4); pap. 7.95 (ISBN 0-668-06265-7). Arco.

--Mime Time: Forty-Five Complete Routines for Everyone. (Illus.). 160p. 1985. 12.95 (ISBN 0-668-06002-6). Arco.

Feder, Harlan & Shelton, Peter. Colorado Winterguide. (Illus.). 343p. (Orig.). 1984. pap. 8.95 (ISBN 0-9608764-2-1). Wayfinder Pr.

Feder, J., et al, eds. National Health Insurance: Conflicting Goals & Policy Choices. LC 80-80045. 721p. 1980. text ed. 28.00x (ISBN 0-87766-035-2); pap. 14.95x (ISBN 0-87766-271-1). Urban Inst.

Feder, Jack. Independent Entertainer: How to Be a Successful Clown, Juggler, Mime, Magician or Puppeteer. LC 81-15352. 146p. 1982. 11.95 (ISBN 0-13-456772-2); pap. 5.95 (ISBN 0-13-456764-1). P-H.

Feder, Jack & Merrick, Kathryn W. Zen of Cubing: In Search of the Seventh Side. LC 82-72610. (Illus.). 120p. (Orig.). 1982. pap. 4.95 (ISBN 0-89708-103-X). And Bks.

Feder, Jan. The Life of a Cat. LC 82-12795. (Animal Lives Ser.). (Illus.). (gr. 2-4). 1982. PLB 10.35 (ISBN 0-516-08931-5); pap. 2.95 (ISBN 0-516-48931-3). Childrens.

--The Life of a Dog. LC 82-9752. (Animal Lives Ser.). (Illus.). (gr. 2-4). 1982. PLB 10.35 (ISBN 0-516-08932-3); pap. 2.95 (ISBN 0-516-48932-1). Childrens.

--The Life of a Hamster. LC 82-12768. (Animal Lives Ser.). (Illus.). (gr. 2-4). 1982. PLB 10.35 (ISBN 0-516-08933-1); pap. 2.95 (ISBN 0-516-48933-X). Childrens.

--The Life of a Rabbit. LC 82-9750. (Animal Lives Ser.). (Illus.). (gr. 2-4). 1982. PLB 10.35 (ISBN 0-516-08934-X); pap. 2.95 (ISBN 0-516-48934-8). Childrens.

Feder, Jane. Beany. LC 78-10416. (ps-1). 1979. PLB 7.99 (ISBN 0-394-93734-1). Pantheon.

--The Night Light. LC 79-20687. (Illus.). (ps-2). 1980. 7.50 (ISBN 0-8037-6604-1). Dial Bks Young.

Feder, Judith. Exploring Careers in Music. (Careers in Depth Ser.). (Illus.). 140p. 1982. lib. bdg. 8.97 (ISBN 0-8239-0557-8). Rosen Group.

--The Student Traveler in Washington, D. C. lib. bdg. cancelled (ISBN 0-8239-0610-8). Rosen Group.

Feder, Judith & Holahan, John. Financing Health Care for the Elderly: Medicare, Medicaid & Private Health Insurance. (Health Policy & the Elderly Ser.). 106p. 1979. pap. 6.00x (ISBN 0-87766-244-4, 24900). Urban Inst.

Feder, Leah H. Unemployment Relief in Periods of Depression: A Study of Measures Adopted in Certain Cities, 1857 Through 1922. LC 75-137165. (Poverty U.S.A. Historical Record Ser). 1971. Repr. of 1936 ed. 29.00 (ISBN 0-405-03104-1). Ayer Co Pubs.

Feder, Lillian. Ancient Myth in Modern Poetry. LC 70-154994. 1972. 36.00x (ISBN 0-691-06207-2); pap. 9.95x (ISBN 0-691-01336-5). Princeton U Pr.

--Madness in Literature. LC 79-3206. 1980. 26.00 (ISBN 0-691-06427-X); pap. 9.95x (ISBN 0-691-01401-9). Princeton U Pr.

Feder, Paula K. Where Does the Teacher Live? LC 78-13157. (gr. k-3). 1979. 7.95 (ISBN 0-525-42586-1, Smart Cat). Dutton.

Feder, Stuart, jt. auth. see Bailey, Norman.

Feder, W. A., jt. auth. see Manning, W. J.

Federal Architecture Project Staff, jt. auth. see Craig, Lois A.

Federal Architecture Project Staff & Craig, Lois A. The Federal Presence: Architecture, Politics, & Symbols in U. S. Government Building. (Illus.). 1978. 55.00x (ISBN 0-262-03057-8); pap. 17.50 (ISBN 0-262-53059-7). MIT Pr.

Federal Aviation Administration. A&P Mechanics Airframe Question Book. (Aviation Maintenance Training Course Ser.). (Illus.). 84p. 1984. pap. 2.75 (ISBN 0-89100-274-X, EA-FFA-T-8080-12). Aviation Maintenance.

--A&P Mechanic's Certification Guide. 4th ed. (Aviation Maintenance Training Course Ser.). 64p. 1976. pap. 4.00 (ISBN 0-89100-082-8, EA-AC65-2D). Aviation Maintenance.

--Advanced Ground Instructor Written Test Guide. 88p. 1980. pap. text ed. 4.50 (ISBN 0-939158-24-8). Flightshops.

--Aircraft Inspection, Repair & Alterations: AC 43.13-1A & 43.13-2a. 449p. pap. 11.50 (ISBN 0-89100-081-X). Aviation Maintenance.

--Airframe & Powerplant Mechanics Airframe Handbook: AC 65-15A. 601p. pap. 13.00x (ISBN 0-89100-080-1). Aviation Maintenance.

--Airframe & Powerplant Mechanics Airframe Writen Test Guide. rev. ed. 109p. 1981. pap. text ed. 5.50 (ISBN 0-939158-20-5). Flightshops.

--Airframe & Powerplant Mechanics Certification Guide: AC 65-2D. pap. 4.00x (ISBN 0-685-46348-6). Aviation.

--Airframe & Powerplant Mechanics General Handbook: AC 65-9A. 549p. pap. 13.00x (ISBN 0-89100-078-X). Aviation Maintenance.

--Airframe & Powerplant Mechanics General Written Test Guide. rev. ed. 95p. 1981. pap. text ed. 5.50 (ISBN 0-939158-19-1). Flightshops.

--Airframe & Powerplant Mechanics Powerplant Handbook: AC 65-12A. 500p. pap. 12.00x (ISBN 0-89100-079-8). Aviation Maintenance.

--Airframe & Powerplant Mechanic's Powerplant Written Test Guide. rev. ed. 90p. 1981. pap. text ed. 5.50 (ISBN 0-939158-21-3). Flightshops.

--Airline Transport Pilot, Airplane, Practical Test Guide (Ac 61-77) 1974. pap. text ed. 3.00 (ISBN 0-686-74081-5, Pub. by Astro). Aviation.

--Airline Transport Pilot-Airplane Written Test Guide: Air Carrier. rev. ed. 189p. 1980. pap. text ed. 7.00 (ISBN 0-939158-16-7). Flightshops.

--Airman's Information Manual, 1985. 20th ed. Winner, Walter P., ed. LC 70-164372. (Illus.). 312p. 1985. pap. 6.75 (ISBN 0-916413-00-4). Aviation.

--Aviation Instructor's Handbook. (Pilot Training Ser.). 120p. 1977. pap. 6.00 (ISBN 0-89100-170-0, EA-AC60-14). Aviation Maintenance.

--Aviation Instructors Handbook. rev. ed. 123p. 1977. pap. text ed. 3.50 (ISBN 0-939158-03-5). Flightshops.

--Aviation Instructor's Handbook (AC-60-14) 1977. pap. text ed. 6.00 (ISBN 0-86677-017-8, Pub. by Cooper Aviation). Aviation.

--Aviation Mechanic Powerplant Question Book. (Aviation Maintenance Training Course Ser.). (Illus.). 79p. 1984. pap. 2.75 (ISBN 0-89100-272-3, EA-FAA-T-8080-11). Aviation Maintenance.

--Aviation Mechanics General Question Book. (Aviation Maintenance Training Course Ser.). 60p. 1984. pap. 2.75 (ISBN 0-89100-268-5, EA-FAA-T-8080-10). Aviation Maintenance.

--Aviation Weather. 2nd ed. (Pilot Training Ser.). (Illus.). 219p. 1975. pap. 8.50 (ISBN 0-89100-160-3, EA-AC61-006A). Aviation Maintenance.

--Aviation Weather: Ac 00-6A. pap. 8.50 (ISBN 0-86677-000-3, Pub. by Cooper). Aviation.

--Aviation Weather Services. 3rd ed. (Pilot Training Ser.). (Illus.). 123p. 1979. pap. 6.00 (ISBN 0-89100-161-1, EA-AC61-0045B). Aviation Maintenance.

--Aviation Weather Services: Ac 00-45b. (Illus.). 1980. pap. 6.00 (ISBN 0-86677-001-1). Aviation.

--Basic Ground Instructor Written Test Guide. 113p. 1980. pap. text ed. 4.75 (ISBN 0-939158-23-X). Flightshops.

--Basic Helicopter Handbook. 3rd ed. (Pilot Training Ser.). (Illus.). 111p. 1978. pap. 5.50 (ISBN 0-89100-162-X, EA-AC61-13B). Aviation Maintenance.

--Basic Helicopter Handbook: Ac 61-13b. pap. 5.50 (ISBN 0-86677-003-8, Pub. by Cooper). Aviation.

--Commercial Pilot-Airplane Flight Test Guide. rev. ed. 70p. 1975. pap. text ed. 4.00 (ISBN 0-939158-10-8). Flightshops.

--Commercial Pilot-Airplane Written Test Guide. rev. ed. 141p. 1979. pap. text ed. 5.50 (ISBN 0-939158-14-0). Flightshops.

--Commercial Pilot Flight Test Guide. 2nd ed. (Pilot Training Ser.: Pilot Training Ser.). 29p. 1975. pap. 4.75 (ISBN 0-89100-172-7, EA-AC61-55A). Aviation Maintenance.

--Commercial Pilot Question Book. (Pilot Training Ser.). (Illus.). 228p. 1984. pap. 6.50 (ISBN 0-89100-260-X, EA-FAA-T-8080-2). Aviation Maintenance.

--Federal Aviation Regulations: Air Taxi Operators & Commerical Operators of Small Aircraft, Pt. 135. Aviation Book Company, ed. 1979. pap. 5.95 (ISBN 0-911720-56-1). Aviation.

--Federal Aviation Regulations for Aircraft Mechanics. 9th ed. (Aviation Maintenance Training Course Ser.). 750p. 1985. pap. 14.95 (ISBN 0-89100-278-2, EA-FAR-1J). Aviation Maintenance.

--Flight Engineer Turboset-Basic Written Test Guide. 144p. 1977. pap. text ed. 4.00 (ISBN 0-939158-18-3). Flightshops.

--Flight Instructor Airplane Written Test Guide. rev. ed. 138p. 1979. pap. text ed. 7.00 (ISBN 0-939158-15-9). Flightshops.

--Flight Instructor Instrument-Airplane Written Test Guide. rev. ed. 86p. 1980. pap. text ed. 4.00 (ISBN 0-939158-13-2). Flightshops.

--Flight Instructor Practical Test Guide. rev. ed. 17p. 1978. pap. text ed. 1.75 (ISBN 0-939158-12-4). Flightshops.

--Flight Instructor Practical Test Guide (AC 61-58A) 1979. pap. 1.75 (ISBN 0-86677-011-9, Pub. by Cooper Aviation). Aviation.

--Flight Instructor Question Book. (Pilot Training Ser.). (Illus.). 150p. 1984. pap. 5.50 (ISBN 0-89100-262-6, EA-FAA-T-8080-3). Aviation Maintenance.

--Flight Test Guide, Instrument, Airplane AC 61-56A) 1976. pap. text ed. 1.75 (ISBN 0-86677-009-7, Pub. by Cooper Aviation). Aviation.

--Flight Training Handbook. 2nd ed. (Pilot Training Ser.). (Illus.). 325p. 1980. pap. 9.00 (ISBN 0-89100-165-4, EA-AC61-21A). Aviation Maintenance.

--Flight Training Handbook. LC 80-70552. (Illus.). 352p. 1981. 15.95 (ISBN 0-385-17599-X). Doubleday.

--Flight Training Handbook. rev. ed. 325p. 1980. pap. text ed. 9.00 (ISBN 0-939158-06-X). Flightshops.

--Flight Training Handbook: Ac 61-21a. pap. 9.00 (ISBN 0-86677-004-6, Pub. by Cooper). Aviation.

--Fundamentals of Instructing Flight & Ground Instructors Written Test Guide. 36p. 1979. pap. text ed. 2.25 (ISBN 0-939158-17-5). Flightshops.

--Instrument Flying Handbook. 3rd ed. (Pilot Training Ser.). (Illus.). 271p. 1980. pap. 8.50 (ISBN 0-89100-257-X, EA-AC61-27C). Aviation Maintenance.

--Instrument Flying Handbook. rev. ed. 268p. 1980. pap. text ed. 8.50 (ISBN 0-939158-07-8). Flightshops.

--Instrument Flying Handbook: Ac 61-27c. 1980. pap. 8.50 (ISBN 0-86677-005-4, Pub. by Cooper). Aviation.

--Instrument Pilot-Airplane Flight Test Guide. rev. ed. 23p. 1976. pap. text ed. 1.75 (ISBN 0-939158-11-6). Flightshops.

--Instrument Rating-Written Test Guide. rev. ed. 200p. 1977. pap. text ed. 4.25 (ISBN 0-939158-04-3). Flightshops.

--Non-Destructive Testing in Aircraft: AC 43-3. 38p. pap. 2.00x (ISBN 0-89100-083-6). Aviation Maint.

--Pilot's Handbook of Aeronautical Knowledge: Ac 61-23b. pap. 11.00 (ISBN 0-86677-012-7, Pub. by Cooper). Aviation.

--Pilot's Handbook of Aeronautical Knowledge. 2nd ed. (Pilot Training Ser.). (Illus.). 257p. 1971. pap. 11.00 (ISBN 0-89100-223-5, EA-AC61-23B). Aviation Maintenance.

--Pilots Weight & Balance Handbook: FAA AC 91-23A. (Illus.). 1977. pap. 5.00 (ISBN 0-939158-22-1, Pub. by Cooper). Aviation.

--Piolt's Weight & Balance Handbook. rev. ed. 68p. 1977. pap. text ed. 4.75 (ISBN 0-939158-22-1). Flightshops.

--Private Pilot (Airplane) Flight Test Guide: AC 61-54a. 1975. pap. 3.50 (ISBN 0-86677-007-0, Pub. by Cooper). Aviation.

--Private Pilot-Airplane Flight Test Guide. rev. ed. 92p. 1975. pap. text ed. 1.75 (ISBN 0-939158-09-4). Flightshops.

--Private Pilot-Airplane Written Test Guide. rev. ed. 148p. 1979. pap. text ed. 3.50 (ISBN 0-939158-08-6). Flightshops.

--Private Pilot Question Book. (Pilot Training Ser.). (Illus.). 138p. 1984. pap. 5.00 (ISBN 0-89100-258-8, EA-FAA-T-8080-1). Aviation Maintenance.

--Private Pilot Question Book & References. (Pilot Training Ser.). (Illus.). 234p. 1984. pap. 9.95 (ISBN 0-89100-259-6, EA-FAA-T-8080-1C). Aviation Maintenance.

--Student Pilot Guide. rev. ed. 36p. 1979. pap. text ed. 2.50 (ISBN 0-939158-05-1). Flightshops.

--Student Pilot Guide (AC 61-12J) 1979. pap. text ed. 3.95 (ISBN 0-939158-05-1, Pub. by Natl Flightshops). Aviation.

--VFR Pilot Exam-O-Grams. Aviation Book Company Staff, ed. (Illus.). 120p. 1982. pap. 3.50 (ISBN 0-911721-78-9). Aviation.

Federal Aviation Administration & Aviation Book Company Editors. IFR Pilot Exam-O-Grams. (Illus.). 96p. 1984. pap. 3.25 (ISBN 0-911721-79-7). Aviation.

Federal Aviation Administration & National Oceanic & Atmospheric Administration. Aviation Weather Services. rev. ed. 123p. 1979. pap. text ed. 5.50 (ISBN 0-939158-02-7). Flightshops.

Federal Aviation Administration, Department of Transportation. Commercial Pilot Question Book. (Illus.). 236p. (Orig.). 1985. pap. text ed. 6.50 (ISBN 0-317-31554-4). Astro Pubs.

Federal Aviation Administration, Dept. of Transportation. Private Pilot-Airplane: Practical Test Standards for Airplane, Single-Engine, Land. 118p. (Orig.). 1984. pap. text ed. 4.95 (ISBN 0-941272-25-7). Astro Pubs.

Federal Aviation Administration of the U.S. Dept of Transportation. Instrument Flying Handbook (AC 61-27c) (Illus.). 272p. 1983. pap. 8.50 (ISBN 0-911721-96-7). Aviation.

Federal Aviation Administration Staff. Federal Aviation Regulations for Pilots, 1985. 9th ed. Winner, Walter P., ed. 216p. 1985. pap. 4.95 (ISBN 0-911721-99-1). Aviation.

--Private Pilot: Practical Test Standards for Airplane, Single-Engine, Land. 112p. 1984. pap. 3.95 (ISBN 0-916413-01-2). Aviation.

--Private Pilot Question Book. rev. ed. (Illus.). 1984. pap. 5.00. Astro Pubs.

Federal Aviation Agency. Pilot Instruction Manual. 1961. 12.95 (ISBN 0-385-01046-X). Doubleday.

Federal Bar Association. Equal Justice under Law. 2nd ed. (Illus.). 151p. 1973. 2.50 (ISBN 0-318-14082-9). Federal Bar.

--Rules of Civil Procedure Conference: Proceedings of the Federal Bar Association, December 1981. 51p. 5.00 (ISBN 0-318-14094-2). Federal Bar.

--U. S. - Mexico Trade Law. 183p. 25.00 (ISBN 0-318-14103-5). Federal Bar.

Federal Bar Association, Annual Conference, 4th, 1979. Administrative Law. 117p. 20.00 (ISBN 0-318-14063-2). Federal Bar.

Federal Bar Association, Annual Convention, August 1980. The Role of Financial Institutions in the 1980's. 207p. 20.00 (ISBN 0-318-14091-8). Federal Bar.

Federal Bar Association, Conference, April 1980. Fifth Annual Indian Law Seminar. 100p. 15.00 (ISBN 0-318-14084-5). Federal Bar.

--Government Contract Litigation. 186p. 20.00 (ISBN 0-318-14087-X). Federal Bar.

Federal Bar Association Conference, April 1981. Sixth Annual Indian Law Conference. 113p. 15.00 (ISBN 0-318-14097-7). Federal Bar.

Federal Bar Association, Conference, April 1979. United States-China Trade Law Conference Summary. 73p. 25.00 (ISBN 0-318-14104-3). Federal Bar.

Federal Bar Association, Conference, December 1980. Accountability & the Management of the Regulatory Process Administrative Law. 85p. 15.00 (ISBN 0-318-14062-4). Federal Bar.

Federal Bar Association, Conference, December 1979. Airline Deregulation. 53p. 10.00 (ISBN 0-318-14064-0). Federal Bar.

Federal Bar Association, Conference, December 1980. Antitrust & Trade Regulation. 159p. 20.00 (ISBN 0-318-14066-7). Federal Bar.

Federal Bar Association, Conference, December 1979. Equal Employment Opportunity Law. 69p. 10.00 (ISBN 0-318-14081-0). Federal Bar.

--Rules of Civil Procedure. 95p. 20.00 (ISBN 0-318-14092-6). Federal Bar.

Federal Bar Association, Conference, December 1980. Rules of Civil Procedure. 93p. 15.00 (ISBN 0-318-14093-4). Federal Bar.

Federal Bar Association, Conference, February 1981. Fourth Annual Seminar on Grant Law. 314p. 35.00 (ISBN 0-318-14086-1). Federal Bar.

Federal Bar Association, Conference, June 1981. Conference on Securities Regulation & the Capital Raising Process for the Small Issuer. 435p. 40.00 (ISBN 0-318-14072-1); members 30.00 (ISBN 0-318-14073-X). Federal Bar.

Federal Bar Association, Conference, June 1979. Report on the United States-Japan Trade Law Conference. 197p. 35.00 (ISBN 0-318-14090-X). Federal Bar.

Federal Bar Association, Conference, March 1981. Fourth Annual Copyright Law Conference. 94p. 10.00 (ISBN 0-318-14085-3). Federal Bar.

--Second Annual Immigration Law Conference. 234p. 30.00 (ISBN 0-318-14095-0). Federal Bar.

Federal Bar Association, Conference, November 1979. Congressional Campaigns & Federal Law. 233p. 35.00 (ISBN 0-318-14075-6). Federal Bar.

Federal Bar Association, Conference, October 1980. Conference on the Proposed Federal Securities Code. 430p. 35.00 (ISBN 0-318-14074-8). Federal Bar.

Federal Bar Association, Conference on Regulatory Reform, May 1980. Current Issues in Regulatory Reform. 304p. 25.00 (ISBN 0-318-14076-4). Federal Bar.

Federal Bar Association, Conference, September 1980. Conference on Broadcast Advertising Law. 158p. 20.00 (ISBN 0-318-14070-5). Federal Bar.

Federal Bar Association, Hartford Regional Conference, April 1980. Bankruptcy Law. 100p. 15.00 (ISBN 0-318-14067-5). Federal Bar.

Federal Bar Association, Midwest Regional Conference, April 1980. Bankruptcy Seminar. 178p. 20.00 (ISBN 0-318-14068-3). Federal Bar.

--Employment Discrimination Seminar. 80p. 15.00 (ISBN 0-318-14080-2). Federal Bar.

Federal Bar Association. Securities Law Committee, jt. auth. see United States. Securities & Exchange Commission.

Federal Bar Association. Securities Law Committee & American Law Institute-American Bar Association Committee on Continuing Professional Education. Broker-Dealer Regulation: ALI-ABA Course of Study Materials. LC 84-118078. (Illus.). xii, 588p. 1984. write for info. Am Law Inst.

Federal Bar Association, Securities Law Committee Staff. Federal Securities Laws: Legislative History, 1933-1982, 4 Vols. 5014p. 1983. text ed. 650.00 (ISBN 0-87179-418-7). BNA.

Federal Bar Association, Seminar, October 1980. Business & Government in United States-Japanese Economic Relations. 106p. 35.00 (ISBN 0-318-14069-1). Federal Bar.

Federal Bar Association, Seminar on Tax Law, January 1980. How Tax Law is Written. 89p. 30.00 (ISBN 0-318-14088-8). Federal Bar.

Federal Bar Association Staff. Dynamics of Pretrial Practice in Contract Litigation: Topics of the Second Annual Seminar on Government Contract Litigation, 1981. 148p. 30.00 (ISBN 0-318-14077-2); members 20.00 (ISBN 0-318-14078-0). Federal Bar.

Federal Bar Association, U.S.-Japan Trade Law Conference, 1979. U. S. - Japan Trade Law Conference. 76p. 15.00 (ISBN 0-318-14102-7). Federal Bar.

Federal Bar Association, Workshop, June 1979. Federal Tort Claims Act: Medical Malpractice. 105p. 25.00 (ISBN 0-318-14083-7). Federal Bar.

Federal Communication Commission. The Northeast Corridor, 3 vols. 1981. Set. pap. 150.00 (ISBN 0-686-39232-9); pap. 50.00 each (ISBN 0-686-39233-7). Info Gatekeepers.

Federal Communications Commission. Annual Reports of the Federal Communications Commission, 1935-1955. LC 72-161167. (History of Broadcasting: Radio to Television Ser). 1971. Repr. of 1935 ed. 144.00 (ISBN 0-405-03577-2). Ayer Co Pubs.

--Competitive Impact Statement on the AT&T Anti-Trust Case. 1982. 50.00 (ISBN 0-686-37962-4). Info Gatekeepers.

--Investigation of the Telephone Industry in the United States. LC 74-4679. (Telecommunications Ser). (Illus.). 668p. 1974. Repr. of 1939 ed. 45.50x (ISBN 0-405-06045-9). Ayer Co Pubs.

--Public Service Responsibility of Broadcast Licensees. LC 74-5225. (Telecommunications Ser). 64p. 1974. Repr. of 1946 ed. 18.00x (ISBN 0-405-06064-5). Ayer Co Pubs.

Federal Communications Commission Planning Conference November 8 & 9, 1976 & Hopewell, Lynn. Computers & Communications: Proceedings. (Illus.). 197p. 1976. pap. 11.50 (ISBN 0-88283-022-8). AFIPS Pr.

Federal Construction Council - Building Research Advisory Board. Crack Control in Concrete Masonry Unit Construction. 1964. pap. 3.00. Natl Acad Pr.

--Evaluation of Components for Underground Heat Distribution Systems. 1964. pap. 2.75 (ISBN 0-309-01196-5). Natl Acad Pr.

--Supplementary Field Investigation of Underground Heat Distribution Systems. 1966. pap. 4.25 (ISBN 0-309-01481-6). Natl Acad Pr.

Federal Council of the Churches of Christ in America. The Public Relations of the Motion Picture Industry: A Report by the Department of Research & Education. LC 76-160231. (Moving Pictures Ser). 156p. 1971. Repr. of 1931 ed. lib. bdg. 11.95x (ISBN 0-89198-032-6). Ozer.

Federal Council on the Arts & Humanities. Cultural Directory II: Federal Funds & Services for the Arts & Humanities. rev. ed. LC 79-20413. 256p. 1980. pap. 8.95x (ISBN 0-87474-323-0). Smithsonian.

Federal Electric Corporation. How to Write Effective Reports. (Communication Ser). (Prog. Bk.). 1965. pap. text ed. 9.95 (ISBN 0-201-02046-7). Addison-Wesley.

--A Programmed Introduction to PERT: Program Evaluation & Review Technique. 145p. 1963. pap. 32.50x (ISBN 0-471-25680-3, Pub. by Wiley-Interscience). Wiley.

Federal Energy Administration. Project Independence Blueprint: Final Task Force Report, Solar Energy. 564p. Repr. of 1974 ed. 59.50x (ISBN 0-89934-062-8, V054-PP). Solar Energy Info.

--Wind Energy Conversion Systems Manufacturing & Sales Activity. Bereny, J. A., ed. 1978. pap. 6.95x (ISBN 0-930978-13-7, W-030). Solar Energy Info.

Federal Energy Administration, jt. auth. see Institute of Real Estate Management.

Federal Institute for Biology in Agriculture & Forestry, Institute for Plant Protection Agent Research, Berlin-Dahlem & Ebing, Winifried. Gaschromatographie der Pflanzenschutzmittel: Tabellarische Literaturreferate, 5 vols. new ed. (Ger.). Vol. I, 1970. 20.00 (ISBN 0-913106-09-7); Vol. II, 1972. 15.00 (ISBN 0-913106-10-0); Vol. III. 15.00 (ISBN 0-913106-11-9); Vol. IV. 15.00 (ISBN 0-913106-12-7); Vol. V, 1975. 15.00 (ISBN 0-913106-13-5). PolyScience.

Federal Institute for Earth Sciences & Raw Materials & German Institute for Economic Research. Cobalt: A Research Report. LC 79-87840. (A World Mining Report). (Illus.). 1979. pap. 295.00 (ISBN 0-87930-120-1). Miller Freeman.

Federal Judicial Center. Manual for Complex Litigation. LC 82-9507. 1982. looseleaf 50.00 (ISBN 0-87632-359-X). Boardman.

Federal Office of Civil Defense, Switzerland. Makeshift Shelters. 1983. 17.50 (ISBN 0-86304-028-4, Pub. by Octagon Pr England). Ins Study Human.

Federal Oil Conservation Board. Oil & Gas Conservation Statutes: Annotated. Ely, Northcutt, ed. 432p. 1982. Repr. of 1933 ed. lib. bdg. 35.00 (ISBN 0-89941-226-2). W S Hein.

--Oil Conservation Through Interstate Agreement. 393p. 1982. Repr. of 1933 ed. lib. bdg. 35.00 (ISBN 0-89941-225-4). W S Hein.

Federal Parliamentary Labor Party. Caucus Minutes Nineteen One to Nineteen Forty-Nine, Vol. 2: 1917-1931. Weller, Patrick & Lloyd, Beverley, eds. (Illus.). 1976. 38.50x (ISBN 0-522-84074-4, Pub. by Melbourne U Pr). Intl Spec Bk.

--Caucus Minutes Nineteen One to Nineteen Forty-Nine, Vol. 3: 1932-1949. Weller, Patrick & Lloyd, Beverley, eds. (Illus.). 1976. 38.50x (ISBN 0-522-84075-2, Pub. by Melbourne U Pr). Intl Spec Bk.

Federal Parliamentary Labor Party, jt. ed. see Weller, Patrick.

Federal Publications Inc. & Boyd, Roger N. Defective Pricing in Government Contracts: Course Manual. LC 85-129612. (Illus.). 226p. 1985. write for info. Fed Pubns Inc.

Federal Publications Inc. & Lifschitz, Judah. Construction Bid Rigging: Course Manual. LC 85-104437. (Illus.). 1984. write for info. Fed Pubns Inc.

Federal Publications Inc., et al. A Contruction Course for Owners. LC 84-229145. (Illus.). write for info. Amer Bar Assn.

Federal Publications Inc. Staff, et al. Emerging Employee Rights. LC 84-249579. write for info. Amer Bar Assn.

Federal Radio Commission. Annual Reports of the Federal Radio Commission, 1927-1933. LC 70-161169. (History of Broadcasting: Radio to Television Ser). 1971. Repr. of 1927 ed. 51.00 (ISBN 0-405-03578-0). Ayer Co Pubs.

Federal Reserve Bank of Atlanta. Growth Industries in the Nineteen Eighties: Conference Proceedings. LC 83-13822. xxii, 196p. 1983. lib. bdg. 35.00 (ISBN 0-89930-069-3, FGI/, Quorum). Greenwood.

Federal Reserve Bank of Atlanta & Emory University Law & Economics Center. Supply-Side Economics in the Nineteen Eighties: Conference Proceedings. LC 82-15025. (Illus.). 572p. 1982. lib. bdg. 35.00 (ISBN 0-89930-045-6, FSU/, Quorum). Greenwood.

Federal Reserve Bank of St. Louis, ed. Financial Innovations. 192p. 1984. 27.95 (ISBN 0-89838-152-5). Kluwer Nijhoff.

Federal Reserve System. Banking Studies. LC 82-48179. (Gold, Money, Inflation & Deflation Ser.). 508p. 1982. lib. bdg. 66.00 (ISBN 0-8240-5231-5). Garland Pub.

Federal Trade Commission. Chain Stores: Nineteen Hundred Thirty-One to Nineteen Hundred Thirty-Four, 4 vols. 1985. Repr. of 1932 ed. Set. lib. bdg. 350.00 (ISBN 0-89941-427-3). W S Hein.

--Report of the Federal Trade Commission on the Radio Industry: In Response to House Resolution 548, 67th Congress, Fourth Session, December 1, 1923. LC 74-4680. (Telecommunications Ser). 360p. 1974. Repr. of 1924 ed. 24.00x (ISBN 0-405-06046-7). Ayer Co Pubs.

Federal Trade Commission, United States. Cooperative Marketing. facsimile ed. McCurry, Dan C. & Rubenstein, Richard E., eds. LC 74-30657. (American Farmers & the Rise of Agribusiness Ser.). 1975. Repr. of 1928 ed. 66.00x (ISBN 0-405-06832-8). Ayer Co Pubs.

--Report of the Federal Trade Commission on Agricultural Income Inquiry, 3 vols. in 2. facsimile ed. McCurry, Dan C. & Rubenstein, Richard E., eds. Incl. Pt. 1. Principal Farm Products; Pt. 2. Fruits & Vegetables; Pt. 3. Supplementary Report. LC 74-30658. (American Farmers & the Rise of Agribusiness Ser.). 1975. Repr. of 1938 ed. Set. 132.00x (ISBN 0-405-06833-6). Ayer Co Pubs.

Federal Writers Program, Florida. Seeing Fernandina: A Guide to the City & Its Industries. LC 73-3604. (American Guide Ser). Repr. of 1940 ed. 20.00 (ISBN 0-404-57908-6). AMS Pr.

Federal Writers' Project. Alabama: A Guide to the Deep South. (American Guidebook Ser.). 1941. Repr. 49.00 (ISBN 0-403-02153-7). Somerset Pub.

--Alaska: A Guide to Alaska, Last American Frontier. LC 72-84457. (American Guidebook Ser.). 1981. Repr. of 1939 ed. lib. bdg. 59.00x (ISBN 0-403-02154-5). Somerset Pub.

Federal Writer's Project. American Stuff. (FDR & the Era of the New Deal Ser.). 1976. Repr. of 1937 ed. lib. bdg. 39.50 (ISBN 0-306-70806-X). Da Capo.

Federal Writers' Project. Arizona: The Grand Canyon State. (American Guidebook Ser.). 532p. 1940. Repr. 59.00 (ISBN 0-403-02155-3). Somerset Pub.

--Arkansas: A Guide to the State. LC 72-84459. (American Guidebook). 1980. Repr. of 1941 ed. lib. bdg. 59.00x (ISBN 0-403-02156-1). Somerset Pub.

--Atlanta: A City of the Modern South. LC 72-84460. (American Guidebook Ser.). 1980. Repr. of 1942 ed. lib. bdg. 49.00x (ISBN 0-403-02200-2). Somerset Pub.

--California: A Guide to the Golden State. LC 72-84461. (American Guidebook Series). 1980. Repr. of 1939 ed. lib. bdg. 69.00x (ISBN 0-403-02157-X). Somerset Pub.

--Cincinnati: A Guide to the Queen City & Its Neighbors. LC 72-84462. (American Guidebook Ser.). 1981. Repr. of 1943 ed. 59.00x (ISBN 0-403-02201-0). Somerset Pub.

--Colorado: A Guide to the Highest State. LC 72-84463. (American Guide Ser.). 1980. Repr. of 1941 ed. lib. bdg. 59.00x (ISBN 0-403-02158-8). Somerset Pub.

--Connecticut: A Guide to Its Roads, Lore & People. LC 72-84463. (American Guidebook Ser.). 1980. Repr. of 1938 ed. lib. bdg. 69.00x (ISBN 0-403-02159-6). Somerset Pub.

--Delaware: A Guide to the First State. (American Guidebook Ser.). 562p. 1938. Repr. 59.00 (ISBN 0-403-02160-X). Somerset Pub.

--Florida: A Guide to the Southernmost State. LC 72-84466. (American Guidebook Ser.). 1981. Repr. of 1939 ed. 69.00x (ISBN 0-403-02161-8). Somerset Pub.

--Georgia: A Guide to Its Towns & Country-Side. LC 72-84467. (American Guidebook Ser.). 1981. Repr. of 1940 ed. 69.00x (ISBN 0-403-02162-6). Somerset Pub.

--Hampton Institute, Hampton VA: A Classified Catalogue of the Negro Collection in the Collis P. Huntington Library. LC 70-129188. (American Guidebook Ser.). 1980. Repr. of 1940 ed. lib. bdg. 39.00x (ISBN 0-403-02209-6). Somerset Pub.

--Hands That Built New Hampshire: The Story of Granite State Craftsmen Past & Present. LC 73-3635. Repr. of 1940 ed. 27.50 (ISBN 0-404-57935-3). AMS Pr.

--Here's New England: A Guide to Vacationland. (American Guidebook Ser.). 1939. Repr. 39.00x (ISBN 0-403-02207-X). Somerset Pub.

--Houston: A History & Guide. (American Guidebook Ser.). 1980. Repr. of 1942 ed. lib. bdg. 59.00x (ISBN 0-686-30668-6). Somerset Pub.

Federal Writers Project. Idaho: A Guide in Word & Picture. 2nd ed. (American Guide Ser). 1950. 22.50x (ISBN 0-19-500589-9). Oxford U Pr.

Federal Writers' Project. Idaho: A Guide in Word & Picture. (American Guidebook Ser.). 1937. Repr. 49.00x (ISBN 0-403-02163-4). Somerset Pub.

Federal Writers Project. Illinois: A Descriptive & Historical Guide. LC 72-145010. (American Guidebook Ser.). (Illus.). 1971. Repr. of 1947 ed. 69.00x (ISBN 0-403-01292-9). Somerset Pub.

Federal Writers' Project. Indiana: A Guide to the Hoosier State. (American Guidebook Ser.). 564p. 1941. Repr. 59.00x (ISBN 0-403-02165-0). Somerset Pub.

--Intracoastal Waterway. LC 73-19778. (American Guidebook Ser.). 1981. Repr. of 1939 ed. 39.00x (ISBN 0-403-02213-4). Somerset Pub.

--Iowa: A Guide to the Hawkeye State. (American Guidebook Ser.). 583p. 1938. Repr. 59.00 (ISBN 0-403-02166-9). Somerset Pub.

--Italians of New York City. LC 72-166660. (American Guidebook Ser.). 1980. Repr. of 1939 ed. lib. bdg. 39.00x (ISBN 0-403-02215-0). Somerset Pub.

--Kansas: A Guide to the Sunflower State. (American Guidebook Ser.). 538p. 1939. Repr. 59.00 (ISBN 0-403-02167-7). Somerset Pub.

--Kentucky: A Guide to the Bluegrass State. (American Guidebook Ser.). 492p. 1939. Repr. 59.00x (ISBN 0-403-02168-5). Somerset Pub.

--Lay My Burden Down: A Folk History of Slavery. (American Guidebook Ser.). 285p. 1945. Repr. 39.00x (ISBN 0-403-02212-6). Somerset Pub.

--Los Angeles: A Guide to the City & Its Environs. (American Guidebook Ser.). 1941. Repr. 49.00x (ISBN 0-403-02202-9). Somerset Pub.

--Louisiana: A Guide to the State. (American Guidebook Ser.). 711p. 1941. Repr. 75.00x (ISBN 0-403-02169-3). Somerset Pub.

--Maine: A Guide Down East. (American Guidebook Ser.). 476p. 1936. Repr. 59.00x (ISBN 0-403-02170-7). Somerset Pub.

--A Maritime History of New York. LC 76-44939. (American Guidebook Ser.). 1980. Repr. of 1941 ed. lib. bdg. 59.00x (ISBN 0-403-03823-5). Somerset Pub.

--Maryland: A Guide to the Old Line State. (American Guidebook Ser.). 1940. Repr. 59.00x (ISBN 0-403-02171-5). Somerset Pub.

--Massachusetts: A Guide to Its Places & People. (American Guidebook Ser.). 675p. 1937. Repr. 69.00x (ISBN 0-403-02150-2). Somerset Pub.

--Michigan: A Guide to the Wolverine State. LC 72-84482. (American Guidebook Ser.). 1981. Repr. of 1941 ed. 69.00x (ISBN 0-403-02172-3). Somerset Pub.

--Minnesota: A State Guide. (American Guidebook Ser.). 545p. 1938. Repr. 59.00x (ISBN 0-403-02173-1). Somerset Pub.

--Mississippi: A Guide to the Magnolia State. (American Guidebook Ser.). 545p. 1938. Repr. 59.00x (ISBN 0-403-02174-X). Somerset Pub.

--Missouri: A Guide to the 'Show Me' State. LC 72-84486. (American Guidebook Ser.). 1981. Repr. of 1941 ed. 69.00x (ISBN 0-403-02175-8). Somerset Pub.

--Montana: A State Guide Book. (American Guidebook Ser.). 430p. 1939. Repr. 49.00x (ISBN 0-403-02176-6). Somerset Pub.

--Nebraska: A Guide to the Cornhusker State. (American Guidebook Ser.). 424p. 1939. Repr. 49.00x (ISBN 0-403-02177-4). Somerset Pub.

--Nebraska: A Guide to the Cornhusker State. LC 78-26756. (Illus.). xxiv, 424p. 1979. 29.95x (ISBN 0-8032-1953-9); pap. 9.95 (ISBN 0-8032-6851-3, BB 690, Bison). U of Nebr Pr.

--Nevada: A Guide to the Silver State. (American Guidebook Ser.). 1940. Repr. 49.00x (ISBN 0-403-02178-2). Somerset Pub.

--New Hampshire: A Guide to the Granite State. (American Guidebook Ser.). 559p. 1938. Repr. 59.00x (ISBN 0-403-02179-0). Somerset Pub.

--New Jersey: A Guide to Its Present & Past. (American Guidebook Ser.). 735p. 1939. Repr. 75.00x (ISBN 0-403-02180-4). Somerset Pub.

--New Mexico: A Guide to the Colorful State. (American Guidebook Ser.). 1940. Repr. 59.00x (ISBN 0-403-02181-2). Somerset Pub.

--New Orleans: A City Guide. (American Guidebook Ser.). 416p. 1938. Repr. 59.00x (ISBN 0-403-02203-7). Somerset Pub.

--New York: A City Guide. LC 39-27593. (American Guidebook Ser.). (Illus.). 708p. 1939. Repr. 75.00x (ISBN 0-403-02921-X). Somerset Pub.

Federal Writers Project. New York: Guide to the Empire State. (American Guide Ser). 1940. 22.50x (ISBN 0-19-500038-2). Oxford U Pr.

Federal Writers' Project. New York Panorama: A Comprehensive View of the Metropolis Presented in a Series of Articles. LC 76-145121. (American Guidebook Ser.). 1981. Repr. of 1941 ed. lib. bdg. 69.00x (ISBN 0-403-02152-9). Somerset Pub.

--New York State: A Guide to the Empire State. (American Guidebook Ser.). 782p. 1940. Repr. 75.00x (ISBN 0-403-02151-0). Somerset Pub.

--North Carolina: A Guide to the Old North State. (American Guidebook Ser.). 649p. 1939. Repr. 69.00x (ISBN 0-403-02182-0). Somerset Pub.

--North Dakota: A Guide to the Northern Prairie State. LC 72-84498. (American Guidebook Ser.). 1980. Repr. of 1938 ed. lib. bdg. 49.00x (ISBN 0-403-02183-9). Somerset Pub.

Federal Writers Project. North Dakota: Guide to the Northern Prairie State. 2nd ed. (American Guide Ser.). 1950. 22.50x (ISBN 0-19-500043-9). Oxford U Pr.

Federal Writers' Project. Ocean Highway. LC 72-10937. (American Guidebook Ser.). 1980. Repr. of 1940 ed. lib. bdg. 39.00x (ISBN 0-403-02183-9). Somerset Pub.

--The Ohio Guide. (American Guidebook Ser.). 634p. 1940. Repr. 69.00x (ISBN 0-403-02184-7). Somerset Pub.

--Oklahoma: A Guide to the Sooner State. (American Guidebook Ser.). 532p. Repr. 59.00x (ISBN 0-403-02185-5). Somerset Pub.

--Oregon: End of the Trail. (American Guidebook Ser.). 548p. 1941. Repr. 59.00 (ISBN 0-403-02186-3). Somerset Pub.

Federal Writers Project. Oregon Trail: The Missouri River to the Pacific Ocean. LC 70-145012. (American Guidebook Ser.). (Illus.). 1971. Repr. of 1939 ed. 39.00x (ISBN 0-403-01290-2). Somerset Pub.

Federal Writers' Project. Pennsylvania: A Guide to the Keystone State. (American Guidebook Ser.). 1980. Repr. of 1940 ed. lib. bdg. 69.00x (ISBN 0-403-02187-1). Somerset Pub.

--Pennsylvania Cavalcade. LC 76-44940. (American Guidebook Ser.). 1980. Repr. of 1942 ed. lib. bdg. 59.00x (ISBN 0-403-03821-9). Somerset Pub.

--Philadelphia: A Guide to the Nation's Birthplace. LC 39-4271. (American Guidebook). 1982. Repr. of 1939 ed. 75.00x (ISBN 0-403-02204-5). Somerset Pub.

--Rhode Island: A Guide to the Smallest State. (American Guidebook Ser.). 500p. 1937. Repr. 59.00x (ISBN 0-403-02188-X). Somerset Pub.

--San Francisco. (American Guidebook Ser.). 538p. 1940. Repr. 11.00 (ISBN 0-403-02205-3). Somerset Pub.

--San Francisco: A Guide to the Bay & Its Cities. new rev. ed. Hansen, Gladys, ed. (American Guide Ser.). 1972. 14.95 (ISBN 0-8038-6692-5). Hastings.

--Santa Barbara: A Guide to the Channel City & Its Environs. LC 73-4574. (American Guidebook Ser.). 1980. Repr. of 1941 ed. lib. bdg. 49.00x (ISBN 0-403-02216-9). Somerset Pub.

Federal Writers Project. Slave Narratives: A Folk History of Slavery in the U.S. from Interviews with Former Slaves, 17 vols. (American Guidebook Ser.). 1941. 699.00x set (ISBN 0-403-02211-8); 49.00 ea. Somerset Pub.

--South Carolina: A Guide to the Palmetto State. (American Guidebook Ser.). 514p. 1941. Repr. 69.00x (ISBN 0-403-02189-8). Somerset Pub.

Federal Writers' Project. South Dakota: A Guide to the State. (American Guidebook Ser.). 421p. 1938. Repr. 59.00x (ISBN 0-403-02190-1). Somerset Pub.

--State & City Guide Books, 61 vols. (American Guidebook Ser.). Repr. of 1942 ed. Set. lib. bdg. 2998.00x (ISBN 0-403-02249-5). Somerset Pub.

--Tennessee: A Guide to the State. 558p. 1939. Repr. 59.00x (ISBN 0-403-02191-X). Somerset Pub.

--Texas: A Guide to the Lone Star State. LC 40-10658. 717p. 75.00x (ISBN 0-403-02192-8). Somerset Pub.

Federal Writers Project. These Are Our Lives. 448p. 1975. pap. 6.95 (ISBN 0-393-00763-4, Norton Lib). Norton.

Federal Writers' Project. Utah: A State Guide. 1941. Repr. 59.00x (ISBN 0-403-02193-6). Somerset Pub.

--Vermont: A Guide to the Green Mountain State. 1937. Repr. 49.00x (ISBN 0-403-02194-4). Somerset Pub.

Federal Writer's Project. Virginia: A Guide to the Old Dominion. LC 72-84513. (American Guidebook Series). 1980. Repr. of 1940 ed. lib. bdg. 75.00x (ISBN 0-403-02195-2). Somerset Pub.

Federal Writers' Project. Washington: A Guide to the Evergreen State. 688p. 1941. Repr. 69.00x (ISBN 0-403-02196-0). Somerset Pub.

--Washington: City & Capital. 528p. 1942. Repr. 79.00x (ISBN 0-403-02237-1). Somerset Pub.

--West Virginia: A Guide to the Mountain State. LC 72-84516. (American Guidebook Ser.). 1980. Repr. of 1941 ed. lib. bdg. 59.00x (ISBN 0-686-34458-8). Somerset Pub.

--Wisconsin: A State Guide. 69.00x (ISBN 0-403-02198-7). Somerset Pub.

Federal Writer's Project. The WPA Guide to Minnesota. (Borealis Bks.). 523p. 1985. pap. 9.95 (ISBN 0-87351-185-9). Minn Hist.

Federal Writers' Project. The WPA Guide to New York City. 1982. 19.50 (ISBN 0-394-52792-5); pap. 8.95 (ISBN 0-394-71215-3). Pantheon.

--Wyoming: A Guide to Its History, Highways & People. 490p. 1941. Repr. 59.00x (ISBN 0-403-02199-5). Somerset Pub.

--Wyoming: A Guide to Its History, Highways, & People. LC 80-23038. (Illus.). xl, 570p. 1981. 31.50x (ISBN 0-8032-1958-X); pap. 9.75 (ISBN 0-8032-6854-8, BB 757, Bison). U of Nebr Pr.

Federal Writer's Project see Hansen, Harry.

Federal Writers' Project, jt. ed. see Hansen, Harry.

Federal Writers' Project, jt. ed. see Truett, Randle B.

Federal Writers' Project, California. Berkeley, the First Seventy-Five Years. LC 73-3596. (American Guide Ser.). Repr. of 1941 ed. 24.50 (ISBN 0-404-57901-9). AMS Pr.

--Death Valley: A Guide. LC 73-3598. (American Guide Ser.). Repr. of 1939 ed. 14.00 (ISBN 0-404-57902-7). AMS Pr.

Federal Writers Project, California. San Diego: A California City. LC 73-3660. (American Guide Ser.). Repr. of 1937 ed. 17.50 (ISBN 0-404-57904-3). AMS Pr.

Federal Writers' Project, Dutchess Co., N. Y. Dutchess County. LC 73-3645. (American Guide Ser). Repr. of 1937 ed. 20.00 (ISBN 0-404-57944-2). AMS Pr.

Federal Writers Project Editors. Whaling Masters. (Sun Dance Reprints: No. 6). 314p. 1986. lib. bdg. 29.95x (ISBN 0-89370-833-X); pap. text ed. 19.95x (ISBN 0-89370-933-6). Borgo Pr.

Federal Writer's Project, Florida. Seeing St. Augustine. LC 73-3605. (American Guide Ser.). Repr. of 1937 ed. 12.50 (ISBN 0-404-57909-4). AMS Pr.

Federal Writers Project, Georgia. Augusta. LC 73-3606. (American Guide Ser.). Repr. of 1938 ed. 12.50 (ISBN 0-404-57910-8). AMS Pr.

Federal Writer's Project, Georgia. Savannah. LC 73-3608. (American Guide Ser.). Repr. of 1937 ed. 12.50 (ISBN 0-404-57912-4). AMS Pr.

Federal Writers' Project, Idaho. Idaho Lore. LC 73-3612. (American Guide Ser). Repr. of 1939 ed. 21.50 (ISBN 0-404-57915-9). AMS Pr.

Federal Writers' Project. Illinois. Cairo Guide. LC 73-3613. Repr. of 1938 ed. 12.00 (ISBN 0-404-57916-7). AMS Pr.

--Galena Guide. LC 73-3615. Repr. of 1937 ed. 14.00 (ISBN 0-404-57918-3). AMS Pr.

Federal Writers Project, Illinois. Nauvoo Guide. LC 73-3616. (American Guide Ser.). Repr. of 1939 ed. 14.00 (ISBN 0-404-57919-1). AMS Pr.

Federal Writers' Project, Indiana. The Calumet Region Historical Guide. LC 73-3619. Repr. of 1939 ed. 29.00 (ISBN 0-404-57921-3). AMS Pr.

Federal Writers' Project, Massachusetts. The Albanian Struggle in the Old World & New. LC 73-3623. Repr. of 1939 ed. 17.50 (ISBN 0-404-57925-6). AMS Pr.

--The Armenians in Massachusetts. LC 73-3624. (American Guide Ser). Repr. of 1937 ed. 17.00 (ISBN 0-404-57926-4). AMS Pr.

--Boston Looks Seaward: The Story of the Port, 1630-1940. LC 73-3627. (American Guide Ser.). Repr. of 1941 ed. 27.50 (ISBN 0-404-57928-0). AMS Pr.

Federal Writers' Project, Minnesota. The Bohemian Flats. LC 73-3628. (American Guide Ser.). Repr. of 1941 ed. 10.00 (ISBN 0-404-57929-9). AMS Pr.

Federal Writers Project, Mississippi. Mississippi Gulf Coast, Yesterday & Today, 1699-1939. LC 73-3631. (American Guide Ser.). Repr. of 1939 ed. 14.00 (ISBN 0-404-57932-9). AMS Pr.

Federal Writers' Project, Montana. Land of Nakoda: The Story of the Assiniboine Indians. LC 73-3634. (American Guide Ser). Repr. of 1942 ed. 20.00 (ISBN 0-404-57934-5). AMS Pr.

Federal Writers' Project, New Jersey. The Swedes & Finns in New Jersey. LC 73-3640. (American Guide Ser.). (Illus.). Repr. of 1938 ed. 20.00 (ISBN 0-404-57940-X). AMS Pr.

Federal Writers' Project of the Work Projects Administration. The WPA Guide to Nineteen Thirties Kansas. LC 84-51694. Orig. Title: Kansas: A Guide to the Sunflower State. (Illus.). 1984. Repr. of 1939 ed. pap. 12.95 (ISBN 0-7006-0249-6). U Pr of KS.

Federal Writers Project, Pennsylvania. Erie: A Guide to the City & County. LC 73-3649. Repr. of 1938 ed. 17.00 (ISBN 0-404-57948-5). AMS Pr.

Federal Writers' Project, South Carolina. South Carolina Folktales. LC 73-3651. (American Guide Ser). Repr. of 1941 ed. 10.00 (ISBN 0-404-57951-5). AMS Pr.

Federal Writers' Project, South Dakota. Legends of the Mighty Sioux. LC 73-3652. Repr. of 1941 ed. 14.00 (ISBN 0-404-57952-3). AMS Pr.

Federal Writers Project Staff, et al. WPA Guide to California. (Illus.). 713p. 1984. pap. 11.95 (ISBN 0-394-72290-6). Pantheon.

Federal Writer's Project, Washington, D.C. Our Washington: A Comprehensive Album of the Nation's Capital in Words & Pictures. LC 73-3602. (American Guide Ser.). Repr. of 1939 ed. 12.00 (ISBN 0-404-57906-X). AMS Pr.

Federal Writers' Projects. U. S. One: Maine to Florida. 344p. 1938. Repr. 39.00x (ISBN 0-403-02208-8). Somerset Pub.

Federated American Engineering Societies. Waste in Industry. LC 73-8508. (Management History Ser.: No. 58). (Illus.). 420p. 1973. Repr. of 1921 ed. 25.00 (ISBN 0-87960-059-4). Hive Pub.

Federation Internationale de la Precontrainte (FIP), ed. FIP Manual of Lightweight Aggregate Concrete. LC 83-12739. 259p. 1983. 39.95x (ISBN 0-470-27484-0). Halsted Pr.

Federation Internationale de la Precontrainte. Multi-Lingual Dictionary of Concrete. 202p. (Eng., Fr., Ger., Span., Rus. & Dutch.). 1976. 53.25 (ISBN 0-444-41237-9). Elsevier.

Federation National des Gites Ruraux de France Staff. Country Welcome. 368p. 1985. pap. 10.95 (ISBN 2-904394-13-3, Pub. by Victoria & Albert Mus UK). Faber & Faber.

Federation of Feminist Women's Health Centers. A New View of a Woman's Body. 1981. (Touchstone Bks); pap. 9.95 (ISBN 0-671-41215-9). S&S.

Federation of Feminist Women's Health Centers Staff & Cassidy-Brinn, Ginny. Woman-Centered Pregnancy & Birth. LC 83-70352. (Illus.). 204p. 1984. pap. 11.95 (ISBN 0-939416-03-4). Cleis Pr.

Federation of German Industries Staff, ed. The German Export Directory. rev. ed. 2490p. (Ger. & Eng. & Fr. & Span.). 1985. 81.00X (ISBN 0-317-14165-1). IR Pubns.

Federation of Societies for Coatings Technology, Educational Committee, ed. see Fuller, W. R.

Federation of Societies for Coatings Technology, Definitions Committee, ed. Glossary of Color Terms. 96p. 6.00 (ISBN 0-686-95498-X). Fed Soc Coat Tech.

--Paint-Coatings Dictionary. 632p. case-bound 30.00 (ISBN 0-686-95495-5); nonmembers 50.00 (ISBN 0-686-99513-9). Fed Soc Coat Tech.

Federer, H. Geometric Measure Theory. LC 69-16846. (Die Grundlehren der Mathematischen Wissenschaften: Vol. 153). 1969. 71.00 (ISBN 0-387-04505-8). Springer-Verlag.

Federer, Herbert & Jonsson, Bjarni. Analytic Geometry & Calculus. LC 61-6325. pap. 160.00 (ISBN 0-317-08413-5, 2012452). Bks Demand UMI.

Federici, Cesare. The Voyage & Travaile of M. C. Frederick into the East India. Hickock, T., tr. LC 70-171758. (English Experience Ser.: No. 340). 84p. 1971. Repr. of 1588 ed. 11.50 (ISBN 90-221-0340-4). Walter J Johnson.

Federici, Silvia, jt. auth. see Cox, Nicole.

Federico, P. J. Descartes on Polyhedra: A Study of the "De Solidorum Elementis". (Sources in the History of Mathematics & Physical Sciences: Vol. 4). (Illus.). 144p. 1982. 39.50 (ISBN 0-387-90760-2). Springer-Verlag.

Federico, Pat A., et al. Management Information Systems & Organizational Behavior. Brun, Kim & McCalla, Douglas B., eds. LC 80-15174. 204p. 1980. 31.95 (ISBN 0-03-057021-2). Praeger.

Federico, Pat Anthony. Management Information Systems & Organization Behavior. 2nd ed. LC 85-6497. 240p. 1985. 37.95 (ISBN 0-03-003969-X). Praeger.

Federico, Ronald, jt. auth. see Berger, Robert.

Federico, Ronald C. An Introduction to the Social Welfare Institution. text ed. 19.95x (ISBN 0-669-97287-8). Heath.

--The Social Welfare Institution. 4th ed. 304p. 1984. text ed. 22.95 (ISBN 0-669-06749-0). Heath.

--The Social Welfare Institution: An Introduction. 4th ed. 1984. text ed. 22.95 (ISBN 0-669-06748-2); instr's manual 1.95 (ISBN 0-669-06749-0). Heath.

Federico, Ronald C. & Schwartz, Janet. Sociology. 3rd ed. LC 82-11375. 592p. 1983. pap. text ed. 17.95 (ISBN 0-394-34867-2, RanC); wkbk. 6.95 (ISBN 0-394-34870-2). Random.

Federico, Ronald C., jt. ed. see Baer, Betty L.

Federighi, Francis & Reilly, Edward D. Weighting for Baudot & Other Problems for You & Your Computer. (Illus.). 1978. 9.95 (ISBN 0-89529-061-8). Avery Pub.

Federlein, Anne C. Play in Preschool Mainstreamed & Handicapped Settings. LC 80-65612. 135p. 1981. perfect bdg. 10.50 (ISBN 0-86548-035-4). R & E Pubs.

Federlin, K. Immunopathology of Insulin: Clinical & Experimental Studies. LC 71-154799. (Monographs on Endocrinology: Vol. 6). (Illus.). 1971. 35.00 (ISBN 0-387-05408-1). Springer-Verlag.

Federlin, Konrad & Pfeifeer, Ernst F. Islet Pancreas Transplantation & Artificial Pancreas. 315p. 48.00 (ISBN 0-86577-062-X). Thieme-Stratton.

Federlin, Konrad F. & Scholtholt, Josef, eds. The Importance of Islets of Langerhans for Modern Endocrinology. (Workshop-Conference HOECHST Ser.: Vol. 12). (Illus.). 254p. 1984. text ed. 45.50 (ISBN 0-89004-939-4). Raven.

Federlin, Tom. A Comprehensive Bibliography on American Sign Language: A Resource Manual. LC 79-54021. 1979. pap. 9.95 (ISBN 0-9603136-0-5). Federlin.

Federman, D., jt. ed. see Rubenstein, E.

Federman, Raymond. Double or Nothing: A Novel. LC 71-171875. 203p. 1971. 10.00x (ISBN 0-8040-0543-5, 82-72783, Pub. by Swallow); pap. 4.95x (ISBN 0-8040-0544-3, 82-72791, Pub. by Swallow). Ohio U Pr.

--Journey into Chaos: Samuel Beckett's Early Fiction. LC 65-25284. 1965. 33.00x (ISBN 0-520-00398-5). U of Cal Pr.

--Me Too. 1976. pap. 1.00 (ISBN 0-915596-13-X). West Coast.

--Rumor Transmissable Ad Infinitum in Either Direction. (Illus.). 1976. pap. 1.00 (ISBN 0-685-53325-5). Assembling Pr.

--Smiles on Washington Square. 154p. 1985. 13.95 (ISBN 0-938410-29-6). Thunder's Mouth.

--Take It or Leave It. LC 75-21556. 426p. 1976. 11.95 (ISBN 0-914590-22-7); pap. 4.95 (ISBN 0-914590-23-5). Fiction Coll.

--The Twofold Vibration. LC 81-47831. 192p. 1982. 10.95 (ISBN 0-253-18989-6). Ind U Pr.

Federman, Raymond, ed. Cinq Nouvelles. LC 70-115011. (Illus., Orig., Fr.). 1970. pap. text ed. 9.95x (ISBN 0-89197-079-7). Irvington.

--Surfiction: Fiction Now & Tomorrow. LC 73-13215. 294p. 1973. 18.00x (ISBN 0-8040-0651-2, 82-73559, Pub. by Swallow). Ohio U Pr.

--Surfiction: Fiction Now & Tomorrow. 2nd ed. LC 80-54657. viii, 316p. 1981. pap. 8.95x (ISBN 0-8040-0652-0, 82-73567, Pub by Swallow). Ohio U Pr.

Federman, Raymond, jt. ed. see Graver, Lawrence.

Federn, Ernst, jt. ed. see Nunberg, Herman.

Federn, Karl. Dante & His Time. LC 78-132439. (Studies in Dante, No. 9). 1970. Repr. of 1902 ed. lib. bdg. 54.95x (ISBN 0-8383-1192-X). Haskell.

--Dante & His Time. LC 70-101026. 1969. Repr. of 1902 ed. 21.00x (ISBN 0-8046-0693-5, Pub. by Kennikat). Assoc Faculty Pr.

--Materialist Conception of History: A Critical Analysis. LC 75-114523. 1971. Repr. of 1939 ed. lib. bdg. 22.25x (ISBN 0-8371-4789-1, FECH). Greenwood.

--Richelieu. LC 72-132440. (World History Ser., No. 48). 1970. Repr. of 1928 ed. lib. bdg. 38.95x (ISBN 0-8383-1222-5). Haskell.

Federn, Robert. Repertoire Bibliographique De la Litterature Francaise Des Origines a 1911, 2 vols. 612p. Repr. of 1913 ed. 58.00 (ISBN 0-384-15401-8). Johnson Repr.

Federoff, Alexander. Falling Through the Night. 1964. 8.95 (ISBN 0-8392-1030-2). Astor-Honor.

--Side of the Angels. 1960. 10.00 (ISBN 0-8392-1103-1). Astor-Honor.

Federoff, S. & Hertz, L., eds. Advances in Cellular Neurobiology, Vol. 2. 1981. 66.00 (ISBN 0-12-008302-7). Acad Pr.

--Advances in Cellular Neurobiology, Vol. 3. (Serial Publication Ser.). 448p. 1982. 70.00 (ISBN 0-12-008303-5). Acad Pr.

Federoff, Serfey, jt. ed. see Zagoren, Joy C.

Federspiel, Howard. Persatuan Islam: Islamic Reform in Twentieth Century Indonesia. (Monograph Ser.). (Orig.). 1970. pap. 7.50 (ISBN 0-87763-013-5). Cornell Mod Indo.

Federspiel, J. F. Ballad of Typhoid Mary. Agee, Joel, tr. LC 83-8938. 171p. 1984. 12.95 (ISBN 0-525-24211-2, 01258-370). Dutton.

--The Ballad of Typhoid Mary. 160p. 1985. pap. 3.50 (ISBN 0-345-31967-2). Ballantine.

--An Earthquake in My Family. Kanes, Eveline, tr. 256p. 1986. 16.95 (ISBN 0-525-24379-8, 01646-490). Dutton.

Fedi, Peter, Jr., ed. The Periodontic Syllabus. LC 84-27787. (Illus.). 190p. 1985. pap. 23.50 (ISBN 0-8121-0982-1). Lea & Febiger.

Fedida, P. Diccionario de Psicoanalisis. (Span.). pap. 6.95 (ISBN 84-206-1730-X, S-32981). French & European.

Fedida, Sam & Malik, Rex. The Viewdata Revolution. 186p. 1979. 44.95 (ISBN 0-470-26879-4). Halsted Pr.

Fedigan, L. M. A Study of Roles in the Arashiyama West Troop of Japanese Monkeys (Macaca Fuscata) Szalay, F. S., ed. (Contributions to Primatology: Vol. 9). (Illus.). 116p. 1976. 21.00 (ISBN 3-8055-2334-3). S Karger.

Fedigan, Linda M. Primate Paradigms: Sex Roles & Social Bonds. (Illus.). 1982. (ISBN 0-920792-03-0); pap. write for info. Eden Pr.

Fedin, K. Early Joys. 398p. 1973. 5.95 (ISBN 0-8285-0963-8, Pub. by Progress Pubs USSR). Imported Pubns.

Fedin, Konstantin. Cities & Years: A Novel. Scammell, Michael, tr. from Rus. LC 75-2695. 415p. 1975. Repr. of 1962 ed. lib. bdg. 45.00x (ISBN 0-8371-8029-5, FECY). Greenwood.

Fedin, Konstantine. Carp. Birkett, G. A., ed. LC 66-25020. (Rus.). 1966. pap. text ed. 1.75x (ISBN 0-89197-487-3). Irvington.

Fedina, L., et al, eds. Mathematical & Computational Methods in Physiology: Proceedings of a Satellite Symposium of the 28th International Congress of Physiological Sciences, Budapest, Hungary, 1980. LC 80-42253. (Advances in Physiological Sciences Ser.: Vol. 34). (Illus.). 400p. 1981. 55.00 (ISBN 0-08-027356-4). Pergamon.

Fedler, Fred. Reporting for the Print Media. 3rd ed. 641p. 1984. pap. text ed. 16.95 (ISBN 0-15-576625-2, HC); instr's manual avail. (ISBN 0-15-576626-0). HarBraceJ.

Fedo, David A. William Carlos Williams: A Poet in the American Theatre. Litz, Walton, ed. LC 83-1132. (Studies in Modern Literature: No. 7). 213p. 1983. 39.95 (ISBN 0-8357-1410-1). UMI Res Pr.

Fedor, Kenneth J., jt. ed. see Dunlop, John T.

Fedor, Thomas S. Patterns of Urban Growth in the Russian Empire During the Nineteenth Century. LC 74-84783. (Research Papers Ser.: No. 163). (Illus.). 1975. pap. 10.00 (ISBN 0-89065-070-5). U Chicago Dept Geog.

Fedorenko, N. P. Optimal Functioning System for a Socialist Economy: A Look at Soviet Economic Planning. 189p. 1975. 12.00x (ISBN 0-8464-0688-8). Beekman Pubs.

Fedoriuk, M. V., jt. auth. see Maslov, V. P.

Fedorjuk, M. V., et al. Eleven Papers on Analysis. LC 51-5559. (Translations, Ser.: No. 2, Vol. 34). 1963. 33.00 (ISBN 0-8218-1734-5, TRANS 2-34). Am Math.

Fedoroff, S. Advances in Cellular Neurobiology, Vol. 5. (Serial Publication Ser.). 1984. 79.50 (ISBN 0-12-008305-1). Acad Pr.

Fedoroff, S. & Hertz, L., eds. Advances in Cellular Neurobiology, Vol. 1. 1980. 65.00 (ISBN 0-12-008301-9). Acad Pr.
--Advances in Cellular Neurobiology, Vol. 4. (Serial Publication Ser.). 420p. 1983. 70.00 (ISBN 0-12-008304-3). Acad Pr.
Fedoroff, S. & Hertz, Leif, eds. Cell, Tissue & Organ Cultures in Neurobiology. 1978. 60.00 (ISBN 0-12-250450-X). Acad Pr.
Fedoroff, Sergey, jt. ed. see Acosta, Enrique V.
Fedorov, A., ed. Chromosome Numbers of Flowering Plants. 926p. 1969. Repr. of 1974 ed. lib. bdg. 77.00x (ISBN 3-87429-067-0). Lubrecht & Cramer.
Fedorov, A. S., jt. auth. see Pavlova, G. E.
Fedorov, E. S. Symmetry of Crystals. LC 75-146982. (American Crystallographic Association Monograph: Vol. 7). 315p. 1971. 4.50 (ISBN 0-686-60371-0). Polycrystal Bk Serv.
Fedorov, Evgenii K. Man & Nature: The Ecological Crisis & Social Progress. 280p. (Orig.). 1981. 8.00 (ISBN 0-7178-0573-5); pap. 2.75 (ISBN 0-7178-0567-0). Intl Pubs Co.
Fedorov, Fedor I. Theory of Elastic Waves in Crystals. LC 65-27349. 375p. 1968. 49.50x (ISBN 0-306-30309-4, Plenum Pr). Plenum Pub.
Fedorov, G. B. & Smirnov, E. A. Diffusion in Reactor Materials. (Diffusion & Defect Monogr Ser.: Vol. 8). 182p. 1984. 36.00 (ISBN 0-87849-531-2). Trans Tech.
Fedorov, K. N., ed. The Thermohaline Finestructure of the Ocean. Brown, D. A. & Turner, J. S., trs. 1978. text ed. 53.00 (ISBN 0-08-021673-0). Pergamon.
Fedorov, V. V. Theory of Optimal Experiments. (Probability & Mathematical Statistics Ser.). 1972. 67.00 (ISBN 0-12-250750-9). Acad Pr.
Fedorov, Y. Polar Diaries. 344p. 1983. 9.95 (ISBN 0-8285-2682-6, Pub. by Progress Pubs USSR). Imported Pubns.
Fedorova, M. P., jt. auth. see Kondratyev, K. Ya.
Fedorovsky, N. Marx's "Civil War in France". 64p. 1985. pap. 1.45 (ISBN 0-8285-2978-7, Pub. by Progress Pubs USSR). Imported Pubns.
Fedorowicz, J. K. England's Baltic Trade in the Early Seventeenth Century. LC 78-67629. (Cambridge Studies in Economic History). (Illus.). 1980. 52.50 (ISBN 0-521-22425-X). Cambridge U Pr.
Fedorowicz, J. K., ed. & tr. A Republic of Nobles: Studies in Polish History to 1864. LC 81-12284. (Illus.). 310p. 1982. 44.50 (ISBN 0-521-24093-X). Cambridge U Pr.
Fedoseyev, P. & Timofeyev, T. Social Problems of Man's Environment: Where We Live & Work. 334p. 1981. 8.50 (ISBN 0-8285-2273-1, Pub. by Progress Pubs USSR). Imported Pubns.
Fedoseyev, P., ed. What Is "Democratic Socialism"? 143p. 1980. pap. 3.50 (ISBN 0-8285-2051-8, Pub. by Progress Pubs USSR). Imported Pubns.
Fedoseyev, P. N. Leninism & the National Question. 504p. 1977. 6.45 (ISBN 0-8285-0400-8, Pub. by Progress Pubs USSR). Imported Pubns.
Fedoseyev, P. N., et al. Karl Marx-a Biography. 635p. 1973. 8.45 (ISBN 0-8285-0063-0, Pub. by Progress Pubs USSR). Imported Pubns.
--Peace & Disarmament: Academic Studies, 1984. 479p. 1984. 7.95 (ISBN 0-8285-2976-0, Pub. by Progress Pubs USSR). Imported Pubns.
Fedotoff White, Dimitri. The Growth of the Red Army. LC 79-2900. 486p. 1980. Repr. of 1944 ed. 36.50 (ISBN 0-8305-0071-5). Hyperion Conn.
Fedotov, S. A. & Markhinin, Y. K., eds. The Great Tolbachik Fissure Eruption: Geological & Geophysical Data, 1975-1976. LC 82-9586. (Cambridge Earth Science Ser.). 300p. 1983. 72.50 (ISBN 0-521-24345-9). Cambridge U Pr.
Fedou, R. Lexique Histoire du Moyen-Age. (Fr.). pap. 16.50 (ISBN 0-686-92260-3, M-8981). French & Eur.
Fedtke, Carl. Biochemistry & Physiology of Herbicide Action. (Illus.). 250p. 1982. 70.00 (ISBN 0-387-11231-6). Springer-Verlag.
Fedtschenko, O. Eremurus: Kritische Uebersicht Ueber Die Gattung. (Plant Monography Ser.: No.3). 1968. pap. 17.50 (ISBN 3-7682-0560-6). Lubrecht & Cramer.
Feduccia, Alan. The Age of Birds. LC 80-11926. (Illus.). 208p. 1980. 20.00 (ISBN 0-674-00975-4). Harvard U Pr.
--Evolutionary Trends in the Neotropical Ovenbirds & Woodhewers. 69p. 1973. 3.50 (ISBN 0-943610-13-3). Am Ornithologists.
--Morphology of the Bony Stapes (Columella) in the Passeriformes & Related Groups: Evolutionary Implications. (Miscellaneous Publications Ser.: No. 63). 34p. 1975. pap. 2.00 (ISBN 0-317-04586-5). U of KS Mus Nat Hist.
--Structure & Evolution of Vertebrates: A Laboratory Text for Comparative Vertebrate Anatomy. new ed. 275p. 1974. pap. 11.95x (ISBN 0-393-09291-7). Norton.
Feduccia, Alan, jt. auth. see Torrey, Theodore W.
Feduchi, L. Spanish Folk Architecture, Vol. 1. (Illus.). 389p. 1982. 59.95 (ISBN 84-7031-017-8, Pub. by Editorial Blume Spain). Intl Spec Bk.
Fedukowicz, Helena B. External Infections of the Eye: Bacterial, Viral & Mycotic. 3rd. ed. (Illus.). 382p. 1984. 58.50 (ISBN 0-8385-2486-9). ACC.
Fedullo, Mick. The Maze. LC 84-81136. 55p. (Orig.). 1985. 6.50 (ISBN 0-913123-06-4); pap. 4.50 (ISBN 0-913123-04-8). Galileo.
Fedyukin, S. A., ed. see Lenin, V. I.
Fee, A. L. Memoires sur la Famille des Fougeres: 1844-66, 11parts in 1 vol. (Illus.). 1966. 245.00 (ISBN 3-7682-0447-2). Lubrecht & Cramer.
Fee, Elizabeth, ed. Women & Health: The Politics of Sex in Medicine. (Baywood Policy, Politics, Health, & Medicine Ser.: Vol. 4). 264p. (Orig.). 1983. pap. text ed. 14.50x (ISBN 0-89503-034-9). Baywood Pub.
Fee, Gordon & Stuart, Douglas. How to Read the Bible for All it's Worth. 272p. 1982. pap. 6.95 (ISBN 0-310-37361-1). Zondervan.
Fee, Gordon D. First & Second Timothy, Titus. LC 83-49061. (Good News Commentary Ser.). 256p. (Orig.). 1984. pap. 9.57 (ISBN 0-06-062333-0, RD 472). Har-Row.
--New Testament Exegesis: A Handbook for Students & Pastors. LC 82-24829. (Illus.). 154p. (Orig.). 1983. pap. 8.95 (ISBN 0-664-24469-6). Westminster.
Fee, Jacqueline. The Sweater Workshop. LC 83-80246. (Illus.). 160p. 1983. spiral bdg. 15.00 (ISBN 0-934026-12-2). Interweave.
Fee, John G. Anti-Slavery Manual, Being an Examination, in the Light of the Bible, & of Facts, into the Moral & Social Wrongs of American Slavery. LC 74-82189. (Anti-Slavery Crusade in America Ser). 1969. Repr. of 1848 ed. 14.00 (ISBN 0-405-00627-6). Ayer Co Pubs.
Fee, Roger D. Basic Ideas About Singing: The Teaching of Theodore Harrison, An American Maestro. LC 78-63254. pap. text ed. 7.50 (ISBN 0-8191-0614-3). U Pr of Amer.
Feeby, C. L. & Ullrich, W. J., eds. Powder Metallurgy in Defense Technology, Vol. 6. 224p. 1985. pap. 52.00 (ISBN 0-918404-62-2). Am Powder Metal.
Feegel, John R. The Dance Card. 320p. 1982. pap. 3.50 (ISBN 0-380-58040-3, 60053-6). Avon.
--Death Sails the Bay. 1978. pap. 1.95 (ISBN 0-380-01972-8, 38570). Avon.
--Not a Stranger. 272p. 1984. pap. 3.50 (ISBN 0-451-12900-8, Sig). NAL.
Feehan, J. M., jt. auth. see Delaney, E. J.
Feehan, John. Bobby Sands & the Tragedy of Northern Ireland. 160p. 1985. 16.95 (ISBN 0-932966-63-2). Permanent Pr.
Feehan, John M. Operation Brogue. 138p. 1984. pap. 6.95 (ISBN 0-85342-729-1, Pub. by Mercier Pr Ireland). Irish Bks Media.
--Tomorrow to Be Brave. 108p. (Orig.). 1973. pap. 4.95 (ISBN 0-85342-300-8, Pub. by Mercier Pr Ireland). Irish Bk Ctr.
--The Wind That Round the Fastnet Sweeps. 1978. pap. 4.95 (ISBN 0-85342-550-7, Co-dist. by Irish Bks Media). Irish Bk Ctr.
Feeley, Falk. A Swarm of WASPS: A Guide to the Manners (Lovely), Mores (Traditional), Morals (Well...), & Way of Life of the Fortunate Few Who Have Always Had Money. LC 82-18884. (Illus.). 132p. (Orig.). 1983. 11.95 (ISBN 0-688-01927-7). Morrow.
Feeley, Mrs. Falk. A Swarm of WASPS: A Guide to the Manners (Lovely), Mores (Traditional), Morals (Well...), & Way of Life of the Fortunate Few Who Have Always Had Money. LC 82-62803. (Illus.). 132p. 1983. pap. 4.70 (ISBN 0-688-02048-8, Quill NY). Morrow.
Feeley, Kathleen. Flannery O'Connor: Voice of the Peacock. 2nd ed. LC 76-163958. xviii, 198p. 1982. pap. 9.00 (ISBN 0-8232-1093-6). Fordham.
Feeley, Malcolm M. Court Reform On Trial: Why Simple Solutions Fail (A Twentieth Century Fund Report) LC 82-72394. 200p. 1983. 14.95 (ISBN 0-465-01437-2). Basic.
--Court Reform on Trial: Why Simple Solutions Fail. LC 82-20674. 251p. 1984. pap. 7.95 (ISBN 0-465-01438-0, CN-5122). Basic.
--The Process Is the Punishment: Handling Cases in a Lower Criminal Court. LC 79-7349. (Illus.). 330p. 1979. 12.95x (ISBN 0-87154-253-6). Russell Sage.
Feeley, Malcolm M. & Krislov, Samuel. Constitutional Law. 1985. text ed. 33.95 (ISBN 0-316-27686-3). Little.
Feeley, Malcolm M., jt. ed. see Becker, Theodore L.
Feeley, Mary A., jt. auth. see Driver, Robienetta.
Feeley-Harnik, Gillian. The Lord's Table: Eucharist & Passover in Early Christianity. 1981. text ed. 22.50x (ISBN 0-8122-7786-4). U of Pa Pr.
Feeling, Durbin, tr. see Ziegenfuss, Mary Lou.
Feelings, Durbin, tr. see Conley, Robert J.
Feelings, Muriel. Jambo Means Hello: Swahili Alphabet Book. LC 73-15441. (Pied Piper Book). (Illus.). 56p. (gr. k-3). 1981. pap. 3.50 (ISBN 0-8037-4428-5). Dial Bks Young.
--Jambo Means Hello: Swahili Alphabet Book. LC 73-15441. (Illus.). 56p. (gr. k-5). 1974. 12.95 (ISBN 0-8037-4346-7, 01258-370); PLB 12.89 (ISBN 0-8037-4350-5). Dial Bks Young.
--Moja Means One: A Swahili Counting Book. LC 76-134856. (Pied Piper Book). (Illus.). 32p. (gr. k up). 1976. pap. 3.95 (ISBN 0-8037-5711-5, 0383-120). Dial Bks Young.
--Moja Means One: A Swahili Counting Book. LC 76-134856. (Illus.). (ps-3). 1971. 11.95 (ISBN 0-8037-5776-X, 01160-350); PLB 11.89 (ISBN 0-8037-5777-8). Dial Bks Young.
Feely, Malcolm & Sarat, Austin. The Policy Dilemma: Federal Crime Policy & the Law Enforcement Assistance Administration. 1981. 17.50x (ISBN 0-8166-0901-2); pap. 7.95x (ISBN 0-8166-0904-7). U of Minn Pr.
Feely, Margot, ed. see O'Neill, John P.
Feely, Terence. Limelight. Lister, Laurie, ed. LC 84-22632. 312p. 1985. 15.95 (ISBN 0-688-04657-6). Morrow.
--Number Ten: The Private Lives of Six Prime Ministers. (Illus.). 224p. 1984. 15.95 (ISBN 0-283-98893-2, Pub. by Sidgwick & Jackson). Merrimack Pub Cir.
Feeman, Jeff & Feeman, Maryellen. Beginning with BASIC: Beginning Computer Skills. (Stick-Out Your Neck Ser.). (Illus.). 64p. (gr. 4-6). 1984. wkbk. 6.95 (ISBN 0-88724-028-3, CD-9040). Carson-Dellos.
--Computer Terms-Hardware. (Stick-Out-Your-Neck Ser.). (Illus.). 32p. (gr. 3up). 1984. pap. 1.99 (ISBN 0-88724-100-X, CD-9045). Carson-Dellos.
--Discovery Learning with LOGO III. (Stick-Out-Your Neck Ser.). (Illus.). 32p. (gr. 3 up). 1984. pap. 1.98 (ISBN 0-88724-111-5, CD-9054). Carson-Dellos.
--Key in on Keyboarding. (Stick-Out-Your-Neck Ser.). (Illus.). (gr. 3-8). 1984. pap. 7.95 spiral bd.-typing-stand-up base (ISBN 0-88724-029-1, CD-9041). Carson-Dellos.
--Keyboarding Activities Workbook. (Stick-Out-Your-Neck Ser.). (Illus.). 32p. (gr. 2-5). 1984. pap. 1.98 (ISBN 0-88724-030-5, CD-9042). Carson-Dellos.
--Problem Solving with BASIC. (Stick-Out-Your-Neck Ser.). (Illus.). 32p. (gr. 5 up). 1984. pap. 1.99 (ISBN 0-88724-105-0, CD-9048). Carson-Dellos.
Feeman, Jeff, jt. auth. see Feeman, Maryellen.
Feeman, Maryellen & Feeman, Jeff. BASIC Programming I. (Stick-Out-Your Neck Ser.). (Illus.). 32p. (gr. 2 up). 1984. pap. 1.98 (ISBN 0-88724-106-9, CD-9049). Carson Dellos.
--BASIC Programming II. (Stick-Out-Your Neck Ser.). (Illus.). 32p. (gr. 2 up). 1984. pap. 1.98 (ISBN 0-88724-107-7, CD-9050). Carson-Dellos.
--BASIC Programming III. (Stick-Our-Your-Neck Ser.). (Illus.). 32p. (gr. 3 up). 1984. pap. 1.98 (ISBN 0-88724-108-5, CD-9051). Carson-Dellos.
--Computer Terms-Software. (Stick-Out-Your-Neck Ser.). (Illus.). 32p. (gr. 2 up). 1984. pap. 1.99 (ISBN 0-88724-101-8, CD-9044). Carson-Dellos.
--Computer Terms-Word-Processing. (Stick-Out-Your-Neck Ser.). (Illus.). 32p. (gr. 2 up). 1984. pap. 1.99 (ISBN 0-88724-102-6). Carson-Dellos.
--Discovery Learning with LOGO I. (Illus.). 32p. (gr. 2 up). 1984. pap. 1.99 (ISBN 0-88724-109-3, CD-9052). Carson-Dellos.
--Discovery Learning with LOGO II. (Stick-Out-Your Neck Ser.). (Illus.). 32p. (gr. 3 up). 1984. pap. 1.98 (ISBN 0-88724-110-7, CD-9053). Carson-Dellos.
--People & Computers. (Illus.). 32p. (gr. 5 up). 1984. pap. 1.98 (ISBN 0-88724-103-4, CD-9046). Carson-Dellos.
--What Computers Can Do. (Stick-Out-Your-Neck Ser.). (Illus.). 32p. (gr. 2 up). 1984. pap. 1.98 (ISBN 0-88724-104-2, CD-9047). Carson-Dellos.
Feeman, Maryellen, jt. auth. see Feeman, Jeff.
Feeman, W. E., Jr. Predicting Hardening of the Arteries. 1985. 10.00 (ISBN 0-533-06601-8). Vantage.
Feenberg, Andrew. Lukacs, Marx & the Sources of Critical Theory. LC 80-22747. (Philosophy & Society Ser.). 300p. 1981. 28.95x (ISBN 0-8476-6272-1). Rowman.
Feenberg, E. Theory of Quantum Fluids. (Pure & Applied Physics Ser.: Vol. 31). 1969. 61.50 (ISBN 0-12-250850-5). Acad Pr.
Feenberg, Eugene. Shell Theory of the Nucleus. LC 54-9017. (Investigations in Physics: No. 3). pap. 55.80 (ISBN 0-317-09267-7, 2000630). Bks Demand UMI.
Feenberg, Eugene & Pake, George E. Notes on the Quantum Theory of Angular Momentum. LC 59-13223. pap. 20.00 (ISBN 0-317-07876-3, 2000789). Bks Demand UMI.
Feeney, Floyd, Jr. The Police & Pretrial Release. LC 79-9629. 240p. 1982. 26.50x (ISBN 0-669-03597-1). Lexington Bks.
Feeney, G. Inquiring About People. (Holt Databank System: Level 1). 1972. text ed. 12.32 (ISBN 0-03-089782-3, HoltE); calendar 14.96 (ISBN 0-03-089788-2); databox s.p. 561.40 (ISBN 0-03-089829-3). HR&W.
Feeney, J., jt. ed. see Emsley, J. W.
Feeney, James H. Divorce & Marriage. 1980. pap. 1.75 (ISBN 0-911739-06-8). Abbott Loop.
Feeney, Joan, jt. auth. see Carter, John M.
Feeney, Joan V., ed. Peasant Literature: A Bibliography of Afro-American Nationalism & Social Protest from the Caribbean, No. 822. 1975. 7.00 (ISBN 0-686-20358-5). CPL Biblios.
Feeney, Leonard. London Is a Place. 1951. 6.00 (ISBN 0-911218-02-5). Ravengate Pr.
--Mother Seton: Saint Elizabeth of New York. LC 75-23224. 212p. 1975. 6.95 (ISBN 0-911218-05-X); pap. 3.95 (ISBN 0-911218-06-8). Ravengate Pr.
--Survival Till Seventeen. LC 79-25067. 1980. 6.95 (ISBN 0-932506-08-9). St Bedes Pubns.
--You'd Better Come Quietly. LC 79-105011. (Essay Index Reprint Ser.). 1939. 36.50 (ISBN 0-8369-1569-0). Ayer Co Pubs.
Feeney, Mary, tr. see Boissard, Janine.
Feeney, Mary, tr. see Follain, Jean.
Feeney, Mary K., jt. auth. see Phillips, Raymond E.
Feeney, Patrick J. Reflection in a Madman's Mirror. LC 82-90264. (Illus.). 51p. (Orig.). 1982. 5.50 (ISBN 0-9608508-0-5); pap. 3.25 (ISBN 0-9608508-1-3). Gravesend Pr.
Feeney, Robert E. & Whitaker, John R., eds. Food Proteins: Improvement Through Chemical & Enzymatic Modification. LC 77-7550. (Advances in Chemistry Ser.: No. 160). 1977. 29.95 (ISBN 0-8412-0339-3). Am Chemical.
--Food Proteins: Improvement Through Chemical & Enzymatic Modifications. LC 77-7550. (American Chemical Society Advances in Chemistry Ser.: No. 160). pap. 80.00 (ISBN 0-317-10649-X, 2021551). Bks Demand UMI.
--Modification of Proteins: Food, Nutritional & Pharmacological Aspects. LC 82-1702. (Advances In Chemistry: No. 198). 402p. 1982. lib. bdg. 59.95 (ISBN 0-8412-0610-4). Am Chemical.
Feeney, Stephanie. A Is for Aloha. LC 80-5462. (Illus.). 64p. (ps-k). 1980. 7.95 (ISBN 0-8248-0722-7). UH Pr.
--Hawaii Is a Rainbow. LC 85-50569. (Illus.). 64p. (ps-3). 1985. 11.95 (ISBN 0-8248-1007-4). UH Pr.
Feeney, Stephanie & Christensen, Doris. Who Am I in the Lives of Children? An Introduction to Early Childhood Education. (Early Childhood Education Ser.). 1978. text ed. 18.50 (ISBN 0-675-08391-5). Merrill.
--Who Am I in the Lives of Children? An Introduction to Teaching Young Children. 416p. 1983. text ed. 22.95 (ISBN 0-675-20056-3). Additional supplements may be obtained from publisher. Merrill.
Feeney, William, ed. Lost Plays of the Irish Renaissance, Vol. 2. 10.00x (ISBN 0-912262-70-2). Proscenium.
Feeney, William J. Drama in Hardwicke Street. LC 82-49315. (Illus.). 320p. 1984. 37.50 (ISBN 0-8386-3188-6). Fairleigh Dickinson.
Feeney, William J., intro. by see Power, Victor.
Feeney, William R., jt. ed. see Tow, William T.
Feengold, G. A. see Wooley, Henry T.
Feenstra, Robert. Catalogue des Imprimes de la Collection Meijers, de la Bibliotheque de l'Universite de Leyde. 479p. (Fr.). 1980. lib. bdg. 45.00 (ISBN 90-271-1654-7). Kluwer Academic.
Feenstra, Robert, ed. see Bhagwati, Jagdish.
Feeny, Maura. A la Mode: Womens Fashion in French Art, 1850-1900. 44p. 1982. pap. 4.00 (ISBN 0-931102-13-8). S & F Clark.
Feer, H. Zwang und Schizophrenie. (Bibliotheca Psychiatrica: No. 150). 108p. 1973. 19.25 (ISBN 3-8055-1546-4). S Karger.
Feer, L. Contes Indiens. LC 78-20115. (Collection de contes et de chansons populaires: Vol. 6). Repr. of 1883 ed. 21.50 (ISBN 0-404-60356-4). AMS Pr.
Feerick, Amalie P., jt. auth. see Feerick, John D.
Feerick, John, et al. NLRB Representation Elections: Law, Practice & Procedure. 1058p. 1980. Supplements avail. press binder 60.00 (ISBN --15-100042-5, H39786); Suppl., 1983. 25.00 (ISBN 0-686-89123-6). HarBraceJ.
Feerick, John D. From Failing Hands: The Story of Presidential Succession. LC 65-14917. xvi, 368p. 1965. 35.00 (ISBN 0-8232-0635-1). Fordham.
--The Twenty-Fifth Amendment: Its Complete History & Earliest Application. LC 75-1719. xiv, 270p. 1975. 25.00 (ISBN 0-8232-0998-9); pap. 12.50x (ISBN 0-8232-0999-7). Fordham.
Feerick, John D. & Feerick, Amalie P. The Vice-Presidents of the United States. (First Books). (Illus.). (gr. 4-6). 1977. PLB 8.90 s&l (ISBN 0-531-02907-7). Watts.
Feerick, John D., jt. auth. see Barbash, Joseph.
Feest, Christian. Native Arts of North America. (World of Art Ser.). (Illus.). 216p. 1985. pap. 9.95f (ISBN 0-500-20179-X); cloth 19.95f. Thames Hudson.
Feest, T., ed. TEQC Nineteen Eighty-Three: Proceedings of the International Conference on Testing, Evaluation & Quality Control of Composites. 300p. 1983. pap. text ed. 49.95 (ISBN 0-408-22162-3). Butterworth.
Feezel, Jerry D. Between Persons: On Becoming an Interpersonal Communicator in Teaching. (Illus.). 48p. 1983. pap. text ed. 4.95x (ISBN 0-89787-312-2). Gorsuch Scarisbrick.
Feezor, Betty. Betty Feezor's Carolina Recipes, Vol. I. 331p. 1964. pap. 6.50 (ISBN 0-915605-01-5). Feezor Betty Bks.
--Betty Feezor's Carolina Recipes, Vol. II. 328p. 1974. pap. 6.50 (ISBN 0-915605-02-3). Feezor Betty Bks.
--A Life That Mattered. 182p. Date not set. 7.95 (ISBN 0-915605-03-1). Feezor Betty Bks.
Feezor, Bob. Betty Feezor's Carolina Recipes, Vol. III. 288p. 1984. pap. 8.50 (ISBN 0-915605-04-X). Feezor Betty Bks.
Fefer, Alexander & Goldstein, Allan, eds. The Potential Role of T-Cells in Cancer Therapy. (Progress in Cancer Research & Therapy Ser.: Vol. 22). 311p. 1982. text ed. 53.50 (ISBN 0-89004-747-2). Raven.
Feferman, S., jt. ed. see Barwise, J.

Feffer, Melvin. The Structure of Freudian Thought: The Problem of Immutability & Discontinuity in Developmental Theory. LC 81-23610. 298p. 1981. text ed. 22.50 (ISBN 0-8236-6185-7). Intl Univs Pr.

Fegan, Lydia, jt. ed. see McCarthy, Wendy.

Fegan, Patrick W. Vineyards & Wineries of America: A Traveler's Guide. LC 82-15806. 1982. pap. 9.95 (ISBN 0-8289-0489-8). Greene.

Fegan, W. R. Becoming a Church Member. 1979. pap. 3.00 (ISBN 0-89536-389-5). CSS of Ohio.

Fegely, Thomas D. Wonders of Geese & Swans. LC 75-38360. (Wonder Ser.). (Illus.). (gr. 4 up). 1976. 9.95 (ISBN 0-396-07307-7). Dodd.

--Wonders of Wild Ducks. LC 75-11443. (Wonders Ser.). (Illus.). 80p. (gr. 3-7). 1975. PLB 9.95 (ISBN 0-396-07226-7). Dodd.

--The World of Freshwater Fish. LC 77-16879. (Illus.). (gr. 5 up). 1978. 7.95 (ISBN 0-396-07562-2). Dodd.

Feger, H., jt. ed. see Lantermann, E. D.

Feger, Hubert, jt. ed. see Lantermann, Ernst.

Feher, Elizabeth. The Psychology of Birth: Roots of Human Personality. 224p. 1981. 12.95 (ISBN 0-8264-0039-6). Assn Birth Psych.

Feher, F., jt. ed. see Butzer, P. L.

Feher, F., jt. ed. see Miller, R. F.

Feher, Ferenc & Heller, Agnes. Hungary, Nineteen Fifty-Six Revisited: The Message of a Revolution a Quarter of a Century After. 192p. 1983. text ed. 28.50x (ISBN 0-04-321031-7). Allen Unwin.

Feher, Ferenc, jt. auth. see Rigby, T. H.

Feher, Ferenc, et al. Dictatorship Over Needs. LC 83-3180. 320p. 1983. 27.50x (ISBN 0-312-20022-6). St Martin.

Feher, G., ed. Electron Paramagnetic Resonance with Applications to Selected Problems in Biology. (Documents in Biology Ser.: Vol. 3). 152p. 1970. 45.25 (ISBN 0-677-02670-6). Gordon.

Feher, K. Digital Communications: Microwave Applications. 1981. 41.95 (ISBN 0-13-214080-2). P-H.

Feher, K., ed. Satellite Communications: Proceedings of the Canadian Domestic & International Conference, 1st, June 15-17, Ottawa, Canada. 670p. 1983. 85.00 (ISBN 0-444-86690-6, North-Holland). Elsevier.

Feher, Kamilo. Digital Communications: Satellite-Earth Station Engineering. (Illus.). 496p. 1983. 41.95 (ISBN 0-13-212068-2). P-H.

--Digital Modulation Techniques in an Interference Environment. White, Donald R., ed. LC 76-52508. (Illus.). 182p. 1977. text ed. 42.00 (ISBN 0-932263-18-6). White Consult.

Feher, Leslie. The Psychology of Birth. 224p. 1985. Repr. of 1980 ed. text ed. 15.00 (ISBN 0-9612182-1-5). Assn Birth Psych.

Feher, Leslie, ed. Birth Psychology. (Illus.). 183p. (Orig.). 1984. pap. 19.50 (ISBN 0-9612182-0-7). Assn Birth Psych.

Feher, Matyas & Erdy, Miklos, eds. Studia Sumiro-Hungarica, 2 vols. Incl. A Sumir Kerdes (the Sumerian Question) Galgoczy, Janos. LC 79-7359. (Vol. 1). 270p (ISBN 0-914246-51-8); Szumirok Es Magyarok (Sumerians & Magyars) Somogyi, Ede. LC 70-7362. (Vol. 2). 270p (ISBN 0-914246-52-6). (Illus.). 1968. Repr. 13.00 ea. Gilgamesh Pub.

Feher, O. & Joo, F., eds. Cellular Analogues of Conditioning & Neural Plasticity: Proceedings of a Satellite Symposium of the 28th International Congress of Physiological Sciences, Szeged, Hungary, 1980. LC 80-41992. (Advances in Physiological Sciences: Vol. 36). (Illus.). 300p. 1981. 44.00 (ISBN 0-08-027372-6). Pergamon.

Fehern, Henry. Is There Anyone Sick among You. 54p. 1984. pap. 2.50 (ISBN 0-916134-59-8). Pueblo Pub Co.

Fehervari, Geza. Islamic Metalwork of the Eighth to the Fifteenth Century. 218p. 1976. 75.00 (ISBN 0-571-09740-5). Faber & Faber.

Fehervari, Istvan H. Bortonvilag Magyarorszagon: The World of Prisons in Hungary. (Illus., Hungarian.). 1978. casebd. 12.00 (ISBN 0-912404-09-4). Alpha Pubns.

Fehervary. Szovjetvilag. 320p. 1984. pap. 16.00 (ISBN 0-936398-26-4). Framo Pub.

Fehl, Fred. Stars of the American Ballet Theatre in Performance Photographs. 144p. 1984. pap. 8.95 (ISBN 0-486-24755-4). Dover.

--Stars of the Ballet & Dance in Performance Photographs. (Illus.). 144p. (Orig.). (gr. 6 up). 1983. pap. 8.95 (ISBN 0-486-24492-X). Dover.

--Stars of the Broadway Stage, 1940-1970. (Illus.). 144p. (Orig.). pap. 8.95 (ISBN 0-486-24398-2). Dover.

Fehl, Fred, et al. On Broadway. (Illus.). xxxv, 419p. 1980. pap. 13.50 (ISBN 0-306-80125-6). Da Capo.

--On Broadway. (Illus.). 456p. 1978. 29.95 (ISBN 0-292-76010-8). U of Tex Pr.

Fehl, Jim, ed. Standard Lesson Commentary. 450p. 1985. text ed. 8.50 (ISBN 0-87239-854-4); kivar 6.95 (ISBN 0-87239-853-6). Standard Pub.

Fehlauer, Adolph. Catechism Lessons: Pupil's Book. Grunze, Richard, ed. 336p. (gr. 5-6). 1981. 6.95 (ISBN 0-938272-09-8). WELS Board.

--Life & Faith of Martin Luther. 1981. pap. 5.95 (ISBN 0-8100-0125-X, 15N0376). Northwest Pub.

Fehlauer, Adolph F. Bible Reader's Guide. 1981. 5.95 (ISBN 0-8100-0146-2, 06N0558). Northwest Pub.

Fehling, Detlef. Quellenangaben bei Herodot: Studien zur Erzaehlkunst Herodots. (Untersuchungen zur Antiken Literatur und Geschichte, 9). 198p. 1971. 20.80x (ISBN 3-11-003634-7). De Gruyter.

Fehm, Sherwood A. The Collaboration of Niccolo Tegliacci & Luca Di Tomme. (J. Paul Getty Museum Publications Ser.). (Illus.). 32p. (Orig.). 1973. pap. 4.00x (ISBN 0-89236-059-3). J P Getty Mus.

Fehmers, Frank, ed. The Twenty-Four Dollar Bargain: Holland & America, 200 Years of Friendship. (Illus.). 225p. (Orig.). 1982. pap. 17.95 (ISBN 90-6151-027-9, Pub. by F Fehmers). Intl Spec Bk.

Fehn, Ann C. Change & Permanence. (Stanford German Studies: Vol. 12). 200p. 1978. pap. 21.45 (ISBN 3-261-02921-8). P Lang Pubs.

Fehr, Barbara. Yankee Denim Dandies. LC 74-79127. (Illus.). 96p. 1974. 15.00 (ISBN 0-87832-014-8). Piper.

Fehr, Lawrence A. Introduction to Personality. 576p. 1983. text ed. write for info. (ISBN 0-02-336700-8). Macmillan.

Fehr, Terry, jt. auth. see Mangan, Doreen.

Fehr, Terry, jt. auth. see Petersen, W. P.

Fehr, W. R., ed. Genetic Contributions to Yield Gains of Five Major Crop Plants. 1984. pap. 12.00 (ISBN 0-89118-517-8). Crop Sci Soc Am.

Fehr, W. R. & Hadley, H. H., eds. Hybridization of Crop Plants. (Illus.). 1980. 25.00 (ISBN 0-89118-034-6). Am Soc Agron.

Fehr, Wayne L. The Birth of the Catholic Tubingen School: The Dogmatics of Johann Sebastian Drey. Raschke, Carl, ed. LC 81-14645. (American Academy of Religion, Dissertation Ser.). 1981. text ed. 14.95 (ISBN 0-89130-544-0, 01-01-37). Scholars Pr GA.

Fehren, Henry, ed. see Liturgical Prayer Magazine.

Fehrenbach, C. G. Marriage in Wittenwiler's Ring. LC 70-140019. (Catholic University Studies in German Ser.: No. 15). Repr. of 1941 ed. 24.00 (ISBN 0-404-50235-0). AMS Pr.

Fehrenbach, Ch., ed. see International Astronomical Union Symposium No. 50, Villa Carlos Paz, Argentina, Oct. 18-24, 1971.

Fehrenbach, Robert J., jt. auth. see Shirley, James.

Fehrenbach, Robert J., et al, eds. A Concordance to the Plays, Poems, & Translations of Christopher Marlowe. LC 81-67175. (A Cornell Concordance). 1710p. 1982. 80.00x (ISBN 0-8014-1420-2). Cornell U Pr.

Fehrenbach, T. R. Comanches. LC 73-20761. 1974. 22.50 (ISBN 0-394-48856-3). Knopf.

--Lone Star: A History of Texas & Texans. 762p. 1985. special edition 100.00 (ISBN 0-02-537210-6). Macmillan.

--Lone Star: A History of Texas & the Texans. (Illus.). 776p. 1980. pap. 9.95 (ISBN 0-02-032190-2, Collier). MacMillan.

--Lone Star: A History of Texas & the Texans. 762p. 1985. pap. 12.95 (ISBN 0-02-032170-8, Collier). Macmillan.

--Lonestar: History of Texas & the Texans. 1983. 9.98 (ISBN 0-517-40280-7, AM Legacy Pr). Crown.

--Seven Keys to Texas. 148p. 1983. 15.00 (ISBN 0-87404-069-8). Tex Western.

--Texas: A Salute from Above. 280p. 1985. 34.95 (ISBN 0-940672-28-6). Texas World Bks.

Fehrenbacher, Don E. Chicago Giant: A Biography of "Long John" Wentworth. (Illus.). 290p. 1983. Repr. of 1957 ed. 12.50x (ISBN 0-252-01035-3). U of Ill Pr.

--The Dred Scott Case: Its Significance in American Law & Politics. LC 78-4665. (Illus.). 1978. 39.95x (ISBN 0-19-502403-6). Oxford U Pr.

--The Leadership of Abraham Lincoln. LC 77-114013. (Problems in American History Ser.). pap. 51.00 (ISBN 0-317-10846-8, 2022598). Bks Demand UMI.

--Manifest Destiny & the Coming of the Civil War, 1840-1861. LC 72-118950. (Goldentree Bibliographies in American History Ser). (Orig.). 1970. pap. 6.95x (ISBN 0-88295-512-8). Harlan Davidson.

--Prelude to Greatness: Lincoln in the 1850's. 1962. 17.50x (ISBN 0-8047-0119-9); pap. 6.95x (ISBN 0-8047-0120-2). Stanford U Pr.

--Slavery, Law, & Politics: The Dred Scott Case in Historical Perspective. (Illus.). 1981. 19.95x (ISBN 0-19-502882-1). Oxford U Pr.

--Slavery, Law & Politics: The Dred Scott Case in Historical Perspective. (Illus.). 1981. pap. 7.95 (ISBN 0-19-502883-X, GB639, GB). Oxford U Pr.

--The South & Three Sectional Crises. Potter, David M., ed. LC 79-18143. viii, 88p. 1980. text ed. 8.95x (ISBN 0-8071-0671-2). La State U Pr.

Fehrenbacher, Don E. & Pease, Otis. The Era of Expansion, 1800-1848. 165p. 1969. pap. text ed. 6.95 (ISBN 0-394-34178-3, RanC). Random.

Fehrenbacher, Don E., ed. Abraham Lincoln: A Documentary Portrait Through His Speeches & Writings. LC 76-53865. 1964. 15.00x (ISBN 0-8047-0942-4); pap. 5.95x (ISBN 0-8047-0946-7). Stanford U Pr.

Fehrenbacher, Don E., jt. ed. see Brown, Richard E.

Fehrenbacher, Don E., ed. see Potter, David M.

Fehrenback, T. R. Texas: A Salute from Above. 280p. 1985. 34.95 (ISBN 0-940672-28-6). Shearer Pub.

Fehrman, Carl. Poetic Creation: Inspiration or Craft. Petherick, Karin, tr. from Swed. 1980. 20.00 (ISBN 0-8166-0899-7). U of Minn Pr.

Fehrman, Cherie. The Complete School Secretary's Desk Book. LC 82-3782. 356p. 1982. 24.50 (ISBN 0-13-163352-X, Busn). P-H.

--School Secretary's Encyclopedic Dictionary. 300p. 24.50 (ISBN 0-13-794446-2, Busn). P-H.

Fei, Edward & Klat, Paul. Balance of Payments of Lebanon, 1951 & 1952. 1954. pap. 11.95x (ISBN 0-8156-6024-3, Am U Beirut). Syracuse U Pr.

Fei, He, tr. see Zhongyi, Yuan.

Fei, Hsiao-Tung. Peasant Life in China: A Field Study of Country Life in the Yangtze Valley. (International Library of Sociology). (Illus.). 1980. 25.00x (ISBN 0-7100-0590-3). Routledge & Kegan.

--Peasant Life in China: A Field Study of Country Life in the Yangtze Valley. (Studies in Chinese History & Civilization). (Illus.). 296p. 1977. Repr. of 1939 ed. 21.00 (ISBN 0-89093-081-3). U Pubns Amer.

Fei, Hsiao-Tung & Redfield, Margaret, eds. China's Gentry: Essays in Rural-Urban Relations with Six Life-Histories of Chinese Gentry Families. LC 53-11440. (Midway Reprint Ser.). 296p. 1980. pap. 11.00x (ISBN 0-226-23957-8). U of Chicago Pr.

Fei, John, et al. Growth with Equity: The Taiwan Case. 1979. 27.50x (ISBN 0-19-520115-9); pap. 12.95x (ISBN 0-19-520116-7). Oxford U Pr.

Fei, John C., jt. auth. see Paauw, Douglas S.

Feia, Marian R., jt. auth. see Christenson, Toni.

Feibel, Charles & Walters, A. A. Ownership & Efficiency in Urban Buses. (Working Paper: No. 371). 19p. 1980. pap. 3.00 (ISBN 0-686-39779-7, WP-0371). World Bank.

Feibelman, Barbara, jt. auth. see Dawson, Barbara.

Feibleman, J. K. Adaptive Knowing. 1976. pap. 34.00 (ISBN 90-247-1890-2, Pub. by Martinus Nijhoff Netherlands). Kluwer Academic.

Feibleman, James. From Hegel to Terrorism & Other Essays on the Dynamic Nature of Philosophy. 144p. 1985. text ed. 14.45x (ISBN 0-391-03057-4). Humanities.

--Technology & Reality. 250p. 1982. 25.00 (ISBN 90-247-2519-4, Pub. by Martinus Nijhoff Netherlands). Kluwer Academic.

Feibleman, James K. Christianity, Communism & the Ideal Society: A Philosophical Approach to Modern Politics. LC 75-3140. Repr. of 1937 ed. 29.50 (ISBN 0-404-59149-3). AMS Pr.

--Collected Poems. 1974. 8.95 (ISBN 0-8180-1571-3). Horizon.

--Conversations: A Kind of Fiction. 360p. 1982. 15.95 (ISBN 0-8180-1134-3). Horizon.

--A Future for Economics: A New Basis for Society. 176p. 1984. 11.95 (ISBN 0-8180-2305-8). Horizon.

--Great April. 5.95 (ISBN 0-8180-0610-2). Horizon.

--Institutions of Society. 1968. Repr. of 1956 ed. text ed. 15.50x (ISBN 0-391-00638-X). Humanities.

--Ironies of History. LC 79-48039. 1980. 9.95 (ISBN 0-8180-0823-7). Horizon.

--Justice, Law, & Culture. LC 84-22671. Date not set. price not set (ISBN 9-02-473105-4, Pub. by Martinus Nijhoff Netherlands). Kluwer Academic.

--New Proverbs for Our Day. LC 77-93933. 1978. 7.95 (ISBN 0-8180-1323-0); pap. 3.95 (ISBN 0-8180-1324-9). Horizon.

--Ontology. LC 68-8333. (Illus.). 1968. Repr. of 1951 ed. lib. bdg. 29.75x (ISBN 0-8371-0072-0, FEON). Greenwood.

--Philosophers Lead Sheltered Lives: A First Volume of Memoirs. LC 75-3141. Repr. of 1952 ed. 27.50 (ISBN 0-404-59150-7). AMS Pr.

--Religious Platonism. LC 78-161628. 236p. Repr. of 1959 ed. lib. bdg. 22.25x (ISBN 0-8371-6184-3, FERP). Greenwood.

--Theory of Human Culture. 1968. Repr. of 1946 ed. text ed. 15.50x (ISBN 0-391-00448-4). Humanities.

--Understanding Civilizations: The Shape of History. 1975. 8.95 (ISBN 0-8180-0816-4). Horizon.

--Understanding Human Nature: A Popular Guide to the Effects of Technology on Man & His Behavior. LC 77-77126. 1978. 8.95 (ISBN 0-8180-1322-2). Horizon.

--Understanding Oriental Philosophy. 1984. pap. 9.95 (ISBN 0-452-00710-0, Mer). NAL.

Feibleman, James K., jt. auth. see Friend, Julius W.

Feibleman, Peter, jt. auth. see Hellman, Lillian.

Feicht, Hieronim. Studia nad Muzyka Polskiego Sredniowiecza. Lissa, Zofia, ed. LC 75-543338. (Opera Musicologica Hieronymi Feicht Ser.: No. 1). (Illus.). 400p. (Eng. & Ger. & Polish.). 1975. 10.00 (ISBN 0-934082-16-2, Pub. by PWM Edition Poland). Theodore Front.

Feichtinger, G., ed. Optimal Control Theory & Economic Analysis: Proceedings of the Viennese Workshop on Economic Applications of Control Theory, First, Vienna, Austria, October 28-30, 1981. 414p. 1982. 68.00 (ISBN 0-444-86428-8, I-285-82, North Holland). Elsevier.

--Optimal Control Theory & Economic Analysis: Workshop on Economic Applications of Control Theory, 2nd, Held in Vienna, 16-18 May, 1984, No. 2. 662p. 1985. 60.00 (ISBN 0-444-87688-X, North-Holland). Elsevier.

Feichtinger, Gustav & Kall, Peter. Operations Research in Progress. 1982. 56.50 (ISBN 90-277-1464-9, Pub. by Reidel Holland). Kluwer Academic.

Feichtner, Rudy, tr. see Alfven, Hannes.

Feidel, Frank, ed. see Buenker, John D.

Feidel, Frank, ed. see Hennings, Robert.

Feidel, Jan, tr. Searching for My Brother. (Illus.). 1973. pap. 5.95 (ISBN 0-685-78994-2, Pub. by Mushinsha Bks). Small Pr Dist.

Feidel, Jan, tr. see Jaquiera, Joaquim & Mansa, Manuel B.

Feidelson, Charles, Jr., ed. Herman Melville: Moby Dick. 775p. 1964. pap. text ed. write for info. (ISBN 0-02-336720-2). Macmillan.

Feidelson, Charles, Jr., jt. ed. see Ellmann, Richard.

Feidelson, Charles, Jr., ed. see Melville, Herman.

Feidelson, Charles N., Jr. Symbolism in American Literature. LC 53-6809. (Midway Reprint Ser.). 1981. pap. 12.00x (ISBN 0-226-24026-6). U of Chicago Pr.

Feiden, Karen L. Basket Weaving. LC 78-73441. 1979. 8.95 (ISBN 0-87523-193-4). Emerson.

Feiden, Margo. The Calorie Factor. 800p. 1984. pap. 14.95 (ISBN 0-671-43646-5, Fireside). S&S.

Feider, Helga, tr. see Pinard, Adrien.

Feider, Paul. Paul's Letters for Today's Christian. LC 81-86678. 128p. 1982. pap. 3.95 (ISBN 0-89622-154-7). Twenty-Third.

Feider, Paul A. The Journey to Inner Peace. LC 84-71863. 112p. (Orig.). 1984. pap. 3.95 (ISBN 0-87793-275-1). Ave Maria.

Feierabend, G., jt. auth. see Korn, K.

Feierabend, Ivo, et al. Political Events Project, Nineteen Forty-Eight to Nineteen Sixty-Five. 1976. write for info., codebk. (ISBN 0-89138-017-5). ICPSR.

Feierman, Steven. The Shambaa Kingdom: A History. LC 72-7985. 250p. 1974. 30.00x (ISBN 0-299-06360-7). U of Wis Pr.

Feierman, Steven, compiled by. Health & Society in Africa: A Working Bibliography. (Archival & Bibliographic Ser.). 1978. pap. 25.00 (ISBN 0-918456-16-9, Crossroads). African Studies Assn.

Feierstein, Ben. Children's Enjoyment Through Poetry. 1982. 4.95 (ISBN 0-533-05121-5). Vantage.

Feifar, Z., ed. see Joint ISC-WHO Symposium, Geneva, 1971.

Feifel, Herman. New Meanings of Death. (Illus.). 1977. 25.00 (ISBN 0-07-020350-4); pap. 17.95 (ISBN 0-07-020349-0). McGraw.

Feiffer, Judy. Lovecrazy. 144p. 1984. pap. 2.25 (ISBN 0-380-84160-6, 84160-6, Flare). Avon.

Feiffer, Jules. Feiffer: Jules Feiffer's America from Eisenhower to Reagan. Heller, Steve, ed. 1982. 25.00 (ISBN 0-394-52846-8); pap. 12.95 (ISBN 0-394-71279-X). Knopf.

--Little Murders. 96p. 1983. pap. 4.95 (ISBN 0-14-048118-4). Penguin.

--Tantrum. LC 79-2207. 1979. 8.95 (ISBN 0-394-50837-8). Knopf.

Feig, B. K. The Parents Guide to Weight Control for Children Ages 5 to 13 Years. (Illus.). 200p. 1980. spiral bdg. 15.75x (ISBN 0-398-03972-0). C C Thomas.

Feig, Barbara K. Now You're Cooking: A Guide to Cooking for Boys & Girls. LC 75-10991. 144p. (YA) 1975. pap. 4.95 (ISBN 0-916836-01-0). J B Pal.

Feig, Gottfried. Wissenschafts- und Praxisorientierung: Eine Analyse und Konzeption fuer die Arbeitslehre. (European University Studies: No. 11, Vol. 165). 374p. (Ger.). 1983. 40.55 (ISBN 3-8204-7731-4). P Lang Pubs.

Feig, Konnilyn G. Hitler's Death Camps. LC 81-140. (Illus.). 548p. 1981. 39.50x (ISBN 0-8419-0675-0); pap. 29.50x (ISBN 0-8419-0676-9). Holmes & Meier.

Feig, Stephen A. & McLelland, Robert, eds. Breast Carcinoma: Current Diagnosis & Treatment. (Illus.). 653p. 1983. 95.00 (ISBN 0-89352-187-7, Co-published by the American College of Radiology). Masson Pub.

Feigel, Marcel. How to Have Sex in Public Without Being Noticed. LC 83-50566. (Illus.). 80p. 1983. pap. 2.95 (ISBN 0-89815-115-5). Ten Speed Pr.

Feigel, William & Zamzow, Dennis. Foot Care Book. (Illus.). 170p. 1982. 9.95 (ISBN 0-89037-245-4). Anderson World.

Feigelman, William. Prescriptions for Better Days: Readings on Policy Alternatives for America's Social Problems. 400p. 1980. pap. text ed. write for info (ISBN 0-697-07561-3). Wm C Brown.

Feigelman, William & Silverman, Arnold R. Chosen Children: New Patterns of Adoptive Relationships. 288p. 1983. 26.95x (ISBN 0-03-062343-X). Praeger.

Feigelson, E. M. & Malkevich, M. S. Calculation of the Brightness of Light in the Case of Anisotropic Scattering. LC 60-8720. (Transactions (Trudy) of the Institute of Atmospheric Physics Ser.: Pt. 1). pap. 27.50 (ISBN 0-317-08290-6, 2020687). Bks Demand UMI.

Feigelson, E. M., ed. Radiation in a Cloudy Atmosphere. 1984. lib. bdg. 64.00 (ISBN 90-277-1803-2, Pub. by Reidel Holland). Kluwer Academic.

Feigelstock, Shalom. Additive Groups of Rings. (Research Notes in Mathematics Ser.: No. 83). 218p. 1983. pap. text ed. 16.95 (ISBN 0-273-08591-3). Pitman Pub MA.

Feigenbaum. Total Quality Control. (Illus.). 630p. 39.50 (ISBN 0-318-13258-3, P65). Am Soc QC.

Feigenbaum, ed. see Kohavi, Zvi.

Feigenbaum, Armand V. Total Quality Control. 3rd ed. (Illus.). 768p. 42.50 (ISBN 0-07-020353-9). McGraw.

Feigenbaum, Ed & Ford, Mark. Emergency Management in the States. Purcell, Le, ed. 56p. (Orig.). 1984. pap. 10.00 (ISBN 0-87292-052-6). Coun State Govts.

Feigenbaum, Edward, ed. see Katzan, Harry.

Feigenbaum, Edward A. Computers & Thought. LC 80-29508. 550p. 1981. Repr. of 1963 ed. lib. bdg. 31.50 (ISBN 0-89874-199-8). Krieger.

Feigenbaum, Edward A. & McCorduck, Pamela. The Fifth Generation: Artificial Intelligence & Japan's Computer Challenge to the World. LC 83-3765. 288p. 1983. 15.95 (ISBN 0-201-11519-0). Addison-Wesley.

Feigenbaum, Gail, jt. auth. see Martin, John R.

Feigenbaum, Harvey. Echocardiography. 3rd. ed. LC 80-20682. (Illus.). 580p. 1981. text ed. 35.00 (ISBN 0-8121-0758-6). Lea & Febiger.

Feigenbaum, Harvey B. The Politics of Public Enterprise: Oil & the French State. LC 84-42883. 184p. 1985. 25.00x (ISBN 0-691-07677-4); pap. 8.95x (ISBN 0-691-02229-1). Princeton U Pr.

Feigenbaum, Irwin, ed. English as a Second Language: Dimensions & Directions. LC 83-51796. 71p. 1984. pap. 7.00 (ISBN 0-88312-929-9); microfiche 1.93 (ISBN 0-88312-544-7). Summer Inst Ling.

Feigenbaum, Joshua & Schulps, David. Rock Quiz. (Illus.). 160p. 1983. pap. 5.95 (ISBN 0-399-50734-5, Perigee). Putnam Pub Group.

Feigenbaum, Rita. American Portraits 1800-1850: A Catalogue of Early Portraits in the Collection of Union College. LC 71-173916. (Illus.). 155p. 1972. text ed. 10.95x (ISBN 0-912756-01-2). Union Coll.

Feigenberg, Loma. Terminal Care: Friendship Contracts with Dying Patients. LC 79-25904. 1980. 25.00 (ISBN 0-87630-224-X). Brunner-Mazel.

Feiger, Allan D., jt. auth. see Dubovsky, Steven L.

Feiger, George & Jacquillat, Bertrand. International Finance: Text & Cases. 496p. 1980. text ed. 31.43 (ISBN 0-205-07137-6, 1071378); tchr's. ed. o.p. avail. (ISBN 0-205-07138-4). Allyn.

Feigert, jt. auth. see Getz.

Feigert, Frank B., jt. auth. see Greenstein, Fred I.

Feighner, John, jt. auth. see Damlouji, Namir F.

Feigin, David S., jt. auth. see Forrest, John V.

Feigin, Ralph D. & Cherry, James D. Textbook of Pediatric Infectious Disease. LC 78-66046. 1981. Vol. 1, 798p. text ed. 73.00 (ISBN 0-7216-3586-5); Vol. 2, 1858p. text ed. 52.00 (ISBN 0-7216-3594-6); text ed. 120.00 (ISBN 0-7216-3596-2). Saunders.

Feigin, Samuel I. Legal & Administrative Texts in the Reign of Samsu-Iluna. LC 78-4032. (Yale Oriental Series-Babylonian Text: No. 12). (Illus.). 1979. text ed. 38.50 (ISBN 0-300-01963-7). Yale U Pr.

Feigl, Dorothy M. & Hill, John W. Foundations of Life, 1983: General, Organic, & Biological Chemistry. 1983. 24.95x (ISBN 0-8087-3000-2). Burgess.

--General, Organic, & Biological Chemistry: Foundations of Life. 2nd, rev. ed. (Illus.). 544p. 1985. text ed. price not set (ISBN 0-8087-3026-6); price not set student guide (ISBN 0-8087-3027-4). Burgess.

Feigl, Dorothy M., jt. auth. see Hill, John W.

Feigl, F. & Anger, Y. Spot Tests in Inorganic Analysis. 6th ed. 669p. 1972. 117.00 (ISBN 0-444-40929-7). Elsevier.

Feigl, Fritz & Anger, Y. Spot Tests in Organic Analysis. 7th ed. 772p. 1966. 117.00 (ISBN 0-444-40209-8). Elsevier.

Feigl, Herbert & Maxwell, G., eds. Scientific Explanation, Space & Time. LC 57-12861. (Studies in the Philosophy of Science Ser: Vol. 3). 1962. 25.00x (ISBN 0-8166-0266-2). U of Minn Pr.

Feigl, Herbert & Scriven, M., eds. Foundations of Science & the Concepts of Psychology & Psychoanalysis. LC 56-11610. (Studies in the Philosophy of Science Ser: Vol. 1). 1956. 22.50x (ISBN 0-8166-0122-4). U of Minn Pr.

Feigl, Herbert & Sellars, Wilfrid, eds. Readings in Philosophical Analysis. x, 593p. 1981. lib. bdg. 25.00x (ISBN 0-917930-29-0); pap. text ed. 15.00x (ISBN 0-917930-09-6). Ridgeview.

Feigl, Herbert, et al, eds. Concepts, Theories & the Mind-Body Problem. LC 57-12861. (Studies in the Philosophy of Science Ser: Vol. 2). 1958. 25.00x (ISBN 0-8166-0158-5). U of Minn Pr.

Feignebaum, Richard & McCorduck, Pamela. The Fifth Generation. 1984. pap. 3.50 (ISBN 0-451-13153-3, Sig). NAL.

Feigon, Lee. Chen Duxiu, Founder of the Chinese Communist Party. LC 83-42556. (Illus.). 304p. 1983. 25.00 (ISBN 0-691-05393-6). Princeton U Pr.

Feigs, Wolfgang. Deskriptive Edition Auf Allograph-, Wort- und Satzniveau, Demonstriert An Handschriftlich Uberlieferten, Deutschsprachigen Briefen Von H. Steffens, Vol. 2. (European University Studies: No. 1, Vol. 523). ix, 699p. (Ger.). 1982. 66.30 (ISBN 3-261-04938-3). P Lang Pubs.

Fei Hsiao Tung. Toward a People's Anthropology. (China Studies). (Illus.). 121p. (Orig.). pap. 5.95 (ISBN 0-8351-0913-5). China Bks.

Fei Hsiao-T'Ung, ed. see Shih Kuo-Heng.

Feijoo, Gladys. Lo Fantastico en los Relatos de Carlos Fuentes: Aproximacion Teorica. LC 84-72570. (Senda de Estudios y Ensayos). 100p. (Orig., Span.). 1985. pap. 11.95 (ISBN 0-918454-43-3). Senda Nueva.

Feil, D. K. Ways of Exchange: The Enga Tee of Papua New Guinea. LC 83-23414. (Illus.). 269p. 1985. text ed. 37.50x (ISBN 0-7022-1994-0). U Of Queensland Pr.

Feil, Ernst. The Theology of Dietrich Bonhoeffer. Rumscheidt, H. Martin, tr. LC 84-47919. 272p. 1985. 19.95 (ISBN 0-8006-0696-5, 1-696). Fortress.

Feil, Hila. The Ghost Garden. LC 75-29277. 256p. (gr. 4-6). 1976. 7.95 (ISBN 0-689-30501-X). Atheneum.

--The Windmill Summer. (Illus.). (gr. 3-7). 1973. pap. 1.50 (ISBN 0-380-43372-9, 43372-9, Camelot). Avon.

Feil, Hila, tr. see Silverstein, Shel.

Feilbogen, Siegmund. Smith & Turgot. LC 78-157162. (Research & Source Works Ser: No. 845). 1971. Repr. of 1892 ed. 20.00 (ISBN 0-8337-4098-9). B Franklin.

Feilchenfeld, Ernst H. The International Economic Law of Belligerent Occupation. xii, 181p. Repr. of 1942 ed. 28.00 (ISBN 0-384-15413-1). Johnson Repr.

Feild, Hubert S. & Bienen, Leigh B. Jurors & Rape: A Study in Psychology & Law. LC 76-48473. (Illus.). 496p. 1980. 39.00x (ISBN 0-669-01148-7). Lexington Bks.

Feild, Lance. Map User's Sourcebook. LC 81-18941. 194p. 1982. lib. bdg. 17.50 (ISBN 0-379-20717-6). Oceana.

Feild, Rachel. Buying Antique Furniture. (Illus.). 176p. 1985. 16.95 (ISBN 0-356-10163-0, Pub. by Salem Hse Ltd). Merrimack Pub Cir.

Feild, Reshad. The Invisible Way: A Sufi Love Story. LC 78-19501. 176p. 1983. pap. 7.64 (ISBN 0-06-062588-0, RD/457, HarpR). Har-Row.

--The Last Barrier. LC 75-9345. 1977. pap. 7.64i (ISBN 0-06-062586-4, RD 202, HarpR). Har-Row.

--Steps to Freedom. LC 83-50115. 176p. (Orig.). 1983. pap. 7.95 (ISBN 0-939660-04-0). Threshold VT.

Feilden. The Conservation of Historic Buildings. 1982. text ed. 135.00 (ISBN 0-408-10782-0). Butterworth.

Feilden, G. B., et al, eds. Prospects for Industrial Electrochemistry. (Illus.). 165p. 1981. lib. bdg. 54.00x (ISBN 0-85403-174-X, Pub. by Royal Soc London). Scholium Intl.

Feilders, John F. Profile: The Role of the Chief Superintendent of Schools. LC 81-85352. 1982. pap. 6.95 (ISBN 0-8224-5555-2). Pitman Learning.

Feilding, Everard. Sittings with Eusapai Palladino & Other Studies. (Illus.). 1963. 10.00 (ISBN 0-8216-0153-9). Univ Bks.

Feiler, Arthur. America Seen Through German Eyes. Goldsmith, Margaret L., tr. LC 73-13128. (Foreign Travelers in America, 1810-1935 Ser.). 300p. 1974. Repr. 20.00x (ISBN 0-405-05451-3). Ayer Co Pubs.

Feiler, Eva, jt. ed. see Barkan, Stanley H.

Feiler, Eva, tr. see Cassian, Nina.

Feiler, Herbert, jt. ed. see Opton, Frank G.

Feiler, Lily, tr. see Kern, Gary.

Feiler, Seymour, tr. see Wiet, Gaston.

Feiling, Keith. British Foreign Policy, Sixteen Sixty to Sixteen Seventy-Two. 385p. 1968. Repr. of 1930 ed. 32.50x (ISBN 0-7146-1473-4, F Cass Co). Biblio Dist.

Feiling, Keith G. Life of Neville Chamberlain. LC 75-95598. (Illus.). xi, 477p. 1970. Repr. of 1946 ed. 35.00 (ISBN 0-208-00970-1, Archon). Shoe String.

--Sketches in Nineteenth Century Biography. LC 73-107698. (Essay Index Reprint Ser.). 1930. 17.00 (ISBN 0-8369-1501-1). Ayer Co Pubs.

Feilitzen, Olof Von see Von Feilitzen, Olof.

Feilmeier, M. Hybridrechnen. (International Ser. of Numerical Mathematics: No. 2). 304p. (Ger.). 1974. 41.95x (ISBN 0-8176-0671-8). Birkhauser.

Feilmeier, M., et al, eds. Parallel Computing: Proceedings of the International Conference, Freie Universitat, Berlin, 26-28, Sept., 1983. 566p. 1984. 74.00 (ISBN 0-444-87528-X, North Holland). Elsevier.

Feiman, Sharon, ed. Teacher Centers: What Place in Education. (Orig.). 1980. pap. 1.50 (ISBN 0-686-29035-6). U Chi Ctr Policy.

Feimer, Nickolaus R. & Geller, Scott, eds. Environmental Psychology: Directions & Perspectives. 368p. 1983. 39.95 (ISBN 0-03-062474-6). Praeger.

Fein & Gatner. University & Community: The New Partnership. LC 75-165286. 1971. 15.00 (ISBN 0-913252-03-4); pap. 8.50 (ISBN 0-913252-04-2). LIU Univ.

Fein, Alan & Levine, Joseph S. Visual System: Proceedings of a Symposium in Honor of Edward F. MacNichol, Jr., Held in Woods Hole, MA, Dec. 2-3, 1983, Vol. 5. LC 84-27828. (MBL Lectures in Biology). 208p. 1985. 44.00 (ISBN 0-8451-2204-5). A R Liss.

Fein, Alan & Szuts, Ete Z. Photoreceptors: Their Role in Vision. LC 81-24209. (International Union of Pure & Applied Physics Biophysics Ser.: No. 5). (Illus.). 1982. 39.50 (ISBN 0-521-24433-1); pap. 15.95 (ISBN 0-521-28684-0). Cambridge U Pr.

Fein, Albert. Frederick Law Olmsted & the American Environmental Tradition. LC 72-75831. (Planning & Cities Ser.). (Illus.). 160p. 1972. 10.00 (ISBN 0-8076-0650-2); pap. 7.95 (ISBN 0-8076-0649-9). Braziller.

Fein, Barbara. MCAT: New Medical College Admissions Test. (Illus.). 288p. (Orig.). 1982. pap. 6.68i (ISBN 0-06-463549-X, EH 549). B&N NY.

--The New Medical College Admission Test. 1982. pap. 6.68i (ISBN 0-06-463549-X, EH-549). Har-Row.

Fein, Bruce E. Significant Decisions of the Supreme Court: 1976-1977 Term. 168p. 1978. pap. 6.25 (ISBN 0-8447-3289-3). Am Enterprise.

--Significant Decisions of the Supreme Court: 1978-1979 Term. 199p. 1980. pap. 6.25 (ISBN 0-8447-3387-3). Am Enterprise.

--Significant Decisions of the Supreme Court, 1979-1980 Term. 248p. (Orig.). 1985. pap. 22.50x (ISBN 0-317-19290-6). Rothman.

--Significant Decisions of the Supreme Court: 1977-78 Term. 162p. 1979. 6.25 (ISBN 0-8447-3360-1). Am Enterprise.

--Significant Decisions of the Supreme Court, 1971-72 Term. 65p. 1972. pap. 4.25 (ISBN 0-8447-1072-5). Am Enterprise.

--Significant Decisions of the Supreme Court: 1975-76 Term. 198p. 1977. pap. 6.25 (ISBN 0-8447-3283-4). Am Enterprise.

Fein, Cheri. New York: Open to the Public. LC 81-21468. (Illus.). 224p. 1982. 19.95 (ISBN 0-941434-00-1); pap. 12.95 (ISBN 0-941434-26-5). Stewart Tabori & Chang.

Fein, David A. Charles 'Orleans. (World Authors Ser.: No. 699). 1983. lib. bdg. 18.95 (ISBN 0-8057-6546-8, Twayne). G K Hall.

--A Reading of Villon's Testament. LC 84-50322. (Illus.). 112p. 1984. pap. 10.95 (ISBN 0-917786-04-1). Summa Pubns.

Fein, Edith, et al. After Foster Care: Outcomes of Permanency Planning in Foster Care. 1983. pap. 4.00 (ISBN 0-87868-223-6). Child Welfare.

Fein, Elizabeth A., ed. Speak for Yourself. 1984. pap. text ed. 8.95 (ISBN 0-88377-460-7). Newbury Hse.

Fein, Gieta & Campbell, Pat. Young Children & Microcomputers. 1985. text ed. 19.95 (ISBN 0-8359-9482-1). Reston.

Fein, Greta. Child Development. (Illus.). 1978. text ed. 28.95 (ISBN 0-13-132571-X); study guide & wkbk. 8.95 (ISBN 0-13-132555-8). P-H.

Fein, Greta G. & Clarke-Stewart, Alison. Day Care in Context. LC 72-8588. 359p. 1973. 47.50x (ISBN 0-471-25695-1, Pub. by Wiley-Interscience). Wiley.

Fein, Harry H. A Harvest of Hebrew Verse: Poems of the Cultural Renaissance & National Revival. Fein, Harry H., tr. from Hebrew. LC 35-233. pap. 37.50 (ISBN 0-317-10147-1, 2017957). Bks Demand UMI.

Fein, Helen. Accounting for Genocide: National Response & Jewish Victimization During the Holocaust. LC 78-53085. (Illus.). 1979. 17.95 (ISBN 0-02-910220-0). Free Pr.

--Accounting for Genocide: National Responses & Jewish Victimization During the Holocaust. LC 83-24219. (Illus.). xxii, 469p. 1984. pap. 13.95 (ISBN 0-226-24034-7). U of Chicago Pr.

--Imperial Crime & Punishment: The Massacre at Jallianwala Bagh & British Judgment, 1919-1920. LC 77-2930. 265p. 1977. text ed. 15.00x (ISBN 0-8248-0506-2). UH Pr.

Fein, J. M. & Flamm, E. S., eds. Cerebrovascular Surgery, Vols. 1-4. 1985. 98.00 ea. Vol. 1, 300p (ISBN 0-387-90995-8). Vol. 2, 300p (ISBN 0-387-90996-6). Vol. 3, 350p (ISBN 0-387-96041-4). Vol. 4, 350p (ISBN 0-387-96026-0). Springer-Verlag.

Fein, J. M. & Reichman, O. H., eds. Microvascular Anastomoses for Cerebral Ischemia. (Illus.). 1978. 63.00 (ISBN 0-387-90240-6). Springer-Verlag.

Fein, Jay S. Boundary Layers in Homogeneous & Stratified Rotating Fluids: Notes on Lectures by Allan R. Robinson & Victor Barcilon. LC 78-400. (Monograph Publishing on Demand: Imprint Ser.: No. 45). pap. 35.50 (ISBN 0-317-29820-8, 2016493). Bks Demand UMI.

Fein, Jess. Godyssey: The True Story of a Young Man's Search for God & Proof of His Existence. LC 80-81677. (Illus.). 236p. (Orig.). 1980. pap. 7.95 (ISBN 0-9604366-0-X). J Fein.

Fein, John M. Modernismo in Chilean Literature: The Second Period. LC 64-25821. pap. 44.30 (ISBN 0-317-26742-6, 2023380). Bks Demand UMI.

Fein, Judith. Are You a Target: A Guide to Self-Protection Personal Safety, & Rape Prevention. (Wadsworth Ser. in Continuing Education). 145p. 1981. pap. text ed. write for info. (ISBN 0-534-00969-7, Continuing Ed). Wadsworth Pub.

Fein, Leah G. The Three-Dimensional Personality Test: Reliability, Validity & Clinical Implications. LC 60-15824. 342p. 1961. text ed. 30.00 (ISBN 0-8236-6520-8). Intl Univs Pr.

Fein, Lois, jt. auth. see Gonzalez, Harvey J.

Fein, Mitchell. Improshare: An Alternative to Traditional Managing. 1981. pap. text ed. 15.00 (ISBN 0-89806-031-1, NO. 129); pap. text ed. 7.50 members. Inst Indus Eng.

--Rational Approaches to Raising Productivity. 1974. pap. text ed. 12.00 (ISBN 0-89806-029-X); pap. text ed. 6.00 members. Inst Indus Eng.

--Wage Incentive Plans. 1970. pap. text ed. 13.00 (ISBN 0-89806-026-5, 42); pap. text ed. 8.00 members. Inst Indus Eng.

Fein, Rashi. Economics of Mental Illness. Grob, Gerald N., ed. LC 78-22559. (Historical Issues in Mental Health Ser.). (Illus.). 1979. Repr. of 1958 ed. lib. bdg. 14.00x (ISBN 0-405-11913-5). Ayer Co Pubs.

Fein, Rashi, jt. auth. see Lewis, Charles E.

Fein, Richard J. Robert Lowell. 2nd ed. (United States Authors Ser.). 1979. lib. bdg. 15.95 (ISBN 0-8057-7279-0, Twayne). G K Hall.

Fein, Sherman E. & Maskell, Arthur M. Selected Cases on the Law of Shoplifting. 92p. 1975. pap. 10.50x spiral bdg. (ISBN 0-398-03355-2). C C Thomas.

Fein, Sylvia. Heidi's Horse. LC 74-76077. (Illus.). 1976. 15.00 (ISBN 0-917388-01-1). Exelrod Pr.

--Heidi's Horse. 2nd ed. LC 83-81900. (Illus.). 1984. 15.00 (ISBN 0-917388-02-X). Exelrod Pr.

Feinberg. Job Search Theory. 1984. lib. bdg. 31.00 (ISBN 0-8240-4152-6). Garland Pub.

--Reason & Responsibility. 6th ed. 1984. write for info. (ISBN 0-534-03873-5). Wadsworth Pub.

Feinberg & Gross. Philosophy of Law. 3rd ed. 1986. text ed. write for info. Wadsworth Pub.

Feinberg, Barbara S. Franklin D. Roosevelt, Gallant President. LC 80-22307. (Illus.). 96p. (gr. 2-6). 1981. 10.00 (ISBN 0-688-00433-4); PLB 10.88 (ISBN 0-688-00434-2). Lothrop.

--Marx & Marxism. (Impact Ser.). (Illus.). 128p. (gr. 7 up). 1985. PLB 9.90 (ISBN 0-531-10065-0). Watts.

Feinberg, Barry. Applied Clinical Engineering. (Illus.). 544p. 1986. text ed. 42.95 (ISBN 0-13-039488-2). P-H.

Feinberg, Barry & Kasrils, Ronald. Bertrand Russell's America: 1945-1970. 1983. 25.00 (ISBN 0-89608-157-5); pap. 10.00 (ISBN 0-89608-156-7). South End Pr.

Feinberg, Barry, ed. Poets to the People. (African Writers Ser.). (Orig.). 1980. pap. text ed. 6.00x (ISBN 0-435-90230-X). Heinemann Ed.

--Poets to the People: South African Freedom Poems. 83p. 1974. 2.50 (ISBN 0-317-20232-4). IDAFSA.

--Poets to the People: South African Freedom Poems. 82p. 1974. 4.50 (ISBN 0-317-36672-6). Africa Fund.

Feinberg, Barry N., jt. auth. see Fleming, David G.

Feinberg, Barry N., ed. Handbook of Clinical Engineering, Vol. 1. 384p. 1980. 66.00 (ISBN 0-8493-0244-7). CRC Pr.

Feinberg, Barry N., jt. ed. see Fleming, David G.

Feinberg, Bill, jt. auth. see Ribowsky, Mark.

Feinberg, Charles L. Daniel, the Kingdom of the Lord. 1984. 9.95 (ISBN 0-88469-157-8). BMH Bks.

--God Remembers: A Study of Zechariah. 4th ed. LC 79-88530. 1979. 8.95 (ISBN 0-930014-33-2). Multnomah.

--Jeremiah. 320p. 1982. 13.95 (ISBN 0-310-45330-5). Zondervan.

--The Minor Prophets. rev ed. LC 76-44088. 384p. 1976. 13.95 (ISBN 0-8024-5306-6). Moody.

--Prophecy of Ezekiel. 1984. 11.95 (ISBN 0-8024-6908-6). Moody.

--Revelation. 1985. 9.95 (ISBN 0-88469-162-4). BMH Bks.

Feinberg, Diane L. Journal of a Transsexual. 21p. 1980. pap. 0.50 (ISBN 0-89567-036-4). World View Pubs.

Feinberg, Gerald. Solid Clues: Quantum Physics, Molecular Biology & the Future of Science. 304p. 1985. 17.95 (ISBN 0-671-45608-3). S&S.

--What Is the World Made of: The Achievements of Twentieth-Century Physics. LC 76-18342. (Illus.). 1978. (Anch); pap. 6.95 (ISBN 0-385-07694-0). Doubleday.

Feinberg, Gerald & Schapiro, Robert. Life Beyond Earth: The Intelligent Earthling's Guide to Extraterrestrial Life. LC 80-14009. (Illus.). 480p. 1980. 16.95 (ISBN 0-688-03642-2). Morrow.

--Life Beyond Earth: The Intelligent Earthling's Guide to Extraterrestrial Life. (Illus.). 480p. 1980. pap. 9.95 (ISBN 0-688-08642-X, Quill NY). Morrow.

Feinberg, Gerald, et al, eds. A Festschrift for Maurice Goldhaber. new ed. LC 80-20599. (Transaction Ser.: Vol. 40). 293p. 1980. 27.00x (ISBN 0-89766-086-2). NY Acad Sci.

Feinberg, H. Cosmetics-Perfumery Thesaurus. 1972. 17.95 (ISBN 0-02-469030-9). Macmillan Info.

Feinberg, Harold. Simon & Schuster Guide to Shells. (Illus.). 1980. pap. 9.95 (ISBN 0-671-25320-4). S&S.

Feinberg, Harold S., jt. auth. see Ryder, Joanne.

Feinberg, Herbert S. All about Hair. LC 77-92355. 1978. 10.00 (ISBN 0-930988-01-9). Wallingford NJ.

Feinberg, Hilda. Title Derivative Indexing Techniques: A Comparative Study. LC 73-2671. 307p. 1973. 27.50 (ISBN 0-8108-0602-9). Scarecrow.

Feinberg, Hilda, ed. Indexing Specialized Formats & Subjects. LC 82-23155. 300p. 1983. 37.50 (ISBN 0-8108-1608-3). Scarecrow.

Feinberg, Joel. Doing & Deserving: Essays in the Theory of Responsibility. 1970. pap. 9.95 (ISBN 0-691-01981-9). Princeton U Pr.

--Harm to Others. (The Moral Limits of Criminal Law Ser.). (Illus.). 1984. 29.95x. Oxford U Pr.

--Offense to Others. 1985. 29.95x (ISBN 0-19-503449-X). Oxford U Pr.
--Problems of Abortion. 1973. pap. write for info. (ISBN 0-534-00334-6). Wadsworth Pub.
--Rights, Justice & the Bounds of Liberty: Essays in Social Philosophy. LC 79-48024. (Princeton Series of Collected Essays). 318p. 1980. 28.00 (ISBN 0-691-07254-X). Princeton U Pr.
--Social Philosophy. 1973. pap. 12.95 ref. ed. (ISBN 0-13-817254-4). P-H.
Feinberg, Joel, ed. Moral Concepts. (Oxford Readings in Philosophy Ser). (Orig.). 1969. pap. text ed. 6.95x (ISBN 0-19-875012-9). Oxford U Pr.
Feinberg, John S. & Feinberg, Paul D. Tradition & Testament. LC 81-11223. 1982. 14.95 (ISBN 0-8024-2544-5). Moody.
Feinberg, Karen. Crown Jewels. LC 82-60559. (Illus.). 64p. 1982. 24.00 (ISBN 0-88014-055-0). Mosaic Pr OH.
--A Small Book of Herbs. LC 83-90112. (Illus.). 64p. 1984. 20.00 (ISBN 0-88014-071-2). Mosaic Pr OH.
Feinberg, Leonard. Introduction to Satire. facsimile ed. 294p. (gr. 11 up). 1967. pap. 9.50 (ISBN 0-8138-2410-9). Iowa St U Pr.
--Introduction to Satire. LC 67-12134. pap. 75.80 (ISBN 0-317-30168-3, 2025350). Bks Demand UMI.
--The Secret of Humor. 1978. pap. text ed. 23.50x (ISBN 90-6203-370-9). Humanities.
Feinberg, M., et al. New Psychology for Managing People. 1982. 17.95 (ISBN 0-13-615302-X). P-H.
Feinberg, Michael, tr. see Treyat, Henri.
Feinberg, Milton. Techniques of Photojournalism. LC 73-96959. pap. 72.80 (ISBN 0-317-10701-1, 2013630). Bks Demand UMI.
Feinberg, Mortimer R. Effective Psychology for Managers. 1975. (Reward); pap. 5.95 (ISBN 0-13-244848-3). P-H.
Feinberg, Mortimer R. & Dempewolff, Richard F. Corporate Bigamy: How to Resolve the Conflict Between Career & Family. LC 79-26322. 1980. 12.95 (ISBN 0-688-03534-5). Morrow.
Feinberg, Murray L. & McHatton, Robert J. How to Increase Profits with Telemarketing. LC 82-60239. 208p. 1982. 39.95 (ISBN 0-914330-53-5, Pub by Pioneer Pub Co). Panorama West.
Feinberg, Nathan. Studies in International Law. 640p. 1981. text ed. 49.50x (ISBN 0-86598-051-9, Pub. by Magnes Israel). Allanheld.
--Studies in International Law. 640p. 1979. text ed. 36.50x (ISBN 965-223-324-2, Pub. by Magnes Israel). Humanities.
Feinberg, Paul. Friends. rev. ed. (Illus.). 58p. 1981. pap. write for info. (ISBN 0-9607144-0-5). T Noble.
Feinberg, Paul, jt. auth. see Geisler, Norman L.
Feinberg, Paul D., jt. auth. see Feinberg, John S.
Feinberg, Renee. Women, Education, & Employment: A Bibliography of Periodical Citations, Pamphlets, Newspapers, & Government Documents, 1970-1980. 274p. 1982. 25.00 (ISBN 0-208-01967-7, Lib Prof Pubns). Shoe String.
Feinberg, Richard. Anuta: Social Structure of a Polynesian Island. 373p. 1981. pap. 14.95 (ISBN 0-939154-23-4). Inst Polynesian.
--Anutan Concepts of Disease: A Polynesian Study. (Monograph Ser.: No. 3). 51p. pap. 6.95 (ISBN 0-939154-03-X). Inst Polynesian.
Feinberg, Richard, et al. Tempest in a Tea House: American Attitudes Toward Breast-Feeding. 50p. (Orig.). 1980. pap. 2.95 (ISBN 0-933522-06-1). Kent Popular.
Feinberg, Richard E. Intemperate Zone: The Third World Challenge to U.S. Foreign Policy. 216p. 1984. pap. 7.95 (ISBN 0-393-30143-5). Norton.
--Subsidizing Success: The Export-Import Bank in the United States Economy. LC 81-4702. (Illus.). 192p. 1982. 39.50 (ISBN 0-521-23427-1). Cambridge U Pr.
Feinberg, Richard E., ed. Central America: International Dimensions of the Crisis. 300p. 1982. 29.50x (ISBN 0-8419-0737-4); pap. 12.50x (ISBN 0-8419-0738-2). Holmes & Meier.
Feinberg, Richard E. & Kallab, Valerina, eds. Adjustment Crisis in the Third World. (U.S. - Third World Policy Perspectives Ser.). 200p. 1984. 19.95 (ISBN 0-88738-040-9); pap. 12.95 (ISBN 0-87855-988-4). Transaction Bks.
--Uncertain Future: Commercial Banks in the Third World. (U.S. - Third World Policy Perspectives Ser.). 146p. 1984. 19.95 (ISBN 0-88738-041-7); pap. 12.95 (ISBN 0-87855-989-2). Transaction Bks.
Feinberg, Richard E., jt. ed. see Sewell, John W.
Feinberg, Samuel. Management's Challenge: The People Problem. 336p. 1976. 12.50 (ISBN 0-87005-141-5). Fairchild.
--The Off-Price Explosion. 80p. 1984. pap. 15.00 (ISBN 0-87005-506-2). Fairchild.
Feinberg, Walter. Reason & Rhetoric: The Intellectual Foundations of Twentieth Century Liberal Educational Policy. LC 74-16009. Repr. of 1975 ed. 57.20 (ISBN 0-8357-9974-3, 2055147). Bks Demand UMI.
--Understanding Education: Towards a Reconstruction of Educational Inquiry. LC 82-12790. (Illus.). 304p. 1983. 39.50 (ISBN 0-521-24864-7); pap. 13.95 (ISBN 0-521-27032-4). Cambridge U Pr.
Feinberg, Walter & Solitis, Jonas F. School & Society. (Thinking about Education Ser.). 160p. 1985. pap. 8.95x (ISBN 0-8077-2785-7). Tchrs Coll.
Feinberg, Walter, ed. Equality & Social Policy. 190p. 1978. 14.50x (ISBN 0-252-00215-6). U of Ill Pr.
Feinberg, Walter & Rosemont, Henry, Jr., eds. Work, Technology, & Education: Dissenting Essays in the Intellectual Foundations of American Education. LC 75-4854. (Illus.). 222p. 1975. 17.95x (ISBN 0-252-00252-0); pap. 6.95 (ISBN 0-252-00649-6). U of Ill Pr.
Feinberg, Walter, jt. ed. see Bredo, Eric.
Feinberg, Wilbert. Lost-Wax Casting: A Practitioner's Manual. Byrne, Jim, ed. (Illus.). 96p. 1983. pap. 11.50x (ISBN 0-903031-88-4, Pub. by Intermediate Tech England). Intermediate Tech.
Feinberg, William H. Ken Stabler. (Sports Superstars Ser). (Illus.). (gr. 3-9). 1978. pap. 3.95 (ISBN 0-89812-170-1). Creative Ed.
Feinberg, William J., ed. Commercial Real Estate Brokers Directory. 350p. 1985. pap. text ed. 77.00 (ISBN 0-938184-15-6). Whole World.
--Directory of Real Estate Investors, 1985. 1985. pap. 115.00 (ISBN 0-938184-14-8). Whole World.
--The Whole World Oil Directory, 1985. 1985. Set. pap. 103.00 (ISBN 0-938184-13-X). Whole World.
Feinblatt. Drawings in the Los Angeles County Museum of Art. treasure trove bdg. 9.95x (ISBN 0-87505-058-1); pap. 4.95 (ISBN 0-87505-211-8). Borden.
Feinblatt, Ebria & Davis, Bruce. Los Angeles Prints: Eighteen Eighty-Three to Nineteen Eighty. (Illus.). 112p. (Orig.). 1980. pap. 10.00x (ISBN 0-87587-097-X). LA Co Art Mus.
--Toulouse Lautrec & His Contemporaries: Posters of the Belle Epoque. (Illus.). 264p. (Orig.). 1985. pap. 24.95 (ISBN 0-87587-125-9, Co-Pub. by Abrams). LA Co Art Mus.
Feinbloom, Richard I. & Forman, Betty Yetta. Pregnancy, Birth & the Early Months: A Complete Guide. LC 84-29458. (Illus.). 384p. 1985. not set 16.95 (ISBN 0-201-10805-4). Addison-Wesley.
Feinburg, Sylvia, jt. auth. see Pitcher, Evelyn G.
Feineman, N. Persistence of Vision: The Films of Robert Altman. LC 77-22906. (Dissertations on Film Ser.). 1978. lib. bdg. 18.00x (ISBN 0-405-10752-8). Ayer Co Pubs.
Feineman, Neil. Lose Fifteen Pounds in Thirty Days. 96p. (Orig.). 1984. pap. 3.95 (ISBN 0-671-47614-9, Wallaby). S&S.
Feinendegen, L. E. Tritium Labeled Molecules in Biology & Medicine. (Atomic Energy Commision Monographs). 1967. 29.50 (ISBN 0-12-251550-1). Acad Pr.
Feinendegen, L. E. & Tisljarlentulis, G., eds. Molecular & Microdistribution of Radioisotopes & Biological Consequences: Proceedings Held in Julich, Federal Republic of Germany, October 1975. (Current Topics in Radiator Research Ser.: Vol. 12). 1978. Repr. 138.50 (ISBN 0-444-85142-9, North-Holland). Elsevier.
Feiner, Arthur & Epstein, Laurence. Countertransference: The Therapist's Contribution to Therapy. LC 79-51929. 476p. 1979. 30.00x (ISBN 0-87668-662-5). Aronson.
Feiner, Benjamin, jt. auth. see Sax, N. Irving.
Feiner, Johannes & Vischer, Lukas, eds. The Common Catechism: A Book of Christian Faith. LC 75-1070. 690p. 1975. 10.95 (ISBN 0-8245-0211-6). Crossroad NY.
Feiner, Ronald R. Operational Financial Analysis: A Practical Handbook with Forms. 288p. 1977. 44.95 (ISBN 0-13-637504-9). P-H.
Feinermann, Emmanuel, jt. auth. see Thalmann, Rita.
Feinglass, Sanford, jt. auth. see Lappin, Myra.
Feingold. Hamlet (Shakespeare) (Book Notes Ser.). 1984. pap. 2.50 (ISBN 0-8120-3417-1). Barron.
--Thirty-Two Warm Weather Dishes. 1983. 4.95 (ISBN 0-8120-5531-4). Barron.
Feingold, Barbara A. & Bank, Caryl L. Developmental Disabilities of Early Childhood. (Illus.). 216p. 1978. 21.00x (ISBN 0-398-03699-3). C C Thomas.
Feingold, Ben. Why Your Child Is Hyperactive. 10.50x (ISBN 0-394-49343-5). Cancer Control Soc.
Feingold, Ben, jt. auth. see Feingold, Helene.
Feingold, Ben F. Introduction to Clinical Allergy. (Illus.). 408p. 1973. 33.50x (ISBN 0-398-02797-8). C C Thomas.
--Why Your Child Is Hyperactive. LC 74-9078. 1974. 10.50 (ISBN 0-394-49343-5, Co-Pub by Bookworks). Random.
--Why Your Child Is Hyperactive. 1985. 7.95 (ISBN 0-394-73426-2). Random.
Feingold, Carl. Fundamentals of Structured COBOL Programming. 4th ed. 880p. 1983. pap. text ed. write for info. (ISBN 0-697-08173-7); instr's. manual avail. (ISBN 0-697-08185-0); student wkbk. avail. (ISBN 0-697-08186-9). Wm C Brown.
--Introduction to Assembler Language Programming. 427p. 1978. pap. text ed. write for info. (ISBN 0-697-08124-9); instrs.' manual avail. (ISBN 0-697-08158-3). Wm C Brown.
--Introduction to Data Processing. 3rd ed. 752p. 1980. pap. text ed. write for info. (ISBN 0-697-08136-2); student wkbk avail. (ISBN 0-697-08140-0); instrs.' manual avail. (ISBN 0-697-08143-5). Wm C Brown.
--RPG II Programming. 720p. 1982. pap. text ed. write for info. (ISBN 0-697-08150-8); instrs.' manual avail. (ISBN 0-697-08152-4). Wm C Brown.
Feingold, Helen. Thirty-Two Better Barbeques. 1983. 4.95 (ISBN 0-8120-5517-9). Barron.
Feingold, Helene & Feingold, Ben. The Feingold Cookbook for Hyperactive Children & Others with Problems Associated with Food Additives & Salicylates. 1979. 10.95 (ISBN 0-394-41232-X); pap. 5.95 (ISBN 0-394-73664-8). Random.
Feingold, Henry L. A Midrash on American Jewish History. (American Jewish History Ser.). 232p. 1982. 34.50x (ISBN 0-87395-637-0); pap. 11.95x (ISBN 0-87395-638-9). State U NY Pr.
--The Politics of Rescue. LC 80-81713. (Illus.). 432p. (Orig.). 1970. pap. 10.95 (ISBN 0-89604-019-4). Holocaust Pubns.
--The Politics of Rescue: The Roosevelt Administration & the Holocaust, 1938-1945. LC 75-127049. 1970. 30.00x (ISBN 0-8135-0664-6). Rutgers U Pr.
--The Politics of Rescue: The Roosevelt Administration & the Holocaust, 1938 to 1945. expanded & updated ed. LC 80-81713. 432p. 1980. pap. 7.95 (ISBN 0-8052-5019-0, Pub. by Holocaust Library). Schocken.
--The Politics of Rescue: The Roosevelt Administration & the Holocaust, 1938-1945. 432p. pap. 7.95 (ISBN 0-686-95080-1). ADL.
--Zion in America. rev. ed. (American Immigrant Ser.). 1981. pap. 10.95 (ISBN 0-88254-592-2). Hippocrene Bks.
Feingold, Jessica, jt. ed. see Faust, Clarence H.
Feingold, M. J., jt. auth. see Perrin, E. V.
Feingold, Marie, jt. auth. see Feingold, S. Norman.
Feingold, Mordechai. The Mathematicians' Apprenticeship: Science, Universities & Society in England, 1560-1640. LC 83-1911. 256p. 1984. 39.50 (ISBN 0-521-25133-8). Cambridge U Pr.
Feingold, Murray & Pashayan, Hermione. Genetics & Birth Defects in Clinical Practice. (Clinical Pediatrics Ser.). 1983. 35.00 (ISBN 0-316-27715-0). Little.
Feingold, Norman & Fins, Alice. Your Future in More Exotic Careers. (Careers in Depth Ser.). 1982. lib. bdg. 8.97 (ISBN 0-8239-0412-1). Rosen Group.
Feingold, Norman & Nicholson, Avis. The Professional & Trade Association Job Finder: A Directory of Employment Resources Offered by Associations & Other Organizations. LC 83-80691. (Illus.). 195p. (Orig.). 1983. 12.95 (ISBN 0-912048-33-6). Garrett Pk.
Feingold, Norman & Perlman, Leonard. Making It On Your Own: What to Know Before You Start Your Own Business. 320p. 1985. pap. 7.95 (ISBN 0-87491-779-4). Acropolis.
Feingold, Norman S. & Nicholson, Avis J. Getting Ahead: A Woman's Guide to Career Success. 275p. 1983. pap. 7.95 (ISBN 0-87491-489-2). Acropolis.
Feingold, Richard. Monarch Notes on Swift's Gulliver's Travels. (Orig.). pap. 2.95 (ISBN 0-671-00648-7). Monarch Pr.
--Nature & Society: Later Eighteenth Century Uses of the Pastoral & Georgic. 1978. 25.00x (ISBN 0-8135-0847-9). Rutgers U Pr.
Feingold, S. Norman. Counseling for Careers in the Nineteen Eighties. LC 78-74700. (Illus.). 186p. 1979. pap. 6.95 (ISBN 0-912048-09-3). Garrett Pk.
--A Counselor's Handbook: Readings in Counseling, Student Aid & Rehabilitation. LC 79-190226. 288p. (gr. 9-12). 1972. text ed. 13.00 (ISBN 0-910328-05-6). Carroll Pr.
--Whither Guidance: Future Directions. LC 81-81749. (Illus.). 155p. (Orig.). 1981. pap. 6.95 (ISBN 0-912048-22-0). Garrett Pk.
Feingold, S. Norman & Evers, Dora. Your Future in Exotic Occupations. Rev. ed. LC 76-182515. (Careers in Depth Ser.). (Illus.). 160p. (gr. 7 up). 1980. PLB 8.97 (ISBN 0-8239-0260-9). Rosen Group.
Feingold, S. Norman & Feingold, Marie. Scholarships, Fellowships & Loans, Vol. 6. LC 49-49180. 518p. 1977. 45.00x (ISBN 0-87442-006-7). Bellman.
--Scholarships, Fellowships & Loans, Vol. 7. LC 49-49180. 804p. 1982. 75.00x (ISBN 0-87442-007-5). Bellman.
Feingold, S. Norman & Fins, Alice. Your Future in More Exotic Occupations. rev. ed. 1982. 8.97. Rosen Group.
Feingold, S. Norman & Hansard-Winkler, Glenda A. Nine Hundred Thousand Plus Jobs Annually: Published Sources of Employment Listings. LC 81-85931. (Illus.). 196p. (Orig.). 1982. pap. 9.95 (ISBN 0-912048-25-5). Garrett Pk.
Feingold, S. Norman & Levin, Shirley. What to Do until the Counselor Comes. (Careers in Depth Ser.). 128p. 1980. lib. bdg. 8.97 (ISBN 0-8239-0506-3). Rosen Group.
--What to Do until the Counselor Comes. rev. ed. (Careers in Depth Ser.). 1983. 8.97. Rosen Group.
Feingold, S. Norman & Miller, Norma R. Emerging Careers: New Occupations for the Year Two Thousand & Beyond. LC 83-80074. 172p. 1983. pap. 11.95 (ISBN 0-912048-32-8). Garrett Pk.
--Your Future: A Guide for the Handicapped Teenager. (Careers in Depth Ser.). 140p. 1982. lib. bdg. 8.97 (ISBN 0-8239-0424-5). Rosen Group.
Feingold, William L. The Revolt of the Tenantry: The Transformation of Local Government in Ireland, 1875-1895. LC 84-4080. (Illus.). 280p. 1984. 24.95x (ISBN 0-930350-55-3). NE U Pr.
Feininger, Andreas. The Anatomy of Nature. (Illus.). 1979. pap. 7.95 (ISBN 0-486-23840-7). Dover.
--The Anatomy of Nature. 16.75 (ISBN 0-8446-5760-3). Peter Smith.
--The Complete Photographer. (Illus.). 1984. pap. 14.95 (ISBN 0-13-162255-2). P-H.
--The Creative Photographer. rev. ed. LC 84-13922. (Illus.). 272p. 1974. 14.95 (ISBN 0-13-190611-9). P-H.
--Feininger's Chicago, Nineteen Forty-One. (Illus.). 14.50 (ISBN 0-8446-5761-1). Peter Smith.
--Feininger's Chicago: 1941. (Illus.). 80p. 1980. pap. 5.00 (ISBN 0-486-23991-8). Dover.
--Industrial America, Nineteen Forty to Nineteen Sixty: One Hundred Seventy-Six Photographs by Andreas Feininger. LC 81-68278. (Illus.). 183p. (Orig.). 1982. pap. 9.95 (ISBN 0-486-24198-X). Dover.
--Nature & Art: A Photographic Exploration. (Photography Ser.). 144p. 1984. pap. 9.95 (ISBN 0-486-24539-X). Dover.
--Nature Close Up: A Fantastic Journey into Reality. rev. ed. (Illus.). 160p. 1981. pap. 9.95 (ISBN 0-486-24102-5). Dover.
--Nature Close Up: A Fantastic Journey into Reality. (Illus.). 18.00 (ISBN 0-8446-5885-5). Peter Smith.
--New York City in the Forties. (Text by John von Hartz). 1983. 14.00 (ISBN 0-8446-5934-7). Peter Smith.
--New York in the Forties. LC 77-8734. (New York Ser.). (Illus.). 1978. pap. 6.95 (ISBN 0-486-23585-8). Dover.
--Shells: Forms & Designs of the Sea. (Illus.). 128p. 1983. pap. 8.95 (ISBN 0-486-24498-9). Dover.
--Stone & Man: A Photographic Exploration. LC 78-73211. (Illus.). 1979. pap. 7.95 (ISBN 0-486-23756-7). Dover.
--Successful Photography. 320p. 1982. pap. 10.95 (ISBN 0-13-864595-7). P-H.
--Total Photography. (Illus.). 252p. 1982. 14.95 (ISBN 0-8174-3531-X, Amphoto). Watson-Guptill.
Feininger, Lyonel. The Kin-der-Kids: All Thirty-One Strips in Full Color. (Illus.). 32p. (Orig.). 1980. pap. 6.95 (ISBN 0-486-23918-7). Dover.
Feinland, Alexander & Iotti, Oscar R. Violin & Violoncello in Duo Without Accompaniment. LC 77-187707. (Detroit Studies in Music Bibliography Ser.: No. 25). (Based on the work of Alexander Feinland). 1973. 5.00 (ISBN 0-911772-48-0); pap. 2.00 (ISBN 0-89990-011-9). Info Coord.
Feinleib, M. E., jt. ed. see Haupt, W.
Feinman, Clarice. Women in the Criminal Justice System. LC 80-12539. 136p. 1980. 24.95 (ISBN 0-03-052561-6); pap. 11.95 (ISBN 0-03-052566-7). Praeger.
Feinman, Clarice, jt. ed. see Schweber, Claudine.
Feinman, Jeffrey. Alternate Forms of Energy. 1981. pap. text ed. 1.95 (ISBN 0-89083-834-8). Zebra.
--Black Narc. (Orig.). 1977. pap. 1.50 (ISBN 0-532-15249-2). Woodhill.
--Freebies for Kids. (gr. 4 up). 1979. pap. 3.95 (ISBN 0-671-33009-8). Wanderer Bks.
--The Newscasters. 1977. pap. 1.50 (ISBN 0-532-15244-1). Woodhill.
Feinman, Jeffrey, jt. auth. see Maller, Dick.
Feinman, Jeffy & Schwartz, Betty. Freebies for Kids. Rev. Updated ed. 208p. 1983. pap. 4.95 (ISBN 0-671-42657-5). Wanderer Bks.
Feinman, Richard D., ed. Chemistry & Biology of A2-Macroglobulin, Vol. 421. 95.00x (ISBN 0-89766-236-9); pap. 95.00 (ISBN 0-89766-237-7). NY Acad Sci.
Feinman, Ronald L. Twilight of Progressivism: The Western Republican Senators & the New Deal. LC 80-20124. (Johns Hopkins Studies in Historical & Political Science). (Illus.). 288p. 1981. text ed. 25.00x (ISBN 0-8018-2373-0). Johns Hopkins.
Feinrider, Martin, jt. ed. see Miller, Arthur S.
Feins, Judith & Lane, Terry S. How Much for Housing? New Perspectives on Affordability & Risk. LC 81-3637. 200p. 1982. 19.00 (ISBN 0-89011-558-3). Abt Bks.
Feins, Judith D. & Lane, Terry S. How Much for Housing? New Perspectives on Affordability & Risk. 206p. 1984. Repr. of 1981 ed. lib. bdg. 19.50 (ISBN 0-8191-4113-5). U Pr of Amer.
Feinschreiber, Robert. Tax Incentives for U. S. Exports. LC 74-23774. 385p. 1975. lib. bdg. 26.00 (ISBN 0-379-00235-3). Oceana.
Feinschreiber, Robert, jt. auth. see Bischel, Jon E.
Feinsilver, A. Aspects of Jewish Belief. 1973. pap. 6.95x (ISBN 0-87068-225-3). Ktav.
Feinsilver, Alexander, ed. The Talmud Today. 320p. 1980. 14.95 (ISBN 0-312-78479-1). St Martin.
Feinsilver, David B., ed. Towards a Comprehensive Model for Schizophrenic Disorders. (Psychoanalytic Inquiry Bk.: Vol. 5). 400p. 1985. text ed. 39.95 (ISBN 0-88163-029-2). Analytic Pr.
Feinsilver, Lillian M. The Taste of Yiddish. LC 70-88260. 480p. 1980. 14.95 (ISBN 0-498-02427-X); pap. 6.95 (ISBN 0-498-02515-2). A S Barnes.
Feinsilver, P. J. Special Functions, Probability Semigroups, & Hamiltonian Flows. (Lecture Notes in Mathematics Ser.: Vol. 696). 1978. pap. 14.00 (ISBN 0-387-09100-9). Springer-Verlag.

Feinsot, Bernice B. Paroles et Pensees Lyriques. LC 55-9916. (Illus.). 127p. (Fr.). 1975. pap. 6.95x (ISBN 0-915526-01-8). B B Feinsot.

Feinstein, A., tr. see Minkhlin, Solomon G.

Feinstein, Alan H., jt. ed. see Becker, Judith.

Feinstein, Alvan R. Clinical Epidemiology: The Architecture of Clinical Research. 450p. Date not set. price not set (ISBN 0-7216-1308-X). Saunders.

--Clinical Judgment. LC 67-19517. 422p. 1974. Repr. of 1967 ed. 26.00 (ISBN 0-88275-141-7). Krieger.

Feinstein, Barbara & Brown, Edwin G. New Partnership: Human Services with Business & Industry. 202p. 1982. text ed. 18.95x (ISBN 0-87073-653-1); pap. text ed. 11.95 (ISBN 0-87073-654-X). Schenkman Bks Inc.

Feinstein, Barbara & Cavanaugh, Catherine. The New Volunteerism: A Community Connection. LC 76-7838. 208p. 1978. pap. 8.95 (ISBN 0-87073-781-3). Schenkman Bks Inc.

Feinstein, C. H. Domestic Capital Formation in the United Kingdom. (Publications of the National Institute of Economic & Social Research & Cambridge Department of Applied Economics: No. 4). 49.00 (ISBN 0-521-04986-5). Cambridge U Pr.

--Domestic Capital Formation in the United Kingdom, 1920-1938. LC 64-21572. (Studies in the National Income & Expenditure of the United Kingdom: No. 4). pap. 70.50 (ISBN 0-317-26397-8, 2024454). Bks Demand UMI.

--National Income, Expenditure & Output of the United Kingdom, 1855-1965. LC 71-163055. (Studies in the National Income & Expenditure of the United Kingdom: Vol. 6). (Illus.). 1972. 85.00 (ISBN 0-521-07230-1). Cambridge U Pr.

--Statistical Tables of National Income Expenditure & Output of the U. K. 1855-1965. LC 76-19627. 1976. limp bdg. 22.95x (ISBN 0-521-21396-7). Cambridge U Pr.

Feinstein, C. H., jt. auth. see Pajestka, Josef.

Feinstein, Charles. The Managed Economy: Essays in British Economic Policy & Performance Since 1929. 1983. 39.95x (ISBN 0-19-828289-3); pap. 17.95x (ISBN 0-19-828290-7). Oxford U Pr.

--York Eighteen Thirty-One to Nineteen Eighty-One: 150 Years of Scientific Endeavour & Social Change. 1981. 100.00x (ISBN 0-686-87292-4, Pub. by Westbury House). State Mutual Bk.

Feinstein, David L., jt. auth. see Nestman, Chadwick H.

Feinstein, Elaine. The Border. 1985. 10.95 (ISBN 0-312-09269-5). St Martin.

--Some Unease & Angels. LC 77-11250. pap. 5.00 (ISBN 0-940580-05-5). Green River.

Feinstein, Elaine, tr. see Tsvetayeva, Marina.

Feinstein, Ellen, jt. auth. see Harris, L. C.

Feinstein, Estelle & Pendery, Joyce. Stamford: An Illustrated History. (Illus.). 192p. 1984. 22.95 (ISBN 0-89781-114-3). Windsor Pubns Inc.

Feinstein, G. Programed Writing Skills. 1976. pap. 15.95 (ISBN 0-13-730523-0); free instr's. manual of tests 0.00 (ISBN 0-13-730515-X). P-H.

Feinstein, George W. Programed Spelling & Vocabulary. 272p. 1983. pap. text ed. 15.95 (ISBN 0-13-729855-2). P-H.

--Programmed College Vocabulary Three Thousand Six Hundred. 2nd ed. 1979. pap. text ed. 15.95 (ISBN 0-13-729806-4). P-H.

--Programmed College Vocabulary 3600. 3rd ed. 336p. 1986. pap. text ed. 14.95 (ISBN 0-13-729427-1). P-H.

--Programmed Spelling Demons. 2nd ed. 240p. 1985. pap. text ed. 15.95 (ISBN 0-13-729211-2). P-H.

Feinstein, Gerry, jt. ed. see Wilhelm, John.

Feinstein, Howard M. Becoming William James. LC 83-45944. (Illus.). 384p. 1984. 24.95 (ISBN 0-8014-1617-5). Cornell U Pr.

Feinstein, Irwin K. & Murphy, Kenneth H. College Algebra: With Problems & Solutions (Pre-Calculus Algebra) 2nd. ed. (Quality Paperback Ser.: No. 39). 486p. (Orig.). 1981. pap. text ed. 6.95 (ISBN 0-8226-0039-0). Littlefield.

Feinstein, Karen W., ed. Working Women & Families. LC 79-639. (Women's Policy Studies Yearbook: Vol. 4). 295p. 1979. 28.00 (ISBN 0-8039-1158-0); pap. 14.00 (ISBN 0-8039-1159-9). Sage.

Feinstein, Lloyd, jt. auth. see Kline, Linda.

Feinstein, Marnin. Basic Hebrew: A Textbook of Contemporary Hebrew. LC 73-77286. 1973. 7.75x (ISBN 0-8197-0287-0). Bloch.

Feinstein, Maurice B. & Levine, Harriet. Pharmacology. 3rd ed. (Nursing Examination Review Bk.: Vol. 6). 1974. spiral bdg. 7.50 (ISBN 0-87488-506-X). Med Exam.

Feinstein, Paul T., jt. auth. see Rosenberg, Kenyon C.

Feinstein, Robert N. Oysters in Love. 104p. (Orig.). 1984. pap. 9.00 (ISBN 0-910429-05-7). Stronghold Pr.

Feinstein, Sherman C. & Giovacchini, Peter L. Adolescent Psychiatry, Vol. 8. LC 70-147017. 544p. 1981. lib. bdg. 25.00x (ISBN 0-226-24053-3). U of Chicago Pr.

Feinstein, Sherman C. & Giovacchini, Peter L., eds. Adolescent Psychiatry, Vol. 7. LC 70-147017. 1979. lib. bdg. 25.00x (ISBN 0-226-24052-5). U of Chicago Pr.

--Adolescent Psychiatry, Vol. 9. LC 70-147017. 5841p. 1982. 30.00x (ISBN 0-226-24054-1). U of Chicago Pr.

Feinstein, Sherman C. & Giovacchini, Peter, eds. Adolescent Psychiatry: Developmental & Clinical Studies, Vol. 6. (Adolescent Psychiatry Ser.). 1979. lib. bdg. 25.00x (ISBN 0-226-24051-7). U of Chicago Pr.

Feinstein, Sherman C. & Looney, John G., eds. Adolescent Psychiatry, Vol. X. LC 70-147017. (Adolescent Psychiatry Ser.). 624p. 1983. lib. bdg. 30.00x (ISBN 0-226-24056-8). U of Chicago Pr.

Feinstein, Sherman C., et al, eds. Adolescent Psychiatry, Vol. 12. LC 70-147017. 570p. 1985. lib. bdg. 32.50x (ISBN 0-226-24058-4). U of Chicago Pr.

Feintech, Lynn D. China's Four Modernizations & the United States. (Headline Ser.: No. 255). (Illus.). 72p. (gr. 11-12). 1982. pap. 3.00 (ISBN 0-87124-070-X). Foreign Policy.

Feintuch, Abraham & Saeks, R. System Theory: A Hilbert Space Approach. LC 82-1816. (Pure & Applied Mathematics Ser.). 1982. 49.50 (ISBN 0-12-251750-4). Acad Pr.

Feipel, J. Elements of Bibliography. 1976. lib. bdg. 59.95 (ISBN 0-8490-1756-4). Gordon Pr.

Feirer. Basic Woodworking. (gr. 9-12). 1978. 10.64 (ISBN 0-02-662630-6); pap. 7.32 (ISBN 0-02-662620-9). Bennett IL.

--Beginning Woodwork. 1984. text ed. 13.32 (ISBN 0-02-662640-3). Bennett IL.

--Industrial Arts Woodworking. rev. ed. (gr. 9-12). 1982. text ed. 17.92 (ISBN 0-02-664670-6). Bennett IL.

--SI Metric Handbook. 1977. text ed. 25.00 (ISBN 0-02-665180-7). Bennett IL.

--Woodworking for Industry. 1979. text ed. 23.72 (ISBN 0-02-666350-3); student guide 7.96 (ISBN 0-02-666360-0); tchr's. ed. 3.96 (ISBN 0-02-666380-5). Bennett IL.

--Woodworking for Industry. 1983. text ed. 25.28 (ISBN 0-02-666390-2). Bennett IL.

Feirer & Hutchings. Advanced Woodwork & Furniture Making. rev. ed. (gr. 9-12). 1982. text ed. 22.20 (ISBN 0-02-662110-X). Bennett IL.

--Advanced Woodwork & Furniture Making. 1978. text ed. 18.60 (ISBN 0-02-662080-4); student guide 5.28 (ISBN 0-02-662120-7); visual masters 20.00 (ISBN 0-02-662070-7); tchr's. guide 3.96 (ISBN 0-02-662150-9). Bennett IL.

--Carpentry & Building Construction. rev. ed. 1981. text ed. 30.60 (ISBN 0-02-662890-2); student guide 6.64 (ISBN 0-02-662900-3); tchrs'. guide 6.64 (ISBN 0-02-662930-5). Bennett IL.

Feirer & Lindbeck. Basic Drafting. (gr. 9-12). 1978. 10.64 (ISBN 0-02-662480-X); pap. 7.32 (ISBN 0-02-662470-2); Activities for Basic Drafting 4.44 (ISBN 0-02-662550-4). Bennett IL.

--Basic Metalwork. (gr. 9-12). 1978. 10.64 (ISBN 0-02-662610-1); pap. 7.32 (ISBN 0-02-662600-4). Bennett IL.

--Metalwork S.I. Metric Edition. 1979. text ed. 15.96 (ISBN 0-02-665150-5); student guide 6.64 (ISBN 0-02-665160-2). Bennett IL.

Feirer, et al. Carpentry & Building Construction: Si Metric Edition. text ed. 31.80 (ISBN 0-02-662940-2). Bennett IL.

Feirer, J. L. & Groneman, C. H. General Metals. 6th ed. 512p. 1985. 26.96 (ISBN 0-07-020398-9); write for info. study guide (ISBN 0-07-020399-7). McGraw.

Feirer, J. L., jt. auth. see Groneman, C. H.

Feirer, John. Cabinetmaking & Millwork. 1982. text ed. 29.28 (ISBN 0-02-662760-4); student guide 6.64 (ISBN 0-02-662740-X); tchr's. guide 3.72 (ISBN 0-02-662770-1). Bennett IL.

--Furniture & Cabinet Making. 1983. text ed. 17.76 (ISBN 0-02-664050-3). Bennett Il.

--Guide to Residential Carpentry. 1983. text ed. 17.08 (ISBN 0-02-665580-2); teacher's guide 5.32 (ISBN 0-02-665590-X); student guide 5.32 (ISBN 0-02-665600-0). Bennett Il.

Feirer, John & Hutchings, Gilbert R. Advanced Woodwork & Furniture-Making. 4th. rev ed. (Illus.). 538p. 1978. 35.00 (ISBN 0-684-17475-8, ScribT). Scribner.

--Carpentry & Building Construction. rev. ed. (Illus.). 1981. 44.50 (ISBN 0-684-16981-9, ScribT). Scribner.

Feirer, John L. Cabinetmaking & Millwork. 2nd, rev. ed. (Illus.). 1983. 42.50 (ISBN 0-684-17941-5, ScribT). Scribner.

--Furniture & Cabinet Making. (Illus.). 512p. 1983. pap. 19.95 (ISBN 0-684-17965-2, ScribT). Scribner.

--General Metals. rev., 5th ed. (Industrial Education Ser.). (Illus.). 480p. (gr. 9-10). 1980. text ed. 24.60 (ISBN 0-07-020380-6). McGraw.

--Industrial Arts Woodworking. (gr. 9-12). 1977. wkbk 5.32 (ISBN 0-02-664650-1); tchr's. ed. 4.24 (ISBN 0-02-664680-3). Bennett IL.

--Machine Tool Metalworking. 2nd ed. Gilmore, D. E., ed. LC 72-10166. (Illus.). 568p. (gr. 10-12). 1973. text ed. 29.20 (ISBN 0-07-020369-5). McGraw.

--Wood: Materials & Processes. 587p. (gr. 7-12). 1975. text ed. 15.96 (ISBN 0-02-666210-8); wkbk. 6.64 (ISBN 0-02-666220-5). Bennett IL.

--Wood: Materials & Processes. rev. ed. (gr. 7-12). 1980. text ed. 21.32 (ISBN 0-02-666240-X). tchr's. ed. 3.96 (ISBN 0-02-666250-7). Bennett IL.

--The Woodworker's Reference Guide & Sourcebook. (Illus.). 384p. 1983. 35.00 (ISBN 0-684-17859-1, ScribT). Scribner.

Feirer, John L. & Hutchings, Gilbert. Guide to Residential Carpentry. (Illus.). 480p. 1983. pap. 17.50 (ISBN 0-684-17966-0, ScribT). Scribner.

Feirer, John L. & Lindbeck. Drawing & Planning for the Industrial Arts. new ed. (Illus.). (gr. 7-12). 1975. text ed. 14.48 (ISBN 0-02-663480-5); tchr's guide, charts & worksheets 7.72 (ISBN 0-02-663490-2). Bennett IL.

Feirer, John L. & Lindbeck, John R. Metalwork. rev. ed. (gr. 7-9). 1970. 15.68 (ISBN 0-02-665190-4); student guide 5.12 (ISBN 0-02-665200-5). Bennett IL.

Feirer, John L., jt. auth. see Groneman, Chris H.

Feiring, Evolyn B. Concatenation: Enoch's Prophecy Fulfilling! Hebrew-Christian Metaphysics Supported by Modern Science. LC 72-96989. 5.00x (ISBN 0-9603386-0-8); pap. 2.00x (ISBN 0-9603386-1-6). Rocky Mtn Bks.

Feirstein, Bruce. Real Men Don't Eat Quiche. (Illus., Orig.). 1983. pap. 4.95 (ISBN 0-671-49228-4). PB.

Feirstein, Bruce, ed. see Redman, Scott.

Feirstein, Frederick. Fathering. 48p. 1982. pap. 4.95 (ISBN 0-918222-33-8). Apple Wood.

--Manhattan Carnival. 60p. 1981. 10.95 (ISBN 0-914378-68-6); pap. 5.95 (ISBN 0-914378-69-4). Countryman.

--Survivors: Poems. LC 74-12385. 1976. 10.00 (ISBN 0-89366-125-2); pap. 5.00 (ISBN 0-89366-126-0). Ultramarine Pub.

Feirtag, Michael, jt. auth. see Nauta, Walle J.

Feirtag, Michael, jt. ed. see Brecher, Kenneth.

Feis, Herbert. Atomic Bomb & the End of World War II. rev. ed. 1966. pap. 8.95x (ISBN 0-691-01057-9). Princeton U Pr.

--Between War & Peace: The Potsdam Conference. LC 83-12966. viii, 367p. 1983. Repr. of 1960 ed. lib. bdg. 45.00x (ISBN 0-313-24219-4, FBWP). Greenwood.

--Changing Pattern of International Economic Affairs. LC 75-137942. (Economic Thought, History & Challenge Ser). 1971. Repr. of 1940 ed. 21.00x (ISBN 0-8046-1445-8, Pub. by Kennikat). Assoc Faculty Pr.

--The China Tangle: The American Effort in China from Pearl Harbor to the Marshall Mission. 456p. 1953. 37.00x (ISBN 0-691-05606-4). Princeton U Pr.

--Churchill, Roosevelt, Stalin: The War They Waged & the Peace They Sought. 2nd ed. 1967. 60.00x (ISBN 0-691-05607-2); pap. 14.95x (ISBN 0-691-01050-1). Princeton U Pr.

--Europe the World's Banker, Eighteen Seventy to Nineteen Fourteen. LC 74-7665. Repr. of 1930 ed. 37.50x (ISBN 0-678-00044-1). Kelley.

--Nineteen Thirty-Three: Characters in Crisis. (FDR & the Era of the New Deal Ser.). 1976. Repr. of 1966 ed. lib. bdg. 39.50 (ISBN 0-306-70807-8). Da Capo.

--Road to Pearl Harbor: The Coming of the War Between the United States & Japan. 1950. pap. 10.95 (ISBN 0-691-01061-7). Princeton U Pr.

--Three International Episodes: Seen from E. A. Orig. Title: Seen from E. 1966. pap. 1.85x (ISBN 0-393-00351-5, Norton Lib). Norton.

Feis, Jacob. Shakespere & Montaigne. LC 73-130615. Repr. of 1884 ed. 17.00 (ISBN 0-404-02375-4). AMS Pr.

Feise, Ernst, tr. see Heine, Heinrich.

Feisner, Edith A. Needlepoint & Beyond: Twenty-Seven Lessons in Advanced Canvas Work. (Illus.). 176p. 1983. pap. 10.95 (ISBN 0-684-17825-7, ScribT). Scribner.

Feist, Joseph R., jt. auth. see Pimm, June B.

Feist, Raymond E. The Magician. LC 80-2957. 552p. 1982. 19.95 (ISBN 0-385-17580-9). Doubleday.

--Magician. LC 80-2957. 552p. 1984. pap. 8.95 (ISBN 0-385-19621-0). Doubleday.

--Silverthorn. LC 83-27471. 360p. 1985. 15.95 (ISBN 0-385-19210-X). Doubleday.

Feist, Robert. Studien zur Rezeption des Franzoesischen Wortschatzes Im Mittelenglischen. 1934. pap. 8.00 (ISBN 0-384-15420-4). Johnson Repr.

Feist, Uwe. German Panzers from Mk. I to Mk. V Panther. LC 66-25077. (Armor Ser.: Vol. 2). (Illus.). 1966. pap. 3.95 (ISBN 0-8168-2004-X). Aero.

--Luftwaffe in World War Two. LC 68-28679. (Aero Pictorials Ser.: Vol. 1). (Illus.). 1968. pap. 4.95 (ISBN 0-8168-0300-5). Aero.

--Luftwaffe in World War Two, Pt. 2. LC 68-28679. (Pictorial Ser.: Vol. 5). 100p. 1980. pap. 6.95 (ISBN 0-8168-0316-1). Aero.

Feist, Uwe & Hirsch, R. S. Heinkel HE100, 112. LC 67-16730. (Aero Ser.: Vol. 12). (Illus.). 1967. pap. 3.95 (ISBN 0-8168-0544-X). Aero.

--Heinkel HE177 Greif. LC 67-16732. (Aero Ser: Vol. 13). (Illus.). 1967. pap. 3.95 (ISBN 0-8168-0548-2). Aero.

--Messerschmitt BF 110. LC 67-21486. (Aero Ser.: Vol. 16). (Illus.). 1967. pap. 3.95 (ISBN 0-8168-0560-1). Aero.

--Messerschmitt ME262. LC 67-16733. (Aero Ser.: Vol. 14). (Illus.). 1967. pap. 3.95 (ISBN 0-8168-0552-0). Aero.

Feist, Uwe & Maloney, Edward T. North American P-Fifty-One Mustang. LC 67-21487. (Aero Ser.: Vol. 15). 1967. pap. 3.95 (ISBN 0-8168-0556-3). Aero.

Feist, Uwe & Weber, Eberhard. Focke Wulf (FW) 190 A, Vol. 18. 2nd ed. (Aero Ser.). (Illus.). 1984. pap. 6.95 (ISBN 0-8168-0569-5). Aero.

Feist, Uwe, jt. auth. see Maloney, Edward T.

Feistcitzer, P. & Kelly, A. Fenwick, eds. Improved Seed Production. (Plant Production & Protection Papers: No. 15). 146p. 1978. pap. 12.25 (ISBN 92-5-100243-6, F1520, FAO). Unipub.

Feister, John, jt. auth. see Quinn, Bernard.

Feistritzer, Emily C. The Condition of Teaching: A State by State Analysis. LC 83-15247. 119p. 1983. pap. text ed. 9.95 (ISBN 0-931050-23-5). Carnegie Found Adv Teach.

Feistritzer, W. P., ed. Cereal Seed Technology: A Manual of Cereal Seed Production, Quality, Control & Distribution. (Plant Production & Protection Papers: No. 10). 238p. (2nd printing, 1977). 1975. pap. 17.00 (ISBN 92-5-100460-9, F94, FAO). Unipub.

Feit, Edward. African Opposition in South Africa: The Failure of Passive Resistance. LC 67-24130. (Publications Ser.: No. 57). 1967. 12.95x (ISBN 0-8179-1571-0). Hoover Inst Pr.

--Governments & Leaders: An Approach to Comparative Politics. LC 77-77977. (Illus.). 1978. text ed. 29.95 (ISBN 0-395-25367-5). HM.

--Urban Revolt in South Africa, 1960-1964: A Case Study. LC 78-138921. pap. 96.80 (ISBN 0-317-11314-3, 2016706). Bks Demand UMI.

--Workers Without Weapons: The South African Congress of Trade Unions & the Organization of the African Workers. 230p. (Orig.). 1975. 19.50 (ISBN 0-208-01496-9, Archon). Shoe String.

Feit, Eugene D. & Wilkins, Cletus, Jr., eds. Polymer Materials for Electronic Applcations. LC 82-1670. (ACS Symposium Ser.: No. 184). 1982. 44.95 (ISBN 0-8412-0715-1). Am Chemical.

Feit, Joseph, jt. auth. see Engelsohn, Harold S.

Feit, Marvin D. Management & Administration of Drug & Alcohol Programs. (Illus.). 152p. 1979. 18.50x (ISBN 0-398-03873-2). C C Thomas.

Feit, W. Representation Theory of Finite Groups. (Mathematical Library: Vol. 25). 502p. 1982. 55.00 (ISBN 0-444-86155-6, North Holland). Elsevier.

Feitelson, Dina, ed. Cross-Cultural Perspectives on Reading & Research. 1978. pap. text ed. 6.50 (ISBN 0-87207-427-7). Intl Reading.

--Mother Tongue or Second Language? On the Teaching of Reading in Multilingual Societies. 1979. pap. text ed. 5.00 (ISBN 0-87207-426-9, 426). Intl Reading.

Feitelson, Mark. Molecular Components of Hepatitis B Virus. (Developments in Molecular Virology Ser.). 1985. lib. bdg. 33.95 (ISBN 0-89838-696-9, Pub. by Martinus Nijhoff Netherlands). Kluwer Academic.

Feitelson, Rose, jt. auth. see Salomon, George.

Feith, Herbert. Decline of Constitutional Democracy in Indonesia. (Illus.). 638p. 1962. 49.95x (ISBN 0-8014-0126-7). Cornell U Pr.

--The Indonesian Elections of 1955: Interim Report. 91p. 1957. pap. 3.50 (ISBN 0-87763-020-8). Cornell Mod Indo.

Feitlowitz. Gulliver's Travels (Swift) (Book Notes Ser.). 1984. pap. 2.50 (ISBN 0-8120-3416-3). Barron.

Feitlowitz, Marguerite, tr. see Atlan, Liliane.

Feito, Francisco E., jt. auth. see Alba-Buffill, Elio.

Feitz, Frank J. Bum Connection. 204p. 1980. 4.95 (ISBN 0-686-98047-6). Telecom Lib.

Feitz, Leland. Colorado Trolley's. (Illus.). 1983. pap. 3.50 (ISBN 0-936564-27-X). Little London.

--Creede, Colorado Boom Town. rev. ed. pap. 2.50 (ISBN 0-936564-03-2). Little London.

--Cripple Creek! (Illus.). pap. 2.95 (ISBN 0-936564-02-4). Little London.

--Cripple Creek Railroads. (Illus.). pap. 1.95 (ISBN 0-936564-15-6). Little London.

--Ghost Towns of the Cripple Creek District. pap. 2.50 (ISBN 0-936564-06-7). Little London.

--Myers Avenue. (Illus.). pap. 1.95 (ISBN 0-936564-16-4). Little London.

--Quartzsite, Arizona: No Ordinary Town. pap. 2.50 (ISBN 0-936564-01-6). Little London.

--Soapy Smith's Creede. pap. 2.50 (ISBN 0-936564-24-5). Little London.

--Victor. (Illus.). pap. 2.50 (ISBN 0-936564-13-X). Little London.

Feitz, Leland, ed. see De Vries, John A.

Feitz, Leland, ed. see Mead, Frances H.

Feitz, Leland, ed. see Munn, Bill.

Feiwel, George R. Growth & Reform in Centrally Planned Economies: The Lessons of the Bulgarian Experience. LC 76-12849. 382p. 1976. text ed. 39.95 (ISBN 0-275-23330-8). Praeger.

--The Intellectual Capital of Michal Kalecki: A Study in Economic Theory & Policy. LC 74-22487. 1975. 32.50x (ISBN 0-87049-161-X). U of Tenn Pr.

--Issues in Contemporary Microeconomics & Welfare. 300p. 1985. lib. bdg. 39.50 (ISBN 0-87395-944-2); pap. text ed. 12.95 (ISBN 0-87395-945-0). State U NY Pr.

--The Soviet Quest for Economic Efficiency: Issues, Controversies, & Reforms. LC 72-145952. (Special Studies in International Economics & Development). 1972. 39.50x (ISBN 0-89197-944-1); pap. text ed. 14.95x (ISBN 0-89197-945-X). Irvington.

Feiwel, George R., ed. Issues in Contemporary Macroeconomics & Distribution. 300p. 1985. lib. bdg. 39.50x (ISBN 0-87395-942-6); pap. text ed. 12.95x (ISBN 0-87395-943-4). State U NY Pr.

--Samuelson & Neo-Classical Economics. (Recent Economic Thought Ser.). 384p. 1981. lib. bdg. 35.00 (ISBN 0-89838-069-3). Kluwer-Nijhoff.

Feiwel, R. J., tr. see Ruppin, Arthur.

Feix, Irmagard & Schlant, Erstine. Gesprache, Diskussionen, Aufsatze. (Ger). 1969. pap. text ed. 16.95 (ISBN 0-03-080020-X, HoltC). HR&W.

Feix, Irmgard & Schlant, Ernestine. Junge Deutsche Prosa. (Rinehart Editions). 1974. text ed. 14.95 (ISBN 0-03-080092-7). HR&W.

Feix, M. R., jt. ed. see Kalman, G.

Fejer, Leopold see Turan, P.

Fejer, M., jt. auth. see Larson, D. H.

Fejer, Paul H. Fundamentals of Dynamic Geometry: The Fejer Vector System. Flemming, Williams, ed. (Illus.). 67p. 1981. 50.00x (ISBN 0-9607422-0-4, TX-808-846). P H Fejer.

--The Measuring Numbers System. Jones, Barbara, ed. (Illus.). 53p. 1975. 60.00x (ISBN 0-9607422-1-2, A-661691). P H Fejer.

--Time in Dynamic Geometry. Meier, Bernadette, ed. (Illus.). 70p. 1984. text ed. 60.00x (ISBN 0-9607422-2-0). P H Fejer.

Fejerskov, Ole & Mjor, Aarhus J. Histology of the Human Tooth. 2nd rev. ed. 174p. 1979. 79.00x (ISBN 0-686-44530-9, Pub. by Munksgaard Denmark). State Mutual Bk.

Fejes, Claire. Villagers. 1981. 14.95 (ISBN 0-394-51673-7). Random.

Fejos, Pal. Archeological Explorations in the Cordillera Vilcabamba, Southeastern Peru. 1944. pap. 19.00 (ISBN 0-384-15430-1). Johnson Repr.

--Ethnography of the Yagua. (Illus.). 1943. pap. 19.00 (ISBN 0-384-15435-2). Johnson Repr.

Fejto, Francois. Dictionnaire des Partis Communistes et des Mouvements Revolutionnaires. 236p. (Fr.). 1971. pap. 12.95 (ISBN 0-686-56857-5, M-6635). French & Eur.

--French Communist Party & the Crisis of International Communism. (Studies in Communism, Revisionism & Revolution). 1967. 30.00x (ISBN 0-262-06017-5). MIT Pr.

--Heine. LC 78-103187. 1970. Repr. of 1946 ed. 24.50x (ISBN 0-8046-0824-5, Pub. by Kennikat). Assoc Faculty Pr.

--Heine, a Biography. 1979. Repr. of 1946 ed. lib. bdg. 30.00 (ISBN 0-8492-4633-4). R West.

Fekete. Real Linear Algebra. (Pure & Applied Mathematics Ser.). 448p. 1985. 39.50 (ISBN 0-8247-7238-5). Dekker.

Fekete, Francois, jt. auth. see Nahum, Henri.

Fekete, Irene & Denyer, Jamine. Mathematics. (The Junior World of Science Ser.). (gr. 7 up). 9.95 (ISBN 0-87196-990-4). Facts on File.

Fekete, Irene & Dorrington, Ward. The World of Science: Disease & Medicine. Date not set. price not set. Facts on File.

Fekete, Irene & Ward, Peter D. Your Body. (The Junior World of Science Ser.). (gr. 7 up). 9.95 (ISBN 0-317-12632-6). Facts on File.

Fekete, Janos. Back to the Realities: Reflections of a Hungarian Banker. 359p. 1982. text ed. 48.00x (ISBN 963-05-2987-4, 41219, Pub. by Kultura Pr Hungary). Humanities.

Fekete, John. The Critical Twilight: Explorations in the Ideology of Anglo-American Literary Theory from Eliot to McLuhan. (The International Library of Phenomenology & Moral Sciences). 1978. 24.95x (ISBN 0-7100-8618-0). Routledge & Kegan.

Fekete, John, ed. The Structural Allegory. LC 83-19878. (Theory & History of Literature Ser.: Vol 11). xxiv, 269p. 1984. 29.50x (ISBN 0-8166-1271-4); pap. 14.95 (ISBN 0-8166-1270-6). U of Minn Pr.

Fekety, Robert, jt. auth. see Pratt, William B.

Fekety, Robert, ed. Reviews of Clinical Infectious Diseases. 1983. 26.50 (ISBN 0-8089-1606-8, 791233). Grune.

--Reviews of Clinical Infectious Diseases, 1984. 528p. 1984. 39.50 (ISBN 0-8089-1684-X, 791234). Grune.

Fekety, Robert, et al, eds. Reviews of Clinical Infectious Diseases. LC 79-1232. 1985. 39.50 (ISBN 0-8089-1748-X). Grune.

Fekrat, M. Ali, jt. auth. see Amuzegar, Jahangir.

Felaco, Vittorio. The Poetry & Selected Prose of Camillo Sbarbaro. Fido, Franco, tr. 1985. 28.50 (ISBN 0-916379-19-1). Scripta.

Felbabov, Vladislava, tr. see Savic, Svenka.

Felbeck, David K. & Atkins, Anthony C. Strength & Fracture of Engineering Solids. (Illus.). 608p. 1984. 41.95 (ISBN 0-13-851709-6). P-H.

Felber, John E. American Tourist Manual for the People's Republic of China. (Illus.). 1980. pap. 8.95. Intl Intertrade.

--American Tourist Manual Lhasa (Xizang) Tibet Sightseeing Guide. LC 73-932101. (Illus.). 8p. 1985. pap. 1.95 (ISBN 0-317-28647-1). Intl Intertrade.

--American's Tourist Manual for Peoples Republic of China. LC 73-93210. 224p. 1980. pap. 8.95. Intl Intertrade.

--American's Tourist Manual for the U. S. S. R. LC 72-78512. (Illus.). 1985. pap. 8.95 (ISBN 0-910794-02-2). Intl Intertrade.

--Beijing (Peking) Restaurant Guide. 24p. 1981. pap. 3.00 (ISBN 0-910794-11-1). Intl Intertrade.

--Guide for Prospective America Importer. 32p. pap. 3.95 (ISBN 0-910794-06-5). Intl Intertrade.

--Kuwait Welcomes Commerce. (Illus.). 48p. 1962. pap. 3.95 (ISBN 0-910794-04-9). Intl Intertrade.

Felber, Paul, ed. see Brucie, Thomas.

Felber, Paul, ed. see Saylor, Lee.

Felber, Ron. The Indian Point Conspiracy. 1977. pap. 1.50 (ISBN 0-532-15267-0). Woodhill.

Felber, Stanley B. & Koch, Arthur. What Did You Say? A Guide to Communications Skills. 2nd ed. (Illus.). 1978. P-H.

Felber, Stanley B., jt. auth. see Koch, Arthur.

Felbinger, Claus, jt. auth. see Ehrenpreis, Andreas.

Feld, Alan L. Tax Policy & Corporate Concentration. LC 81-47277. 176p. 1982. 23.00x (ISBN 0-669-04569-1). Lexington Bks.

Feld, Alan L. & Schuster, J. Mark Davidson. Patrons Depite Themselves: Taxpapers & Arts Policy. LC 83-2234. (A Twentieth Century Fund Report). 246p. 1983. 25.00x (ISBN 0-8147-2572-4); pap. 13.50 (ISBN 0-8147-2574-0). NYU Pr.

Feld, Alan L., et al. Patrons Despite Themselves: Taxpayers & Arts Policy. 263p. 1984. pap. 13.50x (ISBN 0-8147-2574-0). NYU Pr.

Feld, Barry & Levy, Robert J. Standards Relating to Rights of Minors. LC 77-1684. (IJA-ABA Juvenile Justice Standards Project Ser.). 114p. 1980. prof ref 22.50 (ISBN 0-88410-243-2); pap. 12.50 (ISBN 0-88410-810-4). Ballinger Pub.

Feld, Barry C. Neutralizing Inmate Violence: Juvenile Offenders in Institutions. LC 77-21389. (CCJ Series on Massachusetts Youth Correctional Reform). 192p. 1977. prof ref 18.50 (ISBN 0-88410-790-6). Ballinger Pub.

Feld, Benjamin. Manual of Courts-Martial Practice & Appeal. LC 57-6016. 192p. 1957. 10.00 (ISBN 0-379-00134-9). Oceana.

Feld, Bernard, jt. ed. see Epstein, William.

Feld, Bernard T. A Voice Crying in the Wilderness: Essays on the Problem of Science & World Affairs. (Illus.). 1979. pap. text ed. 13.25 (ISBN 0-08-026065-9). Pergamon.

Feld, Bernard T., ed. see Szilard, Leo.

Feld, Bernard T., et al, eds. Impact of New Technologies on the Arms Race. 1971. pap. 5.95x (ISBN 0-262-56010-0). MIT Pr.

Feld, Bruce, jt. auth. see Evatt, Cris.

Feld, Charles, jt. auth. see Char, Rene.

Feld, E. S., et al. Anfang und Fortschrift: An Introduction to German. 2nd ed. 1973. write for info. (ISBN 0-02-336760-1); wkbk. 6.95x (ISBN 0-02-336740-7). Macmillan.

Feld, Ellen. Zielsprache Deutsch: Deutsch. Feld, Von Nardroff, ed. 1981. text ed. write for info. (ISBN 0-02-336810-1). Macmillan.

Feld, Eva. Managing Your Own Secretarial-Word Processing Service for Fun & Profit: A Guide to Greater Financial Success. Michaels, Glen, ed. (Illus.). 36p. (Orig.). 1984. plastic ring bdg. 17.95 (ISBN 0-9614186-0-5). Bullet Pubns.

Feld, Jacob. Construction Failure. LC 68-30908. (Practical Construction Guides Ser.). 1968. 45.95x (ISBN 0-471-25700-1, Pub. by Wiley-Interscience). Wiley.

Feld, Lipman G. Bad Checks & Fraudulent Identity. 112p. 1978. pap. 8.50 (ISBN 0-934914-02-8). NACM.

--Harassment & Other Collection Taboos. 156p. 1976. pap. 8.95 (ISBN 0-934914-08-7). NACM.

Feld, M. S. & Letokhov, V. S., eds. Coherent Nonlinear Optics: Recent Advances. (Topics in Current Physics: Vol. 21). (Illus.). 377p. 1980. 51.00 (ISBN 0-387-10172-1). Springer-Verlag.

Feld, Marilla. I Chose to Live. (Orig.). 1979. pap. 2.25 (ISBN 0-532-22155-9). Woodhill.

Feld, Maury D. The Structure of Violence: Armed Forces as Social Systems. (Armed Forces & Society Ser.). 208p. 1977. 22.50 (ISBN 0-8039-0729-X). Seven Locks Pr.

Feld, Michael S., et al, eds. Fundamental & Applied Laser Physics: Proceedings. LC 73-392. Repr. of 1973 ed. 120.00 (ISBN 0-8357-9896-8, 2012431). Bks Demand UMI.

Feld, Raoul & Cowe, Peter L. Organic Chemistry of Titanium. 213p. 1965. 29.50x (ISBN 0-306-30629-8, Plenum Pr). Plenum Pub.

Feld, Robyn, illus. Color the ABC's of What Should I Be When I Grow up? 1980. pap. 1.35 (ISBN 0-931868-04-1). Beninda.

Feld, Ross. Only Shorter. LC 81-83971. 288p. 1982. 15.00 (ISBN 0-86547-061-8). N Point Pr.

--Philip Guston. LC 79-27425. (Illus.). 152p. 1980. 25.00 (ISBN 0-8076-0975-7); pap. 14.95 (ISBN 0-8076-0962-5). Braziller.

--Plum Poems. LC 79-137210. 1971. pap. 3.00 (ISBN 0-912330-06-6, Dist. by Inland Bk). Jargon Soc.

Feld, Sheila & Radin, Norma. Social Psychology for Social Work. LC 81-17061. 544p. 1982. 21.00x (ISBN 0-231-04190-X). Columbia U Pr.

Feld, Steven. Sound & Sentiment: Birds, Weeping, Poetics, & Song in Kaluli Expression. LC 81-435181. (American Folklore Society Ser.). (Illus.). 224p. (Orig.). 1982. 35.00x (ISBN 0-8122-7829-1); pap. 12.95x (ISBN 0-8122-1124-3). U of Pa Pr.

Feld, Von Nardroff, ed. see Feld, Ellen.

Feld, Warren S. An Organizational Vocabulary & Grammar of Health Planner Influence. LC 84-51577. (Orig.). 1984. pap. text ed. 19.95 (ISBN 0-930791-00-2). Designed Impacts.

Feld, Werner, et al. International Organizations: A Comparative Approach. 352p. 1983. 35.95 (ISBN 0-03-059621-1); pap. 14.95 (ISBN 0-03-059622-X). Praeger.

Feld, Werner J. American Foreign Policy: Aspirations & Reality. LC 83-23274. 336p. 1984. pap. 15.95 (ISBN 0-471-87391-8). Wiley.

--The European Community in World Affairs: Economic Power & Political Influence. LC 83-50811. (Illus.). xiii, 352p. 1985. pap. 30.00x (ISBN 0-86531-750-X). Westview.

--Multinational Enterprises & U. N. Politics: The Quest for Codes of Conduct. (Pergamon Policy Studies). (Illus.). 1980. 33.00 (ISBN 0-08-022488-1). Pergamon.

--West Germany & the European Community: Changing Interests & Competing Policy Objectives. LC 81-8599. 160p. 1981. 29.95 (ISBN 0-03-058019-6). Praeger.

Feld, Werner J. & Coate, Roger A. The Role of International Nongovernmental Organizations in World Politics. (CISE Learning Package Ser.: No. 17). (Illus.). 56p. (Orig.). 1976. pap. text ed. 3.00x (ISBN 0-936876-30-1). Learn Res Intl Stud.

Feld, Werner J. & Wildgen, John K. Congress & National Defense: The Politics of the Unthinkable. LC 84-16007. 144p. 1985. 25.95x (ISBN 0-03-069751-4). Praeger.

--NATO & the Atlantic Defense: Perceptions & Illusions. LC 81-22676. 188p. 1982. 29.95 (ISBN 0-03-059477-4). Praeger.

Feld, Werner J. & Wilgen, John K. Domestic Political Realities of European Unification: A Study of Mass Public & Elites in the European Community Countries. new ed. LC 76-28703. (Westview Replica Editions). 1977. PLB 25.00 (ISBN 0-89158-149-9). Westview.

Feld, Werner J., jt. auth. see Jordan, Robert S.

Feld, Werner J., ed. Energy & Security Concerns in the Atlantic Community. (Monographs in Comparative Public Policy). 107p. 1985. pap. 13.95x (ISBN 0-8133-0205-6). Westview.

--New Directions in Economic & Security Policy: U.S.-West European Relations in a Period of Crisis & Indecision. (Special Studies Ser.). 93p. 1985. pap. 12.85 (ISBN 0-8133-7089-2). Westview.

--Western Europe's Global Reach: Regional Cooperation & Worldwide Aspirations. (Policy Studies). 1980. 35.00 (ISBN 0-08-025130-7). Pergamon.

Feld, Werner J., jt. ed. see Link, Werner.

Feldacker, Bruce. Labor Guide to Labor Law. 2nd ed. 1983. text ed. 27.95 (ISBN 0-8359-3922-7). Reston.

Feldbaum, Eleanor G., jt. auth. see Levitt, Morris J.

Feldbausch, F. Bankwoerterbuch Englisch-Deutsch, Deutsch-Englisch. 400p. (Eng. & Ger., Dictionary of Banking). 38.50 (ISBN 3-478-51240-9, M-7304, Pub. by Vlg. Moderne Industrie). French & Eur.

Feldberg, M. A. Computed Tomography of the Retroperitoneum. (Radiology Ser.). 1983. lib. bdg. 63.00 (ISBN 0-89838-573-3, Pub. by Martinus Nijhoff Netherlands). Kluwer Academic.

Feldberg, Michael. The Philadelphia Riots of Eighteen Forty-Four: A Study of Ethnic Conflict. LC 75-65. (Contributions in American History: No. 43). (Illus.). 209p. 1975. lib. bdg. 29.95 (ISBN 0-8371-7876-2, FGC/). Greenwood.

--The Turbulent Era: Riot & Disorder in Jacksonsian America. 1980. pap. text ed. 5.95x (ISBN 0-19-502678-0). Oxford U Pr.

Feldberg, Michael, jt. auth. see Goldstein, Marc.

Feldberg, Michael, jt. ed. see Elliston, Frederick.

Feldberg, Wilhelm. Fifty Years On: Looking Back on Some Developments in Neurohumoral Physiology. 106p. 1982. 39.00x (ISBN 0-686-92034-1, Pub. by Liverpool Univ England). State Mutual Bk.

Feldblum, E. Y. The American Catholic Press & the Jewish State: 1917-1959. 25.00x (ISBN 0-87068-325-X). Ktav.

Feldbrugge, F. J. The Constitutions of the U.S.S.R. & the Union Republics: Analysis, Texts, Reports, 1979. 381p. 1979. 75.00x (ISBN 90-286-0489-8). Sijthoff & Noordhoff.

--Encyclopedia of Soviet Law. 2nd. Rev. ed. 1985. lib. bdg. 148.00 (ISBN 90-247-3075-9, Pub. by Martinus Nijhoff Netherlands). Kluwer Academic.

Feldbrugge, F. J., ed. Encyclopedia of Soviet Law, 2 vols. LC 73-85236. 900p. 1974. Set. lib. bdg. 100.00 (ISBN 0-379-00481-X). Oceana.

Feldbrugge, F. J. & Simons, William B., eds. Perspectives on Soviet Law of the Nineteen Eighties. 180p. 1981. lib. bdg. 32.50 (ISBN 90-247-2561-5, Pub. by Martinus Nijhoff Netherlands). Kluwer Academic.

Feldbrugge, J. T. & Von Elgg, Y. A., eds. Involuntary Institutionalization: Changing Concepts in the Treatment of Delinquency. (International Congress Ser.: No. 562). 106p. 1981. 23.00 (ISBN 0-444-90233-3, Excerpta Medica). Elsevier.

Feldenkrais, Moshe. Awareness Through Movement: Health Exercises for Personal Growth. LC 74-184419. 192p. 1972. 12.45i (ISBN 0-06-062345-4, HarpR). Har-Row.

--Body & Mature Behavior: A Study of Anxiety, Sex, Gravitation & Learning. 167p. (Orig.). 1970. text ed. 22.50 (ISBN 0-8236-0560-4); pap. text ed. 10.95 (ISBN 0-8236-8009-6, 20555). Intl Univs Pr.

--Elusive Obvious. LC 81-82159. 1981. 20.00x (ISBN 0-916990-09-5). Meta Pubns.

--The Master Moves. LC 84-61647. 1985. 14.95 (ISBN 0-916990-15-X). Meta Pubns.

--The Potent Self: The Dynamics of the Body & the Mind. LC 84-48217. 224p. 1985. 15.34 (ISBN 0-06-250320-0, HarpR). Har-Row.

Felder, David W. The Best Investment: Land In a Loving Community. LC 86-61882. (Illus.). 176p. 1983. pap. 8.50 (ISBN 0-910959-00-5). Wellington Pr.

Felder, Dell, ed. Competency Based Teacher Education: Professionalizing Social Studies Teaching. LC 78-58629. (Bulletin Ser.: No. 56). 1978. pap. 6.95 (ISBN 0-87986-020-0, 498-15272). Nat Coun Soc Studies.

--Competency Based Teacher Education: Professionalizing Social Studies Teaching. LC 78-58629. (National Council for the Social Studies, Bulletin: 56). pap. 32.00 (ISBN 0-317-20141-7, 2023191). Bks Demand UMI.

Felder, Eleanor. Careers in Publishing & Printing. LC 76-5903. (Whole Works Ser). (Illus.). 48p. (gr. 3-7). 1976. PLB 13.31 (ISBN 0-8172-0701-5). Raintree Pubs.

Felder, Emma G. Beginning Phonics for Parents. new ed. LC 77-135316. (Illus.). 1974. pap. 1.75 (ISBN 0-910812-05-5). Johnny Reads.

Felder, Frederick E., jt. auth. see Wishard, William R.

Felder, Henry E. The Changing Patterns of Black Family Income, 1960-1982. LC 84-5654. (Illus.). 67p. (Orig.). 1984. pap. 4.95 (ISBN 0-941410-43-9). Jt Ctr Pol Studies.

Felder, Hilaron. The Ideals of St. Francis of Assisi. 1983. 12.50 (ISBN 0-8199-0845-2). Franciscan Herald.

Felder, Leonard, jt. auth. see Bloomfield, Harold.

Felder, Leonard, jt. auth. see Bloomfield, Harold H.

Felder, Mira B. & Bromberg, Anna B. Light & Lively: A Reader. 191p. 1979. pap. text ed. 9.95 (ISBN 0-15-550900-4, HC). HarBraceJ.

Felder, Paula S. Forgotten Companions: The First Settlers of Spotsylvania County & Fredericksburgh Town. LC 82-81180. (Illus.). 260p. 1982. 20.00 (ISBN 0-9608408-0-X). Hist Pubns.

--Ludwig Borrner & His Sons: The Beginning of the Boatner Family in America. LC 84-81370. (Illus.). 280p. 1985. 25.00 (ISBN 0-9608408-1-8). Hist Pubns.

Felder, Richard M. & Rousseau, Ronald W. Elementary Principles of Chemical Processes. LC 77-12043. 571p. 1978. text ed. 44.00x (ISBN 0-471-74330-5); solutions manual 10.95 (ISBN 0-471-03680-3). Wiley.

Felderer, Ditlieb. Anne Frank's Diary: A Hoax. 1981. lib. bdg. 59.95 (ISBN 0-686-73176-X). Revisionist Pr.

Felderman, Eric. Animal Book. LC 77-5512. 1978. pap. 3.95 (ISBN 0-914974-15-7). Holmgangers.

--The Book of Lies. 1975. 1.00 (ISBN 0-916866-11-4). Cats Pajamas.

--Cheap Laughs. (Illus.). 60p. (Orig.). 1981. pap. 3.00 (ISBN 0-686-30246-X). Praetorius Bks.

--Garden Street. LC 76-907. 60p. (Orig.). 1976. pap. 3.95 (ISBN 0-914974-09-2). Holmgangers.

Feldhake, Susan. For Love Alone. 192p. (Orig.). 1983. pap. 1.95 (ISBN 0-310-46442-0, Serenade-Saga). Zondervan.

--Love's Sweet Promise. 192p. (Orig.). 1983. pap. 1.95 (ISBN 0-310-46462-5, Serenade-Saga). Zondervan.

--Reflection of Love. (Rhapsody Romance Ser.). 92p. 1984. 2.95 (ISBN 0-89081-420-1). Harvest Hse.

Feldhake, Susan C. How to Write & Sell Confessions. 1980. 10.95 (ISBN 0-87116-123-0). Writer.

--In Loves' Own Time. LC 83-15511. (Serenade Saga Ser.: No. 7). 192p. (Orig.). 1984. 1.95 (ISBN 0-310-46512-5, Serenade-Saga). Zondervan.

--Love Beyond Surrender. (Serenade-Saga: No. 10). 192p. (Orig.). 1984. pap. 1.95 (ISBN 0-310-46602-4, 15519P, Serenade-Saga). Zondervan.

Feldhamer, George A., jt. ed. see Chapman, Joseph A.

Feldhaus, Anne. The Religious Systems of the Mahanubhava Sect. 1983. 26.00x (ISBN 0-8364-1005-X). South Asia Bks.

Feldhaus, Anne, ed. The Deeds of God in Rddhipur. LC 83-21949. 211p. 1984. 24.95x (ISBN 0-19-503438-4). Oxford U Pr.

Feldhaus, William R., jt. auth. see Daenzer, Bernard J.

Feldheim, Harold. Five-Card Major Bidding in Contract Bridge. 182p. (Orig.). 1985. pap. 11.95 (ISBN 0-87643-045-0). Barclay Bridge.

--Negative & Responsive Doubles in Bridge. 64p. (Orig.). 1980. pap. 2.95 (ISBN 0-87643-031-0). Barclay Bridge.

--The Weak Two Bid in Bridge. 1971. pap. 4.95 (ISBN 0-87643-005-1). Barclay Bridge.

--Winning Swiss Team Tactics in Bridge. 1976. pap. 7.95 (ISBN 0-87643-027-2). Barclay Bridge.

Feldheym, Len. Pole House Construction. (Orig.). Date not set. pap. 15.75 (ISBN 0-910460-85-X). Craftsman.

Feldhusen, John & Treffinger, Donald J. Creative Thinking & Problem Solving in Gifted Education. (Orig.). 1980. pap. text ed. 8.95 (ISBN 0-8403-2155-4). Kendall-Hunt.

Feldhusen, John, ed. Toward Excellence in Gifted Education. 189p. 1985. pap. text ed. 14.95 (ISBN 0-317-26976-3). Love Pub Co.

Feldhusen, John F. The Three-Stage Model of Course Design. Langdon, Danny G., ed. LC 79-26576. (Instructional Design Library). 96p. 1980. 19.95 (ISBN 0-87778-159-1). Educ Tech Pubns.

Feldhusen, John F. & Richardson, William B. Leadership Education: Developing Skills for Youth. 1984. 9.95 (ISBN 0-89824-085-9). Trillium Pr.

Feldhusen, John F., et al. Creativity Research & Educational Planning: Selected Proceedings of the Second National Conference on Creativity & the Gifted-Talented. 55p. 7.00 (ISBN 0-318-02151-X). NSLTIGT.

Feldkirchner, H L., jt. auth. see Pyrcioch, E J.

Feldman. Nutrition in the Middle & Later Years. (Illus.). 352p. 1982. text ed. 31.00 (ISBN 0-7236-7046-3). PSG Pub Co.

Feldman, jt. auth. see Denhoff.

Feldman, jt. auth. see Scurr.

Feldman, jt. ed. see Newman.

Feldman, Abraham J. The American Jew: A Study of Backgrounds. LC 78-26254. 1979. Repr. of 1937 ed. lib. bdg. 18.75x (ISBN 0-313-20876-X, FEAJ). Greenwood.

Feldman, Alan. Frank O'Hara. (United States Authors Ser.). 1979. lib. bdg. 13.50 (ISBN 0-8057-7277-4, Twayne). G K Hall.

--The Happy Genius. LC 78-15577. 1978. pap. 6.00 (ISBN 0-915342-27-8). SUN.

--Lucy Mastermind. (Illus.). (gr. 3-7). 1985. 10.95 (ISBN 0-525-44155-7, 01063-320). Dutton.

--Lucy Mastermind. (Illus.). 112p. (gr. 3-7). 1985. 10.95 (ISBN 0-525-44155-7, 01063-320). Dutton.

Feldman, Alan S. & Grimes, Charles I. Hearing Conservation in Industry. 352p. 1985. 35.00 (ISBN 0-683-03112-0). Williams & Wilkins.

Feldman, Allan M. Welfare Economics & Social Choice Theory. 1980. lib. bdg. 26.00 (ISBN 0-89838-033-2, Pub. by Martinus Nijhoff Netherlands); pap. text ed. 12.00 (ISBN 0-89838-034-0, Martimus Nijhoff Pubs). Kluwer Academic.

Feldman, Allen & O'Doherty, Eamonn. The Northern Fiddler. (Illus.). 260p. (Orig.). 1979. pap. 13.95 (ISBN 0-85640-155-2, Pub. by Blackstaff Pr Ireland). Irish Bks Media.

Feldman, Anthony. Space. 336p. 1980. 24.95 (ISBN 0-87196-416-3). Facts on File.

Feldman, Anthony & Ford, Peter. Scientists & Inventors. (Horizons of Knowledge Ser.). (Illus.). 1979. 24.95 (ISBN 0-87196-410-4). Facts on File.

Feldman, Anthony & Gunston, Bill. Technology at Work. (Horizons of Knowledge Ser.). (Illus.). 336p. 1980. 24.95 (ISBN 0-87196-413-9). Facts on File.

Feldman, Arnold S., jt. auth. see Moore, Wilbert Ellis.

Feldman, Arnold S., jt. auth. see Tumin, Melvin M.

Feldman, Arnold S., jt. ed. see Moore, Wilbert E.

Feldman, Asher. The Parables & Similes of the Rabbis, Agricultural & Pastoral. LC 75-23127. 1975. Repr. of 1927 ed. lib. bdg. 27.50 (ISBN 0-8414-4229-0). Folcroft.

Feldman, Ben. Best of Ben, 5 vols. 1981. Set. 7.95 (ISBN 0-87863-205-0). Farnswth Pub.

--Creative Selling. LC 79-88528. (Illus.). 1979. 14.95 (ISBN 0-87863-054-6). Farnswth Pub.

Feldman, Bernard. Trigonometry. 1974. write for info. (ISBN 0-534-00354-0). Wadsworth Pub.

Feldman, Beverly N. Homebased Businesses. 3rd ed. 1983. pap. 9.95 (ISBN 0-931208-03-3). Till Pr.

Feldman, Beverly N., ed. Jobs: Careers Serving Children & Youth. 2nd ed. 321p. (Orig.). 1979. tchr's ed. 10.95x (ISBN 0-931208-01-7). Till Pr.

Feldman, Burton & Richardson, Robert D. The Rise of Modern Mythology, 1680-1860. LC 71-135005. (Midland Bks.: No. 188). 592p. 1972. pap. 7.95x (ISBN 0-253-20188-8). Ind U Pr.

Feldman, Burton, ed. see Anquetil-Duperron, A. H.

Feldman, Burton, ed. see Bayle, Pierre.

Feldman, Burton, ed. see Beausobre, Isaac de.

Feldman, Burton, ed. see Bell, John.

Feldman, Burton, ed. see Bryant, Jacob.

Feldman, Burton, ed. see Clavigero, Francesco S.

Feldman, Burton, ed. see Davies, Edward.

Feldman, Burton, ed. see De Camoens, Luis.

Feldman, Burton, ed. see D'Hancarville, Pierre.

Feldman, Burton, ed. see Dupuis, Charles.

Feldman, Burton, ed. see Faber, George S.

Feldman, Burton, ed. see Godwin, William.

Feldman, Burton, ed. see Holbach, Paul H.

Feldman, Burton, ed. see Jones, William.

Feldman, Burton, ed. see Lempriere, John.

Feldman, Burton, ed. see Mallet, Paul H.

Feldman, Burton, ed. see Maurice, Thomas.

Feldman, Burton, ed. see Moor, Edward.

Feldman, Burton, ed. see Owen, William.

Feldman, Burton, ed. see Potter, John.

Feldman, Burton, ed. see Rowlands, Henry.

Feldman, Burton, ed. see Sale, George.

Feldman, Burton, ed. see Stukeley, William.

Feldman, Burton, ed. see Taylor, Thomas.

Feldman, Burton, ed. see Volney, C. F.

Feldman, Carol F., et al. The Development of Adaptive Intelligence: A Cross-Cultural Study. LC 73-22557. (Jossey-Bass Behavioral Science Ser.). pap. 30.10 (ISBN 0-8357-9315-X, 2013920). Bks Demand UMI.

Feldman, Charles F., ed. Executive Compensation Planning. 181p. 1982. text ed. 30.00 (ISBN 0-686-97765-3, J3-1437). PLI.

Feldman, Clarice R. & Silber, Bettina, eds. Alaskan Energy Potential & Constraints to Development. LC 79-91022. (Americans For Energy Independence Energy Policy Ser.). (Orig.). 1979. pap. 5.00 (ISBN 0-934458-01-4). Americans Energy Ind.

Feldman, Clarice R., jt. ed. see Silber, Bettina.

Feldman, Daniel & Arnold, Hugh J. Managing Individual & Group Behavior in Organizations. (Illus.). 560p. 1983. text ed. 30.95 (ISBN 0-07-020386-5). McGraw.

Feldman, David H. Beyond Universals in Cognitive Development. LC 79-24338. (Publications for the Advancement of Theory & History in Psychology Ser.). (Illus.). 1980. 29.50x (ISBN 0-89391-029-5). Ablex Pub.

Feldman, David M. Birth Control in Jewish Law: Marital Relations, Contraception, & Abortion As Set Forth in the Classic Texts of Jewish Law. LC 79-16712. 1980. Repr. of 1968 ed. lib. bdg. 27.50x (ISBN 0-313-21297-X, FEBC). Greenwood.

--Marital Relations, Birth Control, & Abortion in Jewish Law. LC 68-15338. 336p. 1974. pap. 8.95 (ISBN 0-8052-0438-5). Schocken.

Feldman, Duane. Symphony: Advanced Topics. LC 83-60685. (Symphony Ser.). 350p. 1985. pap. 19.95 (ISBN 0-88022-145-3, 172). Que Corp.

--Symphony Tips, Tricks & Traps. LC 84-61398. 360p. 1985. 19.95 (ISBN 0-88022-098-8, 154). Que Corp.

Feldman, Edmund B. The Artist. 200p. 1982. text ed. 15.95 (ISBN 0-13-049031-8); pap. text ed. 14.95 (ISBN 0-13-049023-7). P-H.

--Thinking about Art. (Illus.). 480p. 1985. 26.95 (ISBN 0-13-917493-1). P-H.

--Varieties of Visual Experience. 2nd ed. 536p. 1981. text ed. 26.95 (ISBN 0-13-940585-2). P-H.

Feldman, Edwin B. Housekeeping Handbook for Institutions, Business & Industry. rev. ed. LC 75-83312. 502p. 1979. 29.95 (ISBN 0-8119-0072-X). Fell.

--How to Use Your Time to Get Things Done. LC 68-18138. 273p. 1968. 12.95 (ISBN 0-8119-0110-6). Fell.

Feldman, Edwin B. & Wright, George B. The Supervisor's Handbook. LC 82-71741. 420p. 1982. 29.95 (ISBN 0-8119-0449-0). Fell.

Feldman, Edwin B. & Wright, Goerge B, Sr. The Supervisor's Handbook. 416p. 1983. pap. 7.95 (ISBN 0-671-49349-3, Wallaby). S&S.

Feldman, Edwin B., ed. Programmed Cleaning Guide. rev. ed. (Illus.). 1984. pap. text ed. 9.00 (ISBN 0-9601394-2-7). Soap & Detergent.

--Programmed Cleaning Guide. 188p. 1984. 9.00 (ISBN 0-318-16525-2). Soap & Detergent.

Feldman, Egal. The Dreyfus Affair & the American Conscience, 1895-1906. LC 80-62330. 184p. 1981. 17.95 (ISBN 0-8143-1677-8). Wayne St U Pr.

Feldman, Ellen. AKA Katherine Walden. 324p. 1982. 14.00 (ISBN 0-688-01126-8). Morrow.

--A.K.A. Katherine Wilson. 1983. pap. 3.50 (ISBN 0-440-10219-7). Dell.

Feldman, Elliot & Nevitte, Neil, eds. The Future of North America: Canada, the United States, & Quebec Nationalism. LC 78-71645. (Studies in International Affairs: No. 42). 1979. text ed. 13.95x (ISBN 0-87674-046-8); pap. text ed. 6.95x (ISBN 0-87674-045-X). U Pr of Amer.

Feldman, Elliot J. Concorde & Dissent: Explaining High Technology Project Failures in Britain & France. (Illus.). 192p. 1985. 34.50 (ISBN 0-521-30519-5). Cambridge U Pr.

--A Practical Guide to the Conduct of Field Research in the Social Sciences. 120p. 1981. pap. text ed. 8.00x (ISBN 0-89158-981-3). Westview.

Feldman, Elliot J. & Milch, Jerome. The Politics of Canadian Airport Development: Lessons for Federalism. LC 82-18343. (Duke Press Policy Studies, Commonwealth & Comparative Studies: No. 47). 288p. 1983. 28.50 (ISBN 0-8223-0479-1). Duke.

--Technocracy vs. Democracy: The Comparative Politics of International Airports. (Illus.). 299p. 1981. 24.95 (ISBN 0-86569-063-4). Auburn Hse.

Feldman, Elliot J. & Nevitte, Neil. The Future of North America: Canada, the United States, & Quebec Nationalism. 378p. 1979. pap. text ed. 9.50x (ISBN 0-87674-045-X, Pub. by Inst Res Pub Canada). Brookfield Pub Co.

Feldman, Elliot J. & Nevitte, Neil, eds. The Future of North America: Canada, the United States, & Quebec Nationalism. (Harvard Studies in International Affairs: No. 42). 378p. 1984. lib. bdg. 26.75 (ISBN 0-8191-4057-0); pap. text ed. 12.75 (ISBN 0-8191-4058-9). U Pr of Amer.

Feldman, Evelyn & Driver, Clive E., eds. Cook's Choice: A Selection of Recipes from Rare & Important Cookbooks from the Ninth to the Nineteenth Century. 1982. pap. 5.00 (ISBN 0-939084-13-9, Dist. by U Pr of VA). Rosenbach Mus.

Feldman, Frances L. The Family in Today's Money World. 2nd ed. LC 75-279660. 409p. 1976. 13.95 (ISBN 0-87304-130-5); pap. 10.00 (ISBN 0-87304-131-3). Family Serv.

Feldman, Frances L. & Scherz, Frances H. Family Social Welfare: Helping Troubled Families. LC 67-18276. 1967. 29.95x (ISBN 0-202-36001-6). Aldine Pub.

Feldman, Frayda & Schellmann, Jorg, eds. Andy Warhol Prints. LC 84-13675. (Illus.). 128p. 1985. 35.00 (ISBN 0-89659-580-3). Abbeville Pr.

Feldman, Fred. Introductory Ethics. 1978. text ed. 18.95 (ISBN 0-13-501783-1). P-H.

--Israel. (Orig.). 1984. pap. 4.50 (ISBN 0-440-03842-1). Dell.

Feldman, Fredric J., jt. auth. see Christian, Gary D.

Feldman, G. Iron & Steel in the German Inflation, 1916-1923. 1977. 55.00 (ISBN 0-691-04215-2). Princeton U Pr.

Feldman, Gene & Gartenberg, Max, eds. Beat Generation, & the Angry Young Men. facsimile ed. LC 71-156639. (Essay Index Reprint Ser). Repr. of 1958 ed. 26.50 (ISBN 0-8369-2354-5). Ayer Co Pubs.

Feldman, Gene, jt. ed. see Gartenberg, Max.

Feldman, George B. & Felshman, Anne. The Complete Handbook of Pregnancy. (Illus.). 1985. 17.95 (ISBN 0-399-12957-X). Putnam Pub Group.

Feldman, Gerald D., jt. ed. see Barnes, Thomas G.

Feldman, H., jt. auth. see Feldman, J.

Feldman, H F. & Bair, W G. Production of Pipeline Gas by Hydrogasification of Oil Shale. (Research Bulletin No. 36). iv, 109p. 1966. 5.00 (ISBN 0-317-34312-2). Inst Gas Tech.

Feldman, Harold & Feldman, Margaret. Current Controversies in Marriage & Family. 1985. 25.00 (ISBN 0-8039-2440-2); pap. 12.50 (ISBN 0-8039-2441-0). Sage.

Feldman, Harry, jt. auth. see Feldman, Joseph.

Feldman, Harry A., jt. ed. see Evans, Alfred S.

Feldman, Harvey W., et al, eds. Angel Dust: An Ethnographic Study of Phencyclidine Users. LC 79-8319. 240p. 1979. 18.00x (ISBN 0-669-03379-0). Lexington Bks.

Feldman, Herman. Problems in Labor Relations. LC 78-89732. (American Labor, from Conspiracy to Collective Bargaining Ser., no. 1). 353p. 1969. Repr. of 1937 ed. 20.00 (ISBN 0-405-02120-8). Ayer Co Pubs.

Feldman, Howard & Lopez, Martita A. Developmental Psychology for the Health Care Professions: Young Adult Through Late Aging, Pt. 2. (Behavioral Sciences for Health Care Professionals Ser.). 128p. (Orig.). 1982. 18.50x (ISBN 0-86531-012-2); pap. 9.50x (ISBN 0-86531-013-0). Westview.

Feldman, Howard, jt. auth. see Strang, William A.

Fel'dman, I. A., jt. auth. see Gohberg, I. C.

Feldman, I. A., jt. auth. see Gohberg, I. Z.

Feldman, Irving. Leaping Clear. new ed. LC 76-21052. 80p. 1976. 9.95 (ISBN 0-670-42182-0). Viking.

--New & Selected Poems. 1979. pap. 7.95 (ISBN 0-14-042269-2). Penguin.

--Teach Me, Dear Sister. 80p. 1983. 14.75 (ISBN 0-670-31135-9). Viking.

--Teach Me, Dear Sister: Poems. 80p. 1983. pap. 7.95 (ISBN 0-14-042302-8). Penguin.

Feldman, J. & Feldman, H. An Index to the Films of Jean Vigo. 1976. lib. bdg. 59.95 (ISBN 0-8490-2050-6). Gordon Pr.

Feldman, Jacob J. Dissemination of Health Information: A Case Study in Adult Learning. LC 66-14570. (NORC Monographs in Social Research: No. 11). 1966. 9.95x (ISBN 0-202-27001-7). NORC.

Feldman, Jerome A. The Eloquent Dead: Ancestral Sculpture of Indonesia & Southeast Asia. LC 85-61508. (Illus.). 128p. (Orig.). 1985. text ed. 32.00 (ISBN 0-930741-05-6); pap. text ed. 19.00 (ISBN 0-930741-04-8). UCLA Mus Hist.

Feldman, Jim. Prince. 1985. pap. 2.95 (ISBN 0-345-32325-4). Ballantine.

Feldman, Joan D., jt. ed. see Garrod, David R.

Feldman, Joseph & Feldman, Harry. Dynamics of the Film. LC 73-169342. (Arno Press Cinema Program). (Illus.). 1972. Repr. of 1952 ed. 18.00 (ISBN 0-405-03917-4). Ayer Co Pubs.

Feldman, Kenneth A. & Newcomb, Theodore M. The Impact of College on Students, 2 Vols. LC 79-75940. (Higher Education Ser.). 1969. Set. 37.00x (ISBN 0-87589-036-9). Jossey-Bass.

Feldman, Kenneth A., ed. College & Student: Selected Readings in the Social Psychology of Higher Education. 502p. 1972. pap. text ed. 14.00 (ISBN 0-08-016788-8). Pergamon.

Feldman, L. Mathematical Learning. 224p. 1969. 32.50 (ISBN 0-677-13250-6). Gordon.

Feldman, L. H., ed. see Price, James E. & Krakker, James J.

Feldman, Laurence P. Consumer Protection: Problems & Prospects. 2nd ed. (Illus.). 1980. pap. 17.95 (ISBN 0-8299-0301-1). West Pub.

Feldman, Lawrence, ed. see Bruhns, Karen O.

Feldman, Lawrence, ed. see Collins, Marcia R. & Anderson, Linda.

Feldman, Lawrence H. Riverine Maya: The Torquegua & Other Chols of the Lower Motagua Valley. LC 75-621315. (Museum Brief: No. 15). (Illus.). 25p. 1975. pap. 1.20x (ISBN 0-913134-14-7). Mus Anthro Mo.

Feldman, Lawrence H., ed. Love in the Armpit: Tzeltal Tales of Love, Murder & Cannibalism. Stross, Brian, tr. LC 77-151846. (Museum Briefs: No. 23). (Illus.). 1977. pap. text ed. 1.80x (ISBN 0-913134-23-6). Mus Anthro Mo.

Feldman, Lawrence H. & Walters, Garry R., eds. Excavations in Southeastern Guatemala: 1976-1978. (Miscellaneous Publications in Anthropology Ser.: No. 9, Reports 1 & 2). (Illus.). 1980. pap. 5.60x (ISBN 0-913134-80-5). Mus Anthro Mo.

Feldman, Lawrence H., ed. & pref. by see Gavan, James A.

Feldman, Lawrence H., et al. Jade Workers in the Motagua Valley: The Late Classic Terzuola Site. LC 75-325233. (Museum Brief: No. 17). (Illus.). 1975. pap. 0.85x (ISBN 0-913134-16-3). Mus Anthro Mo.

Feldman, Leonard, et al. Materials Analysis by Ion Channeling: Submicron Crystallography. 1982. 44.00 (ISBN 0-12-252680-5). Acad Pr.

Feldman, Lily G. The Special Relationship Between W. Germany & Israel. 352p. 1984. text ed. 35.00x (ISBN 0-04-327068-9). Allen Unwin.

Feldman, Lionel D. & Graham, Katherine A. Bargaining for Cities, Municipalities & Intergovernmental Relations: An Assessment. 143p. 1979. pap. text ed. 10.95x (ISBN 0-920380-21-2, Pub. by Inst Res Pub Canada). Brookfield Pub Co.

Feldman, Louis H. Josephus: A Supplementary Bibliography. LC 84-48399. (Library of the Humanities). 712p. 1986. lib. bdg. 60.00 (ISBN 0-8240-8792-5). Garland Pub.

--Josephus & Modern Scholarship: 1937-1980. LC 84-1879. xvi, 1055p. 1984. 168.00x (ISBN 3-11-008138-5). De Gruyter.

Feldman, M., jt. ed. see Markl, H.

Feldman, M. Philip. Criminal Behaviour: A Psychological Analysis. LC 76-13229. 1977. 57.95x (ISBN 0-471-99401-4, Pub. by Wiley-Interscience). Wiley.

Feldman, M. Philip & Broadhurst, Anne, eds. Theoretical & Experimental Bases of the Behaviour Therapies. LC 75-20000. pap. 118.80 (ISBN 0-317-07802-X, 2020430). Bks Demand UMI.

Feldman, M. W., jt. auth. see Cavalli-Sforza, L. L.

Feldman, Marc & Christiansen, Fred B. Population Genetics. (Illus.). 150p. 1985. pap. text ed. 14.95 (ISBN 0-86542-307-5). Blackwell Sci.

Feldman, Marc & Mitchison, N. A., eds. Immune Regulation. LC 85-5786. (Experimental Biology & Medicine Ser.). (Illus.). 408p. 1985. 65.00 (ISBN 0-89603-083-0). Humana.

Feldman, Marc, jt. ed. see Pick, Edgar.

Feldman, Margaret, jt. auth. see Feldman, Harold.

Feldman, Martha S., jt. auth. see Bennett, W. Lance.

Feldman, Martin, et al, eds. The Social Studies: Structure, Models & Strategies. LC 83-49166. (History & Historigraphy Ser.). 465p. 1985. lib. bdg. 45.00 (ISBN 0-8240-6362-7). Garland Pub.

Feldman, Marvin J., et al. Fears Related to Death & Suicide. LC 73-12803. (Thanatology Ser.). 221p. 1974. text ed. 27.00x (ISBN 0-8422-7149-X). Irvington.

Feldman, Maurice P. Criminal Behaviour: A Psychological Analysis. LC 76-13229. pap. 86.50 (ISBN 0-317-26340-4, 2025198). Bks Demand UMI.

Feldman, Michael, jt. auth. see Godfrey, Charles.

Feldman, Michael & Globerson, Amiela, eds. Immune Reactivity of Lymphocytes: Development, Expression, & Control. LC 75-42123. (Advances in Experimental Medicine & Biology Ser.: Vol. 66). 751p. 1976. 79.50x (ISBN 0-306-39066-3, Plenum Pr). Plenum Pub.

Feldman, Mildred L. The United States in the International Telecommunication Union & in Pre-ITU Conferences. LC 76-2971. 1976. 10.00 (ISBN 0-9606700-0-9). Feldman.

Feldman, Morris. Salesmanship & Money...the Perfect Pair. (Orig.). pap. write for info. Feldco Ent.

Feldman, Morton, jt. auth. see Hess, Thomas B.

Feldman, N. I., et al. Twelve Papers on Logic & Algebra. LC 51-5559. (Translations Ser.: No. 2, Vol. 59). 1966. 36.00 (ISBN 0-8218-1759-0, TRANS 2-59). Am Math.

Feldman, Nans A. How to Prepare a Personnel Policy Manuel. rev. ed. Cobb, Norman B., ed. 252p. 1982. 3-ring looseleaf binder 47.75 (ISBN 0-910053-00-6). Angus Downs.

Feldman, Nathaniel E. & Kelly, Charles M., eds. Communication Satellites for the Seventies: Systems. LC 74-165161. (Illus.). 657p. 1971. 35.00 (ISBN 0-262-06045-0, PAAS26); members 19.00 (ISBN 0-317-32133-1). AIAA.

--Communication Satellites for the Seventies: Technology. LC 72-163512. (Illus.). 430p. 1971. 35.00 (ISBN 0-262-06044-2, PAAS25); members 18.00 (ISBN 0-317-32134-X). AIAA.

Feldman, Paula R. & Pugh, Diana, eds. The Shelley Journals, 2 vols. (Illus.). 1984. Set. 152.00x (ISBN 0-19-812571-2). Oxford U Pr.

Feldman, Phil, jt. auth. see Rugg, Tom.

Feldman, Philip. Developments in the Study of Criminal Behaviour: Violence, Vol. 2. LC 81-21946. 254p. 1982. 51.95x (ISBN 0-471-10373-X, Pub. by Wiley-Interscience). Wiley.

Feldman, Philip & MacCulloch, Malcolm. Human Sexual Behavior. LC 79-41220. 226p. 1980. 45.95x (ISBN 0-471-27676-6, Pub. by Wiley-Interscience). Wiley.

Feldman, Philip, ed. Developments in the Study of Criminal Behavior: The Prevention & Control of Offending, Vol. I. LC 81-21946. 238p. 1982. 48.95x (ISBN 0-471-10176-1, Pub. by Wiley-Interscience). Wiley.

Feldman, Philip & Orford, Jim, eds. Psychological Problems: The Social Context. 405p. 1980. 63.95x (ISBN 0-471-27741-X, Pub. by Wiley-Interscience). Wiley.

Feldman, Philip S. & Covell, Jamie L. Fine Needle Aspiration Cytology & Its Clinical Application: Breast & Lung. LC 84-11125. 230p. 1985. text ed. 155.00 slide set incl. (ISBN 0-89189-192-7, 15-3-004-00); text ed. 80.00 (ISBN 0-89189-184-6, 16-3-004-00). Am Soc Clinical.

Feldman, R. S. Social Psychology. 608p. 1985. 29.95 (ISBN 0-07-020392-X). McGraw.

Feldman, Richard M., jt. auth. see Curry, Guy L.

Feldman, Richard S., jt. auth. see Salzinger, Kurt.

Feldman, Robert. The Rockhound's Guide to Montana. LC 84-82466. (Illus.). 156p. (Orig.). 1985. pap. 7.95 (ISBN 0-934318-46-8). Falcon Pr MT.

Feldman, Robert, jt. auth. see Levy, Leon.

Feldman, Robert, jt. auth. see Royer, James.

Feldman, Robert, jt. auth. see Young, Ronald.

Feldman, Robert A., tr. see Nakamura, Takafusa.

Feldman, Robert G., jt. ed. see Browne, Thomas R.

Feldman, Robert S. & Quenzer, Linda F. Fundamentals of Neuropsychopharmacology. LC 83-14937. (Illus.). 650p. 1983. 35.00x (ISBN 0-87893-178-3). Sinauer Assoc.

Feldman, Robert S., ed. Development of Nonverbal Behavior in Children. (Illus.). 315p. 1983. 29.50 (ISBN 0-387-90716-5). Springer-Verlag.

Feldman, Robret G., ed. Neurology: The Physician's Guide. (Illus.). 288p. 1984. pap. text ed. 29.00 (ISBN 0-86577-111-1). Thieme-Stratton.

Feldman, Ron, ed. The Jew As Pariah: Jewish Identity & Politics in the Modern Age. 1978. pap. 6.95 (ISBN 0-394-17042-3, E711, Ever). Grove.

Feldman, Ronald A. & Caplinger, Timothy E. The St. Louis Conundrum: The Effective Treatment of Antisocial Youth. (Illus.). 320p. 1983. text ed. 30.95 (ISBN 0-13-786202-4). P-H.

Feldman, Ronald A. & Wodarski, John S. Contemporary Approaches to Group Treatment: Traditional, Behavior-Modification, & Group-Centered. LC 74-27913. (Social & Behavioral Science Ser.). (Illus.). 1975. 23.95x (ISBN 0-87589-249-3). Jossey-Bass.

Feldman, Ruth. The Ambition of Ghosts. LC 78-50052. 1979. 10.00 (ISBN 0-940580-10-1); pap. 5.00 (ISBN 0-940580-11-X). Green River.

Feldman, Ruth, ed. see Zanzotto, Andrea.

Feldman, Ruth, tr. see Bodini, Vittorio.

Feldman, Ruth, tr. see Cattafi, Bartolo.

Feldman, Ruth, tr. see Scotellaro, Rocco.

Feldman, Ruth D. Whatever Happened to the Quiz Kids? Perils & Profits of Growing up Gifted. (Illus.). 375p. 1982. 12.95 (ISBN 0-914091-17-4). Chicago Review.

Feldman, S., jt. ed. see Spierdijk, J.

Feldman, S. Shirley, jt. ed. see Sears, Robert R.

Feldman, Samuel. Home Health Record Book. (Illus.). 96p. (Orig.). 1984. pap. 6.95 (ISBN 0-943392-36-5). Tribeca Comm.

Feldman, Sandor S. Mannerisms of Speech & Gestures in Everyday Life. LC 59-6713. 167p. (Orig.). 1969. text ed. 30.00 (ISBN 0-8236-3100-1); pap. text ed. 10.95 (ISBN 0-8236-8144-0, 023100). Intl Univs Pr.

Feldman, Sari & Feldman, Sharon A. Drugs: A Multimedia Sourcebook for Young Adults. (Selection Guide Ser.: No. 4). 200p. 1980. 22.95 (ISBN 0-87436-281-4). Neal-Schuman.

Feldman, Saul. The Administration of Mental Health Services. 2nd ed. (Illus.). 544p. 1981. 49.75x (ISBN 0-398-03942-9). C C Thomas.

Feldman, Saul D., ed. Deciphering Deviance. 1978. pap. text ed. 13.95 (ISBN 0-316-27757-6). Little.

Feldman, Saul D. & Thielbar, Gerald W., eds. Life Styles: Diversity in American Society. 2nd ed. 482p. 1975. pap. text ed. 13.95 (ISBN 0-316-27756-8). Little.

Feldman, Seth R. Dziga Vertov: A Guide to References & Resources. 1979. lib. bdg. 33.50 (ISBN 0-8161-8085-7, Hall Reference). G K Hall.

Feldman, Seymour, intro. by see Spinoza, Baruch.

Feldman, Seymour, tr. see Gershom, Levi B.

Feldman, Shai. Israeli Nuclear Deterrence: A Strategy for the 1980's. LC 82-9679. 314p. 1983. 27.50x (ISBN 0-231-05546-3); pap. 12.00x (ISBN 0-231-05547-1). Columbia U Pr.

Feldman, Shai & Rechnitz-Kijner, Heda, eds. Deception, Consensus & War: Israel in Lebanon. 75p. 1985. pap. text ed. 8.00x (ISBN 0-8133-0133-5). Westview.

Feldman, Sharon A., jt. auth. see Feldman, Sari.

Feldman, Shel, ed. Cognitive Consistency: Motivational Antecedents & Behavioral Consequents. 1966. 49.00 (ISBN 0-12-252650-3). Acad Pr.

Feldman, Shirley C. & Merrill, Kathleen K. Learning Ways to Read Words, 4 bks. Incl. Bk. 1. Ways to Read Words (ISBN 0-8077-2509-9); Bk. 2. More Ways to Read Words (ISBN 0-8077-2516-1); Bk. 3. Learning About Words (ISBN 0-8077-2517-X); Bk. 4. Learning More About Words (ISBN 0-8077-2518-8). 1978. pap. 14.00 set (ISBN 0-8077-2505-6); 3.50 ea. Tchrs Coll.

Feldman, Silvia. Choices in Childbirth. LC 77-95181. (Illus.). 288p. 1977. pap. 8.95 (ISBN 0-448-14525-1, G&D). Putnam Pub Group.

--Making up Your Mind about Motherhood. 288p. (Orig.). 1985. pap. 3.95 (ISBN 0-553-23862-0). Bantam.

Feldman, Stanley, jt. auth. see Berry, William.

Feldman, Stanley, jt. auth. see Sullivan, John L.

Feldman, Stanley A. Muscle Relaxants. 2nd. ed. LC 79-88002. (Major Problems in Anesthesia Ser.: Vol. I). (Illus.). 1979. text ed. 26.00 (ISBN 0-7216-3592-X). Saunders.

Feldman, Stanley A. & Crawley, Brian E., eds. Trachaeostomy & Artificial Ventilation in the Treatment of Respiratory Failure. 3rd ed. 212p. 1977. pap. 17.50 (ISBN 0-683-03118-X). Krieger.

Feldman, Stephen, jt. auth. see Fabozzi, Frank J.

Feldman, Stephen J. Vocational Training for the Mentally Retarded. (Special Education Ser.). (Illus., Orig.). 1978. pap. text ed. 16.00 (ISBN 0-89568-084-X). Spec Learn Corp.

Feldman, Stephen L. & Wirtshafter, Robert M., eds. On the Economics of Solar Energy: The Public Utility Interface. LC 79-5442. 272p. 1980. 31.50x (ISBN 0-669-03449-5). Lexington Bks.

Feldman, Steven A., jt. auth. see Denhoff, Eric.

Feldman, Sylvia D. Morality-Patterned Comedy of the Renaissance. (De Proprietatibus Litterarum, Ser. Practica: No. 12). (Orig.). 1970. pap. text ed. 13.20x (ISBN 90-2791-547-4). Mouton.

Feldman, Sylvia D., ed. A Yorkshire Tragedy. LC 82-45728. (Malone Society Reprint Ser.: No. 129). 1969. 40.00 (ISBN 0-404-63129-0). AMS Pr.

Feldman, Valentin. L' Esthetique Francaise Contemporaine. Repr. of 1936 ed. 20.00 (ISBN 0-8482-3980-6). Norwood Edns.

Feldman, W. M. Rabbinical Mathematics & Astronomy. rev. ed. LC 78-60816. 1978. 9.75 (ISBN 0-87203-026-1). Hermon.

Feldman, William T. Philosophy of John Dewey: A Critical Analysis. LC 68-19271. 1968. Repr. of 1934 ed. lib. bdg. 15.00x (ISBN 0-8371-0414-9, FEPD). Greenwood.

Feldmann, Doris. Gattungsprobleme des Domestic Drama im Literarhistorischen Kontext des Achtzehnten Jahrhunderts. (Bochum Studies in English: No. 16). 246p. (German.). 1983. pap. 19.00x (ISBN 90-6032-249-5, Pub. by B R Gruener Netherlands). Benjamins North Am.

Feldmann, H. Kompendium der Medizinischen Psychologie. (Illus.). viii, 264p. 1983. pap. 8.75 (ISBN 3-8055-3673-9). S Karger.

--Psychiatrie und Psychotherapie. 9th ed. (Illus.). viii, 420p. 1984. pap. 12.50 (ISBN 3-8055-3754-9). S Karger.

Feldmann, Rodney M. & Heimlich, Richard A. Geology Field Guide: The Black Hills. 208p. (Orig.). 1980. pap. 10.95 (ISBN 0-8403-2193-7). Kendall-Hunt.

Feldmann, Rodney M., et al. Field Guide: Southern Great Lakes. LC 77-75770. (Geology Field Guide Ser). (Illus.). 1977. pap. text ed. 9.95 (ISBN 0-8403-1730-1). Kendall-Hunt.

Feldmann-Mazoyer, Genevieve. Recherches sur les Ceramiaceae de la Mediterranee. 1977. pap. text ed. 61.60x (ISBN 3-87429-120-0). Lubrecht & Cramer.

Feldmeth, Joanne, jt. auth. see Larson, Jim.

Feldon, Leah. Dressing Rich: A Guide to Classic Chic for Women with More Taste than Money. LC 83-23739. (Illus.). 160p. 1984. pap. 7.95 (ISBN 0-399-50980-1, Perigee). Putnam Pub Group.

--Traveling Light: Every Woman's Guide to Getting There in Style. 1985. 13.95 (ISBN 0-399-13042-X). Putnam Pub Group.

--Traveling Light: Every Woman's Guide to Getting There in Style. (Illus.). 160p. 1986. 13.95 (ISBN 0-399-13042-X). Putnam Pub Group.

Feldstein, Donald, jt. auth. see Dolgoff, Ralph.

Feldstein, Leonard C. Choros: The Orchestrating Self. xviii, 502p. 1984. 50.00 (ISBN 0-8232-1075-8). Fordham.

--The Dance of Being: Man's Labyrinthe Rhythms, the Natural Ground of the Human. LC 77-75799. xvi, 302p. 1979. 30.00 (ISBN 0-8232-1032-4). Fordham.

--Homo Quaerens: The Seeker & the Sought Method Become Ontology. LC 76-18464. xviii, 154p. 1978. 25.00 (ISBN 0-8232-1019-7). Fordham.

Feldstein, M., jt. auth. see Auerbach, A. J.

Feldstein, M., jt. ed. see Auerbach, A. J.

Feldstein, M. S., ed. see International Economic Association, Conference, Turin, Italy.

Feldstein, M. S., et al. Resource Allocation Model for Public Health Planning: A Case Study of Tuberculosis Control. (WHO Bulletin Supplement: Vol. 48). (Summary in French). 1973. pap. 6.40 (ISBN 92-4-068481-6). World Health.

Feldstein, Mark. Unseen New York. (Illus.). 11.25 (ISBN 0-8446-5183-4). Peter Smith.

Feldstein, Mark & Fischer, Gael. Who Me Cook? (Illus.). 190p. (Orig.). 1983. 5.95 (ISBN 0-912659-00-9). Damgood Bks.

Feldstein, Mark D., ed. see Ortiz, Joe.

Feldstein, Martin. The American Economy in Transition. LC 80-17450. (National Bureau of Economic Research Ser.). 1980. pap. 13.00x (ISBN 0-226-24082-7, PHOEN). U of Chicago Pr.

--Behavioral Simulation Methods in Tax Policy Analysis. LC 82-21766. (National Bureau of Economic Research-Project Report). 1983. lib. bdg. 47.00x (ISBN 0-226-24084-3). U of Chicago Pr.

--Capital Taxation. (Illus.). 96p. 1983. text ed. 40.00x (ISBN 0-674-09482-4). Harvard U Pr.

--Inflation: Tax Rules & Capital Formation. LC 82-10854. (National Bureau of Economic Research-Monograph). 304p. 1983. lib. bdg. 31.00x (ISBN 0-226-24085-1). U of Chicago Pr.

Feldstein, Martin S. Hospital Costs & Health Insurance. LC 80-18226. (Illus.). 344p. 1981. text ed. 25.00x (ISBN 0-674-40675-3). Harvard U Pr.

--The Rising Cost of Hospital Care. LC 72-171922. (Illus.). viii, 88p. 1971. pap. 7.50 (ISBN 0-87815-004-8). Info Resources.

Feldstein, Paul J. Health Care Economics. 2nd ed. LC 83-6842. (Health Services Ser.: Pt. 1-456). 573p. 1983. 28.50 (ISBN 0-471-87279-2, 83-6842, Pub. by Wiley Med). Wiley.

Feldstein, R. F., compiled by see Brill Koln, E. J.

Feldstein, Ronald F., tr. see Illich-Svitych, Vladislav M.

Feldstein, S., jt. ed. see Siegman, Aron W.

Feldstein, Sandy, ed. see Zorn, Jay & Hanshumaker, James.

Feldstein, Saul, jt. auth. see Ferguson, Tom.

Feldstein, Stanley, jt. auth. see Jaffe, Joseph.

Feldstein, Stanley, jt. ed. see Siegman, Aron W.

Feldstein, Sylvan G. The Dow Jones-Irwin Guide to Municipal Bonds. 1985. 25.00 (ISBN 0-87094-542-4). Dow Jones-Irwin.

Feldstein, Sylvan G. & Fabozzi, Frank J., eds. The Municipal Bond Handbook, Vol. II. LC 83-70058. 550p. 1983. 50.00 (ISBN 0-87094-421-5). Dow Jones-Irwin.

Feldstein, Sylvan G., jt. ed. see Fabozzi, Frank J.

Feldstein, William, Jr. The Lamps of Tiffany Studios. 1983. 120.00 (ISBN 0-8109-1281-3). Abrams.

Feldt, Allan. CLUG: Community Land Use Game. LC 78-190151. Orig. Title: Clug Players Manual. 1972. pap. text ed. 15.95 (ISBN 0-02-910090-9). Free Pr.

Feldt, Robert H., ed. Atrioventricular Canal Defects. LC 76-8574. (Illus.). pap. 29.50 (ISBN 0-8357-9532-2, 2016662). Bks Demand UMI.

Feldvebel, Thomas P. The Ambrotype: Old & New. LC 80-65216. (Illus.). 51p. 1980. pap. 9.95 (ISBN 0-89938-001-8). Tech & Ed Ctr Graph Arts RIT.

Felgar, Robert. Richard Wright. (United States Authors Ser.). 1980. lib. bdg. 13.50 (ISBN 0-8057-7320-7, Twayne). G K Hall.

Felger, Dan. Engineering for the Officer of the Deck. (Illus.). 256p. 1979. 16.95 (ISBN 0-87021-172-2); bulk rates avail. Naval Inst Pr.

--Engineering for the OOD. LC 78-70964. (Illus.). 256p. 1979. 16.95x (ISBN 0-87021-172-2). Naval Inst Pr.

Felger, Donna H., jt. auth. see Rainwater, Dorothy T.

Felger, Donna H., compiled by. Boys' Fashions Eighteen Eighty-Six to Nineteen-Five. (Chronicle for Costume Historians & Doll Costumers Ser.). (Illus.). 113p. (Orig.). 1984. pap. 10.95 (ISBN 0-87588-209-9). Hobby Hse.

Felger, Richard S. & Moser, Mary B. People of the Desert & Sea: Ethnobotany of the Seri Indians. LC 84-16357. 435p. 1985. 65.00x (ISBN 0-8165-0818-6). U of Ariz Pr.

Felheim, Marvin. Theater of Augustin Daly. LC 77-90503. Repr. of 1956 ed. lib. bdg. 19.75x (ISBN 0-8371-2209-0, FETD). Greenwood.

Felheim, Marvin & Traci, Philip. Realism in Shakespeare's Romantic Comedies: "O Heavenly Mingle". LC 80-5580. 239p. 1980. lib. bdg. 22.75 (ISBN 0-8191-1282-8); pap. text ed. 12.50 (ISBN 0-8191-1283-6). U Pr of Amer.

Felheim, Marvin, tr. see Solomos, Alexis.

Felibien Des Avaux, Andre. The Perfect Painting. (Painted Sources of Western Art Ser.). 144p. (Fr.). 1981. pap. 25.00 slipcase (ISBN 0-915346-56-7). A Wofsy Fine Arts.

Felice, Cynthia. Downtime. 1985. 15.95 (ISBN 0-312-94115-3, Dist. by St. Martin). Bluejay Bks.

--Godsfire. 1982. pap. 2.95 (ISBN 0-671-44704-1, Timescape). PB.

Felice, Cynthia & Willis, Connie. Water Witch. 224p. (Orig.). 1984. pap. 2.75 (ISBN 0-441-87380-4). Ace Bks.

Felice, Frank De see De Felice, Frank.

Felice, Louise De see Gray, Juanita & De Felice, Louise.

Felice, Renzo de see De Felice, Renzo.

Felice, Renzo De see De Felice, Renzo.

Felicetti, Barbara, jt. ed. see Warnken, Kelly.

Felicia. I am Felicia. 1983. 14.95 (ISBN 0-934860-38-6). Adventure Pubns.

Feliciano, Alberto R. & Alvarez, Francisco E. Contabilidad Intermedia (I) (Span.). 1985. text ed. write for info. (ISBN 0-538-22410-X, V41). SW Pub.

Feliciaao, Francisco F. Four Asian Contemporary Composers: The Influence of Tradition in Their Works. (Illus.). 148p. 1984. pap. 8.75x (ISBN 971-10-0105-5, Pub. by New Day Philippines). Cellar.

Feliciano, Gloria & Hancock, Alan. The Educational Use of Mass Media, No. 491. v, 124p. 1981. pap. 5.00 (ISBN 0-686-39724-X, WP-0491). World Bank.

Feliciano, Gloria D. Research in Population Communication. (Population Communication Manuals: No. 3). 84p. 1978. pap. 5.25 (ISBN 92-3-101512-5, U854, UNESCO). Unipub.

Feliciano, Margarita. Window on the Sea: Ventana Sobre el Mar. Miller, Yvette E., ed. LC 81-2854. 69p. 1981. pap. 7.95 (ISBN 0-935480-06-4). Lat Am Lit Rev Pr.

Feliciano-Mendoza, Ester. Cajita de Musica. 2nd, rev. ed. LC 82-4910. (Ninos Y Letras Ser.). (Illus.). (gr. 8-12). 1983. pap. 5.00 (ISBN 0-8477-3525-7). U of PR Pr.

--Coqui. LC 82-4884. (Ninos y Letras Ser.). (Illus.). (gr. 4-7). 1982. pap. 5.00 (ISBN 0-8477-3505-2). U of PR Pr.

Feliciano Mendoza, Ester. Nanas. 4.00 (ISBN 0-8477-3200-2). U of PR Pr.

Feliciano-Mendoza, Ester & Rodriquez-Baez, Felix. Ala y Trino: Pajaros De Puerto Rico Libro De Ninos Para Colorear. LC 79-24763. (Orig., Span.). 1980. pap. 4.50 (ISBN 0-8477-3600-8). U of PR Pr.

Felidae, Thomas & Davenport, H. M. Don't Let Them Kiss You: A Cat's Guide to Choosing & Training People. (Illus.). 1984. pap. 3.95 (ISBN 0-87795-575-1). Arbor Hse.

Felig, P., et al. Endocrinology & Metabolism. 1981. 93.00 (ISBN 0-07-020387-3). McGraw.

Feliks, Yehuda. Nature & Man in the Bible. 294p. 1981. 25.00 (ISBN 0-900689-19-6). Soncino Pr NY.

Felimeister, Charles J., jt. ed. see Snyder, Thomas L.

Felins, Yehuda. Nature & Man in the Bible: Chapters in Biblical Ecology. 1982. 25.00x (ISBN 0-900689-19-6). Bloch.

Felipe, Carlos. Requiem Por Yarini. 1978. pap. 3.00 (ISBN 0-685-95271-1). Ediciones.

Felipe, Leon. Leon Felipe the Last Troubador: Selected Poems. Houston, Robert & Cannady, Criss, eds. Franklin, John, et al, trs. from Span. LC 78-73996. 1980. 15.00 (ISBN 0-933188-09-9); pap. 6.95 (ISBN 0-933188-08-0). Blue Moon Pr.

Felitia, Frank De see De Felitta, Frank.

Felitla, Frank de see De Felitta, Frank.

Felitta, Frank De see De Felitta, Frank.

Felitta, Frank de see De Felitta, Frank.

Felix, Amanda M. Trato Personal y Relaciones Humanas. (Span.). 1982. text ed. 3.85 (ISBN 0-538-22170-4, V17). SW Pub.

Felix, Charles. The Notting Hill Mystery. LC 75-32744. (Literature of Mystery & Detection). 1976. Repr. of 1862 ed. 12.00x (ISBN 0-405-07870-6). Ayer Co Pubs.

Felix, David. Marx As Politician. LC 82-10507. 320p. 1983. 27.50x (ISBN 0-8093-1073-2). S Ill U Pr.

Felix, Glenn H., jt. auth. see Riggs, James L.

Felix, H., et al. Dynamic Morphology of Leukemia Cells: A Comparative Study by Scanning Electron Microscopy & Microcinematography. (Illus.). 1978. 63.00 (ISBN 0-387-08495-9). Springer-Verlag.

Felix, J. L. Parenting with Style. LC 79-88029. 1979. pap. 2.95 (ISBN 0-87973-601-1). Our Sunday Visitor.

Felix, James V. Accounting Career Strategies: The Comprehensive Career Planning Guide for Accounting & Financial Professionals. LC 82-73146. (Illus.). 210p. 1982. 14.95 (ISBN 0-910595-00-3). Career Plan.

Felix, John H., et al. The Ukulele: A Portuguese Gift to Hawaii. LC 80-66299. (Illus.). 75p. (Orig.). (gr. 4-12). 1980. pap. 5.95x (ISBN 0-9604190-0-4). Nunes.

Felix, Monique. The Further Adventures of the Little Mouse Trapped in a Book. LC 84-144716. (Illus.). 28p. 1983. 5.95 (ISBN 0-88138-009-1, Star & Elephant Bks.). Green Tiger Pr.

--The Story of a Little Mouse Trapped in a Book. LC 84-146140. (Illus.). 28p. 1981. 5.95 (ISBN 0-914676-52-0). Green Tiger Pr.

Felix, Monique, illus. If I Were a Sheep. (Illus.). 12p. (Orig.). 1982. pap. 2.50 (ISBN 0-914676-67-9, Pub. by Envelope Bks). Green Tiger Pr.

Felix, Pal, tr. see Kadar, Bela.

Felix, R., et al. Contrast Media in Digital Radiography. (Current Clinical Practice Ser.: Vol. 12). 1984. 77.00 (ISBN 0-444-90365-8, I-489-83). Elsevier.

Felix, R. E., et al, eds. Contrast Media in Computed Tomography. (International Congress Ser.: No. 561). 330p. 1981. 55.50 (ISBN 0-444-90225-2, Excerpta Medica). Elsevier.

Felix, Robert H. Mental Illness: Progress & Prospects. LC 67-20278. 110p. 1967. 15.00x (ISBN 0-231-03055-X). Columbia U Pr.

Felix, Sascha M., ed. Second Language Development: Trends & Issues. (Tuebinger Beitraege Zur Linguistik Ser.). (Illus.). 355p. 1979. 33.00x (ISBN 3-87808-125-1); pap. 19.00x (ISBN 3-87808-521-4). Benjamins North Am.

Felix, Sascha W. Psycholinguistische Aspekte des Zweitsprachenerwerbs. (Language Development (LD) Ser.: 2). 340p. (Ger.). 1982. 42.00x (ISBN 3-87808-252-5); pap. 22.00x (ISBN 3-87808-543-5). Benjamins North Am.

Felix, Sascha W. & Wode, Henning, eds. Language Development at the Crossroads. (Language & Development Ser.: 5). 250p. 1983. pap. 28.00x (ISBN 3-87808-571-0). Benjamins North Am.

Felix, Werner. Johann Sebastian Bach. (Illus.). 1985. 25.00 (ISBN 0-393-02232-3). Norton.

Feliz, Jardinera, pseud. Gardening in Spanish: How to Communicate with Your Spanish Speaking Gardener. LC 85-70088. (Illus., Orig.). 1985. pap. 9.95 (ISBN 0-932825-01-X). Ammie Enter.

Felkenes, George. Constitutional Law for Criminal Justice. (Criminal Justice Ser.). 1978. ref. 28.95 (ISBN 0-13-167833-7). P-H.

Felkenes, George T. Criminal Law & Procedure: Text & Cases. LC 75-5735. 480p. 1976. text ed. 27.95 (ISBN 0-13-193441-4). P-H.

--Criminal Law & Procedure: Text & Cases. 2nd ed. 464p. 1985. text ed. 27.95 (ISBN 0-13-193624-7). P-H.

--Michigan Criminal Justice Law Manual. (Criminal Justice Ser.). 300p. 1981. pap. text ed. 18.95 (ISBN 0-8299-0369-0). West Pub.

Felkenes, George T. & Becker, Harold K. Law Enforcement: A Selected Bibliography. 2nd ed. LC 76-50010. 337p. 1977. 20.00 (ISBN 0-8108-0995-8). Scarecrow.

Felker, Charles A. Shop Mathematics. 6th ed. 1984. 14.40 (ISBN 0-02-816310-9); tchrs' man 11.96 (ISBN 0-02-816320-6). Glencoe.

Felker, Donald S., jt. auth. see Castetter, William B.

Felker, Evelyn. Raising Other People's Kids: Successful Child-Rearing in the Restructured Family. 160p. (Orig.). 1981. pap. 4.95 (ISBN 0-8028-1868-4). Eerdmans.

Felker, Evelyn H. Foster Parenting Young Children: Guidelines from a Foster Parent. LC 73-93885. 1974. pap. 5.25 (ISBN 0-87868-119-1, F-51). Child Welfare.

Felker, Rex. Haskell County Texas. (Illus.). 350p. 1975. 17.95 (ISBN 0-89015-097-4). Eakin Pubns.

Felker, Sharon L. Lovely Hull Pottery, Bk. II. 50p. 1985. pap. 2.95 (ISBN 0-87069-204-6). Wallace-Homestead.

Felkin, F. W. The Poet's Craft: An Outline of English Verse Composition for Schools. LC 77-18843. 1973. Repr. of 1916 ed. 10.00 (ISBN 0-8492-0824-6). R West.

Felkin, William. History of the Machine-Wrought Hosiery & Lace Manufactures. (Illus.). 1967. Repr. of 1867 ed. 23.50 (ISBN 0-8337-1104-0). B Franklin.

--History of the Machine-Wrought Hosiery & Lace Manufactures. LC 67-89041. Repr. of 1867 ed. 39.50x (ISBN 0-678-05685-4). Kelley.

Felkner. Microbial Testers: Probing Carcinogenesis. (Microbiology Ser.: Vol. 5). 1981. 45.00 (ISBN 0-8247-1244-7). Dekker.

Felkner, Bruce L., jt. auth. see Taft, Charles P.

Felkner, Mrytle. In the Wigwams of the Wyandots: The Story of Jonathan Pointer. 81p. (Orig.). pap. 6.95 (ISBN 0-941988-02-3). K Q Assocs.

Felknor, Bruce L. Dirty Politics. LC 75-37917. 295p. 1976. Repr. of 1966 ed. lib. bdg. 22.50x (ISBN 0-8371-8148-8, FEDP). Greenwood.

Fell, A. Early Iron Industry of Furness & District. (Illus.). 462p. 1968. Repr. of 1908 ed. 32.50x (ISBN 0-7146-1393-2, F Cass Co). Biblio Dist.

Fell, A. F., ed. Drug Analysis: Keynote & Plenary Papers from the First International Symposium, June 1983, Brussels, Belgium. 200p. 1984. pap. 20.00 (ISBN 0-08-031441-4). Pergamon.

Fell, A. London. Origins of Legislative Sovereignty & the Legislative State: Bodin's Humanistic Legal System & Rejection of "Medieval Political Theology", Vol. 3. LC 82-22332. 400p. 1985. 35.00 (ISBN 0-89946-142-5). Oelgeschlager.

--Origins of Legislative Sovereignty & the Legislative State: Medieval of Renaissance Origins, Vol. 4. LC 82-22332. 400p. 1984. 35.00 (ISBN 0-89946-143-3). Oelgeschlager.

--Origins of Legislative Sovereignty & the Legislative State: Vol. I: Corasius & the Renaissance Systematization of Roman Law. LC 82-22332. 386p. 1982. text ed. 35.00 (ISBN 0-89946-140-9). Oelgeschlager.

--Origins of Legislative Sovereignty & the Legislative State: Vol. II: Classical, Medieval, & Renaissance Foundations of Corasius' Systematic Methodology. LC 82-22332. 336p. 1982. text ed. 35.00 (ISBN 0-89946-141-7). Oelgeschlager.

Fell, Albert, ed. Histories & Historians. LC 68-113015. (History Today Ser). 1968. pap. 5.95 (ISBN 0-05-001654-7). Dufour.

Fell, Alison. Every Move You Make. 288p. 1984. 7.95 (ISBN 0-86068-580-2, Pub. by Virago Pr). Merrimack Pub Cir.

--Kisses for Mayakovsky. 64p. 1985. pap. 4.95 (ISBN 0-86068-593-4, Pub. by Virago Pr). Merrimack Pub Cir.

Fell, Alison, ed. Hard Feelings: Fiction & Poetry from Spare Rib. 4.95 (ISBN 0-7043-3838-6, Pub. by Quartet England). Charles River Bks.

Fell, Barry. America, B.C. 1979. pap. 9.95 (ISBN 0-671-55503-0, Wallaby). PB.

--Bronze-Age America. 1982. 17.95 (ISBN 0-316-27771-1). Little.

--Saga America. LC 79-51440. (Illus.). 1980. 15.00 (ISBN 0-8129-0847-3, Dist. by Har-Row); pap. 8.95 1983 (ISBN 0-8129-6324-5). Times Bks.

Fell, Christine & Clark, Cecily. Women in Anglo-Saxon England & the Impact of 1066. LC 84-48493. (Illus.). 208p. 1985. 24.50x (ISBN 0-253-36607-0). Ind U Pr.

Fell, Derek. Annuals: How to Select, Grow & Enjoy. (Illus.). 160p. 1983. pap. 7.95 (ISBN 0-89586-240-9). H P Bks.

--Annuals, Perennials, & Bulbs. 144p. (Orig.). pap. 7.95 cancelled (ISBN 0-88453-037-X). Countryside Bks.

--House Plants & Crafts: For Fun & Profit. (Fun & Profit Ser.). (Illus.). 1978. 7.95 (ISBN 0-916302-16-4); pap. 5.50 (ISBN 0-916302-04-0). Bookworm Pub.

--How to Photograph Flowers, Plants & Landscapes. LC 80-82571. (Photography Ser.). (Orig.). 1980. pap. 7.95 (ISBN 0-89586-068-6). H P Bks.

--Vegetables: How to Select, Grow & Enjoy. (Illus.). 192p. 1982. pap. 9.95 (ISBN 0-89586-106-2). H P Bks.

Fell, Derek & Shaudys, Phyllis. The Vegetable Spaghetti Cookbook. LC 82-90074. (Illus.). 96p. (Orig.). 1982. pap. 4.95 (ISBN 0-935238-03-4). Pine Row.

Fell, Derek, jt. auth. see Galle, Fred.

Fell, Doris E., jt. auth. see Page, Carole G.

Fell, Edgar T. Recent Problems in Admiralty Jurisdiction. LC 78-63977. (Johns Hopkins University. Studies in the Social Sciences. Fortieth Ser. 1922: 3). Repr. of 1922 ed. 16.50 (ISBN 0-404-61222-9). AMS Pr.

Fell, Elaine, ed. see Wright, David & Scott, Gerald, III.

Fell, G., jt. auth. see McEnhill, S.

Fell, H. B., jt. ed. see Dingle, J. T.

Fell, Henry. Intensive Sheep Management. (Illus.). 248p. 18.95 (ISBN 0-85236-101-7, Pub. by Farming Pr UK). Diamond Farm Bk.

Fell, J. M. Extension of Mackey's Method to Banach-Algebraic Bundles. LC 52-42839. (Memoirs: No. 90). 168p. 1969. pap. 10.00 (ISBN 0-8218-1290-4, MEMO-90). Am Math.

Fell, J. M, et al. Induced Representations & Banach-Algebraic Bundles. (Lecture Notes in Mathematics: Vol. 582). 1977. soft cover 21.00 (ISBN 0-387-08147-X). Springer-Verlag.

Fell, J. R. Ingano Zya Batonga e Zimpangaliko Zimwi. LC 78-67708. (The Folktale). Repr. of 1932 ed. 22.50 (ISBN 0-404-16085-9). AMS Pr.

Fell, James B. Song of Noel & Other Poems. 10.00x (ISBN 0-392-04697-0, LTB). Sportshelf.

Fell, James E., Jr. Ores to Metals: The Rocky Mountain Smelting Industry. LC 79-9093. (Illus.). xvi, 341p. 1979. 24.50x (ISBN 0-8032-1951-2). U of Nebr Pr.

Fell, John. Delegate from New Jersey: The Journal of John Fell. Whisenhunt, Donald W., ed. LC 73-83264. (National University Publications). 222p. 1974. 19.50x (ISBN 0-8046-9041-3, Pub. by Kennikat). Assoc Faculty Pr.

Fell, John L. Film Before Griffith. LC 82-8540. 395p. 1983. cloth 24.50 (ISBN 0-520-04738-9); pap. 10.95 (ISBN 0-520-04758-3, CAL 578). U of Cal Pr.

--A History of Film. LC 78-16203. 1979. pap. text ed. 19.95 (ISBN 0-275-64670-X, HoltC). HR&W.

Fell, Joseph P. Heidegger & Sartre: An Essay on Being & Place. 517p. 1983. 34.00 (ISBN 0-231-04554-9); pap. 16.00x (ISBN 0-231-04555-7). Columbia U Pr.

Fell, Joseph P., 3rd. Emotion in the Thought of Sartre. LC 65-15445. 245p. 1965. 26.00x (ISBN 0-231-02756-7). Columbia U Pr.

Fell, Marian, tr. see Chekhov, Anton P.

Fell, Marian, tr. see Korolenko, Vladimir G.

Fell, Marie L. The Foundations of Nativism in American Textbooks, 1783-1860. LC 76-145480. (The American Immigration Library). ix, 259p. 1971. Repr. of 1941 ed. lib. bdg. 15.95x (ISBN 0-89198-011-3). Ozer.

Fell, Mary. The Persistence of Memory. 1984. pap. 8.95 (ISBN 0-394-72363-5). Random.

--The Triangle Fire. (Shadow Press U.S.A. Poetry Chapbook Ser.: No. 2). 12p. (Orig.). 1983. pap. 2.50 numbered copies (ISBN 0-937724-02-5); pap. 5.00 lettered & signed copies. Shadow Pr.

Fell, Peter J. & Skees, William D. The Doctors' Computer Handbook. (Management Ser.). (Illus.). 290p. 1984. 27.50 (ISBN 0-534-02724-5). Lifetime Learn.

Felldin, Jeanne R. Index to the 1800 Census of Pennsylvania. LC 84-80791. 453p. 1984. 30.00 (ISBN 0-8063-1083-9). Genealog Pub.

--Index to the 1820 Census of Virginia. LC 75-45757. 486p. 1981. Repr. of 1976 ed. 25.00 (ISBN 0-8063-0696-3). Genealog Pub.

Felldin, Jeanne R. & Inman, Gloria K. Index to the 1820 Census of Kentucky. LC 81-80889. 318p. 1981. 22.50 (ISBN 0-8063-0937-7). Genealog Pub.

Fellegy, Joe, et al. Classic Minnesota Fishing Stories: A Rare Collection of First-Hand Accounts, Anecdotes & Reports. 238p. (Orig.). 1983. pap. 8.95 (ISBN 0-931674-04-2). Waldman Hse Pr.

Felleman, Hazel, ed. Best Loved Poems of the American People. 1936. 9.95 (ISBN 0-385-00019-7). Doubleday.

--Poems That Live Forever. LC 65-13987. 1965. 14.95 (ISBN 0-385-00358-7). Doubleday.

Fellendorf, George W., ed. Bibliography on Deafness. rev. ed. LC 77-86323. 1977. softcover 4.95 (ISBN 0-88200-111-6, L9214). Alexander Graham.

--Supplement to Bibliography on Deafness: 1977 to 1979. 1980. pap. text ed. 3.95 (ISBN 0-88200-139-6, L9435). Alexander Graham.

Feller, A. H. Mexican Claims Commissions, 1923-1934. Repr. of 1935 ed. 32.00 (ISBN 0-527-28900-0). Kraus Repr.

Feller, Babara A. & Shipp, Audrey. Health Characteristics of Person with Chronic Activity Limitation: United States 1979. (Series Ten: No. 137). 50p. 1981. pap. text ed. 1.75 (ISBN 0-8406-0229-4). Natl Ctr Health Stats.

Feller, Daniel. The Public Lands in Jacksonian Politics. LC 84-40149. 288p. 1984. text ed. 29.50x (ISBN 0-299-09850-8). U of Wis Pr.

Feller, G., et al, eds. Peace & World Order Studies: A Curriculum Guide. 3rd ed. 1981. pap. 7.95. World Policy.

Feller, I., jt. ed. see Bowden, M. L.

Feller, I., et al. Planning & Designing a Burn Care Facility. LC 80-83418. (Illus.). 350p. 1986. 75.00 (ISBN 0-917478-21-5). Natl Inst Burn.

Feller, Irving. International Bibligraphy on Burns: Supplement 1983. LC 71-94573. 1983. pap. 25.00 (ISBN 0-917478-14-2). Natl Inst Burn.

--International Bibliography on Burns: 1977 Supplement. LC 71-94573. 1977. pap. 25.00 (ISBN 0-917478-08-8). Natl Inst Burn.

--International Bibliography on Burns: 1978 Supplement. LC 71-94573. 1978. pap. 25.00 (ISBN 0-917478-09-6). Natl Inst Burn.

--International Bibliography on Burns: 1979 Supplement. LC 71-94573. 1980. pap. 25.00 (ISBN 0-917478-10-X). Natl Inst Burn.

--International Bibliography on Burns, 1981 Supplement. 1981. pap. 25.00 (ISBN 0-917478-12-6). Natl Inst Burn.

--International Bibliography on Burns: 1970 Supplement. LC 70-137338. 1970. pap. 25.00 (ISBN 0-917478-01-0). Natl Inst Burn.

--International Bibliography on Burns: 1971 Supplement. LC 71-94573. 1971. pap. 25.00 (ISBN 0-917478-02-9). Natl Inst Burn.

--International Bibliography on Burns: 1972 Supplement. LC 71-74573. 1972. pap. 25.00 (ISBN 0-917478-03-7). Natl Inst Burn.

--International Bibliography on Burns: 1973 Supplement. LC 71-94573. 1973. pap. 25.00 (ISBN 0-917478-04-5). Natl Inst Burn.

--International Bibliography on Burns: 1974 Supplement. LC 71-94573. 1974. pap. 25.00 (ISBN 0-917478-05-3). Natl Inst Burn.

--International Bibliography on Burns: 1975 Supplement. LC 71-94573. 1975. pap. 25.00 (ISBN 0-917478-06-1). Natl Inst Burn.

--International Bibliography on Burns: 1976 Supplement. LC 71-94573. 1976. pap. 25.00 (ISBN 0-917478-07-X). Natl Inst Burn.

--International Bibliography on Burns: 1982 Supplement. LC 71-94573. 1983. pap. 25.00 (ISBN 0-917478-13-4). Natl Inst Burn.

--International Bibliography on Burns: 1984, Supplement. 1984. pap. 25.00 (ISBN 0-917478-15-0). Natl Inst Burn.

--International Bibliography on Burns: 1985 Supplement. LC 71-94573. 1985. pap. 25.00 (ISBN 0-917478-16-9). Natl Inst Burn.

--International Bibliography on Burns 1950-1969. LC 71-94573. 1969. 40.00 (ISBN 0-917478-00-2). Natl Inst Burn.

Feller, Irving & Archambeault-Jones, Claudella. Nursing the Burned Patient. LC 77-169193. 1973. 25.00 (ISBN 0-917478-24-X). Natl Inst Burn.

Feller, Irving & Jones, Claudella A. Teaching Basic Burn Care. LC 75-15373. (Illus.). 1975. plastic 3-ring binder 120.00 (ISBN 0-917478-27-4). Natl Inst Burn.

Feller, Irving, jt. auth. see Jones, Claudella A.

Feller, Irving & Grabb, William C., eds. Reconstruction & Rehabilitation of the Burned Patient. LC 78-61362. (Illus.). 1979. text ed. 98.00 (ISBN 0-917478-50-9); text ed. 208.00 genuine leather bdg. (ISBN 0-917478-51-7). Natl Inst Burn.

Feller, Irving, et al. Emergent Care of the Burn Victim. LC 75-15375. (Illus.). 1977. pap. 15.00 (ISBN 0-917478-49-5). Natl Inst Burn.

Feller, J. Yacht Racing Protests & Appeals. 7.95 (ISBN 0-393-60008-4). Norton.

Feller, John Q. Chinese Export Porcelain in the 19th Century: Canton Famille Rose Porcelain. (Illus.). 52p. (Orig.). 1982. pap. 12.50 (ISBN 0-87577-069-X). Peabody Mus Salem.

Feller, L. Lee, jt. auth. see Gish, Oscar.

Feller, Robert, ed. A Pigment Handbook. (Illus.). 320p. Date not set. price not set (ISBN 0-521-30374-5). Cambridge U Pr.

Feller, Robert, et al. On Picture Varnishes & Their Solvents. LC 85-7172. (Illus.). 260p. 1985. write for info. Natl Gallery Art.

Feller, Robert L., et al. On Picture Varnishes & Their Solvents. rev. ed. LC 77-99229. pap. 68.30 (ISBN 0-317-10036-X, 2003003). Bks Demand UMI.

Feller, Steven, jt. auth. see Kasper, Joseph.

Feller, William. Introduction to Probability Theory & Its Applications, Vol. 1. 3rd ed. LC 68-11708. (Probability & Mathematical Statistics Ser.). 509p. 1968. 43.50x (ISBN 0-471-25708-7). Wiley.

--An Introduction to Probability Theory & Its Applications, Vol. 2. 2nd ed. LC 57-10805. (Probability & Mathematical Statistics Ser.). 669p. 1971. 46.00x (ISBN 0-471-25709-5). Wiley.

Fellerer, Karl G. The History of Catholic Church Music. Brunner, Francis A., tr. LC 78-21637. 1979. Repr. of 1951 ed. lib. bdg. 20.75x (ISBN 0-313-21147-7, FECC). Greenwood.

Feller-Roth, Barbara. Country Inns: A Selection of Maine's Distinctive Accommodations. (Maine Geographic Ser.). (Illus.). 48p. 1983. pap. 2.95 (ISBN 0-89933-063-0). DeLorme Pub.

--Day Trips with Children: A Guidebook of Things to See & Do for Children & Adults. Monegain, Bernie, ed. (Maine Geographic Ser.). (Illus.). 48p. 1983. pap. 2.95 (ISBN 0-89933-056-8). DeLorme Pub.

--Hiking: Coastal & Eastern Regions, Vol. I. (Maine Geographic Ser.). (Illus.). 48p. 1983. pap. 2.98 (ISBN 0-89933-047-9). DeLorme Pub.

--Hiking: Western Region, Vol. 2. (Maine Geographic Ser.). (Illus.). 48p. 1983. pap. 2.95 (ISBN 0-89933-048-7). DeLorme Pub.

--Lighthouses: A Guide to Coastal & Offshore Guardians. Monegain, Bernie, ed. (Maine Geographic Ser.). (Illus.). 48p. 1983. pap. 2.95 (ISBN 0-89933-050-9). DeLorme Pub.

--Trees & Shrubs: A Guide to the Beauty in Maine's Fields & Forests. Eastman, L. M., ed. (Maine Geographic Ser.). (Illus.). 48p. 1983. pap. 2.95 (ISBN 0-89933-055-X). Delorme Pub.

--Wildflowers: A Guide to Some of Maine's Most Beautiful Flora. Eastman, L. M., ed. (Maine Geographic Ser.). (Illus.). 48p. 1983. pap. 2.95 (ISBN 0-89933-054-1). Delorme Pub.

Feller-Roth, Barbara, ed. see Bouthillette, Guy.

Feller-Roth, Barbara, ed. see Monegain, Bernie.

Fellers, Frederick P., compiled by. The Metropolitan Opera on Record: A Discography of the Commercial Recordings. LC 83-22587. (Discographies: No. 9). xix, 101p. 1984. lib. bdg. 25.00 (ISBN 0-313-23952-5, FMO/). Greenwood.

Fellers, Frederick P., jt. ed. see Meyers, Betty.

Fellers, Pat. Alphabet Soup: A Complete Curriculum for Your First Week of School. Marson, Ron, ed. (Master Teacher Ser.). (Illus.). 100p. 1985. tchr's. ed. 13.95 (ISBN 0-941008-62-2). Tops Learning.

--Peace-ing It Together: Peace & Justice Activities for Youth. (The Learning Connection Ser.). 160p. (Orig.). 1984. pap. 9.95 (ISBN 0-86683-836-8, 8440). Winston Pr.

--Peaceful Procedures: A Master Teacher's Approach to Classroom Management. Marson, Ron, ed. (Master Teacher Ser.). (Illus.). 100p. 1986. tchr's. ed. 13.95 (ISBN 0-941008-63-0). Tops Learning.

--A Summer Start: How to Organize Your Best School Year Ever. Marson, Ron, ed. (Master Teacher Ser.). (Illus.). 100p. 1985. tchr's. ed. 13.95 (ISBN 0-941008-61-4). Tops Learning.

Felleudorf, George W., ed. Develop & Deliver II: The Proceedings of the Second International Forum on Assistive Listening Devices & Systems for Hearing Impaired Persons. 80p. 1985. 20.00 (ISBN 0-9613033-1-X). Fellendorf Assocs Inc.

Fellhauer, Cheryl, jt. auth. see Goeldner, C. R.

Fellig, Arthur see Weegee, pseud.

Fellin, Phillip, jt. auth. see Tripodi, Tony.

Fellinger, Robert C. & Cook, William J. Introduction to Engineering Thermodynamics. 616p. 1984. text ed. write for info. (ISBN 0-697-08606-2); solutions manual avail. (ISBN 0-697-00195-4). Wm C Brown.

Fellini, Federico. Moraldo in the City & A Journey with Anita. Stubbs, John C., ed. & tr. LC 82-17526. (Illus.). 178p. 1983. 12.95x (ISBN 0-252-01023-X). U of Ill Pr.

Felller-Roth, Barbara, ed. Hiking: Northern Region, Vol. 3. (Maine Geographic Ser.). (Illus.). 48p. 1983. pap. 2.95 (ISBN 0-89933-049-5). DeLorme Pub.

Fellman, Anita C. & Fellman, Michael. Making Sense of Self: Medical Advice Literature in Late Nineteenth-Century America. LC 81-51141. 224p. 1981. 13.95x (ISBN 0-8122-7810-0). U of Pa Pr.

Fellman, David. The Constitutional Right of Association. LC 63-9728. pap. 30.00 (ISBN 0-317-07956-5, 2015755). Bks Demand UMI.

--The Defendant's Rights Today. 462p. 1976. 30.00x (ISBN 0-299-07200-2); pap. 13.50x (ISBN 0-299-07204-5). U of Wis Pr.

--Defendant's Rights Under English Law. 150p. 1966. 20.00x (ISBN 0-299-03860-2). U of Wis Pr.

--The Limits of Freedom. LC 72-9048. 144p. 1973. Repr. of 1959 ed. lib. bdg. 15.00x (ISBN 0-8371-6563-6, FELF). Greenwood.

Fellman, David, ed. Supreme Court & Education. 3rd ed. LC 76-14495. (Classics in Eduation Ser.). 1976. pap. text ed. 8.50x (ISBN 0-8077-2511-0). Tchrs Coll.

Fellman, Gordon & Brandt, Barbara. The Deceived Majority: Politics & Protest in Middle America. LC 72-82197. pap. 69.30 (ISBN 0-317-20612-5, 2024154). Bks Demand UMI.

Fellman, Jack. The Revival of a Classical Tongue: Elizer Ben Yehuda & the Modern Hebrew Language. (Contributions to the Sociology of Language: No. 6). 1973. pap. text ed. 15.60x (ISBN 90-2792-495-3). Mouton.

Fellman, Len. Merchandising by Design. 1981. 20.95 (ISBN 0-86730-237-2). Lebhar Friedman.

Fellman, Michael. The Unbounded Frame: Freedom & Community in Nineteenth Century American Utopianism. LC 72-797. 203p. 1973. lib. bdg. 27.50 (ISBN 0-8371-6369-2, FUF/). Greenwood.

Fellman, Michael, jt. auth. see Fellman, Anita C.

Fellman, Michael, jt. ed. see Perry, Lewis.

Fellman, W., jt. ed. see Baring, G.

Fellmann, Emil, ed. Leonhard Euler, 1707-1783. (Opera Omnia, Complete Works of Leonhard Euler). 500p. (Eng. Fr. & Ger.). 1983. 29.95 (ISBN 0-8176-1343-9). Birkhauser.

Fellmann, Jerome D., jt. auth. see Harris, Chauncy D.

Fellmeth, Robert C. & Folsom, Ralph H. California Regulatory Law & Practice. 480p. 1983. 65.00 (ISBN 0-409-20466-8). Butterworth Legal Pubs.

Fellmeth, Robert C., jt. auth. see Folsom, Ralph H.

Fellner, M. J. Immunology of Skin Diseases. 318p. 1980. 39.50 (ISBN 0-444-00364-9, Biomedical Pr). Elsevier.

Fellner, Rudolph. Opera Themes & Plots. 1961. pap. 9.95 (ISBN 0-671-21215-X, Fireside). S&S.

Fellner, William. Employment Policy at the Crossroads: An Interim Look at Pressures to Be Resisted. 1972. 3.25 (ISBN 0-8447-3091-2). Am Enterprise.

--Monetary Policies & Full Employment. LC 82-48180. (Gold, Money, Inflation & Deflation Ser.). 277p. 1983. lib. bdg. 33.00 (ISBN 0-8240-5232-3). Garland Pub.

--Problems to Keep in Mind When It Comes to Tax Reform. LC 77-84191. 1977. pap. 2.25 (ISBN 0-8447-3266-4). Am Enterprise.

--Towards a Reconstruction of Macroeconomics. LC 76-21162. 1976. pap. 5.25 (ISBN 0-8447-1318-X). Am Enterprise.

--Trends & Cycles in Economic Activity: An Introduction to Problems of Economic Growth. LC 82-48181. (Gold, Money, Inflation & Deflation Ser.). 425p. 1983. lib. bdg. 55.00 (ISBN 0-8240-5233-1). Garland Pub.

Fellner, William, ed. Contemporary Economic Problems: 1976. LC 76-21977. 1976. pap. 8.25 (ISBN 0-8447-1319-8). Am Enterprise.

--Contemporary Economic Problems, 1980. 1980. pap. 9.25 (ISBN 0-8447-1335-X). Am Enterprise.

--Essays in Contemporary Economic Problems: Disinflation. 1983. 19.95 (ISBN 0-8447-1365-1); pap. 10.95 (ISBN 0-8447-1364-3). Am Enterprise.

--Essays in Contemporary Economic Problems: Demand, Productivity, & Population. 1981. 17.25 (ISBN 0-8447-1341-4); pap. 9.25 (ISBN 0-8447-1340-6). Am Enterprise.

Fellner, William, et al. Correcting Taxes for Inflation. LC 75-18713. (Orig.). 1975. pap. 4.25 (ISBN 0-8447-3174-9). Am Enterprise.

Fellner, William J. Competition Among the Few. rev. ed. LC 64-17622. Repr. of 1949 ed. 27.50x (ISBN 0-678-00042-5). Kelley.

Fellner, William J., ed. Contemporary Economic Problems: 1978. 1978. pap. 8.25 (ISBN 0-8447-1330-9). Am Enterprise.

--Contemporary Economic Problems, 1979. 1979. pap. 9.25 (ISBN 0-8447-1334-1). Am Enterprise.

Fellowes, E. H., jt. auth. see Foss, Hubert J.

Fellowes, E. H., jt. ed. see Buck, P. C.

Fellowes, Edmund H. Appendix with Supplementary Notes. (Tudor Church Music Ser.). 1963. Repr. of 1948 ed. 50.00x (ISBN 0-8450-1861-2). Broude.

--English Cathedral Music. 5th, rev. ed. Westrup, J. A., ed. LC 80-24400. (Illus.). xi, 283p. 1981. Repr. of 1973 ed. lib. bdg. 27.50x (ISBN 0-313-22643-1, FEEC). Greenwood.

--English Madrigal. LC 72-6997. (Select Bibliographies Reprint Ser.). 1972. Repr. of 1925 ed. 15.00 (ISBN 0-8369-6929-4). Ayer Co Pubs.

--Orlando Gibbons & His Family: The Last of the Tudor School of Musicians. 2nd ed. (Illus.). 109p. 1970. Repr. of 1951 ed. 12.50 (ISBN 0-208-00848-9, Archon). Shoe String.

Fellowes, Edmund H., ed. English Madrigal Verse: 1588-1632. 3rd ed. 1967. 74.00x (ISBN 0-19-811474-5). Oxford U Pr.

Fellows, Charles. Coins of Ancient Lycia. (Illus.). 1976. 8.00 (ISBN 0-916710-25-4). Obol Intl.

Fellows, D. K. Our Environment: An Introduction to Physical Geography. 3rd ed. 486p. 1985. pap. 22.95 (ISBN 0-471-88193-7). Wiley.

Fellows, Donald K. Our Environment: An Introduction to Physical Geography. 2nd ed. LC 79-18159. 532p. 1980. pap. 29.00 (ISBN 0-471-05755-X). Wiley.

Fellows, E. H., ed. see Beaumont & Fletcher.

Fellows, Henry P. Boat Trips on New England Rivers. 1977. lib. bdg. 59.95 (ISBN 0-8490-1518-9). Gordon Pr.

Fellows, Hugh & Ikeda, Fusaye. Business Speaking & Writing. (Illus.). 352p. 1982. text ed. 26.95 (ISBN 0-13-107854-2). P-H.

Fellows, Jane. Housekeeping Supervision. (Illus.). 256p. 1984. pap. 17.50x (ISBN 0-7121-0820-3). Trans-Atlantic.

Fellows, Jay. The Failing Distance: The Autobiographical Impulse in John Ruskin. LC 74-24374. 202p. 1975. 18.00x (ISBN 0-8018-1671-8). Johns Hopkins.

--Ruskin's Maze: Mastery & Madness in His Art. LC 81-47131. 375p. 1981. 32.00x (ISBN 0-691-06479-2). Princeton U Pr.

Fellows, Julian R., jt. auth. see Severns, William H.

Fellows, Lawrence. A Gentle War: The Story of the Salvation Army. LC 79-14622. (Illus.). 96p. (gr. 5 up). 1979. 9.95 (ISBN 0-02-734430-4, 73443). Macmillan.

Fellows, Len. Cross Facts Puzzles, No. 2. Hook, Henry, ed. (Illus.). 64p. 1984. pap. 6.95 (ISBN 0-671-50319-7, Fireside). S&S.

--Crossfacts. 64p. 1983. spiral bound 6.95 (ISBN 0-671-46874-X, Fireside). S&S.

--Puzzle Blast. (Illus.). 64p. (Orig.). (gr. 3-6). 1983. pap. 1.25 (ISBN 0-590-11894-3). Scholastic Inc.

--Tri-Play Crosswords, No. 1. Hook, Henry, ed. (Illus.). 64p. 1984. 6.95 (ISBN 0-671-50320-0, Fireside). S&S.

Fellows, Len, jt. auth. see Bragdon, Allen.

Fellows, Leonard F. Puzzle Power. (gr. 4-6). 1976. pap. 1.50 (ISBN 0-590-10230-3). Scholastic Inc.

Fellows, Marian, jt. auth. see Parkhurst, Christine.

Fellows, Mary Louise, et al. Public Attitudes About Property Distribution at Death & Interstate Succession Laws in the United States. 73p. (Reprinted from 1978 ABF Res., No. 2). 1978. 2.50 (ISBN 0-317-33353-4). Am Bar Foun.

Fellows of the Royal Society of Literature of the UK. The Eighteen-Eighties, Essays. Mare, Walter De La, ed. LC 77-92514. (Essay Index in Reprint Ser.). 1978. Repr. 25.00x (ISBN 0-8486-3011-4). Core Collection.

--The Eighteen Seventies, Essays. Granville-Barker, Harley, ed. LC 77-92515. (Essay Index in Reprint Ser.). 1978. Repr. 25.00x (ISBN 0-8486-3012-2). Core Collection.

Fellows of the Royal Society of Literature of the U.K. The Eighteen Sixties, Essays. Drinkwater, John, ed. LC 77-92517. (Essays Index in Reprint Ser.). 1978. Repr. 25.00x (ISBN 0-8486-3013-0). Core Collection.

Fellows, Otis, et al. A Livre Ouvert: Premieres Lectures en Francais. 1970. text ed. write for info. (ISBN 0-02-336860-8). Macmillan.

Fellows, Otis E. & Torrey, Norman L. Age of Enlightenment. 2nd ed. LC 73-147121. 1971. text ed. 25.95 (ISBN 0-13-018465-9). P-H.

Fellows, P., jt. auth. see Otten, Paul.

Fellows, Paul E., jt. auth. see Kiefer, E. Kay.

Fellows, Reginald B. London to Cambridge by Train, 1845-1938. (Cambridge Town, Gown, & County Ser.: Vol. 4). (Illus.). 40p. 1976. pap. 4.25 (ISBN 0-902675-65-6). Oleander Pr.

--Railways to Cambridge Actual & Proposed. (Cambridge Town, Gown & County Ser.: Vol. 2). (Illus.). 32p. 1976. pap. 4.00 (ISBN 0-902675-62-1). Oleander Pr.

Fellows, Robert & Eisenbarth, George, eds. Monoclonal Antibodies in Endocrine Research. 212p. 1981. text ed. 34.00 (ISBN 0-89004-687-5). Raven.

Fellows, Ward J. Religions East & West. LC 78-27721. 1979. text ed. 31.95 (ISBN 0-03-019441-5, HoltC). HR&W.

Fellowship Church, Baton Rouge, La, Members. Quickies for Singles. McKee, Gwen, ed. (Cookbook Ser.: No. 4). (Illus.). 80p. 1980. pap. 4.95 (ISBN 0-937552-03-8). Quail Ridge.

Fellowship of Catholic Scholars. Christian Faith & Freedom: Proceedings. Williams, Paul L., ed. LC 82-81072. 128p. (Orig.). 1982. pap. text ed. 4.50 (ISBN 0-686-97454-9). NE Bks.

Fells, John M., jt. auth. see Garcke, Emile.

Fellucci, Mario. The Masterpieces of the Vatican. (A Science of Man Library Bk). (Illus.). 40p. 1975. 97.45 (ISBN 0-913314-54-4). Am Classical Coll Pr.

Felm, Bradford K. & Grady, John C., Jr. Suffering to Silence. (Illus.). 200p. 1975. 9.95 (ISBN 0-89015-098-2). Eakin Pubns.

Felman, Alvin H. The Pediatric Chest: Radiological, Clinical, & Pathological Observations. (Illus.). 576p. 1983. 56.50x (ISBN 0-398-04730-8). C C Thomas.

Felman, Shoshana. The Literary Speech Act. Porter, Catherine, tr. LC 83-45144. 176p. 1983. 19.50x (ISBN 0-8014-1458-X). Cornell U Pr.

--Writing & Madness: Literature-Philosophy-Psychoanalysis. Evans, Martha N. & Massumi, Brian, trs. from Fr. LC 84-19845. 256p. 1985. text ed. 24.95x (ISBN 0-8014-1285-4). Cornell U Pr.

Felman, Shoshana, ed. Literature & Psychoanalysis: The Question of Reading: Otherwise. 512p. 1982. text ed. 30.00x (ISBN 0-8018-2753-1); pap. 9.95x (ISBN 0-8018-2754-X). Johns Hopkins.

Felman, Shoshana, et al. Discours et Pouvoir, Vol. II. Chambers, Ross, ed. LC 81-50963. (Michigan Romance Studies Ser.). 262p. (Orig.). 1982. pap. 8.00 (ISBN 0-939730-01-4). Mich Romance.

Felmeister, Charles J., ed. see Bosmajian, C. Perry & Bosmajian, Linda S.

Felmeister, Charles J., jt. ed. see Snyder, Thomas L.

Felmeister, Charles J., ed. see Snyder, Thomas L. & Bauer, Jeffrey C.

Felmeister, Charles J., ed. see Snyder, Thomas L. & Domer, Larry R.

Felmeister, Charles J., jt. ed. see Synder, Thomas L.

Felner, Joel M. & Schlant, Robert C. Echocardiography: A Teaching Atlas. LC 76-27645. (Illus.). 576p. 1976. 75.00 (ISBN 0-8089-0965-7, 791235). Grune.

Felner, Mira. Apostles of Silence: The Modern French Mimes. LC 83-48682. (Illus.). 216p. 1984. 28.50 (ISBN 0-8386-3196-7). Fairleigh Dickinson.

Felner, Robert D. & Jason, Leonard A., eds. Preventive Psychology: Theory, Research & Practice. 475p. 1983. 24.50 (ISBN 0-08-026340-2). Pergamon.

Felperin, Howard. Beyond Deconstruction: The Uses & Abuses of Literary Theory. 220p. 1985. 19.95 (ISBN 0-19-812839-8). Oxford U Pr.

--Shakespearean Representation: Mimesis & Modernity in Elizabethan Tragedy. LC 77-71982. (Princeton Essays in Literature). 1977. 22.00 (ISBN 0-691-06341-9). Princeton U Pr.

--Shakespearean Romance. LC 70-37575. 336p. 1972. 29.00 (ISBN 0-691-06230-7). Princeton U Pr.

Fels, George. Mastering Pool. LC 77-75726. (Mastering Ser.). (Illus.). 1977. pap. 9.95 (ISBN 0-8092-7895-2). Contemp Bks.

Fels, George, jt. auth. see Columbu, Franco.

Fels, Rendig, et al. Macroeconomic Problems & Policies. 4th ed. 1979. pap. text ed. 9.95 (ISBN 0-8299-0191-4). West Pub.

--Microeconomic Problems & Policies. 4th ed. 1978. pap. text ed. 9.95 (ISBN 0-8299-0192-2). West Pub.

Fels, Rendigs. American Business Cycles, 1865-1897. LC 73-3924. (Illus.). 244p. 1973. Repr. of 1959 ed. lib. bdg. 15.00x (ISBN 0-8371-6863-5, FEAB). Greenwood.

Felsen, Henry G. Boy Gets Car. (Illus.). (gr. 7-11). 1960. PLB 5.39 (ISBN 0-394-90976-3, BYR). Random.

--Handbook for Teen-Age Drivers. pap. 1.25 (ISBN 0-87502-044-5). Benjamin Co.

--Hot Rod. (Literature Ser). (gr. 9-12). 1950. pap. text ed. 4.92 (ISBN 0-87720-754-2). AMSCO Sch.

--Hot Rod. (gr. 5 up). 1950. 8.50 (ISBN 0-525-32245-0). Dutton.

Felsen, Jerry. Cybernetic Approach to Stock Market Analysis vs. Efficient Market Theory. LC 74-34512. 1975. 20.00 (ISBN 0-916376-01-X). CDS Pub.

--Cybernetic Approach to Stock Market Analysis: Versus Efficient Market Theory. LC 74-34512. 1975. 20.00 (ISBN 0-682-48224-2, University). Exposition Pr FL.

--Cybernetic Decision Systems. 350p. 25.00 (ISBN 0-916376-07-9). CDS Pub.

--Decision Making Under Uncertainty: An Artificial Intelligence Approach. LC 75-32712. (Illus.). 150p. 1976. pap. 20.00 (ISBN 0-916376-00-1). CDS Pub.

--How to Double Your Money in Less Than One Year by Trading in Listed Options. LC 78-68049. 1978. pap. 20.00 (ISBN 0-916376-06-0). CDS Pub.

--How to Earn Investment Returns of Fifty Percent to One Hundred Percent A Year: A Guide to Finding the Best Investment Managers, Advisory Services & Trading Systems. (Illus.). 160p. 1982. pap. 20.00 (ISBN 0-916376-08-7). CDS Pub.

--How to Make Money with Computers: A Guide to Thirty High-Profit, Low Capital Computer Business & Investment Opportunities. LC 78-68050. (Illus.). 1979. 20.00 (ISBN 0-916376-05-2). CDS Pub.

--Low-Cost, Personal-Computer-Based Investment Decision Systems. LC 77-83508. 1977. pap. 20.00 (ISBN 0-916376-03-6). CDS Pub.

Felsen, L. B. Hybrid Formulation of Wave Propagation & Scattering. 1984. lib. bdg. 52.00 (ISBN 90-247-3094-5, Pub. by Martinus Nijhoff Netherlands). Kluwer Academic.

Felsen, L. B., contrib. by. Transient Electromagnetic Fields. (Tropics in Applied Physics Ser.: Vol. 10). (Illus.). 340p. 1976. 59.00 (ISBN 0-387-07553-4). Springer-Verlag.

Felsenfeld, Carl & Siegel, Alan. Simplified Consumer Credit Forms. LC 78-50301. 1978. 56.00 (ISBN 0-88262-184-X). Warren.

--Writing Contracts in Plain English. LC 81-12972. 209p. 1981. pap. text ed. 9.95 (ISBN 0-314-60871-0). West Pub.

Felsenfeld, Naomi, jt. auth. see Maclennan, Beryce W.

Felsenfeld, Oscar. Borrelia, Borreliosis & Relapsing Fever: Strains, Vectors, Human & Animal Borreliosis. LC 72-127335. (Illus.). 192p. 1971. 12.50 (ISBN 0-87527-032-8). Green.

--The Cholera Problem. LC 67-26004. (Illus.). 180p. 1967. 10.00 (ISBN 0-87527-008-5). Green.

--The Epidemiology of Tropical Diseases. 504p. 1966. 45.75x (ISBN 0-398-00556-7). C C Thomas.

Felsenstein, Frank, ed. see Smollett, Tobias.

Felsenstein, J., ed. Numerical Taxonomy. (NATO ASI Ser.: Series G, Ecological Sciences, No. 1). (Illus.). 655p. 1983. 66.00 (ISBN 0-387-12293-1). Springer-Verlag.

Felsenstein, Joseph. Bibliography of Theoretical Population Genetics. LC 81-264. 866p. 1981. 50.50 (ISBN 0-87933-397-9). Van Nos Reinhold.

Felshin, J. Perspectives & Principles for Physical Education. LC 67-21329. 233p. 1967. text ed. 10.50 (ISBN 0-471-25717-6, Pub. by Wiley). Krieger.

Felshin, Nina. R. M. Fischer. (Illus.). 1981. 4.00 (ISBN 0-917562-21-6). Contemp Arts.

Felshin, Nina, ed. Disarming Images: Art for Nuclear Disarmament. LC 84-71651. 72p. 1985. pap. 14.95 (ISBN 0-915361-14-0, Dist. by Watts). Adama Pubs Inc.

Felshman, Anne, jt. auth. see Feldman, George B.

Felske, Norma. You Can Teach Young Teens. 48p. 1976. pap. 2.50 (ISBN 0-88207-176-9). Victor Bks.

--You Can Teach Young Teens. 1981. 2.50 (ISBN 0-88207-146-7). Victor Bks.

Felsodriethoma, Tibor P. von see Von Felsodriethoma, Tibor P.

Felson, Benjamin. Chest Roentgenology. LC 73-188387. (Illus.). 1973. text ed. 35.95 (ISBN 0-7216-3591-1). Saunders.

--Radiology of Tuberculosis. (Reprint of Seminars in Roentgenology Ser.). 160p. 1979. 34.00 (ISBN 0-8089-1248-8, 791248). Grune.

Felson, Benjamin, ed. The Acute Abdomen. (Illus.). 212p. 1974. 49.50 (ISBN 0-8089-0831-6, 791244). Grune.

--Interventional Radiology. 176p. 1981. 34.00 (ISBN 0-8089-1414-6, 791250). Grune.

--Roentgen Techniques in Laboratory Animals: Radiography of the Dog & Other Experimental Animals. LC 68-23680. pap. 66.00 (ISBN 0-317-29361-3, 2055940). Bks Demand UMI.

--Roentgenology of Fractures & Dislocations. 192p. 1978. 41.00 (ISBN 0-8089-1131-7, 791246). Grune.

Felson, Benjamin, et al. Principles of Chest Roentgenology: A Programed Text. LC 65-23091. (Illus.). 1965. pap. text ed. 18.95 (ISBN 0-7216-3605-5). Saunders.

Felstiner, John. Translating Neruda: The Way to Macchu Picchu. LC 79-67773. (Illus.). 294p. 1980. 20.00x (ISBN 0-8047-1079-1). Stanford U Pr.

Felstiner, John, tr. see Crow, Mary.

Felt, F. O., jt. auth. see Cape, W. H.

Felt, Jeremy P. Hostages of Fortune: Child Labor Reform in New York State. LC 65-11676. (Illus.). 1965. 12.00x (ISBN 0-8156-2075-6). Syracuse U Pr.

Felt, Joseph B. Customs of New England. 1967. Repr. of 1853 ed. 19.00 (ISBN 0-8337-1105-9). B Franklin.

--Historical Account of Massachusetts Currency. LC 68-57905. (Research & Source Works Ser.: No. 223). (Illus.). 1967. Repr. of 1839 ed. 21.00 (ISBN 0-8337-1106-7). B Franklin.

Felt, Marilyn C. Improving Our Schools: Thirty-Three Studies That Inform Local Action. 224p. 1985. write for info. (ISBN 0-89292-091-2). Educ Dev Ctr.

Felt, Robert L., ed. see Fratkin, Jake.

Felt, Robert L., ed. see Tin-Yau So, James.

Felt, Thomas. Researching Writing & Publishing Local History. 2nd ed. LC 81-10935. (Illus.). 166p. 1981. pap. 9.00 (ISBN 0-910050-53-8). AASLH Pr.

Feltenstein, Rosalie, tr. see Corneille, Pierre.

Feltenstein, Rosalie, tr. see France, Anatole.

Feltenstein, Tom. Restaurant Profits Through Advertising & Promotion: The Indispensable Plan. 156p. 1983. 17.95 (ISBN 0-8436-2262-8). Van Nos Reinhold.

Feltgen, Dennis & Fang, Irving. Smile When the Dewpoint Drops. LC 81-50632. (Illus.). 128p. 1981. pap. 2.50 (ISBN 0-9604212-2-X). Rada Pr.

Feltham, Gerald A. Information Evaluation, Vol. 5. (Studies in Accounting Research). 149p. 1972. 6.00 (ISBN 0-86539-017-7). Am Accounting.

Feltham, Gerald A., jt. auth. see Demski, Joel S.

Feltham, Owen. Resolves, a Duple Century. 3rd ed. LC 74-28853. (English Experience Ser.: No. 734). 1975. Repr. of 1628 ed. 35.00 (ISBN 90-221-0734-5). Walter J Johnson.

Feltham, P. Deformation & Strength of Materials. 142p. 1966. 25.00x (ISBN 0-306-30648-4, Plenum Pr). Plenum Pub.

Feltman, William. Journal of Lieutenant William Feltman, of the First Pennsylvania Regiment, 1781-82 Including the March into Virginia & the Siege of Yorktown. Decker, Peter, ed. LC 77-76559. (Eyewitness Accounts of the American Revolution Ser.: No. 2). 1969. Repr. of 1853 ed. 13.50 (ISBN 0-405-01152-0). Ayer Co Pubs.

Feltner, C. E., Jr. Winning Is Everything--Losing Is Nothing! LC 80-68579. 200p. 1981. 9.95 (ISBN 0-87754-066-7). Chelsea Hse.

Feltner, Charles E. & Feltner, Jeri B. Great Lakes Maritime History: Bibliography & Sources of Information. LC 82-51175. 124p. 1982. pap. 9.95 (ISBN 0-9609014-0-X). Seajay.

Feltner, Helen A., jt. auth. see Smith, Ruth E.

Feltner, Jeri B., jt. auth. see Feltner, Charles E.

Felton, Bruce & Fowler, Mark. Felton & Fowler's Best, Worst & Most Unusual. LC 75-9895. 288p. (YA) 1975. 12.45i (ISBN 0-690-00569-5). T Y Crowell.

--Felton & Fowler's Famous Americans You Never Knew Existed. LC 78-56944. (Illus.). 1981. pap. 9.95 (ISBN 0-8128-6108-6). Stein & Day.

Felton, Craig & Jordan, William B., eds. Jusepe de Ribera: Lo Spagnoletto (1591-1652) LC 82-84144. 246p. 1982. 50.00 (ISBN 0-912804-09-2, Dist by U of Wash Pr); pap. 24.95 (ISBN 0-912804-10-6). Kimbell Art.

Fenn, Elizabeth A. & Wood, Peter H. Natives & Newcomers: The Way We Lived in North Carolina Before 1770. Nathans, Sydney, ed. LC 82-20128. (The Way We Lived in North Carolina Ser.). (Illus.). viii, 98p. 1983. 11.95 (ISBN 0-8078-1549-7); pap. 6.95 (ISBN 0-8078-4101-3). U of NC Pr.

Fenn, Ellenor F. Fables in Monosyllables. LC 21-2685. (Early Children's Bks). 1970. Repr. of 1783 ed. 15.00 (ISBN 0-384-15470-0). Johnson Repr.

Fenn, F. & Wyllie, B. The Fully Illustrated Book of Old British Furniture. (Illus.). 141p. 1982. 77.85 (ISBN 0-86650-022-7). Gloucester Art.

Fenn, Forrest. The African Animals of William R. Leigh. (Illus.). 32p. (Orig.). 1980. pap. 10.00 (ISBN 0-937634-01-8). Fenn Pub Co.

--The Beat of the Drum & the Whoop of the Dance: Biography of Joseph Henry Sharp. LC 83-81832. (Illus.). 360p. 1983. 85.00 (ISBN 0-937634-06-9); limited edition of 227 including Sharp etching 1000.00 (ISBN 0-937634-07-7). Fenn Pub Co.

Fenn, H. C. & Tewksbury, M. G. Read Chinese, Vol. I. 236p. 1961. includes 4 cassettes 55.00x (ISBN 0-88432-090-1, M301). J Norton Pubs.

--Read Chinese, Vol. II. 267p. 1983. includes 3 cassettes 45.00x (ISBN 0-88432-091-X, M310). J Norton Pubs.

Fenn, Henry, et al. Speak Mandarin. Tewksbury, M. Gardner, ed. 238p. 1979. 7 audio cassettes incl. 125.00x (ISBN 0-88432-027-8, M201); 7 audio cassettes incl. J Norton Pubs.

Fenn, Henry C. Review Exercises in Chinese Sentence Structure. 1.50 (ISBN 0-88710-078-3). Far Eastern Pubns.

--Sketch of Chinese History, Pt. I. rev. ed. (Mirror Ser.). 181p. (Chinese.). 1983. pap. text ed. 7.95 (ISBN 0-88710-091-0). Far Eastern Pubns.

--Sketch of Chinese History, Part 2. (Mirror Ser.). 100p. pap. text ed. 4.50 (ISBN 0-88710-092-9). Far Eastern Pubns.

Fenn, Henry C. & Tewksbury, M. Gardner. Speak Mandarin. (Yale Linguistic Ser). 1967. pap. text ed. 12.95x (ISBN 0-300-00084-7); wkbk. 21.00x (ISBN 0-300-00454-0); 10.95x (ISBN 0-300-00085-5); teacher's manual, text ed. o.p. 10.00x (ISBN 0-300-00455-9). Yale U Pr.

Fenn, Henry C., ed. Chinese Characters Easily Confused. 2.50 (ISBN 0-88710-013-9). Far Eastern Pubns.

Fenn, J. B., jt. ed. see Shuler, K. E.

Fenn, John B. Engines, Energy, & Entropy: A Thermodynamics Primer. LC 81-17305. (Illus.). 293p. 1982. text ed. 19.95 (ISBN 0-7167-1281-4); pap. text ed. 12.95 (ISBN 0-7167-1282-2). W H Freeman.

Fenn, Margaret. Making It in Management: A Behavioral Approach for Women Executives. LC 78-17005. (Illus.). 1978. (Spec); pap. 5.95 (ISBN 0-13-547620-8). P-H.

Fenn, P. T., Jr. The Origin of the Right of Fishery in Territorial Waters. 15.00 (ISBN 0-89020-009-2). Brown Bk.

Fenn, Percy T., Jr. The Origin of the Right of Fisheries in Territorial Waters. 245p. 1974. Repr. 15.00x (ISBN 0-89020-009-2). Crofton Pub.

Fenn, R., ed. Topology of Low-Dimensional Manifolds: Proceedings. (Lecture Notes in Mathematics: Vol. 722). 1979. pap. 14.00 (ISBN 0-387-09506-3). Springer-Verlag.

Fenn, Richard K. Liturgies & Trials: The Secularization of Religious Language. LC 81-19250. 256p. 1982. 15.95 (ISBN 0-8298-0495-1). Pilgrim NY.

Fenn, Roger. Low-Dimensional Topology. (London Mathematical Society Lecture Note Ser.: No. 95). 350p. 1985. pap. 27.95 (ISBN 0-521-26982-2). Cambridge U Pr.

Fenn, Roger A. Techniques of Geometric Topology. LC 81-18189. (London Mathematical Society Lecture Note Ser.: No. 57). 208p. 1983. pap. 27.95 (ISBN 0-521-28472-4). Cambridge U Pr.

Fenn, Scott. The Nuclear Power Debate: Issues & Choices. LC 80-28065. 218p. 1981. 31.95 (ISBN 0-03-059074-4). Praeger.

Fenn, Scott A. America's Electric Utilities: Under Siege & in Transition. LC 84-8279. 176p. 1984. 23.95x (ISBN 0-03-070301-8). Praeger.

Fenn, William P. Christian Higher Education in Changing China, 1880-1950. LC 75-43741. (Illus.). pap. 64.00 (ISBN 0-317-07969-7, 2012769). Bks Demand UMI.

Fenn, William W. Theism: The Implication of Experience. 1969. 5.00 (ISBN 0-87233-005-2). Bauhan.

Fenna, D., et al. The Stockholm County Medical Information System. (Lecture Notes in Medical Informatics Ser.: Vol. 2). 1978. pap. 15.00 (ISBN 0-387-08950-0). Springer-Verlag.

Fennah, R. G. Fulgoroidea of Fiji. (BMB). 1950. pap. 8.00 (ISBN 0-527-02310-8). Kraus Repr.

Fennel, Robert A., jt. auth. see Young, Ronald D.

Fennel, T. G. & Gelsen, H. A Grammar of Modern Latvian, 3 vols. (Slavistic Printings & Reprintings: No. 303). 1980. text ed. 144.00x (ISBN 0-686-26963-2). Mouton.

Fennel, William E. A Pig Watcher's Guide to Biology. 88p. 1982. pap. text ed. 8.95 (ISBN 0-8403-2797-8). Kendall-Hunt.

Fennell, Desmond. Beyond Nationalism: The Struggle Against Provinciality in the Modern World. 432p. 1985. cancelled (ISBN 0-906187-57-5, Pub. by Univ Pr of Ireland). Longwood Pub Group.

--Beyond Nationalism: The Struggle Against Provinciality in the Modern World. O'Donoghue, Hilary, ed. (Illus.). 400p. (Orig.). 1985. pap. 15.95 (ISBN 0-907085-88-1, Pub. by Ward River Ireland). Irish Bks Media.

--State of the Nation. rev. ed. 146p. 1984. pap. 5.95 (ISBN 0-907085-61-X, Pub. by Ward River Pr Ireland). Irish Bks Media.

Fennell, Dorothy I., jt. auth. see Raper, Kenneth B.

Fennell, Francis. Writing Now: A College Handbook. 1980. pap. text ed. 12.95 (ISBN 0-574-22050-X, 13-5050); instr's guide avail. (ISBN 0-574-22051-8, 13-5051). SRA.

Fennell, Francis, et al, eds. Selected Papers from the Sixth, Eighth & Ninth National Conference on Diagnostic & Prescriptive Mathematics. Scheer, Jan. (Illus.). 134p. 1985. pap. text ed. 8.40x (ISBN 0-940466-08-2). Research Council.

Fennell, Francis L. Dante Gabriel Rossetti: An Annotated Bibliography. DeVries, Duane, ed. LC 80-9034. 300p. 1981. lib. bdg. 44.00 (ISBN 0-8240-9327-5). Garland Pub.

Fennell, Francis L., Jr., ed. The Rossetti-Leyland Letters: The Correspondence of an Artist & His Patron. LC 75-14552. xxxiv, 111p. 1978. 12.00x (ISBN 0-8214-0207-2, 82-82154). Ohio U Pr.

Fennell, Francis M. Elementary Mathematics Diagnosis & Correction Kit. 1981. pap. 24.95x comb-bound (ISBN 0-87628-295-8). Ctr Appl Res.

--Elementary Mathematics: Priorities for the 1980s. LC 81-80015. (Fastback Ser.: No. 157). 1981. pap. 0.75 (ISBN 0-87367-157-0). Phi Delta Kappa.

Fennell, Frederick. Basic Band Repertory: British Band Classics from the Conductor's Point of View. 1980. pap. 6.00 (ISBN 0-686-29444-0). Instrumental Co.

Fennell, George. La Patrulla Homicida. new ed. Ramiro, Orestes, tr. from Eng. (Compadre Collection). Orig. Title: Killer Patrol. 160p. (Span.). 1974. pap. 0.85 (ISBN 0-88473-605-9). Fiesta Pub.

--Patrulla Sangrienta. new ed. Ramiro, Orestes, tr. from Eng. (Compadre Collection Ser). Orig. Title: Blood Patrol. 160p. (Span.). 1974. pap. 0.75 (ISBN 0-88473-604-0). Fiesta Pub.

Fennell, Geraldine C. A Little Bit of War. 1983. 6.95 (ISBN 0-533-05415-X). Vantage.

Fennell, J. L. Penguin Russian Course. (Reference Ser). 1984. pap. 5.95 (ISBN 0-14-007053-2). Penguin.

Fennell, J. L., et al, eds. Oxford Slavonic Papers, Vol. 14. 1982. 37.50x (ISBN 0-19-815657-X). Oxford U Pr.

Fennell, J. L., jt. ed. see Foote, I. P.

Fennell, James. Apology for the Life of James Fennell. LC 77-82826. 1814. Repr. of 1814 ed. 27.50 (ISBN 0-405-08499-4, Blom Pubns). Ayer Co Pubs.

Fennell, John. The Crisis of Medieval Russia 1200-1304. (Longman History of Russia Ser.). (Illus.). 208p. 1983. pap. text ed. 14.95x (ISBN 0-582-48150-3). Longman.

Fennell, John, ed. Nineteenth-Century Russian Literature: Studies of Ten Russian Writers. (Library Reprint Ser.). 1976. 35.00x (ISBN 0-520-03203-9). U of Cal Pr.

Fennell, John L., et al, eds. Oxford Slavonic Papers, Vol. 12. 1979. 39.00x (ISBN 0-19-815654-5). Oxford U Pr.

Fennell, Robert A., jt. auth. see Young, Ronald D.

Fennell, Rosemary. The Common Agricultural Policy of the European Community. LC 79-2961. 256p. 1980. text ed. 23.50x (ISBN 0-916672-29-8). Allanheld.

Fennell, William O. God's Intention for Man-Essays in Christian Anthropology. (SR Supplement Ser.: No. 4). xii, 56p. 1977. pap. 3.50x (ISBN 0-919812-05-8, Pub. by Wilfrid Laurier U Pr). Humanities.

Fennelly, Catherine see Weaver, Glenn.

Fennelly, Lawrence J. Handbook of Loss Prevention & Crime Prevention. 962p. 1982. text ed. 59.95 (ISBN 0-409-95047-5). Butterworth.

--Museum, Archive, & Library Security. new ed. (Illus.). 912p. 1983. text ed. 59.95 (ISBN 0-409-95058-0). Butterworth.

Fennelly, Lawrence J., jt. auth. see Tyska, Louis A.

Fennelly, Tony. The Glory Hole Murders. 204p. (Orig.). 1985. 14.95 (ISBN 0-88184-180-3). Carroll & Graf.

Fennema, Elizabeth & Ayer, M. Jane. Women & Education: Equity or Equality? LC 83-62772. (A National Society for the Study of Education Publication Ser.). 1984. 21.75 (ISBN 0-8211-0507-8); text ed. 19.50. McCutchan.

Fennema, Elizabeth, ed. Mathematics Education Research: Implications for the 80's. LC 81-67144. 182p. 1981. 6.75 (ISBN 0-87353-196-5). NCTM.

Fennema, Jack. Nurturing Children in the Lord. 1978. kivar 4.95 (ISBN 0-87552-266-1). Presby & Reformed.

Fennema, M. International Networks of Banks & Industry. 1982. lib. bdg. 34.50 (ISBN 90-247-2620-4, Pub. by Martinus Nijhoff Netherlands). Kluwer Academic.

Fennema, O., et al, eds. Low Temperature Preservation of Foods & Living Matter. (Food Science Ser: Vol. 3). 592p. 1973. 95.00 (ISBN 0-8247-1185-8). Dekker.

Fennema, Owen. Principles of Food Science, Pt. 1. (Food Sci. Ser.: Vol. 4). 1976. 79.75 (ISBN 0-8247-6350-5); text ed. 34.75. Dekker.

--Principles of Food Science: Physical Methods of Food Preservation, Pt. 2. (Food Science Ser.: Vol. 4). 1975. 69.75 (ISBN 0-8247-6322-X); text ed. 29.75. Dekker.

Fennema, Owen, ed. Proteins at Low Temperatures. LC 79-16561. (Advances in Chemistry Ser.: No. 180). 1979. 39.95 (ISBN 0-8412-0484-5). Am Chemical.

Fennema, Roger, ed. see Calkins, Michael.

Fennema, Roger, ed. see Chek Chart Staff.

Fennema, Roger, ed. see Leigh, Bob, et al.

Fennema, Roger L., ed. see Chek Chart Staff.

Fennema, Roger L., ed. see Leigh, Bob, et al.

Fenner, Ball. Raising the Veil, or, Scenes in the Courts. LC 77-172580. (Criminology, Law Enforcement, & Social Problems Ser.: No. 168). (Illus.). Date not set. 12.50x (ISBN 0-87585-168-1). Patterson Smith.

Fenner, Carol. Gorilla Gorilla. (gr. 2 up). 1973. (BYR); PLB 6.99 (ISBN 0-394-92069-4). Random.

--Ice Skates. (Illus.). 48p. 1980. pap. 1.50 (ISBN 0-590-30376-7). Scholastic Inc.

--The Skates of Uncle Richard. LC 78-55910. (Illus.). (gr. 2-5). 1978. (BYR); PLB 6.99 (ISBN 0-394-93553-5). Random.

Fenner, Dudley. A Counter-Poyson..., to the Objections & Reproaches, Wherewith the Aunswerer to the Abstract, Would Disgrace the Holy Discipline of Christ. LC 74-28854. (English Experience Ser.: No. 735). 1975. Repr. of 1584 ed. 10.50 (ISBN 90-221-0735-3). Walter J Johnson.

--A Short Treatise of Lawfull & Unlawfull Recreations. LC 77-6740. (English Experience Ser.: No. 870). 1977. Repr. of 1590 ed. lib. bdg. 3.50 (ISBN 90-221-0870-8). Walter J Johnson.

Fenner, Edward T. Rasayana Siddhi: Medicine & Alchemy in the Buddhist Tantras. (Traditional Healing Ser.). 300p. 1984. 39.95 (ISBN 0-932426-28-X). Trado-Medic.

Fenner, F., et al. The Biology of Animal Viruses. 2nd ed. 1974. 83.00 (ISBN 0-12-253040-3). Acad Pr.

Fenner, Frank J. & Ratcliffe, F. N. Myxomatosis. LC 65-17207. pap. 103.00 (ISBN 0-317-28401-0, 2022448). Bks Demand UMI.

Fenner, Frank J. & White, David O. Medical Virology. 1976. 33.00 (ISBN 0-12-253060-8). Acad Pr.

Fenner, James, jt. auth. see Mullings, Llewellyn M.

Fenner, Peter & Armstrong, Martha. Research: A Practical Guide to Finding Information. LC 81-4589. (Illus.). 180p. pap. 9.95 (ISBN 0-86576-010-1). W Kaufmann.

Fenner, Peter G., jt. auth. see Hutch, Richard A.

Fenner, Phyllis R., compiled by. Consider the Evidence, Stories of Mystery & Suspense. LC 73-792. (Illus.). 192p. (gr. 7 up). 1973. 10.00 (ISBN 0-688-20080-X). Morrow.

--The Endless Dark: Stories of Underground Adventure. LC 77-5494. (Illus.). (gr. 7 up). 1977. PLB 11.88 (ISBN 0-688-32122-4). Morrow.

Fenner, Phyllis R., ed. Keeping Christmas: Stories of the Joyous Season. LC 79-15590. (Illus.). 224p. (gr. 7-9). 1979. 11.25 (ISBN 0-688-22206-4); PLB 11.88 (ISBN 0-688-32206-9). Morrow.

Fenner, Phyllis R., compiled by. Midnight Prowlers: Stories of Cats & Their Enslaved Owners. LC 81-3953. (Illus.). 192p. (gr. 7-9). 1981. 11.25 (ISBN 0-688-00704-X); PLB 11.88 (ISBN 0-688-00705-8). Morrow.

Fenner, R. T. Principles of Polymer Processing. 1980. 35.00 (ISBN 0-8206-0285-X). Chem Pub.

Fenner, Roger T. Finite Element Methods for Engineers. (Illus.). 1976. 19.50x (ISBN 0-686-86734-3); pap. text ed. write for info (ISBN 0-333-18656-7). Scholium Intl.

Fenner, Sal. Sea Machines. LC 79-28586. (Machine World). (Illus.). (gr. 2-4). 1980. PLB 14.65 (ISBN 0-8172-1334-1). Raintree Pubs.

Fenner, T. W. & Everett, J. L. Inventor's Handbook. 1968. 17.00 (ISBN 0-8206-0070-9). Chem Pub.

Fenner, Thomas P., ed. see Armstrong, Mrs. M. & Ludlow, Helen W.

Fenner, Thomas P., compiled by. Cabin & Plantation Songs. LC 74-24079. Repr. of 1901 ed. 14.50 (ISBN 0-404-12908-0). AMS Pr.

Fenner, William R. Quick Reference to Veterinary Medicine. (Illus.). 448p. 1982. pap. text ed. 30.75 (ISBN 0-397-50448-9, 65-05937, Lippincott Medical). Lippincott.

Fenney, Mary, tr. see Sihanouk, Nordom.

Fennimore, Donald L. The Knopf Collectors' Guides to American Antiques: Silver & Pewter. 1984. pap. 13.95 (ISBN 0-394-71527-6). Knopf.

Fenning, D., et al. An Encyclopaedia of North & South America 1786. 1984. 60.00x (ISBN 0-905418-02-6, Pub. by Gresham England). State Mutual Bk.

Fenno, Brooks. Helping Your Business Grow. LC 82-71310. 240p. 1984. pap. 8.95 (ISBN 0-8144-7622-8). AMACOM.

--Helping Your Business Grow: 101 Dynamic Ideas in Marketing. LC 82-71310. pap. 58.80 (ISBN 0-317-26708-6, 2023514). Bks Demand UMI.

Fenno, Brooks, Jr. Helping Your Business Grow: One Hundred One Dynamic Ideas in Marketing. 224p. 1982. 15.95 (ISBN 0-8144-5733-9). AMACOM.

Fenno, Frank H. Science & Art of Elocution. facs. ed. LC 78-139760. (Granger Index Reprint Ser). 1878. 23.50 (ISBN 0-8369-6214-1). Ayer Co Pubs.

Fenno, Richard F., Jr. Congressmen in Committees. LC 99-901233. (The Study of Congress Ser.). 320p. 1973. pap. text ed. 10.95 (ISBN 0-316-27807-6). Little.

--Home Style: House Members in Their Districts. 1978. pap. text ed. 10.95 (ISBN 0-316-27809-2). Little.

--United States Senate: A Bicameral Perspective. 1982. pap. 2.95 (ISBN 0-8447-3499-3). Am Enterprise.

Fennow, Karin, tr. see Birket-Smith, Kaj.

Fenoaltea, Doranne. Si Haulte Architecture: The Design of Sceve's Delie. LC 81-71432. (French Forum Monographs: No. 35). 246p. (Orig.). 1982. pap. 15.00x (ISBN 0-917058-34-8). French Forum.

Fenocketti, Mary. Coping with Pain. 80p. 1982. pap. 1.95 (ISBN 0-89243-166-0). Liguori Pubns.

Fenocketti, Mary M. Coping with Discouragement. 64p. 1985. pap. 1.50 (ISBN 0-89243-226-8). Liguori Pubns.

--Learning from Little Ones: Insights from the Gospel. 48p. 1984. pap. 1.95 (ISBN 0-89243-203-9). Liguori Pubns.

Fenoglio. Progress in Surgical Pathology, Vol. III. LC 80-80334. 1981. 65.00x (ISBN 0-89352-122-1). Masson Pub.

Fenoglio, C. M. & Rossini, F. P., eds. Adenomas & Adenomas Containing Carcinoma of the Large Bowel: Advances in Diagnosis & Therapy. 150p. 1985. text ed. 29.50 (ISBN 0-317-19781-9). Raven.

Fenoglio, Cecilia M. & Wolff, Marianne, eds. Progress in Surgical Pathology, Vol. IV. LC 80-80334. 312p. 1981. 65.00x (ISBN 0-89352-143-4). Masson Pub.

--Progress in Surgical Pathology, Vol. II. LC 80-80334. (Illus.). 304p. 1980. 65.00x (ISBN 0-89352-090-X). Masson Pub.

--Progress in Surgical Pathology, Vol. V. (Illus.). 300p. 1983. 65.00 (ISBN 0-89352-198-1). Masson Pub.

Fenoglio, Cecilia M., jt. auth. see King, Donald W.

Fenoglio, John J., Jr., ed. Endomyocardial Biopsy Techniques & Applications. 176p. 1982. 60.00 (ISBN 0-8493-5630-X). CRC Pr.

Fenollosa, Ernest F. East & West. LC 78-104448. Repr. of 1893 ed. lib. bdg. 25.00 (ISBN 0-8398-0553-5). Irvington.

--Epochs of Chinese & Japanese Art: An Outline History of East Asiatic Design, 2 Vols. rev. ed. (Illus.). 30.00 set (ISBN 0-8446-2048-3). Peter Smith.

--Epochs of Chinese & Japanese Art. 2 Vol. (Illus.). 1921. pap. 6.95 ea.; Vol. 1. (ISBN 0-486-20364-6); Vol. 2. 6.95 (ISBN 0-486-20365-4). Dover.

Fenollosa, Ernest F. & Pound, Ezra. The Classic Noh Theatre of Japan. LC 77-4057. 1977. Repr. of 1959 ed. lib. bdg. 45.00x (ISBN 0-8371-9580-2, FECN). Greenwood.

Fenoyl, Pierre De see De Fenoyl, Pierre.

Fenoyl, Pierre de see De Fenoyl, Pierre.

Fensch, Thomas. The Hardest Parts: Techniques for Effective Non-Fiction. 200p. (Orig.). 1984. pap. 15.95 (ISBN 0-930751-01-9). Lander Moore Bks.

--Steinbeck & Covici: The Story of a Friendship. LC 78-26594. 1979. 12.95 (ISBN 0-8397-7888-0); pap. 9.95 (ISBN 0-8397-7889-9). Eriksson.

Fensham, F. Charles. The Books of Ezra & Nehemiah. (The New International Commentary on the Old Testament Ser.). 288p. 1983. 12.95 (ISBN 0-8028-2362-9). Eerdmans.

Fenske, Robert H., et al. Handbook of Student Financial Aid: Programs, Procedures & Policies. LC 83-11336. (Higher Education Ser.). 1983. text ed. 26.95x (ISBN 0-87589-571-9). Jossey-Bass.

Fenske, S. H. My Life in Christ: A Momento of My Confirmation. LC 76-5729. (gr. 8 up). 1976. pap. 2.50 (ISBN 0-8100-0056-3, 16N0514). Northwest Pub.

Fensom, Anthony H., jt. auth. see Benson, Philip F.

Fensom, Rod. America's Grand Resort Hotels: Eighty Classic Resorts in the United States & Canada. LC 84-48888. (Illus.). 224p. (Orig.). 1985. pap. 10.95 (ISBN 0-88742-022-2). East Woods.

Fenson, Harry & Kritzer, Hildreth. Reading, Understanding & Writing about Short Stories. LC 66-15498. (Orig.). 1966. pap. text ed. 15.95 (ISBN 0-02-910120-4). Free Pr.

Fenstad, J. E. General Recursion Theory: An Axiomatic Approach. Gandy, R. O., et al, eds. LC 79-13099. (Perspectives in Mathematical Logic Ser.). 240p. 1980. 48.00 (ISBN 3-540-09349-4). Springer-Verlag.

Fenstad, J. E., et al, eds. Generalized Recursion Theory II: Proceedings of the 1977 Oslo Symposium. (Studies in Logic: Vol. 94). 354p. 1978. 68.00 (ISBN 0-444-85163-1, Biomedical Pr). Elsevier.

Fenster, Robert. Shakespeare Games. (Illus.). 160p. 1982. Outlet 3.98 (ISBN 0-517-54623-X, Harmony); pap. 1.98 Outlet (ISBN 0-517-54624-8). Crown.

Fenster, S. K., jt. auth. see Ugural, A. C.

Fenster, Valmai. Guide to American Literature. 250p. 1983. lib. bdg. 25.00 (ISBN 0-87287-373-0). Libs Unl.

Fensterheim, H. & Baer, J. Stop Running Scared. 1978. pap. 3.95 (ISBN 0-440-17734-0). Dell.
Fensterheim, Herbert & Baer, Jean. Dont Say Yes When You Want to Say No. 1975. pap. 3.95 (ISBN 0-440-15413-8). Dell.
Fensterheim, Herbert & Glazer, Howard I., eds. Behavioral Psychotherapy: Basic Principles & Case Studies in an Integrative Clinical Model. LC 82-20622. 256p. 1983. 25.00 (ISBN 0-87630-325-4). Brunner-Mazel.
Fensterheim, Robert J., jt. ed. see Lederer, William H.
Fenstermacher, Gary D. & Goodlad, John I., eds. Individual Differences in the Common Curriculum, Part I. LC 82-62381. (National Society for the Study of Education Ser.: Bk. 82). 350p. 1984. pap. text ed. 12.00x (ISBN 0-226-60091-2). U of Chicago Pr.
Fenstermaker, John J. Charles Dickens, 1940-1975: An Analytical Subject Index to Periodical Criticism of the Novels & Christmas Books. 1979. lib. bdg. 31.50 (ISBN 0-8161-8064-4, Hall Reference). G K Hall.
--John Forster. (English Authors Ser.: No. 379). 1984. lib. bdg. 18.95 (ISBN 0-8057-6865-3, Twayne). G K Hall.
Fensterwald, Bernard. Coincidence or Conspiracy? (Illus.). 1977. pap. 2.50 (ISBN 0-89083-232-3). Zebra.
Fenten, Barbara & Fenten, D. X. The Team Behind the Great Parades. LC 81-2981. (A Junior Literary Guild Selection). (Illus.). 96p. (gr. 5-9). 1981. 9.95 (ISBN 0-664-32682-X). Westminster.
--Tourism & Hospitality: Careers Unlimited. LC 78-19108. (Illus.). 160p. (gr. 7 up). 1978. 8.95 (ISBN 0-664-32634-X). Westminster.
Fenten, D. X. Ms. Architect. LC 77-7498. (Illus.). 128p. (gr. 7 up). 1977. 7.95 (ISBN 0-664-32615-3). Westminster.
--Ms. Attorney. LC 74-4492. (Illus.). 160p. (gr. 9 up). 1974. 7.50 (ISBN 0-664-32552-1). Westminster.
Fenten, D. X., jt. auth. see Fenten, Barbara.
Fenter, Kenneth. Gaijin! Gaijin! An American Family in Japan. Fenter, Lora, ed. (Illus.). 400p. (Orig.). 1984. pap. 10.45 (ISBN 0-930693-00-0). Cross Press.
Fenter, Kenneth & Fenter, Lora. Mo Ichido-Once More: An American Family in Japan. (Illus.). 400p. (Orig.). 1985. pap. 10.45 (ISBN 0-930693-01-9). Cross Press.
Fenter, Lora, jt. auth. see Fenter, Kenneth.
Fenter, Lora, ed. see Fenter, Kenneth.
Fenton, A. The Northern & Western Isles in the Viking World. (Illus.). 300p. 1984. text ed. 38.50x (ISBN 0-85976-101-0, Pub. by John Donald Scotland). Humanities.
--Review of Scottish Culture One. 112p. 1984. pap. text ed. 10.00x (ISBN 0-85976-106-1, Pub. by John Donald Scotland). Humanities.
--Review of Scottish Culture Two. (Illus.). 120p. 1985. text ed. 9.50x (ISBN 0-85976-138-X, Pub. by Donald Scotland). Humanities.
--The Shape of the Past, Vol. 1. (Illus.). 200p. 1985. text ed. 22.95x (ISBN 0-85976-129-0, Pub. by Donald Scotland). Humanities.
--The Shape of the Past, Vol. 2. (Illus.). 200p. 1985. text ed. 22.95x (ISBN 0-85976-141-X, Pub. by Donald Scotland). Humanities.
Fenton, A. & Kisban, E. Food in Change: Eating Habits from the Middle Ages to the Present Day. (Illus.). 224p. 1985. text ed. 28.50x (ISBN 0-85976-145-2, Pub. by Donald Scotland). Humanities.
Fenton, A. & Stell, G., eds. Loads & Roads in Scotland & Beyond. (Scottish History & Culture Paperback Ser.). (Illus.). 160p. 1984. pap. text ed. 16.75x (ISBN 0-85976-107-X, Pub. by John Donald Scotland). Humanities.
Fenton, Alexander. The Northern Isles: Orkney & Shetland. (Illus.). 1978. text ed. 39.50x (ISBN 0-85976-019-7, Pub. by Donald Scotland). Humanities.
--Scottish Country Life. 266p. 1982. 39.00x (ISBN 0-85976-011-1, Pub. by Donald Pubs Scotland). State Mutual Bk.
Fenton, Alexander & Owen, Trefor. Food in Perspective: Third International Conference of Ethnological Food Research. (Illus.). 425p. 1981. text ed. 50.50x (ISBN 0-85976-044-8). Humanities.
Fenton, Alexander & Walker, Bruce. The Rural Architecture of Scotland. (Illus.). 1981. text ed. 38.00x (ISBN 0-85976-020-0, Pub. by Donald Scotland). Humanities.
Fenton, Ann D., jt. auth. see Peterson, Carolyn S.
Fenton, Barbara, ed. see Zolotow, Charlotte.
Fenton, Calvin W. & Edwards, Charles J. Guide to Federal Grants & Financial Aid 1984. 520p. 1983. pap. 79.00 (ISBN 0-915345-00-5). Fenton Assocs.
Fenton, Carroll L. & Fenton, Mildred. Mountains. facs. ed. LC 70-84305. (Essay Index Reprint Ser). 1942. 22.00 (ISBN 0-8369-1129-6). Ayer Co Pubs.
--Story of the Great Geologists. facs. ed. LC 73-84306. (Essay Index Reprint Ser.). 1945. 22.00 (ISBN 0-8369-1130-X). Ayer Co Pubs.
Fenton, Carroll L. & Kitchen, Hermine B. Plants We Live On: The Story of Grains & Vegetables. rev. ed. LC 78-89322. (Illus.). (gr. 3-6). 1971. PLB 16.89 (ISBN 0-381-99819-3, A61600, JD-J). Har-Row.
Fenton, Charles A. Stephen Vincent Benet: The Life & Times of an American Man of Letters, 1898-1943. LC 77-19015. (Illus.). 1978. Repr. of 1958 ed. lib. bdg. 37.50x (ISBN 0-313-20200-1, FESB). Greenwood.
Fenton, Charles A., ed. see Benet, Stephen V.
Fenton, Doris. Extra Dramatic Moment in Elizabethan Plays. LC 74-16489. 1930. lib. bdg. 20.00 (ISBN 0-8414-4243-6). Folcroft.
Fenton, Edward. The Refugee Summer. LC 81-12593. 272p. (gr. 7 up). 1982. 13.95 (ISBN 0-385-28854-9). Delacorte.
Fenton, Edwin. Immigrants & Unions. LC 74-17926. (Italian American Experience Ser). 672p. 1975. 47.50x (ISBN 0-405-06399-7). Ayer Co Pubs.
Fenton, Edwin, et al. The Americans: A History of the United States. (gr. 7-8). 1975. text ed. 20.72 (ISBN 0-03-089551-0, HoltE); pap. 15.40 (ISBN 0-03-089552-9); wkbk. (dup. masters) 86.80 (ISBN 0-03-089553-7); tests (dup. masters) 50.96 (ISBN 0-03-089554-5); classroom support unit 354.20 (ISBN 0-03-089555-3). HR&W.
--Living in Urban America. (gr. 9-11). 1974. text ed. 18.44 (ISBN 0-03-010466-1, HoltE); wkbk. (dup. masters) 44.80 (ISBN 0-03-010476-9); tchr's. guide 23.24 (ISBN 0-03-010471-8); evaluating component (dup. masters) 48.90 (ISBN 0-03-010481-5); support unit 487.44 (ISBN 0-03-010486-6). HR&W.
Fenton, Elijah. The Life of John Milton. 1978. Repr. of 1977 ed. lib. bdg. 8.50 (ISBN 0-8414-1994-9). Folcroft.
--The Life of John Milton. 8p. 1980. Repr. of 1785 ed. lib. bdg. 10.00 (ISBN 0-8492-4704-7). R West.
Fenton, Fred R., et al. Home & Hospital Psychiatric Treatment: An Interdisciplinary Experiment. LC 81-16354. (Contemporary Community Health Ser.). (Illus.). 240p. 1982. 19.95x (ISBN 0-8229-1142-6). U of Pittsburgh Pr.
Fenton, Frederick. Artistic Anatomy of the Human Figure for Artists, 2 vols. (Illus.). 339p. 1986. Set. 186.50 (ISBN 0-86650-172-X). Gloucester Art.
Fenton, G. L., tr. see Jellinek, S.
Fenton, Geffraie, tr. see Bandello, Matteo.
Fenton, Geoffrey. A Forme of Christian Pollicie. LC 78-38180. (English Experience Ser.: No. 454). 424p. 1972. Repr. of 1574 ed. 42.00 (ISBN 90-221-0454-0). Walter J Johnson.
Fenton, Geoffrey, tr. A Discourse of the Civile Warres in Fraunce, Drawn into Englishe by G. Fenton. LC 76-26510. (English Experience Ser.: No. 248). 1970. Repr. of 1570 ed. 20.00 (ISBN 90-221-0248-3). Walter J Johnson.
--A Form of Christian Policy Gathered Out of French. 504p. Repr. of 1574 ed. 50.00 (ISBN 0-384-15483-2). Johnson Repr.
Fenton, Heike & Hecker, Melvin. The Greeks in America: A Chronology & Fact Book. LC 77-93976. (Ethnic Chronology Ser.). 151p. 1978. lib. bdg. 8.50 (ISBN 0-379-00531-X). Oceana.
Fenton, Irene, ed. see Darwin, Gary.
Fenton, J. C. Saint Matthew. LC 77-81620. (Westminster Pelican Commentaries Ser.). 488p. 1978. Westminster.
Fenton, James. Children in Exile: Poems, 1968-1984. 112p. 1984. 11.95 (ISBN 0-394-53360-7); pap. 5.95 (ISBN 0-394-72387-2). Random.
--A German Requiem. 16p. 1982. 20.00x (ISBN 0-907540-00-7, Pub. by Salamander Pr Scotland). State Mutual Bk.
--You Were Marvelous: Theatre Reviews from the Sunday Times. 272p. 1985. 14.95 (ISBN 0-224-01995-3, Pub. by Jonathan Cape). Merrimack Pub Cir.
Fenton, John. The A to Z of Sales Management. 160p. 1982. 7.95 (ISBN 0-8144-5655-3). AMACOM.
--A-Z Industrial Salesmanship. 1975. text ed. 23.50x (ISBN 0-434-90559-3); pap. text ed. 16.95x (ISBN 0-434-90560-7). Intl Ideas.
--The Gospel of St. Matthew: Commentaries. (Orig.). 1964. pap. 6.95 (ISBN 0-14-020488-1, Pelican). Penguin.
--How to Double Your Profits Within the Year. 192p. 1981. 21.00 (ISBN 0-434-90565-8, Pub. by W Heinemann Ltd). David & Charles.
Fenton, Joseph. Hybrid Buildings. (Pamphlet Architecture Ser.: No. 11). (Illus.). 48p. 1985. pap. 7.00 (ISBN 0-910413-14-2). Princeton Arch.
Fenton, Judith A. & Lifchez, Aaron S. The Fertility Handbook. (Orig.). 1980. 12.95 (ISBN 0-517-53991-8, C N Potter); pap. 5.95 (ISBN 0-517-54125-4, C N Potter Bks). Crown.
Fenton, Loren L. Thirteen Weeks to Riches (Which Could Be Glory!) (Orig.). 1978. pap. 5.00 (ISBN 0-934178-00-3). Christian Success.
Fenton, M. Brock. Communication in the Chiroptera. LC 84-47965. (Animal Communication Ser.). (Illus.). 192p. 1985. 32.50x (ISBN 0-253-31381-3). Ind U Pr.
Fenton, Mildred, jt. auth. see Fenton, Carroll L.
Fenton, N. Brock. Just Bats. (Illus.). 171p. 1983. 25.00x (ISBN 0-8020-2452-1); pap. 9.95 (ISBN 0-8020-6464-7). U of Toronto Pr.
Fenton, Norman. Group Counseling. LC 73-9254. 109p. 1974. Repr. of 1961 ed. lib. bdg. 15.00x (ISBN 0-8371-6997-6, FEGC). Greenwood.
--Human Relations in Adult Corrections. 224p. 1973. 24.75x (ISBN 0-398-02837-0). C C Thomas.
--Self-Direction & Adjustment. 121p. 1980. Repr. of 1926 ed. lib. bdg. 22.50 (ISBN 0-89760-225-0). Telegraph Bks.
Fenton, Norman & Wiltse, Kermit T., eds. Group Methods in the Public Welfare Program. LC 63-18692. 1963. pap. text ed. 7.95x (ISBN 0-87015-121-5). Pacific Bks.
Fenton, Paul, tr. see Maimonides, Obadyah.
Fenton, Robert, ed. see Darwin, Gary.
Fenton, Roger. Roger Fenton, Photographer of the Crimean War: With an Essay on His Life & Work by Helmut & Alison Gernsheim. LC 72-9200. (The Literature of Photography Ser.). Repr. of 1954 ed. 16.00 (ISBN 0-405-04909-9). Ayer Co Pubs.
--A Treatise of Usurie. LC 74-28855. (English Experience Ser.: No. 736). 1975. Repr. of 1611 ed. 13.00 (ISBN 9-0221-0736-1). Walter J Johnson.
Fenton, Ruth M. Adventures in Food, Natural Cooking Made Easy: How to Cook Better for Less Without Adding Oil or Sugar. (Orig.). 1980. pap. 8.50 (ISBN 0-934178-01-1). Christian Success.
Fenton, Sasha. Fortune Telling by Tarot Cards. (Illus., Orig.). 1985. pap. 6.95 (ISBN 0-85030-445-8, Pub. by Aquarian Pr England). Sterling.
Fenton, Steve. Durkheim & Modern Sociology. LC 83-26248. 250p. 1984. 29.95 (ISBN 0-521-25923-1); pap. 14.95 (ISBN 0-521-27763-9). Cambridge U Pr.
Fenton, T., tr. see Colling, Rex.
Fenton, Thomas P. Education for Justice: A Resource Manual. LC 74-83519. 464p. (Orig.). 1975. pap. 7.95 (ISBN 0-88344-119-5). Orbis Bks.
Fenton, Thomas P. & Heffron, Mary J. Third World Resource Directory: A Guide to Organizations & Publications. LC 83-6783. 320p. (Orig.). 1984. pap. 17.95 (ISBN 0-88344-509-3). Orbis Bks.
Fenton, Tom. Growing & Showing Vegetables. (Illus.). 68p. 1984. 9.95 (ISBN 0-7153-8577-1). David & Charles.
Fenton, William, jt. ed. see Jennings, Francis.
Fenton, William N. Contacts Between Iroquois Herbalism & Colonial Medicine. (Shorey Indian Ser.). (Illus.). 34p. pap. 3.95 (ISBN 0-8466-4032-5, 132). Shorey.
--The Roll Call of the Iroquois Chiefs: A Study of a Mnemonic Cane from the Six Nations Reserve. LC 76-43704. (Smithsonian Miscellaneous Collections Ser.: Vol. 3, No. 15). Repr. of 1950 ed. 20.00 (ISBN 0-404-15536-7). AMS Pr.
--Sioux Music. lib. bdg. 29.00 (ISBN 0-403-08975-1). Scholarly.
Fenton, William N., ed. Symposium on Local Diversity in Iroquois Culture. Repr. of 1951 ed. 39.00 (ISBN 0-403-03704-2). Scholarly.
Fenton, William N., ed. see Parker, Arthur C.
Fentress, Alvin K., Jr., jt. auth. see Myerson, Kathleen.
Fenves, Steven J., et al. Numerical & Computer Methods in Structural Mechanics: Proceedings. 1973. 86.50 (ISBN 0-12-253250-3). Acad Pr.
--STRESS: User's Manual. 1964. pap. 16.00x (ISBN 0-262-06029-9). MIT Pr.
Fenwick, Agnes M. My Journey into God's Realm of Light. 1974. 3.50 (ISBN 0-682-47865-2). Exposition Pr FL.
Fenwick, Benedict J. Memoirs to Serve for the Future Ecclesiastical History of the Diocese of Boston. McCarthy, Joseph M., ed. LC 78-64366. (Monograph: No. 35). (Illus.). 270p. 1979. 10.95 (ISBN 0-686-65388-2). US Cath Hist.
Fenwick, Charles G. Foreign Policy & International Law. LC 68-57015. 142p. 1968. 8.50 (ISBN 0-379-00366-X). Oceana.
Fenwick, Daman C. Mobile Home Living: The Money-Saving Guide. (Illus.). 224p. 1981. 14.95 (ISBN 0-8306-9670-9, 1322); pap. 8.95 (ISBN 0-8306-1322-6). TAB Bks.
Fenwick, Dorothy. Directory of Campus Business Linkages. 172p. 1983. 14.95 (ISBN 0-02-910540-4). ACE.
Fenwick, Dorothy C., ed. Directory of Campus-Business Linkages. (Ace Macmillan Higher Education Ser). 192p. 1983. 14.95 (ISBN 0-686-46066-9). Macmillan.
Fenwick, Ian & Quelch, John Q. Consumer Behavior for Marketing Managers. 1984. text ed. 20.72 (ISBN 0-205-08120-7, 138120). Allyn.
Fenwick, R. D. The Advocate Guide to Gay Health. Rev. ed. 240p. 1982. pap. 6.95 (ISBN 0-932870-23-6). Alyson Pubns.
Fenwick, Robert W. Red Fenwick's West, Yesterday & Today. (Illus.). 272p. 1983. Repr. of 1956 ed. 14.95 (ISBN 0-87108-658-1). Pruett.
Fenwick, Sara I., ed. Critical Approach to Children's Literature. LC 60-2341. (Midway Reprint Ser.). 1976. pap. 6.00x (ISBN 0-226-24162-9). U of Chicago Pr.
--New Definitions of School-Library Service: Proceedings of the 24th Annual Conference of the Graduate Library School. LC 60-2341. (University of Chicago Studies in Library Science). 1960. lib. bdg. 6.00x (ISBN 0-226-24163-7). U of Chicago Pr.
Fenwick, Sara I., jt. ed. see Asheim, Lester.
Fenwick, William A. & Practising Law Institute. Computer Litigation 1984, Resolving Computer Related Disputes & Protecting Proprietary Rights. LC 82-63160. (Litigation & Administrative Practice Ser.: No. 216). (Illus.). 1002p. 1984. 35.00 (H4-4933). PLI.
Fenyes, T., jt. auth. see Dombradi, Z. S.
Fenyeves, Marta. From a Distance. (Illus.). 55p. 1981. pap. 3.00 (ISBN 0-942292-06-5). Warthog Pr.
Fenyo, Ivan. North Italian Drawings. LC 66-14731. (Illus.). 1966. 15.00 (ISBN 0-8079-0102-4). October.
Fenyo, M., tr. see Heller, Agnes.
Fenyo, Mario D. Hitler, Horthy, & Hungary: German-Hungarian Relations, 1941-1944. LC 72-75189. (Yale Russian & East European Studies: No. 11). pap. 72.80 (ISBN 0-317-09405-X, 2006156). Bks Demand UMI.
Fenyo, S. Modern Mathematical Methods in Technology, Vol. 2. LC 69-16400. (Applied Mathematics & Mechanics Ser.: Vol. 17). 326p. 1975. 40.50 (ISBN 0-444-10565-4, North-Holland). Elsevier.
Fenyo, S. & Frey, T. Moderne Mathematische Methoden in de Technik, Vol. III. (International Series of Numerical Mathematics: No. 18). 348p. (Ger.). 1980. pap. 64.95x (ISBN 0-8176-1097-9). Birkhauser.
--Moderne Mathematische Methoden in der Technik, 2 vols. Incl. Vol. 1. 409p. 1967. 66.95x (ISBN 0-8176-0192-9); Vol. 2. 336p. 1971. 64.95x (ISBN 0-8176-0529-0). (International Ser. of Numerical Mathematics: Nos. 8 & 11). (Illus.). Birkhauser.
Fenyo, S. & Stolle, H. Theorie und Praxis der Linearen Integralgleichungen: Vol. I. (LMW - MA Ser.: 74). 250p. (Ger.). 1982. text ed. 50.95x (ISBN 0-8176-1164-9). Birkhauser.
--Theorie und Praxis der Linearen Integralgleichungen: Vol. 2. 304p. (Ger.). 1982. text ed. 44.95x (ISBN 0-8176-1165-7). Birkhauser.
Fenyo, Stefan & Stolle, Hans W. Theorie und Praxis der Linearen Integralaleichungen 4. 370p. (Ger.). 1984. text ed. 44.95 (ISBN 3-7643-1167-3). Birkhauser.
Fenyoe, I., jt. ed. see Chatterji, S.
Fenyves, E. & Haiman, O. Physical Principles of Nuclear Radiation Measurements. 1969. 86.50 (ISBN 0-12-253150-7). Acad Pr.
Fenzau, C. J., jt. auth. see Walters, Charles, Jr.
Fenzler, Otto, et al, eds. see Roseman, Mill.
Feofanov, Dmitry, ed. Rare Masterpieces of Russian Piano Music. (Music Scores & Music to Play Ser.). 144p. 1984. pap. 6.95 (ISBN 0-486-24659-0). Dover.
Fer, F. Thermodynamique Macroscopique, 2 Vols. (Fr). 1971. Vol. 1, 300p. 80.95 (ISBN 0-677-50300-8); Vol. 2, 248p. 69.50 (ISBN 0-677-50310-5). Gordon.
Fer, Hugo De see De Fer, Hugo.
Fer, Mehmet & Greco, F. Anthony, eds. Poorly Differentiated Neoplasms & Tumors of Unknown Origin. 1985. price not set (ISBN 0-8089-1755-2). Grune.
Feral, Rex. Hit Man: A Technical Manual for Independent Contractors. (Illus.). 144p. 1983. pap. 10.00 (ISBN 0-87364-276-7). Paladin Pr.
Feramisco, James, et al, eds. Cancer Cells Three: Growth Factors & Transformation. LC 85-3733. (Cancer Cells Ser.: Vol. 3). 460p. (Orig.). 1985. pap. 70.00 (ISBN 0-87969-178-6). Cold Spring Harbor.
Feraru, Anne T. International Conflict. (CISE Learning Package Ser.: No. 5). 67p. (Orig.). 1974. pap. text ed. 3.00x (ISBN 0-936876-22-0). Learn Res Intl Stud.
Feravolo, Rocco V. Junior Science Book of Water Experiments. LC 65-10450. (Jr. Science Ser.). (Illus.). (gr. 2-5). 1965. PLB 7.47 (ISBN 0-8116-6170-9). Garrard.
--Light. LC 61-5489. (Junior Science Ser.). (Illus.). (gr. 2-5). 1961. PLB 7.47 (ISBN 0-8116-6156-3). Garrard.
--Magnets. LC 60-12079. (Junior Science Bks.). (Illus.). (gr. 2-5). 1960. PLB 7.47 (ISBN 0-8116-6155-5). Garrard.
Feray, D. E. & Starnes, J. L. Index to Well Samples. rev. ed. (Pub Ser.: 5015). 148p. 1950. 1.65 (ISBN 0-686-29355-X, PUB 5015). Bur Econ Geology.
Ferazani, Larry. The Last Spartans. LC 85-71764. 185p. 1985. 10.95 (ISBN 0-933341-09-1). Quinlan Pr.
Ferbel, Thomas, ed. Techniques & Concepts of High-Energy Physics I. LC 81-13767. (NATO ASI Series B, Physics: Vol. 66). 554p. 1981. 79.50x (ISBN 0-306-40721-3, Plenum Pr). Plenum Pub.
--Techniques & Concepts of High-Energy Physics II. (NATO ASI Series B, Physics: Vol. 99). 350p. 1983. 49.50x (ISBN 0-306-41385-X, Plenum Pr). Plenum Pub.
Ferber. Solve Your Child's Sleep Problems. Date not set. 13.95. S&S.
Ferber, Al. Gus. 3.50 (ISBN 0-318-04450-1). Pudding.
Ferber, Andrew, et al. The Book of Family Therapy. 1973. pap. 10.95 (ISBN 0-395-17227-6, 77, SenEd). HM.
Ferber, Edna. American Beauty. 3.95 (ISBN 0-385-04014-8). Doubleday.
--American Beauty. 1977. pap. 1.95 (ISBN 0-449-22817-7, Crest). Fawcett.
--American Beauty. 13.95 (ISBN 0-88411-596-8, Pub. by Aeonian Pr). Amereon Ltd.
--Buttered Side Down. facsimile ed. LC 74-169546. (Short Story Index Reprint Ser.). Repr. of 1912 ed. 16.00 (ISBN 0-8369-4008-3). Ayer Co Pubs.

--Cheerful, by Request. facsimile ed. LC 78-169547. (Short Story Index Reprint Ser.). Repr. of 1918 ed. 20.00 (ISBN 0-8369-4009-1). Ayer Co Pubs.
--Cimarron. LC 30-8609. 1951. 14.95 (ISBN 0-385-04069-5). Doubleday.
--Cimarron. 1979. pap. 1.95 (ISBN 0-449-24114-9, Crest). Fawcett.
--Cimarron. 20.95 (ISBN 0-88411-548-8, Pub. by Aeonian Pr). Amereon Ltd.
--Emma McChesney & Co. facs. ed. LC 71-169548. (Short Story Index Reprint Ser.). (Illus.). Repr. of 1915 ed. 16.00 (ISBN 0-8369-4010-5). Ayer Co Pubs.
--Fanny Herself. facsimile ed. LC 74-27979. (Modern Jewish Experience Ser.). (Illus.). 1975. Repr. of 1917 ed. 29.00x (ISBN 0-405-06708-9). Ayer Co Pubs.
--Giant. 1979. pap. 1.95 (ISBN 0-449-24123-8, Crest). Fawcett.
--Gigolo. facsimile ed. LC 75-169549. (Short Story Index Reprint Ser.). Repr. of 1922 ed. 18.00 (ISBN 0-8369-4011-3). Ayer Co Pubs.
--Great Son. 1977. pap. 1.95 (ISBN 0-449-22956-4, Crest). Fawcett.
--Half Portions. facs. ed. LC 74-132115. (Short Story Index Reprint Ser). 1920. 16.00 (ISBN 0-8369-3672-8). Ayer Co Pubs.
--Ice Palace. LC 58-5936. 1958. 6.95 (ISBN 0-385-04799-1). Doubleday.
--Ice Palace. 1979. pap. 1.95 (ISBN 0-449-24124-6, Crest). Fawcett.
--Mother Knows Best. LC 77-110187. (Short Story Index Reprint Ser.). 1927. 17.00 (ISBN 0-8369-3338-9). Ayer Co Pubs.
--One Basket. LC 57-5531. 1957. 3.95. Doubleday.
--Personality Plus: Some Experiences of Emma McChesney & Her Son, Jock. facsimile ed. LC 77-150473. (Short Story Index Reprint Ser.). (Illus.). Repr. of 1914 ed. 15.00 (ISBN 0-8369-3813-5). Ayer Co Pubs.
--Roast Beef, Medium: The Business Adventures of Emma McChesney. facsimile ed. LC 70-169550. (Short Story Index Reprint Ser.). (Illus.). Repr. of 1913 ed. 18.00 (ISBN 0-8369-4012-1). Ayer Co Pubs.
--Saratoga Trunk. 1979. pap. 1.95 (ISBN 0-449-24115-7, Crest). Fawcett.
--Saratoga Trunk. 15.95 (ISBN 0-89190-323-2, Pub. by Am Repr). Amereon Ltd.
--Showboat. 256p. 1977. pap. 1.95 (ISBN 0-449-23191-7, Crest). Fawcett.
--So Big. 1978. pap. 1.95 (ISBN 0-449-23476-2, Crest). Fawcett.
--Spartacus. 19.95 (ISBN 0-88411-547-X, Pub. by Aeonian Pr). Amereon Ltd.
--They Brought Their Women. LC 70-110188. (Short Story Index Reprint Ser.). 1936. 17.00 (ISBN 0-8369-3339-7). Ayer Co Pubs.
Ferber, Ellen, jt. auth. see Fulton, Len.
Ferber, Ellen, jt. ed. see Fulton, Len.
Ferber, Linda S. The New Path Ruskin & the American Preraphaelites. (Illus.). 288p. 1985. pap. 29.95 (ISBN 0-8052-0780-5). Schocken.
--Tokens of a Friendship: Miniature Watercolors by William T. Richards. Hochfield, Sylvia, ed. (Illus.). 118p. (Orig.). 1982. pap. 14.95 (ISBN 0-87099-319-4). Metro Mus Art.
Ferber, Michael. The Social Vision of William Blake. 288p. 1985. text ed. 29.50x (ISBN 0-691-08382-7). Princeton U Pr.
Ferber, Nat J. Sidewalks of New York. LC 74-22781. Repr. of 1927 ed. 22.00 (ISBN 0-404-58428-4). AMS Pr.
Ferber, Richard. Solve Your Child's Sleep Problems. 212p. 1985. 15.95 (ISBN 0-671-46027-7). S&S.
Ferber, Robert. Handbook of Marketing Research. (Illus.). 1344p. 1974. 84.95 (ISBN 0-07-020462-4). McGraw.
--A Study of Aggregate Consumption Functions. 7.00 (ISBN 0-405-18755-6, 16467). Ayer Co Pubs.
Ferber, Robert & Hirsch, Werner Z. Social Experimentation & Economic Policy. LC 81-6146. (Cambridge Surveys of Economic Literature Ser.). (Illus.). 224p. 1981. 42.50 (ISBN 0-521-24185-5); pap. 14.95 (ISBN 0-521-28507-0). Cambridge U Pr.
Ferber, Robert, jt. auth. see Sudman, Seymour.
Ferber, Robert, ed. Motivation & Market Behavior. LC 75-39244. (Getting & Spending: the Consumer's Dilemma). (Illus.). 1976. Repr. of 1958 ed. 33.00x (ISBN 0-405-08018-2). Ayer Co Pubs.
--Readings in Survey Research. LC 78-14428. 1978. 13.00 (ISBN 0-87757-113-9). Am Mktg.
--Readings in the Analysis of Survey Data. LC 80-12975. 249p. (Orig.). 1980. pap. text ed. 24.00 (ISBN 0-87757-140-6). Am Mktg.
Ferber, Robert, et al. A Basic Bibliography on Marketing Research. rev. ed. LC 74-81449. (Bibliography Ser.: No. 2). 1974. pap. 11.00 (ISBN 0-87757-000-0). Am Mktg.
Ferber, Stanley, ed. Islam & the Medieval West. (Illus.). 1975. pap. 26.50x (ISBN 0-87395-802-0). State U NY Pr.
Ferch, Arthur. In the Beginning. Wheeler, Gerald, ed. 128p. (Orig.). 1985. pap. 5.95 (ISBN 0-8280-0282-7). Review & Herald.
Ferch, Arthur J. The Son of Man in Daniel Seven. (Andrews University Seminary Doctoral Dissertation Ser.: Vol. 6). x, 237p. 1983. pap. 9.95 (ISBN 0-943872-38-3). Andrews Univ Pr.
Ferchmin, A. R. & Kobe, S. Amorphous Magnetism & Metallic Magnetic Materials Digest. (Selected Topics in Solid State Physics Ser.: Vol. 17). 345p. 1984. 63.50 (ISBN 0-444-86532-2, North Holland). Elsevier.
Ferderber-Salz, Bertha. And the Sun Kept Shining. LC 80-81684. (Illus.). 240p. (Orig.). 1980. 13.95 (ISBN 0-89604-015-1); pap. 9.95 (ISBN 0-89604-017-8). Holocaust Pubns.
Ferdico. Maine Administrative Procedures. Date not set. price not set (ISBN 0-88063-051-5). Butterworth Legal Pubs.
Ferdico, John M. Criminal Procedure for the Law Enforcement Officer. 2nd ed. (Criminal Justice Ser.). (Illus.). 1979. text ed. 24.95 (ISBN 0-8299-0188-4). West Pub.
Ferdico, John N. Criminal Procedure for the Criminal Justice Professional. 3rd ed. 450p. 1985. text ed. 24.95 (ISBN 0-314-85234-4). West Pub.
Ferdinand, Theodore N., jt. auth. see Cavan, Ruth S.
Ferdinand, Theodore N., ed. Juvenile Delinquency: Little Brother Grows up. LC 77-81152. (Sage Research Progress Series in Criminology: Vol. 2). (Illus.). 160p. 1977. 20.00 (ISBN 0-8039-0916-0). Sage.
Ferdinand, W. The Enzyme Molecule. LC 76-7530. 1976. 58.95x (ISBN 0-471-01822-8, Pub. by Wiley-Interscience); pap. 27.95x (ISBN 0-471-01821-X). Wiley.
Ferdinande. Vacation in London. LC 82-91024. 1984. 12.50 (ISBN 0-533-05681-0). Vantage.
Ferdinandy, Georges. L' Oeuvre Hispanoamericaine de Zsigmond Remengik. (De Proprietatibus Litterarum, Series Practica: No. 86). 191p. (Fr.). 1975. pap. text ed. 18.40x (ISBN 90-2793-356-1). Mouton.
Ferdinandy, Magdalena De see Ferdinandy, Miguel De.
Ferdinandy, Miguel De. Carnaval y Revolucion y Diecinueve Ensayos Mas. De Ferdinandy, Magdalena, et al, trs. from Ger. Port. Hung. (Coleccion Mente y Palabra). (Span.). 1977. 6.25 (ISBN 0-8477-0544-7); pap. 5.00 (ISBN 0-8477-0545-5). U of PR Pr.
Ferdinandy, Miguel de see De Ferdinandy, Miguel.
Ferdman, S., ed. The Second Fifteen Years in Space. (Science & Technology Ser.: Vol. 31). 1973. lib. bdg. 25.00x (ISBN 0-87703-064-2, Pub. by Am Astronaut). Univelt Inc.
Ferdon, Edwin N. Early Tahiti As the Explorers Saw It, 1767-1797. LC 80-26469. 371p. 1981. text ed. 29.50x (ISBN 0-8165-0708-2); pap. 12.50x (ISBN 0-8165-0720-1). U of Ariz Pr.
Ferdowsi. The Epic of the Kings: Shah-Nama. (Persian Heritage Ser.). 1985. pap. 12.95x (ISBN 0-7102-0538-4). Routledge & Kegan.
Fere, Maud. Does Diet Cure Cancer. 5.95x (ISBN 0-7225-0170-6). Cancer Control Soc.
Ferebee, A. S., tr. see Ebbinghaus, H. D., et al.
Ferebee, Ann, ed. Education for Urban Design. (Urban Design Selections Ser.). 183p. 1982. pap. 20.00 (ISBN 0-942468-00-7). Inst Urban Des.
Ferebee, S. Scott, Jr., frwd. by. Award Winning Architecture USA. LC 73-78957. (Illus.). 208p. 1973. 25.00 (ISBN 0-912916-02-8). Foun Adv Artists.
Ferejohn, John A. Pork Barrel Politics: Rivers & Harbors Legislation, 1947-1968. LC 73-89859. 304p. 1974. 22.50x (ISBN 0-8047-0854-1). Stanford U Pr.
Ferenc, Mald. The Law of the European Economic Community. 1978. 23.00 (ISBN 0-9960009-9-2, Pub. by Akademiai Kaido Hungary). Heyden.
Ference, Michael, Jr., et al. Analytical Experimental Physics. 3rd ed. LC 55-5124. (Illus.). 1956. 17.50x (ISBN 0-226-24299-4). U of Chicago Pr.
Ference, Thomas P. & Stoner, James A. Career Development: A Plan for All Seasons. (Illus.). 1978. leader's guide 10.00 (ISBN 0-07-020452-7); wkbk 6.95 (ISBN 0-07-020451-9). McGraw.
Ferencz, B., jt. auth. see Mohilla, R.
Ferencz, Ben. Enforcing International Law: A Way to World Peace, A Documentary History & Analysis, 2 vols. LC 83-42858. 1983. lib. bdg. 90.00 set (ISBN 0-379-12147-6); Vol. 1. lib. bdg. 45.00 (ISBN 0-379-12148-4); Vol. 2, 890 in 2 vols. lib. bdg. 45.00 (ISBN 0-379-12149-2). Oceana.
Ferencz, Benjamin. An International Criminal Court: A Step Toward World Peace, 2 vols. LC 80-10688. 1212p. 1980. Vol. 1. lib. bdg. 75.00 set (ISBN 0-379-20389-8). Oceana.
Ferencz, Benjamin B. Defining International Aggression-the Search for World Peace: A Documentary History & Analysis, 2 vols. LC 75-16473. 1975. 90.00x set (ISBN 0-379-00271-X). Oceana.
--Less Than Slaves: Jewish Forced Labor & the Quest for Compensation. LC 79-10690. 1979. 16.50x (ISBN 0-674-52525-6). Harvard U Pr.
--Less Than Slaves: Jewish Forced Labor & the Quest for Compensation. 280p. 1982. pap. 5.95 (ISBN 0-674-52526-4). Harvard U Pr.
Ferenczi, Imre. International Migrations, Vol. I, Statistics. LC 77-129396. (American Immigration Collection, Ser. 2). 1970. Repr. of 1929 ed. 59.00 (ISBN 0-405-00550-4). Ayer Co Pubs.
Ferenczi, Sandor. The Development of Psychoanalysis. Date not set. price not set (BN#01197). Intl Univs Pr.
--Final Contributions to the Problems & Methods of Psycho-Analysis. Balint, Michael, ed. Mosbacher, Eric, tr. from Ger. LC 80-19817. (Brunner-Mazel Classics in Psychoanalysis Ser.: No. 8). 450p. 1980. Repr. of 1955 ed. 25.00 (ISBN 0-87630-256-8). Brunner-Mazel.
--First Contributions to Psycho-Analysis. Jones, Ernest, tr. from Ger. LC 80-19815. (Brunner-Mazel Classics in Psycholoanalysis Ser.: No. 6). Orig. Title: Sex in Psychoanalysis. 340p. 1980. Repr. 25.00 (ISBN 0-87630-254-1). Brunner-Mazel.
Ferenczy, L., ed. see International Protoplast Symposium, 5th, July 1979, Szeged, Hungary.
Ferendeci, A. M., jt. ed. see McDowell, M. R.
Ferentino, Joseph M., jt. auth. see Metzger, Norman.
Feret, Barbara L. Gastronomical & Culinary Literature: A Survey & Analysis of Historically-Oriented Collections in the U. S. A. LC 78-32098. 128p. 1979. lib. bdg. 15.00 (ISBN 0-8108-1204-5). Scarecrow.
Feret, Edouard. Bordeaux et Ses Vins. 1900p. (Fr.). 1982. 125.00 (ISBN 0-686-46608-X). French & Eur.
Ferge, Zsusza, tr. from Hungarian. A Society in the Making: Hungarian Social & Societal Policy Nineteen Forty-Five to Nineteen Seventy-Five. LC 80-80116. 288p. 1980. 30.00 (ISBN 0-87332-155-3). M E Sharpe.
Fergenson, Laraine, jt. auth. see Matthew, Marie-Louise.
Fergesen, J. E., jt. auth. see Goeldner, C. R.
Fergusson, E. Guatemala. 1977. lib. bdg. 59.95 (ISBN 0-8490-1910-9). Gordon Pr.
Fergus, Andrew. Burn's Scotland. 75p. 10.00x (ISBN 0-85158-129-3, Pub. by Blackwood & Sons England). State Mutual Bk.
Fergus, Hughes & Lloyd, Noppe. Human Development Across the Life Span: A Topical Approach. (Illus.). 650p. 1985. 26.95 (ISBN 0-314-85250-6). West Pub.
Fergus, Jan. Jane Austen & the Didactic Novel: "Northanger Abbey" "Sense & Sensibility" & "Pride & Prejudice". LC 81-12773. 172p. 1983. 28.50x (ISBN 0-389-20228-2, 07010). B&N Imports.
Fergus, Patricia M. Spelling Improvement: A Program for Self-Improvement. 4th ed. 256p. 1983. pap. text ed. 18.95 (ISBN 0-07-020476-4). McGraw.
Ferguson. Advanced Medicine-Twenty. 374p. 1984. 45.00 (ISBN 0-272-79773-1, Pub. by Pitman Bks Ltd UK). Urban & S.
--Criminal Offenses in South Carolina. incl. latest pocket part supplement 54.95 (ISBN 0-686-90971-2); separate pocket part supplement 1984 15.95. Harrison Co GA.
--Introduction to Physiology for Dental Students. 1986. price not set. PSG Pub Co.
--Readings on Concepts of Criminal Law. (Criminal Justice Ser.). 1975. pap. text ed. 20.95 (ISBN 0-8299-0619-3). West Pub.
--Young Widow. 12.00 (ISBN 0-405-13935-7). Ayer Co Pubs.
Ferguson & Adams. Guide to the Antique Shops of Great Britain 1985. (Illus.). 1984. 16.00 (ISBN 0-907462-67-7). Antique Collect.
--Guide to the Antique Shops of Great Britain 1986. (Illus.). 1985. 16.00 (ISBN 0-907462-81-2). Antique Collect.
Ferguson, ed. see Laurence Urdang Associates, Ltd.
Ferguson, A., ed. Natural Philosophy Through the 18th Century & Allied Topics. 172p. 1972. 22.00x (ISBN 0-85066-055-6). Taylor & Francis.
Ferguson, A. B. & Bender, Jay. ABC's of Athletic Injuries & Conditioning. LC 64-18772. 262p. 1970. Repr. of 1964 ed. 9.95 (ISBN 0-88275-017-8). Krieger.
Ferguson, Adam. An Essay on the History of Civil Society. LC 79-64856. (Social Science Classic Ser.). 327p. 1980. 29.95 (ISBN 0-87855-314-2); pap. text ed. 9.95 (ISBN 0-87855-696-6). Transaction Bks.
--Institutes of Moral Philosophy. 2nd rev. ed. LC 75-11219. (British Philosophers & Theologians of the 17th & 18th Centuries Ser.: Vol. 22). 1978. Repr. of 1773 ed. lib. bdg. 51.00 (ISBN 0-8240-1773-0). Garland Pub.
--Principles of Moral & Political Science, 2 Vols. LC 71-147970. Repr. of 1792 ed. Set. 85.00 (ISBN 0-404-08222-X). AMS Pr.
--Principles of Moral & Political Science, 2 vols. Wellek, Rene, ed. LC 75-11218. (British Philosophers & Theologians of the 17th & 18th Centuries Ser.: Vol. 21). 1978. Repr. of 1792 ed. Set. lib. bdg. 101.00 (ISBN 0-8240-1772-2). Garland Pub.
Ferguson, Albert. Orthopaedic Surgery in Infancy & Childhood. 5th ed. (Illus.). 960p. 1981. 85.00 (ISBN 0-683-03167-8). Williams & Wilkins.
Ferguson, Alfred E., et al, eds. see Emerson, Ralph Waldo.
Ferguson, Alfred R. see Emerson, Ralph Waldo.
Ferguson, Alfred R., ed. see Emerson, Ralph Waldo.
Ferguson, Alfred R., jt. ed. see Sealts, Merton M., Jr.
Ferguson, Allen. Comments on Proposed Five-Year Plan for Motor Vehicle Safety & Fuel Economy. 50p. 4.00 (ISBN 0-318-16251-2, B-26). Public Int Econ.
--Economic Impact Analysis of the Proposed OSHA Occupational Noise Regulation. 51p. 4.50 (ISBN 0-318-16260-1, C13). Public Int Econ.
--Hospital Capacity in Somerville. 178p. 14.50 (ISBN 0-318-16277-6, C-4); exec. summary 2.00 (ISBN 0-318-16278-4). Public Int Econ.
--The Potential Economic Benefits of Consumer Education. 61p. 5.00 (ISBN 0-318-16293-8, A-14). Public Int Econ.
--Uniformity in Regulatory Analysis. 97p. 6.80 (ISBN 0-318-16311-X, A-26). Public Int Econ.
--Verified Statement on the Union Pacific-Missouri Pacific & Union Pacific-Western Pacific Consolidations. 54p. 5.70 (ISBN 0-318-16314-4, B-44). Public Int Econ.
Ferguson, Allen & Cook, Zena. The Context of Urban Transportation Policy. 86p. 7.00 (ISBN 0-318-16254-7, B-28). Public Int Econ.
Ferguson, Allen & Snow, Arthur. Variance from Air Quality Regulations: The Criteria for the Grant-Deny Decision. 123p. 10.00 (ISBN 0-318-16313-6, C-2). Public Int Econ.
Ferguson, Allen, jt. auth. see Booth, James.
Ferguson, Allen, jt. auth. see Sumner, Jason.
Ferguson, Allen, jt. auth. see Westernik, Gregory.
Ferguson, Allen, ed. Attacking Regulatory Problems: An Agenda for Research in the 1980's. 256p. 1981. 22.50 (ISBN 0-318-16244-X). Public Int Econ.
--The Benefits of Health & Safety Regulation. 296p. 1981. 26.50 (ISBN 0-318-16247-4). Public Int Econ.
Ferguson, Allen R., ed. see Public Interest Economics Foundation.
Ferguson, Allen R., ed. see Public Interest Economics Foundation, et al.
Ferguson, Andrew. Biochemical Systematics & Evolution. LC 79-20298. 194p. 1980. 64.95x (ISBN 0-470-26856-5). Halsted Pr.
Ferguson, Anne, ed. Advanced Medicine. (Advanced Medicine Ser.: No. 20). 374p. 1984. text ed. 45.00 (ISBN 0-272-79773-1, Pitman Med UK). Urban & S.
Ferguson, Anthony. Annual Review of English Books on Asia: 1976-77. pap. 56.00 (ISBN 0-317-10691-0, 2010359). Bks Demand UMI.
Ferguson, Arthur B. Clio Unbound: Perception of the Social & Cultural Past in Renaissance England. LC 78-67198. (Monographs in Medieval & Renaissance Studies: No. 2). xv, 442p. 1979. 27.75 (ISBN 0-8223-0417-1). Duke.
--The Indian Summer of English Chivalry: Studies in the Decline & Transformation of Chivalric Idealism. LC 78-63497. (Chivalry Ser.). 267p. Repr. of 1960 ed. 32.50 (ISBN 0-404-17145-1). AMS Pr.
--The Indian Summer of English Chivalry: Studies in the Decline & Transformation of Chivalric Idealism. LC 60-8743. pap. 65.00 (ISBN 0-317-08920-X, 2015267). Bks Demand UMI.
Ferguson, Barbara. The Paper Doll: A Collector's Guide with Prices. (Illus.). 151p. pap. 14.95 (ISBN 0-87069-401-4). Wallace-Homestead.
Ferguson, Barbara J., ed. see Ortho Books Staff.
Ferguson, Ben. God, I've Got a Problem. LC 74-80778. (Orig.). 1974. pap. 1.95 (ISBN 0-88449-007-6, A324217). Vision Hse.
Ferguson, Bill & Wonstolen, Ken. A Legislator's Guide to Small-Scale Hydroelectric Development. 50p. 1980. 5.00 (ISBN 0-317-36327-1). Natl Conf State Legis.
Ferguson, Bruce. Canada Video. (Illus.). 112p. 1980. 10.95 (ISBN 0-88884-442-5, 56311-1, Pub. by Natl Mus Canada). U of Chicago Pr.
Ferguson, Bruce, et al. Fly Fishing for Salmon. (Illus.). 120p. 1985. write for info. (ISBN 0-936608-36-6); pap. 17.95 (ISBN 0-936608-35-8). F Amato Pubns.
Ferguson, Bruce K. Index to Landscape Architecture Magazine: 1910-1982. 312p. 1983. pap. 35.00 (ISBN 0-914886-24-X). PDA Pubs.
Ferguson, C., jt. auth. see Snow, Catherine.
Ferguson, C. A., et al, eds. Language in the U. S. A. 650p. 1981. 44.50 (ISBN 0-521-23140-X); pap. 16.95 (ISBN 0-521-29834-2). Cambridge U Pr.
Ferguson, C. E. Neoclassical Theory of Production & Distribution. (Illus.). 1969. 32.50 (ISBN 0-521-07453-3). Cambridge U Pr.
Ferguson, C. E., jt. auth. see Gould, J. P.
Ferguson, Charles A. Language Structure & Language Use: Essays by Charles A. Ferguson. Dil, Anwar S., ed. LC 79-150322. (Language Science & National Development Ser). xiv, 323p. 1971. 27.50x (ISBN 0-8047-0780-4). Stanford U Pr.
Ferguson, Charles A., et al see Sebeok, Thomas A.
Ferguson, Charles B. & Ferguson, Charles B. An Illustrated Catalogue of Known Portraits by Jared B. Flagg, 1820-1899. LC 72-75449. (Illus.). 64p. 1972. pap. 4.00 (ISBN 0-917482-00-X). Stowe-Day.
Ferguson, Charles D. The Experiences of a Forty-Niner in California. Wallace, Frederick T., ed. LC 72-9442. (The Far Western Frontier Ser.). Orig. Title: The Experiences of a Forty-Niner During Thirty-Four Years' Residence in California & Australia. (Illus.). 242p. 1973. Repr. of 1888 ed. 19.00 (ISBN 0-405-04971-4). Ayer Co Pubs.

Ferguson, Charles E. Macroeconomic Theory of Workable Competition. LC 64-11624. Repr. of 1964 ed. 59.30 (ISBN 0-8357-9111-4, 2017902). Bks Demand UMI.

Ferguson, Charles W. Fifty Million Brothers: A Panorama of American Lodges & Clubs. LC 71-125596. 1979. Repr. of 1937 ed. lib. bdg. 26.00x (ISBN 0-8371-5188-0, FMB&). Greenwood.

--Methodists & the Making of America. Orig. Title: Organizing to Beat the Devil. 480p. 1983. 14.95 (ISBN 0-89015-424-4); pap. 9.95 (ISBN 0-89015-405-8). Eakin Pubns.

--Say It with Words. LC 59-8085. x, 219p. 1969. pap. 4.95x (ISBN 0-8032-5058-4, BB 395, Bison). U of Nebr Pr.

Ferguson, Charles W., compiled by. Great Themes of the Christian Faith, As Presented by G. C. Morgan. facs. ed. LC 68-58788. (Essay Index Reprint Ser). 1930. 17.50 (ISBN 0-8369-1034-6). Ayer Co Pubs.

Ferguson, Clara P. Pre-Adolescent Children's Attitudes Toward Television Commercials. new ed. LC 74-22989. (Studies in Marketing: No. 21). (Illus.). 60p. (Orig.). 1974. pap. 5.00 (ISBN 0-87755-201-0). Bureau Busn UT.

Ferguson, Clarence C., Jr., jt. auth. see Blaustein, Albert P.

Ferguson, Colin R. Internal Combustion Engines: Applied Thermosciences. 560p. Date not set. 36.00 (ISBN 0-471-88129-5). Wiley.

Ferguson, D., tr. see Cyzevs'Kyj, Dmytro.

Ferguson, D. B., ed. The Environment of the Teeth. (Frontiers of Oral Physiology: Vol. 3). (Illus.). x, 174p. 1982. 48.75 (ISBN 3-8055-2577-X). S Karger.

--Steroid Hormones in Saliva. (Frontiers of Oral Physiology: Vol. 5). (Illus.). x, 162p. 1984. 69.00 (ISBN 3-8055-3848-0). S Karger.

Ferguson, D. R., tr. see Lembeck, F., et al.

Ferguson, Dale, jt. auth. see Giblin, James.

Ferguson, Dale V., jt. auth. see Buffaloe, Neal D.

Ferguson, David. Tracts. Laing, David, ed. LC 70-168016. (Bannatyne Club, Edinburgh. Publications: No. 110). Repr. of 1860 ed. 20.00 (ISBN 0-404-52864-3). AMS Pr.

Ferguson, David M., ed. The Wrecks of Scapa Flow. 80p. 25.00x (ISBN 0-907618-06-5, Pub. by Orkney Pr Uk). State Mutual Bk.

Ferguson, De Lancey, ed. see Burns, Robert.

Ferguson, DeLancey. Mark Twain, Man & Legend. LC 66-15430. (Illus.). 1966. Repr. of 1943 ed. 18.00x (ISBN 0-8462-0744-3). Russell.

Ferguson, Denzel & Ferguson, Nancy. Oregon's Great Basin Country. (Illus.). 216p. (Orig.). 1979. pap. 8.95 (ISBN 0-89288-033-3). Maverick.

Ferguson, Denzel, jt. auth. see Ferguson, Nancy.

Ferguson, Don. Love Is Always Losing at Tennis. (Illus., Orig.). 1976. pap. 2.95 (ISBN 0-8431-0404-X). Price Stern.

Ferguson, Donald N. A History of Musical Thought. LC 73-5265. 675p. 1975. Repr. of 1959 ed. lib. bdg. 38.75x (ISBN 0-8371-6882-1, FEMT). Greenwood.

--Image & Structure in Chamber Music. LC 77-5586. (Music Reprint Ser.). 1977. Repr. of 1964 ed. lib. bdg. 37.50 (ISBN 0-306-77415-1). Da Capo.

--Image & Structure in Chamber Music. LC 64-18652. pap. 87.30 (ISBN 0-317-09626-5, 2000812). Bks Demand UMI.

--Masterworks of the Orchestral Repertoire: A Guide for Listeners. LC 54-12315. (Illus.). 1968. 15.00x (ISBN 0-8166-0461-4); pap. 5.95 (ISBN 0-8166-0467-3, MP14). U of Minn Pr.

--Music As Metaphor: The Elements of Expression. LC 73-9210. (Illus.). 198p. 1973. Repr. of 1960 ed. lib. bdg. 15.00x (ISBN 0-8371-6981-X, FEMM). Greenwood.

--Piano Music of Six Great Composers. facs. ed. LC 73-111830. (Essay Index Reprint Ser). 1947. 24.50 (ISBN 0-8369-1652-2). Ayer Co Pubs.

--A Short History of Music. LC 73-5266. (Illus.). 500p. 1974. Repr. of 1946 ed. lib. bdg. 22.50x (ISBN 0-8371-6881-3, FEHM). Greenwood.

Ferguson, Dorothy. Black Duck. LC 77-77543. (Illus.). (gr. 1-3). 1978. 6.95 (ISBN 0-8027-6296-4); PLB 6.85 (ISBN 0-8027-6297-2). Walker & Co.

Ferguson, E. James. Power of the Purse: A History of American Public Finance. (Institute of Early American History & Culture Ser.). xvii, 358p. Repr. of 1961 ed. 27.50x (ISBN 0-8078-0804-0). U of NC Pr.

Ferguson, E. James, jt. auth. see Catanzariti, John.

Ferguson, E. James & Catanzariti, John, eds. The Papers of Robert Morris, 1781-1784, Vol. 1: February 7 - July 31, 1781. LC 72-91107. (Robert Morris Papers Ser.). (Illus.). 1973. 26.00x (ISBN 0-8229-3267-9). U of Pittsburgh Pr.

--The Papers of Robert Morris, 1781-1784, Vol. 2: August-September 1781. LC 72-91107. (Robert Morris Papers Ser.). (Illus.). 1975. 25.00x (ISBN 0-8229-3297-0). U of Pittsburgh Pr.

--The Papers of Robert Morris, 1781-1784, Vol. 3: October 1, 1781-January 10, 1782. LC 72-91107. (Robert Morris Papers Ser). (Illus.). 1977. 26.00x (ISBN 0-8229-3324-1). U of Pittsburgh Pr.

--The Papers of Robert Morris, 1781-1784, Vol. 4: January 11-April 15, 1782. LC 72-91107. (Robert Morris Papers Ser). 1978. 37.00x (ISBN 0-8229-3352-7). U of Pittsburgh Pr.

--The Papers of Robert Morris, 1781-1784: Vol. 5; April 16-July 20, 1782. LC 72-91107. (Robert Morris Papers Ser.). 1980. 36.00x (ISBN 0-8229-3420-5). U of Pittsburgh Pr.

Ferguson, E. James, compiled by. Confederation, Constitution, & Early National Period, 1781-1815. LC 74-76969. (Goldentree Bibliographies in American History Ser). (Orig.). 1975. pap. 13.95x (ISBN 0-88295-534-9). Harlan Davidson.

Ferguson, Edith P. The Eighteen Fifty Federal Census: Provincetown, Barnstable Co., Mass. vi, 145p. 1983. pap. 17.50 (ISBN 0-917890-27-2). Heritage Bk.

--The Eighteen Sixty Federal Census: Provincetown, Barnstable County, Massachusetts. iv, 122p. 1984. pap. 16.00 (ISBN 0-917890-52-3). Heritage Bk.

--The Seventeen Ninety to Eighteen Forty Censuses: Provincetown, Barnstable Co., Mass. iv, 123p. 1983. pap. 16.00 (ISBN 0-917890-26-4). Heritage Bk.

Ferguson, Elizabeth R. & Mobley, Emily. Special Libraries at Work. 216p. 1984. 21.50 (ISBN 0-208-01939-1, Lib Prof Pubns); pap. 14.50x (ISBN 0-208-01938-3). Shoe String.

Ferguson, Estelle & Barbaresi, Sara M. How to Raise & Train a Chihuahua. pap. 2.95 (ISBN 0-87666-266-1, DS-1008). TFH Pubns.

Ferguson, Eugene S. Oliver Evans: Inventive Genius of the Industrial Revolution. 72p. 1980. pap. 4.95 (ISBN 0-914650-18-1). Eleutherian Mills-Hagley.

--Truxtun of the Constellation. LC 81-18734. 340p. 1982. 12.95 (ISBN 0-87021-712-7). Naval Inst Pr.

--Truxtun of the Constellation. Michener, James A., frwd. by. 340p. 1982. Repr. of 1956 ed. 12.95 (ISBN 0-87021-712-7); bulk rates avail. Naval Inst Pr.

Ferguson, Eva D. Motivation: An Experimental Approach. LC 82-6559. 470p. 1982. Repr. of 1976 ed. 28.50 (ISBN 0-89874-512-8). Krieger.

Ferguson, Everett. A Cappella Music in the Public Workshop of the Church. LC 72-76963. (Way of Life Ser: No. 125). 1972. pap. text ed. 3.95 (ISBN 0-89112-125-0). Bibl Res Pr.

--Church History, Early & Medieval. 2nd ed. (Way of Life Ser: No. 106). (Orig.). 1966. pap. 3.95 (ISBN 0-89112-106-4). Bibl Res Pr.

--Church History, Reformation & Modern. (Way of Life Ser: No. 107). 1967. pap. 3.95 (ISBN 0-89112-107-2). Bibl Res Pr.

--Demonology of the Early Christian World. LC 84-16681. (Symposium Ser.: Vol. 12). 190p. 1985. 19.95 (ISBN 0-88946-703-X). E Mellen.

--Early Christians Speak. LC 81-68871. 258p. 1981. pap. text ed. 9.95 (ISBN 0-89112-044-0). Bibl Res Pr.

--Message of the New Testament: The Letters of John. (Way of Life Ser.: No. 175). 1984. pap. 3.95 (ISBN 0-89112-175-7). Bibl Res Pr.

--The New Testament Church. LC 68-55790. (Way of Life Ser: No. 108). 1968. pap. 3.95 (ISBN 0-89112-108-0). Bibl Res Pr.

Ferguson, Frances. Wordsworth: Language As Counter-Spirit. LC 76-49932. 1977. 27.00x (ISBN 0-300-02063-5). Yale U Pr.

Ferguson, Francis. Architecture, Cities, & the Systems Approach. LC 74-80660. (Illus.). 192p. 1975. 15.00 (ISBN 0-8076-0763-0); pap. 5.95 (ISBN 0-8076-0764-9). Braziller.

--The Human Image in Dramatic Literature: Essays. 11.25 (ISBN 0-8446-0620-0). Peter Smith.

Ferguson, Frank L. Efficient Drug Store Management. LC 69-17524. (Illus.). 1969. 12.50 (ISBN 0-87005-012-5). Fairchild.

Ferguson, Franklin C. A Pilgrimage in Faith: An Introduction to the Episcopal Church. rev. ed. LC 75-5220. 180p. (Orig.). 1979. pap. 5.95 (ISBN 0-8192-1277-6). Morehouse.

Ferguson, Gary. Freewheeling: Bicycling the Open Road. (Illus.). 204p. (Orig.). 1984. pap. 8.95 (ISBN 0-89886-047-4). Mountaineers.

Ferguson, Gary G. Pathophysiology: Mechanisms & Expressions. (Illus.). 1984. Pp. 400. pap. 24.95 (ISBN 0-7216-3616-0); Pp. 112. student manual 9.95 (ISBN 0-7216-3617-9). Saunders.

Ferguson, George. Britain by Britrail, 1985-1986. 5th ed. (Compleat Traveler Ser.). (Illus.). 320p. (Orig.). 1985. pap. 7.95 (ISBN 0-89102-316-X). B Franklin.

--Europe by Eurail, 1985-1986. 10th ed. (Compleat Traveler Ser.). (Illus.). 640p. (Orig.). 1985. pap. 8.95 (ISBN 0-89102-314-3). B Franklin.

--Signs & Symbols in Christian Art. (Illus.). 1966. pap. 7.95 (ISBN 0-19-501432-4, GB). Oxford U Pr.

Ferguson, George A. Nonparametric Trend Analysis. LC 65-13086. pap. 20.00 (ISBN 0-317-26489-3, 2023830). Bks Demand UMI.

--Statistical Analysis in Psychology & Education. 5th, rev. ed. LC 80-19584. (Psychology Ser.). (Illus.). 560p. 1981. text ed. 31.95x (ISBN 0-07-020482-9). McGraw.

Ferguson, George O. Psychology of the Negro: An Experimental Study. LC 74-107481. Repr. of 1916 ed. 17.50x (ISBN 0-8371-3783-7, FEP&). Greenwood.

Ferguson, George W. Britain by BritRail: How to Tour Britain by Train. 5th ed. Ferguson, LaVerne, ed. (Illus.). 6.95 (ISBN 0-89102-300-3). B Franklin.

--Europe by Eurail: How to Tour Europe by Train. 10th ed. Ferguson, LaVerne, ed. 8.95 (ISBN 0-89102-298-8). B Franklin.

Ferguson, Giovonnia. Handling Small Pets: Step by Step. 1979. 4.00 (ISBN 0-682-49209-4). Exposition Pr FL.

Ferguson, H. L. & Znamensky, V. A., eds. Methods of Computation of the Water Balance of Large Lakes & Reservoirs: Methodology, Vol. 1. (Studies & Reports in Hydrology: No. 31). (Illus.). 120p. (A Contribution to the International Hydrogeological Programme). 1981. pap. 12.25 (ISBN 92-3-101906-6, U1107, UNESCO). Unipub.

Ferguson, Harvie. Essays in Experimental Psychology. (Edinburgh Studies in Sociology). 193p. 1983. text ed. 30.50x (ISBN 0-333-28113-6, Pub by Macmillan England). Humanities.

Ferguson, Helen S. Bring on the Puppets. LC 75-5217. (Illus.). 40p. (Orig.). (gr. k-6). 1975. pap. 4.95 (ISBN 0-8192-1195-8). Morehouse.

Ferguson, Henry. Essays in American History. LC 68-26266. 1969. Repr. of 1894 ed. 19.50x (ISBN 0-8046-0144-5, Pub. by Kennikat). Assoc Faculty Pr.

--Manual for Multi-Cultural & Ethnics Studies. 135p. 49.00 (ISBN 0-317-35817-0, 303). Soc Intercult Ed Train & Res.

Ferguson, Henry L. Fishers Island N. Y., Sixteen Fourteen to Nineteen Twenty-Five. LC 74-17359. (Illus.). 160p. 1974. Repr. of 1925 ed. 15.00 (ISBN 0-916346-11-0). Harbor Hill Bks.

Ferguson, Howard. Keyboard Interpretation from the 14th to the 19th Century: An Introduction. (Music examples). 1975. pap. 11.75x (ISBN 0-19-318419-2). Oxford U Pr.

Ferguson, Howard, jt. auth. see Morris, Reginald O.

Ferguson, Howard, jt. ed. see Lassimonne, Denise.

Ferguson, Howard E. The Edge. (Illus.). 340p. 1983. text ed. 29.95 (ISBN 0-9611180-0-8). H E Ferguson.

Ferguson, Hugh. Superstocks. 1979. 25.00 (ISBN 0-685-49183-8). Windsor.

Ferguson, I. Fantastic Experiences of a Half-Blind & His Interracial Marriage. 1st. ed. LC 81-82422. 520p. 1982. 12.50 (ISBN 0-686-81214-X). Lunan-Ferguson.

Ferguson, I. K. & Muller, J., eds. The Evolutionary Significance of the Exine. (Linnean Society Symposia Ser.: No. 1). 1976. 94.00 (ISBN 0-12-253650-9). Acad Pr.

Ferguson, Ira L. Eighty-Three Practical Philosophical Observations by an Octogenarian Psychologist: An Objective, Frank, Lively, Insightful Discussion of Eighty-Three Timely & Much Discussed Topics. LC 84-81001. 1985. 16.95 (ISBN 0-317-19613-8). Lunan-Ferguson.

--Facing Reality-Functional Blueprint for Living. LC 77-78235. 1977. lib. bdg. 5.45x (ISBN 0-911724-12-5). Lunan-Ferguson.

Ferguson, J. Some Aspects of Bibliography. 1976. lib. bdg. 59.95 (ISBN 0-8490-2624-5). Gordon Pr.

Ferguson, J. G., jt. auth. see Berry, C.

Ferguson, J. Homer. Mammalian Physiology. 544p. 1985. text ed. 34.95 (ISBN 0-675-20384-8). Merrill.

Ferguson, J. M., Jr. The Summerfield Stories. LC 84-16443. 128p. 1985. 14.95 (ISBN 0-87565-000-7); pap. 8.95 (ISBN 0-87565-010-4). Tex Christian.

Ferguson, J. Ray. Air Law, a Selected Bibliography of Articles, 1970-1980. LC 82-202707. (Washington University Law Library Bibliography Ser.: No. 2). 52p. 1982. pap. text ed. 7.50. Wash U Law Lib.

Ferguson, J. Ray, compiled by. Consumer Law - A Selected Bibliography of Articles, 1969-1980. LC 82-202672. (Washington University Law Library Bibliography Ser.: No. 1). vi, 88p. (Orig.). 1982. pap. text ed. 7.50 (ISBN 0-318-01098-4). Wash U Law Lib.

Ferguson, J. Ray, ed. see Reams, Bernard J., Jr.

Ferguson, J. T. & Berry, S. G. The Professional Real Estate Investment Guidebook. LC 81-12912. 1982. text ed. 16.95 (ISBN 0-201-04074-3). Addison-Wesley.

Ferguson, James. The Clan & Name of Ferguson. 32p. 4.50 (ISBN 0-912951-17-6). Scotpr.

--The Compelling Design of Aegyptian, Assyrian & Judean Architecture. (The Masterpieces of World Architecture Library). (Illus.). 145p. 1982. Repr. of 1885 ed. 156.45 (ISBN 0-89901-077-6). Found Class Reprints.

--English Medieval Architecture. (Illus.). 168p. 1984. 117.75 (ISBN 0-86650-116-9). Gloucester Art.

--Fortunes. (Orig.). 1982. pap. 3.95 (ISBN 0-440-12765-3). Dell.

--Student Council Projects. Lucas, Patricia, ed. 104p. 1982. pap. 8.00 (ISBN 0-88210-133-1). Natl Assn Principals.

--The Table in a Roar, Or, If You've Heard It, Try to Stop Me. 303p. 1980. Repr. of 1933 ed. lib. bdg. 15.00 (ISBN 0-8495-1703-6). Arden Lib.

Ferguson, James & Taylor, Craig, eds. The Comprehensive Handbook of Behavioral Medicine, 3 vols. Incl. Vol. 1: Systems Intervention. 364p. 1980 (ISBN 0-89335-078-8); Vol. 2: Syndromes & Special Areas. 308p. 1981 (ISBN 0-89335-111-3); Vol. 3: Extended Applications & Issues. (Illus.). 361p. 1980. text ed. 32.50 ea. (ISBN 0-89335-112-1); 80.00 set (ISBN 0-686-86752-1). LC 79-24021. (Illus.). text ed. 30.00 ea.; 75.00 set. SP Med & Sci Bks.

Ferguson, James G., jt. auth. see Hall, William B.

Ferguson, James M. Habits, Not Diets: The Real Way to Weight Control. LC 76-4098. 1976. pap. 8.95 (ISBN 0-915950-06-5). Bull Pub.

--Learning to Eat: Behavior Modification for Weight Control. 1975. pap. 7.95 student manual (ISBN 0-915950-02-2); leaders' manual 6.95 (ISBN 0-915950-01-4). Bull Pub.

--Public Debt & Future Generations. LC 82-2966. viii, 234p. 1982. Repr. of 1964 ed. lib. bdg. 30.00x (ISBN 0-313-23537-6, FEPU). Greenwood.

Ferguson, James M. & Taylor, C. Barr. A Change for Heart: Your Family & the Food You Eat. 1978. pap. 5.95 (ISBN 0-915950-22-7). Bull Pub.

Ferguson, Jean & Solomon, Rowena. A Toddler in the Family: A Practical Australian Guide for Parents. LC 84-3499. (Illus.). 137p. 1985. pap. 12.95 (ISBN 0-7022-1737-9). U of Queensland Pr.

Ferguson, Jeanne & Miller, Maria B. You're Speaking-Who's Listening? 1980. pap. text ed. 12.95 (ISBN 0-574-22560-9, 13-5560); instr's guide avail. (ISBN 0-574-22561-7, 13-5561). SRA.

Ferguson, Jerry T. Fundamentals of Real Estate Investing. 1984. text ed. 23.80 (ISBN 0-673-15870-5). Scott F.

Ferguson, Jerry T., et al. Real Estate Investment & Management. 1985. pap. 19.95 (ISBN 0-673-15998-1). Scott F.

Ferguson, John. Aristotle. (World Authors Ser.). lib. bdg. 13.50 (ISBN 0-8057-2064-2, Twayne). G K Hall.

--The Arts in Britain in World War I. 137p. 1981. 40.00x (ISBN 0-85249-548-X, Pub. by Stainer & Bell England). State Mutual Bk.

--The Arts in Britain in World War One. (Illus.). 131p. 1980. 26.50x (ISBN 0-8476-6262-4). Rowman.

--Bibliographical Notes on Histories & Inventions & Books of Secrets, 2 vols. in 1. 1983. 60.00 (ISBN 0-87556-494-1). Saifer.

--Biblioteca Chimica; Catalog of the Alchemical & Pharmaceutical Books in the Library of James Young, 2 vols. 1100p. 125.00 (ISBN 0-87556-493-3). Saifer.

--Bibliotheca Chemica: A Catalogue of the Alchemical, Chemical & Pharmaceutical Books in the Collection of the Late James Young of Kelly & Furris, 2 vols. LC 79-8610. Repr. of 1906 ed. 98.50 set (ISBN 0-404-18472-3). AMS Pr.

--Callimachus. (World Authors Ser.). 1980. lib. bdg. 16.95 (ISBN 0-8057-6431-3, Twayne). G K Hall.

--A Companion to Greek Tragedy. LC 74-38380. Repr. of 1972 ed. 120.00 (ISBN 0-8357-9768-6, 2051580). Bks Demand UMI.

--Death Comes to Perigord. 292p. 1983. pap. 5.95 (ISBN 0-486-24434-2). Dover.

--Definitive Quotations. 39p. 1981. pap. 2.95 (ISBN 0-930454-09-X). Verbatim Bks.

--Disarmament: The Unanswerable Case. 112p. 1982. pap. 8.95 (ISBN 0-434-25707-9, Pub by W Heinemann Ltd). David & Charles.

--Encyclopedia of Mysticism & Mystery Religions. (Crossroad Paperback Ser.). (Illus.). 228p. 1982. pap. 9.95 (ISBN 0-8245-0429-1). Crossroad NY.

--Gods Many, Lords Many. 128p. 1982. 39.00x (ISBN 0-7188-2496-2, Pub. by Lutterworth Pr England). State Mutual Bk.

--Moral Values in the Ancient World. Vlastos, Gregory, ed. LC 78-19348. (Morals & Law in Ancient Greece Ser.). 1979. Repr. of 1958 ed. lib. bdg. 19.00x (ISBN 0-405-11542-3). Ayer Co Pubs.

--Pelagius: A Historical & Theological Study. LC 77-84700. Repr. of 1956 ed. 20.00 (ISBN 0-404-16107-3). AMS Pr.

--The Place of Suffering. 137p. 1972. 11.50 (ISBN 0-227-67803-6). Attic Pr.

--The Religions of the Roman Empire. LC 71-110992. (Aspects of Greek & Roman Life Ser). (Illus.). 256p. 1970. 27.50x (ISBN 0-8014-0567-X). Cornell U Pr.

--The Religions of the Roman Empire. LC 71-110992. (Aspects of Greek & Roman Life Ser.). (Illus.). 296p. (Orig.). 1985. 29.95x (ISBN 0-8014-0567-X); pap. text ed. 8.95x (ISBN 0-8014-9311-0). Cornell U Pr.

--Some Aspects of Bibliography. 1978. 25.00 (ISBN 0-685-27170-6). Battery Pk.

--Some Aspects of Bibliography. Lew, Irving, ed. (Bibliographical Reprint Ser.). 1980. Repr. of 1900 ed. text ed. 25.00 ltd. ed. (ISBN 0-89782-004-5). Battery Pk.

--War & Peace in the World's Religions. 1978. pap. 5.95 (ISBN 0-19-520074-8, GB 557). Oxford U Pr.

Ferguson, John & McHenry, Dean. The American Federal Government. 14th ed. Munson, Eric M., ed. 592p. 1981. text ed. 30.95 (ISBN 0-07-020527-2). McGraw.

Ferguson, John, jt. auth. see Chisolm, Kitty.

Ferguson, John, jt. auth. see Johansen, Robert.

Ferguson, John, jt. auth. see Lawrence, Joy.

Ferguson, John, ed. Plato: Republic, Bk. X. (Classical Texts Ser.). 192p. pap. 9.95x (ISBN 0-904679-14-4). Basil Blackwell.

--Political & Social Life in the Great Age of Athens: Open University Course Reader. Chisholm, Kitty. 280p. 1981. 35.00x (ISBN 0-686-79498-2, Pub. by Ward Lock Ed England). State Mutual Bk.

Ferguson, John & Nelson, William, eds. The United Church of Christ Hymnal. LC 74-12571. 1974. spiral bound 12.50x (ISBN 0-8298-0300-9). Pilgrim NY.

Ferguson, John A. Walter Holtkamp: American Organ Builder. LC 78-26500. (Illus.). 140p. 1979. 12.50x (ISBN 0-87338-217-X). Kent St U Pr.

Ferguson, John C. Chinese Mythology. Bd. with Japanese Mythology. Anesaki, Masaharu. LC 63-19093. (Mythology of All Races Ser.: Vol. 8). (Illus.). Repr. of 1932 ed. 30.00 (ISBN 0-8154-0068-3). Cooper Sq.

--Outlines of Chinese Art. facsimile ed. LC 70-37879. (Select Bibliographies Reprint Ser). 1919. 32.00 (ISBN 0-8369-6716-X). Ayer Co Pubs.

Ferguson, John D. American Literature in Spain. LC 74-168017. Repr. of 1916 ed. 22.00 (ISBN 0-404-02377-0). AMS Pr.

--American Literature in Spain. 59.95 (ISBN 0-87968-608-1). Gordon Pr.

Ferguson, John D., et al, eds. Theme & Variation in the Short Story. facsimile ed. LC 74-37541. (Short Story Index Reprint Ser.). Repr. of 1938 ed. 25.00 (ISBN 0-8369-4100-4). Ayer Co Pubs.

Ferguson, John H. & McHenry, Dean E. The American System of Government. 14th ed. Munson, Eric M., ed. (Illus.). 688p. 1981. text ed. 30.95 (ISBN 0-07-020528-0). McGraw.

Ferguson, John P., ed. see Mendelson, E. Michael.

Ferguson, Kathy E. The Feminist Case Against Bureaucracy. (Women in the Political Economy Ser.). 304p. 1984. 24.95 (ISBN 0-87722-357-2). Temple U Pr.

--Self, Society, & Womankind: The Dialectic of Liberation. LC 79-6831. (Contributions in Women's Studies: No. 17). xii, 200p. 1980. lib. bdg. 27.50 (ISBN 0-313-22245-2, FSS/). Greenwood.

Ferguson, LaVerne, ed. see Ferguson, George W.

Ferguson, LeBaron O. Approximation by Polynomials with Integral Coefficients. LC 79-20331. (Mathematical Surveys: Vol. 17). 160p. 1980. 34.00 (ISBN 0-8218-1517-2). Am Math.

Ferguson, Linda. Canada. LC 79-15871. (Illus.). (gr. 7 up). 1979. 10.95 (ISBN 0-684-16080-3, ScribJ). Scribner.

Ferguson, Lorna, jt. auth. see Clark, Terry.

Ferguson, Lucy R., jt. auth. see Young, Harben B.

Ferguson, M. Carr & Freeland, James F. Federal Income Taxation of Estates & Beneficiaries. 776p. 1970. incl. 1985 suppl. 55.00 (ISBN 0-316-27888-2). Little.

Ferguson, M. Carr & Fuller, James P. Research & Development Limited Partnerships 1984. (Tax Law & Estate Planning Ser.: No. 210). (Illus.). 543p. 1984. 35.00 (ISBN 0-317-04102-9, J4-3553). PLI.

Ferguson, M. Carr, et al. Federal Income Taxation of Estates & Beneficiaries. 749p. (Orig.). 1970. text ed. 55.00 (ISBN 0-316-27889-0). Little.

--Federal Income Taxation of Estates & Beneficiaries: 1984 Supplement. LC 70-79882. 195p. 1984. pap. 25.00 (ISBN 0-316-27908-0). Little.

Ferguson, M. Carr, jt. auth. see Eustice, James S.

Ferguson, Madonna A., illus. Quilter's Notebook. 96p. 1985. pap. 6.00 perfect bound (ISBN 0-9612608-5-8). B Boyink.

Ferguson, Margaret W. Trials of Desire: Renaissance Defenses of Poetry. LC 82-8525. (Illus.). 280p. 1983. pap. text ed. 25.00x (ISBN 0-300-02787-7). Yale U Pr.

Ferguson, Marilyn. The Aquarian Conspiracy: Personal & Social Transformation in the 1980s. LC 79-91722. 448p. 1981. 15.00 (ISBN 0-87477-116-1); pap. 8.95 (ISBN 0-87477-191-9). J P Tarcher.

Ferguson, Marion. Service Load of a Staff Nurse in One Official Public Health Agency. LC 71-176768. (Columbia University. Teachers College. Contributions to Education: No. 915). Repr. of 1945 ed. 22.50 (ISBN 0-404-55915-8). AMS Pr.

Ferguson, Marjorie. Forever Feminine: Women's Magazines & the Cult of Femininity. xi, 243p. 1983. text ed. 15.00x (ISBN 0-435-82301-9). Gower Pub Co.

Ferguson, Mark W. The Structured Development & Evolution of Reptiles. (Symposium Zoological Society: No. 52). 1984. 75.00 (ISBN 0-12-613352-2). Acad Pr.

Ferguson, Mary A., compiled by. Bibliography of English Translations from Medieval Sources, Nineteen Forty-Three to Nineteen Sixty-Eight. (Records of Civilization, Sources & Studies: No. 88). 244p. 1974. 29.00x (ISBN 0-231-03435-0). Columbia U Pr.

Ferguson, Mary Anne. Images of Women in Literature. 3rd ed. LC 80-82761. (Illus.). 528p. 1981. pap. text ed. 17.50 (ISBN 0-395-29113-5). HM.

Ferguson, Mary H. Microencapsulation: Selected Papers from the Fourth International Symposium on Microencapsulation. 44p. 1981. pap. text ed. 13.50 (ISBN 0-917330-42-0). Am Pharm Assn.

Ferguson, Mary P. An Introduction to Diabetes for the Young Child. (Illus.). 48p. 1972. 5 copies, spiral 10.75x (ISBN 0-398-02208-9). C C Thomas.

Ferguson, Maxwell. State Regulation of Railroads in the South. LC 75-76711. (Columbia University. Studies in the Social Sciences: No. 162). Repr. of 1916 ed. 18.50 (ISBN 0-404-51162-7). AMS Pr.

Ferguson, Moira & Todd, Janet M. Mary Wollstonecraft. LC 83-18342. (English Author Ser.: No. 381). 158p. 1984. lib. bdg. 17.95 (ISBN 0-8057-6867-X, Twayne). G K Hall.

Ferguson, Moira, ed. First Feminists: British Women Writers, 1578-1799. LC 84-42838. 448p. (Orig.). 1985. 25.00 (ISBN 0-253-32213-8); pap. 12.95 (ISBN 0-253-28120-2). Ind U Pr.

Ferguson, Nancy. Black Coral. 256p. 1985. pap. 3.50 (ISBN 0-441-06518-X, Pub. by Charter Bks). Ace Bks.

Ferguson, Nancy & Ferguson, Denzel. Sacred Cows at the Public Trough. (Illus.). 260p. 1983. pap. 8.95 (ISBN 0-89288-091-0). Maverick.

Ferguson, Nancy, jt. auth. see Ferguson, Denzel.

Ferguson, Nicola. Right Plant, Right Place: The Indispensable Guide to the Successful Garden. McGourty, Fred, ed. (Illus.). 304p. (Orig.). 1984. pap. 14.95 (ISBN 0-671-49983-1). Summit Bks.

Ferguson, Nina. In the Beginning God. 1985. 6.95 (ISBN 0-8062-2430-4). Carlton.

Ferguson, Norman B. Neuropsychology Laboratory Manual. rev. ed. LC 76-45272. 1982. 7.50 (ISBN 0-87735-630-0). Freeman Cooper.

Ferguson, Phil M. Reinforced Concrete Fundamentals. 4th ed. LC 78-21555. 724p. 1979. text ed. 45.45x (ISBN 0-471-01459-1). Wiley.

--Reinforced Concrete Fundamentals: SI Version. 4th ed. LC 80-24409. 694p. 1981. text ed. 45.45x (ISBN 0-471-05897-1). Wiley.

Ferguson, R. Comparative Risks of Electricity Generating Fuel Systems in the UK. 216p. 1981. 80.00 (ISBN 0-906048-66-4). Inst Elect Eng.

Ferguson, R. & King, S. Guide to the Antique Shops of Britain, 1985. 1116p. 1984. 125.00 (ISBN 0-686-87310-6, Pub. by Antique Collectors). State Mutual Bk.

Ferguson, R. Brian. Warfare, Culture, & Environment. LC 83-21452. (Studies in Anthropology). 1984. 49.50 (ISBN 0-12-253780-7). Acad Pr.

Ferguson, R. Fred, jt. auth. see Whisenand, Paul M.

Ferguson, R. J. & Stephenson, Gordon. Physical Planning Report: Murdoch University 1973. LC 73-93913. (Illus.). 72p. 1974. pap. 11.50x (ISBN 0-85564-080-4, Pub. by U of W Austral Pr). Intl Spec Bk.

Ferguson, Rachel. Celebrated Sequels. 1934. 17.50 (ISBN 0-686-18155-7). Havertown Bks.

--Celebrated Sequels: A Book of Parodies. 1934. Repr. 20.00 (ISBN 0-8274-2015-3). R West.

Ferguson, Richard L. Computer Assistance for Individualizing Measurement. 81p. 1971. 1.50 (ISBN 0-318-14701-7). Learn Res Dev.

Ferguson, Robert. Arctic Harpooner: A Voyage on the Schooner Abbie Bradford 1878-1879. Stair, Leslie D., ed. (Seafaring Men: Their Ship & Times Ser.). (Illus.). 1980. Repr. of 1938 ed. text ed. 19.50 (ISBN 0-930576-29-2). E M Coleman Ent.

--The River Road. 64p. 1978. 4.00 (ISBN 0-317-14570-3). Truck Pr.

Ferguson, Robert A. Law & Letters in American Culture. (Illus.). 416p. 1984. text ed. 22.50x (ISBN 0-674-51465-3). Harvard U Pr.

--Psychic Telemetry: Key to Health, Wealth & Perfect Living. (Illus.). 1977. 15.95 (ISBN 0-13-732388-3, Parker). P-H.

--The Universal Law of Cosmic Cycles. 1980. 4.95 (ISBN 0-13-938738-2, Parker). P-H.

Ferguson, Robert J., et al. Preemployment Polygraphy. 184p. 1984. 24.75x (ISBN 0-398-05011-2). C C Thomas.

Ferguson, Robert J., Jr. The Polygraph in Private Industry. (Illus.). 352p. 1966. 28.75x (ISBN 0-398-00557-5). C C Thomas.

--Scientific Informer. (Illus.). 248p. 1971. 28.50x (ISBN 0-398-00558-3). C C Thomas.

Ferguson, Robert J., Jr. & Miller, Allan L. Polygraph for the Defense. 312p. 1974. 25.50x (ISBN 0-398-02877-X). C C Thomas.

--The Polygraph in Court. (Illus.). 372p. 1973. photocopy ed. 28.75x (ISBN 0-398-02679-3). C C Thomas.

Ferguson, Robert W. Artistry in Cabochons. (Illus.). 64p. 1976. pap. 2.00 (ISBN 0-910652-21-X). Gembooks.

Ferguson, Roger. Experiencing Fullness in Christian Living: Studies in Colossians. 36p. 1982. pap. 3.50 (ISBN 0-939298-08-2). J M Prods.

Ferguson, Ronald M., jt. ed. see Schmidtke, Jon R.

Ferguson, Rosalind. Rhyming Dictionary. Date not set. pap. price not set (ISBN 0-14-051136-9). Penguin.

Ferguson, Rosemary & King, Stella, eds. Guide to the Antique Shops of Britain, 1982. 1116p. 1981. 16.00 (ISBN 0-902028-87-1). Antique Collect.

--Guide to the Antique Shops of Britain 1985. (Illus.). 1984. 16.00 (ISBN 0-907462-67-7). Antique Collect.

Ferguson, Rowena. Editing the Small Magazine. 2nd ed. 221p. 1976. 27.50x (ISBN 0-231-03866-6); pap. 12.00x (ISBN 0-231-03970-0). Columbia U Pr.

Ferguson, Royce A. Criminal Practice & Procedure with Forms. LC 84-52217. (Illus.). Date not set. price not set. West Pub.

Ferguson, S. M. & Fitzgerald, H. Studies in the Social Services. 1978. 53.00 (ISBN 0-527-35772-3). Kraus Intl.

Ferguson, Samuel. Congal: A Poem in Five Books. LC 75-28812. Repr. of 1872 ed. Set. 19.50 (ISBN 0-404-13805-5). AMS Pr.

--Lays of the Western Gael, & Other Poems. LC 75-28813. Repr. of 1865 ed. 20.00 (ISBN 0-404-13806-3). AMS Pr.

--Poems of Samuel Ferguson. 1963. 2.95 (ISBN 0-900372-67-2). Irish Bk Ctr.

--Poems of Sir Samuel Ferguson. LC 75-28814. Repr. of 1918 ed. 35.00 (ISBN 0-404-13807-1). AMS Pr.

Ferguson, Sir Samuel. The Hibernian Nights' Entertainment, 3 vols. in 1. LC 79-8420. Repr. of 1887 ed. 44.50 (ISBN 0-404-61845-6). AMS Pr.

Ferguson, Sheila. Growing up in Ancient Egypt. LC 79-56471. (Growing up Ser.). (Illus.). 72p. (gr. 7 up). 1980. text ed. 14.95 (ISBN 0-7134-2683-7, Pub. by Batsford England). David & Charles.

--Growing up in Victorian Britain. (Growing Up Ser.). 1977. 14.95 (ISBN 0-7134-0281-4, Pub. by Batsford England). David & Charles.

--Growing up in Viking Times. (Growing up Ser.). (Illus.). 72p. (gr. 6 up). 1981. 14.95 (ISBN 0-7134-2730-2, Pub. by Batsford England). David & Charles.

--Village & Town Life. (History in Focus Ser.). (Illus.). 72p. (gr. 7-12). 1983. 14.95 (ISBN 0-7134-4301-4, Pub. by Batsford England). David & Charles.

Ferguson, Sherry D., jt. auth. see Ferguson, Stewart.

Ferguson, Sibyl. The Crystal Ball. 1980. pap. 1.50 (ISBN 0-87728-483-0). Weiser.

Ferguson, Simone D., tr. see Baumont, Maurice.

Ferguson, Sinclair. Grow in Grace. LC 83-63370. 192p. (Orig.). 1984. pap. 3.95 (ISBN 0-317-03502-9). NavPress.

--A Heart for God. (Christian Character Library). 1985. text ed. 8.95 (ISBN 0-89109-507-1). NavPress.

--Know Your Christian Life. LC 81-18588. 179p. (Orig.). 1981. pap. 5.95 (ISBN 0-87784-371-6). Inter-Varsity.

--Man Overboard. 1982. pap. 3.95 (ISBN 0-8423-4015-7); leader's guide 2.95 (ISBN 0-8423-4016-5). Tyndale.

Ferguson, Sinclair B. Discovering God's Will. 125p. (Orig.). 1981. pap. 3.95 (ISBN 0-85151-334-4). Banner of Truth.

--Taking the Christian Life Seriously: Biblical Teaching on Christian Maturity. Orig. Title: Add to Your Life. 192p. 1981. pap. 5.95 (ISBN 0-310-43891-8). Zondervan.

Ferguson, Stewart & Ferguson, Sherry D. Intercom: Readings in Organizational Communication. 432p. 1980. 15.00x (ISBN 0-8104-5127-1). Boynton Cook Pubs.

Ferguson, Suzanne. Critical Essays on Randall Jarrell. (Critical Essays on American Literature Ser.). 1983. lib. bdg. 36.50 (ISBN 0-8161-8486-0). G K Hall.

Ferguson, Sybil. The Diet Center Program: Lose Weight Fast & Keep It Off Forever. 424p. 1983. 14.45i (ISBN 0-316-27901-3). Little.

Ferguson, T. J. & Hart, E. Richard. A Zuni Atlas. LC 85-40474. (The Civilization of the American Indian Ser.: Vol. 172). (Illus.). 160p. 1985. 24.95 (ISBN 0-8061-1945-4). U of Okla Pr.

Ferguson, Ted. Sentimental Journey. LC 85-10258. (Illus.). 256p. 1986. 22.95 (ISBN 0-385-23252-7). Doubleday.

Ferguson, Thaddeus. A History of the Romance Vowel Systems Through Paradigmatic Reconstruction. (Janua Linguarum Ser. Practica: No. 176). 1976. pap. text ed. 24.00x (ISBN 90-2793-354-5). Mouton.

Ferguson, Thomas & Rogers, Joel. Right Turn: The Nineteen Eighty-Four Election & the Future of American Politics. 160p. 1985. 14.95 (ISBN 0-8090-8191-1, Pub. by Hill & Wang). FS&G.

--Right Turn: The 1984 Election & the Future of American Politics. 1985. 14.95 (ISBN 0-8090-8191-1). Hill & Wang.

Ferguson, Thomas, ed. The Hidden Election: Politics & Economics in the 1980 Presidential Campaign. 1982. pap. 7.95 (ISBN 0-394-74958-8). Pantheon.

Ferguson, Thomas & Rogers, Joel, eds. The Political Economy: Readings in the Politics & Economics of American Public Economy. 380p. 1984. 35.00x (ISBN 0-87332-276-2); pap. 14.95x (ISBN 0-87332-272-X). M E Sharpe.

Ferguson, Thomas B. The Centrifugal Compressor Stage. LC 64-9032. pap. 40.50 (ISBN 0-317-08541-7, 2051728). Bks Demand UMI.

Ferguson, Thomas M. Taxpayer Alert. 3rd ed. 127p. 1982. 4.95 (ISBN 0-88908-095-X). Self Counsel Pr.

Ferguson, Thomas S. Mathematical Statistics: A Decision Theoretic Approach. (Probability & Mathematical Statistics Ser.: Vol. 1). 1967. text ed. 24.00i (ISBN 0-12-253750-5). Acad Pr.

Ferguson, Thompson B. The Jayhawkers: A Tale of the Border War. LC 71-104449. 415p. Repr. of 1892 ed. lib. bdg. 24.00 (ISBN 0-8398-0554-3). Irvington.

Ferguson, Tom. Medical Self-Care: Access to Health Tools. LC 80-14678. 320p. 1980. 19.95 (ISBN 0-671-40033-9); pap. 8.95 (ISBN 0-671-44816-1). Summit Bks.

Ferguson, Tom & Feldstein, Saul. The Jazz-Rock Ensemble: A Conductor's & Teacher's Guide. LC 76-22566. (Illus.). 150p. 1976. pap. text ed. 9.95x (ISBN 0-88284-044-4). Alfred Pub.

Ferguson, Tom, jt. auth. see Sobel, David.

Ferguson, Valerie, ed. Sayings of the Week. 1978. 8.95 (ISBN 0-7153-7600-4). David & Charles.

Ferguson, W. Scotland's Relations with England: A Survey to 1707. 328p. 1982. 42.00x (ISBN 0-85976-022-7, Pub. by Donald Pubs Scotland). State Mutual Bk.

Ferguson, W., ed. see Van Kaufman, R. & Okigbo, B. N.

Ferguson, W. J. I Saw Booth Shoot Lincoln. LC 70-20379. (Illus.). 8.50 (ISBN 0-8363-0052-1). Jenkins.

Ferguson, W. K. History of the Bureau of Economic Geology, 1909-1960. (Illus.). 329p. 1981. 11.00 (ISBN 0-318-03330-5); pap. 6.00 (ISBN 0-318-03331-3). Bur Econ Geology.

Ferguson, W. Scott. Hellenistic Athens. 512p. 1974. 20.00 (ISBN 0-89005-021-X). Ares.

Ferguson, Wallace K. The Renaissance in Historical Thought: Five Centuries of Interpretation. LC 77-74812. Repr. of 1948 ed. 32.50 (ISBN 0-404-14887-5). AMS Pr.

Ferguson, Wallace K. & Bruun, Geoffrey. A Survey of European Civilization. 4th ed. Incl. Pt. 1. To 1660; Complete. 1969. 32.50 (ISBN 0-395-04425-1). HM.

Ferguson, Walter D. Influence of Flaubert on George Moore. LC 74-10999. 1934. lib. bdg. 10.00 (ISBN 0-8414-4220-7). Folcroft.

Ferguson, William. Freedom & Other Fictions. LC 83-48852. 1984. 11.95 (ISBN 0-394-53391-7). Knopf.

Ferguson, William D. Statutes of Limitation Saving Statutes. 541p. 1978. 35.00 (ISBN 0-87215-214-6). Michie Co.

Ferguson, William M. & Royce, John Q. Maya Ruins in Central America in Color: Tikal, Copan & Quirigua. LC 83-14750. (Illus.). 320p. 1984. 35.00 (ISBN 0-8263-0688-8). U of NM Pr.

--Maya Ruins of Mexico in Color. LC 77-9110. (Illus.). 1977. 29.50 (ISBN 0-8061-1442-8). U of Okla Pr.

--Maya Ruins of Mexico in Color. LC 77-9110. (Illus.). 256p. 1984. pap. 16.95 (ISBN 0-8061-1881-4). U of Okla Pr.

Ferguson, William S. Athenian Archons of the Third & Second Centuries Before Christ. Repr. of 1899 ed. 12.00 (ISBN 0-384-15478-6). Johnson Repr.

--The Athenian Secretaries. Repr. of 1898 ed. 10.00 (ISBN 0-384-15480-8). Johnson Repr.

--Greek Imperialism. LC 63-18045. 1941. 11.00x (ISBN 0-8196-0127-6). Biblo.

Ferguson, Y. H., jt. auth. see Mansbach, R. W.

Ferguson-Lees, James & Hockliffe, Quentin. A Guide to Bird-Watching in Europe. (Illus.). 335p. 9.95 (ISBN 0-684-14475-1). Brown Bk.

Ferguson-Lees, James, et al. The Shell Guide to the Birds of Britain & Ireland. (Illus.). 336p. 1983. pap. 14.95 (ISBN 0-7181-2220-8, Pub. by Michael Joseph). Merrimack Pub Cir.

Ferguson-Lees, James, et al, eds. A Guide to Bird-Watching in Europe. LC 75-329356. 336p. 1979. 14.95 (ISBN 0-370-10476-5, Pub. by the Bodley Head); pap. 6.95 (ISBN 0-370-10477-3). Merrimack Pub Cir.

Ferguson-Wood, E. & Johannes, R., eds. Tropical Marine Pollution. 192p. 1975. 64.00 (ISBN 0-444-41298-0). Elsevier.

Fergusson, Bernard. Beyond the Chindwin. 256p. 1983. pap. 7.50 (ISBN 0-907746-29-2, Pub. by A Mott Ltd). Longwood Pub Group.

Fergusson, Erna. Mexican Cookbook. LC 46-214. (Illus.). 120p. 1983. pap. 6.95 (ISBN 0-8263-0035-9). U of NM Pr.

--New Mexico: A Pageant of Three Peoples. 2nd ed. LC 72-94664. Orig. Title: New Mexico. (Illus.). 408p. 1973. pap. 8.95 (ISBN 0-8263-0271-8). U of NM Pr.

--Our Southwest. 1940. 35.00 (ISBN 0-89984-011-6). Century Bookbindery.

Fergusson, Francis. Dante's Drama of the Mind: A Modern Reading of the Purgatorio. LC 81-4190. x, 231p. 1981. Repr. of 1953 ed. lib. bdg. 27.50x (ISBN 0-313-23034-X, FEDD). Greenwood.

--Idea of a Theater: A Study of Ten Plays, The Art of Drama in Changing Perspective. 1968. 28.50 (ISBN 0-691-06143-2); pap. 9.50 (ISBN 0-691-01288-1). Princeton U Pr.

--Literary Landmarks: Essays on the Theory & Practice of Literature. 1975. 17.50x (ISBN 0-8135-0815-0). Rutgers U Pr.

--Trope & Allegory: Themes Common to Dante & Shakespeare. LC 76-12684. 172p. 1977. 14.00x (ISBN 0-8203-0410-7). U of Ga Pr.

Fergusson, Francis, tr. see Sophocles.

Fergusson, Harvey. The Blood of the Conquerors. Cortes, Carlos E., ed. LC 76-1232. (Chicano Heritage Ser.). 1976. Repr. of 1921 ed. lib. bdg. 16.00x (ISBN 0-405-09500-7). Ayer Co Pubs.

--Grant of Kingdom. LC 75-17378. (Zia Bks). 327p. 1975. pap. 7.95 (ISBN 0-8263-0396-X). U of NM Pr.

--Wolf Song. LC 81-3056. vi, 206p. 1981. pap. 6.50 (ISBN 0-8032-6855-6, BB 780, Bison). U of Nebr Pr.

Fergusson, Harvey, Jr., tr. see Silone, Ignazio.

Fergusson, Heather. Adventures of a Monkey King: Book I. (Adventures of a Monkey King Ser.). (Illus.). 64p. (gr. 4-7). 1982. PLB 8.75 (ISBN 0-942056-01-9). Character Bks.

Fergusson, J. E. Inorganic Chemistry & the Earth: Chemical Resources, Their Extraction, Use & Enivironmental Impact. LC 82-15096. (Pergamon Series on Environmental Science: Vol. 6). (Illus.). 409p. 1982. 44.00 (ISBN 0-08-023995-1); pap. 19.95 (ISBN 0-08-023994-3). Pergamon.

Fergusson, James. The Green Garden: A New Collection of Scottish Poetry. 1979. Repr. of 1946 ed. lib. bdg. 27.50 (ISBN 0-8495-1645-5). Arden Lib.

--An Historical & Illustrated Vision of German Architecture. (Illus.). 127p. 1983. Repr. of 1885 ed. 89.75 (ISBN 0-89901-105-5). Found Class Reprints.

--History of Architecture in All Countries from the Earliest Times to the Present Day, 2 Vols. 1982. Repr. of 1865 ed. Set. lib. bdg. 300.00 (ISBN 0-8495-1732-X). Arden Lib.

--The Palaces of Nineve & Persipolis. 368p. 1981. Repr. text ed. 33.00x (ISBN 0-391-02432-9, Pub. by Concept India). Humanities.

Fergusson, Peter. Architecture of Solitude: Cistercian Abbeys in Twelfth-Century England. LC 83-43072. (Illus.). 370p. 1984. 70.00x (ISBN 0-691-04024-9). Princeton U Pr.

Fergusson, Robert. Poems of Robert Fergusson, 2 Vols. McDiarmid, Matthew P., ed. Repr. of 1954 ed. Set. 50.00 (ISBN 0-384-15487-5); Vol. 1. 19.00 (ISBN 0-384-15485-9); Vol. 2. 32.00 (ISBN 0-384-15486-7). Johnson Repr.

--Works of Robert Fergusson. Grosart, A. B., ed. LC 75-144464. Repr. of 1851 ed. 22.50 (ISBN 0-404-08555-5). AMS Pr.

Fergusson, Robert, jt. auth. see Ramsay, Allan.

Fergusson, Rosalind. The Penguin Rhyming Dictionary Pen. 544p. 1985. 20.00 (ISBN 0-670-80036-8). Viking.

Fergusson, Rosalind, compiled by. The Facts on File Dictionary of Proverbs. 352p. 1983. 21.95x (ISBN 0-87196-298-5). Facts on File.

Fergusson, Thomas G. British Military Intelligence, 1870-1914: The Development of a Modern Intelligence Organization. 1984. 25.00 (ISBN 0-89093-541-6). U Pubns Amer.

Fergusson, William E. The Internal Audit Training Program: How to Organize & Develop a Continuing Education Plan for Your Internal Audit Team. (Research Report: No. 23). (Illus.). 1980. pap. text ed. 10.00 (ISBN 0-89413-084-6, 474). Inst Inter Aud.

Fergusson Of Kilkerran, Sir James. Shakespeare's Scotland. LC 79-15666. Repr. of 1957 ed. lib. bdg. 8.50 (ISBN 0-8414-4164-2). Folcroft.

Ferholt, Deborah L. Clinical Assessment of Children: A Comprehensive Approach to Primary Pediatric Care. LC 79-19625. 331p. 1980. text ed. 22.50 (ISBN 0-397-54329-8, 64-01731, Lippincott Nursing). Lippincott.

Fericano, Paul. Commercial Break. 72p. (Orig.). 1982. 10.00 (ISBN 0-916296-07-5); pap. 4.00 (ISBN 0-916296-08-3). Poor Souls Pr.

--The Condition of Poetry in the Modern World: A Stoogist Manifesto. (Orig.). 1980. 5.00 (ISBN 0-916296-05-9). Poor Souls Pr.

--Loading the Revolver with Real Bullets. LC 77-76905. 1977. pap. 2.50 (ISBN 0-915016-16-8). Second Coming.

--Sinatra, Sinatra. 16p. (Orig.). 1982. Chapbook 200.00 (ISBN 0-916296-06-7). Poor Souls Pr.

Fericano, Paul F. Cancer Quiz. (Orig.). 1977. 10.00 (ISBN 0-916296-00-8). Poor Souls Pr.

Fericano, Paul F., ed. Stoogism Anthology. LC 77-76619. (Illus.). 1977. pap. 15.00 (ISBN 0-916296-01-6). Poor Souls Pr.

Ferkauf, Eugene. Going into Business: How to Do It, by the Man Who Did It. LC 77-3395. (Illus.). 210p. 1980. pap. 5.95 (ISBN 0-87754-135-3). Chelsea Hse.

--Going into Business: How to Do It, by the Man Who Did It. LC 77-3395. (Illus.). 210p. 1977. 8.95 (ISBN 0-87754-049-7). Chelsea Hse.

Ferkiss, Victor C. Africa's Search for Identity. LC 65-25970. 1965. 6.50 (ISBN 0-8076-0322-8). Braziller.

Ferland, Jean B. Cours D'Histoire Du Canada, 2 Vols. (Canadiana Before 1867 Ser). (Fr). 1969. Repr. of 1861 ed. Set. 60.00 (ISBN 0-384-15500-6). Johnson Repr.

--Cours D'histoire Du Canada, 2 vols. (Canadiana Avant 1867: No. 14). 1970. Set. 60.40x (ISBN 0-686-21223-1). Mouton.

Ferland, M. G., jt. auth. see Villeneuve, G. O.

Ferlatte, William J. A Flora of the Trinity Alps. LC 72-635566. (Illus.). 1974. 26.50x (ISBN 0-520-02089-8). U of Cal Pr.

Ferlazzo, Paul. Emily Dickinson. (United States Authors Ser.). 168p. 1984. pap. 5.95 (ISBN 0-8057-7425-4, Twayne). G K Hall.

Ferlazzo, Paul J. Critical Essays on Emily Dickinson. (Critical Essays on American Literature Ser.). 291p. 1984. lib. bdg. 32.50 (ISBN 0-8161-8463-1). G K Hall.

--Emily Dickinson. (United States Authors Ser.). 1976. lib. bdg. 13.50 (ISBN 0-8057-7180-8, Twayne). G K Hall.

Ferleger, Herbert R. David A. Wells & the American Revenue System 1865-1870. LC 77-7106. (Perspectives in American History Ser.: No. 32). 1977. Repr. of 1942 ed. lib. bdg. 25.00x (ISBN 0-87991-356-8). Porcupine Pr.

Ferleger, Lou, jt. auth. see Horwitz, Lucy.

Ferling, John E. The Loyalist Mind: Joseph Galloway & the American Revolution. LC 77-22369. 1977. 19.95x (ISBN 0-271-00514-9). Pa St U Pr.

--A Wilderness of Miseries: War & Warriors in Early America. LC 79-8951. (Contributions in Military History: No. 22). (Illus.). xiv, 227p. 1980. lib. bdg. 29.95 (ISBN 0-313-22093-X, FWW/). Greenwood.

Ferlinghetti, Lawrence. Endless Life: The Selected Poems. LC 80-29127. 224p. 1981. 14.95 (ISBN 0-8112-0796-X); pap. 4.95 (ISBN 0-8112-0797-8, NDP516). New Directions.

--Her. LC 60-9221. 1960. pap. 4.95 (ISBN 0-8112-0042-6, NDP88). New Directions.

--Landscapes of Living & Dying. LC 79-15595. 1979. ltd ed. 45.00 (ISBN 0-8112-0743-9); pap. 2.95 (ISBN 0-8112-0742-0, NDP491). New Directions.

--Leaves of Life: Fifty Drawings from the Model. 1983. pap. 10.95 (ISBN 0-87286-154-6). City Lights.

--Mexican Night: Travel Journal. LC 75-122105. (Illus., Orig.). 1970. pap. 1.50 (ISBN 0-8112-0043-4, NDP300). New Directions.

--Mule Mountain Dreams. 16p. (Orig.). 1980. pap. 2.00x (ISBN 0-938196-01-4). Bisbee Pr.

--Over All the Obscene Boundaries: European Poems & Transitions. LC 84-6919. 128p. 1984. 12.00 (ISBN 0-8112-0919-9); pap. 5.95 (ISBN 0-8112-0920-2, NDP582). New Directions.

--Pictures of the Gone World. LC 64-11470. (Pocket Poets Ser., No. 1). (Orig.). 1955. pap. 2.00 (ISBN 0-87286-040-X). City Lights.

--The Populist Manifestos. LC 80-22105. 56p. 1981. pap. 3.95 (ISBN 0-912516-52-6). Grey Fox.

--Routines. LC 64-23652. (Orig.). 1964. pap. 1.00 (ISBN 0-8112-0044-2, NDP187). New Directions.

--Secret Meaning of Things. LC 69-17826. 1969. pap. 1.00 (ISBN 0-8112-0045-0, NDP268). New Directions.

--Seven Days in Nicaragua Libre. (Illus.). 112p. (Orig.). 1984. pap. 6.95 (ISBN 0-87286-160-0). City Lights.

--Starting from San Francisco. enl. & rev. ed. LC 67-23492. 1967. pap. 1.00 (ISBN 0-8112-0046-9, NDP220). New Directions.

--A Trip to Italy & France. LC 80-36778. 64p. 1981. signed limited ed. 50.00 (ISBN 0-8112-0782-X). New Directions.

--Tyrannus Nix? LC 71-94522. 1969. pap. 1.25 (ISBN 0-8112-0047-7, NDP288). New Directions.

--Unfair Arguments with Existence. LC 63-21384. 1963. pap. 1.00 (ISBN 0-8112-0048-5, NDP143). New Directions.

--Who Are We Now? LC 76-1061. 1976. 4.95 (ISBN 0-8112-0628-9). New Directions.

Ferlinghetti, Lawrence & Ehrlich, J. W., eds. Howl of the Censor: Lawrence Ferlinghetti, Defendant. LC 75-40924. 144p. 1976. Repr. of 1961 ed. lib. bdg. 15.00x (ISBN 0-8371-8685-4, FEHC). Greenwood.

Ferlinghetti, Lawrence, tr. see Prevert, Jacques.

Ferlinghetti, Lawrence, Jr. A Coney Island of the Mind. LC 58-7150. 1968. 9.95 (ISBN 0-8112-0274-7); pap. 3.95 (ISBN 0-8112-0041-8, NDP74). New Directions.

Ferlita, Ernest. Gospel Journey. 120p. (Orig.). 1983. pap. 5.95 (ISBN 0-86683-685-3). Winston Pr.

Ferlito, Alfio, ed. Cancer of the Larynx, 2 vols. 1985. Vol. I, 240pp. 75.00 (ISBN 0-8493-6587-2); Vol. II, 272pp. pap. text ed. 82.00 (ISBN 0-8493-6588-0). CRC Pr.

Ferlosio, Rafael S. Alfanhui. Donald, Ruth M., tr. from Sp. LC 74-82791. (Illus.). 156p. 1975. pap. 3.50 (ISBN 0-911198-39-3). Purdue U Pr.

Ferm, Betty, jt. auth. see Ferm, Max A.

Ferm, Dean W. Alternative Lifestyles Confront the Church. 144p. 1983. pap. 8.95 (ISBN 0-8164-2394-6, Pub. by Seabury). Winston Pr.

Ferm, Deane W. Contemporary American Theologies: A Critical Survey. 192p. (Orig.). 1981. pap. 8.95 (ISBN 0-8164-2341-5, Pub. by Seabury). Winston Pr.

--Contemporary American Theologies II: A Book of Readings. 214p. (Orig.). 1982. pap. 15.95 (ISBN 0-8164-2407-1, Pub. by Seabury). Winston Pr.

Ferm, Max A. & Ferm, Betty. How to Save Dollars with Generic Drugs: A Consumer's Guide to High-Quality, Low-Priced Medicines. LC 84-61113. 1984. 17.95 (ISBN 0-688-03242-7). Morrow.

--How to Save Dollars with Generic Drugs: A Consumer's Guide to High-Quality, Low-Priced Medicines. 1984. pap. 8.95 (ISBN 0-688-02787-3, Quill). Morrow.

Ferm, Robert L., ed. Issues in American Protestantism: A Documentary History from the Puritans to the Present. 15.25 (ISBN 0-8446-2052-1). Peter Smith.

Ferm, Vergilius. The American Church of the Protestant Heritage. LC 76-138228. 481p. 1972. Repr. of 1953 ed. lib. bdg. 20.00x (ISBN 0-8371-5585-1, FEAC). Greenwood.

--An Encyclopedia of Religion. LC 75-36508. 844p. 1976. Repr. of 1945 ed. lib. bdg. 55.00x (ISBN 0-8371-8638-2, FEEOR). Greenwood.

--Memoirs of a College Professor. 1970. 6.95 (ISBN 0-8158-0246-3). Chris Mass.

--Philosophy Beyond the Classroom. 411p. 1974. 12.95 (ISBN 0-8158-0314-1). Chris Mass.

--So You're Going to College. LC 72-85933. (Illus.). 160p. 1972. 6.95 (ISBN 0-8158-0292-7). Chris Mass.

--Toward an Expansive Christian Theology. LC 64-16359. 1964. 5.00 (ISBN 0-8022-0496-1). Philos Lib.

--What Can We Believe. 1952. 5.00 (ISBN 0-8022-0497-X). Philos Lib.

Ferm, Vergilius, ed. Encyclopedia of Morals. LC 70-90504. Repr. of 1956 ed. lib. bdg. 40.00x (ISBN 0-8371-2138-8, FEEM). Greenwood.

--Encyclopedia of Religion. LC 62-18535. 1962. 19.95 (ISBN 0-8022-0490-2). Philos Lib.

Ferm, Vergilius T., ed. Contemporary American Theology. LC 78-86749. (Essay Index Reprint Ser). 1933. 21.50 (ISBN 0-8369-1181-4). Ayer Co Pubs.

--Forgotten Religions. facs. ed. LC 70-128240. (Essay Index Reprint Ser). 1950. 22.00 (ISBN 0-8369-1922-X). Ayer Co Pubs.

--History of Philosophical Systems. facs. ed. LC 73-128241. (Essay Index Reprint Ser). 1950. 33.00 (ISBN 0-8369-1923-8). Ayer Co Pubs.

--Religion in the Twentieth Century. Repr. of 1948 ed. lib. bdg. 20.00x (ISBN 0-8371-2290-2, FERT). Greenwood.

--Religion in Transition. facs. ed. LC 68-29204. (Essay Index Reprint Ser). 1937. 15.50 (ISBN 0-8369-0074-X). Ayer Co Pubs.

Ferm, Virgiulius. Protestant Credo. 1953. 5.00 (ISBN 0-8022-0494-5). Philos Lib.

Fermadig, Mac. Your Michigan Outdoors: An Educational Coloring Book. 1982. pap. 2.00 (ISBN 0-933112-09-2). Mich United Conserv.

Fermaglich, Mollie. Mollie's Rules for the Socially Inept: Guide to Modern Living. LC 83-13918. (Illus.). 192p. (Orig.). 1984. pap. 5.70 (ISBN 0-688-02154-9, Quill NY). Morrow.

Ferman, Barbara. Governing the Ungovernable City: Political Skill, Leadership, & the Modern Mayor. LC 84-16375. 304p. 1985. 34.95 (ISBN 0-87722-376-9). Temple U Pr.

Ferman, Barbara, jt. auth. see Levin, Martin A.

Ferman, Edward, ed. The Best from Fantasy & Science Fiction. 16.95 (ISBN 0-89190-674-6, Pub. by Am Repr). Amereon Ltd.

Ferman, Edward L. The Best From Fantasy & Science Fiction. 24th ed. 288p. 1982. 14.95 (ISBN 0-684-17490-1, ScribT). Scribner.

Ferman, Edward L., ed. The Best from Fantasy & Science Fiction, No. 24. 1983. pap. 2.95 (ISBN 0-441-05485-4, Pub. by Ace Science Fiction). Ace Bks.

--Magazine of "Fantasy & Science Fiction", April 1965. (Alternatives Ser.). (Illus.). 176p. 1981. 16.95 (ISBN 0-8093-1007-4). S Ill U Pr.

Ferman, Gerald S. & Levin, Jack. Social Science Research: A Handbook. 144p. 1977. pap. 8.95 (ISBN 0-87073-219-6). Schenkman Bks Inc.

Ferman, Louis A. Evaluating the War on Poverty. Lambert, Richard D., ed. LC 73-92365. (The Annals of the American Academy of Political & Social Science: No. 385). 1969. 15.00 (ISBN 0-87761-120-3); pap. 7.95 (ISBN 0-87761-119-X). Am Acad Pol Soc Sci.

--Job Development for the Hard-To-Employ. LC 71-626164. (Policy Papers in Human Resources & Industrial Relations Ser.: No. 11). (Orig.). 1969. pap. 2.50 (ISBN 0-87736-111-8). U of Mich Inst Labor.

Ferman, Louis A. & Erfurt, John C. Overview of the Experiences of the ILIR Manpower Laboratory: The Development of a Model Approach to the Retrieval, Dissemination, & Utilization of Information on Manpower Operations. 1973. looseleaf 3.00x (ISBN 0-87736-332-3). U of Mich Inst Labor.

Ferman, Louis A. & Manela, Roger. Agency Company Relationships in Manpower Operations for the Hard to Employ. 1973. pap. 6.50x (ISBN 0-87736-329-3). U of Mich Inst Labor.

Ferman, Louis A. & Gordus, Jeanne P., eds. Mental Health & the Economy. LC 79-25809. 1979. text ed. 19.95 (ISBN 0-911558-69-1); pap. text ed. 13.95 (ISBN 0-911558-68-3). W E Upjohn.

Ferman, Louis A., et al. Agency & Company: Partners in Human Resource Development. LC 80-23246. (Sage Human Services Guides Ser.: Vol. 18). 136p. 1981. 9.95 (ISBN 0-8039-1558-6). Sage.

Ferman, Louis A., et al, eds. Poverty in America: A Book of Readings. rev. ed. LC 68-29261. 1968. 12.50 (ISBN 0-472-31281-2). U of Mich Pr.

Ferme, Deane W., ed. Restoring the Kingdom. LC 83-82671. 226p. 1984. pap. 11.95 (ISBN 0-913757-06-3). Rose Sharon Pr.

Fermi, Enrico. Collected Papers of Enrico Fermi, 2 vols. Segre, Emilio, ed. Incl. Vol. 1. Italy, 1921-38. 60.00x (ISBN 0-226-24359-1); Vol. 2. United States, 1939-54. 60.00x (ISBN 0-226-24360-5). LC 60-12465. 1965. U of Chicago Pr.

--Notes on Quantum Mechanics. LC 64-9447. 1962. pap. 5.00x (ISBN 0-226-24361-3). U of Chicago Pr.

--Notes on Thermodynamics & Statistics. LC 66-20581. (Orig.). 1966. pap. 5.00x (ISBN 0-226-24364-8, P529, Phoen). U of Chicago Pr.

--Nuclear Physics. rev. ed. LC 50-6826. (Midway Reprints Ser). 258p. 1974. pap. text ed. 15.00x (ISBN 0-226-24365-6). U of Chicago Pr.

--Thermodynamics. 1937. pap. 4.00 (ISBN 0-486-60361-X). Dover.

Fermi, G. & Perutz, M. F. Haemoglobin & Myoglobin. (Atlas of Molecular Structures in Biology Ser.: No. 2). (Illus.). 1981. text ed. 49.50x (ISBN 0-19-854706-4). Oxford U Pr.

Fermi, Laura. Atoms for the World: United States Participation in the Conference on the Peaceful Uses of Atomic Energy. LC 57-6977. (Illus.). pap. 50.00 (ISBN 0-317-08772-X, 2011227). Bks Demand UMI.

--Illustrious Immigrants. 2nd ed. LC 76-154689. 1972. pap. 3.95 (ISBN 0-226-24378-8, P444, Phoen). U of Chicago Pr.

--Illustrious Immigrants: The Intellectual Migration from Europe, 1930-41. 2nd ed. LC 76-154689. 1971. 22.00x (ISBN 0-226-24376-1). U of Chicago Pr.

--Mussolini. LC 61-17075. 1966. pap. 13.00x (ISBN 0-226-24375-3, P216, Phoen). U of Chicago Pr.

--The Story of Atomic Energy. (World Landmark Ser.: No. 48). (Illus.). (gr. 7-11). 1961. PLB 5.99 (ISBN 0-394-90548-2). Random.

Fermigier, Andre. Bonnard. Schlanoff, Althea, tr. LC 69-12442. (Library of Great Painters). (Illus.). 1969. 40.00 (ISBN 0-8109-0041-6). Abrams.

Ferminger, Andre. Bonnard. (Master of Art Ser.). 1984. 19.95 (ISBN 0-8109-0732-1). Abrams.

Fermor, Patrick, tr. see Colette.

Fermor, Patrick L. Mani: Travels in the Southern Peloponnese. (Travel Library). 336p. 1984. pap. 5.95 (ISBN 0-14-009503-9). Penguin.

--Roumeli: Travels in Northern Greece. (Travel Library). 366p. 1984. pap. 5.95 (ISBN 0-14-009504-7). Penguin.

--A Time of Gifts. (Travel Library). 304p. 1984. pap. 5.95 (ISBN 0-14-009513-6). Penguin.

--The Violins of Saint Jacques. (Twentieth-Century Classics Ser.). 160p. 1985. pap. 5.95 (ISBN 0-19-281877-5). Oxford U Pr.

Fermor, Patrick L., tr. see Psychoudakis, George.

Fern, Alan & Livingston, Jane. People & Power: Portraits from the Federal Village. (Illus.). 232p. 1985. 29.95 (ISBN 0-8109-1481-6). Abrams.

Fern, Alan & O'Sullivan, Judith. The Complete Prints of Leonard Baskin: A Catalogue Raisonne 1948-1983. LC 84-860. (Illus.). 304p. 1984. 59.00 (ISBN 0-8212-1562-0). NYGS.

Fern, Alan, jt. auth. see Constantine, Mildred.

Fern, Alan, intro. by. Thirty Years of J. L. Steg: Nineteen Forty-Eight to Nineteen Seventy-Eight. LC 78-71034. (Illus.). 1978. pap. 3.95 (ISBN 0-89494-007-4). New Orleans Mus Art.

Fern, Alan & Kaplan, Milton, eds. Viewpoints: The Library of Congress Selection of Pictorial Treasures. new ed. LC 76-5442. (Illus.). 1976. 12.00 (ISBN 0-405-08106-5). Ayer Co Pubs.

Fern, Deane W., ed. Restoring the Kingdom. 240p. (Orig.). 1984. pap. text ed. 10.95 (ISBN 0-913757-06-3, Pub. by New Era Bks). Paragon Hse.

Fern, Lois, jt. ed. see McGuire, Diane K.

Fernadez, Rafael. A Scene of Light & Glory: Approaches to Venice. (Illus.). 48p. 1982. pap. 4.00 (ISBN 0-931102-15-4). S & F Clark.

Fernald, Charles H. Salesmanship. 1933. 15.00 (ISBN 0-686-17730-4). Quest Edns.

Fernald, Charles H., jt. auth. see Forbush, Edward H.

Fernald, Chester B. Cat & the Cherub & Other Stories. LC 70-113660. (Short Story Index Reprint Ser). 1896. 18.00 (ISBN 0-8369-3389-3). Ayer Co Pubs.

Fernald, Edward A., ed. Atlas of Florida. (Illus.). 276p. 1981. 27.50 (ISBN 0-9606708-0-7). Florida State U Found.

Fernald, Edward A. & Patton, Donald J., eds. Water Resources Atlas of Florida. (Illus.). 291p. 1984. 29.50 (ISBN 0-9606708-1-5). Florida State U Found.

Fernald, G. M. see Stanton, George M.

Fernald, James. English Grammar Simplified. Gale, Cedric, rev. by. 320p. (Orig.). 1979. pap. 4.33i (ISBN 0-06-463484-1, EH 484, EH). B&N NY.

Fernald, James C. Connectives of English Speech. 324p. 1981. Repr. of 1904 ed. lib. bdg. 25.00 (ISBN 0-89987-260-3). Darby Bks.

--English Synonyms & Antonyms with Notes on the Correct Use of Prepositions. 727p. 1981. Repr. of 1914 ed. lib. bdg. 40.00 (ISBN 0-8495-1731-1). Arden Lib.

--Expressive English. 463p. 1981. Repr. of 1918 ed. lib. bdg. 35.00 (ISBN 0-8495-1716-8). Arden Lib.

--Funk & Wagnall's Standard Handbook of Synonyms, Antonyms & Prepositions. rev. ed. LC 47-11924. (Funk & W Bk.). (gr. 9-12). 1947. 13.41i (ISBN 0-308-40024-0, 420140). T y Crowell.

--Historic English. 1979. Repr. of 1921 ed. lib. bdg. 30.00 (ISBN 0-8495-1647-1). Arden Lib.

Fernald, John. The Play Produced: An Introduction to the Technique of Producing Plays. 143p. 1983. Repr. of 1983 ed. lib. bdg. 35.00 (ISBN 0-8495-1738-9). Arden Lib.

Fernald, L. D. The Hans Legacy: A Story of Science. LC 83-11539. 241p. 1984. text ed. 29.95x (ISBN 0-89859-301-8). L Erlbaum Assocs.

Fernald, L. Dodge & Fernald, Peter S. Basic Psychology. 5th ed. 528p. 1985. text ed. write for info. (ISBN 0-697-00603-4); pap. text ed. write for info. (ISBN 0-697-00433-3); instr's. manual avail. (ISBN 0-697-00445-7); study guide avail. (ISBN 0-697-00446-5); test item file avail. (ISBN 0-697-00107-5); transparencies avail. (ISBN 0-697-00574-7). Wm C Brown.

Fernald, Mabel R. The Diagnosis of Mental Imagery, 3 vols. in 1. Bd. with Autokinetic Sensations. Adams, H. F. Repr. of 1912 ed; A Study of Cutaneous After-Sensations. Hayes, M. H. Repr. of 1912 ed; On the Relation of the Methods of Just Perceptible Differences & Constant Stimuli. Fernberger, S. W. Repr. of 1913 ed. (Psychology Monographs General & Applied: Vol. 14). pap. 29.00 (ISBN 0-317-15245-9). Kraus Intl.

Fernald, Mabel R., et al. Study of Women Delinquents in New York State. LC 68-55770. (Criminology, Law Enforcement, & Social Problems Ser.: No. 23). 1968. Repr. of 1920 ed. 20.00x (ISBN 0-87585-023-5). Patterson Smith.

Fernald, Mary & Shenton, Eileen. Costume Design & Making. 2nd ed. LC 67-14505. (Illus.). 1967. 15.95 (ISBN 0-87830-021-X). Theatre Arts.

Fernald, Peter S., jt. auth. see Fernald, L. Dodge.

Fernandes. Diccionario de Verbos e Regimes. 606p. (Port.). 35.00 (M-9212). French & Eur.

Fernandes, F. Diccionario Brasileiro Contemporaneo. (Port.). write for info. (M-9322). French & Eur.

--Dicionario da Lingua Portuguesa. (Port.). price not set. French & Eur.

Fernandes, F. & Luft, C. P. Dicionario de Sinonimos e Antonimos da Lingua Portuguesa. 870p. (Port.). 1980. 39.95 (ISBN 0-686-92539-4, M-9321). French & Eur.

Fernandes, Florestan. The Negro in Brazilian Society. LC 78-76247. (Institute of Latin American Studies). 489p. 1969. 39.00x (ISBN 0-231-02979-9). Columbia U Pr.

--Reflections on the Brazilian Counterrevolution. Dean, Warren, pref. by. Vale, Michel & Hughes, Patrick M., trs. from Portuguese. LC 80-5456. 200p. 1981. 30.00 (ISBN 0-87332-177-4). M E Sharpe.

Fernandes, Pracy & Kreacic, Vladimir, eds. Casebook of Public Enterprise Studies. 207p. 1982. pap. 20.00x (ISBN 92-9038-080-2, Pub. by Intl Ctr Pub Yugoslavia). Kumarian Pr.

Fernandes, Praxy, ed. Control Systems for Public Enterprises in Developing Countries. 435p. 1982. pap. 20.00x (ISBN 92-9038-012-8, Pub. by Intl Ctr Pub Yugoslavia). Kumarian Pr.

--Financing of Public Enterprises in Developing Countries. 148p. 1981. pap. 20.00x (ISBN 92-9038-020-9, Pub. by Intl Ctr Pub Yugoslavia). Kumarian Pr.

--State Trading & Development. 277p. 1982. pap. 20.00x (ISBN 92-9038-070-5, Pub. by Intl Ctr Pub Yugoslavia). Kumarian Pr.

Fernandes, Praxy & Sicheri, Pavle, eds. Seeking the Personality of Public Enterprise. 214p. 1981. pap. 20.00x (ISBN 92-9038-030-6, Pub. by Intl Ctr Pub Yugoslavia). Kumarian Pr.

Fernandes, Ron. Come to Think of It, Lord: Personal & Prayerful Reflections. 1977. 5.00 (ISBN 0-682-48851-8). Exposition Pr FL.

Fernandes, Teresa M., tr. see Kashiwara, Masaki.

Fernandes de Queiros, Pedro. Terre Australis Incognita, Or, a New Southerne Discoverie, Lately Found by F. De Quir. LC 68-54659. (English Experience Ser.: No. 246). 28p. 1976. Repr. of 1617 ed. 7.00 (ISBN 90-221-0246-7). Walter J Johnson.

Fernandex, Luis F. A Forgotten American. 56p. 2.50 (ISBN 0-88464-062-0). ADL.

Fernandez, Alejandro M. International Law in Philippine Relations: 1898-1946. 1971. 15.00x (ISBN 0-8248-0439-2). UH Pr.

Fernandez, C. Gandia, jt. auth. see De La Rosa, Angeles.

Fernandez, Celestino. Ethnic Group Insulation, Self-Concept, Academic Standards, & the Failure of Evaluations. LC 79-65269. 115p. 1979. perfect bdg. 10.00 (ISBN 0-88247-581-9). R & E Pubs.

Fernandez, D. S. El Espiritismo. (Coleccion Doctrinas Modernas: No. 1). 32p. pap. 0.75 (ISBN 0-311-05025-5, Edit Mundo). Casa Bautista.

--Los Falsos Testigos De Jehova. 46p. 1983. pap. 1.25 (ISBN 0-311-06351-9). Casa Bautista.

Fernandez, David, jt. auth. see Hamilton, Gavin.

Fernandez, Domingo. En la Escuela de Dios. 148p. 1982. pap. 3.25 (ISBN 0-89922-223-4). Edit Caribe.

--El Mormonismo Revelacion Divina o Invencion Humana. 32p. 1984. pap. 1.00 (ISBN 0-311-05762-4). Casa Bautista.

--Por Que Guardamos el Domingo? 87p. 1981. pap. 2.00 (ISBN 0-311-05603-2). Casa Bautista.

Fernandez, Domingo S. Una Interpretacion Del Apocalipsis. 234p. (Span.). 1983. pap. 3.75 (ISBN 0-311-04312-7). Casa Bautista.

Fernandez, Dominique. The Mother Sea: Travels in South Italy, Sardinia & Sicily. Callum, Michael, tr. from Sp. 236p. 1967. 5.95 (ISBN 0-8090-7100-2). Hill & Wang.

--Rome: Mirror of the Centuries. Lauritzen, Peter, tr. LC 84-7337. (Illus.). 252p. 1984. 50.00 (ISBN 0-86565-049-7). Vendome.

Fernandez, Doreen. Contemporary Theater Arts: Asia & the United States. 81p. (Orig.). 1984. pap. 6.50x (ISBN 971-10-0158-6, Pub. by New Day Philippines). Cellar.

Fernandez, Doreen G. The Iloilo Zarzuela: Nineteen Hundred & Three to Nineteen Thirty. (Illus.). 1979. 22.25x (ISBN 0-686-24651-9, Pub. by Ateneo Univ Pr); pap. 15.00x. Cellar.

Fernandez, Eduardo B., et al. Database Security & Integrity. LC 80-15153. (IBM Systems Programming Ser.). (Illus.). 288p. 1981. text ed. 31.95 (ISBN 0-201-14467-0). Addison-Wesley.

Fernandez, Fernando. Zora & the Hibernauts. (Illus.). 112p. (Orig.). 1984. pap. 11.95 (ISBN 0-87416-001-4). Catalan Communs.

Fernandez, Gaston J., jt. auth. see Zayas-Bazan, Eduardo.

Fernandez, Genevieve. American Traditional: A Comprehensive Guide to Home Decorating the Ethan Allen Way. (Illus.). 320p. 1984. 24.95 (ISBN 0-671-47687-4). S&S.

Fernandez, Happy. The Child Advocacy Handbook. LC 80-24053. 1981. pap. 6.95 (ISBN 0-8298-0403-X). Pilgrim NY.

--Los Padres se Organizan para Mejorar las Escuelas. NCCE, ed. ASPIRA of New York, tr. (Spanish.). 1976. 3.50 (ISBN 0-934460-03-5). NCCE.

Fernandez, Happy & NCCE. Parents Organizing to Improve Schools. NCCE, ed. ASPIRA of New York, tr. 1976. 3.50 (ISBN 0-934460-01-9). NCCE.

Fernandez, J., jt. auth. see Fitzgibbons, R.

Fernandez, J. N. & Ashley, R. Advanced Structured COBOL. (Data Processing Training Ser.). 250p. 1985. pap. 49.95 (ISBN 0-471-89764-7). Wiley.

Fernandez, J. W. Fang Architectonics. LC 76-53553. (Working Papers in the Traditional Arts Ser: No.1). (Illus.). 48p. 1977. pap. text ed. 5.95 (ISBN 0-915980-65-7). ISHI PA.

Fernandez, Jack E. Organic Chemistry: An Introduction. (Illus.). 528p. 1982. text ed. 30.95 (ISBN 0-13-640417-0); solutions manual 9.95 (ISBN 0-13-640425-1). P-H.

Fernandez, James, et al. On Symbols in Anthropology, Essays in Honor of Harry Hoijer, 1980. Maquet, Jacques, ed. LC 81-52797. (Other Realities Ser.: Vol. 3). 140p. 1982. 22.50x (ISBN 0-89003-091-X); pap. 12.50x (ISBN 0-89003-090-1). Undena Pubns.

Fernandez, James W. Bwiti: An Ethnography of the Religious Imagination in Africa. LC 81-47125. (Illus.). 708p. 1982. 92.50x (ISBN 0-691-09390-3); pap. 26.50x LPE (ISBN 0-691-10122-1). Princeton U Pr.

Fernandez, John P. Racism & Sexism in Corporate Life: Changing Values in American Business. LC 80-8945. (Illus.). 384p. 1981. 31.50x (ISBN 0-669-04477-6); pap. 14.00 (ISBN 0-669-05891-2). Lexington Bks.

Fernandez, Jose. Cuarenta Anos De Legislador: Biografia Del Senador Casimiro Barela. Cortes, Carlos E., ed. LC 76-1254. (Chicano Heritage Ser.). (Span.). 1976. Repr. of 1911 ed. 38.50x (ISBN 0-405-09501-5). Ayer Co Pubs.

Fernandez, Jose A. Architecture in Puerto Rico. (Illus.). 1965. 16.95 (ISBN 0-8038-0009-6). Architectural.

Fernandez, Jose B. & Fernandez, Roberto G. Indice Bibliografico de Autores Cubanos: (Diaspora 1959 - 1979) Bilingual ed. LC 80-68771. 106p. (Orig., Eng. & Span.). 1984. pap. 12.00 (ISBN 0-89729-269-3). Ediciones.

Fernandez, Jose B. & Garcia, Nasario. Nuevos Horizontes. 256p. 1981. pap. text ed. 9.95 (ISBN 0-669-04335-4). Heath.

Fernandez, Judi & Ashley, Ruth. Introduction to 8080-8085 Assembly Language Programming. LC 80-39650. (Wiley Self Teaching Guide Ser.: No. 1-581). 303p. 1981. pap. text ed. 12.95 (ISBN 0-471-08009-8, Pub. by Wiley Pr). Wiley.

Fernandez, Judi, jt. auth. see Ashley, Ruth.

Fernandez, Judi N. & Ashley, Ruth. CP-M for the IBM Personal Computer: Using CP-M-86. (A Self-Teaching & Wiley IBM-PC Ser.: No. 1-646). 261p. 1983. pap. text ed. 14.95 (ISBN 0-471-89719-1, Pub. by Wiley Pr). Wiley.

--Introduction to Computer Programming. LC 83-16726. (Data Processing Training Ser.: 1-615). 301p. 1984. pap. 49.95x (ISBN 0-471-87024-2). Wiley.

--Using CP-M. LC 80-36673. (Self-Teaching Guides Ser.: No. 1-581). 243p. 1980. pap. text ed. 15.95 (ISBN 0-471-08011-X, Pub. by Wiley Pr). Wiley.

Fernandez, Judi N., jt. auth. see Ashley, Ruth.

Fernandez, Judi N., jt. ed. see Ashley, Ruth.

Fernandez, Judi N., et al. Assembly Language Programming: 6502. (Wiley Self-Teaching Guides Ser.). 277p. 1983. pap. 14.95 (ISBN 0-471-86120-0, Pub. by Wiley Pr). Wiley.

Fernandez, Justino. Guide to Mexican Art: From Its Beginnings to the Present. Taylor, Joshua C., tr. LC 69-16773. 1969. 20.00x (ISBN 0-226-24420-2); pap. 12.95 (ISBN 0-226-24421-0). U of Chicago Pr.

Fernandez, L., jt. auth. see Fleck, H.

Fernandez, L., jt. auth. see Sallese, N.

Fernandez, Leandro H. Philippine Republic. LC 68-57571. (Columbia University. Studies in the Social Sciences: No. 268). Repr. of 1926 ed. 18.50 (ISBN 0-404-51268-2). AMS Pr.

Fernandez, Magaly, ed. see Roque Dalton Cultural Brigade.

Fernandez, Manuel. Religion y Revolucion en Cuba. (Realidades Ser.). 250p. (Span.). 1984. pap. 14.95 (ISBN 0-917049-00-4). Saeta.

Fernandez, Mendez. Viaje Historico de un Pueblo. 24.95 (ISBN 0-87751-003-2, Pub by Troutman Press). E Torres & Sons.

Fernandez, Oscar. Living Portuguese. 1965. 15.95, with 4 lp records conversation manual & dictionary (ISBN 0-517-03779-3). Crown.

Fernandez, Oscar, jt. auth. see Starnes, George E.

Fernandez, R. C., jt. ed. see Powers, Pauline S.

Fernandez, Rafael. Eastern Winds: The Imprint of Japan on Nineteenth- & Early Twentieth-Century Western Graphics. (Illus.). 32p. (Orig.). 1982. pap. 3.50 (ISBN 0-931102-08-1). S & F Clark Art.

Fernandez, Ramon. Moliere: The Man Seen Through the Plays. LC 79-28249. 212p. 1980. Repr. of 1958 ed. lib. bdg. 16.00x (ISBN 0-374-92739-1). Octagon.

Fernandez, Raul A. The United States-Mexico Border: A Politico-Economic Profile. LC 76-22409. 1978. text ed. 4.95x (ISBN 0-268-01914-2). U of Notre Dame Pr.

Fernandez, Roberto. La Montana Rusa. 120p. (Span.). 1984. 8.00 (ISBN 0-934770-41-7). Arte Publico.

Fernandez, Roberto G. La Vida es un Special. LC 81-69532. (Coleccion Caniqui). (Orig.). pap. 6.95 (ISBN 0-89729-303-7). Ediciones.

Fernandez, Roberto G., jt. auth. see Fernandez, Jose B.

Fernandez, Ron. Excess Profits: The Rise of United Technologies. LC 83-3760. (Illus.). 320p. 1983. 16.95 (ISBN 0-201-10484-9). Addison-Wesley.

Fernandez, Ronald. The I, Me, & You: An Introduction to Social Psychology. LC 76-41957. 430p. 1977. text ed. 20.95 (ISBN 0-275-22080-X, HoltC). HR&W.

--The I, the Me & You: An Introduction to Social Psychology. LC 74-33025. 1977. 20.95 (ISBN 0-275-22080-X). Praeger.

Fernandez, Ronald, et al. The Promise of Sociology. 2nd ed. LC 78-17720. 1979. pap. 18.95 (ISBN 0-275-64840-0, HoltC). HR&W.

Fernandez, Sergio, tr. see Ziglar, Zig.

Fernandez, Sergio L. Foundations of Objective Knowledge. 1985. lib. bdg. 39.50 (ISBN 90-277-1809-1, Pub. by Reidel Holland). Kluwer Academic.

Fernandez, Thomas. Oral Communications for Business. 1984. pap. text ed. 9.95 (ISBN 0-8359-5281-9). Reston.

Fernandez-Armesto, Felip. Sadat & His Statecraft. (Illus.). 196p. 1983. 15.95 (ISBN 0-946041-00-8, Pub. by Salem Hse Ltd). Merrimack Pub Cir.

Fernandez-Armesto, Felipe. The Canary Islands after the Conquest: The Making of a Colonial Society in the Early Sixteenth Century. (Historical Monographs). (Illus.). 1982. 52.00x (ISBN 0-19-821888-5). Oxford U Pr.

--Ferdinand & Isabella. LC 73-14366. (Illus.). 232p. 1975. 15.00 (ISBN 0-8008-2621-3). Taplinger.

Fernandez-Caballero, Carlos & Fernandez-Caballero, Marianne, eds. Emergency Medical Services Systems: A Guide to Information Sources. (Health Affairs Information Guide Series, Gale Information Guide Library: Vol. 9). 250p. 1981. 60.00x (ISBN 0-8103-1503-3). Gale.

Fernandez-Caballero, Marianne, jt. ed. see Fernandez-Caballero, Carlos.

Fernandez De Figueroa, Martin. Spaniard in the Portuguese Indies: The Narrative of Martin Fernandez De Figueroa. McKenna, James B., ed. LC 67-27089. (Studies in Romance Languages: No. 31). 1967. 17.50x (ISBN 0-674-83085-7). Harvard U Pr.

Fernandez De La Torriente, Gaston. Vocabulario Superior. 176p. (Span.). 1975. pap. 8.75 (ISBN 84-359-0124-6). French & Eur.

Fernandez de la Torriente, Gaston, tr. see Montaner, Carlos A.

Fernandez de la Vega, Oscar & Hernandez-Miyares, Julio E. Ortografia en Accion, Con Vocabulario Comercial. (Span.). 1978. text ed. 6.60 wkbk. (ISBN 0-538-22230-1, V23). SW Pub.

Fernandez De Lizardi, Jose J. The Itching Parrot. Porter, Katherine A., tr. & intro. by. LC 80-2479. (Span.). Repr. of 1942 ed. 39.50 (ISBN 0-404-19113-4). AMS Pr.

Fernandez-Florez, Dario. The Spanish Heritage in the United States. Cortes, Carlos E., ed. LC 79-6204. (Hispanics in the United States Ser.). (Illus.). 1981. Repr. of 1965 ed. lib. bdg. 34.50x (ISBN 0-405-13155-0). Ayer Co Pubs.

Fernandez Guardia, Ricardo. Cuentos Ticos: Short Stories of Costa Rica. 3rd ed. Casement, Gray, tr. LC 78-121540. (Short Story Index Reprint Ser). 1925. 24.50 (ISBN 0-8369-3496-2). Ayer Co Pubs.

Fernandez-Kelly, Maria P. For We Are Sold, I & My People: Women & Industry in Mexico's Frontier. LC 82-19249. (SUNY Series in the Anthropology of Work). 217p. 1983. 39.50x (ISBN 0-87395-717-2); pap. 11.95x (ISBN 0-87395-718-0). State U NY Pr.

Fernandez-Kelly, Maria P., jt. ed. see Nash, June.

Fernandez-Marcane, Leonardo. Veinte Cuentistas Cubanos. LC 77-89099. 1978. pap. 6.00 (ISBN 0-89729-164-6). Ediciones.

Fernandez Mendez, Eugenio. Historia Cultural De Puerto Rico 1493-1968. 4th ed. (Illus.). 1980. Repr. of 1970 ed. 10.00 (ISBN 0-8477-0841-1). U of PR Pr.

Fernandez Mendez, Eugenio, ed. Antologia del Pensamiento Puertorriqueno: 1900-1970, 2 vols. (Span.). 1976. Set. 20.00 (ISBN 0-8477-0842-X). Vol. 1 (ISBN 0-8477-0843-8). Vol. 2 (ISBN 0-8477-0844-6). U of PR Pr.

Fernandez-Olmos, Margarite, jt. ed. see Meyer, Doris.

Fernandez-Santamaria, J. A. Reason of State & Statecraft in Spanish Political Thought: 1595-1640. LC 82-25614. 376p. (Orig.). 1983. text ed. 28.25 (ISBN 0-8191-3046-X); pap. text ed. 16.00 (ISBN 0-8191-3047-8). U Pr of Amer.

--The State, War & Peace. LC 76-27903. (Studies in Early Modern History). 1977. 52.50 (ISBN 0-521-21438-6). Cambridge U Pr.

Fernandez-Valledor, Roberto. El Mito De Cofresi En la Narrativa Antillana. LC 77-16653. (Coleccion Mente y Palabra). (Illus.). 1978. 6.25 (ISBN 0-8477-0556-0); pap. 5.00 (ISBN 0-8477-0557-9). U of PR Pr.

Fernandez-Vazquez, Antonio. La Novelistica Cubana De la Revolucion. LC 79-52159. (Coleccion Polymita Ser.). 157p. (Span.). 1980. pap. 10.00 (ISBN 0-89729-228-6). Ediciones.

Fernandez-White, Jessica. Awareness & Stimulation among Squatters & Other Self-Help Builders. 1982. pap. 3.00 (ISBN 0-318-00900-5). Comm Serv Soc NY.

Fernando, Ajith. Leadership Lifestyles: A Study of 1 Timothy. (Living Studies). 224p. 1985. pap. 6.95 (ISBN 0-8423-2130-6); leader's guide 2.95 (ISBN 0-8423-2131-4). Tyndale.

Fernando, Antony & Swidler, Leonard. Buddhism Made Plain: An Introduction for Christians & Jews. LC 84-18880. (Orig.). 1985. pap. 9.95 (ISBN 0-88344-198-5). Orbis Bks.

Fernando, C. H. Ecology & Biogeography of Sri Lanka. (Monographiae Biologicae: No. 57). 520p. 1984. 110.00 (ISBN 90-6193-109-6, Pub. by Junk Pubs Netherlands). Kluwer Academic.

Fernando, Chitra, jt. ed. see Obeyesekere, Ranjini.

Fernando, Enrique M. The Constitution of the Philippines. 931p. 1975. 32.50 (ISBN 0-379-00295-7). Oceana.

Fernando, Lloyd. New Women in the Late Victorian Novel. LC 76-42456. 1977. 22.50x (ISBN 0-271-01241-2). Pa St U Pr.

--Scorpion Orchid. (Writing in Asia Ser.). 1976. pap. text ed. 6.00x (ISBN 0-686-77802-2, 00233). Heinemann Ed.

--Twenty-Two Malaysian Stories. (Writing in Asia Ser.). 1968. pap. text ed. 5.50x (ISBN 0-686-60326-5, 00229). Heinemann Ed.

Fernando, Lloyd, ed. Malaysian Short Stories. (Writing in Asia Ser.). xvii, 302p. (Orig.). 1981. pap. text ed. 7.50x (ISBN 0-686-79034-0, 00264). Heinemann Ed.

Fernando, Quintus & Ryan, Michael D. Calculations in Analytical Chemistry. 241p. 1982. pap. text ed. 12.95 (ISBN 0-15-505710-3, HC). HarbraceJ.

Fernando, Quintus, jt. auth. see Freiser, Henry.

Fernando, Sunimal & Gunaseker, Wickrema. Water Management in the Village of Kelegama in Sri Lanka. (Project on the Sharing of Traditional Technology). 43p. 1983. pap. 5.00 (ISBN 92-808-0382-4, TUNU210, UNU). Unipub.

Fernando, Tissa & Kearney, Robert. Sri Lanka: Profile of an Island Republic. (Nations of Contemporary Ser.). 144p. 1986. 28.00x (ISBN 0-89158-926-0). Westview.

Fernando, Tissa & Kearney, Robert N., eds. Modern Sri Lanka: A Society in Transition. LC 79-13077. (Foreign & Comparative Studies Program, South Asian Ser.: No. 4). (Illus.). 297p. 1979. pap. text ed. 9.00x (ISBN 0-915984-80-6). Syracuse U Foreign Comp.

Fernbach, David. The Spiral Path: A Gay Contribution to Human Survival. 240p. (Orig.). 1981. pap. 6.95 (ISBN 0-932870-12-0). Alyson Pubns.

Fernbach, David, ed. see Marx, Karl.

Fernbach, David, tr. see Buci-Glucksmann, Christine.

Fernbach, David, tr. see Heger, Heinz.

Fernbach, David, tr. see Lukacs, Georg.

Fernbach, David, tr. see Marx, Karl.

Fernbach, S. & Taub, A., eds. Computers & Their Role in the Physical Sciences. 638p. 1970. 113.50 (ISBN 0-677-14030-4). Gordon.

Fernbach, William, jt. auth. see Janssen, Quinith.

Fernberger, Linda M., jt. ed. see Fenn, Dan H.

Fernberger, S. W. see Dearborn, George Van Ness.

Fernberger, S. W. see Fernald, Mabel R.

Ferne, John. The Blazon of Gentrie. LC 72-5986. (English Experience Ser.: No. 513). (Illus.). 488p. 1973. Repr. of 1586 ed. 70.00 (ISBN 90-221-0513-X). Walter J Johnson.

Fernea, Elizabeth W. Guests of the Sheik: An Ethnology of an Iraqi Village. LC 65-13098. 1969. pap. 5.95 (ISBN 0-385-01485-6, A693, Anch). Doubleday.

Fernea, Elizabeth W. & Fernea, Robert A. The Arab World: Personal Encounters. LC 82-45245. (Illus.). 384p. 1985. 19.95 (ISBN 0-385-17123-4, Anchor Pr). Doubleday.

Fernea, Elizabeth W., ed. Women & the Family in the Middle East: New Voices of Change. (Illus.). 368p. 1985. 24.50x (ISBN 0-292-75528-7); pap. 11.95 (ISBN 0-292-75529-5). U of Tex Pr.

Fernea, Elizabeth W. & Bezirgan, Basima Q., eds. Middle Eastern Muslim Women Speak. (Illus.). 452p. 1977. 23.50x (ISBN 0-292-75033-1); pap. 12.50x (ISBN 0-292-75041-2). U of Tex Pr.

Fernea, Elizabeth Warnock. A Street in Marrakech. LC 74-12686. 1976. pap. 8.95 (ISBN 0-385-12045-1, Anch). Doubleday.

Fernea, Robert A., jt. auth. see Fernea, Elizabeth W.
Ferner, Andrew, et al, eds. The Book of Family Therapy. LC 84-24171. 725p. 1983. 30.00 (ISBN 0-87668-671-4). Aronson.
Ferner, Helmut & Staubesand, Jochen, eds. Sobotta: Atlas of Human Anatomy, 2 vols. 10th ed. Incl. Vol. 1. Head, Neck, Upper Extremities. (Illus.). 390p (ISBN 0-8067-1710-6); Vol. 2. Thorax, Abdomen, Pelvis, Lower Extremities, Skin. (Illus.). 375p. 1983 (ISBN 0-8067-1720-3). (Illus.). 1983. text ed. 42.50 ea. Urban & S.
Ferner, Helmut, ed. see Pernkopf, Eduard.
Ferner, Jack D. How to Read, Understand, & Use Financial Reports. (Wiley Self-Teaching Guides). 256p. 1983. pap. 8.95 (ISBN 0-471-09751-9, Pub by Wiley Pr). Wiley.
--Successful Time Management. LC 79-13680. (Self-Teaching Guide Ser.). 296p. 1980. pap. text ed. 10.95x (ISBN 0-471-03911-X, Pub. by Wiley Pr); leaders' guide, 59p 5.00 (ISBN 0-471-07773-9). Wiley.
Ferneti, Casper & Lent, James. Eating. (Project MORE Daily Living Skill Ser.). 96p. 1978. pap. text ed. 10.95 (ISBN 0-8331-1243-0). Hubbard Sci.
--Shaving Your Face. (Project MORE Daily Living Skills Ser.). 68p. (Orig.). 1978. pap. text ed. 9.50 (ISBN 0-8331-1236-8). Hubbard Sci.
Ferneti, Casper, jt. auth. see Ingenthron, Donita.
Ferneti, Casper, jt. auth. see Lewis, Patricia.
Ferneti, Casper, jt. auth. see Stevens, Crystal.
Fernett, Gene. Hollywood's Poverty Row. LC 73-86757. (Film History Ser). (Illus.). 178p. 1973. 9.95 (ISBN 0-914042-01-7). Laura Bks.
Fernholz, H. & Krause, E., eds. Three-Dimensional Turbulaent Boundry Layers, Berlin FRG 1982: Proceedings. (International Union of Theoretical & Applied Mechanics Ser.). (Illus.). 389p. 1982. 42.00 (ISBN 0-387-11772-5). Springer-Verlag.
Fernie, Eric. The Architecture of the Anglo-Saxons. LC 83-12915. (Illus.). 192p. 1983. text ed. 49.50x (ISBN 0-8419-0912-1). Holmes & Meier.
Fernie, J. D., ed. see International Astronomical Union Colloquium No. 21, University of Toronto, Aug. 29-31, 1972.
Fernie, W. T. Precious Stones for Curative Wear & Other Remedial Uses. 69.95 (ISBN 0-8490-0886-7). Gordon Pr.
Fernie, William T. Herbal Remedies Approved for Modern Uses of Cure. 1977. lib. bdg. 59.95 (ISBN 0-8490-1940-0). Gordon Pr.
--The Occult & Curative Powers of Precious Stones. LC 80-8894. (The Harper Library of Spiritual Wisdom). 496p. 1981. pap. 10.53i (ISBN 0-06-062360-8, CN4009, HarpR). Har-Row.
Fernier, Fernand G., et al, trs. see Ciliga, Ante.
Fernig, L. The Role of Information in Educational Development. (Studies & Surveys in Comparative Education). Date not set. pap. price not set (UNESCO). Unipub.
Fernig, Leo. The Place of Information in Educational Development. (IBE Studies & Surveys in Comparative Education). (Illus.). 135p. 1980. pap. 9.25 (ISBN 92-3-101822-1, U1059, UNESCO). Unipub.
Fernig, Leo & Bowen, James, eds. Twenty-Five Years of Educational Practice & Theory. vi, 353p. 1980. lib. bdg. 29.00 (ISBN 90-247-2284-5, Pub. by Martinus Nijhoff Netherlands). Kluwer Academic.
Fernique, X. M., et al, eds. see Ecole de'Ete De Probabilites De Saint-Flour, 4th, 1974.
Fernow, Bernhard E. Economics of Forestry: A Reference Book for Students of Political Economy & Professional & Lay Students of Forestry. LC 72-2836. (Use & Abuse of America's Natural Resources Ser). 536p. 1972. Repr. of 1902 ed. 33.00 (ISBN 0-405-04505-0). Ayer Co Pubs.
Fernow, Bernhard E., et al. Forest Influence. Egerton, Frank N., 3rd, ed. LC 77-74220. (History of Ecology Ser.). 1978. Repr. of 1893 ed. lib. bdg. 16.00x (ISBN 0-405-10391-3). Ayer Co Pubs.
Fernow, Berthold. Ohio Valley in Colonial Days. LC 70-149231. 1971. Repr. of 1890 ed. 21.50 (ISBN 0-8337-1116-4). B Franklin.
--The Records of New Amsterdam: From 1653 to 1674 Anno Domini, 7 vols. LC 76-1195. (Illus.). 2743p. 1976. Repr. of 1897 ed. 125.00 set (ISBN 0-8063-0715-3). Genealog Pub.
Fernow, Berthold, ed. Minutes of the Executive Boards of the Burgomasters of New Amsterdam. LC 71-112544. (Rise of Urban America). 1970. Repr. of 1907 ed. 11.00 (ISBN 0-405-02453-3). Ayer Co Pubs.
Ferns, C. S. Aldous Huxley: Novelist. 240p. 1980. 36.50 (ISBN 0-485-11194-2, Pub. by Athlone Pr Ltd). Longwood Pub Group.
Ferns, G. K. Australian Wheat Varieties. 126p. 1982. 35.00x (ISBN 0-643-00143-3, Pub. by CSIRO Australia). State Mutual Bk.
Ferns, G. K. & Fitzsimmons, R. W. Australian Wheat Varieties. Incl. Supple. 1. (Illus.). 30p. 1978. pap. 13.50 (ISBN 0-643-00325-8, C001, CSIRO); Identification According to Growth, Head & Grain Characteristics. 126p. 1975. pap. 15.50 (ISBN 0-643-00143-3, C008, CSIRO). Unipub.
Ferns, G. K., et al. Australian Wheat Varieties: Identification According to Growth, Head & Grain Characteristics. (Illus.). 1977. pap. 12.00x (ISBN 0-643-00143-3, Pub. by CSIRO). Intl Spec Bk.
--Australian Wheat Varieties: Supplement No. 1. (Illus.). 1979. 11.00x (ISBN 0-643-00325-8, Pub. by CSIRO). Intl Spec Bk.
Ferns, H. S. The Disease of Government. LC 78-17637. 1978. 16.95 (ISBN 0-312-21256-9). St Martin.
--How Much Freedom for Universities? (Institute of Economic Affairs, Occasional Papers: No. 65). pap. 5.95 technical (ISBN 0-255-36158-0). Transatlantic.
--Reading from Left to Right: One Man's Political History. 384p. 1983. 24.95 (ISBN 0-8020-2518-8). U of Toronto Pr.
--Towards an Independent University. (Institute of Economic Affairs, Occasional Papers Ser.: No. 25). pap. 2.50 technical (ISBN 0-255-36010-X). Transatlantic.
Ferns, Henry S. British & Argentina in the Nineteenth Century. Wilkins, Mira, ed. LC 76-29757. (European Business Ser.). 1977. Repr. of 1960 ed. lib. bdg. 40.00x (ISBN 0-405-09772-7). Ayer Co Pubs.
Ferns, John. A. J. M. Smith. (World Authors Ser.). 1979. lib. bdg. 16.95 (ISBN 0-8057-6377-5, Twayne). G K Hall.
Ferns, John, jt. ed. see Crick, Brian.
Ferntheil, Carol. Bible Adventures Basic Bible Reader. 128p. 1985. pap. 4.95 (ISBN 0-317-30639-1, 2757). Standard Pub.
--Noah's Ark Diorama Book. (gr. k-3). 1977. 3.95 (ISBN 0-87239-167-1, 3606). Standard Pub.
Ferntheil, Carol, ed. Garden of Cheer. (Illus.). 16p. (Orig.). 1979. pap. 0.85 (ISBN 0-87239-343-7, 7946). Standard Pub.
--Psalms of Cheer. (Illus.). 16p. (Orig.). 1979. pap. 0.85 (ISBN 0-87239-342-9, 7945). Standard Pub.
--Songs of Cheer. (Illus.). 16p. (Orig.). 1979. pap. 0.85 (ISBN 0-87239-345-3, 7948). Standard Pub.
--Words of Cheer. (Illus.). 16p. (Orig.). 1979. pap. 0.85 (ISBN 0-87239-344-5, 7947). Standard Pub.
Feroe, Paul, ed. Silent Voices: Recent American Poems on Nature. LC 78-54317. 1978. 6.50 (ISBN 0-915408-18-X); pap. 2.95 (ISBN 0-915408-17-1). Ally Pr.
Feroletto, Mia. New York Printmakers: A Dozen Directions, Essay. Liddle, Nancy, ed. (Illus.). 16p. 1985. pap. 2.00 (ISBN 0-910763-01-1). SUNY Albany U Art.
Ferra, B. Chopin & George Sand in Majorca. LC 73-21620. (Studies in French Literature, No. 45). 1974. lib. bdg. 49.95x (ISBN 0-8383-1807-X). Haskell.
Ferrabosco, Alfonso see Arkwright, G. E. P.
Ferrabosco, Alfonso, 2nd. Four Fantasies for String Quartet or Consort of Viols. Edmunds, John, ed. (Penn State Music Series, No. 21). pap. 4.00x (ISBN 0-271-09121-5). Pa St U Pr.
Ferracane, Gerardo, ed. see Dante Alighieri.
Ferracuti, Franco & Wolfgang, Marvin E. Criminological Diagnosis: An International Perspective, 2 vols. LC 77-2686. 1983. Vol. 1. 320p 33.50x (ISBN 0-669-01624-1); Vol. 2. 336p 35.00x (ISBN 0-669-05971-4); 61.00x set (ISBN 0-669-06434-3). Lexington Bks.
Ferracuti, Franco, jt. auth. see Wolfgang, Marvin E.
Ferracuti, Franco, et al. Delinquents & Nondelinquents in the Puerto Rican Slum Culture. LC 75-16465. (Illus.). 265p. 1975. 15.00 (ISBN 0-8142-0239-X). Ohio St U Pr.
Ferrall, Rose N. D. X. V. Prophecy-Dante & the Sabbatum Fidelium. (Studies in Dante, No. 9). 1970. pap. 22.95x (ISBN 0-8383-0090-1). Haskell.
Ferran. L' Esthetique de Baudelaire. 27.95 (ISBN 0-685-34104-6). French & Eur.
Ferrand. Calculus. (College Outline Ser.). 1984. pap. text ed. 10.95 (ISBN 0-15-601556-0, BFP). HarBraceJ.
Ferrand, G. Contes populaires malgaches. LC 78-20127. (Collection de contes et de chansons populaires: Vol. 19). Repr. of 1893 ed. 21.50 (ISBN 0-404-60369-6). AMS Pr.
Ferrando, A., et al, eds. SU3 X SU2 X U1 & Beyond: Proceedings of the XIIIth GIFT International Seminar on Theoretical Physics & Xth Winter Meeting on Fundamentals Physics Masella, Girona, Spain, Jan. 28-Feb. 6, 1982. 516p. 1983. 60.00x (ISBN 9971-950-79-0, Pub. by World Sci Singapore). Taylor & Francis.
Ferrando, Jose, jt. auth. see Carenas, F.
Ferrando, R., ed. see Symposium on Toxicology & Nutrition, Paris, November 1976.
Ferrans, V. J., et al, eds. Cardiac Morphogenesis. 450p. 1985. 54.00 (ISBN 0-444-00983-3). Elsevier.
Ferrante, A. J., jt. auth. see Brebbia, C. A.
Ferrante, J. & Rackoff, C. W. The Computational Complexity of Logical Theories. (Lecture Notes in Mathematics Ser.: Vol. 718). 1979. pap. 19.00 (ISBN 0-387-09501-2). Springer-Verlag.
Ferrante, Joan, ed. see Jackson, W. T.
Ferrante, Joan M. The Conflict of Love & Honor: The Medieval Triston Legend in France, Germany & Italy. LC 73-85773. (De Proprietatibus Litterarum, Ser. Practica: Vol. 78). 157p. 1973. pap. text ed. 17.60x (ISBN 90-2792-604-2). Mouton.
--The Political Vision of the Divine Comedy. LC 82-26906. 400p. 1984. text ed. 35.00x (ISBN 0-691-06603-5). Princeton U pr.
--Woman As Image in Medieval Literature from the Twelfth Century to Dante. 166p. 1985. pap. 8.95 (ISBN 0-939464-43-8). Labyrinth Pr.
Ferrante, Joan M. & Economou, George D., eds. In Pursuit of Perfection: Courtly Love in Medieval Literature. LC 74-80596. 1975. 19.50x (ISBN 0-8046-9092-8, Pub. by Kennikat). Assoc Faculty Pr.
Ferrante, Joan M., ed. see France, Marie De.
Ferrante, Joan M., tr. from Fr. Guillaume D'Orange: Four Twelfth-Century Epics. LC 74-4421. (Records of Civilization Ser). 311p. 1974. 27.50x (ISBN 0-231-03809-7). Columbia U Pr.
Ferranti, M. P. & Fiechter, A., eds. Production & Feeding of Single-Cell Protein: Proceedings of the COST Workshop, Zurich, Switzerland, April 13-15, 1983. (Illus.). 216p. 1983. 37.00 (ISBN 0-85334-243-1, I-337-83, Pub. by Elsevier Applied Sci England). Elsevier.
Ferranti, Phillip. Overcoming Our Obsessions. 1979. 7.95 (ISBN 0-88280-069-8). ETC Pubns.
Ferranti, Wilson. Reina del Amor. (Pimienta Collection Ser). (Orig., Span.). 1977. pap. 1.00 (ISBN 0-88473-269-X). Fiesta Pub.
Ferrar, Carol, ed. Michel Corette & Flute Playing in the 18th Century. (Musical Theorists in Translation Ser.: Vol. 9). 1970. lib. bdg. 20.00 (ISBN 0-912024-29-1). Inst Mediaeval Mus.
Ferrar, H. John Osborne. LC 72-13527. (Columbia Essays on Modern Writers Ser.: No. 67). 48p. 1973. pap. 2.50 (ISBN 0-231-03361-3). Columbia U Pr.
Ferrar, H., et al, eds. The Concise Oxford French Dictionary. 2nd ed. 912p. 1985. pap. 9.95 (ISBN 0-19-864157-5). Oxford U Pr.
Ferrar, Harold, jt. auth. see Clarke, Brenna K.
Ferrar, Jami & Whalley, Elizabeth. English As a Second Language: Manual, Level III-IV. 224p. 1985. pap. text ed. 8.00 ea. (RanC). Level III (ISBN 0-394-33717-4). Level IV (ISBN 0-394-33726-3). Random.
Ferrar, W. J., ed. see Eusebius.
Ferrar, W. L. A Textbook of Convergence. (Illus.). 1980. Repr. of 1938 ed. 19.95x (ISBN 0-19-853176-1). Oxford U Pr.
Ferrar, William J. The Early Christian Books. 1919. Repr. 20.00 (ISBN 0-8274-2211-3). R West.
--The Early Christian Books: A Short Introduction to Christian Literature to the Middle of the Second Century. 1979. Repr. of 1919 ed. lib. bdg. 20.00 (ISBN 0-8495-1637-4). Arden Lib.
Ferrara, Frank. On Being Father: A Divorced Man Talks about Sharing the New Responsibilities of Parenthood. LC 84-4068. 192p. 1985. pap. 7.95 (ISBN 0-385-19128-6, Dolp). Doubleday.
Ferrara, Grace M., ed. Atomic Energy & the Safety Controversy. (Checkmark Bks). 180p. 1978. lib. bdg. 19.95 (ISBN 0-87196-297-7). Facts on File.
--The Disaster File: The Seventies. (Checkmark Ser.). 196p. 1979. 19.95x (ISBN 0-87196-155-5). Facts on File.
--Latin America. LC 73-83047. pap. 48.00 (ISBN 0-317-20491-2, 2022943). Bks Demand UMI.
Ferrara, John A., jt. auth. see Farrell, Kathleen L.
Ferrara, John M. Every Pilot's Guide to Aviation Electronics. 1976. pap. 12.75 (ISBN 0-911720-24-3). Aviation.
Ferrara, Peter. East vs. West in the Middle East. (Impact Ser.). 96p. (gr. 7 up). 1983. PLB 9.90 (ISBN 0-531-04543-9). Watts.
--Natural Remedies. 256p. (Orig.). 1984. pap. 3.95 (ISBN 0-523-42104-4). Pinnacle Bks.
Ferrara, Peter, et al. Solving the Problem of Medicare. Date not set. price not set (ISBN 0-943802-11-3). Natl Ctr Pol.
Ferrara, Peter J. Social Security: Averting the Crisis. abr. ed. (Cato Public Policy Monograph: No. 4). 156p. (Orig.). 1982. pap. 6.95x (ISBN 0-932790-26-7). Cato Inst.
--Social Security: The Inherent Contradiction. LC 80-18949. (Policy Bks.: No. 1). 484p. 1980. 20.00x (ISBN 0-932790-24-0). Cato Inst.
Ferrara, Peter J., ed. Social Security: Prospects for Real Reform. LC 85-9642. 228p. 1985. 20.00 (ISBN 0-932790-45-3); pap. 8.95 (ISBN 0-932790-48-8). Cato Inst.
Ferrara, Peter L. NATO: An Entangled Alliance. (Impact Bks.). 128p. (gr. 7-12). 1984. lib. bdg. 10.90 (ISBN 0-531-04759-8). Watts.
Ferrara, Peter L. & Kahn, Frederick E. Natural Cures for Common Ills. 256p. pap. cancelled (ISBN 0-8329-0111-3). New Century.
Ferrara, S. Supersymmetry. 600p. 1984. 63.00x (ISBN 9971-966-21-2, Pub. by World Sci Singapore); pap. 28.00x (ISBN 9971-966-22-0, Pub. by Sci Singapore). Taylor & Francis.
Ferrara, S. & Taylor, J. G., eds. Supergravity Nineteen Eighty One. LC 82-1204. 512p. 1982. 47.50 (ISBN 0-521-24738-1). Cambridge U Pr.
--Supersymmetry & Supergravity '82: Proceedings of the Trieste Workshop Sept. 1982 School. vi, 334p. 1983. 49.00x (ISBN 9971-950-67-7, Pub. by World Sci Singapore); pap. 21.00x (ISBN 9971-950-68-5, Pub. by World Sci Singapore). Taylor & Francis.
Ferrara, S., et al, eds. Conformal Algebra in Space - Time & Operator Product Expansion. LC 25-9130. (Springer Tracts in Modern Physics: Vol. 67). iv, 69p. 1973. 22.50 (ISBN 0-387-06216-5). Springer-Verlag.
Ferrara, Sergio, jt. ed. see Ellis, John.
Ferrara, Sergio, et al, eds. Unification of the Fundamental Particle Interactions. LC 80-24447. (Ettore Majorana International Science Series-Physical Sciences: Vol. 7). 740p. 1981. 115.00x (ISBN 0-306-40575-X, Plenum Pr). Plenum Pub.
Ferrara, William. Researching the Accounting Curriculum: Strategies for Change, Vol. 2. (Studies in Accounting Education). 227p. 1975. 6.00 (ISBN 0-86539-030-4); members 4.00. Am Accounting.
Ferrare Dtot, Charles De see Dutot, Charles.
Ferrari, A. see Rossini, F. P.
Ferrari, Attilio & Pacholczyk, A. G., eds. Astrophysical Jets. 1983. lib. bdg. 48.00 (ISBN 90-277-1627-7, Pub. by Reidel Holland). Kluwer Academic.
Ferrari, Bernard T., et al. Complications of Colon & Rectal Surgery: Prevention & Management. (Illus.). 450p. 1984. write for info. (ISBN 0-7216-3622-5). Saunders.
Ferrari, C., ed. see CISM (International Center for Mechanical Sciences).
Ferrari, Carlo & Tricomi, Francesco. Transonic Aerodynamics. Cramer, R. H., tr. LC 67-23156. 1968. 94.00 (ISBN 0-12-253950-8). Acad Pr.
Ferrari, D., ed. The Performance of Computer Installations. 342p. 1979. 64.00 (ISBN 0-444-85186-0, North Holland). Elsevier.
Ferrari, D. & Spadoni, H., eds. Experimental Computer Performance Evaluation. 264p. 1981. 47.00 (ISBN 0-444-86129-7, North-Holland). Elsevier.
Ferrari, Dino, tr. see Douhet, Giulio.
Ferrari, Domenico. Computer Systems Performance Evaluation. LC 77-15096. (Illus.). 1978. ed. 425.00ref. (ISBN 0-13-165126-9). P-H.
Ferrari, Domenico & Serazzi, Guiseppe. Measurement & Tuning of Computer Systems. (Illus.). 624p. 1983. text ed. 45.00 (ISBN 0-13-568519-2). P-H.
Ferrari, Ezio & Violini, Galileo, eds. Low & Intermediate Energy Kaon-Nuclear Physics. 424p. 1981. 52.50 (ISBN 90-277-1183-6, Pub. by Reidel Holland). Kluwer Academic.
Ferrari, Gustavo E., jt. auth. see Paz, Alberto C.
Ferrari, Guy. How to Profit from Future Technology: A Guide to Success in the Eighties & Beyond. Adams, Mary, ed. LC 82-73571. 300p. 1983. pap. 14.95 (ISBN 0-911321-01-2). Windsor Hse.
Ferrari, Lorraine D., jt. ed. see Jones, Donald H.
Ferrari, M. & Williams, P. Places "FOR MEN". The Man's Guide, U. S. A., Canada, Caribbean. 349p. 1986. pap. 7.00 (ISBN 0-942586-12-3). Ferrari Pubns.
Ferrari, Marianne & Williams, Pam. Places of Interest: Gay Travel Guide U. S. A., Canada, Caribbean. rev ed. (Illus.). 208p. 1986. pap. 9.00 (ISBN 0-942586-10-7). Ferrari Pubns.
--Places of Interest to Women: U. S. A., Canada, Caribbean. rev. ed. 144p. 1986. pap. 6.00 (ISBN 0-942586-11-5). Ferrari Pubns.
Ferrari, Marianne & Williams, Pamela. Places in Europe, 1986. (Illus.). 96p. (Orig.). 1985. pap. 7.00 (ISBN 0-942586-13-1). Ferrari Pubns.
Ferrari, Mary. The Isle of the Little God. 7.00x (ISBN 0-686-73479-3); pap. 3.50x (ISBN 0-686-73480-7). Kulchur Foun.
Ferrari, Michael R. Profiles of American College Presidents. LC 77-630259. 1970. 7.50 (ISBN 0-87744-094-8). Mich St U Pr.
Ferrari, Nikki & Jett, Adam. How to Get a Man to Give You Everything! (Illus.). 107p. 1984. pap. 4.95 (ISBN 0-917637-00-3). Blithedale.
Ferrari, R. Repertorio dei Sinonimi della Lingua Italiana. 463p. (Ital.). 1980. Leatherette 5.95 (ISBN 0-686-97411-5, M-9181). French & Eur.
Ferrari, R., et al, eds. Myocardial Ischemia & Lipid Metabolism. 328p. 1984. 49.50x (ISBN 0-306-41832-0, Plenum Pr). Plenum Pub.
Ferrari, R. L. & Jonscher, A. K., eds. Problems in Physical Electronics. 1973. 32.00x (ISBN 0-85086-038-5, NO. 2956, Pub. by Pion England). Methuen Inc.
Ferrari, Raffaella, tr. see Meredith, Peter & Tailby, John.
Ferrari, Robert. Days Pleasant & Unpleasant in the Order Sons of Italy. LC 73-21967. 1974. Repr. of 1926 ed. 19.50x (ISBN 0-678-01363-2). Kelley.
Ferrari, Ronald L., jt. auth. see Silvester, Peter P.
Ferrarie, Julia. Swallow Island. (Illus.). 28p. 1981. 25.00 (ISBN 0-939622-14-9); pap. 7.00 (ISBN 0-939622-13-0). Four Zoas Night.
Ferrarini, Elizabeth. Infomania: The Guide to Essential Electronic Services. 320p. 1985. pap. 14.95 (ISBN 0-395-36297-0). HM.
Ferrarini, Elizabeth M. Confessions of an Infomaniac. LC 84-50357. 202p. 1984. 12.95 (ISBN 0-89588-221-3); pap. 6.95 (ISBN 0-89588-186-1). SYBEX.
Ferrario, Carlos, jt. ed. see Buckley, Joseph P.
Ferraris, Luigi V., ed. Report on a Negotiation: Helsinki-Geneva-Helsinki Nineteen Seventy-Two to Nineteen Seventy-Five. Barber, Marie-Claire, tr. from Italian. (Collections De Relations Internationales Ser.). 439p. 1980. 46.00x (ISBN 9-0286-0779-X). Sijthoff & Noordhoff.
Ferrarius Montanus, Joannes. A Work Touching the Good Ordering of a Common Weal. Bauande, William, tr. 430p. Repr. of 1559 ed. 45.00 (ISBN 0-384-15509-X). Johnson Repr.

Ferraro, Bob & Ferraro, Pat. Bottle Collector's Book. LC 65-28887. (Illus.). 1966. 5.25 (ISBN 0-9600212-1-3); pap. 3.00 (ISBN 0-9600212-0-5). Past in Glass.
Ferraro, Geraldine & Franke, Linda B. Geraldine Ferraro. LC 85-47650. (Illus.). 1985. 17.95 (ISBN 0-553-05110-5). Bantam.
Ferraro, J. R., jt. auth. see Rao, C. N.
Ferraro, J. R., ed. see Mid-America Spectroscopy Symposium.
Ferraro, John. Ten Series of Meditations on the Mysteries of the Rosary. (Illus., Orig.). 1964. 5.00 (ISBN 0-8198-0157-7); pap. 4.00 (ISBN 0-8198-0158-5). Dghtrs St Paul.
--Vibrational Spectroscopy at High External Pressures: The Diamond Anvil Cell (Monograph) LC 83-22355. 1984. 59.00 (ISBN 0-12-254160-X). Acad Pr.
Ferraro, John R. Low-Frequency Vibrations in Inorganic & Coordination Compounds. LC 74-107528. 309p. 1971. 39.50x (ISBN 0-306-30453-8, Plenum Pr). Plenum Pub.
Ferraro, John R. & Ziomek, Joseph S. Introductory Group Theory & Its Applications to Molecular Structure. 2nd ed. LC 75-33752. 292p. 1975. 35.00x (ISBN 0-306-30768-5, Plenum Pr). Plenum Pub.
Ferraro, John R., ed. Fourier Transform: Applications to Chemical Systems, Vol. 1. 1978. 59.50 (ISBN 0-12-254101-4). Acad Pr.
Ferraro, John R. & Basile, Louis J., eds. Fourier Transform Infared Spectroscopy, Vol. 3: Techniques Using Fourier Transform Interferometry. 1982. 39.00 (ISBN 0-12-254103-0). Acad Pr.
--Fourier Transform Infrared Spectroscopy: Applications to Chemical Systems, Vol. 2. LC 78-26956. 1979. 55.00 (ISBN 0-12-254102-2). Acad Pr.
--Fourier Transform Infrared Spectroscopy, Vol. 4. 1985. 74.50 (ISBN 0-12-254104-9). Acad Pr.
Ferraro, Pat, jt. auth. see Ferraro, Bob.
Ferraro, R. & Godoy, R., eds. Monitoring Solar Heating Systems: A Practical Handbook. (Illus.). 265p. 1983. pap. 39.50 (ISBN 0-08-029992-X). Pergamon.
Ferrarone, Stephen F., jt. auth. see Schwartz, Steven J.
Ferrarotti, Franco. An Alternative Sociology. Columbaro, Barbara & Columbaro, Pasqualino, trs. 204p. 1979. text ed. 19.50x (ISBN 0-8290-0861-6). Irvington.
--An Alternative Sociology. Columbaro, Barbara & Colmbaro, Pasqualino, trs. from Ital. 204p. 1983. pap. text ed. 9.95x (ISBN 0-8290-1037-8). Irvington.
--Max Weber & the Destiny of Reason. LC 80-5457. Orig. Title: Max Weber e il Destino Ragione. 160p. 1982. 12.95 (ISBN 0-87332-170-7). M E Sharpe.
--The Myth of Inevitable Progress. LC 84-589. (Contributions in Political Science Ser.: No. 115). viii, 208p. 1985. lib. bdg. 35.00 (ISBN 0-313-24329-8, FMY/). Greenwood.
Ferrars, Bertha, jt. auth. see Ferrars, Max.
Ferrars, E. X. Crime & the Crystal. LC 85-1566. (Crime Club Ser.). 192p. 1985. 12.95 (ISBN 0-385-19996-1). Doubleday.
--In at the Kill. 192p. 1980. pap. 3.50 (ISBN 0-14-005644-0). Penguin.
--Root of All Evil. LC 84-6086. (Crime Club Ser.). 192p. 1984. 11.95 (ISBN 0-385-19580-X). Doubleday.
--Root of All Evil. (Large Print Books). 1985. lib. bdg. 14.95 (ISBN 0-8161-3879-6). G K Hall.
--Something Wicked. LC 83-45371. (Crime Club Ser.). 192p. 1984. 11.95 (ISBN 0-385-19254-1). Doubleday.
--Something Wicked. (Nightingale Large Print Ser.). 1985. pap. text ed. 9.95 (ISBN 0-8161-3763-3, Large Print Bks). G K Hall.
Ferrars, Max & Ferrars, Bertha. Burma. LC 77-87077. Repr. of 1900 ed. 42.00 (ISBN 0-404-16818-3). AMS Pr.
Ferrary, Jeannette & Fiszer, Louise. The California-American Cookbook: Innovations on American Regional Dishes. 1985. 16.95 (ISBN 0-671-50503-3). S&S.
Ferrate, G., ed. see IFAC-IFIP Symposium, 3rd, Madrid, Spain, Oct. 1982.
Ferrater, Mora. Diccionario de Filosofia, 2 vols. (Span.). 95.00 set (ISBN 0-686-56658-0, S-31443). French & Eur.
Ferrater, Mora J. Man at the Crossroads. Trask, Willard R., tr. LC 69-10090. Repr. of 1957 ed. lib. bdg. 15.00x (ISBN 0-8371-0415-7, FEMC). Greenwood.
Ferrater Mora, Jose. Diccionario de Filosofia, 4 vols. 3630p. (Span.). 1979. Set. pap. 200.00 (ISBN 84-206-5998-3, S-50051); 240.00 set (ISBN 84-206-5299-7). French & Eur.
--Diccionario de Filosofia Abreviado. 2nd ed. 478p. (Span.). 1978. pap. 9.50 (ISBN 84-350-0141-5, S-50081). French & Eur.
--Unamuno: A Philosophy of Tragedy. Silver, Philip, tr. from Span. LC 81-20162. Orig. Title: Unamuno: Bosquejo De una Filosofia. xx, 136p. 1982. Repr. of 1962 ed. lib. bdg. 18.75x (ISBN 0-313-23341-1, FMUN). Greenwood.
Ferrato, Philip. The Porter Family. LC 80-81265. (Illus.). 23p. 1980. catalogue 1.00 (ISBN 0-943526-04-3). Parrish Art.
Ferraworth, James R. The Major Problems of Our Contemporary Society in the Critical Views of Our Intelligentsia: The Results of a Survey. (Illus.). 129p. 1981. 53.45 (ISBN 0-89266-313-8). Am Classical Coll Pr.
Ferraz-Mello, Sylvio, jt. ed. see Nacozy, Paul E.
Ferrazzi, Guiseppe J. Torquato Tasso: Studi Biografici, Critici, Bibliografici. LC 75-150155. (Bibliography & Reference Ser: No. 432). 1971. Repr. of 1880 ed. lib. bdg. 32.00 (ISBN 0-8337-1119-9). B Franklin.
Ferre see Proust, Marcel.
Ferre, Frederick. Language, Logic, & God. LC 77-9060. 1977. Repr. of 1961 ed. lib. bdg. 20.25x (ISBN 0-8371-9716-3, FELL). Greenwood.
--Language, Logic, & God: With a New Preface. LC 80-27305. viii, 184p. 1981. pap. text ed. 6.50x (ISBN 0-226-24456-3). U of Chicago Pr.
Ferre, Frederick P. & Mataragnon, Rita H., eds. God & Global Justice: Religion & Poverty in an Unequal World. LC 84-26538. (God Ser.). 224p. (Orig.). 1985. text ed. 17.95 (ISBN 0-913757-36-5, Pub. by New Era Bks.); pap. text ed. 12.95 (ISBN 0-913757-37-3, Pub. by New Era Bks.). Paragon Hse.
Ferre, John P. Merrill Guide to the Research Paper. 1983. pap. text ed. 9.95 (ISBN 0-675-20029-6). Additional supplements may be obtained from publisher. Merrill.
Ferre, John P. & Pauley, Steven E. Rhetorical Patterns: An Anthology of Contemporary Essays. (Illus.). 208p. 1981. pap. text ed. 10.95 (ISBN 0-675-08023-1). Merrill.
Ferre, Luis A. The Plea of Puerto Rico. (Studies in Puerto Rican History, Literature & Culture). 1980. lib. bdg. 59.95 (ISBN 0-8490-3087-0). Gordon Pr.
Ferre, Nels. The Christian Understanding of God. LC 78-12234. 1979. Repr. of 1951 ed. lib. bdg. 22.50x (ISBN 0-313-21183-3, FECU). Greenwood.
Ferre, Nels F. Christianity & Society. facs. ed. LC 78-117791. (Essay Index Reprint Ser). 1950. 19.00 (ISBN 0-8369-1924-6). Ayer Co Pubs.
--Evil & the Christian Faith. facsimile ed. LC 71-134075. (Essay Index Reprints - Reason & the Christian Faith Ser.: Vol. 2). Repr. of 1947 ed. 18.00 (ISBN 0-8369-2393-6). Ayer Co Pubs.
--Faith & Reason. facsimile ed. LC 78-142626. (Essay Index Reprints - Reason & the Christian Faith Ser.: Vol. 1). Repr. of 1946 ed. 19.00 (ISBN 0-8369-2392-8). Ayer Co Pubs.
--The Finality of Faith, & Christianity Among the World Religions. LC 78-11979. 1979. Repr. of 1963 ed. lib. bdg. 18.75x (ISBN 0-313-21182-5, FEFF). Greenwood.
--Swedish Contributions to Modern Theology: With Special Reference to Lundensian Thought. 1967. lib. bdg. 17.50x (ISBN 0-88307-092-8). Gannon.
Ferre, Rosario. Cuentos de Juan Bobo. LC 81-69787. (Illus.). 32p. (gr. 7). 1982. pap. 3.75 (ISBN 0-940238-62-4). Ediciones Hura.
--Mona que le Pisaron la Cola. LC 81-69847. (Illus.). 48p. (gr. 7). 1981. pap. 4.95 (ISBN 0-940238-61-6). Ediciones Hura.
--Muneca Menor. (De Orilla a Orilla Ser.). (Illus.). 16p. 1979. pap. 3.00 (ISBN 0-940238-29-2). Ediciones Huracan.
Ferree, C. E. see Brigham, Carl.
Ferree, Myra M. & Hess, Beth. Controversy & Coalition: New Feminist Movement. (Social Movements: Past & Present Ser.). 1985. lib. bdg. 17.95 (ISBN 0-8057-9707-6, Twayne). G K Hall.
Ferreira, E., jt. auth. see Bemporad, M.
Ferreira, J. A. Portuguese-English, English-Portuguese Dictionary. (Port. & Eng.). 30.00 (ISBN 0-685-12039-2). Heinman.
Ferreira, J. Albino. English-Portuguese Dictionary. rev. ed. De Morais, O., ed. (Eng. & Port.). 37.50 (ISBN 0-87559-027-6); thumb indexed 42.50 (ISBN 0-87559-028-4). Shalom.
--Portuguese-English Dictionary. rev. ed. De Morais, A., ed. (Port. & Eng.). 37.50 (ISBN 0-87559-029-2); thumb indexed 42.50 (ISBN 0-87559-030-6). Shalom.
Ferreira, Linda. Express English: Transitions. 1983. pap. text ed. 7.95 (ISBN 0-88377-335-X); 3.95 (ISBN 0-88377-355-4); 9.95 (ISBN 0-88377-350-3). Newbury Hse.
--Notion by Notion. 96p. (Orig.). 1981. pap. text ed. 6.95 (ISBN 0-88377-199-3). Newbury Hse.
--Verbs in Action. LC 77-10886. 1978. pap. text ed. 7.95 (ISBN 0-88377-097-0). Newbury Hse.
Ferreira, Linda A. & Vai, Marjorie. Read on, Speak Out. LC 79-314. 1979. pap. text ed. 8.95 (ISBN 0-88377-133-0). Newbury Hse.
Ferreira, M. Jamie. Doubt & Religious Commitment: The Role of the Will in Newman's Thought. 1980. 29.95x (ISBN 0-19-826654-5). Oxford U Pr.
Ferreira, Nancy. Learning Through Cooking: A Cooking Program for Children Two to Ten. LC 81-86008. 125p. 1982. pap. 6.95 (ISBN 0-88247-658-0). R & E Pubs.
Ferreira, R., et al. Less Abundant Metals. LC 67-11280. (Structure & Bonding Ser.: Vol. 31). (Illus.). 1976. 27.00 (ISBN 0-387-07964-5). Springer-Verlag.
Ferreira, Ruth V., tr. see Getz, Gene.
Ferreira, S. H., jt. ed. see Vane, J. R.
Ferreira-Ibarra, Dario C., ed. The Canon Law Collection of the Library of Congress: A General Bibliography with Selective Annotations. LC 81-607964. (Illus.). xiv, 210p. 1981. 11.00 (ISBN 0-8444-0367-9). Lib Congress.
Ferreiro, Emilia & Teberosky, Ana. Literacy Before Schooling. Castro, Karen G., tr. from Span. LC 82-15839. 324p. text ed. 18.00x (ISBN 0-435-08202-7); pap. text ed. 12.50x (ISBN 0-435-08220-5). Heinemann Ed.
Ferrel, O. C. & Pride, William. Fundamentals of Marketing. LC 81-82558. 1981. 28.95 (ISBN 0-395-31696-0); instr's manual 3.00 (ISBN 0-395-31697-9); study guide 10.50 (ISBN 0-395-31698-7); test bank manual 4.00 (ISBN 0-395-31699-5); color transparencies 100.00 set (ISBN 0-395-32025-9). HM.
Ferrel, Robert H., ed. see Smith, Gaddis.
Ferrell, Anderson. Where She Was. LC 85-40225. 160p. 1985. 13.95 (ISBN 0-394-53521-9). Knopf.
Ferrell, Charles. A Service for Good Friday. 1971. 2.50 (ISBN 0-89536-081-0). CSS of Ohio.
Ferrell, Frank, et al. Trevor's Place: The Story of the Boy Who Brings Hope to the Homeless. LC 84-48768. (Illus.). 160p. 1985. 12.45 (ISBN 0-06-062531-7, HarpR). Har-Row.
Ferrell, Henry C. Claude A. Swanson of Virginia: A Political Biography. LC 84-27031. 304p. 1985. 28.00 (ISBN 0-8131-1536-1, Dist. by Har-Row). U Pr of Ky.
Ferrell, J., jt. auth. see Ehrhardt, Roy.
Ferrell, Jeanne C., ed. see Dexter, Gerry L.
Ferrell, John & Ferrell, MaryAnn. Coaching Flag Football. 56p. 1980. pap. 4.00x (ISBN 0-88035-027-X). Human Kinetics.
Ferrell, John, et al. Family Approach to Youth Sports. 61p. 1978. pap. 4.00 (ISBN 0-88035-032-6). Human Kinetics.
Ferrell, John M. Playing Flag Football. 32p. (gr. 1-6). 1983. pap. 2.00x (ISBN 0-88035-052-0). Human Kinetics.
Ferrell, John M. & McPeak, Clifford T. Youth Volleyball Coaches Manual. 64p. 1983. pap. 3.00x (ISBN 0-88035-065-2). Human Kinetics.
Ferrell, John M., ed. Youth Soccer Coaches Manual. 56p. 1980. pap. 3.00x (ISBN 0-88035-064-4). Human Kinetics.
--Youth Soccer Players Manual. 48p. (gr. 1-6). 1980. pap. 2.00x (ISBN 0-88035-063-6). Human Kinetics.
Ferrell, John M., et al, eds. YMCA Competitive Swimming & Diving Coaches Manual. 1981. 3 ring notebook 18.00x (ISBN 0-88035-028-8). Human Kinetics.
Ferrell, Joseph S., ed. County Government in North Carolina. 2nd. ed. 471p. 1979. 15.00 (ISBN 0-686-39428-3). U of NC Inst Gov.
Ferrell, Kay. Reach Out & Teach: Manual & Reachbook, 2 bks. 1985. Set. spiral bdg. 25.00 (ISBN 0-89128-127-4). Am Foun Blind.
Ferrell, Keith. Ernest Hemingway: The Search for Courage. LC 84-10162. 192p. (gr. 7 up). 1984. 10.95 (ISBN 0-87131-431-2). M Evans.
--George Orwell: The Political Pen. 192p. (gr. 7 up). 11.95 (ISBN 0-317-13300-4). M Evans.
--H. G. Wells: First Citizen of the Future. LC 83-1532. 192p. (gr. 7 up). 1983. text ed. 9.95 (ISBN 0-87131-403-7). M Evans.
Ferrell, Mallory H. Colorado & Southern Narrow Gauge. (Illus.). 1981. 34.95 (ISBN 0-87108-534-8). Pruett.
--Rails, Sagebrush & Pine. LC 67-28315. (Illus.). 1967. 21.95 (ISBN 0-87095-007-X). Golden West.
--The Silver San Juan. LC 77-188633. (Illus.). 1973. 44.95 (ISBN 0-87108-057-5). Pruett.
--Tweetsie Country: The East Tennessee & Western North Carolina Railroad. LC 76-13590. (Illus.). 1976. 25.95 (ISBN 0-87108-082-6). Pruett.
Ferrell, MaryAnn, jt. auth. see Ferrell, John.
Ferrell, Nancy W. The Fishing Industry. (First Books Ser.). (Illus.). 72p. 1984. lib. bdg. 8.90 (ISBN 0-531-04823-3). Watts.
--Passports to Peace: Embassies & the Art of Diplomacy. (Illus.). 96p. (gr. 6 up). 1985. PLB 10.95 (ISBN 0-8225-0644-0). Lerner Pubns.
Ferrell, O. C., jt. auth. see Luck, David J.
Ferrell, O. C., jt. auth. see Pride, William M.
Ferrell, Oliver P. Confidential Frequency List. 6th ed. 320p. 1984. pap. 13.95 (ISBN 0-914542-13-3). Gilfer.
--Guide to RTTY Frequencies. 2nd ed. 192p. 1983. pap. 9.95 (ISBN 0-914542-11-7). Gilfer.
Ferrell, Paul C. & Grabe, Erna F. Subconscious Speaks. 1932. pap. 2.50 (ISBN 0-87516-022-0). De Vorss.
Ferrell, Robert H. American Diplomacy. 3rd ed. (Illus.). 900p. 1975. text ed. 19.95x (ISBN 0-393-09309-3). Norton.
--Frank B Kellogg (1925-29) & Henry L. Stimson (1929-33) (American Secretaries of State & Their Diplomacy, New Ser.: Vol. 11). 1963. 24.50 (ISBN 0-8154-0069-1). Cooper Sq.
--George C. Marshall Nineteen Forty-Seven to Nineteen Forty-Nine. LC 72-197304. (American Secretaries of State & Their Diplomacy, New Ser.: Vol. 15). 1966. 23.50 (ISBN 0-8154-0070-5). Cooper Sq.
--Harry S. Truman & the Modern American Presidency. (Library of American Biographers). 1982. pap. text ed. 6.95 (ISBN 0-316-28123-9). Little.
--Off the Record. 1982. pap. 7.95 (ISBN 0-14-006080-4). Penguin.
--Peace in Their Time: The Origins of the Kellogg-Briand Pact. 1969. pap. 2.95x (ISBN 0-393-00491-0, Norton Lib). Norton.
--Peace in Their Time: The Origins of the Kellogg-Briand Pact. x, 293p. 1968. Repr. of 1952 ed. 22.50 (ISBN 0-208-00653-2, Archon). Shoe String.
--Truman: A Centenary Remembrance of Robert H. Ferrell. (Illus.). 272p. 1984. 25.00 (ISBN 0-670-36196-8). Viking.
--Woodrow Wilson & World War I: 1917-1921. LC 84-48160. (Illus.). 312p. 1985. 17.26 (ISBN 0-06-011229-8, HarpT). Har-Row.
Ferrell, Robert H., ed. America As a World Power, 1872-1945. LC 70-171359. (Documentary History of the United States Ser). xxviii, 306p. 1971. 19.95x (ISBN 0-87249-244-3). U of SC Pr.
--Dear Bess: The Letters from Harry to Bess Truman, 1910-1959. LC 83-8006. (Illus.). 608p. 1983. 19.95 (ISBN 0-393-01822-9); pap. 12.95 1984 (ISBN 0-393-30209-1). Norton.
--The Diary of James C. Hagerty: Eisenhower in Mid-Course, 1954-1955. LC 82-48477. (Illus.). 288p. 1983. 19.50x (ISBN 0-253-11625-2). Ind U Pr.
--Foundations of American Diplomacy, 1775-1872. LC 68-65041. (Documentary History of the United States Ser). xviii, 284p. 1969. 19.95x (ISBN 0-87249-122-6). U of SC Pr.
--Off the Record: The Private Papers of Harry S. Truman. LC 79-3390. (Illus.). 448p. 1980. 15.00i (ISBN 0-06-011281-6, HarpT). Har-Row.
Ferrell, Robert H. & Bowman, John S., eds. The Twentieth Century: An Almanac. (Illus.). 512p. 1985. pap. 12.95. World Almanac.
--The Twentieth Century: An Almanac. 512p. 1984. 24.95 (ISBN 0-345-31708-4). Ballantine.
Ferrell, Robert H., ed. see Eisenhower, Dwight D.
Ferrell, Robert H., ed. see Lawrence, Joseph D.
Ferrell, Robert H., ed. see Truman, Harry S.
Ferrell, Wilfred A. & Salerno, Nicholas A., eds. Strategies in Prose. 5th ed. LC 82-15501. 385p. 1983. pap. text ed. 15.95 (ISBN 0-03-059324-7). HR&W.
Ferren, William P., jt. auth. see Jenson, J. T.
Ferrer, Aldo. Living Within Our Means. 112p. 1985. pap. 28.00 (ISBN 0-8133-0291-9). Westview.
Ferrer, Claire R., ed. see American Ethnological Society.
Ferrer, Cornelio M. Pastor to the Rural Philippines: an Autobiography. 1974. wrps. 2.50x (ISBN 0-686-18697-4). Cellar.
Ferrer, Daniel, jt. ed. see Attridge, Derek.
Ferrer, Eduardo B. Grammatica Storica del Catalano e dei suoi dialetti con speciale riguardo all 'Algherese. xx, 410p. (Orig., Ital.). 1984. pap. 30.00x (ISBN 3-87808-238-X, Pub. by G N Verlag Germany). Benjamins North Am.
Ferrer, Edward B. Operation Puma: The Air Battle of the Bay of Pigs. (Illus.). 242p. 1982. pap. 11.50 (ISBN 0-9609000-0-4). Intl Av Consult.
Ferrer, Jami & De Poleo, Patty W. Bridge the Gap: A Guide to the Development of Acquisition Activities. (Illus.). 148p. 1983. pap. 9.95x (ISBN 0-88084-074-9); text ed. 9.95x. Alemany Pr.
Ferrer, O., ed. see International Symposium on Fluorescin Angiography, Miami, 1970.
Ferrer, Olga M., ed. Symposium on Glaucoma. (Illus.). 296p. 1976. photocopy ed. 34.50x (ISBN 0-398-03294-7). C C Thomas.
Ferrer, Rafael. Al Held: Paintings & Drawings, 1973 - 1978. (Illus.). 1978. pap. 2.50 (ISBN 0-910663-15-7). ICA Inc.
--Rafael Ferrer: Recent Work & an Installation. (Illus.). 1978. pap. 3.00 (ISBN 0-910663-14-9). ICA Inc.
Ferrer Canales, Jose. Imagen De Varona. 2nd ed. 5.00 (ISBN 0-8477-3118-9); pap. 3.75 (ISBN 0-8477-3119-7). U of PR Pr.
Ferreri, Carl A. & Wainright, Richard B. Breakthrough for Dyslexia & Learning Disabilities. (Illus.). 144p. 1984. 14.95 (ISBN 0-317-04550-4). Exposition Pr FL.
Ferrerio, Giovanni. Ferrerii Historia Abbatum De Kynlos. LC 78-168018. (Bannatyne Club, Edinburgh. Publications: No. 63). Repr. of 1839 ed. 15.00 (ISBN 0-404-52774-4). AMS Pr.
Ferrero, G. Ancient Rome & Modern America: A Comparative Study of Morals & Manners. 1977. lib. bdg. 59.95 (ISBN 0-8490-1428-X). Gordon Pr.
--Four Years of Fascism. Dickes, E. W., tr. LC 77-180398. Repr. of 1924 ed. 19.50 (ISBN 0-404-56122-5). AMS Pr.
Ferrero, G. L., et al, eds. Anaerobic Digestion & Carbohydrate Hydrolysis of Waste: Proceedings of an EEC Seminar Held 8-10 May 1984, Luxembourg. 536p. 1984. 72.00 (ISBN 0-85334-324-1, Pub. by Elsevier Applied Sci England). Elsevier.
Ferrero, Guglielmo. The Greatness & Decline of Rome, 5 vols. facsimile ed. Zimmern, Alfred E. & Chayton, H. J., trs. LC 75-169758. (Select Bibliographies Reprint Ser). Repr. of 1909 ed. Set. 110.00 (ISBN 0-8369-5978-7). Ayer Co Pubs.

--Greatness & Decline of Rome, 5 vols. Zimmern, Alfred E., tr. Chayton, H. J., ed. (Select Bibliographies Reprint Ser.). 1982. Repr. of 1909 ed. lib. bdg. 99.00 set (ISBN 0-8290-0848-9). Irvington.

--The Greatness & Decline of Rome, 5 vols. Zimmern, Alfred E. & Chaytor, H. J., trs. 1983. Repr. of 1909 ed. Set. lib. bdg. 250.00 (ISBN 0-89987-285-9). Vol. 1, 382 pgs. Vol. 2, 417 pgs. Vol. 3, 342 pgs. Vol. 4, 291 pgs. Vol. 5, 371 pgs. Darby Bks.

--The Life of Caesar. Zimmern, A. E., tr. LC 77-9520. 1977. Repr. of 1933 ed. lib. bdg. 33.75x (ISBN 0-8371-9090-8, FELC). Greenwood.

--Militarism. LC 73-172547. Repr. of 1902 ed. 15.00 (ISBN 0-405-08500-1). Ayer Co Pubs.

--Militarism. LC 76-147469. (Library of War & Peace; the Character & Causes of War). 1972. lib. bdg. 46.00 (ISBN 0-8240-0260-1). Garland Pub.

--The Most Beautiful Women in Imperial Rome. (Illus.). 1978. deluxe ed. 57.50 (ISBN 0-930582-05-5). Gloucester Art.

--The Nastiest Women in Ancient Rome. (Illus.). 142p. 1983. 74.45x (ISBN 0-86650-083-9). Gloucester Art.

--Peace & War. facs. ed. Pritchard, B., tr. LC 69-18927. (Essay Index Reprint Ser). 1933. 18.00 (ISBN 0-8369-0041-3). Ayer Co Pubs.

--The Principles of Power: The Great Political Crises of History. Jaeckel, Theodore R., tr. LC 72-4274. (World Affairs Ser.: National & International Viewpoints). 346p. 1972. Repr. of 1942 ed. 22.50 (ISBN 0-405-04569-7). Ayer Co Pubs.

--The Principles of Power: The Great Political Crises of History. LC 84-12765. ix, 333p. 1984. Repr. of 1942 ed. lib. bdg. 39.75x (ISBN 0-313-24570-3, FEPP). Greenwood.

--The Women of the Caesars. (Illus.). 1977. 57.15 (ISBN 0-930582-05-5). Am Classical Coll Pr.

--The Women of the Caesars. (Women Ser.). 1911. 35.00 (ISBN 0-8482-4053-7). Norwood Edns.

--The Women of the Caesars. Gause, Christian, tr. 337p. 1978. Repr. of 1911 ed. 18.50 (ISBN 0-87928-093-X). Corner Hse.

Ferrero, Gulielmo. Characters & Events of Roman History. 1909. 25.00. Norwood Edns.

Ferrero, Mercedes V., ed. see Juvarra, Filippo.

Ferrero, William, jt. auth. see Lombroso, Cesar.

Ferrer Y Guardia, Francisco. The Origin & Ideals of the Modern School. McCabe, Joseph, tr. LC 73-161328. (Atheist Viewpoint Ser.). 126p. 1972. Repr. of 1913 ed. 13.00 (ISBN 0-405-03809-7). Ayer Co Pubs.

Ferres, Antonio & Otega, Jose. Literatura Espanola Del Ultimo Exilio. LC 75-20183. 176p. (Orig., Span.). 1975. 9.00x (ISBN 0-87752-203-0); pap. 6.75x (ISBN 0-685-55211-X). Gordian.

Ferres, John, ed. Twentieth Century Interpretations of The Crucible. 128p. 1972. 9.95 (ISBN 0-13-194860-1, Spec). P-H.

Ferres, John, ed. see Anderson, Sherwood.

Ferres, John H. Arthur Miller: A Reference Guide. 1979. lib. bdg. 30.50 (ISBN 0-8161-7822-4, Hall Reference). G K Hall.

Ferres, John H. & Tucker, Martin, eds. Modern Commonwealth Literature. LC 75-35425. (Library of Literary Criticism). 1977. 55.00 (ISBN 0-8044-3080-2). Ungar.

Ferretti, Fred. Afo-A-Kom. LC 73-92800. 1974. 14.95 (ISBN 0-89388-134-1). Okpaku Communications.

--The Great American Book of Sidewalk, Stoop, Dirt, Curb & Alley Games. LC 75-7291. (Illus.). 240p. (gr. 3 up). 1975. pap. 3.95 (ISBN 0-911104-59-3, 080). Workman Pub.

Ferretti, Paolo A. Estetica Gregoriana. LC 77-5498. (Music Reprint Ser.). 1977. Repr. of 1934 ed. lib. bdg. 39.50 (ISBN 0-306-77414-3). Da Capo.

Ferrez, Gilberto & Naef, Weston J. Pioneer Photographers of Brazil. (Illus.). 144p. 1976. 12.50 (ISBN 0-89192-160-5, Pub. by Ctr Inter-Am Rel). Interbk Inc.

--Pioneer Photographs of Brazil, Eighteen Forty to Nineteen Twenty. LC 76-25710. (Center for Inter-American Relations &The American Federation of Arts). (Illus.). 144p. 1980. 16.95x (ISBN 0-295-95737-9). U of Wash Pr.

Ferrez, Gilberto, jt. auth. see Smith, Robert C.

Ferri, E., et al. Biology Learning Guide. 1984. Paladin Hse.

Ferri, Elsa. Disadvantaged Families & Playgroups. 88p. 1977. 8.00x (ISBN 0-85633-133-3, Pub. by NFER Nelson UK). Taylor & Francis.

--Stepchildren: A National Study. 192p. 1984. pap. 16.00x (ISBN 0-7005-0653-5, Pub. by NFER Nelson UK). Taylor & Francis.

Ferri, Elsa & Robinson, Hilary. Coping Alone. (Social Issues Ser.). 80p. 1976. 6.00x (ISBN 0-85633-086-8, Pub. by NFER Nelson UK). Taylor & Francis.

Ferri, Elsa, et al. Combined Nursery Centres. (National Children's Bureau Ser.). 221p. 1981. text ed. 31.75x (ISBN 0-333-29485-8, Pub. by Macmillan England); pap. text ed. 13.00x (ISBN 0-333-29486-6). Humanities.

Ferri, Enrico. Criminal Sociology. LC 67-20717. 1967. Repr. of 1917 ed. 18.50x (ISBN 0-87586-004-4). Agathon.

--Criminal Sociology. 1900. 20.00 (ISBN 0-686-17697-9). Quality Lib.

--The Positive School of Criminology. Untermann, E., tr. 125p. 1981. Repr. of 1913 ed. text ed. 25.00 (ISBN 0-8492-4624-5). R West.

Ferri, Robert & Silverberg, Barry. The Tax Organizer. rev. ed. Dembofsky, Thomas J., ed. 1980. pap. 3.95 (ISBN 0-07-020641-4). McGraw.

Ferri, Roger C. Pedestrian City: A Proposal for an American Architecture & Urbanism in the Post-Petroleum Age. (Illus.). 24p. (Orig.). 1981. pap. text ed. 2.50 (ISBN 0-9605928-0-6). Ferri.

Ferriday, Virginia G. Last of the Handmade Buildings: Glazed Terra Cotta in Downtown Portland. LC 84-62229. (Illus.). 150p. (Orig.). 1984. pap. 22.00 (ISBN 0-9614039-0-X). Mark Pub.

Ferrie, Michel F., jt. auth. see Perez, Roman C.

Ferrier, Carole, ed. Gender, Politics & Fiction: Twentieth Century Australian Women's Novels. LC 84-22051. 262p. 1985. text ed. 32.50 (ISBN 0-7022-1796-4). U of Queensland Pr.

Ferrier, D; see Monro, Alexander.

Ferrier, David. Functions of the Brain. (Contributions to the History of Psychology E, III, Physiological Psychology Ser.). 1978. Repr. of 1886 ed. 30.00 (ISBN 0-89093-176-3). U Pubns Amer.

Ferrier, James F. Philosophical Works: Phenomenology-Background, Foreground & Influences, 3 vols. Natanson, Maurice, ed. LC 78-66732. 1980. lib. bdg. 200.00 set (ISBN 0-8240-9566-9). Garland Pub.

Ferrier, Janet M., jt. ed. see Brereton, Georgine E.

Ferrier, Lucy. Diving the Great Barrier Reef. new ed. LC 75-23411. (Illus.). 32p. (gr. 5-10). 1976. PLB 9.79 (ISBN 0-89375-005-0); pap. 2.50 (ISBN 0-89375-021-2). Troll Assocs.

Ferrier, Ronald W. The History of the British Petroleum Company: The Developing Years 1901-1932, Vol. 1. LC 81-18019. 696p. 1982. 74.50 (ISBN 0-521-24647-4). Cambridge U Pr.

Ferrier, Susan. Works of Susan Ferrier, 4 Vols. LC 74-118948. Repr. of 1929 ed. Set. 150.00 (ISBN 0-404-02380-0); 37.50 ea. Vol. 1 (ISBN 0-404-02381-9). Vol. 2 (ISBN 0-404-02382-7). Vol. 3 (ISBN 0-404-02383-5). Vol. 4 (ISBN 0-404-02384-3). AMS Pr.

Ferrieres, J. C. Mas Puro Que el Diamante. Orig. Title: Purer Than Diamond. 80p. (Span.). 1963. pap. 1.95 (ISBN 0-8254-1227-7). Kregel.

Ferrigno, Carla. For Women Only: Carla Ferrigno's Total Shape-Up Program. 1984. pap. 8.95 (ISBN 0-8092-5659-2). Contemp Bks.

Ferrigno, Lou & Hall, Douglas K. The Incredible Lou Ferrigno. 208p. 1983. pap. 8.95 (ISBN 0-671-49586-0, Wallaby). S&S.

Ferrigno, Lou, jt. auth. see Reynolds, Bill.

Ferrigno, Peter, jt. auth. see Besner, Edward.

Ferril, Thomas H. Anvil of Roses. 2nd ed. Burmaster, Orvis C., ed. LC 82-73829. (Ahsahta Press Modern & Contemporary Poetry of the West Ser.). 50p. (Orig.). 1983. pap. 3.00 (ISBN 0-916272-20-6). Ahsahta Pr.

--High Passage. LC 79-144729. (Yale Series of Younger Poets: No. 22). Repr. of 1926 ed. 18.00 (ISBN 0-404-53822-3). AMS Pr.

Ferrill, Arther. The Origins of War: From the Stone Age to Alexander the Great. LC 84-51642. 68p. 1985. 19.95 (ISBN 0-500-25093-6, Dist. by W. W. Norton). Thames Hudson.

Ferrill, Thomas H. New & Selected Poems. LC 73-104219. Repr. of 1952 ed. lib. bdg. 71.50 (ISBN 0-8371-3336-X, FESP). Greenwood.

Ferriman, David. Human Hair Growth in Health & Disease. (Illus.). 76p. 1971. 11.75x (ISBN 0-398-00560-5). C C Thomas.

Ferriman, Z. Duckett. Turkey & the Turks. LC 77-87627. Repr. of 1911 ed. 26.00 (ISBN 0-404-16452-8). AMS Pr.

Ferrin, Martha. Moments with Martha. LC 83-60477. 1983. pap. text ed. 2.50 (ISBN 0-932050-18-2). New Puritan.

Ferrin, Richard I. & Arbeiter, Solomon. Bridging the Gap: A Selection of Education-to-Work Linkages. 68p. 1975. pap. 4.00 (ISBN 0-87447-007-2, 221763). College Bd.

--Bridging the Gap: A Study of Education-to-Work Linkages. 180p. 1975. pap. 6.00 (ISBN 0-87447-008-0, 221762). College Bd.

Ferring, C. R., et al. An Archaelogical Reconnaissance of Fort Sill, Oklahoma. (Contributions of the Museum of the Great Plains Ser.: No. 6). (Illus.). 1978. pap. 20.30 (ISBN 0-685-91361-9). Mus Great Plains.

Ferring, C. Reid, et al. An Archaelogical Reconnaissance of the Salt Plains Areas of Northwestern Oklahoma. (Contributions of the Museum of the Great Plains Ser.: No. 4). (Illus.). 1976. pap. 3.65 (ISBN 0-685-85503-1). Mus Great Plains.

Ferrini, Vincent. Know Fish. LC 79-20557. (Orig.). 1979. pap. 5.00 (ISBN 0-917590-05-8). Univ Conn Lib.

--Selected Poems. Butterick, George F., ed. & intro. by. LC 76-463360. (Orig.). 1976. pap. 3.95 (ISBN 0-917590-00-7). Univ Conn Lib.

Ferri-Pisani, Camille F. Prince Napoleon in America, 1861: Letters from His Aide-De-Camp. Joyaux, Georges J., tr. from Fr. LC 72-85279. (Illus.). 1973. Repr. of 1959 ed. 27.50x (ISBN 0-8046-1695-7, Pub. by Kennikat). Assoc Faculty Pr.

Ferris, jt. auth. see Bateman.

Ferris, Anthony R., tr. see Gibran, Kahlil.

Ferris, Anthony R, tr. see Gibran, Kahlil.

Ferris, B. G. Mormons at Home. LC 70-134395. Repr. of 1856 ed. 24.00 (ISBN 0-404-08437-0). AMS Pr.

--Utah & the Mormons. LC 77-134394. Repr. of 1856 ed. 27.00 (ISBN 0-404-08436-2). AMS Pr.

Ferris, B. J., jt. auth. see Johnson, H. H.

Ferris, Bill. Images of the South: Visits with Eudora Welty & Walker Evans. Yellin, Carol L., ed. LC 77-89404. (Southern Folklore Reports Ser.: No. I). 1978. pap. 7.50 (ISBN 0-89267-005-3). Ctr South Folklore.

--Ray Lum: Mule Trader -- an Essay. Friedman, Jack, ed. LC 76-53834. (Illus.). 1977. 2.50 (ISBN 0-89267-003-7); film transcript 2.50 (ISBN 0-89267-001-0); record transcript 2.50 (ISBN 0-89267-002-9). Ctr South Folklore.

Ferris, Bill, ed. see Center for Southern Folklore.

Ferris, Brian & Toyne, Peter. World Problems. 236p. 1979. pap. 11.95 (ISBN 0-7175-0509-X). Dufour.

Ferris, Byron, jt. auth. see Nelson, Roy P.

Ferris, Caren. A Hug Just Isn't Enough. LC 80-67696. (Illus.). 106p. 1980. 14.95 (ISBN 0-913580-62-7). Gallaudet Coll.

Ferris, Charles D. & Lloyd, Frank W. Cable Television Law: A Video Communications Practice Guide, 3 vols. 1983. looseleaf 240.00 (148); looseleaf 1984 65.00. Bender.

Ferris, Charles D., et al. Cable Television Law: A Video Communications Practice Guide, 3 vols. 1983. Updates avail. looseleaf 210.00 (ISBN 0-317-09713-X, 148). Bender.

Ferris, Clifford D. Guide to Medical Laboratory Instruments. LC 80-80585. 260p. 1980. text ed. 17.95 (ISBN 0-316-28127-1). Little.

--Introduction to Bioelectrodes. LC 74-19381. (Illus.). 255p. 1974. 32.50x (ISBN 0-306-30780-4, Plenum Pr). Plenum Pub.

--Introduction to Bioinstrumentation with Biological, Environmental & Medical Applications. LC 78-70579. (Contemporary Instrumentation & Analysis Ser.). 330p. 1979. 44.50 (ISBN 0-89603-000-8); soft bdg. 19.50 (ISBN 0-89603-003-2). Humana.

Ferris, Clifford D. & Brown, F. Martin, eds. Butterflies of the Rocky Mountain States. LC 80-22274. (Illus.). 400p. 1981. 39.50 (ISBN 0-8061-1552-1); pap. 17.95 (ISBN 0-8061-1733-8). U of Okla Pr.

Ferris, Elizabeth, ed. Refugees & World Politics. LC 85-495. 240p. 1985. 34.95 (ISBN 0-03-072043-5). Praeger.

Ferris, Elizabeth G. & Lincoln, Jennie I., eds. Latin American Foreign Policies: Global & Regional Dimensions. LC 81-10296. (Special Studies on Latin America). 300p. 1981. pap. text ed. 12.50x (ISBN 0-86531-284-2). Westview.

Ferris, Elizabeth G., jt. ed. see Lincoln, Jennie K.

Ferris, Elvira & Fong, Elizabeth. Microbiology for Health Careers. 2nd ed. LC 81-66764. (Allied Health Ser.). (Illus.). 192p. 1982. pap. text ed. 13.20 (ISBN 0-8273-1901-0); instr's guide 3.00 (ISBN 0-8273-1902-9). Delmar.

Ferris, Elvira B. & Skelley, Esther G. Body Structures & Functions. 5th ed. 1979. 16.95 (ISBN 0-442-21481-2). Van Nos Reinhold.

Ferris, Elvira B., et al. Body Structures & Functions. 6th ed. LC 83-71712. (Illus.). 356p. 1984. text ed. 13.80 (ISBN 0-8273-2185-6); instrs' guide 5.10 (ISBN 0-8273-2186-4). Delmar.

Ferris, Ernest J. & Seibert, J. J. Urinary Tract & Adrenal Glands: Imaging & Diagnosis. (Multiple Imaging Procedures Ser.: Vol. 4). (Illus.). 535p. 1980. 68.50 (ISBN 0-8089-1296-8, 791255). Grune.

Ferris, Forrest G. Law of Extraordinary Legal Remedies. LC 72-136387. Repr. of 1926 ed. 34.50 (ISBN 0-404-02378-9). AMS Pr.

Ferris, G., jt. auth. see Rowland, K.

Ferris, George. Fly Fishing in New Zealand. (Illus.). 116p. 1976. 6.95 (ISBN 0-89955-367-2, Pub. by Heinemann Pubs New Zealand). Intl Spec Bk.

--Flycasting: Techniques for the Flyfisherman. (Illus.). 56p. 1977. pap. 3.95 (ISBN 0-89955-366-4, Pub. by Heinemann Pubs New Zealand). Intl Spec Bk.

--Rivers & Lakes of the North Island: New Zealand Trout Fisherman's Guide. (Illus.). 54p. 1983. pap. 2.95x (ISBN 0-89955-371-0, Pub. by Heinemann Pub New Zealand). Intl Spec Bk.

--Rivers & Lakes of the South Island: New Zealand Trout Fisherman's Guide. (Illus.). 46p. 1983. pap. 2.95x (ISBN 0-908592-04-3, Pub. by Heinemann Pub New Zealand). Intl Spec Bk.

Ferris, George D. Glory & Beauty in the Land of the Pilgrims. (Illus.). 109p. 1983. Repr. of 1899 ed. 79.15 (ISBN 0-89901-106-3). Found Class Reprints.

Ferris, George T. Great Italian & French Composers. 1977. 59.95 (ISBN 0-8490-1899-4). Gordon Pr.

--Great Italian & French Composers. 14.00 (ISBN 0-8369-7260-0, 8059). Ayer Co Pubs.

--Great Singers, 2 Vols. 86.25 (ISBN 0-8369-9362-4, 19733). Ayer Co Pubs.

--Great Singers. 14.00 (ISBN 0-8369-7259-7, 8058). Ayer Co Pubs.

--Great Singers. 12.25 (ISBN 0-8369-7258-9, 8057). Ayer Co Pubs.

--Great Violinists & Pianists. LC 72-6819. (Essay Index Reprint Ser). 1972. Repr. of 1881 ed. 19.00 (ISBN 0-8369-7257-0). Ayer Co Pubs.

--Sketches of Great Pianists & Great Violinists. 1979. Repr. of 1889 ed. lib. bdg. 12.50 (ISBN 0-89341-084-5). Longwood Pub Group.

Ferris, Gerald R., jt. auth. see Rowland, Kendrith.

Ferris, Gerald R., jt. auth. see Rowland, Kendrith M.

Ferris, Gerald R., jt. ed. see Rowland, Kendrith M.

Ferris, Gerald R., jt. auth. see Rowland, Kendrith M.

Ferris, Gordon F. Atlas of the Scale Insects of North America, 7 vols. in 6. Incl. Vol. 1. The Diaspididae. Pt. 1. 40.00 (ISBN 0-404-08501-6); Vols. 2 & 3. The Diaspididae. Pts. 2 & 3. 75.00 (ISBN 0-404-08502-4); Vol. 4. The Diaspididae. Pt. 4, with Index to Pts. 1-4. 40.00 (ISBN 0-404-08503-2); Vol. 5. The Pseudococcidae. Pt. 1. 40.00 (ISBN 0-404-08504-0); Vol. 6. The Pseudococcidae. Pt. 2, with Index to Pts. 1-2. 40.00 (ISBN 0-404-08505-9); Vol. 7. The Families Aclerdidae, Asterolecaniidae Conchaspididae, Dactylopiidae & Lacciferidae, with Index. 40.00 (ISBN 0-404-08506-7). (Illus.). Repr. of 1955 ed. Set. 275.00 (ISBN 0-404-08500-8). AMS Pr.

Ferris, Harry B. Indians of Cuzco & the Apurimac. LC 18-6196. (American Anthro. Society Memoirs). 1916. 15.00 (ISBN 0-527-00513-4). Kraus Repr.

Ferris, Helen, ed. Favorite Poems Old & New. 598p. (gr. 3-7). 1957. 15.95 (ISBN 0-385-07696-7). Doubleday.

Ferris, Helen, compiled by. Love's Enchantment: Story Poems & Ballads. LC 73-86796. (Granger Index Reprint Ser). 1944. 16.00 (ISBN 0-8369-6076-9). Ayer Co Pubs.

Ferris, Helen J., ed. Five Girls Who Dared. LC 77-107699. (Essay Index Reprint Ser.). Repr. of 1931 ed. 20.00 (ISBN 0-8369-2313-8). Ayer Co Pubs.

Ferris, Ina. William Makepeace Thackeray. (English Authors Ser.). 154p. 1983. lib. bdg. 13.50 (ISBN 0-8057-6851-3, Twayne). G K Hall.

Ferris, James J. Inflation: The Ultimate Craven Image. LC 81-83944. 192p. (Orig.). 1982. pap. 4.95 (ISBN 0-89221-087-7). New Leaf.

Ferris, Jean. Amen, Moses Gardenia. 200p. (gr. 7 up). 1983. 10.95 (ISBN 0-374-30252-9). FS&G.

--Music: The Art of Listening. 408p. 1985. pap. text ed. write for info. incl. cassettes (ISBN 0-697-08278-4); instr's. manual avail. (ISBN 0-697-00525-9). Wm C Brown.

--The Stainless-Steel Rule. 192p. (gr. 12 up). 11.95 (ISBN 0-374-37212-8). FS&G.

--The Stainless-Steel Rule. 192p. (gr. 7 up). 1985. 11.95 (ISBN 0-374-37212-8). FS&G.

--The Stainless-Steel Rule: A Novel. 192p. (gr. 7 up). 1985. 11.95 (ISBN 0-374-37212-8). FS&G.

Ferris, John. Participation in Urban Planning. 95p. 1972. pap. text ed. 6.25 (ISBN 0-7135-1714-X, Pub. by Bedford England). Brookfield Pub Co.

Ferris, John A. Financial Economy of the United States Illustrated. LC 68-19359. Repr. of 1867 ed. 35.00x (ISBN 0-678-00472-2). Kelley.

--The Financial Economy of the United States Illustrated & Some of the Causes Which Retard the Progress of California Demonstrated. Bd. with A Searching Analysis of the Action of Paper Money Upon the Trade & Prosperity of the United States, 2 vols. in 1. 71p. 1868. Repr. LC 70-122231. 356p. 1867. Repr. 21.50 (ISBN 0-8337-1120-2). B Franklin.

Ferris, Norman B. Desperate Diplomacy: William H. Seward's Foreign Policy, 1861. LC 75-5509. 1976. 19.95x (ISBN 0-87049-170-9). U of Tenn Pr.

--The Trent Affair: A Diplomatic Crisis. LC 76-28304. 1977. 19.95x (ISBN 0-87049-169-5). U of Tenn Pr.

Ferris, Paul. High Places. cancelled (ISBN 0-698-10799-3, Coward). Putnam Pub Group.

--The Master Bankers: Controlling the World's Finances. LC 84-22598. 320p. 1985. 17.95 (ISBN 0-688-04172-8). Morrow.

--Richard Burton. 288p. 1984. pap. 3.50 (ISBN 0-425-07374-2). Berkley Pub.

Ferris, Roase M. Wild & Tender Magic. (Candlelight Ecstasy Ser.: No. 89). (Orig.). 1982. pap. 1.95 (ISBN 0-440-19411-3). Dell.

Ferris, Robert G. & Morris, Richard E. The Signers of the Declaration of Independence. LC 82-82219. (Illus.). 180p. 1982. 19.95 (ISBN 0-936478-06-3); pap. 5.95 (ISBN 0-936478-07-1). Interpretive Pubns.

Ferris, Robert W. Pupil Personnel Strategies & Systems. (Illus.). 264p. 1975. 19.00x (ISBN 0-398-03370-6). C C Thomas.

Ferris, Rose M. After the Fire. (Candlelight Ecstasy Ser.: No. 37). (Orig.). 1982. pap. 1.75 (ISBN 0-440-10036-4). Dell.

--Bristol's Law. (Candlelight Ecstasy Ser.: No. 207). (Orig.). 1984. pap. 1.95 (ISBN 0-440-10803-9). Dell.

Ferris, Roxana S. Flowers of the Point Reyes National Seashore. (Illus.). 1970. pap. 4.95 (ISBN 0-520-01694-7). U of Cal Pr.

--Native Shrubs of the San Francisco Bay Region. (California Natural History Guides Ser.: No. 24). (Illus.). 1968. pap. 2.85 (ISBN 0-520-00405-1). U of Cal Pr.

Ferris, Roxana S. see Abrams, LeRoy.

Ferris, Roxana S., ed. see Parsons, Mary E.

Ferris, S. D., et al, eds. Laser-Solid Interactions & Laser Processing - 1978: Materials Research Society, Boston. LC 79-51564. (AIP Conference Proceedings Ser.: No. 50). (Illus.). 1979. lib. bdg. 26.00 (ISBN 0-88318-149-5). Am Inst Physics.

Ferris, Seymour W. Handbook of Hydrocarbons. 1955. 56.00 (ISBN 0-12-254050-6). Acad Pr.

Ferris, Sharon P., jt. auth. see Marco, Guy A.

Ferris, Sylvia Van Voast see Van Voast Ferris, Sylvia.

Ferris, Theodoe N., et al, eds. see Educational Research Council of America.

Ferris, Theodore, ed. see Educational Research Council of America.

Ferris, Theodore H., et al, eds. see Educational Research Council of America.

Ferris, Theodore N., ed. see Educational Research Council of America.

Ferris, Theodore N., ed. see Educational Research Council of America Staff.

Ferris, Theodore N., et al, eds. see Educational Research Council of America.

Ferris, Theodore N, et al, eds. see Educational Research Council of America.

Ferris, Theodore N., et al, eds. see Educational Research Council of America Staff.

Ferris, Theodore P. Prayers. 1981. 6.95 (ISBN 0-8164-0483-6, Pub. by Seabury). Winston Pr.

--This Is the Day: Selected Sermons. 2nd ed. LC 76-39640. 368p. 1980. pap. 10.00 (ISBN 0-911658-16-5). Yankee Bks.

Ferris, Thomas F., jt. auth. see Burrow, Gerard N.

Ferris, Timothy. Galaxien. Ehlers, Anita, tr. from Eng. 184p. (Ger.). 1981. 94.00 (ISBN 0-8176-1250-5). Birkhauser.

--Galaxies. LC 80-13139. (Illus.). 200p. 1980. 75.00 (ISBN 0-87156-273-1). Sierra.

--Galaxies. LC 81-21520. (A Sierra Bk.). (Illus.). 192p. 1982. 27.50 (ISBN 0-941434-01-X); pap. 16.95 (ISBN 0-941434-02-8). Stewart Tabori & Chang.

--The Red Limit: The Search for the Edge of the Universe. rev. ed. LC 83-3068. (Illus.). 288p. 1983. pap. 9.70 (ISBN 0-688-01836-X, Quill NY). Morrow.

--Spaceshots: The Beauty of Nature Beyond Earth. LC 84-42705. (Illus.). 143p. 1984. 24.45 (ISBN 0-394-53890-0). Pantheon.

Ferris, Valerie. Promises to Keep. (Candlelight Ecstasy Ser.: No. 30). 192p. (Orig.). 1981. pap. 1.75 (ISBN 0-440-17159-8). Dell.

Ferris, Warren. Life in the Rocky Mountains. rev. ed. Hafen, LeRoy, ed. 1984. 35.00 (ISBN 0-912094-20-6). Old West.

Ferris, William. Blues from the Delta. (Roots of Jazz Ser.). (Illus.). iii, 247p. 1984. Repr. of 1979 ed. lib. bdg. 25.00 (ISBN 0-306-76215-3). Da Capo.

--Local Color: A Sense of Place in Folk Art. 272p. 1983. 19.95 (ISBN 0-07-020652-X); pap. 11.95 (ISBN 0-07-020651-1). McGraw.

Ferris, William & Hart, Mary L., eds. Folk Music & Modern Sound. LC 82-2041. 224p. 1981. pap. 7.95 (ISBN 0-87805-157-0). U Pr of Miss.

Ferris, William, jt. ed. see Vermilye, Dyckman W.

Ferris, William H. The African Abroad, or, His Evolution in Western Civilization, 2 Vols. (Basic Afro-American Reprint Library). 1969. Repr. of 1913 ed. Set. 55.00 (ISBN 0-384-15530-8). Johnson Repr.

Ferris, William R., Jr. Mississippi Black Folklore: A Research Bibliography & Discography. LC 70-158331. 61p. 1971. pap. 2.50x (ISBN 0-87805-001-9). U Pr of Miss.

Ferriss, Abbott L. Indicators of Change in the American Family. LC 76-102385. 170p. 1970. pap. 5.50x (ISBN 0-87154-250-1). Russell Sage.

--Indicators of Trends in American Education. LC 76-92860. 454p. 1969. pap. 6.95x (ISBN 0-87154-251-X). Russell Sage.

--Indicators of Trends in the Status of American Women. LC 76-153996. 452p. 1971. pap. 8.50x (ISBN 0-87154-252-8). Russell Sage.

Ferriss, Hugh. The Metropolis of Tomorrow. (Illus.). 1985. price not set (ISBN 0-910413-11-8). Princeton Arch.

Ferriss, Lloyd. Secrets of a Mountain. Jack, Susan, ed. (Secrets of Ser.). (Illus.). 76p. (Orig.). 1982. pap. 5.95 (ISBN 0-930096-18-5). G Gannett.

Ferriss, Lucy. Philip's Girl. LC 84-22226. 160p. 1985. 14.95 (ISBN 0-8052-3976-6). Schocken.

Ferro, Marc. The Bolshevik Revolution: A Social History of the Russian Revolution. 368p. 1985. pap. 13.95 (ISBN 0-7102-0550-3). Routledge & Kegan.

--Great War, Nineteen Fourteen to Nineteen Eighteen. 1973. pap. 9.95x (ISBN 0-7100-7575-8). Routledge & Kegan.

--October Nineteen Seventeen. (Illus.). 1980. 35.00 (ISBN 0-7100-0534-2). Routledge & Kegan.

--The Use & Abuse of History or How the Past Is Taught. 256p. 1984. 28.95x (ISBN 0-7100-9658-5). Routledge & Kegan.

Ferro, Robert. Blue Star: The Family of Max Desir. 256p. 1985. 16.95 (ISBN 0-525-24321-6, 01646-490). Dutton.

--The Family of Max Desir. LC 83-4906. 217p. 1983. 13.95 (ISBN 0-525-24197-3, 01354-410, Plume). Dutton.

--The Family of Max Desir. 1984. pap. 6.95 (ISBN 0-452-25587-2, Plume). NAL.

Ferro Milone, A. & Giacomo, P. Metrology & Fundamental Constants. (Enrico Fermi Summer School Ser.: No. 68). 820p. 1980. 164.00 (ISBN 0-444-85467-3, North-Holland). Elsevier.

Ferron, Jacques. Dr. Cotnoir. Cloutier, Pierre, tr. LC 73-83339. (French Writers of Canada Ser.). pap. 21.80 (ISBN 0-317-30037-7, 2025046). Bks Demand UMI.

--Selected Tales of Jacques Ferron. Bednarski, Betty, tr. from Fr. (Anansi Fiction Ser.: AF 48). 192p. (Orig.). 1984. pap. 9.95 (ISBN 0-88784-140-6, Pub. by Hse Anansi Pr Canada). U of Toronto Pr.

Ferrone, Frank, jt. auth. see Baker, Thomas.

Ferrone, J., ed. see Calvino, Italo.

Ferrone, J., ed. see Chiaromonte, Nicola.

Ferrone, Soldano & David, Chella S. IA Antigens. 1982. Vol. I, Mice. 264 pp. 73.50, (ISBN 0-8493-6461-2); Vol. II, Man & Other Species. 176 pp.8 55.00, (ISBN 0-8493-6462-0). CRC Pr.

Ferrone, Soldano & Dierich, Manfred P., eds. Handbook of Monoclonal Antibodies: Applications in Biology & Medicine. LC 85-4982. (Illus.). 477p. 1985. 72.00 (ISBN 0-8155-1034-9). Noyes.

Ferrone, Soldano & Solheim, Bjarte G., eds. HLA Typing: Methodology & Clinical Aspects, 2 vols. 1982. 59.00 ea. Vol. I, 208 pp (ISBN 0-8493-6410-8). Vol. II, 200 pp (ISBN 0-8493-6411-6). 59.00. CRC Pr.

Ferrone, Soldano, jt. ed. see Reisfeld, Ralph.

Ferrone, Soldano, jt. ed. see Reisfeld, Ralph A.

Ferroni, Charles D. The Italians in Cleveland: A Study in Assimilation. Cordasco, Francesco, ed. LC 80-855. (American Ethnic Groups Ser.). 1981. lib. bdg. 27.50x (ISBN 0-405-13418-5). Ayer Co Pubs.

Ferronsky, V. I. & Polyakov, V. A. Environmental Isotopes in the Hydrosphere. 466p. 1982. 79.95x (ISBN 0-471-10114-1, Pub. by Wiley-Interscience). Wiley.

Ferrucci, Franco. The Poetics of Disguise: The Autobiography of the Work in Homer, Dante, & Shakespeare. Dunnigan, Ann, tr. from It. LC 80-11242. 178p. 1980. 19.95x (ISBN 0-8014-1262-5). Cornell U Pr.

Ferrucci, Joseph T., jt. auth. see Eaton, S. Boyd, Jr.

Ferrucci, Joseph T., Jr. Interventional Radiology of the Abdomen. 2nd ed. (Illus.). 484p. 1984. 79.95 (ISBN 0-683-03175-9). Williams & Wilkins.

Ferrucci, Piero. What We May Be: Techniques for Psychological & Spiritual Growth. LC 81-51107. (Illus.). 256p. 1982. 6.95 (ISBN 0-87477-262-1). J P Tarcher.

Ferruolo, Stephen C. The Origins of the University: The Schools of Paris & Their Critics, 1100-1215. LC 84-40445. 392p. 1985. 45.00x (ISBN 0-8047-1266-2). Stanford U Pr.

Ferruzzi, Donald R. Human Anatomy & Physiology: A Laboratory Manual, Vol. 1. 4th ed. (Illus.). 226p. 1985. Repr. of 1982 ed. 17.95 (ISBN 0-9609098-1-8). Biomat Pub Co.

--Human Anatomy & Physiology: A Laboratory Manual, Vol. 2. 2nd ed. (Illus.). 241p. 1985. Repr. of 1982 ed. 18.95 (ISBN 0-9609098-4-2). Biomat Pub Co.

Ferry, Anne. Inward Language: Sonnets of Wyatt, Sidney, Shakespeare, Donne. LC 83-1072. 272p. 1983. lib. bdg. 25.00x (ISBN 0-226-24466-0). U of Chicago Pr.

--Milton's Epic Voice: The Narrator in Paradise Lost. LC 83-4839. xx, 188p. 1983. pap. 6.95x (ISBN 0-226-24468-7). U of Chicago Pr.

Ferry, Anne D. Milton & the Miltonic Dryden. LC 68-25608. 1968. 15.00x (ISBN 0-674-57576-8). Harvard U Pr.

Ferry, B. W., et al, eds. Air Pollution & Lichens. (Illus.). 389p. 1973. 70.00 (ISBN 0-485-11140-3, Pub. by Athlone Pr Ltd). Longwood Pub Group.

Ferry, Charles. One More Time. LC 84-20507. 192p. (gr. 7 up). 1985. 11.95 (ISBN 0-395-36692-5). HM.

--Raspberry One. LC 82-25476. 224p. (gr. 7 up). 1983. 11.95 (ISBN 0-395-34069-1). HM.

Ferry, D. K., et al, eds. Physics of Nonlinear Transport in Semiconductors. LC 79-28383. (NATO ASI Series B, Physics: Vol. 52). 634p. 1980. 89.50 (ISBN 0-306-40356-0, Plenum Pr). Plenum Pub.

Ferry, David. The Limits of Mortality: An Essay on Wordsworth's Major Poems. LC 77-15988. 1978. Repr. of 1959 ed. lib. bdg. 24.75x (ISBN 0-313-20020-3, FELM). Greenwood.

--On the Way to the Island. LC 60-13156. (Wesleyan Poetry Program: Vol. 7). (Orig.). 1960. 15.00x (ISBN 0-8195-2007-1); pap. 6.95 (ISBN 0-8195-1007-6). Wesleyan U Pr.

--Strangers: A Book of Poems. LC 83-1163. (Phoenix Poets Ser.). 64p. 1984. 12.95x (ISBN 0-226-24469-5); pap. 5.95 (ISBN 0-226-24470-9). U of Chicago Pr.

Ferry, David K. Gallium Arsenide Technology. Date not set. 44.95 (ISBN 0-672-22375-9, 22375). Sams.

Ferry, Dick. Street of Mansions, No. 12. Spooner, Kerr, ed. 23p. 1983. pap. 3.00 (ISBN 0-932884-11-3). Red Herring.

Ferry, Douglas J. & Brandon, Peter S. Cost Planning of Buildings. 330p. 1980. 17.95x (ISBN 0-8464-1084-2). Beekman Pubs.

--Cost Planning of Buildings. 4th ed. 385p. 1980. pap. text ed. 17.00x (ISBN 0-246-11337-5, Pub. by Granada England). Brookfield Pub Co.

--Cost Planning of Buildings. 5th ed. 398p. 1984. pap. 19.50x (ISBN 0-246-12249-8, Pub. by Granada England). Sheridan.

Ferry, Georgina, ed. The Understanding of Animals. (New Scientist Guides Ser.). (Illus.). 336p. 1984. 24.95x (ISBN 0-85520-729-9); pap. 8.95 (ISBN 0-85520-728-0). Basil Blackwell.

Ferry, J. M., ed. Characterization of Metamorphism Through Mineral Equilibria. (Reviews in Mineralogy: Vol. 10). 397p. 1982. 13.00 (ISBN 0-939950-12-X). Mineralogical Soc.

Ferry, John D. Viscoelastic Properties of Polymers. 3rd ed. LC 79-2866. 641p. 1980. 64.50x (ISBN 0-471-04894-1, Pub. by Wiley-Interscience). Wiley.

Ferry, Peggy C., et al. Seizure Disorders in Children. (Illus.). 320p. 1985. text ed. price not set (ISBN 0-397-50617-1, Lippincott Medical). Lippincott.

Ferry, Ted S. Elements of Accident Investigation. 72p. 1978. spiral 10.75x (ISBN 0-398-03752-3). C C Thomas.

--Modern Accident Investigation & Analysis: An Executive Guide to Accident Investigation. LC 80-21046. 273p. 1981. 38.95x (ISBN 0-471-07776-3, Pub. by Wiley-Interscience). Wiley.

--Safety Management Planning Manual. 1982. 287.00x (ISBN 0-930868-46-3). Merritt Co.

--Safety Management Planning Manual: College Edition. Merritt Company, ed. 200p. 1982. 31.25 (ISBN 0-930868-47-1). Merritt Co.

--Safety Program Administration for Engineers & Managers: A Resource Guide for Establishing & Evaluating Safety Programs. (Illus.). 306p. 1984. 30.50x (ISBN 0-398-05000-7). C C Thomas.

Ferry, Ted S. & Weaver, D. A. Directions in Safety: A Selection of Safety Readings. (Illus.). 498p. 1976. 55.50x (ISBN 0-398-03365-X). C C Thomas.

Ferry, Ted S., ed. Readings in Accident Investigation: Examples of the Scope, Depth & Sources. (Illus.). 302p. 1984. 34.75x (ISBN 0-398-04950-5). C C Thomas.

Ferry, W. Hawkins. Buildings of Detroit: A History. rev. ed. LC 80-15976. (Illus.). 500p. 1980. 40.00 (ISBN 0-8143-1665-4). Wayne St U Pr.

Fersch, Ellsworth A. Psychology & Psychiatry in Courts & Corrections: Controversy & Change. LC 80-11726. (Personality Processes Ser.). 370p. 1980. 37.95x (ISBN 0-471-05604-9, Pub. by Wiley-Interscience). Wiley.

Fersch, Ellsworth A., Jr. Law, Psychology, & the Courts: Rethinking Treatment of the Young & the Disturbed. 184p. 1979. 19.75x (ISBN 0-398-03874-0). C C Thomas.

Fersh, Seymour. Asia: Teaching About, Learning From. LC 77-16458. (Illus.). 1978. pap. text ed. 8.50x (ISBN 0-8077-2539-0). Tchrs Coll.

Fersht, Alan. Enzyme Structure & Mechanism. LC 77-6441. (Illus.). 371p. 1977. pap. text ed. 18.95 (ISBN 0-7167-0188-X). W H Freeman.

--Enzyme Structure & Mechanism. 2nd ed. LC 84-4172. (Illus.). 496p. 1984. text ed. 24.95 (ISBN 0-7167-1614-3). W H Freeman.

Ferson, Jean, ed. see Lurie, H. R.

Ferst, Barton E. & Ferst, Stanley D. Basic Accounting for Lawyers No. B121. 3rd ed. 176p. 1975. pap. 10.00 (ISBN 0-317-30783-5). Am Law Inst.

Ferst, Stanley D., jt. auth. see Ferst, Barton E.

Ferster, Charles & Culbertson, Stuart A. Behavior Principles. 3rd ed. (Illus.). 384p. 1982. reference 28.95 (ISBN 0-13-072520-X). P-H.

Ferster, Dorothy C., jt. auth. see Coben, Lawrence A.

Ferster, J. Chaucer on Interpretation. 194p. 1985. 29.95 (ISBN 0-521-26661-0). Cambridge U Pr.

Ferstle, Jim. Contemporary Jogging. LC 77-91153. 1978. pap. 3.95 (ISBN 0-8092-7575-9). Contemp Bks.

Ferszt, R., jt. ed. see Cervos-Navarro, J.

Fertey, Andre, tr. see Bray, Martha C.

Fertig, James W. Secession & Reconstruction of Tennessee. LC 71-168019. Repr. of 1898 ed. 14.00 (ISBN 0-404-00046-0). AMS Pr.

Fertig, Robert T. The Software Revolution: Trends, Players, Market Dynamics in Personal Computer Software. 400p. 1985. 39.00 (ISBN 0-444-00976-0, North-Holland). Elsevier.

Fertis, Demeter G. Dynamics & Vibration of Structures. LC 83-8416. 504p. 1983. Repr. of 1973 ed. 39.50 (ISBN 0-89874-635-3). Krieger.

Fertl, W. H. Abnormal Formation Pressures. (Developments in Petroleum Science: Vol. 2). 382p. 1976. 47.00 (ISBN 0-444-41328-6). Elsevier.

Ferullo, Dan, jt. auth. see Russell, Harold.

Ferus, D., et al, eds. Global Differential Geometry & Global Analysis: Proceedings. (Lecture Notes in Mathematics: Vol. 838). 299p. 1981. pap. 22.00 (ISBN 0-387-10285-X). Springer-Verlag.

Feruson, David. The Complete Moving Planner. 96p. (Orig.). 1985. pap. 4.50 (ISBN 0-440-51218-2, Dell Trade Pbks). Dell.

Ferval, L., jt. auth. see Lange, K.

Ferziger, Joel H. Numerical Methods for Engineering Application. LC 81-1260. 288p. 1981. 34.95x (ISBN 0-471-06336-3, Pub. by Wiley-Interscience). Wiley.

Fesch, Paul. Constantinople Aux Derniers Jours d'Abdul-Hamid. LC 72-140972. (Research & Source Works Ser.: No. 748). 1971. Repr. of 1907 ed. lib. bdg. 43.00 (ISBN 0-8337-1121-0). B Franklin.

Fesenmaier, Daniel R., jt. ed. see Lieber, Stanley R.

Fesharaki, Fereidum & Isaak, David T. OPEC, the Gulf & the World Petroleum Market: A Study in Government Policy & Downstream Operations. LC 82-17496. (Special Studies in International Economics & Business). 268p. 1983. lib. bdg. 30.00x (ISBN 0-86531-305-9). Westview.

Fesharaki, Fereidun, ed. Critical Energy Issues in the Asia-Pacific Region: The Next Twenty Years. (Special Study). 225p. 1982. 25.50 (ISBN 0-86531-306-7). Westview.

Fesharaki, Fereidun, et al, eds. Earth & the Human Future: Essays in Honor of Harrison Brown. 240p. 1985. 17.85x (ISBN 0-86531-690-2). Westview.

Feshbach, Ann, tr. see Gourfinkel, Nina.

Feshbach, H. & Levin, F. S. Reaction Dynamics, 2 pts. Incl. Pt. 1. Recent Developments in the Theory of Direct Reactions; Pt. 2. Topics in the Theory of Nuclear Reactions. LC 70-183847. (Documents on Modern Physics Ser.). 224p. 1973. Set. 57.75 (ISBN 0-677-04330-9). Gordon.

Feshbach, H., jt. auth. see Morse, Philip M.

Feshbach, Herman, jt. auth. see De Shalit, Amos.

Feshbach, Herman, jt. ed. see Shimony, Abner.

Feshbach, Norma, et al. Learning to Care: Classroom Activities for Social & Affective Development. 1983. pap. 9.95 (ISBN 0-673-15804-7). Scott F.

Feshbach, Seymour & Singer, Roger D. Television & Aggression: An Experimental Field Study. LC 70-138457. (Jossey-Bass Behavioral Science Ser.). pap. 51.00 (ISBN 0-317-26063-4, 2023777). Bks Demand UMI.

Feshbach, Seymour & Weiner, Bernard. Personality. 528p. 1982. text ed. 26.95 (ISBN 0-669-89383-8). Heath.

Feshbach, Seymour & Fraczek, Adam, eds. Aggression & Behavior Change: Biological & Social Processes. LC 79-17934. (Praeger Special Studies Ser.). (Illus.). 316p. 1979. 39.95x (ISBN 0-03-052446-6). Praeger.

Feshbach, Seymour, jt. ed. see Jessor, Richard.

Feshback, Norma D., et al. Early Schooling in England & Israel. (IDEA Reports on Schooling). 224p. 1973. 3.20 (ISBN 0-07-020635-X). McGraw.

Fesler, James. Public Administration: Theory & Practice. (Illus.). 1980. text ed. 27.95 (ISBN 0-13-737320-1). P-H.

Fesler, James W., ed. American Public Administration: Pattern of the Past. (PAR Classics Ser.: Vol. IV). 1982. 11.95 (ISBN 0-936678-05-4). Am Soc Pub Admin.

Fesperman, Francis I. From Torah to Apocalypse: An Introduction to the Bible. 334p. 1983. pap. text ed. 15.00 (ISBN 0-8191-3555-0). U Pr of Amer.

Fesquet, Henri. Has Rome Converted. Salemson, Harold J., tr. 1968. 4.95 (ISBN 0-685-11959-9). Heineman.

Fess & Warren. Managerial Accounting. 1985. text ed. 22.50 (ISBN 0-538-01600-0, A60). SW Pub.

Fess, Elaine, et al. Hand Splinting: Principles & Methods. LC 80-17398. (Illus.). 318p. 1981. text ed. 41.95 (ISBN 0-8016-1569-0). Mosby.

Fess, Philip E. & Warren, Carl S. Accounting Principles. 1984. text ed. 23.00 (ISBN 0-538-01220-X, A22). SW Pub.

--Financial Accounting. 2nd ed. 1985. text ed. 22.50 (ISBN 0-538-01240-4, A24). SW Pub.

Fessard, A., ed. Handbook of Sensory Physiology: Electroreceptors & Other Specialized Receptors in Lower Verterbrates. (Vol. 3, Pt. 1). (Illus.). viii, 333p. 1974. 75.00 (ISBN 0-387-06872-4). Springer-Verlag.

Fessenden, Francis, ed. see Fessenden, William P.

Fessenden, Helen M. Fessenden: Builder of Tomorrows. LC 74-4681. (Telecommunications Ser.). (Illus.). 376p. 1974. Repr. of 1940 ed. 20.00x (ISBN 0-405-06047-5). Ayer Co Pubs.

Fessenden, Joan S., jt. auth. see Fessenden, Ralph J.

Fessenden, Ralph J. & Fessenden, Joan S. Basic Chemistry for the Health Sciences. 3rd ed. 1984. text ed. 37.14 (ISBN 0-205-08016-2, 688016); write for info. instr's. manual (ISBN 0-205-08029-4); student guide 10.22 (ISBN 0-205-08017-0, 688017). Allyn.

--Chemical Principles for the Life Sciences. 2nd ed. 1979. text ed. 32.74 (ISBN 0-205-06506-6, 686506); instr's manual (ISBN 0-205-06533-3). Allyn.

--Techniques & Experiments for Organic Chemistry. 480p. 1983. text ed. write for info. (ISBN 0-87150-755-2, 4401). Brooks-Cole.

Fessenden, W. P., et al, eds. see U. S. 39th Congress 1st Session.

Fessenden, William P. Life & Public Services of William Pitt Fessenden, 2 Vols. Fessenden, Francis, ed. LC 70-87532. (American Public Figures Ser). (Illus.). 1970. Repr. of 1907 ed. Set. lib. bdg. 85.00 (ISBN 0-306-71446-9). Da Capo.

Fessenden-Raden, June & Gert, Bernard. A Philosophical Approach to the Management of Occupational Health Hazards. 43p. 1984. pap. text ed. 2.00x (ISBN 0-88738-641-5). Transaction Bks.

Fessio, Joseph, ed. see Von Balthasar, Hans U.

Fessler, Daniel & Loiseaux, Pierre R. Contracts: Morality, Economics & the Market Place Cases & Materials. LC 82-10927. (American Casebook Ser.). 837p. 1982. 22.95 (ISBN 0-314-66852-7); pap. teacher's manual avail. (ISBN 0-314-71323-9). West Pub.

Fessler, Daniel W. Alternatives to Incorporation for Persons in Quest of Profit: Cases & Materials on Partnerships, Joint Ventures & Related Agency Concepts. LC 80-18481. (American Casebook Ser.). 258p. 1980. pap. text ed. 10.95 (ISBN 0-8299-2102-8). West Pub.

Fessler, Diane M., ed. see Lehman, Charles A.

Fessler, Donald R. Facilitating Community Change: A Basic Guide. LC 76-12768. 146p. 1976. pap. 11.50 (ISBN 0-88390-121-8). Univ Assocs.

Fessler, Edward A. Directed-Energy Weapons: A Juridical Analysis. LC 79-65950. 204p. 1980. 37.95x (ISBN 0-03-053511-5). Praeger.

Fessler, George R. & Westcott, Ray D. The Advanced Real Estate Primer. 22nd, rev. ed. Orig. Title: Real Estate Primer Review. 342p. 1984. pap. text ed. cancelled (ISBN 0-935810-11-0). Primer Pubs.

--The Insurance Primer: Fire & Casuality. 13th rev ed. 172p. 1984. pap. text ed. 7.95 (ISBN 0-935810-10-2). Primer Pubs.

--The Real Estate Primer. 36th, rev. ed. 304p. 1984. pap. text ed. 10.95 (ISBN 0-935810-20-X). Primer Pubs.

Fessler, Loren. Chinese in America: Stereotyped Past, Changing Present. LC 81-90404. 305p. 1983. 12.95 (ISBN 0-533-05154-1). Vantage.

Fessler, Stella L. Chinese Meatless Cooking. 1983. pap. 3.50 (ISBN 0-451-12351-4, Sig). NAL.

--Chinese Seafood Cooking. 1985. pap. 3.95 (ISBN 0-451-13674-8, Sig). NAL.

Fessler, Stella L., tr. see Hatano, Sumi.

Fest, C. & Schmidt, K. J. The Chemistry of Organphosphorous Pesticides. (Illus.). 380p. 1982. 80.00 (ISBN 0-387-11303-7). Springer-Verlag.

Fest, Joachim C. The Face of the Third Reich: Portraits of the Nazi Leadership. Bullock, Michael, tr. LC 66-10412. 1977. pap. 6.95 (ISBN 0-394-73407-6). Pantheon.

--Hitler. 1975. pap. 10.95 (ISBN 0-394-72023-7, Vin). Random.

Fest, Otto. Ueber Surrey's Virgiluebersetzung. 18.00 (ISBN 0-384-15540-5); pap. 13.00 (ISBN 0-685-92693-1). Johnson Repr.

Fest, Wilfried. Dictionary of German History 1806-1945. LC 78-54658. 1979. 13.95x (ISBN 0-312-20103-6). St Martin.

--Peace or Partition: The Habsburg Monarchy & British Policy, 1914-1918. LC 77-92396. 1978. 20.00x (ISBN 0-312-59935-8). St Martin.

Festa-McCormick, Diana. The City As Catalyst: A Study of Ten Novels. LC 77-85595. 261p. 1979. 20.00; pap. 9.95 (ISBN 0-8386-2156-2). Fairleigh Dickinson.

--Proustian Optics of Clothes: Mirrors, Masks, Mores. (Stanford French & Italian Studies: Vol. 29). 224p. 1984. pap. 25.00 (ISBN 0-915838-08-7). Anma Libri.

Festa-McCormick, Diane. Honore De Balzac. (World Authors Ser.). 1979. lib. bdg. 13.50 (ISBN 0-8057-6383-X, Twayne). G K Hall.

Fester, Richard. Machiavelli. LC 77-143655. 204p. 1904. Repr. 21.00 (ISBN 0-8337-3154-8). B Franklin.

Festing, Gabrielle. From the Land of Princes. (Folklore Ser.). 1904. 30.00 (ISBN 0-8482-3985-7). Norwood Edns.

Festing, Jones H., ed. The Note-Books of Samuel Butler. 1978. Repr. of 1915 ed. lib. bdg. 25.00 (ISBN 0-8492-3546-4). R West.

Festing, Michael F. Inbred Strains in Biomedical Research. 1979. text ed. 55.00x (ISBN 0-19-520111-6). Oxford U Pr.

Festing, Michael F., ed. Animal Models of Obesity. 1979. 38.50x (ISBN 0-19-520171-X). Oxford U Pr.

Festing, Sally. Fishermen. 1977. 5.95 (ISBN 0-7153-7448-6). David & Charles.

Festinger, Leon. Conflict, Decision & Dissonance. 1964. 12.50x (ISBN 0-8047-0205-5). Stanford U Pr.

--The Human Legacy. LC 82-22178. 192p. 1983. 21.50 (ISBN 0-231-05672-9). Columbia U Pr.

--A Theory of Cognitive Dissonance. 1957. 25.00x (ISBN 0-8047-0131-8); pap. 7.95x (ISBN 0-8047-0911-4). Stanford U Pr.

Festinger, Leon, jt. auth. see Lawrence, Douglas H.

Festinger, Leon, ed. Retrospections on Social Psychology. (Illus.). 1980. text ed. 18.95x (ISBN 0-19-502751-5). Oxford U Pr.

Festinger, Leon, et al. Social Pressures in Informal Groups: A Study of Human Factors in Housing. 1950. 20.00x (ISBN 0-8047-0173-3); pap. 6.95 (ISBN 0-8047-0174-1, SP57). Stanford U Pr.

--When Prophecy Fails: A Social & Psychological Study of a Modern Group That Predicted the Destruction of the World. pap. 6.95xi (ISBN 0-06-131132-4, TB1132, Torch). Har-Row.

Festinger, Trudy. No One Ever Asked Us: A Postscript to Foster Care. 336p. 1984. 30.00x (ISBN 0-231-05736-9). Columbia U Pr.

Festschrift. Classica et Iberica. 15.00 (ISBN 0-686-23371-9). Classical Folia.

Festugiere, Andre-Jean. Personal Religion among the Greeks. (Sather Classical Lecture Ser.: No. 26). 186p. 1984. Repr. of 1954 ed. lib. bdg. 25.00 (ISBN 0-313-23209-1, FERG). Greenwood.

Fetchko, Peter, jt. auth. see Hickman, Money.

Fete, Ray, jt. auth. see Brown, Jeff.

Feters, L. J., et al. Anionic Polymerization. (Advances in Polymer Science Ser.: Vol.56). (Illus.). 1984. 40.00 (ISBN 0-387-12792-5). Springer-Verlag.

Fetherling, Dale. Mother Jones, the Miners' Angel: A Portrait. LC 73-12444. (Illus.). 280p. 1974. 11.85x (ISBN 0-8093-0643-3). S Ill U Pr.

--Mother Jones, the Miners' Angel: A Portrait. LC 78-16328. (Arcturus Books Paperbacks). (Illus.). 280p. 1979. pap. 8.95 (ISBN 0-8093-0896-7). S Ill U Pr.

Fetherling, Dale & Fetherling, Doug, eds. Carl Sandburg at the Movies: A Poet in the Silent Era 1920-1927. LC 84-14068. 207p. 1985. 16.50 (ISBN 0-8108-1738-1). Scarecrow.

Fetherling, Doug. The Five Lives of Ben Hecht. 1980. 11.95 (ISBN 0-919630-85-5). NY Zoetrope.

--Wheeling, WV: An Illustrated History. (Illus.). 120p. 1983. 19.95 (ISBN 0-89781-071-6). Windsor Pubns Inc.

Fetherling, Doug, jt. ed. see Fetherling, Dale.

Fetherston, Patrick. The World Was a Bubble. (Burning Deck Poetry Ser). 1979. 15.00 (ISBN 0-930900-61-8); pap. 4.00 (ISBN 0-930900-62-6). Burning Deck.

Fethke, Gary C., et al. Investigation of the Conceptual & Qualitative Impact of Employment Tax Credits. LC 78-14292. 1978. pap. 6.95 (ISBN 0-911558-00-4). W E Upjohn.

Fetis, Francis J. Music Explained to the World. (Music Reprint Ser.). 320p. 1985. Repr. of 1842 ed. lib. bdg. 32.50 (ISBN 0-306-76276-5). Da Capo.

Fetis, Francois J. Biographical Notice of Nicolo Paganini. LC 74-24081. (Illus.). Repr. of 1876 ed. 15.00 (ISBN 0-404-12909-9). AMS Pr.

--Biographie Universelle Des Musiciens, 10 Vols. 1964. Repr. of 1873 ed. Set. lea. bdg. 418.00x (ISBN 0-685-05184-6). Adlers Foreign Bks.

--Notice of Anthony Stradivari. Repr. lib. bdg. 25.00 (ISBN 0-403-03807-3). Scholarly.

Fetisov, A. Proof in Geometry. 62p. 1978. pap. 2.45 (ISBN 0-8285-0742-2, Pub. by Mir Pubs USSR). Imported Pubns.

Fetler, Andrew. To Byzantium. LC 76-13854. (Illinois Short Fiction Ser). 115p. 1976. pap. 5.95 (ISBN 0-252-00584-8). U of Ill Pr.

Fetler, James. Impossible Appetites. LC 80-17200. (The Iowa School of Letters Award for Short Fiction Ser.: No. 11). 176p. 1980. 12.95 (ISBN 0-87745-101-X); pap. 7.95 (ISBN 0-87745-102-8). U of Iowa Pr.

Fetner, Gerald. The Contours of Legal Reform in Twentieth Century America. (Law & American Society Ser.). 216p. 1980. pap. text ed. 7.00 (ISBN 0-394-33194-X, RanC). Random.

--Ordered Liberty: Legal Reform in the Twentieth-Century. LC 82-14820. (Borzoi Books in Law & American Society). 1983. text ed. 15.00 (ISBN 0-394-33578-3, KnopfC); pap. text ed. 7.00 (ISBN 0-394-33194-X). Knopf.

Fetridge, Clark & Minor, Robert. Office Administration Handbook. 1000p. 1984. 60.50 (ISBN 0-85013-142-1). Dartnell Corp.

Fetridge, William H. With Warm Regards. LC 75-35055. 1976. 7.95 (ISBN 0-85013-039-5). Dartnell Corp.

Fetridge, William H., ed. Navy Reader. facs. ed. LC 75-134076. (Essay Index Reprint Ser). 1943. 27.50 (ISBN 0-8369-2155-0). Ayer Co Pubs.

--Second Navy Reader. facs. ed. LC 71-142627. (Essay Index Reprint Ser). 1944. 26.50 (ISBN 0-8369-2156-9). Ayer Co Pubs.

Fetros, John. This Day in Sports. 1974. 5.95 (ISBN 0-912318-58-9). N K Gregg.

Fetros, John G. Dictionary of Factual & Fictional Riders & Their Horses. 1979. 10.00 (ISBN 0-682-49417-8). Exposition Pr FL.

Fetrow, Fred M. Robert Hayden. (United States Authors Ser.: No. 471). 181p. 1984. lib. bdg. 17.95 (ISBN 0-8057-7412-2, Twayne). G K Hall.

Fetscher, Iring. Lexikon des Marxismus. (Ger.). 1976. 20.00 (ISBN 3-455-09179-2, M-7207). French & Eur.

Fetsko, J. M., ed. see Walker, W. C., et al.

Fetter, Alexander L. & Walecka, J. Dirk. Theoretical Mechanics of Particles & Continua. (Illus.). 1980. text ed. 39.95 (ISBN 0-07-020658-9). McGraw.

Fetter, B. F., et al. Mycoses of the Central Nervous System. LC 66-28161. 219p. 1967. 14.25 (ISBN 0-683-03185-6, Pub. by Williams & Wilkins). Krieger.

Fetter, Bruce. The Creation of Elizabethville, Nineteen Ten to Nineteen Forty. (Publication Ser.: No. 154). 1976. 10.95x (ISBN 0-8179-6541-6). Hoover Inst Pr.

Fetter, Bruce, ed. Colonial Rule in Africa: Readings from Primary Sources. LC 78-65020. (Illus.). 238p. 1979. 27.50x (ISBN 0-299-07780-2); pap. 11.75x (ISBN 0-299-07784-5). U of Wis Pr.

Fetter, Bruce S. Colonial Rule & Regional Imbalance in Central Africa. LC 83-10556. (Westview Replica Edition Ser.). 235p. 1983. softcover 22.00x (ISBN 0-86531-977-4). Westview.

Fetter, Charles W., Jr. Applied Hydrogeology. (Physics & Physical Science Ser.). 448p. 1980. text ed. 37.50 (ISBN 0-675-08126-2). Merrill.

Fetter, F. W. & Gregory, D. Monetary & Financial Policy in Nineteenth Century Britain. (Government & Society in 19th Century Britain Ser.). 106p. 1973. 25.00x (ISBN 0-7165-2217-9, 02038, Pub. by Irish Academic Pr Ireland); pap. 6.00x o. p. (ISBN 0-7165-2218-7). Biblio Dist.

Fetter, Frank A. Capital, Interest & Rent: Essays in the Theory of Distribution. Rothbard, Murray N., ed. LC 76-25587. (Studies in Economic Theory). 400p. 1976. 25.00x (ISBN 0-8362-0684-3); pap. 10.00x (ISBN 0-8362-0685-1). NYU Pr.

--Masquerade of Monopoly. LC 66-22623. (Illus.). 1971. Repr. of 1931 ed. 37.50x (ISBN 0-678-00291-6). Kelley.

Fetter, Frank W. Development of British Monetary Orthodoxy 1797-1875. LC 76-30912. Repr. of 1965 ed. lib. bdg. 27.50x (ISBN 0-678-01386-1). Kelley.

--The Economist in Parliament, 1780-1868. LC 78-73944. 1980. 23.75 (ISBN 0-8223-0415-5). Duke.

Fetter, Frank W., ed. see Horner, Francis.

Fetter, Helga, tr. see Swokowski, Earl W.

Fetter, Richard. Frontier Boulder. (Illus.). 80p. (Orig.). 1983. pap. 5.95 (ISBN 0-933472-72-2). Johnson Bks.

--Mountain Men of Wyoming. (Wyoming Frontier Ser.). 64p. 1982. pap. 3.95 (ISBN 0-686-97819-6). Johnson Bks.

--Vail: A Connoisseur's Guide. (Illus.). 180p. (Orig.). 1981. pap. 3.95 (ISBN 0-933472-58-7). Johnson Bks.

Fetter, Richard L. Telluride: From Pick to Powder. LC 77-87369. (Illus.). 1979. pap. 7.95 (ISBN 0-87004-265-3). Caxton.

Fetter, Richard L., et al. Front Range Restaurants: The One Hundred Best. LC 80-83139. 1980. pap. 2.50 (ISBN 0-933472-46-3). Johnson Bks.

Fetter, Robert B., ed. see Chien, Chao C.

Fetter, Robert B., ed. see Stair, Ralph M., Jr.

Fetter, Robert B., et al. Cases in Health Policy & Management. 1985. 35.95x (ISBN 0-256-03292-0). Irwin.

Fetterhoff, Dean. Dynamics of Evangelism. pap. 1.00 (ISBN 0-88469-019-9). BMH Bks.

--The Making of a Man of God: Studies in I & II Timothy. pap. 4.95 (ISBN 0-88469-030-X). BMH Bks.

Fetterley, Judith. The Resisting Reader: A Feminist Approach to American Fiction. LC 78-3242. (Midland Bks.: No. 247). 224p. 1978. 20.00x (ISBN 0-253-31078-4); pap. 6.95x (ISBN 0-253-20247-7). Ind U Pr.

Fetterley, Judith, ed. Provisions: A Reader from Nineteenth Century American Women. LC 84-42840. (Everywoman: Studies in History, Literature, & Culture). 480p. 1985. 35.00 (ISBN 0-253-17040-0); pap. 12.95 (ISBN 0-253-20349-X). Ind U Pr.

Fetterman, Elsie. Buying Food. (Consumer Casebook Ser.). (Illus.). 80p. (gr. 10-12). 1981. pap. text ed. 5.00 (ISBN 0-87005-268-3). Fairchild.

Fetterman, Elsie & Jordan. Consumer Credit. (gr. 10-12). 1976. text ed. 13.76 (ISBN 0-02-663000-1); student guide 5.32 (ISBN 0-02-663020-6); tchr's guide 5.32 (ISBN 0-02-663010-9). Bennett IL.

Fetterman, Elsie & Newman, Chris. Consumer Credit. (Consumer Casebook Ser.). (Illus.). 1980. pap. text ed. 5.00 (ISBN 0-87005-266-7). Fairchild.

--Retail Purchases & Mail Order: Terms of Sale. (Consumer Education Casebook). (Illus.). 1979. pap. text ed. 5.00 (ISBN 0-87005-204-7). Fairchild.

Fetterman, Elsie & Schiller, Margery. Let the Buyer Be Aware! Consumer Rights & Responsibilities. LC 75-37093. 228p. 1976. pap. 5.95 (ISBN 0-87005-161-X). Fairchild.

Fetteroll, Eugene, jt. ed. see Nadler, Leonard.

Fetters, Thomas. Palmetto Traction: Electric Railways of South Carolina. (Illus.). 120p. (Orig.). 1978. pap. 9.00 (ISBN 0-911940-28-6). Cox.

Fetters, Thomas T. & Swanson, Peter W. The Piedmont & Northern Railway. LC 74-14801. (Illus.). 170p. 19.95 (ISBN 0-87095-051-7). Golden West.

Fettig, Art. Building Your Child's Self-Esteem & Your Own. LC 85-80482. 80p. 1985. pap. 19.95 with cassette tape (ISBN 0-916927-01-6). Growth Unltd.

--How to Hold an Audience in the Hollow of Your Hand. LC 79-14145. (Illus.). 160p. 1984. pap. 5.95 (ISBN 0-9601334-7-X). Growth Unltd.

--The Pos Activity Book. (Illus.). 48p. 1984. pap. 5.95 (ISBN 0-9601334-5-3). Growth Unltd.

--Remembering. LC 81-90188. (Illus.). 96p. 1982. 4.00 (ISBN 0-9601334-2-9). Growth Unltd.

--Selling Lucky. LC 77-89820. (Illus.). 1977. 7.95 (ISBN 0-9601334-1-0). Growth Unltd.

--Selling Lucky. LC 77-89820. (Illus.). 128p. 1984. pap. 5.95 (ISBN 0-9601334-6-1). Growth Unltd.

--The Three Robots. LC 80-84356. (Illus.). 96p. 1981. PLB 5.95 (ISBN 0-9601334-0-2). Growth Unltd.

--The Three Robots Discover Their Pos-Abilities: A Lesson in Goal Setting. LC 84-81461. 1984. pap. 3.95 (ISBN 0-916927-00-8). Growth Unltd.

--The Three Robots Find a Grandpa. LC 84-80378. (Illus.). 96p. (Orig.). 1984. pap. 3.95 with cassette tape (ISBN 0-9601334-8-8). Growth Unltd.

Fettig, Lester A. Contracting for Audit & Management Advisory Services with the Federal Government. 100p. 1981. 21.00 (ISBN 0-686-84277-4). Am Inst CPA.

Fetting, Art. The Three Robots & the Sandstorm. LC 82-90993. (Illus.). 96p. 1983. pap. 3.95 (ISBN 0-9601334-3-7). Growth Unltd.

Fettis, H. E., et al, trs. see Agrest, M. M. & Maksimov, M. S.

Fettke, Steven M. Messages to a Nation in Crisis: An Introduction to the Prophecy of Jeremiah. LC 82-19997. (Illus.). 72p. (Orig.). 1983. pap. text ed. 7.50 (ISBN 0-8191-2839-2). U Pr of Amer.

Fettner, Ann G. & Check, William A. The Truth about AIDS: Evolution of an Epidemic. LC 83-22799. 320p. 1985. pap. 8.95 (ISBN 0-03-005622-5, Owl Bks.). HR&W.

Fettner, Ann T. Potpourri. LC 77-5931. (Illus.). 130p. 1977. pap. 4.95 (ISBN 0-911104-97-6, 133). Workman Pub.

Fettweis, G. B. World Coal Resources: Methods of Assessment & Results. (Developments in Economic Geology Ser.: Vol. 10). 416p. 1979. 87.25 (ISBN 0-444-99779-2). Elsevier.

Fetz, F. Ski Dictionary: German Definitions with English & French Words. 20.00 (ISBN 3-85-123-0280). Heinman.

Fetzer, James. Scientific Knowledge. 1982. lib. bdg. 49.50 (ISBN 90-277-1335-9, Pub. by Reidel Netherlands); pap. text ed. 14.95 (ISBN 90-277-1336-7, Pub. by Reidel Holland). Kluwer Academic.

Fetzer, James H., ed. Principles of Philosophical Reasoning. LC 83-15985. (American Philosophical Quarterly Library of Philosophy). 292p. 1984. text ed. 32.95x (ISBN 0-8476-7158-5). Rowman & Allanheld.

--Principles of Philosophical Reasoning. LC 83-15985. 304p. 1984. pap. 18.95x (ISBN 0-8476-7341-3). Rowman & Allanheld.

Fetzer, James S. Sociobiology & Epistemology. 1985. lib. bdg. 39.50 (ISBN 90-277-2005-3, Pub. by Reidel Holland); pap. text ed. 14.95 (ISBN 90-277-2006-1). Kluwer Academic.

Fetzer, John. Clemens Brentano. (World Authors Ser.). 16.95 (ISBN 0-8057-6457-7, Twayne). G K Hall.

Fetzer, John F. Romantic Orpheus: Profiles of Clemens Brentano. LC 72-85527. 1974. 31.00x (ISBN 0-520-02312-9). U of Cal Pr.

Fetzer, L., ed. An Anthology of Pre-Revolutionary Russian Science Fiction. 370p. 1981. 35.00 (ISBN 0-88233-594-4); pap. 6.00 (ISBN 0-88233-595-2). Ardis Pubs.

Fetzer, Leland, tr. see Tolstoi, Alexei N.

Fetzer, Ronald & Vogel, Robert A. Designing Messages. 288p. 1982. pap. text ed. 15.95 (ISBN 0-574-22580-3, 13-5580); instr. guide avail. (ISBN 0-574-22581-1, 13-5581). SRA.

Fetzer, Ronald, jt. auth. see Makay, John.

Feuardent, F., jt. auth. see DeRouge, J.

Feucht, D. L., jt. auth. see Milnes, A. G.

Feucht, O. E. Everyone a Minister. 160p. pap. 2.25 (ISBN 0-570-03184-2, 12-2587). Concordia.

Feucht, Oscar E. Guidelines for Women's Groups in the Congregation. 1981. pap. 3.95 (ISBN 0-570-03828-6, 12-2793). Concordia.

Feucht, Oscar E., ed. see Norden, Rudolph F.

Feuchtersleben, Ernst F. Von see Von Feuchtersleben, Ernst F.

Feuchtinger, Eugene. Your Voice: Methods for Strengthening & Developing the Voice. Orig. Title: Voice Development Hints. Nelson-Hall.

Feuchtwang, Stephan, ed. The Chinese Economic Reforms. Hussain, Athar. LC 82-10703. 385p. 1983. 32.50 (ISBN 0-312-13385-5). St Martin.

Feuchtwanger, E. J. & Mason, R. A. Air Power in the Next Generation. 1979. text ed. 26.50x (ISBN 0-333-23609-2). Humanities.

Feuchtwanger, E. J., jt. auth. see Erickson, John.

Feuchtwanger, E. J. & Nailor, E. J., eds. The Soviet Union & the Third World. 1981. 27.50x (ISBN 0-312-74909-0). St Martin.

Feuchtwanger, E. J., jt. ed. see Bessel, Richard.

Feuchtwanger, Lion. Jew Suss. 416p. 1984. 18.95 (ISBN 0-88184-073-4); pap. 8.95 (ISBN 0-88184-047-5). Carroll & Graf.

--Josephus: A Historical Romance. LC 32-28823. (Temple Bks). 1972. pap. 10.95 (ISBN 0-689-70345-7, T25). Atheneum.

--The Oppermanns. 546p. 1983. pap. 8.95 (ISBN 0-88184-063-7). Carroll & Graf.

--Power. Muir, Willa & Muir, Edwin, trs. 424p. 1982. Repr. of 1927 ed. lib. bdg. 20.00 (ISBN 0-89760-238-2). Telegraph Bks.

--Proud Destiny: A Novel. 625p. Date not set. Repr. of 1947 ed. lib. bdg. 25.00 (ISBN 0-8482-4054-5). Norwood Edns.

--Simone: A Novel of Modern France. Hermann, G. A., tr. from Ger. 238p. Date not set. Repr. of 1944 ed. lib. bdg. 20.00 (ISBN 0-8482-4056-1). Norwood Edns.

--Success. 652p. 1984. pap. 10.95 (ISBN 0-88184-078-5). Carroll & Graf.

--Success: Three Years in the Life of a Province. Muir, Willan & Muir, Edwin, trs. from Ger. 743p. Date not set. Repr. of 1930 ed. lib. bdg. 25.00 (ISBN 0-8482-4055-3). Norwood Edns.

--Wahn oder der Teufel in Boston. 1948. 9.00 (ISBN 0-685-57213-7). M S Rosenberg.

Feuer, A. B. The Stairways of My Mind & Other Journeys. 48p. 1984. 5.95 (ISBN 0-89962-398-0). Todd & Honeywell.

Feuer, Alan & Gehani, Narain. Comparing & Assessing Programming Languages: Ada, C & Pascal. (Software Ser.). (Illus.). 256p. 1984. text ed. 18.95; pap. text ed. write for info. (ISBN 0-13-154840-9). P-H.

Feuer, Alan R. The C Puzzle Book. (Illus.). 192p. 1982. text ed. 18.95 (ISBN 0-13-109934-5); pap. text ed. 14.95 (ISBN 0-13-109926-4). P-H.

Feuer, Avrohom C. Tashlich. (Art Scroll Mesorah Ser.). 64p. 1979. 6.95 (ISBN 0-89906-158-3); pap. 4.95 (ISBN 0-89906-159-1). Mesorah Pubns.

Feuer, Carl Henry. Jamaica & the Sugar Worker Cooperatives: The Politics of Reform. (A Westview Replica Edition-Softcover Ser.). 220p. 1984. softcover 19.50x (ISBN 0-86531-897-2). Westview.

Feuer, G. & Iglesia, F. A. de la, eds. Molecular Biochemistry of Human Diseases, Vol. I. 240p. 1985. 90.00 (ISBN 0-8493-6205-9). CRC Pr.

Feuer, Henry, ed. The Chemistry of the Nitro & Nitroso Groups. LC 80-21491. 1981. Repr. of 1969 ed. Pt. 1, 780 P. text ed. (ISBN 0-89874-271-4); Pt. 2, 448 P. text ed. (ISBN 0-89874-272-2); Pts. 1 & 2. text ed. 84.50 (ISBN 0-89874-320-6). Krieger.

Feuer, Jane. The Hollywood Musical. LC 82-48022. (Illus.). 148p. (Orig.). 1982. 22.50x (ISBN 0-253-13822-1); pap. 7.95 (ISBN 0-253-21300-2). Ind U Pr.

Feuer, Jane, ed. see Kerr, Paul & Vahimagi, Tise.

Feuer, Janice. Sweets for Saints & Sinners. LC 80-21934. (Illus.). 144p. 1980. pap. 5.95 (ISBN 0-89286-180-0). One Hund One Prods.

Feuer, K., ed. & tr. see Chernyshevsky, Nikolai.

Feuer, Lewis S. The Case of the Revolutionist's Daughter: Sherlock Holmes Meets Karl Marx. LC 83-61117. (Illus.). 159p. 1983. 15.95 (ISBN 0-87975-245-9). Prometheus Bks.

--Einstein & the Generations of Science. 2nd ed. LC 81-1874. (Illus.). 390p. 1982. pap. 12.95 (ISBN 0-87855-899-3). Transaction Bks.

--Psychoanalysis & Ethics. LC 73-1433. 134p. 1973. Repr. of 1955 ed. lib. bdg. 18.75x (ISBN 0-8371-6795-7, FEPE). Greenwood.

--Spinoza & the Rise of Liberalism. LC 83-18508. x, 323p. 1983. Repr. of 1958 ed. lib. bdg. 39.75x (ISBN 0-313-24250-X, FESR). Greenwood.

Feuerbach, Ludwig. Essence of Christianity. pap. 6.95xi (ISBN 0-06-130011-X, TB11, Torch). Harrow.

--Essence of Christianity. Eliot, George, tr. 1958. 18.25 (ISBN 0-8446-2055-6). Peter Smith.

--The Essence of Christianity. Waring, E. Graham & Strothmann, F. W., eds. LC 57-8650. (Milestones of Thought Ser.). 1975. pap. 3.45 (ISBN 0-8044-6145-7). Ungar.

--Thoughts on Death & Immortality. Massey, James A., tr. from Ger. LC 80-25259. 263p. 1981. 28.50x (ISBN 0-520-04051-1); pap. 6.95 (ISBN 0-520-04062-7, CAL 486). U of Cal Pr.

Feuerbacher, B., et al. Photoemission & the Electronic Properties of Surfaces. 540p. 1978. 103.95x (ISBN 0-471-99555-X). Wiley.

Feuerlicht, Ignace. Alienation: From the Past to the Future. LC 77-87940. (Contributions in Philosophy: No. 11). 1978. lib. bdg. 29.95 (ISBN 0-313-20055-6, FEA/). Greenwood.

--Thomas Mann. (World Authors Ser.). 1969. lib. bdg. 13.50 (ISBN 0-8057-2584-9, Twayne). G K Hall.

Feuerlicht, Roberta S. The Fate of the Jews: The American Jew & Israel. LC 82-40466. 400p. 1983. 18.65 (ISBN 0-8129-1060-5). Times Bks.

Feuerlight, M. M. Where the Jews Fail. 1984. lib. bdg. 79.95 (ISBN 0-87700-569-9). Revisionist Pr.

Feuerstein, G. Bhagavad Gita: A Critical Rendering. 170p. 1981. text ed. 11.25x (ISBN 0-391-02191-5, Pub. by Arnold Heinemann India). Humanities.

--Yoga Sutra: An Exercise in the Methodology of Textual Analysis. 1978. text ed. 10.50x (ISBN 0-391-01091-3). Humanities.

Feuerstein, Georg. Bhagavad Gita: An Introduction. LC 82-42702. 191p. 1983. pap. 6.75 (ISBN 0-8356-0575-2, Quest). Theos Pub Hse.

--The Essence of Yoga. LC 75-42897. 1976. pap. 3.95 (ISBN 0-394-17902-1, E671, Ever). Grove.

Feuerstein, Gunther. New Directions in German Architecture. LC 68-56282. (New Directions in Architecture Ser). (Orig.). 7.95 (ISBN 0-8076-0482-8); pap. 3.95 (ISBN 0-8076-0486-0). Braziller.

Feuerstein, R. Instrumental Enrichment. (Illus.). 462p. 1979. text ed. 28.50 (ISBN 0-8391-1509-1). Univ Park.

Feuerstein, Reuven. The Dynamic Assessment of Retarded Performers: The Learning Potential, Assessment Device, Theory, Instruments & Techniques. (Illus.). 448p. 1979. text ed. 28.50 (ISBN 0-8391-1505-9). Univ Park.

Feuerwerger, Marvin C. Congress & Israel: Foreign Aid Decision-Making in the House of Representatives, Nineteen Sixty-Nine to Nineteen Seventy-Six. LC 78-74654. (Contributions in Political Science Ser.: No. 28). (Illus.). 1979. lib. bdg. 29.95 (ISBN 0-313-21240-6, FCO/). Greenwood.

Feuerwerker, Albert. China's Early Industrialization: Sheng-Hsuan-Huai, 1844-1916 & Mandarin Enterprise. LC 58-12967. 1970. pap. text ed. 3.25x (ISBN 0-689-70220-5, 153). Atheneum.

--Chinese Economy, Ca. Eighteen Seventy to Nineteen Eleven. (Michigan Monographs in Chinese Studies: No. 5). (Illus.). 77p. 1969. pap. 6.00 (ISBN 0-89264-005-7). U of Mich Ctr Chinese.

--Economic Trends in the Republic of China, 1912-1949. (Michigan Monographs in Chinese Studies: No. 31). 1977. pap. 6.00 (ISBN 0-89264-031-6). U of Mich Ctr Chinese.

--The Foreign Establishment in China in the Early Twentieth Century. (Michigan Monographs in Chinese Studies: No. 29). (Illus.). 1976. pap. 6.00 (ISBN 0-89264-029-4). U of Mich Ctr Chinese.

--Rebellion in Nineteenth-Century China. (Michigan Monographs in Chinese Studies: No. 21). 101p. 1975. pap. 6.00 (ISBN 0-89264-021-9). U of Mich Ctr Chinese.

--State & Society in Eighteenth-Century China: The Ch'ing Empire in Its Glory. (Michigan Monographs in Chinese Studies: No. 27). (Illus.). 1976. pap. 6.00 (ISBN 0-89264-027-8). U of Mich Ctr Chinese.

Feuerwerker, Albert & Cheng, Sally. Chinese Communist Studies of Modern Chinese History. LC 61-19595. (East Asian Monographs Ser.: No. 11). 1961. pap. 11.00x (ISBN 0-674-12301-8). Harvard U Pr.

Feuerwerker, Albert, ed. Chinese Social & Economic History from the Song to 1900: Report of the American Delegation to a Sino-American Symposium. LC 83-1789. (Michigan Monographs in Chinese Studies: No. 45). vi, 182p. (Orig.). 1983. pap. 8.00 (ISBN 0-89264-045-6). U of Mich Ctr Chinese.

Feuille, Carolyn. Business Telephone Skills. (Illus.). 90p. 1983. pap. text ed. 5.95 (ISBN 0-88084-072-2); tchr's guide 9.95 (ISBN 0-88084-071-4). Alemany Pr.

Feuillerat, A., ed. Documents Relating to the Office ot the Revels in the Time of Queen Elizabeth. (Mat. for the Study of the Old English Drama Ser. 1: Vol. 21). pap. 56.00 (ISBN 0-317-16141-5). Kraus Repr.

--Documents Relating to the Revels at Court in the Time of King Edward VI & Queen Mary from Loseley Mss. (Mat. for the Study of the Old English Drama Ser. 1: Vol. 44). pap. 56.00 (ISBN 0-317-16164-4). Kraus Repr.

Feuillerat, Albert. Baudelaire et la Belle aux Cheveux D'or. 1941. 39.50x (ISBN 0-686-83483-6). Elliots Bks.

--Comment Marcel Proust A Compose Son Roman. LC 72-1656. (Yale Romanic Studies: No. 7). Repr. of 1934 ed. 32.00 (ISBN 0-404-53207-1). AMS Pr.

--Composition of Shakespeare's Plays. facs. ed. LC 76-128885. (Select Bibliographies Reprint Ser). 1953. 21.00 (ISBN 0-8369-5505-6). Ayer Co Pubs.

--French Life & Ideals. 1925. 49.50x (ISBN 0-685-89753-2). Elliots Bks.

Feuillerat, Albert, ed. see Sidney, Philip.

Feuillet, Andre. Jesus & His Mother. Maluf, Leonard, tr. from Fr. LC 84-6790. (Studies in Scripture Ser.: Vol. I). 266p. (Orig.). 1984. pap. 16.95 (ISBN 0-932506-27-5). St Bedes Pubns.

Feulner, Edwin J. & Berkowitz, Herb B. Looking Back. LC 81-82076. 1981. 4.95. Heritage Found.

Feulner, Edwin J., Jr., ed. China: The Turning Point. 1976. pap. 15.00 (ISBN 0-930690-00-1). Coun Soc Econ.

Feulner, Edwin J., Jr. & Kase, Hideaki, eds. U. S.-Japan Mutual Security: The Next Twenty Years. LC 81-818367. 161p. 1981. 5.00 (ISBN 0-317-07526-8). Heritage Found.

Feulner, Edwin, Jr. Conservatives Stalk the House. 206p. 1983. 14.95 (ISBN 0-89803-112-5, Dist. by Kampmann). Green Hill.

Feulner, Patricia N. Women in the Professions: A Social-Psychological Study. LC 78-68455. 1979. perfect bdg. 9.95 (ISBN 0-88247-561-4). R & E Pubs.

Feunte, Tomas de La see De La Fuente, Tomas.

Feuquieres, Antoine De Pas see Des Pas Feuquieres, Antoine.

Feurer, Kathryn B., ed. Solzhenitsyn: A Collection of Critical Essays. LC 79-34416. 1976. 12.95 (ISBN 0-13-822627-X, Spec). P-H.

Feurmin Industries Staff. Protect Your Dreams, Your Dollars & Your Sanity or How to Deal with Contractors. (Illus.). 51p. (Orig.). 1982. 5.95 (ISBN 0-910531-03-X). Wolcotts.

Feurzeig, W., et al. The LOGO Language: Learning Mathematics Through Programming. 188p. 1977. pap. text ed. 22.95 (ISBN 0-87567-105-5). Entelek.

Feuser, W. F., tr. see Mbiti, John S.

Feuser, Willfried F., tr. see Zahar, Renate.

Feuton, James, tr. see Verdi, Guiseppe & Nicholas, John.

Feutry, Michel, et al, eds. Technological Dictionary: Mechanics, Metallurgy, Hydraulics & Related Industries. (In 4 languages). 1976. lib. bdg. 55.00x (ISBN 2-85608-000-6). Marlin.

Fever, Avrohom C. Tehillim (Psalms, 3 vols. Incl. Vol. 1. Psalms 1-30. 368p. 1977. (ISBN 0-89906-050-1); pap. (ISBN 0-89906-051-X); Vol. 2. Psalms 31-55. 352p. 1978. (ISBN 0-89906-052-8); pap. (ISBN 0-89906-053-6); Vol. 3. Psalms 56-85. 384p. 1979. (ISBN 0-89906-054-4); pap. (ISBN 0-89906-055-2). (Art Scroll Tanach Ser.). 15.95 ea.; pap. 12.95 ea. Mesorah Pubns.

Feville, Peter. Final Offer Arbitration - Concepts, Developments, & Techniques, No. 50. 1975. pap. 10.00 (ISBN 0-685-56577-7). Intl Personnel Mgmt.

Fevin, A. de see Expert, Henry.

Fevre, Ralph. Cheap Labour & Racial Discrimination. LC 84-1522. 226p. 1984. 35.50 (ISBN 0-566-00683-9). Gower Pub Co.

Fevyer, W. H. The Distinguished Service Medal: 1939-1946. 264p. 1982. 75.00 (ISBN 0-903754-90-8, Pub. by Picton England). State Mutual Bk.

Few, H. S. & Hilton, B. C. Fertilizer Procurement. (Fertilizer Bulletins: No. 4). 65p. (Eng. & Fr.). 1981. pap. 7.50 (ISBN 92-5-101077-3, F2194, FAO). Unipub.

Few, Mary D. Azilie of Bordeaux. (Illus.). 286p. 1973. 9.95 (ISBN 0-914056-01-8, Dist. by Sandlapper Pub Co). Carolina Edns.

--Carolina Jewel. (Illus.). 225p. 1973. Repr. of 1970 ed. 9.95 (ISBN 0-914056-02-6, Dist. by Sandlapper Pub Co). Carolina Edns.

--Caroline Jewel Fiction. 2nd ed. LC 73-117160. (Illus.). 255p. 1970. 9.95 (ISBN 0-87667-058-3). Sandlapper Pub CO.

--Under the White Boar. LC 70-161090. (Illus.). 219p. 1973. 9.95 (ISBN 0-87667-069-9, Dist. by sandlapper Pub Co). Carolina Edns.

Few, William P. Papers & Addresses. facs. ed. Woody, Robert H., ed. LC 68-20299. (Essay Index Reprint Ser). 1968. Repr. of 1951 ed. 20.00 (ISBN 0-8369-0439-7). Ayer Co Pubs.

Fewell, Rebecca R., jt. auth. see Garwood, S. Gray.

Fewer, Derek, et al. Brain Tumor Chemotherapy. (Illus.). 224p. 1976. 22.25x (ISBN 0-398-03549-0). C C Thomas.

Fewings, David R. Corporate Growth & Common Stock Risk, Vol. 12. Altman, Edward I. & Walter, Ingo, eds. LC 76-52014. (Contemporary Studies in Economic & Financial Analysis). (Orig.). 1979. lib. bdg. 36.50 (ISBN 0-89232-053-2). Jai Pr.

Fewkes, Jesse W. Aborigines of Puerto Rico & Neighboring Islands. LC 7-35402. (Landmarks in Anthropology Ser). (Illus.). 1970. Repr. of 1907 ed. 30.00 (ISBN 0-384-15550-2). Johnson Repr.

--Designs on Prehistoric Hopi Pottery. (Illus.). 1973. pap. 5.00 (ISBN 0-486-22959-9). Dover.

--Designs on Prehistoric Hopi Pottery. (Illus.). 13.50 (ISBN 0-8446-5107-9). Peter Smith.

--Hopi Katcinas. (American Indians Ser.). 192p. 1985. pap. 5.95 (ISBN 0-486-24842-9). Dover.

--Hopi Katcinas Drawn by Native Artists. LC 62-20282. (Beautiful Rio Grande Classics Ser.). (Illus.). 190p. 1983. Repr. of 1903 ed. lib. bdg. 25.00 (ISBN 0-87380-023-0). Rio Grande.

--Prehistoric Villages Castles & Towers of Southwestern Colorado. Repr. of 1919 ed. 29.00x (ISBN 0-403-03690-9). Scholarly.

Fewkes, Jesse W. & Owens, John G. A Few Summer Ceremonials at the Tusayon Pueblos: Natal Ceremonies of the Hopi Indians,& a Report on the Present Condition of a Ruin in Arizona Called Casa Grande. LC 76-21217. (A Journal of American Ethnology & Archaeology: Vol. 2). 1977. Repr. of 1892 ed. 30.00 (ISBN 0-404-58042-4). AMS Pr.

Fewkes, Jesse W., ed. A Journal of American Ethnology & Archaeology: Hemenway Southwestern Archaeological Expedition, 5 vols. LC 76-17496. Repr. of 1908 ed. Set. 140.00 (ISBN 0-404-19528-8). AMS Pr.

Fewkes, Jesse W., et al. The Snake Ceremonials at Walpi. LC 76-17497. (A Journal of American Ethnology & Archaeology: Vol. 4). Repr. of 1894 ed. 25.00 (ISBN 0-404-58044-0). AMS Pr.

Fewkes, Jessie W. & Gilman, Benjamin I. A Few Summer Ceremonials at Zuni Pueblo: Zuni Melodies, Reconnaissance of Ruins in or Near the Zuni Reservation. LC 76-21216. (A Journal of American Ethnology & Archaeology: Vol. 1). Repr. of 1891 ed. 25.00 (ISBN 0-404-58041-6). AMS Pr.

Fewkes, R. H., jt. auth. see Sorem, R. K.

Fewsmith, Joseph. Party, State & Local Elites in Republican China: Merchant Organizations & Politics in Shanghai, 1890-1930. LC 84-16168. 272p. 1984. text ed. 25.00x (ISBN 0-8248-0913-0). UH Pr.

Fewster, Kevin. Gallipoli Correspondent: The Front Line Diary of C. E. W. Bean. (Illus.). 200p. 1983. 22.50 (ISBN 0-86861-213-8). Allen Unwin.

Fey, H. Colibacillosis in Calves. 147p. 1972. 60.00 (ISBN 3-456-00302-1, Pub. by Holdan Bk Ltd UK). State Mutual Bk.

Fey, Harold E., ed. How My Mind Has Changed. 7.00 (ISBN 0-8446-2056-4). Peter Smith.

Fey, Harold E. & Frakes, Margaret, eds. The Christian Century Reader: Representative Articles, Editorials, & Poems Selected from More Than Fifty Years of the Christian Century. LC 72-331. (Essay Index Reprint Ser.). Repr. of 1962 ed. 24.50 (ISBN 0-8369-2786-9). Ayer Co Pubs.

Fey, James T. Mathematics Teaching Today: Perspectives from Three National Surveys. 31p. 1981. pap. 3.00 (ISBN 0-87353-186-8). NCTM.

Fey, James T., ed. Computing & Mathematics: The Impact on Secondary School Curricula. LC 84-2091. (Illus.). 100p. (Orig.). 1984. pap. 7.50 (ISBN 0-87353-212-0). NCTM.

Fey, Marshall. The Slot Machines: An Illustrated History. (Illus.). 240p. 1983. write for info. (ISBN 0-913814-53-9). Nevada Pubns.

Fey, Venn. Wide Horizon Tales of a Kenya That Has Passed into History. LC 81-90521. (Illus.). 1983. 10.00 (ISBN 0-533-05221-1). Vantage.

Fey, Willard R., jt. auth. see Gutierrez, Luis T.

Fey, William R. Faith & Doubt: The Unfolding of Newman's Thought on Certainty. LC 75-38101. xxii, 229p. 1976. 22.95x (ISBN 0-915762-02-1). Patmos Pr.

Feydeau, Georges. Feydeau, First to Last: Eight One-Act Comedies. Shapiro, Norman R., tr. (Illus.). 320p. 1982. 24.50 (ISBN 0-8014-1295-1). Cornell U Pr.

--Feydeau, First to Last: Eight One-Act Comedies. Shapiro, Norman R., tr. from Fr. LC 81-15182. 320p. 1984. pap. 9.95x (ISBN 0-8014-9271-8). Cornell U Pr.

--Four Farces. Shapiro, Norman R., ed. & tr. LC 78-125164. 1972. pap. 9.95x (ISBN 0-226-24477-6, P474, Phoen). U of Chicago Pr.

--Four Farces. Shapiro, Norman R., tr. from Fr. & intro. by. LC 78-125164. 1970. 22.50x (ISBN 0-226-24476-8). U of Chicago Pr.

--The Lady from Maxim's. Mortimer, John, tr. (National Theatre Plays Ser.). 1977. pap. text ed. 7.50x (ISBN 0-435-23235-5). Heinemann Ed.

--Three Boulevard Farces: A Little Hotel on the Side, a Flea in Her Ear, the Lady from Maxim's Plays. Mortimer, John, tr. 288p. 1985. pap. 5.95 (ISBN 0-14-048191-5). Penguin.

Feyen, Kathleen, jt. auth. see Tobin, John.

Feyerabend, Cessa. Diseases of Budgerigais. 7.95 (ISBN 0-87666-791-4, PS-671). TFH Pubns.

--Parakeets. (Illus.). 80p. 1984. pap. text ed. 3.95 (ISBN 0-86622-233-2, PB-119). TFH Pubns.

Feyerabend, Cessa, jt. auth. see Vriends, Matthew M.

Feyerabend, Cessa & Vriends, Matthew M., eds. Feeding Budgerigars. (Illus.). 1978. pap. 6.95 (ISBN 0-87666-971-2, AP-400). TFH Pubns.

Feyerabend, P. K. Problems of Empiricism: Philosophical Papers, Vol. 2. LC 80-41931. 260p. 1981. 44.50 (ISBN 0-521-23964-8). Cambridge U Pr.

--Realism, Rationalism & Scientific Method: Philosophical Papers, Vol. 1. LC 80-41931. (Illus.). 360p. 1981. 57.50 (ISBN 0-521-22897-2). Cambridge U Pr.

Feyerabend, Paul. Against Method. (Illus.). 1978. pap. 7.95 (ISBN 0-8052-7008-6, Pub by NLB). Schocken.

--The Rise of Western Rationalism. (Philosophy Now. Ser.). 1978. text ed. write for info. (ISBN 0-391-00845-5); pap. text ed. write for info. (ISBN 0-391-00846-3). Humanities.

--Science in a Free Society. 1979. 16.00 (ISBN 0-8052-7043-4, Pub by NLB). Schocken.

Feyerabend, Paul & Maxwell, Grover, eds. Mind, Matter & Method: Essays in Philosophy & Science in Honor of Herbert Feigl. LC 66-13467. 1966. 17.50x (ISBN 0-8166-0379-0). U of Minn Pr.

Feyerabend, Paul K. Philosophical Papers: Problems of Empiricism, Vol. 2. 268p. 1985. pap. 14.95 (ISBN 0-521-31641-3). Cambridge U Pr.

--Philosophical Papers: Realism, Rationalism & Scientific Method, Vol. 1. 367p. 1985. pap. 13.95 (ISBN 0-521-31642-1). Cambridge U Pr.

Feyman, P & Hibbs, A. R. Quantum Mechanics & Path Integrals. (International Earth & Planetary Sciences Ser). 1965. text ed. 45.95 (ISBN 0-07-020650-3). McGraw.

Feynman, R. P. Statistical Mechanics: A Set of Lectures. 1981. pap. 31.95 (ISBN 0-8053-2509-3). Benjamin-Cummings.

Feynman, R. P., et al. Feynman Lectures on Physics, 3 Vols. Vol. 1. text ed. 19.95 (ISBN 0-201-02116-1); Vol. 2. text ed. 19.95 (ISBN 0-201-02117-X); Vol. 3. text ed. 19.95 (ISBN 0-201-02118-8); Set. text ed. 52.95 (ISBN 0-201-02115-3); exercises for vols 2 & 3 o. p. 3.25. Vol. 2 Excercises o. p. Vol. 3 (ISBN 0-201-02019-X). Addison-Wesley.

Feynman, Richard P. Character of Physical Law. (Illus.). 1967. pap. 5.95 (ISBN 0-262-56003-8). MIT Pr.

--QED: The Strange Theory of Light & Matter. LC 85-42685. (Alix G. Mautner Memorial Lectures). (Illus.). 184p. 1985. 18.50 (ISBN 0-691-08388-6). Princeton U Pr.

--Quantum Electrodynamics. LC 61-18179. (Frontiers in Physics Ser.: No. 3). (Illus.). 1961. pap. 24.95 (ISBN 0-8053-2501-8). Benjamin-Cummings.

--Statistical Mechanics. LC 72-1769. (Frontiers in Physics Ser.: No. 36). 354p. 1972. pap. text ed. 31.95 (ISBN 0-8053-2509-3). Benjamin-Cummings.

--Surely You're Joking, Mr. Feynman! Adventures of a Curious Character. Hutchings, Edward, ed. 1985. 16.95 (ISBN 0-393-01921-7). Norton.

--Theory of Fundamental Processes. (Frontiers in Physics Ser.: No. 4). (Illus.). 1961. pap. 31.95 (ISBN 0-8053-2507-7). Benjamin-Cummings.

Feys, J. Sri Aurobindo's Treatment of Hindu Myth. 1984. 7.50x (ISBN 0-8364-1109-9, Pub. by Mukhopadhyay India). South Asia Bks.

Fezandie, Clement. Through the Earth. LC 80-23960. 48p. 1980. Repr. lib. bdg. 14.95x (ISBN 0-89370-028-2). Borgo Pr.
--Through the Earth. 14.95x (ISBN 0-913960-19-5); pap. 2.50x (ISBN 0-913960-00-4). Fax Collect.
Fezler, Lloyd. Adventures at Mountain Haven. LC 84-60868. 1984. pap. 3.95 (ISBN 0-89051-098-9). Master Bks.
--African Adventures. LC 84-60869. 1984. pap. 3.95 (ISBN 0-89051-099-7). Master Bks.
--More African Adventures. 1985. pap. 3.95 (ISBN 0-89051-105-5). Master Bks.
Fezler, William & Field, Eleanor. The Good Girl Syndrome: How Women Are Programmed to Fail in a Man's World & How to Stop It. 224p. 1985. 13.95 (ISBN 0-02-537500-8). Macmillan.
Fezler, William & Shapiro, Jack. Ninety Ways to Leave Your Lover & Survive. 198p. 1980. 9.95 (ISBN 0-934810-01-X). Laurida.
Fezler, William, ed. Breaking Free: Ninety Ways to Leave Your Lover & Survive. LC 84-28399. 160p. 1985. 14.95 (ISBN 0-87491-776-X); pap. 8.95 (ISBN 0-87491-784-0). Acropolis.
Fezler, William D., jt. auth. see Kroger, William S.
Ffolliott, Rosemary. De Bever Hall. (Illus.). 75p. 1976. 8.95x (ISBN 0-7156-1018-X, Pub. by Duckworth England). Biblio Dist.
Ffolliott, Rosemary, jt. auth. see De Breffny, Brian.
Ffolliott, Sheila. Civic Sculpture in the Renaissance: Montorsoli's Fountains at Messina. Harris, Ann S., ed. LC 84-141. (Studies in Renaissance Art History: No. 1). 268p. 1984. 39.95 (ISBN 0-8357-1474-8). UMI Res Pr.
Ffooks, Roger. Natural Gas by Sea: The Development of a New Technology. 248p. 1982. 99.00x (ISBN 0-85614-054-6, Pub. by Gentry England); pap. 50.00x. State Mutual Bk.
Ffoulkes, Charles J. Armourer & His Craft. LC 67-13328. (Illus.). 1967. Repr. of 1912 ed. 24.50 (ISBN 0-405-08501-X). Ayer Co Pubs.
Ffrench, Florence, compiled by. Music & Musicians in Chicago. LC 74-24082. Repr. of 1899 ed. 32.50 (ISBN 0-404-12910-2). AMS Pr.
Ffrench, Florence F. Music & Musicians in Chicago. (Music Reprint Ser.). 1979. Repr. of 1899 ed. lib. bdg. 29.50 (ISBN 0-306-79542-6). Da Capo.
Ffrench, G. E. & Hill, A. G. Kuwait: Urban & Medical Ecology, a Geomedical Study. LC 71-156994. (Geomedical Monograph Ser.: Vol. 4). (Illus.). 1971. 34.30 (ISBN 0-387-05384-0). Springer-Verlag.
Ffrench, Heather, jt. auth. see Ffrench, Jonathan.
Ffrench, Jonathan & Ffrench, Heather. Country Enterprise: Pleasure & Profit from Home Produce. (Illus.). 215p. 1983. 17.50 (ISBN 0-7099-1034-7, Pub. by Croom Helm Ltd). Longwood Pub Group.
Ffrench, Richard. A Guide to the Birds of Trinidad & Tobago. (Illus.). 516p. 1973. 27.50 (ISBN 0-915180-03-0). Livingston.
Ffrench, Yvonne. Mrs. Siddons: Tragic Actress. LC 78-13858. (Illus.). 1981. Repr. of 1954 ed. 25.75 (ISBN 0-88355-791-6). Hyperion Conn.
--Six Great Englishwomen. LC 76-10646. 1953. lib. bdg. 25.00 (ISBN 0-8414-4219-3). Folcroft.
Ffrench Blake, R. L. Dressage for Beginners. 1976. pap. 6.95 (ISBN 0-395-24399-8). HM.
--Intermediate Dressage: Work at Second & Third Levels. 1977. pap. 7.95 (ISBN 0-395-25406-X). HM.
Ffrench-Davis, Ricardo & Tironi, Ernesto. Latin America & the New International Economic Order. LC 81-13525. 1982. 27.50 (ISBN 0-312-47326-5). St Martin.
Fiac, Saint, jt. auth. see Patrick, Saint.
Fiaccadori, Franco, ed. see International Symposium, Parma, May, 1980.
Fiacco. Mathematical Programming with Data Perturbations, Pt. I. (Lecture Notes in Pure & Applied Mathematics Ser.: Vol. 72). 256p. 1982. 39.75 (ISBN 0-8247-1543-8). Dekker.
--Mathematical Programming with Data Perturbations, Pt. II. (Lecture Notes in Pure & Applied Mathematics Ser.). 210p. 1983. 39.75 (ISBN 0-8247-1789-9). Dekker.
Fiacco, A. V., jt. auth. see Falk, J. E.
Fiacco, A. V., ed. Sensitivity, Stability & Parametric Analysis. (Mathematical Programming Studies: Vol. 21). 242p. 1985. pap. 24.00 (ISBN 0-444-87573-5, North-Holland). Elsevier.
Fiacco, A. V. & Kortanek, K. O., eds. Semi-Infinite Programming & Applications. (Lecture Notes in Economics & Mathematical Systems: Vol. 215). 322p. 1983. pap. 23.50 (ISBN 0-387-12304-0). Springer-Verlag.
Fiacco, A. V., et al, eds. Extremal Methods & Systems Analysis. (Lecture Notes in Economics & Mathematical Systems Ser.: Vol. 174). 545p. 1980. pap. 44.00 (ISBN 3-540-09730-9). Springer-Verlag.
Fiacco, Anthony V. Introduction to Sensitivity & Stability Analysis in Nonlinear Programming (Monograph) Analysis in Nonlinear Programming (Monograph) LC 82-11642. (Mathematics in Science & Engineering Ser.). 384p. 1983. 29.50 (ISBN 0-12-254450-1). Acad Pr.
Fiala, Richard & Ortleb, Charles. Le Gay Ghetto. (Illus.). 80p. 1980. pap. 3.95 (ISBN 0-312-47588-8). St Martin.
Fiala, Richard, jt. auth. see Ortleb, Charles.
Fiarotta, Noel, jt. auth. see Fiarotta, Phyllis.
Fiarotta, Phyllis. Phyllis Fiarotta's Nostalgia Crafts Book. LC 75-8812. (Illus.). 224p. 1974. pap. 5.95 (ISBN 0-911104-44-5). Workman Pub.
--Snips & Snails & Walnut Whales. LC 75-9574. (Illus.). 288p. (ps up). 1975. 9.95 (ISBN 0-911104-75-5, 066); pap. 7.95 (ISBN 0-911104-49-6, 065). Workman Pub.
--Sticks & Stones & Ice Cream Cones. LC 74-160843. (Illus.). 322p. (ps up). 1973. pap. 8.95 (ISBN 0-911104-30-5). Workman Pub.
Fiarotta, Phyllis & Fiarotta, Noel. Be What You Want to Be! LC 76-52860. (Illus.). 304p. (gr. k-7). 1977. 10.95 (ISBN 0-911104-94-1, 130); pap. 5.95 (ISBN 0-911104-95-X, 129). Workman Pub.
--Confetti: The Kids' Make-It-Yourself, Do-It-Yourself Party Book. LC 78-7121. (Illus.). 224p. (gr. k-4). 1978. pap. 5.95 (ISBN 0-89480-050-7). Workman Pub.
--Pin It, Tack It, Hang It. LC 75-20211. (Illus.). 288p. (gr. 1 up). 1975. 9.95 (ISBN 0-911104-61-5, 084). Workman Pub.
Fiasconaro, A. L. What Every Woman Wants in a Man. 89p. 1981. 1.95 (ISBN 0-89274-204-6). Harrison Hse.
Fiaux, Louis. Histoire De la Guerre Civile De 1871. LC 76-168020. Repr. of 1879 ed. 47.50 (ISBN 0-404-07126-0). AMS Pr.
Fiber & Wiegle. Applied Business Law. 1983. text ed. 21.95 (ISBN 0-8359-0187-4); wkbk. 9.95 (ISBN 0-8359-0186-6); instr's manual avail. (ISBN 0-8359-0188-2). Reston.
Fiber, Larry, jt. auth. see Huffman, Harry.
Fiber, Larry R. Administrative Office Services. 1985. text ed. 21.95 (ISBN 0-8359-9125-3); instr's. manual avail. (ISBN 0-8359-9126-1). Reston.
Fiberarts Magazine Staff, ed. The Fiberarts Design Book Two. LC 80-67315. (Illus.). 176p. (Orig.). 1980. 24.95 (ISBN 0-937274-00-3); pap. 15.95 (ISBN 0-937274-01-1). Lark Bks.
Fibonacci, Leonardo. The Fibonacci Rhythm Theory As It Applies to Life, History, & the Course of the Stock Market, 2 vols. in one. new exp. ed. Flumiani, C. M., ed. (The Most Meaningful Classics in World Culture Ser.). (Illus.). 1979. Set. 147.75 (ISBN 0-89266-192-5). Am Classical Coll Pr.
--Fibonacci's Visualizations Aimed at Establishing a Mathematical Foundation for Stock Speculation. (Illus.). 119p. 1984. Repr. 107.45 (ISBN 0-89901-183-7). Found Class Reprints.
--Mathematical Curiosities in the Writings of Fibonacci. (Illus.). 113p. 1984. Repr. 77.75 (ISBN 0-89901-186-1). Found Class Reprints.
--The Reconstruction of the Fibonacci Theory of Cycles. (Illus.). 141p. 1982. 77.85x (ISBN 0-86654-029-6). Inst Econ Finan.
Fibonacci, Leonardo & Bradley, Arthur. The Fibonacci Rhythm Theory As It Applies to Life, History & the Stock Market, 2 vols. (Illus.). 177p. 1982. 187.45x (ISBN 0-86654-018-0). Inst Econ Finan.
Fibonacci, Leonardo & Elliott, Ralph N. The Fibonacci Rhythm Theory & Elliott Nature's Law: A Comparative Analysis, 2 vols. Griffith, Clifford, ed. (Illus.). 157p. 1981. 195.00x (ISBN 0-86654-002-4). Inst Econ Finan.
Fibonacci, Leonardo & Fleming, Spencer. The Fibonacci Rhythm Theory As It Applies to Life, History & the Stock Market, 2 vols. (Illus.). 210p. 1985. Set. 210.50 (ISBN 0-86654-163-2). Inst Econ Finan.
Fibonacci, Leonardo & Flumiani, Carlo M. The Fibonacci Rhythm Theory As It Applies to Life, History, & the Future of the Stock Market, 2 vols. (Illus.). 1976. 137.45 (ISBN 0-89266-041-4). Am Classical Coll Pr.
Fibush, Esther & Morgan, Martha. Forgive Me No Longer: The Liberation of Martha. LC 75-27965. 442p. 1977. 14.95 (ISBN 0-87304-148-8). Family Serv.
Fic, Victor M. The Bolsheviks & the Czechoslovak Legion: Origin of Their Armed Conflict. 2nd. rev ed. 1978. 22.50x (ISBN 0-8364-0218-9). South Asia Bks.
--Revolutionary War for Independence & the Russian Question - Czechoslovak Army in Russia, 1914-1918. 1977. 15.00x (ISBN 0-88386-968-3). South Asia Bks.
Ficarra. Medicolegal Handbook: A Guide for Winning Verdicts. 320p. 1983. 39.50 (ISBN 0-8247-7005-6). Dekker.
Ficarra, John & Coker, Paul, Jr. The Mad Book of Fears & Phobias. 192p. (Orig.). 1985. pap. 2.50 (ISBN 0-446-30884-6). Warner Bks.
Ficat & Philippe, eds. Contrast Arthography of the Synovial Joints. LC 81-12391. 184p. 1981. 41.50x (ISBN 0-89352-135-3). Masson Pub.
Ficc, D. C. see Scafer, R. C.
Ficc, D. C. see Schafer, R. C.
Ficc, D. C., jt. auth. see Schafer, R. C.
Ficc, D. C., jt. auth. see Shafer, R. C.
Ficchi, Rocco, ed. Practical Design for Electromagnetic Compatibility. (Illus.). 1971. 17.20 (ISBN 0-8104-5685-0). Hayden.
Ficek, Edmund. Comprehensive CPA Business Law Review. (Illus.). 640p. 1983. text ed. 31.95 (ISBN 0-07-020671-6). McGraw.
Ficek, Edmund F. & Johnson, Ross H. Real Estate Principles & Practices. 3rd ed. 1983. 26.95 (ISBN 0-675-20016-4); study guide 11.95 (ISBN 0-675-20064-4). Additional supplements may be obtained from publisher. Merrill.
Ficher, Miguel, et al, eds. Sexual Arousal: New Concepts in Basic Sciences, Diagnosis, & Treatment. (Illus.). 290p. 1984. 29.50x (ISBN 0-398-04962-9). C C Thomas.
Fichera, G. Numerical & Quantitative Analysis. (Surveys & References Ser.: No. 3). 218p. 1978. text ed. 49.95 (ISBN 0-273-00284-8). Pitman Pub MA.
--Trends in Applications of Pure Mathematics to Mechanics, Vol. 1. (Mongraphs & Studies: No. 2). 459p. 1976. text ed. 54.50 (ISBN 0-273-00129-9). Pitman Pub MA.
Fichman, Martin. Alfred Russel Wallace. (English Authors Ser.). 1981. lib. bdg. 14.50 (ISBN 0-8057-6797-5, Twayne). G K Hall.
Fichner-Rathus, Lois. Understanding Art. (Illus.). 480p. 1986. pap. text ed. 26.95 (ISBN 0-13-935495-6). P H.
Fichte, Immanuel H., ed. see Fichte, Johann G.
Fichte, J. G. Fichte's Critique of All Revelation. Green, G. D., tr. LC 77-77756. 1978. 34.50 (ISBN 0-521-21707-5). Cambridge U Pr.
--The Science of Knowledge: With First & Second Introductions. Heath, Peter & Lachs, John, eds. Heath, Peter & Lachs, John, trs. LC 82-4536. (Texts in German Philosophy Ser.). 298p. 1982. 42.50 (ISBN 0-521-25018-8); pap. 13.95 (ISBN 0-521-27050-2). Cambridge U Pr.
Fichte, Joerg O. Chaucer's (Art Poetical) A Study in Chaucerian Poetics. (Studies & Texts in English: No. 1). (Illus.). 140p. (Orig.). 1980. pap. 18.00x (ISBN 3-87808-441-2). Benjamins North Am.
Fichte, Johann G. Characteristics of the Present Age, Vol. II. Smith, W., tr. Bd. with Way Towards the Blessed Life. (Contributions to the History of Psychology Ser., Pt. A: Orientations). 1978. Repr. of 1889 ed. 30.00 (ISBN 0-89093-151-8). U Pubns Amer.
--Fichtes Werke, 11 vols. Fichte, Immanuel H., ed. 1971. 99.60x (ISBN 3-11-006386-3). De Gruyter.
--Nachgelassene Werke, 3 Vols. Fichte, Immanuel H., ed. (Ger). 1962. Repr. of 1834 ed. Set. 67.20 (ISBN 3-11-005101-X). De Gruyter.
--Saemmtliche Werke, 8 vols. 1965-66. Repr. of 1846 ed. 216.00x (ISBN 3-11-005147-8). De Gruyter.
--The Vocation of Man. Smith, William, tr. LC 56-44104. 1956. pap. 5.99 scp (ISBN 0-672-60220-2, LLA50). Bobbs.
--Vocation of Man. Smith, William, tr. from Ger. xii, 190p. 1965. 16.95 (ISBN 0-87548-074-8); pap. 5.95 (ISBN 0-87548-075-6). Open Court.
Fichtenau, Heinrich. The Carolingian Empire. Munz, Peter, tr. (Mediaeval Academy Reprints for Teaching Ser.). 1979. pap. 7.25 (ISBN 0-8020-6367-5). U of Toronto Pr.
Fichtenholz, G. M. The Definite Integral. Silverman, R. A., tr. from Rus. LC 78-149513. (Pocket Mathematical Library Ser.). (Illus.). 98p. 1973. 30.25 (ISBN 0-677-21090-6). Gordon.
--Functional Series. (Pocket Mathematical Library). 176p. 1970. 32.50 (ISBN 0-677-20950-9). Gordon.
--The Indefinite Integral. Schwartz, Jacob D., ed. Silverman, Richard A., tr. from Rus. LC 76-135120. (Pocket Mathematical Library). (Illus.). 148p. 1971. 45.25 (ISBN 0-677-21030-2). Gordon.
--Infinite Series: Ramifications. (Pocket Mathematical Library). 138p. 1970. 37.25 (ISBN 0-677-20940-1). Gordon.
--Infinite Series: Rudiments. Silverman, Richard A., tr. from Rus. (Pocket Mathematical Library). 144p. 1970. 37.25 (ISBN 0-677-20930-4). Gordon.
Fichter, Andrew. Poets Historical: Dynastic Epic in the Renaissance. LC 81-19795. 237p. 1982. text ed. 20.00x (ISBN 0-300-02721-4). Yale U Pr.
Fichter, George. Iraq. (First Bks). (Illus.). (gr. 4-6). 1978. PLB 8.90 s&l (ISBN 0-531-02236-6). Watts.
Fichter, George, jt. auth. see Kingbay, Keith.
Fichter, George S. American Indian Music & Musical Instruments. (gr. 5-10). 1978. 8.95 (ISBN 0-679-20443-1). McKay.
--Comets & Meteors. (First Bks). (Illus.). 72p. (gr. 4 up). 1982. PLB 8.90 (ISBN 0-531-04382-7). Watts.
--Disastrous Fires. LC 81-2448. (First Bks.). (Illus.). 72p. (gr. 4 up). 1981. lib. bdg. 8.90 (ISBN 0-531-04325-8). Watts.
--The Florida Cookbook. (Illus.). 228p. 1973. pap. 6.95 (ISBN 0-912458-27-5). E A Seemann.
--Florida-In Pictures. LC 78-66310. (Visual Geography Ser.). (Illus.). (gr. 5 up). 1979. PLB 6.69 (ISBN 0-8069-1221-9); pap. 2.95 (ISBN 0-8069-1220-0). Sterling.
--Florida Living Cookbook. LC 85-3704. (Florida Living Ser.). (Illus.). 208p. (Orig.). 1985. pap. 6.95 (ISBN 0-910923-18-3). Pineapple Pr.
--Insect Pests. (Golden Guide Ser). (Illus.). (gr. 5 up). 1966. pap. 2.95 (ISBN 0-307-24016-9, Golden Pr.). Western Pub.
--Karts & Karting. (First Bks). (Illus.). 72p. (gr. 4 up). 1982. PLB 8.90 (ISBN 0-531-04394-0). Watts.
--Keeping Amphibians & Reptiles As Pets. (First Bks.). (Illus.). (gr. 4-6). 1979. PLB 8.90 s&l (ISBN 0-531-02257-9). Watts.
--Poisonous Snakes. (First Bks.). (Illus.). 72p. (gr. 4 up). 1982. PLB 8.90 (ISBN 0-531-04349-5). Watts.
--Racquetball. (First Bks.). (Illus.). (gr. 4 up). 1979. PLB 8.90 s&l (ISBN 0-531-04078-X). Watts.
--Reptiles & Amphibians of North America. LC 81-17733. (Audubon Society Beginner Guide Ser.). (Illus.). 96p. (gr. 2 up). 1982. pap. 2.95 (ISBN 0-394-84769-5). Random.
--Rocks & Minerals. LC 81-17847. (Audubon Society Beginner Guide Ser.). (Illus.). 96p. (gr. 2 up). 1982. pap. 2.95 (ISBN 0-394-84772-5). Random.
--Snakes Around the World. LC 78-9774. (Easy Read Fact Bks.). (Illus.). (gr. 2-4). 1980. PLB 8.60 s&l (ISBN 0-531-02275-7). Watts.
--The Space Shuttle. (First Bks.). (Illus.). 72p. (gr. 4 up). 1981. lib. bdg. 8.90 (ISBN 0-531-04354-1). Watts.
--Wildflowers of North America. LC 81-17760. (Audubon Society Beginner Guide Ser.). (Illus.). 96p. (gr. 2 up). 1982. pap. 2.95 (ISBN 0-394-84770-9). Random.
--Working Dogs. (First Bks.). (Illus.). (gr. 4-6). 1979. PLB 8.90 s&l (ISBN 0-531-02887-9). Watts.
Fichter, George S. & Frances, Phil. Fishing: Guide to Fresh & Saltwater. Zim, Herbert S., ed. (A Golden Guide Ser). 1965. 2.95 (ISBN 0-307-24008-8, Golden Pr). Western Pub.
Fichter, George S., ed. see Brockman, C. Frank.
Fichter, George S., ed. see Levi, Herbert W. & Levi, Lorna R.
Fichter, Harold. VIC-20: Easy Guide to Home Applications. LC 83-51182. 208p. 1984. pap. 8.95 (ISBN 0-672-22224-8, 22224). Sams.
Fichter, Harold O. Wood Heat Is Yours for the Axing. (Illus.). 1980. pap. 4.00 (ISBN 0-918424-02-X). Menaid.
Fichter, Joseph H. The Holy Family of Father Moon. LC 84-82549. 155p. (Orig.). 1985. pap. 7.95 (ISBN 0-934134-13-8). Leaven Pr.
--The Rehabilitation of Clergy Alcoholics: Ardent Spirits Subdued. LC 80-28447. 203p. 1982. 24.95x (ISBN 0-89885-009-6). Human Sci Pr.
--Religion & Pain: The Spiritual Dimensions of Health Care. 128p. 1981. 9.95 (ISBN 0-8245-0102-0). Crossroad NY.
--Religion As an Occupation. (Orig.). 1966. pap. 3.95x (ISBN 0-268-00229-0). U of Notre Dame Pr.
--Social Relations in the Urban Parish. LC 54-11207. pap. 68.00 (ISBN 0-317-07856-9, 2020061). Bks Demand UMI.
--Sociology. 2nd ed. LC 70-143688. 1971. text ed. 12.50x (ISBN 0-226-24633-7); pap. text ed. 4.75x (ISBN 0-226-24634-5). U of Chicago Pr.
Fichter, Joseph H., ed. Dimensions of Authority in the Religious Life. (Religious Life in the Modern World Ser.: Vol. 5). (Orig.). 1966. pap. 1.95x (ISBN 0-268-00079-4). U of Notre Dame Pr.
Fichter, Lynn S. & Farmer, George T., Jr. Earth Materials & Earth Processes: An Introduction. 2nd ed. 1977. spiral bdg. 15.95x (ISBN 0-8087-0633-0). Burgess.
Fichter, Lynn S. & Poche, David J. Ancient Environments & the Interpretation of Geologic History. 1979. pap. 13.95x spiral bdg. (ISBN 0-8087-0669-1). Burgess.
Fichter, William L. Lope De Vega's El castigo del discreto. 280p. (Eng. & Sp.). text ed. 2.00 (ISBN 0-318-14283-X). Hispanic Inst.
Fichter, William L., ed. see De Vega Carpio, L. F.
Fichtl, Frank. The Great Day of the Lord. 256p. 1986. 12.95 (ISBN 0-89962-510-X). Todd & Honeywell.
Fichtner, Hans & Garff, Michael. How to Build Sailboards: Step-by-Step Custom-Made Designs. LC 82-10532. (Illus.). 128p. 1983. pap. 10.00 (ISBN 0-915160-28-5). Seven Seas.
--Sailboards Custom-Made. 136p. 1982. 39.00x (ISBN 0-540-07411-X, Pub. by G Philip Serv England). State Mutual Bk.
Fichtner, Joseph. Proclaim His Word: Homiletic Themes for Sundays & Holy Days - Cycle C, Vol. 1. new ed. LC 73-5726. 238p. (Orig.). 1973. pap. 3.95 (ISBN 0-8189-0274-4). Alba.
--Proclaim His Word: Homiletic Themes for Sundays & Holy Days-Cycle A, Vol. 2. new ed. LC 73-5726. 239p. (Orig.). 1974. pap. 4.95 (ISBN 0-8189-0292-2). Alba.
--To Stand & Speak for Christ. LC 81-10975. 166p. 1981. pap. 6.95 (ISBN 0-8189-0415-1). Alba.
Fichtner, Paula S. Ferdinand I of Austria. (East European Monographs: No. 100). 307p. 1982. 50.00x (ISBN 0-914710-94-X). East Eur Quarterly.
Ficino, Marsilio. The Book of Life. Boer, Charles, tr. from Latin. (Dunquin Ser.: No. 12). xx, 217p. (Orig.). 1980. pap. 12.50 (ISBN 0-88214-212-7). Spring Pubns.
--Commentary on Plato's Symposium on Love. 2nd, rev. ed. Jayne, Sears, tr. LC 84-20255. 213p. (Latin.). 1985. pap. 18.50 (ISBN 0-88214-601-7). Spring Pubns.
--De Vita. Kaske, Carol, tr. LC 77-86226. (The Janus Library). Date not set. 20.00 (ISBN 0-913870-58-7). Abaris Bks.
--The Letters of Marsilio Ficino, 3 vols. 1985. Vol. 3. 23.50s (ISBN 0-8052-6000-5); Vol. 2. 18.95 (ISBN 0-8052-6001-3); Vol. 3. 315 19.95 (ISBN 0-8052-6002-1). Schocken.
Fick, Carl, jt. auth. see Guzman, Jose L.

Fick, D., ed. see Meeting on Polarization Nuclear Physics, Ebermannstadt, Germany, 1973.

Fick, G. & Sprague, R. H., Jr., eds. Decision Support Systems-Issues & Challenges: Proceedings of an International Task Foce Meeting, June 23-25, 1980. (IIASA Proceedings: Vol. 11). (Illus.). 190p. 1980. 35.00 (ISBN 0-08-027321-1). Pergamon.

Fick, Leonard J. Light Beyond: A Study of Hawthorne's Theology. LC 74-8995. 1955. lib. bdg. 22.50 (ISBN 0-8414-4195-2). Folcroft.

Fick, Mike & Richardson, Jim. Control Your Thoughts. 1983. pap. 1.75 (ISBN 0-911739-01-7). Abbott Loop.

Ficke, Arthur D. Chats on Japanese Prints. (Illus.). 1976. Repr. 30.00x (ISBN 0-7158-1091-X). Charles River Bks.

Ficke, Mary M., jt. auth. see Ritch, Barbara A.

Fickeisen, D. H. & Schneider, M. J., eds. Gas Bubble Disease: Proceedings. AEC Technical Information Center. LC 75-619327. 123p. 1967. pap. 11.00 (ISBN 0-87079-023-4, CONF-741033); microfiche 4.50 (ISBN 0-87079-213-X, CONF-741033). DOE.

Fickelson, Maurice. Dodd. 11.95 (ISBN 0-7145-0810-1). Riverrun NY.

Ficken, Carl. God's Story & Modern Literature: Reading Fiction in Community. LC 84-48705. 176p. 1985. pap. 9.95 (ISBN 0-8006-1823-8, 1-1823). Fortress.

Ficken, Robert E. Lumber & Politics: The Career of Mark E. Reed. LC 78-21756. (Illus.). 276p. 1980. 22.50x (ISBN 0-295-95655-0). U of Wash Pr.

Ficker, Nicholas T. Shop Expense: Analysis & Control. Brief, Richard P., ed. LC 80-1492. (Dimensions of Accounting Theory & Practice Ser.). 1981. Repr. of 1917 ed. lib. bdg. 25.50x (ISBN 0-405-13522-X). Ayer Co Pubs.

Ficker, Victor B. & Graves, Herbert S. Social Science & Urban Crisis: Introductory Readings. 2nd ed. 1978. pap. text ed. write for info. (ISBN 0-02-337170-6, 33717). Macmillan.

Ficker, Victor B. & Rigterink, James M. Values in Conflict: A Text Reader in Social Problems. 512p. 1972. pap. text ed. 8.95x (ISBN 0-669-63487-5); instructor's manual 1.95 (ISBN 0-669-81067-3). Heath.

Fickert, Kurt J. Kafka's Doubles. (Utah Studies in Literature & Linguistics: Vol. 15). 105p. 1979. pap. 11.60 (ISBN 3-261-03100-X). P Lang Pubs.

--To Heaven & Back: The New Morality in the Plays of Friedrich Durrenmatt. LC 72-183353. (Studies in Germanic Languages & Literatures: No. 5). 72p. 1972. 8.00x (ISBN 0-8131-1266-4). U Pr of Ky.

Fickes, Clyde P. & Groben, W. Ellis. Building with Logs. (Shorey Lost Arts Ser.). 56p. pap. 4.95 (ISBN 0-8466-6030-X, U30). Shorey.

Fickett, E. D. Meteorology. (Shorey Historical Ser.). 10p. pap. 1.95 (ISBN 0-8466-0029-3, S29). Shorey.

Fickett, Harold. The Holy Fool. LC 82-73658. 360p. 1983. pap. 7.95 (ISBN 0-89107-227-6, Crossway Bks). Good News.

Fickett, Harold & Schaeffer, Franky. A Modest Proposal. 160p. 1984. pap. 7.95 (ISBN 0-8407-5921-5). Nelson.

Fickett, Harold L., Jr. Keep on Keeping On. LC 75-23517. 160p. (Orig.). 1977. pap. 3.50 (ISBN 0-8307-0371-3, S311100). Regal.

Fickett, John D. Confess It, Possess It: Faith's Formula? 40p. 1984. 2.00x (ISBN 0-318-04135-9). Presby Ref Ren.

Fickett, Reginald N. Four, Oh! A Change of Values. LC 84-91274. 123p. 1985. 10.00 (ISBN 0-533-06356-6). Vantage.

Fickett, Wildon & Davis, William C. Detonation. LC 77-85760. (Los Alamos Series in Basic & Applied Sciences). 1979. 42.00x (ISBN 0-520-03587-9). U of Cal Pr.

Fickle, James E. The New South & the "New Competition". Trade Association Development in the Southern Pine Industry. LC 80-12420. 447p. 1980. 17.50x (ISBN 0-252-00788-3). U of Ill Pr.

Ficklen, John R. History of Reconstruction in Louisiana, Series 28. facsimile ed. LC 76-173605. (Black Heritage Library Collection: John Hopkins University Studies in Historical & Political Science). Repr. of 1910 ed. 18.00 (ISBN 0-8369-8898-1). Ayer Co Pubs.

--History of Reconstruction in Louisiana (Through 1868) LC 78-63934. (Johns Hopkins University. Studies in the Social Sciences. Twenty-Eighth Ser. 1910: 1). Repr. of 1910 ed. 13.00 (ISBN 0-404-61183-4). AMS Pr.

--History of Reconstruction in Louisiana: Through 1868. 1910. 11.25 (ISBN 0-8446-1178-6). Peter Smith.

Fickling, David, ed. see Townsend, John R.

Fidanza, F., jt. ed. see Somogyi, J. C.

Fidanza, F., ed. see Symposium of the Group of European Nutritionists, 9th, Chianciano, 1970.

Fiday, Beverly. Jeff's Happy Day. (Happy Day Bks.). (Illus.). 24p. (ps-2). 1984. 1.39 (ISBN 0-87239-740-8, 3710). Standard Pub.

Fiday, David. Kid-Powered Graphics. LC 83-50937. 184p. (gr. 4-6). 1982. pap. 14.95 (ISBN 0-672-22229-9). Sams.

Fiday, David & Christensen, Donald. Kid-Powered LOGO. LC 84-51069. 274p. 1984. pap. 17.95 (ISBN 0-672-22190-X, 22190). Sams.

Fiddes, Angela & Frankl, Ernest. Guide to the City of London. (Color Guides to Britain). (Illus.). 112p. 1984. 13.95 (ISBN 0-13-134529-X); pap. 6.95 (ISBN 0-13-134511-7). P-H.

Fiddian-Green, Richard & Turcotte, Jeremiah, eds. Gastrointestinal Hemorrhage. LC 80-11318. 448p. 1980. 66.00 (ISBN 0-8089-1267-4, 791257). Grune.

Fiddle, Seymour, ed. Uncertainty: Behavioral & Social Dimensions. LC 80-82073. 410p. 1980. 41.95 (ISBN 0-03-057022-0). Praeger.

Fiddy, Rob, ed. In Place of Work: Policy & Practice for the Young Unemployed. 250p. 1983. 28.00x (ISBN 0-8002-3312-3, Pub. by Falmer Pr); pap. 14.00x (ISBN 0-8002-3302-6, Pub. by Falmer Pr). Taylor & Francis.

Fidel, Kenneth, ed. Militarism in Developing Countries. LC 74-20190. (Third World Ser.). 300p. 1975. pap. 5.95x (ISBN 0-87855-585-4). Transaction Bks.

Fidel, Ruth. Primary Drug Abuse Prevention. (Illus.). 50p. 1984. Educational Copy master set 24.00 (ISBN 0-942254-01-5); pap. 1.95 wkbk. (ISBN 0-942254-02-3). Fidelity Hse.

Fidelity & Surety Law Committee, jt. auth. see Forum Committee on the Construction Industry, American Bar Association.

Fidell, Estelle A. see Cook, Dorothy E. & Monro, Isabel S.

Fidell, Jeanette. Jokes, Jokes, Jokes. (gr. 7-12). 1976. pap. 1.50 (ISBN 0-590-02037-4). Scholastic Inc.

Fidell, Linda S. & Delamater, John. Women in the Professions: What's All the Fuss About? LC 73-89940. (Sage Contemporary Social Science Issues Ser.: No. 8). pap. 36.00 (ISBN 0-317-29680-9, 2021898). Bks Demand UMI.

Fidell, Linda S. & Tabachnick, Barbara G. Using Multivariate Statistics. LC 82-11767. 509p. 1982. text ed. 27.50 scp (ISBN 0-06-042045-6, HarpC). Har-Row.

Fidell-Beaufort, Madeleine, et al, eds. see Avery, Samuel P.

Fidez, Ruth. Drug Awareness Day: How Your Community Can Plan One. (Illus.). 25p. 1981. pap. 5.95 (ISBN 0-942254-00-7). Fidelity Hse.

Fidfaddy, Frederick A. The Adventures of Uncle Sam. LC 76-104450. Repr. of 1816 ed. lib. bdg. 14.00 (ISBN 0-8398-0555-1). Irvington.

Fidler, G. R., et al, trs. see Trotsky, Leon.

Fidler, Gail S. Design of Rehabilitation Services in Psychiatric Hospital Settings. 144p. 1984. pap. text ed. 19.50 (ISBN 0-943596-05-X, RAMSCO 00900). Ramsco Pub.

Fidler, Isaac. Observations on Professions: Literature, Manners, & Emigration in the United States & Canada 1832. LC 73-13129. (Foreign Travelers in America, 1810-1935 Ser.). 446p. 1974. Repr. 31.00x (ISBN 0-405-05452-1). Ayer Co Pubs.

Fidler, Isiah & White, Richard. Design of Models for Testing Cancer Therapeutic Agents. (Litton Bionetics Workshop Ser.). 278p. 1982. 38.95 (ISBN 0-442-23897-5). Van Nos Reinhold.

Fidler, J. Havelock. Ley Lines: Their Nature & Properties-A Dowser's Investigation. 144p. 1983. pap. 7.95 (ISBN 0-85500-173-9). Newcastle Pub.

Fidler, J. Havelock, jt. auth. see Wagstaffe, Reginald.

Fidler, Sharon J. & Crump, J. I. Index to the "Chan-kuo Ts'e". 118p. 1974. pap. 1.50 (ISBN 0-89264-900-3). U of Mich Ctr Chinese.

Fidlow, Michael. How to Strengthen Your Memory. LC 83-24199. 128p. (Orig.). 1984. pap. 4.95 (ISBN 0-8069-7808-2). Sterling.

Fido, Franco, tr. see Felaco, Vittorio.

Fido, Martin. Oscar Wilde. LC 85-9028. (Illus.). 144p. 1985. pap. 9.95 (ISBN 0-87226-032-1). P Bedrick Bks.

--Shakespeare. LC 85-9637. (Illus.). 144p. 1985. pap. 9.95 (ISBN 0-87226-031-3). P Bedrick Bks.

Fidone, Salvatore J., jt. auth. see Eyzaguirre, Carlos.

Fieandt, Kai Von see Von Fieandt, Kai & Mousgaard, I. K.

Fiebelkorn, George, jt. auth. see Scott, David L.

Fiebert, Martin S., jt. auth. see Schofield, Carol A.

Fiebig, Denzil, jt. auth. see Theil, Henri.

Fiebre, Henry de see De Fiebre, Henry.

Fiechter, A. Microbial Reactions. (Advances in Biochemical Engineering Ser.: Vol. 23). (Illus.). 200p. 1982. 41.00 (ISBN 0-387-11698-2). Springer-Verlag.

--Space & Terrestrial Biotechnology. (Advances in Biochemical Engineering Ser.: Vol. 22). (Illus.). 230p. 1982. 41.00 (ISBN 0-387-11464-5). Springer-Verlag.

Fiechter, A., ed. Advances in Biochemical Engineering, Vol. 27. (Illus.). 186p. 1983. 39.00 (ISBN 0-387-12182-X). Springer-Verlag.

--Bioenergy. (Advances in Biochemical Engineering Ser.: Vol. 20). (Illus.). 209p. 1981. 40.00 (ISBN 0-387-11018-6). Springer-Verlag.

--Biotechnology. (Advances in Biochemical Engineering: Vol. 7). (Illus.). 1977. 39.00 (ISBN 0-387-08397-9). Springer-Verlag.

--Chromatography. (Advances in Biochemical Engineering Ser.: Vol. 25). (Illus.). 145p. 1982. 27.00 (ISBN 0-387-11829-2). Springer-Verlag.

--Mass Transfer in Biotechnology. LC 72-152360. (Advances in Biochemical Engineering: Vol. 8). (Illus.). 1978. 38.00 (ISBN 0-387-08557-2). Springer-Verlag.

--Microbes & Engineering Aspects. (Advances in Biochemical Engineering Ser.: Vol. 21). (Illus.). 240p. 1982. 41.00 (ISBN 0-387-11019-4). Springer-Verlag.

--Microbial Metabolism. (Advances in Biochemical Engineering Ser.: Vol. 14). (Illus.). 1980. 46.00 (ISBN 0-387-09621-3). Springer-Verlag.

--Microbial Processes. LC 72-152360. (Advances in Biochemical Engineering: Vol. 9). (Illus.). 1978. 38.00 (ISBN 0-387-08606-4). Springer-Verlag.

--New Substrates. LC 72-152360. (Advances in Biochemical Engineering: Vol. 6). (Illus.). 1977. 36.00 (ISBN 0-387-08363-4). Springer-Verlag.

--New Technological Concepts. (Advances in Biochemical Engineering Ser.: Vol. 15). (Illus.). 250p. 1980. 52.00 (ISBN 0-387-09686-8). Springer-Verlag.

--Reaction Engineering. LC 65-6745. (Advances in Biochemical Engineering Ser.: Vol. 24). (Illus.). 150p. 1982. 38.00 (ISBN 0-387-11699-0). Springer-Verlag.

--Reactors & Reactions. (Advances in Biochemical Engineering Ser.: Vol. 19). (Illus.). 250p. 1981. 59.50 (ISBN 0-387-10464-X). Springer-Verlag.

Fiechter, A., jt. ed. see Ferranti, M. P.

Fiechter, A., et al, eds. Advances in Biochemical Engineering, Vol. 2. LC 72-152360. (Illus.). 220p. 1972. 32.50 (ISBN 0-387-06017-0). Springer-Verlag.

--Microbiology, Theory & Application. LC 72-152360. (Advances in Biochemical Engineering Ser.: Vol. 11). 1979. 47.00 (ISBN 0-387-08990-X). Springer-Verlag.

Fieck, G. Symmetry of Polycentric Systems: The Polycentric Tensor Algebra for Molecules. (Lecture Notes in Physics: Vol. 167). 137p. 1982. pap. 10.00 (ISBN 0-387-11589-7). Springer-Verlag.

Fiedelmeier, Leni. Dachshunds. (Pet Care Ser.). 1984. pap. 3.95 (ISBN 0-8120-2888-0). Barron.

Fiedler, Conrad. On Judging Works of Visual Art. Schaefer-Simmern, Henry, tr. from Ger. (Library Reprint Ser.: Vol. 88). 1978. 17.95x (ISBN 0-520-03597-6). U of Cal Pr.

Fiedler, Craig R., jt. auth. see Turnbull, H. Rutherford, III.

Fiedler, Donald B. & Pred, Deborah R. Nebraska Legal Forms: Criminal Law. 175p. 1982. looseleaf 27.50 (ISBN 0-86678-024-6). Butterworth MN.

Fiedler, Fred E. Leader Attitudes & Group Effectiveness. LC 81-1151. (Illus.). 69p. 1981. Repr. of 1958 ed. lib. bdg. 21.75x (ISBN 0-313-22967-8, FILA). Greenwood.

Fiedler, Fred E. & Chemers, Martin M. Improving Leadership Effectiveness: The Leader Match Concept. 2nd ed. (Self-Teaching Guide 1-581). 269p. 1984. pap. 12.95x (ISBN 0-471-89213-0, 1-581, Pub. by Wiley Press). Wiley.

Fiedler, Fred E., jt. auth. see Godfrey, Eleanor P.

Fiedler, George. The Illinois Law Courts in Three Centuries. 1973. 12.75 (ISBN 0-917036-05-0). Physicians Rec.

Fiedler, H. Structure & Mechanisms of Turbulence I: Proceedings of the Symposium on Turbulence Held at the Technische Hochschule Berlin, August 1-5, 1977. (Lecture Notes in Physics: Vol. 75). (Illus.). 1978. pap. 19.00 (ISBN 0-387-08765-6). Springer-Verlag.

Fiedler, H., ed. Structure & Mechanisms of Turbulence II: Proceedings of the Symposium on Turbulence Held at the Technische Hochschule Berlin, August 1-5, 1977. (Lecture Notes in Physics: Vol. 76). (Illus.). 1978. pap. 23.00 (ISBN 0-387-08767-2). Springer-Verlag.

Fiedler, H. G. Textual Studies of Goethe's Faust. LC 73-20371. (Studies in Goethe, No. 61). 1974. lib. bdg. 49.95x (ISBN 0-8383-1809-6). Haskell.

Fiedler, Hermann G. Textual Studies of Goethe's Faust. 92p. 1980. Repr. of 1946 ed. lib. bdg. 15.00 (ISBN 0-8492-4705-5). R West.

Fiedler, J. Michael, jt. ed. see Adams, Robert L.

Fiedler, Jean. The Year the World Was Out of Step with Jancy Fried. LC 81-47530. 156p. 1981. 9.95 (ISBN 0-15-299818-7, HJ). HarBraceJ.

Fiedler, Jean & Mele, Jim. Isaac Asimov. LC 81-70122. (Recognitions Ser.). 180p. 1982. 13.95 (ISBN 0-8044-2203-6); pap. 5.95 (ISBN 0-8044-6147-3). Ungar.

Fiedler, Joseph, ed. Actenstucke Zur Geschichte Franz Rakoczy's und Seiner Verbindung Mit Dem Auslande. Repr. of 1855 ed. 23.00 (ISBN 0-384-15678-9). Johnson Repr.

Fiedler, Judith. Field Research: A Manual for Logistics & Management of Scientific Studies in Natural Settings. LC 78-62562. (Social & Behavioral Science Ser.). (Illus.). 1978. text ed. 22.95x (ISBN 0-87589-381-3). Jossey-Bass.

Fiedler, Leslie. Collected Essays of Leslie Fiedler, 2 Vols. LC 76-122420. 1971. 12.50 ea.; Vol. 1. (ISBN 0-8128-1333-2); Vol. 2. (ISBN 0-8128-1352-9). Stein & Day.

--Cross the Border-Close the Gap. LC 72-81822. pap. 2.95 (ISBN 0-8128-1479-7). Stein & Day.

--End to Innocence. LC 72-82145. 1972. pap. 4.95 (ISBN 0-8128-1478-9). Stein & Day.

--Freaks: Myths & Images of the Secret Self. 368p. 1984. pap. 9.95 (ISBN 0-671-24847-2, Touchstone Bks). S&S.

--Love & Death in the American Novel. LC 66-14948. 1975. pap. 12.95 (ISBN 0-8128-1799-0). Stein & Day.

--No! in Thunder. LC 72-82146. 1972. pap. 4.95 (ISBN 0-8128-1480-0). Stein & Day.

--Nude Croquet. LC 71-87956. 288p. 1974. pap. 1.95 (ISBN 0-8128-1747-8). Stein & Day.

--Return of the Vanishing American. LC 68-15433. (Prog. Bk.). pap. 2.95 (ISBN 0-8128-1236-0). Stein & Day.

--To the Gentiles. LC 72-81821. 1972. pap. 2.95 (ISBN 0-8128-1481-9). Stein & Day.

--Waiting for the End. LC 64-13673. 1970. pap. 4.95 (ISBN 0-8128-1298-0). Stein & Day.

Fiedler, Leslie, et al. Light Rays: James Joyce & Modernism. Ehrlich, Heyward, ed. (Illus.). 1984. 15.95 (ISBN 0-88282-302-7). Horizon.

Fiedler, Leslie A. A Fiedler Reader. LC 76-54437. 1977. pap. 6.95 (ISBN 0-8128-2192-0). Stein & Day.

--Olaf Stapledon: A Man Divided. LC 82-8168. (Science Fiction Writers Ser.). 1983. 19.95x (ISBN 0-19-503086-9); pap. 7.95 (ISBN 0-19-503087-7, GB682). Oxford U Pr.

--What Was Literature? Class Culture & Society. 258p. 1984. pap. 6.95 (ISBN 0-671-24984-3, Touchstone). S&S.

Fiedler, Leslie A., ed. English Literature: Opening up the Canon, Selected Papers from the English Institute, 1979. Baker, Houston A., Jr. LC 80-8863. (New Ser.: No. 4). 176p. 1981. text ed. 8.50x (ISBN 0-8018-2591-1). Johns Hopkins.

Fiedler, Leslie A., et al. Buffalo Bill & the Wild West. LC 81-12198. (Illus.). 96p. 1982. pap. 11.95 (ISBN 0-87273-082-4, Pub. by Brooklyn Mus). U of Pittsburgh Pr.

Fiedorek, Mary B. & Jewell, Diana L. Executive Style: Looking It... Living It. LC 82-25976. (Illus.). 203p. 1983. 12.95 (ISBN 0-8329-0254-3). New Century.

Fiedorowicz, Z. & Priddy, S. Homology of Classical Groups Over Finite Fields & Their Associated Infinite Loop Spaces. LC 78-12091. (Lecture Notes in Mathematics: Vol. 674). 1978. pap. 27.00 (ISBN 0-387-08932-2). Springer-Verlag.

Fieg, John. InterAct: Thailand-U. S. Renwick, George W., ed. LC 80-83909. (Country Orientation Ser.). 82p. 1980. pap. text ed. 10.00x (ISBN 0-933662-15-7). Intercult Pr.

Fieg, John Paul see Renwick, George W.

Fiegehen, G. Companies, Incentives & Senior Managers. (Illus.). 1981. 32.50x (ISBN 0-19-829002-0). Oxford U Pr.

Fiegehen, Guy, et al. Poverty & Progress in Britain, 1953-1973: A Statistical Study of Low Income Households. LC 77-2143. (NIESR, Occasional Paper: No. 29). (Illus.). 1977. 32.50 (ISBN 0-521-21683-4). Cambridge U Pr.

Field & Cameron. The Dusty Universe. 1975. 15.00 (ISBN 0-07-020685-6). McGraw.

Field, A. Today's Greatest Problem: The Jews. 1982. lib. bdg. 59.00 (ISBN 0-87700-390-4). Revisionist Pr.

Field, A. J. Trade & Textiles: An Analysis of the Changing International Division of Labour in the Textile & Clothing Sector, 1963-78. 229p. (Orig.). 1984. pap. 17.50x (ISBN 971-10-0172-1, Pub. by New Day Philippines). Cellar.

Field, A. N. The Bretton Woods Plot: The Twin Evils of the International Monetary Fund & the World Bank for Reconstruction & Development. 1979. lib. bdg. 69.95 (ISBN 0-8490-2879-5). Gordon Pr.

--The Evolution Hoax Exposed. 1971. pap. 3.00 (ISBN 0-89555-049-0). TAN Bks Pubs.

--The Evolution Hoax Exposed. 1982. lib. bdg. 59.95 (ISBN 0-87700-386-6). Revisionist Pr.

Field & Stream. Field & Stream Reader. facs. ed. LC 77-128242. (Essay Index Reprint Ser). 1946. 21.50 (ISBN 0-8369-1875-4). Ayer Co Pubs.

Field, Andrew. Djuna: The Formidable Miss Barnes. (Illus.). 287p. 1985. pap. 8.95 (ISBN 0-292-71546-3). U of Tex Pr.

--Djuna: The Formidable Miss Barnes. (Illus.). 303p. 1985. pap. 8.95 (ISBN 0-292-71546-3). U of Tex Pr.

--Nabokov: His Life in Part. LC 76-47042. 1977. 18.95 (ISBN 0-670-50367-3). Viking.

Field, Anne E. On the Trail of Stoddard Glass. 1975. pap. 4.95 (ISBN 0-87233-021-4). Bauhan.

Field, Annita T. Fingerprint Handbook. (Illus.). 196p. 1976. 23.75x (ISBN 0-398-00562-1). C C Thomas.

Field, Arthur. Recent Discoveries Relating to the Life & Works of William Shakespeare. LC 76-153318. Repr. of 1954 ed. 12.50 (ISBN 0-404-02379-7). AMS Pr.

--Recent Discoveries Relating to the Life & Works of William Shakespeare. LC 73-16466. 1948. lib. bdg. 8.00 (ISBN 0-8414-0851-3). Folcroft.

Field, Arthur W. Cisco & the Twin Foals. LC 83-61713. (Illus.). 160p. (YA) (gr. 8 up). 1983. 12.00 (ISBN 0-935356-06-1). Mills Pub Co.

Field, B. S., Jr. Shakespeare's Julius Caesar: A Production Collection. LC 79-25076. (Illus.). 172p. 1980. text ed. 18.95x (ISBN 0-88229-440-7). Nelson-Hall.

Field, Barry C. & Willis, Cleve E., eds. Environmental Economics: A Guide to Information Sources. (Man & the Environment Information Guide Ser.: Vol. 8). 1979. 60.00x (ISBN 0-8103-1433-9). Gale.

Field, Barry C., jt. ed. see Berndt, Ernst R.

Field, Ben. Piper Tompkins. LC 74-22782. Repr. of 1946 ed. 16.50 (ISBN 0-404-58429-2). AMS Pr.

Field, C. Al-Ghazzali's Al-Chemy of Happiness. 2.50 (ISBN 0-686-18621-4). Kazi Pubns.
--Confessions of Al-Ghazzali. pap. 2.50 (ISBN 0-686-18612-5). Kazi Pubns.
Field, Carol. The Italian Baker. LC 85-42565. (Illus.). 320p. 1985. 19.18 (ISBN 0-06-181266-8, HarpT). Har-Row.
Field, Carol & Kauffman, Richard. The Hill Towns of Italy. (Illus.). 1984. 35.00 (ISBN 0-525-93259-3, 03398-1020). Dutton.
Field, Carolyn. Special Collections in Children's Literature. vii, 257p. 1982. lib. bdg. 18.00x (ISBN 0-8389-0345-2). ALA.
Field, Carolyn, ed. Special Collections in Children's Literature. 272p. 1982. 18.00 (ISBN 0-8389-0345-2). Assn Library Serv.
Field, Charles K. & Irwin, William H. Stanford Stories: Tales of a Young University. LC 71-121541. (Short Story Index Reprint Ser). 1900. 20.00 (ISBN 0-8369-3497-0). Ayer Co Pubs.
Field, Claud. Dictionary of Arabic-Persian Quotes. (Arabic, Persian & Eng.). 18.00x (ISBN 0-86685-168-2). Intl Bk Ctr.
--A Dictionary of Oriental Quotations. 75.00 (ISBN 0-8490-0043-2). Gordon Pr.
Field, Claud, tr. see Gogol, Nikolai V.
Field, Claud H. Dictionary of Oriental Quotations. LC 68-23157. 1969. Repr. of 1911 ed. 38.00x (ISBN 0-8103-3183-7). Gale.
--Jewish Legends of the Middle Ages. LC 76-48141. 1976. Repr. of 1930 ed. lib. bdg. 20.00 (ISBN 0-8414-6771-4). Folcroft.
Field, Claude, tr. see Strindberg, August.
Field, D. Social Psychology for Sociolgists. 1974. pap. 12.95 (ISBN 0-442-30694-6). Van Nos Reinhold.
Field, D. M. Step-by-Step Guide to Tracing Your Ancestors. 64p. 1983. 10.95 (ISBN 0-7095-1258-9, Pub. by Auto Assn-British Tourist Authority England). Merrimack Pub Cir.
Field, D. R., jt. auth. see Dawkins, H. C.
Field, David. Marriage Personalities. 192p. (Orig.). 1985. pap. 5.95 (ISBN 0-89081-476-7). Harvest Hse.
--Projects in Wood. 224p. 1985. 24.95 (ISBN 0-399-13089-6). Putnam Pub Group.
Field, David D., jt. auth. see Wright, Donald K.
Field, David J. & Stroobant, John, eds. Case Studies in Paediatrics. 90p. (Orig.). 1984. pap. text ed. 13.50 (ISBN 0-272-79756-1, Pub. by Pitman Bks Ltd UK). Urban & S.
Field, Donald R., jt. ed. see Machlis, Gary E.
Field, E. J. Multiple Sclerosis in Childhood: Diagnosis & Prophylaxis. (Illus.). 144p. 1980. 12.75x (ISBN 0-398-03919-4). C C Thomas.
Field, Edward. A Full Heart. LC 76-57520. 103p. 1977. pap. 3.95 (ISBN 0-8180-1539-X). Sheep Meadow.
--Stand up, Friend, with Me. 1964. pap. 3.95 (ISBN 0-394-17336-8, E671, Ever). Grove.
--Stars in My Eyes. LC 77-95137. (Illus.). 91p. 1978. pap. 7.95 (ISBN 0-8180-1537-3). Sheep Meadow.
--Sweet Gwendolyn & the Countess. (Illus.). 1974. pap. 12.00 (ISBN 0-916906-03-5); pap. 20.00 signed (ISBN 0-686-86246-5). Konglomerati.
--Variety Photoplays. 1979. 3.50 (ISBN 0-917554-02-7). Maelstrom.
Field, Edward, ed. see Angell, Israel.
Field, Edwin M. Oil Burners. 4th ed. LC 83-22308. (Illus.). 1984. 12.95 (ISBN 0-672-23394-0). Audel.
--Oil Burners. 3rd ed. 320p. 1977. 9.95 (ISBN 0-672-23277-4). Audel.
Field, Eleanor, jt. auth. see Fezler, William.
Field, Elinor W., ed. Horn Book Reflections on Children's Books & Reading. LC 75-89793. 1969. pap. 6.50 (ISBN 0-87675-033-1). Horn Bk.
Field, Elinor W., jt. ed. see Miller, Bertha M.
Field, Elliot, jt. auth. see Field, Mary.
Field, Eugene. Holy Cross & Other Tales. LC 72-94718. (Short Story Index Reprint Ser.). 1893. 18.00 (ISBN 0-8369-3097-5). Ayer Co Pubs.
--Little Book of Profitable Tales. LC 76-98568. (Short Story Index Reprint Ser.). 1889. 18.00 (ISBN 0-8369-3142-4). Ayer Co Pubs.
--A Little Book of Profitable Tales. 286p. 1983. Repr. of 1893 ed. lib. bdg. 25.00 (ISBN 0-89987-271-9). Darby Bks.
--A Little Book of Western Verse. LC 78-74509. (Children's Literature Reprint Ser.). (gr. 5 up). 1979. Repr. of 1889 ed. 19.75x (ISBN 0-8486-0009-6). Core Collection.
--Love Songs of Childhood. LC 74-98081. (Granger Index Reprint Ser.). 1894. 12.00 (ISBN 0-8369-6077-7). Ayer Co Pubs.
--Poems of Childhood. (Classics Ser). (Illus.). (gr. 4 up). 1969. pap. 1.50 (ISBN 0-8049-0211-9, CL-211). Airmont.
--The Temptation of Friar Consol: A Story of the Devil, Two Saints & a Booke. 1900. 25.00 (ISBN 0-932062-56-3). Sharon Hill.
--With Trumpet & Drum. LC 70-116402. (Granger Index Reprint Ser.). 1892. 12.00 (ISBN 0-8369-6143-9). Ayer Co Pubs.
--Wynken, Blynken & Nod. (Illus.). (gr. k-2). 1980. 6.95 (ISBN 0-8038-8046-4). Hastings.
--Wynken, Blynken & Nod. LC 82-2434. (Illus.). 32p. (ps-1). 1982. 11.95 (ISBN 0-525-44022-4, 01160-350). Dutton.
--Wynken, Blynken & Nod. (Illus.). (ps-1). pap. 3.95 (ISBN 0-525-44199-9, 0383-120). Dutton.
--Wynken, Blynken, & Nod. (Pudgy Pal Board Bks.). (Illus.). 18p. (ps). 1986. 3.95 (ISBN 0-448-10225-0, G&D). Putnam Pub Group.
Field, F. Three French Writers & the Great War. LC 35-22982. 1975. 29.95 (ISBN 0-521-20916-1). Cambridge U Pr.
Field, F. H. & Franklin, J. L. Electron Impact Phenomena. rev. ed. (Pure & Applied Physics Ser.: Vol. 1). 1957. 76.50 (ISBN 0-12-255450-7). Acad Pr.
Field, F. W. & Kealey, D. Principles & Practice of Analytical Chemistry. 2nd ed. 462p. pap. text ed. 24.00 (ISBN 0-7002-0283-8, Pub. by Blackie & Son UK). Heyden.
Field, Faye. Walk & Pray. 1982. pap. 3.50 (ISBN 0-8341-0785-6). Beacon Hill.
--Women Who Encountered Jesus. LC 81-65798. 1982. 4.50 (ISBN 0-8054-5182-X). Broadman.
Field, Filip. W. Norman Cooper - a Prophet for Our Time. LC 79-52443. 1979. 7.50 (ISBN 0-87516-417-X); pap. 4.50 (ISBN 0-87516-372-6). De Vorss.
Field, Frank. The Minimum Wage: Its Potential & Dangers. (Policy Studies Institute Ser.). ix, 117p. 1984. text ed. 25.00x (ISBN 0-435-83300-6). Gower Pub Co.
Field, Frank, ed. The Wealth Report Two. (Inequality in Society Ser.). 200p. (Orig.). 1983. pap. 15.95x (ISBN 0-7100-9452-3). Routledge & Kegan.
Field, Frank M. Where Jesus Walked: Through the Holy Land with the Master. Davis, Moshe, ed. LC 77-70681. (America & the Holy Land Ser.). (Illus.). 1977. Repr. of 1951 ed. lib. bdg. 20.00x (ISBN 0-405-10244-5). Ayer Co Pubs.
Field, Frederick V. From Right to Left: An Autobiography. LC 82-23407. 336p. 1983. 16.95 (ISBN 0-88208-162-4); pap. 8.95 (ISBN 0-88208-161-6). Lawrence Hill.
--Pre-Hispanic Mexican Stamp Designs. (Illus.). 12.00 (ISBN 0-8446-5031-5). Peter Smith.
--Thoughts on the Meaning & Use of Pre-Hispanic Mexican Sellos. LC 67-31521. (Studies in Pre-Columbian Art & Archaeology: No.3). (Illus.). 48p. 1967. pap. 4.00x (ISBN 0-88402-017-7). Dumbarton Oaks.
Field, G. Memoirs, Incidents, Reminiscences of the Early History of the New Church in Michigan, Indiana, Illinois, & Adjacent States, & Canada. LC 70-134423. 1972. Repr. of 1879 ed. 27.00 (ISBN 0-404-08463-X). AMS Pr.
Field, G. B., ed. see Greisen, Kenneth.
Field, G. C. Plato & His Contemporaries. LC 74-30008. (Studies in Philosophy, No. 40). 1974. lib. bdg. 75.00 (ISBN 0-8383-1992-0). Haskell.
Field, G. Lowell. Syndical & Corporative Institutions of Italian Fascism. (Columbia University. Studies in the Social Sciences: No. 443). Repr. of 1938 ed. 22.00 (ISBN 0-404-51433-2). AMS Pr.
Field, G. Lowell & Higley, John. Elitism. 1980. 18.50x (ISBN 0-7100-0487-7). Routledge & Kegan.
Field, G. W. The Legal Relations of Infants, Parent & Child, & Guardian & Ward: And a Particular Consideration of Guardianship in the State of New York. xx, 376p. 1981. Repr. of 1888 ed. lib. bdg. 28.50x (ISBN 0-8377-0537-1). Rothman.
Field, Geoffrey G. Evangelist of Race: The Germanic Vision of Houston Stewart Chamberlain. LC 82-23509. 544p. 1981. 31.00x (ISBN 0-231-04860-2). Columbia U Pr.
Field, George B. & Chaisson, Eric J. The Invisible Universe: Probing The Frontiers of Astrophysics. 200p. 1985. 19.95. Birkhauser.
Field, George W. Field's Medico-Legal Guide for Doctors & Lawyers. viii, 291p. 1983. Repr. of 1887 ed. lib. bdg. 25.00x (ISBN 0-8377-0543-6). Rothman.
--Hermann Hesse. (World Authors Ser.). lib. bdg. 13.95 (ISBN 0-8057-2424-9, Twayne). G K Hall.
Field, Greg, et al. Mid-America Trio. LC 81-65138. 1980. 4.95 (ISBN 0-933532-06-7). BKMK.
Field, H. Body-Marking in Southwestern Asia. (Harvard University Peabody Museum of Archaeology & Ethnology Papers). Repr. of 1958 ed. 27.00 (ISBN 0-527-01318-8). Kraus Repr.
--North Arabian Desert Archaeological Survey, 1925-50. (HU PMP). (Orig.). 1960. 32.00 (ISBN 0-527-01319-6). Kraus Repr.
Field, H. John, ed. Toward a Programme of Imperial Life: The British Empire at the Turn of the Century. LC 81-2115. (Contributions in Comparative Colonial Studies: No. 9). xiv, 256p. 1982. lib. bdg. 35.00 (ISBN 0-313-22917-1, FIL/). Greenwood.
Field, Hartry. Science Without Numbers: The Case for Nominalism. LC 80-7560. 100p. 1980. 25.00x (ISBN 0-691-07260-4). Princeton U Pr.
Field, Hazel E. & Taylor, Mary E. Atlas of Cat Anatomy. rev. ed. LC 69-16998. 1969. text ed. 20.00x spiral bdg (ISBN 0-226-24817-8). U of Chicago Pr.
Field, Helen A. Extensive Individual Reading Versus Class Reading: A Study of the Development of Reading Ability in the Transition Grades. LC 75-176769. (Columbia University. Teachers College. Contributions to Education: No. 394). Repr. of 1930 ed. 22.50 (ISBN 0-404-55394-X, CE394). AMS Pr.
Field, Henrey. The Track of Man, Adventures of an Anthropologist: Volume 2: The White House Years, 1941-1945. 134p. 10.95 (ISBN 0-916224-83-X). Banyan Bks.
Field, Henry. Anthropology of Iraq, Pt. 1. (HU PMP). (Illus.). 1940. 41.00 (ISBN 0-527-01890-2). Kraus Repr.
--Contributions to the Anthropology of Iran. (HU PMP). (Illus.). 1939. 51.00 (ISBN 0-527-01889-9). Kraus Repr.
Field, Henry, ed. see Abdushelishvili, M. G., et al.
Field, Henry, ed. see Alekseev, V. P., et al.
Field, Henry, ed. see Beregovaia, N. A., et al.
Field, Henry, ed. see Oshanin, L. V.
Field, Henry, ed. see Tretiakov, P. N. & Mongait, A. L.
Field, Henry M. Bright Skies & Dark Shadows. LC 77-114876. (Select Bibliographies Reprint Ser). 1890. 19.00 (ISBN 0-8369-5280-4). Ayer Co Pubs.
--History of the Atlantic Telegraph. LC 76-38351. (Select Bibliographies Reprint Ser.). Repr. of 1866 ed. 21.00 (ISBN 0-8369-6768-2). Ayer Co Pubs.
--The Story of the Atlantic Telegraph. LC 72-5049. (Technology & Society Ser.). (Illus.). 415p. 1972. Repr. of 1893 ed. 24.00 (ISBN 0-405-04701-0). Ayer Co Pubs.
Field, Hermann H., jt. ed. see Thibodeau, Francis R.
Field, Hugh M. Iowa Legal Froms-Corporations. LC 83-131753. 1982. looseleaf 30.00 (ISBN 0-86678-109-9). Butterworth MN.
Field, Isobel. This Life I've Loved. 353p. 1982. lib. bdg. 35.00 (ISBN 0-89760-233-1). Telegraph Bks.
--This Life I've Loved-Stevenson. 1973. Repr. of 1938 ed. 30.00 (ISBN 0-8274-0532-4). R West.
Field, J. E., ed. The Properties of Diamond. 1979. 89.50 (ISBN 0-12-255350-0). Acad Pr.
Field, James A. Essays on Population & Other Papers. Hohman, Helen F., ed. 1931. 12.50 (ISBN 0-686-33258-X). R S Barnes.
Field, James A., Jr. America & the Mediterranean World, 1776-1882. LC 68-11440. 1969. 47.00x (ISBN 0-691-04590-9). Princeton U Pr.
Field, James A., Jr., tr. see De Belot, Raymond.
Field, James D. IBM PC Guide to Pricing: How to Choose the Best Price Without Losing Sales or Sharing Profits. 320p. 1984. pap. 49.95 incl. disk (ISBN 0-88693-062-6). Banbury Bks.
Field, Jane, jt. auth. see Snyder, Elayne.
Field, Janet N., et al, eds. Graphic Arts Manual. LC 79-6549. (Illus.). 650p. 1980. lib. bdg. 65.00 (ISBN 0-405-12941-6). Ayer Co Pubs.
Field, Joanna. A Life of One's Own. LC 81-50878. (Illus.). 228p. 1981. 12.95 (ISBN 0-87477-201-X); pap. 5.95 (ISBN 0-87477-193-5). J P Tarcher.
--On Not Being Able to Paint. (Illus.). 184p. 1983. pap. 6.95 (ISBN 0-87477-263-X). J P Tarcher.
Field, John. Discovering Place-Names: Their Origins & Meanings. 2nd ed. (Discovering Ser.). 55p. 1978. pap. 2.50 (ISBN 0-913714-18-6). Legacy Bks.
--Discovering Place-names: Their Origins & Meanings. (Discovering Ser.: No. 102). 72p. 1984. pap. 3.95 (ISBN 0-85263-702-0, Pub. by Shire Pubns England). Seven Hills Bks.
--English Field Names: A Dictionary. (Illus.). 291p. 1983. 19.95 (ISBN 0-7153-5710-7). David & Charles.
--A Godly Exhortation. Incl. Sermon Preached at Pawles Crosse, 3 November 1577. White, Thomas. Repr. of 1578 ed. Repr. of 1583 ed. 28.00 (ISBN 0-384-15680-0). Johnson Repr.
--Place-Names of Great Britain & Ireland. (Illus.). 208p. 1980. 24.50x (ISBN 0-389-20154-5, 06924). B&N Imports.
Field, John & Franda, Marc. The Communist Parties of West Bengal. LC 75-904675. (Studies in Electoral Politics in the Indian States Ser.). ix, 158p. 1974. 9.50x (ISBN 0-88386-410-X). South Asia Bks.
Field, John, jt. ed. see Weiner, Myron.
Field, John, et al. Corporate Accounting & Financial Institutions. 1978. 90.00x (ISBN 0-86176-014-X, Pub. by MCB Pubns). State Mutual Bk.
Field, John O. Consolidating Democracy: Politicalization & Partisanship in India. 1981. 22.50x (ISBN 0-8364-0707-5, Pub. by Manohar India). South Asia Bks.
Field, John P. Richard Wilbur: A Bibliographical Checklist. LC 79-626237. (Serif Ser.: No. 16). 95p. 1971. 10.00x (ISBN 0-87338-035-5). Kent St U Pr.
Field, John P. & Weiss, Robert H. Cases for Composition. 2nd ed. 1984. pap. text ed. 12.95 (ISBN 0-316-28175-1); Teachers Manual Avail (ISBN 0-316-28177-8). Little.
Field, John W. Group Practice Development: A Practical Handbook. LC 76-56948. 252p. 1977. 39.50 (ISBN 0-912862-26-2). Aspen Systems.
--Rendezvous with Destiny: The History of the Yale Class of 1937 & Its Times, 2 vols. LC 84-91147. 556p. 1984. Set. 40.00 (ISBN 0-914659-06-5). Phoenix Pub.
Field, Joseph M. The Drama in Pokerville. LC 76-91078. (The American Humorists Ser.). Repr. of 1847 ed. lib. bdg. 18.75 (ISBN 0-8398-0556-X). Irvington.
Field, Joyce & Field, Leslie, eds. Bernard Malamud: A Collection of Critical Essays. (Twentieth Century Views Ser). 192p. 1975. 12.95 (ISBN 0-13-548032-9, Spec). P-H.
Field, Kate. Charles Albert Fechter. LC 70-82827. 1882. 18.00 (ISBN 0-405-08502-8, Blom Pubns). Ayer Co Pubs.
Field, Kent A. Test Your Salvation. 0.60 (ISBN 0-89137-531-7). Quality Pubns.
Field, L. The Forgotten War: Australia's Part in the Boer War. 1979. 27.50x (ISBN 0-522-84149-X, Pub. by Melbourne U Pr Australia). Intl Spec Bk.
Field, Leslie, jt. ed. see Field, Joyce.
Field, Leslie, ed. see Wolfe, Thomas.
Field, Lilian F. Introduction to the Study of the Renaissance. LC 76-110902. 1970. Repr. of 1898 ed. 26.00x (ISBN 0-8046-0885-7, Pub. by Kennikat). Assoc Faculty Pr.
Field, Louise. The Child & His Book. 59.95 (ISBN 0-87968-848-3). Gordon Pr.
--Ellen Glasgow: Novelist of the Old & New South. LC 74-11118. 1923. lib. bdg. 5.00 (ISBN 0-8414-4214-2). Folcroft.
Field, Louise F. Child & His Book. 2nd ed. LC 67-23937. 1968. Repr. of 1892 ed. 40.00x (ISBN 0-8103-3480-1). Gale.
Field, M. J. Search for Security. 478p. 1962. 15.00x (ISBN 0-89771-009-6). State Mutual Bk.
--Several Complex Variables & Complex Manifolds, Pt. II. LC 81-21590. (London Mathematical Society Lecture Note Ser.: No. 66). 220p. 1982. pap. 27.95 (ISBN 0-521-28888-6). Cambridge U Pr.
--Several Complex Variables & Computer Manifolds Part I. LC 81-21590. (London Mathematical Society Lecture Note Ser.: No. 65). 200p. 1982. pap. 22.95 (ISBN 0-521-28301-9). Cambridge U Pr.
Field, Margaret J. Akim-Kotoku: An Oman of the Gold Coast. LC 76-111575. (Illus.). Repr. of 1948 ed. 22.50x (ISBN 0-8371-4600-3, FAK&, Pub. by Negro U Pr). Greenwood.
--Religion & Medicine of the Ga People. LC 76-44718. 1977. Repr. of 1937 ed. 27.50 (ISBN 0-404-15923-0). AMS Pr.
--Search for Security: An Ethno-Psychiatric Study of Rural Ghana. 1970. pap. 2.95x (ISBN 0-393-00508-9, Norton Lib). Norton.
--Search for Security: An Ethno-psychiatric Study of Rural Ghana. LC 60-14408. (Northwestern University African Studies: No. 5). pap. 117.80 (ISBN 0-317-27793-6, 2015294). Bks Demand UMI.
Field, Marilyn J. The Comparative Politics of Birth Control: Determinants of Policy Variation & Change in the Developed Nations. (Landmark Dissertations in Women's Studies). (Illus.). 320p. 1983. 39.95x (ISBN 0-03-069527-9). Praeger.
Field, Mary & Field, Elliot. A Loving Guide to the World as a Two Year-Old Says It. (Illus.). 14p. (Orig.). (ps up). 1983. pap. 5.95 (ISBN 0-914445-00-6). Palm Springs Pub.
Field, Michael. All Manner of Food. LC 82-2321. (Illus.). 382p. 1982. Repr. of 1970 ed. 14.95 (ISBN 0-88001-013-4). Ecco Pr.
--Culinary Classics & Improvisations. LC 83-11542. 270p. 1983. Repr. of 1967 ed. 18.50 (ISBN 0-88001-015-0). Ecco Pr.
--Michael Field's Cooking School. rev. ed. LC 77-1943. 1977. 18.50 (ISBN 0-03-018476-2). HR&W.
Field, Micheal. The Merchants: The Big Business Families of Saudi Arabia & the Gulf States. LC 84-4386. (Illus.). 384p. 1985. 18.95 (ISBN 0-87951-971-1). Overlook Pr.
Field, Minna. The Aged, the Family, & the Community. LC 79-164500. 257p. 1972. 26.00x (ISBN 0-231-03348-6). Columbia U Pr.
--Aging with Honor & Dignity. 224p. 1968. 16.50x (ISBN 0-398-00563-X). C C Thomas.
--Patients Are People: A Medical-Social Approach to Prolonged Illness. 3rd ed. LC 67-31049. 294p. 1967. 31.50x (ISBN 0-231-03108-4). Columbia U Pr.
Field, Moses. Famous Legal Arguments. Mersky, Roy M. & Jacobstein, J. Myron, eds. LC 70-114030. (Classics in Legal History Reprint Ser.: Vol. 6). 196p. 1970. Repr. of 1897 ed. lib. bdg. 35.00 (ISBN 0-89941-005-7). W S Hein.
Field, Nancy & Machlis, Sally. Discovering Mount Rainier. (Illus.). 27p. (Orig.). (gr. 1-6). 1980. pap. 2.50 (ISBN 0-941042-02-2). Dog Eared Pubns.
--Discovering Northwest Volcanoes. (Illus.). 32p. (Orig.). (gr. 2-6). 1980. pap. 2.50 (ISBN 0-941042-03-0). Dog Eared Pubns.
--Discovering Salmon. (Illus.). 32p. (Orig.). (gr. k-6). 1984. pap. 2.75 (ISBN 0-941042-05-7). Dog Eared Pubns.
--Discovering the Princess Marquerite. (Illus.). 27p. (Orig.). 1982. pap. 2.50 (ISBN 0-941042-04-9). Dog Eared Pubns.
--Discovery Book for the Seattle Aquarium. (Illus.). 34p. (Orig.). (gr. 1-6). 1979. pap. 2.50 (ISBN 0-941042-01-4). Dog Eared Pubns.
Field News Syndicate. Boggle Challenge, No. 2. 1983. pap. 1.95 (ISBN 0-451-12411-1, Sig). NAL.
Field, Norma, tr. see Soseki, Natsume.
Field, Norma M., tr. see Soseki, Natsume.
Field, O. P. Effect of an Unconstitutional Statute. LC 74-146273. (American Constitutional & Legal History Ser). 1971. Repr. of 1935 ed. lib. bdg. 42.50 (ISBN 0-306-70118-9). Da Capo.
Field, P. J., ed. see Malory, Sir Thomas.
Field, Pat, jt. auth. see Kery, Pat.

Field, Paul E. Computer-Assisted Home Energy Management. LC 82-50649. 182p. 1982. pap. 15.95 (ISBN 0-672-21817-8, 21817). Sams.

Field, Paul E. & Davies, John A. Computer Interfacing Techniques in Science. LC 84-26714. 224p. 1985. pap. 12.95 (ISBN 0-673-18112-X). Scott F.

Field, Peter. Coyote Gulch. 1976. lib. bdg. 13.50x (ISBN 0-89968-033-X). Lightyear.

Field, Peter & Moore, Alin. Arab Financial Market. 164p. 1981. 88.00 (ISBN 0-8002-3405-7). Intl Pubns Serv.

Field, Phyllis F. The Politics of Race in New York: Struggle for Black Suffrage in the Civil War Era. 256p. 1982. 24.95x (ISBN 0-8014-1408-3). Cornell U Pr.

Field, R. M. A Glossary of Office Automation Terms. 32p. 1982. pap. text ed. 15.00x (ISBN 0-914548-42-5). Univelt Inc.

--A Glossary of Office Automation Terms. Society for Technical Communications, ed. 32p. (Orig.). 1982. pap. text ed. 15.00x (ISBN 0-914548-42-5). Soc Tech Comm.

Field, Rachel. All This & Heaven Too. 320p. 1983. Repr. lib. bdg. 17.95x (ISBN 0-89966-323-0). Buccaneer Bks.

--Hitty: Her First Hundred Years. LC 29-22704. 220p. (gr. 4-6). 1969. 12.95 (ISBN 0-02-734840-7). Macmillan.

--Prayer for a Child. LC 44-47191. 32p. (ps-1). 1968. 7.95x (ISBN 0-02-735190-4); pap. 3.95x 1984 (ISBN 0-02-043050-7). Macmillan.

--Prayer for a Child. LC 84-70991. (Illus.). 32p. (ps-1). 1984. 3.95 (ISBN 0-02-043070-1). Macmillan.

Field Research Corporation. Public Opinion of Criminal Justice in California: A Survey Conducted by Field Research Corporation. LC 75-8959. 156p. 1975. pap. 7.00x (ISBN 0-87772-203-X). Inst Gov Stud Berk.

Field, Richard. In Memorium: A Musician's Collection of Prints & Drawings: Ralph Kirkpatrick. (Illus.). 32p. (Orig.). 1985. pap. 1.00x (ISBN 0-89467-034-4). Yale Art Gallery.

Field, Richard & Baughman, SaraL. American Prints, Nineteen Hundred to Nineteen Fifty. Baier, Leslie K., ed. LC 81-82156. (Illus.). 136p. 1983. pap. 6.00x (ISBN 0-89467-026-3). Yale Art Gallery.

Field, Richard, jt. auth. see Baas, Jacquelynn.

Field, Richard, et al. French Drawings: Acquisitions Nineteen Seventy Nineteen Eighty-Four. (Illus.). 97p. (Orig.). 1984. pap. 5.00x (ISBN 0-89467-033-6). Yale Art Gallery.

Field, Richard H., et al. A Basic Course in Civil Procedure, Materials for. 5th ed. LC 84-6043. (University Casebook Ser.). 1275p. 1984. text ed. 29.50 (ISBN 0-88277-173-6); tchr's manual (ISBN 0-88277-203-1). Foundation Pr.

Field, Richard J. & Burger, Maria. Oscillations & Traveling Waves in Chemical Systems. LC 84-15382. 688p. 1984. pap. text ed. 85.00x (ISBN 0-471-89384-6, Pub. by Wiley Interscience). Wiley.

Field, Richard L. Design Manual for Solar Heating of Buildings & Domestic Hot Water. 3rd ed. (Solar Energy Ser.). (Illus.). 1980. 17.95 (ISBN 0-931912-18-0, 5013H); pap. 9.95 (ISBN 0-931912-19-9, 5013). Solpub.

--The Drapery Solar-Liner. (Solar Energy Ser.: No. 581). (Illus., Orig.). 1978. pap. 3.95 (ISBN 0-931912-12-1). Solpub.

--The Solar Insulator-Insulator TM. (Solar Energy Ser.: No. 580). (Illus., Orig.). 1978. pap. 3.95 (ISBN 0-931912-11-3). Solpub.

--Solar Potpourri-All Our Shorter Works in One. (Solar Energy Ser.: No. 599). (Illus., Orig.). 1977. pap. 9.95 (ISBN 0-931912-03-2). Solpub.

Field, Richard S. The Lithographs & Etchings of Philip Pearlstein. LC 78-52835. (Illus., Orig.). 1978. pap. text ed. 12.95x (ISBN 0-934306-01-X). Springfield.

--Paul Gauguin: Monotypes. LC 73-77306. (Illus.). 148p. 1973. pap. 6.95 (ISBN 0-87633-011-1). Phila Mus Art.

Field, Richard S. & Marrow, James, eds. Picture Atlas of Woodcuts of the Fifteenth Century, 7 Vols. Incl. Vol. 161. Old & New Testament; Vol. 162. New Testament; Vol. 163. Christ & the Holy Family; Vol. 164. Male & Female Saints; Vol. 165. Allegories, Ornaments, Calendars, Portraits, Coats of Arms, etc; Vol. 166. Woodcuts; Vol. 167. Commentary. (Illus.). Date not set. 120.00 ea. (ISBN 0-89835-250-9). Abaris Bks.

Field, Ronald M. A Guide to Micropublishing. 40p. 1975. pap. 10.00x (ISBN 0-914548-18-2); members 6.00. Soc Tech Comm.

Field, Ruth B. Wild Violets. 368p. (Orig.). 1980. pap. 2.50 (ISBN 0-89083-635-3). Zebra.

Field, Sandra. An Attraction of Opposites. (Harlequin Presents Ser.). 192p. 1983. pap. 1.95 (ISBN 0-373-10639-4). Harlequin Bks.

--Jamais Plus de Secrets. (Collection Harlequin). 192p. 1983. pap. 1.95 (ISBN 0-373-49322-3). Harlequin Bks.

--Sight of a Stranger. (Harlequin Romances Ser.). 192p. 1982. pap. 1.50 (ISBN 0-373-02480-0). Harlequin Bks.

--The Storms of Spring. (Harlequin Romances Ser.). 192p. 1982. pap. 1.50 (ISBN 0-373-02457-6). Harlequin Bks.

--The Tides of Summer. (Harlequin Romance Ser.). 192p. 1983. pap. 1.75 (ISBN 0-373-02577-7). Harlequin Bks.

--Walk by My Side. (Harlequin Presents Ser.). 192p. 1983. pap. 1.75 (ISBN 0-373-10568-1). Harlequin Bks.

Field, Stanley, jt. auth. see Hensley, Dennis.

Field, Stephen J. Personal Reminiscences of Early Days in California. LC 68-29601. (American Scene Ser). 1968. Repr. of 1893 ed. lib. bdg. 45.00 (ISBN 0-306-71157-5). Da Capo.

Field Support Service. Family Planning & Population 1982. (Field Support Service Communition & Education Catalogue). (Illus.). 88p. (Orig.). 1982. pap. text ed. price not set (ISBN 0-89836-034-X). Comm & Family.

Field, Syd. The Screenwriter's Workbook. (Orig.). 1984. pap. 7.95 (ISBN 0-440-58225-3, Dell Trade Pbks). Dell.

Field, Syd, ed. Screenplay: The Foundations of Screenwriting. enl. ed. 246p. 1984. pap. 7.95 (ISBN 0-440-57647-4, Dell Trade Pbks). Dell.

Field, T., jt. auth. see Graham, L. J.

Field, T. W. An Essay Towards an Indian Bibliography. 59.95 (ISBN 0-8490-0125-0). Gordon Pr.

--The Schoolmistress in History, Poetry & Romance. 59.95 (ISBN 0-8490-0998-7). Gordon Pr.

Field, Tiffany & Roopnarine, Jaipaul. Friendships in Normal & Handicapped Children. LC 84-11173. 304p. 1984. text ed. 29.50 (ISBN 0-89391-221-2). Ablex Pub.

Field, Tiffany & Sostek, Anita. Infants Born at Risk: Physiological, Perceptual & Cognitive Processes. 368p. 1983. 31.00 (ISBN 0-8089-1563-0, 791258). Grune.

Field, Tiffany & Fox, Nathan, eds. Social Perception in Infants. LC 84-28462. 344p. 1985. text ed. 39.50 (ISBN 0-89391-231-X). Ablex Pub.

Field, Tiffany, jt. ed. see Reite, Martin.

Field, Tiffany, et al, eds. Culture & Early Interactions. 288p. 1981. text ed. 29.95x (ISBN 0-89859-097-3). L Erlbaum Assocs.

--High-Risk Infants & Children: Adult & Peer Interactions. (Developmental Psychology Ser.). 1980. 39.50 (ISBN 0-12-255550-3). Acad Pr.

--Stress & Coping, Vol. I. 350p. 1985. text ed. 36.00 (ISBN 0-89859-564-9). L Erlbaum Assocs.

Field, Tiffany M. & Fogel, Alan, eds. Emotion & Early Interactions. 320p. 1982. text ed. 29.95 (ISBN 0-89859-241-0). L Erlbaum Assocs.

Field, Tiffany M., jt. ed. see Lipsitt, Lewis P.

Field, Tiffany M., et al. Review of Human Development. LC 81-21886. 736p. 1982. 57.95x (ISBN 0-471-08116-7, Pub. by Wiley-Interscience). Wiley.

Field, Tim. Using MacWrite & MacPaint. (Orig.). 1984. pap. 11.95 (ISBN 0-07-881137-6, 137-6). Osborne-McGraw.

Field, Tim, jt. auth. see Graham, Lyle.

Field, Timothy F., et al. Readings in Rehabilitation Counseling. LC 74-11373. 287p. 1975. pap. text ed. 9.50x (ISBN 0-8422-0427-X). Irvington.

Field, Tracey, jt. auth. see Gutowski, Michael.

Field, W. H. Raimon Vidal: Poetry & Prose. (Studies in the Romance Languages & Literatures: No. 110). 196p. 1971. pap. 11.00x (ISBN 0-8078-9110-X). U of NC Pr.

Field, Walter L. Tale of the Horse. LC 76-482750. (Illus.). 50p. 1978. 5.95 (ISBN 0-8143-1607-7). Wayne St U Pr.

Field, Walter T. Fingerposts to Children's Reading. (Educational Ser.). 1911. Repr. 10.00 (ISBN 0-8482-3982-2). Norwood Edns.

Field, Werner. How to Redecorate Your Old Piano... & Make It Look Great. 44p. 1972. pap. 6.95 (ISBN 0-912732-03-2). Duane Shinn.

Field, William P. Basic Economics. 450p. 1983. pap. 21.61 scp (ISBN 0-205-07813-3, 097813). Allyn.

Field, William T., Jr., jt. auth. see Martinello, Marian.

Fieldberg, Alfred & Fluer, Larry. Design Guide to The Semiconductor Facilities Provisions of the Uniform Building Code. (Illus., Orig.). 1985. pap. 125.00 (ISBN 0-9614808-1-5). GRDA Pubns.

Fielden, Christopher, jt. auth. see Price, Pamela V.

Fielden, Christopher D. & Ede, Terence. Energy Management by Computer. 300p. 1981. 60.00x (ISBN 0-7198-2840-6, Pub. by Northwood Bks). State Mutual Bk.

Fielden, F. J., tr. see Hallstrom, Per.

Fielden, F. J., tr. see Nilsson, Martin P.

Fielden, Jean D., jt. auth. see Fielden, John S.

Fielden, John. Curse of the Factory System. 2nd rev. ed. 74p. 1969. 29.50x (ISBN 0-7146-1394-0, F Cass Co). Biblio Dist.

--Curse of the Factory System. LC 68-23399. 1984. Repr. of 1836 ed. 25.00x (ISBN 0-678-05010-4). Kelley.

Fielden, John S. & Dulek, Ronald E. Bottom Line Business Writing. LC 83-19192. 156p. 1983. pap. 6.95 (ISBN 0-13-080283-2, Busn). P-H.

--What Do You Mean I Can't Write? 96p. 1983. pap. 6.95 (ISBN 0-13-952028-7, Busn). P-H.

Fielden, John S. & Fielden, Jean D. The Business Writing Style Book. 152p. 1983. pap. 6.95 (ISBN 0-13-108290-6, Busn). P-H.

Fielden, John S., et al. Elements of Business Writing. LC 83-19206. 332p. 1983. 49.95x (ISBN 0-13-263525-9, Busn). P-H.

Fielden, P. S., jt. auth. see Richards, S. A.

Fielden, Rosemary, jt. auth. see Rosen, Arnold.

Fielder, Hugh, jt. auth. see Sutcliffe, Phil.

Fielder, John. Colorado: Aspens Littlebook. (Illus.). 64p. 1984. 9.95 (ISBN 0-942394-09-7). Westcliffe Pubs Inc.

--Colorado's Hidden Valleys. (Illus.). 172p. 1982. 17.98 (ISBN 0-942394-00-3). Westcliffe Pubs Inc.

Fielder, Mildred. A Guide to Black Hills Ghost Mines. new ed. LC 72-84340. (Illus.). 240p. 1972. 7.95 (ISBN 0-87970-125-0). North Plains.

--Hiking Trails in the Black Hills. LC 73-85969. (Illus.). 1973. pap. 2.95 (ISBN 0-87970-131-5). North Plains.

--Lost Gold. LC 78-71706. (Illus.). 1978. pap. 7.95 (ISBN 0-87970-146-3). North Plains.

--Silver Is the Fortune. LC 78-66268. (Illus.). 1978. pap. 7.95 (ISBN 0-87970-145-5). North Plains.

--The Treasure of Homestake Gold: The Story of Homestake Gold Mine. LC 70-113967. (Illus.). 478p. 1970. 13.95 (ISBN 0-87970-115-3). North Plains.

Fielder, W. R., jt. auth. see Kownslar, A. O.

Fielder, William, jt. auth. see Harris, Howard C., Jr.

Fieldhouse, David, jt. auth. see Madden, Frederick.

Fieldhouse, David, ed. & frwd. by see Graham, G. E. & Floering, Ingrid.

Fieldhouse, David K. Unilever Overseas: The Anatomy of a Multinational. LC 78-20358. (Publications Ser.: No. 205). 1979. 25.00x (ISBN 0-8179-7051-7). Hoover Inst Pr.

Fieldhouse, David K., jt. ed. see Madden, Frederick.

Fieldhouse, Harry. Everyman's Good English Guide. 336p. 1982. 39.00x (Pub. by Dent Australia). State Mutual Bk.

--Everyman's Good English Guide. 284p. 1982. 15.95 (ISBN 0-460-04518-0, Pub. by Evman England). Biblio Dist.

--Everyman's Good English Guide. 284p. 1982. pap. 5.95x (ISBN 0-460-02289-X, BKA-05218, Pub. by Evman England). Biblio Dist.

Fieldhouse, Richard, jt. auth. see Arkin, William M.

Fieldhouse, Roger. Workers' Educational Association: Aims & Achievements 1903-1977. (Landmarks & New Horizons Ser.: No. 4). 1977. pap. 3.50 (ISBN 0-87060-072-9, LHN 4). Syracuse U Cont Ed.

Fieldhouse, W. L. Gun Lust. 208p. (Orig.). 1982. pap. 2.25 (ISBN 0-505-51778-7, Pub. by Tower Bks). Dorchester Pub Co.

--Klaw. (Klaw Ser.: No. 1). (Orig.). 1980. pap. 1.95 (ISBN 0-505-51586-5, Pub. by Tower Bks). Dorchester Pub Co.

--Town of Blood. (Klaw Ser.: No. 2). (Orig.). 1981. pap. 1.75 (ISBN 0-505-51671-3, Pub. by Tower Bks). Dorchester Pub Co.

Fieldhouse, William. Comanchero Kill. (Gun Lust Ser.: No. 2). 224p. 1983. pap. 2.50 (ISBN 0-8439-2027-0, Leisure Bks). Dorchester Pub Co.

--Klaw. 208p. 1984. pap. 2.25 (ISBN 0-8439-2129-3, Leisure Bks). Dorchester Pub Co.

Fielding. Romans: Joseph Andrews, Jonathan Wild, Tom Jones. 1640p. 42.95 (ISBN 0-686-56510-X). French & Eur.

Fielding, A., jt. auth. see Gormulicki, B. R.

Fielding, Alan. Computing for Biologists: An Introduction to BASIC Programming with Applications in the Life Sciences. 1985. pap. 19.95 (ISBN 0-8053-2515-8). Benjamin Cummings.

Fielding, Gabriel. The Birthday King. LC 85-8495. (Phoenix Fiction Ser.). 320p. 1985. 8.95 (ISBN 0-226-24848-8). U of Chicago Pr.

--In the Time of Greenbloom. LC 83-9247. (Phoenix Fiction Ser.). 416p. 1984. pap. 8.95 (ISBN 0-226-24845-3). U of Chicago Pr.

Fielding, Glen D. & Schalock, H. Del. Promoting the Professional Development of Teachers & Principals. LC 85-70936. (Illus.). 110p. (Orig.). 1985. pap. 5.95 (ISBN 0-86552-088-7). U of Oreg ERIC.

Fielding, Henry. The Adventures of Joseph Andrews. De Castro, J. Paul, ed. 1929. 30.00 (ISBN 0-8274-1822-1). R West.

--Amelia, 2 vols. in 1. 1978. Repr. of 1974 ed. 16.95x (ISBN 0-460-10852-2, Evman). Biblio Dist.

--Amelia. 1983. 50.00x (ISBN 0-8195-5084-1); pap. 12.50x (ISBN 0-8195-6114-2). Wesleyan U Pr.

--Apology for the Life of Mrs. Shamela Andrews. Downes, Brian W., ed. LC 76-23319. 1930. lib. bdg. 15.00 (ISBN 0-8414-4201-0). Folcroft.

--An Apology for the Life of Mrs. Shamela Andrews. 80p. 1980. Repr. of 1926 ed. lib. bdg. 12.50 (ISBN 0-8492-4616-4). R West.

--The Author's Farce. Woods, Charles B., ed. LC 65-27454. (Regents Restoration Drama Ser). xx, 151p. 1966. 14.95x (ISBN 0-8032-0359-4); pap. 3.50x (ISBN 0-8032-5358-3, BB 255, Bison). U of Nebr Pr.

--Catalogue of the Entire & Valuable Library of the Books of the Late Henry Fielding Esq. Repr. of 1775 ed. lib. bdg. 19.50 (ISBN 0-404-52315-3). AMS Pr.

--An Enquiry into the Causes of the Late Increase of Robbers. 2nd ed. (Criminology, Law Enforcement, & Social Problems Ser.). (ISBN 0-87585-210-6). Patterson Smith.

--An Enquiry into the Causes of the Late Increase of Robbers, Etc. LC 70-38678. (Foundations of Criminal Justice Ser.). xvi, 128p. 1975. Repr. of 1751 ed. 15.00 (ISBN 0-404-09194-6). AMS Pr.

--Fielding: Selections with Essays by Hazlitt, Scott, Thackeray. 1923. 20.00 (ISBN 0-8274-2342-X). R West.

--Fielding Three Novel Set: The History of Tom Jones; Joseph Andrews, & Amelia. Battestin, Martin, ed. (Wesleyan Field Ser.). text ed. 125.00x (ISBN 0-8195-4046-3); pap. 35.00 members. (ISBN 0-8195-6131-2). Wesleyan U Pr.

--The Grub-Street Opera. Roberts, Edgar V., ed. LC 67-12642. (Regents Restoration Drama Ser). xxiv, 164p. 1968. 15.50x (ISBN 0-8032-0360-8); pap. 4.25x (ISBN 0-8032-5359-1, BB 264, Bison). U of Nebr Pr.

--Henry Fielding: Justice Observed. Simpson, K. G., ed. (Critical Studies Ser.). 224p. 1985. 28.50x (ISBN 0-389-20591-5). B&N Imports.

--The Historical Register for the Year 1736. Appleton, William W., ed. Bd. with Eurydyce Hissed. LC 67-12643. (Regents Restoration Dramas Ser.). xviii, 83p. 1967. 8.50x (ISBN 0-8032-0361-6); pap. 2.50x (ISBN 0-8032-5360-5, BB 265, Bison). U of Nebr Pr.

--The History of the Life of the Late Mr. Jonathan Wild the Great. 294p. 1981. Repr. of 1926 ed. lib. bdg. 20.00 (ISBN 0-89987-262-X). Darby Bks.

--The Jacobite's Journal & Related Writings. Coley, William, ed. LC 73-17020. (Wesleyan Edition of the Works of Henry Fielding Ser.). 1975. 35.00x (ISBN 0-8195-4072-2). Wesleyan U Pr.

--Jonathan Wild. Bd. with Journal of a Voyage to Lisbon. 1973. 12.95x (ISBN 0-460-00877-3, Evman); pap. 4.50x (ISBN 0-460-01877-9, Evman). Biblio Dist.

--Jonathan Wild. pap. 3.50 (ISBN 0-451-51706-7, CE1706, Sig Classics). NAL.

--Jonathan Wild. Nokes, David, ed. (Penguin English Library). 1982. pap. 3.95 (ISBN 0-14-043151-9). Penguin.

--Joseph Andrews. Bd. with Shamela. 1978. pap. 2.95x (Evman). Biblio Dist.

--Joseph Andrews. Battestin, Martin, ed. LC 66-23917. (Works of Henry Fielding). 1984. 45.00x (ISBN 0-8195-3070-0); pap. 12.50x (ISBN 0-8195-6095-2). Wesleyan U Pr.

--Joseph Andrews. Battestin, Martin C., ed. Bd. with Shamela. LC 61-16166. (YA) (gr. 9up). 1961. pap. 5.95 (ISBN 0-395-05150-9, RivEd). HM.

--Joseph Andrews. Battestin, Martin C., ed. 1961. pap. 5.50 (ISBN 0-395-05157-6, RivEd). HM.

--Joseph Andrews. 1958. pap. 6.95x (ISBN 0-393-00274-8, Norton Lib). Norton.

--Joseph Andrews. Brissenden, R. F., ed. (English Library). 1977. pap. 2.95 (ISBN 0-14-043114-4). Penguin.

--Joseph Andrews. 401p. rag paper 25.00 (ISBN 0-913720-25-9, Sandstone); leather bound 45.00 (ISBN 0-913720-24-0). Beil.

--Joseph Andrews & Shamela. 1975. 8.95x (ISBN 0-460-00467-0, Evman); pap. 2.95x (ISBN 0-460-01467-6, Evman). Biblio Dist.

--Joseph Andrews: Movie Edition. 1977. pap. 2.75 (ISBN 0-451-51819-5, Sig Classics). NAL.

--A Journey from This World to the Next. Reginald, R. & Menville, Douglas, eds. LC 75-46270. (Supernatural & Occult Fiction Ser.). (Illus.). 1976. Repr. of 1930 ed. lib. bdg. 15.00x (ISBN 0-405-08127-8). Ayer Co Pubs.

--Miscellanies, Vol. 1. Miller, Henry K., ed. LC 71-184366. (Wesleyan Edition of the Works of Henry Fielding Ser.). 289p. (Textual intro. by Fredson Bowers). 1973. Repr. of 1743 ed. 35.00x (ISBN 0-8195-4046-3). Wesleyan U Pr.

--Tom Jones. (Classic Ser). (gr. 11 up). pap. 2.50 (ISBN 0-8049-0135-X, CL-135). Airmont.

--Tom Jones, 2 Vols. 1974. Repr. of 1909 ed. Vol. 1. 12.95x (ISBN 0-460-00355-0, Evman). Biblio Dist.

--Tom Jones. (Modern Library College Editions Ser.). 1950. pap. 4.50x (ISBN 0-394-30915-4, T15, RanC). Random.

--Tom Jones. pap. 3.95 (ISBN 0-451-51977-9, CE1827, Sig Classics). NAL.

--Tom Jones. Baker, Sheridan, ed. (Critical Editions Ser.). 1973. 17.50 (ISBN 0-393-04359-2); pap. 9.95x (ISBN 0-393-09394-8). Norton.

--Tom Jones. Mutter, Reg, ed. (English Library Ser.). 1966. pap. 3.95 (ISBN 0-14-043009-1). Penguin.

--Tom Jones. pap. 1.25 (ISBN 0-671-48137-1). WSP.

--Tom Jones. 1982. Repr. lib. bdg. 23.95x (ISBN 0-89966-398-2). Buccaneer Bks.

--Tom Jones. Date not set. pap. 10.95 (ISBN 0-394-60519-5). Modern Lib.

--Tom Jones, a Foundling, 2 vols. Bowers, Fredson, ed. LC 73-15009. (Wesleyan Edition of the Works of Henry Fielding Ser.). (Illus.). 1250p. 1974. Set. 50.00x (ISBN 0-8195-4068-4); pap. 12.50x (ISBN 0-8195-6048-0). Wesleyan U Pr.

--Tragedy of the Tragedies for the Life & Death of Tom Thumb the Great with the Annotations of H. Scribblerus Secundus. Hillhouse, James T., ed. LC 71-131704. 1971. Repr. of 1918 ed. 39.00x (ISBN 0-403-00591-4). Scholarly.

--The True Patriot. LC 72-10055. (English Literature Ser., No. 33). 1972. Repr. of 1964 ed. lib. bdg. 66.95x (ISBN 0-8383-1597-6). Haskell.

Fielding, Henry, jt. auth. see Richardson, Samuel.

Fielding, Henry see Swan, D. K.

Fielding, J. W., et al, eds. Gastric Cancer: Proceedings of the International Symposium on Gastric Cancer, Birmingham, 22-23 Sept. 1980. (Advances in the Biosciences: Vol. 32). (Illus.). 260p. 1981. 55.00 (ISBN 0-08-026398-4). Pergamon.

Fielding, Joy. Kiss Mommy Goodbye. 1982. pap. 3.95 (ISBN 0-451-13230-0, AE3230, Sig). NAL.

--Life Penalty. LC 84-4062. 336p. 1984. 15.95 (ISBN 0-385-18871-4). Doubleday.

--Life Penalty. 1985. pap. 3.95 (ISBN 0-451-13848-1, Sig). NAL.

--The Other Woman. 352p. 1983. pap. 3.95 (ISBN 0-451-12550-9, Sig). NAL.

Fielding, K. J; see Bloomfield, Paul.

Fielding, Kathy. Having Your Baby at Home. 1980. softcover 3.95 (ISBN 0-912216-23-9). Angel Pr.

Fielding, Kenneth J., ed. see Dickens, Charles.

Fielding, Kenneth J., jt. ed. see Sanders, Charles R.

Fielding, L. Rotating Machinery Equipment Design: Apple II Plus, IIe, IIc. 176p. 1985. price not set (ISBN 0-07-079368-9). McGraw.

Fielding, L. P., jt. auth. see Todd, Ian P.

Fielding, Leslie. Handheld Calculator Programs for Rotating Equipment Design. LC 82-9962. (Illus.). 480p. 1983. 41.95 (ISBN 0-07-020695-3). McGraw.

Fielding, Mantle. American Engravers upon Copper & Steel. (Illus.). 1964. Repr. of 1917 ed. 34.00 (ISBN 0-8337-1124-5). B Franklin.

--Dictionary of American Painters, Sculptors & Engravers. rev ed. Doran, Genevieve, ed. 480p. 1975. Repr. of 1926 ed. 17.50 (ISBN 0-913274-03-8). Modern Bks.

--Dictionary of American Painters, Sculptors & Engravers. (Illus.). 455p. 25.00 (ISBN 0-913274-03-8). Wallace-Homestead.

--Dictionary of American Painters, Sculptors & Engravers. 1983. pap. 75.00 (ISBN 0-938290-02-9). Apollo.

--Dictionary of American Painters, Sculptors & Engravers: Enlarged. 1974. 25.00 (ISBN 0-685-47043-1). Assoc Bk.

Fielding, Mantle, jt. auth. see Biddle, Edward.

Fielding, Nancy, jt. auth. see Fielding, Temple.

Fielding, Newton. How to Sketch from Nature. (Illus.). 1980. deluxe ed. 46.45 (ISBN 0-930582-66-7). Gloucester Art.

Fielding, Nigel. Probation Practice. LC 84-1543. 174p. 1984. text ed. 42.50x (ISBN 0-566-00730-4). Gower Pub Co.

Fielding, P. PIP College "HELPS". Handicapped & Exceptional Learners Programs & Services. (College Handicapped & Exceptional Programs & Services Ser.: Vol. 3). 1978. pap. 8.95 (ISBN 0-937660-04-3). PIP.

Fielding, P. M. & Alexander, M. E. PIP's Freebie Guide: A Guide to Free & Inexpensive Publications, Products & Aids to Successful Completion of College or Career Training for Learning Disabled Youth. 1978. pap. 5.95 (ISBN 0-937660-06-X). PIP.

Fielding, P. M., ed. A National Directory of Four Year Colleges, Two Year Colleges & Post High School Training Programs for Young People with Learning Disabilities. 5th ed. 1984. 15.95 (ISBN 0-937660-08-6). PIP.

Fielding, P. P. PIP College "HELPS" - Handicapped & Exceptional Learners Programs & Services: (College - Handicapped & Exceptional Learners Programs & Services, Vol. 1. 1976. pap. 6.95 (ISBN 0-937660-02-7). PIP.

--PIP College "HELPS" - Handicapped & Exceptional Learners Programs & Services, Vol. 2. 1977. pap. 7.95 (ISBN 0-937660-03-5). PIP.

Fielding, Raymond. The American Newsreel, 1911-1967. LC 73-177334. (Illus.). 392p. 1981. pap. 10.95 (ISBN 0-8061-1717-6). U of Okla Pr.

--The Technique of Special Effects Cinematography. 3rd rev. & enl. ed. (Library of Communication Techniques). 426p. 1982. 26.95 (ISBN 0-240-50616-2). Focal Pr.

--Technique of Special Effects Cinematography. 4th ed. (Illus.). 448p. 1985. pap. text ed. 29.95 (ISBN 0-240-51234-0). Focal Pr.

Fielding, Raymond, compiled by. A Technological History of Motion Pictures & Television. 1967. 42.50x (ISBN 0-520-03981-5). U of Cal Pr.

Fielding, Raymond, ed. A Technological History of Motion Pictures & Television. (Illus.). 269p. 1983. pap. 10.95 (ISBN 0-520-05064-9). U of Cal Pr.

Fielding, S., jt. auth. see Karpinski, J.

Fielding, Sarah. The Adventures of David Simple, 1744, 2 vols. in 1. 2nd ed. Shugrue, Michael F., ed. (The Flowering of the Novel, 1740-1775 Ser: Vol. 14). 1974. lib. bdg. 61.00 (ISBN 0-8240-1113-9). Garland Pub.

Fielding, Stuart, jt. auth. see Lal, Harbans.

Fielding, Stuart & Effland, Richard C., eds. New Frontiers in Psychotropic Drug Research. LC 79-53620. (Illus.). 240p. 1979. monograph 28.50 (ISBN 0-87993-128-0). Futura Pub.

Fielding, Temple. Fielding's Europe 1983. 1982. 12.95 (ISBN 0-688-01346-5). Morrow.

Fielding, Temple & Fielding, Nancy. Fielding's Low-Cost Europe 1983. 17th, rev. ed. (Illus.). 860p. 1982. pap. 7.25 (ISBN 0-688-01340-6). Morrow.

Fielding, W. J. Boccaccio. 59.95 (ISBN 0-87968-763-0). Gordon Pr.

--Woman: The Eternal Primitive. 59.95 (ISBN 0-8490-1317-8). Gordon Pr.

Fielding, Waldo L. Pregnancy: The Best State of the Union. LC 76-2152. (Illus.). 184p. 1976. pap. 6.95 (ISBN 0-87027-147-4). Cumberland Pr.

Fielding, William J. Strange Customs of Courtship & Marriage. 315p. 1980. Repr. of 1942 ed. lib. bdg. 25.00 (ISBN 0-89987-259-X). Darby Bks.

Fielding, Xan, tr. see Boulle, Pierre.

Fielding-Hall, A. The Theory of the World Soul. (Illus.). 161p. 1985. Repr. of 1910 ed. 88.85 (ISBN 0-89901-235-3). Found Class Reprints.

Fielding-Hall, Harold. The Inward Light. LC 78-72431. Repr. of 1908 ed. 27.00 (ISBN 0-404-17294-6). AMS Pr.

--The Soul of a People. 4th ed. LC 78-72436. Repr. of 1903 ed. 33.50 (ISBN 0-404-17295-4). AMS Pr.

Fields. The Sun. (gr. 2-4). 1980. PLB 8.60 (ISBN 0-531-03243-4, G23). Watts.

Fields, jt. auth. see Campbell.

Fields, A. Nathaniel Hawthorne. LC 74-7223. (American Literature Ser., No. 49). 1974. lib. bdg. 39.95x (ISBN 0-8383-1859-2). Haskell.

Fields, A. A. Charles Dudley Warner. LC 72-4187. (Select Bibliographies Reprint Ser.). 1972. Repr. of 1904 ed. 18.00 (ISBN 0-8369-6878-6). Ayer Co Pubs.

Fields, Alice. Pets. LC 80-20281. (Easy-Read Fact Bks.). (gr. 2-4). 1981. PLB 8.60 (ISBN 0-531-04188-3). Watts.

--Racing Cars. LC 80-15697. (gr. 2-4). 1981. PLB 8.60 (ISBN 0-531-03245-0). Watts.

--Satellites. (Easy Read Fact Bks.). (gr. 2-4). 1981. PLB 8.60 (ISBN 0-531-03246-9). Watts.

--Seals. (gr. 2-4). 1980. PLB 8.60 (ISBN 0-531-03242-6). Watts.

--Television. LC 79-26891. (Easy-Read Fact Bks.). (gr. 2-4). 1981. PLB 8.60 (ISBN 0-531-03248-5). Watts.

Fields, Ann. The Tenth Muse. LC 77-83280. 1977. pap. 4.00 (ISBN 0-686-23277-1). Jaeger.

Fields, Anne. Authors & Friends. LC 5-2567. 16.00x (ISBN 0-403-00092-0). Scholarly.

Fields, Annie. Authors & Friends. (Illus.). 1970. Repr. of 1896 ed. 18.00 (ISBN 0-404-00596-9). AMS Pr.

--Authors & Friends. 1977. Repr. of 1897 ed. lib. bdg. 20.00 (ISBN 0-8414-4251-7). Folcroft.

--Life & Letters of Harriet Beecher Stowe. 1977. Repr. of 1897 ed. lib. bdg. 40.00 (ISBN 0-8495-1606-4). Arden Lib.

--Nathaniel Hawthorne. LC 74-11032. 1899. lib. bdg. 7.50 (ISBN 0-8414-4224-X). Folcroft.

Fields, Annie, ed. James T. Fields: Biographical Notes & Personal Sketches with Unpublished Fragments & Tributes from Men & Women of Letters. LC 73-157501. 1971. Repr. of 1881 ed. 43.00x (ISBN 0-8103-3724-X). Gale.

Fields, Annie A. James T. Fields: Biographical Notes & Personal Sketches. LC 75-122653. 1971. Repr. of 1882 ed. 22.50x (ISBN 0-8046-1301-X, Pub. by Kennikat). Assoc Faculty Pr.

--Whittier. 1978. Repr. of 1893 ed. lib. bdg. 12.50 (ISBN 0-8492-0889-0). R West.

Fields, Armond. George Auriol. LC 85-2511. (Illus.). 192p. (Orig.). 1985. pap. 19.95 (ISBN 0-87905-200-7). Gibbs M Smith.

--Henri Riviere: A Major Discovery. LC 83-13841. (Illus.). 128p. 1983. 17.00 (ISBN 0-87905-133-7, Peregrine Smith). Gibbs M Smith.

Fields, Barbara J. Slavery & Freedom on the Middle Ground: Maryland During the Nineteenth Century. LC 84-20949. (Yale Historical Publications: Misc. 123). 296p. 1985. 27.50x (ISBN 0-300-02340-5). Yale U Pr.

Fields, Belden. Trotskyism & Maoism: Theory & Practice in France & the U. S. (Illus.). 288p. 26.95 (ISBN 0-03-069349-7). Praeger.

Fields, Bernard N., et al, eds. Virology. (Illus.). 1632p. 1985. text ed. 149.50 (ISBN 0-88167-026-X). Raven.

Fields, Beverly. Reality's Dark Dream: Dejection in Coleridge. LC 67-64939. (Kent Studies in English: No. 5). Repr. of 1967 ed. 39.40 (ISBN 0-8357-9374-5, 2011315). Bks Demand UMI.

Fields, Brian A. The Impact of Shifting Ecologies upon the Dental Biology of Precolumbian Populations of the Illinois River Valley: A Case Study in Human Ecosystems Dynamics. Lee, Don Y., ed. LC 84-70885. 384p. 1984. text ed. 62.50x (ISBN 0-939758-08-3). Eastern Pr.

--The Phylogeny of South African Variants of the Australopithecinae: Some Taxonomic Considerations. Lee, Don Y., ed. LC 85-80476. 172p. 1985. 38.50x (ISBN 0-939758-11-3). Eastern Pr.

Fields, Bud & Bertucci, Bob. Big Orange: A Pictorial History of University of Tennessee Football. LC 82-81803. (Illus.). 464p. 1982. 29.95 (ISBN 0-88011-071-6). Leisure Pr.

Fields, Carl. Exploring Careers in Tool & Die Making. 1985. 8.97 (ISBN 0-8239-0633-7). Rosen Group.

Fields, Curtis P. The Forgotten Art of Building a Stone Wall. LC 78-169930. (Forgotten Arts Ser.). (Illus.). 64p. (Orig.). 1971. pap. 4.95 (ISBN 0-911658-52-1). Yankee Bks.

Fields, Daisy. A Woman's Guide to Moving up in Business Government. (Illus.). 182p. 1983. 17.95 (ISBN 0-13-961813-9); pap. 7.95 (ISBN 0-13-961805-8). P-H.

Fields, Dale. Tales of Cedar Lawn Farm. (Illus.). 360p. pap. 9.95 (ISBN 0-87770-278-0). Ye Galleon.

Fields, Dorothy & Kitakoji, Isamitsu. Cherry Blossoms. LC 72-93534. (This Beautiful World Ser: Vol. 40). (Illus.). 138p. 1973. pap. 4.95 (ISBN 0-87011-191-4). Kodansha.

Fields, Francis R. & Horwitz, Rudy J., eds. Psychology & Professional Practice: The Interface of Psychology & the Law. LC 81-19899. (Illus.). 248p. 1982. lib. bdg. 35.00 (ISBN 0-89930-015-4, FIH/, Quorum). Greenwood.

Fields, Frank. Twenty-Eighth Virginia Infantry. (The Virginia Regimental Histories Ser.). (Illus.). 1985. 16.45 (ISBN 0-930919-15-7). H E Howard.

Fields, Gary & Mitchell, Olivia. Retirement, Pensions, & Social Security. (Illus.). 192p. 1985. text ed. 25.00x (ISBN 0-262-06091-4). MIT Pr.

Fields, Gary S. How Segmented is the Bogota Labor Market? (Working Paper: No. 434). 99p. 1980. 5.00 (ISBN 0-686-36146-6, WP-0434). World Bank.

--Poverty, Inequality, & Development. LC 79-21017. (Illus.). 256p. 1980. pap. 11.95 (ISBN 0-521-29852-0). Cambridge U Pr.

Fields, Gary S., ed. Research in Human Capital & Development: Education, Human Capital & Development, Vol. 5. 1984. 42.50 (ISBN 0-89232-417-1). Jai Pr.

Fields, George. From Bonsai to Levi's: When West Meets East. 1985. pap. 4.95 (ISBN 0-451-62379-7, Ment). NAL.

--From Bonsai to Levis-When West Meets East: An Insider's Entertaining, Surprising Account of How the Japanese Live. Forman, Gail, ed. (Illus.). 256p. 1984. 14.95 (ISBN 0-02-537750-7). Macmillan.

Fields, Harvey J. With All Your Heart: Bechol Levavcha, 2 vols. (Illus.). (gr. 7-9). 1977. Set. 10.00 (ISBN 0-8074-0197-8, 142611). UAHC.

Fields, Howard L., et al, eds. World Congress on Pain: Fourth, Proceedings. (Advances in Pain Research & Therapy Ser.: Vol. 9). 1985. text ed. price not set (ISBN 0-88167-121-5). Raven.

Fields, Mrs. Jame T. Memories of a Hostess. De Wolfe Howe, M. A., ed. Repr. 25.00 (ISBN 0-8274-2712-3). R West.

Fields, James T. In & Out of Doors with Charles Dickens. LC 74-148775. 170p. 1976. Repr. of 1876 ed. 21.50 (ISBN 0-404-08749-3). AMS Pr.

--Old Acquaintance: Barry Cornwall & Some of His Friends. LC 74-9554. 1876. 15.00 (ISBN 0-8414-4197-9). Folcroft.

--Old Acquaintance: Barry Cornwall & Some of His Friends. 1978. Repr. of 1876 ed. lib. bdg. 17.50 (ISBN 0-8492-0890-4). R West.

--A Shelf of Old Books. 215p. 1982. Repr. of 1894 ed. lib. bdg. 50.00 (ISBN 0-89987-267-0). Darby Bks.

--A Shelf of Old Books. 1978. Repr. of 1894 ed. lib. bdg. 25.00 (ISBN 0-8414-4309-2). Folcroft.

--Yesterdays with Authors. (Illus.). 1970. Repr. of 1900 ed. 16.50 (ISBN 0-404-00603-5). AMS Pr.

--Yesterdays with Authors. 1977. Repr. of 1882 ed. lib. bdg. 20.00 (ISBN 0-8414-4250-9). Folcroft.

--Yesterdays with Authors. LC 75-108481. (Illus.). 1970. Repr. of 1900 ed. 14.00x (ISBN 0-403-00209-5). Scholarly.

Fields, Mrs. James T. Whittier: Notes on His Life & of His Friendships. LC 73-13954. 1972. Repr. of 1893 ed. lib. bdg. 10.00 (ISBN 0-8414-4154-5). Folcroft.

Fields, Jeanette S., ed. A Guidebook to the Architecture of River Forest. (Illus.). 68p. (Orig.). 1981. pap. 3.50x (ISBN 0-9606314-0-2). River Forest C C.

Fields, Jeff. A Cry of Angels. LC 73-91623. 1979. pap. 2.50 (ISBN 0-345-28204-3). Ballantine.

Fields, Joanne. What Is a Real Person. new ed. 32p. 1975. pap. 0.75 (ISBN 0-87784-152-7). Inter-Varsity.

Fields, Julia. East of Moonlight. 52p. 1973. pap. 3.00x (ISBN 0-911860-60-6). Chatham Bkseller.

--Slow Coins. LC 80-53380. 220p. 1981. 15.00 (ISBN 0-89410-131-5); pap. 8.00 (ISBN 0-89410-132-3). Three Continents.

Fields, Karen E. Revival & Rebellion in Colonial Central Africa. LC 84-42884. (Illus.). 324p. 1985. text ed. 38.50x (ISBN 0-691-09409-8). Princeton U Pr.

Fields, Karen E., jt. auth. see Fields, Mamie G.

Fields, Kenneth. The Odysseus Manuscripts. 9.00 (ISBN 0-318-01983-3). Elpenor.

--Other Walker: A Book of Poems. 1971. 3.95x (ISBN 0-934614-00-8). Talisman Research.

--Sunbelly. Schreiber, Jan, ed. LC 73-81066. (Chapbook Series One). 1974. 5.00 (ISBN 0-87923-078-9). Godine.

Fields, Kenneth, jt. ed. see Winters, Yvor.

Fields, Kent T., jt. auth. see Bonno, John A.

Fields, L. J. Neural Organization. 1979. 32.50 (ISBN 0-8151-3221-2). Year Bk Med.

--Neurotransmitter Function. 1979. 38.50 (ISBN 0-8151-3220-4). Year Bk Med.

Fields, Louis W. Bookkeeping Made Simple. (Made Simple Ser.). 1956. pap. 4.95 (ISBN 0-385-01205-5). Doubleday.

Fields, Mamie G & Fields, Karen E. Lemon Swamp & Other Places: A Carolina Memoir. 1985 ed. 1983. 16.75 (ISBN 0-02-910160-3); pap. 8.95x (ISBN 0-02-910550-1). Free Pr.

Fields, Marion. Fundamentals of Food Microbiology. (Illus.). 1979. text ed. 27.50 (ISBN 0-87055-250-3). AVI.

Fields, Marion L. Laboratory Manual in Food Preservation. 1977. 10.50 (ISBN 0-87055-241-4). AVI.

Fields, Mary E. Foundations of Truth. LC 80-67931. 275p. 1980. 10.00 (ISBN 0-87516-423-4). De Vorss.

Fields, Mike. Getting It Together: The Black Man's Guide to Good Grooming & Fashion. Bailey, A. Peter. LC 83-8919. (Illus.). 143p. 1983. pap. 12.95 (ISBN 0-396-08177-0). Dodd.

Fields, Paul R. & Moeller, Therald, eds. Lanthanide-Actinide Chemistry. LC 67-31656. (Advances in Chemistry Ser: No. 71). 1967. 29.95 (ISBN 0-8412-0072-6). Am Chemical.

Fields, Phyllis, tr. see Oliveira, Nuno.

Fields, Piggie. Why Me? 1979. 4.50 (ISBN 0-682-49259-0). Exposition Pr FL.

Fields, Rick, et al. Chop Wood, Carry Water: A Guide to Finding Spiritual Fulfillment in Everyday Life. LC 84-23942. 304p. 1984. pap. 11.95 (ISBN 0-87477-209-5). J P Tarcher.

Fields, Robert. Our Constitution: Our Government. 1984. 5.95 (ISBN 0-87594-282-2). Book-Lab.

Fields, Robert A. Take Me Out to the Crowd, Ted Turner & the Atlanta Braves. LC 77-71398. (Illus.). 1977. 8.95 (ISBN 0-87397-118-3). Strode.

Fields, Robert R. Survival Primer: The Single Sourcebook for Coping with Crisis. (Illus.). 192p. 1983. pap. 7.95 (ISBN 0-89651-704-7). Icarus.

Fields, Rona M. The Future of Women. LC 84-81427. 182p. (Orig.). 1985. lib. bdg. 25.95x (ISBN 0-930390-60-1); pap. text ed. 8.95 (ISBN 0-930390-59-8). Clin Soc Assn.

--Northern Ireland: Society under Siege. LC 80-80316. 267p. 1980. pap. 5.95 (ISBN 0-87855-806-3). Transaction Bks.

--Society under Siege: A Psychology of Northern Ireland. LC 76-21895. 283p. 1981. 24.95 (ISBN 0-87722-074-3). Temple U Pr.

Fields, Ronald. W. C. Fields: A Life in Film. (Illus.). 288p. 1984. 29.95 (ISBN 0-312-85311-4); pap. 14.95 (ISBN 0-312-85312-2). St Martin.

Fields, S. Helen, ed. see Cuthbertson, John.

Fields, Sue R., et al. The Complete Works of Washington Irving Journals & Notebooks: Vol. 5, 1832-1859. (Critical Editions Program Ser.). 1985. lib. bdg. 45.00 (ISBN 0-8057-8504-3, Twayne). G K Hall.

Fields, Suzanne. Like Father, Like Daughter: How Father Shapes the Woman His Daughter Becomes. 1983. 15.45i (ISBN 0-316-28169-7). Little.

Fields, Sylvia K., jt. ed. see Sherman, Jacques L., Jr.

Fields, T. Windsor. A Re-Examination of the Gibson Paradox. LC 79-53207. (Outstanding Dissertations in Economics Ser.). 235p. 1984. lib. bdg. 31.00 (ISBN 0-8240-4157-7). Garland Pub.

Fields, Terri. Special Someone. (Sweet Dreams Ser.: No. 70). 144p. (Orig.). 1984. pap. 2.25 (ISBN 0-553-24255-5). Bantam.

Fields, Uriah J. Be the Best. LC 83-71413. 255p. 1983. perfect bd. 9.95 (ISBN 0-938844-10-5). Am Mutuality.

--Being in Nothingness. 20p. 1982. pap. 2.95 (ISBN 0-938844-01-6). Am Mutuality.

--Better Living with Less & with Insecurity. 22p. 1982. pap. 2.95 (ISBN 0-938844-03-2). Am Mutuality.

--Happiness Through Consciousness. 54p. 1982. pap. 4.95 (ISBN 0-938844-02-4). Am Mutuality.

--How Lovers Can Become Friends. 26p. 1982. pap. 2.95 (ISBN 0-938844-04-0). Am Mutuality.

--The Magic Power of Positive Ideas. 100p. 1981. pap. 4.50 (ISBN 0-938844-00-8). Am Mutuality.

--The Montgomery Story. 26p. 1982. pap. 7.95 (ISBN 0-938844-05-9). Am Mutuality.

Fields, Victor A. Foundations of the Singer's Art. 2nd ed. 118p. Date not set. pap. 7.50 (ISBN 0-932761-00-3). NAIS.

--Training the Singing Voice: An Analysis of the Working Concepts Contained Contained in Recent Contributions to Vocal Pedagogy. (Music Reprint Ser.). 1979. Repr. of 1966 ed. lib. bdg. 35.00 (ISBN 0-306-79510-8). Da Capo.

Fields, Virginia B. Ezekiel Thomas Eighteen Forty to Nineteen Seventeen & John Thomas Eighteen Forty-Six to Nineteen Twenty-Eight of Georgia & Texas: Their Ancestors & Descendants. LC 85-70026. (Illus.). 125p. 1985. text ed. 19.00 (ISBN 0-9614510-0-9); pap. text ed. 13.00 (ISBN 0-9614510-1-7). Fields.

Fields, W., ed. James Fennimore Cooper: A Collection of Critical Essays. 1979. 12.95 (ISBN 0-13-509943-9, Spec); (Spec). P-H.

Fields, W. C. The Bank Dick. (Lorrimer Classic Screenplay Ser.). (Illus.). pap. 6.95 (ISBN 0-8044-6146-5). Ungar.

--Never Give a Sucker an Even Break; Tillie & Gus. (Lorrimer Classic Screenplay Ser.): (Illus.). o. s. i. 12.95 (ISBN 0-8044-2201-X); pap. 8.95 (ISBN 0-8044-6148-1). Ungar.

Fields, W S., jt. ed. see Rose, Clifford F.

Fields, Weston. Unformed & Unfilled. 1976. pap. 6.95 (ISBN 0-87552-267-X). Presby & Reformed.

Fields, Wilbert J. Unity in Marriage. LC 61-18222. 1962. 5.95 (ISBN 0-570-03191-5, 12-2593). Concordia.

Fields, Wilbur. Exploring Exodus. LC 78-301089. (The Bible Study Textbook Ser.). (Illus.). 1977. 17.50 (ISBN 0-89900-006-1). College Pr Pub.
--The Glorious Church-Ephesians. 2nd ed. LC 71-1065. (The Bible Study Textbook Ser.). (Illus.). 1960. 10.60 (ISBN 0-89900-040-1). College Pr Pub.
--New Testament Backgrounds. 2nd ed. (Bible Student Study Guides Ser). 1977. pap. 5.95 (ISBN 0-89900-156-4). College Pr Pub.
--Philippians, Colossians, Philemon. LC 78-8763. (The Bible Study Textbook Ser.). (Illus.). 1969. 10.60 (ISBN 0-89900-041-X). College Pr Pub.
--Thinking Through Thessalonians. LC 77-1794. (The Bible Study Textbook Ser.). (Illus.). 1963. 10.60 (ISBN 0-89900-042-8). College Pr Pub.
Fields, Wilbur, ed. see Smith, William.
Fields, Willa, jt. auth. see Berger, Karen.
Fields, William S. & Hass, William K. Aspirin, Platelets & Stroke. LC 74-153915. (Illus.). 178p. 1971. 15.00 (ISBN 0-87527-033-6). Green.
Fields, William S. & Spencer, William A. Stroke Rehabilitation: Basic Concepts & Research Trends. LC 67-19383. (Illus.). 184p. 1967. 12.50 (ISBN 0-87527-034-4). Green.
Fields, William S., et al. Stroke Diagnosis & Management: Current Procedures & Equipment. LC 72-13847. (Illus.). 298p. 1973. 18.50 (ISBN 0-87527-101-4). Green.
--The Cerebellum in Health & Disease. LC 78-78016. (Illus.). 588p. 1970. 37.50 (ISBN 0-87527-009-3). Green.
Fields, Williams. The Neural Bases of Violence & Aggression. LC 72-13847. (Illus.). 640p. 1975. 37.50 (ISBN 0-87527-102-2). Green.
Field Stanfield, James. An Essay on the Study & Composition of Biography. (Victorian Muse Ser.). 360p. 1985. lib. bdg. 45.00 (ISBN 0-8240-8618-X). Garland Pub.
Fieldstone, Herrick. What Will Happen to You the Very Moment after You Die: New Discoveries in Spiritistic Occultism. (Illus.). 117p. 1982. 195.00 (ISBN 0-686-31987-7). Am Inst Psych.
Fieler, Frank B. Tamburlaine, Part One, & Its Audience. LC 62-62580. (University of Florida Humanities Monographs: No. 8). 1961. pap. 3.50 (ISBN 0-8130-0077-7). U Presses Fla.
Fieler, Frank B., ed. see Whitney, Geoffrey.
Fielo, Sandra B. & Edge, Sylviac. Technical Nursing of the Adult: Medical, Surgical & Psychiatric Approaches. 2nd ed. 1974. write for info. (ISBN 0-02-337280-X, 33728). Macmillan.
Fienberg, S. Studies in Bayesian Econometrics & Statistics. LC 73-86697. (Contributions to Economic Analysis: Vol. 86). 677p. 1975. 93.75 (ISBN 0-444-10579-4, North-Holland). Elsevier.
Fienberg, S., jt. ed. see Mason, W. M.
Fienberg, S. E. & Hinkley, D. H., eds. R. A. Fisher: An Appreciation. (Lecture Notes in Statistics: Vol. 1). 208p. 1980. pap. 18.00 (ISBN 0-387-90476-X). Springer-Verlag.
Fienberg, S. E. & Zellner, A., eds. Studies in Bayesian Econometrics & Statistics: In Honor of Leonard J. Savage, 2 vols. 1977. Set. pap. 81.00 (North-Holland); Vol. 1. pap. 47.00 (ISBN 0-7204-0562-9); Vol. 2. pap. 47.00 (ISBN 0-7204-0563-7). Elsevier.
Fienberg, S. E., jt. ed. see Atkinson, A. C.
Fienberg, Stephen. The Analysis of Cross-Classified Categorical Data. 2nd ed. 1980. text ed. 18.50x (ISBN 0-262-06071-X). MIT Pr.
Fiene, Donald. Alexander Solzhenitsyn: An International Bibliography of Works by & About Him, 1962-73. 100p. 1973. 25.00 (ISBN 0-88233-042-X). Ardis Pubs.
Fiene, Donald, tr. see Osorgin, Mikhail.
Fiene, Donald M. & Crumb, Robert. R Crumb Checklist. (Illus.). 192p. 1981. 35.95 (ISBN 0-9606654-0-4); pap. 10.95 (ISBN 0-9606654-1-2). Boatner-Norton.
Fiengo, Robert. Surface Structure: The Interface of Autonomous Components. LC 80-14680. (Language & Thought Ser.). 1980. text ed. 22.50x (ISBN 0-674-85725-9). Harvard U Pr.
Fiennes, G. F. I Tried to Run a Railway. text ed. 17.50x (ISBN 0-392-07972-0, SpS). Sportshelf.
Fiennes, R. N., ed. Biology of Nutrition, Pts. 1-2. Incl. Pt. 1. The Evolution & Nature of Living Systems; Pt. 2. The Organizations & Nutritional Methods of Life Forms. 688p. 1972. Set. text ed. 150.00 (ISBN 0-08-016470-6). Pergamon.
--Pathology of Simian Primates, 2 pts. Incl. Pt. 1. General Pathology. 84.75 (ISBN 3-8055-1307-0); Pt. 2. Infectious & Parasitic Diseases. 70.75 (ISBN 3-8055-1308-9). (Illus.). 1972. Set. 139.75 (ISBN 3-8055-1329-1). S Karger.
Fiennes, Ranulph. To the Ends of the Earth: The Transglobe Expedition, the First Pole-to Pole Circumnavigation of the Globe. (Illus.). 1983. 17.95 (ISBN 0-87795-490-9); pap. 12.95 (ISBN 0-87795-614-6). Arbor Hse.
Fiennes, Richard N. Zoonoses & the Origins & Ecology of Human Disease. 1979. 37.50 (ISBN 0-12-256050-7). Acad Pr.
Fiennes, T. W. Infectious Cancers of Animals & Man. 1982. 25.00 (ISBN 0-12-256040-X). Acad Pr.
Fienup-Riordan, Ann. Shape up with Baby: Exercise Games for the New Parent & Child. LC 80-82128. (Illus., Orig.). 1980. pap. 4.50 (ISBN 0-937604-04-6). Pennypress.
Fierabras. Firumbras & Otuel & Roland. (EETS, OS Ser.: No. 198). Repr. of 1935 ed. 20.00 (ISBN 0-527-00198-8). Kraus Repr.
Fierain, Jacques. Les Raffineries de Sucre des Ports en France: XIX Debut de XX Siecles. Bruchey, Stuart, ed. LC 77-77169. (Dissertations in European Economic History Ser.). (Fr.). 1977. lib. bdg. 55.00x (ISBN 0-405-10783-8). Ayer Co Pubs.
Fiering, Myron B. Streamflow Synthesis. LC 67-29625. pap. 39.80 (ISBN 0-317-10931-6, 2001560). Bks Demand UMI.
Fiering, Myron B. & Jackson, Barbara B., eds. Synthetic Streamflows. LC 77-172418. (Water Resources Monograph: Vol. 1). (Illus.). 99p. 1971. pap. 10.00 (ISBN 0-87590-300-2). Am Geophysical.
Fiering, Norman. Jonathan Edward's Moral Thought & Its British Context. LC 80-26755. (Institute of Early American History & Culture Ser.). xiii, 391p. 1981. 30.00x (ISBN 0-8078-1473-3). U of NC Pr.
--Moral Philosophy at Seventeenth-Century Harvard: A Discipline in Transition. LC 80-18282. (Institute of Early American History & Culture Ser.). xiii, 323p. 1981. 24.00x (ISBN 0-8078-1459-8). U of NC Pr.
Fierman, Floyd S. Guts & Ruts: The Jewish Pioneer on the Trail in the American Southwest. (Illus.). 1985. 20.00 (ISBN 0-88125-061-9). Ktav.
--The Schwartz Family of El Paso. (Southwestern Studies: No. 61). 1980. pap. 3.00 (ISBN 0-87404-120-1). Tex Western.
Fierman, L. B., ed. Effective Psychotherapy. LC 65-2314. 1965. 22.95 (ISBN 0-02-910140-9). Free Pr.
Fiermans, L., et al, eds. Electron & Ion Spectroscopy of Solids. LC 78-6171. (NATO ASI Series B, Physics: Vol. 32). 487p. 1978. 75.00x (ISBN 0-306-35732-1, Plenum Pr). Plenum Pub.
Fiero, G. William. Great Basin Geology. (Max C. Fleischmann Series in Great Basin Natural History). (Illus.). 200p. 1985. 22.50 (ISBN 0-87417-083-4); pap. 14.50 (ISBN 0-87417-084-2). U of Nev Pr.
--Nevada's Valley of Fire. LC 75-18136. (Illus.). 1975. 8.95 (ISBN 0-916122-42-5); pap. 3.75 (ISBN 0-916122-17-4). KC Pubns.
Fiero, Gloria K. The Humanistic Tradition: Chapters in the History of Culture to 1650. LC 81-40631. (Illus.). 510p. (Orig.). 1981. lib. bdg. 33.25 (ISBN 0-8191-1755-2); pap. text ed. 20.75 (ISBN 0-8191-1756-0). U Pr of Amer.
Fierro, Alfredo. The Militant Gospel: A Critical Introduction to Political Theologies. Drury, John, tr. from Span. LC 77-1652. Orig. Title: El Evangelio Beligerente. 459p. (Orig.). 1977. pap. 6.95 (ISBN 0-88344-311-2). Orbis Bks.
Fierro, Martin, ed. My Child Is Not Missing. LC 84-71008. (Illus.). 176p. (Orig.). 1984. pap. 12.95 (ISBN 0-917461-00-2). Child Safe.
Fierro, Robert D. The New American Entrepreneur: How to Get off the Fast Track and into a Business of Your Own. LC 81-14218. 320p. 1982. 13.50 (ISBN 0-688-00806-2). Morrow.
--Tax Shelters in Plain English. 1983. pap. 6.95 (ISBN 0-14-006362-5). Penguin.
Fierst, John, jt. auth. see Fried, Lewis.
Fierstein, Harvey. The Torch Song Trilogy. (Illus.). 173p. (Orig.). 1981. pap. 6.95 (ISBN 0-9604724-0-1). Gay Pr NY.
--Torch Song Trilogy. 1983. 9.95 (ISBN 0-394-53428-X, Pub. by Villard Bks). Random.
Fierstein, Jeff. Kid Contracts. (gr. 4-8). 1982. 3.95 (ISBN 0-86653-091-6, GA 442). Good Apple.
Fierstein, Jeff & Lodolce, John. Goal-Directed Program Planning. LC 81-83699. 42p. 1981. wkbk. 19.95 (ISBN 0-941564-00-2). Radicus Comm.
Fierz, H. K., ed. see International Congress of Psychotherapy, 8th, Milan, Aug. 1970.
Fierz, H. K. see International Congress of Psychotherapy, 8th, Milan, 1970.
Fierz, Markus, ed. Girolamo Cardano (1501-1576) Physician, Natural Philosopher, Mathematician, Astrologer & Interpreter of Dreams. Niman, Helga, tr. from Ger. 242p. 1983. 29.95x (ISBN 0-8176-3057-0). Birkhauser.
Fierz, Markus & Weisskopf, V. F., eds. Theoretical Physics in the Twentieth-Century: A Memorial Volume to Wolfgang Pauli. LC 60-15886. pap. 85.00 (ISBN 0-317-08596-4, 2007408). Bks Demand UMI.
Fieschi, C. & Loeb, C. W., eds. Effects of Aging on Regulation of Cerebral Blood Flow & Metabolism: Abstracts. (Journal: European Neurology: Vol. 22, Suppl. 2). (Illus.). x, 64p. 1983. pap. 22.25 (ISBN 3-8055-3732-8). S Karger.
Fieschi, C., ed. see International Symposium on Cerebral Blood Flow Regulation, Acid-Base & Energy Metabolism Acute Brain Injuries, 5th, Roma, Siena, 1971.
Fieschi, C., et al, eds. Effects of Aging on Regulation of Cerebral Blood Flow & Metabolism. (Monographs in Neural Sciences: Vol. 11). (Illus.). xiv, 258p. 1984. 70.00 (ISBN 3-8055-3805-7). S Karger.
Fieser & Fieser's. Reagents for Organic Synthesis, Vol. 11. (Fieser's Reagents for Organic Synthesis Ser.). 669p. 1984. 45.00x (ISBN 0-471-88628-9, Pub. by Wiley-Interscience). Wiley.
Fieser, Louis F. & Fieser, Mary. Reagents for Organic Synthesis, 8 vols. Vol. 1, 1967, 1457p. 74.95 (ISBN 0-471-25875-X); Vol. 2, 1969, 538p. 49.95 (ISBN 0-471-25876-8); Vol. 3, 1972, 401p. 45.95x (ISBN 0-471-25879-2); Vol. 4, 1974, 660p. 51.95 (ISBN 0-471-25881-4); Vol. 5, 1975, 864p. 55.95 (ISBN 0-471-25882-2); Vol. 6, 1977, 765p. 53.50 (ISBN 0-471-25873-3); Vol. 7, 1979, 487p. 49.95 (ISBN 0-471-02918-1); Vol. 8, 1980, 602p. 54.50 (ISBN 0-471-04834-8). Wiley.
Fieser, Louis F. & Williamson, Kenneth L. Organic Experiments. 448p. 1983. 26.95 (ISBN 0-669-05890-4). Heath.
Fieser, Mary. Fieser & Fieser's Reagents for Organic Synthesis, Vol. 10. (Reagents for Organic Synthesis Ser.). 528p. 1982. 44.50 (ISBN 0-471-86636-9, Pub. by Wiley-Interscience). Wiley.
Fieser, Mary & Fieser's. Regents for Organic Synthesis, Vol. 11. (Fieser's Regents for Organic Synthesis Ser.). 669p. 1984. 45.00 (ISBN 0-471-88628-9); Eleven vol. set, 7567p. 520.00 (ISBN 0-471-81521-7). Wiley.
Fieser, Mary, jt. auth. see Fieser, Louis F.
Fieser, Mary, et al. Reagents for Organic Synthesis, Vol. 9. (Reagents for Organic Synthesis Ser.). 596p. 1981. 51.95 (ISBN 0-471-05631-6, Pub. by Wiley-Interscience). Wiley.
Fieser's, jt. auth. see Fieser, Mary.
Fiesta, Janine. The Law & Liability: A Guide for Nurses. 208p. 1983. 16.95 (ISBN 0-471-07879-4, Pub. by Wiley Med). Wiley.
Fiester, M. Blasted Beloved Breckenridge. LC 72-87818. (Illus.). 1973. 29.95 (ISBN 0-87108-059-1). Pruett.
Fiester, Mark. Look for Me in Heaven: The Life of John Lewis Dyer. (Illus.). 400p. 1980. 19.95 (ISBN 0-87108-564-X). Pruett.
Fieux, Michele, jt. auth. see Stommel, Henry.
Fieux, Michele, jt. ed. see Gautier, Catherine.
Fieve, Ronald. Moodswing: The Third Revolution in Psychiatry. 256p. 1976. pap. 3.95 (ISBN 0-553-23014-X). Bantam.
Fieve, Ronald R. & Rosenthal, David, eds. Genetic Research in Psychiatry: Proceedings. LC 74-24394. (American Psychopathological Ser.). (Illus.). 320p. 1975. 30.00x (ISBN 0-8018-1660-2). Johns Hopkins.
Fifadara, Haresh, jt. auth. see Hollo, Reuven.
Fife, Alta & Fife, Austin. Heaven on Horseback. (Western Text Society Ser.: Vol. 1, No. 1). (Illus.). 114p. (Orig.). 1970. pap. 5.95 (ISBN 0-87421-044-5). Utah St U Pr.
Fife, Alta, jt. auth. see Fife, Austin.
Fife, Austin & Fife, Alta. Saints of Sage & Saddle: Folklore Among the Mormons. 375p. 1981. pap. 14.95 (ISBN 0-87480-180-X). U of Utah Pr.
Fife, Austin, jt. auth. see Fife, Alta.
Fife, Austin, et al, eds. Forms Upon the Frontier: Folklife & Folk Arts in the United States. (Illus.). 189p. (Orig.). 1969. pap. 6.50 (ISBN 0-87421-036-4). Utah St U Pr.
Fife, Dale. Destination Unknown. 128p. (gr. 5 up). 1981. 9.95 (ISBN 0-525-28624-1, 0966-290, Unicorn Bk). Dutton.
--Follow That Ghost! LC 79-11370. (Illus.). (gr. 1-5). 1979. 9.75 (ISBN 0-525-30010-4, 0947-280, Unicorn Bk). Dutton.
--North of Danger. (gr. 5 up). 1978. 8.95 (ISBN 0-525-36035-2, Unicorn Bk). Dutton.
--Rosa's Special Garden. Tucker, Kathleen, ed. LC 84-17223. (Illus.). 32p. (ps-1). 1985. PLB 10.75 (ISBN 0-8075-7115-6). A Whitman.
--The Sesame Seed Snatchers. LC 83-12630. (Illus.). 112p. (gr. 2-5). 1983. 8.95 (ISBN 0-395-34826-9). HM.
Fife, Ian & Machin, E. Anthony. Health & Safety at Work. LC 81-182916. Date not set. cancelled (ISBN 0-406-20054-8). Butterworth.
Fife, Iline, jt. auth. see Carter, Elton.
Fife, John, jt. auth. see Pettman, Barrie O.
Fife, Jonathan D., ed. see Austin, Ann E. & Gamson, Zelda F.
Fife, Jonathan D., ed. & frwd. by see Cross, K. Patricia & McCartan, Anne-Marie.
Fife, Jonathan D., ed. & frwd. by see Crosson, Patricia H.
Fife, Jonathan D., ed. & frwd. by see Feasley, Charles E.
Fife, Jonathan D., ed. see Gappa, Judith M.
Fife, Jonathan D., ed. see Guzman, Rafael M. de & Melendez, Winifred A.
Fife, Jonathan D., ed. & frwd. by see Hendrickson, Robert M. & Lee, Barbara A.
Fife, Jonathan D., ed. see Johnson, Lynn G.
Fife, Jonathan D., ed. & frwd. by see Keimig, Ruth T.
Fife, Jonathan D., ed. see Lindgren, J. Ralph, et al.
Fife, Jonathan D., ed. see Marcus, Laurence R., et al.
Fife, Jonathan D., ed. see Moran, Barbara B., et al.
Fife, Jonathan D., ed. see Morse, Suzanne W.
Fife, Jonathan D., ed. see Olswang, Steven G. & Lee, Barbara A.
Fife, Jonathan D., ed. see Preer, Jean L.
Fife, Jonathan D., ed. see Waggaman, John S.
Fife, Jonathan D., ed. & frwd. by see Whitman, Neal A., et al.
Fife, Jonathan D., ed. see Yuker, Harold E.
Fife, Joy L. China's Foreign Policy: Apparent Contradictions - Two Case Studies. 1981. 4.75 (ISBN 0-8062-1821-5). Carlton.
Fife, P. C. Mathematical Aspects of Reacting & Diffusing Systems. LC 79-10216. (Lecture Notes in Biomathematics Ser.: Vol. 28). 1979. pap. text ed. 14.00 (ISBN 0-387-09117-3). Springer-Verlag.
Fife, Robert H. Young Luther. LC 79-131040. 1970. Repr. of 1928 ed. 19.50 (ISBN 0-404-02385-1). AMS Pr.
Fifer, Bill. Metal Projects, Bk. 2. 96p. 1981. 6.00 (ISBN 0-87006-172-0). Goodheart.
Fifer, Charles N., ed. see Farquhar, George.
Fifer, J. Valerie. Bolivia: Land, Location, & Politics Since 1825. LC 72-139713. (Cambridge Latin American Studies: 13). pap. 81.80 (ISBN 0-317-26396-X, 2024453). Bks Demand UMI.
Fifer, Ken. Falling Man. LC 79-15032. 75p. 1979. 4.00 (ISBN 0-87886-105-X). Ithaca Hse.
Fifer, Mike, jt. auth. see Fifer, Peg.
Fifer, Peg & Fifer, Mike. Note from the Fifer's. LC 82-63202. 144p. 1983. write for info. (ISBN 0-9610610-0-6). S F Knapp.
Fified, William. Modigliani. LC 75-41362. (Illus.). 1976. 11.95 (ISBN 0-688-03039-4). Morrow.
Fifield, F. W. & Kealey, D. Principles & Practice of Analytical Chemistry. 1975. text ed. 28.50x (ISBN 0-7002-0257-9). Intl Ideas.
Fifield, L. W. Navigation for Watchkeepers. (Illus.). 416p. 1980. text ed. 32.50x (ISBN 0-434-90564-X). Sheridan.
Fifield, Richard, ed. The Making of the Earth. (New Scientist Guides Ser.). 240p. 1985. 24.95x (ISBN 0-85520-733-7); pap. 8.95 (ISBN 0-85520-732-9). Basil Blackwell.
Fifield, Russel H. National & Regional Interest in Asean: Competition & Cooperation in International Politics. 83p. (Orig.). 1979. pap. text ed. 9.00x (ISBN 0-566-04009-3, Pub. by Inst Southeast Asian Stud). Gower Pub Co.
Fifield, Russell H. Diplomacy of Southeast Asia, 1945-1958. (Illus.). xv, 584p. 1968. Repr. of 1958 ed. 28.00 (ISBN 0-208-00677-X, Archon). Shoe String.
Fifield, Sarah A. Train Whistles. LC 81-51156. (Collaboration of Southwest Writers & Artists Ser.). 53p. 1981. pap. 10.00 (ISBN 0-686-96957-X). SarSan Pub.
--What Does It All Mean? Carlton, Susan, ed. (Illus.). 103p. (Orig.). 1983. pap. 2.50 (ISBN 0-686-45384-0). SarSan Pub.
Fifield, William. In Search of Genius. LC 82-8193. 1982. 13.95 (ISBN 0-688-03717-8). Morrow.
--Jean Cocteau. (Columbia Essays on Modern Writers Ser.: No. 70). 48p. 1974. pap. 2.50 (ISBN 0-231-03369-9). Columbia U Pr.
--Modigliani: The Biography. LC 75-41362. (Illus.). 1978. pap. 3.95 (ISBN 0-688-08039-1). Morrow.
Fifield, William, jt. auth. see Cocteau, Jean.
Fiflis, Ted J., et al. Accounting for Business Lawyers: Teaching Materials. 3rd ed. LC 84-5120. (American Casebook Ser.). 838p. 1984. text ed. 28.95 (ISBN 0-314-80667-9). West Pub.
Fifoot, C. H. Frederic William Maitland: A Life. LC 73-145892. (Studies in Legal History). 1971. 22.50x (ISBN 0-674-31825-0). Harvard U Pr.
Fifoot, Cecil H. History & Sources of the Common Law: Tort & Contract. LC 75-98758. xvii, 446p. Repr. of 1949 ed. lib. bdg. 29.75x (ISBN 0-8371-2814-5, FICL). Greenwood.
Fifoot, Cecil H., ed. see Maitland, Frederick W.
Fifoot, Richard. Bibliography of Edith, Osbert & Sacheverell Sitwell. 2nd ed. 432p. 1971. 27.50 (ISBN 0-208-01233-8, Archon). Shoe String.
Fifteen Southerners. Why the South Will Survive. LC 81-1313. 240p. 1981. pap. 9.00x (ISBN 0-8203-0566-9). U of Ga Pr.
Fifth International Cyclotron Conference. Proceedings. McIlroy, I. W., ed. (Illus.). 1971. 52.50 (ISBN 0-8088-0043-4). Davey.
Fifth International Symposium on Superalloys, Champion, Pennsylvania, Oct. 7-11, 1984, et al. Superalloys Nineteen Eighty-Four. Kortovich, Charles S. & Bricknell, Rodger H., eds. LC 84-61466. (Illus.). 826p. 1984. 70.00 (ISBN 0-89520-478-9); members 45.00. Metal Soc.
Fifth Intl. Conference on Numerical Methods in Fluid Dynamics. Proceedings. Van De Vooren, A. I. & Zandbergen, P. J., eds. (Lecture Notes in Physics Ser.: Vol. 59). 1976. soft cover 23.00 (ISBN 0-387-08004-X). Springer-Verlag.
Fifth Symposium on Chemistry of Nucleic Acids Components, Czechoslovakia. Proceedings. (Nucleic Acids Symposium Ser.: No. 9). 280p. 1981. 25.00 (ISBN 0-904147-31-2). IRL Pr.
Figa-Talamanca & Picardello. Harmonic Analysis on Free Groups. (Lecture Notes in Pure & Applied Mathematics). 224p. 1983. 35.00 (ISBN 0-8247-7042-0). Dekker.
Figes, Eva. Light. LC 83-42819. 91p. 1983. 10.45 (ISBN 0-394-53307-0). Pantheon.
--Light. 160p. 1984. pap. 2.95 (ISBN 0-345-31898-6). Ballantine.
--Tragedy & Social Evolution. 1976. 10.95 (ISBN 0-7145-3516-8); pap. 6.95 (ISBN 0-7145-3639-3). Riverrun NY.
--Waking. 1982. pap. 4.95 (ISBN 0-394-72227-2). Pantheon.
Figg, Royall W. Where Men Only Dare to Go! The Story of a Boy Company, Parker's Battery C. S. A. Repr. of 1885 ed. 19.95 (ISBN 0-317-13714-X). Zenger Pub.
Figge, Frank H., ed. see Sobotta, Johannes.

Figgie, Harry E. The Cost Reduction & Profit Inprovement Handbook. LC 84-29166. 1985. 23.95 (ISBN 0-442-22584-9). Van Nos Reinhold.

Figgins, Ross. The Job Game: Winning the Job That's Right for You. (Illus.). 1980. text ed. 12.95 (ISBN 0-13-510099-2, Spec); pap. text ed. 6.95 (ISBN 0-13-510081-X, Spec). P-H.

Figgins, Ross, jt. auth. see Pearce, C. Glenn.

Figgins, Ross, jt. auth. see Pearce, C. G.

Figgins, Ross F. Techniques of Job Search. 1976. pap. text ed. 9.75 scp (ISBN 0-06-453708-0, HarpC). Har-Row.

Figgis, jt. auth. see Melson.

Figgis, B. N. Introduction to Ligand Fields. LC 84-23371. 362p. 1985. Repr. of 1966 ed. lib. bdg. price not set (ISBN 0-89874-819-4). Krieger.

Figgis, Darrel. A. E. George Russell: A Study of a Man & a Nation. LC 78-102601. (Irish Culture & History Ser). 1970. Repr. of 1916 ed. 26.00x (ISBN 0-8046-0778-8, Pub. by Kennikat). Assoc Faculty Pr.

Figgis, Darrell. Bye-Ways of Study (Thompson, Meredith) LC 73-16281. 1973. lib. bdg. 15.00 (ISBN 0-8414-4170-7). Folcroft.

--Studies & Appreciations. 258p. 1980. Repr. of 1912 ed. lib. bdg. 25.00 (ISBN 0-8495-1711-7). Arden Lib.

--Studies & Appreciations. LC 76-23186. 1976. Repr. of 1912 ed. lib. bdg. 27.50 (ISBN 0-8414-4200-2). Folcroft.

Figgis, Eric. Challenge to Chance. 7.95x (ISBN 0-685-21953-4). Wehman.

Figgis, J. N., ed. see Acton, John E.

Figgis, John B. Keswick from Within. Dayton, Donald W., ed. (The Higher Christian Ser.). 192p. 1985. 25.00 (ISBN 0-8240-6417-8). Garland Pub.

Figgis, John N. The Divine Right of Kings. 14.00 (ISBN 0-8446-0621-9). Peter Smith.

--Studies of Political Thought from Gerson to Grotius, 1414-1625. LC 75-41092. 1976. Repr. of 1907 ed. 21.00 (ISBN 0-404-14540-X). AMS Pr.

--Will to Freedom. LC 68-8236. 1969. Repr. of 1917 ed. 22.50x (ISBN 0-8046-0147-X, Pub. by Kennikat). Assoc Faculty Pr.

Figgis, John N., ed. see Acton, John E.

Figh, M. G. A Word List from 'Bill Arp' & 'Rufus Sanders' (Publications of the American Dialect Society: No. 13). 27p. 1950. pap. 1.10 (ISBN 0-8173-0613-7). U of Ala Pr.

Figh, Margaret G., jt. auth. see Windham, Kathryn T.

Figiel, Richard, jt. auth. see Myers, Stanley.

Figler, Howard. The Complete Job Search Handbook. LC 79-4153. 348p. 1980. 11.95 (ISBN 0-03-044121-8, Owl Bks.); pap. 6.95 (ISBN 0-03-044126-9). HR&W.

Figler, Howard, jt. auth. see Figler, Stephen.

Figler, Howard E. Path: A Career Workbook for Liberal Arts Students. LC 74-12041. 1979. 7.75x (ISBN 0-910328-07-2). Carroll Pr.

Figler, Howard E., jt. auth. see Drum, David J.

Figler, Jeffrey D. Decision Making in Business. (Illus.). 198p. 1981. pap. text ed. 10.95x (ISBN 0-935732-05-5). Roxbury Pub Co.

Figler, Stephen & Figler, Howard. The Athlete's Game Plan for College & Career. LC 83-22112. 279p. (Orig.). 1984. pap. 9.95 (ISBN 0-87866-266-9). Petersons Guides.

Figler, Stephen K. Sport & Play in American Life. 1981. text ed. 26.95 (ISBN 0-03-057672-5, CBS C); instr's manual 19.95 (ISBN 0-03-058247-4). SCP.

Figlewski, Stephen, et al. Hedging with Financial Futures for Institutional Investors: Theory & Practice. 200p. 1985. prof. ref. 29.95x (ISBN 0-88730-083-9). Ballinger Pub.

Figley, Charles R. & Leventman, Seymour. Strangers at Home: Vietnam Veterans Since the War. LC 79-24398. 1980. student edition 17.95 (ISBN 0-03-049776-0). Praeger.

Figley, Charles R., ed. Computers & Family Therapy. LC 85-956. (Journal of Psychotherapy & the Family Ser.: Vol. 1, Nos. 1-2). 216p. 1985. text ed. 29.95 (ISBN 0-86656-375-X); pap. text ed. 19.95 (ISBN 0-86656-408-X). Haworth Pr.

--Stress Disorders Among Vietnam Veterans: Theory, Research, & Treatment Implications. LC 77-94734. 1978. 27.50 (ISBN 0-87630-164-2). Brunner-Mazel.

--Trauma & Its Wake: The Study & Treatment of Post-Traumatic Stress Disorder. (Psychosocial Stress Ser.: Vol. 4). 475p. 1985. 36.00 (ISBN 0-87630-385-8). Brunner-Mazel.

Figley, Charles R. & McCubbin, Hamilton I., eds. Stress & the Family: Vol. II Coping with Catastrophe. LC 83-6048. 272p. 1983. 27.50 (ISBN 0-87630-332-7). Brunner-Mazel.

Figley, Charles R., jt. ed. see McCubbin, Hamilton I.

Figley, Grace E., et al. Elementary School Physical Education: An Educational Experience. 1977. pap. text ed. 13.95 (ISBN 0-8403-1761-1). Kendall-Hunt.

Figliola, Carl L., jt. auth. see Schnall, David J.

Figliuzzi, Richard M. An Aircraft in Trouble. LC 82-90301. 107p. 1983. 7.95 (ISBN 0-533-05401-X). Vantage.

Figueira, Thomas J. Aegina. Connor, W. R., ed. LC 80-2649. (Monographs in Classical Studies). 1981. lib. bdg. 39.00 (ISBN 0-405-14036-3). Ayer Co Pubs.

Figueira, Thomas J. & Nagy, Gregory, eds. Theognis of Megara: Poetry & the Polis. LC 84-21832. 346p. 1985. text ed. 28.50x (ISBN 0-8018-3250-0). Johns Hopkins.

Figueiredo, D. G. de see De Figueiredo, D. G.

Figueiredo, J. L. Progress in Catalyst Deactivation. 1982. lib. bdg. 49.50 (ISBN 90-247-2690-5, Pub. by Martinus Nijhoff Netherlands). Kluwer Academic.

Figueiredo, M. P. De see De Figueiredo, M. P. & Splittstoesser, D. F.

Figueras, P. Decorated Jewish Ossuaries. (Documenta et Monumenta Orientis Antiqui Ser.: No. 20). (Illus.). 119p. 1983. text ed. 35.50x (ISBN 90-04-06579-2, Pub. by E J Brill Holland). Humanities.

Figuerdo, Antonio De see Norman, Jill & De Figuerdo, Antonio.

Figueredo, Luis E. Basic Electricity. 1980. pap. text ed. 14.95 (ISBN 0-89669-053-9). Collegium Bk Pubs.

Figueredo, Luis F., jt. auth. see Siboney, Indian.

Figueroa, Adolfo. Capitalist Development & the Peasant Economy of Peru. LC 83-18861. (Cambridge Latin American Studies: No. 47). (Illus.). 168p. 1984. 29.95 (ISBN 0-521-25397-7). Cambridge U Pr.

Figueroa, Ed & Harshman, Dorothy. Yankee Stranger. (Illus.). 231p. 1982. 11.00 (ISBN 0-682-49902-1). Exposition Pr FL.

Figueroa, Gonzalo, jt. auth. see Mulloy, William.

Figueroa, Jose. A Manifesto to the Mexican Republic. Hutchinson, C. Alan, tr. LC 76-47992. 1978. 24.50 (ISBN 0-520-03347-7). U of Cal Pr.

Figueroa, Martin Fernandez De see Fernandez De Figueroa, Martin.

Figueroa, Oscar & Winkler, Charles. A Business Information Guidebook. 256p. 1980. 19.95 (ISBN 0-8144-5560-3); pap. 9.95 (ISBN 0-8144-7005-X). AMACOM.

Figueroa, Richard A. & Ruiz, Nadeen T. The Bilingual Special Education Dictionary: A Resource for Special Educators & Parents. Diaz-Guerrero, Rogelio, ed. 290p. (Orig.). 1983. pap. text ed. 11.95 (ISBN 0-318-02998-7). Natl His Univ.

Figueroa, William G., ed. Hematology. LC 81-10310. 430p. 1981. 40.00 (ISBN 0-471-09515-X). Krieger.

Figueroa de Thompson, Annie, jt. auth. see Thompson, Donald.

Figueroa Y Miranda, Miguel. La Pintura Cristiana En los Tres Primeros Siglos. (UPREX, Humanidades: No. 12). pap. 1.85 (ISBN 0-8477-0012-7). U of PR Pr.

Figuier, Louis. La Photographie au Salon de 1859 et "La Photographie" et Le Stereoscope", 2 vols. in 1. Bunnell, Peter C. & Sobieszek, Robert A., eds. LC 76-24661. (Sources of Modern Photography Ser.). (Illus., Fr.). 1979. Repr. of 1868 ed. lib. bdg. 28.50x (ISBN 0-405-09639-9). Ayer Co Pubs.

--The World Before the Deluge. 1977. lib. bdg. 69.95 (ISBN 0-8490-2844-2). Gordon Pr.

Figulus, Benedictus. A Golden & Blessed Casket of Nature's Marvels. Waite, Arthur E., tr. from Ger. LC 79-8607. Repr. of 1893 ed. 42.50 (ISBN 0-404-18469-3). AMS Pr.

Figurski, Leszek. Finality & Intelligence. LC 78-62252. 1978. pap. text ed. 11.00 (ISBN 0-8191-0565-1). U Pr of Amer.

Figus. Gastric Precanceroses. 1977. 17.00 (ISBN 0-9960007-3-9, Pub. by Akademiai Kaido Hungary). Heyden.

Fijan, Carol, jt. auth. see Engler, Larry.

Fijoot, Richard. A Bibliography of Edith, Osbert, & Sacherevell Sitwell. 2nd, rev. ed. 432p. 35.00 (ISBN 0-906795-20-6). U Pr of Va.

Fike, Earle W., Jr. Raspberry Seed under God's Denture. 1979. pap. 4.95 (ISBN 0-87178-733-4). Brethren.

Fike, J. L. & Friend, G. E. Understanding Telephone Electronics. 2nd ed. LC 84-50902. (Understanding Ser.). 277p. 1984. pap. text ed. 14.95 (ISBN 0-89512-159-X, LCB7141). Tex Instr Inc.

Fike, Richard A. How to Keep from Being Robbed, Raped, & Ripped Off: A Personal Crime Prevention Manual for You & Your Loved Ones. LC 83-15586. (Illus.). 239p. 1983. 14.95 (ISBN 0-87491-726-3); pap. write for info. (ISBN 0-87491-729-8). Acropolis.

--Personal Crime Prevention: How to Keep from Being Robbed, Raped & Ripped Off. (Illus.). 238p. (Orig.). 1983. pap. 8.95 (ISBN 0-87491-729-8). Acropolis.

Fikentscher, Wolfgang. Draft International Code of Conduct on the Transfer of Technology. (IIC Studies: Vol. 4). 211p. (Orig.). 1980. pap. 30.00x (ISBN 0-89573-030-8). VCH Pubs.

Fikes, R. E., jt. auth. see Walker, D. E.

Fikhtegol'ts, V. S., et al. Ultraviolet Spectra of Elastomers & Rubber Chemicals. LC 66-12889. 170p. 1966. 49.50x (ISBN 0-306-65119-X, IFI Plenum). Plenum Pub.

Fikhtengol'ts, G. M. Fundamentals of Mathematical Analysis, 2 Vols. 1965. Vol. 1. pap. 18.75 (ISBN 0-08-013473-4). Pergamon.

Fikrig, Senih M., ed. Handbook of Immunology for Students & House Staff. LC 82-6878. (Illus.). 203p. 1982. pap. 28.50x (ISBN 0-89573-111-8). VCH Pubs.

Fikusny, Tatiana, et al, trs. see Tesnohlidek, Rudolf.

Fila, Larry V., Jr. Designs Unlimited, Vol. I. Gregg, Chris, ed. LC 82-90955. (Illus.). 68p. (Orig.). 1983. pap. text ed. 15.00 (ISBN 0-9610588-0-3). Filas Des Unltd.

Filarete, Antonio A. Treatise on Architecture: Being the Treatise by Antonio di Piero Averlino, Known As Filarete. Spencer, John R., tr. LC 65-12547. (Yale Publications in the History of Art Ser.: No. 16). Vol. 1 (Translation) pap. 112.50 (ISBN 0-317-10501-9, 2013374); Vol. 2 (Facsimile) pap. 52.50 (ISBN 0-317-10502-7). Bks Demand UMI.

Filaseta, Pat. The Beverly Hills Shopper. Wood, Jayne, ed. (Illus.). 288p. (Orig.). 1984. pap. 5.00 (ISBN 0-9614349-0-2). Golden Tri Pubns.

Filatov, V. P., et al. Lenin the Revolutionary. 1980. 4.00 (ISBN 0-8285-1849-1, Pub. by Progress Pubs USSR). Imported Pubns.

Filbeck, David. The First Fifty Years. LC 80-65966. 336p. 1980. pap. 5.95 (ISBN 0-89900-060-6). College Pr Pub.

--Social Context & Proclamation: A Socio-Cognitive Study in Proclaiming the Gospel Cross Culturally. LC 84-28539. (Illus.). 192p. 1985. pap. text ed. 8.95X (ISBN 0-87808-199-2). William Carey Lib.

Filbee, Marjorie. The Connoisseur Dictionary of Country Furniture. new ed. (Illus.). 1977. 12.95 (ISBN 0-900305-17-7). Hearst Bks.

--Cottage Industries. (Illus.). 192p. 1982. 22.50 (ISBN 0-7153-8286-1). David & Charles.

--Dictionary of Country Furniture. 208p. 1981. 30.00x (ISBN 0-900305-17-7, Pub. by Ebury Pr England). State Mutual Bk.

Filbey, Beverly, ed. see Munz, Elizabeth.

Filbey, John. Natal Charting: How to Master the Techniques of Birth Chart Construction. (Illus.). 192p. 1984. pap. 7.95 (ISBN 0-85030-246-3, Pub. by Aquarian Pr England). Sterling.

Filbey, John & Filbey, Peter. Astronomy for Astrologers. 256p. 1985. pap. 11.95 (ISBN 0-85030-393-1). Newcastle Pub.

Filbey, Peter, jt. auth. see Filbey, John.

Filbrun, J. S. Gemini Rising. 192p. (Orig.). 1982. pap. 2.25 (ISBN 0-449-14493-3, GM). Fawcett.

Filbrun, Jerry A., et al. A Fillbrunn Family History: Various Members of the Families, Fillbrun, Filbrun, Filburn, et al., 1570-1984. LC 85-70102. (Illus.). 300p. Date not set. spiral binding 15.00 (ISBN 0-9614439-0-1). D P Filbrun.

Filby, Birhte. On Disability, the Older Population, Community Service & Volunteerism. (International Exchange of Experts & Information in Rehabilitation Ser.: No. 22). 1983. cancelled (ISBN 0-939986-34-5). World Rehab Fund.

Filby, Frederick A. A History of Food Adulteration & Analysis. LC 75-23707. 1976. Repr. of 1934 ed. 21.00 (ISBN 0-404-13259-6). AMS Pr.

Filby, Jane, jt. ed. see Reid, William.

Filby, Nikola, jt. auth. see Cahen, Leonard.

Filby, P. W. & Howard, Edward G. Star-Spangled Books: Books, Sheet Music, Newspapers, Manuscripts & Persons Associated with the Star-Spangled Banner. LC 70-187215. (Illus.). 200p. 1972. 17.50 (ISBN 0-938420-17-8). Md Hist.

Filby, P. William. American & British Genealogy & Heraldry: A Selected List of Books. 3rd rev. ed. LC 84-865. xix, 940p. 1983. lib. bdg. 49.95 (ISBN 0-88082-004-7). New Eng Hist.

Filby, P. William, ed. Passenger & Immigration Lists Bibliography (1538-1900) Being a Guide to Published Lists of Arrivals in the United States & Canada. 200p. 1981. 90.00x (ISBN 0-8103-1098-8). Gale.

--Passenger & Immigration Lists Bibliography, 1538-1900: Supplement. 125p. 1984. pap. 95.00x (ISBN 0-8103-1098-8). Gale.

--Passenger & Immigration Lists Index: A Reference Guide to Published Lists of About 500,000 Passengers Who Arrived in America in the Seventeenth, Eighteenth & Nineteenth Centuries, 3 vols. 1981. Set. 390.00x (ISBN 0-8103-1099-6). Gale.

--Passenger & Immigration Lists Index: 1983 Supplement. 1984. 120.00x (ISBN 0-8103-1197-6). Gale.

--Passenger & Immigration Lists Index: 1984 Supplement. 800p. 1985. 120.00x (ISBN 0-8103-1791-5). Gale.

--Passenger & Immigration Lists Index: 1985's Supplement. 900p. 1985. 120.00x (ISBN 0-8103-1792-3). Gale.

--Philadelphia Naturalization Records, 1789-1880: Index to Records of Aliens' Declarations of Intention and - or Oaths of Allegiance. 700p. 1982. 285.00x (ISBN 0-8103-1116-X). Gale.

Filby, P. William & Meyer, Mary K., eds. Passenger & Immigration Lists Index 1982: Annual Supplement. 950p. 1983. 120.00x (ISBN 0-317-31590-0). Gale.

--Passenger & Immigration Lists Index: 1982-85 Cumulation. 3100p. 1985. 475.00x (ISBN 0-8103-1795-8). Gale.

Filby, P. William, jt. ed. see Meyer, Mary K.

Filby, Peter. Amazing Mini. (Illus.). cloth hardback 18.95 (ISBN 0-85614-060-0, F395). Haynes Pubns.

--MG 1911 to 1978. (Mini Marque History Ser.). 7.95 (ISBN 0-85429-229-2, F229). Haynes Pubns.

--TVR: Success Against the Odds. 18.95 (ISBN 0-85614-055-4, F408). Haynes Pubns.

Filby, Royston H., et al, eds. Atomic & Nuclear Methods in Fossil Energy Research. LC 81-21169. 518p. 1982. 69.50x (ISBN 0-306-40899-6, Plenum Pr). Plenum Pub.

Fildes, R. & Dews, D., eds. A Bibliography of Business & Economic Forecasting. 432p. 35.00x (ISBN 0-87196-555-0). Facts on File.

Fildes, Valerie. A Social History of Infant Feeding. 400p. 1985. 30.00x (ISBN 0-85224-462-2, Pub. by Edinburgh U Pr Scotland). Columbia U Pr.

Filene, Catherine. Careers for Women. LC 74-3948. (Women in America Ser.). 592p. 1974. Repr. of 1920 ed. 41.00x (ISBN 0-405-06094-7). Ayer Co Pubs.

--Careers for Women. (Women Ser.). 1920. 15.00 (ISBN 0-8482-3970-9). Norwood Edns.

Filene, Edward A. Speaking of Change: A Selection of Speeches & Articles. facsimile ed. LC 76-156640. (Essay Index Reprint Ser). Repr. of 1939 ed. 22.00 (ISBN 0-8369-2355-3). Ayer Co Pubs.

Filene, Peter. Men in the Middle: Coping with the Problems of Work & Family in the Lives of Middle Aged Men. 160p. 1981. 10.95 (ISBN 0-13-574509-8); pap. 5.95 (ISBN 0-13-574491-1). P-H.

Filene, Peter G. Americans & the Soviet Experiment, 1917-1933. LC 67-11669. 1967. 22.50x (ISBN 0-674-03100-8). Harvard U Pr.

Filer, E. W., et al, eds. Microstructural Science, Vol. 4. 370p. 1976. 74.75 (ISBN 0-444-00184-0). Elsevier.

Filesi, Teobaldo. China & Africa in the Middle Ages. Morrison, D. L., tr. (Illus.). 104p. 1972. 28.50x (ISBN 0-7146-2604-X, F Cass Co). Biblio Dist.

Filgate, Macartney. Runway to Death. LC 80-52080. Orig. Title: Bravo Charley. 154p. 1980. 9.95 (ISBN 0-8027-5428-7). Walker & Co.

Filho, Fernando Venancio see Venancio Filho, Fernando.

Filichia, Peter. A Boy's-Eye View of Girls. 128p. (Orig.). (gr. 7 up). 1983. pap. 1.95 (ISBN 0-590-32314-8). Scholastic Inc.

--Cute is not a Compliment. 224p. (Orig.). 1986. pap. 2.50 (ISBN 0-449-70127-1, Juniper). Fawcett.

--Don't Mean to Be Mean. 160p. 1983. pap. 1.95 (ISBN 0-441-15841-2). Ace Bks.

--Everything But Tuesdays & Sundays. 142p. (Orig.). 1984. pap. 1.95 (ISBN 0-449-70047-X, Juniper). Fawcett.

--A Matter of Finding the Right Girl. 208p. (Orig.). 1985. pap. 2.25 (ISBN 0-449-70107-7, Juniper). Fawcett.

--Two by Two Romance, No. 8: Falling in Love Again, No. 8. 192p. (Orig.). 1984. pap. 1.95 (ISBN 0-446-32028-5). Warner Bks.

Filichia, Peter, jt. auth. see Finberg, Pauline.

Filinovskii, V. Yu., jt. auth. see Pleskov, Yu. V.

Filip, Jan. Enzyklopaedisches Hanbuch zur Ur und Fruehgeschichte Europas, Vol. 1. 664p. (Ger.). 1966. 90.00 (ISBN 3-17-084035-5, M-7084). French & Eur.

--Enzyklopaedisches Handbuch zur Ur und Fruehgeschichte Europas, Vol. 2. 1091p. (Ger.). 1969. 90.00 (ISBN 3-17-084036-3, M-7085). French & Eur.

Filipczak, James, jt. auth. see Cohen, Harold L.

Filipek, Nina, jt. auth. see Thorley, David W.

Filipeli, Al. Tanks & Armored Vehicles. (Coloring Experiences Ser.). 48p. (Orig.). 1983. pap. 2.95 (ISBN 0-8431-1025-2). Price Stern.

Filipi, Emily. One Hundred & One Word Puzzles on the Bible. LC 84-21445. 1985. pap. 3.95 (ISBN 0-8054-9110-4). Broadman.

--One Hundred Word Puzzles on the Bible. LC 81-68367. 1982. pap. 2.95 (ISBN 0-8054-9107-4). Broadman.

--Scripture Facts the Easy Way. (Quiz & Puzzle Books). 1980. pap. 1.95 (ISBN 0-8010-3491-4). Baker Bk.

Filipiniana Book Guild & Scott, William H., eds. German Travelers on the Cordillera (1860-1890, Vol. 23. 1975. 20.00x (ISBN 0-686-18669-9). Cellar.

Filipovic, R. Croatian-English, English-Croatian Small Pocket Dictionary. (Langenscheidt.). 1981. pap. 12.00x (ISBN 0-89918-727-7, Y-727). Vanous.

--Deluxe English-Croatian Dictionary. 10th rev. ed. 1980. 75.00 (ISBN 0-317-19025-3, Y779). Vanous.

--Langenscheidt Croatian-English Pocket Dictionary. 1979. 20.00 (ISBN 0-317-19022-9, Y781). Vanous.

--Langenscheidt English-Croatian, Croatian-English Small Pocket Dictionary. pap. 12.00 (ISBN 0-317-19023-7, Y727). Vanous.

--Langenscheidt English-Croatian Pocket Dictionary. 1979. 20.00 (ISBN 0-317-19020-2, Y780). Vanous.

Filipovic, Rudolf. English-Croatian or Serbian Dictionary. 1436p. (Eng. & Serbocroatian.). 1980. 150.00x (ISBN 0-569-08646-9, Pub. by Collets). State Mutual Bk.

Filipovic, Rudolf, et al. English-Serbocroatian Dictionary. 10th ed. (Eng. & Serbocroatian.). 1975. 50.00x (ISBN 0-686-19960-X). Intl Learn Syst.

Filipovitch, Anthony & Reeves, Earl, eds. Urban Community: A Guide to Information Sources. LC 78-13171. (The Urban Studies Information Guide Ser.: Vol. 4). 1978. 60.00x (ISBN 0-8103-1429-0). Gale.

Filippazzo, Vincent. Alessandro. 352p. (Orig.). 1985. pap. 3.95 (ISBN 0-553-24997-5). Bantam.

Filippelli, Ronald L. Labor in the United States. 320p. 1984. pap. text ed. 10.95 (ISBN 0-394-34149-X, RanC). Random.

Filippi, Joseph De. Essai d'une Bibliographie Generale du Theatre. 223p. 1861. Repr. 29.00 (ISBN 0-8337-3312-5). B Franklin.

Filippi, Joseph De see Contant, Clement & De Filippi, Joseph.

Filippi, P., ed. Theoretical Acoustics & Numerical Techniques. (CISM International Centre for Mechanical Sciences, Courses & Lectures Ser.: No. 277). xiv, 348p. 1983. pap. 23.20 (ISBN 0-387-81786-7). Springer-Verlag.

Filippis, Michele de see De Filippis, Michele.

Filippo, Eduardo de see De Filippo, Eduardo.

Filippo, Eduardo De see De Filippo, Eduardo.

Filippov, B. Actors Without Make-up. 278p. 1977. 6.95 (ISBN 0-8285-0926-3, Pub. by Progress Pubs USSR). Imported Pubns.

Filippov, N. D., et al. Ten Papers on Algebra & Functional Analysis. LC 51-5559. (Translations Ser.: No. 2, Vol. 96). 1970. 32.00 (ISBN 0-8218-1796-5, TRANS 2-96). Am Math.

Filippov, S. Theory of Metallurgical Processes. 296p. 1975. 10.00 (ISBN 0-8285-2231-6, Pub. by Mir Pubs USSR). Imported Pubns.

Filippov, V. V. Quality Control Procedures for Meteorological Use. (World Weather Watch Planning Reports: No. 26). 1968. pap. 12.00 (ISBN 0-685-22334-5, W238, WMO). Unipub.

Filisola, Vicente. Memoirs for the History of the War in Texas. Woolsey, Wallace, tr. (Illus.). 256p. (Span.). 1985. 16.95 (ISBN 0-89015-461-9). Eakin Pubns.

Filkens, James P., jt. ed. see Reichard, Sherwood M.

Filkins & Russo. Human Prenatal Diagnosis. 360p. 1985. 75.00 (ISBN 0-8247-7368-3). Dekker.

Filkins, James P., jt. ed. see Reichard, Sherwood M.

Filla, Wilhelm, et al. Am Rande Oesterreichs: Ein Beitrag zur Soziologie der Oesterreichischen Volksgruppen. 126p. 1982. pap. 10.95 (ISBN 3-7003-0307-6). Slavica.

Fillard, J. P. & Van Turnhout, J., eds. Thermally Stimulated Processes in Solids - New Prospects: Proceedings of an International Workshop, Montpellier, June, 1976. 302p. 1977. 72.50 (ISBN 0-444-41652-8). Elsevier.

Fillebrown, C. B. The ABC of Taxation. 1909. 15.00 (ISBN 0-686-17731-2). Quest Edns.

Fillenbaum, Samuel. Syntactic Factors in Memory? (Janua Linguarum Ser. Minor: No. 168). 1973. pap. text ed. 10.80x (ISBN 0-686-22590-2). Mouton.

Fillenbaum, Samuel & Rapoport, Amnon. Structures in the Subjective Lexicon: An Experimental Approach to the Study of Semantic Fields. 1971. 46.00 (ISBN 0-12-256250-X). Acad Pr.

Filler. A Question of Quality. 1976. 13.95 (ISBN 0-87972-077-8); pap. 7.95 (ISBN 0-87972-078-6). Bowling Green Univ.

Filler, Aaron. Apple Thesaurus. 896p. (Orig.). 1984. pap. 29.95 (ISBN 0-88190-346-9, BO346). Datamost.

Filler, Louis. Appointment at Armageddon: Muckraking & Progressivism in American Life. LC 75-23865. (Contributions in American Studies: No. 20). (Illus.). 476p. 1976. lib. bdg. 29.95 (ISBN 0-8371-8261-1, FAR). Greenwood.

--The Crusade Against Slavery, 1830-1860. LC 60-13441. (New American Nation Ser.). (Illus.). 1960. 20.00xi (ISBN 0-06-011235-2, HarpT). Har-Row.

--Dictionary of American Social Change. LC 82-10036. 266p. (Orig.). 1982. 18.50 (ISBN 0-89874-242-0); pap. 10.50 (ISBN 0-89874-564-0). Krieger.

--Dictionary of American Social Reform. LC 74-90505. Repr. of 1963 ed. lib. bdg. 26.25x (ISBN 0-8371-2137-X, FIAS). Greenwood.

--The Muckrakers. rev. ed. LC 75-27152. (Illus.). 466p. 1975. 24.95x (ISBN 0-271-01212-9); pap. 12.50 (ISBN 0-271-01213-7). Pa St U Pr.

--The Rise & Fall of Slavery in America. ix, 165p. 1981. lib. bdg. 10.95x (ISBN 0-89198-122-5); pap. text ed. 6.95x (ISBN 0-89198-123-3). Ozer.

--Seasoned Authors for a New Season: The Search for Standards in Popular Writing. LC 79-90128. 1980. 15.95 (ISBN 0-87972-143-X). Bowling Green Univ.

--Vanguards & Followers: Youth in the American Tradition. LC 78-5893. 268p. 1978. 21.95x (ISBN 0-88229-459-8). Nelson-Hall.

--Voice of the Democracy: A Critical Biography of David Graham Phillips, Journalist, Novelist, Progressive. LC 77-13893. 1978. 22.50x (ISBN 0-271-00528-9). Pa St U Pr.

Filler, Louis, intro. by. Contemporaries: Portraits in the Progressive Era by David Graham Phillips. LC 80-39644. (Contributions in American Studies: No. 56). 232p. 1981. lib. bdg. 29.95 (ISBN 0-313-22487-0, FCP/). Greenwood.

Filler, Louis, ed. Democrats & Republicans: Ten Years of the Republic. 11.50 (ISBN 0-8446-2057-2). Peter Smith.

--From Populism to Progressivism: Representative Selections. LC 77-21444. 312p. 1978. pap. 7.95 (ISBN 0-88275-584-6). Krieger.

--Horace Mann on the Crisis in Education. LC 83-6510. 266p. 1983. pap. text ed. 13.25 (ISBN 0-8191-3164-4). U Pr of Amer.

--The President in the Twentieth Century, Vol. I: The Ascendant President: From William McKinley to Lyndon B. Johnson. 424p. lib. bdg. 22.95x (ISBN 0-89198-127-6); pap. text ed. 12.95x (ISBN 0-89198-128-4). Ozer.

Filler, Louis & Guttmann, Allen, eds. The Removal of the Cherokee Nation: Manifest Destiny or National Dishonor? LC 76-53820. 128p. 1977. pap. 5.50 (ISBN 0-88275-482-3). Krieger.

Filler, Louis, ed. see Hardy, Irene.

Filler, Louis, ed. see Phillips, Wendell.

Filler, Martin. Art & Architecture & Landscape: The Clos Pegase Design Competition. LC 85-8329. (Illus.). 104p. 1985. pap. 15.95 (ISBN 0-918471-03-6). San Fran Mod.

Filler, R. & Kobayashi, Y., eds. Biomedical Aspects of Fluorine Chemistry. 256p. 1983. 74.50 (ISBN 0-444-80466-8, I-133-83, Biomedical Pr). Elsevier.

Filler, Ronald C., jt. auth. see Alexander, J. Estill.

Filler, Trenton. Notes to My Former Lover. 1984. 5.95 (ISBN 0-8062-2365-0). Carlton.

Filley, Alan, jt. auth. see Delbecq, Andre.

Filley, Alan C. The Compleat Manager: What Works When. LC 85-70081. 248p. 1985. pap. 10.95 (ISBN 0-9614511-0-6). Green Briar Pr.

--Interpersonal Conflict Resolution. 180p. 1975. pap. 13.65x (ISBN 0-673-07589-3). Scott F.

Filley, Dorothy M. Recapturing Wisdom's Valley, the Watervliet Shaker Heritage, 1775-1975. (Illus.). 10.00 (ISBN 0-686-32422-6); pap. text ed. 5.00 (ISBN 0-686-32423-4). Albany Hist & Art.

--Recapturing Wisdom's Valley: The Watervliet Shaker Heritage, 1775-1975. Richmond, Mary L., ed. LC 75-27133. (Illus.). 128p. 1975. 10.00 (ISBN 0-89062-010-5, Pub by Albany Institute of History & Art); pap. 5.00 (ISBN 0-89062-029-6). Pub Ctr Cult Res.

Filley, Richard D. & Szoka, Kathryn. Communicating with Graphics: A Series from Industrial Engineering. 1982. pap. text ed. 19.50 (ISBN 0-89806-036-2, 627); pap. text ed. 15.00 members. Inst Indus Eng.

Fillingham, Patricia. Anna's Elephant. (Illus.). 30p. 1983. pap. 5.00 (ISBN 0-942292-02-2). Warthog Pr.

--John Calvin. (Illus.). 42p. 1983. pap. 5.00 (ISBN 0-942292-04-9). Warthog Pr.

--Progress Notes on a State of Mind. 55p. 1980. pap. 2.00 (ISBN 0-942292-07-3). Warthog Pr.

Fillingham, Paul. Basic Guide to Flying. 1977. pap. 5.95 (ISBN 0-8015-0526-7, Hawthorn). Dutton.

--The New Basic Guide to Flying. (Illus.). 1984. 24.95 (ISBN 0-13-611815-1); pap. 9.95 (ISBN 0-13-611807-0). P-H.

--Pilot's Guide to the Lesser Antilles. LC 78-27491. (Illus.). 1979. 15.95 (ISBN 0-07-020815-8). McGraw.

Filliou, Robert. Ample Food for Stupid Thought. LC 65-19530. 1965. 20.00 (ISBN 0-89366-052-3). Ultramarine Pub.

Filliou, Robert, jt. auth. see Brecht, George.

Filliozat, J. The Classical Doctrine of Indian Medicine: Its Origins & Greek Parallels. Chanana, Devraj, tr. from Fr. 320p. 1964. 45.00x (ISBN 0-686-78819-2, Pub. by Bks India England). State Mutual Bk.

Filliozat, V., jt. auth. see Michell, G.

Fillis, James. Breaking & Riding. Hayes, M. H., tr. (Illus.). write for info. (ISBN 0-85131-044-3, NL51, Dist. by Sporting Book Center). J A Allen.

Fillmore, Charles. Atom-Smashing Power of Mind. 1949. 4.95 (ISBN 0-87159-001-8). Unity School.

--Charles Fillmore Concordance. 1975. 3.95 (ISBN 0-87159-015-8). Unity School.

--Christian Healing. 1909. 4.95 (ISBN 0-87159-017-4). Unity School.

--Curacion Cristiana. LC 84-52152. 160p. (Span.). 4.95 (ISBN 0-87159-020-4). Unity School.

--Dynamics for Living. 1967. 4.95 (ISBN 0-87159-025-5). Unity School.

--Guarda una Cuaresma Verdadera. 214p. (Span.). 1983. 4.95 (ISBN 0-87159-076-X). Unity School.

--Jesucristo Sana (Jesus Christ Heals) 200p. (Span.). 1984. 4.95 (ISBN 0-87159-071-9). Unity School.

--Jesus Christ Heals. 1939. 4.95 (ISBN 0-87159-070-0). Unity School.

--Keep a True Lent. 1982. 4.95 (ISBN 0-87159-076-X). Unity School.

--Mysteries of Genesis. 1936. 4.95 (ISBN 0-87159-104-9). Unity School.

--Mysteries of John. 1946. 4.95 (ISBN 0-87159-105-7). Unity School.

--Prosperity. 1936. 4.95 (ISBN 0-87159-130-8). Unity School.

--Revealing Word. 1959. 4.95 (ISBN 0-87159-137-5). Unity School.

--Talks on Truth. 1926. 4.95 (ISBN 0-87159-151-0). Unity School.

--Twelve Powers of Man. 1930. 4.95 (ISBN 0-87159-157-X). Unity School.

Fillmore, Charles & Fillmore, Cora. Teach Us to Pray. 1976. 4.95 (ISBN 0-87159-152-9). Unity School.

Fillmore, Charles F., et al, eds. Individual Differences in Language Ability & Language Behavior. LC 78-20044. (Perspectives in Neurolinguistics & Psycholinguistics Ser.). 1979. 40.00 (ISBN 0-12-255950-9). Acad Pr.

Fillmore, Charles J. & Langendoen, D. Terence, eds. Studies in Linguistic Semantics. LC 74-140383. 307p. 1983. Repr. of 1971 ed. 39.50x (ISBN 0-8290-0982-5). Irvington.

Fillmore, Cora, jt. auth. see Fillmore, Charles.

Fillmore, Cora D. Christ Enthroned in Man. 1981. 4.95. Unity School.

Fillmore, Donna. Let's Teach with Bible Games. (Teaching Helps Ser.). 1979. pap. 2.95 (ISBN 0-8010-3488-4). Baker Bk.

Fillmore, Donna, ed. Leading Children In Worship, Vol. 1, 2, 3. 216p. 1982. pap. 7.95 each (ISBN 0-8341-0767-8). Beacon Hill.

Fillmore, John C. Pianoforte Music: Its History. LC 77-92444. 1978. Repr. of 1884 ed. lib. bdg. 25.00 (ISBN 0-89341-428-X). Longwood Pub Group.

Fillmore, Lowell. Health, Wealth & Happiness. 1964. 4.95 (ISBN 0-87159-055-7). Unity School.

Fillmore, Millard & Severance, F. H., eds. Millard Fillmore Papers, 2 Vols. LC 8-10420. Repr. of 1907 ed. Set. 39.00 ea. (ISBN 0-527-29300-8). Kraus Repr.

Fillmore, Myrtle. Come Dejar Que Dios Te Ayude. 1984. 4.95 (ISBN 0-87159-019-0). Unity School.

--How to Let God Help You. 1956. 4.95 (ISBN 0-87159-057-3). Unity School.

--Myrtle Fillmore's Healing Letters. 1936. 4.95 (ISBN 0-87159-103-0). Unity School.

Fillmore, P. A., ed. see Conference on Operator Theory, Dalhousie Univ., Halifax, 1973.

Fillmore, Parker H. Czechoslovak Fairy Tales. LC 78-67709. (The Folktale). (Illus.). 1980. Repr. of 1919 ed. 23.50 (ISBN 0-404-16086-7). AMS Pr.

Fillmore, Timothy R., ed. The Major Art Works by Frederic Remington with Explanations & Critical Commentaries. (Illus.). 112p. 1981. 81.75 (ISBN 0-86650-008-1). Gloucester Art.

Fillol, Tomas R. Social Factors in Economic Development: The Argentine Case. LC 75-28498. (M.I.T. Research Monograph). 118p. 1975. Repr. of 1961 ed. lib. bdg. 15.00x (ISBN 0-8371-8432-0, FISF). Greenwood.

Filman, Charlotte P. In This Our World. LC 74-3951. (Women in American Ser). (Illus.). 232p. 1974. Repr. of 1899 ed. 18.00x (ISBN 0-405-06098-X). Ayer Co Pubs.

Filman, Robert E. & Friedman, Daniel P. Coordinated Computing: Tools & Techniques for Distributed Software. 320p. 1984. 38.95 (ISBN 0-07-022439-0). McGraw.

Filmer, Richard. Hops & Hop Picking. (History in Camera Ser.). (Illus., Orig.). 1982. pap. 6.95 (ISBN 0-85263-617-2, Pub. by Shire Pubns England). Seven Hills Bks.

Filmer, Robert. Patriarcha & Other Political Works of Sir Robert Filmer. LC 83-48568. (The Philosophy of John Locke Ser.). 326p. 1985. lib. bdg. 40.00 (ISBN 0-8240-5604-3). Garland Pub.

Filmer, Robert see Locke, John.

Filmer-Sankey, Josephine, jt. auth. see Denny, Norman.

Filmore, Charles. Descubre Tu Poder Interno. LC 81-69933. Orig. Title: Discover the Power Within You. 448p. (Eng.). 1983. 4.95 (ISBN 0-87159-026-3). Unity School.

Filmus, Tully. Tully Filmus: Selected Drawings. LC 70-151314. 96p. 1978. pap. 11.95 (ISBN 0-8276-0164-6, 424). Jewish Pubns.

Filon, Augustin. English Stage. Whyte, Frederic, tr. LC 71-102846. 1970. Repr. of 1897 ed. 26.50x (ISBN 0-8046-0753-2, Pub. by Kennikat). Assoc Faculty Pr.

--English Stage: Being an Account of the Victorian Drama. LC 70-81208. 1897. 24.50 (ISBN 0-405-08513-3, Blom Pubns). Ayer Co Pubs.

Filonidov, A. M., jt. auth. see Tret'yakov, A. K.

Filoromo, Tina, jt. auth. see Ziff, Dolores.

Filov, V. A., et al. Quantitative Toxicology: Selected Topics. LC 78-12530. (Environmental Science & Technology Ser.). 462p. 1979. 98.50 (ISBN 0-471-02109-1, Pub. by Wiley-Interscience). Wiley.

Fils, David H. The Developmental Disabilities Handbook. LC 79-57296. (Professional Handbook Ser.). 50p. 1980. pap. 14.50 (ISBN 0-87424-139-1). Western Psych.

Filsinger, Cheryl. Locus. 4th ed. 192p. 1982. pap. 35.00 (ISBN 0-916754-02-2). Filsinger & Co.

--Locus. 5th ed. 236p. 1985. pap. 39.00 (ISBN 0-916754-04-9). Filsinger & Co.

--Locus Select. (Locus Ser.). 120p. 1980. pap. 25.00 (ISBN 0-916754-16-2). Filsinger & Co.

Filsinger, Erik E. & Lewis, Robert A. Assessing Marriages: New Behavioral Approaches. (Sage Focus Editions: Vol. 34). 320p. 1981. 28.00 (ISBN 0-8039-1570-5); pap. 14.00 (ISBN 0-8039-1571-3). Sage.

Filsinger, Erik E., ed. Marriage & Family Assessment: A Sourcebook for Family Therapy. 352p. 1983. 29.95 (ISBN 0-8039-2028-8). Sage.

Filsinger, Tomas. The Aztec Cosmos. 32p. (Orig.). 1984. 9.95 (ISBN 0-89087-352-6). Celestial Arts.

Filskov, Susan B. & Boll, Thomas J., eds. Handbook of Clinical Neuropsychology. LC 80-15392. (Personality Processes Ser.). 806p. 1981. 53.95x (ISBN 0-471-04802-X, Pub. by Wiley-Interscience). Wiley.

Filson, Brent. Exploring with Lasers. (Illus.). 96p. (gr. 4 up). 1984. 8.79 (ISBN 0-671-50573-4). Messner.

--Smoke Jumpers. LC 76-56289. (A Signal Bk.). (gr. 7 up). 1978. pap. 5.95 (ISBN 0-385-12790-1). Doubleday.

Filson, F. V., jt. ed. see Wright, G. Ernest.

Filson, Floyd V. John. LC 59-10454. (Layman's Bible Commentary Ser: Vol. 19). 1963. pap. 4.95 (ISBN 0-8042-3079-X). John Knox.

--A New Testament History: The Story of the Emerging Church. LC 64-15360. (Illus.). 464p. 1964. 12.95 (ISBN 0-664-20525-9). Westminster.

--Yesterday: A Study of Hebrews in the Light of Chapter 13. LC 67-7015. (Studies in Biblical Theology: 2nd Ser., No. 4). 1967. pap. text ed. 10.00x (ISBN 0-8401-3054-6). A R Allenson.

Filson, Floyd V., jt. ed. see Wright, G. Ernest.

Filson, Henry J. Little Hands with First Drawing Practice. (Draw-Sketch Practice Ser.). (Illus.). 28p. (gr. 10 up). 1978. bdg. 2.75plastic (ISBN 0-918554-01-2). Old Violin.

--Senior Hi Artist. (Draw-Sketch Practice Ser.). (Illus.). 44p. (gr. 12 up). 1978. plastic bdg. 3.75 (ISBN 0-918554-02-0). Old Violin.

--Sketch & Draw Today. (Illus.). 1976. plastic bdg. 12.00x (ISBN 0-918554-00-4); library 9.60. Old Violin.

Filson, Wright. Atlas Historico Westminster De la Biblia. 134p. 1981. pap. 19.95 (ISBN 0-311-15030-6). Casa Bautista.

Filstead, William J. & Rossi, Jean J., eds. Alcohol & Alcohol Problems: New Thinking & New Direcitons. 302p. 1976. 17.50 (ISBN 0-318-15275-4). Natl Coun Alcoholism.

Filstead, William J., et al, eds. Alcohol & Alcohol Problems: New Thinking & New Directions. LC 76-7401. 320p. 1976. prof ref 29.95 (ISBN 0-88410-115-0). Ballinger Pub.

Filston, Howard & Izant, Robert. Surgical Neonate: Evaluation & Care. (Illus.). 288p. 1978. pap. 18.95 (ISBN 0-8385-8716-X). ACC.

Filston, Howard C. Surgical Problems in Children: Recognition & Referral. LC 81-11121. (Illus.). 596p. 1982. text ed. 52.95 (ISBN 0-8016-1574-7). Mosby.

Filston, Howard C. & Izant, Robert, Jr. The Surgical Neonate. 2nd ed. 320p. 1985. write for info. (ISBN 0-8385-8717-8). ACC.

Filstrup, Chris & Filstrup, Janie. Beadazzled. LC 81-3426. (Illus.). 192p. (gr. 7 up). 1982. 12.95 (ISBN 0-7232-6204-7). Warne.

--China: From Emperors to Communes. (Discovering Our Heritage Ser.). (Illus.). 144p. (gr. 5 up). 1983. PLB 10.95 (ISBN 0-87518-227-5). Dillon.

Filstrup, Jane. Monday Through Friday: Daycare Alternatives. 1982. pap. 13.95x (ISBN 0-8077-2670-2). Tchrs Coll.

Filstrup, Janie, jt. auth. see Filstrup, Chris.

Filter, Douglas. Demonstrative Evidence Sourcebook. Ward, Gene, et al, eds. (Illus.). 196p. 1985. 129.00 (ISBN 0-932301-00-2). Staffort Hart.

Filter, Maynard D. Communication Disorders: A Handbook for Educators. (Illus.). 192p. 1977. 19.75x (ISBN 0-398-03650-0). C C Thomas.

--Phonatory Voice Disorders in Children. (Illus.). 202p. 1982. 22.75x (ISBN 0-398-04679-4). C C Thomas.

--Speech-Language Clinician's Handbook. (Illus.). 344p. 1979. 38.50x (ISBN 0-398-03899-6). C C Thomas.

Filter Press Staff. Camping Log Book for Trailer, Camper & Motor Home Users. 55p. 1974. pap. 1.50 (ISBN 0-910584-41-9). Filter.

Filthaut, Theodor, ed. Israel in Christian Religious Instruction. (Contemporary Catechetics Ser.: Vol. 3). 1965. pap. 1.25x (ISBN 0-268-00144-8). U of Notre Dame Pr.

Filtzer, Donald, tr. & ed. see Rubin, Isaac Illyich.

Filtzer, Donald A., ed. see Preobrazhensky, E. A.

Filvaroff, Joan, jt. auth. see Hazeltine, Cheryl.

Fimbres, Eric C. Approaching Re-Creation: A Form for Seeing the Delicate Threads. LC 82-90184. (Illus.). 208p. (Orig.). 1982. pap. 5.95 (ISBN 0-9608946-0-8). Life Sustaining.

Fimian, et al. A Teachers Guide to Human Resources in Special Education: Paraprofessionals, Volunteers, & Peer Tutors. 1985. 30.72 (ISBN 0-205-08096-0, 248096). Allyn.

Fimian, Michael J. Managing Human Resources in Special Education. LC 84-17685. 366p. 1984. 32.95 (ISBN 0-03-072063-X). Praeger.

Fimian, Michael J., et al. Guide to Human Resources in Special Education: Paraprofessionals, Volunteers & Peer Tutors. 1984. text ed. 30.72 guidebook (ISBN 0-205-08096-0, 248096). Allyn.

Finacchiaro, Mary & Bonomo, Michael. The Foreign Language Learner: A Guide for Teachers. 1973. pap. text ed. 6.75 (ISBN 0-88345-088-7, 18071, 18072). Regents Pub.

Finan. Exec & Brookings Inst. Options for Tax Reform. 1984. 8.00 (ISBN 0-317-28557-2). Finan Exec.

Finan, Gerard, tr. see Noelle-Neumann, Elisabeth & Neumann, Erich P.

Finan, John J. & Child, John, eds. Latin America: International Relations: A Guide to Information Sources. LC 73-117508. (International Relations Information Guide Ser.: Vol.11). 250p. 1981. 60.00x (ISBN 0-8103-1325-1). Gale.

Finance, Charles. Buffet Catering. (Illus.). 1958. 21.95 (ISBN 0-8104-9401-9). Hayden.

Financial Accounting Standards Board. Accounting Standards: Complete 1984 Edition. 1952p. 1984. 30.90 (ISBN 0-07-079459-6). McGraw.
--Accounting Standards: Current Text-General Standards. 1440p. 1984. 18.95 (ISBN 0-07-020916-2); pap. 11.95 (ISBN 0-07-020917-0). McGraw.
--Accounting Standards: Original Pronouncements-Complete Edition. 2304p. 1984. 30.90 (ISBN 0-07-079460-X). McGraw.
--Accounting Standards: Original Pronouncements; July 1973-June 1, 1984. 1664p. 1984. 20.95 (ISBN 0-07-020919-7). McGraw.
--Accounting Standards: Original Pronouncements-Through June 1973. 640p. 1984. 9.95 (ISBN 0-07-020918-9). McGraw.
--Current Text: 1984-1986 Edition. 1952p. 1984. 275.00 (ISBN 0-07-020912-X). McGraw.
--Field Tests of Financial Reporting in Units of General Purchasing Power. LC 77-76684. (The Financial Accounting Standards Board Research Report). (Illus.). 81p. (Orig.). 1977. pap. 3.00 (ISBN 0-910065-01-2). Finan Acct.
--Financial Accounting Standards Board Current Text 1982-1984: International. 1800p. 1982. loose leaf ed. International 300.00 (ISBN 0-07-020902-2). McGraw.
Financial Acctg Standards Bd. Accounting Standards: Current Text (as of June 1, 1985), Complete Edition. 1985. Set. write for info. shrink-wrapped (ISBN 0-07-020936-7). McGraw.
--Accounting Standards: Current Text (as of June 1, 1985) General Standards. 1985. write for info. (ISBN 0-07-020941-3). McGraw.
--Accounting Standards: Current Text (as of June 1, 1985) Industry Standards. 1985. write for info. (ISBN 0-07-020942-1). McGraw.
--Accounting Standards: Original Pronouncements, Complete Edition. 1985. Set. write for info. (ISBN 0-07-020937-5). McGraw.
--Accounting Standards: Original Pronouncements, July 1973 - June 1, 1985. 1985. write for info. (ISBN 0-07-020938-3). McGraw.
--Accounting Standards: Original Pronouncements, Through June 1973. 1985. write for info. (ISBN 0-07-020939-1). McGraw.
--Accounting Standards: Statements of Financial Accounting Concepts 1-5. 1985. write for info. (ISBN 0-07-020940-5). McGraw.
Financial Consulting Staff. Investment Banking. 1985. 95.00 (ISBN 0-938124-07-2). P R Lees-Haley.
Financial Publishing Co. Bond Yield Tables, Four Percent to Fourteen Percent Nos. 154, 254, 2 vols. 8.50 ea. Finan Pub.
--Mortgage Payment Tables. 5.95; No. 553. 5.75; No. 492. 5.95; No. 592. 5.95. Finan Pub.
--Prepayment Mortgage Yield Table No. 435. 6th ed. 25.00 (ISBN 0-685-02555-1). Finan Pub.
Financial Publishing Company. Advance Payments Table No. 12. 32.00 (ISBN 0-685-41729-8). Finan Pub.
--Continuous Compounding Savings Factor Tables No. 534. 19.50 (ISBN 0-685-02537-3). Finan Pub.
--Coupon Interest Calendar - 360-Day Basis No. 360. 30.25 (ISBN 0-685-02539-X). Finan Pub.
--Discount & Equivalent Interest Tables No. 948. 50.00 (ISBN 0-685-02540-3). Finan Pub.
--Expanded Bond Values Tables. No. 63. pocket ed. 32.00 (ISBN 0-685-02541-1). Finan Pub.
--Financial Compound Interest & Annuity Tables No. 376. 6th ed. 49.95 (ISBN 0-685-02543-8). Finan Pub.
--Financial Constant Percent Amortization Table No. 387. 5.95 (ISBN 0-685-02544-6). Finan Pub.
--Financial Monthly Mortgage Handbook: Ten percent to Twenty-Four percent, No. 158. 4th ed. 19.95 (ISBN 0-685-47820-3). Finan Pub.
--Monthly Payment Direct Reduction Loan Amortization Schedules No. 185. 13th ed. 49.95 (ISBN 0-685-02550-0). Finan Pub.
--Yields If Prepaid, Seventy-Eight's Method No. 841. 12.95 (ISBN 0-685-02561-6). Finan Pub.
Financial Publishing Company, ed. see Mason, James J.
Financial Publishing Company Editors, ed. Financial Pass-Through Yield & Value Tables for GNMA Mortgage-Backed Securities No. 715. 7th ed. 31.50 (ISBN 0-685-47818-1). Finan Pub.
Financial Publishing Company Staff. American Institute of Real Estate Appraisers Financial Tables, No. 373. 29.50 (ISBN 0-317-17317-0). Finan Pub.
--Bond Value Tables, No. 183. 49.95 (ISBN 0-317-17314-6). Finan Pub.
--Constant Prepayment Rate Yield Tables for FNMA Mortgage-Backed Securities, No. 662. 35.00 (ISBN 0-317-17321-9). Finan Pub.
--Constant Prepayment Rate Yield Tables for FHLMC Mortgage Participation Certificates, No. 661. 35.00 (ISBN 0-317-17320-0). Finan Pub.
--Constant Prepayment Rate Yield Tables for GNMA Mortgage-Backed Securities, No. 660. 35.00 (ISBN 0-317-17319-7). Finan Pub.
--The Cost of Personal Borrowing in the United States. Gushee, Charles H., ed. (Illus.). 1985. perfect bound 49.95 (ISBN 0-685-87665-9, 830). Finan Pub.
--Daily Compounding Savings Factor Tables, No. 533. 19.50 (ISBN 0-317-17315-4). Finan Pub.
--FHA & FHA-GPM Mortgage Payment Tables, No. 721. 5.95 (ISBN 0-317-17311-1). Finan Pub.
--Financial Eighth Rate Mortgage Tables, No. 267. 5.95 (ISBN 0-317-17312-X). Finan Pub.
--Net Yield Table for GNMA ARM Mortgage-Backed Securities, No. 663. 35.00 (ISBN 0-317-17322-7). Finan Pub.
--Pass-Through Yield & Value Table for FHLMC Mortgage Participation Certificates, No. 615. 2nd ed. 31.50 (ISBN 0-317-17318-9). Finan Pub.
--Payment Tables for Canadian Mortgages, No. 42. 5.95 (ISBN 0-317-17313-8). Finan Pub.
Finar, I. L. Stereochemistry & the Chemistry of Natural Products. 2nd ed. (Organic Chemistry Ser.: Vol. 2). 834p. 1959. 26.95 (ISBN 0-471-25888-1). Halsted Pr.
Finar, Ivor L. Problems & Their Solutions in Organic Chemistry. LC 73-166074. pap. 92.30 (ISBN 0-317-09079-8, 2010050). Bks Demand UMI.
Finasnd, Mary J. Diabetic High Fiber Cookbook. LC 85-9876. 160p. (Orig.). 1985. 13.95 (ISBN 0-8069-5584-8); pap. 7.95 (ISBN 0-8069-6228-3). Sterling.
Finazzo, Giancarlo. The Notion of Tao in Lao Tzu & Chuang Tsu. 240p. 1980. 11.95 (ISBN 0-89955-146-7, Pub. by Mei Ya China). Intl Spec Bk.
--Principle or Tien. 161p. 1980. 11.95 (ISBN 0-89955-145-9, Pub. by Mei Ya China). Intl Spec Bk.
Finberg. Collection of Accounts. (The Law in Pennsylvania Ser.). 24.95 (ISBN 0-686-90970-4). Harrison Co GA.
--Products Liability. (The Law in Tennessee Ser.). incl. latest pocket part supplement 24.95 (ISBN 0-686-91010-9); separate pocket part supplement, 1982 for usein 1983 11.45 (ISBN 0-686-91011-7). Harrison Co GA.
Finberg & Hightower, Emily. Products Liability. (The Law in North Carolina Ser.). incl. latest pocket part supplement 24.95 (ISBN 0-686-90948-8); separate pocket part supplement, 1981 12.45 (ISBN 0-686-90949-6). Harrison Co GA.
Finberg, jt. auth. see Lee.
Finberg, H. P. The Formation of England 500-1042. 1974. 14.95x (ISBN 0-19-520117-5). Oxford U Pr.
--The Formation of England: 550-1042. (Paladin History of England Ser.). 253p. 1983. pap. 7.95 (ISBN 0-586-08248-4, Pub. by Granada England). Academy Chi Pubs.
--Tavistock Abbey. LC 69-10850. (Illus.). Repr. of 1951 ed. 35.00x (ISBN 0-678-05597-1). Kelley.
--West-Country Historical Studies. LC 69-11235. (Illus.). 1969. 25.00x (ISBN 0-678-05515-7). Kelley.
Finberg, H. P., ed. Agrarian History of England & Wales, Vol. 1, Pt. 2: A.D. 43-1042. LC 66-19763. (Illus.). 600p. 1972. 85.00 (ISBN 0-521-08423-7). Cambridge U Pr.
Finberg, H. P., ed. see Wainwright, Frederick T.
Finberg, H. P., tr. see Villiers De l'Isle-Adam, Jean M.
Finberg, Harris J., ed. Case Studies in Diagnostic Ultrasound, Vol. 9. (Clinics in Diagnostic Ultrasound Ser.). (Illus.). 260p. 1981. 27.00 (ISBN 0-686-37166-6). Churchill.
Finberg, J., tr. see Dobroliubov, Nikolai A.
Finberg, Joscelyne. Exploring Villages. 12.50 (ISBN 0-392-15845-0, SpS). Sportshelf.
Finberg, Laurence, et al. Water & Electrolytes in Pediatrics: Physiology, Pathophysiology & Treatment. (Illus.). 272p. 1982. 39.00 (ISBN 0-7216-3625-X). Saunders.
Finberg, Pauline & Filichia, Peter. Cheerleading! (Illus.). 128p. (Orig.). (gr. 7 up). 1984. pap. 2.25 (ISBN 0-590-33417-4). Scholastic Inc.
Finbow, Malcolm E., jt. ed. see Pitts, John D.
Finby, N., jt. auth. see Chynn, K. Y.
Finch, A. F., ed. Yearbook Nineteen, 1983. (Theilheimer's Synthetic Methods of Organic Chemistry: Vol. 37). xxiv, 576p. 1983. 227.25 (ISBN 3-8055-3600-3). S Karger.
--Yearbook 1982. (Theilheimer's Synthetic Methods of Organic Chemistry: Vol. 36). xxiv, 532p. 1982. 212.00 (ISBN 3-8055-3446-9). S Karger.
--Yearbook, 1985. (Theilheimer's Synthetic Methods of Organic Chemistry Ser.: Vol. 39). xxiv, 548p. 1985. 243.75 (ISBN 3-8055-3987-8). S Karger.
Finch, Alan, ed. Yearbook, 1984. (Theilheimer's Synthetic Methods of Organic Chemistry: Vol. 38). (Illus.). xxiv, 624p. 1984. 246.00 (ISBN 3-8055-3817-0). S Karger.
Finch, Andrew, jt. auth. see Gush, George.
Finch, Anne. Selected Poems of Anne Finch, Countess of Winchilsea. Rogers, Katharine M., ed. 1979. 15.00 (ISBN 0-8044-2741-0). Ungar.
Finch, Anne K. The Poems of Anne, Countess of Winchelsea. Reynolds, Myra, ed. & intro. by. Repr. of 1903 ed. 49.50 (ISBN 0-404-56856-4). AMS Pr.
Finch, Bernard, ed. Multilingual Guide for Medical Personnel. 1967. spiral bdg. 7.50 (ISBN 0-87488-961-8). Med Exam.
Finch, C. A., ed. Chemistry & Technology of Water-Soluble Polymers. 372p. 1983. 59.50x (ISBN 0-306-41251-9, Plenum Pr). Plenum Pub.
Finch, C. E., et al, eds. Parkinson's Disease II: Aging & Neuroendocrine Relationships. LC 79-491. (Advances in Experimental Medicine & Biology Ser.: Vol. 113). 282p. 1979. 39.50x (ISBN 0-306-40156-8, Plenum Pr). Plenum Pub.
Finch, Carol. Dawn's Desire. 1984. pap. 3.50 (ISBN 0-8217-1340-X). Zebra.
--Ecstacy's Embrace. 1985. pap. 3.95 (ISBN 0-8217-1605-0). Zebra.
--Endless Passion. 1983. pap. 3.50 (ISBN 0-8217-1155-5). Zebra.
--Passion's Vixen. 480p. 1984. pap. 3.75 (ISBN 0-8217-1402-3). Zebra.
--Rapture's Dream. 1984. pap. 3.50 (ISBN 0-8217-1037-0). Zebra.
--Rature's Dream. (Orig.). 1982. pap. 3.50 (ISBN 0-8217-1037-0). Zebra.
Finch, Charles W. The Depot Agent. LC 83-90396. (Illus.). 300p. 1983. pap. 12.95 (ISBN 0-914411-01-2). Finch.
Finch, Chas W. Winston Tunnel. LC 83-90396. (Illus.). 85p. 1985. pap. 7.95 (ISBN 0-317-17279-4). Finch.
Finch, Christopher. The Art of Walt Disney: From Mickey Mouse to the Magic Kingdoms. LC 73-4639. (Illus.). 458p. 1973. 29.95 (ISBN 0-8109-8052-5). Abrams.
--Making of the Dark Crystal. (Illus.). 96p. 1983. pap. 10.95 (ISBN 0-03-063332-X). HR&W.
--Norman Rockwell's America. (Illus.). 256p. 1985. 19.95 (ISBN 0-8109-8071-1). Abrams.
--Of Muppets & Men: The Making of "The Muppet Show". LC 81-1374. (Illus.). 160p. 1981. 27.50 (ISBN 0-394-52085-8). Knopf.
--Special Effects. LC 84-9180. (Illus.). 252p. 1984. 49.95 (ISBN 0-89659-452-1); Collector's Ed. 95.00 (ISBN 0-89659-509-9). Abbeville Pr.
--Walt Disney's America. LC 78-16863. (Illus.). 1978. 29.95 (ISBN 0-89659-000-3). Abbeville Pr.
Finch, Christopher & Ramachandran, Srinivasa. Matchmaking: Science Technology & Manufacturing. LC 82-18687. 236p. 1983. 69.95 (ISBN 0-470-27371-2). Halsted Pr.
Finch, Clement A., jt. auth. see Hillman, Robert S.
Finch, Clive F. Food Preparation. 672p. 1984. text ed. 16.95x (ISBN 0-7121-0641-3, Pub. by Macdonald & Evans). Brookfield Pub Co.
Finch, Curtis R. & Crunkilton, John R. Curriculum Development in Vocational & Technical Education: Planning Content, & Implementation. 2nd ed. 352p. 1984. text ed. 26.95 (ISBN 0-205-08116-9, 238116). Allyn.
Finch, Curtis R. & McGough, Robert C. Administering & Supervising Vocational Education. 352p. 1982. 22.95 (ISBN 0-13-004838-0). P-H.
Finch, D. I., et al see Symposium on Temperature, 1971.
Finch, Diana F. & Lira, Hector O. A Course in English Phonetics for Spanish Speakers. 194p. (Orig.). 1982. pap. text ed. 12.50x (ISBN 0-435-28078-3); cassette 15.00x (ISBN 0-435-28079-1). Heinemann Ed.
Finch, Donald G. Georgia. 1976. 5.00 (ISBN 0-87881-053-6). Mojave Bks.
--She Waits for Me. (gr. 8-12). 1977. pap. 1.50 (ISBN 0-912472-16-2). Miller Bks.
Finch, Edward R., Jr. & Moore, Amanda L. Astrobusiness: A Guide to the Commerce & Law of Outer Space. LC 84-18203. 176p. 1984. 29.95x (ISBN 0-03-000537-X). Praeger.
Finch, Eugene D., jt. ed. see Elias, Robert H.
Finch, F. E., et al. Managing for Organizational Effectiveness: An Experiential Approach. (Management Ser). 1975. text ed. 31.50 (ISBN 0-07-020899-9). McGraw.
Finch, George A. The Sources of Modern International Law. ix, 124p. Repr. of 1937 ed. 19.00 (ISBN 0-384-15685-1). Johnson Repr.
Finch, Henry. Law, or a Discourse Thereof. LC 68-57385. Repr. of 1759 ed. 45.00x (ISBN 0-678-04526-7). Kelley.
--Law, Or, a Discourse Thereof: In Four Books. 528p. 1969. Repr. of 1759 ed. 22.50x (ISBN 0-8377-2125-3). Rothman.
Finch, Henry, jt. ed. see Munslow, Barry.
Finch, Henry L. Wittgenstein, the Early Philosophy: An Exposition of the Tractatus. LC 73-135985. 1982. text ed. 18.00x (ISBN 0-391-00123-X). Humanities.
--Wittgenstein-the Later Philosophy: An Exposition of the Philosophical Investigations. LC 76-46421. 1977. text ed. 18.00x (ISBN 0-391-00680-0). Humanities.
Finch, J. H. & Dougall, E. G., eds. Computer Security: A Global Challenge. 1985. 50.00 (ISBN 0-444-87618-9, North-Holland). Elsevier.
Finch, Janet. Married to the Job: Wives' Incorporation in Men's Work. 170p. 1983. text ed. 18.95x (ISBN 0-04-301149-7). Allen Unwin.
--Married to the Job: Wives' Incorporation in Men's Work. 192p. 1983. pap. text ed. 8.95x (ISBN 0-04-301174-8). Allen Unwin.
Finch, Janet & Groves, Dulcie, eds. A Labour of Love: Women, Work, & Caring. 192p. (Orig.). 1983. pap. 9.95x (ISBN 0-7100-9504-X). Routledge & Kegan.
Finch, Jay S., jt. auth. see DeKornfeld, Thomas J.
Finch, Jeremiah S. Sir Thomas Browne: A Doctor's Life of Science & Faith. 319p. 1982. Repr. of 1950 ed. lib. bdg. 40.00 (ISBN 0-89760-237-4). Telegraph Bks.
--Sir Thomas Browne: A Doctor's Life of Science & Faith. LC 83-45917. Repr. of 1950 ed. 33.00 (ISBN 0-404-20298-5). AMS Pr.
Finch, John D. Aspects of Law Affecting the Paramedical Professions. 208p. (Orig.). 1984. pap. 11.95 (ISBN 0-571-13272-3). Faber & Faber.
Finch, John G. Nishkamakarma. LC 82-83498. (Orig.). 1982. pap. 8.50 (ISBN 0-9609928-0-4). Integ Pr.
Finch, M. H. A Political Economy of Uruguay since 1870. LC 80-21047. 1981. 29.95x (ISBN 0-312-62244-9). St Martin.
Finch, Margaret. Style in Art History: An Introduction to Theories of Style & Sequence. LC 73-14705. 178p. 1974. lib. bdg. 14.00 (ISBN 0-8108-0679-7). Scarecrow.
Finch, Minnie. The NAACP: Its Fight for Justice. LC 81-5324. 285p. 1981. 18.50 (ISBN 0-8108-1436-6). Scarecrow.
Finch, Percy, jt. auth. see Smith, Holland M.
Finch, Peter. How to Publish Your Own Poetry. 128p. 1985. pap. 5.95 (ISBN 0-8052-8231-9, Pub. by Allison & Busby England). Schocken.
--Typewriter Poems. 1971. pap. 6.50 (ISBN 0-87110-078-9). Ultramarine Pub.
Finch, Phillip. In a Place Dark & Secret. 384p. 1985. 16.95 (ISBN 0-531-09705-6). Watts.
--The Reckoning. LC 83-27206. 480p. 1984. 14.95 (ISBN 0-517-55398-8). Crown.
Finch, R., jt. auth. see Reed, Jeanne.
Finch, R. C., et al. Lab Studies in Physical Geology. 2nd ed. 276p. 1980. 13.95 (ISBN 0-89459-214-9). Hunter Textbks.
Finch, Richard. Welder's Handbook. 160p. 1985. 12.95 (ISBN 0-89586-257-3). H P Bks.
Finch, Robert. Common Ground: A Naturalist's Cape Cod. LC 80-83953. (Illus.). 144p. 1981. 14.95 (ISBN 0-87923-383-4); ltd. ed. 50.00x (ISBN 0-87923-384-2). Godine.
--Common Ground: A Naturalist's Cape Cod. LC 80-83953. (Illus.). 144p. pap. 8.95 (ISBN 0-87923-427-X). Godine.
--The Primal Place. LC 82-22566. 213p. 1983. 15.00 (ISBN 0-393-01623-4). Norton.
--The Primal Place. 256p. 1985. pap. 5.95 (ISBN 0-393-30228-8). Norton.
Finch, Robert E., jt. auth. see Roman, John.
Finch, Roger. A Cross in the Topsail. (Illus.). 122p. 1979. 14.95 (ISBN 0-85115-113-2, Pub. by Boydell & Brewer). Longwood Pub Group.
--The Ship Painters. (Illus.). 1979. 25.00x (ISBN 0-900963-25-5, Pub. by Terence Dalton England). State Mutual Bk.
--What Is Written in the Wind. (Sparrow Poverty Pamphlet Ser.: No. 47). 32p. 1984. pap. 2.50x (ISBN 0-935552-19-7). Sparrow Pr.
Finch, Sheila. Infinity's Web. 1985. 2.95 (ISBN 0-317-30645-6). Bantam.
Finch, Steven, tr. see Genet, Jean.
Finch, Stuart M. Fundamentals of Child Psychiatry. 1960. 12.50x (ISBN 0-393-01041-4); pap. 4.95 1979 (ISBN 0-393-00958-0). Norton.
Finch, Stuart M., jt. auth. see English, Oliver S.
Finch, T; see Bowen, D. Q.
Finch, Vernor C. & Baker, O. E. Geography of the World's Agriculture. LC 75-118419. 1970. Repr. of 1917 ed. 25.00x (ISBN 0-8046-1375-3, Pub. by Kennikat). Assoc Faculty Pr.
Fincham, A. A. Basic Marine Biology. 157p. 1984. 37.50 (ISBN 0-521-26421-9); pap. 14.95 (ISBN 0-521-26966-0). Cambridge U Pr.
Fincham, F, jt. auth. see Jaspars, J.
Fincham, J. R. Genetic Recombination in Fungi. rev. ed. Head, J. J., ed. LC 77-75593. (Carolina Biology Readers Ser.). (Illus.). 16p. (gr. 10 up). 1983. pap. 1.60 (ISBN 0-89278-202-1, 45-9602). Carolina Biological.
--Microbial & Molecular Genetics. 2nd ed. LC 75-21729. 150p. 1976. pap. 9.95x (ISBN 0-8448-0769-9). Crane-Russak Co.
Fincham, J. R., et al. Fungal Genetics. 4th ed. LC 78-65463. (Botanical Monographs). 1979. 72.50x (ISBN 0-520-03818-5). U of Cal Pr.
Fincham, John. Treatise on Masting Ships & Mastmaking. 384p. 1982. 60.00x (ISBN 0-85177-274-9, Pub. by Conway Marit England). State Mutual Bk.
Fincham, John R. Genetics. 643p. 1983. text ed. write for info (ISBN 0-86720-026-X). Jones & Bartlett.
Fincham, W. H. & Freeman, M. H. Optics. 9th rev. ed. LC 80-40274. (Illus.). 1980. 39.95 (ISBN 0-407-93422-7). Butterworth.
Fincher. American Legal System. (gr. 4 up). 1980. PLB 8.90 (ISBN 0-531-04100-X). Watts.
Fincher, Cameron L., et al. The Closing System of Academic Employment. 1978. pap. text ed. 4.00 (ISBN 0-686-23578-9). S Regional Ed.
Fincher, E. B. Mexico & the United States: Their Linked Destinies. LC 82-45581. (Illus.). 224p. (YA) (gr. 7 up). 1983. 11.06i (ISBN 0-690-04310-4); PLB 11.89g (ISBN 0-690-04311-2). Crowell Jr Bks.
--Spanish-Americans As a Political Factor in New Mexico, 1912-1950. LC 73-14202. (The Mexican American Ser.). 332p. 1974. 23.00x (ISBN 0-405-05676-1). Ayer Co Pubs.
--The Vietnam War. (gr. 7 up). 1980. PLB 9.90 (ISBN 0-531-04112-3, C07). Watts.
--The War in Korea. (First Bks.). (Illus.). 72p. (gr. 4 up). 1981. lib. bdg. 8.90 (ISBN 0-531-04330-4). Watts.
Fincher, Ernest B. Government of the United States. 3rd ed. (Illus.). 384p. 1976. pap. 19.95 (ISBN 0-13-361881-1). P-H.

Fincher, Jack. Lefties: The Origins & Consequences of Being Left-Handed. 1980. pap. 5.95 (ISBN 0-399-50460-5, Perigee). Putnam Pub Group.

Fincher, John H. Chinese Democracy: The Self-Government Movement in Local, Provincial & National Politics 1905-14. 1981. 32.50x (ISBN 0-312-13384-7). St Martin.

Fincher, Terry. Creative Techniques in Photo Journalism. (Illus.). 192p. 1980. 19.18 (ISBN 0-690-01899-1). Har-Row.

Fincher, Terry & Lynch, Tony. The Fincher File. (Illus.). 200p. 1982. 24.95 (ISBN 0-7043-2293-5, Pub. by Quartet Bks). Merrimack Pub Cir.

Finches, T. G. & Strassmaier, J. N. Late Babylonian Astronomical & Related Texts. (Brown University Studies: No. 18). 1955. write for info. U Pr of New Eng.

Finchley, Joan. Audition! A Complete Guide for Actors, with an Annotated Selection of Readings. 1984. 12.95 (ISBN 0-13-052093-4); pap. 6.95 (ISBN 0-13-052085-3). P-H.

Finchy, Mary E. The Wealth of Five Northamptonshire Families 1540-1640. 1966. 50.00x (ISBN 0-686-87136-7, Pub. by Northamptonshire). State Mutual Bk.

Finck, A. Fertilizers & Fertilization: Introduction & Practical Guide to Crop Fertilization. (Illus.). 438p. 1982. 42.50x (ISBN 0-89573-052-9). VCH Pubs.

Finck, Arthur L., Jr., tr. see Von Herff, Ferdinand.

Finck, H. T. My Adventures in the Golden Age of Music. LC 70-87496. (Music Ser.). 462p. 1971. Repr. of 1926 ed. lib. bdg. 49.50 (ISBN 0-306-71448-5). Da Capo.

Finck, Heinrich & Finck, Hermann. Sammlung ausgewaehlter Kompositionen zu vier und fuenf Stimmen. Eitner, Robert, ed. (Publikation aelterer praktischer und theoretischer Musikwerke Ser.: Vol. VIII). (Ger.). 1967. Repr. of 1879 ed. write for info. (ISBN 0-8450-1708-X). Broude.

Finck, Henry T. Chopin, & Other Musical Essays. facsimile ed. LC 78-37471. (Essay Index Reprint Ser). Repr. of 1889 ed. 17.00 (ISBN 0-8369-2548-3). Ayer Co Pubs.

--Fifty Art Songs by Nineteenth Century Masters, for High Voice. 13.25 (ISBN 0-8446-5503-1). Peter Smith.

--Massenet & His Operas. 1976. Repr. of 1910 ed. 21.50 (ISBN 0-404-12912-9). AMS Pr.

--Musical Laughs: Jokes, Tittle-Tattle, & Anecdotes, Mostly Humorous, About Musical Celebrities. LC 79-159955. 1971. Repr. of 1924 ed. 40.00x (ISBN 0-8103-3397-X). Gale.

--Primitive Love & Love-Stories. 1976. lib. bdg. 75.00 (ISBN 0-8490-2476-5). Gordon Pr.

--Richard Strauss. 59.95 (ISBN 0-8490-0955-3). Gordon Pr.

--Songs & Song Writers. 59.95 (ISBN 0-8490-1083-7). Gordon Pr.

--Songs & Song Writers. LC 78-31290. 1979. Repr. of 1902 ed. lib. bdg. 25.00 (ISBN 0-89341-439-5). Longwood Pub Group.

--Songs & Song Writers. 14.25 (ISBN 0-8369-7135-3, 7968). Ayer Co Pubs.

--Wagner & His Works, 2 Vols. LC 68-25287. (Studies in Music, No. 42). 1969. Repr. of 1893 ed. lib. bdg. 79.95x (ISBN 0-8383-0189-4). Haskell.

--Wagner & His Works: The Story of His Life, 2 Vols. LC 68-30999. (Illus.). 1968. Repr. of 1893 ed. Set. lib. bdg. 34.00x (ISBN 0-8371-0419-X, FIWA). Greenwood.

Finck, Henry T., ed. Fifty Art Songs by Nineteenth-Century Masters (for High Voice) LC 75-12131. 208p. 1975. pap. 6.50 (ISBN 0-486-23193-3). Dover.

Finck, Hermann, jt. auth. see Finck, Heinrich.

Finck, Kevin. California Corporation Start-Up Package & Minute Book. 2nd ed. LC 82-81322. (Successful Business Library Ser.). 190p. 1984. 3 ring binder 33.95 (ISBN 0-916378-34-9). PSI Res.

Finckenauer, James O. Juvenile Delinquency & Corrections: The Gap Between Theory & Practice. 1984. text ed. 10.00i (ISBN 0-12-256970-9). Acad Pr.

--Scared Straight: & the Panacea Phenomenon. (Prentice Hall Criminal Justice Ser.). (Illus.). 288p. 1982. pap. 20.95 (ISBN 0-13-791558-6). P-H.

Finckh, Elisabeth. Foundations of Tibetan Medicine, Vol. 1. 1980. 22.50x (ISBN 0-7224-0162-0, Pub. by Watkins England). State Mutual Bk.

Findeisen, Barbara. A Course in Miracles Concordance. 457p. 15.00 (ISBN 0-942494-45-8). Coleman Pub.

Findeisen, Hans. Arbeiten zur Ethnographie Sibiriens und Volkskunde Zentral-Europas. (Asian Folklore & Social Life Monograph: No. 51). 228p. (Ger.). 1973. 14.00 (ISBN 0-89986-048-6). Oriental Bk Store.

Findeisen, W., et al. Control & Coordination in Hierarchical Systems. (IIASA International Ser. on Applied Systems Analysis: No. 9). 467p. 1980. 82.95x (ISBN 0-471-27742-8). Wiley.

Finden, Edward, jt. auth. see Finden, William.

Finden, William & Finden, Edward. Ports & Harbours of Great Britain. (Illus.). 1975. Repr. of 1836 ed. 19.00x (ISBN 0-8464-0738-8). Beekman Pubs.

Finder, Jan H., ed. Alien Encounters. LC 81-50227. 256p. 1982. 11.95 (ISBN 0-8008-0168-7). Taplinger.

Finder, Jan Howard. Finder's Guide to Australterrestrials. (Illus.). 32p. (Orig.). (gr. 1-12). 1981. pap. 6.00 (ISBN 0-686-32294-0). Wombat Ent.

Finder, Joseph. Red Carpet. LC 82-18694. (A New Republic Bk.). (Illus.). 419p. 1983. 16.95 (ISBN 0-03-060484-2). HR&W.

Finder, Morris. Reason & Art in Teaching Secondary-School English. LC 76-9554. 217p. 1976. text ed. 27.95 (ISBN 0-87722-071-9). Temple U Pr.

Findhorn Community. Faces of Findhorn. LC 78-20160. (Illus.). 192p. (Orig.). 1981. pap. 6.97i (ISBN 0-06-090851-3, CN 851, CN). Har-Row.

--The Findhorn Garden. 1976. pap. 10.53i (ISBN 0-06-090520-4, CN520, CN). Har-Row.

--The Findhorn Garden. LC 75-6335. (A Lindisfarne Book). (Illus.). 192p. (YA) 1975. 12.95i (ISBN 0-06-011249-2, HarpT). Har-Row.

Findlater, Jane H. Seven Scots Stories. LC 75-121542. (Short Story Index Reprint Ser). 1913. 19.00 (ISBN 0-8369-3498-9). Ayer Co Pubs.

Findlater, R. Joe Grimaldi: His Life & Theatre. LC 78-7465. 1979. 47.50 (ISBN 0-521-22221-4); pap. 15.95 (ISBN 0-521-29407-X). Cambridge U Pr.

Findlater, Richard. The Player Queens. LC 76-53912. (Illus.). 1977. 10.95 (ISBN 0-8008-6324-0). Taplinger.

--These Our Actors: Theatre Acting of Peggy Ashcroft, John Gielgud, Laurence Olivier, Ralph Richardson. (Illus.). 192p. 1984. 24.95 (ISBN 0-241-11060-2, Pub. by Hamish Hamilton England); pap. 14.95 (ISBN 0-241-11135-8). David & Charles.

--The Unholy Trade. 1978. Repr. of 1952 ed. lib. bdg. 25.00 (ISBN 0-8495-1623-4). Arden Lib.

--The Unholy Trade. 1952. 15.00 (ISBN 0-8482-4052-9). Norwood Edns.

Findlater, Richard, ed. At the Royal Court: Twenty-Five Years of the English Stage Company. LC 80-85375. (Illus.). 256p. 1981. cancelled (ISBN 0-394-51986-8, GP846). Grove.

--Author! Author! 300p. 1984. 16.95 (ISBN 0-571-13377-0); pap. 7.95 (ISBN 0-571-13409-2). Faber & Faber.

Findlater, Richard, et al. The Complete Guide to Britain's National Theatre. 1977. pap. 5.00x (ISBN 0-435-18656-6). Heinemann Ed.

Findlay, Alan, jt. ed. see Lawless, Dick.

Findlay, Alan L. Reproduction & the Fetus. (Illus.). 200p. 1984. pap. text ed. 19.50 (ISBN 0-8391-2074-5, 21997). Univ Park.

Findlay, Alexander. Introduction to Physical Chemistry. 3rd, rev. ed. LC 53-8678. pap. 150.50 (ISBN 0-317-08883-1, 2003640). Bks Demand UMi.

Findlay, Allan M., et al. Tunisia. Collison, Robert L., ed. (World Bibliographical Ser.: Vol. 33). 251p. 1982. 36.00 (ISBN 0-903450-63-1). ABC-Clio.

Findlay, Ann M., et al, eds. Morocco. (World Bibliographical Ser.: No. 47). 311p. 1984. lib. bdg. 45.00. ABC-Clio.

Findlay, Bruce A. & Findlay, Esther B. Your Rugged Constitution. rev. ed. (Illus.). 1969. 17.50x (ISBN 0-8047-0405-8); text ed. 10.95x O.P. (ISBN 0-8047-0406-6); pap. 5.95 (ISBN 0-8047-0407-4). Stanford U Pr.

Findlay, Elsa. Rhythm & Movement: Applications of Dalcroze Eurhythmics. LC 71-169706. 1971. pap. 12.95 (ISBN 0-87487-078-X). Birch Tree Gr.

Findlay, Esther B., jt. auth. see Findlay, Bruce A.

Findlay, Frederick R. N. & Cronwright-Schreiner, S. C. Big Game Shooting & Travel in Southeast Africa: Account of Shooting in the Cheringoma & Gorongoza Divisions of Portuguese South-East Africa & in Zululand. LC 72-4362. (Black Heritage Library Collection Ser.). Repr. of 1903 ed. 44.25 (ISBN 0-8369-9095-1). Ayer Co Pubs.

Findlay, G. G. The Epistles of Paul the Apostle to the Thessalonians. (Thornapple Commentaries Ser.). 319p. 1982. pap. 9.95 (ISBN 0-8010-3503-1). Baker Bk.

Findlay, J. J. The School. (Educational Ser.). 1911. Repr. 15.00 (ISBN 0-8482-3998-9). Norwood Edns.

Findlay, J. N. Ascent to the Absolute: Metaphysical Papers & Lectures. (Muirhead Library of Philosophy). 1970. text ed. 18.00x (ISBN 0-391-00073-X). Humanities.

--Hegel: A Re-Examination. LC 76-12155. 1976. pap. 6.95 (ISBN 0-19-519879-4, 473, GB). Oxford U Pr.

--Plato: The Written & Unwritten Doctrines. (International Library of Philosophy & Scientific Method). 350p. 1974. text ed. 31.75x (ISBN 0-391-00334-8). Humanities.

--Wittgenstein: A Critique. (International Library of Philosophy). 240p. 1984. 29.95x (ISBN 0-7102-0330-6). Routledge & Kegan.

Findlay, J. N., tr. see Hegel, G. W.

Findlay, J. N., tr. see Husserl, Edmund.

Findlay, James A., compiled by. Modern Latin American Art: A Bibliography. LC 83-10743. (Art Reference Collection Ser.: No. 3). xi, 301p. 1983. lib. bdg. 39.95 (ISBN 0-313-23757-3, FIN/). Greenwood.

Findlay, James V. Safety & the Executive. Stephenson, Bette & Hassel, William, eds. LC 79-54954. (Illus.). 128p. 1979. 16.50 (ISBN 0-88061-008-5). Inst Pub GA.

--Safety & the Executive (IS172) 1981. 75.00x (ISBN 0-686-45799-4, Pub. by RoSPA Can Hse England). State Mutual Bk.

Findlay, James V. & Kihlman, Raymond L. Leadership in Safety. LC 80-84097. (Illus.). 197p. 1981. lib. bdg. 14.00 (ISBN 0-88061-002-6). Inst Pub Ga.

Findlay, James V. & Kuhlman, Raymond L. Leadership in Safety (ISa86) 1981. 75.00x (ISBN 0-686-45795-1, Pub. by RoSPA Can Hse England). State Mutual Bk.

Findlay, James V. & Morrison, Richard G. Supervisory Control of Absenteeism. LC 77-77275. (Illus.). 62p. 1977. Incl. transparency masters. 3-ring binder 69.50 (ISBN 0-88061-018-2). Inst Pub GA.

Findlay, Jessie P. Footprints of Robert Burns. LC 77-9341. 1977. lib. bdg. 22.50 (ISBN 0-8414-4303-3). Folcroft.

Findlay, Jessie Patrick. Footprints of Robert Burns. 174p. 1980. Repr. of 1923 ed. lib. bdg. 22.50 (ISBN 0-8492-4725-X). R West.

Findlay, Joann N. Kant & the Transcendental Object. 1981. 27.95x (ISBN 0-19-824638-2). Oxford U Pr.

Findlay, John N. Ascent to the Absolute: Metaphysical Papers & Lectures. LC 72-533364. (Muirhead Library of Philosophy). pap. 67.80 (ISBN 0-317-20115-8). Bks Demand UMI.

--Hegel: A Re-Examination. (Muirhead Library of Philosophy Ser.). 1964. Repr. of 1958 ed. text ed. 18.00x (ISBN 0-391-00893-5). Humanities.

--Language, Mind & Value. (Muirhead Library of Philosophy Ser.). 1978. Repr. of 1963 ed. text ed. 18.00x (ISBN 0-391-00569-3). Humanities.

--Psyche & Cerebrum. (Aquinas Lecture, 1972). 52p. 1972. 7.95 (ISBN 0-87462-137-2). Marquette.

--Transcendence of the Cave: Sequel to the Discipline of the Cave. LC 67-16869. (Muirhead Library of Philosophy Ser.). 1978. text ed. 18.00x (ISBN 0-04-111002-1). Humanities.

Findlay, John N., ed. Studies in Philosophy, British Academy Lectures. (Oxford Paperbacks Ser). (Orig.). 1966. pap. 4.95x (ISBN 0-19-283004-X). Oxford U Pr.

Findlay, John R. Personal Recollections of Thomas De Quincey. LC 76-15258. Repr. of 1886 ed. lib. bdg. 15.00 (ISBN 0-8414-4155-3). Folcroft.

Findlay, L. M., ed. Algernon Charles Swinburne: Selected Poems. (The Fyfield Ser.). 274p. 12.50 (ISBN 0-85635-137-7). Carcanet.

Findlay, M. Chapman & Williams, Edward E. Investment Analysis. (Illus.). 480p. 1974. ref. ed. 32.95 (ISBN 0-13-502633-4). P-H.

Findlay, M. Chapman, III, et al. Real Estate Portfolio Analysis. (Special Series in Real Estate & Urban Land Economics). 240p. 1983. 25.50x (ISBN 0-669-02397-3). Lexington Bks.

Findlay, Mark, et al, eds. Issues in Criminal Justice Administration. 212p. 1983. text ed. 30.00x (ISBN 0-86861-277-4). Allen Unwin.

Findlay, Patrick J. In the Footsteps of R. L. S. 69p. Repr. of 1911 ed. lib. bdg. 75.00 (ISBN 0-918377-59-5). Russell Pr.

Findlay, R., jt. auth. see Brockett, O.

Findlay, R., et al, eds. Theatre Perspectives Two: Contemporary Russian & Polish Theatre & Drama. 1982. 6.75 (ISBN 0-940528-26-6). Am Theatre Assoc.

Findlay, Ronald E. International Trade & Development Theory. LC 73-8623. (Studies in Economics Ser.). 230p. 1973. 25.00x (ISBN 0-231-03546-2). Columbia U Pr.

Findlay, Ted & Beasley, Conger, Jr., eds. Above the Thunder. LC 82-72730. (Orig.). 1982. pap. 9.95 (ISBN 0-89334-031-6). Humanics Ltd.

--Above the Thunder: A Collection of Personal Experiences from Concern Counts. LC 82-72730. (Illus.). 255p. (Orig.). 1982. pap. 6.95 (ISBN 0-686-38089-4). Concern Counts.

Findlay, W. Robert Burns & the Medical Profession. 59.95 (ISBN 0-8490-0961-8). Gordon Pr.

Findlay, W. P. Fungi in Folklore: Fact & Fiction. (Illus.). 112p. (Orig.). 1982. pap. text ed. 12.95x (ISBN 0-916422-42-9, Pub. by Richmond Pub Co). Mad River.

--Timber: Properties & Uses. 224p. 1975. pap. cancelled (ISBN 0-258-97113-4, Pub. by Granada England). Sheridan.

Findlay, W. P., ed. Preservation of Timber in the Tropics. (Forestry Sciences). 1985. lib. bdg. 49.50 (ISBN 90-247-3112-7, Pub. by Martinus Nijhoff Netherlands). Kluwer-Academic.

Findlay, William & Watt, David. Pascal: An Introduction to Methodical Programming. 2nd ed. LC 78-11540. 404p. 1981. pap. 19.95 (ISBN 0-914894-73-0). Computer Sci.

Findlay, William & Watt, David A., eds. Pascal: An Introduction to Methodical Programming. 3rd ed. text ed. 16.95 (ISBN 0-273-02188-5). Pitman Pub MA.

Findler, Nicholas V., ed. Associative Networks: The Representation & Use of Knowledge by Computers. LC 78-31318. 1979. 61.50 (ISBN 0-12-256380-8). Acad Pr.

Findley, Carter V. Bureaucratic Reform in the Ottoman Empire: The Sublime Porte, 1789-1922. LC 79-83987. (Princeton Studies in the Near East). 1980. 38.00x (ISBN 0-691-05288-3). Princeton U Pr.

Findley, D. F., ed. Applied Time Series Analysis, No. 2. LC 78-9007. 1978. 39.50 (ISBN 0-12-257250-5). Acad Pr.

Findley, David, ed. Applied Time Series Analysis, Vol. 2. 1981. 60.00 (ISBN 0-12-256420-0). Acad Pr.

Findley, James F. Dwight L. Moody, American Evangelist, 1837-1899. LC 69-13200. pap. 112.50 (ISBN 0-317-20698-2, 2024113). Bks Demand UMI.

Findley, James S. Pleistocene Soricidae from San Josecito Cave, Nuevo Leon, Mexico. (Museum Ser.: Vol. 5, No. 36). 7p. 1953. 1.00 (ISBN 0-317-04790-6). U of KS Mus Nat Hist.

--Speciation of the Wandering Shrew. (Museum Ser.: Vol. 9, No. 1). 68p. 1955. pap. 3.75 (ISBN 0-686-80279-9). U of KS Mus Nat Hist.

--Taxonomy & Distribution of Some American Shrews. (Museum Ser.: Vol. 7, No. 14). 6p. 1955. pap. 1.25 (ISBN 0-317-05008-7). U of KS Mus Nat Hist.

Findley, James S., jt. auth. see Baker, Rollin H.

Findley, Lesley & Capildeo, Rudy, eds. Movement Disorders: Tremor. 1984. 75.00x (ISBN 0-19-520463-8). Oxford U Pr.

Findley, Myrtle B. Myrtle B. Findley's Real Food. 4th ed. (Illus.). 112p. 1983. pap. 6.00 (ISBN 0-9611550-0-0). Real Food.

Findley, Patricia C. & Yagle, Pamela D. Grammar Game: A Language Skills Workbook for Students. 5th ed. (Illus.). 1984. 8.75 (ISBN 0-930362-04-7). Sch Journal WVU.

Findley, Paul. They Dare to Speak Out: People & Institutions Confront Israel's Lobby. LC 84-28977. 324p. 1985. 16.95 (ISBN 0-88208-179-9). Lawrence Hill.

Findley, Robert. Software Gourmet Guide & Cookbook: 6502. pap. 13.95 (ISBN 0-8104-6277-X, 6277). Hayden.

Findley, Robert & Edwards, Raymond. Eighty-Eighty Software Gourmet Guide & Cookbook. pap. 13.95 (ISBN 0-8104-6280-X, 6280). Hayden.

Findley, Roger W. & Farber, Daniel A. Environmental Law: Cases & Materials. LC 81-1596. (American Casebook Ser.). 738p. 1981. text ed. 23.95 (ISBN 0-314-58802-7). West Pub.

--Environmental Law: Cases & Materials. 2nd ed. (American Casebook Ser.). 1985. text ed. write for info. (ISBN 0-314-90222-8). West Pub.

--Environmental Law, Cases & Materials: 1983 Supplement. (American Casebook Ser.). 179p. 1983. pap. text ed. 5.50 (ISBN 0-314-75711-2). West Pub.

--Environmental Law in a Nutshell. LC 83-6764. (Nutshell Ser.). 343p. 1983. pap. text ed. 8.95 (ISBN 0-314-73633-6). West Pub.

Findley, Rowe. Great American Deserts. LC 72-75382. (Special Publications Ser.). (Illus.). 1972. 6.95 (ISBN 0-87044-107-8). Natl Geog.

Findley, Timothy. Famous Last Words. 1982. 13.95 (ISBN 0-385-28271-0, Sey Lawr). Delacorte.

--Famous Last Words. 1983. pap. 3.95 (ISBN 0-440-32543-9, LE). Dell.

--The Last of the Crazy People. (Orig.). 1985. pap. 4.50 (ISBN 0-440-34670-3, LE). Dell.

--Not Wanted on the Voyage. LC 85-897. 368p. 1985. 17.95 (ISBN 0-385-29415-8). Delacorte.

--The Wars. 1983. pap. 3.95 (ISBN 0-440-39239-X, LE). Dell.

Findley, W., et al. Creep & Relaxation of Nonlinear Viscoelastic Materials. 368p. 1976. 81.00 (ISBN 0-444-10775-4, North-Holland). Elsevier.

Findley, Warren & Bryan, Miriam. The Pros & Cons of Ability Grouping. LC 75-19963. (Fastback Ser.: No. 66). 1975. pap. 0.75 (ISBN 0-87367-066-3). Phi Delta Kappa.

Findley, Warren G. Specialization of Verbal Facility at the College Entrance Level. LC 70-176770. (Columbia University. Teachers College. Contributions to Education: No. 567). Repr. of 1933 ed. 22.50 (ISBN 0-404-55567-5, CE567). AMS Pr.

Findley, Warren G., ed. Impact & Improvement of School Testing Programs. LC 63-5289. (National Society for the Study of Education Yearbooks Ser: No. 62, Pt. 2). 1963. 6.50x (ISBN 0-226-60071-8). U of Chicago Pr.

Findley, William. History of the Insurrection in the Four Western Counties of Pennsylvania: In the Year M.DCC.XCIV. with a Recital of the Circumstances Specially Connected Therewith. 336p. 1984. Repr. of 1796 ed. 27.50 (ISBN 0-87152-394-9, 83-24513). Reprint.

Findling, John E. Dictionary of American Diplomatic History. LC 79-7730. (Illus.). 1980. lib. bdg. 49.95 (ISBN 0-313-22039-5, FDD/). Greenwood.

Findling, Robert L., jt. auth. see Fogel, Danny.

Findly, Ellison B. From the Courts of India: Indian Miniatures in the Collection of the Worcester Art Museum. LC 80-51682. (Illus.). 82p. (Orig.). 1983. pap. 12.50 (ISBN 0-87023-408-0). U of Mass Pr.

Findly, Ellison B., jt. ed. see Haddad, Yvonne Y.

Findon, Benjamin W. Sir Arthur Sullivan: His Life & Music. 1976. Repr. of 1904 ed. 23.00 (ISBN 0-404-12913-7). AMS Pr.

Fine. Talking Sociology. 1985. 10.72 (ISBN 0-205-08358-7, 818358). Allyn.

Fineberg, Jonathan. Kandinsky in Paris, 1906-1907. Foster, Stephen, ed. LC 83-24126. (Studies in the Fine Arts: The Avant-Garde: No. 44). 160p. 1984. 39.95 (ISBN 0-8357-1523-X). UMI Res Pr.

Fineberg, Keith S., et al. Obstetrics-Gynecology & the Law. LC 83-18409. 634p. 1984. text ed. 60.00 (ISBN 0-914904-93-0). Health Admin Pr.

Fineberg, Marjorie. Everyday Math: Tables, Graphs, & Scale. LC 79-730692. (Illus.). 1979. pap. text ed. 135.00 (ISBN 0-89290-129-2, A514-SATC). Soc for Visual.

Fineberg, Marjorie & Shaw, John. Decimals. LC 79-730043. (Illus.). 1978. pap. text ed. 135.00 (ISBN 0-89290-095-4, A511-SATC). Soc for Visual.

Fineberg, Robert G. Jogging-the Dance of Death. Ashton, Sylvia, ed. LC 79-6209. 1980. 14.95 (ISBN 0-87949-174-4). Ashley Bks.

Finegan, Edward. Attitudes Toward English Usage: A History of the War of Words. 1980. pap. 11.95x (ISBN 0-8077-2581-1). Tchrs Coll.

Finegan, Jack. Archaeological History of the Ancient Middle East. (Illus.). 1979. 40.00 (ISBN 0-89158-164-2, Dawson). Westview.

--The Archaeology of the New Testament: The Mediterranean World of the Early Christian Apostles. (Illus.). 400p. 1981. 40.00x (ISBN 0-86531-064-5). Westview.

--Archeology of the New Testament: The Life of Jesus & the Beginning of the Early Church. LC 69-18059. (Illus.). 1970. 57.00x (ISBN 0-691-03534-2); pap. 9.95x (ISBN 0-691-02000-0). Princeton U Pr.

--Discovering Israel: An Archeological Guide to the Holy Land. LC 80-26952. pap. 38.80 (ISBN 0-317-19818-1, 2023211). Bks Demand UMI.

--Encountering New Testament Manuscripts. pap. 8.95 (ISBN 0-8028-1836-6). Eerdmans.

--Light from the Ancient Past, 2 vols. 2nd ed. (Illus.). 1959. Vol. 1 2nd Ed. 50.00 (ISBN 0-691-03550-4); Vol. 1 2nd Edition. pap. 15.50 (ISBN 0-691-00207-X); Vol. 2. 50.00 (ISBN 0-691-03551-2); Vol. 2. pap. 14.50x (ISBN 0-691-00208-8); Set. 90.00 (ISBN 0-686-76901-5). Princeton U Pr.

Finegan, T. A. & Bowen, W. G. Economics of Labor Force Participation. LC 69-17396. (Illus.). 1969. 57.00x (ISBN 0-691-04193-8). Princeton U Pr.

Finegan, Thomas E. Free Schools: A Documentary History of the Free School Movement in New York State. LC 73-165737. (American Education Ser, No. 2). (Illus.). 1972. Repr. of 1921 ed. 49.00 (ISBN 0-405-03606-X). Ayer Co Pubs.

Finegold, jt. auth. see Seitz.

Finegold, Julius J. & Thetford, William N., eds. Choose Once Again. LC 76-20363. (Illus.). 112p. 1981. 6.95 (ISBN 0-89087-413-1). Celestial Arts.

Finegold, Sydney M. & Martin, William J. Bailey & Scott's Diagnostic Microbiology. 6th ed. LC 81-14157. (Illus.). 705p. 1982. text ed. 30.95 (ISBN 0-8016-1577-1). Mosby.

Finegold, Wilfred J. Artificial Insemination. 2nd ed. 156p. 1976. 16.00x (ISBN 0-398-03381-1). C C Thomas.

--Artificial Insemination with Husband Sperm. 112p. 1980. 14.75x (ISBN 0-398-04094-X). C C Thomas.

Finely, Gerald. Turner & George IV In Edinburgh, 1822. 250p. 1982. 30.00 (ISBN 0-85224-432-0, Pub. by Edinburgh U Pr). Columbia U Pr.

Finely, John W. & Schwass, Daniel E., eds. Xenobiotics in Foods & Feeds. LC 83-15685. (ACS Symposium Ser.: No. 234). 421p. 1983. lib. bdg. 49.95 (ISBN 0-8412-0809-3). Am Chemical.

Fineman, Hayim. John Davidson. LC 77-921. 1916. lib. bdg. 15.00 (ISBN 0-8414-4163-4). Folcroft.

--John Davidson: A Study of the Reaction of His Ideas to His Poetry. 51p. 1980. Repr. of 1916 ed. lib. bdg. 12.50 (ISBN 0-8492-4630-X). R West.

--John Davidson: A Study of the Relation of His Ideas to His Poetry. 1978. Repr. of 1916 ed. lib. bdg. 15.00 (ISBN 0-8482-0841-2). Norwood Edns.

Fineman, Irving. Hear, Ye Sons! A Novel. facsimile ed. LC 74-27980. (Modern Jewish Experience Ser.). 1975. Repr. of 1933 ed. 25.50x (ISBN 0-405-06709-7). Ayer Co Pubs.

Fineman, Joel. Shakespeare's Perjured Eye: The Invention of Poetic Subjectivity in the Sonnets. 1985. 29.95x (ISBN 0-520-05486-5). U of Cal Pr.

Fineman, Mark. The Home Darkroom. 2nd ed. LC 72-79608. (Illus.). 96p. 1976. pap. 5.95 (ISBN 0-8174-0555-0, Amphoto). Watson-Guptill.

--The Inquisitive Eye. (Illus.). 1981. pap. text ed. 9.95x (ISBN 0-19-502773-6). Oxford U Pr.

Fineman, Stephen. Social Work Stress & Intervention. LC 84-21268. 174p. 1985. text ed. 29.95 (ISBN 0-566-00664-2). Gower Pub Co.

--White Collar Unemployment: Impact & Stress. (Wiley Series Organizational Change & Development). 154p. 1983. 32.95x (ISBN 0-471-10490-6, Pub. by Wiley-Interscience). Wiley.

Finer, Alex. Deepwater. LC 84-18872. (Crime Club Ser.). 192p. 1985. 11.95 (ISBN 0-385-19944-9). Doubleday.

Finer, Daniel L. The Formal Grammar of Switch-Reference. (Outstanding Dissertations in Linguistics Ser.). 224p. 1985. 25.00 (ISBN 0-8240-5428-8). Garland Pub.

Finer, Herman. America's Destiny. LC 47-12363. 1947. 5.00 (ISBN 0-911090-09-6). Pacific Bk Supply.

--The Presidency: Crisis & Regeneration. 1974. pap. 2.95x (ISBN 0-226-24970-0, P588, Phoen). U of Chicago Pr.

--Road to Reaction. LC 77-9010. 1977. Repr. of 1945 ed. lib. bdg. 19.25x (ISBN 0-8371-9726-0, FIRR). Greenwood.

--The T. V. A. Lessons for International Application. LC 77-172008. (FDR & the Era of the New Deal Ser.). (Illus.). 1972. Repr. of 1944 ed. lib. bdg. 39.50 (ISBN 0-306-70378-5). Da Capo.

--Theory & Practice of Modern Government. rev. ed. LC 69-13895. (Illus.). xiv, 978p. Repr. of 1949 ed. lib. bdg. 48.75x (ISBN 0-8371-1989-8, FIMG). Greenwood.

--The United Nations Economic & Social Council. LC 73-3753. 121p. 1973. Repr. of 1946 ed. lib. bdg. 15.00x (ISBN 0-8371-6849-X, FIUN). Greenwood.

Finer, Leslie, tr. see Spatharis, Sotiris.

Finer, Leslie, tr. see Taktsis, Costas.

Finer, Ruth, jt. auth. see Collins, Judith.

Finer, S. E. Changing British Party System, 1945-1979. 1980. pap. 7.25 (ISBN 0-8447-3368-7). Am Enterprise.

Finer, S. E., ed. Five Constitutions. 1980. text ed. 30.50x (ISBN 0-391-00967-2). Humanities.

Finer, S. E., ed. see Farneti, Paolo.

Finer, S. E., ed. see Pareto, Vilfredo.

Finer, Samuel E. A Primer of Public Administration. LC 77-679. (Man & Society Ser.). 1977. Repr. of 1961 ed. lib. bdg. 22.50x (ISBN 0-8371-9492-X, FIPR). Greenwood.

Fineran, J. M. A Taxonomic Revision of the Genus Entorrhiza C. Weber (Ustilaginales) (Nova Hedwigia Ser.). (Illus.). 1979. pap. text ed. 8.75 (ISBN 3-7682-1211-4). Lubrecht & Cramer.

Fineran, John K. Career of a Tinpot Napoleon: Political Biography of Huey P. Long. 4.50 (ISBN 0-685-08225-3). Claitors.

Finerman, A. see Alt, Franz L., et al.

Finermintz, Ruth. Auguries, Charms, Amulets. LC 82-7431. 95p. 12.50 (ISBN 0-8246-0284-6). Jonathan David.

Finerty, James P. The Population Ecology of Cycles in Small Mammals: Mathematical Theory & Biological Fact. LC 79-23774. (Illus.). 1981. text ed. 24.50x (ISBN 0-300-02382-0). Yale U Pr.

Finerty, John F. War-Path & Bivouac: Or, the Conquest of the Sioux. LC 61-9001. (WFL Ser.). (Illus.). 1977. pap. 7.95 (ISBN 0-8061-1413-4). U of Okla Pr.

--War-Path & Bivouac: The Big Horn & Yellowstone Expedition. Quaife, Milo M., ed. LC 67-89221. (Illus.). xlviii, 375p. 1966. pap. 7.50 (ISBN 0-8032-5059-2, BB 329, Bison). U of Nebr Pr.

Fines, John. Teaching History. 221p. 1983. 35.00x (ISBN 0-7157-2030-9, Pub. by H McDougall UK). State Mutual Bk.

--Tudor People. 1977. 14.95 (ISBN 0-7134-0283-0, Pub. by Batsford England). David & Charles.

--Who's Who in the Middle Ages. LC 72-127225. 232p. (Orig.). 1980. pap. 8.95 (ISBN 0-8128-6074-8). Stein & Day.

Fines, John & Verrier, Raymond. The Drama of History: An Experiment in Cooperative Teaching. (Illus.). 119p. 1974. 13.50 (ISBN 0-85157-512-9, Pub. by Bingley England). Shoe String.

Fineshriber, William H. Stendhal the Romantic Rationalist. LC 72-187169. 1932. lib. bdg. 15.00 (ISBN 0-8414-4254-1). Folcroft.

Finestone, Albert J., ed. Evaluation & Clinical Management of Dizziness & Vertigo. (Illus.). 224p. 1982. casebound 29.00 (ISBN 0-7236-7003-X). PSG Pub Co.

Finestone, Harold. Victims of Change: Juvenile Delinquents in American Society. LC 76-5327. (Contributions in Sociology Ser.: No. 20). (Illus.). 256p. 1976. lib. bdg. 29.95 (ISBN 0-8371-8897-0, FTD/). Greenwood.

Finestone, Jeffery, ed. The Last Courts of Europe: A Royal Family Album: 1860-1914. (Illus.). 256p. 1981. casebound 30.00 (ISBN 0-86565-015-2). Vendome.

Finetti, Bruno, ed. see Bechtolsheim, Lulu.

Fingado, Dorothy & McMillen, Loretta. Richmondtown Receipts - Three Centuries of Staten Island Cookery. (Illus.). 1976. spiral bdg. 5.00 (ISBN 0-686-20333-X). Staten Island.

Fingado, Gail & Jerome, Mary R. English Alive: Grammar, Function & Setting. (Orig.). 1982. pap. text ed. 11.95 (ISBN 0-316-28311-8). Little.

Fingado, Gail, et al. The English Connection: A Text for Speakers as a Second Language. 1981. pap. 14.95 (ISBN 0-316-28312-6). Little.

Fingar, Elmer L., et al. New York Wills & Trusts: Laws, Forms & Taxes, 2 vols. rev. 2nd ed. LC 61-9883. 1971. looseleaf with 1984 supplement 100.00 (ISBN 0-87632-062-0). Boardman.

Fingar, Thomas & Reed, Linda A. An Introduction to Education in the People's Republic of China & U. S.-China Educational Exchanges. 131p. 1982. avail. Natl Assn Foreign Students.

Fingard, Judith. Jack in Port: Sailortowns of Eastern Canada. (Social History in Canada Ser.). (Illus.). 292p. 1982. 35.00x (ISBN 0-8020-2458-0); pap. 13.50 (ISBN 0-8020-6467-1). U of Toronto Pr.

Fingarette, Herbert. Confucius: The Secular As Sacred. 160p. 1972. pap. 4.95xi (ISBN 0-06-131682-2, TB1682, Torch). Har-Row.

--The Meaning of Criminal Insanity. LC 70-165223. 300p. 1972. pap. 6.95x (ISBN 0-520-02631-4). U of Cal Pr.

--Self-Deception. LC 68-58415. (Studies in Philosophical Psychology). 1969. text ed. 17.50x (ISBN 0-7100-6346-6). Humanities.

Fingarette, Herbert & Hasse, Ann F. Mental Disabilities & Criminal Responsibilities. LC 77-91756. 1979. 30.00x (ISBN 0-520-03630-1). U of Cal Pr.

Finger, Alan & Guber, Lynda. Yoga Moves with Alan Finger. (Illus.). 160p. (Orig.). 1984. pap. 9.95 (ISBN 0-671-50064-3, Wallaby). S&S.

Finger, Alexis. Tune in Tonight. 1985. pap. text ed. 9.95 (ISBN 0-88377-286-8); cassettes 25.50 (ISBN 0-88377-979-X). Newbury Hse.

Finger, Anne L., jt. auth. see Bloomenstein, Richard.

Finger, Bill, ed. Here Come A Wind. (Southern Exposure Ser.). (Illus.). 224p. (Orig.). 1976. pap. 4.50 (ISBN 0-943810-05-1). Inst Southern Studies.

Finger, Charles J. Highwaymen. LC 72-105012. (Essay Index Reprint Ser.). 1923. 20.00 (ISBN 0-8369-1570-4). Ayer Co Pubs.

--In Lawless Lands. facsimile ed. LC 79-157776. (Short Story Index Reprint Ser.). Repr. of 1924 ed. 20.00 (ISBN 0-8369-3888-7). Ayer Co Pubs.

--Romantic Rascals. LC 71-90637. (Essay Index Reprint Ser). 1927. 20.00 (ISBN 0-8369-1259-4). Ayer Co Pubs.

--Sailor Chanties & Cowboy Songs. LC 77-27604. 20.00 (ISBN 0-8414-4353-X). Folcroft.

--Tales from Silver Lands. 225p. (gr. 7 up). 1924. 13.95 (ISBN 0-385-07513-8). Doubleday.

--Valiant Vagabonds. facs. ed. LC 68-58789. (Essay Index Reprint Ser). 1936. 20.00 (ISBN 0-8369-0112-6). Ayer Co Pubs.

Finger, Ellis, jt. auth. see Bergethon, K. Roald.

Finger, J. H. & Quell, E. Quell-Finger Dialogues. (Oleander Language & Literature Ser.: Vol. 2). 1.25 (ISBN 0-900891-01-7). Oleander Pr.

Finger, J. M. Industrial Country Policy & Adjustment to Imports from Developing Countries. (Working Paper: No. 470). ii, 20p. 1981. pap. 3.00 (ISBN 0-686-39766-5, WP-0470). World Bank.

Finger, J. M., et al. The Political Economy of Administered Protection. LC 83-919210. (World Bank Reprint Ser.). Date not set. price not set. World Bank.

Finger, J. Michael & Willet, Thomas D., eds. The Internationalization of the American Economy. LC 81-86467. (The Annals of the American Academy of Political & Social Science: Vol. 460). (Illus.). 232p. 1982. 15.00 (ISBN 0-8039-0035-X); pap. 7.95 (ISBN 0-8039-0036-8). Sage.

Finger, Joel L. Age Discrimination Problems in the Context of a Reduction in Work Force. LC 83-60622. (Litigation & Administrative Practice Ser.). 120p. 1983. 30.00 (ISBN 0-317-12896-5). PLI.

Finger, John R. The Eastern Band of Cherokees, 1819-1900. LC 83-10284. (Illus.). 268p. 1984. 24.95x (ISBN 0-87049-409-0); pap. 12.50 (ISBN 0-87049-410-4). U of Tenn Pr.

Finger, Larry W., jt. auth. see Hazen, Robert M.

Finger, Seymour M. American Jewry During the Holocaust. 1984. pap. 14.95x (ISBN 0-9613537-3-2). Am Jewish Holo.

--American Jewry During the Holocaust. 412p. (Orig.). 1984. pap. text ed. 17.95 (ISBN 0-8419-7506-X). Holmes & Meier.

--Your Man at the UN: People, Politics & Bueaucracy in the Making of Foreign Policy. LC 79-3657. 368p. 1980. 15.00x (ISBN 0-8147-2566-X). NYU Pr.

Finger, Seymour M., ed. A New World Balance & Peace in the Middle East - Reality or Mirage? A Colloquium. 308p. 1975. 15.00 (ISBN 0-317-18477-6). Fairleigh Dickinson.

Finger, Seymour M., jt. ed. see Alexander, Yonah.

Finger, Stanley & Stein, Donald. Brain Damage & Recovery: Research & Clinical Perspectives. (Historical & Contemporary Issues Ser.). 352p. 1982. 42.50 (ISBN 0-12-256780-3). Acad Pr.

Finger, Stanley, ed. Recovery from Brain Damage. LC 77-27585. (Illus.). 439p. 1978. 35.00x (ISBN 0-306-31107-0, Plenum Pr). Plenum Pub.

Finger, Stanley, jt. ed. see Almli, C. Robert.

Finger, Stephen. The Trite Report. (Illus.). 96p. (Orig.). 1984. pap. 3.95 (ISBN 0-8092-5358-5). Contemp Bks.

Finger, Susan. Pascal Programming for Engineers Using VPS. 368p. 1983. pap. 12.95 (ISBN 0-8403-3026-X). Kendall-Hunt.

Finger, Thomas. Christian Theology: An Eschatological Approach, Vol. 1. 320p. 1985. text ed. 18.95 (ISBN 0-8407-7505-9). Nelson.

Finger, William R., ed. The Tobacco Industry in Transition: Policies for the Nineteen Eighties. LC 81-47064. 352p. 1981. 27.50x (ISBN 0-669-04552-7). Lexington Bks.

Fingerhut, Astri & Baker, Carol, eds. The Book of Festivals in the Midwest, 1983 & 1984. (Illus.). 220p. 1983. pap. 9.95 (ISBN 0-89651-056-5). Icarus.

Fingerhut, Bruce, ed. Tomorrow Will Be Better: Living with a Parent Who Drinks. 64p. 1985. pap. 9.95 (ISBN 0-89651-786-1). Icarus.

Fingerhut, Bruce M. & Haskin, Steve. Read That Label: How to Tell What's Inside a Wine Bottle from What's on the Outside. (Illus.). 128p. (Orig.). 1983. pap. 4.95 (ISBN 0-89651-652-0). Icarus.

Fingerhut, Eugene R. Survivor: Cadwallader Colden II in Revolutionary America. LC 82-20092. (Illus.). 200p. (Orig.). 1983. lib. bdg. 24.75 (ISBN 0-8191-2868-6); pap. text ed. 12.00 (ISBN 0-8191-2869-4). U Pr of Amer.

--Who First Discovered America? A Critique of Writings on Pre-Colombian Voyages. (Guides to Historical Issues Ser.: No. 1). 147p. 1984. 17.95x (ISBN 0-941690-10-5); pap. 10.95x (ISBN 0-941690-09-1); pap. text ed. 8.75x. Regina Bks.

Fingerhut, Loia A. Changes in Mortality among the Elderly: United States, 1940-1978. Cox, Kaludia, ed. 25p. 1982. pap. text ed. 1.75 (ISBN 0-8406-0245-6). Natl Ctr Health Stats.

Fingerman, Milton. Animal Diversity. 3rd ed. 1981. pap. text ed. 16.95 (ISBN 0-03-049611-X, CBS C). SCP.

Fingesten, Peter. Eclipse of Symbolism. LC 77-86194. (Illus.). 1970. 19.95x (ISBN 0-87249-172-2). U of SC Pr.

Fingleton, B., jt. auth. see Upton, G. J.

Fingleton, Bernard. Models of Category Counts. LC 83-26250. (Illus.). 224p. 1984. 34.50 (ISBN 0-521-25297-0); pap. 12.95 (ISBN 0-521-27283-1). Cambridge U Pr.

Fingleton, David. Kiri Te Kanawa: A Biography. LC 82-73013. 188p. 1983. 13.95 (ISBN 0-689-11345-5). Atheneum.

Fingleton, Eamonn & Turner, Roland, eds. Shareholder Freebies. (Illus.). 40p. (Orig.). 1985. pap. 3.95 (ISBN 0-934867-00-3). Buttonwood Pr.

Finholt, Joan M., jt. auth. see Colvin, Nola R.

Finholt, Richard. American Visionary Fiction: Mad Metaphysics As Salvation Psychology. (National University Publications Literary Criticism Ser.). 1977. 14.95x (ISBN 0-8046-9191-6, Pub by Kennikat). Assoc Faculty Pr.

Finifter, Ada. Using the IBM Personal Computer: IBM Easywriter. 1984. 17.95 (ISBN 0-03-063736-8). HR&W.

Finiguerra, Maso. Florentine Picture Chronicle. Colvin, Sidney, ed. LC 68-56527. (Illus.). 1969. Repr. of 1898 ed. 82.50 (ISBN 0-405-08514-1, Blom Pubns). Ayer Co Pubs.

Finin, Gerard, et al. Strategies for Supporting Local Institutional Development. (Special Series on Local Institutional Development: No. 7). 99p. (Orig.). 1985. pap. text ed. 7.50 (ISBN 0-86731-114-2). RDC Ctr Intl Stud.

Finitskaya, Z. Samarkand. 108p. 1982. 5.45 (ISBN 0-8285-2353-3, Pub. by Progress Pubs USSR). Imported Pubns.

Finizio, Norman & Ladas, Gerasimons. An Introduction to Differential Equations. 608p. 1981. text ed. write for info. (ISBN 0-534-00960-3). Wadsworth Pub.

--Ordinary Differential Equations with Modern Applications. 2nd ed. 432p. 1981. text ed. write for info. (ISBN 0-534-00898-4). Wadsworth Pub.

Fink. Cogenital Heart Disease. 2nd ed. 1985. 19.95 (ISBN 0-8151-3215-8). Year Bk Med.

--Studien Zur Phanomenologie: 1930-1939. (Phaenomenologica Ser: No. 21). 1966. lib. bdg. 24.00 (ISBN 90-247-0253-4, Pub. by Martinus Nijhoff Netherlands). Kluwer Academic.

Fink, A. M. Almost Periodic Differential Equations. (Lecture Notes in Mathematics: Vol. 377). viii, 336p. 1974. pap. 18.00 (ISBN 0-387-06729-9). Springer-Verlag.

Fink, Albert & Kokaska, Charles J., eds. Career Education for Behaviorally Disordered Students. 134p. 1983. pap. 14.95 (ISBN 0-86586-138-2). Coun Exc Child.

Fink, Albert H. International Perspectives on Future Special Education. LC 78-74018. 1979. text ed. 5.00 (ISBN 0-86586-046-7). Coun Exc Child.

Fink, Arlene & Kosecoff, Jacqueline. An Evaluation Primer. LC 77-88461. (Illus.). 99p. 1980. pap. 12.50 (ISBN 0-8039-1480-6). Sage.

--An Evaluation Primer Workbook: Practical Exercises for Educators. LC 77-88462. (Illus.). 57p. 1980. pap. 9.95 (ISBN 0-8039-1481-4). Sage.

--An Evaluation Primer Workbook: Practical Exercises for Health Professionals. LC 77-88463. (Illus.). 89p. 1980. pap. 9.95 (ISBN 0-8039-1482-2). Sage.

Fink, Arlene, jt. auth. see Kosecoff, Jacqueline.

Fink, Arthur E. Causes of Crime. LC 84-22493. xii, 309p. 1985. Repr. of 1938 ed. lib. bdg. 39.75x (ISBN 0-313-24746-3, FICA). Greenwood.

--The Field of Social Work. 7th ed. LC 77-89733. 1978. 23.95 (ISBN 0-03-022196-X, HoltC); inst. manual 25.00 (ISBN 0-03-041721-X). HR&W.

Fink, Augusta. I-Mary: A Biography of Mary Austin. LC 82-21807. 310p. 1983. 17.50 (ISBN 0-8165-0789-9). U of Ariz Pr.

--Monterey County: The Dramatic Story of Its Past. LC 72-76931. 1978. 10.95 (ISBN 0-913548-60-X, Valley Calif); pap. 6.95 (ISBN 0-913548-62-6, Valley Calif). Western Tanager.

--Time & the Terraced Land. LC 66-18957. (Illus.). 1966. 9.95 (ISBN 0-8310-7056-0). Howell-North.

Fink, B. Raymond. The Human Larynx: A Functional Study. LC 74-80536. 207p. 1975. 27.50 (ISBN 0-911216-86-3). Raven.

Fink, B. Raymond & Demarest, Robert J. Laryngeal Biomechanics. LC 77-26937. (Commonwealth Fund Ser.). 1978. 30.00x (ISBN 0-674-51085-2). Harvard U Pr.

Fink, B. Raymond, ed. Molecular Mechanisms of Anesthesia. (Progress in Anesthesiology Ser.: Vol. 2). (Illus.). 528p. 1980. text ed. 83.50 (ISBN 0-89004-456-2). Raven.

--Molecular Mechanisms of Anesthesia. LC 74-14474. (Progress in Anesthesiology Ser.: Vol. 1). 672p. 1975. 69.50 (ISBN 0-911216-94-4). Raven.

Fink, Barbara. Our Neighborhood & Groups: Manual. Hawke, Sharryl D. & Combs, Eunice A., eds. (Illus.). 194p. (gr. 2). 1983. Duplication Masters 69.00 (ISBN 0-943068-51-7); pap. 4.50 Study Book (ISBN 0-943068-73-8). Graphic Learning.

--Our Neighborhoods. Hawke, Sharryl D. & Combs, Eunice A., eds. (And Groups Study Ser.). (Illus.). 1983. pap. 360.00 ser. of 105 (ISBN 0-943068-97-5). Graphic Learning.

Fink, Benjamin. Life of John Kline. 7.95 (ISBN 0-87178-516-1). Brethren.

Fink, Bruce. The Ascomycetes of Ohio, No. I. 1915. 1.50 (ISBN 0-86727-004-7). Ohio Bio Survey.

Fink, Bruce & Corrington, Leafy J. The Ascomycetes of Ohio, No. IV & V. 1921. 1.00 (ISBN 0-86727-009-8). Ohio Bio Survey.

Fink, Carole. The Genoa Conference: European Diplomacy, 1921-1922. LC 83-14724. xxiii, 365p. 1984. 36.00 (ISBN 0-8078-1578-0). U of NC Pr.

Fink, Carole, tr. see Bloch, Marc.

Fink, Carole, et al, eds. German Nationalism & the European Response, 1890-1945. LC 85-1201. (Illus.). 304p. 1985. text ed. 19.95x (ISBN 0-8061-1946-2). U of Okla Pr.

Fink, D. G., jt. auth. see Ryder, J. D.

Fink, Dale B. Mr. Silver & Mr. Gold. LC 79-15924. 32p. (gr. 4-8). 1980. 10.95 (ISBN 0-87705-447-9). Human Sci Pr.

Fink, Diane D., et al. Speedreading: A How-to Book for Every Busy Manager, Executive, & Professional. LC 81-10373. (Wiley Self Teaching Guide Ser.). 195p. 1981. pap. 9.95 (ISBN 0-471-08407-7, Pub. by Wiley Pr). Wiley.

Fink, Donald G. & Beaty, H. Wayne. Standard Handbook for Electrical Engineers. 11th ed. (Illus.). 1978. 79.95 (ISBN 0-07-020974-X). McGraw.

Fink, Donald G. & Christiansen, Donald. Electronics Engineer's Handbook. 2nd ed. 2496p. 1982. 83.50 (ISBN 0-07-020981-2). McGraw.

Fink, Edward J. Building a Career in the Business World. 1984. 10.00 (ISBN 0-533-05968-2). Vantage.

Fink, Eugen, jt. auth. see Heidegger, Martin.

Fink, Gary & Reed, Merl E., eds. Essays in Southern Labor History: Selected Papers, Southern Labor History Conference, 1976. LC 77-85. (Contributions in Economics & Economic History Ser.: No. 16). 1977. lib. bdg. 29.95 (ISBN 0-8371-9528-4, FES/). Greenwood.

Fink, Gary M. Biographical Dictionary of American Labor. LC 84-4687. (Illus.). xvii, 767p. 1984. lib. bdg. 49.95 (ISBN 0-313-22865-5, FLE/). Greenwood.

--Labor Unions. LC 76-8734. (Greenwood Encyclopedia of American Institutions). 544p. 1977. lib. bdg. 49.95 (ISBN 0-8371-8938-1, FLU/). Greenwood.

--Labor's Search for Political Order: The Political Behavior of the Missouri Labor Movement, 1890-1940. LC 73-80582. 238p. 1973. 19.00x (ISBN 0-8262-0149-0). U of Mo Pr.

--Prelude to the Presidency: The Political Character & Legislative Leadership Style of Governor Jimmy Carter. LC 79-7725. (Contributions in Political Science: No. 40). (Illus.). 1980. lib. bdg. 29.95 (ISBN 0-313-22055-7, FPP/). Greenwood.

Fink, Gary M., ed. AFL-CIO Executive Council Statements & Reports, 1956-1975, 5 vols. LC 76-45604. 1977. Set. lib. bdg. 295.00 (ISBN 0-8371-9387-7, AFL/). Greenwood.

Fink, Gary M. & Mills, Mary, eds. State Labor Proceedings: A Bibliography. LC 75-31912. 1975. lib. bdg. 45.00 (ISBN 0-8371-8278-6, FLS/). Greenwood.

Fink, George, ed. Neuropeptides: Basic & Clinical Aspects. (Illus.). 286p. 1982. 59.00 (ISBN 0-443-02537-1). Churchill.

Fink, Hans. Social Philosophy. 128p. 1981. 14.95x (ISBN 0-416-71990-2, NO. 3476); pap. 6.95x (ISBN 0-416-72000-5, NO. 3475). Methuen Inc.

Fink, Harold K. Mind & Performance: A Comparative Study of Learning in Mammals, Birds, & Reptiles. LC 70-138229. (Illus.). 113p. 1972. Repr. of 1954 ed. lib. bdg. 22.50x (ISBN 0-8371-5586-X, FIMI). Greenwood.

Fink, Harold S., ed. see Foucher of Chartres.

Fink, Sr. Harold S., ed. see Fulcher Of Chartres.

Fink, I. Sein, Wahrheit, Welt. (Phaenomenologica Ser.: No. 1). 1958. lib. bdg. 21.00 (ISBN 90-247-0234-8, Pub. by Martinus Nijhoff Netherlands). Kluwer Academic.

Fink, I. & Merriell, C. String Quartet Playing. (Illus.). 191p. 1985. 14.95 (ISBN 0-86622-007-0). Paganiniana Pubns.

Fink, Joanne. Things to Know Before Buying a Bicycle. LC 84-50443. (Look Before You Leap Ser.). 1985. 8.96 (ISBN 0-382-06785-1); pap. 4.75 (ISBN 0-382-06964-1). Silver.

Fink, John W., jt. auth. see Kirkham, E. Bruce.

Fink, Joseph & Sealy, Lloyd G. The Community & the Police - Conflict or Cooperation. LC 84-923. 241p. 1985. Repr. of 1974 ed. price not set (ISBN 0-89874-716-3). Krieger.

Fink, Joseph L. & Siecker, Bruce R. Manager's Guide to Third-Party Programs. 90p. 1982. pap. text ed. 18.00 (ISBN 0-917330-41-2). Am Pharm Assn.

Fink, Joseph L., et al, eds. Pharmacy Law Digest 1984. LC 72-115322. 1984. 41.95 (ISBN 0-932036-06-6). Harwal Pub Co.

Fink, Karl J. & Baeumer, Max L., eds. Goethe As a Critic of Literature. 236p. (Orig.). 1985. lib. bdg. 23.50 (ISBN 0-8191-4280-8); pap. text ed. 12.25 (ISBN 0-8191-4281-6). U Pr of Amer.

Fink, L. Dee. The First Year of College Teaching. LC 83-82743. (Teaching & Learning Ser.: No. 17). (Orig.). 1984. pap. text ed. 8.95x (ISBN 0-87589-790-8). Jossey-Bass.

--Listening to the Learner: An Exploratory Study of Personal Meaning in College Geography Courses. LC 77-15501. (Research Papers: No. 184). (Illus.). 1977. pap. 10.00 (ISBN 0-89065-091-8). U Chicago Dept Geog.

Fink, Larry. Social Graces. LC 83-72660. (Illus.). 80p. 1984. 25.00 (ISBN 0-89381-135-1); ltd. ed. 250.00 (ISBN 0-89381-159-9). Aperture.

--Social Graces. LC 83-72660. (Illus.). 80p. 1985. pap. 12.50 (ISBN 0-89381-201-3). Aperture.

Fink, Lawrence A. & Ducharme, Raymond A., eds. Crisis in Urban Education. LC 73-141258. pap. 87.50 (ISBN 0-8357-9869-0, 2012541). Bks Demand UMI.

Fink, Leon. Workingmen's Democracy: The Knights of Labor & American Politics. LC 82-6902. (Working Class in American History Ser.). 1983. 22.50x (ISBN 0-252-00999-1). U of Ill Pr.

--Workingmen's Democracy: The Knights of Labor & American Politics. LC 82-6902. (Working Class in American History Ser.). 270p. 1985. pap. 10.95x (ISBN 0-252-01256-9). U of Ill Pr.

Fink, Lila, et al. Choices: A Text for Writing & Reading. 1983. pap. text ed. 14.95 (ISBN 0-316-28317-7); tchr's Manual Avail (ISBN 0-316-28318-5). Little.

Fink, Lois Marie, jt. auth. see National Museum of American Art.

Fink, Lorraine. A Parent's Guide to String Instrument Study. LC 77-79565. (Illus.). 1977. pap. 2.50 (ISBN 0-8497-5700-2, WS3, Pub. by Kjos West). Kjos.

Fink, Mary, ed. The Macrophage: Its Role in Tumor Immunology. 1976. 45.00 (ISBN 0-12-256950-4). Acad Pr.

Fink, Mary A., ed. Immune RNA in Neoplasia. 1976. 49.50 (ISBN 0-12-256940-7). Acad Pr.

Fink, Michael. Drawing with Words: A Studio Concept of Composition. LC 81-40709. (Illus.). 64p. (Orig.). 1982. lib. bdg. 19.00 (ISBN 0-8191-2039-1); pap. text ed. 6.75 (ISBN 0-8191-1963-6). U Pr of Amer.

Fink, Michael, jt. auth. see Lofland, John.

Fink, Norman S. & Metzler, Howard C. The Costs & Benefits of Deferred Giving. 224p. 1982. 20.00x (ISBN 0-231-05478-5). Columbia U Pr.

--The Costs & Benefits of Deferred Giving. pap. 24.50 (ISBN 0-686-38899-2). Public Serv Materials.

Fink, Paul. Bits of Mountain Speech. LC 74-8108. 1974. pap. 2.50 (ISBN 0-913239-15-1). Appalach Consortium.

Fink, Peter, illus. New York Nocturnes: Eighty-Six After Dark Photographs. LC 82-1534. (Illus.). 89p. 1982. pap. 6.95 (ISBN 0-486-24299-4). Dover.

Fink, Philip R. Tax Guide for Acquiring, Maintaining & Disposing of Business Equipment. LC 82-503. 310p. 1982. 39.95 (ISBN 0-13-885012-7). P-H.

Fink, Reginald. Introducing the Alto Clef for Trombone. 1969. pap. 4.95 (ISBN 0-918194-04-0). Accura.

Fink, Reginald H. From Treble Clef to Bass Clef Baritone. 1972. pap. 4.95 (ISBN 0-918194-05-9). Accura.

--Introducing the Tenor Clef for Trombone. 1968. pap. 4.95 (ISBN 0-918194-03-2). Accura.

--Studies in Legato for Trombone. 1967. pap. 5.00 (ISBN 0-8258-0245-8, 04767). Fischer Inc NY.

--The Trombonist's Handbook: A Complete Guide to Playing & Teaching. LC 76-55601. (Illus.). 1977. 24.95 (ISBN 0-918194-01-6). Accura.

Fink, Reuben & Moshe, Davis, eds. America & Palestine: The Attitude of Official America & of the American People Toward the Rebuilding of Palestine As a Free & Democratic Jewish Commonwealth. LC 77-70680. (America & the Holy Land Ser.). 1977. Repr. of 1944 ed. lib. bdg. 40.00x (ISBN 0-405-10245-3). Ayer Co Pubs.

Fink, Richard H., intro. by. Supply-Side Economics: A Critical Appraisal. LC 82-51294. (Illus.). 488p. 1982. lib. bdg. 27.50 (ISBN 0-89093-460-6, Aletheia Bks); pap. 12.00. U Pubns Amer.

Fink, Robert O. Roman Military Records on Papyrus. (APA Philological Monographs). 45.00 (ISBN 0-89130-709-5, 40-00-26). Scholars Pr GA.

--Roman Military Records on Papyrus. 566p. 1970. 45.00 (ISBN 0-8295-0174-6, 40-00-26). Scholars Pr GA.

Fink, Robert R. & Ricci, Robert. The Language of Twentieth-Century Music. LC 74-13308. 1975. 17.95 (ISBN 0-02-870600-5). Schirmer Bks.

Fink, Robert S., et al. Tax Fraud: Audits, Investigations, Prosecutions, 2 vols. Abrams, Stuart E. & Silverman, Elliot, eds. 1980. Updates avail. looseleaf 160.00 (305); looseleaf 1983 87.50. Bender.

Fink, S., ed. Das Chronisch Kranke Kind. (Paediatrische Fortbildungskurse fuer die Praxis: Vol. 54). (Illus.). 90p. 1982. pap. 14.25 (ISBN 3-8055-3422-1). S Karger.

Fink, Sam. The Constitution. (Illus.). 1985. 24.50 (ISBN 0-394-54304-1). Random.

Fink, Stephen L. & Jenks, R. Stephen. Designing & Managing Organizations. 1983. 27.95x (ISBN 0-256-02628-9). Irwin.

Fink, Stuart, jt. auth. see Burian, Barbara.

Finkbeiner, Alex E., et al, eds. Pharmacology of the Urinary Tract & the Male Reproductive System. (Illus.). 356p. 1982. 32.00 (ISBN 0-8385-7841-1). ACC.

Finkbeiner, Daniel T., 2nd. Introduction to Matrices & Linear Transformations. 3rd ed. LC 78-18257. (Mathematical Sciences Ser.). (Illus.). 462p. 1978. text ed. 29.95 (ISBN 0-7167-0084-0). W H Freeman.

Finke, Beatrix. Erzahlsituationen und Figurenperspektiven im Detektivroman. (Bochum Studies in English: Vol. 15). 426p. (Orig., German.). 1983. pap. 40.00x (ISBN 90-6032-246-0, Pub. by B R Gruener Netherlands). Benjamins North Am.

Finke, Blythe F. Aleksandr Solzhenitsyn: Beleaguered Literary Giant of the U. S. S. R. Rahmas, D. Steve, ed. (Outstanding Personalities Ser.: No. 60). 32p. (Orig.). 1973. lib. bdg. 3.50 incl catalog cards (ISBN 0-87157-560-4); pap. 1.95 vinyl laminated covers (ISBN 0-87157-060-2). SamHar Pr.

--Angela Davis: Traitor or Martyr of the Freedom of Expression? Rahmas, D. Steve, ed. LC 77-190246. (Outstanding Personalities Ser.: No. 28). 32p. (Orig.). (gr. 7-9). 1972. lib. bdg. 3.50 incl. catalog cards (ISBN 0-87157-528-0); pap. 1.95 vinyl laminated covers (ISBN 0-87157-028-9). SamHar Pr.

--Assassination: Case Studies. Rahmas, Sigurd C., ed. (Topics of Our Times Ser.: No. 17). 32p. (Orig.). 1982. 3.50x (ISBN 0-87157-318-0); pap. text ed. 1.95 (ISBN 0-87157-818-2). SamHar Pr.

--Berlin: Divided City. Rahmas, D. Steve, ed. LC 72-89228. (Topics of Our Times Ser.: No. 1). 32p. (Orig.). (gr. 7-12). 1973. lib. bdg. 3.50 incl. catalog cards (ISBN 0-87157-801-8); pap. 1.95 vinyl laminated covers (ISBN 0-87157-301-6). SamHar Pr.

--Bernard M. Baruch: Speculator & Statesman. Rahmas, D. Steve, ed. LC 78-190249. (Outstanding Personalities Ser.: No. 32). 32p. (Orig.). (gr. 7-12). 1972. lib. bdg. 3.50 incl. catalog cards (ISBN 0-87157-532-9); pap. 1.95 vinyl laminated covers (ISBN 0-87157-032-7). SamHar Pr.

--Charlie Chaplin: Famous Silent Movie Actor & Comic. Rahmas, D. Steve, ed. LC 72-89207. (Outstanding Personalities Ser.: No. 43). 32p. 1973. lib. bdg. 3.50 incl. catalog cards (ISBN 0-87157-539-6); pap. 1.95 vinyl laminated covers (ISBN 0-87157-039-4). SamHar Pr.

--China Joins the U. N. Rahmas, D. Steve, ed. LC 72-89215. (Events of Our Times Ser.: No. 1). 32p. (Orig.). (gr. 7-12). 1973. lib. bdg. 3.50 incl. catalog cards (ISBN 0-87157-701-1); pap. 1.95 vinyl laminated covers (ISBN 0-87157-201-X). SamHar Pr.

--General Patton: Fearless Military Leader. Rahmas, D. Steve, ed. LC 76-190251. (Outstanding Personalities Ser.: No. 34). 32p. (Orig.). (gr. 7-12). 1972. lib. bdg. 3.50 incl. catalog cards (ISBN 0-87157-534-5); pap. 1.95 vinyl laminated covers (ISBN 0-87157-034-3). SamHar Pr.

--George Meany: Modern Leader of the American Federation of Labor. Rahmas, D. Steve, ed. (Outstanding Personalities Ser.: No. 38). 32p. (Orig.). (gr. 7-12). 1972. lib. bdg. 3.50 incl. catalog cards (ISBN 0-87157-548-5); pap. 1.95 vinyl laminated covers (ISBN 0-87157-048-3). SamHar Pr.

--Howard R. Hughes: Twentieth Century Multi-Millionaire & Recluse. Rahmas, D. Steve, ed. (Outstanding Personalities Ser.: No. 69). 32p. (Orig.). (YA) (gr. 7-12). 1974. lib. bdg. 3.50 incl. catalog cards (ISBN 0-87157-569-8); pap. 1.95 vinyl laminated covers (ISBN 0-87157-069-6). SamHar Pr.

--John Foster Dulles: Master of Brinksmanship & Diplomacy. Ramas, D. Steve, ed. LC 77-185666. (Outstanding Personalities Ser.: No. 10). 32p. (Orig.). (YA) (gr. 7-12). 1972. lib. bdg. 3.50 incl. catalog cards (ISBN 0-87157-510-8); pap. 1.95 vinyl laminated covers (ISBN 0-87157-010-6). SamHar Pr.

--Konrad Adenauer: Architect of the New Germany. Rahmas, D. Steve, ed. LC 79-190241. (Outstanding Personalities Ser.: No. 23). 32p. (Orig.). (gr. 7-9). 1972. lib. bdg. 3.50 incl. catalog cards (ISBN 0-87157-523-X); pap. 1.95 vinyl laminated covers (ISBN 0-87157-023-8). SamHar Pr.

--Our Besieged Environment: The Pollution Problem. new ed. Rahmas, D. Steve, ed. (Topics of Our Times Ser.). 32p. 1975. lib. bdg. 3.50 incl. catalog cards (ISBN 0-87157-815-8); pap. 1.95 vinyl laminated covers (ISBN 0-87157-315-6). SamHar Pr.

--W. C. Fields: Renowned Comedian of the Early Modern Picture Industry. Rahmas, D. Steve, ed. (Outstanding Personalities Ser.: No. 48). 32p. (Orig.). (YA) (gr. 7-12). 1972. lib. bdg. 3.50 incl. catalog cards (ISBN 0-87157-552-3); pap. 1.95 vinyl laminated covers (ISBN 0-87157-052-1). SamHar Pr.

Finke, Laurie, jt. ed. see Markley, Robert.

Finke, Marvin, jt. auth. see Verburg, Kenneth.

Finke, Robert C., ed. Electric Propulsion & Its Applications to Space Missions. LC 81-15069. (Illus.). 858p. 1981. 65.00 (ISBN 0-915928-55-8, PAAS79); members 35.00 (ISBN 0-317-32138-2). AIAA.

Finkel, Asher & Frizzell, Lawrence. Standing Before God: Studies on Prayer in Scripture & in Essays in Honor of John M. Oesterreicher. 1981. 39.50x (ISBN 0-87068-708-5). Ktav.

Finkel, Asher J. Hamilton & Hardy's Industrial Toxicology. 446p. 1982. text ed. 49.00 (ISBN 0-7236-7027-7). PSG Pub Co.

Finkel, Donald. Adequate Earth. LC 72-78285. 1972. pap. 2.95 (ISBN 0-689-10512-6). Atheneum.

--The Detachable Man. LC 83-45521. 96p. 1984. 14.95 (ISBN 0-689-11458-3); pap. 7.95 (ISBN 0-689-11459-1). Atheneum.

--Garbage Wars. LC 74-103825. 1970. pap. 3.95 (ISBN 0-689-10310-7). Atheneum.

--Going under & Endurance. LC 78-55020. 1978. pap. 5.95 (ISBN 0-689-10902-4). Atheneum.

--Joyful Noise. LC 66-11396. (Orig.). 1966. pap. 3.95 (ISBN 0-689-10088-4). Atheneum.

--What Manner of Beast. LC 81-66012. 1981. 12.95 (ISBN 0-689-11226-2); pap. 7.95 (ISBN 0-689-11225-4). Atheneum.

Finkel, Donald, et al. Reading Ourselves to Sleep. 24p. 1985. pap. 15.00 (ISBN 0-931757-23-1). Pterodactyl Pr.

Finkel, Herman J., ed. CRC Handbook of Irrigation Technology, Vol. I. 369p. 1982. 66.00 (ISBN 0-8493-3231-1). CRC Pr.

Finkel, J., jt. auth. see Kornfeld, D. S.

Finkel, Jerry B. Consultation-Liaison Psychiatry: Current Trends & New Perspectives. 352p. 1983. 41.50 (ISBN 0-8089-1585-1, 791263). Grune.

Finkel, Jules. Computer-Aided Experimentation: Interfacing to Mini-Computers. LC 74-22060. 422p. 1975. 28.50 (ISBN 0-471-25884-9). Krieger.

Finkel, Kenneth. Nineteenth-Century Photography in Philadelphia. (Illus.). 19.00 (ISBN 0-8446-5762-X). Peter Smith.

Finkel, Kenneth, ed. Nineteenth-Century in Philadelphia: Two Hundred & Fourteen Historic Prints from the Library Company of Philadelphia. (Illus.). 1980. pap. 9.95 (ISBN 0-486-23932-2). Dover.

Finkel, L., jt. auth. see Brown, J. R.

Finkel, LeRoy. Learning Word Processing Concepts Using AppleWriter. (Illus.). 80p. 1983. pap. text ed. 8.48 (ISBN 0-07-020986-3). McGraw.

Finkel, LeRoy & Brown, Jerald R. Apple BASIC: Data File Programming. LC 81-13100. 303p. 1982. pap. 14.95 (ISBN 0-471-09157-X, Pub. by Wiley Pr); software diskette 24.95 (ISBN 0-471-86836-1); pap. 34.90 bk. & disk set (ISBN 0-471-89843-0). Wiley.

--Data File Programming in BASIC. LC 80-39790. (Self-Teaching Guide Ser.). 338p. 1981. pap. text ed. 14.95 (ISBN 0-471-08333-X, Pub. by Wiley Pr). Wiley.

--TRS-80 Data File Programming. (Self-Teaching Guides: No. 1-581). 320p. 1983. pap. text ed. 14.95 (ISBN 0-471-88486-3, Pub. by Wiley Press). Wiley.

Finkel, LeRoy, jt. auth. see Bove, Anthony L.

Finkel, LeRoy, jt. auth. see Brown, Jerald.

Finkel, LeRoy, jt. auth. see Brown, Jerald R.

Finkel, LeRoy, et al. Commodore 64 Data File Programming Book. LC 84-22063. (Self-Teaching Guides Ser.: No. 1-598). 499p. 1985. 14.95 (ISBN 0-471-80734-6, Wiley Professional Software); book & disk 39.90 (ISBN 0-471-80753-2, Wiley Professional Software). Wiley.

Finkel, Leslie G., jt. auth. see Finkel, Norma Y.

Finkel, Madelon, jt. auth. see McCarthy, Eugene.

Finkel, Madelon L., jt. auth. see McCarthy, Eugene G.

Finkel, Maurice. Fresh Hope in Cancer. 117p. 1978. pap. 7.95 (ISBN 0-8464-1065-6). Beekman Pubs.

--Fresh Hope in Cancer. 1980. 15.00x (ISBN 0-85032-159-X, Pub. by Daniel Co England). State Mutual Bk.

--Fresh Hope in Cancer. 128p. 1981. pap. 6.95 (ISBN 0-914794-41-8). Wisdom Garden.

--Fresh Hope with New Cancer Treatments: Over Twenty Natural Methods for Prevention, Treatment, & Control of Cancer. 128p. 1984. 12.95 (ISBN 0-13-330787-5); pap. 5.95 (ISBN 0-13-330779-4). P-H.

Finkel, Norma Y. & Finkel, Leslie G. Kaleidoscopic Designs & How to Create Them. 1980. pap. 2.50 (ISBN 0-486-23935-7). Dover.

Finkel, Norman J. Mental Illness & Health: Its Legacy Tensions, & Changes. 128p. 1976. pap. text ed. write for info. (ISBN 0-02-337700-3, 33770). Macmillan.

--Therapy & Ethics: The Courtship of Law & Psychology. (Current Issues in Behavioral Psychology Ser.). 208p. 1980. 34.00 (ISBN 0-8089-1222-4, 791262). Grune.

Finkel, Nosson. Chessed as an Expression of Emunah: A Schmuess. Kaminetsky, Joseph, ed. 0.50 (ISBN 0-914131-10-9, I30). Torah Umesorah.

Finkel, Raphael A. An Operating Systems Vade Mecum. 320p. 1986. text ed. 32.95 (ISBN 0-13-637455-7). P-H.

Finkel, Robert. The Brainbooster: Your Guide to Rapid Learning & Remembering. (Illus.). 198p. 1983. 13.95 (ISBN 0-13-080895-4); pap. 6.95 (ISBN 0-13-080887-3). P-H.

Finkel, Saul. The Circular Seesaw. LC 76-1779. 269p. 1978. 9.95 (ISBN 0-912282-05-3); pap. 3.95 (ISBN 0-912282-06-1). Pulse-Finger.

Finkel, Sidney R. Cases in Financial Management. 501p. 1986. pap. text ed. price not set (ISBN 0-02-337710-0). Macmillan.

Finkel, Steve. Commodore 16 Users Manual. LC 84-52615. 12.95 (ISBN 0-672-22437-2). Sams.

Finkelhor, David. Child Sexual Abuse: New Theory & Research. LC 84-47889. 304p. 1984. 22.50x (ISBN 0-02-910020-8). Free Pr.

--Sexually Victimized Children. LC 79-7104. 1979. 19.95 (ISBN 0-02-910210-3); pap. text ed. 12.95 (ISBN 0-02-910400-9). Free Pr.

Finkelhor, David & Yllo, Kersti. License to Rape: Sexual Abuse of Wives. 1985. 16.45 (ISBN 0-03-059474-X). HR&W.

Finkelhor, David & Gelles, Richard J., eds. The Dark Side of Families: Current Family Violence Research. 384p. 1983. 29.95 (ISBN 0-8039-1934-4); pap. 14.95 (ISBN 0-8039-1935-2). Sage.

Finkelman, Anita W. Staff Development for the Psychiatric Nurse. LC 78-68711. 100p. 1980. 12.00 (ISBN 0-913590-64-9). Slack Inc.

Finkelman, Jacob & Goldenberg, Shirley. Collective Bargaining in the Public Sector: The Federal Experience in Canada, 2 vols. 600p. (Orig.). 1984. Set. pap. text ed. 29.95x (ISBN 0-920380-79-4, Pub. by Inst Res Pub Canada). Brookfield Pub Co.

Finkelman, Paul. An Imperfect Union: Slavery, Federalism, & Comity. LC 79-27526. (Studies in Legal History). xii, 378p. 1981. 27.50 (ISBN 0-8078-1438-5); pap. 8.95x (ISBN 0-8078-4066-1). U of NC Pr.

--The Law of Freedom & Bondage: A Casebook. (Legal & Constitutional History Ser.). (Orig.). 1985. lib. bdg. 35.00 (ISBN 0-379-20817-2); pap. (ISBN 0-379-20822-9). Oceana.

Finkel'shtein, B. N. Relaxation Phenomena in Metals & Alloys. LC 62-21590. 244p. 1963. 45.00x (ISBN 0-306-10664-7, Consultants). Plenum Pub.

Finkelstein. Statistics at Your Fingertips. 336p. 1985. write for info. (ISBN 0-534-04023-3). Wadsworth Pub.

Finkelstein, et al. Religions of Democracy. 1941. 9.50 (ISBN 0-8159-6708-X). Devin.

Finkelstein, Abe & Holtje, Bert. Handbook of Woodworking Plans, Patterns & Projects. LC 79-26025. 256p. 1980. 12.95 (ISBN 0-13-382853-0, Parker). P-H.

Finkelstein, Adrian. Your Past Lives & the Healing Process. 233p. (Orig.). 1985. pap. 9.95x (ISBN 0-87418-001-5). Coleman Pub.

--Your Past Lives & the Healing Process. 233p. (Orig.). 1985. pap. 9.95x. A Finkelstein.

Finkelstein, Arthur K., jt. auth. see Stein, George N.

Finkelstein, Aryeh, tr. see Mazar, Benjamin & Shanks, Hershel.

Finkelstein, Barbara, ed. Regulated Children-Liberated Children: Education in Psychohistorical Perspective. 230p. 1979. 17.95 (ISBN 0-914434-08-X); pap. 8.95 (ISBN 0-914434-10-1). Psychohistory Pr.

Finkelstein, Bonnie B. Forster's Women: Eternal Differences. LC 74-18418. 183p. 1975. 18.00x (ISBN 0-231-03893-3). Columbia U Pr.

Finkelstein, Haim N. Surrealism & the Crisis of the Object. Foster, Stephen, ed. LC 79-24377. (Studies in the Fine Arts: The Avant-Garde, No. 3). 162p. 1980. 39.95 (ISBN 0-8357-1059-9). UMI Res Pr.

Finkelstein, Honora, jt. auth. see Gross, Gail.

Finkelstein, Irving L. Prints of the High Museum: Image & Process. Morris, Kelly, ed. LC 78-61741. (Illus.). 72p. (Orig.). 1978. pap. 4.00 (ISBN 0-939802-06-6). High Mus Art.

Finkelstein, J. J. The Ox that Gored. LC 80-65852. (Transactions Ser.: Vol. 71, Pt. 2). 1981. 12.00 (ISBN 0-87169-711-4). Am Philos.

Finkelstein, Jacob J. Late Old Babylonian Documents & Letters. LC 72-75190. (Yale Oriental Series. Babylonian Texts: No. 13). pap. 53.60 (ISBN 0-317-10134-X, 2016796). Bks Demand UMI.

Finkelstein, Jacob J., ed. see Speiser, Ephraim A.

Finkelstein, Jesse A., jt. auth. see Balotti, R. Franklin.

Finkelstein, Joseph & Thimm, Alfred L. Economists & Society: The Development of Economic Thought from Aquinas to Keynes. LC 81-51797. 399p. 1981. Repr. of 1973 ed. 9.95 (ISBN 0-912756-11-X). Union Coll.

Finkelstein, L. & Carson, E. R. Mathematical Modelling of Dynamic Biological Systems. 2nd ed. (Medical Computing Ser.). 59.95 (ISBN 0-471-90688-3). Wiley.

Finkelstein, Lawrence, ed. United States & International Organization: The New Setting. 1969. pap. 7.95x (ISBN 0-262-56009-7). MIT Pr.

Finkelstein, Louis. Akiba: Scholar, Saint & Martyr. LC 62-12354. (Temple Bks). 1970. pap. text ed. 6.95x (ISBN 0-689-70230-2, T11). Atheneum.

--Jewish Self-Government in the Middle Ages. LC 74-97277. 390p. 1972. Repr. of 1924 ed. lib. bdg. 20.75x (ISBN 0-8371-2598-7, FIJS). Greenwood.

--Sifre on Deuteronomy. 1969. 25.00x (ISBN 0-685-31422-7, Pub. by Jewish Theol Seminary). Ktav.

--Social Responsibility in an Age of Revolution. 1971. 10.00x (ISBN 0-685-31421-9, Pub. by Jewish Theol Seminary). Ktav.

Finkelstein, Louis see Davies, W. D.

Finkelstein, Louis, ed. The Jews: Their Role in Civilization, Vol. 3. 4th ed. LC 74-107615. 1971. pap. 7.95 (ISBN 0-8052-0273-0). Schocken.

--Thirteen Americans. LC 68-26190. (Essay & General Literature Index Reprint Ser.). 1969. Repr. of 1953 ed. 21.50x (ISBN 0-8046-0219-0, Pub by Kennikat). Assoc Faculty Pr.

Finkelstein, Louis & Katz, Steven, eds. Rab Saadia Gaon: Studies in His Honor. LC 79-7169. (Jewish Philosophy, Mysticism & History of Ideas Ser.). 1980. Repr. of 1944 ed. lib. bdg. 19.00x (ISBN 0-405-12250-0). Ayer Co Pubs.

Finkelstein, Louis, ed. see Kimchi, David B.

Finkelstein, Ludwick & Carson, Ewart R. Mathematical Modeling of Dynamic Biological Systems, Vol. 3. (Medical Computing Ser.). 329p. 1979. 48.95x (ISBN 0-471-27890-4, Research Studies Pr). Wiley.

Finkelstein, M. I., tr. see Rusche, Georg & Kirchheimer, Otto.

Finkelstein, Marina, ed. see Sharp, Gene.

Finkelstein, Mark & McCarty, George. Calculate Basic Statistics. LC 82-82511. 350p. 1982. pap. 14.95 (ISBN 0-936356-01-4). EduCALC Pubns.

Finkelstein, Martin J. The American Academic Profession: A Synthesis of Social Scientific Inquiry Since World War II. LC 84-3613. 304p. 1984. 17.50 (ISBN 0-8142-0371-X). Ohio St U Pr.

Finkelstein, Michael O. Quantitative Methods in Law: Studies in the Application of Mathematical Probability & Statistics to Legal Problems. LC 77-94081. 1978. 22.95 (ISBN 0-02-910260-X). Free Pr.

Finkelstein, Mike. Teach Yourself Rock Drums. 80p. pap. 7.95 (ISBN 0-8256-2211-5). Music Sales.

Finkelstein, Milton, jt. auth. see Basch, Lester D.

Finkelstein, Norman. Remember Not to Forget: A Memory of the Holocaust. (Illus.). 32p. (gr. 1-3). 1985. lib. bdg. 8.90 (ISBN 0-531-04892-6). Watts.

Finkelstein, Norman, tr. see Amin, Samir.

Finkelstein, Raphael, jt. auth. see London, Hymie.

Finkelstein, Robert J. Thermodynamics & Statistical Physics: A Short Introduction. LC 78-94103. (Illus.). 249p. 1970. text ed. 32.95 (ISBN 0-7167-0325-4). W H Freeman.

Finkelstein, Ruth. Mendel the Mouse, Bk. 2. (Illus.). 4.25 (ISBN 0-914131-44-3, D36). Torah Umesorah.

Finkelstein, Sidney. Jazz: A People's Music. LC 74-23386. (Roots of Jazz Ser.). ix, 278p. 1975. Repr. of 1948 ed. lib. bdg. 25.00 (ISBN 0-306-70659-8). Da Capo.

Finkelstein, Victor. Attitudes & Disabled People, No. 5. (International Exchange of Information in Rehabilitation Ser.). 107p. 1980. write for info. (ISBN 0-939986-09-4). World Rehab Fund.

Finkenaur, Robert G. COBOL for Students: A Programmer Primer. 384p. (Orig.). 1977. pap. text ed. 19.95 (ISBN 0-316-28320-7); tchrs'. manual avail. (ISBN 0-316-28321-5). Little.

Finkenstaedt, Thomas & Wolff, Dieter. Ordered Profusion: Studies in Dictionaries & the English Lexicon. 166p. 1973. 29.00x (ISBN 3-5330-2253-6). Adlers Foreign Bks.

Finkentscher, Wolfgang. Schuldrecht. xxvi, 858p. 1985. 47.20x (ISBN 3-11-010527-6); pap. 31.20x (ISBN 3-11-007158-4). De Gruyter.

Finkenzeller, P., jt. ed. see Keidel, W. D.

Finker, Kaja. Spiritualist Healers in Mexico: Successes & Failures of Alternative Therapies. 256p. 1984. 25.95 (ISBN 0-03-063912-3). Praeger.

Finkl, C. W., Jr., jt. ed. see Fairbridge, R. W.

Finkl, Charles, Jr., ed. Soil Classification. LC 81-6214. (Benchmark Papers in Soil Science: Vol. 1). 416p. 1982. 46.50 (ISBN 0-87933-399-5). Van Nos Reinhold.

Finkl, Charles W., Jr., ed. The Encyclopedia of Applied Geology. 832p. 1984. 75.00 (ISBN 0-442-22537-7). Van Nos Reinhold.

Finkle, Bernard J. & Runeckles, Victor C., eds. Phenolic Compounds & Metabolic Regulation. LC 66-29065. 157p. 1967. 19.50x (ISBN 0-306-50023-X, Plenum Pr). Plenum Pub.

Finkle, Jason L. & Gable, Richard W. Political Development & Social Change. 2nd ed. LC 72-149769. pap. 160.00 (ISBN 0-317-19822-X, 2023215). Bks Demand UMI.

Finkle, Robert B. & Jones, William S. Assessing Corporate Talent: A Key to Managerial Manpower Planning. LC 71-120702. pap. 49.40 (ISBN 0-8357-9841-0, 2012353). Bks Demand UMI.

Finkler, Earl. Dissent & Independent Initiative in Planning Offices, 1971. (PAS Reports: No. 269). 64p. 1971. 5.00 (ISBN 0-318-12960-4); members 3.00 (ISBN 0-318-12961-2). Am Plan Assn.

--Nongrowth as a Planning Alternative: A Preliminary Examination of an Emerging Issue. (PAS Reports: No. 283). 65p. 1972. 6.00 (ISBN 0-318-13038-6). Am Plan Assn.

Finkler, Earl, et al. The Design, Regulation, & Location of Service Stations. (PAS Reports: No. 293). 110p. 1973. 5.00 (ISBN 0-318-12957-4); members 3.00 (ISBN 0-318-12958-2). Am Plan Assn.

Finkler, Kaja. Spiritualist Healers in Mexico: Successes & Failures of Alternative Therapeutics. (Illus.). 272p. 1983. text ed. 27.95x (ISBN 0-686-46094-4); pap. text ed. 12.95 (ISBN 0-89789-092-2). Bergin & Garvey.

--Spiritualist Healers in Mexico: Successes & Failures of Alternative Therapeutics. 256p. 1985. pap. 12.95 (ISBN 0-89789-092-2). Bergin & Garvey.

Finkler, Steven A. Budgeting Concepts for Nurse Managers. 208p. 1984. 19.50 (ISBN 0-8089-1638-6, 791261). Grune.

--The Complete Guide to Finance & Accounting for Non-Financial Managers. (Illus.). 222p. 1983. 22.95 (ISBN 0-13-160531-3); pap. 10.95 (ISBN 0-13-160523-2). P-H.

Finklestein, Dorothee M. Melville's Orienda. LC 77-120252. 1970. Repr. lib. bdg. 23.00x (ISBN 0-374-92741-3). Octagon.

Finklestein, Ruth, illus. Mendel the Mouse, 2 bks. Incl. Bk. 1 (ISBN 0-914131-43-5); Bk. 2 (ISBN 0-914131-44-3, D36). 4.25 ea. Torah Umesorah.

Finklin, Arnold I. Weather & Climate of the Selway-Bitterroot Wilderness. LC 83-50098. (GEM Books Ser.). (Illus.). 160p. 1982. 11.95 (ISBN 0-89301-093-6). U Pr of Idaho.

Finks, Lee. Is This a Put-on? 104p. 1985. 3.00 (ISBN 0-682-40233-8). Exposition Pr FL.

Finks, Lee W. How to Quit Smoking Once & for All. vii, 202p. (Orig.). 1984. pap. 5.95 (ISBN 0-9613206-0-5). CCW Pub.

Finks, P. David. Radical Vision of Saul Alinsky. (Orig.). 1984. pap. 9.95 (ISBN 0-8091-2608-7). Paulist Pr.

Finkworth, F. V., jt. auth. see Smith, J. M.

Finlan, Stephen. The Forgotten Teachings of Jesus. (Illus.). 49p. (Orig.). 1984. pap. 3.00 perfect bound (ISBN 0-9614275-0-7). Spiritual.

Finland, M., jt. ed. see Sabath, L. D.

Finland, Maxwell. The Harvard Medical Unit at Boston City Hospital. (Illus.). 903p. 1982. 50.00x (ISBN 0-8139-0977-5, Pub. by Francis A Countway Lib). U Pr of Va.

Finland, Maxwell & Castle, William B., eds. The Harvard Medical Unit, Vol. II. (Illus.). 1441p. 1983. 50.00x (ISBN 0-8139-1000-5, Pub. by Francis A Countway). U Pr of Va.

Finland, Maxwell & Kass, Edward H., eds. Trimethoprim-Sulfamethoxazole. LC 73-92601. viii, 392p. 1974. 17.95x (ISBN 0-226-24916-6). U of Chicago Pr.

Finland, Maxwell, jt. ed. see Charles, David.

Finlason, W. F. Commentaries Upon Martial Law, with Special Reference to Its Regulation & Restraint: With an Introduction, Containing Comments Upon the Charge of the Lord Chief Justice in the Jamaica Case. 287p. 1980. Repr. of 1867 ed. lib. bdg. 28.50x (ISBN 0-8377-0536-3). Rothman.

Finlason, W. F., ed. see Reeves, John.

Finlay, D., jt. auth. see Allen, M.

Finlay, D., jt. auth. see Bell, G.

Finlay, David, et al. MOQ's in Imaging Sciences. 128p. 1982. pap. 9.95 (ISBN 0-7216-0806-X, Pub. by Bailliere-Tindall). Saunders.

Finlay, George. History of Greece, 7 Vols. 1970. Repr. of 1877 ed. Set. 245.00 (ISBN 0-404-02390-8); 35.00 ea. AMS Pr.

Finlay, Holly & Wallace, Judy. The Eatgood Revival. (Illus.). 208p. (gr. 7 up). 1972. pap. 3.95 (ISBN 0-8038-1908-0). Hastings.

Finlay, Iain & Sheppard, Trish. Across the South Pacific: Island-Hopping from Santiago to Sydney. (Illus.). 245p. 1983. 17.95 (ISBN 0-207-14824-4, Pub. by Salem Hse Ltd). Merrimack Pub Cir.

Finlay, Ian. Scottish Crafts. (Illus.). 1977. Repr. of 1948 ed. 29.00x (ISBN 0-7158-1171-1). Charles River Bks.

Finlay, Ian F. Stamp Collecting. (gr. 3-5). 1969. 2.50 (ISBN 0-7214-0235-6). Merry Thoughts.

Finlay, Ian H. A Sailor's Calendar. (Illus.). 1971. pap. 10.00 (ISBN 0-87110-075-4). Ultramarine Pub.

--Selected Ponds. 1975. pap. 10.00 (ISBN 0-915596-10-5). West Coast.

Finlay, Ian H. & Bann, Stephen. Heroic Emblems. (Illus.). 1978. pap. 5.00 (ISBN 0-915990-10-5). Z Pr.

Finlay, J. L. & Sprague, D. N. The Structure of Canadian History 2E. 300p. 1984. pap. text ed. 14.95 (ISBN 0-13-854364-X). P-H.

Finlay, John. Scottish Historical & Romantic Ballads, Chiefly Ancient: With Explanatory Notes & a Glossary. 205p. Repr. of 1808 ed. Set. 250.00 (ISBN 0-89760-275-7). Telegraph Bks.

Finlay, John L. Social Credit: The English Origins. 1972. 15.00x (ISBN 0-7735-0111-8). McGill-Queens U Pr.

Finlay, K. W. & Shepherd, K. W., eds. Wheat Genetics. LC 79-77369. 479p. 1969. 49.50x (ISBN 0-306-30666-2, Plenum Pr). Plenum Pub.

Finlay, M. H. The Lim Family of Singapore. 1982. 7.20 (ISBN 0-686-36254-3). Rod & Staff.

Finlay, Patrick, ed. Jane's Freight Containers 1983. 15th ed. (Jane's Yearbooks). (Illus.). 640p. 1983. 140.00x (ISBN 0-86720-642-X). Jane's Pub Inc.

--Jane's Freight Containers, 1984. 16th ed. (Jane's Yearbooks). (Illus.). 600p. 1984. 125.00x (ISBN 0-7106-0790-3). Jane's Pub Inc.

--Jane's Freight Containers 1985. 17th ed. (Jane's Yearbooks). (Illus.). 630p. 1985. 125.00 (ISBN 0-7106-0808-X). Jane's Pub Inc.

Finlay, Robert. Politics in Renaissance Venice. 1980. 32.00x (ISBN 0-8135-0888-6). Rutgers U Pr.

Finlay, Roger A. Population & Metropolis: The Demography of London, 1580-1650. LC 78-20956. (Cambridge Geographical Studies: No. 12). 224p. 1981. 52.50 (ISBN 0-521-22535-3). Cambridge U Pr.

Finlay, Winifred. Danger at Black Dyke. LC 68-31174. (Illus.). (gr. 7-10). 1968. 10.95 (ISBN 0-87599-150-5). S G Phillips.

Finlay, Winifred & Hancock, Gillian. Clever & Courageous Dogs. (Illus.). (gr. 3-6). 8.95 (ISBN 0-7182-1186-3, Pub. by Kaye & Ward). David & Charles.

Finlay-Freundlich, E. Cosmology. LC 51-4594. (Foundations of the Unity of Science Ser: Vol. 1, No. 8). 1951. pap. 1.50x (ISBN 0-226-57583-7, P407, Phoen). U of Chicago Pr.

Finlayson, A. N. International Wind Energy Symposium. 1982. 60.00 (I00153). ASME.

Finlayson, Angela & McEwen, James. Coronary Heart Disease & Patterns of Living. LC 76-56850. 1977. 22.50 (ISBN 0-88202-110-9). Watson Pub Intl.

Finlayson, Ann. Champions at Bat: Three Power Hitters. LC 74-113838. (Sports Ser.). (Illus.). (gr. 3-6). 1970. PLB 7.12 (ISBN 0-8116-6661-1). Garrard.

--Rebecca's War. LC 78-183735. (Illus.). 280p. (gr. 6 up). 1972. 5.95 (ISBN 0-7232-6090-7). Warne.

Finlayson, B., ed. see International Urinary Stone Conference, Australia, 1979, et al.

Finlayson, Birdwell, jt. auth. see Roth, Robert A.

Finlayson, Birdwell & Thomas, William C., Jr., eds. Colloquium on Renal Lithiasis. LC 77-7779. (Illus.). 1976. 25.00 (ISBN 0-8130-0566-3). U Presses Fla.

Finlayson, Brian, jt. auth. see Statham, Ian.

Finlayson, Bruce A. The Method of Weighted Residuals & Variational Principles. (Mathematics in Science & Engineering Ser.). 1972. 85.00 (ISBN 0-12-257050-2). Acad Pr.

--Nonlinear Analysis in Chemical Engineering. (M-H Chemical Engineering Ser.). (Illus.). 384p. 1980. text ed. 52.00 (ISBN 0-07-020915-4). McGraw.

Finlayson, Iain. The Moth & the Candle: A Life of James Boswell. LC 83-40701. (Illus.). 266p. 1984. 22.50 (ISBN 0-312-54918-0). St Martin.

Finlayson, Niall D., jt. ed. see Shearman, David J.

Finlen, James T. Meet Some Folks. 1984. 12.95 (ISBN 0-8062-1848-7). Carlton.

Finler, Joel. Stroheim. movie ed. LC 68-17757. 1968. pap. 2.45 (ISBN 0-520-00413-2, CAL155). U of Cal Pr.

Finletter, Thomas K. Power & Policy. LC 74-159718. 408p. 1972. Repr. of 1954 ed. lib. bdg. 19.75x (ISBN 0-8371-6189-4, FIPP). Greenwood.

Finley, Blanche. The Structure of the United Nations General Assembly: Its Committees & Other Organisms, 1964-1973, Vol. 3. LC 77-72373. 1463p. 1977. 45.00 (ISBN 0-379-10240-4). Oceana.

--Structure of the United Nations General Assembly, Vol. 3. LC 77-72373. 1977. 45.00 (ISBN 0-379-10243-9). Oceana.

Finley, Charles W. Biology in Secondary Schools & the Training of Biology Teachers. LC 77-176772. (Columbia University. Teachers College. Contributions to Education: No. 199). Repr. of 1926 ed. 22.50 (ISBN 0-404-55199-8). AMS Pr.

Finley, Clarence W., Jr. & Myers, Roy E. Assembly Language for the Applesoft Programmer. 1630p. 1984. pap. 16.95 (ISBN 0-201-05209-1). Addison-Wesley.

Finley, David E. A Standard of Excellence: Andrew W. Mellon Founds the National Gallery of Art at Washington, D. C. LC 73-5676. (Illus.). 200p. 1975. 10.95x (ISBN 0-87474-132-7). Smithsonian.

Finley, Elizabeth. Manual of Procedures for Private Law Libraries. rev. ed. (AALL Publications Ser.: No. 8). xi, 176p. 1966. 17.50x (ISBN 0-8377-0106-6). Rothman.

Finley, George, ed. see Industrial Design Magazine.

Finley, Gerald. George Heriot. (Canadian Artists Ser.). 1980. pap. 5.95 (ISBN 0-88884-369-0, 56363-4, Pub. by Natl Gallery Canada). U of Chicago Pr.

--George Heriot: Postmaster-Painter of the Canadas. 288p. 1983. 37.50x (ISBN 0-8020-5584-2). U of Toronto Pr.

--Landscapes of Memory: Turner As Illustrator to Scott. LC 80-5956. (Illus.). 272p. 1981. 65.00 (ISBN 0-520-04436-3). U of Cal Pr.

Finley, Gerald E. George Heriot Seventeen Fifty-Nine to Eighteen Thirty-Nine. (Canadian Artists Ser.). 1979. pap. 5.95 ea. (Pub. by Natl Mus Canada). French ed (ISBN 0-88884-375-5). English ed (ISBN 0-88884-369-0). Nat Gal Can.

Finley, Glenna. Kiss a Stranger. 1972. pap. 1.95 (ISBN 0-451-11228-8, AJ1228, Sig). NAL.

--Love's Waiting Game. 1985. pap. 2.50 (ISBN 0-451-13328-5, Sig). NAL.

--A Touch of Love. 1985. pap. 2.50 (ISBN 0-451-13564-4, Sig). NAL.

--Treasure of the Heart, No. 3. (Orig.). 1983. pap. 2.95 (ISBN 0-451-13469-9, Sig). NAL.

--Wanted for Love, No. 33. 192p. 1983. pap. 1.95 (ISBN 0-451-12480-4, Sig). NAL.

--A Weekend for Love. 1984. pap. 2.25 (ISBN 0-451-12971-7, Sig). NAL.

--When Love Speaks, No. 8. 1973. pap. 1.95 (ISBN 0-451-11799-9, AJ1799, Sig). NAL.

Finley, Harvey E. & Isbell, Charles D. Biblical Hebrew. 213p. 1975. pap. text ed. 13.95 (ISBN 0-8341-0350-8). Beacon Hill.

Finley, J. M. Practical Wound Management. 1980. 36.50 (ISBN 0-8151-3225-5). Year Bk Med.

Finley, James. The Awakening Call. LC 84-72094. 160p. (Orig.). 1985. pap. 4.95 (ISBN 0-87793-278-6). Ave Maria.

--Merton's Palace of Nowhere. LC 78-58738. 160p. 1978. pap. 3.95 (ISBN 0-87793-159-3). Ave Maria.

--Your Future & You. LC 81-65228. (Illus.). 176p. (Orig.). (gr. 10-12). 1981. pap. 4.50 (ISBN 0-87793-223-9); tchrs. ed. 2.25 (ISBN 0-87793-224-7). Ave Maria.

Finley, James & Pennock, Michael. Your Faith & You. LC 78-53834. (Illus.). 272p. (gr. 11-12). 1978. pap. text ed. 4.95 (ISBN 0-87793-153-4); tchr's manual 2.75 (ISBN 0-87793-154-2). Ave Maria.

Finley, James, jt. auth. see Pennock, Michael.

Finley, James B. Life among the Indians: Or, Personal Reminiscences & Historical Incidents Illustrative of Indian Life & Character. facsimile ed. Clark, D. W., ed. LC 76-160972. (Select Bibliographies Reprint Ser). Repr. of 1857 ed. 31.00 (ISBN 0-8369-5840-3). Ayer Co Pubs.

--Memorials of Prison Life. facsimile ed. LC 74-3823. (Criminal Justice in America Ser.). 1974. Repr. of 1855 ed. 27.50x (ISBN 0-405-06143-9). Ayer Co Pubs.

--Sketches of Western Methodism: Biographical, Historical & Miscellaneous Illustrative of Pioneer Life. LC 79-83419. (Religion in America, Ser. 1). 1969. Repr. of 1954 ed. 30.00 (ISBN 0-405-00244-0). Ayer Co Pubs.

Finley, Jean D., tr. see Perrin, Joseph-Marie.

Finley, Jeanne & Smith, Aileen. Minamata. (Illus.). 24p. 1981. pap. 3.00 (ISBN 0-938262-05-X). U Ariz Ctr Photog.

Finley, John. Considering Plastic Surgery? (Illus., Orig.). 1985. pap. 12.95 (ISBN 0-9614251-9-9). Crescent Bks.

Finley, John, jt. auth. see Sehlinger, Bob.

Finley, John H., Jr. Four Stages of Greek Thought. 1966. 10.00x (ISBN 0-8047-0274-8); pap. 3.95 (ISBN 0-8047-0275-6, SP66). Stanford U Pr.

--Homer's Odyssey. LC 78-9308. 1978. 16.50x (ISBN 0-674-40614-1). Harvard U Pr.

--Pindar & Aeschylus. LC 54-11110. (Martin Classical Lectures Ser.: No. 14). 1955. 20.00x (ISBN 0-674-66800-6). Harvard U Pr.

--Three Essays on Thucydides. LC 67-17308. (Loeb Classical Monographs Ser). 1967. 15.00x (ISBN 0-674-88935-5). Harvard U Pr.

Finley, John M. & McConnell, Richard Y. Emergency Wound Repair. (Illus.). 160p. 1984. pap. text ed. 20.00 (ISBN 0-8391-1960-7, 20583). Univ Park.

Finley, John P. The Sabanu: Studies of a Sub-Visayan Mountain Folk of Mindanao. 1913. 24.00 (ISBN 0-384-15700-9). Johnson Repr.

Finley, Joseph E. White Collar Union: The Story of the OPEIU and Its People. 288p. 1975. lib. bdg. 14.00x (ISBN 0-374-92742-1). Octagon.

Finley, K. T. Triazoles. LC 80-13323. (Chemistry of Heterocyclic Compounds, Series of Monographs: Vol. 39). 349p. 1980. 156.50x (ISBN 0-471-07827-1). Wiley.

Finley, K. Thomas. Triazoles-One-Two-Three. (Chemistry of Heterocyclic Compounds Monographs). 349p. 1980. 179.50 (ISBN 0-471-07827-1). Wiley.

Finley, Kathy, jt. auth. see Finley, Mitch.

Finley, Kay T., jt. auth. see Siegel, Patricia J.

Finley, M. I. The Ancient Economy. (Sather Classical Lectures: Vol. 43). 1973. 24.00x (ISBN 0-520-02436-2); pap. 7.95 (ISBN 0-520-02564-4). U of Cal Pr.

--The Ancient Economy. 2nd. ed. 1985. 8.95 (ISBN 0-520-05452-0, CAL 734). U of Cal Pr.

--Ancient Greeks. 1977. pap. 5.95 (ISBN 0-14-020812-7, Pelican). Penguin.

--Ancient Sicily. rev. ed. (Illus.). 229p. 1979. 16.50x (ISBN 0-8476-6190-3). Rowman.

--Ancient Slavery & Modern Ideology. 208p. 1980. 13.95 (ISBN 0-670-12277-7). Viking.

--Ancient Slavery & Modern Ideology. 1983. pap. 6.95 (ISBN 0-14-022500-5, Pelican). Penguin.

--Aspects of Antiquity. (Illus.). 1977. pap. 6.95 (ISBN 0-14-021509-3, Pelican). Penguin.

--Early Greece: The Bronze & Archaic Ages. 2nd ed. (Ancient Culture & Society). (Illus.). 1982. 14.95 (ISBN 0-393-01569-6); pap. 5.95 (ISBN 0-393-30051-X). Norton.

--Economy & Society in Ancient Greece. Shaw, Brent D. & Saller, Richard P., eds. 352p. 1983. pap. 7.95 (ISBN 0-14-022520-X). Penguin.

--The Legacy of Greece: A New Appraisal. (Illus.). 1981. 22.50x (ISBN 0-19-821915-6); pap. 9.95x (ISBN 0-19-821915-6). Oxford U Pr.

--The World of Odysseus. rev. ed. 1979. pap. 4.95 (ISBN 0-14-020570-5, Pelican). Penguin.

--World of Odysseus. rev. ed. 1978. 13.95 (ISBN 0-670-78764-7). Viking.

Finley, M. I., ed. Portable Greek Historians. (Viking Portable Library: No. 65). 1960. 14.95 (ISBN 0-670-35244-6). Viking.

--Studies in Roman Property. (Classical Studies). (Illus.). 192p. 1976. 17.95 (ISBN 0-521-21115-8). Cambridge U Pr.

Finley, M. I., ed. see Garlan, Yvon.

Finley, M. I., ed. see Lloyd, G. E.

Finley, M. I., ed. see Sandbach, F. H.

Finley, Martha. Elsie at Nantucket. 301p. 1981. Repr. PLB 17.95x (ISBN 0-89966-333-8). Buccaneer Bks.

--Elsie at Nantucket. 302p. 1980. Repr. PLB 17.95x (ISBN 0-89967-011-3). Harmony Raine.

--Elsie Dinsmore. LC 74-15737. (Popular Culture in America Ser.). (Illus.). 342p. 1975. Repr. of 1896 ed. 24.00x (ISBN 0-405-06372-5). Ayer Co Pubs.

--Elsie Dinsmore. 332p. Repr. PLB 17.95x (ISBN 0-89966-332-X). Buccaneer Bks.

--Elsie Dinsmore. 275p. 1980. Repr. lib. bdg. 17.95x (ISBN 0-89967-010-5). Buccaneer Bks.

--Elsie's Children. 243p. 1981. Repr. PLB 17.95x (ISBN 0-89966-336-2). Buccaneer Bks.

--Elsie's Girlhood. 273p. 1981. Repr. PLB 17.95x (ISBN 0-89966-334-6). Buccaneer Bks.

--Elsie's Motherhood. 243p. 1981. Repr. PLB 17.95x (ISBN 0-89966-335-4). Buccaneer Bks.

Finley, Merrill. Christ & Colonel. 120p. pap. cancelled (ISBN 0-911826-51-3). Am Atheist.

Finley, Mike. Lucky You. 1976. perfect bdg. 2.00 (ISBN 0-915214-10-5). Litmus.

--The Movie Under the Blindfold. (Illus.). 1978. pap. 3.50 (ISBN 0-917266-14-5). Vanilla.

Finley, Mitch & Finley, Kathy. Christian Families in the Real World. 1984. 9.95 (ISBN 0-88347-163-9). Thomas More.

Finley, Moses. Politics in the Ancient World. LC 83-1771. 152p. 1983. 29.95 (ISBN 0-521-25489-2); pap. 10.95 (ISBN 0-521-27570-9). Cambridge U Pr.

Finley, Moses, ed. Ancient Economic History Series, 45 bks, Vols. 1-22. 1980. Set. 1860.00 (ISBN 0-405-12345-0). Ayer Co Pubs.

Finley, Moses, jt. ed. see Andreades, A. M.

Finley, Moses, ed. see Babelon, Ernest.

Finley, Moses, ed. see Beloch, Julius.

Finley, Moses, ed. see Blumner, Hugo.

Finley, Moses, ed. see Buchsenschutz, B. & Blumner, Hugo.

Finley, Moses, ed. see Davies, Oliver.

Finley, Moses, ed. see De Robertis, Francesco M. & Norr, Dieter.

Finley, Moses, ed. see Francotte, Henri.

Finley, Moses, ed. see Friedlander, Ludwig.

Finley, Moses, ed. see Fustel De Coulanges, Numa D.

Finley, Moses, ed. see Gernet, Louis.

Finley, Moses, ed. see Graindor, Paul.

Finley, Moses, ed. see Gren, Erik.

Finley, Moses, ed. see Halkin, Leon.

Finley, Moses, ed. see Heichelheim, Fritz M.

Finley, Moses, ed. see Herfst, Pieter.

Finley, Moses, ed. see Jacob, Oscar.

Finley, Moses, ed. see Klima, Otakar.

Finley, Moses, ed. see Korver, Jan.

Finley, Moses, ed. see Krauss, Samuel.

Finley, Moses, ed. see Kuenzi, Adolphe.

Finley, Moses, ed. see Loane, Helen J.

Finley, Moses, ed. see Michwitz, Gunnar.

Finley, Moses, ed. see Mickwitz, Gunnar.

Finley, Moses, ed. see Moritz, L. A.

Finley, Moses, ed. see Mosse, Claude.

Finley, Moses, ed. see Nissen, Heinrich.

Finley, Moses, ed. see Persson, Axel W.

Finley, Moses, ed. see Preaux, Claire.

Finley, Moses, ed. see Reil, Theodor.

Finley, Moses, ed. see Riezler, Kurt.

Finley, Moses, ed. see Rostovtzeff, Michael.

Finley, Moses, ed. see Salvioli, G.

Finley, Moses, ed. see Schmidt, Alfred.

Finley, Moses, ed. see Schneider, Anna.

Finley, Moses, ed. see Thompson, E. A.

Finley, Moses, ed. see Urbach, E. E.

Finley, Moses, ed. see Vandier, Jacques.

Finley, Moses, jt. ed. see Van Groningen, B. A.

Finley, Moses, ed. see Waltzing, J. P.

Finley, Moses, ed. see Weber, Max.

Finley, Moses, ed. see Wilchen, Ulrich.

Finley, Moses I. Studies in Land & Credit in Ancient Athens, 500-200 B. C. The Horos-Inscriptions. LC 72-7890. (Greek History Ser.). Repr. of 1952 ed. 29.00 (ISBN 0-405-04786-X). Ayer Co Pubs.

--Studies in Land & Credit in Ancient Athens, 500-200 B.C. The Horos Inscriptions. 340p. 1985. text ed. 39.95x (ISBN 0-88738-066-2). Transaction Bks.

Finley, Moses I., ed. The Bucher-Meyer Controversy: An Original Anthology. LC 79-4954. (Ancient Economic History Ser.). (Ger.). 1980. lib. bdg. 32.50x (ISBN 0-405-12346-9). Ayer Co Pubs.

--Internationsl Conference of Economic History, Second, Aix-en-Provence, 1962, Volume I: Trade & Politics in the Ancient World. LC 79-5000. (Ancient Economic History Ser.). (Eng. & Fr.). 1980. Repr. of 1965 ed. lib. bdg. 16.00x (ISBN 0-405-12389-2). Ayer Co Pubs.

--Portable Greek Historians. (Viking Portable Library: No. 65). 1977. pap. 7.95 (ISBN 0-14-015065-X). Penguin.

Finley, P. J., ed. Progress in Aerospace Sciences, Vol. 19. (Illus.). 320p. 1982. 130.00 (ISBN 0-08-029097-3, A140, A999). Pergamon.

Finley, P. J., jt. ed. see Bagley, J. A.

Finley, Pete. For Pete's Sake. (Illus.). 114p. (Orig.). 1981. pap. 4.50 (ISBN 0-941718-00-X). Master Writers.

Finley, R. J. Landsat Analysis of the Texas Coastal Zone. (Report of Investigation: RI 93). (Illus.). 71p. 1979. 4.00 (ISBN 0-318-03231-7). Bur Econ Geology.

Finley, R. J. & Gustavson, T. C. Climatic Controls on Erosion in the Rolling Plains along the Caprock Escarpment of the Texas Panhandle: Geological Circular 80-11. (Illus.). 50p. 1980. 1.75 (ISBN 0-686-36578-X). Bur Econ Geology.

Finley, Robert B., Jr. A New Pinon Mouse (Peromyscus Truei) from Durango, Mexico. (Museum Ser.: Vol. 5, No. 20). 5p. 1952. pap. 1.25 (ISBN 0-317-05010-9). U of KS Mus Nat Hist.

--A New Subspecies of Wood Rat (Neotama Mexicana) from Colorado. (Museum Ser.: Vol. 5, No. 30). 8p. 1953. pap. 1.25 (ISBN 0-317-05012-5). U of KS Mus Nat Hist.

--The Wood Rats of Colorado: Distribution & Ecology. (Museum Ser.: Vol. 10, No. 6). 340p. 1958. 17.00 (ISBN 0-686-80280-2). U of KS Mus Nat Hist.

Finley, Robert J. & Gustavson, Thomas C. Lineament Analysis Based on Landsat Imagery, Texas Panhandle. (Geological Circular Ser.: No. 81-5). (Illus.). 37p. 1981. 2.25 (ISBN 0-686-35723-X). Bur Econ Geology.

Finley, Ruth E. The Lady of Godey's: Sara Josephia Hale. LC 74-3949. (Women in America Ser). (Illus.). 378p. 1974. Repr. of 1931 ed. 32.00x (ISBN 0-405-06095-5). Ayer Co Pubs.

--Old Patchwork Quilts. (Illus.). 1971. 9.75 (ISBN 0-8231-5025-9). Branford.

Finley, Sara C., et al. Annual Review of Birth Defects, 1982: Birth Defects: Clinical & Ethical Considerations. LC 83-9338. (Birth Defects: Originial Article Ser.: Vol. 19, No. 5). 254p. 1983. 48.00 (ISBN 0-8451-1056-X). A R Liss.

Finley, Tom. Diabolus Seeks Revenge. LC 82-15069. (Illus.). 96p. (gr. 7 up). 1982. pap. 3.95 (ISBN 0-8307-0839-1, 5416704). Regal.

--Wilbur: Master of the Rats. LC 83-13685. (Illus.). (gr. 7-12). 1983. pap. 3.95 (ISBN 0-8307-0900-2, 5900059). Regal.

Finley, William, jt. auth. see Weinstein, Marion.

Finman, Ted. OEO Legal Service Programs & the Pursuit of Social Change: The Relationship Between Program Ideology & Program Performance. iii, 84p. (Reprinted from 1971 Wisconson Law Review 1001). 1972. pap. 2.00 (ISBN 0-317-33347-X). Am Bar Foun.

Finn. History of Electric Technology. 1985. lib. bdg. 52.00 (ISBN 0-8240-9120-5). Garland Pub.

Finn & O'Gorman. Teaching about Alcohol: Concepts, Methods & Classroom Activities. 27.95 (ISBN 0-205-07195-3, 717195). Allyn.

Finn, Bernard & Sterling, Christopher, eds. Development of Submarine Cable Communications: An Original Anthology, 2 vols. LC 80-482. (Historical Studies in Telecommunications Ser.). (Illus.). 1980. Set. lib. bdg. 71.50x (ISBN 0-405-13192-5). Ayer Co Pubs.

Finn, C. A., ed. Oxford Reviews of Reproductive Biology, Vol. I. (Illus.). 1979. text ed. 79.00x (ISBN 0-19-857534-3). Oxford U Pr.

--Oxford Reviews of Reproductive Biology, Vol. 2. (Illus.). 1980. text ed. 79.00x (ISBN 0-19-857535-1). Oxford U Pr.

--Oxford Reviews of Reproductive Biology, Vol. 3. (Illus.). 1981. text ed. 79.00x (ISBN 0-19-857536-X). Oxford U Pr.

--Oxford Reviews of Reproductive Biology, Vol. 4. (Illus.). 1982. cloth 79.00x (ISBN 0-19-857537-8). Oxford U Pr.

Finn, Catherine, ed. see Ford, Cindy.

Finn, Chester E., jt. ed. see Breneman, David W.

Finn, Chester E, et al, eds. Challenges to the Humanities. 250p. 1985. text ed. 29.50 (ISBN 0-8419-1017-0); pap. 16.50 (ISBN 0-8419-1018-9). Holmes & Meier.

Finn, Chester E., Jr. Scholars, Dollars, & Bureaucrats. LC 78-13363. (Studies in Higher Education Policy). 1978. 26.95 (ISBN 0-8157-2828-X); pap. 9.95 (ISBN 0-8157-2827-1). Brookings.

Finn, Chester E., Jr., et al, eds. Against Mediocrity: The Humanities in America's High Schools. LC 83-22819. 276p. 1984. text ed. 29.50x (ISBN 0-8419-0944-X); pap. text ed. 11.50x (ISBN 0-8419-0945-8). Holmes & Meier.

Finn, Daniel M. Checking Account. (gr. 7-12). 1983. pap. 5.00 (ISBN 0-8224-1363-9). Pitman Learning.

Finn, Daniel P. Managing the Ocean Resources of the United States: The Role of the Federal Marine Sanctuary Program. (Lecture Notes in Coastal & Estuarine Studies: Vol. 2). (Illus.). 193p. 1982. pap. 18.00 (ISBN 0-387-11583-8). Springer-Verlag.

Finn, Daniel R. & Pemberton, Prentiss L. Toward a Christian Economic Ethic. LC 83-25409. 266p. 1985. pap. 10.95 (ISBN 0-86683-876-7, 7919). Winston Pr.

Finn, David. The Corporate Oligarch. LC 83-10449. 320p. 1983. pap. text ed. 11.00 (ISBN 0-8191-3346-9). U Pr of Amer.

--How to Visit a Museum. (Illus.). 144p. 1985. pap. 9.95 (ISBN 0-8109-2297-5). Abrams.

Finn, David & Silverman, Irving. Thoughts & Images: Photographs by David Finn. (Illus.). 15p. 1984. 95.00 (ISBN 0-916523-00-4). Scharf & Sil Publishers.

Finn, David, jt. auth. see Schapiro, Meyer.

Finn, Doug. Heart of a Family. 224p. 1984. 12.95 (ISBN 0-87395-861-6). State U NY Pr.

Finn, Edward E. These Are My Rites: A Brief History of the Eastern Rites of Christianity. LC 79-24937. (Illus.). 104p. 1980. pap. 4.95 (ISBN 0-8146-1058-7). Liturgical Pr.

Finn, Edward J., jt. auth. see Alonso, Marcelo.

Finn, F. Fancy Waterfowl. 2nd ed. (Illus.). 1985. 12.95 (ISBN 0-947647-08-2, Pub. by Fanciers Supplies). Longwood Pub Group.

Finn, F. C. History of Chelsea. 15.00x (ISBN 0-392-07888-0, SpS). Sportshelf.

Finn, F. E. S., compiled by. Poets of Our Time: An Anthology. 160p. 1976. pap. 7.95 (ISBN 0-7195-3243-4). Transatlantic.

Finn, Fes, compiled by. Here & Human: An Anthology of Contemporary Verse. 1977. pap. text ed. 8.50 (ISBN 0-7195-3306-6). Transatlantic.

Finn, Fina. Palestine Peasantry. 1982. 30.00 (ISBN 0-686-45731-5, Pub. by Palestine Explo England). State Mutual Bk.

Finn, James, ed. Global Economics & Religion. 277p. 1983. 26.95 (ISBN 0-87855-477-7). Transaction Bks.

Finn, Jeremy D. Multivariance Six: Univariate & Multivariate Analysis of Variance, Covariance, Regression & Repeated Measures. pap. 15.00 (ISBN 0-89498-003-3). Sci Ware.

Finn, Jeremy D. & Mattsson, Ingrid. Multivariate Analysis in Educational Research. pap. 15.00 (ISBN 0-89498-001-7). Sci Ware.

Finn, Kenneth R. Time Management. (Simulation Game Ser.). 1975. pap. 24.90 (ISBN 0-89401-092-1); pap. 21.50 additional materials (ISBN 0-685-78118-6). Didactic Syst.

Finn, M. C. The Complete Book of International Smuggling. (Illus.). 160p. 1983. 14.95 (ISBN 0-87364-268-6). Paladin Pr.

Finn, Matia. Fundraising for Early Childhood Programs: Getting Started & Getting Results. LC 82-61245. 88p. 1982. pap. text ed. 3.50 (ISBN 0-912674-81-4, NAEYC 120). Natl Assn Child Ed.

Finn, Michael. Art of Shuriken Jutsu. 1984. 27.00 (ISBN 0-901764-65-5, Pub. by P H Crompton Ltd UK). State Mutual Bk.

--Art of Shuriken Jutsu. (Illus.). 86p. (Orig.). 1983. pap. 10.95 (ISBN 0-901764-65-5). Unique Pubns.

--Iaido: The Way of the Sword. 1984. 27.00 (ISBN 0-901764-58-2, Pub. by P H Crompton Ltd UK). State Mutual Bk.

--Police Arrest Techniques. 1984. 20.00x (ISBN 0-901764-39-6, Pub. by P H Crompton Ltd UK). State Mutual Bk.

Finn, Michael H. & Brown, Fred, eds. Training for Clinical Psychology: Proceedings of the Springfield Mt. Sinai Conferences on Intern Training in Clinical Psychology. LC 59-13114. 186p. 1960. text ed. 20.00 (ISBN 0-8236-6620-4). Intl Univs Pr.

Finn, Molly. Feasts for a Farthing. Dinan, Dennis, ed. LC 85-50086. (Illus.). 272p. (Orig.). 1985. pap. 10.95 (ISBN 0-89909-066-4). Yankee Bks.

--Summer Feasts. 1985. pap. 6.95 (ISBN 0-671-55453-0, Fireside). S&S.

Finn, Nancy B. The Electronic Office. (Illus.). 160p. 1983. pap. 15.95 (ISBN 0-13-251819-8). P-H.

--Writing Dynamics: A Guidebook for Communications in the Office of the 80's. 176p. 1982. 17.95 (ISBN 0-8436-0868-4). Van Nos Reinhold.

Finn, P. Irish Coin Values. pap. 4.00 (ISBN 0-686-43400-5, Pub. by Spink & Son England). S J Durst.

Finn, P., jt. auth. see Dowle, A.

Finn, Patrick. Helping Children Learn to Read. 544p. 1985. text ed. 27.95 (ISBN 0-394-32893-0, RanC). Random.

Finn, Patrick T. Pub Games of England. (Oleander Games & Pastimes Ser.: Vol. 5). (Illus.). 156p. 1981. 18.95 (ISBN 0-900891-66-1); pap. 13.50 (ISBN 0-900891-67-X). Oleander Pr.

Finn, Peter & Lawson, Jane. Career Education Activities for Subject Area Teachers, 3 vols. (Illus.). 1975. tchr's eds. 15.00 ea. Grades 1-6 (ISBN 0-89011-479-X, CUM-101). Grades 6-9 (ISBN 0-89011-480-3, CUM-102). Grades 9-12 (ISBN 0-89011-481-1, CUM-103). Abt Bks.

Finn, Peter & O'Gorman, Patricia. Teaching About Alcohol: Concepts, Methods, & Classroom Activities. Date not set. write for info. Allyn.

Finn, Peter, jt. ed. see Pollock, John C.

Finn, R., ed. see Symposium in Applied Mathematics - 17th - New York - 1964.

Finn, R. Weldon. The Norman Conquest & Its Effects on the Economy, 1066-1086. (Illus.). xiv, 322p. 1970. 25.00 (ISBN 0-208-01154-4, Archon). Shoe String.

Finn, Reginald A. Domesday Studies: The Eastern Countries. LC 80-2231. (Illus.). 1981. Repr. of 1967 ed. 37.50 (ISBN 0-404-18759-5). AMS Pr.

--Domesday Studies: The Liber Exoniensis. LC 80-2239. 1981. Repr. of 1964 ed. 32.50 (ISBN 0-404-18760-9). AMS Pr.

Finn, Rex W. The Domesday Inquest & the Making of the Domesday Book. LC 78-2923. 1978. Repr. of 1966 ed. lib. bdg. 20.75x (ISBN 0-313-20344-X, FIDI). Greenwood.

Finn, Richard. Your Fortune in Franchises. rev. ed. 160p. 1980. pap. 4.95 (ISBN 0-8092-7448-5). Contemp Bks.

Finn, Sidney B. Clinical Pedodontics. 4th ed. LC 72-180177. (Illus.). 704p. 1973. text ed. 27.50 (ISBN 0-7216-3637-3). Saunders.

Finn, Timothy. Knapworth at War: Stories from an English Village, 1939-1945. 1982. 30.00 (ISBN 0-686-44511-2, Pub. by Duckworth). State Mutual Bk.

Finn, Virginia S. Pilgrim in the Parish: Spirtuality for Lay Ministers. 272p. (Orig.). 1986. pap. 9.95 (ISBN 0-317-29827-5). Paulist Pr.

Finn, William J. Art of the Choral Conductor, 2 vols. (Illus.). 1960. Vol. 1. pap. text ed. 15.95 (ISBN 0-87487-037-2); Vol. 2. pap. text ed. 15.95 (ISBN 0-87487-038-0). Birch Tree Gr.

Finnane, Mark. Insanity & the Insane in Post-Famine Ireland. LC 81-66330. (Illus.). 242p. 1981. 28.50x (ISBN 0-389-20212-6, 07296). B&N Imports.

Finnegan, David J. Bacterial Conjugation. 48p. 1976. 39.00x (ISBN 0-686-96975-8, Pub. by Meadowfield Pr England). State Mutual Bk.

Finnegan, Ed, ed. see Johnson, Jackie & Culinary Arts Institute Staff.

Finnegan, Edward G. Children's Bible Stories. LC 75-18758. (Treasure House Bks). (Illus.). 256p. (ps-12). 1978. 7.95 (ISBN 0-8326-1803-9, 3602); deluxe ed. 8.95 (ISBN 0-686-66397-7). Delair.

--Historias De la Biblia. LC 75-18758. (Treasure House Bks). (Illus., Span.). (ps-12). 1978. 9.95 (ISBN 0-8326-2601-5, 5180). Delair.

Finnegan, Edward G., ed. New Webster's Crossword Puzzle Dictionary: Vest Pocket Edition. 384p. 1978. pap. 1.95 (ISBN 0-8326-2221-4, 6430). Delair.

--New Webster's Dictionary of the English Language (College Edition) LC 75-18559. (Illus.). 1856p. 1975. 15.95 (ISBN 0-8326-0035-0, 6602). Delair.

--New Webster's Dictionary (Vest Pocket Edition) LC 75-18560. 252p. 1976. pap. 1.95 (ISBN 0-8326-0036-9, 6401). Delair.

--New Webster's English-Spanish Dictionary: Vest Pocket Edition. 224p. 1980. pap. 1.95 (ISBN 0-8326-0050-4, 6454). Delair.

--New Webster's Law for Everyone: Vest Pocket Edition. 192p. 1980. pap. 1.95 (ISBN 0-8326-0049-0, 6452). Delair.

--New Webster's Medical Dictionary: Vest Pocket Edition. 320p. 1980. pap. 1.95 (ISBN 0-8326-0048-2, 6453). Delair.

--New Webster's Secretary's-Student's Guide: Vest Pocket Edition. 192p. 1978. pap. 1.95 (ISBN 0-8326-2220-6, 6451). Delair.

--New Webster's Vest Pocket Thesaurus. LC 78-52347. 256p. 1978. pap. 1.95 (ISBN 0-8326-0045-8, 6440). Delair.

--New Webster's Word Divider: Vest Pocket Edition. LC 76-6038. 352p. 1978. pap. 1.95 (ISBN 0-8326-0041-5, 6450). Delair.

Finnegan, Edward G., ed. see Carter, Linda & Culinary Arts Institute Staff.

Finnegan, Edward G., ed. see Hamelecourt, Juliette & Culinary Arts Institute Staff.

Finnegan, Edward G., ed. see Magida, Phylis & Culinary Arts Institute Staff.

Finnegan, Edward G., ed. see Phillips, Margot & Culinary Arts Institute Staff.

Finnegan, Edward G., ed. see Spitler, Sue & Culinary Arts Inst.

Finnegan, Edward G., ed. see Stover, Annette A. & Culinary Arts Institute Staff.

Finnegan, Frances. Poverty & Prostitution. LC 78-68123. (Illus.). 1979. 39.50 (ISBN 0-521-22447-0). Cambridge U Pr.

Finnegan, Janet A., jt. auth. see LeMaitre, George D.

Finnegan, John P. Against the Specter of a Dragon: The Campaign for American Military Preparedness, 1914-1917. LC 74-288. (Contributions in Military History: No. 7). (Illus.). 1975. lib. bdg. 29.95 (ISBN 0-8371-7376-0, FSD/). Greenwood.

Finnegan, John R. & Hirl, Patricia A. Law & the Media in the Midwest. 1984. pap. 19.95 (ISBN 0-86678-119-6). Butterworth MN.

Finnegan, Marcus B. A Lawyer's Guide to International Business Transactions, Pt. III, Folio 8: Practical & Legal Considerations in the International Licensing of Technoloy. 2nd ed. 51p. 1981. pap. 8.00 (ISBN 0-317-32237-0, B408). Am Law Inst.

--Practical & Legal Considerations in the International Licensing of Technology, Folio 8. 2nd ed. Surrey, Walter S. & Wallace, Don, Jr., eds. (A Lawyer's Guide International Business Transactions Ser.: Part III). 51p. 1981. pap. text ed. 8.00 (ISBN 0-686-32429-3). Am Law Inst.

Finnegan, Richard B. Ireland: The Challenge of Conflict & Change. LC 83-6974. (Profiles-Nations of Contemporary Western Europe Ser.). (Illus.). 166p. 1983. 20.00x (ISBN 0-89158-924-4). Westview.

Finnegan, Richard B., et al. Law & Politics in the International System: Case Studies in Conflict Resolution. LC 79-66153. (Illus.). 1979. pap. text ed. 10.50 (ISBN 0-8191-0793-X). U Pr of Amer.

Finnegan, Rita. ICD-Nine-CM Basic Coding Handbook. rev. ed. 67p. 1980. 9.00 (ISBN 0-318-12847-0, 1015C). Am Med Record Assn.

--Instructor's Guide to ICD-Nine-CM Basic Coding Handbook. 49p. 1979. 5.00 (ISBN 0-318-12848-9, 1016C). Am Med Record Assn.

Finnegan, Robert E. Christ & Satan: A Critical Edition. 169p. 1977. pap. text ed. 15.45x (ISBN 0-88920-041-6, Pub. by Wilfrid Laurier U Pr Canada); pap. text ed. 11.00x (ISBN 0-88920-040-8). Humanities.

Finnegan, Ruth. Oral Literature in Africa. (Oxford Library of African Literature). (Illus.). 1976. pap. text ed. 27.50x (ISBN 0-19-572413-5). Oxford U Pr.

--Oral Poetry: Its Nature, Significance & Social Context. LC 76-11077. (Illus.). 1980. pap. 14.95 (ISBN 0-521-29774-5). Cambridge U Pr.

Finnegan, Ruth, ed. A World Treasury of Oral Poetry. LC 77-88784. 576p. 1978. 18.50x (ISBN 0-253-36665-8). Ind U Pr.

Finnegan, Ruth, et al, eds. New Approaches to Economic Life: Economic Restructuring, Unemployment & the Social Division of Labour. LC 84-19371. 320p. (Orig.). 1985. 30.00 (ISBN 0-7190-1098-5, Pub. by Manchester Univ Pr); pap. 11.00 (ISBN 0-7190-1731-9). Longwood Pub Group.

Finnegan, Ruth H. Limba Stories & Story-Telling. LC 80-25904. (Oxford Library of African Literature). xii, 352p. 1981. Repr. of 1967 ed. lib. bdg. 28.75x (ISBN 0-313-22723-3, FILS). Greenwood.

Finneken, Wouter Van see Van Ginneken, Wouter.

Finnell, Gilbert L., Jr. Coastal Land Management in California. 104p. (Reprinted from 1978 ABF Res. J., No. 4). 1978. 3.25 (ISBN 0-317-33319-4). Am Bar Foun.

--The Federal Regulatory Role in Coastal Land Management. 120p. (Reprinted from 1978 ABF Res. J., No. 2). 1978. 3.25 (ISBN 0-317-33332-1). Am Bar Foun.

Finnell, Joseph T., Jr. The Strictly for Beginners CP-M Book or, How to Talk with Your New Personal Computer. LC 83-51318. (Illus.). 304p. (Orig.). 1984. spiral bdg. 14.95 (ISBN 0-915767-00-7). Topaz Pr.

Finner, Marshall F. Farm Machinery Fundamentals. (Illus.). 1978. pap. text ed. 17.62 (ISBN 0-89534-015-1). Am Pub Co WI.

Finneran, Eugene. Security Supervision: A Handbook for Supervisors & Managers. 300p. 1981. text ed. 24.95 (ISBN 0-409-95025-4). Butterworth.

Finneran, R., ed. Yeats Annual, No. 2. 158p. 1983. text ed. 42.50x (ISBN 0-333-32456-0, Pub. by Macmillan England). Humanities.

Finneran, Richard. The Olympian & the Leprachaun: W. B. Yeats & James Stephens. (New Yeats Papers: No. 16). (Illus.). 1978. pap. text ed. 9.75x (ISBN 0-85105-338-6, Dolmen Pr). Humanities.

Finneran, Richard, ed. Yeats Annual, Number One. (Literary Annuals Ser.). 204p. 1982. text ed. 30.50x (ISBN 0-391-02478-7). Humanities.

Finneran, Richard J. Editing Yeats's Poems. LC 82-21615. 160p. 1983. 20.00 (ISBN 0-312-23694-8). St Martin.

--The Prose Fiction of W. B. Yeats: The Search for Those Simple Forms. (New Yeats Papers: Vol. 4). 1973. pap. text ed. 4.25x (ISBN 0-85105-217-7, Dolmen Pr). Humanities.

Finneran, Richard J., ed. Anglo-Irish Literature: A Review of Research. LC 74-31959. (Reviews of Research). 596p. 1976. 30.00x (ISBN 0-87352-252-4, Z52); pap. 14.00x (ISBN 0-87352-253-2). Modern Lang.

--Yeats: An Annual of Critical & Textual Studies, 1983. (Illus.). 240p. 1983. 27.50x (ISBN 0-8014-1635-3). Cornell U Pr.

--Yeats: An Annual of Critical & Textual Studies, 1984, Vol. II. (Illus.). 304p. 1984. 39.95x (ISBN 0-8014-1761-9). Cornell U Pr.

Finneran, Richard J., jt. ed. see Bornstein, George.

Finneran, Richard J., ed. see Yeats, W. B.

Finneran, Richard J., et al. Recent Research on Anglo-Irish Writers: A Supplement to "Anglo-Irish Literature: A Review of Research". (Reviews of Research Ser.). 361p. 1983. 27.50x (ISBN 0-87352-259-1). Modern Lang.

Finneran, Richard J., et al, eds. Letters to W. B. Yeats, 2 vols. LC 77-5645. 628p. 1977. 60.00x set (ISBN 0-685-81542-0). Vol. 1 (ISBN 0-231-04424-0). Vol. 2 (ISBN 0-231-04425-9). Columbia U Pr.

Finnerty, Gertrude B. & Corbitt, Theodore. Hydrotherapy. LC 60-6593. (Illus.). 1960. 16.50 (ISBN 0-8044-4236-3). Ungar.

Finnerty, J. D. Corporate Financial Analysis: A Comprehensive Guide to Real-World Approaches for Financial Managers. 576p. 1985. price not set (ISBN 0-07-021040-3). McGraw.

Finnerty, Kathleen. Anthology of Verse. 1978. 3.50 (ISBN 0-682-49102-0). Exposition Pr FL.

Finnerty, Mary T. First Complete Report on Data Processing. LC 58-814. (DPR-1: Pt. 1). (Illus.). 53p. 1978. 8.75 (ISBN 0-9602222-3-5). M T Finnerty.

Finnerty, W. Patrick, et al. Community Structure & Trade at Isthmus Cove: A Salvage Excavation on Catalina Island (Calif.) (Pacific Coast Archaeological Society Occasional Papers: No. 1). 81p. 1981. pap. 2.95 (ISBN 0-686-69643-3). Acoma Bks.

Finneson, Bernard E. Low Back Pain. 2nd ed. (Illus.). 597p. 1981. text ed. 49.50i (ISBN 0-397-50493-4). Har-Row.

--Low Back Pain. 2nd ed. (Illus.). 598p. 1981. text ed. 52.50 (ISBN 0-397-50493-4, 65-06356, Lippincott Medical). Lippincott.

Finney, Ben. Once a Marine, Always a Marine. (Illus.). 1978. 6.95 (ISBN 0-517-53275-1). Crown.

--Start Laughing. LC 84-90149. 109p. 1984. 10.00 (ISBN 0-533-06217-9). Vantage.

Finney, Ben R. Big-Men & Business: Entrepreneurship & Economic Growth in the New Guinea Highlands. LC 72-93151. (Illus.). 228p. 1973. 14.00x (ISBN 0-8248-0262-4, Eastwest Ctr). UH Pr.

--Interstellar Migrations & the Human Experience. Jones, Eric M., ed. LC 84-16282. 1985. 24.95 (ISBN 0-520-05349-4). U of Cal Pr.

Finney, Ben R., compiled by. Pacific Navigation & Voyaging. (Illus.). 148p. 1976. text ed. 12.50x (ISBN 0-8248-0584-4). UH Pr.

Finney, Brian. Christopher Isherwood: A Critical Biography. (Illus.). 1979. 22.50x (ISBN 0-19-520134-5). Oxford U Pr.

Finney, Brian, ed. see Lawrence, D. H.

Finney, C. G. The Circus of Dr. Lao. 1976. pap. 3.95 (ISBN 0-380-00750-9, 36368). Avon.

Finney, Charles. Principles of Holiness. LC 83-25769. 274p. 1984. pap. 5.95 (ISBN 0-87123-403-3). Bethany Hse.

--Principles of Union with Christ. Parkhurst, Louis G., ed. 128p. 1985. pap. 5.95 (ISBN 0-87123-447-5). Bethany Hse.

--Reflections on Revival. LC 78-26527. 160p. 1979. pap. 3.95 (ISBN 0-87123-157-3, 210157). Bethany Hse.

Finney, Charles & Parkhurst, L. B. Principles of Liberty. rev. ed. LC 82-20705. (Finney's Sermons on Romans Ser.). 194p. (Orig.). 1983. pap. 4.95 (ISBN 0-87123-475-0). Bethany Hse.

Finney, Charles G. Answers to Prayer. Parkhurst, Louis G., Jr., ed. LC 83-12253. 122p. (Orig.). 1983. pap. 3.95 (ISBN 0-87123-296-0). Bethany Hse.

--The Autobiography of Charles G. Finney. Wessel, Helen S., ed. LC 77-2813. 1977. pap. 4.95 (ISBN 0-87123-010-0). Bethany Hse.

--Charles G. Finney: An Autobiography. 480p. 16.95 (ISBN 0-8007-0095-3). Revell.

--Charles G. Finney Memorial Library, 8 vols. 1975. Set. pap. 31.50 (ISBN 0-8254-2623-5). Kregel.

--The Circus of Dr. Lao. LC 83-3486. 128p. 1983. pap. 3.95 (ISBN 0-394-71617-5, Vin). Random.

--Crystal Christianity: A Guide to Professing Christians. Orig. Title: Lectures to Professing Christians. 330p. Date not set. pap. 3.50 (ISBN 0-88368-171-4). Whitaker Hse.

--Finney on Revival. Shelhamer, E. E., ed. 128p. 1974. pap. 2.95 (ISBN 0-87123-151-4, 200151). Bethany Hse.

--Finney's Systematic Theology. LC 76-3500. Orig. Title: Finney's Lectures on Systematic Theology. 448p. 1976. pap. 7.95 (ISBN 0-87123-153-0, 210153). Bethany Hse.

--God's Love for a Sinning World. LC 66-19200. (Charles G. Finney Memorial Library). 1975. pap. 4.50 (ISBN 0-8254-2620-0). Kregel.

--Guilt of Sin. LC 65-25845. (Charles G. Finney Memorial Library). 1975. pap. 4.50 (ISBN 0-8254-2616-2). Kregel.

--Heart of Truth: Finney's Outlines of Theology. LC 75-46128. Orig. Title: Skeletons of a Course of Theological Lectures. 256p. 1976. pap. 4.95 (ISBN 0-87123-226-X, 210226). Bethany Hse.

--How to Experience Revival. 143p. 1984. pap. text ed. 3.50 (ISBN 0-88368-140-4). Whitaker Hse.

--Lectures to Professing Christians. (The Higher Christian Life Ser.). 348p. 1985. lib. bdg. 45.00 (ISBN 0-8240-6418-6). Garland Pub.

--Love Is Not a Special Way of Feeling. Orig. Title: Attributes of Love. 144p. 1963. pap. 3.50 (ISBN 0-87123-005-4, 200005). Bethany Hse.

--Memoirs of Rev. Charles G. Finney. LC 74-168025. Repr. of 1876 ed. 33.00 (ISBN 0-404-00047-9). AMS Pr.

--The Old China Hands. LC 73-429. (Illus.). 258p. 1973. Repr. of 1961 ed. lib. bdg. 17.75x (ISBN 0-8371-6772-8, FIOC). Greenwood.

--Power from on High. 1962. pap. 2.50 (ISBN 0-87508-190-8). Chr Lit.

--Prevailing Prayer. LC 65-25846. (Charles G. Finney Memorial Library). 1975. pap. 3.50 (ISBN 0-8254-2603-0). Kregel.

--Principles of Prayer. Parkhurst, L. G., ed. LC 80-17856. 112p. (Orig.). 1980. pap. 3.95 (ISBN 0-87123-468-8, 210468). Bethany Hse.

--Principles of Victory. Parkhurst, G., ed. LC 81-15464. 201p. (Orig.). 1981. pap. 4.95 (ISBN 0-87123-471-8, 210471). Bethany Hse.

--The Promise of the Spirit. Smith, Timothy L., ed. LC 79-26286. 272p. (Orig.). 1980. pap. 5.95 (ISBN 0-87123-207-3, 210207). Bethany Hse.

--Revival Lectures. 544p. 15.95 (ISBN 0-8007-0272-7). Revell.

--Sanctification. Allen, W. E., ed. 1963. pap. 2.50 (ISBN 0-87508-191-6). Chr Lit.

--So Great Salvation. LC 65-25844. (Charles G. Finney Memorial Library). 1975. pap. 4.50 (ISBN 0-8254-2621-9). Kregel.

--True & False Repentance. LC 66-10576. (Charles G. Finney Memorial Library). 1975. pap. 4.50 (ISBN 0-8254-2617-0). Kregel.

--True Saints. LC 66-24880. (Charles G. Finney Memorial Library). 1975. pap. 4.50 (ISBN 0-8254-2622-7). Kregel.

--True Submission. LC 66-24881. (Charles G. Finney Memorial Library). 1975. pap. 4.50 (ISBN 0-8254-2618-9). Kregel.

--Victory Over the World. LC 66-24879. (Charles G. Finney Memorial Library). 1975. pap. 4.50 (ISBN 0-8254-2619-7). Kregel.

Finney, Claude L. Evolution of Keats's Poetry, 2 vols in 1. LC 63-11029. (Illus.). 1963. Repr. of 1936 ed. 50.00x (ISBN 0-8462-0372-3). Russell.

Finney Company. Finding Your Job, 6 units. Incl. Unit IC. 1980. (ISBN 0-912486-45-7); Unit 2B. 1974 (ISBN 0-912486-11-2); Unit 3B. 1975 (ISBN 0-912486-12-0); Unit 4B. 1977 (ISBN 0-912486-31-7); Unit 5B. 1978 (ISBN 0-912486-40-6); Unit 6B. 1979 (ISBN 0-912486-42-2). LC 66-40358. (Illus.). (gr. 7 up). Set. 207.00 (ISBN 0-912486-09-0); 34.50 ea. Finney Co.

--Occupational Guidance, 5 units. Incl. Unit 1E. 1984 (ISBN 0-912486-53-8); Unit 2E. 1985 (ISBN 0-912486-54-6); Unit 3D. 1981 (ISBN 0-912486-48-1); Unit 4D. 1982 (ISBN 0-912486-51-1); Unit 5D. 1983 (ISBN 0-912486-52-X). LC 75-20074. (gr. 7 up). Set. 395.00 (ISBN 0-912486-16-3); 79.00 ea. Finney Co.

Finney, D. J. Probit Analysis. 3rd ed. LC 78-134618. (Illus.). 1971. 70.00 (ISBN 0-521-08041-X). Cambridge U Pr.

--Statistics for Mathematicians: An Introduction. 1968. 8.85 (ISBN 0-934454-74-4). Lubrecht & Cramer.

Finney, David. The Power Thyristor & Its Applications. (Illus.). 320p. 1980. 34.95 (ISBN 0-07-084533-6). McGraw.

Finney, David J. Introduction to the Theory of Experimental Design. LC 60-8126. (Midway Reprint Ser.). 1975. pap. 9.00x (ISBN 0-226-25000-8). U of Chicago Pr.

--Statistical Method in Biological Assay. 3rd ed. LC 78-64339. 60.00x (ISBN 0-02-844640-2). Hafner.

Finney, Edwin A. Better Concrete Pavement Serviceability. (Monograph). 1973. 23.85 (ISBN 0-685-85140-0, M-7). ACI.

Finney, Essex E., Jr., ed. Handbook of Transportation & Marketing in Agriculture: Food Commodities, Vol. 1. 464p. 1981. 69.50 (ISBN 0-8493-3851-4). CRC Pr.

--Handbook of Transportation & Marketing in Agriculture, Vol. II: Field Crops. (CRC Ser. in Agriculture). 520p. 1981. 74.50 (ISBN 0-8493-3852-2). CRC Pr.

Finney, Frederick, ed. Aaron's Index, Afro-American, Third World & Alternative Literature. 1979. 32.00 (ISBN 0-89421-021-1); lib. bdg. 35.00 (ISBN 0-89421-020-3). Challenge Pr.

Finney, Frederick M. The City Killers: A Political & Planning Disaster in Dayton, Ohio. LC 77-83463. (Illus.). 1978. 20.00 (ISBN 0-89421-000-9). Challenge Pr.

--Dictionary of Syngraphics & Associated Terms. 96p. 1983. 8.95 (ISBN 0-89421-031-9). Challenge Pr.

Finney, Frederick M., jt. auth. see Curtice, Harlow H.

Finney, Frederick M., ed. Black Voices at Midnight: The Challenge Poets. 1978. 7.00 (ISBN 0-89421-008-4). Challenge Pr.

--Small Press Publishing. LC 78-50210. 1978. 12.00 (ISBN 0-89421-015-7). Challenge Pr.

Finney, Gretchen L. Musical Backgrounds for English Literature 1580-1650. LC 75-35024. 292p. 1976. Repr. of 1962 ed. lib. bdg. 27.50x (ISBN 0-8371-8572-6, FIMB). Greenwood.

Finney, H. A. Consolidated Statements. LC 82-48362. (Accountancy in Transition Ser.). 242p. 1982. lib. bdg. 28.00 (ISBN 0-8240-5313-3). Garland Pub.

Finney, Humphrey S. A Stud Farm Diary. Repr. write for info. (ISBN 0-85131-194-6, NL51, Dist. by Miller). J A Allen.

Finney, J. J., jt. auth. see LeRoy, L. W.

Finney, Jack. Forgotten News: The Crime of the Century & Other Lost Stories. LC 81-43561. (Illus.). 304p. 1983. 14.95 (ISBN 0-385-17721-6). Doubleday.

--The Invasion of the Body Snatchers. 1978. pap. 2.25 (ISBN 0-440-14317-9). Dell.

--Time & Again. 1978. pap. 9.95 (ISBN 0-671-24295-4, Fireside). S&S.

Finney, Jan D. Gene Stratton Porter, the Natural Wonder. 5.95 (ISBN 0-89190-497-2, Pub. by Am Repr). Amereon Ltd.

Finney, Joseph C., ed. Culture Change, Mental Health, & Poverty. LC 68-12967. 368p. 1969. 28.00x (ISBN 0-8131-1172-2). U Pr of Ky.

Finney, Katherine. Interbank Deposits: The Purpose & Effects of Domestic Balances, 1934-54. Bruchey, Stuart, ed. LC 80-1146. (The Rise of Commercial Banking Ser.). (Illus.). 1981. Repr. of 1958 ed. lib. bdg. 14.00x (ISBN 0-405-13649-8). Ayer Co Pubs.

Finney, Nikky. On Wings Made of Gauze. LC 84-29498. 59p. 1985. 14.95 (ISBN 0-688-04796-3); pap. 3.95 (ISBN 0-688-05946-5). Morrow.

Finney, Paul. The Curse of Princess White Lily. (Illus.). 32p. 1982. pap. 5.95 (ISBN 0-89962-285-2). Todd & Honeywell.

Finney, Peter. Fighting Tigers, II: L. S. U. Football, 1893-1980. LC 80-13030. 404p. 1980. 14.95 (ISBN 0-8071-0766-2). La State U Pr.

--Pistol Pete. 1969. pap. 1.95 (ISBN 0-88289-102-2). Pelican.

Finney, Robert T. History of the Air Corps Tactical School 1920-1940. (USAF Historical Studies: No. 100). 90p. 1955. pap. text ed. 10.00 (ISBN 0-89126-137-0). MA AH Pub.

Finney, Ross L. & Ostberg, Donald E. Elementary Differential Equations with Linear Algebra. 2nd ed. LC 75-12096. (Mathematics Ser.). 704p. 1976. text ed. 31.95 (ISBN 0-201-05515-5). Addison-Wesley.

Finney, Ross L., jt. auth. see Thomas, George B., Jr.

Finney, Shan. Basketball. (Easy-Read Sports Bks.). (Illus.). 48p. (gr. 1-3). 1982. PLB 8.60 (ISBN 0-531-04375-4). Watts.

--Cheerleading & Baton Twirling. (First Bks). (Illus.). 72p. 1982. PLB 8.90 (ISBN 0-531-04391-6). Watts.

--Dance. LC 82-17635. (First Bks.). (Illus.). 72p. (gr. 4 up). 1983. PLB 8.90 (ISBN 0-531-04525-0). Watts.

--Noise Pollution. (Impact Bks.). 96p. (gr. 7-12). 1984. lib. bdg. 10.90 (ISBN 0-531-04855-1). Watts.

Finney, Shan, jt. auth. see Dolan, Edward.

Finney, Shan, jt. auth. see Dolan, Edward F., Jr.

Finney, Theodore M. A History of Music. LC 73-17926. (Illus.). 720p. 1976. Repr. of 1947 ed. lib. bdg. 40.75x (ISBN 0-8371-7270-5, FIHM). Greenwood.

Finney, Theodore M., ed. James Warrington: Short Titles of Books, Relating to or Illustrating the History & Practice of Psalmody in the United States,1620-1820. LC 70-18250. (Bibliographia Tripotamopolitana: No.1). 1970. 6.00x (ISBN 0-931222-00-1). C E Barbour.

--James Warrington: Short Titles of Books, Relating to or Illustrating the History & Practice of Psalmody in the United States, 1620-1820. LC 70-18250. 1982. 6.00 (ISBN 0-931222-00-1). Pitts Theolog.

Finnie, David H. Desert Enterprise: The Middle East Oil Industry in Its Local Environment. Bruchey, Stuart, ed. LC 80-559. (Multinational Corporations Ser.). (Illus.). 1980. Repr. of 1958 ed. lib. bdg. 27.50x (ISBN 0-405-13356-1). Ayer Co Pubs.

--Pioneers East: The Early American Experience in the Middle East. LC 67-20875. (Middle Eastern Studies: No. 13). (Illus.). 1967. 20.00x (ISBN 0-674-66900-2). Harvard U Pr.

Finnie, Nancy. Handling the Young Cerebral Palsied Child at Home. rev. ed. (Illus.). 1975. pap. 7.95 (ISBN 0-87690-175-5, 0772-230). Dutton.

Finnie, W. Bruce. Topographic Terms in the Ohio Valley 1748-1800. (Publications of the American Dialect Society: No. 53). 144p. 1970. pap. 8.80 (ISBN 0-8173-0653-6). U of Ala Pr.

Finnigan, Georgia L., ed. see Information Store, Inc. & Institute for Paralegal Training.

Finnigan, Joan. Look! the Land Is Growing Giants. (Illus.). 32p. 1983. 14.95 (ISBN 0-88776-151-8). Tundra Bks.

Finnigan, John. The Right People in the Right Jobs. 2nd ed. 156p. 1983. text ed. 23.50x (ISBN 0-566-02360-1). Gower Pub Co.

Finnigan, Sharon, jt. auth. see Porter-O'Grady, Tim.

Finnin, William M., Jr. & Smith, Gerald A., eds. The Morality of Scarcity: Limited Resources & Social Policy. LC 78-21514. xiv, 138p. 1979. 17.50x (ISBN 0-8071-0485-X). La State U Pr.

Finnis, J. M. Annual Survey of Commonwealth Law Nineteen Seventy-Seven. 1979. 98.00x (ISBN 0-19-825352-4). Oxford U Pr.

Finnis, John. Fundamentals of Ethics. 160p. (Orig.). 1983. 17.95 (ISBN 0-87840-404-X); pap. 8.95 (ISBN 0-87840-408-2). Georgetown U Pr.

--Natural Law & Natural. (Clarendon Law Ser.). 1980. text ed. 49.95x (ISBN 0-19-876098-1); pap. text ed. 14.95x (ISBN 0-19-876110-4). Oxford U Pr.

Finniston, H. M., ed. Structural Characteristics of Materials. (Illus.). 1971. 48.50x (Pub. by Applied Science). Burgess-Intl Ideas.

Finny, D. J. Statistics for Biologists. 1980. pap. 9.95x (ISBN 0-412-21540-3, NO.2963, Pub by Chapman & Hall England). Methuen Inc.

Finocchiaro, Mary. Children's Living Spanish Record. (Living Language Courses Ser). (Illus.). (gr. k-5). 1960. lesson manual & bilingual picture dictionary 15.95 (ISBN 0-517-00136-5). Crown.

--English As a Second Language from Theory to Practice. rev. ed. 230p. 1974. text ed. 5.75 (ISBN 0-88345-222-7, 18137). Regents Pub.

--Hablemos Espanol. 180p. (gr. 9 up). 1976. pap. text ed. 4.50 (ISBN 0-88345-261-8, 18425). Regents Pub.

--Learning to Use English, 2 Bks. (Illus.). (gr. 7 up). 1966. Bk. 1. pap. text ed. 4.95 (ISBN 0-88345-089-5, 17400); Bk. 2. pap. text ed. 4.95 (ISBN 0-88345-090-9, 17401); tchr's manual 5.75 (ISBN 0-88345-091-7, 17402). Regents Pub.

--Teaching English As a Second Language. 2nd ed. LC 68-28195. 1969. 14.37xi (ISBN 0-06-032101-6, HarpT). Har-Row.

Finocchiaro, Mary & Brumfit, Christopher. The Functional-Notional Approach: From Theory to Practice. (Illus.). 1983. pap. 10.95 (ISBN 0-19-434106-2). Oxford U Pr.

Finocchiaro, Mary & Cadoux, Remunda. Living French: Advanced Course. 11.95 (ISBN 0-517-00260-4). Crown.

Finocchiaro, Mary & Lavanda, Violet. Growing in English Language Skills. (gr. 9-12). 1977. pap. text ed. 6.25 (ISBN 0-88345-299-5, 18447); cassettes 25.00 (ISBN 0-686-86690-8, 58444); answer key 1.50 (ISBN 0-685-79305-2, 18443). Regents Pub.

Finocchiaro, Mary & Lavenda, Violet H. Selections for Developing English Language Skills. rev. ed. 230p. (gr. 6 up). 1973. pap. 6.25 (ISBN 0-88345-195-6, 18078); cassettes 25.00 (ISBN 0-685-38987-1, 58193); ans. key 1.50 (ISBN 0-686-66893-6, 18161). Regents Pub.

Finocchiaro, Mary & Sako, Sydney. Foreign Language Testing: A Practical Approach. 1983. pap. text ed. 10.75 (ISBN 0-88345-362-2, 18478). Regents Pub.

Finocchiaro, Maurice A. Galileo & the Art of Reasoning: Rhetorical Foundations of Logic & Scientific Method. (Philosophy of Science Studies: No. 61). 463p. 1980. lib. bdg. 42.00 (ISBN 90-277-1094-5, Pub. by Reidel Holland); pap. 21.00 (ISBN 90-277-1095-3). Kluwer Academic.

--History of Science As Explanation. LC 72-3582. 280p. 1973. 15.95x (ISBN 0-8143-1480-5). Wayne St U Pr.

Finot, Jean. Race Prejudice. facs. ed. Wade-Evans, Florence, tr. LC 72-89413. (Black Heritage Library Collection Ser). 1906. 16.00 (ISBN 0-8369-8570-2). Ayer Co Pubs.

--Race Prejudice. Wade-Evans, Florence, tr. LC 75-100290. Repr. of 1906 ed. 19.75x (ISBN 0-8371-2909-5, FIP&). Greenwood.

Finotti, Joseph. Bibliographia Catholica Americana: A List of Works by Catholic Authors & Published in the United States. LC 74-149232. (Bibliography & Reference Ser.: No. 401). 1971. Repr. of 1872 ed. lib. bdg. 23.50 (ISBN 0-8337-1128-8). B Franklin.

Finree, Judith. The Contemporary Music Performance Directory. LC 75-24697. 1975. write for info (ISBN 0-916052-03-6); pap. write for info (ISBN 0-916052-01-X). Am Music Ctr.

Fins, Alice. Opportunities in Paralegal Careers. (VGM Career Bks.). (Illus.). 160p. 1983. 7.95 (ISBN 0-8442-6594-2, 6594-2, Passport Bks.); pap. 5.95 (ISBN 0-8442-6593-4, 6593-4). Natl Textbk.

--Women in Communications. (Illus.). 160p. 1983. 7.95 (ISBN 0-8442-6645-0, 6645-0, Passport Bks.); pap. 5.95 (ISBN 0-8442-6646-9, 6646-9). Natl Textbk.

--Women in Science. (Illus.). 160p. 1983. 7.95 (ISBN 0-8442-6647-7, 6647-7, Passport Bks.); pap. 5.95 (ISBN 0-8442-6648-5). Natl Textbk.

Fins, Alice, jt. auth. see Feingold, Norman.

Fins, Alice, jt. auth. see Feingold, S. Norman.

Finsaas, Clarence B. They Marched to Heaven's Drumbeat. 1985. pap. 5.95 (ISBN 0-88419-193-1). Creation Hse.

Finsand, Mary J. Barbecue Cookbook. Kuse, James A., ed. (Illus.). pap. 3.50 (ISBN 0-89542-617-X). Ideals.

--Caring & Cooking for the Hyperactive Child. LC 80-54335. 192p. 1981. 12.95 (ISBN 0-8069-5560-0); lib. bdg. 15.69 (ISBN 0-8069-5561-9); pap. 6.95 (ISBN 0-8069-8980-7). Sterling.

--Cooking for Two Cookbook. (Illus.). 64p. (Orig.). 1981. pap. 3.50 (ISBN 0-8249-3004-5). Ideals.

--Diabetic Candy, Cookie & Dessert Cookbook. LC 81-85024. (Illus.). 160p. 1982. 12.95 (ISBN 0-8069-5568-6); lib. bdg. 15.69 (ISBN 0-8069-5569-4); pap. 6.95 (ISBN 0-8069-7586-5). Sterling.

--The Diabetic Chocolate Cookbook. LC 84-8454. 160p. 1985. 14.95 (ISBN 0-8069-5580-5); pap. 7.95 (ISBN 0-8069-7900-3). Sterling.

--The Town that Moved. LC 82-9703. (Carolrhoda on my Own Bks). (Illus.). 48p. (gr. 1-4). 1983. PLB 8.95g (ISBN 0-87614-200-5). Carolrhoda Bks.

Finsand, Mary Jane. Complete Diabetic Cookbook. LC 79-91382. (Illus.). 160p. 1980. pap. 7.95 (ISBN 0-8069-8908-4). Sterling.

Finsinger, Jorg, ed. Economic Analysis of Regulated Markets. LC 82-5769. 224p. 1983. 27.50 (ISBN 0-312-22682-9). St Martin.

--Public Sector Economics. LC 82-42576. 352p. 1983. 25.00 (ISBN 0-312-65567-3). St Martin.

Finsler, P., et al, eds. see Caratheodory, C.

Finson, Bruce. Laura Cares for Pets. (People Working Today Ser.). (Illus.). 40p. (gr. 7-12). 1976. pap. text ed. 2.65 (ISBN 0-915510-11-1). Janus Bks.

Finson, Bruce, ed. Discovering California. (Illus.). 192p. (Orig.). 1983. 25.00 (ISBN 0-940228-13-0); pap. 10.00 (ISBN 0-940228-12-2). Calif Acad Sci.

Finson, Jon & Todd, R. Larry, eds. Mendelssohn & Schumann: Essays on Their Music & Its Context. LC 84-10120. 300p. 1984. lib. bdg. 32.75 (ISBN 0-8223-0569-0). Duke.

Finstad, Suzanne. Heir Not Apparent. Rodriquez, Barbara, ed. (Illus.). 288p. 1984. 17.95 (ISBN 0-932012-57-4). Texas Month Pr.

Finstein, M. S. Pollution Microbiology: A Laboratory Manual. 184p. 1972. 24.75 (ISBN 0-8247-1190-4). Dekker.

Finsten, Jil. Isaac Oliver: Art at the Courts of Elizabeth I & James I, 2 Vols. LC 79-6171. (Outstanding Dissertations in the Fine Arts Ser.: No.5). 775p. 1982. lib. bdg. 100.00 (ISBN 0-8240-3948-3). Garland Pub.

Finsterbusch, Kurt. Understanding Social Impacts: Assessing the Effects of Public Projects. LC 80-17586. (Sage Library of Social Research: Vol. 110). (Illus.). 311p. 1980. 28.00 (ISBN 0-8039-1015-0); pap. 14.00 (ISBN 0-8039-1016-9). Sage.

Finsterbusch, Kurt & Wolf, Charles P., eds. Methodology of Social Impact Assessment. 2nd ed. LC 81-2400. (Community Development Ser.: Vol. 32). 386p. 1981. 35.95 (ISBN 0-87933-401-0). Van Nos Reinhold.

Finsterbusch, Kurt, et al, eds. Social Impact Assessment Methods. 320p. 1983. 29.95 (ISBN 0-8039-2142-X). Sage.

Finston'& Porter. Selected Cases in Labor Relations: An Experiential Approach. 1983. pap. text ed. 19.95 (ISBN 0-8359-6981-9); instr's manual avail. (ISBN 0-8359-6982-7). Reston.

Finston, Charles, jt. auth. see Ragen, Joseph E.

Finston, Harmon L. & Rychtman, Allen C. A New View of Current Acid-Base Theories. LC 81-16030. 216p. 1982. 58.00 (ISBN 0-471-08472-7, Pub. by Wiley-Interscience). Wiley.

Finston, Irving L. & Remsberg, Charles. Inside Badminton. 1979. 9.95 (ISBN 0-8092-7653-4). Contemp Bks.

Fintel, Fred & Fintel, Marilyn. Yesterday's Toys with Today's Prices. LC 84-52273. 208p. 1985. pap. text ed. 14.95 (ISBN 0-87069-438-3). Wallace-Homestead.

Fintel, Marilyn, jt. auth. see Fintel, Fred.

Fintel, Mark. Handbook of Concrete Engineering. 2nd ed. (Illus.). 780p. 1985. 89.50 (ISBN 0-442-22623-3). Van Nos Reinhold.

Finter, N. B., jt. ed. see Billiau, A.

Finter, N. B., jt. ed. see Friedman, R. M.

Finton, Esther. Bulletin Boards Are More Than Something to Look at. (gr. k-6). 1979. 5.95 (ISBN 0-916456-32-3, GA97). Good Apple.

Fintor, Craig, ed. see David, Bruce E.

Finucane, R. C. Appearances of the Dead: A Cultural History of Ghosts. LC 83-62958. (Illus.). 232p. 1984. 19.95 (ISBN 0-87975-238-6). Prometheus Bks.

Finucane, Ronald C. Miracles & Pilgrims: Popular Beliefs in Medieval England. (Illus.). 248p. 1977. 16.00x (ISBN 0-87471-831-7). Rowman.

--Soldiers of the Faith: Crusaders & Moslems at War. (Illus.). 256p. 1984. 19.95 (ISBN 0-312-74256-8). St Martin.

Finuf, Judith L., jt. auth. see Stokes, McNeill.

Finzi, John C., compiled by. Oscar Wilde & His Literary Circle. LC 79-8059. Repr. of 1957 ed. 28.50 (ISBN 0-404-18370-0). AMS Pr.

Fiocco, G., ed. see ESRIN-ESLAB Symposium, 4th, Frascati, Italy, July 6-10, 1970.

Fionn. The Martial Music of the Clans. (Illus.). 164p. (Orig.). 1984. pap. 8.95 (ISBN 0-912951-21-4). ScotPr.

Fiorani, P., et al, eds. Occlusive Arterial Diseases of the Lower Limbs in Young Patients. (Serono Symposia Publications from Raven Press Ser.: Vol. 15). 328p. 1984. text ed. 39.50 (ISBN 0-88167-090-1). Raven.

Fioravanti, Vincenzo. Il Ritorno Di Columella Da Padova Ossia Il Pazzo Per Amore. Gosset, Philip, ed. (Italian Opera Ser., 1810-1840). 85.00 (ISBN 0-8240-6556-5). Garland Pub.

Fioravanzo, Guiseppe. A History of Naval Tactical Thought. LC 78-70966. (Illus.). 312p. 1979. 16.95x (ISBN 0-87021-271-0). Naval Inst Pr.

--A History of Naval Tactical Thought. (Illus.). 312p. 1979. 16.95 (ISBN 0-87021-271-0); bulk rates avail. Naval Inst Pr.

Fiore, Ernest D., Jr. & Ornstein, Melvin. How to Save Time & Taxes Preparing the Federal Partnership Return, Vol. 3. rev. ed. (How to Save Time & Taxes Ser). 1975. Updates avail. 80.00 (ISBN 0-685-02519-5, 733); looseleaf 1983 38.50; looseleaf 1984 38.50. Bender.

Fiore, Evelyn, jt. auth. see Glatzle, Mary.

Fiore, Evelyn L., ed. Low Carbohydrate Diet. (Orig.). 1965. pap. 2.95 (ISBN 0-399-50943-7, G&D). Putnam Pub Group.

Fiore, Frank R. Di see Di Fiore, Frank R.

Fiore, Gaspare de see De Fiore, Gaspare.

Fiore, Jordan D., ed. Mourt's Relation: A Journal of the Pilgrims of Plymouth. (Illus.). 100p. 1985. 12.95 (ISBN 0-942516-07-9). Plymouth Rock Found.

Fiore, Kyle, jt. auth. see Weigle, Marta.

Fiore, Mariano S. di see Di Fiore, Mariano S.

Fiore, N. F. & Berkowitz, B. J., eds. Advanced Techniques for Characterizing Hydrogen in Metals: Proceedings. TMS-AIME Fall Meeting, Louisville, 1981. (Illus.). 260p. 32.00 (ISBN 0-89520-394-4); members 20.00 (ISBN 0-317-36224-0); students 10.00 (ISBN 0-317-36225-9). ASM.

Fiore, Neil A. The Road Back to Health: Coping with the Emotional Side of Cancer. 256p. 1984. pap. 6.95 (ISBN 0-553-34118-9). Bantam.

Fiore, Peter A. Milton & Augustine: Patterns of Augustinian Thought in Milton's Paradise Lost. LC 80-17854. 144p. 1981. 18.95x (ISBN 0-271-00269-7). Pa St U Pr.

Fiore, Peter A., ed. Just So Much Honor: Essays Commemorating the Four-Hundredth Anniversary of the Birth of John Donne. LC 79-157768. 1972. 24.95x (ISBN 0-271-00554-8). Pa St U Pr.

Fiore, Robert, et al, eds. Studies in Honor of William C. McCrary. 220p. 1985. pap. 25.00 (ISBN 0-89295-029-3). Society Sp & Sp-Am.

Fiore, Robert L. Drama & Ethos: Natural-Law Ethics in Spanish Golden Age Theater. LC 74-18931. (Studies in Romance Languages: No. 14). 136p. 1975. 13.00x (ISBN 0-8131-1327-X). U Pr of Ky.

--Lazarillo de Tormes. (World Authors Ser.: No. 714). 150p. 1984. lib. bdg. 15.95 (ISBN 0-8057-6561-1, Twayne). G K Hall.

Fiore, Silvestro. Voices from the Clay: The Development of Assyro-Babylonian Literature. LC 65-11233. pap. 76.00 (ISBN 0-317-09922-1, 2010092). Bks Demand UMI.

Fiore, Vito, et al. Sixty-Eight Hundred Family Book. 1982. text ed. 14.95 (ISBN 0-8359-7005-1). Reston.

Fiore-Donati, L. & Hanna, M. G., eds. Lymphatic Tissue & Germinal Centers in Immune Response. LC 75-82374. (Advances in Experimental Medicine & Biology Ser.: Vol. 5). 552p. 1969. 65.00x (ISBN 0-306-39005-1, Plenum Pr). Plenum Pub.

Fiorelli, Lewis, ed. see De Sales, Francis.

Fiorentino, Mary R. A Basis for Sensorimotor Development-Normal & Abnormal: The Influence of Primitive, Postural Reflexes on the Development & Distribution of Tone. (Illus.). 184p. 1981. 22.75x (ISBN 0-398-04179-2). C C Thomas.

--Normal & Abnormal Development: The Influence of Primitive Reflexes on Motor Development. (Illus.). 80p. 1980. 10.75x (ISBN 0-398-02278-X). C C Thomas.

--Reflex Testing Methods for Evaluating CNS Development. 2nd ed. (Illus.). 72p. 1981. 15.75x (ISBN 0-398-02584-3). C C Thomas.

Fiorenza, Elisabeth S. The Book of Revelation: Justice & Judgment. LC 84-47920. 224p. 1984. pap. 11.95 (ISBN 0-8006-1793-2). Fortress.

--Claiming the Center: A Feminist Critical Theology of Liberation. 200p. 1985. 10.95 (ISBN 0-86683-781-7, 8590, Pub. by Seabury). Winston Pr.

--In Memory of Her: A Feminist Theological Reconstruction of Christian Origins. LC 82-19896. 275p. 1983. 22.50 (ISBN 0-8245-0493-3). Crossroad NY.

Fiorenza, Elisabeth S. & Holmes, Urban T. Lent. Achtemeier, Elizabeth & Krodel, Gerhard, eds. LC 79-7377. (Proclamation 2: Aids for Interpreting the Lessons of the Church Year, Ser. B). 64p. 1981. pap. 3.50 (ISBN 0-8006-4070-5, 1-4070). Fortress.

Fiorenza, Elisabeth S., ed. In Memory of Her: A Feminist Theological Reconstruction of Christian Origins. 384p. 1984. pap. 12.95 (ISBN 0-8245-0667-7). Crossroad NY.

Fiorenza, Elisabeth S. & Collins, Mary, eds. Women: Invisible In Church & Theology. (Concilium Ser.: Vol. 182). 128p. pap. 6.95 (ISBN 0-317-31480-7, 30-30062-1902); pap. 9.05 (ISBN 0-317-31481-5). Fortress.

Fiorenza, Elisabeth S. & Tracy, David, eds. The Holocaust As Event of Interruption. (Concilium Ser.: Vol.175). 128p. pap. 6.95 (ISBN 0-317-31466-1, 30-30055-1902) (ISBN 0-317-31467-X). Fortress.

Fiorenza, Elizabeth S. The Apocalypse. (Read & Pray Ser.). 64p. 1976. pap. 1.25 (ISBN 0-8199-0726-X). Franciscan Herald.

--Bread Not Stone: The Challenge of Feminist Biblical Interpretation. LC 84-14669. 207p. 1985. 17.95 (ISBN 0-8070-1100-2). Beacon Pr.

Fiorenza, Francis S. Foundational Theology: Jesus & the Church. 320p. 1984. 22.50 (ISBN 0-8245-0494-1). Crossroad NY.

Fiorenza, Francis S., tr. see Schleiermacher, Friedrich.

Fiorenza, Joseph, jt. auth. see Perry, Glenn.

Fiorenza, Pierre. Larousse Encyclopedia of Big Game Animals of Africa. Wallace, Ellen, et al, trs. LC 83-80486. (Illus.). 270p. 1983. 100.00 (ISBN 0-88332-319-2, 8043). Larousse.

Fioretti, P. The Menopause: Clinical & Pathophysiological Aspects. (Serono Symposium: No. 39). 1982. 67.00 (ISBN 0-12-256080-9). Acad Pr.

Fiori, Vito, jt. auth. see Streitmatter, Gene.

Fiori, Vittorio E. de see De Fiori, Vittorio E.

Fiorillo, F. Thirty-Six Caprices or Etudes for Violin. Singer, Edmund, ed. (Carl Fischer Music Library: No. 582). 1964. pap. 4.50 (ISBN 0-8258-0075-7, L582). Fischer Inc NY.

Fiorina, Morris P. Congress-Keystone of the Washington Establishment. LC 76-54606. (Fastback Ser.: No. 18). 1977. 15.50x (ISBN 0-300-02132-1); pap. 4.95x (ISBN 0-300-02125-9). Yale U Pr.

--Retrospective Voting in American National Elections. LC 80-24454. 288p. 1981. text ed. 47.00x (ISBN 0-300-02557-2); pap. 11.95x (ISBN 0-300-02703-6). Yale U Pr.

Fiorini, Ettore, ed. Neutrino Physics & Astrophysics. LC 81-11999. (Ettore Majorana International Science Series, Physical Sciences: Vol. 12). 432p. 1982. 62.50x (ISBN 0-306-40746-9, Plenum Pr). Plenum Pub.

Fiorini, S. & Wilson, R. J. Edge-Colourings of Graphs. (Research Notes in Mathematics Ser.: No. 16). 154p. (Orig.). 1977. pap. text ed. 22.95 (ISBN 0-273-01129-4). Pitman Pub MA.

Fiorito, Len, jt. auth. see Marazzi, Rich.

Fiorto, Len, jt. auth. see Marazzi, Rich.

Fiott, Stephen. Tennis Equipment. 2nd rev. ed. (Illus.). 1978. pap. 7.95 (ISBN 0-8019-6716-3). Chilton.

Fippin, Elmer O. Rural New York. LC 79-137943. (Economic Thought, History & Challenge Ser). 1971. Repr. of 1921 ed. 34.00x (ISBN 0-8046-1446-6, Pub. by Kennikat). Assoc Faculty Pr.

Fiquette, Lawerence, ed. see Rose, Louis J.

Firas, Shihab. Healer, Ash-Shafuja, an Ismaili Treatise. Makarem, Sami N., ed. 1966. pap. 15.95x (ISBN 0-8156-6026-X, Am U Beirut). Syracuse U Pr.

Firbank, Ronald. Concerning the Eccentricities of Cardinal Pirelli. 74p. 1977. pap. 6.75 (ISBN 0-7156-1095-3, Pub. by Duckworth England). Biblio Dist.

--Five Novels. Incl. Valmouth; Artificial Princess; Flower Beneath the Foot; Prancing Nigger; Cardinal Pirelli. LC 49-48966. 1981. pap. 8.95 (ISBN 0-8112-0799-4, NDP518). New Directions.

--Five Novels. Incl. Valmouth; Artificial Princess; Flower Beneath the Foot; Prancing Nigger; Cardinal Pirelli. LC 49-48966. 1969. pap. 8.95 (ISBN 0-8112-0799-4, NDP518). New Directions.

--Prancing Nigger. 77p. 1977. pap. 6.75 (ISBN 0-7156-1094-5, Pub. by Duckworth England). Biblio Dist.

--Three More Novels. Incl. Caprice; Inclinations; Vainglory. LC 55-9910. 1951. 6.50 (ISBN 0-8112-0277-1). New Directions.

--Valmouth. 127p. 1977. 20.00 (ISBN 0-7156-1093-7, Pub. by Duckworth England); pap. 6.75 (ISBN 0-7156-1097-X, Pub. by Duckworth England). Biblio Dist.

Firby, P. A. & Gardiner, C. F. Surface Topology. (Mathematics & its Applications Harwood Ser.). 216p. 1982. 54.95X (ISBN 0-470-27528-6). Halsted Pr.

Firchow, Evelyn S., ed. & tr. from Mod. Icelandic. Icelandic Short Stories. LC 74-8735. (Library of Scandinavian Literature Ser.: Vol. 26). 216p. 1975. lib. bdg. 12.00x (ISBN 0-89067-028-5). Am Scandinavian.

Firchow, Evelyn S., ed. Studies for Einar Hauger Presented by Friends & Colleagues. LC 72-889779. (Janua Linguarum, Ser. Major: No. 59). (Illus.). 573p. 1972. text ed. 59.20x (ISBN 90-2792-338-8). Mouton.

Firchow, Evelyn S., et al, eds. Studies by Einar Haugen Presented on the Occasion of His 65th Birthday, April 19, 1971. (Janua Linguarum Ser.: No. 49). 1972. 76.80x (ISBN 0-686-21225-8). Mouton.

Firchow, Irwin & Firchow, Jacqueline. Vocabulary of Rotokas-Pidgin-English. 1973. pap. 6.00x (ISBN 0-88312-669-9). Summer Inst Ling.

Firchow, Jacqueline, jt. auth. see Firchow, Irwin.

Firchow, Peter, tr. Friedrich Schlegel's Lucinde & the Fragments. LC 77-161440. 1971. 15.00x (ISBN 0-8166-0624-2). U of Minn Pr.

Firchow, Peter E. The End of Utopia: A Study of Aldous Huxley's Brave New World. LC 82-74490. 160p. 1984. 23.50 (ISBN 0-8387-5058-3). Bucknell U Pr.

Firdawsi. Suhrab & Rustam: A Poem from the Shah Namah of Firdausi. Atkinson, James, tr. from Persian. LC 72-3772. Orig. Title: Soohrab, a Poem. (Eng. & Persian.). 1972. Repr. of 1814 ed. 30.00x (ISBN 0-8201-1103-1). Schol Facsimiles.

Fire Protection Publications Staff. Command Section. (Incident Command System Position Description Guides Ser.). 16p. pap. text ed. 3.00 (ISBN 0-317-06724-9). Intl Fire Serv.

--Incident Command System Field Operations Pocket Guide. 83p. pap. text ed. 10.00 pkg. of 5 (ISBN 0-317-06722-2). Intl Fire Serv.

--Logistic Section. (Incident Command System Position Description Guides Ser.). 66p. pap. text ed. 5.00 (ISBN 0-317-06727-3). Intl Fire Serv.

--Operation Section. (Incident Command System Position Description Guides Ser.). 47p. pap. text ed. 4.50 (ISBN 0-317-06725-7). Intl Fire Serv.

--Planning Section. (Incident Command System Decription Guides Ser.). 72p. pap. text ed. 5.00 (ISBN 0-317-06726-5). Intl Fire Serv.

Firebaugh, Francille M., jt. auth. see Deacon, Ruth E.

Firebaugh, Morris, jt. ed. see Ruedisili, Lon C.

Firebaugh, W. C. The Inns of Greece & Rome. LC 76-175878. (Illus.). Repr. of 1928 ed. 24.50 (ISBN 0-405-08515-X, Blom Pubns). Ayer Co Pubs.

Firebrace, James & Holland, Stuart. Never Kneel Down: Drought Development & Liberation in Eritrea. LC 85-60323. 1985. text ed. 29.95 (ISBN 0-932415-00-8); pap. 9.95 (ISBN 0-932415-01-6). Red Sea Pr.

Fireman, Bert M. Arizona: Historic Land. LC 82-47807. (Illus.). 305p. 1982. 16.95 (ISBN 0-394-50797-5). Knopf.

Fireman, Bert M., ed. see Theobald, John & Theobald, Lillian.

Fireman, Janet R. The Spanish Royal Corps of Engineers in the Western Borderlands: Instrument of Bourbon Reform, 1764-1815. LC 75-25210. (Spain in the West: Vol. 12). (Illus.). 1977. 16.95 (ISBN 0-87062-116-5). A H Clark.

Fireman, Judy, ed. The Cat Catalog. LC 76-25473. (Illus.). 354p. 1976. 12.50 (ISBN 0-911104-81-X, 111); pap. 8.95 (ISBN 0-911104-82-8, 110). Workman Pub.

--The TV Book. LC 77-5303. (Illus.). 1977. pap. 7.95 (ISBN 0-89480-002-7). Workman Pub.

Firemark, Francis. Firemark. (Illus.). 128p. 1981. 7.95 (ISBN 0-89962-219-4). Todd & Honeywell.

Firenze. Firenze, Pluteo Twenty-Nine, One. Dittmer, Luther, ed. (Veroffentlichungen mittelalterlicher Musikhandschriften - Publications of Mediaeval Musical Manuscripts Ser.: Nos. 10 & 11). 250p. (Eng. & Ger.). prt. 1 80.00 (ISBN 0-912024-10-0); lib. bdg. 80.00 (ISBN 0-912024-11-9). Inst Mediaeval Mus.

Firenze, Robert J. The Process of Hazard Control. (Illus.). 1978. text ed. 25.95 (ISBN 0-8403-8002-X). Kendall-Hunt.

Firer, Benzion. The Long Journey Home. Slae, Bracha, tr. from Hebrew. 211p. 1984. 7.95 (ISBN 0-87306-342-2); pap. 5.95 (ISBN 0-87306-343-0). Feldheim.

--Saadiah Weissman. 140p. (gr. 5-12). 1982. 6.95 (ISBN 0-87306-294-9). Feldheim.

Fireside, Carolyn. Goodbye Again. 336p. 1984. pap. 3.50 (ISBN 0-425-06286-4). Berkley Pub.

Fireside, Harvey. Icon & Swastika: The Russian Orthodox Church Under Nazi & Soviet Control. LC 70-123567. (Russian Research Center Studies: No. 62). 1971. 16.50x (ISBN 0-674-44160-5). Harvard U Pr.

--Icon & Swastika: The Russian Orthodox Church Under Nazi & Soviet Control. LC 70-123567. (Harvard University, Russian Research Center Studies: Vol. 62). pap. 67.00 (ISBN 0-317-08921-8, 2021595). Bks Demand UMI.

--Soviet Psychoprisons. 224p. 1982. pap. 4.95 (ISBN 0-393-00065-6). Norton.

Firestein, Gary S., jt. auth. see Harrell, Robert A.

Firestein, Stephen, jt. ed. see Applebaum, Eleanor G.

Firestein, Stephen K. Terminations in Psychoanalysis. LC 76-46811. 261p. 1978. text ed. 27.50 (ISBN 0-8236-6450-3). Intl Univs Pr.

Firestine, Robert E., jt. auth. see Weinstein, Bernard L.

Firestone, Allan L. Mr. Luckypennys Magic Book. LC 77-71450. (Illus.). (gr. 2-7). 1977. pap. 4.95 (ISBN 0-934682-01-1). Emmett.

Firestone, Bernard J. The Quest for Nuclear Stability: John F. Kennedy & the Soviet Union. LC 81-13257. (Contributions in Political Science Ser.: No. 73). x, 176p. 1982. lib. bdg. 29.95 (ISBN 0-313-23214-8, FPD/). Greenwood.

Firestone, Clark B. Flowing South: Steamboating on the Ohio & Mississippi Rivers. 1977. lib. bdg. 59.95 (ISBN 0-8490-1846-3). Gordon Pr.

Firestone, David B. & Reed, Frank C. Environmental Law for Non-Lawyers. LC 82-70697. (Illus.). 282p. 1983. 29.95 (ISBN 0-250-40529-6). Butterworth.

Firestone, J. M. Federal Receipts & Expenditures During Business Cycles: 1879-1958. (National Bureau of Economic Research, B.9). 1960. 22.00 (ISBN 0-691-04129-6). Princeton U Pr.

Firestone, John M. Federal Receipts & Expenditures During Business Cycles, 1879-1958. (Business Cycles Ser.: No. 9). 192p. 1960. 21.00 (ISBN 0-691-04129-6, Dist. by Princeton U Pr). Natl Bur Econ Res.

Firestone, Laya, et al, trs. see Vinner, Schlomo.

Firestone, Linda & Morse, Whit. Florida's Enchanting Islands: Sanibel & Captiva. 3rd ed. LC 80-67778. (Illus., Orig.). 1980. pap. 4.95 (ISBN 0-917374-08-8). Good Life VA.

--Jefferson's Country: Charlottesville & Albemarle County - a Visitor's Guide. LC 77-82201. (Illus.). 1977. pap. 3.95 (ISBN 0-917374-12-6). Good Life VA.

--Virginia's Favorite Islands: Chincoteague & Assateague. 3rd ed. LC 77-82202. (Illus.). 1982. pap. 3.50t (ISBN 0-917374-02-9). Good Life VA.

Firestone, P., et al. Advances in Behavioral Medicine for Children & Adolescents. 184p. 1983. text ed. 19.95x (ISBN 0-89859-326-3). L Erlbaum Assocs.

Firestone, Philip, jt. ed. see McGrath, Patrick J.

Firestone, R. F., jt. auth. see Yurkewycz, R.

Firestone, Robert & Catlett, Joyce. The Truth: A Psychological Cure. 234p. 1982. pap. 6.95 (ISBN 0-89696-167-2, An Everest House Book). Dodd.

--The Truth: A Psychological Curse. 234p. 1981. 13.95 (ISBN 0-02-538380-9). Macmillan.

Firestone, Ross, jt. auth. see Ashley, Elizabeth.

Firestone, Ross, jt. auth. see Carroll, Diahann.

Firestone, Ross, jt. auth. see Crosby, Gary.

Firestone, Ross, ed. A Book of Men: Visions of the Male Experience. 384p. 1981. 35.00x (ISBN 0-906391-03-2, Pub. by Mainstream). State Mutual Bk.

Firestone, William A. Great Expectations for Small Schools: The Limitations of Federal Projects. LC 80-23199. 234p. 1980. 36.95 (ISBN 0-03-057397-1). Praeger.

Firey, Walter. Man, Mind, & Land: A Theory of Resource Use. LC 77-12902. 1977. Repr. of 1960 ed. lib. bdg. 21.00x (ISBN 0-8371-9834-8, FIMM). Greenwood.

--The Study of Possible Societies. LC 76-55578. (Illus.). 1977. 10.00 (ISBN 0-9603066-0-9). Firey.

Firey, Walter I. Land Use in Central Boston. LC 68-23288. (Harvard Sociological Studies Ser.: Vol. 4). (Illus.). 1968. Repr. of 1947 ed. lib. bdg. 65.00 (ISBN 0-8371-0073-9, FILU). Greenwood.

Firishtah, Muhammed Kasim. History of the Rise of the Mahomedan Power in India till the Year A.D. 1612, 4 Vols. Briggs, John, tr. LC 79-154112. Repr. of 1910 ed. Set. 225.00 (ISBN 0-404-56300-7). AMS Pr.

Firkaly, Susan T. Into the Mouths of Babes: A Natural Foods Cookbook for Infants & Toddlers. LC 84-14620. (Illus.). 168p. (Orig.). 1984. pap. 6.95 (ISBN 0-932620-35-3). Betterway Pubns.

Firkens, Peter, ed. A History of Commerce & Industry in Western Australia. 223p. 1980. 30.00x (ISBN 0-85564-150-9, Pub. by U of West Australia Pr Australia). Intl Spec Bk.

Firkin, B. G. The Platelet & Its Disorders. 350p. 1984. 49.50 (ISBN 0-85200-704-3, Pub. by MTP Pr England). Kluwer Academic.

Firkins, Ina. Index to Plays Eighteen Hundred to Nineteen Twenty-Six. LC 75-144606. (BCL Ser.: I). Repr. of 1927 ed. 24.50 (ISBN 0-404-02386-X). AMS Pr.

Firkins, Ina T. Henrik Ibsen: A Bibliography of Criticism & Biography, with an Index to Characters. LC 72-191605. 1973. lib. bdg. 10.00 (ISBN 0-8414-0816-5). Folcroft.

Firkins, Oscar. Power & Elusiveness in Shelley. LC 70-120253. 1970. Repr. lib. bdg. 17.00x (ISBN 0-374-92745-6). Octagon.

Firkins, Oscar W. Ralph Waldo Emerson. LC 80-2532. Repr. of 1915 ed. 44.50 (ISBN 0-404-19258-0). AMS Pr.

--Selected Essays on Literary Themes. LC 77-86013. (Essay & General Literature Index Reprint Ser). 1969. Repr. of 1933 ed. 23.50x (ISBN 0-8046-0558-0, Pub. by Kennikat). Assoc Faculty Pr.

--Two Passengers for Chelsea & Other Plays. LC 77-94340. (One-Act Plays in Reprint Ser.). 1978. Repr. of 1928 ed. 23.75x (ISBN 0-8486-2038-0). Core Collection.

Firkusny, Tatiana, tr. see Tesnohlidek, Rudolf, et al.

Firmage, D. A., jt. auth. see Heins, C. P.

Firmage, D. Allan. Fundamental Theory of Structures. LC 79-25213. 584p. 1980. 19.50 (ISBN 0-88275-443-2). Krieger.

Firmage, George J. A Checklist of the Published Writings of Gertrude Stein. LC 74-16361. 1974. Repr. of 1954 ed. lib. bdg. 10.00 (ISBN 0-8414-4239-8). Folcroft.

--E. E. Cummings: A Bibliography. LC 73-20969. 129p. 1974. Repr. of 1960 ed. lib. bdg. 18.75x (ISBN 0-8371-5917-2, FIEC). Greenwood.

Firmage, George J., ed. Garland for Dylan Thomas. 1969. 9.50 (ISBN 0-8079-0056-7); pap. 2.95 (ISBN 0-8079-0057-5). October.

Firmage, George J. & Kennedy, Richard S., eds. Etcetera: The Unpublished Poems of E. E. Cummings. (Liveright Bk.). 16.95 (ISBN 0-87140-644-6); pap. 7.95 (ISBN 0-87140-128-2). Norton.

Firmage, George J., ed. see Cummings, E. E.

Firmage, George J., jt. ed. see Kennedy, Richard S.

Firmage, George James, ed. see Cummings, E. E.

Firmage, James, ed. see Cummings, E. E.

Firmage, Robert, tr. see Rilke, Rainer M.

Firmage, William H. Season of Fire, Season of Faith. LC 82-24388. 336p. 1983. 15.95 (ISBN 0-87949-233-3). Ashley Bks.

Firman, I. D. & Waller, J. M. Coffee Berry Diseases & Other Colletotrichum Diseases of Coffee. 53p. 1977. 40.00x (ISBN 0-85198-367-7, Pub. by CAB Bks England). State Mutual Bk.

Firman, James P., et al. Opportunities in Aging: Strategies for Service-Learning. LC 83-25030. (Illus.). 114p. (Orig.). 1983. pap. 10.00 (ISBN 0-910883-01-7). Natl Coun Aging.

Firmin, jt. auth. see Portgate.

Firmin, Peter. Basil Brush & a Dragon. (Illus.). 48p. (gr. 1-4). 1982. pap. 3.95 (ISBN 0-13-066464-2, Pub. by Treehouse). P-H.

--Basil Brush & the Windmills. (Illus.). 48p. 1980. 7.95 (ISBN 0-13-066720-X). P-H.

--Basil Brush at the Beach. (Treehouse Bks). (gr. 1-4). 1981. pap. 3.95 (ISBN 0-13-066746-3). P-H.

--Basil Brush at the Beach. LC 75-40342. (Illus.). 48p. (gr. 1-4). 1976. 7.95 (ISBN 0-13-066654-8). P-H.

--Basil Brush Builds a House. (Illus.). (gr. 1-4). 1981. pap. 3.95 (ISBN 0-13-066597-5). P-H.

--Basil Brush Builds a House. LC 76-44807. (Illus.). (gr. 1-4). 1977. 4.95 (ISBN 0-13-066662-9). P-H.

--Basil Brush Gets a Medal. LC 78-6108. (Illus.). 1978. PLB 5.95 (ISBN 0-13-066688-2). P-H.

--Basil Brush Goes Boating. 48p. 1976. 7.95 (ISBN 0-13-066647-5). P-H.

--Basil Brush Goes Boating. (Basil Brush Ser.). (Illus.). 48p. (gr. 1-4). 1982. pap. 3.95 (ISBN 0-13-066803-6, Pub. by Treehouse). P-H.

--Basil Brush Goes Flying. (Illus.). 48p. (gr. 3-7). 1983. pap. 3.95 (ISBN 0-13-066985-7, Pub. by Treehouse). P-H.

--Basil Brush in the Jungle. (Illus.). (gr. 1-4). 1979. lib. bdg. 7.95 (ISBN 0-13-066621-1). P-H.

--Basil Brush on the Trail. (Illus.). 48p. 1981. 7.95 (ISBN 0-13-066738-2). P-H.

--Chicken Stew: Life with the Badd-Wolfe Family. (Illus.). 32p. 1982. pap. 7.95 (ISBN 0-7207-1299-8, Pub. by Michael Joseph). Merrimack Pub Cir.

--The Winter Diary of a Country Rat. (Illus.). 144p. (gr. 2-5). 1983. 12.95 (ISBN 0-7182-2541-4, Pub. by Kaye & Ward). David & Charles.

Firminger, W. K. Historical Introduction to the Bengal Portion of "The Fifth Report". (ISPP Ser.: Vol. III). 376p. 1977. 10.00 (ISBN 0-88065-084-2, Pub. by Messers Today & Tomorrows Printers & Publishers India). Scholarly Pubns.

Firminger, Walter K., ed. see Great Britain. Parliament. House of Commons.

Firnberg, D. The Information Centre. (Computer State of the Art Report Ser.: Series No. 12, No. 2). (Illus.). 275p. 1984. 460.00 (ISBN 0-08-028586-4). Pergamon.

Firnberg, David. Computer Management & Information. 135p. 1973. 17.95x (ISBN 0-8464-1251-9). Beekman Pubs.

Firor, Ruth A. Folkways in Thomas Hardy. LC 68-25031. 1968. Repr. of 1931 ed. 11.00x (ISBN 0-8462-1143-2). Russell.

Firouz, Eskandar & Harrington, Fred A., Jr. Iran: Concepts of Biotic Community Conservation. (Illus.). 31p. 1976. pap. 8.00 (ISBN 2-88032-048-8, IUCN56, IUCN). Unipub.

Firschein, Oscar, ed. Artificial Intelligence, Vol. VI. (Information Technology Ser.). (Illus.). 250p. 1984. 23.00 (ISBN 0-88283-044-9). AFIPS Pr.

Firsoff, Axel. The New Face of Mars. 1978. 32.00 (ISBN 0-86025-818-1). State Mutual Bk.

Firsoff, V. A. At the Crossroads of Knowledge: The Origins of Life on This Planet & Elsewhere in the Universe. 1981. 16.95x (ISBN 0-86025-812-2). Intl Ideas.

--The New Face of Mars. 1982. 17.95x (ISBN 0-86025-818-1). Intl Ideas.

First Annual Conference on Shock Airlie, Va. June, 1978. Metabolic & Cardiac Alterations in Shock & Trauma: Proceedings. Lefer, Allan M. & Schumer, William, eds. LC 79-2106. 88p. 1979. 24.00x (ISBN 0-8451-0204-4). A R Liss.

First Conference, 1961 see Conferences on Brain & Behavior, Los Angeles.

First Edition Club, London. Bibliographical Catalogue of Lord Byron. LC 74-5102. 1925. lib. bdg. 6.50 (ISBN 0-8414-7743-4). Folcroft.

First Hospital, Shanghai, People's Republic of China, et al. Acupuncture Anesthesia. (Illus.). 1975. 30.00 (ISBN 0-916524-00-0). US Direct Serv.

First International Conference on Prostaglandins & Cancer, Washington, DC, August 30-September 2, 1981. Prostaglandins & Cancer: Proceedings. Powles, Trevor J., et al, eds. LC 82-86. (Prostaglandins & Related Lipids: Vol. 2). 876p. 1982. 84.00 (ISBN 0-8451-2101-4). A R Liss.

First International Congress of Eugenics & Rosenberg, Charles. Problems in Eugenics: Papers Communicated to the First International Congress. LC 83-48620. (The History of Hereditarian Thought Ser.). 679p. 1985. lib. bdg. 80.00 (ISBN 0-8240-5806-2). Garland Pub.

First International Congress of Quantum Chemistry, Menton, France, July 4-10, 1973. The World of Quantum Chemistry: Proceedings. Daudel, R. & Pullman, B., eds. LC 73-91429. 1974. lib. bdg. 58.00 (ISBN 90-277-0421-X, Pub. by Reidel Holland). Kluwer Academic.

First International Symposium, Marburg, West Germany, May 31, 1978. Continuous Transcutaneous Blood Gas Monitoring: Proceedings. Huch, Albert, et al, eds. LC 79-2586. (Birth Defects Original Article Ser.: Vol. XV, No. 4). 664p. 1979. 82.00x (ISBN 0-8451-1027-6). A R Liss.

First, Julia. The Absolute, Ultimate End. 128p. (gr. 7-9). 1985. PLB 10.90 (ISBN 0-531-10075-8). Watts.

--Flat on My Face. (gr. 4-6). 1975. pap. 1.75 (ISBN 0-380-00204-3, 52324-8, Camelot). Avon.

--I Rebekah Take You Lawrence. LC 80-24588. (gr. 6 up). 1981. PLB 8.90 (ISBN 0-531-04256-1). Watts.

--Look Who's Beautiful. (gr. 5 up). 1980. PLB 8.90 (ISBN 0-531-04109-3, B21). Watts.

--Look Who's Beautiful! 128p. (gr. 5-9). 1984. pap. 2.25 (ISBN 0-440-95112-7, LFL). Dell.

First, M. R., jt. auth. see Pesce, A. Z.

First National Foundation-March of Dimes Perinatal Nursing Research Roundtable Conference Chicago, Ill. Newborn Behavioral Organization: Nursing Research & Implications, Proceedings. Anderson, Gene C. & Raff, Beverly, eds. LC 79-2597. (Birth Defects: Original Article Ser.: Vol. XV, No. 7). 240p. 1979. 29.00x (ISBN 0-8451-1032-2). A R Liss.

First of May Group, ed. Towards a Citizens Militia: Anarchist Alternatives to NATO & the Warsaw Pact. 1984. lib. bdg. 79.95 (ISBN 0-87700-631-8). Revisionist Pr.

First, Ruth. Black Gold: The Mozambican Miner, Proletarian & Peasant. LC 82-24042. (Illus.). 320p. 1983. 30.00x (ISBN 0-312-08318-1). St Martin.
--Libya: The Elusive Revolution. LC 75-9944. 294p. 1975. text ed. 30.00x (ISBN 0-8419-0211-9, Africana). Holmes & Meier.
--South West Africa. 12.00 (ISBN 0-8446-2061-0). Peter Smith.
First, Ruth & Scott, Ann. Olive Schreiner. LC 80-13190. (Illus.). 384p. 1980. 20.00 (ISBN 0-8052-3749-6). Schocken.
First Stanford Symposium. Mathematical Methods in the Social Sciences, 1959: Proceedings. Arrow, Kenneth J., et al, eds. 1960. 27.50x (ISBN 0-8047-0021-4). Stanford U Pr.
First Earl of Birkenhead. The Five Hundred Best English Letters. 960p. 1984. Repr. of 1931 ed. lib. bdg. 45.00 (ISBN 0-89760-249-8). Telegraph Bks.
Firt, Vladimir. Statics, Formfinding & Dynamics of Air-Supported Membrane Structures. 1983. lib. bdg. 83.00 (ISBN 90-247-2672-7, Pub. by Martinus Nijhoff Netherlands). Kluwer Academic.
Firtel, Richard A., jt. auth. see Davidson, Eric H.
Firth, jt. auth. see Hooper.
Firth, C. Commentary on Maculay's "History of England". 375p. 1964. Repr. of 1938 ed. 30.00x (ISBN 0-7146-1475-0, BHA-01475, F Cass Co). Biblio Dist.
Firth, C. H. An American Garland. 59.95 (ISBN 0-87968-601-4). Gordon Pr.
--English History in English Poetry from the French Revolution to the Death of Queen Victoria. 59.95 (ISBN 0-8490-0111-0). Gordon Pr.
--Stuart Tracts. LC 64-16747. (Arber's an English Garner Ser.). 1964. Repr. of 1890 ed. 23.50 (ISBN 0-8154-0071-3). Cooper Sq.
Firth, C. H., ed. see Clarke, William.
Firth, C. H., ed. see Ludlow, Edmund.
Firth, C. H., ed. see Macaulay, Thomas B.
Firth, C. H., ed. see Venables, Robert.
Firth, C. H., intro. by. Stuart Tracts, Sixteen Hundred to Three to Sixteen Ninety-Three. Straka, Gerald M., ed. LC 72-83161. (English Studies Ser.). 1972. Repr. of 1903 ed. lib. bdg. 40.00 (ISBN 0-8420-1419-5). Scholarly Res Inc.
Firth, Charles. Sir Walter Raleigh's History of the World. 49p. 1980. Repr. 7.50 (ISBN 0-8492-4707-1). R West.
Firth, Charles H. American Garland, Being a Collection of Ballads Relating to America, 1536-1759. LC 68-20123. 1969. Repr. of 1915 ed. 35.00x (ISBN 0-8103-3411-9). Gale.
--Bibliography of the Writings of Sir Charles Firth. LC 74-13083. 1928. lib. bdg. 15.00 (ISBN 0-8414-4244-4). Folcroft.
--John Bunyan. LC 74-11062. 1911. lib. bdg. 10.00 (ISBN 0-8414-4212-6). Folcroft.
--Milton As an Historian. LC 74-13082. 1908. lib. bdg. 10.00 (ISBN 0-8414-4242-8). Folcroft.
--Political Significance of Gulliver's Travels. LC 74-12166. 1919. lib. bdg. 8.50 (ISBN 0-8414-4236-3). Folcroft.
--The Political Significance of Gulliver's Travels. 6.75 (ISBN 0-8446-1181-6). Peter Smith.
--Sir Walter Raleigh's History of the World. LC 77-1815. 1918. lib. bdg. 10.00 (ISBN 0-8414-4190-1). Folcroft.
Firth, E. W., ed. see Rychtera, M.
Firth, Edith G., ed. The Town of York, Eighteen Fifteen to Eighteen Thirty-Four: A Further Collection of Documents of Early Toronto. (Champlain Society, Toronto, Publications, Ontario Ser.: No. 8). pap. write for info. Bks Demand UMI.
--The Town of York, Seventeen Ninety-Three to Eighteen Fifteen: A Collection of Documents of Early Toronto. LC 62-4422. (Champlain Society, Toronto, Publications, Ontario Ser.: No. 5). pap. 115.50 (ISBN 0-317-26912-7, 2023614). Bks Demand UMI.
Firth, F., ed. see Pirandello, L.
Firth, Grace. Secrets of the Still: A Zesty History & How-To for Making Spirits, Fragrances, Curables, Gasahol & Other Products of the Stillroom. 1983. 17.95 (ISBN 0-914440-66-7). EPM Pubns.
--Stillroom Cookery: The Art of Preserving Foods Naturally, with Recipes, Menus & Metric Measures. LC 76-28240. (Illus.). 1977. 9.95 (ISBN 0-914440-13-6). EPM Pubns.
Firth, J. G., jt. ed. see Cullis, C. F.
Firth, J. R. The Tongues of Man. 1937. 20.00 (ISBN 0-8274-3639-4). R West.
Firth, James. Other Worlds to Conquer. 1982. 10.95 (ISBN 0-533-05376-5). Vantage.
Firth, John B. Augustus Caesar & the Organisation of the Empire of Rome. LC 70-38352. (Select Bibliographies Reprint Ser.). Repr. of 1902 ed. 31.00 (ISBN 0-8369-6769-0). Ayer Co Pubs.
--Augustus Caesar & the Organization of the Empire of Rome. LC 73-14440. (Heroes of the Nations Ser.). Repr. of 1903 ed. 30.00 (ISBN 0-404-58259-1). AMS Pr.
--Constantine the Great: The Reorganization of the Empire & the Triumph of the Church. facsimile ed. LC 77-152983. (Select Bibliographies Reprint Ser). Repr. of 1904 ed. 27.50 (ISBN 0-8369-5735-0). Ayer Co Pubs.
Firth, Katherine R. The Apocalyptic Tradition in Reformation Britain 1530-1645. (Historical Monographs). (Illus.). 1979. 45.00x (ISBN 0-19-821868-0). Oxford U Pr.
Firth, Michael. Forecasting Methods in Business & Management. LC 81-86404. (Illus.). xi, 264p. 1982. pap. text ed. 18.95x (ISBN 0-89563-047-8). Intl Ideas.
--Unit Trusts: Performance & Prospects. 1978. 90.00x (ISBN 0-905440-67-6, Pub. by MCB Pubns). State Mutual Bk.
Firth, R. J. Managing Viewdata Systems. 150p. 1984. pap. text ed. 21.55 (ISBN 0-471-81043-6). Wiley.
--Viewdata Systems: A Practical Evaluation Guide. (Office Technology in the Eighties Ser.). (Illus.). 114p. (Orig.). 1982. pap. 15.00x (ISBN 0-85012-370-4). Taylor & Francis.
--Viewdata Systems: A Practical Evaluation Guide. 100p. 1982. pap. 14.20 (ISBN 0-471-89431-1). Wiley.
Firth, Raymond. Essays on Social Organization & Values. (London School of Economics Monographs on Social Anthropology: No. 28). 328p. 1969. pap. 19.50 (ISBN 0-485-19628-X, Pub. by Athlone Pr Ltd). Longwood Pub Group.
--History & Traditions of Tikopia. 311p. 1961. text ed. 10.00x (ISBN 0-8248-0585-2). UH Pr.
--Human Types. rev. ed. LC 83-13026. (Illus.). 184p. 1983. Repr. of 1975 ed. lib. bdg. 32.50x (ISBN 0-313-24176-7, FIHU). Greenwood.
--Malay Fishermen: Their Peasant Economy. (Illus.). 448p. 1975. pap. 4.95x (ISBN 0-393-00775-8, Norton Lib). Norton.
--Primitive Polynesian Economy. (Illus.). 1975. pap. 4.95x (ISBN 0-393-00774-X, Norton Lib). Norton.
--Rank & Religion in Tikopia. 1970. text ed. 35.00x (ISBN 0-04-200018-1). Allen Unwin.
--Symbols: Public & Private. LC 72-11806. (Symbol, Myth & Ritual Ser). 469p. 1975. pap. 12.95x (ISBN 0-8014-9150-9). Cornell U Pr.
--Symbols: Public & Private. Turner, Victor, ed. (Symbol, Myth & Ritual Ser.). 469p. 1973. 29.50x (ISBN 0-8014-0760-5). Cornell U Pr.
--Tikopia-English Dictionary. 671p. 1985. 22.95 (ISBN 0-19-648037-X). Oxford U Pr.
--We, the Tikopia: A Sociological Study of Kinship in Primitive Polynesia. abr. ed. LC 83-42540. (Illus.). xxviii, 497p. 1963. 35.00x (ISBN 0-8047-1201-8); pap. 10.95x (ISBN 0-8047-1202-6). Stanford U Pr.
--The Work of the Gods in Tikopia. 2nd. ed. (London School of Economics Monographs on Social Anthropology: Nos. 1 & 2). 492p. 1967. 48.50 (ISBN 0-485-19501-1, Pub. by Athlone Pr Ltd). Longwood Pub Group.
Firth, Raymond, ed. Man & Culture: An Evaluation of the Work of Bronislaw Malinowski. 292p. 1980. 28.00x (ISBN 0-7100-1376-0, Pub. by Routledge England). Humanities.
--Themes in Economic Anthropology. (Illus.). 1970. pap. 13.95x (ISBN 0-422-72540-4, NO. 2198, Pub by Tavistock England). Methuen Inc.
Firth, Raymond, et al. Families & Their Relatives, Kinship in a Middle-Class Sector of London: An Anthropological Study. (International Library of Sociology & Social Reconstruction). 1970. text ed. 17.00x (ISBN 0-7100-6431-4). Humanities.
Firth, Raymond W. Art & Life in New Guinea. LC 75-32815. Repr. of 1936 ed. 24.50 (ISBN 0-404-14119-6). AMS Pr.
--Elements of Social Organization. 3rd ed. LC 80-24763. (Josiah Mason Lectures Ser., 1947). (Illus.). xi, 260p. 1981. Repr. of 1961 ed. lib. bdg. 28.50x (ISBN 0-313-22745-4, FIES). Greenwood.
Firth, Robert E., jt. ed. see Phillips, Harold R.
Firth, Robert H. Philippine Invasion Nineteen Forty-One to Nineteen Forty-Two: A Matter of Time. rev. ed. LC 80-68365. 143p. 1981. pap. 6.50 (ISBN 0-9605060-0-4). Firth.
Firth, Stewart. New Guinea Under the Germans. (Illus.). 216p. 26.95x (ISBN 0-522-84220-8, Pub. by Melbourne U Pr Australia). Intl Spec Bk.
Firth, Susanna. Lions Walk Alone. (Harlequin Romances Ser.). 192p. 1983. pap. 1.95 (ISBN 0-373-02564-5). Harlequin Bks.
--Master of Shadows. (Harlequin Presents Ser.). 192p. 1983. pap. 1.95 (ISBN 0-373-10624-6). Harlequin Bks.
--The Overlord. (Harlequin Romances Ser.). 192p. 1982. pap. 1.50 (ISBN 0-373-02493-2). Harlequin Bks.
Firtz, Jean. Will You Sign Here, John Hancock? (Illus.). (gr. 2-6). 1982. pap. 4.95 (ISBN 0-698-20539-1, Coward). Putnam Pub Group.
Firuski, Elvia, ed. see Boulestin, Xavier M.
Firuski, Maurice, ed. see Boulestin, Xavier M.
Fisac, M. Q. Diccionario de Filosofia. 492p. (Span.). 1979. pap. 32.95 (ISBN 84-301-0409-7, S-50135). French & Eur.
Fiscalini, Janet. Evasions. LC 71-185170. 1972. 3.00 (ISBN 0-913270-01-6). Sunstone Pr.
Fisch, et al. Charities & Charitable Foundations. LC 74-76684. 1974. 35.00 (ISBN 0-686-15422-3). Lond Pubns.
Fisch, Allan E. & Redman, Helen C. Blunt & Penetrating Trauma. (Advanced Exercises in Diagnostic Radiology Ser.: Vol. 16). (Illus.). 256p. 1982. pap. 23.95 (ISBN 0-7216-3677-2). Saunders.
Fisch, Charles & Surawicz, Boris. Digitalis. LC 69-15255. (Illus.). 244p. 1969. 62.50 (ISBN 0-8089-0131-1, 791265). Grune.
Fisch, Edith L. Fisch on New York Evidence. 2nd ed. LC 77-77425. 1977. 30.00 (ISBN 0-686-19173-0). Lond Pubns.
Fisch, Edith L., et al. Lawyers in Industry. LC 55-11077. 225p. 1956. 8.50 (ISBN 0-379-00052-0). Oceana.
Fisch, H. Zionist Revolution. LC 78-424. 1978. 19.95x (ISBN 0-312-89886-X). St Martin.
Fisch, Harold. Hamlet & the Word: Covenant Pattern in Shakespeare. LC 70-15840. 1971. 14.50 (ISBN 0-8044-2198-6). Ungar.
--Jerusalem & Albion: The Hebraic Factor in Seventeenth-Century Literature. 301p. 1982. Repr. of 1964 ed. lib. bdg. 35.00 (ISBN 0-89987-268-9). Darby Bks.
--Jerusalem & Albion: The Herbraic Factor in Seventeenth Century Literature. 301p. Date not set. Repr. of 1964 ed. lib. bdg. 40.00 (ISBN 0-918377-39-0). Russell Pr.
--A Remembered Future: A Study in Literary Mythology. LC 83-48899. (Jewish Literature & Culture Ser.). 224p. 1984. 22.50x (ISBN 0-253-35003-4). Ind U Pr.
--S. Y. Agnon. LC 74-76126. (Literature and Life Ser.). 124p. 1975. 12.95 (ISBN 0-8044-2197-8). Ungar.
Fisch, Max, jt. ed. see Peirce, Charles S.
Fisch, Max H., jt. auth. see Anderson, Paul R.
Fisch, Max H., ed. Classic American Philosophers. (Orig.). 1966. pap. text ed. 24.95 (ISBN 0-13-135186-9). P-H.
Fisch, Max H., ed. see Peirce, Charles S., et al.
Fisch, Max H., tr. see Vico, Giambattista.
Fisch, Richard, et al. The Tactics of Change: Doing Therapy Briefly. LC 81-48665. (Social & Behavioral Science Ser.). 1982. text ed. 18.95x (ISBN 0-87589-521-2). Jossey-Bass.
Fisch, U., ed. Aktuelle Probleme der Otorhinolaryngologie. (ORL: Vol. 38, Suppl. 1). 1976. 25.75 (ISBN 3-8055-2394-7). S Karger.
Fisch, U., ed. see International Otoneurological Symposium.
Fischart, Johann. Dichtungen. LC 78-168026. Repr. of 1880 ed. 22.00 (ISBN 0-404-02387-8). AMS Pr.
Fischbach. A Manual of Laboratory Diagnostic Tests. 2nd ed. LC 64-3703. 1984. 17.50 (ISBN 0-397-54429-4, Lippincott Nursing). Lippincott.
Fischbeck, H. J. & Fishbeck, K. H. Formulas, Facts, & Constants for Students & Professionals in Engineering, Chemistry, & Physics. 270p. 1982. pap. 16.00 (ISBN 0-387-11315-0). Springer-Verlag.
Fischbein, E., ed. The Intuitive Sources of Probabilistic Thinking in Children. LC 75-22376. (Synthese Library: No.85). xiii, 201p. 1975. lib. bdg. 39.50 (ISBN 90-277-0626-3, Pub. by Reidel Holland). Kluwer Academic.
Fischborn, Cynthia, ed. see Kibbey, Heather & Long, Cheryl.
Fischborn, Cynthia, ed. see Long, Cheryl.
Fischel, Daniel N. A Practical Guide to Writing & Publishing Professional Books: Business, Technical, Scientific, Scholarly. 300p. 1984. 27.95 (ISBN 0-442-22482-6). Van Nos Reinhold.
Fischel, H. A., intro. by. The First Book of Maccabees. 124p. 1985. pap. 4.95 (ISBN 0-8052-0793-7). Schocken.
Fischel, Jack, jt. ed. see Pinsker, Sanford.
Fischel, Oskar, jt. auth. see Boehn, Max Von.
Fischel, Walter. Jews in the Economic & Political Life of Medieval Islam. rev. ed. LC 68-25719. 1969. Repr. of 1937 ed. 12.50x (ISBN 0-87068-047-1). Ktav.
Fischel, Walter J. Ibn Khaldun in Egypt: His Public Functions & His Historical Research, (1382-1406); A Study in Islamic Historiography. LC 67-11200. 1967. 34.00x (ISBN 0-520-00414-0). U of Cal Pr.
Fischel, Walter J., ed. Semitic & Oriental Studies: A Volume Presented to William Popper, on the Occasion of His 75th Birthday, October 29, 1949. LC 51-9375. (University of California Publications in Semitic Philology Ser.: Vol. 11). pap. 119.00 (ISBN 0-317-29578-0, 2021490). Bks Demand UMI.
Fischel, William A. The Economics of Zoning Laws: A Property Rights Approach to American Land Use Controls. LC 84-21840. 400p. 1985. text ed. 35.00x (ISBN 0-8018-2420-6). Johns Hopkins.
Fischer & Wallis. Federal Local Court Rules, 2 Vols. LC 64-20105. 1972. write for info. Callaghan.
Fischer, jt. auth. see Braune.
Fischer, jt. auth. see Pike.
Fischer, jt. auth. see Schimmel.
Fischer, jt. auth. see SIPRI Staff.
Fischer, A. Lumko English-Xhosa Dictionary. (Eng. & Khosa.). 1984. 39.95x (ISBN 0-19-570290-5). Oxford U Pr.
Fischer, Adam, jt. auth. see Lorentz, Friedrich.
Fischer, Al & Fischer, Mildred. California Favorites Cook Book. 1979. plastic 3.50 (ISBN 0-914846-07-8). Golden West Pub.
--Citrus Recipes from the Citrus Belt. (Illus.). 128p. 1980. plastic comb binding 3.50 (ISBN 0-914846-08-6). Golden West Pub.
Fischer, Al, jt. auth. see Fischer, Mildred.
Fischer, Al, jt. auth. see Fischer, Mildred M.
Fischer, Al & Fischer, Mildred, eds. Arizona Cook Book. 1974. plastic 3.50 (ISBN 0-914846-00-0). Golden West Pub.
Fischer, Alan M., jt. auth. see Reyes-Guerra, David R.
Fischer, Alfred G., et al. Electron Micrographs of Limestones & Their Nannofossils. (Monographs in Geology & Palentology Ser). (Illus.). 1967. 20.00 (ISBN 0-691-07953-6); pap. 9.95 (ISBN 0-691-07954-4). Princeton U Pr.
Fischer, Ann, jt. auth. see Jackson, Hugo.
Fischer, Ann M., jt. auth. see Fischer, John L.
Fischer, Arlene, jt. auth. see Nieburg, Herbert.
Fischer, Asma Z. & Anderson, Joseph C. Pediatric Neurosonography: Clinical Tomographic & Neuropathologic Correlates. 240p. Date not set. 39.95x (ISBN 0-471-89252-1). Wiley.
Fischer, Balthasar. Signs, Words & Gestures. O'Connell, Matthew J., tr. from Ger. 1981. pap. 5.95 (ISBN 0-916134-48-2). Pueblo Pub Co.
Fischer, Barbara. Among the Reeds. (Illus.). 32p. (Orig.). 1974. 3.95x (ISBN 0-912658-89-4). J Mark Pr.
--Poetry Self-Taught. 40p. (Orig.). 1974. 12.95x (ISBN 0-912658-63-0). J Mark Pr.
Fischer, Barbara, ed. see McKinney, Virginia.
Fischer, Barbara, intro. by. The Flaming Sword. (Illus.). 50p. 1976. 4.95x (ISBN 0-912658-25-8). J Mark Pr.
Fischer, Barbara R., jt. auth. see Jones, Lila M.
Fischer, Bela. The Human Exile. LC 74-75081. 1974. 6.00 (ISBN 0-8022-2139-4). Philos Lib.
Fischer, Bernd J. King Zog & the Struggle for Stability in Albania. 352p. 1984. 32.50 (ISBN 0-88033-051-1). East Eur Quarterly.
Fischer, Bill, et al. Growers Weed Identification Handbook. (Illus.). 199p. 1978. 55.00x (ISBN 0-931876-43-5, 4030). Ag & Nat Res.
Fischer, Bob. How You Know When You've Got It. 38p. pap. 5.00 (ISBN 0-942494-31-8). Coleman Pub.
--Toward a New Sexuality. 14p. pap. 3.00 (ISBN 0-942494-42-3). Coleman Pub.
Fischer, Bobby, et al. Bobby Fischer Teaches Chess. (Illus.). 352p. 1972. pap. 3.95 (ISBN 0-553-22906-0). Bantam.
Fischer, Brigitte B. My European Heritage: Life among Great Men of Letters. Zhon, Harry, tr. from Ger. 300p. 1986. 16.95 (ISBN 0-8283-1897-2). Branden Pub Co.
Fischer, C. E., jt. auth. see Gamble, J. S.
Fischer, C. F. The Hartree Fock Method for Atoms: A Numerical Approach. LC 76-50015. 308p. 1977. 44.95 (ISBN 0-471-25990-X). Krieger.
Fischer, C. P., photos by. Classic Dishes Made Easy. (Illus.). 160p. 1983. 19.95 (ISBN 0-688-02489-0). Hearst Bks.
Fischer, C. P., et al. Classic Cooking Made Easy. 120p. 1985. 12.95 (ISBN 0-8120-5663-9). VHS 39.95 (ISBN 0-8120-7340-1); BETA 39.95 (ISBN 0-8120-7373-8). Barron.
Fischer, Carl H., jt. auth. see Menge, Walter O.
Fischer, Carl H., jt. auth. see Rider, Paul R.
Fischer, Christiane. Let Them Speak for Themselves: Women in the American West, 1849-1900. 346p. 1977. 21.00 (ISBN 0-208-01645-7, Archon). Shoe String.
Fischer, Claude S. To Dwell Among Friends: Personal Networks in Town & City. LC 81-11505. 1982. lib. bdg. 35.00x (ISBN 0-226-25137-3); pap. 12.00x (ISBN 0-226-25138-1, Phoen). U of Chicago Pr.
--The Urban Experience. 2nd ed. 371p. 1984. pap. text ed. 11.95 (ISBN 0-15-593498-8, HC). HarBraceJ.
Fischer, Claude S., et al. Human Aggression & Conflict: Interdisciplinary Perspectives. (Illus.). 352p. 1975. pap. 19.95 ref. ed. (ISBN 0-13-444620-8). P-H.
--Networks & Places: Social Relations in the Urban Setting. LC 76-55101. (Illus.). 1977. 22.95 (ISBN 0-02-910240-5). Free Pr.
Fischer, Conan. Stormtroopers: A Social, Economic & Ideological Analysis: 1929-35. 240p. 1983. text ed. 25.00x (ISBN 0-04-943028-9). Allen Unwin.
Fischer, Constance T. Individualizing Psychological Assessment. LC 84-7796. (Psychology Ser.). 416p. 1985. text ed. 23.50 pub net (ISBN 0-534-03981-2). Brooks-Cole.
Fischer, Constance T. & Brodsky, Stanley L., eds. Client Participation in Human Services: The Prometheus Principle. LC 76-1772. 300p. 1978. 12.95 (ISBN 0-87855-131-X). Transaction Bks.
Fischer, Cree J. Piano Tuning: A Simple & Accurate Method for Amateurs. 12.50 (ISBN 0-8446-5477-9). Peter Smith.
Fischer, D., jt. auth. see DeBoer, J. B.
Fischer, D. W., ed. Managing Technological Accidents: Two Blowouts in the North Sea: Proceedings of an IIASA Workshop on Blowout Management. (IIASA Proceedings Ser.: Vol. 16). (Illus.). 242p. 1982. 55.00 (ISBN 0-08-029346-8). Pergamon.
Fischer, David H. Growing Old in America: The Bland-Lee Lectures Delivered at Clark University, Expanded Edition. 1978. pap. 8.95 (ISBN 0-19-502366-8, GB532, GB). Oxford U Pr.
--Historian's Fallacies: Toward a Logic of Historical Thought. 1970. pap. 7.50xi (ISBN 0-06-131545-1, TB1545, Torch). Har-Row.
Fischer, David W. North Sea Oil: An Environment Interface. 332p. (Orig.). 1982. pap. 38.00 (ISBN 82-00-05832-8). Universitet.

Fischer, Debi. The Magic Mountain Natural Dessert Book. (Illus.). 112p. (Orig.). 1983. 18.95 (ISBN 0-89594-117-1); pap. 7.95 (ISBN 0-89594-116-3). Crossing Pr.

Fischer, Dennis A. & Lynn, Russel I. Appeals & Writs in Criminal Cases. (California Criminal Law Practice Ser.). 743p. 1982. 75.00 (ISBN 0-88124-045-1, CR-33480). Cal Cont Ed Bar.

Fischer, Dieter, jt. ed. see Marks, Tobin J.

Fischer, Dietrich. Preventing War in the Nuclear Age. (Illus.). 248p. 1984. 18.95x (ISBN 0-8476-7342-1); pap. 9.95x (ISBN 0-8476-7343-X). Rowman & Allanheld.

Fischer, Donald E. & Jordan, Ronald J. Security Analysis & Portfolio Management. 3rd ed. (Illus.). 672p. 1983. 30.95 (ISBN 0-13-798876-1). P-H.

Fischer, Donald E. CFA, ed. Options & Futures: New Route to Risk-Return Management. LC 85-70373. 1984. 25.00 (ISBN 0-87094-610-2). Dow Jones-Irwin.

Fischer, Doucet D., jt. ed. see Reinman, Donald H.

Fischer, E. Intermediate Real Analysis. (Undergraduate Texts in Mathematics Ser.). (Illus.). 770p. 1983. 32.00 (ISBN 0-387-90721-1). Springer-Verlag.

Fischer, E. H., ed. see International Symposium on Metabolic Interconversion of Enzymes, 3rd, Seattle, 1973.

Fischer, Eberhard & Jain, Jyotindra. Art & Rituals: Twenty Five Hundred Years of Jainism in India. LC 78-670055. (Illus.). 1977. cancelled (ISBN 0-89684-369-6). Intl Pubns Serv.

Fischer, Eberhard, jt. auth. see Brinker, Helmut.

Fischer, Eberhard, jt. auth. see Buhler, Alfred.

Fischer, Ed, jt. auth. see Missinne, Leo E.

Fischer, Edward. Everybody Steals from God: Communication as Worship. LC 77-3711. 1977. text ed. 10.95x (ISBN 0-268-00904-X). U of Notre Dame Pr.

--Fiji Revisited: A Columbian Father's Memories of Twenty-Eight Years in the Islands. LC 81-5365. (Illus.). 1981. 10.95 (ISBN 0-8245-0097-0). Crossroad NY.

--Japan Journey: The Columban Fathers in Nippon. LC 84-14228. 208p. 1984. pap. 9.95 (ISBN 0-8245-0656-1). Crossroad NY.

Fischer, Eileen, jt. auth. see Vollmar, Karen.

Fischer, Eitel, ed. Die Ekloge des Phrynichos: Sammlung Griechischer und Lateinischer Grammitker, Band 1. 1974. text ed. 31.60 (ISBN 3-11-003638-X). De Gruyter.

Fischer, Eric. The Passing of the European Age: A Study of the Transfer of Western Civilization & Its Renewal in Other Continents. 228p. 1983. Repr. of 1948 ed. lib. bdg. 45.00 (ISBN 0-89987-281-6). Darby Bks.

Fischer, Eric & Elliott, Francis E. A German & English Glossary of Geographical Terms. LC 76-20474. (American Geographical Society Library Ser.: No. 5). 111p. (Ger. & Eng.). 1976. Repr. of 1950 ed. lib. bdg. 22.50x (ISBN 0-8371-8994-2, ELGG). Greenwood.

Fischer, Eric, et al. Question of Place. 2nd ed. 1969. 39.50 (ISBN 0-87948-004-1). Beatty.

Fischer, Ernest. Robert Potter, Founder of the Texas Navy. new ed. LC 75-33771. 320p. 1976. 12.95 (ISBN 0-88289-080-8). Pelican.

Fischer, Ernest G. Marxist & Utopias in Texas. 1980. 14.95 (ISBN 0-89015-233-0). Eakin Pubns.

Fischer, Ernst. The Necessity of Art: A Marxist Approach. 1978. pap. 6.95 (ISBN 0-14-055151-4, Peregrine). Penguin.

Fischer, Erwin. The Berlin Indictment. 14.95 (ISBN 0-88411-549-6, Pub. by Aeonian Pr). Amereon Ltd.

Fischer, Farley, jt. ed. see Saxena, Jitendra.

Fischer, Frank. Die Lehnworter Des Altwestnordischen. 27.00; pap. 22.00 (ISBN 0-384-15710-6). Johnson Repr.

--Politics, Values, & Public Policy. (Westview Special Study Ser.). 275p. 1980. lib. bdg. 29.50x (ISBN 0-89158-799-3); pap. 13.00 (ISBN 0-86531-214-1). Westview.

Fischer, Frank & Sirianni, Carmen, eds. Critical Studies in Organization & Bureaucracy. 520p. 1984. lib. bdg. 34.95 (ISBN 0-87722-343-2); pap. text ed. 12.95 (ISBN 0-87722-344-0). Temple U Pr.

Fischer, Fred. In This Corner, Wearing Trunks. Perry, R. Scott, ed. (Illus.). 180p. (Orig.). 1985. pap. 8.95 (ISBN 0-9614190-0-8). High Mount Pub.

Fischer, Fritz. Germany's Aims in the First World War. 1968. pap. 8.95x (ISBN 0-393-09798-6, NortonC). Norton.

--War of Illusions: German Policies, 1911-1914. Jackson, Marion, tr. from German. 578p. 1975. 9.95x (ISBN 0-393-09161-9). Norton.

Fischer, G. Complex Analytic Geometry. (Lecture Notes in Mathematics: Vol. 538). 1976. soft cover 16.00 (ISBN 0-387-07857-6). Springer-Verlag.

Fischer, G. & Weiser, R. J., eds. Hormonally Defined Media: A Tool in Cell Biology. (Proceedings in Life Sciences Ser.). (Illus.). 460p. 1983. 33.00 (ISBN 0-387-12668-6). Springer-Verlag.

Fischer, Gad. Vibronic Coupling. (Theoretical Chemistry Ser.). 1984. 42.00 (ISBN 0-12-257240-8). Acad Pr.

Fischer, Gael, jt. auth. see Feldstein, Mark.

Fischer, George. Russian Liberalism, from Gentry to Intelligentsia. LC 57-13462. (Harvard University Russian Research Center Studies: No. 30). (Illus.). pap. 64.00 (ISBN 0-317-09570-6, 2006417). Bks Demand UMI.

--Soviet Opposition to Stalin, a Case Study in World War Two. LC 70-97344. Repr. of 1952 ed. lib. bdg. 27.50x (ISBN 0-8371-3098-0, FISO). Greenwood.

--Ways of Self Rule. lib. bdg. 14.95 (ISBN 0-86571-042-2). New Soc Pubs.

Fischer, George, ed. Revival of American Socialism: Selected Papers of the Socialist Scholars Conference. (Orig.). 1971. pap. 5.95 (ISBN 0-19-501413-8, GB). Oxford U Pr.

Fischer, Georges. The Non-Proliferation of Nuclear Weapons. Willey, David, tr. LC 72-189811. 270p. 1971. 17.95 (ISBN 0-8290-0190-5). Irvington.

Fischer, Georges, jt. ed. see Morris-Jones, W. H.

Fischer, Gerald C., jt. auth. see Hoffman, Margaret A.

Fischer, Gerd, ed. see Denker, Manfred.

Fischer, Gerhard. The Paris Commune in the Stage Valles, Grieg, Brecht, Adamov. (European University Studies: Series 1, German Language & Literature, Vol. 422). 242p. 1981. pap. 35.25 (ISBN 3-8204-7078-6). P Lang Pubs.

Fischer, Gertrude. The New Complete Golden Retriever. 2nd ed. LC 84-700. (Complete Breed Book Ser.). (Illus.). 304p. 1984. 16.95 (ISBN 0-87605-185-9). Howell Bk.

Fischer, Gretl K. In Search of Jerusalem: Religion & Ethics in the Writings of A. M. Klein. LC 76-367083. pap. 66.50 (ISBN 0-317-26452-4, 2023858). Bks Demand UMI.

Fischer, H. see Hellwege, K. H. & Hellwege, A. M.

Fischer, H. & Hellwege, K. H., eds. Magnetic Properties of Free Radicals: Organic Cation Radicals & Polyradicals. (Landolt-Bernstein Ser. Group II: Vol. 9, Pt. 2). 380p. 1980. 197.40 (ISBN 0-387-09666-3). Springer-Verlag.

Fischer, H. Th., ed. see Kennedy, Raymond.

Fischer, Hal. Eighteenth Street Near Castro. LC 78-78180. (Illus.). 1979. pap. 20.00x (ISBN 0-917986-12-1). NFS Pr.

--Gay Semiotics. LC 77-93056. (Illus.). 1978. pap. 25.00x (ISBN 0-917986-03-2). NFS Pr.

Fischer, Hal see Worth, Don.

Fischer, Hans & Orth, Hans. Chemie Des Pyrrols, 2 Vols. in 3. (Ger). 1969. Repr. Set. 90.00 (ISBN 0-384-15750-5). Johnson Repr.

Fischer, Harry C. The Uses of Accounting in Collective Bargaining. 118p. 1969. 3.00 (ISBN 0-89215-027-0). U Cal LA Indus Rel.

Fischer, Heinz-Dietrich, ed. Outstanding International Press Reporting: Pulitzer Prize Winning Articles in Foreign Correspondence, 3 vols. LC 83-18962. (Illus.). liii, 368p. 1984. Vol. 1, from the Consequences of World War I to the End of World War II, 1928-1945. 39.95 (ISBN 3-11-008918-1). De Gruyter.

--Outstanding International Press Reporting: Pulitzer Prize Winning Articles in Foreign Correspondence, Volume 2, 1946-1962, From the End of World War II to the Various Stations of the Cold War. (Illus.). lxviii, 304p. 1985. 39.95x (ISBN 3-11-009824-5). De Gruyter.

Fischer, Heinz-Dietrich & Melnik, Stefan R., eds. Entertainment: A Cross-Cultural Examination. 1979. 20.50 (ISBN 0-8038-1945-5); pap. text ed. 12.50x (ISBN 0-8038-8047-2). Hastings.

Fischer, Heinz-Dietrich & Merrill, John C., eds. International & Intercultural Communication. (Humanistic Studies in the Communication Arts). 1976. pap. text ed. 12.50x (ISBN 0-8038-3403-9). Hastings.

Fischer, Helmut, tr. see Mehnert, Klaus.

Fischer, Helmut, tr. see Meinecke, Friedrich.

Fischer, Helmut A. & Werner, Gottfried. Autoradiography. Ashworth, M. R., tr. from Ger. LC 70-164842. (Working Methods in Modern Science Ser.). 1971. 31.60x (ISBN 3-1100-3523-5). De Gruyter.

Fischer, Henry G. Ancient Egyptian Calligraphy: A Beginner's Guide to Writing Hieroglyphs. (Illus.). 63p. 1979. 10.00 (ISBN 0-87099-198-1). Metro Mus Art.

Fischer, Henry G., jt. auth. see Caminos, Ricardo A.

Fischer, Henry George. Dendera in the Third Millenium B. C., Down to the Theban Domination of Upper Egypt. LC 66-30543. 20.00 (ISBN 0-685-71725-9). J J Augustin.

Fischer, Henry L., et al. Sex Education for the Developmentally Disabled: A Guide for Parents, Teachers & Professionals. (Illus.). 60p. 1976. pap. text ed. 14.95 (ISBN 0-8391-0750-1). Univ Park.

Fischer, Herbert. Mahatma Gandhi: An East German Marxist Interpretation. 125p. 1984. 15.00 (ISBN 0-934676-66-6). Greenlf Bks.

Fischer, Horst. Produktionsbezogene Kooperationen Zwischen dem Hersteller und dem Verwender Individuell Gefertigter Maschinen. (European University Studies: No. 5, Vol. 428). 370p. (Ger.). 1983. 40.00 (ISBN 3-8204-7683-0). P Lang Pubs.

Fischer, Hugo, ed. Transport Models for Inland & Coastal Waters: Proceedings of a Symposium on Predictive Ability. LC 81-10990. 1981. 49.50 (ISBN 0-12-258152-0). Acad Pr.

Fischer, Hugo B. & List, E. John. Mixing in Inland & Coastal Waters. 1979. 50.00 (ISBN 0-12-258150-4). Acad Pr.

Fischer, I., jt. auth. see Roberts, S.

Fischer, Inge. Christophe in Egypt: The Odyssey of Pharaoh's Cat. LC 68-9214. (Illus.). 154p. (gr. 3-7). 1981. pap. 9.95x (ISBN 0-9610238-0-5, 111). I Fischer.

Fischer, J. Biographisches Lexikon der Hervorragenden Aerzte der Letzten Feunfzig Jahre, 1880-1930: Aaser-Komoto, 2 vols, Vol. 1. 3rd ed. (Ger.). 1962. Set. 375.00 (ISBN 3-541-03723-7, M-7311, Pub. by Urban & Schwarzenberg). French & Eur.

Fischer, J., jt. auth. see Simonyi, J.

Fischer, J. Cree. Piano Tuning: A Simple & Accurate Method for Amateurs. LC 75-14759. 224p. 1976. pap. 3.50 (ISBN 0-486-23267-0). Dover.

Fischer, James. How to Read the Bible. 155p. 1982. 10.95 (ISBN 0-13-430785-2); pap. 4.95 (ISBN 0-13-430777-1). P-H.

Fischer, James A. God Said: Let There Be Woman: A Study of Biblical Women. LC 78-21117. 1979. pap. 4.95 (ISBN 0-8189-0378-3). Alba.

Fischer, James M. Federal Trial Procedure Handbook. LC 84-25784. (Law Publications Ser.). 464p. 1985. 70.00 (ISBN 0-471-88166-X). Wiley.

Fischer, Jean, ed. see Doyle, Nora.

Fischer, Jean, ed. see Lindberg, Karen.

Fischer, Joel. Effective Casework Practice: An Eclectic Approach. LC 77-4069. (Illus.). 1977. 28.95 (ISBN 0-07-021085-3). McGraw.

Fischer, Joel & Gochros, Harvey L. Planned Behavior Change: Behavior Modification in Social Work. LC 74-34554. (Illus.). 1975. 17.95 (ISBN 0-02-910250-2). Free Pr.

--Planned Behavior Change: Behavior Modification in Social Work. LC 74-34554. (Illus.). 1979. pap. text ed. 16.95 (ISBN 0-02-910230-8). Free Pr.

Fischer, Joel, jt. auth. see Bloom, Martin.

Fischer, Joel, jt. auth. see Gochros, Harvey L.

Fischer, Johann K. Saemtliche Werke fuer Klavier und Orgel. Werra, Ernst Von, ed. 142p. (Ger.). 1966. pap. 27.50x (ISBN 0-8450-1007-7). Broude.

Fischer, John. Dark Horse: The Story of a Winner. LC 83-11411. 100p. 1983. pap. 3.95 (ISBN 0-88070-016-5). Multnomah.

--From the High Plains: An Account of the Hard Men, High-Spirited Women -- & a Few Rascals -- Who Settled the Last Frontier of the Old West. LC 78-437. (Illus.). 1978. 12.45i (ISBN 0-06-011269-7, HarpT). Har-Row.

--The Olive Tree Connection: Sharing Israel's Messiah. LC 83-12645. 192p. (Orig.). 1983. pap. 6.95 (ISBN 0-87784-848-3). Inter-Varsity.

Fischer, John, ed. Six in the Easy Chair. LC 73-76273. pap. 69.80 (ISBN 0-317-29089-4, 2020227). Bks Demand UMI.

Fischer, John, jt. ed. see Greenspan, Kalman.

Fischer, John I. On Swift's Poetry. LC 77-12705. 1978. 13.50 (ISBN 0-8130-0583-3). U Presses Fla.

Fischer, John L. & Fischer, Ann M. Eastern Carolines. LC 66-29019. (Area & Country Survey Ser.). 288p. 1970. pap. 12.00x (ISBN 0-87536-310-5). HRAFP.

Fischer, John Paul & Hamline University. Advanced Legal Education. Law Office Management. LC 85-139328. (Illus.). Date not set. price not set. Hamline Law.

Fischer, Josef E. Surgical Nutrition. 1983. 69.95 (ISBN 0-316-28371-1). Little.

--Total Parenteral Nutrition. LC 75-30283. 1976. text ed. 32.50 (ISBN 0-316-28370-3). Little.

Fischer, Joseph. Discoveries of the Norsemen in America. LC 76-140973. (Research & Source Works Ser: No. 643). (Geography & discovery, No. 9). 1971. Repr. of 1903 ed. lib. bdg. 20.00 (ISBN 0-8337-1131-8). B Franklin.

--The Discoveries of the Norsemen in America, with Special Relation to Their Early Cartographical Representation. 1977. lib. bdg. 59.95 (ISBN 0-8490-1728-9). Gordon Pr.

Fischer, Joseph, ed. Foreign Values & Southeast Asian Scholarship. (Research Monographs: No. 11). 326p. 1983. pap. text ed. 14.00 (ISBN 0-8191-3127-X, Co-pub. by Ctr S SE Asia). U Pr of Amer.

Fischer, K. H., jt. auth. see Bass, J.

Fischer, Kathleen B. Political Ideology & Educational Reform in Chile, 1964-1976. LC 79-620018. (Latin American Studies: Vol. 46). 1979. 14.95x (ISBN 0-87903-046-1). UCLA Lat Am Ctr.

Fischer, Kathleen R. The Inner Rainbow: The Imagination in Christian Life. 160p. 1983. pap. 6.95 (ISBN 0-8091-2498-X). Paulist Pr.

--Winter Grace, Spirituality for the Later Years. 1985. pap. 7.95 (ISBN 0-8091-2675-3). Paulist Pr.

Fischer, Kuno. A Commentary on Kant's Critick of Pure Reason. Beck, Lewis W., ed. LC 75-32039. (The Philosophy of Immanuel Kant Ser.: Vol. 3). 1977. Repr. of 1866 ed. lib. bdg. 32.00 (ISBN 0-8240-2327-7). Garland Pub.

Fischer, Kurt & Lazerson, Arlyne. Human Development: From Conception Through Development. (Illus.). 608p. 1984. text ed. 26.95 (ISBN 0-7167-1575-9); write for info. instr's manual (ISBN 0-7167-1576-7); study guide 8.95 (ISBN 0-7167-1577-5). W H Freeman.

Fischer, Kurt W., ed. Levels & Transitions in Children's Development. LC 83-82343. (Child Development Ser.: No. 21). 1983. pap. 8.95x (ISBN 0-87589-933-1). Jossey-Bass.

Fischer, L. Afghanistan. (Geomedical Monograph Ser.: Vol. 2). (Illus., Ger. & Eng.). 1968. 31.30 (ISBN 0-387-04266-0). Springer-Verlag.

--Theory & Practice of Shell Structures. (Illus.). 1968. 76.00x (ISBN 3-4330-0127-8). Adlers Foreign Bks.

Fischer, L. R. Law of Financial Privacy: A Compliance Guide. LC 83-60091. 550p. 1983. 77.00 (ISBN 0-88262-977-8). Warren.

Fischer, Lenore, tr. see Budel, Julius.

Fischer, LeRoy H. Lincoln's Gadfly, Adam Gurowski. (Illus.). 1964. 19.95x (ISBN 0-8061-0621-2). U of Okla Pr.

Fischer, LeRoy H., ed. Civil War Battles in the West. 1981. pap. text ed. 9.95x (ISBN 0-89745-013-2). Sunflower U Pr.

--The Western Territories in the Civil War. 1977. pap. 8.00 (ISBN 0-686-00373-X). AG Pr.

--Western Territories in the Civil War. (Illus.). 113p. 1977. pap. text ed. 9.95x (ISBN 0-89745-000-0). Sunflower U Pr.

Fischer, Louis. The Essential Gandhi. LC 82-48890. 1983. pap. 4.95 (ISBN 0-394-71466-0, Vin). Random.

--Gandhi & Stalin: Two Signs at the World's Crossroads. 1979. Repr. of 1948 ed. lib. bdg. 20.00 (ISBN 0-8495-1642-0). Arden Lib.

--Gandhi: His Life & Message for the World. pap. 2.95 (ISBN 0-451-62142-5, ME2142, Ment). NAL.

--Great Challenge. LC 70-118534. (Essay & General Literature Index Reprint Ser). 1971. Repr. of 1946 ed. 33.00x (ISBN 0-8046-1406-7, Pub. by Kennikat). Assoc Faculty Pr.

--The Life of Mahatma Gandhi. 1983. pap. 8.61i (ISBN 0-06-091038-0, CN1038, CN). Har-Row.

--Men & Politics: An Autobiography. LC 73-111498. vi, 672p. Repr. of 1941 ed. lib. bdg. 25.75x (ISBN 0-8371-4641-0, FIMP). Greenwood.

--Oil Imperialism, the International Struggle for Petroleum. LC 75-6470. (The History & Politics of Oil Ser). 256p. 1976. Repr. of 1926 ed. 19.75 (ISBN 0-88355-289-2). Hyperion Conn.

--Russia's Road from Peace to War: Soviet Foreign Relations, Nineteen Seventeen to Nineteen Forty-One. LC 78-27750. (Illus.). 1979. Repr. of 1969 ed. lib. bdg. 55.00x (ISBN 0-313-20941-3, FIRF). Greenwood.

--Soviet Journey. LC 72-136529. (Illus.). 308p. 1973. Repr. of 1935 ed. lib. bdg. 29.75x (ISBN 0-8371-5450-2, FISJ). Greenwood.

--The Story of Indonesia. LC 72-12633. (Illus.). 341p. 1973. Repr. of 1959 ed. lib. bdg. 19.75x (ISBN 0-8371-6684-5, FISI). Greenwood.

--This Is Our World. LC 74-1514. (Illus.). 522p. 1974. Repr. of 1956 ed. lib. bdg. 25.00x (ISBN 0-8371-7389-2, FIOW). Greenwood.

Fischer, Louis & Schimmel, David. The Rights of Students & Teachers: Resolving Conflicts in the School Community. 447p. 1982. pap. text ed. 13.50 scp (ISBN 0-06-042075-8, HarpC). Har-Row.

Fischer, Louis, ed. see Gandhi, Mohandas K.

Fischer, Louis, et al. Teachers & the Law: A Guide for Educators. LC 80-23394. 448p. 1981. text ed. 25.00x (ISBN 0-582-28135-0); 16.95x (ISBN 0-582-28134-2). Longman.

Fischer, Louise & Sorenson, Gail P. Counselors & the Law. LC 84-15414. Date not set. 30.00 (ISBN 0-582-28451-1); pap. 16.95 (ISBN 0-582-28450-3). Longman.

Fischer, Lucy. Jacques Tati: A Guide to References & Resources. 1983. lib. bdg. 29.00 (ISBN 0-8161-8000-8, Hall Reference). G K Hall.

Fischer, Ludwig, jt. ed. see Daviau, Donald G.

Fischer, Malcolm R. Economic Analysis of Labour. 1972. 25.00 (ISBN 0-312-22680-2). St Martin.

Fischer, Margaret. Calvin Coolidge, Jr. LC 81-69555. (Illus.). 74p. 1981. 10.00 (ISBN 0-914960-42-3); pap. 6.00. Academy Bks.

Fischer, Mark D. The Approaching Five Most Critical Years in World History. (Illus.). 1979. deluxe ed. 48.75x (ISBN 0-930008-28-6). Inst Econ Pol.

Fischer, Martin. Engineering Specifications Writing Guide: An Authoritative Reference for Planning, Writing, & Administrating. 176p. 1983. 17.95 (ISBN 0-13-279208-7); pap. 8.95 (ISBN 0-13-279190-0). P-H.

Fischer, Martin, tr. from Span. Gracian's Manual: A Truth-Telling Manual & the Art of Worldly Wisdom. 2nd ed. 324p. 1979. 7.95x (ISBN 0-398-00581-8). C C Thomas.

Fischer, Marvin J. Pocket Guide to the National Electrical Code. 288p. 1984. 8.95 (ISBN 0-13-683995-9). P-H.

Fischer, Mary, jt. auth. see Boulgarides, James.

Fischer, Mary, et al. The Chocolate Lover's Guide to Silicon Valley. (Illus.). 64p. (Orig.). 1984. pap. 3.95 (ISBN 0-932161-00-6). San Jose Face.

Fischer, Matthias-Johannes. Rueckgriff auf Goethe: Grundlagen einer Kritischen Rezeptionsforschung. (European University Studies: No. 1, Vol. 639). 141p. (Ger.). 1983. 19.45 (ISBN 3-8204-7576-1). P Lang Pubs.

Fischer, Max. One Love Too Many. Ashton, Sylvia, ed. LC 77-78383. 1979. 14.95 (ISBN 0-87949-100-0). Ashley Bks.

Fischer, Maximiliano, ed. Codex Traditionum Ecclesiae Collegiatae Claustroneoburgensis Continens Donationes, Fundationes Commutationesque Hanc Ecclesiam Attinentes Ab Anno Domin: MCCLX Usque Circiter MCCLX. Repr. of 1851 ed. 23.00 (ISBN 0-384-29873-7). Johnson Repr.

Fischer, Michael. Does Deconstruction Make Any Difference? Poststructuralism & the Defense of Poetry in Modern Criticism. LC 84-48044. 160p. 1985. 20.00x (ISBN 0-253-31810-6). Ind U Pr.

Fischer, Michael, tr. see Mallinckrodt, Anita M.

Fischer, Michael M. Iran: From Religious Dispute to Revolution. LC 79-24330. (Harvard Studies in Cultural Anthropology: No. 3). (Illus.). 328p. 1980. text ed. 20.00x (ISBN 0-674-46615-2). Harvard U Pr.

--Iran: From Religious Dispute to Revolution. (Harvard Studies in Cultural Anthropology: Vol. 3). 336p. 1982. pap. 7.95 (ISBN 0-674-46617-9). Harvard U Pr.

Fischer, Michael W. Verheissungen des Gluecks, Vol. 3. (Salzburger Schriften zur Rechts, - Staats - und Sozialphilosophie). 251p. (Ger.). 1982. 27.90 (ISBN 3-8204-6251-1). P Lang Pubs.

Fischer, Mildred. London Theatre Today: A Guide for Travelers. (Illus.). 144p. (Orig.). 1981. pap. 4.50 (ISBN 0-914846-09-4). Golden West Pub.

Fischer, Mildred & Fischer, Al. Chili-Lovers' Cook Book. 1978. pap. 3.50 plastic (ISBN 0-914846-06-X). Golden West Pub.

Fischer, Mildred, jt. auth. see Fischer, Al.

Fischer, Mildred, jt. ed. see Fischer, Al.

Fischer, Mildred M. & Fischer, Al. Arizona Museums. 88p. 1985. pap. 5.00 (ISBN 0-914846-19-1). Golden West Pub.

Fischer, N. & Georgopoulos, N., eds. Continuity & Change in Marxism. 249p. 1982. text ed. 20.45x (ISBN 0-391-02564-3, Pub. by Macmillan England). Humanities.

Fischer, Norma B. Who Could Love an Ugly Toad? (Illus.). 32p. (ps-2). 1972. pap. 3.50 (ISBN 0-8024-9497-8). Moody.

Fischer, Norman. Economy & Self: Philosophy & Economics from the Mercantilists to Marx. LC 78-73799. (Contributions in Economics & Economic History: No. 24). 1979. lib. bdg. 29.95 (ISBN 0-313-20888-3, FIE/). Greenwood.

--Like a Walk Through a Park. new ed. (Orig.). 1980. pap. 3.50 (ISBN 0-931416-02-7). Open Books.

--Why People Lack Confidence in Chairs. (Morning Coffee Chapbook Ser.). (Illus.). 20p. (Orig.). 1984. pap. 7.50 (ISBN 0-918273-07-2). Coffee Hse.

Fischer, O. & Maple, M. B., eds. Superconductivity in Ternary Compounds I: Structural, Electronics & Lattices Properties. (Topics in Current Physics Ser.: Vol. 32). (Illus.). 320p. 1982. 37.00 (ISBN 0-387-11670-2). Springer-Verlag.

Fischer, O., jt. ed. see Maple, M. B.

Fischer, P. Applications of Technical Devices in Archaeology. (Studies in Mediterranean Archaeology: Vol. LXIII). 64p. 1981. pap. text ed. 30.50x (ISBN 91-85058-33-5, Pub. by Paul Astroms Sweden). Humanities.

Fischer, P. C., ed. see Scutte, Joseph F.

Fischer, Paul M. & Frank, Werner G. Cost Accounting: Theory & Application. 1985. text ed. 23.95 (ISBN 0-538-01720-1, A72). SW Pub.

Fischer, Paul M., et al. The Office Laboratory. (Illus.). 325p. 1983. 31.95 (ISBN 0-8385-7243-X). ACC.

Fischer, Peter, ed. A Collection of International Concessions & Related Instruments, Vols. 1-12. LC 75-43707. 1975-1982. text ed. 45.00 ea. (ISBN 0-379-10075-4); Set. text ed. write for info. Oceana.

--A Collection of International Concessions & Related Instruments: Contemporary Series, Vols. 1-5. LC 81-11268. 1981. lib. bdg. 50.00 (ISBN 0-379-20665-X); index 30.00. Oceana.

Fischer, Pieter. Music in Paintings of the Low Countries in the 16th & 17th Centuries. 112p. pap. text ed. 15.50 (ISBN 90-265-0185-4, Pub. by Swets Pub Serv Holland). Swets North Am.

Fischer, Raymond L. Speaking to Communicate: An Introduction to Speech. 145p. pap. text ed. 7.95x (ISBN 0-917974-77-8). Waveland Pr.

Fischer, Raymond P. An Aged Man Remembers April. 80p. 1985. lib. bdg. 10.95 (ISBN 0-87483-000-1); pap. 5.95 (ISBN 0-87483-001-X). August Hse.

Fischer, Robert. Getting Your Act Together: How to Become a Child Actor or Actresss. LC 82-60638. (Illus.). 96p. (gr. 4-7). 1982. lib. bdg. 9.29 (ISBN 0-671-34041-7). Messner.

--Hot Dog! LC 80-201. (Illus.). 64p. (gr. 4 up). 1980. PLB 8.29 (ISBN 0-671-33045-4). Messner.

--Stocks or Options: Programs for Profits. LC 80-11669. 312p. 1980. 50.95x (ISBN 0-471-05599-9, Pub. by Wiley-Interscience). Wiley.

--Trick Photography: Crazy Things You Can Do with Cameras. LC 80-22333. (Illus.). 160p. (gr. 8 up). 1980. 9.95 (ISBN 0-87131-332-4); pap. 5.95 (ISBN 0-87131-335-9). M Evans.

Fischer, Robert, jt. ed. see Architectural Record Magazine.

Fischer, Robert B. Chemical Equilibrium. 1970. pap. text ed. 18.95 (ISBN 0-7216-3705-1, CBS C). SCP.

--God Did It, but How? 128p. 1983. pap. 4.95 (ISBN 0-310-37731-5). Zondervan.

Fischer, Robert H. & Lehmann, Helmut T., eds. Luther's Works: Word & Sacrament III, Vol. 37. LC 55-9893. 1961. 18.95 (ISBN 0-8006-0337-0, 1-337). Fortress.

Fischer, Robert H., tr. see Luther, Martin.

Fischer, Roger A. The Segregation Struggle in Louisiana, 1862-77. LC 74-7230. 180p. 1974. 12.50x (ISBN 0-252-00394-2). U of Ill Pr.

Fischer, Roger A. & Sullivan, Edmund B. American Political Ribbons & Ribbon Badges 1825-1981. LC 84-62281. (Illus.). 409p. 1985. lib. bdg. 65.00x (ISBN 0-88000-138-0). Quarterman.

Fischer, Roland, jt. auth. see Weiers, Werner.

Fischer, Rudolf. Zu den Kunstformen des Mittelalterlichen Epos. 1965. pap. 25.00 (ISBN 0-384-15765-3). Johnson Repr.

Fischer, Rudolph W., ed. see Shepard's & McGraw-Hill.

Fischer, Ruth. Stalin & German Communism: A Study in the Orgins of the State Party. LC 81-3418. (Social Science Classics). 700p. 1982. pap. 19.95 (ISBN 0-87855-822-5). Transaction Bks.

Fischer, Sally, jt. auth. see Keene, Donald.

Fischer, Sandra K. Econolingua: A Glossary of Coins & Economic Language in Renaissance Drama. LC 83-40606. (Illus.). 184p. 1985. 27.50 (ISBN 0-87413-250-9). U Delaware Pr.

Fischer, Stanley & Dornbusch, Rudiger. Economics. (Illus.). 1008p. 1983. 33.95 (ISBN 0-07-017757-0). McGraw.

--Introduction to Macroeconomics. (Illus.). 576p. 1983. 21.95 (ISBN 0-07-021005-5). McGraw.

--Introduction to Microeconomics. (Illus.). 624p. 1983. 21.95 (ISBN 0-07-021006-3). McGraw.

Fischer, Stanley, jt. auth. see Dornbusch, Rudiger.

Fischer, Stanley, ed. Rational Expectations & Economic Policy. LC 79-22661. x, 294p. 1982. pap. text ed. 11.00x (ISBN 0-226-25134-9). U of Chicago Pr.

Fischer, Steven R. The Complete Medieval Dreambook: A Multilingual, Alphabetical "Somnia Danielis" Collation. 172p. 1982. 18.40 (ISBN 3-261-05001-2). P Lang Pubs.

--The Dream in the Middle High German Epic: Introduction to the Study of the Dream as a Literary Device to the Younger Contemporaries of Gottfried & Wolfram. (Australian & New Zealand Studies in German Language & Literature: Vol. 10). (Illus.). 187p. 1978. pap. 22.75 (ISBN 3-261-03138-7). P Lang Pubs.

Fischer, Stuart. Kid's TV: The First 25 Years. (Illus.). 256p. 1984. 19.95 (ISBN 0-87196-794-4); pap. 12.95 (ISBN 0-87196-795-2). Facts on File.

Fischer, Susan K., jt. auth. see Siegel, Carole.

Fischer, Susan M. & Slaga, Thomas J., eds. Arachidonic Acid Metabolism & Tumor Promotion. (Prostaglandins, Leukotrienes, & Cancer Ser.). 1985. lib. bdg. 47.95 (ISBN 0-89838-724-8, Pub. by Martinus Nijhoff Netherlands). Kluwer Academic.

Fischer, T. A. The Scots in Germany. 336p. 1982. 50.00x (ISBN 0-85976-000-6, Pub. by Donald Pubs Scotland). State Mutual Bk.

Fischer, T. E., jt. auth. see Latanision, R. M.

Fischer, Thomas J., jt. auth. see Lawlor, Glenn J., Jr.

Fischer, Ulrich. Eschatologie & Jenseitserwartung Im Hellenistischen Diasporajudentum. (Beiheft 44 Zur Zeitschrift Fuer Die Alttestamentliche Wissenschaft). 1978. 29.20x (ISBN 3-11-007595-4). De Gruyter.

Fischer, Victor. Alaska's Constitutional Convention. LC 74-620165. (Illus.). 277p. 1975. 9.95 (ISBN 0-912006-02-1); pap. 6.50 (ISBN 0-912006-11-0). U of Alaska Pr.

--Alaska's Constitutional Convention. LC 74-620165. (Institute of Social & Economic Research Ser.: No. 46). 302p. 1975. 7.50x (ISBN 0-295-95500-7); pap. 4.00x (ISBN 0-295-95461-2). U of Wash Pr.

--Alaska's Constitutional Convention. 291p. 1975. 1.00 (ISBN 0-318-15789-6). Citizens Forum Gov.

Fischer, Victor, ed. see Twain, Mark.

Fischer, W., jt. auth. see Chodat, R.

Fischer, W. L. F., tr. see Von Vega, Baron.

Fischer, William, ed. see Kelm, Paul.

Fischer, William A. Fischtale Enterprises. 1980. pap. text ed. 11.90x (ISBN 0-673-15414-9). Scott F.

Fischer, William A., jt. auth. see Behrman, Jack N.

Fischer, William B. The Empire Strikes Out: Kurd Lasswitz, Hans Dominik & the Developement of German Science Fiction. LC 83-73123. 335p. 1984. 29.95 (ISBN 0-87972-257-6); pap. 13.95 (ISBN 0-87972-258-4). Bowling Green Univ.

Fischer, William C. & Lohmann, Christopher K. Selected Letters of W. D. Howells: Vol. 5, 1902-1911. (Critical Editions Program Ser.). 1983. lib. bdg. 41.95 (ISBN 0-8057-8531-0, Twayne). G K Hall.

Fischer, William E., ed. see Aderman, James.

Fischer, William E., ed. see Stadler, Richard H.

Fischer, William L. Alternatives. LC 79-67005. 1980. 4.95 (ISBN 0-87159-000-X). Unity School.

--Hidden Secrets of Super Perfect Health at Any Age. McKnight, Juilene, ed. (Illus.). 160p. (Orig.). 1985. pap. 12.95x (ISBN 0-915421-03-8). Fischer Pub.

Fischer-Dieskau, Dietrich. Schubert's Songs: A Biographical Study. 1977. 13.95 (ISBN 0-394-48048-1). Knopf.

--Schubert's Songs: A Biographical Study. Whitton, Kenneth S., tr. from Ger. LC 84-790. 352p. 1984. pap. 8.95 (ISBN 0-87910-005-2). Limelight Edns.

Fischer-Fabian, S. Prussia's Glory: The Rise of a Military State. (Illus.). 314p. 1982. 19.95 (ISBN 0-02-536850-8). Macmillan.

Fischer-Galati, Stephen. The Socialist Republic of Rumania. LC 69-19468. (Integration & Community Building in Eastern Europe Ser: No. 6). (Illus.). 124p. 1969. 12.00x (ISBN 0-8018-1034-5). Johns Hopkins.

--Twentieth Century Rumania. LC 77-108838. (Illus.). 1970. 26.00x (ISBN 0-231-02848-2). Columbia U Pr.

Fischer-Galati, Stephen, jt. auth. see Djordjevic, Dmitrije.

Fischer-Galati, Stephen, ed. The Communist Parties of Eastern Central Europe. LC 79-13016. 1979. 29.00x (ISBN 0-231-04506-9). Columbia U Pr.

--Eastern Europe in the Nineteen Eighties. LC 80-28765. 292p. (Orig.). 1981. lib. bdg. 30.00x (ISBN 0-89158-198-7); pap. 12.50x (ISBN 0-86531-122-6). Westview.

Fischer-Galati, Stephen & Florescu, Radu R., eds. Romania Between East & West. (East European Monographs: No. 103). 414p. 1982. 35.00x (ISBN 0-914710-97-4). East Eur Quarterly.

Fischer-Galati, Stephen A. New Rumania: From People's Democracy to Socialist Republic. (Studies in Communism, Revisionism & Revolution). 1967. 30.00x (ISBN 0-262-06019-1). MIT Pr.

--Rumania: A Bibliographic Guide. LC 63-60076. (Bibliographic Guides Ser). 1969. Repr. of 1963 ed. 10.00 (ISBN 0-405-00057-X). Ayer Co Pubs.

Fischer-Jorgensen, ed. International Congress of Phonetic Sciences, 9th Special Lectures. Copenhagen, August 1979. (Journal: Phonetica: Vol. 37, No 1-2). (Illus.). 108p. 1980. pap. 14.25 (ISBN 3-8055-1414-X). S Karger.

Fischer-Jorgensen, ed. see International Congress of Phonetic Sciences, 9th, Copenhagen, 1979.

Fischer-Lamberg, Hanna, ed. Der Junge Goethe, 6 vols. Incl. Vol. 1, August 1749-Marz 1770. 1963. 52.80x (ISBN 3-11-005119-2); Vol. 2, April 1770-Setember 1772. 1963. 36.80x (ISBN 3-11-005120-6); Vol. 3, Setember 1772-Dezember 1773. 1966. 49.60 (ISBN 3-11-005121-4); Vol. 4, Januar-Dezember 1774. 1968. 38.40x (ISBN 3-11-005122-2); Vol. 5, Januar-Oktober 1775. 1973. 59.20x (ISBN 3-11-004047-6). De Gruyter.

--Der Junge Goethe: Neu Bearbeitete Ausgabe in Fuenf Baenden. Registerband (Namen-, Werk-, und Sachregister zu Den Baenden I-V. viii, 116p. (Ger.). 1974. text ed. 24.80x (ISBN 3-11-004807-8). De Gruyter.

Fischer-Lichte, Erika. Semiotik des Theaters, Vol. 1: Das System der Theatralischen Zeichen. 266p. (Orig., Ger.). 1983. pap. 17.00 (ISBN 3-87808-176-6, Pub by GN Verlag Germany). Benjamins North Am.

--Semiotik des Theaters, Vol. 2: Vom kuenstlichen zum natuerlichen Zeichen Theater des Barock und der Aufklaerung. 211p. (Orig., Ger.). 1983. 15.00x (ISBN 3-87808-177-4, Pub by GN Verlag Germany). Benjamins North Am.

--Semiotik des Theaters, Vol. 3: Die Auffuehrung als Text. 219p. (Orig., Ger.). 1983. pap. 15.00x (ISBN 3-87808-178-2, Pub by GN Verlag Germany). Benjamins North Am.

Fischer-Moller, Knud. Skeletal Remains of the Central Eskimos. Calvert, W. E., tr. LC 76-22524. (Thule Expedition, 5th, 1921-1924: Vol. 3, No. 1). Repr. of 1937 ed. 32.50 (ISBN 0-404-58311-3). AMS Pr.

Fischer-Munstermann, Uta. Jazz Dance: Including Aerobics. rev. ed. (Illus.). 120p. (Orig.). 1983. pap. 9.95 (ISBN 0-8069-7770-1). Sterling.

Fischer-Nagel, Andreas & Fischer-Nagel, Heiderose. Life of the Honeybee. (Nature Watch Bks.). (Illus.). 48p. (gr. 2-5). 1985. lib. bdg. 12.95 (ISBN 0-87614-241-2). Carolrhoda Bks.

--Life of the Ladybug. (Nature Watch Bks.). (Illus.). 48p. (gr. 2-5). 1985. lib. bdg. 12.95 (ISBN 0-87614-240-4). Carolrhoda Bks.

--Season of the White Stork. (Nature Watch Bks.). (Illus.). 48p. (gr. 2-5). 1985. lib. bdg. 12.95 (ISBN 0-87614-242-0). Carolrhoda Bks.

Fischer-Nagel, Andreas, jt. auth. see Fischer-Nagel, Heiderose.

Fischer-Nagel, Heiderose & Fischer-Nagel, Andreas. A Kitten Is Born. (Illus.). (ps-3). 1983. 9.95 (ISBN 0-399-20961-1, Putnam). Putnam Pub Group.

--A Puppy Is Born. (Illus.). 40p. (ps-2). 1985. 10.95 (ISBN 0-399-21234-5, Putnam). Putnam Pub Group.

Fischer-Nagel, Heiderose, jt. auth. see Fischer-Nagel, Andreas.

Fischer-Pap, Lucia, jt. auth. see Berland, Theodore.

Fischer-Theurer, Annette, tr. see Forry, John I. & Theurer, Martin.

Fischer-Theurer, Annette, tr. see Peltzer, Martin & Treumann, Walter.

Fischer-Theurer, Annette, tr. see Riesenkampff, Alexander & Barron, William.

Fischer-Theurer, Annette, tr. see Schurtman, William & Detjen, David W.

Fischer-Theurer, Annette, tr. see Taylor, Robert & Jacobs, Klaus.

Fischer-Theurer, Annette, tr. see Waldmann, Raymond J. & Reichelt, Rainer.

Fischer-Williams, M., ed. see Werner, Percy.

Fischer-Williams, Mariella, et al. A Textbook of Biological Feedback. LC 80-15235. 576p. 1981. 39.95 (ISBN 0-89885-014-2). Human Sci Pr.

Fischgrund, Tom. The Insider's Guide to the Top Ten Business Schools. 228p. 1983. pap. 8.70i (ISBN 0-316-28381-9). Little.

--Match Wits with the Harvard MBA's: The One Hundred Thousand Dollar Inheritance. (Orig.). 1985. pap. 6.95 (ISBN 0-449-90156-4, Columbine). Fawcett.

Fischhoff, Andi. Birth to Three: A Self-Help Network for New Parents. 220p. 1986. 8.95 (ISBN 0-317-31543-9). Castalia Pub.

Fischhoff, Baruch, et al. Acceptable Risk. LC 81-9957. (Illus.). 224p. 1981. 23.95 (ISBN 0-521-24164-2). Cambridge U Pr.

--Acceptable Risk. LC 81-9957. 208p. 1984. pap. 9.95 (ISBN 0-521-27892-9). Cambridge U Pr.

Fischhoff, Joseph & Brohl, Noreen. Before & After My Child Died: A Collection of Parents' Experiences. 247p. (Orig.). 1981. pap. 7.95x (ISBN 0-9607956-0-X). Emmons-Fairfield Pub.

Fischhoff, Martin, ed. Detroit Guide. LC 82-74233. (Illus.). 486p. (Orig.). 1983. pap. 8.95 (ISBN 0-9600448-6-8). Detroit Guide.

Fischietti, Domenico. Il Mercato di Malmantile. Brown, Howard M., ed. LC 80-815. (Italian Opera Ser., 1640-1770: No. II). 260p. 1983. lib. bdg. 83.00 (ISBN 0-8240-4816-4). Garland Pub.

Fischl, Eric & Saltz, Jerry, eds. Make Like an Artist: A Sketchbook. LC 85-40102. 200p. 1985. 12.95 (ISBN 0-912383-16-X). Van der Marck.

Fischl, Josef & Rue, Leonard L., III. After Your Deer Is Down. LC 82-62823. 160p. 1981. pap. 10.95 (ISBN 0-8329-3532-8, Pub. by Winchester Pr). New Century.

Fischl, Viktor, ed. Antonin Dvorak, His Achievement. LC 78-104263. Repr. of 1943 ed. lib. bdg. 27.50 (ISBN 0-8371-3922-8, FIAD). Greenwood.

Fischle, Willy H. The Way to the Centre. Nevill, Tim, tr. from Ger. Orig. Title: Der Weg zur Mitte. (Illus.). 80p. 1982. 17.90 (ISBN 0-7224-0209-0, Dist. by Salem Hse). Robinson & Wat.

--The Way to the Centre: Symbols of Transformation in Tibetan Tankas. (Illus.). 80p. 1984. 24.95 (ISBN 0-7224-0209-0, Pub. by Salem Hse Ltd). Merrimack Pub Cir.

Fischler. Uptown & Downtown. pap. 9.95 (ISBN 0-8015-8196-6, 0966-290, Hawthorn). Dutton.

Fischler, Shirley & Fischler, Stan. Hockey Encyclopedia: The Complete Record of Professional Ice Hockey. 634p. 1983. 24.95 (ISBN 0-02-538400-7). Macmillan.

Fischler, Shirley, jt. auth. see Fischler, Stan.

Fischler, Stan. The Great Gretzky. LC 82-60968. (Illus.). 160p. (Orig.). 1982. pap. 8.70 (ISBN 0-688-01695-2, Quill NY). Morrow.

--Hockey's One Hundred: A Personal Ranking of the Best Players in Hockey History. (Illus.). 256p. 1984. pap. 9.95 (ISBN 0-8253-0245-5). Beaufort Bks NY.

--The New Breed. LC 82-60969. (Illus.). 160p. (Orig.). 1982. pap. text ed. 8.70 (ISBN 0-688-01696-0, Quill NY). Morrow.

Fischler, Stan & Fischler, Shirley. The Best, Worst & Most Unusual in Sports. LC 77-4099. (Illus.). 1977. 12.45i (ISBN 0-690-01457-0). T Y Crowell.

--Everybody's Hockey Book. (Illus.). 400p. 1983. 22.50 (ISBN 0-684-18022-7, ScribT). Scribner.

--Everybody's Hockey Book. (Illus.). 384p. 1985. pap. 12.95 (ISBN 0-684-18507-5, ScribT). Scribner.

Fischler, Stan & Friedman, Richard. Getting into Pro Soccer. (Getting into the Pros Ser.). (Illus.). (gr. 6 up). 1979. PLB 8.40 s&l (ISBN 0-531-02280-3). Watts.

Fischler, Stan, jt. auth. see Cherry, Don.

Fischler, Stan, jt. auth. see Fischler, Shirley.

Fischler, Stan, jt. auth. see Mazer, Bill.

Fischler, Stan, jt. auth. see Potvin, Denis.

Fischman, Joyce. Bible Work & Play, 3 vols. (Illus., Orig.). (gr. 1-3). 1966. pap. text ed. 2.50 ea. Vol. 1 (102610). Vol. 2 (102620). Vol. 3 (102640). UAHC.

--Bible Work & Play, Vol. 2. rev. ed. (Illus.). 80p. 1984. wkbk. 5.00 (ISBN 0-8074-0256-7). UAHC.

--Holiday Work & Play. 1961. pap. 3.00 (ISBN 0-685-02011-8, 101960). UAHC.

Fischman, Leonard L. World Mineral Trends & U. S. Supply Problems. LC 80-8025. (Resources for the Future, Inc. Research Paper R-20). (Illus.). 576p. (Orig.). 1981. pap. text ed. 20.00x (ISBN 0-8018-2491-5). Johns Hopkins.

Fischman, Sheila, tr. see Carrier, Roch.

Fischman, Sheila, tr. see Hebert, Anne.

Fischman, Sheila, tr. see Kattan, Naim.

Fischman, Sheila, tr. see Poulin, Jacques.

Fischman, Sheila, tr. see Tardivel, Jules-Paul.

Fischmeister see Holman, Ralph T., et al.

Fischoff, Ephraim, tr. see Weber, Max.

Fiscina, Salvatore F. Medical Law for the Attending Physician: A Case-Oriented Analysis. LC 82-5559. (Medical Humanities Ser.). 495p. 1982. 45.00x (ISBN 0-8093-1045-7). S Ill U Pr.

Fiscus, Dave. The Birthday Magician's Handbook. Walker, Barbara, ed. (Illus.). viii, 217p. 1980. 22.50 (ISBN 0-915926-44-X). Magic Ltd.

Fiscus, Edward D. & Mandell, Colleen J. Developing Individualized Education Programs (IEP) (Illus.). 350p. 1983. pap. text ed. 14.95 (ISBN 0-314-69648-2); write for info. instr's. manual (ISBN 0-314-72292-0). West Pub.
Fiscus, Edward D., jt. auth. see Mandell, Colleen J.
Fisek, M. Hamit see Berger, Joseph, et al.
Fiser, Emeric. Le Symbole litteraire: Essai sur la signification du symbole chez Wagner, Baudelaire, Mallarme, Bergson, et Marcel Proust. LC 77-10260. Repr. of 1941 ed. 27.50 (ISBN 0-404-16315-7). AMS Pr.
Fiser, Robert H., Jr., ed. see National Foundation-March of Dimes Symposium, April, 1976, New York City.
Fiser, Webb S. Mastery of the Metropolis. LC 80-23244. x, 168p. 1981. Repr. of 1962 ed. lib. bdg. 19.25x (ISBN 0-313-22732-2, FIMAM). Greenwood.
Fisera, Vladimir. Workers' Councils in Czechoslovakia. LC 78-25995. 1979. 25.00x (ISBN 0-312-88959-3). St Martin.
Fisera, Vladimir C., jt. ed. see Cahm, Eric.
Fiserova-Bergerova, Vera, ed. Modeling of Inhalation Exposure to Vapors: Uptake, Distribution. & Elimination, 2 Vols. 1983. Vol. I, 184pp. 54.00 (ISBN 0-8493-6315-2); Vol. II, 208pp. 58.00 (ISBN 0-8493-6316-0). CRC Pr.
Fisge, Rosalie C. & Fotee, Joanne K. Bread Baker's Manual: The Hows & Whys of Creative Bread Making. LC 77-17856. (Creative Cooking Ser.). (Illus.). 1978. 11.95 (ISBN 0-13-081638-8, Spec); pap. 5.95 (ISBN 0-13-081620-5, Spec). P-H.
Fish. Dartmoor: A New Study. 1978. 25.00 (ISBN 0-7153-5041-2). David & Charles.
--One Flew over the Cuckoo's Nest (Kesey) (Book Notes). 1984. pap. 2.50 (ISBN 0-8120-3433-3). Barron.
Fish, Arnold & Lloyd, Norman. Fundamentals of Sight Singing & Ear Training. 1964. pap. text ed. 19.50 scp (ISBN 0-06-042082-0, HarpC). Har-Row.
Fish, Arnold, jt. auth. see Hardy, Gordon.
Fish, Byron, jt. auth. see Lewis, George W.
Fish, Byron, jt. auth. see Spring, Ira.
Fish, C. R. The Civil Service & the Patronage. 1984. lib. bdg. 90.00 (ISBN 0-8490-3237-7). Gordon Pr.
--Guide to the Materials for American History in Roman & Other Italian Archives. 1911. 24.00 (ISBN 0-527-00693-9). Kraus Repr.
Fish, Carl R. The Path of Empire. 1919. 40.00 (ISBN 0-8482-3995-4). Norwood Edns.
--Path of Empire. 1919. 8.50x (ISBN 0-686-83685-5). Elliots Bks.
--The Rise of Common Man: Eighteen Thirty to Eighteen Fifty. LC 83-8561. (Illus.). xix, 391p. 1983. Repr. of 1937 ed. lib. bdg. 45.00 (ISBN 0-313-24065-5, FIRI). Greenwood.
Fish, Carl R see Johnson, Allen & Nevins, Allan.
Fish, Carl R., ed. see Olbrich, Emil.
Fish, Chet, jt. auth. see Swendsen, David H.
Fish, Chet, ed. see Bowring, Dave.
Fish, Chet, ed. see Cadieux, Charles L.
Fish, Chet, ed. see Clede, Bill.
Fish, Chet, ed. see Johnson, Peter H.
Fish, Chet, ed. see Vernon, Steven K.
Fish, Chet, ed. see Wood, J. B.
Fish, D. T. Popular Gardening, 4 vols. 1974. lib. bdg. 600.00 (ISBN 0-685-51357-2). Revisionist Pr.
Fish, Debra, ed. Home-Based Training Resource Handbook. 3rd rev. ed. (Illus.). 392p. 1984. pap. text ed. 29.95 (ISBN 0-934140-13-8). Toys N Things.
Fish, E., jt. auth. see Fish, H.
Fish, Ed. My Life As a Robot. 192p. 1984. 12.95 (ISBN 0-312-92551-4). Congdon & Weed.
Fish, Edwards E. The Past at Present. 4th ed. (Illus.). 201p. 1981. 11.95 (ISBN 0-318-00996-X). H U Fish.
Fish, Enrica. Cat in Art. LC 71-84406. (Fine Art Books). (Illus.). (gr. 5-11). 1970. PLB 5.95g (ISBN 0-8225-0164-3). Lerner Pubns.
Fish, H. & Fish, E. Activities Program for Senior Citizens. cancelled 12.95 (ISBN 0-13-003590-4, Parker). P-H.
Fish, Hamilton. F D R: The Other Side of the Coin. 255p. 1976. pap. 8.00 (ISBN 0-911038-64-7, Inst Hist Rev). Noontide.
--FDR: The Other Side of the Coin. (Illus.). 256p. 1976. 11.00 (ISBN 0-686-76164-2); pap. 8.00 (ISBN 0-911038-64-7). Inst Hist Rev.
--FDR: The Other Side of the Coin. 1977. 8.95 (ISBN 0-533-02220-7). Vantage.
--New York State: The Battleground of the Revolutionary War. 1977. 7.95 (ISBN 0-533-02128-6). Vantage.
--Report of the Select Committee of the Senate of the U.S. on the Sickness & Mortality on Board Emigrant Ships. Rosenkrantz, Barbara G., ed. LC 76-25663. (Public Health in America Ser.). (Illus.). 1977. Repr. of 1854 ed. lib. bdg. 14.00x (ISBN 0-405-09818-9). Ayer Co Pubs.
--Tragic Deception: FDR & America's Involvement in World War II. 1983. 12.95 (ISBN 0-8159-6917-1). Devin.
Fish, Harriet U. Tracks, Trails & Tales in Clallam County State of Washington. (Illus.). 200p. (Orig.). 1983. 15.95 (ISBN 0-9612344-0-7). H U Fish.
--What's Down That Road? 1985. 7.95 (ISBN 0-918146-16-X). H U Fish.
Fish, Helen D. When the Root Children Wake Up. (Illus.). 1976. scroll 7.95 (ISBN 0-914676-06-7). Green Tiger Pr.
Fish, Helen R. Drama & Dramatists: A Handbooks for the High-School Student. 1931. 12.50 (ISBN 0-8482-3978-4). Norwood Edns.
Fish, J. F., jt. ed. see Busnel, R. G.
Fish, John H. Black Power White Control: The Struggle of the Woodlawn Organization in Chicago. LC 72-5379. (Studies in Religion & Society, Center for the Scientific Study of Religion). 360p. 1973. 38.00x (ISBN 0-691-09358-X). Princeton U Pr.
Fish, Joseph, jt. auth. see Fleming, Donald.
Fish, Lydia M. The Folklore of the Coal Miners of the Northeast of England. LC 76-25433. 1976. Set. lib. bdg. 35.00 (ISBN 0-8414-4209-6). Folcroft.
Fish, Margery. Cottage Garden Flowers. 208p. 1980. pap. 7.95 (ISBN 0-571-11462-8). Faber & Faber.
--A Flower for Every Day. 208p. 1981. pap. 7.95 (ISBN 0-571-11738-4). Faber & Faber.
--Gardening in the Shade. LC 83-18523. (Illus.). 160p. (Orig.). 1984. pap. 7.95 (ISBN 0-571-13142-5). Faber & Faber.
--Ground Cover Plants. (Illus.). 144p. 1980. pap. 7.95 (ISBN 0-571-11463-6). Faber & Faber.
--We Made a Garden. LC 83-16489. (Illus.). 120p. (Orig.). 1984. pap. 7.95 (ISBN 0-571-13141-7). Faber & Faber.
Fish, Oscar & Walker, Godfrey. Mobile Health Services. 224p. 1981. 30.00x (ISBN 0-905402-03-0, Pub. by Tri-Med England). State Mutual Bk.
Fish, Peter G. The Politics of Federal Judicial Administration. LC 76-39785. 488p. 1973. 48.00 (ISBN 0-691-09226-5); pap. 18.50 LPEE (ISBN 0-691-10013-6). Princeton U Pr.
Fish, Ray & Trupin, Suzanne. Sexually Transmitted Diseases: Recognition, Prevention, & Treatment. 200p. (Orig.). 1985. pap. 9.95 (ISBN 0-89769-067-2, Dist. by Caroline Hse.). Pine Mntn.
Fish, Raymond M. & Ehrhardt, Melvin E. Malpractice, Managing Your Defense. LC 84-1132. 1985. 24.50 (ISBN 0-87489-388-7). Med Economics.
Fish, Robert. The Incredible Schloch Homes. 1976. pap. 2.95 (ISBN 0-380-00636-7, 28597). Avon.
Fish, Robert L. The Gold of Troy. 368p. 1984. pap. 3.50 (ISBN 0-425-06411-5). Berkley Pub.
--Kek Huuygens, Smuggler. LC 76-7153. 1976. 10.00 (ISBN 0-89296-002-7); limited ed. 20.00 (ISBN 0-89296-003-5). Mysterious Pr.
--The Memoirs of Schlock Holmes. 1975. pap. 3.45 (ISBN 0-380-00367-8, 26062). Avon.
Fish, Roy J. Every Member Evangelism for Today. rev. ed. LC 75-12289. 128p. 1976. pap. 6.68i (ISBN 0-06-061551-6, RD125, HarpR). Har-Row.
--Giving a Good Invitation. LC 74-18043. 1975. pap. 3.25 (ISBN 0-8054-2107-6). Broadman.
Fish, S. M. Aaron Levy Founder of Aaronsburg. LC 51-2554. (Studies in American Jewish History: No. 1). 10.00 (ISBN 0-527-02382-5); pap. 5.00 (ISBN 0-527-02383-3). Kraus Repr.
Fish, Sharon & Shelly, Judith A. Spiritual Care: The Nurse's Role. 2nd ed. LC 83-12604. (Illus.). 192p. 1983. pap. 6.95 (ISBN 0-87784-878-5). Inter-Varsity.
Fish, Sharon, jt. auth. see McCormick, Thomas.
Fish, Sidney M. Aaron Levy, Founder of Aaronsburg. 1951. pap. 2.50 (ISBN 0-911934-00-6). Am Jewish Hist Soc.
--Reshith Binah: A Hebrew Primer. 1976. pap. 3.95x (ISBN 0-8197-0035-5). Bloch.
Fish, Simon. A Supplicacyon for the Beggers. Furnivall, F. J., ed. (EETS, ES Ser.: No. 13). Repr. of 1871 ed. 15.00 (ISBN 0-527-00229-1). Kraus Repr.
--A Supplicacyon for the Beggers. LC 72-5989. (English Experience Ser.: No. 515). 16p. 1973. Repr. of 1529 ed. 6.00 (ISBN 90-221-0515-6). Walter J Johnson.
Fish, Stanley. Is There a Text in This Class? The Authority of Interpretive Communities. 402p. 1980. text ed. 25.00x (ISBN 0-674-46725-6). Harvard U Pr.
--Is There a Text in This Class? The Authority of Interpretive Communities. 408p. 1982. pap. 8.95 (ISBN 0-674-46726-4). Harvard U Pr.
Fish, Stanley E. The Living Temple: George Herbert & Catechizing. LC 73-90664. (Quantum Bks.). 1978. 24.50x (ISBN 0-520-02657-8). U of Cal Pr.
--Self-Consuming Artifacts: The Experience of Seventeenth-Century Literature. LC 76-187747. 1973. pap. 9.95 (ISBN 0-520-02764-7). U of Cal Pr.
--Surprised by Sin: The Reader in Paradise Lost. 1971. pap. 8.95 (ISBN 0-520-01897-4, CAL228). U of Cal Pr.
Fish, Thomas, et al. Financing Community Education: (Community Education "How to" Series) 32p. 1976. pap. 1.50 (ISBN 0-87812-146-3). Pendell Pub.
Fishback, W. T. Projective & Euclidean Geometry. 2nd ed. LC 76-81329. Repr. of 1969 ed. 78.00 (ISBN 0-8357-9967-0, 2051602). Bks Demand UMI.
Fishbane, Joyce O. & Fisher, Glenn W. Politics of the Purse: Revenue & Finance in the Sixth Illinois Constitutional Convention. (Studies in Illinois Constitution Making Ser.). 215p. 1974. pap. 10.00 (ISBN 0-252-00455-8). U of Ill Pr.
Fishbane, Michael. Biblical Interpretation in Ancient Israel. 704p. 1985. 39.95 (ISBN 0-19-826325-2). Oxford U Pr.
--Text & Texture: Close Readings of Selected Biblical Passages. LC 79-14083. 1979. text ed. 12.95x (ISBN 0-8052-3724-0). Schocken.
--Text & Texture: Close Readings of Selected Biblical Texts. LC 79-14083. 154p. 1982. pap. 7.95 (ISBN 0-8052-0726-0). Schocken.
Fishbane, Micheal. Judaism. LC 85-42775. (Religious Traditions of the World Ser.). 128p. (Orig.). 1985. 6.95 (ISBN 0-06-062655-0, HarpR). Har-Row.
Fishbeck, K. H., jt. auth. see Fischbeck, H. J.
Fishbein, Bette K. Social Welfare Abroad: Comparative Data on the Social Insurance & Public Assistance Programs of Selected Industrialized Democracies. LC 75-9028. (Illus.). 35p. 1975. pap. 3.00 (ISBN 0-915312-01-8). Inst Socioecon.
Fishbein, Harold D. The Psychology of Infancy & Childhood: Evolutionary & Cross-Cultural Perspectives. 456p. 1984. 34.95 (ISBN 0-89859-416-2); pap. 19.95 (ISBN 0-89859-510-X). L Erlbaum Assocs.
Fishbein, Justin, jt. ed. see Fishbein, Morris.
Fishbein, L. Chromatography of Environmental Hazards, Vol. 1: Carcinogens, Mutagens & Teratogens. 499p. 1972. 95.75 (ISBN 0-444-40948-3). Elsevier.
--Chromatography of Environmental Hazards, Vol. 2: Metals, Gaseous & Industrial Pollutants. LC 78-180000. 654p. 1974. 117.00 (ISBN 0-444-41059-7). Elsevier.
--Chromatography of Environmental Hazards, Vol. 3: Pesticides. 820p. 1975. 134.00 (ISBN 0-444-41158-5). Elsevier.
--Chromatography of Environmental Hazards, Vol. 4: Drugs of Abuse. 496p. 1982. 106.50 (ISBN 0-444-42024-X). Elsevier.
--Potential Industrial Carcinogens & Mutagens. (Studies in Environmental Science: Vol. 4). 534p. 1979. 106.50 (ISBN 0-444-41777-X). Elsevier.
Fishbein, L. & O'Neill, I. R., eds. Environmental Carcinogens, Selected Methods of Analysis: Some Volatile Halogenated Alkanes & Alkenes, Vol. 7. (Scientific Publications Ser., International Agency for Research on Cancer: No. 68). (Illus.). 450p. 1985. 29.95 (ISBN 0-317-27143-1). Oxford U Pr.
Fishbein, L., et al, eds. Environmental Carcinogens-Selected Methods of Analysis: Some Aromatic Amines & Azo Dyes in the General & Industrial Environment, Vol. 4. (IARC Ser.). (Illus.). 362p. 1981. 35.00x (ISBN 0-19-723040-7). Oxford U Pr.
Fishbein, Lawrence, et al. Chemical Mutagens: Environmental Effects on Biological Systems. LC 71-117078. (Environmental Science Ser.). 1970. 75.00 (ISBN 0-12-257150-9). Acad Pr.
Fishbein, Leslie. Rebels in Bohemia: The Radicals of the Masses, 1911-1917. LC 81-24105. (Illus.). xv, 270p. 1982. 24.50x (ISBN 0-8078-1519-5). U of NC Pr.
Fishbein, M. History of the American Medical Association, 1847-1947. LC 47-46. Repr. of 1947 ed. 51.00 (ISBN 0-527-29450-0). Kraus Repr.
Fishbein, Martin. Reading in Attitude Theory & Measurement. LC 67-22410. (Illus.). 1967. pap. 96.80 (ISBN 0-317-08010-5, 2055145). Bks Demand UMI.
Fishbein, Martin & Ajzen, Icek. Belief, Attitude, Intention, & Behavior: An Introduction to Theory & Research. 544p. 1975. 30.95 (ISBN 0-201-02089-0). Addison-Wesley.
--Understanding Attitudes & Predicting Social Behavior. (Illus.). 1980. pap. text ed. 16.95 (ISBN 0-13-936435-8). P-H.
Fishbein, Martin, ed. Progress in Social Psychology, Vol. 1. LC 79-67453. (Illus.). 240p. 1980. text ed. 24.95x (ISBN 0-89859-005-1). L Erlbaum Assocs.
Fishbein, Morris. Fads & Quackery in Healing. LC 75-23708. Repr. of 1932 ed. 31.00 (ISBN 0-404-13260-X). AMS Pr.
--The Medical Follies. LC 75-23710. Repr. of 1925 ed. 18.00 (ISBN 0-404-13261-8). AMS Pr.
--Medical Writing: The Technic & the Art. 4th ed. (Illus.). 216p. 1978. 20.75x (ISBN 0-398-02279-8). C C Thomas.
--Modern Home Dictionary of Medical Words: With Descriptions, Uses & Standards of Commonly Used Tests. LC 74-18845. 240p. 1976. pap. 1.95 (ISBN 0-385-01105-9, Dolp). Doubleday.
--Modern Home Medical Adviser: Your Health & How to Preserve It. rev. ed. LC 69-10978. 1969. 16.95 (ISBN 0-385-01095-8). Doubleday.
--The New Medical Follies. LC 75-23711. Repr. of 1927 ed. 19.00 (ISBN 0-404-13262-6). AMS Pr.
Fishbein, Morris, ed. Doctors at War. LC 72-4477. (Essay Index Reprint Ser.). Repr. of 1945 ed. 40.00 (ISBN 0-8369-2943-8). Ayer Co Pubs.
--The New Illustrated Medical and Health Encyclopedia: Spanish Language Edition, 2 vols. 1967. 29.95 (ISBN 0-87475-180-2). Stuttman.
Fishbein, Morris & Fishbein, Justin, eds. Fishbein's Illustrated Medical & Health Encyclopedia, 4 vols. LC 77-79746. (Home Library Edition). (Illus.). 1983. 39.95 (ISBN 0-87475-245-0). Stuttman.
--Fishbein's Illustrated Medical & Health Encyclopedia: Family Health Guide Edition. LC 78-53643. 1978. 24.95 (ISBN 0-87475-250-7). Stuttman.
--Fishbein's Illustrated Medical & Health Encyclopedia: International Unified Edition, 22 vols. LC 80-52999. 1981. 131.56 (ISBN 0-87475-200-0). Stuttman.
Fishbein, Warren H. Wage Restraint by Consensus: Britain's Search for an Income Policy Agreement, 1965-1979. 300p. 1984. 35.00x (ISBN 0-7102-0074-9). Routledge & Kegan.
Fishbein, William, ed. Sleep, Dreams & Memory. LC 79-23861. (Advances in Sleep Research Ser.: Vol. 6). (Illus.). 270p. 1981. text ed. 35.00 (ISBN 0-89335-054-0). SP Med & Sci Bks.
Fishberg, Maurice. The Jews: A Study of Race & Environment. facsimile ed. LC 74-27983. (Modern Jewish Experience Ser.). (Illus.). 1975. Repr. of 1911 ed. 52.00x (ISBN 0-405-06710-0). Ayer Co Pubs.
--Materials for the Physical Anthropology of the Eastern European Jews. LC 6-2111. (American Anthro. Association Memoirs). 1905. 14.00 (ISBN 0-527-00500-2). Kraus Repr.
Fishbone, Leslie, tr. see Zel'Dovich, Ya. B. & Novikov, I. D.
Fishburn, Angela. The Batsford Book of Home Furnishings. (Illus.). 144p. 1982. 19.95 (ISBN 0-7134-3466-X, Pub. by Batsford England). David & Charles.
--The Batsford Book of Lampshades. (Illus.). 192p. 1985. 16.95 (ISBN 0-7134-2862-7, Pub. by Batsford England). David & Charles.
--The Batsford Book of Soft Furnishings. (Illus.). 168p. 1985. pap. 11.95 (ISBN 0-7134-1268-2, Pub. by Batsford England). David & Charles.
--Lampshades: Technique & Design. (Illus.). 96p. 1985. pap. cancelled (ISBN 0-7134-3729-4, Pub. by Batsford England). David & Charles.
Fishburn, Janet F. The Fatherhood of God & the Victorian Family: The Social Gospel in America. LC 81-43090. 1982. 21.95 (ISBN 0-8006-0671-X). Fortress.
Fishburn, John P. Analysis of Speedup in Distributed Algorithms. Stone, Harold, ed. LC 83-18307. (Computer Science Ser.: Distributed Database Systems: No. 14). 128p. 1984. 34.95 (ISBN 0-8357-1527-2). UMI Res Pr.
Fishburn, Katherine. The Unexpected Universe of Doris Lessing: A Study of in Narrative Technique. LC 85-9913. (Contributions to the Study of Science Fiction & Fantasy Ser.: No. 17). 208p. 1985. lib. bdg. 27.95 (ISBN 0-313-23424-8, FTW/). Greenwood.
--Women in Popular Culture: A Reference Guide. LC 81-13421. (American Popular Culture Ser.). ix, 267p. 1982. lib. bdg. 29.95 (ISBN 0-313-22152-9, FWC/). Greenwood.
Fishburn, Peter, jt. auth. see Brams, Stephen.
Fishburn, Peter C. The Foundations of Expected Utility. 1982. 39.50 (ISBN 90-277-1420-7, Pub. by Reidel Holland). Kluwer Academic.
--Interval Orders & Interval Sets: A Study of Partially Ordered Sets. (Wiley Interscience Series in Discrete Mathematics). 215p. 1985. text ed. 33.50x (ISBN 0-471-81284-6, Pub. by Wiley-Interscience). Wiley.
--Mathematics of Decision Theory. (Methods & Models in the Social Sciences Ser.: No. 3). 1972. pap. text ed. 9.60x (ISBN 90-2797-142-0). Mouton.
--The Theory of Social Choice. LC 72-1985. (Illus.). 300p. 1973. 29.00x (ISBN 0-691-08121-2). Princeton U Pr.
Fishburn, Peter C., ed. see Mirkin, Boris G., et al.
Fishel, Andrew, jt. ed. see Pottker, Janice.
Fishel, Elizabeth. The Men in Our Lives: Fathers, Lovers, Husbands, Mentors. LC 84-8984. 352p. 1984. 15.95 (ISBN 0-688-03960-X). Morrow.
--Sisters: Love & Rivalry Inside the Family & Beyond. LC 84-22252. 348p. 1985. pap. 7.95 (ISBN 0-688-04227-9, Quill). Morrow.
Fishel, Jeff & C Q Press Staff. Presidents & Promises: From Campaign Pledge to Presidential Performance. LC 84-23782. 226p. 1985. pap. 9.95 (ISBN 0-87187-336-2); 14.95 (ISBN 0-87187-344-3). Congr Quarterly.
Fishel, Jeff, ed. Parties & Elections in an Anti-Party Age: American Politics & the Crisis of Confidence. LC 76-26426. (Midland Bks.: No. 209). 384p. 1978. pap. text ed. 10.95 (ISBN 0-253-20209-4). Ind U Pr.
Fishel, Kent & Rayds, John. Resurrection Evidences. (Cornerstone Ser.). 1985. pap. 2.95 (ISBN 0-310-46102-2). Zondervan.
Fishel, Wesley R. The End of Extraterritoriality in China. 1972. lib. bdg. 21.50x (ISBN 0-374-92749-9). Octagon.
Fishelis, Avraham. Bastion of Faith. 3rd ed. 256p. 1980. 9.00 (ISBN 0-9605560-1-X). A Fishelis.
--Kol Rom, Vol. I. 3rd ed. 208p. (Hebrew.). 5.50 (ISBN 0-9605560-0-1). A Fishelis.
--Kol Rom, Vol. II. 292p. (Hebrew.). 6.50 (ISBN 0-9605560-2-8). A Fishelis.
--Kol Rom, Vol. III. 431p. (Hebrew.). 12.00 (ISBN 0-9605560-3-6). A Fishelis.
Fishelson, Lev. Mysteries of the Red Sea. (Illus.). 144p. 1984. 29.95 (ISBN 0-911378-53-7, Pub. by Massada). Sheridan.
--Tilapia in Aquaculture. (Illus.). 600p. pap. 69.00 (ISBN 0-86689-018-1). Balaban Intl Sci Serv.

Fishenden, Margaret W. & Saunders, O. A. An Introduction to Heat Transfer. LC 50-13872. pap. 53.80 (ISBN 0-317-08880-7, 2051752). Bks Demand UMI.

Fisher. Baby Penguin. (Tiny Bubbles Bks.). Date not set. 1.95. S&S.

--Dancing the Old Testament in Worship & Education. (Illus.). 128p. 1980. 5.95 (ISBN 0-318-16442-6). Sacred Dance Guild.

Fisher & Buettner. Light & Heavy Industrial Buildings. 180p. 1979. 20.00 (ISBN 0-318-12806-3, T113). Am Inst Steel Construct.

Fisher, jt. auth. see Farber.

Fisher, A. Security for Business & Industry. 1979. 22.95 (ISBN 0-13-798967-9). P-H.

Fisher, A. Craig, ed. Psychology of Sport. LC 75-44698. 503p. 1976. text ed. 20.95 (ISBN 0-87484-359-6). Mayfield Pub.

Fisher, A. Garth & Allsen, Philip E. Jogging. (Physical Education Activity Ser.). 96p. 1980. pap. text ed. write for info. (ISBN 0-697-07083-2). Wm C Brown.

Fisher, A. Garth, jt. auth. see Jensen, Clayne R.

Fisher, A. T., jt. auth. see Ayerst, David.

Fisher, Adrian S. & Oliver, Convey T. Restatement of the Law, Second, Foreign Relations Law of the United States. 679p. 1965. 30.00 (ISBN 0-317-30742-8). Am Law Inst.

Fisher, Aileen. All on a Mountain Day. 127p. 5.80 (ISBN 0-686-05600-0). Rod & Staff.

--Anybody Home? LC 78-22508. (Illus.). 32p. (ps-2). 1980. PLB 9.89 (ISBN 0-690-04055-5). Crowell Jr Bks.

--Christmas Plays & Programs. rev. ed. LC 60-6053. (gr. 3 up). 1970. 12.00 (ISBN 0-8238-0017-2). Plays.

--Easter. LC 67-23666. (Holiday Ser.). (Illus.). (gr. k-3). 1968. PLB 10.89 (ISBN 0-690-25236-6). Crowell Jr Bks.

--Going Barefoot. LC 60-6238. (Illus.). (gr. k-3). 1960. Crowell Jr Bks.

--Holiday Programs for Boys & Girls. rev. ed. LC 52-11997. (gr. 2-7). 1980. 12.95 (ISBN 0-8238-0244-2). Plays.

--Like Nothing at All. LC 60-9159. (Illus.). (ps-3). 1979. PLB 10.89 (ISBN 0-690-49379-7). Crowell Jr Bks.

--Listen, Rabbit. LC 64-10860. (Illus.). (gr. k-3). 1964. PLB 11.89 (ISBN 0-690-49592-7). Crowell Jr Bks.

--Once We Went on a Picnic. LC 75-9836. (Illus.). 32p. (gr. k-3). 1975. PLB 11.49i (ISBN 0-690-00956-9). Crowell Jr Bks.

--Out in the Dark & Daylight. LC 78-22492. (Illus.). 176p. (gr. k-5). 1980. 10.53i (ISBN 0-06-021902-5); PLB 10.89 (ISBN 0-06-021903-3). HarpJ.

--Rabbits, Rabbits. LC 82-48849. (A Charlotte Zolotow Bk.). (Illus.). 32p. (gr. k-3). 1983. 9.57i (ISBN 0-06-021896-7); PLB 9.89g (ISBN 0-06-021899-1). HarpJ.

--Year-Round Programs for Young Players. 334p. (Orig.). (gr. 3-7). 1985. 13.95 (ISBN 0-8238-0266-3). Plays.

Fisher, Aileen L. My First Hanukkah Book. LC 84-21510. (My First Bks.). (Illus.). 32p. 1985. lib. bdg. 10.35 (ISBN 0-516-02905-3); pap. 2.95 (ISBN 0-516-42905-1). Childrens.

Fisher, Aimee, tr. see Olesha, Yury.

Fisher, Alan. Country Walks Near Baltimore. (Country Walks Ser.). (Illus.). 214p. 1982. pap. 7.95 (ISBN 0-910146-36-5). Appalach Mtn.

--Country Walks Near Philadelphia. (Country Walks Ser.). (Illus.). 180p. (Orig.). 1983. pap. 7.95 (ISBN 0-910146-42-X). Appalach Mtn.

--Country Walks Near Washington. (Illus.). 220p. (Orig.). 1984. pap. 6.95 (ISBN 0-910146-53-5). Appalach Mtn.

--More Country Walks Near Washington. (Illus.). 219p. 1985. pap. 7.95 (ISBN 0-9614963-0-4). Rambler Bks.

--The Three Passions of Countess Natalya. Black & Boegehold, eds. 352p. 1985. lib. bdg. 15.95 (ISBN 0-02-538460-0). Macmillan.

Fisher, Alan W. Crimean Tartars. LC 76-41085. (Publication Ser: No. 166). (Illus.). 1978. 14.95x (ISBN 0-8179-6661-7). Hoover Inst Pr.

Fisher, Albert K. The Hawks & Owls of the United States in Their Relation to Agriculture. LC 73-17820. (Natural Sciences in America Ser.). (Illus.). 266p. 1974. Repr. 18.00x (ISBN 0-405-05736-9). Ayer Co Pubs.

Fisher, Alden, tr. see Merleau-Ponty, M.

Fisher, Alden L. & Murray, George B., eds. Philosophy & Science As Modes of Knowing: Selected Essays. LC 69-18680. (Orig.). 1969. pap. text ed. 7.95x (ISBN 0-89197-340-0). Irvington.

Fisher, Alec. Formal Number Theory & Computability: A Workbook. (Oxford Logic Guides). 1982. 37.50x (ISBN 0-19-853178-8); pap. 12.50x (ISBN 0-19-853188-5). Oxford U Pr.

Fisher, Alexander. Atlas of Aquatic Dermatology. 120p. 1978. 41.00 (ISBN 0-8089-1139-2, 791270). Grune.

Fisher, Allan C., Jr. America's Inland Waterway. LC 73-831. (Special Publications Ser.). (Illus.). 208p. 1973. 6.95, avail. only from Natl. Geog. (ISBN 0-87044-128-0). Natl Geog.

Fisher, Allan G. Clash of Progress & Security. LC 66-21369. Repr. of 1935 ed. 25.00x (ISBN 0-678-00158-8). Kelley.

--Some Problems of Wages & Their Regulation in Great Britain Since 1918. LC 66-21672. Repr. of 1926 ed. 29.50x (ISBN 0-678-00183-9). Kelley.

Fisher, Allan G., tr. see Nachtigal, Gustav.

Fisher, Allen. PIACE I-XXXVII. 124p. 1976. 4.00 (ISBN 0-916562-04-2). Truck Pr.

Fisher, Andrew, et al. Handbook for Family Planning Operations Research Design. LC 83-13731. 64p. (Orig.). 1983. pap. write for info. (ISBN 0-87834-051-3). Population Coun.

--Manuel de Recherche Operationnell en Matiere de Planification Familiale. Baraket, Irene, tr. (French.). 1985. write for info. Population Coun.

Fisher, Angela. Africa Adorned. LC 84-461. (Illus.). 304p. 1984. 45.00 (ISBN 0-8109-1823-4). Abrams.

Fisher, Anita K., jt. ed. see Srole, Leo.

Fisher, Anne B. Bears, Pirates & Silver Lace. (Illus.). 146p. (gr. 3-7). 1975. pap. 5.95 (ISBN 0-8323-0255-4). Binford.

--No More a Stranger. 1946. Repr. 25.00 (ISBN 0-8274-3039-6). R West.

--Stories California Indians Told. LC 57-8065. (Illus.). (gr. 3-7). 1957. 6.95 (ISBN 0-395-27723-X, Pub. by Parnassus). HM.

Fisher, Anthony C. Economic Efficiency & Air Pollution Control. LC 81-17464. (East-West Environment & Policy Institute Research Report: No. 8). v, 74p. (Orig.). 1981. pap. text ed. 3.00 (ISBN 0-86638-030-2). E W Center HI.

--Resource & Environmental Economics: Natural Resources & the Environment in Economics. LC 81-9951. (Cambridge Surveys of Economic Literature Ser.). 256p. 1981. 44.50 (ISBN 0-521-24306-8); pap. 11.95 (ISBN 0-521-28594-1). Cambridge U Pr.

Fisher, Anthony C., jt. auth. see Krutilla, John V.

Fisher, Antony. Fisher's Concise Guide of Economic Bungling: A Guide for Today's Statesmen. LC 77-15916. 113p. 1978. 8.95 (ISBN 0-916054-63-2, Dist. by Kampmann); pap. 2.95 (ISBN 0-916054-69-1). Green Hill.

Fisher, Aron B., jt. auth. see Fishman, Alfred D.

Fisher, Arthur W. The Jacob Fisher Family, Seventeen Twenty-Seven - Nineteen Fifty-Eight, Vol. I. LC 80-69266. 470p. 1979. Repr. 20.00 (ISBN 0-9612308-1-9). J B Fisher.

Fisher, B. A. Small Group Decision Making: Communication & the Group Process. 2nd ed. Wright, Richard R., ed. (Illus.). 1980. text ed. 28.95x (ISBN 0-07-021091-8). McGraw.

Fisher, B. Aubrey. Perspectives on Human Communication. (Illus.). 1978. text ed. write for info. (ISBN 0-02-337990-1). Macmillan.

Fisher, Barbara. Big Harold & Tiny Enid. (Illus.). 26p. (Orig.). (gr. 1-3). 1975. pap. 2.00 (ISBN 0-934830-01-0). Ten Penny.

--Breathing Room. Pinar, William F., ed. 350p. (Orig.). 1982. pap. 8.00 (ISBN 0-9609642-0-7). Brighton St Pr.

--Car Boy. (Illus.). 29p. (Orig.). (gr. k-2). 1977. pap. 2.00 (ISBN 0-934830-02-9). Ten Penny.

--Dan. (Illus.). 20p. (Orig.). (gr. k-5). 1981. pap. 2.00 (ISBN 0-934830-19-3). Ten Penny.

--Harmony Hurricane Muldoon. (Nutrition Program Ser.). (Illus.). 22p. (Orig.). (gr. 3-5). 1979. pap. 1.00 (ISBN 0-934830-09-6). Ten Penny.

--Jolly Molly Molar. (Nutrition Program Ser.). (Illus.). 44p. (Orig.). (gr. 1-3). 1979. pap. 1.00 (ISBN 0-934830-10-X). Ten Penny.

--Joyce Cary: The Writer & His Theme. 1980. text ed. 29.00x (ISBN 0-391-01763-2). Humanities.

--Linkups. (Illus., Orig.). (ps-3). 1977. pap. 2.00 slipcased (ISBN 0-934830-05-3). Ten Penny.

--Max St. Peter McBride & Theodora. (Illus.). 58p. (Orig.). (gr. k-3). 1981. pap. 2.00 (ISBN 0-934830-20-7). Ten Penny.

--Philpin's Tree. (Illus.). 12p. (Orig.). (gr. 1-3). 1976. pap. 2.00 (ISBN 0-934830-00-2). Ten Penny.

Fisher, Barbara & Spiegel, Richard, eds. Greenwich Village Lore & Chinatown Tales. (Illus.). 112p. (Orig.). (gr. 1-7). 1983. pap. 4.00 (ISBN 0-934830-31-2, Waterways Project). Ten Penny.

--In Search of a Song: Jefferson Market Library, Vol. 3. (Illus.). 64p. (Orig.). (gr. 1-6). 1982. pap. 2.00 (ISBN 0-934830-27-4). Ten Penny.

--In Search of a Song: PS-114, Vol. 1. (Illus.). 90p. (Orig.). (gr. k-6). 1981. pap. 2.00 (ISBN 0-934830-25-8). Ten Penny.

--In Search of a Song: PS-276, Vol. 2. (Illus.). 90p. (Orig.). (gr. k-6). 1981. pap. 2.00 (ISBN 0-934830-26-6). Ten Penny.

--More Poetry Hunter. (Illus.). 92p. (Orig.). 1981. pap. 2.50 (ISBN 0-934830-23-1). Ten Penny.

--Poetry Hunter, No. 1. (Illus.). 92p. (Orig.). (gr. k-6). 1981. pap. 2.50 (ISBN 0-934830-21-5). Ten Penny.

--Still More Poetry Hunter. (Illus.). 36p. (Orig.). (gr. k-6). 1981. pap. 2.00 (ISBN 0-934830-24-X). Ten Penny.

--Subway Slams. (Illus.). 48p. (Orig.). (gr. k-8). 1981. pap. 2.00 (ISBN 0-934830-22-3). Ten Penny.

--Yearning to Breathe Free. 32p. (Orig.). (gr. 4-9). 1984. pap. 2.00 (ISBN 0-934830-33-9). Ten Penny.

Fisher, Barbara, ed. see Day, Adrienne.

Fisher, Barbara, ed. see Mennella, Roxanna.

Fisher, Barbara, ed. see New York Book Fair.

Fisher, Barbara, ed. see Wilkins, Sarah & Mennella, Roxanna.

Fisher, Barbara G. Meridian Markers. (Illus.). 64p. 1984. 7.95 (ISBN 0-89962-377-8). Todd & Honeywell.

Fisher, Barbara L., jt. auth. see Coulter, Harris L.

Fisher, Barbarba, ed. see Wilkins, Sarah.

Fisher, Barry L. & Jenner, Aileen M. Debtor-Creditor Law, 9 vols. LC 81-68420. 1982. Updates avail. 630.00 (216); looseleaf 1983 77.50; looseleaf 1984 267.50. Bender.

Fisher, Barry M. Legal Aspects of Doing Business in Canada. 1020p. 1983. pap. 35.00 (ISBN 0-317-27381-7, A4-4054). PLI.

Fisher, Bart S. & Harte, Kathleen M. Barter in the World Economy. LC 85-6257. 302p. 1985. 39.95 (ISBN 0-03-071609-8). Praeger.

Fisher, Bart S. & Turner, Jeff, eds. Regulating the Multinational Enterprise: National & International Challenges. LC 83-11002. 192p. 1983. 27.95x (ISBN 0-03-063561-6). HR&W.

Fisher, Ben C., ed. New Pathways: A Dialogue in Christian Higher Education. LC 80-80255. 120p. 1980. pap. 4.95x (ISBN 0-86554-000-4). Mercer Univ Pr.

Fisher, Benjamin F. The Very Spirit of Cordiality: The Literary Uses of Alcohol... in the Tales of Edgar Allan Poe. Kadis, Averil, ed. 1978. pap. 2.75 (ISBN 0-910556-10-5). Enoch Pratt.

Fisher, Benjamin F., IV. The Gothic's Gothic: Study Aids to the Tale of Terror. 400p. 1985. lib. bdg. 54.00 (ISBN 0-8240-8784-4). Garland Pub.

Fisher, Berenice M. Industrial Education: American Ideals & Institutions. LC 67-26626. pap. 70.30 (ISBN 0-317-10834-4, 2002754). Bks Demand UMI.

Fisher, Bill. How to Hotrod Corvair Engines. LC 76-28085. (Illus.). 1969. pap. 9.95 (ISBN 0-912656-00-X). H P Bks.

--How to Hotrod Volkswagen Engines. LC 72-28084. (Illus.). 1970. pap. 9.95 (ISBN 0-912656-03-4). H P Bks.

Fisher, Bill & Waar, Bob. How to Hotrod Big-Block Chevys. LC 72-159282. (Illus.). 1971. pap. 9.95 (ISBN 0-912656-04-2). H P Bks.

--How to Hotrod Small-Block Chevys. rev. ed. LC 73-173702. (Illus.). 192p. 1976. pap. 7.95 (ISBN 0-912656-06-9). H P Bks.

Fisher, Bill, jt. auth. see Roe, Doug.

Fisher, Bill, jt. auth. see Urich, Mike.

Fisher, Bob. The Fastnet Disaster & After. (Illus.). 192p. 1981. 15.95 (ISBN 0-7207-1253-X, Pub. by Michael Joseph). Merrimack Pub Cir.

--Great Yacht Races. LC 84-234. (Illus.). 256p. 1984. 45.00 (ISBN 0-941434-57-5). Stewart Tabori & Chang.

Fisher, Bonnie. Bonnie Fisher's Way with Herbs Cookbook. LC 80-82326. 140p. (Orig.). 1980. pap. 2.95 (ISBN 0-87983-205-3). Keats.

Fisher Broadcasting see Wise, Katherine.

Fisher, Bruce. Rebuilding: When Your Relationship Ends. LC 79-24440. 1981. pap. 6.95 (ISBN 0-915166-30-5). Impact Pubs Cal.

--When Your Relationship Ends. 1981. pap. text ed. 6.00 (ISBN 0-9607250-0-8). Family Relations.

Fisher, Bruce D. & Jennings, Marianne M. Law for Business. (Illus.). 800p. 1986. text ed. 27.95 (ISBN 0-314-93178-3). West Pub.

Fisher, Bruce D. & Phillips, Michael J. The Legal Environment of Business. (Illus.). 850p. 1982. text ed. 30.95 (ISBN 0-314-63172-0); study guide 10.95 (ISBN 0-314-71141-4). West Pub.

Fisher, C. D., ed. see Tacitus.

Fisher, Carl, jt. ed. see Baumgartner, Aline.

Fisher, Carl, ed. see Mitchell, Joan & O'Neill, Irene.

Fisher, Carl, ed. see Mitchell, Joan & Sherlock, Therese.

Fisher, Carol & Terry, Ann. Children's Language & the Language Arts. 2nd ed. (Illus.). 368p. 1982. text ed. 28.95x (ISBN 0-07-021108-6). McGraw.

Fisher, Carol M. Letters to God from the Church Secretary. 28p. 1976. pap. 2.50 (ISBN 0-89536-140-X). CSS of Ohio.

Fisher, Caroline, ed. Exporting to Japan: How to Profit from a Growing Market. 35p. 1980. 2.00 (ISBN 0-942286-03-0). Intl Mktg.

Fisher, Charles. The Columnists. 1977. Repr. of 1944 ed. lib. bdg. 35.00 (ISBN 0-686-19801-8). Havertown Bks.

--South-East Asia. 2nd ed. 1966. 69.95x (ISBN 0-416-42480-5, NO.2200). Methuen Inc.

Fisher, Charles A. Central Pennsylvania Marriages, 1700-1896. LC 74-16925. 90p. 1982. pap. 7.50 (ISBN 0-8063-0646-7). Genealog Pub.

--Early Pennsylvania Births: 1675-1875. LC 75-21584. 107p. 1983. pap. 7.50 (ISBN 0-8063-0685-8). Genealog Pub.

--Probate & Orphans Court Records of Snyder County, Pennsylvania, 1772-1855. LC 74-16923. 87p. 1974. pap. 7.50 (ISBN 0-8063-0644-0). Genealog Pub.

Fisher, Charles H. Falconry Reminiscences. 1972. 45.00 (ISBN 0-914802-03-8). Falcon Head Pr.

Fisher, Charles O. & Murray, Richard C. Guide to Maryland Negligence Cases. 449p. 1982. 25.00 (ISBN 0-87215-472-6). Michie Co.

Fisher, Charles W. & Berliner, David C. Perspectives on Instructional Time. LC 84-15398. (Research on Teaching Monograph). 320p. 1985. text ed. 32.95X (ISBN 0-582-28414-7). Longman.

Fisher, Chris. Custom, Work & Market Capitalism: The Forest of Dean Colliers, 1788-1888. (Illus.). 203p. 1981. 27.00 (ISBN 0-7099-1001-0, Pub. by Croom helm). Longwood Pub Group.

Fisher, Clarence S. The Minor Cemetery at Giza. (Eckley B. Coxe Foundation Ser.: Vol. 1). (Illus.). xxiii, 170p. 1924. 25.00X (ISBN 0-686-11902-9). Univ Mus of U PA.

Fisher, Clay. The Apache Kid. 2nd ed. 192p. 1985. pap. 2.50 (ISBN 0-553-25137-6). Bantam.

--The Big Pasture. 192p. (Orig.). 1985. pap. 2.50 (ISBN 0-553-24828-6). Bantam.

Fisher, Clay C. New Concepts of Bible Mysteries & Eschatologies. LC 76-96074. 1969. pap. 2.50 (ISBN 0-686-00510-4). C C Fisher.

Fisher, Constance & Adams, Doug. Dancing with Early Christians. (Illus.). 176p. 1983. pap. 6.95 (ISBN 0-941500-30-6). Sharing Co.

Fisher, Constance L. Dancing the Old Testament: Christian Celebrations of Israelite Heritage for Worship & Education. Adams, Doug, ed. (Illus.). 1980. pap. 5.95 (ISBN 0-941500-07-1). Sharing Co.

--Music & Dance: In the Worship Program of the Church. (Orig.). 1981. pap. 2.50 (ISBN 0-941500-20-9). Sharing Co.

Fisher, D. A. & Burrow, G. N., eds. Perinatal Thyroid Physiology & Disease. LC 75-14333. 291p. 1975. 40.00 (ISBN 0-89004-044-3). Raven.

Fisher, D. A., jt. ed. see Williams, J. H.

Fisher, D. E. Environmental Law in Australia. (Australian Environment Ser.: No. 7). 197p. 1980. text ed. 36.25x (ISBN 0-7022-1456-6); pap. text ed. 18.00x (ISBN 0-7022-1457-4). U of Queensland Pr.

Fisher, D. Havelock, tr. see Boissier, Gaston.

Fisher, D. J. The Anglo-Saxon Age. LC 74-159804. (A History of England Ser.). 350p. 1973. 14.95 (ISBN 0-582-48084-1). Longman.

Fisher, D. J., jt. auth. see Kurz, W.

Fisher, Dalmar. Communication in Organizations. (Illus.). 480p. 1980. text ed. 25.95 (ISBN 0-8299-0374-7). West Pub.

Fisher, Danial, jt. auth. see Smith, Donald E.

Fisher, David. The Book of Madness. 1980. Repr. of 1975 ed. 8.95 (ISBN 0-918222-16-8). Apple Wood.

--Morality & the Bomb: An Ethical & Strategic Assessment. 144p. 1985. 25.00 (ISBN 0-312-54784-6). St Martin.

--Teachings. Monday, Stella, ed. LC 77-71441. (Illus.). 1979. 8.95 (ISBN 0-918510-02-3); signed ed. 10.95 (ISBN 0-685-93990-1); pap. 2.95 (ISBN 0-918510-01-5). Monday Bks.

--Teachings. (Illus.). 40p. lib. bdg. 8.95 (ISBN 0-918510-02-3); pap. 2.95 (ISBN 0-918510-01-5); signed cloth ed. 10.95 (ISBN 0-686-96877-8). Ross-Back Roads.

--The War Magician. 256p. 1983. 16.95 (ISBN 0-698-11140-0, Coward). Putnam Pub Group.

--The War Magician. 416p. 1983. pap. 3.50 (ISBN 0-425-06295-3). Berkley Pub.

Fisher, David & Bragonier, Reg. What's What: A Visual Glossary to the Physical World. 1982. pap. write for info. (ISBN 0-345-30302-4). Ballantine.

Fisher, David, jt. auth. see Bragonier, Reg.

Fisher, David, jt. auth. see Clouser, John W.

Fisher, David, jt. auth. see Lasorda, Tommy.

Fisher, David, jt. auth. see Luciano, Ron.

Fisher, David, jt. auth. see Read, Anthony.

Fisher, David & Bragonier, Reginald, Jr., eds. Qu'est-ce Que C'est. Fantapie, Alain & Brule, Marcel, trs. from Fr. (Illus.). 594p. 1984. 40.00 (ISBN 0-8437-3328-4). Hammond Inc.

--What's What in Sports: The Visual Glossary of the Sports World. LC 84-9082. (Illus.). 256p. 1984. 19.95 (ISBN 0-8437-3528-7); lexotone 14.95 (ISBN 0-8437-3529-5). Hammond Inc.

Fisher, David, jt. ed. see Barrett, Eric C.

Fisher, David A. World History for Christian Schools. (Heritage Studies for Christian Schools). (Illus.). 640p. (gr. 10). 1984. text ed. 26.60 (ISBN 0-89084-243-4); tchr's ed. 19.50 (ISBN 0-89084-244-2). Bob Jones Univ Pr.

Fisher, David E. Katie's Terror. LC 81-22299. 288p. 12.50 (ISBN 0-688-01114-4). Morrow.

--Katie's Terror. 272p. 1984. pap. 2.95 (ISBN 0-441-43126-7). Ace Bks.

--The Third Experiment: Is There Life on Mars? LC 84-21548. 192p. (gr. 7 up). 1985. 12.95 (ISBN 0-689-31080-3). Atheneum.

Fisher, David I. The Corporate Economist. (Report Ser.: No. 655). (Illus.). 55p. (Orig.). 1975. pap. 20.00 (ISBN 0-8237-0074-7); pap. 4.00 member. Conference Bd.

Fisher, David I., ed. Managing in Inflation. LC 78-63420. (Report Ser.: No. 750). 50p. 1978. pap. 15.00 (ISBN 0-8237-0186-7); pap. 5.00 member. Conference Bd.

Fisher, David L. Requiem for Heurtebise: Homage to Jean Cocteau. 1974. pap. 1.00 (ISBN 0-686-18853-5); signed ed. 2.00 (ISBN 0-686-18854-3). Man-Root.

Fisher, David W., jt. auth. see Dixon, Frank.

Fisher, David W., jt. ed. see Dixon, Frank J.

Fisher, Dennis & Peters, Charles W., eds. Comprehension & the Competent Reader: Inter-Specialty Perspectives. LC 80-39686. 176p. 1981. 29.95x (ISBN 0-03-059141-4). Praeger.

Fisher, Dennis, jt. ed. see Nodine, Calvin F.

Fisher, Dennis F., et al, eds. Eye Movements: Cognition & Visual Perception. LC 80-27876. (Eye Movements Ser.). 368p. 1981. text ed. 39.95x (ISBN 0-89859-084-1). L Erlbaum Assocs.

Fisher, Desmond. The Right to Communicate: A Status Report. (Reports & Papers on Mass Communication: No. 94). 55p. 1982. pap. 5.00 (ISBN 92-3-101991-0, U1238, UNESCO). Unipub.

Fisher, Dexter. The Third Woman: Minority Woman Writers of the United States. LC 79-87863. 1980. pap. text ed. 17.50 (ISBN 0-395-27707-8). HM.

Fisher, Dexter, ed. Minority Language & Literature: Retrospective & Perspective. 160p. 1977. pap. 10.00x (ISBN 0-87352-350-4, B101). Modern Lang.

Fisher, Dexter & Stepto, Robert B., eds. Afro-American Literature: The Reconstruction of Instruction. LC 78-62061. viii, 256p. 1979. pap. 12.50x (ISBN 0-87352-351-2, B102). Modern Lang.

Fisher, Dexter, jt. ed. see Brod, Richard I.

Fisher, Diana, jt. auth. see McDermott, Vern.

Fisher, Donald J. A Historical Study of the Migrant in California. LC 73-78057. pap. 11.00 (ISBN 0-88247-225-9). R & E Pubs.

Fisher, Dorothea F. Corneille & Racine in England. (Columbia University. Studies in Romance Philology & Literature: No. 5). Repr. of 1904 ed. 19.00 (ISBN 0-404-50605-4). AMS Pr.

--Four-Square. LC 71-167448. (Short Story Index Reprint Ser.). Repr. of 1949 ed. 18.00 (ISBN 0-8369-3974-3). Ayer Co Pubs.

Fisher, Dorothy C. Understood Betsy. (Illus.). 220p. (gr. 5-9). 1973. pap. 1.75 (ISBN 0-380-01595-1, 49692-5, Camelot). Avon.

--What Mothers Should Know about the Montessori Method of Education, 2 vols. (Illus.). 1985. Set. 117.85 (ISBN 0-89920-084-2). Am Inst Psych.

Fisher, Dorothy C., tr. see Tilgher, Adriano.

Fisher, Doug, ed. Why We Serve: Personal Stories of Catholic Lay Ministers. 176p. (Orig.). 1984. pap. 6.95 (ISBN 0-8091-2640-0). Paulist Pr.

Fisher, Douglas. Macroeconomic Theory: A Survey. LC 82-5767. 320p. 1983. 25.00 (ISBN 0-312-50329-6). St Martin.

--Monetary Theory & the Demand for Money. LC 77-15504. 278p. 1980. pap. 26.95x (ISBN 0-470-27023-3). Halsted Pr.

--Money, Banking & Monetary Policy. LC 79-90544. (Irwin Series in Economics). pap. 126.50 (ISBN 0-317-27999-8, 2055806). Bks Demand UMI.

Fisher, Douglas A. Steel: From the Iron Age to the Space Age. LC 67-8619. (Illus.). (gr. 7 up). 1967. PLB 11.89 (ISBN 0-06-021898-3). HarpJ.

Fisher, Ed L., jt. auth. see Braker, William P.

Fisher, Eddie. Eddie: My Life, My Loves. LC 81-47226. 360p. 1981. 14.38i (ISBN 0-06-014907-8, HarpT). Har-Row.

Fisher, Edgar J. New Jersey As a Royal Province, 1738-1776. LC 75-168028. (Columbia University. Studies in the Social Sciences: No. 107). Repr. of 1911 ed. 23.50 (ISBN 0-404-51107-4). AMS Pr.

Fisher, Edward C. & Reeder, Robert H. Vehicle Traffic Law. LC 74-77463. 360p. 1974. 12.50 (ISBN 0-912642-00-9). Traffic Inst.

Fisher, Edward C., ed. see Donigan, Robert L.

Fisher, Edward C., jt. auth. see Donigan, Robert L.

Fisher, Edward L., ed. Robotics & Industrial Engineering: Selected Readings. 268p. 1983. pap. 34.95 (ISBN 0-89806-045-1). Inst Indus Eng.

Fisher, Elaine Flory. Aesthetic Awareness & the Child. LC 77-83352. 333p. 1978. text ed. 24.95 (ISBN 0-87581-222-8). Peacock Pubs.

Fisher, Elizabeth. This World Does Not Belong to the Old Ladies. 28p. (Orig.). 1976. pap. 5.00 (ISBN 0-686-36716-2). Iron Mtn Pr.

--Woman's Creation. 504p. 1980. pap. 6.95 (ISBN 0-07-021105-1). McGraw.

Fisher, Ellen T. Greater Philadelphia Women's Yellow Pages, 1984-85. 64p. 1984. pap. 2.95 (ISBN 0-9611844-1-8). Greater PWYP.

--The Greater Philadelphia Women's Yellow Pages, 1983-1984. 44p. (Orig.). 1983. pap. 2.50 (ISBN 0-9611844-0-X). Greater PWYP.

--Greater Philadelphia Women's Yellow Pages, 1985-1986. 80p. 1985. pap. 32.95 (ISBN 0-317-29658-2). Greater PWYP.

Fisher, Eric, jt. auth. see Scott, John.

Fisher, Ernest A. Anglo-Saxon Towers. LC 76-77876. (Illus.). 1969. 17.95x (ISBN 0-678-05525-4). Kelley.

Fisher, Esther O., ed. Impact of Divorce on the Extended Family. LC 81-20207. (Journal of Divorce Ser.: Vol. 5, Nos. 1 & 2). 171p. 1982. text ed. 30.00 (ISBN 0-917724-43-7, B43). Haworth Pr.

--Therapists, Lawyers, & Divorcing Spouses. Fisher, Mitchell S. LC 82-15515. (Journal of Divorce Ser.: Vol. 6, Nos. 1-2). 138p. 1982. text ed. 30.00 (ISBN 0-86656-169-2, B169). Haworth Pr.

Fisher, Eugene. Faith Without Prejudice: Rebuilding Christian Attitudes Toward Judaism. LC 77-83550. 196p. 1977. pap. 2.95 (ISBN 0-8091-2064-X). Paulist Pr.

Fisher, Eugene J. Seminary Education & Christian-Jewish Relations: A Curriculum & Resource Handbook. 1983. 4.00 (ISBN 0-686-40267-7). Natl Cath Educ.

Fisher, Eugene J. & Polish, Daniel F., eds. The Formation of Social Policy in the Catholic & Jewish Tradition. new ed. LC 80-50268. 208p. text ed. 17.95 (ISBN 0-268-00953-8); pap. text ed. 8.95 (ISBN 0-268-00951-1). U of Notre Dame Pr.

--Liturgical Foundations of Social Policy in the Catholic & Jewish Traditions. LC 82-40378. 180p. 1983. text ed. 16.95 (ISBN 0-268-01267-9); pap. text ed. 9.95 (ISBN 0-268-01268-7). U of Notre Dame Pr.

Fisher, Eugenia M., jt. auth. see Fisher, Maurice D.

Fisher, Eunice, jt. ed. see Lock, Andrew.

Fisher, Evelyn G. Unfettered Has Nothing to Do with a Nude Bird. (Illus.). 192p. (Orig.). 1984. pap. 5.95 (ISBN 0-9614144-0-5). See-Saw Pr.

Fisher, F. G. International Bonds. 200p. 1981. 88.00 (ISBN 0-8002-3425-1). Intl Pubns Serv.

Fisher, Fay. Narrative Art in Medieval Romances. LC 72-188277. 1938. lib. bdg. 15.00 (ISBN 0-8414-0604-9). Folcroft.

Fisher, Florence. The Search for Anna Fisher. 224p. 1981. pap. 2.50 (ISBN 0-449-23473-8, Crest). Fawcett.

Fisher, Franklin E., jt. auth. see Faupel, Joseph F.

Fisher, Franklin M. Disequilibrium Foundations of Equilibrium Economics. LC 82-25105. (Econometric Society Monographs in Pure Theory). 240p. 1983. 34.50 (ISBN 0-521-24264-9). Cambridge U Pr.

--The Identification Problem in Econometrics. LC 75-23590. 218p. 1976. Repr. of 1966 ed. 14.00 (ISBN 0-88275-344-4). Krieger.

--Supply & Costs in the U. S. Petroleum Industry: Two Econometric Studies. LC 77-86394. (Resources for the Future, Inc. Publications). 192p. Repr. of 1964 ed. 42.50 (ISBN 0-404-60332-7). AMS Pr.

Fisher, Franklin M. & McGowan, John. Folded, Spindled & Mutilated: The Economics of U. S. vs IBM. Schmalensee, ed. (Regulation of Economic Activity Ser.: No. 7). (Illus.). 435p. 1983. 30.00x (ISBN 0-262-06086-8). MIT Pr.

Fisher, Franklin M. & McGowan, John J. Folded, Spindled & Mutilated: Economic Analysis & U. S. vs. IBM. 464p. 1985. pap. text ed. 9.95x (ISBN 0-262-56032-1). MIT Pr.

Fisher, Franklin M. & Shell, Karl. The Economic Theory of Price Indices: Two Essays on the Effects of Taste, Quality & Technological Change. (Economic Theory & Mathematical Economics Ser). 1972. 28.50 (ISBN 0-12-257750-7). Acad Pr.

Fisher, Franklin M., ed. Antitrust & Regulation: Essays in Memory of John J. McGowan. (Illus.). 328p. 1985. text ed. 35.00x (ISBN 0-262-06093-0). MIT Pr.

Fisher, Franklin M., et al. IBM & the U. S. Data Processing Industry: An Economic History. LC 83-3988. (Select Basic Industries Studies). (Illus.). 544p. 1983. 42.95x (ISBN 0-03-063059-2). Praeger.

Fisher, Fred. Brokers Beware: Selling Real Estate Within the Law. 220p. 1981. text ed. 19.95 (ISBN 0-8359-0569-1). Reston.

Fisher, Fred L., jt. auth. see Zicherman, Joseph B.

Fisher, Frederick V. Transformation of Job: A Tale of the High Sierras. facs. ed. LC 70-137729. (American Fiction Reprint Ser). 1900. 14.00 (ISBN 0-8369-7028-4). Ayer Co Pubs.

Fisher, G., jt. ed. see Barnes, J. G.

Fisher, G. H. Stud Poker Blue Book. pap. 2.95x (ISBN 0-685-22117-2). Wehman.

Fisher, G. Lawrence, jt. ed. see Gordon, Gerald.

Fisher, Gail T., jt. auth. see Volhard, Joachim J.

Fisher, Garth A. & Allsen, Philip E. Jogging. (Exploring Sports Ser.). 112p. 1984. pap. 4.95 (ISBN 0-697-00291-8). Wm C Brown.

Fisher, Gene & Chambers, Glen. The Revolution Myth. (Illus.). 161p. (Orig.). 1981. pap. 5.95 (ISBN 0-89084-152-7). Bob Jones Univ Pr.

Fisher, Gene, jt. auth. see Chambers, Glen.

Fisher, George. Fisher's Annual Report 1980: Fisher's Annual Reports. (Illus.). 108p. (Orig.). 1980. pap. 6.95 (ISBN 0-914546-33-3). Rose Pub.

--God Would Have Done It If He'd Had the Money. (Illus.). 1983. pap. 9.95 (ISBN 0-914546-49-X). Rose Pub.

Fisher, George, illus. The Old Guard Rest Home. 64p. 1984. pap. 6.95 (ISBN 0-914546-57-0). Rose Pub.

Fisher, George P. The Colonial Era. 1906. 15.00 (ISBN 0-8482-3972-5). Norwood Edns.

--History of Christian Doctrine. LC 75-41095. Repr. of 1901 ed. 41.50 (ISBN 0-404-14663-5). AMS Pr.

--History of the Christian Church. LC 75-41094. 48.50 (ISBN 0-404-14662-7). AMS Pr.

--The Reformation. LC 83-45660. Date not set. Repr. of 1906 ed. 54.50 (ISBN 0-404-19810-4). AMS Pr.

Fisher, Georgia A., ed. & intro. by. Everybody's Favorites Cookbook. (Illus.). 212p. (Orig.). pap. 8.95 (ISBN 0-930921-00-3). Comm Res OH.

Fisher, Glen. International Negotiation: A Cross Cultural Perspective. LC 81-85716. 69p. (Orig.). 1982. pap. text ed. 6.50 (ISBN 0-933662-24-6). Intercult Pr.

Fisher, Glen, jt. auth. see Jeffries, Ron.

Fisher, Glen W. Financing Local Improvements by Special Assessment. LC 74-18143. (Illus.). 59p. 1974. pap. 6.00 (ISBN 0-686-84375-4). Municipal.

Fisher, Glenn W. & Fairbanks, Robert P. Illinois Municipal Finance: A Political & Economic Analysis. LC 67-21852. (Illus.). 252p. 1968. 19.95x (ISBN 0-252-72373-2). U of Ill Pr.

Fisher, Glenn W., jt. auth. see Fishbane, Joyce O.

Fisher, Glenn W., jt. auth. see Walzer, Norman.

Fisher, Goerge, jt. auth. see Allin, Richard.

Fisher, Graham & Fisher, Heather. Monarch: The Life & Times of Elizabeth II. (Illus.). 220p. 1985. 15.95 (ISBN 0-88162-129-3, Pub. by Salem Hse Ltd). Merrimack Pub Cir.

Fisher, H., et al. Electronic Structure of Organic Compounds. (Topics in Current Chemistry: Vol. 24). 1971. pap. 18.90 (ISBN 0-387-05540-1). Springer-Verlag.

Fisher, H. A. Frederick William Maitland, Downing Professor of the Laws of England: A Bibliographical Sketch. LC 10-25073. (Historical Reprints in Jurisprudence & Classical Legal Literature Ser.). 183p. 1984. Repr. of 1910 ed. lib. bdg. 32.50 (ISBN 0-89941-344-7). W S Hein.

--History of England from the Accession of Henry Seventh to the Death of Henry Eighth, 1485-1547. LC 79-592. Repr. of 1906 ed. 35.00 (ISBN 0-527-00850-8). Kraus Repr.

--Paul Valery. LC 74-8243. 1973. lib. bdg. 8.50 (ISBN 0-8414-4189-8). Folcroft.

Fisher, H. J., jt. auth. see Hart, F. L.

Fisher, Hal, jt. auth. see Merrill, John C.

Fisher, Hank. The Floater's Guide to Montana. LC 79-52411. (Illus.). 160p. (Orig.). 1979. pap. 6.95 (ISBN 0-934318-00-X). Falcon Pr MT.

Fisher, Harold H. Famine in Soviet Russia, 1919-1923: The Operations of the American Relief Administration. facsimile ed. LC 75-148881. (Select Bibliographies Reprint Ser). Repr. of 1927 ed. 33.00 (ISBN 0-8369-5650-8). Ayer Co Pubs.

Fisher, Harold H., jt. auth. see Bunyan, James.

Fisher, Harold H., jt. auth. see Gankin, Olga H.

Fisher, Harold H., ed. American Research on Russia. LC 59-10870. pap. cancelled (ISBN 0-317-09290-1, 2015522). Bks Demand UMI.

Fisher, Harold W., jt. auth. see Williams, Robley C.

Fisher, Harrison. Blank Like Me. LC 79-92351. 52p. (Orig.). 1980. pap. 3.00 (ISBN 0-9602424-2-2). Paycock Pr.

--Collected Works, 6 vols. 600.00 (ISBN 0-87968-889-0). Gordon Pr.

--Curtains for You. LC 79-65656. (Orig.). 1980. pap. 5.95 perfect bdg. (ISBN 0-915380-10-2). Word Works.

--The Text's Boyfriend. (Burning Deck Poetry Ser.). 24p. (Orig.). 1980. pap. 10.00 signed ed (ISBN 0-930900-85-5). Burning Deck.

--U. H. F. O. 60p. (Orig.). 1982. pap. 4.50 (ISBN 0-933442-05-X). Dianas Bimonthly.

Fisher, Harry C. A. Mutt. An Original Compilation: First Collection of the Complete First Years of the Daily Strip, 1907-1908. Blackbeard, Bill, ed. LC 76-53040. (Classic American Comic Strips Ser.). (Illus.). 1977. 18.50 (ISBN 0-88355-635-9); pap. 10.00 (ISBN 0-88355-634-0). Hyperion Conn.

Fisher, Harvey I., jt. auth. see Goodman, Donald C.

Fisher, Harwood. Language & Logic In Personality & Society. 288p. 1985. 30.00x (ISBN 0-231-06012-2). Columbia U Pr.

Fisher, Heather. Riddle of the Runaway. (The Starlight Adventure Ser.). (Illus.). 306p. (gr. 7 up). 1985. pap. 2.95 (ISBN 0-14-031841-0, Puffin). Penguin.

Fisher, Heather, jt. auth. see Fisher, Graham.

Fisher, Helen E. The Sex Contract. LC 82-18126. (Illus.). 256p. 1983. pap. 7.95 (ISBN 0-688-01599-9, Quill NY). Morrow.

--The Sex Contract: The Evolution of Human Behavior. LC 81-11120. (Illus.). 256p. 1982. 13.50 (ISBN 0-688-00640-X). Morrow.

Fisher, Henry. Abroad with Mark Twain & Eugene Field. 1922. 20.00 (ISBN 0-8274-1814-0). R West.

Fisher, Henry G. The Renaissance Sackbut & Its Use Today. LC 84-62233. 71p. 1984. pap. 4.50 (ISBN 0-87099-412-3). Metro Mus Art.

Fisher, Herbert. Studies in Napoleonic Statesmanship: Germany. LC 68-25230. (World History Ser., No. 48). 1969. Repr. of 1903 ed. lib. bdg. 54.95x (ISBN 0-8383-0939-9). Haskell.

Fisher, Herbert A. Common Weal. facs. ed. LC 68-22911. (Essay Index Reprint Ser). 1924. 18.00 (ISBN 0-8369-0440-0). Ayer Co Pubs.

--History of England: From the Accession of Henry Seventh to the Death of Henry Eighth. LC 75-5625. (Political History of England Ser.: No. 5). 22.50 (ISBN 0-404-50775-1). AMS Pr.

--James Bryce, 2 vols. LC 79-114524. (Illus.). Repr. of 1927 ed. Set. lib. bdg. 30.50x (ISBN 0-8371-4797-2, FIJB). Greenwood.

--Medieval Empire, 2 Vols. LC 72-95147. Repr. of 1898 ed. 34.50 (ISBN 0-404-02398-3). AMS Pr.

--Pages from the Past. facs. ed. LC 75-90638. (Essay Index Reprint Ser). 1939. 18.00 (ISBN 0-8369-1260-8). Ayer Co Pubs.

--The Republican Tradition in Europe. facsimile ed. LC 75-179519. (Select Bibliographies Reprint Ser). Repr. of 1911 ed. 21.00 (ISBN 0-8369-6648-1). Ayer Co Pubs.

--Studies in History & Politics. facs. ed. LC 67-26740. (Essay Index Reprint Ser). 1920. 18.00 (ISBN 0-8369-0441-9). Ayer Co Pubs.

Fisher, Hilda B. Improving Voice & Articulation. 2nd ed. 1975. text ed. 25.50 (ISBN 0-395-19232-3). HM.

Fisher, Howard. Mapping Information. 1982. text ed. 35.00 (ISBN 0-89011-571-0). Abt Bks.

Fisher, Howard T. Mapping Information: The Graphic Display of Quantitative Information. (Illus.). 410p. 1984. Repr. of 1982 ed. lib. bdg. 42.50 (ISBN 0-8191-4075-9). U Pr of Amer.

Fisher, Humphrey J., tr. see Nachtigal, Gustav.

Fisher, Ida & Lane, Byron. The Widow's Guide to Life: How to Adjust-How to Grow. 224p. 1981. 13.95 (ISBN 0-13-959452-3, Spec); pap. 6.95 (ISBN 0-13-959445-0). P-H.

Fisher, Iosif Z. Statistical Theory of Liquids. Switz, Theodore M., tr. LC 64-22249. pap. 86.80 suppl. (ISBN 0-317-08823-8, 2020284). Bks Demand UMI.

Fisher, Ira, jt. auth. see Reinhart, Susan H.

Fisher, Irving. Inflation? 1979. Repr. of 1933 ed. lib. bdg. 17.50 (ISBN 0-8482-3955-5). Norwood Edns.

--Making of Index Numbers. 3rd ed. LC 67-28291. Repr. of 1927 ed. 37.50x (ISBN 0-678-00319-X). Kelley.

--Mathematical Investigations in the Theory of Value & Prices. Bd. with Appreciation & Interest (1896) 100p. LC 65-19655. 128p. Repr. of 1892 ed. 27.50x (ISBN 0-678-00082-4). Kelley.

--National Vitality, Its Wastes & Conservation. LC 75-17221. (Social Problems & Social Policy Ser.). 1976. Repr. of 1909 ed. 12.00x (ISBN 0-405-07492-1). Ayer Co Pubs.

--Nature of Capital & Income. LC 65-20921. Repr. of 1906 ed. 37.50x (ISBN 0-678-00112-X). Kelley.

--Purchasing Power of Money. 2nd ed. LC 63-21105. (Illus.). Repr. of 1922 ed. 37.50x (ISBN 0-678-00011-5). Kelley.

--The Rate of Interest: With a New Introduction by Donald Dewey. LC 82-48363. (Accountancy in Transition Ser.). 472p. 1982. lib. bdg. 55.00 (ISBN 0-8240-5314-1). Garland Pub.

--Theory of Interest. LC 56-4884. Repr. of 1930 ed. 37.50x (ISBN 0-678-00003-4). Kelley.

--The Theory of Interest: As Determined by Impatience to Spend Income & Opportunity to Invest It. LC 77-22591. (Illus.). Repr. of 1930 ed. 12.95x (ISBN 0-87991-864-0). Porcupine Pr.

Fisher, Isobel Y. & Dixson, Robert J. Beginning Lessons in English. rev. ed. (Illus.). 128p. 1983. Bk. A. pap. text ed. 4.25 (ISBN 0-88345-530-7, 21155). Bk. B. Regents Pub.

Fisher, J. & Dryer, R. Los Estados Unidos: Programa de Estudios Sociales. Yockstick, Elizabeth, ed. Olivares, Angelina S., tr. from Eng. 126p. (Span.). (gr. 5). 1981. Duplicate Masters 49.00 (ISBN 0-943068-17-7). Graphic Learning.

--United States Studies Program: Activity Manual. 2nd ed. Yockstick, Elizabeth, ed. (Illus.). 126p. (gr. 5). 1981. Duplication Masters 49.00 (ISBN 0-943068-16-9); Teacher's Guide 5.00 (ISBN 0-943068-69-X). Graphic Learning.

--World Studies Program: Activity Manual. Spanish ed. Irvin, J. L. & Yockstick, Elizabeth, eds. Orlando & Miller, M., trs. from Eng. (Illus.). 126p. (Span.). (gr. 6). 1981. Duplicate Masters 49.00 (ISBN 0-943068-08-8). Graphic Learning.

--World Studies Program: Activity Manual. rev. ed. (Illus.). 126p. (gr. 6). 1981. duplication masters 49.00 (ISBN 0-943068-07-X); tchr's. guide 5.00 (ISBN 0-943068-05-3). Graphic Learning.

Fisher, J. & Dryer, Rick. World Studies Program: Work-A-Text. rev. ed. Irvin, J. L. & Yockstick, Elizabeth, eds. (Illus.). 126p. (gr. 6). 1981. wkbk. 3.50 (ISBN 0-943068-06-1). Graphic Learning.

Fisher, J., et al. World Studies Program. Irvin, J. L. & Yockstick, Elizabeth, eds. (Work-A-Text Ser.). (Illus.). 1981. of 105 435.00 set (ISBN 0-943068-24-X). Graphic Learning.

Fisher, J. C. & Guerrerosantos, J., eds. Manual of Aesthetic Surgery. (Comprehensive Manuals of Surgical Specialties Ser.). (Illus.). 115p. 1985. 165.00 (ISBN 0-387-96045-7). Springer-Verlag.

Fisher, J. M. Mystic Gnosis. 1977. lib. bdg. 59.95 (ISBN 0-8490-2316-5). Gordon Pr.

Fisher, J. Patrick. Basic Medical Terminology. 2nd ed. 288p. 1983. pap. text ed. 15.67 scp (ISBN 0-672-61573-8); scp cassettes 290.40 (ISBN 0-672-61575-4); scp instr's. guide 3.67 (ISBN 0-672-61574-6). Bobbs.

Fisher, J. R. Clare Sewell Read, Eighteen Twenty-Six to Nineteen Five: A Farmers' Spokesman of the Late Nineteenth Century. (Occasional Papers in Economic & Social History: No. 8). 39p. 1975. pap. text ed. 4.25x (ISBN 0-900480-38-6). Humanities.

--Government & Society in Colonial Peru: The Intendant System 1784-1814. 289p. 1970. 46.00 (ISBN 0-485-13129-3, Pub. by Athlone Pr Ltd). Longwood Pub Group.

Fisher, J. W., ed. Kidney Hormones: Erythropoietin, Vol. 2. 1978. 99.50 (ISBN 0-12-257652-7). Acad Pr.

Fisher, Jack. Rough Guide to Mexico. (The Routledge Rough Guides Ser.). 232p. (Orig.). 1985. pap. 9.95 (ISBN 0-7102-0059-5). Routledge & Kegan.

Fisher, Jack & Gatland, Bruce. Electronics: From Theory into Practice, 2 vols. 2nd ed. 538p. 1976. Combined Ed. 41.00 (ISBN 0-08-019857-0); Vol. 1. pap. text ed. 17.00 (ISBN 0-08-019855-4); Vol. 2. pap. text ed. 17.00 (ISBN 0-08-019856-2). Pergamon.

Fisher, Jacob. The Response of Social Work to the Depression. 1980. lib. bdg. 25.00 (ISBN 0-8161-8413-5, Univ Bks). G K Hall.

--The Response of Social Work to the Depression. 288p. 1980. pap. 11.95x (ISBN 0-87073-891-7). Schenkman Bks Inc.

Fisher, Jamer E., jt. auth. see Christensen, James E.

Fisher, James. Power of the Presidency. 240p. 1983. 17.95 (ISBN 0-02-910520-X). ACE.

--Thorburn's Birds. (Illus.). 190p. 1985. pap. 12.95 (ISBN 0-7181-2183-X, Pub. by Michael Joseph). Merrimack Pub Cir.

Fisher, James & Flegg, James. Watching Birds. rev. ed. (Illus.). 1974. 10.00 (ISBN 0-85661-005-4, Pub. by T & A D Poyser). Buteo.

Fisher, James, jt. auth. see Lyle, Wes.

Fisher, James, ed. Thorburn's Birds. LC 75-34531. (Illus.). 186p. 1976. 27.95 (ISBN 0-87951-044-7). Overlook Pr.

Fisher, James A., Jr. In Answer to the Play: For Colored Girls...The Virtue of the Black Female Sex. Janrary, Theresa B., ed. LC 80-70834. 196p. (Orig.). 1983. pap. 6.95x (ISBN 0-933886-01-2). Black-A-Moors.

--The Plan of the Snake: A Look at Our Government Today. LC 79-51483. 94p. (Orig.). 1979. pap. 4.95 (ISBN 0-933886-00-4). Black-A-Moors.

Fisher, James E. Democracy & Mission Education in Korea. LC 70-176773. (Columbia University. Teachers College. Contributions to Education: No. 306). Repr. of 1928 ed. 22.50 (ISBN 0-404-55306-0). AMS Pr.

Fisher, James L. Application-Oriented Algebra: An Introduction to Discrete Mathematics. 1977. text ed. 28.95 scp (ISBN 0-7002-2504-8, HarpC). Har-Row.

Fisher, Jane. Home Town in the High Country. (Illus.). 216p. 1985. 15.48 (ISBN 0-912494-36-0); pap. 10.18 (ISBN 0-912494-37-9). Chalfant Pr.

Fisher, Janet Cameron, et al, eds. Building Bridges: Research & Practice in Teaching English As a Second Language. (On TESOL Ser.: '80). 250p. 1981. 9.50 (ISBN 0-318-16634-8). Tchrs Eng Spkrs.

Fisher, Jay M. The Prints of Edouard Manet. Bradley, B. J., ed. LC 85-80175. (Illus.). 128p. (Orig.). 1985. pap. 8.70 (ISBN 0-88397-083-X); pap. text ed. 14.00 (ISBN 0-317-20238-3). Intl Exhibit Foun.

--Theodore Chasseriau: Illustrations for Othello. LC 79-67570. 1980. pap. 13.50 (ISBN 0-912298-50-2). Baltimore Mus.

Fisher, Jay M. & Baxter, Colles. Felix Buhot, Peintre-Graveur: Prints, Drawings, & Paintings. LC 82-74446. (Illus.). 128p. 1983. pap. 15.50 (ISBN 0-912298-55-3). Baltimore Mus.

Fisher, Jean & Reynolds, Patti, eds. Cursive Writing. (Golden Step Ahead Workbooks). (Illus.). 36p. (gr. 2). 1984. 1.95 (ISBN 0-307-23555-6, Golden Bks). Western Pub.

--Manuscript Writing. (Golden Step Ahead Workbks.). (Illus.). 36p. (gr. 1). 1984. 1.95 (ISBN 0-307-23554-8, Golden Bks). Western Pub.

Fisher, Jean-Marie see Aamuna, pseud.

Fisher, Jean-Marie, ed. A Coloring Book of Poetry for Adults, 3 vols. (Illus.). 1976. pap. 3.00 (ISBN 0-685-83505-7); Vol. 1. (ISBN 0-917266-04-8); Vol. 2. (ISBN 0-917266-06-4); Vol. 3. (ISBN 0-917266-05-6). Vanilla.

Fisher, Jeffery. King Henry Fifth Notes. (Orig.). 1981. pap. 2.95 (ISBN 0-8220-0029-6). Cliffs.

--Major Barbara & Saint Joan: Notes. 82p. (Orig.). (gr. 11-12). 1983. pap. text ed. 2.95 (ISBN 0-8220-1154-9). Cliffs.

Fisher, Jeffrey. The Fish Book: How to Buy, Clean, Catch, Cook & Preserve Them. (Illus.). 128p. 1981. 9.95 (ISBN 0-87523-196-9). Emerson.

Fisher, Jeffrey & Roberts, James L. Beckett's Waiting for Godot, Endgame, & Other Plays Notes. (Cliff Notes Ser.). 64p. (Orig.). 1980. pap. text ed. 3.25 (ISBN 0-8220-1354-1). Cliffs.

Fisher, Jeffrey D. & Nadler, Arie, eds. New Directions in Helping: Vol. 1: Recipient Reactions to Aid. 1983. 39.50 (ISBN 0-12-257301-3). Acad Pr.

Fisher, Jeffrey D., et al. Environmental Psychology. 2nd ed. LC 83-12911. 472p. 1984. text ed. 31.95 (ISBN 0-03-059867-2). HR&W.

--New Directions in Helping: Vol. 2: Help Seeking. LC 83-11894. 1983. 39.50 (ISBN 0-12-257302-1). Acad Pr.

Fisher, Jeffrey D., et al, eds. New Directions in Helping: Applied Perspectives on Help-Seeking & Receiving, Vol. 3. 1983. 38.00 (ISBN 0-12-257303-X). Acad Pr.

Fisher, Jennifer. Braid Lace for Today. (Illus.). 112p. 1985. 14.95 (ISBN 0-85219-653-9, Pub. by Batsford England). David & Charles.

--Torchon Lace for Today. (Illus.). 1985. 19.95 (ISBN 0-85219-593-1). Branford.

Fisher, Jeremy, tr. see Potter, Beatrix.

Fisher, John. After Twelve Decades. rev. ed. 1980. pap. 0.75x (ISBN 0-88035-023-7). Human Kinetics.

--Body Magic. 1979. 10.00 (ISBN 0-8128-2330-3); pap. 6.95 (ISBN 0-8128-6088-8). Stein & Day.

--Body Magic. LC 78-6387. (Illus.). 158p. 1980. pap. 6.95 (ISBN 0-8128-6088-8). Stein & Day.

--The English Works of John Fisher, Bishop of Rochester. Mayor, J. E., ed. (EETS, ES Ser.: Nos. 27, 117). 1950. Repr. of 1876 ed. Pt. 1. 78.50 (ISBN 0-527-00239-9); Pt. 2. 12.00 (ISBN 0-527-00240-2). Kraus Repr.

--George Formby. (Entertainers Ser.). (Illus.). 96p. 1975. 8.50x (ISBN 0-7130-0144-5, Pub. by Woburn Pr England). Biblio Dist.

--John Fisher's Magic Book. (Illus.). (gr. 5-8). 1975. pap. 1.95 (ISBN 0-13-510222-7, Pub. by Treehouse). P-H.

--Lexical Affiliations of Vegliote. 249p. 1976. 16.50 (ISBN 0-8386-7796-7). Fairleigh Dickinson.

--This Treatise Concernynge the Fruytfull Saynges of Davyd..Was Made & Compyled by..John Fyssher..Bysshop of Rochester. LC 79-84106. (English Experience Ser.: No. 925). 296p. 1979. Repr. of 1509 ed. lib. bdg. 28.00 (ISBN 90-221-0925-9). Walter J Johnson.

Fisher, John, jt. auth. see Ellingham, Mark.

Fisher, John, ed. Essays on Aesthetics: Perspectives on the Work of Monroe C. Beardsley. 312p. 1983. 29.95 (ISBN 0-87722-287-8). Temple U Pr.

--Perceiving Artworks. (Philosophical Monographs: 3rd Ser.). 246p. 1980. 27.95 (ISBN 0-87722-164-2). Temple U Pr.

Fisher, John, jt. ed. see Wiener, Philip P.

Fisher, John B. & Fisher, Roscoe B. The Jacob Fisher Family, Nineteen Fifty-Nine - Nineteen Seventy-Nine, Vol. II. LC 79-55703. 352p. 1980. 15.00 (ISBN 0-9612308-2-7). J B Fisher.

Fisher, John B., ed. Cheely, Morrison, Gaither, Sharpe, Beall, Chambliss, Jacobs Connections. 700p. 1976. pap. 32.00 (ISBN 0-9612308-0-0). J B Fisher.

Fisher, John B., et al, eds. The Ancestors & Descendants of Abraham (Braun) Brown, The Miller & Jacob (Braun) Brown, The Wagonmaker 1703-1983. 580p. 1984. 37.50 (ISBN 0-9612308-3-5). J B Fisher.

Fisher, John C. Linguistics in Remedial English. (Janua Linguarum, Ser. Practica: No. 47). (Orig.). 1966. pap. text ed. 10.40x (ISBN 90-2790-659-9). Mouton.

Fisher, John H. & Bornstein, Diane. In Forme of Speche Is Chaunge: Readings in the History of the English Language. (Illus.). 384p. 1984. pap. text ed. 13.50 (ISBN 0-8191-3904-1). U Pr of Amer.

Fisher, John H., ed. see Chaucer, Geoffrey.

Fisher, John H., et al. An Anthology of Chancery English. LC 84-3516. 440p. 1984. text ed. 49.50x (ISBN 0-87049-433-3). U of Tenn Pr.

Fisher, John J. Victorious Journey: A Physician-Pilot Battles Cancer During a Worldwide Tour. (Illus.). 188p. 1983. 11.95 (ISBN 0-682-49978-1). Exposition Pr FL.

Fisher, John J., III, jt. auth. see Rubin, Richard R.

Fisher, John S. A Builder of the West: The Life of General William Jackson Palmer. Bruchey, Stuart, ed. LC 80-1306. (Railroads Ser.). (Illus.). 1981. Repr. of 1939 ed. lib. bdg. 35.00x (ISBN 0-405-13775-3). Ayer Co Pubs.

Fisher, John S. & Dolan, Robert, eds. Beach Processes & Coastal Hydrodynamics. (Benchmark Papers in Geology Ser.: Vol. 39). 1977. 63.00 (ISBN 0-12-786471-7). Acad Pr.

Fisher, John Scott. Creative Realities. 64p. 5.50 (ISBN 0-86690-103-5, 1115-01). Am Fed Astrologers.

Fisher, John W. Fatigue & Fracture in Steel Bridges: Case Studies. LC 83-23495. 315p. 1984. 45.95x (ISBN 0-471-80469-X, Pub. by Wiley-Interscience). Wiley.

Fisher, John W. & Struik, John H. Guide to Design Criteria for Bolted & Riveted Joints. LC 73-17158. 314p. 1974. 59.50 (ISBN 0-471-26140-8, Pub. by Wiley-Interscience). Wiley.

Fisher, Jon. The Last Frontiers on Earth. 2nd rev. ed. (Illus.). 1985. pap. 8.95 (ISBN 0-915179-24-5). Loompanics.

--Uninhabited & Deserted Islands. (Illus.). 1983. pap. 7.95 (ISBN 0-317-03309-3). Loompanics.

Fisher, Jon, ed. see Rayo.

Fisher, Joseph, jt. auth. see Rice, Donald E.

Fisher, Julie A. & Putham, Santra T. Gerontologic Nursing Handbook. 1985. write for info. (ISBN 0-87527-340-8). Green.

Fisher, K. D. & Nixon, A. U., eds. The Science of Life: Contributions of Biology to Human Welfare. LC 77-957. 382p. 1977. pap. 11.50x (ISBN 0-306-20025-2, Rosetta). Plenum Pub.

Fisher, Karen. Quick Fix Decorating Ideas. LC 83-23775. 176p. 1984. pap. 8.95 (ISBN 0-452-25519-8, Plume). NAL.

Fisher, Katherine & Kay, Elizabeth. The Craft of Smocking. (Illus.). 1979. pap. 5.95 (ISBN 0-684-16082-X, SL841, ScribT). Scribner.

Fisher, Ken. Isaac Asimov Presents Superquiz II. LC 83-14425. 192p. (Orig.). 1983. pap. 7.95 (ISBN 0-934878-30-7). Dembner Bks.

--Isaac Asimov Presents Superquiz: The Fun Game of Q & A's. LC 81-17386. 192p. (Orig.). 1982. pap. 7.95 (ISBN 0-934878-12-9). Dembner Bks.

--Super Quiz I. Asimov, Isaac, ed. pap. 7.95 (ISBN 0-934878-12-9). Dembner Bks.

--Super Quiz II. Asimov, Isaac, ed. pap. 7.95 (ISBN 0-934878-30-7). Dembner Bks.

Fisher, Kenneth & Nixon, Ann, eds. The Science of Life: Contributions of Biology to Human Welfare. LC 75-5777. 382p. 1975. 37.50x (ISBN 0-306-34501-3, Plenum Pr). Plenum Pub.

Fisher, Kenneth L. Super Stocks. LC 84-70258. 270p. 1984. 19.95 (ISBN 0-87094-552-1). Dow Jones-Irwin.

Fisher, Kenneth P. & Moyer, D. David. Land Parcel Identifiers for Information Systems. 596p. 1973. 15.00 (ISBN 0-910058-59-8, 765-0027); pap. 7.50 (ISBN 0-910058-58-X). Am Bar Foun.

Fisher, L. Foundations for Christian Schools: Teacher's Master Curriculum, 2 vols. (English Skills for Christian Schools Ser.). (Illus.). 1062p. (gr. k-4). 1985. Set. tchr's ed 100.00 (ISBN 0-89084-276-0). Bob Jones Univ Pr.

Fisher, L. E. The Background of the Revolution for Mexican Independence. 1976. lib. bdg. 59.95 (ISBN 0-8490-1469-7). Gordon Pr.

Fisher, Lance J., ed. see Gallaudet, Edward M.

Fisher, Lawrence. Industrial Marketing: An Analytical Approach to Planning & Execution. 2nd ed. 270p. 1975. text ed. 36.75x (ISBN 0-220-66292-4, Pub. by Busn Bks England). Brookfield Pub Co.

Fisher, Lawrence & Lorie, James H. A Half Century of Returns on Stocks & Bonds: Rates of Return on Investments in Common Stocks & on U.S. Treasury Securities, 1926-1976. new ed. (Illus.). 1977. 32.50 (ISBN 0-918584-01-9). U Chicago Grad Sch Busn.

Fisher, Lawrence E. Colonial Madness: Mental Health in the Barbadian Social Order. (Crime, Law & Deviance Ser.). 250p. 1985. 32.00 (ISBN 0-8135-1059-7). Rutgers U Pr.

Fisher, Leonard E. Boxes! Boxes! LC 83-14761. (Illus.). 32p. (ps-1). 1984. 9.95 (ISBN 0-670-18334-2, Viking Kestrel). Viking.

--The Factories. LC 79-2092. (Nineteenth Century America). (Illus.). 64p. (gr. 5 up). 1979. reinforced bdg. 9.95 (ISBN 0-8234-0367-X). Holiday.

--The Hospitals. LC 79-22357. (Nineteenth Century America). (Illus.). 64p. (gr. 5 up). 1980. reinforced bdg. 7.95 (ISBN 0-8234-0405-6). Holiday.

--The Newspapers. LC 80-8812. (Nineteenth Century America). (Illus.). 64p. (gr. 5 up). 1981. reinforced bdg. 7.95 (ISBN 0-8234-0387-4). Holiday.

--Noonan: A Novel about Baseball, ESP, & Time Warps. (Illus.). 128p. (gr. 5 up). 1981. pap. 1.95 (ISBN 0-380-53355-3, 53355-3, Camelot). Avon.

--Olympians: Great Gods & Goddesses of Ancient Greece. LC 84-516. (Illus.). 32p. (gr. 1-4). 1984. reinforced bdg. 14.95 (ISBN 0-8234-0522-2). Holiday.

--The Railroads. LC 79-1458. (A Nineteenth Century America Ser.). (Illus.). 64p. (gr. 5 up). 1979. reinforced bdg. 9.95 (ISBN 0-8234-0352-1). Holiday.

--The Schools. LC 82-18710. (Nineteenth Century America). (Illus.). 64p. (gr. 5 up). 1983. reinforced binding 10.95 (ISBN 0-8234-0477-3). Holiday.

--The Sports. LC 80-16467. (Nineteenth Century America). (Illus.). 64p. (gr. 5 up). 1980. reinforced bdg. 7.95 (ISBN 0-8234-0419-6). Holiday.

--Star Signs. LC 83-305. (Illus.). 32p. (gr. 1-4). 1983. reinforced bdg. 13.95 (ISBN 0-8234-0491-9). Holiday.

--The Statue of Liberty. LC 85-42878. (Illus.). 64p. (gr. 3-7). 1985. reinforced bdg. 12.95 (ISBN 0-8234-0586-9). Holiday.

--Storm at the Jetty. (Illus.). 32p. (gr. k up). 1981. 9.95 (ISBN 0-670-67214-9). Viking.

--Symbol Art. (Illus.). (YA) (gr. 10 up). 1985. 12.95 (ISBN 0-318-12067-4). Four Winds Pr.

--Symbol Art: Thirteen Squares, Circles & Triangles from Around the World. LC 85-42805. (Illus.). 64p. 1985. PLB 12.95 (ISBN 0-02-735270-6, Four Winds Pr). Macmillan.

--The Unions. LC 81-6632. (Nineteenth Century America Bk.). (Illus.). 64p. (gr. 5 up). 1982. reinforced bdg. 9.95 (ISBN 0-8234-0434-X). Holiday.

Fisher, Leonard E., illus. & adapted by. The Seven Days of Creation. LC 81-2952. (Illus.). 32p. (ps-3). 1981. reinforced bdg. 12.95 (ISBN 0-8234-0398-X). Holiday.

Fisher, Leslie E., jt. auth. see Wallace, Benjamin.

Fisher, Lillian E. Intendant System in Spanish America. LC 77-91350. 1970. Repr. of 1929 ed. text ed. 15.00x (ISBN 0-87752-033-X). Gordian.

--Violet Richardson Ward: Founder-President of Soroptimist. 1983. 10.95 (ISBN 0-533-05563-6). Vantage.

Fisher, Lizette A. Mystic Vision in the Grail Legend & in the Divine Comedy. LC 79-168029. Repr. of 1917 ed. 16.50 (ISBN 0-404-02389-4). AMS Pr.

Fisher, Lloyd & McDonald, John. Fixed Effects Analysis of Variance. (Probability & Mathematical Statistics). 1978. 39.50 (ISBN 0-12-257350-1). Acad Pr.

Fisher, Lois. Little White Lies. (Sweet Dreams Ser.). 1983. pap. 2.25 (ISBN 0-553-24293-8). Bantam.

--A Peking Diary. LC 78-21424. 1979. 10.95 (ISBN 0-312-59997-8). St Martin.

Fisher, Lois I. I Can't Forget You. (Sweet Dreams Ser.). 144p. (Orig.). (gr. 5 up). 1984. pap. text ed. 1.95 (ISBN 0-553-23940-6). Bantam.

--Puffy P. Pushycat, Problem Solver. LC 82-19833. (Illus.). 128p. (gr. 4 up). 1983. 8.95 (ISBN 0-396-08119-3). Dodd.

--Rachel Vellars, How Could You? 144p. (gr. 4 up). 1984. PLB 8.95 (ISBN 0-396-08327-7). Dodd.

--Rachel Vellars, How Could You? 160p. (gr. 4 up). 1985. pap. 3.95 (ISBN 0-396-08741-8). Dodd.

--Radio Robert. 128p. (gr. 4 up). 1985. 9.95 (ISBN 0-396-08503-2). Dodd.

--Sarah Dunes, Weird Person. LC 80-2780. 176p. (gr. 5 up). 1981. PLB 7.95 (ISBN 0-396-07929-6). Dodd.

--Wretched Robert. LC 81-17562. 112p. (gr. 4 up). 1982. PLB 7.95 (ISBN 0-396-08039-1). Dodd.

--Wretched Robert. 112p. (gr. 4 up). 1985. pap. 3.50 (ISBN 0-396-08634-9). Dodd.

Fisher, Louis. Constitutional Conflicts Between Congress & the President. LC 83-60462. 390p. text ed. 40.00x (ISBN 0-691-07680-4); pap. 8.95x (ISBN 0-691-02233-X). Princeton U Pr.

--Presidential Spending Power. LC 75-4408. 300p. 1975. 37.50 (ISBN 0-691-07575-1). Princeton U Pr.

Fisher, Louise. President & Congress. LC 78-142362. 1972. 17.00 (ISBN 0-02-910320-7); pap. text ed. 4.95 (ISBN 0-02-910340-1). Free Pr.

Fisher, Lucille. Bible Truths for Christian Schools. (Illus.). 407p. (gr. k-4). 1984. tchr's ed. 34.50 (ISBN 0-89084-241-8). Bob Jones Univ Pr.

--Heritage Studies for Christian Schools, One: Families in America. (Illus.). 127p. (gr. 1). 1979. text ed. 10.60 (ISBN 0-89084-094-6); tchr's ed. 25.50 (ISBN 0-89084-095-4). Bob Jones Univ Pr.

Fisher, Lucretia. The Butterfly & the Stone. LC 80-29260. (Illus.). 48p. (Orig.). (ps up). 1981. pap. 2.95 (ISBN 0-916144-69-0). Stemmer Hse.

--Two Monsters: A Fable. LC 76-21684. (Illus.). 48p. (ps up). 1976. pap. 2.95 (ISBN 0-916144-08-9). Stemmer Hse.

Fisher, M., jt. ed. see Battaglia, J.

Fisher, M. B., ed. see Pliny.

Fisher, M. F. The Art of Eating. 1976. pap. 9.95 (ISBN 0-394-71399-0, Vin). Random.

--Cooking of Provincial France. LC 67-20204. (Foods of the World Ser.). (Illus.). (gr. 7 up). 1968. lib. bdg. 19.94 (ISBN 0-8094-0056-1, Pub. by Time-Life). Silver.

--A Cordiall Water: A Garland of Odd & Old Receipts to Assuage the Ills of Man & Beast. LC 80-28409. 160p. 1981. 12.50 (ISBN 0-86547-035-9); pap. 6.50 (ISBN 0-86547-036-7). N Point Pr.

--Here Let Us Feast. rev. ed. 352p. 1986. pap. 11.50 (ISBN 0-86547-206-8). N Point Pr.

--Not Now, But Now. New ed. LC 82-81499. 264p. 1982. pap. 9.25 (ISBN 0-86547-072-3). N Point Pr.

--Sister Age. LC 82-48880. 1983. 12.95 (ISBN 0-394-53066-7). Knopf.

--Sister Age. 1984. pap. 5.95 (ISBN 0-394-72385-6, Vin). Random.

--With Bold Knife & Fork. LC 79-15562. 1979. pap. 4.95 (ISBN 0-399-50397-8, Perigee). Putnam Pub Group.

Fisher, M. F., jt. auth. see Clancy, Judith.

Fisher, M. F., tr. see Brillat-Savarin.

Fisher, M. F. K. Among Friends. 320p. 1983. pap. 10.00 (ISBN 0-86547-116-9). N Point Pr.

--As They Were. LC 81-48130. 1982. 13.95 (ISBN 0-394-52400-4). Knopf.

Fisher, M. Frances, jt. auth. see Newberry, Lynn.

Fisher, M. K. Two Towns in Provence: Map of Another Town & a Considerable Town. LC 83-6901. (Illus.). 512p. 1983. pap. 7.95 (ISBN 0-394-71631-0, Vin). Random.

Fisher, M. M. & Rankin, J. G., eds. Alcohol & the Liver. LC 77-8648. (Hepatology Ser.: Vol. 3). 414p. 1977. 55.00 (ISBN 0-306-34803-9, Plenum Pr). Plenum Pub.

Fisher, M. M. & Roy, C. C., eds. Pediatric Liver Disease. (Hepatology: Vol. 5). 300p. 1983. 42.50x (ISBN 0-306-41164-4, Plenum Pr). Plenum Pub.

Fisher, M. M., jt. ed. see Goresky, C. A.

Fisher, M. M., et al, eds. Gallstones. LC 79-13122. (Hepatology Ser.: Vol. 4). 453p. 1979. 59.50x (ISBN 0-306-40179-7, Plenum Pr). Plenum Pub.

Fisher, M. Roy. Titian's Assistants During the Later Years. LC 76-23618. (Outstanding Dissertations in the Fine Arts Ser.). 1977. lib. bdg. 68.00 (ISBN 0-8240-2689-6). Garland Pub.

Fisher, Mae. Lively Lipreading Lessons. LC 77-93029. 1978. pap. text ed. 6.00 (ISBN 0-88200-114-0, B0222). Alexander Graham.

Fisher, Margaret. Palm Leaf Patterns: A New Approach to Clothing Design. LC 76-57189. (Illus.). 20p. 1977. pap. 5.95 (ISBN 0-915572-20-6). Panjandrum.

Fisher, Margaret, jt. ed. see Withington, W. A.

Fisher, Margaret B. The Promise of Love in the West: Stories of the Frontier Spirit in America. (Illus.). 50p. (Orig.). 1984. pap. 5.00 (ISBN 0-934996-24-5). Am Stud Pr.

Fisher, Margaret B., jt. auth. see Cooper, Russell M.

Fisher, Margaret E., jt. auth. see O'Brien, Edward L.

Fisher, Margaret W., jt. ed. see Bondurant, Joan V.

Fisher, Marguerite J., ed. Communist Doctrine & the Free World. LC 78-90506. Repr. of 1952 ed. lib. bdg. 15.00x (ISBN 0-8371-2153-1, FICD). Greenwood.

Fisher, Marilyn, jt. auth. see Battaglia, John.

Fisher, Marlene. The Wisdom of the Heart: A Study of the Works of Mulk Raj Anand. xiv, 207p. 1985. text ed. 27.50x (ISBN 0-86590-724-2, Pub. by Sterling Pubs India). APT Bks.

Fisher, Marquita O. Jacqueline Cochran: First Lady of Flight. LC 72-14368. (Americans All Ser.). (Illus.). 96p. (gr. 3-6). 1973. PLB 7.98 (ISBN 0-8116-4580-0). Garrard.

Fisher, Martin & Stricker, George, eds. Intimacy. LC 82-12260. 488p. 1982. 42.50x (ISBN 0-306-40921-6). Plenum Pub.

Fisher, Mary. A Group of French Critics. LC 73-37155. (Essay Index Reprint Ser.). Repr. of 1897 ed. 20.00 (ISBN 0-8369-2496-7). Ayer Co Pubs.

Fisher, Mary, jt. ed. see Miller, Elizabeth W.

Fisher, Mary L. Guide to State Legislative Materials. rev. ed. LC 83-15938. (AALL Publ. Ser.: No. 15). 1983. loose-leaf 32.50x (ISBN 0-8377-0113-9). Rothman.

Fisher, Mary P., jt. auth. see Zelanski, Paul.

Fisher, Maurice D. & Fisher, Eugenia M. The Early Education Connection: An Instructional Resource for Teachers & Parents of Preschool & Kindergarten Children. 54p. (Orig.). 1981. pap. text ed. 9.00 (ISBN 0-910609-01-2). Reading Tutor.

--Gifted Education: Critical Evaluations of Important Books on Identification, Program Development & Research. 40p. (Orig.). 1982. pap. text ed. 9.00 (ISBN 0-910609-02-0). Reading Tutor.

--Identifying & Teaching the Gifted, American Education's Stepchildren. 42p. (Orig.). 1981. pap. text ed. 9.00 (ISBN 0-910609-00-4). Reading Tutor.

Fisher, Maxine. The Indians of New York City. 1980. 17.00x (ISBN 0-8364-0593-5). South Asia Bks.

Fisher, Mike, et al. Mental Health Social Work Observed. (National Institute Social Services Library: No. 45). 240p. 1983. text ed. 28.50x (ISBN 0-04-360061-1); pap. text ed. 12.95x (ISBN 0-04-360062-X). Allen Unwin.

Fisher, Mildred L. Albatross of Midway Island: A Natural History of the Laysan Albatross. LC 75-93881. (Illus.). 171p. 1970. 6.95 (ISBN 0-8093-0426-0). S Ill U Pr.

Fisher, Mitchell S. see Fisher, Esther O.

Fisher, Morris, compiled by. Provinces & Provincial Capitals of the World. 2nd ed. LC 83-22125. 258p. 1985. 19.50 (ISBN 0-8108-1758-6). Scarecrow.

Fisher, Muriel. A Touch of Nature. (Illus.). 91p. 1982. 29.95 (ISBN 0-00-216979-7, Pub. by W Collins New Zealand). Intl Spec Bk.

Fisher, N. M., jt. ed. see Goldsworthy, Peter R.

Fisher, Nancy. Five Years in My Garden. (Orig.). 1981. 9.95 (ISBN 0-938946-00-5). Putterin.

Fisher, Neal F. Context for Discovery. LC 81-7929. (Into Our Third Century Ser.). (Orig.). 1981. pap. 4.95 (ISBN 0-687-09620-0). Abingdon.

Fisher, Nigel. Harold Macmillan: A Biography. LC 81-48509. (Illus.). 416p. 1982. 19.95 (ISBN 0-312-36322-2). St Martin.

Fisher, Nora. Fifteen Hundred Years of Andean Weaving. (Illus.). 1972. pap. 1.25 (ISBN 0-89013-053-1). Museum NM Pr.

Fisher, O. Collector's Guide to Model Aero Engines. (Illus.). 132p. 1985. pap. 7.95 (ISBN 0-85242-492-2, Pub. by Argus). Aztex.

Fisher, O. C. Cactus Jack. 1982. 15.95 (ISBN 0-87244-066-4). Texian.

Fisher, P. S., jt. auth. see Unger, E. A.

Fisher, P. S., et al, eds. Advances in Distributed Processing Management, Vol. 2. LC 81-649059. (Advances in Library EDP Management: 1-604). 298p. 1983. 41.95x (ISBN 0-471-26232-3, Pub. by Wiley Heyden). Wiley.

Fisher, Pat, jt. auth. see Gitter, Kurt A.

Fisher, Patricia, ed. see Considine, Tim.

Fisher, Patricia A. Gingerbread Girl. 192p. (Orig.). 1985. pap. 6.95 (ISBN 0-310-45561-8, 12343P). Zondervan.

Fisher, Patty & Bender, A. E. The Value of Food. 3rd ed. (Illus.). 1979. pap. 8.95x (ISBN 0-19-859465-8). Oxford U Pr.

Fisher, Paul. The Hawks of Fellheath. LC 79-22080. 252p. (gr. 5-9). 1980. 9.95 (ISBN 0-689-30741-1). Atheneum.

--Mont Cant Gold. LC 80-23851. 264p. (gr. 5-9). 1981. PLB 10.95 (ISBN 0-689-30808-6, Argo). Atheneum.

Fisher, Paul, jt. auth. see Berston, Hyman M.

Fisher, Paul, jt. auth. see Rix, Sara E.

Fisher, Paul R. The Ash Staff. (MagicQuest Ser.: No. 4). 176p. 1984. pap. 2.25 (ISBN 0-441-03115-3, Pub. by Tempo). Ace Bks.

--The Hawks of Fellheath. (MagicQuest Ser.: No. 7). 176p. 1984. pap. 2.25 (ISBN 0-441-31906-8, Pub. by Tempo). Ace Bks.

--Mont Cant Gold. (MagicQuest Ser.: No. 14). 224p. 1985. pap. 2.25 (ISBN 0-441-53602-6). Ace Bks.

--The Princess & the Thorn. (MagicQuest Ser.: No. 10). 256p. 1984. pap. 2.25 (ISBN 0-441-67918-8). Ace Bks.

Fisher, Peg. Sucessful Telemarketing Manual. 300p. 1985. 91.50 (ISBN 0-85013-152-9). Dartnell Corp.

Fisher, Pete. Dreamlovers. LC 81-97. 224p. (Orig.). 1982. pap. 8.95x (ISBN 0-933322-07-0). Sea Horse.

Fisher, Peter. Gay Mystique. LC 73-186149. 1972. pap. 1.95 (ISBN 0-8128-7005-0). Stein & Day.

--Prescription for National Health Insurance. LC 72-77266. (Illus.). 158p. 1972. 10.00 (ISBN 0-88427-007-6). North River.

Fisher, Peter & Rubin, Marc. Special Teachers-Special Boys. LC 78-19417. 1979. pap. 4.95 (ISBN 0-312-75152-4). St Martin.

Fisher, Peter, tr. see Davidson, Hilda.

Fisher, Peter, tr. see Davidson, Hilda E.

Fisher, Philip. Hard Facts: Setting & Form in the American Novel. LC 84-18999. 1985. 18.95 (ISBN 0-19-503528-3). Oxford U Pr.

--Making Up Society: The Novels of George Eliot. LC 81-50639. 252p. 1981. 23.95x (ISBN 0-8229-3800-6). U of Pittsburgh Pr.

Fisher, Philip A. Common Stocks & Uncommon Profits. rev. ed. 192p. 1984. Repr. of 1958 ed. 14.95 (ISBN 0-931133-00-9). PSR Pubns.

Fisher, Phyllis K. Los Alamos Experience. (Illus.). 240p. 1985. 12.95 (ISBN 0-87040-623-X, Dist. by Harper & Row). Japan Pubns USA.

Fisher, R. Digital Applications in Television Receivers. Date not set. text ed. cancelled (ISBN 0-408-01149-1). Focal Pr.

--Surgical Treatment on Varicose Veins. 180p. 1981. 60.00 (ISBN 3-456-80764-3, Pub. by Holdan Bk Ltd UK). State Mutual Bk.

Fisher, R. & Kruchten, P. French-English, English-French Dictionary of Computer Science, 2 vols. (Eng. & Fr.). Set. 50.00 (ISBN 0-686-46529-6). Heinman.

Fisher, R. K. Library Services to University Extension Students in the USA. 1978. 30.00x (ISBN 0-905984-17-X, Pub. by Brit Lib England). State Mutual Bk.

Fisher, R. L. Prince of Whales. LC 84-28538. 160p. 1985. 12.95 (ISBN 0-88184-127-7). Carroll & Graf.

Fisher, R. S. & Petty, C. S., eds. Forensic Pathology. 201p. 1980. text ed. 33.00 (ISBN 0-7194-0058-9, Pub. by Castle Hse England). J K Burgess.

Fisher, R. V. & Schmincke, H. U. Pyroclastic Rocks. (Illus.). 350p. 1984. 49.50 (ISBN 0-387-12756-9). Springer-Verlag.

Fisher, Ralph E. Vanishing Markers: Memories of Boston & Maine Railroading 1946-1952. LC 76-15577. 1976. 16.95 (ISBN 0-8289-0287-9). Greene.

Fisher, Randall, ed. Kansas Workers' Compensation Practice Manual. 1984. 100.00 (ISBN 0-318-04149-9). KS Bar CLE.

Fisher, Randall M. Rhetoric & American Democracy: Black Protest Through Vietnam Dissent. LC 84-29115. 314p. (Orig.). 1985. lib. bdg. 26.50 (ISBN 0-8191-4559-9); pap. text ed. 14.25 (ISBN 0-8191-4560-2). U Pr of Amer.

Fisher, Raymond. The Voyage of the Semen Dezhnev in 1648. 1981. 40.00x (ISBN 0-904180-12-3, Pub. by Hakluyt Soc England). State Mutual Bk.

Fisher, Raymond H. Bering's Voyages: Whither & Why. LC 77-73307. (Illus.). 240p. 1978. 25.00x (ISBN 0-295-95562-7). U of Wash Pr.

Fisher, Reginald G. Some Geographic Factors That Influenced the Ancient Populations of the Chaco Canyon, New Mexico. LC 34-27678. 1982. lib. bdg. 19.95x (ISBN 0-89370-734-1). Borgo Pr.

Fisher, Rex, jt. ed. see Hesseltine, William B.

Fisher, Rhoda L., jt. auth. see Fisher, Seymour.

Fisher, Ricahrd B. Aids: Your Questions Answered. 128p. (Orig.). 1984. pap. 3.95 (ISBN 0-907040-29-2, Pub. by GMP England). Alyson Pubns.

Fisher, Richard B. Brain Games: 134 Original Scientific Games That Reveal How the Mind Works. LC 81-84110. (Illus.). 256p. (Orig.). 1982. 16.95 (ISBN 0-8052-3800-X); pap. 7.95 (ISBN 0-8052-0707-4). Schocken.

--A Dictionary of Body Chemistry. (Illus.). 208p. pap. 6.95 (ISBN 0-586-08382-0, Pub. by Granada England). Academy Chi Pubs.

--Dictionary of Mental Health. 268p. (Orig.). 1983. pap. 5.95 (ISBN 0-586-08339-1, Pub. by Granada England). Academy Chi Pubs.

--Syrie Maugham. (Illus.). 104p. 1979. 22.00 (ISBN 0-7156-1307-3, Pub. by Duckworth England). Biblio Dist.

Fisher, Richard B. & Christie, George A. A Dictionary of Drugs: The Medicines You Use. rev. ed. LC 76-12241. 1976. 7.95x (ISBN 0-8052-3638-4). Schocken.

Fisher, Richard H., jt. auth. see Davis, William S.

Fisher, Rick, jt. auth. see Yanda, Bill.

Fisher, Robert. En Espiritu y en Verdad. (Orig., Span.). pap. text ed. 5.95 (ISBN 0-87148-313-0). Pathway Pr.

--The Family & the Church. LC 77-99163. 1978. 5.25 (ISBN 0-87148-334-3); pap. 4.25 (ISBN 0-87148-335-1). Pathway Pr.

--Let the People Decide: Neighborhood Organizing in America. (Social Movements Past & Present Ser.). 295p. 1984. 18.95 (ISBN 0-8057-9706-8, Twayne); pap. 7.95 (ISBN 0-8057-9709-2, Twayne). G K Hall.

Fisher, Robert, ed. Amazing Monsters: Verses to Thrill & Chill. Allen, Rowena, tr. & illus. (Illus.). 96p. (ps-5). 1982. 9.95 (ISBN 0-571-11850-X). Faber & Faber.

--Ghosts Galore: Haunting Verse. (Illus.). 96p. (gr. 2-10). 1983. 10.95 (ISBN 0-571-13100-X). Faber & Faber.

--In Spirit & in Truth. (Orig.). pap. text ed. 5.95 (ISBN 0-87148-438-2). Pathway Pr.

--Pressing Toward the Mark. LC 83-63384. 176p. 1983. pap. text ed. 8.95 (ISBN 0-87148-714-4). Pathway Pr.

Fisher, Robert & Romanofsky, Peter, eds. Community Organization for Urban Social Change: A Historical Perspective. LC 80-21498. (Illus.). 280p. 1981. lib. bdg. 29.95 (ISBN 0-313-21427-1, RCO/). Greenwood.

Fisher, Robert A. An Introduction to RPG: RPG II Programming. LC 74-9537. 393p. 1975. pap. 36.50x (ISBN 0-471-26001-0). Wiley.

--Optical Phase Conjugation. (Quantum Electronics Princples & Applications Ser.). 612p. 1983. 59.50 (ISBN 0-12-257740-X). Acad Pr.

Fisher, Robert C. Japan 1985. (Fisher Annotated Travel Guides Ser.). 448p. 1984. 13.95 (ISBN 0-8116-0073-4, Fisher). NAL.

Fisher, Robert C. & Ziebur, Allen D. Integrated Algebra, Trigonometry & Analytic Geometry. 4th ed. (Illus.). 560p. 1982. 29.95 (ISBN 0-13-468967-4). P-H.

Fisher, Robert C., ed. see Antrobus, Edmund.

Fisher, Robert C., ed. see Bostwick, Jeri.

Fisher, Robert C., ed. see Brooks, Pat & Brooks, Lester.

Fisher, Robert C., ed. see Eliot, Alex.

Fisher, Robert C., ed. see Hesse, Georgia I.

Fisher, Robert C., ed. see Koenig, Helmut.

Fisher, Robert C., ed. see Lawes, Diane N.

Fisher, Robert C., ed. see Lemkowitz, Florence.

Fisher, Robert C., ed. see McNair, Georgia T.

Fisher, Robert C., ed. see Pezzini, Wilma.

Fisher, Robert C., ed. see Sherley, Connie.

Fisher, Robert C., ed. see Turnbull, Robert.

Fisher, Robert C., et al. Europe 1985. (Fisher Annotated Travel Guides Ser.). 800p. 1984. 15.95 (ISBN 0-8116-0064-5). NAL.

Fisher, Robert L., jt. auth. see Edwards, Clifford H.

Fisher, Robert M. Twenty Years of Public Housing. LC 75-29075. (Illus.). 303p. 1975. Repr. of 1959 ed. lib. bdg. 22.50x (ISBN 0-8371-8411-8, FIPH). Greenwood.

Fisher, Robert T. Classical Utopian Theories of Education. 1963. 9.95x (ISBN 0-8084-0394-X); pap. 6.95x (ISBN 0-8084-0395-8). New Coll U Pr.

Fisher, Robin & Johnston, Hugh, eds. Captain James Cook & His Times. LC 78-73989. (Illus.). 288p. 1979. 19.95x (ISBN 0-295-95654-2). U of Wash Pr.

Fisher, Robin, ed. see Walker, Alexander.

Fisher, Roger. Improving Compliance with International Law. LC 80-14616. (Procedural Aspects of International Law Ser.: Vol. 14). 370p. 1981. 35.00x (ISBN 0-8139-0859-0). U Pr of Va.

--International Conflict for Beginners. 15.25 (ISBN 0-8446-5851-0). Peter Smith.

--International Conflicts for Beginners. (Illus.). 1970. pap. 5.50xi (ISBN 0-06-131911-2, TB1911, Torch). Har-Row.

Fisher, Roger & Ury, William. Getting to Yes: Negotiating Agreement Without Giving in. 160p. 1981. 11.95 (ISBN 0-395-31757-6). HM.

--Getting to Yes: Negotiating Agreement Without Giving In. 1983. pap. 5.95 (ISBN 0-14-006534-2). Penguin.

Fisher, Ron. Still Waters, White Waters: Exploring America's Rivers & Lakes. LC 76-56997. (Special Publications Ser.: No.12). (Illus.). 200p. 1976. 14.95 (ISBN 0-295-95988-6). U of Wash Pr.

Fisher, Ron & Whitlock, Charles R. Beyond the Rockies: A Narrative History of Idaho. (Illus.). (gr. 4-9). 1983. text ed. 16.50 (ISBN 0-941734-00-5); write for info. tchr's. ed. Alpha & Omega.

Fisher, Ronald. The Genetical Theory of Natural Selection. 2nd ed. 1958. pap. 7.95 (ISBN 0-486-60466-7). Dover.

Fisher, Ronald A. Statistical Methods & Scientific Inference. rev. ed. 1973. 14.95x (ISBN 0-02-844740-9). Hafner.

--Statistical Methods for Research Workers. 14th ed. (Illus.). 1973. 19.95x (ISBN 0-02-844730-1). Hafner.

Fisher, Ronald J. Social Psychology: An Applied Approach. LC 81-51855. 712p. 1982. text ed. 24.95 (ISBN 0-312-73473-5); instr's. manual avail.; study guide 7.95 (ISBN 0-312-73475-1). St Martin.

Fisher, Ronald M. Animals in Winter. Crump, Donald J., ed. LC 82-47859. (Books for Young Explorers: Set 9). 32p. (gr. 3-8). 1982. PLB 10.95 (ISBN 0-87044-453-0). Natl Geog.

Fisher, Ronald M. see National Geographic Society.

Fisher, Roscoe B., jt. auth. see Fisher, John B.

Fisher, Roscoe B., ed. see Scheer, George F., et al.

Fisher, Rosie. Rooms to Grow Up In. (Illus.). 128p. 1985. 16.95 (ISBN 0-88162-084-X, Pub. by Salem Hse Ltd). Merrimack Pub Cir.

Fisher, Roy. Poems, Nineteen Fifty-Five to Nineteen Eighty. 1980. 27.95x (ISBN 0-19-211935-4). Oxford U Pr.

Fisher, Roy & Wilson, Chas. Authority or Freedom? 222p. 1982. text ed. 36.50x (ISBN 0-566-00593-X). Gower Pub Co.

Fisher, Royal P. Information Systems Security. (Illus.). 208p. 1984. text ed. 34.95 (ISBN 0-13-464727-0). P-H.

Fisher, Rudolph. The Conjure-Man Dies. LC 78-140605. 320p. Repr. of 1932 ed. 9.00 (ISBN 0-405-02800-8). Ayer Co Pubs.

--Walls of Jericho. LC 69-18590. (American Negro: His History & Literature Ser., No. 2). 1969. Repr. of 1928 ed. 25.00 (ISBN 0-405-01862-2). Ayer Co Pubs.

Fisher, Rudolph W., jt. auth. see Shepard's & McGraw-Hill.

Fisher, Russ. Crossovers. (Laughter Library). (Orig.). 1979. pap. 1.95 (ISBN 0-8431-0531-3). Price Stern.

Fisher, Russell S., jt. ed. see Spitz, Werner U.

Fisher, Ruth. Twilight Tales of the Black Baganda: Traditional History of Bunyoro-Kitara. 2nd ed. (Illus.). 198p. 1970. Repr. of 1911 ed. 30.00x (ISBN 0-7146-1868-3, F Cass Co). Biblio Dist.

Fisher, S. & Freedman, A. M., eds. Opiate Addiction: Origins & Treatment. LC 73-19073. (Series in General Psychiatry). 247p. 1974. 11.95x (ISBN 0-470-26153-6). Halsted Pr.

Fisher, S. C. see Haines, Thomas H.

Fisher, S. G. Men, Women & Manners in Colonial Times. 59.95 (ISBN 0-8490-0609-0). Gordon Pr.

Fisher, S. W. & Jerome, J. W. Minimum Norm Extremals in Function Spaces: With Applications to Classical & Modern Analysis. (Lecture Notes in Mathematics: Vol. 479). viii, 209p. (Orig.). 1975. pap. 16.00 (ISBN 0-387-07394-9). Springer-Verlag.

Fisher, Sam S., ed. Rarefied Gas Dynamics: Parts I & II. LC 81-7913. (Illus.). 1248p. 1981. Set. 109.00 (ISBN 0-915928-51-5, PAAS74); members 65.00 (ISBN 0-317-32184-6). AIAA.

Fisher, Sara E. & Stahl, Rachel K. The Amish School. LC 84-81142. (People's Place Booklet: No. 6). (Illus.). 96p. (Orig.). 1985. pap. 3.95 (ISBN 0-934672-17-2). Good Bks PA.

Fisher, Sethard. Black Elected Officials in California. LC 77-90366. 1978. pap. 9.95 perfect bdg. (ISBN 0-88247-512-6). R & E Pubs.

--From Margin to Mainstream: The Social Progress of Black Americans. LC 81-13852. 192p. 1982. 31.95 (ISBN 0-03-059968-7). Praeger.

Fisher, Seymour. Body Consciousness: You Are What You Feel. 192p. 1973. 12.95 (ISBN 0-13-078527-X, Spec). P-H.

--Body Experience in Fantasy & Behavior. LC 71-111878. (Century Psychology Ser). 1970. 34.50x (ISBN 0-89197-046-0); pap. text ed. 10.95x (ISBN 0-89197-683-3). Irvington.

--Development & Structures of the Body Image, 2 vols. Vol. I, 384 pgs. text ed. 39.95 (ISBN 0-89859-684-X); Vol. II, 568 pgs. text ed. 60.00 (ISBN 0-89859-699-8); Set. text ed. 80.00 (ISBN 0-89859-700-5). L Erlbaum Assocs.

Fisher, Seymour & Cleveland, Sidney E. Body Image & Personality. 2nd ed. LC 68-19449. 1968. pap. 7.95 (ISBN 0-486-21947-X). Dover.

--Body Image & Personality. 2nd rev. ed. 12.00 (ISBN 0-8446-2063-7). Peter Smith.

Fisher, Seymour & Fisher, Rhoda L. Pretend the World Is Funny & Forever: A Psychological Analysis of Comedians, Clowns, & Actors. LC 80-7777. 288p. 1981. text ed. 24.95 (ISBN 0-89859-073-6). L Erlbaum Assocs.

Fisher, Seymour & Greenberg, Roger P. The Scientific Credibility of Freud's Theories & Therapy. 502p. 1985. 30.00x (ISBN 0-231-06214-1); pap. 14.50x (ISBN 0-231-06215-X). Columbia U Pr.

Fisher, Sharon G., jt. auth. see Carkhuff, Robert R.

Fisher, Shirley. Stress & the Perception of Control. 288p. 1984. text ed. 39.95 (ISBN 0-86377-006-1). L Erlbaum Assocs.

Fisher, Sidney G. Quaker Colonies. 1919. 8.50x (ISBN 0-686-83720-7). Elliots Bks.

--Trial of the Constitution. LC 70-164511. (American Constitutional & Legal History Ser.). 1972. Repr. of 1864 ed. lib. bdg. 45.00 (ISBN 0-306-70281-9). Da Capo.

--Trial of the Constitution. LC 69-18977. Repr. of 1862 ed. 25.00x (ISBN 0-8371-0896-9, FIC&). Greenwood.

Fisher, Stanley. Standards Relating to Pretrial Court Proceedings. LC 76-12476. (IJA-ABA Juvenile Justice Standards Project Ser.). 160p. 1980. 22.50 (ISBN 0-88410-227-0); pap. 12.50 (ISBN 0-88410-811-2). Ballinger Pub.

Fisher, Stephen. GED Social Studies Test Preparation Guide: High School Equivalency Examination. (Cliff Test Preparation Ser.). 218p. (Orig.). (gr. 10 up). 1980. pap. 3.95 (ISBN 0-8220-2012-2). Cliffs.

Fisher, Stephen D. Function Theory on Planar Domains: A Second Course in Complex Analysis. LC 82-20106. (Pure & Applied Mathematics Ser.). 269p. 1983. 40.25x (ISBN 0-471-87314-4, Pub. by Wiley-Interscience). Wiley.

Fisher, Stephen H. Commonwealth Caribbean. LC 79-53429. (World Education Ser.). (Illus.). 240p. (Orig.). 1979. pap. text ed. 6.00 (ISBN 0-910054-55-X). Am Assn Coll Registrars.

Fisher, Stephen H., jt. auth. see Frey, James S.

Fisher, Steven V. & Helm, Phala A. Comprehensive Rehabilitation of Burns. 440p. 1984. lib. bdg. 40.00 (ISBN 0-683-03242-9). Williams & Wilkins.

Fisher, Sue & Todd, Alexander. The Social Organization of Doctor-Patient Communication. 269p. (Orig.). 1983. pap. 14.95 (ISBN 0-15-599067-5). Ctr Appl Ling.

Fisher, Sue & Todd, Alexander D. Discourse & Institutional Authority. Freedle, Roy O., ed. (Advances in Discourse Processes Ser.: Vol. 19). 288p. 1986. text ed. 32.50 (ISBN 0-89391-367-7); pap. 18.95. Ablex Pub.

Fisher, Susan M., jt. auth. see Apfel, Roberta J.

Fisher, Sydney G. The Making of Pennsylvania. 1896. 30.00 (ISBN 0-8482-3991-1). Norwood Edns.

--Men, Women & Manners in Colonial Times, 2 Vols. LC 70-95776. 1969. Repr. of 1897 ed. Set. 45.00x (ISBN 0-8103-3567-0). Gale.

--The Struggle for American Independence, 2 vols. fascimile ed. LC 78-37341. (Select Bibliographies Reprint Ser). Repr. of 1908 ed. Set. 64.00 (ISBN 0-8369-6688-0). Ayer Co Pubs.

--The Struggle for American Independence, Vol. I. LC 78-37341. (Illus.). 574p. Repr. of 1908 ed. text ed. 28.00 (ISBN 0-8290-0498-X). Irvington.

--The Struggle for American Independence, Vol. II. LC 78-37341. (Illus.). 585p. Repr. of 1908 ed. lib. bdg. 28.00 (ISBN 0-8290-0499-8). Irvington.

Fisher, Sydney G; see Johnson, Allen & Nevins, Allan.

Fisher, Sydney N. The Middle East: A History. 3rd ed. (Illus.). 1978. text ed. 27.00x (ISBN 0-394-32098-0, KnopfC). Knopf.

--The Military in the Middle East: Problems in Society & Government. LC 63-9001. (Ohio State University Graduate Institute for World Affairs Ser.: No. 1). pap. 36.80 (ISBN 0-317-09530-7, 2000511). Bks Demand UMI.

Fisher, Sydney N., ed. France & the European Community. LC 64-64416. 190p. 1965. 5.00 (ISBN 0-8142-0049-4). Ohio St U Pr.

--New Horizons for the United States in World Affairs. LC 66-63003. 174p. 1966. 5.00 (ISBN 0-8142-0050-8). Ohio St U Pr.

--Social Forces in the Middle East. LC 68-23289. (Illus.). 1968. Repr. of 1955 ed. lib. bdg. 20.00x (ISBN 0-8371-0074-7, FIME). Greenwood.

Fisher, T. M. Images. 1978. softcover 1.50 (ISBN 0-686-23104-X). Ghost Dance.

Fisher, T. Richard. Workbook & Manual Introduction to Horticulture. 3rd ed. 1982. pap. text ed. 11.25x (ISBN 0-89917-366-7). TIS Inc.

Fisher, T. W. & Orth, Robert. The Marsh Flies of California: Diptera, Sciomyzidae. (The California Insect Survey Ser.: Vol. 24). 128p. 1982. 21.00x (ISBN 0-520-09665-7). U of Cal Pr.

Fisher, Terry. International Students' Guide to Cooking Without Getting Caught. Carr, Sally B., ed. LC 76-18503. 1976. pap. 9.95 (ISBN 0-87949-055-1). Ashley Bks.

Fisher, Thomas. Negro's Memorial, or Abolitionist's Catechism. LC 74-75809. 1969. Repr. of 1825 ed. 19.00 (ISBN 0-8337-1133-4). B Franklin.

Fisher, Thomas G. Alarm & Interlock Systems. 1984. Instr. Guide: 32p. pap. text ed. 10.00x (ISBN 0-87664-737-9); Student Text: 232p. pap. text ed. 32.95x (ISBN 0-87664-736-0). Instru Soc.

Fisher, Thomas R. Industrial Disputes & Federal Legislation. LC 68-58571. (Columbia University. Studies in the Social Sciences: No. 467). Repr. of 1940 ed. 26.00 (ISBN 0-404-51467-7). AMS Pr.

Fisher, Tom & Smith, Tracey L. Icebreaker: A Manual For Public Speaking. (Illus.). 131p. (Orig.,). 1985. pap. text ed. 7.95x (ISBN 0-88133-126-0). Waveland Pr.

Fisher, Trevor. Communications. (History in Focus Ser.). (Illus.). 72p. (gr. 7-12). 1985. 14.95 (ISBN 0-7134-4631-5, Pub. by Batsford England). David & Charles.

Fisher, Vardis. Children of God. 1977. 12.95 (ISBN 0-918522-50-1). O L Holmes.

--City of Illusion. (Illus.). 400p. 1983. pap. 2.50 (ISBN 0-441-10706-0, Pub. by Charter Bks). Ace Bks.

--Dark Bridwell. 1979. write for info. (ISBN 0-918522-58-7); pap. 5.95 (ISBN 0-686-60831-3). O L Holmes.

--Love & Death. 14.95 (ISBN 0-88411-558-5, Pub. by Aeonian Pr). Amereon Ltd.

--The Mothers. 1976. Repr. of 1943 ed. lib. bdg. 18.95x (ISBN 0-89190-831-5, Pub. by River City Pr). Amereon Ltd.

--The Mothers. 1979. 9.95 (ISBN 0-686-60830-5); pap. 4.95 (ISBN 0-918522-55-2). O L Holmes.

--Mountain Man. 1976. Repr. of 1967 ed. lib. bdg. 17.95 (ISBN 0-89190-832-3, Pub. by River City Pr). Amereon Ltd.

--Mountain Man. 1977. 8.95 (ISBN 0-918522-52-8). O L Holmes.

--Mountain Man. 320p. (gr. 10 up). 1983. pap. 3.50 (ISBN 0-671-47672-6, 42288). PB.

--Pemmican. 341p. Repr. of 1956 ed. lib. bdg. 18.95 (ISBN 0-89190-833-1, Pub. by River City Pr). Amereon Ltd.

--Pemmican. 1977. 8.95 (ISBN 0-918522-54-4). O L Holmes.

--Suicide or Murder. 1978. pap. 2.95 (ISBN 0-918522-57-9). O L Holmes.

--Tale of Valor. 1976. Repr. of 1958 ed. lib. bdg. 23.95 (ISBN 0-89190-834-X, Pub. by River City Pr). Amereon Ltd.

Fisher, Vardis & Holmes, Opal L. Gold Rushes & Mining Camps of the Early American West. LC 68-15028. (Illus.). 1968. 22.95 (ISBN 0-87004-043-X). Caxton.

Fisher, Vardis, et al. Way Out: Libertarian & Mutualist Essays on Free Banking, Free Land & Individualism. 1979. lib. bdg. 59.95 (ISBN 0-87700-267-3). Revisionist Pr.

Fisher, Vera, jt. auth. see Davis, Harold T.

Fisher, W. One Hundred Years of Music Publishing in the U. S. 59.95 (ISBN 0-8490-0768-2). Gordon Pr.

--A String of Chinese Pearls: Ten Tales of Chinese Girls Ancient & Modern. lib. bdg. 79.95 (ISBN 0-87968-518-2). Krishna Pr.

Fisher, W. A. Engineering for Nautical Students. 4th ed. 299p. 1973. 16.50x (ISBN 0-85174-090-1). Sheridan.

Fisher, W. A., jt. ed. see Byrne, D.

Fisher, W. B. The Middle East: A Physical, Social, & Regional Geography. 7th ed. (Illus.). 1978. 25.00x (ISBN 0-416-71520-6, NO. 2778); pap. 25.00x (ISBN 0-416-71510-9, NO. 2817). Methuen Inc.

--The Oil States. (Illus.). 72p. (gr. 9-12). 1980. 14.95 (ISBN 0-7134-2477-X, Pub. by Batsford England). David & Charles.

Fisher, W. B., jt. auth. see Clarke, J. I.

Fisher, W. D. Burns & the Bible: A Series of Parallels to Show Lovers of Burns the Inspiration He Found in the Bible, & to Show Lovers of the Bible How Much of Its Spirit They Will Find in Burns. LC 77-1459. 1977. lib. bdg. 15.00 (ISBN 0-8414-4167-7). Folcroft.

Fisher, W. L. & Brown, L. F., Jr. Clastic Depositional Systems - a Genetic Approach to Facies Analysis an Annotated Outline & Bibliography. 230p. 1972. pap. 7.50. Bur Econ Geology.

Fisher, W. L. & McGowen, J. H. Depositional Systems in the Wilcox Group of Texas & Their Relationship to Occurrence of Oil & Gas. (Geological Circular Ser.: GC 67-4). 1982. Repr. 1.50 (ISBN 0-686-29326-6, GC 67-4). Bur Econ Geology.

Fisher, W. L. & Rodda, P. U. Lower Cretaceous Sands of Texas: Stratigraphy & Resources. (Report of Investigations: RI 59). (Illus.). 116p. 1967. 1.75 (ISBN 0-686-29340-1). Bur Econ Geology.

Fisher, W. L., et al. Delta Systems in the Exploration for Oil & Gas: Syllabus for Research Colloquium Held in Austin, August 1969. (Illus.). 212p. 1982. Repr. of 1969 ed. 6.00 (ISBN 0-318-03366-6). Bur Econ Geology.

--Evolution of Athleta Petrosa Stock (Eocene, Gastropoda) of Texas. (Pub. Ser: 6413). (Illus.). 117p. 1964. 4.00 (ISBN 0-318-03318-6). Bur Econ Geology.

Fisher, W. R., tr. see Schimper, A. F.

Fisher, Wallace E. All the Good Gifts: On Doing Bible Stewardship. LC 79-50077. 1979. pap. 4.95 (ISBN 0-8066-1702-0, 10-0227). Augsburg.

--A New Climate for Stewardship. LC 76-109. 128p. 1976. pap. 4.35 (ISBN 0-687-27723-X). Abingdon.

--Who Dares to Preach? The Challenge of Biblical Preaching. LC 79-54112. 200p. (Orig.). 1979. pap. 7.50 (ISBN 0-8066-1769-1, 10-7076). Augsburg.

Fisher, Walter. Clustering & Aggregation in Economics. LC 68-55610. pap. 52.00 (ISBN 0-317-19876-9, 2023095). Bks Demand UMI.

Fisher, Walter D. Statistics Economized: Basic Statistics for Economics & Business. LC 81-40114. (Illus.). 282p. (Orig.). 1981. pap. text ed. 12.75 (ISBN 0-8191-1745-5). U Pr of Amer.

Fisher, Walter R., ed. Rhetoric: a Tradition in Transition. 315p. 1974. 12.50x (ISBN 0-87013-188-5). Mich St U Pr.

Fisher, Wesley A. The Soviet Marriage Market: Mate Selection in Russia & the USSR. LC 78-19737. 320p. 1980. 42.95 (ISBN 0-03-045346-1). Praeger.

Fisher, Wesley A., jt. ed. see Yanowitch, Murray.

Fisher, William A. Notes on Music in Old Boston. LC 74-27340. Repr. of 1918 ed. 15.00 (ISBN 0-404-12914-5). AMS Pr.

--One Hundred & Fifty Years of Music Publishing in the U. S. 1783--1933. 1981. Repr. lib. bdg. 29.00 (ISBN 0-686-71937-9). Scholarly.

--Seventy Negro Spirituals, for High Voice. LC 72-1637. Repr. of 1926 ed. 29.00 (ISBN 0-404-09921-1). AMS Pr.

Fisher, William E. Transvaal & the Boers, a Brief History. LC 70-98719. Repr. of 1896 ed. 17.50x (ISBN 0-8371-2767-X, FIT&). Greenwood.

Fisher, William H. Free at Last: A Bibliography of Martin Luther King, Jr. LC 77-22202. 175p. 1977. 15.00 (ISBN 0-8108-1081-6). Scarecrow.

--The Invisible Empire: A Bibliography of the Ku Klux Klan. LC 80-10133. 212p. 1980. lib. bdg. 17.50 (ISBN 0-8108-1288-6). Scarecrow.

Fisher, William P., ed. Creative Marketing for the Foodservice Industry: A Practitioner's Handbook. 296p. 1982. 32.95x (ISBN 0-471-08111-6, Pub. by Wiley-Interscience). Wiley.

Fisher, William W. GEO Cepts 1. rev. ed. Charbonneau, Louis, ed. (GEO Cepts Program Ser.). (Illus.). (gr. 5 up). 1977. student wkbk. 7.00x (ISBN 0-87453-111-X, 82011). Denoyer.

--GEO Cepts 1. rev. ed. Charbonneau, Louis, ed. (GEO Cepts Program Ser.). (Illus.). 1977. tchr's ed. 23.00 (ISBN 0-87453-112-8, 82012). Denoyer.

Fisheries Technology Service. Echo Sounding & Sonar for Fishing. 1980. pap. 50.00x (ISBN 0-85238-110-7, Pub. by Fishing News England). State Mutual Bk.

Fishing News Books Ltd., ed. Introduction to Fishery by-Products. 208p. 1981. 70.00x (ISBN 0-686-86774-2, Pub. by Fishing News England). State Mutual Bk.

--Seine Fishing: Bottom Fishing with Rope Warps & Wing Trawls. 224p. 1981. 50.00x (ISBN 0-85238-113-1, Pub. by Fishing News England). State Mutual Bk.

--Study of the Sea: The Development of Marine Research Under the Auspices of the International Council for the Exploration of the Sea. 272p. 1981. 90.00x (ISBN 0-85238-112-3, Pub. by Fishing News England). State Mutual Bk.

Fishing News Books Ltd. Staff, ed. Scallops & the Diver-Fisherman. 144p. 1981. 40.00x (ISBN 0-85238-114-X, Pub. by Fishing News England). State Mutual Bk.

Fishkin, Howard. Taxpayers Survival Manual. 1979. pap. 2.95 (ISBN 0-933586-06-X). Book Promo Pr.

Fishkin, James, jt. ed. see Laslett, Peter.

Fishkin, James S. Beyond Subjective Morality: Ethical Reasoning & Political Philosophy. LC 83-14701. 224p. 1984. 23.50x (ISBN 0-300-03048-7). Yale U Pr.

--Justice, Equal Opportunity & the Family. LC 82-10939. 207p. 1983. text ed. 25.00x (ISBN 0-300-02865-2). Yale U Pr.

--Justice, Equal Opportunity, & the Family. LC 82-10939. 207p. 1984. pap. 8.95x (ISBN 0-300-03249-8, Y-507). Yale U Pr.

--The Limits of Obligation. LC 81-13046. (Illus.). 23.50x (ISBN 0-300-02747-8); pap. 6.95x, 1983 (ISBN 0-300-01523-2, Y-462). Yale U Pr.

--Tyranny & Legitimacy: A Critique of Political Theories. LC 79-11177. 176p. 1979. text ed. 16.00x (ISBN 0-8018-2206-8); pap. text ed. 5.95x (ISBN 0-8018-2256-4). Johns Hopkins.

Fishkin, Lois & Dimarco, Susan. The Not-Strictly Vegetarian Cookbook. 4th ed. LC 82-73064. (Illus.). 260p. (Orig.). 1982. pap. 9.95 (ISBN 0-916870-49-9). Creative Arts Bk.

--The Super Natural Dessert Cookbook. LC 84-45095. (Illus.). 130p. (Orig.). 1984. pap. 6.95 (ISBN 0-916870-61-8). Creative Arts Bk.

Fishkin, Shelley F. From Fact to Fiction: Journalism & Imaginative Writing in America. LC 84-27765. 256p. 1985. 24.50x (ISBN 0-8018-2546-6). Johns Hopkins.

Fishler, S. A; see Newcomb, Franc J.

Fishler, Stan. More Stan Fishler's Sports Stumpers. (Illus.). (gr. 4 up). 1978. pap. 1.50 (ISBN 0-448-16488-4, Pub. by Tempo). Ace Bks.

Fishler, Stanley A. In the Beginning: A Navaho Creation Myth. (Utah Anthropological Papers: No. 13). Repr. of 1953 ed. 26.50 (ISBN 0-404-60613-X). AMS Pr.

Fishlock, Trevor. Gandhi's Children. (Illus.). 208p. 1983. text ed. 16.50x (ISBN 0-87663-436-6, 83-4904). Universe.

--Talking of Wales: A Companion to Wales & the Welsh. 191p. 1978. pap. 4.95 (ISBN 0-586-04555-4, Pub. by Granada England). Academy Chi Pubs.

Fishlow, Albert. American Railroads & the Transformation of the Ante-Bellum Economy. LC 65-22068. (Economic Studies: No. 127). (Illus.). 1965. 27.50x (ISBN 0-674-02850-3). Harvard U Pr.

--The Mature Neighbor Policy: A New United States Economic Policy for Latin America. (Policy Papers in International Affairs: No. 3). 1977. pap. 3.95x (ISBN 0-87725-503-2). U of Cal Intl St.

Fishlow, Albert, jt. auth. see Lowenthal, Abraham F.

Fishlow, Albert, et al. Trade with Manufacturers in Developing Countries: Reinforcing North-South Partnership. 1981. write for info. Trilateral Comm.

Fishman, Alfred D. & Fisher, Aron B. Respiratory System: Section 3, Circulation & Nonrespiratory Functions, Vol. I. 584p. 1985. 136.00 (ISBN 0-683-03244-5). Waverly Pr.

Fishman, Alfred P. Pulmonary Diseases & Disorders, 2 vols. (Illus.). 1696p. 1979. Set. text ed. 150.00 (ISBN 0-07-021116-7). McGraw.

--Pulmonary Diseases & Disorders: Update 1. (Illus.). 496p. 1982. text ed. 50.00x (ISBN 0-07-021119-1). McGraw.

Fishman, Alfred P., ed. Heart Failure. (Illus.). 1978. text ed. 29.95 (ISBN 0-07-021118-3). McGraw.

Fishman, Charles. Mortal Companions. (Illus.). 1977. 7.00x (ISBN 0-918870-02-X). pap. 3.50x (ISBN 0-918870-01-1). Pleasure Dome.

--Warm-Blooded Animals. (Juniper Bk.: No. 22). 1977. 4.00 (ISBN 0-686-61878-5). Juniper Pr WI.

Fishman, Charles, jt. auth. see Vinecour, Earl.

Fishman, Charles, jt. ed. see Rosman, Bernice L.

Fishman, Charles, intro. by see Smith, R. T.

Fishman, Clifford. Wiretapping & Eavesdropping, Vol. 1. LC 78-18629. 1978. 74.50 (ISBN 0-686-29234-0); Suppl. 1984. 20.00; Suppl. 1983. 17.00. Lawyers Co-Op.

Fishman, David. Shopping Centers & the Accessibility Codes. 1979. nonmembers 14.00 (ISBN 0-913598-12-7); members 7.00. Intl Coun Shop.

Fishman, George S. Principles of Discrete Event Simulation. LC 78-17555. (Systems Engineering & Analysis Ser.). 514p. 1978. 49.95x (ISBN 0-471-04395-8, Pub. by Wiley-Interscience). Wiley.

--Spectral Methods in Econometrics. LC 72-78517. (Rand Corporation Research Studies). 1969. text ed. 15.00x (ISBN 0-674-83191-8). Harvard U Pr.

Fishman, H. Charles, jt. auth. see Minuchin, Salvador.

Fishman, Hal & Schiff, Barry. Flight Nine-Zero-Two Is Down! 288p. 1982. 13.95 (ISBN 0-312-29612-6). St Martin.

Fishman, Hal, jt. auth. see Schiff, Barry.

Fishman, Harvey M., jt. ed. see Takashima, Shiro.

Fishman, Hertzel. American Protestantism & a Jewish State. LC 72-3746. (Schaver Publication Fund for Jewish Studies Ser). 254p. 1973. 12.95x (ISBN 0-8143-1481-3). Wayne St U Pr.

Fishman, Howard, ed. Creativity & Innovation: Challenge of the 80's. 408p. (Orig.). 1982. pap. text ed. 21.95 (ISBN 0-942888-03-0). Pyramid Systems.

Fishman, Isadore. Gateway to the Mishnah. LC 76-25367. 10.95 (ISBN 0-87677-139-8); pap. 6.95 (ISBN 0-87677-175-4). Hartmore.

Fishman, Isidore. Gateway to the Mishnah. (gr. 10-12). 1970. 10.95 (ISBN 0-87677-139-8); pap. 6.95 (ISBN 0-87677-175-4). Prayer Bk.

--Remember the Days of Old. (Illus.). (gr. 4-9). 1970. 4.95 (ISBN 0-87677-000-6). Prayer Bk.

--Remember the Days of Old. LC 79-100058. 1969. 4.95 (ISBN 0-87677-000-6). Hartmore.

Fishman, J. Advances in the Creation & Revision of Writing Systems. 1977. 40.40 (ISBN 90-279-7552-3). Mouton.

--Single Issues. (International Journal of the Sociology of Language: No. 22). 1979. 12.40x (ISBN 90-279-7938-3). Mouton.

Fishman, J. A., ed. Advances in the Study of Societal Multilingualism. (Contributions to the Sociology of Language Ser.: No. 9). 1978. 74.00x (ISBN 90-279-7742-9). Mouton.

Fishman, Jack. And the Walls Came Tumbling Down. (Illus.). 384p. 1983. 17.95 (ISBN 0-02-538470-8). Macmillan.

Fishman, Jack, ed. The Bases of Addiction, LSRR 8. (Dahlem Workshop Reports Ser.). 1978. pap. 42.40x (ISBN 0-89573-092-8). VCH Pubs.

Fishman, James J., jt. auth. see Kalodner, Howard I.

Fishman, Jane S. Boerenverdriet: Violence Between Peasants & Soldiers in Early Modern Netherlands Art. Seidel, Linda, ed. LC 81-19655. (Studies in Fine Arts: Iconography: No. 5). 166p. 1982. 39.95 (ISBN 0-8357-1275-3). UMI Res Pr.

Fishman, Jay A., jt. auth. see Austin, Douglas V.

Fishman, Joan & Anrod, Barbara. Something's Got to Taste Good: The Cancer Patient's Cookbook. Graham, Jory, et al, eds. LC 80-26368. 200p. 12.95 (ISBN 0-8362-2102-8); pap. 6.95 (ISBN 0-8362-2103-6). Andrews McMeel Parker.

Fishman, Joanne A., jt. auth. see Bartlett, Michael.

Fishman, Joel & Orsag, Ann. The Legislative History of the Pennsylvania Solid Waste Management Act of 1980. LC 83-110519. (Allegheny Law Library, History & Genealogy Ser.: Vol. 2). 1982. write for info. Allegheny Co Bar.

Fishman, Joseph F. Crucibles of Crime: The Shocking Story of the American Jail. LC 69-14923. (Criminology, Law Enforcement, & Social Problems Ser.: No. 35). 1969. Repr. of 1923 ed. 10.00x (ISBN 0-87585-035-9). Patterson Smith.

Fishman, Joshua A. Language in Sociocultural Change: Essays by Joshua A. Fishman. Dil, Anwar S., ed. LC 72-85699. (Language Science & National Development Ser.). 392p. 1972. 27.50x (ISBN 0-8047-0816-9). Stanford U Pr.

--Yiddish in America: Socio-Linguistic Description & Analysis. LC 65-63395. (General Publications Ser: Vol. 36). (Orig.). 1965. pap. text ed. 5.50x (ISBN 0-87750-110-6). Res Ctr Lang Semiotic.

Fishman, Joshua A., ed. Advances in the Sociology of Language, 2 vols. LC 77-182463. (Contributions to the Sociology of Language Ser.: Nos.1 & 2). 418p. Vol. 1 1976. pap. text ed. 23.60x (ISBN 90-2797-732-1); Vol. 2 1972. pap. text ed. 23.60x (ISBN 90-2792-302-7). Mouton.

--Never Say Die! A Thousand Years of Jewish Life & Letters. (Contributions to the Sociology of Language Ser.). 1980. 47.50x (ISBN 9-0279-7978-2). Mouton.

Fishman, Joshua A., frwd. by. Never Say Die! A Thousand Years of Yiddish in Jewish Life & Letters. LC 81-3957. (Contributions to the Sociology of Language Ser.: No. 30). 763p. 1981. 47.50 (ISBN 0-686-37011-2). Mouton.

Fishman, Joshua A., ed. Readings in the Sociology of Language. LC 68-17892. (Orig.). 1968. pap. text ed. 19.60x (ISBN 90-2791-528-8). Mouton.

--Sociology of Yiddish: International Journal of the Sociology of Language, No. 24. 1980. pap. text ed. 14.40x (ISBN 90-279-3058-9). Mouton.

Fishman, Joshua A. & Keller, Gary D., eds. Bilingual Education for Hispanic Students in the United States. LC 80-27776. (Bilingual Education Ser.). (Orig.). 1981. 24.95x (ISBN 0-8077-2655-9); pap. 18.95x (ISBN 0-8077-2603-6). Tchrs Coll.

Fishman, Joshua A., jt. ed. see Cobarrubias, Juan.

Fishman, Joshua A., ed. see Dillard, J. L.

Fishman, Joshua A., tr. see Weinreich, Max.

Fishman, Joshua A., et al. Language Loyalty in the United States. Cordasco, Francesco, ed. LC 77-90409. (Bilingual-Bicultural Education in the United States Ser.). 1978. Repr. of 1966 ed. lib. bdg. 43.00x (ISBN 0-405-11078-2). Ayer Co Pubs.

--Ethnicity in Action: The Communtiy Resources of Ethnic Languages in the United States. LC 84-73315. 128p. 1985. 15.00x (ISBN 0-916950-53-0). Biling Rev-Pr.

Fishman, Judith. Responding to Prose: A Reader for Writers. (Illus.). 480p. (Orig.). 1982. pap. text ed. 12.04 scp (ISBN 0-672-61569-X); scp instr's. guide 3.67 (ISBN 0-672-61566-5). Bobbs.

--Responding to Prose: A Reader for Writers. 480p. 1983. pap. text ed. write for info. (ISBN 0-02-337900-6). Macmillan.

Fishman, Judith & Summerfield, Geoffrey. Frames of Mind: A Course in Composition. (Illus.). 300p. 1986. text ed. 14.95 (ISBN 0-394-33795-6, RanC). Random.

Fishman, Judith, jt. auth. see Schor, Sandra.

Fishman, Judith, jt. auth. see Summerfield, Geoffery.

Fishman, K. D. The Computer Establishment. 480p. 1982. pap. 7.95 (ISBN 0-07-021127-2). McGraw.

Fishman, Katharine D. The Computer Establishment. LC 80-8202. (Illus.). 400p. 1981. 21.10 (ISBN 0-06-011283-2, HarpT). Har-Row.

Fishman, Katherine D. The Computer Establishment. 468p. 1981. 20.95 (ISBN 0-686-98079-4). Telecom Lib.

Fishman, Ken. Paradise. (Orig.). 1980. pap. 2.25 (ISBN 0-440-16796-5). Dell.

Fishman, L., jt. auth. see Brambilla, R.

Fishman, Lew & Golf Magazine Editors, eds. Golf Magazine's Shortcuts to Better Golf. LC 78-19559. (Illus.). 1979. 14.37 (ISBN 0-06-011273-5, HarpT). Har-Row.

Fishman, Marck C., et al. Medicine. 2nd ed. (Illus.). 500p. 1985. pap. text ed. price not set (ISBN 0-397-50696-1, Lippincott Medical). Lippincott.

Fishman, Mark. Manufacturing the News. 189p. 1980. text ed. 15.95x (ISBN 0-292-75054-4). U of Tex Pr.

Fishman, Mark C., et al. Medicine. (Illus.). 500p. 1981. pap. text ed. 19.75 (ISBN 0-397-50436-5, 65-05622, Lippincott Medical). Lippincott.

Fishman, Meryl & Horwich, Kathleen. Living with Your Teenage Daughter & Liking it. 1983. 8.95 (ISBN 0-671-46880-4, Fireside). S&S.

Fishman, N. H. Thoracic Drainage: Manual of Procedures. 1983. 19.95 (ISBN 0-8151-3259-X). Year Bk Med.

Fishman, P. A. Assessment of Pulmonary Function. 1980. text ed. 30.00 (ISBN 0-07-021117-5). McGraw.

Fishman, Priscilla. Learn Mishnah Notebook. 128p. (gr. 7-8). 1983. pap. 3.50x (ISBN 0-87441-369-9). Behrman.

Fishman, Priscilla, ed. see Frankel, Max & Hoffman, Judy.

Fishman, Richard, ed. Housing for All under Law: New Directions in Housing, Land Use & Planning Law. LC 77-810. 720p. 1977. prof ref 29.95 (ISBN 0-88410-751-5). Ballinger Pub.

Fishman, Robert. Urban Utopias in the Twentieth Century: Ebenezer Howard, Frank Lloyd Wright & Le Corbusier. LC 76-43457. 1977. 15.00x (ISBN 0-465-08933-X). Basic.

--Urban Utopias in the Twentieth Century. (Illus.). 384p. 1982. pap. 8.95 (ISBN 0-262-56023-2). MIT Pr.

Fishman, Robert A. Cerebrospinal Fluid in Diseases of the Nervous System. LC 79-67304. (Illus.). 384p. 1980. text ed. 41.500 (ISBN 0-7216-3686-1). Saunders.

Fishman, Ross. Alcohol & Alcoholism. (Encyclopedia of Psychoactive Drugs Ser.). (Illus.). 1985. PLB 15.95x (ISBN 0-87754-762-9). Chelsea Hse.

Fishman, Sam. The Restless Mind. 120p. 1982. 6.00 (ISBN 0-8184-0323-3). Citadel Pr.

Fishman, Samuel Z. & Saypol, Judyth R., eds. Jewish Studies at American & Canadian Universities: A Catalog of Academic Programs. 2nd ed. LC 79-54250. 1979. pap. 3.95 (ISBN 0-9603058-2-3). B'nai B'rith-Hillel.

Fishman, Sterling. The Struggle for the Mind of German Youth, 1890-1914. 1974. lib. bdg. 59.95 (ISBN 0-87700-229-0). Revisionist Pr.

Fishman, W. J. & Breach, N. The Streets of East London. (Illus.). 1980. pap. 20.00 (ISBN 0-7156-1416-9). Heinman.

Fishman, Walda. The New Right: Unraveling the Opposition to Women's Equality. 224p. 1985. 22.95t (ISBN 0-03-060611-X). Praeger.

Fishman, William H., jt. auth. see Stigbrand, Torgny.

Fishman, William H., ed. Metabolic Conjugation & Metabolic Hydrolysis, 3 vols. LC 79-107556. Vol. 1, 1970. 90.00 (ISBN 0-12-257601-2); Vol. 2, 1971. 95.00 (ISBN 0-12-257602-0); Vol. 3, 1973. 90.00 (ISBN 0-12-257603-9). Acad Pr.

--On Codevelopmental Markers: Biologic Diagnostic & Monitoring Aspects, Vol. 1. 1983. 70.00 (ISBN 0-12-257701-9). Acad Pr.

Fishman, William H. & Sell, Stewart, eds. Onco-Developmental Gene Expression. 1976. 75.00 (ISBN 0-12-257660-8). Acad Pr.

Fishner, Stanley. Costing for Negotiated Government Contracts. 100p. (Orig.). 1981. pap. 28.00 (ISBN 0-9606848-0-8). Fishner Bks.

Fishof, David & Shapiro, Eugene D. Putting It on the Line: The Negotiation Secrets, Tactics, & Techniques of a Top Sports & Entertainment Agent. LC 83-62246. (Illus.). 256p. 1983. 14.95 (ISBN 0-688-02447-5). Morrow.

Fishtein, Ruth. Classroom Psychology. LC 74-79108. 72p. 1974. pap. 2.95 (ISBN 0-87594-115-X). Book-Lab.

Fishwick, ed. Shakespearian Addresses: Delivered at the Arts Club, Manchester 1886 to 1912. 400p. 1983. Repr. of 1912 ed. lib. bdg. 75.00 (ISBN 0-317-01344-0). Century Bookbindery.

Fishwick & Ditchfield, P. H., eds. Memorials of Old Lancashire, 2 vols. 1979. Repr. of 1909 ed. Set. lib. bdg. 125.00 (ISBN 0-8495-1628-5). Arden Lib.

Fishwick, Frank. Labour Economics. 1979. 45.95x (ISBN 0-905440-14-5). State Mutual Bk.

Fishwick, Marshall. Parameters: Man-Media Mosaic. LC 78-61074. 1978. 12.95 (ISBN 0-87972-093-X); pap. 6.95 (ISBN 0-87972-092-1). Bowling Green Univ.

--Popular Architecture. 1975. pap. 2.50 (ISBN 0-87972-164-2). Bowling Green Univ.

--Ronald Revisited: The World of Ronald McDonald. LC 83-72235. 1983. 19.95 (ISBN 0-87972-247-9); pap. 9.95 (ISBN 0-87972-248-7). Bowling Green Univ.

--Springlore in Virginia. LC 78-70459. 1978. 25.00 (ISBN 0-87972-128-6); pap. 12.95 (ISBN 0-87972-190-1). Bowling Green Univ.

Fishwick, Marshall W. American Heroes, Myth & Reality. LC 72-10695. 242p. 1975. Repr. of 1954 ed. lib. bdg. 18.50x (ISBN 0-8371-6610-1, FIAH). Greenwood.

--Common Culture & the Great Tradition: The Case for Renewal. LC 81-4232. (Contributions to the Study of Popular Culture Ser.: No. 2). (Illus.). x, 230p. 1982. lib. bdg. 27.50 (ISBN 0-313-23042-0, FCC/). Greenwood.

--Lee After the War. LC 73-7102. (Illus.). 242p. 1973. Repr. of 1963 ed. lib. bdg. 22.50 (ISBN 0-8371-6911-9, FILW). Greenwood.

--Seven Pillars of Popular Culture. LC 84-8994. (Contributions to the Study of Popular Culture Ser.: No. 10). (Illus.). 224p. lib. bdg. 29.95 (ISBN 0-313-23263-6, FIF/). Greenwood.

Fishwick, Marshall W., jt. auth. see Browne, Ray B.

Fishwick, Nina M. Liberated for Life: A Christian Declaration of Independence. (Study & Grow Electives Ser.). 64p. 1985. pap. 3.95 (ISBN 0-8307-1039-6, 6102095). Regal.

Fishwick, Wilfred. Strengthening Co-operation Between Engineering Schools & Industry. (Studies in Engineering Education: No. 8). 167p. 1983. pap. text ed. 13.25 (ISBN 92-3-101989-9, U1284, UNESCO). Unipub.

Fisiak, Jacek, ed. Contrastive Linguistics: Prospects & Problems. LC 83-19430. (Trends in Linguistics Studies & Monographs: No. 22). x, 449p. 1984. 69.95x (ISBN 90-279-3260-3). Mouton.

--Historical Morphology: Papers Prepared for the Conference, Held at Boszkovo, Poland, March 1978. (Trends in Linguisitics, Studies & Monographs: No. 17). 1980. text ed. 54.00 (ISBN 90-279-3038-4). Mouton.

--Historical Syntax. LC 84-8208. (Trends in Linguistics. Studies & Monographs: No. 23). xii, 636p. 1984. 79.95x (ISBN 90-279-3250-6). Mouton.

--Recent Developments in Historical Phonology. (Trends in Linguistics Ser.). 1978. pap. text ed. 52.40x (ISBN 90-279-7706-2). Mouton.

--Theoretical Issues in Contrastive Linguistics. (Current Issues in Linguistic Theory Ser.). x, 430p. 1980. 48.00x (ISBN 90-272-3502-3, 12). Benjamins North Am.

Fisichella, Anthony J. Metaphysics: Science of Life. 2nd ed. LC 82-9726. (New Age Ser.). (Illus.). 320p. 1985. pap. 9.95 (ISBN 0-87542-229-2). Llewellyn Pubns.

Fisk, Albert. A New Look at Senility. (Illus.). 112p. 1981. pap. 11.75x (ISBN 0-398-04436-8). C C Thomas.

Fisk, Anette. First Fifty Years of the Waltham Training School for Nurses. Reverby, Susan, ed. LC 83-49127. (The History of American Nursing Ser.). 482p. 1985. lib. bdg. 30.00 (ISBN 0-8240-6514-X). Garland Pub.

Fisk, D. J. Thermal Control of Buildings. (Illus.). xvii, 245p. 1981. 69.95x (ISBN 0-85334-950-9). Intl Ideas.

Fisk, Donald, et al. Private Provision of Public Services: An Overview. 105p. 1978. pap. 9.00 (ISBN 0-87766-221-5, 18300). Urban Inst.

Fisk, E. K. Aboriginal Economy in Town & Country. 160p. 1985. text ed. 22.50x (ISBN 0-317-31540-4). Allen Unwin.

Fisk, E. K., ed. The Adaption of Traditional Agriculture: Socioeconomic Problems of Urbanization. new ed. (Development Studies Centre Monograph: No. 11). pap. text ed. 9.00 (ISBN 0-909150-58-3, Pub. by ANUP Australia). Australia N U P.

Fisk, E. K. & Rani, Osman, eds. The Political Economy of Malaysia. 1982. 55.00x (ISBN 0-19-582501-2). Oxford U Pr.

Fisk, E. K., ed. see Howie-Willis, Ian.

Fisk, E. K., ed. see Robinson, Neville K.

Fisk, E. K., jt. ed. see Young, E. A.

Fisk, Edward R. Construction Engineer's Form Book. LC 80-22395. 624p. 1981. text ed. 59.95 (ISBN 0-471-06307-X). Wiley.

--Construction Project Administration. 2nd ed. 434p. 1982. 29.95 (ISBN 0-471-09186-3). Wiley.

Fisk, Elizabeth C., jt. auth. see Rossman, Mark H.

Fisk, Erma J. Parrot's Wood. 1985. 15.95 (ISBN 0-393-01997-7). Norton.

--The Peacocks of Baboquivari: A Journal. (Illus.). 1983. 14.95 (ISBN 0-393-01758-3). Norton.

Fisk, Erma J., tr. see Koepcke, Maria.

Fisk, Frank S., ed. see Thiers, Adolphe.

Fisk, George & Korsvold, Pal E. Social Responsibility in Business: Scandinavian Viewpoint. 170p. (Orig.). 1979. pap. text ed. 17.95x (ISBN 0-317-03038-8, Pub. by Chartwell-Bratt England). Brookfield Pub Co.

Fisk, George & Nason, Robert W., eds. Macromarketing, Vol. III: New Steps on the Learning Curve. 421p. 1979. 12.00 (ISBN 0-686-69387-6). U CO Busn Res Div.

Fisk, George, et al, eds. Macromarketng, Vol. IV: Evolution of Thought. 1980. 12.00 (ISBN 0-686-64748-3). U CO Busn Res Div.

Fisk, George M. Continental Opinion Regarding a Proposed Middle European Tariff-Union. LC 78-63892. (Johns Hopkins University. Studies in the Social Sciences. Twentieth Ser. 1902: 11-12). 64p. 1983. Repr. of 1902 ed. 24.50 (ISBN 0-404-61146-X). AMS Pr.

Fisk, James W. A Practical Guide to Management of the Painful Neck & Back: Diagnosis, Manipulation, Exercises, Prevention. (Illus.). 248p. 1977. photocopy ed. 29.50x (ISBN 0-398-03640-3). C C Thomas.

--A Simple Answer to Fitness for All Ages: How to Lose Weight without Dieting--with Practical Reasons Why--Easily Explainable to Laypersons & Physicans. (Illus.). 132p. 1984. pap. 12.75x (ISBN 0-398-04995-5). C C Thomas.

Fisk, Jim & Barron, Robert. Buzzwords: The Official MBA Dictionary. 1983. pap. 5.95 (ISBN 0-671-47006-X, Wallaby). S&S.

--The Official MBA Directory. 1983. 5.95 (ISBN 0-686-44931-2, Wallaby). S&S.

--The Official MBA Handbook. 1982. 4.95 (ISBN 0-671-44358-5, Wallaby). S&S.

--The Official MBA Handbook of Great Business Quotations. (Orig.). 1984. pap. 5.95 (ISBN 0-671-50318-9, Fireside). S&S.

Fisk, Lori & Lindgren, Henry C. Learning Centers. 1974. pap. 7.95 (ISBN 0-914420-54-2). Exceptional Pr Inc.

Fisk, Marion J. & Anderson, H. William. Introduction to Solar Technology. LC 80-29599. (Engineering Ser.). (Illus.). 640p. 1982. text ed. 28.95 (ISBN 0-201-04713-6); solution manual 1.50 (ISBN 0-201-14591-X). Addison-Wesley.

Fisk, Mary B. Baby Gourmet Cookbook. (Illus.). 1978. pap. 4.95 (ISBN 0-915696-09-6). Determined Prods.

Fisk, Michael D. Treason with Glory: Or, What Happened at Paradize, Nevada? 1985. 10.95 (ISBN 0-533-05234-3). Vantage.

Fisk, Milton. Ethics & Society: A Marxist Interpretation of Value. LC 79-3513. 1980. 20.00x (ISBN 0-8147-2564-3). NYU Pr.

--Nature & Necessity: An Essay in Physical Ontology. LC 72-85605. (Indiana University Humanities Ser.: No. 73). pap. 79.00 (ISBN 0-317-09316-9, 2055220). Bks Demand UMI.

Fisk, Nicholas. Grinny. 112p. (gr. 2-5). 9.50 (ISBN 0-434-93856-4, Pub. by W Heinemann Ltd). David & Charles.

--A Rag, a Bone & a Hank of Hair. 128p. (gr. 3-5). 1982. 1.98 (ISBN 0-517-54635-3). Crown.

--Time Trap. 1976. 10.95 (ISBN 0-575-02195-0, Pub. by Gollancz England). David & Charles.

Fisk, P. R. Stochastically Dependent Equations. (Griffin's Statistical Monographs: No. 21). 110p. 1967. pap. 14.25x (ISBN 0-85264-177-X). Lubrecht & Cramer.

Fisk, Raymond P., jt. auth. see Brown, Stephen W.

Fisk, Robert. In Time of War. (Illus.). 672p. 1985. pap. 9.95 (ISBN 0-586-08498-3, Pub. by Granada England). Academy Chi Pubs.

--In Time of War: Ireland, Ulster, & the Price of Neutrality, 1939-45. (Illus.). 565p. 1983. 27.50x (ISBN 0-8122-7888-7). U of Pa Pr.

Fisk, Robert S., jt. auth. see Duryea, E. D.

Fisk, Samuel. Divine Healing Under the Searchlight. LC 78-15083. 1978. pap. 2.25 (ISBN 0-87227-057-2). Reg Baptist.

--Divine Sovereignty & Human Freedom. LC 73-81550. 1973. pap. 3.75 (ISBN 0-87213-166-1). Loizeaux.

--Letters to Teresa. 91p. 1973. pap. 1.95 (ISBN 0-87398-516-8, Pub. by Bibl Evang Pr). Sword of Lord.

Fisk, Theophilus. Orations on the Freedom of the Press. LC 73-125692. (American Journalists Ser). 1970. Repr. of 1837 ed. 16.00 (ISBN 0-405-01669-7). Ayer Co Pubs.

Fisk University Library (Nashville) Dictionary Catalog of the Negro Collection of the Fisk University Library, 6 vols. 1974. Set. lib. bdg. 510.00 (ISBN 0-8161-1055-7, Hall Library). G K Hall.

Fisk, W. J., jt. auth. see Hekmat, D.

Fisk, Wilbur. Anti-Rebel: The Civil War Letters of Wilbur Fisk. LC 83-17774. 380p. 1983. 25.95 (ISBN 0-9610060-1-3). E Rosenblatt.

Fiske, Amos. The Story of the Phillipines. 59.95 (ISBN 0-8490-1141-8). Gordon Pr.

Fiske, Amos K. The Modern Bank. Bruchey, Stuart, ed. LC 80-1147. (The Rise of Commercial Banking Ser.). (Illus.). 1981. Repr. of 1904 ed. lib. bdg. 32.00x (ISBN 0-405-13650-1). Ayer Co Pubs.

Fiske, Bradley A. The Navy As a Fighting Machine. 1977. lib. bdg. 59.95 (ISBN 0-8490-2333-5). Gordon Pr.

Fiske, Charles. Confessions of a Puzzled Parson, & Other Pleas for Reality. facs. ed. LC 68-54345. (Essay Index Reprint Ser). 1968. Repr. of 1928 ed. 18.00 (ISBN 0-8369-0442-7). Ayer Co Pubs.

Fiske, Donald W. Strategies for Personality Research: The Observation Versus Interpretation of Behavior. LC 78-1150. (Social & Behavioral Science Ser.). (Illus.). 1978. text ed. 29.95x (ISBN 0-87589-373-2). Jossey-Bass.

Fiske, Donald W., jt. auth. see Duncan, Starkey.

Fiske, Donald W., jt. auth. see Kelly, Everett L.

Fiske, Edward B. Selective Guide to Colleges 1984-85. LC 83-45117. 483p. 1983. 19.95 (ISBN 0-8129-1091-5); pap. 9.95 (ISBN 0-8129-1087-7). Times Bks.

--Selective Guide to Colleges 1986-87. rev. ed. LC 85-40267. 524p. (Orig.). Date not set. pap. 10.95 (ISBN 0-8129-1263-2). Times Bks.

Fiske, Edward B. & Michalak, Joseph M. The Best Buys in College Education. LC 85-40266. 468p. (Orig.). 1985. pap. 9.95 (ISBN 0-8129-6345-8). Times Bks.

Fiske, Frank S., tr. see Thiers, Adolphe.

Fiske, George C. Lucilius & Horace, a Study in Classical Theory of Imitation. LC 78-109732. 524p. Repr. of 1920 ed. lib. bdg. 24.75x (ISBN 0-8371-4222-9, FILH). Greenwood.

Fiske, George W. Boy Life & Self-Government. (Educational Ser.). 1911. Repr. 8.50 (ISBN 0-8482-3969-5). Norwood Edns.

Fiske, Henry W. Consistent Profits in the Psychological Mastery of the Stock Market. (Illus.). 1979. 62.50x (ISBN 0-918968-35-6). Inst Econ Finan.

Fiske, Horace S. Provincial Types in American Fiction. LC 67-27596. 1968. Repr. of 1903 ed. 21.00x (ISBN 0-8046-0148-8, Pub. by Kennikat). Assoc Faculty Pr.

Fiske, Irving. Bernard Shaw's Debt to William Blake. LC 74-120730. 1974. Repr. of 1951 ed. lib. bdg. 7.50 (ISBN 0-8414-4233-9). Folcroft.

--Bernard Shaw's Debt to William Blake. 1982. pap. 12.50 (ISBN 0-686-45096-5). Porter.

Fiske, J., jt. auth. see Wilson, J. G.

Fiske, Jane F., ed. see Woodworth-Barnes, Esther L.

Fiske, John. The Beginnings of New England. 1978. lib. bdg. 25.00 (ISBN 0-8492-0899-8). R West.

--The Critical Period of American History: 1783-1789. 1901. Repr. 27.50 (ISBN 0-8482-3974-1). Norwood Edns.

--Darwinism & Other Essays. LC 28-2631. 1913. 17.00 (ISBN 0-527-29500-0). Kraus Repr.

--Edward Livingston Youmans. LC 72-4171. (Select Bibliographies Reprint Ser.). 1972. Repr. of 1894 ed. 32.00 (ISBN 0-8369-6879-4). Ayer Co Pubs.

--Essays Historical & Literary, 2 vols. facsimile ed. LC 70-156641. (Essay Index Reprint Ser). Repr. of 1902 ed. 39.00 (ISBN 0-8369-2314-6). Ayer Co Pubs.

--Historical Writings of John Fiske, 12 vols. 1902. Repr. Set. 300.00 (ISBN 0-8482-3986-5). Norwood Edns.

--Introduction to Communication Studies. LC 81-16908. (Studies in Communication). 1982. pap. 7.95x (ISBN 0-416-74570-9, NO. 3588). Methuen Inc.

--Italians, French, British & Dutch in the Colonization of North America, 2 vols. (Illus.). 1985. Set. 117.50 (ISBN 0-89266-518-1). Am Classical Coll Pr.

--The Miscellaneous Writings of John Fiske, 12 vols. 1902. Repr. Set. 150.00 (ISBN 0-8482-3993-8). Norwood Edns.

--Myths & Myth-Makers: Old Tales & Superstitions Interpreted by Comparative Mythology. LC 77-85618. 1977. Repr. of 1890 ed. lib. bdg. 30.00 (ISBN 0-89341-304-6). Longwood Pub Group.

--The Origin & Destiny of Man. (Illus.). 111p. Repr. of 1891 ed. 69.85 (ISBN 0-89901-042-3). Found Class Reprints.

--Outlines of Cosmic Philosophy: Based on the Doctrine of Evolution with Criticisms on the Positive Philosophy, 2 Vols. (American Studies). 1969. Repr. of 1875 ed. Set. 60.00 (ISBN 0-384-15780-7). Johnson Repr.

--Unpublished Orations: The Discovery of the Columbia River & the Whitman Controversy, the Crispus Attucks Memorial & Columbus Memorial. LC 77-168031. Repr. of 1909 ed. 14.00 (ISBN 0-404-02403-3). AMS Pr.

--Writings, 24 vols. LC 70-168032. Repr. of 1902 ed. Set. 1080.00 (ISBN 0-404-02410-6); 45.00 ea. AMS Pr.

Fiske, John & Hartley, John. Reading Television. (New Accents Ser.). 1978. pap. 8.95x (ISBN 0-416-85560-1, NO. 2781). Methuen Inc.

Fiske, Kenneth & Harter, James H. Direct Current Circuit Analysis through Experimentation. 4th ed. 240p. 1982. pap. 9.50x (ISBN 0-911908-17-X). Tech Ed Pr.

Fiske, Kenneth A. & Harter, James H. Alternating Current Circuit Analysis through Experimentation. 3rd ed. 176p. 1982. pap. 8.50x (ISBN 0-911908-41-2). Tech Ed Pr.

Fiske, Loring. How to Beat Better Tennis Players. pap. 4.00 (ISBN 0-87980-262-6). Wilshire.

Fiske, Majorie. Book Selection & Censorship: A Study of School & Public Libraries in California. LC 59-10464. (California Library Reprint: No. 1). 1968. 25.00x (ISBN 0-520-00418-3). U of Cal Pr.

Fiske, Patricia. Prayer Rugs from Private Collections. (Illus.). 139p. 1974. pap. 2.50 (ISBN 0-87405-003-0). Textile Mus.

Fiske, Patricia, ed. Irene Emery Roundtable on Museum Textiles: 1975 Proceedings, Imported & Domestic Textiles in 18th Century America. LC 76-56646. (Illus.). 196p. 1976. pap. 17.50 (ISBN 0-87405-006-5). Textile Mus.

Fiske, Patricia, ed. see Archaeological Textiles.

Fiske, Patricia, ed. see Lamb, Venice & Lamb, Alastair.

Fiske, Patricia L., et al, eds. From the Far West: Carpets & Textiles of Morocco. LC 80-54883. (Illus.). 192p. 1980. 37.50 (ISBN 0-87405-015-4). Textile Mus.

Fiske, Richard, jt. ed. see Simkin, Tom.

Fiske, Roger. Beethoven Concertos & Overtures. LC 70-110118. (BBC Music Guides Ser.). (Illus.). 1971. pap. 4.95 (ISBN 0-295-95112-5). U of Wash Pr.

--Score Reading, 4 vols. Incl. Vol. 1. Orchestration. 1958. 6.75 (ISBN 0-19-321301-X); Vol. 2. Musical Form. 1958. 6.75 (ISBN 0-19-321302-8); Vol. 3. Concertos. 1960. 6.75 (ISBN 0-19-321303-6); Vol. 4. Oratorios. 1955. 6.75 (ISBN 0-19-321304-4). (YA) (gr. 9up). Oxford U Pr.

--Scotland in Music. LC 82-14583. (Illus.). 300p. 1983. 34.50 (ISBN 0-521-24772-1). Cambridge U Pr.

Fiske, Roger, ed. The Eighteenth Century. (Athlone History of Music in Britain Ser.). 400p. 1986. 95.00 (ISBN 0-485-13004-1, Pub. by Athlone Pr Ltd). Longwood Pub Group.

Fiske, Stephen. Off-Hand Portraits of Prominent New Yorkers. facsimile ed. LC 75-1847. (Leisure Class in America Ser.). 1975. Repr. of 1884 ed. 23.50x (ISBN 0-405-06914-6). Ayer Co Pubs.

Fiske, Susan T. & Taylor, Shelley E. Social Cognition. (Illus.). 512p. 1984. pap. text ed. 11.95 (ISBN 0-394-34801-X, RanC). Random.

Fiske, Susan T., jt. auth. see Clark, Margaret S.

Fiske, Thomas S. Low Cost Costing: Product Costing with Your Microcomputer. (Illus.). 94p. (Orig.). 1984. pap. 24.95 spiral bound (ISBN 0-88006-084-0); Apple II, II Plus, IIe. spiral bound incl. disk 24.95 (ISBN 0-88006-067-0, CC7399); IBM-PC. spiral bound incl. disk 24.95 (ISBN 0-88006-071-9, CC7402); TRS-80 Model I, Model III. spiral bound incl. disk 24.95 (ISBN 0-88006-072-7, CC7403); spiral bound incl. disk 24.95 (ISBN 0-88006-092-1, CC7421). Green Pub Inc.

Fiske, Turbese L. & Lummis, Keith. Charles F. Lummis: The Man & His West. LC 74-15910. (Illus.). 250p. 1975. 21.95 (ISBN 0-8061-1228-X). U of Okla Pr.

Fiske, Willard M. The Fully Scientific Book of Old British Furniture. (Illus.). 151p. 1981. 99.75 (ISBN 0-86650-012-X). Gloucester Art.

Fiske, William F., jt. auth. see Howard, Leland O.

Fisketjon, G. & Galassi, J., eds. Random Review 1982. 336p. 1982. pap. 3.95 (ISBN 0-345-30224-9). Ballantine.

Fisler, George F. Keys to Identification of the Orders & Families of Living Mammals of the World. (Science Ser.: No. 25). (Illus.). 29p. 1970. 2.25 (ISBN 0-938644-04-1). Nat Hist Mus.

Fison, J. E. Understanding the Old Testament: The Way of Holiness. LC 78-21116. 1979. Repr. of 1952 ed. lib. bdg. 24.75x (ISBN 0-313-20839-5, FIUO). Greenwood.

Fison, Lois A. Merry Suffolk, Master Archie & Other Tales. (Folklore Ser). 12.50 (ISBN 0-8482-3992-X). Norwood Edns.

Fison, Lorimer. Tales from Old Fiji. LC 75-32816. Repr. of 1904 ed. 20.00 (ISBN 0-404-14120-X). AMS Pr.

Fiss, Owen M. The Civil Rights Injunction. LC 78-2052. pap. 30.80 (ISBN 0-317-27816-9, 2056034). Bks Demand UMI.

Fiss, Owen M. & Rendleman, Doug. Injunctions. 2nd ed. LC 83-20573. (University Casebook Ser.). 1241p. 1983. text ed. 34.50 (ISBN 0-88277-151-5). Foundation Pr.

Fissan, H., ed. Aerosols in Science, Medicine & Technology: Proceedings of the Tenth Annual Conference of the Association for Aerosol Research (Gesellschaft fur Aerosolforschung), Bologna, Italy, 14-17 September 1982. 225p. 1983. pap. 29.50 (ISBN 0-08-030260-2). Pergamon.

Fisse, Brent. The Impact of Publicity on Corporate Offenders. Braithewaite, John, ed. LC 82-19643. (Critical Issues in Criminal Justice Ser.). 252p. 1983. 49.50x (ISBN 0-87395-732-6); pap. 17.95x (ISBN 0-87395-733-4). State U Ny Pr.

Fisse, Brent & French, Peter A., eds. Corrigible Corporation & Unruly Law. 272p. (Orig.). 1985. text ed. 30.00 (ISBN 0-939980-12-6); pap. text ed. 14.95 (ISBN 0-939980-13-4). Trinity U Pr.

Fissinger. Billy Joel. (Rock 'N Pop Stars Ser.). (Illus.). 32p. 1983. 7.95 (ISBN 0-89813-104-9). Creative Ed.

--Bruce Springsteen. (Rock 'n Pop Stars Ser.). (Illus.). 32p. (gr. 4-12). PLB 7.95 (ISBN 0-317-31120-4). Creative Ed.

--Hall & Oates. (Rock & Pop Stars Ser.). (Illus.). 32p. (gr. 4-12). PLB 7.95 (ISBN 0-317-31130-1). Creative Ed.

--John Cougar. (Rock & Pop Stars Ser.). (Illus.). 32p. (gr. 4-12). PLB 7.95 (ISBN 0-317-31133-6). Creative Ed.

--Linda Ronstadt. (Rock 'n Pop Stars Ser.). (Illus.). 32p. (gr. 4-12). PLB 7.95 (ISBN 0-317-31135-2). Creative Ed.

--Pat Benatar. (Rock 'n Pop Stars Ser.). (Illus.). 32p. (gr. 4-12). PLB 7.95 (ISBN 0-317-31137-9). Creative Ed.

Fissinger, Laura. Tina Turner. 1985. pap. 2.95 (ISBN 0-345-32642-3). Ballantine.

Fistedis, S. H., ed. Structural Mechanics in Reactor Technology: Transactions of the 7th International Conference. (Structural Mechanics in Reactor Technology: Vol. 7). 1983. 332.00 (ISBN 0-444-86703-1). Elsevier.

Fistell, Ira. America by Train, Nineteen Eighty-Five to Nineteen Eighty-Six. 3rd ed. (Compleat Traveler Ser.). (Illus.). 512p. (Orig.). 1985. pap. 8.95 (ISBN 0-89102-315-1). B Franklin.

Fistul, V. I. Heavily Doped Semiconductors. LC 68-28095. (Monographs in Semiconductor Physics: Vol. 1). 418p. 1969. 42.50x (ISBN 0-306-30352-3, Plenum Pr). Plenum Pub.

Fisz, Marek. Probability Theory & Mathematical Statistics. 3rd ed. LC 80-12455. 696p. 1980. Repr. of 1963 ed. lib. bdg. 39.50 (ISBN 0-89874-179-3). Krieger.

Fiszdon, W., ed. Rarefied Gas Flows: Theory & Experiment. (CISM-International Centre for Mechanical Sciences, Courses & Lectures: Vol. 224). (Illus.). 524p. 1982. pap. 45.60 (ISBN 0-387-81595-3). Springer-Verlag.

Fiszel, H. Investment Efficiency in a Socialist Economy. 1966. 16.25 (ISBN 0-08-011760-0). Pergamon.

Fiszer, Louise, jt. auth. see Ferrary, Jeannette.

Fiszman, Joseph R. Revolution & Tradition in People's Poland: Education & Socialization. LC 70-166369. 400p. 1972. 46.00 (ISBN 0-691-05194-1); pap. 15.50x LPE (ISBN 0-691-10009-8). Princeton U Pr.

Fit Magazine Editors. Aloe Vera: The Miracle Plant. 64p. 1983. pap. 3.95 (ISBN 0-89037-261-6). Anderson World.

--Breast Care. (Fit Self-Improvement Ser.: No. 2). 96p. 1983. pap. 7.95 (ISBN 0-89037-259-4). Anderson World.

--Figure Maintenance. (Fit Self-Improvement Ser.: No. 1). 96p. 1983. pap. 7.95 (ISBN 0-89037-255-1). Anderson World.

--Legs & Thighs. (Fit Self-Improvement Ser.: No. 3). 96p. 1983. pap. 7.95 (ISBN 0-89037-260-8). Anderson World.

--Waist & Stomach. (Fit Self Improvement Ser.: No. 5). 96p. (Orig.). 1983. pap. 7.95 (ISBN 0-89037-264-0). Anderson World.

Fit Magazine Editors, ed. Hair Care. (Fit Self Improvement Ser.: Bk. 4). (Illus.). 96p. (Orig.). 1983. pap. 7.95 (ISBN 0-89037-263-2). Anderson World.

Fitch, jt. auth. see Simpson.

Fitch, A. A., ed. Developments in Geophysical Exploration Methods, Vol. 1. (Illus.). 310p. 1979. 50.00 (ISBN 0-85334-835-9, Pub. by Elsevier Applied Sci England). Elsevier.

--Developments in Geophysical Exploration Methods, Vol. 2. (Illus.). 235p. 1981. 40.75 (ISBN 0-85334-930-4, Pub. by Elsevier Applied Sci England). Elsevier.

--Developments in Geophysical Exploration Methods, Vol. 3. (Illus.). 320p. 1982. 57.50 (ISBN 0-85334-126-5, Pub. by Elsevier Applied Sci England). Elsevier.

--Developments in Geophysical Exploration Methods, Vol. 4. (Illus.). 200p. 1983. 37.00 (ISBN 0-85334-174-5, I-454-82, Pub. by Elsevier Applied Sci England). Elsevier.

--Developments in Geophysical Exploration Methods, Vol. 5. 262p. 1983. 63.00 (ISBN 0-85334-216-4, Pub. by Elsevier Applied Sci England). Elsevier.

--Developments in Geophysical Exploration Methods Six. (Illus.). 280p. 1985. 57.00 (ISBN 0-85334-334-9, Pub. by Elsevier Applied Sci England). Elsevier.

Fitch, Albert A. Seismic Reflection Interpretation. (Geo-Exploration Monographs: Ser. 1, No. 8). (Illus.). 1976. text ed. 27.30x (ISBN 0-686-31719-X). Lubrecht & Cramer.

Fitch, Alger. Claiming God's Promises. 144p. (Orig.). 1984. pap. 2.95 (ISBN 0-87239-750-5, 41028). Standard Pub.

Fitch, Alger M., Jr. Afterglow of Christ's Resurrection. LC 75-14692. (New Life Bks). (Illus.). 136p. 1975. pap. 3.95 (ISBN 0-87239-055-1, 40030). Standard Pub.

Fitch, Asa. Their Own Voices: Oral Accounts of Early Settlers in Washington County, New York. Adler, Winston, ed. 160p. 1983. 15.00 (ISBN 0-932334-59-8); pap. 8.95 (ISBN 0-932334-60-1). Heart of the Lakes.

Fitch, B. L' Etranger de Camus: Un Texte, ses lecteurs, leurs lectures. new ed. (Collection L). 176p. (Orig., Fr.). 1972. pap. 13.95 (ISBN 2-03-036005-8). Larousse.

Fitch, Bob. My Eyes Have Seen. LC 79-176238. (Illus., Orig.). 1972. 9.95 (ISBN 0-912078-22-7); pap. 5.95 (ISBN 0-912078-18-9). Volcano Pr.

Fitch, Bob & Fitch, Lynne. Grandfather's Land. LC 75-190188. (gr. 5-9). 1970. PLB 7.95 (ISBN 0-87191-049-7). Creative Ed.

--Mark Will Ward - a Black Family in the City. LC 74-190185. (gr. 5-9). 1970. PLB 7.95 (ISBN 0-87191-051-9). Creative Ed.

Fitch, Brian T. The Narcissitic Text: A Reading of Camus' Fiction. (Romance Ser.: No. 42). 128p. 1982. 20.00x (ISBN 0-8020-2426-2). U of Toronto Pr.

Fitch, Charles M. All about Orchids. LC 80-1806. (Illus.). 288p. 1981. 15.95 (ISBN 0-385-15848-3). Doubleday.

--The Complete Book of Miniature Roses. (Illus.). 352p. 1980. pap. 10.95 (ISBN 0-8015-1507-6, Hawthorn). Dutton.

--Rodale Book of Garden Photography. (Illus.). 176p. 1981. pap. 12.95 (ISBN 0-8174-5781-X, Amphoto). Watson-Guptill.

Fitch, Clyde, jt. auth. see Gernsback, Hugo.

Fitch, D. In Pursuit of Productivity: Making Things Happen in the Microcomputer Age. 1982. 16.95 (ISBN 0-201-04072-7). Addison-Wesley.

Fitch, Donald. Increasing Productivity in the Microcomputer Age. 386p. 1981. 16.95 (ISBN 0-201-04072-7). Addison-Wesley.

Fitch, Ed. Castle of Deception. Weschcke, Carl L., ed. LC 83-80166. (Llewellyn's Magical Fantasy Ser.). (Illus.). 290p. (Orig.). 1983. pap. 6.95 (ISBN 0-87542-231-4, L 231). Llewellyn Pubns.

Fitch, Ed & Renee, Janine. Magical Rites from the Crystal Well. Weschcke, Carl L., ed. LC 83-80134. (Practical Magick Ser.). (Illus.). 166p. 1984. pap. 13.00 (ISBN 0-87542-230-6, L-230). Llewellyn Pubns.

Fitch, Ed, jt. auth. see Rene'e, Janine.

Fitch, Frederick B. Elements of Combinatory Logic. LC 73-86892. pap. 32.30 (ISBN 0-317-08731-2, 2013383). Bks Demand UMI.

Fitch, George. Petey Simmons at Siwash. (Illus.). 10.25 (ISBN 0-8446-5185-0). Peter Smith.

Fitch, George A. My Eighty Years in China. 470p. 1980. (Pub. by Mei Ya China). Intl Spec Bk.

Fitch, George H. Comfort Found in Good Old Books. facs. ed. LC 76-121466. (Essay Index Reprint Ser). 1911. 19.00 (ISBN 0-8369-1805-3). Ayer Co Pubs.

--Comfort Found in Good Old Books. 1977. lib. bdg. 59.95 (ISBN 0-8490-1646-0). Gordon Pr.

--Comfort in Good Old Books: Shakespeare, Milton, Dr. Johnson, Cervantes. 1973. Repr. of 1911 ed. 17.50 (ISBN 0-8274-0665-7). R West.

--The Critic in the Occident. 1973. Repr. of 1913 ed. 20.00 (ISBN 0-8274-0666-5). R West.

--Great Spiritual Writers of America. LC 76-105013. (Essay Index Reprint Ser.). 1916. 19.00 (ISBN 0-8369-1464-3). Ayer Co Pubs.

--Great Spiritual Writers of America. 1973. lib. bdg. 20.00 (ISBN 0-8414-4257-6). Folcroft.

--Great Spiritual Writers of America. 1977. lib. bdg. 59.95 (ISBN 0-8490-1904-4). Gordon Pr.

--Modern English Books of Power. facs. ed. LC 70-121467. (Essay Index Reprint Ser). 1912. 19.00 (ISBN 0-8369-1706-5). Ayer Co Pubs.

Fitch, Grace E. & Larson, Margaret A. Basic Arithmetic Review & Drug Therapy for Practical-Vocational Nurses. 4th ed. (Illus.). 192p. 1977. pap. text ed. write for info. (ISBN 0-02-338010-1, 33801). Macmillan.

Fitch, H. S. & Henderson, Robert W. Reproduction: Age & Sex Differences, & Conservation of Iguana Iguana. 21p. 1977. 0.75 (ISBN 0-89326-026-6). Milwaukee Pub Mus.

Fitch, Harry N. Analysis of the Supervisory Activities & Techniques of the Elementary School Training Supervisor in State Normal Schools & Teachers Colleges. LC 74-176774. (Columbia University Teachers College Contributions to Education: No. 476). Repr. of 1931 ed. 22.50 (ISBN 0-404-55476-8). AMS Pr.

Fitch, Helen F., ed. see Chapuis, Alfred.

Fitch, Henry S. Aspects of Reproduction & Development in the Prairie Vole (Microtus Ochrogaster) (Museum Ser.: Vol. 10, No. 4). 33p. 1957. pap. 1.75 (ISBN 0-686-80283-7). U of KS Mus Nat Hist.

--Autecology of the Copperhead, Vol. 13, No. 4. 2nd ed. Hall, Raymond E. & Wilson, Robert W., eds. (Illus.). 288p. 1980. pap. 12.00 (ISBN 0-89338-016-4). U of KS Mus Nat Hist.

--A Demographic Study of the Ringneck Snake (Diadophis Punctatus) in Kansas. (Miscellaneous Publications Ser.: No. 62). 53p. 1975. pap. 2.75 (ISBN 0-686-80359-0). U of KS Mus Nat Hist.

--Observations on the Mississippi Kite in Southwestern Kansas. (Museum Ser.: Vol. 12, No. 11). 17p. 1963. pap. 1.25 (ISBN 0-317-04587-3). U of KS Mus Nat Hist.

--Population Structure & Survivorship in Some Costa Rican Lizards. (Occasional Papers: No. 18). 41p. 1973. pap. 2.25 (ISBN 0-686-80356-6). U of KS Mus Nat Hist.

--Reproductive Cycles in Tropical Reptiles. (Occasional Papers: No. 96). 53p. 1982. 3.25 (ISBN 0-317-04861-9). U of KS Mus Nat Hist.

--Sexual Size Differences in Reptiles. (Miscellaneous Publications: No. 70). 72p. 1981. 5.25 (ISBN 0-317-04862-7). U of KS Mus Nat Hist.

--Sexual Size Differences in the Mainland Anoles. (Occasional Papers: No. 50). 21p. 1976. pap. 1.25 (ISBN 0-686-80357-4). U of KS Mus Nat Hist.

--Spiders of the University of Kansas Natural History Reservation & Rockefeller Experimental Tract. (Miscellaneous Publications: No. 33). 202p. 1963. pap. 8.00 (ISBN 0-686-79810-4). U of KS Mus Nat Hist.

--Two New Anoles (Reptilia: Iguanidae) From Oaxaca with Comments on Other Mexican Species. 15p. 1978. 1.00 (ISBN 0-89326-034-7). Milwaukee Pub Mus.

--The University of Kansas Natural History Reservation, 1965. (Miscellaneous Publications: No. 42). 60p. 1965. pap. 3.50 (ISBN 0-686-79806-6). U of KS Mus Nat Hist.

Fitch, Henry S. & McGregor, Ronald L. The Forest Habitat of the University of Kansas Natural History Reservation. (Museum Ser.: Vol. 10, No. 3). 51p. 1956. pap. 3.00 (ISBN 0-686-79804-X). U of KS Mus Nat Hist.

Fitch, Henry S. & Maslin, T. Paul. Occurrence of the Garter Snake, Thamnophis Sirtalis, in the Great Plains & Rocky Mountains. (Museum Ser.: Vol. 13, No. 5). 20p. 1961. pap. 1.25 (ISBN 0-686-80355-8). U of KS Mus Nat Hist.

Fitch, Henry S. & Rainey, Dennis G. Ecological Observations on the Woodrat, Neotoma Floridana. (Museum Ser.: Vol. 8, No. 9). 35p. 1956. pap. 2.00 (ISBN 0-686-80282-9). U of KS Mus Nat Hist.

Fitch, Henry S. & Sandridge, Lewis L. Ecology of the Opossum on a Natural Area in Northeastern Kansas. (Museum Ser.: Vol. 7, No. 2). 34p. 1953. pap. 2.00 (ISBN 0-686-80281-0). U of KS Mus Nat Hist.

Fitch, Henry S. & Seigel, Richard A. Ecological & Taxonomic Notes on Nicaraguan Anoles. 1984. 4.95 (ISBN 0-89326-104-1). Milwaukee Pub Mus.

Fitch, Henry S., jt. auth. see LaVal, Richard K.

Fitch, Henry S., et al. Variation in the Central American Iguanid Lizard, Anolis Cupreus, with the Description of a New Subspecies. (Occasional Papers: No. 8). 20p. 1972. 1.25 (ISBN 0-317-04857-0). U of KS Mus Nat Hist.

Fitch, Howard M., ed. see Chapuis, Alfred.

Fitch, J. Eurosam 84: International Symposium on Symbolic & Algebraic Computation, Cambridge, England, July 9-11, 1984. (Lecture Notes in Computer Science Ser.: Vol. 174). xi, 396p. pap. 21.00 (ISBN 0-387-13350-X). Springer-Verlag.

Fitch, James M. American Building: The Environmental Forces That Shape It, Vol. II. 2nd ed. LC 75-10857. (Illus.). 368p. 1975. pap. 9.95 (ISBN 0-8052-0503-9). Schocken.

--American Building: The Historical Forces That Shaped It. (Illus.). 1966. 15.00 (ISBN 0-395-07680-3). HM.

--American Building: The Historical Forces That Shaped It, Vol. I. 2nd. ed. LC 65-10689. (Illus.). 1973. pap. 10.95 (ISBN 0-8052-0392-3). Schocken.

--American Building Two: The Environmental Forces That Shape It. 1972. 20.00 (ISBN 0-395-12681-9). HM.

--Architecture & the Esthetics of Plenty. LC 84-27922. (Illus.). xii, 304p. 1985. Repr. of 1961 ed. lib. bdg. 55.00x (ISBN 0-313-24798-6, FIAR). Greenwood.

--Historic Preservation. (Illus.). 448p. 1982. 41.50 (ISBN 0-07-021121-3). McGraw.

Fitch, Janet. Foreign Devil: Reminiscences of a China Missionary Daughter, 1909-1935. (Asian Library Ser.: No. 39). 1982. 28.75x (ISBN 0-686-37543-2). Oriental Bk Store.

Fitch, John. The Original Steam-Boat Supported: Or, Reply to Mr. James Rumsey's Pamphlet. facsimile ed. LC 73-165631. (Select Bibliographies Reprint Ser). Repr. of 1788 ed. 15.00 (ISBN 0-8369-5938-8). Ayer Co Pubs.

Fitch, John A. The Steel Worker. LC 70-89757. (American Labor, from Conspiracy to Collective Bargaining Ser., No. 1). 393p. 1969. Repr. of 1910 ed. 21.00 (ISBN 0-405-02121-6). Ayer Co Pubs.

Fitch, John E. & Lavenberg, Robert J. Marine Food & Game Fishes of California. (California Natural History Guides: No. 28). (Illus.). 1971. pap. 5.95 (ISBN 0-520-01831-1). U of Cal Pr.

--Tidepool & Nearshore Fishes of California. (Illus.). 1976. pap. 3.95 (ISBN 0-520-02845-7). U of Cal Pr.

Fitch, John S., 3rd. The Military Coup D'etat As a Political Process: Ecuador, 1948-1966. LC 76-47381. (SHPS Ser.: No. 1, 95th Ser.). (Illus.). 264p. 1977. text ed. 25.00x (ISBN 0-8018-1915-6). Johns Hopkins.

Fitch, Joshua. Thomas & Matthew Arnold & Their Influence on English Education. 1973. Repr. of 1910 ed. 25.00 (ISBN 0-8274-0719-X). R West.

Fitch, Kenneth L., jt. auth. see Cockrum, E. Lendell.

Fitch, Lynne, jt. auth. see Fitch, Bob.

Fitch, Noel R. Sylvia Beach & the Lost Generation: A History of Literary Paris in the Twenties & Thirties. (Illus.). 1983. 25.00 (ISBN 0-393-01713-3). Norton.

--Sylvia Beach & the Lost Generation: A History of Literary Paris in the Twenties & Thirties. (Illus.). 448p. 1985. pap. 9.95 (ISBN 0-393-30231-8). Norton.

Fitch, Phillip. Computer Ethics: A Philosophical Problem Book. 1983. 9.95 (ISBN 0-89824-082-4). Trillium Pr.

Fitch, Rachel F. The Bride's Little Black Book. 128p. 1983. 16.95 (ISBN 0-9611414-0-9). RFF Assocs.

Fitch, Raymond E. The Poison Sky: Myth & Apocalypse in Ruskin. LC 70-122097. (Illus.). xii, 722p. 1982. 35.00x (ISBN 0-8214-0090-8, 82-80943). Ohio U Pr.

Fitch, Richard D. & Porter, Edward A. Accidental or Incendiary. (Illus.). 224p. 1975. photocopy ed. 23.75x (ISBN 0-398-00582-6). C C Thomas.
Fitch, Robert. London, A Pictorial & Literary Map. 1952. 3.00 (ISBN 0-911218-04-1). Ravengate Pr.
Fitch, Robert, jt. auth. see Duffee, David.
Fitch, Robert E. Certain Blind Man: And Other Essays on the American Mood. facsimile ed. LC 75-142628. (Essay Index Reprint Ser). Repr. of 1944 ed. 19.00 (ISBN 0-8369-2549-1). Ayer Co Pubs.
--The Decline & Fall of Sex, with Some Curious Digressions on the Subject of True Love. LC 72-12555. 114p. 1973. Repr. of 1957 ed. lib. bdg. 22.50x (ISBN 0-8371-6722-1, FIDS). Greenwood.
Fitch, Robert M. & Svengalis, Cordell M. Futures Unlimited: Teaching about Worlds to Come. LC 79-52124. (Bulletin Ser.: No. 59). 88p. (Orig.). 1979. pap. 7.25 (ISBN 0-87986-023-5). Nat Coun Soc Studies.
Fitch, Robert M., ed. Polymer Colloids, I. LC 70-153721. 187p. 1971. 39.50 (ISBN 0-306-30536-4, Plenum Pr). Plenum Pub.
--Polymer Colloids, II. LC 80-112. 695p. 1980. 95.00 (ISBN 0-306-40350-1, Plenum Pr). Plenum Pub.
Fitch, Stanley K. The Science of Child Development. 496p. 1985. 18.00x (ISBN 0-256-03156-8). Dorsey.
Fitch, W. H., illus. Refugium Botanicum or Figurs & Descriptions from Living Specimens of Little Known or New Plants of Botanical Interest, Vol. II. (Orchid Ser.). (Illus.). 1980. Repr. text ed. 27.50 (ISBN 0-930576-19-5). E M Coleman Ent.
Fitch, W. S., ed. Multiple Periodic Variable Stars. 1976. 25.00 (ISBN 0-9960008-9-5, Pub. by Akademiai Kaido Hungary). Heyden.
Fitch, Walter S., ed. see I.A.U. Colloquium, 29th, Budapest, 1975.
Fitch, William D. Study of the Oboe. 1984. 10.00 (ISBN 0-685-21807-4). Wahr.
Fitchen, F. C., jt. auth. see Motchenbacher, C. D.
Fitchen, Janet M. Poverty in Rural America: A Cast Study. (Special Studies in Contemporary Social Issues). 266p. (Orig.). 1981. pap. text ed. 11.50x (ISBN 0-89158-901-5). Westview.
Fitchen, John. The Construction of Gothic Cathedrals: A Study of Medieval Vault Erection. LC 80-26291. (Illus.). 1977. pap. 12.50 (ISBN 0-226-25203-5, Phoen). U of Chicago Pr.
--New World Dutch Barn: A Study of Its Characteristics, Its Structural System & Its Probable Erectional Procedures. LC 68-20485. (New York State Studies). (Illus.). 1968. 15.00x (ISBN 0-8156-2126-4). Syracuse U Pr.
Fitcher. Bulge of Africa. 1981. 8.90 (ISBN 0-531-04270-7). Watts.
Fitcher, George S. Birds of North America. LC 81-15788. (Audubon Society Beginner Guide Ser.). (Illus.). 96p. (gr. 2 up). 1982. pap. 3.95 (ISBN 0-394-84771-7). Random.
Fitchett, Allan E., jt. ed. see Hobbs, Harry J.
Fitchett, W. H. The Tale of the Great Mutiny. Repr. of 1909 ed. 25.00 (ISBN 0-686-19880-8). Ridgeway Bks.
Fitchett, W. H., ed. Wellington's Men: Some Soldier Autobiographies. 1977. Repr. of 1900 ed. 27.00 (ISBN 0-7158-1151-7). Charles River Bks.
Fite, David. Harold Bloom: The Rhetoric of Romantic Vision. LC 85-5864. 256p. 1985. lib. bdg. 25.00x (ISBN 0-87023-484-6). U of Mass Pr.
Fite, Emerson D. Social & Industrial Conditions in the North During the Civil War. LC 74-22742. 328p. 1983. Repr. of 1910 ed. 32.50 (ISBN 0-404-58493-4). AMS Pr.
--Social & Industrial Conditions in the North During the Civil War. 318p. 1976. Repr. of 1910 ed. 16.50 (ISBN 0-87928-070-0). Corner Hse.
Fite, Gilbert C. American Farmers: The New Minority. LC 80-8843. (Illus.). 288p. 1981. 22.50x (ISBN 0-253-30182-3); pap. 7.95x (ISBN 0-253-20321-X, 321, MB). Ind U Pr.
--Beyond the Fence Rows: A History of Farmland Industries Inc., 1929-1978. LC 78-62287. 336p. 1978. text ed. 27.00x (ISBN 0-8262-0258-6). U of Mo Pr.
--Cotton Fields No More: Southern Agriculture, 1865-1980. LC 84-7439. (New Perspectives on the South Ser.). (Illus.). 288p. 1984. 28.00x (ISBN 0-8131-0306-1); pap. 10.00x (ISBN 0-8131-0160-3). U PR of KY.
--Mount Rushmore. (Illus.). pap. 8.95 (ISBN 0-8061-0959-9). U of Okla Pr.
Fite, Gilbert C., jt. auth. see Moody, J. Carroll.
Fite, Katherine V., ed. The Amphibian Visual System: A Multidisciplinary Approach. 1976. 67.00 (ISBN 0-12-257450-8). Acad Pr.
Fite, R., jt. auth. see Blair, T.
Fite, W. see Marton, L.
Fiter, Donald, tr. see Rubin, Isaac I.
Fithian, Janet, ed. Understanding the Child with a Chronic Illness in the Classroom. LC 83-43250. 264p. 1984. lib. bdg. 37.50 (ISBN 0-89774-083-1). Oryx Pr.
Fithian, Marilyn, jt. auth. see Hartman, William.
Fithian, Marilyn A., jt. auth. see Hartman, William.
Fithian, Marilyn A., jt. auth. see Hartman, William E.
Fithian, Philip V. Journal & Letters Seventeen Sixty-Seven to Seventeen Seventy-Four. Williams, John R., ed. LC 78-102269. (Select Bibliographies Reprint Ser). 1900. 29.00 (ISBN 0-8369-5023-2). Ayer Co Pubs.
Fitouss, Jean-Paul, jt. ed. see Malinvaud, Edmond.
Fitoussi, Jean-Paul, ed. Modern Macroeconomic Theory. LC 83-7139. 220p. 1983. 29.95x (ISBN 0-389-20411-0, 07296). B&N Imports.
Fitt, A. P. Life of D. L. Moody. pap. 2.95 (ISBN 0-8024-4727-9). Moody.
Fitt, Arthur P. The Shorter Life of D. L. Moody. 143p. 1982. pap. 2.00 (ISBN 0-89323-014-6). Bible Memory.
Fitt, Mary. Death & the Pleasant Voices. (Detective Stories). 224p. 1984. pap. 4.50 (ISBN 0-486-24603-5). Dover.
Fitt, Sally & Riordan, Anne, eds. Dance for the Handicapped: Focus on Dance IX. 104p. 198C. 8.65 (ISBN 0-88314-071-3). Natl Dance Assn.
Fitt, William C., ed. Steam & Stirling: Engines You Can Build. LC 80-50602. (Illus.). 160p. 1980. 24.95 (ISBN 0-914104-06-3). Wildwood Pubns MI.
--Union Pacific FEF-3 Class 4-8-4 Locomotive Drawings. LC 75-27822. (Illus.). 54p. 1975. pap. 15.50 (ISBN 0-914104-02-0). Wildwood Pubns MI.
Fitt, Yann, et al. The World Economic Crisis: American Imperialism at Bay. 224p. (Orig.). 1980. 31.00x (ISBN 0-905762-53-3, Pub. by Zed Pr England); pap. 8.50x (ISBN 0-905762-54-1, Pub. by Zed Pr England). Biblio Dist.
Fittbogen, Gottfried. Die Religion Lessings. 1967. 36.00; pap. 31.00 (ISBN 0-685-13575-6). Johnson Repr.
Fitter. Collins Pocket Guide to Bird Watching. 29.95 (ISBN 0-00-219171-7, Collins Pub England). Greene.
--Finding Wild Flowers. 29.95 (ISBN 0-00-219366-3, Collins Pub England). Greene.
Fitter & Blamey. The Wild Flowers of Britain & Northern Europe. pap. 14.95 (ISBN 0-00-219069-9, Collins Pub England). Greene.
Fitter & Richardson. Collins Pocket Guide to British Birds. 26.95 (ISBN 0-00-219174-1, Collins Pub England). Greene.
--Collins Pocket Guide to Nests & Eggs. 26.95 (ISBN 0-00-219306-X, Collins Pub England). Greene.
Fitter, jt. auth. see Arlott.
Fitter, jt. auth. see Blamey.
Fitter, jt. auth. see Heinzel.
Fitter, jt. auth. see McClintock.
Fitter, A. H. & Hay, R. K. Environmental Physiology of Plants. (Experimental Botany Ser.). 1981. 55.00 (ISBN 0-12-257760-4); pap. 27.00 (ISBN 0-12-257762-0). Acad Pr.
Fitter, A. H., ed. Ecological Interactions in the Soil Environment. (Illus.). 400p. 1985. pap. text ed. 57.00x (ISBN 0-632-01386-9). Blackwell Pubns.
Fitter, Richard, ed. see Clare, John.
Fitterer, G. Applications of Fundamental Thermodynamics to Metallurgical Processes. 434p. 1967. pap. 119.25 (ISBN 0-677-10815-X). Gordon.
Fitti, Charles J. Between God & Man. LC 78-50527. 48p. 1978. 6.75 (ISBN 0-8022-2225-0). Philos Lib.
--A Poetry Series. LC 76-181333. 1972. 3.75 (ISBN 0-8022-2079-7). Philos Lib.
Fitting, Dale & Adler, Laszlo. Ultrasonic Spectral Analysis for Nondestructive Evaluation. LC 80-14991. 364p. 1981. 59.50x (ISBN 0-306-40484-2, Plenum Pr). Plenum Pub.
Fitting, Frances, ed. see DeLaurentis, Rocky.
Fitting, Frances, ed. see Partain, Katherine.
Fitting, Frances, ed. see Thomson, T. L.
Fitting, James E. The Archaeology of Michigan: A Guide to the Prehistory of the Great Lakes Region. LC 75-14773. (Bulletin Ser.: No. 56). (Illus.). 274p. 1975. pap. text ed. 7.50x (ISBN 0-87737-033-8). Cranbrook.
--The Prehistory of the Burnt Bluff Area. (Illus.). 140p. 1968. pap. 3.00 (ISBN 0-932206-32-8). U Mich Mus Anthro.
Fitting, James E., ed. The Development of North American Archaeology. LC 73-5862. 312p. 1973. 16.00x (ISBN 0-271-01161-0). Pa St U Pr.
--The Pre-History of the Burnt Bluff Area. (Anthropological Papers: No. 34). 1968. pap. 3.00x (ISBN 0-932206-32-8). U Mich Mus Anthro.
--The Schultz Site at Green Point: A Stratified Occupation Area in the Saginaw Valley of Michigan. (Memoirs Ser: No. 4). (Illus.). 1972. pap. 8.00x (ISBN 0-932206-66-2). U Mich Mus Anthro.
Fitting, M. Fundamentals of Generalized Recursion Theory. (Studies in Logic & the Foundations of Mathematics: Vol. 105). 308p. 1982. 64.00 (ISBN 0-444-86171-8, North-Holland). Elsevier.
Fitting, Marjorie A. & Dubisch, Roy. Bases & Computation. pap. 4.75 (ISBN 0-317-05289-6). Midwest Pubns.
--Bites & Memory. pap. 4.75 (ISBN 0-317-05288-8). Midwest Pubns.
--Bits & Codes. pap. 4.75 (ISBN 0-317-05287-X). Midwest Pubns.
--Computer Literacy Series, 6 Bks. 1983. 4.75 ea. Midwest Pubns.
Fitting, Melvin. Proof Methods for Modal & Intuitionistic Logic. 1983. lib. bdg. 65.00 (ISBN 90-277-1573-4, Pub. by Reidel Holland). Kluwer Academic.
Fittipaldi, Emerson & Hayward, Elizabeth. Flying on the Ground. (Illus.). 256p. 1973. 9.95 (ISBN 0-7183-0013-0). Motorbooks Intl.
Fittipaldi, F., jt. ed. see Palz, W.
Fittipaldi, Silvio. How to Pray Always: Without Always Praying. LC 85-80599. (Orig.). 1985. pap. 2.95 (ISBN 0-89243-237-3). Liguori Pubns.
Fitton, A. O. & Smalley, R. K. Practical Heterocyclic Chemistry. LC 68-19255. 1968. 26.00 (ISBN 0-12-257850-3). Acad Pr.
Fitton, Mary, tr. see Lanez, Manuel M.
Fitton, R. S. & Wadsworth, A. P. Strutts & the Arkwrights, 1758-1830. LC 72-375. Repr. of 1958 ed. 35.00x (ISBN 0-678-06758-9). Kelley.
Fitton, R. S., ed. see Collier, Frances.
Fitts, Bob. When You Pray - Things Happen. LC 82-82018. 144p. 1982. 2.95 (ISBN 0-89221-089-3). New Leaf.
Fitts, Dudley, jt. auth. see Taggard, Genevieve.
Fitts, Dudley, ed. Anthology of Contemporary Latin American Poetry. LC 76-17656. 1976. Repr. of 1947 ed. lib. bdg. 47.50x (ISBN 0-8371-8905-5, FIAC). Greenwood.
--Aristophanes: Four Comedies. Incl. Lysistrata; The Frogs; The Birds; Ladies' Day. LC 62-19595. 343p. 1962. pap. 4.95 (ISBN 0-15-607900-3, Harv). HarBraceJ.
--Four Greek Plays. 17.95 (ISBN 0-89190-699-1, Pub. by Am Repr). Amereon Ltd.
--The Oedipus Cycle of Sophocles. Fitzgerald, Robert, tr. Incl. Oedipus Rex; Antigone; Oedipus at Colonus. 243p. 1955. pap. 3.95 (ISBN 0-15-683838-9, Harv). HarBraceJ.
Fitts, Dudley, tr. Four Greek Plays. Incl. Agamemnon. Aeschylus; Oedipus Rex. Sophocles; Alcestis. Euripides; The Birds. Aristophanes. LC 60-1871. 310p. 1960. pap. 5.95 (ISBN 0-15-632777-5, Harv). HarBraceJ.
Fitts, Dudley, tr. see Anthologia Graeca Selections.
Fitts, Gary. Module XI: Graphing Functions. Ablon, Leon J., ed. LC 76-62884. (Ser. in Mathematics Modules). 1977. pap. 8.95 (ISBN 0-8465-0265-8). Benjamin-Cummings.
Fitts, Gary, ed. Module X: Functions & Word Problems. Ablon, Leon J. LC 76-1055. (Mathematics Modules Ser.). 1976. pap. 7.95 (ISBN 0-8465-0264-X). Benjamin-Cummings.
Fitts, Henry. Winnowings from the Granite State. LC 82-2074. (Illus.). 123p. (Orig.). 1982. pap. 5.95 (ISBN 0-936988-06-1, Pub. by Tompson & Rutter). Shoe String.
Fitts, Henry K. Winnowings from the Granite State: Reflections on Country Living. LC 82-2074. (Illus.). 123p. (Orig.). 1982. pap. 5.95 (ISBN 0-936988-06-1). Tompson & Rutter.
Fitts, Leroy. A History of Black Baptists. LC 84-1851. 1985. pap. 9.95 (ISBN 0-8054-6580-4). Broadman.
--Lott Carey: First Black Missionary to Africa. 1978. pap. 6.95 (ISBN 0-8170-0820-9). Judson.
Fitts, Paul M. & Posner, Michael I. Human Performance. LC 79-4253. (Illus.). 1979. Repr. of 1967 ed. lib. bdg. 24.75x (ISBN 0-313-21245-7, FIHP). Greenwood.
Fitts, Richard E., ed. The Strategy of Electromagnetic Conflict. 1979. Repr. of 1978 ed. 21.95 (ISBN 0-932146-02-3). Peninsula CA.
Fitz, Earl E. Clarice Lispector. (World Author Ser.). 1985. lib. bdg. 19.95 (ISBN 0-8057-6605-7). G K Hall.
Fitz, Franklin H. A Gardener's Guide to Propagating Food Plants. (Illus.). 160p. 1983. 11.95 (ISBN 0-684-17655-6, ScribT). Scribner.
Fitz, J., ed. Limes: Proceedings 11th Intl. Lime Congress. 1977. 55.00 (ISBN 0-9960002-8-3, Pub. by Akademiai Kaido Hungary). Heyden.
Fitz, Jean D. Devon Maze. LC 70-93120. Orig. Title: Devon House. 1969. 4.95 (ISBN 0-87672-102-1). Geron-X.
--Viper's Bite. LC 72-87226. 1969. 4.95 (ISBN 0-87672-101-3). Geron-X.
Fitz, Virginia W. Spirit of Shady Side: Peninsula Life 1664-1984. LC 84-52251. (Illus.). 122p. 1984. pap. 9.50 (ISBN 0-9614295-0-X). Shady Side Pen.
Fitzaimmons, Thomas, ed. see Yoshioka, Minoru & Iijima, Koichi.
Fitzalan, C. W. Motley Heraldry by the Fool of Arms. 1976. Repr. 10.00x (ISBN 0-901951-33-1). Charles River Bks.
FitzBarnard, L. Fighting Sports. 334p. 1983. 26.95 (ISBN 0-904558-09-6). Triplegate.
Fitzell, John. Hermit in German Literature: From Lessing to Eichendorff. LC 74-168033. (North Carolina. University. Studies in the Germanic Languages & Literatures: No. 30). Repr. of 1961 ed. 27.00 (ISBN 0-404-50930-4). AMS Pr.
Fitzell, Lincoln. Selected Poems. 88p. 1955. 5.95 (ISBN 0-8040-0269-X, 82-71884, Pub. by Swallow). Ohio U Pr.
Fitzell, Philip B. Private Labels: Store Brands & Generic Products. (Illus.). 1982. lib. bdg. 32.50 (ISBN 0-87055-415-8). AVI.
Fitz-enz, J. How to Measure Human Resources Management. 1984. 29.95 (ISBN 0-07-021131-0). McGraw.
Fitzer, Donald, ed. see Rubin, Isaac I.
Fitzer, Joseph. Moehler & Baur in Controversy Eighteen Thirty-Two to Thirty-Eight: Romantic-idealist Assesment of the Reformation & Counter-Reformation. LC 74-77619. (American Academy of Religion. Studies in Religion). 1974. 9.95 (ISBN 0-88420-111-2, 010007). Scholars Pr GA.
Fitzergerald, Joseph. Black Gold with Grit. 240p. 1978. 16.95 (ISBN 0-686-74129-3). Superior Pub.
Fitzgerald. ABC. (Dear God Kids Ser.). Date not set. 3.95 (ISBN 0-671-50677-3). S&S.
--Animal Friends. (Dear God Kids Ser.). Date not set. 3.95 (ISBN 0-671-50679-X). S&S.
--Count Their Blessings. (Dear God Kids Ser.). Date not set. 3.95 (ISBN 0-671-50678-1). S&S.
--Fundamentals of Systems Analysis. 3rd ed. 1986. pap. price not set wkbk. (ISBN 0-471-82509-3). Wiley.
--Lifespan: Topical Approach. 1986. pap. text ed. write for info. Wadsworth Pub.
--Rainbow. (Dear God Kids Ser.). Date not set. 3.95 (ISBN 0-671-50681-1). S&S.
Fitzgerald, A. E., et al. Basic Electrical Engineering. 5th ed. 1981. text ed. 42.00 (ISBN 0-07-021154-X). McGraw.
--Electric Machinery. 4th ed. (McGraw-Hill Series in Electrical Engineering). (Illus.). 640p. 1983. text ed. 42.00 (ISBN 0-07-021145-0). McGraw.
Fitzgerald, Adolf A. Current Accounting Trends. Brief, Richard P., ed. LC 77-87271. (Development of Contemporary Accounting Thought Ser). 1978. Repr. of 1952 ed. lib. bdg. 29.00x (ISBN 0-405-10899-0). Ayer Co Pubs.
Fitzgerald, Alan J. The Italian Farming Soldiers: Prisoners of War in Australia, 1941 to 1947. (Illus.). 200p. 1981. 25.00x (ISBN 0-522-84211-9, Pub. by Melbourne U Pr Australia). Intl Spec Bk.
Fitzgerald, Alice I. Missouri's Literary Heritage for Children & Youth: An Annotated Bibliography of Books About Missouri. LC 81-3030. 272p. 1981. text ed. 21.00x (ISBN 0-8262-0346-9). U of Mo Pr.
FitzGerald, Ann, jt. ed. see McPhee, Carol.
Fitzgerald, Anne & Lane, Saunders M., eds. Pure & Applied Math in People's Republic of China. LC 77-79329. (CSCPRC Report: No. 3). 1977. pap. 9.75 (ISBN 0-309-02609-1). Natl Acad Pr.
Fitzgerald, Anne & Slichter, Charles, eds. Solid State Physics in the People's Republic of China: A Trip Report of the American Solid State Physics Delegation. LC 76-49402. (People's Republic of China Ser.: No. 1). 1976. pap. 11.95 (ISBN 0-309-02523-0). Natl Acad Pr.
Fitzgerald, Annie. Dear God, Bless Our Food. (Dear God Bks.). 16p. (Orig.). 1984. pap. 1.50 (ISBN 0-8066-2108-7, 10-1859). Augsburg.
--Dear God, Good Morning. (Dear God Bks.). 16p. (Orig.). 1984. pap. 1.50 (ISBN 0-8066-2104-4, 10-1860). Augsburg.
--Dear God, Good Night. (Dear God Bks.). 16p. 1984. pap. 1.50 (ISBN 0-8066-2105-2, 10-1861). Augsburg.
--Dear God, I Just Love Birthdays. (Dear God Bks.). 16p. (Orig.). 1984. pap. 1.50 (ISBN 0-8066-2107-9, 10-1862). Augsburg.
--Dear God, Let's Play. LC 83-70495. 16p. (Orig.). (gr. 3-6). 1983. pap. 1.50 (ISBN 0-8066-2001-3, 10-1852). Augsburg.
--Dear God, Thanks for Friends. (Dear God Bks.). 16p. (Orig.). 1984. pap. 1.50 (ISBN 0-8066-2109-5, 10-1863). Augsburg.
--Dear God, Thanks for Making Me. (Dear God Bks.). 16p. (Orig.). 1984. pap. 1.50 (ISBN 0-8066-2106-0, 10-1864). Augsburg.
--Dear God, Thanks for Thinking up Love. LC 83-70499. 16p. (gr. 3-6). 1983. pap. 1.50 (ISBN 0-8066-2005-6, 10-1853). Augsburg.
--Dear God, Thanks for Your Help. LC 83-70496. 16p. (gr. 3-6). 1983. pap. 1.50 (ISBN 0-8066-2002-1, 10-1854). Augsburg.
--Dear God, We Just Love Christmas. LC 83-70494. 16p. (Orig.). (gr. 3-6). 1983. pap. 1.50 (ISBN 0-8066-2000-5, 10-1855). Augsburg.
--Dear God, Where Do You Live? LC 83-70497. 16p. (gr. 3-6). 1983. pap. 1.50 (ISBN 0-8066-2003-X, 10-1856). Augsburg.
--Dear God, Your World Is Wonderful. LC 83-70498. 16p. (gr. 3-6). 1983. pap. 1.50 (ISBN 0-8066-2004-8, 10-1857). Augsburg.
Fitzgerald, Anselm. Song of a Happy Man. LC 81-369. 1981. pap. 4.95 (ISBN 0-932506-12-7). St Bedes Pubns.
Fitzgerald, Ardra F., jt. auth. see Fitzgerald, Jerry.
Fitzgerald, Arlene. Windfire. (Orig.). 1983. pap. 3.50 (ISBN 0-8217-1216-0). Zebra.
Fitzgerald, Arthur. Prix de L'Arc de Triomphe: The Official History. (Illus.). 240p. 1983. 29.95 (ISBN 0-283-99036-8, Pub. by Sidgwick & Jackson). Merrimack Pub Cir.
Fitzgerald, Barbara. Footprint upon Water. 216p. 1983. pap. 8.95 (ISBN 0-85640-291-5, Pub. by Blackstaff Pr). Longwood Pub Group.
Fitzgerald, Barbara, jt. auth. see Aronson, Virginia.
Fitzgerald, Bob. Practical Sign Shop Operation. (Illus.). 1982. 25.00 (ISBN 0-911380-58-2). Signs of Times.
Fitzgerald, Brian. The Anglo-Irish: Three Representative Types, Cork, Ormonde, Swift, 1602-1745. LC 76-22190. 1976. Repr. of 1952 ed. lib. bdg. 25.00 (ISBN 0-8414-4211-8). Folcroft.

--Daniel Defoe. 1973. Repr. of 1954 ed. 25.00 (ISBN 0-8274-1116-2). R West.
--Daniel Defoe: A Study in Conflict. 1978. Repr. of 1954 ed. lib. bdg. 25.00 (ISBN 0-8495-1615-3). Arden Lib.
--Daniel Defoe: A Study in Conflict. LC 74-26788. 1976. Repr. of 1954 ed. lib. bdg. 25.00 (ISBN 0-8414-4231-2). Folcroft.
Fitzgerald, Brian T., ed. Guide Book of the Long Trail. 23rd ed. (Illus.). 175p. (Orig.). 1985. pap. 8.50 (ISBN 0-318-12118-2). Green Mtn Club.
Fitzgerald, Bridget. Little Dark Cloud. LC 78-189877. (Story & Its Verse Ser.). (Illus.). 44p. (gr. 1-2). 1973. 2.50 (ISBN 0-87884-012-5). Unicorn Ent.
--Winkie, the Cross-Eyed Witch. LC 71-189878. (Story & Verse Ser.). (Illus.). (gr. 1-2). 1973. 2.50 (ISBN 0-87884-020-6). Unicorn Ent.
Fitzgerald, Brigid, jt. auth. see Young, Lynne.
Fitzgerald, C. P. China: A Short Cultural History. 1942. 20.00 (ISBN 0-686-19902-2). Quaker City.
--China: A Short Cultural History. 644p. 1985. pap. 45.00 (ISBN 0-8133-0279-X). Westview.
--Revolution in China. (Westview Encore Edition Ser.). 300p. 1985. pap. 25.00 (ISBN 0-8133-0280-3). Westview.
Fitzgerald, Caroline G. Crossword Puzzles for Religious Education, Vol.1. 1980. pap. 7.55 (ISBN 0-88479-030-4). Arena Lettres.
Fitzgerald, Catharine, jt. auth. see Young, Rosamond.
Fitzgerald, Charles P. Mao Tse-Tung & China. LC 76-3700. (Illus.). 175p. 1976. text ed. 19.50x (ISBN 0-8419-0268-2). Holmes & Meier.
--Son of Heaven: A Biography of Li Shih-Min, Founder of the T'ang Dynasty. LC 74-136382. Repr. of 1933 ed. 20.00 (ISBN 0-404-02404-1). AMS Pr.
--The Tower of Five Glories: A Study of the Min Chia of Ta Li. LC 73-872. (China Studies: from Confucius to Mao Ser.). (Illus.). 280p. 1973. Repr. of 1941 ed. 21.50 (ISBN 0-88355-067-9). Hyperion Conn.
Fitzgerald, David, photos by. Oklahoma. LC 79-92730. (Belding Imprint Ser.). (Illus.). 128p. (Text by Bill Burchardt). 1980. 32.50 (ISBN 0-912856-57-2). Graphic Arts Ctr.
--Ozarks. LC 85-71194. (Illus.). 160p. (Text by Clay Anderson). 1985. 37.50 (ISBN 0-912856-94-7). Graphic Arts Ctr.
Fitzgerald, Don. Hawaii Cook Book. (Illus., Orig.). pap. 3.50 (ISBN 0-911098-00-3). Pacifica.
Fitzgerald, Don, jt. auth. see Roy, Mike.
Fitzgerald, Don, ed. Hawaii Cookbook. 1973. pap. 3.50 (ISBN 0-911098-00-3). Borden.
Fitzgerald, Dorothy H. Unicorn Country. 65p. (Orig.). 1985. pap. 6.95 (ISBN 0-932269-13-3). Wyndham Hall.
Fitzgerald, E. P., ed. Proceedings of the Eighth Annual Meeting of the French Colonial Historical Society, 1982. (Illus.). 246p. (Orig.). 1985. lib. bdg. 24.75 (ISBN 0-8191-4408-8, French Colonial Hist Soc); pap. text ed. 12.25 (ISBN 0-8191-4409-6). U Pr of Amer.
FitzGerald, E. V. The Political Economy of Peru, Nineteen Fifty-Six to Nineteen Seventy-Seven. LC 78-72086. (Illus.). 1980. 59.50 (ISBN 0-521-22289-3). Cambridge U Pr.
--Public Sector Investment Planning for Developing Countries. 200p. 1978. text ed. 28.50x (ISBN 0-8419-5027-X). Holmes & Meier.
--The State & Economic Development: Peru Since 1968. LC 75-30443. (Department of Applied Economics, Occasional Papers Ser.: No. 49). (Illus.). 140p. 1976. pap. 13.95x (ISBN 0-521-29054-6). Cambridge U Pr.
Fitzgerald, Ed. A Nickel an Inch: A Memoir. LC 85-47777. 384p. 1985. 17.95 (ISBN 0-689-11590-3). Atheneum.
Fitzgerald, Edith. Straight Language for the Deaf. rev. ed. LC 49-4933. 1949. pap. text ed. 7.75 (ISBN 0-88200-076-4, C1771). Alexander Graham.
Fitzgerald, Edmond J. Marine Painting in Watercolor. (Illus.). 176p. 1972. 22.50 (ISBN 0-8230-3008-3). Watson-Guptill.
Fitzgerald, Edward. Dictionary of Madame De Sevigne, 2 Vols. Kerrich, Mary E., ed. LC 74-130598. 1971. Repr. of 1914 ed. lib. bdg. 43.00 (ISBN 0-8337-1140-7). B Franklin.
--Edward Fitzgerald & Bernard Barton: Letters Written by Fitzgerald. Barton, F. R., ed. 1924. lib. bdg. 25.00 (ISBN 0-8414-4258-4). Folcroft.
--A Fitzgerald Friendship: Being Hitherto Unpublished Letters of Edward Fitzgerald to William Bodham Donne. Hannay, Neilson C., ed. LC 73-12992. 1932. lib. bdg. 30.00 (ISBN 0-8414-4752-7). Folcroft.
--Fitzgerald to His Friends. Hayer, Alethea, ed. 1979. pap. 9.95 (ISBN 0-85967-499-1). Scolar.
--Letters, 2 vols. Wright, William A., ed. LC 72-5597. (Select Bibliographies Reprint Ser.). 1972. Repr. of 1894 ed. Set. 42.00 (ISBN 0-8369-6906-5). Ayer Co Pubs.
--Letters & Literary Remains of Edward Fitzgerald, 7 Vols. Wright, William A., ed. LC 78-168035. Repr. of 1903 ed. Set. 280.00 (ISBN 0-404-02440-8). AMS Pr.
--Letters & Literary Remains of Edward Fitzgerald, 3 vols. Wright, William A., ed. 1889. Set. lib. bdg. 65.00 (ISBN 0-8414-4259-2). Folcroft.
--Letters from Edward Fitzgerald to Bernard Qwaritch: 1853-1883. Wrentmore, C. Qwaritch, ed. LC 73-13547. 1926. lib. bdg. 25.00 (ISBN 0-8414-9428-2). Folcroft.
--Letters of Edward Fitzgerald, 2 vols. 1889. Set. lib. bdg. 30.00 (ISBN 0-8414-4260-6). Folcroft.
--The Letters of Edward Fitzgerald, 4 vols. Terhune, Alfred M. & Terhune, Annabelle B., eds. Incl. Vol. 1. 1830-1850. 55.00 (ISBN 0-691-06383-4); Vol. 2. 1851-1866. 55.00 (ISBN 0-691-06386-9); Vol. 3. 1867-1876. 55.00 (ISBN 0-691-06387-7); Vol. 4. 1877-1883. 55.00 (ISBN 0-691-06388-5). LC 78-23221. (Illus.). 1980. 195.00 set (ISBN 0-686-60727-9). Princeton U Pr.
--Letters of Edward Fitzgerald to Fanny Kremble, 1871-1883. LC 72-2502. (Select Bibliographies Reprint Ser). 1972. Repr. of 1902 ed. 19.00 (ISBN 0-8369-6854-9). Ayer Co Pubs.
--Miscellanies. 1900. lib. bdg. 12.50 (ISBN 0-8414-4261-4). Folcroft.
--More Letters of Edward Fitzgerald. 1977. Repr. of 1901 ed. lib. bdg. 22.50 (ISBN 0-8495-1608-0). Arden Lib.
--More Letters of Edward Fitzgerald. Wright, William A., ed. 1901. lib. bdg. 25.00 (ISBN 0-8414-4262-2). Folcroft.
--Rubaiyat of Omar Khayyam. LC 77-27060. 1978. Repr. of 1902 ed. lib. bdg. 22.50 (ISBN 0-8414-4357-2). Folcroft.
--Rubaiyat of Omar Khayyam. (Illus.). 112p. 1985. pap. 8.95 (ISBN 0-245-54234-5). Beaufort Bks NY.
--Rubaiyat of Omar Khayyam: A Comparative Printing of the First Four-Quaritch-Editions of Edward Fitzgerald's Renderings into English Verse with Notes Showing the Variants in That Fifth-Wright-Edition. 1915. lib. bdg. 25.00 (ISBN 0-8414-4357-2). Folcroft.
--Some New Letters of Edward Fitzgerald. Barton, F. R., ed. LC 73-13605. 1923. lib. bdg. 22.50 (ISBN 0-8414-3241-4). Folcroft.
--Writings of Edward Fitzgerald, 7 Vols. variorum ed. LC 67-18645. Repr. of 1903 ed. Set. 75.00x (ISBN 0-87753-015-7). Phaeton.
Fitzgerald, Edward, tr. Rubaiyat of Omar Khayyam. (Illus.). 1930. 10.95 (ISBN 0-385-00146-0, C28, Dolp); pap. 2.95 (ISBN 0-385-09499-X). Doubleday.
--Rubaiyat of Omar Khayyam. 128p. 1983. 8.95 (ISBN 0-312-69527-6). St Martin.
Fitzgerald, Edward, tr. see Khayyam, Omar.
Fitzgerald, Edward, tr. see Loewenstein, Prince H. & Von Zuhlsdorff, Volkmar.
Fitzgerald, Edward, tr. see Renn, Ludwig.
Fitzgerald, Edward, tr. see Siegfried, Andre.
Fitzgerald, Edward, tr. see Sternberg, Fritz.
Fitzgerald, Elisa B., ed. see Leroe, Ellen.
Fitzgerald, Ellen. The Dangerous Dr. Langhorne. 1985. pap. 2.50 (ISBN 0-451-13855-4, Sig). NAL.
--Lord Caliban. 1985. pap. 2.50 (ISBN 0-451-13476-1, Sig). NAL.
--A Novel Alliance. 1984. pap. 2.50 (ISBN 0-451-13274-2, Sig). NAL.
Fitzgerald, Ellen, tr. see Bazalgette, Leon.
Fitzgerald, Ernest A. Diamonds Everywhere: Appreciating God's Gifts. 112p. (Orig.). 1983. pap. 7.75 (ISBN 0-687-10734-2). Abingdon.
Fitzgerald, F. S. The Last Tycoon. 12.95 (ISBN 0-89190-604-5, Pub. by Am Repr). Amereon Ltd.
--Six Tales of the Jazz Age & Other Stories. 13.95 (ISBN 0-88411-597-6, Pub. by Aeonian Pr). Amereon Ltd.
Fitzgerald, F. Scott. Afternoon of an Author. (Hudson River Edition Ser.). 1981. 20.00 (ISBN 0-684-16469-8, ScribT). Scribner.
--Afternoon of an Author. 1957. (ScribT); pap. 2.95 (ISBN 0-684-12734-2, SL332, ScribT). Scribner.
--The Basil & Josephine Stories. (The Library of Contemporary Classics). 320p. 1985. pap. 8.95 (ISBN 0-684-14693-2, ScribT). Scribner.
--The Basil & Josephine Stories. Kuehl, John & Bryer, Jackson R., eds. LC 73-1120. 320p. 1973. 8.95 (ISBN 0-684-13398-9, ScribT). Scribner.
--Beautiful & Damned. 1920. lib. rep. ed. 25.00 (ISBN 0-684-15153-7, ScribT); pap. 7.95 (ISBN 0-684-71758-1, SL90, ScribT). Scribner.
--The Crack-Up. Wilson, Edmund, ed. LC 56-13361. 1956. pap. 6.95 (ISBN 0-8112-0051-5, NDP54). New Directions.
--The Cruise of the Rolling Junk. 1976. 25.00 (ISBN 0-89723-008-6). Bruccoli.
--F. Scott Fitzgerald on Writing. Phillips, Larry, ed. 160p. 1985. 12.95 (ISBN 0-684-18516-4, ScribT). Scribner.
--F. Scott Fitzgerald's St. Paul Plays: 1911-1914. Margolies, Alan, ed. LC 78-56379. (Illus.). 166p. 1978. 12.00 (ISBN 0-87811-022-4). Princeton Lib.
--The Fitzgerald Reader. Mizener, Arthur, ed. 509p. 1978. pap. text ed. price not set (ISBN 0-02-381830-1, Pub. by Scribner). Macmillan.
--Great Gatsby. (Hudson River Edition Ser.). 1981. 20.00 (ISBN 0-684-16498-1, ScribT). Scribner.
--Great Gatsby. (gr. 9-12). 1920. (ScribT); (ScribC); pap. 4.95 (ISBN 0-684-71760-3, SL1, ScribT); pap. text ed. 5.95 (ISBN 0-684-51516-4, SSP2, ScribC); ScribT. pap. 2.95 rack size (ISBN 0-684-16325-X). Scribner.
--The Great Gatsby. 179p. 1984. 400.00 (ISBN 0-910457-05-0). Arion Pr.
--The Great Gatsby. 13.95 (ISBN 0-317-28492-4, Pub. by Am Repr). Amereon Ltd.
--The Great Gatsby. 282p. 1925. pap. text ed. price not set (ISBN 0-02-338120-5, Pub. by Scribner). Macmillan.
--Last Tycoon. 1941. lib. rep. ed. 20.00 (ISBN 0-684-15311-4, ScribT); pap. 5.95 (ISBN 0-684-71764-6, SL242, ScribT). Scribner.
--The Last Tycoon. 176p. 1983. pap. 2.95 rack-size (ISBN 0-684-17953-9, ScribT). Scribner.
--The Letters of F. Scott Fitzgerald. (Hudson River Edition Ser.). 1981. 40.00 (ISBN 0-684-16476-0, ScribT). Scribner.
--Pat Hobby Stories. 1962. (ScribT); 17.50 (ISBN 0-684-16477-9). Scribner.
--Screenplay for "Three Comrades" by Erich Maria Remarque. Bruccoli, Matthew J., ed. LC 77-28077. (Screenplay Library). (Illus.). 303p. 1978. 12.95x (ISBN 0-8093-0854-1); pap. 7.95x (ISBN 0-8093-0853-3). S Ill U Pr.
--Six Tales of the Jazz Age & Other Stories. 1968. (ScribT); pap. 5.95 (ISBN 0-684-71762-X, ScribT). Scribner.
--The Stories of F. Scott Fitzgerald. 512p. 1984. 27.50 (ISBN 0-684-15366-1, ScribT); pap. 9.95 (ISBN 0-684-71737-9). Scribner.
--Taps at Reveille. 1935. lib. rep. ed. 20.00 (ISBN 0-684-14742-4, ScribT); (ScribT). Scribner.
--Tender Is the Night. 1960. lib. rep. ed. 22.00x (ISBN 0-684-15151-0, ScribT); pap. 7.95 (ISBN 0-684-71763-8, SL2, ScribT). Scribner.
--Tender Is the Night. 320p. 1985. pap. 4.95 (ISBN 0-684-17817-6, ScribT). Scribner.
--Tender Is the Night. 17.95 (ISBN 0-89190-600-2, Pub. by Am Repr). Amereon Ltd.
--This Side of Paradise. 1920. lib. rep. ed. 20.00x (ISBN 0-684-15601-6, ScribT); pap. 6.95 (ISBN 0-684-71765-4, SL60, ScribT); pap. 4.95 rack size (ISBN 0-684-17468-5). Scribner.
--Three Novels of F. Scott Fitzgerald. Bd. with The Great Gatsby; Tender is the Night; The Last Tycoon. 634p. 1979. pap. text ed. price not set (ISBN 0-02-337980-4, Pub. by Scribner). Macmillan.
--The Vegetable, or, From President to Postman. LC 76-2633. 1976. 7.95 (ISBN 0-684-14622-3, ScribT); pap. 2.95 (ISBN 0-684-14623-1, ScribT). Scribner.
Fitzgerald, F. Scott & Fitzgerald, Zelda. Bits of Paradise. LC 74-4648. 392p. 1974. encore ed. 2.49 (ISBN 0-684-13902-2, ScribT). Scribner.
FitzGerald, Frances. America Revised. LC 80-11239. 256p. 1980. pap. 3.95 (ISBN 0-394-74439-X, Vin). Random.
--Fire in the Lake: The Vietnamese & the Americans in Vietnam. (YA) 1973. pap. 4.95 (ISBN 0-394-71927-1, V927, Vin). Random.
Fitzgerald, Frank J. I Saw a Century Blossom. LC 84-7622. 255p. 1985. 15.00 (ISBN 0-8022-2453-9). Philos Lib.
FitzGerald, G. M. Sixth Century Monastery at Beth-Shan (Scythopolis) (Publications of the Palestine Section Ser.: Vol. 4). (Illus.). xiv, 19p. 1939. 18.75 (ISBN 0-686-24094-4). Univ Mus of U.
Fitzgerald, Garret, et al. The Middle East & the Trilateral Countries. 1981. write for info. Trilateral Comm.
Fitzgerald, Gavin H. The Moors, the Women & the Beauties of Spain, 2 vols. (Illus.). 256p. 1985. Set. 187.45 (ISBN 0-86650-143-6). Gloucester Art.
Fitzgerald, George. Handbook of the Mass. 128p. 1982. pap. 2.95 (ISBN 0-8091-2401-7). Paulist Pr.
--A Practical Guide to Preaching. LC 79-67742. 160p. (Orig.). 1980. pap. 4.95 (ISBN 0-8091-2281-2). Paulist Pr.
Fitzgerald, Gerald, jt. ed. see Peltz, Mary E.
Fitzgerald, Glenna W. Do You Think the Rain Will Hurt the Rhubarb? (Illus.). 230p. 1984. write for info (ISBN 0-933776-14-4). Perdido Bay.
Fitzgerald, H., jt. auth. see Ferguson, S. M.
Fitzgerald, Hiram & McGreal, Cathleen E., eds. Fathers & Infants: A Special Issue of Infant Mental Health Journal, Vol. 2, No. 4. LC 81-82739. 88p. 1981. pap. 9.95 (ISBN 0-89885-121-1). Human Sci Pr.
Fitzgerald, Hiram E. & Gage, Patricia, eds. Child Nurturance, Vol. 3: Studies of Development in Nonhuman Primates. 288p. 1982. 29.50x (ISBN 0-306-41176-8, Plenum Pr). Plenum Pub.
Fitzgerald, Hiram E., et al. Developmental Psychology: The Infant & Young Child. 1982. pap. 16.00x (ISBN 0-256-02406-5). Dorsey.
Fitzgerald, Hiram E., et al, eds. Theory & Research in Behavioral Pediatrics, Vol. 1. 308p. 1982. 29.50x (ISBN 0-306-40851-1, Plenum Pr). Plenum Pub.
--Theory & Research in Behavioral Pediatrics, Vol. 2. 266p. 1984. 39.50x (ISBN 0-306-41566-6, Plenum Pr). Plenum Pub.
Fitz-Gerald, J. D. & Taylor, P., eds. Todd Memorial Volumes: Philological Studies, 2 Vols. facs. ed. LC 68-22950. (Essay Index Reprint Ser). 1968. Repr. of 1930 ed. 28.00 (ISBN 0-8369-0948-8). Ayer Co Pubs.
Fitzgerald, Jack D., jt. auth. see Cox, Steven M.
Fitzgerald, James, jt. ed. see Boswell, John.
FitzGerald, James A. Don Carlos & Other Stories. LC 81-65342. 168p. 1981. 9.95 (ISBN 0-939296-00-4). Bond Pub Co.
Fitzgerald, Janet A. Alfred North Whitehead's Early Philosophy of Space & Time. LC 79-63849. (Illus.). 1979. 12.00 (ISBN 0-8191-0747-6). U Pr of Amer.
Fitzgerald, Jerry. Business Data Communications: Basic Concepts, Security & Design. LC 83-14798. (Wiley Series in Computers & Information Processing Systems for Business: 1-661). 502p. 1984. 33.45x (ISBN 0-471-89549-0); tchr's. ed. avail. (ISBN 0-471-88327-1). Wiley.
--Designing Controls into Computerized Systems. LC 81-67870. (Illus.). 157p. 1981. pap. 16.95 (ISBN 0-932410-36-7). FitzGerald & Assocs.
--Internal Controls for Computerized Systems. LC 78-69677. (Illus.). 93p. 1978. pap. text ed. 14.95 (ISBN 0-932410-04-9). FitzGerald & Assocs.
Fitzgerald, Jerry & Eason, Tom. Fundamentals of Data Communications. 260p. 1978. 23.95 (ISBN 0-686-98098-0). Telecom Lib.
Fitzgerald, Jerry & Fitzgerald, Ardra F. Student Workbook & Wellright Office Supply Company Case to Accompany Fundamentals of Systems Analysis. 354p. 1983. pap. 14.95 (ISBN 0-471-87105-2). Wiley.
Fitzgerald, Jerry, et al. Fundamentals of Systems Analysis. 2nd ed. LC 80-11769. 590p. 1981. 35.45 (ISBN 0-471-04968-9, Pub. by Wiley Heyden); text ed. 29.50 members (ISBN 0-471-08117-5). Assn Inform & Image Mgmt.
Fitzgerald, Jim. Boxing for Beginners. LC 79-1989. (Illus.). 1983. pap. 6.95 (ISBN 0-689-70661-8, 304). Atheneum.
--The Joys of Smoking Cigarettes. (Illus.). 144p. 1983. pap. 6.95 (ISBN 0-03-063357-5). HR&W.
Fitzgerald, Jim & Boswell, John. The First Family Paper Doll & Cut Out Book. (Orig.). 1981. pap. 5.95 (ISBN 0-440-52632-9, Dell Trade Pbks). Dell.
Fitzgerald, Jim, jt. auth. see Jonland, Einar.
Fitzgerald, Joe, jt. auth. see Auerbach, Red.
Fitzgerald, John & Murcer, Bill. Building New Families: Through Adoption & Fostering. (The Practice of Social Work Ser.: No. 10). 128p. 1981. text ed. 28.95x (ISBN 0-631-13148-5); pap. text ed. 11.95x (ISBN 0-631-13193-0). Basil Blackwell.
Fitzgerald, John & White, Michael. The Tabula of Cebes. LC 82-19118. (SBL Texts & Translations). 236p. 1983. pap. 14.25 (ISBN 0-89130-601-3, 06 02 24). Scholars Pr GA.
Fitzgerald, John D. Great Brain. (Illus.). 192p. (gr. 7 up). 1971. pap. 2.50 (ISBN 0-440-43071-2, YB). Dell.
--Great Brain. LC 67-22252. (Illus.). (gr. 4-8). 1967. PLB 11.89 (ISBN 0-8037-3076-4). Dial Bks Young.
--Great Brain at the Academy. 164p. (gr. 3-7). 1973. pap. 2.50 (ISBN 0-440-43113-1, YB). Dell.
--The Great Brain at the Academy. LC 72-712. (The Great Brain Ser). (Illus.). 176p. (gr. 4-7). 1972. PLB 11.89 (ISBN 0-8037-3040-3). Dial Bks Young.
--The Great Brain Does It Again. LC 74-18600. (Illus.). (gr. 4-7). 1975. PLB 11.89 (ISBN 0-8037-5066-8). Dial Bks Young.
--Great Brain Reforms. 176p. 1975. pap. 2.75 (ISBN 0-440-44841-7, YB). Dell.
--The Great Brain Reforms. LC 72-7601. (The Great Brain Ser.). (Illus.). 176p. (gr. 4-7). 1973. 9.95 (ISBN 0-8037-3067-5); PLB 9.89 (ISBN 0-8037-3068-3). Dial Bks Young.
--Me & My Little Brain. 144p. (gr. 4-7). 1972. pap. 2.50 (ISBN 0-440-45533-2, YB). Dell.
--Me & My Little Brain. LC 71-153732. (Illus.). (gr. 4-7). 1971. PLB 11.89 (ISBN 0-8037-5532-5). Dial Bks Young.
--More Adventures of the Great Brain. 144p. 1971. pap. 2.50 (ISBN 0-440-45822-6, YB). Dell.
--More Adventures of the Great Brain. LC 73-85547. (Illus.). (gr. 4-8). 1969. 11.95 (ISBN 0-8037-5819-7); PLB 11.89 (ISBN 0-8037-5821-9). Dial Bks Young.
--Papa Married a Mormon. 1976. Repr. 9.95 (ISBN 0-914740-21-0). Western Epics.
--The Return of the Great Brain. 180p. (gr. 3-5). 1975. pap. 2.50 (ISBN 0-440-45941-9, YB). Dell.
--The Return of the Great Brain. LC 73-15443. (Illus.). 176p. (gr. 4-7). 1974. PLB 11.89 (ISBN 0-8037-7413-3). Dial Bks Young.
Fitz-Gerald, John D. Versification of the Cuaderna Via as Found in Berceo's Vida de Santo Domingo de Silos. LC 71-168035. (Columbia University Studies in Romance Philology & Literature: No. 7). Repr. of 1905 ed. 15.00 (ISBN 0-404-50607-0). AMS Pr.
Fitzgerald, John D., jt. auth. see Meredith, Robert C.
FitzGerald, John L. Congress & the Separation of Powers. LC 85-12187. Date not set. price not set (ISBN 0-03-004634-3). Praeger.
Fitzgerald, Julia. Beyond Ecstasy. 368p. (Orig.). 1985. pap. 3.50 (ISBN 0-317-18143-2, 424817). Pinnacle Bks.
--Scarlet Woman. 352p. 1981. pap. 2.75 (ISBN 0-8439-0967-6, Leisure Bks). Dorchester Pub Co.
--Silken Trade. 432p. (Orig.). 1985. pap. 3.50 (ISBN 0-523-42482-5). Pinnacle Bks.
Fitzgerald, Kath, et al. Locality Studies: A Bibliography & Index. (Public Administration Ser.: P-1425). 171p. 1984. pap. 18.75 (ISBN 0-88066-925-X). Vance Biblios.

FitzGerald, Kathleen. Architecture Napa: A Guide to the Land, the Buildings & Styles of Napa County. LC 79-90702. (Illus., Orig.). 1979. pap. 3.95 (ISBN 0-935360-03-4). Napa Landmarks.

Fitzgerald, Laurie & Murphy, Joseph. Installing Quality Circles: A Strategic Approach. LC 82-50353. 134p. 1982. 13.95 (ISBN 0-88390-174-9). Univ Assocs.

Fitzgerald, Lawrence. Rain in Her Voice. 24p. 1978. 10.00 (ISBN 0-913719-05-6); pap. 3.50 (ISBN 0-913719-04-8). High-Coo Pr.

Fitzgerald, Lee A. Time Wounds All Heels. 182p. 1980. 10.00 (ISBN 0-682-49621-9). Exposition Pr FL.

Fitzgerald, Louise S. & Kearney, Elizabeth I. The Continental Novel: A Checklist of Criticism in English 1967-1980. LC 82-20454. 510p. 1983. 29.50 (ISBN 0-8108-1598-2). Scarecrow.

Fitzgerald, M. R. An Introduction to Osiris III at the University of Oklahoma. 1975. 2.50 (ISBN 0-686-18645-1). Univ OK Gov Res.

Fitzgerald, Margaret M. First Follow Nature: Primitivism in English Poetry, 1725-1750. 1976. Repr. of 1947 ed. lib. bdg. 20.00x (ISBN 0-374-92748-0). Octagon.

Fitzgerald, Mark J. Britain Views Our Industrial Relations. 1955. 14.95 (ISBN 0-268-00025-5). U of Notre Dame Pr.

--Common Market's Labor Programs. 1966. 22.95 (ISBN 0-268-00053-0). U of Notre Dame Pr.

FitzGerald, Mary, ed. Selected Plays of Lady Gregory. LC 82-22013. (Irish Drama Selections Ser.: No. 3). 376p. 1983. 29.95x (ISBN 0-8132-0582-4); pap. 9.95 (ISBN 0-8132-0583-2). Cath U Pr.

Fitzgerald, Maurice. Embriologia. (Span.). 1981. pap. text ed. 14.20 (ISBN 0-06-313120-X, Pub. by HarLA Mexico). Har-Row.

Fitzgerald, Maurice H., intro. by see Southey, Robert.

Fitzgerald, Maurice H., ed. see Southey, Robert.

Fitzgerald, Michael, jt. auth. see Dionne, Rene.

Fitzgerald, Michael N. Tax Shelter Alternatives: Measuring the Risks. LC 84-72812. 1985. 35.00 (ISBN 0-87094-538-6). Dow Jones-Irwin.

Fitzgerald, Michael R., jt. auth. see Rechichar, Stephen J.

Fitzgerald, Michael R., jt. auth. see Watson, Richard A.

Fitzgerald, Michael R., et al. Intragovernmental Regulation & the Public Interest: Air Pollution Control in the Tennessee Valley. (Studies in the Politics & Administration of the Tennessee Valley Ser.). (Orig.). 1983. pap. 4.50 (ISBN 0-914079-11-5). Bureau Pub Admin U Tenn.

Fitzgerald, Mike & Muncie, John. System of Justice. 200p. 1984. 34.95x (ISBN 0-631-13248-1); pap. 14.95x (ISBN 0-631-13249-X). Basil Blackwell.

Fitzgerald, Mike & Sim, Joe. British Prisons. 2nd ed. (Illus.). 192p. 1982. pap. 14.95x (ISBN 0-631-12606-6). Basil Blackwell.

Fitzgerald, Mollie. On Campus Cookbook. 96p. (Orig.). 1984. pap. 4.95 (ISBN 0-89480-775-7, 775). Workman Pub.

Fitzgerald, Nancy. Chelsea. 1980. lib. bdg. 13.95 (ISBN 0-8161-3059-0, Large Print Bks). G K Hall.

--Down Into the Water. 52p. 1984. 1.95 (ISBN 0-89900-143-2). College Pr Pub.

--Grover Square. 272p. 1984. pap. 2.95 (ISBN 0-515-07639-2). Jove Pubns.

Fitzgerald, Nicholas. Brian Jones: The Inside Story of the Original Rolling Stone. (Illus.). 304p. 1985. 17.95 (ISBN 0-399-13061-6). Putnam Pub Group.

Fitzgerald, Nigel. Suffer a Witch. Barzun, J. & Taylor, W. H., eds. LC 81-47411. (Crime Fiction 1950-1975 Ser.). 256p. 1983. lib. bdg. 18.00 (ISBN 0-8240-5001-0). Garland Pub.

Fitzgerald, Oscar P. Three Centuries of American Furniture. (Illus.). 323p. 1981. 34.95 (ISBN 0-13-920371-0); pap. 16.95 (ISBN 0-13-920363-X). P-H.

Fitzgerald, P. The History of Pickwick. 59.95 (ISBN 0-8490-0343-1). Gordon Pr.

--Pickwickian Manners & Customs. LC 73-21619. (Studies in Dickens, No. 52). 1974. lib. bdg. 49.95x (ISBN 0-8383-1822-3). Haskell.

--This Law of Ours. 1977. 12.70 (ISBN 0-13-919274-3); pap. 6.40 study guide (ISBN 0-13-919266-2); pap. 8.50 tchr's guide (ISBN 0-13-919282-4). P-H.

Fitzgerald, Patrick. Industrial Combination in England. Wilkins, Mira, ed. LC 76-29996. (European Business Ser.). 1977. Repr. of 1927 ed. lib. bdg. 21.00x (ISBN 0-405-09754-9). Ayer Co Pubs.

Fitzgerald, Patrick, jt. auth. see Bloch, Jonathan.

Fitzgerald, Patrick W., ed. Handbook of Personal Finance: A Prescription for Financial Health. 200p. (Orig.). 1983. pap. 8.95x (ISBN 0-910649-06-5). Energy Textbks.

FitzGerald, Paul A. Governance of Jesuit Colleges in the United States, 1920-1970. LC 83-25927. 328p. 1984. text ed. 20.00 (ISBN 0-268-01010-2, 85-10109). U of Notre Dame Pr.

Fitzgerald, Penelope. At Freddie's. LC 82-3143. 224p. 1985. 14.95 (ISBN 0-87923-439-3). Godine.

Fitzgerald, Percy. Bardell vs. Pickwick. LC 78-26151. 1978. Repr. of 1902 ed. lib. bdg. 17.50 (ISBN 0-8414-4172-3). Folcroft.

--The Book Fancier or the Romance of Book Collecting. 1973. Repr. of 1887 ed. 35.00 (ISBN 0-8274-0663-0). R West.

--Boswell's Autobiography. 1973. Repr. of 1912 ed. 20.00 (ISBN 0-8274-0706-8). R West.

--Chronicles of a Bow Street Police-Office, 2 vols. in 1. LC 78-129313. (Criminology, Law Enforcement, & Social Problems Ser.: No. 136). (Illus.). 816p. (With intro. & index added). 1972. Repr. of 1888 ed. 30.00x (ISBN 0-87585-136-3). Patterson Smith.

--A Critical Examination of Dr. G. Birkbeck Hill's "Johnsonian" Editions. 1898. Repr. 30.00 (ISBN 0-8274-2118-4). R West.

--The Garrick Club. 1973. Repr. of 1904 ed. 45.00 (ISBN 0-8274-0664-9). R West.

--Jane Austen: A Criticism & Appreciation. LC 72-10357. 1973. lib. bdg. 15.00 (ISBN 0-8414-0466-6). Folcroft.

--Kembles, 2 Vols. LC 73-89712. (Illus.). 1871. Set. 40.00 (ISBN 0-405-08516-8, Blom Pubns); 20.00 ea. Vol. 1 (ISBN 0-405-08517-6). Vol. 2 (ISBN 0-405-08518-4). Ayer Co Pubs.

--Life of Charles Dickens, 2 vols. LC 72-4115. (Studies in Dickens, No. 52). 1972. Repr. of 1905 ed. lib. bdg. 79.95x (ISBN 0-8383-1607-7). Haskell.

--The Life of Charles Dickens, 2 vols. 1973. Repr. of 1905 ed. 50.00 (ISBN 0-8274-0416-6). R West.

--The Life of Charles Dickens: As Revealed in His Writings, 2 vols. 309p. 1982. Repr. of 1905 ed. Set. lib. bdg. 65.00 (ISBN 0-8495-1734-6). Arden Lib.

--Life of James Boswell (of Auchinleck, 2 vols. 1891. Repr. Set. 100.00 (ISBN 0-8274-2887-1). R West.

--The Life of Laurence Sterne. 1977. Repr. of 1906 ed. lib. bdg. 35.00 (ISBN 0-8495-1609-9). Arden Lib.

--The Life of Laurence Sterne, 2 vols. 1973. Repr. of 1864 ed. 85.00 (ISBN 0-8274-0406-9). R West.

--The Life of Laurence Sterne. 436p. 1982. Repr. of 1906 ed. lib. bdg. 30.00 (ISBN 0-89760-231-5). Telegraph Bks.

--The Life of Laurence Sterne. 436p. 1983. Repr. of 1906 ed. text ed. 35.00 (ISBN 0-89984-218-6). Century Bookbindery.

--Live & Adventures of Alexander Dumas, 2 vols. 1979. Repr. of 1873 ed. Set. lib. bdg. 100.00 (ISBN 0-8495-1632-3). Arden Lib.

--Memories of an Author. 1895. Repr. 45.00 (ISBN 0-8274-2714-X). R West.

--The Pickwickian Dictionary & Cyclopedia. LC 74-7473. Repr. of 1900 ed. lib. bdg. 50.00 (ISBN 0-8414-4179-0). Folcroft.

--Pickwickian Manners & Customs. LC 78-2620. 1975. 16.50 (ISBN 0-8492-0836-X). R West.

--Principles of Comedy & Dramatic Effect. LC 76-7982. 1973. Repr. of 1870 ed. lib. bdg. 25.00 (ISBN 0-8414-4221-5). Folcroft.

--Recreations of a Literary Man. 1973. Repr. of 1883 ed. 35.00 (ISBN 0-8274-0661-4). R West.

--Samuel Foote: A Biography. LC 72-84512. 1910. 18.00 (ISBN 0-405-08519-2, Blom Pubns). Ayer Co Pubs.

--The Sheridans, 2 vols. 1973. Repr. of 1886 ed. 85.00 (ISBN 0-8274-0417-4). R West.

--Victoria's London, Vol. 2: The Suburbs. 312p. 1984. 59.00 (ISBN 0-946619-20-4, Pub. by Alderman Pr Pubs UK). State Mutual Bk.

Fitzgerald, Percy, ed. see Lamb, Charles.

Fitzgerald, Percy H. Charles Lamb: His Friends, His Haunts & His Books. LC 78-2784. Repr. of 1866 ed. lib. bdg. 30.00 (ISBN 0-8414-4359-9). Folcroft.

--Charles Lamb: His Friends, His Haunts & His Books. 228p. 1979. Repr. of 1866 ed. lib. bdg. 30.00 (ISBN 0-8482-0849-8). Norwood Edns.

--Charles Lamb: His Friends, His Haunts & His Books. 228p. 1980. Repr. of 1866 ed. lib. bdg. 30.00 (ISBN 0-8492-4629-6). R West.

--The Great Canal at Suez: Its Political, Engineering & Financial History, 2 vols. LC 74-15037. Repr. of 1876 ed. Set. 65.00 (ISBN 0-404-12042-3). AMS Pr.

--The History of Pickwick. LC 77-21911. 1977. Repr. of 1891 ed. lib. bdg. 40.00 (ISBN 0-8414-4350-5). Folcroft.

--The History of Pickwick. 1980. Repr. of 1891 ed. lib. bdg. 45.00 (ISBN 0-8492-4631-8). R West.

--Memories of Charles Dickens. LC 75-148778. Repr. of 1913 ed. 29.00 (ISBN 0-404-08779-5). AMS Pr.

--The Pickwickian Dictionary & Cyclopaedia. LC 71-148777. Repr. of 1902 ed. 27.50 (ISBN 0-404-08778-7). AMS Pr.

--Pickwickian Dictionary & Encyclopedia. 1973. Repr. of 1902 ed. 25.00 (ISBN 0-8274-1274-6). R West.

--Pickwickian Studies. LC 77-916. 1977. lib. bdg. 20.00 (ISBN 0-8414-4188-X). Folcroft.

Fitzgerald, Peter J. The Basis of Sex Education. 1981. 7.95 (ISBN 0-533-04636-X). Vantage.

Fitzgerald, R., tr. see Perse, St. John.

Fitzgerald, R. S. Liverpool Road Station, Manchester. 1980. 20.00 (ISBN 0-7190-0765-8, Pub. by Manchester Univ Pr); pap. 9.50 (ISBN 0-7190-0790-9). Longwood Pub Group.

Fitzgerald, R. V. Conjoint Marital Therapy. LC 73-81208. 256p. 1973. 25.00x (ISBN 0-87668-091-0). Aronson.

Fitzgerald, R. W. Mechanics of Materials. 2nd ed. LC 81-4737. 1982. 36.95 (ISBN 0-201-04073-5); avail. solutions manual 4.00 (ISBN 0-201-04573-7). Addison-Wesley.

Fitzgerald, Randall & Lipson, Gerald. Porkbarrel: The Unexpurgated Grace Commission Story of Congressional Profligacy. 114p. 1984. 7.95 (ISBN 0-932790-44-5). Cato Inst.

Fitzgerald, Ray. Touching All Bases: The Collected Ray Fitzgerald 1971-1982. LC 83-17191. 224p. 1983. 14.95 (ISBN 0-8289-0507-X). Greene.

Fitzgerald, Richard. Art & Politics: Cartoonists of the "Masses" & "Liberator". LC 72-609. (Contributions in American Studies: No. 8). 288p. 1973. lib. bdg. 29.95 (ISBN 0-8371-6006-5, FR1/). Greenwood.

Fitzgerald, Robert. Enlarging the Change: The Princeton Seminars in Literary Criticism, 1949-1951. 261p. 1984. 19.95x (ISBN 0-930350-62-6). NE U Pr.

--In the Rose of Time: Poems, Nineteen Thirty-Nine to Nineteen Fifty-Six. LC 56-13349. 6.00 (ISBN 0-8112-0279-8). New Directions.

--Spring Shade: Poems 1931-1970. LC 74-145931. 1971. 6.50 (ISBN 0-8112-0280-1); pap. 2.75 (ISBN 0-8112-0052-3, NDP311). New Directions.

Fitzgerald, Robert, ed. see O'Connor, Flannery.

Fitzgerald, Robert, tr. see Fitts, Dudley.

Fitzgerald, Robert, tr. see Homer.

Fitzgerald, Robert see Sophocles.

Fitzgerald, Robert, tr. see Virgil.

Fitzgerald, Robert H., ed. Musculoskeletal Infections: Recognition, Prevention & Management. (Illus.). 48p. (Orig.). 1982. write for info. (ISBN 0-911741-00-3). Advanced Thera Comm.

Fitzgerald, Robert, Jr., ed. see Brause, B., et al.

Fitzgerald, Robert, Jr., et al. Musculoskeletal Infections: Recognition, Prevention & Management-Antimicrobial Prophylaxis in Musculoskeletal Surgery. 47p. 1983. write for info. (ISBN 0-911741-07-0). Advanced Thera Comm.

Fitzgerald, Robert S., et al, eds. The Regulation of Respiration During Sleep & Anesthesia. LC 78-6658. (Advances in Experimental Medicine & Biology Ser.: Vol. 99). 460p. 1978. 59.50x (ISBN 0-306-32699-X, Plenum Pr). Plenum Pub.

Fitzgerald, Rosemary. This Splendid Peril. (Orig.). 1982. pap. 3.50 (ISBN 0-440-18810-5). Dell.

Fitzgerald, Ross. From Nineteen Fifteen to the Early Nineteen Eighties: A History of Queensland. LC 83-10260. (Illus.). 653p. 1984. text ed. 25.00x (ISBN 0-7022-1734-4). U of Queensland Pr.

--From the Dreaming to Nineteen Fifteen: A History of Queensland. LC 81-11532. (Illus.). 354p. 1982. text ed. 29.50x (ISBN 0-7022-1634-8). U of Queensland Pr.

Fitzgerald, Ross, ed. Comparing Political Thinkers. 320p. 1980. 34.00 (ISBN 0-08-024800-4); pap. 17.50 (ISBN 0-08-024799-7). Pergamon.

--Human Needs & Politics. 1978. 17.50 (ISBN 0-08-021401-0). Pergamon.

Fitzgerald, Ruth C. A Different Story: A Black History of Fredericksburg, Stafford & Spotsylvania, Virginia. LC 79-67534. (Illus.). 336p. 1980. 11.95 (ISBN 0-9604564-2-2). Unicorn VA.

Fitzgerald, S. J. The Story of the Savoy Opera in Gilbert & Sullivan Days. (Music Reprint Ser.). 1979. Repr. of 1925 ed. lib. bdg. 29.50 (ISBN 0-306-79543-4). Da Capo.

Fitzgerald, Sally, ed. The Habit of Being: Letters of Flannery O'Connor. LC 79-23319. 1980. pap. 10.95 (ISBN 0-394-74259-1, Vin). Random.

Fitzgerald, Sally, ed. & intro. by see O'Connor, Flannery.

Fitzgerald, Sally, ed. see O'Connor, Flannery.

Fitzgerald, Scott F. The Pat Hobby Stories. 12.95 (ISBN 0-317-28237-9, Pub. by Am Repr). Amereon Ltd.

--Taps at Reveille. 18.95 (ISBN 0-89190-602-9, Pub. by Am Repr). Amereon Ltd.

--This Side of Paradise. 16.95 (ISBN 0-89190-603-7, Pub. by Am Repr). Amereon Ltd.

Fitzgerald, Sheila, jt. ed. see Harris, Laurie L.

Fitzgerald, Stephan & Hewitt, Pamela, eds. China in the Seventies: Australian Perspectives. (Contemporary China Paper: No. 15). 187p. 1981. pap. text ed. 5.95 (ISBN 0-908160-92-5, 0026, Pub. by ANUP Australia). Australia N U P.

Fitzgerald, Sue. CIS COBOL: A Structured Programming Approach. 1985. 15.95 (ISBN 0-471-90504-6). Wiley.

Fitzgerald, T. H. Money Market Directory of Pension Funds & Their Managers: 1985. 1985. 435.00 (ISBN 0-939712-02-4). Money Mkt.

Fitzgerald, T. J., jt. auth. see Lee, H.

Fitzgerald, Theodore C. The Coturnix Quail: Anatomy & Histology. (Illus.). 1970. 12.95x (ISBN 0-8138-0356-X). Iowa St U Pr.

Fitzgerald, Thomas K., ed. Nutrition & Anthropology in Action. (Studies of Developing Countries: No. 21). (Orig.). 1976. pap. text ed. 16.50x (ISBN 90-232-1447-1). Humanities.

--Social & Cultural Identity: Problems of Persistence & Change. LC 73-90848. (Southern Anthropological Society Proceedings Ser.: No. 8). 136p. 1974. pap. 5.25x (ISBN 0-8203-0329-1). U of Ga Pr.

Fitzgerald, Tom. Chocolate Charlie. Young, Billie, ed. LC 72-91129. 1973. 11.95 (ISBN 0-87949-006-3). Ashley Bks.

--Get Tough! The U. S. Special Forces Physical Conditioning Program. (Illus.). 256p. 1985. pap. 10.95 (ISBN 0-312-32629-7). St Martin.

Fitzgerald, Tonie. Gardening in the Inland Northwest. 126p. pap. 6.95 (ISBN 0-87770-343-4). Ye Galleon.

Fitzgerald, W., jt. auth. see Brackin, I. L.

Fitzgerald, W. L. & Huffman, D. C. Guidelines for Financial Planning. 59p. (Orig.). 1983. pap. 12.00 (ISBN 0-910769-15-X). Am Coll Apothecaries.

Fitzgerald, W. L., et al. Advertising & Promotion for Professional Pharmacy Practice. 238p. 1983. pap. 25.00 (ISBN 0-910769-20-6). Am Coll Apothecaries.

FitzGerald, W. N. The Harness Makers Illustrated Manual. (Illus.). 1974. 20.00 (ISBN 0-918778-17-4). Printed Horse.

Fitzgerald, W. W., et al. Ferrari: The Sports & Gran Tursimo Cars. 4th enlarged ed. (Illus.). 1979. 39.95 (ISBN 0-393-01276-X). Norton.

Fitzgerald, Walter. The New Europe: An Introduction to Its Political Geography. LC 80-24065. (Illus.). xiii, 298p. 1980. Repr. of 1946 ed. lib. bdg. 32.50x (ISBN 0-313-21006-3, FINE). Greenwood.

Fitzgerald, Walter L., Jr. Guidelines for Community Pharmacy Security. 51p. (Orig.). 1984. pap. 12.00 (ISBN 0-910769-18-4). Am Coll Apothecaries.

Fitz-Gerald, William. The Harness Makers' Illustrated Manual. (Illus.). 1977. Repr. of 1875 ed. 20.00x (ISBN 0-88427-014-9). North River.

Fitzgerald, William, jt. auth. see Brackin, Ivan L.

Fitzgerald, William G., ed. Can America Last? From the Wilderness to World-Power. LC 73-13131. (Foreign Travelers in America, 1810-1935 Ser.). 324p. 1974. Repr. 24.50x (ISBN 0-405-05453-X). Ayer Co Pubs.

Fitzgerald, Zelda. Save Me the Waltz. LC 32-30021. (Arcturus Books Paperbacks). 224p. 1967. pap. 8.95 (ISBN 0-8093-0255-1). S Ill U Pr.

--Scandalabra. limited ed. 1980. 35.00x (ISBN 0-89723-022-1). Bruccoli.

Fitzgerald, Zelda, jt. auth. see Fitzgerald, F. Scott.

Fitzgerald-Finch, O. P. Renal Radiology & Imaging. (Topics in Renal Disease Ser.). 96p. 1982. 17.95 (ISBN 0-85200-423-0, Pub. by MTP Pr England). Kluwer Academic.

Fitz-Gibbon, Carol T. & Morris, Lynn L. How to Calculate Statistics. LC 78-58659. (Program Evaluation Kit: Vol. 7). 142p. 1978. pap. 9.95 (ISBN 0-8039-1072-X). Sage.

--How to Design a Program Evaluation. LC 78-57011. (Program Evaluation Kit: Vol. 3). 1978. pap. 8.50 (ISBN 0-8039-1068-1). Sage.

Fitz-Gibbon, Carol T., jt. auth. see Morris, Lynn L.

FitzGibbon, Constantine. The Irish in Ireland. (Illus.). 1983. 19.95 (ISBN 0-393-01745-1). Norton.

FitzGibbon, Constantine, ed. see Thomas, Dylan.

Fitzgibbon, Constantine, tr. see Von Salomon, Ernst.

Fitzgibbon, Dan. All about Your Money. LC 83-15608. (Illus.). 148p. (gr. 6 up). 1984. 11.95 (ISBN 0-689-31031-5). Atheneum.

Fitzgibbon, Dan, jt. auth. see Carlson, Dale.

Fitzgibbon, H. Macaulay. Famous Elizabethan Plays, Expurgated & Adapted for Modern Readers. 1979. Repr. of 1890 ed. lib. bdg. 50.00 (ISBN 0-8495-1631-5). Arden Lib.

Fitzgibbon, H. Macauley. Early English & Scottish Poetry. 1888. lib. bdg. 25.00 (ISBN 0-8414-4264-9). Folcroft.

--Famous Elizabethan Plays. 1890. 30.00 (ISBN 0-8482-3981-4). Norwood Edns.

Fitzgibbon, John F. Ethics: Fundamental Principles of Moral Philosophy. LC 83-1178. 92p. (Orig.). 1983. lib. bdg. 20.00 (ISBN 0-8191-3064-8); pap. text ed. 8.50 (ISBN 0-8191-3065-6). U Pr of Amer.

Fitzgibbon, Louis. The Betrayal of the Somalis. 29.00x (ISBN 0-86036-194-2, Pub. by R Collings UK). State Mutual Bk.

--Katyn. (Illus.). 285p. 1978. 12.00 (ISBN 0-911038-25-6); pap. 8.00 (ISBN 0-911038-60-4). Inst Hist Rev.

--Katyn. (Illus.). 1979. 12.00 (ISBN 0-911038-25-6, Inst Hist Rev); pap. 8.00 (ISBN 0-911038-60-4). Noontide.

Fitzgibbon, Marie, jt. auth. see Muclcahy, Michael.

Fitzgibbon, R. Legal Guidelines for the Clinical Laboratory. 1981. 24.95 (ISBN 0-87489-243-0). Med Economics.

Fitzgibbon, Robert J. & Statland, Bernard E., eds. DRG Survival Manual for the Clinical Lab. 275p. 1985. pap. 19.95 (ISBN 0-87489-413-1). Med Economics.

Fitzgibbon, Russell H. The Agatha Christie Companion. LC 78-61075. 1980. 15.95 (ISBN 0-87972-137-5); pap. 8.95 (ISBN 0-87972-138-3). Bowling Green Univ.

Fitzgibbon, Russell H., ed. Argentina: A Chronology & Fact Book (1516-1973) LC 73-20375. (World Chronology Ser.). 148p. 1974. 8.50 (ISBN 0-379-16308-X). Oceana.

Fitzgibbon, Russell H., ed. & Brazil: A Chronology & Fact Book. LC 73-17058. (World Chronology Ser.). 150p. 1974. lib. bdg. 8.50 (ISBN 0-379-16309-8). Oceana.

Fitzgibbon, Snyder. Laboratory Manager's Problem Solver. 400p. 1985. 16.95 (ISBN 0-87489-386-0). Med Economics.

Fitzgibbon, Theodora. Irish Traditional Food. 240p. 1983. 14.95 (ISBN 0-312-43631-9). St Martin.

--A Taste of Ireland: In Food & in Pictures. (Illus.). 122p. 1970. pap. 8.95 (ISBN 0-330-02458-2, Pub. by Pan Bks England). Irish Bk Ctr.

--A Taste of Scotland: In Food & in Pictures. (Illus.). 122p. 1971. pap. 8.95 (ISBN 0-330-02872-3, Pub. by Pan Bks England). Irish Bk Ctr.

--A Taste of the Lake District. (A "Taste of" Cookbooks). (Illus.). 128p. (Orig.). 1980. pap. 8.95 (ISBN 0-330-26046-4, Pub. by Pan Bks England). Irish Bk Ctr.

--A Taste of the West Country. (A "Taste of" Cookbooks Ser.). (Illus.). 120p. 1975. pap. 8.95 (ISBN 0-330-24364-0, Pub. by Pan Bks England). Irish Bk Ctr.

--A Taste of Wales: In Food & in Pictures. (Illus.). 122p. 1973. pap. 8.95 (ISBN 0-330-23624-5, Pub. by Pan Bks England). Irish Bk Ctr.

Fitzgibbon, Theodora, compiled by. The Pleasures of the Table. (Small Oxford Books). (Illus.). 1981. 9.95 (ISBN 0-19-214120-1). Oxford U Pr.

Fitzgibbon, W. E., ed. Partial Differential Equations & Dynamical Systems. (Research Notes in Mathematics Ser.: No. 101). 384p. (Orig.). 1984. pap. 24.95 (ISBN 0-273-08644-8). Pitman Pub MA.

Fitzgibbon, W. E., jt. ed. see Walker, H. F.

Fitzgibbons, Gloria. U. D. A. G. A Public - Private Partnership. 168p. (Orig.). 1982. pap. text ed. 14.95x (ISBN 0-940438-01-1). Innovations Pr.

Fitzgibbons, Patricia, jt. auth. see Russell, Anne.

Fitzgibbons, R. & Fernandez, J. Latin America: Political Culture & Development. 2nd ed. 1981. pap. 17.95 (ISBN 0-13-524348-3). P-H.

Fitzgibbons, Robert E. Making Educational Decisions: An Introduction to Philosophy of Education. 261p. 1981. pap. text ed. 13.95 (ISBN 0-15-554621-X, HC). HarBraceJ.

Fitzhardinge, L. F. The Spartans. LC 79-66136. (Ancient Peoples & Places Ser.). (Illus.). 180p. 1985. pap. 10.95 (ISBN 0-500-27364-2). Thames Hudson.

Fitzharris, Tim. The Wild Prairie: A Natural History of the Western Plains. (Illus.). 1984. 27.50 (ISBN 0-19-540438-6). Oxford U Pr.

Fitzharris, Timothy L. The Desirability of a Correctional Ombudsman. LC 72-13057. 114p. (Orig.). 1973. pap. 4.00x (ISBN 0-87772-155-6). Inst Gov Stud Berk.

Fitzhenry, Robert I., ed. Barnes & Noble Book of Quotations. 340p. 1983. pap. 4.76i (ISBN 0-06-463571-6, EH 571). B&N NY.

Fitzherbert, Anthony, tr. from Fr. The Newe Boke of Justices of the Peas. LC 72-195. (English Experience Ser.: No. 109). 1969. Repr. of 1538 ed. 21.00 (ISBN 90-221-0109-6). Walter J Johnson.

Fitzherbert, John. Boke of Surveying, Here Begynneth a Ryght Frutefull Mater: And Has to Name the Boke of Surveying. LC 74-80175. (English Experience Ser.: No. 657). (Illus.). 131p. 1974. Repr. of 1523 ed. 13.00 (ISBN 90-221-0657-8). Walter J Johnson.

--Fitzherberts Booke of Husbandrie: Newlie Corrected. LC 79-84107. (English Experience Ser.: No. 926). 220p. 1979. Repr. of 1598 ed. lib. bdg. 21.00 (ISBN 90-221-0926-7). Walter J Johnson.

Fitzhugh, George. Cannibals All!, or, Slaves Without Masters. Woodward, C. Vann, ed. LC 60-5400. (The John Harvard Library). 1960. pap. 6.95x (ISBN 0-674-09451-4). Harvard U Pr.

Fitzhugh, Louise. Harriet the Spy. 304p. (gr. 5 up). 1978. pap. 2.50 (ISBN 0-440-93447-8, LFL). Dell.

--Harriet the Spy. 304p. (gr. 5 up). 1984. pap. 2.95 (ISBN 0-440-43447-5, YB). Dell.

--Harriet the Spy. LC 64-19711. (gr. 5 up). 1964. 11.49i (ISBN 0-06-021910-6); PLB 11.89 (ISBN 0-06-021911-4). HarpJ.

--I Am Four. LC 82-70309. (Illus.). 48p. (ps-k). 1982. 9.95 (ISBN 0-385-28444-6); PLB 9.95 (ISBN 0-385-28445-4). Delacorte.

--I Am Three. LC 81-15218. 48p. (ps). 1982. 8.95 (ISBN 0-440-04035-3); PLB 8.89 (ISBN 0-440-04039-6). Delacorte.

--I Am Three. LC 81-15218. (Illus.). 48p. (ps-3). 1982. 9.95 (ISBN 0-385-28454-3); PLB 9.95 (ISBN 0-385-28455-1). Delacorte.

--The Long Secret. 240p. (gr. 5 up). 1978. pap. 2.25 (ISBN 0-440-94977-7, LFL). Dell.

--The Long Secret. 240p. (gr. 3-7). 1984. pap. 2.95 (ISBN 0-440-44977-4, YB). Dell.

--Long Secret. LC 65-23370. (Illus.). (gr. 5 up). 1965. 12.98i (ISBN 0-06-021410-4); PLB 13.89 (ISBN 0-06-021411-2). HarpJ.

--Nobodys Family Is Going to Change. 224p. (gr. 3-7). 1975. pap. 1.50 (ISBN 0-440-46454-4, YB). Dell.

--Nobody's Family Is Going to Change. LC 74-19152. 256p. (gr. 3 up). 1974. 11.95 (ISBN 0-374-35539-8). FS&G.

--Nobody's Family Is Going to Change. 224p. (gr. 3-7). 1985. pap. 2.50 (ISBN 0-440-96454-7, LFL). Dell.

--Sport. LC 78-72861. 250p. (gr. 4-6). 1978. 10.95 (ISBN 0-385-28908-1). Delacorte.

--Sport. 224p. (gr. 7 up). 1980. pap. 2.25 (ISBN 0-440-98350-9, LFL). Dell.

--Sport. 224p. (gr. 7 up). 1982. pap. 2.50 (ISBN 0-440-48221-6, YB). Dell.

Fitzhugh, Louise & Scoppettone, Sandra. Bang Bang You're Dead. LC 69-14440. 32p. (ps-3). 1969. PLB 12.89 (ISBN 0-06-021914-9). HarpJ.

Fitzhugh, Percy K. Roy Blakely on the Mohawk Trail. LC 74-15738. (Popular Culture in America Ser.). 222p. 1975. Repr. of 1925 ed. 20.00x (ISBN 0-405-06373-3). Ayer Co Pubs.

Fitzhugh, Robert J. & Chadwick, Martin M. Integrated Macro Package: The LRDC Integrated Macro Package. (Illus.). 100p. 1971. 1.50 (ISBN 0-318-14717-3, ED 049 613). Learn Res Dev.

Fitzhugh, Robert J., jt. auth. see Wang, Margaret C.

FitzHugh, Terrick. Dictionary of Genealogy: A Guide to British Ancestry Research. LC 85-1220. (Illus.). 384p. 1985. 28.50x (ISBN 0-389-20565-6). B&N Imports.

Fitzhugh, William. William Fitzhugh & His Chesapeake World, 1676-1701: The Fitzhugh Letters & Other Documents. Davis, Richard B., ed. (Virginia Historical Society: No. 3). (Illus.). 399p. 1963. 20.00x (ISBN 0-8139-0080-8). U Pr of Va.

Fitzhugh, William W. Environmental Archaeology & Cultural Systems in Hamilton Inlet, Labrador: A Survey of the Central Labrador Coast from 3000 B.C. to the Present. LC 79-171589. (Smithsonian Contributions to Anthropology Ser.: No. 16). pap. 68.00 (ISBN 0-317-28679-X, 2051626). Bks Demand UMI.

Fitzhugh, William W. & Kaplan, Susan. Inua: Spirit World of the Bering Sea Eskimo. LC 82-5542. (Illus.). 296p. 1982. 35.00 (ISBN 0-87474-430-X); pap. 15.00 (ISBN 0-87474-429-6). Smithsonian.

Fitzhugh, William W., ed. Cultures in Contact: The European Impact on Native Cultural Institutions in Eastern North America, A.D. 1000-1800. LC 85-40400. (Anthropological Society of Washington Ser.). (Illus.). 360p. 1985. 29.95x (ISBN 0-87474-438-5, FICC). Smithsonian.

Fitzkee, Daniel. The Card Expert Entertains. 10.00 (ISBN 0-87505-272-X). Borden.

--The Card Expert Entertains. (Illus.). 171p. 1978. Repr. of 1948 ed. 10.00 (ISBN 0-915926-25-3). Magic Ltd.

--Magic by Misdirection. 15.00 (ISBN 0-87505-239-8). Borden.

--Magic by Misdirection. (Illus.). 227p. 1978. 13.50 (ISBN 0-915926-03-2). Magic Ltd.

--Rings in Your Fingers. 1977. 10.00 (ISBN 0-87505-253-3). Borden.

--Showmanship for Magicians. 15.00 (ISBN 0-87505-256-8). Borden.

--Showmanship for Magicians. 1980. 12.50 (ISBN 0-915926-02-4). Magic Ltd.

--The Trick Brain. 15.00 (ISBN 0-87505-260-6). Borden.

--The Trick Brain. (Illus.). 316p. 1978. 15.00 (ISBN 0-915926-01-6). Magic Ltd.

FitzLyon, April. Lorenzo da Ponte. 288p. 1982. pap. 7.95 (ISBN 0-7145-3783-7). Riverrun NY.

--A Month in the Country. (Orig.). pap. 6.95 (ISBN 0-905209-44-3, Pub. by Victoria & Albert Mus UK). Faber & Faber.

--The Price of Genius. 1981. pap. 5.95 (ISBN 0-7145-0488-2). Riverrun NY.

Fitzlyon, April, tr. see Bokov, Nikolai.

FitzLyon, April, tr. see De Mandiargues, Andre P.

Fitzlyon, April, jt. tr. see Fitzlyon, Kyril.

Fitzlyon, Kyril & Browning, Tatiana. Before the Revolution: A View of Russia under the Last Czar. LC 78-56075. (Illus.). 1979. pap. 11.95 (ISBN 0-87951-167-2). Overlook Pr.

Fitzlyon, Kyril & Fitzlyon, April, trs. Leo Tolstoy: A Landowner's Morning Family Happiness & the Devil. 216p. 1984. 13.95 (ISBN 0-7043-2426-1, Pub. by Quartet Bks). Merrimack Pub Cir.

Fitzmaurice, E. B., jt. auth. see Little, A. G.

FitzMaurice, Eugene. The Indulgence. 336p. 1985. 16.95 (ISBN 0-88191-010-4). Freundlich.

--Shadows: The Saga of an American Interracial Family. 1984. 14.95 (ISBN 0-88015-026-2). Empire Bks.

Fitzmaurice, George. Plays of George Fitzmaurice: Folkplays, Vol. 2. 1970. 12.00 (ISBN 0-85105-013-1). Dufour.

--Plays of George Fitzmaurice: Realistic Plays, Vol. 3. Slaughter, Howard K., ed. 1970. 12.00 (ISBN 0-85105-174-X). Dufour.

Fitzmaurice, George & Guinan, John. The Wonderful Wedding. (Lost Play Ser.). pap. 1.95x (ISBN 0-912262-52-4). Proscenium.

Fitzmaurice, Joan, et al. Rheumatic Heart Disease & Mitral Valve Disease. (Cont. Education in Cardiovascular Nursing Ser.). (Illus.). 70p. 1980. pap. 6.95x (ISBN 0-8385-8439-X). ACC.

Fitzmaurice, John. Politics in Denmark. 1981. 26.00x (ISBN 0-312-62663-0). St Martin.

--The Politics of Belgium: Crisis & Compromise in a Plural Society. LC 82-24056. 300p. 1983. 25.00x (ISBN 0-312-62639-8). St Martin.

--Quebec & Canada: Past, Present & Future. 240p. 1985. 37.50 (ISBN 0-312-65921-0). St Martin.

Fitzmaurice, John W. The Shanty Boy. LC 70-104451. Repr. of 1889 ed. lib. bdg. 14.00 (ISBN 0-8398-0557-8). Irvington.

--The Shanty Boy. (Michigan Heritage Library: Vol. 2). 245p. 1979. Repr. of 1889 ed. 12.00 (ISBN 0-915056-11-9). Hardscrabble Bks.

Fitzmaurice, Robert. The New Energy. 1982. 10.00 (ISBN 0-533-05096-0). Vantage.

Fitzmaurice-Kelly, J. Chapters on Spanish Literature. 1973. lib. bdg. 45.00 (ISBN 0-8414-4265-7). Folcroft.

Fitzmaurice-Kelly, James. Chapters on Spanish Literature. LC 9-18715. 1908. 17.00 (ISBN 0-527-29600-7). Kraus Repr.

--A History of Spanish Literature. 423p. 1983. Repr. of 1898 ed. lib. bdg. 50.00 (ISBN 0-89987-270-0). Darby Bks.

--The Life of Miguel de Cervantes Saavedra. LC 77-20915. Repr. of 1892 ed. text ed. 45.00 (ISBN 0-8414-1987-6). Folcroft.

--Lope de Vega & Spanish Drama. LC 79-115860. (Studies in European Literature Ser., No. 56). 1970. Repr. of 1902 ed. lib. bdg. 22.95x (ISBN 0-8383-1073-7). Haskell.

--Some Masters of Spanish Verse. facs. ed. LC 67-23217. (Essay Index Reprint Ser). 1924. 15.00 (ISBN 0-8369-0443-5). Ayer Co Pubs.

Fitzmaurice-Kelly, Jas. The Life of Miguel De Cervantes Saavedra: A Biographical, Literary, & Historical Study of a Tentative Bibliography from 1585 to 1892, & an Annotated Appendix on the Canto De Galiope. 1973. 45.00 (ISBN 0-8274-0541-3). R West.

Fitzmaurice-Kelly, Julia. Antonio Perez. 1922. pap. 4.00 (ISBN 0-87535-011-9). Hispanic Soc.

Fitzmayer, Joseph A. A Christological Catechism: New Testament Answers. 160p. (Orig.). 1982. pap. 4.95 (ISBN 0-8091-2453-X). Paulist Pr.

Fitzmyer, J. A. To Advance the Gospel: New Testament Essays. 320p. 1981. 19.50 (ISBN 0-8245-0008-3). Crossroad NY.

Fitzmyer, Joseph A. The Dead Sea Scrolls: Major Publications & Tools for Study. LC 75-5987. (Society of Biblical Literature. Sources for Biblical Study Ser.). xiv, 171p. 1975. pap. 10.50 (ISBN 0-88414-053-9, 060308). Scholars Pr GA.

--Essays on the Semitic Background of the New Testament. LC 74-83874. (Society of Biblical Literature. Sources for Biblical Study). 1974. pap. 13.50 (ISBN 0-89130-309-X, 060305). Scholars Pr GA.

--Gospel According to Luke I-IX, Vol. 28. LC 80-702. Date not set. 18.00 (ISBN 0-385-00515-6). Doubleday.

--Gospel According to Luke X-XXIV, Vol. 28A. LC 82-45882. (Anchor Bible Ser.). 840p. 1985. 18.00 (ISBN 0-385-15542-5). Doubleday.

--A Wandering Aramean: Collected Aramaic Essays. LC 77-21379. (Society of Biblical Literature. Monograph: No. 25). 317p. 1984. pap. 12.00 (ISBN 0-89130-152-6, 06 00 25). Scholars Pr GA.

Fitzmyer, Joseph F. Pauline Theology: A Brief Sketch. (Orig.). 1967. pap. text ed. 13.95 (ISBN 0-13-654525-4). P-H.

Fitzpatrick. Zhou Enlai. 1984. pap. 4.95 (ISBN 0-318-01310-X). U of Queensland Pr.

Fitzpatrick, A. J., jt. ed. see Vaughan, W. E.

Fitzpatrick, Brian. The Australian People, Seventeen Eighty-Eight to Nineteen Forty-Five. LC 81-13255. (Illus.). viii, 279p. 1982. Repr. of 1951 ed. lib. bdg. 32.50x (ISBN 0-313-23016-1, FIAU). Greenwood.

--Catholic Royalism in the Department of the Gard: 1814-1852. LC 82-14564. (Illus.). 224p. 1983. 47.50 (ISBN 0-521-22454-3). Cambridge U Pr.

Fitzpatrick, Clare L., ed. see AKempis, Thomas.

Fitzpatrick, Daniel J. Confusion, Call, Commitment: The Spiritual Exercises & Religious Education. LC 76-3801. 178p. 1976. pap. 4.95 (ISBN 0-8189-0327-9). Alba.

Fitz-Patrick, David G. & Kimbuna, John. Bundi: The Culture of a Papua New Guinea People. (Illus.). 178p. 1983. 29.95 (ISBN 0-295-96233-X). U of Wash Pr.

Fitzpatrick, Doyle C. Mormon: The King Strang Story. LC 70-140603. 1970. 7.95 (ISBN 0-685-57226-9). Natl Heritage.

FitzPatrick, E. A. Micromorphology of Soils. (Illus.). 330p. 1984. 59.95 (ISBN 0-412-24200-1, 5067, Pub. by Chapman & Hall England). Methuen Inc.

--Soils: Their Formation, Classification & Ditribution. LC 82-12669. (Illus.). 384p. 1983. pap. text ed. 23.00x (ISBN 0-582-30116-5). Longman.

Fitzpatrick, Edward A. Educational Views & Influence of DeWitt Clinton. LC 78-176775. (Columbia University. Teachers College. Contributions to Education: No. 44). Repr. of 1911 ed. 22.50 (ISBN 0-404-55044-4). AMS Pr.

--Educational Views & Influence of DeWitt Clinton. LC 76-89177. (American Education: Its Men, Institutions & Ideas, Ser. 1). 1969. Repr. of 1911 ed. 8.00 (ISBN 0-405-01415-5). Ayer Co Pubs.

Fitzpatrick, Edward A., ed. St. Ignatius & the Ratio Studiorum. Mayer, Mary H. & Ball, A. R., trs. LC 83-45593. Date not set. Repr. of 1933 ed. 31.50 (ISBN 0-404-19886-4). AMS Pr.

Fitzpatrick, F. L. & Hole, J. W. Modern Life Science. (gr. 7-9). 1974. text ed. 21.24 (ISBN 0-03-005661-6, HoltE); tchrs' ed. 31.04 (ISBN 0-03-005666-7). HR&W.

Fitzpatrick, F. L., et al. Living Things. (gr. 7-9). 1970. text ed. 21.80 (ISBN 0-03-080068-4, HoltE); tchrs' ed. 33.00 (ISBN 0-03-083445-7); exercises 7.52 (ISBN 0-686-66456-6); transparencies o.p. 86.50 (ISBN 0-686-66457-4). HR&W.

Fitzpatrick, H. M. The Lower Fungi, Phycomycetes. Repr. of 1930 ed. 32.00 (ISBN 0-384-15810-2). Johnson Repr.

Fitzpatrick, J. Puerto Rican Americans: The Meaning of Migration to the Mainland. 1971. pap. 15.95 ref. ed. (ISBN 0-13-740100-0). P-H.

Fitzpatrick, J. B. Ireland & the Making of Britain. 59.95 (ISBN 0-8490-0422-5). Gordon Pr.

Fitzpatrick, J. C., ed. see Washington, George.

Fitzpatrick, James F., et al. The Law & Roadside Hazards. 550p. 1974. 35.00 (ISBN 0-87215-170-0). Michie Co.

Fitzpatrick, James K. God, Country, & the Supreme Court. 212p. 1985. 18.95 (ISBN 0-89526-610-5). Regnery-Gateway.

Fitzpatrick, James M., jt. auth. see Simon, Thomas G.

Fitzpatrick, Jean G. Pregnancy & Work. 256p. 1984. pap. 7.95 (ISBN 0-380-88666-9, 88666-9). Avon.

Fitzpatrick, Jim, jt. auth. see Roget, Daniel.

Fitzpatrick, John. The Merchant of Manchac: The Letterbooks of John Fitzpatrick, 1768-1790. Dalrymple, Margaret F., ed. LC 77-28801. 480p. 1978. text ed. 35.00x (ISBN 0-8071-0268-7). La State U Pr.

Fitzpatrick, John, ed. see Van Buren, Martin.

Fitzpatrick, John C. George Washington Himself. LC 75-18398. (Illus.). 544p. 1975. Repr. of 1933 ed. lib. bdg. 25.75x (ISBN 0-8371-8338-3, FIGW). Greenwood.

--Spirit of the Revolution. LC 71-120875. (American Bicentennial Ser). 1970. Repr. of 1924 ed. 22.50x (ISBN 0-8046-1268-4, Pub. by Kennikat). Assoc Faculty Pr.

Fitzpatrick, John C., ed. The Last Will & Testament of George Washington. 67p. 1.50 (ISBN 0-317-34931-7). Mt Vernon Ladies.

Fitzpatrick, John C., ed. see Van Buren, Martin.

Fitzpatrick, John W., jt. auth. see Woolfendon, Glen E.

FitzPatrick, Joseph A., jt. ed. see Freeman, Mark P.

Fitzpatrick, Joseph F., Jr. How to Know the Freshwater Crustacea. (Pictured Key Nature Ser.). 240p. 1982. write for info wire coil (ISBN 0-697-04783-0). Wm C Brown.

Fitzpatrick, Joyce & Whall, Ann. Conceptual Models of Nursing & Analysis Evaluation: Applications. LC 82-17913. (Illus.). 352p. 1983. pap. text ed. 16.95 (ISBN 0-89303-233-6). Brady Comm.

Fitzpatrick, Joyce, jt. auth. see Werley, Harriet.

Fitzpatrick, Joyce, et al. Nursing Models & Their Psychiatric Mental Health Applications. LC 81-10108. (Illus.). 128p. 1981. pap. text ed. 15.95 (ISBN 0-89303-026-0). Brady Comm.

Fitzpatrick, Joyce J., jt. auth. see Werley, Harriet H.

Fitzpatrick, Julie. In the Air. LC 84-40839. (Illus.). 32p. (gr. 2-5). PLB 6.95 (ISBN 0-382-09060-8). Silver.

--Magnets. LC 84-40838. (Illus.). 32p. (gr. 2-5). PLB 6.95 (ISBN 0-382-09061-6). Silver.

--Mirrors. LC 84-40837. (Illus.). 32p. (gr. 2-5). PLB 6.95 (ISBN 0-382-09059-4). Silver.

--On the Water. LC 84-40836. (Illus.). 32p. (gr. 2-5). PLB 6.95 (ISBN 0-382-09058-6). Silver.

Fitzpatrick, Kathryn. Commandments: Twenty-Eight Family Times to Respond in Love. (Familytime - Faithtime: A Home-Based Approach to Religious Education Ser.). (Illus.). 52p. (Orig.). 1982. pap. text ed. 3.50 (ISBN 0-86716-013-6). St Anthony Mess Pr.

--Creed: Twenty-Nine Family Times to Explore Belief, 3 Vols. (Family Time - Faith Time: A Home-Based Approach to Religious Education Ser.). (Illus.). 70p. (Orig.). 1982. pap. text ed. 3.50 (ISBN 0-86716-012-8). St Anthony Mess Pr.

--Family Time, Faith Time, 3 Vols. (Illus.). 307p. (Orig.). 1982. Set. pap. text ed. 8.95 (ISBN 0-86716-030-6). St Anthony Mess Pr.

--Sacraments: Twenty-Eight Family Times to Celebrate Life. (Family Time - Faith Time: A Home-Based Approach to Religious Education Ser.). (Illus.). 70p. (Orig.). 1982. pap. 3.50 (ISBN 0-86716-010-1). St Anthony Mess Pr.

Fitzpatrick, Lilian L. Nebraska Place-Names. Fairclough, G. Thomas, ed. LC 60-15471. xii, 227p. 1960. pap. 5.95 (ISBN 0-8032-5060-6, BB 107, Bison). U of Nebr Pr.

Fitzpatrick, Lois, jt. ed. see Morin-Kabatut, G.

Fitzpatrick, Lorenzo. Seasons of My Mind. 48p. (Orig.). 1984. pap. 3.00 (ISBN 0-9613323-0-1). Pat Pub Co.

Fitzpatrick, M. Louise. Prologue to Professionalism. LC 83-2526. 288p. 1983. pap. text ed. 14.95 (ISBN 0-89303-773-7). Brady Comm.

Fitzpatrick, M. Louise, ed. Historical Studies in Nursing. LC 78-12192. 1978. text ed. 9.95x (ISBN 0-8077-2527-7). Tchrs Coll.

--Present Realities: Future Imperatives in Nursing Education. LC 76-55404. 1977. pap. text ed. 7.95x (ISBN 0-8077-2513-7). Tchrs Coll.

Fitzpatrick, Mariana, jt. ed. see Cunningham, Ann Marie.

Fitzpatrick, Mariana, tr. see Berrondo, Marie.

Fitzpatrick, Marianna, tr. see Satprem.

Fitzpatrick, Mary C., tr. see Thomas Aquinas, Saint.

Fitzpatrick, Merrilyn. Zhou Enlai. (Leaders of Asia Ser.). 1984. pap. 4.95 (ISBN 0-318-12094-1). U of Queensland Pr.

Fitzpatrick, Nancy H., ed. All-Time Baking Favorites. LC 74-76331. (Family Circle Books). (Illus.). 144p. 1976. 7.98x (ISBN 0-405-06686-4). Ayer Co Pubs.

--Great Desserts. LC 74-76331. (Family Circle Books). (Illus.). 144p. 1976. 9.98x (ISBN 0-405-11404-4). Ayer Co Pubs.

Fitzpatrick, Paul. Rugby League Review, Nineteen Eighty-Four to Nineteen Eighty-Five. (Illus.). 144p. 1985. 19.95 (ISBN 0-571-13687-7); pap. 9.95 (ISBN 0-571-13690-7). Faber & Faber.
--Rugby League Review, 1983-84. (Illus.). 150p. 1984. 21.95 (ISBN 0-571-13402-5); pap. 10.95 (ISBN 0-571-13403-3). Faber & Faber.
--Rugby League Review, 1984-1985. LC 85-12852. (Illus.). 144p. 1985. 19.95 (ISBN 0-571-13687-7); pap. 9.95 (ISBN 0-571-13690-7). Faber & Faber.
Fitzpatrick, Peter. Law & State in Papua, New Guinea. LC 80-49982. (Law, State & Society Ser.). 1981. 38.50 (ISBN 0-12-257880-5). Acad Pr.
Fitzpatrick, Ray & Hinton, John. The Experience of Illness. 288p. 1985. pap. 16.95x (ISBN 0-422-78530-X, 9266, Pub. by Tavistock England). Methuen Inc.
Fitzpatrick, Sheila. Education & Social Mobility in the Soviet Union: 1921-1934. LC 78-58788. (Soviet & East European Studies). 1979. 44.50 (ISBN 0-521-22325-3). Cambridge U Pr.
--The Russian Revolution. 1984. 19.95x (ISBN 0-19-219162-4); pap. 6.95 (ISBN 0-19-289148-0). Oxford U Pr.
Fitzpatrick, Sheila, ed. Cultural Revolution in Russia, 1928-1931. LC 77-74439. (Studies of the Russian Institute, Columbia University Ser.). 352p. 1978. 17.50 (ISBN 0-253-31591-3). Ind U Pr.
--Cultural Revolution in Russia, 1928-1931. LC 77-74439. 320p. (Orig.). 1984. 27.50x (ISBN 0-253-31591-3); pap. 10.95 (ISBN 0-253-20337-6). Ind U Pr.
Fitzpatrick, Shelia, ed. Cultural Revolution in Russia, 1928-1931. LC 77-74439. (Columbia Uniservity Russian Institute Studies). pap. cancelled (ISBN 0-317-08642-1, 2055497). Bks Demand UMI.
Fitzpatrick, T. B., et al. Biology & Diseases of Dermal Pigmentation. 376p. 1981. 75.00x (ISBN 0-86008-292-X, Pub. by U of Tokyo Japan). Columbia U Pr.
--Dermatology in General Medicine. 2nd ed. LC 78-9850. (Illus.). 1979. text ed. 115.00 (ISBN 0-07-021196-5). McGraw.
Fitzpatrick, T. J. Fitzpatrick's Rafinesque: A Sketch of His Life with Bibliography. rev. ed. Boewe, Charles, ed. (Illus.). 360p. 1982. Repr. of 1911 ed. lib. bdg. 30.00x (ISBN 0-87730-011-9). M&S Pr.
Fitzpatrick, Thomas. Bloody Bridge. LC 71-102602. (Irish Culture & History Ser). 1970. Repr. of 1903 ed. 24.50x (ISBN 0-8046-0779-6, Pub. by Kennikat). Assoc Faculty Pr.
Fitzpatrick, Thomas B. & Polano, Machiel K. Color Atlas & Synopsis of Clinical Dermatology. (Illus.). 352p. 1982. pap. text ed. 34.00 (ISBN 0-07-021197-3). McGraw.
Fitzpatrick, Thomas B., et al. Dermatology in General Medicine: Update One. (Illus.). 320p. 1982. text ed. 54.00 (ISBN 0-07-021198-1). McGraw.
Fitzpatrick, William J. Monarch Notes on Austen's Emma & Mansfield Park. (Orig.). pap. 3.50 (ISBN 0-671-00704-1). Monarch Pr.
Fitz-Randolph, Jane, jt. auth. see Jespersen, James.
Fitz-Randolph, Jane, jt. auth. see Jesperson, James.
Fitzroy, A. T., pseud. Despised & Rejected. LC 75-12314. (Homosexuality Ser.). 1975. Repr. of 1917 ed. 17.00x (ISBN 0-405-07389-5). Ayer Co Pubs.
Fitz-Roy, Robert, et al. Narrative of the Surveying Voyages of His Majesty's Ships Adventure & Beagle, 3 Vols. in 4 Pts. Repr. of 1839 ed. Set. 295.00 (ISBN 0-404-09900-9). Vol. 1 (ISBN 0-404-09901-7). Vol. 2 Pt. 1 (ISBN 0-404-09902-5). Vol. 2 Pt. 2 (ISBN 0-404-09903-3). Vol. 3 (ISBN 0-404-09904-1). AMS Pr.
Fitzsimmons, Ada. Character Dressed Kewpies. (Illus.). 44p. 1982. pap. 7.00 (ISBN 0-915195-02-X). Paper Pile.
--Old Paper Collectibles: An Evolving Value Guide. (Illus.). Date not set. pap. 12.50 (ISBN 0-915195-03-8). Paper Pile.
Fitzsimmons, Ada, compiled by. American Collectibles As Advertised, 1860-1899. (Illus.). 210p. 1982. 17.95 (ISBN 0-915195-00-3). Paper Pile.
Fitzsimmons, J. A. & Sullivan, R. S. Service Operations Management. 464p. 1982. 34.95x (ISBN 0-07-021215-5). McGraw.
Fitzsimmons, John, ed. Manning: Anglican & Catholic. LC 78-11571. 1979. Repr. of 1951 ed. lib. bdg. 18.75x (ISBN 0-313-21005-5, FIMA). Greenwood.
Fitzsimmons, Michele & Schmidt, Diane. The Chicago Exhibition. 112p. 1985. 24.95 (ISBN 0-932735-01-0). Melrose Pub Inc.
Fitzsimmons, Muriel. Cooking for Absolute Beginners. LC 75-35405. Orig. Title: You Can Cook If You Can Read. 380p. 1976. pap. 4.95 (ISBN 0-486-23311-1). Dover.
Fitzsimmons, R. W. & Wrigley, C. W. Australian Barley. 62p. 1980. 20.00x (ISBN 0-643-00344-4, Pub. by CSIRO Australia). State Mutual Bk.
--Australian Barleys. 86p. 1980. 9.95x (ISBN 0-643-00344-4, Pub. by CSIRO Australia). Intl Spec Bk.
--Australian Barleys: Identifications of Varieties, Grain Defects & Foreign Seeds. 62p. 1979. pap. 13.50 (ISBN 0-643-00344-4, C002, CSIRO). Unipub.
Fitzsimmons, R. W., jt. auth. see Ferns, G. K.
Fitzsimmons, Raymund. Death & the Magician. large print ed. LC 81-8957. 326p. 1981. Repr. of 1980 ed. 10.95 (ISBN 0-686-78414-6). Thorndike Pr.
Fitzsimmons, Stephen J. & Freedman, Abby J. Rural Community Development: A Comprehensive Model for Programs, Policy, & Research. LC 80-69664. (Illus.). 544p. 1981. text ed. 28.00 (ISBN 0-89011-556-7). Abt Bks.
Fitzsimmons, Stephen J. & Freeman, Abby J. Rural Community Development: A Program, Policy & Research Model. (Illus.). 540p. 1984. Repr. of 1981 ed. lib. bdg. 34.75 (ISBN 0-8191-4107-0). U Pr of Amer.
Fitzsimmons, Stephen J. & Salama, Ovadia A. Man & Water: A Social Report. 1973. pap. 20.00x (ISBN 0-89011-485-4, ECR-102). Abt Bks.
Fitzsimmons, Thomas. Meditation Seeds. 1971. pap. 0.75 (ISBN 0-685-01053-8). Stone-Marrow Pr.
--RSFSR, Russian Soviet Federated Socialist Republic, 2 vols. LC 74-12008. (Country Survey Ser.). (Illus.). 681p. 1974. Repr. of 1957 ed. lib. bdg. 50.00x (ISBN 0-8371-7668-9, FIRS). Greenwood.
Fitzsimmons, Thomas, et al. U. S. S. R. It's People, Its Society, Its Culture. LC 74-12074. (Illus.). 590p. 1974. Repr. of 1960 ed. lib. bdg. 45.00x (ISBN 0-8371-7667-0, FIUS). Greenwood.
Fitz-Simon, Christopher. The Arts in Ireland: A Chronological Survey. 256p. 1982. text ed. 40.50x (ISBN 0-391-02578-3, Pub. by Gill & Macmillan Ireland). Humanities.
--The Irish Theatre. LC 82-74547. (Illus.). 208p. 1983. 24.95f (ISBN 0-500-01300-4). Thames Hudson.
--Irish Theatre. (Irish Heritage Ser.). (Illus.). 26p. 1983. pap. 3.95 (ISBN 0-900346-37-X, Pub. by Salem Hse Ltd). Merrimack Pub Cir.
Fitzsimons. A Field Guide to the Snakes of Southern Africa. 29.95 (ISBN 0-00-219327-2, Collins Pub England). Greene.
Fitzsimons, Bernard. U. S. Air Force. LC 84-6502. (Illus.). 144p. 1984. 16.95 (ISBN 0-668-06201-0, 6201). Arco.
Fitzsimons, Cecilia. My First Birds. LC 84-48347. (Illus.). 12p. (gr. k-4). 1985. 8.61i (ISBN 0-06-021892-4). HarpJ.
--My First Butterflies. LC 84-48348. (Illus.). 12p. (gr. k-4). 1985. 8.61i (ISBN 0-06-021893-2). HarpJ.
Fitzsimons, Christopher. Early Warning. 256p. 1981. pap. 2.25 (ISBN 0-380-50179-1, 50179). Avon.
--Reflex Action. 224p. 1981. pap. 2.50 (ISBN 0-449-24414-8, Crest). Fawcett.
Fitzsimons, J. O'C. Pheasants & Their Enemies. (Illus.). 112p. 1979. 13.50 (ISBN 0-904558-56-8). Saiga.
Fitzsimons, J. T. The Physiology of Thirst & Sodium Appetite. LC 78-16212. (Physiological Society Monographs: No. 35). 1979. 95.00 (ISBN 0-521-22292-3). Cambridge U Pr.
Fitzsimons, M. A. Catholic Church Today: Western Europe. 1969. 19.95x (ISBN 0-268-00307-6). U of Notre Dame Pr.
--The Past Recaptured: Great Historians & the History of History. LC 83-1168. 240p. 1983. 16.95x (ISBN 0-268-01550-3, 85-15504). U of Notre Dame Pr.
Fitzsimons, M. A., jt. auth. see Kertesz, Stephen D.
Fitzsimons, M. A., jt. ed. see Kertesz, Stephen D.
Fitzsimons, M. A., et al, eds. see Review of Politics.
Fitz-Simons, Marian J. Some Parent-Child Relationships As Shown in Clinical Case Studies. LC 71-176776. (Columbia University. Teachers College. Contributions to Education: No. 643). Repr. of 1935 ed. 22.50 (ISBN 0-404-55643-4). AMS Pr.
Fitzsimons, Matthew A. Empire by Treaty: Britain & the Middle East in the Twentieth Century. (International Studies Ser). 1964. 21.95x (ISBN 0-268-00088-3). U of Notre Dame Pr.
FitzSimons, Neal, ed. see Jervis, John B.
FitzSimons, Raymund. Death & the Magician: The Mystery of Houdini. LC 80-21071. 216p. 1985. pap. 7.95 (ISBN 0-689-70694-4, 331). Atheneum.
FitzSimons, Ruth M. & Murphy, Albert T. Guess What! 1.50 (ISBN 0-686-08734-8). Expression.
--Let's Play Hide & Seek. 7.50 (ISBN 0-686-11822-7); includes manual (ISBN 0-686-11823-5). Expression.
Fitzsimons, Ruth M., jt. auth. see Murphy, Albert T.
Fitzsimons, Virginia, jt. auth. see Forbes, Elizabeth.
Fitz-Thedmar, Arnold. De Antiquis Legibus Liber. Stapleton, Thomas, ed. (Camden Society, London. Publications, First Ser.: No. 34). Repr. of 1846 ed. 55.00 (ISBN 0-404-50134-6). AMS Pr.
--De Antiquis Legibus Liber. Repr. of 1846 ed. 55.00 (ISBN 0-384-15820-X). Johnson Repr.
Fitzwalter, Raymond & Taylor, David. Web of Corruption: The Story of J. G. L. Poulson & T. Dan Smith. LC 82-138863. (Illus.). 282p. 1981. cancelled (ISBN 0-246-10915-7, Pub. by Granada England). Sheridan.
Fitzwarren, Albert E. The Nature of Nature from Alpha to Zeta. (Illus.). 32p. 1981. pap. 1.50 (ISBN 0-942788-07-9). Marginal Med.
Fitzwater, Eva. Cry the Beloved Country Notes. (Orig.). 1970. pap. 2.95 (ISBN 0-8220-0339-2). Cliffs.
--Doctor Faustus Notes. (Orig.). 1967. pap. 3.25 (ISBN 0-8220-0406-2). Cliffs.
--Pearl Notes. (Orig.). 1981. pap. 2.75 (ISBN 0-8220-0994-3). Cliffs.
--Pride & Prejudice Notes. (Orig.). 1982. pap. 3.50 (ISBN 0-8220-1084-4). Cliffs.
--To Kill a Mockingbird Notes. (Orig.). 1966. pap. 2.75 (ISBN 0-8220-1282-0). Cliffs.
Fitzwater, Ivan W. Failproof Children. LC 82-192705. (Illus.). 178p. 1979. 13.00x (ISBN 0-941420-02-7). Mandel Pubns.
--Finding Time for Success & Happiness: Through Time Management. rev. ed. LC 77-670026. (Illus.). 115p. 1979. pap. 7.00x (ISBN 0-941420-00-0). Mandel Pubns.
--You Can Be a Powerful Leader. LC 78-55516. (Illus.). 155p. 1984. pap. 10.00x (ISBN 0-941420-04-3). Mandel Pubns.
Fitzwater, J. Water Borne Coatings Buyer's Guide. 28p. 1984. pap. text ed. 25.00 (ISBN 0-318-01980-9). Tech Marketing.
Fitzwater, Perry B. La Mujer: Su Mision, Posicion y Ministerio. Orig. Title: Woman: Mission, Position, Ministry. 76p. (Span.). 1972. pap. 2.25 (ISBN 0-8254-1233-1). Kregel.
Fitzwilliam Museum. All for Art: The Ricketts & Shannon Collection. Darracott, J., ed. LC 79-51597. (Illus.). 1979. 39.50 (ISBN 0-521-22841-7); pap. 12.95 (ISBN 0-521-29674-9). Cambridge U Pr.
--Drawings & Watercolours by Peter De Wint. LC 79-4652. (Illus.). pap. 9.95 (ISBN 0-521-29631-5). Cambridge U Pr.
Fivars, Grace, ed. The Critical Incident Technique: A Bibliography. 2nd ed. 1980. pap. 7.50 (ISBN 0-89785-662-7). Am Inst Res.
Fix, jt. ed. see Eads.
Fix, Alan G. The Demography of the Semai Senoi. (Anthropological Papers Ser.: No. 62). (Illus., Orig.). 1977. pap. 5.00x (ISBN 0-932206-60-3). U Mich Mus Anthro.
Fix, G. J., jt. auth. see Coffman, C. V.
Fix, George J., jt. auth. see Strang, G.
Fix, James. Atlas of the Human Brain Stem & Spinal Cord. 2ND ed. 1985. pap. text ed. 23.00 (ISBN 0-8391-2085-0, 22136). Univ Park.
Fix, James A., jt. auth. see Becker, R. Frederick.
Fix, James D. & Punte, Carroll S. Atlas of the Human Brain Stem & Spinal Cord. (Illus.). 104p. 1981. pap. text ed. 20.00 (ISBN 0-8391-1666-7). Univ Park.
Fix, Janet & Levitt, Zola. For Singles Only. 128p. 1978. pap. 4.95 (ISBN 0-8007-5034-9, Power Bks). Revell.
Fix, Michael, jt. auth. see Eads, George C.
Fix, Penn, ed. Adventures of a Gentleman Traveler. 20p. 1974. pap. 1.50 (ISBN 0-87770-152-0). Ye Galleon.
Fix, William R. The Bone Peddlers: The Selling of Evolution. (Illus.). 368p. 1984. 18.95 (ISBN 0-02-538480-5). Macmillan.
--Pyramid Odyssey. LC 78-14540. (Illus.). 291p. 1984. pap. 9.95 (ISBN 0-932487-00-9). Mercury Media.
--Star Maps. (Octopus Bk.). (Illus.). 1979. 14.95 (ISBN 0-7064-1066-1, Mayflower Bks); pap. 8.95 (ISBN 0-7064-1085-8). Smith Pubs.
Fixel, Albert W. How to Detect False Entries in Financial Statements. (Illus.). 119p. 1982. 89.85x (ISBN 0-86654-038-5). Inst Econ Finan.
Fixel, Lawrence. The Edge of Something. 1976. pap. 2.50 (ISBN 0-685-82995-2, Pub. by Cloud Marauder). Small Pr Dist.
--Time to Destroy-To Discover. 1972. regular ed 3.00 (ISBN 0-915572-09-5); ltd. signed, numbered ed 7.00 (ISBN 0-915572-58-3). Panjandrum.
Fixman, Adeline. Aim for a Job in Cartooning. (Aim High Vocational Guidance Ser.). (gr. 7 up). 1976. PLB 8.97 (ISBN 0-8239-0355-9). Rosen Group.
--Your Future As a Designer. (Careers in Depth Ser.). (Illus.). 140p. 1980. lib. bdg. 7.97 (ISBN 0-8239-0509-8). Rosen Group.
--Your Future in Creative Careers. (YA) 1978. PLB 7.97 (ISBN 0-8239-0402-4). Rosen Group.
Fixx, James. Games for the Super Intelligent. 128p. 1982. pap. 2.75 (ISBN 0-446-31032-8). Warner Bks.
--More Games for the Super-Intelligent. 144p. 1982. pap. 2.75 (ISBN 0-446-31044-1). Warner Bks.
--Solve It. 128p. 1983. pap. 2.95 (ISBN 0-446-31080-8). Warner Bks.
Fixx, James F. The Complete Book of Running. (Illus.). 1977. 13.95 (ISBN 0-394-41159-5). Random.
--Games for the Superintelligent. LC 73-180074. (Illus.). 120p. 1972. 9.95 (ISBN 0-385-05768-7). Doubleday.
--Jim Fixx's Second Book of Running. 320p. 1980. 11.95 (ISBN 0-394-50898-X). Random.
--More Games for the SuperIntelligent. LC 76-7695. 1976. 8.95 (ISBN 0-385-11039-1). Doubleday.
Fixx, James F., jt. auth. see Nike Sport Research Laboratory.
Fixx, James F., ed. Drugs. LC 78-169196. (Great Contemporary Issues Ser). (Illus.). 757p. 1971. 35.00 (ISBN 0-405-01290-X, New York Times) (ISBN 0-685-27570-1). Ayer Co Pubs.
--The Mass Media & Politics. LC 76-183137. (Great Contemporary Issues Ser). (Illus.). 600p. 1971. 35.00 (ISBN 0-405-01291-8, New York Times) (ISBN 0-685-27572-8). Ayer Co Pubs.
Fizdale, Robert, jt. auth. see Gold, Arthur.
Fizer, John. Psychologism & Psychoaesthetics: A Historical & Critical View of Their Relations. (Linguistic & Literary Studies in Eastern Europe: Vol. 6). 278p. 1981. 33.00x (ISBN 90-272-1506-5). Benjamins North Am.
Fjallbrant, Nancy & Malley, Ian. User Education in Libraries. 2nd ed. 190p. 1984. 19.50 (ISBN 0-85157-361-4, Pub. by Bingley England). Shoe String.
Fjallbrant, Nancy, jt. auth. see Gilbert, J. K.
Fjeld, Jon, jt. auth. see Damsgaard, Kristen.
Fjeld, Per-Olaf. Sverere Fehn: The Thought of Consturction. LC 82-42845. (Illus.). 192p. 1983. pap. 25.00 (ISBN 0-8478-0471-2). Rizzoli Intl.
Fjelde, Rolf, tr. see Ibsen, Henrik.
Fjelstul, Alice, et al. More Early American Stencils in Color. (Illus.). 144p. 1985. 29.95 (ISBN 0-525-24240-6, 02908-870); pap. 15.95 (ISBN 0-525-48114-1, 01549-460). Dutton.
Fjermedal, Grant. Magic Bullets: A Revolution in Cancer Treatment. LC 84-12251. 288p. 1984. 15.95 (ISBN 0-02-538550-X). Macmillan.
Flaccus, Edward. North Country Cabin. LC 78-21638. (Illus.). 122p. 1979. pap. 5.95 (ISBN 0-87842-111-4). Mountain Pr.
Flaccus, Kimball. A Poet's View. 64p. 1984. 10.00 (ISBN 0-8059-2913-4). Dorrance.
Flaccus, Louis W. Artists & Thinkers. facs. ed. LC 67-23218. (Essay Index Reprint Ser). 1916. 17.00 (ISBN 0-8369-0444-3). Ayer Co Pubs.
Flaceliere, Robert. Love in Ancient Greece. Cleugh, James, tr. LC 72-13866. (Illus.). 224p. 1973. Repr. of 1962 ed. lib. bdg. 22.50x (ISBN 0-8371-6758-2, FLLA). Greenwood.
Flach, Frederic F. & Draghi, Suzanne C. The Nature & Treatment of Depression. LC 74-28265. Repr. of 1975 ed. 108.50 (ISBN 0-8357-9939-5, 2055169). Bks Demand UMI.
Flach, George. Changes in the Nineteen Eighty-One National Electrical Code. 145p. 1981. 18.95 (ISBN 0-13-127860-6, Reward); pap. 9.95 (ISBN 0-13-127852-5). P-H.
Flach, George W. Changes in the Nineteen Eighty-Four National Electrical Code. Revised ed. (Illus.). 176p. 1984. pap. text ed. 12.95 (ISBN 0-13-127762-6). P-H.
Flach, George W., jt. auth. see Osborn, Richard W.
Flach, Jacques. Origines De L'ancienne France, 4 Vols. LC 69-18612. (Research & Source Works: No. 391). (Fr). 1970. Repr. of 1917 ed. Set. text ed. 135.00 (ISBN 0-8337-1148-2). B Franklin.
Flach, Johannes. Der Deutsche Professor der Gegenwart: The German Professor Today. Metzger, Walter P., ed. LC 76-55203. (The Academic Profession Ser.). (Ger.). 1977. Repr. of 1886 ed. lib. bdg. 19.00x (ISBN 0-405-10035-3). Ayer Co Pubs.
Flach, M., jt. ed. see Stanton, W. R.
Flachman, Leonard. Christmas: The Annual of Christmas Literature & Art, Vol. 55. 64p. 1985. text ed. 13.50 (ISBN 0-8066-8967-6, 17-0131); pap. text ed. 6.95 (ISBN 0-8066-8966-8, 17-0130). Augsburg.
Flachmann, Charles R. Bethlehem's Brightest Star. (Arch Book Ser.: No. 21). 1984. pap. 0.99 (59-1283). Concordia.
Flachmann, Kim. Focus: A College English Handbook. LC 80-82699. (Illus.). 448p. 1981. pap. text ed. 14.95 (ISBN 0-395-29728-1); instr's. manual 1.00 (ISBN 0-395-29729-X). HM.
Flachmann, Michael, jt. auth. see Appel, Libby.
Flachsmeyer, J., et al, eds. Contributions to Extension Theory of Topological Structures: Proceedings. 1969. 68.00 (ISBN 0-12-258050-8). Acad Pr.
Flack, Dora & Erickson, Karly. Gifts Only You Can Give. Lyon, Jack, ed. LC 84-70591. 125p. 1984. 7.95 (ISBN 0-87747-993-3). Deseret Bk.
Flack, Dora, jt. auth. see Betenson, Lula P.
Flack, Dora D. Dry & Save. LC 77-72665. (Illus., Orig.). 1977. pap. 4.95 (ISBN 0-912800-41-0). Woodbridge Pr.
--Fun with Fruit Preservation: Leather, Drying, & Other Methods. LC 74-78025. (Illus.). 98p. 1973. pap. 5.95 (ISBN 0-88290-023-4). Horizon Utah.
--What About Christmas? A Family Storybook for December. (Illus.). 1971. pap. 4.95 (ISBN 0-88290-000-5). Horizon Utah.
Flack, Elmer E., ed. see Melanchthon, Philipp.
Flack, H., ed. see Taft, William H.
Flack, Horace E. The Adoption of the Fourteenth Amendment. LC 78-64271. (Johns Hopkins University. Studies in the Social Sciences. Extra Volumes: 26). Repr. of 1908 ed. 11.50 (ISBN 0-404-61373-X). AMS Pr.
--Adoption of the Fourteenth Amendment. 1908. 11.75 (ISBN 0-8446-1182-4). Peter Smith.
--Spanish-American Diplomatic Relations Preceding the War of 1898. LC 78-63912. (Johns Hopkins University. Studies in the Social Sciences. Twenty-Fourth Ser. 1906: 1-2). Repr. of 1906 ed. 14.50 (ISBN 0-404-61164-8). AMS Pr.
Flack, J. A. Douglas. Bird Populations of Aspen Forests in Western North America. 97p. 1976. 7.50 (ISBN 0-943610-19-2). Am Ornithologists.
Flack, J. Ernest. Urban Water Conservation: Increasing Efficiency-in-Use Residential Water Demand. LC 82-70113. 111p. 1982. pap. 13.25x (ISBN 0-87262-296-7). Am Soc Civil Eng.

Flack, J. Kirkpatrick. Desideratum in Washington: The Intellectual Community in the Capitol City, 1870-1900. 200p. 1976. text ed. 16.95 (ISBN 0-87073-114-9). Schenkman Bks Inc.

Flack, J. Kirkpatrick, ed. Records of the Columbia Historical Society of Washington, D.C, Vol. 51. (Illus.). 225p. 1984. text ed. 20.00x (ISBN 0-8139-0866-3). U Pr of Va.

Flack, Marjorie. Angus & the Ducks. (ps-k). 7.95 (ISBN 0-385-07213-9). Doubleday.

--Angus Y el Gato. Palacios, Argentina, tr. from Span. (gr. k-3). 1979. pap. 2.25 (ISBN 0-590-12068-9). Scholastic Inc.

--Ask Mister Bear. LC 58-8370. 32p. (gr. k-3). 1932. 9.95 (ISBN 0-02-735390-7); pap. 3.95x (ISBN 0-02-043090-6). Macmillan.

--Story About Ping. (gr. k-2). 1977. pap. 3.95 (ISBN 0-14-050241-6, Puffin). Penguin.

--Story about Ping. (Illus.). (ps-2). 1933. PLB 10.95 (ISBN 0-670-67223-8). Viking.

--Wait for William. (Illus.). (gr. k-3). PLB 6.95 (ISBN 0-395-15484-7). HM.

--Walter the Lazy Mouse. LC 62-16500. (gr. 2-5). 6.95a (ISBN 0-385-02772-9); pap. 2.50 (ISBN 0-385-01078-8, Zephyr). Doubleday.

Flackes, W. D. Northern Ireland: A Political Directory 1968-79. 1980. 26.00 (ISBN 0-312-57905-5). St Martin.

Flacks, Niki & Rasberry, Robert W. Power Talk: How to Use Theater Techniques to Win Your Audience. LC 81-69632. 256p. 1982. text ed. 12.95 (ISBN 0-02-910390-8). Free Pr.

Flad, H. D., et al, eds. Immunodiagnosis & Immunotherapy of Malignant Tumors: Relevance to Surgery. Proceedings of a Workshop Held at Reisenburg, Nov. 2-4, 1977. (Illus.). 1979. pap. 45.00 (ISBN 0-387-09161-0). Springer-Verlag.

Fladby, Berit. Household Viability & Economic Differentiation in Gama, Sri Lanka. (Bergen Studies in Social Anthropology: No. 28). 445p. 1985. pap. text ed. 9.95x (ISBN 0-936508-61-2, Pub. by Dept Soc Anthropology, Unuversity of Bergen, Norway). Barber Pr.

Fladeland, Betty. Abolitionists & Working-Class Problems in the Age of Industrialization. 220p. 1984. text ed. 22.50x (ISBN 0-8071-1167-8). La State U Pr.

--Men & Brothers: Anglo-American Antislavery Cooperation. LC 78-186343. 492p. 1972. 35.50x (ISBN 0-252-00225-3). U of Ill Pr.

Fladeland, Betty L. James Gillespie Birney: Slaveholder to Abolitionist. LC 70-88985. (Illus.). 323p. Repr. of 1955 ed. lib. bdg. 15.00x (ISBN 0-8371-2312-7, FIJB). Greenwood.

Flader, Susan L. Thinking Like a Mountain: Aldo Leopold & the Evolution of an Ecological Attitude Toward Deer, Wolves & Forests. LC 78-17667. (Illus.). xxvi, 284p. 1978. pap. 5.95 (ISBN 0-8032-6850-5, BB 668, Bison). U of Nebr Pr.

Flader, Susan L., ed. The Great Lakes Forest: An Environmental & Social History. (Illus.). 369p. 1983. 29.50x (ISBN 0-8166-1089-4). U of Minn Pr.

Flag, Phyllis M. Neither Chart nor Cross. 1978. 5.00 (ISBN 0-8233-0277-6). Golden Quill.

Flagel, Clarice. Avoiding Burnout: Time Management for D. R. E. 's. 60p. (Orig.). 1981. pap. 5.95 (ISBN 0-697-01782-6). Wm C Brown.

--The DRE Mininstry: Issues & Answers. 112p. 1983. pap. 4.25 (ISBN 0-697-01842-3). Wm C Brown.

Flagella, P. N., jt. auth. see Conway, J. B.

Flageul, G., jt. auth. see Elbaz, Jean S.

Flagg, Andrew S. The Story of Cape Cod Cooking. LC 79-67317. (Illus., Orig.). softcover 11.95 (ISBN 0-88492-033-X). W S Sullwold.

Flagg, Charles A. An Index of Pioneers from Massachusetts to the West, Especially the State of Michigan. LC 74-29148. 86p. 1980. Repr. of 1915 ed. 8.50 (ISBN 0-8063-0660-2). Genealog Pub.

Flagg, Fannie. Coming Attractions. LC 80-29451. 320p. 1981. 12.95 (ISBN 0-688-00472-5). Morrow.

Flagg, Isaac, ed. see Autenrieth, Georg.

Flagg, Jared B. Life & Letters of Washington Allston. LC 72-82002. (Illus.). Repr. of 1892 ed. 32.00 (ISBN 0-405-08521-4, Blom Pubns). Ayer Co Pubs.

--Life & Letters of Washington Allston. LC 68-27719. (Library of American Art Ser.). 1969. Repr. of 1892 ed. lib. bdg. 45.00 (ISBN 0-306-71168-0). Da Capo.

Flagg, John F., ed. Chemical Processing of Reactor Fuels. (Nuclear Science and Technology Ser.: Vol. 1). 1961. 76.00 (ISBN 0-12-258250-0). Acad Pr.

Flagg, John S. Prometheus Unbound & Hellas: An Approach to Shelley's Lyrical Dramas. (Salzburg Studies in English Literature, Romantic Reassessment: No. 14). 1972. pap. text ed. 25.50x (ISBN 0-391-01375-0). Humanities.

Flagg, Oscar H. Review of the Cattle Business in Johnson County Wyoming, Since 1822, & the Causes That Led to the Recent Invasion. LC 79-90174. (Mass Violence in America Ser). Repr. of 1892 ed. 6.50 (ISBN 0-405-01309-4). Ayer Co Pubs.

Flagg, Paul, jt. auth. see Reynolds, Allan.

Flagg, William. The Clam Lover's Cookbook. 3rd ed. pap. 6.95 (ISBN 0-88427-054-8). Dodd.

--The Shrimp Lover's Cookbook. LC 84-7957. 128p. 1984. pap. 6.95 (ISBN 0-88427-055-6, Dist. by Dodd, Mead). North River.

--The Shrimp Lover's Cookbook. 128p. 1984. pap. 6.95 (ISBN 0-88427-055-6). Dodd.

Flagg, William G. The Clam Lover's Cookbook. 3rd ed. LC 83-2445. (Illus.). 160p. (Orig.). 1983. pap. 6.95 (ISBN 0-88427-054-8, Dist. by Dodd, Mead). North River.

--Cookin' in the Keys. (Illus.). 128p. (Orig.). 1985. pap. 7.95 (ISBN 0-88427-058-0). North River.

--The Mushroom Lover's Cookbook. LC 80-39496. (Illus.). 160p. (Orig.). 1983. pap. 6.95 (ISBN 0-88427-044-0, Dist. by Dodd, Mead). North River.

Flagler, John J. Modern Trade Unionism. LC 79-84424. (Real World of Economics Ser.). (Illus.). (gr. 5-11). 1970. PLB 4.95 (ISBN 0-8225-0621-1). Lerner Pubns.

Flahault, C., jt. auth. see Bornet, E.

Flahault, D., jt. ed. see Pitcairn, D. M.

Flaherty, ed. Baldwin's Ohio Domestic Relations Law, 1 vol. 1492p. 1984. annual 90.00 (ISBN 0-8322-0080-8). Banks-Baldwin.

Flaherty, Alice E. Hope of Heaven: Joy of Earth. LC 83-72222. 1983. pap. 4.95 (ISBN 0-88270-550-4, Haven Bks). Bridge Pub.

Flaherty, Anne. Women Without Warranties. 288p. 1985. 13.95 (ISBN 0-8092-5436-0). Contemp Bks.

Flaherty, Bernard E., ed. see Symposium on Psychophysiological Aspects of Space Flight, Brooks Air Force Base, Texas, 1960.

Flaherty, Carolyn, jt. ed. see Labine, Clem.

Flaherty, Charles. Animal Cognition. 450p. 1985. text ed. 26.00 (ISBN 0-394-33042-0, KnopfC). Knopf.

Flaherty, Cornelia M. Go with Haste into the Mountains. 144p. (Orig.). 1984. write for info. (ISBN 0-934318-42-5); pap. write for info. Falcon Pr MT.

Flaherty, Daniel, jt. auth. see Ciszek, Walter J.

Flaherty, Daniel L., jt. auth. see Ciszek, Walter J.

Flaherty, Dave C., jt. auth. see Rabe, Fred W.

Flaherty, David H. Essays in the History of Canadian Law, Vol. 2. (Publications of the Osgoode Society). 607p. 1983. 45.00x (ISBN 0-8020-3391-1). U of Toronto Pr.

--Privacy & Data Protection: An International Bibliography. LC 84-15415. (Professional Librarian Ser.). 276p. 1984. 37.50 (ISBN 0-86729-121-4, 244-BW). Knowledge Indus.

--Privacy & Government Data Banks: An International Perspective. 352p. 1979. 43.00x (ISBN 0-7201-0930-2). Mansell.

--Privacy in Colonial New England, 1630-1776. LC 76-154804. (Illus.). 287p. 1972. 17.50x (ISBN 0-8139-0339-4). U Pr of Va.

--Protecting Privacy in Two-Way Electronic Services. LC 84-15492. (Communications Library). 184p. 1985. professional 34.95 (ISBN 0-86729-107-9, 428-BW). Knowledge Indus.

Flaherty, David H., ed. see Strachey, William.

Flaherty, David H., et al, eds. Privacy & Access to Government Data for Research: An International Bibliography. 208p. 1979. 43.00x (ISBN 0-7201-0920-5). Mansell.

Flaherty, Donald L., et al, eds. Grape Pest Management. LC 80-70846. (Illus.). 312p. (Orig.). 1981. pap. 25.00x (ISBN 0-931876-44-3, 4105). Ag & Nat Res.

Flaherty, Doug. Computers & Culture: A Cure for the Deadly Embrace. 300p. 1985. pap. text ed. write for info. (ISBN 0-534-05436-6). Wadsworth Pub.

--A Love-Tangle of Roots. LC 77-3018. 65p. 1977. 3.50 (ISBN 0-87886-080-0). Ithaca Hse.

--To Keep the Blood from Drowning. 1976. pap. 2.95 (ISBN 0-915016-07-9). Second Coming.

Flaherty, F. J., ed. Asymptotic Behavior of Mass & Spacetime Geometry. (Lecture Notes in Physics Ser.: Vol. 202). 213p. 1984. pap. 13.50 (ISBN 0-387-13351-8). Springer-Verlag.

Flaherty, Frances H. Odyssey of a Film-Maker: Robert Flaherty's Story. LC 77-169343. (Arno Press Cinema Program). (Illus.). 66p. 1972. Repr. of 1960 ed. 12.00 (ISBN 0-405-03918-2). Ayer Co Pubs.

--Odyssey of a Film-Maker: Robert Flaherty's Story. (Illus.). 80p. 1984. ltd. ed. 15.00 (ISBN 0-939660-15-6); pap. 8.00 (ISBN 0-939660-14-8). Threshold VT.

Flaherty, Gerald. Filthy the Man: Stories by Gerald Flaherty. LC 84-21893. (Breakthrough Ser.: No. 46). 128p. 1985. pap. 8.95 (ISBN 0-8262-0463-5). U of Mo Pr.

Flaherty, Gloria. Opera in the Development of German Critical Thought. LC 78-51163. 1978. 37.50x (ISBN 0-691-06370-2). Princeton U Pr.

Flaherty, J. E., jt. ed. see Chandra, J.

Flaherty, John E. Managing Change: Today's Challenge to Management. 188p. 1984. pap. 7.95x (ISBN 0-8290-1575-2). Irvington.

Flaherty, Joseph. Tin Wife. 256p. 1984. 16.95 (ISBN 0-671-47280-1). S&S.

Flaherty, Joseph A., jt. auth. see Rezler, Agnes G.

Flaherty, Linda, jt. auth. see Cassidy, Hope.

Flaherty, M. Josephine, jt. auth. see Curtin, Leah.

Flaherty, Martin C., jt. auth. see Gayley, Charles M.

Flaherty, Maureen. The Care of the Elderly Person: A Guide for the Licensed Practical Nurse. 3rd. ed. LC 80-11236. (Illus.). 218p. 1980. pap. text ed. 12.95 (ISBN 0-8016-3706-6). Mosby.

Flaherty, Patricia, jt. ed. see Davis, Bernard D.

Flaherty, Patrick F. & Ziegler, Richard. Estate Planning for Everyone. rev. ed. LC 80-8314. 160p. 1981. 14.37i (ISBN 0-690-01943-2, HarpT). Har-Row.

Flaherty, Patrick F., jt. auth. see Ziegler, Richard S.

Flaherty, Richard, jt. auth. see Chasteen, Lanny.

Flaherty, Richard E., ed. The Core of the Curriculum for Accounting Majors, Vol. 3. (Studies in Accounting Education). 234p. 1979. nonmember 8.00 (ISBN 0-86539-031-2); 6.00. Am Accounting.

Flahiff, F. T., jt. ed. see Colie, Rosalie L.

Flaig, W., et al. Organic Materials & Soil Productivity. (Soils Bulletins: No. 35). 127p. (2nd Printing). 1977. pap. 9.50 (ISBN 92-5-100510-9, F1404, FAO). Unipub.

Flaim, Stephen & Zelis, Robert F., eds. Calcium Blockers: Mechanisms of Action & Clinical Applications. LC 82-8548. (Illus.). 313p. 1982. text ed. 44.50 (ISBN 0-8067-0611-2). Urban & S.

Flake, Carol. Redemptorama. LC 82-45356. 288p. 1984. 15.95 (ISBN 0-385-18241-4, Anchor Pr). Doubleday.

--Redemptorama: Culture, Politics & the New Evangelicalism. (Nonfiction Ser.). 320p. 1985. pap. 6.95 (ISBN 0-317-19383-X). Penguin.

Flake, Chad J., ed. A Mormon Bibliography, 1830-1930: Books, Pamphlets, Periodicals, & Broadsides Relating to the First Century of Mormonism. LC 74-22639. (Illus.). 1978. 80.00x (ISBN 0-87480-016-1). U of Utah Pr.

Flake, Janice L., et al. Fundamentals of Computer Education. 416p. 1985. write for info. (ISBN 0-534-04764-5). Wadsworth Pub.

Flakser, David. Marxism Ideology & Myths. LC 70-164908. 1971. 6.95 (ISBN 0-8022-2059-2). Philos Lib.

Flam, Henry, jt. ed. see Persky, Stan.

Flam, Jack, jt. auth. see Ashton, Dore.

Flam, Jack D., ed. Matisse on Art. 1978. pap. 11.95 (ISBN 0-525-47490-0, 01160-350). Dutton.

Flamant, R. & Fohanno, C., eds. Evaluation of Methods of Treatment & Diagnostic Procedures in Cancer. (Technical Report Ser.: Vol. 70). 156p. 1982. pap. text ed. 14.80 (ISBN 92-9018-070-6, Pub. by Intl Union Against Cancer Switzerland). J K Burgess.

Flame. Flame: A Life on the Game. 176p. (Orig.). 1984. pap. 6.50 (ISBN 0-907040-23-3, Pub. by GMP England). Alyson Pubns.

Flamenbaum, Walter. Nephrology: An Approach to the Patient with Renal Disease. (Illus.). 640p. 1982. text ed. 39.50 (ISBN 0-397-50533-7, 65-06802, Lippincott Medical). Lippincott.

Flament, C. L'analyse Booleenne de Questionnaire. 1977. 46.00x (ISBN 90-279-7733-X). Mouton.

Flament, Claude. Theorie Des Graphes et Structures Sociales. (Mathematiques et Sciences De L'homme: No. 2). 1968. pap. 10.80x (ISBN 90-2796-312-6). Mouton.

Flamholtz, et al. Financial Accounting. 1600p. 1986. text ed. price not set (ISBN 0-02-338150-7). Macmillan.

Flamholtz, Eric G. & Lacey, John M. Personnel Management, Human Capital Theory, & Human Resource Accounting. (Monograph & Research Ser.: No. 27). 112p. 1981. 7.00 (ISBN 0-89215-111-0). U Cal LA Indus Rel.

Flamholtz, Eric G., ed. Human Resource Productivity in the 1980s. (Monograph & Research Ser.: No. 31). 250p. 1982. 9.00 (ISBN 0-89215-115-3). U Cal LA Indus Rel.

Flamholtz, Eric G. & Das, T. K., eds. Human Resource Management & Productivity; State of the Art & Future Prospects: Focus on the U. S, Vol. 1. (Monograph & Research Ser.: No. 39). 175p. 1985. 9.50 (ISBN 0-89215-124-2). U Cal La indus Rel.

Flamigni, C. & Givens, J. R., eds. The Gonadotropins. (Serono Symposium Ser.: No. 42). 512p. 1982. 66.00 (ISBN 0-12-258550-X). Acad Pr.

Flamini, Roland. Ava. (Illus.). 352p. 1983. 14.95 (ISBN 0-698-11123-0, Coward). Putnam Pub Group.

--Ava. 272p. 1984. pap. 3.50 (ISBN 0-425-07510-9). Berkley Pub.

Flamion, Allen. Jack up Your "C" Power. LC 79-67011. (Orig.). 1979. pap. 5.95 (ISBN 0-935248-00-5). Simplex Comm.

Flamm, D. & Schoberl, F. Quantum Numbers, Gauge Theories & Hadron Spectroscopy. (Quark Models in Elementary Particles Ser.). 384p. 1982. 77.25 (ISBN 0-677-16270-7). Gordon.

Flamm, E. S., jt. ed. see Fein, J. M.

Flamm, Jerry. Good Life in Hard Times: San Francisco's '20s & '30s. LC 76-30524. (Illus.). 1977. pap. 7.95 (ISBN 0-87701-092-7). Chronicle Bks.

Flamm, Kenneth, jt. auth. see Grunwald, Joseph.

Flamm, Steven, jt. auth. see Miller, Ed.

Flamma, Thomas. Metaphysics, a Bridge to ECKANKAR. LC 81-80177. 232p. 1981. pap. 3.95 (ISBN 0-914766-65-1, 0193). IWP Pub.

Flammanc, Solveng, tr. see McDowell, Josh.

Flammang, C. J. Police & the Underprotected Child. 324p. 1970. 18.50x (ISBN 0-398-00583-4). C C Thomas.

--Police Juvenile Enforcement. 284p. 1972. 29.75x (ISBN 0-398-02280-1). C C Thomas.

Flammang, James M. How to Make Your Old Car Run Like New. (Illus., Orig.). 1980. pap. 7.95 (ISBN 0-8306-2062-1, 2062). TAB Bks.

Flammang, Janet A. Political Women: Current Roles in State & Local Government. LC 84-6922. (Yearbooks in Women's Policy Studies: Vol. 8). 320p. 1984. 29.95 (ISBN 0-8039-2139-X); pap. 14.95 (ISBN 0-8039-2140-3). Sage.

Flammang, Robert. U. S. Programs That Impede U. S. Export Competitiveness: The Regulatory Environment, Vol. II. LC 80-80933. (Significant Issues Ser.: No. 3). 58p. 1980. 5.95 (ISBN 0-89206-017-4). CSI Studies.

Flammang, Susann. Changes of Heart. Woodward, Stuart, ed. LC 85-8066. 92p. 1985. pap. 4.95 (ISBN 0-932873-24-3). Family Man.

Flammang, Susann & Woodward, Stuart. Autumn Leaves... 92p. 1985. pap. 4.95 (ISBN 0-932873-20-0). Family Man.

Flammarion, Camille. Haunted Houses. LC 76-159957. (Tower Bks.). 1971. Repr. of 1924 ed. 43.00x (ISBN 0-8103-3911-0). Gale.

--Omega: The Last Days of the World. LC 74-15971. (Science Fiction Ser). (Illus.). 287p. 1975. Repr. of 1894 ed. 22.00x (ISBN 0-405-06291-5). Ayer Co Pubs.

Flammer, A. & Kintsch, W., eds. Discourse Processing: An Edited Selection of Papers Presented at the International Symposium, Fribourg, Switzerland. (Advances in Psychology Ser.: Vol. 8). 614p. 1982. 66.00 (ISBN 0-444-86515-2, North Holland). Elsevier.

Flammer, Philip M. Vivid Air: The Lafayette Escadrille. LC 80-22059. (Illus.). 264p. 1981. 19.00 (ISBN 0-8203-0537-5). U of Ga Pr.

Flammer, R. Differentialdiagnosen der Pilzvergiftungen, mit Bestimmungsschluesselein fuer Mediciner und Mykologen. (Illus.). 92p. (Ger.). 1980. text ed. 11.60 (ISBN 3-437-10636-8). Lubrecht & Cramer.

Flamming, Peter J. God & Creation. LC 85-6647. 1985. 5.95 (ISBN 0-8054-1635-8). Broadman.

Flammonde, Paris. Mystic Healers. LC 73-91856. (Illus.). 256p. 1974. 8.95 (ISBN 0-8128-1680-3). Stein & Day.

Flanagan, Bernard J. A Lenten Pastoral Letter. 1976. pap. 0.50 (ISBN 0-685-77497-X). Franciscan Herald.

Flanagan, Cathleen C. Books & Other Printed Materials. Duane, James E., ed. LC 80-23053. (The Instructional Media Library: Vol. 1). 112p. 1981. 19.95 (ISBN 0-87778-161-3). Educ Tech Pubns.

Flanagan, Cathleen C. & Flanagan, John T. American Folklore: A Bibliography, 1950-1974. LC 77-23381. 412p. 1977. 24.50 (ISBN 0-8108-1073-5). Scarecrow.

Flanagan, Dale. The HP Touchscreen. LC 84-60132. 280p. 1984. pap. 19.95 (ISBN 0-88022-105-4, 124). Que Corp.

--The HP 110 Portable: Power to Go! LC 84-61401. 250p. 1985. 16.95 (ISBN 0-88022-135-6, 165). Que Corp.

Flanagan, Donal. Evolving Church. 1966. 4.95 (ISBN 0-8189-0047-4). Alba.

Flanagan, Dorothy B. Dark Certainty. LC 79-144737. (Yale Series of Younger Poets: No. 30). Repr. of 1931 ed. 18.00 (ISBN 0-404-53830-4). AMS Pr.

Flanagan, Edward M., Jr. Before the Battle: A Commonsense Guide to Leadership & Management. (Illus.). 240p. (Orig.). 1985. pap. 10.95 (ISBN 0-89141-210-7). Presidio Pr.

Flanagan, Floyd. MacCats: Ninety Nine Ways to Paint a Cat with MacPaint. 1985. pap. 9.95 (ISBN 0-673-18143-X). Scott F.

Flanagan, G. T. Feed Water Systems & Treatment. (Marine Engineering Ser.). 144p. 1978. pap. 9.95x (ISBN 0-540-07343-1). Sheridan.

--Marine Boilers: Questions & Answers. 2nd ed. (Marine Engineering Ser.). 102p. 1980. pap. 9.95x (ISBN 0-540-07348-2). Sheridan.

Flanagan, Geraldine L. The First Nine Months of Life. 1982. 16.95 (ISBN 0-671-45974-0); pap. 6.95 (ISBN 0-671-45975-9). S&S.

Flanagan, Hallie. Arena. (Illus.). 492p. 1985. 12.95 (ISBN 0-87910-033-8). Limelight Edns.

--Arena: The History of the Federal Theatre. LC 65-23693. (Illus.). Repr. of 1940 ed. 29.00 (ISBN 0-405-08521-4, Blom Pubns). Ayer Co Pubs.

--Shifting Scenes of the Modern European Theatre. LC 79-187832. (Illus.). Repr. of 1929 ed. 31.00 (ISBN 0-405-08522-2, Blom Pubns). Ayer Co Pubs.

Flanagan, J. L. Speech Analysis, Synthesis & Perception. 2nd rev. ed. LC 70-172068. (Communications & Cybernetics: Vol. 3). (Illus.). 440p. 1972. 39.00 (ISBN 0-387-05561-4). Springer-Verlag.

Flanagan, J. L. & Rabiner, L. R., eds. Speech Synthesis. LC 73-9728. (Benchmark Papers in Acoustics: Vol. 3). 511p. 1973. 57.95 (ISBN 0-87933-044-9). Van Nos Reinhold.

Flanagan, James F. Spitalfields Silks of the Eighteenth & Nineteenth Centuries. 1981. 25.00x (ISBN 0-85317-360-5, Pub. by Lewis Pubs). State Mutual Bk.

Flanagan, James W. & Robinson, Anita W., eds. No Famine in the Land: Studies in Honor of John L. McKenzie. (AAR Homage Ser.). pap. 11.95 (ISBN 0-89130-051-1, 00-16-02). Scholars Pr GA.

--No Famine in the Land: Studies in Honor of John L. McKenzie. 349p. 1975. pap. 11.95 (ISBN 0-89130-051-1, 00-16-02); pap. 7.95 members (ISBN 0-317-35709-3). Scholars Pr GA.

Flanagan, Jim. The Crossing. 224p. 1983. pap. 2.50 (ISBN 0-449-12428-2, GM). Fawcett.

Flanagan, Joan. The Grass Roots Fund Raising Book. 1981. pap. 12.00 (ISBN 0-686-31965-6). Public Serv Materials.

--Grass Roots Fund Raising Book: How to Raise Money in Your Community. 320p. 1982. pap. 11.95 (ISBN 0-8092-5746-7). Contemp Bks.

--The Grass Roots Fundraising Book: How to Raise Money in Your Community. 344p. 1982. pap. 9.35 (ISBN 0-318-17145-7, B2). Natl Ctr Cit Involv.

--The Successful Volunteer Organization. 320p. 1981. pap. 11.95 (ISBN 0-8092-5837-4). Contemp Bks.

--The Successful Volunteer Organization: Getting Started & Getting Results in Nonprofit, Charities, Grass Roots, & Community Groups. 376p. 1981. pap. 9.50 (ISBN 0-318-17155-4, C78). Natl Ctr Cit Involv.

Flanagan, John C. & Russ-Eft, Darlene. An Empirical Study to Aid in Formulating Educational Goals. 1975. pap. 4.50 (ISBN 0-89785-517-5). Am Inst Res.

Flanagan, John C., ed. Perspectives on Improving Education: Project Talent's Young Adults Look Back. LC 78-13600. (Praeger Special Studies). 1978. 29.95 (ISBN 0-03-043481-5). Praeger.

Flanagan, John R. How to Prepare Patent Applications: A Self-Study Course Book Using Actual Inventions. LC 83-61896. 260p. 1983. pap. 29.95 (ISBN 0-913995-00-2). Patent Ed.

--How to Prosecute Patent Applications: A Self-Study Course Using Actual Inventions. LC 84-60154. 250p. 1985. pap. 29.95 (ISBN 0-913995-01-0). Patent Ed.

Flanagan, John T. Edgar Lee Masters: The Spoon River Poet & His Critics. LC 74-20530. 183p. 1974. 16.50 (ISBN 0-8108-0741-6). Scarecrow.

Flanagan, John T., jt. auth. see Flanagan, Cathleen C.

Flanagan, John T., ed. America Is West: An Anthology of Middle-Western Life & Literature. LC 71-106687. (Illus.). vii, 677p. Repr. of 1945 ed. lib. bdg. 32.50x (ISBN 0-8371-3358-0, FLAW). Greenwood.

--Folklore in American Literature. LC 74-138230. (Illus.). 511p. 1972. Repr. of 1958 ed. lib. bdg. 33.00x (ISBN 0-8371-5587-8, FLFH). Greenwood.

Flanagan, Martin J. The Passing Parade: The Story of Somersworth, NH, 1910-1981. LC 82-62138. (Illus.). 285p. 1983. 10.00 (ISBN 0-89725-036-2). NE History.

Flanagan, Mary. Bad Girls. LC 84-24493. 240p. 1985. 14.95 (ISBN 0-689-11593-8). Atheneum.

Flanagan, Neal. Jeremia, 2 pts. (Bible Ser.). Pt. 1. pap. 1.00 (ISBN 0-8091-5071-9); Pt. 2. pap. 1.00 (ISBN 0-8091-5072-7). Paulist Pr.

Flanagan, Neal M. The Gospel According to John VII the Johannine Epistles, No. 4. Karris, Robert J., ed. LC 82-22908. (Collegeville Bible Commentary Ser.). 128p. 1983. pap. 2.50 (ISBN 0-8146-1304-7). Liturgical Pr.

Flanagan, Owen J., Jr. The Science of the Mind. (Illus.). 384p. (Orig.). 1984. text ed. 25.00x (ISBN 0-262-06090-6, Pub. by Bradford Bks); pap. text ed. 12.50x (ISBN 0-262-56031-3). MIT Pr.

Flanagan, Padraig, ed. A New Missionary Era. LC 81-9595. 192p. (Orig.). 1982. pap. 9.95 (ISBN 0-88344-331-7). Orbis Bks.

Flanagan, Patrick, jt. auth. see Southwood, Julie.

Flanagan, Robert. Maggot. 272p. 1971. pap. 3.50 (ISBN 0-446-30523-5). Warner Bks.

--Three Times Three. 38p. 1977. pap. 2.50 (ISBN 0-87886-086-X). Ithaca Hse.

Flanagan, Robert J. & Soskice, David W. Unionism, Economic Stabilization & Incomes Policy: European Experience. LC 83-71459. 705p. 1983. 36.95 (ISBN 0-8157-2856-5); pap. 18.95 (ISBN 0-8157-2855-7). Brookings.

Flanagan, Robert J. & Weber, Arnold R. Bargaining Without Boundaries: The Multinational Corporation & International Labor Relations. LC 74-5724. (Studies in Business & Society Ser). xviii, 258p. 1974. text ed. 20.00x (ISBN 0-226-25312-0). U of Chicago Pr.

Flanagan, Robert J., et al. Perspectives on Availability: A Symposium on Determining Protected Group Representation in Internal & External Labor Markets. LC 78-63628. 243p. (Orig.). 1977. pap. 12.75 (ISBN 0-937856-02-9). Equal Employ.

--Labor Economics & Labor Relations. 1984. 28.95 (ISBN 0-673-15620-6). Scott F.

Flanagan, Roy K. What a Duet! Bayes, Ronald H., ed. 80p. (Orig.). 1977. pap. 3.00 (ISBN 0-932662-20-X). St Andrews NC.

Flanagan, Scott C., jt. auth. see Richardson, Bradley M.

Flanagan, Sue. Sam Houston's Texas. LC 64-22338. (Illus.). 231p. 1973. Repr. of 1964 ed. 19.95 (ISBN 0-292-73363-1). U of Tex Pr.

--Trailing the Longhorns: A Century Later. LC 74-77510. (Illus.). 290p. 1974. 16.50 (ISBN 0-89052-008-9). Madrona Pr.

Flanagan, Terrence, jt. auth. see Milman, David.

Flanagan, Thomas. Louis David Riel: Prophet of the New World. LC 78-18497. pap. 56.50 (ISBN 0-317-27051-6, 2023617). Bks Demand UMI.

--The Year of the French. LC 78-23539. 1979. 12.95 (ISBN 0-03-044591-4). HR&W.

--The Year of the French. 1980. pap. 3.75 (ISBN 0-671-83301-4). PB.

Flanagan, Thomas D., jt. ed. see Milgrom, Felix.

Flanagan, Thomas J. The Irish Novelists, 1800-1850. LC 76-21874. 362p. 1976. Repr. of 1959 ed. lib. bdg. 27.50x (ISBN 0-8371-9004-5, FLIN). Greenwood.

Flanagan, Vincent. George Washington: First President of the United States. Kurland, Gerald & Rahmas, D. Steve, eds. LC 73-87623. (Outstanding Personalities Ser.: No. 6). 32p. (Orig.). (YA) (gr. 7-12). 1973. lib. bdg. 3.50 incl. catalog cards (ISBN 0-87157-561-2); pap. 1.95 vinyl laminated covers (ISBN 0-87157-061-0). SamHar Pr.

Flanagan, W., jt. auth. see Gugler, J.

Flanagan, W. M. Handbook of Transformer Applications. 448p. 1985. price not set (ISBN 0-07-021290-2). McGraw.

Flanagan, William. The Chairman. (Orig.). 1981. pap. 2.50 (ISBN 0-440-11546-9). Dell.

Flanagan, William G. The Executive's Guide to Major American Cities. 1979. pap. 3.95 (ISBN 0-346-12372-0). Cornerstone.

Flanagin, Michael, jt. ed. see Haddick, Vern.

Flanary, David A. Champfleury: The Realist Writer as Art Critic. Kuspit, Donald B., ed. LC 80-17475. (Studies in Fine Arts: Criticism: No. 1). 96p. 1980. 34.95 (ISBN 0-8357-1087-4). UMI Res Pr.

Flandermeyer, Kenneth L. Clear Skin: A Step by Step Program to Stop Pimples, Blackheads, Acne. LC 79-486. 1979. 12.95 (ISBN 0-316-28545-5); pap. 6.70i (ISBN 0-316-28546-3). Little.

Flanders, Allan. Management & Unions. 318p. (Orig.). 1975. pap. 4.95 (ISBN 0-571-10711-7). Faber & Faber.

Flanders, Claire, jt. auth. see Kopp, Sheldon.

Flanders, Dennis. BASIC Programming for the IBM PC. 1985. cancelled (ISBN 0-89303-240-9). Brady Comm.

--Britannia. (Illus.). 240p. 1984. 32.00 (ISBN 0-85362-206-X, Oriel); (Oriel). Routledge & Kegan.

Flanders, Dennis, jt. auth. see Flanders, Robert.

Flanders, G. M. Ebony Idol. facs. ed. LC 75-83915. (Black Heritage Library Collection Ser). 1860. 15.00 (ISBN 0-8369-8571-0). Ayer Co Pubs.

Flanders, H., jt. auth. see Pierce, E.

Flanders, H. F. Hydrological. (Operational Hydrology Reports: No. 14). 34p. 1981. pap. 6.00 (ISBN 92-63-10559-6, W499, WMO). Unipub.

Flanders, Harley. Calculus. LC 84-18773. (Illus.). 1129p. 1985. text ed. 38.95 (ISBN 0-7167-1643-7); pap. text ed. instr's. manual avail. (ISBN 0-7167-1645-3); student guide 8.95 (ISBN 0-7167-1644-5). W H Freeman.

--Scientific Pascal. 1983. text ed. 29.95 (ISBN 0-8359-6932-0); pap. text ed. 21.95 (ISBN 0-8359-6931-2). Reston.

--Single Variable Calculus. 672p. (Orig.). pap. text ed. 26.95 (ISBN 0-7167-1752-2). W H Freeman.

Flanders, Harley & Price, Justin J. Algebra. 2nd ed. 1981. text ed. 27.95 (ISBN 0-03-057801-9, CBS C); instr's manual 11.95 (ISBN 0-03-058633-X); study guide 11.95 (ISBN 0-03-058634-8). SCP.

--Algebra & Trigonometry. 2nd ed. 1981. text ed. 29.95 (ISBN 0-03-057779-9, CBS C); instr's manual 12.95 (ISBN 0-03-058249-0); study guide 11.95 (ISBN 0-03-058252-0). SCP.

--Precalculus Mathematics. 2nd ed. 1981. text ed. 29.95 (ISBN 0-03-057723-3, CBS C); instr's manual 13.95 (ISBN 0-03-058251-2); study guide 11.95 (ISBN 0-03-058253-9). SCP.

--Trigonometry. 2nd ed. 1982. text ed. 27.95 (ISBN 0-03-057802-7, CBS C). SCP.

Flanders, Helen H. & Brown, George. Vermont Folk-Songs & Ballads. LC 68-20768. iv, 256p. 1968. Repr. of 1931 ed. 40.00x (ISBN 0-8103-5010-6). Gale.

Flanders, Helen H. & Olney, Marguerite, eds. Ballads Migrant in New England. facs. ed. LC 68-58825. (Granger Index Reprint Ser.). 1953. 17.00 (ISBN 0-8369-6015-7). Ayer Co Pubs.

Flanders, Helen H., compiled by. Vermont Chapbook. facs. ed. LC 70-76935. (Granger Index Reprint Ser). 1941. 13.00 (ISBN 0-8369-6016-5). Ayer Co Pubs.

Flanders, Henry. The Chief Justices of the Supreme Court in the United States, 2 vols. Mersky, Roy M. & Jacobstein, J. Myron, eds. (Classics in Legal History Reprint Ser.: Vols. 7 & 8). 1972. Repr. of 1881 ed. Vol. 1, 664p. lib. bdg. 32.50 (ISBN 0-89941-006-5); Vol. 2, 572p. lib. bdg. 32.50 (ISBN 0-89941-007-3); Set. lib. bdg. write for info. (ISBN 0-89941-259-9). W S Hein.

Flanders, Henry, ed. see Cumberland, Richard.

Flanders, Henry J., Jr., et al. Introduction to the Bible. 588p. 1973. text ed. 31.95 (ISBN 0-394-34416-2, RandC). Random.

Flanders, Jane. The Students of Snow. LC 82-8461. 68p. 1982. lib. bdg. 8.00x (ISBN 0-87023-378-5); pap. 4.00 (ISBN 0-87023-379-3). U of Mass Pr.

Flanders, Jesse K. Legislative Control of the Elementary Curriculum. LC 75-176777. (Columbia University. Teachers College. Contributions to Education: No. 195). Repr. of 1925 ed. 22.50 (ISBN 0-404-55195-5). AMS Pr.

Flanders, John. The Craftsman's Way: Canadian Expressions. (Illus.). 256p. 1981. 37.50 (ISBN 0-8020-2433-5). U of Toronto Pr.

Flanders, John A., jt. ed. see Crenshaw, Floyd D.

Flanders, M. June. The Demand for International Reserves. LC 72-158967. (Princeton Studies in International Finance Ser.: No. 27). pap. 20.00 (ISBN 0-317-30069-5, 2019245). Bks Demand UMI.

Flanders, M. June & Razin, Assaf, eds. Development in an Inflationary World. LC 80-28548. (Economic Theory, Econometrics & Mathematical Economics Ser.). 1981. 66.00 (ISBN 0-12-259750-8). Acad Pr.

Flanders, Michael & Swann, Donald. The Songs of Michael Flanders & Donald Swann. LC 77-82055. (Illus.). 1977. 15.00 (ISBN 0-312-74495-1). St Martin.

Flanders, Peter. A Thematic Index to the Works of Benedetto Pallavicino. (Music Indexes & Bibliographies: No. 11). 1974. pap. 9.00 (ISBN 0-913574-11-2). Eur-Am Music.

Flanders, Rebecca. Best of Friends. (Harlequin American Romance Ser.). 256p. 1983. pap. 1.95 (ISBN 0-373-16024-0). Harlequin Bks.

--Falkone's Promise. (Harlequin Presents Ser.). 192p. 1984. pap. 1.95 (ISBN 0-373-10666-1). Harlequin Bks.

--The Key. 1984. pap. 2.25 (ISBN 0-318-01323-1). Harlequin Bks.

--A Matter of Trust. (American Romance Ser.). 192p. 1983. pap. 2.25 (ISBN 0-373-16006-2). Harlequin Bks.

--Morning Song. (Harlequin Presents Ser.). 192p. 1983. pap. 1.95 (ISBN 0-373-10632-7). Harlequin Bks.

--Suddenly Love. (Harlequin American Romance Ser.). 256p. 1984. pap. 2.25 (ISBN 0-373-16041-0). Harlequin Bks.

Flanders, Rebecca, jt. auth. see Gallant, Felicia.

Flanders, Robert & Flanders, Dennis. Systems Made Simple on the IBM PC: How to Design & Develop Applications Programs. 1984. cancelled (ISBN 0-89303-242-5). Brady Comm.

Flanders, Robert B. Nauvoo: Kingdom on the Mississippi. LC 65-19110. (Illus.). 374p. 1975. pap. 7.95x (ISBN 0-252-00561-9). U of Ill Pr.

Flanders, Robert G. Learn to Type. 2nd ed. LC 78-54788. (Illus.). 1978. pap. 6.95 (ISBN 0-89709-036-5). Liberty Pub.

Flanders, W. Austin. Structures of Experience: History, Society & Personal Life in the 18th Century British Novel. 308p. 1984. 19.95x (ISBN 0-87249-419-5). U of SC Pr.

Flandrau, Charles M. Harvard Episodes. LC 76-94719. (Short Story Index Reprint Ser.). 1897. 19.00 (ISBN 0-8369-3098-3). Ayer Co Pubs.

--Loquacities. facs. ed. LC 68-22912. (Essay Index Reprint Ser). Repr. of 1931 ed. 17.00 (ISBN 0-8369-0445-1). Ayer Co Pubs.

--Viva Mexico! Gardiner, C. Harvey, ed. LC 64-18223. 327p. 1964. pap. 6.95x (ISBN 0-252-72701-0). U of Ill Pr.

Flandrau, Claude M. Viva Mexico! A Traveller's Account of Life in Mexico. (Eland Travel Classics Ser.). 294p. 1985. pap. 8.95 (ISBN 0-907871-20-8, Pub. by Eland Bks UK). Hippocrene Bks.

Flandrau, Grace. Frontier Days Along the Upper Missouri. (Shorey Historical Ser.). (Illus.). 40p. Repr. pap. 3.95 (ISBN 0-8466-0209-1, SJS209). Shorey.

--Glance at the Lewis & Clark Expedition. (Shorey Historical Soc.). (Illus.). 29p. Repr. pap. 3.95 (ISBN 0-8466-0211-3, S211). Shorey.

--Lewis & Clark Expedition. (Shorey Historical Ser.). (Illus.). 64p. pap. 5.95 (ISBN 0-8466-0210-5, S210). Shorey.

--Story of Marias Pass. (Illus.). 23p. pap. 3.95 (ISBN 0-8466-0212-1, S212). Shorey.

--Verendrye Overland Quest of Pacific. 64p. pap. 3.95 (ISBN 0-8466-0213-X, S213). Shorey.

Flandrin, J. L. Families in Former Times. LC 78-18095. (Themes in the Social Sciences Ser.). (Illus.). 1979. pap. 13.95 (ISBN 0-521-29449-5). Cambridge U Pr.

Flango, Victor E., ed. see Task Force on Principles for Assessing Judicial Resources.

Flango, Victor E., et al. The Business of State Trial Courts. LC 83-17436. (Illus.). 143p. (Orig.). 1983. pap. text ed. 10.00 (ISBN 0-89656-070-8, R-083). Natl Ctr St Courts.

Flanigan, Francis J. Complex Variables: Harmonic & Analytic Functions. (Illus.). 353p. 1983. pap. 7.00 (ISBN 0-486-61388-7). Dover.

Flanigan, James. History of Gwinnett County, Georgia, 1818-1943, Vol. I. 464p. 1975. 25.00 (ISBN 0-87797-071-8). Cherokee.

Flanigan, James C. History of Gwinnett County, Ga. 1818-1960, Vol. II. (Illus.). 637p. 1984. Repr. of 1959 ed. 25.00 (ISBN 0-914923-05-6). Gwinnett Hist.

Flanigan, Karen C. Those Magnificent Clydesdales: The Gentle Giants. 1977. 6.95 (ISBN 0-517-53426-6). Crown.

Flanigan, Michael C. & Boone, Robert S. Using Media in the Language Arts: A Source Book. LC 76-9550. (Language Arts for Children Ser.). 123p. 1977. pap. text ed. 7.50 (ISBN 0-87581-194-9). Peacock Pubs.

Flanigan, Patrick J., et al. Orientation to Mental Retardation: A Programmed Text. (Illus.). 216p. 1973. 22.50x (ISBN 0-398-00584-2). C C Thomas.

Flanigan, William, jt. auth. see Dahl, Robert A.

Flanigan, William H. & Zingale, Nancy H. American Voting Behavior: Presidential Elections from 1952 to 1980. LC 82-83324. 1982. write for info. casebook (ISBN 0-89138-920-2, ICPSR 7581). ICPSR.

--Political Behavior of the American Electorate. 5th ed. 1983. pap. text ed. 15.00 (ISBN 0-205-07980-6, 767980). Allyn.

Flanigen, E. M. & Sand, Leonard B., eds. Molecular Sieve Zeolites I & II, 2 pts. LC 77-156974. (Advances in Chemistry Ser.: Nos. 101-102). 1971. Set. 64.95 (ISBN 0-8412-0617-1); Pt. 1. 39.95 (ISBN 0-8412-0114-5); Pt. 2. 36.95 (ISBN 0-8412-0115-3). Am Chemical.

Flaningam, Barbara & Miller, Gaylier. Wordworking. 144p. 1982. pap. text ed. 9.50 (ISBN 0-8403-2732-3). Kendall-Hunt.

Flank, William H., ed. Adsorption & Ion Exchange with Synthetic Zeolites. LC 80-18916. (ACS Symposium Ser.: No. 135). 1980. 34.95 (ISBN 0-8412-0582-5). Am Chemical.

Flannagan, John F. & Marshall, K. Eric, eds. Advances in Ephemeroptera Biology. LC 79-27713. 565p. 1980. 69.50x (ISBN 0-306-40357-9, Plenum Pr). Plenum Pub.

Flannagan, Roy C. Paradise Lost Notes. 1970. pap. 3.25 (ISBN 0-8220-0977-3). Cliffs.

Flannelly, Kevin J., et al. Biological Perspectives on Aggression. (Progress in Clinical & Biological Research Ser.: Vol. 169). 372p. 1984. 48.00 (ISBN 0-8451-5019-7). A R Liss.

Flanner, Hildegarde. Brief Cherishing: A Napa Valley Harvest. 112p. 1985. pap. 10.00 (ISBN 0-317-30650-2). J Daniel.

--Hearkening Eye. 2nd. ed. Trusky, Tom, ed. LC 79-51631. (Modern & Contemporary Poets of the West Ser.). 1979. pap. 3.00 (ISBN 0-916272-12-5). Ahsahta Pr.

--A Vanishing Land. 60p. (Orig.). 1980. pap. 6.00 (ISBN 0-931832-15-2). No Dead Lines.

Flanner, Janet. The Cubical City: A Novel. LC 74-8655. (Lost American Fiction Ser). 440p. 1974. Repr. of 1926 ed. 13.95 (ISBN 0-8093-0700-6). S Ill U Pr.

--Janet Flanner's World: Uncollected Writings 1932-1975. Drutman, Irving, ed. LC 79-1820. 384p. 1981. pap. 8.95 (ISBN 0-15-645971-X, Harv). HarBraceJ.

--Men & Monuments. facs. ed. LC 73-121468. (Essay Index Reprint Ser). 1957. 21.50 (ISBN 0-8369-1876-2). Ayer Co Pubs.

--Paris Journal: Vol. I, 1944-1965. Shawn, William, ed. LC 76-45462. 1977. pap. 8.95 (ISBN 0-15-670950-3, Harv). HarBraceJ.

--Paris Journal: Vol. II, 1965-1971. Shawn, William, ed. LC 76-45462. 1977. pap. 9.95 (ISBN 0-15-670951-1, Harv). HarBraceJ.

Flanner, Janet, pseud. Paris Was Yesterday: Nineteen Twenty-Five to Nineteen Thirty-Nine. Drutman, Irving, ed. 1979. pap. 3.95 (ISBN 0-14-005068-X). Penguin.

Flanner, Janet, tr. from Fr. Cheri: Colette. 112p. 1983. 215.00x (ISBN 0-686-46592-X). G F Ritchie.

Flanner, Janet, tr. see Colette.

Flanner, Janet, tr. see Leblanc, Georgette.

Flannery, Austin. Vatican Council II: The Conciliar & Post Conciliar Documents, Vol. 2. 994p. 1983. pap. 9.95 (ISBN 0-8146-1299-7). Liturgical Pr.

Flannery, Austin, ed. Vatican Council II. 1976. pap. 7.95 (ISBN 0-685-77498-8). Franciscan Herald.

Flannery, Austin P. Document of Vatican 11. 1975. pap. 7.95 (ISBN 0-8028-1623-1). Eerdmans.

Flannery, Austin P., ed. Vatican II: More Postconciliar Documents. 944p. (Orig.). 1983. pap. 9.95 (ISBN 0-8028-1638-X). Eerdmans.

Flannery, Edward. The Anguish of the Jews. rev. ed. 352p. 1985. pap. 12.95 (ISBN 0-8091-2702-4). Paulist Pr.

Flannery, Gerald V., jt. auth. see Hoppe, Arthur.

Flannery, John B. The Irish Texans. (Illus.). 174p. 1980. 11.95 (ISBN 0-933164-33-5); pap. 7.95 (ISBN 0-933164-58-0). U of Tex Inst Tex Culture.

Flannery, Kent, ed. Maya Subsistence. (Studies in Archaeology). 1982. 39.50 (ISBN 0-12-259780-X). Acad Pr.

Flannery, Kent V. Guila Naquitz: Arcahic Foraging & Early Agriculture in Oaxaca, Mexico. Date not set. price not set (ISBN 0-12-259830-X). Acad Pr.

Flannery, Kent V., ed. The Early Mesoamerican Village. LC 82-6737. 250p. 1982. pap. 19.50 (ISBN 0-12-259852-0). Acad Pr.

Flannery, Kent V. & Blanton, Richard, eds. Prehistory & Human Ecology of the Valley of Oaxaca: Memoirs, 1 vol, No. 10. Incl. Part 1. The Vegetational History of the Oaxaca Valley. Smith, C. Earle; Part 2. Zapotec Plant Knowledge: Classification, Uses & Communication About Plants in Mitla, Oaxaca, Mexico. Messer, Ellen. (Illus.). 1978. pap. 8.00x (ISBN 0-932206-72-7). U Mich Mus Anthro.

Flannery, Kent V. & Marcus, Joyce, eds. The Cloud People: The Divergent Evolution of the Zapotic & Mixte Civilizations. 1983. 74.50 (ISBN 0-12-259860-1). Acad Pr.

Flannery, Kent V., ed. see Drennan, Robert D.

Flannery, Kent V., ed. see Lees, Susan.

Flannery, Mary C. Yeats & Magic: The Earlier Works. LC 77-244. (Irish Literary Studies: No. 2). 165p. 1977. text ed. 24.75x (ISBN 0-06-492102-6). B&N Imports.

Flannery, Peter. Our Friends in the North. 56p. 1982. pap. 4.95 (ISBN 0-413-50090-X, NO. 3641). Methuen Inc.

Flannery, Regina. An Analysis of Coastal Algonquian Culture. LC 76-43705. (Catholic University of America, Anthropological Ser.: No. 7). 1983. Repr. of 1939 ed. 22.50 (ISBN 0-404-15537-5). AMS Pr.

--Gros Ventre of Montana, 2 vols. Incl. Vol. 1. Social Life; Vol. 2. Religion & Ritual. (Illus.). 1956. Repr. 21.00 set (ISBN 0-686-10282-7). Gros Ventre Treaty.

Flannery, Sean. Broken Idols. 400p. 1985. pap. 3.95 (ISBN 0-441-08126-6, Pub. By Charter Bks). Ace Bks.

--Eagles Fly. 320p. 1982. pap. 3.50 (ISBN 0-441-18019-1, Pub. by Charter Bks). Ace Bks.

--False Prophets. 320p. 1985. pap. 3.50 (ISBN 0-441-22695-7, Pub. by Charter Bks). Ace Bks.

--The Hollow Men. 388p. 1982. pap. 3.50 (ISBN 0-441-34232-9, Pub. by Charter Bks). Ace Bks.

--The Kremlin Conspiracy. 288p. (Orig.). 1979. pap. 3.25 (ISBN 0-441-45502-6, Pub. by Charter Bks). Ace Bks.

--The Trinity Factor. 418p. (Orig.). 1982. pap. 2.95 (ISBN 0-441-82402-1, Pub. by Charter Bks). Ace Bks.

Flannigan, Arthur. Les Desordres de L'Amour: Madame de Villedieu: A Critical Edition. LC 82-16138. (Illus.). 130p. 1983. lib. bdg. 21.75 (ISBN 0-8191-2730-2); pap. text ed. 8.75 (ISBN 0-8191-2731-0). U Pr of Amer.

--Me De Villedieu's Les Desordres Del L'amour: History, Literature & the Nouvelle Historique. LC 81-43835. 206p. 1983. lib. bdg. 25.50 (ISBN 0-8191-2696-9); pap. text ed. 12.25 (ISBN 0-8191-2697-7). U Pr of Amer.

Flannigan, B., et al. MRI of the Posterior Cranial Fossa: Functional Anatomy & Pathology. 225p. 1987. 49.50 (ISBN 0-943432-57-X). Slack Inc.

Flans, Bobyn. Inside Duran Duran. (Star Bks.). (Illus.). 64p. 1984. pap. 4.95 (ISBN 0-89531-084-8). Sharon Pubns.

Flans, Robyn. Musicmania. Lee, Sharon, ed. (Star Bks.). (Illus.). 96p. 1983. pap. 5.95 (ISBN 0-89531-038-4). Sharon Pubns.

Flantz, Richard, tr. see Kaniuk, Yoram.

Flantz, Richard, tr. see Tammuz, Benjamin.

Flanz, Gisbert H. Comparative Women's Rights & Political Participation in Europe. LC 82-19317. (Comparative Women's Rights Ser.). 520p. 1983. lib. bdg. 50.00 (ISBN 0-941320-02-2). Transnatl Pubs.

Flanz, Gisbert H., jt. ed. see Blaustein, Albert P.

Flanz, Gisbert R. Comparative Women's Rights & Politcal Participation in Europe. (Comparative Women's Rights). 520p. 1984. pap. 25.00 (ISBN 0-941320-23-5). Transnatl Pubs.

Flanzer, Jerry P. The Many Faces of Family Violence. 142p. 1982. 23.75x (ISBN 0-398-04612-3). C C Thomas.

Flapan, Dorothy. Children's Understanding of Social Interaction. LC 67-25065. 1968. pap. text ed. 4.75x (ISBN 0-8077-1357-0). Tchrs Coll.

Flapan, Dorothy & Neubauer, Peter B. Assessment of Early Child Development. LC 84-4513. (Illus.). 168p. 1983. 17.50 (ISBN 0-87668-659-5, 9564). Aronson.

Flapan, Simha. Zionism & the Palestinians. LC 78-26044. (Illus.). 361p. 1979. text ed. 26.50x (ISBN 0-06-492104-2). B&N Imports.

Flapan, Simha, ed. When Enemies Dare to Talk: An Israeli-Palestinian Debate (5-6 September 1978) Organised by "New Outlook". 129p. 1979. 25.00 (ISBN 0-7099-0174-7, Pub. by Croom Helm Ltd). Longwood Pub Group.

Flasche, Rainer. Die Religionswissenschaft Joachim Wachs. (Theologische Bibliothek Toeelmann: Vol. 35). 1978. 35.20x (ISBN 3-11-007238-6). De Gruyter.

Flaschka, H. A. & Barnard, A. V. Quantitative Analytical Chemistry. 2nd ed. LC 80-18555. 614p. 1981. text ed. 24.00 pub net (ISBN 0-87150-707-2, 4251). Brooks-Cole.

Flaschka, H. A., et al. Quantitative Analytical Chemistry: An Introduction to Practice. 2nd ed. 225p. 1981. pub net Lab manual. 12.00 (ISBN 0-87150-731-5, 4252). Brooks-Cole.

Flaschka, Hermenegild A., et al, eds. Chelates in Analytical Chemistry, Vol. 1. LC 67-17003. (Illus.). pap. 108.00 (ISBN 0-317-07987-5, 2055074). Bks Demand UMI.

--Chelates in Analytical Chemistry, Vol. 2. LC 67-17003. (Illus.). pap. 103.00 (ISBN 0-317-07986-7, 2055075). Bks Demand UMI.

Flash, Edward S., Jr. Economic Advice & Presidential Leadership. LC 65-24587. 1965. 33.00x (ISBN 0-231-02827-X). Columbia U Pr.

Flash, J. Basic Bartending Made Easy: The Bartender's School in a Book. 1984. 14.00 (ISBN 0-533-06039-7). Vantage.

Flashar, Hellmut, et al, eds. Geisteswissensschaft Als Aufgabe: Kulturpolitische Perspektiven und Aspekte. 1978. 13.60x (ISBN 3-11-007456-7). De Gruyter.

Flaskerud, Jacqueline. Community Mental Health Nursing Theories & Methods. 320p. 1984. pap. 19.95 (ISBN 0-8385-1179-1). ACC.

Flasschoen, Marie. Fires at Midnight. (Velvet Glove Ser.: No. 12). 176p. 1984. pap. 2.25 (ISBN 0-380-89482-3). Avon.

Flast, Lauren, jt. auth. see Flast, Robert.

Flast, R. Fifty-four VisiCalc Models: Finance-Statistics-Mathematics. 240p. 1984. pap. 15.95 (Osborne-McGraw). McGraw.

Flast, Robert & Flast, Lauren. Macintosh Spreadsheets: Using Microsoft Multiplan, Chart, & File. 200p. (Orig.). 1985. pap. 16.95 (ISBN 0-07-881187-2). Osborne-McGraw.

--One-Two-Three Run! Forty-One Ready to Use Lotus 1-2-3 Models. 255p. (Orig.). 1984. pap. 17.95 (ISBN 0-07-881142-2, 142-2). Osborne-McGraw.

Flast, Robert H. Fifty-Four SuperCalc Models: Finance, Statistics, Mathematics. 288p. (Orig.). 1983. pap. 15.95 (ISBN 0-07-881118-X, 118-X). Osborne-McGraw.

--VisiCalc Models: Finance-Statistics-Mathematics. 240p. 1984. 15.95 (Osborne-Mcgraw). Mcgraw.

Flaste, Richard, jt. auth. see Franey, Pierre.

Flaste, Richard, et al. The New York Times Guide to the Return of Halley's Comet. LC 84-40420. (Illus.). 288p. 1985. 16.95 (ISBN 0-8129-1148-2); pap. 7.95 (ISBN 0-8129-6347-4). Times Bks.

Flaster, Donald J. Malpractice: A Guide to the Legal Rights of Doctors & Patients. 256p. 1983. 15.95 (ISBN 0-684-17903-2, ScribT). Scribner.

Flaster, Nancy, jt. auth. see Gnap, John L.

Flaster, Richard J. Tax Aspects of Separation & Divorce. LC 83-121014. (Illus.). x, 303p. 1982. write for info. NJ Inst CLE.

Flatauer, S., tr. see Levy, J.

Flatauer, Susanne, tr. see Schneede, Uwe M., et al.

Flaten, Essye P. Come Ride "The Rails " with Me: All over the United States & Norway, England, & Wales. (Illus.). 1985. 5.50 (ISBN 0-682-40214-1). Exposition Pr FL.

Flaten, Essye Price. All Aboard for Wales! 1979. 4.00 (ISBN 0-682-49265-5). Exposition Pr FL.

--Our Farm Years. 1981. 5.00 (ISBN 0-682-49737-1). Exposition Pr FL.

Flath, Arnold, ed. Athletics in America: Proceedings of the 1972 Conference Held at Oregon State University. LC 72-86319. (Illus.). 92p. 1973. pap. 5.95x (ISBN 0-87071-444-9). Oreg St U Pr.

Flathman, Richard E. The Practice of Political Authority: Authority & the Authoritative. LC 79-26431. 228p. 1980. lib. bdg. 20.00x (ISBN 0-226-25319-8). U of Chicago Pr.

Flatley, Joannis K., jt. auth. see England, David A.

Flato, M., jt. ed. see Cahen, M.

Flato, Moshe, et al, eds. Applications of Group Theory in Physics & Math. Incl. Large-Scale Computations in Fluid Mechanics. Osher, Stanley, ed. (Lectures in Applied Mathematics: Vol. 21). 1984. write for info. Am Math.

Flatt, Adrian E. The Care of Minor Hand Injuries. 4th ed. LC 79-12082. (Illus.). 340p. 1979. text ed. 49.95 (ISBN 0-8016-1581-X). Mosby.

--Care of the Arthritic Hand. 4th ed. LC 82-6428. (Illus.). 305p. 1982. text ed. 41.95 (ISBN 0-8016-1585-2). Mosby.

Flatt, Bill. Since You Asked. pap. 5.95 (ISBN 0-89137-408-6). Quality Pubns.

--You Can Overcome Grief. 0.75 (ISBN 0-8010-3501-5). Baker Bk.

Flatt, Bill & Flatt, Dowell. Counseling the Homosexual. 11.00 (ISBN 0-934916-49-7). Natl Christian Pr.

Flatt, Carol, jt. auth. see Edeen, Susan.

Flatt, Dowell, jt. auth. see Flatt, Bill.

Flattau, John. Bridges. (Illus.). 80p. 1985. 15.00 (ISBN 0-912810-50-5). Lustrum Pr.

Flatte, S. M., ed. Sound Transmission Through a Fluctuating Ocean. LC 77-88676. (Cambridge Monographs on Mechanics & Applied Mathematics). (Illus.). 1979. 54.50 (ISBN 0-521-21940-X). Cambridge U Pr.

Flattem, Ardell. But First... Pioneering in Twentieth Century America. (Illus.). 56p. (Orig.). 1984. pap. 5.00 (ISBN 0-934996-27-X). Am Stud Pr.

Flatter, Charles H., jt. auth. see Rice, Mary F.

Flatter, Richard. Moor of Venice. LC 74-10586. 1950. lib. bdg. 15.00 (ISBN 0-8414-4208-8). Folcroft.

--Shakespeare's Producing Hand. LC 79-94583. Repr. of 1948 ed. lib. bdg. 18.75x (ISBN 0-8371-2454-9, FLSH). Greenwood.

--Shakespeare's Producing Hand. 1973. Repr. of 1948 ed. 25.00 (ISBN 0-8274-0540-5). R West.

Flatters, F. & Lipsey, R. G. Common Ground for the Canadian Common Market. (Essays in International Economics Ser.). 60p. (Orig.). 1984. pap. text ed. 6.00x (ISBN 0-920380-92-1, Pub. by Inst Res Pub Canada). Brookfield Pub Co.

Flattery, George M. Teaching for Christian Maturity. 126p. 1968. 1.50 (ISBN 0-88243-618-X, 02-0618). Gospel Pub.

Flatto, Edwin. Conquer Constipation-The Father & Mother of All Diseases: Confidential Report. pap. 8.95 (ISBN 0-935540-00-8). Plymouth Pr.

--Dr. Flatto's Weight & Blood Pressure Reduction Diet. 1984. pap. 6.95 (ISBN 0-317-20245-6). Plymouth Pr.

--Exercise Your Way to Health & Beauty. 1977. pap. 8.95 (ISBN 0-935540-01-6). Plymouth Pr.

--Look Younger, Think Clearer, Live Longer. 1978. pap. 2.95 (ISBN 0-935540-04-0). Plymouth Pr.

--Manual for Midwives: Step by Step Instructions for Natural Home & Emergency Childbirth. 1979. pap. 8.95 (ISBN 0-935540-02-4). Plymouth Pr.

--The Restoration of Health: Nature's Way. 1970. 500 copies or more only 2.95 (ISBN 0-935540-03-2). Plymouth Pr.

--Warning: How Sex May Be Hazardous to Your Health. 1983. pap. 5.95 (ISBN 0-935540-07-5). Plymouth Pr.

Flatto, Edwin & Allerhand, Annette. Asbestos: The Unseen Peril in Our Environment. 1983. pap. 4.95 (ISBN 0-935540-10-5). Plymouth Pr.

Flatto, Janice S. Insomnia: Why Some People Can't Sleep. 1985. pap. 4.95 (ISBN 0-317-20243-X). Plymouth Pr.

Flaubert, G. Letters: Gustave Flaubert. 248p. 1980. Repr. lib. bdg. 40.00 (ISBN 0-8495-1705-2). Arden Lib.

Flaubert, Gustave. Best Known Works of Gustave Flaubert. 637p. 1985. Repr. of 1904 ed. lib. bdg. 45.00 (ISBN 0-8482-4057-X). Norwood Edns.

--Bouvard & Pecuchet. Earp, T. W. & Stonier, G. W., trs. LC 78-12046. 1979. Repr. of 1954 ed. lib. bdg. 27.50x (ISBN 0-313-21189-2, FLBP). Greenwood.

--Bouvard & Pecuchet. Krailsheimer, A. J., tr. (Classics Ser.). 336p. 1976. pap. 4.95 (ISBN 0-14-044320-7). Penguin.

--Bouvard et Pecuchet. Maynial, ed. 1954. pap. 4.50 (ISBN 0-685-11054-0). French & Eur.

--Correspondance, 2 vols. 1220p. Vol. 1, 1830-1851. 37.50 (ISBN 0-686-56511-8); Vol. 2, 1851-1858. write for info. French & Eur.

--Dictionary of Accepted Ideas. LC 68-15880. 1954. pap. 4.95 (ISBN 0-8112-0054-X, NDP230). New Directions.

--L' Education Sentimentale. Maynial, ed. (Class. Garnier). pap. 9.95 (ISBN 0-685-34897-0). French & Eur.

--L' Education Sentimentale. Maynial, ed. (Coll. Prestige). 27.95 (ISBN 0-685-34898-9). French & Eur.

--Education Sentimentale. Suffel, ed. (Coll. G.F). 1961. pap. 4.95 (ISBN 0-685-11155-5). French & Eur.

--L' Education Sentimentale, 2 Vols. (Fr). pap. 2.95 ea. Larousse.

--The First Sentimental Education. Garman, Douglas, tr. LC 77-149947. 275p. 1972. 29.50x (ISBN 0-520-01967-9). U of Cal Pr.

--Golden Tales from Flaubert. facsimile ed. LC 73-38720. (Short Story Index Reprint Ser.). Repr. of 1928 ed. 18.00 (ISBN 0-8369-4133-0). Ayer Co Pubs.

--La Legende De Saint Julien l'Hospitalier. (Illus.). 144p. 1945. 4500.00 (ISBN 0-686-55984-3). French & Eur.

--The Letters of Gustave Flaubert, Eighteen Thirty to Eighteen Fifty-Seven. Steegmuller, Francis, ed. LC 79-13503. (Harvard Paperbacks Ser.). 272p. 1981. pap. 5.95 (ISBN 0-674-52637-6, Belknap Pr). Harvard U Pr.

--The Letters of Gustave Flaubert: Eighteen Thirty to Eighteen Fifty-Seven, Vol. I. Steegmuller, Francis, ed. (Illus.). 267p. 1980. 16.50x (ISBN 0-674-52636-8, Belknap Pr). Harvard U Pr.

--The Letters of Gustave Flaubert, 1857-1880, Vol. II. Steegmuller, Francis, ed. & tr. from Fr. (Illus.). 336p. 1982. 16.50 (ISBN 0-674-52640-6, Belknap Pr). Harvard U Pr.

--Madame Bovary. (Classics Ser.). (gr. 11 up). pap. 1.50 (ISBN 0-8049-0089-2, CL-89). Airmont.

--Madame Bovary. (Literature Ser.). (gr. 10-12). 1970. pap. text ed. 5.00 (ISBN 0-87720-744-5). AMSCO Sch.

--Madame Bovary. Bersani, Leo & Bair, Lowell, eds. (Bantam Classics Ser.). 424p. (gr. 9-12). 1981. pap. 2.50 (ISBN 0-553-21101-3). Bantam.

--Madame Bovary. (Span.). pap. 4.50 (ISBN 0-685-11300-0). French & Eur.

--Madame Bovary. (Coll. GF). (Fr.). pap. 4.50 (ISBN 0-685-34900-4). French & Eur.

--Madame Bovary. Gothot-Mesch, ed. 1961. pap. 12.95 (ISBN 0-685-11301-9). French & Eur.

--Madame Bovary. Gothot-Mesch, ed. (Coll. Prestige). (Fr.). 27.95 (ISBN 0-685-34899-7). French & Eur.

--Madame Bovary. Bree, Germaine, ed. Lawrence, Merloyd, tr. 1969. pap. 5.50 (ISBN 0-395-05210-6, RivEd). HM.

--Madame Bovary. (Documentation Thematique Ser.). (Fr). pap. 2.95 (ISBN 0-685-13975-1, 100). Larousse.

--Madame Bovary. Steegmuller, Frances, tr. LC 57-5214. 1957. 6.95 (ISBN 0-394-60460-1). Modern Lib.

--Madame Bovary. Steegmuller, Francis, tr. (YA) 1981. pap. 3.50 (ISBN 0-394-32986-4, T17, Mod LibC). Modern Lib.

--Madame Bovary. Marmur, Mildred, tr. (Orig.). 1964. pap. 2.50 (ISBN 0-451-51914-0, Sig Classics). NAL.

--Madame Bovary. De Man, Paul, ed. (Critical Editions). (gr. 9-12). 1965. pap. text ed. 5.95x (ISBN 0-393-09608-4, NortonC). Norton.

--Madame Bovary. Russell, Alan, tr. (Classics Ser.). (Orig.). 1951. pap. 2.95 (ISBN 0-14-044015-1). Penguin.

--Madame Bovary. Steegmuller, Francis, tr. (Modern Library College Editions Ser.). 396p. 1982. pap. text ed. 3.95 (ISBN 0-394-32986-4, MLCE). Random.

--Madame Bovary. (gr. 9 up). pap. 1.25. WSP.

--Madame Bovary. 320p. 1983. Repr. lib. bdg. 17.95x (ISBN 0-89966-324-9). Buccaneer Bks.

--Madame Bovary. (Book Notes Ser.). 1985. pap. 2.50 (ISBN 0-8120-3524-0). Barron.

--Madame Bovary. (Illus.). 400p. 1985. 12.95 (ISBN 0-396-08689-6). Dodd.

--Oeuvres, 2 tomes. Thibaudet & Dumesnil, eds. (Bibl. de la Pleiade). Set. 71.90 (ISBN 0-685-11438-4). French & Eur.

--Oeuvres Completes, 2 tomes. Masson, ed. (Coll L'Integrale). Set. 31.90 (ISBN 0-685-34896-2). French & Eur.

--Par les Champs et par les Greves. deluxe ed. 1137.50 (ISBN 0-685-34906-3). French & Eur.

--Preface a la Vie d'Ecrivain. 1963. 16.50 (ISBN 0-686-55986-X). French & Eur.

--La Premiere Education Sentimentale. 1963. 14.95 (ISBN 0-686-55987-8). French & Eur.

--La Queue de la Poire de la Boule de Monseigneur. (Illus.). 53p. 1958. 13.50 (ISBN 0-686-55988-6). French & Eur.

--Salammbo. (Coll. GF). 1961. pap. 4.50 (ISBN 0-685-11553-4, 2794). French & Eur.

--Salammbo. Maynial, ed (Class. Garnier). (Fr.). pap. 9.95 (ISBN 0-685-34901-2). French & Eur.

--Salammbo. Maynial, ed. (Coll. Prestige). (Fr.). 27.95 (ISBN 0-685-34902-0). French & Eur.

--Salammbo. (Noveaux Classique Larousse). (Fr). pap. 2.95 (ISBN 0-685-14072-5, 102). Larousse.

--Salammbo. Krailsheimer, A. J., tr. (Classics Ser.). 1977. pap. 3.95 (ISBN 0-14-044328-2). Penguin.

--La Second Volume de Bouvard et Pecuchet. 5.95 (ISBN 0-686-55989-4). French & Eur.

--Selected Letters. facsimile ed. Steegmuller, Francis, tr. LC 78-160919. (Biography Index Reprint Ser.). Repr. of 1953 ed. 17.50 (ISBN 0-8369-8082-4). Ayer Co Pubs.

--Sentimental Education. Baldick, Robert, tr. (Classics Ser.). (Orig.). 1964. pap. 3.95 (ISBN 0-14-044141-7). Penguin.

--The Sentimental Education. 1984. pap. 3.95 (ISBN 0-452-00719-4, Mer). NAL.

--Souvenirs, Notes et Pensees Intimes. 109p. 1965. 4.95 (ISBN 0-686-55990-8). French & Eur.

--The Temptation of Saint Anthony. Mrosovsky, Kitty, tr. LC 80-70452. (Illus.). 288p. 1981. 27.50x (ISBN 0-8014-1239-0). Cornell U Pr.

--The Temptation of St. Anthony. Mrosovsky, Kitty, tr. from Fr. (Penguin Classics Ser.). 272p. 1983. pap. 4.95 (ISBN 0-14-044410-6). Penguin.

--La Tentation de Saint Antoine. Maynial, ed. (Class. Garnier). pap. 6.95 (ISBN 0-685-34903-9). French & Eur.

--Three Tales. Baldick, Robert, tr. Incl. A Simple Heart; Legend of Saint Julian Hospitator; Herodias. (Classics Ser.). (Orig.). 1961. pap. 2.95 (ISBN 0-14-044106-9). Penguin.

--Trois Contes. (Coll. GF). 1963. pap. 2.95 (ISBN 0-685-11604-2, 1958). French & Eur.

--Trois Contes. Maynial, ed. (Class. Garnier). pap. 6.95 (ISBN 0-685-34904-7). French & Eur.

--Trois Contes. Maynial, ed. (Coll. Prestige). 27.95 (ISBN 0-685-34905-5). French & Eur.

--Trois Contes. (Documentation Thematique). (Fr). pap. 2.95 (ISBN 0-685-14088-1, 103). Larousse.

Flaubert, Gustave & Douyere, Sylvia E. Un Coeur Simple. 220p. 1974. 12.50 (ISBN 0-686-55983-5). French & Eur.

Flaubert, Gustave & Naaman, Antoine Y. Lettres d'Egypte. 480p. 1965. 22.50 (ISBN 0-686-55985-1). French & Eur.

Flaud, J. M. & Camy-Peyret, C. Water Vapour Line Parameters from Microwave to Medium Infrared: An Atlas of H2 to the Sixteenth, O; H2 to the Seventeenth, O; H2 to the Eighteenth, O; Line Positions & Intensities Between O & 4350 Cm to the -1. (International Tables of Constants Ser.: Vol. 19). xvi, 259p. 1981. 83.00 (ISBN 0-08-026181-7). Pergamon.

Flaumenhaft, Mera J., tr. see Machiavelli, Niccolo.

Flautz, John. Life: The Gentle Satirist. 1972. 7.95 (ISBN 0-87972-043-3). Bowling Green Univ.

Flavel, John. The Mystery of Providence. 1976. pap. 3.45 (ISBN 0-85151-104-X). Banner of Truth.

Flavell, John & Ross, Lee, eds. Social Cognitive Development: Frontiers & Possible Futures. (Cambridge Studies in Social & Emotional Development). (Illus.). 336p. 1981. 42.50 (ISBN 0-521-23687-8); pap. 15.95 (ISBN 0-521-28156-3). Cambridge U Pr.

Flavell, John H. Cognitive Development. 2nd ed. 336p. 1985. text ed. 25.95 (ISBN 0-13-139791-5); pap. text ed. 17.95 (ISBN 0-13-139783-4). P-H.

Flavell, John H., jt. ed. see Elkind, David.

Flavell, John H., ed. see Mussen, Paul.

Flavell, John H., et al. The Development of Role-Taking & Communication Skills in Children. LC 74-22477. 250p. 1975. Repr. of 1968 ed. 14.00 (ISBN 0-88275-238-3). Krieger.

Flavell, R. B., jt. ed. see Dover, G. A.

Flavian, C. The College Student Introduction to the World of Wall Street. (Illus.). 84p. 1974. text ed. 47.85 (ISBN 0-913314-31-5). Am Classical Coll Pr.

Flavier, Juan M. Back to the Barrios (Balikbario) 1979. pap. 4.00 (ISBN 0-686-25216-0, Pub. by New Day Pub). Cellar.

--Back to the Barrios: Balikbaryo. 150p. 1978. 4.00 (ISBN 0-318-14573-1). Intl Inst Rural.

--Doctor to the Barrios: Experiences with the Philippine Rural Reconstruction Movement. 1970. wrps. 3.50x (ISBN 0-686-18698-2). Cellar.

--Doctor to the Barrios: Experiences with the Philippine Rural Reconstruction Movement. 208p. 1970. 4.00 (ISBN 0-318-14574-X). Intl Inst Rural.

--My Friends in the Barrios. 1974. wrps. 3.50x (ISBN 0-686-18699-0). Cellar.

--My Friends in the Barrios. 190p. 1974. 3.00 (ISBN 0-318-14579-0). Intl Inst Rural.

Flavin, Christopher. Electricity from Sunlight: The Future of Photovoltaics. LC 82-62631. (Worldwatch Papers). 1982. pap. 2.00 (ISBN 0-916468-50-X). Worldwatch Inst.

--Electricity from Sunlight: The Future of Photovoltaics. (Worldwatch Institute Papers: No. 52). 63p. 1982. pap. 2.95 (ISBN 0-916468-50-X, WW52, WW). Unipub.

--Electricity in the Eighties. (Worldwatch Papers). 1984. pap. 4.00. Worldwatch Inst.

--Electricity's Future: The Shift to Efficiency & Small Scale Power. (Worldwatch Papers). 1984. pap. 4.00 (ISBN 0-916468-61-5). Worldwatch Inst.

--Energy & Architecture: The Solar & Conservation Potential. LC 80-54002. (Worldwatch Papers). 1980. pap. 2.00 (ISBN 0-916468-39-9). Worldwatch Inst.

--The Future of Synthetic Materials: The Petroleum Connection. LC 80-51137. (Worldwatch Papers Ser.). 1980. pap. 2.00 (ISBN 0-916468-35-6). Worldwatch Inst.

--Nuclear Power: The Market Test. LC 83-51433. (Worldwatch Papers). 1983. pap. 2.00 (ISBN 0-916468-56-9). Worldwatch Inst.

--Nuclear Power: The Market Test World Watch Paper, No. 57. 81p. 1983. pap. text ed. 2.95 (ISBN 0-916468-56-9, WW57, WW). Unipub.

--Wind Energy: A Turning Point. LC 81-52516. (Worldwatch Papers). 1981. pap. 2.00 (ISBN 0-916468-44-5). Worldwatch Inst.

Flavin, Christopher, jt. auth. see Deudney, Daniel.

Flavin, Martin. Journey in the Dark. LC 78-104220. Repr. of 1943 ed. lib. bdg. 22.50x (ISBN 0-8371-3337-8, FLJD). Greenwood.

Flavin, Martin, ed. see Shirley, James.

Flavin, Matt. Fundamental Concepts of Information Modeling. (Illus.). 136p. (Orig.). 1981. pap. 17.50 (ISBN 0-917072-22-7). Yourdon.

Flavin, Sean, jt. auth. see Ehrman, Kenneth.

Flavius, Josephus see Josephus, Flavius.

Flawn, P. T., et al. The Ouachita System. (Illus.). 401p. 1982. Repr. of 1980 ed. 12.00 (ISBN 0-318-03315-1, PUB 6120). Bur Econ Geology.

Flaws, Bob. Path of Pregnancy. rev. ed. 113p. pap. 9.95 (ISBN 0-912111-01-1). Paradigm Pubns.

Flaws, Bob & Wolfe, Honora L. Prince Wen Hui's Cook. 208p. (Orig.). 1985. pap. 12.95 (ISBN 0-912111-05-4). Paradigm Pubns.

Flax, Brian D. Best of the Hammer, Vol. II. (Illus.). vi, 280p. (Orig.). 1985. pap. 6.00 (ISBN 0-943228-05-0). Raymonds Quiet Pr.

Flax, Brian D., ed. Best of the Hammer, Vol. I. (Illus.). vi, 200p. (Orig.). 1985. pap. 6.00 (ISBN 0-943228-04-2). Raymonds Quiet Pr.

Flax, Oriel. Rock the Tower. LC 84-90521. 107p. 1985. 10.95 (ISBN 0-533-06456-2). Vantage.

Flax, Zena, ed. The Old Fashioned Children's Storybook. LC 82-80875. (Illus.). 64p. 1982. 6.95 (ISBN 0-448-12537-4, G&D). Putnam Pub Group.

Flaxman, Andrew. New York City Superguide. (Illus.). 32p. 1983. soft cover 3.95 (ISBN 0-89345-953-4, Biograf Pubns). Garber Comm.

Flaxman, Edward. Great Feats of Modern Engineering. facs. ed. rev. ed. LC 67-23219. (Essay Index Reprint Ser). 1938. 20.00 (ISBN 0-8369-0446-X). Ayer Co Pubs.

Flaxman, Erwin, et al, eds. Readings in Equal Education: An AMS Anthology, Vol. 7. 440p. 1984. 47.50 (ISBN 0-404-10107-0). AMS Pr.

Flaxman, John. Drawings by John Flaxman in the Huntington Collection. Wark, Robert R., notes by. LC 73-128363. (Illus.). 94p. 1970. pap. 5.00 (ISBN 0-87328-047-4). Huntington Lib.

Flaxman, Seymour L., ed. Modern Language Teaching in Schools & Colleges. 72p. 1961. pap. 7.95x (ISBN 0-915432-61-7). NE Conf Teach Foreign.

Flay, Joseph C. Hegel's Quest for Certainty. (Hegelian Studies). 560p. 1984. 49.50x (ISBN 0-87395-877-2); pap. 24.50x (ISBN 0-87395-878-0). State U NY Pr.

Flayerman, Norm, ed. Flayderman's Guide to Antique American Firearms. 3rd ed. LC 75-36418. (Illus.). 624p. 1983. pap. 19.95 (ISBN 0-910676-58-5). DBI.

Flayhart, William H., III & Warwick, Ronald. QE Two. (Illus.). 1985. 19.95 (ISBN 0-393-01885-7). Norton.

Flayhart, William J., III, jt. auth. see Shaum, John H., Jr.

Flayton, Linda. He & I. LC 85-90943. 1985. 10.00 (ISBN 0-87212-192-5). Libra.

Fleagle, jt. auth. see Ciochon.

Fleagle, Fred K. Social Problems in Puerto Rico. LC 74-14233. (The Puerto Rican Experience Ser). (Illus.). 152p. 1975. Repr. 12.00x (ISBN 0-405-06222-2). Ayer Co Pubs.

Fleagle, Robert G. An Introduction to Atmospheric Physics. 2nd ed. LC 80-766. (International Geophysics Ser.). 1980. 34.00 (ISBN 0-12-260355-9). Acad Pr.

Fleagle, Robert G., ed. Weather Modification: Science & Public Policy. LC 68-8511. (Public Policy Issues in Resource Management Ser.: Vol. 3). (Illus.). 158p. 1968. 20.00x (ISBN 0-295-78551-9). U of Wash Pr.

Fleagle, Robert G., et al. Weather Modification in the Public Interest. LC 74-590. (Illus.). 98p. 1974. 17.50x (ISBN 0-295-95321-7). U of Wash Pr.

Fleay, Frederick G. Biographical Chronicle of the English Drama, 1559-1642, 2 vols. 1973. Repr. of 1891 ed. lib. bdg. 47.00 (ISBN 0-8337-1151-2). B Franklin.

--Chronicle History of London Stage, 1559-1642. 1964. Repr. of 1890 ed. 24.50 (ISBN 0-8337-1152-0). B Franklin.

--Chronicle History of the Life & Work of Shakespeare. LC 70-139614. Repr. of 1886 ed. 26.00 (ISBN 0-404-02405-X). AMS Pr.

--Guide to Chaucer & Spenser. LC 72-168038. Repr. of 1877 ed. 14.25 (ISBN 0-404-02406-8). AMS Pr.

--Introduction to Shakespearian Study. LC 76-130613. Repr. of 1877 ed. 14.50 (ISBN 0-404-02407-6). AMS Pr.

--Shakespeare Manual. LC 76-130621. Repr. of 1876 ed. 14.00 (ISBN 0-404-02408-4). AMS Pr.

--Shakespeare Manual. 1973. Repr. of 1878 ed. 13.95 (ISBN 0-8274-1600-8). R West.

Flechas, Genaro. Handbook of Speech Improvement for Spanish-Speaking Students. Mergal, Margaret Z., ed. LC 77-9954. 1978. pap. 9.00 (ISBN 0-8477-3320-3). U of PR Pr.

Fleche, Francis La see La Fleche, Francis.

Fleck, David L., jt. auth. see Montero, James P.

Fleck, David L., et al. Design Supplement: 1979. 1979. saddle stitch 35.00x (ISBN 0-686-24886-4). Archinform.

Fleck, G. Peter. The Mask of Religion. LC 79-9644. (Library of Liberal Religion). 204p. 1980. 12.95 (ISBN 0-87975-125-8). Prometheus Bks.

Fleck, George, jt. ed. see Senechal, Marjorie.

Fleck, Glen, ed. see Eames, Charles & Eames, Ray.

Fleck, H. & Fernandez, L. Exploring Home Making & Personal Living. 4th ed. 1977. text ed. 21.28x (ISBN 0-13-297051-1). P-H.

Fleck, Henrietta. Introduction to Nutrition. 4th ed. 1981. text ed. write for info. (ISBN 0-02-338280-5). Macmillan.

--Toward Better Teaching of Home Economics. 3rd ed. (Illus.). 1980. text ed. write for info. (ISBN 0-02-338240-6). Macmillan.

Fleck, J. Roland & Carter, John D., eds. Psychology & Christianity: Integrative Readings. LC 81-7911. 400p. (Orig.). 1981. pap. 15.95 (ISBN 0-687-34740-8). Abingdon.

Fleck, James N., ed. see TMS-AIME Spring Meeting, Pittsburgh, 1976.

Fleck, Jeffrey. Character & Context: Studies in the Fiction of Abramovitsh, Brenner & Agnon. LC 83-9068. (Brown Judaic Studies). 136p. 1984. pap. 14.00 (14 00 45). Scholars Pr GA.

Fleck, Ludwig. Genesis & Development of a Scientific Fact. Trenn, Thaddeus J. & Merton, Robert K., eds. Bradley, Fred, tr. from Ger. LC 79-12521. 224p. 1981. pap. 8.00x (ISBN 0-226-25325-2). U of Chicago Pr.

Fleck, Paul A. Solar Energy Handbook, Special California Edition: How to Save Three Thousand Dollars on State Income Taxes with Solar Energy. (Illus.). 1977. pap. 5.95 (ISBN 0-918826-03-9). Time-Wise.

Fleck, Paul A., ed. Solar Energy Handbook. rev. ed. (Illus.). 1976. pap. 4.45 (ISBN 0-918826-01-2). Time-Wise.

Fleck, Raymond F. & Hollaender, Alexander, eds. Genetic Toxicology: An Agricultural Perspective. (Basic Life Sciences: Vol. 21). 560p. 1982. 65.00x (ISBN 0-306-41135-0, Plenum Pr). Plenum Pub.

Fleck, Richard. Clearing of the Mist. (The American Dust Ser.: No. 10). 1979. 7.95 (ISBN 0-913218-86-3); pap. 2.95 (ISBN 0-913218-85-5). Dustbooks.

Fleck, Richard, ed. John Muir: The Mountaineering Essays. (Literature of the American Wilderness Ser.). (Illus.). 208p. 1984. pap. 4.95 (ISBN 0-87905-169-8, Peregrine Smith). Gibbs M Smith.

Fleck, Richard F. Cottonwood Moon. 1979. 4.00 (ISBN 0-936204-06-0). Jelm Mtn.

--Henry Thoreau & John Muir among the Indians. 1985. text ed. 17.50 (ISBN 0-208-02112-4, Archon Bks). Shoe String.

--Palms, Peaks & Prairies. 1967. 4.00 (ISBN 0-8233-0024-2). Golden Quill.

Fleck, Richard F., ed. see Thoreau, Henry D.

Fleck, Stephen, jt. auth. see Lidz, Theodore.

Fleckenstein, Albrect. Calcium-Antagonism in Heart & Smooth Muscle: Experimental Facts & Therapeutic Prospects. LC 82-15990. 399p. 1983. 60.00x (ISBN 0-471-05435-6, Pub. by Wiley-Interscience). Wiley.

Fleckenstein, Alfred C. The Prince of Gravas: A Story of the Past. Reginald, R. & Melville, Douglas, eds. LC 77-84233. (Lost Race & Adult Fantasy Ser.). (Illus.). 1978. Repr. of 1898 ed. lib. bdg. 24.50x (ISBN 0-405-10976-8). Ayer Co Pubs.

Fleckenstein, Henry A. Decoys of the Mid-Atlantic Region. LC 79-52438. (Illus.). 256p. 1979. 19.95 (ISBN 0-916838-24-2). Schiffer.

Fleckenstein, Henry A., Jr. American Factory Decoys. LC 81-51466. (Illus.). 240p. 1981. 37.50 (ISBN 0-916838-53-6). Schiffer.

--Southern Decoys of Virginia & the Carolinas. LC 83-61650. (Illus.). 232p. 1983. 39.50 (ISBN 0-916838-86-2). Schiffer.

Fleckenstein, Henry, Jr. New Jersey Decoys. LC 82-62952. (Illus.). 272p. 1983. text ed. 37.50 (ISBN 0-916838-75-7). Schiffer.

--Shore Bird Decoys. LC 80-52024. (Illus.). 144p. 1980. 35.00 (ISBN 0-916838-32-3). Schiffer.

Fleckenstein, J. Early Medieval Germany. (Europe in the Middle Ages, Selected Studies: Vol. 16). 212p. 1978. 47.00 (ISBN 0-444-85134-8, North-Holland). Elsevier.

Flecker, James E. Collected Prose. LC 75-41096. (BCL Ser.: II). Repr. of 1920 ed. 21.50 (ISBN 0-404-14541-8). AMS Pr.

Fleckles, Elliot. Willie Speaks Out. LC 73-23123. (Illus.). 225p. 1974. 7.95 (ISBN 0-87542-233-0). Llewellyn Pubns.

Fleckner, John A. Archives & Manuscripts: Surveys. rev. ed. LC 77-14554. (SAA Basic Manual Ser.). 28p. 1977. pap. 5.00 (ISBN 0-931828-05-8). Soc Am Archivists.

Flecknoe, Richard. Love's Kingdom: With a Short Treatise of the English Stage. LC 74-170431. (The English Stage Ser.: Vol. 17). 1973. lib. bdg. 61.00 (ISBN 0-8240-0600-3). Garland Pub.

Flecknoe, Richard see Wright, James.

Flectcher, Alice C. & La Flesche, Francis. The Omaha Tribe. LC 11-31959. 1971. Repr. of 1911 ed. 50.00 (ISBN 0-384-16000-X). Johnson Repr.

Flecther, Rivers. Jaguar XJS. (Illus.). 144p. 14.95 (ISBN 0-85429-418-X, B1418). Haynes Pubns.

--MG: Past & Present. (Illus.). 250p. 18.95 (P402). Haynes Pubns.

Fledelius, H. C., et al, eds. see Myopia International Conference, 3rd, Copenhagen, 1980.

Fledelius, H. C., et al, eds. see Third International Conference on Myopia, Copenhagen, 1980.

Fleder, jt. auth. see Levy.

Flee, Kenn, jt. auth. see Jerome, Judson.

Fleeman, J. D., ed. see Johnson, Samuel.

Fleeman, J. E., ed. see Boswell, James.

Fleeman, Stephen. Electronic Principles. 1985. text ed. 28.95 (ISBN 0-8359-1587-5); solutions manual avail. (ISBN 0-8359-1588-3). Reston.

Fleener-Marzec, Nickieann. D. W. Griffith's the Birth of a Nation: Controversy, Suppression, & the First Amendment As It Applies to Filmic Expression, 1915-1973. Joewtt, Garth S., ed. LC 79-6675. (Dissertations on Film Ser.). 564p. 1980. lib. bdg. 56.50 (ISBN 0-405-12909-2). Ayer Co Pubs.

Fleenor, C. Patrick, jt. auth. see Knudson, Harry R.

Fleenor, Juliann, ed. The Female Gothic. 250p. (Orig.). pap. write for info. (ISBN 0-920792-06-5). Eden Pr.

Fleeson, Tyler. Limbo Zoning. 1976. pap. 1.50 (ISBN 0-685-79282-X). Stone-Marrow Pr.

Fleet, Betsy & Fuller, John D. Green Mount: A Virginia Plantation Family During the Civil War. LC 62-19375. (Illus.). 374p. 1977. Repr. of 1962 ed. 14.95x (ISBN 0-8139-0752-7). U Pr of Va.

Fleet, Betsy, ed. Green Mount After the War: The Correspondence of Maria Louisa Wacker Fleet & Her Family, 1865-1900. LC 77-24079. 374p. 1978. 14.95x (ISBN 0-8139-0730-6). U Pr of Va.

Fleet, Beverly. Henrico County, Virginia Records, Vol. 21. (Virginia Colonial Abstracts Ser.). 100p. 1944. 15.00 (ISBN 0-89308-371-2, VA 94). Southern Hist Pr.

--Northumberland, Virginia Records, Vols. 2 & 3. (Virginia Colonial Abstracts Ser.). 265p. 1938. 26.50 (ISBN 0-89308-389-5, VA 73). Southern Hist Pr.

--Richmond County, Virginia Records, Vols. 16 & 17. (Virginia Colonial Abstracts Ser.). 265p. 1942-43. 26.50 (ISBN 0-89308-391-7, VA 75). Southern Hist Pr.

--Virginia Colonial Abstracts, Vols. 1, 9, 19, 20. LC 63-568. 1961-67. pap. 5.00 ea. (ISBN 0-8063-0112-0). Genealog Pub.

--The Virginia Company of London 1607-1624, Vol. 3. Fleet, Beverly, compiled by. (Series 2, the Virginia Company of London 1607-1624). 1978. Repr. 15.00 (ISBN 0-89308-064-0). Southern Hist Pr.

--Washington County, Virginia Records, Vol. 34. (Virginia Colonial Abstracts Ser.). 83p. 1949. 15.00 (ISBN 0-89308-392-5, VA 76). Southern Hist Pr.

Fleet, David D. van see Albanse, Robert & Van Fleet, David D.

Fleet, David D. Van see Van Fleet, David D.

Fleet, F. R. Theory of Wit & Humour. LC 71-105785. 1970. Repr. of 1890 ed. 19.50x (ISBN 0-8046-0951-9, Pub by Kennikat). Assoc Faculty Pr.

Fleet, James K. Van see Van Fleet, James K.

Fleet, James Van see Van Fleet, James.

Fleet, Michael. The Rise & Fall of Chilean Christian Democracy. LC 84-42885. 292p. 1985. text ed. 35.00x (ISBN 0-691-07684-7); pap. 14.50x (ISBN 0-691-02217-8). Princeton U Pr.

Fleet Owner Magazine Staff. Fleet Owners Maintenance Shop Design Book. 256p. 1981. 31.50 (ISBN 0-07-021260-0). McGraw.

Fleet, Robert R. Red-tailed Tropicbird on Kure Atoll. 64p. 1974. 5.50 (ISBN 0-943610-16-8). Am Ornithologists.

Fleetcroft, C. The Musculo-Skeletal System. (Penguin Library of Nursing). (Illus.). 1983. pap. text ed. 7.00 (ISBN 0-443-01611-9). Churchill.

Fleetwood, Hugh. A Dance to the Glory of God. 192p. 1983. 16.95 (ISBN 0-241-11088-2, Pub. by Hamish Hamilton England). David & Charles.

--The Girl Who Passed for Normal. LC 72-95909. 288p. 1973. 2.25 (ISBN 0-8128-7034-4). Stein & Day.

--The Godmother. 152p. 1980. 16.95 (ISBN 0-241-10126-3, Pub. by Hamish Hamilton England). David & Charles.

Fleetwood, Janet, jt. ed. see Rainbolt, Martha.

Fleetwood, Jucker & Elver, Erin. Sweden's Capital Imports & Exports. Wilkins, Mira, ed. LC 76-29743. (European Business Ser.). (Illus.). 1977. Repr. of 1947 ed. lib. bdg. 37.50x (ISBN 0-405-09760-3). Ayer Co Pubs.

Fleetwood, William. Chronicon Precosium. LC 68-55711. (Illus.). Repr. of 1745 ed. 29.50x (ISBN 0-678-00492-7). Kelley.

--The Relative Duties of Parents & Children, Husbands & Wives, Masters & Servants. LC 83-48607. (Marriage, Sex & the Family in England Ser.). 495p. 1985. lib. bdg. 55.00 (ISBN 0-8240-5933-6). Garland Pub.

Fleey, David. Living with Animals. (Illus.). (gr. 2 up). 8.50x (ISBN 0-392-03825-0, ABC). Sportshelf.

Fleg, Edmond. The Jewish Anthology. Samuel, Maurice, tr. LC 72-142934. 399p. 1975. Repr. of 1925 ed. lib. bdg. 17.50x (ISBN 0-8371-5824-9, FLJA). Greenwood.

--Why I Am a Jew. 2nd facsimile ed. Wise, Louise W., tr. from Fr. LC 74-27984. (Modern Jewish Experience Ser.). (Eng.). 1975. Repr. of 1945 ed. 13.00 (ISBN 0-405-06711-9). Ayer Co Pubs.

--Why I Am a Jew. Wise, Louise W., tr. from Fr. LC 75-4124. 1985. pap. 4.95 (ISBN 0-8197-0009-6). Bloch.

Flegal, Sharon, jt. auth. see Azarnoff, Pat.

Flegenheimer, Walter V. Techniques of Brief Psychotherapy. LC 82-13891. 224p. 1982. 25.00 (ISBN 0-87668-496-7). Aronson.

Flegg, Graham. Numbers: Their History & Meaning. LC 82-19134. (Illus.). 288p. 1983. 14.95 (ISBN 0-8052-3847-6). Schocken.

Flegg, H. Graham. From Geometry to Topology. LC 74-78155. 150p. 1974. 19.50x (ISBN 0-8448-0364-2). Crane-Russak Co.

Flegg, James, jt. auth. see Fisher, James.

Flegg, Jim. Discovering Bird Watching. (Discovering Ser.: No. 155). 1984. pap. text ed. 4.50 (ISBN 0-85263-674-1, Pub. by Shire Pubns England). Seven Hills Bks.

--Garden Birds. (Picture-Perfect Miniatures Ser.). (Illus.). 48p. 1983. 4.95 (ISBN 0-8253-0172-6). Beaufort Bks NY.

--Parasitic Worms. (Shire Natural History Ser.: No. 5). (Orig.). 1985. pap. 3.95 (ISBN 0-85263-761-6, Pub. by Shire Pubns England). Seven Hills Bks.

--The Puffin. (Shire Natural History Ser.: No. 2). (Orig.). 1985. pap. 3.95 (ISBN 0-85263-744-6, Pub. by Shire Pubns England). Seven Hills Bks.

Flegg, Jim, jt. auth. see Hosking, Eric.

Flegg, Jim, annotations by. Just a Lark! LC 84-45555. (Illus.). 160p. 1984. 15.00 (ISBN 0-7099-1049-5, Pub. by Croom Helm Ltd). Longwood Pub Group.

Flegg, Jim, ed. see Hosking, Eric.

Flegg, P. B., et al. The Biology & Technology of the Cultivated Mushroom. Date not set. price not set. Wiley.

Flegm, Eugene H. Accounting: How to Meet the Challenges of Relevance & Regulation. LC 83-12333. (Modern Accounting Perspectives & Practices Ser.). 261p. 1984. 29.95x (ISBN 0-471-09326-2, Pub. by Ronald Pr). Wiley.

Flegmann, G. W. & George, R. A. Soils & Other Growth Media. 1977. text ed. 13.00 (ISBN 0-87055-240-6). AVI.

Flegmann, Vilma. Called to Account: The Public Accounts Committee of the House of Commons. 328p. 1980. text ed. 39.95x (ISBN 0-566-00371-6). Gower Pub Co.

Flegmann, Wilma. Public Expenditure & Select Committees of the Commons. 160p. 1985. text ed. price not set. Gower Pub Co.

Fleharty, Eugene D. & Hulett, Gary K., eds. The Vital Continuum. rev. ed. LC 80-50300. (Illus.). 500p. 1980. pap. 12.95 (ISBN 0-936352-00-0, B511). U of KS Cont Ed.

Fleicher, Becca, jt. ed. see Fleischer, Sidney.

Fleichits, Ye & Makovsky, A. The Civil Codes of the Soviet Republics. 1976 ed. 288p. 14.95 (ISBN 0-686-37387-1). Beekman Pubs.

Fleisch, H., et al, eds. Urolithiasis Research. LC 76-47019. 598p. 1976. 75.00x (ISBN 0-306-30988-2, Plenum Pr). Plenum Pub.

Fleisch, Herbert, jt. ed. see Massry, Shaul G.

Fleisch, Paul. Die Moderne Gemeinschaftsbewegung in Deutschland. Dayton, Donald W., ed. (The Higher Christian Life Ser.). 605p. 1985. 75.00 (ISBN 0-8240-6419-4). Garland Pub.

Fleischauer, Paul D., jt. ed. see Adamson, Arthur W.

Fleischauer, Warren, ed. see Johnson, Samuel.

Fleischer, Arthur C. & James, A. Everette. Introduction to Diagnostic Sonography. LC 79-19065. 339p. 1980. 44.00 (ISBN 0-471-05473-9, Pub. by Wiley-Medical). Wiley.

--Real-Time Sonography. 431p. 1983. 57.50 (ISBN 0-8385-8270-2). ACC.

Fleischer, Arthur, Jr. Tender Offers: Defenses, Responses, & Planning, 3 vols. 2nd ed. 1200p. 1983. 210.00 (ISBN --15-100055-7, H39492). HarBraceJ.

Fleischer, Arthur, Jr., et al, eds. Eleventh Annual Institute on Securities Regulation. LC 70-125178. 593p. 1980. text ed. 25.00 (ISBN 0-686-69167-9, B2-1275). PLI.

--Tenth Annual Institute on Securities Regulation. LC 70-125178. 1979. text ed. 25.00 (ISBN 0-686-58549-6, B2-1266). PLI.

--Twelfth Annual Institute on Securities Regulation. 611p. 1981. text ed. 30.00 (ISBN 0-686-76238-X, B2-1280). PLI.

Fleischer, Becca see Fleischer, Sidney.

Fleischer, Becca, jt. ed. see Fleischer, Sidney.

Fleischer, Belton M. Minimum Wage Regulation in Retail Trade. 1981. 12.25 (ISBN 0-8447-3419-5); pap. 5.25 (ISBN 0-8447-3420-9). Am Enterprise.

Fleischer, D. Digital Logic Elements. 228p. 1979. pap. 35.95 (ISBN 0-471-25675-7, Pub. by Wiley Heyden). Wiley.

Fleischer, D., et al, eds. Therapeutic Laser Endoscopy in Gastrointestinal Disease. 1983. lib. bdg. 43.50 (ISBN 0-89838-577-6, Pub. by Martinus Nijhoff Netherlands). Kluwer Academic.

Fleischer, David, jt. ed. see Wesson, Robert.

Fleischer, Eugene & Goodman, Helen. Cataloguing Audiovisual Materials: A Manual Based on the AACR II. LC 80-18782. (Illus.). 387p. 1981. pap. 29.95 (ISBN 0-918212-39-1). Neal-Schuman.

Fleischer, Eugene B. A Style Manual for Citing Microform & Nonprint Media. LC 78-9375. 76p. 1978. pap. 6.00x (ISBN 0-8389-0268-5). ALA.

Fleischer, G. Evolutionary Principles of the Mammalian Middle Ear. (Advances in Anatomy, Embriology & Cell Biology: Vol. 55, Pt. 5). (Illus.). 1978. pap. 29.00 (ISBN 0-387-09140-8). Springer-Verlag.

Fleischer, G. A. Contingency Table Analysis for Road Safety Studies. (NATO Advanced Study Institute Series - Applied Science: No. 42). 300p. 1981. 29.00x (ISBN 90-286-0960-1). Sijthoff & Noordhoff.

Fleischer, H. Kleines Textbuch der kommunistischen Ideologie: Auszuege aus dem Lehrbuch Osnovy Marksizma-Leninizma. (Sovietica Ser.: No. 11). 116p. (Ger.). 1963. 16.00 (ISBN 90-277-0052-4, Pub. by Reidel Holland). Kluwer Academic.

--Short Handbook of Communist Ideology: Synopsis of the Osnovy Marksizma-Leninizma. Blakeley, T. J., tr. from Ger. (Sovietica Ser.: No. 20). 98p. 1965. lib. bdg. 16.00 (ISBN 90-277-0053-2, Pub. by Reidel Holland). Kluwer Academic.

Fleischer, Herbert O., jt. auth. see Youngquist, Wally G.

Fleischer, Jane. Pontiac, Chief of the Ottawas. LC 78-18050. (Illus.). 48p. (gr. 4-6). 1979. PLB 7.89 (ISBN 0-89375-156-1); pap. 1.95 (ISBN 0-89375-146-4); cassette avail. Troll Assocs.

--Sitting Bull, Warrior of the Sioux. new ed. LC 78-18047. (Illus.). 48p. (gr. 4-6). 1979. PLB 7.89 (ISBN 0-89375-154-5); pap. 1.95 (ISBN 0-89375-144-8). Troll Assocs.

--Tecumseh, Shawnee War Chief. new ed. LC 78-18046. (Illus.). 48p. (gr. 4-6). 1979. PLB 7.89 (ISBN 0-89375-153-7); pap. 1.95 (ISBN 0-89375-143-X). Troll Assocs.

Fleischer, Julie, ed. see Hurwitz, Sadie W.

Fleischer, Lenore. The Cat's Pajamas. LC 82-47907. (Illus.). 192p. 1982. pap. 6.68i (ISBN 0-06-090974-9, CN 974, CN). Har-Row.

--It Came upon the Midnight Clear. 224p. (Orig.). 1985. pap. 2.95 (ISBN 0-345-32163-4). Ballantine.

Fleischer, Leonore. Blind Sunday. 171p. (gr. 7 up). 1982. pap. 1.95 (ISBN 0-590-32155-2, Wishing Star Bks). Scholastic Inc.

--Breathless. 1983. pap. 2.95 (ISBN 0-440-10804-7). Dell.

--The Chicken Soup Book. LC 77-76040. 1978. pap. 4.95 (ISBN 0-8008-1441-X). Taplinger.

--Fame. 1980. pap. 2.25 (ISBN 0-449-14359-7, GM). Fawcett.

--Ice Castles. 224p. (gr. 7 up). 1981. pap. 1.95 (ISBN 0-449-70012-7, Juniper). Fawcett.

--Making Love. 1982. pap. 2.50 (ISBN 0-345-30162-5). Ballantine.

--Staying Alive. (Illus., Orig.). 1983. pap. 2.95 (ISBN 0-671-47786-2). PB.

Fleischer, Margot. Hermeneutische Anthropologie: Platon - Aristoteles. 1976. 60.00x (ISBN 3-11-006714-5). De Gruyter.

Fleischer, Martha H. The Iconography of the English History Play. (Salzburg Studies in English Literature, Elizabethan & Renaissance Studies: No. 10). 363p. 1974. pap. text ed. 25.50x (ISBN 0-391-01376-9). Humanities.

Fleischer, Max. Betty Boop. 1975. pap. 3.45 (ISBN 0-380-00294-9, 24133). Avon.

Fleischer, Nathaniel S. Fifty Years at Ringside. LC 77-90144. Repr. of 1958 ed. lib. bdg. 18.25x (ISBN 0-8371-2164-7, FLFY). Greenwood.

Fleischer, Neil T. & Gates, Calvin. The Micro Editor. (gr. 9-12). 1983. text ed. 2.35 wkbk. (ISBN 0-538-23670-1, W67). SW Pub.

Fleischer, Richard. The Narrow Margin. (RKO CLassic Screenplay Ser.). 1985. o. s. i. 14.95 (ISBN 0-8044-2191-9); pap. 8.95 (ISBN 0-8044-6135-X). Ungar.

Fleischer, Rita M., jt. auth. see Dunmore, Charles W.

Fleischer, Rita M., jt. auth. see Moreland, Floyd L.

Fleischer, Robert L., et al. Nuclear Tracks in Solids. LC 73-90670. 1975. 62.50x (ISBN 0-520-02665-9); pap. 17.50x (ISBN 0-520-04096-1). U of Cal Pr.

Fleischer, S. see Colowick, Sidney P. & Kaplan, Nathan O.

Fleischer, S., et al, eds. The Molecular Biology of Membranes. LC 78-2207. (Illus.). 363p. 1978. 42.50x (ISBN 0-306-31114-3, Plenum Pr). Plenum Pub.

Fleischer, Sidney, ed. Methods in Enzymology: Biomembranes: Membrane Biogenesis: Assembly & Targeting (General Methods Eukaryotes, Vol. 96, Pt. J. Fleischer, Becca. 1983. 79.00 (ISBN 0-12-181996-5). Acad Pr.

Fleischer, Sidney & Fleicher, Becca, eds. Methods in Enzymology: Biomembranes: Membrane Biogenesis: Proceedings & Recycling, Vol. 98, Pt. L. 1983. 73.00 (ISBN 0-12-181998-1). Acad Pr.

Fleischer, Sidney & Fleischer, Becca, eds. Methods in Enzymology: Biomembranes: Membrane Biogenesis: Assembly & Targeting, Vol. 97. (Prokaryotes, Mitochondria & Chloroplasts Ser.: Pt. K). 1983. 69.50 (ISBN 0-12-181997-3). Acad Pr.

Fleischer, Victor. Rienzo: The Rise & Fall of a Dictator. LC 76-112801. 1970. Repr. of 1948 ed. 12.00x (ISBN 0-8046-1067-3, Pub. by Kennikat). Assoc Faculty Pr.

Fleischhacker, Daniel & Kerr, Rose N. Interpretive Costume Design. 1984. 15.00 (ISBN 0-932826-18-0). New Issues MI.

Fleischhacker, Hedwig. Die Staats und Voelkerrechtlichen Grundlagen der Moskauischen Aussenpolitik. Repr. of 1938 ed. 14.00 (ISBN 0-384-15970-2). Johnson Repr.

Fleischhacker, R. V., ed. see Lanfranco Of Milan.

Fleischhauer-Hardt, Helga, jt. auth. see McBride, Will.

Fleischmajer, Raul, ed. Progress in Diseases of the Skin, Vol. I. 288p. 1981. 47.00 (ISBN 0-8089-1412-X, 791272). Grune.

--Progress in Diseases of the Skin, Vol. II. 288p. 1984. 49.50 (ISBN 0-8089-1623-8, 791273). Grune.

Fleischman, Charles & Helberg, Kristin. The Victorian Seaside Hotel Coloring Book. (Illus.). 48p. (gr. 3 up). 1983. pap. 2.50 (ISBN 0-486-24399-0). Dover.

Fleischman, Marjorie R. Dosage Calculation: Method & Workbook. (League Exchange Ser.: No. 106). 106p. 1975. 5.95 (ISBN 0-88737-141-8, 20-1560). Natl League Nurse.

Fleischman, Matthew J., et al. Troubled Families: A Treatment Program. LC 82-62573. 284p. (Orig.). 1983. pap. text ed. 19.95 (ISBN 0-87822-271-5). Res Press.

Fleischman, Paul. The Animal Hedge. LC 82-2404. (Illus.). 32p. (gr. 2-5). 1983. 9.95 (ISBN 0-525-44002-X, 0966-290). Dutton.

--The Birthday Tree. LC 78-22155. (Illus.). (gr. k-3). 1979. 10.53i (ISBN 0-06-021915-7). HarpJ.

--Coming-&-Going Men: Four Tales. LC 84-48336. (Charlotte Zolotow Bk.). (Illus.). 160p. (gr. 6 up). 1985. 11.06i (ISBN 0-06-021883-5); PLB 10.89g (ISBN 0-06-021884-3). HarpJ.

--Finzel the Farsighted. LC 83-1416. (Illus.). 48p. (gr. 1-5). 1983. 9.95 (ISBN 0-525-44057-7, 0966-290, Unicorn Bk). Dutton.

--Graven Images. LC 81-48649. (A Charlotte Zolotow Bk.). (Illus.). 96p. (gr. 6 up). 1982. 10.53i (ISBN 0-06-021906-8); PLB 10.89g (ISBN 0-06-021907-6). HarpJ.

--The Half-a-Moon Inn. LC 79-2010. (Illus.). 96p. (gr. 5 up). 1980. PLB 10.89 (ISBN 0-06-021918-1). HarpJ.

--I Am Phoenix: Poems for Two Voices. LC 85-42615. (A Charlotte Zolotow Bk.). (Illus.). 64p. (ps up). 1985. 11.06i (ISBN 0-06-021881-9); PLB 10.89g (ISBN 0-06-021882-7). HarpJ.

--Path of the Pale Horse. LC 82-48611. (Charlotte Zolotow Bk). 160p. (gr. 6 up). 1983. 10.53i (ISBN 0-06-021904-1); PLB 10.89g (ISBN 0-06-021905-X). HarpJ.

--Phoebe Danger, Detective, in the Case of the Two-Minute Cough. LC 82-15616. (Illus.). 64p. (gr. 2-5). 1983. 8.95 (ISBN 0-395-33226-5). HM.

Fleischman, Richard K., Jr. Conditions of Life among the Cotton Workers of Southeastern Lancashire During the Industrial Revolution: 1780-1850. LC 84-46001. 475p. 1985. lib. bdg. 50.00 (ISBN 0-8240-6681-2). Garland Pub.

Fleischman, Sid. The Bloodhound Gang in The Case of the Secret Message. LC 80-28469. (Bloodhound Gang Bks.). (Illus.). 64p. (gr. 2-4). 1981. PLB 4.99 (ISBN 0-394-94764-9); pap. 1.50 (ISBN 0-394-84764-4). Random.

--The Bloodhound Gang in the Case of the 264-Pound Burglar. LC 81-12066. (Bloodhound Gang Bks.). (Illus.). 64p. (gr. 2-5). 1982. PLB 4.99 (ISBN 0-394-95108-5); pap. 1.50 (ISBN 0-394-85108-0). Random.

--The Bloodhound Gang's Secret Code Book. LC 82-3682. (A Three-Two-One Contact Bk.). (Illus.). 64p. (gr. 3-7). 1983. pap. 3.95 (ISBN 0-394-85231-1). Random.

--By the Great Horn Spoon. (Illus.). (gr. 4-6). 8.95 (ISBN 0-316-28577-3, Pub. by Atlantic Monthly Pr). Little.

--The Case of Princess Tomorrow. LC 80-19518. (The Bloodhound Gang Ser.). (Illus.). 64p. (gr. 2-5). 1981. PLB 4.99 (ISBN 0-394-94674-X); pap. 1.50 (ISBN 0-394-84674-5). Random.

--The Case of the Cackling Ghost. LC 80-20059. (The Bloodhound Gang Ser.). (Illus.). 64p. (gr. 2-4). 1981. PLB 4.99 (ISBN 0-394-94673-1); pap. 1.50 (ISBN 0-394-84673-7). Random.

--The Case of the Flying Clock. LC 80-28056. (Bloodhound Gang Bks.). (Illus.). 64p. (gr. 2-4). 1981. PLB 4.99 (ISBN 0-394-94765-7); pap. 1.50 (ISBN 0-394-84765-2). Random.

--Chancy & the Grand Rascal. (Illus.). (gr. 4-6). 1966. 7.95 (ISBN 0-316-28575-7, Pub. by Atlantic Monthly Pr). Little.

--The Ghost in the Noonday Sun. (Illus.). (gr. 4-6). 1965. 7.95 (ISBN 0-316-28576-5, Pub. by Atlantic Monthly Pr). Little.

--The Ghost on Saturday Night. (Illus.). 64p. (gr. 4-6). 1974. 7.95 (ISBN 0-316-28583-8, Pub. by Atlantic Monthly Pr.). Little.

--The Hey Hey Man. (Illus.). (gr. 1-3). 1979. 7.95g (ISBN 0-316-26001-0, Pub. by Atlantic Monthly Pr). Little.

--Humbug Mountain. LC 78-9419. (Illus.). (gr. 4-6). 1978. 8.95 (ISBN 0-316-28569-2, Pub. by Atlantic Monthly Pr). Little.

--Jingo Django. (gr. 4-6). 1971. 9.95 (ISBN 0-316-28580-3, Pub. by Atlantic Monthly Pr). Little.

--Kate's Secret Riddle Book. (Illus.). (gr. k-3). 1978. pap. 1.50 (ISBN 0-380-40253-X, 51987-9, Camelot). Avon.

--McBroom & the Beanstalk. LC 77-22177. (Illus.). (gr. 4-6). 1978. 7.95 (ISBN 0-316-28570-6, Atlantic-Little, Brown). Little.

--McBroom & the Big Wind. (Illus.). 48p. (gr. 3 up). 1982. 8.95 (ISBN 0-316-28543-9, Pub. by Atlantic Monthly Pr); pap. 3.95 (ISBN 0-316-28544-7). Little.

--McBroom & the Great Race. (Illus.). 64p. (gr. 3-7). 1980. 7.95 (ISBN 0-316-28568-4, Atlantic-Little Brown). Little.

--McBroom Tells a Lie. (Illus.). 64p. (gr. 4-6). 1976. 7.95 (ISBN 0-316-28572-2, Pub. by Atlantic Monthly Pr). Little.

--McBroom Tells the Truth. LC 81-1035. (Illus.). 48p. (gr. 3-7). 1981. 7.95 (ISBN 0-316-28550-1, Pub. by Atlantic Pr); pap. 3.95 (ISBN 0-316-28552-8). Little.

--McBroom the Rainmaker. (Illus.). 48p. (gr. 3 up). 1982. 10.45i (ISBN 0-316-28541-2, Pub. by Atlantic Monthly Pr); pap. 3.95 (ISBN 0-316-28542-0). Little.

--McBroom's Almanac. (Illus.). (gr. 3-7). 1984. 12.45i (ISBN 0-316-26009-6, Pub. by Atlantic Monthly Pr). Little.

--McBroom's Ear. LC 81-15636. (Illus.). (gr. 3 up). 1982. 8.95 (ISBN 0-316-28539-0, Pub. by Atlantic Monthly Pr); pap. 3.95 (ISBN 0-316-28540-4). Little.

--McBroom's Ghost. LC 81-1118. (Illus.). 48p. (gr. 3-7). 1981. 7.95 (ISBN 0-316-28547-1, Pub. by Atlantic Monthly Pr); pap. 3.95 (ISBN 0-316-28549-8). Little.

--McBroom's Ghost. LC 81-1118. (Illus.). (gr. 3 up). 1981. 8.95 (ISBN 0-316-28547-1, Pub. by Atlantic Monthly Pr); pap. 3.95 (ISBN 0-316-28549-8). Little.

--McBroom's Zoo. (Illus.). 48p. (gr. 3 up). 1982. 8.95g (ISBN 0-316-28536-6, Pub. by Atlantic Monthly Pr); pap. 3.95 (ISBN 0-316-28538-2). Little.

--Me & the Man on the Moon-Eyed Horse. (Illus.). (gr. 3 up). 1977. 7.95 (ISBN 0-316-28571-4, Pub. by Atlantic Monthly Pr). Little.

--Mr. Mysterious & Company. (Illus.). (gr. 4-6). 1962. 10.45i (ISBN 0-316-28578-1, Pub. by Atlantic Monthly Pr). Little.

--Mr. Mysterious's Secrets of Magic. (Illus.). 96p. (gr. 4-6). 1975. 6.95 (ISBN 0-316-28584-6, Pub. by Atlantic Monthly Pr). Little.

Fleischman, Suzanne. The Future in Thought & Language: Diachronic Evidence from Romance. LC 81-15438. (Cambridge Studies in Linguistics: No. 36). 230p. 1981. 44.50 (ISBN 0-521-24389-0). Cambridge U Pr.

Fleischman, Ted. Half a Bottle of Catsup. 40p. (Orig.). 1978. pap. 3.00 (ISBN 0-917658-09-4). BPW & P.

Fleischman, W. M., ed. see Conference on Set-Valued Mappings, SUNY, Buffalo, 1969.

Fleischmann, Arnold. A Bibliography of Texas Governmwent & Politics. (Policy Research Ser.: No. 2). 118p. 1985. 12.00 (ISBN 0-89940-151-1). LBJ Sch Pub Aff.

Fleischmann, Joel, ed. The Future of American Political Parties. (Illus.). 179p. 1982. 14.95 (ISBN 0-13-345595-5); pap. 6.95 (ISBN 0-13-345587-4). P-H.

Fleischmann, Kaspar M., jt. auth. see Gernsheim, Helmut.

Fleischmann, Otto, et al, eds. see Aichhorn, August.

Fleischmann, W. B., ed. Encyclopedia of World Literature in the 20th Century, 4 vols. rev. & enl. ed. Incl. Vol. 1. A-F. (Illus.). 425p. 85.00 (ISBN 0-8044-3092-6); Vol. 2. G-N. 469p. 85.00 (ISBN 0-8044-3093-4); Vol. 3. O-Z. 590p. 85.00 (ISBN 0-8044-3094-2); Vol. 4. Supplement & Index. Ungar, Frederick & Mainiero, Lina, eds. 85.00 (ISBN 0-8044-3095-0). LC 67-13615. Set. 300.00 (ISBN 0-8044-3091-8). Ungar.

Fleischner, E., ed. Auschwitz - Beginning of a New Era? Reflections on the Holocaust. 35.00x (ISBN 0-87068-499-X). Ktav.

Fleischner, Eva. Judaism in German Christian Theology since 1945: Christianity & Israel Considered in Terms of Mission. LC 75-22374. (ATLA Monograph: No. 8). 205p. 1975. 16.00 (ISBN 0-8108-0835-8). Scarecrow.

Fleisher, Arthur, Jr. Tender Offers: Defenses, Responses & Planning, 3 vols. 2nd ed. 1720p. 1983. 210.00 (ISBN 0-15-004361-9, Law & Business). HarBraceJ.

Fleisher, Belton J. & Kniesner, Thomas J. Economics. 528p. 1985. pap. write for info. (ISBN 0-697-08253-9); instr's. manual avail. (ISBN 0-697-00547-X); transparencies avail. (ISBN 0-697-00709-X); study guide avail. (ISBN 0-697-00631-X). Wm C Brown.

Fleisher, Belton M. & Kniesner, Thomas J. Labor Economics: Theory, Evidence & Policy. 2nd ed. (Illus.). 1980. text ed. 27.95 O.P. (ISBN 0-13-517433-3). P-H.

--Labor Economics: Theory, Evidence, & Policy. 3rd ed. (Illus.). 640p. 1984. 29.95 (ISBN 0-13-517417-1). P-H.

Fleisher, D. William Godwin. 69.95 (ISBN 0-87968-276-0). Gordon Pr.

Fleisher, David. William Godwin: A Study in Liberalism. LC 73-1838. (Illus.). 154p. 1973. Repr. of 1951 ed. lib. bdg. 15.00x (ISBN 0-8371-6807-4, FLWG). Greenwood.

Fleisher, David & Freedman, David M. Death of an American: The Killing of John Singer. (Illus.). 248p. 1983. 15.95 (ISBN 0-8264-0231-3). Crossroad NY.

Fleisher, Gary & Ludwig, Stephen. Textbook Pediatric Emergency Medicine. (Illus.). 1381p. 1983. text ed. 97.50 (ISBN 0-683-03253-4). Williams & Wilkins.

Fleisher, Leonore. Annie. 1982. pap. 2.50 (ISBN 0-345-30451-9). Ballantine.

Fleisher, Martin, ed. The Clinical Biochemistry of Cancer: Proceedings of the Second Arnold O. Beckman Conference in Cliniical Chemistry. LC 79-14027. 405p. 1979. 30.00 (ISBN 0-915274-09-4); members 20.00. Am Assn Clinical Chem.

Fleisher, Michael L. Encyclopedia of the Comic Book Heroes: Wonder Woman, Vol. 2. (Illus.). 1976. pap. 7.95 (ISBN 0-02-080080-0, Collier). Macmillan.

Fleisher, p. J., jt. ed. see Costa, J. E.

Fleisher, Rita M., jt. auth. see Dunmore, Charles W.

Fleisher, Wilfrid. Sweden, the Welfare State. LC 72-10696. (Illus.). 255p. 1973. Repr. of 1956 ed. lib. bdg. 22.50x (ISBN 0-8371-6611-X, FLSW). Greenwood.

Fleishman, Alfred. Common Sense Management. LC 84-80765. 75p. 1984. 2.00 (ISBN 0-918970-33-4). Intl Gen Semantics.

--Dialogue with Street Fighters. LC 81-80600. 140p. 1981. 5.95x (ISBN 0-918970-29-6). Intl Gen Semantics.

--Sense & Nonsense: A Study in Human Communication. LC 77-156304. 1971. pap. 2.95x (ISBN 0-918970-07-5). Intl Gen Semantics.

Fleishman, Alfred & Meyer, William D. Troubled Talk. 2nd ed. LC 73-90145. 75p. (gr. 9 up). 1978. pap. 2.95x (ISBN 0-918970-16-4). Intl Gen Semantics.

Fleishman, Avrom. Conrad's Politics: Community & Anarchy in the Fiction of Joseph Conrad. LC 67-19479. 256p. 1967. 24.50x (ISBN 0-8018-0199-0). Johns Hopkins.

--The English Historical Novel: Walter Scott to Virginia Woolf. LC 71-150040. 288p. 1971. pap. 6.95x (ISBN 0-8018-1433-2). Johns Hopkins.

--Fiction & the Ways of Knowing: Essays on British Novels. LC 78-4896. 236p. 1978. text ed. 17.50x (ISBN 0-292-72422-5). U of Tex Pr.

--Figures of Autobiography: The Language of Self-Writing in Victorian & Modern England. LC 81-23163. 512p. 1983. text ed. 29.50x (ISBN 0-520-04666-8). U of Cal Pr.

--A Reading of Mansfield Park: An Essay in Critical Synthesis. 109p. 1970. pap. 3.95x (ISBN 0-8018-1149-X). Johns Hopkins.

--Virginia Woolf: A Critical Reading. LC 74-24375. (Illus.). 248p. 1977. pap. 7.95 (ISBN 0-8018-1958-X). Johns Hopkins.

Fleishman, Edwin A. & Quaintance, Marilyn A. Taxonomies of Human Performance: The Description of Human Tasks. 1984. 55.00 (ISBN 0-12-260450-4). Acad Pr.

Fleishman, Edwin A., jt. ed. see Alluisi, Earl A.

Fleishman, Edwin A., jt. ed. see Dunnette, Marvin D.

Fleishman, Edwin A., jt. ed. see Howell, William C.

Fleishman, Joel L. The Future of the Postal Service. LC 82-12314. 334p. 1983. 42.95 (ISBN 0-03-059921-0). Praeger.

Fleishman, Joel L. & Payne, Bruce L. Ethical Dilemmas & the Education of Policymakers. LC 80-10230. (The Teaching of Ethics Ser.). 76p. 1980. pap. 4.00 (ISBN 0-916558-05-3). Hastings Ctr Inst Soc.

Fleishman, Joel L., et al, eds. Public Duties: The Moral Obligation of Government Officials. (Illus.). 320p. 1981. text ed. 22.50x (ISBN 0-674-72231-0). Harvard U Pr.

Fleishman, Neil M. The X Factor: An American Cultural Dilemma. 1985. 14.95 (ISBN 0-533-06460-0). Vantage.

Fleishman, Seymour. Printcrafts for Fun & Profit. Rubin, Caroline, ed. LC 76-78907. (How to Ser.). (Illus.). (gr. 3-6). 1977. PLB 10.25 (ISBN 0-8075-6633-0). A Whitman.

--Too Hot in Potzburg. LC 81-11498. (Illus.). 32p. (ps-3). 1981. PLB 10.75 (ISBN 0-8075-8024-4). A Whitman.

Fleishman, Thelma, jt. auth. see Ritter, Priscilla R.

Fleisig, Heywood. Long Term Capital Flows & the Great Depression: The Role of the United States, 1927-1933. facsimile ed. LC 75-2580. (Dissertations in American Economic History). 1975. 35.50x (ISBN 0-405-07200-7). Ayer Co Pubs.

Fleisig, R., ed. see American Astronautical Society.

Fleiss, Joseph L. Statistical Methods for Rates & Proportions. 2nd ed. LC 80-26382. (Probability & Statistics Ser.: Applied Probability & Statistics). 321p. 1981. 37.50x (ISBN 0-471-06428-9, Pub. by Wiley-Interscience). Wiley.

Fleissner, E. M., jt. ed. see Fleissner, Otto S.

Fleissner, Else M. Herman Hesse: Modern German Poet & Writer. Rahmas, D. Steve, ed. LC 70-190244. (Outstanding Personalities Ser.: No. 26). 32p. (Orig.). (gr. 7-9). 1972. lib. bdg. 3.50 incl. catalog cards (ISBN 0-87157-526-4); pap. 1.95 vinyl laminated covers (ISBN 0-87157-026-2). SamHar Pr.

--Inflation. Rahmas, D. Steve, ed. LC 72-89225. (Topics of Our Times Ser.: No. 3). 32p. (Orig.). (YA) (gr. 7-12). 1973. lib. bdg. 3.50 incl. catalog cards (ISBN 0-87157-803-4); pap. 1.95 vinyl laminated covers (ISBN 0-87157-303-2). SamHar Pr.

Fleissner, Otto S. & Fleissner, E. M., eds. Kleine Anthologie Deutscher Lyrik. (Ger.). 1935. text ed. 12.95x (ISBN 0-89197-257-9); pap. text ed. 4.95x (ISBN 0-89197-258-7). Irvington.

--Kunst der Prosa. 1941. text ed. 15.95x (ISBN 0-89197-260-9); pap. text ed. 8.95x (ISBN 0-89197-261-7). Irvington.

Fleissner, Robert F. Dickens & Shakespeare: A Study in Histrionic Contrasts. LC 65-28337. (Studies in Comparative Literature, No. 35). 1969. Repr. of 1965 ed. lib. bdg. 49.95x (ISBN 0-8383-0549-0). Haskell.

--Resolved to Love: The 1592 Edition of Henry Constable's Diana. (Salzburg Elizabethan Studies: No. 92). 1980. pap. text ed. 25.50x (ISBN 0-391-01903-1). Humanities.

Fleiszar, K. A. & Hicks, B. J. Introductory Experiments in Cell Biology. 168p. (Orig.). 1983. lab manual 10.95x (ISBN 0-89459-205-X). Hunter Textbks.

Fleiszar, Kathleen, jt. auth. see Daniel, William.

Flekkoy, Kjell. Biological Aspects of Schizophrenia. 112p. 1982. pap. 22.00 (ISBN 82-00-05688-0). Universitet.

Flemal, R. C., jt. ed. see Melhorn, W. N.

Flemans, R. J., jt. auth. see Hayhoe, F. G.

Fleming, et al. Piling Engineering. 1985. 69.95 (ISBN 0-470-20144-4). Wiley.

Fleming, A., tr. see Caius, John.

Fleming, A. F., ed. Sickle-Cell Disease: A Handbook for the General Clinician. (Illus.). 145p. 1982. pap. 12.50 (ISBN 0-443-02037-X). Churchill.

Fleming, A. P. Industrial Research in the United States of America: Science & Industry, a Series of Papers Bearing on Industrial Research, No. 1. LC 72-5050. (Technology & Society Ser.). (Illus.). 68p. 1972. Repr. of 1917 ed. 15.00 (ISBN 0-405-04702-9). Ayer Co Pubs.

Fleming, A. William & Bloom, Joel A. Paddleball & Racquetball. LC 72-90984. (Physical Activities Ser.). 1973. pap. text ed. 8.65x (ISBN 0-673-16193-5). Scott F.

Fleming, Alex. Private Capital Flows to Developing Countries & Their Determinations: Historical Perspective, Recent Experience, & Future Prospects. (Working Paper: No. 484). 484p. 1981. pap. 3.00 (ISBN 0-686-39747-9, WP-0484). World Bank.

Fleming, Alice. America Is Not All Traffic Lights: Poems of the Midwest. 84p. (gr. 7 up). 1976. 6.95 (ISBN 0-316-28590-0). Little.

--Welcome to Grossville. 112p. (gr. 5-7). 1985. 11.95 (ISBN 0-684-18289-0). Scribner.

--What to Say When You Don't Know What to Say. LC 82-5782. 128p. (gr. 7 up). 1982. 10.95 (ISBN 0-684-17626-2, ScribJ). Scribner.

Fleming, Arnold. Scottish & Jacobite Glass. (Illus.). 1977. Repr. of 1938 ed. 35.00x (ISBN 0-7158-1207-6). Charles River Bks.

Fleming, Austin H. Preparing for Liturgy: A Theology & Spirituality. (Orig.). 1985. pap. write for info. (ISBN 0-912405-16-3). Pastoral Pr.

Fleming, Berry. The Affair at Honey Hill. LC 81-65833. 104p. 1981. 5.95 (ISBN 0-9604810-2-8). Cotton Lane.

--The Affair at Honey Hill. LC 81-65833. 93p. 1981. 5.95 (Pub. by Cotton Lane). Pelican.

--The Bookman's Tale. 104p. Date not set. 12.95x (ISBN 0-9604810-7-9). Cotton Lane.

--Country Wedding. 128p. 1983. 8.95 (ISBN 0-932298-29-X). Copple Hse.

--Country Wedding. 198p. 1983. 8.95 (ISBN 0-9604810-3-6). Cotton Lane.

--The Make-Believers. LC 77-121887. 428p. 1972. 12.95 (ISBN 0-911116-81-8). Pelican.

--Notes for a Now-&-Then Painter. LC 84-70286. (Illus.). 60p. (Orig.). 1984. pap. 6.95x (ISBN 0-9604810-6-0). Cotton Lane.

--Once There Was a Fisherman. 187p. 1984. 11.95 (ISBN 0-9604810-5-2). Cotton Lane.

--Two Tales for Autumn. LC 79-88065. 332p. 1979. 9.95 (ISBN 0-9604810-0-1); pap. 4.95 (ISBN 0-9604810-1-X). Cotton Lane.

Fleming, Berry, compiled by. Autobiography of a City in Arms: Augusta, Georgia, 1861-1865. LC 76-12661. (Illus.). 1976. 14.50 (ISBN 0-686-15796-6); pap. 6.50 (ISBN 0-686-15797-4). Richmond Cty Hist Soc.

Fleming, Bruce C. E. Contextualization of Theology: An Evangelical Assessment. 1981. pap. 5.95 (ISBN 0-87808-431-2). William Carey Lib.

Fleming, C. A., jt. auth. see Muir-Wood, A. M.

Fleming, C. A., ed. George Edward Lodge: Unpublished Bird Paintings. (Illus.). 408p. 1984. 150.00 (ISBN 0-7181-2212-7, Pub. by Michael Joseph). Merrimack Pub Cir.

Fleming, Charles. Executive Pursuit. 1984. pap. 3.95 (ISBN 0-451-62339-8, Ment). NAL.

Fleming, Charlotte M. Adolescence: Its Social Psychology. 1969. pap. text ed. 9.95 (ISBN 0-8236-8004-5, 020060). Intl Univs Pr.

--Adolescence, Its Social Psychology: With an Introduction to Recent Findings from the Fields of Anthropology, Physiology, Medicine, Psychometrics & Sociometry. LC 49-900. pap. 51.30 (ISBN 0-317-10600-7, 2010710). Bks Demand UMI.

Fleming, D. R., jt. ed. see Gamlin, Peter J.

Fleming, Daniel B., Jr., jt. auth. see Cline, Paul C.

Fleming, David & Ko, Wen H., eds. Indwelling & Implantable Pressure Transducers. LC 76-48168. (Uniscience Ser.). 224p. 1977. 66.00 (ISBN 0-8493-5195-2). CRC Pr.

Fleming, David A., ed. Religious Life at the Crossroads. 208p. (Orig.). 1985. pap. 8.95 (ISBN 0-8091-2709-1). Paulist Pr.

Fleming, David G. & Feinberg, Barry N. Handbook of Engineering in Medicine & Biology, CRC: Section B-Instruments & Measurements, Vol. 2. (Engineering in Medicine & Biology Ser.). 446p. 1978. 66.00 (ISBN 0-8493-0242-0). CRC Pr.

Fleming, David G. & Feinberg, Barry N., eds. Handbook of Engineering in Medicine & Biology, CRC. LC 75-44222. (Handbook Ser.). 1976. General Date, Vol. 1, 432 Pgs. 64.00 (ISBN 0-87819-285-9). CRC Pr.

Fleming, David H., ed. The Reformation in Scotland, Causes, Characteristics, Consequences: Stone Lectures at Princeton Theological Seminary, 1907-1908. LC 83-45579. Date not set. Repr. of 1910 ed. 67.50 (ISBN 0-404-19897-X). AMS Pr.

Fleming, David L. A Contemporary Reading of the Spiritual Exercises: A Companion to St. Ignatius' Text. 2nd ed. Ganss, George E., ed. LC 80-81812. (Study Aids on Jesuit Topics Ser.:. No.2). 112p. 1980. pap. 3.00 (ISBN 0-912422-47-5); smyth sewn 4.00 (ISBN 0-912422-48-3). Inst Jesuit.

--Modern Spiritual Exercises: A Contemporary Reading of the Spiritual Exercises of St. Ignatius. LC 82-46055. 152p. 1983. pap. 3.95 (ISBN 0-385-18853-6, Im). Doubleday.

--The Spiritual Exercises of St. Ignatius: A Literal Translation & a Contemporary Reading. Ganss, George E., ed. LC 77-93429. (Study Aids on Jesuit Topics Ser.: No. 7). 290p. 1978. 12.00 (ISBN 0-912422-32-7); smythe sewn 8.50 (ISBN 0-912422-31-9). Inst Jesuit.

Fleming, Denise, illus. The Charmkins Sniffy Adventure. (Sniffy Bks.). (Illus.). 24p. (gr. 3-5). 1983. 3.95 (ISBN 0-394-86115-9). Random.

--Ernie's Sesame Street Friends. (Illus.). 12p. (gr. 1-4). 1985. 3.95 (ISBN 0-394-87515-X, BYR). Random.

--It Feels Like Christmas! A Book of Surprises to Touch, See & Sniff. LC 84-60622. (Illus.). (ps). 1984. bds. 5.95 (ISBN 0-394-86862-5, Pub. by BYR). Random.

Fleming, Denna F. Treaty Veto of the American Senate. LC 76-168039. Repr. of 1930 ed. 25.00 (ISBN 0-404-02409-2). AMS Pr.

--Treaty Veto of the American Senate. LC 72-147598. (Library of War & Peace; International Law). 1972. lib. bdg. 46.00 (ISBN 0-8240-0359-4). Garland Pub.

--United States & World Organization, 1920-1933. LC 70-168040. Repr. of 1938 ed. 41.50 (ISBN 0-404-02435-1). AMS Pr.

Fleming, Don A. How to Stop the Battle with Your Child. Lupiani, Millicent, ed. LC 82-90682. (Illus.). 139p. (Orig.). 1982. pap. 11.95x (ISBN 0-9609264-0-2). D Fleming Sem.

Fleming, Donald. John William Draper & the Religion of Science. LC 74-120254. 1970. Repr. lib. bdg. 16.50x (ISBN 0-374-92750-2). Octagon.

Fleming, Donald & Fish, Joseph. Science & Technology in Providence, 1760-1914: An Essay in the History of Brown University in the Metropolitan Community. LC 52-9555. (Illus.). 54p. 1952. pap. 4.00x (ISBN 0-87057-031-5). U Pr of New Eng.

Fleming, Donald, ed. see Loeb, Jacques.

Fleming, Donald H. & Bailyn, Bernard, eds. The Intellectual Migration: Europe & America, 1930-1960. LC 78-75432. pap. 160.00 (ISBN 0-317-09993-0, 2002964). Bks Demand UMI.

Fleming, E. McClung. R. R. Bowker: Militant Liberal. LC 52-11604. 395p. 1952. 10.95 (ISBN 0-8352-0273-9, Pub. by U of Oklahoma Pr). Bowker.

Fleming, Elizabeth. Believe the Heart: Our Dyslexic Days. (Illus.). 160p. 1984. pap. 7.95 (ISBN 0-89407-061-4). Strawberry Hill.

Fleming, Esther, jt. auth. see Fleming, Robert E.

Fleming, Farold, ed. see Krause, Tina.

Fleming, Francis. Southern Africa. 1981. Repr. lib. bdg. 19.00x (ISBN 0-403-00408-X). Scholarly.

Fleming, Frank. Being Better Than You've Ever Been: 13 Uncommon People Tell You How to Solve 13 of Life's Most Common Problems. 218p. 1983. 16.95 (ISBN 0-13-071795-9); pap. 7.95 (ISBN 0-13-071787-8). P-H.

Fleming, G. H. The Dizziest Season: The Gashouse Gang Chases the Pennant. LC 84-60213. (Illus.). 311p. 1984. 15.95 (ISBN 0-688-03097-1). Morrow.

--Murderer's Row: The 1927 New York Yankees. LC 84-25385. (Illus.). 388p. 1985. 19.95 (ISBN 0-688-04804-8). Morrow.

--The Unforgettable Season. LC 80-18299. (Illus.). 336p. 1981. 16.95 (ISBN 0-03-056221-X). HR&W.

--The Unforgettable Season. Schaap, Dick, ed. (Penguin Sports Library). (Illus.). 368p. 1982. pap. 5.95 (ISBN 0-14-006273-4). Penguin.

Fleming, George. Computer Simulation Techniques in Hydrology. (Environmental Science Ser.). 352p. 1975. 42.50 (ISBN 0-444-00157-3). Elsevier.

Fleming, Gerald. Hitler & the Final Solution. LC 83-24535. (Illus.). 219p. 1984. 15.95 (ISBN 0-520-05103-3). U of Cal Pr.

Fleming, Geranna. Starting with Coquille. Gale, Vi, ed. LC 77-95426. (First Book Ser.). (Illus.). 1978. ltd. ed. 20.00 (ISBN 0-915986-07-8); pap. 5.00 (ISBN 0-915986-08-6). Prescott St Pr.

Fleming, Gerry, ed. see Peaslee, Ann.

Fleming, Gladys A. Creative Rhythmic Movement: Boys & Girls Dancing. (Illus.). 432p. 1976. pap. 22.95 (ISBN 0-13-191106-6). P-H.

Fleming, Glenn, et al. Wild Flowers of Florida. LC 76-43050. (Illus.). 1976. pap. 6.95 (ISBN 0-916224-08-2). Banyan Bks.

Fleming, Harold. Elizabeth Newt. LC 67-17786. (Orig.). 1967. 4.95 (ISBN 0-87376-006-9); pap. 3.00 (ISBN 0-87376-007-7). Red Dust.

--A Needed Path. (Black Willow Chapbook Ser.: BW/2). 20p. (Orig.). 1982. pap. 2.50 (ISBN 0-910047-00-6). Black Willow.

Fleming, Harold, ed. see DeFoe, Mark.

Fleming, Harold, ed. see McClane, Kenneth A.

Fleming, Harold, ed. see Smith, R. T.

Fleming, Harold, ed. see Witt, Harold.

Fleming, Harold L. Love Letters to the South. Davenport, Eileen, ed. (Black Willow Pamphlet Ser.: BW/11). 10p. 1984. pap. text ed. 1.50 (ISBN 0-910047-09-X). Black Willow.

--A Million Yellow Holes in Snow. Davenport, Eileen, ed. (Black Willow Pamphlet Ser.: BW/9). 12p. 1984. pap. text ed. 2.00 (ISBN 0-910047-10-3). Black Willow.

Fleming, Harold M. Gasoline Prices & Competition. LC 65-26736. 1966. 27.00x (ISBN 0-89197-187-4). Irvington.

--States, Contracts & Progress. LC 60-10207. 128p. (Orig.). 1960. 7.50 (ISBN 0-379-00053-9). Oceana.

--Ten Thousand Commandments: A Story of the Antitrust Laws. LC 75-172211. (Right Wing Individualist Tradition in America Ser). 1972. Repr. of 1951 ed. 16.00 (ISBN 0-405-00420-6). Ayer Co Pubs.

Fleming, Howard. Narrow Gauge Railways in America. 140p. 1985. 14.95 (ISBN 0-912113-05-7); pap. 8.95 (ISBN 0-912113-04-9). Railhead Pubns.

Fleming, Howard A. Canada's Arctic Outlet: A History of the Hudson Bay Railway. LC 78-5665. (Illus.). 129p. 1978. Repr. of 1957 ed. lib. bdg. 18.75x (ISBN 0-313-20392-X, FLCA). Greenwood.

Fleming, I., jt. auth. see Williams, D. H.

Fleming, I. A. The Small Business Case Book. 144p. 1985. text ed. 24.50 (ISBN 0-566-00841-6). Gower Pub Co.

Fleming, Ian. Berlin Escapes. 10.95 (ISBN 0-88411-872-X, Pub. by Aeonian Pr). Amereon Ltd.

--Casino Royale. pap. 3.95 fr. ed (ISBN 0-685-11066-4). French & Eur.

--Casino Royale. 192p. 1985. pap. 3.50 (ISBN 0-425-08162-1). Berkley Pub.

--Chitty Chitty Bang Bang. 159p. Repr. of 1964 ed. lib. bdg. 13.95 (ISBN 0-88411-983-1, Pub. by Aeonian Pr). Amereon Ltd.

--The Diamond Smugglers. 12.95 (ISBN 0-88411-873-8, Pub. by Aeonian Pr). Amereon Ltd.

--Diamonds Are Forever. pap. 3.91 fr. ed. (ISBN 0-685-11138-5); pap. 2.95 Sp. ed. (ISBN 0-685-11139-3). French & Eur.

--Diamonds Are Forever. 224p. 1985. pap. 2.95 (ISBN 0-425-06393-3). Berkley Pub.

--Doctor No. pap. 3.95 fr. ed (ISBN 0-685-11147-4); pap. 2.95 span. ed. (ISBN 0-685-11148-2). French & Eur.

--Doctor No. 240p. 1985. pap. 2.95 (ISBN 0-425-06394-1). Berkley Pub.

--For Your Eyes Only. pap. 3.95 fr. ed (ISBN 0-685-11195-4). French & Eur.

--For Your Eyes Only. 192p. 1985. pap. 3.50 (ISBN 0-425-08167-2). Berkley Pub.

--From Russia with Love. pap. 3.95 fr. ed. (ISBN 0-685-11210-1); pap. 2.95 span. ed. (ISBN 0-685-11211-X). French & Eur.

--From Russia with Love. 256p. 1985. pap. 3.50 (ISBN 0-425-08164-8). Berkley Pub.

--Frontier Orbitals & Organic Chemical Reactions. LC 76-3800. 249p. 1976. pap. 19.95x (ISBN 0-471-01819-8, Pub. by Wiley-Interscience). Wiley.

--Goldfinger. pap. 4.50 fr. ed. (ISBN 0-685-11216-0); pap. 2.95 span. ed. (ISBN 0-685-11217-9). French & Eur.

--Goldfinger. 272p. 1985. pap. 3.50 (ISBN 0-425-08165-6). Berkley Pub.

--Live & Let Die. (Fr. & Sp.). fr. ed. 4.50 (ISBN 0-685-11295-0); pap. 2.95 span. ed. (ISBN 0-685-11296-9). French & Eur.

--Live & Let Die. 224p. 1985. pap. 3.50 (ISBN 0-425-08163-X). Berkley Pub.

--The Man with the Golden Gun. fr. ed. 4.50 (ISBN 0-685-11338-8); pap. 2.95 span. ed. (ISBN 0-685-11339-6). French & Eur.

--Man with the Golden Gun. pap. 2.95 (ISBN 0-451-13705-1, AE2106, Sig). NAL.

--Octopussy. pap. 4.50 fr. ed. (ISBN 0-685-11430-9); pap. 2.95 Span. ed. (ISBN 0-685-11431-7). French & Eur.

--Octopussy. 1983. pap. 1.95 (ISBN 0-451-11878-2, Sig). NAL.

--On Her Majesty's Secret Service. pap. 4.50 fr. ed. (ISBN 0-685-11468-6). French & Eur.

--On Her Majesty's Secret Service. pap. 2.95 (ISBN 0-451-13707-8, AE2107, Sig). NAL.

--Selected Organic Syntheses: A Guidebook for Organic Chemists. LC 72-615. 227p. 1973. 49.95x (ISBN 0-471-26390-7); pap. 32.95 (ISBN 0-471-26391-5, Pub. by Wiley-Interscience). Wiley.

--Spy Who Loved Me. pap. 4.50 fr ed (ISBN 0-685-11575-5). French & Eur.

--The Spy Who Loved Me. 192p. 1985. pap. 2.95 (ISBN 0-425-06399-2). Berkley Pub.

--The Spy Who Loved Me. 192p. 1986. pap. 3.50 (ISBN 0-425-08637-2). Berkley Pub.

--Thrilling Cities. 14.95 (ISBN 0-88411-874-6, Pub. by Aeonian Pr). Amereon Ltd.

--Thunderball. pap. 4.50 fr ed (ISBN 0-685-11597-6); pap. 2.95 span. ed. (ISBN 0-685-11598-4). French & Eur.

--Thunderball. 240p. 1983. pap. 2.95 (ISBN 0-425-06428-X). Berkley Pub.

--Thunderball. 240p. 1985. pap. 3.50 (ISBN 0-425-08634-8). Berkley Pub.

--You Only Live Twice. pap. 4.50 fr. ed (ISBN 0-685-11630-1); pap. 2.95 span. ed (ISBN 0-685-11631-X). French & Eur.

--You Only Live Twice. pap. 2.95 (ISBN 0-451-13708-6, AE2108, Sig). NAL.

Fleming, Ian, jt. auth. see Barrowclough, Christine.

Fleming, J. Authenticity in Art (The Scientific Detection of Forgery) 1976. 20.00 (ISBN 0-9960026-1-8, Pub. by A Hilger England). Heyden.

Fleming, J., jt. auth. see Ball, K. P.

Fleming, J. B., jt. auth. see Lenihan, J.

Fleming, J. Clifton. Tax Aspects of Buying & Selling Corporate Businesses. LC 83-20291. (Tax & Estate Planning Ser.). 612p. 1984. 75.00 (ISBN 0-07-021298-8, Shepards-McGraw). McGraw.

Fleming, J. Marcus. Essays in International Economics. 1971. 22.50x (ISBN 0-674-26435-5). Harvard U Pr.

--Essays on Economic Policy. LC 77-15991. 1978. 36.00x (ISBN 0-231-04366-X). Columbia U Pr.

Fleming, Jacqueline. Blacks in College: A Comparative Study of Students' Success in Black & in White Institutions. LC 84-47984. (Higher Education Ser.). 1984. 20.95x (ISBN 0-87589-616-2). Jossey-Bass.

Fleming, James. Interpreting the Electrocardiogram. new ed. (Illus.). 1979. text ed. 16.50 (ISBN 0-906141-05-2, Pub. by Update Pubns, England). Kluwer Academic.

Fleming, James, ed. see Negri, Antonio.

Fleming, James E. The Blacksmith's Source Book: An Annotated Bibliography. LC 80-18560. 116p. 1980. 19.95x (ISBN 0-8093-0989-0). S Ill U Pr.

Fleming, James, Jr. & Hazard, Geoffrey C., Jr. Civil Procedure. 3rd ed. LC 84-81753. 1985. text ed. 28.00 (ISBN 0-316-45693-4). Little.

Fleming, Jane L. & Gilman, Irene P., eds. The Collected Poems of Peter Lott: Unionville Farmer Poet. (Illus.). 192p. 1983. pap. 11.50 (ISBN 0-9612800-0-X). J L Gilman.

Fleming, Jean. Between Walden & the Whirlwind. 1985. pap. price not set (ISBN 0-89109-520-9). NavPress.
--A Mother's Heart. LC 81-85727. 224p. 1982. 3.95 (ISBN 0-89109-489-X). NavPress.
Fleming, Jo. His Affair: The Powerful True Story of One Woman's Confrontation with Every Woman's Nightmare. LC 76-15245. 204p. 1976. 6.95 (ISBN 0-87131-216-6). M Evans.
Fleming, Jo Ellen & Goplerud, Dena. Mainstreaming with Learning Sequences. 1980. pap. 10.95 (ISBN 0-8224-4260-4). Pitman Learning.
Fleming, Joan & Benedek, Therese. Psychoanalytic Supervision. Chicago Institute for Psychanalysis, ed. LC 83-22763. (Classics in Psychoanalysis Monograph Ser.: No. 1). xii, 252p. 1983. Repr. of 1966 ed. text ed. 27.50x (ISBN 0-8236-5041-3). Intl Univs Pr.
Fleming, John. Desert Hiking Guide. (Illus.). 28p. (Orig.). 1979. pap. 3.95 (ISBN 0-937794-01-5). Nature Trails.
--The Lengthening Shadow of Slavery: A Historical Justification for Affirmative Action for Blacks in Higher Education. LC 76-21656. 158p. 1976. pap. 5.95 (ISBN 0-88258-074-4). Howard U Pr.
--Robert Adam & His Circle. (Illus.). 1979. 30.00 (ISBN 0-7195-0000-1). Transatlantic.
Fleming, John, jt. auth. see Honour, Hugh.
Fleming, John, ed. see Heydenreich, Ludwig H.
Fleming, John, et al. Catch Seventy-Six. (Occasional Paper: No. 47). 1977. pap. 5.95 technical (ISBN 0-255-36080-0). Transatlantic.
--Chaucer & the Craft of Fiction. Arrathoon, Leigh A., ed. (Illus.). 400p. 1985. pap. 20.00 (ISBN 0-933760-05-1). Solaris Pr.
--The Penguin Dictionary of Architecture. rev. ed. (Reference Ser.). 1966. pap. 6.95 (ISBN 0-14-051013-3). Penguin.
Fleming, John A. The Troubadours of Provence. LC 77-806. 1977. Repr. of 1952 ed. lib. bdg. 27.00 (ISBN 0-685-76861-9). Folcroft.
Fleming, John E., et al. The Case for Affirmative Action for Blacks in Higher Education. LC 78-19553. 1978. 15.00 (ISBN 0-88258-076-0); pap. 8.95 (ISBN 0-88258-075-2). Howard U Pr.
Fleming, John G. An Introduction to the Law of Torts. (Clarendon Law Ser.). 1967. pap. 11.95x (ISBN 0-19-876079-5). Oxford U Pr.
--An Introduction to the Law of Torts. 2nd ed. (Clarendon Law Ser.). 200p. 1985. 22.95 (ISBN 0-19-876154-6); pap. 12.95 (ISBN 0-19-876155-4). Oxford U Pr.
Fleming, John V. From Bonaventure to Bellini: An Essay in Franciscan Exegesis. LC 82-47593. (Princeton Essays on the Arts Ser.: No. 14). (Illus.). 192p. 1982. 26.50x (ISBN 0-691-07270-1); pap. 13.50 L.P.E. (ISBN 0-691-10143-4). Princeton U Pr.
--An Introduction to the Franciscan Literature of the Middle Ages. 274p. 1977. 10.95 (ISBN 0-8199-0651-4). Franciscan Herald.
--Reason & the Lover. LC 83-42557. 244p. 1984. 20.00x (ISBN 0-691-06578-0). Princeton U Pr.
Fleming, Juanita W., jt. ed. see Downs, Florence S.
Fleming, June. Games & More for Backpackers. (Illus.). 112p. 1983. pap. 4.95 (ISBN 0-399-50712-4, Perigee). Putnam Pub Group.
--Outdoor Idea Book. LC 78-6514. (Illus.). 1978. write for info. (ISBN 0-918480-06-X). Victoria Hse.
--Staying Found: The Complete Map & Compass Handbook. LC 81-52429. (Illus.). 192p. (Orig.). 1982. pap. 4.95 (ISBN 0-394-75152-3, Vin). Random.
--The Well-Fed Backpacker. LC 81-40197. (Illus.). 112p. 1981. pap. 3.95 (ISBN 0-394-74897-2, Vin). Random.
--The Well-Fed Backpacker. Date not set. 7.95 (ISBN 0-394-73804-7, Vin). Random.
Fleming, Kathleen. Lovers in the Present Afternoon. LC 83-19413. 416p. (Orig.). 1984. pap. 8.50 (ISBN 0-930044-46-0). Naiad Pr.
Fleming, Kenneth C. God's Voice in the Stars: Zodiac Signs & Bible Truth. LC 80-27700. 144p. 1981. pap. 3.95 (ISBN 0-87213-175-0). Loizeaux.
Fleming, L. S. Le see Chekhov, Anton P.
Fleming, Launcelot, et al, photos by. Portrait of Antarctica. (Illus.). 168p. 1983. 19.95 (ISBN 0-540-01075-8, Pub. by G Philip). Sheridan.
Fleming, Laurence & Gore, Alan. The English Garden. (Illus.). 256p. 1983. pap. 10.95 (ISBN 0-7181-2191-0, Pub by Michael Joseph). Merrimack Pub Cir.
Fleming, Linda L., jt. auth. see Fleming, Robert L.
Fleming, Lizanne, ed. California Water Resources Directory: A Guide to Organizations & Information Resources. LC 82-70810. (California Information Guides Ser.). (Illus., Orig.). 1984. pap. 20.00x (ISBN 0-912102-60-8). Cal Inst Public.
Fleming, Lizanne, ed. see California Institute of Public Affairs.
Fleming, Louise & Boshart-McCleary, Jane. Forkner Dictation & Transcription for College. 384p. 1984. 21.95 (ISBN 0-7715-0750-X); instr's. resource guide 8.94 (ISBN 0-7715-0752-6); Set. cassettes 400.00x (ISBN 0-7715-0751-8). Forkner.
Fleming, M., jt. auth. see Merrill, John.
Fleming, M. C. Construction & the Related Professions. (Illus.). 1980. 155.00 (ISBN 0-08-024034-8). Pergamon.
Fleming, Malcolm & Levie, W. Howard. Instructional Message Design: Principles from the Behavioral Sciences. LC 77-26089. (Illus.). 320p. 1978. 27.95 (ISBN 0-87778-104-4). Educ Tech Pubns.
Fleming, Malcolm L. & Hutton, Deane W., eds. Mental Imagery & Learning. LC 82-20917. 160p. 1983. 26.95 (ISBN 0-87778-185-0). Educ Tech Pubns.
Fleming, Margaret. Language All Around Us. 84p. 6.00 (ISBN 0-8141-2577-8). NCTE.
Fleming, Margaret, ed. Teaching the Epic. LC 74-84481. 120p. 1974. pap. 5.20 (ISBN 0-8141-5205-8). NCTE.
Fleming, Margaret & McGinnis, Jo, eds. Portraits: Biography & Autobiography in the Secondary School. 104p. 1985. pap. 7.20 (ISBN 0-8141-3648-6); pap. 6.00 members. NCTE.
Fleming, Marie. The Anarchist Way to Socialism: Elisee Reclus & Nineteenth Century European Anarchism. 299p. 1979. 26.50x (ISBN 0-8476-6158-X). Rowman.
Fleming, Mary M. Managerial Accounting & Control Techniques for the Non-Accountant. 392p. 1984. 32.50 (ISBN 0-442-22573-3). Van Nos Reinhold.
Fleming, Michael & Manvell, Roger. Images of Madness: The Depiction of Insanity in the Feature Film. LC 82-49022. (Illus.). 368p. 1985. 49.50 (ISBN 0-8386-3112-6). Fairleigh Dickinson.
Fleming, Michael, tr. see Jenne, Michael.
Fleming, N. C., jt. auth. see Kent, Peter.
Fleming, N. C., ed. see Masters, P. M.
Fleming, Nicholas. August: 1939. (Illus.). 242p. 1980. 19.50x (ISBN 0-8419-7200-1). Holmes & Meier.
Fleming, Patricia H. Villagers & Strangers: An English Proletarian Village Over Four Centuries. 256p. 1979. 15.50x (ISBN 0-87073-818-6); pap. 9.95x (ISBN 0-87073-819-4). Schenkman Bks Inc.
Fleming, Paul. Paul Fleming Book Reviews, Vol. 3. 200p. 1979. 10.00 (ISBN 0-915926-37-7). Magic Ltd.
--Principles of Switching, Vol. X. 1979. 15.00 (ISBN 0-686-98066-2). Telecom Lib.
Fleming, Paul, ed. see Gaultier, Camille.
Fleming, Peggy, ed. see Continental Assocation of Funeral & Memorial Societies, Inc.
Fleming, Peter. Bayonets to Lhasa. LC 73-16737. (Illus.). 1974. Repr. of 1961 ed. lib. bdg. 22.50x (ISBN 0-8371-7216-0, FLBL). Greenwood.
--Brazilian Adventure. 1978. Repr. of 1933 ed. lib. bdg. 25.00 (ISBN 0-8482-0822-6). Norwood Edns.
--Brazilian Adventure. 1934. 25.00 (ISBN 0-686-17234-5). Scholars Ref Lib.
--Brazilian Adventure. LC 82-17036. (Library of Travel Classics). 376p. pap. 9.95 (ISBN 0-87477-246-X). J P Tarcher.
--News from Tartary: Library of Travel Classics. LC 82-5872. 1982. pap. 9.50 (ISBN 0-87477-234-6). J P Tarcher.
--Operation Sea Lion: The Projected Invasion of England in 1940: An Account of the German Preparations & the British Countermeasures. LC 76-56777. (Illus.). 1977. Repr. of 1957 ed. lib. bdg. 24.25x (ISBN 0-8371-9429-6, FLOS). Greenwood.
Fleming, Phyllis J. Language of Physics. LC 77-76110. (Physics Ser.). 1978. text ed. 23.95 (ISBN 0-201-02472-1); 5.95 (ISBN 0-201-02474-8). Addison-Wesley.
Fleming, Quentin W. A Guide to Doing Business in the Arabian Peninsula. LC 80-69703. pap. 40.00 (ISBN 0-317-20746-6, 2023900). Bks Demand UMI.
--A Guide to Doing Business on the Arabian Peninsula. 128p. 1981. 29.95 (ISBN 0-8144-5666-9); comb-bound 29.95 (ISBN 0-8144-7012-2). AMACOM.
--Put Earned Value into Your Management Control System. LC 83-3054. (Illus.). 380p. (Orig.). 1983. 29.95x (ISBN 0-942280-04-0); pap. 15.95x (ISBN 0-942280-03-2). Pub Horizons.
Fleming, R. F., tr. see Kratzsch, H.
Fleming, R. H., ed. Minutes of Council Northern Department of Rupert Land, 1821-1831. (Hudson's Bay Record Society Publications Ser.: Vol. 3). pap. 52.00 (ISBN 0-317-17864-4). Kraus Repr.
Fleming, R. W. The Labor Arbitration Process. LC 65-19569. 233p. 1965. pap. 6.50x (ISBN 0-252-74536-1). U of Ill Pr.
Fleming, Ray. Diplomatic Relations. LC 81-82660. 59p. 1981. pap. 4.00x perfect bd. (ISBN 0-916418-34-0). Lotus.
Fleming, Robert E. Charles F. Lummis. LC 81-67304. (Western Writers Ser.: No.50). (Illus.). 52p. (Orig.). 1981. pap. 2.00x (ISBN 0-88430-074-9). Boise St Univ.
Fleming, Robert E. & Fleming, Esther. Sinclair Lewis: A Reference Guide. 1980. lib. bdg. 21.00 (ISBN 0-8161-8094-6, Hall Reference). G K Hall.
Fleming, Robert E., ed. James Weldon Johnson & Arna Wendell Bontemps: A Reference Guide. 1978. lib. bdg. 17.00 (ISBN 0-8161-7932-8, Hall Reference). G K Hall.
Fleming, Robert L. Justice League of America. (A Super Power Which Way Bk.: No. 3). 128p. (Orig.). (gr. 3-6). 1984. pap. 2.50 (ISBN 0-671-47567-3). Archway.
Fleming, Robert L. & Fleming, Linda L. Kathmandu Valley. LC 77-15371. (This Beautiful World Ser.: No. 61). (Illus.). 1978. pap. 5.25 (ISBN 0-87011-328-3). Kodansha.
Fleming, Ronald L. Facade Stories: The Saving & Renovation of Fifty American Commercial Buildings & Shop Fronts. (Illus.). 128p. 1982. pap. 13.50 (ISBN 0-8038-2398-3). Hastings.
Fleming, Ronald L. & Halderman, Lauri A. On Common Ground: Caring for Shared Land from Town Common to Urban Park. 1982. 25.00 (ISBN 0-916782-24-7); pap. text ed. 12.95 (ISBN 0-916782-25-5). Harvard Common Pr.
Fleming, Ronald L. & Von Tsharner, Renata. Place Makers. (Illus.). 128p. (Orig.). 1981. pap. 9.95 (ISBN 0-8038-5894-9). Hastings.
Fleming, S. J. Thermoluminescence Techniques in Archaeology. (Illus.). 1979. 52.00x (ISBN 0-19-859929-3). Oxford U Pr.
Fleming, Sanford. Children & Puritanism: The Place of Children in the Life & Thought of the New England Churches, 1620-1847. LC 70-89178. (American Education: Its Men, Institutions & Ideas Ser). 1969. Repr. of 1933 ed. 15.00 (ISBN 0-405-01416-3). Ayer Co Pubs.
Fleming, Sarah L. Clouds & Sunshine. facsimile ed. LC 70-173606. (Black Heritage Library Collection Ser.). Repr. of 1920 ed. 10.75 (ISBN 0-8369-8916-3). Ayer Co Pubs.
--Hope's Highway. LC 76-144607. Repr. of 1918 ed. 16.00 (ISBN 0-404-00158-0). AMS Pr.
Fleming, Spencer. The Approaching Inevitable Catastrophe of the International Monetary System & What to Do about It. (Illus.). 153p. 1985. 157.45 (ISBN 0-86654-156-X). Inst Econ Finan.
--The Cylinder Theory As an Absolutely Guaranteed Method for the Maximization of Profits in the Stock Market. (Illus.). 89p. 1984. pap. 22.75x (ISBN 0-86654-132-2). Inst Econ Finan.
--Economic & Political Complications in the Rivalry for Supremacy Between the United States & Soviet Russia with Their Repercussions for the Future of Mankind, 2 vols. (Illus.). 287p. 1985. Set. 259.75 (ISBN 0-86722-118-6). Inst Econ Finan.
--The Failure of the American Democracy: Degenerative Forces in Contemporary United States Society. enl ed. LC 72-88744. (Illus.). 65p. 1973. 57.50 (ISBN 0-913314-13-7). Am Classical Coll Pr.
--The Five Power Nuclei Which Control the Life & Destinies of the United States. (Illus.). 200p. 1976. 51.50 (ISBN 0-913314-71-4); lib. bdg. 67.50 (ISBN 0-685-59176-X). Am Classical Coll Pr.
--The Full Discovery of the Theory of Reversals As a Major Speculative Instrument for the Gaining of Maximal Profits in the Stock Market. (Illus.). 158p. 1982. 72.45x (ISBN 0-86654-035-0). Inst Econ Finan.
--How to Become a Master Manipulator in a Complex, Dangerous & Inimical World. (Illus.). 111p. 1984. 90.00x (ISBN 0-86654-124-1). Inst Econ Finan.
--How to Develop the Creative Powers of your Imagination. (Human Development Library Book). (Illus.). 63p. (Orig.). 1983. pap. 26.45 (ISBN 0-89266-388-X). Am Classical Coll Pr.
--How to Stimulate the Forces of Your Imagination for the Development of a Creative Mentality. (A Human Development Library). (Illus.). 107p. 1981. 49.75 (ISBN 0-86650-006-5). Gloucester Art.
--Power Anatomy of the Economic Forces Dominating the Business & the Political World. (Illus.). 137p. 1983. 99.75x (ISBN 0-86722-032-5). Inst Econ Pol.
--The Psychological Foundation of Managerial Action, 2 vols. (Illus.). 259p. 1985. 227.45 (ISBN 0-86654-182-9). Inst Econ Finan.
--The Silent & the Thunderous Wall Street Warning Signals. (The New Stock Market Library). (Illus.). 1978. deluxe ed. 61.75x (ISBN 0-918968-15-1). Inst Econ Finan.
--Stimulative Educational Games for the Mentally Perplexed. (Illus.). 98p. 1984. 37.45 (ISBN 0-89266-461-4); pap. 19.75 (ISBN 0-89266-462-2). Am Classical Coll Pr.
--Swiss Banks - How Safe Are They? Strange Speculative Diversions of Switzerland's Presumably Astute World Bankers. (Illus.). 1977. 55.75 (ISBN 0-89266-021-X). Am Classical Coll Pr.
--The Twenty Most Valuable Books for Speculative Success in the Stock Market with Elucidations Sufficient to Master the Content of Each Single Book. (Illus.). 97p. 1984. pap. 23.75 (ISBN 0-86654-133-0). Inst Econ Finan.
Fleming, Spencer, jt. auth. see Fibonacci, Leonardo.
Fleming, Spencer, ed. The Compelling Process of the Historical Inevitabilities at the End of the 20th Century. exp. ed. (Illus.). 187p. 1982. 67.85x (ISBN 0-86722-002-3). Inst Econ Pol.
Fleming, Stuart. Dating in Archaeology: A Guide to Scientific Techniques. (Illus.). 1977. text ed. 27.50 (ISBN 0-312-18305-4). St Martin.
Fleming, Stuart, et al. The Egyptian Mummy: Secrets & Science. (University Museum Handbook Ser.: No. 1). (Illus.). x, 93p. (Orig.). 1980. pap. 10.00x (ISBN 0-934718-38-5). Univ Mus of U Pa.
Fleming, Susan. Countdown at Thirty-Seven Pinecrest Drive. LC 82-8337. (Illus.). 132p. (gr. 3-5). 9.95 (ISBN 0-664-32694-3). Westminster.
--The Pig at Thirty-Seven Pinecrest Drive. LC 80-22391. (Illus.). 130p. (gr. 3-5). 1981. 9.95 (ISBN 0-664-32676-5). Westminster.
Fleming, Suzie. The Family Allowance Under Attack. 2nd ed. 12p. 1973. pap. 1.25 (ISBN 0-905046-01-3). Falling Wall.
Fleming, Suzie, jt. ed. see Broad, Richard.
Fleming, Suzie, jt. ed. see Edmond, Wendy.
Fleming, Theodore, jt. auth. see Kendrick, Frank.
Fleming, Thomas. Dreams of Glory. 496p. 1983. pap. 3.95 (ISBN 0-446-80655-2). Warner Bks.
--New Jersey. (States & the Nation Ser.). (Illus.). 1977. 14.95 (ISBN 0-393-05639-2). Norton.
--New Jersey: A History. (States & the Nation Ser.). (Illus.). 1984. pap. 7.95 (ISBN 0-393-30180-X). Norton.
--The Officers' Wives. 720p. 1982. pap. 4.95 (ISBN 0-446-32557-0). Warner Bks.
--The Spoils of War. LC 84-18270. 528p. 1985. 18.95 (ISBN 0-399-12968-5, Putnam). Putnam Pub Group.
Fleming, Thomas J. All Good Men. LC 76-6341. (Irish Americans Ser.). 1976. Repr. of 1961 ed. 31.00 (ISBN 0-405-09336-5). Ayer Co Pubs.
--First in Their Hearts: A Biography of George Washington. (Illus.). 136p. 1984. Repr. of 1963 ed. 11.95 (ISBN 0-8027-0809-9). Walker & Co.
Fleming, Thomas P. Communicating Issues in Thanatology. 17.50 (ISBN 0-405-12512-7). Ayer Co Pubs.
Fleming, Thomas P., et al. Communicating Issues in Thanatology. 1976. text ed. 29.50x (ISBN 0-8422-7272-0). Irvington.
Fleming, Tom. Voices Out of the Air: The Royal Christmas Broadcasts 1932-1981. 1981. 19.95 (ISBN 0-434-26680-9, Pub. by W Heinemann Ltd). David & Charles.
Fleming, W. G. Education: Ontario's Preoccupation. LC 78-186280. 1972. 10.00x (ISBN 0-8020-3274-5). U of Toronto Pr.
--Ontario's Educative Society, 7 vols. Incl. Vol. 1. The Expansion of the Educational System. xxv, 367p. 12.50x (ISBN 0-8020-3267-2); Vol. 2. The Administrative Structure. xii, 565p. 17.50x (ISBN 0-8020-3268-0); Vol. 3. Schools, Pupils & Teachers. 622p. 20.00x (ISBN 0-8020-3269-9); Vol. 4. Post-Secondary & Adult Education. 771p. 22.50x (ISBN 0-8020-3270-2); Vol. 5. Supporting Institutions & Services. 545p. 17.50x (ISBN 0-8020-3271-0); Vol. 6. Significant Developments in Local School Systems. 12.50x (ISBN 0-8020-3272-9); Vol. 7. Educational Contributions of Associations. 14.00x (ISBN 0-8020-3273-7). LC 77-166928. 1971-72. vol. 1-7 with Education: Ontario's Preoccupation 90.00x (ISBN 0-8020-3284-2). U of Toronto Pr.
Fleming, W. G. & Sliwinski, Z. J. The Use & Influence of Bentonite in Bored Pile Construction. 93p. 1977. 35.00x (ISBN 0-86017-031-4, Pub. by Ciria Pubns Dept). State Mutual Bk.
Fleming, W. H. Functions of Several Variables. 2nd ed. LC 76-40029. (Undergraduate Texts in Mathematics Ser.). (Illus.). 1977. Repr. 33.00 (ISBN 3-540-90206-6). Springer-Verlag.
--Shakespeare's Plots. 59.95 (ISBN 0-8490-1046-2). Gordon Pr.
Fleming, W. H. & Rishel, R. W. Deterministic & Stochastic Optimal Control. LC 75-28391. (Applications of Mathematics Ser.: Vol. 1). (Illus.). xi, 222p. 1975. 44.00 (ISBN 0-387-90155-8). Springer-Verlag.
Fleming, W. H. & Gorostiza, L. G., eds. Advances in Filtering & Optimal Stochastic Control: Proceedings; Cocoyoc, Mexico 1982. (Lecture Notes in Control & Information Science: Vol. 42). 392p. 1982. pap. 19.50 (ISBN 0-387-11936-1). Springer-Verlag.
Fleming, W. P. Crisp County, Georgia: Historical Sketches, Vol. 1. LC 80-13477. (Illus.). 288p. 1980. Repr. of 1932 ed. 15.00 (ISBN 0-87152-319-1). Reprint.
Fleming, Wallace B. History of Tyre. LC 74-168041. (Columbia University. Oriental Studies: No. 10). Repr. of 1915 ed. 17.50 (ISBN 0-404-50500-7). AMS Pr.
Fleming, Walter & Varberg, Dale. Algebra & Trigonometry. 2nd ed. (Illus.). 576p. 1984. text ed. 29.95 (ISBN 0-13-021535-X). P-H.
--College Algebra. 2nd ed. (Illus.). 496p. 1984. text ed. 28.95 (ISBN 0-13-141630-8). P-H.
--Precalculus Mathematics. (Illus.). 480p. 1984. 29.95 (ISBN 0-13-694851-0). P-H.
Fleming, Walter & Varberg, Dale E. Plane Trigonometry. 1980. text ed. 28.95 (ISBN 0-13-679043-7). P-H.
Fleming, Walter L. Civil War & Reconstruction in Alabama. (Illus.). 16.50 (ISBN 0-8446-1183-2). Peter Smith.
--Civil War & Reconstruction in Alabama. LC 78-2231. (Illus.). 1978. Repr. of 1911 ed. 21.00 (ISBN 0-87152-257-8). Reprint.
--Documentary History of Reconstruction: Political, Military, Social, Religious, Educational & Industrial, 2 vols. in 1. 26.00 (ISBN 0-8446-1184-0). Peter Smith.
--Freedman's Savings Bank: A Chapter in the Economic History of the Negro Race. LC 75-109324. Repr. of 1927 ed. 17.50x (ISBN 0-8371-3590-7, FLF&, Pub. by Negro U Pr). Greenwood.
--Sequel of Appomattox. 1919. 8.50x (ISBN 0-686-83736-3). Elliots Bks.
Fleming, Walter L see Johnson, Allen & Nevins, Allan.

Fleming, William. Arts & Ideas. 6th ed. LC 79-20123. 502p. 1980. pap. text ed. 26.95 (ISBN 0-03-046531-1, HoltC). HR&W.

Fleming, William H. How to Study Shakespeare. LC 78-168042. Repr. 27.50 (ISBN 0-404-02436-X). AMS Pr.

--How to Study Shakespeare, 3 vols. 1979. Repr. of 1898 ed. Set. lib. bdg. 125.00 (ISBN 0-8495-1800-8). Arden Lib.

--Shakespeare's Plots. LC 75-131512. Repr. of 1902 ed. 30.00 (ISBN 0-404-02437-8). AMS Pr.

Fleming, William W., et al, eds. Neuronal & Extraneuronal Events in Autonomic Pharmacology. 280p. 1984. text ed. 57.00 (ISBN 0-88167-001-4). Raven.

Fleming-Mitchell, Leslie. Astrology Terms. LC 77-597. (Orig.). 1977. lib. bdg. 12.90 (ISBN 0-914294-69-5); pap. 2.95 (ISBN 0-914294-70-9). Running Pr.

Fleming-Redish. The U. S. McMaster Glossary of FORTRAN-77. 64p. 1983. pap. text ed. 3.95 (ISBN 0-8403-3052-9). Kendall-Hunt.

Flemings, jt. auth. see Taylor.

Flemings, Merton. Solidification Processing. (Materials Sciences Ser.). (Illus.). 1974. text ed. 50.00 (ISBN 0-07-021283-X). McGraw.

Fleming-Williams, Ian. Constable: Landscape Watercolours & Drawings. (Illus.). 128p. 22.95 (ISBN 0-905005-10-4, Pub by Salem Hse Ltd). Merrimack Pub Cir.

Fleming-Williams, Ian & Parris, Leslie. The Discovery of Constable. LC 84-10795. (Illus.). 262p. 1984. text ed. 39.50x (ISBN 0-8419-0980-6). Holmes & Meier.

Fleming-Williams, Ian, jt. auth. see Parris, Leslie.

Flemmen, Asbjorn & Grosvold, Olav. Teaching Children to Ski. Brady, Michael, tr. from Norwegian. LC 83-80708. (Illus.). 176p. 1983. pap. 8.95 (ISBN 0-88011-165-8). Leisure Pr.

--Teaching Children to Ski. Brady, Michael, tr. from Norwegian. LC 83-80708. 176p. 1983. pap. text ed. 8.95x (ISBN 0-931250-60-9, BFLE0165). Human Kinetics.

Flemming, Albert E., tr. from Ger. Rainer Maria Rilke: Selected Poems. (Illus.). 224p. (Orig.). 1985. pap. 9.95 (ISBN 0-416-01191-8, 9681). Methuen Inc.

Flemming, Bonnie M., et al. Resources for Creative Teaching in Early Childhood Education. (Illus.). 636p. (Orig., Songs & Parodies by Joanne D. Hicks). 1977. pap. text ed. 22.95 (ISBN 0-15-576624-4, HC). HarBraceJ.

Flemming, Cecile W. Detailed Analysis of Achievement in the High School: Comparative Significance of Certain Mental, Physical & Character Traits for Success. LC 79-176778. (Columbia University. Teachers College. Contributions to Education Ser.: No. 196). Repr. of 1925 ed. 22.50 (ISBN 0-404-55196-3). AMS Pr.

Flemming, Donald N. & Mowry, Robert G. Sobre Heroes y Rumbos: Modelo Para Explicar. LC 81-40620. 240p. (Orig.). 1982. lib. bdg. 24.00 (ISBN 0-8191-2027-8); pap. text ed. 12.50 (ISBN 0-8191-2028-6). U Pr of Amer.

Flemming, Hanns T., ed. Bruno Bruni. (Illus.). 159p. 1978. 25.00 (ISBN 0-936598-00-X). J Szoke Graphics.

Flemming, J. Arnold. Scottish Pottery. (Illus.). 1976. Repr. 24.00x (ISBN 0-85409-778-3). Charles River Bks.

Flemming, John. Inflation. (Illus.). 1976. pap. 7.95x (ISBN 0-19-877086-3). Oxford U Pr.

Flemming, K., jt. ed. see Di Luzio, N. R.

Flemming, Laraine. Reading for Results. 2d ed. 468p. 1983. pap. text ed. 15.95 (ISBN 0-395-32605-2); instr's. manual 2.00 (ISBN 0-395-32606-0). HM.

Flemming, Leslie A. Another Lonely Voice: The Urdu Short Stories of Saadat Hasan Manto. (Monograph Ser.: No. 18). 144p. 1983. pap. text ed. 12.25 (ISBN 0-8191-3130-X, Co-pub. by Ctr S SE Asia). U Pr of Amer.

Flemming, Louis A. Putnam's Word Book: A Practical Aid in Expressing Ideas Through the Use of an Exact & Varied Vocabulary. 709p. 1983. Repr. of 1913 ed. text ed. 40.00 (ISBN 0-89984-217-8). Century Bookbindery.

Flemming, Williams, ed. see Fejer, Paul H.

Flemmons, Jerry. Plowboys, Cowboys & Slanted Pigs: A Collection. LC 84-2421. (Illus.). 230p. 1984. 15.95 (ISBN 0-912646-90-X); pap. 8.95 (ISBN 0-912646-95-0). Tex Christian.

Flemyng, Francis P. Southern Africa: A Geography & Natural History of the Country, Colonies & Inhabitants from the Cape of Good Hope to Angola. LC 73-76479. (Illus.). Repr. of 1856 ed. 24.00x (ISBN 0-8371-1134-X, FLS&, Pub. by Negro U Pr). Greenwood.

Flender, Harold. Rescue in Denmark. LC 80-81716. (Illus.). 280p. 1980. pap. 5.95 (ISBN 0-8052-5016-6, Pub. by Holocaust Library). Schocken.

--Rescue in Denmark. (Illus.). 280p. pap. 5.95 (ISBN 0-686-95083-6). ADL.

--Rescue in Denmark. LC 80-81716. (Illus.). 281p. (Orig.). 1963. pap. 8.95 (ISBN 0-89604-018-6). Holocaust Pubns.

--To Be... 256p. 1972. pap. 0.95 (ISBN 0-532-95199-9). Woodhill.

Flenley, D. C., ed. Recent Advances in Respiratory Medicine, No. 2. (Recent Advances Ser.). (Illus.). 272p. 1981. text ed. 42.50 (ISBN 0-443-02012-4). Churchill.

Flenley, David C. Respiratory Diseases. (Illus.). 276p. (Orig.). 1981. pap. text ed. 17.95x (ISBN 0-7216-0724-1, Bailliere-Tindall). Saunders.

Flenley, J., jt. ed. see Neale, J.

Flenley, Ralph. Makers of Nineteenth Century Europe. LC 77-108637. (Essay Index Reprint Ser.). 1927. 16.00 (ISBN 0-8369-1571-2). Ayer Co Pubs.

Flercher, Francis. The Murder Sonata. 1980. pap. 1.95 (ISBN 0-8439-0847-5, Pub. by Nordon Pubns). Dorchester Pub Co.

Flere, W. A. Handy Guide to Stowage. 1970. 11.50 (ISBN 0-85288-005-7). Heinman.

Flerko, B., et al, eds. Reproduction & Development: Proceedings of the 28th International Congress of Physiological Sciences, Budapest, 1980. LC 80-41877. (Advances in Physiological Sciences: Vol. 15). (Illus.). 200p. 1981. 28.00 (ISBN 0-08-027336-X). Pergamon.

Fleron, Frederic J., Jr., jt. ed. see Hoffmann, Erik P.

Fles, Berthold, tr. see Krenek, Ernst.

Flesch, Carl. The Art of Violin Playing, Bk. 1. rev. ed. Martens, Frederick H., tr. (Illus.). 188p. 1924. pap. 19.95 (ISBN 0-8258-0135-4, 01317). Fischer Inc NY.

--The Art of Violin Playing: Artistic Realization & Instruction, Book 2. Martens, Frederick H., tr. 237p. 1930. pap. 19.95 (ISBN 0-8258-0136-2, 0 2046). Fischer Inc NY.

--The Memoirs of Carl Flesch. (Music Reprint Ser.). 1979. Repr. of 1957 ed. lib. bdg. 39.50 (ISBN 0-306-77574-3). Da Capo.

--Scale System. 120p. (Ger. & Fr.). 1926. pap. 11.95 (ISBN 0-8258-0178-8, 01509). Fischer Inc NY.

--Scale System. 112p. 1942. pap. 11.95 (ISBN 0-8258-0231-8, 02921). Fischer Inc NY.

--Violin Fingering: It's Theory & Practice. (Music Reprint Ser.). Repr. of 1960 ed. lib. bdg. 39.50 (ISBN 0-306-79573-6). Da Capo.

Flesch, Ed. The Sour Prince. 24p. 1972. pap. 1.75 (ISBN 0-88680-180-X); 20.00 (ISBN 0-317-03629-7). I E Clark.

--Sour Prince. 20p. (Piano-Vocal Score by Ed Flesch). 1972. pap. 4.50 (ISBN 0-88680-181-8). I E Clark.

Flesch, Janos. Planning in Chess. (Illus.). 96p. 1983. pap. 12.95 (ISBN 0-7134-1597-5, Pub. by Batsford England). David & Charles.

Flesch, Rudolf. The ABC of Style: A Guide to Plain English. LC 64-25139. 1980. pap. 2.95i (ISBN 0-06-080083-6, P 83, PL). Har-Row.

--The Art of Clear Thinking. (Illus.). 212p. 1973. pap. 4.33i (ISBN 0-06-463369-1, EH 369, EH). B&N NY.

--The Art of Clear Thinking. 1951. 12.45i (ISBN 0-06-001440-7, HarpT). Har-Row.

--Art of Plain Talk. 224p. 1962. pap. 3.95 (ISBN 0-02-046380-4, Collier). Macmillan.

--Art of Readable Writing. 1962. pap. 3.95 (ISBN 0-02-046460-6, Collier). Macmillan.

--The Art of Readable Writing, 25th Anniversary Edition. rev. & enl. ed. LC 73-14260. (Illus.). 288p. (YA) 1974. 13.41i (ISBN 0-06-011293-X, HarpT). Har-Row.

--How to Write Plain English: A Book for Lawyers & Consumers. LC 76-26225. (Illus.). 144p. 1981. pap. 4.09i (ISBN 0-06-463536-8, EH 536, EH). B&N NY.

--How to Write, Speak & Think More Effectively. 1964. pap. 3.95 (ISBN 0-451-13357-9, AE2168, Sig). NAL.

--Johnny Still Can't Read: A New Look at the Scandal of Our Schools. LC 80-8686. 224p. 1983. pap. 4.76i (ISBN 0-06-091031-3, CN 1031, CN). Har-Row.

--Lite English: Popular Words That Are OK to Use No Matter What William Safire, John Simon, Edwin Newman & Other Purists Say! 1983. 10.95 (ISBN 0-517-55139-X). Crown.

--Look It up: A Deskbook of American Spelling & Style. LC 75-23880. 1977. 13.41i (ISBN 0-06-011292-1, HarpT). Har-Row.

--Rudolf Flesch on Business Communications: How to Say What You Mean in Plain English. pap. 4.76i (ISBN 0-06-463393-4, EH 393, EH). B&N NY.

--Say What You Mean. LC 72-79664. 256p. (YA) 1972. 13.41i (ISBN 0-06-011291-3, HarpT). Har-Row.

--Why Johnny Can't Read & What You Can Do About It. 1966. pap. 2.84i (ISBN 0-06-080088-7, P88, PL). Har-Row.

--Why Johnny Still Can't Read: A New Look at the Scandal of Our Schools. LC 80-8686. 192p. 1981. 12.45i (ISBN 0-06-014842-X, HarpT). Har-Row.

Flesch, Rudolf & Lass, A. H. A New Guide to Better Writing. 1982. pap. 3.50 (ISBN 0-446-31304-1). Warner Bks.

Flesch, Rudolf F. Marks of Readable Style: A Study in Adult Education. LC 72-176779. (Columbia University. Teachers College. Contributions to Education: No. 897). Repr. of 1943 ed. 22.50 (ISBN 0-404-55897-6). AMS Pr.

Flesch, U., jt. auth. see Stuttgen, G.

Flesch, Y. Julian Lennon. (Illus.). 80p. (Orig.). (gr. 6 up). 1985. lib. bdg. 12.90 (ISBN 0-89471-397-3); pap. 4.95 (ISBN 0-89471-396-5). Running Pr.

Flesch, Yolande. Free Things for Homeowners. 96p. (Orig.). 1981. pap. 4.95 (ISBN 0-346-12533-2). Cornerstone.

Flesche, Francis La see Flectcher, Alice C. & La Flesche, Francis.

Flesche, Francis La see Fletcher, Alice C. & La Flesche, Francis.

Flesche, Francis La see La Flesche, Francis.

Flesher, Dale L. Accounting for Advertising Assets. 1979. pap. 4.50 (ISBN 0-938004-01-8). U MS Bus Econ.

Flesher, Dale L. & Flesher, Tonya K. Accounting for the Middle Manager. 462p. 1980. 16.95 (ISBN 0-442-23875-4). Van Nos Reinhold.

Flesher, Dale L. & Siewert, Stewart. Independent Auditor's Guide to Operational Auditing. LC 81-19726. (Modern Accounting Perspectives & Practice). 265p. 1982. 45.00x (ISBN 0-471-09368-8, Pub. by Ronald Pr). Wiley.

Flesher, Dale L., ed. Tax Tactics for Small Business: Pay Less Taxes Legally. 100p. (Orig.). 1980. pap. 4.00 (ISBN 0-938004-06-9). U MS Bus Econ.

Flesher, Irene. Pressed Flower Art: Greeting Cards, Pictures & Other Decorative Projects. LC 84-16632. (Illus.). 1984. pap. 14.95 (ISBN 0-8329-0305-1). New Century.

Flesher, Stanley M. Developing Baseball Skills Indoors in the Off-Season: A Coach's Guide. 1983. 7.95 (ISBN 0-533-05715-9). Vantage.

Flesher, Tonya K., jt. auth. see Flesher, Dale L.

Flesher, Vivienne, jt. auth. see Crumpacker, Emily.

Fleshin, Senya, jt. auth. see Steimer, Mollie.

Fleshman, Bob & Fryrear, Jerry L. The Arts in Therapy. LC 80-20334. 240p. 1981. text ed. 21.95x (ISBN 0-88229-520-9); pap. text ed. 11.95x (ISBN 0-88229-762-7). Nelson-Hall.

Fleshman, Robert, jt. auth. see Fryrear, Jerry L.

Fleshman, Ruth P., jt. auth. see Archer, Sarah E.

Flesor, C. N., ed. How to Read a Financial Report. rev. ed. (Financial Planning & Accounting Ser.). 140p. 1985. pap. 16.00 (ISBN 0-932905-02-1). Penton IPC.

Flesseman-Van Leer, E. A Faith for Today. Steely, John E., tr. LC 79-56514. (Special Studies Ser.: No. 7). 1980. pap. 6.95 (ISBN 0-932180-06-X). NABPR.

Fletcher. Iris Murdoch. 1985. lib. bdg. 65.00 (ISBN 0-8240-8910-3). Garland Pub.

--Quasi-Uniform Spaces. (Lecture Notes in Pure & Applied Mathematics Ser.: Vol. 77). 232p. 1982. 35.00 (ISBN 0-8247-1839-9). Dekker.

Fletcher, jt. auth. see Beaumont.

Fletcher, A. & Clark, G. Management & Mathematics. (Illus.). 1972. 29.95x (ISBN 0-8464-0589-X). Beekman Pubs.

Fletcher, A. D. & Jugenheimer, D. W. Problems & Practices in Advertising Research: Readings & Workbook. 215p. 1982. pap. 19.95 (ISBN 0-471-84159-5). Wiley.

Fletcher, A. F. MG: Past & Present. 2nd ed. (Illus.). 280p. 1986. 17.95 (ISBN 0-85429-425-2, Pub. by G T Foulis Ltd). Interbook.

Fletcher, A. J. The Outbreak of the English Civil War. 384p. 1981. 60.00x (ISBN 0-7131-6320-8, Pub. by E Arnold England). State Mutual Bk.

Fletcher, Aaron. Blood Money. (Bounty Hunter Ser.: No. 2). 176p. 1981. pap. 1.95 (ISBN 0-8439-1018-6, Leisure Bks). Dorchester Pub Co.

--Bloody Sunday. 192p. 1981. pap. 1.95 (ISBN 0-8439-1014-3, Leisure Bks). Dorchester Pub Co.

--Bounty Hunter. 160p. 1981. pap. 1.75 (ISBN 0-8439-1006-2, Leisure Bks). Dorchester Pub Co.

--Capricorn People. 512p. 1983. pap. 3.95 (ISBN 0-8439-2012-2, Leisure Bks). Dorchester Pub Co.

--The Card Game. 1980. pap. 1.75 (ISBN 0-505-51456-7, Pub. by Tower Bks). Dorchester Pub Co.

--The Castaway. (The New Zealanders Ser.: No. 1). (Orig.). 1984. pap. 3.95 (ISBN 0-440-11125-0). Dell.

--Cowboy. 224p. 1982. pap. 2.25 (ISBN 0-8439-1107-7, Leisure Bks). Dorchester Pub Co.

--Cowboy. (Orig.). 1977. pap. 1.50 (ISBN 0-505-51152-5, BT51152, Pub. by Tower Bks). Dorchester Pub Co.

--Dangerous Desire. 1978. pap. 2.25 (ISBN 0-532-22135-4). Woodhill.

--The Flame of Chandrapore. 1979. pap. 2.25 (ISBN 0-505-51342-0, Pub. by Tower Bks). Dorchester Pub Co.

--Flame of Chandrapore. 352p. 1983. pap. 3.50 (ISBN 0-8439-2033-5, Leisure Bks). Dorchester Pub Co.

--The Founders. (The New Zealanders Ser.: No. 2). 496p. (Orig.). 1984. pap. 3.95 (ISBN 0-440-12691-6). Dell.

--Icepick. 208p. 1982. pap. 2.25 (ISBN 0-8439-1026-7, Leisure Bks). Dorchester Pub Co.

--The Labyrinth. 1977. pap. 1.95 (ISBN 0-505-51121-5, BT51121, Pub. by Tower Bks). Dorchester Pub Co.

--Love's Gentle Agony. 1978. pap. 2.25 (ISBN 0-440-04972-5). Dell.

--Love's Gentle Agony. 496p. 1984. pap. 3.75 (ISBN 0-8439-2084-X). Dorchester Pub Co.

--The Microwave Factor. 304p. pap. 3.25 (ISBN 0-8439-2010-6, Leisure Bks). Dorchester Pub Co.

--Outback. 448p. (Orig.). 1982. pap. 3.25 (ISBN 0-8439-1028-3, Leisure Bks). Dorchester Pub Co.

--Outback. 1978. pap. 2.25 (ISBN 0-8439-0533-6, Leisure Bks). Dorchester Pub Co.

--Outback. 448p. 1983. pap. 3.50 (ISBN 0-8439-2013-0, Leisure Bks). Dorchester Pub Co.

--Project Jael. 480p. (Orig.). 1985. pap. 3.95 (ISBN 0-8439-2236-2, Leisure Bks). Dorchester Pub Co.

--The Reckoning. 192p. 1981. pap. 1.95 (ISBN 0-8439-0963-3, Leisure Bks). Dorchester Pub Co.

--Treasure of the Lost City. 1976. pap. 1.25 (ISBN 0-685-73461-7, LB391, Leisure Bks). Dorchester Pub Co.

Fletcher Aircraft Company Staff. Standard Aircraft Workers' Manual. spiral bdg. 7.50x (ISBN 0-911721-29-0, Pub. by Fletcher). Aviation.

Fletcher, Alan, ed. American Academy of Advertising Annual Meeting, 24th: Proceedings. 1982. pap. 15.00 (ISBN 0-931030-05-6). Am Acad Advert.

Fletcher, Alan & Phillips, Lorraine, eds. Australian Buying Reference. 5th ed. 650p. 1984. 180.00x (ISBN 0-317-02375-6). Gale.

--Business Who's Who of Australia 1983. 17th ed. 769p. 1983. 245.00x (ISBN 0-317-02378-0). Gale.

Fletcher, Alan D. & Bowers, Thomas A. Fundamentals of Advertising Research. 2nd ed. LC 82-24217. (Advertising & Journalism Ser.). 334p. 1983. 32.50 (ISBN 0-471-84158-7, Pub. by Grid); text ed. 26.95 (ISBN 0-88244-260-0). Wiley.

Fletcher, Alan D. & Jugenheimer, Donald W. Problems & Practices in Advertising Research: Readings & Workbook. (Advertising & Journalism Ser.). 210p. 1982. pap. text ed. 16.95 (ISBN 0-88244-237-6, Pub. by Grid). Wiley.

Fletcher, Alice C. Home Life Among the Indians. (Shorey Indian Ser.). 16p. pap. 2.95 (ISBN 0-8466-4068-6, I68). Shorey.

--Indian Games & Dances with Native Songs. LC 75-136369. Repr. of 1915 ed. 14.50 (ISBN 0-404-07229-1). AMS Pr.

--Indian Story & Song from North America. LC 76-136396. Repr. of 1900 ed. 9.50 (ISBN 0-404-07880-X). AMS Pr.

--Indian Story & Song from North America. LC 1432. (American Studies). 1970. Repr. of 1900 ed. 16.00 (ISBN 0-384-15990-7). Johnson Repr.

Fletcher, Alice C. & La Flesche, Francis. Omaha Tribe, 2 vols. Incl. Vol. 1. 312p (ISBN 0-8032-5756-2, BB 549, Bison); Vol. 2. viii, 347p (ISBN 0-8032-5757-0, BB 550, Bison). LC 72-175503. (Illus.). 1972. pap. 7.95 ea. U of Nebr Pr.

Fletcher, Alice C. & LaFlesche, Francis. Study of Omaha Indian Music with a Report of the Structural Peculiarities of the Music by J. C. Fillmore. (HU PMP). 1893. 18.00 (ISBN 0-527-01187-8). Kraus Repr.

Fletcher, Angus. Allegory: The Theory of a Symbolic Mode. LC 64-11415. (Illus.). 464p. 1982. 9.95x (ISBN 0-8014-9238-6). Cornell U Pr.

--The Prophetic Moment: An Essay on Spenser. LC 73-130587. 1971. 20.00x (ISBN 0-226-25332-5). U of Chicago Pr.

Fletcher, Angus, ed. The Literature of Fact: Selected Papers from the English Institute. LC 76-25582. (Essays of the English Institute). 172p. 1976. 20.00x (ISBN 0-231-04144-6). Columbia U Pr.

Fletcher, Ann. Belgium. (World Education Ser.). (Illus.). 144p. (Orig.). 1985. pap. write for info. (ISBN 0-910054-82-7). Am Assn Coll Registrars.

Fletcher, Anne. Guidance & Counselling in Secondary Schools in Scotland. 120p. 1980. 18.00 (ISBN 0-08-025722-4); pap. 9.00 (ISBN 0-08-025721-6). Pergamon.

Fletcher, Anne B., jt. auth. see Henig, Robin M.

Fletcher, Anne M., jt. auth. see Family Circle Food Staff.

Fletcher, Anthony. Elizabethan Village. Reeves, Marjorie, ed. (Then & There Ser.). (Illus.). 92p. (YA) (gr. 7-12). 1972. pap. text ed. 3.75 (ISBN 0-582-20409-7). Longman.

--The Outbreak of the English Civil War. 384p. 1981. 47.50x (ISBN 0-8147-2569-4). NYU Pr.

--Tudor Rebellions. 2nd rev. ed. (Seminar Studies in History). (Illus.). 176p. 1973. pap. text ed. 6.25x (ISBN 0-582-35255-X). Longman.

Fletcher, Anthony & Stevenson, John, eds. Order & Disorder in Early Modern England. 300p. Date not set. price not set. (ISBN 0-521-25294-6). Cambridge U Pr.

Fletcher, Arnold. Afghanistan: Highway of Conquest. LC 81-20233. (Illus.). vii, 325p. 1982. Repr. of 1965 ed. lib. bdg. 35.00x (ISBN 0-313-23349-7, FLAF). Greenwood.

--Oil Painting Step by Step. (Illus.). 1971. 12.95 (ISBN 0-571-06411-6). Transatlantic.

Fletcher, Arthur. The Silent Sellout. LC 73-83161. 121p. 1973. 7.95 (ISBN 0-89388-100-7). Okpaku Communications.

Fletcher, B. Universities in the Modern World. 1968. pap. 7.75 (ISBN 0-08-012762-2). Pergamon.

Fletcher, Banister. History of Architecture. 18th ed. Palmes, J. C., ed. LC 74-25545. (Illus.). 1975. text ed. 70.00 (ISBN 0-684-14207-4, ScribR). Scribner.

Fletcher, Barbara J., et al. Exercise for Heart & Health. Hull, Nancy R., ed. (Illus.). 76p. (Orig.). 1985. pap. text ed. 5.00 (ISBN 0-939838-19-2). Pritchett & Hull.

Fletcher, J. G. John Smith - Also Pocahontas. LC 28-25141. Repr. of 1928 ed. 29.00 (ISBN 0-527-29700-3). Kraus Repr.
Fletcher, J. H., et al, eds. Nomenclature of Organic Compounds: Principles & Practice. LC 73-92675. (Advances in Chemistry Ser.: No. 126). 337p. 1972. 49.95 (ISBN 0-8412-0191-9); pap. 9.00 (ISBN 0-8412-0234-6). Am Chemical.
Fletcher, J. M., jt. auth. see Ott, H.
Fletcher, J. R., jt. auth. see Charlesworth, A. S.
Fletcher, J. S. The Middle Temple Murder. 1980. Repr. of 1910 ed. 4.50 (ISBN 0-486-23910-1). Dover.
--Reformation in Northern England. LC 71-118469. 1971. Repr. of 1925 ed. 21.50x (ISBN 0-8046-1218-8, Pub. by Kennikat). Assoc Faculty Pr.
Fletcher, J. T. Diseases of Greenhouse Plants. (Illus.). 1984. text ed. 39.95 (ISBN 0-582-44263-X). Longman.
Fletcher, James, ed. Handbook of Radio & T V Broadcasting. 352p. 1981. 32.50 (ISBN 0-442-22417-6). Van Nos Reinhold.
Fletcher, James C., jt. auth. see Kidder, Daniel P.
Fletcher, James E., jt. ed. see Dominick, Joseph R.
Fletcher, Janet K., jt. auth. see Donnelly, Hallie.
Fletcher, Jefferson B. Dante. 1916. 25.00 (ISBN 0-8274-2130-3). R West.
--Dante. 1965. pap. 3.95x (ISBN 0-268-00071-9). U of Notre Dame Pr.
--Religion of Beauty in Woman: Essays on Platonic Love in Poetry & Society. LC 68-925. (Studies in Poetry, No. 38). 1969. Repr. of 1911 ed. lib. bdg. 49.95x (ISBN 0-8383-0550-4). Haskell.
--Symbolism of the Divine Comedy. LC 71-168043. Repr. of 1921 ed. 19.00 (ISBN 0-404-02438-6). AMS Pr.
Fletcher, Jerry, ed. Rural Education. LC 82-80482. (Dialogue Bks.). 400p. (Orig.). 1982. pap. 15.75 (ISBN 0-89881-009-4). Intl Dialogue Pr.
Fletcher, Jerry L., ed. Human Growth Games: Explorations & Research Prospects. LC 77-94067. (Sage Contemporary Social Science Issues Ser.: 41). pap. 39.00 (ISBN 0-317-08219-1, 2021899). Bks Demand UMI.
Fletcher, Jesse C. Bill Wallace of China. LC 63-17522. (Illus.). (gr. 7-10). 1963. pap. 2.25 (ISBN 0-8054-1113-5). Broadman.
--Practical Discipleship. LC 79-54763. 1980. 6.95 (ISBN 0-8054-5595-7). Broadman.
Fletcher, John. Alain Robbe-Grillet. LC 83-13077. (Contemporary Writers Ser.). 92p. 1983. pap. 4.75 (ISBN 0-416-34420-8, NO.3749). Methuen Inc.
--The Bloody Brother: A Tragedy. LC 79-25641. (English Experience Ser.: No. 179). 82p. 1969. Repr. of 1639 ed. 11.50 (ISBN 90-221-0179-7). Walter J Johnson.
--Bonduca. LC 82-45697. (Malone Society Reprint Ser.: No. 94). Repr. of 1961 ed. 40.00 (ISBN 0-404-63094-4). AMS Pr.
--Cars & Trucks. (Gateway Facts Bks.). (Illus.). 96p. (gr. 4-6). PLB 8.90 (ISBN 0-531-09214-3). Watts.
--Claude Simon: And Fiction Now. 240p. 1978. pap. 7.95 (ISBN 0-7145-1015-7, Dist by Scribner). M Boyars.
--Demetrius & Enanthe, or the Humorous Lieutenant. LC 82-45695. (Malone Society Reprint Ser.: No. 92). Repr. of 1950 ed. 40.00 (ISBN 0-404-63092-8). AMS Pr.
--The Elder Brother, a Comedie. LC 77-25437. (English Experience Ser.: No. 247). 72p. 1970. Repr. of 1637 ed. 9.50 (ISBN 90-221-0247-5). Walter J Johnson.
--Information Sources in Economics. (Butterworths Guide to Information Sources Ser.). 382p. 1984. 59.95 (ISBN 0-408-11471-1). Butterworth.
--Interview at Work. 1973. 19.95x (ISBN 0-7156-0727-8). Intl Ideas.
--Novel & Reader. LC 79-56842. 196p. 1983. 16.00 (ISBN 0-7145-2620-7, Dist. by Scribner); pap. 8.95 (ISBN 0-7145-2621-5). M Boyars.
--The Painted Churches of Romania: A Vistor's Impressions. (Illus.). 52p. 1971. 22.95 (ISBN 0-88010-062-1, Pub. by Steinerbooks). Anthroposophic.
--Portrait of a Preacher. 8.95 (ISBN 0-686-12902-4). Schmul Pub Co.
--Studies on Slavery, in Easy Lessons. facs. ed. LC 70-83962. (Black Heritage Library Collection Ser). 1851. 27.50 (ISBN 0-8369-8572-9). Ayer Co Pubs.
--The Two Noble Kinsmen. 71. Bd. with Quarto of 1634, Pt. 1. rev. ed. (New Shakespeare Soc., London, Ser. 2). pap. 59.00 (ISBN 0-317-16175-X). Kraus Repr.
--The Wild-Goose Chase: A Modern Critical Edition with Commentary and Notes Based on the 1652 Folio. Lister, Rota H. & Orgel, Stephen, eds. LC 79-54349. (Renaissance Drama Second Ser.). 200p. 1980. lib. bdg. 26.00 (ISBN 0-8240-4466-5). Garland Pub.
Fletcher, John & Massinger, Philip. The Tragedy of Sir John Van Olden Barnavelt. LC 82-45736. (Malone Society Reprint Ser.: No. 140). Repr. of 1979 ed. 40.00 (ISBN 0-404-63141-X). AMS Pr.
Fletcher, John & Miller, David R. A Wife for a Month. LC 83-115198. (Costerus New Ser.: No. 36). 286p. 1983. pap. text ed. 28.25x (ISBN 90-6203-894-8, Pub. by Rodopi Holland). Humanities.
Fletcher, John & Shakespeare, William. Two Noble Kinsmen. LC 72-133736. (Tudor Facsimile Texts. Old English Plays: No. 141). Repr. of 1910 ed. 49.50 (ISBN 0-404-53441-4). AMS Pr.
--The Two Noble Kinsmen. Proudfoot, G. R., ed. LC 74-80902. (Regents Renaissance Drama Ser). xxvi, 141p. 1970. 14.50x (ISBN 0-8032-0286-5); pap. 3.95x (ISBN 0-8032-5287-0, BB 234, Bison). U of Nebr Pr.
Fletcher, John & Spurling, John. Beckett the Playwright. rev. ed. 192p. pap. 6.95 (ISBN 0-8090-0551-4). Hill & Wang.
Fletcher, John see Bald, Robert C.
Fletcher, John, jt. auth. see Beaumont, Francis.
Fletcher, John, ed. Reader Services in Polytechnic Libraries. 200p. 1985. text ed. write for info. (ISBN 0-566-03528-6). Gower Pub Co.
Fletcher, John, ed. see Schindler, Maria.
Fletcher, John, tr. see Simon, Claude.
Fletcher, John, et al. A Student's Guide to the Plays of Samuel Beckett. 288p. 1985. 19.95 (ISBN 0-571-13418-1); pap. 8.95 (ISBN 0-571-13419-X). Faber & Faber.
Fletcher, John C. Coping with Genetic Disorders: A Guide for Counselling. LC 81-48207. 192p. 1982. 14.37i (ISBN 0-06-062665-8, HarpR). Har-Row.
Fletcher, John G. Goblins & Pagodas. LC 78-64023. (Des Imagistes: Literature of the Imagist Movement). 128p. Repr. of 1916 ed. 18.50 (ISBN 0-404-17096-X). AMS Pr.
--Irradiations: Sand & Spray. LC 78-64024. (Des Imagistes: Literature of the Imagist Movement). Repr. of 1915 ed. 18.00 (ISBN 0-404-17097-8). AMS Pr.
--Life Is My Song: The Autobiography of John Gould Fletcher. LC 78-64024. (Des Imagistes: Literature of the Imagist Movement). 416p. Repr. of 1937 ed. 38.50 (ISBN 0-404-17098-6). AMS Pr.
--Some Contemporary American Poets. 1978. Repr. of 1920 ed. lib. bdg. 10.00 (ISBN 0-8495-1620-X). Arden Lib.
--Some Contemporary American Poets. LC 75-1170. 1973. lib. bdg. 8.50 (ISBN 0-8414-4223-1). Folcroft.
Fletcher, John M. The Problem of Stuttering. 1928. 25.00 (ISBN 0-8274-3206-2). R West.
Fletcher, Joseph. Humanhood: Essays in Biomedical Ethics. LC 79-1756. 204p. 1979. 17.95 (ISBN 0-87975-112-6); pap. 10.95 (ISBN 0-87975-123-1). Prometheus Bks.
--Moral Responsibility: Situation Ethics at Work. LC 67-14515. 256p. (Orig.). 1967. pap. 4.95 (ISBN 0-664-24770-9). Westminster.
--Morals & Medicine: The Moral Problems of the Patient's Right To Know the Truth. LC 54-9019. 1979. 27.00 (ISBN 0-691-07234-5); pap. 8.95 (ISBN 0-691-02004-3). Princeton U Pr.
--The Poems of Joseph Fletcher. LC 73-21063. (Fuller Worthies' Library). 272p. 1983. Repr. of 1869 ed. 50.00 (ISBN 0-404-11482-2). AMS Pr.
--Situation Ethics: The New Morality. LC 66-11917. 176p. 1966. pap. 6.95 (ISBN 0-664-24691-5). Westminster.
Fletcher, Joseph & Montgomery, John W. Situation Ethics: True or False. 90p. (Orig.). 1972. pap. 2.95 (ISBN 0-87123-525-0, 200525). Bethany Hse.
Fletcher, Joseph F. William Temple, Twentieth-Century Christian. LC 63-12587. 1963. text ed. 10.00x (ISBN 0-8401-0741-2). A R Allenson.
Fletcher, Joseph S. At the Blue Bell Inn. LC 79-122697. (Short Story Index Reprint Ser). 1898. 14.00 (ISBN 0-8369-3530-6). Ayer Co Pubs.
--Behind the Monocle, & Other Stories. LC 72-122698. (Short Story Index Reprint Ser). 1930. 17.00 (ISBN 0-8369-3531-4). Ayer Co Pubs.
--Massingham Butterfly, & Other Stories. LC 76-122699. (Short Story Index Reprint Ser). 1926. 17.00 (ISBN 0-8369-3532-2). Ayer Co Pubs.
--Secret of the Barbican, & Other Stories. LC 79-121543. (Short Story Index Reprint Ser). 1925. 19.00 (ISBN 0-8369-3499-7). Ayer Co Pubs.
Fletcher, Julia C. Kismet. facsimile ed. LC 72-164560. (American Fiction Reprint Ser). Repr. of 1877 ed. 24.50 (ISBN 0-8369-7036-5). Ayer Co Pubs.
Fletcher, K. Fun, Fitness & Fundamentals of Soccer. (Illus.). Date not set. pap. 8.95 (ISBN 0-88826-093-8). Superior Pub.
Fletcher, Kenneth, et al. Extend: Youth Reaching Youth. LC 74-77684. 112p. (Orig.). 1974. pap. 6.50 (ISBN 0-8066-1435-8, 10-2150). Augsburg.
Fletcher, L. S. & Shoup, T. E. Introduction to Engineering Including FORTRAN Programming. (Illus.). 1978. pap. 26.95 ref. ed. (ISBN 0-13-501858-7). P-H.
Fletcher, L. S., ed. Aerodynamic Heating & Thermal Protection Systems. LC 78-5187. (Illus.). 424p. 1978. 45.00 (ISBN 0-915928-23-X, PAAS59); 25.00 (ISBN 0-317-32126-9). AIAA.
--ASME Conference on Mechanical Engineering Education-1980: Proceedings. 181p. 1982. 15.00 (I00145). ASME.
Fletcher, Laadan, ed. Pioneers of Education in Western Australia. (Illus.). 360p. 1983. 52.50x (ISBN 0-85564-220-3, Pub. by U of W Austral Pr); pap. 29.50x (ISBN 0-85564-222-X). Intl Spec Bk.
Fletcher, Lehman B., et al. Guatemala's Economic Development: The Role of Agriculture. facsimile ed. LC 74-114800. (Orig.). 1970. pap. 8.20x (ISBN 0-8138-2240-8). Iowa St U Pr.
Fletcher, Leon. How to Design & Deliver a Speech. 2nd ed. LC 78-9851. 1979. pap. text ed. 13.95 scp (ISBN 0-06-042091-X, HarpC). Har-Row.
--How to Design & Deliver a Speech. 3rd ed. 403p. 1985. scp 13.50 (ISBN 0-06-042089-8, HarpC). Har-Row.
--How to Speak Like a Pro. 272p. (Orig.). 1983. pap. 2.95 (ISBN 0-345-30171-4). Ballantine.
Fletcher, Leonard, et al. Construction Contract Dictionary. LC 81-16935. 128p. 1981. 25.00x (ISBN 0-902132-65-2, 6632, Pub. by E & Fn. Spon England). Methuen Inc.
Fletcher, Leslie. Florida's Fantastic Fauna & Flora. LC 77-78032. 1977. pap. 3.50 (ISBN 0-911980-09-1). Beau Lac.
Fletcher, Lucille. Eighty Dollars to Stamford. (Crime Ser). 1978. pap. 2.95 (ISBN 0-14-004788-3). Penguin.
Fletcher, Madilyn M. & Floodgate, George D., eds. Bacteria in Their Natural Environments. (Society for General Microbiology Special Publications: Vol. 16). Date not set. price not set (ISBN 0-12-260560-8). Acad Pr.
Fletcher, Madilyn M., jt. ed. see Savage, Dwayne C.
Fletcher, Margaret C., ed. see Thompson, Paul W.
Fletcher, Marilyn. Science Fiction Story Index: 1950-1979. 2nd ed. LC 80-28685. 622p. 1981. pap. 20.00x (ISBN 0-8389-0320-7). ALA.
Fletcher, Marjorie. Thirty-Three. LC 75-32642. 72p. 1976. pap. 6.95 (ISBN 0-914086-12-X). Alicejamesbooks.
--Us Women. LC 73-86245. 59p. 1973. pap. 6.95 (ISBN 0-914086-00-6). Alicejamesbooks.
Fletcher, Mark & Birt, David. Newsflash: Twenty Picture Stories & Activities for Students of English. 1979. pap. 14.95x (ISBN 0-7131-8004-8). Intl Ideas.
Fletcher, Marvin E. The Black Soldier & Officer in the United States Army, 1891-1917. LC 73-93640. 224p. 1974. 18.00x (ISBN 0-8262-0161-X). U of Mo Pr.
Fletcher, Mary. My Very First Prayer-Time Book. (Very First Bible Stories Ser.). 1984. 1.59 (ISBN 0-87162-274-2, D8503). Warner Pr.
Fletcher, Mary A. & MacDonald, Mhairi G. Atlas of Procedures in Neonatology. (Illus.). 348p. 1983. 59.00 (ISBN 0-397-50535-3, 65-06828, Lippincott Medical). Lippincott.
Fletcher, Max E. Economics & Social Problems. LC 78-69590. (Illus.). 1979. pap. text ed. 20.95 (ISBN 0-395-26508-8); instr's. manual 1.00 (ISBN 0-395-26509-6). HM.
Fletcher, Miles. The Search for a New Order: Intellectuals & Fascism in Prewar Japan. LC 81-16198. x, 226p. 1982. 24.00x (ISBN 0-8078-1514-4). U of NC Pr.
Fletcher, Nancy M. Separation of Singapore from Malaysia. (Data Papers: No. 73). 98p. 1969. pap. text ed. 2.50 (ISBN 0-87727-073-2). Cornell SE Asia.
Fletcher, Neville. The Physics of Music. (The Fundamentals of Senior Physics Ser.). 1976. pap. text ed. 4.95x (ISBN 0-85859-085-9, 00509); cassette 8.50x (ISBN 0-686-65412-9, 00510). Heinemann Ed.
Fletcher, Neville H. Chemical Physics of Ice. LC 74-75825. (Monographs on Physics). (Illus.). 1970. 49.50 (ISBN 0-521-07597-1). Cambridge U Pr.
--The Physics of Rainclouds. pap. 101.00 (ISBN 0-317-08923-4, 2051499). Bks Demand UMI.
Fletcher, Norma, jt. auth. see Ainsworth-Land, Vaune.
Fletcher, Omar. Black Against the Mob. rev. ed. (Orig.). 1984. pap. 2.25 (ISBN 0-87067-240-1, BH240). Holloway.
--Black Godfather. rev. ed. (Orig.). 1984. pap. 2.25 (ISBN 0-87067-068-9, BH244). Holloway.
--Escape from Death Row. (Orig.). 1979. pap. 2.25 (ISBN 0-87067-052-2, BH052). Holloway.
--Hurricane Man. (Orig.). 1976. pap. 1.50 (ISBN 0-87067-815-9, BH815). Holloway.
--Miss Annie. rev. ed. (Orig.). 1984. pap. 2.25 (ISBN 0-87067-242-8, BH242). Holloway.
--Walking Black & Tall. rev. ed. (Orig.). 1984. pap. 2.25 (ISBN 0-87067-241-X, BH241). Holloway.
Fletcher, P., ed. see Virginia Polytechnic Institute & State University, March 22-24, 1973.
Fletcher, Paul & Garman, Michael, eds. Language Acquisition. LC 78-67305. 1980. 72.50 (ISBN 0-521-22521-3); pap. 19.95x (ISBN 0-521-29536-X). Cambridge U Pr.
Fletcher, Pauline. Gardens & Grim Ravines: The Language of Landscape in Victorian Poetry. LC 82-24130. (Illus.). 275p. 1983. 27.50 (ISBN 0-691-06556-X). Princeton U Pr.
Fletcher, Peter, jt. auth. see Walker, Kenneth.
Fletcher, Phineas. The Purple Island. LC 72-196. (English Experience Ser.: No. 313). 132p. 1971. Repr. of 1633 ed. 42.00 (ISBN 90-221-0313-7). Walter J Johnson.
--The Spenser of His Age Being Selected Works of Phineas Fletcher. 1979. Repr. of 1905 ed. lib. bdg. 40.00 (ISBN 0-8495-1629-3). Arden Lib.
Fletcher, Phineas, jt. auth. see Fletcher, Giles.
Fletcher, R. Practical Methods of Optimization: Constrained Optimization, Vol. 2. 224p. 1981. 37.95x (ISBN 0-471-27828-9, Pub. by Wiley Interscience). Wiley.
--Practical Methods of Optimization: Unconstrained Optimization, Vol. 1. LC 79-41486. 120p. 1980. 34.95x (ISBN 0-471-27711-8, Pub. by Wiley-Interscience). Wiley.
Fletcher, R. & Voke, J. Detective Color Vision. 580p. 1985. 72.00 (ISBN 0-85274-395-5, 990300269, Pub. by A Hilger England). Heyden.
Fletcher, R. A. The Episcopate in the Kingdom of Leon in the Twelfth Century. (Historical Monographs). (Illus.). 1978. 38.00x (ISBN 0-19-821869-9). Oxford U Pr.
--St. James Catapult: The Life & Times of Diego Gelmirez of Santiago de Compostela. (Illus.). 341p. 1984. 54.00x (ISBN 0-19-822581-4). Oxford U Pr.
--Warships & Their Story. 1977. lib. bdg. 69.95 (ISBN 0-8490-2808-6). Gordon Pr.
Fletcher, Raymond & Howes, David. Rothmans Rugby League Yearbook, 1982. 400p. 1982. 40.00x (ISBN 0-907574-16-5, Pub. by Rothmans Pubns England); limp 30.00x (ISBN 0-907574-15-7). State Mutual Bk.
Fletcher, Richard M. The Stylistic Development of Edgar Allen Poe. LC 72-94467. (Janua Linguarum, Ser. Practica: No. 55). 192p. 1974. pap. text ed. 20.80x (ISBN 90-2792-508-9). Mouton.
Fletcher, Rivers. Bentley: Past & Present. (Illus.). 18.95 (ISBN 0-85614-082-1, F399). Haynes Pubns.
--MG: Past & Present. (Illus.). 256p. Date not set. 25.95 (ISBN 0-85614-074-0, Pub. by Wilton Hse England). Motorbooks Intl.
--MG: Past & Present. 18.95 (ISBN 0-85614-074-0, F402). Haynes Pubns.
Fletcher, Robert. Arthurian Material in the Chronicles of Great Britain & France. LC 68-2114. (Arthurian Legend & Literature Ser., No. 1). 1969. Repr. of 1906 ed. lib. bdg. 75.00 (ISBN 0-8383-0551-2). Haskell.
--A Briefe & Familiar Epistle Shewing His Maiesties Title to All His Kingdomes. LC 72-5991. (English Experience Ser.: No. 516). 14p. 1973. Repr. of 1603 ed. 6.00 (ISBN 90-221-0516-4). Walter J Johnson.
Fletcher, Robert H. Arthurian Material in the Chronicles, Especially Those of Great Britain & France... Expanded by a Bibliography & Critical Essay for the Period 1905-1965 by Roger Sherman Loomis. new ed. LC 66-20679. 344p. 1973. lib. bdg. 28.50 (ISBN 0-8337-1153-9). B Franklin.
--A History of English Literature. 1973. Repr. of 1916 ed. 25.00 (ISBN 0-8274-0662-2). R West.
Fletcher, Robert S. History of Oberlin College: From Its Foundation Through the Civil War, 2 vols. in 1. LC 75-165716. (American Education Ser, No. 2). 1971. Repr. of 1943 ed. 60.50 (ISBN 0-405-03705-8). Ayer Co Pubs.
Fletcher, Roger. Revisionism & Empire: Socialist Imperialism in Germany 1897-1914. (Illus.). 224p. 1984. text ed. 29.95 (ISBN 0-04-943031-9). Allen Unwin.
Fletcher, Ronald. In a Country Churchyard. (Illus.). 155p. 1982. pap. 4.95 (ISBN 0-586-08342-1, Pub. by Granada England). Academy Chi Pubs.
--Instinct in Man. rev. ed. 348p. 1974. text ed. 30.00 (ISBN 0-8236-2700-4). Intl Univs Pr.
--The Making of Sociology, 2 vols. Incl. Vol. 1. Beginnings & Foundations. 726p (ISBN 0-684-13316-4); Vol. 2. Developments. 884p (ISBN 0-684-13317-2). 1973. 12.50 ea. (ScribT). Scribner.
Fletcher, S. G., et al, eds. Turning, Vol. 2. (Engineering Craftsmen: No. H23). 1969. spiral bdg. 37.50x (ISBN 0-85083-038-9). Intl Ideas.
Fletcher, Samuel, jt. ed. see Berg, Frederick S.
Fletcher, Samuel G. Diagnosing Speech Disorders from Cleft Palate. (Illus.). 240p. 1978. 45.50 (ISBN 0-8089-1074-4, 791280). Grune.
Fletcher, Sara. Christian Babysitter's Handbook. 1985. pap. 3.95 (ISBN 0-570-03948-7, 12-2881). Concordia.
Fletcher, Sarah. Bible Story Book: New Testament. LC 56-1427. (Continued Applied Christianity Ser.). 1983. 9.95 (ISBN 0-570-04080-9). Concordia.
--Bible Story Book: Old Testament. LC 83-1801. (Continued Applied Christianity Ser.). 1983. 9.95 (ISBN 0-570-04079-5, 56-1426). Concordia.
--My Bible Story Book. LC 73-91810. (Illus.). 72p. (ps-3). 1974. 8.50 (ISBN 0-570-03423-X, 56-1171). Concordia.
--My Stories About God's People. (Illus.). 32p. (ps-3). 1974. pap. 1.25 (ISBN 0-570-03426-4, 56-1181). Concordia.
--My Stories About Jesus. (Illus.). 32p. (ps-3). 1974. 5.95 (ISBN 0-570-03428-0, 56-1183); pap. 1.25 (ISBN 0-570-03427-2, 56-1182). Concordia.
--Prayers for Little People. (Illus.). 32p. (gr. 3-7). 1974. pap. 1.50 (ISBN 0-570-03429-9, 56-1184). Concordia.
--Stewardship: Taking Care of God's World. (Illus.). (gr. k-4). 1984. pap. 3.95 (ISBN 0-570-04106-6, 56-1498). Concordia.
Fletcher, Sheila. Feminists & Bureaucrats. LC 79-20630. 1980. 39.50 (ISBN 0-521-22880-8). Cambridge U Pr.
--Women First: The Female in English Physical Education, 1880-1980. 208p. cancelled (ISBN 0-8052-3942-1). Schocken.
--Women First: The Female Tradition in English Physical Education, 1880-1980. LC 84-70367. (Illus.). 194p. 1984. 36.50 (ISBN 0-485-11248-5, Pub. by Athlone Pr Ltd). Longwood Pub Group.

Fletcher, Stevenson W. Pennsylvania Agriculture & Country Life: 1640-1840. LC 50-9470. 605p. 1971. 9.50 (ISBN 0-911124-33-0). Pa Hist & Mus.
--Pennsylvania Agriculture & Country Life: 1840-1940. LC 50-9470. 630p. 1955. 9.50 (ISBN 0-911124-34-9). Pa Hist & Mus.
Fletcher, Susan, jt. auth. see Stone, L. O.
Fletcher, Sybil M., jt. auth. see Keane, Claire B.
Fletcher, T. J. Some Lessons in Mathematics. pap. 12.95x (ISBN 0-521-09248-5). Cambridge U Pr.
Fletcher, Tom. One Hundred Years of the Negro in Show Business. (Music Reprint Ser.). (Illus.). xxii, 337p. 1984. Repr. of 1954 ed. lib. bdg. 39.50 (ISBN 0-306-76219-6). Da Capo.
Fletcher, Tyler, jt. auth. see Braswell, Michael.
Fletcher, Valentine. Chimney Pots & Stacks: An Introduction to Their History, Variety & Identification. LC 77-387517. (Centaur Monographs). (Illus.). pap. 21.90 (ISBN 0-317-09964-7, 2051319). Bks Demand UMI.
Fletcher, Valerie J. Dreams & Nightmares: Utopian Visions in Modern Art. LC 83-16651. (Illus.). 201p. 1983. 42.50 (ISBN 0-87474-432-6, FLDV). Smithsonian.
Fletcher, W., jt. auth. see Richardson, G.
Fletcher, W. K. Analytical Methods in Geochemical Prospecting. (Handbook of Exploration Geochemistry Ser.: Vol. 1). 256p. 1981. 64.00 (ISBN 0-444-41930-6). Elsevier.
Fletcher, W. W. The Pest War. LC 74-11440. 218p. 1978. pap. 21.95x (ISBN 0-470-26345-8). Halsted Pr.
Fletcher, W. W. & Kirkwood, R. C. Herbicides & Plant Growth Regulation. (Illus.). 384p. 1983. 49.95x (ISBN 0-412-00271-X, NO. 5028, Pub. by Chapman & Hall England). Methuen Inc.
Fletcher, Walter. Dogs of the World. (All Color Guides). 1977. pap. 3.95 (ISBN 0-553-23525-7). Bantam.
Fletcher, Walter R. My Times with Dogs. LC 79-24575. (Illus.). 320p. 1980. 14.95 (ISBN 0-87605-664-8). Howell Bk.
Fletcher, William. The Second Greatest Commandment. LC 83-62501. 156p. 1983. pap. 4.95 (ISBN 0-89109-502-0). NavPress.
--Soviet Believers: The Religious Sector of the Population. LC 80-25495. 276p. 1981. 27.50x (ISBN 0-7006-0211-9). U Pr of KS.
Fletcher, William, jt. auth. see Kelley, Patrick.
Fletcher, William, jt. ed. see Lenihan, John.
Fletcher, William A. Rebel Private, Front & Rear. 1983. Repr. of 1908 ed. 16.95 (ISBN 0-89201-107-6). Zenger Pub.
Fletcher, William c. Soviet Charismatics: The Pentecostals in the U. S. S. R. (American University Studies VII (Theology & Religion): Vol. 9). 287p. 1986. text ed. 25.20 (ISBN 0-8204-0226-5). P Lang Pubs.
Fletcher, William D., frwd. by. Clare Leighton an Exhibition: American Sheaves English Seed Corn. (Illus.). pap. 3.00 (ISBN 0-685-85775-1). Boston Public Lib.
Fletcher, William H., ed. Papers for the First Interdisciplinary Conference on Netherlandic Studies: Held at the University of Maryland 11-13 June 1982. LC 85-9006. 248p. (Orig.). 1985. lib. bdg. 25.75 (ISBN 0-8191-4707-9, Amer Assoc Netherlandic Studies); pap. text ed. 14.25 (ISBN 0-8191-4708-7). U Pr of Amer.
Fletcher, William I. An Engineering Approach to Digital Design. (Illus.). 1980. text ed. 40.95 (ISBN 0-13-277699-5). P-H.
Fletcher, William I., compiled by see Brinley, George.
Fletcher, William Y. English Book Collectors. Pollard, Alfred, ed. 1969. 29.00 (ISBN 0-8337-1154-7). B Franklin.
Fletcher, Winston. Meetings, Meetings: How to Manipulate Them & Make Them More Fun. LC 83-17284. 192p. 1984. 10.95 (ISBN 0-688-02650-8). Morrow.
Fletcher, Wyndham. Port: An Introduction to Its History & Delights. (Illus.). 124p. 1978. 22.50 (ISBN 0-85667-044-8, Pub. by Sotheby Pubns England). Biblio Dist.
--Port: An Introduction to Its Histroy & Delights. (Illus.). 128p. 22.50 (ISBN 0-85667-044-8). Sotheby Pubns.
Fletcher-Allen, E., tr. see Gafencu, Grigore.
Fletcher-Watson, John. Subject & Place for Watercolour Landscapes. (Illus.). 144p. 1985. 22.50 (ISBN 0-7134-3748-0, Pub. by Batsford England). David & Charles.
Flett, D. S., ed. Ion Exchange Membranes. LC 83-4343. 210p. 1983. 52.95 (ISBN 0-470-27452-2). Halsted Pr.
Flett, J. P., jt. auth. see Flett, T. M.
Flett, T. M. Differential Analysis. Pym, J. S., ed. LC 78-67303. (Illus.). 1980. 59.50 (ISBN 0-521-22420-9). Cambridge U Pr.
Flett, T. M. & Flett, J. P. Traditional Dancing in Scotland. (Illus.). 313p. 1985. pap. 8.95 (ISBN 0-7102-0731-X). Routledge & Kegan.
Fletterick, Robert J., et al. Molecular Structure: Macromolecules in Three Dimensions. (Illus.). 216p. 1985. pap. text ed. 19.95 (ISBN 0-86542-300-8). Blackwell Pubns.
Flettrich, Terry. House in the Bend of Bourbon Street. (Illus.). 1974. pap. 2.95 (ISBN 0-88289-015-8). Pelican.
Flettrich, Terry & Carr, Jan. Creole Cajun Cooking Cards from an Old New Orleans Bag. 1973. 2.95 (ISBN 0-88289-014-X). Pelican.
Fleu, Richard. Indian Rassle & Other Poems. (Stone Country Poetry Ser.: No. 10). (Illus.). 44p. 1980. pap. 5.95x (ISBN 0-930020-09-X). Stone Country.
Fleure, H. F. & Peake, Harold. Priests & Kings. (Corridors of Time Ser.: No. 4). 1927. 29.50x (ISBN 0-686-83710-X). Elliots Bks.
Fleure, H. J. An Introduction to Geography. 1978. Repr. of 1929 ed. lib. bdg. 12.50 (ISBN 0-8492-0895-5). R West.
--The Races of Mankind. 1979. Repr. of 1927 ed. lib. bdg. 12.50 (ISBN 0-8495-1649-8). Arden Lib.
Fleure, H. J. & Peake, Harold. Hunters & Artists. (Corridors of Time Ser.: No. 2). 1927. 29.50x (ISBN 0-686-83573-5). Elliots Bks.
--Merchant Ventures in Bronze. (Corridors of Time Ser.: No. 7). 1931. 29.50x (ISBN 0-686-83625-1). Elliots Bks.
--Peasants & Potters. (Corridors of Time Ser.: No. 3). 1927. 29.50x (ISBN 0-686-83689-8). Elliots Bks.
--Steppe & the Sown. (Corridors of Time Ser.: No.5). 1928. 29.50x (ISBN 0-686-83785-1). Elliots Bks.
--Way of the Sea. (Corridors of Time Ser.: No. 6). 1929. 29.50x (ISBN 0-686-83850-5). Elliots Bks.
Fleure, H. J., jt. auth. see Peake, Harold.
Fleure, Herbert J. The Peoples of Europe. LC 76-44717. Repr. of 1922 ed. 14.00 (ISBN 0-404-15922-2). AMS Pr.
Fleurian, Dominique de. Dictionnaire National des Communes de France. 20th ed. Simond, Jacques & Frenay, Jacques, eds. 1150p. (Fr.). 1977. 39.95 (ISBN 0-686-57184-3, M-6254). French & Eur.
Fleury, C. Rohault. La Messe: Etudes Archeologiques sur ses Monuments, 8 vols. (Illus.). 1722p. (Fr.). Repr. of 1889 ed. lib. bdg. 600.00x (ISBN 0-89241-153-8). Caratzas.
Fleury, C. Rohault de see De Fleury, C. Rohault.
Fleury, C. Rohault de see Fleury, C. Rohault.
Fleury, Mai L. The Healing Bond: Human Relations Skills for Nurses & Other Health Care Professionals. 208p. 1984. 16.95 (ISBN 0-13-384735-7); pap. 8.95 (ISBN 0-13-384727-6). P-H.
Fleury, P. J., ed. Advances in Non-Communicative Ring-Theory, Plattsburg, 1981. (Lecture Notes in Mathematics: Vol. 951). 142p. 1982. pap. 11.00 (ISBN 0-387-11597-8). Springer-Verlag.
Fleury, Paul A. & Golding, Brage, eds. Coherence & Energy Transfer in Glasses. (NATO Conference Series VI, Materials Science: Vol. 9). 416p. 1984. 62.50x (ISBN 0-306-41638-7, Plenum Pr). Plenum Pub.
Flew, A. G., ed. Logic & Language. (First Ser.). 214p. 1968. pap. 11.95x (ISBN 0-631-03420-X). Basil Blackwell.
--Logic & Language. (Second Ser.). 250p. 1973. pap. 11.95 (ISBN 0-631-17300-5). Basil Blackwell.
Flew, A. G. N., jt. ed. see Warren, Thomas B.
Flew, Anthony. A Dictionary of Philosophy. 2nd, rev. ed. LC 78-68699. 393p. 1984. 22.50x (ISBN 0-312-20924-X). St Martin.
--A Rational Animal: & Other Philosophical Essays on the Nature of Man. 1978. 24.95x (ISBN 0-19-824576-9). Oxford U Pr.
Flew, Anthony, jt. ed. see Carter, Curtis I.
Flew, Antony. A Dictionary of Philosophy. 2nd. ed. 388p. 1984. pap. 8.95 (ISBN 0-312-20923-1). St Martin.
--God: A Critical Inquiry. 210p. 1984. pap. 7.95 (ISBN 0-87548-371-2). Open Court.
--God, Freedom & Immortality: A Critical Analysis. LC 84-42543. 183p. 1984. pap. text ed. 9.95 (ISBN 0-87975-251-3). Prometheus Bks.
--Philosophy: An Introduction. LC 79-93076. 194p. 1980. pap. text ed. 9.95 (ISBN 0-87975-127-4). Prometheus Bks.
--The Politics of Procrustes: Contradictions of Enforced Equality. 216p. 1981. text ed. 19.95 (ISBN 0-87975-150-9). Prometheus Bks.
--The Politics of Procrustes: Contradictions of Enforced Equality. 1980. 40.00x (ISBN 0-85117-204-0, Pub. by M Temple Smith). State Mutual Bk.
--The Presumption of Atheism & Other Philosophical Essays on God, Freedom & Immortality. LC 75-43411. 183p. 1976. text ed. 24.50 (ISBN 0-06-492119-0). B&N Imports.
--Thinking Straight. LC 76-56674. 127p. 1977. pap. 8.95 (ISBN 0-87975-088-X). Prometheus Bks.
Flew, Antony, ed. Body, Mind & Death. 1964. pap. 3.95 (ISBN 0-02-084840-4). Macmillan.
--Dictionary of Philosophy. LC 78-68699. 351p. 1979. 20.00x (ISBN 0-312-20921-5). St Martin.
Flew, Antony G. Hume's Philosophy of Belief. (International Library of Philosophy & Scientific Method). 1961. 28.00x (ISBN 0-7100-1370-1). Humanities.
Flew, Antony G., ed. Essays in Conceptual Anaylsis. LC 81-6295. xi, 265p. 1981. Repr. of 1966 ed. lib. bdg. 25.00x (ISBN 0-313-23057-9, FLES). Greenwood.
Flew, Josiah. Studies in Browning. LC 74-115859. (Studies in Browning, No. 4). 1970. Repr. of 1904 ed. lib. bdg. 39.95x (ISBN 0-8383-1071-0). Haskell.
--Studies in Browning. 1979. Repr. lib. bdg. 22.50 (ISBN 0-8492-4608-3). R West.
Flew, Robert N. & Davies, Rupert E., eds. The Catholicity of Protestantism: Being a Report Presented to His Grace the Archbishop of Canterbury by a Group of Free Churchmen. LC 80-29108. 159p. 1981. Repr. of 1950 ed. lib. bdg. 19.25x (ISBN 0-313-22825-6, FLCAT). Greenwood.
Flewelling, Ralph T. Creative Personality: A Study in Philosophical Reconciliation. LC 75-3146. Repr. of 1926 ed. 22.00 (ISBN 0-404-59153-1). AMS Pr.
--The Forest of Yggdrasill. LC 61-8735. 180p. 1962. 6.00 (ISBN 0-88474-005-6). U of S Cal Pr.
--Personalism & the Problems of Philosophy: An Appreciation of the Works of Borden Parker Bowne. LC 75-3147. Repr. of 1915 ed. 14.00 (ISBN 0-404-59154-X). AMS Pr.
--The Reason in Faith. LC 75-3148. Repr. of 1924 ed. 17.00 (ISBN 0-404-59155-8). AMS Pr.
--Survival of Western Culture. LC 68-15825. 1968. Repr. of 1943 ed. 23.00x (ISBN 0-8046-0152-6, Pub by Kennikat). Assoc Faculty Pr.
Flewett, H. W. & Pantin, William E. First Book of Latin Poetry with Vocabulary. (Illus., Lat.). 1977. pap. text ed. 11.95 (ISBN 0-312-29226-0). St Martin.
Flewin, Arthur. Electrognathographics: Atlas of Diagnostic Procedures & Interpretation. (Illus.). 168p. 1985. pap. text ed. 68.00 (ISBN 0-86715-156-0). Quint Pub CO.
Flewitt, P. E. & Wild, R. K. Microstructural Characterisation of Metals & Alloys. 212p. 1984. pap. text ed. 22.40x (ISBN 0-904357-53-8, Pub. by Metals Soc). Brookfield Pub Co.
Flewitt, Peter. Pocket Guide: The Philips P5020 Word Processor. (Pitman Word Processing Pocket Guides Ser.). 64p. (Orig.). 1984. pap. 6.95 (ISBN 0-273-02074-9). Pitman Pub MA.
Flexer, Abraham S., jt. auth. see Prescott, David.
Flexer, Abraham S., jt. auth. see Prescott, David M.
Flexner, Abraham. American College: A Criticism. LC 73-89179. (American Education: Its Men, Institutions & Ideas Ser). 1969. Repr. of 1908 ed. 19.00 (ISBN 0-405-01417-1). Ayer Co Pubs.
--The Flexner Report on Medical Education in the United States & Canada. 346p. 1910. text ed. 38.00 (ISBN 0-89443-354-7). Aspen Systems.
--Medical Education in the United States & Canada. LC 78-180575. (Medicine & Society in America Ser). 368p. 1972. Repr. of 1910 ed. 22.00 (ISBN 0-405-03952-2). Ayer Co Pubs.
--Prostitution in Europe. LC 69-14924. (Criminology, Law Enforcement, & Social Problems Ser.: No. 30). 1969. Repr. of 1914 ed. 18.00x (ISBN 0-87585-030-8). Patterson Smith.
--Universities: American, English, German. 381p. 1980. Repr. of 1930 ed. lib. bdg. 30.00 (ISBN 0-89984-200-3). Century Bookbindery.
Flexner, Abraham & Bailey, Esther S. Funds & Foundations: Their Policies, Past & Present. LC 75-22817. (America in Two Centuries Ser). 1976. Repr. of 1952 ed. 13.00x (ISBN 0-405-07689-4). Ayer Co Pubs.
Flexner, Eleanor. American Playwrights: Nineteen Eighteen to Nineteen Thirty-Eight. LC 77-99634. (Essay Index Reprint Ser.). 1938. 32.00 (ISBN 0-8369-1412-0). Ayer Co Pubs.
--Century of Struggle: The Woman's Rights Movement in the United States. rev. ed. LC 74-34542. (Illus.). 531p. 1975. (Belknap Pr); pap. 7.95 (ISBN 0-674-10652-0). Harvard U Pr.
Flexner, J. T., jt. auth. see Flexner, S.
Flexner, James. The Hudson River & the Highlands: Photographs by Robert Glenn Ketchum. price not set. Aperture.
Flexner, James T. An American Saga: The Story of Helen Thomas & Simon Flexner. (Illus.). 488p. 1984. 24.45i (ISBN 0-316-28611-7). Little.
--America's Old Masters. rev. ed. (McGraw-Hill Paperback Ser.). (Illus.). 1982. pap. 9.95 (ISBN 0-07-021285-6). McGraw.
--George Washington: A Biography, 4 vols. Incl. Vol. 1. The Force of Experience, 1732-1775. 1965. 22.00i (ISBN 0-316-28597-8); Vol. 2. In the American Revolution, 1775-1783. LC 68-11529. 1968. 22.00i (ISBN 0-316-28595-1); Vol. 3. And the New Nation, 1783-1793. LC 78-117042. 1970. 22.00i (ISBN 0-316-28600-1); Vol. 4. Anguish & Farewell, 1793-1799. 1972. 22.00i (ISBN 0-316-28602-8). (Illus.). Little.
--George Washington: A Biography in Four Volumes, Special 250th Anniversary Edition. 1982. 75.00 (ISBN 0-316-28610-9). Little.
--The Light of Distant Skies: 1760-1835. LC 68-54703. (Illus.). 1969. pap. 5.00 (ISBN 0-486-22179-2). Dover.
--Lord of the Mohawks: A Biography of Sir William Johnson. rev. ed. LC 77-13877. 1979. 16.95 (ISBN 0-316-28609-5). Little.
--States Dyckman: An American Loyalist. 1980. 15.95 (ISBN 0-316-28603-6). Little.
--Steamboats Come True. LC 78-69953. 1978. 12.95 (ISBN 0-316-28608-7). Little.
--That Wilder Image: The Paintings of America's Native School from Thomas Cole to Winslow Homer. (Illus.). 13.25 (ISBN 0-8446-0093-8). Peter Smith.
--Washington: The Indispensable Man. LC 74-7235. (Illus.). 1974. 16.45i (ISBN 0-316-28605-2). Little.
--Washington: The Indispensable Man. 1979. pap. 3.95 (ISBN 0-451-62213-8, ME2213, Ment). NAL.
--Washington: The Indispensable Man. 1984. pap. 3.95 (ISBN 0-451-12890-7, Sig). NAL.
--Washington: The Indispensable Man. pap. 8.95 (ISBN 0-452-25542-2, Plume). NAL.
--The Young Hamilton: A Biography. LC 77-13877. (Illus.). 1978. 17.45i (ISBN 0-316-28594-3). Little.
Flexner, James T., et al. Institute to University: A Seventy-Fifth Anniversary Colloquium. LC 77-24825. 116p. 1977. pap. 2.95x (ISBN 0-87470-025-6). Rockefeller.
Flexner, Jean A., jt. auth. see Lorwin, Lewis L.
Flexner, S. & Flexner, J. T. William Henry Welch & the Heroic Age of American Medicine. (Illus.). 11.75 (ISBN 0-8446-2068-8). Peter Smith.
Flexner, Stuart B. Listening to America: An Illustrated History of Words & Phrases from Our Lively & Splendid Past. 592p. 1984. pap. 13.95 (ISBN 0-671-52798-3, Touchstone Bks). S&S.
Flexner, Stuart B., jt. auth. see Wentworth, Harold.
Flexner, Stuart B., ed. The Random House College Dictionary. (Illus.). 1979. 19.93 (ISBN 0-394-05433-4); thumbed index 20.60 (ISBN 0-394-05434-2). Random.
--The Random House School Dictionary. (Illus.). 966p. 1983. 17.32 (ISBN 0-676-39289-X). Random.
Flexner, William, et al. Strategic Planning in Health Care Management. LC 81-2488. 408p. 1981. text ed. 39.50 (ISBN 0-89443-298-2). Aspen Systems.
Flicek, Barbara D., jt. auth. see Gross, John A.
Flick, Alcyon R. Brand from the Burning. LC 60-8299. (Dest Ser.). 1984. pap. 4.95 (ISBN 0-317-28307-3). Pacific Pr Pub Assn.
Flick, Alexander. History in Rhyme & Jingles. 59.95 (ISBN 0-8490-0314-8). Gordon Pr.
Flick, Alexander C. Decline of the Medieval Church, 2 vols. (Bibliography & Reference Ser: No. 133). 1968. Repr. of 1930 ed. Set. 48.00 (ISBN 0-8337-1158-X). B Franklin.
--Loyalism in New York During the American Revolution. LC 75-120214. (Columbia University. Studies in the Social Sciences: No. 37). Repr. of 1901 ed. J0.00 (ISBN 0-404-51037-X). AMS Pr.
--Loyalism in New York During the American Revolution. LC 72-90175. (Mass Violence in America Ser). Repr. of 1901 ed. 15.00 (ISBN 0-405-01310-8). Ayer Co Pubs.
--Rise of the Medieval Church & Its Influence on the Civilization of Western Europe from the 1st to the 13th Century. 636p. 1973. Repr. of 1909 ed. lib. bdg. 33.50 (ISBN 0-8337-1159-8). B Franklin.
Flick, Alexander C. & Lobrano, Gustav. Samuel Jones Tilden: A Study in Political Sagacity. LC 73-7103. (Illus.). 597p. 1973. Repr. of 1939 ed. lib. bdg. 31.00x (ISBN 0-8371-6912-7, FLST). Greenwood.
Flick, Art. Art Flick's Master Fly Tying Guide. rev. ed. LC 83-63027. (Illus.). 208p. 1983. pap. 12.95 (ISBN 0-8329-0243-8, Pub. by Winchester Pr). New Century.
Flick, Art, et al, eds. Art Flick's Master Fly-Tying Guide. (Illus.). 220p. 1972. pap. 8.95 (ISBN 0-517-52135-0). Crown.
Flick, Carlos T. The Birmingham Political Union & the Movements for Reform in Britain, 1830-1839. (Illus.). 206p. 1978. 19.00 (ISBN 0-208-01752-6, Archon). Shoe String.
Flick, Ella M. The Life of Bishop McDevitt. Repr. of 1940 ed. lib. bdg. 20.00 (ISBN 0-8495-1619-6). Arden Lib.
Flick, Ernest W. Adhesive & Sealant Compound Formulations. 2nd ed. LC 83-22016. 366p. 1984. 48.00 (ISBN 0-8155-0966-9). Noyes.
--Contemporary Industrial Coatings: Environmentally Safe Formulations. LC 85-4905. (Illus.). 333p. 1985. 48.00 (ISBN 0-8155-1025-X). Noyes.
--Cosmetic & Toiletry Formulations. LC 84-14771. (Illus.). 596p. 1985. 64.00 (ISBN 0-8155-0995-2). Noyes.
--Exterior Water-Based Trade Paint Formulations. LC 80-19212. 349p. 1981. 36.00 (ISBN 0-8155-0820-4). Noyes.
--Handbook of Adhesive Raw Materials. LC 82-2251. (Illus.). 303p. 1982. 45.00 (ISBN 0-8155-0897-2). Noyes.
--Handbook of Paint Raw Materials. LC 81-18937. 340p. (Orig.). 1982. 45.00 (ISBN 0-8155-0881-6). Noyes.
--Household, Automotive & Industrial Chemical Formulations. 2nd ed. LC 83-22115. 360p. 1984. 48.00 (ISBN 0-8155-0970-7). Noyes.
--Institutional & Industrial Cleaning Product Formulations. LC 85-4961. (Illus.). 338p. 1985. 48.00 (ISBN 0-8155-1026-8). Noyes.
--Interior Water-Based Trade Paint Formulations. LC 80-12814. 364p. 1980. 36.00 (ISBN 0-8155-0803-4). Noyes.
--Printing Ink Formulations. LC 84-22636. 184p. 1985. 36.00 (ISBN 0-8155-1014-4). Noyes.
Flick, Ernest W., ed. Industrial Solvents Handbook, 1985. 3rd ed. LC 84-22637. (Illus.). 650p. 1985. 86.00 (ISBN 0-8155-1010-1). Noyes.
Flick, Jim, jt. auth. see Toski, Bob.
Flick, Lawrence F. Development of Our Knowledge of Tuberculosis. LC 75-23712. Repr. of 1925 ed. 63.00 (ISBN 0-404-13263-4). AMS Pr.
Flick, Maurizio, jt. auth. see Alszeghy, Zoltan.
Flick, Pauline. Children's China. 1982. 45.00x (ISBN 0-09-463880-2, Pub. by Constable & Co England). State Mutual Bk.

--Discovering Toys & Toy Museums. 2nd ed. (Discovering Ser.). (Illus.). 72p. (Orig.). (gr. 6 up). 1977. pap. 2.50 (ISBN 0-913714-38-0). Legacy Bks.
--Old Toys. (Shire Album Ser.: No. 147). (Orig.). 1985. pap. 3.50 (ISBN 0-85263-754-3, Pub. by Shire Pubns England). Seven Hills Bks.
Flicke, Wilhelm F. War Secrets in the Ether, 2 vols. LC 77-88801. (Cryptographic Ser.). 1977. Vol. 1. 17.80 (ISBN 0-89412-021-2); Vol. 2. 18.80 (ISBN 0-89412-023-9). Aegean Park Pr.
Flicker, Barbara. Standards for Juvenile Justice: A Summary & Analysis. LC 77-14497. (Juvenile Justice Standards Project Ser.). 336p. 1982. prof ref 35.00 (ISBN 0-88410-758-2); pap. 17.50 prof ref (ISBN 0-88410-831-7). Ballinger Pub.
Flicker, Y. Z. The Trace Formula & Base Change for GL(3) (Lecture Notes in Mathematics: Vol. 927). 204p. 1982. pap. 15.00 (ISBN 0-387-11500-5). Springer-Verlag.
Flickinger, Charles J. & Brown, Jay C. Medical Cell Biology. LC 77-16987. pap. 143.50 (ISBN 0-317-26429-X, 2024985). Bks Demand UMI.
Flickinger, Charles J., et al. Medical Cell Biology. (Illus.). 566p. 1979. 27.50 (ISBN 0-7216-3721-3). Saunders.
Flickinger, Roy C. Greek Theatre & Its Drama. 4th ed. LC 36-11686. 1960. 30.00x (ISBN 0-226-25369-4). U of Chicago Pr.
Fliegel, C. P., jt. ed. see Stalder, G.
Fliegel, Carl J., compiled by. Index to the Records of the Moravian Mission Among the Indians of North America, 2 vols. 1407p. 1970. Set. 400.00 (ISBN 0-89235-018-0). Res Pubns Conn.
Fliegel, Norris, jt. auth. see Rosenberg, Bernard.
Fliegelman, Avra, ed. see Broadcast Information Bureau, Inc.
Fliegelman, Jay. Prodigals & Pilgrims: The American Revolution Against Patriarchal Authority, 1750-1800. LC 81-10179. 420p. 1981. 27.95 (ISBN 0-521-23719-X). Cambridge U Pr.
--Prodigals & Pilgrims: The American Revolution Against Patriarchal Authority, 1750-1800. 420p. 1985. pap. 12.95 (ISBN 0-521-31726-6). Cambridge U Pr.
Flieger, Verlyn. Splintered Light: Logos & Language in Tolkien's World. 144p. 1983. pap. 6.95 (ISBN 0-8028-1955-9). Eerdmans.
Flieger, Wilhelm & Pagtolun-an, Imelda. An Assessment of Fertility & Contraception in Seven Philippine Provinces: 1975. LC 81-17443. (Papers of the East-West Population Institute: No.77). x, 154p. (Orig.). 1981. pap. text ed. 3.00 (ISBN 0-86638-014-0). E W Center HI.
Flieger, Wilhelm, jt. auth. see Keyfitz, Nathan.
Flieger, Wilhelm, et al. One the Road to Longevity: 1970 National, Regional & Provincial Mortality for the Philippines. 333p. 1981. pap. 15.75x (ISBN 0-686-34625-4, Pub. by San Carlos Philippines). Cellar.
Flier, Michael. Slavic Forum: Essays in Linguistics & Literature. LC 72-88178. (Slavistic Printings & Reprintings Ser.: No. 277). 169p. 1974. text ed. 23.20x (ISBN 90-2792-713-8). Mouton.
Flier, Michael, ed. American Contributions to the Ninth International Congress of Slavists, Vol. 1: Linguistics. 381p. (Orig., Eng. & Slavic.). 1983. pap. 19.95 (ISBN 0-89357-112-1). Slavica.
Flier, Michael S. Aspects of Nominal Determination in Old Church Slavonic. LC 72-88186. (Slavistic Printing & Reprinting Ser.: No. 172). 248p. 1974. text ed. 28.80x (ISBN 90-2793-242-5). Mouton.
Flier, Michael S., jt. auth. see Stepanoff, N. C.
Flier, Michael S. & Brecht, Richard, eds. Issues in Russian Morphosyntax. (UCLA Slavic Studies: Vol. 10). 208p. (Orig.). 1985. pap. 12.95 (ISBN 0-89357-139-3). Slavica.
Flier, Michael S., jt. ed. see Birnbaum, Henrik.
Fliess, Peter J. International Relations in the Bipolar World. 8.25 (ISBN 0-8446-2069-6). Peter Smith.
--Thucydides & the Politics of Bipolarity. LC 66-17215. (Illus.). xiv, 194p. 1966. 20.00x (ISBN 0-8071-0448-5). La State U Pr.
Fliess, Robert. Ego & Body Ego. 2nd ed. LC 61-16641. (Psychoanalytic Ser.: Vol. 2). 390p. 1971. text ed. 30.00 (ISBN 0-8236-1538-3); pap. text ed. 8.95 (ISBN 0-8236-8033-9, 21538). Intl Univs Pr.
--Erogeneity & Libido. LC 57-9327. (Psychoanalytic Ser.: Vol. 1). 325p. 1970. text ed. 27.50 (ISBN 0-8236-1700-9); pap. text ed. 7.95 (ISBN 0-8236-8039-8, 217000). Intl Univs Pr.
--Revival of Interest in the Dream. 164p. 1953. text ed. 17.50 (ISBN 0-8236-5820-1). Intl Univs Pr.
--Symbol, Dream & Psychosis. LC 72-184212. (Psychoanalytic Ser.: Vol. 3). 435p. 1973. text ed. 35.00 (ISBN 0-8236-6287-X). Intl Univs Pr.
Fliess, Robert, ed. The Psychoanalytic Reader: An Anthology of Essential Papers with Critical Introductions. 358p. (Orig.). 1969. text ed. 30.00 (ISBN 0-8236-4480-4); pap. text ed. 9.95 (ISBN 0-8236-8230-7, 24480). Intl Univs Pr.
Fligel', D. S., jt. auth. see Al'pert, Y. L.
Flight, Nancy, ed. see Leung, Sophia R.
Flight Safety Foundation. What Is Safe: Corporate Aviation Safety Seminar Proceedings, 28th Annual Meeting, April 17-19, 1983, Fairmont Hotel, New Orleans, Louisiana. pap. 53.00 (ISBN 0-317-29629-9, 2021549). Bks Demand UMI.
Fligstein, Neil. Going North: Migration of Blacks & Whites from the South, 1900-1950. LC 81-14901. (Quantitative Studies in Social Relations). 1981. 30.00 (ISBN 0-12-260720-1). Acad Pr.
Flik, T. & Liebig, H. The Sixteen-Bit Microprocessor Systems. 300p. 1985. pap. 34.50 (ISBN 0-387-15164-8). Springer-Verlag.
Flikeid, Karin. La Variation Phonetique dans le Parler Acadien du Nordest du Nouveau Brunswick: Etude Socio-Linguistique. (American University Studies XIII: Vol. 1). 496p. (Orig., Fr.). 1984. pap. text ed. 39.00 (ISBN 0-8204-0066-1). P Lang Pubs.
Flinders, Matthew & Ingleton, Geoffrey. Matthew Flinders: Navigator & Chartmaker. ltd. ed. (Illus.). 700p. 1983. hand bound leather 460.00 (ISBN 0-904351-13-0). Genesis Pubns.
Fling, Fred M. Outline of the Historical Method. LC 76-147836. (Research & Source Works Ser.: No. 726). 1971. Repr. of 1899 ed. lib. bdg. 15.00 (ISBN 0-8337-1160-1). B Franklin.
Fling, Helen. Marionettes: How to Make & Work Them. (Illus.). 192p. 1973. pap. 3.95 (ISBN 0-486-22909-2). Dover.
--Marionettes: How to Make & Work Them. (Illus.). 14.25 (ISBN 0-8446-4736-5). Peter Smith.
Fling, Paul N. & Puterbaugh, Donald L. The Basic Manual of Fly Tying. LC 77-80194. (Illus.). 1979. pap. 9.95 (ISBN 0-8069-8146-6). Sterling.
--Expert Fly-Tying. LC 81-85025. (Illus.). 160p. (Orig.). 1982. pap. 8.95 (ISBN 0-8069-7580-6). Sterling.
Fling, Paul N. & Puterbaugh, Donald N. Fly-Fisherman's Primer. LC 84-26737. (Illus.). 164p. (Orig.). 1985. pap. 8.95 (ISBN 0-8069-7890-2). Sterling.
Fling, Robert Michael, ed. Basic Music Library: Essential Scores & Books. 2nd. ed. LC 83-2768. xii, 357p. 1983. pap. 12.00x (ISBN 0-8389-0375-4). ALA.
Flink, James J. America Adopts the Automobile, 1895-1910. 1970. 25.00x (ISBN 0-262-06036-1). MIT Pr.
--The Car Culture. LC 74-31191. 280p. 1975. o. p. 25.00x (ISBN 0-262-06059-0); pap. 6.95x (ISBN 0-262-56015-1). MIT Pr.
Flink, Salomon J. Equity Financing of Small Manufacturing Companies in New Jersey. Bruchey, Stuart & Carosso, Vincent P., eds. LC 78-18960. (Small Business Enterprise in America Ser.). (Illus.). 1979. Repr. of 1963 ed. lib. bdg. 12.00x (ISBN 0-405-11464-8). Ayer Co Pubs.
--German Reichsbank & Economic Germany. LC 70-95097. Repr. of 1930 ed. lib. bdg. 15.00x (ISBN 0-8371-2542-1, FLGR). Greenwood.
Flinker, Susan. Hip Hair: From Mohawks to Dreadlocks & Beyond. (Illus.). 64p. (Orig.). 1985. pap. 3.95 (ISBN 0-440-53660-X, Dell Trade Pbks). Dell.
Flinn, Avril & Almand, Joan. Come into My Parlor. LC 79-55652. 1979. pap. 2.50 (ISBN 0-88270-396-X, Pub. by Logos). Bridge Pub.
Flinn, D. E., jt. auth. see West, L. J.
Flinn, E., ed. Scientific Results of Viking Project. (Illus.). 725p. 1977. 15.00 (ISBN 0-87590-207-3). Am Geophysical.
Flinn, Frank, ed. Hermeneutics & Horizons: The Shape of the Future. LC 82-50053. 445p. (Orig.). 1982. pap. 12.95 (ISBN 0-932894-11-9). Rose Sharon Pr.
Flinn, Frank K., ed. Hermeneutics & Horizons: The Shape of the Future. LC 82-50053. (Conference Ser.: No. 11). xvii, 445p. (Orig.). 1982. pap. text ed. 11.95 (ISBN 0-932894-11-9, Pub. by New Era Bks). Paragon Hse.
--Religious Liberty in Peril. (Orig.). Date not set. text ed. price not set (ISBN 0-913757-34-9, Pub. by New Era Bks.); pap. text ed. price not set (ISBN 0-913757-35-7, Pub. by New Era Bks.). Paragon Hse.
Flinn, Frank K. & Hendricks, Tyler, eds. Religion in the Pacific Era. (Orig.). 1985. text ed. 17.95 (ISBN 0-913757-18-7, Pub. by New Era Bks.); pap. text ed. 12.95 (ISBN 0-913757-19-5, Pub. by New Era Bks.). Paragon Hse.
Flinn, Frank K., jt. ed. see DeGraeve, Frank P.
Flinn, J. E. Rapid Solidification Technology for Reduced Consumption of Strategic Materials. LC 85-4769. (Illus.). 215p. 1985. 32.00 (ISBN 0-8155-1032-2). Noyes.
Flinn, J. E., ed. Membrane Science & Technology: Industrial, Biological, & Waste Treatment Processes. LC 77-118126. 234p. 1970. 35.00x (ISBN 0-306-30484-8, Plenum Pr). Plenum Pub.
Flinn, Jane Z., ed. Reflections on Writing: Programs & Strategies for Classrooms K-12. 99p. 1981. 6.00 (ISBN 0-8141-3983-3). NCTE.
Flinn, John J. History of the Chicago Police; from the Settlement of the Community to the Present Time. LC 77-156016. Repr. of 1887 ed. 20.00 (ISBN 0-404-09116-4). AMS Pr.
--History of the Chicago Police: From the Settlement of the Community to the Present Time. LC 75-172577. (Criminology, Law Enforcement, & Social Problems Ser.: No. 164). (Illus.). 750p. (With intro. & index added). 1973. Repr. of 1887 ed. lib. bdg. 20.00x (ISBN 0-87585-164-9). Patterson Smith.
Flinn, John J. & Wilkie, John E. History of the Chicago Police: From the Settlement of the Community to the Present Time. LC 72-156280. (Police in America Ser). 1971. Repr. of 1887 ed. 35.00 (ISBN 0-405-03369-9). Ayer Co Pubs.
Flinn, M., ed. see Chadwick, E.
Flinn, M. W. & Smout, T. C., eds. Essays in Social History. (Illus.). 1974. pap. 15.95x (ISBN 0-19-877017-0). Oxford U Pr.
Flinn, Michael W. The European Demographic System: Fifteen Hundred to Eighteen Twenty. LC 80-19574. (Studies in Comparative History: No. 11). 192p. 1981. text ed. 18.50x (ISBN 0-8018-2426-5). Johns Hopkins.
--The European Demographic System, Fifteen Hundred to Eighteen Twenty. LC 80-19574. (Symposia in Comparative History Ser.). 192p. 1985. pap. text ed. 8.95x (ISBN 0-8018-3155-5). Johns Hopkins.
--Scottish Population History: From the Seventeenth Century to the 1930s. LC 76-11060. (Illus.). 1978. 79.50 (ISBN 0-521-21173-5). Cambridge U Pr.
Flinn, Michael W. & Stoker, David. The History of the British Coal Industry: Vol. 2 - 1700-1830, The Industrial Revolution. (Illus.). 1984. 67.00x (ISBN 0-19-828283-4). Oxford U Pr.
Flinn, Nancy. The Prison Garden Book. 56p. Date not set. pap. price not set (ISBN 0-915873-05-2). Natl Gardening Assn.
Flinn, Richard A. Fundamentals of Metal Casting. 324p. text ed. 20.95 (ISBN 0-317-32629-5, OS6304). Am Foundrymen.
Flinn, Richard A. & Trojan, Paul K. Engineering Materials & Their Applications. 2nd ed. (Illus.). 753p. 1981. text ed. 34.95 (ISBN 0-395-29645-5); solutions manual 7.50 (ISBN 0-395-29646-3). HM.
Flinn, Thomas A. Local Government & Politics: Analyzing Decision-Making Systems. 1970. pap. 10.80 (ISBN 0-673-05562-0). Scott F.
Flint, A. P., et al, eds. Embryonic Diapause in Mammals. 260p. 1981. 60.00x (ISBN 0-906545-04-8, Pub. by Journals Repro England). State Mutual Bk.
Flint, Aili. Say It in Finnish. (Language & Linguistics Ser.). 192p. (Orig.). 1984. pap. 3.50 (ISBN 0-486-24591-8). Dover.
Flint, Albert S. Madison Catalogue of Two Thousand Seven Hundred Eighty-Six Stars for the Epoch 1910 from Meridian Observations. Roy, Arthur J., ed. LC 39-33947. (Carnegie Institution of Washington Ser.: No. 515). pap. 20.00 (ISBN 0-317-09020-8, 2007906). Bks Demand UMI.
Flint, Austin. Insights: A Contemporary Reader. 176p. (Orig.). 1981. pap. text ed. 8.95 (ISBN 0-88377-185-3). Newbury Hse.
Flint, Betty M. The Security of Infants. LC 59-40393. (Illus.). 1959. pap. 36.00 (ISBN 0-317-08106-3, 2014209). Bks Demand UMI.
Flint, Brian. Suffolk Windmills. (Illus.). 1979. 13.50 (ISBN 0-85115-112-4, Pub. by Boydell & Brewer). Longwood Pub Group.
Flint, Carol. Flat in Bliss. 1980. 2.00 (ISBN 0-936814-06-3). New Collage.
Flint, Christine E. & Conway, Stephen M., eds. The Company Data Directory. 823p. 1983. looseleaf 180.00 (RC100, RC). Unipub.
Flint, D. A True & Fair View in Company Accounts. 1982. pap. 12.95 (ISBN 0-85258-223-4). Van Nos Reinhold.
Flint, David C. The Data Ring Main: An Introduction to Local Area Networks. LC 82-23738. (Computing Science Ser.: I-652). 375p. 1983. 39.95x (ISBN 0-471-26251-X, Pub. by Wiley Heyden). Wiley.
Flint, E. Essentials of Crystallography. 2nd ed. MIR Publishers, tr. from Rus. (Illus.). 231p. 1974. text ed. 15.00x (ISBN 0-8464-0389-7). Beekman Pubs.
Flint, Emily P., ed. Creative Editing & Writing Workbook. 279p. 1979. 40.00 (ISBN 0-89964-038-9). Coun Adv & Supp Ed.
--Creative Editing & Writing Workbook. 279p. 1979. 40.00 (ISBN 0-89964-038-9). Coun Adv & Supp Ed.
Flint, Emily P., ed. see Williams, Doone & Williams, Greer.
Flint, F. Cudworth. Amy Lowell. (Pamphlets on American Writers Ser: No. 82). (Orig.). 1969. pap. 1.25x (ISBN 0-8166-0544-0, MPAW82). U of Minn Pr.
Flint, F. S. Cadences. LC 78-64026. (Des Imagistes: Literature of the Imagist Movement). (Illus.). Repr. of 1915 ed. 15.00 (ISBN 0-404-17099-4). AMS Pr.
--In the Net of the Stars. LC 78-64027. (Des Imagistes: Literature of the Imagist Movement). Repr. of 1909 ed. 11.50 (ISBN 0-404-17106-0). AMS Pr.
--Otherworld. LC 78-64028. (Des Imagistes: Literature of the Imagist Movement). Repr. of 1920 ed. 12.50 (ISBN 0-404-17107-9). AMS Pr.
--Some Modern French Poets. Bd. with The Younger French Poets. LC 78-64029. (Des Imagistes: Literature of the Imagist Movement). Repr. of 1920 ed. 14.00 (ISBN 0-404-17108-7). AMS Pr.
Flint, F. S., tr. see Fulop-Miller, Rene.
Flint, Harrison. The Country Journal Book of Hardy Trees & Shrubs. (Illus.). 176p. (Orig.). 1983. pap. 10.00 (ISBN 0-918678-02-1). Historical Times.
Flint, Harrison L. Landscape Plants for Eastern North America: Exclusive of Florida & the Immediate Gulf Coast. LC 82-16068. 677p. 1983. 59.95x (ISBN 0-471-86905-8, Pub. by Wiley-Interscience). Wiley.
Flint, Helen, ed. see Beckley, John L.
Flint, Henry M. The Railroads of the United States. LC 75-22818. (America in Two Centuries Ser). 1976. Repr. of 1868 ed. 34.50x (ISBN 0-405-07690-8). Ayer Co Pubs.
Flint, James. Letters from America: Containing Observations on the Climate & Agriculture of the Western States, the Manners of the People & the Prospects of Emigrants. 1971. Repr. of 1822 ed. 21.00 (ISBN 0-384-16028-X). Johnson Repr.
Flint, Janet. The Prints of Louis Lozowick: A Catalogue Raisonne. LC 82-6223. (Illus.). 224p. 1982. 50.00 (ISBN 0-933920-30-X). Hudson Hills.
Flint, Jeremy & Greenwood, David. Instructions for the Defence. (Illus.). 125p. 1981. 11.50 (ISBN 0-370-30032-7, Pub. by the Bodley Head). Merrimack Pub Cir.
Flint, Joe, jt. auth. see Brown, Toni S.
Flint, John E., ed. see Kent, Tom & McAllister, Ian.
Flint, John W. Stop the Clock: The Tao of Time & Timelessness. LC 84-51562. 85p. 1985. pap. 6.95 (ISBN 0-87516-546-X). De Vorss.
Flint, Kate. Impressionists in England: The Critical Reception. (Schools of Art Ser.). (Illus.). 400p. 1984. 29.95 (ISBN 0-7100-9470-1). Routledge & Kegan.
Flint, Kenneth C. Champions of the Sidhe. 1984. pap. 2.95 (ISBN 0-553-24543-0). Bantam.
--Master of the Sidhe. 1985. pap. 2.95 (ISBN 0-317-31350-9). Bantam.
--Riders of Sidhe. 272p. 1984. pap. 2.95 (ISBN 0-553-24175-3). Bantam.
Flint, Lucy. The Peggy Guggenheim Collection. Messer, Thomas M., selected by. (Illus.). 224p. 1983. 30.00 (ISBN 0-8109-0959-6). Abrams.
Flint, Lucy, tr. see Rowell, Margit.
Flint, Mary L. & Kobbe, Brunhilde. Integrated Pest Management for Citrus. LC 83-82076. (Illus.). 100p. (Orig.). 1983. pap. 15.00x (ISBN 0-931876-65-6, 3303). Ag & Nat Res.
Flint, Mary L. & Van Den Bosch, Robert. Introduction to Integrated Pest Management. LC 80-28479. 255p. 1981. 19.95x (ISBN 0-306-40682-9, Plenum Pr). Plenum Pub.
Flint, Mary L., jt. auth. see IPM Manual Group.
Flint, Mary L., jt. auth. see IPM Manual Group Staff.
Flint, Mary L., ed. Integrated Pest Management for Alfalfa Hay. LC 81-65780. (Illus.). 96p. (Orig.). 1981. pap. 15.00x (ISBN 0-931876-46-X, 4104). Ag & Nat Res.
--Integrated Pest Management for Tomatoes. LC 82-70536. 112p. 1982. pap. text ed. 15.00x (ISBN 0-931876-56-7, 3274). Ag & Nat Res.
--Integrated Pest Management for Walnuts. LC 81-69166. (Illus.). 96p. (Orig.). 1982. pap. text ed. 12.00x (ISBN 0-931876-50-8, 3270). Ag & Nat Res.
Flint, Mary L., et al, eds. Integrated Pest Management for Rice. LC 82-73445. (Illus.). 85p. (Orig.). 1983. pap. text ed. 15.00x (ISBN 0-931876-61-3, 3280). Ag & Nat Res.
Flint, Oliver S. The Genus Brachycentrus in North America, with a Proposed Phylogeny of the Genera of Brachycentridae (Trichoptera) LC 84-600157. (Smithsonian Contributions to Zoology Ser.: No. 398). pap. 20.00 (ISBN 0-317-26339-0, 2024229). Bks Demand UMI.
Flint, R. W., tr. see Marinetti, Filippo T.
Flint, R. Warren & Rabalais, Nancy N., eds. Environmental Studies of a Marine Ecosystem: South Texas Outer Continental Shelf. 268p. 1981. text ed. 35.00x (ISBN 0-292-72030-0). U of Tex Pr.
Flint, Richard F. Earth & Its History. (Illus.). 500p. 1973. text ed. 13.95x (ISBN 0-393-09377-8). Norton.
--Glacial & Quaternary Geology. LC 74-141198. (Illus.). 892p. 1977. 52.95x (ISBN 0-471-26435-0). Wiley.
Flint, Richard F. & Skinner, Brian J. Physical Geology. 2nd ed. LC 76-23206. 671p. 1977. text ed. 35.45 (ISBN 0-471-26442-3); study guide, 185p. 11.45 (ISBN 0-471-02593-3); tchrs.' manual avail. (ISBN 0-471-03075-9). Wiley.
Flint, Robert. History of the Philosophy of History. 59.95 (ISBN 0-8490-0360-1). Gordon Pr.
--Philosophy As Scientia Scientiarum: A History of Classifications of the Sciences. LC 74-26261. (History, Philosophy & Sociology of Science Ser). 1975. Repr. 25.00x (ISBN 0-405-06589-2). Ayer Co Pubs.
--Vico. Mayer, J. P., ed. & intro. by. LC 78-67355. (European Political Thought Ser.). 1979. Repr. of 1901 ed. lib. bdg. 16.00x (ISBN 0-405-11697-7). Ayer Co Pubs.
Flint, Roland. And Morning. LC 74-11608. 1975. pap. 5.95 (ISBN 0-931848-02-4). Dryad Pr.
--Say It. LC 78-5149. 1979. pap. 5.95 (ISBN 0-931848-21-0). Dryad Pr.
Flint, Russ, jt. auth. see Mason, Alice L.
Flint, Timothy. Biographical Memoir of Daniel Boone. Folsom, James K., ed. (Masterworks of Literature Ser). 1967. 7.95x (ISBN 0-8084-0061-4); pap. 4.95x (ISBN 0-8084-0062-2). New Coll U Pr.

--Condensed Geography & History of the Western States or the Mississippi Valley 1828, 2 Vols. LC 70-119865. 1970. Repr. of 1828 ed. 130.00x set (ISBN 0-8201-1076-0). Schol Facsimiles.
--Indian Wars of the West, Containing Biographical Sketches of Those Pioneers Who Headed the Western Settlers in Repelling the Attacks of the Savages. LC 74-146395. (First American Frontier Ser). 1971. Repr. of 1833 ed. 20.00 (ISBN 0-405-02848-2). Ayer Co Pubs.
--Little Henry: the Stolen Child. LC 73-104452. Repr. of 1830 ed. lib. bdg. 27.00 (ISBN 0-8398-0558-6). Irvington.
--Recollections of the Last Ten Years in the Valley of the Mississippi. 2nd ed. LC 68-24891. (American Scene Ser). 1968. Repr. of 1826 ed. lib. bdg. 49.50 (ISBN 0-306-71136-2). Da Capo.
--Recollections of the Last Ten Years in the Valley of the Mississippi. Brooks, George R., ed. LC 68-21413. (Travels on the Western Waters Ser). (Illus.). 367p. 1968. 15.00x (ISBN 0-8093-0332-9). S Ill U Pr.
--Recollections of the Last Ten Years: Passed in Occasional Residences & Journeyings in the Valley of the Mississippi. (American Studies). 1968. Repr. of 1826 ed. 24.00 (ISBN 0-384-16030-1). Johnson Repr.
Flint, Timothy, ed. see Pattie, James O.
Flint, Tommy & Griffin, Neil. Gospel Guitar. 48p. 1976. wkbk 2.95 (ISBN 0-89228-018-2). Impact Bks MO.
Flint, V. E., et al. A Field Guide to Birds of the U. S. S. R. Bourso-Leland, Natalia, tr. from Russian. LC 83-42558. (Illus.). 353p. 1984. 65.00 (ISBN 0-691-08244-8). Princeton U Pr.
Flint, W. Russell, tr. see Thomas A'Kempis.
Flint, William W. Use of Myth to Create Suspense. (Studies in Comparative Literature, No. 35). 1970. pap. 24.95x (ISBN 0-8383-0030-8). Haskell.
Flinter, George D. View of the Present Condition of the Slave Population in the Island of Puerto Rico Under the Spanish Government. LC 76-110011. Repr. of 1832 ed. 10.00x (ISBN 0-8371-4161-3). Greenwood.
Flintoff, F. & Millard, R. Public Cleansing. (Illus.). 475p. 1969. 44.50 (ISBN 0-85334-004-8, Pub. by Elsevier Applied Sci England). Elsevier.
Flipovic, R., et al. Yugoslavic Deluxe Dictionary: English-Croation or Serbian. 11th ed. 1436p. (Eng. & Serbocroatian.). 1983. 75.00x (ISBN 0-89918-779-X, Y-779). Vanous.
--Yugoslavic Pocket Dictionary: Croation-English. 468p. 1979. 15.00x (ISBN 0-89918-781-1). Vanous.
--Yugoslavic Pocket Dictionary: English-Croation. 564p. (Eng. & Croatian.). 1979. 20.00x (ISBN 0-89918-780-3, Y-780). Vanous.
Flippen, Charles C. Liberating the Media: The New Journalism. LC 73-22086. 300p. 1974. 9.95 (ISBN 0-87491-361-6); pap. 5.95 (ISBN 0-87491-362-4). Acropolis.
Flipper, Henry O. Colored Cadet at West Point. LC 69-18551. (American Negro: His History & Literature, Ser. No. 2). 1969. Repr. of 1878 ed. 11.50 (ISBN 0-405-01863-0). Ayer Co Pubs.
--The Colored Cadet at West Point: First Graduate of Color from the U.S. Military Academy. (Basic Afro-American Reprint Library). (Illus.). 1969. Repr. of 1878 ed. 20.00 (ISBN 0-384-16040-9). Johnson Repr.
Flippin, Percy S. The Financial Administration of the Colony of Virginia. LC 78-63952. (Johns Hopkins University. Studies in the Social Sciences. Thirty-Third Ser. 1915: 2). 416p. 1983. Repr. of 1915 ed. 24.50 (ISBN 0-404-61200-8). AMS Pr.
--Royal Government in Virginia, 1624-1775. LC 76-168047. (Columbia University. Studies in the Social Sciences: No. 194). Repr. of 1919 ed. 27.50 (ISBN 0-404-51194-5). AMS Pr.
Flippo, Chet. David Bowie's Serious Moonlight: The World Tour. LC 83-40140. (Illus.). 256p. 1984. 35.00 (ISBN 0-385-19265-7, Dolp); pap. 16.95 (ISBN 0-385-19266-5). Doubleday.
--On the Road with the Rolling Stones. LC 84-28764. 192p. 1985. pap. 6.95 (ISBN 0-385-19374-2, Dolp). Doubleday.
--Your Cheatin' Heart: A Biography of Hank Williams. LC 84-16693. (Illus.). 272p. 1985. pap. 8.95 (ISBN 0-385-19737-3, Dolp). Doubleday.
Flippo, Edwin B. Personnel Management. 6th ed. (Management Ser.). 608p. 1984. text ed. 31.95 (ISBN 0-07-021321-6). McGraw.
Flippo, Edwin B. & Munsinger, Gary M. Management. 5th ed. 625p. 1982. pap. 31.43 (ISBN 0-205-07681-5, 087681X); tchr's ed. free (ISBN 0-205-07682-3, 0876828). Allyn.
Flipse, J. E., ed. Deep Ocean Mining. (OED: Vol. 8). 80p. 1975. 8.00 (ISBN 0-317-33470-0, G00162); members 4.00 (ISBN 0-317-33471-9). ASME.
Fliss, Tiffany, tr. see Bazin, Andre.
Flisser, Ana, et al, eds. Cysticercosis: Symposium. 1982. 60.00 (ISBN 0-12-260740-6). Acad Pr.
Fliszar, S. Charge Distributions & Chemical Effects. (Illus.). 225p. 1983. 42.80 (ISBN 0-387-90854-4). Springer-Verlag.
Flitch, J. Crawford, tr. see Unamuno, Miguel.
Flitch, J. E., tr. from Ger. see Selesius, Angelus.
Flitcroft, John E. Outline Studies in American Literature. 1979. Repr. of 1930 ed. lib. bdg. 20.00 (ISBN 0-8492-4613-X). R West.
Flitner, Arthur L., jt. auth. see Malecki, Donald S.
Flitsch, Wilhelm, jt. auth. see Valters, Raimonds E.
Flloyd, Thomas & Swammerdam, John. The Book of Nature: The History of Insects. Sterling, Keir B., ed. LC 77-83844. (Biologists & Their World Ser.). (Illus.). 1978. Repr. of 1758 ed. lib. bdg. 51.00x (ISBN 0-405-10742-0). Ayer Co Pubs.
Floan, Howard R. The South in Northern Eyes. LC 72-6774. (American History & Americana Ser., No. 47). 1972. Repr. of 1958 ed. lib. bdg. 42.95x (ISBN 0-8383-1647-6). Haskell.
--William Saroyan. (U. S. Authors Ser.: No. 100). 1966. lib. bdg. 10.95 (ISBN 0-8057-0652-6, Twayne). G K Hall.
Floating Eaglefeather, ed. As One Is, So One Sees - Stories, Poems, & Epigrams: A Literary & Graphic Medicine Bundle from Many World Cultures. LC 83-90132. (Illus.). 90p. (Orig.). 1983. pap. 6.00 (ISBN 0-9611360-0-6). Renaissance Art Writ Assn.
Floberg, Marilyn. Practice in Real Estate Mathematics. 3rd ed. 1975. text ed. 18.50 scp (ISBN 0-06-453617-3, HarpC); scp instructors manual 2.95 (ISBN 0-06-453621-1). Har-Row.
Floc'h, F., jt. ed. see Werner, G. H.
Floch, Martin H. Nutrition & Diet Therapy in Gastrointestinal Diseases. (Topics in Gastroenterology Ser.). 502p. 1981. 39.50x (ISBN 0-306-40508-3, Plenum Med. Bks.). Plenum Pub.
Flock, Emil & Flock, Miriam. BASIC Primer for the Macintosh. 1985. pap. 17.95 (ISBN 0-452-25639-9, Plume). NAL.
Flock, Miriam, jt. auth. see Flock, Emil.
Flock, Warren L. Electromagnetics & the Environment: Remote Sensing & Telecommunications. (Illus.). 1979. ref. 38.95 (ISBN 0-13-248997-X). P-H.
Flocker, William J. & Hartmann, Hudson T. Plant Science: Growth, Development & Utilization of Cultivated Plants. (Illus.). 688p. 1981. text ed. 32.95 (ISBN 0-13-681056-X). P-H.
Flocks, R. H. & Culp, David A. Surgical Urology: A Handbook of Operative Surgery. 4th ed. (Illus.). 575p. 1974. 47.50 (ISBN 0-8151-3262-X). Year Bk Med.
Flodin, N. W. Vitamin-Trace Mineral-Protein Interactions, Vol. 1. Horrobin, D. F., ed. (Annual Research Reviews). 1979. 26.40 (ISBN 0-88831-042-0). Eden Pr.
--Vitamin-Trace Mineral-Protein Interactions, Vol. 2. Horrobin, D. F., ed. (Annual Research Reviews). 1980. 30.00 (ISBN 0-88831-062-5, Dist. by Pergamon). Eden Pr.
Flodin, Nestor W. Vitamin-Trace Mineral-Protein Interactions. (Annual Research Reviews Ser.: Vol. 4). 386p. 1981. 38.00 (ISBN 0-88831-114-1). Eden Pr.
--Vitamin-Trace Mineral-Protein Interactions, Vol. 3. Horribin, David F., ed. (Annual Research Reviews). 362p. 1980. 38.00 (ISBN 0-88831-085-4). Eden Pr.
Flodstrom, John H., tr. see Ey, Henri.
Floegel, Ekkehard. The Apple in Your Hand. 220p. 12.95 (ISBN 3-88963-178-9). Blue Cat.
--FORTH on the Atari. 118p. 8.00 (ISBN 0-936200-38-3). Mountain View Pr.
--FORTH on the Atari: Learning by Using. 118p. 7.95 (ISBN 0-936200-38-3). Blue Cat.
--ZX-81 Timex: Programming in BASIC & Machine Language. 139p. 9.95 (ISBN 0-317-05097-4). Elcomp.
--ZX-81 Timex: Programming in BASIC & Machine Language. 139p. 9.95 (ISBN 3-921682-98-3). Blue Cat.
Floegel, Ekkehard, jt. auth. see Hofacker, Winfried.
Floering, Ingrid, jt. auth. see Graham, G. E.
Floethe, Louise L. Farmer & His Cows. (Illus.). (gr. 1-5). 1957. reinforced bdg. 5.95 (ISBN 0-684-12396-7, ScribJ). Scribner.
Flogel, Carl F. Geschichte Des Menschlichen Verstandes. 1973. Repr. of 1776 ed. 50.00 (ISBN 0-384-16050-6). Johnson Repr.
Flohe, L., et al. Glutathione. 1974. 71.50 (ISBN 0-12-260750-3). Acad Pr.
Flohn, H. General Climatology. Landsberg, H. E., ed. (World Survey of Climatology Ser.: Vol. 2). 266p. 1970. 102.25 (ISBN 0-444-40702-2). Elsevier.
--Investigations on the Climatic Conditions of the Advancement of the Tunisian Sahara. (Technical Note Ser.: No. 116). x, 32p. (Orig., Engl. & Fr.). 1971. pap. 10.00 (ISBN 0-685-25260-4, W92, WMO). Unipub.
Flohn, Hermann & Fantachi, Roberto, eds. The Climate of Europe: Past, Present & Future. 1984. lib. bdg. 49.00 (ISBN 90-277-1745-1, Pub. by Reidel Holland). Kluwer Academic.
Flohn, N. Climate & Weather. (Illus., Orig.). 1968. pap. 3.95 (ISBN 0-07-021325-9). McGraw.
Flohr, H. & Precht, W., eds. Lesion-Induced Neuronal Plasticity in Sensorimotor Systems. (Proceedings in Life Sciences Ser.). (Illus.). 400p. 1981. 52.00 (ISBN 0-387-10747-9). Springer-Verlag.
Flohr, John W., jt. auth. see Smith, Robert B.
Flohr, John W., et al. Study of the Guitar. (Illus.). 36p. (Orig.). 1986. pap. text ed. 5.95 (ISBN 0-914487-01-9). Troostwyk Pr.
Flohr, Scott. Handicapping to Win. pap. 5.95 (ISBN 0-87067-801-9). Borden.
--Memory Without Pain. (Orig.). 1969. pap. 1.75 (ISBN 0-87067-177-4, BH177). Holloway.
Floistad, Gutton. Contemporary Philosophy: A New Survey. 1983. lib. bdg. 58.50 (ISBN 90-247-2632-8, Pub. by Martinus Nijhoff Netherlands). Kluwer Academic.
Floistad, Guttorm. Contemporary Philosophy: A New Survey, (Philosophy of Science, Vol. II. 1982. 78.50 (ISBN 90-247-2518-6, Pub. by Martinus Nijhoff Netherlands). Kluwer Academic.
Floistad, Guttorm & Von Wright, G. H., eds. Philosophy of Language: Philosophical Logic. (Contemporary Philosophy: a New Survey Ser.: No. 1). 320p. 1981. 43.20 (ISBN 0-686-31875-7, Pub. by Martinus Nujhoff Netherlands). Kluwer Academic.
Flom, George T. The Language of the Konungs Skuggsja Speculum Regale, 2 Vols. 1921-1923. Vol. 7, No. 3. 12.00 ea. (ISBN 0-384-16060-3); Vol. 8, No. 4. (ISBN 0-384-16070-0). Johnson Repr.
--The Phonology of the Dialect of Aurland Norway, Vol. 1 Nos. 1-2. pap. 8.00 (ISBN 0-384-16080-8). Johnson Repr.
--Scandinavian Influence on Southern Lowland Scotch. LC 70-168048. (Columbia University. Germanic Studies, Old Ser.: No. 1). Repr. of 1900 ed. 14.00 (ISBN 0-404-50401-9). AMS Pr.
Flomenbaum, Neal & Goldfrank, Lewis, eds. Diagnostic Testing in the Emergency Department. 340p. 1984. 42.00 (ISBN 0-89443-592-2). Aspen Systems.
Flomenhaft, Eleanor. The Roots & Development of Cobra Art. (Illus.). 128p. 1985. 55.00 (ISBN 0-933535-00-7). Fine Arts Muse LI.
Flomenhaft, Kalman & Christ, Adolpf E., eds. The Challenge of Family Therapy: A Dialogue for Child Psychiatric Educators. LC 80-18943. (Downstate Series of Research in Psychiatry & Psychology: Vol. 3). 234p. 1980. 32.50x (ISBN 0-306-40553-9, Plenum Pr). Plenum Pub.
Flomenhaft, Kalman, jt. ed. see Christ, Adolf E.
Flomenhaft, Kalman, jt. ed. see Christ, Adolph E.
Flood & Lapp. Teaching Students to Read. 642p. 1986. pap. 15.00 (ISBN 0-02-338450-6). Macmillan.
Flood, Aaron. The Goddess Stick. (Orig.). 1969. pap. 1.25 (ISBN 0-87067-174-X, BH174). Holloway.
Flood, Barbara & Witiak, Joanne, eds. Challenges to an Information Society, 1984: Proceedings of the 47th ASIS Annual Meeting 1984, Vol. 21. LC 64-8303. 256p. 1984. pap. 22.50 (ISBN 0-86729-115-X, 351-BW). Knowledge Indus.
Flood, Bob. Moody Church History. (Orig.). 1985. pap. price not set. Moody.
Flood, C. R., jt. auth. see Parkin, N.
Flood, Charles B. Lee: The Last Years. (Illus.). 352p. 1981. 14.95 (ISBN 0-395-31292-2); 8.95 (ISBN 0-395-34637-1). HM.
Flood, David. Franciscan Women. 64p. 1976. pap. 0.95 (ISBN 0-8199-0593-3). Franciscan Herald.
Flood, David & Matura, Thadee. The Birth of a Movement. LaChance, Paul & Schwartz, Paul, trs. 168p. 1975. 6.95 (ISBN 0-8199-0567-4). Franciscan Herald.
Flood, E. A., ed. The Solid-Gas Interface, Vols. 1 & 2. 1967. Vol. 1. 125.00 (ISBN 0-8247-1200-5); Vol. 2. 125.00 (ISBN 0-8247-1201-3). Dekker.
Flood, Edmund. Making More of Holy Week. 1984. pap. 3.95 pamphlet (ISBN 0-8091-5184-7). Paulist Pr.
--More Parables For Now. 4.95 (ISBN 0-87193-192-3). Dimension Bks.
--Parables for Now. 4.95 (ISBN 0-87193-186-9). Dimension Bks.
Flood, J. The Moth Hunters: Aboriginal Prehistory of the Australian Alps. (AIAS New Ser.). (Illus.). 1980. text ed. 25.50x (ISBN 0-391-00993-1); pap. text ed. 18.00x (ISBN 0-391-00994-X). Humanities.
Flood, J. L., ed. see King, K. C.
Flood, James & Salus, Peter H. Language & the Language Arts. (Illus.). 320p. 1984. 24.95 (ISBN 0-13-522979-0). P-H.
Flood, James, jt. auth. see Lapp, David.
Flood, James, jt. auth. see Lapp, Diane.
Flood, James, ed. Promoting Reading Comprehension. 320p. 1984. 18.00 (ISBN 0-87207-737-3). Intl Reading.
--Understanding Reading Comprehension. 16.00 (ISBN 0-87207-736-5). Intl Reading.
Flood, James E. & Lapp, Diane. Language-Reading Instruction for the Young Child. (Illus.). 1981. text ed. write for info. (ISBN 0-02-338470-0). Macmillan.
Flood, Jeanne. Brian Moore. (Irish Writers Ser.). 98p. 1975. 4.50 (ISBN 0-8387-7823-2); pap. 1.95 (ISBN 0-8387-7972-7). Bucknell U Pr.
Flood, John A. Barristers' Clerks: The Law's Middlemen. LC 83-912. 164p. 1983. 22.00 (ISBN 0-7190-0928-6, Pub. by Manchester Univ Pr). Longwood Pub Group.
Flood, John L., ed. Modern Swiss Literature: Unity & Diversity. LC 84-27707. 192p. 1985. 25.00 (ISBN 0-312-54237-2). St Martin.
Flood, Josephine. Archaeology of the Dreamtime: The Story of Prehistoric Australia & Her People. (Illus.). 288p. 1983. text ed. 19.95x (ISBN 0-8248-0897-5). UH Pr.
Flood, Kenneth U. & Callson, Oliver G. Transportation Management. 4th ed. 736p. 1984. text ed. write for info. (ISBN 0-697-08514-7). Wm C Brown.
Flood, Kenneth U., ed. Research in Transportation: Legal-Legislative & Economic Sources & Procedures. LC 72-118792. (Management Information Guides Ser.: No. 20). 1970. 60.00x (ISBN 0-8103-0820-7). Gale.
Flood, R. B. Home Fruit & Vegetable Production. LC 78-4214. 175p. 1978. 16.00 (ISBN 0-8108-1132-4). Scarecrow.
Flood, Robert. The Book of Fascinating Christian Facts. LC 84-71633. 206p. (Orig.). 1985. pap. 6.95 (ISBN 0-89636-145-4). Accent Bks.
Flood, Robert G. The Christian Kids Almanac. 224p. (gr. 4 up). 1983. 9.95 (ISBN 0-89191-715-2). Cook.
--The Christian's Vacation & Travel Guide. 224p. 1982. pap. 9.95 (ISBN 0-8423-0260-3). Tyndale.
--Thirty Minute Panorama of the Bible. (Orig.). 1984. pap. 1.95 (ISBN 0-8024-8747-5). Moody.
Flood, Robert G. & Jenkins, Jerry B. Men Behind Moody. (Orig.). 1984. pap. 1.95 (ISBN 0-8024-5393-7). Moody.
--Teaching the Word, Reaching the World. 1985. text ed. 14.95 (ISBN 0-8024-8567-7). Moody.
Flood, Robert J. Clay Tobacco Pipes in Cambridgeshire. (Cambridge Town, Gown & County Ser.: Vol. 6). (Illus.). 40p. 1976. pap. 4.25 (ISBN 0-902675-70-2). Oleander Pr.
Flood, W. E. Scientific Words: Their Structure & Meaning. LC 74-6707. 220p. 1974. Repr. of 1960 ed. lib. bdg. 22.50x (ISBN 0-8371-7541-0, FLOW). Greenwood.
Flood, William G. The Story of the Bagpipe. LC 76-22332. (Illus.). 1976. Repr. of 1911 ed. lib. bdg. 25.00 (ISBN 0-89341-009-8). Longwood Pub Group.
Flood, William Grattan. The Story of the Harp. LC 76-42036. 1977. Repr. of 1905 ed. lib. bdg. 25.00 (ISBN 0-89341-057-8). Longwood Pub Group.
Flood, William H. Early Tudor Composers: Biographical Sketches of Thirty-Two Musicians & Composers of the Period 1485-1555. facs. ed. LC 68-25603. (Essay Index Reprint Ser). 1925. 14.00 (ISBN 0-8369-0447-8). Ayer Co Pubs.
Flood, Wm. H. A History of Irish Music. 1979. Repr. of 1905 ed. lib. bdg. 85.00 (ISBN 0-8495-1639-0). Arden Lib.
--Introductory Sketch of Irish Musical History. LC 77-75229. 1977. Repr. of 1921 ed. lib. bdg. 15.00 (ISBN 0-89341-085-3). Longwood Pub Group.
Floodgate, George D., jt. ed. see Fletcher, Madilyn M.
Floodplains & Wetlands-Legal Constraints & Options Institute & Loyola University of Chicago. The Law of Floodplains & Wetlands: Cases & Materials. 2nd ed. American Bar Association Special Committee on Housing & Urban Development Law, ed. (Illus.). 591p. 1982. looseleaf 25.00 (391-0001). Amer Bar Assn.
Flook, Maria. Reckless Wedding. 1982. 12.95 (ISBN 0-395-32507-2); pap. 5.95 (ISBN 0-395-32508-0). HM.
Flooke, jt. auth. see Morris.
Floors, O. Rosemaling Designs (8) Nordmore. pap. 10.00x (ISBN 0-89918-422-7, N422). Vanous.
--Rosemaling Designs (8) Sunnmore. pap. 10.00x (ISBN 0-89918-423-5, N423). Vanous.
Floors, Telmark O. Rosemaling Designs (Eight) 10.00x (ISBN 0-89918-421-9, N-421). Vanous.
Flora, Cornelia B. Pentecostalism in Colombia: Baptism by Fire & Spirit. LC 74-4974. 288p. 1976. 26.50 (ISBN 0-8386-1578-3). Fairleigh Dickinson.
Flora, James. The Day the Cow Sneezed. LC 75-8746. (Illus.). 42p. (gr. k-1). 1975. pap. 1.95 (ISBN 0-15-624213-3, VoyB). HarBraceJ.
--Grandpa's Ghost Stories. 1980. pap. 1.95 (ISBN 0-689-70469-0, A-98, Aladdin). Atheneum.
--Grandpa's Ghost Stories. LC 78-51999. (Illus.). 32p. (ps-4). 1978. 12.95 (ISBN 0-689-50112-9, McElderry Bk); pap. 1.95 (ISBN 0-689-70469-0). Atheneum.
--Grandpa's Witched-Up Christmas. LC 81-12843. (Illus.). 32p. (ps-4). 1982. 12.95 (ISBN 0-689-50232-X, McElderry Bk). Atheneum.
--The Great Green Turkey Creek Monster. LC 75-43894. (Illus.). 32p. (ps-4). 1976. 9.95 (ISBN 0-689-50060-2, McElderry Bk); pap. 1.95 (ISBN 0-689-70459-3). Atheneum.
--My Friend Charlie. LC 64-16265. (Illus.). (gr. 1-4). 1972. pap. 1.25 (ISBN 0-15-662330-7, VoyB). HarBraceJ.
--Wanda & the Bumbly Wizard. LC 79-54683. (Illus.). 32p. (ps-4). 1980. 9.95 (ISBN 0-689-50154-4, McElderry Bk). Atheneum.
Flora, Joseph M. The English Short Story, Eighteen Eighty to Nineteen Forty-Five: A Critical History. (Critical History of the Short Story Ser.). 1985. lib. bdg. 17.95 (ISBN 0-8057-9357-7, Twayne). G K Hall.
--Frederick Manfred. LC 74-1972. (Western Writers Ser: No. 13). 1974. pap. 2.00x (ISBN 0-88430-012-9). Boise St Univ.
--Hemingway's Nick Adams. LC 81-14284. xvi, 272p. 1982. text ed. 25.00x (ISBN 0-8071-0993-2). La State U Pr.

--Vardis Fisher. (Twayne's United States Authors Ser.). 1965. pap. 5.95x (ISBN 0-8084-0311-7, T76, Twayne). New Coll U Pr.

--William Ernest Henley. LC 72-120015. (Twayne's English Authors Ser.). 1970. lib. bdg. 15.95 (ISBN 0-89197-977-8); pap. text ed. 4.95x (ISBN 0-89197-994-8). Irvington.

Flora, Joseph M., ed. see Cabell, James B.

Flora, Peter & Heidenheimer, Arnold J., eds. Development of Welfare States in Europe & America. LC 79-65227. 420p. 1981. pap. 12.95 (ISBN 0-87855-920-5). Transaction Bks.

Flora, Peter, et al. State, Economy & Society in Western Europe, 1815-1975: A Data Handbook, 2 vols. Incl. Vol. 1. The Growth of Mass Democracies & Welfare States. 1983 (ISBN 0-912289-00-7); Vol. 2. The Growth of Industrial Societies & Capitalist Economies. 1985 (ISBN 0-912289-06-6). (Illus.). 650p. lib. bdg. 72.50x ea. St James Pr.

Flora, Philip C. International CAD-CAM Software Directory. (Illus.). 140p. (Orig.). Date not set. pap. text ed. 35.00 (ISBN 0-910747-06-7). Tech Data TX.

--International Computer Aided Design Directory. (Illus.). 240p. (Orig.). pap. text ed. 35.00 (ISBN 0-910747-01-6). Tech Data TX.

--International Computer Aided Manufacturing Directory. (Illus., Orig.). Date not set. pap. text ed. 35.00 (ISBN 0-910747-00-8). Tech Data TX.

--International Computer Vision Directory. (Illus.). 160p. (Orig.). Date not set. pap. text ed. 35.00 (ISBN 0-910747-08-3). Tech Data TX.

--International Engineering-Scientific Software Directory. (Illus., Orig.). Date not set. pap. text ed. 35.00 (ISBN 0-910747-05-9). Tech Data TX.

--International Industrial Sensor Directory. (Illus.). 280p. (Orig.). Date not set. pap. text ed. 35.00 (ISBN 0-910747-19-9). Tech Data TX.

--International Programmable Controllers Directory. (Illus.). 136p. (Orig.). Date not set. pap. text ed. 35.00 (ISBN 0-910747-07-5). Tech Data TX.

Flora, Philip C., ed. International Robotics Industry Directory, 1984. 4th ed. (Illus.). 348p. 1984. pap. 35.00 (ISBN 0-444-86890-9). Tech Data Corp.

Flora, Sherrill. Preschool Teacher's Daily Plan Book. 32p. 1985. 2.95 (ISBN 0-513-01792-5). Denison.

Flora, Snowden D. Hailstorms of the United States. (Illus.). 216p. 1956. 13.50x (ISBN 0-8061-0359-0). U of Okla Pr.

Flora, Steven R., jt. auth. see Barnett, Timothy L.

Florance, A. Geographical Lexicon of Greek Coin Inscriptions. (Gr.). 1978. pap. 10.00 (ISBN 0-89005-232-8). Ares.

Florance, Cheri L., jt. auth. see Shames, George H.

Florance, Chris. Carolina Home Gardener. LC 75-23480. vi, 140p. 1976. 4.95 (ISBN 0-8078-1258-7). U of NC Pr.

Florant, J., jt. auth. see Bach, H.

Florczyk, Sandra E., jt. auth. see Bednarski, Mary W.

Flore, Frances. Love's Wine. (Candlelight Ecstasy Ser.: No. 61). (Orig.). 1982. pap. 1.75 (ISBN 0-440-14785-9). Dell.

Flore, Ron Le see Le Flore, Ron & Hawkins, Jim.

Florea, J. H. ABC of Poultry Raising. 6.00 (ISBN 0-685-48057-7). Assoc Bk.

--The ABC of Poultry Raising: A Complete Guide for the Beginner or Expert. 3rd ed. LC 75-8092. 256p. 1977. pap. 3.50 (ISBN 0-486-23201-8). Dover.

--ABC of Poultry Raising: A Complete Guide for the Beginner or Expert. (Illus.). 12.75 (ISBN 0-8446-5186-9). Peter Smith.

Florea, Vasile. Romanian Painting. LC 82-23740. (Illus.). 154p. 1983. 13.50x (ISBN 0-8143-1731-6). Wayne St U Pr.

Floren, Lee. Bonanza at Wishbone. 1977. pap. 1.50 (ISBN 0-505-51183-5, Pub. by Tower Bks). Dorchester Pub Co.

--Boothill Brand. 192p. 1983. pap. 2.25 (ISBN 0-8439-2059-9, Leisure Bks). Dorchester Pub Co.

--Boothill Riders. 1978. pap. 1.25 (ISBN 0-532-12584-3). Woodhill.

--Broken Creek. 1981. pap. 1.95 (ISBN 0-8439-0939-0). Dorchester Pub Co.

--Broomtail Basin. 1981. pap. 1.95 (ISBN 0-8439-0941-2). Dorchester Pub Co.

--The Bushwhackers. (Orig.). 1980. pap. 1.75 (ISBN 0-505-51531-8, Pub. by Tower Bks). Dorchester Pub Co.

--Callahan Rides Alone. 192p. 1981. pap. 1.95 (ISBN 0-505-51749-3, Pub. by Tower Bks). Dorchester Pub Co.

--A Double Cross Ranch. (Orig.). 1981. pap. 1.95 (ISBN 0-8439-0922-6, Leisure Bks). Dorchester Pub Co.

--Fast Gun Grass. (Orig.). 1979. pap. 1.75 (ISBN 0-532-23214-3). Woodhill.

--Fighting Ramrod. 1978. pap. 1.25 (ISBN 0-8439-0547-6, Leisure Bks). Dorchester Pub Co.

--Gambler With a Gun. 13.95 (ISBN 0-88411-129-6, Pub. by Aeonian Pr). Amereon Ltd.

--Gun Chore. 1979. pap. 1.25 (ISBN 0-532-12590-8). Woodhill.

--Gun Lords of Stirrup Basin. 1977. pap. 1.25 (ISBN 0-532-12526-6). Woodhill.

--Gun to Gun. 1977. pap. 1.25 (ISBN 0-532-12521-5). Woodhill.

--Gun Wolves of Lobo Basin. 1978. pap. 1.25 (ISBN 0-532-12568-1). Woodhill.

--Gunpowder Grass. 1978. pap. 1.25 (ISBN 0-532-12572-X). Woodhill.

--Gunpowder Mesa. 1978. pap. 1.25 (ISBN 0-532-12588-6). Woodhill.

--Guns of Montana. 192p. 1981. pap. 1.95 (ISBN 0-8439-0965-X, Leisure Bks). Dorchester Pub Co.

--Hangman's Range. 1975. pap. 0.95 (ISBN 0-685-53131-7, LB279NK, Leisure Bks). Dorchester Pub Co.

--The Hard Riders. 1978. pap. 1.25 (ISBN 0-8439-0522-0, Leisure Bks). Dorchester Pub Co.

--High Border Riders. (Orig.). 1979. pap. 1.50 (ISBN 0-532-15391-X). Woodhill.

--High Gun. (Orig.). 1979. pap. 1.50 (ISBN 0-532-23110-4). Woodhill.

--Law of the West. 1977. pap. 1.50 (ISBN 0-8439-0497-6, Leisure Bks). Dorchester Pub Co.

--The Outlaw Breed. Orig. Title: Wild Border Guns. 1977. pap. 1.25 (ISBN 0-8439-0481-X, Leisure Bks). Dorchester Pub Co.

--Pinon Mesa. 1978. pap. 1.50 (ISBN 0-505-51266-1, Pub. by Tower Bks). Dorchester Pub Co.

--Powdersmoke Lawyer. (Orig.). 1979. pap. 1.50 (ISBN 0-532-15390-1). Woodhill.

--Puma Pistoleers. (Orig.). 1981. pap. 1.95 (ISBN 0-8439-0920-X, Leisure Bks). Dorchester Pub Co.

--Rails West to Glory. 1978. pap. 1.25 (ISBN 0-532-12559-2). Woodhill.

--The Rawhide Men. (Orig.). 1979. pap. 1.50 (ISBN 0-532-15399-5). Woodhill.

--The Renegade Rancher. 1978. pap. 1.25 (ISBN 0-532-12575-4). Woodhill.

--Ride the Wild Country. 176p. 1983. pap. 1.95 (ISBN 0-8439-2034-3, Leisure Bks). Dorchester Pub Co.

--Rifles on the Range. 1978. pap. 1.25 (ISBN 0-8439-0531-X, Leisure Bks). Dorchester Pub Co.

--Rimrock Renegade. 1978. pap. 1.25 (ISBN 0-505-51247-5, Pub. by Tower Bks). Dorchester Pub Co.

--Rope the Wild Wind. (Orig.). 1979. pap. 1.75 (ISBN 0-532-23149-X). Woodhill.

--Rough Country. 1976. pap. 0.95 (ISBN 0-685-69149-7, LB362NK, Leisure Bks). Dorchester Pub Co.

--The Saddle Tramps. 1977. pap. 1.25 (ISBN 0-532-12520-7). Woodhill.

--Shootout at Milk River. 1977. pap. 1.50 (ISBN 0-505-51185-1, Pub. by Tower Bks). Dorchester Pub Co.

--This Grass, This Gun. 1978. pap. 1.25 (ISBN 0-532-12531-2). Woodhill.

--Wolf Dog Range. 1978. pap. 1.25 (ISBN 0-8439-0530-1, Leisure Bks). Dorchester Pub Co.

--Wyoming Saddles. 1977. pap. 1.25 (ISBN 0-532-12522-3). Woodhill.

Floren, Myron & Floren, Randee. Accordion Man. LC 81-6583. (Illus.). 256p. 1981. 12.95 (ISBN 0-8289-0400-6). Greene.

Floren, Randee, jt. auth. see Floren, Myron.

Florence, A. T. & Attwood, D. Physicochemical Principles of Pharmacy. (Illus.). 509p. 1982. 29.95x (ISBN 0-412-00131-4, NO. 5000). Methuen Inc.

Florence, A. T., jt. auth. see Attwood, D.

Florence, A. T., ed. Materials Used in Pharmaceutical Formulation. (Critical Reports on Applied Chemistry Ser.). (Illus.). 160p. 1984. text ed. 39.00x (ISBN 0-632-01257-9, Pub. by Blackwell Sci UK). Blackwell Pubns.

Florence, Alan. Information Management with dBASE II. cancelled (ISBN 0-89303-550-5). Brady Comm.

--Information Management with dBASE II. (Illus.). 320p. 19.95 (ISBN 0-317-13065-X). P-H.

Florence, Barbara M., ed. Lella Secor: A Diary in Letters, 1915-1922. (American Women's Diary Ser). (Illus.). 1978. lib. bdg. 14.95 (ISBN 0-89102-071-3); pap. 5.95 (ISBN 0-89102-114-0). B Franklin.

Florence, Bob. College: What Every Athlete Needs to Know. LC 80-65921. 213p. 1980. 12.95 (ISBN 0-8092-7109-5). Contemp Bks.

Florence, David & Hegedus, Frank. Coping with Chronic Pain: A Patient's Guide to Wellness. 26p. 1982. 5.25 (ISBN 0-88440-037-9, 705). Sis Kenny Inst.

Florence, Mal. Trojan Heritage: A Pictorial History of USC Football. LC 80-84556. (Illus.). 184p. 1980. 16.95 (ISBN 0-938694-01-4). JCP Corp VA.

Florence of Worcester. Chronicle. Forester, Thomas, tr. LC 68-55550. (Bohn's Antiquarian Library Ser). 1968. Repr. of 1854 ed. 27.50 (ISBN 0-404-50008-0). AMS Pr.

Florence, P. Sargant. Economics of Fatigue & Unrest & the Efficiency of Labour in English & American Industry. LC 83-49109. (Accounting History & the Development of a Profession Ser.). 415p. 1984. lib. bdg. 50.00 (ISBN 0-8240-6325-2). Garland Pub.

Florence, Philip S. Economics of Fatigue & Unrest & the Efficiency of Labour in English & American Industry. LC 77-136530. 426p. Repr. of 1924 ed. lib. bdg. 19.75x (ISBN 0-8371-5451-0, FLEF). Greenwood.

--Use of Factory Statistics in the Investigation of Industrial Fatigue. LC 76-76627. (Columbia University. Studies in the Social Sciences: No. 190). Repr. of 1918 ed. 16.50 (ISBN 0-404-51190-2). AMS Pr.

Florence, Ronald. The Gypsy Man. Jaffe, Marc, ed. LC 84-40484. 336p. 1985. 16.45 (ISBN 0-394-53751-3, Pub. by Villard Bks). Random.

--Zeppelin. LC 81-66959. 416p. 1982. 14.95 (ISBN 0-87795-327-9). Arbor Hse.

Florens, J. P., et al, eds. Specifying Statistical Models, From Parametric to Non-Parametric, Using Bayesian or Non-Bayesian Approaches: Proceedings, Louvain-la-Neuve, Belgium, 1981. (Lecture Notes in Statistics Ser.: Vol. 16). (Illus.). 204p. 1983. pap. 15.00 (ISBN 0-387-90809-9). Springer-Verlag.

Flores, A. Spanish Literature in English Translation: A Bibliographical Syllabus. 59.95 (ISBN 0-8490-1103-5). Gordon Pr.

Flores, Angel. Bibliografía de Escritores Hispanoamericanos, 1609-1974. LC 74-30319. 328p. 1975. 35.00x (ISBN 0-87752-183-2). Gordian.

--Ibsen: Four Essays. (Studies in Comparative Literature, No. 35). 1970. pap. 27.95x (ISBN 0-8383-0091-X). Haskell.

--A Kafka Bibliography 1908-1976. LC 76-21333. 256p. 1976. 15.00x (ISBN 0-87752-206-5). Gordian.

--Lope de Vega, Monster of Nature. LC 74-95098. Repr. of 1930 ed. lib. bdg. 18.75x (ISBN 0-8371-2541-3, FLLV). Greenwood.

--Lope de Vega: Monster of Nature. LC 79-93062. 1969. Repr. of 1930 ed. 19.50x (ISBN 0-8046-0675-7, Pub. by Kennikat). Assoc Faculty Pr.

--The Problem of the Judgment: Eleven Approaches to Kafka's Story. LC 76-48958. 1977. 12.50x (ISBN 0-87752-210-3). Gordian.

Flores, Angel & Benardete, M. J. Cervantes Across the Centuries: A Quadricentennial Volume. LC 79-90367. (Corrected Ed.). 1969. Repr. of 1947 ed. text ed. 15.00x (ISBN 0-87752-036-4). Gordian.

Flores, Angel, ed. Anthology of German Poetry from Holderlin to Rilke. 12.75 (ISBN 0-8446-1185-9). Peter Smith.

--Explain to Me: Some Stories of Kafka. LC 83-11648. 160p. (Orig.). 1983. pap. text ed. 6.95 (ISBN 0-87752-228-6). Gordian.

--The Kafka Debate: New Perspectives for Our Time. LC 77-2699. 1977. 20.00x (ISBN 0-87752-211-1). Gordian.

--The Kafka Problem: An Anthology of Criticism About Franz Kafka. LC 77-2699. 1976. Repr. of 1963 ed. 17.50x (ISBN 0-87752-204-9). Gordian.

--Nineteenth Century French Tales. LC 63-31051. pap. 5.95 (ISBN 0-8044-6150-3). Ungar.

--Spanish Writers in Exile. 1977. 12.50 (ISBN 0-685-74168-0). Porter.

Flores, Angel & Flores, Kate, eds. The Defiant Muse: Hispanic Feminist Poems from the Middle Ages to the Present. 275p. (Orig., Span.). 1985. text ed. 24.95 (ISBN 0-935312-47-1); pap. text ed. 9.95 (ISBN 0-935312-54-4). Feminist Pr.

Flores, Angel & Swander, Homer, eds. Franz Kafka Today. LC 77-23982. 1977. Repr. of 1958 ed. 13.50x (ISBN 0-87752-207-3). Gordian.

Flores, Angel, tr. see Neruda, Pablo.

Flores, Angel, tr. see Sabartes, Jaime.

Flores, Anthony. Basic Borders. 1984. pap. 7.95 (ISBN 0-8224-2144-5). Pitman Learning.

--Instant Borders. 1979. pap. 6.95 (ISBN 0-8224-3899-2). Pitman Learning.

--Instant Bulletin Boards: Month by Month Classroom Graphics. 1983. pap. 10.95 (ISBN 0-8224-3900-X). Pitman Learning.

Flores, Bess, jt. ed. see Coppell, William.

Flores, Carlos F., jt. auth. see Winograd, Terry.

Flores, Dan L., ed. Journal of an Indian Trader: Anthony Glass & the Texas Trading Frontier, 1790-1810. LC 85-40049. (Southwestern Studies: No. 4). (Illus.). 152p. 1985. 19.50 (ISBN 0-89096-235-9). Tex A&M Univ Pr.

Flores, Dan L., ed. see Freeman, Thomas & Custis, Peter.

Flores, David, jt. ed. see Wallace, Don.

Flores, E., ed. see Wells, Robert.

Flores, Eliezer. Full-Auto. (Illus.). 32p. (Orig.). 1981. pap. 8.00 (ISBN 0-918751-00-4). J O Flores.

Flores, Eliezer, ed. How to Make Disposable Silencers, Vol. II. (Illus.). 120p. (Orig.). 1985. pap. 12.00 (ISBN 0-918751-03-9). J O Flores.

Flores, Ernest Y. The Mini-Guide to Leadership. LC 80-83627. 90p. 1981. perfect bdg. 6.50 (ISBN 0-86548-037-0). R & E Pubs.

--The Nature of Leadership for Hispanics & Other Minorities. LC 80-69239. 140p. 1981. perfect bdg. 10.95 (ISBN 0-86548-036-2). R & E Pubs.

--Teaching Your Child to Lead: A Parents Guide. LC 81-51217. (Illus.). 60p. 1981. perfect bound 4.95 (ISBN 0-88247-592-4). R & E Pubs.

Flores, Evelina V. El Yugo de los Infieles. 116p. (Sp.). 1981. pap. 2.20 (ISBN 0-311-37008-X). Casa Bautista.

Flores, F., jt. auth. see Garcia-Moliner, F.

Flores, Issac M. An American Legacy. (Illus.). 317p. 1982. write for info. (ISBN 0-89305-047-4); pap. write for info. (ISBN 0-89305-048-2). Anna Pub.

Flores, Ivan. Data Base Architecture. 480p. 1981. 28.50 (ISBN 0-442-22729-9). Van Nos Reinhold.

--Data Structure & Management. 2nd ed. 1977. 32.95 (ISBN 0-13-197335-5). P-H.

--The Professional Microcomputer Handbook. (Illus.). 752p. 1985. 49.50 (ISBN 0-442-22497-4). Van Nos Reinhold.

--Word Processing Handbook. 512p. 1982. 37.95 (ISBN 0-442-22526-1). Van Nos Reinhold.

Flores, Ivan & Terry, Christopher. Microcomputer Systems. 290p. 1982. 24.50 (ISBN 0-442-26141-1). Van Nos Reinhold.

Flores, Ivan, jt. auth. see Seidman, Arthur.

Flores, John. Poetry in East Germany: Adjustments, Visions & Provocations 1945-1970. LC 77-115368. (Yale Germanic Studies: No. 5). Repr. of 1971 ed. 70.00 (ISBN 0-8357-9442-3, 2016777). Bks Demand UMI.

Flores, Jose. Profecia y Carisma, Que de las Lenguas? Orig. Title: Prophecy & Charisma. 68p. (Span.). 1974. pap. 1.95 (ISBN 0-8254-1238-2). Kregel.

Flores, Jose, tr. see Collins, Gary.

Flores, Jose, tr. see Karo, Nancy & Mickelson, Alvera.

Flores, Jose, tr see Manley & Robinson.

Flores, Juan. Insularismo e ideologia burguesa. 128p. 1980. pap. 3.75 (ISBN 0-940238-20-9). Ediciones Huracan.

Flores, Juan, tr. see Iglesias, Cesar A.

Flores, Kate. Relativity & Consciousness: A New Approach to Evolution. LC 84-24674. 186p. (Orig.). 1985. pap. text ed. 10.00 (ISBN 0-87752-230-8). Gordian.

Flores, Kate, jt. ed. see Flores, Angel.

Flores, Miguel C. El Charro en U. S. A. LC 84-70211. (Illus., Span.). 1984. pap. 10.00 (ISBN 0-9608806-1-5, 00291). Assoc Pubns.

Flores, P. V. Educational Innovation in the Philippines: A Case Study of Project Impact. 88p. 1981. pap. 9.00 (ISBN 0-88936-294-7, IDRCTS36, IDRC). Unipub.

Flores, Ralph. The Rhetoric of Doubtful Authority: Deconstructive Readings of Self-Questioning Narratives, St. Augustine to Faulkner. LC 83-15297. 176p. 1984. 17.50x (ISBN 0-8014-1625-6). Cornell U Pr.

Flores, Raymond J. The Socio-Economic Status Trends of the Mexican People Residing in Arizona. pap. 10.00 (ISBN 0-88247-211-9). R & E Pubs.

Flores, Robert M. The Compositers of the First & Second Madrid Editions of Don Quixote. (Publications of the Modern Humanities Research Association: Vol. 7). x, 148p. 1975. avail. Modern Humanities Res.

Flores, Romeo M., jt. ed. see Rahmani, Ray A.

Flores, Solomon H. The Nature & Effectiveness of Bilingual Education Programs for the Spanish-Speaking Child in the United States. Cordasco, Francesco, ed. LC 77-92296. (Bilingual-Bicultural Education in the U. S. Ser.). 1978. lib. bdg. 21.00x (ISBN 0-405-11082-0). Ayer Co Pubs.

Flores, Xavier. Agricultural Organizations & Economic & Social Development in Rural Areas. (Studies & Reports, New Ser.: No. 77). 1971. 14.85 (ISBN 92-2-100104-0, NS77). Intl Labour Office.

Flores, Zella K. The Relation of Language Difficulty to Intelligence & School Retardation in a Group of Spanish-Speaking Children. LC 74-833371. 1975. Repr. of 1926 ed. soft bdg. 10.95 (ISBN 0-88247-355-7). R & E Pubs.

Flores Caballero, Romeo. Counterrevolution: The Role of the Spaniards in the Independence of Mexico, 1804-1838. Rodriquez O., Jaime E., tr. LC 75-172037. (Illus.). xiv, 186p. 1974. 16.95x (ISBN 0-8032-0805-7). U of Nebr Pr.

Florescu, Radu R. Magyar Culture in Socialist Romania. (Ethnology Ser.: No. 1). (Illus.). 1976. pap. 2.50 (ISBN 0-89304-005-3, CCC103). Cross Cult.

Florescu, Radu R., jt. ed. see Fischer-Galati, Stephen.

Flores d'Arcais, G. B. & Jarvella, R. J., eds. The Process of Language Understanding. LC 82-23754. 340p. 1983. 64.95x (ISBN 0-471-90129-6, Pub. by Wiley-Interscience). Wiley.

Flores-Esteves, Manuel. Life after Shakespeare: Careers for Liberal Arts Majors. (Handbooks Ser.). 192p. (Orig.). 1985. pap. 6.95 (ISBN 0-14-046662-2). Penguin.

Flores Magon, Ricardo. Ricardo Flores Magon: Writings, 5 vols. 1979. Set. lib. bdg. 500.00 (ISBN 0-8490-2999-6). Gordon Pr.

Flores-Ochoa, Jorge A. Pastoralists of the Andes: The Alpaca Herders of Paratia. Bolton, Ralph, tr. from Spanish. LC 78-31360. (Illus.). 144p. 1979. text ed. 15.00x (ISBN 0-915980-89-4). ISHI PA.

Florestano & Marando. The States & the Metropolis. (Public Administration & Public Policy: a Comprehensive Publication Program Ser.: Vol. 9). 176p. 1981. 19.75 (ISBN 0-8247-1287-0). Dekker.

Floret, C., jt. ed. see Mabbutt, J. A.

Floret, K. Weekly Compact Sets. (Lecture Notes in Mathematics Ser.: Vol. 801). 123p. 1980. pap. 13.00 (ISBN 0-387-09991-3). Springer-Verlag.

Florey, Francis G. Elementary Linear Algebra with Applications. LC 78-9412. (Illus.). 1979. ref. ed. 28.95 (ISBN 0-13-258251-1). P-H.

Florey, Klaus, ed. Analytical Profiles of Drug Substances, Vol. 8. LC 79-187259. 1979. 60.00 (ISBN 0-12-260808-9). Acad Pr.

--Analytical Profiles of Drug Substances, Vol. 9. 1980. 50.00 (ISBN 0-12-260809-7). Acad Pr.

--Analytical Profiles of Drug Substances, Vol. 10. 1981. 60.00 (ISBN 0-12-260810-0). Acad Pr.

--Analytical Profiles of Drug Substances, Vol. 11. LC 70-187259. 1982. 55.00 (ISBN 0-12-260811-9). Acad Pr.

--Analytical Profiles of Drug Substances, Vol. 12. 1983. 53.50 (ISBN 0-12-260812-7). Acad Pr.
--Analytical Profiles of Drug Substances, Vol. 13. 1984. 46.50 (ISBN 0-12-260813-5). Acad pr.

Florey, Klaus, et al, eds. Analytical Profiles of Drug Substances, Vols. 1-6. Vol. 1, 1972. 70.00 (ISBN 0-12-260801-1); Vol. 2. 1973. 70.00 (ISBN 0-12-260802-X); Vol. 3, 1974. 70.00 (ISBN 0-12-260803-8); Vol. 4, 1975. 75.00 (ISBN 0-12-260804-6); Vol. 5, 1976. 70.00 (ISBN 0-12-260805-4); Vol. 6, 1977. 70.00 (ISBN 0-12-260806-2). Acad Pr.

Florey, R. A. The General Strike of Nineteen Twenty-Six. 1981. 28.95 (ISBN 0-7145-3698-9); pap. 12.95 (ISBN 0-7145-3813-2). Riverrun NY.

Flor-Henry. Cerebral Bases of Psychopathology. 384p. 1983. text ed. 41.50 (ISBN 0-7236-7034-X). PSG Pub Co.

Flor-Henry, P., jt. auth. see Gruzelier, J. H.

Flor-Henry, P. & Gruzelier, J., eds. Laterality & Psychopathology. (Developments in Psychiatry Ser.: Vol. 6). 600p. 1983. 64.00 (ISBN 0-444-80481-1, I-360-83, Biomedical Pr). Elsevier.

Florian. Transportation Planning Models. 1984. 55.00 (ISBN 0-444-87581-6). Elsevier.

Florian, David J. The Phenomenon of Language: Tabula Latina. (Illus.). 243p. (Orig.). (gr. 6-9). 1979. 7.00x (ISBN 0-88334-124-7); tests 5.00 (ISBN 0-88334-150-6). Ind Sch Pr.

Florian, Doug. People Working. LC 82-45188. (Illus.). 32p. (ps-3). 1983. 10.53i (ISBN 0-690-04263-9); PLB 10.89g (ISBN 0-690-04264-7). Crowell Jr Bks.

Florian, Douglas. Airplane Ride. LC 83-45048. (Illus.). 32p. (ps-2). 1984. 10.53i (ISBN 0-690-04364-3); PLB 10.89g (ISBN 0-690-04365-1). Crowell Jr Bks.

Florian, Jorge E. Amor Gemelo. (Romance Real Ser.). 189p. 1981. pap. 1.50 (ISBN 0-88025-002-X). Roca Pub.

Florian, M., ed. Practice of Transportation Planning: Proceedings Relating to the Course Given at the International Center for Transportation Studies (ICTS), Amalfi, Italy, 4-8 October, 1983. 286p. 1985. 70.50 (ISBN 0-444-87668-5, North-Holland). Elsevier.

Florian, Michael & Gaudry, Marc, eds. Transportation Supply Models. 225p. 1981. 31.00 (ISBN 0-08-026075-6). Pergamon.

Florian, Tibor. Defense & Counter-Attack. (Pergamon Chess Ser.). (Illus.). 124p. 1984. 13.95 (ISBN 0-08-024143-3). Pergamon.

Florida Anthropological Society. Florida Anthropological Society Publications, Nos. 1-5. Set. pap. 35.00 (ISBN 0-384-16110-3). Johnson Repr.

Florida Atlantic University Conference. Management Problems in Serials Work: Proceedings. Spyers-Duran, Peter & Gore, Daniel, eds. LC 73-10775. 1974. lib. bdg. 27.50 (ISBN 0-8371-7050-8, SSW/). Greenwood.

Florida Bar Continuing Legal Education. Comparative Negligence & Contribution in Florida. 2nd ed. LC 82-83853. (Illus.). vii, 111p. 1982. 20.00. CLE Pubns.

Florida Flair Books Staff. The Everglades Coloring Book. (Illus.). 32p. 1982. pap. 2.50 (ISBN 0-916224-75-9). Banyan Bks.

Florida Solar Energy Center. Performance Monitoring of Active Solar Energy Systems. Yarosh, Marvin, ed. 327p. 1984. pap. 34.95 (H047). Solar Energy Info.

Florida Trend Magazine, ed. Florida Facts & Figures. 18th rev ed. LC 66-13567. (Illus.). 1984. pap. 1.25 (ISBN 0-88251-079-7). Trend House.

Floridi, Alexis. Moscow & the Vatican. 365p. 1985. 23.50 (ISBN 0-88233-647-9). Ardis Pubs.

Floridi, Alexis U. & Stiefbold, Annette E. The Uncertain Alliance: The Catholic Church & Labor in Latin America. LC 73-92382. (Monographs in International Affairs). 108p. 1973. text ed. 7.95 (ISBN 0-933074-22-0); pap. text ed. 4.95 (ISBN 0-933074-23-9). AISI.

Floridis, Ronald G. Comprehensive Split Dollar. 180p. (Orig.). 1983. pap. 19.00 (ISBN 0-87218-424-2). Natl Underwriter.

Florin, Gustav. Interpretation of Shear & Bond in Reinforced Concrete. (Structural Engineering Ser.: Vol. 1). (Illus.). 86p. 1980. pap. 24.00x (ISBN 0-87849-033-7). Trans Tech.
--Theory & Design of Surface Structures Slabs & Plates. (Structural Engineering Ser.: Vol. 2). (Illus.). 222p. 1980. 38.00x (ISBN 0-87849-034-5); pap. 24.00 (ISBN 0-87849-035-3). Trans Tech.

Florin, J. W., jt. auth. see Birdsall, S. S.

Florin, John W., ed. see Birdsall, Stephen S.

Florin, Lambert. Guide to Western Ghost Towns. LC 67-26049. (Illus.). pap. 4.95 (ISBN 0-87564-307-8). Superior Pub.
--Victorian West. LC 78-23760. (Illus.). 1978. 15.95 (ISBN 0-87564-341-8). Superior Pub.

Florin, Lambert F. Alaska Ghost Towns-British Columbia-Yukon. LC 72-160186. 1971. pap. 4.95 (ISBN 0-87564-330-2). Superior Pub.
--California Ghost Towns. LC 70-160180. (Illus.). 1971. pap. 4.95 (ISBN 0-87564-324-8). Superior Pub.
--Nevada Ghost Towns. LC 78-160182. (Illus.). 1971. pap. 4.95 (ISBN 0-87564-326-4). Superior Pub.
--New Mexico-Texas Ghost Towns. LC 79-160185. (Illus.). 1971. pap. 4.95 (ISBN 0-87564-329-9). Superior Pub.
--Oregon Ghost Towns. LC 76-160179. (Illus.). 1971. pap. 4.95 (ISBN 0-87564-323-X). Superior Pub.

Florini, James R., ed. Handbook of Biochemistry in Aging. 320p. 1981. 59.00 (ISBN 0-8493-3141-2). CRC Pr.

Florini, James R., et al, eds. Rates of Protein Synthesis During Aging. 253p. 1974. text ed. 34.50x (ISBN 0-8422-7221-6). Irvington.

Florinskij, T. Juznye Slavjane I Vizantija: Vo Vtoroj Cetverti XIV Veka. 444p. 1973. 50.00x (ISBN 0-902089-53-6, Pub. by Variorum). State Mutual Bk.

Florinsky, Michael T. Fascism & National Socialism: A Study of the Economic & Social Policies of the Totalitarian State. LC 78-63667. (Studies in Fascism: Ideology & Practice). Repr. of 1936 ed. 29.50 (ISBN 0-404-16934-1). AMS Pr.
--Integrated Europe? LC 78-712. 1978. Repr. of 1955 ed. lib. bdg. 19.00x (ISBN 0-313-20279-6, FLIE). Greenwood.

Florinsky, N. I. Soslasno li c Evangelijem Dejstvoval i uchil Ljuter? 166p. 1975. pap. text ed. 6.00 (ISBN 0-317-30257-4). Holy Trinity.

Florio, A. E. & Alles. Safety Education. 4th, rev. ed. (Illus.). 1979. text ed. 34.95 (ISBN 0-07-021371-2). McGraw.

Florio, Anthony. You Can Make Your Marriage Stronger. (Christian Counseling Aids Ser). 1978. pap. 1.25 (ISBN 0-8010-3484-1). Baker Bk.

Florio, C., jt. auth. see Cross, W.

Florio, Carol. Collegiate Programs for Older Adults: A Summary Report on a 1976 Survey. LC 78-51940. (Academy Occasional Papers: No. 7). 52p. (Orig.). 1978. pap. 3.00 (ISBN 0-89492-003-0). Acad Educ Dev.

Florio, Carol, jt. auth. see Murphy, Judith.

Florio, Giovanni. Florios Second Frutes. LC 72-197. (English Experience Ser.: No. 157). 208p. 1969. Repr. of 1591 ed. 42.00 (ISBN 90-221-0157-6). Walter J Johnson.

Florio, J., tr. see Cartier, Jacques.

Florio, John. Florio His Firste Fruites: A Perfect Induction to the Italian & English Tongues. LC 72-6214. (English Experience Ser.: No. 95). 1969. Repr. of 1578 ed. 42.00 (ISBN 90-221-0095-2). Walter J Johnson.
--Second Frutes. LC 53-11448. 1977. Repr. of 1591 ed. 35.00x (ISBN 0-8201-1222-4). Schol Facsimiles.

Florio, John, tr. see De Montaigne, Michel.

Florio, John, tr. see De Montaigne, Michel E.

Florio, John, tr. see Montaigne, Michel D.

Florio, John A. World of Words: A Sixteenth Century Italian-English Dictionary. 1971. Repr. of 1598 ed. 66.50x (ISBN 3-4870-4227-4). Adlers Foreign Bks.

Floris, Christopher. The Floris Book of Cakes. (Illus.). 192p. 1981. 14.95 (ISBN 0-233-96978-0). Andre Deutsch.
--The Floris Book of Cakes. (Illus.). 192p. 1981. 14.95 (ISBN 0-233-96978-0, Pub. by A Deutsch England). David & Charles.

Florisoone, Michel. Dictionnaire des Cathedrales de France. 256p. (Fr.). 1971. pap. 6.95 (ISBN 0-686-56834-6, M-6612). French & Eur.

Floristan, Casiano & Duquoc, Christian. Francis of Assisi Today, Vol. 149. (Concilium 1981). 128p. (Orig.). 1981. pap. 6.95 (ISBN 0-8164-2349-0, Pub. by Seabury). Winston Pr.

Floristan, Casiano, jt. auth. see Duquoc, Christian.

Floristan, Casiano & Duquoc, Christian, eds. Charisms in the Church Concilium, Vol. 109. 1978. pap. 4.95 (ISBN 0-8245-0269-8). Crossroad NY.

Floristan, Casiano, jt. ed. see Duquoc, Christian.

Florit, E., jt. auth. see Anderson-Imbert, E.

Florit, Engenio. Poema Mio 1920-1944. 503p. (Sp.). 4.50 (ISBN 0-318-14300-3). Hispanic Inst.

Florit, Eugenio. Obras Completas, Vol. 1. 180p. 1985. pap. text ed. 30.00 (ISBN 0-89295-037-4). Society SP & Sp-Am.
--Obras Completas, Vol. 2. LC 82-60407. (Illus.). 150p. (Orig.). 1983. pap. 25.00 (ISBN 0-89295-021-8). Society Sp & Sp-Am.
--Obras Completas, Vol. 3. LC 80-53822. 370p. 1982. pap. 35.00 (ISBN 0-89295-017-X). Society Sp & Sp-Am.
--Poesia, Casi Siempre. (Span.). 1978. pap. 10.00 (ISBN 84-399-8746-3). Edit Mensaje.
--Poesia En Jose Marti, Juan Ramon Jimenez, Alfonso Reyes, Federico Garcia Lorca y Pablo Neruda. LC 78-55266. 1978. pap. 10.95 (ISBN 0-89729-207-3). Ediciones.
--Versos Pequenos (Nineteen Thirty-Eight to Nineteen Seventy-Five) LC 78-66030. (Senda Poetica Ser.). (Orig., Span.). 1979. pap. 3.95 (ISBN 0-918454-13-1). Senda Nueva.

Florit, Eugenio & Patt, B. P., eds. Retratos de Hispanoamerica. (Span.). 1962. text ed. 16.95x (ISBN 0-03-017135-0). Irvington.

Florit, Patricia C. Shadows in the Sun (Poems) 32p. (Orig.). 1985. pap. 5.00 (ISBN 0-89729-362-2). Ediciones.

Florkin, M. & Stotz, E. E. History of Molecular Interpretation of Physical & Biological Concepts & Origins of Conception. 1984. write for info. Elsevier.

Florkin, M. & Stotz, E. H. Comprehensive Biochemistry, Section 6: History of Biochemistry, Vols. 30-32. Incl. Vol. 30. Part 1: Proto-Biochemistry; Part 2: From Proto-Biochemistry to Biochemistry. 1972. 82.75 (ISBN 0-444-41024-4); Vol. 31. Pt. 3 History of Indentification of the Sources of Free Energy in Organisms. 1975. 119.75 (ISBN 0-444-41145-3); Vol. 32. Pt. 4 Early Studies on Biosynthesis. 73.75 (ISBN 0-444-41544-0). 1972-77. 0.00 (North Holland). Elsevier.

Florkin, M. & Neuberger, A., eds. Comprehensive Biochemistry, Vol. 19B, Pt. 1: Part 1: Protein Metabolism, Vol.19B. 528p. 1980. 101.50 (ISBN 0-444-80171-5, Biomedical Pr). Elsevier.

Florkin, M. & Stotz, eds. Comprehensive Biochemistry, Vol. 33A: Unravelling of Biosynthetic Pathways. 434p. 1979. 96.50 (ISBN 0-444-80067-0, Biomedical Pr). Elsevier.

Florkin, M. & Stotz, E., eds. Comprehensive Biochemistry: Amino Acids Metabolism & Sulphur Metabolism, Vol. 19A. 482p. 1981. 103.50 (ISBN 0-444-80257-6, Biomedical Pr). Elsevier.
--Comprehensive Biochemistry: Unraveling of Biosynthetic Pathways, Vol. 33B. 320p. 1979. 78.50 (ISBN 0-444-80068-9, Biomedical Pr). Elsevier.
--Comprehensive Biochemistry, Vol. 34A: The Recognition of Molecular Correlate of Biological Concepts. 1984. write for info. (ISBN 0-444-41544-0, Biomedical Pr). Elsevier.
--Comprehensive Biochemistry, Vol. 34B: From Ordered Polymers to Molecular Complementarities. 200p. 1984. write for info. (Biomedical Pr). Elsevier.

Florkin, M. & Stotz, E. E., eds. Comprehensive Biochemistry, Vol. 34: From Biological Biochemistry to Molecular Biology. Date not set. write for info. Elsevier.

Florkin, M. & Stotz, E. H., eds. Comprehensive Biochemistry: Pyruvates & Fatty Acid Metabolism, Vol. 18S. LC 62-10359. (Illus.). 125p. 1971. 39.25 (ISBN 0-444-40950-5, North Holland). Elsevier.
--Comprehensive Biochemistry, Section 1: Physico-Chemical & Organic Aspects of Biochemistry, Vols. 1-4. Incl. Vol. 1. Atomic & Molecular Structure; Vol. 2. Organic & Physical Chemistry. o. p. 78.50 (ISBN 0-444-40215-2); Vol. 3. Methods for the Study of Molecules. 78.50 (ISBN 0-444-40216-0); Vol. 4. Separation Methods. o. p. 78.50 (ISBN 0-444-40217-9). 1962 (North Holland). Elsevier.
--Comprehensive Biochemistry, Section 3: Biochemical Reaction Mechanics, Vols. 12-16. Incl. Vol. 12. Enzymes - General Considerations. 3rd ed. 1964. o. p. 71.00 (ISBN 0-444-40225-X); Vol. 13. Nomenclature of Enzymes & Coenzymes. 1973. o. p. 104.75 (ISBN 0-444-41140-2); Vol. 14. Biological Oxidations. 1966. 121.75 (ISBN 0-444-40229-2); Vol. 15. Group-Transfer Reactions. 1964. o. p. 59.75 (ISBN 0-444-40230-6); Vol. 16. Hydrolytic Reactions, Cobamide & Biotin Coenzymes. 1965. o. p. 64.25 (ISBN 0-444-40231-4). North Holland). Elsevier.
--Comprehensive Biochemistry, Section 5: Chemical Biology, Vols. 22-29. Incl. Vol. 22. Bioenergetics. 1967. 53.00 (ISBN 0-444-40233-0); Vol. 23. Cytochemistry. 1969. o. p. 41.50 (ISBN 0-444-40687-5); Vol. 25. Regulatory Functions - Mechanisms of Hormone Action. 1975. 39.25 (ISBN 0-444-41281-6); Vol. 26. Extracellular & Supporting Structures, 3 pts. 1968-71. Pt. A. 71.00 (ISBN 0-444-40234-9); Pt. B. 71.00 (ISBN 0-444-40235-7); Pt. C. o. p. 73.75 (ISBN 0-444-40870-3); Vol. 27. Photobiology, Ionizing Radiation. 1967. o. p. 93.00 (ISBN 0-444-40236-5); Vol. 28. Morphogenesis, Differentiation & Development. o. p. 69.00 (ISBN 0-444-40237-3); Vol. 29. Comparative Biochemistry, Molecular, 2 pts. 1980. Pt. A. o. p. 87.25 (ISBN 0-444-41192-5); Pt. B. 69.00 (ISBN 0-444-41282-4); Vol. 24. Biological Information Transfer. 1977. 74.50 (ISBN 0-444-41583-1). 1967-71 (North Holland). Elsevier.

Florkin, M., et al, eds. Comprehensive Biochemistry, Vol. 19B, Pt. 2: Protein Metabolism. 514p. 1982. 74.50 (ISBN 0-444-80346-7, Biomedical Pr). Elsevier.

Florkin, Marcel & Schoffeniels, Ernest. A Molecular Approaches to Ecology. 1969. 49.00 (ISBN 0-12-261046-6). Acad Pr.

Florkin, Marcel & Mason, Howard S., eds. Comparative Biochemistry: A Comprehensive Treatise, 7 vols. Incl. Vol. 1. Sources of Free Energy. 1960. 76.50 (ISBN 0-12-261001-6); Vol. 2. Free Energy & Biological Function. 1960. 78.00 (ISBN 0-12-261002-4); Vol. 3. Constituents of Life. 1962. 95.00 (ISBN 0-12-261003-2); Vol. 4. Constituents of Life. 1962. 97.50 (ISBN 0-12-261004-0); Vol. 5. Constituents of Life. 1963. 78.00 (ISBN 0-12-261005-9); Vol. 6. Cells & Organisms. 1963. 78.00 (ISBN 0-12-261006-7); Vol. 7. Supplementary Volume. 1964. 76.50 (ISBN 0-12-261007-5). LC 67-23158. Acad Pr.

Florkin, Marcel & Sheer, Bradley T., eds. Chemical Zoology, 11 vols. Incl. Vol. 1. 1967. 90.00 (ISBN 0-12-261031-8); Vol. 2. 1968. 86.00 (ISBN 0-12-261032-6); Vol. 3. 1969. 94.50 (ISBN 0-12-261033-4); Vol. 4. 1969. 80.50 (ISBN 0-12-261034-2); Vol. 5. 1970. 70.00 (ISBN 0-12-261035-0); Vol. 6. 1971. 75.00 (ISBN 0-12-261036-9); Vol. 7. 1972. 78.00 (ISBN 0-12-261037-7); Vol. 8. 1974. 92.00 (ISBN 0-12-261038-5); Vol. 9. 1974. 85.00 (ISBN 0-12-261039-3); Vol. 10. 1978. 72.00 (ISBN 0-12-261040-7); Vol. 11. Mammalia. 1979. 60.50 (ISBN 0-12-261041-5). LC 67-23158. Set. 750.00. Acad Pr.

Florman, Monte & Consumer Reports Books Editors. Consumer Reports Guide to Electronics in the Home. LC 84-80383. (Illus.). 256p. 1984. pap. 12.95 (ISBN 0-316-15339-7). Little.

Florman, Samuel. Blaming Technology: The Irrational Search for Scapegoats. 224p. 1982. pap. 6.95 (ISBN 0-312-08363-7). St Martin.
--Blaming Technology: The Retreat from Responsibility. LC 81-5818. 256p. 1981. 12.95 (ISBN 0-312-08362-9). St Martin.
--The Existential Pleasures of Engineering. LC 75-9480. 1977. pap. 4.95 (ISBN 0-312-27546-3). St Martin.

Florman, Samuel C. Engineering & the Liberal Arts: A Technologist's Guide to History, Literature, Philosophy, Art & Music. LC 81-23607. 288p. 1982. Repr. of 1968 ed. 24.50 (ISBN 0-89874-402-4). Krieger.

Florus. Roman History. Bd. with Lives. Cornelius Nepus. (Loeb Classical Library: No. 231). 12.50x (ISBN 0-674-99254-7). Harvard U Pr.

Flory, C. D., jt. auth. see Freeman, Frank N.

Flory, Charles, ed. Managers for Tomorrow. 1971. pap. 2.75 (ISBN 0-451-61938-2, ME1938, Ment). NAL.

Flory, Charles D. Osseous Development in the Hand As an Index of Skeletal Development. 1936. 15.00 (ISBN 0-527-01488-5). Kraus Repr.
--Physical Growth of Mentally Deficient Boys. (SRCD M). 1936. 11.00 (ISBN 0-527-01491-5). Kraus Repr.

Flory, Claude. Economic Criticism in American Fiction 1792-1900. LC 72-195217. 1972. lib. bdg. 27.50 (ISBN 0-8414-4245-2). Folcroft.

Flory, Esther V. see Cook, Dorothy E. & Monro, Isabel S.

Flory, Jane. The Bear on the Doorstep. (Illus.). 32p. (gr. k-3). 1980. PLB 6.95 (ISBN 0-395-29239-5). HM.
--The Great Bamboolzlement. (Illus.). 160p. (gr. 5-9). 1982. 7.95 (ISBN 0-395-31859-9). HM.
--Miss Plunkett to the Rescue. LC 82-15797. (Illus.). 84p. (gr. 3-6). 1983. 7.95 (ISBN 0-395-33072-6). HM.
--We'll Have a Friend for Lunch. (Illus.). (gr. k-3). 1981. pap. 3.45 (ISBN 0-395-31126-8). HM.
--We'll Have a Friend for Lunch. LC 73-18452. (Illus.). 32p. (gr. k-3). 1974. PLB 6.95 (ISBN 0-395-18448-7). HM.

Flory, M. A. A Book about Fans: The History of Fans & Fan-Painting. LC 72-174940. (Illus.). xiv, 141p. 1975. Repr. of 1895 ed. 37.00x (ISBN 0-8103-4049-6). Gale.

Flory, M. A. & Jones, Mary C. A Book about Fans: The History of Fans & Fan-Painting. LC 77-23572. 1977. Repr. of 1895 ed. lib. bdg. 25.00 (ISBN 0-89341-204-X). Longwood Pub Group.

Flory, P. J. Statistical Mechanics of Chain Molecules. LC 68-21490. 1969. 51.50x (ISBN 0-470-26495-0, Pub. by Wiley-Interscience). Wiley.

Flory, Paul J. Principles of Polymer Chemistry. (Illus.). 688p. 1953. 44.50x (ISBN 0-8014-0134-8). Cornell U Pr.
--Selected Works of Paul J. Flory, 3 vols. Mandelkern, Leo, et al, eds. LC 84-51712. 2644p. 1985. Set. 165.00x (ISBN 0-8047-1277-8). Stanford U Pr.

Flory, Phoebe, et al. Watercolor Portraiture: A Practical Guide. 192p. 1985. pap. 4.95 (ISBN 0-486-24972-7). Dover.

Flory, Randall K. & Sherman, J. Gilmour. Student Laboratory Experiments in Operant Conditioning. (Illus.). 100p. (Orig.). 1974. pap. text ed. 4.00 (ISBN 0-914044-02-8). Scholars Pr Ltd.

Flory, Sheldon. A Winter's Journey. (Illus., Orig.). 1979. pap. 4.50 (ISBN 0-914278-22-3). Copper Beech.

Flory, Thomas. Judge & Jury in Imperial Brazil, 1808-1871: Social Control & Political Stability in the New State. (Latin American Monographs: No. 53). 284p. 1981. text ed. 22.50x (ISBN 0-292-74015-8). U of Tex Pr.

Flory, Thomas, tr. see Petras, James & Zemelman Merino, Hugo.

Flory, Wayne E. Clete. 144p. 1985. pap. 7.95 (ISBN 0-89962-447-2). Todd & Honeywell.

Flory, Wendy S. Ezra Pound & the Cantos: A Record of Struggle. LC 79-23904. (Illus.). 1980. 33.00x (ISBN 0-300-02392-8). Yale U Pr.

Flosch, Doz U., jt. auth. see Creutzfeldt, Werner.

Floss, Michael M., jt. auth. see Cass, David B.

Flosso, Al. Great Magicians Mysteries. 1.95 (ISBN 0-685-38462-4). Wehman.

Floto, Igwa. Colonel House in Paris: A Study of American Policy at the Paris Peace Conference, 1919. LC 79-24059. (The Papers of Woodrow Wilson Suppl Vol.). 376p. 1981. Repr. of 1973 ed. 26.00x (ISBN 0-691-04662-X). Princeton U Pr.
Flottes. Vigny et sa Fortune Litteraire. 10.50 (ISBN 0-685-37143-3). French & Eur.
Floud, J. E., et al. Social Class & Educational Opportunity. LC 73-7195. (Illus.). 152p. 1973. Repr. of 1957 ed. lib. bdg. 21.00x (ISBN 0-8371-6918-6, FLSC). Greenwood.
Floud, Jean & Young, Warren. Dangerousness & Criminal Justice. LC 82-1762. (Cambridge Studies in Criminology: Vol. XLVII). 246p. 1982. text ed. 28.50 (ISBN 0-389-20286-X, 07106). B&N Imports.
--Dangerousness & Criminal Justice. 246p. 1982. 26.50 (ISBN 0-318-02911-1). Biblio Dist.
Floud, Roderick. The British Machine-Tool Industry, 1850-1914. LC 75-46205. (Illus.). 180p. 1976. 34.50 (ISBN 0-521-21203-0). Cambridge U Pr.
--Introduction to Quantitative Methods for Historians. 2nd ed. 1980. 12.95x (ISBN 0-416-71660-1, NO.2979); pap. 12.95x (ISBN 0-416-71670-9, NO.2978). Methuen Inc.
Floud, Roderick, ed. & intro. by. Essays in Quantitative Economic History. 1974. 21.95x (ISBN 0-19-877018-9). Oxford U Pr.
Floud, Roderick & McCloskey, Donald, eds. The Economic History of Britain Since 1700: Volume 2: 1860 to the 1970s. LC 79-41645. (Illus.). 504p. 1981. 69.50 (ISBN 0-521-23167-1); pap. text ed. 19.95 (ISBN 0-521-29843-1). Cambridge U Pr.
--The Economic History of Britain since 1700: 1700-1860, Vol. 1. LC 79-41645. 323p. 1981. 52.50 (ISBN 0-521-23166-3); pap. 16.95 (ISBN 0-521-29842-3). Cambridge U Pr.
Flournoy & Gibbs, Inc., ed. see Ohio Veterinary Medical Association.
Flournoy, Don M. The Rationing of American Higher Education. 202p. 1982. pap. text ed. 9.95 (ISBN 0-87073-989-1). Schenkman Bks Inc.
Flournoy, Don M., et al. The New Teachers. LC 77-184957. (Jossey-Bass Higher Education Ser.). Repr. of 1972 ed. 56.00 (ISBN 0-8357-9339-7, 2013817). Bks Demand UMI.
Flournoy, Fran. The Very Best Book of All. LC 82-80032. (Happy Day Bk.). (Illus.). 24p. (Orig.). (ps-3). 1982. pap. 1.39 (ISBN 0-87239-545-6, 3591). Standard Pub.
Flournoy, Francis R. British Policy Towards Morocco in the Age of Palmerston, 1830-1865. LC 74-106835. Repr. of 1935 ed. 19.75x (ISBN 0-8371-3457-9, FBP&, Pub. by Negro U Pr). Greenwood.
Flournoy, Mary H. Essays: Historical & Critical. facs. ed. LC 67-23220. (Essay Index Reprint Ser). 1967. Repr. of 1928 ed. 12.00 (ISBN 0-8369-0448-6). Ayer Co Pubs.
Flournoy, Richard L., et al. One Hundred Ways to Obtain Peace: Overcoming Anxiety. Anderson, Marty, ed. 100p. (Orig.). pap. 3.50 (ISBN 0-933629-04-4). Today Pubs.
Flournoy, Richard W., Jr. & Hudson, Manley O., eds. A Collection of Nationality Laws of Various Countries as Contained in Constitutions, Statutes & Treaties. xxiii, 776p. 1983. Repr. of 1929 ed. lib. bdg. 60.00x (ISBN 0-8377-0544-4). Rothman.
Flournoy, Roy. New Crime Controls: Savings for Taxpayers & Victims. LC 77-70445. (Illus.). 1977. 10.00x (ISBN 0-9601178-2-2); pap. 5.00 (ISBN 0-9601178-1-4). Church Cross.
Flournoy, Sheryl. Destiny's Embrace. (Tapestry Romance Ser.: No. 33). (Orig.). 1984. pap. 2.95 (ISBN 0-671-49665-4). PB.
--Flames of Passion. (Tapestry Romance Ser.). (Orig.). 1982. pap. 2.50 (ISBN 0-671-46195-8). PB.
Flournoy, T. Philosophy of William James. LC 78-99658. (Select Bibliographies Reprint Ser). 1917. 22.00 (ISBN 0-8369-5087-9). Ayer Co Pubs.
Flournoy, Theodore, jt. auth. see James, William.
Flournoy, Valerie. The Best Time of Day. LC 77-91641. (Picturebacks Ser.). (Illus.). (ps-2). 1979. PLB 4.99 (ISBN 0-394-93799-6, BYR). Random.
--The Patchwork Quilt. LC 84-1711. (Illus.). (gr. 4-8). 1985. 10.95 (ISBN 0-8037-0097-0, 01063320); PLB 10.89 (ISBN 0-8037-0098-9). Dial Bks Young.
--The Twins Strike Back. LC 79-21960. (Illus.). (ps-4). 1980. 7.95 (ISBN 0-8037-8691-3). Dial Bks Young.
Flow Resources Corporation. Potential Health & Safety Impacts of High-BTU Coal Gasification: Occupational. 200p. 1978. pap. 3.50 (ISBN 0-318-12669-9, F00687). Am Gas Assn.
Flower & Garden Magazine. The Gardener's Answer Book. LC 83-11394. 64p. (Orig.). 1984. pap. 2.95 (ISBN 0-86675-601-9, 6019). Mod Handcraft.
Flower, B. O. The Century of Sir Thomas More. 1896. Repr. 50.00 (ISBN 0-8274-2018-8). R West.
--Whittier: Prophet, Seer & Man. 1896. Repr. 30.00 (ISBN 0-8274-3701-3). R West.
Flower, Benjamin O. Progressive Men, Women & Movements of the Past Twenty-Five Years. LC 75-313. (The Radical Tradition in America Ser.). 316p. 1975. Repr. of 1914 ed. 25.85 (ISBN 0-88355-217-5). Hyperion Conn.
Flower, C. Radiology of the Respiratory System. (Topics in Respiratory Disease Ser.). 128p. 1981. 17.95 (ISBN 0-85200-429-X, Pub. by MTP Pr England). Kluwer Academic.
Flower, Cedric & Fortney, Alan. Puppets: Methods & Materials. LC 82-74004. (Illus.). 137p. 1983. 16.95 (ISBN 0-87192-142-1, Pub. by Davis Mass). Sterling.
Flower, David, ed. Planetary Nebulae. 1983. 65.00 (ISBN 90-277-1557-2, Pub. by Reidel Holland). Kluwer Academic.
Flower, Dean. Henry James in Northhampton: Vision & Revision. (Illus.). 28p. 1971. pap. 3.00 (ISBN 0-87391-027-3). Smith Coll.
Flower, Dean, ed. see James, Henry.
Flower, Dean S., ed. Eight Short Novels. 1979. pap. 2.50 (ISBN 0-449-30842-1, Prem). Fawcett.
Flower, Desmond. Pursuit of Poetry. LC 72-194978. 1939. lib. bdg. 20.00 (ISBN 0-8414-4266-5). Folcroft.
--Voltaire's Essay on Milton. LC 77-918. 1954. lib. bdg. 9.50 (ISBN 0-8414-4186-3). Folcroft.
Flower, Desmond, ed. The Poetry of Ernest Dowson. LC 75-88560. 165p. 1970. 24.50 (ISBN 0-8386-7551-4, 8386-7551-4). Fairleigh Dickinson.
Flower, Desmond, ed. see Dowson, Ernest.
Flower, Desmond, tr. see Panassie, Hugues & Gautier, Madeleine.
Flower, Elizabeth & Murphey, Murray G. A History of Philosophy in America, 2 vols. LC 75-40254. Vol. 1 488pp. 17.50 (ISBN 0-399-11650-8); Vol. 2 544pp. 17.50 (ISBN 0-399-11743-1). Vols. 1 & 2. Hackett Pub.
Flower Essence Society. The Flower Essence Journal, Issue 1. rev. ed. Katz, Richard A., ed. (Illus.). 36p. 1982. pap. 3.00 (ISBN 0-943986-01-X). Gold Circle.
--The Flower Essence Journal, Issue 2. rev. ed. Katz, Richard A., ed. (Illus.). 36p. 1983. pap. 3.00 (ISBN 0-943986-02-8). Gold Circle.
--The Flower Essence Journal, Issue 3. rev. ed. Katz, Richard A., ed. (Illus.). 48p. 1983. pap. 3.00 (ISBN 0-943986-03-6). Gold Circle.
--The Flower Essence Journal, Issue 4. Katz, Richard A. & Kaminski, Patricia A., eds. (Illus.). 80p. (Orig.). 1982. pap. 7.00 (ISBN 0-943986-04-4). Gold Circle.
Flower, Frank A. Edwin McMasters Stanton, the Autocrat of Rebellion, Emancipation & Reconstruction. LC 78-169090. Repr. of 1905 ed. 34.50 (ISBN 0-404-04590-1). AMS Pr.
Flower, George. The Errors of Emigrants. facsimile ed. LC 75-100. (Mid-American Frontier Ser.). 1975. Repr. of 1841 ed. 13.50 (ISBN 0-405-06868-9). Ayer Co Pubs.
Flower, J. E. Literature & the Left in France. 240p. 1985. pap. text ed. 11.95 (ISBN 0-416-39640-2, 9488). Methuen Inc.
--Literature & the Left in France: Society, Politics & the Novel since the Late Nineteenth Century (The Humanities Research Centre/Macmillan) LC 76-2895. 1984. text ed. 29.50x (ISBN 0-389-20285-1, 06466). B&N Imports.
Flower, J. E., ed. France Today: Introductory Studies. 5th ed. 259p. 1983. pap. 9.95x (ISBN 0-416-35010-0, NO. 4036). Methuen Inc.
Flower, J. E., et al. Writers & Politics in Modern Britain, France, & Germany. LC 77-7595. 280p. 1977. 34.50 (ISBN 0-8419-0320-4). Holmes & Meier.
Flower, John, jt. auth. see Daiches, David.
Flower, John, jt. auth. see Daitches, David.
Flower, Margaret. The Wonderful Discoveries of the Witchcrafts of M. & P. Flower. LC 72-5992. (English Experience Ser.: No. 517). 50p. 1972. Repr. of 1619 ed. 6.00 (ISBN 90-221-0517-2). Walter J Johnson.
Flower, Mary & Russell, Pugh. Growing Up in Lousiana, Nineteen Thirteen to Nineteen Thirty-Three. 1984. pap. 10.00 (ISBN 0-911051-13-9). Plain View.
Flower, Milton E. John Dickinson: Conservative Revolutionary. LC 82-11151. 360p. 1983. 27.50x (ISBN 0-8139-0966-X). U Pr of Va.
Flower, Newman. Handel, His Personality & His Times. 383p. 1972. pap. 5.95 (ISBN 0-586-03778-0, Pub. by Granada England). Academy Chi Pubs.
--Just As It Happened: Thomas Hardy, Arnold Bennett. 1973. Repr. of 1950 ed. 20.00 (ISBN 0-8274-0660-6). R West.
Flower, Phyllis. The Barn Owl. LC 77-58686. (Science I Can Read Bk.). (Illus.). 64p. (gr. k-3). 1978. 8.64i (ISBN 0-06-021919-X). HarpJ.
Flower, R. Catalogue of Irish Manuscripts, Vol. III. (Illus.). 290p. 1953. 22.50 (ISBN 0-7141-0419-1, Pub. by British Lib). Longwood Pub Group.
Flower, R. & Smith, A. H., eds. The Parker Chronicle & Laws: Facsimile. rev. ed. (EETS OS Ser.: Vol. 208). 1973. Repr. of 1937 ed. 42.00 (ISBN 0-317-15849-X). Kraus Repr.
Flower, Raymond & Jones, Michael W. Lloyd's of London: An Illustrated History. (Illus.). 1974. 16.50 (ISBN 0-8038-4290-2). Hastings.
--One Hundred Years of Motoring: An RAC Social History of the Car. 224p. 1981. 50.00x (ISBN 0-86211-018-1, Pub. by Biblios Pubs). State Mutual Bk.
Flower, Richard M. Delivery of Speech-Language Pathology & Audiology Services. (Illus.). 376p. 1983. lib. bdg. 28.00 (ISBN 0-683-03299-2). Williams & Wilkins.
Flower, Robin. Irish Tradition. 1947. pap. 5.95x (ISBN 0-19-815216-7). Oxford U Pr.
--Western Island or the Great Basket. (Oxford Paperbacks Ser.). (Illus.). 1978. pap. 4.95x (ISBN 0-19-281234-3). Oxford U Pr.
Flower, Robin, tr. Love's Bitter Sweet. 52p. 1971. Repr. of 1925 ed. 12.50x (ISBN 0-7165-1363-3, BBA 02052, Pub. by Cuala Press Ireland). Biblio Dist.
Flower, Robin, tr. see O'Crohan, Thomas.
Flower, S. J. Bulwer-Lytton. (Clarendon Biography Ser.). (Illus.). 1973. pap. 3.50 (ISBN 0-912728-60-4). Newbury Bks.
Flower, Sibylla J. Bulwer-Lytton. (Lifelines Ser.: No. 9). (Illus.). 64p. (Orig.). 1983. pap. 3.50 (ISBN 0-85263-187-1, Pub. by Shire Pubns England). Seven Hills Bks.
--Debrett's the Stately Homes of Britain. 1985. pap. 14.95 (ISBN 0-03-002843-4, Owl Bks). HR&W.
Flower, Sybilla J., compiled by. Debrett's Stately Homes of Great Britain. (Illus.). 240p. 1982. 24.95 (ISBN 0-03-061993-9). HR&W.
Flower, Wickham. Dante: A Defense of the Ancient Text of the Divina Commedia. 1897. 25.00 (ISBN 0-8274-2132-X). R West.
Flower, William H. Essays on Museums. LC 72-6793. (Essay Index Reprint Ser). 1972. Repr. of 1898 ed. 20.75 (ISBN 0-8369-7255-4). Ayer Co Pubs.
--The Horse: A Study in Natural History. 1978. Repr. of 1892 ed. lib. bdg. 25.00 (ISBN 0-8482-0824-2). Norwood Edns.
Flower, William H. & Lydekker, Richard. An Introduction to the Study of Mammals, Living & Extinct. Sterling, Keir B., ed. LC 77-81075. (Biologists & Their World Ser.). (Illus.). 1978. Repr. of 1891 ed. lib. bdg. 59.50x (ISBN 0-405-10644-0). Ayer Co Pubs.
Flowerdew, Robin, ed. Institutions & Geographical Patterns. LC 82-42541. 331p. 1982. 27.50x (ISBN 0-312-41886-8). St Martin.
Flowers. Dermatology in Ambulatory & Emergency Medicine. 1984. 49.95 (ISBN 0-8151-3263-8). Year Bk Med.
--Return of the Native (Hardy) (Book Notes Ser.). 1984. pap. 2.50 (ISBN 0-8120-3439-2). Barron.
Flowers, Ann M. The Big Book of Language Through Sounds. 2nd ed. LC 79-92515. 314p. 1980. pap. text ed. 8.75x (ISBN 0-8134-2114-4, 2114). Interstate.
--The Big Book of Sounds. 3rd ed. LC 80-81413. 352p. 1980. pap. text ed. 8.75x (ISBN 0-8134-2142-X, 2142). Interstate.
--Helping the Child with a Learning Disability-Suggestions for Parents. 2nd ed. 10p. 1982. pap. text ed. 0.40x (ISBN 0-8134-2247-7, 2247); pap. text ed. 7.00 25 copies; pap. text ed. 24.00 100 copies. Interstate.
--Language Building Cards: Matching of Color & Form. 1968. text ed. 11.00 (ISBN 0-8134-1007-X). Interstate.
--Language-Building Cards: Serial Speech. 1968. text ed. 11.00 (ISBN 0-8134-1006-1). Interstate.
--Language Development Through Perceptual-Motor Activities. 1975. text ed. 10.95x (ISBN 0-8134-1761-9). Interstate.
Flowers, Arthur. Auditory Perception, Speech, Language & Learning. 215p. 1983. 19.95 (ISBN 0-9612654-0-X). Perceptual Learn Sys.
--De Mojo Blues. 192p. 1986. 15.95 (ISBN 0-525-24376-3, 01559-460). Dutton.
Flowers, Charles. It Never Rains in Los Angeles. 1973. pap. 1.25 (ISBN 0-380-01308-8, 16766). Avon.
Flowers, Charles E., Jr. & Abrams, Maxine. A Woman Talks with Her Doctor. 1981. pap. 2.95 (ISBN 0-425-04613-3). Berkley Pub.
Flowers, Charles M., jt. ed. see Callaway, Cason J., Jr.
Flowers, Damon B., ed. The Photography Index for Nineteen Eighty, Vol. IV. LC 80-640225. 160p. (Orig.). 1981. pap. 8.95 (ISBN 0-934918-03-1). Photo Res.
--The Photography Index for Nineteen Seventy-Eight, Vol. II. 106p. (Orig.). 1980. pap. 8.95 (ISBN 0-934918-01-5). Photo Res.
--The Photography Index for Nineteen Seventy-Nine, Vol. III. 125p. (Orig.). 1980. pap. 8.95 (ISBN 0-934918-02-3). Photo Res.
--The Photography Index for Nineteen Seventy-Seven, Vol. I. 96p. (Orig.). 1979. pap. 8.95 (ISBN 0-934918-00-7). Photo Res.
Flowers, H. D. Speech As an Art. 1978. pap. text ed. 11.95 (ISBN 0-8403-1939-8). Kendall-Hunt.
Flowers, Helen L. A Classification of the Folktales of the West Indies by Types & Motifs. Dorson, Richard M., ed. LC 80-726. (Folklores of the World Ser.). 1980. lib. bdg. 63.00x (ISBN 0-405-13313-8). Ayer Co Pubs.
Flowers, James L. A Complete Preparation for the New MCAT: Knowledge & Comprehension of Science, Vol. 1. (Illus.). 456p. 1982. pap. text ed. 17.00 (ISBN 0-941406-01-6); Set of 2 vols. pap. text ed. 35.00 (ISBN 0-941406-03-2). Betz Pub Co Inc.
Flowers, James L. & Jenkins-Murphy, Andrew. A Complete Preparation for the Health Professions: Dentistry, Optometry, Pharmacy, Veterinary Medicine. (Illus.). 500p. (Orig.). Date not set. pap. text ed. price not set (ISBN 0-941406-04-0). Betz Pub Co Inc.
Flowers, John, et al. Helping Your Children Be Self-Confident. (Illus.). 157p. 1982. pap. 4.95 (ISBN 0-13-386938-5). P-H.
--Are You Neurotic? A Guide to Fashionable Psychological Disorders. (Illus.). 96p. 1984. 12.95 (ISBN 0-13-045436-2); pap. 4.95 (ISBN 0-13-045428-1). P-H.
Flowers, John G. Content of Student-Teaching Courses Designed for the Training of Secondary Teachers in State Teachers Colleges. LC 77-176780. (Columbia University. Teachers College. Contributions to Education: No. 538). Repr. of 1932 ed. 22.50 (ISBN 0-404-55538-1). AMS Pr.
Flowers, John H., ed. Nebraska Symposium on Motivation Ser., 1980: Cognitive Processes. LC 53-11655. (Nebraska Symposium on Motivation Ser.: Vol. 28). xvi, 249p. 1981. 19.95x (ISBN 0-8032-0620-8); pap. 8.95x (ISBN 0-8032-0621-6). U of Nebr Pr.
Flowers, Marilyn R. Women & Social Security: An Institutional Dilemma. LC 77-23075. 41p. 1977. pap. 3.25 (ISBN 0-8447-3259-1). Am Enterprise.
Flowers, Marilyn R., jt. auth. see Buchanan, James M.
Flowers, Mary L. Sentence Structure & Characterization in the Tragedies of Jean Racine: A Computer-Assisted Study. LC 76-50284. 223p. 1978. 20.00 (ISBN 0-8386-2056-6). Fairleigh Dickinson.
Flowers, Michael, jt. auth. see Wilson, David H.
Flowers, Montaville. The Japanese Conquest of American Opinion. Daniels, Roger, ed. LC 78-54815. (Asian Experience in North America Ser.). 1979. Repr. of 1917 ed. lib. bdg. 20.00x (ISBN 0-405-11271-8). Ayer Co Pubs.
Flowers, Ronald B. Criminal Jurisdiction Allocation in Indian Country. LC 83-6424. 126p. 1983. 14.50x (ISBN 0-8046-9324-2). Assoc Faculty Pr.
--Religion in Strange Times: The 1960s & 1970s. 275p. 1984. 18.50x (ISBN 0-86554-127-2, MUP-H118). Mercer Univ Pr.
Flowers, Ronald B., jt. auth. see Miller, Robert T.
Flowers, Ruth C. Voltaire's Stylistic Transformation of Rabelaisian Satirical Devices. LC 72-94182. (Catholic University of America. Studies in Romance Languages & Literatures: No. 41). 1969. Repr. of 1951 ed. 21.00 (ISBN 0-404-50341-1). AMS Pr.
Flowers, Seville. Mosses: Utah & the West. Holmgren, Arthur, ed. LC 72-96422. (Illus.). 567p. 1973. text ed. 7.95 (ISBN 0-8425-1524-0). Brigham.
Flowers, Seville, et al. Ecological Studies of the Flora & Fauna of Flaming Gorge Reservoir Basin, Utah & Wyoming. (Upper Colorado Ser: No. 3). 42.00 (ISBN 0-404-60648-2). AMS Pr.
Flowers, T. J., jt. auth. see Hall, J. L.
Floy, Michael. The Diary of Michael Floy Jr., Bowery Village, Eighteen Thirty-Three to Eighteen Thirty-Seven. Brooks, R. A., ed. 1941. 49.50x (ISBN 0-686-51371-1). Elliots Bks.
Floyd, Ann. Cognitive Development in the School Years. LC 78-9155. 383p. 1979. 35.95x (ISBN 0-470-26429-2). Halsted Pr.
Floyd, Barry. Jamaica: An Island Microcosm. (Illus.). 1979. 19.95 (ISBN 0-312-43953-9). St Martin.
Floyd, Beth, jt. ed. see Floyd, Steve.
Floyd, Bryan. Prayerfully Sinning. LC 83-63239. 96p. 1985. pap. 8.95 (ISBN 0-932966-48-9). Permanent Pr.
Floyd, Bryan A. The Long War Dead. LC 83-63243. 1984. pap. 8.95 (ISBN 0-932966-45-4). Permanent Pr.
--Prayerfully Sinning. LC 83-63239. 100p. 1984. text ed. 16.95 (ISBN 0-932966-49-7). Permanent Pr.
Floyd, C. M., jt. ed. see Berry, M. F.
Floyd, Carol M. Anybody Listening? 1982. 2.50 (ISBN 0-89536-572-3). CSS of Ohio.
Floyd, Charles F. Real Estate Principles. 584p. 1981. text ed. 26.95 (ISBN 0-88462-514-1, Real Estate Ed). Longman USA.
Floyd, Dale E. The World Bibliography of Armed Land Conflict: From Waterloo to World War I, 2 vols. 800p. 1980. Set. 65.00 (ISBN 0-89453-147-6). M Glazier.
Floyd, Dale R. Actions with Indians. 1983. pap. 4.95 (ISBN 0-88342-248-4). Old Army.
Floyd, David, tr. see Anatoli, A.
Floyd, E. E., jt. auth. see Conner, Pierre E.
Floyd, E. E., jt. auth. see Connor, Pierre E.
Floyd, Elizabeth S. A Winning Heart... Tender & Courageous. (Illus.). 80p. (Orig.). 1983. pap. 6.95 (ISBN 0-9613238-0-9). Impex Pub Co.
Floyd, James C. Some Gentle Moving Thing. 2nd ed. LC 82-60198. (Illus.). 70p. (gr. 7-9). 1982. 5.95 (ISBN 0-938232-11-8). Winston-Derek.
Floyd, James J. Listening: A Practical Approach. 1985. pap. text ed. 7.30x (ISBN 0-673-15789-X). Scott F.
Floyd, Jesse M. International Fish Trade of Southeast Asian Nations. LC 84-10168. (East-West Environment & Policy Institute Research Report Ser.: No. 16). 66p. 1984. pap. text ed. 3.00 (ISBN 0-318-03783-1). E W Center HI.
Floyd, Jo. Instruction Manual for Use with the Labanotation: IBM Selectric Typewriter Element. (Illus.). 33p. (Orig.). 1974. pap. text ed. 5.00x (ISBN 0-932582-14-1). Dance Notation.
Floyd, Joe S., Jr., jt. auth. see Maclachlan, John M.
Floyd, John A., Jr., jt. auth. see Southern Living Gardening Staff.

Floyd, John A., Jr., ed. Southern Living Growing Vegetables & Herbs. LC 83-60426. (Illus.). 272p. 1984. 19.18i (ISBN 0-8487-0542-4). Oxmoor Hse.

Floyd, John E. World Monetary Equilibrium: International Monetary Theory in an Historical-Institutional Context. (Illus.). 224p. 1985. text ed. 25.00 (ISBN 0-8122-7983-2). U of Pa Pr.

Floyd, John E. & Block, Walter E. Focus: On the Canadian Dollar. (Focus Ser.: No. 14). 88p. 1985. 5.00 (ISBN 0-88975-080-7). Fraser Inst.

Floyd, Lois G., jt. auth. see Quintana, Bertha B.

Floyd, M., ed. see Dickens, Charles.

Floyd, Margaret H., ed. see Bunting, Bainbridge.

Floyd, Mary K. Abortion Bibliography for 1970. LC 72-78877. (Abortion Bibliography Ser.: No. 2). 120p. 1972. 7.50x (ISBN 0-87875-024-X). Whitston Pub.

--Abortion Bibliography for 1971. LC 72-78877. (Abortion Bibliography Ser.: No. 3). 125p. 1973. 11.00x (ISBN 0-87875-030-4). Whitston Pub.

--Abortion Bibliography for 1972. LC 72-78877. (Abortion Bibliography Ser.: No. 4). xx, 223p. 1973. 11.00x (ISBN 0-87875-044-4). Whitston Pub.

--Abortion Bibliography for 1973. LC 72-78877. (Abortion Bibliography Ser.: No. 5). xxiii, 237p. 1974. 11.00x (ISBN 0-87875-056-8). Whitston Pub.

--Abortion Bibliography for 1974. LC 72-78877. (Abortion Bibliography Ser.: No. 6). 1975. 15.00x (ISBN 0-87875-079-7). Whitston Pub.

--Abortion Bibliography for 1976. LC 72-78877. (Abortion Bibliography Ser.: Vol. 7). 1978. 17.00x (ISBN 0-87875-126-2). Whitston Pub.

--Abortion Bibliography for 1977. LC 72-78877. (Annual Bibliography Ser.: No. 8). 306p. 1979. 19.50x (ISBN 0-87875-175-0). Whitston Pub.

--A Bibliography of Noise for 1971. LC 72-87107. 150p. 1973. 10.00x (ISBN 0-87875-031-2). Whitston Pub.

--Bibliography of Noise for 1972. LC 72-87107. xvii, 126p. 1974. 10.00x (ISBN 0-87875-054-1). Whitston Pub.

--A Bibliography of Noise for 1973. LC 72-87107. 1975. 10.00x (ISBN 0-87875-055-X). Whitston Pub.

--A Bibliography of Noise, 1965-1970. LC 72-87107. xxx, 375p. 1973. 17.00x (ISBN 0-87875-029-0). Whitston Pub.

Floyd, Michael. Policymaking & Planning in Local Government: A Cybernetic Perspective. LC 84-13665. (Illus.). 138p. 1984. text ed. 31.50x (ISBN 0-566-00787-8). Gower Pub Co.

Floyd, Olive. James Neale Thorne, American Ace in the RAF. (Illus.). 1956. 35.00 (ISBN 0-913076-04-X). Beachcomber Bks.

Floyd, P., ed. see Dickens, Charles.

Floyd, Robert A., ed. Free Radicals & Cancer. (Illus.). 552p. 1982. 75.00 (ISBN 0-8247-1551-9). Dekker.

Floyd, Robert H., et al. Public Enterprise in Mixed Economics: Some Macroeconomic Aspects. xiv, 196p. 1984. pap. 12.00 (ISBN 0-939934-30-2). Intl Monetary.

--Public Enterprise in Mixed Economics: Some Macroeconomic Aspects. pap. 53.50 (ISBN 0-317-26168-1, 2024270). Bks Demand UMI.

Floyd, Samuel A., Jr. & Reisser, Marsha J. Black Music in the United States: An Annotated Bibliography of Selected Reference & Research Materials. LC 82-49044. 230p. 1983. lib. bdg. 35.00 (ISBN 0-527-30164-7). Kraus Intl.

Floyd, Silas X. Floyd's Flowers. LC 78-168050. (Illus.). Repr. of 1905 ed. 23.50 (ISBN 0-404-00048-7). AMS Pr.

--Life of Charles T. Walker D.D. LC 70-97423. Repr. of 1902 ed. 17.50x (ISBN 0-8371-2708-4, FLW&, Pub. by Negro U Pr). Greenwood.

Floyd, Steve & Floyd, Beth, eds. Handbook of Interactive Video. LC 82-12690. (Video Bookshelf Ser.). 168p. 1982. professional 34.95 (ISBN 0-86729-019-6, 505-BW). Knowledge Indus.

Floyd, Thomas. The Picture of a Perfit Common Wealth. LC 72-5993. (English Experience Ser.: No. 518). 338p. 1973. Repr. of 1600 ed. 22.00 (ISBN 90-221-0518-0). Walter J Johnson.

Floyd, Thomas L. Digital Fundamentals. 2nd ed. Orig. Title: Digital Logic Fundamentals. 624p. 1982. text ed. 29.95 (ISBN 0-675-09876-9). Additional Supplements May Be Obtained From Publisher. Merrill.

--Electric Circuits: Electron Flow Version. 1983. text ed. 28.95 (ISBN 0-675-20037-7). Additional supplements may be obtained from publisher. Merrill.

--Electronic Devices. 1984. Additional supplements may be obtained from publisher. text ed. 29.95 (ISBN 0-675-20157-8). Merrill.

--Essentials of Electronic Devices. 1983. pap. text ed. 11.50 (ISBN 0-675-20062-8). Merrill.

--Principles of Electric Circuits. (Illus.). 768p. 1981. text ed. 28.95 (ISBN 0-675-08081-9). Additional supplements may be obtained from publisher. Merrill.

--Principles of Electric Circuits. 2nd ed. 832p. 1985. text ed. 28.95 (ISBN 0-675-20402-X). Additional supplements may be obtained from publisher. Merrill.

Floyd, Tim. Welcome to the Real World. LC 84-5876. 1984. pap. 5.95 (ISBN 0-8054-5001-7). Broadman.

Floyd, Tom. Lost Trails & Forgotten People: The Story of Jones Mountain. 1981. pap. 5.50 (ISBN 0-317-06956-X). Potomac Appalach.

Floyd, Virginia. Eugene O'Neill: A World View. LC 79-4826. 1980. 15.50 (ISBN 0-8044-2204-4). Ungar.

--The Plays of Eugene O'Neill: A New Assessment. (Literature & Life Ser.). (Illus.). 350p. 1984. 19.50 (ISBN 0-8044-2206-0); pap. 9.95 (ISBN 0-8044-6153-8). Ungar.

Floyd, Virginia, ed. Eugene O'Neill at Work: Newly Released Ideas for Plays. LC 81-40460. (Illus.). 448p. 1981. 30.00 (ISBN 0-8044-2205-2). Ungar.

Floyd, Virginia H., jt. ed. see Doyle, Esther M.

Floyd, W. F. & Welford, A. T., eds. Symposium on Fatigue & Symposium on Human Factors in Equipment Design, 2 vols. in one. LC 77-70494. (Work Ser.). (Illus.). 1977. Repr. of 1954 ed. lib. bdg. 32.00x (ISBN 0-405-10165-1). Ayer Co Pubs.

Floyd, Wayne. The Double Exposure Book. (Illus.). 88p. (Orig.). 1985. pap. text ed. 9.95 (ISBN 0-9613160-0-4). W Floyd.

Floyer, A. M. Evolution of Ancient Buddhism. 59.95 (ISBN 0-8490-0143-9). Gordon Pr.

Floyer, John. Medicina Gerocomica. Kastenbaum, Robert, ed. LC 78-22199. (Aging & Old Age Ser.). 1979. Repr. of 1724 ed. lib. bdg. 14.00x (ISBN 0-405-11838-4). Ayer Co Pubs.

Fluchere, Henri, tr. see Giono, Jean.

Fluck, E. & Goldanskii, V. I. Modern Physics in Chemistry, Vol. 1. 1977. 67.00 (ISBN 0-12-261201-9). Acad Pr.

--Modern Physics in Chemistry, Vol. 2. 1980. 99.50 (ISBN 0-12-261202-7). Acad Pr.

Fluck, E., et al. Inorganic Chemistry. Boschke, F., ed. LC 51-5497. (Topics in Current Chemistry: Vol. 35). (Illus.). 129p. 1973. pap. 23.60 (ISBN 0-387-06080-4). Springer-Verlag.

Fluck, Edward J., jt. auth. see Robinson, David M.

Fluck, Richard C. & Baird, C. Direlle. Agricultural Energetics. (Illus.). 1980. text ed. 22.50 (ISBN 0-87055-346-1). AVI.

Flucke, Paul, ed. Facing Death: A Guide for Christians. 1980. 3.25 (ISBN 0-89536-418-2). CSS of Ohio.

Fluckiger, W. Lynn. Unique Advantages of Being a Mormon. pap. 3.95 (ISBN 0-89036-138-X). Hawkes Pub Inc.

Fludd, Robert. Robert Fludd & His Philosophicall Key. (Illus.). 156p. 1979. 45.00 (ISBN 0-88202-037-4). Watson Pub Intl.

Flude, Michael, jt. ed. see Ahier, John.

Flude, Ray & Parrott, Allen. Education & the Challenge of Change. 176p. 1979. pap. 11.00x (ISBN 0-335-00257-9, Pub. by Open Univ Pr). Taylor & Francis.

Fluegel, Erik. Microfacies Analysis of Limestones. (Illus.). 550p. 1982. 69.50 (ISBN 0-387-11269-3). Springer-Verlag.

Fluegelman, Andrew & Hewes, Jeremy J. Writing in the Computer Age: Word Processing Skills & Style for Every Writer. LC 81-43852. 256p. 1983. 19.95 (ISBN 0-385-18124-8, Quantum Pr); pap. 10.95 (ISBN 0-385-18125-6, Quantum Pr). Doubleday.

Fluegelman, Andrew, ed. see New Games Foundation.

Fluegge, C. A., ed. Handbook of Physics, 54 vols, Vol. 6a, Pt. 4. (Illus.). 430p. 1974. 109.20 (ISBN 0-387-06097-9). Springer-Verlag.

Fluegge, E., ed. Encyclopedia of Physics, 54 vols, Vols. 11-12, 14-19. Incl. Vol. 11, Pt. 1. Acoustics One. (Illus.). 1961. 123.90 (ISBN 0-387-02686-X); Vol. 11, Pt. 2. Acoustics Two. (Illus.). 1962. 97.40 (ISBN 0-387-02841-2); Vol. 12. Thermodynamics of Gases. (Illus.). 1958. 147.50 (ISBN 0-387-02292-9); Vol. 14. Low Temperature Physics One. (Illus.). 1956. 70.80 (ISBN 0-387-02037-3); Vol. 15. Low Temperature Physics Two. (Illus.). 1956. 109.20 (ISBN 0-387-02038-1); Vol. 16. Electric Fields & Waves. (Illus.). 1958. 153.40 (ISBN 0-387-02293-7); Vol. 17. Dielectrics. (Illus.). 1956. 94.40 (ISBN 0-387-02039-X); Vol. 18, Pt. 1. Magnetism. Wijn, H. P., ed. (Illus.). 1969. 153.40 (ISBN 0-387-04164-8); Vol. 18, Pt. 2. Ferromagnetism. Wijn, H. P., ed. (Illus.). 1966. 153.40 (ISBN 0-387-03548-6); Vol. 19. Electrical Conductivity One. (Illus.). 1956. 82.60 (ISBN 0-387-02040-3). Springer-Verlag.

--Encyclopedia of Physics, 54 vols, Vols. 21-23, 25, 27, 28, 30, 32, 34-35. Incl. Vol. 21. Electron Emission. Gas Discharges One. (Illus.). 1956. 129.80 (ISBN 0-387-02041-1); Vol. 22. Gas Discharges Two. (Illus.). 1956. 126.90 (ISBN 0-387-02042-X); Vol. 23. Electrical Instruments. Pannenborg, A. E., ed. (Illus.). 1967. 153.40 (ISBN 0-387-03852-3); Vol. 25, Pt. 1. Crystal Optics, Diffraction. (Illus.). 1961; Vol. 25, Pts. 2a-2c. Light & Matter. Genzel, L., ed. (Illus.). Pt. 2a, 1967. 88.50 (ISBN 0-387-03853-1); Pt. 2b, 1974. 116.90 (ISBN 0-387-06638-1); Pt. 2c, 1970. 94.40 (ISBN 0-387-04856-1); Vol. 27. Spectroscopy One. (Illus.). 1964. 115.10 (ISBN 0-387-03153-7); Vol. 28. Spectroscopy Two. 1957. 97.40 (ISBN 0-387-02167-1); Vol. 30. X-Rays. (Illus.). 1957. 88.50 (ISBN 0-387-02168-X); Vol. 32. Structural Research. (Illus.). 1957. 141.60 (ISBN 0-387-02169-8); Vol. 34. Corpuscles & Radiation in Matter Two. (Illus.). 1958. 76.70 (ISBN 0-387-02295-3); Vol. 35. Atoms One. (Illus.). 1957. 97.40 (ISBN 0-387-02170-1). Springer-Verlag.

--Encyclopedia of Physics, 54 vols, Vols. 46-49, 51-54. Incl. Vol. 46, Pt. 1. Cosmic Rays One. 1961. 97.40 (ISBN 0-387-02689-4); Vol. 46, Pt. 2. Cosmic Rays Two. Sitte, K., ed. 1967. 159.30 (ISBN 0-387-03855-8); Vol. 47. Geophysics One. 1956. 116.90 (ISBN 0-387-02046-2); Vol. 48. Geophysics Two. 1957. 194.70 (ISBN 0-387-02174-4); Vol. 49. Geophysics Three, 4 pts. Bartels, J. & Rower, K., eds. (Illus.). Pt. 1, 1966. 112.10 (ISBN 0-387-03549-4); Pt. 2, 1967. 112.10 (ISBN 0-686-96891-3); Pt. 3, 537p, 1971. 159.30 (ISBN 0-387-05570-3); Pt. 4, 592p, 1972. 140.50 (ISBN 0-387-05583-5); Vol. 51. Astrophysics Two: Stellar Structure. (Illus.). 1958. 171.10 (ISBN 0-387-02299-6); Vol. 52. Astrophysics Three: The Solar System. (Illus.). 1959. 141.60 (ISBN 0-387-02416-2); Vol. 53. Astrophysics Four: Stellar Systems. (Illus.). 1959. 141.60 (ISBN 0-387-02417-4); Vol. 54. Astrophysics Five: Miscellaneous. (Illus.). 1962. 97.40 (ISBN 0-387-02844-7). Springer-Verlag.

Fluegge, S. Encyclopedia of Physics, Vol. 49, Pt. 5: Geophysics 3, Pt. 5. LC 56-2942. (Illus.). 420p. (Eng, Fr, & Ger.). 1976. 116.90 (ISBN 0-387-07512-7). Springer-Verlag.

--Practical Quantum Mechanics. LC 74-23732. (Illus.). xiv, 623p. 1974. pap. 26.00 (ISBN 0-387-07050-8). Springer-Verlag.

--Practical Quantum Mechanics One. rev. ed. (Die Grundlehren der Mathematischen Wissenschaften: Vol. 177). 1971. 52.00 (ISBN 0-387-05276-3). Springer-Verlag.

--Practical Quantum Mechanics Two. rev. ed. (Grundlehren der Mathematischen Wissenschaften: Vol. 178). 1971. 49.60 (ISBN 0-387-05277-1). Springer-Verlag.

Fluegge, S., ed. Encyclopedia of Physics, 54 vols, Vols. 3-4, 6, 8-10. Incl. Vol. 3, Pt. 1. Principles of Classical Mechanics & Field Theory. (Illus.). viii, 902p. 1960; Vol. 3, Pt. 3. The Non-Linear Field Theories of Mechanics. Truesdell, C. & Noll, W. (Illus.). viii, 602p. 1965. 174.10 (ISBN 0-387-03313-0); Vol. 4. Principles of Electrodynamics & Relativity. (Illus.). vi, 290p. 1962. 97.40 (ISBN 0-387-02840-4); Vol. 6. Elasticity & Plasticity. (Illus.). viii, 642p. 1958. 141.60 (ISBN 0-387-02290-2); Vol. 6a, Pt. 1. Mechanics of Solids One. Truesdell, C., ed. (Illus.). 1973. 175.90 (ISBN 0-387-05873-7); Vol. 6a, Pt. 2. Mechanics of Solids Two. Truesdell, C., ed. (Illus.). 1972. 205.40 (ISBN 0-387-05535-5); Vol. 6a, Pt. 3. Mechanics of Solids Three. Truesdell, C., ed. (Illus.). 1973. 164.10 (ISBN 0-387-05536-3); Vol. 8, Pt. 1. Fluid Dynamics One. (Illus.). 1959. 129.80 (ISBN 0-387-02411-5); Vol. 8, Pt. 2. Fluid Dynamics Two. (Illus.). 1963. 182.90 (ISBN 0-387-02997-4); Vol. 9. Fluid Dynamics Three. (Illus.). 1960. 194.70 (ISBN 0-387-02548-0); Vol. 10. Structure of Liquids. (Illus.). vi, 686p. 1960. 94.40 (ISBN 0-387-02549-9). (Eng., Fr & Ger.). Springer-Verlag.

--Encyclopedia of Physics, 54 vols, Vols. 37-42, 44-45. Incl. Vol. 37, Pt. 1. Atoms Three - Molecules One. (Illus.). vi, 439p. 1959. 118.00 (ISBN 0-387-02412-3); Vol. 37, Pt. 2. Molecules Two. (Illus.). vi, 303p. 1961. 97.40 (ISBN 0-387-02688-6); Vol. 38, Pt. 2. Neutrons & Related Gamma Ray Problems. (Illus.). vi, 868p. 1959. 171.10 (ISBN 0-387-02413-1); Vol. 39. Structure of Atomic Nuclei. (Illus.). vi, 566p. 1971. 123.90 (ISBN 0-387-02171-X); Vol. 40. Nuclear Reactions One. (Illus.). vi, 553p. 1957. 123.90 (ISBN 0-387-02172-8); Vol. 41, Pt. 1. Nuclear Reactions Two: Theory. (Illus.). viii, 580p. 1959. 141.60 (ISBN 0-387-02414-X); Vol. 41, Pt. 2. Beta Decay. (Illus.). vi, 117p. 1962. 47.20 (ISBN 0-387-02843-9); Vol. 42. Nuclear Reactions Three. (Illus.). viii, 626p. 1957. 129.80 (ISBN 0-387-02173-6); Vol. 44. Nuclear Instrumentation One. Creutz, E., ed. (Illus.). viii, 473p. 1959. 123.90 (ISBN 0-387-02415-8); Vol. 45. Nuclear Instrumentation Two. Creutz, E., ed. (Illus.). viii, 544p. 1958. 129.80 (ISBN 0-387-02297-X). Springer-Verlag.

--Geophysics Three. (Encyclopedia of Physics Ser.: Vol. 49, Pt. 6). (Illus.). 429p. 1982. 118.60 (ISBN 0-387-07080-X). Springer-Verlag.

Fluegge, W. Stresses in Shells. 2nd ed. LC 74-183604. (Illus.). 525p. 1973. 38.00 (ISBN 0-387-05322-0). Springer-Verlag.

--Tensor Analysis & Continuum Mechanics. LC 74-183541. (Illus.). vii, 207p. 1972. 29.00 (ISBN 0-387-05697-1). Springer-Verlag.

Fluegge-Lotz, Irmgard. Discontinuous Automatic Control. LC 52-13156. (Illus.). pap. 44.00 (ISBN 0-317-10759-3, 2000032). Bks Demand UMI.

Fluer, Larry, jt. auth. see Fieldberg, Alfred.

Flug, Phyllis O. & Miller, Michael J., eds. Catline & the Roman Conspiracy: Two Accounts. LC 77-39300. (Conspiracy: Historical Perspectives). 1972. 16.00 (ISBN 0-405-04151-9). Ayer Co Pubs.

--Conspiracy of Arnold & Sir Henry Clinton Against the United States & Against General Washington. LC 77-39299. (Conspiracy: Historical Perspectives). 1972. Repr. of 1817 ed. 16.00 (ISBN 0-405-04152-7). Ayer Co Pubs.

--The Conspiracy Trial for the Murder of the President: And the Attempt to Overthrow the Government by the Assassination of Its Principal Officers. LC 70-39301. (Conspiracy: Historical Perspectives). 1972. Repr. of 1865 ed. Set. 70.00 (ISBN 0-405-04153-5); Vol. 1. 24.00 (ISBN 0-405-04158-6); Vol. 2. 23.00 (ISBN 0-405-04159-4); Vol. 3. 28.00 (ISBN 0-405-04160-8). Ayer Co Pubs.

--Legal Concepts of Conspiracy: A Law Review Trilogy 1922-1970. LC 71-39304. (Conspiracy: Historical Perspectives). 1972. 16.00 (ISBN 0-405-04156-X). Ayer Co Pubs.

Flugel, E. Thomas Carlyle's Moral & Religious Development. LC 74-116793. (Studies in Philosophy, No. 40). 1970. Repr. of 1891 ed. lib. bdg. 46.95x (ISBN 0-8383-1035-4). Haskell.

Flugel, E., ed. Fossil Algae: Recent Results & Developments. LC 76-46461. (Illus.). 1977. 54.00 (ISBN 0-387-07974-2). Springer-Verlag.

Flugel, Ewald. Thomas Carlyle's Moral & Religious Development. LC 72-195908. 1891. lib. bdg. 9.75 (ISBN 0-8414-4268-1). Folcroft.

Flugel, Ewald, ed. Middle English Literature, 4 vols. (Belles Lettres Ser.: Sec. 2). Repr. of 1913 ed. write pub. for prices (ISBN 0-404-53611-5). AMS Pr.

Flugel, J. C. Man, Morals & Society. 328p. 1970. text ed. 30.00 (ISBN 0-8236-3085-4); pap. text ed. 10.95 (ISBN 0-8236-8139-4, 23085). Intl Univs Pr.

--The Psychological of Clothes. (Illus.). 257p. 27.50 (ISBN 0-8236-5580-6, BN#05580). Intl Univs Pr.

Flugel, John C. Psychoanalytic Study of the Family. 1960. text ed. 13.00x (ISBN 0-7012-0103-7). Humanities.

--The Psychology of Clothes. LC 75-41097. Repr. of 1930 ed. 32.50 (ISBN 0-404-14721-6). AMS Pr.

Flugel, Karl H. Invasion of the Strip. 520p. 1982. 29.50 (ISBN 0-933136-01-3). Academie Pr.

--Salons Success Society. LC 78-73478. 330p. 1981. lib. bdg. 50.00 (ISBN 0-933136-00-5). Academie Pr.

Flugge, Wilhelm, ed. Handbook of Engineering Mechanics. 1962. 89.50 (ISBN 0-07-021392-5). McGraw.

Fluharty, George W. & Ross, Harold R. Public Speaking. 2nd ed. (Illus.). 416p. (Orig.). 1981. pap. 5.95 (ISBN 0-06-463525-2, EH 525, EH). B&N NY.

Fluharty, Vernon L. Dance of the Millions: Military Rule & the Social Revolution in Colombia. LC 75-26918. (Illus.). 336p. 1975. Repr. of 1957 ed. lib. bdg. 22.50x (ISBN 0-8371-8368-5, FLDM). Greenwood.

Fluiani, Carlo M. The Elliot Wave Theory Flow of Speculative Matter into the Active Cylinder Theory Stream. (The Recondite Sources of Stock Market Action Library). (Illus.). 137p. 1983. 91.45x (ISBN 0-86654-043-1). Inst Econ Finan.

Fluid Film Bearing Committee of the Lubrication Division. Topics in Fluid Film Bearing & Rotor Bearing Systems Design & Optimization: Presented at the Design Engineering Conference, Chicago, Ill., April 17-20, 1978. Rohde, S. M., et al, eds. LC 78-52526. pap. 70.00 (ISBN 0-317-11248-1, 2017648). Bks Demand UMI.

Fluid Logic Conference - 1st - Milwaukee - 1969. Proceedings. 1970. Fluidics Quarterly, Vol. 2, Issue 3 26.00 (ISBN 0-88232-009-2). Delbridge Pub Co.

Fluid Power Symposium, 1st. Proceedings. 1969. text ed. 27.00x (ISBN 0-900983-03-5, Dist. by Air Science Co.). BHRA Fluid.

Fluid Power Symposium, 2nd. Proceedings. 1971. text ed. 43.00x (ISBN 0-900983-11-6, Dist. by Air Science Co.). BHRA Fluid.

Fluid Power Symposium, 3rd. Proceedings. 1973. text ed. 47.00x (ISBN 0-900983-30-2, Dist. by Air Science Co.). BHRA Fluid.

Fluid Power Symposium, 4th. Proceedings. 1975. text ed. 50.00x (ISBN 0-900983-45-0, Dist. by Air Science Co.). BHRA Fluid.

Fluid Power Symposium, 5th. Proceedings, 2 vols. Stephens, H. S. & Stapleton, C. A., eds. (Illus.). 1979. Set. lib. bdg. 69.00x (ISBN 0-900983-96-5, Dist by Air Science Co.). BHRA Fluid.

Fluid-Solid Interaction Symposium (1967: Pittsburgh) Fluid-Solid Interaction. LC 67-31132. pap. 67.30 (ISBN 0-317-08708-8, 2013310). Bks Demand UMI.

Fluidics Symposium, Chicago, 1967. Advances in Fluidics. Brown, Forbes T., ed. LC 67-23027. (Illus.). pap. 116.50 (ISBN 0-317-11130-2, 2013308). Bks Demand UMI.

Fluitt, John L., jt. auth. see Gifford, Charles S.

Fluke, Joanne. Cold Judgement. (Orig.). 1985. pap. 3.50 (ISBN 0-440-11311-3). Dell.

--The Stepchild. (Orig.). 1980. pap. 2.25 (ISBN 0-440-18408-8). Dell.

--Winter Chill. 208p. (Orig.). 1984. pap. 3.50 (ISBN 0-440-19617-5). Dell.

Fluker, Anne & Fluker, Winifred. Confederate Gold. LC 84-16231. 1984. 10.95 (ISBN 0-916913-01-5). Tullous.

Fluker, Winifred, jt. auth. see Fluker, Anne.

Flukinger, Roy. The Formative Decades: Photography in Great Britain, 1839-1920. (Illus.). 168p. 1985. 15.95 (ISBN 0-292-72450-0). U of Tex Pr.

Flukinger, Roy, jt. auth. see Downs, Fane.

Flukinger, Roy, intro. by. Victoria's World: An Exhibition from the Gernsheim Collection. 3rd ed. 1980. 2.50 (ISBN 0-87959-008-4). U of Tex H Ransom Ctr.
Flukinger, Roy, et al. Paul Martin: Victorian Photographer. LC 77-4764. (Illus.). 235p. 1977. 24.95 (ISBN 0-292-76436-7). U of Tex Pr.
Flukinger, Roy, jt. auth. see Brettell, Richard.
Flum, J. & Ziegler, M. Topological Model Theory. (Lecture Notes in Mathematics: Vol. 769). 151p. 1980. pap. 15.00 (ISBN 3-540-09732-5). Springer-Verlag.
Flume, Violet S. The Last Mountain: The Life of Robert Wood. 1983. 19.95 (ISBN 0-8283-1829-8); pap. 10.50 (ISBN 0-8283-1878-6). Branden Pub Co.
Flumiani, C. M. The Amazing Stock Market Trading Adventures of a Teenager in Wall Street. (Illus.). 109p. 1984. pap. 27.75x (ISBN 0-89266-449-5). Am Classical Coll Pr.
--The Best Critical Stock Market Studies of the Fibonacci-Elliot Research Foundation, 3 vols. (Illus.). 418p. 1983. Set. 575.00x (ISBN 0-86654-070-9). Inst Econ Finan.
--The Best Critical Studies Issued by the Stock Market Chartists Club of America, 3 vols. (Illus.). 365p. 1983. 237.45x (ISBN 0-89266-401-0). Am Classical Coll Pr.
--The Best Critical Studies of the Cylinder Theory Research Foundation, 2 vols. (Illus.). 1979. Set. deluxe ed. 185.50x (ISBN 0-685-67254-9). Inst Econ Finan.
--The Chart Encyclopedia of Wall Street Technical Action. (Illus.). 300p. 1975. 65.00 (ISBN 0-913314-49-8). Am Classical College Pr.
--The Collapse of Gold & the Tragic Dilemma of the Swiss Banks. (Illus.). 205p. 1976. 49.50 (ISBN 0-918968-18-6). Am Classical Coll Pr.
--The Compelling Process of the Historical Inevitabilities at the Close of the 20th Century. (The Institute for Economic & Political World Strategic Studies). (Illus.). 1978. 57.85 (ISBN 0-89266-092-9). Am Classical Coll Pr.
--The Decline & Decay of American Education. (Illus.). 200p. 1976. 67.50 (ISBN 0-913314-79-X). Am Classical Coll Pr.
--Economics: The Essential Knowledge Which Everybody, but Absolutely Everybody Ought to Possess of Economics & Economic Forecasting. (Essential Knowledge Ser.). (Illus.). 1978. plastic spiral bdg. 49.45. Am Classical Coll.
--The Elliott Wave Theory Flow of Speculative Matter into the Active Cylinder Theory Stream. (Illus.). 1977. 95.85 (ISBN 0-89266-045-7). Am Classical Coll Pr.
--Elliott Wave Theory in Projection Charts, 2 vols. in one. rev. & enl ed. (Institute for Economic & Financial Research Ser.). (Illus.). 89p. 1975. Set. 187.75 (ISBN 0-913314-64-1). Am Classical Coll Pr.
--Fast Stock Market Profits with the Application of the Theory of the Stock Market Extremes. (Illus.). 143p. 1982. 63.45x (ISBN 0-86654-034-2). Inst Econ Finan.
--The Financial Education of Children & Teenagers. (Idea Books Ser.). (Illus.). 1978. 41.95 (ISBN 0-89266-127-5). Am Classical Coll Pr.
--The Gyrations of the Dollar & the Deceit of Gold, 2 Vols. LC 73-85330. 30p. 1971. 147.75 (ISBN 0-913314-03-X). Am Classical Coll Pr.
--The Gyrations of the Dollar & the Deceit of Gold. (Illus.). 1978. deluxe ed. 87.75x (ISBN 0-930008-16-2). Inst Econ Pol.
--The Hidden & Mysterious Life of Stock Market Syndicates. (A New Stock Market Library Bk.). (Illus.). 116p. 1983. 59.85x (ISBN 0-86654-057-1). Inst Econ Finan.
--History's Key to Stock Market Profits. (Illus.). 87p. 1974. 62.40 (ISBN 0-913314-28-5). Am Classical Coll Pr.
--How to Gain Exposure to the Possibility of Gaining Thousands upon Thousands of Dollars in the Stock Market by Following a Simple Method Recently Discovered. (A New Stock Market Library Bk.). (Illus.). 77p. 1983. pap. 26.45 (ISBN 0-89266-393-6). Am Classical Coll Pr.
--How to Make a Fortune in a Bear Market. LC 72-89241. (Illus.). 35p. 1972. 49.15 (ISBN 0-913314-09-9). Am Classical Coll Pr.
--How to Protect Your Money from the Destructive Powers of Inflation, Business Depressions, Political Turmoil, Wars, Revolutions & How to Double Your Patrimony Safely Every Five Years. (Illus.). 114p. 1974. 60.00 (ISBN 0-913314-37-4). Am Classical Coll Pr.
--How to Read Financial Statements: For Better Stock Market Performance. LC 73-90531. (Illus.). 1975. 52.80 (ISBN 0-913314-33-1). Am Classical Coll Pr.
--How to Select a Stock with the Power to Make You Wealthy Almost Overnight. LC 76-168997. (Illus.). 35p. 1972. 49.45 (ISBN 0-913314-07-2). Am Classical Coll Pr.
--The Iron Laws of the Historical Inevitabilities. (Illus.). 1977. 42.75 (ISBN 0-89266-081-3). Am Classical Coll Pr.
--The Large Corporation, the Perversion of the Democratic Order & the Corporate State. (Illus.). 1977. 49.50 (ISBN 0-89266-073-2). Am Classical Coll Pr.
--The Laws of History & the Caprice of Men. (Illus.). 1977. 49.75 (ISBN 0-89266-018-X). Am Classical Coll Pr.
--The Lessons of a Famous Course in the Techniques of Stock Market Charts. (Illus.). 125p. 1981. 81.85x (ISBN 0-86654-006-7). Inst Econ Finan.
--The Logical Powers of Stock Market Action. (Illus.). 1977. 65.85x (ISBN 0-918968-01-1). Inst Econ Finan.
--The Method. (Illus.). 1977. 47.75 (ISBN 0-89266-083-X). Am Classical Coll Pr.
--The New Dictionary of Strange & Ingenious Stock Market Tricks the Experts Follow in Their Search for Wealth. 215p. 1976. 57.50 (ISBN 0-89266-002-3). Am Classical Coll Pr.
--The New Expanded Dictionary of Stock Market Charts. new ed. (Illus.). 1977. 65.25 (ISBN 0-89266-050-3). Am Classical Coll Pr.
--The New Historical Function of the Large Corporation, 2 vols. in one. (Illus.). 200p. 1976. Set. 71.40 (ISBN 0-913314-73-0). Am Classical Coll Pr.
--New Technical Discoveries in Stock Market Chart Analysis. (A Stock Market Chartists Club of America Book). (Illus.). 1978. 67.50 (ISBN 0-89266-093-7). Am Classical Coll Pr.
--New Techniques for Profit with Stock Market Formula Plans. LC 72-87299. (Illus.). 40p. 1972. 51.15 (ISBN 0-913314-05-6). Am Classical Coll Pr.
--The Physiology & Psychology of Stock Market Charts. (Illus.). 103p. 1981. 67.85x (ISBN 0-918968-84-4). Inst Econ Finan.
--The Power Anatomy of the Economic Forces Dominating the Business & Political World. LC 73-92272. (Illus.). 142p. 1974. 52.75 (ISBN 0-913314-44-7). Am Classical Coll Pr.
--Power Anatomy of the Economic Forces Dominating the Business & the Political World. (Illus.). 1979. deluxe ed. 67.50x (ISBN 0-918968-22-4). Inst Econ Finan.
--Seven Unusual Business Careers: Guaranteed Maximal Profit Potential for the Intelligent College Graduate & the Daring Businessman. LC 76-115460. (Illus.). 90p. 1974. 47.50 (ISBN 0-913314-47-1). Am Classical Coll Pr.
--Silver, Gold & the Approaching Revolution in the International Monetary System. LC 74-28459. (Illus.). 90p. 1974. 67.50 (ISBN 0-913314-42-0). Am Classical Coll Pr.
--Silver, Gold & the Approaching Revolution in the International Monetary System. (Illus.). 1978. deluxe ed. 79.75x (ISBN 0-930008-10-3). Inst Econ Pol.
--Stock Market & Wall Street: The Essential Knowledge for Everyone Who Is Eager to Speculate for Profits in Stocks & Bonds. (An Essential Knowledge Library Bk.). (Illus.). 119p. 1983. 61.85x (ISBN 0-89266-408-8). Am Classical Coll Pr.
--Stock Market Charts: How to Interpret & Apply Them for the Making of Money in Wall Street. (An Essential Knowledge Library Bk.). (Illus.). 119p. 1983. 66.55x (ISBN 0-89266-407-X). Am Classical Coll Pr.
--Stock Market Charts: The Essential Knowledge of Stock Market Charts, How to Interpret & Apply Them Which Everyone, but Absolutely Everybody Who Is Interested in Speculation Ought to Know. (Essential Knowldge Ser. Books). (Illus.). 1978. 59.85 (ISBN 0-89266-119-4). Am Classical Coll Pr.
--Stock Market Manual for Teenagers. LC 72-89684. (Illus.). 70p. (YA) 1973. 26.50 (ISBN 0-913314-14-5). Am Classical Coll Pr.
--Stock Market Mastery Through the Application of the First Elliott Wave. (Illus.). 1976. 57.85 (ISBN 0-89266-005-8). Am Classical Coll Pr.
--The Strange Elliott Wave Theory Flow of Speculative Matter into the Active Cylinder Theory Stream Resulting in the Dominion of the Averages. (Illus.). 181p. 1983. 115.50x (ISBN 0-86654-083-0). Inst Econ Finan.
--The Subtle Art of Reading Stock Market Charts As a Guide to Successful Scalping Operations. (Illus.). 1977. 57.50 (ISBN 0-89266-077-5). Am Classical Coll Pr.
--The Subtle Operative Techniques on How to Make a Fortune in a Bear Market When Prices Decline Sharply & May Prepare the Ground for a Robust Advance. (Illus.). 1977. 47.50 (ISBN 0-89266-062-7). Am Classical Coll Pr.
--Teenager's Guide to Economics & Finance, 2 vols. in one. LC 72-91789. (Illus.). 70p. (gr. 10-12). 1973. Set. 47.50 (ISBN 0-913314-16-1). Am Classical Coll Pr.
--The Teenager's Life Extension Financial Test. (The Seminar for Human Development Books). (Illus.). 1978. plastic spiral bdg. 12.00 (ISBN 0-89266-124-0). Am Classical Coll Pr.
--The Theory of Inventiveness. LC 68-23100. (Illus.). 32p. 1972. 49.45 (ISBN 0-913314-15-3). Am Classical Coll Pr.
--Three Ways for an Investor with Very Little Money to Make a Killing in the Stock Market. (Illus.). 210p. 1976. 41.50 (ISBN 0-913314-82-X). Am Classical Coll Pr.
--The Twenty Major Wall Street Classics with Pertinent Commentaries which, Properly Applied, Will Guide You to the Accumulation of the Fortune You are After. (Illus.). 117p. 1986. 57.75 (ISBN 0-86654-187-X). Inst Econ Finan.
--The Wall Street Manual for Teenagers. (Illus.). 80p. (gr. 7-12). 1973. 19.75 (ISBN 0-913314-24-2). Am Classical Coll Pr.
--The Wall Street Manual for Teenagers. (Illus.). 99p. 1981. 23.75 (ISBN 0-89266-287-5). Am Classical Coll Pr.
--The Wave Theory Flow of Speculative Matter into the Active Cylinder Theory Stream. (Illus.). 1980. deluxe ed. 94.75x (ISBN 0-918968-48-8). Inst Econ Finan.
--The Winning Power of Stock Market Charts, 2 vols. (Illus.). 1985. Set. 198.75 (ISBN 0-86654-176-4). Inst Econ Finan.
Flumiani, C. M., jt. auth. see Elliott, Ralph N.
Flumiani, C. M., ed. The Wall Street Library, 3 vols. (The New Stock Market Library Book). (Illus.). Set. deluxe ed. 175.00x (ISBN 0-918968-26-7). Inst Econ Finan.
Flumiani, C. M., jt. ed. see Elliott, Ralph N.
Flumiani, C. M., ed. see Fibonacci, Leonardo.
Flumiani, Carlo M. The Advanced Course in Stock Market Charts, 2Vols. (The New Stock Market Library). (Illus.). 1979. 147.50 (ISBN 0-89266-173-9). Am Classical Coll Pr.
--Advanced Discoveries in Stock Market Charts, 3 vols. (Illus.). 477p. 1984. Set. 327.55x (ISBN 0-89266-436-3). Am Classical Coll Pr.
--The Chart Encyclopedia of the Wall Street Technical Action. (Illus.). 154p. 1984. 88.45x (ISBN 0-86654-099-7). Inst Econ Finan.
--Comparative Analysis of the Elliott Wave Theory & of the Cylinder Theory: Affinities & Divergencies, 2 vols. in one. (Illus.). 1977. Set. 64.35 (ISBN 0-89266-031-7). Am Classical Coll Pr.
--The Cylinder Theory As the Expression of the Fibonacci Theory of Cycles. (Illus.). 198p. 1984. 107.75x (ISBN 0-86654-120-9). Inst Econ Finan.
--The Deepening Moral Degeneration in Our Colleges & Universities. (Illus.). 1978. 47.50 (ISBN 0-89266-102-X). Am Classical Coll Pr.
--The Dynamic Substance & Power of the Theory of Inventiveness. (Illus.). 141p. 1982. 57.85 (ISBN 0-89266-333-2). Am Classical Coll Pr.
--The Economic Philosophy of History & Basic Patterns in the Growth & Decline of Nations. (Illus.). 117p. 1981. 79.85x (ISBN 0-930008-77-4). Inst Econ Finan.
--The Economic Philosophy of History & Basic Patterns in the Growth & Decline of Nations. (Illus.). 127p. 1983. 97.45x (ISBN 0-86722-053-8). Inst Econ Pol.
--The Economic Philosophy of History & the Science of Maximal Prediction. (The International Foundation for Social, Historical & Political Studies Ser.). (Illus.). 1978. 51.75 (ISBN 0-89266-094-5). Am Classical Coll Pr.
--How to Make Money in the Stock Market: A Guide to the Perplexed. (Illus.). 159p. 1985. 27.50 (ISBN 0-89266-511-4). Am Classical Coll Pr.
--Managing the Large Corporation in a World of Conflicting & Antagonistic Forces. (Illus.). 1977. 47.15 (ISBN 0-89266-039-2). Am Classical Coll Pr.
--The New Expanded Dictionary of Stock Market Charts. (Illus.). 179p. 1983. 81.75x (ISBN 0-86654-091-1). Inst Econ Finan.
--The Nine Deceits & the Collapse of Gold. (Illus.). 1977. 69.75 (ISBN 0-89266-051-1). Am Classical Coll Pr.
--The Survival of the Leadership Corporation & the Corporate State. (Illus.). 273p. 1977. 42.25 (ISBN 0-89266-042-2). Am Classical Coll Pr.
--The Technical Wall Street Encyclopedia. (The Library). 198p. 1982. 68.15x (ISBN 0-86654-041-5). Inst Econ Finan.
--The Teenager's Guidebook to Wall Street & the Stock Market. (Illus.). 143p. 1984. 49.75x (ISBN 0-89266-433-9). Am Classical Coll Pr.
--The Theory of Inventiveness in Schematic Representations. (Illus.). 141p. 1982. 62.55x (ISBN 0-86654-027-X). Inst Econ Finan.
--What a Teenager Ought to Know About God. (Illus.). 1978. 42.50 (ISBN 0-89266-140-2). Am Classical Coll Pr.
--The Winning Power of Stock Market Charts, 2 Vols. (The New Stock Market Library). (Illus.). 1977. 157.85 (ISBN 0-89266-071-6). Am Classical Coll Pr.
--Your Financial I. Q. Personal Test. (New Stock Market Library Bks.). 91p. 1983. 21.75x (ISBN 0-86654-044-X). Inst Econ Finan.
Flumiani, Carlo M., jt. auth. see Fibonacci, Leonardo.
Flumiani, Carlo Maria. The Cylinder Theory & the Metaphysics of Catastrophe. (Illus.). 1978. deluxe ed. 74.75x (ISBN 0-918968-09-7). Inst Econ Finan.
Flumiani, Carlo Maria de see De Flumiani, Carlo M.
Flumiani, Carlo Maria De see De Flumiani, Carlo M.
Flumiani, D. M. The Collapse of Gold & the Tragic Dilemma of the Swiss Bankers, 2 vols. in 1. (Illus.). 1978. deluxe ed. 65.15x (ISBN 0-918968-18-6). Inst Econ Finan.
Flurry, Robert L., Jr. Quantum Chemistry: An Introduction. (Illus.). 480p. 1983. 39.95 (ISBN 0-13-747832-1). P-H.
--Symmetry Groups: Theory & Chemical Applications. (Illus.). 1980. text ed. 44.95 (ISBN 0-13-880013-8). P-H.
Flurscheim, C. H., ed. Industrial Design in Engineering: A Marriage of Techniques. (Illus.). 400p. 1983. 49.00 (ISBN 0-387-12627-9). Springer-Verlag.
--Power Circuit Breaker Theory & Design. rev. ed. (IEE Power Engineering Ser.: No. 1). 602p. 1982. pap. 75.00 (ISBN 0-906048-70-2, P0001, Pub. by Peregrinus England). Inst Elect Eng.
--Power Circuit Breaker Theory & Design, No. 17. (IEE Monograph Series). 573p. 1975. 69.00 (ISBN 0-901223-62-X). Inst Elect Eng.
Flurscheim, M. The Economic & Social Problem. 69.95 (ISBN 0-87968-401-1). Gordon Pr.
Flury, Patricia A. Environmental Health & Safety in the Hospital Laboratory. (Illus.). 200p. 1978. 24.75x (ISBN 0-398-03773-6). C C Thomas.
Flusche, Della M. & Korth, Eugene H. Forgotten Females: Women of African & Indian Descent in Colonial Chile, 1535-1800. LC 82-24269. 112p. 1983. 16.50 (ISBN 0-87917-085-9). Ethridge.
Flusser, Alan. Making the Man: The Insider's Guide to Buying & Wearing Men's Clothes. 224p. 1981. pap. 9.95 (ISBN 0-671-79147-8, Wallaby). S&S.
Flusser, David. Die Rabbinischen Gleichnisse und der Gleichniserzaehler Jesus. (Judaica et Christiana: Vol. 4). 322p. (Ger.). 1981. 31.60 (ISBN 3-261-04778-X). P Lang Pubs.
Fly, J. Mark, jt. auth. see Marans, Robert W.
Fly, Richard. Shakespeare's Mediated World. LC 75-32486. 192p. 1976. 15.00x (ISBN 0-87023-199-5). U of Mass Pr.
Flygare, Thomas. The Legal Rights of Students. LC 75-19956. (Fastback Ser.: No. 59). 50p. (Orig.). 1975. pap. 0.75 (ISBN 0-87367-059-0). Phi Delta Kappa.
Flygare, Thomas J. Collective Bargaining in the Public Schools. LC 77-84041. (Fastback Ser.: No. 99). 49p. 1977. pap. 0.75 (ISBN 0-87367-099-X). Phi Delta Kappa.
--The Legal Rights of Teachers. LC 76-16878. (Fastback Ser.: No.83). (Orig.). 1976. pap. 0.75 (ISBN 0-87367-083-3). Phi Delta Kappa.
Flygare, W. H. Molecular Structure & Dynamics. LC 77-16786. (Illus.). 1978. ref. 48.95 (ISBN 0-13-599753-4). P-H.
Flygare, William. Presence. 120p. 12.50 (ISBN 0-933704-14-3). Dawn Pr.
Flygt, Sten G. Friedrich Hebbel. LC 68-20810. (World Authors Ser.). 1968. lib. bdg. 15.95 (ISBN 0-8057-2412-5). Irvington.
--Friedrich Hebbel's Conception of Movement in the Absolute & in History. LC 71-168051. (North Carolina. University. Studies in the Germanic Languages & Literatures: No. 7). Repr. of 1952 ed. 27.00 (ISBN 0-404-50907-X). AMS Pr.
--Notorious Doctor Bahrdt. LC 63-14648. (Illus.). 1963. 17.50x (ISBN 0-8265-1066-3). Vanderbilt U Pr.
Flying Magazine Editors. More I Learned about Flying from That. (Illus.). 256p. 1984. 18.95 (ISBN 0-02-579350-0). Macmillan.
Flynn. About the House. LC 76-48842. 144p. 1977. 6.95 (ISBN 0-916752-21-6). Dorison Hse.
Flynn, Bernice, jt. auth. see Flynn, Leslie.
Flynn, Beverly, jt. ed. see Miller, Michael H.
Flynn, Bobby. Differentiated Staffing for Urban Schools. 1985. 5.00 (ISBN 0-682-40216-8). Exposition Pr FL.
Flynn, Brian. Compute's Easy BASIC Programs for the Apple. Compute Editors, ed. 400p. (Orig.). 1985. pap. 14.95 (ISBN 0-942386-88-4). Compute Pubns.
--Easy BASIC Programs for the IBM PC & PCjr. (Orig.). 1984. pap. 14.95 (ISBN 0-942386-58-2). Compute Pubns.
--Thirty-Three Programs for the TI 99-4A. 199p. (Orig.). 1984. pap. 12.95 (ISBN 0-942386-42-6). Compute Pubns.
Flynn, Carol H. Samuel Richardson: A Man of Letters. LC 81-47916. (Illus.). 342p. 1982. 29.00x (ISBN 0-691-06506-3). Princeton U Pr.
Flynn, Charles. After the Beyond: Human Transformation & the Near-Death Experience. 1985. 14.95 (ISBN 0-13-018359-8); pap. 7.95 (ISBN 0-13-018342-3). P-H.
Flynn, Charles L., Jr. White Land, Black Labor: Caste & Class in Late Nineteenth-Century Georgia. LC 83-721. 208p. 1983. text ed. 20.00x (ISBN 0-8071-1097-3). La State U Pr.
Flynn, Charles P. Insult & Society: Patterns of Comparative Interaction. 1976. 13.50x (ISBN 0-8046-9152-5, Pub. by Kennikat). Assoc Faculty Pr.
Flynn, Charles P., jt. auth. see Greyson, Bruce.
Flynn, Charlotte. Dangerous Beat. (Moonstone Ser.: No. 3). (Orig.). (gr. 5 up). 1985. pap. 2.25 (ISBN 0-671-50783-4). Archway.
--Dangerous Beat. (gr. 5 up). 1985. pap. 2.25 (ISBN 0-317-19325-2). PB.
Flynn, Christopher. Compute's Guide to Extended BASIC Home Applications on the TI 99-4A. 172p. 1984. pap. 12.95 (ISBN 0-942386-41-8). Compute Pubns.
--Home Applications in BASIC for the IBM PC & PCjr. Compute Editors, ed. (Illus., Orig.). 1985. pap. 12.95 (ISBN 0-942386-60-4). Compute Pubns.
Flynn, David H., jt. auth. see Pancheri, Michael.

Flynn, Deborah. Introduction to Real Estate Law. 2nd ed. (Illus.). 475p. Date not set. text ed. price not set (ISBN 0-314-77984-1). West Pub.

Flynn, Dennis, ed. On Irish Themes: James T. Farrell. LC 82-60301. 256p. (Orig.). 1982. 27.50x (ISBN 0-8122-7860-7); pap. 11.95x (ISBN 0-8122-1132-4). U of Pa Pr.

Flynn, Dennis J. The Secrets of Soil-Less Indoor Gardening. LC 83-90240. (Illus.). 112p. 1983. pap. 6.95 (ISBN 0-934318-19-0). Falcon Pr Mt.

--The Secrets of Soil-less Indoor Gardening. (Illus.). 112p. (Orig.). 1983. pap. 6.95 (ISBN 0-934318-19-0). Valley Farms.

Flynn, Don. Murder Isn't Enough. 192p. 1983. 12.95 (ISBN 0-8027-5495-3). Walker & Co.

--Murder on the Hudson. 192p. 1985. 13.95 (ISBN 0-8027-5609-3). Walker & Co.

Flynn, Edith E. & Conrad, John P., eds. The New & the Old Criminology. LC 76-14130. (Praeger Special Studies). 350p. 1978. 42.95 (ISBN 0-03-040891-1). Praeger.

Flynn, Edward J. You're the Boss. LC 82-24156. x, 244p. 1983. Repr. of 1947 ed. lib. bdg. 29.75x (ISBN 0-313-23627-5, FLYB). Greenwood.

Flynn, Edwin H., ed. Cephalosporins & Penicillins: Chemistry & Biology. 1972. 76.50 (ISBN 0-12-261450-X). Acad Pr.

Flynn, Eileen P. Human Fertilization "In Vitro". A Catholic Moral Perspective. LC 83-27343. 202p. (Orig.). 1984. lib. bdg. 22.50 (ISBN 0-8191-3819-3); pap. text ed. 12.00 (ISBN 0-8191-3820-7). U Pr of Amer.

--My Country Right or Wrong? Selective Conscientious Objection in the Nuclear Age. 1985. pap. 3.95 (ISBN 0-317-18110-6). Loyola.

Flynn, Elizabeth A. & Donaldson, Christine F. Alternative Careers for Ph.D.s in the Humanities: A Selected Bibliography. LC 82-3399. 41p. (Orig.). 1982. pap. 6.50x (ISBN 0-87352-099-8). Modern Lang.

Flynn, Elizabeth G. The Alderson Story: My Life as a Political Prisoner. new ed. LC 63-10863. 223p. 1972. pap. 2.25 (ISBN 0-7178-0002-4). Intl Pubs Co.

--The Rebel Girl: An Autobiography. My First Life. new ed. LC 72-94154. (Illus.). 368p. 1973. pap. 5.95 (ISBN 0-7178-0368-6). Intl Pubs Co.

Flynn, Errol. Beam Ends. 1976. Repr. of 1937 ed. lib. bdg. 17.95 (ISBN 0-89966-092-4). Buccaneer Bks.

--From a Life of Adventure: The Writings of Errol Flynn. Thomas, Tony, ed. (Illus.). 1980. 12.95 (ISBN 0-8065-0690-3). Citadel Pr.

--My Wicked, Wicked Ways. 1983. pap. 2.95 (ISBN 0-425-06479-4). Berkley Pub.

--My Wicked, Wicked Ways. 1976. Repr. of 1959 ed. lib. bdg. 18.95x (ISBN 0-89966-093-2). Buccaneer Bks.

--Showdown. 1976. Repr. of 1946 ed. lib. bdg. 17.95x (ISBN 0-89966-094-0). Buccaneer Bks.

Flynn, Fletcher & McGuire, Thomas G. Design: Rhetoric & Anthology for College English. 3rd ed. 512p. 1981. pap. text ed. write for info. (ISBN 0-534-00993-X). Wadsworth Pub.

Flynn, George. Zingers: Twenty Five Poems. 32p. 6.00 (ISBN 0-686-00335-7). G Flynn.

Flynn, George, Jr. Experts Sports Quiz Book. (Illus.). 192p. (Orig.). 1979. pap. 1.95 (ISBN 0-916800-23-7). Chapter & Cask.

Flynn, George Q. American Catholics & the Roosevelt Presidency, 1932-1936. LC 68-12968. 288p. 1968. 26.00x (ISBN 0-8131-1165-X). U Pr of Ky.

--Lewis B. Hershey, Mr. Selective Service. LC 84-10397. (Illus.). 380p. 1985. 24.95x (ISBN 0-8078-1621-3). U of NC Pr.

--The Mess in Washington: Manpower Mobilization in World War II. LC 78-4027. (Contributions in American History: No. 76). xi, 294p. 1979. lib. bdg. 29.95 (ISBN 0-313-20418-7, FMW/). Greenwood.

--Roosevelt & Romanism: Catholics & American Diplomacy, 1937-1945. LC 75-35343. (Contributions in American History: No. 47). 272p. 1976. lib. bdg. 29.95 (ISBN 0-8371-8581-5, FRR/). Greenwood.

Flynn, Gerard. Sor Juana Ines de la Cruz. LC 75-120482. (World Authors Ser.). 1971. lib. bdg. 15.95 (ISBN 0-8057-2256-4). Irvington.

Flynn, Gerard C., ed. see Baroja, Pio.

Flynn, Gregory, ed. Economic Interests in the Nineteen Eighties: Convergence or Divergence? (Atlantic Papers Ser.: No. 44-45). (Illus.). 126p. 1982. pap. text ed. 13.00x (ISBN 0-86598-103-5). Allanheld.

--Nato's Northern Allies: The National Security Policies of Belguim, the Netherlands, Norway & Denmark. (Atlantic Institute Research Volume Ser.). 220p. 1985. 45.00x (ISBN 0-8476-7444-4). Rowman.

Flynn, Gregory & Rattinger, Hans, eds. The Public & Atlantic Defense. LC 84-15894. (Atlantic Institute Research Ser.). (Illus.). 416p. 1985. 45.00x (ISBN 0-8476-7365-0). Rowman & Allanheld.

Flynn, Gregory A., et al. The Internal Fabric of Western Security: (An Atlantic Institute Research Volume) LC 81-65011. 264p. 1981. text ed. 32.50x (ISBN 0-86598-039-X). Allanheld.

Flynn, J. & Heffron, P. Nursing: From Concept to Practice. LC 83-15918. (Illus.). 704p. 1984. pap. text ed. 24.95 (ISBN 0-89303-719-2). Brady Comm.

Flynn, J. G., tr. see Shahrastani, Muhammad B.

Flynn, J. M. Danger Zone. (Inflation Fighters Ser.). 192p. 1982. pap. 1.50 (ISBN 0-8439-1139-5, Leisure Bks). Dorchester Pub Co.

--Danger Zone. 1977. pap. 1.50 (ISBN 0-505-51171-1, Pub. by Tower Bks). Dorchester Pub Co.

Flynn, James & Glaser, Joseph. Writer's Handbook. 460p. 1983. pap. text ed. write for info. (ISBN 0-02-471580-8). Macmillan.

Flynn, James, ed. Understanding Celine. LC 84-10281. 270p. (Orig.). 1984. pap. 12.50x (ISBN 0-915781-00-X). Genitron Press.

Flynn, James H., Jr. Building the Balalaika, a Russian Folk Instrument. LC 84-90311. (Illus.). 55p. 1984. spiral bound 9.95 (ISBN 0-9613258-0-1). J H Flynn.

Flynn, James R. Race, I. Q. & Jensen. 320p. 1980. 29.95x (ISBN 0-7100-0651-9). Routledge & Kegan.

Flynn, Jay. Bannerman. 1976. pap. 1.25 (ISBN 0-8439-0389-9, LB389, Leisure Bks). Dorchester Pub Co.

--Bannerman. 192p. 1982. pap. 2.25 (ISBN 0-8439-1119-0, Leisure Bks). Dorchester Pub Co.

--Bannerman. 192p. 1983. pap. 2.25 (ISBN 0-8439-2030-0, Leisure Bks). Dorchester Pub Co.

--Blood on Frisco Bay. 1976. pap. 1.25 (ISBN 0-8439-0360-0, LB36OZK, Leisure Bks). Dorchester Pub Co.

--Trouble Is My Business. 1976. pap. 1.25 (ISBN 0-685-72358-5, LB384ZK, Leisure Bks). Dorchester Pub Co.

Flynn, Jean. Jim Bowie: A Texas Legend. (Stories for Young Americans Ser.). 1980. 5.95 (ISBN 0-89015-241-1). Eakin Pubns.

--Remember Goliad Fannin: James W. Fannin, Jr. 64p. 1984. 5.95 (ISBN 0-89015-444-9). Eakin Pubns.

--Stephen F. Austin: The Father of Texas. (Stories for Young Americans Ser.). (Illus.). 64p. 1981. 5.95 (ISBN 0-89015-285-3). Eakin Pubns.

--William Barret Travis. 1982. 5.95 (ISBN 0-89015-348-5). Eakin Pubns.

Flynn, Jean P., jt. auth. see Mahoney, Elizabeth A.

Flynn, Joe B. The Design of Executive Protection Systems. (Illus.). 100p. 1979. 14.75x (ISBN 0-398-03894-5). C C Thomas.

Flynn, Johanna & Canfield, Anita. Visiting Teaching: A Call to Serve. 80p. (Orig.). 1984. pap. 3.95 (ISBN 0-934126-42-9). Randall Bk Co.

Flynn, John, jt. auth. see Lapper, Ivan.

Flynn, John D. Federalism & State Antitrust Regulations. LC 64-64967. (Michigan Legal Publications Ser.). vii, 312p. 1984. Repr. of 1964 ed. lib. bdg. 30.00 (ISBN 0-89941-322-6). W S Hein.

Flynn, John J., jt. auth. see Schwartz, Louis B.

Flynn, John P., jt. auth. see Constable, Robert T.

Flynn, John S. Influence of Puritanism. LC 72-102569. 1970. Repr. of 1920 ed. 21.00x (ISBN 0-8046-0729-X, Pub. by Kennikat). Assoc Faculty Pr.

Flynn, John T. As We Go Marching. LC 79-172212. (Right Wing Individualist Tradition in America Ser). 1972. Repr. of 1944 ed. 18.00 (ISBN 0-405-00421-4). Ayer Co Pubs.

--Can Hitler Invade America? A Myth Exposed. 1984. lib. bdg. 79.95 (ISBN 0-87700-593-1). Revisionist Pr.

--Decline of the American Republic. 1955. 9.95 (ISBN 0-8159-5303-8). Devin.

--God's Gold: The Story of Rockefeller & His Times. LC 78-138231. (Illus.). 1971. Repr. of 1932 ed. lib. bdg. 26.00x (ISBN 0-8371-5588-6, FLGG). Greenwood.

--Investment Trusts Gone Wrong! facsimile ed. LC 75-2629. (Wall Street & Security Market Ser.). 1975. Repr. of 1930 ed. 23.50x (ISBN 0-405-06955-3). Ayer Co Pubs.

--Men of Wealth. facs. ed. LC 79-142629. (Essay Index Reprint Ser). 1941. 27.50 (ISBN 0-8369-2047-3). Ayer Co Pubs.

--The Smear Terror. 1982. lib. bdg. 59.95 (ISBN 0-87700-367-X). Revisionist Pr.

--The Truth about Pearl Harbor. 1984. lib. bdg. 79.95 (ISBN 0-87700-613-X). Revisionist Pr.

--While You Slept: Our Tragedy in Asia & Who Made It. 1951. 6.50 (ISBN 0-8159-7207-5). Devin.

Flynn, John T. & Rothbard, Murray. The Roosevelt Myth: A Critical Account of the New Deal & Its Creator. 454p. 1985. pap. cancelled (ISBN 0-8159-6713-6). Devin.

Flynn, John Thomas. Country Squire in the White House. LC 77-167846. (FDR & the Era of the New Deal Ser). 122p. 1972. Repr. of 1940 ed. lib. bdg. 22.50 (ISBN 0-306-70324-6). Da Capo.

Flynn, Joseph M. Massachusetts Tax Handbook 1985. price not set. P-H.

Flynn, Kathlee M., jt. auth. see Dunn, Donald J., Jr.

Flynn, Kathleen, jt. auth. see Marram, Gwen.

Flynn, Leslie. The Twelve. 156p. 1982. pap. 4.95 (ISBN 0-88207-310-9). Victor Bks.

Flynn, Leslie & Flynn, Bernice. Humorous Notes, Quotes, & Anecdotes. (Direction Bks.). 1980. pap. 3.95 (ISBN 0-8010-3493-0). Baker Bk.

Flynn, Leslie B. Dare to Care Like Jesus. LC 81-51949. 119p. 1982. pap. 3.95 (ISBN 0-88207-348-6). Victor Bks.

--Nineteen Gifts of the Spirit. LC 74-91027. 204p. 1974. pap. 5.95 (ISBN 0-88207-701-5). Victor Bks.

--The Sustaining Power of Hope. 132p. 1985. pap. 4.95 (ISBN 0-89693-600-7). Victor Bks.

--What Is Man? 132p. 1983. pap. 4.50 (ISBN 0-88207-104-1). Victor Bks.

--What Is Man. Chao, Lorna Y., tr. (Chinese.). 1985. pap. price not set (ISBN 0-941598-27-6). Living Spring Pubns.

--Worship: Together We Celebrate. 132p. 1983. pap. 4.50 (ISBN 0-88207-608-6). Victor Bks.

--You Don't Have to Go It Alone. LC 80-66722. 160p. (Orig.). 1981. pap. 4.95 (ISBN 0-89636-058-X). Accent Bks.

--Your Inner You. 156p. 1984. pap. 4.95 (ISBN 0-89693-378-4). Victor Bks.

Flynn, Lucine H. Dogs for Protection. (Illus.). 96p. 1983. 4.95 (ISBN 0-87666-813-9, PS-802). TFH Pubns.

--Talk Dog. (Other Dog Bks). (Illus.). 1985. write for info. (ISBN 0-87714-120-7). Denlingers.

Flynn, M. J., et al. Operating Systems: An Advanced Course. (Springer Study Editions). 593p. 1979. pap. 23.00 (ISBN 0-387-09812-7). Springer-Verlag.

Flynn, M. J., et al, eds. Microcomputer System Design: An Advanced Course, Dublin, 1981. 2nd ed. (Springer Study Edition). vii, 397p. 1984. pap. 19.95 (ISBN 0-387-13545-6). Springer-Verlag.

--Microcomputer System Design: An Advanced Course. (Lecture Notes in Computer Science Ser.: Vol. 126). 397p. 1981. pap. 22.00 (ISBN 0-387-11172-7). Springer-Verlag.

Flynn, Mannix. Nothing to Say. 172p. 1983. pap. 7.95 (ISBN 0-907085-52-0, Pub. by Ward River Pr Ireland). Irish Bks Media.

Flynn, Mary A., jt. auth. see Walls, Betsy.

Flynn, Mary A., jt. auth. see Walls, Elizabeth.

Flynn, Michael. Structure Building Operations & Word Order. Hankamer, Jorge, ed. (Outstanding Dissertations in Linguistics Ser.). 150p. 1985. 25.00 (ISBN 0-8240-5447-4). Garland Pub.

Flynn, Michael J., jt. auth. see Waser, Shlomo.

Flynn, Nancy. Pearl. (La Mer Press Ser.). 24p. (Orig.). 1985. pap. 5.00 (ISBN 0-917573-02-1). CAO Times.

Flynn, Norman, et al. Abolition or Reform? The Metropolitan Counties & the GLC. LC 84-24384. (Local Government Briefings Ser.). 120p. 1985. text ed. 20.00x (ISBN 0-04-352119-3); cancelled (ISBN 0-04-352121-5). Allen Unwin.

Flynn, Patricia, jt. auth. see Burbach, Roger.

Flynn, Patricia, jt. ed. see Burbach, Roger.

Flynn, Patricia, tr. see Burbach, R.

Flynn, Patricia A. Holistic Health: The Art & Science of Care. LC 79-27671. (Illus.). 259p. 1980. pap. text ed. 17.95 (ISBN 0-87619-626-1). Brady Comm.

Flynn, Peter. Brazil: A Political Analysis. (Nations of the Modern World Ser.). (Illus.). 1979. pap. 25.00x (ISBN 0-89158-694-6). Westview.

Flynn, Philip. Francis Jeffrey. LC 76-27915. 218p. 1978. 22.50 (ISBN 0-87413-123-5). U Delaware Pr.

Flynn, Richard B., jt. ed. see Coates, Edward.

Flynn, Robert. And Holy Is His Name. 1983. 5.95 (ISBN 0-87193-197-4). Dimension Bks.

--North to Yesterday. LC 85-4688. (The Texas Tradition Ser.: No. 4). 352p. 1985. 16.95 (ISBN 0-87565-014-7); pap. 9.95 (ISBN 0-87565-015-5). Tex Christian.

Flynn, Robert J. Carpenter's Shopping Center Management: Principles & Practices. 208p. 1984. avail. (ISBN 0-913598-23-2). Intl Coun Shop.

--Normalization Social Integration & Community Services. LC 79-26670. (Illus.). 448p. 1980. pap. 16.00 (ISBN 0-8391-1524-5). Pro Ed.

--Parasites of Laboratory Animals. LC 77-171165. (Illus.). 884p. 1973. 37.00x (ISBN 0-8138-0470-1). Iowa St U Pr.

Flynn, Rose. Quicksilver Love. (YA) 1980. 8.95 (ISBN 0-686-73941-8, Avalon). Bouregy.

Flynn, Suzanne K. How to Save Your Hair: A Complete Guide to the Prevention & Treatment of Baldness. LC 84-12453. (Orig.). 1984. pap. 6.95 (ISBN 0-87795-579-4). Arbor Hse.

Flynn, T. Geoffrey & Weiner, Henry. Enzymology of Carbonyl Metabolism, Vol. 2: Aldehyde Dehydrogenase, Aldo-Keto Reductase & Alcohol Dehydrogenase. LC 84-27828. (Progress in Clinical & Biological Research Ser.: Vol. 174). 336p. 1985. 46.00 (ISBN 0-8451-5024-3). A R Liss.

Flynn, Thomas R. Sartre & Marxist Existenialism: The Test Case of Collective Responsibility. LC 83-4994. 265p. 1984. lib. bdg. 27.50x (ISBN 0-226-25465-8). U of Chicago Pr.

Flynn, Vincent J., jt. auth. see Rizvi, Saiyid A.

Flynt, Candace. Sins of Omission. LC 84-42629. 304p. 1984. 15.45 (ISBN 0-394-53955-9). Random.

Flynt, Dorothy S., jt. auth. see Flynt, J. Wayne.

Flynt, Faye D. They Dared to Cross Frontiers. (Orig.). (gr. 4-6). 1975. pap. 1.95 (ISBN 0-377-00029-9). Friend Pr.

Flynt, Henry N., jt. auth. see Chamberlain, Samuel.

Flynt, J. Wayne. Dixie's Forgotten People: The South's Poor Whites. LC 78-20613. (Midland Bks: Minorities in Modern America Ser.: No. 244). (Illus.). 224p. 1979. 15.00x (ISBN 0-253-19765-1); pap. 6.95x (ISBN 0-253-20244-2). Ind U Pr.

Flynt, J. Wayne & Flynt, Dorothy S. Southern Poor Whites: A Selected, Annotated Bibliography of Published Sources. LC 80-9035. 1981. lib. bdg. 61.00 (ISBN 0-8240-9314-3). Garland Pub.

Flynt, Josiah. Notes of an Itinerant Policeman. LC 72-5504. (Select Bibliographies Reprint Ser.). 1972. Repr. of 1900 ed. 20.00 (ISBN 0-8369-6907-3). Ayer Co Pubs.

--World of Graft. facs. ed. LC 72-150181. (Select Bibliographies Reprint Ser.). 1901. 18.00 (ISBN 0-8369-5694-X). Ayer Co Pubs.

Flynt, Suzanne L. George Fuller: At Home. (Illus.). 24p. (Orig.). 1984. pap. 2.00 (ISBN 0-9612876-2-4). Pocumtuck Valley Mem.

Flynt, Wayne. Cracker Messiah: Governer Sidney J. Catts of Florida. LC 76-57664. (Southern Biography Ser). (Illus.). 360p. 1977. 30.00x (ISBN 0-8071-0263-6). La State U Pr.

--Duncan Upshaw Fletcher: Dixie's Reluctant Progressive. LC 73-149954. 213p. 1971. 10.00. U Presses Fla.

--Montgomery: An Illustrated History. 200p. 1980. 17.95 (ISBN 0-317-12311-4). Windsor Pubns Inc.

FMLN-FDR Political-Diplomatic Commission. Massacre in El Salvador's Morazan Province. (Illus.). 58p. 1983. pap. 2.00 (ISBN 0-942638-00-X, 13L). Solidarity.

Fo, Dario. Accidental Death of an Anarchist. pap. 4.95 (ISBN 0-86104-217-4). Pluto Pr.

--Gli Imbianchini Non Hanno Ricordi. (Easy Readers a). 1977. pap. 3.25 (ISBN 0-88436-296-5, 55251). EMC.

--We Can't Pay? We Won't Pay! 72p. (Orig.). 1981. pap. 4.95 (ISBN 0-86104-204-2). Pluto Pr.

Fo, Dario & Rame, Franca R. Female Parts: One Woman Plays. 48p. (Orig.). 1981. pap. 3.95 (ISBN 0-86104-220-4). Pluto Pr.

Foa, Edna B., jt. auth. see Goldstein, Alan.

Foa, Edna B. & Emmelkamp, Paul M., eds. Failures in Behavior Therapy. LC 82-17644. (Personality Processes Ser.). 446p. 1983. 45.00x (ISBN 0-471-09238-X, Pub. by Wiley-Interscience). Wiley.

Foa, P. P. & Bajaj, J. S., eds. Glucagon. LC 77-13657. (Its Role in Physiology & Clinical Medicine). 1977. 40.00 (ISBN 0-387-90297-X). Springer-Verlag.

Foa, Piero P., jt. auth. see Cohen, Margo P.

Foa, Piero P., jt. ed. see Cohen, Margo P.

Foad, E. V. Purpose-Made Joinery. 1982. 27.95 (ISBN 0-442-30470-6). Van Nos Reinhold.

Foakes, Joanne S. Tolley's European Community Institutions. 1982. 50.00x (ISBN 0-85459-060-9, Pub. by Tolley Pub England). State Mutual Bk.

Foakes, R. A. Coleridge on Shakespeare: The Text of the Lectures of 1811-12. (Monographs). 1978. 12.95x (ISBN 0-918016-54-1). Folger Bks.

--Illustrations of the English Stage, 1580-1642. LC 83-40517. (Illus.). xviii, 180p. 1985. 45.00x (ISBN 0-8047-1236-0). Stanford U Pr.

--Shakespeare, the Dark Comedies to the Last Plays: From Satire to Celebration. LC 70-146536. 200p. 1971. 14.95x (ISBN 0-8139-0327-0). U Pr of Va.

Foakes, R. A., ed. A Midsummer Night's Dream. Date not set. price not set. Cambridge U Pr.

--Romantic Criticism: 1800-1850. LC 76-116476. (English Library). 224p. 1970. pap. text ed. 4.95x (ISBN 0-87249-165-X). U of SC Pr.

Foakes, R. A. & Gibson, J. C., eds. The Telltale. LC 82-45711. (Malone Society Reprint Ser.: No. 110). 1959. 40.00 (ISBN 0-404-63111-8). AMS Pr.

Foakes, R. A., ed. see Shakespeare, William.

Foakes, R. A., ed. see Tourneur, Cyril.

Foale, Marion. Marion Foale's Classic Knitwear: A Beautiful Collection of 30 Original Patterns. Hylton, Bill, ed. (Illus.). 128p. 1985. 21.95 (ISBN 0-87857-583-9); pap. 12.95 (ISBN 0-87857-584-7). Rodale Pr Inc.

Foard, Walker, tr. see Zamiatin, Evgeny.

Foat, Ginny. Presumption of Guilt. LC 85-6261. 1985. 19.45 (ISBN 0-394-54141-3). Random.

Foat, Ginny & Foreman, Laura. Never Guilty, Never Free. 1985. 17.95 (ISBN 0-394-54141-3). Random.

Foata, D., ed. Combinatoire et Representation Du Groupe Symetrique. (Lecture Notes in Mathematics Ser: Vol. 579). 1977. pap. 20.40 (ISBN 0-387-08143-7). Springer-Verlag.

Fobel, J. Beautiful Food Book. 1983. 17.95 (ISBN 0-442-22730-2). Van Nos Reinhold.

Fobes, F. H., ed. see Averroes.

Fobes, F. H., jt. ed. see Ross, W. D.

Fobes, Francis H. Philosophical Greek: An Introduction. LC 57-8580. 1957. 25.00x (ISBN 0-226-25620-0). U of Chicago Pr.

Fobes, Harriet K. Mystic Gems. 1977. 59.95 (ISBN 0-8490-2315-7). Gordon Pr.

Fobes, Jacqueline. A Papago Boy & His Friends. 1980. pap. 1.50 (ISBN 0-686-32641-5). Impresora Sahuaro.

Fobes, James & King, James, eds. Primate Behavior. (Communication & Behavior Ser.). 385p. 1982. 35.00 (ISBN 0-12-261320-1). Acad Pr.

Fobes, Walter K., ed. Five-Minute Declamations, First Pt. facs. ed. LC 71-139761. (Granger Index Reprint Ser). 1885. 43.00 (ISBN 0-8369-6215-X). Ayer Co Pubs.

--Five-Minute Declamations, Second Pt. facs. ed. LC 71-139761. (Granger Index Reprint Ser). 1890. 35.00 (ISBN 0-8369-6216-8). Ayer Co Pubs.

Foch, Ferdinand. Principles of War. De Morinni, J., tr. LC 70-128436. Repr. of 1918 ed. 27.00 (ISBN 0-404-02439-4). AMS Pr.

Fochs, Arnold. Advertising That Won Elections. 272p. 1980. pap. 14.92 (ISBN 0-914190-03-2). A J Pub.

--The Very Idea: A Collection of Unusual Retail Advertising Ideas, Vol. 2. rev. ed. 272p. (Orig.). 1980. pap. 13.50 (ISBN 0-914190-02-4). A J Pub.

Fochs, Arnold, ed. Best Local-Retail Ads. rev. ed. 248p. 1981. pap. 14.92 (ISBN 0-685-99089-3). A J Pub.

Fochs, Arnold, compiled by. Prize-Winning Ads Used by Night Clubs, Cafes, Drive-Ins, & Hotels-Motels. rev. ed. 1982. pap. 14.92 (ISBN 0-685-58280-9). A J Pub.

Fochtman, Dianne & Raffensperger, John G. Principles of Nursing Care for the Pediatric Surgery Patient. 2nd ed. LC 75-30297. 1976. pap. text ed. 13.95 (ISBN 0-316-28681-8). Little.

Fochtman, Edward G., et al, eds. Forum on Ozone Disinfection. LC 76-51563. 1977. text ed. 18.00 (ISBN 0-918650-01-1); text ed. 25.00 non-members (ISBN 0-918650-00-3). Intl Ozone.

Focillon, Henri. The Art of the West in the Middle Ages: Vol. 2, Gothic. King, Donald, tr. from Fr. (Landmarks in Art History Ser.). (Illus.). 388p. 1980. pap. 12.95x (ISBN 0-8014-9192-4). Cornell U Pr.

--The Art of the West in the Middle Ages: Vol. 1, Romanesque. King, Donald, tr. from Fr. (Landmarks in Art History Ser.). (Illus.). 332p. 1980. pap. 12.95x (ISBN 0-8014-9191-6). Cornell U Pr.

Focillon, Henri, et al. Dumbarton Oaks Inaugural Lectures, November 2nd & 3rd, 1940. 1966. Repr. of 1941 ed. 16.00 (ISBN 0-384-13255-3). Johnson Repr.

Fock, V. Fundamentals of Quantum Mechanics. 375p. 1978. 8.45 (ISBN 0-8285-5197-9, Pub. by Mir Pubs USSR). Imported Pubns.

Fock, V. A. The Theory of Space, Time & Gravitation. 2nd ed. 1964. 62.00 (ISBN 0-08-010061-9). Pergamon.

Focsa, Marcela, jt. auth. see Irimie, Cornel.

Foda, Ezzeldin. The Projected Arab Court of Justice: A Study in Regional Jurisdiction with Specific Reference to the Muslim Law of Nations. LC 79-2858. 258p. 1981. Repr. of 1957 ed. 24.75 (ISBN 0-8305-0031-6). Hyperion Conn.

Fodell, Beverly. Cesar Chavez & the United Farm Workers: A Selective Bibliography. LC 73-6365. 116p. 1974. pap. text ed. 4.95x (ISBN 0-8143-1502-X). Wayne St U Pr.

Foden, Frank. Philip Magnus: Victorian Educational Pioneer. 298p. 1970. 15.00x (ISBN 0-85303-044-8, Pub. by Vallentine Mitchell England). Biblio Dist.

Foderaro, Anthony. Elements of Neutron Interaction Theory. LC 79-103896. 1971. text ed. 40.00x (ISBN 0-262-06033-7). MIT Pr.

Fodor, Alexander. Tolstoy & the Russians: Reflections on a Relationship. 200p. 1984. 22.50 (ISBN 0-88233-891-9). Ardis Pubs.

Fodor, D. The Neutrals. LC 82-10388. (World War II Ser.). 1982. lib. bdg. 22.60 (ISBN 0-8094-3432-6, Pub. by Time-Life). Silver.

Fodor, Denis. The Neutrals. (World War II Ser.). (Illus.). 176p. 1983. 14.95 (ISBN 0-8094-3431-8). Time Life.

Fodor, Gabor, jt. auth. see Szetsko, Tamas.

Fodor, Illie L. Shock: Medical Subject Analysis & Research Bibliography. LC 84-45663. 150p. 1985. 29.95 (ISBN 0-88164-202-9); pap. 21.95 (ISBN 0-88164-203-7). ABBE Pubs Assn.

Fodor, Istvan. A Fallacy of Contemporary Linquistics. 114p. (Orig.). 1981. pap. text ed. 14.00x (ISBN 3-87118-421-7, Pub. by Helmut Buske Verlag Hamburg). Benjamins North Am.

--Film Dubbing: Phonetic Semiotic, Esthetic & Psychological Aspects. 110p. (Orig.). 1976. pap. text ed. 10.00x (ISBN 3-87118-209-5, Pub. by Helmut Buska Verlag Hamburg). Benjamins North Am.

--Introduction to the History of Umbundu: L. Magyar's Records (1859) & the Later Sources. 327p. 1983. 34.00x (ISBN 3-87118-554-X, Pub. by Helmut Buske Verlag Hamburg). Benjamins North Am.

Fodor, Istvan & Hagege, Claude. Language Reform: History & Future, Vol. 3. (Illus.). xi, 586p. (Eng. Fr. & Ger.). 1984. 114.00x (ISBN 3-87118-678-3, H Buske). Benjamins North Am.

Fodor, Istvan & Hagege, Claude, eds. K Language Reform, History & Future-La Reforme des Langues, Histoire et Avenir-Sprachreform, Geschichte und Zukunft, Vol. 2. (Illus.). 521p. (Fr. & Ger. & Eng.). 1983. 112.00x (ISBN 3-87118-572-8, 6065, Pub. by Helmut Buske Verlag Hamburg). Benjamins North Am.

--Language Reform: History & Future, 3 vols. (Illus.). xliv, 1651p. (Eng. Fr. & Ger.). 1983. Set. 343.00x (ISBN 3-87118-572-8, H Buske). Benjamins North Am.

--Language Reform: History & Future, Vol. 1. (Illus.). 544p. (Ger., Rus. & Fr.). 1983. 115.00x (ISBN 3-87118-676-7, Pub. by Helmut Buske Verlag Hamburg). Benjamins North AM.

Fodor, Janet D. The Linguistic Description of Opaque Contexts. Hankamer, Jorge, ed. LC 78-66537. (Outstanding Dissertations in Linguistics Ser.). 1985. 51.00 (ISBN 0-8240-9686-X). Garland Pub.

--Semantics: Theories of Meaning in Generative Grammar. (Language & Thought Ser.). 240p. 1980. pap. 8.95x (ISBN 0-674-80134-2). Harvard U Pr.

Fodor, Jerry A. The Language of Thought. 1979. pap. text ed. 8.95x (ISBN 0-674-51030-5). Harvard U Pr.

--Modularity of Mind: Faculty Psychology. (Bradford Monograph Ser.). 216p. 1983. text ed. 19.00x (ISBN 0-262-06084-1); pap. text ed. 8.50x (ISBN 0-262-56025-9). MIT Pr.

--Psychological Explanation: An Introduction to the Philosophy of Psychology. 1968. pap. text ed. 6.95 (ISBN 0-394-30663-5, RanC). Random.

--Representations: Philosophical Essays on the Foundations of Cognitive Science. LC 81-24313. (Illus.). 384p. 1981. 27.50x (ISBN 0-262-06079-5, Pub. by Bradford); pap. 9.95x (ISBN 0-262-56027-5). MIT Pr.

Fodor, John T. & Dalis, Gus T. Health Instruction: Theory & Application. 3rd ed. LC 80-24484. (Illus.). 150p. 1981. text ed. 9.75 (ISBN 0-8121-0776-4). Lea & Febiger.

Fodor, Nandor. Encyclopaedia of Psychic Science. 416p. 1974. pap. 8.95 (ISBN 0-8065-0428-5). Citadel Pr.

--Encyclopaedia of Psychic Science. (Illus.). 1966. 17.50 (ISBN 0-8216-0073-7). Univ Bks.

--New Approaches to Dream Interpretations. 308p. 1972. 7.95 (ISBN 0-8216-0126-1). Univ Bks.

Fodor, Nandor, ed. see Freud, Sigmund.

Fodor, R. F. & Taylor, G. J. Junior Body Building: Growing Strong. LC 82-50552. (Illus.). 144p. (gr. 9 up). 1982. pap. 4.95 (ISBN 0-8069-7676-4). Sterling.

Fodor, R. V. Chiseling the Earth: How Erosion Shapes the Land. LC 82-18227. (Illus.). 96p. (gr. 5-12). 1983. PLB 11.95 (ISBN 0-89490-074-9). Enslow Pubs.

--Earth in Motion: The Concept of Plate Tectonics. LC 77-12568. (Illus.). (gr. 3-7). 1978. 10.00 (ISBN 0-688-22135-1); PLB 10.88 (ISBN 0-688-32135-6). Morrow.

--Frozen Earth: Explaining the Ice Ages. LC 80-21588. (Illus.). 64p. (gr. 7-12). 1981. PLB 10.95 (ISBN 0-89490-036-6). Enslow Pubs.

--Meteorites: Stones from the Sky. LC 76-12513. (Illus.). (gr. 2-5). 1976. 7.95 (ISBN 0-396-07369-7). Dodd.

--Nickels, Dimes & Dollars, How Currency Works. LC 79-22539. (Illus.). 96p. (gr. 4-6). 1980. 10.00 (ISBN 0-688-22220-X); PLB 10.88 (ISBN 0-688-32220-4). Morrow.

--What Does a Geologist Do? LC 77-6483. (Illus.). (gr. 5 up). 1977. 6.95 (ISBN 0-396-07481-2). Dodd.

--Winning Weightlifting. LC 83-6749. (Illus.). 160p. (Orig.). 1983. pap. 6.95 (ISBN 0-8069-7758-2). Sterling.

Fodor, R. V. & Taylor, G. J. Impact! 1979. pap. 1.95 (ISBN 0-8439-0648-0, Leisure Bks). Dorchester Pub Co.

Fodor, Ronald V. Complete Do-It-Yourself Handbook for Auto Maintenance: With the Repair-O-Matic Guide. 228p. cancelled 12.95 (ISBN 0-686-92143-7, Parker). P-H.

--Earth Afire! Volcanoes & Their Activity. LC 81-3984. (Junior Bks.). (Illus.). 96p. (gr. 4-6). 1981. 11.25 (ISBN 0-688-00706-6); PLB 11.88 (ISBN 0-688-00707-4). Morrow.

--What to Eat & Why: The Science of Nutrition. LC 78-24086. (Illus.). (gr. 4-6). 1979. PLB 10.88 (ISBN 0-688-32189-5). Morrow.

Foe, Daniel De see Defoe, Daniel.

Foege, Richard H. Stewardship Preaching: Series C. 56p. (Orig.). 1985. pap. 4.95 (ISBN 0-8066-2152-4, 10-6003). Augsburg.

Foehn, Carla. Directions. (Illus.). (gr. 2-5). 1978. pap. text ed. 6.50 (ISBN 0-918932-56-4). Activity Resources.

Foehr, Dieter, jt. auth. see Drochner, Karl Heinz.

Foelix, Rainer F. Biology of Spiders. (Illus.). 320p. 1982. text ed. 30.00x (ISBN 0-674-07431-9). Harvard U Pr.

Foell, W. K. National Perspectives on Management of Energy-Environment Systems. LC 82-7025. (International Series on Applied Systems Analysis). 343p. 1983. 64.95x (ISBN 0-471-10022-6, Pub. by Wiley-Interscience). Wiley.

Foell, Wesley K. Management of Energy-Environment Systems: Methods & Case Studies. LC 78-13617. (International Institute Series on Applied Systems Analysis). 487p. 1979. 64.95x (ISBN 0-471-99721-8, Pub. by Wiley-Interscience). Wiley.

--Small-Sample Reactivity Measurements in Nuclear Reactors. LC 74-144051. (ANS Monographs). 272p. 1972. 23.50 (ISBN 0-89448-003-0, 300005). Am Nuclear Soc.

Foelsch, D. & Vestergaard, K. Das Verhalten von Huehnern. (Animal Management Ser.: 12). 176p. 1981. 17.95x (ISBN 0-8176-1240-8). Birkhauser.

Foenander, Orwell Der see Der Foenander, Orwell.

Foerester, Bernd & Heritage Commission. Independence, Missouri. LC 78-2287. (Illus.). 1978. 15.00 (ISBN 0-8309-0203-1). Ind Pr MO.

Foerst, W. Newer Methods of Preparative Organic Chemistry, 3 vols. LC 48-6233. 1968. Vol. IV. 43.60x (ISBN 3-527-25087-5); Vol. V. 43.60x (ISBN 3-527-25088-3); Vol. VI. 53.00x (ISBN 3-527-25338-6). VCH Pubs.

Foerster, Donald M. The Fortunes of Epic Poetry. 250p. 1962. 13.95x (ISBN 0-8132-0331-7). Cath U Pr.

Foerster, Friedrich W. Europe & the German Question. LC 70-180399. Repr. of 1940 ed. 34.50 (ISBN 0-404-56123-3). AMS Pr.

Foerster, H. Von see Von Foerster, H. & Beauchamp, James W.

Foerster, Heinz von see Von Foerster, Heinz.

Foerster, Iris, tr. see Wodehouse, P. G.

Foerster, K. Beitrag zur Desmidieenflora von Sued-Holstein und der Hansestadt Hamburg. (Illus.). 160p. 1970. pap. text ed. 7.00x (ISBN 3-7682-0676-9). Lubrecht & Cramer.

--Desmidieen aus dem Suedosten der Vereinigten Staaten von Amerika. (Illus.). 132p. 1972. pap. text ed. 14.00x (ISBN 3-7682-0874-5). Lubrecht & Cramer.

Foerster, Lloyd, frwd. by. The Aging in Rural Mid-America: A Symposium on Values for an Evolving Quality of Life, June 5-6, 1978. LC 78-19579. 1978. pap. 3.00x (ISBN 0-916030-04-0). Bethany Coll KS.

Foerster, Norman. American Prose & Poetry, 2 vols. 1977. Repr. of 1934 ed. Set. 20.00 (ISBN 0-89984-181-3). Century Bookbindery.

--American Scholar. LC 65-18604. 1965. Repr. of 1929 ed. 14.50x (ISBN 0-8046-0155-0, Pub by Kennikat). Assoc Faculty Pr.

--The Chief American Prose Writers. 1977. Repr. of 1916 ed. 20.00 (ISBN 0-89984-182-1). Century Bookbindery.

--Future of the Liberal College. LC 78-89180. (American Education: Its Men, Institutions & Ideas, Ser. 1). 1969. Repr. of 1938 ed. 9.00 (ISBN 0-405-01418-X). Ayer Co Pubs.

--Image of America: Our Literature from Puritanism to the Space Age. 1962. pap. 4.95x (ISBN 0-268-00127-8). U of Notre Dame Pr.

--The Intellectual Heritage of Thoreau. LC 74-19264. 1974. Repr. lib. bdg. 12.50 (ISBN 0-8414-4235-5). Folcroft.

--Toward Standards. LC 66-13476. 1928. 10.00x (ISBN 0-8196-0166-7). Biblo.

Foerster, Norman, jt. auth. see Clark, H. H.

Foerster, Norman, ed. Humanism & America: Essays on the Outlook of Modern Civilisation. 294p. 1983. Repr. of 1930 ed. lib. bdg. 38.50 (ISBN 0-89987-273-5). Darby Bks.

--Humanities After the War, by Wendell L. Willkie. facs. ed. LC 77-76898. (Essay Index Reprint Ser). 1944. 13.50 (ISBN 0-8369-1035-4). Ayer Co Pubs.

Foerster, Norman & Lampe, M. Willard, eds. College Bible. 1938. 29.50x (ISBN 0-89197-086-X); pap. text ed. 14.95x (ISBN 0-89197-087-8). Irvington.

Foerster, Norman & Pierson, William W., eds. American Ideals. facs. ed. LC 70-128243. (Essay Index Reprint Ser). 1917. 21.00 (ISBN 0-8369-1925-4). Ayer Co Pubs.

Foerster, Norman, et al, eds. American Poetry & Prose, 2 pts. 5th ed. LC 70-137981. 1970. 21.95 ea. Pt. 1 (ISBN 0-395-04458-8). Pt. 2 (ISBN 0-395-04459-6). one-vol. ed. 27.50 (ISBN 0-395-30471-7). HM.

--Introduction to American Poetry & Prose. LC 72-140999. 1971. text ed. 25.50 (ISBN 0-395-04457-X). HM.

Foerster, Robert F. Italian Emigration of Our Times. LC 69-18774. (American Immigration Collection Ser., No. 1). 1969. Repr. of 1919 ed. 22.50 (ISBN 0-405-00522-9). Ayer Co Pubs.

Foerster, Rolf, tr. see Wodehouse, P. G.

Foerster, Werner. From the Exile to Christ: Historical Introduction to Palestinian Judaism. Harris, Gordon E., ed. LC 64-18151. 264p. 1964. pap. 10.95 (ISBN 0-8006-0978-6, 1-978). Fortress.

Foerster-Nietzsche, Elizabeth, ed. see Nietzsche, Friedrich & Wagner, Richard.

Foerstner, U. & Wittman, G. T. Metal Pollution in the Aquatic Environment. 2nd ed. (Illus.). 486p. 1983. pap. 31.00 (ISBN 0-387-12856-5). Springer-Verlag.

Foerstner, U. & Wittmann, G. T. Metal Pollution in the Aquatic Environment. rev., 2nd ed. (Illus.). 486p. 1981. 56.00 (ISBN 0-387-10724-X). Springer-Verlag.

Foerstner, U., jt. auth. see Salomons, W.

Foesig, Harry, et al. Trolleys of Bucks County, Pennsylvania. (Illus.). 72p. (Orig.). 1985. pap. 10.00 (ISBN 0-911940-41-3). Cox.

Fog, Mogens H. & Nadkarni, Kishore L. Energy Efficiency & Fuel Substitution in the Cement Industry with Emphasis on Developing Countries. 94p. 3.00 (ISBN 0-318-02822-0, WP0270). World Bank.

Fogarty, Daniel. Roots for a New Rhetoric. LC 68-15175. (Illus.). 1968. Repr. of 1959 ed. 18.00x (ISBN 0-8462-1144-0). Russell.

Fogarty, Donald W. Aggregate Inventory Management Training Aid. LC 83-73024. 18p. 1984. 24.00 (ISBN 0-935406-38-7). Am Prod & Inventory.

--Discrete, Static, & Other Order Quantity Models Training Aid. LC 83-73023. 26p. 1984. 24.00 (ISBN 0-935406-37-9). Am Prod & Inventory.

--Distribution Inventory Management Training Aid. LC 83-73025. 14p. 1984. tchr's ed. 15.00 (ISBN 0-935406-39-5). Am Prod & Inventory.

--Inventory Management: An Introduction. LC 83-73021. 23p. 1983. 27.00 (ISBN 0-935406-35-2). Am Prod & Inventory.

--Inventory Management: Basic Models & Systems. LC 83-73022. 32p. 1983. 27.00 (ISBN 0-935406-36-0). Am Prod & Inventory.

Fogarty, Donald W. & Hoffman, Thomas R. Production & Inventory Management. 1983. text ed. 29.95 (ISBN 0-538-07040-4, G04). SW Pub.

Fogarty, J., jt. ed. see Mumford, D.

Fogarty, John, ed. see Milkovich, J.

Fogarty, M. P. Prospects of the Industrial Areas of Great Britain. (English Workers Ser.). 492p. 1985. lib. bdg. 60.00 (ISBN 0-8240-7611-7). Garland Pub.

Fogarty, Marna S. The Cat Yellow Pages: The Cat Owner's Guide to Goods & Services. (Illus.). 224p. 1984. 19.95 (ISBN 0-684-18094-4, ScribT); pap. 12.95 (ISBN 0-684-18158-4). Scribner.

Fogarty, Michael. Forty to Sixty-How We Waste the Middle Aged. 250p. 1975. pap. text ed. 9.75x (ISBN 0-7199-0904-X, Pub. by Bedford England). Brookfield Pub Co.

Fogarty, Michael, ed. Retirement Policy: The Next Fifty Years. (NIESR, PSI, RII A Joint Studies in Public Policy Ser.). viii, 216p. 1982. text ed. 28.00x (ISBN 0-435-83320-0). Gower Pub Co.

Fogarty, Michael, et al. Women in Top Jobs, 1968 to 1979. (Policy Studies Institute Ser.). vii, 273p. 1981. text ed. 37.50x (ISBN 0-435-83806-7). Gower Pub Co.

Fogarty, Michael P. Christian Democracy in Western Europe, 1820-1953. LC 73-11997. (Illus.). 448p. 1974. Repr. of 1957 ed. lib. bdg. 26.75x (ISBN 0-8371-7114-8, FOCH). Greenwood.

--The Just Wage. LC 75-29076. 309p. 1975. Repr. of 1961 ed. lib. bdg. 18.00x (ISBN 0-8371-8404-5, FOJW). Greenwood.

Fogarty, Michael P., et al. Sex, Career & Family: Including an International Review of Women's Roles. LC 70-158823. pap. 145.50 (ISBN 0-317-29679-5, 2021900). Bks Demand UMI.

Fogarty, Nancy. Shelley in the Twentieth Century: A Study of the Development of Shelley Criticism in England & America, 1916-71. (Salzburg Studies in English Literature, Romantic Reassessment: No. 56). 179p. 1976. pap. text ed. 25.50x (ISBN 0-391-01377-7). Humanities.

Fogarty, Robert S. Dictionary of American Communal & Utopian History. LC 79-7476. 320p. 1980. lib. bdg. 39.95 (ISBN 0-313-21347-X, FDA/). Greenwood.

--The Righteous Remnant: The House of David. LC 80-84666. (Illus.). 208p. 1981. 17.50 (ISBN 0-87338-251-X). Kent St U Pr.

Fogarty, William M., ed. Microbial Enzymes & Biotechnology. (Illus.). 382p. 1983. 63.00 (ISBN 0-85334-185-0, Pub. by Elsevier Applied Sci England). Elsevier.

Fogdall, Alberta B. Royal Family of the Columbia. (Illus.). 1978. 14.95 (ISBN 0-87770-168-7). Ye Galleon.

--Royal Family of the Columbia: Dr. John McLoughlin & His Family. 2nd ed. LC 78-17170. (Illus.). 1982. 16.95 (ISBN 0-8323-0413-1). Binford.

Fogdall, Richard P., jt. ed. see Ream, Allen K.

Foged, N. Diatom Fora in Springs in Jutland Denmark. (Illus.). 344p. 1984. lib. bdg. 35.00x (ISBN 3-7682-1378-1). Lubrecht & Cramer.

--Diatoms Found in a Bottom Sediment Sample from a Small Deep Lake in the Northern Slope, Alaska. 1971. pap. text ed. 10.50 (ISBN 3-7682-0824-9). Lubrecht & Cramer.

--Diatoms in Eastern Australia. (Bibliotheca Phycologica Ser.: No. 41). (Illus.). 1979. 21.00 (ISBN 3-7682-1203-3). Lubrecht & Cramer.

--Diatoms in New Zealand, the North Island. (Bibliotheca Phycologica: No. 47). (Illus.). 1979. pap. text ed. 21.00x (ISBN 3-7682-1253-X). Lubrecht & Cramer.

--Freshwater Diatoms in Ireland. (Bibliotheca Phycologica Ser.: No. 34). (Illus.). 1977. lib. bdg. 17.50x (ISBN 3-7682-1155-X). Lubrecht & Cramer.

Foged, Niels. Diatoms in Alaska. (Bibliotheca Phycologica). (Illus.). 318p. 1981. text ed. 28.00x (ISBN 3-7682-1303-X). Lubrecht & Cramer.

--Diatoms in Bornholm, Denmark. (Bibliotheca Phyc. 59). (Illus.). 104p. 1982. 17.50 (ISBN 3-7682-1328-5). Lubrecht & Cramer.

--Diatoms in Oland, Sweden. (Bibliotheca Phycologica Ser.: No. 49). (Illus.). 194p. 1980. pap. 17.50 (ISBN 3-7682-1269-6). Lubrecht & Cramer.

--Diatoms in Samos, a Greek Island in the Aegean: Diatoms in Kos & Kalymnos, Two Greek Islands. (Bibliotheca Diatomologica Ser.: No. 10). (Illus.). 226p. 1985. lib. bdg. 28.00 (ISBN 3-7682-1443-5). Lubrecht & Cramer.

--Freshwater & Littoral Diatoms from Cuba. (Bibliotheca Diatomologica Ser.: Vol. 5). (Illus.). 248p. 1984. lib. bdg. 35.00x (ISBN 3-7682-1407-9). Lubrecht & Cramer.

Fogedby, Hans C. Theoretical Aspects of Mainly Low Dimensional Magnetic Systems. (Lecture Notes in Physics Ser.: Vol. 131). 163p. 1980. pap. 15.00 (ISBN 0-387-10238-8). Springer Verlag.

Fogel, Aaron. Coercion to Speak: Conrad's Poetics of Dialogue. 304p. 1985. text ed. 22.50x (ISBN 0-674-13639-X). Harvard U Pr.

Fogel, Alan. Infancy: Infant, Family, & Society. (Illus.). 350p. 1983. pap. text ed. 19.95 (ISBN 0-314-77998-1); tchrs' manual avail. (ISBN 0-314-78000-9). West Pub.
Fogel, Alan & Melson, Gail F., eds. Origins of Nurturance. 304p. 1986. text ed. 32.50 (ISBN 0-89859-643-2). L Erlbaum Assocs.
Fogel, Alan, jt. ed. see Field, Tiffany M.
Fogel, Barbara. Energy: Choices for the Future. (Impact Ser.). (Illus.). 96p. (gr. 7-12). 1985. PLB 10.90 (ISBN 0-531-10060-X). Watts.
Fogel, Barbara R. Design for Change. 80p. 1977. pap. 5.00 (ISBN 0-89192-238-5, Pub. by ICED). Interbk Inc.
Fogel, Barbara R., jt. ed. see Thompson, Kenneth W.
Fogel, Catherine I. & Woods, Nancy F. Health Care of Women: A Nursing Perspective. LC 80-17400. (Illus.). 643p. 1981. pap. text ed. 29.95 (ISBN 0-8016-1605-0). Mosby.
Fogel, Daniel. Africa in Struggle: National Liberation & Proletarian Revolution. LC 82-82655. (Illus.). 428p. (Orig.). 1982. pap. 8.00 (ISBN 0-910383-00-6). Ism Pr.
--Revolution in Central America. LC 84-27805. (Illus.). 241p. 1985. pap. 6.00 (ISBN 0-910383-08-1). Ism Pr.
Fogel, Daniel M. Henry James & the Structure of the Romantic Imagination. LC 81-4824. xvi, 208p. 1981. 20.00x (ISBN 0-8071-0789-1). La State U Pr.
--A Trick of Resilience. LC 75-324199. 55p. 1975. 3.50 (ISBN 0-87886-063-0). Ithaca Hse.
Fogel, Danny & Findling, Robert L. Real Estate Is Now...Investment Analysis & Exchange. 3rd ed. 256p. (Orig.). 1983. pap. text ed. 19.95 (ISBN 0-8403-3037-5, 40303701). Kendall-Hunt.
Fogel, David. We Are Living Proof: The Justice Model for Corrections: 2nd ed. 338p. 1979. softcover 14.95 (ISBN 0-87084-284-6). Anderson Pub Co.
Fogel, David & Hudson, Joe, eds. Justice As Fairness: Perspectives on the Justice Model. 300p. 1981. pap. text ed. 15.95 (ISBN 0-87084-287-0). Anderson Pub Co.
Fogel, Ephim, jt. ed. see Di Cesare, Mario A.
Fogel, Johua A., ed. Recent Japanese Studies of Modern Chinese History. 235p. 1984. pap. 18.95 (ISBN 0-87332-308-4). M E Sharpe.
Fogel, Joshua A. Politics & Sinology: The Case of Naito Konan (1866-1934) (Harvard East Asian Monographs: No. 114). 1984. text ed. 20.00x (ISBN 0-674-68790-6). Harvard U Pr.
Fogel, Marvin & Walker, Mort. How to Get into Medical School: A Comprehensive Guide. 196p. 1981. pap. 7.25 (ISBN 0-8015-3670-7, 0704-210, Hawthorn). Dutton.
Fogel, Norm, ed. see Mollica, Peter.
Fogel, P. H., jt. auth. see Whitney, G. T.
Fogel, Robert, et al, eds. Aging: Stability & Change in the Family. LC 81-12804. 1981. 40.00 (ISBN 0-12-040003-0); pap. 20.00 (ISBN 0-12-040023-5). Acad Pr.
Fogel, Robert W. Railroads & American Economic Growth: Essays in Econometric History. LC 64-25069. (Illus.). 311p. 1970. pap. 6.95x (ISBN 0-8018-1148-1). Johns Hopkins.
--The Union Pacific Railroad: A Case in Premature Enterprise. LC 78-64234. (Johns Hopkins University. Studies in the Social Sciences. Seventy-Eighth Ser. 1960: 2). Repr. of 1960 ed. 24.50 (ISBN 0-404-61339-X). AMS Pr.
Fogel, Robert W. & Elton, G. R. Which Road to the Past? Two Views of History. LC 83-3573. 160p. 1983. 20.00x (ISBN 0-300-03011-8). Yale U Pr.
--Which Road to the Past? Two Views of History. LC 83-3573. 160p. 1984. pap. 6.95x (ISBN 0-300-03278-1, Y-512). Yale U Pr.
Fogel, Robert W. & Engerman, Stanley. Time on the Cross: The Economics of Negro Slavery, 2vols. Incl. The Economics of American Negro Slavery. 286p. pap. text ed. 9.95 (ISBN 0-316-28701-6); Vol. 2. Evidence & Methods, a Supplement. 288p. 1974. pap. text ed. 9.95 vol.1 (ISBN 0-316-28701-6); pap. text ed. 8.95 vol. 2 (ISBN 0-316-28699-0). Little.
Fogel, Robert W. & Engerman, Stanley L. Time on the Cross: The Economics of American Negro Slavery. (Illus.). 304p. 1985. pap. text ed. 13.00 (ISBN 0-8191-4331-6). U Pr of Amer.
Fogel, Ruby. Of Apes & Angels. LC 72-179833. (New Poetry Ser.). Repr. of 1966 ed. 16.00 (ISBN 0-404-56033-4, NP33). AMS Pr.
Fogel, Walter. California Farm Labor Relations & Law. (Monograph & Research Ser.: No. 41). 224p. 1985. 10.00 (ISBN 0-89215-129-3). U Cal La Indus Rel.
--Mexican Illegal Alien Workers in the United States. (Monograph & Research Ser.: No. 20). 204p. 1978. 7.50 (ISBN 0-89215-091-2). U Cal LA Indus Rel.
Fogel, Walter, ed. Current Research in Labor Economics. (Monograph & Research Ser.: No. 38). 159p. 1984. pap. 8.00 (ISBN 0-89215-122-6). U Cal LA Indus Rel.
--Job Equity & Other Studies in Industrial Relations: Essays in Honor of Frederic Meyers. (Monograph Ser.: No. 30). 250p. 1981. 8.50 (ISBN 0-89215-114-5). U Cal LA Indus Rel.
Fogel, Walter A. The Equal Pay Act: Implications for Comparable Worth. LC 84-11594. 140p. 1984. 25.95 (ISBN 0-03-071789-2). Praeger.
Fogeleson, Robert M., ed. see Governor's Conference on Crime, the Criminal & Society, Sep 30-Oct 3, 1935, New York.
Fogelin, Maria B. The Vow. 272p. (Orig.). 1980. pap. 2.50 (ISBN 0-89083-653-1). Zebra.
Fogelin, Robert J. Hume's Skepticism: In the Treatise of Human Nature. (International Library of Philosophy). 192p. 1985. 25.00x (ISBN 0-7102-0368-3). Routledge & Kegan.
--Understanding Arguments: An Introduction to Informal Logic. 2nd ed. 430p. 1982. pap. text ed. 15.95 (ISBN 0-15-592858-9, HC); instr's manual avail. (ISBN 0-15-592859-7). HarBraceJ.
Fogelklou, Emilia. Reality & Radiance: Selected Autobiographical Works of Emilia Fogelklou. Lutz, Howard T., ed. & tr. from Swedish. 176p. (Orig.). 1985. pap. 10.95 (ISBN 0-913408-89-1). Friends United.
Fogelklou-Norlind, Emilia. Atonement of George Fox. Mather, Eleanore P., ed. LC 75-84675. (Orig.). 1969. pap. 2.30x (ISBN 0-87574-166-5). Pendle Hill.
Fogelman, E., jt. auth. see Ebenstein, W.
Fogelman, Edwin, jt. auth. see Ebenstein, William.
Fogelman, Floyd, jt. auth. see Kline, Richard.
Fogelman, K. R. Piagetian Tests for the Primary School. 72p. 1970. 7.00x (ISBN 0-901225-50-9, Pub. by NFER Nelson UK). Taylor & Francis.
Fogelman, Ken. Growing Up in Great Britain: National Children's Bureau. 352p. 1983. text ed. 37.50x (ISBN 0-333-34394-8, Pub. by Macmillan England). Humanities.
Fogelman, Martin. Business Corporation Law, BCL. LC 85-125095. (McKinney's Forms Ser.). Date not set. price not set. West Pub.
Fogelman, Morris J., jt. auth. see Vanatta, John C.
Fogelson, Genia. Harry Belafonte. (Orig.). 1980. pap. 1.95 (ISBN 0-87067-680-6, BH680). Holloway.
--Jewel: Undercover Cop. (Orig.). 1980. pap. 1.95 (ISBN 0-87067-665-2, BH665). Holloway.
Fogelson, Gina. Charity Memorial Hospital: The Fire. 1985. pap. 3.25 (ISBN 0-87067-719-5, BH919). Holloway.
Fogelson, Ginia. Charity Memorial Hospital: The Fire. 1985. pap. 2.95 (ISBN 0-87067-716-0). Holloway.
--Tides of Passion. (Orig.). 1984. pap. 1.95 (ISBN 0-87067-235-5, BH235). Holloway.
Fogelson, Raymond D. & Adams, Richard N., eds. The Anthropology of Power: Ethnographic Studies from Asia, Oceania & New World. (Studies in Anthropology). 1977. 47.50 (ISBN 0-12-261550-6). Acad Pr.
Fogelson, Robert, ed. Los Angeles Riots. LC 70-90205. (Mass Violence in America Ser). Repr. of 1969 ed. 14.00 (ISBN 0-405-01311-6). Ayer Co Pubs.
Fogelson, Robert M. Big-City Police: An Urban Institute Study. 1979. 22.50x (ISBN 0-674-07281-2); pap. 8.95x (ISBN 0-674-07295-2). Harvard U Pr.
--Pensions, the Hidden Costs of Public Safety. LC 84-1919. 1984. 25.00x (ISBN 0-231-05958-2). Columbia U Pr.
--Violence As Protest: A Study of Riots & Ghettos. LC 80-36808. xviii, 265p. 1980. Repr. of 1971 ed. lib. bdg. 24.75x (ISBN 0-313-22642-3, FOVP). Greenwood.
Fogelson, Robert M., ed. Police in Great Britain, 6 vols. 1971. Repr. Set. 281.00 (ISBN 0-405-03405-9). Ayer Co Pubs.
--Reform of the Criminal Law & Procedure. facsimile ed. LC 74-3816. (Criminal Justice in America). 1974. Repr. of 1911 ed. 18.00 (ISBN 0-405-06165-X). Ayer Co Pubs.
--Selections from the Court Reports Originally Published in the Boston Morning Post from 1834 to 1837. f ed. LC 74-3850. (Criminal Justice in America Ser.). 1974. Repr. 21.00x (ISBN 0-405-06166-8). Ayer Co Pubs.
--Wiretapping in New York City. LC 74-3843. (Criminal Justice in America Ser.). 1974. Repr. 12.00x (ISBN 0-405-06180-3). Ayer Co Pubs.
Fogelson, Robert M. & Rubenstein, Richard, eds. Mass Violence in America, 43 vols. 1970. Set. 678.25 (ISBN 0-405-01299-3). Ayer Co Pubs.
Fogelson, Robert M., ed. see National Conference on Bail & Criminal Justice, May 27-29, 1964, & May, 1964-Apr 1965.
Fogelson, Robert M., et al, eds. American Federalism Series: The Urban Dimension, 37 vols. 1978. lib. bdg. 1092.50xet (ISBN 0-405-10474-X). Ayer Co Pubs.
--Federal Aid to the Cities: An Original Anthology. LC 77-74925. (American Federalism-the Urban Dimension). (Illus.). 1978. lib. bdg. 45.50x (ISBN 0-405-10481-2). Ayer Co Pubs.
--Federal-City Relations in the Nineteen Thirties: An Original Anthology. LC 77-74963. (American Federalism-the Urban Dimension). 1978. lib. bdg. 20.00x (ISBN 0-405-10506-1). Ayer Co Pubs.
Fogerty, James E., compiled by. Manuscripts Collections of the Minnesota Regional Research Centers: Guide No. 2. LC 80-25374. 92p. 1979. pap. 4.50 (ISBN 0-87351-150-6). Minn Hist.
Fogerty, James E., jt. ed. see Johnson, Lila.
Fogerty, Robert P. Biographical Data on Air Force General Command, 1917-1952. (USAF Historical Studies: No. 91). 1953. pap. text ed. 100.00 set (ISBN 0-317-20162-X); Vol. 1, A-K. pap. text ed. 53.00x, 519p. (ISBN 0-89126-132-X); Vol. 2, L-Z. pap. text ed. 58.50x, 584p. (ISBN 0-89126-133-8). MA-AH Pub.
Fogg, A. S. Australian Town Planning: Uniformity & Change. Rev., 2nd ed. 601p. 1983. text ed. 27.50x (ISBN 0-7022-1951-7). U of Queensland Pr.
Fogg, A. S. & Young. Ammonia Amines, Phosphides, Arsin. 1985. 100.00 (ISBN 0-08-026177-9). Pergamon.
Fogg Art Museum, ed. see Harvard University.
Fogg, Bob & Goettsche, Ron. Down to Earth II: A Guide for Daily Living. 300p. (Orig.). 1985. pap. 8.95x (ISBN 0-915223-12-0). Synergy Pubs.
Fogg, Bob, jt. auth. see Goettsche, Ron.
Fogg, Charles. Chains & Chainmaking. (Album Ser.: No. 69). (Illus.). 32p. pap. 2.95 (ISBN 0-85263-561-3, Pub. by Shire Pubns England). Seven Hills Bks.
Fogg, G. E. Algal Cultures & Phytoplankton Ecology. 2nd ed. LC 74-27308. (Illus.). 192p. 1975. 22.50x (ISBN 0-299-06760-2). U of Wis Pr.
Fogg, G. E. & Kreitler, C. W. Ground-Water Hydraulics & Hydrochemical Facies in Eocene Aquifers of the East Texas Basin. (Report of Investigations Ser.: RI 127). (Illus.). 75p. 1982. 3.00 (ISBN 0-318-03274-0). Bur Econ Geology.
Fogg, G. E., et al. Three-Dimensional Ground-Water Modeling in Depositional Systems, Wilcox Group, Oakwood Salt Dome Area, East Texas. (Report of Investigations Ser.: RI 133). (Illus.). 55p. 1983. 3.25 (ISBN 0-318-03289-9). Bur Econ Geology.
Fogg, George. Art at Auction 1984-85. LC 67-30652. (Illus.). 416p. 1985. 45.00 (ISBN 0-85667-303-X, Pub. by P Wilson Pubs). Sotheby Pubns.
Fogg, H. G. Soft Fruit Growing. 160p. 1981. pap. 12.00x (ISBN 0-906379-01-6, Pub. by Jupiter England). State Mutual Bk.
Fogg, H. Witham. Salad Crops All Year Round. (Illus.). 200p. 1983. 16.95 (ISBN 0-7153-8411-2). David & Charles.
Fogg, Stephen. Imperial Sportswear, Inc. An Audit Case Problem. 65p. 1980. pap. text ed. 16.50 scp (ISBN 0-06-042107-X, HarpC); solution manual avail. (ISBN 0-06-362205-X). Har-Row.
Fogg, Walter. One Thousand Sayings of History, Presented as Pictures in Prose. LC 79-143634. 1971. Repr. of 1929 ed. 53.00x (ISBN 0-8103-3779-7). Gale.
Fogg, Walter L. & Richter, Peyton E. Philosophy Looks to the Future: Confrontation, Commitment & Utopia. 2nd ed. 1978. pap. text ed. 25.72 (ISBN 0-205-06030-7, 6060307). Allyn.
Fogg, Walter L., jt. auth. see Richter, Peyton E.
Fogh, Jorgen & Giovanella, Beppino. The Nude Mouse in Experimental & Clinical Research, Vol. II. 1982. 65.00 (ISBN 0-12-261862-9). Acad Pr.
Fogh, Jorgen, ed. Contamination in Tissue Culture. 1973. 64.50 (ISBN 0-12-261850-5). Acad Pr.
--Human Tumor Cells in Vitro. LC 74-26959. (Illus.). 576p. 1975. 59.50x (ISBN 0-306-30810-X, Plenum Pr). Plenum Pub.
Fogh, Jorgen & Giovanella, Beppino, eds. The Nude Mouse in Experimental & Clinical Research, Vol. 1. 1978. 61.50 (ISBN 0-12-261860-2). Acad Pr.
Fogh, Jorgen, et al. Transformation of Tissue Culture Cells by SV - 40 Viruses. LC 72-13562. (Illus.). 220p. 1973. text ed. 28.00x (ISBN 0-8422-7065-5). Irvington.
Fogiel, M., pref. by. The Algebra & Trigonometry Problem Solver. rev. ed. LC 76-334. (Illus.). 928p. 1984. pap. text ed. 19.85 (ISBN 0-87891-508-7). Res & Educ.
--The Physics Problem Solver. rev. ed. LC 76-332. (Illus.). 1120p. 1984. pap. text ed. 19.85 (ISBN 0-87891-507-9). Res & Educ.
Fogiel, Max. How to Pay Lots Less for Life Insurance. LC 76-22597. 1971. 12.95 (ISBN 0-87891-502-8). Res & Educ.
Fogiel, Max, intro. by. The Biology Problem Solver. rev. ed. LC 78-63610. (Illus.). 1984. pap. text ed. 19.85 (ISBN 0-87891-514-1). Res & Educ.
--Problem Solver in Business, Management & Finance. rev. ed. LC 78-64582. (Illus.). 1984. pap. text ed. 19.85 (ISBN 0-87891-516-8). Res & Educ.
--The Statistics Problem Solver: A Supplement to Any Class Text. rev. ed. LC 78-64581. (Illus.). 1056p. 1984. pap. text ed. 19.85 (ISBN 0-87891-515-X). Res & Educ.
Fogle, Bruce. Interrelations Between People & Pets. (Illus.). 370p. 1981. 32.75x (ISBN 0-398-04169-5). C C Thomas.
--Pets & Their People. (Illus.). 240p. 1984. 14.95 (ISBN 0-670-55052-3). Viking.
--Pets & Their People. (Nonfiction Ser.). 256p. 1985. pap. 5.95 (ISBN 0-14-007786-3). Penguin.
Fogle, French see Milton, John.
Fogle, French, ed. see Vaughan, Henry.
Fogle, Jeanne S. Signs of God's Love: Baptism & Communion. Duckert, Mary J. & Lane, W. Ben, eds. (Illus.). 32p. (Orig.). (gr. 3-8). 1984. pap. 4.50 (ISBN 0-664-24636-2). Geneva Pr.
Fogle, Lerry W. Revelation Explained. LC 80-84975. 269p. 1981. (Haven Bks). Bridge Pub.
Fogle, Richard H. Idea of Coleridge's Criticism. LC 77-26232. (Perspectives in Criticism Ser.: No. 9). 1978. Repr. of 1962 ed. lib. bdg. 22.50x (ISBN 0-313-20086-6, FOIC). Greenwood.
Fogle, Richard H., compiled by. Romantic Poets & Prose Writers. LC 66-29743. (Goldentree Bibliographies in Language & Literature Ser.). (Orig.). 1967. pap. 13.95x (ISBN 0-88295-513-6). Harlan Davidson.
Fogle, Sonja, et al, eds. Recent Advances in Leather Conservation: Proceedings of a Refresher Course Sponsored by FAIC, June 1984, Harpers Ferry, West Virginia. LC 85-80203. (Illus.). 181p. 1985. pap. text ed. 15.00 (ISBN 0-933098-04-9); until 08/31/85 10.00 (ISBN 0-317-20398-3). Am Inst Cons.
Fogle, Willa. Beside the Still Waters. 1979. pap. 4.00 (ISBN 0-87516-282-7). De Vorss.
--Thinking Does It. pap. 1.50 (ISBN 0-87516-136-7). De Vorss.
Fogler, H. S., ed. Energy Balances. LC 80-25594. (ALCHEMI Modular Instruction F-Ser.: Vol. 3). 74p. 1982. pap. 30.00 (ISBN 0-8169-0213-5, J-18); pap. 15.00 members. Am Inst Chem Eng.
Fogler, H. S., jt. ed. see Crynes, B. L.
Fogler, H. Scott. The Elements of Chemical Kinetics & Reactor Calculations: A Self-Paced Approach. (Illus.). 512p. 1974. pap. 31.95 ref. ed. (ISBN 0-13-263442-2). P-H.
Fogler, H. Scott, ed. Chemical Reactors. LC 81-12672. (ACS Symposium Ser: No. 168). 1981. 39.95 (ISBN 0-8412-0658-9). Am Chemical.
Fogler, Russell & Bayston, Darwin M. CFA, eds. Improving the Investment Decision Process: Quantitative Assistance for the Practitioner--& the Firm. LC 84-72361. 1984. 25.00x (ISBN 0-87094-648-X). Dow Jones-Irwin.
Fogleson, Robert M., ed. Police in America, 35 Bks. 1971. Repr. Set. 628.00 (ISBN 0-405-03360-5). Ayer Co Pubs.
Foglesong, Elizabeth C., ed. The Means Family of America. (Illus.). 1004p. 1972. 50.00x (ISBN 0-686-32458-7). C V Barnes.
Foglio, Frank. Hey God! A Large Italian Family's Amazing Experience with God. LC 72-87328. 1972. pap. 4.95 (ISBN 0-88270-007-3, Pub. by Logos). Bridge Pub.
Fogoros, Anne W., ed. Where to Turn: The Directory of Health, Welfare & Community Services in Allegheny County. rev. ed. 402p. (Orig.). 1984. pap. 30.00x (ISBN 0-930053-00-1). Helpline.
Foh, Susan. Women & the Word of God. 6.95 (ISBN 0-87552-268-8). Presby & Reformed.
Fohanno, C., jt. ed. see Flamant, R.
Foher, E. Europe by Rail. 580p. 1984. pap. 12.95 (ISBN 3-92327-825-X, Pub. by M Muller West Germany). Bradt Ent.
Fohl, Mark E. An Assembly Course. (Illus.). 216p. 1982. 17.50 (ISBN 0-89433-149-3). Petrocelli.
--A Microprocessor Course. (Illus.). 218p. text ed. 16.50 (ISBN 0-89433-072-1). Petrocelli.
Fohrer, Georg. Geschichte der Israelitischen Religion. xvi, 367p. (Ger.). 1969. 20.80x (ISBN 3-11-002652-X). De Gruyter.
--Theologische Grundstrukturen des Alten Testaments. (Theologische Bibliothek Toepelmann, 24). 1972. pap. 23.20x (ISBN 3-11-003874-9). De Gruyter.
Fohrer, Georg, et al, eds. Hebrew & Aramaic Dictionary of the Old Testament. Johnstone, W. A., tr. from Ger. LC 73-82430. viii, 344p. (Hebrew & Aramaic.). 1973. text ed. 12.80 (ISBN 3-11-004572-9). De Gruyter.
Foias, C., jt. auth. see Colojoara, I.
Foias, C., jt. auth. see Nagy, B. Sz.
Foighel, Isi. Nationalization: A Study in the Protection of Alien Property in International Law. LC 82-6263. 136p. 1982. Repr. of 1957 ed. lib. bdg. 25.00x (ISBN 0-8371-7675-1, FONA). Greenwood.
Foik, Paul J. Pioneer Catholic Journalism. LC 78-95099. Repr. of 1930 ed. lib. bdg. 18.75x (ISBN 0-8371-2540-5, FOCJ). Greenwood.
Foin, Theodore C. Ecological Energetics. Head, J. J., ed. LC 83-70605. (Carolina Biology Readers Ser.). (Illus.). 16p. (gr. 10 up). 1984. pap. 1.60 (ISBN 0-89278-291-9, 45-9691). Carolina Biological.
Foisberg, R. A., ed. Triticale. 82p. 1985. 12.00 (ISBN 0-89118-519-4). Crop Sci Soc Am.
Fokke, Erik, tr. see Jackins, Harvey.
Fokkelman, J. P. Narrative Art & Poetry in the Books of Samuel: King David, Vol. 1. 536p. 1981. text ed. 47.75x (ISBN 90-232-1852-3, Pub. by Van Gorcum Holland). Humanities.
Fokkema, D. C. Introduction to Dutch Law. Lisser, E. C. & Hondius, E. H., eds. 710p. 1978. lib. bdg. 66.00 (ISBN 90-26-8089-76, Pub. by Kluwer Law Netherlands). Kluwer Academic.
Fokkema, D. W. Literary Doctrine in China & Soviet Influence, 1956-1960. 1965. text ed. 28.80x (ISBN 90-2790-994-6). Mouton.
Fokkema, Douwe W. General Problems of Literary History: Proceedings of the Tenth Congress of the International Comparative Literature Association. LC 84-48468. 375p. 1985. lib. bdg. 60.00 (ISBN 0-8240-4011-2). Garland Pub.

--Literary History, Modernism & Postmodernism. LC 84-23498. (Utrecht Publications in Literature (UPAL): 19). vi, 63p. 1984. 20.00x (ISBN 0-317-14850-8); pap. 10.00x (ISBN 90-272-2204-5); lib. bdg. 20.00x. Benjamins North Am.

Fokkens, O., et al, eds. Medinfo Seminars, 1983: Proceedings of the MEDINFO '83 Seminars, Amsterdam, Aug. 22-26, 1983. 370p. 1983. 57.50 (ISBN 0-444-86749-X, I-412-83, North Holland). Elsevier.

Fokker, A. A. & Smolikowska, Emilia. Anatomy of Word Class: A Chapter of Polish Grammar. (Slavistic Printings & Reprintings Ser.: No. 254). 108p. 1971. text ed. 15.20x (ISBN 90-2792-049-4). Mouton.

Fokker, Anthony H. & Gould, Bruce. Flying Dutchman: The Life of Anthony Fokker. LC 70-169415. (Literature & History of Aviation Ser). 1972. Repr. of 1931 ed. 21.00 (ISBN 0-405-03760-0). Ayer Co Pubs.

Fokker, Nicolas. The Tamer. LC 78-2056. 1979. 10.00i (ISBN 0-06-011299-9, HarpT). Har-Row.

Foladare, Joseph. Boswell's Paoli. (Connecticut Academy of Arts & Sciences Transaction Ser.: Vol. 48). 290p. 1979. 25.00 (ISBN 0-208-01765-8, Archon). Shoe String.

Folami, Takiu. The History of Lagos, Nigeria: The Shaping of an African City. (Illus.). 256p. 1982. 8.50 (ISBN 0-682-49772-X, University). Exposition Pr FL.

Folan, William J., et al. Coba: A Classical Maya Metropolis. (Studies in Archaeology). 224p. 1983. 70.00 (ISBN 0-12-261880-7). Acad Pr.

Folarin, jt. auth. see Shyllon, Folarin.

Folb, Edith A. Black Vernacular Vocabulary: A Study of Intra-Inter-Cultural Concerns & Usage. (CAAS Monographs: No. V). 53p. (Orig.). 1972. pap. 3.95x (ISBN 0-934934-14-2). Ctr Afro-Am Stud.

--Runnin' Down Some Lines: The Language & Culture of Black Teenagers. LC 79-26708. 1980. text ed. 17.50x (ISBN 0-674-78039-6). Harvard U Pr.

Folb, P. I. Drug Safety in Clinical Practice. (Illus.). 210p. 1984. pap. 19.00 (ISBN 0-387-12811-5). Springer Verlag.

--Safety of Medicines: Evaluation & Prediction. (Illus.). 120p. 1980. pap. 18.50 (ISBN 0-387-10143-8). Springer-Verlag.

Folberg, Jay & Taylor, Alison. Mediation: A Comprehensive Guide to Resolving Conflict Without Litigation. LC 83-49259. (Social & Behavioral Science Ser.). 1984. text ed. 22.95x (ISBN 0-87589-594-8). Jossey-Bass.

Folberg, Jay, ed. Joint Custody & Shared Parenting. 350p. 1984. pap. 25.00 (ISBN 0-87179-449-7). BNA.

Folberg, Neil. Sinai. (Illus.). 1984. 60.00 (ISBN 0-915361-05-1, Dist. by Watts); deluxe ed. 200.00. Adama Pubs Inc.

Folberth, D. G. & Grobman, W. D., eds. VLSI-Technology & Design. LC 84-15848. 1984. 41.95 (ISBN 0-87942-180-0, PC01743). Inst Electrical.

Folcarelli, Ralph F., et al. The Microform Connection: A Basic Guide for Libraries. 210p. 1982. 39.95 (ISBN 0-8352-1475-3). Bowker.

Folco, G., jt. ed. see Berti, F.

Folda, Jaroslav. Crusader Manuscript Illumination at Saint-Jean D'Acre, 1275-1291. LC 75-2991. (Illus.). 646p. 1975. 67.00 (ISBN 0-691-03907-0). Princeton U Pr.

Folda, Jaroslav, et al, eds. see Buchthal, Hugo.

Foldeak, Arpad. Chess Olympiads. (Illus.). 1966. 12.00 (ISBN 0-8283-1175-7). Branden Pub Co.

--Chess Olympiads: 1927-1968. LC 78-68173. (Illus.). 1979. pap. 5.95 (ISBN 0-486-23733-8). Dover.

Foldes, F. F., ed. Enzymes in Anesthesiology. (Illus.). 1978. 49.50 (ISBN 3-540-90241-4). Springer-Verlag.

Foldiak, G. Radiation Chemistry of Hydrocarbons. (Studies in Physical & Theoretical Chemistry: Vol. 14). 476p. 1982. 83.00 (ISBN 0-444-99746-6). Elsevier.

Folds. Laboratory Procedures in Diagnostic Immunology. Date not set. write for info. (ISBN 0-444-00855-1). Elsevier.

Foldvar, Maria V. Theory & Practice of Regional Geochemical Exploration. 1978. 26.50 (ISBN 0-9960009-3-3, Pub. by Akademiai Kaido Hungary). Heyden.

Foldvary, Fred E. The Soul of Liberty: The Universal Ethic of Freedom & Human Rights. LC 79-56782. (Illus.). 330p. 1980. pap. 6.75 (ISBN 0-9603872-1-8). Gutenberg.

Folejewski, Z., ed. Canadian Contributions to the International Congress of Slavists, 8th International Congress. 10.00 (ISBN 0-318-03290-2). Centre for E E S.

--Canadian Contributions to the International Congress of Slavists, 9th International Congress. 10.00 (ISBN 0-318-03291-0). Centre for E E S.

Folejewski, Zbigniew. Maria Dabrowska. LC 67-12267. (World Authors Ser.). 1967. lib. bdg. 15.95 (ISBN 0-8057-2260-2). Irvington.

Folejewski, Zbigniew, jt. auth. see Birkenmayer, Sigmund.

Folejewski, Zbigniew, ed. Canadian Contributions to the International Congress of Slavists, 7th International Congress. (Slavistic Printings & Reprintings: No. 285). 1973. 41.60x (ISBN 90-2792-543-7). Mouton.

Folena, G., ed. see Palazzi, F.

Foley, et al. Building Math Skills. Incl. Level 1. text ed. 11.96 (ISBN 0-201-13350-4); tchr's. manual with answers 8.64 (ISBN 0-201-13359-8); avail. test & practice duplicating masters 14.44 (ISBN 0-201-13360-1); Level 2. text ed. 11.96 (ISBN 0-201-13370-9); tchr's. manual with anwers 8.64 (ISBN 0-201-13379-2); test & practice duplicating masters avail.. (Gr. 7-12 Basal, Gr. 9-12 Remedial, Gr. 7-12 Supplemental). 1981. Addison-Wesley.

Foley, Albert S. Bishop Healy: Beloved Outcaste. LC 79-94130. (American Negro: His History & Literature, Ser. No. 3). 1970. Repr. of 1954 ed. 17.00 (ISBN 0-405-01925-4). Ayer Co Pubs.

--Dream of an Outcaste: The Slave-Born Georgian Who Became the Second Founder of America's Great Catholic University, Georgetown. (Illus.). 1985. 17.80 (ISBN 0-916620-31-X). Portals Pr.

--God's Men of Color: The Colored Catholic Priest of the U. S. 1854-1954. LC 69-18569. (American Negro: His History & Literature, Ser. No. 2). 1969. Repr. of 1955 ed. 14.00 (ISBN 0-405-01864-9). Ayer Co Pubs.

Foley, Allen R. What the Old-Timer Said: (& Then Some) To the Feller from Down Country & Even to His Neighbor (When He Had It Coming) LC 83-11635. (Illus.). 160p. 1983. pap. 5.95 (ISBN 0-8289-0516-9). Greene.

Foley, Anne E. Lincoln on the Greensprings. (Illus.). 30p. 1985. pap. 3.95 (ISBN 0-943388-07-4). South Oregon.

Foley, Arthur L. You Can Cure Yourself. LC 85-70166. 152p. 1985. 11.95 (ISBN 0-8323-0440-9); pap. 5.95 (ISBN 0-8323-0441-7). Binford.

Foley, Barbara. Listen to Me! 1985. pap. text ed. 8.95 (ISBN 0-88377-272-8); cassettes 48.95 (ISBN 0-88377-977-3). Newbury Hse.

--Now Hear This! Listening Comprehension For High Beginners & Intermediates. 1983. pap. text ed. 8.95 (ISBN 0-88377-410-0). Newbury Hse.

Foley, Barbara, jt. auth. see Pomann, Howard.

Foley, Bernard & Maunders, Keith. Accounting Information Disclosure & Collective Bargaining. LC 78-31148. 210p. 1979. text ed. 36.00x (ISBN 0-8419-0481-2). Holmes & Meier.

Foley, Bernice W. The Gazelle & the Hunter. LC 79-18880. (Illus.). (gr. 2-5). 1980. PLB 6.50 (ISBN 0-89565-104-1). Childs World.

--Spaceships of the Ancients. LC 78-59116. (Illus.). (gr. 3-6). 1978. 6.95 (ISBN 0-915964-04-X). Veritie Pr.

--A Walk Among Clouds. LC 79-18295. (Illus.). (gr. 2-5). 1980. PLB 6.50 (ISBN 0-89565-105-X). Childs World.

--Why the Cock Crows Three Times. LC 79-19088. (Illus.). (gr. k-4). 1980. PLB 6.50 (ISBN 0-89565-106-8). Childs World.

Foley, Betsy. Green Bay: Gateway to the Great Waterway. (Illus.). 168p. 1983. 22.95 (ISBN 0-89781-076-7). Windsor Pubns Inc.

Foley, C. W., jt. ed. see Johnson, A. D.

Foley, C. W., et al. Abnormalities of Companion Animals: Analysis of Heritability. (Illus.). 270p. 1979. text ed. 14.95x (ISBN 0-8138-0940-1). Iowa St U Pr.

Foley, Charles & Scobie, W. I. The Struggle for Cyprus. LC 74-10837. (Publications Ser.: No. 137). 187p. 1975. 9.95x (ISBN 0-8179-6371-5). Hoover Inst Pr.

Foley, D. Creating an Energy Empire. 1986. cancelled (ISBN 0-442-22766-3). Van Nos Reinhold.

Foley, Daniel J. Gardening by the Sea. (Illus.). 304p. 1982. pap. 9.95 (ISBN 0-940160-13-7). Parnassus Imprints.

--Ground Covers for Easier Gardening. (Illus.). 224p. 1972. pap. 5.00 (ISBN 0-486-20124-4). Dover.

--Nursing Home Estimates for California, Illinois, Massachusetts, New York & Texas from the 1977 National Nursing Home Survey. Olmsted, Mary, ed. (Ser. 13-48). 50p. 1980. pap. text ed. 1.75 (ISBN 0-8406-0190-5). Natl Ctr Health Stats.

Foley, David R., jt. auth. see Solovay, Norman.

Foley, Donald L. Governing the London Region: Reorganization & Planning in the 1960's. LC 76-157822. (Institute of Governmental Studies, UC Berkeley & Lane Studies in Regional Environment). 1972. 28.50x (ISBN 0-520-02040-5); pap. 7.95x (ISBN 0-520-02248-3, CAMPUS81). U of Cal Pr.

Foley, Doris, jt. ed. see Morely, Jim.

Foley, Douglas E., et al. From Peones to Politicos: Ethnic Relations in a South Texas Town, 1900-1977. LC 77-93094. (Mexican American Monographs: No. 3). 287p. 1978. pap. 7.50x (ISBN 0-292-72423-3, Pub. by Ctr Mex Am Stud). U of Tex Pr.

Foley, Duncan K. Money, Accumulation & Crisis. (Fundamentals of Pure & Applied Economics Ser.: Vol. 1, pt. 2). 88p. 1985. pap. text ed. 14.00 (ISBN 3-7186-0280-6). Harwood Academic.

Foley, Frank J., Jr. Requiem for Innocence. LC 75-9425. 61p. 1975. 5.00 (ISBN 0-8233-0221-0). Golden Quill.

Foley, Frederic J. The Great Formosan Imposter. 126p. 1980. (Pub. by Mei Ya China). Intl Spec Bk.

Foley, Grover, tr. see Barth, Karl.

Foley, Hamilton, ed. see Wilson, Woodrow.

Foley, Helen S. Abstracts of Wills & Estates, Barbour County, Ala., 1852-1856, Vol. 3. 122p. 1976. pap. 12.50 (ISBN 0-89308-183-3). Southern Hist Pr.

--Bible Records, Barbour County, Ala, Vol. 1. 80p. 1983. pap. 10.00 (ISBN 0-89308-180-9). Southern Hist Pr.

--Bible Records, Barbour County, Ala, Vol. 2. 84p. 1983. pap. 10.00 (ISBN 0-89308-181-7). Southern Hist Pr.

--The Eighteen Thirty-Three State Census of Barbour County, Ala. 66p. 1976. pap. 9.00 (ISBN 0-89308-177-9). Southern Hist Pr.

--Marriage & Death Notices from Alabama Newspapers, 1819 to 1890. 200p. 1981. 25.00 (ISBN 0-89308-208-2). Southern Hist Pr.

--Obituaries from Babour County Newspapers, 1890-1905. 146p. 1976. pap. 15.00 (ISBN 0-89308-182-5). Southern Hist Pr.

--The U. S. Census of Eighteen Fifty, Barbour County, Ala. 178p. 1976. 15.00 (ISBN 0-89308-178-7). Southern Hist Pr.

--U. S. Census of Eighteen Sixty, Barbour County, Ala. 228p. 1976. pap. 15.00 (ISBN 0-89308-179-5). Southern Hist Pr.

Foley, Helene P. Reflections of Women in Antiquity. 420p. 1982. 42.00 (ISBN 0-677-16370-3). Gordon.

--Ritual Irony: Poetry & Sacrifice in Euripides. LC 84-17470. 288p. 1985. text ed. 25.00x (ISBN 0-8014-1692-2). Cornell U Pr.

Foley, Henry. Records of the English Province of the Society of Jesus, 7 Vols. in 8. (Illus.). Repr. of 1883 ed. Set. 690.00 (ISBN 0-384-16310-6). Johnson Repr.

Foley, Henry A. & Sharfstein, Steven. Madness & Government. LC 83-2824. 304p. 1983. 19.95x (ISBN 0-88048-001-7). Am Psychiatric.

Foley, J. & Maneker, M. National Service & the American Future. 1983. pap. cancelled (ISBN 0-8159-6315-7). Devin.

Foley, J. D. & Van Dam, A. Fundamentals of Interactive Computer Graphics. 1982. 41.95 (ISBN 0-201-14468-9). Addison-Wesley.

Foley, James. Foundations of Theoretical Phonology. LC 76-27904. (Cambridge Studies in Linguistics Monographs: No. 2). 1977. 32.50 (ISBN 0-521-21466-1). Cambridge U Pr.

--Theoretical Morphology of the French Verb. iv, 292p. 1979. 34.00x (ISBN 90-272-0502-7, LIS 1). Benjamins North Am.

Foley, Jeanne M., jt. auth. see DePalma, David J.

Foley, Joan, jt. auth. see Foley, Joseph.

Foley, John F. Self-Assessment of Current Knowledge in Oncology. 1975. spiral bdg. 17.00 (ISBN 0-87488-284-2). Med Exam.

Foley, John M. Oral-Formulaic Theory & Research: An Introduction & Annotated Bibliography. LC 82-49146. (Reference Library of the Humanities). 734p. 1984. lib. bdg. 48.00 (ISBN 0-8240-9148-5). Garland Pub.

Foley, John M., ed. Oral Traditional Literature: A Festschrift for Albert Bates Lord. (Illus.). 461p. 1981. 24.95 (ISBN 0-89357-073-7). Slavica.

Foley, John P., ed. The Jefferson Encyclopedia. 75.00 (ISBN 0-8490-0441-1). Gordon Pr.

Foley, Joseph & Foley, Joan. The Chesapeake Bay Fish & Fowl Cookbook: A Treasury of Old & New Recipes from Maryland's Eastern Shore. (Illus.). 192p. 1981. 17.95 (ISBN 0-02-539560-2). Macmillan.

Foley, Joyce P., jt. auth. see Bagley, Michael T.

Foley, June. It's No Crush, I'm in Love. LC 81-15214. 224p. (gr. 7 up). 1982. 12.95 (ISBN 0-385-28465-9). Delacorte.

--It's No Crush, I'm in Love! (Young Love Romance Ser.). 224p. (YA) (gr. 7-12). 1983. pap. 2.50 (ISBN 0-440-94212-8, LFL). Dell.

--Love by Any Other Name. LC 82-72752. 224p. (gr. 7 up). 1982. 13.95 (ISBN 0-385-29245-7). Delacorte.

--Love by Any Other Name. (Young Love Romance Ser.). 224p. (YA) (gr. 7-12). 1983. pap. 2.50 (ISBN 0-440-94738-3, LFL). Dell.

Foley, K. Sue. The Political Blacklist in the Broadcasting Industry. Sterling, Christopher H., ed. LC 78-21718. (Dissertations in Broadcasting Ser.). 1979. lib. bdg. 37.00x (ISBN 0-405-11757-4). Ayer Co Pubs.

Foley, Kathleen M. & Inturrisi, Charles, eds. Opioid Analgesics in the Management of Clinical Pain. (Advances in Pain Research & Therapy Ser.: Vol. 8). 1985. text ed. price not set (ISBN 0-88167-108-8). Raven.

Foley, Kathryn, et al. The Good Apple Guide to Creative Drama. (gr. 2-6). 1981. 8.95 (ISBN 0-86653-030-4, GA 258). Good Apple.

Foley, Kathy & Herder, Mark. Nuclear Chic. 96p. (Orig.). 1984. pap. 3.95 (ISBN 0-523-42299-7). Pinnacle Bks.

Foley, Lawrence. Phonological Variation in Western Cherokee. LC 79-6621. (Outstanding Dissertations in Linguistics Ser.). 250p. 1985. 33.00 (ISBN 0-8240-4552-1). Garland Pub.

Foley, Lawrence M. A Phonological & Lexical Study of the Speech of Tuscaloosa County. (Publications of the American Dialect Society: No. 58). 68p. 1972. pap. 7.45 (ISBN 0-8173-0658-7). U of Ala Pr.

Foley, Leonard. Believing in Jesus: A Popular Overview of the Catholic Faith. (Illus.). 185p. (Orig.). 1981. pap. text ed. 4.95 (ISBN 0-912228-79-2). St Anthony Mess Pr.

--From Eden to Nazareth: Finding Our Story in the Old Testament. (Illus.). 103p. (Orig.). 1983. pap. text ed. 3.50 (ISBN 0-86716-020-9). St Anthony Mess Pr.

--God Never Says, "Yes, but...". (Illus.). 74p. (Orig.). 1979. pap. 1.50 (ISBN 0-912228-53-9). St Anthony Mess Pr.

--Saint of the Day: A Life & Lesson for Each of the 173 Saints of the New Missal, Vol. 2. (Illus.). 160p. 1975. pap. 2.95 (ISBN 0-912228-20-2). St Anthony Mess Pr.

--Signs of Love: The Sacraments of Christ. (Illus.). 1976. pap. 1.95 (ISBN 0-912228-32-6). St Anthony Mess Pr.

Foley, Leonard, ed. Saint of the Day. (Illus.). 354p. 1981. text ed. 10.95 (ISBN 0-912228-96-2). St Anthony Mess Pr.

--Saint of the Day: A Life & Lesson for Each of the 173 Saints of the New Missal, Vol. 1. (Illus.). 1974. pap. 2.95 (ISBN 0-912228-16-4). St Anthony Mess Pr.

Foley, Louise M. The Lost Tribe, No. 23. (Choose Your Own Adventure Ser.). (Illus.). 128p. 1984. pap. 1.95 (ISBN 0-553-23366-1). Bantam.

--The Mystery of Echo Lodge. 128p. (gr. 4 up). 1985. pap. 1.95 (ISBN 0-553-24720-4). Bantam.

--The Mystery of the Highland Crest. (Choose Your Own Adventure Ser.: No. 34). (gr. 4 up). 1984. pap. 1.95 (ISBN 0-553-24344-6). Bantam.

--The Sinister Studios of KESP-TV. (Twistaplot Bks.: No. 5). (Illus.). 96p. (Orig.). (gr. 7 up). 1983. pap. 1.95 (ISBN 0-590-32827-1). Scholastic Inc.

--Tackle Twenty-Two. (Illus.). 48p. (ps-3). 1981. pap. 1.95 (ISBN 0-440-48484-7, YB). Dell.

--The Train of Terror. (Twistaplot Bks.: No. 2). (Illus.). 96p. (Orig.). (gr. 7 up). pap. 1.95 (ISBN 0-590-32499-3). Scholastic Inc.

Foley, Louise P. Early Virginia Families Along the James River: Henrico County, Goochland County, Vol. I. LC 79-88216. (Illus.). 138p. 1983. Repr. of 1974 ed. 15.00 (ISBN 0-8063-0849-4). Genealog Pub.

Foley, Louise P. H. Early Virginia Families Along the James River: Their Deep Roots & Tangled Branches: Charles City County, Prince George County, Vol. II. LC 79-88216. (Illus.). 201p. 1980. Repr. of 1978 ed. 20.00 (ISBN 0-8063-0877-X). Genealog Pub.

Foley, Martha. The Story of Story Magazine. 1980. 12.95 (ISBN 0-393-01348-0). Norton.

Foley, Martha, ed. Best American Short Stories 1973. 1973. 8.95 (ISBN 0-395-17119-9). HM.

--The Best American Short Stories 1974. LC 16-11387. 400p. 1974. 9.95 (ISBN 0-395-19415-6). HM.

--The Best American Short Stories 1977. 1977. 10.00 (ISBN 0-395-25701-8). HM.

--Two Hundred Years of Great American Short Stories. LC 75-1107. 960p. 1975. 14.95 (ISBN 0-395-20447-X). HM.

Foley, Martha & Burnett, David, eds. Best American Short Stories, 1971. 1971. 7.50 (ISBN 0-395-12709-2). HM.

Foley, Mary D. Kentucky in Fiction: An Annotated Bibliography 1951-1980. (University of Kentucky Libraries Occasoinal Papers: No. 2). 38p. 1981. pap. 5.00 (ISBN 0-317-27427-9). U of KY Libs.

Foley, Mary M. The American House. LC 79-1662. (Illus.). 304p. 1981. pap. 14.90i (ISBN 0-06-090831-9, CN 831, CN). Har-Row.

--The American House. LC 79-1662. (Illus.). 1980. 20.00i (ISBN 0-06-011296-4, HarpT). Har-Row.

Foley, Matthew. Commodore PET for the Beginning Beginner. (Illus.). 144p. (gr. 5 up). 1983. C-64, VIC-20, Pet-64 & P-128. pap. 8.95 (ISBN 0-86582-120-8, EN79223). Enrich.

Foley, Matthew, jt. auth. see Russ, Flora.

Foley, Michael. The Go Situation. 64p. (Orig.). 1982. pap. 7.95 (ISBN 0-85640-263-X, Pub. by Blackstaff Pr). Longwood Pub Group.

--The New Senate: Liberal Influence on a Conservation Institution. LC 79-27751. 360p. 1980. 27.50x (ISBN 0-300-02440-1). Yale U Pr.

--True Life Love Stories. 40p. (Orig.). 1976. pap. 1.50 (ISBN 0-85640-088-2, Pub. by Blackstaff Pr). Longwood Pub Group.

Foley, N. Nadine, intro. by. Preaching & the Non-Ordained: An Interdisciplinary Study. 1983. pap. 6.95 (ISBN 0-8146-1291-1). Liturgical Pr.

Foley, Patrick K. American Authors, Seventeen Ninety-Five to Eighteen Ninety-Five. 59.95 (ISBN 0-8490-1412-3). Gordon Pr.

Foley, Rae. Girl On a High Wire. pap. 3.50 (ISBN 0-396-08163-0). Dodd.

Foley, Richard N. Criticism in American Periodicals of the Works of Henry James. LC 76-43043. lib. bdg. 20.00 (ISBN 0-8414-4165-0). Folcroft.

Foley, Rita. Create! 2nd ed. (Catechist Training Ser.). 1982. 3.95 (ISBN 0-8215-1230-7). Sadlier.

Foley, Robert. Hominid Evolution & Community Ecology. LC 83-77271. (Studies in Archaeology). 1984. 37.50 (ISBN 0-12-261920-X). Acad Pr.

Foley, Robert, jt. auth. see Randall, Anne.

Foley, Robert L. Late Pleistocene (Woodfordian) Vertebrates from the Driftless Area of Southwestern Wisconsin, the Moscow Fissure Local Fauna. (Reports of Investigations Ser.: No. 39). (Illus.). x, 50p. (Orig.). 1984. pap. text ed. 5.00 (ISBN 0-89792-102-X). Ill St Museum.

Foley, Ruth H. Some Chatham Neighbors of Yesterday. (Illus.). 76p. 1984. pap. 4.95 (ISBN 0-9613694-0-X). Thompson & Forbes Co.
Foley, Stepehn, ed. see More, Thomas.
Foley, Sue, jt. auth. see Ingrassia, Sara.
Foley, Suzanne. Space-Time-Sound Conceptual Art in the San Francisco Bay Area: The 1970's. (Illus.). 208p. pap. 15.00x (ISBN 0-295-95879-0). U of Wash Pr.
Foley, Suzanne, jt. auth. see Marshall, Richard.
Foley, Theresa S. & Davies, Marilyn A. Rape: Nursing Care of Victims. LC 82-18764. (Illus.). 489p. 1983. pap. text ed. 14.95 (ISBN 0-8016-1620-4). Mosby.
Foley, Tom, illus. Sakshi Gopal: A Witness for the Wedding. (Illus.). 16p. (gr. 1-4). 1981. pap. 2.00 (ISBN 0-89647-010-5). Bala Bks.
Foley, Vernard. The Social Physics of Adam Smith. LC 76-5710. 282p. 1976. 11.95 (ISBN 0-911198-43-1). Purdue U Pr.
Foley, Vincent D. An Introduction to Family Therapy. 207p. 1974. 19.50 (ISBN 0-8089-0846-4, 791290). Grune.
Foley, W. T. Advances in the Management of Cardiovascular Disease, Vol. 3. 1982. 39.95 (ISBN 0-8151-3256-5). Year Bk Med.
Foley, Ward. God Didn't Make Me a Woman Because I Had Enough Problems. 153p. 1985. pap. 7.95 (ISBN 0-318-12023-2). Ward Pubns.
Foley, William A. & Van Valin, Robert D., Jr. Functional Syntax & Universal Grammar. (Studies in Linguistics: No. 38). (Illus.). 375p. 1984. 59.50 (ISBN 0-521-25956-8); pap. 17.95 (ISBN 0-521-29704-4). Cambridge U Pr.
Foley, William E. History of Missouri: Volume 1: 1673 T0 1820. LC 70-15584. (Missouri Sesquicentennial History Ser.: Vol. 1). (Illus.). 266p. (gr. 9-12). 1971. text ed. 20.00x (ISBN 0-8262-0108-3). U of Mo Pr.
Foley, William E. & Rice, C. David. The First Chouteaus: River Barons of Early St. Louis. LC 83-1325. (Illus.). 258p. 1983. 22.50 (ISBN 0-252-01022-1). U of Ill Pr.
Foley, William T. Advances in the Management of Cardiovascular Disease, Vol. 2. 1981. 47.95 (ISBN 0-8151-3255-7). Year Bk Med.
Foley, Winifred. As the Twig Is Bent: Sketches of a Bittersweet Life. LC 77-92766. 1978. 9.95 (ISBN 0-8008-0421-X). Taplinger.
--A Child in the Forest. LC 85-8455. (Illus.). 192p. 1985. 17.95 (ISBN 0-03-005857-0). HR&W.
Folgelson, Robert M., ed. Administration of Justice in the United States. facsimile ed. LC 73-3813. (Criminal Justice in America Ser.). 1974. Repr. of 1910 ed. 18.00x (ISBN 0-405-06136-6). Ayer Co Pubs.
--Capital Punishment: Nineteenth-Century Arguments. facsimile ed. LC 74-3834. (Criminal Justice in America Ser.). 1974. Repr. of 1974 ed. 20.00x (ISBN 0-405-06138-2). Ayer Co Pubs.
Folger, Franklin. The Girls Again. new ed. LC 75-186491. (The Girls Ser.). (Illus.). 80p. 1972. pap. 1.50 (ISBN 0-87884-101-6). Unicorn Ent.
--The Girls from Day to Day. new ed. LC 74-176076. (The Girls Ser.). (Illus.). 80p. 1971. pap. 1.50 (ISBN 0-87884-100-8). Unicorn Ent.
--The Girls on the Go. new ed. LC 71-186490. (The Girls Ser.). (Illus.). 80p. 1972. pap. 1.50 (ISBN 0-87884-102-4). Unicorn Ent.
Folger, H. Scott & Brown, Lee F. Fundamentals of Chemical Reaction Engineering. (Illus.). 752p. 1986. text ed. 42.95 (ISBN 0-13-334558-0). P-H.
Folger, John K. & Nam, Charles B. Education of the American Population. LC 75-22814. (America in Two Centuries Ser). 1976. Repr. of 1967 ed. 23.50x (ISBN 0-405-07687-8). Ayer Co Pubs.
Folger, John K., et al. Human Resources & Higher Education: Staff Report on the Commission on Human Resources & Advanced Education. LC 68-58129. 476p. 1970. 20.00x (ISBN 0-87154-258-7). Russell Sage.
Folger, Joseph P. & Poole, Marshall S. Working Through Conflict. 1984. pap. text ed. 10.80 (ISBN 0-673-15836-5). Scott F.
Folger, Mary. Depression Recipes: Nineteen Thirties Good Food for Hard Times. LC 84-29380. (Illus.). 64p. 1985. pap. 7.50 (ISBN 0-932769-00-4). Bumper Crop Pr.
Folger, Robert G., ed. The Sense of Injustice: A Social Psychological Perspective. LC 84-2068. (Critical Issues in Social Justice Ser.). 1984. 29.50x (ISBN 0-306-41459-7). Plenum Pub.
Folger Shakespeare Library, Washington, D. C. Catalog of Manuscripts of the Folger Shakespeare Library, 3 vols. (Library Catalogs). 1970. Set. lib. bdg. 270.00 (ISBN 0-8161-0888-9, Hall Library). G K Hall.
--Catalog of Printed Books of the Folger Shakespeare Library, 28 vols. 1970. Set. lib. bdg. 2340.00 (ISBN 0-8161-0887-0, Hall Library). G K Hall.
Foli. Fortune Telling with Cards. pap. 4.00 (ISBN 0-87980-035-6). Wilshire.
Foli, P. R. Fortune Telling by Cards. 1.00 (ISBN 0-685-02613-2, 00545223). Stein Pub.
Foligno, Angela Da see Da Foligno, Angela.
Foligno, C. The Story of Padua. (Mediaeval Towns Ser.: Vol. 4). pap. 35.00 (ISBN 0-317-16168-7). Kraus Repr.
Foligno, Cesare. Dante. 1929. lib. bdg. 10.00 (ISBN 0-8414-4269-X). Folcroft.
--Epochs of Italian Literature. LC 78-103223. 1970. Repr. of 1920 ed. 15.00x (ISBN 0-8046-0860-1, Pub. by Kennikat). Assoc Faculty Pr.
Foligno, Cesare, tr. see Malaparte, Curzio.
Folinsbee, Lawrence J., et al, eds. Environmental Stress: Individual Human Adaptations. 1978. 43.00 (ISBN 0-12-261350-3). Acad Pr.
Folio Editors, ed. see Ellenthal, Ira.
Folio, M. Rhonda. Teaching Psychomotor Skills to Exceptional Learners: A Practical Approach. 1985. pap. text ed. price not set (ISBN 0-87189-243-X). Aspen Systems.
Foliot, G. The Letters & Charters of Gilbert Foliot. Morey, A. & Brooke, C. N., eds. 1967. Cambridge U Pr.
Folk, Dean. External Neuroanatomy of Old World Monkeys (Cercopithecoidea) Szalay, F. S., ed. (Contributions to Primatology: Vol. 15). (Illus.). 1978. 25.25 (ISBN 3-8055-2834-5). S Karger.
Folk, Edgar E., jt. auth. see Shaw, Bynum.
Folk, Eileen, illus. Needlework Designs for Miniature Projects. (Dolls, Miniatures Ser.). 48p. 1984. pap. 2.75 (ISBN 0-486-24660-4). Dover.
Folk, Ernest L., III. The Delaware General Corporation Law: A Commentary & Analysis. 1972. 60.00 (ISBN 0-316-28780-6). Little.
Folk, George E. Textbook of Environmental Physiology. 2nd ed. LC 73-8683. pap. 119.80 (ISBN 0-317-28604-8, 2055425). Bks Demand UMI.
Folk, Jerry. Worldly Christians: A Call to Faith, Prayer & Action. LC 82-72652. 144p. 1983. pap. 6.95 (ISBN 0-8066-1959-7, 10-7343). Augsburg.
Folk, Jerry L., jt. auth. see Lutz, Charles P.
Folk, Karen R., jt. auth. see Wolf, Carolyn E.
Folk, R. L. Field Excursion, Central Texas: Tertiary Bentonites of Central Texas. 53p. 1978. Repr. of 1961 ed. 1.25 (ISBN 0-686-29312-6, GB 3). Uranium-Bearing Clays & Tuffs of South-Central Texas, by D. H. Eargle & A. D. Weeks. Vermiculite Deposits Near Liano, by V. E. Barnes & S. E. Clabaugh. Bur Econ Geology.
Folk, Robert L. Petrology of Sedimentary Rocks. 4th ed. LC 80-83557. (Illus.). 1980. 15.95x (ISBN 0-914696-14-9). Hemphill.
Folk-Song Society Of The Northeast. Bulletin of the Folk-Song Society of the Northeast, Nos. 1-12. (American Folklore Society Bibliographical & Special Ser.). Repr. of 1960 ed. 24.00 (ISBN 0-527-01129-0). Kraus Repr.
Folkard, Frederick. Rare Sex. 16.50 (ISBN 0-392-04344-0, ABC). Sportshelf.
Folkard, Simon & Monk, Timothy H., eds. Hours of Work: Temporal Factors in Work Scheduling (Controlled Drug Bioavailability) 1985. 39.95 (ISBN 0-471-10524-4). Wiley.
Folke, Ann & Harden, Richard. Opportunities in Theatrical Design & Production. (VGM Career Bks.). (Illus.). 160p. 1983. 7.95 (ISBN 0-8442-6256-0, 6256-0, Passport Bks.); pap. 5.95 (ISBN 0-8442-6257-9, 6257-9). Natl Textbk.
Folkenflik, Robert, ed. The English Hero, 1660-1800. LC 80-53894. 288p. 1982. 27.50 (ISBN 0-87413-174-X). U Delaware Pr.
Folkenflik, Robert, ed. see Swift, Jonathan.
Folkening, John. Handbells in the Liturgical Service. (Illus.). 52p. (Orig.). 1984. pap. 3.00 (ISBN 0-570-01328-3, 99-1254). Concordia.
Folkers, George F., et al, trs. The Complete Narrative Prose of Conrad Ferdinand Meyer, 2 vols. 754p. 1976. Vol. 1, 1872-1879. 45.00 (ISBN 0-8387-1036-0); Vol. 2, 1881-1891. 45.00 (ISBN 0-8387-1547-8). Bucknell U Pr.
Folkers, K., jt. auth. see Wagner, A. F.
Folkers, K. & Yamamura, Y., eds. Biomedical & Clinical Aspects of Coenzyme Q: Proceedings of the International Symposium Held in Lake Yamanaka, Japan, 1976 & 1979, Vols. 1 & 2. 1977. Vol. 1. 61.50 (ISBN 0-444-41576-9, North Holland); Vol. 2. 68.00 (ISBN 0-444-80238-X). Elsevier.
--Biomedical & Clinical Aspects of Coenzyme Q: Proceedings of the International Symposium, 3rd, Texas, January 1981, Vol. 3. 414p. 1981. 69.50 (ISBN 0-444-80319-X, Biomedical Pr). Elsevier.
--Biomedical & Clinical Aspects of Coenzyme Q: Proceedings of the International Symposium on Coenzyme Q, 4th, Held in Martinsried, Munich, West Germany, 6-9 November, 1983, Vol. 4. 432p. 1984. 83.00 (ISBN 0-444-80380-7, I-480-84, Biomedical Pr). Elsevier.
Folkerts, George W., jt. auth. see Mason, William H.
Folkerts-Landau, O. F. Intertemporal Planning, Exchange, & Macroeconomics. LC 81-38501. (Illus.). 308p. 1982. 34.50 (ISBN 0-521-23067-5). Cambridge U Pr.
Folkes. Processing, Structure & Properties of Block Co-Polymers. (Illus.). 224p. 1985. 45.00 (ISBN 0-85334-323-3, Pub. by Elsevier Applied Sci England). Elsevier.
Folkes, M. J. Short Fibre Reinforced Thermoplastics. (Polymer Engineering Research Studies Ser.). 176p. 1982. 39.95x (ISBN 0-471-10209-1, Pub. by Res Stud Pr). Wiley.
--Short Fibre Reinforced Thermoplastics. (Illus.). 186p. 1982. 40.00 (ISBN 0-686-48236-0, 0808). T-C Pubns CA.
Folkestad, K., ed. Ionospheric Radio Communications. LC 68-20271. 468p. 1968. 42.50x (ISBN 0-306-30336-1, Plenum Pr). Plenum Pub.
Folkingham, William. Brachigraphy: Or, The Art of Short Writing. LC 79-3818. (English Experience Ser.: No. 455). 24p. 1972. Repr. of 1620 ed. 7.00 (ISBN 90-221-0455-9). Walter J Johnson.
Folkins, John W., jt. auth. see Kahane, Joel C.
Folkman, D. & Folkman, E. Dictionary of Races or Peoples. 75.00 (ISBN 0-8490-0045-9). Gordon Pr.
Folkman, David I., Jr. The Nicaragua Route. LC 73-180827. (University of Utah Publications in the American West: Vol. 8). 1976. pap. 9.95 (ISBN 0-87480-117-6). U of Utah Pr.
Folkman, E., jt. auth. see Folkman, D.
Folkman, Jane & Hollerorth, Hugo J. A Guide for Women with Diabetes Who Are Pregnant or Plan to Be. 147p. 24.50 (ISBN 0-318-17813-3). Joslin CTR.
Folkman, Steven L., jt. auth. see Batty, J. Clair.
Folkman, Susan, jt. auth. see Lazarus, Richard S.
Folkow, Bjoern & Neil, Eric. Circulation. (Illus., Orig.). 1971. text ed. 39.95x (ISBN 0-19-501343-3). Oxford U Pr.
Folks, Homer. Care of Destitute, Neglected, & Delinquent Children. LC 72-137167. (Poverty U.S.A. Historical Record Ser.). 1971. Repr. of 1900 ed. 13.00 (ISBN 0-405-03105-X). Ayer Co Pubs.
--The Care of Destitute, Neglected & Delinquent Children. LC 78-51849. (NASW Classics Ser.). 262p. 1978. pap. 5.95x (ISBN 0-87101-076-3). Natl Assn Soc Wkrs.
--The Care of the Destitute, Neglected & Delinquent Children. (Social Welfare Ser.). 1970. Repr. of 1900 ed. 14.00 (ISBN 0-384-16320-3). Johnson Repr.
Folks, J. Leroy. Ideas of Statistics. LC 80-14723. 368p. 1981. text ed. 30.00 (ISBN 0-471-02099-0). study guide avail. (ISBN 0-471-07972-3); tchrs.' manual avail. (ISBN 0-471-07969-3). Wiley.
Folks, Leroy, jt. auth. see Kempthorne, Oscar.
Folk-Williams, John A., et al. Western Water Flows to the Cities. Deardorff, Anna, ed. (Water in the West Ser.). (Illus.). 184p. (Orig.). 1985. pap. 25.00 (ISBN 0-933280-28-9). Island CA.
Follain, James & Struyk, Raymond. Homeownership Effects of Alternative Mortgage Instruments. 95p. 1977. pap. 6.00x (ISBN 0-87766-193-6, 18900). Urban Inst.
Follain, James, et al. Place to Place Indexes of the Price of Housing: Some New Estimates & a Comparative Analysis. 98p. 1979. pap. text ed. 6.00x (ISBN 0-87766-265-7). Urban Inst.
Follain, James R., Jr. & Malpezzi, S. Dissecting Housing Value & Rent. 132p. (Orig.). pap. text ed. 8.50 (ISBN 0-87766-276-2). Urban Inst.
Follain, Jean. Canisy. Guiney, Louise & Follain, Madeleine, trs. from Fr. 96p. 1981. text ed. 12.00 (ISBN 0-937406-06-6); pap. 5.00 (ISBN 0-937406-05-8); ltd. ed. 50.00 (ISBN 0-937406-07-4). Logbridge-Rhodes.
--D'Apres Tout: Poems by Jean Follain. McHugh, Heather, tr. from Fr. LC 81-47126. (Lockert Library of Poetry in Translation). 192p. 1981. 13.00 (ISBN 0-691-06476-8); pap. 6.95 (ISBN 0-691-01372-1). Princeton U Pr.
--Selected Prose. Feeney, Mary & Guiney, Louise, trs. from Fr. 1985. 14.00 (ISBN 0-937406-32-5); pap. 5.00 (ISBN 0-937406-34-1). Logbridge-Rhodes.
--A World Rich in Anniversaries. rev. ed. Feeney, Mary & Matthews, William, trs. (Illus.). 96p. (Fr.). 1981. text ed. 12.00 (ISBN 0-937406-01-5); deluxe ed. 50.00 (ISBN 0-937406-02-3); pap. 5.00 (ISBN 0-937406-00-7). Logbridge-Rhodes.
Follain, Madeleine, tr. see Follain, Jean.
Folland, G. B. Partial Differential Equations. (Tata Institute Lectures on Mathematics). 160p. 1983. pap. 10.00 (ISBN 0-387-12280-X). Springer-Verlag.
Folland, G. B. & Kohn, J. J. The Neumann Problem for the Cauchy-Riemann Complex. LC 72-1984. (Annals of Mathematics Studies: No. 75). 180p. 1972. lib. bdg. 22.00 (ISBN 0-691-08120-4). Princeton U Pr.
Folland, G. B. & Stein, E. M. Hardy Spaces on Homogeneous Groups. 1982. 15.00 (ISBN 0-691-08310-X). Princeton U Pr.
Folland, Gerald B. Introduction to Partial Differential Equations. LC 76-3029. (Mathematical Notes Ser.: No. 17). 349p. (Orig.). 1976. pap. 20.00 (ISBN 0-691-08177-8). Princeton U Pr.
--Real Analysis: Modern Techniques & Their Applications. LC 84-10435. (Pure & Applied Mathematics Ser.: 1-237). 350p. 1984. text ed. 34.95 (ISBN 0-471-80958-6, Pub. by Wiley-Interscience). Wiley.
Follendore, Joan S. You Can Learn Metric Easily. (Illus., Orig.). 1976. pap. 1.00 (ISBN 0-916546-01-2). Racz Pub.
Follendore, Joan S., compiled by. From Our Immigrants with Love. LC 76-20977. (Illus.). 1977. 14.00 (ISBN 0-916546-03-9). Racz Pub.
Follet, Robert J. The Financial Side Of Book Publishing: Correspondence Course for the Non-Accountant. 296p. 1982. 50.00 (ISBN 0-933636-03-2). AAP.
Follett, B. K. & Follett, D. E. Biological Clocks in Seasonal Reproductive Systems. LC 81-4614. 292p. 1981. 54.95x (ISBN 0-470-27175-2). Halsted Pr.
Follett, B. K., jt. ed. see Reiter, R. J.
Follett, B. K., et al, eds. The Endocrine System & the Environment. (Illus.). xiii, 329p. 1985. 49.50 (ISBN 0-387-15101-X). Springer-Verlag.
Follett, Barbara Lee. Checklist for a Perfect Wedding. rev. ed. LC 72-97272. 120p. 1973. pap. 2.45 (ISBN 0-385-04251-5, Dolp). Doubleday.
Follett, D. E., jt. auth. see Follett, B. K.
Follett, Frederick. History of the Press in Western New York: From the Beginning to the Middle of the Nineteenth Century. LC 73-6520. (Illus.). 80p. 1973. Repr. of 1920 ed. 8.50 (ISBN 0-916346-03-X). Harbor Hill Bks.
Follett, Helen T. & Follett, Wilson. Some Modern Novelists: Appreciations & Estimates. facs. ed. LC 67-26741. (Essay Index Reprint Ser). 1918. 21.50 (ISBN 0-8369-0449-4). Ayer Co Pubs.
Follett, Helen T., et al. Arnold Bennett. LC 73-15532. lib. bdg. 6.50 (ISBN 0-8414-4162-6). Folcroft.
Follett, James. Dominator. 264p. 1986. 15.95 (ISBN 0-385-19778-0). Doubleday.
Follett, Ken. The Big Needle. 1981. pap. 2.25 (ISBN 0-89083-787-2). Zebra.
--Eye of the Needle. LC 77-90670. 1978. 17.95 (ISBN 0-87795-186-1). Arbor Hse.
--Eye of the Needle. movie ed. (Illus.). 1981. pap. 3.95 (ISBN 0-451-12430-8, AE2430, Sig). NAL.
--The Key to Rebecca. 1981. lib. bdg. 16.95 (ISBN 0-8161-3151-1, Large Print Bks). G K Hall.
--The Key to Rebecca. LC 80-16760. 1980. 12.95 (ISBN 0-688-03734-8). Morrow.
--Key to Rebecca. 1981. pap. 4.50 (ISBN 0-451-13509-1, AE2788, Sig). NAL.
--The Man from St. Petersburg. LC 81-22550. 320p. 1982. 14.50 (ISBN 0-688-01150-0). Morrow.
--The Man from St. Petersburg. (General Ser.). 1982. lib. bdg. 15.95 (ISBN 0-8161-3412-X, Large Print Bks). G K Hall.
--The Man from St. Petersburg. 1983. pap. 3.95 (ISBN 0-451-12438-3, Sig). NAL.
--The Modigliani Scandal. Golbitz, Pat, ed. LC 84-27278. 224p. 1985. Repr. of 1977 ed. 15.95 (ISBN 0-688-05119-7). Morrow.
--The Modigliani Scandal. 1985. pap. 3.50 (ISBN 0-451-13640-3, Sig). NAL.
--On Wings of Eagles. LC 83-9328. 1983. 16.95 (ISBN 0-688-02371-1). Morrow.
--On Wings of Eagles. 664p. 1984. lib. bdg. 16.95 (ISBN 0-8161-3642-4, Large Print Bks). G K Hall.
--On Wings of Eagles. 1984. pap. 4.50 (ISBN 0-451-13151-7, Sig). NAL.
--Triple. LC 78-73869. 1980. 10.95 (ISBN 0-87795-223-X). Arbor Hse.
--Triple. 1980. pap. 4.50 (ISBN 0-451-13988-7, AE2790, Sig). NAL.
Follett, Ken, jt. auth. see Maurice.
Follett, Ken, jt. auth. see Maurice, Rene L.
Follett, Mary P. The New State: Group Organization the Solution of Popular Government. 11.75 (ISBN 0-8446-1187-5). Peter Smith.
--The Speaker of the House of Representatives. LC 72-81995. 1974. Repr. of 1902 ed. lib. bdg. 23.50 (ISBN 0-8337-4567-0). B Franklin.
Follett, Muriel. New England Year: A Journal of Vermont Farm Life. LC 73-145711. 1971. Repr. of 1939 ed. 35.00x (ISBN 0-8103-3393-7). Gale.
Follett, Richard. Birds of Yellowstone & Grand Teton National Parks. 1985. pap. 5.95 (ISBN 0-911797-14-9). R Rinehart Inc.
Follett, Robert. How to Keep Score in Business. LC 78-9401. 1978. 12.95 (ISBN 0-695-81101-0). Alpine Guild.
--How to Keep Score in Business: Accounting & Financial Analysis for the Non-Accountant. 1980. pap. 2.95 (ISBN 0-451-62259-6, ME2259, Ment). NAL.
--What to Take Backpacking--& Why. (Illus.). 1978. pap. 3.95 (ISBN 0-931712-01-7). Alpine Guild.
Follett, Robert J. R. The Financial Side of Book Publishing. 288p. 1985. 55.00x (ISBN 0-931712-04-1). Alpine Guild.
Follett, Wilson. Modern American Usage: A Guide. Barzun, Jacques, ed. (American Century Ser.). 443p. 1966. pap. 9.95 (ISBN 0-8090-0139-X). Hill & Wang.
Follett, Wilson, jt. auth. see Follett, Helen T.
Follett, Wilson, ed. see Beer, Thomas.
Follette, Daniel. Machining Fundamentals. Williams, Roy & Weller, E. J., eds. LC 80-51218. (Illus.). 400p. 1980. 27.50 (ISBN 0-87263-054-4). SME.
Follette, John W. Broken Bread: Sermons & Poems. 216p. 1957. pap. 4.95 (ISBN 0-88243-474-8, 02-0474). Gospel Pub.
Follette, Marcel C. La see La Follette, Marcel C.
Follette, Marcel la. Creationism, Science, & the Law: Arkansas Case Documents & Commentaries. LC 82-21646. 232p. (Orig.). 1983. pap. 9.95x (ISBN 0-262-62041-3). MIT Pr.
Follette, Robert M. La see La Follette, Robert M.
Follette, Suzanne La see La Follette, Suzanne.
Folley. American Law Enforcement: Police, Courts, Corrections. 3rd ed. 1985. 30.54 (ISBN 0-205-06651-8, 826651). Allyn.
Folley, K. W., ed. Semigroups: Proceedings. 1969. 66.00 (ISBN 0-12-261950-1). Acad Pr.
Folley, T. Spanish Aide-Memoire: English-Spanish Vocabulary. pap. 7.50x (ISBN 0-392-08443-0, SpS). Sportshelf.

Folley, Vern L. Police Patrol Techniques & Tactics. 192p. 1974. photocopy ed. 20.50x (ISBN 0-398-02842-7). C C Thomas.

Folliet, jt. auth. see Watson.

Folliet, Joseph. The Evening Sun. 1983. 12.50 (ISBN 0-8199-0817-7). Franciscan Herald.

--Finding Peace of Heart. 1983. pap. 10.50 (ISBN 0-8199-0840-1). Franciscan Herald.

Follin, Marion G., III & Smith, Norman B. Collections: A North Carolina Law Practice System. (Law Practice Systems Ser.). 436p. 1984. looseleaf 75.00 (ISBN 0-87215-760-1). Michie Co.

Folliot, Denise, tr. see Castelot, Andre.

Folliot, Denise, tr. see Valery, Paul.

Follis, Anne B. I'm Not a Women's Libber, But... LC 81-1241. 128p. 1981. 8.75 (ISBN 0-687-18687-0). Abingdon.

Follis, Joan J., jt. auth. see Fordney, Marilyn T.

Follis, John & Hammer, Dave. Architectural Signing & Graphics. (Illus.). 232p. 1979. 32.50 (ISBN 0-8230-7051-4, Whitney Lib). Watson-Guptill.

Follis, Richard H., Jr. The Pathology of Nutritional Disease: Physiological & Morphological Changes Which Result from Deficiencies of the Essential Elements, Amino Acids, Vitamins, & Fatty Acids. (Illus.). 306p. 1948. photocopy ed. 24.50x (ISBN 0-398-04255-1). C C Thomas.

Follmann, Joseph F. The Economics of Industrial Health: History, Theory, Practice. LC 77-25077. pap. 123.50 (ISBN 0-317-20735-0, 2023893). Bks Demand UMI.

--Helping the Troubled Employee. LC 78-23474. pap. 68.00 (ISBN 0-317-26846-5, 2023546). Bks Demand UMI.

Follmann, Joseph F., Jr. Alcoholics & Business: Problems, Costs, Solutions. new ed. LC 75-40270. 256p. 1976. 12.95 (ISBN 0-8144-5410-0). AMACOM.

Followell, Virginia, jt. auth. see Waldron, Rodney K.

Follweiler, Joanne M. & Sherma, Joseph, eds. Handbook of Chromatography, Pesticides & Related Organic Chemicals. 368p. 1984. 67.00 (ISBN 0-8493-4010-1). CRC Pr.

Folly, Dennis. Hear My Story. 48p. 1982. pap. 3.95 (ISBN 0-917658-19-1). BPW & P.

Folmar, John K., ed. From That Terrible Field: The Civil War Letters of James M. Williams, Twenty-First Alabama Volunteers. LC 80-27672. (Illus.). 224p. 1981. text ed. 18.95 (ISBN 0-8173-0068-6). U of Ala Pr.

Folmar, Leroy C. So She's Coming to Dinner: A Cookbook for Men. 120p. (Orig.). 1985. pap. 8.95 (ISBN 0-913629-01-4). Alex Collection.

Folmer, A. P. Fabulous Holiday Ornaments. (Illus.). 16p. (Orig.). (gr. k up). 1985. pap. 2.95 (ISBN 0-590-33841-2). Scholastic Inc.

--Fabulous Sticker Masks. (Illus.). 24p. (Orig.). (ps-5). 1984. pap. 2.95 (ISBN 0-590-33367-4). Scholastic Inc.

Folmer, Hendrik & Oosterhaven, Jan. Spatial Inequalities & Regional Development. 1979. lib. bdg. 34.50 (ISBN 0-89838-006-5, Pub. by Martins Nijhoff Netherlands). Kluwer Academic.

Folmsbee, Beulah. Little History of the Horn-Book. LC 42-36336. (Illus.). 1942. 9.00 (ISBN 0-87675-085-4). Horn Bk.

Folmsbee, Stanley J. Historical Highlights of Tennessee. 1981. pap. 2.95 (ISBN 0-686-32032-8). Upper Country.

Folomkina, S. & Weiser, H. Learner's English-Russian Dictionary. (Eng. & Rus.). 1963. pap. 9.95 (ISBN 0-262-56002-X). MIT Pr.

--The Learner's English-Russian Dictionary. 471p. (Eng. & Rus.). 1975. leatherette 9.95 (ISBN 0-686-92469-X, M-9118). French & Eur.

Folomkina, V. & Weiser, T. Learner's English-Russian Dictionary. 655p. (Eng. & Rus.). 1980. 15.00x (ISBN 0-569-05869-4, Pub. by Collet's). State Mutual Bk.

Folon, Jean M. Flowers by Giorgio Morandi. LC 85-60992. (Illus.). 84p. 1985. 30.00 (ISBN 0-8478-0639-1). Rizzoli Intl.

Folon, Jean-Michel, jt. auth. see Glaser, Milton.

Folprecht, William. Write the Word: A Creative Writing Text. LC 76-18091. (Illus.). 220p. (gr. 10-12). 1976. pap. text ed. 5.95 (ISBN 0-915134-15-2). Mott Media.

Folsch, D. W., ed. The Ethology & Ethics of Farm Animal Production. (Animal Management Ser.: No. 6). 144p. (Ger. & Eng.). 1978. pap. 22.95x (ISBN 0-8176-1004-9). Birkhauser.

Folsch, D. W. & Nabholz, A., eds. Ethologische Aussagen zur Artgerechten Nutztierhaltung. (Animal Management Ser.: Vol. 13). 184p. 1982. pap. 16.95 (ISBN 0-8176-1338-2). Birkhauser.

Folse, Henry J., Jr. The Philosophy of Niels Bohr: Framework of Complementarity. (Personal Library: Vol. 4). 296p. 1985. 46.50 (ISBN 0-444-86914-X, North-Holland); pap. 19.50 (ISBN 0-444-86938-7, North-Holland). Elsevier.

Folse, Keith S. English Structure Practices. 384p. 1983. pap. text ed. 6.95x (ISBN 0-472-08034-2). U of Mich Pr.

--Intermediate Reading Practices: Building Reading & Vocabulary Skills. LC 84-52414. 320p. 1985. pap. text ed. 8.95x (ISBN 0-472-08057-1). U of Mich Pr.

Folse, Lois J., jt. auth. see Ingram, Marilyn W.

Folse, Nancy & Henrion, Marilyn. Careers in the Fashion Industry: What the Jobs Are & How to Get Them. LC 80-8852. 224p. 1981. pap. 12.45i (ISBN 0-06-014886-1, HarpT, EH510, HarpT). Har-Row.

Folse, Nancy M. & Henrion, Marilyn. Careers in Fashion Industry: What the Jobs Are & How to Get Them. LC 80-8852. 288p. 1981. pap. 5.72i (ISBN 0-06-463510-4, EH 510, EH). B&N NY.

Folsom, Burton W., Jr. Urban Capitalists: Entrepreneurs & City Growth in Pennsylvania's Lackawanna & Lehigh Valleys, 1800-1920. LC 80-8864. (Studies in Industry & Society: No. 1). (Illus.). 208p. 1981. text ed. 19.50x (ISBN 0-8018-2520-2). Johns Hopkins.

Folsom, Ezekiel G. Folsom's Logical Bookkeeping: The Logic of Accounts. LC 75-18469. (History of Accounting Ser.). 1976. 32.00x (ISBN 0-405-07552-9). Ayer Co Pubs.

Folsom, Franklin. Some Basic Rights of Soviet Citizens. 1983. 4.95 (ISBN 0-8285-2656-7, Pub. by Progress Pubs USSR). Imported Pubns.

--Some Basic Rights of Soviet Citizens. LC 84-109382. 165p. 1983. write for info. Progress Pubs.

Folsom, Franklin & Folsom, Mary E. America's Ancient Treasures. 3rd, rev. & enl. ed. (Illus.). 448p. 1983. 35.00x (ISBN 0-8263-0650-0); pap. 17.50 (ISBN 0-8263-0651-9). U of NM Pr.

Folsom, G. History of Saco & Biddeford. rev. ed. 352p. 1984. Repr. of 1830 ed. 25.00 (ISBN 0-917890-47-7). Heritage Bk.

Folsom, Gwendolyn B. Legislative History: Research for the Interpretation of Laws. viii, 136p. 1979. Repr. of 1972 ed. lib. bdg. 17.50x (ISBN 0-8377-0532-0). Rothman.

Folsom, James K. Man's Accidents & God's Purposes: Multiplicity in Hawthorne's Fiction. 1963. pap. 6.95x (ISBN 0-8084-0208-0). New Coll U Pr.

--Timothy Flint. (Twayne's United States Authors Ser.). 1965. pap. 5.95x (ISBN 0-8084-0301-X, T83, Twayne). New Coll U Pr.

Folsom, James K., ed. The Western: A Collection of Critical Essays. (Twentieth Century Views Ser.). 1978. text ed. 12.95 (ISBN 0-13-950717-5, Spec). P-H.

Folsom, James K., ed. see Flint, Timothy.

Folsom, James K., jt. ed. see Slotkin, Richard.

Folsom, Joseph K. Culture & Social Progress. 1928. 17.50 (ISBN 0-8482-3975-X). Norwood Edns.

--Social Psychology. 1978. Repr. of 1931 ed. lib. bdg. 35.00 (ISBN 0-8482-0842-0). Norwood Edns.

Folsom, Le Roi A., ed. see Culinary Institute of America.

Folsom, M. H., jt. auth. see Kelling, H. W.

Folsom, M. M. & Kirschner, L. H. By Women. 1975. pap. text ed. 15.96 (ISBN 0-395-20500-X); instr's. resource bk. 6.60 (ISBN 0-395-20494-1). HM.

Folsom, Mary E., jt. auth. see Folsom, Franklin.

Folsom, Merrill. Great American Mansions & Their Stories. (Illus.). 1976. pap. 12.95 (ISBN 0-8038-2681-8). Hastings.

--More Great American Mansions: And Their Stories. (Illus.). 1979. pap. 12.95 (ISBN 0-8038-4723-8). Hastings.

Folsom, Michael, jt. auth. see Elting, Mary.

Folsom, Michael B. & Lubar, Steven D., eds. The Philosophy of Manufactures: Early Debates Over Industrialization in the United States. (Documents in American Industrial History Ser.). 512p. 1982. 50.00x (ISBN 0-262-06076-0). MIT Pr.

Folsom, Rachel, jt. auth. see Moll, Robert.

Folsom, Ralph H. & Fellmeth, Robert C. California Antitrust Law & Practice. 271p. 1983. 65.00 (ISBN 0-317-12917-1). Butterworth Legal Pubs.

Folsom, Ralph H., jt. auth. see Fellmeth, Robert C.

Folsom, Robert S. Attic Black-Figured Pottery. LC 75-13568. (Illus.). 219p. 1975. 9.95 (ISBN 0-8155-5035-9, NP). Noyes.

--Attic Red-Figured Pottery. LC 76-41132. (Illus.). 219p. 1977. 9.95 (ISBN 0-8155-5049-9, NP). Noyes.

--I Diomedes. 1984. 14.95 (ISBN 0-8158-0421-0). Chris Mass.

Folsome, Clair E. The Origin of Life: A Warm Little Pond. LC 78-10809. (Biology Ser.). (Illus.). 168p. 1979. text ed. 22.95 (ISBN 0-7167-0294-0); pap. text ed. 11.95 (ISBN 0-7167-0293-2). W H Freeman.

Folsome, Clair E., intro. by. Life: Origin & Evolution: Readings from Scientific American. LC 78-15129. (Illus.). 148p. 1979. text ed. 22.95 (ISBN 0-7167-1033-1); pap. text ed. 11.95 (ISBN 0-7167-1032-3). W H Freeman.

Folson, Marcia & Folson, Michael. Easy As Pie: A Guessing Game of Saying. LC 84-14978. (Illus.). 64p. (Orig.). (ps-3). 1985. 11.95 (ISBN 0-89919-303-X, Clarion); pap. 4.95 (ISBN 0-89919-351-X). HM.

Folson, Michael, jt. auth. see Folson, Marcia.

Folson, Rachel, jt. auth. see Moll, Robert.

Folsor, DeFrancias. Our Police: A History of the Baltimore Police from the First Watchman to the Latest Appointee. LC 75-172585. (Criminology, Law Enforcement, & Social Problems Ser.: No. 175). (Illus.). Date not set. Repr. of 1888 ed. o. p. 17.50 (ISBN 0-87585-175-4). Patterson Smith.

Folta, J. & Deck, E., eds. Sociological Framework for Patient Care. 2nd ed. LC 78-12073. 510p. 1979. pap. 21.00 (ISBN 0-471-04496-2, Pub. by Wiley Medical). Wiley.

Folta, Richard C. Rush of Eagle Wings. LC 82-6810. 1985. 15.95 (ISBN 0-87949-219-8). Ashley Bks.

Foltin, Bela, jt. auth. see Nettl, Bruno.

Foltin, Lore B. & Heinen, Hubert, eds. Paths to German Poetry: An Introductory Anthology. (Orig., Ger.). 1969. pap. text ed. 14.75 scp (ISBN 0-06-042112-6, HarpC). Har-Row.

Foltiny, Stephen. Hungarian Archaeological Collection of the American Museum of Natural History in New York. LC 67-66165. (Uralic & Altaic Ser: Vol. 77). (Illus.). 1969. pap. text ed. 9.50x (ISBN 0-87750-028-2). Res Ctr Lang Semiotic.

Foltman, Felician F. Manpower Information for Effective Management, 2 pts. Incl. Pt. 1. Collecting & Managing Employee Information (ISBN 0-87546-217-0); Pt. 2. Skills Inventories & Manpower Planning (ISBN 0-87546-218-9). (Key Issues Ser.: Nos. 10 & 14). 1973. pap. 2.00 ea. ILR Pr.

--White & Blue-Collars in a Mill Shutdown: A Case Study in Relative Redundancy. LC 68-63931. (Paperback Ser.: No. 6). 136p. 1968. pap. 3.00 (ISBN 0-87546-031-3). ILR Pr.

Folts, Betty, ed. see Nisbet, James D.

Folts, Betty, ed. see Nisbet, James D., et al.

Folts, Franklin E. Introduction to Industrial Management. LC 77-22994. 686p. 1979. Repr. of 1963 ed. 35.50 (ISBN 0-88275-566-8). Krieger.

Folts, Harold C. & Dally, Kathleen L. X.25 & Related Protocols. 250p. 1984. 38.50 (ISBN 0-07-606872-2). McGraw.

Folts, Harold C., ed. McGraw-Hill's Compilation of Data Communications Standards. 2nd, rev. ed. 1923p. 1983. 295.00 (ISBN 0-07-606775-0). McGraw.

Folts, Jim, jt. auth. see Beekman, George.

Foltz, Anne-Marie. An Ounce of Prevention: Child Health Politics Under Medicaid. (Health & Public Policy Ser.). 272p. 1982. 35.00x (ISBN 0-262-06082-5). MIT Pr.

Foltz, Floyd M., jt. auth. see Matzke, Howard A.

Foltz, John, et al, eds. Microwave Cooking: It's Not Magic. LC 77-20466. (Illus.). 1977. 15.00 (ISBN 0-930380-03-7). Quail Run.

Foltz, Roger, jt. auth. see Edmister, Jane.

Foltz, Roger E., jt. auth. see DeZeeuw, Anne M.

Foltz, William J. From French West Africa to the Mali Federation. LC 65-11178. (Yale Studies in Political Science: No. 12). pap. 62.80 (ISBN 0-317-10987-1, 2003063). Bks Demand UMI.

Foltz, William J. & Bienen, Henry S., eds. Arms & the African: The Military Influences of Africa's International Relations. LC 84-40670. (A Council on Foreign Relations Bks.). 240p. 1985. 22.50X (ISBN 0-300-03347-8). Yale u Pr.

Folus, Alice. Alice, Where Are You? (Illus.). 43p. 1984. 4.95 (ISBN 0-533-04522-3). Vantage.

Folwell, William W. A History of Minnesota, 4 vols. rev. ed. Incl. Vol. 1, 1956. LC 28-20894. 533p. 7.95 (ISBN 0-87351-000-3); Vol. 2, 1961. LC 21-20894. 477p. 7.95 (ISBN 0-87351-001-1); Vol. 3, 1969. LC 56-57334. 605p. 7.95 (ISBN 0-87351-002-X); Vol. 4, 1969. LC 56-57334. 575p. 7.95 (ISBN 0-87351-003-8). LC 21-20894. 1956-69. 29.95 set (ISBN 0-87351-151-4). Minn Hist.

--Minnesota, the North Star State. LC 72-3767. (American Commonwealths: No. 19). Repr. of 1908 ed. 34.00 (ISBN 0-404-57219-7). AMS Pr.

Folz, Joe. Psychic Healers of the Philippines. LC 81-80418. 1981. pap. 2.95 (ISBN 0-88270-508-3, Pub. by Logos). Bridge Pub.

Folz, Robert. The Concept of Empire in Western Europe from the Fifth to the Fourteenth Century. Ogilvie, Sheila A., tr. from French. LC 80-18796. xv, 250p. 1980. Repr. of 1969 ed. lib. bdg. 32.50x (ISBN 0-313-22453-6, FOCO). Greenwood.

Fombrun, Charles, et al. Strategic Human Resource Management. 550p. 1984. 24.95 (ISBN 0-471-81079-7, Pub. by Wiley-Interscience). Wiley.

Fomby, T. B., et al. Advanced Econometric Methods. (Illus.). 600p. 1984. 54.00 (ISBN 0-387-90908-7). Springer-Verlag.

Fomenko, V. T., et al. Twelve Papers on Functional Analysis & Geometry. LC 51-5559. (Translations Ser.: No. 2, Vol. 85). 1969. 34.00 (ISBN 0-8218-1785-X, TRANS 2-85). Am Math.

Fomenko, Vadim S. Handbook of Thermionic Properties: Electronic Work Functions & Richardson Constants of Elements & Compounds. LC 65-23385. 151p. 1966. 42.50x (ISBN 0-306-65117-3, IFI Plenum). Plenum Pub.

Fomin, Aleksandr G. Putevoditel' Po Bibliografii. Repr. of 1934 ed. 24.00 (ISBN 0-384-16350-5). Johnson Repr.

Fomin, S., et al. Nine Papers on Foundations, Measure Theory, & Analysis. (Translations Ser.: No. 2, Vol. 57). 1966. 37.00 (ISBN 0-8218-1757-4, TRANS 2-57). Am Math.

Fomin, S. V. Number Systems. 2nd ed. Teller, Joan W. & Branson, Thomas P., trs. from Rus. LC 73-89787. (Popular Lectures in Mathematics Ser). 48p. 1975. pap. text ed. 3.50x (ISBN 0-226-25669-3). U of Chicago Pr.

--Sistemas De Numeracion. 46p. (Span.). 1975. pap. 1.45 (ISBN 0-8285-1692-8, Pub. by Mir Pubs USSR). Imported Pubns.

Fomin, S. V., jt. auth. see Budak, B. M.

Fomin, S. V., jt. auth. see Gelfand, Izrail M.

Fomin, S. V., jt. auth. see Kolmogorov, A. N.

Fomon, Samuel & Bell, Julius. Rhinoplasty: New Concepts, Evaluation & Application. (Illus.). 332p. 1970. photocopy ed. 37.75x (ISBN 0-398-00592-3). C C Thomas.

Fomon, Samuel J. Infant Nutrition. 2nd ed. LC 74-4560. (Illus.). 575p. 1974. text ed. 42.00 (ISBN 0-7216-3809-0). Saunders.

Fon, Neal La see Ratkevich, Ron & La Fon, Neal.

Fonagy, Ivan. Situation et Signification. (Pragmatics & Beyond Ser.: III: 1). 160p. (Orig., Fr.). 1982. pap. 20.00 (ISBN 90-272-2504-4). Benjamins North Am.

Fonagy, Peter & Higgitt, Anna. Personality Theory & Clinical Practice. 194p. 1985. pap. 7.95 (ISBN 0-416-35630-3, NO. 9182). Methuen inc.

Fonarrow, Jerry. Coming of a God. (Orig.). 1969. pap. 0.95 (ISBN 0-87067-201-0, BH201). Holloway.

Fonash, Stephen J. Solar Cell Device Physics. LC 81-14934. (Energy Science & Engineering Ser.: Resources, Technology, Management). 1981. 49.50 (ISBN 0-12-261980-3). Acad Pr.

Fonblanque, Edward B. De see DeFonblanque, Edward B.

Fonda, Jane. Jane Fonda's Workout Book. LC 81-13553. 256p. 1981. 19.95 (ISBN 0-671-43217-6). S&S.

--Jane Fonda's Workout Book. 1984. pap. 9.95 (ISBN 0-671-50896-2). S&S.

--Jane Fonda's Year of Fitness, Health & Nutrition, 1985. 1984. 9.95 (ISBN 0-671-47649-1). S&S.

Fonda, Jane & McCarthy, Mignon. Women Coming of Age. (Illus.). 444p. 1984. 19.95 (ISBN 0-671-46997-5). S&S.

Fonda, L. & Ghirardi, G. C. Symmetry Principles in Quantum Physics. (Theoretical Physics Ser: Vol. 1). 1970. 45.00 (ISBN 0-8247-1213-7). Dekker.

Fondakinadee, Joi. The La-La Means I'm Hungry: Also Known As the MJ Diet. 1985. 8.50 (ISBN 0-8062-2459-2). Carlton.

Fondane, Benjamin. La Conscience Malheureuse. LC 78-65073. (Phenomenology-Background, Foreground & Influences Ser.). 1980. lib. bdg. 40.00 (ISBN 0-8240-9565-0). Garland Pub.

Fondaneche, Pierre, jt. auth. see Brosset, Raymond.

Fondation des Sciences Politiques, Paris, France. Bibliographie Courante D'Articles de Periodiques Posterieurs a 1944 Sur les Problems Politiques, Economiques et Sociaux: Dixieme Supplement, 2 vols. (Library Catalogs Bib.Guides). Orig. Title: Index to Post-1944 Periodical Articles on Political Economic & Social Problems - Tenth Supplement. 1979. Set. lib. bdg. 290.00 (ISBN 0-8161-0298-8, Hall Library). G K Hall.

Fondation Le Corbusier & Architectural History Foundation. Le Corbusier Sketchbooks: Vol. 1, 1914-1948. LC 80-28987. (Architectural History Foundation Ser.). (Illus.). 456p. (Fr. & Eng.). 1981. 165.00x (ISBN 0-262-03078-0). MIT Pr.

Fondation Le Corbusier & Architectural History Foundation, eds. Le Corbusier Sketchbooks: Volume 4, 1957-1964. (Illus.). 520p. (Fr. & Eng.). 1982. 165.00x (ISBN 0-262-12093-3). MIT Pr.

--Le Corbusier Sketchbooks: Vol. 3, 1954-1957. (Illus.). 520p. (Fr. & Eng.). 1982. 165.00x (ISBN 0-262-12092-5). MIT Pr.

Fondation Le Corbusier & the Architectural History Foundation, ed. Le Corbusier Sketchbooks: Vol. 2, 1950-1954. (Illus.). 444p. (Fr. & Eng.). 1981. 165.00x (ISBN 0-262-12090-9). MIT Pr.

Fondation Nationale Des Sciences Politique, Paris. Bibliographie Courante D'Articles De Periodiques Posterieurs a 1944 Sur les Problems Poliiques, Economiques, et Sociaux, Suppl 6, 2 vols. 1974. Set. lib. bdg. 225.00 (ISBN 0-8161-1171-5, Hall Library). G K Hall.

Fondation Nationale des Sciences Politiques. Bibliographie Courante d'Articles de Periodiques Posterieurs a 1944 sur les Problemes Politiques. Economiques et Sociaux, 17 Vols. 1968. Set. lib. bdg. 1680.00 (ISBN 0-8161-0769-6, Hall Library); first suppl., 1969, 2 vols. 225.00 (ISBN 0-8161-0803-X); second suppl., 1970, 2 vols. 225.00 (ISBN 0-8161-0917-6); third suppl., 1971, 2 vols. 225.00 (ISBN 0-8161-0981-8); fourth suppl., 1972, 2 vols. 225.00 (ISBN 0-8161-1056-5). G K Hall.

Fondation Nationale Des Sciences Politiques, Paris. Bibliographie Courante D'Articles De Periodiques Posterieurs a, 1944 Sur les Problems, Economiques et Sociaux, Fifth Supplement, 2 vols. 1345p. 1973. Set. lib. bdg. 225.00 (ISBN 0-8161-1122-7, Hall Library). G K Hall.

Fondation Nationale Des Sciences Politiques (Paris) Bibliographie Courante d'Articles de Periodiques Posterieurs a 1944 Sur les Problemes Politiques, Economiques et Sociaux: Seventh Supplement, 2 vols. 1976. Set. lib. bdg. 225.00 (ISBN 0-8161-0035-7, Hall Library). G K Hall.

Fondation Nationale Des Sciences Politiques. Index to Post-Nineteen Forty-Four Periodical Articles on Political, Economic & Social Problems, Supplement Eleven. 1981. lib. bdg. 290.00 (ISBN 0-8161-0357-7, Hall Library). G K Hall.

Fonderen, C. A. A Brief History of the Military Career of Carpenter's Battery from Its Organization As a Rifle Company under the Name of the Alleghany Roughs to the Ending of the War Between the States. 88p. 1911. Repr. of 1911 ed. 15.00 (ISBN 0-913419-02-8). Butternut Pr.

Fondiller, Harvey. The Best of Popular Photography. (Illus.). 432p. 1979. 29.95 (ISBN 0-87165-037-1, Amphoto). Watson-Guptill.

Fondiller, Harvey V., ed. Popular Photography Answer Book. 256p. 1980. 14.95 (ISBN 0-87165-039-8, Amphoto). Watson-Guptill.

Fondiller, Shirley H. The Entry Dilemma: The National League for Nursing & the Higher Education Movement, 1952-1972, with an Epilogue to 1983. 144p. 1983. 12.95 (ISBN 0-88737-261-9, 41-1896). Natl League Nurse.

Fondren. Mississippi Criminal Trial Practice. incl. latest pocket part supplement 59.95 (ISBN 0-686-90601-2); separate pocket part supplement, 1984 24.95 (ISBN 0-686-90602-0); Supplement 1984. 24.95. Harrison Co GA.

--Mississippi Criminal Trial Practice Forms. incl. latest pocket part supplement 59.95 (ISBN 0-686-90605-5); separate pocket part supplement, 1982 18.95 (ISBN 0-686-90606-3); Supplement 1982. 18.95. Harrison Co GA.

Fondren, Louis. Mississippi Civil Trial Practice Forms. LC 83-231747. xx, 349p. 1983. 54.95 (ISBN 0-317-01696-2). Harrison Co GA.

Fondu, M. Food Additives Tables, Pt. 2: Classes V-VIII. updated ed. (Vol. 1). 1983. 138.50 (ISBN 0-444-42069-X). Elsevier.

Fondu, M., ed. Lipids & Lipoproteins. (Journal: Nutrition & Metabolism: Vol. 24, Supplement 1). (Illus.). iv, 212p. 1980. 21.00 (ISBN 3-8055-1266-X). S Karger.

Fondu, M., et al, eds. Food Additive Tables III: Classes IX-XII, Vol. 1. rev. ed. 224p. 1985. 166.75 (ISBN 0-444-42286-2). Elsevier.

Fondu, M. H., et al, eds. Food Additives Tables, Pt. 1: Updated Edition, Classes I-IV. (Vol. 1). 162p. 1981. 117.00 (ISBN 0-444-41937-3). Elsevier.

Fondu, P. Haemostatic Failure in Liver Disease. (Developments in Hematology & Immunology Ser.). 1984. lib. bdg. 34.50 (ISBN 0-89838-640-3, Pub. by Martinus Nijhoff Netherlands). Kluwer Academic.

Fone, Byrne R., ed. The Gay Experience: Fiction & Non-Fiction from the Homosexual Tradition, 45 vols. Repr. of 1959 ed. write for info. (ISBN 0-404-61500-7). AMS Pr.

--Hidden Heritage: History & the Gay Imagination, an Anthology. 323p. 1979. 24.50 (ISBN 0-934200-00-9); pap. 12.95 (ISBN 0-8290-0401-7). Irvington.

Foner, Anne. Aging & Old Age: New Perspectives. 200p. 1986. text ed. 13.95 (ISBN 0-13-018656-2). P-H.

Foner, Anne & Schwab, Karen. Aging & Retirement. LC 80-24765. (Social Gerontology Ser.). 192p. (Orig.). 1981. pap. text ed. 9.00 pub net (ISBN 0-8185-0444-7). Brooks-Cole.

Foner, Anne, jt. auth. see Riley, Matilda W.

Foner, Eric. Free Soil, Free Labor, Free Men: The Ideology of the Republican Party Before the Civil War. 1970. pap. 8.95 (ISBN 0-19-501352-2, 342, GB). Oxford U Pr.

--Nothing But Freedom: Emancipation & Its Legacy. LC 83-7906. (Walter Lynwood Fleming Lectures in Southern History Ser.). 152p. 1983. 14.95 (ISBN 0-8071-1118-X); pap. 5.95x (ISBN 0-8071-1189-9). La State U Pr.

--Nothing But Freedom: Emancipation & Its Legacy. 142p. 1984. 14.95 (ISBN 0-8071-1118-X); pap. text ed. 5.95x (ISBN 0-8071-1189-9). La State U Pr.

--Politics & Ideology in the Age of the Civil War. LC 80-13024. 1980. 19.95x (ISBN 0-19-502781-7). Oxford U Pr.

--Politics & Ideology in the Age of the Civil War. 1980. pap. 8.95 (ISBN 0-19-502926-7, GB 646, GB). Oxford U Pr.

--Tom Paine & the American Revolution. LC 75-25456. (Illus.). 1976. pap. 8.95 (ISBN 0-19-502182-7). Oxford U Pr.

Foner, Eric, ed. see Clinton, Catherine.

Foner, Eric, ed. see Countryman, Edward.

Foner, Eric, ed. see Green, James R.

Foner, Eric, ed. see Kaestle, Carl.

Foner, Mathew, ed. see Kupferman, Theodore R.

Foner, Moe & Vassil, Pamela, eds. Images of Labor. LC 80-28820. (Illus.). 94p. 1981. pap. 16.95 (ISBN 0-8298-0452-8). Pilgrim NY.

Foner, Nancy. Ages in Conflict: A Cross-Cultural Perspective on Inequality Between Old & Young. Monk, Abraham, ed. LC 83-26157. (New Columbia Studies of Social Gerontology & Aging). 350p. 1984. 37.50x (ISBN 0-231-05696-6, King's Crown Paperbacks); pap. 17.50x (ISBN 0-231-05697-4). Columbia U Pr.

--Jamaica Farewell: Jamaican Migrants in London. LC 77-80471. 1978. 28.50x (ISBN 0-520-03544-5). U of Cal Pr.

--Status & Power in Rural Jamaica: A Study of Educational & Political Change. LC 72-5943. (Illus.). 1973. text ed. 11.50x (ISBN 0-8077-2366-5); pap. text ed. 7.95x (ISBN 0-8077-2408-4). Tchrs Coll.

Foner, Philip, ed. W. E. B. Du Bois Speaks, 2 vols. Incl. 1890-1919. Vol. 1. 24.00 (ISBN 0-87348-181-X); Vol. 1. pap. 7.95 (ISBN 0-87348-125-9); 1920-1963. 1970. Vol. 2. 24.00 (ISBN 0-87348-182-8); Vol. 2. pap. 7.95 (ISBN 0-87348-126-7). LC 78-108719. Set. 44.00 (ISBN 0-87348-351-0); Set. pap. 15.90 (ISBN 0-87348-262-X). Path Pr NY.

Foner, Philip, ed. see Marti, Jose.

Foner, Philip S. American Socialism & Black Americans: From the Age of Jackson to World War II. LC 77-71858. (Contributions in Afro-American & African Studies: No. 33). 1977. lib. bdg. 35.00 (ISBN 0-8371-9545-4, FAS/). Greenwood.

--Antonio Maceo: The "Bronze Titan" of Cuba's Struggle for Independence. LC 77-76163. 340p. 1978. 15.00 (ISBN 0-85345-423-X); pap. 5.95 (ISBN 0-85345-480-9). Monthly Rev.

--The Autobiographies of the Haymarket Martyrs. LC 77-85125. 1978. pap. 5.95 (ISBN 0-913460-58-3). Monad Pr.

--Blacks in the American Revolution. (Contributions in American History: No. 55). 224p. (Orig.). 1976. pap. text ed. 3.95 (ISBN 0-8371-8946-2, FBR/). Greenwood.

--British Labor & the American Civil War. LC 80-26162. 130p. 1981. text ed. 24.50x (ISBN 0-8419-0671-8). Holmes & Meier.

--Case of Joe Hill. LC 65-26742. (Illus.). 1965. pap. 2.75 (ISBN 0-7178-0022-9). Intl Pubs Co.

--Essays in Afro American History. LC 78-16944. 1978. 27.95 (ISBN 0-87722-140-5). Temple U Pr.

--First Facts of American Labor. LC 81-7074. 237p. 1984. 29.75x (ISBN 0-8419-0742-0). Holmes & Meier.

--Frederick Douglass on Women's Rights. LC 76-5326. (Contributions in Afro-American & African Studies: No. 25). (Orig.). 1976. lib. bdg. 29.95 (ISBN 0-8371-8895-4, FFD/). Greenwood.

--Great Labor Uprising of 1877. LC 77-80725. 1978. 23.00 (ISBN 0-913460-56-7); pap. 6.95 (ISBN 0-913460-57-5). Monad Pr.

--History of Black Americans: From Africa to the Emergence of the Cotton Kingdom, 4 vols, Vol. 1. LC 74-5987. (Contributions in American History Ser.: Vol. 1, No. 40). 680p. 1975. lib. bdg. 55.00 (ISBN 0-8371-7529-1, FBA/1). Greenwood.

--A History of Cuba & Its Relations with the United States, 2 vols. Incl. Vol. 1. 1492-1845, From the Conquest of Cuba to la Escalera. 255p. 1962. pap. 8.00 (ISBN 0-7178-0089-X); Vol. 2. 1845-1895, From the Annexationist Era to the Second War for Independence. 384p. 1963 (ISBN 0-7178-0090-3). Intl Pubs Co.

--History of the Labor Movement in the U.S. 1985-1986, Vol. 7. 1986. write for info. (ISBN 0-7178-0637-5); pap. write for info. (ISBN 0-7178-0627-8). Intl Pubs Co.

--History of the Labor Movement in the United States, 6 vols. Incl. Vol. 1. From Colonial Times to the Founding of the American Federation of Labor. 576p. 1947. 19.00 (ISBN 0-7178-0091-1); pap. 6.95 (ISBN 0-7178-0376-7); Vol. 2. From the Founding of the American Federation of Labor to the Emergence of American Imperialism. 480p. 1955. 19.00 (ISBN 0-7178-0092-X); pap. 4.95 (ISBN 0-7178-0388-0); Vol. 3. The Policies & Practices of the A.F.of L., 1900-1909. 480p. 1964. 19.00 (ISBN 0-7178-0093-8); pap. 4.95 (ISBN 0-7178-0389-9); Vol. 4. The Industrial Workers of the World. 608p. 1965. 19.00 (ISBN 0-7178-0094-6); pap. 4.95 (ISBN 0-7178-0396-1); Vol. 5. The AFL in the Progressive Era, Nineteen Hundred Ten - Nineteen Hundred Thirteen. 300p. 1979. 19.00 (ISBN 0-7178-0570-0); pap. 4.95 (ISBN 0-7178-0562-X); Vol. 6. On the Eve of America's Entrance into World War I, 1915-1916. 300p. 1982. 19.00 (ISBN 0-7178-0602-2); pap. 5.75 (ISBN 0-7178-0595-6). LC 47-19381. pap. Intl Pubs Co.

--Mark Twain: Social Critic. LC 58-11505. 335p. 1972. pap. 2.25 (ISBN 0-7178-0356-2). Intl Pubs Co.

--Organized Labor & the Black Worker, 1619-1981. 504p. (Orig.). 1982. 17.00 (ISBN 0-7178-0601-4); pap. 6.50 (ISBN 0-7178-0594-8). Intl Pubs Co.

--The Social Writings of Jack London. new ed. 1984. pap. 8.95 (ISBN 0-8065-0886-8). Citadel Pr.

--The Spanish-Cuban-American War & the Birth of American Imperialism, 1895-1902, 2 vols. Incl. LC 79-187595. 386p. 1973. Set. 22.50 (ISBN 0-85345-229-6). Monthly Rev.

--U. S. Labor in Latin America: A History of Workers' Response to Intervention. 304p. (Orig.). 1985. 25.95 (ISBN 0-89935-050-X); pap. 9.95 (ISBN 0-89935-049-6). Synthesis Pubns.

--Women & the American Labor Movement: From Colonial Times to the Eve of World War I. LC 79-63035. 1979. 29.95 (ISBN 0-02-910370-3). Free Pr.

--Women & the American Labor Movement: From the First Trade Unions to the Present. 1982. pap. 15.95x (ISBN 0-317-30519-0). Free Pr.

--Women & the American Labor Movement: From World War I to the Present. LC 80-753. (Illus.). 1980. 29.95 (ISBN 0-02-910380-0); pap. 15.95 2 vol. abbreviated edition (ISBN 0-02-910470-X). Free Pr.

--The Workingmen's Party of the United States. LC 83-26553. (Studies in Marxism: Vol. 14). 148p. 1984. 19.95x (ISBN 0-930656-35-0); pap. 6.95 (ISBN 0-930656-36-9). MEP Pubns.

Foner, Philip S. & Pacheco, Josephine F. Three Who Dared: Prudence Crandall, Margaret Douglass, Myrtilla Miner-Champions of Antebellum Black Education. LC 83-12830. (Contributions in Women's Studies: No. 47). xviii, 234p. 1984. lib. bdg. 29.95 (ISBN 0-313-23584-8, FTH/). Greenwood.

Foner, Philip S., ed. American Labor Songs of the Nineteenth Century. LC 74-20968. (Music in American Life Ser.). (Illus.). 373p. 1975. 22.50x (ISBN 0-252-00187-7). U of Ill Pr.

--Black Socialist Preacher: The Teachings of Rev. George Washington Woodbey & His Disciple Reverened George W. Slater, Jr. LC 83-17927. 363p. (Orig.). 1983. 19.95 (ISBN 0-89935-026-7); pap. 8.95 (ISBN 0-89935-025-9). Synthesis Pubns.

--The Black Worker: The Era of Post-War Prosperity & the Great Depression, 1920 to 1936, Vol. VI. Lewis, Ronald L. 632p. 1981. 39.95 (ISBN 0-87722-196-0). Temple U Pr.

--Black Worker: The Era of the AFL, the Railroad Brotherhood & the UMW, 1880-1903, Vol. IV. Lewis, Ronald L. LC 78-2875. 416p. 1979. 39.95 (ISBN 0-87722-139-1). Temple U Pr.

--The Democratic-Republican Societies, 1790-1800: A Documentary Sourcebook. LC 76-5260. (Orig.). 1976. lib. bdg. 39.95 (ISBN 0-8371-8907-1, FLT/). Greenwood.

--The Factory Girls: A Collection of Writings on Life & Struggles in the New England Factories of the 1840s. LC 77-22410. 387p. 1977. 22.50x (ISBN 0-252-00422-1). U of Ill Pr.

--Fellow Workers & Friends: I.W.W. Free-Speech Fights As Told by Participants. LC 80-23621. (Contributions in American History Ser.: No. 92). 224p. 1981. lib. bdg. 29.95 (ISBN 0-313-20660-0, FFW/). Greenwood.

--Karl Marx Remembered: Comments at the Time of His Death. 2nd. rev. ed. 304p. (Orig.). 1983. pap. 9.95 (ISBN 0-89935-020-8, 83-346). Synthesis Pubns.

--Life & Major Writings of Thomas Paine. 689p. 1974. pap. 6.95 (ISBN 0-8065-0414-5). Citadel Pr.

--Paul Robeson Speaks. (Illus.). 625p. 1982. pap. 9.95 (ISBN 0-8065-0815-9). Citadel Pr.

--Paul Robeson Speaks: Writing, Speeches, Interviews 1918-1974. LC 78-17590. (Illus.). 1978. 27.50 (ISBN 0-87630-179-0). Brunner-Mazel.

--We, the Other People: Alternative Declarations of Independence, by Labor Groups, Farmers, Woman's Rights Advocates, Socialists, & Blacks, 1829-1975. LC 76-10736. 224p. 1976. 19.95x (ISBN 0-252-00623-2); pap. 4.95x (ISBN 0-252-00624-0). U of Ill Pr.

--Wilhelm Liebknecht: Letters to the Chicago Workingmen's Advocate (1870-1871) 190p. 1983. text ed. 32.50x (ISBN 0-8419-0743-9). Holmes & Meier.

Foner, Philip S. & Chamberlin, Brewster, eds. Friedrich A. Sorge's Labor Movement in the United States: A History of the American Working Class from Colonial Times to 1890. LC 76-15319. (Illus.). 1977. lib. bdg. 35.00 (ISBN 0-8371-9028-2, FLM/). Greenwood.

Foner, Philip S. & Lewis, Ronald L., eds. The Black Worker: A Documentary History from Colonial Times to the Present: The Black Worker from the Founding of the CIO to the AFL-CIO Merger, 1937-1955, Vol. VII. 1983. 39.95 (ISBN 0-87722-197-9). Temple U Pr.

--The Black Worker: A Documentary History from Colonial Times to the Present: The Black Worker Since the AFL-CIO Merger, 1955-1980, Vol. VIII. 400p. 1984. 39.95 (ISBN 0-87722-198-7). Temple U Pr.

--The Black Worker: From Colonial Times to 1869, Vol. 1. LC 78-2875. 432p. 1979. 39.95 (ISBN 0-87722-136-7). Temple U Pr.

--The Black Worker: From Nineteen Hundred to Nineteen Nineteen, Vol. V. 450p. 1980. 39.95 (ISBN 0-87722-184-7). Temple U Pr.

--Black Worker: The Era of the Knights of Labor, Vol. III. LC 78-2875. 416p. 1979. 39.95 (ISBN 0-87722-138-3). Temple U Pr.

--The Black Worker: The Era of the National Labor Union, Vol. II. LC 78-2875. 416p. 1980. 39.95 (ISBN 0-87722-137-5). Temple U Pr.

Foner, Philip S. & Miller, Sally M., eds. Kate Richards O'Hare: Selected Writings & Speeches. LC 81-15667. 372p. 1982. text ed. 35.00x (ISBN 0-8071-0988-6); pap. text ed. 9.95x (ISBN 0-8071-1010-8). La State U Pr.

Foner, Philip S. & Walker, George E., eds. Black National & State Conventions, 1865-1900: Proceedings, Vol. 1. 400p. 1985. 39.95 (ISBN 0-87722-324-6). Temple U Pr.

--Proceedings of the Black National & State Conventions, 1865-1900. 400p. 1985. text ed. 39.95 (ISBN 0-87722-324-6). Temple U Pr.

--Proceedings of the Black State Conventions, Eighteen Forty to Eighteen Sixty-Five, 2 vols. 39.95 ea.; Vol. 1, 1979, 387p. (ISBN 0-87722-145-6); Vol. 2, 1980, 336p. (ISBN 0-87722-149-9). Temple U Pr.

Foner, Philip S. & Winchester, Richard C., eds. The Anti-Imperialist Reader: A Documentary History of Anti-Imperialism in the United States, Vol. 1: From the Mexican War to the Election of 1900. 520p. 1984. 42.50x (ISBN 0-8419-0768-4). Holmes & Meier.

Foner, Philip S., ed. see Brawley, Benjamin.

Foner, Philip S., ed. see Douglass, Frederick.

Foner, Philip S., ed. see Marti, Jose.

Foner, Philip S., ed. see Mother Jones.

Foner, Philip S., ed. see Zetkin, Clara.

Foner, Philip S., et al, eds. The Black Worker: The Black Worker Since the AFL-CIO Merger, 1955-1980, Vol. VIII. 1985. 39.95 (ISBN 0-317-30217-5). Temple U Pr.

Foner, Phillip S. History of Black Americans: From the Compromise of 1850 to the End of the Civil War, Vol. III. LC 82-11702. (Contributions in American History Ser.: No. 103). viii, 539p. 1983. lib. bdg. 39.95 (ISBN 0-8371-7967-X, FBA/3). Greenwood.

--History of Black Americans: From the Emergence of the Cotton Kingdom to the Eve of the Compromise of 1850, Vol II. LC 74-5987. (Contributions in American History Ser.: No. 102). viii, 656p. 1983. lib. bdg. 45.00 (ISBN 0-8371-7966-1, FBA/2). Greenwood.

--Labor & the American Revolution. LC 76-18034. 1976. lib. bdg. 29.95 (ISBN 0-8371-9003-7, FLA/). Greenwood.

Foner, S. Magnetism: Selected Topics. LC 72-121047. 768p. 1976. 180.50 (ISBN 0-677-15390-2). Gordon.

Foner, S. & Schwartz, B., eds. Superconducting Machines & Devices: Large Systems Applications. LC 74-624. (NATO ASI Series B, Physics: Vol. 1). 692p. 1974. 89.50x (ISBN 0-306-35701-1, Plenum Pr). Plenum Pub.

Foner, Simon & Schwartz, Brian B., eds. Superconductor Materials Science: Metallurgy, Fabrication, & Applications. LC 81-8669. (NATO ASI Series: Series B: Physics: Vol. 68). 1000p. 1981. 135.00x (ISBN 0-306-40750-7, Plenum Pr). Plenum Pub.

Foner, Simon, jt. ed. see Schwartz, Brian B.

Fonfrias, Ernesto J. Puerto Rican Danza, with an Essay on la Borinquena. (Puerto Rico Ser.). 1979. lib. bdg. 59.95 (ISBN 0-8490-2988-0). Gordon Pr.

Fong, Caroline K. Y., ed. see Hsiung, G. D.

Fong, Chan O. Technological Leap: Malaysian Industry in Transition. (Illus.). 250p. 1985. pap. 16.95x (ISBN 0-19-582615-9). Oxford U Pr.

Fong, Donna. The Coaches Collection of Field Hockey Drills. LC 81-86506. (Illus.). 100p. 1982. pap. 7.95 (ISBN 0-88011-040-6). Leisure Pr.

Fong, Elizabeth, jt. auth. see Ferris, Elvira.

Fong, F. K., ed. Light Reaction Path of Photosynthesis. (Molecular Biology, Biochemistry & Biophysics Ser.: Vol. 35). (Illus.). 350p. 1982. 66.00 (ISBN 0-387-11379-7). Springer-Verlag.

--Radiationless Processes in Molecules & Crystals. (Topics in Applied Physics: Vol. 15). (Illus.). 1976. 61.00 (ISBN 0-387-07830-4). Springer-Verlag.

Fong, Francis K. Theory of Molecular Relaxation: Applications in Chemistry & Biology. LC 75-17814. (Illus.). pap. 83.00 (ISBN 0-317-09104-2, 2017400). Bks Demand UMI.

Fong, H. D. Terminal Marketing of Tientsin Cotton: An Analysis of the Accounts of the Principal Chinese Banks, 1932-1934. Myers, Ramon H., ed. LC 80-8821. (China During the Interregnum 1911-1949, The Economy & Society Ser.). 142p. 1982. lib. bdg. 24.00 (ISBN 0-8240-4676-5). Garland Pub.

Fong, H. Gifford & Fabozzi, Frank J. Fixed Income Portfolio Management. LC 84-71127. 400p. 1984. 37.50 (ISBN 0-87094-245-X). Dow Jones-Irwin.

Fong, J. T., ed. Inservice Data Reporting & Analysis: PVP-Vol. 35, Vol. 11. 236p. 1979. 30.00 (ISBN 0-317-33550-2, H00149); members 15.00 (ISBN 0-317-33551-0). ASME.

Fong, J. T. & Tashjian, B. J., eds. Inservice Data Reporting & Analysis, PVP-PB-32. (Pressure Vessel & Piping Division Ser.). 1978. 30.00 (ISBN 0-685-66802-9, H00137). ASME.

Fong, J. T., et al, eds. Critical Issues in Materials & Mechanical Engineering. (PVP Ser.: Vol. 47). 276p. 1981. 40.00 (ISBN 0-686-34517-7, H00183). ASME.

Fong, L. Power Training in Kung-Fu & Karate. 9.50x (ISBN 0-685-63773-5). Wehman.

Fong, L. T. Sil Lum Kung-Fu. 8.95x (ISBN 0-685-38451-9). Wehman.

Fong, Leo. Aggressive Defensive Fighting. Date not set. pap. 5.95 (ISBN 0-86635-014-4). Koinonia Prods.

--Combat Kung-Fu: Streetfighting Art. Date not set. pap. 5.95 (ISBN 0-86635-003-9). Koinonia Prods.

--Hitting Without Getting Hit. Date not set. pap. 5.95 (ISBN 0-86635-015-2). Koinonia Prods.

--Iron Palm-Open Hand Fighting. Date not set. pap. 5.95 (ISBN 0-86635-002-0). Koinonia Prods.

--Kung Fu Free Fighting Technique. Date not set. pap. 5.95 (ISBN 0-86635-007-1). Koinonia Prods.

--Modified Wing Chun: Sticking Techniques, Vol. 3. Date not set. pap. 5.95 (ISBN 0-86635-012-8). Koinonia Prods.

--Modified Wing Chun: Trapping Hands, Vol. 2. Date not set. pap. 5.95 (ISBN 0-86635-010-1). Koinonia Prods.

--Modified Wing Chun, Vol. 1: Basic Techniques. Date not set. pap. 5.95 (ISBN 0-86635-009-8). Koinonia Prods.

--Offensive Fighting. Date not set. pap. 5.95 (ISBN 0-86635-013-6). Koinonia Prods.

--Power Kicking. Date not set. pap. 5.95 (ISBN 0-86635-004-7). Koinonia Prods.

--Strategies for Winning in Kung Fu. Date not set. pap. 5.95 (ISBN 0-86635-001-2). Koinonia Prods.

--The Theory & Practice of Knockout Punching. Date not set. pap. 5.95 (ISBN 0-86635-000-4). Koinonia Prods.

--Tiger Claw Training & Techniques. Date not set. pap. 5.95 (ISBN 0-86635-006-3). Koinonia Prods.

--Wei Kuen Do: The Psychodynamic Art of Free Fighting. Date not set. pap. 5.95 (ISBN 0-86635-005-5). Koinonia Prods.

--Winning by Deception. Date not set. pap. 5.95 (ISBN 0-86635-016-0). Koinonia Prods.

Fong, Leo, jt. auth. see Marchini, Ron.

Fong, Leo T. Choy Lay Fut Kung-Fu. Alston, Pat, ed. LC 70-181999. (Ser. 307). (Illus.). 1972. pap. text ed. 9.95 (ISBN 0-89750-035-0). Ohara Pubns.

--Sil Lum Kung-Fu: The Chinese Art of Self Defense. Alston, Pat, ed. LC 76-157045. (Ser. 304). (Illus.). 1971. pap. text ed. 8.95 (ISBN 0-89750-032-6). Ohara Pubns.

Fong, Mak Lau see Mak Lau Fong.

Fong, Pang E., jt. auth. see Lim, Linda.

Fong, Paul, ed. see Brauer, Richard.

Fong, Peter. Physical Science, Energy & Our Environment. (Illus.). text ed. write for info. (ISBN 0-02-338660-6). Macmillan.

--Statistical Theory of Nuclear Fission. (Documents on Modern Physics Ser.). 228p. (Orig.). 1969. 69.50 (ISBN 0-677-01850-9). Gordon.

Fong, Wen. Returning Home: Tao-Chi's Album of Landscapes & Flowers. LC 76-15911. (Illus.). 1982. 15.00 (ISBN 0-8076-1040-2). Braziller.

Fong, Wen, ed. The Great Bronze Age of China. (Illus.). 1980. 40.00 (ISBN 0-394-51256-1). Knopf.

--The Great Bronze Age of China: An Exhibition from the People's Republic of China. (Illus.). xviii, 404p. 1980. 9.50 (ISBN 0-87099-226-0). Metro Mus Art.

Fong, Wen, intro. by see Fong Wen.

Fong, Wen C. Images of the Mind: Selections from the Edward L. Elliott Family & John B. Elliott Collections of Chinese Calligraphy. LC 83-43056. (The Art Museum Ser.). (Illus.). 400p. 1984. text ed. 65.00x (ISBN 0-691-04027-3). Princeton U Pr.

Fong-Torres, Ben, ed. Rolling Stone Interviews: 1967-1980. (Illus.). 400p. 1981. 24.95 (ISBN 0-312-68954-3); pap. 12.95 (ISBN 0-312-68955-1). St Martin.

Fong Wen, tr. from Chinese. Returning Home: Tao-Chi's Album of Landscapes and Flowers. Fong, Wen, intro. by. LC 76-15911. (Illus.). 92p. 1976. slipcase 25.00 (ISBN 0-8076-0827-0). Braziller.

Fonkalsrud, Alfred O. The Scandinavian-American. 13.00 (ISBN 0-88247-026-4). R & E Pubs.

Fonkalsrud, E. W. Undescended Testes. 1980. 41.95 (ISBN 0-8151-3257-3). Year Bk Med.

Fonken, G. & Johnson, R. Chemical Oxidations with Microorganisms. (Oxidation in Organic Chemistry Ser.: Vol. 2). 1972. 75.00 (ISBN 0-8247-1211-0). Dekker.

Fonnum, Frade, ed. Amino Acids As Chemical Transmitters. LC 78-2362. (NATO ASI A, Life Sciences: Vol. 16). 759p. 1978. 75.00x (ISBN 0-306-35616-3, Plenum Pr). Plenum Pub.

Fonosch, Gail & Kvitka, Elaine. Meal Management Concepts. 1978. text ed. 20.50 scp (ISBN 0-06-453520-7, HarpC); scp instructor's manual 1.50 (ISBN 0-06-453523-1). Har-Row.

Fons, Marianne & Porter, Liz. Classic Quilted Vests. 48p. 1982. pap. 9.00 (ISBN 0-932946-07-0). Yours Truly.

Fons, Marianne, jt. auth. see Porter, Liz.

Fonseca, A. J., ed. The Marxian Dilemma: Transformation of Values to Prices. 1980. 10.00x (ISBN 0-8364-0654-0, Pub. by Manohar India). South Asia Bks.

Fonseca, F. Peixoto Da see Da Fonseca, F. Peixoto.

Fonseca, Jaime M. Communication Policies in Costa Rica. (Communication Policy Studies). 89p. 1977. pap. 6.25 (ISBN 92-3-101348-3, U80, UNESCO). Unipub.

Fonseca, John R. Consumer Credit Compliance Manual. 2nd ed. LC 84-81909. 1984. 69.50. Lawyers Co-Op.

Fonseca, John R., jt. auth. see Squillante, Alphonse M.

Fonseca, John R., jt. auth. see Woodroof, M. G., 3rd.

Fonseca, Mabel. Sox & the Teenager. 3rd ed. 1983. pap. 5.95x (ISBN 0-7069-2434-7, Pub. by Vikas India). Advent NY.

Fonsecae, Petri. Commentariorvm in Metaphysicorvm Aristotelis Stagiritae Libros. 1978. Repr. of 1964 ed. 200.00 (ISBN 0-8492-4600-8). R West.

Fonstad, Karen W. Atlas of Middle-Earth. 224p. 1981. 18.95 (ISBN 0-395-28665-4). HM.

--The Atlas of Pern. LC 84-6511. (Orig.). 1984. 19.95 (ISBN 0-345-31432-8, Del Rey); pap. 9.95 (Del Rey). Ballantine.

--The Atlas of the Land. 1985. 19.95 (ISBN 0-345-31431-X, Del Ray); pap. 9.95 (ISBN 0-345-31433-6, Del Ray). Ballantine.

Fontain, Jan. Masterpieces From the Boston Museum. (Illus.). 112p. 1981. 29.95 (ISBN 0-87846-202-3); pap. 19.95 (ISBN 0-87846-201-5). Mus Fine Arts Boston.

Fontaine & Bourgoignie. Consumer Legislation in Belgium & Luxemburg. 1982. 42.50 (ISBN 0-442-30418-8). Van Nos Reinhold.

Fontaine, Arthur. French Industry During the War. (Economic & Social History of the World War Ser.). 1926. 75.00x (ISBN 0-317-27471-6). Elliots Bks.

Fontaine, Carol R. Traditional Sayings in the Old Testament: A Contextual Study. (Bible & Literature Ser.: No. 5). 1982. text ed. 24.95x (ISBN 0-907459-08-0, Pub. by Almond Pr England); pap. text ed. 14.95x (ISBN 0-907459-09-9, Pub. by Almond Pr England). Eisenbrauns.

Fontaine, Claude, jt. auth. see Fourastie, Jean.

Fontaine, Elizabeth L. Reading Aloud to Your Child. LC 84-60976. 125p. (Orig.). 1985. pap. text ed. 5.50 (ISBN 0-88247-732-3). R & E Pubs.

Fontaine, J. R. Le see Le Fontaine, J. R.

Fontaine, Jacob, III & Burd, Gene. Jacob Fontaine: From Slavery to the Greatness of the Pulpit, Press, & Public Service. 96p. 1984. 6.95 (ISBN 0-89015-438-4). Eakin Pubns.

Fontaine, Jan. The Spaghetti Tree. (Illus.). (gr. k-4). 1979. pap. 1.50 (ISBN 0-934926-00-X). Talespinner.

Fontaine, Jean de la. Fables de-la Fontaine. Marsh, Edward, tr. from Fr. LC 81-67110. (Illus.). 36p. 1981. 45.00 (ISBN 0-940032-00-7). Alphabet MA.

Fontaine, Jean De La see De La Fontaine, Jean.

Fontaine, Jean de la see La Fontaine, Jean de.

Fontaine, Jean de La Fontaine see De La Fontaine, Jean & Calder, Alexander.

Fontaine, Jean La see La Fontaine, Jean.

Fontaine, John. Journal of John Fontaine: An Irish Huguenot Son in Spain & Virginia, 1710-1719. Alexander, Edward P., ed. LC 74-165362. (Colonial Williamsburg Eyewitness to History Ser.). (Illus.). pap. 39.00 (ISBN 0-8357-9806-2, 2017256). Bks Demand UMI.

Fontaine, Maurice. Physiologie. (Methodique Ser.). 1956p. 52.50 (ISBN 0-686-56432-4). French & Eur.

Fontaine, Patrick. Little Talks About Life. 1956. 4.50 (ISBN 0-8198-0082-1). Dghtrs St Paul.

Fontaine, Paul. Proficiency in Counterpoint: A College Worktext. LC 67-13407. (Illus., Orig.). 1967. pap. text ed. 16.95x (ISBN 0-89197-360-5). Irvington.

Fontaine, Pierre-Michel, jt. ed. see Alpers, Edward A.

Fontaine, Roger W. Brazil & the United States. 1974. pap. 5.25 (ISBN 0-8447-3145-5). Am Enterprise.

--On Negotiating with Cuba. LC 75-39898. 1975. pap. 4.25 (ISBN 0-8447-3191-9). Am Enterprise.

Fontaine, Thomas D., III & Bartell, Steven M., eds. Dynamics of Lotic Ecosystems. LC 82-48641. (Illus.). 450p. 1983. 34.95 (ISBN 0-250-40612-8). Butterworth.

Fontaine, William T. Reflections on Segregation, Desegregation, Power & Morals. 176p. 1967. 17.75x (ISBN 0-398-00593-1). C C Thomas.

Fontainerie, Francois De La see La Fontainerie.

Fontaines, Una Des see Des Fontaines, Una.

Fontana, Andrea. The Last Frontier: The Social Meaning of Growing Old. LC 77-23186. (Sage Library of Social Researc: Vol. 42). 1977. 24.00 (ISBN 0-8039-0832-6); pap. 12.00 (ISBN 0-8039-0833-4). Sage.

Fontana, Andrea, jt. auth. see Smith, Ronald W.

Fontana, Andrea, jt. ed. see Kotarba, Joseph A.

Fontana, Bernard, intro. by see Russell, Frank.

Fontana, Bernard L. Of Earth & Little Rain: The Papago Indians. (Illus.). 145p. 1981. 27.50 (ISBN 0-87358-287-X). Northland.

Fontana, Bernard L., jt. ed. see Matson, Daniel S.

Fontana, D. C. The Questor Tapes. 1976. Repr. of 1974 ed. lib. bdg. 13.95x (ISBN 0-88411-091-5, Pub. by Aeonian Pr). Amereon Ltd.

Fontana, David. Behaviorism & Learning Theory in Education. (British Journal of Educational Psychology Monograph). 208p. 1985. 20.00x (ISBN 0-7073-0391-5, Pub. by Scottish Academic Pr Scotland). Columbia U Pr.

--Psychology for Teachers. (Psychology for Professional Groups Ser.). 350p. 1981. text ed. 23.75x (ISBN 0-333-31858-7, Pub. by Macmillan England); pap. text ed. 9.75x (ISBN 0-333-31880-3). Humanities.

Fontana, David, ed. The Education of the Young Child. 2nd ed. 300p. 1984. 34.95x (ISBN 0-631-13584-7); pap. 9.95x (ISBN 0-631-13585-5). Basil Blackwell.

Fontana, Frank. Patchwork Quilt Designs for Needlepoint. (Needlework Ser.). (Illus.). 40p. 1976. pap. 2.25 (ISBN 0-486-23300-6). Dover.

Fontana, Frank, jt. auth. see Drayton, Grace.

Fontana, Frank, jt. auth. see Gross, Nancy D.

Fontana, John M. Mankind's Greatest Invention. LC 64-5232. 112p. 1964. 4.95 (ISBN 0-9600034-1-X). J M Fontana.

--Thank Gutenberg for Shakespeare & Ben Franklin. 24p. 1964. pap. 1.25 (ISBN 0-685-26780-6). J M Fontana.

Fontana, Luke. Save the Wetlands. (Illus.). 1982. 14.00 (ISBN 0-942494-20-2). Coleman Pub.

Fontana, M. G. & Staehle, R. W., eds. Advances in Corrosion Science & Technology. Incl. Vol. 1. 384p. 1970 (ISBN 0-306-39501-0); Vol. 2. 354p. 1972 (ISBN 0-306-39502-9); Vol. 3. 431p. 1973 (ISBN 0-306-39503-7); Vol. 4. 340p. 1974 (ISBN 0-306-39504-5); Vol. 5. 407p. 1976 (ISBN 0-306-39505-3); Vol. 6. 277p. 1976 (ISBN 0-306-39506-1); Vol. 7. 375p. 1980 (ISBN 0-306-39507-X). LC 76-107531. (Illus.). each 59.50 (Plenum Pr). Plenum Pub.

Fontana, M. P., jt. auth. see Farge, Y.

Fontana, Marjorie A. & Larson, Jean L. Cup of Fortune. LC 78-67289. (Illus.). 61p. (Orig.). 1979. pap. 3.95 (ISBN 0-9603596-2-1). Fontastic.

--Say Cheese & Milk Please. LC 78-67289. (Illus.). 62p. (Orig.). 1978. 7.95 (ISBN 0-9603596-0-5); pap. 5.95 (ISBN 0-9603596-1-3). Fontastic.

Fontana, Mars G. & Greene, Norbert D. Corrosion Engineering. 2nd ed. (Materials Sciences & Engineering). (Illus.). 1978. text ed. 48.00 (ISBN 0-07-021461-1). McGraw.

Fontana, Peter. Atomic Radiative Processes. (Pure & Applied Physics Ser.). 1982. 35.00 (ISBN 0-12-262020-8). Acad Pr.

Fontana, Vincent J. Somewhere a Child Is Crying: Maltreatment-Causes & Prevention. 1976. pap. 4.50 (ISBN 0-451-62429-7, ME2196, Ment). NAL.

Fontana, Vincent J. & Besharov, Douglas J. Maltreated Child: The Maltreatment Syndrome in Children - A Medical, Legal & Social Guide. 4th ed. (Illus.). 192p. 1979. 17.50x (ISBN 0-398-03904-6). C C Thomas.

Fontana, Vincent J., et al, eds. Asthma: Current Studies in Therapy. 1978. 29.00x (ISBN 0-8422-7289-5). Irvington.

Fontanay, Elisabeth de see De Fontenay, Elisabeth.

Fontane, Theodor. Before the Storm. Hollingdale, R. J., ed. (The World's Classics (Paperback)). 560p. 1985. pap. 6.95 (ISBN 0-19-281649-7). Oxford U Pr.

--Effi Briest. Parmee, Douglas, tr. (Classics Ser.). 1976. pap. 3.95 (ISBN 0-14-044190-5). Penguin.

--Effi Briest. abr. ed. Cooper, W. A., tr. LC 66-25107. pap. 5.95 (ISBN 0-8044-6156-2). Ungar.

--Jenny Treibel. Zimmermann, Ulf, tr. from Ger. LC 76-15648. 1977. pap. 4.95 (ISBN 0-8044-6154-6). Ungar.

--A Man of Honor. Valk, E. M., tr. LC 74-78439. 206p. 1975. 12.50 (ISBN 0-8044-2207-9); pap. 4.95 (ISBN 0-8044-6155-4). Ungar.

--Short Novels & Other Writings. Demetz, Peter, ed. LC 81-17505. (The German Library: Vol. 46). 326p. 1982. 19.50x (ISBN 0-8264-0250-X); pap. 8.95 (ISBN 0-8264-0260-7). Continuum.

Fontane, Theodor, tr. The Women Taken in Adultery & The Poggenpuhl Family. LC 78-31371. 1979. lib. bdg. 15.00x (ISBN 0-226-25680-4). U of Chicago Pr.

Fontannza, Luciennec & Wilson, Barbara K. The Willow Pattern Story. (Illus.). 1984. 10.95 (ISBN 0-207-13848-6, Pub. by Salem Hse Ltd). Merrimack Pub Cir.

Fontanosa, Napoleon E., II. Shoes Story. 32p. 1984. 5.95 (ISBN 0-89962-373-5). Todd & Honeywell.

Fontbrune, Jean-Charles de. Nostradamus: Countdown to Apocalypse. 512p. 1983. 18.95 (ISBN 0-03-064177-2). HR&W.

Fontein, J. Pilgrimage of Sudhana. 1967. text ed. 35.60x (ISBN 90-2796-387-8). Mouton.

Fontenay, Charles L. Epistle to the Babylonians: An Essay on the Natural Inequality of Man. LC 68-9778. pap. 55.80 (ISBN 0-317-29312-5, 2022214). Bks Demand UMI.

--Estes Kefauver: A Biography. LC 79-28299. (Illus.). 440p. 1980. 24.50x (ISBN 0-87049-262-4). U of Tenn Pr.

--The Keyen of Fu Tze: The Wise Sayings of Confucious. 1977. 5.95 (ISBN 0-900306-50-5, Pub. by Coombe Springs Pr). Claymont Comm.

Fonteneau, M. & Theureau, S. Mon Premier Larousse en couleurs. (Illus., Fr.). 28.95 (3795). Larousse.

Fonteneau, M., et al. Larousse English-French, French-English Dictionary for Beginners. (Illus.). 352p. 1984. 9.95 (ISBN 0-88332-351-6, 3789). Larousse.

Fonteneau, Marthe. Mon Larousse en Images. (Illus.). 17.25 (ISBN 0-686-65648-2, 3796). Larousse.

Fonteneau, Marthe, et al. Larousse English-French, French-English Dictionary: Bilingual Dictionary for the Beginner. (Illus.). 352p. 1984. 9.95 (ISBN 0-88332-351-6). Larousse.

Fontenelle, Don H. How to Live with Your Children: A Guide for Parents Using a Positive Approach to Child Behavior. LC 80-21261. 264p. 1981. pap. 9.95 (ISBN 0-930256-07-7). Almar.

--Understanding & Managing Overactive Children: A Guide for Parents & Teachers. 200p. 1983. 13.95 (ISBN 0-13-936765-9); pap. 6.95 (ISBN 0-13-936757-8). P-H.

Fontenelle, Don, 2nd, jt. auth. see Collins, Mallary M.

Fontenelle, Maurice De see De Fontenelle, Maurice.

Fontenelle Bernard Le, Bovier De see Le Bovier De Fontenelle, Bernard.

Fontenilles, Alfred & Heimerdinger, Mark C. Le Francais des Affaires. 1981. pap. text ed. write for info. (ISBN 0-02-338700-9). Macmillan.

Fontenilles, Alfred & Marambaud, Pierre. Dictionnaire des Oeuvres et des Themes de la Litterature Americane. 282p. (Fr.). 1976. pap. 8.95 (ISBN 0-686-56854-0, M-6632). French & Eur.

Fontenot, Chester, jt. auth. see Wexlmann, Joe.

Fontenot, Mary A. Clovis Crawfish & Etienne Escargot. 32p. (gr. k-6). 1982. 10.95 (ISBN 0-88289-368-8). Pelican.

--Clovis Crawfish & His Friends. 1962. 4.95 (ISBN 0-87511-045-2). Claitors.

--Clovis Crawfish & His Friends. rev. ed. (Clovis Crawfish Ser.). (Illus.). 32p. (gr. k-6). Date not set. write for info. (ISBN 0-88289-479-X). Pelican.

--Clovis Crawfish & Michelle Mantis. 4.95 (ISBN 0-87511-050-9). Claitors.

--Clovis Crawfish & Petit Papillon. (Illus.). 52p. (gr. k-5). 1985. Repr. 10.95 (ISBN 0-88289-448-X). Pelican.

--Clovis Crawfish & the Big Betail. 1963. 4.95 (ISBN 0-87511-046-0). Claitors.

--Clovis Crawfish & the Orphan Zozo. LC 81-17740. (Clovis Crawfish Ser.). (Illus.). 32p. (gr. k-2). 1983. 10.95 (ISBN 0-88289-312-2). Pelican.

--Clovis Crawfish & the Singing Cigales. LC 81-5608. 32p. 1981. 10.95 (ISBN 0-88289-270-3). Pelican.

--Ghost of Bayou Tigre. 1965. 4.95 (ISBN 0-87511-051-7). Claitors.

Fontenrose, Joseph. The Delphic Oracle: Its Responses & Operations. LC 76-47969. 1978. pap. 10.95 (ISBN 0-520-04359-6, CAL 490). U of Cal Pr.

--Python. 1959. 25.00x (ISBN 0-8196-0285-X). Biblo.

--Python: A Study of Delphic Myth & Its Origins. 637p. 1981. 34.00x (ISBN 0-520-04106-2); pap. 8.95 (ISBN 0-520-04091-0, CAL 449). U of Cal Pr.

Fontes, J. C., jt. auth. see Fritz, P.

Fontes, M. E. Existentialism & Its Implications for Counseling. pap. 0.75 (ISBN 0-8199-0382-5, L38138). Franciscan Herald.

Fontes, Marthe S. Collection de Fil en Images. Incl. Cherchez-Moi (ISBN 2-03-652151-7, 2921); A Cause D'une Goutte D'Eau (ISBN 2-03-652152-5, 2920); Ensemble a la Noce (ISBN 2-03-652154-1, 2923); De Deux Choses L'une (ISBN 2-03-652155-X, 2922); Le Long Voyage D'une Lettre (2924); La Bouilloire a un Secret (ISBN 2-03-652158-4, 2919). (Fr.). 1984. 6.95 ea. Larousse.

Fontes, Norman E., jt. auth. see Miller, Gerald R.

Fontet, M. & Mehlhorn, K., eds. STACS 84: Symposium of Theoretical Aspects of Computer Science Paris, April 11-13, 1984. (Lecture Notes in Computers Science: Vol. 166). vi, 338p. (Eng. & Fr.). 1984. pap. 18.00 (ISBN 0-387-12920-0). Springer Verlag.

Fonteyn, Margot. The Magic of Dance. LC 79-2221. (Illus.). 1982. 22.95 (ISBN 0-394-52906-5). Knopf.

--Margot Fonteyn: Autobiography. (Illus.). 1976. 16.95 (ISBN 0-394-48570-X). Knopf.

--Pavlova: Self-Portrait of a Dancer. LC 83-40658. (Illus.). 160p. 1984. 25.00 (ISBN 0-670-54394-2). Viking.

Fontgalland, Bernard De see De Fontgalland, Bernard.

Fontham, M. R. Written & Oral Advocacy. (General Practice Library). 462p. 1985. 75.00 (ISBN 0-471-87119-2); pap. 25.00 (ISBN 0-471-87121-4). Wiley.

Fontijn, A., ed. Gas-Phase Chemiluminescence & Chemi-Ionization. 370p. 1985. 40.75 (ISBN 0-444-86950-6, North-Holland). Elsevier.

Fontijn, A. & Clyne, M. A., eds. Reactions of Small Transient Species, Kinetics & Energetics. 1984. 89.00 (ISBN 0-12-262040-2). Acad Pr.

Fontoura, Marco. The Real Chant of the Rolling Wheels. Leach, Jennifer & Reyes, Fred, eds. Orig. Title: Canto real das Rodas Rolantes. (Illus.). 168p. (Orig.). 1985. 10.95 (ISBN 0-934169-01-2); pap. 5.95 (ISBN 0-934169-00-4). Rolling Hse.

Fonts, Alfredo R. Histology & Embryology Notes for Dental Assistants & Dental Hygienists. 1980. pap. text ed. 8.50 (ISBN 0-89669-029-6). Collegium Bk Pubs.

Fonvizin, Dennis. Political Writings. Gleason, Walter, tr. from Rus. 170p. 1985. 22.50 (ISBN 0-88233-799-8). Ardis Pubs.

Fonvizin, I. The Minor. Harrison, W., ed. (Library of Russian Classics). 168p. pap. text ed. 9.95x (ISBN 0-900186-51-8). Basil Blackwell.

Fonyam, John, ed. see Kopf, Ebs Dumm.

Food & Agricultural Organization. Food Aid in Figures: December, 1983. 91p. (Orig.). 1984. pap. 7.50 (ISBN 92-5-101499-X, F2588, FAo). Unipub.

Food & Agriculture Organization. Drought in the Sahel: International Relief Operations, 1973-1975. 48p. 1976. pap. 7.50 (ISBN 0-685-66344-2, F751, FAO). Unipub.

--Soil Map of the World: Europe, Vol. 5. 199p. 1981. pap. 22.00 (ISBN 0-686-83161-6, M134, UNESCO). Unipub.

Food & Agriculture Organization of the United Nations. Per Capita Fibre Consumption 1967-1969: Cotton, Wool, Flax, Silk & Man-Made Fibres. Incl. Per Capita Fibre Consumption 1970-1972: Cotton, Wool, Flax, & Man-Made Fibres. Food & Agriculture Organization of the United Nations. pap. 15.50 (F1188); Per Capita Fibre Consumption 1971-1973: Cotton, Wool, Flax, Silk, & Man Made Fibre. 188p. 1975. pap. 16.25 (F1189); Per Capita Fibre Consumption 1973-1974: Cotton, Wool & Man-Made Fibres. 1977. pap. 8.25 (ISBN 92-5-000102-9, F1190). pap. 15.50 (F1187, FAO). Unipub.

Food & Agriculture Organization of the U.N., et al. Protection of the Public in the Event of Radiation Accidents: Proceedings. (Illus.). 370p. (Eng, Fr, & Rus.). 1965. 14.40 (ISBN 92-4-156025-8). World Health.

Food & Agriculture Organization of the United Nations. Sixteenth Regional Conference for Asia & the Pacific: Report, Jakarta, June 1-11, 1982. xiv, 56p. 1982. 7.50 (ISBN 92-5-101255-5, FAO). Unipub.

Food & Drug Administration. Animal Drugs Analytical Manual. Markus, John R. & Sherma, Joseph, eds. LC 85-9147. (Illus.). 350p. 1985. write for info. (ISBN 0-935584-30-7). Assoc Official.

--FDA Device Inspections Manual. Hadley, Richard D., ed. 141p. 1983. pap. text ed. 27.00 (ISBN 0-914176-21-8). Wash Busn Info.

--FDA Executive Information Manual. Hadley, Richard D., ed. 294p. 1982. pap. text ed. 35.00 (ISBN 0-914176-19-6). Wash Busn Info.

--FDA Inspections Operations Manual for Drugs, Devices, & Cosmetics. Hadley, Richard D., ed. 162p. 1983. pap. text ed. 39.00 (ISBN 0-914176-22-6). Wash Busn Info.

--Macroanalytical Procedures Manual. rev. ed. (FDA Technical Bulletin Ser.: No. 5). (Illus.). 176p. 1984. three hole drill with binder 29.00 (ISBN 0-935584-28-5); foreign 30.50. Assoc Official.

Food & Drug Book Company. The Pill Book of High Blood Pressure. 208p. (Orig.). 1985. pap. 3.95 (ISBN 0-553-24489-2). Bantam.

Food & Drug Book Company, Inc. The Pill Book of Arthritis. 208p. (Orig.). 1985. pap. 3.95 (ISBN 0-553-24626-7). Bantam.

Food & Nutrition Board. Folic Acid: Biochemistry & Physiology in Relation to the Human Nutrition Requirement. LC 77-8182. 1977. 14.50 (ISBN 0-309-02605-9). Natl Acad Pr.

--Food Chemicals Codex. 3rd ed. (Illus.). 768p. 1981. 50.00 (ISBN 0-309-03090-0). Natl Acad Pr.

--Human Vitamin B-Six Requirements. 1978. pap. 14.75 (ISBN 0-309-02642-3). Natl Acad Pr.

--Laboratory Indices of Nutritional Status in Pregnancy. 1978. pap. 10.75 (ISBN 0-309-02729-2). Natl Acad Pr.

--Nutrition and Fertility Interrelationships. 1975. pap. 5.95 (ISBN 0-309-02341-6). Natl Acad Pr.

--Radionuclides in Foods. 2nd rev. ed. LC 62-60075. (Illus.). 104p. 1973. pap. 6.75 (ISBN 0-309-02113-8). Natl Acad Pr.

--Recommended Dietary Allowances: Ninth Edition. (Illus.). 1980. pap. 8.50 (ISBN 0-309-02941-4). Natl Acad Pr.

--Toxicants Occurring Naturally in Foods. rev. 2nd ed. (Illus.). 704p. 1973. 19.25 (ISBN 0-309-02117-0). Natl Acad Pr.

Food & Nutrition Board - Division of Biology & Agriculture. Maternal Nutrition & the Course of Pregnancy. LC 72-605179. (Illus., Orig.). 1970. pap. text ed. 9.95 (ISBN 0-309-01761-0). Natl Acad Pr.

Food & Nutrition Board, National Research Council. Prevention of Microbial & Parasitic Hazard Associated with Processed Foods: A Guide for the Food Processor. 1975. pap. 7.25 (ISBN 0-309-02345-9). Natl Acad Pr.

--A Selected Annotated Bibliography on Breast Feeding 1970-1977. 1978. pap. text ed. 7.95 (ISBN 0-309-02796-9). Natl Acad Pr.

Food & Nutrition Board, Natural Research Council, jt. auth. see Agricultural & Renewable Resources Board.

Food & Nutrition Group. Feed, Need, Greed. Tafler, Sue & Phillips, Connie, eds. (Illus.). 108p. (Orig.). 1980. pap. 5.00 (ISBN 0-9607314-0-7). Sci People.

Food & Wine, ed. Best of "Food & Wine". LC 84-12415. (Illus.). 240p. 1984. 19.95 (ISBN 0-385-19619-9). Doubleday.

Food Industry Instrumentation Symposium. Instrumentation in the Food Industry, Vol. 3: Proceedings of the 3rd Food Industry Instrumentation Symposium. 60p. pap. text ed. 15.00x (ISBN 0-87664-472-8). Instru Soc.

Food Processors Institute. The A-to-Z of Container Corrosion: Another Path to Productivity. 48p. 1982. pap. text ed. 15.00 (ISBN 0-937774-06-5). Food Processor.

--Canned Foods: Principles of Thermal Process Control, Acidification & Container Closure Evaluation. 4th, rev. ed. 256p. 1982. pap. 40.00 (ISBN 0-937774-07-3). Food Processors.

--Guide for Waste Management in the Food Processing Industry, 2 vols. Incl. Vol. I. Katsuyama, Allen M., ed. 276p (ISBN 0-937774-01-4); Vol. 2. 555p (ISBN 0-937774-00-6). LC 79-115086. 1979. Set. pap. text ed. 15.00. Food Processors.

--A New Market...Nutrition & Quality. 40p. (Orig.). 1983. pap. 15.00 (ISBN 0-937774-08-1). Food Processors.

--Principles of Food Processing Sanitation. Katsuyama, Allen, ed. LC 79-57624. 303p. (Orig.). 1980. pap. 40.00 (ISBN 0-937774-03-0). Food Processors.

--Proceedings: Quality (Concepts) from Start to Finish. 39p. (Orig.). 1984. pap. 10.00 (ISBN 0-937774-10-3). Food Processors.

--Shelf Life: A Key to Sharpening Your Competitive Edge; Proceedings. 64p. (Orig.). 1981. pap. 10.00 (ISBN 0-937774-05-7). Food Processors.

Food Processors Institute Staff. Capitalizing on Aseptic. 96p. (Orig.). 1984. pap. 50.00 (ISBN 0-937774-09-X). Food Processors.

Food Products & Drink Industries, Second Tripartite Technical Meeting, Geneva, 1978. Appropriate Technology for Employment Creation in the Food Processing & Drink Industries of Developing Countries: Report III. 88p. 1978. 8.55 (ISBN 92-2-101880-6, FAD/2/III). Intl Labour Office.

Food Safety Council, Columbia, U. S. A., ed. Proposed System for Food Safety Assessment: A Comprehensive Report on the Issues of Food Ingredient Testing. new ed. LC 78-40901. (Illus.). 1979. 25.00 (ISBN 0-08-023752-5). Pergamon.

Food Staff of the Los Angeles Times. The Los Angeles Times California Cookbook. (Illus.). 400p. 1981. 25.00 (ISBN 0-8109-1277-5). Abrams.

Fooden, Myra & Gordon, Susan, eds. Genes & Gender Four: The Second X & Women's Health. LC 83-5552. 203p. 1983. pap. text ed. 8.95 (ISBN 0-87752-223-5). Gordian.

Fookes, P. G. & Vaughan, P. R., eds. A Handbook of Engineering Geomorphology. (Illus.). 320p. 1985. 66.00 (ISBN 0-412-00591-3, 9022, Pub by Chapman & Hall). Methuen Inc.

Fookes, P. J. & Collis, L. Concrete in the Middle East, Pt. I. 1982. pap. 5.00x (ISBN 0-86310-001-5). Scholium Intl.

Fookes, P. J. & Pollock, D. J. Concrete in the Middle East, Pt. II. 1982. pap. 19.75x (ISBN 0-86310-007-4). Scholium Intl.

Foon, Chew S. & MacDougall, John A. Forever Plural: The Perception & Practice of Inter-Communal Marriage in Singapore. LC 77-620031. (Papers in International Studies: Southeast Asia Ser.: No. 45). (Illus.). 1977. pap. 6.00x (ISBN 0-89680-030-X, 82-90462, Ohio U Ctr Intl). Ohio U Pr.

Foonberg, Jay. How to Start & Build A Law Practice. 272p. pap. 14.95 (ISBN 0-89707-130-1). Chicago Review.

Foonberg, Jay G. How to Start & Build a Law Practice. 2nd ed. LC 83-734564. (Economics of Law Practice Section & Law Student Division). 256p. 1984. pap. text ed. 14.95x (ISBN 0-89707-130-1, 527-0080); sect. or div members 9.95. Amer Bar Assn.

Foont, Ronnie, jt. auth. see Kustanowitz, Shulamit.

Foord, Archibald S. His Majesty's Opposition, Seventeen Fourteen to Eighteen Thirty. LC 79-14245. 1979. Repr. of 1964 ed. lib. bdg. 42.50x (ISBN 0-313-21974-5, FOHM). Greenwood.

Foord, H. The Carboniferous Cephalopoda of Ireland, Vols. 55, 57, Nos. 259, 269. Repr. of 1901 ed. 25.00 ea. Johnson Repr.

Foord, J. Decorative Plant & Flower Studies. 1983. 13.75 (ISBN 0-8446-5956-8). Peter Smith.

--Decorative Plant & Flower Studies for Artists & Craftsmen. (Illus.). 144p. 1982. pap. 5.50 (ISBN 0-486-24276-5). Dover.

Foorman, Barbara R. & Siegel, Alexander W., eds. Learning to Read: Cognitive Universals & Cultural Constraints. 192p. 1985. text ed. 22.50. L Erlbaum Assocs.

Foorman, V. Olympic Stamps. 195p. 1981. 5.95 (ISBN 0-8285-2514-5, Pub. by Progress Pubs USSR). Imported Pubns.

Foos, Anya. One Soul, Rising. LC 76-29097. (Illus., Orig.). 1976. pap. 4.95 (ISBN 0-685-84856-6). Thadian Pubns.

--Slycleaver. LC 74-33966. 1975. 9.95 (ISBN 0-685-84857-4). Thadian Pubns.

Foose, Sandra L. More Scrap Savers Stitchery. LC 80-2740. 1981. 14.95 (ISBN 0-385-17526-4). Doubleday.

Foose, Sandy. Scrap Saver's Stitchery Book: A Farm Journal Book. (Illus.). 1978. 14.95 (ISBN 0-385-13437-1). Doubleday.

Foos-Graber, Anya. Deathing: An Intelligent Alternative for the Final Moments of Life. 1984. 16.95 (ISBN 0-201-11388-0, 1630); pap. 9.95 (ISBN 0-201-11389-9, 957). Addison-Wesley.

Fooshee, George, Jr. You Can Be Financially Free. (Illus.). 128p. 1977. pap. 4.95 (ISBN 0-8007-5000-4, Power Bks). Revell.

Fooshee, George, Jr. & Fooshee, Marjean. You Can Beat the Money Squeeze. 176p. pap. 4.95 (ISBN 0-8007-5030-6). Revell.

Fooshee, Marjean, jt. auth. see Fooshee, George, Jr.

Foot, D. K. Provincial Public Finance in Ontario: An Empirical Analysis of the Last Twenty-Five Years. (Ontario Economic Council Research Studies). 1977. 8.50 (ISBN 0-8020-3350-4). U of Toronto Pr.

Foot, David. Harold Gimblett: Tormented Genius of Cricket. (Illus.). 192p. (Orig.). 1982. 19.95 (ISBN 0-434-26820-8, Pub. by W Heinemann Ltd). David & Charles.

--Operational Urban Models. (Illus.). 1982. 27.00x (ISBN 0-416-73320-4, NO. 3531); pap. 12.95x (ISBN 0-416-73330-1, NO. 3532). Methuen Inc.

Foot, David, jt. auth. see Richards, Viv.

Foot, David K. Public Employment & Compensation in Canada: Myths & Realities. 188p. 1978. pap. text ed. 10.95x (ISBN 0-409-88600-9, Pub. by Inst Res Pub Canada). Brookfield Pub Co.

--Public Employment in Canada: Statistical Series. 217p. 1979. pap. text ed. 15.00x (ISBN 0-409-88603-3, Pub. by Inst Res Pub Canada). Brookfield Pub Co.

Foot, Hugh, et al, eds. Road Safety: Research & Practice. LC 81-191962. 244p. 1981. 38.95 (ISBN 0-03-060054-5). Praeger.

Foot, Hugh C., et al, eds. Friendship & Social Relations in Children. LC 79-40637. 396p. 1980. 69.95x (ISBN 0-471-27628-6, Pub. by Wiley-Interscience). Wiley.

Foot, Isaac. John Milton, Selections from His Works & Tributes to His Genius. 151p. 1982. Repr. of 1935 ed. lib. bdg. 65.00 (ISBN 0-89987-279-4). Darby Bks.

Foot, M. R. Resistance: European Resistance to Nazism 1940-45. LC 76-49521. 360p. 1977. 15.00 (ISBN 0-07-021475-1). McGraw.

--S.O.E. in France: An Account of the Work of the British Special Operations Executive in France, 1940-1944. 596p. 1984. 29.50x (ISBN 0-89093-594-7). U Pubns Amer.

Foot, M. R. & Langley, J. M. MI Nine: Escape & Evasion, 1939-1945. (Illus.). 384p. 1980. 13.95 (ISBN 0-316-28840-3). Little.

Foot, M. R., ed. see Gladstone, William E.

Foot, Michael. Debts of Honour: Profiles in Autobiography. LC 81-47227. 240p. 1981. 13.95i (ISBN 0-06-039001-8, HarpT). Har-Row.

Foot, Mirjam M. The Henry Davis Gift: A Collection of Bookbindings. (Studies in the History of Bookbindings: Vol. 1). 352p. 1980. 250.00x (ISBN 0-7141-0391-8, Pub. by Brit Lib England). State Mutual Bk.

--The Henry Davis Gift: A Collection of Bookbindings, Vol. I: Studies in the History of Bookbinding. 2nd ed. 352p. 1979. lib. bdg. 120.00 (ISBN 0-904654-72-9, Pub. by British Lib). Longwood Pub Group.

--The Henry Davis Gift: A Collection of Bookbindings, Vol. 2: British, German & Dutch Bindings. (Illus.). 446p. 1983. lib. bdg. 150.00 (ISBN 0-904654-73-7, Pub. by British Lib). Longwood Pub Group.

Foot, Philippa, ed. Theories of Ethics. (Oxford Readings in Philosophy Ser.). 1967. pap. 8.95x (ISBN 0-19-875005-6). Oxford U Pr.

Foot, Philippa R. Virtues & Vices & Other Essays in Moral Philosophy. LC 78-54794. 1979. 28.50x (ISBN 0-520-03686-7); pap. 5.95 (ISBN 0-520-04396-0). U of Cal Pr.

Foot, Rosemary. The Wrong War: American Policy & the Dimensions of the Korean Conflict, 1950-1953. LC 84-29305. (Cornell Studies in Security Affairs). 296p. 1985. text ed. 29.95x (ISBN 0-8014-1800-3). Cornell U Pr.

Foote, jt. auth. see Oxorn, Harry.

Foote, ed. Thesaurus of Entomology. 1977. 15.00 (ISBN 0-686-22689-5); members 9.00. Entomol Soc.

Foote, A. Edward. Chotankers: A Family History. LC 82-6989. 336p. 1982. 19.95 (ISBN 0-943054-13-3). Thornwood Bk.

Foote, Andrea & Erfurt, John C. Cost Effectiveness of Occupational Employee Assistance Programs: Test of an Evaluation Method. 110p. 1978. 7.00 (ISBN 0-87736-328-5). U of Mich Inst Labor.

--Occupational Employee Assistance Programs for Substance Abuse & Mental Health Problems. 1977. pap. 7.00x (ISBN 0-87736-327-7). U of Mich Inst Labor.

Foote, Andrea, jt. auth. see Erfurt, John C.

Foote, Andrea E. & Erfurt, John C. Development & Dissemination of Model Systems for Hypertension Control in Organizational Settings. 1974. 3.50x (ISBN 0-87736-322-6). U of Mich Inst Labor.

Foote, Andrew H. Africa & the American Flag. (Illus.). 390p. 1970. Repr. of 1854 ed. 19.95x (ISBN 0-8464-0121-5). Beekman Pubs.

--Africa & the American Flag. LC 71-82050. Repr. of 1854 ed. cancelled (ISBN 0-8371-1543-4, FOA&, Pub. by Negro U Pr). Greenwood.

Foote, Arthur. Arthur Foote, 1853-1937: An Autobiography. LC 78-2021. (Music Reprint Ser.,1978). (Illus.). 1978. Repr. of 1946 ed. lib. bdg. 29.50 (ISBN 0-306-77531-X). Da Capo.

--Quintet for Piano & Strings in A Minor,(Opus 38) (Earlier American Music Ser.: No.26). 108p. 1983. Repr. of 1898 ed. lib. bdg. 22.50 (ISBN 0-306-76145-9). Da Capo.

--Suite in E Major, op.63 & Serenade in E Major, op.25. (Earlier American Music Ser.: No.24). 65p. 1983. Repr. of 1909 ed. lib. bdg. 18.50 (ISBN 0-306-76091-6). Da Capo.

Foote, Arthur W. Modulation & Related Harmonic Questions. LC 78-98. (Illus.). 1978. Repr. of 1919 ed. lib. bdg. 22.50x (ISBN 0-313-20301-6, FOMR). Greenwood.

Foote, Arthur W. & Spalding, Walter R. Foote & Spalding: Harmony. LC 78-176. 1978. Repr. of 1969 ed. lib. bdg. 25.75x (ISBN 0-313-20265-6, FOHA). Greenwood.

Foote, Caleb & Levy, Robert J. Criminal Law: Cases & Materials. 950p. 1981. text ed. 32.00 (ISBN 0-316-28853-5). Little.

Foote, Caleb & Meyer, Henry. The Culture of the University: Governance & Education. LC 68-54947. (Jossey-Bass Higher Education Ser.). pap. 58.60 (ISBN 0-8357-9312-5, 2013793). Bks Demand UMI.

Foote, Caleb, et al. Cases & Materials on Family Law. 2nd ed. 1975. 29.95 (ISBN 0-316-28850-0); Supplement, 1980. pap. 7.95 1980 suppl. (ISBN 0-316-28852-7); Statutory Appendix. text ed. 5.50 (ISBN 0-316-28849-7). Little.

--Cases & Materials on Family Law. 3rd ed. LC 84-82456. 1985. text ed. write for info. (ISBN 0-316-28847-0); Statutory Supplement, 1985. text ed. write for info. (ISBN 0-316-28855-1). Little.

--Cases & Materials on Family Law: 1985 Statutory Supplement. 3rd ed. Date not set. pap. text ed. write for info. Little.

Foote, Carolyn. Carolyn Foote: Selected Poems. Wright, Judith, et al, eds. LC 84-71629. (Cold-Drill Bks.). 75p. (Orig.). 1984. pap. 6.95 (ISBN 0-916272-26-5, Pub. by Cold-drill Bks Boise State Univ). Ahsahta Pr.

Foote, Don C., et al. St. Paul Community Study: An Economic & Social Analysis of St. Paul, Pribilof Islands, Alaska. (Joint Institute of Social & Economic Research Ser.: No. 18). (Illus.). 188p. 1968. pap. 5.00x (ISBN 0-295-95115-X). U of Wash Pr.

Foote, Evelyn C. Time with God: Devotional Readings for Youth. LC 72-97604. 1978. pap. 2.75 (ISBN 0-8054-5164-1, 4251-64). Broadman.

Foote, Evelyn Carter. A Very Special Spring. LC 81-67749. (YA) (gr. 7-12). 1982. pap. 3.95 (ISBN 0-8054-7317-3). Broadman.

Foote, G. W. & Ball, W. P. The Bible Handbook. 362p. 1983. pap. 6.95 (ISBN 0-910309-10-8). Am Atheist.

Foote, G. W. & Ball, W. P., eds. Bible Handbook. 11th ed. 196p. 1985. pap. 10.00 (ISBN 0-89005-535-1). Ares.

--The Bible Handbook: For Freethinkers & Inquiring Christians. 11th ed. LC 71-161330. (Atheist Viewpoint Ser). 176p. 1972. Repr. of 1961 ed. 20.00 (ISBN 0-405-03797-X). Ayer Co Pubs.

Foote, G. W. & Wheeler, J. M., eds. The Jewish Life of Christ: Being Sepher Toldoth Jeshu. (Illus.). 49p. 1982. pap. 3.00 (ISBN 0-910309-02-7). Am Atheist.

Foote, Geoffrey. The Labour Party's Political Thought: A History. LC 85-4151. 384p. 1985. 43.00 (ISBN 0-7099-1075-4, Pub. by Croom Helm Ltd). Longwood Pub Group.

Foote, Henry S. Casket of Reminiscences. LC 68-58057. Repr. of 1874 ed. 21.50x (ISBN 0-8371-0421-1, FOR&, Pub. by Negro U Pr). Greenwood.

Foote, Henry W. John Smilbert, Painter. LC 78-87537. (Library of American Art Ser). 1969. Repr. of 1930 ed. lib. bdg. 32.50 (ISBN 0-306-71453-1). Da Capo.

--Robert Feke, Colonial Portrait Painter. LC 72-75357. (Library of American Art Ser). 1969. Repr. of 1950 ed. lib. bdg. 32.50 (ISBN 0-306-71319-5). Da Capo.

Foote, Henry W., jt. auth. see Clarke, Herman F.

Foote, Horton. Courtship. 1984. pap. 3.35x (ISBN 0-317-17212-3). Dramatists Play.

Foote, Horton & Faulkner, William. Three Plays. 145p. Date not set. pap. 1.45 (ISBN 0-15-691275-9). HarBraceJ.

Foote, I. P. & Fennell, J. L., eds. Oxford Slavonic Papers: New Series, Vol. 15. 1982. 39.50x (ISBN 0-19-815658-8). Oxford U Pr.

Foote, John A. & Mersky, Roy M., eds. Pie Powder by a Circuit Tramp. (Classics in Legal History Reprint Ser.: Vol. 1). 216p. 1967. Repr. of 1911 ed. lib. bdg. 30.00 (ISBN 0-89941-000-6). W S Hein.

Foote, John P. Schools of Cincinnati & Its Vicinity. LC 75-112545. (Rise of Urban America). (Illus.). 1970. Repr. of 1855 ed. 15.00 (ISBN 0-405-02454-1). Ayer Co Pubs.

Foote, John T. The Look of Eagles. (Illus.). 14.95 (ISBN 0-85131-019-2, NL51, Dist. by Miller). J A Allen.

--Look of Eagles: Racing Story. 1970. 12.50x (ISBN 0-87556-090-3). Saifer.

--Sporting Days. LC 72-121544. (Short Story Index Reprint Ser). (Illus.). 1937. 14.50 (ISBN 0-8369-3500-4). Ayer Co Pubs.

Foote, Kenneth E. Color in Public Spaces: Toward a Communication-Based Theory of the Urban Built Environment. LC 83-5809. (Research Papers Ser.: No. 205). 1983. pap. 10.00 (ISBN 0-89065-111-6). U Chicago Dept Geog.

Foote, L. B., compiled by. Bibliography of the Official Publications of Louisana, 1803-1934. (Historical Records Survey Ser: No. 19). Repr. of 1942 ed. 37.00 (ISBN 0-527-01916-X). Kraus Repr.

Foote, Leonard E., jt. auth. see Duncan, Wilbur H.

Foote, Mary. Cup of Trembling & Other Stories. LC 74-110189. (Short Story Index Reprint Ser.). 1895. 18.00 (ISBN 0-8369-3340-0). Ayer Co Pubs.

--In Exile & Other Stories. 1972. Repr. of 1894 ed. lib. bdg. 18.25 (ISBN 0-8422-8045-6). Irvington.

Foote, Mary, pseud. A Touch of Sun: And Other Stories. LC 72-4422. (Short Story Index Reprint Ser.). Repr. of 1903 ed. 18.00 (ISBN 0-8369-4175-6). Ayer Co Pubs.

Foote, Mary. A Touch of Sun & Other Stories. 1972. Repr. of 1903 ed. lib. bdg. 17.00 (ISBN 0-8422-8046-4). Irvington.

Foote, Mary H. Coeur D'Alene. LC 74-22783. (Labor Movement in Fiction & Non-Fiction). Repr. of 1895 ed. 20.00 (ISBN 0-404-58430-6). AMS Pr.

--The Led-Horse Claim. LC 68-20012. (Americans in Fiction Ser.). 1979. lib. bdg. 19.50 (ISBN 0-8398-0559-4); pap. text ed. 7.95x (ISBN 0-8290-0135-2). Irvington.

--A Victorian Gentlewoman in the Far West: The Reminiscences of Mary Hallock Foote. Paul, Rodman, ed. LC 72-86535. (Illus.). 416p. 1980. pap. 7.00 (ISBN 0-87328-057-1). Huntington Lib.

--A Victorian Gentlewoman in the Far West: The Reminiscences of Mary Hallock Foote. Rodman, Paul, ed. LC 72-86535. (Illus.). 416p. 1983. pap. 10.00. Huntington Lib.

Foote, Nancy, et al. Drawings: The Pluralist Decade. LC 80-83653. (Illus.). 1979. pap. 12.00 (ISBN 0-88454-057-X). U of Pa Contemp Art.

Foote, Nelson N. & Cottrell, Leonard S., Jr. Identity & Interpersonal Competence: A New Direction in Family Research. LC 56-11957. 1955. 25.00x (ISBN 0-226-25685-5). U of Chicago Pr.

Foote, P. Aurvandilsta: Norse Studies. Barnes, M., et al, eds. (Viking Collection Ser.: Vol. 2). 311p. 1984. text ed. 45.50x (ISBN 87-7492-478-8, Pub. by Odense U Denmark). Humanities.

Foote, P. G., tr. see Winsnes, Andreas H.

Foote, Patricia. Girls Can Be Anything They Want. LC 79-24903. (Illus.). 96p. (gr. 5 up). 1980. PLB 9.29 (ISBN 0-671-33013-6). Messner.

Foote, Paul, tr. see Lermontov.

Foote, Paul, tr. see Tolstoy, Leo.

Foote, Peter G. & Wilson, David M. The Viking Achievement: The Society & Culture of Early Medieval Scandinavia. (The Great Civilization Ser.). (Illus.). 481p. (Orig.). 1983. pap. 12.95 (ISBN 0-283-97926-7, Pub. by Sidgwick & Jackson). Merrimack Pub Cir.

Foote, R. B. Prehistory & Protohistoric Antiquities of India. 1979. text ed. 23.00x (ISBN 0-391-01865-5). Humanities.

Foote, Rosslyn F. Running An Office for Fun & Profit: Business Techniques for Small Design Firms. LC 78-15912. (Illus.). 1978. 19.95 (ISBN 0-87933-317-0). Van Nos Reinhold.

Foote, Samuel. Dramatic Works of Samuel Foote, 2 Vols. LC 68-20223. 1968. 55.00 (ISBN 0-405-08523-0, Blom Pubns); 27.50. Vol. I (ISBN 0-405-08524-9). Ayer Co Pubs.

--A Treatise on the Passions, So Far As They Regard the Stage. LC 72-144608. Repr. of 1747 ed. 11.50 (ISBN 0-404-02448-3). AMS Pr.

Foote, Samuel & Murphy, Arthur. Plays. Taylor, George, ed. LC 83-18930. (British & American Playwrights Ser.). 220p. 1984. 44.50 (ISBN 0-521-24132-4); pap. 15.95 (ISBN 0-521-28467-8). Cambridge U Pr.

Foote, Shelby. The Civil War: A Narrative, 3 vols. Incl. Vol. 1. Fort Sumter to Perryville. 1958 (ISBN 0-394-41948-0); Vol. 2. Fredericksburg to Meridian. 1963 (ISBN 0-394-41951-0); Vol. 3. Red River to Appomattox. LC 58-988. (Illus.). 1974 (ISBN 0-394-46512-1). (Illus.). Set. 104.50 (ISBN 0-394-49517-9); 35.00 ea. Random.

--Follow Me Down. 1978. 10.95 (ISBN 0-394-40875-6). Random.

--Love in a Dry Season. 1979. 10.00 (ISBN 0-394-40877-2). Random.

--Shiloh. 1985. 16.95 (ISBN 0-8488-0158-X, Pub. by J M C & Co). Amereon Ltd.

Foote, Ted. Jewelry Making: A Guide for Beginners. LC 80-67547. (Illus.). 112p. 1981. 16.95 (ISBN 0-87192-130-8). Davis Mass.

Foote, Timothy. The Great Ringtail Garbage Caper. (Illus.). 80p. (gr. 3-6). 1980. 5.95 (ISBN 0-395-28759-6). HM.

--The Great Ringtail Garbage Caper. (Illus.). (gr. 4-6). 1983. pap. 1.95 (ISBN 0-590-32121-8, Apple Paperbacks). Scholastic Inc.

--World of Bruegel. LC 68-31677. (Library of Art Ser.). (Illus.). (gr. 7 up). 1968. 19.94 (ISBN 0-8094-0275-0, Pub. by Time-Life). Silver.

Foote, Victoria. Snow Princess. (Tapestry Romance Ser.). (Orig.). 1983. pap. 2.75 (ISBN 0-671-49333-7). PB.

Foote, Warren E., jt. auth. see Pedde, Lawrence D.

Foote, Wilder, jt. ed. see Cordier, Andrew W.

Foote, William H. Sketches of North Carolina. 3rd ed. 593p. 1965. 12.00. Synod NC Church.

Foote, Y., et al. CARES: Criterion Arithmetic Remediation & Enrichment System. Kit. 82.50 (ISBN 0-87879-121-3). Acad Therapy.

Foote-Smith, Elizabeth. Opportunities in Writing Careers. (VGM Career Bks.). (Illus.). 160p. 1983. 7.95 (ISBN 0-8442-6348-6, 6348-6, Passport Bks.); pap. 5.95 (ISBN 0-8442-6349-4, 6349-4). Natl Textbk.

Footman, D. Antonin Besse of Aden. 256p. 1985. text ed. 36.50x (ISBN 0-333-38508-X, Pub by MacMillan England). Humanities.

Footman, David. The Alexander Conspiracy: A Life of A. I. Zhelybov. LC 74-57. Orig. Title: Red Prelude. (Illus.). 370p. 1974. Repr. of 1944 ed. 19.95 (ISBN 0-912050-47-0, Library Pr). Open Court.

--Red Prelude: The Life of the Russian Terrorist Zhelyabov. LC 78-14119. (Illus.). 1980. Repr. of 1945 ed. 24.00 (ISBN 0-88355-792-4). Hyperion Conn.

Footner, Hulbert. Rivers of the Eastern Shore. (Illus.). 381p. 1979. Repr. of 1944 ed. 14.95 (ISBN 0-87033-092-6). Tidewater.

Foott, Bethia. Dismissal of a Premier: The Philip Game Papers. 17.50x (ISBN 0-392-02674-0, ABC). Sportshelf.

Foppl, August. Drang und Zwang: Eine Hoehere Festigkeitslehre Fuer Ingeneure, 3 Vols. LC 69-20268. (Ger). 1969. Repr. of 1941 ed. Set. 70.00 (ISBN 0-384-16275-4). Johnson Repr.

Foquette, M. J., Jr., jt. auth. see Duellman, William E.

Foraker, Alvan G., jt. auth. see Anderson, A. E., Jr.

Foraker, Joseph W. What You Should Know about Earthquakes: It Could Save Your Life. (Illus.). 64p. (Orig.). 1983. pap. 5.95 (ISBN 0-912287-00-4). SJB Pub Co.

Foraker, Julia B. I Would Live It Again: Memories of a Vivid Life. facsimile ed. LC 75-1848. (Leisure Class in America Ser.). (Illus.). 1975. Repr. of 1932 ed. 24.50 (ISBN 0-405-06915-4). Ayer Co Pubs.

Foran, Heather M., jt. auth. see Foran, Max.

Foran, Mary, tr. see Aletrino, L.

Foran, Max & Foran, Heather M. Calgary: Canada's Frontier Metropolis. (Illus.). 368p. 1982. 29.95 (ISBN 0-89781-055-4). Windsor Pubns Inc.

Foran, Thomas J. Puerto Rico: Pupil's Edition. LC 76-40992. (gr. k-3). 1976. pap. text ed. 5.64 (ISBN 0-07-021477-8). McGraw.

Foran, William L. The Golfer's Diary: Tips, Log, Statistics. (Illus.). 72p. (Orig.). 1983. pap. 2.95 (ISBN 0-912941-01-4). Foran Pubn.

Forastiere, Arlene A., ed. Gynecologic Cancer. (Contemporary Issues in Clinical Oncology Ser.: Vol. 2). (Illus.). 312p. 1984. text ed. 38.00 (ISBN 0-443-08274-X). Churchill.

Forastieri-Braschi, Eduardo & Guiness, Gerald. On Text & Context: Methodological Approaches to the Context of Literature. LC 79-18001. 1980. pap. 12.00 (ISBN 0-8477-3194-4). U of PR Pr.

Foray, Cyril P. Historical Dictionary of Sierra Leone. LC 77-3645. (African Historical Dictionaries Ser.: No. 12). 336p. 1977. 25.00 (ISBN 0-8108-1035-2). Scarecrow.

Forbes, jt. auth. see Harris.

Forbes, A. Dean, jt. auth. see Andersen, Francis I.

Forbes, Adrienne & Debease, Gloria. Regents Competency Tests. LC 80-14348. 250p. (Orig.). 1980. pap. 6.95 (ISBN 0-668-04815-8, 4815-8). Arco.

Forbes, Alec. The Bristol Detox Diet for Cancer Patients. LC 84-52563. 196p. Date not set. pap. 3.95 (ISBN 0-87983-419-6). Keats.

--Try Being Healthy. 184p. 1976. pap. 5.50x (ISBN 0-8464-1057-5). Beekman Pubs.

--Try Being Healthy. 1980. 15.00x (ISBN 0-85032-140-9, Pub. by Daniel Co England). State Mutual Bk.

Forbes, Alexander. California: A History of Upper & Lower California. LC 72-9443. (The Far Western Frontier Ser.). (Illus.). 384p. 1973. Repr. of 1839 ed. 24.50 (ISBN 0-405-04972-2). Ayer Co Pubs.

Forbes, Allan. The Boston French. (Illus.). 1976. Repr. 7.50 (ISBN 0-686-20855-2). Polyanthos.

Forbes, Andrew D. W. Warlords & Muslims in Chinese Central Asia: A Political History of Republican Sinkiang, 1911-1949. 220p. Date not set. price not set. (ISBN 0-521-25514-7). Cambridge U Pr.

Forbes, Andrew F., jt. auth. see Bartholomew, David J.

Forbes, Archibald. Life of Napoleon the Third. LC 70-112802. 1970. Repr. of 1898 ed. 24.50x (ISBN 0-8046-1068-1, Pub. by Kennikat). Assoc Faculty Pr.

Forbes, Bertie C. Men Who Are Making the West. LC 72-330. (Essay Index Reprint Ser.). Repr. of 1923 ed. 24.50 (ISBN 0-8369-2793-1). Ayer Co Pubs.

Forbes, Bertie C. & Foster, Orline D. Automotive Giants of America: Men Who Are Making Our Motor Industry. LC 72-5603. (Essay Index Reprint Ser.). 1972. Repr. of 1926 ed. 19.00 (ISBN 0-8369-2989-6). Ayer Co Pubs.

Forbes, Brian. The Rewrite Man. 320p. 1985. 16.95 (ISBN 0-671-50610-2). S&S.

Forbes, Bryan. That Despicable Race: The History of the British Acting Tradition. (Illus.). 326p. 1981. 29.95 (ISBN 0-241-10164-6, Pub. by Hamish Hamilton England). David & Charles.

Forbes, C. D. Unresolved Problems in Haemophilia. (Illus.). 245p. 1981. text ed. 29.95 (ISBN 0-85200-388-9, Pub. by MTP Pr England). Kluwer Academic.

Forbes, Calvin. Blue Monday. LC 73-15011. (Wesleyan Poetry Program: Vol. 70). 1974. pap. 6.95 (ISBN 0-8195-1070-X). Wesleyan U Pr.

--From the Book of Shine. (Burning Deck Poetry Ser.). 1979. pap. 10.00 signed ed. (ISBN 0-930900-70-7). Burning Deck.

Forbes, Charles D., jt. ed. see Ratnoff, Oscar D.

Forbes, Charles G. Aviation Gasoline Production & Control. (USAF Historical Studies: No. 65). 95p. 1947. pap. text ed. 10.00x (ISBN 0-89126-146-X). MA-AH Pub.

Forbes, Cheryl. The Religion of Power. 176p. 1983. 9.95 (ISBN 0-310-45770-X). Zondervan.

Forbes, Christopher. Faberge Eggs: Imperial Russian Fantasies. (Illus., Orig.). 1980. pap. 12.95 (ISBN 0-8109-2227-4). Abrams.

Forbes, Christopher, ed. see Von Solodkoff, Alexander, et al.

Forbes, Clarence A. Greek Physical Education. LC 78-136383. 312p. Repr. of 1929 ed. 27.50 (ISBN 0-404-02449-1). AMS Pr.

Forbes, Clarence A., ed. The Teaching of Classical Subjects in English. 98p. (Gr., Lat., Eng.). 4.50 (ISBN 0-318-12463-7, B20). Amer Classical.

Forbes, Clarence A., ed. see Vida, Marco G.

Forbes, Colin. Avalanche Express. 1979. pap. 2.50 (ISBN 0-449-24252-8, Crest). Fawcett.

--Avalanche Express. LC 83-48948. 256p. 1984. pap. 2.84i (ISBN 0-06-080699-0, P 699, PL). Har-Row.

--The Leader & the Damned. LC 84-2883. 480p. 1984. 15.95 (ISBN 0-689-11469-9). Atheneum.

--The Stone Leopard. LC 84-48946. 256p. 1984. pap. 2.84i (ISBN 0-06-080700-8, P 700, PL). Har-Row.

--Terminal. LC 85-47601. 320p. 1985. 15.95 (ISBN 0-689-11589-X). Atheneum.

--Year of the Golden Ape. LC 83-48950. 320p. 1984. pap. 3.80i (ISBN 0-06-080701-6, P 701, PL). Har-Row.

Forbes, Colleen, ed. see Kelley, Bruce K. & Cundall, Alan W.

Forbes, D. Hume's Philosophical Politics. LC 75-9282. 400p. 1975. 54.50 (ISBN 0-521-20754-1). Cambridge U Pr.

Forbes, D., jt. auth. see Shumway, Nicholas.

Forbes, D., ed. see Hegel, Georg W.

Forbes, Dean K. The Geography of Underdevelopment. LC 84-47903. (Studies in Development). 224p. 1985. text ed. 22.50x (ISBN 0-8018-2526-1). Johns Hopkins.

Forbes, Dee, jt. auth. see Solie, Gordon.

Forbes, Duncan. August Autumn. 64p. 1984. 12.95 (ISBN 0-436-16138-9, Pub. by Secker & Warburg UK). David & Charles.

--Hume's Philosophical Politics. 350p. 1985. pap. 14.95 (ISBN 0-521-31997-8). Cambridge U Pr.

--Life Before Man: The Story of Fossils. LC 68-29359. (Junior Reference Bks). (Illus.). (gr. 6 up). 1967. 8.95 (ISBN 0-8023-1153-9). Dufour.

--The Peacemakers. (Heinemann Guided Readers Ser.: Int 29). (Orig.). 1981. pap. text ed. 2.00x (ISBN 0-435-27077-X). Heinemann Ed.

Forbes, Duncan see Milne, John.

Forbes, E. The Echinoderms of the Crag, London Clay, Etc. pap. 10.00 (ISBN 0-384-16390-4). Johnson Repr.

Forbes, Edward & Godwin-Austen, Robert. The Natural History of the European Seas. Egerton, Frank N., 3rd, ed. LC 77-74221. (History of Ecology Ser.). 1978. Repr. of 1859 ed. lib. bdg. 24.50x (ISBN 0-405-10392-1). Ayer Co Pubs.

Forbes, Elizabeth. Mario & Grisi. (Illus.). 208p. 1985. 26.00 (ISBN 0-575-03606-0, Pub. by Gollancz England). David & Charles.

Forbes, Elizabeth & Fitzsimons, Virginia. The Older Adult: A Process for Wellness. LC 80-39513. 333p. 1981. pap. text ed. 16.95 (ISBN 0-8016-1631-X). Mosby.

Forbes, Elliot, ed. Thayer's Life of Beethoven, 2 Vols. rev ed. 1967. Set. 87.50x (ISBN 0-691-09103-X); pap. 17.50 1 vol. ed. (ISBN 0-691-02702-1). Princeton U Pr.

Forbes, Elliot, jt. ed. see Beethoven.

Forbes, Eric G., et al. Greenwich Observatory, 3 Vols. LC 75-15269. 1975. Boxed set. 60.00x (ISBN 0-684-14456-5). Scribner.

Forbes, Ernest R. The Maritime Rights Movement, 1919-1927: A Study in Canadian Regionalism. 1979. 25.00x (ISBN 0-7735-0321-8); pap. 12.95 (ISBN 0-7735-0330-7). McGill-Queens U Pr.

Forbes, Esther. America's Paul Revere. (Illus.). 48p. (gr. 4-6). 1946. PLB 8.95 (ISBN 0-395-06767-7); pap. 2.95 (ISBN 0-395-24907-4). HM.

--Johnny Tremain. 305p. 1981. Repr. lib. bdg. 16.95x (ISBN 0-89966-306-0). Buccaneer Bks.

--Johnny Tremain. 1969. pap. 2.75 (ISBN 0-440-94250-0, LFL). Dell.

--Johnny Tremain. (Illus.). 272p. (gr. 7 up). pap. 3.25 (ISBN 0-440-44250-8, YB). Dell.

--Johnny Tremain. (Illus.). (gr. 7-9). 1943. 11.95 (ISBN 0-395-06766-9). HM.

--A Mirror for Witches. 215p. 1985. pap. 7.95 (ISBN 0-89733-154-0). Academy Chi Pubs.

--A Mirror for Witches. 14.95 (ISBN 0-8488-0079-6, Pub. by Amereon Hse). Amereon Ltd.

--Paul Revere & the World He Lived In. (Illus.). (gr. 4-8). 1962. 12.95 (ISBN 0-395-07695-1); pap. 12.95 (ISBN 0-395-08370-2, SenEd). HM.

Forbes, Fred W., ed. see Gov. Rockefeller Symposium Winrock, Arkansas, Oct. 1970.

Forbes, Frederick E. Dahomey & the Dahomans: Being the Journals of Two Missions, 2 vols. (Illus.). 1966. Repr. of 1851 ed. Set. 85.00x (ISBN 0-7146-1807-1, BHA-01807, F Cass Co). Biblio Dist.

Forbes, G. H., jt. auth. see Neale, John M.

Forbes, George. The Earth, the Sun, & the Moon. 1928. 15.00 (ISBN 0-686-17422-4). Ridgeway Bks.

--The Earth, the Sun & the Moon. 1928. 15.00 (ISBN 0-932062-57-1). Sharon Hill.

--The Stars. 1928. 15.00 (ISBN 0-686-17423-2). Ridgeway Bks.

--The Stars. 1928. 15.00 (ISBN 0-932062-58-X). Sharon Hill.

Forbes, George F. Digital Differential Analyzers. 4th ed. LC 57-903. 1957. pap. text ed. 25.00 (ISBN 0-685-10947-X). G F Forbes.

--System Analyzer. 1961. pap. text ed. 2.25 (ISBN 0-685-10948-8). G F Forbes.

Forbes, Geraldine, ed. A Pattern of Life in India: Autobiography of an Indian Woman. 1977. 12.50x (ISBN 0-8364-0009-7); pap. text ed. 7.00x (ISBN 0-8364-0014-3). South Asia Bks.

Forbes, Geraldine H. Positivism in Bengal. LC 76-18730. 1976. 9.00 (ISBN 0-88386-535-1). South Asia Bks.

Forbes, Gordon. Goodbye to Some. (War Library). 272p. 1982. pap. 2.50 (ISBN 0-345-30641-4). Ballantine.

--A Handful of Summers. LC 78-21618. (Illus.). 1979. 12.50 (ISBN 0-8317-4362-X, Mayflower Bks). Smith Pubs.

Forbes, Graeme. The Metaphysics of Modality. 1985. 29.95 (ISBN 0-19-824432-0). Oxford U Pr.

Forbes, H. A. Chinese Export Silver, Seventeen Eighty-Five to Eighteen Eighty-Five. LC 85-12401. (Illus.). 1975. 75.00 (ISBN 0-937650-02-1). Mus Am China Trade.

Forbes, H. A. & Lee, Henry. Massachusetts Help to Ireland During the Great Famine. LC 67-24085. (Illus.). 1967. 6.00x (ISBN 0-937650-00-5). Mus Am China.

Forbes, H. Crosby. Chinese Export Silver: A Legacy of Luxury. LC 84-82443. (Illus.). 20p. (Orig.). 1984. pap. 5.00 (ISBN 0-88397-082-1). Intl Exhibit Foun.

--Hills & Streams: Landscape Decoration on Chinese Export Blue & White Porcelain. Walker, Janet, ed. LC 82-81634. 20p. (Orig.). 1982. pap. 5.00x (ISBN 0-88397-041-4). Intl Exhibit Foun.

Forbes, Harold M. West Virginia History: Bibliography & Guide to Studies. 359p. 1981. 9.00 (ISBN 0-937058-03-3). West Va U Pr.

Forbes, Harrie R. Mission Tales in the Days of the Dons. LC 71-128735. (Short Story Index Reprint Ser). (Illus.). 1909. 20.00 (ISBN 0-8369-3626-4). Ayer Co Pubs.

Forbes, Harriette M. Gravestones of Early New England: And the Men Who Made Them. (Thanatology Service Ser.). 150p. 1986. Repr. of 1927 ed. 15.00 (ISBN 0-930194-03-9). Ctr Thanatology.

Forbes, Harrison, ed. Reflections from the Son: For Men. (Orig.). 1985. pap. 5.00 (ISBN 0-915541-07-6). Star Bks Inc.

Forbes, Henry O. A Handbook to the Primates, 2 vols. LC 78-72715. Repr. of 1894 ed. Set. 84.50 (ISBN 0-404-18288-7). Vol. 1 (ISBN 0-404-18289-5). Vol. 2 (ISBN 0-404-18290-9). AMS Pr.

--A Naturalist's Wanderings in the Eastern Archipelago: A Narrative of Travel & Exploration from 1878 to 1883. LC 77-86991. (Illus.). Repr. of 1885 ed. 41.50 (ISBN 0-404-16708-X). AMS Pr.

Forbes, Hugh D. Nationalism, Ethnocentrism, & Personality: Social Science & Critical Theory. LC 85-1202. 264p. 1985. lib. bdg. 27.50x (ISBN 0-226-25703-7). U of Chicago Pr.

Forbes, Ian & Smith, Steve. Politics & Human Nature. LC 83-42531. 250p. 1984. 25.00 (ISBN 0-312-62625-8). St Martin.

Forbes, J. A., jt. auth. see Clark, Ewen M.

Forbes, J. C. & Watson, R. D. Agricultural Botany. 250p. 1986. pap. text ed. write for info. (ISBN 0-7131-2891-7). E Arnold.

Forbes, J. M., jt. ed. see Carovillano, R. L.

Forbes, J. T. Socrates. 1913. Repr. 25.00 (ISBN 0-8274-3447-2). R West.

--Socrates: The World's Epoch-Makers. LC 78-31513. 1978. lib. bdg. 27.50 (ISBN 0-8414-4312-2). Folcroft.

Forbes, Jack. The Gordon Treasure & McDonald Gold. (Illus.). 200p. 1985. 12.50 (ISBN 0-941402-03-7). Devon Pub.

--Native Americans & Nixon: Presidential Politics & Minority Self Determination, 1969-1972. 2nd ed. 148p. 1984. pap. 12.00 (ISBN 0-935626-06-9). U Cal AISC.

Forbes, Jack D. Apache, Navaho, & Spaniard. LC 79-17069. (Illus.). 1980. Repr. of 1960 ed. lib. bdg. 27.50x (ISBN 0-313-22021-2, FOAN). Greenwood.

--Apache, Navaho, & Spaniard. (Civilization of the American Indian Ser.: Vol. 115). (Illus.). 304p. 1960. pap. 8.95 (ISBN 0-8061-1092-9). U of Okla Pr.

--Native Americans of California & Nevada. rev. ed. LC 82-7906. (Illus.). 240p. 1982. lib. bdg. 13.95 (ISBN 0-87961-118-9); pap. 7.95 (ISBN 0-87961-119-7). Naturegraph.

Forbes, James. Philosophie De la Science Economique. LC 72-150157. 32p. 1973. Repr. of 1897 ed. lib. bdg. 13.50 (ISBN 0-8337-1172-5). B Franklin.

Ford, Burnette G. The Blessing of Infinite Reflections. 48p. 1985. 6.95 (ISBN 0-89962-489-8). Todd & Honeywell.

Ford, C. Quentin, ed. Space Technology & Earth Problems. (Science & Technology Ser.: Vol. 23). (Illus.). 1970. lib. bdg. 35.00x (ISBN 0-87703-051-0, Pub. by Am Astronaut); microfiche suppl. 20.00x (ISBN 0-87703-134-7). Univelt Inc.

Ford, Camie & Hale, Sunny. Two Too Thin: Two Women Who Triumphed over Anorexia Nervosa. LC 83-61378. 400p. 1983. pap. 5.95 (ISBN 0-941478-15-7). Paraclete Pr.

Ford, Carol K. & Silverman, Ann M. American Cultural Encounters. Olsen, Judy E., ed. (Illus.). 124p. 1981. pap. text ed. 4.95x (ISBN 0-88084-054-4). Alemany Pr.

Ford, Caroline. Less Traveled Road, Study of Robert Frost. LC 74-12496. 1935. lib. bdg. 15.00 (ISBN 0-8414-4238-X). Folcroft.

Ford, Caroline, jt. auth. see Frost, Robert.

Ford, Charles & Tyler, Parker. The Young & Evil: Homosexuality. LC 75-12351. 1975. Repr. of 1933 ed. 14.00x (ISBN 0-405-07392-5). Ayer Co Pubs.

Ford, Charles, ed. Making Musical Instruments: Strings & Keyboard. LC 77-88774. (Illus.). 1979. pap. 10.95 (ISBN 0-394-73561-7). Pantheon.

Ford, Charles H. Om Krishna I. LC 78-16142. 1979. 50.00x set (ISBN 0-916156-37-0); pap. 3.50x (ISBN 0-916156-36-2). Cherry Valley.

--Om Krishna II: From the Sickroom of the Walking Eagles. LC 80-13972. 1981. pap. 4.00x (ISBN 0-916156-47-8); 50.00 (ISBN 0-916156-48-6). Cherry Valley.

--Silver Flower Coo. pap. 3.50x (ISBN 0-686-73475-0). Kulchur Foun.

--The Super Executive's Guide to Getting Things Done. 272p. 1983. 14.95 (ISBN 0-8144-5724-X). AMACOM.

--Think Smart, Move Fast: Decision Making-Problem Solving for Super Executives. LC 82-71321. 272p. 1984. pap. 9.95 (ISBN 0-8144-7624-4). AMACOM.

Ford, Charles V. The Somatizing Disorders: Illness As a Way of Life. 165p. 1983. 31.50 (ISBN 0-444-00752-0, Biomedical Pr). Elsevier.

Ford, Charles W. How to Study the Bible. LC 77-99213. (Radiant Life Ser.). 128p. 1978. pap. text ed. 2.50 (ISBN 0-88243-912-X, 02-0912); tchr's ed. 2.50 (ISBN 0-88243-183-8, 32-0183). Gospel Pub.

--The Inspired Scriptures. LC 78-60267. (Radiant Life Ser.). 128p. 1978. pap. 1.50 (ISBN 0-88243-914-6, 02-0914); tchr's ed. 2.50 (ISBN 0-88243-185-4, 32-0185). Gospel Pub.

--Learning from Hebrews. LC 80-67467. (Radiant Life Ser.). 127p. (Orig.). 1980. 2.50 (ISBN 0-88243-915-4, 02-0915); teacher's ed 3.95 (ISBN 0-88243-188-9, 32-0188). Gospel Pub.

Ford, Charlotte. Charlotte Ford's Book of Modern Manners. 512p. 1982. pap. 9.95 (ISBN 0-671-45769-1, Fireside). S&S.

Ford, Cindy. Daisy Leaders Guide Handbook. Finn, Catherine, ed. 128p. (Orig.). 1983. pap. 2.50. GS.

Ford, Clebert & McPherson, Cynthia. A Guide to the Black Apple. (Illus.). 1977. pap. 2.95 (ISBN 0-916800-12-1). L J Martin.

Ford, Clellan S. Smoke from Their Fires: The Life of a Kwakiutl Chief. (Illus.). 248p. 1968. Repr. of 1941 ed. 18.50 (ISBN 0-208-00336-3, Archon). Shoe String.

Ford, Clellan S. & Beach, Frank A. Patterns of Sexual Behavior. LC 80-159. (Illus.). vii, 307p. 1980. Repr. of 1951 ed. lib. bdg. 32.75x (ISBN 0-313-22355-6, FOPS). Greenwood.

Ford, Clellan S., ed. Cross-Cultural Approaches: Readings in Comparative Research. LC 66-27876. (Comparative Studies). 375p. 1967. 14.50x (ISBN 0-87536-103-X); pap. 9.50x (ISBN 0-87536-104-8). HRAFP.

Ford, Curtis B. How to Establish an Estate Analysis Practice. 2nd ed. LC 78-69946. 208p. 1982. 21.50 (ISBN 0-87218-024-7). Natl Underwriter.

Ford, D., jt. auth. see Eckenfelder, W. W.

Ford, D. H., ed. see International Society of Psychoneuroendocrinology-Brooklyn-1970.

Ford, D. H., et al. Atlas of the Human Brain. 3rd ed. 1978. 34.00 (ISBN 0-444-80008-5). Elsevier.

Ford, D. M. & Ford, Mary A., eds. The Romance of Chivalry in Italian Verse. 657p. 1984. Repr. of 1904 ed. lib. bdg. 65.00 (ISBN 0-89760-242-0). Telegraph Bks.

Ford, Daniel. The Country Northward: A Hiker's Journal. LC 76-11306. (Illus.). 208p. 1976. pap. 6.95 (ISBN 0-912274-60-3). Backcountry Pubns.

--The Cult of the Atom: The Secret Papers of the Atomic Energy Commission. 1984. pap. 6.95 (ISBN 0-671-25302-6). S&S.

Ford, Daniel, jt. auth. see Ford, Sally.

Ford, Daniel, et al. Is Nuclear Power Safe? LC 75-34738. 1975. pap. 3.75 (ISBN 0-8447-2068-2). Am Enterprise.

--Beyond the Freeze: The Road to Nuclear Sanity. LC 82-72504. (Orig.). 1982. pap. 6.95 (ISBN 0-8070-0484-7, BP646). Beacon Pr.

Ford, Daniel F. The Button: The Pentagon's Strategic Command & Control System. 1985. 16.95 (ISBN 0-671-50068-6). S&S.

--Three Mile Island: Thirty Minutes to Meltdown. 1982. pap. 5.95 (ISBN 0-14-006048-0). Penguin.

--Three Mile Island. 30 Minutes to Melt Down, 261p. 1981. 4.95 (ISBN 0-14-006048-0). Union Conc Sci.

Ford, Daniel F. & Schuster, Simon. Cult of the Atom. 240p. 1982. 5.95 (ISBN 0-671-25301-8). Union Conc Sci.

Ford, David. Developments in Industrial Marketing. 1980. 90.00x (ISBN 0-86176-065-4, Pub. by MCB Pubns). State Mutual Bk.

Ford, David F., jt. auth. see Hardy, Daniel W.

Ford, Desmond. The Abomination of Desolation in Biblical Eschatology. LC 79-64195. 1979. pap. text ed. 14.00 (ISBN 0-8191-0757-3). U Pr of Amer.

Ford, Donald H. & Rue, Joseph. Standard FORTRAN Programming. 4th ed. 1982. pap. 19.95x (ISBN 0-256-02608-4). Irwin.

Ford, Donald H. & Urban, Hugh B. Systems of Psychotherapy: A Comparative Study. LC 63-20630. 712p. 1963. 54.95x (ISBN 0-471-26580-2). Wiley.

Ford, Donna, jt. auth. see Ford, Bud.

Ford, Doug. Getting Started in Golf. 124p. 1964. pap. 2.50 (ISBN 0-346-12354-2). Cornerstone.

--Start Golf Young. LC 77-93324. 160p. (gr. 5 up). 1978. 8.95 (ISBN 0-8069-4126-X); PLB 10.99 (ISBN 0-8069-4127-8). Sterling.

--The Wedge. 160p. 1965. pap. 2.95 (ISBN 0-346-12357-7). Cornerstone.

Ford, E. B. Ecological Genetics. 4th ed. 1979. 29.95x (ISBN 0-412-16130-3, NO.6110, Pub. by Chapman & Hall). Methuen Inc.

--Understanding Genetics. LC 79-63132. (Illus.). 1979. text ed. 15.00x (ISBN 0-87663-728-4, Pica Pr). Universe.

Ford, E. David, jt. ed. see MacFadyen, A.

Ford, Edna P., jt. auth. see Bannister, Barbara.

Ford, Edna P., jt. ed. see Bannister, Barbara.

Ford, Edsel. Looking for Shiloh: Poems. LC 68-9420. 64p. 1969. pap. 5.95 (ISBN 0-8262-8012-9). U of Mo Pr.

Ford, Edward. Bibliography of Australian Medicine Seventeen Ninety to Nineteen Hundred. (Illus.). 1976. 48.00x (ISBN 0-424-00022-9, Pub. by Sydney U Pr). Intl Spec Bk.

Ford, Edward E. Choosing to Love: A New Way to Respond. 168p. 1983. 14.95 (ISBN 0-86683-749-3, AY8400); pap. 7.95 (ISBN 0-86683-695-0, AY8280). Winston Pr.

Ford, Edward E. & Englund, Steven. Permanent Love: Practical Steps to a Lasting Relationship. 1979. pap. 4.95 (ISBN 0-86683-770-1). Winston Pr.

Ford, Eileen & Heilman, Joan. The Ford Models' Crash Course in Looking Great. 1985. 18.95 (ISBN 0-671-49961-0). S&S.

Ford, Elaine. Missed Connections. 1984. pap. 3.95 (ISBN 0-440-35680-6, LE). Dell.

Ford, Emily E. Notes on the Life of Noah Webster, 2 Vols. LC 14-150160. 1971. Repr. of 1912 ed. lib. bdg. 53.00 (ISBN 0-8337-1196-2). B Franklin.

Ford, Emma. Birds of Prey. (Illus.). 1982. pap. 8.95 (ISBN 0-686-98031-X). Branford.

--Falconry. (Shire Album Ser.: No. 115). (Illus.). 32p. (Orig.). 1984. pap. 2.95 (ISBN 0-85263-667-9, Pub. by Shire Pubns England). Seven Hills Bks.

--Falconry in Mews & Field. (Illus.). 1982. 32.00 (ISBN 0-7134-4047-3). Branford.

Ford, F., jt. auth. see Ford, Percy.

Ford, Ford M. A Call. (Neglected Books of the Twentieth Century). 1985. pap. 8.50 (ISBN 0-317-17525-4). Ecco Pr.

--The English Novel, from the Earliest Days to the Death of Joseph Conrad. Repr. of 1929 ed. 39.00x (ISBN 0-403-03879-0). Somerset Pub.

--The Rash Act. 348p. 1985. 14.95 (ISBN 0-85635-399-X); pap. 8.50 (ISBN 0-85635-529-1). Carcanet.

Ford, Ford M., jt. auth. see Conrad, Joseph.

Ford, Ford Maddox. A Man Could Stand Up: A Novel. 347p. 1985. Repr. of 1926 ed. lib. bdg. 40.00 (ISBN 0-89987-287-5). Darby Bks.

Ford, Ford Madox. Between Saint Denis & Saint George. LC 73-153640. (English Literature Ser., No. 33). 1971. Repr. lib. bdg. 38.95x (ISBN 0-8383-1244-6). Haskell.

--The Brown Owl. LC 66-12908. (Illus.). (gr. 1-4). 1966. Braziller.

--Collected Poems. LC 78-64033. (Des Imagistes: Literature of the Imagist Movement). Repr. of 1914 ed. 21.00 (ISBN 0-404-17114-1). AMS Pr.

--Critical Attitude. facs. ed. LC 67-30187. (Essay Index Reprint Ser). 1911. 15.00 (ISBN 0-8369-0450-8). Ayer Co Pubs.

--Critical Writings of Ford Madox Ford. MacShane, Frank, ed. LC 64-11356. (Regents Critics Ser). xiv, 168p. 1964. 14.95x (ISBN 0-8032-0455-8); pap. 3.95x (ISBN 0-8032-5454-7, BB 401, Bison). U of Nebr Pr.

--The English Novel. 1979. Repr. of 1930 ed. lib. bdg. 20.00 (ISBN 0-8495-1635-8). Arden Lib.

--English Novel. LC 76-29036. 1929. lib. bdg. 18.00 (ISBN 0-8414-4180-4). Folcroft.

--The English Novel. 148p. pap. 8.50 (ISBN 0-85635-480-5). Carcanet.

--Fifth Queen. LC 63-13786. 592p. (Consists of: Fifth Queen, Privy Seal, & Fifth Queen Crowned). 1963. 19.50 (ISBN 0-8149-0099-2). Vanguard.

--Ford Madox Brown: A Record of His Life & Work. LC 76-144609. (Illus.). Repr. of 1896 ed. 37.00 (ISBN 0-404-02459-9). AMS Pr.

--Good Soldier. (YA) 1951. pap. 3.95 (ISBN 0-394-71386-9, Vin, V45). Random.

--Hans Holbein the Younger: A Critical Monograph. 1980. Repr. lib. bdg. 30.00 (ISBN 0-89341-370-4). Longwood Pub Group.

--Henry James. 1964. lib. bdg. 18.00x (ISBN 0-374-92775-8). Octagon.

--It Was the Nightingale. 1972. lib. bdg. 29.00x (ISBN 0-374-92782-0). Octagon.

--Joseph Conrad. 1965. lib. bdg. 23.00x (ISBN 0-374-92793-6). Octagon.

--A Last Post. 1928. lib. bdg. 40.00 (ISBN 0-8414-4270-3). Folcroft.

--Memories & Impressions. (Neglected Books of the Twentieth Century). 335p. 1985. pap. 9.50 (ISBN 0-88001-087-8). Ecco Pr.

--No Enemy. LC 84-6090. 302p. 1984. pap. 8.50 (ISBN 0-88001-062-2). Ecco Pr.

--No More Parades: A Novel. 1979. Repr. of 1925 ed. lib. bdg. 25.00 (ISBN 0-8495-1646-3). Arden Lib.

--Parade's End. rev. ed. 1961. 18.95 (ISBN 0-394-43972-4). Knopf.

--Parade's End: Consisting of "Some Do Not", "No More Parades", "A Man Could Stand up", & "The Last Post". LC 79-2158. 1979. pap. 6.95 (ISBN 0-394-74108-0, Vin). Random.

--Provence. LC 78-16071. (Neglected Books of the 20th Century Ser.). (Illus.). 1979. pap. 6.95 (ISBN 0-912946-63-6). Ecco Pr.

--The Queen Who Flew. LC 65-23176. (Illus.). (gr. 4-6). 1965. Braziller.

--The Rash Act. 348p. 1982. Repr. of 1933 ed. lib. bdg. 35.00 (ISBN 0-89984-206-2). Century Bookbindery.

--Return to Yesterday. 416p. 1972. 12.95 (ISBN 0-87140-563-6); pap. 7.95(f) (ISBN 0-87140-271-8). Liveright.

--Romance. Conrad, Joseph, ed. (Neglected Books of the Twentieth Century). (Illus.). 428p. 1985. pap. 9.50 (ISBN 0-88001-086-X). Ecco Pr.

--Rossetti: A Critical Essay on His Art. LC 76-40417. 1976. Repr. of 1914 ed. lib. bdg. 25.00 (ISBN 0-8414-4939-2). Folcroft.

--Selected Poems. 135p. 1971. pap. 3.00 (ISBN 0-913219-17-7). Pym-Rand Pr.

--The Soul of London. LC 72-91. (English Literature Ser., No. 33). 1972. Repr. of 1911 ed. lib. bdg. 39.95x (ISBN 0-8383-1407-4). Haskell.

Ford, Ford Madox, jt. auth. see Pound, Ezra.

Ford, Ford Madox see Shipp, Horace.

Ford Foundation. City High Schools: A Recognition of Progress. LC 84-10258. (Ford Foundation Report Ser.). 107p. (Orig.). 1984. pap. 4.50 (ISBN 0-916584-23-2). Ford Found.

--Financial Support of Women's Programs in the 1970's: A Review of Private & Government Funding in the United States & Abroad (A Report for the Ford Foundation) LC 79-88287. 67p. 1979. 4.50 (ISBN 0-916584-10-0). Ford Found.

--Litigation on Behalf of Women: A Review for the Ford Foundation. Berger, Margaret A., ed. LC 80-66052. 72p. 1980. pap. 4.50 (ISBN 0-916584-15-1). Ford Found.

--The Political Economy of Education: A Bibliography of Ford Foundation-Supported Publications, 1968-1980. LC 81-2303. 92p. (Orig.). 1981. pap. text ed. 4.50 (ISBN 0-916584-17-8, AACR2). Ford Found.

--Student Aid & the Urban Poor. Washington Office of the College Board, ed. LC 80-29114. (Ford Foundation Series on Higher Education in the Cities). 48p. (Orig.). 1981. pap. text ed. 3.50 (ISBN 0-916584-16-X). Ford Found.

Ford Foundation & Atwater, James D. Better Testing, Better Writing: A Report to the Ford Foundation. LC 81-15136. (Papers on Research About Learning Ser.). 36p. (Orig.). 1981. pap. text ed. 4.00 (ISBN 0-916584-20-8). Ford Found.

Ford Foundation & Lynton, Ernest. A Tale of Three Cities: Boston, Birmingham, Hartford. LC 81-9790. (Ford Foundation Series on Higher Education in the Cities). 80p. (Orig.). 1981. pap. text ed. 4.00 (ISBN 0-916584-18-6). Ford Found.

Ford Foundation & Orfield, Gary. Toward a Strategy for Urban Integration: Lessons in School & Housing Policy from Twelve Cities: A Report to the Ford Foundation. LC 81-19447. 87p. (Orig.). 1982. pap. text ed. 4.50 (ISBN 0-916584-19-4). Ford Found.

Ford Foundation, jt. auth. see Rand Corporation.

Ford Foundation Program Tulane University, Jan. to May, 1947. Partial Differential Equations & Related Topics. Goldstein, J. A., ed. LC 75-6604. (Lecture Notes in Mathematics Ser: Vol. 446). iv, 389p. 1975. pap. 21.00 (ISBN 0-387-07148-2). Springer-Verlag.

Ford Foundation Staff. Grass-Roots Environmentalists. LC 77-24992. 32p. 1977. pap. 3.00 (ISBN 0-916584-06-2). Ford Found.

Ford, Frank & Buckingham, Jamie. The Coming Food Crisis. 140p. 1982. pap. 4.95 (ISBN 0-310-60121-5, Pub by Chosen Bks). Zondervan.

Ford, Frank, ed. see Sack, Allan & Yourman, Jack.

Ford, Frank R. Diseases of the Nervous System: In Infancy, Childhood & Adolescence. 6th ed. (Illus.). 1584p. 1973. 50.00x (ISBN 0-398-02845-1). C C Thomas.

Ford, Franklin L. Europe, Seventeen Eighty to Eighteen Thirty. (General History of Europe Ser.). 1971. pap. text ed. 13.95x (ISBN 0-582-48346-8). Longman.

--Political Murder: From Tyrannicide to Terrorism. (Illus.). 456p. 1985. 29.50 (ISBN 0-674-68635-7). Harvard U Pr.

--Robe & Sword: The Regrouping of the French Aristocracy After Louis 14. LC 52-12261. (Historical Studies: No. 64). (Illus.). 1953. 17.50x (ISBN 0-674-77415-9). Harvard U Pr.

Ford, G., jt. auth. see Ford, P.

Ford, G., et al. The Use of Medical Literature: A Preliminary Survey. 1980. 45.00x (ISBN 0-905984-51-X, Pub. by Brit Lib England). State Mutual Bk.

Ford, G. A., jt. auth. see Ford, P.

Ford, G. B., Jr., tr. see Meillet, A.

Ford, G. H., ed. see Dickens, Charles.

Ford, Gary A., jt. auth. see Wiener, Richard S.

Ford, Gary T., ed. Marketing & the Library. LC 84-668. (Journal of Library Administration Ser.: Vol. 4, No. 4). 80p. 1984. text ed. 19.95 (ISBN 0-86656-307-5, B307). Haworth Pr.

Ford, Gene. Ford's Illustrated Guide to Wines, Brews, & Spirits. 382p. 1983. pap. 18.95 (ISBN 0-697-08227-X). Wm C Brown.

Ford, George. Baby's First Picture Book. LC 79-62941. (Cloth Bks.). (Illus.). (ps). 1979. 2.95 (ISBN 0-394-84245-6, BYR). Random.

--Gator. 176p. 1980. pap. 1.95 (ISBN 0-441-27419-6, Pub. by Charter Bks). Ace Bks.

Ford, George & Kane, Jim. Go for Goal: Winning Drills & Exercises for Soccer. 186p. 1984. 17.95x (ISBN 0-205-08065-0, Pub. by Longwood Div). Allyn.

Ford, George, jt. auth. see Williamson, Mel.

Ford, George A. & Ford, Kathleen H. Analysis of Sex Role Traits. 1982. programmed wkbk. 1.95 (ISBN 0-934698-15-5). BDR Learn Prods.

Ford, George A. & Lippitt, Gordon L. Planning Your Future: A Workbook for Personal Goal Setting. LC 76-11357. Orig. Title: Life Planning Workbook for Guidance in Planning & Personal Goal Setting. 49p. 1976. pap. 7.50 (ISBN 0-88390-120-X). Univ Assocs.

Ford, George A., jt. auth. see Hall, Anna H.

Ford, George H. Dickens & His Readers. LC 74-3059. 318p. 1974. Repr. of 1955 ed. 15.00x (ISBN 0-87752-176-X). Gordian.

Ford, George H., ed. The Dickens Critics. LC 72-152596. 417p. 1972. Repr. of 1961 ed. lib. bdg. 42.50 (ISBN 0-8371-6029-4, FODC). Greenwood.

--Victorian Fiction: A Second Guide to Research. xxv, 401p. 1978. 25.00x (ISBN 0-87352-254-0, Z43); pap. 14.50x (ISBN 0-87352-255-9, Z44). Modern Lang.

Ford, George H., ed. see Dickens, Charles.

Ford, George H., ed. see Keats, John.

Ford, Gerald R. Churchill Lecture. LC 83-83406. 25p. 1984. deluxe ed. 100.00 Signed Ed. (ISBN 0-935716-30-0). Lord John.

--Global Stability. 25p. 1982. limited signed ed. 50.00 (ISBN 0-935716-14-9). Lord John.

--A Time to Heal: The Autobiography of Gerald R. Ford. LC 78-20162. (Illus.). 1979. 14.37i (ISBN 0-06-011297-2, HarpT). Har-Row.

--A Vision for America. (YA) 1981. Deluxe signed ed. 50.00 (ISBN 0-935716-08-4). Lord John.

Ford, Gordon. Sign Here Please. 1981. 25.00x (ISBN 0-7223-1377-2, Pub. by Stockwell). State Mutual Bk.

Ford, Gordon B., Jr., tr. from Lat. Ruodlieb: The First Medieval Epic of Chivalry from 11th Century Germany. 1965. pap. 20.00x (ISBN 0-685-05284-2). Adlers Foreign Bks.

Ford, Gordon, Jr., tr. see Mayrhofer, Manfred.

Ford, Guy S. Hanover & Prussia, 1795-1803. LC 72-168054. (Columbia University. Studies in the Social Sciences: No. 48). 18.00 (ISBN 0-404-51048-5). AMS Pr.

--Stein: The Era of Reform in Prussia, 1807-1815. 1922. 11.25 (ISBN 0-8446-1189-1). Peter Smith.

Ford, H. Collation of the Ben Jonson Folios, 1616-31-1640. LC 72-6295. (English Literature Ser., No. 33). 1972. Repr. of 1932 ed. lib. bdg. 41.95x (ISBN 0-8383-1624-7). Haskell.

Ford, H. J. The Scotch-Irish in America. 59.95 (ISBN 0-8490-1004-7). Gordon Pr.

Ford, H. L. Collation of the Ben Jonson Folios. LC 73-12916. Repr. of 1932 ed. lib. bdg. 15.00 (ISBN 0-8414-4152-9). Folcroft.

--Shakespeare: A Collection of the Editions & Separate Plays with Some Account of T. Johnson & R. Walker. 1935. lib. bdg. 12.50 (ISBN 0-8414-4273-8). Folcroft.

Ford, H. V., jt. ed. see Coffee, J. M.

Ford, Harold. Shakespeare, His Ethical Teaching. 112p. 1980. Repr. lib. bdg. 30.00 (ISBN 0-89987-257-3). Century Bookbindery.

--Shakespeare's Hamlet, a New Theory or What Was the Poets Intention in the Play. LC 72-12903. 1900. lib. bdg. 15.00 (ISBN 0-8414-0984-6). Folcroft.

Ford, Harold W. A History of the Restoration Plea. 2nd ed. 1967. pap. 3.95 (ISBN 0-89900-110-6). College Pr Pub.

Ford, Harry E. Modern Provencal Phonology & Morphology Studied in the Language of Frederic Mistral. LC 72-168117. (Columbia University. Studies in Romance Philology & Literature: No. 30). Repr. of 1921 ed. 15.00 (ISBN 0-685-05898-0). AMS Pr.

Ford, Harvey. A Nothern Lasse. LC 79-54339. (Renaissance Drama Ser.). 200p. 1982. lib. bdg. 26.00 (ISBN 0-8240-4457-6). Garland Pub.

Ford, Henry. An American Foreign Policy. 1979. lib. bdg. 59.95 (ISBN 0-8490-2864-7). Gordon Pr.

--Good Morning: After a Sleep of 25 Years, Old-Fashioned Dancing Is Being Revived by Mr. & Mrs. Henry Ford. (Ballroom Dance Ser.). 1985. lib. bdg. 79.95 (ISBN 0-87700-828-0). Revisionist Pr.

--Henry Ford on U. S. Finance. 1984. lib. bdg. 79.95 (ISBN 0-87700-588-5). Revisionist Pr.

--The International Jew. 59.95 (ISBN 0-8490-0418-7). Gordon Pr.

--The International Jew. 1978. pap. 5.00x (ISBN 0-911038-45-0). Noontide.

--The International Jew, 4 vols. 1984. lib. bdg. 500.95 (ISBN 0-87700-586-9). Revisionist Pr.

Ford, Henry & Crowther, Samuel. My Life & Work. LC 73-2507. (Big Business; Economic Power in a Free Society Ser.). Repr. of 1922 ed. 23.50 (ISBN 0-405-05088-7). Ayer Co Pubs.

Ford, Henry C. Observations on the Language of Chaucer's "House of Fame". LC 76-168118. Repr. 12.50 (ISBN 0-404-02511-0). AMS Pr.

Ford, Henry J. Cleveland Era. 1919. 8.50x (ISBN 0-686-83504-2). Elliots Bks.

--The Cost of Our National Government: A Study in Political Pathology. LC 73-19145. (Politics of People Ser.). 164p. 1974. Repr. 13.00x (ISBN 0-405-05869-1). Ayer Co Pubs.

--The Natural History of the State: An Introduction to Political Science. LC 79-1628. 1981. Repr. of 1915 ed. 19.75 (ISBN 0-88355-932-3). Hyperion Conn.

--Rise & Growth of American Politics. 2nd ed. LC 67-23377. (Law, Politics, & History Ser). 1967. Repr. of 1898 ed. lib. bdg. 35.00 (ISBN 0-306-70946-5). Da Capo.

--Scotch-Irish in America. LC 69-18775. (American Immigration Collection Ser., No. 1). 1969. Repr. of 1915 ed. 20.00 (ISBN 0-405-00523-7). Ayer Co Pubs.

--Washington & His Colleagues. 1918. 8.50x (ISBN 0-686-83847-5). Elliots Bks.

Ford, Henry J see Johnson, Allen & Nevins, Allan.

Ford, Herbert. Flee the Captor. (Orion Ser). 1979. pap. 4.50 (ISBN 0-8127-0219-0). Review & Herald.

Ford, Herbert L. Shakespeare Seventeen Hundred & Seventeen Forty. 1973. Repr. of 1935 ed. 12.45 (ISBN 0-8274-0539-1). R West.

--Shakespeare; Seventeen Hundred to Seventeen Forty. LC 68-56498. 1969. Repr. of 1935 ed. 22.00 (ISBN 0-405-08526-5, Blom Pubns). Ayer Co Pubs.

Ford, Herschel W. Simple Sermons for Funeral Services. 54p. 1985. pap. 2.95 (ISBN 0-8010-3514-7). Baker Bk.

Ford, Hildegard. My Go to Bed Book. (Illus.). 1976. 5.95 (ISBN 0-8054-4151-4, 4241-51). Broadman.

Ford, Hildegarde. Baby's Animal Book. (Illus.). 1976. 5.95 (ISBN 0-8054-4150-6, 4241-50). Broadman.

Ford, Hugh. Four Lives in Paris. (Illus.). 288p. 1984. 19.95 (ISBN 0-8180-0234-4). Horizon.

--Published in Paris. 1980. pap. 14.95 (ISBN 0-916366-09-X). Pushcart Pr.

Ford, Hugh, jt. auth. see Cody, Morrill.

Ford, Hugh, ed. The Left Bank Revisited: Selections from the Paris Tribune, 1917-1934. LC 76-136964. 1972. 28.50 (ISBN 0-271-01144-0). Pa St U Pr.

Ford, Hugh, jt. ed. see Cunard, Nancy.

Ford, Hugh, ed. see Stearns, Harold.

Ford, Hugh, et al. Fracture Mechanics in Design & Service. (Phil Trans of the Royal Soc., Series A: Vol. 299). (Illus.). 239p. 1981. lib. bdg. 67.00x (ISBN 0-85403-152-9, Pub. by Royal Soc London). Scholium Intl.

Ford, Ian. Buying & Running Your Own Business. 184p. 1974. 17.95x (ISBN 0-8464-0230-0). Beekman Pubs.

Ford, Ira W. Traditional Music of America. (Music Reprint Ser., 1978). 1978. Repr. of 1940 ed. lib. bdg. 42.50 (ISBN 0-306-77588-3). Da Capo.

Ford, Isaac N. Tropical America. LC 70-168119. Repr. of 1893 ed. 24.50 (ISBN 0-404-02512-9). AMS Pr.

Ford, J., ed. see Volta Memorial Conference, Como, Italy, 1977.

Ford, J. D., jt. auth. see Al-Alak, B.

Ford, J. D., ed. Old Spanish Readings Selected on the Basis of Critically Edited Texts. 1977. lib. bdg. 59.95 (ISBN 0-8490-2371-8). Gordon Pr.

--A Spanish Anthology: A Collection of Lyrics from the Thirteenth Century to the Present Time. 1977. lib. bdg. 59.95. Gordon Pr.

Ford, J. E., jt. auth. see Newton, A.

Ford, J. F., et al. Deaf Smith Country Cookbook. 1973. pap. 6.95 (ISBN 0-02-009500-7, Collier). Macmillan.

Ford, J. L. Choice, Expectation & Uncertainty: An Appraisal of G. L. S. Shackle's Theory. LC 83-10011. 224p. 1983. 29.50x (ISBN 0-389-20415-3, 07300). B&N Imports.

Ford, J. L., jt. ed. see Carter, C. F.

Ford, J. Massingberd. Trilogy on Wisdom & Celibacy. 1967. 16.95x (ISBN 0-268-00285-1). U of Notre Dame Pr.

Ford, J. Massyngbaerd. My Enemy Is My Guest. LC 84-5812. 1984. pap. 9.95 (ISBN 0-88344-348-1). Orbis Bks.

Ford, J. Massyngberd. Pentecostal Experience. LC 72-116869. 64p. (Orig.). 1970. pap. 1.95 (ISBN 0-8091-1655-3). Paulist Pr.

Ford, J. Massyngberde, tr. Revelation. LC 74-18796. (Anchor Bible Ser.: Vol. 38). (Illus.). 504p. 1975. 18.00 (ISBN 0-385-00895-3). Doubleday.

Ford, J. W., ed. A Seaman's Guide to the Rule of the Road. 3rd ed. (Illus.). 300p. 1984. pap. 13.95 (ISBN 0-87021-865-4). Naval Inst Pr.

Ford, James. Slums & Housing, with Special Reference to New York City. LC 76-142935. (Illus.). 1972. Repr. of 1936 ed. 64.00x (ISBN 0-8371-5936-9, FOS&). Greenwood.

Ford, James, ed. see President's Conference On Home Building & Home Ownership.

Ford, James A. Analysis of Indian Village Site Collections from Louisiana & Mississippi. LC 37-27887. 1975. Repr. of 1937 ed. 23.00 (ISBN 0-527-03231-X). Kraus Repr.

--Ceramic Decoration Sequence at an Old Indian Village Site Near Sicily Island, Louisiana. LC 36-19610. 1975. Repr. of 1935 ed. 12.00 (ISBN 0-527-03230-1). Kraus Repr.

--A Comparison of Formative Cultures in the Americas: Diffusion or the Psychic Unity of Man. LC 69-60004. (Illus.). 211p. 1969. 45.00x (ISBN 0-87474-159-9). Smithsonian.

--Quantitative Method for Deriving Cultural Chronology. LC 75-24231. (Museum Brief Ser.: No. 9). vi, 62p. 1972. pap. 3.25 (ISBN 0-913134-08-2). Mus Anthro Mo.

Ford, James A. & Willey, Gordon. Crooks Site, a Marksville Period Burial Mound in the LaSalle Parish, Louisiana. LC 40-28710. 1975. Repr. of 1940 ed. 15.00 (ISBN 0-527-03232-8). Kraus Repr.

Ford, James L. Every Day in the Year. 59.95 (ISBN 0-8490-0140-4). Gordon Pr.

--Forty-Odd Years in the Literary Shop: William Dean Howells, Etc. 1973. Repr. of 1921 ed. 15.00 (ISBN 0-8274-0656-8). R West.

Ford, James L. & Stark, T. Long & Short-Term Interest Rates. LC 67-9408. (Illus.). 1967. 10.00x (ISBN 0-678-06255-2). Kelley.

Ford, James L. & Ford, Mary K., eds. Every Day in the Year: A Political Epitome of the World's History. LC 68-17941. 1969. Repr. of 1902 ed. 40.00x (ISBN 0-8103-3105-5). Gale.

Ford, Jeremiah & Lansing, Ruth. Cervantes: A Tentative Bibliography. LC 77-13539. 1977. Repr. of 1931 ed. lib. bdg. 20.00 (ISBN 0-89341-454-9). Longwood Pub Group.

Ford, Jeremiah D. Main Currents of Spanish Literature. LC 68-13689. 1968. Repr. of 1919 ed. 10.00x (ISBN 0-8196-0213-2). Biblo.

--Old Spanish Readings. LC 67-21713. 1967. Repr. of 1911 ed. 9.50x (ISBN 0-87752-037-2). Gordian.

Ford, Jeremiah D., ed. Old Spanish Readings. LC 11-11753. Repr. of 1911 ed. 22.00 (ISBN 0-527-30420-4). Kraus Repr.

Ford, Jeremiah D., ed. see De Camoes, L.

Ford, Jessie. The Burning Woman. (Orig.). 1985. pap. 3.95 (ISBN 0-345-31046-2). Ballantine.

--Searching. (Love & Life Romance Ser.). 176p. (Orig.). 1982. pap. 1.75 (ISBN 0-345-30696-1). Ballantine.

Ford, Jill. Human Behavior: Towards a Practical Understanding. (Library of Social Work Ser.). 160p. 1983. pap. 8.95x (ISBN 0-7100-9218-0). Routledge & Kegan.

Ford, Jo Ann G., et al. Applied Decision Making for Nurses. LC 78-15713. (Illus.). 140p. 1979. pap. text ed. 15.95 (ISBN 0-8016-1624-7). Mosby.

Ford, John. The Broken Heart. Spencer, T. J. P., ed. (Revels Plays Ser.). 256p. 1981. 22.00x (ISBN 0-8018-2479-6). Johns Hopkins.

--The Broken Heart. Morris, Brian, ed. (New Mermaid Ser.). 1976. pap. 2.95x (ISBN 0-393-90036-3). Norton.

--The Broken Heart. Anderson, Donald K., Jr., ed. LC 68-10354. (Regents Renaissance Drama Ser). xxiv, 117p. 1968. 11.95x (ISBN 0-8032-0259-8); pap. 2.95x (ISBN 0-8032-5259-5, BB 227, Bison). U of Nebr Pr.

--The Broken Heart: A Tragedy. LC 72-38184. (English Experience Ser.: No. 456). 80p. 1972. Repr. of 1633 ed. 11.50 (ISBN 90-221-0456-7). Walter J Johnson.

--The Chronicle Historie of Perkin Warbeck. LC 72-5994. (English Experience Ser.: No. 447). 82p. 1972. Repr. of 1634 ed. 11.50 (ISBN 90-221-0447-8). Walter J Johnson.

--Dramatic Works from the Old English Quarto, Vol. 1. Bd. with Forde's Contribution to the Decadence of the Drama & Reprint of Dekker' Penny-Wise, Pound-Foolish. Bang, W., ed. (Mat. for the Study of the Old English Drama Ser. 1: Vol. 23). pap. 53.00. Kraus Repr.

--Fames Memoriall, or the Earle of Devonshire Deceased. LC 70-25888. (English Experience Ser.: No. 188). 56p. 1969. Repr. of 1606 ed. 8.00 (ISBN 90-221-0188-6). Walter J Johnson.

--The Fancies, Chast & Noble. LC 73-6128. (English Experience Ser.: No. 594). 76p. 1973. Repr. of 1638 ed. 8.00 (ISBN 90-221-0594-6). Walter J Johnson.

--The Ladies Trial. LC 75-25789. (English Experience Ser.: No. 285). 80p. 1971. Repr. of 1639 ed. 11.50 (ISBN 90-221-0285-8). Walter J Johnson.

--A Line of Life. LC 70-38186. (English Experience Ser.: No. 457). 144p. 1972. Repr. of 1620 ed. 14.00 (ISBN 90-221-0457-5). Walter J Johnson.

--The Lovers Melancholy. LC 70-25576. (English Experience Ser.: No. 271). 88p. 1970. Repr. of 1629 ed. 13.00 (ISBN 90-221-0271-8). Walter J Johnson.

--The Lover's Melancholy. Hill, R. F., ed. LC 84-12263. (The Revels Plays Ser.). 1985. 35.00 (ISBN 0-7190-1533-2, Pub. by Manchester Univ Pr). Longwood Pub Group.

--Loves Sacrifice. LC 76-25887. (English Experience Ser.: No. 314). 88p. 1971. Repr. of 1633 ed. 13.00 (ISBN 90-221-0314-5). Walter J Johnson.

--Perkin Warbeck. Anderson, Donald K., Jr., ed. LC 65-15338. (Regents Renaissance Drama Ser). xx, 114p. 1965. 10.95x (ISBN 0-8032-0260-1); pap. 2.75x (ISBN 0-8032-5260-9, BB 213, Bison). U of Nebr Pr.

--The Role of the Trypanosomiases in African Ecology: A Study of the Tsetse Fly Problem. LC 76-23168. pap. 145.50 (ISBN 0-317-29955-7, 2051719). Bks Demand UMI.

--Stagecoach. (Lorrimer Classic Screenplay Ser.). (Illus.). 10.95 (ISBN 0-8044-2210-9); pap. 6.95 (ISBN 0-8044-6157-0). Ungar.

--Tis Pity She's a Whore. Stavig, Mark, ed. LC 66-16498. (Crofts Classics Ser.). 1966. pap. text ed. 3.75x (ISBN 0-88295-036-3). Harlan Davidson.

--Tis Pity She's a Whore. Morris, Brian, ed. (New Mermaid Ser.). 1978. pap. 2.95x (ISBN 0-393-90011-8). Norton.

--Tis Pity She's a Whore. Sherman, S. P., ed. Bd. with The Broken Heart. 287p. 1980. Repr. lib. bdg. 25.00 (ISBN 0-8492-4625-3). R West.

--Tis Pity She's a Whore. Bawcutt, N. W., ed. LC 65-15339. (Regents Renaissance Drama Ser). xxii, 110p. 1966. pap. 4.25x (ISBN 0-8032-5261-7, BB 215, Bison). U of Nebr Pr.

--Tis Pity She's A Whore. Roper, Derek, ed. (The Revels Plays Ser.). 146p. 1975. 25.00 (ISBN 0-7190-1511-1, Pub. by Manchester Univ Pr). Longwood Pub Group.

--Wagonmaster. (RKO Classic Screenplay Ser.). (Illus.). 125p. (Orig.). 1985. o. s. i. 14.95 (ISBN 0-8044-2213-3); pap. 8.95 (ISBN 0-8044-6166-X). Ungar.

Ford, John see Bald, Robert C.

Ford, John, jt. auth. see Webster, John.

Ford, John G. Chinese Snuff Bottles. (Edward Choate O'Dell Collection). (Illus.). 80p. (Orig.). 1982. 32.95x (ISBN 0-9609668-0-3). Intl Chi Snuff.

Ford, John K. A Framework for Financial Analysis. 176p. 1981. pap. text ed. 17.95 (ISBN 0-13-330241-5). P-H.

Ford, John L., jt. auth. see Eddy, Cristen C.

Ford, John M. Cestus Dei. (Tor Bks.). 256p. (Orig.). 1983. pap. 2.75 (ISBN 0-523-48584-0). Pinnacle Bks.

--The Dragon Waiting. 400p. 1985. pap. 3.50 (ISBN 0-380-69887-0). Avon.

--The Final Reflection. (A Star Trek Novel Ser.). 256p. (Orig.). 1984. pap. 2.95 (ISBN 0-671-47388-3). PB.

--The Final Reflection. (Gregg Fiction Star Trek Ser.). 1985. lib. bdg. 11.95 (ISBN 0-8398-2885-3, Gregg). G K Hall.

Ford, John W., ed. see Company for the Propagation of the Gospel in New England & the Parts Adjacent in America, London.

Ford, Julienne. Paradigms & Fairy Tales: An Introduction to the Science of Meanings, 2 vols. 1975. Vol. 1. pap. 8.95x (ISBN 0-7100-8248-7); Vol. 2. pap. 8.95x (ISBN 0-7100-8249-5); Set. pap. 16.95x (ISBN 0-7100-8250-9). Routledge & Kegan.

Ford, Julienne, et al. Special Education & Social Control: Invisible Disasters. 192p. 1982. pap. 19.95x (ISBN 0-7100-0951-8). Routledge & Kegan.

Ford, K. W., ed. Brandeis University Summer Institute in Theoretical Physics: 1963 Lectures, 2 vols. Incl. Vol. 1. Strong & Electromagnetic Interactions. 352p. 93.75 (ISBN 0-677-10630-0); Vol. 2. Astrophysics & Weak Interactions. 478p. 99.00 (ISBN 0-677-10640-8). 1964. Gordon.

Ford, K. W., et al. Efficient Use of Energy. LC 75-18227. (AIP Conference Proceedings Ser.: No. 25). 304p. 1975. 20.00 (ISBN 0-88318-124-X). Am Inst Physics.

Ford, K. W., et al, eds. Efficient Use of Energy: A Physics Perspective. LC 75-18227. (AIP Conference Proceedings Ser.: No. 25). 305p. 1975. 20.00 (ISBN 0-88318-124-X). Am Inst Physics.

Ford, Karen C. Las Yerbas de la Gente: A Study of Hispano-American Medicinal Plants. (Anthropological Papers: No. 60). (Illus.). 1975. pap. 5.00x (ISBN 0-932206-58-1). U Mich Mus Anthro.

Ford, Katherine & Buskirk, Phyllis. Selected Population, Housing & Economic Characteristics in Kalamazoo County by Tracts: 1960-1970. 63p. 1973. pap. 0.50 (ISBN 0-911558-46-2). W E Upjohn.

Ford, Kathleen. Contraceptive Utilization: United States 1973. Akers, Karen, ed. (Ser. 23-2). 1978. pap. 1.75 (ISBN 0-8406-0148-4). Natl Ctr Health Stats.

Ford, Kathleen H., jt. auth. see Ford, George A.

Ford, Kenneth. Classical & Modern Physics, 3 vols. Incl. Vol. 1. 1972; Vol. 2. Ford, Kenneth W. 1972. text ed. 33.50x (ISBN 0-471-00724-2); answer manual o.p. 7.50 (ISBN 0-471-00945-8); Vol. 3. 1974. text ed. 35.50x (ISBN 0-471-00878-8); answer manual o.p. 6.95 (ISBN 0-471-00946-6). LC 76-161385. 1973. combined ed. for vols. 1 & 2 o.p. 35.95 (ISBN 0-471-00666-1). Wiley.

Ford, Kenneth W. see Ford, Kenneth.

Ford, Kristina, ed. Remote Sensing for Planners. LC 78-31594. (Illus.). 272p. 1979. text ed. 25.00 (ISBN 0-88285-058-X). Ctr Urban Pol Res.

Ford, L. The Christian Persuader. LC 66-22043. 160p. 1976. pap. 6.68i (ISBN 0-06-062679-8, RD/157, HarpR). Har-Row.

Ford, Lana J. I'm Just That Kind of Woman. 1981. 5.75 (ISBN 0-8062-1822-3). Carlton.

Ford, Lauren. Little Book About God. LC 81-43749. (Illus.). 48p. (ps-3). 1985. 9.95 (ISBN 0-385-17691-0). Doubleday.

Ford, Lee E. Animal Welfare Encyclopedia. Incl. Vol. 12. Model State Bills on Animal Welfare (ISBN 0-88017-088-3); Vol. 13. Existing Animal Laws in Various States (ISBN 0-88017-089-1); Vol. 14. More State Bills Re Animal Welfare (ISBN 0-88017-090-5). (Orig.). 1975. pap. 10.00 ea. Ford Assocs.

--Animal Welfare Encyclopedia. 1983. pap. text ed. 12.00 ea. vol. Ford Assocs.

--Animal Welfare Encyclopedia: Breeder's Journal for 1958, Vols. 7, 7A, 7B, 7C. 100p. 1975. Set. pap. 40.00 (ISBN 0-88017-068-9); Vol. 7. pap. (ISBN 0-88017-069-7); Vol. 7A. pap. (ISBN 0-88017-070-0); Vol. 7B. pap. (ISBN 0-88017-071-9); Vol. 7C. pap. (ISBN 0-88017-072-7). Ford Assocs.

--Animal Welfare Encyclopedia: Breeder's Journal for 1959, Vols. 8, 8A, 8B, 8C. 100p. 1975. Set. pap. 40.00 (ISBN 0-88017-114-6); Vol. 8. pap. (ISBN 0-88017-073-5); Vol. 8A. pap. (ISBN 0-88017-074-3); Vol. 8B. pap. (ISBN 0-88017-075-1); Vol. 8C. pap. (ISBN 0-88017-076-X). Ford Assocs.

--Animal Welfare Encyclopedia: Breeder's Journal for 1960, Vols. 9, 9A-9E. 100p. 1975. Set. pap. 60.00 (ISBN 0-88017-115-4); Vol. 9. pap. (ISBN 0-88017-077-8); Vol. 9A. pap. (ISBN 0-88017-078-6); Vol. 9B. pap. (ISBN 0-88017-079-4); Vol. 9C. pap. (ISBN 0-88017-080-8); Vol. 9D. pap. (ISBN 0-88017-081-6); Vol. 9E. pap. (ISBN 0-88017-082-4). Ford Assocs.

--Animal Welfare Encyclopedia: Breeder's Journal for 1961, Vols. 10, 10A, 10B, 10C. 100p. 1975. Set. pap. 40.00 (ISBN 0-88017-116-2); Vol. 10. pap. (ISBN 0-88017-083-2); Vol. 10A. pap. (ISBN 0-88017-084-0); Vol. 10B. pap. (ISBN 0-88017-085-9); Vol. 10C. pap. (ISBN 0-88017-086-7). Ford Assocs.

--Animal Welfare Encyclopedia: Guide Dog Training & Schools in U. S. A. & Abroad. 1975. Set. pap. 30.00 (ISBN 0-88017-117-0); Vol. 16. pap. (ISBN 0-88017-094-8); Vol. 16A. pap. (ISBN 0-88017-095-6); Vol. 16B. pap. (ISBN 0-88017-096-4). Ford Assocs.

--Animal Welfare Encyclopedia: Legislation & Litigation of Interest to Dog Owners, Vols. 4-6. 300p. (Orig.). 1975. Vol. 4. pap. 10.00 (ISBN 0-88017-064-6); Vol. 5. pap. 10.00 (ISBN 0-88017-065-4); Vol. 6. pap. 10.00 (ISBN 0-88017-066-2). Ford Assocs.

--Animal Welfare Encyclopedia: Notice & Advanced Obedience Training for Dogs. (Orig.). 1975. Set. pap. 30.00 (ISBN 0-88017-118-9); Vol. 15. pap. (ISBN 0-88017-091-3); Vol. 15A. pap. (ISBN 0-88017-092-1); Vol. 15B. pap. (ISBN 0-88017-093-X). Ford Assocs.

--Animal Welfare Encyclopedia, Vol. 17: Legislation-Litigation of Interest to Dog Owners. 100p. 1976. pap. 10.00 (ISBN 0-88017-067-0). Ford Assocs.

--Job & Sex Discrimination: Justice Ser, Vol. 1. (The Justice Ser.: No. 6). pap. 12.00x (ISBN 0-88017-123-5). Ford Assocs.

--Women's Legal Handbook, State Commissions on Women. rev. ed. Incl. Set. pap. 140.00 (ISBN 0-88017-008-5); Vol. 6A. pap. (ISBN 0-88017-009-3); Vol. 6B. pap. (ISBN 0-88017-010-7); Vol. 6C. pap. (ISBN 0-88017-011-5); Vol. 6D. pap. Vol. 6E. pap. (ISBN 0-88017-013-1); Vol. 6F. pap. (ISBN 0-88017-014-X); Vol. 6G. pap. (ISBN 0-88017-015-8); Vol. 6H. pap. (ISBN 0-88017-016-6); Vol. 6I. pap. (ISBN 0-88017-017-4). Vol. 6J (ISBN 0-88017-018-2). Vol. 6K. pap. (ISBN 0-88017-019-0); Vol. 6L. pap. (ISBN 0-88017-020-4); Vol. 6M. pap. (ISBN 0-88017-021-2). 100p. 1976. pap. Ford Assocs.

Ford, Lee E., ed. Animal Welfare Encyclopedia, 5 vols. (Series 22). 500p. 1985. Set. pap. 60.00 (ISBN 0-88017-397-1); Vol. 1. pap. 12.00 (ISBN 0-88017-398-X); Vol. 2. pap. 12.00 (ISBN 0-88017-399-8); Vol. 3. pap. 12.00 (ISBN 0-88017-400-5); Vol. 4. pap. 12.00 (ISBN 0-88017-401-3); Vol. 5. pap. 12.00 (ISBN 0-88017-402-1). Ford Assocs.

--Animal Welfare Encyclopedia: Dog Genetics & Legislation, 28 vols. 100p. (Orig.). 1975. Set. pap. 280.00. Ford Assocs.

--Animal Welfare Encyclopedia, Vol. 11: Anthology of Dog Genetics & Breeding. 100p. 1975. pap. 7.00 (ISBN 0-88017-087-5). Ford Assocs.
--Indiana Directory of Humane Societies. 100p. 1980. pap. 10.00 (ISBN 0-88017-099-9). Ford Assocs.
--Indiana Dog Laws. 100p. 1980. pap. 10.00x (ISBN 0-88017-098-0). Ford Assocs.
--Job & Sex Discrimination, 10 vols. (The Justice Ser.: No. 6). Set. pap. write for info. (ISBN 0-88017-122-7). Ford Assocs.
--Job & Sex Discrimination, 10 vols. (The Eighties Woman Ser.: No. 7). 1983. Set. pap. write for info. (ISBN 0-88017-133-2). Ford Assocs.
--Job & Sex Discrimination, 10 vols. (Advocate for the Handicapped Ser.: No. 8). 1983. Set. pap. write for info. (ISBN 0-88017-144-8). Ford Assocs.
--Job & Sex Discrimination: As a Boss, Vol. 7. (The Eighties Woman Ser.: No. 7). 1983. pap. 12.00x (ISBN 0-88017-140-5). Ford Assocs.
--Job & Sex Discrimination: As a Parent, Vol. 8. (The Eighties Woman Ser.: No. 7). 1983. pap. 12.00x (ISBN 0-88017-141-3). Ford Assocs.
--Job & Sex Discrimination: As a Person, Vol. 6. (The Eighties Woman Ser.: No. 7). 1983. pap. 12.00x (ISBN 0-88017-139-1). Ford Assocs.
--Job & Sex Discrimination: Blind Children of the 60's, Vol. 1. (Advocates for the Handicapped Ser.: No. 8). 1983. pap. 12.00x (ISBN 0-88017-145-6). Ford Assocs.
--Job & Sex Discrimination: Hidden Discrimination, Vol. 3. (The Eighties Woman Ser.: No. 7). 1983. pap. 12.00x (ISBN 0-88017-136-7). Ford Assocs.
--Job & Sex Discrimination: In the Community, Vol. 10. (The Eighties Woman Ser.: No. 7). 1983. pap. 12.00x (ISBN 0-88017-143-X). Ford Assocs.
--Job & Sex Discrimination: In the Media, Vol. 9. (The Eighties Woman Ser.: No. 7). 1983. pap. 12.00x (ISBN 0-88017-142-1). Ford Assocs.
--Job & Sex Discrimination: Justice for the Poor, Vol. 7. (The Justice Ser.: No. 6). 1983. pap. 12.00x (ISBN 0-88017-129-4). Ford Assocs.
--Job & Sex Discrimination: Justice for the Animals. (The Justice Ser.: No. 6). 1983. pap. 12.00x (ISBN 0-88017-131-6). Ford Assocs.
--Job & Sex Discrimination: Justice for the Alcoholic, Vol. 6. (The Justice Ser.: No. 6). 1983. pap. 12.00x (ISBN 0-88017-128-6). Ford Assocs.
--Job & Sex Discrimination: Justice for the Handicapped, Vol. 4. (The Justice Ser.: No. 6). pap. 12.00x (ISBN 0-88017-126-X). Ford Assocs.
--Job & Sex Discrimination: Justice for the Juvenile, Vol. 8. (The Justice Ser.: No. 6). 1983. pap. 12.00x (ISBN 0-88017-130-8). Ford Assocs.
--Job & Sex Discrimination: Justice in Our Courts, Vol. 10. (The Justice Ser.: No. 6). 1983. pap. 12.00x (ISBN 0-88017-132-4). Ford Assocs.
--Job & Sex Discrimination: Justice in State Agencies, Vol. 2. (The Justice Ser.: No. 6). pap. 12.00x (ISBN 0-88017-124-3). Ford Assocs.
--Job & Sex Discrimination: Justice in Support & Custody, Vol. 5. (The Justice Ser.: No. 6). pap. 12.00x (ISBN 0-88017-127-8). Ford Assocs.
--Job & Sex Discrimination: Justice in State Legislatures, Vol. 3. (The Justice Ser.: No. 6). pap. 12.00x (ISBN 0-88017-125-1). Ford Assocs.
--Job & Sex Discrimination: Migrants in the 70's, Vol. 10. (Advocates for Handicapped Ser.: No. 8). 1983. pap. 12.00x (ISBN 0-88017-154-5). Ford Assocs.
--Job & Sex Discrimination: New Networks, Vol. 2. (The Eighties Woman Ser.: No. 7). 1983. pap. 12.00x (ISBN 0-88017-135-9). Ford Assocs.
--Job & Sex Discrimination: No Hypocrite, Vol. 4. (The Eighties Woman Ser.: No. 7). 1983. pap. 12.00x (ISBN 0-88017-137-5). Ford Assocs.
--Job & Sex Discrimination: No Longer the Loner, Vol. 1. (The Eighties Woman Ser.: No. 7). 1983. pap. 12.00x (ISBN 0-88017-134-0). Ford Assocs.
--Job & Sex Discrimination: Poor in the 80's, Vol. 9. (Advocates for Handicapped Ser.: No. 8). 1983. pap. 12.00x (ISBN 0-88017-153-7). Ford Assocs.
--Job & Sex Discrimination: Prognosis for 80's, Vol. 3. (Advocates for Handicapped Ser.: No. 8). 1983. pap. 12.00x (ISBN 0-88017-147-2). Ford Assocs.
--Job & Sex Discrimination: Retarded in the 70's, Vol. 2. (Advocates for Handicapped Ser.: No. 8). 1983. pap. 12.00x (ISBN 0-88017-146-4). Ford Assocs.
--Job & Sex Discrimination: Right to Education in 70's, Vol. 5, Pt. 1. (Advocates for Handicapped Ser.: No. 8). 1983. pap. 12.00x (ISBN 0-88017-149-9). Ford Assocs.
--Job & Sex Discrimination: Right to Education in 70's, Vol. 6, Pt. 2. (Advocates for Handicapped Ser.: No. 8). 1983. pap. 12.00x (ISBN 0-88017-150-2). Ford Assocs.
--Job & Sex Discrimination: Right to Education in 70's, Vol. 7, Pt. 3. (Advocates for Handicapped Ser.: No. 8). 1983. pap. 12.00x (ISBN 0-88017-151-0). Ford Assocs.
--Job & Sex Discrimination: Right to Education in 70's, Vol. 8, Pt. 4. (Advocates for Handicapped Ser.: No. 8). 1983. pap. 12.00x (ISBN 0-88017-152-9). Ford Assocs.
--Job & Sex Discrimination: Right to Treatment in 70's, Vol. 4. (Advocates for Handicapped Ser.: No. 8). 1983. pap. 12.00x (ISBN 0-88017-148-0). Ford Assocs.
--Job & Sex Discrimination: What Price Popularity, Vol. 5. (The Eighties Woman Ser.: No. 7). 1983. pap. 12.00x (ISBN 0-88017-138-3). Ford Assocs.
--Women of the Eighties, 10 vols. 100p. (Orig.). 1981. Set. pap. 120.00 (ISBN 0-88017-101-4). Ford Assocs.
--Women of the Eighties: Vol. 1: the Family Woman. 100p. (Orig.). 1981. pap. 12.00 (ISBN 0-88017-103-0). Ford Assocs.
--Women of the Eighties: Vol. 10: Women in the World. 100p. (Orig.). 1981. pap. 12.00 (ISBN 0-88017-111-1). Ford Assocs.
--Women of the Eighties: Vol. 2: the Legal Oriented Woman. 100p. (Orig.). 1981. pap. 12.00 (ISBN 0-88017-103-0). Ford Assocs.
--Women of the Eighties: Vol. 3: the Woman in Research. 100p. (Orig.). 1981. pap. 12.00 (ISBN 0-88017-104-9). Ford Assocs.
--Women of the Eighties: Vol. 4: Social Security & the Woman. 100p. (Orig.). 1981. pap. 12.00 (ISBN 0-88017-105-7). Ford Assocs.
--Women of the Eighties: Vol. 5: Economics & Women. 100p. (Orig.). 1981. pap. 12.00 (ISBN 0-88017-106-5). Ford Assocs.
--Women of the Eighties: Vol. 6: the Political Woman. 100p. (Orig.). 1982. pap. 12.00 (ISBN 0-88017-107-3). Ford Assocs.
--Women of the Eighties: Vol. 7: the Woman Criminal. 100p. (Orig.). 1981. pap. 12.00 (ISBN 0-88017-108-1). Ford Assocs.
--Women of the Eighties: Vol. 8: Women Play to Win. 100p. (Orig.). 1981. pap. 12.00 (ISBN 0-88017-109-X). Ford Assocs.
--Women of the Eighties: Vol. 9: Women in Religion. 100p. (Orig.). 1981. pap. 12.00 (ISBN 0-88017-110-3). Ford Assocs.
--Women's Legal Handbook Series on the Protection of the Right of Privacy in Public-Private Records. Incl. Vols. 17, 17A, 17B. Introduction NJ Study. Set. pap. 30.00 (ISBN 0-88017-041-7); Vol. 17. pap. (ISBN 0-88017-042-5); Vol. 17A. pap. (ISBN 0-88017-043-3); Vol. 17B. pap. (ISBN 0-88017-044-1); Vols. 18 & 18A. Privacy Bills & Statutes, Etc. Set. pap. 20.00 (ISBN 0-88017-257-6); Vol. 18. pap. (ISBN 0-88017-045-X); Vol. 18a. pap. (ISBN 0-88017-046-8); Vol. 19 & 19A. Privacy Bills & Statutes, Etc. Set. pap. 20.00 (ISBN 0-88017-258-4); Vol. 19. pap. (ISBN 0-88017-047-6); Vol. 19A. pap. (ISBN 0-88017-048-4); Vol. 20 & 20A. Privacy Bills & Statutes, Etc. Set. pap. 20.00 (ISBN 0-88017-259-2); Vol. 20. pap. (ISBN 0-88017-049-2); Vol. 20A. pap. (ISBN 0-88017-050-6); Vols. 21, 21A, 21B. Privacy Bills & Statutes, Etc. Set. pap. 30.00 (ISBN 0-686-34377-8); Vol. 21. pap. (ISBN 0-88017-051-4); Vol. 21A. pap. (ISBN 0-88017-052-2); Vol. 21B. pap. (ISBN 0-88017-053-0). 1975. Privacy Set. pap. (ISBN 0-88017-256-8). Ford Assocs.

Ford, Lee Ellen, ed. Animal Welfare Handbooks, 3 Vol. (Animal Welfare Encyclopedia Ser.: 20). 300p. (Orig.). 1984. Set. pap. text ed. 36.00 (ISBN 0-88017-228-2). Ford Assocs.
--Canine Genetics & Breeding, 5 Vols. (Animal Welfare Encyclopedia Ser.: 19). 100p. (Orig.). 1984. Set. pap. text ed. 60.00 (ISBN 0-318-01272-3). Ford Assocs.
--Christian Caring vs. Politics & the Poor, 3 Vols. (Women's Legal Handbook Ser.: 13). (Orig.). 1984. Set. pap. text ed. 36.00 (ISBN 0-88017-234-7). Ford Assocs.
--Directory of Women Attorneys U. S. A., 1977, 5 Vols. (Women's Legal Handbook Ser.: 9). (Orig.). 1984. Set. pap. text ed. 60.00 (ISBN 0-318-01274-X). Ford Assocs.

Ford, Lee Ellen, ed. & intro. by. Directory of Women Law Graduates & Attorneys in the USA, 1977, 5 vols. 1977. pap. 46.50 (ISBN 0-88017-054-9). Ford Assocs.

Ford, Lee Ellen, ed. Family Justice, 6 Vols. (Women's Legal Handbook Ser.: 16). (Orig.). 1984. Set. pap. text ed. 72.00 (ISBN 0-88017-260-6). Ford Assocs.
--Guide Dogs for Blind Children, 5 Vols. (Animal Welfare Encyclopedia Ser.: 18). 100p. (Orig.). 1984. Set. pap. text ed. 60.00 (ISBN 0-318-01273-1). Ford Assocs.
--Justice & the Law: For People & Women, 3 Vols. (Orig.). 1984. Set. pap. text ed. 36.00 (ISBN 0-88017-318-1). Ford Assocs.
--Justice: The Family, the Church & Society, 3 Vols. (Women's Legal Handbook Ser.: 20). (Orig.). 1984. Set. pap. text ed. 36.00 (ISBN 0-88017-314-9). Ford Assocs.
--Legal Rights of Blind & Disabled, 3 Vols. (Women's Legal Handbook Ser.: 14). (Orig.). 1984. Set. pap. text ed. 36.00 (ISBN 0-88017-243-6). Ford Assocs.
--The Reformation Woman: Jobs, 2 Vols. (Women's Legal Handbook Ser.: 24). (Orig.). 1984. Set. pap. text ed. 24.00 (ISBN 0-88017-280-0). Ford Assocs.
--Right of Privacy, Vol. 22. (Women's Legal Handbook Ser.: 12). (Orig.). 1984. pap. text ed. 12.00 (ISBN 0-88017-239-8). Ford Assocs.
--Status of Women in Religion, Law, Probate, Government & Employment, 6 Vols. (Women's Legal Handbook Ser.: 15). (Orig.). 1984. Set. pap. text ed. 72.00 (ISBN 0-88017-244-4). Ford Assocs.
--Township Trustee & Poor Relief, 3 Vols. (Women's Legal Handbook Ser.: 11). (Orig.). 1984. Set. pap. text ed. 36.00 (ISBN 0-88017-232-0). Ford Assocs.
--The Welfare Problem in U. S. A., 1971: Or St. Thomas Aquinas vs. the Dandridge Case, 6 Vols. (Women's Legal Handbook Ser.: 10). (Orig.). 1984. pap. text ed. 72.00 (ISBN 0-88017-227-4). Ford Assocs.
--Women Addicts, 5 Vols. (Women's Legal Handbook Ser.: 18). (Orig.). 1984. Set. pap. text ed. 60.00 (ISBN 0-88017-272-X). Ford Assocs.
--Women & Power, 4 Vols. (Women's Legal Handbook Ser.: 17). 1984. Set. pap. text ed. 48.00 (ISBN 0-88017-267-3). Ford Assocs.
--Women in Public Eye, 3 Vols. (Women's Legal Handbook Ser.: 22). 1984. Set. pap. text ed. 36.00 (ISBN 0-88017-322-X). Ford Assocs.
--Women: Problems in Education, 3 Vols. (Women's Legal Handbook Ser.: 23). (Orig.). 1984. Set. pap. text ed. 36.00 (ISBN 0-88017-276-2). Ford Assocs.
--Youth: Education, Jobs & Motivation, 10 Vols. (Women's Legal Handbook Ser.: 19). (Orig.). 1984. Set. pap. text ed. 120.00 (ISBN 0-88017-303-3). Ford Assocs.

Ford, Leighton. Good News Is for Sharing. LC 77-78496. 1977. 6.95 (ISBN 0-89191-083-2). Cook.
--Sandy: A Heart for God. LC 85-52. 192p. (Orig.). 1985. 9.95 (ISBN 0-87784-824-6). Inter-Varsity.

Ford, LeRoy. Capacitese Como Lider. Blair, Guillermo, tr. 64p. (Span.). 1982. pap. 3.75 (ISBN 0-311-17023-4, Edit Mundo). Casa Bautista.
--Pedagogia Ilustrada: La Conferecia en la Ensenanza. Using Problem Solving in Teaching & Training, Tomo 3. 132p. 1983. pap. 4.95 (ISBN 0-311-11040-1). Casa Bautista.
--Pedagogia Ilustrada: Tomo I Principios Generales. Orig. Title: A Primer for Teachers & Leaders. (Illus.). 144p. 1982. pap. 2.75 (ISBN 0-311-11001-0, Edit Mundo). Casa Bautista.
--Pedagonia Ilustrada: La Conferencia en la Ensenanza, Tomo 2. Orig. Title: Using the Lecture in Teaching & Training. 136p. (Span.). pap. 3.25 (ISBN 0-311-11027-4). Casa Bautista.
--Primer for Teachers & Leaders. LC 63-19069. (Orig.). 1963. pap. 4.95 (ISBN 0-8054-3404-6). Broadman.
--A Sourcebook of Learning Activities. LC 83-27223. 1984. pap. 5.95 (ISBN 0-8054-3430-5). Broadman.
--Tools for Teaching & Training. LC 61-5630. (Orig.). 1961. pap. 4.95 (ISBN 0-8054-3411-9). Broadman.
--Using Problem Solving in Teaching & Training. LC 77-178060. (Multi-Media Teaching & Training Ser.). (Orig.). 1972. pap. 5.50 (ISBN 0-8054-3415-1). Broadman.
--Using the Case Study in Teaching & Training. LC 71-105324. (Multi-Media Teaching & Training Ser.). (Illus.). 1970. pap. 5.50 (ISBN 0-8054-3413-5). Broadman.
--Using the Lecture in Teaching & Training. LC 68-20673. (Multi-Media Teaching & Training Ser.). (Orig.). 1968. pap. 5.50 (ISBN 0-8054-3412-7). Broadman.
--Using the Panel in Teaching & Training. McCormick, Joe, tr. LC 79-127196. (Multi-Media Teaching & Training Ser.). (Orig.). 1971. pap. 5.50 (ISBN 0-8054-3414-3). Broadman.

Ford, Lester R. Automorphic Functions. LC 52-8647. Chelsea Pub.

Ford, Lester R., Jr. & Fulkerson, D. R. Flows in Networks. (Rand Corp. Research Studies Ser.). 1962. 20.00 (ISBN 0-691-07962-5). Princeton U Pr.

Ford, Lewis S. The Emergence of Whitehead's Metaphysics, 1925-29. (Philosophy Ser.). 368p. 1984. 39.50x (ISBN 0-87395-856-X); pap. 19.95x (ISBN 0-87395-857-8). State U NY Pr.

Ford, Lewis S. & Kline, George L., eds. Explorations in Whitehead's Philosophy. LC 77-75800. x, 353p. 1983. 35.00 (ISBN 0-8232-1102-9); pap. 20.00 (ISBN 0-8232-1103-7). Fordham.

Ford, Linda S., jt. auth. see Campbell, Jonathan A.

Ford, Louis R. Practical Marine Diesel Engineering. 4th ed. LC 43-4152. (Illus.). 1948. 7.00 (ISBN 0-911090-11-8). Pacific Bk Supply.

Ford, Madox. Great Trade Route. 448p. 1983. Repr. of 1937 ed. lib. bdg. 40.00 (ISBN 0-89987-274-3). Darby Bks.

Ford, Madox B. The Diary of Madox Brown. Surtees, Virginia, ed. LC 81-51344. (Paul Mellon Centre for Studies in British Art). (Illus.). 320p. 1981. 32.50x (ISBN 0-300-02743-5). Yale U Pr.

Ford, Marcus P. William James's Philosophy: A New Perspective. LC 81-16314. 136p. 1982. lib. bdg. 13.50x (ISBN 0-87023-366-1). U of Mass Pr.

Ford, Mark, jt. auth. see Feigenbaum, Ed.

Ford, Marvin, et al. On the Other Side. LC 78-52065. 1978. pap. 2.50 pocketsize (ISBN 0-88270-310-2, Pub. by Logos). Bridge Pub.

Ford, Mary. The Application of the Rorschach Test to Young Children. LC 70-141545. (Univ. of Minnesota Institute of Child Welfare Monographs: No. 23). (Illus.). 114p. 1975. Repr. of 1946 ed. lib. bdg. 18.75x (ISBN 0-8371-5892-3, CWFR). Greenwood.

Ford, Mary & Ford, Michael. Mary Ford's Cake Designs: Another 101 with Step-by-Step Instructions. (Illus.). 320p. 1985. 24.95 (ISBN 0-946429-01-4, Pub. by M Ford Cake Artistry Centre). Interbook.
--One Hundred & One Cake Designs: Step-by-Step Instruction. (Illus.). 320p. 1985. 24.95 (ISBN 0-946429-00-6, Pub. by M Ford Cake Artistry Centre). Interbook.

Ford, Mary A., jt. ed. see Ford, D. M.

Ford, Mary K., jt. ed. see Ford, James L.

Ford, Mary K., tr. see Halevy, Ludovic.

Ford, Michael, jt. auth. see Ford, Mary.

Ford, Michael C. Goddess Latitudes & the Great American Grab-Bag of 1945; Two American Plays. 40p. (Orig.). 1982. pap. 3.95 (ISBN 0-89807-027-9). Illuminati.

Ford, Michael J. The Changing Climate: Responses of the Natural Flora & Fauna. (Illus.). 192p. 1982. text ed. 27.50x (ISBN 0-04-574017-8). Allen Unwin.

Ford, Michael J. & Munro, John F. Practical Procedures in Clinical Medicine. (Illus.). 144p. 1981. pap. text ed. 12.00 (ISBN 0-443-02120-1). Churchill.

Ford, Miriam A. De see De Ford, Miriam A.

Ford, Miriam A. de see De Ford, Miriam A. & Jackson, Joan S.

Ford Motor Co. Ford Passenger Car Shop Manual: 1952-1954. (Illus.). 560p. 1977. 28.95 (ISBN 0-911160-37-X). Post-Era.

Ford Motor Company. Ford Model GP Prototype Jeep: TM-10-1101. Post, Dan R., ed. LC 72-185934. (Illus.). 128p. 1971. pap. 12.95 (ISBN 0-911160-46-9). Post-Era.
--Ford Passenger Car Shop Manual: 1949-1951. (Illus.). 320p. 1977. 21.95 (ISBN 0-911160-36-1). Post-Era.
--Ford V-8 Service Bulletins 1932-1937 Complete. Post, Dan R., ed. LC 76-8817. (Illus.). 544p. 1968. 21.95 (ISBN 0-911160-32-9). Post-Era.
--Ford V-8 Service Bulletins 1938-1940 Complete. Post, Dan R., ed. (Illus.). 576p. 1970. Post-Era.
--Ford V-8 Service Bulletins: 1941-1948, Complete. Post, Dan R., ed. LC 76-26325. (Illus.). 1977. 21.95 (ISBN 0-911160-34-5). Post-Era.
--Matchless Model A, a Tour Through the Factory. Post, Dan R., ed. (Illus.). 1961. pap. 3.00 (ISBN 0-911160-29-9). Post-Era.
--Model A Ford Service Bulletins Complete. Post, Dan R., ed. LC 72-90821. (Illus.). 320p. 1957. 13.95 (ISBN 0-911160-28-0). Post-Era.
--Model T Ford Service Bulletin Essentials. Post, Dan R., ed. LC 73-89603. (Illus.). 520p. 1966. 21.95 (ISBN 0-911160-19-1). Post-Era.

Ford Motor Company, Airplane Division. Ford Tri-Motor Monoplane Instruction Book. Post, Dan R., ed. LC 76-57054. (Illus.). 1977. 12.95 (ISBN 0-911160-71-X). Post-Era.

Ford, Neil M., et al. Sales Force Performance. LC 84-17166. 480p. 1984. 35.00x (ISBN 0-669-09376-9). Lexington Bks.

Ford, Nelson. Business Graphics for the IBM PC. LC 83-51567. (Illus.). 259p. 1984. pap. 18.95 (ISBN 0-89588-124-1). SYBEX.

Ford, Newell F. The Prefigurative Imagination of John Keats: A Study of the Beauty-Truth Identification & Its Implications. LC 74-24643. (Stanford University. Stanford Studies in Language & Literature: No. 2). Repr. of 1951 ed. 18.00 (ISBN 0-404-51818-4). AMS Pr.

Ford, Newell F., intro. by see Shelley, Percy B.

Ford, Nick A. Seeking a Newer World: Memoirs of a Black American Teacher. (Illus.). 320p. 1982. 12.95 (ISBN 0-89962-277-1). Todd & Honeywell.

Ford, Nick A., ed. Language in Uniform: A Reader on Propaganda. LC 67-18746. (Orig.). 1967. pap. 4.68 scp (ISBN 0-672-63054-0). Odyssey Pr.

Ford, Nick A., jt. ed. see Faggett, H. L.

Ford, Norman. Good Night: The Easy & Natural Way to Sleep the Whole Night Through. LC 83-60060. 208p. 1983. pap. 8.95 (ISBN 0-914918-47-8). Para Res.
--How to Eat Away Arthritis & Gout. 248p. 1982. 17.95 (ISBN 0-13-405647-7, Parker). P-H.
--Lifestyle for Longevity How to Extend Your Life with Moderation Joy & Ease. McKeigue, Emily & Ren, Marah, eds. 176p. 1984. pap. 9.95 (ISBN 0-914918-63-X). Para Res.
--Sleep Well, Live Well. 1985. pap. 3.50 (ISBN 0-8217-1579-8). Zebra.

Ford, Norman D. America by Car. 18th ed. (Illus.). 1984. pap. 5.95 (ISBN 0-685-65735-3). Harian.
--Fabulous Mexico: Where Everything Costs Less. 14th rev. ed. 192p. (Orig.). 1978. pap. 2.50 (ISBN 0-685-31471-5, 6957). Harian.
--Florida. 1985. pap. 6.95 (ISBN 0-686-42888-9). Harian.
--Investing to Beat Inflation. 169p. 1979. 4.95 (ISBN 0-686-63829-8). Harian.
--Natural Ways to Relieve Pain. 169p. 1980. 4.95 (ISBN 0-686-64248-1). Harian.
--Off the Beaten Path. 19th, rev. ed. (Illus.). 272p. 1985. pap. text ed. 5.95 (ISBN 0-686-46670-5). Harian.
--Retirement Paradises of the World. 18th ed. (Illus.). 184p. 5.95 (ISBN 0-686-63828-X). Harian.
--Where to Retire on a Small Income. 24th, rev. ed. (Illus.). 327p. 1985. pap. text ed. 6.95 (ISBN 0-686-46668-3). Harian.

Ford, Olive E. The Gospel According to Mother Goose. LC 80-70931. 1981. 8.95 (ISBN 0-9607786-0-8). Larksong Dayspring.
--The Gospel According to Mother Goose. Incl. Vol. 6. Indices I-IV Continens. 1983. 192.00 (ISBN 3-11-009530-0). 71p. (Orig.). 1979. pap. 6.95 (ISBN 0-9607786-1-6). Larksong Dayspring.

Ford, P. Social Theory & Social Practice: An Exploration of Experience. (Bibliography on Parliamentary Papers Ser.). 348p. 1969. 25.00x (ISBN 0-7165-0500-2, Pub. by Irish Academic Pr Ireland). Biblio Dist.

Ford, P. & Ford, G. Select List of British Parliamentary Papers 1833-1899. 188p. 1969. Repr. of 1953 ed. 25.00x (ISBN 0-7165-0574-6, Pub. by Irish Academic Pr Ireland). Biblio Dist.

--A Select List of Reports of Inquiries of the Irish Dail & Senate: Fifty Years of Policy Making, 1922-72. 64p. 1974. 20.00x (ISBN 0-7165-2254-3, Pub. by Irish Academic Pr Ireland). Biblio Dist.

Ford, P. & Ford, G. A. Breviate of Parliamentary Papers 1900-1916. 520p. 1969. Repr. of 1957 ed. 40.00x (ISBN 0-7165-0575-4, Pub. by Irish Academic Pr Ireland). Biblio Dist.

--Breviate of Parliamentary Papers 1917-1939. 624p. 1969. Repr. of 1951 ed. 40.00x (ISBN 0-7165-0576-2, Pub. by Irish Academic Pr Ireland). Biblio Dist.

Ford, P., et al. Select List of British Parliamentary Papers 1955-1964. 128p. 1970. 20.00x (ISBN 0-7165-0884-2, Pub. by Irish Academic Pr Ireland). Biblio Dist.

Ford, P. J. George Buchanan: Prince of Poets. 224p. 1982. 30.00 (ISBN 0-08-028458-2). Pergamon.

Ford, P. L., ed. see Dickinson, John.

Ford, P. R. The Oriental Carpet: A History & Guide to Traditional Motifs, Patterns, & Symbols. (Illus.). 352p. 1981. 75.00 (ISBN 0-8109-1405-0). Abrams.

Ford, Pat, ed. see Sandford, Michael.

Ford, Patricia. Women Political Leaders. (Illus.). 1985. pap. 5.95 (ISBN 0-913290-56-4). Camaro Pub.

Ford, Patrick J., jt. auth. see Mayhew, Lewis B.

Ford, Patrick K. The Poetry of Llywarch Hen: Introduction, Text & Translation. LC 73-87249. 1974. 25.00x (ISBN 0-520-02601-2). U of Cal Pr.

Ford, Patrick K., ed. Mabinogi & Other Medieval Welsh Tales. LC 76-3885. 1977. pap. 5.95 (ISBN 0-520-03414-7). U of Cal Pr.

Ford, Patrick K. & Borst, Karen G., eds. Connections Between Old English & Medieval Celtic Literature: Three Essays by Daniel Frederick Melia, Joseph Falaky Nagy, & Sarah Lynn Higley. (Old English Colloquium Ser.: No. 2). 76p. 1985. pap. text ed. 7.25 (ISBN 0-8191-4511-4). U Pr of Amer.

Ford, Paul L. Bibliotheca Hamiltoniana. LC 74-168120. Repr. of 1886 ed. 11.50 (ISBN 0-404-02513-7). AMS Pr.

--Bibliotheca Hamiltoniana. Repr. of 1886 ed. 12.50 (ISBN 0-8363-0013-0). Jenkins.

--Franklin Bibliography: A List of Book Written by or Relating to Benjamin Franklin. 1966. Repr. of 1889 ed. 31.50 (ISBN 0-8337-1187-3). B Franklin.

--Franklin Bibliography: A List of Books Written by, or Relating to Benjamin Franklin. LC 77-13526. 1977. Repr. of 1889 ed. lib. bdg. 25.00 (ISBN 0-89341-455-7). Longwood Pub Group.

--George Washington. LC 75-120876. (American Bicentennial Ser). 1970. Repr. of 1896 ed. 26.00x (ISBN 0-8046-1269-2, Pub. by Kennikat). Assoc Faculty Pr.

--The Honorable Peter Sterling. LC 68-20013. 1977. lib. bdg. 13.50 (ISBN 0-8398-0560-8); pap. text ed. 4.95x (ISBN 0-89197-791-0). Irvington.

--The Honorable Peter Sterling. 1969. Repr. of 1896 ed. 18.00 (ISBN 0-384-16410-2). Johnson Repr.

--Janice Meredith. (Classics Ser). (gr. 11 up). pap. 0.95 (ISBN 0-8049-0148-1, CL-148). Airmont.

--Josiah Tucker & His Writings. LC 77-182124. (Bibliography & Reference Ser.). 24p. 1972. Repr. of 1894 ed. lib. bdg. 10.00 (ISBN 0-8337-1188-1). B Franklin.

--List of Some Briefs in Appeal Causes Which Relate to America Tried Before the Lord Commissioners of Appeals of Prize Causes of His Majesty's Privy Council, 1736-58. LC 70-182125. (Historical Printing Club Publications: No. 25). 20p. 1972. Repr. of 1889 ed. lib. bdg. 10.00 (ISBN 0-8337-1189-X). B Franklin.

--List of Treasury Reports & Circulars Issued by Alexander Hamilton, 1789-1795. LC 72-131451. (Bibliography & Reference Ser.: No. 390). 1971. Repr. of 1886 ed. lib. bdg. 13.50 (ISBN 0-8337-1200-4). B Franklin.

--The Many-Sided Franklin. LC 73-38353. (Select Bibliographies Reprint Ser). Repr. of 1898 ed. 34.00 (ISBN 0-8369-6770-4). Ayer Co Pubs.

--The Many Sided Franklin. 1899. 30.00 (ISBN 0-8274-2671-2). R West.

--Pamphlets on the Constitution of the United States. LC 68-22228. (American History, Politics & Law Ser). 1968. Repr. of 1888 ed. lib. bdg. 35.00 (ISBN 0-306-71144-3). Da Capo.

--Short History & Description of Fort Niagara with an Account of Its Importance to Great Britain. LC 72-173994. (Research & Source Works Ser.: No. 847). 1971. pap. text ed. 10.00 (ISBN 0-8337-1199-7). B Franklin.

--Some Notes Towards an Essay on the Beginnings of American Dramatic Literature, 1606-1789. LC 70-140974. 1971. Repr. of 1893 ed. lib. bdg. 10.00 (ISBN 0-8337-1197-0). B Franklin.

--Tattletales of Cupid. LC 70-94720. (Short Story Index Reprint Ser.). 1898. 17.00 (ISBN 0-8369-3099-1). Ayer Co Pubs.

--The True George Washington. 1981. Repr. of 1896 ed. lib. bdg. 30.00 (ISBN 0-8495-1622-6). Arden Lib.

--The True George Washington. facsimile ed. LC 70-160973. (Select Bibliographies Reprint Ser). Repr. of 1896 ed. 26.50 (ISBN 0-8369-5841-1). Ayer Co Pubs.

--Washington & the Theater. LC 77-130099. (Dunlap Society, N. Ser.: No. 8). 1970. Repr. of 1899 ed. 13.00 (ISBN 0-8337-1204-7). B Franklin.

--Washington & the Theatre. LC 67-13345. (Illus.). 1967. Repr. of 1899 ed. 11.00 (ISBN 0-405-08527-3). Ayer Co Pubs.

--Who Was the Mother of Franklin's Son? An Historical Conundrum, Hitherto Given up-Now Partly Answered. LC 78-182127. (Historical Printing Club, Publications: No. 26). 16p. 1972. Repr. of 1889 ed. lib. bdg. 10.00 (ISBN 0-8337-1203-9). B Franklin.

Ford, Paul L., ed. Bibliotheca Chaunciana: List of the Writings of Charles Chauncy. LC 74-182126. (Bibliography & Reference Ser.: No. 442). 50p. (History of Education Ser., No. 9). 1972. pap. text ed. 10.00 (ISBN 0-8337-1179-2). B Franklin.

--Essays on the Constitution of the United States Published During Its Discussion by the People, 1787-1788. LC 79-123599. (Research & Source Ser.: No. 494). 1970. Repr. of 1892 ed. 26.50 (ISBN 0-8337-1186-5). B Franklin.

--New England Primer. LC 62-20977. (Classics in Education Ser.). (Orig.). 1962. pap. text ed. 4.95x (ISBN 0-8077-1368-6). Tchrs Coll.

--Pamphlets on the Constitution of the U. S. 1971. Repr. of 1888 ed. lib. bdg. 24.00 (ISBN 0-8337-4568-9). B Franklin.

Ford, Percy & Ford, F. A Guide to Parliamentary Papers. 3rd rev. & enl. ed. 87p. 1972. 13.75x (ISBN 0-87471-100-2). Rowman.

Ford, Peter, jt. auth. see Feldman, Anthony.

Ford, Peter, jt. auth. see Howell, Michael.

Ford, Peter, ed. Catalytic Activation of Carbon Monoxide. LC 81-1885. (ACS Symposium Ser.: No. 152). 1981. 39.95 (ISBN 0-8412-0620-1). Am Chemical.

Ford, Peter, tr. see Amanuddin, Syed.

Ford, Philip, jt. auth. see Palfreman, David.

Ford, Phyllis. Eco-Acts. rev. 2nd ed. 259p. 1983. 10.00 (ISBN 0-943272-04-1). Inst Recreation Res.

--Informal Recreation Activities: A Leader's Guide. 119p. 1977. pap. 6.95 (ISBN 0-87603-026-6). Am Camping.

Ford, Phyllis & Blanchard, James. Leadership & Administration of Outdoor Pursuits. (Illus.). 400p. 1985. 22.95 (ISBN 0-317-30656-1). Venture Pub PA.

Ford, Phyllis, ed. Provocative Facts for West Coast Interpreters. 194p. 1983. 7.00 (ISBN 0-943272-05-X). Inst Recreation Res.

Ford, Phyllis, et al. Apertures to Anywhere. LC 79-84675. (Salon Ser: No. 1). (Illus.). 1979. 10.00 (ISBN 0-933908-06-7); pap. 3.95 (ISBN 0-933908-07-5). Harper Sq Pr.

Ford, Phyllis M. Principles & Practices of Outdoor-Environmental Education. LC 80-23200. 348p. 1981. text ed. 28.45 (ISBN 0-471-04768-6). Wiley.

Ford, Phyllis M., jt. auth. see Edington, Christopher R.

Ford, Phyllis M., jt. auth. see Rodney, Lyn S.

Ford, Ray. Day Hikes of Santa Barbara. Malin, Kathrine, ed. 96p. 1984. pap. 6.50 (ISBN 0-87461-056-7). McNally.

Ford, Regina D. Health Assessment Handbook. (Illus.). 470p. 1985. 18.95 (ISBN 0-916730-88-3). Springhouse Corp.

Ford, Regina D., ed. Cardiovascular Handbook. (Illus.). 480p. 1985. pap. 18.95 (ISBN 0-916730-98-0). Springhouse Corp.

--CCRN Review Workbook. 250p. pap. 16.95 (ISBN 0-87434-000-4). Springhouse Corp.

--Handbook of Emergency Care. 500p. pap. text ed. 18.95 (ISBN 0-916730-99-9). Springhouse Corp.

--MediQuik Cards. 200p. 1985. 12.95 (ISBN 0-916730-92-1). Springhouse Corp.

--Nursing Diagnosis Cards. 120p. 1985. pap. 12.95 (ISBN 0-87434-001-2). Springhouse Corp.

--Nursing MediQuik Cards Eighty-Six. 224p. 1985. pap. 13.95 (ISBN 0-87434-009-8). Springhouse Corp.

Ford, Regina Daley see Daley Ford, Regina.

Ford, Richard. Children in the Cinema. LC 70-160232. (Moving Pictures Ser). viii, 232p. 1971. Repr. of 1939 ed. lib. bdg. 16.95x (ISBN 0-89198-033-4). Ozer.

--Gatherings from Spain. 1976. 17.50 (ISBN 0-8495-1729-X). Arden Lib.

--Gatherings from Spain. 1970. Repr. of 1906 ed. 12.95x (ISBN 0-460-00152-3, Evman). Biblio Dist.

--Handbook for Travellers in Spain, 2 vols. 1977. Set. lib. bdg. 250.00 (ISBN 0-8490-1930-3). Gordon Pr.

--Handbook for Travellers in Spain, 2 vols. 1983. Set. 170.00x (ISBN 0-900000-29-5, Pub. by Centaur Pr England). State Mutual Bk.

--Handbook for Travellers in Spain & Readers at Home, 3 Vols. Robertson, Ian, ed. LC 65-10028. (Centaur Classics Ser.). (Illus.). 1543p. 1966. Set. 50.00x (ISBN 0-8093-0213-6). S Ill U Pr.

--A Piece of My Heart. (Vintage Contemporaries Ser.). 1985. pap. 5.95 (ISBN 0-394-72914-5, Vin). Random.

--Quest for the Faradawn. (Illus.). 1982. 14.95 (ISBN 0-385-28815-8, E Friede). Delacorte.

--Quest for the Faradawn. 320p. 1983. pap. 3.95 (ISBN 0-440-17182-2). Dell.

--Sea Green Primer. (Illus.). 64p. pap. 3.95 (ISBN 0-916870-65-0). Creative Arts Bk.

Ford, Richard & Andersen, Juel. Juel Andersen's Sea Green Primer. (Illus.). 64p. (Orig.). 1983. pap. 3.95 (ISBN 0-916870-65-0). Creative Arts Bk.

Ford, Richard A., jt. auth. see Gordon, Arnold J.

Ford, Richard I. An Ethnobiology Sourcebook. LC 83-47625. (The North American Indian Ser.). 510p. 1985. lib. bdg. 60.00 (ISBN 0-8240-5894-1). Garland Pub.

Ford, Richard I., ed. The Ethnographic American Southwest: Myth, Clan & Kinship. LC 83-47640. (The North American Indian Ser.). 611p. 1985. lib. bdg. 75.00 (ISBN 0-8240-5893-3). Garland Pub.

--The Prehistoric American Southwest: History, Chronology, Ecology & Technology. LC 83-47641. (The North American Indian Ser.). 627p. 1985. lib. bdg. 75.00 (ISBN 0-8240-5892-5). Garland Pub.

Ford, Richard I., et al, eds. The Nature & Status of Ethnobotany. (Anthropological Papers Ser.: No. 67). (Illus., Orig.). 1978. pap. 10.00x (ISBN 0-932206-79-4). U Mich Mus Anthro.

Ford, Richard J. & Maizel, Abby L., eds. Mediators in Cell Growth & Differentiation. (M. D. Anderson Cancer Research Symposium Ser.: No. 37). 388p. 1985. text ed. 90.50 (ISBN 0-88167-071-5). Raven.

Ford, Richard J., Jr., et al, eds. Hodgkin's Disease & Non-Hodgkin's Lymphoma: New Perspectives in Immunopathology, Diagnosis & Treatment. 27th ed. (M. D. Anderson Clinical Conference on Cancer Ser.). 496p. 1984. text ed. 98.00 (ISBN 0-88167-039-1). Raven.

Ford, Richard K., jt. auth. see Lewis, Bruce R.

Ford, Robert. Children's Rhymes, Children's Games, Children's Songs & Stories. 59.95 (ISBN 0-87968-852-1). Gordon Pr.

--Vagabond Songs & Ballads in Scotland, 2 vols. LC 74-13895. 1975. Repr. of 1901 ed. Set. lib. bdg. 50.00 (ISBN 0-88305-206-7). Norwood Edns.

--Vagabond Songs & Ballads of Scotland: Many Old & Familiar Melodies, 2 Vols. 1978. Repr. of 1899 ed. lib. bdg. 50.00 (ISBN 0-8495-1737-0). Arden Lib.

Ford, Robert, et al. Fire Protection Handbook Study Guide. 1976. pap. 15.00x (ISBN 0-89368-300-0). Davis Pub Co.

Ford, Robert E. Engineers, Pump Operators, Drivers Handbook, Vol. 3. 1977. pap. 9.00x (ISBN 0-89368-310-8). Davis Pub Co.

--Fire Command Officer's Handbook, Vol. 1. 1978. pap. 6.50x (ISBN 0-89368-311-6). Davis Pub Co.

--Fire Lieutenant's-Captain's Handbook, Vol. 3. 1977. pap. 9.00x (ISBN 0-89368-307-8). Davis Pub Co.

--Firefighter's Entrance Handbook. 1977. pap. 11.00x (ISBN 0-89368-312-4). Davis Pub Co.

--Police Entrance Examinations. 1968. pap. 10.00 (ISBN 0-89368-018-4). Davis Pub Co.

Ford, Robert N. Why Jobs Die & What to Do about It: Job Redesign & Future. LC 79-11307. pap. 59.50 (ISBN 0-317-26950-X, 2023583). Bks Demand UMI.

Ford, Robert S. Stale Food vs. Fresh Food: Cause & Cure of Choked Arteries. 6th ed. 48p. 1977. pap. 7.00 (ISBN 0-686-09051-9). Magnolia Lab.

Ford, Roger & Strimpel, Oliver. The World of Science: Computers-An Introduction. Date not set. price not set. Facts on File.

Ford, S. F. & Campos, S. Summary of Validity Data from the Admissions Testing Program Validity Study Service. 1977. 2.00 (ISBN 0-87447-089-7, 251713). College Bd.

Ford, Sallie R. Mary Bunyan: Blind Daughter of John Bunyan. 9.95 (ISBN 0-685-00748-0). Reiner.

Ford, Sally & Ford, Daniel. Twenty-Five Ski Tours in the White Mountains: A Guide to New Hampshire's Backcountry Trails. 2nd, rev ed. LC 83-7651. (Twenty Five Ski Tours Ser.). (Illus.). 128p. 1983. pap. 5.95 (ISBN 0-942440-15-3). Backcountry Pubns.

Ford, Samuel E., ed. see Alameda Poets.

Ford, Sara De see De Ford, Sara, et al.

Ford, Scott. Design B: How to Play Tennis in the Zone. (Illus.). 130p. 1984. 12.95 (ISBN 0-89651-153-7). Icarus.

Ford, Sewell. Horses Nine: Stories of Harness & Saddle. LC 70-122701. (Short Story Index Reprint Ser). 1903. 17.00 (ISBN 0-8369-3534-9). Ayer Co Pubs.

--Just Horses. LC 76-121545. (Short Story Index Reprint Ser). (Illus.). 1910. 17.00 (ISBN 0-8369-3501-2). Ayer Co Pubs.

--On with Torchy. LC 75-125210. (Short Story Index Reprint Ser). (Illus.). 1914. 19.00 (ISBN 0-8369-3577-2). Ayer Co Pubs.

--Shorty McCabe Gets the Hail. LC 79-125211. (Short Story Index Reprint Ser). 1919. 18.00 (ISBN 0-8369-3578-0). Ayer Co Pubs.

--Shorty McCabe Looks 'em Over. LC 73-122702. (Short Story Index Reprint Ser). (Illus.). 1917. 19.00 (ISBN 0-8369-3535-7). Ayer Co Pubs.

--Side Stepping with Shorty. 18.00 (ISBN 0-8369-4242-6, 6053). Ayer Co Pubs.

--Truegate of Mogador. facs. ed. LC 76-142261. (Short Story Index Reprint Ser). 1906. 20.00 (ISBN 0-8369-3745-7). Ayer Co Pubs.

--Wilt Thou Torchy. LC 77-122703. (Short Story Index Reprint Ser.). (Illus.). 1917. 18.00 (ISBN 0-8369-3536-5). Ayer Co Pubs.

Ford, Sondra. The ABC's of Managing with Employee Teams. 109p. (Orig.). 1983. pap. text ed. 9.95 (ISBN 0-913043-00-1). S Ford & Assoc.

Ford, Steven & Hart, Fred. A Color Pictorial of Northeastern Railfaning. (Illus.). 36p. 1982. pap. 9.98 (ISBN 0-934088-07-1). NJ Intl Inc.

Ford, T. D., ed. The Science of Speleology. 1976. 55.00 (ISBN 0-12-262550-1). Acad Pr.

Ford, Tamara de see De Ford, Tamara.

Ford, Tamara De see De Ford, Tamara.

Ford, Thomas K., jt. auth. see Walket, John J., Jr.

Ford, Thomas K., jt. auth. see Walklet, John J.

Ford, Thomas K., jt. auth. see Walklet, John J., Jr.

Ford, Thomas R., ed. Rural U.S.A. Persistence & Change. (Illus.). 1978. text ed. 12.95x (ISBN 0-8138-1345-X). Iowa St U Pr.

Ford, Thomas R., et al, eds. A Legacy of Knowledge: Sociological Contributions of T. Lynn Smith. 1980. text ed. 30.00x (ISBN 0-7069-0791-4, Pub. by Vikas India). Advent NY.

Ford, Thomas W. A. B. Guthrie, Jr. (United States Authors Ser.). 1981. 13.50 (ISBN 0-8057-7327-4, Twayne). G K Hall.

--Heaven Beguiles the Tired: Death in the Poetry of Emily Dickinson. LC 66-24138. Repr. of 1966 ed. 52.00 (ISBN 0-8357-9617-5, 2050449). Bks Demand UMI.

Ford, Thornton. Every Other Thursday. Date not set. 7.00 (ISBN 0-8062-2417-7). Carlton.

Ford, Tommy. Bama under Bear: Alabama's Family Tides. rev. ed. (College Sports Ser.: Football). (Illus.). 288p. 1983. 10.95 (ISBN 0-87397-251-1). Strode.

Ford, Trevor D. Limestone & Caves of the Peak District. 469p. 1981. 50.00x (ISBN 0-86094-005-5, Pub. by GEO Abstracts England). State Mutual Bk.

--Limestone & Caves of the Peak District. 469p. 1980. pap. 26.45x (ISBN 0-86094-004-7, Pub. by GEO Abstracts England). State Mutual Bk.

Ford, W. B., jt. auth. see Steinberg, W. F.

Ford, W. E., jt. auth. see Dana, E. S.

Ford, W. Herschel. Sermons You Can Preach. (Simple Sermon Ser.). 384p. 1983. pap. 10.95 (ISBN 0-310-46971-6). Zondervan.

--Sermons You Can Preach on Matthew. 240p. (Orig.). 1985. pap. 8.95 (ISBN 0-310-45521-9, Pub. by Minister Res Lib). Zondervan.

--Simple Sermons for Saints & Sinners. 152p. 1986. price not set. Baker Bk.

--Simple Sermons for Special Days & Occasions. 140p. 1985. pap. 4.50 (ISBN 0-8010-3515-5). Baker Bk.

--Simple Sermons for Sunday Morning. 128p. 1986. price not set. Baker Bk.

--Simple Sermons for Time & Eternity. 120p. 1985. pap. 3.95 (ISBN 0-8010-3516-3). Baker Bk.

--Simple Sermons of Great Christian Doctrines. 138p. 1985. pap. 4.50 (ISBN 0-8010-3519-8). Baker Bk.

--Simple Sermons on Evangelistic Themes. 128p. 1986. price not set. Baker Bk.

--Simple Sermons on Grace & Glory. 92p. 1986. price not set. Baker Bk.

--Simple Sermons on Prayer. 88p. 1985. pap. 3.50 (ISBN 0-8010-3520-1). Baker Bk.

--Simple Sermons on Salvation & Service. 136p. 1986. price not set. Baker Bk.

--Simple Sermons on the New Testament Texts. 112p. 1985. pap. 3.95 (ISBN 0-8010-3517-1). Baker Bk.

Ford, Walter B. Studies in Divergent Series & Summability, & the Asymptotic Development of Functions. LC 60-16836. 371p. 1985. text ed. 19.50 (ISBN 0-8284-0143-8). Chelsea Pub.

Ford, Washington C. see Sumner, Charles.

Ford, Wendell H. The Public Papers of Governor Wendell H. Ford: 1971-1974. Jones, W. Landis, ed. (The Public Papers of the Governors of Kentucky). 722p. 1978. 28.00x (ISBN 0-8131-0602-8). U Pr of Ky.

Ford, Wendy W., jt. auth. see Resnick, Lauren B.

Ford, Willard S. Some Administrative Problems of the High School Cafeteria. LC 70-176781. (Columbia University. Teachers College. Contributions to Education: No. 238). Repr. of 1926 ed. 22.50 (ISBN 0-404-55238-2). AMS Pr.

Ford, William W. Bacteriology. LC 75-23671. (Clio Medica Ser.: No. 22). (Illus.). Repr. of 1939 ed. 18.00 (ISBN 0-404-58922-7). AMS Pr.

Ford, Worthington, ed. see Jones, Joseph.

Ford, Worthington, ed. see Lee, William.

Ford, Worthington, ed. see Webb, Samuel B.

Ford, Worthington C. Boston Book Market, Sixteen Seventy-Nine to Seventeen Hundred. LC 72-81997. (Club of Odd Volumes Publications: No. 25). (Illus.). 197p. 1973. Repr. of 1917 ed. lib. bdg. 21.00 (ISBN 0-8337-1181-4). B Franklin.

--British Officers Serving in America, 1754-1774. 59.95 (ISBN 0-87968-792-4). Gordon Pr.

--Washington As an Employer & Importer of Labor. (Research & Source Works Ser.: No. 848). 1971. pap. text ed. 15.50 (ISBN 0-8337-1201-2). B Franklin.

Ford, Worthington C., ed. Defences of Philadelphia in 1777. LC 71-146145. (Era of the American Revolution Ser). 1971. Repr. of 1897 ed. lib. bdg. 39.50 (ISBN 0-306-70140-5). Da Capo.

Ford, Worthington C., ed. see Adams, John Q.

Ford, Worthington C., ed. see Lee, William.

Fordam, R. & Biggs, A. G. Principles of Vegetable Crop Production. 250p. (Orig.). 1985. pap. text ed. 22.50x (ISBN 0-00-383014-4, Pub. by Collins England). Sheridan.

Forde, C. Daryll. Ancient Mariners: The Story of Ships & Sea Routes. 88p. 1982. Repr. of 1928 ed. lib. bdg. 20.00 (ISBN 0-89760-236-6). Telegraph Bks.

Forde, Daryll. Yoruba-Speaking Peoples of South-Western Nigeria. LC 70-575491. 1969. cancelled (ISBN 0-85302-023-X). Intl Pubns Serv.

Forde, Daryll, ed. African Worlds. (International African Institute Ser.). 1954. pap. 12.95x (ISBN 0-19-724156-5). Oxford U Pr.

Forde, Daryll & Kaberry, P. M., eds. West African Kingdoms in the Nineteenth-Century. 1967. pap. 14.95x (ISBN 0-19-724187-5). Oxford U Pr.

Forde, Daryll, ed. see International African Institute.

Forde, Daryll, et al. Essays on the Ritual of Social Relations. Gluckman, Max, ed. 1962. text ed. 23.00x (ISBN 0-7190-0255-9). Humanities.

Forde, Emanuel. Montelyon Knight of the Oracle. (Salzburg - Elizabethan & Renaissance Studies: No. 99). 300p. 1981. pap. text ed. 25.50x (ISBN 0-391-02555-4, Pub. by Inst Eng Lit Austria). Humanities.

Forde, Eustace. Land of Riches. 256p. 1984. 12.95 (ISBN 0-89962-413-8). Todd & Honeywell.

Forde, Frank. The Long Watch. 1981. 35.00x (ISBN 0-7171-1126-1, Pub. by Gill & Macmillan Ireland). State Mutual Bk.

Forde, Gerhard O. Justification by Faith: A Matter of Death & Life. LC 81-70663. 112p. 1982. pap. 5.95 (ISBN 0-8006-1634-0, 1-1634). Fortress.

--Where God Meets Man: Luther's Down-to-Earth Approach to the Gospel. LC 72-78569. 128p. 1972. pap. 5.95 (ISBN 0-8066-1235-5, 10-7060). Augsburg.

Forde, Nels W. Nebraska Cuneiform Texts of the Sumerian Ur III Dynasty. 1972. 12.50x (ISBN 0-87291-040-7). Coronado Pr.

Forde, Terry. Easy-to-Make Wooden Toys. LC 84-2678. (Illus.). 136p. (Orig.). 1985. pap. 9.95 (ISBN 0-8069-7918-6). Sterling.

Forde-Johnston. Hillforts of the Iron Age in England & Wales. 370p. 1982. 90.00x (ISBN 0-85323-381-0, Pub. by Liverpool Univ England). State Mutual Bk.

Forde-Johnston, J. Hillforts of the Iron Age in England & Wales: A Survey of the Surface Evidence. (Illus.). 331p. 1976. 55.00x (ISBN 0-87471-802-3). Rowman.

Forde-Johnston, James. Great Medieval Castles of Britain. (Illus.). 208p. 1980. 16.95 (ISBN 0-370-30236-2, Pub. by the Bodley Head). Merrimack Pub Cir.

--Hadrian's Wall. (Illus.). 240p. 1980. 15.95 (ISBN 0-7181-1652-6, Pub. by Michael Joseph). Merrimack Pub Cir.

Forder, Anthony, et al. Theories of Welfare. 256p. (Orig.). 1984. pap. 14.95x (ISBN 0-7100-9625-9). Routledge & Kegan.

Forder, Anthony, ed. see Hall, Penelope.

Forder, Archibald. With the Arabs in Tent & Town: An Account of Missionary Work, Life, & Experiences in Moab & Edom & the First Missionary Journey into Arabia from the North. LC 77-87658. (Illus.). Repr. of 1902 ed. 24.00 (ISBN 0-404-16405-6). AMS Pr.

Forder, Henry G. Calculus of Extension. LC 59-1178. 25.00 (ISBN 0-8284-0135-7). Chelsea Pub.

Forder, Reg A. SoulWinning: An Action Handbook for Christians. 264p. 1984. 15.95 (ISBN 0-13-822826-4); pap. 6.95 (ISBN 0-13-822818-3). P-H.

Fordham Corporate Law Institute & Hawk, Barry E. Antitrust, Technology Transfers, & Joint Ventures in International Trade: Annual Proceedings of the Fordham Corporate Law Institute. New York, N.Y. & Fordham University. School of Law, eds. LC 83-189452. xi, 407p. Date not set. price not set. Bender.

Fordham, Derek. Eskimos. LC 79-65843. (Surviving Peoples Ser.). PLB 12.68 (ISBN 0-382-06305-8). Silver.

Fordham, Edward W., ed. Notable Cross-Examinations. LC 79-98759. xxii, 202p. Repr. of 1951 ed. lib. bdg. 15.00x (ISBN 0-8371-3099-9, FOCE). Greenwood.

Fordham, Frieda. Introduction to Jung's Psychology. (Orig.). 1953. pap. 4.95 (ISBN 0-14-020273-0, Pelican). Penguin.

Fordham, Mary W. Magnolia Leaves: Poems. LC 71-168122. Repr. of 1897 ed. 12.50 (ISBN 0-404-00050-9). AMS Pr.

Fordham, Michael. Children As Individuals. LC 75-80467. (Illus.). 1969. 9.00 (ISBN 0-913430-09-9). C G Jung Foun.

--The Self & Autism. (Library of Analytical Psychology: Vol. 3). 1981. 33.00 (ISBN 0-12-262163-8). Acad Pr.

Fordham, Michael, ed. Analytical Psychology. (Library of Analytical Psychology: Vol. 1). 1981. 27.00 (ISBN 0-12-262161-1). Acad Pr.

Fordham, Michael, et al, eds. Techniques in Jungian Analysis. (Library of Analytical Psychology: Vol. 2). 1981. 27.00 (ISBN 0-12-262162-X). Acad Pr.

Fordham, Michael S. Jungian Psychotherapy: A Study in Analytical Psychology. LC 77-26331. (Wiley Series on Methods in Psychotheraphy). pap. 48.80 (ISBN 0-317-08432-1, 2022400). Bks Demand UMI.

Fordham, Morva, jt. auth. see Wilson-Barnett, J.

Fordham, S. High Explosives & Propellants. 2nd ed. 1966. pap. 14.50 (ISBN 0-08-023833-5). Pergamon.

Fordham, Sheldon L. & Leaf, Carol A. Physical Education & Sports: An Introduction to Alternative Careers. LC 77-19115. 385p. 1978. text ed. 35.45 (ISBN 0-471-26622-1). Wiley.

Fordham University. School of Law, ed. see Fordham Corporate Law Institute & Hawk, Barry E.

Ford-Hutchinson, A & Rainsford, K., eds. Prostaglandins & Inflammation. (Agents & Actions Supplements: No. 6). (Illus.). 242p. 1979. pap. 34.95x (ISBN 0-8176-1132-0). Birkhauser.

Fordin, Hugh. Getting to Know Him: A Biography of Oscar Hammerstein II. (Illus.). 400p. 1985. pap. 11.95 (ISBN 0-8044-6200-3). Ungar.

--The Movies' Greatest Musicals. 2nd ed. 1985. pap. 11.95 (ISBN 0-8044-6168-6). Ungar.

--The Movies' Greatest Musicals: Produced in Hollywood U. S. A. by the Freed Unit. (Illus.). 576p. 1984. Repr. of 1975 ed. 22.95 (ISBN 0-8044-5369-1). Ungar.

--The World of Entertainment. (Illus.). 1976. pap. 4.95 (ISBN 0-380-00754-1, 30338). Avon.

Fordney, Marilyn T. Insurance Handbook for the Medical Office. 2nd ed. (Illus.). 475p. 1981. pap. text ed. 19.95 (ISBN 0-7216-3814-7); wkbk. 11.95 (ISBN 0-7216-3816-3). Saunders.

Fordney, Marilyn T. & Follis, Joan J. Administrative Medical Assisting. LC 81-2141. 668p. 1982. 21.50 (ISBN 0-471-86240-1, Pub. by Wiley Med); pap. 24.50 (ISBN 0-471-06380-0); instr's. manual avail. Wiley.

Fordney, Marilyn T., jt. auth. see Diehl, Marcy O.

Fordriner, Gustav H. Italian Fascism & American New Deal. (Illus.). 134p. 1981. 66.75x (ISBN 0-930008-92-8). Inst Econ Pol.

Ford-Robertson, F. C. & Winters, Robert K., eds. Terminology of Forest Science, Technology, Practice & Products. rev. ed. LC 82-61327. (The Multilingual Forestry Terminology Ser.). 370p. 1983. pap. 15.00 (ISBN 0-939970-16-3, SAF 83-01). Soc Am Foresters.

Fords, et al. Poganuc People. (Illus.). 416p. 1977. pap. 7.95 (ISBN 0-317-35972-X). Stowe-Day.

Fordtran, John S., jt. auth. see Sleisenger, Marvin H.

Fordwor, Kwame D. The African Development Bank: Problems of International Cooperation. LC 80-24607. (Pergamon Policy Studies on International Development). 300p. 1981. 33.00 (ISBN 0-08-026339-9). Pergamon.

Fordyce, Beth see Eldridge, James, pseud.

Fordyce, C. J. & Knox, T. M. The Library of Jesus College, Oxford: With an Appendix on the Books Bequeathed Thereto by Lord Herbert of Cherbury. rev. ed. (Oxford Bible Society Ser.: Vol. 5, Pt. 2). Repr. of 1937 ed. 13.00 (ISBN 0-317-16190-3). Kraus Repr.

Fordyce, C. J., ed. Catullus: A Commentary. 1961. 25.00x (ISBN 0-19-814430-X). Oxford U Pr.

Fordyce, Edward, jt. ed. see Beach, Charles.

Fordyce, Jack K. & Weil, Raymond. Managing with People: A Manager's Handbook of Organization Development. 2nd ed. 1979. pap. text ed. 12.95 (ISBN 0-201-02031-9). Addison-Wesley.

Fordyce, M. W., jt. auth. see Fordyce, Wodehouse.

Fordyce, Rachel. Children's Theatre & Creative Dramatics: An Annotated Bibliography of Critical Works. 1975. lib. bdg. 27.50 (ISBN 0-8161-1161-8, Hall Reference). G K Hall.

Fordyce, Rachel, ed. Caroline Drama: A Bibliographic History of Criticism. 1978. lib. bdg. 28.50 (ISBN 0-8161-7952-2, Hall Reference). G K Hall.

Fordyce, Wodehouse & Fordyce, M. W. GRC in Buildings. 1983. text ed. 39.95 (ISBN 0-408-00395-2). Butterworth.

Forecasting & Assessment of Science & Technology Team. Eurofutures: The Challenge of Innovations. 220p. 1984. text ed. 49.95 (ISBN 0-408-01556-X). Butterworth.

Forece, Roland W. & Force, Maryanne, eds. The Fuller Collection of Pacific Artifacts. 376p. 1980. pap. 95.00x (ISBN 0-85331-281-8, Pub. by Lund Humphries England). State Mutual Bk.

Forecki, Marcia C. Speak to Me. LC 84-28740. 146p. (Orig.). 1985. pap. 8.50 (ISBN 0-913580-95-3). Gallaudet Coll.

Forefront Corporation Staff. Framework: A Developer's Handbook. (Framework Bks.). 300p. 1985. pap. 24.95 (ISBN 0-912677-24-4). Ashton-Tate Bks.

--Framework: A Programmer's Reference. Ashton-Tate, ed. 300p. 1984. pap. 24.95 (ISBN 0-912677-21-X). Ashton-Tate Bks.

--Framework: An Introduction to Programming. (Framework Bks.). 300p. 1985. pap. 24.95 (ISBN 0-912677-23-6). Ashton-Tate Bks.

Forehand, David, jt. auth. see Cross, Frank L., Jr.

Forehand, David, jt. ed. see Cross, Framk L., Jr.

Forehand, David, jt. ed. see Cross, Frank L, Jr.

Forehand, David, jt. ed. see Cross, Frank L., Jr.

Forehand, G. A., et al. Psychology for Living. 4th ed. 1977. 22.56 (ISBN 0-07-021520-0). McGraw.

Forehand, Garlie A., ed. Applications of Time Series Analysis to Evaluation. LC 81-48580. (Program Evaluation Ser.: No. 16). 1982. 8.95x (ISBN 0-87589-918-8). Jossey-Bass.

Forehand, Mary A. Love Lives Here. (Orig.). (gr. 1-3). 1975. pap. 1.95 (ISBN 0-377-00028-0). Friend Pr.

Forehand, Mary A., jt. auth. see Schirer, Marshall E.

Forehand, Rex L. & McMahon, Robert J. Helping the Non-Compliant Child: A Clinician's Guide to Parent Training. LC 81-6629. 253p. 1981. text ed. 20.00 (ISBN 0-89862-611-0, 2611). Guilford Pr.

Forehand, Walter E. Terence. (World Author Ser.). 1985. lib. bdg. 24.95 (ISBN 0-8057-6593-X, Twayne). G K Hall.

Forehlich, Walter. Spacelab: An International Short-Stay Orbiting Laboratory. (NASA EP Ser.: No. 165). 82p. 1983. pap. 7.00 (ISBN 0-318-11750-9). Gov Printing Office.

Foreign Affairs & Bundy, William P., eds. America & the World, 1982. 300p. 1983. 30.00 (ISBN 0-08-030132-0); pap. 7.95 (ISBN 0-08-030131-2). Pergamon.

Foreign & Commonwealth Office, London. Catalogue of the Colonial Office Library: Third Supplement, 4 vols. 1979. Set. lib. bdg. 545.00 (ISBN 0-8161-0010-1, Hall Library). G K Hall.

--Catalogue of the Foreign Office Library, 1926-1968, 8 vols. 6208p. 1972. lib. bdg. 790.00 (ISBN 0-8161-0998-2, Hall Library). G K Hall.

Foreign & Commowealth Office, London. Catalogue of the Colonial Office Library, London, 15 vols. 1964. Set. 1485.00 (ISBN 0-8161-0688-6, Hall Library); First Suppl. 1963-67. 140.00 (ISBN 0-8161-0729-7); Second Suppl. 1972. 2 Vols. 220.00 (ISBN 0-8161-0843-9). G K Hall.

Foreign Office of the Federal Republic of Germany Staff, ed. International Organisationen - International Organizations: Designations, Abbreviations, Acronyms (German, English, French, Spanish, Dutch, Italian, Russian) LC 84-28751. (Terminological Ser.: Vol. 2). xiv, 640p. 1985. pap. 51.20x (ISBN 3-11-010042-8). De Gruyter.

Foreign Policy Association. Global Resources: Challenges of Interdependence. Glassner, Martin I., ed. 692p. 1983. 39.95 (ISBN 0-317-06804-0); pap. 22.95 (ISBN 0-317-06805-9). Foreign Policy.

--Great Decisions Nineteen Eighty-Four Teacher's Guide. (Illus.). 24p. (Orig.). 1984. pap. 2.00 (ISBN 0-87124-087-4). Foreign Policy.

--Great Decisions Nineteen Eighty-One. (Illus.). 96p. (Orig.). 1981. pap. 6.00 (ISBN 0-87124-066-1). Foreign Policy.

--Great Decisions Nineteen Eighty Two. (Illus.). 96p. 1982. pap. 6.00 (ISBN 0-87124-072-6). Foreign Policy.

--Great Decisions Nineteen Seventy Eight. LC 58-59828. (Great Decisions Ser.). (Illus.). 1978. pap. 6.00 (ISBN 0-87124-044-0). Foreign Policy.

--Great Decisions Nineteen Seventy Nine. LC 58-59828. (Illus.). 1979. pap. 6.00 (ISBN 0-87124-049-1). Foreign Policy.

Foreign Policy Association & Irwin, Wallace, Jr. America in the World: A Guide to U. S. Foreign Policy. 246p. 1983. 31.95 (ISBN 0-317-06806-7); pap. 10.95 (ISBN 0-317-06807-5). Foreign Policy.

Foreign Policy Association, ed. Foreign Policy Choices for Americans: A Nonpartisan Focus on Facts, Policies & Alternatives. LC 84-80976. 160p. 1984. pap. 5.95 (ISBN 0-87124-090-4). Foreign Policy.

Foreign Policy Association Editors, jt. auth. see Kojm, Christopher A.

Foreign Policy Association Editors. Great Decisions-Eighty-Three. LC 58-59828. (Illus.). 96p. 1983. pap. 6.00 (ISBN 0-87124-080-7). Foreign Policy.

--Great Decisions Nineteen Eighty. LC 58-59828. (Illus.). 1980. pap. 6.00 (ISBN 0-87124-056-4). Foreign Policy.

--Guide to Careers in World Affairs. LC 82-82538. 104p. 1982. pap. 4.95 (ISBN 0-87124-077-7). Foreign Policy.

--Israel & the U. S. Friendship & Discord. 1982. pap. 1.50 (ISBN 0-686-43902-3). Foreign Policy.

--Trade & the Dollar: Coping with Interdependence. (Headline Ser.: No. 242). (Illus.). 1978. pap. 3.00 (ISBN 0-87124-052-1). Foreign Policy.

Foreign Policy Association Staff. Great Decisions Nineteen Eighty-Three Teacher's Guide. (Illus.). 20p. (Orig.). 1983. pap. 2.00 (ISBN 0-87124-081-5). Foreign Policy.

Foreign Policy Research Institute Staff. The Three Percent Solution & the Future of NATO. LC 80-27824. 118p. (Orig.). 1981. pap. 6.95 (ISBN 0-910191-02-6). For Policy Res.

Foreign Service Institute. Advanced French. 572p. (Fr.). 1980. Pt. A, 567p. 18 audio cassettes & text 185.00x (ISBN 0-88432-023-5, F260); Pt. B, 567p. 18 audio cassettes incl. 185.00x (ISBN 0-88432-024-3, F290). J Norton Pubs.

--Advanced French, 2 pts. 1980. Pt. A, 567. text & 18 cassettes 185.00x (ISBN 0-88432-067-7, F260, Audio-Forum); Pt. B. text & 18 cassettes 185.00x (ISBN 0-88432-068-5, F290). J Norton Pubs.

--Advanced German Course. 375p. 1980. plus 18 audio-cassettes 185.00x (ISBN 0-88432-043-X, G160). J Norton Pubs.

--Advanced Spanish, Pt. C. 472p. 1980. includes 18 cassettes 185.00x (ISBN 0-88432-102-9, S170). J Norton Pubs.

--Advanced Spanish, Pt. A. 699p. 1980. plus 16 audio cassettes 175.00x (ISBN 0-88432-057-X, S 131). J Norton Pubs.

--Advanced Spanish, Pt. B. 614p. 1980. plus 12 audio-cassettes 145.00x (ISBN 0-88432-058-8, S 153). J Norton Pubs.

--Basic Cantonese, Vol. II. 410p. (Chinese.). 1980. plus 15 cassettes 175.00 (ISBN 0-88432-033-2, C140); 15 audio cassettes incl. J Norton Pubs.

--Basic Cantonese, Vol. I. 392p. (Chinese.). 1979. plus 8 audio cassettes 125.00x (ISBN 0-88432-020-0, C131). J Norton Pubs.

--Basic Hungarian, Vol. I. 266p. 1980. plus 24 audio-cassettes 195.00 (ISBN 0-88432-046-4, U500). J Norton Pubs.

--Basic Saudi Arabic Course: Urban Hijazi Dialect. 288p. (Arabic.). 1980. 135.00x (ISBN 0-88432-037-5, A234); 10 audiocassettes incl. J Norton Pubs.

--Basic Thai, Vol. 1. 427p. 1980. plus 12 audio-cassettes 175.00x (ISBN 0-88432-050-2, D300). J Norton Pubs.

--Basic Thai, Vol. 2. 410p. 1970. with 17 cassettes 185.00x (ISBN 0-88432-104-5, D350). J Norton Pubs.

--Basic Turkish, Vol. I. 385p. 1980. plus 14 audio-cassettes 175.00x (ISBN 0-88432-049-9, T700). J Norton Pubs.

--Basic Turkish Course, Vol. II. 358p. 1968. with 13 cassettes 175.00x (ISBN 0-88432-105-3, T750). J Norton Pubs.

--Basic Vietnamese, Vol. I. 328p. 1980. plus 22 audio-cassettes 225.00x (ISBN 0-88432-051-0, V401). J Norton Pubs.

--Basic Vietnamese Course, Vol. II. 321p. 1967. with 10 cassettes 185.00x (ISBN 0-88432-108-8, V450). J Norton Pubs.

--Bulgarian Basic Course. 487p. 1980. with 23 cassettes 225.00x (ISBN 0-88432-089-8, L450). J Norton Pubs.

--French & Spanish Testing Kit. 140p. 1981. with 8 cassettes 60.00x (ISBN 0-88432-060-X, X100). J Norton Pubs.

--French Basic Course, 2 pts. (Fr.). 1979. Pt.A, 194p. 12 audio cassettes incl. 125.00x (ISBN 0-88432-021-9, F170); Pt. B, 290p. 18 audio cassettes incl. 149.00x (ISBN 0-88432-022-7, F181). J Norton Pubs.

--French Phonology. 394p. (Fr.). 1980. 85.00x (ISBN 0-88432-032-4, F250); 8 audiocassettes incl. J Norton Pubs.

--Greek Basic Course, Vol. I. 327p. (Gr.). 1980. 12 cassettes plus text 145.00x (ISBN 0-88432-034-0, R301, Audio-Forum). J Norton Pubs.

--Greek Basic Course, Vol. II. 199p. (Gr.). 12 cassettes plus text 145.00x (ISBN 0-88432-035-9, R318, Audio-Forum). J Norton Pubs.

--Greek Basic Course, Vol. III. 201p. (Gr.). 1980. 6 cassettes plus text 75.00x (ISBN 0-88432-036-7, R338, Audio-Forum). J Norton Pubs.

--Hausa Basic Course. 420p. 1980. with 15 cassettes 175.00x (ISBN 0-88432-109-6, HA1). J Norton Pubs.

--Hebrew Basic Course. 552p. (Hebrew.). 1980. plus 24 cassettes 195.00x (ISBN 0-88432-040-5, H345). J Norton Pubs.

--Khmer Cambodian Basic Course, 2 vols. 1970. Vol. I, 453p. with 13 cassettes 185.00x (ISBN 0-88432-097-9, KH1); Vol. II, 363p. with 29 cassettes 245.00x (ISBN 0-88432-098-7, KH50). J Norton Pubs.

--Korean, Vol. 1. 553p. 1980. plus 18 audio-cassettes 185.00x (ISBN 0-88432-047-2, Q800). J Norton Pubs.

--Korean, Vol. 2. 560p. 1980. plus 16 audio-cassettes 175.00x (ISBN 0-88432-048-0, Q850). J Norton Pubs.

--Levantine Arabic: Pronunciation. 100p. (Arabic.). 1980. 10 cassettes incl. 85.00x (ISBN 0-88432-038-3, A244). J Norton Pubs.

--Modern Written Arabic, Vol. I. 419p. (Arabic.). 1980. 185.00x (ISBN 0-88432-039-1, A269); 18 audiocassettes incl. J Norton Pubs.

--Modern Written Arabic, Vol. II. 385p. 1980. with 8 cassettes 125.00x (ISBN 0-88432-088-X, A320). J Norton Pubs.

--Programmatic German, 2 vols. (Ger.). 1978. Vol. 1, 647. 10 audio cassettes incl. 125.00x (ISBN 0-88432-017-0, G141); Vol. 2, 179p. 8 audio cassettes incl. 110.00x (ISBN 0-88432-018-9, G151). J Norton Pubs.

--Programmatic Portuguese, Vol. I. 783p. (Port.). 1982. plus 16 audio cassettes incl. 149.00x (ISBN 0-88432-019-7, P151). J Norton Pubs.

--Programmatic Portuguese, Vol. 2. 618p. 1982. with 22 cassettes 190.00x (ISBN 0-88432-100-2, P180). J Norton Pubs.

--Programmatic Spanish, 2 vols. (Span.). 1978. Vol. I, 464p. plus 12 audio cassettes 125.00x (ISBN 0-88432-015-4, S101); Vol. II, 614p. 8 audio cassettes incl. 110.00x (ISBN 0-88432-016-2, S121). J Norton Pubs.

--Serbo-Croatian, Vol. I. 633p. (Serbo-Croatian.). 1980. 185.00x (ISBN 0-88432-042-1, Y601); 22 audio cassettes incl. J Norton Pubs.

--Serbo-Croatian Basic Course, Vol. II. 677p. 1981. includes 24 cassettes 195.00x (ISBN 0-88432-101-0, Y650). J Norton Pubs.

--Spanish to Portugese. 91p. 1980. 2 cassettes incl. 35.00x (ISBN 0-88432-059-6, SP500). J Norton Pubs.

--Swahili: Active Introduction-General Conversation. 159p. 1966. with 2 cassettes 39.00x (ISBN 0-88432-110-X, W300). J Norton Pubs.

--Swahili Basic Course. 560p. (Swahili.). 1980. 215.00x (ISBN 0-88432-041-3, W426); 20 audio-cassettes incl. J Norton Pubs.

--Swedish Basic Course. 261p. 1980. plus 28 audio-cassettes 245.00x (ISBN 0-88432-045-6, K381). J Norton Pubs.

--Twi Basic Course. 240p. 1963. with 9 cassettes 125.00x (ISBN 0-88432-111-8, TW1). J Norton Pubs.

--Yoruba Basic Course. 381p. 1963. with 36 cassettes 295.00x (ISBN 0-88432-112-6, YR1). J Norton Pubs.

Forel, August. Hypnotism Suggestion. 9.95 (ISBN 0-685-21984-4). Wehman.

Forel, Francois A. La Faune Profonde Des Lags Suisses: The Bottom Fauna of Swiss Lakes. Egerton, Frank N., 3rd, ed. LC 77-74224. (History of Ecology Ser.). 1978. Repr. of 1884 ed. lib. bdg. 19.00x (ISBN 0-405-10394-8). Ayer Co Pubs.

--Handbuch der Seenkunde, Allgemeine Limnologie: Handbook of Lake Studies. Egerton, Frank N., 3rd, ed. LC 77-74225. (History of Ecology Ser.). 1978. Repr. of 1901 ed. lib. bdg. 21.00x (ISBN 0-405-10395-6). Ayer Co Pubs.

Forell, Betty & Wind, Betty. Little Benjamin & the First Christmas. (Arch Bks: Set 1). (Illus.). (ps-3). 1964. laminated bdg. 0.99 (ISBN 0-570-06005-2, 59-1113). Concordia.

Forell, George W. Augsburg Confession: A Contemporary Commentary. LC 68-25798. (Orig.). 1968. pap. 5.50 (ISBN 0-8066-0815-3, 10-0518). Augsburg.

--Christian Social Teachings. LC 71-159003. 1971. pap. 6.50 (ISBN 0-8066-1126-X, 10-1179). Augsburg.

--Ethics of Decision: An Introduction to Christian Ethics. LC 55-7767. 176p. 1955. pap. 4.50 (ISBN 0-8006-1770-3, 1-1770). Fortress.

--Faith Active in Love. LC 15-5702. 1954. pap. 6.50 (ISBN 0-8066-0186-8, 10-2165). Augsburg.

--History of Christian Ethics: From the New Testament to Augustine, Vol. 1. LC 79-50096. 248p. 1979. 14.95 (ISBN 0-8066-1715-2, 10-3042). Augsburg.

--The Luther Legacy: An Introduction to Luther's Life & Thought for Today. LC 83-72106. 80p. 1983. pap. 4.50 (ISBN 0-8066-2050-1, 104142). Augsburg.

--The Protestant Faith. LC 74-26341. 320p. 1975. pap. 8.95 (ISBN 0-8006-1095-4, 1-1095). Fortress.

Forell, George W. & McCue, James F. Confessing One Faith: A Joint Commentary on the Augsburg Confession by Lutheran & Catholic Theologians. LC 80-65557. 368p. 1981. pap. 15.00 (ISBN 0-8066-1802-7, 10-1637). Augsburg.

Forell, George W., ed. & tr. from Ger. Zinzendorf: Nine Public Lectures on Important Subjects in Religion. LC 74-93784. 170p. 1973. text ed. 6.12.00x (ISBN 0-87745-036-6). U of Iowa Pr.

Forell, George W. & Lazareth, William H., eds. Corporation Ethics: The Quest for Moral Authority. rev. ed. LC 79-8899. (Justice Bks.). 1980. pap. 1.50 (ISBN 0-8006-1556-5, 1-1556). Fortress.

--Crisis in Marriage. LC 77-20538. (Justice Bks). 64p. (Orig.). 1978. pap. 1.50 (ISBN 0-8006-1552-2, 1-1552). Fortress.

Forell, George W. & Lehmann, Helmut T., eds. Luther's Works: Career of the Reformer II, Vol. 32. LC 55-9893. 1958. 16.95 (ISBN 0-8006-0332-X, 1-332). Fortress.

Foreman. Landscape Ecology. 448p. Date not set. price not set (ISBN 0-471-87037-4). Wiley.

Foreman, jt. auth. see Allen.

Foreman, Alexa L. Women in Motion. LC 83-72435. 248p. 1983. 19.95 (ISBN 0-87972-266-5). Bowling Green Univ.

Foreman, Ann. Femininity As Alienation: Women & the Family in Marxism & Psychoanalysis. 168p. 1977. pap. 5.95 (ISBN 0-904383-62-8). Pluto Pr.

Foreman, Brian & Schultze, Peter. A New Gymnarthrid Microsaur from the Lower Permian of Kansas with a Review of the Tuditanomorph Microsaurs (Amphibia) (Occasional Papers: No. 91). 25p. 1981. 1.50 (ISBN 0-317-04814-7). U of KS Mus Nat Hist.

Foreman, Carolyn T. Indian Women Chiefs. LC 75-37860. 1976. Repr. of 1954 ed. 10.50 (ISBN 0-89201-019-3). Zenger Pub.

Foreman, Clark. The New Internationalism. facsimile ed. LC 71-37342. (Select Bibliographies Reprint Ser). Repr. of 1934 ed. 15.00 (ISBN 0-8369-6689-9). Ayer Co Pubs.

Foreman, Dale I. & Allen, Sally. Reading Skills for Social Studies: Understanding Concepts, Level C. (Skillbooster Ser.). 64p. (gr. 3). 1980. 2.80 (ISBN 0-87895-351-5). Modern Curr.

--Reading Skills for Social Studies: Understanding Concepts, Level E. (Skillbooster Ser.). 64p. (gr. 5). 1981. wkbk. 2.80 (ISBN 0-87895-555-0). Modern Curr.

--Reading Skills for Social Studies: Understanding Concepts, Level F. (Skillbooster Ser.). 64p. (gr. 6). 1981. wkbk. 2.80 (ISBN 0-87895-657-3). Modern Curr.

--Reading Skills for Social Studies: Understanding Concepts, Level D. (Skillbooster Ser.). 64p. (gr. 4). 1980. wkbk. 2.80 (ISBN 0-87895-452-X). Modern Curr.

--Reading Skills for Social Studies: Using Maps, Charts & Graphs, Level C. (Skillbooster Ser.). 64p. (gr. 3). 1980. wkbk. 2.80 (ISBN 0-87895-350-7). Modern Curr.

--Reading Skills for Social Studies: Using Maps, Charts & Graphs. (Skillbooster Ser.: Level D). 64p. (gr. 4). 1980. wkbk. 2.80 (ISBN 0-87895-452-X). Modern Curr.

--Reading Skills for Social Studies: Using Maps, Charts & Graphs, Level E. (Skillbooster Ser.). 64p. (gr. 5). 1981. wkbk. 2.80 (ISBN 0-87895-554-2). Modern Curr.

--Reading Skills for Social Studies: Using Maps, Charts & Graphs, Level F. (Skillbooster Ser.). 64p. (gr. 6). 1981. wkbk. 2.80 (ISBN 0-87895-656-5). Modern Curr.

Foreman, Dave, ed. Ecodefense: A Field Guide to Monkeywrenching. (Illus.). 184p. (Orig.). 1985. pap. 10.00 (ISBN 0-933285-01-9). Earth First.

Foreman, Gail H., jt. auth. see Zollers, Frances E.

Foreman, George C., jt. auth. see O'Neil, Barbara T.

Foreman, Gloria. Busy Hands. (Illus.). (gr. 3-8). 1959. pap. 1.00 (ISBN 0-915198-01-0). G Foreman.

--Four Hundred-Twenty Handicrafts Illustrated in Simple Steps. 30th ed. (Illus.). (gr. 1-3). 1964. pap. 3.50 (ISBN 0-915198-02-9). G Foreman.

Foreman, Grant. Five Civilized Tribes. (Civilization of the American Indian Ser.: No. 8). (Illus.). 1971. pap. 9.95 (ISBN 0-8061-0923-8). U of Okla Pr.

--Fort Gibson: A Brief History. LC 36-15038. (Historic Oklahoma Ser.: No. 1). pap. 20.00 (ISBN 0-317-29294-3, 2055511). Bks Demand UMI.

--Indian Removal: The Emigration of the Five Civilized Tribes of Indians. (Civilization of the American Indian Ser.: Vol. 2). (Illus.). 424p. 1976. 19.95 (ISBN 0-8061-0019-2); pap. 10.95 (ISBN 0-8061-1172-0). U of Okla Pr.

--Last Trek of the Indians. LC 73-173536. (Illus.). 1972. Repr. of 1946 ed. 26.00x (ISBN 0-8462-1197-1). Russell.

--Sequoyah. (Civilization of the American Indian Ser.: No. 16). (Illus.). 85p. 1938. pap. 3.95 (ISBN 0-8061-1056-2). U of Okla Pr.

Foreman, J. K. & Stockwell, P. B., eds. Topics in Automatic Chemical Analysis, Vol. 1. LC 79-40239. (Series in Analytical Chemistry). 313p. 1979. 79.95x (ISBN 0-470-26600-7). Halsted Pr.

Foreman, James. The Pumpkin Shell. LC 81-7774. 156p. (gr. 7 up). 1981. 9.95 (ISBN 0-374-36159-2). FS&G.

--The Pumpkin Shell. 160p. 1983. pap. 1.95 (ISBN 0-449-70054-2, Juniper). Fawcett.

Foreman, John. Prime of Life Beauty Book. LC 78-19957. (Helena Rubinstein Library). (Illus.). 1980. 12.95 (ISBN 0-8128-2536-5). Stein & Day.

Foreman, John, jt. auth. see Greggains, Joanie.

Foreman, Ken. Coaching Track & Field Techniques. 4th ed. 250p. 1982. pap. write for info. (ISBN 0-697-07187-1). Wm C Brown.

--Track & Field. 2nd ed. (Physical Education Ser.). 112p. 1983. pap. text ed. write for info. (ISBN 0-697-07213-4); tchr's manual o.p. avail. (ISBN 0-697-07226-6). Wm C Brown.

Foreman, Kenneth J. From This Day Forward: Thoughts about a Christian Marriage. pap. 2.95x (ISBN 0-685-02584-5). Outlook.

--Romans, First & Second Corinthians. LC 59-10454. (Layman's Bible Commentary Ser: Vol. 21). 1961. pap. 4.95 (ISBN 0-8042-3081-1). John Knox.

Foreman, Kenneth J., et al. Introduction to the Bible. Kelly, Balmer H., et al, eds. LC 59-10454. (Layman's Bible Commentary, Vol. 1). 1959. pap. 4.95 (ISBN 0-8042-3061-7). John Knox.

Foreman, Kenny. Spiritual Authority. 128p. (Orig.). 1983. pap. 3.75 (ISBN 0-88144-014-0, CPS-014). Christian Pub.

Foreman, L. L. Desperado's Gold. 1979. pap. 1.50 (ISBN 0-505-51431-1, Pub. by Tower Bks). Dorchester Pub Co.

--The Mustang Trail. 192p. 1982. pap. 1.95 (ISBN 0-441-54722-2). Ace Bks.

--The Road to San Jancinto. 1977. pap. 1.25 (ISBN 0-505-51117-7, Pub. by Tower Bks). Dorchester Pub Co.

Foreman, Laura, jt. auth. see Foat, Ginny.

Foreman, Laure, jt. auth. see Mirkin, Gabe.

Foreman, Lewis, ed. Bax: A Composer & His Times. (Illus.). 464p. 1984. 55.00 (ISBN 0-85967-643-9). Scolar.

Foreman, Martin & Gilbert, John. Factoring & Finance. 160p. 1976. 13.95 (ISBN 0-434-90568-2, Pub. by W Heinemann Ltd). David & Charles.

Foreman, Mary D., jt. ed. see Fundaburk, Emma L.

Foreman, Max L. Rx for Living: Take as Needed. 1982. 20.00x (ISBN 0-8197-0490-3). Bloch.

Foreman, Michael. Cat & Canary. LC 84-9568. (Illus.). (ps-3). 1985. 11.95 (ISBN 0-8037-0137-3, 01160350). Dial Bks Young.

--Land of Dreams. LC 82-11889. (Illus.). 32p. (gr. k-3). 1982. 11.95 (ISBN 0-03-062053-8). HR&W.

--War & Peas. LC 74-10368. (Illus.). (ps-3). 1974. 11.49i (ISBN 0-690-00628-4); PLB 11.89 (ISBN 0-690-00629-2). Crowell Jr Bks.

Foreman, Michael, jt. auth. see Newman, Nanette.

Foreman, Michael, jt. auth. see Wright, Freire.

Foreman, Michael, jt. auth. see Wright, Friere.

Foreman, Monte & Wyse, Patrick. Monte Foreman's Horse-Training Science. LC 82-40450. (Illus.). 156p. 1983. 24.95 (ISBN 0-8061-1583-1). U of Okla Pr.

Foreman, Nancy. Bound for Success. 1985. 6.95 (ISBN 0-671-55547-2, Pub. by Fireside). S&S.

Foreman, Paul. Quanah, the Serpent Eagle. LC 82-62545. (Illus.). 144p. pap. 8.95 (ISBN 0-87358-324-8); 60.00 (ISBN 0-87358-330-2). Northland.

--Redwing Blackbird. 1973. pap. 2.50x (ISBN 0-914476-15-7). Thorp Springs.

--Texas Liveoak. LC 78-17104. 1977. o.s. 7.50 (ISBN 0-914476-67-X); pap. 5.00x (ISBN 0-914476-66-1). Thorp Springs.

Foreman, Richard. Reverberation Machines: The Later plays & Essays. (Illus.). 212p. (Orig.). 1985. 19.95 (ISBN 0-88268-001-3); pap. 10.95 (ISBN 0-88268-000-5). Station Hill Pr.

Foreman, Richard L. Indian Water Rights. 233p. 1980. pap. text ed. 8.95x (ISBN 0-8134-2160-8, 2160). Interstate.

Foreman, Robert L. Communicating the Appraisal: A Guide to Report Writing. 85p. 1982. pap. 10.00 (ISBN 0-911780-61-0). Am Inst Real Estate Appraisers.

Foreman, Roberta & Frederick, Marti. Domestic Violence: A Training Manual for Mental Health Professionals. LC 82-61475. 125p. (Orig.). 1985. pap. text ed. 6.95 (ISBN 0-88247-716-1). R & E Pubs.

Foreman, Roberto, jt. auth. see Moore, Robin.

Foreman, Thomas E. Discrimination Against the Negro in American Athletics. LC 74-76466. 1975. soft bdg. 10.95 (ISBN 0-88247-340-9). R & E Pubs.

Foreman, Velma. Grammar of Yessan-Mayo. (Language Data--Asia-Pacific Ser.: No. 4). 300p. (Orig.). 1974. pap. 4.75 (ISBN 0-88312-204-9); microfiche (4) 4.73 (ISBN 0-88312-304-5). Summer Inst Ling.

Foreman, Walter C., Jr. The Music of the Close: The Final Scenes of Shakespeare's Tragedies. LC 77-75484. 240p. 1978. 22.00x (ISBN 0-8131-1366-0). U Pr of Ky.

Foreman-Peck, James. A History of the World Economy: International Economic Relations since 1850. LC 82-24295. 408p. 1983. text ed. 28.50x (ISBN 0-389-20337-8). B&N Imports.

Foren, R. & Bailey, R. Authority in Social Casework. 1968. 11.25 (ISBN 0-08-012962-5). Pergamon.

Forer, Bruce, jt. auth. see Atwan, Robert.

Forer, Lois G. Criminals & Victims. 1980. 14.95 (ISBN 0-393-01349-9). Norton.

--Money & Justice: Who Owns the Courts? LC 83-25004. 237p. 1984. 16.95 (ISBN 0-393-01869-5). Norton.

Forer, Lois J. Criminals & Victims: A Trial Judge Reflects on Crime & Punishment. 352p. 1984. pap. 6.95 (ISBN 0-393-30190-7). Norton.

Forer, Lucille K. Birth Order & Life Roles. 184p. 1969. 15.75x (ISBN 0-398-00596-6). C C Thomas.

Forer, Pip. Applied Apple Graphics. 368p. 1984. pap. 18.95 (ISBN 0-13-039289-8); incl. disk 31.95 (ISBN 0-13-039330-4). P-H.

Foresi, Pascal. Celibacy Put to the Gospel Test. 33p. 1969. pap. 1.15 (ISBN 0-911782-16-8). New City.

--Reaching for More. Moran, Hugh J., tr. from Ital. 128p. (Orig.). 1982. pap. 4.95 (ISBN 0-911782-40-0). New City.

Foresman, Ethel. Health & Happiness Are Twins. 1961. 6.95 (ISBN 0-8315-0034-4). Speller.

Forest & Tracey, eds. Automation & Informatics Technology: Effects on Labour & Employment. (OECD Library Special Annotated Bibliography: 51, 1981). 99p. (Eng. & Fr.). 1981. pap. write for info. OECD.

Forest, Antonia. Run Away Home. 224p. (YA) (gr. 7-10). 1982. 12.95 (ISBN 0-571-11837-2). Faber & Faber.

Forest, David, jt. auth. see Stone, Michael H.

Forest, Grant E. De see De Forest, Grant E.

Forest History Society. Encyclopedia of American Forest & Conservation History, 2 vols. Davis, Richard C., ed. (Illus.). 1983. lib. bdg. 150.00X encyclopedia set (ISBN 0-02-907350-2). Macmillan.

Forest Industries Commission on Timber Valuation & Taxation. Timber Tax Journal, Vol. 18. 335p. 1982. 30.00 (ISBN 0-686-43165-0, Pub. by FICTVT). Intl Spec Bk.

Forest Industries Committee on Timber Taxation & Valuation, ed. Timber Tax Journal, Vol. 16. 335p. 1980. 25.00x (ISBN 0-914272-19-5, Pub. by Forest Industries). Intl Spec Bk.

Forest Industries Committee on Timber Valuation & Taxation. Timber Tax Journal, Vol. 19. 450p. 1983. 35.00x (ISBN 0-914272-22-5, Pub. by FICTVT). Intl Spec Bk.

--Timber Tax Journal, Vol. 20. 360p. 1985. 35.00x (ISBN 0-914272-23-3). Forest Ind Comm.

Forest, Izette. The Leaven of Love. (Psychoanalysis: Examined & Re-Examined Ser.). 220p. 1983. Repr. of 1954 ed. lib. bdg. 22.50 (ISBN 0-306-76234-X). Da Capo.

Forest, Izette de see De Forest, Izette.

Forest, Izette De see Forest, Izette.

Forest, J. W. De see De Forest, J. W.

Forest, Jack D. The New Commandment. (Orig.). 1975. pap. 3.00 (ISBN 0-89536-166-3). CSS of Ohio.

Forest, James H. Thomas Merton: A Pictorial Biography. LC 80-82249. (Illus.). 112p. (Orig.). 1980. pap. 5.95 (ISBN 0-8091-2284-7). Paulist Pr.

Forest, Jean see Otten, Anna.

Forest, John W. De see De Forest, John W.

Forest, Leon. Two Wings to Veil My Face. LC 83-42777. 297p. 1984. 15.95 (ISBN 0-394-52965-0). Random.

Foresta, Ronald. Open Space Policy: New Jersey's Green Acres Program. 173p. (Orig.). 1981. 18.00x (ISBN 0-8135-0923-8). Rutgers U Pr.

Foresta, Ronald A. America's National Parks & Their Keepers. LC 83-43262. 382p. 1984. lib. bdg. 45.00x (ISBN 0-915707-02-0); pap. text ed. 11.95x (ISBN 0-915707-03-9). Resources Future.

Forestal, Sean. Dark Angel. (Orig.). 1982. pap. 3.25 (ISBN 0-440-12033-0). Dell.

Forestell, J. T. Targumic Traditions. LC 79-19293. (Society of Biblical Literature Aramaic Studies: No. 4). 151p. 1984. pap. 12.00 (ISBN 0-89130-352-9, 06-13-04). Scholars Pr GA.

Forestell, J. Terrence. Proverbs. (Bible Ser.). 1.00 (ISBN 0-8091-5122-7). Paulist Pr.

Forester, Bruce. Signs & Omens. 256p. 1984. 15.95 (ISBN 0-396-08392-7). Dodd.

Forester, Bruce M. In Strict Confidence. LC 81-4779. 1982. 14.95 (ISBN 0-87949-206-6). Ashley Bks.

Forester, C. S. Admiral Hornblower in the West Indies. 1958. 9.95 (ISBN 0-316-28901-9). Little.

--Admiral Hornblower in the West Indies. (Hornblower Saga Ser.: No. 10). 320p. 1980. pap. 2.50 (ISBN 0-523-41395-5). Pinnacle Bks.

--The African Queen. 1977. lib. bdg. 14.95 (ISBN 0-89244-065-1, Queens Hse). Amereon Ltd.

--The Baby Pirates. 13.95 (ISBN 0-88411-927-0, Pub. by Aeonian Pr). Amereon Ltd.

--Beat to Quarters. (Hornblower Saga Ser.: No. 5). 224p. 1982. pap. 2.50 (ISBN 0-523-41390-4). Pinnacle Bks.

--Brown on Resolution. 13.95 (ISBN 0-88411-631-X, Pub. by Aeonian Pr). Amereon Ltd.

--The Captain from Connecticut. (gr. 7 up). 1941. 12.95 (ISBN 0-316-28892-6). Little.

--Captain Horatio Hornblower, 1 vol. ed. Incl. Beat to Quarters; Ship of the Line; Flying Colours. (Illus.). 1939. 12.95 (ISBN 0-316-28893-4). Little.

--Commodore Hornblower. (gr. 7 up). 1945. 13.95 (ISBN 0-316-28894-2). Little.

--Commodore Hornblower. (Hornblower Saga Ser.: No. 8). 320p. 1981. pap. 2.50 (ISBN 0-523-41393-9). Pinnacle Bks.

--Commodore Hornblower. 17.95 (ISBN 0-317-27950-5, Pub. by Aeonian Pr). Amereon Ltd.

--Death to the French. 188p. 1978. 7.95 (ISBN 0-370-00684-4, Pub. by the Bodley Head). Merrimack Pub Cir.

--Death to the French. 13.95 (ISBN 0-88411-632-8, Pub. by Aeonian Pr). Amereon Ltd.

--Flying Colors. (Hornblower Saga Ser.: No. 7). 224p. 1981. pap. 2.50 (ISBN 0-523-41392-0). Pinnacle Bks.

--The General. LC 82-80140. (Great War Stories Ser.). 260p. 1982. Repr. 14.95 (ISBN 0-933852-27-4). Nautical & Aviation.

--The General. 15.95 (ISBN 0-89190-609-6, Pub. by Am Repr). Amereon Ltd.

--Gold from Crete. LC 73-121441. 263p. (gr. 8 up). 1970. 7.95 (ISBN 0-316-28919-1). Little.

--The Good Shepherd. 1982. pap. 2.50 (ISBN 0-523-41861-2). Pinnacle Bks.

--The Gun. 13.95 (ISBN 0-88411-634-4, Pub. by Aeonian Pr). Amereon Ltd.

--Hornblower & the Atropos. 1953. 12.95 (ISBN 0-316-28911-6); pap. 6.70i (ISBN 0-316-28929-9). Little.

--Hornblower & the Atropos. (Hornblower Saga Ser.: No. 4). 1981. pap. 2.50 (ISBN 0-523-41389-0). Pinnacle Bks.

--Hornblower & the Hotspur. 1962. 14.45 (ISBN 0-316-28899-3); pap. 6.70i (ISBN 0-316-28928-0). Little.

--Hornblower & the Hotspur. (Hornblower Saga Ser.: No. 3). 352p. 1981. pap. 2.75 (ISBN 0-523-41790-X). Pinnacle Bks.

--Hornblower During the Crisis. (Illus.). 1967. 11.95 (ISBN 0-316-28915-9). Little.

--Hornblower During the Crisis. (Hornblower Saga Ser.: No. 11). 176p. 1981. pap. 2.50 (ISBN 0-523-41396-3). Pinnacle Bks.

--Hornblower Goes to Sea. 13.95 (ISBN 0-88411-635-2, Pub. by Aeonian Pr). Amereon Ltd.

--Hornblower In Captivity. 14.95 (ISBN 0-88411-636-0, Pub. by Aeonian Pr). Amereon Ltd.

--Hornblower Takes Command. 14.95 (ISBN 0-88411-636-0, Pub. by Aeonian Pr.). Amereon Ltd.

--Hornblower's Triumph. 14.95 (ISBN 0-88411-638-7, Pub. by Aeonian Pr). Amereon Ltd.

--Hunting the Bismarck. 118p. 1983. pap. 2.95 (ISBN 0-583-10388-X, Pub. by Granada England). Academy Chi Pubs.

--Indomitable Hornblower. Bd. with Commodore Hornblower; Lord Hornblower; Admiral Hornblower in the West Indies. 17.50 (ISBN 0-316-28904-3). (Illus.). 1963. Little.

--The Last Nine Days of the Bismarck. (gr. 7 up). 1959. 8.95 (ISBN 0-316-28905-1). Little.
--The Last Nine Days of the Bismark. 11.95 (ISBN 0-89190-606-1, Pub. by Am Repr). Amereon Ltd.
--Lieutenant Hornblower. (gr. 7 up). 1952. 12.95 (ISBN 0-316-28907-8). Little.
--Lieutenant Hornblower. (Hornblower Saga Ser.: No. 2). 320p. 1980. pap. 2.50 (ISBN 0-523-41387-4). Pinnacle Bks.
--Long Before Forty. 15.95 (ISBN 0-89190-605-3, Pub. by Am Repr). Amereon Ltd.
--Lord Hornblower. (gr. 7 up). 1946. 11.95 (ISBN 0-316-28908-6). Little.
--Lord Hornblower. (Hornblower Saga Ser.: No. 9). 256p. 1981. pap. 2.50 (ISBN 0-523-41394-7). Pinnacle Bks.
--Mr. Midshipman Hornblower. (gr. 7 up). 1950. 12.95 (ISBN 0-316-28909-4). Little.
--Mr. Midshipman Hornblower. (Hornblower Saga Ser.: No. 1). 172p. 1981. pap. 2.50 (ISBN 0-523-41672-5). Pinnacle Bks.
--Mr. Midshipman Hornblower. (The Hornblower Saga Ser., No. 1). 1974. pap. 1.50 (ISBN 0-523-23381-7). Pinnacle Bks.
--Mr. Midshipman Hornblower. 288p. 1984. Repr. 6.70i (ISBN 0-316-28912-4). Little.
--Payment Deferred. 302p. Repr. of 1926 ed. lib. bdg. 16.95x (ISBN 0-88411-925-4, Pub. by Aeonian Pr). Amereon Ltd.
--Payment Deferred. 188p. 1978. 7.95 (ISBN 0-370-00657-7, Pub. by the Bodley Head). Merrimack Pub Cir.
--Plain Murder. 1978. 7.95 (ISBN 0-370-00650-X, Pub. by the Bodley Head). Merrimack Pub Cir.
--Plain Murder. 13.95 (ISBN 0-8488-0097-4, Pub. by Amereon Hse). Amereon Ltd.
--Randall & the River of Time. 19.95 (ISBN 0-89190-610-X, Pub. by Am Repr). Amereon Ltd.
--Ship of the Line. (Hornblower Saga Ser.: No. 6). 256p. 1980. pap. 2.50 (ISBN 0-523-41391-2). Pinnacle Bks.
--The Sky & the Forest. 1978. pap. 1.95 (ISBN 0-523-40382-8, Dist. by Independent News Co.). Pinnacle Bks.
--To the Indies. 206p. Repr. of 1940 ed. lib. bdg. 12.70x (ISBN 0-88411-926-2, Pub. by Aeonian Pr). Amereon Ltd.

Forester, C. S see Swan, D. K.

Forester, Frank. The Complete Manual for Young Sportsmen. LC 74-15739. (Popular Culture in America Ser.). (Illus.). 1975. Repr. 36.50x (ISBN 0-405-06374-1). Ayer Co Pubs.

Forester, John. Bicycle Transportation. 2nd ed. (Illus.). 275p. 1983. 20.00x (ISBN 0-262-06085-X). MIT Pr.
--Effective Cycling. 5th ed. (Illus.). 424p. 1983. text ed. 32.50x (ISBN 0-262-06088-4); pap. text ed. 15.00 (ISBN 0-262-56026-7). MIT Pr.
--Effective Cycling at the Intermediate Level. (Illus.). 27p. (gr. 3-7). 1981. 3-ring binder 1.50 (ISBN 0-940558-01-7). CCF.
--Effective Cycling: Instructors Manual. (Illus.). 158p. 1982. pap. 6.00 (ISBN 0-940558-02-5). CCF.

Forester, John, ed. Critical Theory & Public Life. (Studies in Contemporary German Social Theory). (Illus.). 376p. 1985. text ed. 30.00x (ISBN 0-262-06097-3). MIT Pr.

Forester, Larry. Fly for Your Life. 1978. pap. 3.95 (ISBN 0-553-24656-9). Bantam.

Forester, Marie-Christine. Let's Face It! (Illus.). 100p. (Orig.). 1984. pap. 6.95 (ISBN 0-917043-05-7). Press on Pr.

Forester, R. J., jt. ed. see Campbell, D. J.

Forester, T., ed. see Henry of Huntingdon.

Forester, Thomas, tr. see Florence of Worcester.

Forester, Tom. The British Labour Party & the Working Class. LC 75-19474. 225p. 1976. 19.50x (ISBN 0-8419-0217-8). Holmes & Meier.

Forester, Tom, ed. The Information Technology Revolution. 678p. (Orig.). 1985. text ed. 30.00x (ISBN 0-262-06095-7); pap. 14.95 (ISBN 0-262-56033-X). MIT Pr.
--The Microelectronics Revolution: The Complete Guide to the New Technology & Its Impact on Society. (Illus.). 589p. 1981. 37.50x (ISBN 0-262-06075-2); pap. 13.50 (ISBN 0-262-56021-6). MIT Pr.

Forestier, J., et al. Ankylosing Spondylitis: Clinical Considerations -- Roentgenology -- Pathologic Anatomy -- Treatment. Desjardins, A. U., tr. (Illus.). 392p. 1956. photocopy ed. 34.75x (ISBN 0-398-04256-X). C C Thomas.

Forestier, Louis, ed. see Rimbaud, Arthur.

Forestiero, Saverio, jt. auth. see Sbordoni, Valerio.

Foret, Nancy C. De see De Foret, Nancy C.

Foreville, Raymonde. Gouvernment et Vie de L'Eglise au Moyen-Age. 418p. 1979. 60.00x (ISBN 0-86078-040-6, Pub. by Variorum). State Mutual Bk.
--Thomas Beckett Dans La Tradition Historique et Hagiographique. 348p. 1981. 60.00x (ISBN 0-86078-076-7, Pub. by Variorum). State Mutual Bk.

Forey, P. L., ed. The Evolving Biosphere. (Chance, Change & Challenge Ser.). (Illus.). 350p. 1981. 89.50 (ISBN 0-521-23811-0); pap. 32.50 (ISBN 0-521-28230-6). Cambridge U Pr.

Forey, Pamela. Fungi. (Shire Natural History Ser.: No. 4). (Orig.). 1985. pap. 3.95 (ISBN 0-85263-746-2, Pub. by Shire Pubns England). Seven Hills Bks.

Foreyt, John P. & Rathjen, Diana P. Cognitive-Behavior Therapy: Research & Application. LC 78-15948. (Illus.). 265p. 1978. 27.50x (ISBN 0-306-31145-3, Plenum Pr). Plenum Pub.

Foreyt, John P., jt. auth. see Davis, Julian C.

Foreyt, John P., ed. Behavioral Treatments of Obesity: A Practical Handbook. 1977. text ed. 25.00 (ISBN 0-08-019902-X). Pergamon.

Foreyt, John P., jt. ed. see Rathjen, Diana P.

Foreyt, John P., jt. ed. see Williams, Ben J.

Forfar, John O. & Arneil, Gavin C. Textbook of Paediatrics, 2 vols. 3rd ed. (Illus.). 1984. text ed. 180.00 (ISBN 0-443-02426-X); pap. text ed. 139.00 (ISBN 0-443-02400-6). Churchill.

Forgacs, David, ed. see Gramsci, Antonio.

Forgacs, Paul. Lung Sounds. (Illus.). 84p. 1983. pap. 8.95 (ISBN 0-7216-0819-1, Pub. by Bailliere-Tindall). Saunders.
--Problems in Respiratory Medicine. Fry, J., et al, eds. LC 81-68106. (Problems in Practice Ser.: Vol. 2). (Illus.). 158p. 1982. text ed. 20.00x (ISBN 0-8036-3684-9). Davis Co.

Forgacs, S. Bones & Joints in Diabetes Mellitus. 1982. lib. bdg. 34.00 (ISBN 90-247-2395-7, Pub. by Martinus Nijhoff Netherlands). Kluwer Academic.

Forgan, Harry & Striebel, Bonnie. Phorgan's Phonics. LC 77-13945. (Illus.). 1978. 14.95 (ISBN 0-673-16365-2); pap. 12.95 (ISBN 0-673-16366-0). Scott F.

Forgan, Harry W. Reading Skillbuilder: Comprehension Skills. 1982. pap. 6.95 (ISBN 0-673-16549-3). Scott F.
--Reading Skillbuilder: Functional Reading Skills. 1982. pap. 6.95 (ISBN 0-673-16550-7). Scott F.
--Reading Skillbuilder: Prereading Skills. 1982. pap. 6.95 (ISBN 0-673-16547-7). Scott F.
--Reading Skillbuilder: Word Recognition Skills. 1982. pap. 6.95 (ISBN 0-673-16548-5). Scott F.

Forgan, Harry W. & Mangrum, Charles T., II. Teaching Content Area Reading Skills. 3rd ed. 328p. 1984. pap. 18.95 (ISBN 0-675-20308-2). Merrill.

Forgan, Henry & Christman-Rothlein, Liz. Getting Ready to Read. 1980. Bk. 2. pap. 9.95 (ISBN 0-673-16373-3). Scott F.

Forgan, Henry W. The Reading Corner: Ideas, Games & Activities for Individualizing Reading. LC 76-28292. (Illus.). 1977. pap. 12.95 (ISBN 0-673-16419-5). Scott F.

Forgan, James B. Recollections of a Busy Life. facsimile ed. LC 75-2632. (Wall Street & the Security Market Ser.). (Illus.). 1975. Repr. of 1924 ed. 29.00x (ISBN 0-405-06957-X). Ayer Co Pubs.

Forgan, Ruth A., jt. auth. see Striebel, Bonnie.

Forgas, J. P. Language & Social Situations. (Springer Series in Social Psychology). (Illus.). 250p. 1985. 33.00 (ISBN 0-387-96090-2). Springer-Verlag.

Forgas, Joseph. Social Episodes: The Study of Interaction Routines. LC 79-40925. (European Monographs in Social Psychology). 1980. 59.50 (ISBN 0-12-263550-7). Acad Pr.

Forgas, Joseph, ed. Social Cognition: Perspectives on Everyday Understanding. LC 81-66400. (European Monographs in Social Psychology: No. 26). 1981. 44.00 (ISBN 0-12-263560-4); pap. 22.50 (ISBN 0-12-263562-0). Acad Pr.

Forgatch, jt. auth. see Patterson.

Forgatsch, Olive H. A World of Wonder: Poetry for Children. LC 82-90106. (Illus.). 60p. (gr. 2-5). 1982. lib. bdg. 14.95 (ISBN 0-9608784-0-8). Rainbow Child Bks.

Forgays, Donald G., ed. Environmental Influences & Strategies in Primary Prevention. LC 77-95398. (Primary Prevention Psychopathology Ser.: Vol. 2). (Illus.). 277p. 1978. 25.00x (ISBN 0-87451-153-4). U Pr of New Eng.

Forge, Andrew, jt. auth. see Ades, Dawn.

Forge, Andrew, jt. auth. see Gordon, Robert.

Forge, Andrew, ed. The Townsend Journals: An Artists Record of His Times 1928-51. (Illus.). 112p. 12.95 (ISBN 0-900874-97-X, Pub. by Salem Hse Ltd). Merrimack Pub Cir.

Forge, P. G. La see La Forge, P. G.

Forge, Suzanne. Victorian Splendour: Australian Interior Decoration, 1837-1901. (Illus.). 1981. 70.00x (ISBN 0-19-554299-1). Oxford U Pr.

Forges, Roger V. Des see Des Forges, Roger V.

Forget, Bernard G., jt. auth. see Bunn, H. Franklin.

Forget, C. Elsevier's Dictionary of Jewellery & Watchmaking. 1984. 106.00 (ISBN 0-444-42279-X, I-031-84). Elsevier.

Forget, Claude E. China's External Trade: A Canadian Perspective. (Illus.). 81p. 1971. 2.00 (ISBN 0-88806-088-2). Inst C D Howe.

Forget, Claude E., ed. La Caisse de Depot et Placement du Quebec: Sa Mission, son Impact et sa Performance. 163p. 1984. 8.00 (ISBN 0-88806-119-6). Inst C D Howe.

Forgey, William W. Campfire Stories: Things That Go Bump in the Night. LC 85-2429. 160p. (Orig.). 1985. pap. 9.95 (ISBN 0-934802-23-8). ICS Bks.
--Hypothermia. LC 84-19803. (Illus.). 180p. (Orig.). 1985. pap. 9.95 (ISBN 0-934802-10-6). ICS Bks.
--Wilderness Medicine. LC 79-89027. (Illus.). 1979. pap. 9.95 (ISBN 0-934802-02-5). ICS Bks.

Forgie, George B. Patricide in the House Divided: A Psychological Interpretation of Lincoln & His Age. 1979. 14.95x (ISBN 0-393-05695-3). Norton.
--Patricide in the House Divided: A Psychological Interpretation of Lincoln & His Age. 320p. 1981. pap. 5.95 (ISBN 0-393-00035-4). Norton.

Forgione, Albert G., et al. Fear: Learning to Cope. 1978. 11.95 (ISBN 0-442-26388-0). Van Nos Reinhold.

Forgione, Louis. The River Between. LC 74-17927. (Italian American Experience Ser). 262p. 1975. Repr. 18.00x (ISBN 0-405-06400-4). Ayer Co Pubs.

Forgionne, Guisseppi A. Quantitative Decision-Making. 768p. 1985. text ed. write for info. (ISBN 0-534-05364-5). Wadsworth Pub.

Forgo, F., jt. auth. see Szep, J.

Forgue, Guy J., ed. Letters of H. L. Mencken. LC 81-5086. 531p. 1981. 20.95 (ISBN 0-930350-17-0); pap. 10.95 (ISBN 0-930350-18-9). NE U Pr.

Forgus, Ronald, jt. auth. see Shulman, Bernard H.

Foriegn Policy Association. Great Decisions 1985. LC 58-59828. (Illus.). 96p. (Orig.). 1985. 15.00 (ISBN 0-87124-095-5); pap. 6.00 (ISBN 0-87124-085-8). Foreign Policy.

Forintos, Gyozo & Haag, Ervin. Petroff's Defence: Competitive & Master Level. (Illus.). 192p. 1982. pap. 21.00 (ISBN 0-7134-3202-0, Pub. by Batsford England). David & Charles.

Foris, Andreas. Charted Folk Designs for Cross-Stitch Embroidery. LC 75-9175. 1975. lib. bdg. 11.50x (ISBN 0-88307-591-1). Gannon.

Foris, Andreas, jt. auth. see Foris, Maria.

Foris, Maria & Foris, Andreas. Charted Folk Designs for Cross-Stitch Embroidery. LC 75-9175. Orig. Title: Susann Folk Cross-Stitch Charts. (Illus.). 1975. pap. 3.95 (ISBN 0-486-23191-7). Dover.

Forish, Joseph J., jt. auth. see Chiappa, Joseph A.

Forisha, Barbara. Experience of Adolescence: Development in Context. 1983. text ed. 23.80x (ISBN 0-673-15353-3). Scott F.
--Power & Love: How to Work for Success & Still Care for Others. (Illus.). 196p. 1982. 11.95 (ISBN 0-13-687293-X); pap. 5.95 (ISBN 0-13-687285-9). P-H.

Forisha, Barbara L. Sex Roles. 1978. pap. text ed. 13.65x (ISBN 0-673-15307-X). Scott F.

Forisha-Koavach, Barbara. Organizational Sync: Making Your Job Work for You. (Illus.). 208p. 1983. 16.95 (ISBN 0-13-641456-7); pap. 7.95 (ISBN 0-13-641449-4). P-H.

Forisha-Kovach, Barbara. The Flexible Organization: A Unique New Approach to Organizational Effectiveness & Success. (Illus.). 160p. 1984. 16.95 (ISBN 0-13-322321-3); pap. 7.95 (ISBN 0-13-322313-2). P-H.

Forizs, Loran. Loops & Interfaces of Man. LC 76-24283. 1977. 7.95 (ISBN 0-87212-072-4). Libra.

Forke, Alfred. The World-Conception of the Chinese: Their Astronomical Cosmological & Physico-Philosophical Speculations. LC 74-26262. (History, Philosophy & Sociology of Science Ser). 1975. Repr. 24.50x (ISBN 0-405-06590-6). Ayer Co Pubs.

Forkel, Johann N. Johann Sebastian Bach. Terry, Charles S., ed. (Music Ser: Practice & Theory). (Illus.). 1970. Repr. of 1920 ed. 17.00 (ISBN 0-384-16420-X). Johnson Repr.
--Johann Sebastian Bach: His Life, Art, & Work. LC 75-125044. (Music Ser). 1970. Repr. of 1920 ed. lib. bdg. 35.00 (ISBN 0-306-70010-7). Da Capo.
--Johann Sebastian Bach: His Life, Art, & Work. Terry, Charles S., tr. LC 74-77496. 353p. 1974. pap. 15.00x (ISBN 0-8443-0021-7). Vienna Hse.

Forker, et al. Henry V: An Annotated Bibliography. Godshalk, William L., ed. (Garland Shakespeare Bibliographies Ser.). 1983. lib. bdg. 72.00 (ISBN 0-8240-9323-2). Garland Pub.

Forker, Charles, jt. auth. see Calder, Daniel G.

Forker, Dom. The Ultimate Baseball Quiz Book. (Orig.). 1981. pap. 2.50 (ISBN 0-451-09679-7, E9679, Sig). NAL.
--The Ultimate World Series Quiz Book. 1982. pap. 2.50 (ISBN 0-451-11788-3, AJ1788, Sig). NAL.

Forker, Frank X. Hey Coach, Thanks. (Illus.). 1982. 7.95 (ISBN 0-533-05152-5). Vantage.

Forker, Gregory N. Deliverance. 1977. pap. text ed. 2.50 (ISBN 0-916556-07-7). Desert First.

Forkner, Ben, ed. Modern Irish Short Stories. 546p. 1980. pap. 6.95 (ISBN 0-14-005669-6). Penguin.
--Modern Irish Short Stories. 512p. 1980. 15.95 (ISBN 0-670-48324-9). Viking.

Forkner, Ben & Samway, Patrick, eds. Stories of the Modern South. 464p. 1981. pap. 6.95 (ISBN 0-14-005848-6). Penguin.
--Stories of the Modern South. 1984. 15.25 (ISBN 0-8446-6171-6). Peter Smith.

Forkner, Hamden L., jt. auth. see Brown, Francis A.

Forkner, Hamden L., et al. Forkner Shorthand. 4th ed. 206p. 10.24x (ISBN 0-912036-10-9); tchr's. manual 7.42x (ISBN 0-912036-14-1). Forkner.
--Forkner Shorthand: Study Guide. 4th ed. 121p. 1968. pap. 6.12x (ISBN 0-912036-12-5). Forkner.

Forkner, Hamden L., Jr. & Brown, Frances A. Forkner Shorthand. 5th ed. LC 81-65399. 224p. (gr. 10-12). 1981. text ed. 10.24x (ISBN 0-912036-31-1); tchr's. ed. 7.42x (ISBN 0-912036-35-4); study guide, 128p 6.12x (ISBN 0-912036-33-8); 18 cassettes 300.00 (ISBN 0-912036-36-2). Forkner.

Forkner, Irvine, jt. auth. see Bentley, Trevor.

Forkner, Irvine, jt. auth. see McLeod, Raymond.

Forkner, Irvine F. BASIC Programming for Business. (Illus.). 288p. 1978. pap. text ed. 21.95x (ISBN 0-13-066423-5). P-H.

Forkner, Irvine H. Pascal Programming. LC 84-17467. (Computer Science Ser.). 300p. 1985. pap. text ed. 14.50 pub net (ISBN 0-534-04215-5). Brooks-Cole.
--Pascal Programming Business, Management Science, & Social Science Applications. 250p. 1984. pap. write for info. Wadsworth Pub.

Forkner, Jerry & Schatz, Gail. Consumer Education Learning Activities. 120p. (Orig.). 1981. pap. 15.95 (ISBN 0-89994-252-0). Soc Sci Ed.

Forkosch, Morris D. Anti-Trust & the Consumer. LC 56-6738. xi, 521p. 1956. lib. bdg. 25.00 (ISBN 0-89941-368-4). W S Hein.
--Outer Space & Legal Liability. 1982. lib. bdg. 43.50 (ISBN 90-247-2582-8, Pub. by Martinus Nijhoff Netherlands). Kluwer Academic.

Forkuo, Peter C. A Successful Approach to Your Venture Capital Needs: Your Key to a Venture Capital Fortune. (Home Entrepreneurs Success Library). 1982. 29.95 (ISBN 0-941928-00-4). P C Forkuo World Ent.

Forlag, P. A., jt. ed. see Bergendahl, Goran.

Forland, Marvin. Concise Textbook of Nephrology. 1983. pap. text ed. 30.00 (ISBN 0-87488-177-3). Med Exam.

Forlano, George. School Learning, with Various Methods of Practice & Rewards. LC 74-176782. (Columbia University. Teachers College. Contributions to Education: No. 688). Repr. of 1936 ed. 22.50 (ISBN 0-404-55688-4). AMS Pr.

Forley, Maurice. Practical Guide to Public Speaking. pap. 5.00 (ISBN 0-87980-121-2). Wilshire.

Forlines, F. Leroy. Christian Standards & Convictions Without Legalism. 1981. pap. 2.25 (ISBN 0-89265-074-5). Randall Hse.
--Survey of the Minor Prophets. 1977. pap. 1.95 (ISBN 0-89265-041-9). Randall Hse.

Forlines, Leroy. Biblical Ethics. 1973. pap. 4.95 (ISBN 0-89265-014-1). Randall Hse.
--Biblical Ethics. 1980. 7.95 (ISBN 0-89265-068-0). Randall Hse.
--Biblical Systematics. 1975. 7.95 (ISBN 0-89265-025-7); pap. 4.95 (ISBN 0-89265-038-9). Randall Hse.

Forlines, Leroy & Picirilli, Robert. A Survey of the Pauline Epistles. 1976. pap. 3.75 (ISBN 0-89265-035-4). Randall Hse.

Forlini, Gary, jt. auth. see Leo, Miriam.

Forliti, John. Faith Without Anger. (Infinity Ser.: No. 2). 1972. text ed. 2.50 (ISBN 0-03-004021-3, 229); tchr's guide 1.15 (ISBN 0-03-004026-4, 230). Winston Pr.

Forliti, John E. Program Planning for Youth Ministry. LC 75-143. 1975. pap. 4.50 (ISBN 0-88489-061-9). St Marys.
--Reverence for Life & Family Program: Parent-Teacher Resource. 1981. pap. 4.50 176 pp (ISBN 0-697-01789-3); tchr. training tape 9.95 (ISBN 0-697-01837-7). Wm C Brown.

Form, William. Divided We Stand: Working-Class Stratification in America. 304p. 1986. 28.95x (ISBN 0-252-01168-6). U of Ill Pr.

Form, William H. Blue-Collar Stratification: Auto Workers in Four Countries. LC 75-17525. 1976. 38.50x (ISBN 0-691-09366-0). Princeton U Pr.

Form, William H., jt. auth. see D'Antonio, William V.

Form, William H., jt. auth. see Huber, Joan.

Form, William H., jt. auth. see Miller, Delbert C.

Form, William H. & Blum, Albert A., eds. Industrial Relations & Social Change in Latin America. LC 65-18667. 1965. 7.50 (ISBN 0-8130-0079-3). U Presses Fla.

Formaad, William. Articulation Therapy Through Play. 1974. pap. 7.95 (ISBN 0-914420-51-8). Exceptional Pr Inc.

Formacarr, Jack. True Horror Stories of Science: Research & Medicine in American College Education. LC 83-48722. 171p. 1984. 19.95 (ISBN 0-88164-077-8); pap. 14.95 (ISBN 0-88164-074-3). ABBE Pubs Assn.

Formacek & Kuboczka. Essential Oils Analysis by Carbon-13 NMR Spectroscopy. 1981. 112.00x (ISBN 0-471-26218-8). Wiley.

Formacek, V. & Kubeczka, K. H. Essential Oils Analysis by Capillary Gas Chromatography & Carbon-13 NMR Spectroscopy. 373p. 1982. 124.95x (ISBN 0-471-26218-8, Pub. by Wiley Heyden). Wiley.

Forman. Divine Comedy (Dante) (Book Notes). 1984. pap. 2.50 (ISBN 0-8120-3411-2). Barron.
--Fascism: The Meaning & Experience of Reactionary Revolution. 156p. (YA) (gr. 7 up). pap. 1.75 (ISBN 0-440-94707-3, LFL). Dell.
--The Tempest (Shakespeare) (Book Note Ser.). 1985. pap. 2.50 (ISBN 0-8120-3545-3). Barron.

Forman & Weeks. Whey Cookery (Treats Made with Milk Sugar) (Illus.). pap. 2.95 (ISBN 0-89036-064-2). Hawkes Pub Inc.

Forman, Arthur S., jt. auth. see Denison, David O.

Forman, B. Fred. Local Stresses in Pressure Vessels. 3rd ed. 1981. 60.00 (ISBN 0-914458-08-6). Pressure.
--Local Stresses in Vessels: Computer Programs. 1981. 40.00 (ISBN 0-914458-09-4); with 6 magnetic cards 100.00 (ISBN 0-686-86661-4). Pressure.

Forman, Bedrich. Borobudur: The Buddhist Legend in Tone. (Illus.). 1980. 16.95 (ISBN 0-686-70134-8, Mayflower Bks). Smith Pubs.
Forman, Bedrich, et al. Bali: The Split Gate to Heaven. (Illus.). 118p. 1984. 20.00 (ISBN 0-85613-513-5, Pub. By Salem Hse Ltd). Merrimack Pub Cir.
Forman, Betty Yetta, jt. auth. see Feinbloom, Richard I.
Forman, Charles C. Four Early Bibles in Pilgrim Hall. (Pilgrim Society Notes: No. 9). 1959. 1.00 (ISBN 0-940628-17-1). Pilgrim Hall.
Forman, Charles W. A Faith for the Nations. LC 57-9601. (Layman's Theological Library). 1957. pap. 1.00 (ISBN 0-664-24007-0). Westminster.
--The Island Churches of the South Pacific: Emergence in the Twentieth Century. LC 81-18666. 304p. (Orig.). 1982. pap. 17.50 (ISBN 0-88344-218-3). Orbis Bks.
Forman, Charles W., ed. Christianity in the Non-Western World. facs. ed. LC 71-117792. (Essay Index Reprint Ser). 1967. 17.00 (ISBN 0-8369-1806-1). Ayer Co Pubs.
Forman, D. T., ed. Essential & Non-Essential Metals-Metabolism with Antibiotic Activity-Pharmacology of Benzodiazepines-Intefron Gamma Research. (Progress in Clinical Biochemistry & Medicine Ser.: Vol. 1). (Illus.). 240p. 1984. 35.50 (ISBN 0-387-13605-3). Springer-Verlag.
Forman, Denis. Mozart's Concerto Form: The First Movements of the Piano Concertos. (Music Reprint Ser.). 303p. 1983. Repr. of 1971 ed. lib. bdg. 32.50 (ISBN 0-306-76197-1). Da Capo.
Forman, Donald T. & Mattoon, Richard W., eds. Clinical Chemistry. LC 76-49983. (ACS Symposium Ser.: No. 36). 1976. 26.95 (ISBN 0-8412-0345-8). Am Chemical.
Forman, F. Mastering British Politics. 320p. 1985. text ed. 18.50x (ISBN 0-333-36650-6, Pub. by Macmillan England); pap. text ed. 6.50x (ISBN 0-333-36651-4). Humanities.
Forman, Gail, ed. see Fields, George.
Forman, George E. & Kushner, David S. The Childs Construction of Knowledge: Piaget for Teaching Children. LC 77-8676. 244p. 1983. pap. 6.00 (ISBN 0-8185-0231-2, NAEYC116). Natl Assn Child Ed.
Forman, George E., ed. Action & Thought: From Sensorimotor Schemes to Symbolic Operations. LC 81-12730. (Developmental Psychology Ser.). 1981. 44.00 (ISBN 0-12-262220-0). Acad Pr.
Forman, H. B. The Books of William Morris. 45.00x (ISBN 0-87556-290-6). Saifer.
Forman, H. Buxton. The Books of William Morris Described with Some Account of His Doings in Literature & in the Allied Crafts. (Illus.). xvi, 224p. 1976. Repr. of 1897 ed. 40.00 (ISBN 0-900470-74-7). Oak Knoll.
--The Shelley Library, an Essay in Bibliography. LC 74-30296. (Shelley Society, Fourth Ser.: No. 1). Repr. of 1886 ed. 24.00 (ISBN 0-404-11513-6). AMS Pr.
Forman, H. Buxton, ed. see Keats, John.
Forman, H. Buxton, ed. see Shelley, Percy B.
Forman, H. Buxton, ed. see Trelawny, Edward J.
Forman, H. Chandlee. Old Buildings, Gardens & Furniture in Tidewater, Maryland. LC 67-17538. (Illus.). 341p. 1967. 12.50 (ISBN 0-87033-075-6). Tidewater.
Forman, Harrison. Report from Red China. LC 74-28417. (China in the 20th Century Ser). (Illus.). iv, 250p. 1975. Repr. of 1945 ed. lib. bdg. 29.50 (ISBN 0-306-70676-8). Da Capo.
--Through Forbidden Tibet. 1984. lib. bdg. 90.00 (ISBN 0-8490-3240-7). Gordon Pr.
Forman, Harry B. Books of William Morris Described with Some Account of His Doings in Literature & in the Allied Arts. LC 68-58235. (Research & Source Ser.: No. 104). (Illus.). 1969. Repr. of 1897 ed. 23.50 (ISBN 0-8337-1205-5). B Franklin.
--Our Living Poets: An Essay in Criticism. (The Victorian Muse Ser.). 60.00 (ISBN 0-8240-8605-8). Garland Pub.
Forman, Henry C. The Architecture of the Old South: The Medieval Style, 1585-1850. LC 66-27071. (Illus.). 1967. Repr. of 1948 ed. 15.00x (ISBN 0-8462-0925-X). Russell.
--Early Manor & Plantation Houses of Maryland: Arch History. (Illus.). 272p. 1982. Repr. 35.00 (ISBN 0-910254-16-8). Bodine.
Forman, Henry J. In the Footprints of Heine. 15.75 (ISBN 0-8369-6930-8, 7811). Ayer Co Pubs.
--Our Movie Made Children. LC 72-124028. (Literature of Cinema Ser: Payne Fund Studies of Motion Pictures & Social Values). Repr. of 1935 ed. 17.00 (ISBN 0-405-01646-8). Ayer Co Pubs.
--The Story of Prophecy. 388p. 1981. pap. 12.00 (ISBN 0-89540-103-7, SB-089). Sun Pub.
Forman, James. A Ballad for Hogskin Hill. LC 79-16563. 246p. (gr. 7 up). 1979. 10.95 (ISBN 0-374-30497-1). FS&G.
--Code Name Valkyrie: Count Claus von Stauffenberg & the Plot to Kill Hitler. LC 72-12581. (Illus.). 256p. (gr. 9-12). 1973. PLB 12.95 (ISBN 0-87599-188-2). S G Phillips.
--Communism: From Marx's Manifesto to 20th-Century Reality. (Studies in Contemporary Politics Ser.). 158p. (gr. 7 up). 1976. pap. 2.25 (ISBN 0-440-94611-5, LFL). Dell.
--Fascism. (Studies in Contemporary Politics Ser.). 156p. (gr. 7 up). 1976. pap. 1.75 (ISBN 0-440-94707-3, LFL). Dell.
--A Fine, Soft Day. LC 78-11127. 224p. (gr. 7 up). 1978. 10.95 (ISBN 0-374-32301-1). FS&G.
--The Life & Death of Yellow Bird. LC 73-82697. 224p. (gr. 7 up). 1973. 10.95 (ISBN 0-374-34408-6). FS&G.
--The Making of Black Revolutionaries. 2nd ed. 592p. 1985. pap. 12.95 (ISBN 0-940880-10-5). Open Hand.
--My Enemy, My Brother. (gr. 7-12). 1972. pap. 2.25 (ISBN 0-590-04477-X). Scholastic Inc.
--Nazism. (Studies in Contemporary Politics Ser.). 176p. (gr. 7 up). 1980. pap. 1.50 (ISBN 0-440-95772-9, LFL). Dell.
--People of the Dream. LC 76-188271. (Illus.). 240p. (gr. 7 up). 1972. 8.95 (ISBN 0-374-35804-4). FS&G.
--Self-Determination: An Examination of the Question & its Application to African-American People. 2nd ed. (Illus.). 116p. 1984. 15.00 (ISBN 0-940880-09-1); pap. 6.00 (ISBN 0-940880-08-3). Open Hand.
--Song of Jubilee. LC 74-149224. 192p. (gr. 7 up). 1971. 10.95 (ISBN 0-374-37142-3). FS&G.
--The Survivor. LC 76-2478. 288p. (gr. 7 up). 1976. 11.95 (ISBN 0-374-37312-4). FS&G.
Forman, James D. Call Back Yesterday. 192p. (gr. 7 up). 1981. 10.95 (ISBN 0-684-17168-6, ScribJ). Scribner.
--Call Back Yesterday. pap. 1.95 (ISBN 0-451-11851-0, AJ1851, Sig). NAL.
--Doomsday Plus Twelve. LC 84-20220. 224p. (gr. 7 up). 1984. 14.95 (ISBN 0-684-18221-1, ScribJ). Scribner.
--Freedom's Blood. (Illus.). (gr. 7 up). 1979. PLB 6.90 s&l (ISBN 0-531-02866-6). Watts.
--That Mad Game: War & the Chances for Peace. LC 80-11600. (gr. 7 up). 1980. 10.95 (ISBN 0-684-16509-0, ScribJ). Scribner.
Forman, James D. & Gross, Nancy E. Anarchism: Teacher's Guide. 1976. pap. 1.75 (ISBN 0-440-90189-8). Dell.
--Capitalism: Teacher's Guide. 1976. pap. 1.50 (ISBN 0-440-94622-0). Dell.
--Communism: Teacher's Guide. 1976. pap. 2.25 (ISBN 0-440-94611-5). Dell.
--Facism: Teacher's Guide. 1976. pap. 1.75 (ISBN 0-440-94707-3). Dell.
--Socialism: Teacher's Guide. 1976. pap. 1.75 (ISBN 0-440-98318-5). Dell.
Forman, Joan. The Romans. (Peoples of the Past Ser.). 80p. (gr. 4 up). 1985. pap. 5.75 (ISBN 0-382-06914-5). Silver.
Forman, Joan & Strongman, Harry. The Romans. LC 77-86188. (Peoples of the Past Ser.). (Illus.). 61p. 1977. PLB 13.72 (ISBN 0-382-06120-9). Silver.
Forman, Keith & Schafer, Walt. Stress, Distress & Growth: A Student Manual. LC 82-82154. (Dialogue Bks.). 120p. 1978. 7.75 (ISBN 0-89881-001-9). Intl Dialogue Pr.
Forman, L. Ronald, et al. Audubon Park: An Urban Eden. 176p. 29.95 (ISBN 0-9612038-4-6). D K Gleason.
Forman, Ludovico L. & Siegmund, Preuss. Index Andocideus, Lycurgeus, Dinarcheus & Index Aeschineus, 2 vols. in one. Vlastos, Gregory, ed. LC 78-14614. (Morals & Law in Ancient Greece Ser.). (Gr. & Lat.). 1979. Repr. of 1896 ed. lib. bdg. 23.00x (ISBN 0-405-11589-X). Ayer Co Pubs.
Forman, M. B., ed. see Keats, John.
Forman, M. Buxton. Letters of Edward John Trelawny. 1972. Repr. of 1910 ed. lib. bdg. 25.00 (ISBN 0-8414-4274-6). Folcroft.
--Some Letters & Miscellanea of Charles Brown, the Friend of John Keats & Thomas Richards. LC 76-26940. 1937. lib. bdg. 15.00 (ISBN 0-8414-4205-3). Folcroft.
Forman, Marc, jt. auth. see Hetznecker, William.
Forman, Maurice B. Bibliography of Writings of George Meredith & Meredithiana. LC 78-122982. (Studies in George Meredith, No. 21). (2 vol set). 1970. Repr. lib. bdg. 89.95x (ISBN 0-8383-1114-8). Haskell.
--George Meredith: Some Early Appreciations. LC 70-86014. 1969. Repr. of 1909 ed. 24.50x (ISBN 0-8046-0609-9, Pub. by Kennikat). Assoc Faculty Pr.
--John Keats & His Family. LC 77-1149. 1973. lib. bdg. 20.00 (ISBN 0-8414-4198-7). Folcroft.
--Shelley Library. LC 78-116794. (Studies in Shelley, No. 25). 1970. Repr. of 1886 ed. lib. bdg. 28.95x (ISBN 0-8383-1036-2). Haskell.
Forman, Maurice B., ed. see Keats, John.
Forman, Max L., ed. World's Greatest Quotations. 1969. 18.95 (ISBN 0-682-46844-4). Exposition Pr FL.
Forman, Michael L. Kapampangan Dictionary. McKaughan, Howard P., ed. LC 75-152464. (University of Hawaii, Honolulu. Pacific & Asian Linguistics Institute. PALI Language Texts: Philippines). Repr. of 1971 ed. 64.80 (ISBN 0-8357-9824-0, 2016106). Bks Demand UMI.
--Kapampangan Grammar Notes. LC 79-152465. (University of Hawaii, Honolulu. Pacific & Asian Linguistics Institute. PALI Language Texts: Philipines). pap. 27.80 (ISBN 0-317-10125-0, 2017217). Bks Demand UMI.
Forman, Peter N. Flying Hawaii: A Pilot's Guide to the Islands. (Illus.). 160p. (Orig.). 1983. pap. 10.25 (ISBN 0-8306-2361-2, 2361). TAB Bks.
Forman, Rachel Z. Let Us Now Praise Obscure Women: A Comparative Study of Publicly Supported Unmarried Mothers in Government Housing in the United States & Britain. LC 82-17579. 240p. (Orig.). 1983. lib. bdg. 25.00 (ISBN 0-8191-2813-9); pap. text ed. 12.25 (ISBN 0-8191-2814-7). U Pr of Amer.
Forman, Richard R., ed. Pine Barrens: Ecosystem & Landscape. LC 79-9849. (Natural Resource Management Ser.). 1979. 55.00 (ISBN 0-12-263450-0). Acad Pr.
Forman, Robert. How to Control Your Allergies. 256p. (Orig.). 1979. pap. 3.95 (ISBN 0-915962-29-2). Larchmont Bks.
Forman, Samuel E. Political Activities of Philip Freneau. LC 77-125693. (American Journalists Ser). 1970. Repr. of 1902 ed. 14.00 (ISBN 0-405-01670-0). Ayer Co Pubs.
--The Political Activities of Phillip Freneau. LC 78-63891. (Johns Hopkins University. Studies in the Social Sciences. Twentieth Ser. 1902: 9-10). Repr. of 1902 ed. 11.50 (ISBN 0-404-61145-1). AMS Pr.
Forman, Samuel S. Narrative of a Journey Down the Ohio & Mississippi in 1789-90 With a Memoir & Illustrative Notes by Lyman C. Draper. LC 78-146396. (First American Frontier Ser.). 1971. Repr. of 1888 ed. 11.00 (ISBN 0-405-02850-4). Ayer Co Pubs.
Forman, Shepard. The Brazilian Peasantry. LC 75-16156. 319p. 1975. 30.00x (ISBN 0-231-03106-8); pap. 15.00x (ISBN 0-231-08366-1). Columbia U Pr.
Forman, Sidney. Billie Is Black. LC 79-89331. 1980. 5.95 (ISBN 0-87212-107-0). Libra.
Forman, Sidney, jt. auth. see Allen, Virginia F.
Forman, Stephen. Travel & Tourism Research: A Guide of Information Sources in the Washington, D. C. Area. 1982. pap. text ed. 10.00 (ISBN 0-89478-057-3). U CO Busn Res Div.
Forman, Sylvia H., et al. New Approaches to the Study of Migration. Guillet, David & Uzzell, Douglas, eds. (Rice University Studies, Vol. 62: No. 3). 181p. 1976. pap. 10.00x (ISBN 0-89263-229-1). Rice Univ.
Forman, Werner & Lewis, David. The Maori: Heirs of Tane. (Illus.). 128p. 1984. 20.00 (ISBN 0-85613-343-4, Pub. by Salem Hse Ltd). Merrimack Pub Cir.
Forman, Werner, jt. auth. see Bancroft-Hunt, Norman.
Forman, Werner, jt. auth. see Brett, Michael.
Forman, Werner, jt. auth. see Burland, Cottie.
Forman, Werner, jt. auth. see Hetherington, Paul.
Forman, Werner, jt. auth. see Lyttleton, Margaret.
Forman, William & Gavurin, Lester L. Elements of Arithmetic: Algebra & Geometry. LC 78-159159. 318p. 1972. text ed. 30.50x (ISBN 0-471-00654-8). Wiley.
Formanek, Ruth & Gurian, Anita. Charting Intellectual Development: A Practical Guide to Piagetian Tasks. 2nd ed. (Illus.). 136p. 1981. 15.75x (ISBN 0-398-04476-7). C C Thomas.
Formations Editorial Collective, ed. Formations of Nations & People. (Routledge Formations Ser.). (Illus.). 240p. (Orig.). 1983. pap. 14.95 (ISBN 0-7102-0044-7). Routledge & Kegan.
Formento, Dan. Rock Chronicle: Today in Rock History. (Illus.). 372p. (Orig.). 1982. pap. 9.95 (ISBN 0-933328-41-9). Delilah Bks.
Formey, Ronald R. The Historical Foundations of Modern Company Law. 59.95 (ISBN 0-8490-0308-3). Gordon Pr.
Formhals, Hugh. The Jolliest Game under the Sun: A Beginner's Guide to Cricket. LC 83-60379. (Illus.). 128p. 1984. 10.95 (ISBN 0-911265-04-X). Western Mtn.
Formisano, Ronald P. Birth of Mass Political Parties: Michigan, Eighteen Twenty-Seven to Eighteen Sixty-One. LC 73-154995. 1971. 35.00x (ISBN 0-691-04605-0); pap. 9.95 (ISBN 0-691-04605-0). Princeton U Pr.
--The Transformation of Political Culture: Massachusetts Parties, 1790s-1840s. (Illus.). 1983. 35.00x (ISBN 0-19-503124-5); pap. 9.95x (ISBN 0-19-503509-7). Oxford U Pr.
Formisano, Ronald P. & Burns, Constance K., eds. Boston 1700-1980: The Evolution of Urban Politics. LC 83-18415. (Contributions in American History Ser.: No. 106). (Illus.). ix, 296p. 1984. lib. bdg. 35.00 (ISBN 0-313-23336-5, FOB). Greenwood.
Formisano, V., ed. see Neil Brice Memorial Symposium, Frascati, Italy, May 28-June 1 1974.
Formstecher, Salomon. Die Religion des Geistes. Katz, Steven, ed. LC 79-7129. (Jewish Philosophy, Mysticism & History of Ideas Ser.). 1980. Repr. of 1841 ed. lib. bdg. 40.00x (ISBN 0-405-12251-9). Ayer Co Pubs.
Formwalt, Lee W. Benjamin Henry Latrobe & the Development of Internal Improvements in the New Republic, 1796-1820. 35.00 (ISBN 0-405-14080-0). Ayer Co Pubs.
Formwalt, Lee W., ed. see Latrobe, Benjamin H.
Fornaess, John, ed. Recent Developments on Several Variables. LC 80-8548. (Annals of Mathematical Studies: No. 100). 565p. 1981. 40.00 (ISBN 0-691-08285-5); pap. 16.50 (ISBN 0-691-08281-2). Princeton U Pr.
Fornander, Abraham. An Account of the Polynesian Race: Its Origin & Migration, 3 vols. in 1. LC 69-13505. (Illus.). 1980. Repr. of 1878 ed. Set. 37.50 (ISBN 0-8048-0002-2). C E Tuttle.
Fornara, Charles W. The Nature of History in Ancient Greece & Rome. LC 82-21888. (Eidos: Studies in Classical Kinds). 264p. 1983. text ed. 22.00x (ISBN 0-520-04910-1). U of Cal Pr.
Fornara, Charles W., ed. Archaic Times to the End of the Peloponnesian War. LC 79-54018. (Translated Documents of Greece & Rome Ser.: No. 1). 232p. 1983. 42.50 (ISBN 0-521-25019-6); pap. 12.95 (ISBN 0-521-29946-2). Cambridge U Pr.
Fornari, Franco. The Psychoanalysis of War. Pfeifer, Alenka, tr. from It. LC 74-17458. 20.00 (ISBN 0-253-34632-0, Indiana U Pr). Lib Soc Sci.
Fornari, Harry. The Story of Peace. 1977. 5.95 (ISBN 0-87695-191-4). Aurora Pubs.
Fornaro, Carlo De see De Fornaro, Carlo.
Fornatale, Peter. Radio in the Television Age. LC 79-67675. 240p. 1983. 17.95 (ISBN 0-87951-106-0); pap. 8.95 (ISBN 0-87951-172-9). Overlook Pr.
Fornatora, Nancy. Planetanimals: Mission Zapton. Lewis, Jean, ed. LC 84-61163. (Illus.). 48p. (ps-3). 1984. 5.95 (ISBN 0-448-18965-8). Putnam Pub Group.
Fornell. A Second Generation of Multivariate Analysis: Measurement & Evaluation, 2 Vols. LC 82-11273. 444p. 1982. Vol. 1. 48.00 (ISBN 0-03-061604-2); Vol. 2. 49.00 (ISBN 0-03-062627-7); 86.50 set (ISBN 0-03-062632-3). Praeger.
Fornell, Earl W. The Galveston Era: The Texas Crescent on the Eve of Secession. (Illus.). 371p. 1976. pap. 9.95x (ISBN 0-292-72710-0). U of Tex Pr.
--The Unhappy Medium: Spiritualism & the Life of Margaret Fox. LC 64-10317. pap. 55.00 (ISBN 0-317-10609-0, 2000824). Bks Demand UMI.
Forneron, Henri. Histoire generale des emigres pendant la Revolution francaise, 3 vols. 2nd ed. LC 75-168123. Repr. of 1890 ed. Set. 135.00 (ISBN 0-404-07190-2). AMS Pr.
Fornes, et al. Wordplays I: New American Drama. LC 80-83855. 1981. 14.95 (ISBN 0-933826-10-9); pap. 7.95 (ISBN 0-933826-11-7). Performing Arts.
Forness, Steven, jt. auth. see Kavale, Kenneth.
Forness, Steven R., jt. auth. see Hewett, Frank M.
Forney, J. W. Anecdotes of Public Men, 2 Vols. in 1. LC 70-87540. (American Scene Ser). 1970. Repr. of 1873 ed. lib. bdg. 95.00 (ISBN 0-306-71456-6). Da Capo.
Forney, James L., jt. auth. see Forney, Lianne.
Forney, John. Crimson Memories, Golden Days & Other Short Stories. LC 81-52624. 1982. pap. 8.95 (ISBN 0-87397-225-2). Strode.
Forney, Lianne & Forney, James L. Pie in the Sky: Profiling Portland Bakeries. LC 81-81595. (Illus.). 140p. (Orig.). 1981. pap. 5.95 (ISBN 0-939930-00-5). Hampshire Pacific.
Forney, Matthias, ed. The Car Builder's Dictionary. (Illus.). 544p. 1971. Repr. of 1879 ed. lib. bdg. 14.95 buckram (ISBN 0-912318-16-3). N K Gregg.
Forney, Matthias N. The Railroad Car Builders Pictorial Dictionary. (Illus.). 13.25 (ISBN 0-8446-5187-7). Peter Smith.
Forney, Robert & Hughes, Francis. Combined Effects of Alcohol & Other Drugs. 132p. 1968. 12.75x (ISBN 0-398-00597-4). C C Thomas.
Forni, Luigi. The Dove & the Bear. 160p. 1983. 12.95 (ISBN 0-88254-833-6). Hippocrene Bks.
Fornia, Alice, jt. auth. see Parker, Page.
Forno, Lawrence J. Robert Challe: Intimations of the Enlightenment. LC 77-139993. 199p. 1972. 18.50 (ISBN 0-8386-7846-7). Fairleigh Dickinson.
Fornoff, Frederick, tr. see Alban, Laureano.
Fornoff, Fredrick H., tr. see Alban, Laureano.
Foroulis, Z. A., ed. Environment-Sensitive Fracture of Engineering Materials. 672p. 50.00 (ISBN 0-89520-353-7, 176); members 32.00 (ISBN 0-317-37171-1); student members 16.00 (ISBN 0-317-37172-X). Metal Soc.
--High Temperature Metallic Corrosion of Sulfur & Its Compounds. LC 71-120299. pap. 68.80 (ISBN 0-317-08511-5, 2051581). Bks Demand UMI.
Forpe & McCollister. The Sunshine Book. LC 78-19150. 1979. 12.50 (ISBN 0-8246-0229-3). Jonathan David.
Forpe, Will. The Best of the Old Farmer's Almanac. (Illus.). 1977. 16.95 (ISBN 0-8246-0209-9). Jonathan David.
Forquer, Nancy. Trial of the Christmas Bells. 1984. pap. 4.95 (ISBN 0-912963-05-0). Eldridge Pub.
Forrai, Jeno. Radiology of Haemophilic. 1979. lib. bdg. 26.00x (ISBN 9-0247-2130-X, Pub. by Martinus Nijhoff Netherlands). Kluwer Academic.
Forrai, Katalin, et al. Music Education in Hungary. 3rd, enl. ed. Macnicol, Fred, tr. from Hungarian. LC 80-123375. 310p. 1975. 15.00 (ISBN 0-85162-025-6). Boosey & Hawkes.
Forrer, Gordon R. Adventure of Tangerine Island. LC 81-81615. 1982. 7.95 (ISBN 0-87212-148-8). Libra.
--Dear Brother. LC 79-93051. 1980. 7.95 (ISBN 0-87212-128-3). Libra.

--Psychiatric Self-Help. LC 72-85870. 1973. 5.00 (ISBN 0-87212-029-5). Libra.
--The Technique of Psychiatric Self Help. LC 75-42601. 1975. 7.95 (ISBN 0-87212-039-2). Libra.
--Weaning & Human Development. LC 72-79731. 1969. 5.95 (ISBN 0-87212-020-1). Libra.
Forrer, L., ed. see Sydenham, Edward A.
Forrer, Matthi. Egoyomi & Surimono: Their History & Development. (Illus.). 1977. pap. text ed. 23.50x (ISBN 90-70265-01-X). Humanities.
Forrer, Matthi, et al, eds. A Sheaf of Japanese Papers: In Tribute to Heinz Kaempfer on His Seventy-Fifth Birthday. 1980. pap. text ed. 20.50x (ISBN 90-70265-71-0). Humanities.
Forrest. The Fragmented Fiber of Society. write for info. Dghtrs St Paul.
Forrest, A. C. The Unholy Land. (Illus.). 1972. Devin.
Forrest, A. D. & Affleck, James, eds. New Perspectives in Schizophrenia. (Illus.). 272p. 1975. text ed. 21.50 (ISBN 0-443-01247-4). Churchill.
Forrest, Alan. The French Revolution & the Poor. LC 80-29105. 280p. 1981. 25.00x (ISBN 0-312-30524-9). St Martin.
--Society & Politics in Revolutionary Bordeaux. (Oxford Historical Monographs). 1975. 52.00x (ISBN 0-19-821859-1). Oxford U Pr.
Forrest, Anthony. A Balance of Dangers: A Captain Justice Story. 232p. 1984. 14.95 (ISBN 0-8090-2800-X). Hill & Wang.
--Captain Justice. 307p. 1981. 13.95 (ISBN 0-8090-3357-7). Hill & Wang.
--Captain Justice, Bk. 1. 320p. 1983. pap. 3.95 (ISBN 0-515-08301-1). Jove Pubns.
--The Pandora Secret. (Captain Justice Ser.: No. 2). 320p. 1984. pap. 3.50 (ISBN 0-515-07394-6). Jove Pubns.
--The Pandora Secret: A Captain Justice Story. 303p. 1982. 15.50 (ISBN 0-8090-7504-0). Hill & Wang.
Forrest, Arthur T. Microcomputers for the Professional Accountant. 108p. (Orig.). 1983. pap. 38.50x (ISBN 0-566-03441-7). Gower Pub Co.
Forrest, D. W. Francis Galton: The Life & Work of a Victorian Genius. LC 74-5819. (Illus.). 280p. 1974. 14.95 (ISBN 0-8008-2682-5). Taplinger.
Forrest, David M. Eel Capture, Culture, Processing & Marketing. 1978. 40.00 (ISBN 0-685-63399-3). State Mutual Bk.
--Eel Capture, Culture, Processing & Marketing. (Illus.). 206p. 30.00 (ISBN 0-85238-070-4, FN9, FNB). Unipub.
Forrest, Denys. The World Tea Trade. 272p. 1985. 37.50 (ISBN 0-85941-259-8, Pub. by Woodhead-Faulkner). Longwood Pub Group.
Forrest, Diane. The Adventurers: Ordinary People with Special Callings. 1984. pap. 5.95 (ISBN 0-317-13951-7). Upper Room.
Forrest, Donna-Lynn, et al, eds. Meta-Cognition, & Cognition & Human Performance, Vol. 1. Date not set. 46.50 (ISBN 0-12-262301-0). Acad Pr.
Forrest, Douglas F. Odyssey in Gray: A Diary of Confederate Service, 1863-1865. Still, William N., ed. LC 78-31757. ix, 352p. 1979. 15.00 (ISBN 0-88490-005-3). VA State Lib.
Forrest, E. & Johnson, R. H. CAE, CAD, CAD-CAM Service Bureaus: Directory, Review, & Outlook, 1983. (Illus.). 130p. 1983. cancelled (ISBN 0-938484-09-5). Daratech.
Forrest, Earle R. Arizona's Dark & Bloody Ground. LC 84-124. (Illus.). 385p. 1984. pap. 11.95 (ISBN 0-8165-0853-4). U of Ariz Pr.
--Missions & Pueblos of the Old Southwest. LC 79-468. (Beautiful Rio Grande Classics Ser.). 398p. 1983. Repr. of 1929 ed. lib. bdg. 17.50 (ISBN 0-87380-128-8). Rio Grande.
--The Snake Dance of the Hopi Indians. LC 61-15835. (Illus.). 8.95 (ISBN 0-87026-018-9). Westernlore.
Forrest, G. Topham, jt. auth. see Cox, Montagu H.
Forrest, Gary. How to Live with a Problem Drinker & Survive. LC 79-55620. 1980. 8.95 (ISBN 0-689-11038-3). Atheneum.
Forrest, Gary G. Alcoholism & Human Sexuality. 408p. 1983. 35.50x (ISBN 0-398-04691-3). C C Thomas.
--Alcoholism, Narcissism & Psychopathology. 320p. 1983. 28.50x (ISBN 0-398-04815-0). C C Thomas.
--Confrontation in Psychotherapy with the Alcoholic. rev. ed. LC 81-83559. 45p. 1982. pap. text ed. 4.95 (ISBN 0-918452-32-5). Learning Pubns.
--The Diagnosis & Treatment of Alcoholism. 2nd ed. 362p. 1978. spiral 24.75x (ISBN 0-398-03780-9). C C Thomas.
--How to Cope with a Teenage Drinker: New Alternatives & Hope for Parents & Families. LC 82-73023. 128p. 1983. 10.95 (ISBN 0-689-11346-3). Atheneum.
--How to Cope with a Teenage Drinker: New Alternatives & Hope for Parents & Families. 250p. 1984. pap. 2.95 (ISBN 0-449-20535-5, Crest). Fawcett.
--Intensive Psychotherapy of Alcoholism. 230p. 1984. 24.50x (ISBN 0-398-04994-7). C C Thomas.
Forrest, Gary G., jt. ed. see Bratter, Thomas E.
Forrest, H. T. The Original "Venus & Adonis". 132p. 1981. Repr. of 1930 ed. lib. bdg. 35.00 (ISBN 0-89760-227-7). Telegraph Bks.
Forrest, Herbert E. & Anderson, Howard C. Implementing the AT&T Settlement: The New Telecommunications Era. LC 84-100988. (Patents, Copyrights, Trademarks, & Literary Property Course Handbook Ser.: No. 172). (Illus.). 1983. 35.00. PLI.
Forrest, Herbert E. & Wiley, Richard E. Regulation & Deregulation after the AT & T Divestiture. LC 85-110902. (Patents, Copyrights, Trademarks, & Literary Property Course Handbook Ser.: No. 192). 1984. 40.00. PLI.
Forrest, Irene, jt. auth. see Usdin, Carl.
Forrest, Irene S., et al, eds. Phenothiazines & Structurally Related Drugs. LC 73-88571. (Advances in Biochemical Psychopharmacology Ser.: Vol. 9). 840p. 1974. 88.00 (ISBN 0-911216-61-8). Raven.
Forrest, J. O. Preventive Dentistry. 2nd ed. (Dental Practitioner Handbook Ser.: No. 22). (Illus.). 140p. 1981. pap. text ed. 16.00 (ISBN 0-7236-0553-X). PSG Pub Co.
Forrest, J. S. The Breeder Reactor. 1977. pap. 7.50x (ISBN 0-7073-0216-1, Pub. by Scottish Academic Pr Scotland). Columbia U Pr.
Forrest, James, jt. ed. see Burnley, Ian.
Forrest, James F. & Greaves, Richard L. John Bunyan: A Reference Guide. 1982. lib. bdg. 52.00 (ISBN 0-8161-8267-1, Hall Reference). G K Hall.
Forrest, James F., ed. see Bunyan, John.
Forrest, John C., et al. Principles of Meat Science. LC 75-8543. (Food & Nutrition Ser.). (Illus.). 417p. 1975. text ed. 35.95 (ISBN 0-7167-0743-8). W H Freeman.
Forrest, John F. Explorations in Australia, 3 vols. in 1. Incl. Vol. 1. Explorations in Search of Dr. Leichardt & Party; Vol. 2. From Perth to Adelaide, Around the Great Australian Bight; Vol. 3. From Champion Bay, Across the Desert to the Telegraph & to Adelaide. LC 68-55186. 1968. Repr. of 1875 ed. lib. bdg. 17.75x (ISBN 0-8371-1648-1, FOAU). Greenwood.
Forrest, John V. & Feigin, David S. Essentials of Chest Radiology. (Illus.). 176p. 1982. pap. 13.95 (ISBN 0-7216-3818-X). Saunders.
Forrest, Katherine, jt. auth. see Swanson, Janice.
Forrest, Katherine V. Amateur City. 224p. 1984. pap. 7.95 (ISBN 0-930044-55-X). Naiad Pr.
--Curious Wine. LC 82-24663. 176p. (Orig.). 1983. pap. 7.50 (ISBN 0-930044-43-6). Naiad Pr.
--Daughters of a Coral Dawn. LC 83-21964. 230p. (Orig.). 1984. 7.95 (ISBN 0-930044-50-9). Naiad Pr.
Forrest, Kenton & Albi, Charles. Denver's Railroads, the Story of Union Station & the Railroads of Denver. (Illus.). 256p. 1981. 27.50 (ISBN 0-918654-31-9). CO RR Mus.
Forrest, Kenton, jt. auth. see Albi, Charles.
Forrest, Kenton, jt. auth. see Jones, William C.
Forrest, Kenton, jt. auth. see Patterson, Steve.
Forrest, Lewis C., Jr. Training for the Hospitality Industry: Techniques to Improve. Harless, Marjorie, ed. 1983. text ed. 34.95 (ISBN 0-86612-009-2). Educ Inst Am Hotel.
Forrest, Linn A., jt. auth. see Garfield, Viola E.
Forrest, M., ed. see Cambridge School Classics Project Foundation Course.
Forrest, M. D. Chats with Converts: Complete Explanation of Catholic Belief. 31st ed. LC 78-56979. 1978. pap. 5.00 (ISBN 0-89555-069-5). TAN Bks Pubs.
Forrest, Mary, pseud. Women of the South Distinguished in Literature. 1972. Repr. of 1861 ed. lib. bdg. 24.00 (ISBN 0-8422-8047-2). Irvington.
Forrest, Mary & Olson, Margot. Exploring Speech Communication: An Introduction. 433p. 1981. pap. text ed. 16.95 (ISBN 0-8299-0381-X). West Pub.
Forrest, Ray & Henderson, Jeff. Urban Political Economy & Social Theory. 232p. 1982. text ed. 32.00x (ISBN 0-566-00493-3). Gower Pub Co.
Forrest, Richard. A Child's Garden of Death. (Scene of the Crime Ser.: No. 44). 1982. pap. 2.25 (ISBN 0-440-11325-3). Dell.
--The Death at Yew Corner. (Suspense Novel Ser.). 228p. 1981. 10.95 (ISBN 0-03-053386-4). HR&W.
--The Death at Yew Corner: Scene of the Crime. 176p. 1984. pap. 2.95 (ISBN 0-440-11782-8). Dell.
--Death under the Lilacs. LC 84-22886. 208p. 1985. 13.95 (ISBN 0-312-18878-1). St Martin.
--The Killing Edge. (Orig.). 1980. pap. text ed. 1.75 (ISBN 0-505-51567-9, Pub. by Tower Bks). Dorchester Pub Co.
Forrest, Rose A. Welcome to Paradise. (Illus.). 96p. 1981. pap. 1.95 (ISBN 0-380-76901-8, 76901). Avon.
Forrest, Steven. The Inner Sky: The Dynamic New Astrology for Everyone. 368p. 1984. pap. 3.95 (ISBN 0-553-24351-9). Bantam.
Forrest, Theodore R., Jr., jt. auth. see Brown, Stanford H.
Forrest, W. G. History of Sparta, Nine Fifty to One Ninety-Two B.C. 1969. pap. 4.95x (ISBN 0-393-00481-3, Norton Lib). Norton.
Forrestal, Dan. Public Relations Handbook. 2nd ed. 1979. 56.50 (ISBN 0-85013-104-9). Dartnell Corp.
Forrestal, Peter, tr. Benavides' Memorial of Sixteen Thirty. (Documentary Ser.). (Illus.). 1954. 10.00 (ISBN 0-88382-001-3). AAFH.
Forrester, Alice M., jt. ed. see Harbin, Denise.
Forrester, D. A., jt. ed. see Wanless, P. T.
Forrester, D. M., et al. The Radiology of Joint Disease. 2nd ed. LC 77-27747. (Monographs in Clinical Radiology: Vol. 2). 1978. text ed. 49.95 (ISBN 0-7216-3822-8). Saunders.
Forrester, David A. Schmalenbach & After: A Study of the Evolution of German Business Economics. 1978. 14.95x (ISBN 0-906161-00-2, Pub. by Strathclyde Convergencies). Intl Spec Bk.
Forrester, Donald J., et al, eds. Pediatric Dental Medicine. LC 80-10694. (Illus.). 692p. 1981. text ed. 48.50 (ISBN 0-8121-0663-6). Lea & Febiger.
Forrester, Duncan B. Caste & Christianity. 1980. text ed. 15.50x (ISBN 0-391-01785-3). Humanities.
Forrester, Frank. The Double Trust: A Tax-Haven for Saving All Taxes. (Illus.). 340p. 1984. Repr. of 1984 ed. 250.00 (ISBN 0-9608962-0-1). Am Dynamics NY.
Forrester, Frank H. One Thousand & One Questions Answered about the Weather. (Illus.). 15.50 (ISBN 0-8446-5886-3). Peter Smith.
--One Thousand One Questions Answered about the Weather. (Illus.). 448p. 1982. pap. 5.95 (ISBN 0-486-24218-8). Dover.
Forrester, Helen. By the Waters of Liverpool. 280p. 15.95 (ISBN 0-370-30909-X, Pub. by the Bodley Head). Merrimack Pub Cir.
--Minerva's Stepchild. LC 80-26968. 320p. 1981. 10.95 (ISBN 0-8253-0017-7). Beaufort Bks NY.
Forrester, I., et al, trs. German Civil Code: As Ammended to January 1, 1975. 442p. 1977. 80.75 (ISBN 0-7204-8036-1, North Holland). Elsevier.
Forrester, Ian S. & Ilgen, Hans-Michael. The German Legal System. v, 25p. 1972. pap. 2.95x (ISBN 0-8377-0529-0). Rothman.
Forrester, Ian S., ed. Introductory Act to the German Civil Code & Marriage Law of the Federal Republic of Germany. Goren, Simon L., tr. from Ger. x, 54p. 1976. pap. text ed. 12.50x (ISBN 0-8377-0604-1). Rothman.
Forrester, Ian S., jt. tr. see Goren, Simon L.
Forrester, Ian S., et al, trs. from Ger. German Civil Code of August 18, 1896: Amended As of January 1, 1975. xxxvii, 434p. 1975. text ed. 60.00x (ISBN 0-8377-0601-7). Rothman.
Forrester, J. S. The Sinister Twilight. 352p. (Orig.). 1984. pap. 3.50 (ISBN 0-440-08056-8). Dell.
Forrester, Jan S., jt. tr. see Goren, Simon L.
Forrester, Jay W. Collected Papers of Jay W. Forrester. LC 73-89547. (Illus.). 1975. 55.00x (ISBN 0-262-06065-5). MIT Pr.
--Industrial Dynamics. (Illus.). 1961. pap. 25.00x (ISBN 0-262-56001-1). MIT Pr.
--Principles of Systems. 2nd ed. 1968. pap. 17.50x (ISBN 0-262-56017-8). MIT Pr.
--Urban Dynamics. 1969. 35.00x (ISBN 0-262-06026-4). MIT Pr.
Forrester, Jeffrey. The Stooge Chronicles. (Illus.). 112p. 1982. pap. 8.95 (ISBN 0-8092-5666-5). Contemp Bks.
--The Stoogephile Trivia Book. (Illus., Orig.). 1982. pap. 6.95 (ISBN 0-8092-5613-4). Contemp Bks.
Forrester, Jeffrey, jt. auth. see Hansen, Tom.
Forrester, John. Bestiary Mountain. LC 85-5685. 176p. (gr. 7 up). 1985. 11.95 (ISBN 0-02-735530-6). Bradbury Pr.
--Language & the Origins of Psychoanalysis. LC 80-13755. 304p. 1980. 30.00x (ISBN 0-231-05136-0). Columbia U Pr.
Forrester, Kent & Herndon, Jerry A. The Freshman Reader: Essays & Casebook. 1983. pap. text ed. 15.95 (ISBN 0-03-059296-8). HR&W.
Forrester, Marian. Farewell to Thee. 1978. pap. 2.25 (ISBN 0-505-51309-9, Pub. by Tower Bks). Dorchester Pub Co.
Forrester, Mary G. Moral Language. 240p. 1982. 25.00x (ISBN 0-299-08630-5). U of Wis Pr.
Forrester, Nathan B. The Life Cycle of Economic Development. LC 73-86760. (Illus.). 1973. 35.00x (ISBN 0-262-06067-1). MIT Pr.
Forrester, Ray & Moye, John E. Federal Jurisdiction & Procedure: Cases & Materials Nineteen Eighty-One Supplement. 3rd ed. (American Casebook Ser.). 87p. 1981. pap. text ed. 3.95 (ISBN 0-314-58804-3). West Pub.
Forrester, Rex. Trout Fishing in New Zealand. 204p. 1982. 40.00x (ISBN 0-7233-0612-5, Pub. by Whitcoulls New Zealand). State Mutual Bk.
Forrester, Roy & Moye, John E. Federal Jurisdiction & Procedure, Cases & Materials 1985 Supplement. 3rd ed. (American Casebook Ser.). 138p. 1985. pap. text ed. write for info. (ISBN 0-314-90493-X). West Pub.
Forrester, T., tr. see Ordericus Vitalis.
Forrester, Victoria. Bears & Theirs: A Book for Bear Lovers. LC 81-15071. (Illus.). 96p. (gr. k up). 1982. PLB 7.95 (ISBN 0-689-30913-9). Atheneum.
--The Candlemaker & Other Tales. LC 83-15658. (Illus.). 64p. (ps up). 1984. 10.95 (ISBN 0-689-31013-7). Atheneum.
--A Latch Against the Wind. LC 84-21526. (Illus.). 48p. (gr. 7up). 1985. 9.95 (ISBN 0-689-31091-9). Atheneum.
--The Magnificent Moo. LC 82-13781. (Illus.). 40p. (gr. k-1). 1983. 10.95 (ISBN 0-689-30954-6). Atheneum.
--Oddward. LC 81-12908. (Illus.). 48p. (gr. k up). 1982. PLB 6.95 (ISBN 0-689-30912-0). Atheneum.
--The Touch Said Hello. LC 82-3894. (Illus.). 32p. (ps-2). 1982. 11.95 (ISBN 0-689-30947-3). Atheneum.
--Words to Keep Against the Night. LC 83-2624. (Illus.). 40p. (gr. k up). 1983. PLB 6.95 (ISBN 0-689-30984-8). Atheneum.
Forrester, W. World Dynamics. 2nd ed. 1973. 22.50x (ISBN 0-262-06066-3); pap. 8.95x (ISBN 0-262-56018-6). MIT Pr.
Forrest-Pressley, D. L. & Waller, T. G. Cognition, Metacognition & Reading. (Springer Series in Language & Communication: Vol. 18). (Illus.). 440p. 1984. 32.00 (ISBN 0-387-90983-4). Springer-Verlag.
Forrest-Thompson, Veronica. On the Periphery. (Illus.). 1976. pap. 4.00 (ISBN 0-685-83036-5, Pub. by St Edns). Small Pr Dist.
--Poetic Artifice: A Theory of Twentieth Century Poetry. 1979. 26.00 (ISBN 0-312-61798-4). St Martin.
Forrette, J. E., ed. see Mid-America Spectroscopy Symposium (14th; 1963; Chicago, IL).
Forristal, Desmond. Black Man's Country. (The Irish Play Ser.). Date not set. pap. 1.95x (ISBN 0-912262-39-7). Proscenium.
--Kolbe: A Saint in Auschwitz. (Patron Bk.). Orig. Title: Maximillian of Auschwitz. 191p. (Orig.). 1983. pap. 2.95 (ISBN 0-89944-066-5, P066-5). Don Bosco Multimedia.
Forry, John I. & Theurer, Martin. Geschaeftstaetigkeit und Investitionen in Den U. S. A. German American Chamber of Commerce, ed. Fischer-Theurer, Annette, tr. from Eng. 796p. (Ger.). 1981. 56.00 (ISBN 0-86640-016-8). German Am Chamber.
Forry, John I., ed. Differences in Tax Treatment: Between a Domestic Subsidiary & a Domestic Branch of a Non-Resident Company. 175p. 1983. bound volume 40.00 (ISBN 0-686-41017-3). Kluwer Academic.
--Differences in Tax Treatment of Foreign Investors: Domestic Subsidiaries & Domestic Branches. LC 84-751. 1984. lib. bdg. 52.00 (ISBN 90-654-4074-7, Pub. by Kluwer Law Netherlands). Kluwer Academic.
Forry, Samuel. The Climate of the United States & Its Endemic Influences. LC 77-10224. Repr. of 1842 ed. 27.50 (ISBN 0-404-16205-3). AMS Pr.
Forsander, O. & Eriksson, K. Biological Aspects of Alcohol Consumption. (The Finnish Foundation for Alcohol Studies: Vol. 20). 1972. pap. 6.50 (ISBN 951-9192-09-3). Rutgers Ctr Alcohol.
Forsberg, Gerald. Brown's Pocket-Book for Seamen. 1981. 50.00x (ISBN 0-85174-391-9, Pub. by Brown Son Ferguson). State Mutual Bk.
Forsberg, Howard K. An Approach to Figure Painting for Beginners. LC 79-19504. (Illus.). 144p. 1979. 17.95 (ISBN 0-89134-023-8). North Light Pub.
Forsdale, Louis. Perspectives on Communication. (Illus.). 320p. 1981. pap. text ed. 16.95 (ISBN 0-394-34975-X, RanC). Random.
Forsdyke, A. G. Meteorological Factors of Air Pollution. (Technical Note Ser.: No. 114). (Illus.). 32p. 1970. pap. 10.00 (ISBN 0-685-02472-5, W86, WMO). Unipub.
Forsen, S., et al. Chlorine, Bromine & Iodine NMR Physico-Chemicall & Biological Applications. Diehl, P., et al, eds. (Basic Principles & Progress: Vol. 12). (Illus.). 1976. 59.00 (ISBN 0-387-07725-1). Springer-Verlag.
Forset, Edward. A Comparative Discourse of the Bodies Natural & Politique. LC 72-5995. (English Experience Ser.: No. 520). 116p. 1973. Repr. of 1606 ed. 13.00 (ISBN 90-221-0520-2). Walter J Johnson.
Forseth, Kevin. Glide Projection: Lateral Architectural Drawing. LC 84-7559. (Illus.). 128p. 1984. 24.95 (ISBN 0-442-22674-8); pap. 14.95 (ISBN 0-442-22672-1). Van Nos Reinhold.
--Graphics for Architecture. (Illus.). 288p. 1979. pap. 12.95 (ISBN 0-442-26390-2). Van Nos Reinhold.
Forseth, Pat, jt. auth. see Cavanaugh, Joan.
Forseth, Sonia D. Creative Math-Art Activities for the Primary Grades. LC 83-26918. 270p. 1984. 17.95 (ISBN 0-13-190109-5, Busn). P-H.
Forseth, Sonia D., et al. E-Z Microcomputer Handbook for Elementary Teachers: Programs in BASIC for Mathematics, Science & Reading-Language Arts. 256p. 1984. pap. 24.95 (ISBN 0-13-298415-6). P-H.
Forsett, Edward. A Comparative Discourse of Boides Natural & Politique London 1606 & a Defence of the Right of Kings. 210p. 1982. Repr. of 1624 ed. 100.00x (ISBN 0-576-53170-7, Pub. by Gregg Intl Dist Ctr England). State Mutual Bk.
Forsey, Eugene A. Trade Unions in Canada, Eighteen Twelve to Nineteen Two. 736p. 1982. 70.00x (ISBN 0-8020-5485-4). U of Toronto Pr.
Forsh, Olga D. Palace & Prison. Solaske, Fainna, tr. LC 75-38498. (Soviet Literature in English Translation Ser.). (Illus.). 261p. 1976. Repr. of 1958 ed. 19.00 (ISBN 0-88355-401-1). Hyperion Conn.
Forsham, Peter H., jt. ed. see Greenspan, Francis S.
Forshaw, Alec. Smithfield, Past & Present. 1980. 18.95 (Pub. by W Heinemann Ltd). David & Charles.
Forshaw, Chas F. Holroy's Collection on Yorkshire Ballads. 318p. 1983. Repr. of 1892 ed. lib. bdg. 37.50 (ISBN 0-8492-5351-9). R West.
Forshaw, Joseph M. Australian Parrots. 2nd ed. (Illus.). 224p. 1980. 75.00 (ISBN 0-686-62188-3); write for ltd. ed. Eastview.

--Parrots of the World. (Illus.). 1977. Repr. of 1973 ed. 34.95 (ISBN 0-87666-959-3, PS-753). TFH Pubns.

Forshay-Lundford, Cin. Walk Through Cold Fire. LC 84-17643. 224p. (gr. 7 up). 1985. 14.95 (ISBN 0-385-29395-X). Delacorte.

Forshee, Kenneth J. The Eternal Triangle. 272p. 1975. 10.95 (ISBN 0-934914-10-9). NACM.

Forshufvud, S. & Weider, B. Assassination at St. Helena: The Poisoning of Napoleon Bonaparte. (Illus.). 1978. 25.00 (ISBN 0-686-91775-8). Heinman.

Forsky, V., ed. see Romen, A. S.

Forslin, Jan, et al, eds. Automation & Industrial Workers: A Fifteen Nation Study, 2 pts, Vol. 1. (Publications of the Vienna Centre). (Illus.). 721p. 1979-81. Vol. 1, Pt. 1. 73.00 (ISBN 0-08-023339-2); Vol. 1, Pt. 2. 62.00 (ISBN 0-08-024310-X). Pergamon.

Forsling, Mary. Anti-Diuretic Hormone, Vol. 3. Horrobin, D. F., ed. (Annual Research Reviews Ser.). 1979. 26.00 (ISBN 0-88831-044-7). Eden Pr.

Forsling, Mary L. Anti-Diuretic Hormone, Vol. 1. (Annual Research Reviews Ser.). 1977. 19.20 (ISBN 0-904406-51-2). Eden Pr.

--Anti-Diuretic Hormone, Vol. 2. LC 78-309279. (Annual Research Reviews). 1978. 24.00 (ISBN 0-88831-016-1). Eden Pr.

--Antidiuretic Hormone, Vol. 4. Horrobin, D. F., ed. (Annual Research Reviews Ser.). 165p. 1980. 26.00 (ISBN 0-88831-072-2). Eden Pr.

--Pocket Examiner in Endocrinology. 172p. (Orig.). 1984. pap. text ed. 8.00 (ISBN 0-272-79682-4, Pub. by Pitman Books Ltd UK). Urban & S.

Forsman, John, ed. Recipe Index, Nineteen Seventy-One: The Eater's Guide to Periodical Literature. LC 72-884. 1972. 48.00x (ISBN 0-8103-0526-7). Gale.

--Recipe Index, Nineteen Seventy: The Eater's Guide to Periodical Literature. LC 72-884. 1972. 48.00x (ISBN 0-8103-0525-9). Gale.

Forss, Derek. South Wales in Cameracolour. (Illus.). 112p. 1985. 14.95 (ISBN 0-86364-028-1, Pub. by Town & Country Bks England). Hippocrene Bks.

Forss, George, jt. auth. see Duncan, David D.

Forssberg, K. S., ed. Flotation of Sulphide Minerals: Developments in Mineral Processing. (No. 8). 480p. 1985. 102.00 (ISBN 0-444-42494-6). Elsevier.

Forsse, Ken. The Airship: Teddy Ruxpin Adventure Ser. (Illus.). 26p. (ps). 1985. incl. audio-cassette 6.95 (ISBN 0-934323-00-3). Alchemy Comms.

--All about Bears. (Teddy Ruxpin Adventure Ser.). (Illus.). 26p. (ps). 1985. incl. audio-cassette 6.95 (ISBN 0-934323-09-7). Alchemy Comms.

--The Faded Fobs. (Teddy Ruxpin Adventure Ser.). (Illus.). 26p. (ps). 1985. incl. audio-cassette 6.95 (ISBN 0-934323-02-X). Alchemy Comms.

--Grubby's Romance. (Teddy Ruxpin Adventure Ser.). (Illus.). 26p. (ps). 1985. incl. audio-cassette 6.95 (ISBN 0-934323-04-6). Alchemy Comms.

--Grunge Music. (Teddy Ruxpin Adventure Ser.). (Illus.). 26p. (ps). 1985. incl. audio-cassette 6.95 (ISBN 0-934323-06-2). Alchemy Comms.

--The Missing Princess. (Teddy Ruxpin Adventure Ser.). (Illus.). 26p. (ps). 1985. incl. audio-cassette 6.95 (ISBN 0-934323-11-9). Alchemy Comms.

--Take a Good Look. (Teddy Ruxpin Adventure Ser.). (Illus.). 26p. (ps). 1985. incl. audio-cassette 6.95 (ISBN 0-934323-08-9). Alchemy Comms.

--Teddy Ruxpin & the Mudblups. (Teddy Ruxpin Adventure Ser.). (Illus.). 26p. (ps). 1985. incl. audio-cassette 6.95 (ISBN 0-934323-03-8). Alchemy Comms.

--Teddy Ruxpin Lullabies. (Teddy Ruxpin Adventure Ser.). (Illus.). 26p. (ps). 1985. incl. audio-cassette 6.95 (ISBN 0-934323-01-1). Alchemy Comms.

--Teddy Ruxpin's Workout. (Teddy Ruxpin Adventure Ser.). (Illus.). 26p. (ps). 1985. incl. audio-cassette 6.95 (ISBN 0-934323-07-0). Alchemy Comms.

--Teddy's Rurpin's Birthday. (Teddy Rurpin Adventure Ser.). (Illus.). 26p. (ps). 1985. write for info. incl. audio-cassette (ISBN 0-934323-13-5). Alchemy Comms.

--Teddy's Winter Adventure. (Teddy Rurpin Adventure Ser.). (Illus.). 26p. (ps). 1985. write for info. incl. audio-cassette (ISBN 0-934323-12-7). Alchemy Comms.

--Tweeg & the Bounders. (Teddy Ruxpin Adventure Ser.). (Illus.). 26p. (ps). 1985. incl. audio-cassette 6.95 (ISBN 0-934323-10-0). Alchemy Comms.

--The Wooly What's-It. (Teddy Ruxpin Adventure Ser.). (Illus.). 26p. (ps). 1985. incl. audio-cassette 6.95 (ISBN 0-934323-05-4). Alchemy Comms.

Forssell, Nils. Fouche, the Man Napoleon Feared. LC 71-112299. Repr. of 1928 ed. 19.50 (ISBN 0-404-02514-5). AMS Pr.

Forssman, Erik. The Palazzo da Festa in Vicenza. Enggass, Catherine, tr. from Ital. LC 75-20027. (Corpus Palladianum Ser.: Vol. 8). (Illus.). 186p. 1980. lib. bdg. 56.00x (ISBN 0-271-01202-1). Pa St U Pr.

Forssman, S. & Coppee, G. H. Occupational Health Problems of Young Workers. 2nd ed. (Occupational Safety & Health Ser.: No. 26). 1975. 5.70 (ISBN 92-2-101051-1). Intl Labour Office.

Forssmann, W. G., jt. ed. see Coupland, R. E.

Forssmann, W. G., jt. ed. see Heym, C.

Forsstrom, G. The Verb "To Be" in Middle English: A Survey of the Forms. (Lund Studies in English: Vol. 15). pap. 22.00 (ISBN 0-317-16135-0). Kraus Repr.

Forst, G., jt. auth. see Berg, C.

Forst, Martin L., jt. auth. see Estrella, Manuel M., Jr.

Forst, Martin L., ed. Sentencing Reform: Experiments in Reducing Disparity. (Sage Criminal Justice System Annuals: Vol. 17). (Illus.). 288p. 1982. 28.00 (ISBN 0-8039-1858-5); pap. 14.00 (ISBN 0-8039-1859-3). Sage.

Forst, Wendell. Theory of Unimolecular Reactions. (Physical Chemistry Ser.). 1973. 81.00 (ISBN 0-12-262350-9). Acad Pr.

Forst-Battaglia, Otto, ed. Dictatorship on Trial. LC 72-99635. (Essay Index Reprint Ser.). 1930. 27.50 (ISBN 0-8369-1607-7). Ayer Co Pubs.

Forstchen, William R. A Darkness upon the Ice. 288p. 1985. pap. 2.95 (ISBN 0-345-31682-7, Del Rey). Ballantine.

--The Flame upon the Ice. 288p. 1985. pap. 2.95 (ISBN 0-345-31137-X, Del Rey). Ballantine.

Forstemann, E. Commentary on the Maya Manuscript in the Royal Public Library of Dresden. (HU PMP). 1906. 25.00 (ISBN 0-527-01202-5). Kraus Repr.

Forsten, Charlene A. Cobblestone Companion: A Teacher's Activity Guide. (Illus.). 128p. (gr. 4-9). 1985. pap. 7.95 (ISBN 0-9607638-4-8). Cobblestone Pub.

Forstenberg, Frank F., Jr. & Spanier, Graham B. Recycling the Family: Remarriage after Divorce. LC 83-24699. 288p. 1984. 25.00 (ISBN 0-8039-2260-4). Sage.

Forstenzer, Thomas R. French Provincial Police & the Fall of the Second Republic: Social Fear & Counterrevolution. LC 80-8549. 384p. 1981. 32.00 (ISBN 0-691-05318-9). Princeton U Pr.

Forster, A. S., tr. see Crouzet, Francois.

Forster, Angela & Palastanga, Nigel. Clayton's Electrotherapy: Theory & Practice. 8th ed. (Illus.). 232p. 1982. 25.95 (ISBN 0-7216-0726-8, Pub. by Bailliere-Tindall). Saunders.

Forster, Anthony, tr. see Zonabend, Francoise.

Forster, Arnold. Report from Israel. 72p. pap. 1.25 (ISBN 0-686-74976-6). ADL.

Forster, Arnold & Epstein, Benjamin R. Cross-Currents. LC 72-591. 382p. 1956. Repr. lib. bdg. 16.25x (ISBN 0-8371-5993-8, FOCC). Greenwood.

--Danger on the Right. LC 76-10992. 1976. Repr. of 1964 ed. lib. bdg. 22.50x (ISBN 0-8371-8147-X, FODR). Greenwood.

Forster, Arthur B. & Lenoir, Lucille, eds. French Songs, Poems & Proverbs. 1934. pap. text ed. 1.75x (ISBN 0-89197-502-0). Irvington.

Forster, C. Oxidation Ditches. (Water Resources Engineering Ser.). 300p. 1983. text ed. 65.95 (ISBN 0-273-08527-1). Pitman Pub MA.

Forster, C. F. Biotechnology & Wastewater Treatment. (Cambridge Studies in Biotechnology: No. 2). (Illus.). 392p. Date not set. 59.50 (ISBN 0-521-25723-9). Cambridge U Pr.

Forster, C. S. Lieutenant Hornblower. 320p. 1984. Repr. 6.70i (ISBN 0-316-28921-3). Little.

Forster, Charles. The Monuments of Assyria, Babylonia & Persia. LC 77-94577. 1979. Repr. of 1859 ed. lib. bdg. 40.00 (ISBN 0-89341-261-9). Longwood Pub Group.

Forster, Cornelius P. The Uncontrolled Chancellor: Charles Townshend & His American Policy. LC 78-63017. 155p. 1978. 9.95 (ISBN 0-917012-16-X). RI Pubns Soc.

Forster, D. F. see Pickersgill, J. W.

Forster, Daniel. The Sailor's Edge. (Illus.). 192p. 1985. 35.00 (ISBN 0-03-006057-5). HR&W.

Forster, Donald F., jt. ed. see Saywell, John T.

Forster, E. M. Abinger Harvest. LC 36-10167. 1966. pap. 6.95 (ISBN 0-15-602610-4, Harv). HarBraceJ.

--Albergo Empedocle & Other Writings. LC 79-162435. 273p. 1971. 17.50 (ISBN 0-87140-540-7). Ultramarine Pub.

--Alexandria. 320p. 1981. (Pub. by M Haag); pap. 20.00x (ISBN 0-686-91569-0, Pub. by M Haag). State Mutual Bk.

--Alexandria: A History & a Guide. (Illus.). 17.00 (ISBN 0-8446-0625-1). Peter Smith.

--Arctic Summer & Other Fiction. (The Abinger Edition of E. M. Forster: Vol. 9). 342p. 1981. text ed. 49.50x (ISBN 0-8419-0670-X). Holmes & Meier.

--Aspects of the Novel. LC 27-23181. 1956. pap. 2.95 (ISBN 0-15-609180-1, Harv). HarBraceJ.

--The Celestial Omnibus & Other Stories. LC 76-10586. (YA) 1976. pap. 2.45 (ISBN 0-394-72176-4, Vin). Random.

--Collected Tales of E. M. Forster. 1947. 14.95 (ISBN 0-394-41978-2). Knopf.

--Commonplace Book. 1978. 300.00 (ISBN 0-85967-492-4). Scolar.

--A Commonplace Book. Gardner, Philip, ed. LC 85-50099. (Illus.). 376p. 1985. Repr. of 1978 ed. 35.00 (ISBN 0-8047-1280-8). Stanford U Pr.

--Eternal Moment & Other Stories. LC 28-11816. 1970. pap. 3.95 (ISBN 0-15-629125-8, Harv). HarBraceJ.

--Goldsworthy Lowes Dickinson. Stallybrass, Oliver, ed. (Abinger Edition of E. M. Forster Ser.). 294p. 1978. text ed. 17.75x (ISBN 0-8419-5810-6). Holmes & Meier.

--Goldsworthy Lowes Dickinson. 277p. 1981. Repr. of 1934 ed. lib. bdg. 25.00 (ISBN 0-89760-229-3). Telegraph Bks.

--The Hill of Devi. LC 53-9224. (Illus.). 1971. pap. 4.95 (ISBN 0-15-640265-3, Harv). HarBraceJ.

--The Hill of Devi & Other Indian Writings. Stallybrass, Oliver, ed. (The Abinger Edition of E. M. Forster Ser.). 400p. 1983. text ed. 55.00x (ISBN 0-8419-5828-9). Holmes & Meier.

--Howard's End. 391p. 1981. Repr. lib. bdg. 17.95x (ISBN 0-89966-301-X). Buccaneer Bks.

--Howards End. Stallybrass, Oliver, ed. (Abinger Edition of E. M. Forster Ser.). 276p. 1978. text ed. 29.50x (ISBN 0-8419-5806-8). Holmes & Meier.

--The Life to Come & Other Stories. 1976. pap. 2.95 (ISBN 0-380-00870-X, 48611-3, Bard). Avon.

--The Life to Come & Other Stories. 264p. 1973. 7.95 (ISBN 0-393-08381-0). Norton.

--Longest Journey. 1922. 3.95 (ISBN 0-394-70040-6). Knopf.

--The Longest Journey. Heine, Elizabeth, ed. (Abinger Edition of E. M. Forster: Vol. 2). 400p. 1985. 69.50 (ISBN 0-8419-5832-7). Holmes & Meier.

--Maurice. 256p. 1981. pap. 6.95 (ISBN 0-393-00026-5). Norton.

--Nordic Twilight. LC 77-28146. Repr. of 1940 ed. lib. bdg. 17.50 (ISBN 0-8414-4358-0). Folcroft.

--Passage to India. 429p. 1981. Repr. lib. bdg. 16.95x (ISBN 0-89966-300-1). Buccaneer Bks.

--A Passage to India. LC 43-1812. (Modern Classic Ser.). 1949. 11.95 (ISBN 0-15-171141-0). HarBraceJ.

--A Passage to India. LC 43-1812. 1985. pap. 5.95 (ISBN 0-15-671142-7, Harv). HarBraceJ.

--A Passage to India. Stallybrass, Oliver, ed. LC 78-26692. (The Abinger Edition of E. M. Forster Ser.: Vol. 6). 671p. 1978. text ed. 64.50x (ISBN 0-8419-0469-3). Holmes & Meier.

--A Passage to India. 450p. 1981. Repr. lib. bdg. 14.95 (ISBN 0-89968-223-5). Lightyear.

--Pharos & Pharillon. LC 62-1459. 101p. 1980. pap. 4.95 (ISBN 0-916870-28-6). Creative Arts Bk.

--Selected Letters of E. M. Forster: Vol. II, 1921-1970. Lago, Mary & Furbank, P. N., eds. (Illus.). 352p. 1984. 20.00 (ISBN 0-674-79827-9, Belknap). Harvard U Pr.

--Two Cheers for Democracy. LC 51-13652. 1962. pap. 7.95 (ISBN 0-15-692025-5, Harv). HarBraceJ.

--Two Cheers for Democracy. Stallybrass, Oliver, ed. (Abinger Edition of E. M. Forster Ser.). 424p. 1978. text ed. 39.50x (ISBN 0-8419-5808-4). Holmes & Meier.

--Where Angels Fear to Tread. Stallybrass, Oliver, ed. (Abinger Edition of E. M. Forster Ser.). 200p. 1978. text ed. 29.50x (ISBN 0-8419-5803-3). Holmes & Meier.

--Where Angels Fear to Tread. 402p. 1981. Repr. lib. bdg. 14.95 (ISBN 0-89968-224-3). Lightyear.

Forster, E. M. & Stallybrass, Oliver, eds. The Manuscripts of a Passage to India. LC 78-26698. (The Abinger Edition of E. M. Forster Ser.). 589p. 1979. text ed. 125.00x (ISBN 0-8419-0470-7). Holmes & Meier.

Forster, E. S., ed. Homer: Illiad, Bk. XI. (Classical Texts Ser.). 100p. pap. 9.95x (ISBN 0-904679-17-9). Basil Blackwell.

Forster, Edward M. Anonymity: An Enquiry. LC 76-44266. 1976. Repr. of 1925 ed. lib. bdg. 10.00 (ISBN 0-8414-4207-X). Folcroft.

--Howards End. 1954. pap. 3.95 (ISBN 0-394-70007-4, V7, Vin). Random.

--Longest Journey. 1962. pap. 3.95 (ISBN 0-394-70040-6, V40, Vin). Random.

--Room with a View. 1961. pap. 3.95 (ISBN 0-394-70187-9, V187, Vin). Random.

--Where Angels Fear to Tread. 1958. pap. 2.95 (ISBN 0-394-70061-9, V61, Vin). Random.

Forster, Edward M., ed. see Virgil.

Forster, Edward S. A Short History of Modern Greece, 1821-1956. Dakin, Douglas, ed. 1977. Repr. of 1958 ed. lib. bdg. 22.50x (ISBN 0-8371-9803-8, FOMG). Greenwood.

Forster, Edward S., ed. see Isocrates.

Forster, Elborg, tr. see Charlotte, Elisabeth.

Forster, Elborg, tr. see Duby, Georges.

Forster, Elborg, tr. see Forster, Robert & Ranum, Orest.

Forster, Elborg, tr. see Furet, Francois.

Forster, Elborg, tr. see Jardin, Andre & Tudesq, Andre-Jean.

Forster, Elizabeth. Himalayan Solo. 220p. 1981. 20.00x (ISBN 0-904614-03-4, Pub. by Nelson Ltd). State Mutual Bk.

Forster, Francis M. Clinical Neurology. 4th ed. LC 78-7343. 242p. 1978. pap. text ed. 11.45 (ISBN 0-8016-1637-9). Mosby.

--Reflex Epilepsy, Behavioral Therapy & Conditional Reflexes. (Illus.). 328p. 1977. 29.00x (ISBN 0-398-03614-4). C C Thomas.

Forster, Georg. Zweite Teil der Kurtzweiligen Guten Frischen Deutschen Liedlein. Eitner, Robert, ed. (Publikation aelterer praktischer und theoretischer Musikwerke Ser.: Vol. XXIX). (Ger.). 1967. Repr. of 1905 ed. write for info. (ISBN 0-8450-1729-2). Broude.

Forster, George. A Voyage Round the World in H. M. S. Resolution 1772-1775, 2 vols. (Illus.). 300p. 1985. 49.00 (ISBN 0-904573-38-9, Pub. by Caliban Bks). Longwood Pub Group.

Forster, Jackie, jt. auth. see Hanscombe, Gillian E.

Forster, Janet & Sheppard, Julia. British Archives: A Guide to Archive Resources in the United Kingdom. 1982. 129.00 (ISBN 0-317-20303-7, Pub. by Pinhorns UK). State Mutual Bk.

Forster, John. Charles Dickens. LC 77-1326. 1977. 10.00 (ISBN 0-685-00009-5). Folcroft.

--Charles Dickens: Some Notes on His Life & Writings, with Eight Portraits, Thirty-Seven Illustrations & Facsimilies of His Handwriting & Autographs. LC 77-1326. 1973. lib. bdg. 15.00 (ISBN 0-8414-4192-8). Folcroft.

--Daniel Defoe. LC 73-12454. 1955. lib. bdg. 20.00 (ISBN 0-8414-1983-3). Folcroft.

--The Life & Adventures of Oliver Goldsmith: A Biography, 4 bks. 704p. 1982. Repr. of 1848 ed. Set. lib. bdg. 100.00 (ISBN 0-89984-209-7). Century Bookbindery.

--The Life & Time of Oliver Goldsmith. 1973. Repr. of 1890 ed. 40.00 (ISBN 0-8274-1806-X). R West.

--The Life & Times of Oliver Goldsmith, 2 vols. 1979. Repr. of 1877 ed. Set. lib. bdg. 50.00 (ISBN 0-8495-1749-4). Arden Lib.

--The Life & Times of Oliver Goldsmith. LC 70-145020. (Literature Ser). (Illus.). 496p. 1972. Repr. of 1890 ed. 40.00x (ISBN 0-403-00967-7). Scholarly.

--Life of Dickens, Vol. 1. 1976. 14.95x (ISBN 0-460-00781-5, Evman). Biblio Dist.

--Life of Dickens, Vol. 2. 1976. 14.95x (ISBN 0-460-00782-3, Evman). Biblio Dist.

--Life of Jonathan Swift. LC 74-9746. 1875. lib. bdg. 40.00 (ISBN 0-8414-4199-5). Folcroft.

--Life of Oliver Goldsmith. abr. ed. Ingpen, Roger, ed. LC 78-98835. 1971. Repr. of 1903 ed. lib. bdg. 24.75x (ISBN 0-8371-3100-6, FOOG). Greenwood.

--Walter Savage Landor: A Biography, 2 vols. 1979. Repr. of 1869 ed. lib. bdg. 100.00 (ISBN 0-8492-4612-1). R West.

--Walter Savage Landor: A Biography, 8 Bks. LC 79-115241. 1971. Repr. of 1869 ed. 59.00x (ISBN 0-403-00407-1). Scholarly.

Forster, John, tr. see Jaime I King Of Aragon.

Forster, Joseph. Great Teachers: Burns, Shelley, Coleridge, Tennyson, Ruskin, Carlyle, Emerson, Browning. LC 76-30419. 1898. lib. bdg. 30.00 (ISBN 0-8414-4153-7). Folcroft.

Forster, K., ed. Boundary Algorithms for Multi-Dimensional Inviscid Hyperbolic Flow, No. 1. (Notes on Numerical Fluid Mechanics). 1978. casebound 22.00 (ISBN 0-9940011-9-3, Pub. by Vieweg & Sohn Germany). Heyden.

Forster, Klaus. Pronouncing Dictionary of English-Place Names. 308p. 1981. 30.00 (ISBN 0-7100-0756-6). Routledge & Kegan.

Forster, Lancelot. The New Culture in China. LC 79-2823. 240p. 1981. Repr. of 1936 ed. 19.75 (ISBN 0-8305-0003-0). Hyperion Conn.

Forster, Leonard, ed. Penguin Book of German Verse. (Poets Ser.). (Orig., Ger., With prose translations). (YA) (gr. 9 up). 1957. pap. 5.95 (ISBN 0-14-042036-3). Penguin.

Forster, M., et al. Reading about Science II: SI Metric. (Reading about Science Ser.). (YA) (gr. 8-9). Date not set. text ed. price not set (ISBN 0-03-920069-8, Pub. by HR&W Canada). HR&W.

Forster, M. C., jt. auth. see Beck, P. G.

Forster, Margaret. Significant Sisters: The Grassroots of Active Feminism, 1839-1939. LC 84-48536. (Illus.). 368p. 1985. 17.95 (ISBN 0-394-54153-7). Knopf.

--The Travels of Maudie Tipstaff. 251p. 1981. pap. 2.75 (ISBN 0-8128-7058-1). Stein & Day.

Forster, Merlin H. Fire & Ice: The Poetry of Xavier Villaurruti. (Studies in the Romance Languages & Literatures Ser.: No. 169). 178p. 1976. pap. 10.50x (ISBN 0-8078-9169-X). U of NC Pr.

--Historia De la Poesia Hispanoamericana. (Span.). 1981. 24.95x (ISBN 0-89217-006-9); pap. 14.95x (ISBN 0-89217-007-7). American Hispanist.

Forster, Merlin H., ed. Tradition & Renewal: Essays on Twentieth-Century Latin American Literature & Culture. LC 74-31179. (Office of International Programs & Studies Ser.: Vol. 2). 250p. 1975. 19.50x (ISBN 0-252-00440-X). U of Ill Pr.

Forster, Meta & Zappa, Winifred. Robert Browning Bibliographie. LC 77-975. 1939. lib. bdg. 15.00 (ISBN 0-8414-4194-4). Folcroft.

Forster, O. Lectures on Riemann Surfaces. (Graduate Texts in Mathematics Ser.: Vol. 81). (Illus.). 254p. 1981. 41.00 (ISBN 0-387-90617-7). Springer-Verlag.

Forster, O. & Landy, M., eds. Heterogeneity of Mononuclear Phagocytes. LC 81-66367. 1981. 53.00 (ISBN 0-12-262360-6). Acad Pr.

Forster, Pannell K. Isle of Man: Basic Business Information. 1980. 45.00x (ISBN 0-686-44509-0, Pub. by Oyez Longman Pub England). State Mutual Bk.

Forster, Peter G. The Esperanto Movement. (Contributions to the Sociology of Language Ser.: No. 32). xiv, 413p. 1982. 48.00 (ISBN 90-279-3399-5). Mouton.

Forster, R. H., jt. auth. see O'Kelly, Elizabeth.

Forster, Richard R. Planning for Man & Nature in National Parks: Reconciling Perpetuation & Use. (Illus.). 84p. 1973. pap. 12.00 (ISBN 2-88032-035-6, IUCN54, IUCN). Unipub.

Forster, Robert. The House of Saulx-Tavanes: Versailles & Burgundy, 1700-1830. LC 75-150041. (Illus.). 292p. 1971. 27.00x (ISBN 0-8018-1247-X). Johns Hopkins.

--Merchants, Landlords, Magistrates: The Depont Family in Eighteenth-Century France. LC 80-14944. (Illus.). 320p. 1981. text ed. 27.00x (ISBN 0-8018-2406-0). Johns Hopkins.

--The Nobility of Toulouse in the Eighteenth Century. LC 78-64233. (Johns Hopkins University. Studies in the Social Sciences. Seventy-Eighth Ser. 1960: 1). Repr. of 1960 ed. 11.50 (ISBN 0-404-61338-1). AMS Pr.

Forster, Robert & Ranum, Orest. Rural Society in France. Forster, Elborg & Ranum, Patricia, trs. from Fr. LC 76-47373. (Selections from the Annales, Economics, Societies, Civilizations Ser: Vol. 3). (Illus.). 1977. pap. 5.95x (ISBN 0-8018-1917-2). Johns Hopkins.

Forster, Robert & Greene, Jack P., eds. Preconditions of Revolution in Early Modern Europe. LC 76-122010. (The Johns Hopkins Symposia in History Ser.). pap. 56.00 (ISBN 0-317-29826-7, 2019820). Bks Demand UMI.

Forster, Robert & Ranum, Orest, eds. Biology of Man in History, Vol. 1: Selections from the Annales: Economies-Societies, Civilistions. LC 74-24382. 1975. text ed. 18.50x (ISBN 0-8018-1690-4). Johns Hopkins.

--Deviants & the Abandoned in French Society. LC 77-17253. (Selections from the Annales, Economies, Societes, Civilisations: Vol. 4). pap. 64.80 (ISBN 0-317-20668-0, 2024146). Bks Demand UMI.

--Family & Society: Selections from the Annales: Economies, Societes, Civilisations, Vol. 2. Ranum, Patricia, tr. from Fr. LC 76-17299. (Illus.). 288p. 1976. text ed. 20.00x (ISBN 0-8018-1780-3). Johns Hopkins.

--Food & Drink in History. LC 78-21920. pap. 46.50 (ISBN 0-317-27778-2, 2055957). Bks Demand UMI.

--Medicine & Society in France. Forster, Elborg & Ranum, Patricia M., trs. LC 79-16851. (Annales Ser.: Vol. 6). 1980. 16.50x (ISBN 0-8018-2305-6); pap. text ed. 5.95x (ISBN 0-8018-2306-4). Johns Hopkins.

Forster, Roger & Marston, Paul. That's a Good Question. 2nd ed. Sun, Hugo S. & Chan, Silas, trs. 204p. (Chinese.). 1982. pap. write for info (ISBN 0-941598-01-2). Living Spring Pubns.

Forster, Roger T. & Marston, V. Paul. God's Strategy in Human History. 304p. 1984. pap. 6.95 (ISBN 0-87123-434-3). Bethany Hse.

Forster, Roger V. & Marston, V. Paul. God's Strategy in Human History. Tseng, Chen C., tr. from Eng. (Chinese.). 1984. pap. write for info. (ISBN 0-941598-09-8). Living Spring Pubns.

Forster, S., tr. see Janssen, W.

Forster, S., tr. see Krstic, R. V.

Forster, W. Prison Education in England & Wales. 1982. 35.00x (ISBN 0-900559-44-6, Pub. by Natl Inst Adult Ed England). State Mutual Bk.

Forster, Walter. Numerical Solution of Highly Nonlinear Problems. 440p. 1980. 68.00 (ISBN 0-444-85427-4, North-Holland). Elsevier.

Forster, Werner, et al. Prostaglandins & Thromboxins: Proceedings of the Third International Symposium on Prostaglandins & Thromboxanes in the Cardiovascular System, Hale-Salle, GDR, 5-7 May 1980. LC 80-41802. (Illus.). 500p. 1981. 80.00 (ISBN 0-08-027369-6). Pergamon.

Forsthoefel, John. Utilizing Problem Solving in Math. (Illus.). 40p. (Orig.). (gr. 3-8). 1984. 4.95 (ISBN 0-88047-039-9, 8405). DOK Pubs.

Forsthoefel, John & Ransick, Gary. Discovering Botany. (The Discovering Ser.). (Illus.). 84p. (gr. 3-6). 1982. 5.95 (ISBN 0-88047-005-4, 8206). DOK Pubs.

Forstman, H. Jackson. Word & Spirit: Calvin's Doctrine of Biblical Authority. 1962. 20.00x (ISBN 0-8047-0070-2). Stanford U Pr.

Forstman, Jack, tr. see Schleiermacher, Friedrich.

Forstmann, Dorothy L. Fragments. LC 83-63388. (Illus.). 64p. 1983. pap. 14.95 (ISBN 0-87100-197-7, 2197). Morgan.

Forstner, G. G., ed. Mucus Secretions & Cystic Fibrosis. (Modern Problems in Paediatrics: Vol. 19). (Illus.). 1977. 47.25 (ISBN 3-8055-2678-4). S Karger.

Forstner, H., jt. ed. see Gnaiger, E.

Forstner, Lorne, jt. ed. see Elkins, A. C.

Forsund, Finn R., ed. Topics in Production Theory. LC 83-40610. 220p. 1984. 27.50 (ISBN 0-312-80914-X). St Martin.

Forsund, Finn R. & Honkapohja, Seppo, eds. Limits & Problems of Taxation. 208p. 1985. 27.50 (ISBN 0-312-48684-7). St Martin.

Forsyth, Adrian. A Natural History of Sex. 256p. 1986. 16.95 (ISBN 0-684-18338-2, ScribT). Scribner.

Forsyth, Adrian & Miyata, Ken. Tropical Nature: Life & Death in the Rain Forests of Central & South America. (Illus.). 272p. 1984. 16.95 (ISBN 0-684-17964-4, ScribT). Scribner.

Forsyth, Alastair. Building for the Age: New Building Types 1900-1939. 1982. pap. 25.00x (ISBN 0-317-20305-3, Pub. by Pinhorns UK). State Mutual Bk.

Forsyth, Alice D. Louisiana Marriages: Vol. 1: 1784-1806. 1977. 20.00 (ISBN 0-686-20419-0). Polyanthos.

Forsyth, Benjamin. Unified Design of Reinforced Concrete Members. 2nd. ed. LC 80-16123. 520p. 1982. 42.50 (ISBN 0-89874-189-0). Krieger.

Forsyth, Cecil. Music & Nationalism: A Study of English Opera. LC 80-2276. Repr. of 1911 ed. 37.00 (ISBN 0-404-18844-3). AMS Pr.

--Orchestration. (Music Ser.). (Illus.). 50p. 1982. pap. 8.95 (ISBN 0-486-24383-4). Dover.

--Orchestration. 1983. 15.25 (ISBN 0-8446-6014-0). Peter Smith.

Forsyth, Donelson R. An Introduction to Group Dynamics. LC 82-12783. (Psychology Ser.). 512p. 1982. text ed. 24.25 pub net (ISBN 0-534-01225-6). Brooks-Cole.

Forsyth, Elizabeth R. & Ramirez, Gilberto, eds. Development & Equity in Mexico: An Annotated Bibliography. 196p. 1981. pap. text ed. 12.50x (ISBN 0-292-71530-7, Pub. by the Mexico-U.S. Border Development Program). U of Tex Pr.

Forsyth, Ella M. Building a Chamber Music Collection: A Descriptive Guide to Published Scores. LC 79-4587. 211p. 1979. 15.00 (ISBN 0-8108-1215-0). Scarecrow.

Forsyth, Frederick. The Day of the Jackal. 1979. pap. 3.95 (ISBN 0-553-23535-4). Bantam.

--The Devil's Alternative. 416p. 1981. pap. 3.95 (ISBN 0-553-23159-6). Bantam.

--The Devil's Alternative. 1980. 12.95 (ISBN 0-670-27081-4). Viking.

--The Dogs of War. 448p. 1975. pap. 3.95 (ISBN 0-553-23272-X). Bantam.

--The Dogs of War. LC 73-19103. 416p. 1974. 11.95 (ISBN 0-670-27753-3). Viking.

--Forsyth's Three. 1152p. 1980. 15.95 (ISBN 0-670-52410-7). Viking.

--The Fourth Protocol. 456p. 1984. 17.95 (ISBN 0-670-32637-2). Viking.

--The Fourth Protocol. 400p. 1985. deluxe ed. 50.00 signed (ISBN 0-88733-009-6). Underwood-Miller.

--The Fourth Protocol. (Large Print Bks.). 1985. lib. bdg. 19.95 (ISBN 0-8161-3825-7); pap. 9.95 (ISBN 0-8161-3890-7). G K Hall.

--No Comebacks. LC 81-71238. 228p. 1982. 13.95 (ISBN 0-670-51420-9). Viking.

--No Comebacks. 1983. pap. 3.95 (ISBN 0-553-23105-7). Bantam.

--The Odessa File. pap. 3.95 (ISBN 0-553-23737-3). Bantam.

--The Shepherd. 1977. pap. 2.95 (ISBN 0-553-22551-0). Bantam.

--The Shepherd. 10.95 (ISBN 0-88411-563-1, Pub. by Aeonian Pr). Amereon Ltd.

--Three Complete Novels. 31.95 (ISBN 0-88411-564-X, Pub. by Aeonian Pr). Amereon Ltd.

Forsyth, George H. & Weitzmann, Kurt. The Monastery of Saint Catherine at Mount Sinai: The Church & Fortress of Justinian: Plates. LC 68-29257. (Illus.). 236p. 1973. 65.00 (ISBN 0-472-33000-4). U of Mich Pr.

Forsyth, Gordon. Doctors & State Medicine. 1973. pap. text ed. 65.00 (ISBN 0-272-00178-3). State Mutual Bk.

--Doctors & State Medicine in England. 224p. 1973. pap. text ed. 12.50x (ISBN 0-8464-0339-0). Beekman Pubs.

Forsyth, J. Grammar of Aspect, Usage & Meaning in the Verb. (Studies in the Modern Language). 64.50 (ISBN 0-521-07514-9). Cambridge U Pr.

Forsyth, J., ed. see Vinokur, G. O.

Forsyth, J. B., jt. auth. see Brown, P. Jane.

Forsyth, J. Bruce, jt. ed. see Convert, Pierre.

Forsyth, James. Heloise. (Orig.). 1959. pap. 1.00x (ISBN 0-87830-542-4). Theatre Arts.

--Tyrone Guthrie: The Authorized Biography. (Illus.). 1978. 19.95 (ISBN 0-241-89471-9, Pub. by Hamish Hamilton England). David & Charles.

Forsyth, James, ed. see Gogol, N. V.

Forsyth, James, ed. see Pushkin, A. S.

Forsyth, Jane, jt. auth. see Forsyth, Robert.

Forsyth, John & Tynan, Meg. The Best Country Cafes in Texas: The East. LC 83-50953. (Illus.). 160p. (Orig.). 1983. pap. 7.95 (ISBN 0-915101-00-9). Texas Geograph.

--The Best Country Cafes in Texas: The West. (Illus.). 160p. (Orig.). 1984. pap. 6.95 (ISBN 0-915101-01-7). Texas Geograph.

Forsyth, John D. The Aggies & the 'Horns. (Illus.). 160p. 1981. 15.95 (ISBN 0-932012-14-0). Texas Month Pr.

Forsyth, Karen. Ariadne Auf Naxos by Hugo Von Hofmannsthall & Richard Strauss: Its Genesis & Meaning. (Oxford Modern Languages & Literature Monographs). (Illus.). 1982. 49.95x (ISBN 0-19-815536-0). Oxford U Pr.

Forsyth, Lucy, tr. see Martos, Jean-Francois & Sanguinetti, Gianfranco.

Forsyth, Lucy, tr. see Sanguinetti, Gianfranco.

Forsyth, Michael. Buildings for Music: The Architect, the Musician, & the Listener from the Seventeenth Century to the Present Day. (Illus.). 236p. 1985. 30.00 (ISBN 0-262-06089-2). MIT Pr.

Forsyth, Murray G. Unions of States: Theory & Practice of Confederation. LC 80-29044. 360p. 1981. text ed. 35.00 (ISBN 0-8419-0691-2); pap. text ed. 19.50x (ISBN 0-8419-0729-3). Holmes & Meier.

Forsyth, Patrick. Running An Effective Sales Office. 160p. 1980. text ed. 37.25x (ISBN 0-566-02185-4). Gower Pub Co.

Forsyth, Patrick, jt. auth. see Hoy, Wayne.

Forsyth, Patrick, ed. Managing Sales & Marketing Training. LC 83-25381. 352p. 1984. text ed. 41.95x (ISBN 0-566-02410-1). Gower Pub Co.

Forsyth, Peter T. The Cruciality of the Cross. 104p. 1983. pap. 5.95 (ISBN 0-913029-00-9). Chanticleer Pub.

--Religion in Recent Art. 3rd ed. LC 73-148780. Repr. of 1905 ed. 24.50 (ISBN 0-404-02515-3). AMS Pr.

Forsyth, Phyllis Y. Atlantis: The Making of Myth. (Illus.). 256p. 1980. 22.50x (ISBN 0-7735-0355-2). McGill-Queens U Pr.

Forsyth, R. A. The Lost Pattern: Essays on the Emergent City Sensibility in Victorian England. 1976. 21.95x (ISBN 0-85564-115-0, Pub. by U of W Austral Pr). Intl Spec Bk.

Forsyth, Richard. The BASIC Idea: An Introduction to Computer Programming. 1978. pap. 8.95 (ISBN 0-412-21470-9, NO.6111, Pub. by Chapman & Hall). Methuen Inc.

Forsyth, Richard & Naylor, Chris. The Hitch-Hiker's Guide to Artificial Intelligence. 184p. 1985. pap. 15.95 (ISBN 0-412-27090-0, Pub. by Chapman & Hall England). Methuen Inc.

Forsyth, Richard S. Pascal at Work & Play. 250p. 1982. 35.00 (ISBN 0-412-23370-3, NO. 6638, Pub. by Chapman & Hall); pap. 12.95 (ISBN 0-412-23380-0, NO. 6639). Methuen Inc.

Forsyth, Robert & Forsyth, Jane. Forsyth Guide to Successful Dog Showing. LC 75-25418. (Illus.). 96p. 1983. 11.95 (ISBN 0-87605-523-4). Howell Bk.

Forsyth, Robert A., jt. auth. see Blommers, Paul J.

Forsyth, Roger, et al. Family Pactice Self Assessment & Review. 3rd ed. 1982. 30.00 (ISBN 0-87488-261-3). Med Exam.

Forsyth, Travis. Sweet Seduction. (Orig.). 1982. pap. 2.95 (ISBN 0-440-18017-1). Dell.

Forsyth, William. The History of Lawyers, Ancient & Modern. 1977. lib. bdg. 59.95 (ISBN 0-8490-1976-1). Gordon Pr.

--History of Trial by Jury. 2nd ed. LC 77-168705. (Research & Source Works Ser.: No. 807). 1971. Repr. of 1878 ed. lib. bdg. 23.50 (ISBN 0-8337-1215-2). B Franklin.

--Hortensius the Advocate: An Historical Essay on the Office & Duties of an Advocate. xvii, 404p. 1982. Repr. of 1882 ed. lib. bdg. 35.00x (ISBN 0-8377-0617-3). Rothman.

--Life of Marcus Tullius Cicero. 1877. 35.00 (ISBN 0-8274-2936-3). R West.

--The Novels & Novelists of the Eighteenth Century in Illustration of the Manners & Morals of the Age. 1978. Repr. of 1871 ed. lib. bdg. 30.00 (ISBN 0-8495-1613-7). Arden Lib.

--Novels & Novelists of the Eighteenth Century. LC 74-9784. 1871. lib. bdg. 42.50 (ISBN 0-8414-4202-9). Folcroft.

Forsyth, William H. Entombment of Christ: French Sculptures of the Fifteenth & Sixteenth Centuries. LC 70-99523. (Illus., Pub. for the Metropolitan Museum of Art). 1970. 17.50x (ISBN 0-674-25775-8). Harvard U Pr.

Forsythe, A. I., et al. Computer Science: A First Course. 2nd ed. LC 74-34244. 876p. 1975. 40.45 (ISBN 0-471-26681-7); tchrs.' manual avail. (ISBN 0-471-26682-5). Wiley.

Forsythe, Alexandra I., et al. Computer Science: Programming in FORTRAN IV with WATFOR-WATFIV. LC 74-96044. 210p. 1975. pap. 14.00x (ISBN 0-471-26685-X). Wiley.

Forsythe, Charles E. & Keller, Irwin A. Administration of High School Athletics. 6th ed. (Illus.). 1979. 27.95 (ISBN 0-13-005710-X). P-H.

Forsythe, Charles E., jt. auth. see Keller, Irvin.

Forsythe, Dall W. Taxation & Political Change in the Young Nation 1781-1833. LC 77-822. 167p. 1977. 19.00x (ISBN 0-231-04192-6). Columbia U Pr.

Forsythe, David P. Human Rights & World Politics. LC 82-13360. (Illus.). xiv, 309p. 1983. 25.95x (ISBN 0-8032-1962-8); pap. 8.50x (ISBN 0-8032-6856-4, BB818, Bison). U of Nebr Pr.

Forsythe, David P., ed. American Foreign Policy in an Uncertain World. LC 83-27370. xviii, 575p. 1984. 18.95x (ISBN 0-8032-1964-4); pap. 9.95x (ISBN 0-8032-6858-0). U of Nebr Pr.

Forsythe, Elizabeth. The High-Fibre Gourmet. (Orig.). 1983. pap. 6.95 (ISBN 0-7207-1420-6, Pub. by Michael Joseph). Merrimack Pub Cir.

--Living with Multiple Sclerosis. 144p. 1979. 11.95 (ISBN 0-571-11293-5); pap. 6.95 (ISBN 0-571-11294-3). Faber & Faber.

--The Low-Fat Gourmet. 156p. 1981. 14.95 (ISBN 0-7207-1226-2, Pub. by Michael Joseph). Merrimack Pub Cir.

Forsythe, Elizabeth, ed. see Riley, P. A. & Cunningham, P. J.

Forsythe, George E. & Moler, C. Computer Solution of Linear Algebraic Systems. 1967. ref. ed. 30.00 (ISBN 0-13-165779-8). P-H.

Forsythe, George E., et al. Computer Methods for Mathematical Computations. (Illus.). 1977. ref. ed. 41.95 (ISBN 0-13-165332-6). P-H.

Forsythe, J. History of Ancient Manuscripts. lib. bdg. 59.95 (ISBN 0-8490-1967-2). Gordon Pr.

Forsythe, J. M., jt. ed. see Anderson, J.

Forsythe, John. Death Sentence. Wesnick, Richard J., ed. (Illus., Orig.). 1983. pap. cancelled (ISBN 0-913311-00-6). Unicorn Comm.

--Death Sentence: Murder on the Prairie. rev. ed. Wesnick, Richard J., ed. (Illus.). 1984. pap. 7.95 (ISBN 0-913311-02-2). Unicorn Comm.

Forsythe, Marie Branigan. In Those Days. 1983. 5.95 (ISBN 0-8062-1997-1). Carlton.

Forsythe, Peter W. Expanding Management Technology & Professional Account Ability in Social Service Programs. 62p. 5.00 (ISBN 0-317-35040-4, 5613); 5-20 copies 4.00 ea.; 21 or more 3.50 ea. Natl Conf Soc Welfare.

Forsythe, Richard. Bishop's Landing. 1980. pap. 2.75 (ISBN 0-8439-0824-6). Dorchester Pub Co.

--Bishop's Landing. 368p. 1983. pap. 3.50 (ISBN 0-8439-2053-X, Leisure Bks). Dorchester Pub Co.

Forsythe, Robert S. Bernard DeVoto: A New Force in American Letters. LC 74-17306. 1974. Repr. of 1928 ed. lib. bdg. 7.50 (ISBN 0-8414-4246-0). Folcroft.

--Relations of Shirley's Plays to the Elizabethan Drama. LC 65-19615. 1914. 27.50 (ISBN 0-405-08528-1, Blom Pubns). Ayer Co Pubs.

Forsythe, Robert S., ed. see Melville, Herman.

Forsythe, Sidney A. An American Missionary Community in China, 1895-1905. LC 70-178077. (East Asian Monographs Ser: No. 43). 1971. pap. 11.00x (ISBN 0-674-02626-8). Harvard U Pr.

Fort, Charles. Collected Writings, 4 vols. 400.00 (ISBN 0-87968-902-1). Gordon Pr.

--The Complete Books of Charles Fort, 4 vols. in 1. Incl. The Book of the Damned. Repr. of 1919 ed; New Lands. Repr. of 1923 ed; Lo! Repr. of 1931 ed; Wild Talents. Repr. of 1932 ed. 1975. 17.50 (ISBN 0-486-23094-5). Dover.

--LO! Del Rey, Lester, ed. LC 75-407. (Library of Science Fiction). 1975. lib. bdg. 21.00 (ISBN 0-8240-1412-X). Garland Pub.

--New Lands. Del Rey, Lester, ed. LC 75-409. (Library of Science Fiction). 1975. lib. bdg. 21.00 (ISBN 0-8240-1413-8). Garland Pub.

--The Town Clock Burning. 53p. (Orig.). 1985. pap. 7.95 (ISBN 0-932662-54-4). St Andrews NC.

--Wild Talents. Del Ray, Lester, ed. LC 75-409. (Library of Science Fiction). 1975. lib. bdg. 21.00 (ISBN 0-8240-1414-6). Garland Pub.

Fort, George F. Medical Economy During the Middle Ages. LC 71-95625. Repr. of 1883 ed. 37.50x (ISBN 0-678-03758-2). Kelley.

Fort, Gertrud von Le see Von Le Fort, Gertrud.

Fort, Gertrud Von Le see Von Le Fort, Gertrud.

Fort, J. A. Compendio de Anatomia Descriptiva. 546p. (Espn.). pap. 8.95 (ISBN 84-252-0222-1, S-50272). French & Eur.

Fort, Joel. The Addicted Society. LC 81-8918. 160p. 1982. pap. 5.95 (ISBN 0-394-17889-0, E814, Ever). Grove.

--The Addicted Society: Pleasure-Seeking & Punishment Revisited. LC 80-8918. 224p. 1981. 10.95 (ISBN 0-394-52234-6, GP848). Grove.

--Alcohol: Our Biggest Drug Problem. (Illus.). 180p. 1973. 24.95 (ISBN 0-07-021598-7); pap. 20.95 (ISBN 0-07-021599-5). McGraw.

Fort, Joel & Salin, Lothar. To Dream the Perfect Organization. LC 80-53829. (Illus.). 144p. 1981. text ed. 14.95x (ISBN 0-89914-005-X); pap. text ed. 7.95x. Third Party Pub.

Fort Sedgwick Historical Society, compiled by. The History of Sedgwick County, Colorado, Vol. II. (Illus.). 527p. 1982. 58.00 (ISBN 0-88107-003-3). Natl ShareGraphics.

Forte, Allan & Gilbert, Steven E. Introduction to Schenkerian Analysis: Form & Content in Tonal Music. (Illus.). 350p. 1982. text ed. 27.95x (ISBN 0-393-95192-8); instr's. manual avail. (ISBN 0-393-95230-4). Norton.

Forte, Allen. The Compositional Matrix. LC 73-4337. 1974. Repr. of 1961 ed. lib. bdg. 18.50 (ISBN 0-306-70577-X). Da Capo.

--The Harmonic Organization of the Rite of Spring. LC 77-90946. 1978. 24.50x (ISBN 0-300-02201-8). Yale U Pr.

--The Structure of Atonal Music. LC 72-91295. 1977. pap. 24.50x (ISBN 0-300-01610-7); pap. 11.95x (ISBN 0-300-02120-8). Yale U Pr.

--Tonal Harmony in Concept & Practice. 3rd ed. LC 78-12229. 1979. text ed. 26.95 (ISBN 0-03-020756-8, HoltC). HR&W.

Forte, B. Rome & the Romans as the Greeks Saw Them. (Papers & Monographs: No. 24). 730p. 1972. 24.50 (ISBN 0-318-12333-9). Am Acad Rome.

Forte, Cecile, jt. auth. see Lewis, Stephen.

Forte, Frances, jt. ed. see Peacock, Alan.

Forte, Francesco, jt. ed. see Roskamp, Karl W.

Forte, Imogene. Arts & Crafts: From Things Around the House. LC 83-80961. (The Tabletop Learning Ser.). (Illus.). 80p. (gr. k-6). 1983. pap. text ed. 3.95 (ISBN 0-86530-090-9, IP909). Incentive Pubns.

--Backyard: Adventures for Outdoor Explorers. LC 83-80959. (The Tabletop Learning Ser.). (Illus.). 80p. (gr. k-6). 1983. pap. text ed. 3.95 (ISBN 0-86530-091-7, IP 917). Incentive Pubns.

--Comprehension Corral. (Skills Stretchers Ser.). (Illus.). 32p. (gr. 2-5). 1981. pap. 3.95 (ISBN 0-86530-032-1, IP 32-1). Incentive Pubns.

Fortescue, William. Alphonse de Lamartine: A Political Biography. LC 82-42927. 304p. 1983. 29.95x (ISBN 0-312-02138-0). St Martin.

Fortescue-Foulkes, J. Seasonal Breeding & Migrations of the Desert Locust (Schistocerca Gregaria Forskal) in South-Western Asia. 1953. 35.00x (ISBN 0-85135-015-1, Pub. by Centre Overseas Research). State Mutual Bk.

Fortesque, Michael. West Greenlandic. LC 84-19862. (Descriptive Grammars Ser.). 384p. 1984. 52.50 (ISBN 0-7099-1069-X, Pub. by Croom Helm Ltd). Longwood Pub Group.

Fortet, R. Elements of Probability Theory. 544p. 1977. 113.50 (ISBN 0-677-02110-0). Gordon.

Fortet, R., jt. auth. see Blanc-LaPierre, Andre.

Fortey, R. A. The Ordovician Trilobites of Spitsbergen I. Olenidae. (Norsk Polarinstitutt Ser: No. 162). 1974. 16.00x (ISBN 8-200-29180-4, Dist. by Columbia U Pr). Universitet.

--The Ordovician Trilobites of the Spitsbergen. (Norsk Polarinstitutt Skrifter: Vol. 171). (Illus.). 163p. 1980. pap. 19.00x (ISBN 82-00-29189-8). Universitet.

Fortey, R. A., jt. auth. see Morris, S. F.

Forth, Inc. Staff & Brodie, Leo. Starting FORTH: An Introduction to the FORTH Language & Operating Systems for Beginners & Professionals. LC 81-11837. (Software Ser.). (Illus.). 384p. 1982. text ed. 24.95 (ISBN 0-13-842930-8); pap. text ed. 21.95 (ISBN 0-13-842922-7). P-H.

FORTH Standards Team. FORTH-83 Standard. 84p. (Orig.). 1983. pap. 15.00 (ISBN 0-914699-03-2). Mountain View Pr.

FORTH Standards Team, ed. FORTH-83 Standard. 82p. 1983. pap. 12.50 (ISBN 0-914593-01-3). Inst Appl Forth.

Forthal, Sonya. Cogwheels of Democracy: A Study of the Precinct Captain. LC 71-138232. 106p. 1972. Repr. of 1946 ed. lib. bdg. 22.50x (ISBN 0-8371-5589-4, FOCD). Greenwood.

Forthergill, Brian, ed. Essays by Divers Hands XLI. 147p. 1980. 11.25 (ISBN 0-85115-132-9, Pub. by Boydell & Brewer). Longwood Pub Group.

Forthergill, John, jt. auth. see Berden, John M.

Forthofer, Ronald H. & Lehnen, Robert G. Public Program Analysis: A New Approach to Categorical Data. 294p. 1981. 31.95 (ISBN 0-534-97974-2). Van Nos Reinhold.

Forthofer, Ronald N. & Lehnen, Robert G. Public Program Analysis: A New Categorical Data Approach. (Illus.). 294p. 1981. 31.95 (ISBN 0-534-97955-6); solutions manual 4.95 (ISBN 0-534-01133-0). Lifetime Learn.

Forti, jt. auth. see Cook.

Forti, Augusto. Research & Human Needs: A Search for a New Development Paradigm. (Illus.). 176p. 1981. 33.00 (ISBN 0-08-027417-X). Pergamon.

Forti, Augusto, ed. Scientific Forecasting & Human Needs: Trends, Methods & Message. 204p. 1984. pap. 33.75 (ISBN 92-3-102134-6, U1403 5071, UNESCO). Unipub.

Forti, Gianni, jt. ed. see Rodbard, David.

Forti, Kathleen J. The Door to the Secret City. (Freddie Bks.). (Illus.). 144p. (gr. 2 up). 1984. 9.95 (ISBN 0-913299-10-3, Pub. by Angelfood Bks). Stillpoint.

Forti, Simone. Handbook in Motion: An Account of an Ongoing Personal Discourse & Its Manifestations in Dance. LC 74-15415. (The Nova Scotia Ser). (Illus.). 140p. 1974. 27.50x (ISBN 0-8147-2557-0); pap. 15.00x (ISBN 0-8147-2556-2). NYU Pr.

Fortie, Marius. Black & Beautiful. facsimile ed. LC 78-168515. (Black Heritage Library Collection). Repr. of 1938 ed. 27.75 (ISBN 0-8369-8867-1). Ayer Co Pubs.

Fortier, Alcee. History of Louisiana. rev. ed. Carrigan, J. A., ed. Vols. 1 & 2. 20.00 (ISBN 0-87511-137-8); text ed. 20.00 (ISBN 0-87511-138-6). Claitors.

Fortier, Alcee, ed. Louisiana Folk-Tales in French Dialect & English Translation. LC 9-47. (AFS M). Repr. of 1895 ed. 15.00 (ISBN 0-527-01054-5). Kraus Repr.

Fortier, Andrew C. & Emerson, Thomas E. The Go-Kart North Site, & the Dyroff & Levin Sites. LC 84-8900. (American Bottom Archaeology: FAI-270 Site Reports Ser.: Vol. 9). (Illus.). 376p. 1985. pap. 15.95x (ISBN 0-252-01071-X). U of Ill Pr.

Fortier, Andrew C., jt. auth. see McElrath, Dale L.

Fortier, Andrew C., et al. The Mund Site. LC 83-17867. (American Bottom Archaeology: Selected FAI-270 Site Reports Ser.: Vol. 5). (Illus.). 448p. 1983. 13.95x (ISBN 0-252-01067-1). U of Ill Pr.

--The Fish Lake Site. LC 84-4607. (American Bottom Archaeology: FAI-270 Site Reports Ser.: Vol. 8). (Illus.). 256p. 1984. pap. 12.50x (ISBN 0-252-01069-8). U of Ill Pr.

Fortier, Ed. One Survived. LC 78-10530. (Illus.). 1979. pap. 2.95 (ISBN 0-88240-118-1). Alaska Northwest.

Fortier, P. J. Design & Analysis of Distributed Real-Time Systems. 1985. 36.95 (ISBN 0-07-021619-3). McGraw.

Fortin, A., et al. Petit Lexique du Soudage. Anglais-Francais. Chartrand, P., ed. 47p. (Eng. & Fr.). 1974. pap. 2.95 (ISBN 0-686-92078-3, M-9227). French & Eur.

Fortin, Carlos, jt. ed. see Anglade, Christian.

Fortin, Karen. Accounting One - Introduction to Financial Accounting. 227p. 1981. 15.95 (ISBN 0-318-13856-5). Credit Union Natl Assn.

Fortin, M. & Glowinski, R. Augmented Lagrangian Methods: Applications to the Numerical Solution of Boundary-Value Problems. (Studies in Mathematics & Its Applications: Vol. 15). 340p. 1983. 59.75 (ISBN 0-444-86680-9, I-168-83, North Holland). Elsevier.

Fortin, Pierre. Chomage, infaltion et regulation de la conjoncture au Quebec. 144p. 1980. 6.00 (ISBN 0-88806-063-7, AQ-13). Inst C D Howe.

--Unemployment, Inflation, & Economic Stabilization in Quebec. (Accent Quebec). 132p. (Eng. & Fr.). 1980. 6.00 (ISBN 0-88806-064-5, AQ13). Inst C D Howe.

Fortina, Carl. Accordion, As Written. LC 61-3658. (Illus.). 1961. pap. 3.00 (ISBN 0-910736-02-2). Holly-Pix.

Fortiner, Virginia J. Science-Hobby Book of Archaeology. rev. ed. LC 62-11633. (Science Hobby Bks). (Illus.). (gr. 5-10). 1968. PLB 4.95 (ISBN 0-8225-0552-5). Lerner Pubns.

Fortini, Arnaldo. Francis of Assisi. Moak, Helen, tr. 900p. 1980. 39.50 (ISBN 0-8245-0003-2). Crossroad NY.

Fortini, Peter, et al, trs. see Sobol, I. M.

Fortino, Andre. Fundamentals of Computer Aided Analysis of Integrated Circuits Devices & Processes. 1983. pap. text ed. 18.95 (ISBN 0-8359-2120-4). Reston.

Fortino, Andres. Fundamentals of Integrated Circuit Technology. 1984. text ed. 28.95 (ISBN 0-8359-2135-2); instr's manual avail. (ISBN 0-8359-2136-0). Reston.

Fortino, Andres G. Workbench Guide to Microelectronics. 1984. text ed. 19.95 (ISBN 0-8359-8819-8); pap. 14.95 (ISBN 0-8359-8820-1). Reston.

Fortino, Denise, jt. auth. see Haberman, Fredric.

Fortis, Alberto. Travels into Dalmatia. LC 70-135806. (Eastern Europe Collection Ser). 1970. Repr. of 1778 ed. 37.50 (ISBN 0-405-02748-6). Ayer Co Pubs.

Fortman, E. J., tr. see De Margerie, Bertrand.

Fortman, Edmund J. The Triune God: A Historical Study of the Doctrine of the Trinity. (Twin Brooks Ser.). 408p. 1982. pap. 10.95 (ISBN 0-8010-3505-8). Baker Bk.

Fortman, Jan. Creatures of Mystery. LC 77-24705. (Great Unsolved Mysteries). (Illus.). (gr. 4-5). 1977. PLB 14.25 (ISBN 0-8172-1063-6). Raintree Pubs.

--Houdini & Other Masters of Magic. LC 77-12638. (Myth, Magic & Superstition). (Illus.). (gr. 4-5). 1977. PLB 14.25 (ISBN 0-8172-1032-6). Raintree Pubs.

Fortman, Janis L. Creatures of Mystery. LC 77-24705. (Great Unsolved Mysteries Ser.). (Illus.). 48p. (gr. 4up). 1983. pap. 9.27 (ISBN 0-8172-2157-3). Raintree Pubs.

Fortmann, Louise. Peasants, Officials & Participation in Rural Tanzania: Experience with Villagization & Decentralization. (Special Series on Rural Local Organization: No. 1). 136p. (Orig.). 1980. pap. text ed. 6.95 (ISBN 0-86731-028-6). RDC Ctr Intl Stud.

Fortmann, Louise & Riddell, James. Trees & Tenure: An Annotated Bibliography for Agroforesters & Others. xvii, 135p. (Orig.). 1985. pap. 8.00 (ISBN 0-934519-00-5). U of Wis Land.

Fortmann, Louise & Roe, Emery. Water Use in Rural Botswana. 150p. (Orig.). 1982. pap. text ed. 5.50 (ISBN 0-86731-059-6). RDC Ctr Intl Stud.

Fortmann, Louise, jt. auth. see Roe, Emery.

Fortmann, Thomas E. & Hitz, Konrad L. Introduction to Linear Control Systems. (Control & Systems Theory: Vol. 5). 1977. 37.75 (ISBN 0-8247-6512-5). Dekker.

Fortna, Nancy L. & Suran, Frank M., eds. Guide to County & Municipal Records in the Pennsylvania State Archives. (Illus.). 50p. (Orig.). 1982. lib. bdg. 4.95 (ISBN 0-89271-022-5). Pa Hist & Mus.

Fortner, Ethel. Nervous on the Curves. Bayes, Ronald H., ed. LC 82-62748. 60p. (Orig.). 1982. pap. 7.95 (ISBN 0-932662-40-4). St Andrews NC.

Fortner-Frazier, Carrie L. Social Work & Dialysis: The Medical & Psychosocial Aspects of Kidney Disease. LC 78-51754. 224p. 1981. 18.50x (ISBN 0-520-03674-3). U of Cal Pr.

Fortney, Alan, jt. auth. see Flower, Cedric.

Forto, Rocco Z. Anatomy & Health Sciences: Medical Analysis Index with Research Bibliography. LC 85-47861. 150p. 1985. 29.95 (ISBN 0-88164-264-9); pap. 21.95 (ISBN 0-88164-265-7). ABBE Pubs Assn.

--Famous Persons Index I: Habits, History, Medical Syndromes, Psychology & Behavior. LC 84-45872. 150p. 1985. 29.95 (ISBN 0-88164-276-2); pap. 21.95 (ISBN 0-88164-277-0). ABBE Pubs Assn.

Forto, Rocco Z. de see De Forto, Rocco Z.

Fortschen, William R. Ice Prophet. 304p. (Orig.). 1985. pap. 2.95 (ISBN 0-345-30790-9, Del Rey). Ballantine.

Fortson, E. N., jt. ed. see VanDyke, R. S., Jr.

Fortson, James C., jt. auth. see Clutter, Jerome L.

Fortuin, Nicholas J. Current Therapy in Cardiovascular Disease 1984-1985. 420p. 1984. casebound 48.00 (ISBN 0-317-01504-4, D1651-4). Mosby.

Fortuine, Robert, ed. Circumpolar Health '84: Proceedings of the Sixth International Symposium. LC 85-50874. (Illus.). 496p. 1985. 40.00 (ISBN 0-295-96202-X). U of Wash Pr.

Fortun, Clara. Artes Populares. (Lecturas Faciles). 68p. (Spanish.). 1983. pap. text ed. 3.75 (ISBN 0-88345-521-8, 21256). Regents Pub.

Fortun, Michael, jt. ed. see Nader, Ralph.

Fortuna, James L., Jr. The Unsearchable Wisdom of God: A Study of Providence in Richardson's Pamela. LC 80-14919. (University of Florida Humanities Monographs: No. 49). vii, 130p. 1980. pap. 6.50 (ISBN 0-8130-0676-7). U Presses Fla.

Fortunato, Connie. Music Is for Children. LC 78-50962. 1978. pap. 1.50 (ISBN 0-89191-128-6). Cook.

Fortunato, Donald J. Two Thousand Miles on the Appalachian Trail. (Illus.). 153p. (Orig.). 1984. pap. 6.95 (ISBN 0-9613494-0-9). D J Fortunato.

Fortunato, John. Embracing the Exile: Healing Journeys of Gay Christians. 156p. (Orig.). 1984. pap. 7.95 (ISBN 0-8164-2637-6, 6338, Pub. by Seabury). Winston Pr.

Fortunato, P. When We Were Young: An Album of Stars. 1980. 8.95 (ISBN 0-13-956482-9); pap. 2.50 (ISBN 0-13-956474-8). P-H.

Fortunato, Pat. A Colonial Williamsburg Activities Book: Fun Activities for Children 7 & up. (Illus.). 48p. (Orig.). (gr. 1-4). 1982. pap. 2.95 (ISBN 0-87935-062-8). Williamsburg.

--Foozles. 1978. pap. 1.25 (ISBN 0-440-92740-4). Dell.

Fortunato, Pat, jt. auth. see Chaback, Elaine.

Fortunato, Peter. A Bell or a Hook. LC 77-22186. 45p. 1977. 3.50 (ISBN 0-87886-087-8). Ithaca Hse.

Fortunato, Ray T. & Waddell, D. Geneva. Personnel Administration in Higher Education: Handbook of Faculty & Staff Personnel Practices. LC 81-47769. (Higher Education Ser.). 416p. 1981. text ed. 26.95x (ISBN 0-87589-506-9). Jossey-Bass.

Fortune. Guide to Landscaping. LC 64-472. 1963. pap. 2.95 (ISBN 0-8200-0403-0). Great Outdoors.

Fortune, Anne. Task-Centered Practice with Families & Groups. (Springer Series on Social Work: Vol. 6). 272p. 1985. text ed. 23.95 (ISBN 0-8261-4460-8). Springer Pub.

Fortune, Dion. Applied Magic. 18p. 1973. pap. 6.95 (ISBN 0-85030-218-8). Weiser.

--Aspects of Occultism. 88p. 1973. 5.95 (ISBN 0-85030-153-X). Weiser.

--The Cosmic Doctrine. 160p. 1976. pap. 6.95 (ISBN 0-85030-194-7). Weiser.

--Demon Lover. 1972. pap. 6.95 (ISBN 0-87728-499-7). Weiser.

--The Esoteric Orders & Their Work. 144p. 1975. 7.95. Weiser.

--Esoteric Philosophy of Love & Marriage. 96p. 1982. pap. 5.95 (ISBN 0-85030-121-1). Weiser.

--Goat-Foot God. (Orig.). 1980. pap. 7.95 (ISBN 0-87728-500-4). Weiser.

--The Machinery of the Mind. 1980. pap. 5.95 (ISBN 0-87728-505-5). Weiser.

--Moon Magic. (Orig.). 1979. pap. 7.95 (ISBN 0-87728-423-7). Weiser.

--Mystical Qabalah. 311p. 1984. 7.95 (ISBN 0-87728-596-9). Weiser.

--Practical Occultism in Daily Life. 64p. (Orig.). 1972. pap. 5.95 (ISBN 0-85030-133-5). Weiser.

--The Problem of Purity. 1980. pap. 5.95 (ISBN 0-87728-506-3). Weiser.

--Psychic Self-Defense. 210p. (Orig.). 1977. pap. 6.95 (ISBN 0-85030-151-3). Weiser.

--Sane Occultism. 192p. 1973. pap. 7.95 (ISBN 0-85030-105-X). Weiser.

--The Sea Priestess. (Orig.). 1979. pap. 7.95 (ISBN 0-87728-424-5). Weiser.

--Secrets of Dr. Taverner. 4th rev. ed. 277p. 1979. pap. 3.95 (ISBN 0-87542-227-6). Llewellyn Pubns.

--Through the Gates of Death. 94p. 1972. pap. 5.95 (ISBN 0-85030-091-6). Weiser.

--Training & Work of an Initiate. 128p. 1973. 6.95 (ISBN 0-85030-154-8). Weiser.

--Winged Bull. 328p. (Orig.). 1980. pap. 6.95 (ISBN 0-87728-501-2). Weiser.

Fortune, Dion, ed. The Esoteric Orders & Their Work. 144p. 1983. pap. 7.95 (ISBN 0-85030-310-9). Newcastle Pub.

Fortune Editorial Staff. The Exploding Metropolis. LC 76-5781. (Illus.). 193p. 1976. Repr. of 1958 ed. lib. bdg. 17.50x (ISBN 0-8371-8823-7, FMEM). Greenwood.

Fortune Editors. Fabulous Future: America in Nineteen Eighty. facsimile ed. LC 79-134077. (Essay Index Reprint Ser). Repr. of 1956 ed. 18.00 (ISBN 0-8369-2315-4). Ayer Co Pubs.

Fortune, J. J. Danger: Due North. (Race Against Time Ser.: No. 10). 144p. (Orig.). (gr. k-12). 1985. pap. 2.25 (ISBN 0-440-91865-0, LFL). Dell.

--Escape from Raven Castle. (Race Against Time Ser.: No. 2). 160p. (Orig.). (gr. 3-9). 1984. pap. 2.25 (ISBN 0-440-92406-5, LFL). Dell.

--Evil in Paradise. (Race Against Time Ser.: No. 6). (Illus.). 140p. (gr. 5-9). 1984. pap. 2.25 (ISBN 0-440-92430-8). Dell.

--Journey to Atlantis. (Race Against Time Ser.: No. 9). 144p. (Orig.). (gr. k-12). 1985. pap. 2.25 (ISBN 0-440-94272-1, LFL). Dell.

--Pursuit of the Deadly Diamonds. (Race Against Time Ser.: No. 3). 160p. (Orig.). (YA) (gr. 3-9). 1984. pap. 2.25 (ISBN 0-440-97181-0, LFL). Dell.

--Race Against Time. 144p. (gr. 5-9). Date not set. price not set (YB). Dell.

--Revenge in the Silent Tomb. (Race Against Time Ser.: No. 1). 160p. (Orig.). (YA) (gr. 7-12). 1984. pap. 2.25 (ISBN 0-440-97707-X, LFL). Dell.

--Search for Mad Jack's Crown. (Race Against Time Ser.: No. 4). 160p. (Orig.). (YA) (gr. 7-12). 1984. pap. 2.25 (ISBN 0-440-97685-5, LFL). Dell.

--The Secret of the Third Watch. (Race Against Time Ser.: No. 7). 128p. (Orig.). (gr. 3-9). 1984. pap. 2.25 (ISBN 0-440-97745-2, LFL). Dell.

--Trapped in the U. S. S. R. (Race Against Time Ser.: No. 8). 144p. (Orig.). (gr. 7-12). 1984. pap. 2.25 (ISBN 0-440-99058-0, LFL). Dell.

Fortune, J. J., et al. Duel for the Samurai Sword. (No. 5). 160p. (Orig.). (YA) (gr. 7-12). 1984. pap. 2.25 (ISBN 0-440-92172-4, LFL). Dell.

Fortune, Jim C., et al. Understanding Testing in Occupational Licensing: Establishing Links Between Principles of Measurement & Practices of Licensing. LC 84-43026. (Social & Behavioral Science Ser.). 1985. text ed. 21.95x (ISBN 0-87589-644-8). Jossey-Bass.

Fortune, Joyce, jt. auth. see Bignell, Victor.

Fortune, Katie. How to Avoid the Pitfalls of a Passive Mind. 32p. 1977. pap. 0.95 (ISBN 0-930756-25-8, 4240-PM). Aglow Pubns.

--Receive All God Has to Give. 1971. pap. write for info. color booklet (ISBN 0-930756-01-0, 541001); pap. 0.95 color booklet (ISBN 0-317-03288-7). Aglow Pubns.

Fortune Magazine. Fortune's Favorites: Portraits of Some American Corporations, An Anthology. facs. ed. LC 68-20300. (Essay Index Reprint Ser). 1931. 18.00 (ISBN 0-8369-0451-6). Ayer Co Pubs.

Fortune Magazine & Davenport, Russell W. U. S. A., the Permanent Revolution. LC 80-15776. 267p. 1980. Repr. of 1951 ed. lib. bdg. 24.75x (ISBN 0-313-22500-1, FMUS). Greenwood.

Fortune Magazine Editors. Markets of the Sixties. LC 74-167340. (Essay Index Reprint Ser.). Repr. of 1960 ed. 26.50 (ISBN 0-8369-2769-9). Ayer Co Pubs.

--Working Smarter. LC 81-24074. 198p. 1982. 13.95 (ISBN 0-670-78293-9). Viking.

Fortune, Marie M. Sexual Abuse Prevention: A Study for Teenagers. (Orig.). 1984. pap. 3.95 (ISBN 0-8298-0711-X). Pilgrim NY.

--Sexual Violence: The Unmentionable Sin: An Ethical & Pastoral Perspective. 256p. (Orig.). 1983. pap. 9.95 (ISBN 0-8298-0652-0). Pilgrim NY.

Fortune, Nigel & Lewis, Anthony, eds. New Oxford History of Music, Vol. 5: Opera & Church Music 1630-1750. (Illus.). 1975. 49.95x (ISBN 0-19-316305-5). Oxford U Pr.

Fortune, Nigel, jt. ed. see Arnold, Denis.

Fortune, Nigel, ed. see Chater, James.

Fortune, Nigel, ed. see Cross, Eric.

Fortune, Nigel, ed. see Dunsby, Jonathan M.

Fortune, Nigel, ed. see Jones, Andrew V.

Fortune, Nigel, ed. see Kirwan-Mott, Anne.

Fortune, Nigel, ed. see Lawson, Colin.

Fortune, Nigel, ed. see Whenham, John.

Fortune, R. F. Sorcerers of Dobu: The Social Anthropology of the Dobu Islanders of the Western Pacific. 1979. Repr. of 1932 ed. lib. bdg. 25.00 (ISBN 0-8495-1736-2). Arden Lib.

Fortune, Raymond, tr. see Sumarokov, A. P.

Fortune, Reo F. Arapesh. LC 75-32817. (American Ethnological Society. Publications: No. 19). Repr. of 1942 ed. 30.00 (ISBN 0-404-14121-8). AMS Pr.

--Omaha Secret Societies. LC 70-82351. (Columbia Univ. Contributions to Anthropology Ser.: Vol. 14). Repr. of 1932 ed. 27.50 (ISBN 0-404-50564-3). AMS Pr.

Fortune, Richard. Alexander Sukhovo-Kobylin. (World Authors Ser.). 1982. lib. bdg. 19.95 (ISBN 0-8057-6515-8, Twayne). G K Hall.

Fortune, Richard, tr. see Sumarokov, A. P.

Fortune, Robert & Myers, Ramon H. Three Years' Wanderings in the Northern Provinces of China. LC 78-74307. (Modern Chinese Economy Ser.: Vol. 4). 1979. 53.00 (ISBN 0-8240-4253-0). Garland Pub.

Fortune, Sarah D. & Gray, Barbara Q. Experience to Exposition: Patterns of Basic Writing. 464p. 1984. pap. text ed. 11.50scp (ISBN 0-06-042132-0, HarpC); instr. manual avail. (ISBN 0-06-362215-7). Har-Row.

Fortune Staff, ed. Working Smarter. 228p. 1984. pap. 6.95 (ISBN 0-14-006894-5). Penguin.

Fortune, Stephen A. Merchants & Jews: The Struggle for British West Indian Commerce, 1650-1750. LC 83-25903. (University of Florida Latin American Monographs: No. 26). 1984. 18.00 (ISBN 0-8130-0735-6). U Presses Fla.

Fortune, Timothy T. Black & White: Land, Labor & Politics in the South. LC 68-28995. (American Negro: His History & Literature, Ser. No. 1). 1968. Repr. of 1884 ed. 13.00 (ISBN 0-405-01814-2). Ayer Co Pubs.

--Dreams of Life. LC 72-168125. Repr. of 1905 ed. 9.00 (ISBN 0-404-00051-7). AMS Pr.

--Dreams of Life: Miscellaneous Poems. facs. ed. LC 77-89433. (Black Heritage Library Collection Ser). 1905. 12.00 (ISBN 0-8369-8573-7). Ayer Co Pubs.

Fortune, William L. The Moment. LC 79-87489. 8.95 (ISBN 0-934168-00-8). Progeny Pr.

Forty, Ann. Treen & Earthenware. (Illus.). 1981. 25.00x (Pub. by Midas Bks England). State Mutual Bk.
Forty, Anne. Treen & Earthenware. 1979. pap. 10.50 (ISBN 0-85936-074-1, Pub. by Midas Bks England). Intl Spec Bk.
Forty, George. At War in Korea. (Illus.). 144p. 1982. 25.00 (ISBN 0-7110-1116-8, Pub. by Ian Allan England). Hippocrene Bks.
--Missile Systems. (Illus.). 120p. 1985. 14.95 (ISBN 0-87052-153-5, Pub. by Ian Allan England). Hippocrene Bks.
--Photo History of Armoured Cars in Two World Wars. (Illus.). 288p. 1985. 17.95 (ISBN 0-317-17109-7, Pub. by Blandford England). Sterling.
--A Photo History of Tanks in Two World Wars. (Illus.). 191p. 1984. 16.95 (ISBN 0-7137-1216-3, Pub. by Blandford Pr England). Sterling.
Forty, George & Batchelor, John. United States Tanks of World War II in Action. (Illus.). 160p. 1983. 16.95 (ISBN 0-7137-1214-7, Pub. by Blandford Pr England). Sterling.
Forucci, Samuel L. A Folk Song History of America: America Through it's Songs. LC 83-24610. 256p. 1984. 22.95 (ISBN 0-13-323130-5); pap. 14.95 (ISBN 0-13-323122-4). P-H.
Forum. Forum Papers, First Series. Heydrick, Benjamin A., ed. LC 72-86750. (Essay Index Reprint Ser.). 1924. 18.00 (ISBN 0-8369-1465-1). Ayer Co Pubs.
--Forum Papers, Second Series. Gaston, C. R., ed. LC 73-152170. (Essay Index Reprint Ser.). Repr. of 1925 ed. 18.00 (ISBN 0-8369-2224-7). Ayer Co Pubs.
Forum Comm. on the Construction Industry. Construction Contract Documents for Private Work. 500p. 1981. 50.00 (ISBN 0-686-47814-2). Amer Bar Assn.
Forum Committee on the Construction Industry, American Bar Association & Fidelity & Surety Law Committee. Bankruptcy-Crisis in the Construction Industry, Thursday, January 27, 1983, the New York Hilton, New York, New York. LC 83-128770. 270p. 1983. 35.00 (557-0008). ABA Prof Educ Pubns.
Forum Committee on the Construction Industry Staff. Bankruptcy: Crisis in the Construction Industry. 270p. 1983. looseleaf 35.00 (ISBN 0-317-30630-8). Amer Bar Assn.
Forum Committee on the Construction Industry. Contract Administration Seminar. 507p. 1981. 50.00 (ISBN 0-686-47813-4). Amer Bar Assn.
Forum on Forest Policy for the Future. Forest Policy for the Future-Conflict, Compromise, Consensus: Papers & Discussions from a Forum on Forest Policy for the Future, 1974. Clawson, Marion, ed. LC 74-13169. (Resources for the Future, RFF Working Paper: LW-1). pap. 91.50 (ISBN 0-317-26456-7, 2023791). Bks Demand UMI.
Forum Quorum. Forum Feasts. 300p. 1968. 10.00 (ISBN 0-9606778-0-1). Forum Quorum.
Forve, Guy. Alexander MacKenzie: Lone Courage. (American Explorers Ser.: No. 12). 320p. (Orig.). 1983. pap. 2.95 (ISBN 0-440-00066-1, Emerald). Dell.
Forwald, Haakon. Mind, Matter, & Gravitation. LC 72-97212. (Parapsychological Monograph No. 11). 1969. pap. 3.50 (ISBN 0-912328-15-0). Parapsych Foun.
Forward, J., jt. auth. see Dillon, T. S.
Forward, Jane. Make Your Own Machine Applique Baby Quilts. (Illus.). 120p. 1984. text ed. 15.00x (ISBN 0-87663-445-5); pap. 8.95 (ISBN 0-87663-599-0). Universe.
Forward, Robert. Dragon's Egg. 352p. 1981. 9.95 (ISBN 0-345-28646-4, Del Rey); pap. 2.25 (ISBN 0-345-28349-X, Del Rey). Ballantine.
--The Flight of the Dragonfly: A Novel. 17.95 (ISBN 0-671-49939-4); pap. 7.95 (ISBN 0-671-49944-0). S&S.
Forward, Robert L. The Flight of the Dragonfly. 1984. 17.45 (ISBN 0-671-49939-4, Timescape); pap. 7.70 (ISBN 0-671-49944-0, Timescape). PB.
--Starquake. 1985. 14.95 (ISBN 0-345-31232-5, Dey Rey). Ballantine.
Forward, Susan & Buck, Craig. Betrayal of Innocence: Incest & Its Devastation. 1979. pap. 5.95 (ISBN 0-14-005264-X). Penguin.
Fosback, Norman G. Stock Market Logic: A Sophisticated Approach to Profits on Wall Street. LC 76-28826. (Illus.). 1976. 40.00 (ISBN 0-917604-48-2); pap. 30.00 (ISBN 0-917604-49-0). Inst Econometric.
Fosbenner, Al. The Westphal Empire. (Orig.). 1980. pap. 2.75 (ISBN 0-440-19492-X). Dell.
Fosberg, F. R. Genus Gouldia. (BMB). Repr. of 1937 ed. 14.00 (ISBN 0-527-02255-1). Kraus Repr.
--Polynesian Species of Hedyotis. Repr. of 1943 ed. 12.00 (ISBN 0-527-02282-9). Kraus Repr.
Fosbroke, G. E. Character Reading Through Analysis of the Features. 1977. lib. bdg. 59.95 (ISBN 0-8490-1594-4). Gordon Pr.
Fosburgh. Old Money. Date not set. pap. 3.95 (ISBN 0-671-52622-7). PB.
Fosburgh, Lacey. Old Money. LC 82-45246. (Illus.). 432p. 1983. 17.95 (ISBN 0-385-15310-4). Doubleday.
Fosburgh, Liza. Bella Arabella. (Illus.). (gr. 9-12). 1985. 10.95 (ISBN 0-02-735430-X). Four Winds Pr.
--With Friends Like These... (Orig.). 1983. pap. text ed. 3.50 (ISBN 0-671-45258-4). PB.
Foscue, Virginia O. The Place Names of Sumter County, Alabama. Hartman, James W., ed. (Publication of the American Dialect Society Ser.: No. 65). (Illus.). 75p. 1978. pap. 5.90 (ISBN 0-8173-0663-3). U of Ala Pr.
--A Preliminary Survey of the Vocabulary of White Alabamians. (Publications of the American Dialect Society Ser., No. 56). 48p. 1971. pap. 3.10 (ISBN 0-8173-0656-0, Am Dialect Soc). U of Ala Pr.
Fosdick, Harry E. As I See Religion. LC 75-11835. 201p. 1975. Repr. of 1932 ed. lib. bdg. 45.00x (ISBN 0-8371-8142-9, FOAI). Greenwood.
--Great Time to Be Alive: Sermons on Christianity in Wartime. LC 78-167341. (Essay Index Reprint Ser.). Repr. of 1944 ed. 18.00 (ISBN 0-8369-2688-9). Ayer Co Pubs.
--The Man from Nazareth: As His Contemporaries Saw Him. LC 78-16469. 1978. Repr. of 1949 ed. lib. bdg. 24.25x (ISBN 0-313-20603-1, FOMN). Greenwood.
--The Meaning of Faith. (Festival Bks). 352p. 1982. pap. 3.95 (ISBN 0-687-23959-1). Abingdon.
--The Meaning of Prayer. 1982. pap. 2.95 (ISBN 0-687-23960-5, Festival). Abingdon.
--The Meaning of Prayer. LC 76-50560. 1976. Repr. of 1946 ed. lib. bdg. 18.50 (ISBN 0-8414-4159-6). Folcroft.
--The Meaning of Service. 224p. 1983. pap. 4.35 (ISBN 0-687-23961-3). Abingdon.
--The Modern Use of the Bible. 1925. 25.00 (ISBN 0-8274-2758-1). R West.
--A Pilgrimage to Palestine. Davis, Moshe, ed. LC 77-70688. (America & the Holy Land Ser.). 1977. Repr. of 1927 ed. lib. bdg. 30.00x (ISBN 0-405-10247-X). Ayer Co Pubs.
Fosdick, Howard. Computer Basics for Librarians & Information Scientists. LC 81-80539. (Illus.). x, 203p. 1981. text ed. 22.50 (ISBN 0-87815-034-X). Info Resources.
--Structured PL-I Programming: For Textual & Library Processing. 350p. 1982. lib. bdg. 25.00 (ISBN 0-87287-328-5). Libs Unl.
Fosdick, L., ed. Performance Evaluation of Numerical Software. 340p. 1979. 42.75 (ISBN 0-444-85330-8, North Holland). Elsevier.
Fosdick, Lucian J. The French Blood in America. LC 73-279. (Illus.). 448p. 1973. Repr. of 1906 ed. 20.00 (ISBN 0-8063-0552-5). Genealog Pub.
Fosdick, Raymond B. American Police Systems. LC 69-14925. (Criminology, Law Enforcement, & Social Problems Ser.: No. 53). (With intro. added). 1969. o. p. 18.00 (ISBN 0-87585-053-7); pap. 8.50x (ISBN 0-87585-909-7). Patterson Smith.
--European Police Systems. LC 69-14926. (Criminology, Law Enforcement, & Social Problems Ser.: No. 54). (With intro. added). 1969. 18.00x (ISBN 0-87585-054-5); pap. 8.50 (ISBN 0-87585-910-0). Patterson Smith.
--Letters on the League of Nations. (The Papers of Woodrow Wilson). 1966. 23.50 (ISBN 0-691-04523-2). Princeton U Pr.
FOSECO, see Foundry Services Ltd.
Foseco Minsep Group. The Business Traveller's Handbook: How to Get along with People in 100 Countries. 310p. 1983. 15.95 (ISBN 0-13-107797-X); pap. 7.95 (ISBN 0-13-107789-9). P-H.
Fosegan, Joseph S. Alphabetic Indexing Rules: Application by Computer. 1984. pap. 3.70 (ISBN 0-538-11640-4, K64). SW Pub.
Fosgate, Blanchard. Sleep Psychologically Considered. (Hypnosis & Altered States of Consciousness Ser.). 188p. 1982. Repr. of 1850 ed. lib. bdg. 22.50 (ISBN 0-306-76165-3). Da Capo.
Fosh, P. The Active Trade Unionist: A Study of Motivation & Participation at Branch Level. (DAE Papers in Industrial Relations & Labour). (Illus.). 1981. 32.50 (ISBN 0-521-23700-9). Cambridge U Pr.
Fosh, Patricia & Littler, Craig. Industrial Relations & the Law in the 1980's. 256p. 1985. text ed. write for info. (ISBN 0-566-00978-1). Gower Pub Co.
Foshay, Arthur W., ed. Considered Action for Curriculum Improvement. LC 80-50621. 201p. (Orig.). 1980. pap. text ed. 9.75 (ISBN 0-87120-099-6, 610-80186). Assn Supervision.
Foshay, Ella M. Reflections of Nature: Flowers in American Art. LC 83-48823. (Illus.). 1984. 29.95 (ISBN 0-394-53490-5). Knopf.
Foshay, Toby, ed. see Lewis, Wyndham.
Foshee, Howard. Broadman Church Manual. LC 72-94629. 192p. 1973. 8.95 (ISBN 0-8054-2525-X). Broadman.
Foshee, Howard B. Now That You're a Deacon. LC 74-79488. 128p. 1975. 7.50 (ISBN 0-8054-3506-9). Broadman.
Foshee, John. Alabama Canoe Rides & Float Trips. LC 75-26074. 1976. pap. 6.95 (ISBN 0-87397-087-X). Strode.
--You, Too, Can Canoe. LC 76-58244. 1977. 9.95 (ISBN 0-87397-116-7). Strode.
Fosheim, Robin M., jt. ed. see Bailey, Richard W.
Foskett, A. C. The Subject Approach to Information. 4th ed. 480p. 1982. 27.50 (ISBN 0-85157-313-4, Pub. by Bingley England); pap. 18.50 (ISBN 0-85157-339-8, Pub. by Bingley England). Shoe String.
Foskett, D. J. Notes on Compiling Bibliographies. 3rd ed. 1977. 29.00x (ISBN 0-900008-22-9, Pub. by U of London England). State Mutual Bk.
Foskett, D. J., ed. Reader in Comparative Librarianship. LC 76-10124. 333p. 1976. 28.50 (ISBN 0-313-24037-X, ZRE/). Greenwood.
Foskett, D. J., ed. & intro. by see Shera, Jesse H.
Foskett, Daphne. Collecting Miniatures. (Illus.). 500p. 1980. 62.50 (ISBN 0-902028-79-0). Antique Collect.
--John Smart: The Man & His Miniatures. (Illus.). 1965. 9.50 (ISBN 0-8079-0071-0). October.
Fosler, R. Scott, ed. see Committee for Economic Development.
Fosler, Scott & Berger, Renee A. Public-Private Partnership in American Cities: Seven Case Studies. LC 82-48016. 368p. 1982. 27.50x (ISBN 0-669-05834-3). Lexington Bks.
Foslien, Dagmar. The Fantastic Fashion Show. (Rose-Petal Place Ser.). (Illus.). 40p. (ps-3). 1984. 5.95 (ISBN 0-910313-50-4). Parker Bro.
--A Garden of Love to Share. (Rose-Petal Place Ser.). 1984. incl. cassette 7.95 (ISBN 0-910313-63-6). Parker Bro.
Fosmire, Bea. Growing Pains: The Risks & Rewards of Love. 144p. 1983. pap. 4.95 (ISBN 0-310-29331-6). Zondervan.
Foss. Basic Metallurgy. text ed. write for info. (ISBN 0-685-67274-3). Bennett IL.
Foss, Brian, ed. Psychology Survey, Vol. 1. (Psychology Yearbook Ser.). 1978. text ed. 22.50x (ISBN 0-04-150065-2). Allen Unwin.
Foss, Charles R. Evening Before the Diesel: A History of the Grand Trunk Western Railroad. (Illus.). 1980. 49.95 (ISBN 0-87108-552-6). Pruett.
Foss, Christopher. Armoured Fighting Vehicles of the World. 192p. 1981. 35.00x (ISBN 0-7110-0778-0, Pub. by Ian Allan). State Mutual Bk.
--Artillery of the World. 3rd, rev. ed. 1981. 17.50 (ISBN 0-684-16722-0, ScribT). Scribner.
--Jane's Light Tanks & Armoured Cars. (Illus.). 192p. 1984. 18.95 (ISBN 0-7106-0322-3). Jane's Pub Inc.
--Jane's World Armoured Fighting Vehicles. LC 76-57887. 1977. 25.00 (ISBN 0-312-44047-2). St Martin.
Foss, Christopher, ed. Jane's Military Vehicles & Ground Support Equipment 1985. 6th ed. Gander, Terry. (Jane's Yearbooks). (Illus.). 875p. 1985. 125.00 (ISBN 0-7106-0811-X). Jane's Pub Inc.
Foss, Christopher F. The Illustrated Guide to Modern Tanks & Fighting Vehicles. LC 80-65165. (Illustrated Military Guides Ser.). (Illus.). 160p. 1980. 9.95 (ISBN 0-668-04965-0, 4965-0). Arco.
--Jane's Main Battle Tanks. (Illus.). 205p. 1984. 18.95 (ISBN 0-7106-0277-4). Jane's Pub Inc.
Foss, Christopher F., ed. Jane's Armour & Artillery 1984-85. (Jane's Yearbooks). (Illus.). 950p. 1984. 125.00 (ISBN 0-7106-0800-4). Jane's Pub Inc.
--Jane's Armour & Artillery 1985-86. 6th ed. (Jane's Yearbooks). (Illus.). 900p. 1985. 125.00x (ISBN 0-7106-0820-9). Jane's Pub Inc.
--Jane's Military Vehicle & Ground Support Equipment, 1984. 5th ed. (Jane's Yearbooks). (Illus.). 850p. 1984. 125.00x (ISBN 0-7106-0794-6). Jane's Pub Inc.
Foss, Clive. Byzantine & Turkish Sardis. (Archaeological Exploration of Sardis Monograph: No. 4). (Illus.). 288p. 1976. 14.00x (ISBN 0-674-08969-3). Harvard U Pr.
--Ephesus After Antiquity. LC 78-1152. (Illus.). 1980. 44.50 (ISBN 0-521-22086-6). Cambridge U Pr.
Foss, Clive & Magdalino, Paul. Rome & Byzantium. 1981. 30.00x (ISBN 0-7290-0012-5, Pub. by Phaidon Pr). State Mutual Bk.
Foss, Daniel A., jt. auth. see Larkin, Ralph.
Foss, Dennis C. The Value Controversy in Sociology: A New Orientation for the Profession. LC 77-82915. (Social & Behavioral Science Ser). 1977. text ed. 22.95x (ISBN 0-87589-348-1). Jossey-Bass.
Foss, Donald J. & Hakes, David T. Psycholinguistics: An Introduction to the Psychology of Language. LC 77-27826. (Experimental Psychology Ser.). (Illus.). 1978. ref. 28.95 (ISBN 0-13-732446-4). P-H.
Foss, Edward. Judges of England, 9 Vols. LC 76-168126. Repr. of 1864 ed. Set. 400.00 (ISBN 0-404-02580-3). AMS Pr.
Foss, F. F. Ragweed the Pixie & Other Tales. (Illus.). 48p. 1983. pap. 4.00 (ISBN 0-682-49923-4). Exposition Pr FL.
Foss, George R. What the Author Meant. 196p. 1980. Repr. of 1932 ed. lib. bdg. 25.00 (ISBN 0-89984-204-6). Century Bookbindery.
--What the Author Meant (Shakespeare) 196p. 1979. Repr. of 1932 ed. lib. bdg. 25.00 (ISBN 0-89987-022-8). Darby Bks.
Foss, Hannen. The Home Video Book: How to Make Your Own Home Video Programmes. 128p. 30.00x (ISBN 0-241-10572-2, Pub. by Hamish Hamilton England). State Mutual Bk.
--How to Make Your Own Video Programmes: For Family, Educational & Business Use. (Illus.). 128p. 1982. 19.95 (ISBN 0-241-10572-2, Pub. by Hamish Hamilton England). David & Charles.
Foss, Hubert. Ralph Vaughan Williams: A Study. LC 74-9042. (Illus.). 219p. 1974. Repr. of 1950 ed. lib. bdg. 22.50x (ISBN 0-8371-7610-7, FORW). Greenwood.
Foss, Hubert J. & Fellowes, E. H. Heritage of Music, Vol. 2. facsimile ed. LC 73-156642. (Essay Index Reprint Ser.). Repr. of 1934 ed. 19.00 (ISBN 0-8369-2356-1). Ayer Co Pubs.
Foss, Hubert J., ed. Heritage of Music. LC 73-93338. (Essay Index Reprint Ser.). 1927. 19.00 (ISBN 0-8369-1292-6). Ayer Co Pubs.
Foss, J. F., jt. auth. see Potter, M. C.
Foss, Joseph J. & Simmons, Walter. Joe Foss, Flying Marine. LC 79-19902. Repr. of 1943 ed. 12.95 (ISBN 0-89201-080-0). Zenger Pub.
Foss, Kenelm. Here Lies Richard Brinsley Sheridan. LC 72-13661. 1940. lib. bdg. 20.00 (ISBN 0-8414-1250-2). Folcroft.
Foss, Lukas. Quintets for Orchestra: Study Score. 60p. (Orig.). 1980. pap. 20.00 (ISBN 0-8258-0065-X, PCB115). Fischer Inc NY.
--Thirteen Ways of Looking at a Blackbird. 1979. pap. 7.50 (ISBN -08258-0064-1, PCB114). Fischer Inc NY.
Foss, Martin. Death, Sacrifice, & Tragedy. LC 66-16513. pap. 33.80 (ISBN 0-317-08120-9, 2001980). Bks Demand UMI.
--Logic & Existence. LC 61-18687. 1962. 4.75 (ISBN 0-8022-0521-6). Philos Lib.
Foss, Mildred B. Creative Embroidery with Your Sewing Machine. LC 76-7588. 1976. (Spec); pap. 3.95 (ISBN 0-13-189357-2, Spec). P-H.
Foss, Murray F. Changes in the Workweek of Fixed Capital. 1981. 12.25 (ISBN 0-8447-3422-5); pap. 5.25 (ISBN 0-8447-3423-3). Am Enterprise.
--Changing Utilization of Fixed Capital. 1984. 14.95 (ISBN 0-8447-3559-0). Am Enterprise.
--The U. S. National Income & Product Accounts: Selected Topics. LC 82-11081. (National Bureau of Economic Research-Studies in Income & Wealth: No. 47). (Illus.). 1983. lib. bdg. 47.00x (ISBN 0-226-25728-2). U of Chicago Pr.
Foss, Phillip, Jr. Somata. (Illus.). 1983. 50.00x (ISBN 0-931460-18-2). Bieler.
Foss, Phillip O. Politics & Grass: The Administration of Grazing on the Public Domain. LC 75-90508. (Illus.). ix, 236p. Repr. of 1960 ed. lib. bdg. 15.00x (ISBN 0-8371-2136-1, FOPG). Greenwood.
Foss, Sonja K., et al. Contemporary Perspectives on Rhetoric. 321p. (Orig.). 1985. pap. text ed. 12.95X (ISBN 0-88133-129-5). Waveland Pr.
Foss, Thomas C. & Sutberry, Thomas D., eds. State Budgeting in Florida: A Handbook for Budget Analysts. 272p. 1984. 25.00 (ISBN 0-932143-00-8). FL Ctr Public.
Foss, William O. The United States Navy in Hampton Roads. Morgan, Nancy, ed. LC 83-16471. (Illus.). 1984. 19.95 (ISBN 0-89865-337-1). Donning Co.
Fossard, Esta de, jt. auth. see Rinsky, Lee A.
Fossat, Guy De see Du Fossat, Guy.
Fossati, P., jt. ed. see Lemarchand-Beraud.
Fosse, E. S. Del see Del Fosse, E. S.
Fossedal, Gregory A., jt. auth. see Graham, Daniel O.
Fossel, Peter V. Keeping Cool: A Sensible Guide to Beating the Heat. LC 83-21975. 144p. 1984. pap. 7.95 (ISBN 0-399-50990-9, GD Perigee). Putnam Pub Group.
--Keeping Warm: A Sensible Guide to Heat Conservation. (Illus.). 196p. (Orig.). 1983. pap. 7.95 (ISBN 0-399-50845-7, GD Perigee). Putnam Pub Group.
Fossen, Richard W. Van see Marlowe, Christopher.
Fossett, Frank. Colorado: Its Gold & Silver Mines, Farms & Stock Ranges, & Health & Pleasure Resorts. LC 72-9444. (The Far Western Frontier Ser.). (Illus.). 544p. 1973. Repr. of 1879 ed. 32.00 (ISBN 0-405-04973-0). Ayer Co Pubs.
Fossett, James W. Federal Aid to Big Cities: The Politics of Dependence. LC 82-74098. 64p. 1983. pap. 6.95 (ISBN 0-8157-2895-6). Brookings.
Fossey, Bernard M. de, jt. auth. see Blacque-Belair, Alain.
Fossey, Dian. Gorillas in the Mist. 1984. pap. 10.95 (ISBN 0-317-11488-3). HM.
--Gorillas in the Mist: A Remarkable Woman's Thirteen Year Adventure in Remote African Rain Forests with the Greatest of the Great Apes. LC 82-23332. (Illus.). 325p. 1983. 19.95 (ISBN 0-395-28217-9); pap. 10.95. HM.
Fossey, John, jt. auth. see Pearson, Roy.
Fossgreen, Judith C. Doing What's Right. (Character Foundation Curriculum Ser.). (gr. 1). 1981. pap. 2.95 (ISBN 0-8007-7027-7); tchr's ed. wkbk. 7.00 (ISBN 0-8007-7028-5). Revell.
Fosshage, James L. & Olsen, Paul T. Healing: Implications for Psychotherapy. LC 77-25917. (New Directions in Psychotherapy Ser.: Vol.II). 388p. (Series editor Paul T. Olsen). 1978. 29.95 (ISBN 0-87705-359-6). Human Sci Pr.
Fosso, D. R. Parabola Rasa. LC 84-51413. 72p. 1984. pap. 6.00 (ISBN 0-913773-14-X). S Wright.
Fosson, Abe R. & Kaak, H. Otto. Child Abuse & Neglect Case Studies. 1977. 18.50 (ISBN 0-87488-062-9). Med Exam.
Fossum, Eystein. Computerisation of Working Life. (Computers & Their Applications Ser.). 148p. 1983. 42.95x (ISBN 0-470-27409-3). Halsted Pr.
Fossum, John A. Labor Relations: Development, Structure, Process. 3nd ed. 1985. 27.95x (ISBN 0-256-03291-2). Business Pubns.
Fossum, John A., ed. Horizons of Industrial Productivity, Vol. II. (Illus.). 102p. 1980. 12.00 (ISBN 0-938654-22-5, HOR II). Indus Dev Inst Sci.

Fossum, Paul R. The Agrarian Movement in North Dakota. LC 78-64116. (Johns Hopkins University. Studies in the Social Sciences. Forty-Third Ser. 1925: 1). 184p. Repr. of 1925 ed. 24.50 (ISBN 0-404-61231-8). AMS Pr.

Fossum, R. M. The Divisor Class Group of a Krull Domain. LC 72-918901. (Ergebnisse der Mathematik und Ihrer Grenzgebiete: Vol. 74). (Illus.). 148p. 1973. 31.00 (ISBN 0-387-06044-8). Springer-Verlag.

Fossum, R. M., et al. Trivial Extensions of Abelian Categories: Homological Algebra of Trivial Extensions of Abelian Categories with Applications to Ring Theory. (Lecture Notes in Mathematics Ser.: Vol. 456). xi, 122p. (Orig.). 1975. pap. 13.00 (ISBN 0-387-07159-8). Springer-Verlag.

Fossum, Robert H. Hawthorne's Inviolable Circle: The Problem of Time. 2nd ed. LC 74-172791. 229p. 1973. lib. bdg. 12.00 (ISBN 0-912112-10-7). Everett-Edwards.

Fossum, Timothy V. & Gatterdam, Ronald W. Calculus & the Computer: An Approach to Problem Solving. 1980. pap. text ed. 13.65x (ISBN 0-673-15158-1). Scott F.

Foste. Guide to Painting. (Hobby Guides Ser.). (gr. 2-5). 1981. 7.95 (ISBN 0-86020-547-9, Usborne-Hayes); PLB 12.95 (ISBN 0-88110-026-9); pap. 4.95 (ISBN 0-86020-546-0). EDC.

Foster. Aegean Faience of the Bronze Age. LC 79-4132. 1979. 37.50x (ISBN 0-300-02316-2). Yale U Pr.

--Introduction to Earth Science. 1982. 31.95 (ISBN 0-8053-2660-X); instr's manual 6.95 (ISBN 0-8053-2661-8). Benjamin-Cummings.

--A Very First Book. 9.95 (ISBN 0-19-916051-1, Pub. by Oxford U Pr Childrens). Merrimack Pub Cir.

--A Very First Poetry Book. pap. 4.95 (ISBN 0-19-916050-3, Pub. by Oxford U Pr Childrens). Merrimack Pub Cir.

Foster, jt. auth. see Griffin.

Foster, ed. see Nee, Watchman.

Foster, et al. Mathematics for Developmental Students. 464p. (gr. 10-12). 1983. pap. 19.95 (ISBN 0-8403-3016-2). Kendall-Hunt.

--Let the Sunshine in: Learning Activities for Multiply Handicapped Deaf Children, Pt. 1. 1973. pap. 3.50 (ISBN 0-913072-15-X). Natl Assn Deaf.

Foster, A. B. Carbohydrate Chemistry, Vol. 9. 1979. 50.00 (ISBN 0-08-022354-0). Pergamon.

Foster, Mrs. A. F. French Literature. 1979. Repr. of 1860 ed. lib. bdg. 40.00 (ISBN 0-8482-3958-X). Norwood Edns.

Foster, Abram J. The Coming of the Electrical Age to the United States. Bruchey, Stuart, ed. LC 78-22680. (Energy in the American Economy Ser.). 1979. lib. bdg. 28.50x (ISBN 0-405-11983-6). Ayer Co Pubs.

Foster, Adriance S. & Gifford, Ernest M. Comparative Morphology of Vascular Plants. 2nd ed. LC 73-22459. (Illus.). 751p. 1974. text ed. 37.95 (ISBN 0-7167-0712-8). W H Freeman.

Foster, Alan D. Alien. 272p. (Orig.). 1979. pap. 3.25 (ISBN 0-446-30577-4). Warner Bks.

--The Black Hole. LC 79-53894. (Illus., Orig.). 1979. pap. 1.95 (ISBN 0-345-28538-7). Ballantine.

--Bloodhype. 1977. pap. 2.25 (ISBN 0-345-29476-9). Ballantine.

--Cachalot. (Orig.). 1980. pap. 2.25 (ISBN 0-345-28066-0). Ballantine.

--The Day of the Dissonance. 1984. 17.00 (ISBN 0-932096-30-1). Phantasia Pr.

--The End of the Matter. 1982. pap. 2.25 (ISBN 0-345-29594-3, Del Rey). Ballantine.

--Flinx of the Commonwealth, 3 vols. 1982. pap. 6.25 (ISBN 0-345-26200-X, Del Rey). Ballantine.

--For Love of Mother-Not. 256p. (Orig.). 1983. pap. 2.95 (ISBN 0-345-30511-6, Del Rey). Ballantine.

--The I Inside. 320p. (Orig.). 1984. pap. 2.95 (ISBN 0-446-32027-7). Warner Bks.

--Icerigger. 1978. pap. 2.25 (ISBN 0-345-29454-8, Del Rey Bks). Ballantine.

--Krull. (Illus.). 240p. 1983. pap. 2.95 (ISBN 0-446-30642-8). Warner Bks.

--The Last Starfighter. 224p. 1984. pap. 2.95 (ISBN 0-425-07255-X). Berkley Pub.

--The Man Who Used the Universe. 320p. (Orig.). 1983. pap. 2.95 (ISBN 0-446-32819-7). Warner Bks.

--Midworld. 1976. pap. 2.25 (ISBN 0-345-25364-7). Ballantine.

--Midworld. 213p. 1975. 15.00 (ISBN 0-354-04154-1). Ultramarine Pub.

--Mission to Moulokin. 1979. pap. 2.50 (ISBN 0-345-29661-3, Del Rey Bks.). Ballantine.

--The Moment of the Magician. 17.00 (ISBN 0-932096-33-6). Phantasia Pr.

--Nor Crystal Tears. 240p. 1982. pap. 2.75 (ISBN 0-345-29141-7, Del Rey). Ballantine.

--Orphan Star. 1982. pap. 2.50 (ISBN 0-345-29903-5, Del Rey). Ballantine.

--Pale Rider. 1985. pap. 2.95 (ISBN 0-446-32767-0). Warner Bks.

--Sentenced to Prism. 288p. (Orig.). 1985. pap. 3.50 (ISBN 0-345-31980-X, Del Rey). Ballantine.

--Shadowkeep. 256p. (Orig.). 1984. pap. 2.95 (ISBN 0-446-32553-8). Warner Bks.

--Slipt. 272p. 1984. pap. 2.95 (ISBN 0-425-08011-0). Berkley Pub.

--Spellsinger. 352p. pap. 2.95 (ISBN 0-446-90352-3). Warner Bks.

--Spellsinger Four: The Moment of the Magician. 320p. (Orig.). 1985. pap. 3.50 (ISBN 0-446-32326-8). Warner Bks.

--Spellsinger II: The Hour of the Gate. 304p. pap. 2.95 (ISBN 0-446-32609-7). Warner Bks.

--Spellsinger III: The Day of the Dissonance. 304p. (Orig.). 1984. pap. 2.95 (ISBN 0-446-32133-8). Warner Bks.

--Splinter of the Mind's Eye. 1981. 7.95 (ISBN 0-345-27566-7, Del Rey). Ballantine.

--Star Trek Log Eight. 1976. lib. bdg. 15.95x (ISBN 0-88411-088-5, Pub. by Aeonian Pr). Amereon Ltd.

--Star Trek Log Five. 1975. Repr. of 1974 ed. lib. bdg. 15.95x (ISBN 0-88411-085-0, Pub. by Aeonian Pr). Amereon Ltd.

--Star Trek Log Four. 1975. Repr. of 1974 ed. lib. bdg. 15.95x (ISBN 0-88411-084-2, Pub. bv Aeonian Pr). Amereon Ltd.

--Star Trek Log Nine. 195p. Repr. of 1976 ed. lib. bdg. 15.95x (ISBN 0-88411-089-3, Pub. by Aeonian Pr). Amereon Ltd.

--Star Trek Log One. 1975. Repr. of 1974 ed. lib. bdg. 15.95x (ISBN 0-88411-081-8, Pub. by Aeonian Pr). Amereon Ltd.

--Star Trek Log Seven. 1976. lib. bdg. 15.95x (ISBN 0-88411-087-7, Pub. by Aeonian Pr). Amereon Ltd.

--Star Trek Log Six. 1976. Repr. of 1975 ed. lib. bdg. 15.95x (ISBN 0-88411-086-9, Pub. by Aeonian Pr). Amereon Ltd.

--Star Trek Log Ten. 215p. Repr. of 1977 ed. lib. bdg. 15.95x (ISBN 0-88411-090-7, Pub. by Aeonian Pr). Amereon Ltd.

--Star Trek Log Three. 1975. Repr. of 1974 ed. lib. bdg. 15.95x (ISBN 0-88411-083-4, Pub. by Aeonian Pr). Amereon Ltd.

--Star Trek Log Two. 1975. Repr. of 1974 ed. lib. bdg. 15.95x (ISBN 0-88411-082-6, Pub. by Aeonian Pr). Amereon Ltd.

--Starman. (Orig.). 1984. pap. 2.95 (ISBN 0-446-32598-8). Warner Bks.

--The Tar-Aiym Krang. 1982. pap. 2.50 (ISBN 0-345-30280-X, Del Rey). Ballantine.

--Voyage to the City of the Dead. (Commonwealth Ser.). 256p. (Orig.). 1984. pap. 2.95 (ISBN 0-345-31215-5, Del Rey). Ballantine.

--Who Needs Enemies? 1984. pap. 2.95 (ISBN 0-345-31657-6, Del Rey). Ballantine.

--With Friends Like These... (A Del Rey Bk). 1977. pap. 1.75 (ISBN 0-345-25701-4). Ballantine.

--With Friends Like These... 256p. Date not set. pap. 2.75 (ISBN 0-345-31189-2, Del Rey). Ballantine.

Foster, Albert B. & Bosworth, Duane. Approved Practices in Soil Conservation. 5th ed. (Illus.). 470p. 1982. 19.95 (ISBN 0-8134-2170-5, 2170); text ed. 14.95x. Interstate.

Foster, Albert J. Bunyan's Country. LC 77-9082. 1977. Repr. of 1901 ed. lib. bdg. 25.00 (ISBN 0-8414-4304-1). Folcroft.

Foster, Allen C., et al. Construction & Design Law Digest. 395.00 (ISBN 0-87215-823-3); Separate bound volume, 1984. 125.00 (ISBN 0-87215-912-4). Michie Co.

Foster, Ann T. Theodore Roethke's Meditative Sequences: Contemplation & the Creative Process. LC 85-3041. (Studies in Art & Religious Interpretation: Vol. 4). 210p. 1985. 49.95x (ISBN 0-88946-555-X). E Mellen.

Foster, Annie H. Makers of History. LC 76-38544. (Biography Index Reprint Ser.). Repr. of 1946 ed. 16.25 (ISBN 0-8369-8121-9). Ayer Co Pubs.

Foster, Anthony M. The Book of Hitchin. 1981. 40.00x (ISBN 0-86023-138-0, Pub. by Barracuda England). State Mutual Bk.

Foster, Arthur L., ed. The House Church Evolving. LC 76-4198. (Studies in Ministry & Parish Life). 126p. 1976. 13.95x (ISBN 0-913552-04-6); pap. 6.95x (ISBN 0-913552-05-4). Exploration Pr.

Foster, Arthur R. & Wright, Robert L., Jr. Basic Nuclear Engineering. 4th ed. 1983. text ed. 44.26x (ISBN 0-205-07886-9, 327886) (ISBN 0-205-05698-9). Allyn.

Foster, Augustus J. Jeffersonian America: Notes on the United States of America Collected in the Years 1805-1807 & 1811-1812. Davis, Richard B., ed. LC 79-17928. 1980. Repr. of 1954 ed. lib. bdg. 32.50x (ISBN 0-313-22076-X, FOJA). Greenwood.

Foster, B. Frank, jt. auth. see Mambert, W. A.

Foster, Benjamin, jt. auth. see Bennett, James A.

Foster, Benjamin R. UMMA in the Sargonic Period. (Connecticut Academy of Arts & Sciences Transaction Ser.: No. 49). (Illus.). xiv, 228p. 1981. 39.50 (ISBN 0-208-01951-0). Shoe String.

Foster, Benjamin R. & Donbaz, Veysel. Sargonic Texts from Telloh in the Istanbul Archaeological Museums. (Publications of the Babylonian Fund: No. 5). (Illus.). xi, 17p. 1982. 20.00 (ISBN 0-934718-44-X). Univ Mus of U PA.

Foster, Betty J. Herculy. 1984. 10.95 (ISBN 0-8062-2337-5). Carlton.

Foster, Betty J., jt. auth. see Krahn, John H.

Foster, Bill. Conditioning for Basketball: A Guide for Coaches & Athletes. LC 81-82403. (Illus.). 208p. (Orig.). 1983. pap. 7.95 (ISBN 0-918438-79-9). Leisure Pr.

Foster, Birket, illus. Christmas with the Poets. (Illus.). 1978. Repr. of 1851 ed. 50.00 (ISBN 0-8492-0090-3). R West.

Foster, Blair. Love's Unearthly Power. 352p. 1983. pap. 3.50 (ISBN 0-8439-2039-4, Leisure Bks). Dorchester Pub Co.

Foster, Blanche F. East Central Africa. LC 80-2684. (First Bks.). (gr. 4 up). 1981. PLB 8.90 (ISBN 0-531-04272-3). Watts.

Foster, Brad, illus. Aesop's Fables Color & Story Album. Townsend, George F., tr. (Illus.). 32p. (Orig.). (gr. 3-8). 1982. pap. 3.95 (ISBN 0-8431-4087-9). Troubador Pr.

Foster, Brian. Commerce & Ethnic Differences: The Case of the Mons in Thailand. (Papers in International Studies: Southeast Asia Ser.: No. 59). 100p. 1982. pap. 10.00x (ISBN 0-89680-112-8, 82-90603, Ohio U Ctr Intl). Ohio U Pr.

Foster, Bruce D., jt. auth. see Stark, Rodney.

Foster, Bryan. Scenic Models. 192p. 1980. 32.95x (ISBN 0-85177-168-8, Pub. by Conway Maritime England). State Mutual Bk.

Foster, Bryan, jt. auth. see Foster, Maureen.

Foster, C. C. Real Time Programming: Neglected Topics. 1981. 9.95 (ISBN 0-201-01937-X). Addison-Wesley.

Foster, C. D., et al. Local Government Finance in a Unitary State. (Illus.). 640p. 1980. text ed. 60.00x (ISBN 0-04-336066-1). Allen Unwin.

Foster, C. E. Showcasing Your Stamp Collection. LC 78-62408. (Illus.). 1978. plastic bdg. 12.00 (ISBN 0-917922-09-3); pap. 10.00 (ISBN 0-917922-08-5). Hobby Pub Serv.

Foster, C. R., et al. Modern Guidance Practices in Teaching. (Illus.). 294p. 1980. 19.75x (ISBN 0-398-03990-9); pap. 14.50x (ISBN 0-398-04040-0). C C Thomas.

Foster, C. W., ed. Calendar of Lincoln Wills, Vol. 1: 1320-1600. (British Record Society Index Library Ser.: Vol. 28). pap. 30.00 (ISBN 0-317-16003-6). Kraus Repr.

--Calendar of Lincoln Wills, Vol. 2: Consistory Court Wills, 1601-1652. (British Record Society Index Library Ser.: Vol. 41). pap. 19.00 (ISBN 0-317-16095-8). Kraus Repr.

--Calendars of Administrations in the Consistory Court of Lincoln: A. D. 1540-1659. (British Record Society Index Library Ser.: Vol. 52). pap. 52.00 (ISBN 0-317-16104-0). Kraus Repr.

--Calendars of Wills & Administrations at Lincoln, Vol. 4: Archdeaconry of Stow. Peculiar Courts & Miscellaneous Courts. (British Record Society Index Library Ser.: Vol. 57). pap. 52.00 (ISBN 0-317-16109-1). Kraus Repr.

Foster, Carno A. Justice in Man. LC 79-190197. 270p. 1972. 12.00 (ISBN 0-8022-2084-3). Philos Lib.

Foster, Carol. Developing Self-Control. 136p. 1974. pap. text ed. 7.00 (ISBN 0-917472-02-0). F Fournies.

Foster, Carol, et al, eds. Gambling-Crime or Recreation? (Instructional Aides Ser.). 78p. 1984. pap. 13.95 (ISBN 0-936474-38-6). Instruct Aides TX.

--Minorities: A Changing Role in American Society. (Instructional Aides Ser.). 90p. 1984. pap. 13.95 (ISBN 0-936474-42-4). Instruct Aides TX.

--Social Welfare: Help or Hindrance. (Instrutional Aides Ser.). 82p. 1984. pap. 13.95 (ISBN 0-936474-43-2). Instruct Aides TX.

Foster, Catherine O. The Organic Gardener. pap. 8.95 (ISBN 0-394-71785-6, V-785, Vin). Random.

Foster, Caxton. Cryptanalysis for Microcomputers. 1983. pap. 16.50 (ISBN 0-8104-5174-3, 5174). Hayden.

Foster, Caxton C. Content Addressable Parallel Processors. (Computer Science Ser.). 233p. 1976. 19.95 (ISBN 0-442-22433-8). Van Nos Reinhold.

--Programming a Microcomputer: 6502. 1978. pap. text ed. 9.95 (ISBN 0-201-01995-7). Addison-Wesley.

Foster, Caxton C. & Iberall, Thea. Computer Architecture. 3rd ed. (Illus.). 384p. 1985. 38.95 (ISBN 0-442-27219-7). Van Nos Reinhold.

Foster, Charles. Dial Artemis. 40p. (Orig.). 1975. pap. 1.95 (ISBN 0-917744-19-5). Aldebaran Rev.

--Home Wine Making, Brewing & Other Drinks. (Illus.). 80p. 1983. pap. 8.95 (ISBN 0-88266-354-2). Garden Way Pub.

--Home Winemaking. (Illus.). 128p. 1975. pap. 7.95x (ISBN 0-8464-0488-5). Beekman Pubs.

--Peyote Toad. LC 75-44699. 1976. perfect bdg. 2.00 (ISBN 0-915214-09-1). Litmus.

--Victoria Mundi. LC 72-96445. (Illus.). 80p. 1973. 4.50 (ISBN 0-912292-29-6). The Smith.

Foster, Charles A., et al. Introduction to the Administration of Justice. 2nd ed. LC 78-13498. (Administration of Justice Ser.). 347p. 1979. text ed. 29.95 (ISBN 0-471-04079-7); study guide 9.95 (ISBN 0-471-05316-3). Wiley.

Foster, Charles H. The Cape Cod National Seashore: A Landmark Alliance. LC 84-40583. (Illus.). 144p. (Orig.). 1985. pap. 8.95 (ISBN 0-87451-346-4). U Pr of New Eng.

--Experiments in Bioregionalism: The New England River Basins Story. LC 83-40554. (Futures of New England Ser.). (Illus.). 249p. 1984. 22.50x (ISBN 0-87451-301-4). U Pr of New Eng.

--Rungless Ladder: Harriet Beecher Stowe & New England Puritanism. LC 79-114086. 278p. 1970. Repr. of 1954 ed. lib. bdg. 18.50 (ISBN 0-8154-0319-4). Cooper Sq.

Foster, Charles H., ed. Benjamin Browne Foster's Down East Diary. 1975. 13.95 (ISBN 0-89101-030-0). U Maine Orono.

--Beyond Concord: Selected Writings of David Atwood Wasson. LC 72-85317. 352p. 1973. Repr. of 1965 ed. 26.00x (ISBN 0-8046-1737-6, Pub. by Kennikat). Assoc Faculty Pr.

Foster, Charles K. The Unknown History of the Jewish People, 2 vols. (Illus.). 247p. 1986. Set. 187.45 (ISBN 0-89901-243-4). Found Class Reprints.

Foster, Charles R. Editorial Treatment of Education in the American Press. LC 71-136384. Repr. of 1938 ed. 24.50 (ISBN 0-404-02519-6). AMS Pr.

--Teaching in the Community of Faith. 160p. (Orig.). 1982. pap. 8.75 (ISBN 0-687-41086-X). Abingdon.

Foster, Charles R., ed. Comparative Public Policy & Citizen Participation: Energy, Education, Health & Local Governance in the U. S. A. & Germany. (Pergamon Policy Studies). 1980. 35.00 (ISBN 0-08-024624-9). Pergamon.

--Nations Without a State: Ethnic Minorities in Western Europe. LC 80-20900. 224p. 1980. 29.95 (ISBN 0-03-056807-2). Praeger.

Foster, Charles R. & Valdman, Albert, eds. Haiti-Today & Tomorrow: An Interdisciplinary Study. (Illus.). 404p. 1985. lib. bdg. 28.50 (ISBN 0-8191-4325-1). U Pr of Amer.

--Haiti-Today & Tomorrow: An Interdisciplinary Study. (Illus.). 404p. (Orig.). 1985. pap. text ed. 17.50 (ISBN 0-8191-4326-X). U Pr of Amer.

Foster, Charles W. The Phonology of the Conjure Tales of Charles W. Chesnutt. (Publications of the American Dialect Society Ser., No. 55). 1971. pap. 5.25 (ISBN 0-8173-0655-2, Am Dialect). U of Ala Pr.

Foster, Christopher & Heath, J. Lessons of Maplin. (Institute of Economic Affairs, Occasional Papers Ser.: No. 40). 1975. technical 4.25 (ISBN 0-255-36053-3). Transatlantic.

Foster, Claude R., et al, trs. see Roehrich, Gustave G.

Foster, Clifford D., jt. auth. see Jarolimek, John.

Foster, Craig. The Scissor Reflex Golf Swing. (Illus.). 124p. (Orig.). 1985. pap. 9.95 (ISBN 0-317-11367-4). Golf Sports Pub.

Foster, Cullison, jt. auth. see Foster, Levy.

Foster, D., jt. auth. see Beek, M.

Foster, D. Lynn & Erven, Bernard L. Foundations for Managing the Farm Business. LC 80-20832. (Agricultural Economics Ser.). 366p. 1981. text ed. 34.95 (ISBN 0-471-84160-9, Pub. by Grid). Wiley.

Foster, David. Dog Rock: A Postal Pastoral. 176p. 1985. pap. 4.95 (ISBN 0-14-007652-2). Penguin.

--Innovation & Employment. 1980. o. p. 29.00 (ISBN 0-08-022500-4); pap. 12.00 (ISBN 0-08-022499-7). Pergamon.

--A Primer for Writing Teachers: Theories, Theorists, Issues, Problems. 192p. (Orig.). 1983. pap. text ed. 9.75x (ISBN 0-86709-053-7). Boynton Cook Pubs.

Foster, David, ed. Latin American Government Leaders. LC 75-15809. 135p. 1975. 8.00x. ASU Lat Am St.

Foster, David E. Revision of North American Trichodes (Herbst) (Coleoptera: Cleridae) (Special Publications: No. 11). (Illus.). 86p. 1976. pap. 4.00 (ISBN 0-89672-037-3). Tex Tech Pr.

Foster, David W. Alternate Voices in the Contemporary Latin American Narrative. LC 85-1411. 192p. 1985. text ed. 22.00x (ISBN 0-8262-0481-3). U of Mo Pr.

--The Argentine Teatro Independiente, 1930-1955. LC 84-50801. (Illus.). 180p. 1985. 19.00x (ISBN 0-938972-08-1). Spanish Lit Pubns.

--Christian Allegory in Early Hispanic Poetry. LC 76-111508. (Studies in Romance Languages: No. 4). 148p. 1970. 14.00x (ISBN 0-8131-1230-3). U Pr of Ky.

--Cuban Literature: An Annotated Bibliography. LC 84-48099. (Reference Library of the Humanities). 1984. lib. bdg. 72.50 (ISBN 0-8240-8903-0). Garland Pub.

--Currents in the Contemporary Argentine Novel: Arlt, Mallea, Sabato, & Cortazar. LC 74-30083. 167p. 1975. 13.00x (ISBN 0-8262-0176-8). U of Mo Pr.

--The Early Spanish Ballad. (World Authors Ser.). lib. bdg. 14.50 (ISBN 0-8057-2288-2, Twayne). G K Hall.

--Estudios sobre Teatro Mexicano Contemporaneo: Semiologia de la Competencia Teatral. LC 84-47536. (Utah Studies in Literature & Linguistics: Vol. 25). (Orig., Span.). 1984. text ed. 19.00 (ISBN 0-8204-0125-0). P Lang Pubs.

--Jorge Luis Borges: An Annotated Primary & Secondary Bibliography. LC 83-48271. (Reference Library of the Humanities). 250p. 1984. lib. bdg. 36.00 (ISBN 0-8240-9075-6). Garland Pub.

--Mexican Literature: A Bibliography of Secondary Sources. LC 81-8871. 412p. 1981. 25.00 (ISBN 0-8108-1449-8). Scarecrow.

--The Myth of Paraguay in the Fiction of Augusto Roa Bastos. (Studies in the Romance Languages & Literatures: No. 80). 88p. 1969. pap. 6.00x (ISBN 0-8078-9080-4). U of NC Pr.

--Peruvian Literature: A Bibliography of Secondary Sources. LC 81-6957. 352p. 1981. lib. bdg. 45.00 (ISBN 0-313-23097-8, FPL/). Greenwood.

--Puerto Rican Literature: A Bibliography of Secondary Sources. LC 82-6198. xxiii, 232p. 1982. lib. bdg. 35.00 (ISBN 0-313-23419-1, FPR/). Greenwood.

--Research Guide ot Argentine Literature. LC 82-3035. 788p. 1982. lib. bdg. 110.00 (ISBN 0-8240-9397-6). Garland Pub.

--Sourcebook of Hispanic Culture in the U. S. A. 1982p. lib. bdg. 32.00x (ISBN 0-8389-0354-1). ALA.

--Studies in the Contemporary Spanish-American Short Story. LC 79-1558. 144p. 1979. text ed. 15.50x (ISBN 0-8262-0279-9). U of Mo Pr.

--Twentieth Century Spanish-American Novel: A Bibliographic Guide. LC 75-25787. 234p. 1975. 16.00 (ISBN 0-8108-0871-4). Scarecrow.

--Unamuno & the Novel as Expressionistic Conceit. LC 73-75405. 52p. (Orig.). 1973. pap. 2.50 (ISBN 0-913480-15-0). Inter Am U Pr.

Foster, David W. & Foster, Virginia R. Manual of Hispanic Bibliography. 2nd ed. (Reference Library of the Humanities: Vol. 85). (LC 76-052672). 1977. lib. bdg. 48.00 (ISBN 0-8240-9888-9). Garland Pub.

Foster, David W., jt. auth. see Rosales, F. Arturo.

Foster, David W., ed. Chilean Literature: A Working Bibliography of Secondary Sources. (Reference Publications). 1978. lib. bdg. 32.50 (ISBN 0-8161-8180-2, Hall Reference). G K Hall.

--Dictionary of Contemporary Latin American Authors. LC 75-17988. 250p. 1975. pap. 6.95x (ISBN 0-87918-021-8). ASU Lat Am St.

Foster, David W. & Foster, Virginia R., eds. Modern Latin American Literature, 2 vols. LC 72-81710. (A Library of Literary Criticism). 1100p. 1975. Set. 120.00 (ISBN 0-8044-3139-6). Ungar.

Foster, David W. & Reis, Roberto, eds. A Dictionary of Contemporary Brazilian Authors. LC 79-29686. 152p. 1982. 18.95x (ISBN 0-87918-051-X); pap. 11.95x (ISBN 0-686-97323-2). ASU Lat Am St.

Foster, David W., tr. from Span. The Duke: Memories & Anti-Memoirs of a Participant in the Repression. (Third World Literature Ser.). 128p. 1985. pap. 6.95 (ISBN 0-86232-410-6, Pub. by Zed Pr England). Biblio Dist.

Foster, Dennis. Career Synthesis: The Art & Science of Work Fulfillment. 185p. (Orig.). 1984. pap. 9.95 (ISBN 0-89769-081-8, Dist. by Caroline Hse). Pine Mntn.

Foster, Dennis L. The Practical Guide to the IBM Personal Computer AT. LC 85-1249. 1985. 19.95 (ISBN 0-201-12040-2). Addison-Wesley.

Foster, Dennis L. & D. L. Foster Book Company Editors. The Addison-Wesley Book of Apple Software 1985. 416p. 1985. pap. 19.95 (ISBN 0-201-12018-6). Addison-Wesley.

--The Addison-Wesley Book of Atari Software 1985. 416p. 1985. pap. 19.95 (ISBN 0-201-12019-4). Addison-Wesley.

--The Addison-Wesley Book of Commodore Software 1985. 416p. 1985. pap. 19.95 (ISBN 0-201-12020-8). Addison-Wesley.

--The Addison-Wesley Book of IBM Software 1985. 416p. 1985. pap. 19.95 (ISBN 0-201-12021-6). Addison-Wesley.

Foster, Don. Three Oaks. 1976. 7.95 (ISBN 0-915626-08-X). Yellow Jacket.

Foster, Donald L. Managing the Catalog Department. 2nd ed. LC 81-16694. 244p. 1982. 16.00 (ISBN 0-8108-1486-2). Scarecrow.

Foster, Douglas. Marketing Imperative. 1974. 16.95x (ISBN 0-8464-0609-8). Beekman Pubs.

Foster, Durwood, jt. ed. see Bryant, Darrol.

Foster, Durwood, jt. ed. see Mojzes, Paul.

Foster, E. M., et al. Dairy Microbiology. xviii, 492p. 1983. lib. bdg. 32.00x (ISBN 0-917930-78-9); pap. text ed. 20.00x (ISBN 0-917930-64-9). Ridgeview.

Foster, Edgar E. An Outline of Foreign Policy for the United States. 1949. 9.50 (ISBN 0-912314-02-8); pap. 2.25 (ISBN 0-912314-01-X). Academy Santa Clara.

Foster, Edward. Mary E. Wilkins Freeman. 238p. 1956. 10.00 (ISBN 0-87532-058-9). Hendricks House.

Foster, Edward H. The Civilized Wilderness: Backgrounds to American Literature, 1817-1860. LC 74-33091. (Illus.). 1975. 12.95 (ISBN 0-02-910350-9). Free Pr.

--Josiah Gregg & Lewis H. Garrard. LC 77-76324. (Western Writers Ser: No. 28). (Illus.). 1977. pap. 2.00x (ISBN 0-88430-052-8). Boise St Univ.

--Richard Brautigan. (United States Authors Ser.). 1983. lib. bdg. 15.95 (ISBN 0-8057-7378-9, Twayne). G K Hall.

--William Saroyan. LC 84-70249. (Western Writers Ser.: No. 61). (Orig.). 1984. pap. 2.00x (ISBN 0-88430-035-8). Boise St Univ.

Foster, Elizabeth. Gigi in America: The Further Adventures of a Merry-Go-Round Horse. (Illus.). 130p. (gr. 4-8). pap. 9.95 (ISBN 0-913028-69-X). North Atlantic.

--Gigi: The Story of a Merry-Go-Round Horse. (Illus.). 124p. (gr. 4-8). pap. 9.95 (ISBN 0-913028-55-X). North Atlantic.

Foster, Elizabeth A., tr. see Motolinia, Toribio.

Foster, Elizabeth R. The House of Lords, 1603-1649: Structure, Procedure, & the Nature of Its Business. LC 82-6909. x, 347p. 1983. 32.00x (ISBN 0-8078-1533-0). U of NC Pr.

--The Painful Labour of Mr. Elsyng. LC 72-89400. (Transactions Ser.: Vol. 62, Pt. 8). 1972. pap. 3.00 (ISBN 0-87169-628-2). Am Philos.

Foster, Elizabeth R., ed. Proceedings in Parliament Sixteen Ten, 2 vols. Incl. Vol. 1. The House of Lords. (Illus.). lxix, 366p; Vol. 2. The House of Commons. (Illus.). xxi, 422p. (Historical Publications, Manuscripts & Edited Texts Ser.: No. 22 & 23). 1966. Yale U Pr.

Foster, Elizabeth S. Tutoring: Learning by Helping. rev. ed. Sorenson, Don L., ed. LC 83-80004. (Illus.). 224p. (YA) (gr. 9 up). 1983. pap. text ed. 7.95x (ISBN 0-932796-13-3). Ed Media Corp.

Foster, Elizabeth S., ed. see Melville, Herman.

Foster, Ellery. The Coming Age of Conscience. (Illus.). 1977. pap. 2.00 (ISBN 0-686-21778-0). Sandrock & Foster.

Foster, Ellwood. Inspirationally Yours. LC 80-53330. 1984. 5.95 (ISBN 0-533-04843-5). Vantage.

Foster, Elma W. Sound of Shadows. LC 71-179822. (New Poetry Ser.). Repr. of 1960 ed. 16.00 (ISBN 0-404-56022-9). AMS Pr.

Foster, Eric & Ralston, Trudy. How to Display It: A Basic Guide to Window & Interior Displays. LC 84-72470. 123p. 1985. 12.50 (ISBN 0-88108-017-9). Art Dir.

Foster, Ethan see Cartland, Fernando G.

Foster, Ethel M., ed. see Foster, Joshua J.

Foster, Eugene S. Understanding Broadcasting. 2nd ed. (Illus.). 544p. 1982. pap. text ed. 25.95 (ISBN 0-394-35000-6, RanC). Random.

Foster, F. F. The Politics of Stability: A Portrait of the Rulers in Elizabethan London. (Royal Historical Society-Studies in History Ser.: Vol.1). 209p. 1977. text ed. 29.00x (ISBN 0-901050-31-8, Pub. by Swiftbks England). Humanities.

Foster, F. Gordon. Ferns to Know & Grow. (Illus.). 228p. 1984. Repr. of 1964 ed. 29.95 (ISBN 0-917304-98-5). Timber.

Foster, Finley M. English Translations from the Greek. LC 70-168127. Repr. of 1918 ed. 15.00 (ISBN 0-404-02541-2). AMS Pr.

Foster, Frances S., ed. Witnessing Slavery: The Development of the Ante-Bellum Slave Narratives. LC 78-22137. (Contributions in African & Afro-American Studies: No. 46). lib. bdg. 27.50 (ISBN 0-313-20821-2, FWS/). Greenwood.

Foster, Frank, jt. auth. see Mambert, W. A.

Foster, Frank H. Modern Movement in American Theology. facs. ed. LC 76-86751. (Essay Index Reprint Ser). 1939. 14.50 (ISBN 0-8369-1131-8). Ayer Co Pubs.

Foster, Fred B. & Foster, Linda. Guardian One: The Answers. 224p. 1984. pap. 9.95 (ISBN 0-9613762-0-1). F B Foster Pubns.

--Guardian Two: The Answers Continued. (Orig.). Date not set. pap. price not set (ISBN 0-9613762-1-X). F B Foster Pubns.

Foster, Fred J. Their Story: Twentieth Century Pentecostals. Wallace, Mary H., ed. (Illus.). 192p. 1983. pap. 4.95 (ISBN 0-912315-05-9). Word Aflame.

Foster, G. Allen. Eyes & Ears of the Civil War. LC 63-19084. (Illus.). (gr. 7 up). 1963. 10.53i (ISBN 0-200-00087-X, 322410, AbS-J). Har-Row.

Foster, G. M. Tzintzuntzan. rev. ed. 416p. 1979. pap. 15.50 (ISBN 0-444-99070-4). Elsevier.

Foster, G. M., et al. Medical Anthropology. 354p. 1978. text ed. 30.95 (ISBN 0-394-34403-0, RandC). Random.

Foster, Genevieve. George Washington's World. 344p. 15.00 (ISBN 0-317-34930-9). Mt Vernon Ladies.

--Nineteen Hundred Three: Year of the Flying Machine. LC 77-9074. (Encore Edition). (Illus.). (gr. 2-6). 1977. reinforced bdg. 2.49 (ISBN 0-684-17735-8, ScribJ). Scribner.

--Theodore Roosevelt: An Initial Biography. (Illus.). (gr. 5-7). 1954. 5.95 (ISBN 0-684-12690-7, ScribJ). Scribner.

--The World Was Flooded with Light: A Mystical Experience Remembered. LC 84-22013. 216p. 1985. 14.95 (ISBN 0-8229-3512-0). U of Pittsburgh Pr.

--Year of Columbus, 1492. LC 77-85268. (Illus.). (gr. 2-6). 1969. 5.95 (ISBN 0-684-12695-8, ScribJ). Scribner.

--Year of the Horseless Carriage. LC 74-29161. (Encore Edition). (Illus.). 96p. (gr. 4-7). 1975. reinforced bdg. 1.79 (ISBN 0-684-14198-1, ScribJ). Scribner.

Foster, Genevieve W., et al. Child Care Work with Emotionally Disturbed Children. LC 74-158185. (Contemporary Community Health Ser.). 1971. 23.95x (ISBN 0-8229-3231-8). U of Pittsburgh Pr.

--Child Care Work with Emotionally Disturbed Children. LC 74-158185. (Contemporary Community Health Ser.). 310p. 1982. pap. 7.95x (ISBN 0-8229-5335-8). U of Pittsburgh Pr.

Foster, George. Financial Statement Analysis. (Illus.). 1978. 35.95 (ISBN 0-13-316273-7). P-H.

Foster, George, jt. auth. see Drucker, Malka.

Foster, George, et al, eds. Long-Term Field Research in Social Anthropology. (Academic Press Studies in Anthropology Ser.). 1979. 39.50 (ISBN 0-12-263350-4). Acad Pr.

Foster, George B. & Reese, Curtis W. Friedrich Nietzsche. 250p. 1981. Repr. of 1931 ed. lib. bdg. 40.00 (ISBN 0-89760-226-9). Telegraph Bks.

Foster, George E. Se-Quo-Yah, the American Cadmus & Modern Moses. LC 76-43709. (Illus.). Repr. of 1885 ed. 23.50 (ISBN 0-685-77713-8). AMS Pr.

Foster, George M. Empire's Children: The People of Tzintzuntzan. LC 73-118760. (Illus.). 297p. 1973. Repr. of 1948 ed. lib. bdg. 35.00x (ISBN 0-8371-5077-9, SMIG). Greenwood.

--Pops Foster: The Autobiography of a New Orleans Jazzman. Stoddard, Tom, as told to. LC 75-132414. 1971. 16.95 (ISBN 0-520-01826-5); pap. 3.45 (ISBN 0-520-02355-2). U of Cal Pr.

--A Primitive Mexican Economy. LC 81-23759. (Monographs of the American Ethnological Society: No. 5.). (Illus.). vii, 115p. 1982. Repr. of 1966 ed. lib. bdg. 22.50x (ISBN 0-313-23405-1, FOPM). Greenwood.

--Problems in Intercultural Health Programs. LC 58-10873. 1958. pap. 1.00 (ISBN 0-527-03300-6). Kraus Repr.

--Traditional Societies & Technological Change. 2nd ed. 300p. 1973. pap. text ed. 14.50 scp (ISBN 0-06-042129-0, HarpC). Har-Row.

Foster, George N. Lawyers Legal Search. LC 85-60263. (Legal Bibliographic & Research Reprint Ser.: Vol. 6). v, 104p. 1985. Repr. of 1920 ed. lib. bdg. 28.50 (ISBN 0-89941-399-4). W S Hein.

Foster, Gerald. Cult of the Harley-Davidson. (Osprey Color Ser.). (Illus.). 128p. 1982. pap. 11.95 (ISBN 0-85045-463-8, Pub. by Osprey England). Motorbooks Intl.

--Ride It: The Complete Book of Flat Track Racing. (Drive it! Ride it! Ser.). 155p. 9.95 (ISBN 0-85429-232-2, F232). Haynes Pubns.

Foster, Gregory D., jt. auth. see Yarmolinsky, Adam.

Foster, H. Daily Thoughts on Bible Characters. 1971. pap. 4.95 (ISBN 0-87508-196-7). Chr Lit.

--A Gringo in Manana Land. 1976. lib. bdg. 59.95 (ISBN 0-8490-1907-9). Gordon Pr.

Foster, H. D. Disaster Planning: The Preservation of Life & Property. (Springer Series on Environmental Management). (Illus.). 275p. 1981. 36.00 (ISBN 0-387-90498-0). Springer-Verlag.

Foster, H. Lincoln. Rock Gardening: A Guide to Growing Alpines & Other Wildflowers in the American Garden. LC 82-16994. (Illus.). 466p. 1982. pap. 22.95 (ISBN 0-917304-29-2). Timber.

Foster, H. S. Activism Replaces Isolationism: U. S. Public Attitudes 1940-1975. LC 83-81284. 420p. 1983. 14.95 (ISBN 0-9611128-1-6). Foxhall Pr.

Foster, Hal. The Minks' Cry. LC 83-70650. (Illus.). 108p. (Orig.). (gr. 3 up). 1982. 8.95 (ISBN 0-941920-00-3). Bay Pr.

--Prince Valiant-An American Epic, Vol. I. LC 82-17919. (Prince Valiant Ser.). 56p. 1982. 100.00 (ISBN 0-936414-04-9). Manuscript Pr.

--Prince Valiant: An American Epic, Vol. 2. Norwood, Rick, ed. (The Complete Prince Valiant Ser.: Bk. 2). (Illus.). 60p. (Orig.). 1984. pap. 100.00 (ISBN 0-936414-05-7). Manuscript Pr.

--Prince Valiant: Queen of the Misty Isles. Kaler, David, ed. LC 77-73489. (Illus.). 1978. 14.95 (ISBN 0-87897-023-1). Nostalgia Pr.

--Recodings: Art, Spectacle, Cultural Politics. LC 85-70184. (Illus.). 176p. 1985. 14.95 (ISBN 0-941920-03-8); pap. 9.95 (ISBN 0-941920-04-6). Bay Pr.

Foster, Hal & Kardon, Janet. Connections: Ladders, Bridges, Staircases. (Illus.). 1983. 10.00 (ISBN 0-88454-032-4). U of PA Contemp Art.

Foster, Hal & Trell, Max. Prince Valiant & the Golden Princess. LC 77-89913. (Illus.). 120p. 1976. 7.95 (ISBN 0-87897-005-3). Nostalgia Pr.

--Prince Valiant & the Three Challenges, Vol. 7. LC 77-89916. (Illus.). 1978. 7.95 (ISBN 0-87897-007-X). Nostalgia Pr.

--Prince Valiant Fights Attila the Hun, Vol. 2. LC 77-89910. (Illus.). 1978. 7.95 (ISBN 0-87897-048-7). Nostalgia Pr.

--Prince Valiant in the Days of King Arthur, Vol. 1. LC 77-89908. (Illus.). 1978. 7.95 (ISBN 0-87897-001-0). Nostalgia Pr.

--Prince Valiant in the New World. LC 77-89915. (Illus.). 128p. 1976. 7.95 (ISBN 0-87897-006-1). Nostalgia Pr.

--Prince Valiant on the Inland Sea, Vol. 3. LC 77-89911. (Illus.). 1978. 7.95 (ISBN 0-87897-003-7). Nostalgia Pr.

--Prince Valiant's Perilous Voyage. LC 77-89912. (Illus.). 128p. 1976. 7.95 (ISBN 0-87897-004-5). Nostalgia Pr.

Foster, Hal, ed. The Anti-Aesthetic: Essays on Postmodern Culture. LC 83-70650. (Illus.). 176p. (Orig.). 1983. o.s.i 13.95 (ISBN 0-941920-02-X); pap. 8.95 (ISBN 0-941920-01-1). Bay Pr.

Foster, Hannah see Brown, William H.

Foster, Hannah W. The Coquette. LC 72-78707. 1797. Repr. 39.00x (ISBN 0-403-01949-4). Somerset Pub.

Foster, Harold. Prince Valiant: Adventures in Two Worlds. Kaler, David A., ed. LC 77-73490. (Illus.). 1978. 14.95 (ISBN 0-87897-024-X). Nostalgia Pr.

Foster, Harold M. The New Literacy: The Language of Film & Television. LC 79-141592. 1979. pap. 3.85 (ISBN 0-8141-3333-9). NCTE.

Foster, Harry. The Secret of Daniel's Strength. Fang, Carl, tr. from Eng. 97p. (Chinese.). 1983. pap. write for info (ISBN 0-941598-05-5). Living Spring Pubns.

Foster, Helen. It's Hard to Look Graceful When You're Dragging Your Feet. 134p. 1983. 9.95 (ISBN 0-8138-0811-1). Iowa St U Pr.

Foster, Henry & Fox, James, eds. The Mouse in Biomedical Research: Vol. 3, Normative Biology, Immunology & Husbandry. 390p. 1983. 83.00 (ISBN 0-12-262503-X). Acad Pr.

Foster, Henry, et al, eds. The Mouse in Biomedical Research: Vol. 2, Diseases. LC 80-70669. (American College of Laboratory Animal Medicine Ser.). 1982. 80.00 (ISBN 0-12-262502-1). Acad Pr.

Foster, Henry H. & Freed, Doris J. Law & the Family-New York, 2 Vols. LC 66-5920. 1885p. 139.00. Lawyers Co-Op.

Foster, Henry H., jt. auth. see Davis, Floyd J.

Foster, Henry H., Jr., ed. A Practical Guide to the New York Equitable Distribution Divorce Law. 771p. 1980. 35.00 (ISBN 0-686-89094-9, C00566, Law & Business). HarBraceJ.

Foster, Henry Hubbard & Brown, Ronald L. Contemporary Matrimonial Law Issues: A Guide to Divorce Economics & Practice. LC 85-10894. 1985. 49.00 (ISBN 0-15-004394-5). HarBraceJ.

Foster, Henry, Jr. A Bill of Rights for Children. 96p. 1974. pap. 7.75x (ISBN 0-398-02986-5). C C Thomas.

Foster, Henry L., et al, eds. The Mouse in Biomedical Research: Vol. 4, Experimental Biology & Oncology. 545p. 1982. 90.00 (ISBN 0-12-262504-8). Acad Pr.

--The Mouse in Biomedical Research: Vol. 1, History Genetics & Wild Mice. LC 80-70669. (ACLAM Ser.). 1981. 65.00 (ISBN 0-12-262501-3). Acad Pr.

Foster, Herbert L. Ribbin' Jivin & Playin' the Dozens: The Persistence Dilemma of Inner City. 2nd ed. 3776p. 1985. pap. 16.95 (ISBN 0-88410-982-8). Ballinger Pub.

--Ribbin', Jivin', & Playin' the Dozens: The Unrecognized Dilemma of Inner-City Schools. LC 74-7393. 384p. 1974. pap. 12.95 (ISBN 0-88410-163-0). Ballinger Pub.

Foster, Hope S., jt. auth. see Halper, H. Robert.

Foster, J. & Robinson, H., eds. Essays on Berkeley. 224p. 1985. 29.95 (ISBN 0-19-824734-6). Oxford U Pr.

Foster, J., jt. ed. see Colwell, Rita R.

Foster, J. B., jt. ed. see Horler, A. R.

Foster, J. Bristol, jt. auth. see Dagg, Anne I.

Foster, J. J., jt. auth. see Bridger, J. P.

Foster, J. M. Automatic Syntactic Analysis. (Computer Monograph Ser.: Vol. 7). 65p. 1970. 40.00 (ISBN 0-444-19725-7). Elsevier.

Foster, J. R. History of the Pre-Romantic Novel in England. (MLA MS). 1949. 24.00 (ISBN 0-527-30600-2). Kraus Repr.

Foster, J. R., tr. see Frossard, Andre & Pope John Paul II.

Foster, J. R., tr. see Gernet, Jacques.

Foster, J. R., tr. see Mayeur, Jean-Marie & Reberioux, Madeleine.

Foster, Jack S. Structure & Fabric, 2 pts. LC 78-53853. (Mitchell's Building Construction Ser.). 1978. Pt. 1, 264p. pap. 17.95x (ISBN 0-470-26348-2). Halsted Pr.

Foster, James C. The Ideology of Apolitical Politics: Elite Lawyers' Response to the Crisis of Liberal-Capitalism, 1870-1920. LC 84-6172. 136p. Date not set. text ed. 14.00x (ISBN 0-8046-9363-3, 9363, Natl U). Assoc Faculty Pr.

--The Union Politic: The CIO Political Action Committee. LC 74-22240. 257p. 1975. 21.00x (ISBN 0-8262-0171-7). U of Mo Pr.

Foster, James C., ed. American Labor in the Southwest: The First 100 Years. LC 81-21819. 236p. 1982. 18.50x (ISBN 0-8165-0741-4); pap. 9.85x (ISBN 0-8165-0758-9). U of Ariz Pr.

Foster, James C., et al. Elusive Equality: Liberalism, Affirmative Action, & Social Change in America. 163p. 1983. 16.50x (ISBN 0-8046-9309-9, 5309, Natl U). Assoc Faculty Pr.

Foster, James S. Outlines of History of the Territory of Dakota: And Emigrant's Guide to the Free Lands of the Northwest. facsimile ed. LC 77-165632. (Select Bibliographies Reprint Ser). Repr. of 1870 ed. 13.00 (ISBN 0-8369-5939-6). Ayer Co Pubs.

Foster, James W. George Calvert: The Early Years. 110p. 1983. 4.95 (ISBN 0-938420-24-0). Md Hist.

Foster, Jan. An Unamerican Lady. (Illus.). 253p. 1983. (Pub. by Sidgwick & Jackson); pap. 7.95 (ISBN 0-283-98711-1). Merrimack Pub Cir.

Foster, Jean & Eckard, Eugenia. Family Planning Visits by Teenagers: United States,1978. Cox, Klaudia, ed. (Series Thirteen: No. 58). 45p. 1981. pap. 1.75 (ISBN 0-8406-0227-8). Natl Ctr Health Stats.

Foster, Jean & Kleinman, Joel. Adjusting Neonatal Mortality Rates for Birth Weight: Series 2, No. 94. Shipp, Audrey, ed. 55p. 1982. pap. text ed. 1.75 (ISBN 0-8406-0254-5). Natl Ctr Health Stats.

Foster, Jeanne. Deborah Leigh. (Frontier Women Saga: No. 2). 352p. 1981. pap. 2.95 (ISBN 0-449-14437-2, GM). Fawcett.

--Missouri Flame: Deborah Leigh. (Frontier Woman Saga Ser.: No. 2). 1982. pap. 2.95 (ISBN 0-686-87391-2, GM). Fawcett.

--Woman of Three Worlds. 320p. (Orig.). 1984. pap. 3.50 (ISBN 0-449-12500-9, GM). Fawcett.

--Wyoming Glory. (Eden Richards, The Frontier Women Saga Ser.: Vol. IV). 288p. (Orig.). 1982. pap. 2.95 (ISBN 0-449-14482-8, GM). Fawcett.

Foster, Jeanne R. Awakening Grace, Poems at the Feet of the Silent Master. Shaw, Jeanne & Shaw, Darwin, eds. (Illus.). 1977. 4.95x (ISBN 0-913078-28-X). Sheriar Pr.

Foster, Jeannette H. Sex Variant Women in Literature. 448p. 1985. pap. 8.95 (ISBN 0-930044-65-7). Naiad Pr.

Foster, Jeannette H., tr. see Vivien, Renee.

Foster, Jerry, jt. auth. see Berkeley, William D.

Foster, Joan. Reader in Children's Librarianship. 450p. 1978. 28.50 (ISBN 0-313-24039-6, ZRG/). Greenwood.

Foster, John. Ayer. (Arguments of the Philosophers Ser.). 384p. 1985. 32.95x (ISBN 0-7102-0602-X). Routledge & Kegan.

--The Case for Idealism: International Library of Philosophy. 280p. 1982. 25.00x (ISBN 0-7100-9019-6). Routledge & Kegan.

--Critical Essays, 2 vols. 1860. 75.00 set (ISBN 0-932062-59-8). Sharon Hill.

--Napoleon's Marshal: The Life of Michel Ney. (Illus.). (gr. 7 up). 1968. 11.25 (ISBN 0-688-21606-4). Morrow.

--A Second Poetry Book. (Illus.). 128p. 1982. 10.95 (ISBN 0-19-918137-3, Pub. by Oxford U Pr Childrens); pap. 4.95 (ISBN 0-19-918136-5). Merrimack Pub Cir.

Foster, John & Goldsborough, June. Christian ABC Book. (Illus.). 1982. 6.95 (ISBN 0-911346-05-8). Christianica.

Foster, John, compiled by. Shakespeare Word-Book, Being a Glossary of Archaic Forms & Varied Usages of Words Employed by Shakespeare. LC 68-15123. 1969. Repr. of 1908 ed. 17.50x (ISBN 0-8462-1234-X). Russell.

Foster, John, et al. Energy for Development: An International Challenge. LC 81-8683. 304p. 1981. 43.95x (ISBN 0-03-059917-2). Praeger.

--Energy for Development: An International Challenge. 304p. 1981. 29.95 (ISBN 0-318-16148-6); pap. 9.95 (ISBN 0-318-16149-4). Overseas Dev Council.

Foster, John B. The Theory of Monopoly Capitalism: An Elaboration of Marxian Political Economy. 288p. (Orig.). 1985. 26.00 (ISBN 0-85345-688-7); pap. 10.00 (ISBN 0-85345-689-5). Monthly Rev.

Foster, John B. & Szlajfer, Henryk. The Faltering Economy: The Problem of Accumulation under Monopoly Capitalism. 320p. 1984. 28.00 (ISBN 0-85345-603-8); pap. 12.50 (ISBN 0-85345-604-6). Monthly Rev.

Foster, John B., Jr. Heirs to Dionysus: A Nietzschean Current in Literary Modernism. LC 81-47127. 450p. 1981. 30.00 (ISBN 0-691-06480-6). Princeton U Pr.

Foster, John L. A First Poetry Book. (Illus.). 128p. 1982. 10.95 (ISBN 0-19-918113-6, Pub. by Oxford U Pr Childrens); pap. 4.95 (ISBN 0-19-918112-8). Merrimack Pub Cir.

--A Fourth Poetry Book. (Poetry Anthologies). (Illus.). 144p. (gr. 4-7). 1983. 10.95 (ISBN 0-19-918152-7, Pub by Oxford U Pr Childrens); pap. 4.95 (ISBN 0-19-918151-9). Merrimack Pub Cir.

--A Third Poetry Book. (Poetry Anthologies). (Illus.). 144p. (gr. 3-6). 1983. 10.95 (ISBN 0-19-918140-3, Pub by Oxford U Pr Childrens); pap. 4.95 (ISBN 0-19-918139-X). Merrimack Pub Cir.

Foster, John L., jt. auth. see Henderson, Thomas A.

Foster, John L., ed. Reluctant to Read? 176p. 1981. 18.00x (ISBN 0-7062-3642-4, Pub. by Ward Lock Ed England). State Mutual Bk.

Foster, John L., et al. National Policy Game: A Simulation of the American Political Process. LC 74-3411. 108p. 1975. text ed. 16.50x (ISBN 0-471-26775-9). Wiley.

Foster, John M. Hell in the Heavens: A Marine Fighter Pilot's Story. 1983. Repr. of 1961 ed. 16.95 (ISBN 0-89201-098-3). Zenger Pub.

Foster, John S. & Harington, Raymond. Structure & Fabric. (Mitchell's Building Ser.). (Illus., Orig.). 1983. Vol. 1 288 pgs. pap. 16.95 (ISBN 0-7134-3863-0, Pub. by Batsford England); Vol. 2 456 pgs. pap. 21.00 (ISBN 0-7134-3865-7, Pub. by Batsford England). David & Charles.

Foster, John T. Savannah. (Orig.). 1982. pap. 3.50 (ISBN 0-89083-953-0). Zebra.

--Vicksburg. 1981. pap. 2.95 (ISBN 0-89083-789-9). Zebra.

Foster, John W. American Diplomacy in the Orient. LC 74-112309. (Law, Politics, & History Ser). 1970. Repr. of 1903 ed. lib. bdg. 55.00 (ISBN 0-306-71915-0). Da Capo.

--Arbitration & the Hague Court. vi, 148p. 1980. Repr. of 1904 ed. lib. bdg. 18.50x (ISBN 0-8377-0535-5). Rothman.

--Century of American Diplomacy. LC 79-87542. (American History, Politics & Law Ser). 1970. Repr. of 1900 ed. lib. bdg. 55.00 (ISBN 0-306-71458-2). Da Capo.

Foster, Mrs. Jonathan, tr. see Conde, Jose A.

Foster, Joseph, tr. see Obaldia, Rene de.

Foster, Joseph G., tr. see Glissant, Edouard.

Foster, Joseph J., III & Foster, T. L. How To Change Your Life for the Better. LC 85-70676. 104p. 1985. pap. 6.95 (ISBN 0-931494-69-9). Brunswick Pub.

Foster, Joseph W., 3rd, et al. Reliability, Availability & Maintainability: RAM. LC 80-81873. 272p. 1982. Repr. of 1981 ed. 39.95 (ISBN 0-930206-05-3). M-A Pr.

Foster, Josephine & Anderson, John. The Young Child & His Parents. LC 73-141546. (Univ. of Minnesota Institute of Child Welfare Monographs: No. 1). (Illus.). 190p. 1975. Repr. of 1927 ed. lib. bdg. 17.50x (ISBN 0-8371-5893-1, CWFY). Greenwood.

Foster, Joshua J. A Dictionary of Painters of Miniatures, 1525-1850 with Some Account of Exhibitions, Collections, Sales, Etc. Foster, Ethel M., ed. 1967. Repr. of 1926 ed. 29.50 (ISBN 0-8337-1218-7). B Franklin.

Foster, Judy, jt. auth. see Porter, Kay.

Foster, Julia A., jt. auth. see Lund, Shirley.

Foster, K. Minoan Ceramic Relief. (Studies in Mediterranean Archaeology: No. LXIV). 196p. 1982. pap. text ed. 69.50x (ISBN 91-86098-08-X, Pub. by Paul Astroms Sweden). Humanities.

Foster, K. Neill. The Discerning Christian. 104p. (Orig.). 1982. 6.95 (ISBN 0-87509-312-4); pap. 3.95 (ISBN 0-87509-316-7). Chr Pubns.

Foster, Kenelm. Petrarch: An Introduction to the Canzoniere. 194p. 1984. 18.00 (ISBN 0-85224-485-1, Pub. by Edinburgh Pr Scotland). Columbia U Pr.

--The Two Dantes & Other Studies. LC 76-24581. 1978. 31.00x (ISBN 0-520-03326-4). U of Cal Pr.

Foster, Kenelm & Boyde, Patrick, eds. Cambridge Readings in Dante's Comedy. LC 81-3861. 220p. 1982. 44.50 (ISBN 0-521-24140-5). Cambridge U Pr.

Foster, Kurt, ed. Oppositions 25: Monument-Memory. 144p. 1982. pap. 15.00 (ISBN 0-8478-5359-4). Rizzoli Intl.

Foster, Laurence. Negro-Indian Relationships in the Southeast. LC 76-43708. Repr. of 1935 ed. 14.50 (ISBN 0-404-15543-X). AMS Pr.

Foster, Lawrence. Religion & Sexuality: The Shakers, the Mormons, & the Oneida Community. LC 83-18315. 384p. 1984. pap. 9.95x (ISBN 0-252-01119-8). U of Ill Pr.

--Religion & Sexuality: Three American Communal Experiments of the Nineteenth Century. 1981. 21.95x (ISBN 0-19-502794-9). Oxford U Pr.

Foster, Lawrence, jt. auth. see Foster, Lynn V.

Foster, Lawrence & Swanson, J. W., eds. Experience & Theory. LC 77-103472. 176p. 1970. 12.00x (ISBN 0-87023-055-7). U of Mass Pr.

Foster, Lawrence J. & Foster, Pauline E. Teaching Preschool Language Arts. (Illus.). 272p. 1982. pap. text ed. 12.95x (ISBN 0-8425-1933-5). Brigham.

Foster, Lee. Backyard Farming. LC 81-4449. (Urban Life Practical Solutions to the Challenges of the 80's Ser.). 96p. (Orig.). 1982. pap. 4.95 (ISBN 0-87701-224-5). Chronicle Bks.

--Basic Gardening Techniques. Smith, Michael D., ed. LC 84-61503. (Illus.). 192p. (Orig.). 1985. pap. 9.95 (ISBN 0-89721-031-X). Ortho.

--The Beautiful California Missions. Shangle, Robert D., ed. LC 78-102341. (Illus.). 72p. 1977. 12.95 (ISBN 0-915796-23-6); pap. 7.95 (ISBN 0-915796-22-8). Beautiful Am.

--Beautiful San Francisco. LC 78-102340. (Illus.). 80p. 1985. 15.95 (ISBN 0-915796-19-8); pap. 8.95 (ISBN 0-89802-433-1). Beautiful Am.

--Beautiful Southern California. Shangle, Robert D., ed. LC 78-8532. (Illus.). 72p. 1978. pap. 6.95 (ISBN 0-915796-37-6). Beautiful Am.

--Making the Most of the Peninsula: A California Guide to San Mateo, Santa Clara, & Santa Cruz Counties. (Illus.). 304p. (Orig.). 1983. pap. 8.95 (ISBN 0-89141-164-X). Presidio Pr.

Foster, Levy & Foster, Cullison. Let the Sunshine in: Learning Activities for Multiply Handicapped Deaf Children, Pt. 2. 1975. pap. 3.50 (ISBN 0-913072-35-4). Natl Assn Deaf.

Foster, Lewis. The Only Way. LC 77-83658. 96p. (Orig.). 1978. pap. 2.25 (ISBN 0-87239-193-0, 40048). Standard Pub.

--The True Life. LC 77-83656. 96p. (Orig.). 1978. pap. 2.25 (ISBN 0-87239-192-2, 40047). Standard Pub.

Foster, Lewis & Stedman, Jon. Selecting a Translation of the Bible. LC 83-4689. (Illus.). 128p. (Orig.). 1983. pap. 3.95 (ISBN 0-87239-645-2, 39975). Standard Pub.

Foster, Lillian. Way-Side Glimpses, North & South. LC 68-58058. Repr. of 1860 ed. cancelled (ISBN 0-8371-4980-0). Greenwood.

Foster, Linda, jt. auth. see Foster, Fred B.

Foster, Lorn S. The Voting Rights Act: Cosequences & Implications. LC 85-6600. Date not set. price not set (ISBN 0-03-070684-X). Praeger.

Foster, Lorraine. Lost Summers. 424p. (Orig.). 1984. pap. 7.95x (ISBN 0-931290-80-5). Alchemy Bks.

Foster, Lorri & Gitchel, Sam. Hablemos Acerca del...S-E-X-O: Un Libro para Toda la Familia Acerca de la Pubertad. (Illus.). 90p. (Span. & Eng.). (gr. 4-8). 1985. pap. 4.95 (ISBN 0-9610122-1-8). Plan Par Fresno.

Foster, Lorri, jt. auth. see Gitchel, Sam.

Foster, Lowell W. Geo-Metrics II: The Application of Geometric Tolerancing Techniques (Using Customary System) Rev. ed. LC 82-11655. (Illus.). 320p. 1983. pap. text ed. 19.95 (ISBN 0-201-11520-4); pap. 2.00. Addison-Wesley.

--Geo-Metrics II: The Application of Geometric Tolerancing Techniques (Using Cusomary Inch System) rev. ed. LC 85-4032. 352p. 1985. pap. 19.95x (ISBN 0-201-11527-1). Addison-Wesley.

--Geo-Metrics: The Metric Application of Geometric Tolerancing. rev. ed. LC 85-3990. 352p. 1985. pap. 19.95x (ISBN 0-201-11526-3). Addison-Wesley.

--Instructor's Guide to Modern Geometric Dimensioning & Telerancing. (Geometrics, Measuring & Gaging). 64p. 9.95 (ISBN 0-318-15894-9, 502). Natl Tool Die & Precision.

--Modern Geometric Dimensioning & Tolerancing. (Geometrics, Measuring & Gaging). 170p. 16.95 (ISBN 0-318-15895-7, CAT. NO. 5021). Natl Tool Die & Precision.

--Modern Geometric Dimensioning & Tolerancing: With Workbook Section. (Illus.). 170p. 16.95 (ISBN 0-318-15882-5, 5021); 9.95, instr's guide (ISBN 0-318-15883-3, 5022). Natl Tool & Mach.

Foster, Lynn & Boast, Carol. Subject Compilations of State Laws: Research Guide & Annotated Bibliography. LC 80-1788. 473p. 1981. lib. bdg. 45.00 (ISBN 0-313-21255-4, FOS). Greenwood.

Foster, Lynn & Slusser-Kelly, Elizabeth. Legal Research Exercises to Accompany How to Find the Law: 1983. 8th ed. (American Casebook Ser.). 318p. 1983. pap. text ed. write for info. (ISBN 0-314-77633-8). West Pub.

--Legal Research Exercises to Accompany How to Find the Law: Instructor's Manual for 1983. 8th ed. (American Casebook Ser.). 318p. 1983. pap. text ed. 7.50 (ISBN 0-314-77634-6). West Pub.

Foster, Lynn V. & Foster, Lawrence. Fielding's Mexico 1984. (Illus.). 688p. (Orig.). 1984. pap. 12.95 FPT (ISBN 0-688-02439-4). Morrow.

--Fielding's Mexico, 1985. (Illus.). 704p. 1984. 12.95 (ISBN 0-688-03959-6). Fielding Travel Bks.

--Fielding's Mexico, 1986. rev. ed. (Illus.). 704p. (Orig.). 1985. pap. 12.95 (ISBN 0-688-04758-0). Fielding Travel Bks.

Foster, Lynne. Mountaineering Basics. LC 82-61637. (Illus.). 255p. (Orig.). 1982. pap. 9.95 (ISBN 0-932238-24-6, Pub. by Avant Bks). Slawson Comm.

Foster, M. A. The Day of the Klesh. (Daw Science Fiction Ser.). 1979. pap. 2.95. Daw Bks.

--The Gameplayers of Zan. (Science Fiction Ser.). 1977. pap. 3.95 (UE1497). DAW Bks.

--Magnetic Resonance in Medicine & Biology. (Illus.). 330p. 1983. 55.00 (ISBN 0-08-025913-8); pap. 25.00 (ISBN 0-08-030770-1). Pergamon.

--The Morphodite. (Science Fiction Ser.). 1981. pap. 2.95 (ISBN 0-88677-017-3, U E 1669). DAW Bks.

--Owl Time: A Collection of Fictions. 256p. 1985. pap. 2.95 (ISBN 0-87997-992-5). DAW Bks.

--Preserver. 1985. pap. 3.50 (ISBN 0-88677-095-5). DAW Bks.

--Transformer. 256p. 1983. pap. 2.50 (ISBN 0-87997-814-7). DAW Bks.

--Warriors of Dawn. (Science Fiction Ser.). pap. 3.25 (ISBN 0-87997-994-1). DAW Bks.

--Waves. (Science Fiction Ser.). 1983. pap. 2.50 (ISBN 0-87997-819-8). DAW Bks.

Foster, M. W., ed. Recent Antarctic & Subantarctic Brachiopods. LC 74-9234. (Antarctic Research Ser.: Vol. 21). (Illus.). 1974. 39.00 (ISBN 0-87590-121-2). Am Geophysical.

Foster, Marcia S. OJT Payroll Clerk Resource Materials. 2nd ed. (Gregg Office Job Training Program). (Illus.). 112p. (gr. 11-12). 1980. soft cover 6.88 (ISBN 0-07-021641-X). McGraw.

Foster, Margery S. Out of Smalle Beginings: An Economic History of Harvard College in the Puritan Period, 1636-1712. LC 62-13266. (Illus.). 1962. 15.00x (ISBN 0-674-64800-5, Belknap Pr). Harvard U Pr.

Foster, Mark. The Denver Bears: From Sandlots to Sellouts. LC 82-24066. (Illus.). 1983. 14.95 (ISBN 0-87108-643-3). Pruett.

Foster, Mark S. From Streetcar to Superhighway: American City Planners & Urban Transportation, 1900-1940. LC 80-27202. (Technology & Urban Growth Ser.). (Illus.). 263p. 1981. 34.95 (ISBN 0-87722-210-X). Temple U Pr.

Foster, Marshall E. & Swanson, Mary E. The American Covenant: The Untold Story. rev. ed. (Illus.). 186p. (Orig.). 1982. limited, signed 19.95; pap. text ed. 9.95 (ISBN 0-941370-00-3). Foun Chr Self Govt.

Foster, Mary F. Doty Dontcare. facsimile ed. LC 78-39082. (Black Heritage Library Collection). Repr. of 1895 ed. 15.50 (ISBN 0-8369-9020-X). Ayer Co Pubs.

Foster, Mary L., jt. ed. see Rubenstein, Robert A.

Foster, Maureen. Creating Patterns from Grasses, Seedheads & Cones. (Illus.). 48p. 1983. 9.95 (ISBN 0-7207-1397-8, Pub. by Michael Joseph). Merrimack Pub Cir.

--Making Animal & Bird Collages: With Grasses, Leaves, Seedheads & Cones. (Illus.). 88p. 1981. 14.95 (ISBN 0-7207-1251-3, Pub. by Michael Joseph). Merrimack Pub Cir.

Foster, Maureen & Foster, Bryan. The Art of Preserved Flower Arrangement. (Illus.). 160p. 1985. 18.95 (ISBN 0-00-411625-9, Pub. by Salem Hse Ltd). Merrimack Pub Cir.

Foster, Michael. Freedom's Thunder. 1976. pap. 1.95 (ISBN 0-380-00660-X, 29058). Avon.

Foster, Michael B. Mystery & Philosophy. LC 79-8721. (The Library of Philosophy & Theology). 96p. 1980. Repr. of 1957 ed. lib. bdg. 24.75x (ISBN 0-313-20792-5, FOMP). Greenwood.

--The Political Philosophy of Plato & Hegel. LC 83-48506. (The Philosophy of Hegel Ser.). 220p. 1984. lib. bdg. 30.00 (ISBN 0-8240-5629-9). Garland Pub.

Foster, Michael J. Energy in Law Enforcement. LC 81-67133. 327p. 1982. lib. bdg. 19.95 (ISBN 0-917882-14-8). Maryland Hist Pr.

--Energy in Law Enforcement. LC 81-67133. 327p. 19.95 (ISBN 0-917882-14-8). Energy Forum.

Foster, Michael K., et al, eds. Extending the Rafters: Interdisciplinary Approaches to Iroquois Studies. 396p. 1984. 48.50x (ISBN 0-87395-780-6); pap. 16.95x (ISBN 0-87395-781-4). State U NY Pr.

Foster, Michael S., jt. auth. see Dawson, E. Yale.

Foster, Michael S. & Weigand, Phil C., eds. The Archaeology of West & Northwest America. (A Westview Special Study). 325p. 1985. softcover 30.00x (ISBN 0-8133-0201-3). Westview.

Foster, Mike, ed. see Rhoda, Franklin.

Foster, Mrs. A. French Literature. 1860. Repr. 30.00 (ISBN 0-8274-2372-1). R West.

Foster, Muriel. Days on Sea, Loch & River. (Illus.). 124p. 1981. 4.95 (ISBN 0-7181-1788-3, Pub. by Michael Joseph). Merrimack Pub Cir.

Foster, Myles B. Anthems & Anthem Composers. LC 76-125047. (Music Ser). 1970. Repr. of 1901 ed. lib. bdg. 25.00 (ISBN 0-306-70012-3). Da Capo.

Foster, Nancy A. Cheap Thrills: A Guide to Thrift Stores & Consignment Shops in the Baltimore Area, 1984-85. (Illus.). 112p. (Orig.). 1984. pap. 3.00 (ISBN 0-9614278-0-9). Pathfinder Pr MD.

Foster, Nancy H. The Alamo & Other Texas Missions to Remember. LC 84-647. (Illus.). 96p. (Orig.). 1984. pap. 9.95x (ISBN 0-88415-033-X, Lone Star Bks). Gulf Pub.

Foster, Nancy H. & Fairbank, Ben. San Antonio: The Texas Monthly Guidebook. Rodriguez, Barbara, ed. (Texas Monthly Guidebooks Ser.). 320p. (Orig.). 1983. pap. 9.95 (ISBN 0-932012-62-0). Texas Month Pr.

Foster, Nora R. A Synopsis of the Marine Prosobranch Gastropod & Bivalve Mullusks in Alaskan Waters. (IMS Report Ser.: No. R81-3). 499p. 37.50 (ISBN 0-914500-14-7). U of Ak Inst Marine.

Foster, Norman. Construction Estimates from Take off to Bid. 2nd ed. (Modern Structure Ser.). (Illus.). 288p. 1973. 46.50 (ISBN 0-07-021632-0). McGraw.

Foster, Norman G., jt. auth. see Hamming, Mynard C.

Foster, Orline D. Stimulating the Organization. LC 73-7994. (Management History Ser.: No. 38). (Illus.). 429p. 1973. Repr. of 1923 ed. 23.75 (ISBN 0-87960-041-1). Hive Pub.

Foster, Orline D., jt. auth. see Forbes, Bertie C.

Foster, P., jt. auth. see Clignet, Remi.

Foster, P. W., jt. auth. see Weber, C. U.

Foster, Patience. Guide to Drawing. (Hobby Guides Ser.). (gr. 2-5). 1981. 7.95 (ISBN 0-86020-541-X, Usborne-Hayes); PLB 12.95 (ISBN 0-88110-025-0); pap. 4.95 (ISBN 0-86020-540-1). EDC.

Foster, Paul. Balls. 1984. 9.95 (ISBN 0-7145-0105-0); pap. cancelled. Riverrun NY.

--Elizabeth I. 1980. pap. 4.95 (ISBN 0-7145-1029-7). Riverrun NY.

--Marcus Brutus & The Silver Queen Saloon. 1981. pap. 4.95 (ISBN 0-7145-3570-2). Riverrun NY.

Foster, Pauline E., jt. auth. see Foster, Lawrence J.

Foster, Pearl B. Classic American Cooking. (Illus.). 512p. 1983. 17.95 (ISBN 0-671-44303-8). S&S.

--Classic American Cooking. 416p. 1984. pap. 9.95 (ISBN 0-671-53027-5, Fireside). S&S.

Foster, Philip & Zolberg, Aristide R., eds. Ghana & the Ivory Coast: Perspectives on Modernization. LC 70-159784. 1971. 25.00x (ISBN 0-226-25752-5). U of Chicago Pr.

Foster, Philip E. A Study of Lorenzo De'Medici's Villa at Poggio a Caiano, 2 vols. LC 77-94695. (Outstanding Dissertations in the Fine Arts Ser.). 776p. 1978. lib. bdg. 88.00 Set (ISBN 0-8240-3227-6). Garland Pub.

Foster, Phyllis M., ed. Activities & the "Well Elderly". LC 83-4326. (Activities, Adaptation & Aging Ser.: Vol. 3, No. 2). 120p. 1983. text ed. 19.95 (ISBN 0-86656-230-3, B230). Haworth Pr.

Foster, R. Introduction to Earth Science. 1982. text ed. 29.95 (ISBN 0-8053-2660-X); instr's guide 6.95 (ISBN 0-8053-2661-8). Benjamin-Cummings.

--Organic Charge-Transfer Complexes. (Organic Chemistry Ser.). 1969. 79.00 (ISBN 0-12-262650-8). Acad Pr.

Foster, R. B., et al, eds. Strategy for the West: American-Allied Relations in Transition. LC 73-91532. 258p. 1974. 19.50x (ISBN 0-8448-0274-3). Crane-Russak Co.

Foster, R. C. Studies in the Life of Christ. 1979. Repr. 29.95 (ISBN 0-8010-3452-3). Baker Bk.

Foster, R. C., et al. Ultrastructure of the Root-Soil Interface. (Illus.). 157p. 1983. 36.00 (ISBN 0-89054-051-9). Am Phytopathol Soc.

Foster, R. E. The Influence of Freud on the Autobiographical Novel. 59.95 (ISBN 0-8490-0407-1). Gordon Pr.

Foster, R. F. Lord Randolph Churchill: A Political Life. (Illus.). 1982. pap. 16.95x (ISBN 0-19-822756-6). Oxford U Pr.

Foster, R. L. The Nature of Enzymology. 384p. 1980. 79.00x (ISBN 0-85664-434-X, Pub. by Croom Helm England). State Mutual Bk.

Foster, R. P., ed. Gold: Proceedings of the International Symposium, Zimbabwe, May 1982. 500p. 1983. lib. bdg. 40.00 (ISBN 90-6191-504-X, Pub. by Balkema RSA). IPS.

Foster, R. R. Charles Stewart Parnell: The Man & His Family. 320p. 1976. text ed. 31.75x (ISBN 0-391-00909-5); pap. 13.50x (ISBN 0-391-00910-9). Humanities.

Foster, Ray. Real Estate Ideas from Ray Foster. 1980. 9.95 (ISBN 0-8359-6524-4). Reston.

Foster, Raymond. The Garden in Autumn & Winter. (Illus.). 192p. 1983. 24.95 (ISBN 0-7153-8416-3). David & Charles.

--The Overlook Guide to Growing Rare & Exotic Plants. LC 83-22057. Orig. Title: The Gardener's Guide to Rare, Exotic & Difficult Plants. (Illus.). 216p. 1985. 17.95 (ISBN 0-87951-968-1). Overlook Pr.

--Rock Garden & Alpine Plants. LC 81-67009. (Illus.). 272p. 1981. 31.50 (ISBN 0-7153-8203-9). David & Charles.

--Trees & Shrubs in Garden Design. (Illus.). 253p. 1982. 27.50 (ISBN 0-7153-8271-3). David & Charles.

Foster, Richard. Discovering English Churches: A Beginner's Guide to the Story of the Parish Church from Before the Conquest to the Gothic Revival. (Illus.). 1982. 30.00x (ISBN 0-19-520366-6). Oxford U Pr.

--The S-Curve: Profiting from Technological Change. 384p. 1984. 19.95 (ISBN 0-671-50918-7). Summit Bks.

Foster, Richard, ed. Six American Novelists of the Nineteenth Century: An Introduction. LC 68-17305. (Library on American Writers: No. 3). vi, 270p. 1968. 17.50x (ISBN 0-8166-0463-0). U of Minn Pr.

Foster, Richard, jt. ed. see Sutton, Walter.

Foster, Richard B., et al, eds. Strategy & Security in Northeast Asia. LC 79-9977. 315p. 1979. 24.50x (ISBN 0-8448-1326-5). Crane-Russak Co.

Foster, Richard D. A Pictorial Record of London & North Western Railways Signalling. 280p. 60.00x (ISBN 0-86093-147-1, Pub. by ORPC Ltd UK). State Mutual Bk.

Foster, Richard H. & Edington, Robert V. Viewing International Relations & World Politics. (Illus.). 192p. 1985. pap. text ed. 17.95 (ISBN 0-13-942087-8). P-H.

Foster, Richard J. The Celebration of Discipline: Paths to Spiritual Growth. LC 77-20444. 1978. 12.95 (ISBN 0-06-062831-6, HarpR). Har-Row.

--Celebration of Discipline Study Guide. LC 77-20444. 96p. (Orig.). 1983. pap. 4.76i (ISBN 0-06-062833-2, RD/390, HarpR). Har-Row.

--Freedom of Simplicity. LC 80-8351. 192p. 1981. 12.95 (ISBN 0-06-062832-4, HarpR). Har-Row.

--Money, Sex & Power: Study Guide. LC 84-48785. 96p. (Orig.). 1985. pap. 4.76 (ISBN 0-06-062827-8, HarpR). Har-Row.

--Money, Sex & Power: The Challenge of the Disciplined Life. LC 84-48769. 192p. 1985. 13.41 (ISBN 0-06-062826-X, HarpR). Har-Row.

Foster, Rick, ed. West Coast Plays: A Collection of Complete Scripts of New Plays. (Illus.). 186p. (Orig.). 1981. pap. 6.00 (ISBN 0-934782-09-1). CA Thea-Westcoast.

--West Coast Plays: A Collection of Eight Complete Scripts of New Plays, Nos. 11 & 12. (Illus.). 369p. (Orig.). 1982. pap. 9.95 (ISBN 0-934782-11-3). CA Thea-Westcoast.

--West Coast Plays: A Collection of Eight Complete Scripts of New Plays, Nos. 13 & 14. (Illus.). 300p. (Orig.). 1982. pap. 9.95 (ISBN 0-317-18251-X). CA Thea-Westcoast.

--West Coast Plays 10. (Illus.). 185p. (Orig.). 1981. pap. 6.00 (ISBN 0-317-18245-5). CA Thea-Westcoast.

Foster, Robert. The Complete Guide to Middle Earth: From "the Hobbit" to "the Silmarillion". LC 77-26825. 1985. pap. 3.95 (ISBN 0-345-32436-6, Del Rey Bks). Ballantine.

--A Guide to Middle Earth. 1975. pap. 2.95 (ISBN 0-345-24936-4). Ballantine.

--Wilderness Trail Cemeteries in Kentucky, Tennessee & Virginia. text ed. 24.00 (ISBN 0-686-32899-X); pap. text ed. 19.00 (ISBN 0-686-32900-7). West Cent KY Family Re Assoc.

Foster, Robert, jt. auth. see Glass, Charles.

Foster, Robert D. The Navigator. LC 83-60287. 240p. 1983. pap. 3.95 (ISBN 0-89109-495-4). NavPress.

Foster, Robert E. Multiple Option: Marching Band Techniques. LC 75-4595. (Illus.). 250p. 1975. pap. text ed. 12.95x spiral bdg. (ISBN 0-88284-027-4). Alfred Pub.

Foster, Robert J. General Geology. 3rd ed. (Physical Science Ser.). 1978. study guide 8.95 (ISBN 0-675-08447-4). Merrill.

--General Geology. 4th ed. 672p. 1983. text ed. 28.50 (ISBN 0-675-20020-2). Merrill.

--Geology. 5th, rev. ed. 224p. 1985. pap. text ed. 9.95 (ISBN 0-675-20414-3). Merrill.

--Physical Geology. 4th ed. 460p. 1983. text ed. 25.95 (ISBN 0-675-20021-0). Additional supplments may be obtained from publisher. Merrill.

Foster, Robin, jt. auth. see Chilvers, Lloyd.

Foster, Roland. The Role of the Presiding Bishop. (Orig.). 1982. pap. 1.90 (ISBN 0-88028-017-4). Forward Movement.

Foster, Rory C. Dr. Wildlife: The Crusade of a Northwoods Veterinarian. LC 84-22114. (Illus.). 182p. 1985. 14.95 (ISBN 0-531-09788-9). Watts.

Foster, Rose L. Vitamin & Herb Almanac. 4.95 (ISBN 0-89557-055-6). Bi World Indus.

Foster, Roy, ed. Molecular Association: Including Molecular Complexes, Vol. 1. 1975. 65.00 (ISBN 0-12-262701-6). Acad Pr.

--Molecular Association: Including Molecular Complexes, Vol. 2. 1979. 95.00 (ISBN 0-12-262702-4). Acad Pr.

Foster, Ruel E., jt. auth. see Campbell, Harry M.

Foster, S. G. Colonial Improver: A Life of Edward Deas Thomson. 1978. 22.00x (ISBN 0-522-84136-8, Pub. by Melbourne U Pr). Intl Spec Bk.

Foster, Sally. A Pup Grows up. LC 83-25474. (Illus.). 64p. (gr. 1-3). 1984. PLB 10.95 (ISBN 0-396-08314-5). Dodd.

Foster, Sheila. Victorian Women's Fiction: Marriage, Freedom & the Individual. LC 84-24367. 248p. 1985. 26.75x (ISBN 0-389-20551-6, 08113). B&N Imports.

Foster, Stephanie. First Summer Love. (Sweet Dreams Ser.: No. 75). 144p. (Orig.). 1984. pap. 2.25 (ISBN 0-553-24382-9). Bantam.

--Love Times Two. (Sweet Dreams Ser.: No. 66). 192p. 1984. pap. 2.25 (ISBN 0-553-24153-2). Bantam.

--A Penny for Your Dreams. (First Romance Ser.: No. 1). 192p. (Orig.). (YA) (gr. 6-12). 1982. pap. 1.95 (ISBN 0-8439-1116-6, Leisure Bks). Dorchester Pub Co.

--Rhythm of Love, No. 58. (Sweet Dreams Ser.). 160p. 1984. pap. 2.25 (ISBN 0-553-23970-8). Bantam.

--Star Light, Star Bright. (First Romance Ser.: No. 4). 192p. (YA) (gr. 6-12). 1982. pap. 1.95 (ISBN 0-8439-1144-1, Leisure Bks). Dorchester Pub Co.

Foster, Stephen. The Critics of Abstract Expressionism. Kuspit, Donald B., ed. LC 80-17239. (Studies in the Fine Arts: Criticism: No. 2). 146p. 1980. 34.95 (ISBN 0-8357-1088-2). UMI Res Pr.

--Dada-Dimensions. LC 84-28089. (Studies in the Fine Arts Ser.: The Avant-Garde: No. 48). 305p. 1985. 34.95 (ISBN 0-8357-1625-2). UMI Res Pr.

--Household Songs: Eighteen Forty-Four to Eighteen Sixty-Four. LC 76-169647. (Earlier American Music Ser.: No. 12). (Illus.). 1973. Repr. of 1862 ed. lib. bdg. 21.50 (ISBN 0-306-77312-0). Da Capo.

--Notes from the Caroline Underground: Alexander Leighton, the Puritan Triumvirnate, & the Laudian Reaction to Nonconformity. (Conference on British Studies: Vol. VI). xviii, 126p. 1978. 16.50 (ISBN 0-208-01758-5, Archon). Shoe String.

--The Social Orchestra for Flute or Violin: A Collection of Popular Melodies Arranged As Duets, Trios, & Quartets. Hitchcock, H. Wiley, ed. LC 79-169645. (Earlier American Music Ser.: Vol. 13). (Illus.). 96p. 1973. Repr. of 1854 ed. lib. bdg. 21.50 (ISBN 0-306-77313-9). Da Capo.

--Stephen Foster Song Book. 224p. (Orig.). 1974. pap. 6.50 (ISBN 0-486-23048-1). Dover.

--Stephen Foster Songbook. 224p. 10.75 (ISBN 0-318-14905-2, E115). Midwest Old Settlers.

--Their Solitary Way: The Puritan Social Ethic in the First Century of Settlement in New England. LC 76-151573. (Yale Historical Publications Miscellany Ser.: No. 94). pap. 59.50 (ISBN 0-317-29587-X, 2021997). Bks Demand UMI.

Foster, Stephen, ed. see Adcock, Craig E.

Foster, Stephen, ed. see Allen, Roy F.

Foster, Stephen, ed. see Ball, Susan L.

Foster, Stephen, ed. see Banes, Sally.

Foster, Stephen, ed. see Bantens, Robert J.

Foster, Stephen, ed. see Barton, Brigid S.

Foster, Stephen, ed. see Bassin, Joan.

Foster, Stephen, ed. see Bernstein, Roberta.

Foster, Stephen, ed. see Block, Jane.

Foster, Stephen, ed. see Bock, Catherine C.

Foster, Stephen, ed. see Bohan, Ruth L.

Foster, Stephen, ed. see Buckberrough, Sherry A.

Foster, Stephen, ed. see Chadwick, Whitney.

Foster, Stephen, ed. see Charernbhak, Wichit.

Foster, Stephen, ed. see Cohn, Sherrye.

Foster, Stephen, ed. see Cox, Annette.

Foster, Stephen, ed. see DeShong, Andrew.

Foster, Stephen, ed. see Dittmann, Reidar.

Foster, Stephen, ed. see Douglas, Charlotte C.

Foster, Stephen, ed. see Fineberg, Jonathan.

Foster, Stephen, ed. see Finkelstein, Haim N.

Foster, Stephen, ed. see Frank, Suzanne S.

Foster, Stephen, ed. see Glover, J. Garrett.

Foster, Stephen, ed. see Greenberg, Allan C.

Foster, Stephen, ed. see Harrington, Kevin.

Foster, Stephen, ed. see Hedrick, Hannah.

Foster, Stephen, ed. see Held, Roger L.

Foster, Stephen, ed. see Hirsh, Sharon L.

Foster, Stephen, ed. see Howe, Jeffery W.

Foster, Stephen, ed. see Isdebsky-Pritchard, Aline.

Foster, Stephen, ed. see Kaplan, Julius D.

Foster, Stephen, ed. see Kush, Thomas.

Foster, Stephen, ed. see Leavens, Ileana B.

Foster, Stephen, ed. see Ligo, Larry L.

Foster, Stephen, ed. see McGreevy, Linda.

Foster, Stephen, ed. see Mansbach, Steven A.

Foster, Stephen, ed. see Melzer, Annabelle.

Foster, Stephen, ed. see Moore, Richard A.

Foster, Stephen, ed. see O'Connor, Timothy E.

Foster, Stephen, ed. see Pokinski, Deborah F.

Foster, Stephen, ed. see Prestiano, Robert.

Foster, Stephen, ed. see Robinson, Susan B.

Foster, Stephen, ed. see Samaltanos, Katia.

Foster, Stephen, ed. see Santomasso, Eugene A.

Foster, Stephen, ed. see Seaman, David W.

Foster, Stephen, ed. see Siegel, Jeanne.

Foster, Stephen, ed. see Slatkin, Wendy.

Foster, Stephen, ed. see Steiner, Frances H.

Foster, Stephen, ed. see Taylor, Christiana J.

Foster, Stephen, ed. see Tower, Beeke S.

Foster, Stephen, ed. see Watts, Harriet A.

Foster, Stephen, ed. see Zinder, David G.

Foster, Stephen, ed. see Zygas, Kestutis P.

Foster, Stephen C. Biography, Songs, & Musical Compositions of Stephen C. Foster. LC 74-24086. Repr. of 1896 ed. 40.00 (ISBN 0-404-12915-3). AMS Pr.

Foster, Stephen C., ed. see Becherer, Richard.

Foster, Stephen C., ed. see Evett, Elisa.

Foster, Stephen C., ed. see Gibbs, Kenneth T.

Foster, Stephen C., ed. see Ross, Novelene.

Foster, Stephen C., ed. see Teilhet-Fisk, Jehanne.

Foster, Stephen Ch. & Kuenzli, Rudolf E., eds. Dada Spectrum: The Dialectics of Revolt. LC 78-13448. 259p. 1979. write for info. (ISBN 0-930956-01-X). U Iowa Lab Poli Sci.

Foster, Stephen S. Brotherhood of Thieves, or a True Picture of the American Church & Clergy. LC 79-82190. (Anti-Slavery Crusade in America Ser). 1969. Repr. of 1886 ed. 9.00 (ISBN 0-405-00628-4). Ayer Co Pubs.

Foster, Steven. Herbal Bounty: The Gentle Art of Herb Cultivation. (Illus.). 200p. 1984. pap. 11.95 (ISBN 0-87905-156-6, Peregrine Smith). Gibbs M Smith.

--Minstrel-Show Songs. (Earlier American Music Ser.: No. 14). 1980. Repr. of 1863 ed. lib. bdg. 22.50 (ISBN 0-306-77314-7). Da Capo.

Foster, Steven & Little, Meredith. The Book of the Vision Quest. 2nd ed. LC 80-22810. (Illus.). 160p. pap. 8.95 (ISBN 0-943404-04-5). Bear Tribe.

Foster, Steven E. The Easy Money Formula. rev. ed. 32p. 1984. pap. 15.00 (ISBN 0-930567-00-5). S Foster Fin.

Foster, Sunny & Billionis, Cynthia. Using a Sanitary Napkin. (Project MORE Daily Living Skills Ser.). 48p. 1978. pap. text ed. 7.95 (ISBN 0-8331-1245-7). Hubbard Sci.

Foster, Susan. Escape from Dependency: New State Directions for Social Policy. 80p. Date not set. price not set (ISBN 0-934842-40-X). Coun State Plan.

Foster, T. L., jt. auth. see Foster, Joseph J., III.

Foster, Ted J., jt. auth. see Whitman, Richard F.

Foster, Teree E. Oklahoma Remedies Practice Manual. Date not set. price not set looseleaf (ISBN 0-409-25088-0). Butterworth TX.

Foster, Theodora C. Women, Religion, & Development in the Third World. LC 83-13670. 288p. 1984. 28.95 (ISBN 0-03-064108-X). Praeger.

Foster, Theodore. Rhode Island Constitutional Convention of Seventeen Ninety: Theodore Foster's Minutes. Cotner, Robert C., ed. 99p. 1967. 8.50 (ISBN 0-917012-31-3). RI Hist Soc.

--Theodore Foster's Minutes of the Convention. facs. ed. LC 79-137375. (Select Bibliographies Reprint Ser). 1929. 12.00 (ISBN 0-8369-5576-5). Ayer Co Pubs.

Foster, Timothy. How to Deal with Depression. 132p. 1984. pap. 4.50 (ISBN 0-88207-610-8). Victor Bks.

--Investor's Catalog. 1986. cancelled (ISBN 0-442-22548-2); pap. cancelled (ISBN 0-442-22547-4). Van Nos Reinhold.

Foster, Timothy R. Flying in Congested Airspace. (Illus.). 192p. 1983. pap. 10.25 (ISBN 0-8306-2358-2, 2358). TAB Bks.

--How to Become an Airline Pilot. (Illus.). 192p. 1982. pap. 10.95 (ISBN 0-8306-2308-6, 2308). TAB Bks.

--Upgrading Your Airplane's Avionics. (Illus.). 112p. 1982. 9.95 (ISBN 0-8306-9620-2); pap. 5.95 (ISBN 0-8306-2301-9, 2301). TAB Bks.

--Word Processing for Executives & Professionals. 160p. 1983. 22.95 (ISBN 0-442-22717-5). Van Nos Reinhold.

Foster, V., jt. auth. see Walkley, Christina.

Foster, Vanda. Bags & Purses. (Illus.). 96p. 1982. text ed. 13.95x (ISBN 0-7134-3772-3). Drama Bk.

--A Visual History of Costume: The Nineteenth Century. LC 83-14120. (Visual History of Costume Ser.). (Illus.). 152p. 1984. text ed. 17.95x (ISBN 0-89676-079-0). Drama Bk.

Foster, Virginia. The Botany Laboratory: A Manual for a First Course in Botany. 153p. 1981. pap. 8.95 lab manual (ISBN 0-89459-049-9). Hunter Textbks.

Foster, Virginia R., jt. auth. see Foster, David W.

Foster, Virginia R., jt. ed. see Foster, David W.

Foster, W. The Church Before Covenants. 1975. 12.50x (ISBN 0-7073-0184-X, Pub. by Scottish Academic Pr Scotland). Columbia U Pr.

Foster, W. E. Town Government in Rhode Island. 1973. pap. 9.00 (ISBN 0-384-16455-2). Johnson Repr.

Foster, Warren D., ed. Heroines of Modern Religion. LC 77-107700. (Essay Index Reprint Ser.). 1913. 20.00 (ISBN 0-8369-1572-0). Ayer Co Pubs.

Foster, William. Build-It Book of Solar Heating Projects. (Illus.). 1977. pap. 5.95 (ISBN 0-8306-1006-5, 1006). TAB Bks.

--Descriptive Catalogue of the Paintings, Statues, etc. in the India Office. 5th ed. 142p. (Orig.). 1924. pap. 3.00 (ISBN 0-7123-0603-X, Pub. by British Lib). Longwood Pub Group.

Foster, William, compiled by. Early Travels in India: Fifteen Eighty-Three to Sixteen Nineteen. LC 70-179196. (Illus.). Repr. of 1921 ed. 26.00 (ISBN 0-404-54825-3). AMS Pr.

Foster, William, ed. The Embassy of Sir Thomas Roe to the Court of the Great Mogul, 1615-1619, 2 vols. in 1. (Hakluyt Society Works Ser.: No. 2, Vols. 1 & 2). (Illus.). Repr. of 1899 ed. 72.00 (ISBN 0-317-15681-0). Kraus Repr.

--The Journal of John Jourdain, 1608-1617, Describing His Experiences in Arabia, India & the Malay Archipelago. (Hakluyt Society Works Ser.: No. 2, Vol. 16). (Illus.). Repr. of 1905 ed. 52.00 (ISBN 0-317-15684-5). Kraus Repr.

--The Red Sea & Adjacent Countries at the Close of the Seventeenth Century as Described by Joseph Pitts, William Daniel, & Charles Jacques Poncet. (Hakluyt Society Works Ser. 2: Vol. 1001). (Illus.). Repr. of 1949 ed. 32.00 (ISBN 0-317-15819-8). Kraus Repr.

--The Travels of John Sanderson in the Levant, 1584-1602. (Hakluyt Society Works Ser. 2: No. 2, Vol. 67). (Illus.). Repr. of 1930 ed. 38.00 (ISBN 0-317-15691-8). Kraus Repr.

--The Voyage of Nicholas Downton to the East Indies, 1614-1615. (Hakluyt Society Works Ser.: No. 2 Vol. 82). (Illus.). Repr. of 1938 ed. 32.00 (ISBN 0-317-15697-7). Kraus Repr.

Foster, William, compiled by. The Voyage of Sir Henry Middleton to the Moluccas: 1604-1606. (Hakluyt Society Works Ser.: No. 2, Vol. 88). (Illus.). Repr. of 1943 ed. 32.00 (ISBN 0-317-15812-0). Kraus Repr.

Foster, William, ed. The Voyage of Thomas Best to the East Indies, 1612-1614. (Hakluyt Society Works Ser.: No. 2, Vol. 75). (Illus.). Repr. of 1934 ed. 38.00 (ISBN 0-317-15693-4). Kraus Repr.

Foster, William, compiled by. The Voyages of Sir James Lancaster to Brazil & the East Indies: 1591-1603. (Hakluyt Society Works Series 1: No. 56). (Illus.). Repr. of 1940 ed. 25.00 (ISBN 0-317-15808-2). Kraus Repr.

Foster, William, ed. see Herbert, Thomas.

Foster, William, ed. see Priestley, Joseph.

Foster, William E. Town Government in Rhode Island. LC 78-6359. (John Hopkins University. Studies in the Social Sciences. Fourth Ser. 1886: 2). Repr. of 1886 ed. 11.50 (ISBN 0-404-61027-7). AMS Pr.

Foster, William H. New England Grouse Shooting. 193p. 1983. 45.00 (ISBN 0-932558-15-1). Willow Creek.

Foster, William L. Vicksburg: Southern City Under Siege. Urquhart, Kenneth T., ed. LC 80-84685. (Illus.). xxv, 82p. 1980. 15.00x (ISBN 0-917860-02-0). Historic New Orleans.

--Vicksburg: Southern City Under Siege. Urquhart, Kenneth T., ed. LC 80-84685. (Illus.). xxv, 82p. 1982. pap. text ed. 6.95 (ISBN 0-917860-12-8). Historic New Orleans.

Foster, William M. The Backyard Energy Projects Handbook. (Illus.). 192p. 1982. 13.95 (ISBN 0-8306-2512-7, 1412); pap. 8.95 (ISBN 0-8306-1412-5). TAB Bks.

Foster, William T., jt. ed. see Sarret, Lew.

Foster, William Z. Great Steel Strike & Its Lessons. LC 76-90176. (Mass Violence in America). Repr. of 1920 ed. 15.00 (ISBN 0-405-01312-4). Ayer Co Pubs.

--Great Steel Strike & Its Lessons. LC 70-139202. (Civil Liberties in American History Ser). (Illus.). 1971. Repr. of 1920 ed. lib. bdg. 37.50 (ISBN 0-306-70079-4). Da Capo.

--History of the Communist Party of the United States. LC 68-30821. 1968. Repr. of 1952 ed. lib. bdg. 30.50x (ISBN 0-8371-0423-8, FOHC). Greenwood.

--History of the Three Internationals: The World Socialist & Communist Movements from 1848 to the Present. LC 68-30822. (Illus.). 1968. Repr. of 1955 ed. lib. bdg. 34.25x (ISBN 0-8371-0076-3, FOTI). Greenwood.

--The Negro People in American History. 1970. 8.50 (ISBN 0-7178-0275-2); pap. 4.95 (ISBN 0-7178-0276-0). Intl Pubs Co.

--Pages from a Worker's Life. LC 72-130864. (Illus.). 1970. o. p. 7.50 (ISBN 0-7178-0297-3); pap. 3.25 (ISBN 0-7178-0149-7). Intl Pubs Co.

--Toward Soviet America. LC 75-315. (The Radical Tradition in America Ser). 350p. 1975. Repr. of 1932 ed. 23.50 (ISBN 0-88355-218-3). Hyperion Conn.

Foster-Carter, Aidan. The Sociology of Development. (Themes & Perspectives in Sociology Ser.). 96p. (Orig.). 1985. pap. text ed. 6.95x (ISBN 0-946183-08-2, Pub. by Causeway Pr Ltd England). Sheridan.

Foster-Harris, William. Basic Formulas of Fiction. rev. ed. 1977. Repr. of 1960 ed. 12.95x (ISBN 0-8061-0135-0). U of Okla Pr.

--The Basic Patterns of Plot. 128p. 1981. pap. 5.95x (ISBN 0-8061-1769-9). U of Okla Pr.

Fosterling, Charles D., jt. auth. see Colbach, Edward M.

Fostieris, Andonis. The Devil Sang in Tune. Friar, Kimon, tr. from Gr. (Contemporary Poets Ser.: No. 3). (Illus.). 64p. (Orig.). 1983. pap. 3.95 (ISBN 0-916982-28-9, RL228). Realities.

Fosu, Kojo. Trends in African Contemporary Art. LC 79-51527. (Illus.). 1980. 45.00 (ISBN 0-933184-02-6); pap. 35.00 (ISBN 0-933184-03-4). Flame Intl.

Fotee, Joanne K., jt. auth. see Fisge, Rosalie C.

Foth. Soil Fertility. Date not set. pap. price not set (ISBN 0-471-82507-7). Wiley.

--Study Guide for Federal Tax Course, 1984. 428p. pap. 9.50 (ISBN 0-317-04203-3). Commerce.

Foth, et al. Kansas Appellate Practice Manual. 1985. 35.00 (ISBN 0-318-04140-5). KS Bar CLE.

Foth, Henry D. Fundamentals of Soil Science. 1977. pap. text ed. 9.50 study guide (ISBN 0-8403-2790-0, 40279001). Kendall-Hunt.

--Fundamentals of Soil Science. 7th ed. LC 83-23383. 435p. 1984. text ed. 35.45 (ISBN 0-471-88926-1). Wiley.

Foth, Henry D. & Schafer, John. Soil Geography & Land Use. LC 79-27731. 484p. 1980. text ed. 43.50 (ISBN 0-471-01710-8). Wiley.

Foth, Henry D., et al. Laboratory Manual for Introductory Soil Science. 6th ed. 224p. 1982. write for info wire coil bdg (ISBN 0-697-05855-7). Wm C Brown.

Foth, Margaret. Life Is Too Short. 144p. (Orig.). 1985. pap. 5.95 (ISBN 0-310-42681-2, Pub. by Daybreak). Zondervan.

Fotherby, K., ed. Hormones in Normal & Abnormal Human Tissues, Vol. 3. 297p. 1983. 60.00x (ISBN 3-11-008616-6). De Gruyter.

Fotherby, K. & Pal, S. B., eds. Hormones in Normal & Abnormal Human Tissues, Vol. 1. 1980. 58.00x (ISBN 3-11-008031-1). De Gruyter.

--The Role of Drugs & Electrolytes in Hormonogenesis. LC 84-7611. (Illus.). xii, 360p. 1984. 72.00x (ISBN 3-11-008463-5). De Gruyter.

--Steroid Converting Enzymes & Diseases. LC 84-17034. (Illus.). ix, 261p. 1984. 82.00x (ISBN 3-11-009556-4). De Gruyter.

Fothergill, Augusta B. Wills of Westmoreland County, Virginia, 1654-1800. 238p. (Orig.). 1982. pap. 22.50 (ISBN 0-89308-323-2). Southern Hist Pr.

Fothergill, Brian. The Strawberry Hill Set. 208p. 1983. 25.95 (ISBN 0-571-10609-9). Faber & Faber.

Fothergill, Brian, ed. Essays by Divers Hands: Being the Transactions of the Royal Society of Literature. (New Series: Vol. XLI). 147p. 1980. 22.50x (ISBN 0-8476-3530-9). Rowman.

--Essays by Divers Hands: Being the Transactions of the Royal Society of Literature. (New Ser.: Vol. XLI). 147p. 1980. 11.25 (ISBN 0-85115-132-9, BAB 03530, Pub. by Boydell & Brewer). Longwood Pub Group.

Fothergill, Chuck & Sterling, Bob. The Colorado Angling Guide. (Illus.). 238p. 1985. pap. 13.95 (ISBN 0-9614704-0-2). Stream Stalker.

Fothergill, D. Russia & Her People. 198p. 1982. 4.95 (ISBN 0-8285-2301-0, Pub. by Progress Pubs USSR). Imported Pubns.

Fothergill, Gerald. Emigrants from England, 1773-1776. LC 64-19752. 206p. 1976. Repr. of 1913 ed. 13.50 (ISBN 0-8063-0148-1). Genealog Pub.

Fothergill, J., ed. see Penn, W.

Fothergill, John. Chain of Friendship: Selected Letters of Dr. John Fothergill of London, 1735-1780. Corner, Betsy C. & Booth, Christopher C., eds. LC 75-127877. (Illus.). 1971. 32.50x (ISBN 0-674-10660-1, Belknap Pr). Harvard U Pr.

--Mr. Fothergill's Plot: His Conspirators Martin Armstrong, H. R. Barbor, Elizabeth Bowen & Others. 19.00 (ISBN 0-8369-4243-4, 6054). Ayer Co Pubs.

Fothergill, John W., jt. auth. see Klote, John H.

Fothergill, Richard & Butchart, Ian. Non-Book Materials in Libraries: A Practical Guide. 2nd ed. 228p. 1984. 23.00 (ISBN 0-85157-345-2, Pub By Bingley England). Shoe String.

Fothergill, Stephen & Gudgin, Graham. Unequal Growth: Urban & Regional Employment Change in the U. K. 210p. 1982. text ed. 35.00x (ISBN 0-435-84370-2). Gower Pub Co.

Fotheringham, A. Stewart, jt. auth. see Haynes, Kingsley E.

Fotheringham, J. Studies in the Mind & Art of Robert Browning. LC 72-756. (Studies in Browning, No. 4). 1972. Repr. of 1898 ed. lib. bdg. 54.95x (ISBN 0-8383-1416-3). Haskell.

--Studies in the Mind & Art of Robert Browning. 1973. Repr. of 1898 ed. 13.45 (ISBN 0-8274-1737-3). R West.

Fotheringham, James. Wordsworth's Prelude As a Study of Education. LC 74-12210. 1899. lib. bdg. 8.50 (ISBN 0-8414-4234-7). Folcroft.

Fotheringham, John K., jt. auth. see Brodrick, George C.

Fotheringham, Nick, et al. Beachcomber's Guide to Gulf Coast Marine Life. LC 80-10607. (Illus.). 124p. (Orig.). 1980. pap. 9.95x (ISBN 0-88415-062-3, Lone Star Bks). Gulf Pub.

Fotia, Ralph. Does Anyone Listen? 1976. 3.25 (ISBN 0-317-04046-4, 0404). CSS of Ohio.

Fotine, Larry. Contemporary Musician's Handbook & Dictionary. LC 80-82353. (Illus.). 1984. softcover 12.50 (ISBN 0-933830-03-3). Poly Tone.

--Cowboys, Indians & Other Characters. LC 80-82354. Date not set. pap. 7.50 (ISBN 0-933830-09-2). Poly Tone.

--Maelzel's Metronome Tempo Chart Is Outmoded. 1983. pap. 1.50 (ISBN 0-933830-12-2). Poly Tone.

--The Metamorphosis of Music by Interception. LC 82-82164. Date not set. pap. 10.00 (ISBN 0-933830-11-4). Poly Tone.

--Musicians & Other Noisemakers. LC 79-93016. (Illus.). 142p. 1980. pap. 4.95 (ISBN 0-933830-05-X). Poly Tone.

--Pieces of Life. LC 79-93017. 1984. pap. 10.00 (ISBN 0-933830-07-6). Poly Tone.

--Pieces of Life. LC 79-93017. 1985. write for info. (ISBN 0-933830-06-8). Poly Tone.

--Theory & Technique of Twelve Tone Composition. 1967. 10.00 (ISBN 0-933830-00-9). Poly Tone.

Fotinis, Athanasios P. The De Anima of Alexander of Aphrodisias: A Translation & Commentary. LC 80-5062. 362p. 1980. text ed. 25.75 (ISBN 0-8191-1032-9); pap. text ed. 15.00 (ISBN 0-8191-1033-7). U Pr of Amer.

Fotinos, S. Douglas, jt. auth. see Carver, Tina K.

Fotinos, Sandra, jt. auth. see Carver, Tina.

Fotion, N. Moral Situations. LC 68-31034. 135p. 1968. 8.00x (ISBN 0-87338-076-2); pap. 4.95x (ISBN 0-87338-077-0). Kent St U Pr.

Fotitch, Tatiana. Anthology of Old Spanish. LC 70-83406. 253p. 1969. 13.95x (ISBN 0-8132-0260-4). Cath U Pr.

--Narrative Tenses in Chretien De Troyes: A Study in Syntax & Stylistics. LC 75-94180. (Catholic University of America Studies in Romance Languages & Literatures Ser: No. 38). 1969. Repr. of 1950 ed. 19.00 (ISBN 0-404-50338-1). AMS Pr.

Fotonovel Publication Staff, ed. Heaven Can Wait. (Illus., Orig.). 1978. pap. 2.50 (ISBN 0-89752-001-7). Fotonovel.

--Ice Castles. (Illus., Orig.). 1979. pap. 2.50 (ISBN 0-686-52698-8). Fotonovel.

--Nightwing. (Illus., Orig.). 1979. pap. 2.75 (ISBN 0-686-52702-X). Fotonovel.

Fotonovel Publications Staff, ed. Americathon. (Illus., Orig.). 1979. pap. 2.75 (ISBN 0-686-52692-9). Fotonovel.

--The Best of Rocky, the Complete Rocky II. (Illus., Orig.). 1979. pap. 2.95 (ISBN 0-686-52693-7). Fotonovel.

--Buck Rogers in the Twenty-Fifth Century. (Illus., Orig.). 1979. pap. 2.75 (ISBN 0-686-52694-5). Fotonovel.

--The Champ. (Illus., Orig.). 1979. pap. 2.75 (ISBN 0-686-52695-3). Fotonovel.

--Grease. (Illus.). 1979. pap. 2.75 (ISBN 0-686-52696-1). Fotonovel.

--Hair. (Illus., Orig.). 1979. pap. 2.75 (ISBN 0-686-52697-X). Fotonovel.

--Invasion of the Body Snatchers. (Illus., Orig.). 1979. pap. 2.50 (ISBN 0-686-52699-6). Fotonovel.

--Love at First Bite. (Illus., Orig.). 1979. pap. 2.75 (ISBN 0-686-52701-1). Fotonovel.

--Revenge of the Pink Panther. (Illus., Orig.). 1979. pap. 2.75 (ISBN 0-686-52703-8). Fotonovel.

Fotonovel Publications Staff, ed. see Tolkien, J. R.

Fotos, J., jt. auth. see Cattell, J.

Fototeca Unione & Einaudi, Karen, eds. Ancient Roman Architecture: A Text-Fiche, 2 Vols. (Illus.). 1982. Vol. I, 24p. ring binder 850.00x (ISBN 0-686-97828-5, 69040-7); Vol. II, 40p. ring binder 850.00x (ISBN 0-686-97829-3, 69041-5). U of Chicago Pr.

Fottler, Myron D. Manpower Substitution in the Hospital Industry: A Study of New York City Voluntary & Municipal Hospital Systems. LC 73-173280. (Special Studies in U.S. Economic, Social & Political Issues). 1972. 39.50x (ISBN 0-275-06150-7). Irvington.

Fottler, Myron D., jt. auth. see Smith, Howard L.

Fottrell, Eamon. Case Histories in Psychiatry. LC 82-25512. 328p. 1983. pap. text ed. 13.50 (ISBN 0-443-02362-X). Churchill.

Fouad, A. A., jt. auth. see Anderson, P. M.

Foucar, Emile C. I Lived in Burma. 1956. 10.95 (ISBN 0-234-77386-3). Dufour.

Foucart, Paul F. Des Associations Religieuses chez les Grecs: Thiases, Eranes, Orgeons. facsimile ed. LC 75-10637. (Ancient Religion & Mythology Ser.). (Fr.). 1976. Repr. of 1873 ed. 20.00x (ISBN 0-405-07014-4). Ayer Co Pubs.

--Les Mysteres d'Eleusis. facsimile ed. LC 75-10636. (Ancient Religion & Mythology Ser.). (Fr.). 1976. Repr. of 1914 ed. 37.50x (ISBN 0-405-07013-6). Ayer Co Pubs.

Foucault, Michael. Birth of the Clinic: An Archeology of Medical Perception. LC 74-3389. 1974. pap. 3.95 (ISBN 0-394-71097-5, V-97, Vin). Random.

Foucault, Michel. Archaeology of Knowledge: Includes the Discourse on Language. Sheridan-Smith, A. M., tr. LC 72-1135. 1972. 29.50x (ISBN 0-394-47118-0). Irvington.

--Birth of the Clinic: An Archaeology of Medical Perception. LC 73-3493. 1973. 8.95 (ISBN 0-394-48321-9). Pantheon.

--Discipline & Punish: The Birth of the Prison. Sheridan, Alan, tr. LC 78-11257. 1979. pap. 6.95 (ISBN 0-394-72767-3, Vin). Random.

--A History of Sexuality, Vol. I: An Introduction. LC 79-7460. 1980. pap. 4.95 (ISBN 0-394-74026-2, Vin). Random.

--The History of Sexuality, Vol. 1: An Introduction. Hurley, Robert, tr. from Fr. LC 78-51804. 1978. 8.95 (ISBN 0-394-41775-5). Pantheon.

--Language, Counter-Memory, Practice: Selected Essays & Interviews. Bouchard, Donald F., ed. Simon, Sherry, tr. from Fr. LC 77-4561. (Cornell Paperbacks Ser.). 240p. 1980. pap. 7.95 (ISBN 0-8014-9204-1). Cornell U Pr.

--Language, Counter-Memory, Practice: Selected Essays and Interviews. Bouchard, Donald F., ed. & tr. from Fr. LC 77-4561. (Illus.). 240p. 1977. 27.95x (ISBN 0-8014-0979-9). Cornell U Pr.

--Madness & Civilization: A History of Insanity in the Age of Reason. 320p. 1973. pap. 4.95 (ISBN 0-394-71914-X, Vin). Random.

--Order of Things: An Archaeology of the Human Sciences. 1973. pap. 5.95 (ISBN 0-394-71935-2, V935, Vin). Random.

--Power-Knowledge: Selected Interviews & Other Writings, 1972-1977. 1981. 12.95 (ISBN 0-394-51357-6); pap. 5.95 (ISBN 0-394-73954-X). Pantheon.

--Power, Truth, Strategy. Morris, M. & Patton, P., eds. 184p. 1979. pap. text ed. 9.45x (ISBN 0-9596143-1-1, Pub. by Stonemass Trad Co Australia). Humanities.

--This Is Not a Pipe: With Illustrations & Letters by Rene Magritte. Harkness, James, tr. LC 80-26627. (Art Quantum). (Illus.). 112p. 1982. 14.95 (ISBN 0-520-04232-8); pap. 4.95 (ISBN 0-520-04916-0). U of Cal Pr.

Foucault, Michel, ed. I, Pierre Riviere, Having Slaughtered My Mother, My Sister, & My Brother: A Case Of Parricide in the Nineteenth Century. Jellinek, Frank, tr. from Fr. LC 82-8580. xiv, 289p. 1982. pap. 7.50 (ISBN 0-8032-6857-2, BB 819, Bison). U of Nebr Pr.

Foucault, Michel, intro. by. Herculine Barbin: Being the Recently Discovered Memoirs of a Nineteenth-Century French Hermaphodite. McDougall, Richard, tr. 1980. 8.95 (ISBN 0-394-50821-1); pap. 4.95 (ISBN 0-394-73862-4). Pantheon.

Fouchard, Jean. The Haitian Maroons: Liberty or Death. Watts, A. Faulkner, tr. from Fr. 500p. 1982. 25.00x (ISBN 0-914110-11-X). Blyden Pr.

Foucher, A. The Beginnings of Buddhist Art. 1972. 20.00 (ISBN 0-89684-370-X). Orient Bk Dist.

Foucher, Alfred C. The Life of the Buddha. Boas, Simone B., tr. LC 72-6195. 272p. 1972. Repr. of 1963 ed. lib. bdg. 22.50x (ISBN 0-8371-6476-1, FOLB). Greenwood.

Foucher, G. Treatise on the History & Construction of the Violin. LC 77-94578. 1978. Repr. of 1897 ed. lib. bdg. 15.00 (ISBN 0-89341-407-7). Longwood Pub Group.

Foucher, Simon. Critique De La Recherche De La Verite. (Texts in Early Modern Philosophy Ser). (Fr). 1970. Repr. of 1675 ed. 20.00 (ISBN 0-384-16480-3). Johnson Repr.

Foucher De Chartres. Chronicle of the First Crusade. McGinty, Martha E., tr. LC 76-29823. Repr. of 1941 ed. 14.00 (ISBN 0-404-15417-4). AMS Pr.

Foucher of Chartres. A History of the Expedition to Jerusalem, 1095-1127. Fink, Harold S., ed. LC 78-77847. pap. 90.50 (ISBN 0-317-29723-6, 2019678). Bks Demand UMI.

Fouchet, M. & Menant, N. India. 147p. 1979. text ed. 46.00x (ISBN 0-391-02909-6, Pub. by Roli Pubns India). Humanities.

Fouchier, J. & Billet, F. Chemical Dictionary. 3rd ed. 1464p. (Fr., Ger. & Eng.). 1972. 117.00 (ISBN 0-444-41090-2). Elsevier.

Foudray, Elbertie & U. S. Dept. of Commerce, Bureau of the Census. United States Abridged Life Tables: 1919-1920. LC 75-37268. (Demography Ser.). (Illus.). 1976. Repr. of 1923 ed. 14.00x (ISBN 0-405-08000-X). Ayer Co Pubs.

Fouere, Rene. Krishnamurti: The Man & His Teaching. 1974. lib. bdg. 69.95 (ISBN 0-8490-0477-2). Gordon Pr.

Fougereau, M. & Dausset, J., eds. Immunology Eighty: Progress in Immunology IV (Fourth International Congress of Immunology) 1500p. 1981. pap. 98.00 (ISBN 0-12-262940-X). Acad Pr.

Fougereau, M. & Daussett, J., eds. Immunology, 1980. LC 80-49682. 1981. Vol. 1. 63.00 (ISBN 0-12-262901-9); Vol. 2. 63.00 (ISBN 0-12-262902-7); Vol. 3. 63.00 (ISBN 0-12-262903-5). Acad Pr.

Fougeres, Regine Dalchow. Modern Russian Adjectives Correlative with the Past Passive Participles: Slavonic Languages & Literatures. (European University Studies: Series 16, Vol. 3). 170p. 1974. pap. 18.25 (ISBN 3-261-01085-1). P Lang Pubs.

Fought, J. G., jt. auth. see Hymes, D.

Fought, John G. Chorti (Mayan) Texts: I. LC 72-80380. (Folklore & Folklife Ser). 592p. 1973. 25.00x (ISBN 0-8122-7667-1). U of Pa Pr.

Fought, Sharon G. & Throwe, Anita N. Psychosocial Nursing Care of the Emergency Patient. LC 84-12024. 256p. 1984. pap. text ed. 16.95 (ISBN 0-471-87562-7, Pub by Wiley Med). Wiley.

Fouillee, A., et al. Modern French Legal Philosophy. (Modern Legal Philosophy Ser: Vol. 7). lxvi, 578p. 1969. Repr. of 1916 ed. 37.50x (ISBN 0-8377-2126-1). Rothman.

Fouk al-Ada, Samuhi. English-French-Arabic Dictionary of Diplomacy & International Affairs. 30.00x (ISBN 0-86685-114-3). Intl Bk Ctr.

Fouke, George R. A First Book of Space Form Making. (Illus.). 64p. (Orig.). (gr. 4-8). 1974. pap. 2.95 (ISBN 0-914462-01-6). GeoBooks.

Foulard, C., jt. auth. see El-Fattah, Y. M.

Foulche-Delbosc, R., ed. see Quevedo Villegas, Francisco de.

Foulche-Delbosc, Raymond, ed. see De Gongoray Argote, Luis.

Foulds, Elfrida V. The Candle of the Lord. pap. 2.30x (ISBN 0-87574-248-3, 248). Pendle Hill.

--Let Your Lives Speak. 1983. pap. 5.00x (ISBN 0-87574-071-5, 071). Pendle Hill.

Foulds, G. A., ed. The Hierarchical Nature of Personal Illness. 1976. 35.00 (ISBN 0-12-263250-8). Acad Pr.

Foulds, Jervis. The Lady Dudley Challenge Cup. (Illus.). 1978. 10.95 (ISBN 0-85131-294-2, NL51, Dist. by Miller). J A Allen.

Foulds, L. Combinatorial Optimization. (Undergraduate Texts in Mathematics Ser.). (Illus.). 280p. 1984. 36.00 (ISBN 0-387-90977-X). Springer-Verlag.

--Neoplastic Development. Vol. 1. 1969. 70.00 (ISBN 0-12-262801-2); Vol. 2. 1975. 90.00 (ISBN 0-12-262802-0). Acad Pr.

Foulds, L. R. Optimization Techniques: An Introduction. (Undergraduate Text in Mathematics). (Illus.). 502p. 1981. 39.00 (ISBN 0-387-90586-3). Springer-Verlag.

Foulds, L. R., jt. auth. see Robinson, D. F.

Foulds, Sam & Harris, Paul. America's Soccer Heritage: A History of the Game. LC 79-63981. (Illus.). 1979. pap. 8.95 (ISBN 0-916802-14-0). Soccer for Am.

Foulet, Alfred & Speer, Mary B. On Editing Old French Texts. 1979. 19.95x (ISBN 0-7006-0182-1). U Pr of KS.

Foulet, Lucien see Roach, William.

Foulger, R. J. Programming Embedded Microprocessors: A High-Level Language Solution. (Illus.). 240p. (Orig.). 1983. 28.00x (ISBN 0-85012-336-4). Intl Pubns Serv.

--Programming Embedded Microprocessors: A High-Level Language Solution. 240p. 1982. pap. 27.35 (ISBN 0-471-89421-4). Wiley.

Foulger, Richard & Routledge, Edward. The Food Poisoning Handbook. 104p. (Orig.). 1981. pap. text ed. 8.95x (ISBN 0-86238-019-7, Pub. by Chartwell-Bratt England). Brookfield Pub Co.

Foulis, D. J., jt. auth. see Munem, M. A.

Foulke, Adrienne, tr. see Condominas, Georges.

Foulke, Adrienne, tr. see Malurie, Jean.

Foulke, Adrienne, tr. see Masi, Edoarda.

Foulke, Arthur T. Mr. Typewriter. 1975. 6.95 (ISBN 0-8158-0094-0). Chris Mass.

--My Danville: Where the Bright Waters Meet. (Illus.). 1969. 9.75 (ISBN 0-8158-0020-7). Chris Mass.

--Picture-Book for Proud Lovers of Danville, Montour County & Riverside, PA. LC 75-32061. (Illus.). 320p. 1976. 15.00 (ISBN 0-8158-0334-6). Chris Mass.

--What Makes a Year Anyway? 144p. 1980. 8.95 (ISBN 0-8158-0391-5). Chris Mass.

Foulke, D., ed. Electroplaters' Process Control Handbook. rev. ed. LC 74-13010. 444p. 1975. 31.50 (ISBN 0-88275-213-8). Krieger.

Foulke, Emerson, jt. ed. see Schiff, William.

Foulke, J. Focusing on Gebruder Heubach Dolls. 64p. 1980. pap. 6.95 (ISBN 0-87588-148-3). Hobby Hse.

Foulke, Jan. Blue Book Dolls & Values. 4th ed. (Illus.). 350p. 1980. pap. 5.95 (ISBN 0-87588-162-9). Hobby Hse.

--Blue Book of Dolls & Values. 5th ed. 364p. 1982. pap. 5.95 (ISBN 0-87588-189-0). Hobby Hse.

--Focusing on Effanbee Composition Dolls. Blau, Clare, ed. (Focusing On). 48p. 1978. pap. 4.95 (ISBN 0-87588-137-8). Hobby Hse.

--Kestner: King of Dollmakers. 236p. 1982. 19.95 (ISBN 0-87588-185-8). Hobby Hse.

--Simon & Halbig Dolls: The Artful Aspect. (Illus.). 236p. 1984. 22.95 (ISBN 0-87588-219-6). Hobby Hse.

--Sixth Blue Book of Dolls & Values. (Illus.). 364p. (Orig.). 1984. pap. 12.95 (ISBN 0-87588-228-5). Hobby Hse.

--Treasury of Mme. Alexander Dolls. (Illus.). 102p. pap. 9.95 (ISBN 0-87588-147-5). Hobby Hse.

Foulke, O. G. Electroplaters Process Control Handbook. 438p. 1975. 29.50 (ISBN 0-318-12530-7); members 22.50 (ISBN 0-318-12531-5). Am Electroplate.

Foulke, Patricia & Foulke, Robert. Fielding's Motoring & Camping Europe. (Illus.). 256p. (Orig.). 1985. pap. 8.95 (ISBN 0-688-04807-2). Fielding Travel Bks.

Foulke, Patricia, jt. auth. see Foulke, Robert.

Foulke, Patricia N. & Foulke, Robert D. Europe Under Canvas: A Guide to Camping for Singles, Couples & Families. (Illus.). 1980. 11.95 (ISBN 0-13-292094-8, Spec). P-H.

Foulke, Paul, tr. see Boltzmann, Ludwig.

--Salesman Performance Appraisal: A National Study. 1975. 25.00 (ISBN 0-917472-01-2). F Fournies.

Fournival, Richard de see De Fournival, Richard.

Fournol, Etienne M. Bodin, Predecesseur de Montesquieu; Etude sur Quelques Theories Politiques de la Republique et de l'Esprit des Lois. LC 79-157157. 176p. (Fr.). 1972. Repr. of 1896 ed. lib. bdg. 17.50 (ISBN 0-8337-4115-2). B Franklin.

Fourquin, G. The Anatomy of Popular Rebellion in the Middle Ages. (Europe in the Middle Ages - Selected Studies: Vol. 9). 182p. 1978. 42.75 (ISBN 0-444-85006-6, North-Holland). Elsevier.

Fourrier, M., jt. auth. see Auvray, J.

Fourt, Lyman E. & Hollies, Norman R. Clothing: Comfort & Function. LC 70-134699. (Fiber Science Ser.). (Illus.). pap. 65.80 (ISBN 0-317-08345-7, 2017851). Bks Demand UMI.

Fourteen International Universitaetswochen Fuer Kernphysik 1975 der Karlfranzens-Universitaet at Schladming. Electromagnetic Interactions & Field Theory: Proceedings. Urban, P., ed. (Acta Physica Austriaca: No. 14). (Illus.). v, 681p. 1975. 87.40 (ISBN 0-387-81333-0). Springer-Verlag.

Fourteenth Inter-University Geological Congress. Geology & Shelf Seas: Proceedings. Donovan, D. T., ed. 1968. 11.75 (ISBN 0-934454-43-4). Lubrecht & Cramer.

Fourth Australian Conference, University of Adelaide, 27-29 Aug. 1976. Combinatonal Mathematics, IV: Proceedings. Casse, L. R. & Wallis, W. D., eds. (Lecture Notes in Mathematics Ser.: Vol. 560). 1976. soft cover 17.00 (ISBN 3-540-08053-8). Springer-Verlag.

Fourth Conference Held at Dundee, Scotland, Mar 30-Apr 2, 1976. Ordinary & Partial Differential Equations, Dundee 1976: Proceedings. Everitt, W. N. & Sleeman, B. D., eds. (Lecture Notes in Mathematics Ser.: Vol. 564). 1976. soft cover 29.00 (ISBN 0-387-08058-9). Springer-Verlag.

Fourth International Conference on the Origin of Life, 1973, Invited Papers & Contributed Papers, et al. Cosmochemical Evolution & the Origins of Life, 2 vols. Oro, J. & Miller, S. L., eds. LC 74-77967. vii, 755p. 1974. Vol. 1. lib. bdg. 59.00 (ISBN 90-277-0519-4, Pub. by Reidel Holland); Vol. 2. lib. bdg. 36.00 (ISBN 9-0277-0518-6). Kluwer Academic.

Fourth International Exhibition of Twentieth Century Botanical Art & Illustration. Catalogue. Secrist, S. & Howard, N., eds. (Illus.). 1977. 12.00x (ISBN 0-913196-19-3). Hunt Inst Botanical.

Fourth National Conference on Business Ethics. Ethics & the Management of Computer Technology: Proceedings. Hoffman, Michael & Moore, Jennifer, eds. LC 82-3562. 384p. 1982. text ed. 30.00 (ISBN 0-89946-144-1). Oelgeschlager.

Fourth Symposium, Oct. 22-25, 1975. Social Work in Practice: Proceedings. Khinduka, S. K. & Ross, Bernard, eds. LC 76-39587. 270p. 1976. 10.00x (ISBN 0-87101-073-9). Natl Assn Soc Wkrs.

Fourtner, Charles R., jt. ed. see Herreid, Clyde F., II.

Fourtouni, Eleni. Monovassia 1976. (Greek Women Poets Ser.). (Illus.). 110p. (Orig.). 1979. pap. text ed. 6.50 (ISBN 0-915017-01-6). Thelphini Pr.

--Watch the Flame. (Greek Women Poets Ser.). (Orig.). 1983. pap. 6.50 (ISBN 0-915017-04-0). Thelphini Pr.

Foussard, Michael. Guitares. (Illus.). 320p. 1979. text ed. 70.00 (ISBN 0-686-44084-6). Bold Strummer Ltd.

Foust, Alan S., et al. Principles of Unit Operations. 2nd ed. LC 78-12449. 768p. 1980. 54.00x (ISBN 0-471-26897-6). Wiley.

Foust, Brady, jt. auth. see DeSouza, Anthony.

Foust, Clement E. The Life & Dramatic Works of Robert Montgomery Bird. 725p. 1981. Repr. of 1919 ed. lib. bdg. 100.00 (ISBN 0-8495-1730-3). Arden Lib.

Foust, Clement E., ed. Life & Dramatic Works of Robert Montgomery Bird, 1806-54, 2 vols. in 1. (Research & Source Works Ser.: No. 716). 1971. Repr. of 1919 ed. lib. bdg. 40.50 (ISBN 0-8337-0294-7). B Franklin.

Foust, Cleon H. & Webster, D. Robert, eds. An Anatomy of Criminal Justice: A System Overview. LC 79-3908. 352p. 1980. 31.00x (ISBN 0-669-02854-1). Lexington Bks.

Foust, Cleon H., jt. ed. see Dutile, Fernand N.

Foust, James D. The Yeoman Farmer & Westward Expansion of U. S. Cotton Production. facsimile ed. LC 75-2581. (Dissertations in American Economic History). (Illus.). 1975. 23.00x (ISBN 0-405-07201-5). Ayer Co Pubs.

Foust, Juana. Searching for Fifth Mesa. LC 78-31284. (Orig.). 1979. pap. 4.95 (ISBN 0-913270-81-4). Sunstone Pr.

Foust, O. J. Sodium-Nak Engineering Handbook: Vol. 1-Sodium Chemistry & Physical Properties. LC 70-129473. (U. S. Atomic Energy Commission Monographs). 340p. 1972. 89.25 (ISBN 0-677-03020-7). Gordon.

Foust, O. J., ed. Sodium-Nak Engineering Handbook, 5 vols. 1730p. 1979. Set. 404.25 (ISBN 0-677-03070-3). Gordon.

--Sodium-Nak Engineering Handbook, Vol. 2. LC 70-129473. (U. S. Atomic Energy Commission Monographs). (Illus.). 402p. 1976. 103.95 (ISBN 0-677-03030-4). Gordon.

--Sodium-Nak Engineering Handbook, Vols. 3-4. (U.S. Atomic Energy Commission Monograhs). (Illus.). 1978. Vol. 3, 348p. 93.75 (ISBN 0-677-03040-1); Vol. 4, 298p. 89.25 (ISBN 0-677-03050-9). Gordon.

--Sodium Nak Engineering Handbook: Vol. 5-Sodium Purification, Materials, Heaters, Coolers, & Radiators. 342p. 1979. 93.75 (ISBN 0-677-03060-6). Gordon.

Foust, Paul. Reborn to Multiply. LC 73-9110. 1973. pap. 2.75 (ISBN 0-570-03170-2, 12-2573). Concordia.

Foust, Paul & Kortals, Richard. Reach Out. 1984. pap. 3.95 (ISBN 0-570-03933-9, 12-2868). Concordia.

Fout, John C., ed. German Women in the Nineteenth Century: A Social History. 450p. 1984. text ed. 39.50x (ISBN 0-8419-0843-5); pap. text ed. 24.50x (ISBN 0-8419-0844-3). Holmes & Meier.

Fout, John C., jt. ed. see Riemer, Eleanor S.

Fouts, Raymond P. Marriages of Bertie County, North Carolina, 1762-1868. LC 81-86325. 130p. 1982. 15.00 (ISBN 0-8063-0976-8). Genealog Pub.

Foutz, Susan L., jt. auth. see Morris, George G.

Fovoledo, Elena, jt. auth. see Pirrotta, Nino.

Foward, Robert. The Owl. 256p. (Orig.). 1984. pap. 2.95 (ISBN 0-523-42194-X). Pinnacle Bks.

Foward, Susan & Buck, Craig. Betrayal of Innocence: Incest & Its Devastation. 198p. 1978. postpaid 6.00 (ISBN 0-318-17073-6). Kemper Nat Ctr.

Fowden, L. see Blaxter, K.

Fowden, L. & Graham-Bryce, I. J., eds. Crop Protection Chemicals: Directions of Future Development. (Illus.). 212p. 1981. lib. bdg. 63.00x (ISBN 0-85403-175-8, Pub. by Royal Soc London). Scholium Intl.

Fowden, L., et al, eds. Trace Element Deficiency: Metabolic & Physiological Consequences. (Royal Society of London Ser.). (Illus.). 213p. 1982. lib. bdg. 65.50x (ISBN 0-85403-171-5, Pub. by Royal Soc London). Scholium Intl.

Fowden, Leslie & Miflin, B. J., eds. Seed Storage Proteins. (Philosophical Transactions of The Royal Society of London: Ser. B, Vol. 304). (Illus.). 137p. 1984. Repr. lib. bdg. 52.00x (ISBN 0-85403-225-8, Pub. by Royal Soc London). Scholium Intl.

Fowden, Leslie, et al, eds. Clay Minerals: Their Structure, Behavior & Use. (Illus.). 212p. 1984. lib. bdg. 70.00x (ISBN 0-85403-232-0, Pub. by Royal Soc London). Scholium Intl.

Fowell, Frank. Censorship in England. (Illus.). 1967. Repr. of 1913 ed. 18.50 (ISBN 0-8337-1227-6). B Franklin.

Fowell, Frank & Palmer, Frank. Censorship in England. LC 74-82828. Repr. of 1913 ed. 27.50 (ISBN 0-405-08529-X, Blom Pubns). Ayer Co Pubs.

Foweraker, J. The Struggle for Land. (Illus.). 304p. 1981. 47.50 (ISBN 0-521-23555-3). Cambridge U Pr.

Fowke, Edith. Sea Songs & Ballads from Nineteenth Century Nova Scotia: The William H. Smith & Fenwick Hatt Manuscripts. Goldstein, Kenneth S., ed. LC 81-68624. (Publications in Folksong & Balladry Ser.). 118p. 1982. pap. 14.95 (ISBN 0-939544-04-0). Folklorica Pr.

Fowke, Edith & Carpenter, Carole H. A Bibliography of Canadian Folklore in English. 232p. 1981. 30.00x (ISBN 0-8020-2394-0). U of Toronto Pr.

Fowke, Edith & Glazer, Joe. Songs of Work & Protest. Orig. Title: Songs of Work & Freedom. 290p. 1973. Repr. of 1960 ed. 6.50 (ISBN 0-486-22899-1). Dover.

--Songs of Work & Protest. 14.25 (ISBN 0-8446-4737-3). Peter Smith.

Fowke, Edith, ed. Sea Songs & Ballads from Nineteenth Century Nova Scotia: The William B. Smith & Fenwick Hatt Manuscripts. LC 81-68629. (Folksong & Balladry: No. 5). 118p. pap. 12.95 (ISBN 0-939544-04-0). Wildman Pr.

Fowke, Edith, ed. see Kane, Alice.

Fowke, Frank R. The Bayeux Tapestry: A History & Description. LC 75-131705. 308p. 1972. Repr. of 1913 ed. 49.00x (ISBN 0-403-00592-2). Scholarly.

Fowke, Gerard, jt. auth. see Smith, Harlan I.

Fowke, L. C. & Constabel, F., eds. Plant Protoplasts. 256p. 1985. price not set (ISBN 0-8493-6473-6). CRC Pr.

Fowke, V. C., jt. auth. see Britnell, George E.

Fowke, Vernon C. Canadian Agricultural Policy: The Historical Pattern. LC 47-2754. 1978. pap. 7.50 (ISBN 0-8020-6352-7). U of Toronto Pr.

Fowkes, Ben. Communism in Germany under the Weimar Republic. LC 83-40169. 256p. 1984. 25.50 (ISBN 0-312-15274-4). St Martin.

Fowkes, Ben, tr. see Marx, Karl.

Fowkes, F. M., ed. Hydrophobic Surfaces: Proceedings. 1969. 52.50 (ISBN 0-12-263050-5). Acad Pr.

Fowkes, Robert A., jt. auth. see Brody, Elaine.

Fowkes, William I. A Hegelian Account of Contemporary Art. Kuspit, Donald, ed. LC 81-2972. (Studies in the Fine Arts: Art Theory, No. 3). 126p. 1981. 34.95 (ISBN 0-8357-1187-0). UMI Res Pr.

Fowle, Eleanor. Cranston, the Senator from California. LC 83-24232. 1984. pap. 7.95 (ISBN 0-87477-320-2). J P Tarcher.

Fowle, T. W. The Poor Law: The English Citizen: His Rights & Responsibilities. vi, 175p. 1979. Repr. of 1893 ed. lib. bdg. 17.50x (ISBN 0-8377-0534-7). Rothman.

Fowler. Infant & Child Care: A Guide to Education in Group Settings. 1985. 32.86 (ISBN 0-205-06514-7, 236514). Allyn.

Fowler & May. Neurology. (Management of Common Diseases in Family Practice Ser.). 1985. 15.00 (ISBN 0-317-28882-2). PSG Pub Co.

Fowler, A., ed. see Lewis, Clive S.

Fowler, Alastair. From the Domain of Arnheim. 64p. (Orig.). 1982. 12.50 (ISBN 0-436-16180-X, Pub. by Secker & Warburg UK). David & Charles.

--John Milton: Paradise Lost. (Longman Annotated English Poets Ser.). (Illus.). 1974. pap. text ed. 12.95x (ISBN 0-582-48455-3). Longman.

--Kinds of Literature: An Introduction to the Theory of Genres & Modes. 368p. 1985. pap. text ed. 8.95x (ISBN 0-674-50356-2). Harvard U Pr.

--Kinds of Literature: Introduction to the Theory of Genres & Modes. (Illus.). 368p. 1982. text ed. 20.00x (ISBN 0-674-50355-4). Harvard U Pr.

--Triumphal Forms, Structural Patterns in Elizabethan Poetry. LC 75-105498. (Illus.). 1970. 49.50 (ISBN 0-521-07747-8). Cambridge U Pr.

Fowler, Alastair, jt. auth. see Carey, John.

Fowler, Albert. Two Trends in Modern Quaker Thought. 1983. pap. 5.00x (ISBN 0-87574-112-6, 112). Pendle Hill.

Fowler, Albert, ed. Cranberry Lake from Wilderness to Adirondack Park. LC 68-17845. (Adirondack Museum Bks.). (Illus.). 1968. 13.75 (ISBN 0-8156-0059-3). Syracuse U Pr.

Fowler, Albert V., ed. Cranberry Lake, from Wilderness to Adirondack Park. (Illus.). 256p. 1968. 13.75 (ISBN 0-686-74841-7). Adirondack Mus.

Fowler, Albert Vann, ed. Cranberry Lake, from Wilderness to Adirondack Park. (Illus.). 256p. 1968. bds. 13.75 (ISBN 0-317-32103-X). Adirondack Mus.

Fowler, Alex D. Splinters from the Past: Discovering History in Old Houses. Meyer, Lucy & Adams, Anne, eds. (Illus.). 208p. 1984. 15.00 (ISBN 0-910301-08-5). M C H S.

Fowler, Ann & Walters, D. K., eds. Charles Morgan on Retrievers. (Illus.). 1968. 20.00 (ISBN 0-8079-0026-5). October.

Fowler, Arlen L. The Black Infantry in the West, 1869-1891. LC 78-105985. (Contributions in Afro-American & African Studies: No. 6). (Illus.). 1971. 27.50 (ISBN 0-8371-3313-0, FON&, Pub. by Negro U Pr). Greenwood.

Fowler, Austin. Monarch Notes on Camus' Major Works. (Orig.). pap. 3.95 (ISBN 0-671-00552-9). Monarch Pr.

--Monarch Notes on Hemingway's the Snows of Kilimanjaro. (Orig.). pap. 3.50 (ISBN 0-671-00839-0). Monarch Pr.

--Monarch Notes on Tolstoy's War & Peace. (Orig.). pap. 2.95 (ISBN 0-671-00572-3). Monarch Pr.

Fowler, B. A., ed. Biological & Environmental Effects of Arsenic. (Topics in Environmental Health: Vol. 6). 288p. 1984. 81.00 (ISBN 0-444-80513-3, I-379-83, Biomedical Pr). Elsevier.

Fowler, Barney. Adirondack Album, Vol. 1. (Illus.). 200p. (Orig.). 1974. pap. 10.25 (ISBN 0-9605556-1-7). Outdoor Assocs.

--Adirondack Album, Vol. 2. (Illus.). 200p. (Orig.). 1980. pap. 10.25 (ISBN 0-9605556-0-9). Outdoor Assocs.

--Adirondack Album, Vol. 3. (Illus.). 192p. (Orig.). 1982. pap. 10.25 (ISBN 0-9605556-2-5). Outdoor Assocs.

Fowler, Carol. Contributions of Women: Art. LC 76-3479. (Contributions of Women Ser.). (Illus.). (gr. 6 up). 1976. PLB 8.95 (ISBN 0-87518-115-5). Dillon.

--Contributions of Women: Dance. LC 78-10313. (Contributions of Women Ser.). (Illus.). (gr. 6 up). 1979. PLB 8.95 (ISBN 0-87518-169-4). Dillon.

Fowler, Carolyn. A Knot in the Thread: The Life & Work of Jacques Roumain. LC 76-53817. 1980. 14.95 (ISBN 0-88258-057-4). Howard U Pr.

Fowler, Charles, ed. see Bitz, Gregory W.

Fowler, Charles B. Dance As Education. 1977. pap. text ed. 5.20x (ISBN 0-88314-051-9). AAHPERD.

Fowler, Charles H. Historical Romance of the American Negro. Repr. of 1902 ed. 27.00 (ISBN 0-384-16530-3). Johnson Repr.

Fowler, Charles W. & Smith, Tim D. Dynamics of Large Mammal Populations. LC 81-115. 477p. 1981. 48.50x (ISBN 0-471-05160-8, Oub. by Wiley-Interscience). Wiley.

Fowler, Cheryl A., jt. ed. see Robinson, Jan.

Fowler, Clarence M., jt. ed. see Erber, Thomas.

Fowler, D. H., tr. see Thom, R.

Fowler, David C. The Bible in Early English Literature. LC 76-7786. (Illus.). 274p. 1976. 18.95x (ISBN 0-295-95438-8). U of Wash Pr.

--The Bible in Middle English Literature. LC 84-7453. (Illus.). 336p. 1984. 25.00x (ISBN 0-295-96130-9). U of Wash Pr.

--A Literary History of the Popular Ballad. LC 68-19917. pap. 90.00 (ISBN 0-317-28961-6, 2023761). Bks Demand UMI.

--Piers the Plowman: Literary Relations of the A & B Texts. LC 61-11575. (Publications in Language & Literature: No. 16). 260p. 1961. 15.00x (ISBN 0-295-73879-0). U of Wash Pr.

Fowler, David C., jt. ed. see Knott, Thomas A.

Fowler, David C., ed. see Langland, William.

Fowler, David G. Briefcase. 1979. pap. 2.50 (ISBN 0-930324-15-3). Wings Pr.

--Dream Turf Ravers. 32p. (Orig.). 1979. lib. bdg. 20.00 (ISBN 0-916908-34-8); pap. 3.00 (ISBN 0-916908-13-5). Place Herons.

Fowler, Don D. Excavations, Harris Wash, Utah, 1961. (Glen Canyon Ser: No. 19). Repr. of 1963 ed. 25.00 (ISBN 0-404-60664-4). AMS Pr.

--In a Sacred Manner We Live: Photographs of the American Indian at the Beginning of the Twentieth Century. LC 73-185614. (Illus.). 196p. 1972. pap. 5.95 (ISBN 0-517-51735-3). Barre.

Fowler, Don D. & Aikens, C. Melvin. Excavations, Kaiparowits Plateau, Utah, 1961. (Glen Canyon Ser: No. 20). Repr. of 1963 ed. 24.00 (ISBN 0-404-60666-0). AMS Pr.

Fowler, Don D. & Matley, John F. Material Culture of the Numa: The John Wesley Powell Collection, 1867-1880. LC 78-22066. (Smithsonian Contributions to Anthropology Ser.: No. 26). pap. 46.80 (ISBN 0-317-28871-7, 2020307). Bks Demand UMI.

Fowler, Don D., ed. Photographed All the Best Scenery: Jack Hillers's Diary of the Powell Expeditions 1871-1875. LC 78-189755. (University of Utah Publications in the American West: Vol. 9). (Illus.). 1971. 19.95 (ISBN 0-87480-066-8). U of Utah Pr.

Fowler, Don D., jt. ed. see Condie, Carol J.

Fowler, Don D., et al. The Glen Canyon Archeological, 3 vols. (Glen Canyon Ser: No. 6). Repr. of 1959 ed. Set. 136.00 (ISBN 0-404-60639-3); Pt, I. 52.00 (ISBN 0-404-60711-X); Pt. II. 59.00 (ISBN 0-404-60712-8); Pt, III. 25.00 (ISBN 0-404-60713-6). AMS Pr.

Fowler, Doreen. Faulkner's Changing Vision: From Outrage to Affirmation. Litz, Walton, ed. LC 83-7010. (Studies in Modern Literature: No. 14). 102p. 1983. 34.95 (ISBN 0-8357-1423-3). UMI Res Pr.

Fowler, Doreen & Abadie, Ann, eds. A Cosmos of My Own: Faulkner & Yoknapatawpha. LC 81-7430. (Faulkner & Yoknapatawpha Ser.). 324p. 1981. 17.95x (ISBN 0-87805-142-2); pap. 9.95 (ISBN 0-87805-143-0). U Pr of Miss.

Fowler, Doreen & Abadie, Ann J., eds. Faulkner & Humor. LC 85-40518. (Faulkner & Yoknapatawpha Ser.). (Orig.). 1986. price not set (ISBN 0-87805-281-X); pap. price not set (ISBN 0-87805-282-8). U Pr of Miss.

--Faulkner & the Southern Renaissance. LC 82-6982. (Faulkner & Yoknapatawpha Ser.). 296p. 1982. 18.95x (ISBN 0-87805-163-5). U Pr of Miss.

--Faulkner: International Perspectives. LC 84-5096. (Faulkner & Yoknapatawpha Ser.). 368p. 1984. 22.50 (ISBN 0-87805-216-X); pap. text ed. 12.95 (ISBN 0-87805-217-8). U Pr of Miss.

--Fifty Years of Yoknapatawpha: Faulkner & Yoknapatawpha, 1979. LC 80-12255. (Faulkner & Yoknapatawpha Ser.). 1980. 15.95x (ISBN 0-87805-121-X); pap. 7.95 (ISBN 0-87805-122-8). U Pr of Miss.

--New Directions in Faulkner Studies. LC 84-40306. (Faulkner & Yoknapatawpha Ser.). 416p. 1984. 25.00x (ISBN 0-87805-220-8); pap. 14.95 (ISBN 0-87805-221-6). U Pr of Miss.

Fowler, Dorothy G. Cabinet Politician: The Postmasters General, 1829-1909. Repr. of 1943 ed. 26.00 (ISBN 0-404-02542-0). AMS Pr.

Fowler, Douglas. Reading Nabokov. LC 82-17342. 224p. 1983. pap. text ed. 11.75 (ISBN 0-8191-2721-3). U Pr of Amer.

--S. J. Perelman. (United States Authors Ser.). 1983. lib. bdg. 13.50 (ISBN 0-8057-7376-2, Twayne). G K Hall.

Fowler, E. P., tr. see Benedikt, Moriz.

Fowler, Earle B. Spenser & the System of Courtly Love. LC 72-194882. 1934. lib. bdg. 8.50 (ISBN 0-8414-4276-2). Folcroft.

--Spenser & the System of Courtly Love. LC 67-30903. 1967. Repr. of 1934 ed. 7.50x (ISBN 0-87753-016-5). Phaeton.

Fowler, Elaine W. English Sea Power in the Early Tudor Period, 1485-1558. LC 65-22933. (Folger Guides to the Age of Shakespeare). 1966. pap. 3.95 (ISBN 0-918016-15-0). Folger Bks.

Fowler, Elaine W., jt. ed. see Wright, Louis B.

Fowler, Elizabeth M. Ninety Days to Fortune. 1965. 8.95 (ISBN 0-8392-1137-6). Astor-Honor.

Fowler, Ellen T. Sirius: A Volume of Fiction. facsimile ed. LC 73-150543. (Short Story Index Reprint Ser.). Repr. of 1901 ed. 22.00 (ISBN 0-8369-3840-2). Ayer Co Pubs.

Fowler, Ethel L., ed. Daffodil Poetry Book. facs. ed. LC 70-128153. (Granger Index Reprint Ser). 1920. 18.00 (ISBN 0-8369-6180-3). Ayer Co Pubs.

--Second Daffodil Poetry Book. facs. ed. LC 75-123389. (Granger Index Reprint Ser). 1931. 17.00 (ISBN 0-8369-6177-3). Ayer Co Pubs.

Fowler, Everett W. Evaluating Versions of the New Testament. LC 80-81607. (Illus.). 80p. (Orig.). 1981. pap. 2.95 (ISBN 0-937136-03-4). Maranatha Baptist.

Fowler, F. G., jt. auth. see Fowler, H. W.

Fowler, F. G., jt. auth. see Fowler, Henry W.

Fowler, F. Parker, Jr. Basic Mathematics for Administration. LC 83-94. 358p. 1983. Repr. of 1962 ed. text ed. 24.95 (ISBN 0-89874-613-2). Krieger.

Fowler, Flora C. Materials Book for Reading Games for Middle & Upper Grades. (Illus.). 100p. 1974. pap. text ed. 4.95x (ISBN 0-8422-0430-X). Irvington.

Fowler, Flora C., ed. Reading Games for Middle & Upper Grades. LC 74-8367. 198p. 1975. pap. text ed. 6.95x (ISBN 0-8422-0430-X). Irvington.

Fowler, Frank. Southern Lights & Shadows. 1976. 16.00x (ISBN 0-424-00017-2, Pub. by Sydney U Pr). Intl Spec Bk.

Fowler, Frederick, jt. ed. see Appleby, William.

Fowler, G. N., jt. ed. see Conn, G. K.

Fowler, G. T., et al. Decision-Making in British Education: Theory & Practice. 1973. pap. text ed. 6.00x (ISBN 0-435-80311-5). Heinemann Ed.

Fowler, Gene. Beau James. 248p. Repr. of 1949 ed. lib. bdg. 15.95x (ISBN 0-89190-482-4, Pub. by River City Pr). Amereon Ltd.

--Beau James. LC 70-122073. Repr. of 1949 ed. 35.00x (ISBN 0-678-03154-1). Kelley.

--Father Goose. 1974. pap. 1.95 (ISBN 0-380-01179-4, 15966). Avon.

--Felon's Journal. 1975. pap. 2.50 (ISBN 0-915016-01-X). Second Coming.

--Fires. rev. ed. LC 75-19185. (Illus.). 1975. 10.00 (ISBN 0-914476-51-3); pap. 5.00x (ISBN 0-914476-01-7). Thorp Springs.

--Good Night, Sweet Prince. 1978. Repr. of 1944 ed. 21.95x (ISBN 0-89966-095-9). Buccaneer Bks.

--The Great Mouthpiece. 316p. 1984. Repr. lib. bdg. 21.95x (ISBN 0-89966-511-X). Buccaneer Bks.

--Minutes of the Last Meeting. 287p. Repr. of 1954 ed. lib. bdg. 16.95x (ISBN 0-89190-496-4, Pub. by River City Pr). Amereon Ltd.

--The Quiet Poems. 70p. (Orig.). 1982. pap. 5.00 (ISBN 0-932112-13-7). Carolina Wren.

--Return of the Shaman. 64p. (Orig.). 1981. pap. 4.00 (ISBN 0-915016-29-X). Second Coming.

--Timber Line. 416p. 1974. pap. 2.75 (ISBN 0-89174-007-4). Comstock Edns.

--Timber Line. 1981. Repr. lib. bdg. 17.95x (ISBN 0-89966-424-5). Buccaneer Bks.

--Waking the Poet. LC 81-52886. (Illus.). 272p. 1982. pap. 13.50 (ISBN 0-941386-00-7). Re-Geniusing.

Fowler, Gene & Meredyth, Bess. The Mighty Barnum. Kupelnick, Bruce S., ed. LC 76-52100. (Classics of Film Literature Ser.). 1978. lib. bdg. 22.00 (ISBN 0-8240-2873-2). Garland Pub.

Fowler, George B. Intellectual Interests of Engelbert of Admont. LC 75-168131. (Columbia University. Studies in the Social Sciences: No. 530). Repr. of 1947 ed. 20.00 (ISBN 0-404-51530-4). AMS Pr.

Fowler, George L., ed. Locomotive Dictionary. (Illus.). 684p. 1972. Repr. of 1906 ed. lib. bdg. 24.95 buckram (ISBN 0-912318-20-1). N K Gregg.

Fowler, Godfrey, jt. ed. see Gray, Muir.

Fowler, Gus. Getting What You Pay For. LC 82-74187. (Illus.). 248p. 1983. 10.95 (ISBN 0-9610432-1-0); pap. 9.95 (ISBN 0-9610432-0-2). Amistad Brands.

Fowler, H., jt. ed. see Hulse, S. H.

Fowler, H. R. The Fishes of Oceania: With Supplements 1-3. 1967. Repr. of 1881 ed. 105.00 (ISBN 3-7682-0444-8). Lubrecht & Cramer.

Fowler, H. Ramsey, et al. The Little, Brown Handbook. 2nd ed. 1982. text ed. 12.95 (ISBN 0-316-28981-7); tchr's. manual avail. (ISBN 0-316-28978-7); correction chart (ISBN 0-316-28976-0); answer booklet (ISBN 0-316-28975-2); diagnostic test A avail. (ISBN 0-316-28977-9); diagnostic test B avail. (ISBN 0-316-28974-4). Little.

Fowler, H. Seymour, jt. auth. see Palmer, E. Lawrence.

Fowler, H. W. Archaeological Fishbones Collected by E. W. Gifford in Fiji. (BMB). pap. 10.00 (ISBN 0-527-02322-1). Kraus Repr.

--A Dictionary of Modern English Usage. 2nd ed. 1983. pap. 8.95 (ISBN 0-19-281389-7, GB 725, GB). Oxford U Pr.

--Fishes of Guam, Hawaii, Samoa, & Tahiti. (BMB). pap. 8.00 (ISBN 0-527-02125-3). Kraus Repr.

--The Fishes of Oceania, 1927. (BMB). (Orig.). Repr. of 1949 ed. 98.00 (ISBN 0-527-01664-0). Kraus Repr.

--Fishes of the Tropical Central Pacific. (BMB). pap. 8.00 (ISBN 0-527-02141-5). Kraus Repr.

--Modern English Usage. 752p. 1985. 28.50 (ISBN 0-317-19969-2). Porter.

Fowler, H. W. & Ball, S. C. Fishes of Hawaii, Johnston Island, & Wake Island. (BMB). pap. 8.00 (ISBN 0-527-02129-6). Kraus Repr.

Fowler, H. W. & Fowler, F. G. The King's English. 3rd ed. 384p. 1985. pap. 6.95 (ISBN 0-19-881330-9). Oxford U Pr.

Fowler, H. W., et al. Metaphor. Commager, Steele, ed. Incl. English Idioms; English Influence on the French Vocabulary; Briton, British, Britisher; The Split Infinitive; Logic & Grammar; Four Words; Subjunctives; Medium Aevum & the Middle Age; Index to Tracts I-XIX. (Society for Pure English Ser.: Vol. 2). 1979. lib. bdg. 46.00 (ISBN 0-8240-3666-2). Garland Pub.

Fowler, Harlan D. Behold the Flaming Sword: A Biography of John & Jesus. 1983. 35.00 (ISBN 0-533-05059-6). Vantage.

--Three Caravans to Yuma: The Untold Story of Bactrian Camels in Western America. LC 80-66268. (Illus.). 173p. 1980. 25.00 (ISBN 0-87062-131-9). A H Clark.

Fowler, Harold. The Gospel of Matthew, Vol. I. LC 78-1064. (The Bible Study Textbook Ser.). (Illus.). 1975. 14.30 (ISBN 0-89900-029-0). College Pr Pub.

--The Gospel of Matthew, Vol. II. (The Bible Study Textbook Ser.). (Illus.). 1972. 15.90 (ISBN 0-89900-030-4). College Pr Pub.

--The Gospel of Matthew, Vol. III. (The Bible Study Textbook Ser.). (Illus.). 1978. 17.50 (ISBN 0-89900-031-2). College Pr Pub.

Fowler, Harold N. Greek Coins. 94p. 3.50 (ISBN 0-86516-017-1). Bolchazy-Carducci.

Fowler, Harold N. & Wheeler, James R. Handbook of Greek Archaeology. (Illus.). Repr. of 1909 ed. 19.50 (ISBN 0-404-02543-9). AMS Pr.

Fowler, Helen, jt. ed. see Fowler, Laurence.

Fowler, Henry T. The History & Literature of the New Testament. LC 78-12516. 1979. Repr. of 1925 ed. lib. bdg. 27.50x (ISBN 0-313-21188-4, FOHL). Greenwood.

Fowler, Henry W. Dictionary of Modern English Usage. 2nd ed. Gowers, Ernest, ed. (YA) (gr. 9 up). 1965. 17.95 (ISBN 0-19-500153-2); with thumb index 21.95 (ISBN 0-19-500154-0). Oxford U Pr.

--The Fishes of Oceania, 4 Vols. in 1. (Illus.). Repr. of 1949 ed. 140.00 (ISBN 0-384-16535-4). Johnson Repr.

--The Fishes of the George Vanderbilt South Pacific Expedition, 1937. (Monograph: No. 2). (Illus.). 349p. (Orig.). 1938. pap. 23.00 (ISBN 0-910006-09-1). Acad Nat Sci Phila.

--A Study of the Fish of the Southern Piedmont & Coastal Plain. (Monograph: No. 7). (Illus.). 408p. (Orig.). 1945. pap. 26.00 (ISBN 0-910006-16-4). Acad Nat Sci Phila.

Fowler, Henry W. & Fowler, F. G. King's English. 3rd ed. 384p. 1931. 18.95x (ISBN 0-19-869105-X). Oxford U Pr.

Fowler, Herbert A. & Bittinger, Ross T. Modern Creative Design & Its Application. 1951. 10.00 (ISBN 0-686-78144-9). Wahr.

Fowler, Ila E. Kentucky Pioneers & Their Descendants. LC 67-16864. 460p. 1978. Repr. of 1951 ed. 20.00 (ISBN 0-8063-0150-3). Genealog Pub.

Fowler, Ira. Human Anatomy. 615p. write for info. (ISBN 0-534-02746-6). Wadsworth Pub.

Fowler, J. B., Jr. Living Illustrations. 1985. pap. 5.95 (ISBN 0-8054-2260-9). Broadman.

Fowler, J. H. De Quincey As Literary Critic. LC 74-11177. 1974. Repr. of 1922 ed. lib. bdg. 6.00 (ISBN 0-8414-4216-9). Folcroft.

--Novels of Thomas Hardy. LC 77-873. 1928. lib. bdg. 8.50 (ISBN 0-8414-4184-7). Folcroft.

Fowler, Jacob. Journal Narrating an Adventure from Arkansas Through Indian Territory Etc. Coues, Elliot, ed. 1965. Repr. 8.75 (ISBN 0-87018-019-3). Ross.

--The Journal of Jacob Fowler. Coues, Elliott, ed. LC 77-110152. x, 152p. 1970. 13.95x (ISBN 0-8032-0756-5). U of Nebr Pr.

Fowler, James, ed. Images of Show Business: From the Theatre Museum, V. & A. (Illus.). 106p. 1983. pap. 12.95 (ISBN 0-413-39990-7, NO. 3827). Methuen Inc.

Fowler, James W. Becoming Adult, Becoming Christian: Adult Development & Christian Faith. LC 83-48987. 144p. 1984. 13.41 (ISBN 0-06-062841-3, HarpR). Har-Row.

--Stages of Faith: The Psychology of Human Development & the Quest for Meaning. LC 80-7757. 224p. 1981. 18.22 (ISBN 0-06-062840-5, HarpR). Har-Row.

Fowler, Jay B., Jr. Psalmbook of the White Butterfly. 64p. (Orig.). 1985. pap. 5.00 (ISBN 0-914061-03-8). Orchises Pr.

Fowler, Jennifer. Heinemann Modern Dictionary for Dental Students. 184p. (Eng. & Fr.). 1973. 29.95 (ISBN 0-686-56750-1, M-6257). French & Eur.

Fowler, Jim & Keen, Sam. Life Maps. 276p. 1985. 9.95 (ISBN 0-8499-0493-5, 0493-5); pap. 6.95 (ISBN 0-8499-3029-4, 3029-4). Word Bks.

Fowler, John. The IBM PC XT Graphics Book. (Illus.). 300p. 1984. 16.95 (ISBN 0-13-448408-8); pap. 34.95 incl. disk (ISBN 0-13-448416-9). P-H.

--Journal of a Tour in the State of New York in the Year 1830. LC 70-122073. Repr. of 1831 ed. 35.00x (ISBN 0-678-00582-6). Kelley.

--MGB '62 - '80. (Haynes Owners Workshop Manuals: No. 111). 1982. 12.95 (ISBN 0-85696-623-1, Pub by J H Haynes England). Haynes Pubns.

Fowler, John, jt. auth. see Cornforth, John.

Fowler, John F. Nuclear Particles in Cancer Treatment. (Medical Physics Handbook: No. 8). 216p. 1981. 28.00 (ISBN 0-9960020-7-3, Pub. by A. Hilger England). Heyden.

Fowler, John F., Jr. American Investment Trusts. facsimile ed. LC 75-2633. (Wall Street & the Security Market Ser.). 1975. Repr. of 1928 ed. 35.50x (ISBN 0-405-06958-8). Ayer Co Pubs.

Fowler, John M. Energy & the Environment. 2nd ed. 672p. 1984. pap. text ed. 27.95 (ISBN 0-07-021722-X). McGraw.

--Energy-Environment Source Book: Energy, Society, & the Environment; Energy, Its Extraction, Conversion, & Use, 2 vols. rev. ed. (Illus.). 1980. Set. pap. 9.00 (ISBN 0-87355-022-6). Natl Sci Tchrs.

Fowler, John S. Movement Education. 1981. text ed. 27.95 (ISBN 0-03-057881-7, CBS C). SCP.

Fowler, Kathryn M. Hunger: The World Food Crisis, An NSTA Environmental Materials Guide. 1977. pap. 5.00 (ISBN 0-87355-005-6). Natl Sci Tchrs.

--Population Growth: The Human Dilemma, An NSTA Environmental Materials Guide. 1977. pap. 5.00 (ISBN 0-87355-008-0). Natl Sci Tchrs.

Fowler, Kenneth. Jackal's Gold. 1981. pap. 1.95 (ISBN 0-440-14237-7). Dell.

Fowler, L., ed. Gas Chromatography. 1963. 65.00 (ISBN 0-12-263150-1). Acad Pr.

Fowler, L. N. How to Measure the Quality & Intensity of Your Mental Powers from the Physical Structure of Your Cranial Capacity. (Illus.). 1980. Repr. of 1842 ed. deluxe ed. 57.45 (ISBN 0-89901-000-8). Found Class Reprints.

--Phrenology Applied to Marriage & to the Major Social Relations of Mankind. (Illus.). 1978. Repr. of 1842 ed. 47.75 (ISBN 0-89266-109-7). Am Classical Coll Pr.

Fowler, Laurence & Fowler, Helen, eds. Cambridge Commemorated: An Anthology of University Life. (Illus.). 400p. 1984. 27.50 (ISBN 0-521-25743-3). Cambridge U Pr.

Fowler, Laurence H. & Baer, Elizabeth, eds. The Fowler Architectural Collection of the Johns Hopkins University. 1982. 100.00 (ISBN 0-89235-059-8). Res Pubns Conn.

Fowler, Lea. Precious in the Sight of God. 1983. pap. 4.95 (ISBN 0-89137-428-0). Quality Pubns.

Fowler, Loretta. Arapahoe Politics, 1851-1978: Symbols in Crises of Authority. LC 81-10368. (Illus.). xxii, 373p. 1982. 26.50x (ISBN 0-8032-1956-3). U of Nebr Pr.

Fowler, Marian. The Embroidered Tent: Five Gentlewomen in Early Canada. (Illus.). 240p. 1982. pap. 9.95 (ISBN 0-88784-091-4, Pub. by Hse Anansi Pr Canada). U of Toronto Pr.

--Redney: A Life of Sara Jeannette Duncan. (Illus.). 336p. 1983. 19.95 (ISBN 0-88784-099-X, Pub. by Hse Anansi Pr Canada). U of Toronto Pr.

Fowler, Mark, jt. auth. see Felton, Bruce.

Fowler, Melvin L. Ferry Site, Hardin County, Illinois. facsimile ed. (Scientific Papers Ser.: Vol. VIII, No. 1). (Illus.). 36p. 1974. pap. 2.00 (ISBN 0-89792-016-3). Ill St Museum.

--Rutherford Mound, Hardin County, Illinois. facsimile ed. (Scientific Papers Ser.: Vol. VII, No. 1). (Illus.). 44p. 1974. pap. 2.00 (ISBN 0-89792-015-5). Ill St Museum.

--Summary Report of the Modoc Rock Shelter, 1952-1956. facsimile ed. (Reports of Investigations Ser.: No. 8). (Illus.). 72p. 1971. pap. 3.00 (ISBN 0-89792-019-8). Ill St Museum.

Fowler, Michael. Winston S. Churchill: Philosopher & Statesman. LC 84-29122. (The Credibility of Institutions, Policies & Leadership Ser.: Vol. 19). 92p. (Orig.). 1985. lib. bdg. 16.50 (ISBN 0-8191-4416-9, Co-pub. by White Miller Center); pap. text ed. 6.75 (ISBN 0-8191-4417-7). U Pr of Amer.

Fowler, Murray E. Restraint & Handling of Wild & Domestic Animals. (Illus.). 332p. 1978. text ed. 28.95x (ISBN 0-8138-1890-7). Iowa St U Pr.

Fowler, Nathaniel C. The Boy: How to Help Him Succeed. (Educational Ser.). 1912. Repr. 8.00 (ISBN 0-685-43499-0). Norwood Edns.

--The Story of Story Writing: Facts & Information about Literary Work of Practical Value to Both Amateur & Professional Writers. 255p. 1982. Repr. of 1913 ed. lib. bdg. 40.00 (ISBN 0-89984-207-0). Century Bookbindery.

Fowler, Noble O. The Pericardium in Health & Disease. (Illus.). 376p. 1984. 47.50 (ISBN 0-87993-229-5). Futura Pub.

Fowler, Noble O., ed. Diagnostic Methods in Cardiology. LC 74-12055. (Cardiovascular Clinics Ser.: Vol. 6, No. 3). (Illus.). 455p. 1975. text ed. 35.00x (ISBN 0-8036-3710-1). Davis Co.

--Myocardial Diseases. LC 73-1685. (Clinical Cardiology Monograph). (Illus.). 392p. 1973. 75.00 (ISBN 0-8089-0799-9, 791300). Grune.

--Noninvasive Diagnostic Methods in Cardiology. LC 82-23646. (Cardiovascular Clinics: Vol.13, No. 3). (Illus.). 411p. 1983. 50.00x (ISBN 0-8036-3712-8). Davis Co.

Fowler, Orson. Hereditary Descent: Its Laws & Facts Applied to Human Improvement. Rosenberg, Charles, ed. LC 83-48538. (The History of Hereditarian Thought Ser.). 288p. 1985. Repr. of 1847 ed. lib. bdg. 35.00 (ISBN 0-8240-5812-7). Garland Pub.

Fowler, Orson S. Amativeness. LC 78-72339. (Free Love in America). Repr. of 1844 ed. 12.50 (ISBN 0-404-60953-8). AMS Pr.

--Creative & Sexual Science. LC 78-72340. (Free Love in America). Repr. of 1870 ed. 69.50 (ISBN 0-404-60954-6). AMS Pr.

--The Octagon House: A Home for All. LC 72-93768. Orig. Title: A Home for All. (Illus.). 198p. 1973. pap. 4.95 (ISBN 0-486-22887-8). Dover.

Fowler, P. B., jt. ed. see Keynes, W. Milo.

Fowler, P. H., ed. see International Conference on Solid State Nuclear Track Detectors, 11th, Bristol, UK, Sept. 1981.

Fowler, Peter. The Farming of Prehistoric Britain. LC 83-1808. 256p. 1983. pap. 15.95 (ISBN 0-521-27369-2). Cambridge U Pr.

Fowler, Peter J., ed. Recent Work in Rural Archaeology. (Illus.). 160p. 1975. 15.00x (ISBN 0-87471-596-2). Rowman.

Fowler, R. UFOs: Interplanetary Visitors. 1979. pap. 4.95 (ISBN 0-13-935569-3, Reward). P-H.

Fowler, R. F. The Depreciation of Capital, Analytically Considered. (London School of Econ. & Pol. Sci. Studies in Economics & Commerce: Vol. 3). pap. 17.00 (ISBN 0-317-16227-6). Kraus Repr.

Fowler, R. J. Electricity: Principles & Applications. 2nd ed. 336p. 1984. 25.56 (ISBN 0-07-021707-6); activities manual 12.76 (ISBN 0-07-021708-4). McGraw.

Fowler, Ralph H. Statistical Mechanics. rev., 2nd ed. (Illus.). 875p. 1980. 110.00 (ISBN 0-521-05025-1); pap. 44.50 (ISBN 0-521-09377-5). Cambridge U Pr.

Fowler, Ralph H. & Guggenheim, E. A. Statistical Thermodynamics: A Version of Statistical Mechanics for Students of Physics & Chemistry. pap. 160.00 (ISBN 0-317-08661-8, 2051495). Bks Demand UMI.

Fowler, Raymond E. The Andreasson Affair, Phase Two: The Continuing Investigation of a Woman's Abduction by Alien Beings. (Illus.). 278p. 1983. pap. 5.95 (ISBN 0-13-036624-2). P-H.

--Casebook of a UFO Investigator. 1981. 10.95 (ISBN 0-13-117432-0). P-H.

Fowler, Richard. Amazing Journey of Space Ship H-20. (Slot Bks.). 24p. (ps-1). 1984. pap. 8.95 (ISBN 0-88110-156-7). EDC.

--Bear's Story. (Stand-Up Stories Ser.). (Illus.). 24p. (gr. k). 1985. pap. 1.95 (ISBN 0-448-07854-6, G&D). Putnam Pub Group.

--Cat's Story. (Stand-Up Stories Ser.). (Illus.). 24p. (gr. k). 1985. pap. 1.95 (ISBN 0-448-07851-1, G&D). Putnam Pub Group.

--Dog's Story. (Stand-Up Stories Ser.). (Illus.). 24p. (gr. k-1). 1985. pap. 1.95 (ISBN 0-448-07852-X, G&D). 15.60 (ISBN 0-448-81837-X). Putnam Pub Group.

--Fun on the Beach. (Unfold-A-Story Ser.). (Illus.). 1984. 2.95 (ISBN 0-8431-0983-1). Price Stern.

--Inspector Smart Gets the Message! LC 82-82623. (Illus.). 16p. (gr. 1-3). 1983. 7.95i (ISBN 0-316-28983-3). Little.

--Inspector Smart's International Mystery Tour. (Illus.). (gr. 1-3). 1984. 8.70i (ISBN 0-316-28988-4). Little.

--Let's Find the Treasure. (Unfold-A-Story Ser.). (Illus.). 1984. 2.95 (ISBN 0-8431-0985-8). Price Stern.

--Let's Go to the Zoo. (Unfold-a-Story Ser.). 8p. 1984. pap. 2.95 (ISBN 0-8431-0984-X). Price Stern.

--Let's Have a Picnic. (Unfold-A-Story Ser.). (Illus.). 1984. 2.95 (ISBN 0-8431-0986-6). Price Stern.

--Mouse about the House. (Slot Bks.). 24p. (ps-1). 1984. 8.95 (ISBN 0-88110-154-0). EDC.

--Owl's Story. (Stand-Up Stories Ser.). (Illus.). 24p. (gr. k-1). 1985. pap. 1.95 (ISBN 0-448-07853-8, G&D). Putnam Pub Group.

--Squirrel's Tale. (Slot Bks.). 24p. 1984. 8.95 (ISBN 0-88110-157-5). EDC.

--Ted & Dolly's Magic Carpet Ride. (Slot Bks.). 24p. (ps-1). 1984. 8.95 (ISBN 0-88110-155-9). EDC.

Fowler, Richard A. & House, H. Wayne. The Christian Confronts His Culture. 228p. (Orig.). 1983. pap. 7.95 (ISBN 0-8024-0232-1). Moody.

Fowler, Richard J. Electricity: Principles & Applications. Schuler, Charles, ed. (Basic Skills in Electricity & Electronics). (Illus.). 1979. text ed. 25.54 (ISBN 0-07-021704-1). McGraw.

Fowler, Robert A., ed. Buyerism: How to Buy or Start & Successfully Run Your Own Small Business. 1971. pap. 5.95 (ISBN 0-317-11969-9). WWWWW Info Serv.

--Buyerism: Survival & Tactics to Help You Buy or Start & Successfully Run Your Own Small Business. 1982. pap. 2.95 (ISBN 0-317-11982-6). WWWWW Info Serv.

--Creative Winemaking. 1972. pap. 12.95 (ISBN 0-317-11984-2). WWWWW Info Serv.

Fowler, Robert A & Hummel, T. W., eds. Buyerism: How to Buy a Franchise or Small Business. new ed. 1979. pap. 5.95 (ISBN 0-685-48362-2). WWWWW Info Serv.

Fowler, Robert B. Believing Skeptics: American Political Intellectuals, 1945-1964. LC 77-87967. (Contributions in Political Science Ser.: No. 5). 1978. lib. bdg. 29.95 (ISBN 0-313-20026-2, FAP/). Greenwood.

--A New Engagement: Evangelical Political Thought, 1966-1976. 298p. (Orig.). 1983. pap. 13.95 (ISBN 0-8028-1929-X). Eerdmans.

Fowler, Robert B. & Orenstein, Jeffrey R. Contemporary Issues in Political Theory. rev. ed. LC 84-26280. 176p. 1985. 28.95x (ISBN 0-03-000838-7); pap. 13.95x (ISBN 0-03-000839-5). Praeger.

Fowler, Robert Booth. Religion & Politics in America. LC 84-20237. (Atla Monograph: No. 21). 365p. 1984. 25.00 (ISBN 0-8108-1752-7). Scarecrow.

Fowler, Robert D., ed. see Ryback, Ralph S., et al.

Fowler, Robert H. The Spoils of Eden. 352p. 1985. 16.95 (ISBN 0-396-08490-7). Dodd.

Fowler, Robert M. Loaves & Fishes: The Function of the Feeding Stories in the Gospel of Mark. Baird, William, ed. LC 81-2749. (Society of Biblical Literature Dissertation Ser.). 1981. pap. 15.00 (ISBN 0-89130-486-X, 06-01-54). Scholars Pr GA.

Fowler, Roe. Christmas Was. 88p. 1982. pap. 6.95 (ISBN 0-686-38093-2). Fig Leaf Pr.

Fowler, Roger. Introduction to Transformational Syntax. 1971. pap. 9.95x (ISBN 0-7100-6976-6). Routledge & Kegan.

--Linguistics & the Novel. (New Accents Ser.). 160p. 1977. 9.95 (ISBN 0-416-83820-0, NO. 2242). Methuen Inc.

--Literature as Social Discourse: The Practice of Linguistic Criticism. LC 81-47761. 216p. 1982. 17.50x (ISBN 0-253-33511-6). Ind U Pr.

Fowler, Roger, ed. A Dictionary of Modern Critical Terms. 218p. 1973. pap. 7.95 (ISBN 0-7100-7544-8). Routledge & Kegan.

--Style & Structure in Literature: Essays in the New Stylistics. LC 74-24277. 257p. 1975. 24.95 (ISBN 0-8014-0949-7). Cornell U Pr.

Fowler, Roger, et al. Language & Control. (Illus.). 1979. 25.00x (ISBN 0-7100-0288-2). Routledge & Kegan.

Fowler, Ron. Flying Precision Maneuvers. 1982. 10.95 (ISBN 0-02-540350-8). Macmillan.

--Making Perfect Landings in Light Airplanes. (Illus.). 128p. 1984. 12.95 (ISBN 0-8138-1081-7). Iowa St U Pr.

--Pre-Flight Planning. (Illus.). 320p. 1983. 17.95 (ISBN 0-02-540300-1). Macmillan.

Fowler, Ruth, ed. see Soon Man Rhim.

Fowler, Steve, ed. see Center for Business & Economic Research.

Fowler, Stewart H. Beef Production in the South. LC 78-55815. (Illus.). 932p. (gr. 9-12). 1979. 38.00 (ISBN 0-8134-2035-0); text ed. 28.50x (2035). Interstate.

Fowler, T. & May, R., eds. Neurology. (Management of Common Diseases in Family Practice Ser.). 1985. lib. bdg. 19.00 (ISBN 0-85200-758-2, Pub. by MTP Pr England). Kluwer-Academic.

Fowler, Thomas. Locke. Morley, John, ed. LC 68-58378. (English Men of Letters). Repr. of 1888 ed. lib. bdg. 12.50 (ISBN 0-404-51710-2). AMS Pr.

--Locke. 1973. Repr. of 1880 ed. 12.00 (ISBN 0-8274-1339-4). R West.

Fowler, Thomas, ed. see Bacon, Francis.

Fowler, Thomas, ed. see Locke, John.

Fowler, Thomas B., Jr., tr. see Zubiri, Xavier.

Fowler, Virginia C. Henry James's American Girl: The Embroidery on the Canvas. LC 83-51050. 192p. 1984. 22.50x (ISBN 0-299-09570-3). U of Wis Pr.

Fowler, Virginie. Christmas Crafts & Customs Around the World. LC 84-9770. (Illus.). 160p. (gr. 5 up). 1984. 10.95 (ISBN 0-13-133661-4). P-H.

--Folk Arts Around the World. (Illus.). 168p. (gr. 5 up). 1984. pap. 5.95 (ISBN 0-13-322975-0). P-H.

--Folk Arts Around the World: And How to Make Them. (YA) (gr. 5 up). 1981. 7.95 (ISBN 0-13-323014-7). P-H.

--Folk Toys Around the World & How to Make Them. 160p. 1984. 10.95 (ISBN 0-13-323148-8). P-H.

--Paperworks: Colorful Crafts from Picture Eggs to Fish Kites. (Illus.). 162p. (Orig.). (gr. 5 up). 1982. 10.95 (ISBN 0-13-648543-X). P-H.

--Paperworks: Colorful Crafts from Picture Eggs to Fish Kites. (Illus.). (gr. 5 up). 1985. pap. 7.95 (ISBN 0-13-648551-0). P-H.

Fowler, W. Beall. Physics of Color Centers. LC 68-18667. (Illus.). 1968. 83.00 (ISBN 0-12-262950-7). Acad Pr.

Fowler, W. W. Coleoptera: General Introduction & Cicindelidae & Paussidae. (Fauna of British India Ser.). xx, 530p. 1973. Repr. of 1912 ed. 20.00 (ISBN 0-88065-085-0, Pub. by Messers Today & Tomorrows Printers & Publishers India). Scholarly Pubns.

Fowler, W. Warde. The Roman Festivals of the Period of the Republic. 1977. lib. bdg. 59.95 (ISBN 0-8490-2532-X). Gordon Pr.

--Social Life at Rome in the Age of Cicero. 1916. 65.00 (ISBN 0-8274-3444-8). R West.

Fowler, Washington. Histories & Mysteries of the Money: Kings of Wall Street, 2 vols. (Illus.). 546p. 1984. Set. 237.45x (ISBN 0-86654-121-7). Inst Econ Finan.

Fowler, Will. The Second Handshake. (Illus.). 1980. 12.50 (ISBN 0-8184-0287-3). Lyle Stuart.

Fowler, William, ed. see Coyle, E. Wallace.

Fowler, William, et al. Potentials of Childhood: Studies in Early Developmental Learning, 2 vols. LC 80-8839. 1983. Set. 71.00x (ISBN 0-669-06432-7); Vol. I. 39.00x (ISBN 0-669-04387-7); Vol. II. 39.00x (ISBN 0-669-06433-5). Lexington Bks.

Fowler, William A. Nuclear Astrophysics. LC 67-18204. (Memoirs Ser.: Vol. 67). (Illus.). 1967. 5.00 (ISBN 0-87169-067-5). Am Philos.

Fowler, William C. Local Law in Massachusetts & Connecticut. facsimile ed. LC 70-161259. (Black Heritage Library Collection). Repr. of 1875 ed. 16.00 (ISBN 0-8369-8818-3). Ayer Co Pubs.

Fowler, William L. Advanced Chord Progressions. LC 84-71709. (Guitar Ser.: Bk. 4). (Illus.). 84p. 1985. pap. text ed. 10.00 (ISBN 0-943894-07-7). Fowler Music.

--Advanced Chord Ser. Guitar Ser. LC 84-71709. (Bk. 3). (Illus.). 76p. 1984. pap. text ed. 10.00 (ISBN 0-943894-06-9). Fowler Music.

--Chord Progression Systems: Session Systems. LC 84-71709. (Guitar Ser.: Bk. 2). (Illus.). 84p. 1984. pap. text ed. 10.00 (ISBN 0-943894-05-0). Fowler Music.

--Chord Voicing Systems. LC 84-71709. (Guitar Ser.: Bk. 1). (Illus.). 84p. 1984. pap. text ed. 10.00 (ISBN 0-943894-04-2). Fowler Music.

--Take Another Look at Linear Bass Patterns. LC 82-90965. (Illus.). 82p. 1983. pap. text ed. 10.00 (ISBN 0-943894-01-8). Fowler Music.

--Take Another Look at the Keyboard. LC 82-90364. (Illus.). 100p. 1982. pap. text ed. 12.00 (ISBN 0-943894-00-X). Fowler Music.

--Visual Keyboard Chord Progressions, Bk. I. LC 83-81908. (Illus.). 75p. 1983. pap. text ed. 10.00 (ISBN 0-943894-02-6). Fowler Music.

--Visual Keyboard Chord Progressions, Bk. II. LC 83-81908. (Illus.). 76p. 1984. pap. text ed. 10.00 (ISBN 0-943894-03-4). Fowler Music.

--Visual Keyboard Chord Progressions, Bk. III. LC 83-81908. (Illus.). 84p. 1985. pap. text ed. 10.00 (ISBN 0-943894-08-5). Fowler Music.

Fowler, William M. & Coyle, Wallace, eds. The American Revolution: Changing Perspectives. LC 79-88424. (Illus.). 231p. 1979. 20.95x (ISBN 0-930350-03-0). NE U Pr.

Fowler, William M., Jr. Jack Tars & Commodores: The American Navy, 1783-1815. (Illus.). 310p. 1984. 19.95 (ISBN 0-395-35314-9). HM.

Fowler, William P. Sunset Wings. 96p. 1981. 8.50 (ISBN 0-914339-03-6). P E Randall Pub.

Fowler, William S. A Study in Radicalism & Dissent. LC 72-11684. (Illus.). 192p. 1973. Repr. of 1961 ed. lib. bdg. 15.00x (ISBN 0-8371-6673-X, FOSR). Greenwood.

Fowler, William W. Inside Life in Wall Street. LC 75-174397. (Illus.). Repr. of 1874 ed. 27.50 (ISBN 0-405-08503-6, Blom Pubns). Ayer Co Pubs.

--Julius Caesar & the Foundation of the Roman Imperial System. LC 73-14443. (Heroes of the Nations Ser.). Repr. of 1892 ed. 30.00 (ISBN 0-404-58261-3). AMS Pr.

--Religious Experience of the Roman People: From the Earliest Times to the Age of Augustus. LC 71-145870. 504p. 1971. Repr. of 1911 ed. lib. bdg. 40.00 (ISBN 0-8154-0372-0). Cooper Sq.

--Roman Ideas of Deity in the Last Century Before the Christian Era. LC 75-102236. (Select Bibliographies Reprint Ser). 1914. 19.00 (ISBN 0-8369-5121-2). Ayer Co Pubs.

--Ten Years in Wall Street: Or, Revelations of Inside Life & Experience on Change. (Illus.). 1870. 26.00 (ISBN 0-8337-4643-X). B Franklin.

--Virgil's Gathering of the Clans. Steele, Commager, ed. (Latin Poetry Ser.). 52.00 (ISBN 0-8240-2969-0). Garland Pub.

--Woman of the American Frontier. 59.95 (ISBN 0-8490-1316-X). Gordon Pr.

--Woman on the American Frontier. LC 73-12867. 1974. Repr. of 1878 ed. 56.00x (ISBN 0-8103-3702-9). Gale.

--Woman on the American Frontier. 527p. Repr. of 1877 ed. 59.00 (ISBN 0-932051-33-2). Am Repr Serv.

--Women on the American Frontier. 527p. 1976. Repr. of 1876 ed. 21.00 (ISBN 0-87928-074-3). Corner Hse.

Fowler, Wilton B. British-American Relations, Nineteen Seventeen to Nineteen Eighteen: The Role of Sir William Wiseman. (The Papers of Woodrow Wilson). 1969. 35.00x (ISBN 0-691-04594-1). Princeton U Pr.

--American Diplomatic History Since 1890. LC 74-76971. (Goldentree Bibliographies in American History Ser). (Orig.). 1975. pap. 13.95x (ISBN 0-88295-544-6). Harlan Davidson.

Fowler, Zinita. Ghost Stories of Old Texas. (Illus.). 68p. 1983. 6.95 (ISBN 0-89015-407-4). Eakin Pubns.

--Monster Magic: A Reading Activities Idea Book for Use with Children. LC 82-12492. (A Fun with Reading Bk.). (Illus.). 78p. (Orig.). 1983. pap. 9.95x (ISBN 0-89774-044-0). Oryx Pr.

Fowler-Clark, Margaret W. Tchaikovsky: The Lonely Way. 1981. 12.50 (ISBN 0-317-02278-4); pap. 7.95 (ISBN 0-317-02279-2). Dietz.

Fowles, jt. auth. see Cartmell.

Fowles, A. J. Complex Sequencing by Programmable Logic Controller, 1977. 1981. 35.00x (ISBN 0-686-97049-7, Pub. by W Spring England). State Mutual Bk.

Fowles, A. J., jt. auth. see Jones, Kathleen.

Fowles, D. E., jt. auth. see Willmott, A. S.

Fowles, Don C., ed. Clinical Applications of Psychophysiology. LC 75-15609. (Illus.). 238p. 1975. 26.00x (ISBN 0-231-03931-X). Columbia U Pr.

Fowles, G. M. Down in Puerto Rico. 1976. lib. bdg. 69.95 (ISBN 0-8490-1380-1). Gordon Pr.

Fowles, Grant. Analytical Mechanics. 3rd ed. LC 76-57839. 1977. text ed. 41.95 (ISBN 0-03-089725-4, HoltC). HR&W.

--Analytical Mechanics. 4th ed. 1986. text ed. 41.95 (ISBN 0-03-004124-4, CBS C). SCP.

Fowles, Jib. Television Viewers vs. Media Snobs. LC 82-40007. 288p. 1982. 16.95 (ISBN 0-8128-2879-8). Stein & Day.

Fowles, Jib, ed. Handbook of Futures Research. LC 77-84767. (Illus.). 1978. lib. bdg. 55.00x (ISBN 0-8371-9885-2, FHF/). Greenwood.

Fowles, John. The Aristos. rev. ed. 1970. 14.45i (ISBN 0-316-29094-7). Little.

--The Aristos. 1975. pap. 5.95 (ISBN 0-452-25354-3, Z5354, Plume). NAL.

--The Collector. 256p. 1975. pap. 3.95 (ISBN 0-440-31335-X). Dell.

--The Collector. 1963. 15.45i (ISBN 0-316-29096-3). Little.

--Daniel Martin. 1977. 15.00 (ISBN 0-316-28959-0). Little.

--Daniel Martin. 1978. pap. 4.50 (ISBN 0-451-12210-0, AE2210, Sig). NAL.

--The Ebony Tower. 1974. 12.95 (ISBN 0-316-29093-9). Little.

--The Ebony Tower. 320p. 1975. pap. 3.95 (ISBN 0-451-13464-8, AE2354, Sig). NAL.

--The French Lieutenant's Woman. LC 77-86616. 1969. 14.95 (ISBN 0-316-29099-8). Little.

--The French Lieutenant's Woman. 1981. pap. 3.95 (ISBN 0-451-11095-1, Sig). NAL.

--Islands. (Illus.). 1979. 10.95 (ISBN 0-316-28960-4). Little.

--A Maggot. 1985. 19.95 (ISBN 0-317-20676-1); ltd. ed. 100.00 (ISBN 0-316-29115-3). Little.

--The Magus. rev. ed. 1979. pap. 4.95 (ISBN 0-440-35162-6). Dell.

--The Magus. rev. ed. 1978. 12.95 (ISBN 0-316-29092-0). Little.

--Mantissa. LC 82-7234. 192p. 1982. 13.95 (ISBN 0-316-28980-9); deluxe ed. 75.00 (ISBN 0-316-28982-5). Little.

--Mantissa. LC 83-10526. 208p. 1983. pap. 6.95 (ISBN 0-452-25429-9, Plume). NAL.

--Poems. LC 72-96853. 100p. 1973. 7.50 (ISBN 0-912946-02-4). Ecco Pr.

--Shipwreck. LC 74-196873. (Illus.). 48p. 1979. 8.95 (ISBN 0-224-01053-0, Pub. by Jonathan Cape). Merrimack Pub Cir.

--Shipwreck. (Illus.). 48p. 1983. pap. 9.70i (ISBN 0-316-29091-2). Little.

--A Short History of Lyme Regis. (Illus.). 56p. 1983. 13.00 (ISBN 0-316-28987-6). Little.

--The Tree. (Illus.). 1980. 24.95 (ISBN 0-316-28957-4). Little.

--The Tree. 125p. (Orig.). 1983. 13.50 (ISBN 0-88001-033-9); pap. 7.95 (ISBN 0-88001-040-1). Ecco Pr.

Fowles, John & Huffaker, Robert. Fowles John. (English Authors Ser.). 1980. 13.50 (ISBN 0-8057-6785-1, Twayne). G K Hall.

Fowles, John, ed. see Aubrey, John.

Fowles, John, tr. from Fr. Cinderella. (Illus.). 32p. (gr. 1-3). 1976. 5.95 (ISBN 0-316-29101-3). Little.

Fowles, John, et al. Britain: A World by Itself; Reflections on the Landscape by Eminent British Writers. LC 84-81453. (Illus.). 160p. 1984. 27.50 (ISBN 0-316-91776-1). Little.

Fowles, John V. Skeletal Trauma Notes. 509p. 1985. 42.00 (ISBN 0-683-03318-2). Williams & Wilkins.

Fowles, Robert B. Mass Advertising As Social Forecast: A Method for Futures Research. LC 75-35344. (Illus.). 160p. 1976. lib. bdg. 27.50 (ISBN 0-8371-8595-5, FMA/). Greenwood.

Fowley, John. John Aubrey's Monumenta Britannica. 600p. 250.00x (ISBN 0-686-75655-X, Pub. by Dorset). State Mutual Bk.

--Steep Holm: Case History in the Study of Evolution. 228p. 40.00x (ISBN 0-686-75653-3, Pub. by Dorset). State Mutual Bk.

Fowlie, Wallace. Aubade: A Teacher's Notebook. LC 83-14095. 216p. 1983. 30.00 (ISBN 0-8223-0566-6); pap. 12.95 (ISBN 0-8223-0588-7). Duke.

--Characters from Proust: Poems. LC 82-18641. 50p. 1983. 13.95x (ISBN 0-8071-1070-1); pap. 5.95 (ISBN 0-8071-1071-X). La State U Pr.

--Clowns & Angels: Studies in Modern French Literature. LC 72-93684. 162p. 1973. Repr. of 1943 ed. lib. bdg. 20.00 (ISBN 0-8154-0467-0). Cooper Sq.

--Clown's Grail, Study of Love in Its Literary Expression. LC 73-11380. 1947. lib. bdg. 17.50 (ISBN 0-8414-1981-7). Folcroft.

--Dionysus in Paris: A Guide to Contemporary French Theatre. (Illus.). 11.25 (ISBN 0-8446-0096-2). Peter Smith.

--Guide to Contemporary French Literature from Valery to Sartre. 11.00 (ISBN 0-8446-2077-7). Peter Smith.

--Journal of Rehearsals: A Memoir. LC 77-79809. 1977. 16.50x (ISBN 0-8223-0401-5). Duke.

--Love in Literature: Studies in Symbolic Expression. facsimile ed. LC 70-37836. (Essay Index Reprint Ser). Repr. of 1965 ed. 18.00 (ISBN 0-8369-2589-0). Ayer Co Pubs.

--Mallarme. 1953. Repr. 15.00 (ISBN 0-8274-2667-4). R West.

--Mallarme. LC 53-9931. (Illus.). 1962. pap. 2.45 (ISBN 0-226-25881-5, P93, Phoen). U of Chicago Pr.

--Pantomime, a Journal of Rehearsals. LC 74-29632. 246p. 1975. Repr. of 1951 ed. lib. bdg. 19.75x (ISBN 0-8371-7981-5, FOPA). Greenwood.

--A Reading of Dante's Inferno. LC 80-19025. 248p. 1981. lib. bdg. 18.00x (ISBN 0-226-25887-4); pap. 6.50x (ISBN 0-226-25888-2). U of Chicago Pr.

--A Reading of Proust. 11.00 (ISBN 0-8446-0627-8). Peter Smith.

--A Reading of Proust. 2nd ed. LC 75-14766. xii, 324p. 1975. pap. 14.00 (ISBN 0-226-25885-8). U of Chicago Pr.

Fowlie, Wallace, ed. see Rimbaud, Jean N.

Fowlie, Wallace, tr. see Moliere, Jean B.

Fowlie, Wallace, tr. see Rimbaud, Arthur.

Fowlkes, Diane L. & McClure, Charlotte S. Feminist Visions: Toward a Transformation of the Liberal Arts Curriculum. LC 83-6539. (Illus.). viii, 220p. 1984. text ed. 22.50 (ISBN 0-8173-0172-0). U of Ala Pr.

Fowlkes, Martha R. Behind Every Successful Man: Wives of Medicine & Academe. LC 79-24901. (Illus.). 232p. 1980. 25.00x (ISBN 0-231-04776-2). Columbia U Pr.

Fox & Buckley. Pathology for Gynecologists. (Illus.). 288p. 1983. text ed. 49.50 (ISBN 0-8391-1818-X, 19836). Univ Park.

Fox, jt. auth. see Dixson.

Fox, jt. auth. see Odeh.

Fox, jt. auth. see Parkinson.

Fox, jt. auth. see Sokolow.

Fox, et al. Fitness for Life. 369p. 1986. pap. price not set (ISBN 0-02-339190-1). Macmillan.

Fox, A. Sociology of Work in Industry. 1971. pap. text ed. 2.45x (ISBN 0-02-973610-2). Macmillan.

Fox, A. F. World of Oil. 1964. pap. 7.75 (ISBN 0-08-010686-2). Pergamon.

Fox, Aileen. Prehistoric Maori Fortifications in the North Island of New Zealand. new ed. (New Zealand Archaeological Association Monographs: No. 6). (Illus.). 1976. text ed. 15.00x (ISBN 0-582-71746-9). Longman.

--Roman Britain. LC 68-23081. (Illus.). (gr. 7 up). 1968. 9.50 (ISBN 0-8023-1143-1). Dufour.

Fox, Alan. History & Heritage: The Social Origins of the British Industrial Relations System. 440p. 1985. text ed. 42.50X (ISBN 0-04-331099-0). Allen Unwin.

--Man Mismanagement. 2nd ed. 224p. 1985. 15.95x (ISBN 0-915938-08-1, Pub. by Busn Bks England). Brookfield Pub Co.

Fox, Alistair. Thomas More: History & Providence. LC 82-11178. 288p. 1983. text ed. 27.50x (ISBN 0-300-02951-9). Yale U Pr.

--Thomas More: History & Providence. LC 82-11178. 288p. 1985. Repr. of 1983 ed. pap. text ed. 10.95x (ISBN 0-300-03415-6, Y-536). Yale U Pr.

Fox, Ann M. S., jt. auth. see Dodd, Sue A.

Fox, Anne C. The Foxie Reference: A Guide to the Readability Levels of Stories in Thirty-Two Basal Reading Series from 1970-1978, Vol. I. LC 78-67799. 1979. 95.00 (ISBN 0-686-26183-6). Fox Reading Res.

Fox, Annette B. The Politics of Attraction: Four Middle Powers & the United States. LC 76-27291. (Institute of War & Peace Studies). 371p. 1977. 29.00x (ISBN 0-231-04116-0). Columbia U Pr.

Fox, Annette B., jt. auth. see Fox, William T.

Fox, Annie & Fox, David. Armchair BASIC: An Absolute Beginner's Guide to Programming in BASIC. 264p. (Orig.). 1982. pap. 12.95 (ISBN 0-07-047858-9, 858-9). Osborne-McGraw.

Fox, Anthony. German Intonation: An Outline. LC 83-24399. 120p. 1984. 19.95x (ISBN 0-19-815794-0). Oxford U Pr.

Fox, Anthony, jt. auth. see Crewe, Ivor.

Fox, Arnold & Fox, Barry. DLPA to End Pain & Depression. (Orig.). 1985. pap. 6.95 (ISBN 0-671-54503-5, Long Shadow Bks). PB.

Fox, Arthur W. Ennyson's "Idylls of the King," Six Studies. LC 73-12602. Repr. of 1909 ed. lib. bdg. 5.50 (ISBN 0-8414-4150-2). Folcroft.

--Tennyson's Idylls of the King. LC 79-113334. 1970. Repr. of 1909 ed. 14.00x (ISBN 0-8046-1017-7, Pub by Kennikat). Assoc Faculty Pr.

Fox, Arturo A. Espana: Ida y Vuelta. 224p. 1981. pap. text ed. 9.95 (ISBN 0-15-522868-4, HC). HarBraceJ.

Fox, Augustus H. Fundamentals of Numerical Analysis. LC 63-10639. pap. 38.30 (ISBN 0-317-08686-3, 2012453). Bks Demand UMI.

Fox, Austin M., ed. see Irving, Washington.

Fox, B. W. & Fox, M., eds. Antitumor Drug Resistance. (Handbook of Experimental Pharmacology: Vol. 72). (Illus.). 745p. 1984. 198.00 (ISBN 0-387-13069-1). Springer-Verlag.

Fox, Barry, jt. auth. see Fox, Arnold.

Fox, Bernard H. & Newberry, Benjamin H., eds. Impact of Psychoendocrine Systems in Cancer & Immunity. 314p. (Orig.). 1984. text ed. 36.00 (ISBN 0-88937-005-2). Hogrefe Intl.

Fox, Bertrand, jt. auth. see Smith, Dan T.

Fox, Brian A. & Cameron, Allan G. Food Science: A Chemical Approach. 382p. 1982. pap. 19.50x (ISBN 0-8448-1451-2). Crane-Russak Co.

Fox, C. A. Notes on William Shakespeare & Robert Tofte. LC 74-10779. 1957. lib. bdg. 8.50 (ISBN 0-8414-4210-X). Folcroft.

--Notes on William Shakespeare & Robert Tofte. 70p. 1983. Repr. of 1957 ed. lib. bdg. 10.00 (ISBN 0-8492-4632-6). R West.

Fox, C. A., jt. auth. see Holmes, R. L.

Fox, C. D. & Silver, Milton L. Who's Who on the Screen. 95.00 (ISBN 0-87968-277-9). Gordon Pr.

Fox, C. Fred & Chabner, Bruce A., eds. Rational Basis for Chemotherapy. LC 82-12921. (UCLA Symposium on Molecular & Cellular Biology Ser.: Vol. 4). 524p. 1983. 54.00 (ISBN 0-8451-2603-2). A R Liss.

Fox, C. Fred & Fox, C. Fred, eds. Membrane Research: ICN-UCLA Symposium in Molecular Biology, 1972. 1972. 70.00 (ISBN 0-12-263650-3). Acad Pr.
Fox, C. Fred, jt. ed. see Alberts, Bruce.
Fox, C. Fred, jt. ed. see Gale, Robert P.
Fox, C. Fred, jt. ed. see Hynes, R.
Fox, C. Fred, ed. see ICN-UCLA Symposium, Keystone, Colo., February 1979.
Fox, C. Fred, jt. ed. see Oxender, Dale.
Fox, C. J., ed. see Lewis, Wyndham.
Fox, C. J., Jr. C. J. Understanding. 261p. 1982. 10.95 (ISBN 0-89962-286-0). Todd & Honeywell.
--C J's Quest: Or Last Winter I Visited Detroit. 288p. 1980. 8.95 (ISBN 0-89962-024-8). Todd & Honeywell.
Fox, C. Lynn. Communicating to Make Friends: A Program for the Classroom Teacher. (Illus.). 130p. (Orig.). 1980. pap. 10.95x (ISBN 0-935266-04-6). B L Winch.
--Handicapped...How Does It Feel. Lovelady, Janet, ed. (Illus.). 48p. 1982. pap. 5.95 elementary (ISBN 0-935266-12-7, MS-20); pap. 5.95 secondary (ISBN 0-935266-13-5, MS-21). B L Winch.
Fox, C. Lynn & Malian, Ida. Social Acceptance: Key to Mainstreaming. (Illus.). 64p. (Orig.). 1983. pap. 5.95 (ISBN 0-935266-05-4, MS-32). B L Winch.
Fox, C. Lynn & Weaver, Francine L. Unlocking Doors to Friendship. LC 83-60148. 150p. (Orig.). 1983. pap. 12.95 (ISBN 0-935266-14-3, MS-09). B L Winch.
Fox, Caroline. Memories of Old Friends. 1884. Repr. 25.00 (ISBN 0-8274-3869-9). R West.
--Sea Spell. 224p. 1981. pap. 2.50 (ISBN 0-449-24454-7, Crest). Fawcett.
Fox, Charles. The Noble Enemy. 400p. 1982. pap. 3.50 (ISBN 0-446-90672-7). Warner Bks.
--Portrait in Oil. LC 82-45287. 384p. 1984. 16.95 (ISBN 0-385-17127-7). Doubleday.
Fox, Charles & Nahas, Gabriel. Body Fluid Replacement in the Surgical Patient: A Symposium. 392p. 1970. 110.00 (ISBN 0-8089-0638-0, 791314). Grune.
Fox, Charles, jt. auth. see Gammond, Peter.
Fox, Charles D. Famous Film Folk. 1976. lib. bdg. 95.00 (ISBN 0-8490-1802-1). Gordon Pr.
--Mirrors of Hollywood: Hollywood Studios of 1925. 1976. lib. bdg. 59.95 (ISBN 0-8490-2260-6). Gordon Pr.
Fox, Charles J. History of the Old Township of Dunstable: Including Nashua, Nashville, Hollis, Hudson, Litchfield & Merrimack, N.H.; Dunstable & Tyngsborough, Mass. (Illus.). 293p. 1983. Repr. of 1846 ed. 30.00 (ISBN 0-917890-35-3). Heritage Bk.
--Memorials & Correspondence of Charles James Fox, 4 Vols. Russell, John, ed. LC 75-115362. Repr. of 1857 ed. Set. 190.00 (ISBN 0-404-05470-6). Vol. 1. Vol. 2 (ISBN 0-404-05472-2). Vol. 3 (ISBN 0-404-05473-0). Vol. 4 (ISBN 0-404-05474-9). AMS Pr.
--Speeches During the French Revolution. 415p. 1982. Repr. of 1924 ed. lib. bdg. 20.00 (ISBN 0-89984-210-0). Century Bookbindery.
Fox, Charles K. The Book of Lures. (Illus.). 256p. 1975. 14.95 (ISBN 0-88395-019-7). Freshet Pr.
Fox, Charles K., jt. auth. see Hitchcock, John C.
Fox, Charles P. American Circus Posters in Full Color. 1978. pap. 6.95 (ISBN 0-486-23693-5). Dover.
--Circus Baggage Stock: A Tribute to the Percheron Horse. LC 82-7631. (Illus.). 250p. 1983. 34.95 (ISBN 0-87108-625-5). Pruett.
Fox, Charles P. & Freeman, L. Big Top Circus Days. LC 64-7599. 1964. 20.00 (ISBN 0-87282-038-6). CHB-ALF.
Fox, Charles P. & Kelly, F. Beverly. The Great Circus Street Parade in Pictures. (Illus.). 16.50 (ISBN 0-8446-5664-X). Peter Smith.
Fox, Charles P. & Parkinson, Tom. Billers, Banners & Bombast: The Story of Circus Advertising. (Illus.). 300p. write for info. (ISBN 0-87108-609-3). Pruett.
Fox, Charles P., jt. auth. see Parkinson, Tom.
Fox, Charles P., ed. Old Time Circus Cuts: A Pictorial Archive of Two Hundred & Two Illustrations. LC 79-50262. (Pictorial Archive Ser.). (Illus.). 1979. pap. 4.50 (ISBN 0-486-23653-6). Dover.
--Old-Time Circus Cuts: A Pictorial Archive of 202 Illustrations. 13.25 (ISBN 0-8446-5763-8). Peter Smith.
Fox, Christopher J. Information & Misinformation: An Investigation of the Notions of Information, Misinformation, Informing & Misinforming. LC 83-5545. (Contributions in Librarianship & Information Science Ser.: No. 45). xii, 223p. 1983. lib. bdg. 29.95 (ISBN 0-313-23928-2, FOI/). Greenwood.
Fox, Claire R. Syndicating Single-Family Homes. Golomb, Patricia C., ed. LC 81-86370. (Illus.). 256p. 1982. pap. 16.95 (ISBN 0-9601530-6-3, Dist. by Har-Row). Impact Pub.
Fox, Clayton. Prairie Empire. 192p. 1982. pap. 2.25 (ISBN 0-505-51823-6, Pub. by Tower Bks). Dorchester Pub Co.
--A Sweet Bait of Money. 1977. pap. 1.50 (ISBN 0-532-15284-0). Woodhill.
Fox, Con-e-wago. I Don't Kill No Butterflies. LC 84-90086. 127p. 1985. 7.95 (ISBN 0-533-06157-1). Vantage.
Fox, Connie. The Dream of the Black Topaze Chamber: The Poem Cycle. (Illus., Orig.). 1983. pap. 3.00 (ISBN 0-941160-06-8). Ghost Pony Pr.
Fox, Cyril F. The Personality of Britain, Its Influence on Inhabitant & Invader in Prehistoric & Early Historic Times. LC 78-27272. Repr. of 1947 ed. 30.00 (ISBN 0-404-14728-3). AMS Pr.
Fox, Cyril S. Water. LC 75-138233. (Illus.). 148p. 1972. Repr. of 1951 ed. lib. bdg. 15.00x (ISBN 0-8371-5590-8, FOWA). Greenwood.
Fox, D. R. Theory of Stochastic Processes. 1965. 20.00x (ISBN 0-412-15170-7, NO. 6430, Pub. by Chapman & Hall). Methuen Inc.
Fox, D. R., jt. ed. see Schlesinger, A. M.
Fox, Dan, ed. The John Denver Songbook. (Illus.). 112p. 1971. pap. 7.95 (ISBN 0-89524-114-5, 9003). Cherry Lane.
Fox, Dan, jt. ed. see Okun, Milton.
Fox, Dan, ed. see Okun, Milton.
Fox, Dan, jt. ed. see Okun, Milton.
Fox, Daniel E. Traces of Texas History: The Archeological Evidence of 450 Years. LC 83-70811. (Illus.). 1983. lib. bdg. 22.00 (ISBN 0-931722-24-1); pap. 12.95 (ISBN 0-931722-23-3). Corona Pub.
Fox, Daniel M. Economists & Health Care: From Reform to Relativism. 1979. 8.95 (ISBN 0-88202-128-1). Watson Pub Intl.
Fox, Daniel M., ed. see Patten, Simon N.
Fox, David. Garden of Eagles: The Life & Times of a Falconer. (Illus.). 216p. 1984. 16.95 (ISBN 0-85059-706-4, Pub. by Salem Hse Ltd). Merrimack Pub Cir.
--Saint George: The Saint with Three Faces. (Illus.). 188p. 1984. 17.50 (ISBN 0-946041-13-X, Pub. by Salem Hse Ltd). Merrimack Pub Cir.
Fox, David & Waite, Mitch. Computer Animation Primer. (Illus.). 208p. 1984. pap. 22.95 (ISBN 0-07-021742-4, BYTE Bks). McGraw.
Fox, David & Waite, Mitchell. Pascal Primer. LC 80-53275. 208p. 1981. pap. 17.95 (ISBN 0-672-21793-7, 21793). Sams.
Fox, David, jt. auth. see Fox, Annie.
Fox, David, jt. auth. see Steinmann, Anne.
Fox, David J. Fundamentals of Research in Nursing. 4th ed. (Illus.). 468p. 1982. 19.95 (ISBN 0-8385-2797-3). ACC.
--Graduate Record Examination in Education. LC 84-258. 160p. (Orig.). 1984. pap. 7.95 (ISBN 0-668-05759-9). Arco.
--National Teacher Examination (NTE) 288p. 1984. pap. 8.00 (ISBN 0-668-05783-1). Arco.
--NTE: National Teacher Examination. 8th ed. 352p. pap. 8.00 (ISBN 0-668-05783-1). Arco.
Fox, David J. & Leeser, Ilse, eds. Readings on the Research Process in Nursing. (Illus.). 232p. 1981. pap. 19.95 (ISBN 0-8385-8266-4). ACC.
Fox, Denis. Animal Biochromes & Structural Colours. LC 72-89801. 1976. 46.00x (ISBN 0-520-02347-1). U of Cal Pr.
Fox, Denis L. Biochromy: Natural Coloration of Living Things. LC 78-57309. (Illus.). 1979. 36.50x (ISBN 0-520-03699-9). U of Cal Pr.
Fox, Denton, intro. by. The Bannatyne Manuscript: National Library of Scotland Advocates' MS 1.1.6. (Medieval Manuscripts Ser.). 1980. 340.00 (ISBN 0-85967-540-8). Scolar.
Fox, Denton, ed. see Henryson, Robert.
Fox, Denton & Palsson, Herman, trs. Grettir's Saga. LC 72-90746. (Illus.). 1974. 20.00x (ISBN 0-8020-1925-0); pap. 8.95 (ISBN 0-8020-6165-6). U of Toronto Pr.
Fox, Derek. Growing Lilies. LC 85-6665. (Illus.). 264p. 1985. 29.00 (ISBN 0-7099-1039-8, Pub. by Croom Helm Ltd). Longwood Pub Group.
Fox, Dickie L. Directory of Dividend Reinvestment Plans. LC 80-19078. 240p. (Orig.). 1980. pap. 15.00 (ISBN 0-930256-06-9). Almar.
Fox, Dixon R. Caleb Heathcote, Gentleman Colonist. LC 74-164523. (Illus.). viii, 301p. 1972. Repr. of 1926 ed. lib. bdg. 24.50 (ISBN 0-8154-0392-5). Cooper Sq.
--The Decline of Aristocracy in the Politics of New York. LC 70-161764. (Columbia University. Studies in the Social Sciences: No. 198). (Illus.). Repr. of 1919 ed. 24.50 (ISBN 0-404-51198-8). AMS Pr.
--Yankees & Yorkers. LC 79-15575. (Illus.). 1980. Repr. of 1940 ed. lib. bdg. 24.75x (ISBN 0-8371-5720-X, FOYY). Greenwood.
Fox, Dixon R., jt. auth. see Krout, John A.
Fox, Donald H., ed. see Fox, Frederic E.
Fox, Donald S. The White Fox of Andhra. 216p. 1978. 6.95 (ISBN 0-8059-2432-9). Dorrance.
Fox, Donald T. Human Rights in Guatemala: Report of A Mission to Guatemala in June 1979 on Behalf of the International Commission of Jurists. pap. 20.00 (ISBN 0-317-29859-3, 2051905). Bks Demand UMI.
Fox, Donald T., ed. The Cambodian Incursion: Legal Issues. LC 79-141325. (Hammarskjold Forum Ser.: No. 15). 89p. 1971. 10.00 (ISBN 0-379-11815-7). Oceana.
Fox, Donna R. & Blechman, Mark. Clinical Management of Voice Disorders. LC 73-91493. (Speech & Hearing Ser.). 82p. (Orig.). 1975. pap. text ed. 4.95 (ISBN 0-8220-1803-9). Cliffs.
Fox, Donna R., ed. Private Practice. LC 78-151465. viii, 34p. 1971. pap. text ed. 1.50x (ISBN 0-8134-6256-8, 6256). Interstate.
Fox, Donna R., jt. ed. see Battin, R. Ray.
Fox, Douglas. Managing the Public's Interest: A Results-Oriented Approach. LC 78-11399. 1979. pap. text ed. 18.95 (ISBN 0-03-041911-5, HoltC). HR&W.
Fox, Douglas A. What Do You Think about God. 96p. 1985. pap. 5.95 (ISBN 0-8170-1077-7). Judson.
Fox, Douglas C., jt. auth. see Frobenius, Leo.
Fox, Douglas J. The Matthew-Luke Commentary of Philoxenus. LC 78-12852. 1979. 14.50 (ISBN 0-89130-350-2); pap. 9.95 (ISBN 0-89130-266-2, 060143). Scholars Pr GA.
Fox, Early L. American Colonization Society, 1817-1840. Repr. of 1919 ed. 14.00 (ISBN 0-404-00159-9). AMS Pr.
Fox, Edward. Lifetime Fitness. 1983. pap. text ed. 10.95 (ISBN 0-03-059738-2, CBS C). SCP.
--Sports Physiology. 2nd ed. 1984. text ed. 29.95 (ISBN 0-03-063771-6, CBS C). SCP.
--The True Differences Between the Regal Power & the Ecclesiastical Power. LC 73-6129. (English Experience Ser.: No. 595). 108p. 1973. Repr. of 1548 ed. 9.50 (ISBN 90-221-0595-4). Walter J Johnson.
Fox, Edward & Mathews, Donald K. The Physiological Basis of Physical Education & Athletics. 3rd ed. 1981. text ed. 29.95 (ISBN 0-03-057676-8, CBS C). SCP.
Fox, Edward, ed. see Johnson, Jerah & Percy, William A.
Fox, Edward J. & Moore, Malcolm T. Junior Words, Phrases, Clauses: Exercises in Elementary Grammar. 89p. (Orig.). (gr. 4-6). 1980. pap. 4.50x (ISBN 0-88334-127-1). Ind Sch Pr.
--Words, Phrases, Clauses: Exercises in English Grammar. 3rd ed. 120p. (gr. 6-12). 1980. pap. text ed. 4.75x (ISBN 0-88334-128-X). Ind Sch Pr.
Fox, Edward J. & Wheatley, Edward W. Modern Marketing: Principles & Practice. 1978. text ed. 24.95x (ISBN 0-673-15045-3). Scott F.
Fox, Edward L. & Mathews, Donald K. Interval Training for Lifetime Fitness. (Illus.). 194p. 1980. 8.95 (ISBN 0-385-27065-8, Dial). Doubleday.
Fox, Edward W. History in Geographic Perspective: The Other France. LC 79-140754. (Illus.). 1972. pap. 2.45x (ISBN 0-393-00650-6, Norton Lib). Norton.
Fox, Elaine. The Marriage-Go-Round: An Exploratory Study of Multiple Marriage. 198p. (Orig.). 1983. lib. bdg. 23.50 (ISBN 0-8191-3376-0); pap. text ed. 11.25 (ISBN 0-8191-3377-9). U Pr of Amer.
Fox, Elliot M. & Urwick, L., eds. Dynamic Administration: The Collected Papers of Mary Parker Follett. 1982. pap. 8.95 (ISBN 0-88254-452-7); 16.95 (ISBN 0-88254-703-8). Hippocrene Bks.
Fox, Emmet. Alter Your Life. 1950. 10.53i (ISBN 0-06-062850-2, HarpR). Har-Row.
--Around the Year with Emmet Fox. LC 58-13248. 1958. 10.53i (ISBN 0-06-062870-7, HarpR). Har-Row.
--Diagrams for Living: The Bible Unveiled. LC 69-10475. 1968. 8.95i (ISBN 0-06-062851-0, HarpR). Har-Row.
--The Emmet Fox Treasury, 5 bks. 1979. Set. pap. 15.34i (ISBN 0-06-062860-X, RD 237, HarpR). Har-Row.
--Find & Use Your Inner Power. 1941. 10.53i (ISBN 0-06-062890-1, HarpR). Har-Row.
--Make Your Life Worthwhile. LC 83-48456. 256p. 1984. pap. 7.64 (ISBN 0-06-062913-4, RD 508, HarpR). Har-Row.
--Power Through Constructive Thinking. 1940. 9.95i (ISBN 0-06-062930-4, HarpR). Har-Row.
--El Sermon del Monte. 1984. 4.95 (ISBN 0-87159-034-4). Unity School.
--Sermon on the Mount. 1934. 10.53i (ISBN 0-06-062950-9, HarpR). Har-Row.
--Stake Your Claim. LC 52-11683. 1952. 8.95i (ISBN 0-06-062970-3, HarpR). Har-Row.
--The Ten Commandments. LC 53-8369. 1953. 10.53 (ISBN 0-06-062990-8, HarpR). Har-Row.
Fox, Eugene R., jt. auth. see Sysler, Barry.
Fox, Everett. In the Beginning: A New English Rendition of the Book of Genesis. 288p. 1983. 14.95 (ISBN 0-8052-3870-0). Schocken.
Fox, Frances M. The Little Cat That Could Not Sleep. LC 72-89335. (Illus.). 32p. (gr. k-4). 1973. 6.95 (ISBN 0-87592-030-6). Scroll Pr.
Fox, Frank. Great Ships: The Battlefleet of King Charles the Second. 208p. 1980. 69.75x (ISBN 0-85177-166-1, Pub. by Conway Maritime England). State Mutual Bk.
--Mastery of the Pacific. LC 75-111757. (American Imperialism: Viewpoints of United States Foreign Policy, Ser. 1898-1941). 1970. Repr. of 1928 ed. 18.00 (ISBN 0-405-02020-1). Ayer Co Pubs.
Fox, Frank W. J. Reuben Clark: The Public Years. LC 80-17903. (J. Reuben Clark Three Vol. Ser.). (Illus.). 706p. 1980. 10.95 (ISBN 0-8425-1832-0). Brigham.
--J. Reuben Clark: The Public Years. LC 80-17903. (Illus.). 702p. 10.95 (ISBN 0-87747-834-1). Deseret Bk.
Fox, Fred. Essentials of Brass Playing. LC 77-85127. 1978. pap. 6.00 (ISBN 0-913650-03-X). Columbia Pictures.
Fox, Fred C., ed. Virus Research: Second ICN-UCLA Symposium on Molecular Biology. Robinson, William S. 1973. 65.00 (ISBN 0-12-263660-0). Acad Pr.
Fox, Fred K., jt. auth. see Cannon, William A.
Fox, Frederic E. Seven Sermons & One Eulogy as Preached in the Chapel of Princeton University from 1965 to 1980. Fox, Donald H., ed. LC 82-90693. 88p. (Orig.). 1982. pap. 5.95 (ISBN 0-910521-02-6). Fox Head.
Fox, G. K., jt. auth. see Anderson, V. R.
Fox, Gail. Making Your Children's Clothes. (Penny Pinchers Ser.). 1978. 2.95 (ISBN 0-7153-7549-0). David & Charles.
Fox, Gardner. Blood Trail. 1979. pap. 1.50 (ISBN 0-505-51367-6, Pub. by Tower Bks). Dorchester Pub Co.
--Hurricane. 1976. pap. 1.50 (ISBN 0-685-69510-7, LB375DK, Leisure Bks). Dorchester Pub Co.
--Savage Passage. 1978. pap. 1.95 (ISBN 0-505-51270-X, Pub. by Tower Bks). Dorchester Pub Co.
Fox, Gardner F. Kyrik & the Lost Queen. 1976. pap. 1.25 (ISBN 0-685-74571-6, LB420ZK, Leisure Bks). Dorchester Pub Co.
--Kyrik & the Wizards Swords. (Orig.). 1976. pap. 1.25 (ISBN 0-685-64011-6, Leisure Bks). Dorchester Pub Co.
--Kyrik Fights the Demon World. (Orig.). 1975. pap. 0.95 (ISBN 0-685-53902-4, LB284NK, Leisure Bks). Dorchester pub Co.
--Kyrik: Warlock Warrior. (Orig.). 1975. pap. 0.95 (ISBN 0-685-52180-X, LB252NK, Leisure Bks). Dorchester Pub Co.
--The Liberty Sword. 1976. pap. 1.25 (ISBN 0-685-69145-4, LB358ZK, Leisure Bks). Dorchester Pub Co.
Fox, Geoffrey E. Working-Class Emigres from Cuba. LC 78-57993. 1979. perfect bdg. 11.00 (ISBN 0-88247-550-9). R & E Pubs.
Fox, George. Amok. 1979. pap. 2.50 (ISBN 0-449-23995-0, Crest). Fawcett.
--George Fox's Book of Miracles. Cadbury, Henry J., ed. LC 73-735. 161p. 1973. Repr. of 1948 ed. lib. bdg. 16.50x (ISBN 0-374-92825-8). Octagon.
--Warlord's Hill. 1982. 14.50 (ISBN 0-8129-1022-2). Times Bks.
--The Works of George Fox, Vols. 1-8. Incl. Vols. 1 & 2. A Journal or Historical Account of the Life, Travels, Sufferings, Christian Experiences & Labour of Love in the Work of the Ministry, of That Ancient, Eminent, & Faithful Servant of Jesus Christ, George Fox. LC 75-16194. Vol. 1 (ISBN 0-404-09351-5). Vol. 2 (ISBN 0-404-09352-3); Vol. 3. The Great Mystery of the Great Whore Unfolded. LC 75-16195. 616p (ISBN 0-404-09353-1); Vols. 4-6. Gospel Truth Demonstrated, in a Collection of Doctrinal Books, Given Forth by That Faithful Minister of Jesus Christ, George Fox. LC 75-16199. Vol. 4 (ISBN 0-404-09354-X). Vol. 5 (ISBN 0-404-09355-8). Vol. 6 (ISBN 0-404-09356-6); Vols. 7 & 8. A Collection of Many Select & Christian Epistles, Letters & Testimonies. LC 75-16207. Vol. 7 (ISBN 0-404-09357-4). Vol. 8 (ISBN 0-404-09358-2). Repr. of 1831 ed. Set. 320.00 (ISBN 0-404-09350-7); 40.00 ea. AMS Pr.
Fox, George & Puffer, Lela. Okemos: Story of a Fox Indian in His Youth. (Indian Culture Ser.). (gr. 3-9). 1976. 1.95 (ISBN 0-89992-036-5). Coun India Ed.
Fox, George G. Medieval Sciences in the Works of John Gower. LC 65-21089. (Studies in Poetry, No. 38). 1969. Repr. of 1931 ed. lib. bdg. 49.95x (ISBN 0-8383-0553-9). Haskell.
Fox, George M. The Vanishing Gods. 1983. 10.95 (ISBN 0-533-05801-5). Vantage.
Fox, Gerald, jt. auth. see Chandler, Tertius.
Fox, Grace, ed. The Hairy Brown Angel & Other Animal Tails. LC 76-45040. 132p. (gr. 8-12). 1977. pap. 2.95 (ISBN 0-88207-475-X). Victor Bks.
Fox, Grace E. British Admirals & Chinese Pirates, 1832-1869. LC 73-873. (China Studies: from Confucius to Mao Ser.). (Illus.). xiv, 227p. 1973. Repr. of 1940 ed. 21.50 (ISBN 0-88355-068-7). Hyperion Conn.
Fox, Grayson C. Oil & Gas Drilling Funds: A Primer for Attorneys & Investors. LC 83-60327. 169p. 1983. 30.00 (ISBN 0-938160-32-X, 6208). State Bar TX.
Fox, Greer L., ed. The Childbearing Decision: Fertility Attitudes & Behavior. LC 82-3354. (New Perspectives on Family Ser.). (Illus.). 288p. 1982. 25.00 (ISBN 0-8039-0136-4); pap. 12.50 (ISBN 0-8039-0137-2). Sage.
Fox, Greg & Anderson, Roy. Midland Railway Architecture. 96p. 42.00x (ISBN 0-86093-320-2, Pub. by ORPC Ltd UK). State Mutual Bk.
Fox, H. Tumors of the Ovary. (Illus.). 1976. 33.50 (ISBN 0-8151-3269-7). Year Bk Med.
--The Years in My Herb Garden. 1973. pap. 1.95 (ISBN 0-686-66885-5). Macmillan.
Fox, H. & Buckley, C. H. Atlas of Gynecological Pathology, Vol. 5. (Current Histopathology Ser.). (Illus.). 166p. 1983. text ed. 62.50 (ISBN 0-397-58288-9, 65-73166, Lippincott Medical). Lippincott.
--Pathology for Gynaecologists. 256p. 1982. 95.00x (ISBN 0-7131-4402-5, Pub. by E Arnold). State Mutual Bk.

Fox, H. & Langley, F. A. Postgraduate Obstetrical & Gynaecological Pathology. 596p. 1973. 105.00 (ISBN 0-08-016992-9). Pergamon.

Fox, H., ed. Harry Smith: Early Poems. 1978. softcover 1.50 (ISBN 0-686-23103-1). Ghost Dance.

Fox, H. B. Murder in a Small Town (Perhaps) 120p. 1983. pap. 7.95 (ISBN 0-89015-406-6). Eakin Pubns.

--The Two Thousand Mile Turtle & Other Episodes from Editor Harold Smith's Private Journal. LC 75-1600. (Illus.). 128p. 1975. 7.95 (ISBN 0-89052-014-3). Madrona Pr.

Fox, H. R., jt. auth. see Crowell, H. R.

Fox, H. S. A. & Butlin, R. A., eds. Change in the Countryside: Essays on Rural England, 1500-1900. (The Special Publication of the Institute of British Geographers Ser.: No. 10). 1980. 25.00 (ISBN 0-12-264280-5). Acad Pr.

Fox, Harland. Top Executive Compensation: 1976 Edition. LC 76-55480. (Report Ser.: No. 706). (Illus.). 1976. pap. 75.00 (ISBN 0-8237-0140-9); pap. 25.00 member. Conference Bd.

--Top Executive Compensation: 1978 Edition. LC 78-65443. (Report Ser.: No. 753). (Illus.). 79p. 1978. pap. 45.00 (ISBN 0-8237-0189-1); pap. 15.00 member. Conference Bd.

--Top Executive Compensation: 1980. (Report Ser.: No. 793). (Illus.). vii, 73p. (Orig.). 1980. pap. 75.00 (ISBN 0-8237-0229-4); pap. 15.00 member. Conference Bd.

--Top Executive Compensation 1982. (Report No. 827). (Illus.). ix, 66p. (Orig.). 1982. pap. 75.00 (ISBN 0-8237-0266-9); pap. 15.00 member. Conference Bd.

--Top Executive Compensation: 1983. (Report: No. 840). (Illus.). vi, 66p. pap. 125.00 (ISBN 0-8237-0280-4); pap. 25.00 member. Conference Bd.

--Top Executive Compensation: 1985 Edition. (Report Ser.: No. 854). 73p. 1984. 125.00 (ISBN 0-8237-0296-0); members 25.00 (ISBN 0-317-36908-3). Conference Bd.

Fox, Harland, jt. auth. see Meyer, Mitchell.

Fox, Harold. Amphibian Morphogenesis. LC 83-26526. (Bioscience Ser.). 320p. 1984. 54.50 (ISBN 0-89603-043-1). Humana.

--Pathology of the Placenta. (Major Problems in Pathology Ser.: Vol. 7). (Illus.). 491p. 1978. 20.00 (ISBN 0-7216-3831-7). Saunders.

Fox, Harold G. Monopolies & Patents: A Study of the History & Future of the Patent Monopoly. LC 47-28708. (University of Toronto Legal Ser.: Extra vol.). pap. 106.00 (ISBN 0-317-27644-1, 2014210). Bks Demand UMI.

Fox, Harrison W. & Hammond, Susan W. Congressional Staffs: The Invisible Force in American Lawmaking. LC 77-72041. (Illus.). 1977. 12.95 (ISBN 0-02-910420-3). Free Pr.

Fox, Harrison W., Jr. & Hammond, Susan W. Congressional Staffs: The Invisible Force in American Lawmaking. LC 77-72041. (Illus.). 1979. pap. text ed. 12.95 (ISBN 0-02-910430-0). Free Pr.

Fox, Harrison W., Jr., ed. Contemporary Issues in Civil Rights & Liberties. 319p. 1972. pap. text ed. 9.75x (ISBN 0-8422-0191-2). Irvington.

Fox, Harry W., Jr. Master OP Amp Applications Handbook. (Illus.). 1977. pap. 13.95 (ISBN 0-8306-6856-X, 856). TAB Bks.

Fox, Helen, jt. auth. see Steiner, Rudolf.

Fox, Helen, tr. see Steiner, Rudolf.

Fox, Helen M. Gardening with Herbs for Flavor & Fragrance. (Illus.). 1972. pap. 4.95 (ISBN 0-486-22540-2). Dover.

Fox, Herbert, jt. auth. see Dixson, Robert J.

Fox, Hero N., et al. Canada & the United States: Transnational & Transgovernmental Relations. LC 75-45495. (Illus.). 443p. 1976. 37.00x (ISBN 0-231-04025-3); pap. 16.00x (ISBN 0-231-04026-1). Columbia U Pr.

Fox, Howard N. Directions. LC 79-14499. (Illus.). 103p. 1979. 19.95 (ISBN 0-87474-434-2). Smithsonian.

--Kenneth Snelson. LC 81-66596. (Illus.). 88p. 1981. pap. 10.00 (ISBN 0-914782-39-8). Buffalo Acad.

Fox, Howard N., jt. ed. see Messerli, Douglas.

Fox, Howard N., et al. Content: A Contemporary Focus Nineteen Seventy-Four to Nineteen Eighty-Four. LC 84-10624. (Illus.). 184p. 1984. 29.95 (ISBN 0-87474-436-9, FOCC). Smithsonian.

Fox, Hugh. Charles Bukowski: A Critical & Biographical Study. LC 72-129088. 1968. pap. 3.75 (ISBN 0-911856-01-3). Abyss.

--The Guernica Cycle: The Year Franco Died. LC 84-12643. 80p. cancelled (ISBN 0-916156-60-5); pap. 5.00x (ISBN 0-916156-61-3). Cherry Valley.

--Happy Deathday. (Chapbook: No. 7). 28p. 1977. pap. 1.00 (ISBN 0-912824-16-6). Vagabond Pr.

--Henry James, a Critical Introduction. LC 65-57412. (Comparative Literature Studies). (Illus.). 109p. 1968. pap. 5.00 (ISBN 0-87423-005-5). Westburg.

--Honeymoon-Mom. LC 78-73822. (Illus.). 177p. 1978. pap. 5.95x (ISBN 0-913204-10-2). December Pr.

--Huaca. 1977. pap. 2.50 (ISBN 0-686-20609-6). Ghost Dance.

--Leviathan. LC 80-39823. 1981. pap. 5.95x (ISBN 0-914140-10-8). Carpenter Pr.

--The Living Underground: A Critical Overview. LC 78-134764. 1970. 6.50x (ISBN 0-87875-005-3). Whitston Pub.

--Lyn Lifshin: A Critical Study. LC 84-52092. 184p. 1985. 15.00x (ISBN 0-87875-299-4). Whitston Pub.

--The Poetry of Charles Potts. (American Dust Ser.: No. 12). 1979. pap. 2.95 (ISBN 0-913218-44-8). Dustbooks.

Fox, Hugh see Smith Experimental Fiction Project.

Fox, Hugh, ed. The Living Underground: An Anthology of Contemporary American Poetry. LC 72-87105. (Illus.). 479p. 1973. 15.00x (ISBN 0-87875-034-7). Whitston Pub.

Fox, Hugh, ed. see Seixas, Cid.

Fox, I. Private Schools & Public Issues. 220p. 1984. text ed. 36.50x (ISBN 0-333-36328-0, Pub. by Macmillan England). Humanities.

Fox, Ira L. Ins & Outs of Ups & Downs. LC 82-90730. 1983. 10.95 (ISBN 0-87212-170-4). Libra.

Fox, Ivan & Raphael, Jesse. College Law Guide. 5.85 (ISBN 0-914770-05-5). Littoral Develop.

Fox, J. The Hydraulic Analysis of Unsteady Flow in Pipe Networks. 216p. 1977. 49.95 (ISBN 0-470-27037-3). Halsted Pr.

Fox, J., ed. Expert Systems. (Computer State of the Art Report: Ser. 12, No. 8). (Illus.). 300p. 1984. 460.00 (ISBN 0-08-028592-9). Pergamon.

--Microwave Research Institute Symposia. Incl. Vol. 1. Modern Network Synthesis. 1952; Vol. 4. Modern Advances in Microwave Techniques. LC 55-12897. 1955. o.p. (ISBN 0-470-27192-2); Vol. 5. Modern Network Synthesis. LC 56-2590. 1956; Vol. 6. Nonlinear Circuit Analysis. LC 55-3575. 1956; Vol. 9. Millimeter Waves. LC 60-10073. 1960; Vol. 11. Electromagnetics & Fluid Dynamics of Gaseous Plasma. LC 62-13174. 1962. 38.95 (ISBN 0-470-27423-9); Vol. 13. Optical Lasers. LC 63-22084; Vol. 15. System Theory. LC 65-28522. 1965; Vol. 17. Modern Optics. LC 67-31757. 1967. o.p. (ISBN 0-470-27433-6); Vol. 19. Computer Processing in Communications. LC 77-122632. 1970; Vol. 20. Submillimeter Waves. 1971; Vol. 21. Computers & Automata. 1972; Vol. 22. Computer Communications. 1972. 46.95 (ISBN 0-471-27439-9); Vol. 24. Computer Software Engineering. 1977. Pub. by Wiley-Interscience). Wiley.

Fox, J. C. A History of Contempt of Court. 100.00 (ISBN 0-686-96584-1, Pub. by Prof Bks England). State Mutual Bk.

Fox, J. C., jt. ed. see Singleton, W. T.

Fox, J. D., jt. ed. see Robson, D.

Fox, J. DeWitt. Why Not Smoke? Woolsey, Raymond H., ed. LC 83-23015. (Better Living Ser.). (Illus.). 63p. (Orig.). 1984. pap. 0.99 (ISBN 0-8280-0239-8). Review & Herald.

Fox, J. G. see Drury, C. G.

Fox, J. J. Indonesia: The Making of a Culture. 288p. 1981. pap. text ed. 10.00 (ISBN 0-909596-59-X, 1145, Pub. by ANUP Australia). Australia N U P.

Fox, J. J., et al. Indonesia: Australian Perspectives. 772p. (Orig.). 1981. pap. text ed. 24.00 (ISBN 0-909596-65-4, 1133, Pub. by ANUP Australia). Australia N U P.

Fox, J. L. Intracranial Aneurysms, Vol. 1. (Illus.). 676p. 1983. 139.00 (ISBN 0-387-90717-3). Springer Verlag.

--Intracranial Aneurysms, Vol. 3. 360p. 1983. 115.00 (ISBN 0-387-90864-1). Springer Verlag.

Fox, J. L., ed. Intracranial Aneurysms, Vol. 2. (Illus.). 497p. 1983. 149.00 (ISBN 0-387-90863-3). Springer Verlag.

Fox, J. L., et al, eds. Protein Structure & Evolution. 1976. 85.00 (ISBN 0-8247-6386-6). Dekker.

Fox, J. Ronald. Managing Business-Government Relationships. 1982. 28.95x (ISBN 0-256-02900-8). Irwin.

Fox, Jack. Illustrated History of Sprint Car Racing. (Illus.). 340p. 1985. lib. bdg. 69.95 (ISBN 0-915088-40-1). C Hungness.

--Illustrated History of the Five Hundred. (Illus.). 384p. 1985. lib. bdg. 69.95 (ISBN 0-915088-05-3). C Hungness.

Fox, Jack & Liberman, Paul S. Government Backed Loans: Forms Packet. (Illus., Orig.). 1983. pap. 25.00x (ISBN 0-913885-01-0). Madison Financial.

--How to Obtain Your Own SBA Loan. (Orig.). 1983. pap. 45.00x (ISBN 0-913885-00-2). Madison Financial.

Fox, Jack, ed. Starting & Building Your Own Accounting Business. LC 84-7336. (Wiley-Ronald National Association of Accounts Professional Bks.: 1-700). 280p. 1984. text ed. 39.95x (ISBN 0-471-80053-8, Pub. by Ronald Pr). Wiley.

Fox, Jack & Hungness, Carl, eds. Indianapolis Five Hundred Yearbook: 1982. 224p. 1982. 18.95 (ISBN 0-915088-32-0); pap. 12.95 (ISBN 0-915088-31-2). C Hungness.

Fox, Jack C. The Mighty Midgets: The Illustrated History of Midget Auto Racing. (Illus.). 304p. 1985. lib. bdg. 49.95 (ISBN 0-915088-08-8). C Hungness.

Fox, James. Comeback: An Actor's Direction. LC 83-1545. pap. 37.80 (ISBN 0-317-30138-1, 2025321). Bks Demand UMI.

--White Mischief. LC 82-42800. (Illus.). 299p. 1983. 19.95 (ISBN 0-394-50918-8). Random.

--White Mischief. 1984. pap. 4.95 (ISBN 0-394-72366-X, Vin). Random.

Fox, James, jt. ed. see Foster, Henry.

Fox, James A., jt. auth. see Levin, Jack.

Fox, James A., ed. Methods in Quantitative Criminology. LC 80-29695. (Quantitative Studies in Social Relations Ser.). 1981. 24.50 (ISBN 0-12-263952-9). Acad Pr.

--Models in Quantitative Criminology. LC 80-1782. (Quantitative Studies in Social Relations). 1981. 26.00 (ISBN 0-12-263950-2). Acad Pr.

Fox, James G. Organizational & Racial Conflict in Maximum-Security Prisons. LC 81-47710. (Illus.). 288p. 1982. 28.50x (ISBN 0-669-04727-9). Lexington Bks.

Fox, James G., et al, eds. Laboratory Animal Medicine. LC 83-21477. 1984. 60.00 (ISBN 0-12-263620-1). Acad Pr.

Fox, James J. Harvest of the Palm: Ecological Change in Eastern Indonesia. 1977. 20.00x (ISBN 0-674-38111-4). Harvard U Pr.

--Religion & Morality: Their Nature & Mutual Relations. 334p. 1983. Repr. of 1899 ed. 20.00x (ISBN 0-939738-09-0). Zubal Inc.

Fox, James J., ed. The Flow of Life: Essays on Eastern Indonesia. LC 79-9552. (Harvard Studies in Classical Anthropology: No. 2). (Illus.). 1980. 30.00x (ISBN 0-674-30675-9). Harvard U Pr.

Fox, James J., tr. see Mauss, Marcel & Beuchat, Henri.

Fox, Jane. Primary Health Care of the Young. (Illus.). 1024p. 1981. text ed. 45.00 (ISBN 0-07-021741-6). McGraw.

Fox, Joe. Trapped in the Organization. 1980. 2.50 (ISBN 0-8431-0689-1). Price Stern.

--What If... 1979. pap. 1.50 (ISBN 0-8431-0483-X). Price Stern.

Fox, John. The Boys on the Rock. LC 83-24681. 160p. 1984. 11.95 (ISBN 0-312-09419-1). St Martin.

--The Boys on the Rock. 1985. pap. 5.95 (ISBN 0-452-25753-0, Plume). NAL.

--Christmas Eve on Lonesome, & Other Stories. LC 70-121546. (Short Story Index Reprint Ser). (Illus.). 1904. 19.00 (ISBN 0-8369-3502-0). Ayer Co Pubs.

--Crittenden: A Kentucky Story of Love & War. 1976. lib. bdg. 12.95x (ISBN 0-89968-035-6). Lightyear.

--Cumberland Vendetta, & Other Stories. LC 73-121547. (Short Story Index Reprint Ser). 1895. 17.00 (ISBN 0-8369-3503-9). Ayer Co Pubs.

--Foxe's Christian Martyrs of the World. 1985. 5.99 (ISBN 0-916441-12-1). Barbour & Co.

--The Greatest Season Ever Played. 1983. 9.95 (ISBN 0-940416-05-0). Bacchus Pr.

--Home Poker: Who Wins, Who Loses, & Why. 9.95 (ISBN 0-940416-02-6). Bacchus Pr.

--The Kentuckians. 1976. lib. bdg. 13.50x (ISBN 0-89968-038-0). Lightyear.

--Linear Statistical Models & Related Methods: With Applications to Social Research. LC 83-23278. (Probability & Mathematical Statistics Ser.: 1-346). 496p. 1984. 39.95x (ISBN 0-471-09913-9, NO. 1-346, Pub. by Wiley-Interscience). Wiley.

--The Little Shepherd of Kingdom Come. 1976. lib. bdg. 17.95x (ISBN 0-89968-039-9). Lightyear.

--Play Poker, Quit Work & Sleep till Noon. 14.95 (ISBN 0-940416-01-8). Bacchus Pr.

--The Poetry of Villon. 174p. 1981. Repr. of 1962 ed. lib. bdg. 35.00 (ISBN 0-8495-1728-1). Arden Lib.

--The Poetry of Villon. LC 76-43255. 1976. Repr. of 1962 ed. lib. bdg. 19.75x (ISBN 0-8371-9291-9, FOPV). Greenwood.

--Scholarmanship: Or How to Succeed in College Without Really Trying. 9.95 (ISBN 0-940416-04-2). Bacchus Pr.

--The Trail of the Lonesome Pine. 1976. lib. bdg. 19.95x (ISBN 0-89968-040-2). Lightyear.

Fox, John, jt. auth. see Anderson, Carl.

Fox, John C. The Byron Mystery. LC 78-9397. 1973. Repr. of 1924 ed. 25.00 (ISBN 0-8492-0880-7). R West.

--The Byron Mystery. LC 72-131707. (Illus.). 262p. 1972. Repr. of 1924 ed. 29.00x (ISBN 0-403-00594-9). Scholarly.

Fox, John C., jt. auth. see Murg, Gary E.

Fox, John D. & Robson, D., eds. Isobaric Spin in Nuclear Physics: Proceedings. 1966. 76.00 (ISBN 0-12-263850-6). Acad Pr.

Fox, John F. Roman Coins & How to Collect Them. LC 82-20363. (Illus.). 224p. (Orig.). 1984. 11.95 (ISBN 0-582-50309-4). Longman.

Fox, John, Jr Hell Fer Sartain & Other Stories. 1972. Repr. of 1897 ed. 9.95 (ISBN 0-8422-8048-0). Irvington.

--Little Shepard of Kingdom Come. 1973. pap. 1.25 (ISBN 0-380-01330-4, 17707). Avon.

--The Trail of the Lonesome Pine. LC 84-2234. 440p. 1984. 20.00 (ISBN 0-8131-1508-6); pap. 10.00 (ISBN 0-8131-0156-5). U Pr of KY.

Fox, John P. Germany & the Far Eastern Crisis 1931-1938: A Study in Diplomacy & Ideology. 1982. 49.95x (ISBN 0-19-822573-3). Oxford U Pr.

--Germany & the Far Eastern Crisis 1931-1938: A Study in Diplomacy and Ideology. (Illus.). 464p. 1985. pap. 14.95 (ISBN 0-19-821975-X). Oxford U Pr.

Fox, John P. & Hall, Carrie E. Viruses in Families. LC 75-12023. (Illus.). 462p. 1980. 44.00 (ISBN 0-88416-042-4). PSG Pub Co.

Fox, John P., et al. Epidemiology: Man & Disease. (Illus.). 1970. text ed. write for info. (ISBN 0-02-339170-7). Macmillan.

Fox, John W., Jr. The Kentuckians: A Novel. facsimile ed. LC 76-164561. (American Fiction Reprint Ser). Repr. of 1898 ed. 21.00 (ISBN 0-8369-7037-3). Ayer Co Pubs.

Fox, Josef. A Faith in Reason. 118p. 1982. pap. 7.95 (ISBN 0-915996-08-1). North Am Rev.

Fox, Joseph F. Executive Qualities. LC 75-40902. (Illus.). 300p. 1976. text ed. 12.95 (ISBN 0-201-02437-3). Addison-Wesley.

Fox, Joseph L. Captain John Smith: Hero & Conqueror. (Illus.). 176p. 1985. 8.75 (ISBN 0-89962-466-9). Todd & Honeywell.

Fox, Joseph M. Software & Its Development. (Illus.). 336p. 1982. text ed. 34.95 (ISBN 0-13-822098-0). P-H.

Fox, Judith H. Furniture, Furnishings: Subject & Object. LC 83-63474. (Illus.). 64p. (Orig.). 1984. pap. 10.00 (ISBN 0-911517-01-4). Mus of Art RI.

Fox, Judy, et al. An Illuminated I Ching. LC 84-452. (Illus.). 160p. (Orig.). 1984. pap. 6.95 (ISBN 0-668-06090-5, 6090-5). Arco.

Fox, Judy, jt. auth. see Tampion, John.

Fox, Julian. A Cup of Coffee. (Origins Ser.). (gr. 4-6). 1984. PLB 8.90 (ISBN 0-531-04692-3). Watts.

Fox, K. A., et al. Theory of Quantitative Economic Policy: With Applications to Economic Growth, Stabilization & Planning. 2nd rev. ed. (Studies in Mathematical & Managerial Economics: Vol. 5). (Illus.). 290p. 1974. 42.75 (ISBN 0-444-10544-1, North-Holland). Elsevier.

Fox, Karen F., jt. auth. see Kotler, Philip.

Fox, Karl A. Econometric Analysis for Public Policy. facsimile ed. 1958. pap. 11.95x (ISBN 0-8138-2430-3). Iowa St U Pr.

Fox, Karl A., jt. auth. see Ezekiel, Mordecai.

Fox, Kenneth F., Jr. & Rinehart, C. Dean. Distribution of Copper & Other Metals in Gully Sediments of Part of Okanogan County, Washington. (Bulletin Ser.: No. 65). (Illus.). 38p. 1972. 2.00 (ISBN 0-686-34715-3). Geologic Pubns.

Fox, Kenneth F., Jr., jt. auth. see Rinehart, C. Dean.

Fox, Kenneth P. Better City Government: Innovation in American Urban Politics, 1850-1937. LC 77-71957. 244p. 1977. 29.95 (ISBN 0-87722-099-9). Temple U Pr.

Fox, L. Raymond & Elliott, Paul R. Heredity & You. LC 76-51113. 1983. pap. text ed. 9.50 (ISBN 0-8403-3215-7). Kendall-Hunt.

Fox, Larry. Football Basics. (Illus.). (gr. 3-7). 1981. 9.95 (ISBN 0-13-323998-5). P-H.

Fox, Lauren. A Clash of Wills. (Second Chance at Love Ser.: No. 248). 192p. 1985. pap. 1.95 (ISBN 0-317-13681-X). Berkley Pub.

--Country Pleasures. (Second Chance at Love Ser.: No. 197). 192p. 1984. pap. 1.95 (ISBN 0-515-07813-1). Jove Pubns.

--Passions Dance. (Second Chance At Love Ser.: No. 266). 192p. 1985. pap. 1.95 (ISBN 0-425-08154-0). Berkley Pub.

--Sparring Partners. 192p. 1984. pap. 1.95 (ISBN 0-515-07592-2). Jove Pubns.

--The Storm & Starlight. (Second Chance at Love: No. 282). 192p. 1985. pap. 2.25 (ISBN 0-425-08463-9). Berkley Pub.

Fox, Laurie A. Sweeping Beauty; Or, Notes on Cinderella. (Pictograms Ser.). (Illus.). 32p. (Orig.). 1984. pap. 2.95 (ISBN 0-89807-114-3). Illuminati.

Fox, Leland, ed. see Cowden, Robert H.

Fox, Leland, ed. see Goldovsky, Boris & Wolf, Thomas.

Fox, Leland, ed. see Hunt, Jon L.

Fox, Leland, ed. see Wu, Arlouine.

Fox, Len. Passages: An Intermediate-Advanced Writing Book. 143p. 1983. pap. text ed. 9.95 (ISBN 0-15-568227-X, HC). HarBraceJ.

--Perspectives: An Intermediate Reader. 179p. 1980. pap. text ed. 10.95 (ISBN 0-15-570486-9, HC). HarBraceJ.

Fox, Leonard. The Jew's Harp: A Comprehensive Anthology. (Illus., Orig.). 1985. pap. 25.00 (ISBN 0-932329-01-2). Intl Fanorona.

Fox, Leonard, tr. see Chauvicourt, J. & Chauvicourt, S.

Fox, Leslie. Introduction to Numerical Linear Algebra. (Monographs on Numerical Analysis Ser.). 1965. 19.95x (ISBN 0-19-500325-X). Oxford U Pr.

Fox, Leslie A. & Joseph, Eric. A DRG & Prospective Pricing Action Plan for Medical Records. (Prospective Pricing Action Plans Ser.). 80p. (Orig.). 1984. pap. 22.50 (ISBN 0-916499-09-X). Care Comm Inc.

Fox, Lilla M. Folk Costume of Eastern Europe. LC 76-51358. (Illus.). 1977. 7.95 (ISBN 0-8238-0213-2). Plays.

Fox, Lloyd A. Asbestos Abatement & Removal: Legal Considerations & Planning. 75p. (Orig.). 1985. pap. 19.95 (ISBN 0-917097-02-5). SourceFinders.

Fox, Louise M. The Adventures of Pickie & Brownie. LC 84-90107. 65p. 1985. 4.95 (ISBN 0-533-06256-X). Vantage.

Fox, Lucia. Forms-Formas. Bilingual ed. Fox, Lucia, tr. (Illus.). 110p. (Eng., Span.). Date not set. pap. price not set. Shambala Pubns.

Fox, Luke. North-West Fox, Or, Fox from the North-West Passage. (Illus.). 1965. Repr. of 1635 ed. 24.00 (ISBN 0-384-16550-8). Johnson Repr.

Fox, Lynn H. & Durden, William G. Educating Verbally Gifted Youth. LC 81-86308. (Fastback Ser.: No. 176). 50p. (Orig.). 1982. pap. 0.75 (ISBN 0-87367-176-7). Phi Delta Kappa.

Fox, Lynn H., ed. see Hyman Blumberg Symposium on Research in Early Childhood Education, 1976.

Fox, Lynn H., et al. Learning Disabled-Gifted Children. LC 83-5930. (Illus.). 304p. 1983. 23.00 (ISBN 0-8391-1881-3). Pro Ed.

Fox, M., jt. ed. see Fox, B. W.

Fox, M. W. Canine Behavior. (Illus.). 152p. 1978. photocopy ed. 15.75x (ISBN 0-398-00599-0). C C Thomas.

--Canine Pediatrics: Development, Neonatal & Congenital Diseases. (Illus.). 160p. 1966. photocopy ed. 15.75x (ISBN 0-398-00600-8). C C Thomas.

--Concepts in Ethology: Animal & Human Behavior. LC 73-93834. (Wesley W. Spink Lectures on Comparative Medicine Ser: Vol. 2). (Illus.). 160p. 1974. 8.50x (ISBN 0-8166-0723-0). U of Minn Pr.

Fox, M. W., ed. The Wild Canids: Their Systematics, Behavioral Ecology & Evolution. LC 83-268. 526p. 1984. Repr. of 1975 ed. text ed. 27.50 (ISBN 0-89874-619-1). Krieger.

Fox, Madeline J. Questions & Answers for the Laryngectomee & the Family. 1979. pap. 0.75x (ISBN 0-8134-2078-4, 2078). Interstate.

Fox, Malcom, et al. Bibliography on Engine Lubricating Oil: 1968-1983. 300p. 1985. text ed. price not set (ISBN 0-566-02616-3). Gower Pub Co.

Fox, Marcia R. Put Your Degree to Work: Job-Hunting Success for the New Professional. 1979. pap. 6.95 (ISBN 0-393-00938-6). Norton.

Fox, Margaret S. & Bear, John. Cafe Beaujolais. LC 84-51172. (Illus.). 224p. (Orig.). 1984. 17.95 (ISBN 0-89815-150-3); pap. 9.95 (ISBN 0-89815-134-1). Ten Speed Pr.

Fox, Mark & Quist, Norman, eds. Hearings of the Nuclear Regulatory Commision, Part 1. 1980. 1520.00 (ISBN 0-89093-281-6). U Pubns Amer.

Fox, Martin, jt. auth. see Odeh, Robert E.

Fox, Marvin, ed. Modern Jewish Ethics: Theory & Practice. LC 74-28395. 274p. 1975. 14.50 (ISBN 0-8142-0192-X). Ohio St U Pr.

Fox, Mary F. & Hesse-Biber, Sharlene. Women at Work. LC 83-61533. (Illus.). 276p. (Orig.). 1983. 11.95 (ISBN 0-87484-525-4, 525). Mayfield Pub.

Fox, Mary Frank, ed. Scholarly Writing & Publishing: Issues, Problems, & Solutions. 130p. 1985. 30.00x (ISBN 0-8133-0038-X); pap. 15.00x (ISBN 0-8133-0039-8). Westview.

Fox, Mary V. Jane Goodall: Living Chimp Style. LC 80-27542. (Taking Part Ser.). (Illus.). 48p. (gr. 3 up). 1981. PLB 8.95 (ISBN 0-87518-204-6). Dillon.

--Justice Sandra Day O'Connor. LC 82-8857. (Illus.). 96p. (gr. 5-11). 1983. PLB 11.95 (ISBN 0-89490-073-0). Enslow Pubs.

--Lady for the Defense. LC 74-27460. 160p. 1975. PLB 6.50 (ISBN 0-15-243400-3, HJ). HarBraceJ.

--Mister President: The Story of Ronald Reagan. LC 81-12491. (Illus.). 128p. (gr. 5-12). 1982. PLB 11.95 (ISBN 0-89490-053-6). Enslow Pubs.

--The Skating Heidens. LC 80-23066. (Illus.). 128p. (gr. 5-12). 1981. PLB 11.95 (ISBN 0-89490-046-3). Enslow Pubs.

--The Statue of Liberty. (Illus.). 64p. (gr. 3 up). 1985. 9.79 (ISBN 0-671-60482-1); pap. 6.95 (ISBN 0-671-60481-3). Messner.

--Women Astronauts: Aboard the Shuttle. (Illus.). 160p. (gr. 7 up). 1985. 9.79 (ISBN 0-671-53105-0). Messner.

Fox, Matt & Swimme, Brian. Manifesto for a Global Civilization. LC 82-71450. 54p. (Orig.). 1982. pap. 3.50 (ISBN 0-939680-05-X). Bear & Co.

Fox, Matthew. Meditations with TM Meister Eckhart. LC 82-71451. (Meditations with TM Ser.). (Illus.). 133p. (Orig.). 1982. pap. 6.95 (ISBN 0-939680-04-1). Bear & Co.

--On Becoming a Musical Mystical Bear: Spirituality American Style. LC 75-34842. 192p. 1976. pap. 3.95 (ISBN 0-8091-1913-7). Paulist Pr.

--Original Blessing. LC 82-71452. 349p. (Orig.). 1983. pap. 10.95 (ISBN 0-939680-07-6). Bear & Co.

--A Spirituality Named Compassion, & the Healing of the Global Village, Humpty Dumpty, & Us. 1979. pap. 7.95 (ISBN 0-86683-751-5). Winston Pr.

--A Spiritually Named Compassion. 290p. pap. 7.95 (ISBN 0-86683-751-5, AY8986). Winston Pr.

--Western Spirituality: Historical Roots, Ecumenical Routes. LC 81-67364. 440p. 1981. pap. 11.95 (ISBN 0-939680-01-7). Bear & Co.

Fox, Matthew, intro. By. Breakthrough: Meister Eckhart's Creation Spirituality. LC 80-909. 600p. 1980. pap. 8.95 (ISBN 0-385-17034-3, Im). Doubleday.

Fox, Matthew, frwd. by. Whee! We, Wee All the Way Home: A Guide to a Sensual Prophetic Spirituality. 257p. 1981. pap. 8.95 (ISBN 0-939680-00-9). Bear & Co.

Fox, Matthew H., jt. auth. see Barker, Carol M.

Fox, Mem. Wilfrid Gordon McDonald Partridge. (Illus.). 32p. (gr. k-4). 1985. 9.95 (ISBN 0-916291-04-9). Kane Miller Bk.

Fox, Michael. Dr. Fox's Fables: Lessons from Nature. LC 80-18345. (Illus.). 1980. 9.95 (ISBN 0-87491-291-1); pap. 4.95 (ISBN 0-87491-516-3). Acropolis.

--Ninety-Nine Programming Tips & Tricks for the IBM Personal Computer. 128p. 1984. 8.95 (ISBN 0-86668-046-2). ARCsoft.

--Practical IBM Personal Computer Programs for Beginners. 96p. 1984. 8.95 (ISBN 0-86668-045-4). ARCsoft.

--Quick 'n Fun Games for the IBM Personal Computer. 96p. 1984. 8.95 (ISBN 0-86668-044-6). ARCsoft.

--The Way of the Dolphin. LC 81-12743. (Illus.). 64p. 1981. 8.95 (ISBN 0-87491-466-3). Acropolis.

Fox, Michael & Groarke, Leo. Nuclear War: Philosophical Perspectives. 286p. 1985. text ed. 23.00 (ISBN 0-8204-0209-5). P Lang Pubs.

Fox, Michael, ed. Schopenhauer: His Philosophical Achievement. 276p. 1980. 29.50x (ISBN 0-389-20097-2). B&N Imports.

Fox, Michael & Mickley, Linda, eds. Advances in Animal Welfare Science, 1984. 1985. lib. bdg. 42.50 (ISBN 0-89838-699-3, Pub. by Martinus Nijhoff Netherlands). Kluwer Academic.

Fox, Michael W. The Animal Doctor's Answer Book. (Illus.). 320p. (Orig.). 1984. 17.95 (ISBN 0-937858-37-4); pap. 10.95 (ISBN 0-937858-38-2). Newmarket.

--Behavior of Wolves, Dogs & Related Canids. LC 83-18706. 220p. 1984. Repr. of 1971 ed. lib. bdg. 15.75 (ISBN 0-89874-686-8). Krieger.

--Between Animal & Man. LC 85-12574. 224p. 1985. Repr. of 1976 ed. lib. bdg. price not set (ISBN 0-89874-827-5). Krieger.

--The Dog: Its Domestication & Behavior. LC 76-57852. 1978. 40.00 (ISBN 0-8240-9858-7). Garland Pub.

--Farm Animals: Husbandry, Behavior, & Veterinary Practice. (Illus.). 288p. 1983. pap. 25.00 (ISBN 0-8391-1769-8). Univ Park.

--The Healing Touch. LC 82-22476. Orig. Title: Dr. Michael Fox's Massage Program for Cats & Dogs. 160p. 1983. pap. 6.95 (ISBN 0-937858-18-8). Newmarket.

--Love Is a Happy Cat. LC 82-14216. (Illus.). 112p. 1983. 7.95 (ISBN 0-937858-16-1); pap. 3.95 (ISBN 0-937858-34-X). Newmarket.

--One Earth One Mind. LC 84-3929. 264p. 1984. Repr. of 1980 ed. lib. bdg. 16.50 (ISBN 0-89874-752-X). Krieger.

--Returning to Eden: Animal Rights & Human Responsibility. LC 79-56281. 300p. 1980. 13.95 (ISBN 0-670-12722-1). Viking.

--The Soul of the Wolf. (Illus.). 144p. 1980. 12.95 (ISBN 0-316-29109-9). Little.

--The Touchlings: The Adventures of the Fantasy Creatures That Who Live on Love, Sunshine & Giving. LC 80-27959. 64p. 1981. 7.95 (ISBN 0-87491-293-8). Acropolis.

--Understanding Your Cat. (YA) (gr. 8 up). 1977. pap. 3.50 (ISBN 0-553-24693-3). Bantam.

--The Whistling Hunters: Field Studies of the Asiatic Wild Dog (Cuon Alpinus) (Animal Behavior Ser.). 224p. 1984. 29.50x (ISBN 0-87395-842-X); pap. 9.95x (ISBN 0-87395-843-8). State U NY Pr.

Fox, Michael W. & Gates, Wende D. What Is Your Cat Saying? LC 81-4884. (Illus.). 80p. 1982. 9.95 (ISBN 0-698-20443-3, Coward). Putnam Pub Group.

Fox, Micheal & McDonough, Kathleen. Wisconsin Municipal Records Manual. 102p. pap. 5.00 (ISBN 0-686-31607-X). State Hist Soc Wis.

Fox, Micheal V. The Song of Songs & the Ancient Egyptian Love Songs. LC 84-40494. (Illus.). 544p. 1985. text ed. 32.50x (ISBN 0-299-10090-1). U of Wis Pr.

Fox, Mike & Smith, Steve. Rolls-Royce: The Complete Works-The Best 599 Rolls-Royce Stories. 1984. 19.95 (ISBN 0-571-13363-0); pap. 9.95 (ISBN 0-571-13364-9). Faber & Faber.

Fox, Milden J., Jr. & Howard, Patsy C. Labor Relations & Collective Bargaining: A Bibliographic Guide to Doctoral Research. LC 83-4612. 297p. 1983. 19.50 (ISBN 0-8108-1632-6). Scarecrow.

Fox, Nancy. You, Your Parent & the Nursing Home. 1984. 13.95 (ISBN 0-9601874-3-X); pap. 8.95 (ISBN 0-9601874-4-8). Caroline Hse.

Fox, Nathan, jt. ed. see Field, Tiffany.

Fox, Nathan A. & Davidson, Richard J., eds. The Psychobiology of Affective Development. 424p. 1984. text ed. 39.95x (ISBN 0-89859-269-0). L Erlbaum Assocs.

Fox, Norm C. The Trivia Challenge. (Orig.). 1984. pap. 4.95 (ISBN 0-671-53224-3, Wallaby). PB.

Fox, Norman. Fossils: Hard Facts from the Earth. LC 81-68315. 1981. pap. 3.95 (ISBN 0-89051-077-6); tchr's guide 2.95x (ISBN 0-686-33037-4). Master Bks.

Fox, Oliver. Astral Projection. 160p. 1974. pap. 2.95 (ISBN 0-8065-0463-3). Citadel Pr.

Fox, P. F., ed. Developments in Dairy Chemistry, Vol. 2. (Illus.). 436p. 1984. 85.25 (ISBN 0-85334-224-5, Pub. by Elsevier Applied Sci England). Elsevier.

--Developments in Dairy Chemistry, Vol. 1: Proteins. (Illus.). x, 409p. 1982. 85.00 (ISBN 0-85334-142-7, I-361-82, Pub. by Elsevier Applied Sci England). Elsevier.

Fox, P. F. & Condon, J. J., eds. Food Proteins. (Illus.). xi, 361p. 1982. 76.00 (ISBN 0-85334-143-5, Pub. by Elsevier Applied Sci England). Elsevier.

Fox, P. W. Politics: Canada. 5th ed. 672p. 1982. 16.95 (ISBN 0-07-548024-7). McGraw.

Fox, Paul. Poles in America. LC 70-129397. (American Immigration Collection, Ser. 2). (Illus.). 1970. Repr. of 1922 ed. 12.00 (ISBN 0-405-00551-2). Ayer Co Pubs.

--Reformation in Poland. LC 72-136395. Repr. of 1924 ed. 24.50 (ISBN 0-404-02544-7). AMS Pr.

--Reformation in Poland, Some Social & Economic Aspects. LC 71-104272. Repr. of 1924 ed. lib. bdg. 15.00x (ISBN 0-8371-3924-4, FORP). Greenwood.

Fox, Paula. Blowfish Live in the Sea. LC 75-122740. 128p. (gr. 5-7). 1970. 8.95 (ISBN 0-02-735610-8). Bradbury Pr.

--Desperate Characters. LC 79-90373. 176p. 1980. pap. 8.95 (ISBN 0-87923-309-5, Nonpareil Bks). Godine.

--How Many Miles to Babylon? LC 79-25802. (Illus.). 128p. (gr. 5-7). 1980. 8.95 (ISBN 0-02-735590-X). Bradbury Pr.

--The King's Falcon. LC 69-13322. (Illus.). 64p. (gr. 4-6). 1969. 6.95 (ISBN 0-02-735580-2). Bradbury Pr.

--The Little Swineherd & Other Tales. (gr. k-6). 1981. pap. 1.75 (ISBN 0-440-45302-X, YB). Dell.

--Maurice's Room. LC 85-7200. (Illus.). 64p. (gr. 2-6). 1985. PLB 9.95 (ISBN 0-02-735490-3). Macmillan.

--One-Eyed Cat. LC 84-10964. 192p. (gr. 6-8). 1984. 11.95 (ISBN 0-02-735540-3). Bradbury Pr.

--One-Eyed Cat. (gr. k-6). 1985. pap. 3.25 (ISBN 0-440-46641-5, YB). Dell.

--A Place Apart. LC 80-36717. 192p. (gr. 6 up). 1980. 10.95 (ISBN 0-374-35985-7). FS&G.

--A Place Apart. 1982. pap. 1.95 (ISBN 0-451-11283-0, AJ1283, Sig). NAL.

--Portrait of Ivan. LC 74-93085. (Illus.). 144p. (gr. 5-7). 1969. 8.95 (ISBN 0-13-685362-5). P-H.

--Portrait of Ivan. LC 84-20476. (Illus.). 144p. (gr. 5-7). 1985. 10.95 (ISBN 0-02-735510-1). Bradbury Pr.

--A Servant's Tale. 330p. 1984. 16.50 (ISBN 0-86547-164-9). N Point Pr.

--The Slave Dancer. LC 73-80642. (Illus.). 192p. (gr. 5-8). 1973. 10.95 (ISBN 0-02-735560-8). Bradbury Pr.

--Slave Dancer. 128p. (gr. 7 up). 1975. pap. 2.25 (ISBN 0-440-96132-7, LFL). Dell.

--The Stone-Faced Boy. LC 68-9053. (Illus.). 112p. (gr. 4-6). 1968. 8.95 (ISBN 0-02-735570-5). Bradbury Pr.

Fox, Peter. The Trail of the Reaper. 224p. 1983. 11.95 (ISBN 0-312-81366-X). St Martin.

Fox, Peter D., et al. Health Care Cost Management: Private Sector Initiatives. LC 84-12993. (Illus.). 214p. 1984. pap. 22.50 (ISBN 0-910701-00-8, 00787). Health Admin Pr.

Fox, Philip G., jt. auth. see Sharp, Frank C.

Fox, Phyllis W. & Coleman, David. Cinderella. (Musical Children's Theatre Playscript Ser.). 1978. pap. 2.50x (ISBN 0-88020-002-2); vocal & instrumental score 9.00x (ISBN 0-88020-003-0). Coach Hse.

Fox, R. M. & Real, H. G. A Monograph of the Ithomiidae: Napeogenini, Pt. 4. (Memoirs Ser: No. 15). (Illus.). 368p. 1971. 30.00x (ISBN 0-686-01270-4). Am Entom Inst.

Fox, R. M., jt. ed. see Tattersall, M. H.

Fox, R. W. & McDonald, A. T. Introduction to Fluid Mechanics. 3rd ed. 741p. 1985. 39.95 (ISBN 0-471-88598-3). Wiley.

Fox, Ralph, tr. see Bukharin, Nikolai I., et al.

Fox, Ray E. Angela Ambrosia. LC 78-20386. 1979. 10.95 (ISBN 0-394-50096-2). Knopf.

Fox, Renee C. Essays in Medical Sociology: Journeys into the Field. LC 79-10413. (Health, Medicine & Society: a Wiley Interscience Ser.). 548p. 1979. 42.95x (ISBN 0-471-27040-7, Pub. by Wiley-Interscience). Wiley.

--Experiment Perilous. LC 59-6816. 264p. 1974. pap. 9.95x (ISBN 0-8122-1040-9). U of Pa Pr.

Fox, Renee C. & Swazey, Judith P. The Courage to Fail: A Social View of Organ Transplants & Dialysis. 2nd ed. LC 78-56332. 1979. pap. 6.95x (ISBN 0-226-25944-7, P778, Phoen). U of Chicago Pr.

--The Courage to Fail: A Social View of Organ Transplants & Dialysis. 2nd rev. ed. LC 78-56332. (Illus.). 1979. lib. bdg. 25.00x (ISBN 0-226-25943-9). U of Chicago Pr.

Fox, Renee C., jt. auth. see De Craemer, Willy.

Fox, Renee C. & Lambert, Richard D., eds. The Social Meaning of Death. LC 79-53669. (Annals of the American Academy of Political & Social Science: No. 447). 1980. 15.00 (ISBN 0-87761-246-3); pap. 7.95 (ISBN 0-87761-247-1). Am Acad Pol Soc Sci.

Fox, Richard & Freiberg, Arie. Sentencing in Victoria: State & Federal Law. 600p. 1985. 62.00 (ISBN 0-19-554656-3). Oxford U Pr.

Fox, Richard C. The Adductor Muscles of the Jaw in Some Primitive Reptiles. (Museum Ser.: Vol. 12, No. 15). 24p. 1964. pap. 1.50 (ISBN 0-686-79816-3). U of KS Mus Nat Hist.

--Chorda Tympani Branch of the Facial Nerve in the Middle Ear of the Tetrapods. (Museum Ser.: Vol. 17, No. 2). 7p. 1965. 1.25 (ISBN 0-317-04773-6). U of KS Mus Nat Hist.

--Two New Pelycosaurs from the Lower Permian of Oklahoma. (Museum Ser.: Vol. 12, No. 6). 11p. 1962. 1.25 (ISBN 0-317-04792-2). U of KS Mus Nat Hist.

Fox, Richard G. Kin, Clan, Raja, & Rule: State-Hinterland Relations in Preindustrial India. LC 76-129614. (Center for South & Southeast Asia Studies, UC Berkeley). 1971. 30.00x (ISBN 0-520-01807-9). U of Cal Pr.

--Lions of the Punjab: Culture in the Making. LC 84-28016. 1985. 29.95x (ISBN 0-520-05491-1). U of Cal Pr.

Fox, Richard H. & Cunningham, Carl L. Crime Scene Search & Physical Evidence Handbook. 206p. 1973. pap. 7.00 (ISBN 0-318-11772-X). Gov Printing Office.

Fox, Richard L. Optimization Methods for Engineering Design. LC 78-127891. (Engineering Ser). 1971. 31.95 (ISBN 0-201-02078-5). Addison-Wesley.

Fox, Richard M., jt. auth. see Azrin, Nathan.

Fox, Richard S. & Ruppert, Edward E., eds. Shallow-Water Marine Benthic Macro-Invertebrates of South Carolina. (Belle W. Baruch Library in Marine Science: No. 14). 1985. 39.95x (ISBN 0-87249-473-X). U of SC Pr.

Fox, Richard W. So Far Disordered in Mind: Insanity in California, 1870-1930. LC 77-93479. 1979. 19.95x (ISBN 0-520-03653-0). U of Cal Pr.

Fox, Richard W. & Lears, T. Jackson, eds. The Culture of Consumption: Critical Essays in American History, 1860-1960. LC 83-2391. 288p. 1983. 19.50 (ISBN 0-394-51131-X); pap. 9.95 (ISBN 0-394-71611-6). Pantheon.

Fox, Robert. Bob's Letters. 1980. 5.95 (ISBN 0-87881-086-2). Mojave Bks.

--Caloric Theory of Gases from Lavoisier to Regnault. (Illus.). 1971. 32.00x (ISBN 0-19-858131-9). Oxford U Pr.

--Destiny News. LC 76-44192. (Illus.). 100p. 1976. pap. 5.95x (ISBN 0-913204-07-2). December Pr.

--Teenagers & Purity, Teenagers & Going Steady, Teenagers & Looking Ahead to Marriage. 1978. pap. 0.75 (ISBN 0-8198-0370-7). Dghtrs St Paul.

Fox, Robert, jt. auth. see Rotatori, Anthony F.

Fox, Robert, ed. Poems, Nineteen Seventy-Eight to Nineteen Eighty-Three. LC 83-13163. 176p. (Orig.). 1983. pap. 6.00x (ISBN 0-913335-00-2). OH Arts Council.

--Something I Wrote Myself. LC 83-12156. (Anthologies from Artists in Education Program Ser.). (Illus.). 312p. 1983. pap. 5.00x (ISBN 0-913335-01-0). OH Arts Council.

Fox, Robert & Weisz, George, eds. The Organisation of Science & Technology in France 1808-1914. LC 80-40227. (Illus.). 336p. 1980. 44.50 (ISBN 0-521-23234-1). Cambridge U Pr.

Fox, Robert B. Walks Two Worlds. LC 83-513. (Illus.). 62p. (Orig.). (gr. 4-6). 1983. pap. 6.95 (ISBN 0-86534-015-3). Sunstone Pr.

Fox, Robert F. Catechism of the Catholic Church. 1979. 8.95 (ISBN 0-685-94958-3). Franciscan Her.

Fox, Robert J. Call of Heaven: Brother Gino, Stigmatist. (Illus.). 206p. (Orig.). 1982. pap. 3.95 (ISBN 0-931888-06-9). Christendom Pubns.

--The Catholic Faith. LC 83-61889. 360p. (Orig.). 1983. pap. 7.95 (ISBN 0-87973-614-3, 614). Our Sunday Visitor.

--A Catholic Prayer Book. LC 74-75133. 128p. 1974. pap. 3.95 (ISBN 0-87973-771-9). Our Sunday Visitor.

--Catholic Truth for Youth. (Illus.). 448p. (gr. 5-12). 1978. pap. 5.95 (ISBN 0-911988-05-X). AMI Pr.

--Fatima Today. (Illus.). 263p. (Orig.). pap. 6.95 (ISBN 0-931888-11-5). Christendom Pubns.

--Francisco of Fatima: His Life As He Might Tell It. 14p. 1982. pap. 1.00 (ISBN 0-911988-53-X). Ami Pr.

--Jacinta of Fatima: Her Life as She Might Tell It. 22p. 1982. pap. 1.00 (ISBN 0-911988-52-1). Ami Pr.

--Opus Sanctorum Angelorum: Work of the Holy Angels. 1.50 (ISBN 0-911988-49-1). AMI Pr.

--A Prayer Book for Young Catholics. LC 82-81318. 168p. (gr. 4-8). 1982. pap. 5.50 Leatherette (ISBN 0-87973-370-5, 370). Our Sunday Visitor.

--Prayerbook for Catholics. 112p. (Orig.). 1982. 6.00 (ISBN 0-931888-08-5); pap. 3.95. Christendom Pubns.

--Rediscovering Fatima. LC 82-60667. (Illus.). 144p. (Orig.). 1982. pap. 4.50 (ISBN 0-87973-657-7, 657). Our Sunday Visitor.

--Religious Education: Its Effects, Its Challenges Today. 1972. pap. 0.95 (ISBN 0-8198-0344-8). Dghtrs St Paul.

--St. Joseph: His Life As He Might Tell It. 1983. pap. 1.00 (ISBN 0-317-02286-5). AMI Pr.

--St. Louis Grignon de Montfort. 20p. 1983. 1.00 (ISBN 0-911988-62-9). Ami Pr.

--St. Therese of Lisieux: Her Life As She Might Tell It. 20p. 1982. pap. 1.00 (ISBN 0-911988-54-8). AMI Pr.

--Saints & Heroes Speak. 512p. 1983. 7.95 (ISBN 0-911988-43-2). Ami Pr.

--A World at Prayer. LC 78-74623. 1979. pap. 3.95 (ISBN 0-87973-633-X). Our Sunday Visitor.

Fox, Robert W. & McDonald, Alan T. Introduction to Fluid Mechanics. 2nd ed. LC 77-20839. 684p. 1978. text ed. 43.45x (ISBN 0-471-01909-7). Wiley.

Fox, Robin. Kinship & Marriage: An Anthropological Perspective. (Cambridge Studies in Social Anthropology: No. 50). 288p. 1984. 32.50 (ISBN 0-521-26073-6); pap. 7.95 (ISBN 0-521-27823-6). Cambridge U Pr.

--Poulet: A Rooster Who Laid Eggs. (Illus., Fr.). 3.50 (ISBN 0-685-11509-7). French & Eur.

--The Red Lamp of Incest: An Enquiry into the Origins of Mind & Society. LC 83-16686. 284p. 1983. pap. text ed. 7.95 (ISBN 0-268-01620-8, 85-16205). U of Notre Dame Pr.

--The Tory Islanders. LC 77-83992. (Illus.). 1978. 37.50 (ISBN 0-521-21870-5); pap. 11.95 (ISBN 0-521-29298-0). Cambridge U Pr.

Fox, Robin, jt. auth. see Mehler, Jacques.

Fox, Robin, jt. auth. see Palazzo, Tony.

Fox, Robin, ed. Biosocial Anthropology. LC 75-4110. (Association of Social Anthropologists, Ser. No. 1). 169p. 1975. 29.95x (ISBN 0-470-27033-0). Halsted Pr.

Fox, Robin L. The Search for Alexander. (Illus.). 432p. 1980. 29.45 (ISBN 0-316-29108-0). Little.

Fox, Ronald F. The Biological Energy Transduction: The Uroboros. LC 81-11556. 279p. 1982. 42.95x (ISBN 0-471-09026-3, Pub. by Wiley-In terscience). Wiley.

Fox, Ross A. Quebec & Related Silver at the Detroit Institute of Arts. LC 77-4850. (Illus.). 160p. 1978. 12.00 (ISBN 0-8143-1575-5). Wayne St U Pr.

Fox, Roy. Technology. (Science in Today's World Ser.). (Illus.). 72p. (YA) (gr. 7-12). 1985. 14.95 (ISBN 0-7134-3710-3, Pub. by Batsford England). David & Charles.

Fox, Ruth. The Tangled Chain: The Structure of Disorder in the Anatomy of Melancholy. LC 75-17296. 1976. 25.00x (ISBN 0-520-03085-0). U of Cal Pr.

Fox, Ruth, jt. auth. see Bourne, Peter G.

Fox, Ruth, jt. ed. see Bourne, Peter G.

Fox, Ruth B. A Catch or Key: New England Poems. 1969. 5.95 (ISBN 0-87233-012-5). Bauhan.

Fox, S. Transparencies. 1978. pap. 2.95 (ISBN 0-942396-23-5). Blackberry ME.

Fox, S., jt. auth. see Lawless, Gary.

Fox, S. L. Industrial & Occupational Ophthalmology. (Illus.). 224p. 1973. photocopy ed. 17.25x (ISBN 0-398-02827-3). C C Thomas.

Fox, Sally. The Medieval Woman: An Illuminated Book of Days. 1985. 12.95 (ISBN 0-8212-1587-6, Dist. by Little). Little.

--Tasty Adventures in Science. (Illus.). (gr. 3-6). 1962. PLB 6.19 (ISBN 0-8313-0037-X). Lantern.

Fox, Samuel. King Alfred's Anglo-Saxon Version of Boethius' De Consolatione Philosophiae. 1890. 40.00 (ISBN 0-8274-2650-X). R West.

--Management & the Law. LC 66-20469. 1980. pap. text ed. 6.95x (ISBN 0-89197-288-9). Irvington.

Fox, Samuel E., et al, eds. The CLS Book of Squibs & Cumulative Index 1968-1977. LC 77-83905. 174p. 1977. pap. 6.00 (ISBN 0-914203-08-8). Chicago Ling.

Fox, Sandi. Small Endearments: Nineteenth Century Quilts for Children. (Illus.). 160p. 1985. 24.95 (ISBN 0-684-18185-1). Scribner.

Fox, Sandra S., jt. auth. see Bassuk, Ellen L.

Fox, Sanford. Economic Control & Free Enterprise. LC 63-19700. 1963. 4.50 (ISBN 0-8022-0526-7). Philos Lib.

--A New Deal in Economics. LC 80-65256. (Illus.). 144p. (Orig.). 1980. pap. 2.50 (ISBN 0-9603854-0-1). S Fox.

Fox, Sanford J. The Law of Juvenile Courts in a Nutshell. 3rd ed. LC 83-21876. (Nutshell Ser.). 291p. 1984. pap. text ed. 7.95 (ISBN 0-314-79306-2). West Pub.

--Modern Juvenile Justice Cases & Materials. 2nd ed. LC 81-11615. (American Casebook Ser.). 960p. 1981. text ed. 25.95 (ISBN 0-314-60129-5). West Pub.

--Science & Justice: The Massachusetts Witchcraft Trials. LC 68-18771. (Illus.). Repr. of 1968 ed. 27.40 (ISBN 0-8357-9285-4, 2016570). Bks Demand UMI.

Fox, Seymour. Freud & Education. 272p. 1975. 16.50x (ISBN 0-398-03009-X). C C Thomas.

Fox, Seymour, ed. Philosophy for Education. 120p. 1983. text ed. 10.45x (ISBN 0-686-46590-3, Pub. by Van Leer Jerusalem Found Israel). Humanities.

Fox, Sharon E. & Allen, Virginia G. The Language Arts: An Integrated Approach. 1983. text ed. 30.95 (ISBN 0-03-054046-1). HR&W.

Fox, Shirley R. Great Resources & Opportunities for Working Women. 114p. 1980. 10.00 (ISBN 0-318-15741-1). Natl Inst Work.

--Progress Report, Vol. I. (The Michigan Interagency Collaborative Initiative). 110p. 15.00 (ISBN 0-318-15749-7). Natl Inst Work.

Fox, Sidney. Labor Law. 124p. 1968. pap. 4.00x (ISBN 0-87526-042-X). Gould.

Fox, Sidney A. Lid Surgery: Current Concepts. LC 72-4704. (Illus.). 177p. 1972. 75.00 (ISBN 0-8089-0774-3, 791316). Grune.

--Ophthalmic Plastic Surgery. 5th ed. LC 76-28427. (Illus.). 688p. 1976. 99.50 (ISBN 0-8089-0966-5, 791312). Grune.

--Surgery of Ptosis. LC 67-29565. (Illus.). 248p. 1968. 75.00 (ISBN 0-8089-0134-6, 791310). Grune.

Fox, Sidney W. & Dose, Klaus. Molecular Evolution & the Origins of Life. 2nd expanded ed. LC 77-21434. (Biology-a Series of Textbooks: Vol. 2). 1977. 49.75 (ISBN 0-8247-6619-9). Dekker.

Fox, Sidney W., ed. Individuality & Determinism: Chemical & Biological Bases. 236p. 1984. 35.00x (ISBN 0-306-41621-2, Plenum Pr). Plenum Pub.

Fox, Siv. Joys of Fantasy: The Book for Sexual Couples. LC 76-53561. (Illus.). 1978. pap. 11.95 (ISBN 0-8128-2182-3). Stein & Day.

--Mother Is. LC 74-30145. 80p. 1975. pap. 2.95 (ISBN 0-8128-1809-1). Stein & Day.

Fox, Siv C. Cup of Cold Water. 1973. 15.00, signed ltd ed (ISBN 0-685-37300-2); pap. 3.00 (ISBN 0-685-37301-0). New Rivers Pr.

--How to Eat a Fortune Cookie. 1977. perfect bound in wrappers 3.50 (ISBN 0-685-80000-8). New Rivers Pr.

Fox, Siv C., tr. Letters from Helge. 1975. signed 25.00 (ISBN 0-685-56240-9); pap. 3.00 (ISBN 0-685-56241-7). New Rivers Pr.

Fox, Sol. Thinking Big: The Education of a Gambler. LC 84-45620. 320p. 1985. 15.95 (ISBN 0-689-11551-2). Atheneum.

Fox, Stephen. The Mirror Makers: A History of Twentieth Century American Advertising. LC 83-19326. 435p. 1984. 17.95 (ISBN 0-688-02256-1). Morrow.

--The Mirror Makers: A History of Twentieth-Century American Advertising. 1985. 4.95 (ISBN 0-394-73246-4, Vin). Random.

Fox, Stephen R. Guardian of Boston: William Monroe Trotter. LC 78-108822. (Studies in American Negro Life). 1971. pap. text ed. 3.45x (ISBN 0-689-70256-6, NL26). Atheneum.

--John Muir & His Legacy: The American Conservation Movement. (Illus.). 416p. 1981. 22.00 (ISBN 0-316-29110-2). Little.

Fox, Steve, ed. see Parsons, James.

Fox, Stuart I. Human Physiology. 736p. 1984. text ed. write for info. (ISBN 0-697-08232-6); lab manual avail. (ISBN 0-697-04724-5); instr's manual avail. (ISBN 0-697-00254-3); transparencies avail. (ISBN 0-697-04942-6). Wm C Brown.

--Laboratory Guide to Human Physiology: Concepts & Clinical Applications. 3rd ed. 336p. 1984. write for info wire coil (ISBN 0-697-04724-5); write for info. Wm C Brown.

Fox, Stuart I., jt. auth. see Van De Graaff, Kent M.

Fox, Susan. Poetic Form in Blake's Milton. LC 75-53417. 260p. 1976. 24.50x (ISBN 0-686-86666-5). Princeton U Pr.

--Rats. (Illus.). 96p. 1984. 4.95 (ISBN 0-87666-933-X, KW-128). TFH Pubns.

Fox, Ted. Showtime at the Apollo. LC 83-4299. (Illus.). 336p. 1983. 16.95 (ISBN 0-03-060533-4, Owl Bks.); pap. 9.95 (ISBN 0-03-060534-2). HR&W.

Fox, Theron. Eastern California Treasure Hunter's Ghost Town Guide. (Illus.). 1979. pap. 1.95 (ISBN 0-913814-24-5). Nevada Pubns.

--Utah Treasure Hunter's Ghost Town Guide. (Illus.). 1983. pap. 1.95 (ISBN 0-913814-53-9). Nevada Pubns.

Fox, Theron, ed. see Gravatt, Glenn.

Fox, Theron, ed. see Gravattt, Glenn.

Fox, Theron, jt. ed. see Walker, Barbara.

Fox, Theron L. Arizona Treasure Hunter's Ghost Town Guide. (Illus.). 1964. pap. 2.50 (ISBN 0-913814-17-2). Nevada Pubns.

--Nevada Treasure Hunter's Ghost Town Guide. (Illus.). 1960. pap. 2.50 (ISBN 0-913814-16-4). Nevada Pubns.

Fox, Truman B. History of Saginaw County. (Local History Reprints Ser.). 1965. pap. 3.25 (ISBN 0-317-11565-0). Clarke His.

Fox, Valerie. Abigail to Zachariah. LC 82-7681. 352p. 1983. 18.00 (ISBN 0-86628-021-9). Ridgefield Pub.

Fox, Vernon. Correctional Institutions. (Illus.). 336p. 1983. 25.95 (ISBN 0-13-178228-2). P-H.

--Introduction to Corrections. 3rd ed. (Illus.). 528p. 1985. text ed. 26.95 (ISBN 0-13-480484-8). P-H.

--Introduction to Criminology. (Illus.). 416p. 1976. 24.95. P-H.

--Violence Behind Bars. LC 73-13414. 317p. 1973. Repr. of 1956 ed. lib. bdg. 20.00x (ISBN 0-8371-7131-8, FOVB). Greenwood.

Fox, Vernon, jt. auth. see Wright, Burton.

Fox, Vernon B. Introduction to Corrections. 2nd ed. (Illus.). 1977. text ed. 24.95. P-H.

--Introduction to Criminology. 2nd ed. LC 84-3314. 1985. 27.95 (ISBN 0-13-479940-2). P-H.

Fox, Virgil. A Basic Book of Self-Instruction on How to Draw & Paint Successfully Both in the Fine & in the Commercial Art. (Illus.). 201p. 1982. 67.85 (ISBN 0-86650-035-9). Gloucester Art.

Fox, Vivian. The Winding Trail: The Alabama-Coushatta Indians. (Illus.). 1983. 7.95 (ISBN 0-89015-397-3). Eakin Pubns.

Fox, Vivian C. & Quitt, Martin H. Loving, Parenting, & Dying: The Family Cycle in England & America, Past & Present. 503p. 1981. 39.50 (ISBN 0-914434-14-4); pap. 12.95 (ISBN 0-914434-15-2). Psychohistory Pr.

Fox, W., ed. Serology of Tuberculosis & BCG Vaccination. (Advances in Tuberculosis Research: Vol. 21). (Illus.). viii, 192p. 1983. 70.25 (ISBN 3-8055-3855-3). S Karger.

Fox, W., jt. ed. see Birkhaeuser, H.

Fox, W. J., jt. auth. see McBirnie, S. C.

Fox, W. Randolph. After the Apocalypse. (Orig.). 1980. pap. 1.95 (ISBN 0-532-23118-X). Woodhill.

Fox, Walter. Writing the News: Print Journalism in the Electronic Age. 1977. 9.95 (ISBN 0-8038-8081-2); pap. text ed. 6.50x (ISBN 0-8038-8082-0). Hastings.

Fox, Wayne L., jt. auth. see Wheeler, Alan H.

Fox, Wesley. Golden State Rails. LC 80-65624. (Illus.). 76p. 1980. pap. 8.95 (ISBN 0-9604122-0-4). W Fox.

--Overland to the Rockies. LC 84-81564. (Illus.). 104p. (Orig.). 1984. pap. 14.95 (ISBN 0-9604122-2-0). W Fox.

Fox, William. At the Sea's Edge: An Introduction to Coastal Oceanography for the Amateur Naturalist. LC 82-23074. (Illus.). 317p. 1983. 21.95 (ISBN 0-13-049783-5); pap. 12.95 (ISBN 0-13-049775-4). P-H.

--Every Man His Own Doctor: The Botanic System Guide to Better Health. 1974. lib. bdg. 69.95 (ISBN 0-685-51387-4). Revisionist Pr.

--Tin: The Working of a Commodity Agreement. 1977. 40.00 (ISBN 0-685-87560-1). State Mutual Bk.

Fox, William & Stein, Emanuel. Cardiac Rhythm Disturbances: A Step by Step Approach. LC 82-12727. (Illus.). 287p. 1983. text ed. 34.50 (ISBN 0-8121-0838-8). Lea & Febiger.

Fox, William, jt. auth. see Shepard's & McGraw-Hill.

Fox, William F. Federal Regulation of Energy. LC 83-20027. 920p. 1983. 75.00 (ISBN 0-07-021757-2). McGraw.

--History of the Lumber Industry in the State of New York. LC 76-7561. (Illus.). 1976. Repr. of 1901 ed. 14.95 (ISBN 0-916346-23-4). Harbor Hill Bks.

--Regimental Losses in the American Civil War, 1861-1865. 595p. 1985. 50.00 (ISBN 0-89029-007-5). Pr of Morningside.

Fox, William L. Time by Distance. Robertson, Kirk, ed. (Windriver Ser.). (Illus.). 72p. (Orig.). 1985. lettered & signed 25.00 (ISBN 0-916918-29-7); pap. 6.00 (ISBN 0-916918-28-9). Duck Down.

--Twenty-One, & Over. Robertson, Kirk, ed. 36p. 1982. pap. 3.00 (ISBN 0-916918-18-1); pap. 10.00 (ISBN 0-916918-19-X). Duck Down.

Fox, William L., jt. auth. see Laws, Edward R., Jr.

Fox, William L., jt. ed. see Walsh, Richard.

Fox, William P. Chitlin Strut & Other Madrigals. LC 83-61916. 200p. 1983. 9.95 (ISBN 0-931948-46-0). Peachtree Pubs.

--Dixiana Moon. LC 80-51770. 256p. 1981. 11.95 (ISBN 0-670-27453-4). Viking.

--Doctor Golf. 180p. 1984. Repr. of 1963 ed. 12.95 (ISBN 0-87249-448-9). U of SC Pr.

--Southern Fried Plus Six. 1980. pap. 2.25 (ISBN 0-89176-030-X, 6030). Mockingbird Bks.

Fox, William P. & Ashley, Franklin. How 'bout Them Gamecocks! (Illus.). 240p. 1985. 24.95 (ISBN 0-87249-463-2). U of Sc Pr.

Fox, William P., ed. Contemporary Sources: Readings from the "Writer's Workshop". LC 82-12038. 280p. 1982. pap. text ed. 13.95 (ISBN 0-03-062186-0). HR&W.

Fox, William S. Greek & Roman Mythology, Vol. I. LC 63-19086. (Mythology of All Races Ser.). (Illus.). Repr. of 1932 ed. 30.00 (ISBN 0-8154-0073-X). Cooper Sq.

Fox, William T. A Continent Apart: The United States & Canada in World Politics. 208p. 1985. 10.95 (ISBN 0-8020-6575-9). U of Toronto Pr.

Fox, William T. & Fox, Annette B. NATO & the Range of American Choice. LC 67-11560. (Institute for War & Peace Studies). 352p. 1967. 33.00x (ISBN 0-231-03001-0). Columbia U Pr.

Fox, William T., ed. Theoretical Aspects of International Relations. (International Studies Ser). 1959. 7.95x (ISBN 0-268-00273-8). U of Notre Dame Pr.

Fox, William T. & Lambert, Richard D., eds. How Wars End. LC 70-130999. (Annals of the American Academy of Political & Social Science: No. 392). 1970. 15.00 (ISBN 0-87761-132-7); pap. 7.95 (ISBN 0-87761-131-9, 87761). Am Acad Pol Soc Sci.

Fox, William T. & Schilling, Warner R, eds. European Security & the Atlantic System. LC 72-4248. (Institute for War & Peace Studies). 276p. 1973. 26.50x (ISBN 0-231-03640-X). Columbia U Pr.

Fox, Zeni, et al. Leadership for Youth Ministry. (Illus.). 200p. (Orig.). 1984. pap. 8.95 (ISBN 0-88489-157-7). St Mary's.

Foxall, Gordon. Corporate Innovation: Marketing & Strategy. LC 83-40096. 240p. 1984. 25.00 (ISBN 0-312-16995-7). St Martin.

--Marketing Behaviour: Issues in Managerial & Buyer Decision Making. 200p. 1981. text ed. 35.50x (ISBN 0-566-00434-8). Gower Pub Co.

Foxall, Gordon, jt. auth. see Driver, John.

Foxall, Gordon, ed. Marketing in the Service Industries. (Illus.). 222p. 1985. 27.50x (ISBN 0-7146-3270-8, F Cass Co). Biblio Dist.

Foxall, Gordon R. Co-Operative Marketing in European Agriculture. 116p. 1982. text ed. 35.00 (ISBN 0-566-00512-3). Gower Pub Co.

--Consumer Behavior: A Pratical Guide. LC 79-25979. 207p. 1980. 32.95x (ISBN 0-470-26914-6). Halsted Pr.

--Consumer Choice. LC 83-2897. 260p. 1983. 27.50x (ISBN 0-312-16612-5). St Martin.

--Strategic Marketing Management. LC 81-6828. 273p. 1981. pap. 24.95x (ISBN 0-470-27265-1). Halsted Pr.

Foxall, Raymond. The Silver Goblet. 1976. pap. 1.50. WSP.

Fox-Ashrei, Meir, tr. see Zevin, Shlomo Y.

Fox Bourne, H. R. English Merchants. xvi, 492p. Repr. of 1886 ed. 59.00 (ISBN 0-932051-31-6). Am Repr Serv.

Foxcroft, jt. auth. see Cole.

Foxcroft, G. E., jt. auth. see Taylor, Charles A.

Foxcroft, H. C. The Life & Letters of Sir George Savile, First Marquis of Halifax, 2 vols. Straka, Gerald M., ed. LC 72-83170. (English Studies Ser.). 1972. Repr. of 1898 ed. Set. lib. bdg. 65.00 (ISBN 0-8420-1427-6). Scholarly Res Inc.

Foxcroft, Helen C. Life & Letters of Sir George Savile, 2 Vols. LC 4-35272. 1969. Repr. of 1898 ed. Set. 70.00 (ISBN 0-384-16573-7). Johnson Repr.

Foxcroft, Thomas. The Sermons of Thomas Foxcroft of Boston: 1697-1769. LC 82-10457. 1983. 50.00x (ISBN 0-8201-1387-5). Schol Facsimiles.

Fox-Davies, A. C. The Mauleverer. 1976. lib. bdg. 14.95x (ISBN 0-89968-163-8). Lightyear.

Fox-Davies, Arthur C. Art of Heraldry: An Encyclopaedia of Armory. LC 68-56481. (Illus.). 1968. Repr. of 1904 ed. 60.00 (ISBN 0-405-08530-3, Blom Pubns). Ayer Co Pubs.

Fox-Davies, Arthur C., ed. Armorial Families: A Directory of Gentlemen of Coat-Armour, Vol. 1 & 2. LC 76-94029. (Illus.). 1970. Repr. Set. 85.00 (ISBN 0-8048-0721-3). C E Tuttle.

Foxe, Barbara. Long Journey Home. 239p. pap. 6.50 (ISBN 0-317-36126-0). Vedanta Pr.

Foxe, John. Acts & Monuments, 8 Vols. Cattley, S. R. & Townsend, George, eds. LC 79-168132. Repr. of 1849 ed. Set. 400.00 (ISBN 0-404-02590-0). AMS Pr.

--The English Sermons of John Foxe. LC 77-29100. 1978. Repr. of 1578 ed. 60.00x (ISBN 0-8201-1267-4). Schol Facsimiles.

--Foxe's Book of Martyrs. Berry, W. Grinton, ed. (Giant Summit Bks). 1978. pap. 7.95 (ISBN 0-8010-3483-3). Baker Bk.

--Foxe's Book of Martyrs. 400p. pap. 3.95 (ISBN 0-8007-8013-2, Spire Bks). Revell.

--Foxe's Book of Martyrs. 1981. pap. 3.50 (ISBN 0-88368-095-5). Whitaker Hse.

--John Foxe the Martyrologist: Two Latin Comedies: Titus & Gesippus, Christus Triumphans. Smith, John H., ed. 1973. 35.00 (ISBN 0-318-11899-8). Renaissance Soc Am.

Foxe, Richard W. The Subtle Art of Discovering Major Bargains in Wall Street Capable of Doubling Your Money in Less Than One Year. (Illus.). 167p. 1981. 73.45x (ISBN 0-86654-011-3). Inst Econ Finan.

Foxe, Sonja & Miles, Barbara. Essential Chicago: An Astrological Portrait of the Windy City. (Illus.). 1982. pap. 3.80 (ISBN 0-933646-21-6). Aries Pr.

Foxen, E. H. Lecture Notes on Diseases of the Ear, Nose & Throat. 5th. ed. (Illus.). 240p. 1981. pap. text ed. 12.75 (ISBN 0-632-00652-8, B 1642-5). Mosby.

Fox-Genovese, Elizabeth & Genovese, Eugene D. Fruits of Merchant Capital: Slavery & Bourgeois Property in the Rise & Expansion of Capitalism. 1983. 35.00x (ISBN 0-19-503157-1, GB694); pap. 10.95 (ISBN 0-19-503158-X). Oxford U Pr.

Fox-Genovese, Elizabeth, tr. The Autobiography of Du Pont De Nemours. LC 84-10645. Orig. Title: Fr. (Illus.). 304p. 1984. 24.95 (ISBN 0-8420-2132-9). Scholarly Res Inc.

Foxglove, Lady. We've got the Power: Witches among Us. LC 81-11098. (A Jem Book Ser.). (Illus.). 64p. (Teens reading on a 2-3rd grade level). 1981. lib. bdg. 9.29 (ISBN 0-671-43604-X). Messner.

Fox-Hutchinson, Juliet. Remembering Vernon. 112p. (Orig.). 1984. pap. 12.95x (ISBN 0-85362-209-4, Oriel). Routledge & Kegan.

Foxley, A., et al. Redistributive Effects of Government Programmes: The Chilean Case. (Illus.). 1979. 37.00 (ISBN 0-08-023130-6). Pergamon.

Foxley, Alejandro. Latin American Experiments in Neo-Conservative Economics. (Campus Ser.: No. 317). (Illus.). 228p. 1984. pap. text ed. 7.95x (ISBN 0-520-05134-3). U of Cal Pr.

--Latin American Experiments in Neoconservative Economics. LC 82-20252. 1983. text ed. 28.50x (ISBN 0-520-04807-5). U of Cal Pr.

Foxley, Alejandro & Whitehead, Laurence, eds. Economic Stabilization in Latin America: Political Dimensions. 120p. 1980. pap. 18.25 (ISBN 0-08-026788-2). Pergamon.

Foxley, Cecilia H. Locating, Recruiting, & Employing Women: An Equal Opportunity Approach. LC 76-7236. 358p. (Orig.). 1976. pap. 8.50 (ISBN 0-912048-66-2). Garrett Pk.

Foxley, William C. Frontier Spirit: Catalog of the Collection of the Museum of Western Art. LC 83-62850. xiv, 200p. 1985. 90.00x (ISBN 0-914965-00-X); deluxe ed. 500.00 limited ed. (ISBN 0-914965-01-8). Mus W Art.

Fox-Lockert, Lucia. Women Novelists in Spain & Spanish America. LC 79-23727. 356p. 1979. 22.50 (ISBN 0-8108-1270-3). Scarecrow.

Foxman, Loretta D. The Key to Your Successful Resume: How to Sell Yourself on Paper. Mulligan, Michael V. & Polsky, Walter L., eds. 96p. (Orig.). 1982. pap. 7.50 (ISBN 0-9610946-0-5). Foxman.

Foxman, Loretta D. & Polsky, Walter L. Resumes That Work: How to Sell Yourself on Paper. (General Trade Bks.). 96p. 1984. pap. 8.95 (ISBN 0-471-80608-0, Pub. by Wiley Pr). Wiley.

Foxman, S. Classified Love: A Guide to the Personals. 120p. 1982. pap. 5.95 (ISBN 0-07-021756-4). McGraw.

Foxon, D. F. English Verse, 1701-50. Incl. Vol. 1. Catalogue; Vol. 2. Indexes. 1975. 600.00 (ISBN 0-521-08144-0). Cambridge U Pr.

Foxon, David. Libertine Literature in England 1660-1745. (Illus.). 1965. 6.00 (ISBN 0-8216-0106-7). Univ Bks.

Fox-Strangways, Arthur H. Music Observed: The Selection Made by Steuart Wilson. facs. ed. LC 68-16931. (Essay Index Reprint Ser). 1936. 17.00 (ISBN 0-8369-0452-4). Ayer Co Pubs.

Foxwell, H. S., ed. see Jevons, William S.

Foxworth, Jo. Wising up. 1981. pap. 5.95 (ISBN 0-385-29159-0, Delta). Dell.

Foxworth, Joe. Boss Lady. 1979. pap. 2.50 (ISBN 0-446-91252-2). Warner Bks.

Foxworth, Thomas, ed. see Matt, Paul, et al.

Foxworth, Thomas G., ed. see Matt, Paul R.

Foxworthy, Nancy, jt. auth. see Shiffman, Yvette.

Foxx, Richard M. Decreasing Behaviors of Severely Retarded & Autistic Persons. LC 82-60088. 191p. (Orig.). 1982. pap. text ed. 12.95 (ISBN 0-87822-264-2, 2642); pap. text ed. 22.50 Increasing & Decreasing, set (ISBN 0-87822-265-0). Res Press.

--Increasing Behaviors of Severely Retarded & Autistic Persons. LC 82-60087. 221p. (Orig.). 1982. pap. text ed. 12.95 (ISBN 0-87822-263-4, 2634); pap. text ed. 21.50 set of increasing & decreasing (ISBN 0-87822-265-0). Res Press.

Foxx, Richard M. & Azrin, Nathan H. Toilet Training the Retarded: A Rapid Program for Day & Nighttime Independent Toileting. 156p. 1973. pap. 9.95; program set 13.95 (ISBN 0-87822-025-9); program forms only 5.95. Res Press.

Foxx, Rosalind. Flame Against the Wind. 320p. (Orig.). 1983. pap. 3.25 (ISBN 0-440-12450-6). Dell.

--Reluctant Ward. (Coventry Romance Ser.: No. 194). 192p. 1982. pap. 1.50 (ISBN 0-449-50296-1, Coventry). Fawcett.

Foxx, Teralene S. & Hoard, Dorothy. Flowers of the Southwestern Forests & Woodlands. (Illus.). 210p. (Orig.). 1984. pap. 12.95 (ISBN 0-317-14837-0). Los Alamos Hist Soc.

--Flowers of the Southwestern Forests & Woodlands. (Illus.). 210p. (Orig.). 1985. pap. 12.95 (ISBN 0-941232-04-2). U of NM Pr.

Foy, Charles. Pigeons for Pleasure & Profit. (Illus.). 1972. pap. 4.00 (ISBN 0-911466-19-3). Swanson.

Foy, David A. For You the War Is Over: American Prisoners of War in Nazi Germany. LC 83-42633. (Illus.). 224p. 1984. 18.95 (ISBN 0-8128-2925-5). Stein & Day.

Foy, Felician A. & Avato, Rose, eds. Concise Guide to the Catholic Church. LC 83-63170. 80p. (Orig.). 1984. pap. 6.95 (ISBN 0-87973-616-X, 616). Our Sunday Visitor.

Foy, Felician A. & Avato, Rose M., eds. Catholic Almanac, 1986. LC 73-64101. 650p. (Orig.). 1985. pap. 13.95 (ISBN 0-87973-256-3, 256). Our Sunday Visitor.

Foy, George. The Asia Rip. 336p. 1984. 16.95 (ISBN 0-670-13804-5). Viking.

--Asia Rip. 1985. pap. 3.95 (ISBN 0-671-55240-6). PB.

Foy, George, jt. auth. see Lawrence, Sidney.

Foy, Gretchen. A New Beginning. Foy, Richard & Walleen, Gayle, eds. LC 80-50611. (Illus.). 152p. 1980. pap. 4.95 (ISBN 0-89142-036-3). Sant Bani Ash.

Foy, Leslie. The City Bountiful: Utah's Second Settlement from Pioneers to Present. (Illus.). 350p. 1975. 10.95 (ISBN 0-88290-057-9). Horizon Utah.

Foy, Marcia & Nicholas, Anna K. The Beagle. (Illus.). 320p. 1985. text ed. 14.95 (ISBN 0-317-27058-3, PS-811). TFH Pubns.

Foy, Marcia, jt. auth. see Nicholas, Anna K.

Foy, Marcia A. & Nicholas, Anna K. The Basset Hound. (Illus.). 320p. 1985. text ed. 14.95 (ISBN 0-86622-044-5, PS-815). TFH Pubns.

Foy, Nancy. Management Education: Current Action & Future Trends. 1979. 90.00x (ISBN 0-686-79293-9, Pub. by MCB Pubns). State Mutual Bk.

Foy, Richard, ed. see Foy, Gretchen.

Foy, Sally & Oxford Scientific Films. The Grand Design: Form & Color in Animals. (Illus.). 238p. 1983. 24.95 (ISBN 0-13-362574-5). P-H.

Foy, Thomas. Richard Crashaw Poet & Saint. LC 74-9797. 1933. lib. bdg. 8.50 (ISBN 0-8414-4204-5). Folcroft.

Foy, Tom. A Guide to Archery. (Illus.). 176p. 1981. 14.95 (ISBN 0-7207-1245-9, Pub. by Michael Joseph). Merrimack Pub Cir.

Foye, Arthur B. Haskins & Sells: Our First Seventy-Five Years. LC 83-49430. (Accounting History & the Development of a Profession Ser.). 185p. 1984. lib. bdg. 25.00 (ISBN 0-8240-6326-0). Garland Pub.

Foye, Raymond, ed. see Kaufman, Bob.

Foye, Raymond, ed. see Poe, Edgar Allan.

Foye, Raymond, ed. see Smith, Duncan.

Foye, Raymond, ed. see Wieners, John.

Foye, William O., ed. Principles of Medicinal Chemistry. 2nd ed. LC 80-23838. (Illus.). 931p. 1981. text ed. 49.50 (ISBN 0-8121-0722-5). Lea & Febiger.

Foyer, Christine. Photosynthesis: Cell Biology. LC 83-21764. (A Series of Monographs). 219p. 1984. 29.95x (ISBN 0-471-86473-0, 1-570, Pub. by Wiley-Interscience). Wiley.

Foyle, Christina. So Much Wisdom: A Commonplace Book. 144p. 1984. 11.95 (ISBN 0-233-97568-3, Pub. by A Deutsch England). David & Charles.

Foyo, Maria, jt. auth. see Owre, H. B.

Foyt, A. J. & Neeley, William. A. J. My Life as America's Greatest Race Car Driver. (Illus.). 1984. pap. 3.50 (ISBN 0-446-32418-3). Warner Bks.

Foyt, A. J. & Neely, William. A. J. LC 83-45036. (Illus.). 233p. 1983. 14.95 (ISBN 0-8129-1077-X). Times Bks.

Fozzard, Harry A., et al. The Heart. 1985. text ed. price not set (ISBN 0-88167-126-6). Raven.

Fozzarrd, Harry A. Effects of Anesthesia. 232p. 1985. 39.95 (ISBN 0-683-02146-X). Waverly Pr.

FPP, ed. see IFSTA Committee.

Fraade, David J., ed. The Aster Guide to Computer Applications in the Pharmaceutical Industry: An Overview of System Manufacturers' Hardware & Software. (Illus.). 250p. (Orig.). 1984. pap. 45.00x (ISBN 0-943330-05-X). Aster Pub Corp.

--Automation of Pharmaceutical Operations. 360p. 1983. 57.50 (ISBN 0-943330-02-5). Aster Pub Corp.

--Automation of Pharmaceutical Operations: Supplement. (Illus.). 150p. (Orig.). 1985. pap. 27.00x (ISBN 0-943330-06-8). Aster Pub Corp.

Fraade, Steven D. Enosh & His Generation: Pre-Israelite Hero & History in Post-Biblical Interpretation. LC 83-27137. (Society of Biblical Literature-Monograph Ser.). 1984. 29.95 (ISBN 0-89130-724-9, 06 00 30); pap. 19.95 (ISBN 0-89130-725-7). Scholars Pr GA.

Fraas, Arthur P. Energy Evaluation of Energy Systems. (Energy, Combustion & Environment Ser.). (Illus.). 704p. 1982. 40.00x (ISBN 0-07-021758-0). McGraw.

Fraas, John W. Basic Concepts in Educational Research. LC 83-6843. (Illus.). 328p. (Orig.). 1983. pap. text ed. 13.75 (ISBN 0-8191-3220-9). U Pr of Amer.

--Basic Concepts in Educational Research: A Workbook. 176p. (Orig.). 1983. pap. 13.00 (ISBN 0-8191-3221-7). U Pr of Amer.

Fraas, Karl N. Geschichte Der Landbau-Und Forstwissenschaft. Repr. of 1865 ed. 50.00 (ISBN 0-384-16660-1). Johnson Repr.

Fraassen, Bas C. Van see Beltrametti, E. & Van Fraassen, Bas C.

Frabetti, P. Portolan Charts: Carte Nautiche Italiane. (Illus.). 1983. pap. 65.00 (ISBN 0-87556-599-9). Saifer.

Frable, William J. Thin Needle Aspiration Biopsy. (Major Problems in Pathology: Vol. 14). (Illus.). 384p. 1983. 49.95 (ISBN 0-7216-3835-X). Saunders.

Frable, William J., jt. auth. see Johnston, William W.

Fracastorius. Syphilis; Or a Poetical History of the French Disease. 69.95 (ISBN 0-8490-1170-1). Gordon Pr.

Fracht, J. A. & Robinson, E. Singer's & Speaker's Handbook. 1978. text ed. 15.00 (ISBN 0-8206-0238-8). Chem Pub.

Frachtenberg, Leo J. Coos Texts. LC 74-82355. (Columbia Univ. Contributions to Anthropology Ser.: Vol. 1). 1969. Repr. of 1913 ed. 27.50 (ISBN 0-404-50551-1). AMS Pr.

--Lower Umpqua Texts & Notes on the Kusan Dialects. LC 72-82341. (Columbia Univ. Contributions to Anthropology Ser.: Vol. 4). 1969. Repr. of 1914 ed. 24.00 (ISBN 0-404-50554-6). AMS Pr.

Frackenpohl, Arthur. Harmonization at the Piano. 5th. ed. 288p. 1985. write for info. plastic comb bdg. (ISBN 0-697-03574-3). Wm C Brown.

Fracker, Stanley B. The Classification of Lepidopterous Larvae. (Illus.). Repr. of 1915 ed. 15.00 (ISBN 0-384-16670-9). Johnson Repr.

Frackman Becker, Lucille. Francoise Mallet-Joris. (World Author Ser.). 1985. lib. bdg. 22.95 (ISBN 0-8057-6610-3, Twayne). G K Hall.

Fraczek, Adam, jt. ed. see Feshbach, Seymour.

Fradas, Stan, jt. auth. see Updegraff, Robert R.

Fradenburg, Leo G. United States Airlines: Trunk & Regional Carriers, Their Operations & Management. (Orig.). 1980. pap. text ed. 21.95 (ISBN 0-8403-2128-7). Kendall-Hunt.

Fradin, Dennis. Alabama: In Words & Pictures. LC 80-15135. (Young People's Stories of Our States Ser.). (Illus.). 48p. (gr. 2-5). 1980. PLB 11.25 (ISBN 0-516-03901-6). Childrens.

--Alaska: In Words & Pictures. LC 77-4353. (Young People's Stories of Our States). (Illus.). 48p. (gr. 2-5). 1977. PLB 11.25 (ISBN 0-516-03902-4). Childrens.

--Arizona: In Words & Pictures. LC 79-21480. (Young People's Stories of Our States Ser.). (Illus.). 48p. (gr. 2-5). 1980. PLB 11.25 (ISBN 0-516-03903-2). Childrens.

--Arkansas: In Words & Pictures. LC 80-11995. (Young People's Stories of Our States Ser.). (Illus.). 48p. (gr. 2-5). 1980. PLB 11.25 (ISBN 0-516-03904-0). Childrens.

--California: In Words & Pictures. LC 76-50600. (Young People's Stories of Our States). (Illus.). 48p. (gr. 2-5). 1977. PLB 11.25 (ISBN 0-516-03905-9). Childrens.

--Colorado: In Words & Pictures. LC 80-15778. (Young People's Stories of Our States Ser.). (Illus.). 48p. (gr. 2-5). 1980. PLB 11.25 (ISBN 0-516-03906-7). Childrens.

--Connecticut: In Words & Pictures. LC 79-23292. (Young People's Stories of Our States). (Illus.). 48p. (gr. 2-5). 1980. PLB 11.25 (ISBN 0-516-03907-5). Childrens.

--Delaware: In Words & Pictures. LC 80-5842. (Young Peoples Stories of Our States Ser.). (Illus.). 48p. (gr. 2-5). 1980. PLB 11.25 (ISBN 0-516-03908-3). Childrens.

--Disaster! Earthquakes. LC 81-12263. (Illus.). 64p. (gr. 3 up). 1982. PLB 11.35 (ISBN 0-516-00853-6); pap. text ed. 3.95 (ISBN 0-516-40853-4). Childrens.

--Disaster! Fires. LC 82-9404. (Illus.). (gr. 3 up). 1982. PLB 11.35 (ISBN 0-516-00855-2); pap. 3.95 (ISBN 0-516-40855-0). Childrens.

--Disaster! Floods. LC 82-9402. (Illus.). (gr. 3 up). 1982. PLB 11.35 (ISBN 0-516-00856-0); pap. 3.95 (ISBN 0-516-40856-9). Childrens.

--Disaster! Hurricanes. LC 81-38553. (Illus.). (gr. 3 up). 1982. PLB 11.35 (ISBN 0-516-00852-8); pap. 3.95 (ISBN 0-516-40852-6). Childrens.

--Disaster! Tornadoes. LC 81-12277. (Illus.). 64p. (gr. 3 up). 1982. PLB 11.35 (ISBN 0-516-00854-4); pap. text ed. 3.95 (ISBN 0-516-40854-2). Childrens.

--Disaster! Volcanoes. LC 81-12294. (Disaster Ser.). (Illus.). 64p. (gr. 3 up). 1982. PLB 11.35 (ISBN 0-516-00851-X); pap. text ed. 3.95 (ISBN 0-516-40851-8). Childrens.

--Explorers. LC 84-7077. (New True Bks.). (Illus.). 48p. (gr. k-4). 1984. lib. bdg. 10.60 (ISBN 0-516-01926-0); pap. 3.95 (ISBN 0-516-41926-9). Childrens.

--Farming. LC 83-15110. (New True Bks.). (Illus.). 48p. (gr. k-4). 1983. PLB 10.60 (ISBN 0-516-01693-8). Childrens.

--Florida: In Words & Pictures. LC 80-16681. (Young People's Stories of Our States Ser.). (Illus.). 48p. (gr. 2-5). 1980. PLB 11.25 (ISBN 0-516-03909-1). Childrens.

--Georgia: In Words & Pictures. LC 80-26768. (Young People's Stories of Our States Ser.). (Illus.). 48p. (gr. 2-5). 1981. PLB 11.25 (ISBN 0-516-03910-5); pap. 3.95 (ISBN 0-516-43910-3). Childrens.

--Hawaii: In Words & Pictures. LC 79-25605. (Young People's Stories of Our States Ser.). (Illus.). 48p. (gr. 2-5). 1980. PLB 11.25 (ISBN 0-516-03913-X). Childrens.

--Idaho: In Words & Pictures. LC 80-14660. (Young People's Stories of Our States Ser.). (Illus.). 48p. (gr. 2-5). 1980. PLB 11.25 (ISBN 0-516-03914-8). Childrens.

--Illinois: In Words & Pictures. LC 76-7389. (Young People's Stories of Our States). (Illus.). 48p. (gr. 2-5). 1976. PLB 11.25 (ISBN 0-516-03911-3). Childrens.

--Indiana: In Words & Pictures. LC 79-21383. (Young People's Stories of Our States Ser.). (Illus.). 48p. (gr. 2-5). 1980. PLB 11.25 (ISBN 0-516-03912-1). Childrens.

--Iowa: In Words & Pictures. LC 79-19399. (Young People's Stories of Our States Ser.). (Illus.). 48p. (gr. 2-5). 1980. PLB 11.25 (ISBN 0-516-03915-6). Childrens.

--Kansas: In Words & Pictures. LC 80-12576. (Young People's Stories of Our States Ser.). (Illus.). 48p. (gr. 2-5). 1980. PLB 11.25 (ISBN 0-516-03916-4). Childrens.

--Kentucky: In Words & Pictures. LC 80-25810. (Young People's Stories of Our States Ser.). (Illus.). 48p. (gr. 2-5). 1981. PLB 11.25 (ISBN 0-516-03917-2). Childrens.

--Louisiana: In Words & Pictures. LC 80-28609. (Young People's Stories of Our States Ser.). (Illus.). 48p. (gr. 2-5). 1981. PLB 11.25 (ISBN 0-516-03918-0); pap. 3.95 (ISBN 0-516-43918-9). Childrens.

--Maine: In Words & Pictures. LC 79-25122. (Young People's Stories of Our States Ser.). (Illus.). 48p. (gr. 2-5). 1980. PLB 11.25 (ISBN 0-516-03919-9). Childrens.

--Maryland: In Words & Pictures. LC 80-15185. (Young People's Stories of Our States Ser.). (Illus.). 48p. (gr. 2-5). 1980. PLB 11.25 (ISBN 0-516-03920-2). Childrens.

--Massachusetts: In Words & Pictures. LC 80-26161. (Young People's Stories of Our States Ser.). (Illus.). 48p. (gr. 2-5). 1981. PLB 11.25 (ISBN 0-516-03921-0). Childrens.

--Michigan: In Words & Pictures. LC 79-225356. (Young People's Stories of Our States Ser.). (Illus.). 48p. (gr. 2-5). 1980. PLB 11.25 (ISBN 0-516-03922-9). Childrens.

--Minnesota: In Words & Pictures. LC 79-21543. (Young People's Stories of Our States Ser.). (Illus.). 48p. (gr. 2-5). 1980. PLB 11.25 (ISBN 0-516-03923-7). Childrens.

--Mississippi: In Words & Pictures. LC 80-36855. (Young People's Stories of Our States Ser.). (Illus.). 48p. (gr. 2-5). 1980. PLB 11.25 (ISBN 0-516-03924-5). Childrens.

--Missouri: In Words & Pictures. LC 80-12249. (Young People's Stories of Our States Ser.). (Illus.). 48p. (gr. 2-5). 1980. PLB 11.25 (ISBN 0-516-03925-3). Childrens.

--Montana: In Words & Pictures. LC 80-25023. (Young People's Stories of Our States Ser.). (Illus.). 48p. (gr. 2-5). 1981. PLB 11.25 (ISBN 0-516-03926-1). Childrens.

--Moon Flights. (Illus.). 48p. (gr. k-4). 1985. 3.95 (ISBN 0-516-41940-4). Childrens.

--Nebraska: In Words & Pictures. LC 79-19456. (Young People's Stories of Our States Ser.). (Illus.). 48p. (gr. 2-5). 1980. PLB 11.25 (ISBN 0-516-03927-X). Childrens.

--Nevada: In Words & Pictures. LC 80-24179. (Young People's Stories of Our States Ser.). (Illus.). 48p. (gr. 2-6). 1981. PLB 11.25 (ISBN 0-516-03928-8). Childrens.

--New Hampshire: In Words & Pictures. LC 80-25421. (Young People's Stories of Our States Ser.). (Illus.). 48p. (gr. 2-5). 1981. PLB 11.25 (ISBN 0-516-03929-6). Childrens.

--New Jersey: In Words & Pictures. LC 80-19688. (Young People's Stories of Our States Ser.). (Illus.). 48p. (gr. 2-5). 1980. PLB 11.25 (ISBN 0-516-03930-X). Childrens.

--New Mexico: In Words & Pictures. LC 81-298. (Young People's Stories of Our States Ser.). (Illus.). 48p. (gr. 2-5). 1981. PLB 11.25 (ISBN 0-516-03931-8). Childrens.

--New York: In Words & Pictures. LC 81-28366. (Young People's Stories of Our States Ser.). (Illus.). 48p. (gr. 2-5). 1981. PLB 11.25 (ISBN 0-516-03932-6). Childrens.

--North Carolina: In Words & Pictures. LC 79-25291. (Young People's Stories of Our States Ser.). (Illus.). 48p. (gr. 2-5). 1980. PLB 11.25 (ISBN 0-516-03933-4); pap. 3.95 (ISBN 0-516-43933-2). Childrens.

--North Dakota: In Words & Pictures. LC 80-26480. (Young People's Stories of Our States Ser.). (Illus.). 48p. (gr. 2-5). 1981. PLB 11.25 (ISBN 0-516-03934-2). Childrens.

--Ohio: In Words & Pictures. LC 76-46941. (Young People's Stories of Our States Ser.). (Illus.). 48p. (gr. 2-5). 1977. PLB 11.25 (ISBN 0-516-03935-0); pap. 3.95 (ISBN 0-516-43935-9). Childrens.

--Oklahoma: In Words & Pictures. LC 80-26961. (Young People's Stories of Our States Ser.). (Illus.). 48p. (gr. 2-5). 1981. PLB 11.25 (ISBN 0-516-03936-9). Childrens.

--Oregon: In Words & Pictures. LC 80-15183. (Young People's Stories of Our States Ser.). (Illus.). 48p. (gr. 2-5). 1980. PLB 11.25 (ISBN 0-516-03937-7). Childrens.

--Pennsylvania: In Words & Pictures. LC 79-24942. (Young People's Stories of Our States Ser.). (Illus.). 48p. (gr. 2-5). 1980. PLB 11.25 (ISBN 0-516-03938-5). Childrens.

--Pioneers. LC 84-9418. (New True Bks.). (Illus.). 48p. (gr. k-4). 1984. lib. bdg. 10.60 (ISBN 0-516-01927-9); pap. 3.95 (ISBN 0-516-41927-7). Childrens.

--The Republic of Ireland. LC 83-20960. (Enchantment of the World Ser.). (Illus.). 128p. (gr. 5-9). 1984. lib. bdg. 19.95 (ISBN 0-516-02767-0). Childrens.

--Rhode Island: In Words & Pictures. LC 80-22497. (Young People's Stories of Our States Ser.). (Illus.). 48p. (gr. 2-5). 1981. PLB 11.25 (ISBN 0-516-03939-3). Childrens.

--South Carolina: In Words & Pictures. LC 79-22550. (Young People's Stories of Our States Ser.). (Illus.). 48p. (gr. 2-5). 1980. PLB 11.25 (ISBN 0-516-03940-7). Childrens.

--South Dakota: In Words & Pictures. LC 80-25349. (Young People's Stories of Our States Ser.). (Illus.). 48p. (gr. 2-5). 1981. PLB 11.25 (ISBN 0-516-03941-5). Childrens.

--Tennessee: In Words & Pictures. LC 79-19218. (Young People's Stories of Our States Ser.). (Illus.). 48p. (gr. 2-5). 1980. PLB 11.25 (ISBN 0-516-03942-3). Childrens.

--Texas: In Words & Pictures. LC 80-27497. (Young People's Stories of Our States Ser.). (Illus.). 48p. (gr. 2-5). 1981. PLB 11.25 (ISBN 0-516-03943-1); pap. 3.95 (ISBN 0-516-43943-X). Childrens.

--Utah: In Words & Pictures. LC 80-15177. (Young People's Stories of Our States Ser.). (Illus.). 48p. (gr. 2-5). 1980. PLB 11.25 (ISBN 0-516-03944-X). Childrens.

--Vermont: In Words & Pictures. LC 79-22069. (Young People's Stories of Our States Ser.). (Illus.). 48p. (gr. 2-5). 1980. PLB 11.25 (ISBN 0-516-03946-6). Childrens.

--Virginia in Words & Pictures. LC 76-7387. (Young People's Stories Ofour States). (Illus.). 48p. (gr. 2-5). 1976. PLB 11.25 (ISBN 0-516-03945-8). Childrens.
--The Voyager Space Probes. (Illus.). 48p. (gr. k-4). 1985. 3.95 (ISBN 0-516-41944-7). Childrens.
--Washington: In Words & Pictures. LC 80-14745. (Young People's Stories of Our States Ser.). (Illus.). 48p. (gr. 2-5). 1980. PLB 11.25 (ISBN 0-516-03947-4). Childrens.
--West Virginia: In Words & Pictures. LC 80-12133. (Young People's Stories of Our States Ser.). (Illus.). 48p. (gr. 2-5). 1980. PLB 11.25 (ISBN 0-516-03949-0). Childrens.
--Wisconsin: In Words & Pictures. LC 77-5330. (Young People's Stories of Our States). (Illus.). 48p. (gr. 2-5). 1977. PLB 11.25 (ISBN 0-516-03948-2). Childrens.
--Wyoming: In Words & Pictures. LC 79-26511. (Young People's Stories of Our States Ser.). (Illus.). 48p. (gr. 2-5). 1980. PLB 11.25 (ISBN 0-516-03950-4). Childrens.
Fradin, Dennis B. Archaeology. LC 83-7309. (New True Bks). 48p. (gr. k-4). 1983. PLB 10.60 (ISBN 0-516-01691-1); pap. 3.95 (ISBN 0-516-41691-X). Childrens.
--Astronomy. LC 82-19722. (New True Bks.). (Illus.). 48p. (gr. k-4). 1983. PLB 10.60 (ISBN 0-516-01673-3); pap. 3.95 (ISBN 0-516-41673-1). Childrens.
--Comets, Asteroids, & Meteors. LC 83-23231. (New True Bks.). (Illus.). 48p. (gr. k-4). 1984. lib. bdg. 10.60 (ISBN 0-516-01723-3); pap. 3.95 (ISBN 0-516-41723-1). Childrens.
--Disaster! Blizzards & Winter Weather. LC 83-10074. (Disaster Ser.). (Illus.). 64p. (gr. 3 up). 1983. PLB 11.35 (ISBN 0-516-00857-9); pap. 3.95 (ISBN 0-516-40857-7). Childrens.
--Disaster! Droughts. LC 83-10073. (Disaster Ser.). (Illus.). 64p. (gr. 3 up). 1983. PLB 11.35 (ISBN 0-516-00858-7); pap. 3.95 (ISBN 0-516-40858-5). Childrens.
--Movies. LC 83-7261. (New True Bks.). (Illus.). 48p. (gr. k-4). 1983. PLB 10.60 (ISBN 0-516-01699-7). Childrens.
--The Netherlands. LC 82-17896. (Enchantment of the World Ser.). (Illus.). 128p. (gr. 5-9). 1983. PLB 19.95 (ISBN 0-516-02779-4). Childrens.
--Olympics. LC 83-7214. (New True Bks.). (Illus.). 48p. (gr. k-4). 1983. PLB 10.60 (ISBN 0-516-01703-9). Childrens.
--One Winter. (gr. 6-10). 1985. 9.95 (ISBN 0-8038-5401-3). Hastings.
--Skylab. LC 83-23180. (Illus.). 48p. (gr. k-4). 1984. lib. bdg. 10.60 (ISBN 0-516-01727-6); pap. 3.95 (ISBN 0-516-41727-4). Childrens.
Fradin, Morris. Hey, Ey, Ey, Lock! Adventure on the Chesapeake & Ohio Canal. LC 73-91394. (Illus.). 120p. 1977. pap. 4.95 (ISBN 0-87033-244-9). Tidewater.
Fradkin, Helen, ed. see Arden House Conference, October, 1966.
Fradkin, Philip L. A River, No More: The Colorado River & the West. LC 80-2713. (Illus.). 384p. 1981. 15.95 (ISBN 0-394-41579-5). Knopf.
--A River No More: The Colorado River & the West. LC 83-18053. (Illus.). 360p. 1984. pap. 10.95 (ISBN 0-8165-0823-2). U of Ariz Pr.
Frados, Joel. Plastics Engineering Handbook of the SPI. 4th ed. 1976. 49.50 (ISBN 0-442-22469-9). Van Nos Reinhold.
Frados, Joel, ed. Plastics Engineering Handbook of the SPI. 4th ed. 909p. 1976. 49.50 (ISBN 0-686-48143-7, 0208). T-C Pubns CA.
Fra Draco. The Mysteries of Draco & Leona. (Illus.). 40p. 1981. pap. 7.00 (ISBN 0-939622-22-X). Four Zoas Night.
Frady. Wallace. rev. ed. 1976. pap. 3.95 (ISBN 0-452-00442-X, F442, Mer). NAL.
Frady, Marshall. Southerners. 1981. pap. 6.95 (ISBN 0-452-00566-3, Mer). NAL.
Frady, Marshall, et al. To Save Our Schools, to Save Our Children. (Illus.). 260p. 1985. 16.95 (ISBN 0-88282-013-3). New Horizon NY.
Frady, Steve. Red Shirts & Leather Helmets: Volunteer Fire Fighting on the Comstock Lode. LC 84-2335. (Illus.). 261p. 1984. 19.95x (ISBN 0-87417-086-9); pap. 12.95 (ISBN 0-87417-087-7). U of Nev Pr.
Fraembs, Dorothy G. My Mother Told Me. (Illus.). 32p. 1984. 18.00 (ISBN 0-88014-068-2). Mosaic Pr OH.
Franckelscher, Stiftung. Festschrift Seventy-Five Jahrigen Bestehen Des Judich-Theologischen Seminars, 2 vols. Katz, Steven, ed. LC 79-7159. (Jewish Philosophy, Mysticism & History of Ideas Ser.). 1980. Repr. of 1929 ed. Set. lib. bdg. 80.00x (ISBN 0-405-12243-8). Ayer Co Pubs.
Fraenger, Wilhelm. Hieronymus Bosch. Sebba, Helen, tr. LC 81-48072. (Illus.). 526p. 1983. 39.95 (ISBN 0-399-12713-5, Putnam). Putnam Pub Group.
Fraenkel, C. E., jt. auth. see Brookes, H. F.
Fraenkel, C. E., ed. see Brecht, Bertolt.
Fraenkel, C. E., ed. see Grass, Gunter.
Fraenkel, Eduard. Horace. 1957. pap. 25.95x (ISBN 0-19-814376-1). Oxford U Pr.
Fraenkel, Eduard, ed. see Aeschylus.
Fraenkel, Ernst. Dual State. LC 78-86276. 1969. Repr. of 1941 ed. lib. bdg. 19.00x (ISBN 0-374-92831-2). Octagon.
--Litauisches Etymologisches Woerterbuch, Vol. 1. (Lithuanian & Ger.). 1960. 152.00 (ISBN 3-533-00650-6, M-7541, Pub. by Westdeutscher Verlag/VVA). French & Eur.
--Litauisches Etymologisches Woerterbuch, Vol. 2. (Lithuanian & Ger.). 1965. 195.00 (ISBN 3-533-00651-4, M-7542, Pub. by Westdeutscher Verlag/VVA). French & Eur.
Fraenkel, G. S. Decorative Music Title Pages: 201 Examples from 1500 to 1800. (Illus.). 12.00 (ISBN 0-8446-2079-3). Peter Smith.
Fraenkel, Gideon, jt. auth. see Kaplan, Jerome I.
Fraenkel, Gottfried S. Decorative Music Title Pages: 201 Examples from 1500-1800. (Pictorial Archive Series). (Illus., Orig.). 1968. pap. 8.95 (ISBN 0-486-21915-1). Dover.
Fraenkel, Jack R. Crime & Criminals: What Should We Do About Them. (gr. 10-12). 1977. text ed. 12.80 (ISBN 0-13-192872-4); pap. text ed. 9.24 (ISBN 0-13-192880-5). P-H.
--How to Teach About Values: An Analytic Approach. (Illus.). 176p. 1977. pap. text ed. 15.95x (ISBN 0-13-435453-2). P-H.
Fraenkel, Jack R., ed. see Durfee, David A.
Fraenkel, Jack R., ed. see Eckenrod, James S.
Fraenkel, Jack R., jt. ed. see Ubbelohde, Carl.
Fraenkel, Jack R., et al. Decision-Making in American Government. (gr. 9-12). 1980. text ed. 22.64 (ISBN 0-205-06845-6, 7668457); tchr's. guide 15.00 (ISBN 0-205-06852-9, 766852-X). Allyn.
Fraenkel, Michael. Day Face & Night Face. 74p. 1947. 12.50 (ISBN 0-87556-093-8). Saifer.
Fraenkel, P., et al. Foundations of Set Theory. 2nd ed. (Studies in Logic: Vol. 67). 1973. 36.25 (ISBN 0-7204-2270-1). Elsevier.
Fraenkel, Peter. Food from Windmills. (Illus.). 75p. (Orig.). 1975. pap. 4.50x (ISBN 0-903031-25-6, Pub. by Intermediate Tech England). Intermediate Tech.
Fraenkel, R. Technik und Handhabung der Funktionsregler. (Illus.). 124p. 1984. 17.50 (ISBN 3-8055-3924-X). S Karger.
Fraenkel, Richard, et al, eds. The Role of U. S. Agriculture on Foreign Policy. LC 78-19761. 270p. 1979. 36.95 (ISBN 0-03-043101-8). Praeger.
Fraenkel-Conrat, H. & Wagner, R. R., eds. Comprehensive Virology, Vol. 1: Descriptive Catalogue of Viruses. LC 74-5493. (Illus.). 200p. 1974. 29.50x (ISBN 0-306-35141-2, Plenum Pr). Plenum Pub.
--Comprehensive Virology, Vol. 10: Viral Gene Expression & Integeration. (Illus.). 512p. 1977. 55.00x (ISBN 0-306-35150-1, Plenum Pr). Plenum Pub.
--Comprehensive Virology, Vol. 11: Genetics of Plant Viruses. LC 77-7908. (Illus.). 364p. 1977. 39.50x (ISBN 0-306-35151-X, Plenum Pr). Plenum Pub.
--Comprehensive Virology, Vol. 12: Newly Characterized Protist & Invertebrate Viruses. (Illus.). 359p. 1978. 39.50x (ISBN 0-306-35152-8, Plenum Pr). Plenum Pub.
--Comprehensive Virology, Vol. 13: Primary, Secondary, Tertiary & Quaternary Structures. LC 79-6. (Illus.). 672p. 1979. 65.00x (ISBN 0-306-40137-1, Plenum Pr). Plenum Pub.
--Comprehensive Virology, Vol. 14: Newly Characterized Vertebrate Viruses. LC 79-810. (Illus.). 562p. 1979. 55.00x (ISBN 0-306-40231-9, Plenum Pr). Plenum Pub.
--Comprehensive Virology, Vol. 15: Virus - Host Interactions - Immunity to Viruses. LC 79-26533. (Illus.). 309p. 1979. 35.00x (ISBN 0-306-40262-9, Plenum Pr). Plenum Pub.
--Comprehensive Virology, Vol. 2: Reproduction of Small & Intermediate RNA Viruses. LC 74-13471. (Illus.). 354p. 1974. 39.50x (ISBN 0-306-35142-0, Plenum Pr). Plenum Pub.
--Comprehensive Virology, Vol. 3: Reproduction of DNA Animal Viruses. LC 74-17457. (Illus.). 502p. 1974. 49.50x (ISBN 0-306-35143-9, Plenum Pr). Plenum Pub.
--Comprehensive Virology, Vol. 4: Reproduction of Large RNA Viruses. LC 74-20501. (Illus.). 359p. 1975. 39.50x (ISBN 0-306-35144-7, Plenum Pr). Plenum Pub.
--Comprehensive Virology, Vol. 5: Structure & Assembly of Virions, Pseudovirions, & Intraviral Nucleic Acids. LC 74-5494. (Illus.). 236p. 1975. 35.00x (ISBN 0-306-35145-5, Plenum Pr). Plenum Pub.
--Comprehensive Virology, Vol. 6: Reproduction of Small RNA Viruses. LC 75-46506. (Illus.). 236p. 1976. 35.00x (ISBN 0-306-35146-3, Plenum Pr). Plenum Pub.
--Comprehensive Virology, Vol. 7: Reproduction of Bacterial DNA Viruses. (Illus.). 312p. 1977. 35.00x (ISBN 0-306-35147-1, Plenum Pr). Plenum Pub.
--Comprehensive Virology, Vol. 8: Genetics of Bacterial DNA Viruses. (Illus.). 362p. 1977. 39.50x (ISBN 0-306-35148-X, Plenum Pr). Plenum Pub.
--Comprehensive Virology, Vol. 9: Genetics of Animal Viruses. LC 77-1176. (Illus.). 630p. 1977. 65.00x (ISBN 0-306-35149-8, Plenum Pr). Plenum Pub.
Fraenkel-Conrat, Heinz. Design & Function at the Threshold of Life: The Viruses. (Orig.). 1962. pap. 21.50 (ISBN 0-12-265168-5). Acad Pr.
--The Viruses: Catalogue, Characterization & Classification. 268p. 1985. 49.50x (ISBN 0-306-41766-9, Plenum Pr). Plenum Pub.
Fraenkel-Conrat, Heinz & Kimball, Paul. Virology. (Illus.). 432p. 1982. 40.95 (ISBN 0-13-942144-0). P-H.
Fraenkel-Conrat, Heinz & Wagner, Robert, eds. Comprehensive Virology, Vol. 16: Virus-Host Interactions, Viral Invasion, Persistence & Disease. 385p. 1980. 45.00x (ISBN 0-306-40488-5, Plenum Pr). Plenum Pub.
--Comprehensive Virology, Vol. 17: Methods Used in the Study of Viruses. LC 80-21841. 479p. 1981. 49.50x (ISBN 0-306-40418-4). Plenum Pub.
Fraenkel-Conrat, Heinz & Wagner, Robert R., eds. Comprehensive Virology, Vol. 18: Virus-Host Interactions: Receptors, Persistence, & Neurological Diseases. 214p. 1983. 32.50x (ISBN 0-306-41158-X, Plenum Pr). Plenum Pub.
Fraenkel-Conrat, Heinz & Wagner, Robert, eds. Comprehensive Virology, Vol. 19: Viral Cytopathology: Cellular Macromolecular Synthesis & Cytocidal Viruses. 556p. 1984. 69.50x (ISBN 0-306-41698-0, Plenum Pr). Plenum Pub.
Fraenkel Von Velson, Ruth, tr. see Ehrenberg, Victor.
Fraga, S. & Muszynska, J. Atoms in External Fields. (Physical Sciences Data Ser.: Vol. 8). 558p. 1981. 106.50 (ISBN 0-444-41936-5). Elsevier.
Fraga, S., et al. Handbook of Atomic Data. (Physical Sciences Data Ser.: Vol. 5). 552p. 1976. 106.50 (ISBN 0-444-41461-4). Elsevier.
--Atomic Energy Levels: Data for Parametric Calculations, Vol. 4. (Physical Sciences Data Ser.). 482p. 1979. 106.50 (ISBN 0-444-41838-5). Elsevier.
--Biomolecular Information Theory. (Studies in Physical & Theoretical Chemistry: Vol. 4). 272p. 1978. 59.75 (ISBN 0-444-41736-2). Elsevier.
Fragala, Ignzio L., jt. ed. see Marks, Tobin J.
Frager, Dorothy. The Book of Sampler Quilts. LC 82-83540. (Illus.). 276p. 1983. 16.95 (ISBN 0-8019-7267-1); pap. 12.95 (ISBN 0-8019-7268-X). Chilton.
--The Book of Sampler Quilts. (Illus.). 250p. 1985. pap. 12.95 (ISBN 0-8019-7268-X). Wallace-Homestead.
--Cloth Hats, Bags 'n Baggage. LC 77-6116. (Creative Crafts Ser.). (Illus.). 1978. 12.50 (ISBN 0-8019-6367-2, 6367); pap. 6.95 (ISBN 0-8019-6368-0, 6368). Chilton.
--The Quilting Primer. 2nd ed. LC 78-22118. (Creative Crafts Ser.). (Illus.). 1979. 19.95 (ISBN 0-8019-6826-7); pap. 12.95 (ISBN 0-8019-6827-5, 6827). Chilton.
Frager, Robert & Fadiman, James. Personality & Personal Growth. 2nd ed. 522p. 1984. text ed. 23.95 scp (ISBN 0-06-041964-4, HarpC); write for info. instr's manual (ISBN 0-06-361981-4). Har-Row.
Frager, Robert, jt. auth. see Fadiman, James.
Frager, Ruth L., jt. auth. see Paternoster, Lewis M.
Fragermont, Stephan C. The Secret Art of Successful Tape Reading. 1980. 69.45x (ISBN 0-918968-52-6). Inst Econ Finan.
Fragiacomo, C., jt. auth. see Noseda, G. F.
Fragiadakis, Helen. All Clear! Idioms in Context. (Illus.). 208p. (Orig.). 1985. pap. text ed. 12.50 (ISBN 0-8384-1299-8); cassette 11.00 (ISBN 0-8384-1300-5). Heinle & Heinle.
Fraginals, Manuel M. The Sugarmill. Belfrage, Cedric, tr. from Sp. LC 73-90074. (Illus.). 1978. pap. 10.95 (ISBN 0-85345-432-9). Monthly Rev.
Fraginals, Manuel M., ed. Africa in Latin America. Blum, Leonor, tr. 350p. 1984. 45.00x (ISBN 0-8419-0748-X). Holmes & Meier.
Fraginals, Manuel Moreno. Sugarmill: The Socioeconomic Complex of Sugar in Cuba. Belfrage, Cedric, tr. from Span. LC 73-90074. 182p. 1976. 23.50 (ISBN 0-85345-319-5). Monthly Rev.
Fragment, Ariel, ed. see Blotnick, Elihu.
Fragment, Ariel, ed. see Blotnick, Elihu & Robinson, Barbara.
Fragniere, Gabriel, ed. Education Without Frontiers: A World Program of Educational Reform. 1976. 18.95x (ISBN 0-7156-0988-2). Intl Ideas.
Fragnoli, Raymond R. The Transformation of Reform: Progressivism in Detroit & After, 1912-1933. LC 80-8464. (Modern American History Ser.). 420p. 1981. lib. bdg. 61.00 (ISBN 0-8240-4856-3). Garland Pub.
Fragomen, Austin L., ed. see Annual Legal Conference on the Representation of Aliens 1978-1983.
Fragomen, Austin T. & Rey, Alfred J. Immigration Procedures Handbook. 1984. 55.00 (ISBN 0-87632-456-1). Boardman.
Fragomen, Austin T., ed. Seventeeth Annual Immigration & Naturalization Institute. (Litigation & Administrative Practice Ser.). 519p. 1984. 35.00 (ISBN 0-686-80141-5, H4-4957). PLI.
Fragomen, Austin T., et al. Immigration Law & Business. LC 83-11315. 1983. 2 looseleaf vols. 150.00 (ISBN 0-87632-344-1). Boardman.
Fragomen, Austin T., Jr., ed. Tenth Annual Immigration & Naturalization Institute. LC 79-53161. 1979. text ed. 25.00 (ISBN 0-686-58199-7, H2-2947). PLI.
Fragomeni, Lydia, jt. auth. see Columbu, Franco.
Fragoso, Heleno C. Report on the Situation of Defence Lawyers in Argentina, March, 1975. pap. 20.00 (ISBN 0-317-29847-X, 2051909). Bks Demand UMI.
Fragoso, Heleno C. & Artucio, Alejandlo. Human Rights in Nicaragua, Yesterday & Today: Report of a Mission for the International Commission of Jurists. pap. 22.30 (ISBN 0-317-29856-9, 2051906). Bks Demand UMI.
Frahn, W. E. Diffractive Processes in Nuclear Physics. (Oxford Studies in Nuclear Physics). (Illus.). 200p. 1985. 32.50 (ISBN 0-19-851512-X). Oxford U Pr.
Fraiberg, Louis. Psychoanalysis & American Literary Criticism. LC 74-12171. 263p. 1974. Repr. of 1960 ed. lib. bdg. 23.00x (ISBN 0-374-92837-1). Octagon.
Fraiberg, Louis, jt. auth. see Fraiberg, Selma.
Fraiberg, Selma. Clinical Studies in Infant Mental Health: The First Year of Life. (Illus.). 279p. 1980. text ed. 21.95x (ISBN 0-465-01170-5). Basic.
Fraiberg, Selma & Fraiberg, Louis. Insights from the Blind: Comparative Studies of Blind & Sighted Infants. 1979. pap. 4.95 (ISBN 0-452-00502-7, F502, Mer). NAL.
Fraiberg, Selma H. Magic Years: Understanding & Handling the Problems of Early Childhood. LC 59-6073. 320p. 1984. pap. 7.95 (ISBN 0-684-71768-9, ScribT). Scribner.
Fraiburg, Selma, ed. Clinical Studies in Infant Mental Health: The First Year of Life. 279p. (Orig., AS). 1980. 21.50 (ISBN 0-318-17079-5). Kemper Nat Ctr.
Frailey, David. An Early Miocene (Arikareean) Fauna from North-Central Florida (the Sb-1a Local Fauna) (Occasional Papers: No. 75). 20p. 1978. pap. 1.25 (ISBN 0-686-79817-1). U of KS Mus Nat Hist.
Frailey, Lester E. Handbook of Business Letters. rev. ed. 1965. 32.50 (ISBN 0-13-375972-5). P-H.
Frain, John. Introduction to Marketing. 238p. 1981. pap. text ed. 18.50x (ISBN 0-7121-0959-5). Trans-Atlantic.
--Marketing: Principles & Practice. 288p. (Orig.). 1985. pap. text ed. 19.95x (ISBN 0-7121-2808-5). Trans-Atlantic.
Frain, John D. De see DeFrain, John D., et al.
Fraioli, F., et al, eds. Opioid Peptides in the Periphery: Proceedings of the International Symposium on Opioid Peptides in Periphery under the Patronage of the Italian National Council of Research Held in Rome, Italy, 23-25 May, 1984. (Developments in Neuroscience Ser.: Vol. 18). 298p. 1985. 58.00 (ISBN 0-444-80624-5). Elsevier.
Frair, John & Ardoin, Birthney. Effective Photography. (Illus.). 496p. 1982. 26.95 (ISBN 0-13-244459-3); pap. 23.95 (ISBN 0-13-244442-9). P-H.
Fraire, Isabel. Isabel Fraire: Selected Poems. new ed. Hoeksema, Thomas, tr. from Sp. LC 74-33066. 104p. (Eng. & Span.). 1975. pap. 7.00 (ISBN 0-8214-0214-5). Mundus Artium.
--Poems in the Lap of Death: English & Spanish. Hoekema, Thomas, tr. LC 81-3724. (Discoveries Ser.). 99p. 1980. pap. 8.50 (ISBN 0-935480-04-8). Lat Am Lit Rev Pr.
Fraissard, Jacques P. & Resing, Henry A., eds. Magnetic Resonance in Colloid & Interface Science. (NATO Advanced Study Institutes C. Mathematical & Physical Sciences Ser.: No. 61). 710p. 1980. lib. bdg. 76.00 (ISBN 90-277-1153-4, Pub. by Reidel Holland). Kluwer Academic.
Fraissard, Jacques P., jt. ed. see Petrakis, Leonidas.
Fraisse, jt. ed. see Groner.
Fraisse, Paul. The Psychology of Time. Leith, Jennifer, tr. from Fr. LC 75-37653. 343p. 1976. Repr. of 1963 ed. lib. bdg. 27.50x (ISBN 0-8371-8556-4, FRPT). Greenwood.
Fraisse, R. Course in Mathematical Logic, Vol. 1: Relation & Logical Formula. Louvish, D., tr. from Fr. LC 72-95893. (Synthese Library: No. 54). Orig. Title: Cours De Logique Mathematique, Tome 1. 210p. 1973. lib. bdg. 34.00 (ISBN 90-277-0268-3, Pub. by Reidel Holland); pap. 16.00 (ISBN 90-277-0403-1). Kluwer Academic.
--Course of Mathematical Logic: Model Theory, Vol. 2. Louvish, David, tr. from Fr. LC 72-95893. (Synthese Library: No. 69). Orig. Title: Cours De Logique Mathematique. 212p. 1974. lib. bdg. 34.00 (ISBN 90-277-0269-1); pap. text ed. 16.00 (ISBN 90-277-0510-0). Kluwer Academic.
Fraistat, Neil. The Poem & the Book: Interpreting Collections of Romantic Poetry. LC 84-10381. (Illus.). 241p. 1985. 19.95x (ISBN 0-8078-1615-9). U of NC Pr.
Fraistat, Neil, ed. Shelley's Prometheus Unbound, with Other Poems: A Facsimile Text. 1984. lib. bdg. 44.00 (ISBN 0-8240-9405-0). Garland Pub.
Fraistat, Rose A. Caroline Gordon As Novelist & Woman of Letters. LC 83-19963. (Southern Literary Studies). 224p. 1984. text ed. 20.00x (ISBN 0-8071-1151-1). La State U Pr.
Fraizer, Dale W. Alain Robbe-Grillet: An Annotated Bibliography of Critical Studies, 1953-1972. LC 73-13874. (Author Bibliographies Ser.: No. 13). 286p. 1973. 20.00 (ISBN 0-8108-0645-2). Scarecrow.
Frajese, G., et al, eds. Oligozoospermia: Recent Progress in Andrology. 496p. 1981. text ed. 70.50 (ISBN 0-89004-589-5). Raven.

--Seven Wives of Bluebeard. facsimile ed. LC 73-144154. (Short Story Index Reprint Ser.). Repr. of 1923 ed. 17.00 (ISBN 0-8369-3769-4). Ayer Co Pubs.
--Sur la Voie Glorieuse. 102p. 1916. 25.00 (ISBN 0-686-55878-2). French & Eur.
--Tales from a Mother-of-Pearl Casket. facsimile ed. Pene Du Bois, Henri, tr. from Fr. LC 78-37542. (Short Story Index Reprint Ser.). Repr. of 1896 ed. 15.50 (ISBN 0-8369-4101-2). Ayer Co Pubs.
--Thais. (Coll. Bleue). 1960. pap. 14.95 (ISBN 0-685-11585-2). French & Eur.
--Thais. Gulati, Basia, tr. from Fr. LC 75-20893. pap. 3.95 (ISBN 0-226-25989-7, P711, Phoen). U of Chicago Pr.
--Vaux-le-Vicomte. 1950. 3.95 (ISBN 0-686-55880-4). French & Eur.
--La Vie En Fleur. 280p. 1966. 7.95 (ISBN 0-686-55881-2). French & Eur.
--La Vie Litteraire. 5th ed. 336p. 1950. 8.95 (ISBN 0-686-55882-0). French & Eur.
--Well of Saint Clare. Allinson, Alfred, tr. LC 70-121549. (Short Story Index Reprint Ser). 1909. 19.00 (ISBN 0-8369-3505-5). Ayer Co Pubs.
--Works of Anatole France, 40 vols. 1975. 2700.00 (ISBN 0-8490-1329-1). Gordon Pr.

France, Anatole & Aveline, Claude. Oeuvres Completes: Vers les Temps Meilleurs. Trente Ans de Vie Sociale (Introduction Generale 1897-1904, Vol. 1. (Illus.). 329p. 1969. 15.95 (ISBN 0-686-55868-5). French & Eur.

France, Anatole, et al. Trente Ans de Vie Sociale: Vers les Temps Meileurs, 1915-1925, Vol. 4. 216p. 1973. 12.50 (ISBN 0-686-55879-0). French & Eur.

France, Anna K. Boris Pasternak's Translations of Shakespeare. LC 76-52027. 1978. 28.50x (ISBN 0-520-03432-5). U of Cal Pr.

France Armee Etat Major. Afrique Francaise du Nord: Bibliographie Militaire Des Ouvrages Francaise Ou Traduits En Francais et Des Articles Des Principales Revues Francaises Relatifs a L'algerie, a la Tunisie et Au Maroc De 1830-1927, 4 parts in 2 vols. (Fr.). Repr. of 1935 ed. Set. 155.00 (ISBN 0-404-56206-X). AMS Pr.

France Chambre des Deputes, 1814-1848 Staff. Report Made to the Chamber of Deputies on the Abolition of Slavery in the French Colonies, July 23, 1869. De Tocqueville, Alexis, ed. LC 70-106787. Repr. of 1849 ed. lib. bdg. 15.00x (ISBN 0-8371-3556-7, TRD&, Pub. by Negro U Pr). Greenwood.

France, Charles E., ed. see Baryshnikov, Mikhail.

France, Edires, ed. Arabanks: The International Yearbook, 1981-1982. 322p. 1981. 165.00xcancelled (ISBN 2-86255-002-7). Intl Pubns Serv.

France, Edward E. Some Aspects of the Migration of the Negro to the San Francisco Bay Area Since 1940. LC 74-76465. 1974. Repr. of 1962 ed. soft bdg. 12.00 (ISBN 0-88247-291-7). R & E Pubs.

France, Galeriede de see De France, Galeriede.

France, J. & Thornley, J. H. Mathematical Models in Agriculture: A Quantitative Approach to Problems in Agriculture & Related Sciences. 352p. 1984. text ed. 79.95 (ISBN 0-408-10868-1). Butterworth.

France, J. F. De see Chronister, R. B. & De France, J. F.

France, Joseph B. Crisis Therapy. LC 80-83967. 118p. 1980. pap. text ed. 8.75x (ISBN 0-918970-28-8). Intl Gen Semantics.

France, Kenneth. Body Conditioning: A Thinking Person's Guide to Aerobic Fitness. 184p. (Orig.). 1985. pap. 12.95 (ISBN 0-89334-080-4). Humanics Ltd.
--Crisis Intervention: A Handbook of Immediate Person-to-Person Help. 252p. 1982. 24.75x (ISBN 0-398-04535-6). C C Thomas.

France, Lillian E. Challenge, I Dare You. 1984. 5.75 (ISBN 0-8062-1803-7). Carlton.

France, Marie De. The Lais of Marie De France. Hanning, Robert W. & Ferrante, Joan M., eds. 256p. (Eng.). 1982. pap. text ed. 7.95x (ISBN 0-939464-02-0). Labyrinth Pr.

France, Marie de see De France, Marie.

France, Ministere de la Guerre. Rules & Regulations for the Field Exercise & Manoeuvres of the French Infantry: Issued August 1, 1791, 2 vols. 2nd ed. MacDonald, John, tr. from Fr. LC 68-54795. (Illus.). Repr. of 1806 ed. cancelled (ISBN 0-8371-2336-4). Greenwood.

France, Ministere Des Affaires Etrangeres. Les Combattants Francais De la Guerre Americaine, 1778-1783. LC 68-9149. (Illus.). 453p. 1969. Repr. of 1905 ed. 40.00 (ISBN 0-8063-0151-1). Genealog Pub.

France, P. W. Experiments in Elementary Physics. 2nd ed. 1981. pap. text ed. 12.95x (ISBN 0-89917-331-X). TIS Inc.

France, Peter. Diderot. (Past Masters Ser.). 1983. 12.95x (ISBN 0-19-287551-5); pap. 3.95 (ISBN 0-19-287550-7). Oxford U Pr.
--Poets of Modern Russia. LC 82-4264. (Cambridge Studies in Russian Literature). 256p. 1983. 39.50 (ISBN 0-521-23490-5); pap. 13.95 (ISBN 0-521-28000-1). Cambridge U Pr.

France, Peter, tr. see Pasternak, Boris.

France, Peter, tr. see Rousseau, Jean J.

France, R. H. Germs of Mind in Plants. Simons, A. M., tr. from Ger. (Science for the Workers Ser.). (Illus.). 151p. 9.95 (ISBN 0-88286-083-6). C H Kerr.

France, R. T. Jesus & the Old Testament: Application of Old Testament Passages to Himself & His Mission. (Twin Brooks Ser.). 286p. 1982. pap. 9.95 (ISBN 0-8010-3508-2). Baker Bk.

France, R. T., ed. A Bibliographical Guide to New Testament Research. 56p. (Orig.). 1979. pap. text ed. 3.95x (ISBN 0-905774-19-1, Pub. by JSOT Pr England). Eisenbrauns.

France, R. T. & Wenham, David, eds. Gospel Perspectives: Studies of History & Tradition in the Four Gospels, Vol. II. 375p. 1981. text ed. 14.75x (ISBN 0-905774-31-0, Pub. by JSOT Pr England). Eisenbrauns.
--Gospel Perspectives: Studies of History & Tradition in the Four Gospels, Vol. 1. 263p. 1980. text ed. 14.75x (ISBN 0-905774-21-3, Pub. by JSOT Pr England). Eisenbrauns.
--Gospel Perspectives, Vol. III: Studies of History & Tradition in the Four Gospels. 299p. 1983. text ed. 14.75x (ISBN 0-905774-56-6, Pub. by JSOT Press England). Eisenbrauns.

France, Richard. First Word & the Last. (Illus.). 30p. (Director's Production Script). 1974. pap. 5.00 (ISBN 0-88680-055-2). I E Clark.
--Sherlock Holmes in the Adventure of the Dying Detective. (Illus.). 29p. (Director's Production Script). 1974. pap. 5.00 (ISBN 0-88680-177-X). I E Clark.
--Station J: An American Play. LC 82-14936. 170p. (Orig.). 1983. pap. 8.95 (ISBN 0-8290-0538-2). Irvington.

France, Richard & Canty, Jerome. Healing Naturally: A Macrobiotic Philosophy of Nutrition for Better Health. (Illus.). 144p. 1985. pap. 6.95 (ISBN 0-8283-1906-5). Branden Pub Co.

France, Wilmer C. The Emperor Julian's Relation to the New Sophistic & Neo-Platonism: With a Study of His Style. LC 78-66599. (Ancient Philosophy Ser.). 113p. 1982. lib. bdg. 18.00 (ISBN 0-8240-9598-7). Garland Pub.

Francello, Joseph A. The Seneca World of Ga-No-Say-Yeh (Peter Crouse, White Captive) LC 80-1358. 227p. 1980. pap. text ed. 12.25 (ISBN 0-8191-1141-4). U Pr of Amer.

Frances, Allen, et al. Differential Therapeutics in Psychiatry: The Art & Science of Treatment Selection. LC 84-5883. 424p. 1984. 30.00 (ISBN 0-87630-360-2). Brunner-Mazel.

Frances, Allen J., jt. ed. see Hales, Robert.

Frances, Carol, ed. Successful Responses to Financial Difficulty. LC 81-48570. (Higher Education Ser.: No. 38). 1982. 8.95x (ISBN 0-87589-896-3). Jossey-Bass.

Frances, E., jt. auth. see Calderon De La Barca.

Frances, Jane. A Prophet's Story. 1982. 8.95 (ISBN 0-533-04971-7). Vantage.

Frances, Marian. Mr. Mac-A-Doodle. (Illus.). (gr. 1). 1972. pap. 1.50 (ISBN 0-89375-045-X). Troll Assocs.
--Witch on a Motorcycle. new ed. (Illus.). (gr. 3-4). 1972. pap. 1.50 (ISBN 0-89375-047-6). Troll Assocs.

Frances, Michael, jt. ed. see Pinner, R.

Frances, Osvald, jt. auth. see Costa, Vasco.

Frances, Phil, jt. auth. see Fichter, George S.

Frances, Richard J. Self-Assessment of Current Knowledge in Psychiatry. 5th ed. 1985. pap. text ed. write for info. (ISBN 0-87488-644-9). Med Exam.

Frances, Robert & Roubertoux, Pierre, eds. Culture Artistique et Enseignement Superieur: La Structure Des Interets Artistiques Deloisir Chez les Etudiants. (Textes De Sciences Sociales: No. 15). 1976. pap. 15.20x (ISBN 0-686-22364-0). Mouton.

Francesca, Rosina. How to Marry Somebody Else's Housebroken Husband. Young, Billie, ed. LC 73-76538. 128p. 1973. 12.95 (ISBN 0-87949-008-X). Ashley Bks.

Francesca, Sal Di see Di Francesca, Sal.

Franceschetti, A., et al. Chorioretinal Heredodegenerations: An Updated Report of La Societe Francaise d'Ophtalmologie. (Illus.). 1496p. 1974. 221.50x (ISBN 0-398-02705-6). C C Thomas.

Francesco, Armand Di. The Shut-Ins: A Survival Manual. LC 84-62171. 160p. (Orig.). 1985. pap. 5.50 (ISBN 0-87973-599-6, 599). Our Sunday Visitor.

Francesco, Giovanni, jt. auth. see Mirandola, Pico D.

Francesco, Grete de. The Power of the Charlatan. Beard, Miriam, tr. from Ger. LC 79-8609. Repr. of 1939 ed. 31.50 (ISBN 0-404-18471-5). AMS Pr.

Francesco, M., ed. & intro. by see U. S. Congress. Senate Select Committee on Equal Opportunity.

Francesconi, Mario. Bishop John B. Scalabrini: An Insight into His Spirituality. Cinquino, J. & Monaco, Vincent, trs. from It. LC 73-75230. (Illus.). 107p. 1973. pap. 3.00 (ISBN 0-913256-50-1). Ctr Migration.
--John B. Scalabrini: An Insight into His Spirituality. Cinquino, J., tr. (Pastoral Series). 106p. 1973. pap. 2.25 (ISBN 0-913256-50-1, 501). Ctr Migration.

Francesconi, Mario, jt. auth. see Caliaro, Marco.

Frances D'Assisi, Saint The Writings of Saint Francis of Assisi. Robinson, Paschal, tr. 1977. lib. bdg. 59.95 (ISBN 0-8490-2822-1). Gordon Pr.

Franch, Jose A. Pre-Columbian Art. (Illus.). 618p. 1983. 125.00 (ISBN 0-8109-0645-7). Abrams.

Franchak, Stephen J. & Desy, Jeanne. Involving Business-Industry-Labor: Guidelines for Planning & Evaluating Vocational Education Programs. 86p. 1984. 8.00 (ISBN 0-318-17787-0, RD250). Natl Ctr Res Voc Ed.

Franchak, Stephen J. & Kean, Michael H. Using Evaluation Results: Guidelines & Practice for Using Vocational Evaluation Effectively. 86p. 1981. 6.25 (ISBN 0-318-15584-2, RD212). Natl Ctr Res Voc Ed.

Franchak, Stephen J. & Smiley, Larry L. Evaluating Employer Satisfaction: Measurement of Satisfaction with Training & Job Performance of Former Vocational Education Students. 79p. 1981. 5.50 (ISBN 0-318-15463-3, RD210). Natl Ctr Res Voc Ed.

Franchak, Stephen J. & Spirer, Janet E. Evaluation Handbook: Guidelines & Practices for Follow-up Studies of Former Vocational Students, Vol. 1. 230p. 1978. 13.00 (ISBN 0-318-15466-8, RD 171). Natl Ctr Res Voc Ed.
--Evaluation Handbook: Guidelines & Practices for Follow-up Studies of Special Population, Vol. 2. 273p. 1979. 14.25 (ISBN 0-318-15465-X, RD 172). Natl Ctr Res Voc Ed.

Franchak, Stephen J., et al. Specifications for Longitudinal Studies. 126p. 1980. 6.75 (ISBN 0-318-15567-2, RD191). Natl Ctr Res Voc Ed.

Franchak, Stephen J., jt. auth. see Ponce, Eliseo R.

Franchere, Hoyt C. & O'Donnell, Thomas F. Harold Frederic. (Twayne's United States Authors Ser). 1961. pap. 5.95x (ISBN 0-8084-0149-1, T3, Twayne). New Coll U Pr.

Franchere, Ruth. Cesar Chavez. LC 78-101927. (Crocodile Paperbacks Ser). (Illus.). 48p. (gr. 2-6). 1973. pap. 2.95 (ISBN 0-690-18385-2); lib. bdg. 10.89 (ISBN 0-690-18384-4). Crowell Jr Bks.
--Hannah Herself. (YA) (gr. 7-11). 1977. pap. 1.25 (ISBN 0-380-01647-8, 33050). Avon.
--The Wright Brothers. LC 70-158689. (Biography Ser). (Illus.). (gr. 1-5). 1972. PLB 10.89 (ISBN 0-690-90701-X). Crowell Jr Bks.

Franchet, A. R. Plantae Davidiane Ex Sinarum Imperio, 2 pts. (Illus.). 1970. Repr. of 1884 ed. 105.00 (ISBN 3-7682-0670-X). Lubrecht & Cramer.

Franchi, G., jt. ed. see Garattini, S.

Franchimont, P., ed. Articular Synovium. (Illus.). viii, 184p. 1982. pap. 48.75 (ISBN 3-8055-3461-2). S Karger.

Franchimont, P. & Channing, C. P., eds. Intragonadal Regulation of Reproduction. LC 81-66365. 1981. 55.00 (ISBN 0-12-265280-0). Acad Pr.

Franchini, Antonello, et al. Atlas of Stomal Pathology. (Illus.). 124p. 1983. text ed. 85.00 (ISBN 8-88503-737-2). Raven.

Francia, Arthur J. & Strawser, Robert H. Accounting for Managers. LC 82-71152. 1982. text ed. 28.95x (ISBN 0-931920-38-8). Dame Pubns.
--Managerial Accounting. 5th ed. (Illus.). 651p. 1985. pap. text ed. 28.95 (ISBN 0-931920-70-1); practice problems 4.95x (ISBN 0-931920-53-1); study guide 8.95x (ISBN 0-931920-55-8); work papers 8.95x (ISBN 0-686-70446-0). Dame Pubns.

Francia, Peter de see De Francia, Peter.

Francia, Rubio De see Peral, I & De Francia, Rubio J.

Francillen, R. McDonnell Douglas F-15A-B: Minigraph 2. write for info. (ISBN 0-942548-07-8). Aerofax.
--McDonnell F-40: Minigraph 4. write for info. (ISBN 0-942548-09-4). Aerofax.

Francillon, R. Lockheed F-94 Variants: Minigraph 14. write for info. (ISBN 0-942548-19-1). Aerofax.

Francillon, Rene. Aerograph 2: The Air Guard. (Aerograph Ser.). (Illus.). 180p. 1983. pap. 24.95 (ISBN 0-942548-03-5). Aerofax.
--Grumman F-14, (Minigraph Ser.: No. 3). (Illus.). 40p. 1984. pap. 4.95 (ISBN 0-317-18392-3, Pub. by Aerofax TX). Motorbooks Intl.
--Japanese Aircraft of the Pacific War. 2nd ed. (Illus.). 548p. 1980. 31.95 (ISBN 0-370-30251-6, Pub. by the Bodley Head). Merrimack Pub Cir.

Francillon, Rene J. Lockheed Aircraft since 1913. (Illus.). 512p. 1982. 39.95 (ISBN 0-370-30329-6, Pub. by the Bodley Head). Merrimack Pub Cir.
--McDonnell Douglas Aircraft Since Nineteen Twenty. LC 79-314590. (Putnam Aeronautical Bks.). (Illus.). 696p. 1979. 40.00 (ISBN 0-370-00050-1, Pub. by the Bodley Head). Merrimack Pub Cir.

Francin, Rudy. The Turbulent History of the North Adriatic Archipelago. (Illus.). 304p. 1983. 13.00 (ISBN 0-682-49977-3). Exposition Pr FL.

Franciose, Helen E. & Swanson, Nancy C. Your Norwegian Elkhound. LC 73-84513. (Your Dog Bk.). (Illus.). 160p. 1974. 12.95 (ISBN 0-87714-014-6). Denlingers.

Francis. Cement Industry: 1796-1914. 1978. 25.00 (ISBN 0-7153-7386-2). David & Charles.

Francis, A. J. Introducing Structures. (International Series in Structure & Solid Body Mechanics). 1980. 41.00 (ISBN 0-08-022701-5); pap. 12.00 (ISBN 0-08-022702-3). Pergamon.

Francis, Alfred W. Handbook of Components in Solvent Extraction. LC 72-78013. 544p. 1972. 132.95 (ISBN 0-677-03080-0). Gordon.

Francis, Andre. Jazz. LC 76-6983. (Roots of Jazz Ser.). 1976. Repr. of 1960 ed. lib. bdg. 22.50 (ISBN 0-306-70812-4). Da Capo.

Francis, Anna B. Pleasant Dreams. (Illus.). 32p. (gr. k-2). 1983. 11.95 (ISBN 0-03-060574-1). HR&W.

Francis, Anne F. Hieronimus Bosch: The Temptation of Saint Anthony. (Illus.). 1980. 12.50 (ISBN 0-682-48910-7, University). Exposition Pr FL.
--Voyage of Re-Discovery: The Veneration of St. Vincent. 1978. 15.00 (ISBN 0-682-48429-6, University). Exposition Pr FL.

Francis, Arthur, jt. auth. see Wainwright, Judith.

Francis, Arthur, et al, eds. Power, Efficiency & Institutions. 217p. 1983. text ed. 35.00x (ISBN 0-435-82315-9). Gower Pub Co.

Francis, Austin. Catskill Rivers. LC 83-4164. (Illus.). 224p. 1983. 24.95 (ISBN 0-8329-0282-9, Pub. by Winchester Pr). New Century.
--Smart Squash. 1979. pap. 2.95 (ISBN 0-346-12385-2). Cornerstone.

Francis, Azalia S., jt. auth. see Barbe, Walter B.

Francis, C. W. Radiostrontium Movement in Soils & Uptake in Plants. LC 78-19051. (DOE Critical Review Ser.). 139p. 1978. pap. 11.50 (ISBN 0-87079-110-9, TID-27564); microfiche 4.50 (ISBN 0-87079-332-2, TID-27564). DOE.

Francis, Carol A. Study Skills. pap. text ed. 2.95 (ISBN 0-933892-14-4). Child Focus Co.

Francis, Carol B. Europe Dimensions: A Study-Activity Guide. (Orig.). 1981. pap. 3.95 (ISBN 0-377-00108-2). Friend Pr.

Francis, Carolyn. Music Reading & Theory Skills: A Sequential Method for Pratice & Mastery, Level 3. 90p. 1984. tchrs. manual 23.95 (ISBN 0-931303-00-1); student wkbk. 7.95 (ISBN 0-931303-01-X). Innovative Learn.

Francis, Charles. Charles Francis Adams. (The Works of Charles Francis Adams Ser.). vii, 426p. Repr. of 1900 ed. lib. bdg. 49.00 (ISBN 0-932051-05-7, Pub. by Am Repr Serv). Am Biog Serv.

Francis, Charles E. Tuskegee Airmen: The Story of the Negro in the U. S. Air Force. 1968. 12.95 (ISBN 0-8283-1386-5). Branden Pub Co.

Francis, Chester & Auerbach, Stanley I., eds. Environment & Solid Wastes: Characterization, Treatment, & Disposal. LC 82-71528. (Illus.). 450p. 1983. 49.95 (ISBN 0-250-40583-0). Butterworth.

Francis, Clare. Night Sky. LC 83-17351. 600p. 1984. 16.95 (ISBN 0-688-02633-8). Morrow.
--Night Sky. 640p. 1985. pap. 4.50 (ISBN 0-446-32550-3). Warner Bks.

Francis, Clark & Archer, Stephen H. Portfolio Analysis. 2nd ed. (Foundations of Finance Ser.). (Illus.). 1979. text ed. 28.95 (ISBN 0-13-686675-1). P-H.

Francis, Claude, tr. see De Beauvoir, Simone.

Francis, Claude, et al. Le Francais de Nos Jours. LC 77-17062. (Illus.). 428p. 1978. 11.85x (ISBN 0-8093-0841-X). S Ill U Pr.

Francis, Connie. Who's Sorry Now? (Illus.). 400p. 1985. pap. 3.95 (ISBN 0-312-90386-3). St Martin.
--Who's Sorry Now? Connie Francis Tells Her Own Story. LC 84-11759. (Illus.). 352p. 1984. 14.95 (ISBN 0-312-87088-4). St Martin.

Francis, Convers. Life of John Eliot: The Apostle to the Indians. 1972. Repr. of 1854 ed. lib. bdg. 24.00 (ISBN 0-8422-8049-9). Irvington.

Francis, D., jt. ed. see Bryant, J. A.

Francis, D. Pitt. Statistical Method for Accounting Students. 1978. pap. text ed. 21.00x (ISBN 0-434-90580-1). Intl Ideas.

Francis, Dale, ed. see Seeley, Burns K.

Francis, Daniel. Battle for the West: Fur Traders & the Birth of Western Canada. (Illus.). 192p. 1982. text ed. 18.95x (ISBN 0-295-96020-5, Pub. by Hurtig Publishers). U of Wash Pr.

Francis, Daniel & Morantz, Toby. Partners in Furs: A History of the Fur Trade in Eastern James Bay, 1600-1870. 200p. 1983. 25.00x (ISBN 0-7735-0385-4); pap. 11.95 (ISBN 0-7735-0386-2). McGill-Queens U Pr.

Francis, Dave & Woodcock, Mike. The Unblocked Boss: A Guidebook for Managers. LC 81-51806. 274p. 1981. pap. 14.95 (ISBN 0-88390-169-2). Univ Assocs.

Francis, Dave & Young, Don. Improving Work Groups: A Practical Manual for Team Building. LC 78-64978. 261p. 1979. pap. 19.50 (ISBN 0-88390-149-8). Univ Assocs.

Francis, Dave, jt. auth. see Woodcock, Mike.

Francis, David & Sobel, Raoul. Chaplin: Genesis of a Clown. 5.95 (ISBN 0-7043-3134-9, Pub. by Quartet England). Charles River Bks.

Francis, David, ed. see Permanent International Altaistic Conference, Indiana University, 1962.

Francis, David P., jt. auth. see O'Muircheartaigh, Colm.

Francis, David R. Russia from the American Embassy April, 1916 - November, 1918. LC 78-115537. (Russia Observed, Series I). 1970. Repr. of 1921 ed. 24.50 (ISBN 0-405-03026-6). Ayer Co Pubs.

Francis, Deak. American International Law Cases: 1971-1978, Vols. 1-20. Incl. Vols. 21- Ruddy, F. 1980. LC 78-140621. 50.00 ea. (ISBN 0-379-20075-9). Oceana.

Francis, Devon. Flak Bait: The Story of the B-26 Bombers & the Men Who Flew Them in World War II. LC 79-15574. Repr. of 1948 ed. 19.95 (ISBN 0-89201-044-4). Zenger Pub.

Francis, Dick. Banker. (General Ser.). 456p. 1983. lib. bdg. 15.50 (ISBN 0-8161-3579-7, Large Print Bks). G K Hall.
--Banker. 1984. pap. 3.95 (Del Rey). Ballantine.
--Banker. 1984. pap. 3.95 (ISBN 0-449-20262-3, Crest). Fawcett.
--Blood Sport. 1985. pap. 3.50 (ISBN 0-671-50738-9). PB.
--Bonecrack. 1983. pap. 3.50 (ISBN 0-671-50739-7). PB.
--The Danger. LC 83-13973. 1984. 15.95 (ISBN 0-399-12890-5, Putnam). Putnam Pub Group.
--The Danger. (General Ser.). 1984. lib. bdg. 17.95 (ISBN 0-8161-3724-2, Large Print Bks); pap. 9.95 (ISBN 0-8161-3767-6). G K Hall.
--The Danger. 352p. 1985. pap. 3.95 (ISBN 0-449-20263-1, Crest). Fawcett.
--Dead Cert. 256p. 1983. pap. 3.50 (ISBN 0-671-50730-3). PB.
--Dead Cert. Barzun, J. & Taylor, W. H., eds. LC 81-47383. (Crime Fiction 1950-1975 Ser.). 220p. 1982. lib. bdg. 18.00 (ISBN 0-8240-4991-8). Garland Pub.
--Enquiry. 1984. pap. 3.50 (ISBN 0-671-54362-8). PB.
--Flying Finish. 1984. pap. 3.50 (ISBN 0-671-50926-8). PB.
--For Kicks. 1985. pap. 3.50 (ISBN 0-671-53265-0). PB.
--Forfeit. 1985. pap. 3.50 (ISBN 0-671-54692-9). PB.
--High Stakes. LC 75-25082. (Harper Novel of Suspense Ser.). 224p. (YA) 1976. 9.95i (ISBN 0-06-011307-3, HarpT). Har-Row.
--High Stakes. 1982. pap. 2.95 (ISBN 0-671-46423-X). PB.
--High Stakes. 1985. pap. 3.50 (ISBN 0-671-55268-6). PB.
--In the Frame. LC 76-47255. 1977. 9.95i (ISBN 0-06-011341-3, HarpT). Har-Row.
--In the Frame. 1985. pap. 3.50 (ISBN 0-671-50754-0). PB.
--Knockdown. LC 74-15870. (Harper Novel of Suspense). (Illus.). 224p. 1975. 11.49i (ISBN 0-06-011339-1, HarpT). Har-Row.
--Knockdown. 1984. pap. 3.50 (ISBN 0-671-50760-5). PB.
--Nerve. 1975. pap. 2.95 (ISBN 0-671-45072-7). PB.
--Nerve. 1984. pap. 3.50 (ISBN 0-671-52522-0). PB.
--Proof. 324p. 1985. 16.95 (ISBN 0-399-13036-5, Putnam). Putnam Pub Group.
--The Racing Game (Odds Against) 1984. pap. 3.50 (ISBN 0-671-53086-0). PB.
--Rat Race. 224p. 1984. pap. 3.50 (ISBN 0-671-53026-7). PB.
--Reflex. (General Ser.). 1981. lib. bdg. 14.95 (ISBN 0-8161-3255-0, Large Print Bks). G K Hall.
--Reflex. 320p. 1984. pap. 3.95 (ISBN 0-449-20713-7, Crest). Fawcett.
--Risk. 1984. pap. 3.50 (ISBN 0-671-50755-9). PB.
--Slayride. 1984. pap. 3.50 (ISBN 0-671-50731-1). PB.
--Smokescreen. 224p. 1984. pap. 3.50 (ISBN 0-671-50737-0). PB.
--Trial Run. LC 78-20204. (Harper Novel of Suspense). 1979. 13.41i (ISBN 0-06-011383-9, HarpT). Har-Row.
--Trial Run. 1985. pap. 3.50 (ISBN 0-671-50732-X). PB.
--Twice Shy. (General Ser.). 1982. lib. bdg. 14.95 (ISBN 0-8161-3445-6, Large Print Bks). G K Hall.
--Twice Shy. 320p. 1985. pap. 3.95 (ISBN 0-449-20756-0, Crest). Fawcett.
--Two By Francis. LC 82-48488. 512p. 1983. 14.37i (ISBN 0-06-015126-9, HarpT). Har-Row.
--Whip Hand. LC 79-3408. 1980. 9.95i (ISBN 0-06-011384-7, HarpT). Har-Row.
--Whip Hand. 336p. 1982. pap. 3.50 (ISBN 0-671-46404-3). PB.
Francis, Doris. Will You Still Need Me, Will You Still Feed Me, When I'm 84? LC 82-49351. (Illus.). 272p. 1984. 18.50x (ISBN 0-253-36545-7). Ind U Pr.
Francis, Dorothy. The Ghost of Graydon Place. 192p. (Orig.). (gr. 7 up). 1982. pap. 1.95 (ISBN 0-590-32545-0, Windswept). Scholastic Inc.
--The Warning. 192p. (Orig.). (gr. 7-12). 1984. pap. 1.95 (ISBN 0-590-33250-3, Windswept Bks). Scholastic Inc.
Francis, Dorothy & Dixon, Daphne. Diets for Sick Children. 3rd ed. 432p. 1975. 20.25 (ISBN 0-8016-1648-4, Blackwell). Mosby.
Francis, Dorothy B. Blink of the Mind. (Twilight Ser.: No. 5). (gr. 5 up). 1982. pap. 1.95 (ISBN 0-440-90496-X, LFL). Dell.
--Piggy Bank Minds & Other Object Lessons for Children. LC 76-49639. 1977. pap. 5.50 (ISBN 0-687-31420-8). Abingdon.
--Promises & Turtle Shells: And Forty-Nine Other Object Lessons for Children. 112p. (Orig.). 1984. pap. 7.50 (ISBN 0-687-34337-2). Abingdon.
--Shoplifting: The Crime Everybody Pays for. LC 79-20807. 1980. 10.95 (ISBN 0-525-66658-3, 01063-320). Lodestar Bks.
--Vandalism: The Crime of Immaturity. 128p. (gr. 12 up). 1983. 10.95 (ISBN 0-525-66774-1, 01063-320). Lodestar Bks.
Francis, E. K. Interethnic Relations: An Essay in Sociological Theory. LC 75-8271. 448p. 1976. 35.00 (ISBN 0-444-99011-9, FIR/, Pub. by Elsevier). Greenwood.
Francis, Edward L., ed. see Ruggles, Philip K.
Francis, Edward P. & DeAngelis, George. The Early Ford V-8 As Henry Built It. LC 82-22955. (Illus.). 220p. 1982. 21.95 (ISBN 0-911383-01-8). Motor Cities.
Francis, Edward P., jt. auth. see De Angelis, George.
Francis, Emily. Elena. 1977. pap. 1.50 (ISBN 0-8439-0502-6, Leisure Bks). Dorchester Pub Co.
Francis, F. J. & Clydesdale, F. M. Food Colorimetry: Theory & Applications. (Illus.). 1975. text ed. 60.00 (ISBN 0-87055-183-3). AVI.
Francis, F. J., jt. auth. see Clydesdale, F. M.
Francis, F. J., jt. auth. see Clydesdale, Fergus S.
Francis, Frank. A Bibliographical Ghost Revisits His Old Haunts. LC 72-619563. (Bibliographical Monograph: No. 5). 1972. 5.95 (ISBN 0-87959-046-7). U of Tex H Ransom Ctr.
Francis, Fred O. & Sampley, J. Paul. Pauline Parallels. rev. ed. LC 83-48920. (Foundations & Facets: New Testament Ser.). 416p. 1984. 29.95 (ISBN 0-8006-2103-4, 1-2103). Fortress.
Francis, Fred O. & Wallace, Raymond P., eds. Tradition As Openness to the Future: Essays in Honor of Willis W. Fisher. (Illus.). 236p. (Orig.). 1984. lib. bdg. 22.50 (ISBN 0-8191-3722-7); pap. text ed. 12.00 (ISBN 0-8191-3723-5). U Pr of Amer.
Francis, Frederick J., jt. auth. see Clydesdale, Fergus M.
Francis, G. James. Organization Development: A Practical Approach. 200p. 1982. text ed. 19.95 (ISBN 0-8359-5301-7). Reston.
Francis, G. James & Milbourn, Gene, Jr. Human Behavior in the Work Environment. 1980. text ed. 23.80x (ISBN 0-673-16086-6). Scott F.
Francis Galton Laboratory for National Eugenics Staff, et al. Eugenics Laboratory Lecture Series. Rosenberg, Charles, ed. LC 83-48563. (The History of Hereditarian Thought Ser.). 434p. 1985. lib. bdg. 52.00 (ISBN 0-8240-5815-1). Garland Pub.
Francis Galton Laboratory for National Eugenics Staff & Pearson, Karl. Questions of the Day & of the Fray. Rosenberg, Charles, ed. LC 83-48539. (The History of Hereditarian Thought Ser.). 350p. 1985. Repr. lib. bdg. 45.00 (ISBN 0-8240-5813-5). Garland Pub.
Francis Galton Laboratory for National Eugenics Staff, et al. Selected Eugenics Laboratory Memoirs. Rosenberg, Charles, ed. LC 83-48540. (The History of Hereditarian Thought Ser.). 330p. 1985. Repr. lib. bdg. 45.00 (ISBN 0-8240-5814-3). Garland Pub.
Francis, Gary S., jt. auth. see Alpert, Joseph S.
Francis, George. She Died, She Lives: In Search of Maria Orsola. 176p. 1977. pap. 4.95 (ISBN 0-232-51392-9). Attic Pr.
Francis, Gloria A. & Lozynsky, Artem, eds. Whitman at Auction: 1899-1972. LC 77-16647. (Authors at Auction Ser.). (Illus.). 444p. 1978. 44.00x (ISBN 0-8103-0921-1, Bruccoli Clark). Gale.
Francis, Gloria A. & Lozynsky, Artemcompiled by. Whitman at Auction. (Illus.). 1977. 34.00 (ISBN 0-8103-0921-1). Bruccoli.
Francis, Gloria M. & Munjas, Barbara A. Manual of Socialpsychologic Assessment. 219p. 1976. pap. 13.95 (ISBN 0-8385-6127-6). ACC.
--Promoting Psychological Comfort. 3rd ed. (Foundations of Nursing Ser.). 120p. 1979. pap. text ed. write for info. (ISBN 0-697-05544-2). Wm C Brown.
Francis, H. E. A Disturbance of Gulls & Other Stories. LC 83-2676. 150p. 1983. 12.95 (ISBN 0-8076-1071-2). Braziller.
--The Itinerary of Beggars. LC 73-80957. (The Iowa School of Letters Award for Short Fiction Ser.: No. 4). 278p. 1973. 17.50 (ISBN 0-87745-039-0). U of Iowa Pr.
--Naming Things. LC 80-19543. (Illinois Short Fiction Ser.). 157p. 1980. pap. 5.95 (ISBN 0-252-00831-6). U of Ill Pr.
Francis, Hazel. Language in Childhood: Form & Function in Language Learning. LC 75-4393. 200p. 1975. 26.00 (ISBN 0-312-46725-7). St Martin.
--Learning to Read: Literate Behavior & Orthographic Knowledge. 192p. 1983. text ed. 29.50x (ISBN 0-04-372037-4); pap. text ed. 12.50x (ISBN 0-04-372038-2). Allen Unwin.
Francis, Hazel, jt. auth. see Chanan, Gabriel.
Francis, Hazel, ed. Learning to Teach: Psychology in Teacher Training. 200p. 1985. 27.00x (ISBN 1-85000-041-7, Falmer Pr); pap. 15.00x (ISBN 1-85000-042-5, Falmer Pr). Taylor & Francis.
Francis, Hywel. Miners Against Fascism: Wales & the Spanish Civil War. (Illus.). 304p. 1984. 20.00 (ISBN 0-85315-576-3, Pub. by Salem Hse Ltd). Merrimack Pub Cir.
Francis, Ivor. Statistical Software: A Comparative Review. 542p. 1981. 75.00 (ISBN 0-444-00658-3, North-Holland). Elsevier.
Francis, J. C. Investments: Analysis & Management. 4th ed. (Finance Ser.). 896p. 1985. price not set (ISBN 0-07-021803-X). McGraw.
--Readings in Investments. 1980. 20.95 (ISBN 0-07-019963-9). McGraw.
Francis, J. D., ed. see Raudkivi, A. J.
Francis, J. De see De Francis, J.
Francis, J. R. The Encyclopedia of Death. large type ed. (Illus.). pap. 7.00 (ISBN 0-910122-47-4). Amherst Pr.
--Fluid Mechanics for Engineering Students. 4th ed. 1975. text ed. 37.50x (ISBN 0-7131-3331-7); pap. text ed. 23.95x (ISBN 0-7131-3332-5). Intl Ideas.
Francis, Jack C. Investments: Analysis & Management. 3rd ed. 1980. 34.95 (ISBN 0-07-021789-0). McGraw.
--Management of Investments. (Finance Ser.). (Illus.). 608p. 1983. text ed. 33.50 (ISBN 0-07-021805-6). McGraw.
Francis, Jack C., jt. auth. see Alexander, Gordon J.
Francis, Jean. The Doctor in Ward B. 1978. pap. 1.50 (ISBN 0-532-15320-0). Woodhill.
Francis, Jessie D. An Economic & Social History of Mexican California (1822-1846) Chiefly Economic, Vol. 1, 2 Vols. in 1. Cortes, Carlos E., ed. LC 76-1238. (Chicano Heritage Ser.). 1976. Repr. lib. bdg. 64.00x (ISBN 0-405-09502-3). Ayer Co Pubs.
Francis, John. History of the Bank of England from 1694 to 1844. 1981. lib. bdg. 75.00 (ISBN 0-686-71629-9). Revisionist Pr.
--History of the English Railway, 2 Vols. in One. LC 68-20087. Repr. of 1851 ed. 45.00x (ISBN 0-678-00344-0). Kelley.
Francis, John De see De Francis, John.
Francis, John De see Ma, Ho-t'ien.
Francis, John F. De see De Francis, John F.
Francis, John G. & Ganzel, Richard, eds. Western Public Lands: The Management of Natural Resources in a Time of Declining Federalism. 320p. 1984. 39.50x (ISBN 0-86598-147-7). Rowman & Allanheld.
Francis, John H. From Caxton to Carlyle. LC 76-15217. 1976. Repr. of 1937 ed. lib. bdg. 20.00 (ISBN 0-8414-4213-4). Folcroft.
Francis, John J., jt. ed. see Marcus, Irwin M.
Francis, Leslie J. Experience of Adulthood: A Profile of Twenty-Six to Thirty-Nine Year Olds. 228p. 1982. text ed. 32.00x (ISBN 0-566-00562-X). Gower Pub Co.
--Youth in Transit: A Profile of 16-25 year olds. 202p. 1982. text ed. 32.00x (ISBN 0-566-00530-1). Gower Pub Co.
Francis, Linda & Hartzel, John. What's in a Name? (Orig.). 1982. pap. 2.95 (ISBN 0-8423-7935-5). Tyndale.
Francis, Marilyn A. Water & Windfall. (Illus.). 48p. 1982. 20.00 (ISBN 0-88014-039-9). Mosaic Pr OH.
Francis, Marjorie. Three R's of Life Language. (gr. k-6). 1971. 3.25 (ISBN 0-933892-11-X). Child Focus Co.
Francis, Mark, ed. The Viennese Enlightenment. LC 84-18385. 192p. 1985. 25.00 (ISBN 0-312-84583-9). St Martin.
Francis, Mark, et al. Community Open Spaces: Greening Neighborhoods through Community Action & Land Conservation. rev. ed. (Illus.). 204p. 1984. 24.95 (ISBN 0-933280-27-0). Island CA.
Francis, Mary. But I Have Called You Friends. 1974. 4.95 (ISBN 0-8199-0500-3). Franciscan Herald.
Francis, Mother Mary. Strange Gods Before Me. 199p. 1976. pap. 4.95 (ISBN 0-8199-0599-2). Franciscan Herald.
Francis, Sr. Mary. Variations on a Theme. 1977. 5.00 (ISBN 0-8199-0664-6). Franciscan Herald.
--Where Caius Is & Other Poems. (Spirit & Life Ser). 1955. 3.00 (ISBN 0-686-11570-8). Franciscan Inst.
Francis, Michael J. The Limits of Hegemony: United States Relations with Argentina & Chile During World War II. LC 77-89754. (International Studies Ser). 1977. text ed. 24.95x (ISBN 0-268-01260-1). U of Notre Dame Pr.
Francis, P. G. Mathematics for Chemists. 176p. (Orig.). 1984. text ed. 29.95 (ISBN 0-412-24980-4, 9193, Pub. by Chapman & Hall England); pap. text ed. 11.95 (ISBN 0-412-24990-1, Pub. by Chapman & Hall England). Methuen Inc.
Francis, P. H. The Straight Line & the Conic Section. (Oleander Mathematics Ser.: Vol. 2). (Illus.). 1975. pap. 13.50 (ISBN 0-902675-76-1). Oleander Pr.
Francis, Peter. Images of Earth. (Illus.). 160p. 1984. 24.95 (ISBN 0-13-451394-0). P-H.
--Volcanoes. 1976. pap. 7.95 (ISBN 0-14-021897-1, Pelican). Penguin.
Francis, Philip. Legal Status of Women. 2nd ed. 128p. 1978. 5.95 (ISBN 0-317-30364-3). Oceana.
--Mathematics of the Universe: The Universe of the Mind. (Oleander Mathematics Ser.: Vol. 1). (Illus.). 1977. pap. 13.50 (ISBN 0-902675-75-3). Oleander Pr.
Francis, Philip see Callahan, Parnell J.
Francis, Philip H. Cartesian & Argand Values. (Oleander Manthematics Ser.: Vol. 3). (Illus.). 1978. pap. 13.50 (ISBN 0-900891-47-5). Oleander Pr.
--Principles of R & D Management. LC 77-24179. pap. 60.00 (ISBN 0-317-27075-3, 2023534). Bks Demand UMI.
Francis, Philip H. & Lindholm, Ulric S. Advanced Experimental Techniques in the Mechanics of Materials. 462p. 1973. 101.25 (ISBN 0-677-12570-4). Gordon.
Francis, R. D., jt. auth. see Borchardt, D. H.
Francis, R. L. A Simple Graphical Procedure to Estimate the Minimum Time to Evacuate a Building. 1979. 3.50 (ISBN 0-686-25955-6, TR 79-5). Society Fire Protect.
Francis, R. Mabel. Filled with the Spirit-Then What? 1974. 1.25 (ISBN 0-87509-082-6). Chr Pubns.
Francis, Ray, jt. ed. see Pons, Valdo.
Francis, Rell G. The Utah Photographs of George Edward Anderson. LC 79-1123. (Illus.). xii, 155p. 1979. 23.50 (ISBN 0-8032-1952-0). U of Nebr Pr.
Francis, Rene. Egyptian Aesthetics. LC 72-80144. Repr. of 1911 ed. 20.00 (ISBN 0-405-08531-1, Blom Pubns). Ayer Co Pubs.
Francis, Richard. Jasper Johns. LC 84-3065. (Modern Masters Ser.). (Illus.). 1984. 29.95 (ISBN 0-89659-443-2); pap. 16.95 (ISBN 0-89659-444-0). Abbeville Pr.
Francis, Richard H. The Whispering Gallery. 251p. 1984. 13.95 (ISBN 0-393-01926-8). Norton.
Francis, Richard L., jt. auth. see White, John A.
Francis, Robert. A Certain Distance. Kaplan, Peter, ed. LC 76-28159. 1976. 3.00x (ISBN 0-915176-15-7). Pourboire.
--Come Out into the Sun: Poems New & Selected. LC 65-26243. 156p. 1968. 12.00x (ISBN 0-87023-015-8); pap. 6.50 (ISBN 0-87023-057-3). U of Mass Pr.
--Frost: A Time to Talk, Conversations & Indiscretions Recorded by Robert Francis. LC 72-77570. (New England Writers Ser.). 104p. 1972. 9.00x (ISBN 0-87023-106-5). U of Mass Pr.
--God Believes in Jewelry. (Quest Ser.). 1985. pap. 0.99 (ISBN 0-8163-0590-0). Pacific Pr Pub Assn.
--Like Ghosts of Eagles. LC 73-93273. 94p. 1974. 8.00x (ISBN 0-87023-156-1); pap. 4.50 (ISBN 0-87023-157-X). U of Mass Pr.
--The Orb Weaver. LC 60-7255. (Wesleyan Poetry Program: Vol. 5). (Orig.). 1960. 15.00x (ISBN 0-8195-2005-5); pap. 6.95 (ISBN 0-8195-1005-X). Wesleyan U Pr.
--Pot Shots at Poetry. (Poets on Poetry Ser.). 1980. pap. 7.95 (ISBN 0-472-06318-9). U of Mich Pr.
--Robert Francis: Collected Poems, 1936-1976. LC 76-8753. (Illus.). 304p. 1976. 17.50x (ISBN 0-87023-211-8). U of Mass Pr.
--The Satirical Rogue on Poetry. LC 68-13940. 136p. 1968. 9.00x (ISBN 0-87023-034-4). U of Mass Pr.
--Social Security Disability Claims: Practice & Procedure. LC 82-24286. 828p. 1983. 75.00 (ISBN 0-317-12004-2). Callaghan.
--The Trouble with Francis. LC 75-150313. (New England Writers Ser.). 256p. 1971. 15.00x (ISBN 0-87023-083-2). U of Mass Pr.
Francis, Robin. Memories of Love. (Harlequin American Romance). 256p. 1984. pap. 2.25 (ISBN 0-373-16038-0). Harlequin Bks.
Francis, Ronald D. Migrant Crime in Australia. (Illus.). 217p. 1981. text ed. 19.25x (ISBN 0-7022-1561-9). U of Queensland Pr.
Francis, Roy G. Sociology in a Different Key: Essays in Non-Linear Sociology. LC 82-72534. 164p. 1983. text ed. 19.95x (ISBN 0-88105-000-8); pap. text ed. 12.95x (ISBN 0-88105-007-5). Cap & Gown.
Francis, Russell. Teach to the Difference: Cross-Cultural Studies in Australian Education. 1982. text ed. 27.95x (ISBN 0-7022-1542-2); pap. text ed. 15.95x (ISBN 0-7022-1543-0). U of Queensland Pr.
Francis, Sally, jt. auth. see Droske, Susan C.
Francis, Sam. Aphorisms. 40p. (Orig.). 1985. signed & ltd. ed. 25.00 (ISBN 0-932499-02-3). Lapis Pr.
Francis, Samuel N. & Rutter, Thomas M., Jr. Pennsylvania School Law 1970-1985: The Complete Guide to Law & Fiscal Procedure for Pennsylvania Educators & Their Legal Counsel, 3 vols. 1985. Set. 200.00 (ISBN 0-8322-0024-7). Banks-Baldwin.
Francis, Samuel T. Power & History: The Political Thought of James Burnham. 154p. (Orig.). 1984. lib. bdg. 19.50 (ISBN 0-8191-3752-9); pap. text ed. 9.00 (ISBN 0-8191-3753-7). U Pr of Amer.
Francis, Sharon. Earthly Splendor. 192p. 1983. pap. 1.95 (ISBN 0-515-07576-0). Jove Pubns.
--Silken Longings. (Second Chance at Love Ser.: No. 212). 192p. 1984. pap. 1.95 (ISBN 0-515-07960-X). Jove Pubns.
--Vintage Moments. (Second Chance at Love Ser.: No. 228). 192p. 1984. pap. 1.95 (ISBN 0-515-08202-3). Jove Pubns.
Francis, Sydney, et al. The Revised Technique of Latin American Dancing. 4th, rev. ed. Pearson, Peter & Romain, Elizabeth, eds. (Illus.). 188p. 1981. pap. text ed. 24.50x (ISBN 0-392-16686-0, SpS). Sportshelf.
--The Revised Technique of Latin American Dancing. 5th, enl. ed. (Illus.). 192p. 1984. pap. text ed. 24.50x (ISBN 0-392-17000-0, SpS). Sportshelf.
Francis, Thadys J. & Daniels, Dewar. Programmed Proofreading. 1982. text ed. 3.50 wkbk. (ISBN 0-538-23010-X, W01). SW Pub.
Francis, Thomas J., et al. Planning, Budgeting & Control for Data Processing: Making Zero Base Budgeting Work for You. 248p. 1984. 24.95 (ISBN 0-442-22550-4). Van Nos Reinhold.
Francis, Trevor & Miller, David. The World to Play For. (Illus.). 215p. 1983. 14.95 (ISBN 0-283-98825-8, Pub. by Sidgwick & Jackson). Merrimack Pub Cir.

Francis, W. Fuels & Fuel Technology, 2 Vols. 2nd ed. 1965. Vol. 1. 125.00 (ISBN 0-08-025249-4); Vol. 2. text ed. 125.00 (ISBN 0-08-025250-8); Vol. 1. pap. 38.00 (ISBN 0-08-010753-2); Vol. 2. pap. 34.50 (ISBN 0-08-010755-9). Pergamon.

Francis, W. & Peters, M. C. Fuels & Fuel Technology. 2nd ed. (Illus.). 608p. 1980. 125.00 (ISBN 0-08-025249-4); pap. 38.00 (ISBN 0-08-025250-8). Pergamon.

Francis, W. Nelson. History of English. (Orig.). 1963. pap. text ed. 2.95x (ISBN 0-393-09709-9, NortonC). Norton.

Francis, W. Nelson & Kucera, Henry. Frequency Analysis of English Usage: Lexicon & Grammar. LC 82-901. 561p. 1982. 40.00 (ISBN 0-395-32250-2). HM.

Francis, William, tr. see Ohm, G. S.

Francis, William H., jt. auth. see Choate, Robert A.

Franciscan Fathers. Ethnologic Dictionary of the Navaho Language. (Navaho.). 1968. pap. 25.00 (ISBN 0-686-32648-2). St Michaels.

Franciscans, Saint Michaels, Arizona. An Ethnologic Dictionary of the Navaho Language. LC 76-43710. 536p. (Navaho.). Repr. of 1910 ed. 49.50 (ISBN 0-404-15766-1). AMS Pr.

Francisco, Al, et al. Cost Accounting: Study Guide. (Illus.). 1977. pap. 10.50 (ISBN 0-8299-0145-0). West Pub.

Francisco, Albert K. & Smith, Albert A. CPA Review of Business Law: 1983-1984. LC 83-1573. 1983. 18.95 (ISBN 0-201-07813-9). Addison-Wesley.

Francisco, Albert K. & Smith, Kenneth A. CPA Review of Auditing, 1983-1984. LC 83-15710. 384p. (Orig.). 1984. pap. text ed. 18.95 (ISBN 0-201-07812-0). Addison-Wesley.

Francisco, C. T. Introduccion Al Antiguo Testamento. Lacue, Juan J., tr. from Eng. 350p. (Span.). 1983. pap. 5.25 (ISBN 0-311-04010-1). Casa Bautista.

Francisco, Cesar P. De see World Congress of Psychiatry, 6th, Honolulu, Hawaii, August-September 1977.

Francisco, Charles. Gentleman: The William Powell Story. 1985. 15.95 (ISBN 0-312-32103-1). St Martin.

--You Must Remember This: The Filming of Casablanca. LC 80-18176. 1980. 10.00 (ISBN 0-13-977058-5). P-H.

Francisco, Clyde T. Introducing the Old Testament. rev. ed. LC 76-24060. 1977. bds. 13.95 (ISBN 0-8054-1213-1, 4212-13). Broadman.

--Un Varon Llamado Job. Glaze, Jack A., tr. from Eng. (Reflexiones Teologicas Ser.). Orig. Title: A Man Called Job. 64p. 1981. pap. 1.95 (ISBN 0-311-04659-2). Casa Bautista.

Francisco De Jesus. El Hecho De los Tratados Del Matrimonio Pretendido Pro el Principe De Gales Con la Serenissima Infa De Espana, Maria. Gardiner, Samuel R., tr. Repr. of 1869 ed. 28.00 (ISBN 0-384-16690-3). Johnson Repr.

--Narrative of the Spanish Marriage Treaty. Gardiner, Samuel R., tr. LC 72-168133. (Camden Society, London, Publications, First Ser.: No. 101). Repr. of 1869 ed. 28.00 (ISBN 0-404-50201-6). AMS Pr.

Francisco, Garcia & Pavon. Las Hermanas Coloradas. (Easy Readers, C Ser.). 1977. pap. 4.25 (ISBN 0-88436-295-7, 70271). EMC.

Francisco, Lazaro. Maganda Pa ang Daigdig. 304p. (Orig.). 1983. pap. 8.75x (ISBN 971-04-0009-6, Pub. by Atenco De Manila U Pr Philippines). Cellar.

Francisco, Leia. Common Sense Writing. 80p. 1983. pap. text ed. 8.95 (ISBN 0-8403-3061-8). Kendall-Hunt.

Francisco, Martha N., ed. see American Water Resources Association.

Francisco, Ronald & Merritt, Richard L. Berlin Between Two Worlds. (Special Studies Ser.). 140p. 1985. pap. 16.50 (ISBN 0-8133-7131-7). Westview.

Franciscus, Marie L. & Abbott, Marguerite. Opportunities in Occupational Therapy. rev. ed. LC 78-60522. (VGM Career Bks.). (gr. 8 up). 1979. 7.95 (6585-4); pap. 5.95 (6585-0). Natl Textbk.

Francis Of Assisi, Saint Words of Saint Francis. Meyer, J., ed. pap. 6.00 (ISBN 0-8199-0105-9, L39005). Franciscan Herald.

Franck, Adolph. The Kabbalah or the Religious Philosophy of the Hebrews. LC 73-2199. (The Jewish People; History, Religion, Literature Ser.). Repr. of 1926 ed. 30.00 (ISBN 0-405-05264-2). Ayer Co Pubs.

Franck, Adolphe. The Kabbalah. 1979. pap. 5.95 (ISBN 0-8065-0708-X). Citadel Pr.

Franck, Carl L. Villas of Frascati, 1650-1750. (Illus.). 1966. 20.00 (ISBN 0-85458-669-5). Transatlantic.

Franck, Cesar. Selected Piano Compositions. D'Indy, Vincent, ed. LC 75-27672. 192p. 1976. pap. 6.50. (ISBN 0-486-23269-7). Dover.

--Selected Piano Compositions. D'Indy, Vincent, ed. 10.25 (ISBN 0-8446-5457-4). Peter Smith.

Franck, Cesar, ed. see Philidor, Francois A. D.

Franck, Frederick. Art As a Way: A Return to the Spiritual Roots. LC 81-7853. (Illus.). 160p. (Orig.). 1981. pap. 9.95 (ISBN 0-8245-0076-8). Crossroad NY.

--The Awakened Eye. pap. 4.95 (ISBN 0-394-74021-1, V-21, Vin). Random.

--The Book of Angelus Silesius. 160p. 1985. pap. 10.95 (ISBN 0-939680-20-3). Bear & Co.

--The Buddha Eye: An Anthology of the Kyoto School. 256p. 1982. 14.95 (ISBN 0-8245-0410-0). Crossroad NY.

--Echoes from the Bottomless Well. 1985. pap. 8.95 (ISBN 0-394-72995-1, Vin). Random.

--Exploding Church. pap. 2.95 (ISBN 0-440-52432-6). Dell.

--Pilgrimage to Now - Here. LC 73-78933. (Illus.). 192p. (Orig.). 1974. pap. 3.95 (ISBN 0-88344-387-2). Orbis Bks.

--The Supreme Koan: An Artist's Spiritual Journey. LC 81-22037. (Illus.). 1982. pap. 12.95 (ISBN 0-8245-0430-5). Crossroad NY.

--Zen of Seeing. 1973. pap. 8.95 (ISBN 0-394-71968-9, V968, Vin). Random.

Franck, Frederick, ed. Zen & Zen Classics: Selections from R. H. Blyth. (Illus.). 1978. pap. 4.95 (ISBN 0-394-72489-5, Vin). Random.

Franck, Harry A. Zone Policeman 88: A Close Range Study of the Panama Canal & Its Workers. LC 71-111713. (American Imperialism: Viewpoints of United States Foreign Policy, 1898-1941). 1970. Repr. of 1913 ed. 20.00 (ISBN 0-405-02019-8). Ayer Co Pubs.

Franck, Irene M. To the Ends of the Earth: The Great Travel & Trade Routes of History. (Illus.). 388p. 1984. 35.00 (ISBN 0-87196-647-6). Facts on File.

Franck, Irene M., jt. auth. see Brownstone, David M.

Franck, Lavina M. History of Costume. 1977. spiral bdg. 11.95x (ISBN 0-916434-27-3). Plycon Pr.

Franck, Marga, jt. ed. see Afflerbach, Lois.

Franck, Phyllis & Price, Marjorie. Nursing Management: A Programmed Text. 2nd ed. 1980. pap. text ed. 14.95 (ISBN 0-8261-1663-9). Springer Pub.

Franck, Pierre, jt. auth. see Balzac, Honore De.

Franck, Richard. The Admirable & Indefatigable Adventures of the Nine Pious Pilgrims... Written in America. LC 72-170515. (Foundations of the Novel Ser.: Vol. 11). 1973. lib. bdg. 61.00 (ISBN 0-8240-0523-6). Garland Pub.

Franck, Susana see Mehler, Jacques & Walker, Edward.

Franck, T. M. & Carey, J. The Legal Aspects of the United Nations in the Congo. LC 63-14451. (Hammarskjold Forum Ser: No. 2). 137p. 1963. 10.00 (ISBN 0-379-11802-5). Oceana.

Franck, Thomas M. Control of Sea Resources by Semi-Autonomous States. LC 78-69499. 1978. pap. 1.75 (ISBN 0-87003-032-9). Carnegie Endow.

--Human Rights in Third World Perspective, Vol. 1-3. LC 82-6489. 1982. 150.00 (ISBN 0-379-20725-7). Set. Oceana.

--Nation Against Nation: What Happened to the U. N. Dream & What the U. S. Can Do about It. 384p. 1985. 19.95 (ISBN 0-19-503587-9). Oxford U Pr.

--Race & Nationalism: The Struggle for Power in Rhodesia-Nyasaland. LC 73-11853. 369p. 1973. Repr. of 1960 ed. lib. bdg. 20.00x (ISBN 0-8371-7074-5, FRRN). Greenwood.

--Race & Nationalism: The Struggle for Power in Rhodesia-Nyasaland. 1960. 10.00 (ISBN 0-685-99549-6). Univ Place.

Franck, Thomas M. & Renninger, John P. Diplomats' Views on the United Nations System: An Attitude Survey. (Unitar Policy & Efficacy Studies). 38p. 1982. 5.00 (ISBN 0-686-97633-9, E.82.XV.PE/7). UN.

Franck, Thomas M. & Weisband, Edward. Word Politics: Verbal Strategy among the Superpowers. 1971. 17.95x (ISBN 0-19-501460-X); pap. 7.95x (ISBN 0-19-501459-6). Oxford U Pr.

Franck, Thomas M., jt. auth. see El Baradei, Mohamed.

Franck, Thomas M., jt. auth. see Glennon, Michael J.

Franck, Thomas M., ed. The Tethered Presidency: A Study of New Congressional Restraints on Presidential Power & Their Effect on America's Ability to Conduct an Effective Foreign Policy. 272p. 1981. 30.00x (ISBN 0-8147-2567-8). NYU Pr.

Franck, Thomas M. & Weisband, Edward, eds. Secrecy & Foreign Policy. 1974. 29.95x (ISBN 0-19-501746-3). Oxford U Pr.

Francke, A. H. Ladakh, the Mysterious Land. 191p. 1978. Repr. of 1907 ed. 21.00 (ISBN 0-89684-106-5, Pub. by Cosmo Pubns India). Orient Bk Dist.

Francke, Arthur E., Jr. Fort Mellon: Microcosm of the Second Seminole War 1837-1842. LC 77-11918. (Illus.). 1977. 8.95 (ISBN 0-916224-17-1). Banyan Bks.

Francke, Donald E., ed. Handbook of I.V. Additive Reviews. Incl. 1970. (Illus.). 50p (ISBN 0-914768-03-4); 1971. (Illus.). 60p (ISBN 0-914768-04-2); 1972. (Illus.); 1973. (Illus.). 68p (ISBN 0-914768-06-9). pap. 6.00 ea. Drug Intl Pubns.

Francke, K. Emerson in German Ideals of Today. 1973. Repr. of 1928 ed. 30.00 (ISBN 0-8274-0409-3). R West.

Francke, Kuno. Glimpses of Modern German Culture. 1978. Repr. of 1898 ed. lib. bdg. 25.00 (ISBN 0-8492-4603-2). R West.

--History of German Literature As Determined by Social Forces. 4th ed. LC 73-100524. Repr. of 1901 ed. 37.50 (ISBN 0-404-02545-5). AMS Pr.

--Personality in German Literature Before Luther. LC 72-141480. 221p. 1973. Repr. of 1916 ed. lib. bdg. 18.75x (ISBN 0-8371-5865-6, FRPG). Greenwood.

--Social Forces in German Literature. 59.95 (ISBN 0-8490-1064-0). Gordon Pr.

Francke, Kuno, ed. German Classics, 20 Vols. Repr. of 1914 ed. Set. 900.00 (ISBN 0-404-02600-1); 45.00 ea. AMS Pr.

Francke, Linda B. The Ambivalence of Abortion. 1978. 10.00 (ISBN 0-394-41080-7). Random.

--Growing up Divorced. 304p. 1984. pap. 3.50 (ISBN 0-449-20570-3, Crest). Fawcett.

--Growing up Divorced: Children of the Eighties. 1983. 15.95 (ISBN 0-671-25516-9, Linden Pr). S&S.

Francke, O. F., jt. auth. see Moody, J. V.

Francke, Oscar F. Systematic Revision of Diplocentrid Scorpions (Diplocentridae) from Circum - Caribbean Lands. (Special Publications: No. 14). (Illus.). 92p. (Orig.). 1978. pap. 7.00 (ISBN 0-89672-062-4). Tex Tech Pr.

Francki, R. I. Atlas of Plant Viruses, Vol. I. 240p. 1985. 73.00 (ISBN 0-8493-6501-5). CRC Pr.

Francki, R. I., ed. The Plant Viruses: Polyhedral Virions with Tripartite Genomes, Vol. 1. (The Viruses Ser.). 297p. 1985. 49.50x (ISBN 0-306-41958-0, Plenum Pr). Plenum Pub.

Francki, R. I., et al, eds. Atlas of Plant Viruses, Vol. II. 304p. 1985. 87.00 (ISBN 0-8493-6502-3). CRC Pr.

Francklyn, G. Answer to the Rev. Mr. Clarkson's Essay on the Slavery & Commerce of the Human Species. facs. ed. LC 74-83963. (Black Heritage Library Collection Ser). 1789. 13.50 (ISBN 0-8369-8574-5). Ayer Co Pubs.

Francko, Daird. Runner's World Health Club Book. 220p. 1982. sprial bdg. 11.95 (ISBN 0-89037-177-6). Anderson World.

Francks, Olive R., jt. ed. see Ashby-Davis, Claire.

Francks, Penelope. Technology & Agricultural Development in Pre-War Japan. LC 82-20306. 352p. 1984. 32.00x (ISBN 0-300-02927-6). Yale U Pr.

Francl, Joseph. Overland Journey of Joseph Francl. LC 75-6184. 1968. 35.00x (ISBN 0-9600574-1-2). Wreden.

Franco. Cuentos Escogido H Quiroga. Franco, Jean, ed. 1968. pap. 6.50 (ISBN 0-08-012791-6). Pergamon.

Franco, Eloise. Little Stories. (Illus.). 1979. pap. 2.25 (ISBN 0-87516-384-X). De Vorss.

--The Young Look. (Illus.). (gr. 3-7). 1979. pap. 4.95 (ISBN 0-87516-294-0). De Vorss.

Franco, Eloise & Franco, Johan. Making Music. (Illus.). (gr. 1-5). 1976. pap. 4.25 (ISBN 0-87516-212-6). De Vorss.

Franco, Fabiola. El Concierto Siniestro. (Illus.). 56p. (Span.). 1983. pap. text ed. 2.95 (ISBN 0-8219-0030-7, 70279); wkbk 1.75 (ISBN 0-8219-0031-5, 70655). EMC.

--El Novio Robado. (Illus.). 56p. (Span.). 1983. pap. text ed. 2.95 (ISBN 0-8219-0033-1, 70278); wkbk 1.75 (ISBN 0-8219-0034-X, 70654). EMC.

Franco, G. E., jt. auth. see Villamizar, M.

Franco, Jean. Introduction to Spanish-American Literature. LC 69-12927. 1969. 44.50 (ISBN 0-521-07374-X); pap. 13.95 (ISBN 0-521-09891-2). Cambridge U Pr.

Franco, Jean, ed. Spanish Short Stories. (YA) (gr. 9 up). 1966. pap. 3.95 (ISBN 0-14-002500-6). Penguin.

Franco, Jean, ed. see Franco.

Franco, Johan, jt. auth. see Franco, Eloise.

Franco, Juan, jt. auth. see Levine, Elaine.

Franco, Lawrence G., et al. The Petroleum Industry in Western Europe: A Guide to Information Sources. LC 75-20065. (Reference Library of Social Science: Vol. 13). 178p. 1975. lib. bdg. 34.00 (ISBN 0-8240-9990-7). Garland Pub.

Franco, Marjorie. Genevieve & Alexander. large print ed. LC 82-16924. 375p. 1982. Repr. of 1982 ed. 13.95 (ISBN 0-89621-400-1). Thorndike Pr.

--Love in a Different Key. LC 83-10653. 160p. (gr. 7up). 1983. 9.95 (ISBN 0-395-34827-7). HM.

--Love in a Different Way. (gr. 7-12). 1985. pap. 2.50 (ISBN 0-440-95065-1, LFL). Dell.

Franco, Ribeiro R. see Ribeiro Franco, Rui.

Franco, Sylvia, et al. The World of Cosmetology: A Professional Text. LC 79-20678. (Illus.). 512p. 1980. text ed. 22.88 (ISBN 0-07-021791-2). McGraw.

Francoeur, Robert T. Becoming a Sexual Person. LC 81-19782. 840p. 1982. text ed. write for info. (ISBN 0-02-338840-4). Macmillan.

--Becoming a Sexual Person. 840p. 1984. 27.95 (ISBN 0-471-07848-4); pap. 19.45 brief ed. (ISBN 0-471-89546-6); 12.45 (ISBN 0-471-09893-0). Wiley.

--Biomedical Ethics: A Guide to Decision Making. LC 83-6812. 341p. 1983. pap. 17.50 (ISBN 0-471-09827-2, Pub. by Wiley Med). Wiley.

Franco Grande, Xose L. Diccionario Galego-Castelan e Vocabulario Castelan-Galego. 4th ed. 970p. (Span.). 1978. 23.95 (ISBN 84-7154-024-X, S-50436). French & Eur.

--Vocabulario Galego-Castelan. 336p. (Gallic & Span.). 1972. pap. 9.50 (ISBN 84-7154-283-8, S-50437). French & Eur.

Francois. Mass Media Law & Regulation. 4th ed. 1986. price not set (ISBN 0-471-82376-7). Wiley.

Francois, ed. see Marguerite De Navarre.

Francois, Antoine. Memoirs of a Man of Honour, 1747. (Novel in England, 1700-1775 Ser). 1975. lib. bdg. 61.00 (ISBN 0-8240-1119-8). Garland Pub.

Francois, Bernard & Perrin, Paul. Urinary Infections. text ed. 79.95 (ISBN 0-407-00257-X). Butterworth.

Francois, Carlo. Raison et Deraison dans le Theatre de Pierre Corneille. 178p. (Fr.). 1979. 13.95 (ISBN 0-917786-17-3). Summa Pubns.

Francois, D. Advances in Fracture Research: Proceedings of the 5th International Conference on Fracture, 1981, Cannes, France, 6 vols. LC 80-41879. (International Series on the Strength & Fracture of Materials & Structures). 3000p. 1981. Set. text ed. 495.00 (ISBN 0-08-025428-4). Pergamon.

Francois, D., jt. ed. see Sih, G. C.

Francois, H., et al, eds. see International Conference on Solid State Nuclear Track Detectors, 10th, Lyon, France, July 1979.

Francois, J. & Victoria-Troncoso, V. The Cornea in Normal Condition & in Groenouw's Macular Dystrophy. (Illus.). x, 198p. 1980. lib. bdg. 45.00 (ISBN 90-6193-161-4, Pub. by Junk Pubs Netherlands). Kluwer Academic.

Francois, J. & De Rouck, A., eds. Electrodiagnosis, Toxic Agents & Vision. 1978. lib. bdg. 58.00 (ISBN 90-6193-155-X, Pub. by Junk Pubs. Netherlands). Kluwer Academic.

Francois, J. & Maione, M., eds. Paediatric Opthalmology: Proceedings of International Society for Paediatric Opthalmology, 2nd Meeting. 600p. 1982. 50.00x (ISBN 0-471-10040-4, Pub. by Wiley-Interscience). Wiley.

Francois, J., ed. see International Congress on Cataract Surgery, 1st Florence, 1978.

Francois, J., ed. see International Congress on Neuro-Genetics & Neuro-Ophthalmology, 3rd, Brussels, 1970.

Francois, J., ed. see International Society for Ultrasonic Diagnosis in Ophthalmology, Ghent, May 1973.

Francois, J., et al, eds. Proceedings of the Symposium of the International Society for Corneal Research. (Documenta Ophthalmologica Proceedings Ser.: No. 20). 1979. pap. text ed. 47.50 (ISBN 90-6193-157-6, Pub. by Junk Pubs Netherlands). Kluwer Academic.

Francois, Jules, et al. Oculomycoses. (Illus.). 444p. 1972. 43.75x (ISBN 0-398-02282-8). C C Thomas.

Francois, Louis. The Right to Education: From Proclamation to Achievement, 1948-1968. 1968. pap. 2.25 (ISBN 92-3-100700-9, U558, UNESCO). Unipub.

Francois, Michel. La France et les Francais. (Historique Ser.). 1696p. 53.95 (ISBN 0-686-56462-6). French & Eur.

Francois, Victor E. Two Deaf Men. (Silver Series of Puppet Plays). pap. 1.50 (ISBN 0-8283-1243-5). Branden Pub Co.

Francois, W. E. Yearbook for Mass Media, 1983: Law & Regulation. 3rd ed. 1983. pap. 8.00 (ISBN 0-471-86053-0). Wiley.

Francois, William E. Beginning News Writing. LC 74-16752. (Journalism & Advertising Ser.). pap. 41.30 (ISBN 0-8357-9138-6, 2016565). Bks Demand UMI.

--Beginning News Writing: A Programmed Text. LC 82-45063. (Illus.). 164p. 1982. Repr. of 1975 ed. 11.00 (ISBN 0-8191-1823-0). U Pr of Amer.

--Mass Media Law & Regulation. 3rd ed. LC 81-6628. (Journalism & Advertising). 732p. 1982. text ed. 31.95 (ISBN 0-88244-241-4, Pub. by Grid); pap. 35.50 (ISBN 0-471-84161-7). Wiley.

Francois De Sales. Oeuvres: Introduction a la Vie Devote & Traite de l'Amour de Dieu, etc. (Saint). 2024p. 46.95 (ISBN 0-686-56512-6). French & Eur.

Francom, Lane A. Lanes One Walks Thru. 19p. 1985. 5.95 (ISBN 0-533-06247-0). Vantage.

Francombe, Maurice H. see Hass, Georg, et al.

Francombe, Maurice H., jt. ed. see Hass, Georg.

Francome, Colin. Abortion Freedom: A Worldwide Movement. LC 83-15558. 234p. 1984. text ed. 19.95x (ISBN 0-04-179001-4). Allen Unwin.

--Abortion Freedom: A Worldwide Movement. 248p. 1984. pap. text ed. 7.95x (ISBN 0-04-179002-2). Allen Unwin.

Francon, M. Halography. 1974. 35.00 (ISBN 0-12-265750-0). Acad Pr.

--Laser Speckle & Application in Optics. LC 79-50215. 1979. 29.50 (ISBN 0-12-265760-8). Acad Pr.

--Optical Image Formation & Processing. 1979. 29.50 (ISBN 0-12-264850-1). Acad Pr.

Francon, M., et al. Experiences d'Optique Physique. 294p. (Fr). 1969. 102.95 (ISBN 0-677-50040-8). Gordon.

--Experiments in Physical Optics. 284p. 1970. 57.75 (ISBN 0-677-30040-9). Gordon.

Francon, Marcel, ed. see De Montaigne, Michel.

Francon, Maurice. Optical Interferometry. 1966. 35.00 (ISBN 0-12-266350-0). Acad Pr.

Francon, Maurice & Mallick, S. Polarization Interferometers: Applications in Microscopy & Macroscopy. LC 75-147194. (Wiley Ser. in Pure & Appied Optics). pap. 43.00 (ISBN 0-317-29330-3, 2024021). Bks Demand UMI.

Francone, Clarice A., jt. auth. see Jacob, Stanley W.

Franconi, Cafiero. Magnetic Resonances in Biological Research. (Illus.). 420p. 1971. 106.50 (ISBN 0-677-14780-5). Gordon.

Franco-Oppenheimer, Felix. Imagen De Puerto Rico En su Poesia. 4.35 (ISBN 0-8477-3122-7); pap. 3.10 (ISBN 0-8477-3123-5). U of PR Pr.

Francotte, Henri. Les Finances des Cites Grecques. Finley, Moses, ed. LC 79-4971. (Ancient Economic History Ser.). (Fr.). 1980. Repr. of 1909 ed. lib. bdg. 26.50x (ISBN 0-405-12357-4). Ayer Co Pubs.

--L' Industrie dans la Grece Ancienne, 2 vols. Finley, Moses, ed. LC 79-4972. (Ancient Economic History Ser.). (Fr.). 1980. Repr. of 1901 ed. Set. lib. bdg. 61.00x (ISBN 0-405-12358-2); lib. bdg. 30.50x ea. Vol. 1 (ISBN 0-405-12433-3). Vol. 2 (ISBN 0-405-12434-1). Ayer Co Pubs.

--Le Polis Greccue. pap. 19.00 (ISBN 0-384-16710-1). Johnson Repr.

Francovich, Allan, tr. see Salles Gomes, P. E.

Francuch, Peter D. Four Concepts of the Spiritual Structure of Creation. LC 82-62630. 119p. 1983. pap. 7.95 (ISBN 0-939386-05-4). TMH Pub.

--Fundamentals of Human Spirituality. LC 81-16660. 483p. 1982. 24.95x (ISBN 0-939386-01-1). TMH Pub.

--Major Ideas of the New Revelation. LC 84-51914. 266p. 1985. pap. 14.95 (ISBN 0-939386-08-9). TMH Pub.

--Messages from Within. LC 82-60513. 220p. 1982. pap. 9.95 (ISBN 0-939386-03-8). TMH Pub.

--Principles of Spiritual Hypnosis. LC 81-50059. 240p. 1981. cancelled (ISBN 0-939386-00-3). TMH Pub.

--Principles of Spiritual Hypnosis. rev. ed. LC 81-50059. (Illus.). 256p. 1982. Repr. of 1981 ed. 19.95x (ISBN 0-939386-02-X). TMH Pub.

--Reality, Myths & Illusions. LC 83-51193. 513p. 1984. 24.95 (ISBN 0-939386-06-2). TMH Pub.

--Understanding & Fulfillment of Our Earthly Life. LC 84-52358. 200p. 1985. pap. 12.95 (ISBN 0-939386-09-7). TMH Pub.

--Who Are You & Why Are You Here? LC 83-51781. 256p. (Orig.). 1984. pap. 14.95 (ISBN 0-939386-07-0). TMH Pub.

Francuch, Peter D. & Jones, Arthur E. Intensive Spiritual Hypnotherapy. LC 82-62015. 543p. 1983. 34.95 (ISBN 0-939386-04-6). TMH Pub.

Franda, Marc, jt. auth. see Field, John.

Franda, Marcus. Bangladesh: The First Decade. 1982. 24.00x (ISBN 0-8364-0891-8). South Asia Bks.

--Bangladesh: The First Decade. LC 81-19639. 1981. 9.95 (ISBN 0-88333-006-7). U Field Staff Intl.

--India's Rural Development: An Assessment of Alternatives. LC 79-2177. (Illus.). 320p. 1980. 20.00x (ISBN 0-253-19315-X). Ind U Pr.

--Punjabis, War & Women: The Short Stories of Gulzar Singh Sandhu. 1983. 17.00x (ISBN 0-8364-0936-1, Pub. by Heritage India). South Asia Bks.

--The Seychelles: Unquiet Islands. LC 82-1979. (Nations of Contemporary Africa Ser.). (Illus.). 140p. 1982. lib. bdg. 20.00x (ISBN 0-86531-266-4). Westview.

Franda, Marcus F. Radical Politics in West Bengal. (Studies in Communism, Revisionism, & Revolution). 1971. 30.00x (ISBN 0-262-06040-X). MIT Pr.

--West Bengal & the Federalizing Process in India. LC 68-10391. 1968. 28.00x (ISBN 0-691-03068-5). Princeton U Pr.

Franda, Marcus F., jt. ed. see Brass, Paul R.

Frandin, F., jt. auth. see Herman, Herbert.

Frandon, Ramona & Hunt, Dave. The Story of Superman: Four Little Library Books. LC 79-67574. (Illus.). (ps). 1980. Set. 6.95 (ISBN 0-394-84416-5, BYR). Random.

Frandsen & Benson. MODCOM: Nonverbal Communication. 2nd ed. Applbaum, Ronald & Hart, Roderick, eds. 1984. pap. text ed. 3.25 (ISBN 0-574-22585-4, 13-5585). SRA.

Frandsen, ed. Public & Health Aspects of Periodontal Disease. (Illus.). 220p. 1984. text ed. 34.00 (ISBN 0-86715-153-6). Quint Pub Co.

Frandsen, Asger, ed. Dental Health Care in Scandinavia. (Illus.). 260p. (Orig.). 1982. 14.00 (ISBN 0-931386-46-2). Quint Pub Co.

Frandsen, Betty R., et al. Where's Mom Now That I Need Her? Surviving Away from Home. 1983. 12.95 (ISBN 0-318-04698-9). Aspen West Pub.

Frandsen, Joy. Birds of the South Western Cape. (Illus.). 236p. 1985. 24.95 (ISBN 0-88072-067-0, Pub. by Tanager). Longwood Pub Group.

Frandsen, Karen G. I Started School Today. LC 83-23169. (Childhood Fantasies & Fears Ser.). (Illus.). 32p. (ps-2). 1984. lib. bdg. 10.35 (ISBN 0-516-03495-2). Childrens.

Frandsen, Katherine, jt. auth. see Hafen, Brent.

Frandsen, Kathryn J., jt. auth. see Hafen, Brent Q.

Frandsen, Maude L. High in the Rockies. 3.75x (ISBN 0-686-67777-3). Johnson Bks.

Frandson, R. D. Anatomy & Physiology of Farm Animals. 3rd ed. LC 80-25775. (Illus.). 553p. 1981. text ed. 24.50 (ISBN 0-8121-0759-4). Lea & Febiger.

Frane, Jeff. Fritz Leiber. LC 81-21652. (Starmont Reader's Guide Ser.: No. 8). 64p. 1980. lib. bdg. 13.95x (ISBN 0-89370-039-8). Borgo Pr.

--Reader's Guide to Fritz Leiber. Scholbin, Roger C., ed. LC 80-22107. (Starmont Reader's Guides to Contemporary Science Fiction & Fantasy Authors Ser.: Vol. 8). (Illus., Orig.). 1980. 13.95x (ISBN 0-916732-02-9); pap. text ed. 5.95x (ISBN 0-916732-10-X). Starmont Hse.

Franey, Pierre. More Sixty-Minute Gourmet. 304p. 1983. pap. 6.95 (ISBN 0-449-90038-X, Columbine). Fawcett.

--The New York Times More Sixty-Minute Gourmet. LC 81-50078. 1981. 15.95 (ISBN 0-8129-0982-8). Times Bks.

--The New York Times More 60-Minute Gourmet. 1983. pap. 7.95 (ISBN 0-449-90038-X, Columbine). Fawcett.

--The New York Times Sixty Minute Gourmet. 352p. 1981. pap. 6.95 (ISBN 0-449-90045-2, Columbine). Fawcett.

--The New York Times Sixty-Minute Gourmet. LC 79-51427. 1979. 15.95 (ISBN 0-8129-0834-1, Dist. by Har-Row). Times Bks.

--The New York Times Sixty-Minute Gourmet. Large-Type ed. LC 84-40113. 288p. 1984. 18.95 (ISBN 0-8129-1126-1). Times Bks.

Franey, Pierre & Flaste, Richard. Pierre Franey's Kitchen. (Illus.). 304p. 14.95 (ISBN 0-8129-1023-0). Times Bks.

--Pierre Franey's Kitchen. 288p. 1984. pap. 7.95 (ISBN 0-449-90095-9, Columbine). Fawcett.

--Pierre Franey's Low-Calorie Dessert: The New York Times 60-Minute Gourmet's Lighter Approach to Classic Cuisine. 14.95 (ISBN 0-317-18179-3). Times Bks.

--Pierre Franey's Low-Calorie Gourmet. LC 84-40099. 288p. 1984. 14.95 (ISBN 0-8129-1121-0). Times Bks.

Franey, Pierre, jt. auth. see Claiborne, Craig.

Frangen, Ute. Oekonoemische Analyse des Markts fuer Malerei in der Bundesrepublik Deutschland. (European University Studies: No. 5, Vol. 444). 315p. (Ger.). 1983. 37.35 (ISBN 3-8204-7776-4). P Lang Pubs.

Frangi, Abdallah. The PLO & Palestine. (Illus.). 256p. 1983. 26.25x (ISBN 0-86232-194-8, Pub. by Zed Pr England); pap. 9.25 (ISBN 0-86232-195-6, Pub. by Zed Pr England). Biblio Dist.

Frangiamore, Roy & Grady, James. A Thing of Beauty: Art Nouveau, Art Deco, Arts & Crafts Movement, & Aesthetic Movement Objects in Atlanta Collections. Morris, Kelly, ed. (Illus.). 91p. 1980. pap. 10.50 (ISBN 0-939802-04-X). High Mus Art.

Frangipane, E. De Fraga see Pearson, E. A. & De Fraga Frangipane, E.

Frangsmyr, Tore, ed. see Lindroth, Stan, et al.

Franhauser, Jerry. Everybody Is Your Teacher. 16p. 1979. pap. 3.00 (ISBN 0-686-89070-1). Coleman Pub.

Frank. Alcohol & the Family: Three Sure Ways to Solve the Problem. 1978. pap. 1.50 (ISBN 0-89243-086-9). Liguori Pubns.

Frank, A. G. Mexican Agriculture: Fifteen Twenty-One to Sixteen Thirty. LC 78-6201. (Studies in Modern Capitalism Ser.). 1979. 22.95 (ISBN 0-521-22209-5). Cambridge U Pr.

Frank, A. L. A Guide for Software Entrepreneurs. (Illus.). 208p. 1982. text ed. 35.00 (ISBN 0-13-370726-1). P-H.

--A Workbook for Software Entrepreneurs. (Illus.). 128p. 1985. text ed. 30.00 (ISBN 0-13-965302-3). P-H.

Frank, Agnes. Quilting for Beginnners: Patchwork & Applique Projects. (Illus.). 128p. (Orig.). 1985. 20.00 (ISBN 0-915590-73-5); pap. 12.95 (ISBN 0-915590-72-7). Main Street.

Frank, Alan. The Horror Film Handbook. LC 81-22882. (Illus.). 194p. 1982. 26.95 (ISBN 0-389-20260-6). B&N Imports.

--The Science Fiction & Fantasy Film Handbook. LC 82-8802. (Illus.). 194p. 1982. 26.95 (ISBN 0-389-20319-X). B&N Imports.

Frank, Alan R. & McFarland, Thomas. Coin Skills Curriculum. (Illus.). 80p. (Orig.). 1983. pap. text ed. 14.00 (ISBN 0-936104-28-7, 0360). Pro Ed.

Frank, Alan R. & Meyer, John L. An Introduction to Songwriting for the Beginner. LC 84-20827. (Illus.). 156p. (Orig.). 1985. pap. text ed. 12.00 (ISBN 0-8191-4358-8). U Pr of Amer.

Frank, Albert J. Von see Von Frank, Albert J.

Frank, Alfred L. & Abou-Rass, Marwan, eds. Clinical & Surgical Endodontics: Concepts in Practice. (Illus.). 288p. 1983. text ed. 34.50 (ISBN 0-397-50567-1, 65-07263, Lippincott Medical). Lippincott.

Frank, Allan D. Communicating on the Job. 1982. text ed. 19.50x (ISBN 0-673-15275-8). Scott F.

Frank, Andre F. On Capitalist Underdevelopment. 1975. pap. 7.95x (ISBN 0-19-560475-X). Oxford U Pr.

Frank, Andre G. Capitalism & Underdevelopment in Latin America. rev. ed. LC 65-14271. 1969. pap. 8.50 (ISBN 0-85345-093-5). Monthly Rev.

--Crisis: In the Third World. LC 80-239444. 375p. 1981. text ed. 17.50x (ISBN 0-8419-0584-3); pap. text ed. 14.50x osi (ISBN 0-8419-0597-5). Holmes & Meier.

--Crisis: In the World Economy. LC 80-14540. 382p. 1980. text ed. 34.50x (ISBN 0-8419-0583-5); pap. text ed. 14.50x (ISBN 0-8419-0596-7). Holmes & Meier.

--Dependent Accumulation & Underdevelopment. LC 78-13913. 226p. 1979. 15.00 (ISBN 0-85345-468-X); pap. 7.95 (ISBN 0-85345-492-2). Monthly Rev.

--The European Challenge: Peace & Recovery from Atlantic Alliance to Pan-European Entente. 96p. 1984. pap. 5.95 (ISBN 0-88208-173-X). Lawrence Hill.

--Lumpenbourgeoisie: Lumpendevelopment: Dependence, Class, & Politics in Latin America. Berdicio, Marion D., tr. from Span. LC 72-81764. 160p. 1973. pap. 6.50 (ISBN 0-85345-285-7). Monthly Rev.

--Reflections on the World Economic Crisis. LC 80-29270. 192p. 1981. 13.50 (ISBN 0-85345-563-5); pap. 5.50 (ISBN 0-85345-564-3). Monthly Rev.

--World Accumulation, Fourteen Ninety-Two to Seventeen Eighty-Nine. LC 77-91746. 1980. pap. 5.95 (ISBN 0-85345-493-0). Monthly Rev.

--World Accumulation, 1492-1789. LC 77-91746. 303p. 1978. 16.50 (ISBN 0-85345-442-6). Monthly Rev.

Frank, Andre Gunder. Kampuchea, Viet Nam, China: Observations & Reflections: Project on Goals, Processes & Indicators of Development. 17p. 1982. pap. 5.00 (ISBN 92-808-0320-4, TUNU201, UNU). Unipub.

Frank, Anne. Anne Frank: The Diary of a Young Girl. rev. ed. Mooyaart, B. M., tr. 312p. (YA) (gr. 7 up). 1967. 15.95 (ISBN 0-385-04019-9); PLB (ISBN 0-385-09190-7). Doubleday.

--Anne Frank: The Diary of a Young Girl. pap. 2.50 272p (ISBN 0-671-42636-2); enriched classic ed. 320p 2.95 (ISBN 0-671-46199-0). WSP.

--Anne Frank: The Diary of a Young Girl. 13.95 (ISBN 0-89190-223-6, Pub. by Am Repr). Amereon Ltd.

--Anne Frank's Tales from the Secret Annex. 160p. 1983. pap. 2.95 (ISBN 0-671-45857-4). WSP.

--Anne Frank's Tales from the Secret Annex. Manheim, Ralph & Mok, Michael, trs. LC 82-45871. (Illus.). 1984. 14.95 (ISBN 0-385-18715-7). Doubleday.

--Diary of a Young Girl. LC 58-11474. 1958. o.s. 5.95 (ISBN 0-394-60451-2). Modern Lib.

--The Works of Anne Frank. LC 73-16643. (Illus.). 332p. 1974. Repr. of 1959 ed. lib. bdg. 32.50x (ISBN 0-8371-7206-3, FRWO). Greenwood.

Frank, Arlen W. The Cotton Gazetteer. LC 84-91851. xii, 194p. 1985. 19.75 (ISBN 0-9614531-0-9). Arlen Frank.

Frank, Armin P. Kenneth Burke. LC 74-79213. (United States Authors Ser.). 1969. lib. bdg. 15.95 (ISBN 0-89197-816-X). Irvington.

--Literaturwissenschaft Zwischen Extremen. (De Gruyter Studienbuch). 1977. 12.80x (ISBN 3-11-007025-1). De Gruyter.

Frank, Arthur D. Development of the Federal Program of Flood Control on the Mississippi River. LC 68-58572. (Columbia University. Studies in the Social Sciences: No. 323). Repr. of 1930 ed. 21.00 (ISBN 0-404-51323-9). AMS Pr.

Frank, Barbara, jt. auth. see Frank, Jerome.

Frank, Ben. No Aging Diet. 1981. 17.95 (ISBN 0-686-76745-4). B Of A.

--No Aging Diet. Orig. Title: Ben Frank's No Aging Diet. 200p. 1984. 18.95x (ISBN 0-911238-17-4, Regent House); pap. 8.95x (ISBN 0-317-06949-7). B of A.

Frank, Benjamin, ed. Contemporary Corrections: A Concept in Search of Content. LC 73-20072. 272p. 1974. pap. 16.95 (ISBN 0-87909-151-7). Reston.

Frank, Bernhard, tr. from Heb. & intro. by. Modern Hebrew Poetry. LC 80-20037. (Iowa Translations Ser.). 248p. 1980. text ed. 20.00x (ISBN 0-87745-106-0); pap. 9.95 (ISBN 0-87745-107-9). U of Iowa Pr.

Frank, Beryl. A Pictorial History of Pikesville, Maryland. (Baltimore County Heritage Publication). (Illus.). 140p. 1982. 9.95 (ISBN 0-937076-02-3). Baltimore Co Pub Lib.

Frank, Beryl, ed. Encyclopedia of U. S. Government Benefits. 11th ed. (Illus.). 1000p. 1985. 22.95 (ISBN 0-396-08438-9). Dodd.

Frank, Beryl, ed. see National Square Dancers Convention, Inc.

Frank, Bruno. Days of the King. Lowe-Porter, H. T., tr. LC 75-121550. (Short Story Index Reprint Ser). 1927. 14.00 (ISBN 0-8369-3506-3). Ayer Co Pubs.

--A Man Called Cervantes. 1935. 20.00 (ISBN 0-8274-2668-2). R West.

Frank, Bryn. Drives Around Oxford. 1983. 19.00x (ISBN 0-86334-009-1, Pub. by Macdonald Pub UK). State Mutual Bk.

--Drives Around York. 1983. 19.00x (ISBN 0-86334-007-5, Pub. by Macdonald Pub UK). State Mutual Bk.

--Everyman's England. LC 84-47568. (Illus.). 325p. 1984. 19.23 (ISBN 0-06-015361-X, HarpT). Har-Row.

Frank, Bryn & Wickers, David. Drives Around Chester. 1983. 19.00x (ISBN 0-86334-010-5, Pub. by Macdonald Pub UK). State Mutual Bk.

Frank, C. P., tr. see Robert, Charles.

Frank, C. W. Maximizing Hospital Cash Resources. LC 78-14271. 250p. 1979. text ed. 34.95 (ISBN 0-89443-076-9). Aspen Systems.

Frank, C. W., et al. Spectroscopy: NMR, Fluorescence, FT-IR. (Advances in Polymer Science Ser.: Vol. 54). (Illus.). 170p. 1984. 41.00 (ISBN 0-387-12591-4). Springer-Verlag.

Frank, Camilla Mays. Far from Eden. 1982. 12.00 (ISBN 0-8059-2824-3). Dorrance.

Frank, Charles. Liquid Crystals: Their Physics, Chemistry & Applications. (Series A: Vol. 309). (Illus.). 169p. 1983. text ed. 55.00x (ISBN 0-85403-210-X, Pub. by Royal Soc London). Scholium Intl.

Frank, Charles R., Jr. Adjustment Assistance: American Jobs & Trade with the Developing Countries. LC 73-84869. (Development Papers: No. 13). 50p. 1973. pap. 1.00 (ISBN 0-686-28678-2). Overseas Dev Council.

--Foreign Trade & Domestic Aid. LC 76-51821. 1977. 16.95 (ISBN 0-8157-2914-6). Brookings.

--Production Theory & Indivisible Commodities. LC 68-29383. (Studies in Mathematical Economics Ser.: No. 3). 1968. 23.50x (ISBN 0-691-04192-X). Princeton U Pr.

Frank, Charles R., Jr. & Webb, Richard C., eds. Income Distribution & Growth in the Less-Developed Countries. LC 77-86494. 1977. pap. 17.95 (ISBN 0-8157-2915-4). Brookings.

Frank, Charles W., Jr. Anatomy of a Waterfowl: For Carvers & Painters. LC 81-10657. (Illus.). 128p. 1982. 45.00 (ISBN 0-88289-290-8). Pelican.

--Wetland Heritage: The Louisiana Duck Decoy. 192p. 1985. 49.95 (ISBN 0-88289-398-X). Pelican.

Frank, Chuck, jt. auth. see Combs, Steve.

Frank, Claudia. Enzyklopaedie der Minerale und Edelsteine. 304p. (Ger.). 1977. 80.00 (ISBN 3-451-17622-X, M-7058). French & Eur.

Frank, Clyde, jt. auth. see Pietrzyk, Donald J.

Frank, Cynthia. A Sea-Lulled Rocky Mountain Isle. Monday, Stella, ed. (Illus.). 1977. pap. 2.00 (ISBN 0-918510-00-7). Monday Bks.

Frank, Daniel B. Deep Blue Funk & Other Stories: Portraits of Teenage Parents. LC 83-3965. 1983. pap. 3.95 (ISBN 0-226-25994-3, 25994-3 ORDER #, Dist. by Ounce of Prevention Fund). U of Chicago Pr.

Frank, Daniel H. The Arguments 'From the Sciences' in Aristotle's Peri Ideon. LC 83-48711. (American University Studies, Series V, Philosophy: Vol. 2). 154p. (Orig.). 1984. pap. 15.25 (ISBN 0-8204-0035-1). P Lang Pubs.

Frank, Darlene. Silicon English: Business Writing Tools for the Computer Age. LC 84-8081. (Illus., Orig.). 1985. pap. 12.95 (ISBN 0-914735-00-4). Royall Pr.

Frank, Diana. No Time to Cook Cookbook. (Illus.). 340p. 1981. pap. 11.95 spiral bdg. (ISBN 0-89037-172-5). Anderson World.

--Runner's World No Time to Cook Cookbook. 340p. 1981. spiral bdg. 11.95 (ISBN 0-89037-172-5). Anderson World.

Frank, Diane, ed. see Fries, Michael, et al.

Frank, Diane, ed. see Fries, Michael & Taylor, C. Holland.

Frank, Edgar. Talmudic & Rabbinical Chronology. 1978. 5.50 (ISBN 0-87306-050-4). Feldheim.

--Zemanim. 6.00 (ISBN 0-87306-063-6). Feldheim.

Frank, Elizabeth. Jackson Pollock. LC 83-3856. (Modern Masters Ser.). (Illus.). 128p. 1983. 29.95 (ISBN 0-89659-383-5); pap. 16.95 (ISBN 0-89659-384-3). Abbeville Pr.

--Louise Bogan: A Portrait. LC 83-48853. (Illus.). 496p. Date not set. 24.95 (ISBN 0-394-52484-5). Knopf.

Frank, Elke, jt. auth. see Irish, Marion D.

Frank, Ellen, jt. auth. see Boller, Francois.

Frank, Ellen E. Literary Architecture: Essays Toward a Tradition-Walter Pater, Gerard Manley Hopkins, Marcel Proust, Henry James. (Illus.). 328p. 1982. 15.95 (ISBN 0-520-03352-3); pap. 8.95 (ISBN 0-520-04772-9). U of Cal Pr.

Frank, Eric & Palmer, John. Just Who Do You Think You Are... & Where Are You Going? 86p. (Orig.). 1981. pap. text ed. 6.25x (ISBN 0-86238-008-1, Pub. by Chartwell-Bratt England). Brookfield Pub Co.

Frank, Erich. Philosophical Understanding & Religious Truth. LC 82-8476. 220p. 1982. pap. text ed. 12.25 (ISBN 0-8191-2510-5). U Pr of Amer.

Frank, Ernest. Electrical Measurement Analysis. LC 77-3508. (Electrical & Electronic Engineering Ser.). (Illus.). 458p. 1977. Repr. of 1959 ed. lib. bdg. 30.50 (ISBN 0-88275-554-4). Krieger.

Frank, Francine & Anshen, Frank. Language & the Sexes. 120p. 1984. 24.95x (ISBN 0-87395-881-0); pap. 7.95x (ISBN 0-87395-882-9). State U NY Pr.

Frank, Frederick S. Guide to the Gothic: An Annotated Bibliography of Criticism. LC 83-24507. 437p. 1984. 30.00 (ISBN 0-8108-1669-5). Scarecrow.

Frank, Fredric D., jt. auth. see Jaffee, Cabot L.

Frank, G. The Wechsler Enterprise: An Assessment of the Development, Structure & Use of the Wechsler Tests of Intelligence. (International Series in Experimental Psychiatry). 176p. 1983. 30.00 (ISBN 0-08-027973-2). Pergamon.

Frank, Gelya F., jt. auth. see Langness, L. L.

Frank, George. Eighty-Eight Rue de Charonne: Adventures in Wood Finishing. LC 80-54431. (Illus.). 128p. 1981. 9.95 (ISBN 0-918804-06-X, Dist. by W W Norton). Taunton.
--Psychiatric Diagnosis: A Review of Research. LC 74-13884. 1975. text ed. 28.00 (ISBN 0-08-017712-3). Pergamon.
Frank, Gerald W. Gerry Frank's "Where to Find It, Buy It, Eat It in New York". rev., 4th ed. 1985. pap. 10.95 (ISBN 0-9612578-3-0); pap. 5.95 pocket ed. (ISBN 0-9612578-2-2). G's Frankly Speaking.
Frank, Grace. Medieval French Drama. 1954. 34.95x (ISBN 0-19-815317-1). Oxford U Pr.
Frank, Grace, tr. see Sudermann, Hermann.
Frank, H. & Torgeson, R., eds. Science Fiction & Fantasy Magazine Checklist & Price Guide, 1977. 1977. pap. 8.95 (ISBN 0-918364-00-0). Sci Fiction.
Frank, H. D. Polypropylene. LC 68-24786. (Polymer Monographs Ser.: Vol. 2). (Illus.). 144p. 1968. 27.95 (ISBN 0-677-01540-2). Gordon.
Frank, Harold H. Women in the Organization. LC 76-20167. 1977. 16.95x (ISBN 0-8122-7715-5); manual 3.50x (ISBN 0-686-77158-3). U of Pa Pr.
Frank, Harry T. Atlas of the Bible Lands. rev. ed. LC 77-6292. (Illus.). 48p. 1984. 6.95 (ISBN 0-8437-7056-2); pap. 4.99 (ISBN 0-8437-7055-4). Hammond Inc.
--Discovering the Biblical World. LC 74-7044. (Illus.). 228p. 1977. 19.95 (ISBN 0-8437-3624-0); pap. 12.95 (ISBN 0-8437-3625-9). Hammond Inc.
Frank, Harry T., ed. Atlas of the Bible Lands. 1979. pap. 3.95 (ISBN 0-8054-1136-4). Broadman.
Frank, Harvey. ERC Closely-Held Corporation Guide. 1981. 99.50 (ISBN 0-13-160515-1). Exec Reports.
Frank, Harvey, jt. auth. see Executive Reports Corporation.
Frank, Helena, tr. see Perez, Isaac L.
Frank, Helena, tr. see Rischin, Moses.
Frank, Helmut J. Arizona's Energy Future: Making the Transition to a New Mix. LC 82-6941. 154p. 1982. pap. 9.95 (ISBN 0-8165-0773-2). U of Ariz Pr.
Frank, Henley M. The Origins & Substance of Roman Literature. (Illus.). 133p. 1984. 67.50 (ISBN 0-89266-460-6). Am Classical Coll Pr.
Frank, Irmgard. Althochdeutschen Glossen der Handschrift Leipzig Rep. II. 6. (Arbeiten zur Fruehmittelalterforschung, Vol. 7). 294p. 1973. 45.60x (ISBN 3-11-004370-X). De Gruyter.
Frank, Isaiah. Foreign Enterprise in Developing Countries. 218p. 1980. 18.50x (ISBN 0-8018-2343-9); pap. 6.95x (ISBN 0-8018-2378-1). Johns Hopkins.
--Trade Policy Issues for the Developing Countries in the 1980's. (Working Paper Ser.: No. 478). 52p. 1981. 5.00 (ISBN 0-686-36203-9, WP-0478). World Bank.
Frank, Isaiah, ed. The Japanese Economy in International Perspective. LC 74-15567. (Committee for Economic Development Ser). (Illus.). 314p. 1975. o. p. 25.00x (ISBN 0-8018-1629-7); pap. 8.95x (ISBN 0-8018-1630-0). Johns Hopkins.
--The Japanese Economy in International Perspective. 306p. 1975. 3.95 (ISBN 0-317-33990-7, 240). Comm Econ Dev.
Frank, Isaiah, jt. ed. see Hirono, Ryokichi.
Frank, J. American Law: The Case for Radical Reform. 1969. 5.95 (ISBN 0-02-896020-3). Macmillan.
Frank, J., et al, eds. Accretion Power in Astrophysics. 273p. 1985. 59.50 (ISBN 0-521-24530-3). Cambridge U Pr.
Frank, J. H., ed. Phytotelmata: Terrestrial Plants As Hosts of Aquatic Insect Communities. Lounibos, L. P. 304p. 1983. pap. text ed. 24.95 (ISBN 0-937548-05-7). Plexus Pub.
Frank, J. W., et al. Effects & Significance of Replacement Cost Disclosure. LC 78-59300. 1978. 8.00 (ISBN 0-910586-25-X). Finan Exec.
Frank, Jacqueline. No One Took a Country from Me. LC 81-72095. 64p. (Orig.). 1982. pap. text ed. 6.95 (ISBN 0-914086-37-5). Alicejamesbooks.
Frank, Jerome. Courts on Trial: Myth & Reality in American Justice. LC 72-11942. 454p. 1949. 45.00 (ISBN 0-691-09205-2); pap. 12.95 (ISBN 0-691-02755-2). Princeton U Pr.
--Law & the Modern Mind. 15.75 (ISBN 0-8446-0629-4). Peter Smith.
--A Man's Reach: The Philosophy of Judge Jerome Frank. Kristein, Barbara F., ed. LC 77-7288. xxvii, 450p. 1977. Repr. of 1965 ed. lib. bdg. 27.75x (ISBN 0-8371-9669-8, FRMR). Greenwood.
Frank, Jerome & Frank, Barbara. Not Guilty. LC 72-138495. (Civil Liberties in American History Ser.). 1971. Repr. of 1957 ed. lib. bdg. 32.50 (ISBN 0-306-70072-7). Da Capo.
Frank, Jerome D. Persuasion & Healing: A Comparative Study of Psychotherapy. rev. ed. LC 74-10146. 368p. 1974. pap. 8.95 (ISBN 0-8052-0470-9). Schocken.
--Psychotherapy & the Human Predicament: A Psychosocial Approach. Dietz, Park E., ed. LC 78-54396. 1979. 16.95 (ISBN 0-8052-3696-1). Schocken.
--Sanity & Survival in the Nuclear Age. LC 82-9872. 1982. pap. text ed. 6.95 (ISBN 0-394-33229-6, RanC). Random.
Frank, Jerome D., jt. auth. see Powdermaker, Florence B.
Frank, Johann P. A System of Complete Medical Police: Selections from Johann Peter Frank. Lesky, Erna, ed. LC 75-39820. pap. 123.30 (ISBN 0-317-07932-8, 2020757). Bks Demand UMI.
Frank, John P. Justice Daniel Dissenting: A Biography of Peter V. Daniel, 1784-1860. xii, 336p. 1964. 8.00x (ISBN 0-8377-2127-X). Rothman.
--Justice Daniel Dissenting 1784-1860. 1964. 25.00x (ISBN 0-678-08028-3). Kelley.
Frank, Jori, jt. auth. see Sherman, Sylvia.
Frank, Joseph. Cromwell's Press Agent: A Critical Biography of Marchamont Nedham, 1620-1678. LC 80-5637. 213p. 1980. lib. bdg. 22.50 (ISBN 0-8191-1193-7); pap. text ed. 11.25 (ISBN 0-8191-1194-5). U Pr of Amer.
--Dostoevsky: The Seeds of Revolt, 1821-1849. 1976. 37.50 (ISBN 0-691-06260-9); pap. 9.95x (ISBN 0-691-01355-1). Princeton U Pr.
--Dostoevsky: The Years of Ordeal, 1850-1859. LC 76-3704. (Illus.). 320p. 1983. 25.00x (ISBN 0-691-06576-4). Princeton U Pr.
--Levellers: John Lilburne, Richard Overton, William Walwyn. LC 68-27058. 1969. Repr. of 1955 ed. 12.00x (ISBN 0-8462-1278-1). Russell.
Frank, Josette. Television: How to Use It Wisely with Children. rev ed. 30p. 1976. pap. 1.75 (ISBN 0-87183-076-0). Jewish Bd Family.
--What Books for Children? Guideposts for Parents. 363p. 1981. Repr. of 1937 ed. lib. bdg. 25.00 (ISBN 0-89987-266-2). Darby Bks.
Frank, Josette, ed. Poems to Read to the Very Young. LC 82-518. (Illus.). 48p. (ps-3). 1982. PLB 6.99 (ISBN 0-394-95188-3); pap. 6.95 (ISBN 0-394-85188-9). Random.
Frank, Josette, adapted by see Barrie, J. M.
Frank, Julia. Alzheimer's Disease: The Silent Epidemic. (Illus.). 80p. (gr. 5 up). 1985. PLB 9.95 (ISBN 0-8225-1578-4). Lerner Pubns.
Frank, Kenneth A., ed. The Human Dimension in Psychoanalytic Practice. 224p. 1977. 37.00 (ISBN 0-8089-1039-6, 791350). Grune.
Frank, L. K. Projective Methods. 96p. 1948. 9.75x (ISBN 0-398-04257-8). C C Thomas.
Frank, Larry & Harlow, Francis. Historic Pottery of the Pueblo Indians, 1600-1880. LC 73-89957. (Illus.). 224p. 1975. 32.50 (ISBN 0-8212-0586-2, 365017). NYGS.
Frank, Larry & Holbrook, Millard J. Indian Silver Jewelry of the Southwest, 1868-1930. LC 78-7071. (Illus.). 1979. 34.95 (ISBN 0-8212-0740-7, 417947). NYGS.
Frank, Lawrence. Charles Dickens & the Romantic Self. LC 84-3601. viii, 283p. 1984. 23.95x (ISBN 0-8032-1965-2). U of Nebr Pr.
--Playing Hardball: The Dynamics of Baseball Folk Speech. LC 83-48834. 150p. (Orig.). 1984. text ed. 9.60 (ISBN 0-8204-0061-0). P Lang Pubs.
Frank, Lawrence K. Society As the Patient. LC 72-86568. (Essay & General Literature Index Reprint Ser). 1969. Repr. of 1948 ed. 32.25x (ISBN 0-8046-0559-9, Pub. by Kennikat). Assoc Faculty Pr.
Frank, Lawrence K., et al. Personality Development in Adolescent Girls. (SRCD M). 1951. 16.00 (ISBN 0-527-01552-0). Kraus Repr.
Frank, Leonard, ed. The History of Shock Treatment. 206p. 7.00 (ISBN 0-318-17659-9). NAPA.
Frank, Leonard R., jt. auth. see Chaudhuri, Haridas.
Frank, Leonard R., ed. The History of Shock Treatment. LC 78-13550. (Illus.). 206p. 1978. 10.00 (ISBN 0-9601376-1-0). L R Frank.
Frank, Lewis A. Soviet Nuclear Planning. LC 76-57804. (Orig.). 1976. pap. 4.25 (ISBN 0-8447-3237-0). Am Enterprise.
Frank, Luanne T. & George, Emery E., eds. Husbanding the Golden Grain: Studies in Honor of Henry W. Nordmeyer. 337p. 1973. 12.50x (ISBN 0-913950-01-7). M S Rosenberg.
Frank, M. Modern English: Exercises for Non Native Speakers, 2 pts. Incl. Pt. 1. Parts of Speech. 1972. pap. text ed. 12.95 (ISBN 0-13-593806-6); Pt. 2. Sentences & Complex Structures (ISBN 0-13-593814-7). 1972. pap. text ed. 12.95 (ISBN 0-686-86555-3). P-H.
Frank, Marcella. Modern English: A Practical Reference Guide. (Illus.). 1972. pap. text ed. 16.95 (ISBN 0-13-594002-8). P-H.
--Writer's Companion. 144p. 1983. pap. text ed. 9.95 (ISBN 0-13-969790-X). P-H.
--Writing from Experience. 288p. 1983. pap. text ed. 12.95 (ISBN 0-13-970285-7). P-H.
Frank, Marge. Fraction Action. (Choose-a-Card Ser.). (Illus.). 32p. (gr. 3-6). 1981. pap. text ed. 5.95 (ISBN 0-86530-015-1, IP 15-1). Incentive Pubns.
--If You're Trying to Teach Kids How to Write, You've Gotta Have This Book! LC 78-70901. (Illus.). 218p. (gr. 2 up). 1979. pap. 8.95 (ISBN 0-913916-62-5, IP625). Incentive Pubns.
Frank, Marge & Linton, Nancy. Better, Better Body Book. 1985. pap. 9.95 (ISBN 0-310-42741-X, Pub. by Pyranee). Zondervan.
Frank, Marge, jt. auth. see Forte, Imogene.
Frank, Marjorie. I Can Make a Rainbow. LC 76-506. (Illus.). 300p. (gr. k up). 1976. pap. 12.95 (ISBN 0-913916-19-6, IP 19-6). Incentive Pubns.
--Kids' Stuff Math. LC 74-18907. (The Kids' Stuff Set). 307p. (gr. 2-6). 1974. 10.95 (ISBN 0-913916-12-9, IP 12-9). Incentive Pubns.
Frank, Marjorie, ed. see Institute of Modern Languages.
Frank, Marjorie, ed. see Ozaeta, Pablo.
Frank, Marjorie S. Building Language Power with Cloze: Level B. Hutchins, R. J., ed. (Skillbooster Ser.). 64p. (gr. 2). 1981. text ed. write for info. (ISBN 0-87895-520-8). Modern Curr.
Frank, Marjorie S. & Hutchins, P. J. Building Language Power with Cloze: Level C. (Skillbooster Ser.). 64p. (gr. 3). 1981. write for info. wkbk. (ISBN 0-87895-516-X). Modern Curr.
--Building Language Power with Cloze: Level D. (Skillbooster Ser.). 64p. (gr. 4). 1981. write for info. (ISBN 0-87895-517-8). Modern Curr.
--Building Language Power with Cloze: Level E. (Skillbooster Ser.). 64p. (gr. 5). 1981. write for info. wkbk. (ISBN 0-87895-518-6). Modern Curr.
--Building Language Power with Cloze, Level F. (Skillbooster Ser.). 64p. (gr. 6). 1981. write for info. (ISBN 0-87895-519-4). Modern Curr.
Frank, Martin J. & Alvarez-Mena, Sergio C. Cardiovascular Physical Diagnosis. 2nd ed. (Illus.). 1982. 19.95 (ISBN 0-8151-3331-6). Year Bk Med.
Frank, Mary, ed. Child Care: Emerging Legal Issues. LC 83-12929. (Journal of Children in Contemporary Society Ser.: Vol. 15, No. 4). 104p. 1983. text ed. 19.95 (ISBN 0-86656-182-X, B182). Haworth Pr.
--Children of Exceptional Parents. LC 82-25481. (Journal of Children in Contemporary Society Ser.: Vol. 15, No. 1). 99p. 1983. text ed. 20.00 (ISBN 0-917724-96-8, B96); pap. text ed. 6.95 (ISBN 0-86656-210-9). Haworth Pr.
--A Child's Brain: The Impact of Advanced Research on Cognitive & Social Behaviors. LC 84-678. (Journal of Children in Contemporary Society Ser.: Vol. 16, Nos. 1-2). 243p. 1984. text ed. 22.95 (ISBN 0-86656-269-9, B269); pap. text ed. 14.95 (ISBN 0-86656-366-0). Haworth Pr.
--Infant Intervention Programs: Truths & Untruths. LC 82-22427. (Journal of Children in Contemporary Society Ser.: Vol 17 No. 1). 160p. 1985. text ed. 19.95 (ISBN 0-86656-329-6). Haworth Pr.
--Marketing Child Care Programs: Why & How. LC 84-27948. (Journal of Children in Contemporary Society Ser.: Vol. 17, No. 2). 128p. 1985. text ed. 19.95 (ISBN 0-86656-330-X). Haworth Pr.
--Newcomers to the United States: Children & Families. LC 83-8402. (Journal of Children in Contemporary Society Ser.: Vol. 15, No. 3). 89p. 1983. text ed. 19.95 (ISBN 0-86656-181-1, B181). Haworth Pr.
--Primary Prevention for Children & Families. LC 81-17858. (Journal of Children in Contemporary Society Ser.: Vol. 14, Nos. 2 & 3). 119p. 1982. text ed. 20.00 (ISBN 0-86656-107-2, B107). Haworth Pr.
--The Puzzling Child: From Recognition to Treatment. LC 82-11692. (Journal of Children in Contemporary Society Ser.: Vol. 14, No. 4). 109p. 1982. text ed. 20.00 (ISBN 0-86656-119-6, B119). Haworth Pr.
--Young Children in a Computerized Environment. LC 81-20028. (Journal of Children in Contemporary Society Ser.: Vol. 14, No. 1). 96p. 1981. text ed. 20.00 (ISBN 0-86656-108-0, B108). Haworth Pr.
Frank, Mary I., ed. Teacher: Economic Growth & Society. LC 84-6621. (Journal of Children in Contemporary Society Ser.: Vol. 16, Nos. 3-4). 200p. 1984. text ed. 24.95 (ISBN 0-86656-286-9). Haworth Pr.
Frank, Maude M. Short Plays About Famous Authors. 1979. Repr. lib. bdg. 20.00 (ISBN 0-8495-1630-7). Arden Lib.
Frank, Mel & Rosenthal, Ed. The Indoor-Outdoor Highest Quality Marijuana Grower's Guide. rev. ed. LC 81-10942. 96p. 1982. pap. 5.95 (ISBN 0-915904-59-4). And-Or Pr.
--Marijuana Grower's Guide. LC 77-82452. 1978. deluxe ed. 14.95 (ISBN 0-915904-26-8); spiral bdg. 17.95 (ISBN 0-915904-75-6). And-Or Pr.
Frank, Mel, jt. auth. see Rosenthal, Ed.
Frank, Michael. My Autograph Book. (My Bks.). 48p. (Orig.). 1982. pap. 1.75 (ISBN 0-8431-0912-2). Price Stern.
Frank, Michael B., ed. see Blair, Walter.
Frank, Michael R. The Effective EDP Manager. 288p. 1981. 17.95 (ISBN 0-8144-5635-9). AMACOM.
--The Effective EDP Manager. LC 80-65876. pap. 51.80 (ISBN 0-317-20737-7, 2023895). Bks Demand UMI.
Frank, Milo. How to Get Your Point Across in Thirty Seconds-or Less. 1985. 14.95. S&S.
Frank, Morry. Every Young Man's Dream: Confessions of a Southern League Shortstop. LC 84-50312. 562p. (Orig.). 1984. lib. bdg. 15.95 (ISBN 0-916747-01-8); pap. 9.95 (ISBN 0-916747-02-6). Silverback.
Frank, Myra G. Speech Activity Card File. 1972. text ed. 12.95x (ISBN 0-8134-1427-X). Interstate.
--Speech Tic-Tac-Toe: A Game Providing Practice in the S & R Sounds. 1973. text ed. 6.00x (ISBN 0-8134-1602-7). Interstate.
--Switch, R Sound. 1978. 4.75x (ISBN 0-8134-2005-9). Interstate.
--Switch, S Sound. 1976. text ed. 4.75x (ISBN 0-8134-1790-2, 1790). Interstate.
Frank, Myra G., jt. auth. see Egerer, Marlene M.
Frank, Nancy K. Crimes Against Health & Safety. (Special Edge Supplementary Texts Ser.). 100p. (Orig.). 1986. pap. text ed. 4.99 (ISBN 0-911577-05-X). Harrow & Heston.
Frank, Nathalie D. & Ganly, John V. Data Sources for Business & Market Analysis. 3rd ed. LC 83-3214. 484p. 1983. 32.50 (ISBN 0-8108-1618-0). Scarecrow.
Frank, Nathaniel H., jt. auth. see Slater, John C.
Frank, Neil A., jt. auth. see Kram, Shirley W.
Frank, Newton, jt. ed. see LaPlaca, Peter J.
Frank, Oscar, jt. auth. see Baker, Herman.
Frank, P. El Alcohol y la Familia. 1981. pap. 1.50 (ISBN 0-89243-139-3). Liguori Pubns.
Frank, P., ed. see Von Mises, Richard.
Frank, P. M. Introduction to System Sensitivity Theory. 1978. 47.50 (ISBN 0-12-265650-4). Acad Pr.
Frank, Pat. Alas, Babylon. 320p. (YA) (gr. 8 up). 1976. pap. 3.50 (ISBN 0-553-25212-7). Bantam.
Frank, Perry & Moore, Michele, eds. Public Welfare Directory, 1975. LC 41-4981. 1975. pap. 25.00x (ISBN 0-910106-06-1). Am Pub Welfare.
--Public Welfare Directory, 1976-1977. LC 41-4981. 1976. pap. 25.00x (ISBN 0-910106-07-X). Am Pub Welfare.
Frank, Peter. Mapped Art: Charts, Routes, Regions. LC 81-80985. (Illus.). 48p. 1981. 6.00 (ISBN 0-916365-07-7). Ind Curators.
--Nineteen Artists: Emergent Americans - 1981 National Exhibition. LC 80-54018. (Illus.). 92p. 1981. cover museum catologue 8.50soft (ISBN 0-89207-026-9). S R Guggenheim.
--Something Else Press: An Annotated Bibliography. LC 82-25892. 96p. 1983. 17.50 (ISBN 0-914232-40-1, Documentext); pap. 8.00 (ISBN 0-914232-39-8). McPherson & Co.
--The Travelogues. LC 82-80710. (Contemporary Literature Ser.: No. 12). 48p. (Orig.). 1982. pap. 4.00 (ISBN 0-940650-15-0). Sun & Moon MD.
Frank, Peter & Wilson, Martha. Artist's Books U. S. A. 148p. 1978. 6.00 (ISBN 0-916365-11-5). Ind Curators.
Frank, Peter, jt. auth. see Hill, Ronald J.
Frank, Philipp. Foundations of Physics. LC 46-4908. (Foundations of the Unity of Science Ser: Vol. 1, No. 7). 1946. pap. 1.95x (ISBN 0-226-57582-9, P406, Phoen). U of Chicago Pr.
--Modern Science & Its Philosophy. LC 74-26263. (History, Philosophy & Sociology of Science Ser). 1975. Repr. 27.00x (ISBN 0-405-06591-4). Ayer Co Pubs.
Frank, Pierre. The Fourth International: The Long March of the Trotskyists. Schein, Ruth, tr. (Ink Link Ser.). 192p. 1980. 11.95 (ISBN 0-906133-08-4); pap. 6.95 (ISBN 0-906133-09-2). Pluto Pr.
--The Fourth International: The Long March of the Trotskyists. Schein, Ruth, tr. from Fr. Orig. Title: La Quartrieme Internationale. 192p. 1980. 11.95 (ISBN 0-906133-08-4, Pub. by Ink Links Ltd.); pap. 6.95 (ISBN 0-906133-09-2). Longwood Pub Group.
Frank, R. I. Scholae Palatinae: The Palace Guards of the Later Roman Empire. (Papers & Monographs: No. 23). 260p. 1969. 15.00 (ISBN 0-318-12334-7). Am Acad Rome.
Frank, R. I., tr. see Bengtson, Hermann.
Frank, R. M. & Leach, S. A., eds. Surface & Colloid Phenomena in the Oral Cavity: Methodological Aspects. Proceedings. (Illus.). 288p. 1982. pap. 34.00 (ISBN 0-904147-36-3). IRL Pr.
Frank R. Walker Company, ed. see Bourgeois, G. Patrick, et al.
Frank R. Walker Company, ed. see Crespin, Vick S., et al.
Frank, Raymond. Forty-Nine Steps to Sainthood. 50p. (Orig.). 1984. pap. 2.00 (ISBN 0-932588-08-5). Jakubowsky.
--God Looked Down & Saw a Baby. 69p. (Orig.). (ps). 1984. pap. 2.00 (ISBN 0-932588-07-7). Jakubowsky.
Frank, Richard M. Beings & Their Attributes. LC 78-6957. 1978. 49.50x (ISBN 0-87395-378-9). State U NY Pr.
Frank, Robert. Don't Call Me Gentle Charles: Discourses on Charles Lamb's Essays of Elia. (Oregon State Studies in Literature: No. 2). 144p. 1976. 9.95x (ISBN 0-87071-082-6). Oreg St U Pr.
Frank, Robert & Model, Lisette. Charles Pratt: Photographs. LC 82-71396. (Illus.). 88p. 1983. pap. 25.00 (ISBN 0-89381-111-4). Aperture.
Frank, Robert, jt. auth. see Norton, Thomas E.
Frank, Robert G., Jr. Harvey & the Oxford Physiologists: Scientific Ideas & Social Interaction. LC 79-63553. (Illus.). 1981. 34.00x (ISBN 0-520-03906-8). U of Cal Pr.
Frank, Robert H. Choosing the Right Pond: Human Behavior & the Quest for Status. (Illus.). 320p. 1985. 22.95 (ISBN 0-19-503520-8). Oxford U Pr.
Frank, Robert H. & Freeman, Richard T. Distributional Consequences of Direct Foreign Investment. (Economic Theory, Econometrics & Mathematical Economic Ser.). 1978. 37.50 (ISBN 0-12-265050-6). Acad Pr.
Frank, Robert J., jt. ed. see Robbins, William G.
Frank, Robert W., Jr. Chaucer & the Legend of Good Women. LC 72-81271. 249p. 1973. 15.00x (ISBN 0-674-11190-7). Harvard U Pr.

--Faith of Reason. LC 71-86277. 1969. Repr. of 1948 ed. lib. bdg. 17.00x (ISBN 0-374-92850-9). Octagon.
--Human Rights & Foreign Policy. LC 78-65548. (Headline Ser.: No. 241). (Orig.). 1978. pap. 3.00 (ISBN 0-87124-048-3). Foreign Policy.
--Morality & U. S. Foreign Policy. (Headline Ser.: No. 224). (Orig.). 1975. pap. 3.00 (ISBN 0-87124-029-7). Foreign Policy.
--The Neglected Aspects of Foreign Affairs: American Educational & Cultural Policy Abroad. LC 65-28724. pap. 42.00 (ISBN 0-317-20463-7, 2023004). Bks Demand UMI.
Frankel, Charles, ed. Controversies & Decisions: The Social Sciences & Public Policy. LC 75-28514. 310p. 1976. 10.00x (ISBN 0-87154-262-5). Russell Sage.
--Issues in University Education: Essays by Ten American Scholars. LC 76-48978. 1977. Repr. of 1959 ed. lib. bdg. 15.00x (ISBN 0-8371-9353-2, FRIU). Greenwood.
Frankel, Dave. Self-Determination in the Mideast: A Debate. 1974. pap. 0.60 (ISBN 0-87348-335-9). Path Pr NY.
Frankel, David. Corpus of Cypriote Antiquities. (Studies in Mediterranean Archaeology: Vol. XX-7). 187p. 1983. pap. text ed. 35.00x (ISBN 9-18505-827-0, Pub. by Paul Astroms Sweden). Humanities.
--Middle Cypriote White Painted Pottery: An Analytical Study of the Decoration. (Studies in Mediterranean Archaeology Ser.: No. XLII). (Illus.). 1974. pap. text ed. 11.75x (ISBN 91-85058-60-2). Humanities.
Frankel, Edith R. Novy Mir: A Case Study in the Politics of Literature 1952-1958. LC 80-42152. (Cambridge Studies in Russian Literature: No. 1). (Illus.). 220p. 1981. 42.50 (ISBN 0-521-23438-7). Cambridge U Pr.
Frankel, Edward. DNA: The Ladder of Life. 2nd ed. (Illus.). (gr. 7 up). 1978. 10.95 (ISBN 0-07-021883-8). McGraw.
--Ferns: A Natural History. LC 81-6700. (Illus.). 256p. 1981. 17.50 (ISBN 0-8289-0429-4). Greene.
Frankel, Emily. The Splintered Heart. 320p. 1985. pap. 3.50 (ISBN 0-553-22930-3). Bantam.
Frankel, Eric, jt. auth. see Merkin, Lisa.
Frankel, Ernst G. Management & Operations of American Shipping. 256p. 1982. 28.00 (ISBN 0-86569-100-2). Auburn Hse.
--Regulation & Policies of American Shipping. 352p. 1982. 28.00 (ISBN 0-86569-099-5). Auburn Hse.
--Systems Reliability & Risk Analysis. 1984. lib. bdg. 40.00 (ISBN 90-247-2895-9, Pub. by Martinus Nijhoff Netherlands). Kluwer Academic.
Frankel, F. H. & Zamansky, H., eds. Hypnosis at Its Bicentennial. LC 78-16605. 320p. 1978. 34.50x (ISBN 0-306-40029-4, Plenum Pr). Plenum Pub.
Frankel, Francine. India's Political Economy, Nineteen Forty-Seven to Nineteen Seventy-Five: The Gradual Revolution. LC 78-51164. 1978. 60.00 (ISBN 0-691-03120-7). Princeton U Pr.
Frankel, Francine R. India's Green Revolution: Political Costs of Economic Growth. LC 74-132237. (Center of International Studies Ser.). 1971. 26.50 (ISBN 0-691-07536-0). Princeton U Pr.
Frankel, Fred H., ed. Hypnosis: Trance As a Coping Mechanism. LC 76-14856. 195p. 1976. 24.50x (ISBN 0-306-30932-7, Plenum Pr). Plenum Pub.
Frankel, Hans H. The Flowering Plum & the Palace Lady: Interpretations of Chinese Poetry. LC 75-8203. 288p. 1976. 27.50x (ISBN 0-300-01889-4); pap. 8.95x (ISBN 0-300-02242-5). Yale U Pr.
Frankel, Hans H., compiled by. Catalogue of Translations from the Chinese Dynastic Histories for the Period 220-960. LC 74-9395. (Chinese Dynastic Studies. Translations. U of Cal Pr). 295p. 1974. Repr. of 1957 ed. lib. bdg. 19.75x (ISBN 0-8371-7661-1, FRDH). Greenwood.
Frankel, Harry. Sam Adams & the American Revolution. pap. 0.75 (ISBN 0-87348-197-6). Path Pr NY.
Frankel, Haskel, jt. auth. see Fyodorova, Victoria.
Frankel, Haskel, jt. auth. see Hagen, Uta.
Frankel, Hermann. Early Greek Poetry & Philosophy. Hadas, Moses & Willis, James, trs. from Ger. LC 74-10724. 576p. 1975. 34.50 (ISBN 0-8290-0985-X). Irvington.
Frankel, Israel & Nelson, Rod. Shoe Machinery Maintenance. (Illus.). 1983. pap. text ed. 10.00 (ISBN 0-931424-11-9). Shoe Serv Inst.
Frankel, Jack B. Helping Students Think & Value: Strategies for Teaching Social Studies. 2nd ed. 1980. text ed. 27.95 (ISBN 0-13-386375-1). P-H.
Frankel, Jeffrey A. The Yen-Dollar Agreement: Liberalizing Japanese Capital Markets. LC 84-27842. (Policy Analyses in International Economics Ser.: No. 9). 86p. (Orig.). 1984. pap. 10.00x (ISBN 0-88132-035-8). MIT (ISBN 0-262-56034-8, FRAYP). Inst Intl Eco.
Frankel, Jonathan. Prophecy & Politics: Socialism, Nationalism, & the Russian Jews, 1862-1917. LC 80-14414. (Illus.). 816p. 1981. 69.50 (ISBN 0-521-23028-4). Cambridge U Pr.
--Prophecy & Politics: Socialism, Nationalism, & the Russian Jews, 1862-1917. LC 80-14414. 686p. 1984. pap. 18.95 (ISBN 0-521-26919-9). Cambridge U Pr.
Frankel, Jonathan, ed. see Akimov, Vladimir.
Frankel, Joseph. International Relations in a Changing World. 3rd ed. 1979. 15.95x (ISBN 0-19-219147-0); pap. text ed. 6.95x (ISBN 0-19-289128-6). Oxford U Pr.
Frankel, Julie & Scheier, Michael. The Wildfire Romance Fill-In Book. (Wildfire Extra Ser.). (Illus.). 80p. (Orig.). (gr. 7 up). 1984. pap. 2.25 (ISBN 0-590-33214-7, Wildfire). Scholastic Inc.
Frankel, Julie, jt. auth. see Sheier, Michael.
Frankel, Lawrence, jt. ed. see Harris, Raymond.
Frankel, Leon A. Gastric Surgery & the Dumping Syndrome: The "Mirror-Image" Concept. (Illus.). 352p. 1975. photocopy ed. 57.75x (ISBN 0-398-03195-9). C C Thomas.
Frankel, Linda, jt. auth. see Bart, Pauline.
Frankel, Lionel H., et al. Commercial Transactions: Payment Systems. (Contemporary Legal Education Ser.). 322p. 1982. pap. text ed. 11.00 (ISBN 0-87215-469-6). Michie Co.
--Commercial Transactions: Sales. (Contemporary Legal Education Ser.). 463p. pap. text ed. 15.00 (ISBN 0-87215-470-X). Michie Co.
--Commercial Transactions: Secured Financing. (Contemporary Legal Education Ser.). 389p. 1982. pap. text ed. 14.00 (ISBN 0-87215-468-8). Michie Co.
Frankel, Mark, jt. auth. see Rudestam, Kjell E.
Frankel, Mark D., jt. auth. see Gates, Sam.
Frankel, Martin R. Inference from Survey Samples: An Empirical Investigation. LC 72-161550. 173p. 1971. 12.00x (ISBN 0-87944-013-9). Inst Soc Res.
Frankel, Martin R., jt. auth. see Occhiogrosso, Michael G.
Frankel, Marvin. British & American Manufacturing Productivity: A Comparison & Interpretation, Vol. 54. LC 82-2868. (University of Illinois Bulletin: No. 49). 130p. 1982. Repr. of 1957 ed. lib. bdg. 22.50x (ISBN 0-313-23487-6, FRAB). Greenwood.
--Partisan Justice. 142p. 1980. 9.95 (ISBN 0-8090-7547-4); pap. 5.95 (ISBN 0-8090-1395-9). Hill & Wang.
Frankel, Marvin E. Criminal Sentences: Law Without Order. LC 72-95111. (American Century Ser.). 134p. 1973. pap. 5.25 (ISBN 0-8090-1374-6). Hill & Wang.
Frankel, Maurice. Social Audit Pollution Handbook: How to Assess Environmental & Workplace Pollution. 1978. text ed. 26.50x (ISBN 0-333-21646-6); pap. text ed. 10.50x (ISBN 0-333-21647-4). Humanities.
Frankel, Max & Hoffman, Judy. I Live in Israel. Fishman, Priscilla, ed. LC 79-12833. (Illus.). (gr. 3-4). 1979. pap. text ed. 4.95x (ISBN 0-87441-317-6). Behrman.
Frankel, Max G., et al. Functional Teaching of the Mentally Retarded. 2nd ed. (Illus.). 288p. 1975. photocopy ed. 30.75x (ISBN 0-398-03361-7). C C Thomas.
Frankel, Nat & Smith, Larry. Patton's Best. 240p. 1985. pap. 3.50 (ISBN 0-515-08312-7). Jove Pubns.
Frankel, Norman, ed. The Grants Register, 1985-1987. 9th ed. LC 77-12055. 870p. 1984. 39.95x (ISBN 0-312-34409-0). St Martin.
Frankel, O. H. & Soule, M. E. Conservation & Evolution. LC 80-40528. (Illus.). 300p. 1981. 59.50 (ISBN 0-521-23275-9); pap. 22.95 (ISBN 0-521-29889-X). Cambridge U Pr.
Frankel, O. H. & Hawkes, J. G., eds. Crop Genetic Resources for Today & Tomorrow. LC 74-82586. (International Biological Programme Ser.: Vol. 2). (Illus.). 544p. 1975. 95.00 (ISBN 0-521-20575-1). Cambridge U Pr.
Frankel, Paul H. Essentials of Petroleum: A Key to Oil Economics. 2nd, rev. ed. 188p. 1969. 28.50x (ISBN 0-7146-1220-0, F Cass Co). Biblio Dist.
Frankel, Philip H. Pretoria's Praetorians: Civil-Military Relations in South Africa. (Illus.). 230p. 1985. 44.50 (ISBN 0-521-26440-5). Cambridge U Pr.
Frankel, Phillip & Gras, Ann. The Software Sifter: An Intelligent Shopper's Guide to Software. 250p. 1983. pap. 24.95 spiral bound (ISBN 0-02-949330-7). Macmillan.
Frankel, R. & Galun, E. Pollination Mechanisms, Reproduction & Plant Breeding. (Monographs on Theoretical & Applied Genetics: Vol. 2). 1977. 39.00 (ISBN 0-387-07934-3). Springer-Verlag.
Frankel, R., ed. Heterosis. (Monographs on Theoretical & Applied Genetics: Vol. 6). (Illus.). 320p. 1983. 63.00 (ISBN 0-387-12125-0). Springer-Verlag.
Frankel, Richard B., jt. auth. see Freeman, Arthur J.
Frankel, Robert. Radiation Protection for Radiologic Technologists. (Illus.). 1976. text ed. 27.95 (ISBN 0-07-021875-7). McGraw.
Frankel, S., jt. auth. see Chalk, Rosemary.
Frankel, S. Herbert. Investment & the Return to Equity Capital in the South African Gold Mining Industry, 1887-1965: An International Comparison. LC 68-1574. (Illus.). 1967. 12.00x (ISBN 0-674-46550-4). Harvard U Pr.
--Money & Liberty. 1980. pap. 4.25 (ISBN 0-8447-3398-9). Am Enterprise.
Frankel, Saul J. Staff Relations in the Civil Service: The Canadian Experience. LC 63-4271. pap. 86.00 (ISBN 0-317-20715-6, 2023829). Bks Demand UMI.
Frankel, Sidney. Multiconductor Transmission Line Analysis. LC 77-28230. (Illus.). 1978. 36.00x (ISBN 0-89006-054-1). Artech Hse.
Frankel, Steven. The Complete Kaypro: Kaypro II, IV, & 10. 1983. pap. text ed. 16.95 (ISBN 0-8359-0802-X). Reston.
Frankel, Tamar. The Regulation of Money Managers, 4 vols. LC 77-1577. 1980. Vol. 1. 60.00 (ISBN 0-316-29191-9); Vol. 2. 60.00 (ISBN 0-316-29192-7); 60.00 (ISBN 0-316-29193-5); Vol. 3. 60.00 ea. (ISBN 0-316-29194-3); 225.00 set (ISBN 0-316-29190-0). Little.
--Regulation of Money Managers: 1983 Supplement. 1983. pap. 36.00 (ISBN 0-316-29197-8). Little.
--Regulation of Money Managers: 1984 Supplement. 1984. pap. write for info. (ISBN 0-316-29198-6). Little.
Frankel, Theodore. Tables for Traffic Management & Design. 1977. 8.95 (ISBN 0-686-98071-9). Telecom Lib.
Frankel, Theodore T. Gravitational Curvature: An Introduction to Einstein's Theory. LC 78-12092. (Illus.). 1979. text ed. 23.95 (ISBN 0-7167-1006-4); pap. text ed. 14.95 (ISBN 0-7167-1062-5). W H Freeman.
Frankel, Victor H. & Burstein, Albert H. Orthopaedic Biomechanics: The Application of Engineering to the Musculoskeletal System. LC 77-78537. pap. 49.00 (ISBN 0-317-30000-8, 2051852). Bks Demand UMI.
Frankel, Victor H. & Nordin, Margareta, eds. Basic Biomechanics of the Skeletal System. LC 79-24593. (Illus.). 303p. 1980. text ed. 20.00 (ISBN 0-8121-0708-X). Lea & Febiger.
Frankel, Viktor E. Man's Search for Meaning. 3rd ed. 1984. pap. 5.95 (ISBN 0-671-24422-1, Touchstone Bks). S&S.
Frankel, William. Israel Observed: An Anatomy of the State. 288p. 1981. 18.95 (ISBN 0-500-01247-4). Thames Hudson.
--Israel Observed: An Anatomy of the State. rev. ed. 1982. pap. 9.95 (ISBN 0-500-27258-1). Thames Hudson.
Frankel, William, ed. Survey of Jewish Affairs 1982. LC 83-48732. 289p. 1984. 25.00 (ISBN 0-8386-3206-8). Fairleigh Dickinson.
--Survey of Jewish Affairs 1983. 320p. 1985. 25.00 (ISBN 0-8386-3244-0). Fairleigh Dickinson.
Frankell, Charles, ed. see Rousseau, Jean-Jacques.
Franken, Darrell. Healing Through Stress Management. 352p. 1985. pap. 14.95 (ISBN 0-934957-02-9); Set of 6 cassettes. 49.95 (ISBN 0-934957-09-6). Wellness Pubns.
--Health Through Stress Reduction. 392p. 1985. pap. 12.95 (ISBN 0-934957-01-0). Wellness Pubns.
Franken, Edmund A., et al, eds. Gastrointestinal Imaging in Pediatrics, 2-e. (Illus.). 909p. 1982. text ed. 83.75 (ISBN 0-06-140833-6, 14-08228, Harper Medical). Lippincott.
Franken, Peter, et al. Queues & Point Processes. (Probability & Mathematical Statistics Ser.). 208p. 1982. 32.95x (ISBN 0-471-10074-9, Pub. by Wiley-Interscience). Wiley.
Franken, Robert E. Human Motivation. LC 81-9937. 512p. 1981. text ed. 21.50 pub net (ISBN 0-8185-0461-7). Brooks-Cole.
Frankena, Frederick. Solar Energy Directories. (Architecture Ser.: Bibliography: No. A-1136). 50p. 1984. pap. 7.50 (ISBN 0-88066-846-6). Vance Biblios.
Frankena, M. W. & Scheffman, D. T. Economic Analysis of Provincial Land Use Policies in Ontario. (Ontario Economic Council Research Studies). 1980. pap. 7.50 (ISBN 0-8020-3364-4). U of Toronto Pr.
Frankena, Mark W. Urban Transportation Financing: Theory & Policy in Ontario. (Ontario Economic Council Research Studies). 248p. 1982. pap. 12.50 (ISBN 0-8020-3380-6). U of Toronto Pr.
Frankena, William K. Ethics. 2nd ed. (Foundations of Philosophy Ser.). 144p. 1973. pap. text ed. 11.95 (ISBN 0-13-290478-0). P-H.
--Philosophy of Education. 1965. pap. write for info. (ISBN 0-02-339490-0, 33949). Macmillan.
--Thinking about Morality. (Michigan Faculty Ser.). 112p. 1980. pap. 4.95 (ISBN 0-472-06316-2). U of Mich Pr.
Frankena, William K. & Granrose, John T. Introductory Readings in Ethics. 496p. 1974. text ed. 29.95 (ISBN 0-13-502112-X). P-H.
Frankena, William K., ed. The Philosophy & Future of Graduate Education. LC 80-14804. (Michigan Faculty Ser.). 272p. 1980. text ed. 15.00x (ISBN 0-472-09321-5); pap. 8.50x (ISBN 0-472-06321-9). U of Mich Pr.
Frankena, William K., ed. see Edwards, Jonathan.
Frankenberg, Lloyd. Pleasure Dome: On Reading Modern Poetry. LC 68-57701. 1968. Repr. of 1949 ed. 15.00x (ISBN 0-87752-038-0). Gordian.
--The Stain of Circumstance: Selected Poems. LC 73-85448. 237p. 1974. 12.95 (ISBN 0-8214-0138-6, 82-81412). Ohio U Pr.
Frankenberg, Lloyd, ed. Invitation to Poetry: A Round of Poems from John Skelton to Dylan Thomas. LC 68-8061. (Illus.). 1968. Repr. of 1956 ed. lib. bdg. 42.50 (ISBN 0-8371-0077-1, FRIP). Greenwood.
Frankenberg, Ronald, ed. Custom & Conflict in British Society. 361p. 1982. text ed. 21.50x (ISBN 0-7190-0855-7, 40671, Pub. by Manchester England). Humanities.
Frankenburg, Frank Von see Von Frankenburg, Richard & Cotton, Michael.
Frankenburg, W. G., et al. Advances in Catalysis & Related Subjects, 28 vols. Incl. Vol. 1. 1948. 80.00 (ISBN 0-12-007801-5); Vol. 2. 1950. 80.00 (ISBN 0-12-007802-3); Vol. 3. 1951. 80.00 (ISBN 0-12-007803-1); Vol. 4. 1952. 80.00 (ISBN 0-12-007804-X); Vol. 5. 1953. 80.00 (ISBN 0-12-007805-8); Vol. 6. 1954. 80.00 (ISBN 0-12-007806-6); Vol. 7. 1955. 80.00 (ISBN 0-12-007807-4); Vol. 8. 1956. 80.00 (ISBN 0-12-007808-2); Vol. 9. Proceedings. International Congress on Catalysis - Philadelphia - 1956. Eley, D. D., et al, eds. 1957. 80.00 (ISBN 0-12-007809-0); Vol. 10. 1958. 80.00 (ISBN 0-12-007810-4); Vol. 11. Eley, D. D., et al, eds. 1959. 80.00 (ISBN 0-12-007811-2); Vol. 12. 1960. 80.00 (ISBN 0-12-007812-0); Vol. 13. 1962. 80.00 (ISBN 0-12-007813-9); Vol. 14. Eley, D. D., et al, eds. 1963. 80.00 (ISBN 0-12-007814-7); Vol. 15. 1965. 80.00 (ISBN 0-12-007815-5); Vol. 16. 1966. 80.00 (ISBN 0-12-007816-3); Vol. 17. 1967. 80.00 (ISBN 0-12-007817-1); Vol. 18. 1968. 80.00 (ISBN 0-12-007818-X); Vol. 19. 1969. 80.00 (ISBN 0-12-007819-8); Vol. 20. 1969. 80.00 (ISBN 0-12-007820-1); Vol. 21. 1970. 80.00 (ISBN 0-12-007821-X); Vol. 22. 1972. 80.00 (ISBN 0-12-007822-8); Vol. 24. 1975. 90.00 (ISBN 0-12-007824-4); Vol. 25. 1976. 90.00 (ISBN 0-12-007825-2); Vol. 26. 1977. 90.00 (ISBN 0-12-007826-0); Vol. 27. 1979. 90.00 (ISBN 0-12-007827-9); Vol. 28. 1979. 90.00 (ISBN 0-12-007828-7). Vol. 23. 80.00 (ISBN 0-12-007823-6). Acad Pr.
--Advances in Catalysis & Related Subjects, Vol. 29. 1980. 70.00 (ISBN 0-12-007829-5). Acad Pr.
Frankenburg, William K., jt. auth. see Thorton, Susan M.
Frankenburg, William K. & Camp, Bonnie, eds. Pediatric Screening Tests. (Illus.). 564p. 1975. 31.25x (ISBN 0-398-03211-4). C C Thomas.
Frankenburg, William K. & Thornton, Susan M., eds. Child Health Care Communication. LC 84-13270. 400p. 1984. 39.95x (ISBN 0-03-072021-4). Praeger.
Frankenburg, William K., jt. ed. see Thornton, Susan M.
Frankenfield, T. C. Using Industrial Hydraulics. LC 84-81279. (Illus.). 406p. 1985. 35.00 (ISBN 0-932905-01-3). Penton IPC.
Frankenhoff, Charles A, et al. Environmental Planning & Development in the Caribbean. LC 76-56379. (Planning Series: A-1). (Illus.). 1976. 4.00 (ISBN 0-8477-2440-9). U of PR Pr.
Frankenstein, Alfred. After the Hunt. LC 68-31417. (Illus.). 1975. 65.00x (ISBN 0-520-02936-4). U of Cal Pr.
--Karel Appel. (Contemporary Artists Ser.). 1985. 65.00 (ISBN 0-8109-0364-4). Abrams.
--World of Copley. LC 74-113381. (Library of Art Ser.). (Illus.). (gr. 7 up). 1970. 19.94 (ISBN 0-8094-0284-X, Pub. by Time-Life). Silver.
Frankenstein, C. Impaired Intelligence: Pathology & Rehabilitation. 256p. 1970. 48.75 (ISBN 0-677-02810-5). Gordon.
--Varieties of Juvenile Delinquency. 264p. 1970. 48.75 (ISBN 0-677-02820-2). Gordon.
Frankenstein, Carl. They Think Again: Restoring Cognitive Abilities Through Teaching. 320p. 1979. pap. 14.95 (ISBN 0-442-22549-0). Van Nos Reinhold.
Frankenstein, Diane, jt. auth. see Frankenstein, George.
Frankenstein, George & Frankenstein, Diane. Brand Names: Who Owns What. 384p. 1981. 45.00 (ISBN 0-87196-420-1). Facts on File.
Frankenstein, John. American Art: Its Awful Attitude. Coyle, William, ed. 136p. 5.00 (ISBN 0-87972-037-9). Bowling Green Univ.
Frankenstein, Louise. Dialect Play-Readings. 125p. 1937. 5.00 (ISBN 0-573-60065-1). French.
--Junior Play-Readings. 137p. 1935. 5.00 (ISBN 0-573-69032-4). French.
--Playreadings. 132p. 1933. 5.00 (ISBN 0-573-60074-0). French.
Frankenstein, Marilyn. Basic Algebra. (Illus.). 1979. pap. text ed. 27.95 (ISBN 0-13-056788-4). P-H.
Frankenthaler, Marilyn R. Skills for Bilingual Legal Personnel. (Span. & Eng.). 1982. text ed. 9.30 wkbk. (ISBN 0-538-22680-3, V68). SW Pub.
Frankenthaler, Marilyn R., jt. auth. see Vanson, George N.
Frankfather, Dwight. The Aged in the Community: Managing Senility & Deviance. LC 77-8327. (Praeger Special Studies). 236p. 1977. 39.95x (ISBN 0-03-021936-1); pap. 18.95x (ISBN 0-03-021931-0). Praeger.
Frankfather, Dwight L., et al. Family Care of the Elderly: Public Initiatives & Private Obligations. LC 80-7577. 144p. 1981. 21.00x (ISBN 0-669-03759-1). Lexington Bks.
Frankfort, jt. auth. see Dye.
Frankfort, Ellen. Kathy Boudin & the Dance of Death. LC 83-40082. 226p. 1983. 14.95 (ISBN 0-8128-2946-8). Stein & Day.

--Kathy Boudin & the Dance of Death. 288p. 1984. pap. 3.95 (ISBN 0-8128-8108-7). Stein & Day.

Frankfort, H. A. Greek Tragedy. 3rd ed. LC 78-18440. 233p. 1979. pap. 8.95x (ISBN 0-06-494192-2). B&N Imports.

Frankfort, Hans, tr. see Schafer, Harald.

Frankfort, Henri. Ancient Egyptian Religion: An Interpretation. pap. 5.95xi (ISBN 0-06-130077-2, TB77, Torch). Har-Row.

--Ancient Egyptian Religion: An Interpretation. 16.00 (ISBN 0-8446-2084-X). Peter Smith.

--Art & Architecture of the Ancient Orient. (History of Art Ser: No. 7). (Illus.). 1977. pap. 18.95x (ISBN 0-14-056107-2, Pelican). Penguin.

--Art & Architecture of the Ancient Orient. rev. ed. (Pelican History of Art Ser.: No. 7). (Illus.). 1955. 50.00 (ISBN 0-670-13379-5, Pelican). Viking.

--Kingship & the Gods: A Study of Ancient Near Eastern Religion As the Integration of Society & Nature. LC 48-5158. 1978. pap. 12.95 (ISBN 0-226-26011-9, P766, Phoen). U of Chicago Pr.

Frankfort, Henri, et al. The Intellectual Adventure of Ancient Man: An Essay on Speculative Thought in the Ancient Near East. LC 47-1318. 1977. pap. 11.95 (ISBN 0-226-26008-9, P725, Phoen). U of Chicago Pr.

Frankfort, Nancy see Warshawsky & Constinett.

Frankfort, Roberta. Collegiate Women: Domesticity & Career in Turn of the Century America. LC 76-53614. 1977. 20.00x (ISBN 0-8147-2563-5). NYU Pr.

Frankforter, A. Daniel. A History of the Christian Movement: The Development of Christian Institutions. LC 77-8071. 332p. 1978. text ed. 22.95x (ISBN 0-88229-292-7); pap. 11.95x (ISBN 0-88229-568-3). Nelson-Hall.

Frankfurt am Main, jt. ed. see Stadt und Universitatsbibiliothek.

Frankfurt am Main, jt. ed. see Stadt und Universitatsbibliothek.

Frankfurt am Main, jt. ed. see Stadt und Universitatsbucherei.

Frankfurt Book Fair Editors. Who' Who at the Frankfurt Book Fair 1985: An Internationl Publishers' Guide. 16th ed. Albertshauser, Marianne, compiled by. 500p. 1985. lib. bdg. 20.00 (ISBN 3-598-21885-0). K G Saur.

Frankfurter, Felix. Commerce Clause Under Marshall, Taney & Waite. 11.25 (ISBN 0-8446-2086-6). Peter Smith.

--Felix Frankfurter on the Supreme Court: Extrajudicial Essays on the Court & the Constitution. Kurland, Philip B., ed. LC 70-99518. (Illus.). 1970. 30.00x (ISBN 0-674-29835-7, Belknap Pr). Harvard U Pr.

--Felix Frankfurter Reminisces. LC 78-5896. ix, 304p. 1978. Repr. of 1960 ed. lib. bdg. 23.50x (ISBN 0-313-20466-7, FRFF). Greenwood.

--Law & Politics. Prichard, E. F., Jr. & Macleish, A., eds. 11.25 (ISBN 0-8446-0097-0). Peter Smith.

--Of Law & Life & Other Things That Matter: Papers & Addresses of Felix Frankfurter, 1956-1963. Kurland, Philip B., ed. LC 65-7916. 1969. pap. 2.95 (ISBN 0-689-70076-8). Atheneum.

--Of Law & Life & Other Things That Matter: Papers & Addresses of Felix Frankfurter, 1956-1963. Kurland, Philip B., ed. LC 65-13221. (Illus.). 1965. 17.50x (ISBN 0-674-63100-5, Belknap Pr). Harvard U Pr.

Frankfurter, Felix & Greene, Nathan. The Labor Injunction. 1963. 12.75 (ISBN 0-8446-1190-5). Peter Smith.

Frankfurter, Felix & Landis, James M. Business of the Supreme Court: A Study in the Federal Judicial System. LC 26-24024. 1971. Repr. of 1928 ed. 35.00 (ISBN 0-384-16730-6). Johnson Repr.

Frankfurter, Felix, ed. Mr. Justice Brandeis. LC 73-37766. (American Constitutional & Legal History Ser). (Illus.). 232p. 1972. Repr. of 1932 ed. lib. bdg. 27.50 (ISBN 0-306-70430-7). Da Capo.

Frankfurter, Felix, ed. see Cleveland Foundation.

Frankfurter, Marion & Jackson, Gardner, eds. Letters of Sacco & Vanzetti. 412p. 1984. pap. 8.95 (ISBN 0-8065-0894-9). Citadel Pr.

Frankfurter, Marion D., ed. see Sacco, Nicola & Vanzetti, Bartolomeo.

Frankhauser, Eduard. Nudism, Obscenity & the Law. Knapp, Alozis, tr. (Illus.). 1.95 (ISBN 0-910550-09-3). Elysium.

Frankhouser, William L., et al. Gasless Combustion Synthesis of Refractory Compounds. LC 84-22640. (Illus.). 152p. 1985. 24.00 (ISBN 0-8155-1015-2). Noyes.

Franki, M. & Hillstrom, J. America's First Unfinished Revolution. (Illus.). 53p. (Orig.). 1976. pap. 1.00x (ISBN 0-686-32884-1). News & Letters MN.

Frankie, G. W. & Koehler, C. S., eds. Perspectives in Urban Entomology. 1978. 49.50 (ISBN 0-12-265250-9). Acad Pr.

Frankie, Gordon W. & Koehler, Carl S., eds. Urban Entomology: Interdisciplinary Perspectives. 512p. 1983. 45.00x (ISBN 0-03-057572-9). Praeger.

Frankiel, Ruth V., jt. auth. see Family Service Association of America, Research Dept.

Frankiel, Sandra S. Christianity: A Way of Salvation. LC 84-48770. 144p. (Orig.). 1985. pap. 6.68 (ISBN 0-06-063015-9, RD 498, HarpR). Har-Row.

Frankis, G., jt. auth. see Anderson, R. C.

Frankis, G., jt. auth. see Anderson, Roy C.

Frankis, G. G., jt. auth. see Anderson, R. C.

Frank-Kamenetskii, D. A. Diffusion & Heat Transfer in Chemical Kinetics. LC 68-26770. 574p. 1969. 45.00x (ISBN 0-306-30349-3, Plenum Pr). Plenum Pub.

--Plasma: The Fourth State of Matter. LC 71-165695. 159p. 1972. 35.00x (ISBN 0-306-30523-2, Plenum Pr). Plenum Pub.

Frankl, Daniel R. Electromagnetic Theory. (Illus.). 480p. 1986. text ed. 33.95 (ISBN 0-13-249095-1). P-H.

Frankl, Ernest, jt. auth. see Fiddes, Angela.

Frankl, Ernest, jt. auth. see Hall, Michael.

Frankl, F. Dictionnaire de Droit Social Francais-Allemand. 258p. (Fr. & Ger.). 1970. write for info. (ISBN 3-19-006279-X, M-7099). French & Eur.

Frankl, Ludwig A. The Jews in the East, 2 vols. Beaton, P., tr. LC 78-97278. 1975. Repr. of 1859 ed. Set. lib. bdg. 28.50x (ISBN 0-8371-2596-0, FRJE). Greenwood.

Frankl, Paul. Principles of Architectural History. O'Gorman, James F., tr. LC 68-18236. 1968. pap. 8.95 (ISBN 0-262-56013-5). MIT Pr.

Frankl, Paul T. New Dimensions: The Decorative Arts of Today in Words & Pictures. LC 75-15851. (Architecture and Decorative Arts Ser.). (Illus.). 122p. 1975. Repr. of 1928 ed. lib. bdg. 39.50 (ISBN 0-306-70741-1). Da Capo.

Frankl, Victor. The Unconscious God. 1976. pap. 5.95 (ISBN 0-671-22426-3, Touchstone Bks). S&S.

--Will to Meaning. pap. 6.95 (ISBN 0-452-25712-3, Z5472, Plume). NAL.

Frankl, Victor E. Psychotherapy & Existentialism. 1968. pap. 8.95 (ISBN 0-671-20056-9, Touchstone Bks). S&S.

--The Unheard Cry for Meaning. 1979. pap. 8.95 (ISBN 0-671-24736-0, Touchstone Bks). S&S.

Frankl, Viktor. Man's Search for Meaning. 1984. pap. 3.95 (ISBN 0-671-82161-X). PB.

--Man's Search for Meaning. 1985. 3.95 (ISBN 0-671-83465-7). WSP.

--Psychotherapy & Existentialism. 1985. pap. write for info. (ISBN 0-671-54729-1). WSP.

--The Unconscious God. 1985. pap. 3.50 (ISBN 0-671-54728-3). WSP.

--The Unheard Cry for Meaning. 1985. pap. 3.95 (ISBN 0-671-54163-3). WSP.

Frankl, Viktor E. The Doctor & the Soul: From Psychotherapy to Logotherapy. 320p. 1973. pap. 4.95 (ISBN 0-394-71866-6, Vin). Random.

Frankl, William S. & Brest, Albert N., eds. Valvular Heart Disease: Comprehensive Evaluation & Management. (Cardiovascular Clinics Ser.: Vol. 16, No. 2). (Illus.). 505p. 1985. text ed. 90.00 (ISBN 0-8036-3791-8). Davis Co.

Frankland, B., jt. auth. see Kendrick, R. E.

Frankland, F. W. The Story of Euclid. 59.95 (ISBN 0-8490-1132-9). Gordon Pr.

Frankland, J. C., et al. Decomposer Basidiomycetes: Their Biology & Ecology. LC 81-18145. (British Mycological Society Symposium Ser.: No. 4). (Illus.). 250p. 1982. 82.50 (ISBN 0-521-24634-2). Cambridge u Pr.

Frankland, Mark. Khrushchev. LC 67-16690. 1969. pap. 4.95 (ISBN 0-8128-1234-4). Stein & Day.

Frankland, Noble. Prince Henry: Duke of Gloucester. (Illus.). 343p. 1980. 25.00x (ISBN 0-297-77705-X, GWN 03582, Pub. by Weidenfeld & Nicolson England). Biblio Dist.

Frankland, Noble, ed. see Allen, Louis.

Frankland, Noble, ed. see Bond, Brian.

Frankland, Noble, ed. see Callahan, Raymond A.

Frankland, Noble, ed. see Cruickshank, Charles.

Frankland, Noble, ed. see Jackson, William.

Frankland, Noble, ed. see Upton, Anthony F.

Frankland, Noble, ed. see Warner, Geoffrey.

Frankland, Phillip & Airola, Stephen. Atlas of Selected Iowa Services. LC 78-16807. 160p. 1978. pap. text ed. 6.95x (ISBN 0-87745-085-4). U of Iowa Pr.

Frankland, Thomas N. The Pipe Fitter's & Pipe Welder's Handbook. 175p. 1981. 25.00x (ISBN 0-561-00012-3, Pub. by Bailey & Swinfen South Africa). State Mutual Bk.

Frankland, Thomas W. Pipe Fitter's & Welder's Handbook. (Illus., Orig.). 1984. pap. 6.95 (ISBN 0-02-802490-7). Glencoe.

--Pipe Template Layout. (Illus., Orig.). 1967. pap. 6.95 (ISBN 0-02-802400-1). Glencoe.

--Pipe Trades Pocket Manual. (Illus., Orig.). 1969. pap. 7.25 (ISBN 0-02-802410-9). Glencoe.

Frankland, William B. Theories of Parallelism. LC 72-7224. (Select Bibliographies Reprint Ser.). 1972. Repr. of 1910 ed. 13.00 (ISBN 0-8369-6931-6). Ayer Co Pubs.

Frankle, John T., jt. auth. see Klapper, Jacob.

Frankle, Reva T. Nutrition Education in the Medical School: A Curriculum Design. 56p. 6.00 (ISBN 0-935368-13-2). Nutrition Found.

Frankle, Reva T. & Owen, Anita Y. Nutrition in the Community: The Art of Delivering Services. LC 78-9144. 396p. 1978. text ed. 22.95 (ISBN 0-8016-1666-2). Mosby.

Franklin. Rat Race. 5.00 (ISBN 0-686-00480-9); pap. 2.00 (ISBN 0-686-00481-7). Fantasy Pub Co.

Franklin, et al, eds. Creep of Zirconium Alloys in Nuclear Reactors- STP 815. 284p. 1983. 42.00 (ISBN 0-8031-0259-3, 04-815000-35). ASTM.

Franklin, A. C. & Franklin, D. P. The J & P Transformer Book. 11th ed. Woth, C. A., ed. (Illus.). 320p. 1983. text ed. 99.95 (ISBN 0-408-00494-0). Butterworth.

Franklin, Afred L. Dictionnaire Historique Des Arts, Metiers & Professions Exerces Dans Paris Depuis Le Treizieme Siecle. (Biblio. & Ref. Ser.: No. 198). (Fr.). 1968. Repr. of 1906 ed. 49.00 (ISBN 0-8337-1231-4); 40.00 (ISBN 0-685-06747-5). B Franklin.

Franklin, Alan D., jt. ed. see Olin, Jacquelin S.

Franklin, Alexander. Seven Miracle Plays. 1963. pap. 7.95x (ISBN 0-19-831391-8). Oxford U Pr.

Franklin, Alfred L. Corporations Ouvrieres de Paris du Douzieme au Dix-Huitieme Siecle. LC 72-164481. (Research & Source Works Ser: No. 776). 1971. lib. bdg. 29.00 (ISBN 0-8337-1229-2). B Franklin.

Franklin, Alfred W., ed. The Challenge of Child Abuse. 310p. 1977. 40.00 (ISBN 0-8089-1056-6, 791360). Grune.

Franklin, Allan. The Principle of Inertia in the Middle Ages. LC 76-10515. 100p. (Orig.). 1976. pap. 7.95x (ISBN 0-87081-069-3). Colo Assoc.

Franklin, Anderson J. see Boykin, A. Wade, et al.

Franklin, B. A. The Industrial Executive. LC 73-10346. (Management History Ser.: No. 39). 153p. Repr. of 1926 ed. 17.50 (ISBN 0-87960-043-8). Hive Pub.

Franklin, Barbara A., tr. see Glissant, Edouard.

Franklin, Benjamin. Advice to a Young Man on the Choice of a Mistress. 59.95 (ISBN 0-87968-097-0). Gordon Pr.

--Anais Nin: A Bibliography. LC 72-619701. (Serif Series, Bibliographies & Checklists: No. 29). pap. 31.30 (ISBN 0-317-10335-0, 2051212). Bks Demand UMI.

--An Apology for Printers. Goodman, Randolph, ed. LC 72-12396. (Illus.). 40p. 1973. pap. 3.95 (ISBN 0-87491-146-X). Acropolis.

--Autobiography & Other Writings. Nye, Russel B., ed. LC 58-59440. (YA) (gr. 9 up). 1958. pap. 5.50 (ISBN 0-395-05130-4, RivEd). HM.

--Autobiography & Other Writings. 1961. pap. 2.75 (ISBN 0-451-51625-7, CE1625, Sig Classics). NAL.

--Autobiography & Selected Writings. Wecter, Dixon & Ziff, Larzer, eds. LC 59-14521. (Rinehart Editions Ser.). 1949. pap. text ed. 10.95 (ISBN 0-03-009890-4, HoltC). HR&W.

--Autobiography & Selected Writings. 1981. pap. 3.95 (T18, Mod LibC). Modern Lib.

--Autobiography of Benjamin Franklin. (Classics Ser.). (gr. 8 up). pap. 1.50 (ISBN 0-8049-0071-X, CL-71). Airmont.

--Autobiography of Benjamin Franklin. 1962. pap. 3.95 (ISBN 0-02-002910-1, Collier). Macmillan.

--Autobiography of Benjamin Franklin. Labaree, Leonard W., et al, eds. (Illus.). 1964. 30.00x (ISBN 0-300-00648-9); pap. 7.95x (ISBN 0-300-00147-9, Y117). Yale U Pr.

--Autobiography of Benjamin Franklin. 1981. Repr. lib. bdg. 18.95x (ISBN 0-89966-416-4). Buccaneer Bks.

--The Autobiography of Benjamin Franklin. May, J. A., et al, eds. (Norton Critical Editions Ser.). 1984. pap. 6.95x (ISBN 0-393-95294-0). Norton.

--The Autobiography of Benjamin Franklin. Wilson, R. Jackson, ed. LC 80-26312. (Modern Library College Editions). 223p. 1981. pap. text ed. 3.95 (ISBN 0-394-32669-5, RanC). Random.

--The Autobiography of Benjamin Franklin: A Genetic Text. Lemay, J. A. & Zall, P. M., eds. LC 78-25907. 352p. 1981. 29.95x (ISBN 0-87049-256-X). U of Tenn Pr.

--Bagatelles from Passy. LC 67-28990. 1967. 15.00x (ISBN 0-87130-005-2). Eakins.

--Benjamin Franklin's Letters to the Press, 1758-1775. Crane, Verner W., ed. (Institute of Early American History & Culture Ser.). lxv, 308p. 1950. 24.00x (ISBN 0-8078-0592-0). U of NC Pr.

--Essays on General Politics, Commerce & Political Economy. Sparks, Jared & Phillips, W., eds. LC 66-21673. Repr. of 1836 ed. 35.00 (ISBN 0-678-00292-4). Kelley.

--Historical Review of the Constitution & Government of Pennsylvania, from Its Origin. LC 75-141087. (Research Library of Colonial Americana). 1972. Repr. of 1759 ed. 37.50 (ISBN 0-405-03286-2). Ayer Co Pubs.

--The Old Mistresses' Apologue. Bell, Whitfield, ed. 1956. pap. 3.50 (ISBN 0-939084-05-8). Rosenbach Mus and Lib.

--On the Choice of a Mistress. 1976. 4.95 (ISBN 0-88088-187-9). Peter Pauper.

--The Papers of Benjamin Franklin, 18 vols. Incl. Vol. 1. January 6, 1706 Through December 31, 1734. Labaree, Leonard W., ed. (Illus.). lxxxviii, 400p. 1959 (ISBN 0-300-00650-0); Vol. 2. January 1, 1735 Through December 31, 1744. Labaree, Leonard W., ed. (Illus.). xxv, 471p. 1960 (ISBN 0-300-00651-9); Vol. 3. January 1, 1745 Through June 30, 1750. Labaree, Leonard W., ed. (Illus.). xxv, 513p. 1961 (ISBN 0-300-00652-7); Vol. 4. July 1, 1750 Through June 30, 1753. Labaree, Leonard W., ed. (Illus.). xxviii, 544p. 1961 (ISBN 0-300-00653-5); Vol. 5. July 1, 1753 Through March 31, 1755. Labaree, Leonard W., ed. (Illus.). xxvi, 575p. 1962 (ISBN 0-300-00654-3); Vol. 6. April 1, 1755 Through September 24, 1756. Labaree, Leonard W., ed. (Illus.). xxix, 581p. 1963 (ISBN 0-300-00655-1); Vol. 7. October 1, 1756 Through March 31, 1758. Lambaree, Leonard W., ed. (Illus.). xxvi, 427p. 1963 (ISBN 0-300-00657-8); Vol. 8. April 1, 1758 Through December 31, 1759. Labaree, Leonard W., ed. (Illus.). xxiv, 489p. 1965 (ISBN 0-300-00658-6); Vol. 9. January 1, 1760 Through December 31, 1761. Labaree, Leonard W., ed. (Illus.). xxvi, 429p. 1966 (ISBN 0-300-00659-4); Vol. 10. January 1, 1762 Through December 31, 1763. Labaree, Leonard W., ed. (Illus.). xxix, 459p. 1966 (ISBN 0-300-00660-8); Vol. 11. January 1, 1764 Through December 31, 1764. Labaree, Leonard W., ed. (Illus.). xxviii, 593p. 1967 (ISBN 0-300-00661-6); Vol. 12. January 1, 1765 Through December 31, 1765. Labaree, Leonard W., ed. (Illus.). 1968 (ISBN 0-300-01073-7); Vol. 13. January 1, 1766 Through December 31, 1766. Labaree, Leonard W., ed. (Illus.). 544p. 1969 (ISBN 0-300-01132-6); Vol. 14. January 1, 1767 Through December 31, 1767. Labaree, Leonard W., ed. (Illus.). 600p. 1970 (ISBN 0-300-01317-5); Vol. 15. January 1, 1768 Through December 31, 1768. Willcox, William B., ed. (Illus.). 1972 (ISBN 0-300-01469-4); Vol. 16. Papers of Benjamin Franklin: January 1 1769 Through December 31, 1769. Willcox, William B., ed. LC 59-12697. (Illus.) (ISBN 0-300-01570-4); Vol. 17. January 1, 1770 Through December 31, 1770. (Illus.). 1973 (ISBN 0-300-01596-8); Vol. 18. January 1, 1771 Through December 31, 1771. Willcox, William B., ed. LC 59-12697. 1974 (ISBN 0-300-01685-9); Vol. 19. January 1, 1792 Through December 31, 1772. 1976 (ISBN 0-300-01865-7); Vol. 20. January 1, 1773 Through December 31, 1773. 1976 (ISBN 0-300-01966-1); Vol. 21. January 1, 1774 Through March 22, 1775. 1978 (ISBN 0-300-02224-7). LC 59-12697. 55.00x ea. Yale U Pr.

--The Papers of Benjamin Franklin: March 23, 1775 Through October 27, 1776; October 27, 1776-April 30, 1977, 2 Vols, Vols. 22, 23. Willcox, William B., ed. LC 59-12697. 1982, 768 55.00x (ISBN 0-300-02618-8); text ed. 55.00x 1983 752pp (ISBN 0-300-02897-0). Yale U Pr.

--The Papers of Benjamin Franklin: May 1 Through September 30, 1777, Vol. 24. Willcox, William B., et al, eds. LC 59-12697. (Illus.). 672p. 1984. text ed. 55.00x (ISBN 0-300-03162-9). Yale U Pr.

--Poor Richard's Almanac: An Almanac. facsimile ed. 1977. pap. 3.50x (ISBN 0-939084-07-4). U Pr of Va.

--Poor Richard's Almanack. (Classics Ser.). (gr. 7 up). dust jacket 8.95 (ISBN 0-88088-918-7). Peter Pauper.

--Poor Richard's Almanack. 28p. 1983. pap. 3.50 (ISBN 0-939084-07-4). U Pr of Va.

--The Sayings of Poor Richard: The Prefaces, Proverbs & Poems of Benjamin Franklin. Leicester, Paul, compiled by. LC 74-23378. 1975. Repr. of 1890 ed. 24.50 (ISBN 0-8337-1198-9). B Franklin.

--Writings of Benjamin Franklin, 10 Vols. Smyth, Albert H., et al, eds. LC 68-24976. (American History & Americana Ser., No. 47). 1969. Repr. of 1907 ed. lib. bdg. 350.00x (ISBN 0-8383-0194-0). Haskell.

Franklin, Benjamin & Schneider, Duane. Anais Nin: An Introduction. LC 79-10635. 1980. 20.00x (ISBN 0-8214-0395-8, 82-82857); pap. 12.00x (ISBN 0-8214-0432-6, 82-82865). Ohio U Pr.

Franklin, Benjamin, ed. Poetry of the Minor Connecticut Wits, 1791-1818. LC 68-17015. 1970. 90.00x (ISBN 0-8201-1066-3). Schol Facsimiles.

--The Prose of the Minor Connecticut Wits, 3 vols. LC 74-11124. 1500p. 1974. Repr. 200.00x set (ISBN 0-8201-1132-5). Schol Facsimiles.

Franklin, Benjamin E. How to Become a Successful Investment Advisor. (Illus.). 129p. 1984. 77.75x (ISBN 0-86654-110-1); pap. 19.75x (ISBN 0-86654-111-X). Inst Econ Finan.

Franklin, Beverly A. The Fun & Hassles of Adoption. 1983. 6.95 (ISBN 0-533-05620-9). Vantage.

Franklin, Carolyn, jt. auth. see Rubey, Jane A.

Franklin, Charles A. The Bearing of Coat-Armour by Ladies. LC 73-8999. (Illus.). 144p. 1973. Repr. of 1923 ed. 12.50 (ISBN 0-8063-0574-6). Genealog Pub.

Franklin, Charles L. Negro Labor Unionist of New York. LC 68-58573. (Columbia University. Studies in the Social Sciences: No. 420). Repr. of 1936 ed. 27.50 (ISBN 0-404-51420-0). AMS Pr.

Franklin, Clay. Anybody We Know. 1982. 5.00 (ISBN 0-573-60080-5). French.

--I Step from a Famous Story. 126p. 1966. 5.00 (ISBN 0-573-60067-8). French.

--Mixed Company. 100p. 1959. 5.00 (ISBN 0-573-60070-8). French.
--Skits for the Young in Heart. 1977. pap. 3.00 (ISBN 0-686-38386-9). Eldridge Pub.
Franklin, Clyde W. Theoretical Perspectives in Social Psychology. 1982. text ed. 21.95 (ISBN 0-316-29199-4). Little.
Franklin, Clyde W., II. The Changing Definition of Masculinity. (Perspectives in Sexuality Ser.). 246p. 1984. 29.50x (ISBN 0-306-41554-2, Plenum Pr). Plenum Pub.
Franklin Co. Chapter OGS & Martin, W. I. Franklin County, Ohio, History. 1.50 (ISBN 0-318-04652-0). OH Genealogical.
Franklin Conference, 4th. Innovation & the American Economy. 140p. 1980. pap. text ed. 8.95 (ISBN 0-89168-033-0). L Erlbaum Assocs.
Franklin, D. & Adamson, R. B. Zirconium in the Nuclear Industry - STP 824: Sixth International Symposium. LC 83-71644. 850p. 1984. text ed. 84.00 (ISBN 0-8031-0270-4). ASTM.
Franklin, D., ed. Zirconium in the Nuclear Industry, Fifth Conference - STP 754. 498p. 1981. 52.00 (ISBN 0-8031-0754-4, 04-754000-35). ASTM.
Franklin, D. P., jt. auth. see Franklin, A. C.
Franklin, Donald. Sonnets. 84p. (Orig.). 1973. pap. 3.95 (ISBN 0-914714-00-7). Donald Franklin.
Franklin, Doug. Keep the Change. (Illus.). 100p. (Orig.). 1985. pap. 7.95 (ISBN 0-930867-02-5). S O S Pubs.
Franklin, Douglas & Jankowski, Thaddeus. Massachusetts Property Re-Evaluation: Taxpayers' Rights & Legal Procedures. LC 82-73442. 176p. (Orig.). 1983. pap. 13.00 (ISBN 0-88063-030-2). Butterworth Legal Pubs.
Franklin, E. C. Clinical Immunology Update, 1981: Reviews for Physicians. 428p. 1980. 42.50 (ISBN 0-444-00416-5, Biomedical Pr). Elsevier.
Franklin, E. C., ed. Clinical Immunology Update 1979: Reviews for Physicians. 352p. 1979. 42.50 (ISBN 0-444-00312-6, Biomedical Pr). Elsevier.
--Clinical Immunology Update, 1983. 410p. 1983. 48.50 (ISBN 0-444-00711-3, Biomedical Pr). Elsevier.
Franklin, Elizabeth. Shortcuts. 256p. 1984. 15.95 (ISBN 0-8119-0703-1). Fell.
Franklin, Eric N., jt. auth. see Watkins, William H.
Franklin, Fay, jt. auth. see Conil, Jean.
Franklin, Francis, ed. see Bowers, Claude G. & Browder, Earl.
Franklin, Frank G. Legislative History of Naturalization in the United States: From the Revolutionary War to 1861. LC 69-18776. (American Immigration Collection Ser., No. 1). 1969. Repr. of 1906 ed. 13.00 (ISBN 0-405-00524-5). Ayer Co Pubs.
--Legislative History of Naturalization in the United States from the Revolutionary War to 1861. LC 75-119538. Repr. of 1906 ed. 27.50x (ISBN 0-678-00689-X). Kelley.
Franklin, G. E. Palestine Depicted & Described. 1976. lib. bdg. 69.95 (ISBN 0-8490-2399-8). Gordon Pr.
Franklin, Gene F. & Powell, J. David. Digital Control of Dynamic Systems. LC 79-16377. 1980. text ed. 34.95 (ISBN 0-201-02891-3); solution manual 2.00 (ISBN 0-201-02892-1). Addison-Wesley.
Franklin, George E. From Cotswolds to High Sierras. LC 66-20373. (Illus.). 167p. 1966. 4.00 (ISBN 0-87004-046-4). Caxton.
Franklin, George, Jr., jt. auth. see Voight, Randall L.
Franklin, Grace A. & Ripley, Randall B. CETA: Politics & Policy, 1973-1982. LC 84-5145. 268p. 1984. text ed. 24.95x (ISBN 0-87049-437-6). U of Tenn Pr.
Franklin, Grace A., jt. auth. see Ripley, Randall B.
Franklin, Grace A., jt. ed. see Ripley, Randall B.
Franklin, H. Bruce. American Prisoners & Ex-Prisoners: Their Writings: An Annotated Bibliography of Published Works, 1798-1981. LC 82-11682. 64p. 1982. pap. 5.95 (ISBN 0-88208-147-0). Lawrence Hill.
--Future Perfect: American Science Fiction of the Nineteenth Century. rev. ed. 1978. pap. 9.95 (ISBN 0-19-502323-4, GB241, GB). Oxford U Pr.
--Prison Literature in America: The Victim As Criminal & Artist. 303p. 1982. pap. 8.95 (ISBN 0-88208-146-2). Lawrence Hill.
--Robert A. Heinlein: America As Science Fiction. (Science Fiction Writers Ser.). (Illus.). 1980. 25.00x (ISBN 0-19-502746-9, GB); pap. 7.95 (ISBN 0-19-502747-7, GB 610). Oxford U Pr.
--The Wake of the Gods: Melville's Mythology. 1963. pap. 15.95x (ISBN 0-8047-0137-7). Stanford U Pr.
Franklin, H. Bruce, ed. Countdown to Midnight. 288p. 1984. pap. 2.95 (ISBN 0-87997-983-6). DAW Bks.
--Future Perfect: American Science Fiction of the Nineteenth Century. 1978. 25.00x (ISBN 0-19-502322-6). Oxford U Pr.
Franklin, Harold L. see Alimayo, Chikuyo, pseud.
Franklin, Herbert M., jt. auth. see Brenner, Joel F.
Franklin, Howard. A Flowers Arrangers Guide to Showing. 1979. 14.95 (ISBN 0-7134-3321-3, Pub by Batsford England). David & Charles.
Franklin, Howard M., et al. Golden Delicious Games for the Apple Computer. LC 81-23074. (Self Teaching Guides Ser.: No. 1-704). 150p. 1982. pap. 12.95 (ISBN 0-471-09083-2); Avail. software disk set 47.90 (ISBN 0-471-89842-2); disk 34.95 (ISBN 0-471-86837-X). Wiley.
Franklin Institute. ENGUIDE: A Guide to Bibliographic Data for Users of Environmental Information. 100p. 1980. pap. text ed. 8.95 (ISBN 0-686-70970-5). L Erlbaum Assocs.
Franklin Institute Laboratories. Investigation of Copper-Containing Catalysts for Catalytic Afterburners. 76 ed. 76p. 1963. 11.40 (ISBN 0-317-34532-X, 11). Intl Copper.
Franklin, J. Methods of Mathematical Economics, Linear & Nonlinear Economics: Fixed-Point Theories. (Undergraduate Texts in Mathematics Ser.). (Illus.). 297p. 1980. 29.00 (ISBN 0-387-90481-6). Springer-Verlag.
Franklin, J. E. Black Girl from Genesis to Revelations. LC 74-30386. 1977. 9.95 (ISBN 0-88258-019-1). Howard U Pr.
Franklin, J. L., jt. auth. see Field, F. H.
Franklin, J. L., ed. Ion-Molecule Reactions, 2 vols. LC 77-179758. 393p. 1972. Vol. 1, 362p. 59.50x (ISBN 0-306-30551-8, Plenum Pr); Vol. 2. 59.50x (ISBN 0-306-30552-6). Plenum Pub.
Franklin, Jack L. & Thrasher, Jean H. An Introduction to Program Evaluation. LC 76-4789. 246p. 1976. 16.50 (ISBN 0-471-27519-0). Krieger.
Franklin, Jacque. Where Do I Look? (Illus.). 40p. (Orig.). pap. 6.95 (ISBN 0-938216-20-1). GCNHA.
Franklin, James. New German Cinema. (Filmmakers Ser.). 1983. lib. bdg. 20.95 (ISBN 0-8057-9288-0, Twayne). G K Hall.
--Present State of Hayti (Saint Domingo) 412p. 1972. Repr. of 1828 ed. 35.00x (ISBN 0-7146-2707-0, F Cass Co). Biblio Dist.
--Present State of Hayti: Saint Domingo-with Remarks on Its Agriculture, Commerce, Laws, Regligion, Finance & Population. LC 79-109325. Repr. of 1828 ed. 25.00x (ISBN 0-8371-3591-5, FRH&). Greenwood.
Franklin, James C. Mystical Transformations: The Imagery of Liquids in the Work of Mechthild Von Magdeburg. LC 75-5248. 192p. 1976. 18.50 (ISBN 0-8386-1738-7). Fairleigh Dickinson.
Franklin, James L. Pompeii: The Electoral Programmata, Campaigns & Politics. 141p. write for info. Am Acad Rome.
Franklin, James T. Mid-Day Gleanings: A Book for Home & Holiday Readings. LC 76-168134. Repr. of 1893 ed. 16.00 (ISBN 0-404-00052-5). AMS Pr.
Franklin, Jane, jt. ed. see Gettleman, Marvin E.
Franklin, Jerome L., ed. Human Resource Development in the Organization: A Guide to Information Sources. LC 76-28289. (Management Information Guide Ser.: No. 35). 1978. 60.00x (ISBN 0-8103-0835-5). Gale.
Franklin, Jessie M. Grandparents Are Special. LC 79-51761. 1979. 8.95 (ISBN 0-8054-5639-2). Broadman.
Franklin, Jill. The Gentleman's Country House & Its Plan 1835-1914. (Illus.). 272p. 1981. 42.50 (ISBN 0-7100-0622-5). Routledge & Kegan.
Franklin, Jimmie L. The Blacks in Oklahoma. LC 79-24318. (Newcomers to a New Land Ser.: Vol. 5). (Illus.). 96p. (Orig.). 1980. pap. 3.95 (ISBN 0-8061-1671-4). U of Okla Pr.
--Journey Toward Hope: A History of Blacks in Oklahoma. LC 82-7101. 270p. 1982. 19.95 (ISBN 0-8061-1810-5). U of Okla Pr.
Franklin, Joe. Classics of the Silent Screen. (Illus.). 256p. 1983. pap. 9.95 (ISBN 0-8065-0181-2). Citadel Pr.
--Encyclopedia of Comedians. 1979. 14.95 (ISBN 0-8065-0566-4). Citadel Pr.
--Joe Franklin's Awfully Corny Joke Book. LC 80-66450. 230p. (Orig.). 1980. pap. 4.95 (ISBN 0-87754-142-6). Chelsea Hse.
--Joe Franklin's Encyclopedia of Comedians. (Illus.). 384p. 1981. pap. 7.95 (ISBN 0-8065-0774-8). Citadel Pr.
--Seventy Years of Great Comics. Smith, Ron, ed. (Celebrity Photo Scrapbooks Ser.). (Illus.). 72p. 1981. pap. 6.95 (ISBN 0-938294-06-7). Global Comm.
Franklin, Joel N. Matrix Theory. 1968. ref. ed. 33.95 (ISBN 0-13-565648-6). P-H.
Franklin, John. Narrative of a Journey to the Shores of the Polar Sea, in the Years 1819 - 1822. LC 68-55187. 1968. Repr. of 1823 ed. lib. bdg. 40.25x (ISBN 0-8371-1447-0, FRPS). Greenwood.
--Narrative of a Journey to the Shores of the Polar Sea in the Years 1819-20-21-22. 1978. Repr. lib. bdg. 20.00 (ISBN 0-8492-4700-4). R West.
--Narrative of a Second Expedition to the Shores of the Polar Sea. LC 71-133871. (Illus.). 1971. Repr. 35.00 (ISBN 0-8048-1008-7). C E Tuttle.
Franklin, John, et al, trs. see Felipe, Leon.
Franklin, John H. Free Negro in North Carolina, Seventeen Ninety to Eighteen Sixty. (Illus.). 1971. pap. 2.25x (ISBN 0-393-00579-8, Norton Lib). Norton.
--From Slavery to Freedom: A History of Negro Americans. 5th ed. 554p. 1980. pap. text ed. 22.00 (ISBN 0-394-50774-6, KnopfC); pap. 15.00 (ISBN 0-394-32256-8); wkbk. 4.95 (ISBN 0-394-32474-9). Knopf.
--George Washington Williams: A Biography. LC 85-5800. (Illus.). 384p. 1985. 24.95 (ISBN 0-226-26083-6). U of Chicago Pr.
--George Washington Williams: The Massachusetts Years. 1983. pap. 3.50 (ISBN 0-912296-58-5, Dist. by U Pr of Va). Am Antiquarian.
--Militant South, Eighteen Hundred to Eighteen Sixty-One. LC 56-10160. 1970. Repr. 20.00t (ISBN 0-674-57450-8, Belknap Pr). Harvard U Pr.
--Racial Equality in America. LC 76-26168. 1976. 7.95x (ISBN 0-226-26073-9). U of Chicago Pr.
--Reconstruction after the Civil War. LC 61-15931. (Chicago History of American Civilization Ser). (Illus.). 1962. 22.00x (ISBN 0-226-26075-5); pap. 8.00x (ISBN 0-226-26076-3, CHAC6). U of Chicago Pr.
--A Southern Odyssey - Travelers in the Antebellum North. LC 74-27190. (Illus.). 320p. 1976. 27.50x (ISBN 0-8071-0161-3); pap. 6.95x (ISBN 0-8071-0351-9). La State U Pr.
Franklin, John H., ed. Three Negro Classics. Incl. Up from Slavery. Washington, Booker T; The Souls of Black Folk. Du Bois, William E; The Autobiography of an Ex-Colored Man. Johnson, James W. (YA) (gr. 7 up). 1965. pap. 4.95 (ISBN 0-380-01581-1, 60260-1, Discus). Avon.
Franklin, John H. & Meier, August, eds. Black Leaders of the Twentieth Century. LC 81-11454. (Illus.). 390p. 1982. 19.95x (ISBN 0-252-00870-7); pap. 7.95 (ISBN 0-252-00939-8). U of Ill Pr.
--Black Leaders of the Twentieth Century. 1983. pap. 7.95 (ISBN 0-252-00939-8). U of Ill Pr.
Franklin, John H., ed. see Dubofsky, Melvyn.
Franklin, John H., ed. see Horsman, Reginald.
Franklin, John H., ed. see Levy, Eugene.
Franklin, John H., ed. see Lynch, John R.
Franklin, John H., ed. see Mohl, Raymond A.
Franklin, John H., ed. see Tourgee, Albion W.
Franklin, John H., et al. Ethnicity in American Life. 47p. 2.95 (ISBN 0-88464-012-4). ADL.
Franklin, John Hope, jt. auth. see Clark, Kenneth B.
Franklin, Jon & Doelp, Alan. Shocktrauma. 256p. 1981. pap. 2.95 (ISBN 0-449-24387-7, Crest). Fawcett.
Franklin, Jon & Sutherland, John. Guinea Pig Doctors: The Drama of Medical Research Through Self-Experimentation. LC 83-19477. (Illus.). 317p. 1984. 17.95 (ISBN 0-688-02666-4). Morrow.
Franklin, Joseph. African: A Photographic Essay on Black Women of Ghana & Nigeria. LC 77-81436. 1977. 9.95 (ISBN 0-685-99392-2, Pub. by Wallingford Bks). Chulainn Press.
--African: A Photographic Essay on Black Women of Ghana & Nigeria. LC 77-81456. (Illus.). 138p. 1977. pap. 12.00 (ISBN 0-317-07102-5, Pub. by Wallingford Bks). Three Continents.
Franklin, Julia, tr. see Brink, Bernhard A. Ten.
Franklin, Julia, tr. see Rodbertus, Johann K.
Franklin, Julian H. Jean Bodin & the Rise of Absolutist Theory. (Cambridge Studies in the History & Theory of Politics). 1973. 21.95 (ISBN 0-521-20000-8). Cambridge U Pr.
--Jean Bodin & the Sixteenth-Century Revolution in the Methodology of Law & History. LC 77-1187. 163p. 1977. Repr. of 1963 ed. lib. bdg. 22.50x (ISBN 0-8371-9525-X, FRJEB). Greenwood.
--John Locke & the Theory of Sovereignty: Mixed Monarchy & the Right of Resistance in the Political Thought of the English Revolution. LC 77-80833. (Cambridge Studies in the History & Theory of Politics). 160p. 1981. pap. 10.95 (ISBN 0-521-28547-X). Cambridge U Pr.
--John Locke & the Theory of Soverenity. LC 77-80833. (Studies in the History & Theory of Politics). 1978. 32.50 (ISBN 0-521-21758-X). Cambridge U Pr.
Franklin, Julian H., ed. Constitutionalism & Resistance in the Sixteenth Century: Three Treatises by Holtman, Beza & Mornay. LC 71-77131. 1969. 28.50x (ISBN 0-672-53519-X). Irvington.
Franklin, Justin D. & Bouchard, Robert F., eds. Guidebook to the Freedom of Information & Privacy Acts. LC 79-27406. 1980. 50.00 (ISBN 0-87632-310-7). Boardman.
Franklin, Karl, et al. Tolai Language Course. (Asia-Pacific Ser.: No. 7). 140p. 1974. pap. 4.25x o. p. (ISBN 0-88312-207-3); microfiche 2.25x (ISBN 0-88312-307-X). Summer Inst Ling.
Franklin, Kay & Schaeffer, Norma. Duel for the Dunes: Land Use Conflict on the Shores of Lake Michigan. LC 82-25601. (Illus.). 302p. 1983. 18.95 (ISBN 0-252-01034-5); pap. 7.95 (ISBN 0-252-00939-8). U of Ill Pr.
Franklin, Kay, jt. auth. see Schaeffer, Norma.
Franklin, Kenneth H. The Executive's Guide to Health & Fitness. (Illus.). 1985. 14.95 (ISBN 0-910187-04-5). Economics Pr.
Franklin, Kenneth J. A Monograph on Veins. (Illus.). 410p. 1937. photocopy ed. 36.50x (ISBN 0-398-04258-6). C C Thomas.
Franklin, Kenneth J., ed. see Harvey, William.
Franklin, Kenneth R. & Cross, H. Russell, eds. Meat Science & Technology Proceedings: An International Symposium. 398p. 1983. 7.00 (ISBN 0-88700-000-2). Natl Live Stock.
Franklin, Leslie, tr. see Egolz, W.
Franklin, Linda. Antiques & Collectibles: A Bibliography of Works in English, 16th Century to 1976. LC 77-25026. (Illus.). 1115p. 1978. 45.00 (ISBN 0-8108-1092-1). Scarecrow.
--Library Display Ideas. 1985. 13.95 (ISBN 0-317-18417-2). McFarland & Co.
Franklin, Linda C. Address Book. (Old Fashioned Keepbook). (Illus.). 128p. 1981. 16.00 (ISBN 0-934504-07-5). Tree Comm.
--A Baby Book for... (Old Fashioned Keepbook Ser.). (Illus.). 96p. 1980. 12.00 (ISBN 0-934504-03-2). Tree Comm.
--A Birthday Book. (Old Fashioned Keepbook). (Illus.). 128p. 1980. 12.00 (ISBN 0-934504-06-7). Tree Comm.
--Display & Publicity Ideas for Small & Mid-Sized Libraries. LC 84-43229. 272p. 1985. pap. 14.95 (ISBN 0-89950-168-0). McFarland & Co.
--Food Lovers' Notebook. (Old Fashioned Keepbook Ser.). (Illus.). 96p. 1984. 12.00 (ISBN 0-934504-35-0). Tree Comm.
--Library Display Ideas. LC 80-17036. (Illus.). 244p. 1980. lib. bdg. 12.95x (ISBN 0-89950-008-0); pap. 9.95x (ISBN 0-89950-009-9). McFarland & Co.
--Our Old Fashioned Country Diary for 1986. (Old Fashioned Keepbk.). (Illus.). 144p. 1982. 12.00 (ISBN 0-934504-20-2). Tree Comm.
--Three Hundred Years of Kitchen Collectibles. 2nd ed. (Illus.). 599p. (Orig.). 1984. pap. 10.95 (ISBN 0-89689-041-4). Bks Americana.
--Travel Diary. (Old Fashioned Keepbook Ser.). (Illus.). 96p. 1983. 8.00 (ISBN 0-934504-19-9). Tree Comm.
--Wedding Memory Keepbook. (Illus.). 60p. 1985. 20.00 (ISBN 0-317-27419-8). Tree Comm.
--Wedding Notebook for the Bride. (Old Fashioned Keepbook Ser.). (Illus.). 128p. 1980. 12.00 (ISBN 0-934504-02-4). Tree Comm.
Franklin, Linda Campbell. Three Hundred Years of Kitchen Collectibles. (Illus.). 300p. 11.75 (ISBN 0-318-14907-9, A157). Midwest Old Settlers.
Franklin, Louis M. The CB PLL Data Book. (Illus.). 130p. (Orig.). 1982. pap. 14.95 (ISBN 0-943132-05-3). CB City Intl.
Franklin, Lynn & Harrison, Shirley. The Psychic Search. Swenson, Allan, ed. 280p. (Orig.). 1981. pap. 7.95 (ISBN 0-930096-16-9). G Gannett.
--Psychic Search. 280p. 1981. 12.95 (ISBN 0-930096-22-3). G Gannett.
Franklin, M. & Dotts, Maryann J. Clues to Creativity, Vol. 1: A-I. (Orig.). 1974. pap. 4.95 (ISBN 0-377-00015-9). Friend Pr.
--Clues to Creativity, Vol. 2: J-P. (Orig.). 1975. pap. 4.95 (ISBN 0-377-00041-8). Friend Pr.
--Clues to Creativity, Vol. 3: R-Z. (Orig.). 1976. pap. 4.95 (ISBN 0-377-00042-6). Friend Pr.
Franklin, M. B., jt. ed. see Smith, N. R.
Franklin, M. J. British Biscuit Tins. (Illus.). 220p. 1984. 60.00 (ISBN 0-904568-11-3, Pub. by New Cavendish England). Schiffer.
--British Biscuit Tins, 1868-1939: An Aspect of Decorative Packaging. 1980. 99.95 (ISBN 0-904568-11-3, NO.0224, Pub. by New Cavendish). Methuen Inc.
Franklin, M. M. Refreshing English Poems. 1983. 5.95 (ISBN 0-533-05405-2). Vantage.
Franklin, Marc A. The First Amendment & the Fourth Estate, Communications Law for Undergraduates. 2nd ed. LC 81-5055. 715p. 1981. text ed. 17.75 (ISBN 0-88277-025-X). Foundation Pr.
--Mass Media Law, Cases & Materials On. 2nd ed. LC 82-7272. (University Casebook Ser.). 946p. 1982. text ed. 26.00 (ISBN 0-88277-060-8). Foundation Pr.
--Mass Media Law, Cases & Materials On: 1985 Supplement. 2nd ed. (University Casebook Ser.). 180p. 1984. pap. text ed. write for info (ISBN 0-88277-215-5). Foundation Pr.
Franklin, Marc A. & Carter, Barton T. The First Amendment & the Fourth Estate: The Dynamics of Communication Law. 3rd ed. LC 85-6929. 116p. 1985. write for info. (ISBN 0-88277-240-6). Foundation Pr.
Franklin, Marc A. & Rabin, Robert L. Tort Law & Alternatives, Cases & Materials on. 3rd ed. LC 83-5583. (University Casebook Ser.). 1006p. 1983. text ed. 28.00 (ISBN 0-88277-118-3). Foundation Pr.
Franklin, Margery B. & Barten, Sybil S., eds. Development Process: Selected Papers of Heinz Werner, 2 vols. LC 77-92187. 1978. Set. 80.00 (ISBN 0-8236-8405-9). Intl Univs Pr.
Franklin, Margery B., jt. ed. see Barten, Sybil S.
Franklin, Margery B., jt. ed. see Smith, Nancy R.
Franklin, Marian P., ed. Classroom Centers & Stations in America & Britain. LC 73-10240. 1973. 29.50x (ISBN 0-8422-5120-0); pap. text ed. 12.50x (ISBN 0-8422-0327-3). Irvington.
Franklin, Mark. Programming the IBM Personal Computer: Organization & Assembly Language Programming. 1984. 19.95 (ISBN 0-03-062862-8). HR&W.
Franklin, Max. Vegas. 1978. pap. 1.75 (ISBN 0-345-28051-2). Ballantine.
Franklin, Meine J., jt. ed. see Blair, Walter.
Franklin, Michael. British Biscuit Tins. 1984. 9.95 (ISBN 0-905209-62-1, Pub. by Victoria & Albert Mus UK). Faber & Faber.

Franklin, Michael, et al. A Reader's Guide to Fantasy. 224p. 1982. pap. 2.95 (ISBN 0-380-80333-X, 80333-X). Avon.

Franklin, Miles. Bring the Monkey. LC 84-17360. 248p. 1985. 15.95 (ISBN 0-7022-1817-0). U of Queensland Pr.

--The End of My Career. 1984. pap. 3.95 (ISBN 0-671-49937-8). WSP.

--My Brilliant Career. 252p. 1980. 9.95 (ISBN 0-312-55599-7). St Martin.

--My Brilliant Career. 272p. 1981. pap. 3.95 (ISBN 0-671-45915-5). WSP.

--On Dearborn Street. LC 81-11570. 224p. (YA) 1982. 14.95 (ISBN 0-7022-1636-4). U of Queensland Pr.

Franklin, Miriam A. & Dixon, James G., III. Rehearsal: The Principles & Practice of Acting for the Stage. 6th ed. (Illus.). 272p. 1983. pap. 21.95 (ISBN 0-13-771550-1). P-H.

Franklin, Myrtle & Bor, Michael. Sir Moses Montefiore 1784-1885. (Illus.). 129p. 1985. 24.50 (ISBN 0-8149-0902-7). Vanguard.

Franklin, N. N. Economics in South Africa. 2nd ed. LC 55-4788. Repr. of 1954 ed. 17.00 (ISBN 0-527-31200-2). Kraus Repr.

Franklin, P., ed. see Bauer-Lechner, Natalie.

Franklin, Patrick. The Uncertainty of Strangers & Other Stories. LC 85-7653. 152p. 1985. pap. 7.95 (ISBN 0-912516-91-7). Grey Fox.

Franklin, Paul L. Educational Information & Advisement Services: A Resource Guide for Creating Local Services & Building Statewide Networks. 222p. 5.50 (ISBN 0-318-15738-1). Natl Inst Work.

Franklin, Paula. Indians of North America: Survey of Tribes That Inhabit the Continent. (Illus.). 1979. 9.95 (ISBN 0-679-20700-7). McKay.

--The Unwatched Pot. LC 75-79991. (Illus.). 144p. 1975. 9.95 (ISBN 0-916752-00-3). Dorison Hse.

Franklin, Paula & Franklin, Richard. Tomorrow's Track. 1976. pap. 4.95 (ISBN 0-934698-09-0). BDR Learn Prods.

Franklin, Paula, retold by. The Seventh Night of July. LC 84-40798. (Stories from Around the World Ser.). (Illus.). 28p. (ps-3). 1985. pap. 3.95 (ISBN 0-382-09047-0). Silver.

Franklin, Paula, tr. see Aka, Masago.

Franklin, Paula, tr. see Nagasaki, Gennosuke.

Franklin, Peter, jt. auth. see Franklin, Walt.

Franklin, Peter J. & Woodhead, Caroline. The U. K. Life Assurance Industry: A Study in Applied Economics. (Illus.). 390p. 1980. 80.00x (ISBN 0-85664-654-7, Pub. by Croom Helm Ltd). Longwood Pub Group.

Franklin, Phyllis, jt. auth. see Brod, Richard I.

Franklin, Phyllis, jt. ed. see Brod, Richard I.

Franklin, Phyllis, et al. Sexual & Gender Harassment in the Academy: A Guide for Faculty, Students, & Administrators. LC 81-14059. iii, 75p. (Orig.). 1981. pap. 6.00x (ISBN 0-87352-333-4, B811). Modern Lang.

Franklin, R. N., tr. see Gekker, I. R.

Franklin, R. N., tr. see Lifshitz, E. M. & Pitaevskii, L. P.

Franklin, R. W. Editing of Emily Dickinson: A Reconsideration. (Illus.). 206p. 1967. 17.00x (ISBN 0-299-04380-0). U of Wis Pr.

Franklin, R. W., ed. see Williams, George H.

Franklin, Ralph W., ed. see Dickinson, Emily.

Franklin, Raoul N. Plasma Phenomena in Gas Discharges. (Oxford Engineering Science Ser.). (Illus.). 1976. 59.00x (ISBN 0-19-856113-X). Oxford U Pr.

Franklin, Raymond S. American Capitalism: Two Visions. 1977. pap. text ed. 6.95 (ISBN 0-394-31261-9, RanC). Random.

Franklin, Rena. Soups of Hakafri Restaurant: Kosher Edition. LC 81-16011. (Illus.). 144p. 1981. 12.95 (ISBN 0-937404-13-6). Triad Pub FL.

--Soups of Hakafri Restaurant: Original Version. LC 82-2678. (Illus.). 144p. 1982. 12.95 (ISBN 0-937404-12-8). Triad Pub FL.

Franklin, Richard. Comeback City. 1982. pap. 4.95 (ISBN 0-932616-11-9). New Poets.

Franklin, Richard, jt. auth. see Franklin, Paula.

Franklin, S. Harvey. Trade, Growth & Anxiety: New Zealand Beyond the Welfare State. (Illus.). 1978. 36.00x (ISBN 0-456-02320-8, NO. 2830). Methuen Inc.

Franklin, Shirley A. Perilous Homecoming. 192p. (YA) 1975. 8.95 (ISBN 0-685-53497-9, Avalon). Bouregy.

Franklin, Stanley & Thomas, Barbara S. Topology: Proceedings of the Memphis State University Conference. (Lecture Notes in Pure and Applied Math Ser.: Vol. 24). 1976. 55.00 (ISBN 0-8247-6460-9). Dekker.

Franklin, Stephen G., jt. auth. see Terry, George R.

Franklin, Sterling C., jt. auth. see Beserra, Sarah S.

Franklin, Steven C., jt. auth. see Fulmer, Robert M.

Franklin, T. J. & Snow, G. A., eds. Biochemistry of Antimicrobial Action. 3rd ed. 1981. 35.00x (ISBN 0-412-22440-2, NO. 2239, Pub. by Chapman & Hall); pap. 17.95x (ISBN 0-412-22450-X, NO. 6540). Methuen Inc.

Franklin, Thomas B. Climates in Miniature: A Study in Micro-Climate & Environment. LC 79-138234. 137p. 1972. Repr. of 1955 ed. lib. bdg. 18.75x (ISBN 0-8371-5591-6, FRCM). Greenwood.

Franklin, Ursula. Anatomy of Poesis: The Prose Poems of Stephane Mallarme. (Studies in the Romance Languages & Literatures Ser: No. 167). 267p. 1976. pap. 14.00x (ISBN 0-8078-9167-3). U of NC Pr.

--The Broken Angel: Myth & Method in Valery. (Studies in the Romance Languages & Literatures: No. 222). 160p. pap. 11.00 (ISBN 0-8078-9226-2). U of NC Pr.

--The Rhetoric of Valery's Prose "Aubades". LC 78-13044. (Romance Ser.). 1979. 20.00x (ISBN 0-8020-5427-7). U of Toronto Pr.

Franklin, V. P. Black Self-Determination: A Cultural History of the Faith of the Fathers. 1985. 18.95 (ISBN 0-88208-177-2); pap. 9.95 (ISBN 0-88208-178-0). Lawrence Hill.

Franklin, Vincent P. The Education of Black Philadelphia: The Social & Educational History of a Minority Community, 1900-1950. LC 79-5045. (Illus.). 1979. 10.95x (ISBN 0-8122-7769-4). U of Pa Pr.

Franklin, Vincent P. & Anderson, James D., eds. New Perspectives on Black Educational History. 1978. lib. bdg. 23.00 (ISBN 0-8161-8114-4, Hall Reference). G K Hall.

Franklin, Walt. Encyclopedia of Self-Publishing: Complete Reference for Self-Publishing Writers. rev. ed. Walton, S. F., ed. (Illus.). 256p. 1979. 24.95 (ISBN 0-686-63393-8). Media Unltd.

--Little Water Company. 1985. 4.00 (ISBN 0-934834-64-4). White Pine.

--Talking to the Owls. (Illus.). 64p. 1984. pap. 4.00 (ISBN 0-9613465-0-7). Great Elm.

Franklin, Walt & Franklin, Peter. The Glass also Rises. 44p. 1985. pap. 4.50 (ISBN 0-318-12117-4). Great Elm.

Franklin, Wayne. Discoverers, Explorers, Settlers: The Diligent Writers of Early America. LC 79-4390. 1979. 15.00x (ISBN 0-226-26071-2). U of Chicago Pr.

--The New World of James Fenimore Cooper. LC 81-16121. 1982. 17.00x (ISBN 0-226-26080-1). U of Chicago Pr.

Franklin, William M. Protection of Foreign Interests, a Study in Diplomatic and Consular Practice. Repr. of 1947 ed. lib. bdg. 18.00x (ISBN 0-8371-0426-2, FRFI). Greenwood.

Franklin, Woodman B. Guatemala. (World Bibliographical Ser.: No. 9). 109p. 1981. lib. bdg. 21.00 (ISBN 0-903450-24-0). ABC-Clio.

Frankl-Lundborg, Otto. What Is Anthroposophy? Wetzl, Joseph, tr. 1977. pap. 2.95 (ISBN 0-916786-14-5). St George Bk Serv.

Franklyn, Julian. A Dictionary of Rhyming Slang. rev ed. 1975. pap. 8.95 (ISBN 0-7100-8052-2). Routledge & Kegan.

Franklyn, Julian, ed. A Dictionary of the Occult. Repr. of 1935 ed. 45.00x (ISBN 0-685-32596-2). Gale.

Franko, David A. & Wetzel, Robert G. To Quench Our Thirst. (Illus.). 176p. 1983. text ed. 20.00x (ISBN 0-472-10032-7); pap. text ed. 8.50x (ISBN 0-472-08037-7). U of Mich Pr.

Franko, Ivan. Fox Mykyta. Melnyk, Bohdan, tr. from Ukrainian. (Illus.). 1978. 4.95 (ISBN 0-88776-112-7). Tundra Bks.

Franko, Lawrence & Stephenson, Sherry. French Export Behavior in Third World Markets, No. 6. LC 80-66695. (Significant Issues Ser.: Vol. II). 106p. 1980. 5.95 (ISBN 0-89206-021-2). CSI Studies.

Franko, Lawrence G. A Survey of the Impact of Manufactured Exports from Industrializing Countries in Asia & Latin America: Must Export-Oriented Growth Be Disruptive? LC 79-91759. (Committee on Changing International Realities Ser.). 56p. 1979. 4.50 (ISBN 0-89068-051-5). Natl Planning.

--The Threat of Japanese Multinationals: How the West Can Respond. LC 83-10599. (Wiley IRM Series on Multinationals: I-659). 148p. 1984. 24.95x (ISBN 0-471-90232-2, Pub. by Wiley Interscience). Wiley.

Franko, Robert M. Export-Import Operations: A Manager's "How to" & "Why" Guide. LC 79-89772. (Orig.). 1979. pap. 35.00 (ISBN 0-935154-13-2). Prof Busn Serv.

Frankowitz, Eugene von see Von Frankowitz, Eugene.

Franks, A. H. Ballroom Dancer's Handbook. (Ballroom Dance Ser.). 1985. lib. bdg. 69.00 (ISBN 0-87700-762-4). Revisionist Pr.

--Social Dance: A Short History. (Ballroom Dance Ser.). 1985. lib. bdg. 64.00 (ISBN 0-87700-761-6). Revisionist Pr.

--Svetlana Beriosova: A Biography. (Series in Dance). 1978. Repr. of 1958 ed. 19.50 (ISBN 0-306-79537-X). Da Capo.

Franks, A. H., ed. Ballet: A Decade of Endeavour. (Series in Dance). (Illus.). 223p. 1981. Repr. of 1955 ed. lib. bdg. 22.50 (ISBN 0-306-76112-2). Da Capo.

--Pavlova: A Collection of Memoirs. (Quality Paperbacks Ser.). (Illus.). 144p. 1981. pap. 6.95 (ISBN 0-306-80149-3). Da Capo.

--Pavlova (Eighteen Eighty-One to Nineteen Thirty-One) A Biography. LC 79-1053. (Series in Dance). (Illus.). 144p. 1979. Repr. of 1956 ed. 22.50 (ISBN 0-306-79538-8). Da Capo.

Franks, Alan. Boychester's Bugle. 245p. 1983. 14.95 (ISBN 0-434-27060-1, Pub. by W. Heinemann Ltd). David & Charles.

Franks, Arthur H. Twentieth Century Ballet. LC 71-97382. (Illus.). 228p. 1972. Repr. of 1954 ed. lib. bdg. 15.00x (ISBN 0-8371-3926-0, FRBA). Greenwood.

Franks, Betty B. & Howard, Mary K. People, Law & the Futures Perspective. 56p. 1979. pap. 4.95 (ISBN 0-8106-1676-9). NEA.

Franks, C. E. The Canoe & White Water: From Essential to Sport. LC 77-2611. 1977. 20.00 (ISBN 0-8020-2236-7); pap. 10.95 (ISBN 0-8020-6294-6). U of Toronto Pr.

Franks, C. M., jt. ed. see Rubin, R. D.

Franks, C. S. The Fiction of Radclyffe Hall. 1983. 50.00x (ISBN 0-686-79108-8, Pub. by Avebury Pub England). State Mutual Bk.

Franks, Claudia S. Beyond the 'Well of Loneliness' 192p. 1982. text ed. 34.25x (ISBN 0-86127-210-2, Pub. by Avebury England); pap. text ed. 19.50x (ISBN 0-86127-221-8, Pub. by Avebury England). Humanities.

Franks, Cyril M. & Wilson, G. Terence. Annual Review of Behavior Therapy, Vol. 8. LC 76-126864. 417p. 1982. text ed. 27.50 (ISBN 0-89862-612-9, 2612). Guilford Pr.

Franks, Cyril M., jt. auth. see Mays, Daniel T.

Franks, Cyril M., ed. The New Developments in Behavior Therapy: From Research to Clinical Application. LC 83-26402. (Supplement to Child & Family Behavior Therapy Ser.: Vol. 6). 589p. 1984. text ed. 45.00 (ISBN 0-86656-241-9, B241); pap. text ed. 24.95 (ISBN 0-86656-178-1, B178). Haworth Pr.

Franks, Cyril M., jt. ed. see Wilson, G. Terence.

Franks, Cyril M., et al. Annual Review of Behavior Therapy, Vol. 9. LC 76-126864. 437p. 1984. text ed. 27.50 (ISBN 0-89862-618-8, 2618). Guilford Pr.

--Annual Review of Behavior Therapy: Theory & Practice. (Vol. 10). 400p. 1985. text ed. write for info. (ISBN 0-89862-750-8). Guilford Pr.

Franks, Felix. Biophysics & Biochemistry at Low Temperatures. (Illus.). 224p. 1985. 44.50 (ISBN 0-521-26320-4). Cambridge U Pr.

--Polywater. (Illus.). 200p. 1981. 20.00x (ISBN 0-262-06073-6). MIT Pr.

--Polywater. 224p. 1981. pap. 5.95 (ISBN 0-262-56029-1). MIT Pr.

Franks, Felix & Mathias, S. F. Biophysics of Water: Proceedings of a Working Conference Held at Girton College Cambridge, June 29 - July 3, 1981. 400p. 1982. 69.95x (ISBN 0-471-10229-6, Pub. by Wiley-Interscience). Wiley.

Franks, Felix, ed. Water: A Comprehensive Treatise, 6 vols. Incl. Vol. 1. The Physics & Physical Chemistry of Water. LC 78-165694. 596p. 1972. 75.00x (ISBN 0-306-37181-2); Vol. 2. Water in Crystalline Hydrates. LC 78-165694. 681p. 1973. 75.00x (ISBN 0-306-37182-0); Vol. 3. Aqueous Solutions of Simple Electrolytes. LC 78-165694. 472p. 1973. 75.00x (ISBN 0-306-37183-9); Vol. 4. Aqueous Solutions of Amphiphiles & Macromolecules. LC 74-17244. 839p. 1975. 85.00x (ISBN 0-306-37184-7); Vol. 5. Water in Disperse Systems. LC 74-17190. 366p. 1975. 59.50x (ISBN 0-306-37185-5); Vol. 6. Recent Advances. LC 78-165694. 465p. 1979. 69.50x (ISBN 0-306-40139-8); Vol. 7. Water & Aqueous Solutions at Subzero Temperatures. 400p. 1982. 69.50 (ISBN 0-306-40710-8). (Illus., Plenum Pr). Plenum Pub.

Franks, Hugh. Will to Live. 1979. 15.00x (ISBN 0-7100-0181-9). Routledge & Kegan.

Franks, J. Building Sub-Contract Management. (Illus.). 208p. 1984. 49.95 (ISBN 0-582-30518-7). Longman.

Franks, J. R. & Broyles, J. E. Modern Managerial Finance. LC 79-83955. 376p. 1979. 57.95 (ISBN 0-471-99751-X); pap. 27.95x (ISBN 0-471-27563-8, Pub. by Wiley-Interscience). Wiley.

Franks, J. R. & Scholefield, H. H. Corporate Financial Management. 2nd ed. 332p. 1977. text ed. 43.00x (ISBN 0-566-02054-8). Gower Pub Co.

Franks, Jacqueline & Levine, Michael S., eds. MSIS Proceedings of the Eighth Annual National Users Group Conference, October 18-19, 1984. (Orig.). 1984. pap. 10.00 (ISBN 0-936934-04-2). N S Kline Inst.

Franks, John. Company Director & the Law. 1981. 40.00x (ISBN 0-686-44514-7, Pub. by Oyez Longman Pub England). State Mutual Bk.

Franks, John M. Homology & Dynamical Systems. LC 82-8897. (Conference Board of the Mathematical Sciences Ser.: Vol. 49). 120p. 1982. pap. 15.00 (ISBN 0-8218-1700-0). Am Math.

Franks, Judith, jt. auth. see Samskriti.

Franks, Julian R., et al. Corporate Finance: Concepts & Applications. LC 84-23357. 832p. 1985. text ed. write for info. (ISBN 0-534-04095-0). Kent Pub Co.

Franks, Kenny, et al. Early Oklahoma Oil: A Photographic History, 1859-1936. LC 80-26043. (The Montague History of Oil Ser.: No. 2). (Illus.). 260p. 1981. 27.95 (ISBN 0-89096-110-7). Tex A&M Univ Pr.

Franks, Kenny A. Citizen Soldiers: Oklahoma's National Guard. LC 83-40326. (Illus.). 264p. 1984. 24.95 (ISBN 0-8061-1862-8). U of Okla Pr.

--The Oklahoma Petroleum Industry. LC 80-5242. (Oklahoma Horizons Ser.: Vol. 4). (Illus.). 320p. 1980. 21.95 (ISBN 0-8061-1625-0). U of Okla Pr.

--Stand Watie & the Agony of the Cherokee Nation. LC 79-124380. 1979. 14.95x (ISBN 0-87870-063-3). Memphis St Univ.

Franks, Kenny A. & Lambert, Paul F. Early California Oil: A Photographic History, 1865-1940. LC 84-40134. (The Montague History of Oil Ser.: No. 4). (Illus.). 260p. 1985. 34.50 (ISBN 0-89096-206-5). Tex A&M Univ Pr.

--Early Louisiana & Arkansas Oil: A Photographic History, 1901-1946. LC 82-40313. (The Montague History of Oil Ser.: No. 3). (Illus.). 260p. 1982. 27.95 (ISBN 0-89096-134-4). Tex A&M Univ Pr.

Franks, Kenny A., jt. ed. see Lambert, Paul F.

Franks, L. E., ed. Data Communication: Fundamentals of Baseband Transmission. LC 74-12338. (Benchmark Papers in Electrical Engineering & Computer Science Ser.: Vol. 9). 1975. 64.50 (ISBN 0-12-786480-6). Acad Pr.

Franks, L. M. & Wigley, C. B., eds. Neoplastic Transformation in Differentiated Epithelial Cell Systems in Vitro. LC 79-41276. 1980. 48.50 (ISBN 0-12-266260-1). Acad Pr.

Franks, Lloyd. The Book of Morbid. 112p. (Orig.). 1982. pap. 5.95 (ISBN 0-942264-01-0). Jon-Juan.

Franks, Lloyd & Bonafide, John. The Juan Book. (Illus.). 112p. (Orig.). 1982. pap. 5.95 (ISBN 0-942264-00-2). Jon-Juan.

Franks, Maurice R. Winning Custody. LC 82-24114. 185p. 1983. 16.95 (ISBN 0-13-961011-1, Busn); pap. 7.95 (ISBN 0-13-961003-0). P-H.

Franks, Norman L. The Battle of the Airfields. 1982. 40.00x (ISBN 0-686-82339-7, Pub. by W Kimber). State Mutual Bk.

Franks, R. & Swartz, H. Simplified Medical Dictionary. 1977. 19.95 (ISBN 0-87489-054-3). Med Economics.

Franks, Ray. The Ol' Coach on the Banquet Circuit. (Illus.). 80p. 1984. pap. 7.95 (ISBN 0-943976-01-4). R Franks Ranch.

--What's in a Nickname? LC 82-90195. (Illus.). 208p. (Orig.). 1982. pap. 12.95 (ISBN 0-943976-00-6). R Franks Ranch.

Franks, Roger G. Modeling & Simulation in Chemical Engineering. LC 72-39717. 411p. 1972. 54.95x (ISBN 0-471-27535-2, Pub. by Wiley-Interscience). Wiley.

Franks, Ronald & Dowd, Thomas. The Will, a Modern Day Treasure Hunt. 2nd ed. 1981. pap. text ed. 6.95 (ISBN 0-9607132-0-4). Tricore Assoc.

Franks, Violet & Rothblum, Esther D. The Stereotyping of Women: Its Effects on Mental Health. (Springer Series-Focus on Women: No. 5). 1983. 23.95x (ISBN 0-8261-3820-9). Springer Pub.

Franksen, O. I., et al. Qualitative Aspects of Large Systems. (Lecture Notes in Control & Information Science: Vol. 17). 1979. pap. 13.00 (ISBN 0-387-09609-4). Springer-Verlag.

Franksen, Ole I. Mr. Babage's Secret: The Tale of a Cipher-& APL. (Illus.). 320p. 1985. text ed. 32.00 (ISBN 0-13-604729-7). P-H.

Franquin, P., jt. auth. see Cocheme, J.

Franquesa, Manuel. Diccionari De Sinonims. 1248p. (Catalan.). 1970. 40.50 (ISBN 0-686-57365-X, S-50185). French & Eur.

Franqui, Carlos. Diary of the Cuban Revolution. Kerrigan, Elaine, et al, trs. from Sp. (Richard Seaver Bk.). 546p. 1980. 25.00 (ISBN 0-670-27217-5). Viking.

--Family Portrait with Fidel: A Memoir. MacAdam, Alfred, tr. from Span. LC 83-42774. 256p. 1984. 17.95 (ISBN 0-394-53260-0). Random.

--Family Portrait with Fidel: A Memoir. LC 84-40054. 256p. 1984. pap. 8.95 (ISBN 0-394-72620-0, Vin). Random.

--Twelve. Teicher, Albert, tr. LC 68-10011. 1968. 4.50 (ISBN 0-8184-0089-7). Lyle Stuart.

Fransecky, Roger B. Telecommunications & Community Services. 1974. pap. 3.00x (ISBN 0-89011-468-4, TEC-102). Abt Bks.

Fransecky, Roger B. & Debes, John L. Visual Literacy: A Way to Learn, a Way to Teach. 1972. pap. 2.45 sale (ISBN 0-89240-024-2, 904). Assn Ed Comm Tech.

Fransella, F. Personal Change & Reconstruction: Research on a Treatment of Stuttering. 1973. 44.00 (ISBN 0-12-266150-8). Acad Pr.

Fransella, F. & Bannister, D. A Manual for Repertory Grid Technique. 1977. 36.00 (ISBN 0-12-265450-1); pap. 18.00 (ISBN 0-12-265456-0). Acad Pr.

Fransella, F., jt. auth. see Bannister, D.

Fransella, Fay. Need to Change. (Essential Psychology Ser.). 1975. pap. 4.50x (ISBN 0-416-82180-4, NO. 2782). Methuen Inc.

--On Being a Woman. (Tavistock Women's Studies). 1977. pap. 9.95 (ISBN 0-422-76080-3, NO. 2783, Pub. by Tavistock England). Methuen Inc.

--Personality. (Psychology in Progress Ser.). 1981. 26.50x (ISBN 0-416-72770-0, NO. 2226); pap. 11.95x (ISBN 0-416-72780-8, NO. 2236). Methuen Inc.

--Psychology for Occupational Therapists. (Psychology for Professional Groups Ser.). 320p. 1982. text ed. 23.75x (ISBN 0-333-31859-5, Pub. by Macmillan England); pap. text ed. 9.75x (ISBN 0-333-31883-8). Humanities.

Fransella, Fay, ed. Personal Construct Psychology 1977. 1978. 39.50 (ISBN 0-12-265460-9). Acad Pr.
Fransen, L., jt. auth. see Cardon, A.
Fransen, P. Intelligent Theology, Vol. 1: The Trinity Lives in Us As We Celebrate Life. pap. 2.50 (ISBN 0-8199-0400-7). Franciscan Herald.
--Intelligent Theology, Vol. 2: Confirmation & Priesthood. pap. 2.50 (ISBN 0-8199-0401-5). Franciscan Herald.
--Intelligent Theology, Vol. 3: A Universal Theology. pap. 2.50 (ISBN 0-8199-0402-3). Franciscan Herald.
Fransman, Martin, ed. Industry & Accumulation in Africa. (Studies in the Economics of Africa). (Illus.). 1982. text ed. 40.00x (ISBN 0-435-97139-5); pap. text ed. 15.00x (ISBN 0-435-97140-9). Heinemann Ed.
Fransman, Martin & King, Kenneth, eds. Technological Capability in the Third World. LC 83-13737. 256p. 1984. 30.00 (ISBN 0-312-78792-8). St Martin.
Franson, Gwyn & Bradshaw, Annette. Friends Forever. 32p. (Orig.). 1983. pap. 3.95 (ISBN 0-88290-214-8). Horizon Utah.
--Garden Goodies. 32p. (Orig.). 1983. pap. 3.95 (ISBN 0-88290-215-6). Horizon Utah.
--Sweet & Sassy. 32p. (Orig.). 1983. pap. 4.50 (ISBN 0-88290-216-4). Horizon Utah.
--A Woman's Gift. (Monuments to Womanhood Ser.). 48p. (Orig.). 1982. pap. 4.95 (ISBN 0-88290-204-0, 2805). Horizon Utah.
--A Woman's Love. (Monuments to Womanhood Ser.). 48p. (Orig.). 1982. pap. 4.95 (ISBN 0-88290-205-9, 2806). Horizon Utah.
Franson, Gwyn, jt. auth. see Bradshaw, Annette.
Franson, J. Earl, jt. auth. see Dube, Anthony.
Franson, John K., ed. Milton Reconsidered: Essays in Honour of Arthur E. Baker. (Salzburg Studies in English Literature: Elizabethan & Renaissance Studies: No. 49). (Illus.). 215p. 1976. pap. text ed. 25.50x (ISBN 0-391-01378-5). Humanities.
Franson, Robert T. The Legal Aspects of Ecological Reserve Creation & Management in Canada. (Environmental Policy & Law Papers: No. 9). 108p. 1975. pap. 10.00 (ISBN 2-88032-079-8, IUCN12, IUCN). Unipub.
Franson, Robert W. The Shadow of the Ship. 288p. (Orig.). 1983. pap. 2.75 (ISBN 0-345-30688-0, Del Rey). Ballantine.
Franssen, Herman, et al. World Energy Supply & International Security. LC 82-49243. (Special Reports Ser.). 93p. 1983. 7.50 (ISBN 0-89549-048-X). Inst Foreign Policy Anal.
--World Energy Supply & International Security: Special Report 1983. (Special Report Ser.). 96p. 1983. pap. text ed. 7.50 (ISBN 0-89549-048-X, IFPA31, IFPA). Unipub.
Fransson, G. Middle English Surnames of Occupation: 1100-1350. (Lund Studies in English: Vol. 3). pap. 22.00 (ISBN 0-317-16134-2). Kraus Repr.
Fransu, A., jt. auth. see Magureanu, R.
Fransz, H. G. The Functional Response to Prey Density in an Acarine System. New ed. (Simulation Monographs). 143p. 1974. pap. 16.00 (ISBN 90-220-0509-7, PDC37, PUDOC). Unipub.
Franta, G. E., ed. Progress in Solar Energy: Proceedings of the American Section of the International Solar Energy Society, Vol. 6. 1500p. 1984. pap. 135.00x Preprints (ISBN 0-89553-126-7). Am Solar Energy.
Franta, Gregory E. & Glenn, Barbara H., eds. Twenty-Five Years of the Sun at Work: Proceedings of the Annual Meeting of the American Section of the International Solar Energy Society, Phoenix 1980, 2 vols. 1980. Set. pap. 150.00x (ISBN 0-89553-021-X). Am Solar Energy.
Franta, Gregory E. & Haggard, Keith W., eds. Progress in Solar Energy: Vol. 5, The Renewable Challenge. 1985. pap. text ed. 185.00x (ISBN 0-89553-034-1). Am Solar Energy.
Franta, Gregory E., ed. see International Solar Energy Society, American Section, Annual Meeting, Denver, 1978.
Franta, Gregory E., ed. see National Passive Solar Conference, 4th, Kansas City, 1979.
Franta, Gregroy E., ed. see International Solar Energy Society, American Section, Annual Meeting, Philadelphia, 1981.
Franta, W. R. & Chlamtac, Imrich. Local Networks: Motivation, Technology & Performance. LC 80-7725. (Illus.). 512p. 1982. 44.50x (ISBN 0-669-03779-6). Lexington Bks.
Franta, W. R., et al. Formal Methods of Program Verification & Specification. (Illus.). 224p. 1982. text ed. 22.50. P-H.
Frantsevich, I. N. Silicon Carbide. LC 69-12512. 276p. 1970. 40.00x (ISBN 0-306-10838-0, Consultants). Plenum Pub.
Frantz, A. The Well Adult, Vol. 1. (RN Nursing Assessment Ser.). 152p. 1982. pap. 12.95 (ISBN 0-87489-281-3). Med Economics.
Frantz, Albert T. How Courts Decide. LC 68-54164. iii, 111p. 1968. lib. bdg. 35.00 (ISBN 0-930342-12-7). W S Hein.
Frantz, Alison. The Church of the Holy Apostles. LC 76-356003. (Athenian Agora Ser: Vol. 20). (Illus.). xiii, 45p. 1972. 15.00x (ISBN 0-87661-220-6). Am Sch Athens.
--The Middle Ages in the Athenian Agora. LC 69-68253. (Excavations of the Athenian Agora Picture Bks.: No. 7). (Illus.). 1961. pap. 1.50x (ISBN 0-87661-607-4). Am Sch Athens.
Frantz, Charles, ed. Ideas & Trends in World Anthropology. (ICAES Ser.: No. 4). 278p. 1981. pap. text ed. 14.75x (ISBN 0-391-02280-6, Pub. by Concept India). Humanities.
Frantz, Eusebius. The Psychology of Fear & the Obsessive Ideas of Action. (Illus.). 143p. 1985. 97.15 (ISBN 0-89920-077-X). Am Inst Psych.
Frantz, Evelyn. A Bonnet for Virginia. mass market ed. 1978. pap. 1.95 (ISBN 0-87178-101-8). Brethren.
Frantz, Forest H. Successful Small Business Management. LC 77-14385. 1978. text ed. 24.95 (ISBN 0-13-872119-X). P-H.
Frantz, Gilda, ed. Cooking-The Art of Innocent Alchemy: A Guide to the Mundane & the Unusual in Cooking. 1975. pap. 7.00 (ISBN 0-9600936-0-5). Analytic Psych.
Frantz, Joe B. Aspects of the American West: Three Essays. LC 76-17973. (Essays on the American West Ser.-Elma Dill Russell Spencer: No. 1). 88p. 1976. 5.00 (ISBN 0-89096-023-2). Tex A&M Univ Pr.
--The Forty-Acre Follies. Okrent, Daniel, ed. (Illus.). 254p. 1983. 17.95 (ISBN 0-932012-38-8). Texas Month Pr.
--Texas. (States & the Nation). (Illus.). 1976. 14.95 (ISBN 0-393-05580-9, Co-Pub by AASLH). Norton.
--Texas: A History. (States & the Nation Ser.). (Illus.). 1984. pap. 7.95 (ISBN 0-393-30173-7). Norton.
Frantz, Joe B. & Choate, Julian E., Jr. The American Cowboy: The Myth & the Reality. LC 81-6580. (Illus.). xiii, 232p. 1981. Repr. lib. bdg. 25.00x (ISBN 0-313-23109-5, FRAMC). Greenwood.
Frantz, Joe B., jt. auth. see Duke, Cordia S.
Frantz, Ray W. English Traveller & the Movement of Ideas, 1660-1732. 1967. lib. bdg. 18.00x (ISBN 0-374-92870-3). Octagon.
Frantzen, Allen J. The Literature of Penance in Anglo-Saxon England. 395p. 1983. 27.50x (ISBN 0-8135-0955-6). Rutgers U Pr.
Frantzen, Trond & McEvoy, Ken. A Game Plan for Systems Development. (Orig.). 1985. pap. text ed. price not set (ISBN 0-917072-54-5). Yourdon.
Frantzeskakis, Ion F., ed. Zygos. Cullen, Timothy & Duckworth, Eddie, trs. from Greek. (Illus.). 216p. 1982. (Pub. by Zygos Greece). Intl Spec Bk.
Frantzich, Stephen E. Computers in Congress: The Politics of Information. (Managing Information Ser.: Vol. 4). (Illus.). 288p. 1982. 25.00 (ISBN 0-686-97289-9). Sage.
Frantzis, Nicholas. The Seven Popular Games of Backgammon. 1979. 6.00 (ISBN 0-682-49295-7). Exposition Pr FL.
Frantzve, Jerri L. Behaving in Organizations: Cases & Exercises. 304p. 1983. pap. 16.51 scp (ISBN 0-205-07853-2, 797853). Allyn.
Franz, A. Johann Klaj. pap. 19.00 (ISBN 0-384-16740-3). Johnson Repr.
Franz, Carl. Color Me Macho. (Illus.). 112p. 1985. pap. 6.95 (ISBN 0-912528-46-X). John Muir.
--The People's Guide to Camping in Mexico. (Illus.). 416p. (Orig.). 1982. pap. 10.00 (ISBN 0-912528-24-9). John Muir.
Franz, Carl & Havens, Lorena. The On & Off the Road Cookbook: Planning, Preparation & Recipes for the Complete Outdoor Kitchen. (Illus.). 272p. (Orig.). 1982. pap. 8.50 (ISBN 0-912528-27-3). John Muir.
Franz, Carol. If Not for Love. 352p. 1984. pap. 3.50 (ISBN 0-8439-2127-7, Leisure Bks). Dorchester Pub Co.
Franz, David R., jt. auth. see Jacobson, Morris K.
Franz, Eckjart G., jt. ed. see Boberach, Heinz.
Franz, Erich & Growe, Bernd. Georges Seurat: Drawings. LC 84-80902. (Illus.). 204p. 1984. 45.00 (ISBN 0-8212-1575-2, 332488). NYGS.
Franz, Gunther. Urkundliche Quellen zur Hessischen Reformationsgeschichte. 571p. (Ger.). 1951. 6.00x (ISBN 0-8361-1153-2). Herald Pr.
Franz, H. E., jt. ed. see Rosenthal, J.
Franz, L. Lexikon Zur - und Fruehgeschichtlicher Fundstaetten Oesterreichs. (Ger.). 1965. 47.00 (ISBN 3-7749-0255-0, M-7193). French & Eur.
Franz, Marie-Louise Von see Jung, Emma & Von Franz, Marie-Louise.
Franz, Marie-Louise von see Thomas Aquinas, Saint.
Franz, Marie-Louise Von see Von Franz, Marie-Louise.
Franz, Marie-Louise von see Von Franz, Marie-Louise.
Franz, Marie Louise von see Von Franz, Marie-Louise.
Franz, Marie-Louise von see Von Franz, Marie-Louise.
Franz, Marie-Louise Von see Von Franz, Marie-Louise.
Franz, Marie-Louise von see Von Franz, Marie-Louise & Hillman, James.
Franz, Martin & Good, Phillip I. Writing Business Programs in C Language. LC 84-45695. 200p. (Orig.). 1985. spiral incl. disk o.p. 59.95 (ISBN 0-8019-7612-X); pap. 16.95 (ISBN 0-8019-7611-1). Chilton.
Franz, Mary-Louise von see Von Franz, Marie-Louise.
Franz, Philip. Gogol Bibliography. 300p. 1984. 30.00 (ISBN 0-88233-809-9). Ardis Pubs.
Franz, Raymond. Crisis of Conscience: The Struggle between Loyalty to God & Loyalty to One's Religion. LC 83-62637. (Illus.). 384p. 1983. 10.95 (ISBN 0-914675-00-1); pap. 7.95 (ISBN 0-914675-03-6). Comment Pr.
Franz, Richard see Pritchard, Peter C.
Franz, S. I. Handbook of Mental Examination Methods. (Nervous & Mental Disease Monographs: No. 10). Repr. of 1912 ed. 19.00 (ISBN 0-384-16750-0). Johnson Repr.
Franz, S. I. see American Psychological Association Committee on the Standardizing of Procedure in Experimental Tests.
Franz, Sharon L., jt. auth. see Schrutt, Harold.
Franz, Shepherd I. On the Function of the Cerebrum. Bd. with The Psycho-Physiological Effect of the Elements of Speech in Relation to Poetry. Givler, R. C. Repr. of 1916 ed; Standardization of Tests for Defective Children. Schmitt, C. Repr. of 1915 ed; A Study of Retroactive Inhibition. De Camp, J. E. Repr. of 1915 ed. (Psychology Monographs General & Applied Ser.: Vol. 19). pap. 36.00 (ISBN 0-317-15244-0). Kraus Repr.
Franz, Shepherd I. see Breese, B. B.
Franzblau, Abraham N. Religious Belief & Character Among Jewish Adolescents. LC 78-176783. (Columbia University. Teachers College. Contributions to Education: No. 634). Repr. of 1934 ed. 22.50 (ISBN 0-404-55634-5). AMS Pr.
Franzblau, Bettie, jt. auth. see Bechtel, Judith.
Franzel, David. Sailing: The Basics. (Illus.). 160p. 1985. pap. 14.95 (ISBN 0-87742-201-X). Intl Marine.
Franzen, Cola, tr. see Agosin, Marjorie.
Franzen, Cola, tr. see Yurkievich, Saul, et al.
Franzen, Gosta. Prose & Poetry of Modern Sweden: An Intermediate Swedish Reader. LC 70-78815. x, 155p. 1969. 13.95x (ISBN 0-8032-0047-1). U of Nebr Pr.
Franzen, Lavern G. Good News from Luke: Visual Messages for Children. LC 76-3869. 112p. (Orig.). 1976. pap. 5.50 (ISBN 0-8066-1528-1, 10-2813). Augsburg.
--Smile God Loves You: 59 Gospel Talks for Children to See & Hear. LC 72-90257. 128p. (Orig.). 1973. pap. 5.50 (ISBN 0-8066-1304-1, 10-5840). Augsburg.
--Smile! Jesus Is Lord: Fifty Messages for Children to See & Hear. LC 74-14175. 112p. (Orig.). (gr. 3 up). 1975. pap. 5.50 (ISBN 0-8066-1458-7, 10-5842). Augsburg.
Franzen, Nils-Olof. Agaton Sax & Lispington's Grandfather Clock. (gr. 2-7). 1979. 8.95 (ISBN 0-233-96964-0). Andre Deutsch.
Franzen, Raymond H. Accomplishment Ratio: A Treatment of the Inherited Determinants of Disparity in School Product. LC 71-176784. (Columbia University. Teachers College. Contributions to Education: No. 125). Repr. of 1922 ed. 22.50 (ISBN 0-404-55125-4). AMS Pr.
Franzen, Sixten, jt. ed. see Linsk, Joseph A.
Franzen, William L., jt. auth. see Bonaparte, T. H.
Franzini, J. B., jt. auth. see Daughtery, R. L.
Franz Joseph, I. Incredible Friendship: Letters of Emperor Franz Joseph to Frau Katharina Schratt. De Bourgoing, Jean, ed. LC 66-63789. 1966. 39.50x (ISBN 0-87395-019-4). State U NY Pr.
Franzke, Andreas. Dubuffet. Wolf, Robert E., tr. (Illus.). 340p. 1982. 95.00 (ISBN 0-8109-0815-8). Abrams.
Franzlin, F., jt. ed. see Breitenbach, J.
Franzmann, jt. auth. see Roehrs.
Franzmann, Martin H. The Revelation to John. 136p. 1976. 7.50 (ISBN 0-570-03728-X, 12-2630). Concordia.
Franzmann, Werner H. Bible History Commentary: Old Testament. LC 80-53145. (Illus.). 616p. 1981. 15.95 (ISBN 0-938272-04-7). WELS Board.
Franzmeyer, Fritz. Approaches to Industrial Policy Within the EC & Its Impact on European Integration. 180p. 1982. text ed. 41.50x (ISBN 0-566-00358-9). Gower Pub Co.
Franzoi, Barbara. At the Very Least She Pays the Rent: Women & German Industrialization, 1871-1914. LC 84-22455. (Contributions in Women's Studies: No. 57). (Illus.). 224p. 1985. lib. bdg. 29.95 (ISBN 0-313-24487-1, FAV/). Greenwood.
Franzoni, T. & Vesentini, E. Holomorphic Maps & Invariant Distances. (Mathematics Studies: Vol. 40). 226p. 1980. 42.75 (ISBN 0-444-85436-3, North Holland). Elsevier.
Franzos, Karl E. The Jews of Barnow. facsimile ed. Macdowall, M. W., tr. from Ger. LC 74-27985. (Modern Jewish Experience Ser.). (Eng.). 1975. Repr. of 1883 ed. 30.00x (ISBN 0-405-06712-7). Ayer Co Pubs.
Franzosa, Bill, ed. The UNIX System Encyclopedia. 2nd ed. (Illus.). 1985. pap. 44.95 (ISBN 0-917195-01-9). Yates Vent.
Franzosa, Susan D. & Mazza, Karen A., eds. Integrating Women's Studies into the Curriculum: An Annotated Bibliography. LC 84-12815. (Bibliographies & Indexes in Education Ser.: No. 1). xiv, 100p. 1984. lib. bdg. 29.95 (ISBN 0-313-24482-0, FIW/). Greenwood.
Franzosini, P. & Sanesi, P., eds. Thermodynamic & Transport Properties of Organic Salts. (IUPAC Chemical Data Ser.: No. 28). 376p. 1980. 110.00 (ISBN 0-08-022378-8). Pergamon.
Franz Von Siebold, Phillip. Ukiyo-e Collection, 3 Vols. (Illus.). Set. limited edition 1250.00 (ISBN 0-384-64941-6). Johnson Repr.
Franzwa, Gregory, ed. see Haines, Aubrey L.
Franzwa, Gregory M. History of the Hazelwood School District. (Illus.). 1977. 9.95 (ISBN 0-935284-08-7). Patrice Pr.
--Maps of the Oregon Trail. 2nd ed. North, Arielle, ed. LC 82-675039. (Illus.). 299p. 1982. 24.95 (ISBN 0-935284-30-3); looseleaf 27.95 (ISBN 0-935284-31-1); pap. 14.95 (ISBN 0-935284-32-X). Patrice Pr.
--The Old Cathedral. 2nd ed. LC 80-15885. (Illus.). 1980. 14.95 (ISBN 0-935284-18-4). Patrice Pr.
--The Oregon Trail Revisited. 2nd ed. (Illus.). 1978. pap. 12.95 (ISBN 0-935284-07-9). Patrice Pr.
--The Story of Old Ste. Genevieve. (Illus.). 2nd ed. 1977 8.95 (ISBN 0-935284-02-8); pap. 3.95 3rd ed. (ISBN 0-935284-03-6). Patrice Pr.
Franzwa, Gregory M., ed. Oregon Trail Revisited. 3rd ed. (Illus.). 1978. pap. 6.95 (ISBN 0-935284-29-X). Patrice Pr.
Franzwa, Gregory M., ed. see Hanson, William L.
Franzwa, Gregory M., ed. see Kelley, F. Beverly.
Franzwa, Gregory M., ed. see Start, Clarissa.
Frapa, Pierre, jt. auth. see Aubert, Claude.
Frape, D. L., tr. see Pirchner, Franz.
Frappier, Jean. Chretien De Troyes: The Man & His Work. Cormier, Raymond J., tr. from Fr. LC 81-9475. (Illus.). xx, 241p. 1982. lib. bdg. 22.95x (ISBN 0-8214-0603-5, 82-83889). Ohio U Pr.
Frappier, William. Steamboat Yesterdays on Casco Bay. 384p. Date not set. price not set (ISBN 0-933858-11-6). Kennebec River.
Fraprie, Frank R. Photographic Amusements Including Tricks & Unusual or Novel Effects Obtainable with the Camera. 10th ed. LC 72-9199. (The Literature of Photography Ser.). Repr. of 1931 ed. 29.00 (ISBN 0-405-04908-0). Ayer Co Pubs.
Frary, Dave. How to Build Realistic Model Railroad Scenery. Hayden, Bob, ed. (Illus.). 100p. (Orig.). 1981. pap. 8.95 (ISBN 0-89024-037-X). Kalmbach.
Frary, Ihna T. They Built the Capitol. LC 76-99660. (Select Bibliographies Reprint Ser). 1940. 33.00 (ISBN 0-8369-5089-5). Ayer Co Pubs.
Frary, L. T. Early Homes of Ohio. (Illus.). 13.25 (ISBN 0-8446-0631-6). Peter Smith.
Frary, Louise G. Studies in the Syntax of the Old English Passive. (LD). 1929. pap. 16.00 (ISBN 0-527-00751-X). Kraus Repr.
Frary, Michael. Impressions of the Texas Panhandle. LC 77-89515. (Joe & Betty Moore Texas Art Ser.: No. 2). (Illus.). 114p. 1977. 35.00 (ISBN 0-89096-037-2). Tex A&M Univ Pr.
--Watercolors of the Rio Grande. LC 84-40128. (Illus.). 120p. 1984. 37.50 (ISBN 0-89096-207-3). Tex A&M Univ Pr.
Frary, Michael & Owens, William A. Impressions of the Big Thicket. LC 73-1674. (Blaffer Ser. of Southwestern Art: No. 2). (Illus.). 112p. 1973. 22.50 (ISBN 0-292-70706-1). U of Tex Pr.
--Impressions of the Big Thicket. (Illus.). 112p. 1983. pap. 12.95 (ISBN 0-292-73831-5). U Of Tex Pr.
Frary, Thomas D., jt. auth. see Dondero, John P.
Frasca, Albert J. & Hill, Robert H. The Forty Five - Seventy Springfield. Suydam, Charles R., ed. LC 80-51230. (Illus.). 396p. 1980. deluxe ed. 49.50 (ISBN 0-937500-11-9); deluxe ed. 99.50x limited ed. (ISBN 0-937500-10-0). Springfield Pub Co.
Frasch, Gisela. Kommunale Politik und Offentliche Bibliothek. 200p. (Ger.). 1984. pap. text ed. 17.50 (ISBN 3-598-10428-6). K G Saur.
Frasche, Dean F. Southeast Asian Ceramics: Ninth Through Seventeenth Centuries. LC 76-20204. (Illus.). 144p. 1976. 25.00 (ISBN 0-87848-047-1). Asia Soc.
Frascina & Harrison. Modern Art & Modernism. 320p. 1982. text ed. 20.00 (ISBN 0-06-318234-3, Pub. by Har-Row Ltd England); pap. text ed. 9.95 (ISBN 0-06-318233-5, Pub. by Har-Row Ltd England). Har-Row.
Frascina, Francis & Harrison, Charles. Modern Art & Modernism: An Anthology of Critical Texts from Manet to Pollock. LC 82-48153. (Icon Editions). (Illus.). 352p. 1983. 19.23i (ISBN 0-06-433215-2, HarpT). Har-Row.
Frascina, Francis, intro. by. Pollack & After: The Critical Debate. LC 84-48596. (Illus.). 320p. 1985. 19.23 (ISBN 0-06-433126-1, Icon Edns). Har-Row.
Frascino, Ed. Eddie Spaghetti on the Home Front. LC 82-48847. (Illus.). 128p. (gr. 3-7). 1983. 9.57i (ISBN 0-06-021894-0); PLB 9.89g (ISBN 0-06-021895-9). HarpJ.
Frascino, Edward. Eddie Spaghetti. LC 77-11850. (Illus.). 1978. 10.53i (ISBN 0-06-021908-4). HarpJ.
--My Cousin the King. (Illus.). 32p. (gr. k-3). 1985. 12.95 (ISBN 0-13-608423-0). P-H.
Frascino, Edward, jt. auth. see Warren, William.
Frascogna, X. M., Jr. & Hetherington, H. Lee. Successful Artist Management. 224p. 1978. 17.50 (ISBN 0-8230-5000-9, Billboard Bks). Watson-Guptill.
Frascogna, Xavier M. & Hetherington, H. Lee. Negotiation Strategy for Lawyers. LC 84-11776. 1984. 29.95 (ISBN 0-13-611237-4). P-H.

Frascona, Joseph L. C. P. A. Law Review Under 1978 Uniform Commercial Code. 6th ed. 1981. 34.50 (ISBN 0-256-02465-0). Irwin.
--C.P.A. Law Review: Under the 1978 Uniform Commercial Code: Text, Previous C.P.A. Law Examination Questions, & the Author's Model Answers. 7th ed. LC 84-81123. (Illus.). 1984. 36.95 (ISBN 0-256-03208-4). Irwin.
Frascona, Joseph L., et al. Business Law; Text & Cases: The Legal Environment of Business. 2nd ed. 1184p. 1984. text ed. write for info (ISBN 0-697-08229-6); study guide avail. (ISBN 0-697-08226-1); instr's manual avail. (ISBN 0-697-08236-9); transparencies avail. (ISBN 0-697-00276-4); test item file avail. (ISBN 0-697-00273-X). Wm C Brown.
Frasconi, Antonio. Antonio Frasconi's World. 1974. pap. 5.95 (ISBN 0-685-42855-9). Macmillan.
Frase, Marianne, jt. auth. see Hunt, Linda.
Frase, Richard S. Criminal Evidence: Constiutional, Statutory & Rules Limitations. LC 85-142116. (Minnesota Criminal Law Ser.). Date not set. price not set (ISBN 0-86678-351-2). Butterworth.
Frase, Richard S., jt. auth. see Zimring, Franklin E.
Frase, Richard S., et al. Minnesota Misdemeanors & Moving Traffic Violations. 2nd ed. 1982. looseleaf 85.00 (ISBN 0-917126-81-5). Butterworth MN.
Frase, Robert W., jt. auth. see McKinley, Charles.
Fraser. Ethology of Farm Animals. Date not set. price not set (ISBN 0-444-42359-1). Elsevier.
Fraser, ed. International Catalogue of Recorded Folk Music. 201p. 1954. 5.00 (ISBN 0-318-17464-2). Intl Coun Trad.
Fraser, A. F. Farm Animal Behaviour. 2nd ed. (Illus.). 304p. 1980. pap. 14.75 (ISBN 0-7216-0787-X, Pub. by Bailliere-Tindall). Saunders.
Fraser, A. F., ed. Reproductive & Developmental Behavior in Sheep: An Anthology from "Applied Animal Ethology". (Developments in Animal & Veterinary Sciences Ser.: Vol. 18). 478p. 1985. 59.25 (ISBN 0-444-42444-X). Elsevier.
Fraser, A. Ian. The Clowes Collection. (Illus.). 1973. 4.00 (ISBN 0-317-29197-1). Ind Mus Art.
Fraser, Adlyn. Understanding Financial Statements: Through the Maze of a Corporate Annual Report. 1984. 24.95 (ISBN 0-8359-8042-1); pap. 16.95 (ISBN 0-8359-8041-3). Reston.
Fraser, Al, jt. auth. see Gillespie, Dizzy.
Fraser, Alexander C. Berkeley. 1899. 12.50 (ISBN 0-8274-1926-0). R West.
--Locke. LC 71-103188. 1970. Repr. of 1890 ed. 22.50x (ISBN 0-8046-0825-3, Pub. by Kennikat). Assoc Faculty Pr.
--Philosophy of Theism. LC 77-27228. (Gifford Lectures: 1894-95). Repr. of 1895 ed. 24.50 (ISBN 0-404-60453-6). AMS Pr.
--Philosophy of Theism: Second Series. LC 77-27227. (Gifford Lectures: 1895-96). Repr. of 1896 ed. 22.50 (ISBN 0-404-60454-4). AMS Pr.
--Rational Philosophy in History & in System: An Introduction to a Logical & Metaphysical Course. LC 73-21803. 1974. Repr. of 1858 ed. lib. bdg. 21.00 (ISBN 0-8337-1235-7). B Franklin.
Fraser, Alexander C., ed. see Locke, John.
Fraser, Alistair & Thear, Katie, eds. Small Farmer's Guide to Raising Livestock & Poultry. (Illus.). 240p. 1981. 14.95 (ISBN 0-668-04687-2). Arco.
Fraser, Alistair, jt. ed. see Thear, Katie.
Fraser, Allan & Stamp, John. Sheep Husbandry & Diseases. 6th ed. 350p. 1986. 24.00x (ISBN 0-246-11209-3, Pub. by Granada England). Sheridan.
Fraser, Amy S. The Hills of Home. (Illus.). 250p. 1973. pap. 8.95 (ISBN 0-7102-0540-6). Routledge & Kegan.
Fraser, Andrew A. Essays on Music. facs. ed. LC 68-16932. (Essay Index Reprint Ser). 1930. 15.00 (ISBN 0-8369-0454-0). Ayer Co Pubs.
Fraser, Andrew F. Reproductive Behaviour in Ungulates. 1968. 39.00 (ISBN 0-12-266450-7). Acad Pr.
Fraser, Angus, jt. auth. see Collie, Michael.
Fraser, Angus M. The People's Liberation Army: Communist China's Armed Forces. LC 73-76898. (Strategy Paper Ser.: No. 19). 72p. 1973. pap. 2.45x (ISBN 0-8448-0223-9). Crane-Russak Co.
Fraser, Antonia. Cool Repentance. 224p. 1985. pap. 3.95 (ISBN 0-393-30264-4). Norton.
--Cool Repentance: A Jemima Shore Mystery. 1983. 12.95 (ISBN 0-393-01625-0). Norton.
--Mary Queen of Scots. 736p. 1984. pap. 5.95 (ISBN 0-440-35476-5, LE). Dell.
--Quiet As a Nun. 1982. pap. 3.95 (ISBN 0-393-30120-6). Norton.
--Royal Charles: Charles II & the Restoration. 544p. 1980. pap. 8.95 (ISBN 0-385-28788-7, Delta). Dell.
--Royal Charles: Charles II & the Restoration. LC 79-2208. (Illus.). 1979. 19.95 (ISBN 0-394-49721-X). Knopf.
--A Splash of Red. 1984. pap. 3.50 (ISBN 0-393-30213-X). Norton.
--The Weaker Vessel: Woman's Lot in Seventeenth-Century England. LC 84-47751. (Illus.). 560p. 1984. 19.95 (ISBN 0-394-51351-7). Knopf.
--The Weaker Vessel: Woman's Lot in Seventeenth-Century England. (Illus.). 550p. 1985. pap. 9.95 (ISBN 0-394-73251-0, Vin). Random.
--The Wild Island: A Mystery. 1978. 8.95 (ISBN 0-393-08831-6). Norton.
Fraser, Antonia & Yorke, Margaret. John Creasey's Crime Collection, 1983. Harris, Herbert, ed. 192p. 1983. 12.95 (ISBN 0-312-44297-1). St Martin.
Fraser, Antonia, ed. see Marshall, Dorothy.
Fraser, Antonia, ed. see Miller, John.
Fraser, Antonia, ed. see Senior, Michael.
Fraser, Antonia, ed. see Watson, D. R.
Fraser, Antonio, ed. see Lacey, Robert.
Fraser, Arvonne. Looking Forward to a Career: Government. 2nd ed. LC 75-5819. (Looking Forward to a Career Ser.). (Illus.). (gr. 6 up). 1975. PLB 6.95 (ISBN 0-87518-117-1). Dillon.
Fraser Associates. PAC Handbook: Political Action for Business. 432p. 1982. prof ref 29.95 (ISBN 0-88410-879-1). Ballinger Pub.
Fraser, B. Kay. Creative Bottle Cutting. (Arts & Crafts Ser.). (Illus.). 96p. 1972. pap. 3.95 (ISBN 0-517-50214-3). Crown.
--Decorative Tole Painting: A Basic Course in Folk Art for Beginners & Craftsmen. (Arts & Crafts Ser.). (Illus.). 96p. 1972. pap. 6.95 (ISBN 0-517-50373-5). Crown.
--Modern Stitchery: Stitches, Patterns, Free-Form Designing. 1976. 6.95 (ISBN 0-517-51864-3). Crown.
Fraser, Beverly, et al. Gross Motor Management of Severely Multiply Impaired Students, Vol. II: Curriculum Model. LC 79-16187. (Illus.). 128p. 1980. pap. 13.00 (ISBN 0-8391-1508-3). Pro Ed.
Fraser, Beverly A. & Hensinger, Robert N. Managing Physical Handicaps: A Practical Guide for Parents, Care Providers & Educators. LC 82-19716. (Illus.). 256p. 1983. text ed. 19.95 (ISBN 0-933716-30-3, 303). P H Brookes.
Fraser, Bruce. Weekend Navigator. 1981. 18.50 (ISBN 0-8286-0090-2). J De Graff.
Fraser, Bryna S. The Structure of Adult Learning, Education & Training. 88p. 1980. 10.00 (ISBN 0-318-15752-7). Natl Inst Work.
Fraser, C. M. China: Past, Present & Personal. LC 80-67728. 141p. 1980. 8.95 (ISBN 0-8059-2736-0). Dorrance.
Fraser, C. M. & Emsley, K. Tyneside. 1974. 3.50 (ISBN 0-7153-5764-6). David & Charles.
Fraser, Catherine C. Problems in a New Medium: Autobiographies by Three Artists. LC 84-47906. (American University Studies I (Germanic Languages & Literature): Vol. 33). 150p. 1985. text ed. 19.00 (ISBN 0-8204-0160-9). P Lang Pubs.
Fraser, Cecil E. & Teetle, Stanley F., eds. Industry Goes to War. facs. ed. LC 75-142630. (Essay Index Reprint Ser). 1941. 17.00 (ISBN 0-8369-2048-1). Ayer Co Pubs.
Fraser, Charles, tr. see Naima.
Fraser, Chelsea. Famous American Flyers. Gilbert, James, ed. LC 79-7254. (Flight: Its First Seventy-Five Years Ser.). (Illus.). 1979. Repr. of 1941 ed. lib. bdg. 32.50x (ISBN 0-405-12165-2). Ayer Co Pubs.
Fraser, Clarence M., jt. ed. see Siegmund, Otto H.
Fraser, Claud L. A Book of Simple Toys: A Facsimile. (Illus.). 72p. 1983. 50.00 (ISBN 0-8139-1014-5). U Pr of Va.
--Old Broadside Ballads. LC 74-17468. 1975. Repr. of 1920 ed. lib. bdg. 15.00 (ISBN 0-88305-208-3). Norwood Edns.
Fraser, Colin. Tractor Pioneer: The Life of Harry Ferguson. LC 73-85451. (Illus.). vi, 294p. 1973. 15.00x (ISBN 0-8214-0134-3, 82-81370). Ohio U Pr.
Fraser, Colin & Scherer, Klaus R., eds. Advances in the Social Psychology of Language. LC 81-15551. (European Studies in Social Psychology). (Illus.). 280p. 1982. 44.50 (ISBN 0-521-23192-2); pap. 14.95 (ISBN 0-521-29857-1). Cambridge U Pr.
Fraser, D., jt. auth. see Yuen, C. K.
Fraser, D. A. The Physics of Semiconductor Devices. 3rd ed. (Oxford Physics Ser.). 1983. pap. text ed. 13.95x (ISBN 0-19-851860-9). Oxford U Pr.
Fraser, D. G., jt. auth. see Wood, B. J.
Fraser, D. J. Conceptual Design & Preliminary Analysis of Structures. LC 81-760. 320p. 1981. text ed. 34.95 (ISBN 0-273-01645-8). Pitman Pub MA.
Fraser, D. M. Class Warfare. 2nd ed. 169p. 1974. pap. 5.95 (ISBN 0-88978-012-9). Left Bank.
--Voice of Emma Sachs. 137p. 1983. pap. 7.95 (ISBN 0-88978-138-9). Left Bank.
Fraser, D. R., jt. auth. see Cooper, S. K.
Fraser, David. The Adventurers: 1484-1760. (Wales in History: Vol. 3). 336p. 1976. text ed. 5.75x (ISBN 0-7083-0610-1, Pub. by Univ of Wales Pr England). Humanities.
--And We Shall Shock Them: The British Army in the Second World War. (Illus.). 429p. 1984. 27.00 (ISBN 0-340-27085-3, Hodder & Stoughton UK). David & Charles.
--Blitz. 544p. 1981. pap. 2.95 (ISBN 0-449-24419-9, Crest). Fawcett.
--The Defenders: One Thousand Sixty-Three to Fourteen Eighty-Five. (Wales in History Ser.: Vol. II). 253p. 1975. text ed. 4.75x (ISBN 0-7083-0099-5, Pub. by Univ of Wales England). Humanities.
--The Fortunes of War. 1985. 15.95 (ISBN 0-393-01973-X). Norton.
--The Invaders (To Ten Sixty-Six) (Wales in History Ser.: Vol. I). 209p. 1965. text ed. 5.75 (ISBN 0-7083-0098-7, Pub. by Univ of Wales Pr England). Humanities.
Fraser, David, jt. auth. see Dayton, Edward.
Fraser, David, jt. ed. see Bronner, Edwin.
Fraser, Dean. People Problem: What You Should Know about Growing Population & Vanishing Resources. LC 77-143245. (Midland Bks.: No. 167). pap. cancelled (ISBN 0-8357-9229-3, 2015817). Bks Demand UMI.
Fraser, Derek & Sutcliffe, Anthony. The Pursuit of Urban History. 512p. 1983. text ed. 69.50 (ISBN 0-7131-6383-6). E Arnold.
Fraser, Derek, ed. A History of Modern Leeds. (Illus.). 488p. 1982. 25.00 (ISBN 0-7190-0747-X, Pub. by Manchester Univ Pr); pap. 8.50 (ISBN 0-7190-0781-X). Longwood Pub Group.
--Municipal Reform & the Industrial City. LC 81-21302. 1982. 32.50 (ISBN 0-312-55268-8). St Martin.
--The New Poor Law in the Nineteenth Century. LC 75-43484. (Problems in Focus Ser.). 250p. 1976. 25.00 (ISBN 0-312-56910-6). St Martin.
Fraser, Donald. African Idylls: Portraits & Impressions of Life on a Central African Mission Station. LC 78-94477. (Illus.). Repr. of 1923 ed. 17.50x (ISBN 0-8371-2354-2, FRA&, Pub. by Negro U Pr). Greenwood.
--Autobiography of an African. LC 78-138006. Repr. of 1925 ed. 17.50x (ISBN 0-8371-5653-X, FAU&, Pub. by Negro U Pr). Greenwood.
--Future of Africa. LC 77-137231. (Illus.). Repr. of 1911 ed. 25.00x (ISBN 0-8371-4113-3, FFA&, Pub. by Negro U Pr). Greenwood.
--New Africa. LC 78-89034. (Illus.). Repr. of 1927 ed. 17.50x (ISBN 0-8371-1914-6, FRN&, Pub. by Negro U Pr). Greenwood.
--Winning a Primitive People. LC 78-107474. (Illus.). Repr. of 1914 ed. 22.50x (ISBN 0-8371-3752-7, FPP&). Greenwood.
Fraser, Donald, jt. auth. see Crofton, Ian.
Fraser, Donald, ed. Thermodynamics in Geology. (Nato Adv. Study Inst. Ser. C: No. 30). 1977. lib. bdg. 50.00 (ISBN 90-277-0794-4, Pub. by Reidel Holland); pap. 16.00 (ISBN 90-277-0834-7). Kluwer Academic.
Fraser, Donald, jt. ed. see Crofton, Ian.
Fraser, Donald C., ed. Journal of Guidance, Control, & Dynamics, Vol. 8. 128p. (J). 1985. 90.00 (ISBN 0-317-36784-6); foreign 94.00 (ISBN 0-317-36785-4). AIAA.
Fraser, Donald R. & Kolari, James W. The Future of Small Banks in a Deregulated Environment. 280p. 1985. 29.95 ea. (ISBN 0-88730-014-6). Ballinger Pub.
Fraser, Donald R. & Rose, Peter S. Financial Institutions & Markets in a Changing World. 2nd ed. 1984. 17.50 (ISBN 0-256-03061-8). Business Pubns.
Fraser, Donald R., jt. auth. see Cooper, S. Kerry.
Fraser, Donald R., jt. auth. see Rose, Peter S.
Fraser, Douglas, ed. Early Chinese Art & the Pacific Basin: A Photographic Exhibition. LC 68-28018. (Illus.). 152p. 1968. pap. 5.00 (ISBN 0-913456-17-9). Interbk Inc.
Fraser, Douglas & Cole, Herbert M., eds. African Art & Leadership. LC 72-157391. (Illus.). pap. 87.50 (ISBN 0-317-10171-4, 2007667). Bks Demand UMI.
Fraser, Douglas, jt ed. see Barker, Philip J.
Fraser, Douglas A. & Byrom, Fletcher L. Failing Industries: The Role of Government. 90p. 1981. 14.00x (ISBN 0-915604-49-3). Columbia U Pr.
Fraser, Douglas F. Torres Straits Sculpture: A Study in Oceanic Primitive Art. LC 77-94696. (Outstanding Dissertations in the Fine Arts Ser.). 1978. lib. bdg. 58.00 (ISBN 0-8240-3228-4). Garland Pub.
Fraser, Duncan. Edinburgh in Olden Times. 1981. 35.00x (ISBN 0-686-78871-0, Pub. by Standard Scotland). State Mutual Bk.
--The Flower People. 36p. 1981. 35.00x (ISBN 0-900871-26-1, Pub. by Standard Scotland). State Mutual Bk.
--Glen of the Rowan Trees. 1981. 35.00x (ISBN 0-900871-12-1, Pub. by Standard Scotland). State Mutual Bk.
--Highland Perthshire. 5th ed. 1980. 30.00x (ISBN 0-900871-09-1, Pub. by Standard Scotland). State Mutual Bk.
--Historic Fife. 1980. 35.00x (ISBN 0-900871-36-9, Pub. by Standard Scotland). State Mutual Bk.
--Portrait of a Parish. 144p. 1981. 35.00x (ISBN 0-900871-35-0, Pub. by Standard Scotland). State Mutual Bk.
--The Smugglers. 1981. 35.00x (ISBN 0-900871-34-2, Pub. by Standard Scotland). State Mutual Bk.
Fraser, Duncan, ed. see Carnegie, David.
Fraser, Edward & Gibbons, John. Soldier & Sailor Words & Phrases. LC 68-30635. 1968. Repr. of 1925 ed. 46.00x (ISBN 0-8103-3281-7). Gale.
Fraser, Elizabeth. Quick Cuisine. LC 83-82661. 144p. 1984. pap. 6.95 (ISBN 0-89709-130-2). Liberty Pub.
Fraser, Esther. The Canadian Rockies: Early Travels & Explorations. (Illus.). 256p. 1969. pap. 8.95 (ISBN 0-295-95978-9, Pub. by Hurtig Pubs). U of Wash Pr.
Fraser, F., jt. ed. see Wilson, James G.
Fraser, F. C. British Whales, Dolphins & Porpoises. 5th ed. (Illus.). (gr. 7 up). 1976. pap. text ed. 2.00x (ISBN 0-8277-4825-6, Pub. by Brit Mus Nat Hist). Sabbot-Natural Hist Bks.
--Odonata: Vol. 1 - Coenagriidae. (Fauna of British India Ser.). (Illus.). xiv, 424p. 1977. Repr. of 1933 ed. 30.00 (ISBN 0-88065-086-9, Pub. by Messers Today & Tomorrows Printers & Publishers India). Scholarly Pubns.
--Odonata: Vol. 2 - Agriidae & Gomphida. (Illus.). xxiv, 416p. 1977. Repr. of 1934 ed. 30.00 (ISBN 0-88065-087-7, Pub. by Messers Today & Tomorrows Printers & Publishers India). Scholarly Pubns.
--Odonata: Vol. 3 - Cordulegasteridae, Aeshnidae, Labellulidae. (Fauna of British India Ser.). (Illus.). xii, 472p. 1977. Repr. of 1936 ed. 30.00 (ISBN 0-88065-088-5, Pub. by Messers Today & Tomorrows Printers & Publishers India). Scholarly Pubns.
Fraser, F. Clark, jt. auth. see Nora, James J.
Fraser, G. M. & Blockley, J. The Language Disordered Child. Berse, P. A., ed. 56p. 1974. 6.00x (ISBN 0-85633-031-0, Pub. by NFER Nelson UK). Taylor & Francis.
Fraser, G. S. Metre, Rhyme, & Free Verse. (Critical Idiom Ser.). 1970. pap. 5.50x (ISBN 0-416-17300-4, NO. 2203). Methuen Inc.
--A Short History of English Poetry. 396p. 1981. 28.50x (ISBN 0-389-20174-X); pap. 14.95x (ISBN 0-389-20175-8, 06951). B&N Imports.
--A Short History of English Poetry. 400p. 1981. 60.00x (ISBN 0-7291-0077-4, Pub. by Open Bks England); pap. 30.00x (ISBN 0-7291-0072-3). State Mutual Bk.
--A Stranger & Afraid: Memoirs. LC 83-134906. 240p. 1983. text ed. 19.50x (ISBN 0-85635-460-0, Pub. by Carcanet New Pr England). Humanities.
Fraser, G. S; see Bradbrook, M. C.
Fraser, G. S., ed. Selected Poems of Robert Burns. (The Poetry Bookshelf). 1960. pap. text ed. 5.00x (ISBN 0-435-15025-1). Heinemann Ed.
Fraser, G. S., tr. see Moreux, Serge.
Fraser, George. Essays on Twentieth-Century Poets. 255p. 1977. pap. 12.50x (ISBN 0-87471-876-7). Rowman.
Fraser, George M. Flash for Freedom! 1985. 6.95 (ISBN 0-452-25677-1, Plume). NAL.
--Flashman. 1984. pap. 6.95 (ISBN 0-452-25588-0, Plume). NAL.
--Flashman & the Redskins. LC 82-47828. 1982. 14.95 (ISBN 0-394-52852-2). Knopf.
--Flashman & the Redskins. LC 84-6781. 480p. 1983. pap. 7.95 (ISBN 0-452-25431-0, Plume). NAL.
--The Pyrates. LC 84-47771. 416p. 1984. 16.95 (ISBN 0-394-53837-4). Knopf.
--The Pyrates. 1985. pap. 7.95 (ISBN 0-452-25764-6, Plume). NAL.
--Royal Flash. 1985. pap. 6.95 (ISBN 0-452-25676-3, Plume). NAL.
--Sir Walter Scott & the Aberdonians. LC 76-44855. 1976. Repr. of 1908 ed. lib. bdg. 12.50 (ISBN 0-8414-4182-0). Folcroft.
Fraser, George R. The Causes of Profound Deafness in Childhood. LC 75-36954. (Illus.). 432p. 1976. 28.00x (ISBN 0-8018-1685-8). Johns Hopkins.
Fraser, George S. Essays on Twentieth-Century Poets. LC 78-300315. pap. 64.00 (ISBN 0-317-28253-0, 2022637). Bks Demand UMI.
--The Modern Writer & His World. LC 75-32457. 426p. 1976. Repr. of 1965 ed. lib. bdg. 70.00x (ISBN 0-8371-8549-1, FRMW). Greenwood.
--W. B. Yeats. LC 83-45432. Repr. of 1954 ed. 16.50 (ISBN 0-404-20099-0). AMS Pr.
Fraser, Gordon. Bill Brandt: Nudes Nineteen Forty-Five to Nineteen Eighty. 132p. 1982. 55.00x (ISBN 0-86092-064-X, Pub. by Fraser Bks). State Mutual Bk.
--Modern Transportation & Internatonal Crime. (Illus.). 120p. 1970. photocopy ed. 14.50x (ISBN 0-398-00604-0). C C Thomas.
Fraser, Gordon H. Is Mormonism Christian? 1977. pap. 3.95 (ISBN 0-8024-4169-6). Moody.
Fraser, Gordon S. Physical Processes of Stratigraphy. (Illus.). 325p. 1986. text ed. write for info. (ISBN 0-934634-86-6). Intl Human Res.
Fraser, Hamish, jt. auth. see Ward, J. T.
Fraser, Hermia. Tall Brigade. 1956. 8.95 (ISBN 0-8323-0058-6); pap. 5.95 (ISBN 0-8323-0284-8). Binford.
Fraser, Hugh, jt. ed. see Barnett, Herbert E.
Fraser, Hugh, jt. ed. see Barnett, Hert E.
Fraser, Hugh R. Democracy in the Making: The Jackson-Tyler Era. LC 38-25891. 1969. Repr. of 1938 ed. 32.00 (ISBN 0-527-31300-9). Kraus Repr.
Fraser, I., jt. auth. see Marshall, D.
Fraser, Iain, et al, trs. see Trotsky, Leon.
Fraser, Ian, tr. see Brohm, Jean-Marie.
Fraser, Ian F. Spirit of French Canada: A Study of the Literature. LC 70-168135. Repr. of 1939 ed. 17.50 (ISBN 0-404-02548-X). AMS Pr.
Fraser, J. C. Determining Discharges for Fluvial Resources. (Fisheries Technical Papers: No. 143). (Illus.). 102p. 1975. pap. 7.50 (ISBN 92-5-101909-6, F873, FAO). Unipub.
Fraser, J. D. & Allbutt, Mary E., eds. Prayer of Faith. pap. 1.00 (ISBN 0-85363-106-9). OMF Bks.
Fraser, J. H. British Pelagic Fauna Tunicates. LC 80-42174. (Synopses of the British Fauna Ser.: No. 20). 65p. 1982. pap. 14.95 (ISBN 0-521-28367-1). Cambridge U Pr.
Fraser, J. M. Industrial Psychology. 1962. 19.50 (ISBN 0-08-009649-2). Pergamon.

Fraser, J. Nelson & Marathe, K. B., eds. Poems of Tukarama. Fraser, J. Nelson & Marathe, K. B., trs. 1981. Repr. of 1909 ed. 15.00x (ISBN 0-8364-0747-4, Pub. by Motilal Banarsidass). South Asia Bks.

Fraser, J. Nelson, tr. see Fraser, J. Nelson & Marathe, K. B.

Fraser, J. T. The Genesis & Evolution of Time: A Critique of Interpretation in Physics. LC 82-8622. (Illus.). 224p. 1982. lib. bdg. 20.00x (ISBN 0-87023-370-X). U of Mass Pr.

--Of Time, Passion & Knowledge: Reflections on the Strategy of Existence. LC 74-12783. 544p. 1975. 20.00 (ISBN 0-8076-0770-3). Braziller.

--Time As Conflict: A Scientific & Humanistic Study. (Science & Culture Ser.: No. 35). 356p. 1978. 26.95x (ISBN 0-8176-0950-4). Birkhauser.

Fraser, J. T., ed. The Voices of Time: A Cooperative Survey of Man's Views of Time As Expressed by the Sciences & by the Humanities. 2nd ed. LC 81-3025. (Illus.). 772p. 1981. pap. text ed. 15.95x (ISBN 0-87023-337-8). U of Mass Pr.

Fraser, J. T., et al, eds. Study of Time IV: Proceedings. (Illus.). 286p. 1981. 46.00 (ISBN 0-387-90594-4). Springer-Verlag.

--Study of Time II: 2nd Conference of the International Society for the Study of Time, Summer, 1973. (Illus.). ix, 487p. 1975. 39.50 (ISBN 0-387-07321-3). Springer-Verlag.

--Study of Time III: 3rd Conference of the International Society for the Study of Time. 1978. 37.00 (ISBN 0-387-90311-9). Springer-Verlag.

Fraser, James. Death in a Pheasant's Eye. 1984. pap. 2.95 (ISBN 0-8027-3093-0). Walker & Co.

--Investment Sources. 1979. 7.00 (ISBN 0-87034-057-3). Fraser Pub Co.

Fraser, James, jt. auth. see Scott, Ronald B.

Fraser, James, ed. Society & Children's Literature. 218p. (Publishes by Godine). 1979. pap. 8.00 (ISBN 0-8389-3213-4). Assn Library Serv.

Fraser, James A. Outcomes of a Study Excursion. LC 75-176785. (Columbia University. Teachers College. Contributions to Education: No. 778). Repr. of 1939 ed. 22.50 (ISBN 0-404-55778-3). AMS Pr.

Fraser, James B. The Himala Mountains. 548p. 1983. text ed. 75.00x (ISBN 0-86590-149-X). Apt Bks.

--Narrative of a Journey into Khorasan in the Years 1821 & 1822. 824p. 1985. 29.95x (ISBN 0-19-561627-8). Oxford U Pr.

--Narrative of the Residence of the Persian Princes in London in 1835 & 1836, 2 vols. in 1. LC 73-6280. (The Middle East Ser.). Repr. of 1838 ed. 45.50 (ISBN 0-405-05336-3). Ayer Co Pubs.

--A Winter's Journey (Tatar) from Constantinople to Tehran, 2 vols. in 1. LC 73-6281. (The Middle East Ser.). Repr. of 1838 ed. 58.00 (ISBN 0-405-05339-8). Ayer Co Pubs.

Fraser, James F. Dr. Jimmy: Some Reminiscences by James Fowler Fraser 1893-1979. 150p. 1982. pap. 8.00 (ISBN 0-08-025737-2). Pergamon.

Fraser, James H., ed. Society & Children's Literature. LC 77-94110. 1978. 20.00 (ISBN 0-87923-236-6). Godine.

Fraser, James L. The Art of Selling Stocks. 1982. 2.00 (ISBN 0-87034-066-2). Fraser Pub Co.

--P. S. What Do You Think of the Market. (Orig.). 1966. Repr. of 1920 ed. 5.00 (ISBN 0-87034-023-9). Fraser Pub Co.

--Ten Rules for Investing. 1964. 2.00 (ISBN 0-87034-030-1). Fraser Pub Co.

--Ten Ways to Become Rich. (Illus.). 1967. flexible cover 2.00 (ISBN 0-87034-031-X). Fraser Pub Co.

Fraser, James R. & Weber, Renee K., eds. Children's Authors & Illustrators: A Guide to the Manuscript Collections in United States Research Libraries. 199p. 1980. lib. bdg. 10.00 (ISBN 3-598-40504-9). K G Saur.

Fraser, James W. Cremation: Is It Christian? 1965. pap. 1.50 (ISBN 0-87213-180-7). Loizeaux.

Fraser, James W., et al, eds. From Common School to Magnet School: Selected Essays in the History of Boston Schools. 1979. 5.00 (ISBN 0-89073-059-8). Boston Public Lib.

Fraser, Janet, jt. auth. see May, Ernest R.

Fraser, John. America & the Patterns of Chivalry. LC 81-6180. 272p. 1982. 22.95 (ISBN 0-521-24183-9). Cambridge U Pr.

--Introduction to the Thought of Galvano Della Volpe. 1977. text ed. 8.50x (ISBN 0-85315-389-2). Humanities.

--Italy: Society in Crisis-Society in Transformation. 288p. 1981. 27.50x (ISBN 0-7100-0771-X). Routledge & Kegan.

--The Name of Action: Critical Essays. 272p. 1985. 44.50 (ISBN 0-521-25876-6); pap. 14.95 (ISBN 0-521-27745-0). Cambridge U Pr.

--Violence in the Arts. LC 73-84319. 208p. 1976. pap. 11.95 (ISBN 0-521-29029-5). Cambridge U Pr.

Fraser, John, frwd. By. Resource-Constrained Economies: The North American Dilemma. LC 80-16502. xvi, 307p. (Orig.). 1980. pap. text ed. 8.50 (ISBN 0-935734-05-8). Soil Conservation.

Fraser, John, tr. see Della Volpe, Galvano.

Fraser, John F. Round the World on a Wheel. 336p. 1982. 36.00x (ISBN 0-7011-2609-4, Pub. by Chatto Bodley Head England). State Mutual Bk.

Fraser, John M. Employment Interviewing. 5th ed. (Illus.). 224p. 1978. pap. 14.95x (ISBN 0-7121-0570-0, Pub. by Macdonald & Evans England). Trans-Atlantic.

Fraser, John W. Tips on Having a Successful Sale, etc. LC 82-60525. 125p. (Orig.). 1983. pap. 4.95 (ISBN 0-88247-679-3). R & E Pubs.

Fraser, John W. see Calvin, John.

Fraser, John W., tr. see Calvin, John.

Fraser, Kathleen. My Brazen Heart. 1985. pap. 3.75 (ISBN 0-451-13516-4, Sig). NAL.

--Something (Even Human Voices) in the Foreground, a Lake. Rosenwasser, Rena, ed. LC 83-22200. (Illus.). 48p. 1984. pap. 6.25 (ISBN 0-932716-18-0). Kelsey St Pr.

Fraser, Kennedy. The Fashionable Mind: Reflections on Fashion. LC 81-47479. 256p. 1981. 14.50 (ISBN 0-394-51775-X). Knopf.

--Fashionable Mind: Reflections on Fashion, 1970-1983. LC 81-47479. 320p. 1984. pap. 10.95 (ISBN 0-87923-543-8). Godine.

Fraser, Kit. Toff Down Pitt. 130p. 1985. 12.95 (ISBN 0-7043-2513-6, Pub. by Quartet Bks). Merrimack Pub Cir.

Fraser, L. M., et al, trs. see Hasbroeck, J.

Fraser, L. P. Contemporary Staffing Techniques in Nursing. 1983. pap. 18.00 (ISBN 0-8385-1186-4). ACC.

Fraser, Leon. Testimony of Leon Fraser on the Bretton Woods Agreement Act. LC 84-80692. 84p. pap. 8.00 (ISBN 0-87034-073-5). Fraser Pub Co.

Fraser, Lindley M. Economic Thought & Language. LC 76-156825. 1971. Repr. of 1937 ed. 37.50x (ISBN 0-8046-1620-5, Pub. by Kennikat). Assoc Faculty Pr.

Fraser, Lionel M. History of Trinidad from 1781-1839, 2 vols. 776p. 1971. Repr. of 1896 ed. 95.00x set (ISBN 0-7146-1937-X, F Cass Co). Biblio Dist.

Fraser, Lisa, ed. see Graham, Winifred.

Fraser, Malcolm. Self Therapy for the Stutterer. rev. ed. LC 81-84674. 184p. 1981. pap. 2.50 (ISBN 0-933388-17-9). Speech Found Am.

--Self Therapy for the Stutterer. 5th ed. LC 84-52792. 192p. 1985. pap. 2.50 (ISBN 0-933388-21-7). Speech Found Am.

--Self-Therapy for the Stutterer. 3.00 (ISBN 0-87980-415-7). Wilshire.

Fraser, Malcolm, intro. by. To the Stutterer. LC 76-376781. 116p. 1972. pap. 1.50 (ISBN 0-933388-07-1). Speech Found Am.

Fraser, Marie. In Stevenson's Samoa. 1973. Repr. of 1895 ed. 25.00 (ISBN 0-8274-0410-7). R West.

Fraser, Mary. Custom of the Country. LC 70-101811. (Short Story Index Reprint Ser.). 1899. 19.00 (ISBN 0-8369-3199-8). Ayer Co Pubs.

Fraser, Mary C. & Cortazzi, Hugh. A Diplomat's Wife in Japan: Sketches at the Turn of the Century. LC 82-2589. (Illus.). 392p. 1982. 29.95 (ISBN 0-8348-0172-8). Weatherhill.

Fraser, Mitchell W. English Pulpit Oratory from Andrews to Tillotson: A Study of Its Literary Aspects. 516p. 1982. Repr. of 1932 ed. lib. bdg. 85.00 (ISBN 0-89760-564-0). Telegraph Bks.

Fraser, Morris. E. C. T. A Clinical Guide. LC 82-2666. 150p. 1982. 20.00x (ISBN 0-471-10416-7, Pub. by Wiley Med). Wiley.

--Moped Maintenance & Repair. (Illus.). 256p. (Orig.). 1985. pap. 14.95 (ISBN 0-8306-1847-3, 1847). TAB Bks.

Fraser, N. M., jt. auth. see Bates, R. W.

Fraser, N. M. & Hipel, K. W., eds. Conflict Analysis: Models & Resolutions. (Series in System Science & Engineering: Vol. 11). 1984. 34.50 (ISBN 0-444-00921-3). Elsevier.

Fraser, Nicholas & Navarro, Marysa. Eva Peron. (Illus.). 1981. 17.95 (ISBN 0-393-01457-6). Norton.

--Eva Peron. 144p. 1985. pap. 6.95 (ISBN 0-393-30238-5). Norton.

Fraser, P. M. Ptolemaic Alexandria, 3 vols. 2136p. 1985. Repr. of 1972 ed. Set. 149.00x (ISBN 0-317-19690-1). Oxford U Pr.

--Rhodian Funerary Monuments. (Illus.). 1978. text ed. 74.00x (ISBN 0-19-813192-5). Oxford U Pr.

Fraser, P. M. see Lehmann, Karl & Lehmann, P. W.

Fraser, P. M., ed. see Butler, Alfred J.

Fraser, P. M., tr. see Lofstedt, Einar.

Fraser, Peter. The Portrait Series: Suzanne. 176p. 1982. pap. 2.50 (ISBN 0-523-41810-8). Pinnacle Bks.

--Puppet Circus. 1971. 10.00 (ISBN 0-8238-0119-5). Plays.

--Puppets & Puppetry. LC 81-40328. (Illus.). 172p. 1982. 16.95 (ISBN 0-8128-2830-5); pap. 8.95 (ISBN 0-8128-6201-5). Stein & Day.

--Vanessa. (The Portrait Ser.). 176p. (Orig.). 1983. pap. 2.50 (ISBN 0-523-41817-5). Pinnacle Bks.

Fraser, Peter, tr. see Kjellberg, Ernst & Saflund, Gosta.

Fraser, Phyllis see Wise, Herbert A.

Fraser, Phyllis, jt. ed. see Wise, Herbert.

Fraser, R. The Novels of Ayi Kwei Armah. 1980. text ed. 17.50x (ISBN 0-435-91300-X); pap. text ed. 9.50x (ISBN 0-435-91301-8). Heinemann Ed.

Fraser, R. D. & MacRae, T. P. Conformation in Fibrous Protein & Related Synthetic Polypeptides. (Molecular Biology: An International Series of Monographs & Textbooks). 1973. 94.50 (ISBN 0-12-266850-2). Acad Pr.

Fraser, R. D., et al. Keratins: Their Composition, Structure & Biosynthesis. (Illus.). 320p. 1972. 24.75 (ISBN 0-398-02283-6). C C Thomas.

Fraser, Raymond. The Fighting Fisherman: The Life of Yvon Durelle. LC 80-703. (Illus.). 1981. 13.95 (ISBN 0-385-15863-7). Doubleday.

Fraser, Robert, jt. auth. see Pare, J. A.

Fraser, Robert D. International Banking & Finance. 6th ed. (A Comprehensive Overview: Vol. 1). 500p. 1984. 26.00 (ISBN 0-935246-00-2). R & H Pubs.

--International Banking & Finance: Vol. 2 - Global Management of Assets Liabilities. 2nd ed. 500p. 1978. 35.00 (ISBN 0-935246-01-0). R & H Pubs.

Fraser, Robert G. & Pare, J. A. Diagnosis of Diseases of the Chest, Vol. 1. 2nd ed. LC 76-20932. (Illus.). 1977. text ed. 42.00 (ISBN 0-7216-3852-X). Saunders.

--Diagnosis of Diseases of the Chest, Vol. 2. 2nd ed. LC 76-20932. (Illus.). 1978. pap. 47.00 (ISBN 0-7216-3853-8). Saunders.

--Diagnosis of Diseases of the Chest, Vol. 3. 2nd ed. LC 76-20932. (Illus.). 1979. 47.00 (ISBN 0-7216-3854-6). Saunders.

--Diagnosis of Diseases of the Chest, Vol. 4. 2nd ed. LC 76-20932. (Illus.). 1979. text ed. 37.00 (ISBN 0-7216-3855-4). Saunders.

--Structure & Function of the Lung with Emphasis on Roentgenology. 2nd ed. LC 76-20933. (Illus.). 1977. text ed. 9.50 (ISBN 0-7216-3859-7). Saunders.

Fraser, Robert G. & Pave, J. A. Organ Physiology: Structure & Function of the Lung. 2nd ed. LC 76-20933. pap. 59.50 (ISBN 0-317-26430-3, 2024986). Bks Demand UMI.

Fraser, Robert S., ed. Essays on the Rossettis. (Illus.). 117p. 1972. 10.00 (ISBN 0-686-79072-3). Princeton Lib.

Fraser, Ron. Championship Baseball. (Illus.). 144p. (Orig.). 1984. pap. 6.95 (ISBN 0-87670-089-X, Sterling). Athletic Inst.

Fraser, Ronald. Blood of Spain: An Oral History of the Spanish Civil War. LC 78-20416. 1979. 15.95 (ISBN 0-394-48982-9). Pantheon.

--Blood of Spain: An Oral History of the Spanish Civil War. 1980. pap. 7.95 (ISBN 0-394-73854-3). Pantheon.

--Consolidations: A Simplified Approach. LC 80-83431. 128p. 1981. pap. text ed. 8.95 (ISBN 0-8403-2713-7). Kendall-Hunt.

--In Search of a Past: The Rearing of an English Gentleman 1933-45. LC 84-45049. 192p. 1984. 12.95 (ISBN 0-689-11480-X). Atheneum.

Fraser, Ronald, tr. see Schwaller De Lubicz, Isha.

Fraser, Russel A. & Rabkin, Norman. Drama of the English Renaissance: The Tudor Period, Vol. 1. 1976. write for info. (ISBN 0-02-339570-2, 33957). Macmillan.

--Drama of the English Renaissance: The Stuart Period, Vol. 2. 736p. 1976. pap. text ed. write for info. (ISBN 0-02-339580-X, 33958). Macmillan.

Fraser, Russell. The Dark Ages & the Age of Gold. LC 70-29786. 472p. 1973. 43.00 (ISBN 0-691-06216-1). Princeton U Pr.

--The Language of Adam: On the Limits and Systems of Discourse. LC 77-3528. 288p. 1977. 26.50x (ISBN 0-231-04256-6). Columbia U Pr.

--A Mingled Yarn: The Life of R. P. Blackmur. LC 81-47554. (Illus.). 320p. 1981. 19.95 (ISBN 0-15-160138-0). HarBraceJ.

--The Three Romes. 352p. 1985. 17.95 (ISBN 0-15-190186-4). HarBraceJ.

--The War Against Poetry. LC 71-113001. 1970. 23.50x (ISBN 0-691-06190-4). Princeton U Pr.

Fraser, Russell, ed. see Shakespeare, William.

Fraser, Russell A., jt. auth. see Hall, John.

Fraser, Russell A., ed. Essential Shakespeare: Nine Major Plays & the Sonnets. (Illus.). 544p. 1972. pap. text ed. write for info. (ISBN 0-02-339550-8). Macmillan.

Fraser, Samantha. Word Processing for the Wang Professional Computer: Principles & Applications. 1984. pap. text ed. 15.95 (ISBN 0-8359-8804-X). Reston.

Fraser, Sir William. Hic et Ubique. 1978. Repr. of 1893 ed. lib. bdg. 25.00 (ISBN 0-8495-1618-8). Arden Lib.

Fraser, Stewart E. British Commentary on American Education. 1970. 30.00x (ISBN 0-900008-03-2, Pub. by U of London England). State Mutual Bk.

--One Hundred Great Chinese Posters. (Illus.). 1977. 19.95 (ISBN 0-89545-006-2); pap. 8.95 (ISBN 0-89545-007-0). Images Graphiques.

Fraser, Stewart E. & Hsu, Kuang-Liang. Chinese Education & Society: A Bibliographic Guide, the Cultural Revolution & Its Aftermath. LC 72-77206. pap. 53.50 (ISBN 0-317-10233-8, 2015407). Bks Demand UMI.

Fraser, Stewart E. & Hsu Kuang-Liang. China; the Cultural Revolution: Its Aftermath & Effects on Education & Society; a Select & Partially Annotated Bibliography. 1972. 30.00x (ISBN 0-900008-05-9, Pub. by U of London England). State Mutual Bk.

Fraser, Stewart E., jt. auth. see Bjork, Robert M.

Fraser, Stewart E., et al. North Korean Education & Society: A Select & Partially Annotated Bibliography Pertaining to the Democratic People's Republic of Korea. 1972. 30.00x (ISBN 0-900008-16-4, Pub. by U of London England). State Mutual Bk.

Fraser, T. G. The Middle East: 1914-1979. 1980. 22.50 (ISBN 0-312-53181-8). St Martin.

--Partition in Ireland, India, & Palestine: Theory & Practice. LC 84-6960. 256p. 1984. 27.50 (ISBN 0-312-59752-5). St Martin.

Fraser, T. M. Ergonomic Principles in the Design of Hand Tools. International Labour Office, ed. (Occupational Safety & Health Ser.: No. 44). (Illus.). vii, 93p. (Orig.). 1980. pap. 8.55 (ISBN 92-2-102356-7). Intl Labour Office.

--Ergonomic Principles in the Design of Hand Tools. (Occupational Safety & Health Ser.: No. 44). 97p. 1981. pap. 8.55 (ISBN 92-2-102356-7, ILO155, ILO). Unipub.

--Human Stress, Work & Job Satisfaction: A Critical Approach. International Labour Office, ed. (Occupational Safety & Health Ser.: No. 50). 72p. (Orig.). 1984. pap. 9.75 (ISBN 92-2-103042-3). Intl Labour Office.

Fraser, Theodore P. & Kopp, Richard L. The Moralist Tradition in France. LC 81-69245. 286p. (Orig.). 1982. text ed. 18.50x (ISBN 0-86733-017-1). Assoc Faculty Pr.

Fraser, Theodore P. & Whipple, Alan L. Le Pot au Feu. (Illus.). 218p. (gr. 7-10). 1975. pap. text ed. 6.25x (ISBN 0-88334-068-2). Ind Sch Pr.

Fraser, Theodore P., jt. auth. see Kopp, Richard D.

Fraser, Thomas G. Captain Fraser's Voyages. Gee, Marjory, ed. (Illus.). 1979. 17.50 (ISBN 0-393-01254-9). Norton.

Fraser, Thomas H. & Lachner, Ernest A. A Revision of the Cardinalfish Subgenera Pristiapogon & Zoramia (Genus Apogon) of the Indo-Pacific Region (Teleostei: Apogonidae) LC 84-600287. (Smithsonian Contributions to Zoology Ser.: No. 412). pap. 20.00 (ISBN 0-317-30175-6, 2025357). Bks Demand UMI.

Fraser, Thomas M., Jr. Culture & Change in India: The Barpali Experiment. LC 68-19671. (Illus.). 472p. 1968. 20.00x (ISBN 0-87023-041-7); pap. 12.00x (ISBN 0-87023-061-1). U of Mass Pr.

--Fishermen of South Thailand: The Malay Villagers. Spindler, George & Spindler, Louise, eds. (Case Studies in Cultural Anthropology). (Illus.). 130p. (Orig.). pap. text ed. cancelled (ISBN 0-8290-0324-X). Irvington.

--Fishermen of South Thailand: The Malay Villagers. (Illus.). 110p. 1984. pap. text ed. 6.95x (ISBN 0-88133-081-7). Waveland Pr.

Fraser, Tony, jt. auth. see Phillips, Keri.

Fraser, W. Telecommunications. 2nd ed. 812p. 1969. 119.25 (ISBN 0-677-61240-0). Gordon.

Fraser, W. Hamish. The Coming of the Mass Market 1850-1914. (Illus.). 336p. 1981. 27.50 (ISBN 0-208-01960-X, Archon). Shoe String.

Fraser, W. I. & Grieve, R., eds. Communicating with Normal & Retarded Children. (Illus.). 208p. 1981. pap. text ed. 13.00 (ISBN 0-7236-0572-6). PSG Pub Co.

Fraser, W. R. Residential Education. LC 68-24064. 1968. pap. 12.75 (ISBN 0-08-012908-0). Pergamon.

Fraser, Walter J., Jr. & Moore, Winfred B., Jr., eds. From the Old South to the New: Essays on the Traditional South. LC 80-23315. (Contributions in American History Ser.: No. 93). (Illus.). 320p. 1981. lib. bdg. 35.00 (ISBN 0-313-22534-6, FFO/). Greenwood.

--The Southern Enigma: Essays on Race, Class, & Folk Culture. LC 82-20966. (Contributions in American History Ser.: No. 105). (Illus.). x, 240p. 1983. lib. bdg. 35.00 (ISBN 0-313-23640-2, FSE/). Greenwood.

Fraser, Walter J., Jr., et al, eds. The Web of Southern Social Relations: Women, Family, & Education. LC 85-1054. 280p. 1985. text ed. 25.00 (ISBN 0-8203-0787-4). U of Ga Pr.

Fraser, William. Disraeli & His Day. 1891. 65.00 (ISBN 0-8274-2191-5). R West.

Fraser, William A. Brave Hearts. LC 76-103508. (Short Story Index Reprint Ser.). 1904. 19.00 (ISBN 0-8369-3250-1). Ayer Co Pubs.

--Eye of a God, & Other Tales of East & West. LC 79-121551. (Short Story Index Reprint Ser.). 1899. 18.00 (ISBN 0-8369-3507-1). Ayer Co Pubs.

--Red Meekins. LC 72-125212. (Short Story Index Reprint Ser). 1921. 18.00 (ISBN 0-8369-3579-9). Ayer Co Pubs.

--Thirteen Men. LC 72-4423. (Short Story Index Reprint Ser.). Repr. of 1906 ed. 20.00 (ISBN 0-8369-4176-4). Ayer Co Pubs.

Fraser, William I., jt. auth. see Hallas, Charles H.

Fraser, William R. White Stone. 1956. 3.50 (ISBN 0-8022-0533-X). Philos Lib.

Fraser-Gruss, Jane, jt. auth. see Ainsworth, Stanley.

Fraser-Gruss, Jane, ed. Stuttering Therapy: Prevention & Intervention with Children, No. 20. 152p. pap. 1.50 (ISBN 0-933388-22-5). Speech Found Am.

Fraser-Harris, D. Shakespeare & the Influence of the Stars. 69.95 (ISBN 0-8490-1031-4). Gordon Pr.

Frasers. Frasers Canadian Trade Directory. 1985. write for info. (ISBN 0-8002-3896-6). Intl Pubns Serv.

Fraser-Simon, H., jt. auth. see Milne, A. A.

Fraser-Tytler, William K., Sr. Afghanistan: A Study of Political Developments in Central and Southern Asia. 5th ed. LC 80-1931. 1981. 42.50 (ISBN 0-404-18962-8). AMS Pr.

Frasier, Carl. Inspiring Poems. 6.00 (ISBN 0-8062-2493-2). Carlton.

Frasier, Jane. Women Composers: A Discography. LC 83-22563. (Detroit Studies in Music Bibliography: No. 50). 1983. 18.50 (ISBN 0-89990-018-6). Info Coord.

Frasier, Mary M., et al, eds. Dictionary of Gifted, Talented, & Creative Education Terms. 135p. 1984. 15.00 (ISBN 0-89824-021-2). Trillium Pr.

Frasier, S. Douglas. Pediatric Endocrinology. 373p. 1980. 42.50 (ISBN 0-8089-1272-0, 791363). Grune.

Frassanito, Elaine, jt. auth. see Arias, Toby.

Frassanito, William. Gettysburg: A Journey in Time. LC 74-10597. 1976. pap. 12.95 (ISBN 0-684-14696-7, ScribT). Scribner.

Frassanito, William A. Antietam: The Photographic Legacy of America's Bloodiest Day. LC 78-2336. (Encore Edition). (Illus.). 1978. 5.95 (ISBN 0-684-16835-9, ScribT); pap. 14.95 (ISBN 0-684-17645-9). Scribner.

--Grant & Lee: The Virginia Campaigns, 1864-1865. (Illus.). 448p. 1983. 24.95 (ISBN 0-684-17873-7, ScribT). Scribner.

Frassen, Bas C. van see Van Fraassen, Bas C.

Frassica, Pietro & Carrara, Antonio. Per Modo Di Dire: A First Course in Italian. 544p. 1981. text ed. 23.95 (ISBN 0-669-02068-0); wkbk. 9.95 (ISBN 0-669-02070-2); cassette 25.00 (ISBN 0-669-02073-7); tapes-reels 40.00 (ISBN 0-669-02072-9); instr's manual 1.95 (ISBN 0-669-02069-9); tapescript 1.95 (ISBN 0-669-02074-5); demo tape 1.95 (ISBN 0-669-02075-3); transcripts 1.95 (ISBN 0-669-02074-5). Heath.

Frasure, David. Mary. 128p. (Orig.). 1982. pap. 5.95 (ISBN 0-932298-26-5). Copple Hse.

Frasure, David W. Bluebirds. 1978. pap. 4.95 (ISBN 0-932298-08-7). Copple Hse.

Frasure, William W., jt. auth. see Rossell, James H.

Fratangelo, Robert A., jt. auth. see Connelly, James F.

Fratcher, William F. Scott on Trusts: 1984 Supplement. LC 66-25719. 875p. 1984. pap. 70.00 (ISBN 0-316-29219-2). Little.

--Scott on Trusts: 1985 Supplement. 1985. pap. text ed. price not set. Little.

Frate, Frank. Bridgewalker. 12p. 1982. pap. 1.00 (ISBN 0-686-37934-9). Samisdat.

--Investigations, Pt. II. 1981. pap. 1.00. Samisdat.

--Watchers. 12p. 1983. pap. 1.00 (ISBN 0-686-89394-8). Samisdat.

Frater, Alexander. Stopping Train Britain. (Illus.). 168p. 1985. pap. 16.95 (ISBN 0-340-38441-7, Pub. by Hodder & Stoughton UK). David & Charles.

--Stopping Train Britain: A Railway Odyssey. (Illus.). 192p. 1984. 22.50 (ISBN 0-340-32451-1, Pub. by Hodder & Stoughton UK). David & Charles.

Frater, Alexander, ed. Great Rivers of the World. LC 83-83383. (Illus.). 224p. 1984. 24.95 (ISBN 0-316-29222-2). Little.

Frates, Jeffrey. Programming in BASIC: Communicating with Computers. (Illus.). 304p. 1985. pap. text ed. 19.95 (ISBN 0-13-729369-0). P-H.

Frates, Jeffrey & Molrup, William. Introduction to the Computer: An Integrative Approach. 2nd ed. (Illus.). 496p. 1984. 26.95 (ISBN 0-13-480319-1). P-H.

Frates, Jeffrey E. & Moldrup, William. Computers & Life: An Integrative Approach. (Illus.). 448p. 1983. pap. 25.95 (ISBN 0-13-165084-X). P-H.

Fratianni, Michele & Peeters, Theo, eds. One Money for Europe. LC 78-67228. (Praeger Special Studies). 225p. 1979. 39.95 (ISBN 0-03-047526-0). Praeger.

Fratkin, Jake. WQ-Ten Electro Acupuncture Machine. Felt, Robert L., ed. 48p. (Orig.). pap. 7.95 (ISBN 0-912111-03-8). Paradigm Pubns.

Fratti, Mario, ed. Nuovo Teatro Italiano: Plays by Nine Modern Young Italian Playwrights. 1972. pap. 5.95x (ISBN 0-913298-25-5). S F Vanni.

Fratzke, Bob. Taking Trophy Whitetails. Helgeland, Glenn, ed. LC 83-50905. (On Target Ser.). (Illus.). 132p. (Orig.). 1983. pap. 10.00 (ISBN 0-913305-02-2). Target Comm.

Frauchiger, Fritz & Van Buskirk, William R. Spoken Swedish. 261p. 1980. Sold only with cassettes. pap. text ed. 10.00x (ISBN 0-87950-704-7); cassettes 24 dual track 140.00x (ISBN 0-87950-705-5); bk. & cassettes 145.00x (ISBN 0-87950-706-3). Spoken Lang Serv.

Frauchimont, Paul, jt. auth. see Odell, William D.

Frauen, Janice, jt. auth. see Kranz, Joe.

Frauenfelder, Hans & Henley, Ernest M. Subatomic Physics. (Illus.). 544p. 1974. 43.95 (ISBN 0-13-859082-6). P-H.

Frauenglas, Robert A. The Brooklyn Bum Again. rev. ed. LC 81-84685. 128p. Date not set. pap. cancelled (ISBN 0-9603950-2-4). Somrie Pr.

Frauenglas, Robert A., ed. Brooklyn Prospects: The First Brooklyn Book Fair Anthology. 80p. (Orig.). 1984. pap. 6.00 (ISBN 0-9603950-7-5). Somrie Pr.

Frauenglas, Robert A., ed. see Houston, Lee.

Frauenthal, J. C. Introduction to Population Modeling. (UMAP Monographs). 186p. 1979. pap. 9.95x (ISBN 0-8176-3015-5). Birkhauser.

--Mathematical Modeling in Epidemiology. (Universitexts Ser.). 118p. 1980. pap. 18.00 (ISBN 0-387-10328-7). Springer-Verlag.

--Smallpox: When Should Routine Vaccination Be Discontinued. 55p. 1981. pap. text ed. 8.75x (ISBN 0-8176-3042-2). Birkhauser.

Frauhofer, J. A. Von see Von Fraunhofer, J. A. & Banks, C. H.

Fraumann, L. K., ed. see Keatley, Lu.

Fraumeni, Joseph F., jt. auth. see Schottenfeld, David.

Fraumeni, Joseph F., Jr., jt. ed. see Boice, John D., Jr.

Fraunce, Abraham. The Arcadian Rhetorike. Seton, Ethel, intro. by. LC 78-14120. (Illus.). 1980. Repr. of 1950 ed. 21.45 (ISBN 0-88355-794-0). Hyperion Conn.

--Victoria: A Latin Comedy. Smith, G. C., ed. (Mat. for the Study of the Old English Drama Ser. 1: Vol. 14). pap. 16.00 (ISBN 0-317-16139-3). Kraus Repr.

Fraunce, Abraham see Batman, Stephen.

Fraunfelder, F. T. Drug-Induced Ocular Side Effects & Drug Interactions. 2nd ed. LC 82-146. 544p. 1982. text ed. 30.00 (ISBN 0-8121-0850-7). Lea & Febiger.

Fraunfelder, Frederick T. & Roy, F. Hampton. Current Ocular Therapy. 600p. 1980. text ed. 55.00 (ISBN 0-7216-3860-0). Saunders.

--Current Ocular Therapy Two. 880p. 1984. write for info. (ISBN 0-7216-3849-X). Saunders.

Fraunhofer, J. A., et al. Protective Paint Coatings for Metals. 118p. 1981. 40.00x (ISBN 0-901994-89-8, Pub. by Portcullio Pr). State Mutual Bk.

Fraunhofer, J. A. von see Boxall, J. & Von Fraunhofer, J. A.

Fraunhofer, J. A. von see Von Fraunhofer, J. A.

Fraunhofer, J. A. Von see Von Fraunhofer, J. A. & Murray, J. J.

Frausto, Fernando A. Improve Your Grammatical Knowledge. (Span. & Eng.). 1983. text ed. 6.80 (ISBN 0-538-22390-1, V39). SW Pub.

Frausto, Tomas Y., jt. auth. see Wagner, Nora E.

Frautschi, R. L. Barron's Simplified Approach to Voltaire's Candide. LC 68-31479. 1969. pap. text ed. 01.95 (ISBN 0-8120-0366-7). Barron.

Frautschi, Richard L. & Bouygues, Claude. Pour et Contre: Manuel De Conversations Graduees. 2nd ed. LC 78-20794. 1979. scp 20.95 (ISBN 0-06-042164-9, HarpC). Har-Row.

Frautschi, Steven C., et al. The Mechanical Universe: Mechanics & Heat, Advanced Edition. (Illus.). 450p. Date not set. price not set (ISBN 0-521-30432-6). Cambridge U Pr.

Frauwallner, Erich. History of Indian Philosophy, 2 vols. Bedeker, V. M., tr. 1973. 22.50 set (ISBN 0-89684-219-3). Orient Bk Dist.

Frawley, Honora M. Certain Procedures of Studying Poetry in the Fifth Grade. LC 79-178799. (Columbia University. Teachers College. Contributions to Education: No. 539). Repr. of 1932 ed. 22.50 (ISBN 0-404-55539-X). AMS Pr.

Frawley, R. W. Blackjack: How to Play & Win Like an Expert. 32p. 1985. pap. 5.95 (ISBN 0-934650-09-8). Sunnyside.

Frawley, William, ed. Linguistics & Literacy. (Topics in Language & Linguistics). 504p. 1982. 55.00x (ISBN 0-306-41174-1, Plenum Pr). Plenum Pub.

--Translation: Literary, Linguistic & Philosophical Approaches. LC 82-40479. (Illus.). 224p. 1984. 27.50 (ISBN 0-87413-226-6). U Delaware Pr.

Frawley, William, tr. see Bosquet, Alain.

Fray, G. I. & Saxton, R. G. The Chemistry of Cyclo-Octatetraene & Its Derivatives. LC 76-57096. 1978. Cambridge U Pr.

Fraydas, Stan. Professional Cartooning: A Complete Course in Graphic Humor. LC 72-81126. (Illus.). 160p. 1977. Repr. of 1972 ed. cloth 12.50 (ISBN 0-88275-064-X). Krieger.

Fraydas, Stan, illus. The Strawberry Storybook to Color. (Strawberry Shortcake Bks.). (Illus.). 80p. (ps-3). 1980. pap. 1.95 saddle stitch (ISBN 0-394-84574-9). Random.

Frayer, W. E., et al, eds. Inventory Design & Analysis. (Illus.). 368p. 1974. pap. 6.50 (ISBN 0-939970-11-2). Soc Am Foresters.

Frayer, William C. Congenital Anomalies & the Phakomatoses. LC 80-720244. (Lancaster Course in Opthalmic Histopathology Ser.). (Illus.). 16p. text ed. 65.00 (includes 45 slides) (ISBN 0-8036-3830-2). Davis Co.

--Diseases of the Optic Nerve. LC 80-720251. (Lancaster Course in Ophthalmic Histopathology Ser.). (Illus.). 15p. text ed. 58.00 (includes 41 slides) (ISBN 0-8036-3837-X). Davis Co.

--Pathology of the Crystalline Lens. LC 80-720250. (Lancaster Course in Ophthalmic Histopathology Ser.). (Illus.). 8p. text ed. 43.00 incl. 27 slides (ISBN 0-8036-3836-1). Davis Co.

Frayer, William C., ed. Lancaster Course in Ophthalmic Histopathology. (Illus.). 320p. 1980. Text, Slides, Cassette tapes & Fourteen Units with Lectures. 936.00x (ISBN 0-8036-3840-X). Davis Co.

Frayling, Christopher. Spaghetti Westerns: Cowboys & Europeans from Karl May to Sergio Leone. LC 80-40822. (Cinema & Society Ser.). (Illus.). 304p. 1981. pap. 13.95 (ISBN 0-7100-0504-0). Routledge & Kegan.

Frayn, J. Subsistence Farming in Roman Italy. 1981. 40.00x (ISBN 0-900000-92-9, Pub. by Centaur Pr). State Mutual Bk.

Frayn, Michael. Alphabetical Order & Donkeys' Years. 165p. 1977. pap. 6.95 (ISBN 0-413-37990-6, NO.3003). Methuen Inc.

--Benefactors. 80p. 1984. pap. 6.95 (ISBN 0-413-54160-6, NO.4109). Methuen Inc.

--Clouds. 84p. 1977. pap. 6.95 (ISBN 0-413-38010-6, NO.3001). Methuen Inc.

--Make & Break. 1980. pap. 6.95 (ISBN 0-413-47790-8, NO. 2567). Methuen Inc.

--Noises Off. (Modern Play Ser.). 60p. 1982. pap. 6.95 (ISBN 0-413-50670-3, NO. 3757). Methuen Inc.

Frayn, Michael, tr. see Chekhov, Anton.

Frayn, Michael, tr. see Tolstoy, Lev.

Frayne, John P. Sean O'Casey- Columbia Essays on Modern Writers, No. 73. 1976. pap. 2.50 (ISBN 0-231-03655-8). Columbia U Pr.

Frayne, John P., ed. see Yeats, W. B.

Fraysse, Mike, jt. auth. see Honig, Daniel T.

Frazee, Charles A. Catholics & Sultans: The Church & the Ottoman Empire 1453-1923. LC 82-4562. 384p. 1983. 62.50 (ISBN 0-521-24676-8). Cambridge U Pr.

--Orthodox Church in Independent Greece 1821-52. LC 69-10488. 1969. 42.50 (ISBN 0-521-07247-6). Cambridge U Pr.

Frazee, Irving A. & Billiet, Walter. Automotive Brakes & Power Transmission Systems. LC 56-7199. (Automotive Ser.). (Illus.). pap. 69.30 (ISBN 0-317-11020-9, 2004568). Bks Demand UMI.

Frazee, Irving A. & Landon, William. Automotive Fuel & Ignition Systems. LC 53-1714. (Automotive Ser.). (Illus.). pap. 128.00 (ISBN 0-317-11015-2, 2004569). Bks Demand UMI.

Frazee, Jane. Singing in the Season. 1983. pap. 4.00 (ISBN 0-918812-24-0). MMB Music.

Frazee, Steve. He Road Alone. 160p. 1981. pap. 1.75 (ISBN 0-449-14103-9, Crest). Fawcett.

--Many Rivers to Cross. 176p. 1981. pap. 1.75 (ISBN 0-449-14012-1, GM). Fawcett.

Frazee, W. D. Ransom & Reunion: Through the Sanctuary. LC 77-76135. (Horizon Ser.). 1977. pap. 5.95 (ISBN 0-8127-0138-0). Review & Herald.

Frazen, Lavern G. Good News from Matthew: Visual Messages for Children. LC 77-72463. (gr. 1-4). 1977. pap. 5.50 (ISBN 0-8066-1597-4, 10-2814). Augsburg.

Frazer, A. C., et al. Current Topics in Microbiology & Immunology, Vol. 69. (Illus.). 200p. 1975. 46.00 (ISBN 0-387-07195-4). Springer-Verlag.

Frazer, August H. High Temperature Resistant Polymers. LC 68-21491. pap. 88.00 (ISBN 0-317-09197-2, 2006348). Bks Demand UMI.

Frazer, F., jt. auth. see Corti, G.

Frazer, F. W., ed. Rehabilitation Within the Community. 208p. 1983. pap. 7.95 (ISBN 0-571-11901-8). Faber & Faber.

Frazer, Felix J. Parallel Paths to the Unseen Worlds. 1967. pap. 5.50 (ISBN 0-87516-298-3). De Vorss.

Frazer, J. F. Amphibians. (The Wykeham Science Ser.: No. 25). 128p. 1972. pap. cancelled (ISBN 0-85109-330-2). Taylor & Francis.

Frazer, J. F. & Frazer, O. H. Amphibians. (Wykeham Science Ser.: No. 25). 128p. 1972. 9.95x (ISBN 0-8448-1152-1). Crane Russak Co.

Frazer, J. G. Psyche's Task: A Discourse Concerning the Influence of Superstition on the Growth of Institutions. 2nd ed. 1979. Repr. of 1913 ed. lib. bdg. 27.50 (ISBN 0-8495-1636-6). Arden Lib.

Frazer, J. G., ed. see Cowper, William.

Frazer, J. G., tr. see Pausanias.

Frazer, J. W. & Kunz, F. W., eds. Computerized Laboratory Systems, STP 578. LC 75-2512. (Special Technical Publications Ser.: No. 578). 278p. 1984. 24.00 (ISBN 0-8031-0268-2, 04-578000-34). ASTM.

Frazer, James. The New Golden Bough. rev. ed. Gaster, Theodore, ed. 832p. 1975. pap. 5.95 (ISBN 0-451-62208-1, ME2208, Ment). NAL.

Frazer, James G. Aftermath: A Supplement to The Golden Bough. LC 75-41104. Repr. of 1937 ed. 34.00 (ISBN 0-404-14543-4). AMS Pr.

--Anthologia Anthropologica: The Native Races of America. LC 73-21267. Repr. of 1939 ed. 47.50 (ISBN 0-404-11423-7). AMS Pr.

--Anthologia Anthropologica: The Native Races of Australasia. LC 73-21269. Repr. of 1939 ed. 47.50 (ISBN 0-404-11425-3). AMS Pr.

--Anthologia Anthropologica: The Native Races of Africa & Madagascar: a Copious Selection of Passages for the Study of Social Anthropology. Downie, Robert A., ed. LC 73-21266. Repr. of 1938 ed. 67.50 (ISBN 0-404-11422-9). AMS Pr.

--Anthologia Anthropologica: The Native Races of Asia & Europe. LC 73-21268. Repr. of 1939 ed. 47.50 (ISBN 0-404-11424-5). AMS Pr.

--Creation & Evolution in Primitive Cosmogonies & Other Pieces. facs. ed. LC 67-26742. (Essay Index Reprint Ser). 1935. 15.00 (ISBN 0-8369-0456-7). Ayer Co Pubs.

--The Fear of the Dead in Primitive Religion, 3 vols. in one. Kastenaum, Robert, ed. LC 76-19571. (Death & Dying Ser.). 1977. Repr. of 1936 ed. lib. bdg. 57.50x (ISBN 0-405-09566-X). Ayer Co Pubs.

--Garnered Sheaves: Essays, Addresses, Reviews. facs. ed. LC 67-30212. (Essay Index Reprint Ser). 1931. 21.50 (ISBN 0-8369-0457-5). Ayer Co Pubs.

--Golden Bough. abr ed. 19.95 (ISBN 0-02-095560-X); pap. 8.95 (ISBN 0-685-15196-4). Macmillan.

--The Golden Bough, 13 vols. Incl. Pt. I. The Magic Art & the Evolution of Kings, 2 vols; Pt. II. Taboo & the Perils of the Soul; Pt. III. The Dying God; Pt. IV. Adonis, Attis, Osiris, 2 vols; Pt. V. Spirits of the Corn & of the Wild, 2 vols; Pt. VI. The Scapegoat; Pt. VII. Balder the Beautiful; The Fire Festivals of Europe & the Doctrines of the Eternal Soul, 2 vols; Pt. VIII. Bibliography & General Index; Pt. IX. Aftermath: A Supplement. 5380p. 1980. Repr. of 1890 ed. Set Only. 375.00 (ISBN 0-312-33215-7). St Martin.

--Gorgon's Head, & Other Literary Pieces. facs. ed. LC 67-23221. (Essay Index Reprint Ser). 1927. 26.50 (ISBN 0-8369-0458-3). Ayer Co Pubs.

--Growth of Plato's Ideal Theory: An Essay. LC 66-27072. 1967. Repr. of 1930 ed. 6.50x (ISBN 0-8462-0840-7). Russell.

--New Golden Bough. abridged ed. Gaster, Theodor H., ed. LC 59-6125. 1959. 21.95 (ISBN 0-87599-036-3). S G Phillips.

--The Origin of Fire in North America. 1984. pap. 5.95 (ISBN 0-916411-39-7, Pub. by Sure Fire). Holmes Pub.

--Sir Roger De Coverley & Other Literary Pieces. 1978. Repr. of 1920 ed. lib. bdg. 40.00 (ISBN 0-8482-0816-1). Norwood Edns.

--The Worship of Nature. LC 73-21271. (Gifford Lectures: 1924-25). Repr. of 1926 ed. 41.50 (ISBN 0-404-11427-X). AMS Pr.

Frazer, Joan, et al. Thirty-Thousand Selected Words Organized by Letter, Sound & Syllable. 1978. text ed. 16.95 (ISBN 0-88450-799-8, 3083-B); pap. text ed. 11.95 (ISBN 0-88450-798-X, 2506-B). Communication Skill.

Frazer, Joan, jt. auth. see Blockcolsky, Valeda.

Frazer, Joan M. & Smith, Cynthia J. Adjectives-Comparatives & Superlatives, Pt. III. (Shape Up Your Language Ser.). 225p. (gr. k-6). 1983. spiral bdg. 24.95 (ISBN 0-88450-863-3, 7026-B). Communication Skill.

--Nouns-Plurals, Pt. II. (Shape Up Your Language Ser.). 300p. (gr. k-6). 1983. spiral bound 24.95 (ISBN 0-88450-857-9, 7025-B). Communication Skill.

--Verbs, Pt. I. (Shape Up Your Language). 1982. spiral wire 24.95 (ISBN 0-88450-828-5, 7024-B). Communication Skill.

Frazer, Joan M., jt. auth. see Blockcolsky, Valeda.

Frazer, John. Artificially Arranged Scenes: The Films of Georges Meiles. 1979. lib. bdg. 29.50 (ISBN 0-8161-8368-6, Hall Reference). G K Hall.

Frazer, Lilly G. Dancing: A Handbook. 59.95 (ISBN 0-87968-991-9). Gordon Pr.

Frazer, Louise. Ballet: The Art Defined. 2nd ed. LC 83-62154. 130p. 1984. pap. 8.95 (ISBN 0-914447-01-7). Physical Stud.

Frazer, Marjory K. A Life of Song. Muirhead, May K., ed. 200p. 1985. Repr. of 1929 ed. 12.95 (ISBN 0-930623-02-9), Anro Comm.

Frazer, O. H., jt. auth. see Frazer, J. F.

Frazer, P. M., ed. see Rostovtzeff, Mikhail.

Frazer, Percifor. Bibliotics, or the Study of Documents: Determinations of the Individual Character of Handwriting & Detection of Fraud & Forgery. 1977. lib. bdg. 59.95 (ISBN 0-8490-1504-9). Gordon Pr.

Frazer, Persifor. Bibliotics. LC 70-156017. (Illus.). Repr. of 1901 ed. 23.75 (ISBN 0-404-09117-2). AMS Pr.

Frazer, R. M., tr. & intro. by. The Poems of Hesiod. LC 82-40451. (Illus.). 160p. 1983. 14.95x (ISBN 0-8061-1837-7); pap. 4.95 (ISBN 0-8061-1846-6). U of Okla Pr.

Frazer, R. W. Literary History of India. LC 78-128001. (Studies in Asiatic Literature, No. 57). 1970. Repr. of 1898 ed. lib. bdg. 58.95x (ISBN 0-8383-1150-4). Haskell.

Frazer, Ray & Kelling, Harold D., eds. Literature in Four Aspects. 1965. pap. text ed. 14.95x (ISBN 0-669-20628-8). Heath.

Frazer, Robert A., et al. Elementary Matrices & Some Applications to Dynamics & Differential Equations. LC 76-29426. (BCL Ser.: II). Repr. of 1946 ed. 38.50 (ISBN 0-404-15334-8). AMS Pr.

Frazer, Robert W. British India. LC 70-39404. (Select Bibliographies Reprint). 1972. Repr. of 1896 ed. 26.75 (ISBN 0-8369-9904-5). Ayer Co Pubs.

--Forts & Supplies: The Role of the Army in the Economy of the Southwest, 1846-1861. LC 83-17051. (Illus.). 296p. 1983. 22.50x (ISBN 0-8263-0630-6). U of NM Pr.

--Forts of the West: Military Forts & Presidios & Posts Commonly Called Forts West of the Mississippi to 1898. LC 65-24196. (Illus.). 1977. pap. 7.95 (ISBN 0-8061-1250-6). U of Okla Pr.

Frazer, Robert W., ed. Over the Chihuahua & Sante Fe Trails, 1847-1848: George Rutledge Gibson's Journal. LC 81-52054. (Illus.). 96p. 1981. 7.95 (ISBN 0-8263-0590-3). U of NM Pr.

Frazer, Susan, tr. see Rouge, Jean.

Frazer, William. Expectations, Forecasting & Control: A Provisional Textbook of Macroeconomics: Vol. II, Prices, Market & Turning Points. LC 80-1361. 439p. 1980. lib. bdg. 32.00 (ISBN 0-8191-1290-9); pap. text ed. 19.00 (ISBN 0-8191-1291-7). U Pr of Amer.

--Expectations, Forecasting & Control: A Provisional Textbook of Macroeconomics, Vol. I: Monetary Matters, Keynesian & Other Models. LC 80-1361. 493p. 1980. pap. 32.25 (ISBN 0-8191-1144-9); pap. text ed. 19.50 (ISBN 0-8191-1145-7). U Pr of Amer.

Frazer, William & Henyey, Frank, eds. Quantum Chromodynamics. LC 79-54969. (AIP Conference Ser.; Particles & Fields Sub-Ser.: No. 55; No. 18). (Illus.). 1979. lib. bdg. 20.50 (ISBN 0-88318-154-1). Am Inst Physics.

Frazer, William J., Jr. Crisis in Economic Theory: A Study of Monetary Policy, Analysis, & Economic Goals. LC 73-16273. 1973. 20.00 (ISBN 0-8130-0392-X); pap. 14.50x (ISBN 0-8130-0445-4). U Presses Fla.

--Liquidity Structure of Firms & Monetary Economics. LC 65-63999. (University of Florida Social Sciences Monographs: No. 27). (Illus.). 1965. pap. 3.50 (ISBN 0-8130-0080-7). U Presses Fla.

Frazer, Winifred L. E.G. & E.G.O. Emma Goldman & "The Iceman Cometh". LC 74-7361. (University of Florida Humanities Monographs: No. 43). 105p. 1974. pap. 4.00 (ISBN 0-8130-0504-3). U Presses Fla.

--Mabel Dodge Luhan. (United States Authors Ser.: No. 477). 1984. lib. bdg. 17.95 (ISBN 0-8057-7418-1, Twayne). G K Hall.

Frazer Clark, C. E., ed. The Nathaniel Hawthorne Journal, Nineteen Seventy-Two. (Illus.). 1973. 25.00 (ISBN 0-910972-33-8). Bruccoli.

Frazer Clark, C. E., Jr., ed. The Nathaniel Hawthorne Journal, Nineteen Seventy-Six. (Illus.). 1978. 25.00 (ISBN 0-910972-60-5). Bruccoli.

Frazer Clark, C. E., Jr., compiled by. Hawthorne at Auction. (Illus.). 32.00 (ISBN 0-685-77411-2). Bruccoli.

Frazer Clark, C. E., Jr. see Bruccoli, Matthew J.

Frazetta, Eleanor, jt. auth. see Frazetta, Frank.

Frazetta, Frank. Frank Frazetta, Bk. 5. 1985. 12.95 (ISBN 0-553-34175-8). Bantam.

Frazetta, Frank & Frazetta, Eleanor. Frank Frazetta: The Living Legend. (Illus.). 96p. 1980. pap. 9.95 (ISBN 0-9607060-0-3). Sun Litho Frazetta.

Frazier, Alexander. Adventuring, Mastering, Associating: New Strategies for Teaching Children. new ed. Leeper, Robert R., ed. LC 76-11655. 1976. pap. 5.00 (ISBN 0-87120-079-1, 611-76080). Assn Supervision.

--Values, Curriculum & the Elementary School. LC 79-87862. 1980. pap. text ed. 17.50 (ISBN 0-395-26739-0). HM.

Frazier, Allie M., ed. Readings in Eastern Religious Thought, 3 vols. Incl. Vol. 1. Hinduism; Vol. 2. Buddhism; Vol. 3. Chinese & Japanese Religions. (ISBN 0-664-24848-9). LC 69-14197. 1969. Westminster.

Frazier, Anitra & Eckroate, Norma. It's a Cat's Life: True Stories with Practical Help for Your Cat from Birth to Old Age. (Illus.). 224p. 1985. 14.95 (ISBN 0-8253-0302-8). Beaufort Bks NY.

--The Natural Cat: A Holistic Guide for Finicky Owners. rev. ed. (Illus.). 208p. 1981. pap. 9.95 (ISBN 0-936602-12-0). Kampmann.

Frazier, Bessie. Poems, Short Stories & Plays for Youth. 80p. 1980. 5.00 (ISBN 0-682-49591-3). Exposition Pr FL.

Frazier, Beverly. Nature Crafts & Projects. (Illus.). 40p. (gr. 1-8). 1979. pap. 2.95 (ISBN 0-8431-1748-6). Troubador Pr.

Frazier, C. Psychosomatic Aspects of Allergy. 1977. 26.50 (ISBN 0-317-12939-2). Van Nos Reinhold.

Frazier, Carl & Frazier, Rosalie. The Lincoln Country-In Pictures. (Illus.). (gr. 4-6). 1963. 6.95 (ISBN 0-8038-4238-4). Hastings.

Frazier, Charles & Hatfield, Alan. Using the Computer for Offensive Football Scouting. (Illus.). 256p. 1984. 24.95 (ISBN 0-13-940198-9). P-H.

Frazier, Charles & Secreast, Donald. Adventuring in the Andes: The Sierra Club Travel Guide to Ecuador, Peru, Bolivia, the Amazon Basin, & Galapagos Islands. LC 84-22219. (Illus.). 384p. (Orig.). 1985. pap. 10.95 (ISBN 0-87156-833-0). Sierra.

Frazier, Charles, jt. auth. see Hatfield, Alan.

Frazier, Charles R., jt. auth. see Ingram, Robert W.

Frazier, Claude A. Bi-Annual Review of Allergy, 1983. 1983. 48.00 (ISBN 0-87488-294-X). Med Exam.

--Coping & Living with Allergies: A Complete Guide to Help Allergy Patients of All Ages. (Illus.). 272p. 1980. 11.95 (ISBN 0-13-172304-9, Spec); pap. 5.95 (ISBN 0-13-172296-4). P-H.

--Coping with Food Allergy. rev. ed. LC 84-40419. 352p. 1985. Repr. of 1974 ed. pap. 8.95 (ISBN 0-8129-1149-0). Times Bks.

--Coping with Food Allergy: Symptoms & Treatment. LC 73-89471. 192p. 1974. pap. 7.95 (ISBN 0-8129-6278-8). Times Bks.

--Insect Allergy: Allergic & Toxic Reactions to Insects & Other Arthropods. 2nd ed. (Illus.). 480p. 1985. 42.50 (ISBN 0-87527-324-6). Green.

--Occupational Asthma. 384p. 1980. 34.95 (ISBN 0-442-21687-4). Van Nos Reinhold.

--Self-Assessment of Current Knowledge in Allergy & Clinical Immunology. 1981. 24.00 (ISBN 0-87488-296-6). Med Exam.

--Sniff, Sniff Al-er-gee. new ed. LC 76-27985. (Illus.). (gr. k-3). 1978. 6.75 (ISBN 0-910812-19-5); pap. 3.25 (ISBN 0-910812-24-1). Johnny Reads.

Frazier, Claude A. & Brown, F. K. Insects & Allergy: And What to Do About Them. LC 79-6706. (Illus.). 350p. 1980. 17.95 (ISBN 0-8061-1518-1); pap. 9.95 (ISBN 0-8061-1706-0). U of Okla Pr.

Frazier, Claude A., ed. Dentistry & the Allergic Patient. (Illus.). 456p. 1973. photocopy ed. 46.75x (ISBN 0-398-02585-1). C C Thomas.

--Is It Moral to Modify Man? 252p. 1973. 24.50x (ISBN 0-398-02632-7). C C Thomas.

Frazier, David. AG Pilot Flight Training Guide-Including FAA Rules Part 137. (Illus.). 1979. o.p 8.95 (ISBN 0-8306-9860-4); pap. 5.95 (ISBN 0-8306-2247-0, 2247). TAB Bks.

Frazier, David A. How to Master Precision Flight. (Illus.). 60p. (Orig.). 1984. pap. 9.95 (ISBN 0-8306-2354-X, 2354). TAB Bks.

Frazier, Dianne M., jt. auth. see Frazier, James R.

Frazier, E. Franklin. Black Bourgeoisie. 1965. pap. 11.95 (ISBN 0-02-910580-3). Free Pr.

--Black Bourgeoisie: The Rise of a New Middle Class in the United States. (Orig.). 1962. pap. 3.95 (ISBN 0-02-095600-2, Collier). Macmillan.

--E. Franklin Frazier on Race Relations. Edwards, G. Franklin, ed. LC 68-8586. (Heritage of Sociology Ser). (Orig.). 1968. pap. 3.95x (ISBN 0-226-18744-6, P324, Phoen). U of Chicago Pr.

--Free Negro Family: A Study of Family Origins Before the Civil War. LC 68-28996. (American Negro: His History & Literature Ser.: No. 1). 1968. Repr. of 1932 ed. 10.00 (ISBN 0-405-01815-0). Ayer Co Pubs.

--Negro Family in the United States. rev. & abr ed. LC 66-13868. 1966. pap. 9.00x (ISBN 0-226-26141-7). U of Chicago Pr.

Frazier, E. Franklin & Lincoln, C. Eric. The Negro Church in America. Bd. with The Black Church Since Frazier. LC 72-96201. (Sourcebooks in Negro History Ser.). 1973. pap. 4.95 (ISBN 0-8052-0387-7). Schocken.

Frazier, Edward F. Race & Culture Contacts in the Modern World. LC 78-17087. 1978. Repr. of 1957 ed. lib. bdg. 24.00x (ISBN 0-313-20579-5, FRRC). Greenwood.

Frazier, Greg. San Francisco Scenes. (City Scenes Ser.). (Illus.). 32p. 1972. pap. 3.95 (ISBN 0-8431-4048-8, 29-9). Troubador Pr.

Frazier, Harriet C., ed. A Babble of Ancestral Voices: Shakespeare, Cervantes, & Theobald, No. 73. (Studies in English Literature). 162p. 1974. text ed. 20.80x (ISBN 0-686-27740-6). Mouton.

Frazier, Harry. Recollections. 100p. 1938. 1.00 (ISBN 0-318-13698-8). Ches & OH Hist.

Frazier, Howard, ed. Uncloaking the CIA. LC 77-87573. 1978. 14.95 (ISBN 0-02-910590-0). Free Pr.

Frazier, Ian. Dating Your Mom. 128p. 1986. 11.95 (ISBN 0-374-13508-8). FS&G.

Frazier, J. The Marijuana Farmers: Hemp Cults & Cultures. (Illus.). 1973. pap. 6.95 (ISBN 0-914304-00-3). Solar Age Pr.

Frazier, Jack. Automobile Fuels of the 1980's: A Survey. (Illus.). 1978. pap. 4.95 (ISBN 0-685-87593-8). Solar Age Pr.

Frazier, James R. & Frazier, Dianne M. Exceptional Children: Biological & Psychological Perspectives. LC 74-12092. 339p. 1974. text ed. 29.50x (ISBN 0-8422-5198-7); pap. text ed. 14.95x (ISBN 0-8422-0428-8). Irvington.

Frazier, James R. & Routh, Donald K., eds. Readings on the Behavior Disorders of Childhood. LC 72-86267. 320p. 1972. pap. text ed. 12.50x (ISBN 0-8422-0202-1). Irvington.

Frazier, John W., ed. Applied Geography: Selected Perspectives. (Illus.). 352p. 1982. 30.95 (ISBN 0-13-040451-9). P-H.

Frazier, K. Solar Systems. LC 84-16117. (Planet Earth Ser.). 1985. lib. bdg. 19.94 (ISBN 0-8094-4530-1, Pub. by Time-Life). Silver.

Frazier, Kendrick. Our Turbulent Sun. LC 81-5883. (Illus.). 198p. 1982. 16.95 (ISBN 0-13-644500-4); pap. 7.95 (ISBN 0-13-644492-X). P-H.

--The Skeptical Inquirer. Orig. Title: The Zetetic. 96p. (J). ann. subscr. 18.00, quarterly (ISBN 0-318-16886-3). Comm Sci Investigation.

Frazier, Kendrick, ed. Paranormal Borderlands of Science. LC 80-84403. (Science & the Paranormal Ser.). 469p. 1981. pap. 15.95 (ISBN 0-87975-148-7). Prometheus Bks.

--Science Confronts the Paranormal. 450p. 1985. pap. 15.95 (ISBN 0-87975-314-5). Prometheus Bks.

Frazier, Lois E., jt. auth. see Moon, Harry R.

Frazier, Lois E., ed. see Frye, Marianne E., et al.

Frazier, Margaret A., jt. auth. see Saperstein, Arlyne B.

Frazier, Margaret Mendenhall see Mendenhall, Margaret F.

Frazier, Mary & Long, Dean. Old Georgia Privies. (Illus.). 40p. (Orig.). 1984. pap. text ed. 6.00 (ISBN 0-9614192-0-2). Frazier-Long.

Frazier, Mary J. Cry a Little, Laugh a Lot. 64p. 1985. 4.95 (ISBN 0-310-45510-3, Pub. by Daybreak). Zondervan.

Frazier, N. W., ed. Virus Diseases of Small Fruits & Grapevines. 1970. 7.50x (ISBN 0-931876-21-4, 4056). Ag & Nat Res.

Frazier, Nancy. Special Museums of the Northeast: A Guide to Uncommon Collections from Maine to Washington, DC. LC 85-8027. (Illus.). 288p. (Orig.). 1985. pap. 9.95 (ISBN 0-87106-869-9). Globe Pequot.

Frazier, Nancy & Sadker, Myra. Sexism in School & Society. (Fischer Ser). (Illus.). 150p. 1973. pap. text ed. 12.00 scp (ISBN 0-06-042172-X, HarpC). Har-Row.

Frazier, Raymond L., jt. auth. see Cox, Keller.

Frazier, Richard, et al. What's the Good Word? 1979. pap. 4.00 (ISBN 0-89536-384-4). CSS of Ohio.

Frazier, Richard H., et al. Magnetic & Electric Suspensions. (Monographs in Modern Electrical Technology). 416p. 1974. 45.00x (ISBN 0-262-06054-X). MIT Pr.

Frazier, Robert, ed. see Disch, Thomas, et al.

Frazier, Robert C., et al. The Humanities: A Quest for Meaning in Twentieth Century America. 352p. 1982. pap. text ed. 19.95. Kendall-Hunt.

Frazier, Rosalie, jt. auth. see Frazier, Carl.

Frazier, Shervert & Carr, Arthur C. An Introduction to Psychopathology. LC 84-45111. 168p. 1983. 17.50x (ISBN 0-87668-702-8). Aronson.

Frazier, Shervert, ed. Aggression. (ARNMD Research Publications Ser.: Vol. 52). 360p. 1974. 50.50 (ISBN 0-683-00246-5). Raven.

Frazier, Thomas, jt. ed. see Merrill, Reed B.

Frazier, Thomas R., ed. The Underside of American History, Other Readings. 4th ed. Incl. Vol. 1. To 1877. 441p. pap. (ISBN 0-15-592850-3); Vol. 2. Since 1865. 375p. pap. (ISBN 0-15-592851-1). (Illus., Orig.). 1982. pap. text ed. 12.95 ea. (HC). HarBraceJ.

Frazier, Thomas R., jt. ed. see Nash, Gary B.

Frazier, Tyrone. Life Lights: Troilus on the Battlefield. 1982. 5.95 (ISBN 0-533-05307-2). Vantage.

Frazier, William A. & Glaser, Luis, eds. Cellular Recognition. LC 82-6555. (UCLA Symposia on Molecular & Cellular Biology Ser.: Vol. 3). 966p. 1982. 152.00 (ISBN 0-8451-2602-4). A R Liss.

Frazier, William C. & Westhoff, Dennis. Food Microbiology. 3rd ed. (Illus.). 1978. text ed. 44.95 (ISBN 0-07-021917-6). McGraw.

Frazin, Judith R. A Translation Guide to Nineteenth-Century Polish-Language Civil-Registration Documents (Birth, Marriage & Death Records) (Illus.). 128p. (Orig.). 1984. pap. 10.00 (ISBN 0-9613512-0-9). Jewish Genealogical.

Freakley, P. K. & Payne, A. R. Theory & Practice of Engineering with Rubber. (Illus.). 666p. 1978. 96.25 (ISBN 0-85334-772-7, Pub. by Elsevier Applied Sci England). Elsevier.

Freakley, Philip K. Rubber Processing & Production Organization. 472p. 1985. 59.50x (ISBN 0-306-41745-6, Plenum Pr). Plenum Pub.

Fream, Donald. A Chain of Jewels from James & Jude. LC 71-1073. (The Bible Study Textbook Ser.). (Illus.). 1965. 12.20 (ISBN 0-89900-045-2). College Pr Pub.

--Thirteen Lessons on James & Jude. (Bible Student Study Guides). 1979. pap. 2.95 (ISBN 0-89900-161-0). College Pr Pub.

Fream, William C. Notes on Obstetrics. LC 76-19020. (Livingston Nursing Notes). 1977. pap. 9.75 (ISBN 0-443-01451-5). Churchill.

Frean, D. Board & Management Development. 1977. 22.50x (ISBN 0-8464-0201-7). Beekman Pubs.

Frean, David. The Board & Management Development. 202p. 1977. text ed. 36.75x (ISBN 0-220-66304-1, Pub. by Busn Bks England). Brookfield Pub Co.

Frear, Walter F. Mark Twain & Hawaii. 519p. 1980. Repr. of 1947 ed. lib. bdg. 50.00 (ISBN 0-8492-4636-9). R West.

Frears, J. C. & Parodi, Jean-Luc. War Will Not Take Place: The French Parliamentary Elections March, 1978. LC 79-527. (Illus.). 148p. 1979. text ed. 22.50x (ISBN 0-8419-0478-2). Holmes & Meier.

Frears, J. R. France in the Giscard Presidency. 224p. 1981. pap. text ed. 10.95x (ISBN 0-04-354026-0). Allen Unwin.

--Political Parties & Elections in the French 5th Republic. LC 77-82043. 1978. 25.00 (ISBN 0-312-62331-3). St Martin.

Freas, Frank K. Frank Kelly Freas: The Art of Science Fiction. LC 77-8644. (Illus.). 1977. pap. 9.95 (ISBN 0-915442-37-X). Donning Co.

--A Separate Star. (Illus.). 128p. (Orig.). 1985. slipcased limited ed., signed & numbered 39.95 (ISBN 0-917431-00-6); lib. bdg. 24.95 (ISBN 0-917431-01-4); pap. 14.95 (ISBN 0-917431-02-2). Greenswamp.

Freas, Kelly, ed. see Asprin, Robert.

Freas, Kelly, ed. see Garrett, Randall.

Freas, Kelly, ed. see Whelan, Michael.

Freas, Polly, ed. see Asprin, Robert.

Freas, Polly, ed. see Garrett, Randall.

Freas, Polly, ed. see Whelan, Michael.

Freburger, William. Baptism. 1970. pap. 0.95 (ISBN 0-8189-0425-9). Alba.

--This Is the Word of the Lord. rev. ed. LC 83-72480. 176p. 1984. spiral bound 6.95 (ISBN 0-87793-309-X). Ave Maria.

Freburger, William & Haas, James E. Eucharistic Prayers for Children. LC 75-39414. 88p. 1976. pap. 2.95 (ISBN 0-87793-109-7). Ave Maria.

Freburger, William J. Birthday Blessings. (Greeting Book Line Ser.). 32p. (Orig.). 1985. pap. 1.50 (ISBN 0-89622-242-X). Twenty-Third.

--Liturgy: Work of the People. 112p. (Orig.). 1984. pap. 4.95 (ISBN 0-89622-214-4). Twenty-Third.

Freccero, Yvonne, tr. see Girard, Rene.

Freccero, Yvonne, tr. see Verlinden, Charles.

Frech, H. E. & Ginsburg, Paul B. Public Insurance in Private Medical Markets: Some Problems of National Health Insurance. 1978. pap. 4.25 (ISBN 0-8447-3303-2). Am Enterprise.

Frech, Mary, jt. ed. see Swindler, William F.

Frechet, Alec. John Galsworthy: A Reassessment. Mahaffey, Denis, tr. from French. LC 81-22900. 242p. 1982. text ed. 29.50x (ISBN 0-389-20277-0, 07095). B&N Imports.

Frechet, Rene. George Borrow Eighteen Three to Eighteen Eighty-One, Vagabond Polyglotte, Agent Biblique, Eorivain. 378p. Date not set. Repr. of 1956 ed. lib. bdg. 85.00 (ISBN 0-8414-4293-2). Folcroft.

Frechette, V. D., ed. Ceramic Engineering & Science-Emerging Priorities. LC 74-19304. (Materials Science Research Ser.: Vol. 8). 289p. 1974. 49.50x (ISBN 0-306-38508-2, Plenum Pr). Plenum Pub.

Frechette, V. D., et al, eds. Quality Assurance in Ceramic Industries. LC 79-14166. 275p. 1979. 49.50 (ISBN 0-306-40183-5, Plenum Pr). Plenum Pub.

--Surfaces & Interfaces of Glass & Ceramics. LC 74-17371. (Materials Science Research Ser.: Vol. 7). 558p. 1974. 79.50x (ISBN 0-306-38507-4, Plenum Pr). Plenum Pub.

Frechtman, tr. see Celine, Louis-Ferdinand.

Frechtman, A. Bernard. Employment Agency Law: A Guide for the Personnel Professional. LC 81-68390. 224p. 35.00 (ISBN 0-9611608-0-2). NAPC.

Frechtman, Bernard, tr. see Genet, Jean.

Frechtman, Bernard, tr. see Gide, Andre.

Frechtman, Bernard, tr. see Sartre, Jean-Paul.

Frechtman, Bernard, tr. see Simenon, Georges.

Freck, P. G., et al. Intra-Airport Transportation Systems: An Examination of Technology & Evaluation Methodology. LC 73-135078. 152p. 1969. 19.00 (ISBN 0-403-04500-2). Scholarly.

Freckman, Diana W., ed. Nematodes in Soil Ecosystems. (Illus.). 220p. 1982. text ed. 20.00x (ISBN 0-292-75526-0). U of Tex Pr.

Fred Brown Associates Staff, ed. The Brown Book: Industry Guide for Microcomputer Pricing. (Orig.). 1985. 395.00 (ISBN 0-318-04409-9). Adventure Cap Corp.

Fred R. Weber Co. Real Estate Math Using the Pocket Calculator-Computer. 1979. pap. 13.95 (ISBN 0-8359-6554-6). Reston.

Freddi, Chris. The Elder. Wilson, Victoria, ed. LC 85-40119. 336p. 1985. 16.95 (ISBN 0-394-53914-1). Knopf.

Freddi, Cris. Pork. 224p. 1983. pap. 6.95 (ISBN 0-525-48064-1, 0674-210). Dutton.

--Pork & Others. LC 80-39853. 1981. 10.95 (ISBN 0-394-51889-6). Knopf.

Freddoso, Alfred J., ed. The Existence & Nature of God. LC 83-47521. (Notre Dame Studies in Philosophy of Religion). 190p. 1984. 16.95x (ISBN 0-268-00910-4, 85-09119); pap. text ed. 9.95x (ISBN 0-268-00911-2). U of Notre Dame Pr.

Freddoso, Alfred J., tr. see Ockham, William.

Frede, Ellen. Getting Involved: Workshops for Parents. 306p. (Orig.). 1984. pap. 12.00 (ISBN 0-931114-31-4). High Scope.

Frede, Michael, ed. see Galen.

Frede, Richard. The Nurses. 480p. 1985. 17.95 (ISBN 0-395-38169-X). HM.

Frede-Lynn, Ellen. Getting Involved: Workshops for Parents. 200p. 1984. 15.00 (ISBN 0-318-17824-9). High Scope.

Fredeman, W. E., ed. see Nadel, Ira B.

Fredeman, W. E., ed. see Stasny, John F.

Fredeman, W. E., et al, eds. see Buchanan, Robert.

Fredeman, William, ed. see Nadel, Ira B.

Fredeman, William D., ed. see Rossetti, William M.

Fredeman, William E. The Victorian Poets: An Alphabetical Compilation of the Bio-Critical Introductions of the Victorian Poets from A. H. Miles's The Poets & The Victorian Muse. Nadel, I. B. & Stashy, J. F., eds. 150.00 (ISBN 0-8240-8631-7). Garland Pub.

Fredeman, William E. & Nadel, Ira B., eds. Victorian Poets After 1850. (Dictionary of Literary Biography Ser.: Vol. 35). 400p. 1985. 88.00x (ISBN 0-8103-1713-3). Gale.

--Victorian Poets Before 1850. (Dictionary of Literary Biography Ser.: Vol. 32). 300p. 1984. 88.00x (ISBN 0-8103-1710-9). Gale.

Fredeman, William E., jt. ed. see Nadel, Ira B.

Fredeman, William E., et al, eds. see Kendal, Madge.

Fredeman, William E., et al, eds. see Knight, Joseph A.

Fredeman, William E., et al, eds. see Scott, Clement.

Freden, Lars. Psychosocial Aspects of Depression: No Way Out? 240p. 1982. 42.95x (ISBN 0-471-10023-4, Pub. by Wiley-Interscience). Wiley.

Fredenberg, D. Van see Van Fredenberg, D.

Fredenslund, et al. Vapor-Liquid Equilibria Using UNIFAC: A Group Contribution Method. 380p. 1977. 89.50 (ISBN 0-444-41621-8). Elsevier.

Frederic, Harold. Collected Works, 14 vols. Incl. Seth's Brother's Wife. 1887. Repr. 6.00x (ISBN 0-686-01530-4); The Lawton Girl. 1890. Repr. 40.00 (ISBN 0-686-01531-2); In the Valley. 1890. Repr. 36.00x (ISBN 0-686-01532-0); The Young Emperor: William the Second of Germany. 1891. Repr. 19.00 (ISBN 0-686-01533-9); The Return of O'Mahony. 1892. Repr. 27.00 (ISBN 0-686-01534-7); The New Exodus. 1892. Repr. 25.00 (ISBN 0-686-01535-5); The Copperhead. 1893. Repr. 20.00 (ISBN 0-686-01536-3); Marsena & Other Stories of the Wartime. 1894. Repr. 16.00x (ISBN 0-686-01537-1); Mrs. Albert Grundy. 1896. Repr. 21.00 (ISBN 0-686-01538-X); The Damnation of Theron Ware. 1896. Repr. 49.00x (ISBN 0-686-01539-8); March Hares. 1896. Repr. 29.00x (ISBN 0-686-01540-1); The Deserter & Other Stories. 1898. Repr. 19.00 (ISBN 0-686-01541-X); Gloria Mundi. 1898. Repr. 47.00 (ISBN 0-686-01542-8); The Market Place. 1899. Repr. 23.00x (ISBN 0-686-01543-6). Set. 300.00 (ISBN 0-686-01529-0). Somerset Pub.

--The Copperhead. 1972. Repr. of 1893 ed. 8.00 (ISBN 0-8422-8050-2). Irvington.

--Copperhead & Other Stories of the North During the American War. LC 70-144610. Repr. of 1894 ed. 10.00 (ISBN 0-404-02571-4). AMS Pr.

--The Damnation of Theron Ware. Carter, Everett, ed. LC 60-11553. (The John Harvard Library). 355p. 1974. pap. 6.95x (ISBN 0-674-19001-7). Harvard U Pr.

--Damnation of Theron Ware. LC 60-13818. (Rinehart Editions). 1960. pap. text ed. 11.95 (ISBN 0-03-010200-6, HoltC). HR&W.

--The Damnation of Theron Ware; or, Illumination. Dodge, Charlyne & Garner, Stanton, eds. LC 84-25790. x, 506p. 1985. 25.00x (ISBN 0-8032-1967-9). U Of Nebr Pr.

--Deserter & Other Stories, a Book of Two Wars. LC 77-99245. (BCL Ser.: I). Repr. of 1898 ed. 15.00 (ISBN 0-404-02572-2). AMS Pr.

--Deserter & Other Stories: A Book of Two Wars. LC 79-110190. (Short Story Index Reprint Ser.). 1898. 23.50 (ISBN 0-8369-3341-9). Ayer Co Pubs.

--In the Sixties. LC 74-144611. Repr. of 1897 ed. 21.50 (ISBN 0-404-02573-0). AMS Pr.

--Major Works, 5 vols. LC 68-59013. (Illus.). 1887-1900. Repr. Set. lib. bdg. 150.75x (ISBN 0-8371-2990-7, FRF). Greenwood.

--Marsena & Other Stories of the Wartime. LC 72-110191. (Short Story Index Reprint Ser.). 1894. 17.00 (ISBN 0-8369-3342-7). Ayer Co Pubs.

--New Exodus: A Study of Israel in Russia. LC 71-115538. (Russia Observed, Series I). 1970. Repr. of 1892 ed. 19.00 (ISBN 0-405-03027-4). Ayer Co Pubs.

--Seth's Brother's Wife. LC 68-23720. (Americans in Fiction Ser.). lib. bdg. 14.50 (ISBN 0-8398-0565-9); pap. text ed. 7.50x (ISBN 0-89197-934-4). Irvington.

Frederic, Louis. Encyclopaedia of Asian Civilizations, Vols. 1-9. 2229p. 1984. Set. 650.00 (ISBN 0-917056-11-6). Cheng & Tsui.

Frederick. Origins & Evolution of Eukaryotic Intracellular Organalles, Vol. 361. 1981. 101.00x (ISBN 0-89766-111-7); pap. 101.00x (ISBN 0-89766-112-5). NY Acad Sci.

Frederick, A. Bruce. Gymnastics for Men. (Physical Education Activities Ser.). 80p. 1969. pap. text ed. write for info. (ISBN 0-697-07014-X); tchr's manual (ISBN 0-697-07219-3). Wm C Brown.

--Gymnastics for Women. (Physical Education Activities Ser.). 94p. 1966. pap. text ed. write for info. (ISBN 0-697-07015-8); write for info. tchr's. manual (ISBN 0-697-07220-7). Wm C Brown.

Frederick, A. Bruce, ed. Two Hundred Twelve Ideas for Making Low-Cost Physical Education Equipment. LC 79-187903. 219p. 1972. 7.95x (ISBN 0-685-24216-1). Sch Aid.

Frederick, A. W., jt. auth. see Wiley, S. T.

Frederick, Brooks, pseud. A Happy Christmas Carol. (Writers Workshop Redbird Book Ser.). 35p. 1975. 9.00 (ISBN 0-88253-554-4); pap. text ed. 4.00 (ISBN 0-88253-553-6). Ind-US Inc.

--Rocket to the Moon. (Redbird Ser). 118p. 1975. 15.00 (ISBN 0-88253-616-8); pap. text ed. 4.80 (ISBN 0-88253-615-X). Ind-US Inc.

Frederick, C., jt. auth. see Lonergan, T.

Frederick, C. Schwan & Boling, Joseph E. World War II Military Currency. LC 78-60306. (Illus.). 1978. pap. 19.50 (ISBN 0-931960-00-2). BNR Pr.

Frederick, Carlton. Carlton Fredericks' Nutrition Guide for the Prevention & Cure of Common Ailments & Diseases. LC 82-10705. (Illus.). 224p. 1981. pap. 8.95 (ISBN 0-671-44509-X, Fireside). S&S.

Frederick, Clara M., ed. see Cedar Bog Symposium, Urbana College, Nov. 3, 1973.

Frederick, Dean K. & Carlson, A. Bruce. Linear Systems in Communication & Control. LC 71-155118. 575p. 1971. 46.50x (ISBN 0-471-27721-5). Wiley.

Frederick, Dean K., jt. auth. see Close, Charles M.

Frederick, Donald. That Crazy, Mixed-up Cube. rev. ed. (Illus.). 72p. 1981. pap. 1.95 (ISBN 0-9607180-0-1). Frederick Ent.

Frederick, E. C. Teaching Content Through Reading: A Human Experience. (Illus.). 214p. 1984. Spiral 18.75x (ISBN 0-398-04901-7). C C Thomas.

Frederick, E. C., ed. Sport Shoes & Playing Surfaces: Biomechanical Properties. LC 83-83166. 1984. text ed. 24.95x (ISBN 0-931250-51-X, BFRE0051). Human Kinetics.

Frederick, E. D., ed. see Clayton, W. E.

Frederick, E. D., ed. see Kaddar, T., et al.

Frederick, E. D., ed. see Lupin, M. S. & Le, N. D.

Frederick E. Jones Memorial Symposium in Thoracic Surgery, Columbus, Ohio, October 1976. Perspectives in Lung Cancer: Proceedings. Williams, T. E., et al, eds. (Illus.). 1977. 18.75 (ISBN 3-8055-2649-0). S Karger.

Frederick, Ernest D., ed. see Martinez, Adolfo, et al.

Frederick, Filis, ed. see Schloss, Malcolm & Purdom, Charles.

Frederick, Franz J. Guide to Microcomputers. Assn Ed Comm Tech, ed. LC 80-68716. (Orig.). 1980. pap. 11.50 (ISBN 0-89240-038-2); pap. 9.50 members. Assn Ed Comm Tech.

Frederick, Gary E., jt. auth. see Weaver, Betsy.

Frederick, Guy. One Hundred One Best Magic Tricks. 1985. pap. 2.95 (ISBN 0-451-14010-9, Sig). NAL.

Frederick, J. George. The Long Island Seafood Cookbook. Joyce, Jean, ed. 1971. pap. 4.95 (ISBN 0-486-22677-8). Dover.

--Masters of Advertising Copy. 1977. Repr. of 1926 ed. lib. bdg. 25.00 (ISBN 0-8492-0810-6). R West.

--Masters of Advertising Copy. Assel, Henry & Craig, C. Samuel, eds. (The History of Advertising Ser.). 45.00 (ISBN 0-8240-6746-0). Garland Pub.

--The Pennsylvania Dutch Cookbook. abr. ed. Orig. Title: Pennsylvania Dutch & Their Cookery. 1971. pap. 3.50 (ISBN 0-486-22676-X). Dover.

--Pennsylvania Dutch Cookbook. 12.75 (ISBN 0-8446-0099-7). Peter Smith.

Frederick, J. George & Joyce, Jean. Long Island Seafood Cook Book. 11.75 (ISBN 0-8446-0098-9). Peter Smith.

Frederick, John, tr. see Chardenon, Ludo.

Frederick, John B. Lineage Book of the British Army: Mounted Corps & Infantry. LC 72-10747. pap. 93.50 (ISBN 0-317-08183-7, 2055319). Bks Demand UMI.

Frederick, John H. Commercial Air Transportation. 5th ed. LC 54-42. pap. 127.30 (ISBN 0-317-09208-1, 2000127). Bks Demand UMI.

--Industrial Marketing. Assael, Henry, ed. LC 78-223. (Century of Marketing Ser.). (Illus.). 1978. Repr. of 1934 ed. lib. bdg. 32.00x (ISBN 0-405-11187-8). Ayer Co Pubs.

Frederick, John T. The Darkened Sky: Nineteenth-Century American Novelists & Religion. LC 69-14811. pap. 72.50 (ISBN 0-317-29688-4, 2022068). Bks Demand UMI.

Frederick, Justus G. Modern Sales Management. Assael, Henry, ed. LC 78-327. (Century of Marketing Ser.). 1978. Repr. of 1921 ed. lib. bdg. 33.00x (ISBN 0-405-11185-1). Ayer Co Pubs.

Frederick, Kenneth D. Water for Western Agriculture. LC 82-47985. (A Resources for the Future Research Paper Ser.). (Illus.). 256p. (Orig.). 1982. pap. text ed. 15.00x (ISBN 0-8018-2832-5). Johns Hopkins.

--Water Management & Agricultural Development: A Case Study of the Cuyo Region of Argentina. LC 74-24402. (Resources for the Future Research Ser). (Illus.). 208p. 1975. 16.50x (ISBN 0-8018-1701-3). Johns Hopkins.

--Water Management & Agriculture Development: A Case Study of the Cuyo Region of Argentina. 204p. 1975. 16.50 (ISBN 0-8018-1701-3). Resources Future.

Frederick, Lawrence W., jt. auth. see Berg, Rebecca M.

Frederick, M. T. & Smith, R. T. Bolivia Fertilizer Situation & Recommendations. (Technical Bulletin Ser.: No. T-15). (Illus., Orig.). 1979. pap. 4.00 (ISBN 0-88090-014-8). Intl Fertilizer.

Frederick, M. Terry. Pollution Control & Environmental Protection. LC 83-198. (Paper Series International Fertilizer Development Center: Pt. 3). 1983. 4.00 (ISBN 0-88090-043-1). Intl Fertilizer.

Frederick, Marti, jt. auth. see Foreman, Roberta.

Frederick, Norris, jt. auth. see Moore, Thomas.

Frederick, Olivia M. Henry P. Fletcher & United States-Latin American Policy, 1910-1930. 25.00 (ISBN 0-405-14081-9). Ayer Co Pubs.

Frederick, Peter J. Knights of the Golden Rule: The Intellectual As Christian Social Reformer in the 1890s. LC 76-9497. 344p. 1976. 28.00x (ISBN 0-8131-1345-8). U Pr of Ky.

Frederick, Portia M. & Kinn, Mary E. The Medical Office Assistant: Administrative & Clinical. 5th ed. (Illus.). 707p. 1981. text ed. 25.95 (ISBN 0-7216-3863-5). Saunders.

Frederick, Richard. North Pacific Frontiers. LC 76-53366. (Illus.). 91p. 1976. 20.00 (ISBN 0-917048-02-4). Wash St Hist Soc.

Frederick, Richard & Engerman, Jeanne. Asahel Curtis: Photographs of the Great Northwest. (Illus.). 72p. (Orig.). 1983. pap. 7.95 (ISBN 0-917048-56-3). Wash St Hist Soc.

Frederick, Richard G., jt. auth. see Roe, Keith E.

Frederick, Robert A., ed. Writing Alaska's History: A Guide to Research. (Alaska Historical Commission Studies in History: No. 1). 160p. (Orig.). 1974. pap. 6.00 (ISBN 0-943712-00-9). Alaska Hist.

Frederick, S. H. & Capper, H., eds. Materials for Marine Machinery. 1977. 45.00x (ISBN 0-900976-42-X, Pub. by Inst Marine Eng). Intl Spec Bk.

Frederick, Stella. I Can Be a Machinist. McFadden, S. Michele, ed. (Reach High Career Awareness Ser.). (Illus.). (gr. 1-4). 1979. pap. text ed. 4.95x (ISBN 0-89262-020-X). Career Pub.

--I Can Be a Marine Biologist. McFadden, S. Michele, ed. (Reach High Career Awareness Ser.). (Illus.). (gr. 1-4). 1978. pap. 4.95x (ISBN 0-89262-018-8). Career Pub.

Frederick, Sven & Svensson, Fischer. Dynamic Astrology. 224p. 1982. 32.00x (ISBN 0-85435-065-9, Pub. by Neville Spearman Ltd England). State Mutual Bk.

Frederick, Thea. Beloved Adversary. (Second Chance at Love Ser.: No. 204). 192p. 1984. pap. 1.95 (ISBN 0-515-07820-4). Jove Pubns.

Frederick, Wayne A. & Lyons, Thomas T. The Expansion of the Federal Union Eighteen Hundred One to Eighteen Forty-Eight. (Illus.). 296p. (Orig.). (gr. 10-12). 1978. pap. text ed. 6.25 (ISBN 0-88334-116-6). Ind Sch Pr.

Frederick, William, jt. auth. see McGlynn, John.

Frederick, William H., tr. & intro. by see Hatta, Mohammad.

Frederick II Of Hohenstaufen. The Art of Falconry. Wood, Casey A. & Fyfe, F. Marjorie, eds. (Illus.). 1943. 49.50 (ISBN 0-8047-0374-4). Stanford U Pr.

Frederick Of Prussia. The Refutation of Machiavelli's Prince or Anti-Machiavel. Sonnino, Paul, tr. LC 80-15801. viii, 174p. 1981. 16.95x (ISBN 0-8214-0559-4, 82-83541); pap. 7.95x (ISBN 0-8214-0598-5, 82-83558). Ohio U Pr.

Fredericks, Anne, ed. see Spencer, John H.

Fredericks, Anthony D. Raising Bookworms: A Parents Guide to Reading Success. LC 84-60980. 125p. (Orig.). 1985. pap. text ed. 5.95 (ISBN 0-88247-733-1). R & E Pubs.

--The Reading Comprehension Idea Book. 1984. pap. 9.95 (ISBN 0-673-15950-7). Scott F.

--Your Child & Reading: A Practical Guide for Parents. 50p. 1981. pap. 3.50 (ISBN 0-939690-00-4). Fredericks Pub.

Fredericks, Anthony D. & Taylor, David. Parent Programs in Reading: Guidelines for Success. 85p. 1985. pap. 6.00 (ISBN 0-317-30079-2). Intl Reading.

Fredericks, Carlton. Arthritis: Don't Learn to Live with it. 1981. 12.95x (ISBN 0-448-14028-4). Cancer Control Soc.

--Arthritis: Don't Learn to Live with It. 224p. (Orig.). 1985. pap. 7.95 (ISBN 0-399-51133-4, Perigee). Putnam Pub Group.

--Calorie & Carbohydrate Guide. 1982. pap. 2.95 (ISBN 0-671-46941-X, 43059). PB.

--Carlton Fredericks' High-Fiber Way to Total Health. 1983. pap. 2.95 (ISBN 0-671-49621-2). PB.

--Carlton Fredericks' New Low Blood Sugar & You. (Illus.). 192p. 1985. pap. 6.95 (ISBN 0-399-51087-7, Perigee). Putnam Pub Group.

--Carlton Fredericks' Nutrition Guide for Prevention & Cure of Common Ailments & Disease. 1982. 8.95x (ISBN 0-671-44509-X). Cancer Control Soc.

--Carlton Fredericks' Nutrition Planner. 1984. pap. 7.95 (ISBN 0-671-44511-1). S&S.

--Carlton Fredericks' Program for Living Longer. 224p. 1983. 9.50 (ISBN 0-671-47237-2, Fireside). S&S.

--Eat Well, Get Well, Stay Well. LC 79-91618. 1981. (G&D); pap. 5.95 (ISBN 0-448-12023-2, G&D). Putnam Pub Group.

--Look Younger, Feel Healthier. 1982. 6.95x (ISBN 0-686-40232-4). Cancer Control Soc.

--Look Younger, Feel Healthier: A Safe, Professional, Step-by-Step Guide to Total Nutritional Health. 320p. 1982. pap. 6.75 (ISBN 0-671-44948-6, Fredericks). S&S.

--Low Blood Sugar & You. 4.95x (ISBN 0-448-12246-4). Cancer Control Soc.

--Program for Living Longer. 1983. 9.95 (ISBN 0-686-44866-9, Fireside). S&S.

--Psycho-Nutrition. (Health, Nutrition & Well Being Bks). 224p. 1983. pap. 5.95 (ISBN 0-399-50789-2, G&D). Putnam Pub Group.

Fredericks, Carlton & Goodman, Herman. Low Blood Sugar & You. 256p. 1983. pap. 2.95 (ISBN 0-441-49764-0, Pub. by Charter Bks). Ace Bks.

--Low Blood Sugar & You. 1969. pap. 4.95 (ISBN 0-399-51043-5, G&D); PLB 13.50 (ISBN 0-448-13341-5, Today Press). Putnam Pub Group.

Fredericks, Casey. The Future of Eternity: Mythologies of Science Fiction & Fantasy. LC 81-47773. (Midland Bks.: No. 295). 256p. (Orig.). 1982. 22.50x (ISBN 0-253-32530-7); pap. 9.95x (ISBN 0-253-20295-7). Ind U Pr.

Fredericks, Claude see Corrigan, Robert W.

Fredericks, H. D., et al. The Teaching Research Curriculum for Moderately & Severely Handicapped. (Illus.). 340p. 1978. photocopy ed. spiral 24.75x (ISBN 0-398-03330-7). C C Thomas.

--The Teaching Research Curriculum for Moderately & Severely Handicapped: Gross & Fine Motor. (Illus.). 264p. 1980. pap. 17.75x (ISBN 0-398-04035-4); developmental chart 3.50x. C C Thomas.

--The Teaching Research Curriculum for Moderately & Severely Handicapped: Self-Help & Cognitive. (Illus.). 280p. 1980. pap. 17.75x (ISBN 0-398-04034-6); developmental chart 3.50x. C C Thomas.

--Teaching Research Motor-Development Scale: For Moderately & Severely Retarded Children. (Illus.). 80p. 1972. 9.75x (ISBN 0-398-02284-4). C C Thomas.

Fredericks, Karen. Modern Love. (Illus.). 1984. pap. 6.95 (ISBN 0-87795-635-9, Pub. by Priam). Arbor Hse.

Fredericks, Laura. Chastity Belt. 8.95 (ISBN 0-8315-0071-9). Speller.

Fredericks, Lee & Wells, R. G. Rice Processing in Peninsula Malaysia. (Illus.). 1983. 25.95x (ISBN 0-19-582522-5). Oxford U Pr.

Fredericks, Leo Brooks see Frederick, Brooks, pseud.

Fredericks, Lipner & Fredericks, Robert. Cloze for Comprehension: Leaders of the Old West, Bk. 1. (Illus.). pap. text ed. 16.95 set of 10 (ISBN 0-87594-202-4). Book-Lab.

Fredericks, Marcel, et al. Citizen Jesuit: Life & Reflections of Ralph A. Gallagher S. J. on Chicago & the Nation. LC 83-127922. (Illus.). 58p. 1982. pap. 3.00 (ISBN 0-911531-10-6). Loyola U Ctr Urban.

Fredericks, Marcel A. & Mundy, Paul. Making It in Med School: Biography of a Medical Student. 144p. 1980. pap. 4.95 (ISBN 0-8294-0302-7). Loyola.

Fredericks, Marcel A., et al. Dental Care in Society: The Sociology of Dental Health. LC 80-15985. (Illus.). 194p. 1980. text ed. 18.95 (ISBN 0-89950-001-3). McFarland & Co.

Fredericks, Pierce G. The Civil War As They Knew It. 13.95 (ISBN 0-88411-268-3, Pub. by Aeonian Pr). Amereon Ltd.

Fredericks, Robert, jt. auth. see Fredericks, Lipner.

Fredericks, Robert, jt. auth. see Lipner, Barbara.

Fredericks, Robert F., jt. auth. see Lipner, Barbara E.

Fredericksen, Burton, ed. The J. Paul Getty Museum Journal, Vol. 3. LC 76-642750. (Illus.). 124p. (Orig.). 1976. pap. 10.00 (ISBN 0-89236-005-4). J P Getty Mus.

Fredericksen, Burton B. Alma Tadema's Spring. rev. ed. LC 78-78201. (Illus.). 32p. 1979. pap. 5.00 (ISBN 0-89236-013-5). J P Getty Mus.

--Giovanni di Francesco & the Master of Pratovecchio. (Illus.). 1974. pap. text ed. 9.00 (ISBN 0-89236-014-3). J P Getty Mus.

--Masterpieces of Painting in the J. Paul Getty Museum. LC 79-54099. (Illus.). 120p. 1980. 29.95 (ISBN 0-89236-022-4); pap. 19.95 (ISBN 0-89236-028-3). J P Getty Mus.

Fredericksen, Burton B. & Davisson, Darrell D. Benvenuto di Giovanni & Girolamo di Benvenuto: Their Altarpieces in the J. Paul Getty Museum. (J. Paul Getty Museum Publications Ser.). (Illus.). 64p. (Orig.). 1966. pap. 4.00x (ISBN 0-89236-046-1). J P Getty Mus.

Fredericksen, Burton B. & Zeri, Federico. Census of Pre-Nineteenth-Century Italian Paintings in North American Public Collections. LC 73-182813. 809p. 1972. 45.00x (ISBN 0-674-10491-9). Harvard U Pr.

Fredericksen, Hazel & Mulligan, Raymond A. The Child & His Welfare. 3rd ed. LC 70-172242. (Illus.). 1972. text ed. 25.95 (ISBN 0-7167-0905-8). W H Freeman.

Fredericksen, Thomas M. Intuitive IC Electronics: A Sophisticated Primer for Engineers & Technicians. (Illus.). 208p. 1981. 27.95 (ISBN 0-07-021923-0). McGraw.

Fredericks-Mundy. Making of a Physician. 1976. 9.95 (ISBN 0-8294-0244-6). Loyola.

Frederickson, C. J., et al. The Neurobiology of Zinc: Proceedings of a Satellite Symposium to the Annual Meeting, Society for Neuroscience, Boston, Massachusetts, November, 4-6, 1983. LC 84-11235. (Neurology & Neurobiology Ser.: Vols. 11A & 11B). 1984. Pt. A: Physiochemistry, Anatomy, & Techniques, 404 pgs. 58.00 (ISBN 0-8451-2712-8); Pt. B: Deficiency, Toxicity, & Pathology, 360 pgs. 54.00 (ISBN 0-8451-2713-6). A R Liss.

Frederickson, F. M., ed. Snubber Design Applications & Minimization Methods. (PVP Ser.: Vol. 55). 75p. 1981. 14.00 (ISBN 0-686-34515-0, H00191). ASME.

Frederickson, G., jt. auth. see Pettigrew, T.

Frederickson, George M., ed. see Helper, Hinton R.

Frederickson, H. George. New Public Administration. LC 80-10569. (Illus.). 144p. 1980. 13.75 (ISBN 0-8173-0040-6); pap. 5.75 (ISBN 0-8173-0041-4). U of Ala Pr.

Frederickson, H. George & Chandler, Ralph Clark, eds. Citizenship & Public Administration. 1984. 6.00 (ISBN 0-317-06621-8). Am Soc Pub Admin.

Frederickson, H. George & Wise, Charles, eds. Administering Public Policy. 1976. pap. 8.00 (ISBN 0-918592-16-X). Policy Studies.

Frederickson, H. George, et al. Public Personnel Administration: Threshold or Crossroad? 1970. 3.00 (ISBN 0-87373-282-0, PR 703). Intl Personnel Mgmt.

Frederickson, J. M., ed. see Barany Society Meeting, Toronto, Aug. 1971.

Frederickson, Jaye & Gibb, Sandra. The Covenant Chain: Indian Ceremonial & Trade Silver. (Illus.). 168p. 1980. 24.95 (ISBN 0-660-10347-8, 56313-8, Pub. by Natl Gallery Canada); pap. 19.95 (ISBN 0-660-10348-6, 56314-6). U of Chicago Pr.

Frederickson, Jeffreys, jt. auth. see Hegel, Georg F.

Frederickson, Keville. Opportunities in Nursing. LC 76-42886. (VGM Career Bks.). (Illus.). (YA) (gr. 8 up). 1977. lib. bdg. 7.95 (ISBN 0-8442-6273-0, 6273-0); pap. 5.95 (ISBN 0-8442-6274-9, 6274-9). Natl Textbk.

Frederickson, Lars. History of Weston, Idaho. Simmonds, A. J., ed. (Western Text Society Ser.: No. 5). (Illus.). 78p. 1972. pap. 5.50 (ISBN 0-87421-051-8). Utah St U Pr.

Frederickson, Mary, jt. ed. see Kornbluh, Joyce L.

Frederick The Great. Musical Works of Frederick the Great, 4 Vols. in 3. Spitta, Philip, ed. LC 67-27453. (Music Ser). 1967. Repr. of 1889 ed. Set. lib. bdg. 125.00 (ISBN 0-306-70980-5). Da Capo.

Frederick Van, Der Meer see Van Der Meer, Frederick.

Frederico Da Guena, Rafael, jt. auth. see Grisolia, Santiago M.

Fredericq. Electric Dichroism & Electric Birefringence. (Monographs in Physical Biochemistry). (Illus.). 1973. 47.50x (ISBN 0-19-854616-5). Oxford U Pr.

Fredericq, Paul. The Study of History in England & Scotland. LC 78-63776. (Johns Hopkins University. Studies in the Social Sciences. Fifth Ser. 1887: 10). Repr. of 1887 ed. 11.50 (ISBN 0-404-61042-0). AMS Pr.

--The Study of History in England & Scotland. 1973. pap. 9.00 (ISBN 0-384-16755-1). Johnson Repr.

--The Study of History in Germany & France. LC 78-63795. (Johns Hopkins University. Studies in the Social Sciences. Eighth Ser. 1890: 5-6). Repr. of 1890 ed. 11.50 (ISBN 0-404-61060-9). AMS Pr.

--The Study of History in Holland & Belgium. LC 78-63797. (Johns Hopkins University. Studies in the Social Sciences. Eighth Ser. 1890: 10). Repr. of 1890 ed. 11.50 (ISBN 0-404-61062-5). AMS Pr.

Fredericq, Paul see McIlvain, James W.

Fredericq, Paul see Mason, Otis T.

Frederics, Diana. Diana: A Strange Autobiography. LC 75-12315. (Homosexuality). 1976. Repr. of 1939 ed. 17.00x (ISBN 0-405-07359-3). Ayer Co Pubs.

Frederiks, J. A., jt. ed. see Vinken, P. J.

Frederiksen, A. K. The Finer Points of Riding. rev. ed. (Illus.). pap. 5.95 (ISBN 0-85131-323-X, BL2403, Dist. by Miller). J A Allen.

--Finer Points of Riding. (Illus.). 1970. 10.00x (ISBN 0-87556-094-6). Saifer.

Frederiksen, Alan. Love & Guilt. LC 84-80898. 387p. (Orig.). 1985. 14.50 (ISBN 0-910783-02-0). Green Key Pr.

--Red Roe Run. LC 82-82810. 258p. 1983. 12.95 (ISBN 0-910783-00-4). Green Key Pr.

Frederiksen, C. H. & Dominic, J. F., eds. Writing: The Nature, Development, & Communication, Vol. 2. 256p. 1982. 24.95x (ISBN 0-89859-158-9). L Erlbaum Assocs.

Frederiksen, Carl H. & Dominic, Joseph F., eds. Writing: The Nature, Development, & Teaching of Written Communication, Vol. 2. (Illus.). 256p. 1982. text ed. 24.95x (ISBN 0-89859-158-9). L Erlbaum Assocs.

Frederiksen, Christian P. Budgeting for Nonprofits. 2nd ed. LC 79-89135. 1980. 3 ring binder 59.00x (ISBN 0-916664-13-9, 42A). Public Management.

--Nonprofit Financial Management. LC 79-89135. 1979. 3 ring binder 59.00x (ISBN 0-916664-12-0). Public Management.

Frederiksen, D. W., jt. ed. see Colowick, Sidney P.

Frederiksen, Lee W. Handbook of Organizational Behavior Management. LC 82-4741. 604p. 1982. 39.95 (ISBN 0-471-09109-X, Pub. by Wiley-Interscience). Wiley.

Frederiksen, Lee W., jt. auth. see Eisler, Richard M.

Frederiksen, Lee W. & Riley, Anne W., eds. Computers, People & Productivity. LC 84-25281. (Journal of Organizational Behavior Management: Vol. 6, Nos. 3 & 4). 205p. 1985. text ed. 19.95 (ISBN 0-86656-339-3). Haworth Pr.

--Improving Staff Effectivness in Human Service Settings: Organizational Behavior Management Approaches. LC 84-722. (Journal of Organizational Behavior Management Ser.: Vol. 5, Nos. 3/4). 195p. 1984. text ed. 24.95 (ISBN 0-86656-282-6, B282). Haworth Pr.

Frederiksen, Lee W., et al, eds. Marketing Health Behavior: Principles, Techniques, & Applications. 216p. 1984. 24.50x (ISBN 0-306-41523-2, Plenum Pr). Plenum Pub.

Frederiksen, N., et al. Prediction of Organizational Behavior. 344p. 1973. pap. text ed. 14.50 (ISBN 0-08-017189-3). Pergamon.

Frederiksen, Thomas M. Intuitive IC CMOS Evolution: From Early ICs to Micro CMOS Technology & CAD for VLSI. 200p. 14.95 (ISBN 0-317-13071-4). P-H.

Frederiske, Julie. None But Ourselves: Masses vs. Media in the Making of Zimbabwe. 376p. 1984. pap. 16.95 (ISBN 0-14-007222-5). Penguin.

Frederking, T. H., et al, eds. Cryogenic Processes & Equipment, Nineteen Eighty-Two. LC 83-11414. (AIChE Symposium: Vol. 79). 143p. 1983. pap. 40.00 (ISBN 0-8169-0249-6); pap. 20.00 members (ISBN 0-317-03720-X). Am Inst Chem Eng.

Fredersdorff, C. G. Von see Von Fredersdorff, C. G.

Fredet, Jean, jt. auth. see Maybon, Charles B.

Fredgant, Don. Collecting Art Nouveau, Identification & Values. (Illus.). 300p. (Orig.). 1982. pap. 10.95 (ISBN 0-89689-036-8). Bks Americana.

--Electrical Collectibles: Relics of the Electrical Age. LC 81-2449. (Illus.). 160p. 1981. pap. 9.95 (ISBN 0-914598-04-X). Padre Prods.

Frediksson, Don. Plumbing for Dummies: A Guide to the Maintenance & Repair of Everything Including the Kitchen Sink. LC 82-17790. (Illus.). 256p. 1983. pap. 10.95 (ISBN 0-672-52738-3). Bobbs.

Fredland, J. Eric & MacRae, C. Duncan. Econometric Models of the Housing Sector: A Policy-Oriented Survey. 109p. 1978. pap. 6.00x (ISBN 0-87766-232-0, 23600). Urban Inst.

Fredland, Richard A., jt. ed. see Potholm, Christian P.

Fredlee. The Magic of Sea Shells. LC 76-12931. (Illus.). 36p. (Orig.). (gr. 1-3). 1976. pap. 2.95 (ISBN 0-89317-010-0). Windward Pub.

Fredlein, R. A., jt. auth. see Bockris, J. O'M.

Fredman, A., jt. auth. see Adby, P.

Fredman, Alice. Anthony Trollope. LC 74-136496. (Columbia Essays on Modern Writers Ser.: No. 56). 48p. 1971. pap. 2.50 (ISBN 0-231-03081-9). Columbia U Pr.

Fredman, Alice G. Diderot & Sterne. LC 72-13743. xii, 264p. 1972. Repr. lib. bdg. 22.00x (ISBN 0-374-92884-3). Octagon.

Fredman, L. E. Australian Ballot: The Story of an American Reform. x, 150p. 1968. 5.75 (ISBN 0-87013-121-4). Mich St U Pr.

Fredman, Lionel E. James Madison: American President & Constitutional Author. Rahmas, D. Steve, ed. LC 74-14592. (Outstanding Personalities Ser.). 32p. 1974. lib. bdg. 3.50 incl. catalog cards (ISBN 0-87157-578-7); pap. 1.95 vinyl laminated covers (ISBN 0-87157-078-5). SamHar Pr.

--John Dickinson: American Revolutionary Statesman. LC 74-14599. (Outstanding Personalities Ser.). 32p. 1974. lib. bdg. 3.50 incl. catalog cards (ISBN 0-87157-575-2); pap. 1.95 vinyl laminated covers (ISBN 0-87157-075-0). SamHar Pr.

Fredman, Lionel E. & Kurland, Gerald. John Adams: American Revolutionary Leader & President. Rahmas, D. Steve, ed. LC 73-87627. (Outstanding Personalities Ser.: No. 65). 32p. (Orig.). (YA) (gr. 7-12). 1973. lib. bdg. 3.50 incl. catalog cards (ISBN 0-87157-565-5); pap. 1.95 vinyl laminated covers (ISBN 0-87157-065-3). SamHar Pr.

Fredman, Ruth G. The Passover Seder. 1982. pap. 5.95 (ISBN 0-452-00606-6, Mer). NAL.

--The Passover Seder: Afikoman in Exile. 1981. 21.00x (ISBN 0-8122-7788-0). U of Pa Pr.

--The Passover Seder: Afikoman in Exile. 192p. 19.00 (ISBN 0-686-95143-3). ADL.

Fredman, Ruth G., ed. Jewish Life on Campus: A Directory of B'nai B'rith Hillel Foundations & Other Campus Agencies. 1985. pap. 7.95 (ISBN 0-9603058-4-X). B'nai B'rith Hillel.

Fredman, Stephen. Poet's Prose: The Crisis in American Verse. LC 83-7549. (Cambridge Studies in American Literature & Culture). 176p. 1983. 19.95 (ISBN 0-521-25722-0). Cambridge U Pr.

Fredman, Stephen, tr. see Alegria, Fernando.

Fredman, Stephen, et al, trs. see Huidobro, Vicente.

Fredman, William E. Victorian Prefaces & Introductions: A Facimile Collection. Nadel, I. B. & Stashy, J. F., eds. (The Victorian Muse Ser.). 55.00 (ISBN 0-8240-8627-9). Garland Pub.

Fredoville, Jean C. Dictionnaire civilisation Romaine. (Dictionnaires de l'homme du vingtieme siecle). (Illus., Fr.). 1968. 8.50 (ISBN 0-685-13862-3, 3716). Larousse.

Fredrich, Carl. Hippokratische Untersuchungen. facsimile ed. LC 75-13264. (History of Ideas in Ancient Greece Ser.). (Ger.). 1976. Repr. of 1899 ed. 16.00x (ISBN 0-405-07306-2). Ayer Co Pubs.

Fredrichs, Dave. Automobile Maintenance Organization: A "How-To" Paper. 1982p. 1982. 3.50 (ISBN 0-318-17947-4, M09C). NASCO.

Fredrick, Edna C. The Plot & Its Construction in Eighteenth Century Criticism of French Comedy: A Study of the Theory with Relation to the Practice of Beaumarchais. LC 72-82001. 132p. 1973. Repr. of 1934 ed. lib. bdg. 21.00 (ISBN 0-8337-4118-7). B Franklin.

Fredrick, Laurence W. & Baker, Robert H. An Introduction to Astronomy. 9th ed. LC 78-69754. 512p. (Orig.). 1981. 18.50 (ISBN 0-442-22422-2). Krieger.

Fredricks, Darlene. Wham! 160p. 1986. pap. 2.95 (ISBN 0-345-32998-8). Ballantine.

Fredricks, Marci. Rob Lowe. (Teen Dreams Ser.). 112p. (Orig.). 1985. pap. 2.95 (ISBN 0-523-42570-8). Pinnacle Bks.

Fredricks, Marjorie W., ed. see Spehr, Paul.

Fredricksen, Burton B. Cassone Paintings of Francesco di Giorgio. (Illus.). 45p. 1969. pap. 4.00 (ISBN 0-89236-062-3). J P Getty Mus.

Fredrickson, Carl, ed. Church Soloists Favorites, 2 bks. (Illus.). 1963. Bk. 1, High Voice, 64p. pap. 6.95 (ISBN 0-8258-0228-8, RB-65); Bk. 2, Low Voice, 85p. pap. 6.95 (ISBN 0-8258-0229-6, RB-66). Fischer Inc NY.

Fredrickson, George, ed. William Lloyd Garrison. (Great Lives Observed Ser). 1968. 8.95 (ISBN 0-13-346858-5, Spec); pap. 1.95 (ISBN 0-13-346841-0, Spec). P-H.

Fredrickson, George M. The Black Image in the White Mind: The Debate on Afro-American Character & Destiny, 1817-1914. 1977. pap. 8.95xi (ISBN 0-06-131688-1, TB 1688, Torch). Har-Row.

--Black Image in the White Mind: The Debate on Afro-American Character & Destiny, 1817-1914. LC 71-138721. 1971. text ed. 27.50x (ISBN 0-8290-0136-0). Irvington.

--Inner Civil War: Northern Intellectuals & the Crisis of the Union. 1968. pap. 5.95xi (ISBN 0-06-131358-0, TB1358, Torch). Har-Row.

--White Supremacy: A Comparative Study in American & South African History. (Galaxy Bk.: No. 665). 1981. pap. 9.95 (ISBN 0-19-503042-7, GB). Oxford U Pr.

--White Supremacy: A Comparative Study of American & South African History. (Illus.). 1981. 29.95x (ISBN 0-19-502759-0). Oxford U Pr.

Fredrickson, George M., ed. see Tourgee, Albion W.

Fredrickson, Helene. Baudelaire: Heros et Fils: Dualite et Problemes du Travail Dans les Lettres a Sa Mere. (Stanford French & Italian Studies: No. 8). 138p. 1978. pap. 25.00 (ISBN 0-915838-36-2). Anma Libri.

Fredrickson, Jack M. Cost Reduction in the Office. LC 83-73036. 288p. 1984. 24.95 (ISBN 0-317-12696-2). AMACOM.

Fredrickson, Olive A. & East, Ben. Silence of the North. 208p. 1973. pap. 2.75 (ISBN 0-446-85559-6). Warner Bks.

Fredrickson, Ronald H. Career Information. (Illus.). 416p. 1982. reference 28.95 (ISBN 0-13-114744-7). P-H.

Fredrickson, Terry L. & Wedel, Paul F., Jr. English by Newspaper. 1983. pap. text ed. 8.95 (ISBN 0-88377-375-9). Newbury Hse.

Fredrik, Alan S., tr. see Beroul.

Fredriksen, John C. Free Trade & Sailors' Rights: A Bibliography of the War of 1812. LC 84-15743. (Bibliographies & Indexes in American History Ser.: No. 2). xiii, 399p. 1985. lib. bdg. 45.00 (ISBN 0-313-24313-1, FFT/). Greenwood.

Fredrikson, Roger & Garver, John J. It Costs Your Life, 2 Bks. Bk. 1. Pupils' Ed. pap. 1.25 (ISBN 0-8170-0237-5); Bk. 2. Teacher's Ed. pap. 1.00 (ISBN 0-8170-0238-3). Judson.

Fredrikson, Roger L. The Communicator's Commentary-John, Vol. 4. Ogilvie, Lloyd J., ed. (The Communicator's Commentaries Ser.). 1983. 15.95 (ISBN 0-8499-0157-X). Word Bks.

Fredriksson, Don. The Home Buyer's & Owners Checklist: The Original Residential Real Estate Inspection & Evaluation Manual. Poropat, Kathy, ed. (Illus.). 137p. (Orig.). 1984. pap. 14.95 (ISBN 0-931751-00-4). Writers Pub Coop.

Fredriksson, H. & Hillert, M., eds. Physical Metallurgy of Cast Iron: Materials Research Society Symposia Proceedings, Vol. 34. xxi, 500p. 1985. 95.00 (ISBN 0-444-00938-8, North-Holland). Elsevier.

Fredriksson, Kristine. American Rodeo: From Buffalo Bill to Big Business. LC 83-40501. (Illus.). 248p. 1985. 18.95 (ISBN 0-89096-181-6). Tex A&M Univ Pr.

Fredro, Alexandro. The Major Comedies of Alexander Fredro. Segel, Harold B., tr. (Columbia Slavic Studies Ser). 1969. 42.00 (ISBN 0-691-06151-3). Princeton U Pr.

Fred R. von, der Mehden see Mehden, Fred R. von der.

Free, jt. ed. see Birnbaum.

Free, Alfred H. & Free, Helen M. Urinalysis in Clinical Laboratory Practice. LC 75-29484. (Uniscience Ser.). 284p. 1975. 52.00 (ISBN 0-8493-5104-9). CRC Pr.

Free, Anne R. Social Usage. 2nd ed. (Illus.). 1969. pap. text ed. 18.95 (ISBN 0-13-819607-9). P-H.

Free Church. Ministers Service Manual. 1981. 5.95 (ISBN 0-911802-33-9). Free Church Pubns.

Free Church Authors. You & Your Church. 3rd ed. 1978. pap. 1.95 (ISBN 0-911802-41-X). Free Church Pubns.

Free Convention, Rutland, Vermont. Proceedings of the Free Convention, Held at Rutland, Vermont, July 25th, 26th, & 27th, 1858. LC 78-22163. (Free Love in America). Repr. of 1858 ed. 19.00 (ISBN 0-404-60963-5). AMS Pr.

Free, Helen M., jt. auth. see Free, Alfred H.

Free, James L. Just One More. 193p. 1977. 4.95 (ISBN 0-318-15335-1). Natl Coun Alcoholism.

--Training Your Retriever. 7th rev. ed. (Illus.). 1980. 13.95 (ISBN 0-698-11009-9, Coward). Putnam Pub Group.

Free, Jessica. Dolls. 408p. (Orig.). 1982. pap. 3.50 (ISBN 0-441-15217-1). Ace Bks.

Free, John B. Bees & Mankind. (Illus.). 174p. 1982. 17.95 (ISBN 0-04-638001-9). Allen Unwin.

--Insect Pollination of Crops. 1971. 84.00 (ISBN 0-12-266650-X). Acad Pr.

--Social Organization of Honeybees. (Studies in Biology: No. 81). 74p. 1977. pap. text ed. 8.95 (ISBN 0-7131-2655-8). E Arnold.

Free, John Da see Da Free, John.

Free, John Da see John, Da Free.

Free Library Of Philadelphia. Catalog of the Hampton L. Carson Collection Illustrative of the the Growth of the Common Law, 2 Vols. 1962. Set. 200.00 (ISBN 0-8161-0490-5, Hall Library). G K Hall.

Free, Michael J., jt. auth. see Goldstein, Norman N.

Free, Montague. All about African Violets: The Complete Guide to Success with America's Favorite House Plant. rev. ed. LC 78-60289. (Illus.). 1979. 12.95 (ISBN 0-385-14521-7). Doubleday.

Free Public Library Commission of Vermont, ed. Index to the Vermonter, 1914-1939: Volumes 18-44. 1941. pap. 2.50x (ISBN 0-934720-08-8). VT Hist Soc.

Freeberg, Lori. My Big FunThinker Book of Step-by-Step Drawing. (FunThinkers Ser.). (Illus.). 56p. (Basic Set includes: 8" x 10" activity book with step-by-step directions for drawing pets, wild animals, farm animals & vehicles, 2 wipe-off cards, 50-sheet pad of paper, soft lead drawing pencil, pencil eraser parent's manual & box. Ensemble includes: Basic Set plus 4 boxed wipe-off crayons, 8 colored pencils, pencil sharpener & carrying case.). (gr. 3-6). 1983. pap. 6.00 Basic Set (ISBN 0-88679-014-X, EI-5627); pap. 10.00 Ensemble (ISBN 0-88679-013-1, EI-5607). Educ Insights.

Freeborn, Richard. The Russian Revolutionary Novel. 302p. 1985. pap. 17.95 (ISBN 0-521-31737-1). Cambridge U Pr.

--The Russian Revolutionary Novel: Turgenev to Pasternak. LC 82-4259. (Cambridge Studies in Russian Literature). 220p. 1983. 49.50 (ISBN 0-521-24442-0). Cambridge U Pr.

--Turgenev: The Novelist's Novelist, a Study. 1978. Repr. of 1960 ed. lib. bdg. 24.75x (ISBN 0-313-20187-0, FRTU). Greenwood.

Freeborn, Richard, tr. see Turgenev, Ivan.

Freeborn, Richard, et al. Russian Literary Attitudes from Pushkin to Solzhenitsyn. LC 76-15796. 158p. 1976. text ed. 26.50x (ISBN 0-06-492260-X). B&N Imports.

Freeburg, Victor O. Art of Photoplay Making. LC 72-124006. (Literature of Cinema Ser.). Repr. of 1918 ed. 13.00 (ISBN 0-405-01612-3). Ayer Co Pubs.

--Disguise Plots in Elizabethan Drama. LC 65-19616. 1965. Repr. of 1915 ed. 17.00 (ISBN 0-405-08532-X, Blom Pubns). Ayer Co Pubs.

--Pictorial Beauty on the Screen. LC 76-124007. (Literature of Cinema, Ser. 1). Repr. of 1923 ed. 12.50 (ISBN 0-405-01613-1). Ayer Co Pubs.

Freed, Alice. The Semantics of English: Aspectual Complementation. 1979. lib. bdg. 26.50 (ISBN 90-277-1010-4, Pub. by Reidel Holland); pap. 10.50 (ISBN 90-277-1011-2, Pub. by Reidel Holland). Kluwer Academic.

Freed, Alvyn & Freed, Margaret. TA for Kids (& Grownups Too) 3rd rev ed. LC 77-81761. (Transactional Analysis for Everybody Ser.). (Illus.). (gr. 4-7). 1977. pap. 9.95 (ISBN 0-915190-09-5). Jalmar Pr.

Freed, Alvyn M. TA for Teens (& Other Important People) LC 76-19651. (Transactional Analysis for Everybody Ser). (Illus.). (YA) (gr. 8-12). 1976. pap. 9.95 (ISBN 0-915190-03-6). Jalmar Pr.

--TA for Tots, Vol. II. LC 76-19650. (Transactional Analysis for Everybody Ser.). (Illus., Orig.). (ps-3). 1980. pap. 9.95 (ISBN 0-915190-25-7). Jalmar Pr.

--TA for Tots (& Other Prinzes) LC 76-19650. (Transactional Analysis for Everybody Ser.). (Illus.). (ps-3). 1973. pap. 9.95 (ISBN 0-915190-12-5). Jalmar Pr.

--TA for Tots Coloring Book. (Transactional Analysis for Everybody Ser.). 1976. pap. 2.95 (ISBN 0-915190-33-8). Jalmar Pr.

Freed, Alvyn M. & Michelson, Herb. Please Keep on Smoking: We Need the Money. (Orig.). 1980. pap. 2.95 saddle stitch (ISBN 0-915190-27-3). Jalmar Pr.

Freed, Anne O., jt. ed. see Blau, David.

Freed, Barbara F. From the Community to the Classroom: Gathering Second Language Speech Samples. (Language in Education Ser.: No. 6). 26p. 1978. pap. 3.95x (ISBN 0-15-599069-1). Ctr Appl Ling.

Freed, Barbara F., jt. auth. see Lambert, Richard D.

Freed, Clarence L. A Sigh, a Tear. (Illus.). 36p. 1983. 14.95 (ISBN 0-914715-00-3). Spectracolor Reynolds.

--A Sigh, a Tear. (Illus.). 36p. 1984. Repr. 14.95 (ISBN 0-914715-01-1). Spectracolor-Reynolds.

Freed, D. S. & Uhlenbeck, K. K. Instantons & Four-Manifolds. (Mathematical Sciences Research Institute Publications Ser.: Vol. 1). (Illus.). x, 232p. 1984. 15.00 (ISBN 0-387-96036-8). Springer-Verlag.

Freed, Daniel J. & Terrell, Timothy P. Standards Relating to Interim Status: The Release, Control & Detention of Accused Juvenile Offenders Between Arrest & Disposition. LC 77-2318. (IJA-ABA Juvenile Justice Standards Project Ser.). 144p. 1980. prof ref 22.50 (ISBN 0-88410-244-0); pap. 12.50 prof ref (ISBN 0-88410-812-0). Ballinger Pub.

Freed, Debbie, jt. auth. see Darling, Kathy.

Freed, Donald. China Card. LC 80-66506. 1980. 12.95 (ISBN 0-87795-281-7). Arbor Hse.

--Spymaster. LC 78-72922. 1980. 12.95 (ISBN 0-87795-211-6). Arbor Hse.

Freed, Donald & Landis, Fred S. Death in Washington: The Murder of Orlando Letelier. 274p. 1980. 12.95 (ISBN 0-88208-123-3); pap. 7.95 (ISBN 0-88208-124-1). Lawrence Hill.

Freed, Donald, jt. auth. see Ross, Joan.

Freed, Donald, ed. see Citizens Research & Investigation Committee & Tackwood, Louis.

Freed, Doris J., jt. auth. see Foster, Henry H.
Freed, Earl X., ed. Interfaces Between Alcoholism & Mental Health. LC 79-620039. (NIAAA-RUCAS Alcoholism Treatment Ser.: No. 4). 1982. pap. 15.00 (ISBN 0-911290-50-8). Rutgers Ctr Alcohol.
Freed, Edwin D. The New Testament: A Critical Introduction. 600p. 1985. text ed. write for info. (ISBN 0-534-05388-2). Wadsworth Pub.
Freed, J. A., jt. ed. see Dorio, M. M.
Freed, John B. The Counts of Falkenstein: Noble Self-Consciousness in Twelfth-Century Germany. LC 83-73282. (Transactions Ser.: Vol. 74, Pt. 6). 1984. 10.00 (ISBN 0-87169-746-7). Am Philos.
--The Friars & German Society in the Thirteenth Century. LC 75-36480. 1977. 14.00x (ISBN 0-910956-60-X). Medieval Acad.
Freed, Josh & Kalina, Jon, eds. The Anglo Guide to Survival in Quebec. 148p. 1983. pap. 9.95 (ISBN 0-920792-33-2). Eden Pr.
Freed, Karl F., jt. ed. see Rice, Stuart A.
Freed, Lewis. T. S. Eliot: Aesthetics & History. LC 61-11289. xvi, 251p. 1962. pap. 7.95 (ISBN 0-87548-011-X). Open Court.
--T. S. Eliot: The Critic As Philosopher. LC 77-85598. 291p. 1979. 11.95 (ISBN 0-911198-54-7). Purdue U Pr.
Freed, Margaret, jt. auth. see Freed, Alvyn.
Freed, Margaret M. A Time to Teach, a Time to Dance: A Creative Approach to Teaching Dance. new ed. LC 76-19647. (NO Ser). 1976. 8.95 (ISBN 0-915190-04-4). Jalmar Pr.
Freed, Margaret M., jt. auth. see Bird, Harriet.
Freed, Ned & Glover, Fred. Simple but Powerful Goal Programming Formula for Problems of Statistical Discrimination & Multi-Dimensional Classification. 1977. 2.50 (ISBN 0-686-64911-7). U CO Busn Res Div.
--Simple but Powerful Goal Programming Models for Discriminant Problems. 1978. 2.50 (ISBN 0-686-64183-3). U CO Busn Res Div.
Freed, Paul. The General Ledger Software Consultant. 80p. 1985. spiral bdg. 24.95 (ISBN 0-931281-06-7). Mykro.
Freed, Ray. Moom. (Backstreet Editions Ser.). 16p. 1980. pap. 3.00 (ISBN 0-935252-13-4); o. p. 10.00 (ISBN 0-686-61077-6). Street Pr.
--Shinnecock Bay. 2nd, Rev. ed. 16p. 1978. pap. 2.00 (ISBN 0-935252-08-8). Street Pr.
Freed, Ray & Tyack, Jim, eds. On Good Ground: Poems & Photographs of Eastern Long Island. LC 81-50936. (Illus., Orig.). 1981. pap. 6.95 (ISBN 0-935252-28-2). Street Pr.
Freed, Ray, ed. see Aehegma, Aelbert C.
Freed, Shervin & Lichko, Joseph. Measuring Union Climate. LC 81-66402. 319p. 1981. 8.95 (ISBN 0-910436-20-7). Conway Data.
Freed, Stanley A., ed. Anthropology & the Climate of Opinion, Vol. 293. (Annals of the New York Academy of Sciences). 274p. 1977. 23.00x (ISBN 0-89072-039-8). NY Acad Sci.
Freed, V. H. see Haque, Rizwanel.
Freedberg, Catherine Blanton see Blanton Freedberg, Catherine.
Freedberg, David. Rubens: The Life of Christ after the Passion, Pt. VII. (Corpus Rubenianum Ludwig Burchand). (Illus.). 1983. 74.00 (ISBN 0-19-921032-2). Oxford U Pr.
Freedberg, S. J. Circa Sixteen Hundred: A Revolution of Style in Italian Painting. (Illus.). 176p. 1983. text ed. 25.00x (ISBN 0-674-13156-8). Harvard U Pr.
--Painting in Italy: 1500 to 1600. (Pelican History of Art Ser.: No. 35). 1978. 50.00 (ISBN 0-670-53637-7). Viking.
--Painting in Italy: 1500-1600. (History of Art Ser.). (Illus.). 1975. pap. 18.95x (ISBN 0-14-056135-8, Pelican). Penguin.
--Painting of the High Renaissance in Rome & Florence, 2 vols. 3rd, rev. ed. LC 84-82388. (Illus.). 1158p. 1985. Repr. of 1961 ed. lib. bdg. 120.00 (ISBN 0-87817-301-3). Hacker.
Freedberg, S. J., ed. see Amishai-Maisels, Ziva.
Freedberg, S. J., ed. see Benezra, Neal D.
Freedberg, S. J., ed. see Blanton Freedberg, Catherine.
Freedberg, S. J., ed. see Blumenthal, Arthur.
Freedberg, S. J., ed. see Boyd, Sterling.
Freedberg, S. J., ed. see Bruntjen, Sven H.
Freedberg, S. J., ed. see Burr Carter, Jane.
Freedberg, S. J., ed. see Caroselli, Susan L.
Freedberg, S. J., ed. see Ceen, Allan.
Freedberg, S. J., ed. see Cheney, Liana.
Freedberg, S. J., ed. see Covi, Dario A.
Freedberg, S. J., ed. see Davis, Bruce.
Freedberg, S. J., ed. see De Sabato Swinton, Elizabeth.
Freedberg, S. J., ed. see Gaber-Saletan, Pamela.
Freedberg, S. J., ed. see Gibert, Creighton E.
Freedberg, S. J., ed. see Grove, Nancy.
Freedberg, S. J., ed. see Hibbs, Vivian A.
Freedberg, S. J., ed. see Hyland, Douglas K.
Freedberg, S. J., ed. see Kowal, David M.
Freedberg, S. J., ed. see Lieberman, Ralph E.
Freedberg, S. J., ed. see McGough, Stephen C.
Freedberg, S. J., ed. see Martone, Thomas.
Freedberg, S. J., ed. see Michael, Erika.
Freedberg, S. J., ed. see Mitchell-Grizzard, Mary F.
Freedberg, S. J., ed. see Osborne, Carol M.
Freedberg, S. J., ed. see Paradise, JoAnne.
Freedberg, S. J., ed. see Quimby, Ian.
Freedberg, S. J., ed. see Quint Platt, Arlene.
Freedberg, S. J., ed. see Rosasco, Besty.
Freedberg, S. J., ed. see Schreiber-Jacoby, Beverly.
Freedberg, S. J., ed. see Sheppard, Jennifer M.
Freedberg, S. J., ed. see Ten Grotenhuis, Elizabeth.
Freedberg, S. J., ed. see Trilling, James.
Freedberg, S. J., ed. see Von Barghahn, Barbara.
Freedberg, S. J., ed. see Wilkins, David G.
Freedberg, S. J., ed. see Yard, Sally.
Freedberg, Sydney J. Andrea Del Sarto: Catalogue Raisonne. LC 63-17198. (Illus.). 1963. 17.50x (ISBN 0-674-03552-6, Belknap Pr). Harvard U Pr.
--Parmigianino: His Works in Painting. LC 72-95120. (Illus.). 1971. Repr. of 1950 ed. lib. bdg. 29.75x (ISBN 0-8371-3717-9, FRPA). Greenwood.
Freedberg, Sydney J., ed. see Erhart, Katherine P.
Freedberg, Sydney J., ed. see Lamoureux, Richard E.
Freedberg, Sydney J., ed. see Lichtenstein, Sara.
Freedberg, Sydney J., ed. see Passavant, Johann D.
Freedberg, Sydney J., ed. see Sale, J. Russell.
Freedeman, Charles E. Conseil d'Etat in Modern France. LC 68-59225. (Columbia University. Studies in the Social Sciences: No. 603). Repr. of 1961 ed. 18.50 (ISBN 0-404-51603-3). AMS Pr.
--Joint Stock Enterprise in France, 1807-1867: From Privileged Company to Modern Corporation. LC 78-26674. xvi, 234p. 1979. 22.50 (ISBN 0-8078-1359-1). U of NC Pr.
Freeden, Michael. The New Liberalism: An Ideology of Social Reform. 1978. 39.95x (ISBN 0-19-822463-X). Oxford U Pr.
Freeden, Michael, ed. see Hobson, J. A.
Freedland, Mark, jt. auth. see Davies, Paul.
Freedland, Mark R. The Contract of Employment. 1976. 42.00x (ISBN 0-19-825306-0). Oxford U Pr.
Freedland, Michael. Jerome Kern. (Illus.). 182p. 1978. 13.25x (ISBN 0-8476-3126-5). Rowman.
--Jerome Kern: A Biography. LC 80-6160. 200p. 1981. 11.95 (ISBN 0-8128-2776-7). Stein & Day.
--Katherine Hepburn. (Illus.). 250p. 1984. 16.95 (ISBN 0-491-03421-0, Pub. by Salem Hse Ltd). Merrimack Pub Cir.
--Peter O'Toole. (Illus.). 237p. 1983. 12.95 (ISBN 0-312-60362-2). St Martin.
--Sophie: The Sophie Tucker Story. (Illus.). 221p. 1978. 15.00x (ISBN 0-7130-0153-4, Pub. by Woburn Pr England). Biblio Dist.
--The Warner Brothers. LC 83-9747. (Illus.). 240p. 1983. 13.95 (ISBN 0-312-85620-2). St Martin.
Freedland, R. A. & Briggs, S. A Biochemical Approach to Nutrition. 1977. pap. 7.50 (ISBN 0-412-13040-8, NO.6113, Pub. by Chapman & Hall). Methuen Inc.
Freedle, R. O., jt. ed. see Carroll, J. B.
Freedle, Roy, ed. see Benson, James & Greaves, William.
Freedle, Roy O., jt. auth. see Fine, Jonathan.
Freedle, Roy O., ed. Discourse Production & Comprehension. (Advances in Discourse Processes Ser.: Vol. 1). (Illus.). 1977. text ed. 39.50 (ISBN 0-89391-001-5); pap. text ed. 24.50. Ablex Pub.
--New Directions in Discourse Processing. (Advances in Discourse Processes: Vol. 2). 1979. text ed. 39.50x (ISBN 0-89391-003-1). Ablex Pub.
Freedle, Roy O., ed. see Beaugrande, Robert de.
Freedle, Roy O., ed. see Benson, James & Greaves, William.
Freedle, Roy O., ed. see DiPietro, Robert J.
Freedle, Roy O., ed. see Fisher, Sue & Todd, Alexander D.
Freedle, Roy O., ed. see Hedley, Carolyn & Baratta, Anthony.
Freedle, Roy O., ed. see Pellegrini, Anthony D. & Yawkey, Thomas D.
Freedle, Roy O., ed. see Tannen, Deborah.
Freedle, Roy O., ed. see Verschueren, Jef.
Freedley, Edwin T. A Practical Treatise on Business. LC 73-2508. (Big Business; Economic Power in a Free Society Ser.). Repr. of 1853 ed. 23.50 (ISBN 0-405-05089-5). Ayer Co Pubs.
Freedley, George, jt. auth. see Gilder, Rosamond.
Freedley, George, ed. Three Plays about Crime & Criminals. Incl. Arsenic & Old Lace. Kesselring, Joseph; Detective Story. Kingsley, Sidney; Kind Lady. Chodorov, Edward. 279p. pap. 3.95 (ISBN 0-671-47229-1). WSP.
Freedman. Yearbook of Psychiatry & Applied Mental Health, 1985. 1985. 45.95 (ISBN 0-8151-6027-5). Year Bk Med.
Freedman, A. L. & Lees, R. A. Real-Time Computer Systems. LC 76-22844. (Computer Systems Engineering Ser.). 277p. 1977. 27.50x (ISBN 0-8448-1003-7). Crane-Russak Co.
Freedman, A. M., jt. ed. see Fisher, S.
Freedman, Abby J., jt. auth. see Fitzsimmons, Stephen J.
Freedman, Alan. The Computer Glossary: It's Not Just a Glossary. 3rd ed. (Illus.). 324p. 1983. 14.95 (ISBN 0-941878-02-3). Computer Lang.
--The dBASE II for the First Time User. LC 84-194501. 174p. 1984. pap. 19.95 (ISBN 0-912677-08-2). Ashton-Tate Bks.
--The dBASE II for the First-Time User: A Visual Guide. 1984. 19.95 (ISBN 0-8359-1244-2). Reston.
Freedman, Alan & Morrison, Irma L. The Computer Glossary: It's Not Just a Glossary! 320p. 1983. pap. 15.95 (ISBN 0-13-164483-1). P-H.
Freedman, Alan & Morrison, Irma Lee. The Computer Coloring Book: It's Not Just a Coloring Book. 80p. 1983. pap. 6.95 (ISBN 0-13-164632-X). P-H.
Freedman, Alfred, ed. see American Psychopathological Association Publications.
Freedman, Ann E. & Freedman, P. E. The Psychology of Political Control. LC 75-10556. 224p. 1975. pap. text ed. 13.95 (ISBN 0-312-65310-7). St Martin.
Freedman, Ann. E., jt. auth. see Babcock, Barbara A.
Freedman, Anne, jt. auth. see Smith, Constance.
Freedman, Ariva & Pringle, Ian, eds. Reinventing the Rhetorical Tradition. 197p. 1981. 13.00 (ISBN 0-8141-3987-6). NCTE.
Freedman, Arthur M., jt. ed. see Lee, Robert J.
Freedman, Audrey. Industry Response to Health Risk. (Report Ser.: No. 811). (Illus.). viii, 72p. (Orig.). 1981. pap. 100.00 (ISBN 0-8237-0248-0); pap. 20.00 member. Conference Bd.
--Managing Labor Relations. LC 79-55275. (Report Ser.: No. 765). (Illus.). 92p. (Orig.). 1979. pap. 30.00 (ISBN 0-8237-0201-4); pap. 10.00 member. Conference Bd.
--Security Bargains Reconsidered: SUB Severance Pay Guaranteed Work. LC 77-93684. (Report Ser: No. 736). (Illus.). 64p. 1978. 30.00 (ISBN 0-8237-0170-0); member 10.00. Conference Bd.
Freedman, B. Markov Chains. (Illus.). 382p. 1983. Repr. of 1971 ed. 30.00 (ISBN 0-387-90808-0). Springer-Verlag.
Freedman, Ben. Sanitarian's Handbook: Theory & Administrative Practice for Environmental Health. 1977. 69.50 (ISBN 0-930234-02-2). Peerless.
Freedman, Benedict. Mrs. Mike. 1981. Repr. lib. bdg. 16.95x (ISBN 0-89966-396-6). Buccaneer Bks.
Freedman, Benedict & Freedman, Nancy. Mrs. Mike. (gr. 7 up). 1984. pap. 2.95 (ISBN 0-425-07986-4). Berkley Pub.
Freedman, Benjamin. Facts Are Facts. 1979. lib. bdg. 59.95 (ISBN 0-8490-2912-0). Gordon Pr.
Freedman, Benjamin, jt. auth. see Baumrin, Bernard.
Freedman, Benjamin H. Facts Are Facts. 1954. pap. 2.00 (ISBN 0-911038-15-9). Noontide.
Freedman, Carleton H. Manhood Redux: Standing Up to Feminism. Leiman, J., ed. 294p. (Orig.). 1985. pap. 7.95 (ISBN 0-318-12138-7). Samson Pubns.
Freedman, D. Approximating Countable Markov Chains. (Illus.). 140p. 1983. Repr. of 1972 ed. 24.00 (ISBN 0-387-90804-8). Springer-Verlag.
--Brownian Motion & Diffusion. (Illus.). 231p. 1983. Repr. of 1971 ed. 26.00 (ISBN 0-387-90805-6). Springer-Verlag.
Freedman, D., ed. Biology of Major Psychosis. 1975. 25.75 (ISBN 0-7204-7560-0). Elsevier.
Freedman, D. N. Pottery, Poetry & Prophecy: Studies in Early Hebrew Poetry. 1980. text ed. 18.75x (ISBN 0-931464-04-8). Eisenbrauns.
Freedman, D. N. & Mathews, K. A. The Paleo-Hebrew Leviticus Scroll. (Illus.). xii, 135p. 1985. text ed. 19.95x (ISBN 0-89757-007-3). Am Sch Orient Res.
Freedman, D. N. & Campbell, E. F., Jr., eds. The Biblical Archaeologist Reader, No. 4. (Illus.). xiii, 390p. 1983. text ed. 24.95x (ISBN 0-907459-34-X, Pub. by Almond Pr England); pap. text ed. 9.95x (ISBN 0-907459-35-8). Eisenbrauns.
Freedman, D. X., ed. see Association for Research in Nervous & Mental Disease.
Freedman, D. Z., jt. ed. see Van Nieuwenhuizen, P.
Freedman, Daniel G. Human Sociobiology: A Holistic Approach. LC 78-73025. (Illus.). 1979. 16.95 (ISBN 0-02-910660-5). Free Pr.
Freedman, Daniel P. & Weinberg, Gerald M. Handbook of Walkthroughs, Inspections, & Technical Reviews. 3rd ed. 448p. 1982. text ed. 38.00 (ISBN 0-316-29282-6). Little.
Freedman, Daniel P., jt. auth. see Weinbert, Gerald M.
Freedman, Daniel X., jt. auth. see Redlich, Frederick C.
Freedman, Daniel X., ed. Year Book of Psychiatry & Applied Mental Health 1981. 1981. 42.95 (ISBN 0-8151-3328-6). Year Bk Med.
--The Year Book of Psychiatry & Applied Mental Health, 1983. 1983. 42.95 (ISBN 0-8151-6025-9). Year Bk Med.
Freedman, Daniel X. & Dyrud, Jarl E., eds. American Handbook of Psychiatry, Vol. 5: Treatment. 2nd ed. LC 72-89185. 1975. text ed. 42.50x (ISBN 0-465-00151-3). Basic.
Freedman, Daniel X., et al, eds. Year Book of Psychiatry & Applied Mental Health, 1982. 1982. 42.95 (ISBN 0-8151-3329-4). Year Bk Med.
Freedman, David & Love, David. Mathematical Methods in Statistics: A Workbook. 1981. 6.95x (ISBN 0-393-95223-1). Norton.
Freedman, David, jt. auth. see Running, Leona.
Freedman, David, ed. see Morton, A. Q., et al.
Freedman, David, ed. see Parunak, Van Dyke H.
Freedman, David, ed. see Radday, Yehuda & Levi, Yaakov.
Freedman, David, et al. Statistics. (Illus.). 608p. 1978. text ed. 26.95x (ISBN 0-393-09076-0); instr's. manual 2.95 (ISBN 0-393-09041-8). Norton.
Freedman, David A. Approximating Countable Markov Chains. LC 76-142943. 140p. 1972. 38.00x (ISBN 0-8162-3034-X). Holden-Day.
Freedman, David H., ed. see International Labour Office, Geneva.
Freedman, David M., jt. auth. see Fleisher, David.
Freedman, David M., ed. Employment: Outlook & Insights. vi, 146p. 1979. pap. 11.50 (ISBN 92-2-102155-6, ILO137, ILO). Unipub.
Freedman, David N., jt. auth. see Cross, Frank M., Jr.
Freedman, David N., ed. Archaeological Reports from the Tabqa Dam Project--Euphrates Valley, Syria. LC 78-12251. (Annual of the American Schools of Oriental Research: Vol. 44). 182p. 1979. text ed. 20.00x (ISBN 0-89757-044-8, Am Sch Orient Res). Eisenbrauns.
--Preliminary Excavation Reports: Bab edh-Dhra, Sardis, Meiron, Tell el-Hesi, Carthage. LC 77-13341. (Annual of the American Schools of Oriental Research: Vol. 43). 190p. 1978. 17.50x (ISBN 0-89757-043-X, Am Sch Orient Res). Eisenbrauns.
Freedman, David N. & Graf, David F., eds. Palestine in Transition: The Emergence of Ancient Israel. (Social World of Biblical Antiquity Ser.: No. 2). ix, 108p. 1983. text ed. 22.95x (ISBN 0-907459-32-3, Pub. by Almond Pr England); pap. text ed. 10.95x (ISBN 0-907459-33-1). Eisenbrauns.
Freedman, David N., intro. by see Charlesworth, James H.
Freedman, David N., jt. ed. see Cornfeld, Gaalyah.
Freedman, David N., ed. see Morton, A. Q. & Michaelson, S.
Freedman, David Noel, ed. see Morton, A. Q. & Michaelson, Sidney.
Freedman, David Noel, ed. see Tyson, Joseph B. & Longstaff, Thomas R. W.
Freedman, Deborah A., jt. auth. see Freedman, George.
Freedman, Estelle B. Their Sister's Keepers: Women's Prison Reform in America, 1830-1930. LC 80-24918. (Women & Culture Ser.). 272p. 1981. text ed. 18.50x (ISBN 0-472-10008-4). U of Mich Pr.
Freedman, Estelle B., et al, eds. The Lesbian Issue: Essays from Signs. LC 84-16246. 300p. 1985. lib. bdg. 20.00x (ISBN 0-226-26151-4); pap. 10.95 (ISBN 0-226-26152-2). U of Chicago Pr.
Freedman, Florence B. Brothers. LC 85-42616. (Illus.). 40p. (gr. k-3). 1985. 9.57i (ISBN 0-06-021871-1); PLB 9.89g (ISBN 0-06-021872-X). HarpJ.
--William Douglas O'Connor: Walt Whitman's Chosen Knight. LC 84-25451. (Illus.). xiv, 368p. 1985. text ed. 35.00x (ISBN 0-8214-0767-8). Ohio U Pr.
Freedman, Gabriel & Haller, M. A. Verbal Workbook for the S.A.T. College Entrance Examinations. LC 81-22751. 288p. 1981. pap. 6.00 (ISBN 0-668-04853-0, 4853). Arco.
Freedman, George & Freedman, Deborah A. The Technical Editor's & Secretary's Desk Guide. 1985. 29.95 (ISBN 0-07-021918-4). McGraw.
Freedman, H. I. & Strobeck, C., eds. Population Biology. (Lecture Notes in Biomathematics Ser.: Vol. 52). 440p. pap. 26.00 (ISBN 0-387-12677-5). Springer-Verlag.
Freedman, Helen R. Big Apple Baby. (Illus.). 240p. (Orig.). 1985. pap. 8.95 (ISBN 0-933649-00-2). Laurel Howard.
Freedman, Helen R. & Krieger, Karen. The Writer's Guide to Magazine Markets: Nonfiction. 384p. 1983. pap. 8.95 (ISBN 0-452-25452-3, Plume). NAL.
Freedman, Hy. Sex Link: The Three-Billion-Year-Old Urge & What the Animals Do About It. LC 77-8546. (Illus.). 224p. 1977. 8.95 (ISBN 0-87131-242-5). M Evans.
Freedman, Jacob. Polychrome Historical Prayerbook: Siddur 'Bet Yosef' (Illus.). 400p. 1984. 125.00x (ISBN 0-686-12113-9). J Freedman Liturgy.
Freedman, James O. Crisis & Legitimacy. LC 78-51683. 1978. 37.50 (ISBN 0-521-22063-7); pap. 13.95 (ISBN 0-521-29380-4). Cambridge U Pr.
Freedman, Janet L. & Bantly, Harold A., eds. Information Searching: A Handbook for Designing & Creating Instructional Programs. Rev. ed. LC 81-21417. 208p. 1982. 16.00 (ISBN 0-8108-1509-5). Scarecrow.
Freedman, Johnathan, jt. auth. see Goleman, Daniel.
Freedman, Jonathan. Crowding & Behavior. LC 75-20217. (Psychology Ser.). 1975. pap. text ed. 9.95 (ISBN 0-7167-0750-0). W H Freeman.
Freedman, Jonathan, et al. Readings in Social Psychology. (Personality, Clinical & Social Psychology Ser). 1971. pap. text ed. 18.95 (ISBN 0-13-761072-6). P-H.
Freedman, Jonathan L. Introductory Psychology. 2nd ed. 672p. 1982. text ed. 26.95 (ISBN 0-394-34775-7, RanC); 7.95 (ISBN 0-394-34777-3). Random.
Freedman, Jonathan L., jt. auth. see Sears, David O.
Freedman, Jonathan N. & Doob, Anthony. Deviancy: The Psychology of Being Different. LC 68-14666. (Social Psychology Ser). 1968. 32.00 (ISBN 0-12-266550-3). Acad Pr.
Freedman, Kenneth. Management of the Geriatric Dental Patient. (Illus.). 148p. 1980. 48.00 (ISBN 0-931386-05-5). Quint Pub Co.
Freedman, Lawrence. Britain & Nuclear Weapons. 1981. text ed. 28.00x (ISBN 0-333-30494-2). Humanities.
--The Evolution of Nuclear Strategy. 1981. 35.00x (ISBN 0-312-27269-3). St Martin.
--The Evolution of Nuclear Strategy. 473p. 1983. pap. 10.95 (ISBN 0-312-27270-7). St Martin.

--Strategic Lessons of the Falklands. 1984p. 28.00 (ISBN 0-317-02799-9). Abt Bks.
Freedman, Lawrence, ed. The Troubled Alliance: Atlantic Relations in the 1980s. LC 83-40188. 224p. 1984. 25.00 (ISBN 0-312-81990-0). St Martin.
Freedman, Lawrence R. Infective Endocarditis & Other Intravascular Infections. (Current Topics in Infectious Diseases Ser.). (Illus.). 260p. 1982. 35.00x (ISBN 0-306-40937-2, Plenum Med Bk). Plenum Pub.
Freedman, Lawrence Z., ed. By Reason of Insanity: Essays on Psychiatry & the Law. LC 83-3314. 253p. 1983. lib. bdg. 30.00 (ISBN 0-8420-2203-1). Scholarly Res Inc.
Freedman, Lawrence Z. & Alexander, Yonah, eds. Perspectives on Terrorism. LC 83-3011. 258p. 1983. lib. bdg. 30.00 (ISBN 0-8420-2201-5). Scholarly Res Inc.
Freedman, Leon D., jt. auth. see Doak, George D.
Freedman, Leonard. Power & Politics in America. 4th ed. LC 82-12867. 500p. 1982. pap. text ed. 16.00 pub net (ISBN 0-534-01252-3). Brooks-Cole.
Freedman, M. David & Evans, Lansing B. Designing Systems with Microcomputers: A Systematic Approach. (Illus.). 320p. 1983. text ed. 36.95 (ISBN 0-13-201350-9). P-H.
Freedman, M. H. Surgery on Codimension 2 Submanifolds. LC 77-23944. (Memoirs Ser.: No. 191). 93p. 1977. pap. 13.00 (ISBN 0-8218-2191-1, MEMO 191). Am Math.
Freedman, Marcia. The Process of Work Establishment. LC 71-76248. (Illus.). 135p. 1969. 18.00x (ISBN 0-231-03225-0). Columbia U Pr.
Freedman, Marcia & Maclachlan, Gretchen. Labor Markets: Segments & Shelters. LC 76-470. (Conservation of Human Resources Ser: No. 1). 220p. 1976. 8.95x (ISBN 0-916672-00-X). Allanheld.
Freedman, Marlene. Molokai: The Friendly Isle. LC 80-109617. (Illus.). 32p. 1977. pap. text ed. 3.50 (ISBN 0-930081-00-5); write for info. braille (ISBN 0-930081-01-3). Molokai Bk Pubs.
Freedman, Matt, jt. auth. see Hoffman, Paul.
Freedman, Maurice. Chinese Family & Marriage in Singapore. (Colonial Research Studies). pap. 28.00 (ISBN 0-384-16760-8). Johnson Repr.
--Chinese Lineage & Society: Fukien & Kwantung. (London School of Economics Monographs on Social Anthropology: No. 33). 206p. 1971. pap. 18.95 (ISBN 0-485-19633-6, Pub. by Athlone Pr Ltd). Longwood Pub Group.
--Lineage Organization in South Eastern China. (London School of Economics Monographs on Social Anthropology: No. 18). 153p. 1965. pap. 16.95 (ISBN 0-485-19618-2, Pub. by Athlone Pr Ltd). Longwood Pub Group.
--Main Trends in Social & Cultural Anthropology. LC 79-12927. (Main Trends in the Social & Human Sciences Ser.). 176p. 1979. pap. text ed. 12.50x (ISBN 0-8419-0504-5). Holmes & Meier.
--The Study of Chinese Society: Essays by Maurice Freedman. Skinner, G. William, ed. LC 78-65395. 1979. 35.00x (ISBN 0-8047-0964-5). Stanford U Pr.
Freedman, Maurice, ed. Family & Kinship in Chinese Society. (Studies in Chinese Society). 274p. 1970. 22.50x (ISBN 0-8047-0713-8). Stanford U Pr.
--Social Organization: Essays Presented to Raymond Firth. 300p. 1967. 32.50x (ISBN 0-7146-1059-3, F Cass Co). Biblio Dist.
Freedman, Maurice, tr. see Granet, Marcel.
Freedman, Maurice J., ed. see Information Science & Automation Institutes on the Catalog.
Freedman, Melvin H. & Silver, Samuel M. How to Enjoy This Moment. rev. ed. Ettinger, Andrew & Bafaro, Johanna, eds. 192p. pap. 8.95 (ISBN 0-911665-00-5, EN982). Entre Prods.
Freedman, Melvin H., jt. ed. see Bafaro, Johanna.
Freedman, Mervin. Academic Culture & Faculty Development. LC 79-84482. 1979. pap. 11.95 (ISBN 0-917430-02-6). Montaigne.
Freedman, Mervin B., ed. Facilitating Faculty Development. LC 73-2589. (New Directions for Higher Education: Vol. 1, No. 1). pap. 33.00 (ISBN 0-317-26060-X, 2023778). Bks Demand UMI.
Freedman, Michael. The Diamond Book: A Practical Guide for Successful Investing. LC 80-70145. 160p. 1981. 16.95 (ISBN 0-87094-223-9). Dow Jones-Irwin.
Freedman, Miriam & Perl, Teri. A Sourcebook for Substitutes...& Other Teachers. (gr. k-8). 1974. 12.50 (ISBN 0-201-05786-7). Addison-Wesley.
Freedman, Morris. Moral Impulse: Modern Drama from Ibsen to the Present. LC 67-10025. (Crosscurrents-Modern Critiques Ser.). 148p. 1967. 6.95 (ISBN 0-8093-0235-7). S Ill U Pr.
Freedman, Nancy. Prima Donna. (General Ser.). 1981. lib. bdg. 16.95 (ISBN 0-8161-3266-6, Large Print Bks). G K Hall.
Freedman, Nancy, jt. auth. see Freedman, Benedict.
Freedman, Norbert & Grand, Stanley, eds. Communicative Structures & Psychic Structures. LC 77-9574. (The Downstate Research in Psychiatry & Psychology Ser: Vol. 1). 492p. 1977. 49.50x (ISBN 0-306-34361-4, Plenum Pr). Plenum Pub.
Freedman, P. E., jt. auth. see Freedman, Ann E.
Freedman, Paul H. The Diocese of Vic: Tradition & Regeneration in Medieval Catalonia. 232p. 1983. 25.00 (ISBN 0-8135-0970-X). Rutgers U Pr.
Freedman, Paul I. Oh Brother, Oh Friend. (Illus.). 128p. 1982. 7.95 (ISBN 0-89962-220-8). Todd & Honeywell.
Freedman, Philip, et al. Nephrology. 2nd ed. (Medical Examination Review Book: Vol. 34). 1981. 28.50 (ISBN 0-87488-176-5). Med Exam.
Freedman, Philip M. Etude in Black. LC 83-90811. 39p. 1984. 6.95 (ISBN 0-533-05820-1). Vantage.
Freedman, Ralph. Herman Hesse: Pilgrim of Crisis. LC 78-51795. (Illus.). 1979. 15.00 (ISBN 0-394-41981-2). Pantheon.
--Lyrical Novel: Studies in Hermann Hesse, Andre Gide, & Virginia Woolf. 1963. pap. 10.95 (ISBN 0-691-01267-9, 62). Princeton U Pr.
Freedman, Ralph, ed. & intro. by. Virginia Woolf: Revaluation & Continuity, a Collection of Essays. 1980. pap. 4.95 (ISBN 0-520-03980-7). U of Cal Pr.
Freedman, Richard A. Travels & Life in Ashanti & Jaman. 559p. 1967. Repr. of 1898 ed. 42.50x (ISBN 0-7146-1808-X, BHA-01808, F Cass Co). Biblio Dist.
Freedman, Richard D. Management Education: Issues in Theory, Research & Practice. Cooper, Cary L., ed. Stumpf, Stephen A., tr. LC 81-14666. 278p. 1982. text ed. 41.95x (ISBN 0-471-10078-1). Wiley.
Freedman, Rita. Beauty Bound. (Illus.). 1985. 14.95 (ISBN 0-669-11141-4). Lexington Bks.
Freedman, Rita J., jt. ed. see Golub, Sharon.
Freedman, Robert. The Mind of Karl Marx: Economic, Political, & Social Perspectives. (Chatham House Studies in Political Thinking). (Illus.). 192p. 1985. pap. text ed. 8.95x (ISBN 0-934540-31-4). Chatham Hse Pubs.
Freedman, Robert & Hawkins, H. G., eds. The Enzymology of Post-Translational Modification of Proteins, Vol. I. (Molecular Biology Ser.). 1981. 96.00 (ISBN 0-12-266501-5). Acad Pr.
Freedman, Robert L., compiled by. Human Food Uses: A Cross-Cultural, Comprehensive Annotated Bibliography. LC 81-469. xxxvii, 552p. 1981. lib. bdg. 75.00 (ISBN 0-313-22901-5, FHU/). Greenwood.
--Human Food Uses: A Cross-Cultural Comprehensive Annotated Bibliography Supplement. LC 82-25163. xxxii, 387p. 1983. lib. bdg. 65.00 (ISBN 0-313-23434-5, FUS/). Greenwood.
Freedman, Robert O. Israel in the Begin Era. 288p. 1982. 35.95 (ISBN 0-03-059376-X). Praeger.
Freedman, Robert O., ed. Soviet Jewry in the Decisive Decade, 1971-1980. LC 83-20592. (Duke Press Policy Studies). 192p. 1984. text ed. 34.75 (ISBN 0-8223-0544-5). Duke.
--World Politics & the Arab-Israeli Conflict. (Pergamon Policy Studies). 1979. 46.00 (ISBN 0-08-023380-5). Pergamon.
Freedman, Ronald. The Sociology of Human Fertility: An Annotated Bibliography. LC 73-12272. 283p. 1975. 16.50 (ISBN 0-470-27732-7, Pub. by Wiley). Krieger.
Freedman, Ronald & Coombs, Lolagene C. Cross-Cultural Comparisons: Data on Two Factors in Fertility Behavior. LC 74-80928. 94p. (Orig.). 1974. pap. text ed. 3.95 (ISBN 0-87834-022-X). Population Coun.
Freedman, Roy S. Programming Concepts with the Ada Reference Manual. (Illus.). 128p. 1982. pap. text ed. 12.00 (ISBN 0-89433-190-6). Petrocelli.
--Programming with APSE Software Tools. (Illus.). 276p. 1985. text ed. 27.50 (ISBN 0-89433-220-1). Petrocelli.
Freedman, Russell. Animal Games. LC 76-10975. (Illus.). 32p. (gr. 1-4). 1976. 5.95 (ISBN 0-8234-0284-3). Holiday.
--Animal Superstars: Biggest, Strongest, Fastest, Smartest. (Illus.). 112p. (gr. 5 up). 1984. pap. 5.95 (ISBN 0-13-037615-9). P-H.
--Can Bears Predict Earthquakes? Unsolved Mysteries of Animal Behavior. (Illus.). 96p. (gr. 5 up). 1982. 10.95 (ISBN 0-13-114009-4). P-H.
--Children of the Wild West. LC 83-5133. (Illus.). 128p. (gr. 3-6). 1983. PLB 12.95 (ISBN 0-89919-143-6, Clarion). HM.
--Cowboys of the Wild West. LC 85-4200. (Illus.). 128p. (gr. 3-7). 1985. 14.95 (ISBN 0-89919-301-3, Clarion). HM.
--Dinosaurs & Their Young. LC 83-6160. (Illus.). 32p. (gr. 1-4). 1983. reinforced bdg. 9.95 (ISBN 0-8234-0496-X). Holiday.
--Farm Babies. LC 81-2898. (Illus.). 40p. (gr. k-3). 1981. reinforced bdg. 9.95 (ISBN 0-8234-0426-9). Holiday.
--The First Days of Life. LC 74-7573. (Illus.). 64p. (gr. 3-6). 1974. 5.50 (ISBN 0-8234-0249-5). Holiday.
--Getting Born. LC 78-6673. (Illus.). 40p. (gr. 1-4). 1978. reinforced bdg. 9.95 (ISBN 0-8234-0336-X). Holiday.
--Hanging on: How Animals Carry Their Young. LC 76-41822. (Illus.). 40p. (gr. 1-4). 1977. reinforced bdg. 5.95 (ISBN 0-8234-0292-4). Holiday.
--Holiday House: The First Fifty Years. LC 84-48744. (Illus.). 160p. 1985. 25.00 (ISBN 0-8234-0562-1). Holiday.
--How Birds Fly. LC 77-555. (Illus.). 64p. (gr. 4-6). 1977. 8.95 (ISBN 0-8234-0301-7). Holiday.
--Immigrant Kids. LC 79-20060. 64p. (gr. 3-7). 1980. 11.95 (ISBN 0-525-32538-7, 01160-350). Dutton.
--Killer Fish. LC 81-85089. (Illus.). 40p. (gr. 1-4). 1982. reinforced bdg. 9.95 (ISBN 0-8234-0449-8). Holiday.
--Killer Snakes. LC 82-80821. (Illus.). 40p. (gr. 1-4). 1982. Reinforced bdg. 9.95 (ISBN 0-8234-0460-9). Holiday.
--Rattlesnakes. LC 84-4602. (Illus.). 40p. (gr. 1-3). 1984. reinforced 10.95 (ISBN 0-8234-0536-2). Holiday.
--Rattlesnakes. (Illus.). (gr. 1-4). 10.95 (ISBN 0-317-13385-3). HR&W.
--Scouting with Baden-Powell. (Illus.). 224p. (gr. 6 up). 1967. 4.95 (ISBN 0-8234-0101-4). Holiday.
--Sharks. LC 85-42881. (Illus.). 40p. (gr. 1-4). 1985. reinforced 11.95 (ISBN 0-8234-0582-6). Holiday.
--They Lived with the Dinosaurs. LC 80-15851. (Illus.). 40p. (gr. 1-4). 1980. reinforced bdg. 9.95 (ISBN 0-8234-0424-2). Holiday.
--Two Thousand Years of Space Travel. (Illus.). 256p. (YA) (gr. 7 up). 1963. 4.95 (ISBN 0-8234-0123-5). Holiday.
--When Winter Comes. LC 80-22831. (Illus.). (gr. 1-3). 1981. 8.25 (ISBN 0-525-42583-7, 0801-240, Smart Cat). Dutton.
Freedman, Russell & Morriss, James E. The Brains of Animals & Man. LC 71-151754. (Illus.). 160p. (gr. 4-6). 1972. 8.95 (ISBN 0-8234-0205-3). Holiday.
Freedman, Ruth, jt. auth. see Doucette, John.
Freedman, Sally. Monster Birthday Party. Tucker, Kathleen, ed. LC 83-17088. (Just for Fun Bks.). (Illus.). 32p. (gr. k-3). 1983. PLB 10.75 (ISBN 0-8075-5259-3). A Whitman.
Freedman, Samuel S. & Naughton, Pamela J. ERA: May a State Change Its Vote? LC 78-10821. 256p. 1978. 14.00x (ISBN 0-8143-1623-9); pap. 6.95x (ISBN 0-8143-1624-7). Wayne St U Pr.
Freedman, Sanford & Taylor, Carole A. Roland Barthes: A Bibliographical Reader's Guide. LC 81-43338. (Modern Critics & Critical Schools Ser.). 445p. 1982. lib. bdg. 55.00 (ISBN 0-8240-9292-9). Garland Pub.
Freedman, Sarah W. The Acquisition of Written Language: Response & Revision. Farr, Marcia, ed. (Writing Research Ser.). 308p. 1985. text ed. 39.50 (ISBN 0-89391-227-1); pap. 24.95 (ISBN 0-89391-324-3). Ablex Pub.
Freedman, Stephany J., jt. ed. see Close, Arthur C.
Freedman, Stephany J., jt. ed. see Colgate, Craig, Jr.
Freedman, Stephen, jt. ed. see Lucas, Barbara A.
Freedman, T. Birch. Journal of Various Visits to the Kingdoms of Ashanti, Aku & Dahomi in Western Africa. 3rd ed. (Illus.). 298p. 1968. Repr. of 1844 ed. 42.50x (ISBN 0-7146-1869-1, F Cass Co). Biblio Dist.
Freedman, Warren. Product Liability for Corporate Counsels, Controllers & Product Safety Executives. 1984. 39.95 (ISBN 0-442-22493-1). Van Nos Reinhold.
--Societal Behavior: New & Unique Rights of the Person. 356p. 1965. 27.50x (ISBN 0-398-00609-1). C C Thomas.
--World Guide for the Jewish Traveler. 360p. 1984. pap. 8.95 (ISBN 0-525-48095-1, 0869-260). Dutton.
Freedman, Warren & Sklaren, Cary S. Contemporary Social Problems: Selcted Readings in Sociology & the Law. 352p. 1972. 28.50x (ISBN 0-398-02285-2). C C Thomas.
Freedman, William. Laurence Sterne & the Origins of the Musical Novel. LC 77-7082. 224p. 1978. 19.50x (ISBN 0-8203-0429-8). U of Ga Pr.
Freedman, William, ed. see Dallas, Eneas S.
Freedman, William, et al, eds. see Carnegie, James.
Freedomways Associates. Paul Robeson: The Great Forerunner. (Illus.). 400p. 1985. pap. 10.95 (ISBN 0-7178-0625-1). Intl Pubs Co.
Freedy, Amos see Hopple, Gerald W. & Andriole, Stephen J.
Freedy, Amos, et al. The Application of a Theoretical Learning Model to a Remote Handling Control System. LC 73-141073. 104p. 1970. 19.00 (ISBN 0-403-04501-0). Mgmt Info Serv.
Freegel, John R. Not a Stranger. 272p. 1983. 14.95 (ISBN 0-453-00435-0). NAL.
FreeHand, Julianna. Elizabeth's Dream: A Photographic Tapestry of Woman...Her Relationships Her Life. LC 83-61953. (Illus.). 104p. 1984. 75.00 (ISBN 0-9605700-2-0); deluxe ltd. ed., 106p. 500.00 (ISBN 0-9605700-3-9). Menses.
--Treason in the American Revolution. LC 80-149497. (Westchester Treasure Hunt Tour: Guide 1). (Illus., Orig.). (gr. 7-12). 1980. pap. 8.95 (ISBN 0-9605700-0-4). Menses.
Freehill, Maurice F. Gifted Children, Their Psychology & Education. (Perspective Through a Retrospective Ser.: Vol. 4). 412p. 15.50 (ISBN 0-318-02149-8). NSLTIGT.
--Gifted Children, Their Psychology & Education: A Perspective Through a Retrospective, Vol. 4. 412p. 15.50 (ISBN 0-318-16004-8, 31). NSLTIGT.
Freehling, Alison G. Drift Toward Dissolution: The Virginia Slavery Debate of 1831-1832. LC 82-6517. 306p. 1982. text ed. 32.50x (ISBN 0-8071-1035-3). La State U Pr.
Freehling, William. Prelude to Civil War: The Nullification Controversy in South Carolina, 1816-1836. (Illus.). 1968. pap. 7.95xi (ISBN 0-06-131359-9, TB1359, Torch). Har-Row.
Freehling, William H., ed. see Rose, Willie L.
Freehling, William W., ed. see Rose, Willie L.
Freehof, S. Reform Jewish Practice. 8.95x (ISBN 0-685-55600-X). Ktav.
Freehof, S. B. Reform Responsa for Our Time. 15.00x (ISBN 0-87820-111-4, HUC Pr). Ktav.
Freehof, Soloman B. Book of Isaiah: A Commentary. Syme, Daniel B., ed. LC 72-2156. (Jewish Commentary for Bible Readers Ser.). 1972. 15.00 (ISBN 0-8074-0042-4, 383015). UAHC.
Freehof, Solomon. Contemporary Reform Response. 15.00x (ISBN 0-87820-108-4, Pub. by Hebrew Union College Press). Ktav.
--Ezekiel: A Commentary. 1979. 15.00 (ISBN 0-8074-0033-5, 380010). UAHC.
--Isaiah: A Commentary. 1972. 15.00 (ISBN 0-8074-0042-4, 383015). UAHC.
Freehof, Solomon B. The Book of Jeremiah: A Commentary. LC 77-8259. 1977. 15.00 (ISBN 0-8074-0008-4, 381610). UAHC.
--Current Reform Responsa. 1969. 15.00x (ISBN 0-87820-102-5, Pub. by Hebrew Union). Ktav.
--Modern Reform Response. 1971. 15.00x (ISBN 0-87820-101-7, Pub. by Hebrew Union). Ktav.
--Preaching the Bible. 1974. 15.00x (ISBN 0-87068-244-X). Ktav.
Free John, Da. The Knee of Listening. rev. ed. LC 78-53863. (Illus.). 1978. pap. 8.95 (ISBN 0-913922-43-9). Dawn Horse Pr.
--The Method of the Siddhas. rev. ed. LC 78-53869. (Illus.). 1978. pap. 8.95 (ISBN 0-913922-44-7). Dawn Horse Pr.
--The Paradox of Instruction: An Introduction to the Esoteric Spiritual Teaching of Da Free John. LC 77-81836. 9.95 (ISBN 0-913922-32-3). Dawn Horse Pr.
Freeland, Al. Uncle Al: The Life & Times of Inventor-Marksman Albin Freeland. (Illus.). 304p. 1982. 8.95 (ISBN 0-940286-51-3). Quest Pub IL.
Freeland, Howard J., et al, eds. Fjord Oceanography. LC 80-12273. (NATO Conference Series IV, Marine Science: Vol. 4). 730p. 1980. 95.00x (ISBN 0-306-40439-7, Plenum Pr). Plenum Pub.
Freeland, James F., jt. auth. see Ferguson, M. Carr.
Freeland, James J., et al. Cases & Materials on Fundamentals of Federal Income Taxation. LC 85-12943. (University Casebook Ser.). Date not set. price not set (ISBN 0-88277-251-1). Foundation Pr.
--Fundamentals of Federal Income Taxation, Cases & Materials. 5th ed. (University Casebook Ser.). 1070p. 1985. text ed. write for info (ISBN 0-88277-251-1). Foundation Pr.
--Fundamentals of Federal Income Taxation, Cases & Materials on. 4th ed. LC 82-7271. (University Casebook Ser.). 1026p. 1982. text ed. 26.50 (ISBN 0-88277-063-2). Foundation Pr.
--Fundamentals of Federal Income Taxation Cases & Material On. 5th ed. (University Casebook Ser.). 419p. 1985. pap. write for info. (ISBN 0-88277-307-0). Foundation Pr.
--Fundamentals of Federal Income Taxation: 1983 Teacher's Manual to Accompany Cases & Materials. Rev., 4th ed. (University Casebook Ser.). 362p. 1983. pap. text ed. write for info. (ISBN 0-88277-141-8). Foundation Pr.
Freeland, James R., jt. auth. see Landel, Robert D.
Freeland, Jeanne H., jt. auth. see Peckham, Gladys C.
Freeland, Kenneth H. High School Work Study Program for the Retarded: Practical Information for Teacher Preparation & Program Organization & Operation. (Illus.). 120p. 1974. 11.50x (ISBN 0-398-00611-3). C C Thomas.
Freeland, Richard M. The Truman Doctrine & the Origins of McCarthyism: Foreign Policy, Domestic Policy, & Internal Security, 1946-48. 448p. 1985. 30.00x (ISBN 0-8147-2575-9); pap. 14.50x (ISBN 0-8147-2576-7). NYU Pr.
Freeland, William. Love & Treason, 3 vols. in 2. LC 79-8264. Repr. of 1872 ed. Set. 84.50 (ISBN 0-404-61849-9). AMS Pr.
Freelander, Iris see Carr, Clare.
Freeley, Austin J. Argumentation & Debate: Reasoned Decision Making, 6th ed. 400p. 1985. text ed. write for info (ISBN 0-534-05526-5). Wadsworth Pub.
Freeling, Nicholas. The Bugles Blowing. LC 79-23078. (An Henri Castang Suspense Novel Ser.). 1980. pap. 1.95 (ISBN 0-394-74551-5, Vin). Random.
--No Part in Your Death. (Henri Castang Mystery Ser.). 240p. 1984. 13.95 (ISBN 0-670-51441-1). Viking.
--Sabine. LC 79-23077. (An Henri Castang Suspense Novel Ser.). 1980. pap. 1.95 (ISBN 0-394-74553-1, Vin). Random.
Freeling, Nicolas. Arlette. 1981. pap. 2.95 (ISBN 0-394-75260-0). Pantheon.
--Aupres de Ma Blonde. 1979. pap. 2.95 (ISBN 0-394-74550-7, Vin). Random.
--The Back of the North Wind. LC 83-47994. 192p. 1983. 13.95 (ISBN 0-670-14398-7). Viking.
--The Back of the North Wind. (Crime Monthly Ser.). 224p. 1984. pap. 3.50 (ISBN 0-14-006953-4). Penguin.

--Because of the Cats. (Crime Ser.). 192p. 1975. pap. 3.50 (ISBN 0-14-002282-1). Penguin.

--Castang's City. LC 81-40075. (Henri Castang Novels of Suspense). 304p. 1981. pap. 2.95 (ISBN 0-394-74747-X, Vin). Random.

--A City Solitary. (Mystery Ser.). 224p. 1985. 14.95 (ISBN 0-670-80607-2). Viking.

--Criminal Conversation. LC 80-6127. (Inspector Van der Valk Suspense Novel Ser.). 213p. 1981. pap. 2.50 (ISBN 0-394-74692-9, V-692, Vin). Random.

--Double Barrel. LC 80-6128. (Inspector Van der Valk Suspense Novel Ser.). 224p. 1981. pap. 2.50 (ISBN 0-394-74693-7, V-693, Vin). Random.

--Gadget. (Penguin Crime Ser.). 1979. pap. 2.95 (ISBN 0-14-004898-7). Penguin.

--The King of the Rainy Country. (Crime Ser.). 160p. 1985. pap. 3.50 (ISBN 0-14-002853-6). Penguin.

--Love in Amsterdam. (Crime Ser.). 192p. 1985. pap. 3.50 (ISBN 0-14-002281-3). Penguin.

--The Lovely Ladies. LC 80-6129. (Inspector Van der Valk Suspense Novel). 1981. pap. 3.95 (ISBN 0-394-74694-5, V-694, Vin). Random.

--Strike Out Where Not Applicable. (Crime Ser.). 176p. 1985. pap. 3.50 (ISBN 0-14-003009-3). Penguin.

--The Widow. LC 80-10634. 256p. 1980. pap. 3.95 (ISBN 0-394-74467-5, Vin). Random.

--Wolfnight. LC 82-40427. (Henri Castang Ser.). 288p. 1983. pap. 2.95 (ISBN 0-394-71381-8, Vin). Random.

Freeling, Paul & Barry, Susan. In-Service Training: A Study of the Nuffield Course of the Royal College of Practitioners. 224p. 1982. 18.00x (ISBN 0-317-17964-0, Pub. by NFER Nelson UK). Taylor & Francis.

Freelove, William F. Victorian Horses & Carriages: Personal Sketch Book. 1980. 1.49 (ISBN 0-517-53984-5, C N Potter Bks). Crown.

Freely, J., jt. auth. see Sumner-Boyd, H.

Freely, John. Boston & Cambridge. (Blue Guide Ser.). (Illus.). 1984. 29.95 (ISBN 0-393-01560-2); pap. 15.95 (ISBN 0-393-30012-9). Norton.

--Istanbul. (Blue Guides Ser.). (Illus.). 400p. 1983. 25.95 (ISBN 0-393-01558-0); cloth 14.95. Norton.

Freely, John, jt. auth. see Sumner-Boyd, Hilary.

Freely, Maureen. The Life of the Party. 416p. 1985. 17.95 (ISBN 0-671-50614-5). S&S.

Freeman. Handbook of Bible Manners & Customs. Date not set. Repr. of 1870 ed. price not set cancelled. Guildhall Pubs.

--Writing Resumes, Locating Jobs, Handling Job Interviews. (Plain Ser.). 1976. pap. 7.95 (ISBN 0-256-01871-5). Dow Jones-Irwin.

Freeman & Bracegirdle. Atlas de Histologia. 140p. (Span.). 1975. write for info. (S-37584). French & Eur.

Freeman & Krieger. Writer's Guide to Magazine Markets: Fiction. 1983. pap. 8.95 (ISBN 0-452-25451-5, Plume). NAL.

Freeman see Wood, S.

Freeman, ed. & intro. by see Ovid.

Freeman, A. Glosario de Computation. 396p. 1985. 19.95 (ISBN 0-07-021920-6). McGraw.

Freeman, A. J. & Lander, G. Handbook on the Physics & Chemistry of the Actinides, Pt. 1: Physics, Vol. 2. 504p. 1985. 111.00 (ISBN 0-444-86907-7, North-Holland). Elsevier.

Freeman, A. J. & Schmid, H. Magnetoelectric Interaction Phenomena in Crystals. 236p. 1975. 76.50 (ISBN 0-677-15985-4). Gordon.

Freeman, A. J., ed. Proceedings of the Arbeitsgemeinschaft Magnetismus Conference, 1974. 503p. 1975. 59.75 (ISBN 0-444-10900-5, North-Holland). Elsevier.

Freeman, A. J. & Darby, J. B., eds. The Actinides: Electronic Structure & Related Properties, 2 vols. Vol. 1. 1974. 75.00 (ISBN 0-12-266701-8); Vol. 2. 1974. 75.00 (ISBN 0-12-266702-6). Acad Pr.

Freeman, A. J. & Lander, G. H., eds. Handbook on the Physics & Chemistry of the Actinides, Vol. 1. 530p. 1984. 115.50 (ISBN 0-444-86903-4, North-Holland). Elsevier.

Freeman, A. M., III. Intermediate Microeconomic Analysis. 558p. 1983. text ed. 27.50 scp (ISBN 0-06-042185-1, HarpC); instr's manual avail. (ISBN 0-06-362223-8). Har-Row.

Freeman, A. Martin. Thomas Love Peacock: A Critical Study. LC 74-11329. 1911. lib. bdg. 17.50 (ISBN 0-8414-4226-6). Folcroft.

--Vanessa & Her Correspondence with Jonathan Swift. LC 74-9722. 1921. lib. bdg. 15.00 (ISBN 0-8414-4206-1). Folcroft.

Freeman, A. Myrick. Air & Water Pollution Control: A Benefit Cost Assessment. LC 82-8409. (Environmental Science & Technology Monographs). 186p. 1982. 39.95x (ISBN 0-471-08985-0, Pub. by Wiley-Interscience). Wiley.

--Benefits of Environmental Improvement. LC 78-20532. (Resources for the Future Ser.). 1979. text ed. 23.00x (ISBN 0-8018-2163-0); pap. text ed. 7.95x (ISBN 0-8018-2195-9). Johns Hopkins.

--The Benefits of Environmental Improvement: Theory & Practice. 288p. 1979. 23.00 (ISBN 0-8018-2163-0); pap. 7.95 (ISBN 0-8018-2195-9). Resources Future.

Freeman, A. Myrick, et al. The Economics of Environmental Policy. LC 72-7249. 184p. 1973. pap. text ed. 15.50x (ISBN 0-471-27786-X). Wiley.

Freeman, A. Myrick, III, et al. The Economics of Environmental Policy. LC 84-4663. 198p. 1984. Repr. of 1973 ed. lib. bdg. 13.25 (ISBN 0-89874-741-4). Krieger.

Freeman, A. Myrick, 3rd, jt. ed. see Enthoven, Alain C.

Freeman, A. V. International Responsibility of States for Denial of Justice. LC 39-17013. Repr. of 1938 ed. 36.00 (ISBN 0-527-31400-5). Kraus Repr.

Freeman, Aaron E. Astro Blue: A Member of Our Family. LC 83-73197. (Illus.). 144p. (gr. 6 up). 1984. lib. bdg. 9.95x (ISBN 0-915509-00-8); pap. 6.95x (ISBN 0-915509-01-6). Argos Pub Co.

Freeman, Abby J., jt. auth. see Fitzsimmons, Stephen J.

Freeman, Allen G. Railways: Past, Present, & Future. LC 82-60816. (Illus.). 304p. 1982. 40.00 (ISBN 0-688-00636-1). Morrow.

Freeman, Arnold. Boy Life & Labour: The Manufacture of Inefficiency. LC 79-56956. (The English Working Class Ser.). 267p. 1980. lib. bdg. 33.00 (ISBN 0-8240-0110-9). Garland Pub.

--The Riddle of Goethe's Faust. LC 76-46931. 1976. Repr. of 1954 ed. lib. bdg. 10.00 (ISBN 0-8414-4151-0). Folcroft.

Freeman, Arnold, tr. see Steiner, Rudolf.

Freeman, Arthur. Assays of Bias. LC 70-143384. 1971. 12.95 (ISBN 0-87923-017-7); pap. 5.95 (ISBN 0-87923-018-5). Godine.

--Elizabeth's Misfits. LC 74-2067. (Illus.). 1977. lib. bdg. 31.00 (ISBN 0-8240-1051-5). Garland Pub.

Freeman, Arthur, ed. Cognitive Therapy with Couples & Groups. 350p. 1983. 35.00x (ISBN 0-306-41149-0, Plenum Pr). Plenum Pub.

Freeman, Arthur, jt. ed. see Mahoney, Michael J.

Freeman, Arthur J. & Frankel, Richard B. Hyperfine Interactions. 1967. 76.50 (ISBN 0-12-266750-6). Acad Pr.

Freeman, Arthur M., et al, eds. Psychiatry for the Primary Care Physician. LC 78-18737. 432p. (Orig.). 1979. pap. 23.00 (ISBN 0-686-47376-0). Krieger.

Freeman, Austin R. Mr. Pottermack's Oversight. (Detective Stories Ser.). 352p. 1985. pap. 5.95 (ISBN 0-486-24780-5). Dover.

--The Penrose Mystery. 274p. 1977. Repr. lib. bdg. 13.95x (ISBN 0-89966-275-7). Buccaneer Bks.

Freeman, B. M. Physiology & Biochemistry of the Domestic Fowl, Vol. 5. 1984. 79.95 (ISBN 0-12-267105-8). Acad Pr.

Freeman, B. M., ed. Physiology & Biochemistry of the Domestic Fowl, Vol. 4. 1983. 59.50 (ISBN 0-12-267104-X). Acad Pr.

Freeman, Barbara. Mirror, Mirror, on the Wall. 1978. pap. 1.50 (ISBN 0-532-15367-7). Woodhill.

Freeman, Barbara, jt. auth. see Freeman, Bob.

Freeman, Bill. Gaining Christ in Daily Life. 12p. 1983. pap. 0.25 (ISBN 0-914271-02-4). NW Christian Pubns.

--God's Eternal Purpose. (Illus.). 14p. 1983. pap. 0.25 (ISBN 0-914271-01-6). NW Christian Pubns.

Freeman, Bill, jt. auth. see Dellinger, Bill.

Freeman, Bill, ed. see Bunyan, John, et al.

Freeman, Bob & Freeman, Barbara. Wanta Bet? A Study of the Pari-Mutuals Systems in the United States, How it Works-& the Sports Involved. (Illus.). 302p. (Orig.). 1982. 15.00 (ISBN 0-9608022-1-5); pap. 12.00 (ISBN 0-9608022-0-7). Freeman Mutuels.

Freeman, Bob A. Burrows Textbook of Microbiology. 21st ed. LC 77-16986. (Illus.). 1979. text ed. 39.50 (ISBN 0-7216-3869-4). Saunders.

--Burrows Textbook of Microbiology. 22nd ed. (Illus.). 1100p. Date not set. price not set (ISBN 0-7216-3868-6). Saunders.

Freeman, Bud. You Don't Look Like a Musician. LC 73-89352. 135p. 1974. 5.95 (ISBN 0-913642-05-3). Balamp Pub.

Freeman, C. & Holdsworth, D. Arts & Crafts of Papua & New Guinea. (Illus.). 8.00 (ISBN 0-912728-02-7). Newbury Bks.

Freeman, C. & Jahoda, M. Progress & Problems in Social Forecasting. 85p. 1976. 20.00x (ISBN 0-900296-40-2, Pub. by Social Sci Res). State Mutual Bk.

Freeman, C. E. & Lowe, W. D., eds. Greek Reader for Schools. 1917. pap. 6.95x (ISBN 0-19-831831-6). Oxford U Pr.

Freeman, C. E., jt. ed. see Lowe, W. D.

Freeman, Carroll B. The Senior Adult Years. LC 79-51137. 1979. 7.95 (ISBN 0-8054-5421-7). Broadman.

Freeman, Caryl, jt. auth. see Mascolini, Marcia.

Freeman, Cecilia, jt. auth. see Dieterich, Thomas G.

Freeman, Charles. Defence. (Today's World Ser.). (Illus.). 72p. (gr. 7-12). 1983. 14.95 (ISBN 0-7134-0969-X, Pub. by Batsford England). David & Charles.

--Living Through History: Britain in the 1930's. (Living Through History Ser.). (Illus.). 72p. (gr. 7-12). 1985. 14.95 (ISBN 0-7134-4354-5, Pub. by Batsford England). David & Charles.

--Terrorism in Today's World. LC 79-56474. (Illus.). 96p. 1980. 14.95 (ISBN 0-7134-1230-5, Pub. by Batsford England). David & Charles.

Freeman, Christopher. The Economics of Industrial Innovation. 2nd ed. 320p. 1983. 30.00x (ISBN 0-262-06083-3). MIT Pr.

Freeman, Christopher, ed. Long Waves in the World Economy. LC 84-42649. 246p. 1984. 25.75 (ISBN 0-86187-466-8, Pub. by Frances Pinter); pap. 12.50 (ISBN 0-86187-467-6). Longwood Pub Group.

Freeman, Christopher, et al. Unemployment & Technical Innovation: A Study of Long Waves & Economic Development. (Illus.). 252p. 1984. pap. 10.95 (ISBN 0-86187-342-4). F Pinter Pubs.

Freeman, Christopher, et al, eds. Unemployment & Technical Innovation: A Study of Long Waves & Economic Development. LC 82-1113. (Contributions in Economics & Economic History Ser.: No. 50). (Illus.). xiii, 214p. 1982. lib. bdg. 29.95 (ISBN 0-313-23601-1, FUN/). Greenwood.

Freeman, Christopher J. Encyclopedia of World Air Power. (Illus.). 1980. 19.95 (ISBN 0-517-53754-0, Pub. by Crescent). Outlet Bk Co.

Freeman, Cortlandt. Steve Rieschl's Ski Touring for the Fun of It. LC 73-13891. (A Sports Illustrated Book). (Illus.). 1974. pap. 6.95 (ISBN 0-316-74562-6). Little.

Freeman, Cynthia. Come Pour the Wine. LC 80-66501. 1980. 12.95 (ISBN 0-87795-276-0). Arbor Hse.

--Come Pour the Wine. 368p. 1985. pap. 3.95 (ISBN 0-553-20026-7). Bantam.

--Come Pour the Wine. (General Ser.). 1981. lib. bdg. 15.95 (ISBN 0-8161-3201-1, Large Print Bks). G K Hall.

--Cynthia Freeman: A World Full of Strangers, the Days of Winter, Portraits, & Come Pour the Wine. 1981. boxed set 50.00 (ISBN 0-87795-353-8). Arbor Hse.

--The Days of Winter. LC 77-79533. 1978. 9.95 (ISBN 0-87795-171-3). Arbor Hse.

--The Days of Winter. 1985. pap. 3.95 (ISBN 0-553-20523-4). Bantam.

--The Days of Winter. (General Ser.). 1983. lib. bdg. 18.95 (ISBN 0-8161-3527-4, Large Print Bks). G K Hall.

--Fairytales. LC 76-50340. 1977. 8.95 (ISBN 0-87795-163-2). Arbor Hse.

--Fairytales. (General Ser.). 562p. 1983. lib. bdg. 17.95 (ISBN 0-8161-3593-2, Large Print Bks). G K Hall.

--Illusions of Love. LC 84-8392. 276p. 1985. 16.95 (ISBN 0-399-13009-8, Putnam). Putnam Pub Group.

--No Time for Tears. LC 80-70542. 448p. 1981. 14.95 (ISBN 0-87795-317-1). Arbor Hse.

--No Time for Tears. 448p. 1982. pap. 3.95 (ISBN 0-553-22656-8). Bantam.

--Portraits. LC 78-73865. 1979. 11.95 (ISBN 0-87795-219-1). Arbor Hse.

--Portraits. 608p. 1980. pap. 4.50 (ISBN 0-553-24790-5). Bantam.

--Seasons of the Heart. 312p. 1986. 16.95 (ISBN 0-399-13107-8). Putnam Pub Group.

--A World Full of Strangers. LC 74-18154. 1975. 8.95 (ISBN 0-87795-102-0). Arbor Hse.

--A World Full of Strangers. 640p. 1985. pap. 4.50 (ISBN 0-553-25088-4). Bantam.

--A World Full of Strangers. (General Ser.). 1984. lib. bdg. 17.95 (ISBN 0-8161-3640-8, Large Print Bks). G K Hall.

Freeman, Dan. Beautiful Bodies. LC 83-25723. 44p. 1984. 10.95 (ISBN 0-911745-52-1). P Bedrick Bks.

Freeman, Daniel B. Speaking of Survival. (Illus.). 1982. pap. 6.50x (ISBN 0-19-503110-5). Oxford U Pr.

Freeman, Darlene. A New Way to Use Your Bean: Developing Thinking Skills in Children. LC 80-54766. (Illus.). 161p. 1981. pap. 10.00 (ISBN 0-89824-019-0). Trillium Pr.

Freeman, Darlene & Stuart, Virginia. Resources for Gifted Children in the New York Area. LC 79-91434. 350p. (Orig.). 1980. pap. 10.00 (ISBN 0-89824-005-0). Trillium Pr.

Freeman, David. Choosing the Right School: A Parents' Guide. 246p. (Orig.). 1984. pap. 16.95x (ISBN 0-7102-0036-6). Routledge & Kegan.

--Creeps. LC 72-191690. (Canadian Play Ser.). pap. 20.00 (ISBN 0-317-27049-4, 2023618). Bks Demand UMI.

--The Handbook on Private Foundations. LC 81-5331. (Illus.). 452p. 1981. pap. 14.95x (ISBN 0-932020-07-0). Seven Locks Pr.

--Know Your Self. 1976. pap. 3.95 (ISBN 0-934532-11-7). Presby & Reformed.

--The Last Days of Alfred Hitchcock. LC 84-42672. (Illus.). 280p. 1984. 17.95 (ISBN 0-87951-984-3). Overlook Pr.

Freeman, David F. The Handbook on Private Foundations. (Illus.). 1981. pap. 20.00 (ISBN 0-932020-07-0). Coun Found.

Freeman, David H. Tillich. (Modern Thinkers Ser.). 1960. pap. 2.00 (ISBN 0-87552-589-X). Presby & Reformed.

Freeman, David S. Techniques of Family Therapy. LC 80-69669. 350p. 1981. 30.00 (ISBN 0-87668-431-2). Aronson.

Freeman, Denne. That Good Old Baylor Line. LC 75-260701. (College Sports Ser.). 1975. 9.95 (ISBN 0-87397-063-2). Strode.

Freeman, Denne H. Hook'em Horns: A Story of Texas Football. LC 74-84329. (College Sports Ser.). Orig. Title: Texas Football. 1980. 9.95 (ISBN 0-87397-054-3). Strode.

Freeman, Derek. Margaret Mead & Samoa: The Making & Unmaking of an Anthropological Myth. (Illus.). 375p. 1983. 20.00 (ISBN 0-674-54830-2). Harvard U Pr.

--Report on the Iban. (London School of Economics Monographs on Social Anthropology: No. 41). 320p. 1970. 45.00 (ISBN 0-485-19541-0, Pub. by Athlone Pr Ltd). Longwood Pub Group.

Freeman, Devery. Father Sky. LC 79-18562. 1979. 9.95 (ISBN 0-688-03557-4). Morrow.

Freeman, Don. Beady Bear. (Illus.). (gr. 3-6). 1977. pap. 3.95 (ISBN 0-14-050197-5, Puffin). Penguin.

--Beady Bear. LC 54-12295. (Illus.). 48p. (ps-1). 1954. PLB 11.95 (ISBN 0-670-15056-8). Viking.

--Bearymore. (Picture Puffins Ser). (Illus.). 1979. pap. 2.95 (ISBN 0-14-050279-3, Puffin). Penguin.

--Bearymore. LC 76-94. (Illus.). 40p. (gr. k-3). 1976. PLB 12.50 (ISBN 0-670-15174-2). Viking.

--The Chalk Box Story. LC 76-10169. (ps-2). 1976. 7.95i (ISBN 0-397-31699-2). HarpJ.

--Corduroy. (Picture Puffin Ser). (Illus.). (gr. k-1). 1976. pap. 3.50 (ISBN 0-14-050173-8, Puffin). Penguin.

--Corduroy. LC 68-16068. (Illus.). 32p. 1968. PLB 9.95 (ISBN 0-670-24133-4). Viking.

--Corduroy. (gr. k-3). 1982. incl. cass. 19.95 (ISBN 0-941078-08-6); pap. 12.95 incl. cass. (ISBN 0-941078-06-X); user's guide incl. 4 pbs. & cass. 27.95 (ISBN 0-941078-07-8). Live Oak Media.

--Corduroy's Day. LC 84-40477. 14p. (ps). 1985. 2.95 (ISBN 0-670-80521-1, Viking Kestrel). Viking.

--Corduroy's Party. LC 84-40476. (Illus.). 14p. (ps). 1985. 2.95 (ISBN 0-670-80520-3, Viking Kestrel). Viking.

--Corduroy's Toys. LC 84-40478. 24p. 1985. 2.95 (ISBN 0-670-80522-X). Viking.

--Dandelion. LC 64-21472. (Illus.). (ps-2). 1977. pap. 3.50 (ISBN 0-14-050218-1, VS4, Puffin). Penguin.

--Dandelion. LC 64-21472. (Illus.). 48p. (ps-2). 1964. PLB 11.95 (ISBN 0-670-25532-7). Viking.

--Dandelion. (gr. k-3). 1982. incl. cassette 19.95 (ISBN 0-941078-11-6); pap. 12.95 incl. cassette (ISBN 0-941078-09-4); user's guide incl. 4 pbs. & cassette 27.95 (ISBN 0-941078-10-8). Live Oak Media.

--Guard Mouse. (Illus.). (ps-2). 1967. PLB 12.95 (ISBN 0-670-35639-5). Viking.

--In a Flea's Navel: A Critic's Love Affair with Television. LC 80-16781. 224p. 1980. 8.95 (ISBN 0-498-05030-0). A S Barnes.

--Mop Top. (Picture Puffins Ser.). 1978. pap. 3.95 (ISBN 0-14-050326-9, Puffin). Penguin.

--Mop Top. (Illus.). (ps-1). 1955. PLB 11.95 (ISBN 0-670-48882-8). Viking.

--Mop Top. (gr. k-3). 1982. incl. cass. 19.95 (ISBN 0-941078-14-0); pap. 12.95 incl. cass. (ISBN 0-941078-12-4); user's guide incl. 6 pbs. & cass. 27.95 (ISBN 0-941078-13-2). Live Oak Media.

--Norman the Doorman. (Picture Puffins Ser.). (Illus.). (ps-3). 1981. pap. 3.50 (ISBN 0-14-050288-2, Puffin). Penguin.

--Norman the Doorman. (Illus.). (ps-2). 1959. PLB 11.50 (ISBN 0-670-51515-9). Viking.

--The Paper Party. (Picture Puffin Ser.). (Illus.). (gr. 1 up). 1977. pap. 2.50 (ISBN 0-14-050212-2, Puffin). Penguin.

--Penguins, of All People. (Illus.). (gr. k-3). 1971. 12.50 (ISBN 0-670-54617-8). Viking.

--A Pocket for Corduroy. (Illus.). (gr. 3-5). 1978. 10.95 (ISBN 0-670-56172-X). Viking.

--A Pocket for Corduroy. (gr. k-3). 1982. incl. cass. 19.95 (ISBN 0-941078-17-5); pap. 12.95 incl. cass. (ISBN 0-941078-15-9); user's guide incl. 4 pbs. & cass. 27.95 (ISBN 0-941078-16-7). Live Oak Media.

--Quiet! There's a Canary in the Library. (Easy Reading Picture Bks.). (Illus.). 48p. (gr. k-3). 1969. 10.35 (ISBN 0-516-08737-1). Childrens.

--A Rainbow of My Own. 32p. (ps-2). 1978. pap. 3.95 (ISBN 0-14-050328-5, Puffin). Penguin.

--Rainbow of My Own. (Illus.). (gr. k-3). 1966. PLB 9.95 (ISBN 0-670-58928-4). Viking.

--A Rainbow of My Own. (gr. k-3). 1982. incl. cass. 19.95 (ISBN 0-941078-20-5); pap. 12.95 incl. cass. (ISBN 0-941078-18-3); user's guide incl. 4 pbs. & cass. 27.95 (ISBN 0-941078-19-1). Live Oak Media.

--Space Witch. (Picture Puffins Ser.). (Illus.). (gr. k-3). 1979. pap. 3.95 (ISBN 0-14-050346-3, Puffin). Penguin.

--Space Witch. (Illus.). (gr. k-3). 1959. PLB 11.95 (ISBN 0-670-65995-9). Viking.

--Tilly Witch. (Picture Puffins Ser.). 1978. pap. 3.95 (ISBN 0-14-050262-9, Puffin). Penguin.

--Tilly Witch. (Illus.). (gr. k-3). 1969. 9.95 (ISBN 0-670-71303-1). Viking.

--Will's Quill. (Illus.). (gr. k-3). 1977. pap. 2.95 (ISBN 0-14-050215-7, Puffin). Penguin.

--Will's Quill. (Illus.). 32p. (gr. k-3). 1975. PLB 12.50 (ISBN 0-670-76922-3). Viking.

Freeman, Don, illus. A Pocket for Corduroy. (Illus.). 1980. pap. 3.50 (ISBN 0-14-050352-8, Puffin). Penguin.

Freeman, Donald, jt. auth. see Ray, Arthur J.

Freeman, Donald B. International Trade, Migration & Capital Flows: A Quantitative Analysis of Spatial Economic Interaction. LC 73-75154. (Research Papers Ser.: No. 146). (Illus.). 201p. 1973. pap. 10.00 (ISBN 0-89065-053-5). U Chicago Dept Geog.

Freeman, Donald B. & Norcliffe, Glen B. Rural Enterprise in Kenya: Development & Spatial Organization of the Nonfarm Sector. LC 85-1037. (Research Papers: No. 214). 180p. 1985. pap. 10.00 (ISBN 0-89065-119-1). U Chicago Dept Geog.

Freeman, Donald C., ed. Essays in Modern Stylistics. 424p. 1981. pap. 15.95x (ISBN 0-416-74430-3, NO. 3024). Methuen Inc.

Freeman, Donald E. & Perry, Olney R. I-O Design: Data Management in Operating Systems. (Illus.). 1977. text ed. 25.95x (ISBN 0-8104-5789-X). Hayden.

Freeman, Donald M., ed. Foundation of Political Science: Research, Methods & Scope. LC 76-43130. 1978. 40.00 (ISBN 0-02-910670-2). Free Pr.

Freeman, Dorothy. From Copper to Gold: The Life of Dorothy Baker. (Illus.). 368p. 15.95 (ISBN 0-85398-177-9); pap. 7.95 (ISBN 0-85398-178-7). G Ronald Pub.

Freeman, Dorothy R. Marital Crisis & Short-Term Counseling: A Casebook. LC 81-429. 304p. 1982. 22.95 (ISBN 0-02-910680-X). Free Pr.

Freeman, Douglas. R. E. Lee, 4 vols. (Illus.). 1935. Set. lib. rep. ed. 150.00 (ISBN 0-684-15629-6, ScribT). Scribner.

Freeman, Douglas K. Estate Tax Freeze: Tools & Techniques. LC 84-72696. 1985. looseleaf 95.00 (128). Bender.

Freeman, Douglas S. George Washington: A Biography, 7 vols. Incl. Vol. 1. Young Washington 1732-54. (ISBN 0-678-02827-3); Vol. 2. Young Washington 1754-58. (ISBN 0-678-02828-1); Vol. 3. Planter & Patriot. (ISBN 0-678-02829-X); Vol. 4. Leader of the Revolution 1776-78. (ISBN 0-678-02830-3); Vol. 5. Victory with the Help of France 1778-83. (ISBN 0-678-02831-1); Vol. 6. Patriot & President 1784-93. (ISBN 0-678-02832-X); Vol. 7. First in Peace 1793-99. Carroll, John A. & Ashworth, Mary W. (ISBN 0-678-02833-8). LC 75-4504. (Illus.). 1975. Repr. of 1957 ed. lib. bdg. 27.50 ea. Kelly.

--George Washington: A Biography, Vol. 4. LC 75-4504. (Illus.). viii, 736p. 1981. Repr. of 1951 ed. lib. bdg. 37.50x (ISBN 0-317-20095-X). Kelley.

--George Washington: A Biography Planter & Patriot, Vol. 3. LC 75-4504. (Illus.). xxxviii, 600p. 1981. Repr. of 1951 ed. lib. bdg. 37.50 (ISBN 0-317-20100-X). Kelley.

--George Washington: A Biography Victory with the Help of France, Vol. 5. LC 75-4504. (Illus.). xvi, 570p. 1981. Repr. of 1951 ed. lib. bdg. 37.50x (ISBN 0-678-02831-1). Kelley.

--George Washington: A One-Volume Abridgement. Harwell, Richard, ed. 1985. pap. 17.50 (ISBN 0-684-18354-4). Scribner.

--Lee. Harwell, Richard, abridged by. (Illus.). 656p. 1982. pap. 17.50 (ISBN 0-684-17427-8, ScribT). Scribner.

--Lee's Lieutenants, 3 vols. 1942-1944. Set. lib. rep. ed. 105.00 (ISBN 0-684-17926-1, ScribT). Scribner.

--R. E. Lee: An Abridgement. (Illus.). 1961. lib. rep. ed. 30.00x (ISBN 0-684-15489-7, ScribT). Scribner.

--The South to Posterity. Rev. ed. (Illus.). xxix, 235p. 1983. Repr. of 1951 ed. 25.00 (ISBN 0-916107-05-1). Broadfoot.

Freeman, Douglas S., ed. see Confederate Memorial Literary Society - Richmond - 1908.

Freeman, E., ed. Proceedings of the Arbeitsgemeinschaft Magnetismus Conference, 1975. 76. Repr. 68.00 (ISBN 0-7204-0441-X, North Holland). Elsevier.

Freeman, E., ed. see Anouilh, Jean.

Freeman, E., ed. see Cocteau, Jean.

Freeman, E. A. An Introduction to American Institutional History. 1973. pap. 9.00 (ISBN 0-384-16766-7). Johnson Repr.

--William the Conqueror. 59.95 (ISBN 0-8490-1307-0). Gordon Pr.

Freeman, E. A. & Bury, J. B. The Historical Geography of Europe. 612p. 1974. 20.00 (ISBN 0-89005-045-7). Ares.

Freeman, E. M., ed. Campfire Chillers. LC 79-28318. (Illus.). 192p. (Orig.). 1980. pap. 7.95 (ISBN 0-914788-23-X). East Woods.

Freeman, Edith M., ed. Social Work Practice with Clients Who Have Alcohol Problems. 404p. 1985. 37.50x (ISBN 0-398-05107-0). C C Thomas.

Freeman, Edward A. The Epoch of Negro Baptists & the Foreign Mission Board. Gaustad, Edwin S., ed. LC 79-52593. (The Baptist Tradition Ser.). 1980. Repr. of 1953 ed. lib. bdg. 26.50x (ISBN 0-405-12460-0). Ayer Co Pubs.

--Historical Essays, 4 Vols. 1871-92. Set. 170.00 (ISBN 0-404-02630-3); 42.50 ea. Vol. 1 (ISBN 0-404-02631-1). Vol. 2 (ISBN 0-404-02632-X). Vol. 3 (ISBN 0-404-02633-8). Vol. 4 (ISBN 0-404-02634-6). AMS Pr.

--History of Federal Government in Greece & Italy. 2nd ed. Bury, J. B., ed. LC 72-39670. (Select Bibliographies Reprint Ser.). 1972. Repr. of 1893 ed. 31.25 (ISBN 0-8369-9936-3). Ayer Co Pubs.

--History of Sicily from Earliest Times, 4 Vols. (Illus.). 1965. 161.00 (ISBN 0-8337-1241-1). B Franklin.

--History of the Norman Conquest of England: Its Causes & Its Results, 5 Vols. Repr. of 1879 ed. Set. 295.00 (ISBN 0-404-07980-6). AMS Pr.

--An Introduction to American Institutional History. LC 78-63730. (Johns Hopkins University, Studies in the Social Sciences. First Ser. 1882-1883: 1). Repr. of 1882 ed. 11.50 (ISBN 0-404-61001-3). AMS Pr.

--Reign of William Rufus & the Accession of Henry the First, 2 Vols. Repr. of 1882 ed. Set. 85.00 (ISBN 0-404-00620-5); 42.50 ea. Vol. 1 (ISBN 0-404-00621-3). Vol. 2 (ISBN 0-404-00622-1). AMS Pr.

--Some Impressions of the United States. facs. ed. LC 76-117875. (Select Bibliographies Reprint Ser). 1883. 21.50 (ISBN 0-8369-5328-2). Ayer Co Pubs.

Freeman, Eileen E. The Holy Week Book. new ed. LC 78-73510. 1979. pap. 19.95 (ISBN 0-89390-007-9). Resource Pubns.

Freeman, Elizabeth W. You'll Never Come Back. LC 79-66735. 1979. pap. write for info. (ISBN 0-87930-124-4). Miller Freeman.

Freeman, Ernest R. Interference Suppression Techniques for Microwave Antennas & Transmitters. (Artech Microwave Library). (Illus.). 400p. 1982. 48.00 (ISBN 0-89006-110-6). Artech Hse.

Freeman, Ernest R. & Sechs, Michael. Electromagnetic Compatibility Design Guide for Avionics & Related Ground Support Equipment. LC 81-71923. pap. 69.80 (ISBN 0-317-30047-4, 2025049). Bks Demand UMI.

Freeman, Eugene, ed. The Abdication of Philosophy: Philosophy & the Public Good. LC 72-93357. 328p. 1976. 19.95 (ISBN 0-87548-274-0). Open Court.

--The Relevance of Charles Peirce. (Monist Library of Philosophy). 412p. 1983. cloth 29.95 (ISBN 0-914417-00-2). Hegeler Inst.

Freeman, Eugene & Mandelbaum, Maurice, eds. Spinoza: Essays in Interpretation. LC 72-84079. (The Monist Library of Philosophy Ser.). 329p. 1974. pap. 8.95 (ISBN 0-87548-196-5). Open Court.

Freeman, Eugene & Sellars, Wilfrid, eds. Basic Issues in the Philosophy of Time. LC 73-128197. (The Monist Library of Philosophy Ser.). 241p. 1971. 19.95 (ISBN 0-87548-078-0). Open Court.

Freeman, Eugene, jt. ed. see Reese, William L.

Freeman, Evelyn, jt. auth. see Freeman, Will.

Freeman, F. W. Robert Ferguson & the Poetry of Compromise: A Study of Eighteenth Century Scottish Humanism. 249p. 1983. 25.00x (ISBN 0-85224-474-6, Pub. by Edinburgh U Pr Scotland). Columbia U Pr.

Freeman, Farley. And the Angels Wept. 1985. 9.95 (ISBN 0-533-06597-6). Vantage.

Freeman, Frank H. The CEO: An Annotated Bibliography. (Special Report Ser.). 21p. 1983. 12.00 (ISBN 0-912879-53-X). Ctr Creat Leader.

Freeman, Frank N. & Flory, C. D. Growth in Intellectual Ability As Measured by Repeated Tests. (SRCD M). 1937. 11.00 (ISBN 0-527-01495-8). Kraus Repr.

Freeman, Fred, jt. auth. see Freeman, Janet W.

Freeman, Frederick. Africa's Redemption, the Salvation of Our Country. LC 76-106873. Repr. of 1852 ed. 19.75x (ISBN 0-8371-3290-8, FRR&, Pub. by Negro U Pr). Greenwood.

--Africa's Redemption, the Salvation of Our Country. LC 70-92427. 1852. 17.00x (ISBN 0-403-00160-9). Scholarly.

--Yaradee: A Plea for Africa. LC 70-79807. Repr. of 1836 ed. 25.00x (ISBN 0-8371-1505-1, FRP&). Greenwood.

Freeman, G. D. Midnight & Noonday: Or the Incidental History of Southern Kansas & the Indian Territory, 1871-1890. Lane, Richard L., ed. LC 83-40330. (Illus.). 400p. 1984. 24.95 (ISBN 0-8061-1875-X). U of Okla Pr.

Freeman, G. L. Early American Currier & Ive's Battle Prints. LC 60-15562. (Illus.). 1961. 12.50 (ISBN 0-87282-039-4). CHB-ALF.

--Self-Fulfillment in Aging: Avocational Psychology in the Management of a Tri-Powered Life. LC 73-88439. (Illus.). 224p. 1973. 15.00 (ISBN 0-87282-040-8). CHB-ALF.

Freeman, Gage E. & Salvin, Francis H. Falconry: Its Claims, History & Practice. 1972. 25.50 (ISBN 0-914802-05-4); deluxe ed. 45.00, limited (ISBN 0-914802-06-2). Falcon Head Pr.

Freeman, Gail. Alien Thunder. LC 82-9578. 192p. (YA) (gr. 8 up). 1982. 10.95 (ISBN 0-02-735620-5). Bradbury Pr.

--Out from Under. LC 81-18154. 192p. (YA) (gr. 7 up). 1982. 9.95 (ISBN 0-02-735400-8). Bradbury Pr.

Freeman, Gary P. Immigrant Labor & Racial Conflict in Industrial Societies: The French & British Experience, 1945-1975. LC 78-70292. 1979. 38.00 (ISBN 0-691-07603-0). Princeton U Pr.

Freeman, Geoffrey, jt. auth. see Gabszewicz, Anton.

Freeman, Gillian. Confessions of Elizabeth Von S. 316p. 1982. pap. 2.95 (ISBN 0-441-11702-3). Ace Bks.

--The Marriage Machine. LC 74-30237. 256p. 1975. pap. 1.95 (ISBN 0-8128-7017-4). Stein & Day.

--The Marriage Machine. 1984. pap. 3.50 (ISBN 0-8128-8017-X). Stein & Day.

Freeman, Grace & Sugarman, Joan. Inside the Synagogue. rev. ed. (Illus.). 64p. (gr. 1-3). 1984. pap. 6.00 (ISBN 0-8074-0268-0, 301785). UAHC.

Freeman, Grace & Sugarman, Joan G. Inside the Synagogue. LC 62-19996. (Illus.). (gr. 3-5). 1963. 5.00 (ISBN 0-8074-0041-6, 301782). UAHC.

Freeman, Grace B. Children Are Poetry. 3rd ed. (Illus.). 16p. 1982. pap. 2.00 (ISBN 0-9607730-3-7). Johns Pr.

--Firekeeping Poems. (Illus.). 48p. (Orig.). Date not set. pap. 4.95 (ISBN 0-9607730-1-0). Johns Pr.

--No Costumes or Masks. (Red Clay Reader Ser.: Vol. 10, No. 2). 48p. 1983. pap. 4.95 (ISBN 0-9607730-2-9). Johns Pr.

--Stars & the Land. 16p. (Orig.). 1983. pap. 2.95 (ISBN 0-9607730-7-X). Johns Pr.

Freeman, Grace B., ed. see Freeman, John A.

Freeman, Gustave & Milman, Harry. Markers of Chemically Induced Cancer. LC 83-23617. (Illus.). 239p. 1984. 36.00 (ISBN 0-8155-0972-3). Noyes.

Freeman, H. A Glossary of Technical Concepts Containing 4300 Din Definitions. 703p. 1983. pap. 87.00 (ISBN 0-686-40807-1, Pub. by DIN Germany). Heyden.

--Taschenwoerterbuch Eisen und Stahl. 600p. (Ger. & Eng., Dictionary of Iron and Steel). 1966. 12.50 (ISBN 3-19-006215-3, M-7634, Pub. by M. Hueber). French & Eur.

--Taschenwoerterbuch Kraftfahrzeugtechnik. 377p. (Ger. & Eng., Dictionary of Automotive Engineering). 1968. 12.50 (ISBN 3-19-006270-6, M-7635, Pub. by M. Hueber). French & Eur.

--Technisches Taschenwoerterbuch. 3rd ed. 584p. (Ger. & Eng., German-English Technical Dictionary). 1972. 12.50 (ISBN 3-19-006212-9, M-7648, Pub. by M. Hueber). French & Eur.

Freeman, H., jt. auth. see Diringer, David.

Freeman, H. G. Special Dictionary Machinery. 8th ed. 207p. (Eng. & Ger.). 1971. 44.25x (ISBN 3-7736-5031-0). Adlers Foreign Bks.

--Two Thousand Six Hundred Definitions of Technical Terms According to Din: English-German, German-English. 1977. 53.00 (ISBN 0-686-39804-1, 10804-1, Pub. by DIN Germany). Heyden.

Freeman, H. W. Joseph & His Brethren. 359p. pap. 7.95 (ISBN 0-85115-217-1, Pub. by Boydell & Brewer). Academy Chi Pubs.

Freeman, Harold. If You Give a Damn about Life. 96p. 1985. pap. 3.95 (ISBN 0-396-08615-2). Dodd.

--Toward Socialism in America. 2nd ed. LC 79-12410. 256p. 1982. text ed. 14.50x (ISBN 0-87073-911-5); pap. text ed. 9.95x (ISBN 0-87073-912-3). Schenkman Bks Inc.

Freeman, Harold, Jr., jt. auth. see Richardson, Ellis.

Freeman, Harrop A. Counseling in the United States. LC 67-24526. 322p. 1967. 15.00 (ISBN 0-379-00308-2). Oceana.

Freeman, Harrop A. & Freeman, Norman D. Tax Practice Desk Book. 1973. 64.00 (ISBN 0-88262-061-4). Warren.

Freeman, Harry A., jt. auth. see Bray, Olin H.

Freeman, Harvey A. & Thurber, Kenneth J. Microcomputer Networks. (Tutorial Texts Ser.). 268p. 1981. 27.00 (ISBN 0-8186-0395-X, Q395). IEEE Comp Soc.

Freeman, Harvey A., jt. auth. see Larson, James A.

Freeman, Harvey A., jt. auth. see Thurber, Kenneth J.

Freeman, Harvey A. & Thurber, Kenneth J., eds. Local Network Equipment. LC 85-60466. (Tutorial Text Ser.). 370p. (Orig.). 1985. 36.00 (ISBN 0-8186-0605-3, 605); microfiche 36.00 (ISBN 0-8186-4605-5). IEEE Comp Soc.

Freeman, Heather, jt. auth. see Wootton, I. D.

Freeman, Henry G. Dictionary of Metal-Cutting Machine Tools. 561p. (Eng. & Ger.). 1965. leatherette 72.00 (ISBN 3-7736-5095-7, M-7110). French & Eur.

--Fachenglisch Fur Technik und Industrie. 303p. (Ger. & Eng., English for Engineering and Industry). 1974. 22.50 (ISBN 3-452-17766-1, M-7376, Pub. by Carl Heymanns Verlag KG). French & Eur.

--Fachwoerterbuch Spanende Werkzeugmaschinen. 527p. (Ger. & Eng., Dictionary of Machine Tools). 1965. leatherette 72.00 (ISBN 3-7736-5090-6, M-7403, Pub. by Verlag W. Gerardet). French & Eur.

--Spanende Werkzeugmaschinen, Deutsch-Englische Begriffserlauterungen und Kommentare. 617p. (Ger. & Eng., Machine Tools, German-English Explanations and Comments). 1973. 75.00 (ISBN 3-7736-5082-5, M-7624, Pub. by Verlag W. Girardet). French & Eur.

--Spezialwoerterbuch Maschinenwesen. 207p. (Ger. - Eng., Dictionary of Mechanical Engineering). 1971. write for info (M-7625, Pub. by Verlag W. Girardet). French & Eur.

--Technical Pocket Dictionary, English-German, German-English, 2 vols. 2nd ed. (Eng. & Ger.). 12.00x ea. Ger.-Eng (ISBN 3-1900-6212-9). Eng.-Ger (ISBN 3-1900-6213-7). Adlers Foreign Bks.

--Technisches Englisch. 7th ed. (Ger. -Eng.). 1975. 48.00 (ISBN 3-7736-5011-6, M-7647, Pub. by Girardet). French & Eur.

--Tool Dictionary. 2nd ed. (Ger. & Eng.). 1960. 78.00x (ISBN 3-7736-5052-3). Adlers Foreign Bks.

--Woerterbuch Werkzeuge. 2nd ed. (Ger. & Eng., Dictionary of Tools). 1960. leatherette 92.00 (ISBN 3-7736-5052-3, M-6908). French & Eur.

Freeman, Henry P. The Unjust & Deceitful Man: An Autobiography, 1 vol. LC 79-53743. 304p. (Orig.). 1979. 9.00 (ISBN 0-9609920-0-6); pap. 6.00 (ISBN 0-9609920-1-4). Freeman Sr.

Freeman, Henry P., Sr. How to Succeed at Vegetable Gardening: Sound, Successful Directions for Home Gardening. LC 81-90616. (Illus.). 256p. 1981. 12.00 (ISBN 0-9609920-2-2); pap. 8.75x (ISBN 0-9609920-3-0). Freeman Sr.

--Mr. Editor, "What's Happening?". Compilation of Letters by a Philosopher. LC 82-90970. 352p. 1984. 12.00x (ISBN 0-9609920-4-9); pap. 8.75x (ISBN 0-9609920-5-7). Freeman Sr.

Freeman, Herbert. Discrete-Time Systems. LC 80-15357. 256p. 1980. Repr. of 1965 ed. lib. bdg. 19.25 (ISBN 0-89874-228-5). Krieger.

--Interactive Computer Graphics. (Tutorial Texts Ser.). 415p. 1980. 30.00 (ISBN 0-8186-0266-X, Q266). IEEE Comp Soc.

Freeman, Herbert & Lewis, P. M., II, eds. Software Engineering. 1980. 31.50 (ISBN 0-12-267160-0). Acad Pr.

Freeman, Herbert & Pieroni, Goffredo G., eds. Map Data Processing. 1980. 39.00 (ISBN 0-12-267180-5). Acad Pr.

Freeman, Hobart. Angels of Light? Deliverance from Occult Oppression. 1969. pap. 2.95 small type ed. (ISBN 0-912106-63-8, Pub. by Logos). Bridge Pub.

--Nahum, Sofonias, Habacuc (Comentario Biblico Portavoz) Orig. Title: Nahum, Zephaniah & Habakkuk (Everyman's Bible Commentary) 112p. (Span.). 1980. pap. 3.50 (ISBN 0-8254-1246-3). Kregel.

Freeman, Howard E. & Jones, Wyatt C. Social Problems. 3rd ed. 1979. 27.50 (ISBN 0-395-30594-2). HM.

Freeman, Howard E., jt. auth. see Bernstein, Ilene N.

Freeman, Howard E. see Brim, Orville G., Jr., et al.

Freeman, Howard E., jt. auth. see Lambert, Camille, Jr.

Freeman, Howard E., jt. auth. see Rossi, Peter H.

Freeman, Howard E., ed. Policy Studies Review Annual, Vol. 2. 752p. 1978. text ed. 37.50 (ISBN 0-8039-1100-9). Transaction Bks.

Freeman, Howard E. & Dynes, Russell R., eds. Applied Sociology: Roles & Activities of Sociologists in Diverse Setting. LC 82-49035. (Social & Behavioral Science Ser.). 1983. text ed. 25.95x (ISBN 0-87589-563-8). Jossey-Bass.

Freeman, Howard E. & Solomon, Marian A., eds. Evaluation Studies Review Annual, Vol. 6. (Illus.). 751p. 1981. 40.00 (ISBN 0-8039-1656-6). Sage.

Freeman, Howard E., et al. Handbook of Medical Sociology. 3rd ed. 1979. 32.95 (ISBN 0-13-380253-1). P-H.

--Evaluating Social Projects in Developing Countries. 239p. (Orig.). 1980. pap. text ed. 9.00x (ISBN 92-64-12040-8). OECD.

Freeman, Huey. Judge, Jury & Executioner. LC 84-52398. 404p. (Orig.). 1985. pap. 5.00 (ISBN 0-932077-01-3). Talking Leaves Pub.

Freeman, Hugh, ed. Progress in Mental Health. 346p. 1970. 43.50 (ISBN 0-8089-0587-2, 791384). Grune.

Freeman, Ira, jt. auth. see Freeman, Mae.

Freeman, Ira M. Physics Made Simple. rev. ed. LC 65-13090. (Made Simple Ser.). pap. 4.95 (ISBN 0-385-08727-6). Doubleday.

Freeman, Ira M., jt. auth. see Freeman, Mae.

Freeman, Ira M., jt. auth. see Freeman, Mae B.

Freeman, J. Forgotten Rebel: Mission Furniture. LC 65-28083. 1966. 50.00 (ISBN 0-87282-041-6). CHB-ALF.

Freeman, J. C. Old Cars of the Twenties. 1959. 4.50 (ISBN 0-87282-088-2). CHB-ALF.

Freeman, J. D. Iban Agriculture: A Report on the Shifting Cultivation of Hill Rice by the Iban of Sarawak. LC 77-86974. Repr. of 1955 ed. 25.00 (ISBN 0-404-16709-8). AMS Pr.

Freeman, J. Leiper. Political Change in Tennessee, Nineteen Forty-Eight to Nineteen Seventy-Eight: Party Politics Trickles Down. (Studies in Tennessee Politics). 57p. (Orig.). 1980. pap. 3.50 (ISBN 0-914079-04-2). Bureau Pub Admin U Tenn.

Freeman, J. W. Discovering Surnames: Their Origins & Meanings. 4th ed. (Discovering Ser.). 72p. (gr. 6 up). 1979. pap. 2.50 (ISBN 0-913714-36-4). Legacy Bks.

Freeman, J. W., ed. Solar Power Satellites: Proceedings of the International Symposium, Toulouse, France, June 1980. 200p. 1981. pap. 39.00 (ISBN 0-08-027592-3). Pergamon.

Freeman, James A. Milton & the Martial Muse: Paradise Lost & European Traditions of War. LC 80-7519. 1981. 26.00 (ISBN 0-691-06435-0). Princeton U Pr.

Freeman, James A. & Beeler, Myrton F., eds. Laboratory Medicine-Urinalysis & Medical Microscopy. 2nd ed. LC 82-17254. (Illus.). 611p. 1983. text ed. 47.50 (ISBN 0-8121-0822-1). Lea & Febiger.

Freeman, James A. & Low, Anthony, eds. Milton Studies, Vol. XIX: Urbane Milton: The Latin Poetry. LC 69-12335. (Milton Studies Ser.). (Illus.). 320p. 1984. 32.95x (ISBN 0-8229-3492-2). U of Pittsburgh Pr.

Freeman, James A., et al. Pathology of Leprosy. LC 80-720434. 16p. 1980. pap. 50.00 (ISBN 0-89189-101-3, 15-7-011-00). Am Soc Clinical.

Freeman, James D. Be. 1955. 4.95 (ISBN 0-87159-007-7). Unity School.

--Of Time & Eternity. LC 81-51069. 200p. 1981. 4.95 (ISBN 0-87159-122-7). Unity School.

--Once Upon a Christmas. LC 78-53345. (Illus.). 1978. 5.95 (ISBN 0-87159-119-7). Unity School.

--Prayer: The Master Key. 1975. 4.95 (ISBN 0-87159-128-6). Unity School.

--The Story of Unity. rev. ed. (Illus.). 1978. 4.95 (ISBN 0-87159-145-6). Unity School.

--Tu Puedes! LC 82-70490. 256p. 1982. 4.95 (ISBN 0-87159-158-8). Unity School.

--What God Is Like. 1974. 4.95 (ISBN 0-87159-172-3). Unity School.

Freeman, James M. Manners & Customs of the Bible. (Illus.). 515p. 1972. (Pub. by Logos); pap. 8.95 (ISBN 0-88270-022-7). Bridge Pub.

--Scarcity & Opportunity in an Indian Village. (Illus.). 177p. 1985. pap. text ed. 7.95x (ISBN 0-88133-165-1). Waveland Pr.

--Untouchable: An Indian Life History. LC 78-55319. (Illus.). 1979. 30.00x (ISBN 0-8047-1001-5); pap. 10.00 (ISBN 0-8047-1103-8, SP40). Stanford U Pr.

Freeman, Janet W. & Freeman, Fred. Trial Handbook for New Jersey Lawyers. LC 72-76294. 520p. 69.50; Suppl. 1984. 21.50; Suppl. 1983. 19.50. Lawyers Co-Op.

Freeman, Jean K. This Angry Loving Land. 184p. (Orig.). 1981. pap. 3.95 (ISBN 0-87123-568-4, 210568). Bethany Hse.

Freeman, Jean K., jt. ed. see Haikalis, Peter D.

Freeman, Jeff. How to Attach An Interface Card to An Apple IIe Computer. (Illus.). 36p. 1984. pap. 8.95 (ISBN 0-915509-05-9). Argos Pub Co.

Freeman, Jim. California Steelhead. LC 84-11373. (Illus.). 160p. (Orig.). 1984. pap. 7.95 (ISBN 0-87701-268-7). Chronicle Bks.

--California Trout. (Illus.). 224p. 1983. pap. 6.95 (ISBN 0-87701-251-2). Chronicle Bks.

Freeman, Jim, jt. auth. see Best, Don.

Freeman, Jo. The Politics of Women's Liberation: A Case Study of an Emerging Social Movement & Its Relation to the Policy Process. LC 74-25208. 1975. text ed. 17.95x (ISBN 0-679-30284-0); pap. text ed. 13.95x (ISBN 0-582-28009-5). Longman.

--Women: A Feminist Perspective. 3rd ed. (Orig.). 1984. pap. text ed. 18.95 (ISBN 0-87484-568-8). Mayfield Pub.

Freeman, Joan. Lettering & Calligraphy. (Illus.). 128p. 1984. 12.95 (ISBN 0-668-06193-6, 6193-6). Arco.

Freeman, Joan, ed. The Psychology of Gifted Children. (Developmental Psychology & Its Applications Ser.). 1985. 50.95 (ISBN 0-471-10255-5). Wiley.

Freeman, Joanna M. How to Minister in Nursing Homes. 40p. 1983. pap. text ed. 3.95 (ISBN 0-87148-410-2). Pathway Pr.

Freeman, John. Collected Poems. 1971. Repr. of 1928 ed. 29.00 (ISBN 0-403-00596-5). Scholarly.

--English Portraits & Essays. 244p. 1981. Repr. lib. bdg. 30.00 (ISBN 0-89987-261-1). Darby Bks.

--English Portraits & Essays. LC 74-131710. 1971. Repr. of 1924 ed. 14.00x (ISBN 0-403-00597-3). Scholarly.

--Herman Melville. LC 73-18099. (American Literature, No. 49). 1974. lib. bdg. 75.00x (ISBN 0-8383-1733-2). Haskell.

--Moderns: Essays in Literary Criticism. 1973. Repr. of 1917 ed. 10.75 (ISBN 0-8274-0593-6). R West.

--Oliver Goldsmith. LC 74-5386. 1952. lib. bdg. 25.00 (ISBN 0-8414-4185-5). Folcroft.

--Poems, New & Old. 319p. 1920. Repr. 39.00x (ISBN 0-403-01761-0). Scholarly.

--Portrait of George Moore in a Study of His Work. LC 74-4125. 1973. lib. bdg. 38.50 (ISBN 0-8414-4177-4). Folcroft.

--Portrait of George Moore in a Study of His Work. LC 78-131711. 1971. Repr. of 1922 ed. 23.00x (ISBN 0-403-00598-1). Scholarly.

--Super Machines. LC 85-40204. (Let's Look Up Ser.). (Illus.). 32p. (gr. 3-6). PLB 5.95 (ISBN 0-382-09076-4). Silver.

Freeman, John & Hollis, Martin. Mechanics. LC 83-50224. (Visual Science Ser.). 48p. (gr. 6 up). 1983. 13.72 (ISBN 0-382-06716-9); pap. 6.75 (ISBN 0-382-09001-2). Silver.

Freeman, John, ed. Prisons Past & Future. LC 79-304504. (Cambridge Studies in Criminology). 1978. text ed. 48.95x (ISBN 0-435-82308-6). Gower Pub Co.

Freeman, John, ed. see Jones, C. S. & Williams, H. T.

Freeman, John A. Survival Gardening Cookbook: Low Cost Nutritious. Freeman, Grace B., ed. (Illus.). 104p. (Orig.). 1985. pap. 10.95 (ISBN 0-9607730-8-8). Johns Pr.

--Survival Gardening: Enough Nutrition to Live on... Just in Case. 2nd ed. (Illus.). 104p. 1983. pap. 8.95 (ISBN 0-9607730-5-3). Johns Pr.

Freeman, John F. & Smith, Murphy D. Guide to Manuscripts Relating to the American Indian in the Library of the American Philosophical Society. LC 65-23435. (Memoirs Ser.: Vol. 65). 1966. 12.00 (ISBN 0-87169-065-9). Am Philos.

Freeman, John R. The Politics of Indebted Economic Growth. (World Affairs Ser.: Vol. 21, Bk. 3). 130p. (Orig.). 1985. pap. 6.95 (ISBN 0-87940-078-1). Monograph Series.

Freeman, John W. The Metropolitan Opera Stories of the Great Operas. LC 84-8030. 565p. 1984. 20.00 (ISBN 0-393-01888-1). Norton.

Freeman, Joseph. An American Testament. LC 72-13741. x, 678p. 1972. Repr. lib. bdg. 43.00x (ISBN 0-374-92887-8). Octagon.

--The Soviet Worker. LC 73-841. (Russian Studies: Perspectives on the Revolution Ser.). 408p. 1973. Repr. of 1932 ed. 27.50 (ISBN 0-88355-036-9). Hyperion Conn.

Freeman, Joseph, jt. auth. see Nearing, Scott.

Freeman, Joseph T. Aging: Its History & Literature. LC 79-11839. 161p. 1979. 19.95 (ISBN 0-87705-251-4). Human Sci Pr.

--Clinical Features of the Older Patient. (Illus.). 512p. 1965. 42.50x (ISBN 0-398-00612-1). C C Thomas.

Freeman, Joy. The Last Frost Fair. 258p. 1985. 13.95 (ISBN 0-312-47084-3). St Martin.

--The Last Frost Fair. 1985. pap. 2.50 (ISBN 0-317-27030-3, Sig). NAL.

Freeman, Judy. Books Kids Will Sit Still For: A Guide to Using Children's Literature for Librarians, Teachers, & Parents. LC 83-21414. (Illus.). 224p. (Orig.). 1984. pap. 11.95 (ISBN 0-913853-02-X, 115-007). Freline.

Freeman, Judy, ed. see Jones, C. S. & Williams, H. T.

Freeman, Julia D. see Forrest, Mary, pseud.

Freeman, Kathleen. Ancilla to the Pre-Socratic Philosophers: A Complete Translation of the Fragments in Diels, Fragmente Der Vorsokratiker. LC 48-9987. 1948. 14.00x (ISBN 0-674-03500-3). Harvard U Pr.

--Ancilla to the Pre-Socratic Philosophers. 176p. 1983. pap. text ed. 5.95x (ISBN 0-674-03501-1). Harvard U Pr.

--God, Man & State. LC 79-101039. 1969. Repr. of 1952 ed. 25.00x (ISBN 0-8046-0705-2, Pub. by Kennikat). Assoc Faculty Pr.

--God, Man & State: Greek Concepts. Repr. of 1952 ed. lib. bdg. 27.50 (ISBN 0-8371-2821-8, FRGM). Greenwood.

--The Work & Life of Solon, with a Translation of His Poems. facsimile ed. LC 75-13265. (History of Ideas in Ancient Greece Ser.). 1976. Repr. of 1926 ed. 13.00x (ISBN 0-405-07307-0). Ayer Co Pubs.

Freeman, Kenneth J. Schools of Hellas. LC 73-101040. 1969. Repr. of 1907 ed. 26.00x (ISBN 0-8046-0706-0, Pub. by Kennikat). Assoc Faculty Pr.

Freeman, Kenneth J., ed. Schools of Hellas. LC 73-7994. (Classics in Education Ser.). (Illus.). 1969. text ed. 11.00 (ISBN 0-8077-1391-0); pap. text ed. 6.00x (ISBN 0-8077-1390-2). Tchrs Coll.

Freeman, L. Collecting Prang Mark Greeting Cards. 1974. pap. 3.50 (ISBN 0-87282-042-4). CHB-ALF.

--How to Buy & Sell Old Books. LC 64-66000. (Orig.). 1965. pap. 5.00x (ISBN 0-87282-043-2, 66000). CHB-ALF.

Freeman, L., jt. auth. see Fox, Charles P.

Freeman, Larry. The Big Top Circus Days. LC 64-7599. (Illus.). 132p. 1974. 20.00 (ISBN 0-87282-053-X, 87282). CHB-ALF.

--Early American Plated Silver: Flat & Holloware. new ed. LC 72-97475. Orig. Title: American Plated Silver. (Illus.). 160p. 1973. text ed. 15.00x (ISBN 0-87282-044-0); pap. text ed. 6.95x (ISBN 0-87282-106-4). CHB-ALF.

--Grand Old American Bottles. LC 63-23066. 1964. 25.00 (ISBN 0-87282-045-9). CHB-ALF.

--Historical Cities Prints. (Illus.). 1952. 6.00 (ISBN 0-87282-046-7). CHB-ALF.

--Hope Paintings. LC 60-13415. (Illus.). 1961. deluxe ed. 8.50 (ISBN 0-87282-047-5). CHB-ALF.

--How to Price Antiques. 1964 ed. LC 60-15559. pap. 4.50 (ISBN 0-87282-048-3). CHB-ALF.

--How to Restore Antiques. LC 60-13416. 1960. pap. 4.50 (ISBN 0-87282-049-1). CHB-ALF.

--Louis Prang, Color Lithographer. LC 70-145867. (Library of Victorian Culture Ser.). (Illus.). 1971. 25.00 (ISBN 0-87282-050-5, 87282). CHB-ALF.

--New Light on Old Lamps. 7th ed. LC 68-12854. (Illus.). 1984. 14.95 (ISBN 0-87282-051-3). CHB-ALF.

--Nursery Americana. (Orig.). 1947. pap. 5.50 (ISBN 0-87282-052-1, 20). CHB-ALF.

--Southern Tier Yesterdays: New York & Upstate Cinderella. 1972. pap. 3.50 (ISBN 0-87282-054-8). CHB-ALF.

--Victorian Posters. LC 68-30049. (Victorian Culture Ser.). (Illus.). 1969. 15.00 (ISBN 0-87282-055-6). CHB-ALF.

--Victorian Silver: Hollow & Flatware, Sterling & Plated. LC 67-12052. (Victorian Culture Series). (Photos). 1967. 25.00 (ISBN 0-87282-056-4). CHB-ALF.

Freeman, Larry & Freeman, Ruth. Yesterday's Toys. LC 61-15922. (Illus., Orig.). 1962. 5.00 (ISBN 0-87282-057-2). CHB-ALF.

Freeman, Larry, ed. A Centennial Guide to Postcard Collecting. new ed. LC 75-21439. (Illus.). 180p. 1976. 14.95 (ISBN 0-87282-000-9); pap. 9.95 (ISBN 0-87282-114-5). CHB-ALF.

Freeman, Larry G. Iridescent Glass. (Illus.). 1956. 8.50 (ISBN 0-87282-058-0). CHB-ALF.

--Merry Old Mobiles. (Illus.). 1949. 13.95 (ISBN 0-87282-060-2). CHB-ALF.

Freeman, Larry G. & Freeman, Ruth. Child & His Picture Book. rev. ed. LC 66-29514. (Head Start Program Ser.). 1967. 7.00 (ISBN 0-87282-062-9). CHB-ALF.

Freeman, Larry G., jt. auth. see Freeman, Ruth.

Freeman, Lawrence H., jt. auth. see Bacon, Terry R.

Freeman, Lenore & Stahmer, Jean. D-O-G W-A-S-H. LC 79-13976. (Illus., Orig.). 1979. pap. 3.95 (ISBN 0-9600472-4-7). Triad Pub FL.

Freeman, Leonard, ed. Freeman & Johnson's Clinical Radionuclide Imaging, 2 vols. 3rd ed. 1648p. 1984. Set. 179.00 (ISBN 0-8089-1597-5, 791393). Grune.

Freeman, Leonard M. & Blaufox, Donald, eds. Cardiovascular Nuclear Medicine: Current Methodology & Practice. (Seminars in Nuclear Medicine Reprint Ser.). 304p. 1980. 49.50 (ISBN 0-8089-1292-5, 791392). Grune.

Freeman, Leonard M. & Blaufox, M. Donald, eds. Nuclear Medicine & Ultrasound. 176p. 1976. 43.50 (ISBN 0-8089-0968-1, 791376). Grune.

--Pediatric Nuclear Medicine. 224p. 1975. 49.50 (ISBN 0-8089-0920-7, 7913-70). Grune.

--Radioimmunoassay. (Seminars in Nuclear Medicine Reprint Ser.). 176p. 1975. 49.50 (ISBN 0-8089-0933-9, 791374). Grune.

--Radionuclide Studies of the Genitourinary System. (Seminars in Nuclear Medicine Reprint Ser.). 224p. 1975. 49.50 (ISBN 0-8089-0921-5, 791372). Grune.

Freeman, Leonard M. & Weissman, Heidi S., eds. Nuclear Medicine Annual, 1982. 420p. 1982. text ed. 70.50 (ISBN 0-89004-726-X). Raven.

Freeman, Leonard M. & Weissmann, Heidi S., eds. Nuclear Medicine Annual, 1980. 440p. 1980. text ed. 62.00 (ISBN 0-89004-472-4). Raven.

--Nuclear Medicine Annual, 1983. (Nuclear Medicine Annual Ser.). (Illus.). 408p. 1983. text ed. 48.00 (ISBN 0-89004-930-0). Raven.

--Nuclear Medicine Annual, 1984. LC 80-645231. (Illus.). 360p. 1984. text ed. 51.50 (ISBN 0-89004-453-8). Raven.

--Nuclear Medicine Annual, 1985. (Illus.). 368p. 1985. text ed. 59.50 (ISBN 0-88167-086-3). Raven.

Freeman, Leslie G., jt. ed. see Butzer, Karl.

Freeman, Leslie J. Nuclear Witnesses: Insiders Speak Out. (Illus.). 1981. 16.95 (ISBN 0-393-01456-8). Norton.

--Nuclear Witnesses: Insiders Speak Out. (Illus.). 360p. 1982. pap. 7.95 (ISBN 0-393-30033-1). Norton.

Freeman, Linton, ed. Research Methods in Social Networks Analysis. (Illus.). 574p. Date not set. lib. bdg. 34.95x (ISBN 0-8304-1094-5). Nelson-Hall.

Freeman, Linton C. A Bibliography of Social Networks, Nos. 1170-1171. 1976. 12.50 (ISBN 0-686-20415-8). CPL Biblios.

--Metropolitan Decision-Making Further Analysis from the Syracuse Study of Local Community Leadership. 1962. 2.50 (ISBN 0-87060-079-6, PUC 27). Syracuse U Cont Ed.

--Patterns of Local Community Leadership. LC 68-23259. 1968. pap. text ed. 3.95x (ISBN 0-672-60838-3). Irvington.

Freeman, Linton C., et al. Local Community Leadership. 1960. 2.50 (ISBN 0-87060-083-4, PUC 15). Syracuse U Cont Ed.

Freeman, Lory. It's My Body. (Illus.). 32p. (ps-3). 1983. lib. bdg. 8.95 (ISBN 0-943990-02-5); pap. 3.00 (ISBN 0-943990-03-3). Parenting Pr.

--A Kid's Guide to First Aid. (ps-5). 1983. PLB 10.95 (ISBN 0-943990-00-9); pap. 4.95 (ISBN 0-943990-01-7). Parenting Pr.

--Loving Touches. (Illus.). 32p. (Orig.). (ps). 1985. PLB 8.95 (ISBN 0-943990-21-1); pap. 3.50 (ISBN 0-943990-20-3). Parenting Pr.

--Mi Cuerpo es Mio. Dunn, Lois, tr. from Eng. (Illus.). 32p. (Orig., Span.). (ps). 1985. pap. 3.00 (ISBN 0-943990-19-X). Parenting Pr.

Freeman, Louis. Modular Typewriting. (gr. 10-11). 1978. wkbk. 9.50 (ISBN 0-87720-405-5). AMSCO Sch.

Freeman, Lucy. Fight Against Fears. LC 81-20075. xiv, 332p. 1982. Repr. of 1951 ed. lib. bdg. 27.50x (ISBN 0-313-23352-7, FRFE). Greenwood.

--Freud Rediscovered. LC 79-52251. 1980. 11.95 (ISBN 0-87795-227-2). Arbor Hse.

--The Murder Mystique: Crime Writers on Their Art. (Recognitions Ser.). 200p. 1982. 11.95x (ISBN 0-8044-2212-5); pap. 6.95 (ISBN 0-8044-6162-7). Ungar.

--The Psychiatrist Says Murder. LC 73-82190. 1973. 6.95 (ISBN 0-87795-045-8). Arbor Hse.

--What Do Women Want? Self Discovery Through Fantasy. LC 77-28003. 197p. 1978. 19.95 (ISBN 0-87705-298-0). Human Sci Pr.

--Who Is Sylvia? LC 78-57327. 1979. 9.95 (ISBN 0-87795-197-7). Arbor Hse.

Freeman, Lucy & Strean, Herbert S. Freud & Women. LC 81-40461. 266p. 1981. 14.95 (ISBN 0-8044-5374-8). Ungar.

Freeman, Lucy, ed. Listening to the Inner Self. LC 83-9988. 206p. 1984. 16.95 (ISBN 0-87668-640-4). Aronson.

Freeman, Lucy, et al. Dear Heart: The Biography of Belle Case La Follette. (Illus.). 224p. 1986. 17.95 (ISBN 0-8253-0314-1). Beaufort Bks NY.

Freeman, M. A. Adult Articular Cartilage. LC 73-10772. (Illus.). 341p. 1974. 73.50 (ISBN 0-8089-0826-X, 791388). Grune.

Freeman, M. A., ed. Arthritis of the Knee. (Clinical Features & Surgical Management Ser.). (Illus.). 320p. 1980. 125.00 (ISBN 0-387-09699-X). Springer-Verlag.

Freeman, M. D. The Rights & the Wrongs of Children. LC 83-124532. 295p. 1983. 19.95 (ISBN 0-903804-20-4); pap. 10.50 (ISBN 0-86187-226-6). F Pinter Pubs.

Freeman, M. H., jt. auth. see Fincham, W. H.

Freeman, M. Herbert & Graf, David K. Money Management: A Consumer's Guide to Savings, Spending, & Investing. 1980. pap. 21.17 scp (ISBN 0-672-97181-X); scp tchrs. manual 3.67 (ISBN 0-672-97182-8). Bobbs.

Freeman, M. Herbert & Salser, Carl W. Personal Shorthand for the Administrator, Executive, Manager & Supervisor. 136p. 1984. pap. text ed. 15.70 incl. key to exercises (ISBN 0-89420-237-5, 420125). Natl Book.

Freeman, M. Herbert, jt. auth. see Logan, William B.

Freeman, Mae & Freeman, Ira. The Sun, the Moon, & the Stars. rev. ed. LC 78-64604. (Illus.). (gr. 2-4). 1979. 5.95 (ISBN 0-394-80110-5, BYR); PLB 5.99 (ISBN 0-394-90110-X). Random.

Freeman, Mae & Freeman, Ira M. You Will Go to the Moon. LC 75-158389. (gr. 1-2). 1971. PLB 7.99 (ISBN 0-394-92340-5). Beginner.

Freeman, Mae B. Fun with Ballet. (Illus.). (gr. 4-6). 1952. 7.95 (ISBN 0-394-80276-4, BYR). Random.

--Fun with Cooking. rev ed. (Illus.). (gr. 4-6). 1947. (BYR); PLB 4.99 (ISBN 0-394-90278-5). Random.

Freeman, Mae B. & Freeman, Ira M. The Story of Chemistry. (Gateway Ser: No. 26). (gr. 3-6). 1962. PLB 5.99 (ISBN 0-394-90126-6, BYR). Random.

--You Will Go to the Moon. rev. ed. (Illus.). 60p. (gr. 1-3). 1971. (BYR); PLB 7.99 (ISBN 0-394-92340-5). Random.

Freeman, Margaret. Hidden Treasure: Parables for Kids. LC 81-16669. (Illus.). 96p. (Orig.). (gr. 4-9). 1982. pap. 3.95 (ISBN 0-87239-499-9, 2728). Standard Pub.

Freeman, Margaret B. Herbs for the Mediaeval Household, for Cooking, Healing & Divers Uses. LC 43-18177. (Illus.). 1943. 7.95 (ISBN 0-87099-067-5, Pub. by Metro Mus Art). NYGS.

--The Unicorn Tapestries. LC 76-2466. (Illus.). 1983. 60.00 (ISBN 0-525-22643-5, 05825-1750). Dutton.

Freeman, Margaret C., jt. auth. see Park, Charles F., Jr.

Freeman, Margaret H., ed. see Patterson, Rebecca.

Freeman, Marie E. & Davis, Maria H. Alpine to Alkali. LC 83-80807. (Nevada: Its Land & Communities). (Illus.). 150p. (Orig.). (gr. 7-12). 1983. pap. text ed. 9.50 (ISBN 0-913205-01-X); tchrs. ed. 1.75 (ISBN 0-913205-06-0). Grace Dangberg.

Freeman, Marion H. Whispering Wind. 96p. 1982. 6.00 (ISBN 0-682-49880-7). Exposition Pr FL.

Freeman, Mark P. & FitzPatrick, Joseph A., eds. Theory, Practice & Process Principles for Physical Separation. LC 81-68949. 750p. 1981. pap. 50.00 (ISBN 0-8169-0204-6, P-32); pap. 40.00 members (ISBN 0-317-03776-5). Am Inst Chem Eng.

Freeman, Martin. Forecasting by Astrology. 160p. 1983. pap. 7.95 (ISBN 0-85030-297-8). Newcastle Pub.

--Forecasting by Astrology: A Comprehensive Manual of Interpretation & Technique. (Illus.). 160p. (Orig.). 1983. pap. 7.95 (ISBN 0-85030-297-8, Pub. by Aquarian Pr Emgland). Sterling.

--How to Interpret a Birth Chart. 128p. 1981. pap. 6.95 (ISBN 0-85030-249-8). Newcastle Pub.

Freeman, Mary E. Copy-Cat, & Other Stories. LC 71-122707. (Short Story Index Reprint Ser). 1914. 19.00 (ISBN 0-8369-3540-3). Ayer Co Pubs.

--Evelina's Garden. Date not set. lib. bdg. 7.95 (ISBN 0-915864-74-6); pap. 3.95 (ISBN 0-915864-73-8). Academy Chi Pubs.

--The Givers. 1972. Repr. of 1904 ed. 26.50 (ISBN 0-8422-8051-0). Irvington.

--Humble Romance & Other Stories. LC 71-130991. Repr. of 1899 ed. 17.50 (ISBN 0-404-02574-9). AMS Pr.

--A Humble Romance & Other Stories. 1972. Repr. of 1887 ed. 15.50 (ISBN 0-8422-8052-9). Irvington.

--Jane Field. LC 78-104456. (Illus.). Repr. of 1893 ed. lib. bdg. 19.00 (ISBN 0-8398-0566-7). Irvington.

--Love of Parson Lord, & Other Stories by Mary E. Wilkins. facs. ed. LC 76-75776. (Short Story Index Reprint Ser.). 1900. 17.00 (ISBN 0-8369-3001-0). Ayer Co Pubs.

--Pembroke. Westbrook, Perry D., ed. (Masterworks of Literature Ser.). 1971. 8.95x (ISBN 0-8084-0022-3); pap. 5.95x (ISBN 0-8084-0023-1). New Coll U Pr.

--People of Our Neighborhood by Mary E. Wilkins. LC 76-110192. (Short Story Index Reprint Ser.). 1898. 14.50 (ISBN 0-8369-3343-5). Ayer Co Pubs.

--The Portion of Labor. LC 67-29267. (Americans in Fiction Ser.). (Illus.). lib. bdg. 19.50 (ISBN 0-8398-0568-3); pap. text ed. 7.95x (ISBN 0-89197-897-6). Irvington.
--Pot of Gold & Other Stories. LC 74-113661. (Short Story Index Reprint Ser.). 1892. 19.50 (ISBN 0-8369-3390-7). Ayer Co Pubs.
--Shoulders of Atlas. Date not set. 9.95 (ISBN 0-915864-76-2); pap. 5.00 (ISBN 0-915864-75-4). Academy Chi Pubs.
--Silence & Other Stories by Mary E. Wilkins. LC 74-101812. (Short Story Index Reprint Ser.). 1898. 18.00 (ISBN 0-8369-3200-5). Ayer Co Pubs.
--Six Trees. LC 74-94721. (Short Story Index Reprint Ser.). 1903. 18.00 (ISBN 0-8369-3100-9). Ayer Co Pubs.
--Understudies. facs. ed. LC 70-86141. (Short Story Index Reprint Ser.). 1901. 19.00 (ISBN 0-8369-3045-2). Ayer Co Pubs.
--The Wind in the Rose Bush & Other Stories of the Supernatural. 1972. Repr. of 1903 ed. lib. bdg. 24.00 (ISBN 0-8422-8053-7). Irvington.
--Young Lucretia & Other Stories by Mary E. Wilkins. LC 79-106287. (Short Story Index Reprint Ser.). 1892. 18.00 (ISBN 0-8369-3324-9). Ayer Co Pubs.
Freeman, Mary E., jt. auth. see Freeman, Mary Eleanor Wilkins.
Freeman, Mary Eleanor Wilkins & Freeman, Mary E. The Shoulders of Atlas. LC 76-51665. (Rediscovery Fiction by American Women Ser.). 1977. Repr. of 1908 ed. lib. bdg. 30.00x (ISBN 0-405-10044-2). Ayer Co Pubs.
Freeman, Mary Wilkens. Best Stories of Mary E. Wilkins. Lanier, Henry W., ed. LC 70-145023. 1971. Repr. of 1927 ed. 59.00x (ISBN 0-403-00970-7). Scholarly.
Freeman, Mary Wilkins. Pembroke. 350p. 1979. o. p. 13.95 (ISBN 0-915864-72-X); pap. 6.95 (ISBN 0-89733-014-5). Academy Chi Pubs.
Freeman, Michael. Achieving Photographic Style. (Illus.). 224p. 1984. 27.50 (ISBN 0-8174-3508-5, Amphoro). Watson-Guptill.
--Edmund Burke & the Critique of Political Radicalism. LC 80-16266. 264p. 1980. lib. bdg. 25.00x (ISBN 0-226-26175-1). U of Chicago Pr.
--How to Take Great Nature & Wildlife Photos. (Illus.). 224p. 1983. pap. 14.95 (ISBN 0-89586-294-8). H P Bks.
--Instant Film Photography. (Illus.). 224p. 1985. 17.95 (ISBN 0-88162-117-X, Pub. by Salem Hse Ltd). Merrimack Pub Cir.
--Instant Photography: A Creative Handbook. (Illus.). 1985. 17.95 (ISBN 0-318-04516-8, Pub. by Salem Hse Ltd). Merrimack Pub Cir.
--Photo School: A Step by Step Course in Photography. (Illus.). 224p. 1982. 24.95 (ISBN 0-8174-5402-0, Amphoto). Watson-Guptill.
--The Photographer's Studio Manual. (Illus.). 224p. 1984. 24.95 (ISBN 0-8174-5462-4, Amphoto). Watson-Guptill.
--Salem House Concise Guide to Photography: The Professional Manual for the Amateur Photographer. (Illus.). 176p. 1985. pap. 11.95 (ISBN 0-88162-096-3, Pub. by Salem Hse Ltd). Merrimack Pub Cir.
--The State, the Law & the Family: Critical Perspectives. 328p. (Orig.). 1985. pap. 16.95 (ISBN 0-422-79080-X, 9332, Pub. by Tavistock England). Methuen Inc.
--The Thirty-Five Millimeter Handbook. (Illus.). 320p. 1980. 25.00 (ISBN 0-87165-093-2, Amphoto). Watson-Guptill.
--The Thirty-Five Millimeter Handbook: A Complete Course from Basic Techniques to Professional Applications. 1985. 14.98 (ISBN 0-89471-339-6). Running Pr.
--The Wildlife & Nature Photographer's Field Guide. (Illus.). 223p. 1984. 14.95 (ISBN 0-89879-128-6). Writers Digest.
Freeman, Michael & Aldcroft, Derek. Atlas of British Railway History. 128p. 1985. 20.50 (ISBN 0-7099-0542-4, Pub. by Croom Helm Ltd). Longwood Pub Group.
Freeman, Michael, compiled by. Critical Quarterly: Index to Volumes 1-25, 1959-83. LC 84-3881. 1984. 19.50 (ISBN 0-7190-1078-0, Pub. by Manchester Univ Pr). Longwood Pub Group.
Freeman, Michael & Robertson, David, eds. Frontiers of Political Theory: Essays in a Revitalized Discipline. LC 79-27449. 224p. 1980. 32.50x (ISBN 0-312-30920-1). St Martin.
Freeman, Michael D. & Lyon, Christina M. Cohabitation Without Marriage. 256p. 1983. text ed. 35.50x (ISBN 0-566-00455-0). Gower Pub Co.
Freeman, Michael J., jt. ed. see Aldcroft, Derek H.
Freeman, Michelle A. The Poetics of Translatio Studii & Conjointure: Chretien de Troyes's Cliges. LC 78-54262. (French Forum Monographs: No. 12). 199p. (Orig.). 1979. pap. 12.50x (ISBN 0-917058-11-9). French Forum.
Freeman, Morton. A Treasury for Word Lovers. (Professional Writing Ser.). 333p. 1983. 19.95 (ISBN 0-89495-026-6); pap. 14.95 (ISBN 0-89495-027-4). ISI Pr.
Freeman, Morton S. The Grammatical Lawyer. LC 79-50329. 350p. 1979. 20.00. Am Law Inst.
--The Story Behind the Word. (Professional Writing Ser.). 285p. 1985. 19.95 (ISBN 0-89495-046-0); pap. 14.95 (ISBN 0-89495-047-9). ISI Pr.
Freeman, Muriel, et al. The Complete Rottweiler. LC 83-22688. (Illus.). 288p. 1985. 15.95 (ISBN 0-87605-269-3). Howell Bk.
Freeman, N. T. & Whiteman, J. Introduction to Safety in the Chemical Laboratory. 1983. 33.00 (ISBN 0-12-267220-8). Acad Pr.
Freeman, Nona. The Adventures of Bug & Me. Clanton, Charles, ed. 128p. (Orig.). 1977. pap. 4.95 (ISBN 0-912315-28-8). Word Aflame.
--Box 44, Monrovia. Wallace, Mary H., ed. (Illus.). 224p. 1983. pap. 5.95 (ISBN 0-912315-09-1). Word Aflame.
--Bug & Nona on the Go. Clanton, Charles, ed. 176p. (Orig.). 1979. pap. 4.95 (ISBN 0-912315-27-X). Word Aflame.
--This Is the Day. Clanton, Charles, ed. 256p. (Orig.). 1978. pap. 4.95 (ISBN 0-912315-36-9). Word Aflame.
Freeman, Norman. Strategies of Representation in Young Children: Analysis of Spatial Skills & Drawing Processes. LC 79-40900. 1980. 59.50 (ISBN 0-12-264750-5). Acad Pr.
Freeman, Norman D., jt. auth. see Freeman, Harrop A.
Freeman, Orville. The Multinational Company: Instrument for World Growth. LC 81-717. 144p. 1981. 29.95 (ISBN 0-03-059052-3). Praeger.
Freeman, P., ed. see Interface Workshop.
Freeman, Patricia K. A Comparative Analysis of State-Local Relations. (Studies in Tennessee Politics Ser.). (Orig.). 1984. pap. 3.50 (ISBN 0-914079-10-7). Bureau Pub Admin U Tenn.
Freeman, Patricia K. & McClellan, E. Fletcher. The Consequences of Increased Legislative Oversight of Federal Funds: The Case of Tennessee. 66p. (Orig.). 1981. pap. 3.00 (ISBN 0-914079-08-5). Bureau Pub Admin U Tenn.
Freeman, Paul & De Meillon, Botha. Simuliide of the Ethiopian Region. (Illus.). vii, 224p. 1953. Repr. of 1968 ed. 24.00x (ISBN 0-565-00194-9, Pub. by Brit Mus Nat Hist). Sabbot-Natural Hist Bks.
Freeman, Paul, ed. Common Insect Pests of Stored Food Products: A Guide to Their Identification. rev., 6th ed. (Illus.). 69p. 1980. pap. 4.50x (ISBN 0-565-00830-7, Pub. by Brit Mus Nat Hist England). Sabbot-Natural Hist Bks.
Freeman, Peggotty, ed. see Center for Contemporary European Studies.
Freeman, Peter. Software Systems Principles: A Survey. LC 75-1440. (Computer Science Ser). (Illus.). 600p. 1975. text ed. 31.95 (ISBN 0-574-18000-1, 13-4000). SRA.
Freeman, Peter & Wasserman, Anthony I. Software Design Techniques. 4th ed. (Tutorial Texts Ser.). 719p. 1983. 36.00 (ISBN 0-8186-0514-6). IEEE Comp Soc.
Freeman, Phyllis, et al, eds. New Art. (Illus.). 208p. 1984. pap. 17.95 (ISBN 0-8109-2287-8). Abrams.
Freeman, R. & Pescar, S. Safe Delivery: Protect Your Baby During High Risk Pregnancy. 320p. 1983. pap. 7.95 (ISBN 0-07-022048-4). McGraw.
Freeman, R. A. Socialism & Private Enterprise in Equatorial Asia. LC 67-31386. (Studies Ser.: No. 20). 1968. 6.95x (ISBN 0-8179-3201-1). Hoover Inst Pr.
Freeman, R. Austin. The Best Dr. Thorndyke. Bleiler, E. F., ed. 14.25 (ISBN 0-8446-4739-X). Peter Smith.
--The Best Dr. Thorndyke Detective Stories. Bleiler, E. F., ed. 274p. 1973. pap. 3.95 (ISBN 0-486-20388-3). Dover.
--John Thorndyke's Cases. LC 74-10486. (Milestones of Mystery Ser). (Illus.). xi, 288p. 1975. Repr. of 1909 ed. 12.50 (ISBN 0-88355-201-9). Hyperion Conn.
--John Thorndykes Cases. 1976. lib. bdg. 12.95x (ISBN 0-89968-169-7). Lightyear.
--The Singing Bone. LC 75-44972. (Crime Fiction Ser.). 1976. Repr. of 1912 ed. lib. bdg. 21.00 (ISBN 0-8240-2367-6). Garland Pub.
--The Singing Bone. 1976. lib. bdg. 12.95x (ISBN 0-89968-168-9). Lightyear.
--The Stoneware Monkey. Bleiler, E. F., ed. Bd. with The Penrose Mystery. 1973. pap. 5.00 (ISBN 0-486-22963-7). Dover.
--The Stoneware Monkey & the Penrose Mystery: Two Dr. Thorndyke Novels. 11.25 (ISBN 0-8446-5108-7). Peter Smith.
--Uttermost Farthing. 1974. 8.50 (ISBN 0-685-41690-9). Bookfinger.
Freeman, R. B. British Natural History Books from the Beginning to Nineteen Hundred: A Handlist. LC 80-50228. 437p. 1980. 39.50 (ISBN 0-208-01790-9, Archon). Shoe String.
--The Works of Charles Darwin: An Annotated Bibliographical Handlist. rev. & 2nd ed. LC 76-30002. 235p. 1977. 24.75x (ISBN 0-208-01658-9, Pub. by St. Pauls Biblios England). U Pr of Va.
Freeman, R. D., ed. Developmental Neurobiology of Vision. LC 79-19389. (NATO ASI Series A, Life Sciences: Vol. 27). 460p. 1979. 59.50x (ISBN 0-306-40306-4, Plenum Pr). Plenum Pub.
Freeman, R. Edward. Strategic Management: A Stakeholder Approach. (Business & Public Policy Ser.). 288p. 1983. text ed. 19.95 (ISBN 0-273-01913-9). Pitman Pub MA.
Freeman, R. G. & Knox, J. M. Treatment of Skin Cancer. (Recent Results in Cancer Research: Vol. 11). (Illus.). 1967. 15.00 (ISBN 0-387-03959-7). Springer-Verlag.
Freeman, R. M. The New Boswell. 1923. Repr. 20.00 (ISBN 0-8274-3015-9). R West.
--Samuel Pepys & the Minxes. 1973. 20.00 (ISBN 0-8274-0538-3). R West.
--Samuel Pepys, Listener. 1973. Repr. of 1931 ed. 20.00 (ISBN 0-8274-0537-5). R West.
Freeman, R. R., ed. see AIP Conference Proceedings No. 90 Boulder, 1982.
Freeman, R. S. Children's Picture Books. LC 66-29514. (Victorian Culture Series). (Illus.). 1967. 15.00 (ISBN 0-87282-063-7); pap. 7.50 (ISBN 0-87282-107-2). CHB-ALF.
Freeman, Ralph E., ed. Postwar Economic Trends in the United States. LC 72-10884. (Essay Index Reprint Ser.). 1973. Repr. of 1960 ed. 19.00 (ISBN 0-8369-7216-3). Ayer Co Pubs.
Freeman, Richard. Black Elite: The New Market for Highly Educated Black Americans. LC 76-28702. pap. 67.50 (ISBN 0-317-29020-7, 2020890). Bks Demand UMI.
--How to Study Effectively. 93p. 1982. 29.00x (ISBN 0-902404-10-5, Pub. by Natl Ext England). State Mutual Bk.
Freeman, Richard B. Charles Darwin: A Companion. (Illus.). 309p. 1978. 27.50 (ISBN 0-208-01739-9, Archon). Shoe String.
--Labor Economics. 2nd ed. (Foundations of Economics Ser.). (Illus.). 1979. pap. text ed. 14.95 (ISBN 0-13-517474-0). P-H.
--Market for College-Trained Manpower: A Study in the Economics of Career Choice. LC 70-139726. 1971. 17.50x (ISBN 0-674-54976-7). Harvard U Pr.
--The Market for College-Trained Manpower: A Study in the Economics of Career Choice. LC 70-139726. pap. 73.00 (ISBN 0-317-29617-5, 2021593). Bks Demand UMI.
Freeman, Richard B. & Medoff, James L. What Do Unions Do? LC 81-68407. 293p. 1984. 22.95 (ISBN 0-465-09133-4). Basic.
--What Do Unions Do? LC 81-68407. 293p. 1985. pap. 9.95 (ISBN 0-465-09134-2, CN-5148). Basic.
Freeman, Richard B., ed. The Overeducated American. 1976. 29.50 (ISBN 0-12-267250-X); pap. 10.00 (ISBN 0-12-267252-6). Acad Pr.
Freeman, Richard H. & Wise, David A., eds. The Youth Labor Market Problem: Its Nature, Causes, & Consequences. LC 81-11438. (National Bureau of Economic Research Conference Ser.). 608p. 1982. lib. bdg. 48.00x (ISBN 0-226-26161-1). U of Chicago Pr.
Freeman, Richard T., jt. auth. see Frank, Robert H.
Freeman, Robert. Opera Without Drama: Currents of Change in Italian Opera, 1675-1725. Buelow, George, ed. LC 80-29133. (Studies in Musicology: No. 35). 358p. 1981. 84.95 (ISBN 0-8357-1152-8). UMI Res Pr.
--Yesterday-The Beatles 1963-1965. (Illus.). 96p. 1983. 10.95 (ISBN 0-03-064033-4, Owl Bks); pap. 6.95 (ISBN 0-03-000094-7). HR&W.
Freeman, Robert & Lasky, Vivienne. Hidden Treasure: Public Sculpture in Providence, Rhode Island. (Illus.). 50p. (Orig.). 1981. pap. 4.95 (ISBN 0-917012-23-2). RI Pubns Soc.
Freeman, Robert H. Requiem for a Fleet. 260p. 1984. 15.00 (ISBN 0-931099-00-5). Shellback Pr.
--Sea Tramps. 250p. 1985. write for info. (ISBN 0-931099-01-3). Shellback Pr.
Freeman, Robert H., ed. see Twain, Mark.
Freeman, Robert J., jt. auth. see Lynn, Edward S.
Freeman, Robert N. Franz Schneider (Seventeen Thirty-Seven to Eighteen Twelve) A Thematic Catalogue of His Works. (Thematic Catalogues Ser.: No. 5). 1979. lib. bdg. 36.00 (ISBN 0-918728-13-4). Pendragon NY.
Freeman, Roger. B-24 Liberator at War. (Illus.). 128p. 16.95 (ISBN 0-7110-1264-4, Pub. by Ian Allen England). Motorbooks Intl.
--A Preview & Summary of "The Wayward Welfare State". (Publication Ser.: No. 257). (Illus.). 122p. 1981. pap. 8.95x (ISBN 0-8179-7572-1). Hoover Inst Pr.
--Telecommunication System Engineering: Analog & Digital Network Design. LC 79-26661. 480p. 1980. 45.95 (ISBN 0-471-02955-6, Pub. by Wiley-Interscience). Wiley.
--The Wayward Welfare State. (Publications Ser.: No. 249). (Illus.). 544p. 1981. pap. 13.50x (ISBN 0-8179-7492-X). Hoover Inst Pr.
Freeman, Roger A. The Growth of American Government: A Morphology of the Welfare State. LC 75-10553. (Publications Ser.: No. 148). 1975. pap. 7.95x (ISBN 0-8179-6482-7). Hoover Inst Pr.
--Mighty Eighth: A History of the U. S. Eighth Air Force. LC 72-76496. 1970. 19.95 (ISBN 0-385-01168-7). Doubleday.
--Mighty Eighth War Diary. (Illus.). 240p. 1981. 29.50 (ISBN 0-86720-560-1). Jane's Pub Inc.
--Mighty Eighth War Manual. (Illus.). 320p. 1984. 29.95 (ISBN 0-7106-0325-8). Jane's Pub Inc.
Freeman, Roger D., et al. Can't Your Child Hear? LC 81-4993. (Illus.). 368p. 1981. pap. 15.00 (ISBN 0-936104-56-2). Pro Ed.
--Can't Your Child Hear? (Illus.). 368p. 1981. pap. text ed. 17.95 (ISBN 0-8391-1616-0). Univ Park.
Freeman, Roger K. & Pescar, Susan. Safe Delivery: Protecting Your Baby During High Risk Pregnancy. 320p. 1982. 14.95 (ISBN 0-87196-666-2). Facts on File.
Freeman, Roger L. English-Spanish, Spanish-English Dictionary of Communications & Electronic Terms. LC 78-152639. pap. 54.00 (ISBN 0-317-26395-1, 2024452). Bks Demand UMI.
--Reference Manual for Telecommunications. LC 84-13207. 1500p. 1984. text ed. 75.00 (ISBN 0-471-86753-5, Pub. by Wiley-Interscience). Wiley.
--Telecommunication System Engineering. 480p. 1980. 38.50 (ISBN 0-686-91743-X). Telecom Lib.
--Telecommunication Transmission Handbook. 2nd ed. LC 81-7499. 706p. 1981. 61.95x (ISBN 0-471-08029-2, Pub. by Wiley-Interscience). Wiley.
--Telecommunications Transmission Handbook. 700p. 1980. 49.50 (ISBN 0-686-98109-X). Telecom Lib.
Freeman, Roland L. Southern Roads-City Pavements: Photographs of Black Americans. 1981. pap. 12.95 (ISBN 0-933642-04-0). Intl Ctr Photo.
Freeman, Roland L., jt. ed. see Black, Patti C.
Freeman, Ronald E., ed. Bibliographies of Studies in Victorian Literature: For the Ten Years 1965-1974. LC 79-8838. 1981. 57.50 (ISBN 0-404-19562-8). AMS Pr.
Freeman, Ronald G. Intercambios: An Activities Manual. 209p. 1980. pap. text ed. 8.95 (ISBN 0-394-32425-0, RanC). Random.
Freeman, Rosemary. English Emblem Books. 1966. lib. bdg. 20.00x (ISBN 0-374-92888-6). Octagon.
Freeman, Rosemary see Muir, Kenneth.
Freeman, Russell. Animal Superstars: Biggest, Strongest, Fastest, Smartest. (Illus.). (gr. 5 up). 1981. 10.95 (ISBN 0-13-037648-5). P-H.
Freeman, Ruth. Cavalcade of Dolls: A Basic Sourcebook for Collectors. LC 75-30167. (Illus.). 200p. 1978. lib. bdg. 35.00 (ISBN 0-87282-001-7, 78282). CHB-ALF.
--Child's First Picture Book. rev. ed. 1946. 6.50 (ISBN 0-87282-064-5). CHB-ALF.
--How to Repair & Dress Dolls. LC 60-15559. (Orig.). pap. 5.00 (ISBN 0-87282-065-3, 21). CHB-ALF.
Freeman, Ruth & Freeman, Larry G. O Promise Me Picture Album. 1954. 12.00 (ISBN 0-87282-067-X). CHB-ALF.
--Yesterday's School & Yesterday's School Books, 2 Vols. LC 62-16427. 1962. Set. 15.00 (ISBN 0-686-66391-8). Vol. 1 (ISBN 0-87282-068-8). Vol. 2 (ISBN 0-87282-069-6). CHB-ALF.
Freeman, Ruth, jt. auth. see Freeman, Larry.
Freeman, Ruth, jt. auth. see Freeman, Larry G.
Freeman, Ruth B. & Heinrich, Janet. Community Health Nursing Practice. 2nd ed. (Illus.). 500p. 1981. text ed. 17.95 (ISBN 0-7216-3877-5). Saunders.
Freeman, Ruth S. Encyclopedia of American Dolls. new ed. LC 62-18403. (Illus.). 112p. 1972. 8.50 (ISBN 0-87282-070-X); pap. 4.95 (ISBN 0-87282-108-0). CHB-ALF.
Freeman, Ruth S., ed. see Johl, Janet.
Freeman, S. Natural Lifestyles Library, Vol. 2, 4 pts. pap. 12.95 ea. Pt. 1, 1972, 80p (ISBN 0-677-42005-6). Pt. 2, 1973, 80p (ISBN 0-677-42015-3). Pt. 3, 1973, 80p (ISBN 0-677-42025-0). Pt. 4, 1974, 80p (ISBN 0-677-16005-4). Gordon.
Freeman, S. David. Energy: The New Era. LC 74-9174. 1974. pap. 2.45 (ISBN 0-394-71316-8, V-316, Vin). Random.
--Energy: The New Era. LC 74-77980. 1974. 14.50 (ISBN 0-8027-0460-3). Walker & Co.
Freeman, S. T. & Walters, L. R. Europeanist Social Anthropologists in North America: A Directory. 1975. pap. 1.50 (ISBN 0-686-36564-X). Am Anthro Assn.
Freeman, Sean. Parables, Psalms, Prayers. 1985. 10.95 (ISBN 0-88347-185-X). Thomas More.
Freeman, Stanley K. Application of Laser Raman Spectroscopy. LC 73-12688. 350p. 1974. 25.00 (ISBN 0-471-27788-6). Krieger.
Freeman, Stephen A. Middlebury College Foreign Language Schools, Nineteen Fifteen to Nineteen Seventy: The Story of a Unique Idea. (Orig.). 1975. pap. 5.95x (ISBN 0-910408-17-3). Coll Store.
Freeman, Stephen A; see Bishop, G. Reginald, Jr.
Freeman, Stephen A; see Kellenberger, Hunter.
Freeman, Stephen W. Does Your Child Have a Learning Disability? Questions Answered for Parents. 128p. 1974. spiral 13.75x (ISBN 0-398-03073-1). C C Thomas.
--The Epileptic in Home, School & Society: Coping with the Invisible Handicap. 304p. 1979. 30.50x (ISBN 0-398-03870-8). C C Thomas.
Freeman, Susan T. Neighbors: The Social Contract in a Castilian Hamlet. LC 70-125548. 1970. 17.50x (ISBN 0-226-26169-7). U of Chicago Pr.
--The Pasiegos: Spaniards in No Man's Land. LC 78-13928. (Illus.). 1979. lib. bdg. 26.00x (ISBN 0-226-26173-5). U of Chicago Pr.
Freeman, T. L., jt. auth. see Delves, L. M.
Freeman, T. M. & Gregg, O. W, eds. Sodium Intake: Dietary Concerns. LC 81-71372. 161p. 1982. member 18.00 (ISBN 0-913250-26-0); non-member 24.00. Am Assn Cereal Chem.
Freeman, T. W. Geographers: Bibliographical Studies. (The Geographers Ser.: Vol. 8). 159p. 1984. pap. 34.00x (ISBN 0-7201-1705-4). Mansell.
--Geographers: Biobibliographical Studies, Vol. 7. 176p. 1983. 34.00x (ISBN 0-7201-1684-8). Mansell.

--The Geographer's Craft. 215p. 1967. text ed. 13.50 (ISBN 0-7190-0055-6, Pub. by Manchester Univ Pr). Longwood Pub Group.

Freeman, T. W., ed. Geographers: Biobibliographical Studies, Vol. 5. 160p. 1982. 34.00 (ISBN 0-7201-1635-X). Mansell.

--Geographers: Biobibliographical Studies, Vol. 6. (Illus.). 152p. 1983. pap. 34.00x (ISBN 0-7201-1664-3). Mansell.

Freeman, T. W. & Pinchemel, Philippe, eds. Geographers: Biobibliographical Studies, Vol. 2. (Illus.). 160p. 1978. pap. 34.00x (ISBN 0-7201-0710-5). Mansell.

--Geographers: Biobibliographical Studies, Vol. 4. (Illus.). 168p. 1980. pap. text ed. 34.00x (ISBN 0-7201-1584-1). Mansell.

Freeman, T. W., et al, eds. Geographers Biobibliographical Studies, Vol. 1. Oughton, Marguerita & Pinchemel, Philippe. (Illus.). 138p. 1977. pap. 34.00x (ISBN 0-7201-0637-0). Mansell.

--Geographers: Biobibliographical Studies, Vol. 3. (Illus.). 184p. 1979. pap. 34.00x (ISBN 0-7201-0927-2). Mansell.

Freeman, Thomas. Childhood Psychopathology & Adult Psychoses. LC 75-31854. 1976. text ed. 30.00 (ISBN 0-8236-0775-5). Intl Univs Pr.

--A Psychoanalytic Study of the Psychoses. LC 72-80551. 1973. text ed. 30.00 (ISBN 0-8236-4977-6). Intl Univs Pr.

--Psychopathology of the Psychoses. LC 72-86647. 1969. text ed. 30.00 (ISBN 0-8236-5670-5). Intl Univs Pr.

Freeman, Thomas & Custis, Peter. An Account of the Red River in Louisiana. 12.00 (ISBN 0-87770-328-0). Ye Galleon.

--Jefferson & Southwestern Exploration: The Freeman & Custis Accounts of the Red River Expedition of 1806. Flores, Dan L., ed. LC 83-47833. (The American Exploration & Travel Ser.: Vol. 67). (Illus.). 406p. 1984. 48.50x (ISBN 0-8061-1748-6). U of Okla Pr.

Freeman, Thomas, et al. Chronic Schizophrenia. 1966. text ed. 20.00 (ISBN 0-8236-0860-3). Intl Univs Pr.

--Studies on Psychosis: Descriptive, Psychoanalytic, & Psychological Aspects. LC 65-25672. 1966. text ed. 20.00 (ISBN 0-8236-6220-9). Intl Univs Pr.

Freeman, Tina. The Photographs of Mother St. Croix. LC 82-61400. (Illus.). 39p. 1982. pap. 8.95 (ISBN 0-89494-015-5). New Orleans Mus Art.

Freeman, Tony. Aircraft That Work for Us. LC 80-23078. (On the Move Ser.). (Illus.). 48p. (gr. 3-6). 1981. PLB 10.60 (ISBN 0-516-03888-5); pap. 2.95 (ISBN 0-516-43888-3). Childrens.

--Beginning Backpacking. LC 80-12379. (Sports for Everyone Ser.). (Illus.). 48p. (gr. 3 up). 1980. PLB 10.60 (ISBN 0-516-04372-2); pap. 2.95 (ISBN 0-516-44372-0). Childrens.

--Beginning Bicycle Motocross. LC 82-17822. (Sports For Everyone Ser.). (Illus.). 48p. (gr. 3 up). 1983. PLB 10.60 (ISBN 0-516-04374-9). Childrens.

--Beginning Surfing. LC 79-26609. (Sports for Everyone Ser.). (Illus.). 48p. (gr. 3 up). 1980. PLB 10.60 (ISBN 0-516-04373-0). Childrens.

--Blimps. LC 78-38826. (On the Move Ser.). (Illus.). 48p. (gr. 3-6). 1979. PLB 10.60 (ISBN 0-516-03882-6); pap. 2.95 (ISBN 0-516-43882-4). Childrens.

--Hot Air Balloons. LC 82-22087. (On the Move Ser.). (Illus.). 48p. (gr. 3-6). 1983. PLB 10.60 (ISBN 0-516-03891-5). Childrens.

--Photography. LC 83-7359. (New True Bks.). (Illus.). 48p. (gr. k-4). 1983. PLB 10.60 (ISBN 0-516-01704-7). Childrens.

Freeman, Vicki & Adams, Suzy. Why Won't My Teeter-Totter? (Illus.). 48p. (YA) 1972. 2.50 (ISBN 0-8065-0269-X). Citadel Pr.

Freeman, Victoria. You Thought I Would Never Leave You. (Illus.). 64p. 1973. 4.00 (ISBN 0-8065-0366-1). Citadel Pr.

Freeman, Vivian & Callahan, Betsy N. Career Planning for Women. LC 78-53905. (Workshop Models for Family Life Education Ser.). 151p. 1978. Plastic comb 14.95 (ISBN 0-87304-159-3). Family Serv.

Freeman, W. H. & Bracegirdle, Brian. An Advanced Atlas of Histology. (Heinemann Biology Atlases Ser.). 1976. text ed. 17.50x (ISBN 0-435-60317-5). Heinemann Ed.

--An Atlas of Embryology. 3rd ed. (Heinemann Biology Atlases Ser.). 1978. text ed. 15.50x (ISBN 0-435-60318-3). Heinemann Ed.

--An Atlas of Histology. 2nd ed. (Heinemann Biology Atlases Ser.). 1967. 12.50x (ISBN 0-435-60324-8). Heinemann Ed.

--An Atlas of Invertebrate Structure. (Heinemann Biology Atlases Ser.). 1971. 12.50x (ISBN 0-435-60319-1). Heinemann Ed.

Freeman, W. H., jt. auth. see Keller, Evelyn F.

Freeman, Walter & Watts, James W. Psychosurgery: In the Treatment of Mental Disorders & Intractable Pain. 2nd ed. (Illus.). 638p. 1951. photocopy ed. 54.75x (ISBN 0-398-00614-8). C C Thomas.

Freeman, Walter J. Mass Action in the Nervous System: Examination of the Neurophysiological Basis of Adaptive Behavior Through the EEG. 1975. 78.00 (ISBN 0-12-267150-3). Acad Pr.

Freeman, Warren S., jt. auth. see Barbour, Harriet.

Freeman, Will & Freeman, Evelyn. Plyometrics. 54p. (Orig.). 1984. pap. 5.95 (ISBN 0-89279-068-7). Championship Bks.

Freeman, William. The Human Approach to Literature. 1973. lib. bdg. 12.50 (ISBN 0-8414-4252-7). Folcroft.

--Human Approach to Literature. LC 72-105788. 1970. Repr. of 1933 ed. 22.50x (ISBN 0-8046-0953-5, Pub. by Kennikat). Assoc Faculty Pr.

--The Life of Lord Alfred Douglas: Spoilt Child of Genius. 1948. Repr. 20.00 (ISBN 0-8274-2893-6). R West.

Freeman, William, compiled by. Dictionary of Fictional Characters. rev. ed. 1973. 13.95 (ISBN 0-87116-085-4). Writer.

Freeman, William H. Physical Education & Sports in a Changing Society. 2nd ed. LC 81-67688. 1982. text ed. 14.95x (ISBN 0-8087-0690-X). Burgess.

Freeman-Grenville, G. The East African Coast: Select Documents. 39.00x (ISBN 0-317-20261-8, Pub. by R Collings UK). State Mutual Bk.

Freeman-Grenville, G. S. Atlas of British History. (Illus.). 92p. 1979. 16.50x (ISBN 0-8476-6197-0); pap. 8.95x (ISBN 0-8476-6198-9). Rowman.

--The Beauty of Cairo. (Illus.). 130p. 1984. pap. 8.95 (ISBN 0-317-06379-0, 6193-7). Ungar.

--The Beauty of Jerusalem. (Illus.). 127p. 1984. pap. 8.95 (ISBN 0-317-06378-2, 6197-X). Ungar.

--Chronology of World History: A Calendar of Principal Events from 3000 BC to AD 1976. 2nd ed. 746p. 1978. 45.00x (ISBN 0-8476-6040-0). Rowman.

--The Mombasa Rising Against the Portuguese, Sixteen Thirty-One: From Sworn Evidence. (British Academy-Fontes Historiae Africanae). (Illus.). 1980. 102.00x (ISBN 0-19-725992-8). Oxford U Pr.

--The Muslim & Christian Calendars: Being Tables for the Conversion of Muslim & Christian Dates from the Hijra to the Year A. D. 2000. 2nd ed. 87p. 1977. 7.50x (ISBN 0-8476-1482-4). Rowman.

Freeman-Grenville, G. S., tr. The Wonders of India. 124p. 1982. 35.00x (ISBN 0-85692-063-0, Pub. by E-W Pubns England). State Mutual Bk.

Freeman-Grenville, G. S. P., ed. Memoirs of An Arabian Princess. (Illus.). 308p. 1982. 17.95 (ISBN 0-85692-062-2, Pub. by Salem Hse). Merrimack Pub Cir.

Freeman-Moir, John D., jt. auth. see Broughton, John M.

Freemantle. The Lost American. 3.50 (ISBN 0-317-31799-7). Tor Bks.

Freemantle, Alfred, tr. see Leonid, Sobolev.

Freemantle, Brian. Charlie M. 1982. pap. 2.25 (ISBN 0-345-30611-2). Ballantine.

--Charlie Muffin U. S. A. 208p. 1982. pap. 2.50 (ISBN 0-345-29440-8). Ballantine.

--CIA. (Illus.). 224p. 1983. 17.95 (ISBN 0-8128-2947-6). Stein & Day.

--Deaken's War. 288p. 1985. pap. 3.50 (ISBN 0-8125-8252-7). Tor Bks.

--Here Comes Charlie M. 1979. pap. 1.95 (ISBN 0-345-28337-6). Ballantine.

--The Inscrutable Charlie Muffin. 182p. 1981. pap. 2.25 (ISBN 0-345-28854-8). Ballantine.

--KGB. LC 81-23205. (Illus.). 192p. 1982. 14.95 (ISBN 0-03-062458-4); pap. 6.95 (ISBN 0-03-071059-6). HR&W.

--The Lost American. (Orig.). 1984. pap. 3.50 (ISBN 0-8125-8250-0). Tor Bks.

--Vietnam Legacy. 384p. (Orig.). 1984. pap. 3.50 (ISBN 0-8125-0284-1). Tor Bks.

Freemantle, David. Superboss: The A-Z of Managing People Successfully. 300p. 1985. text ed. 23.50x (ISBN 0-566-02588-4). Gower Pub Co.

Freemesser, Bernard. An Oregon Experience. Beltran, George, ed. LC 78-73426. (Illus.). 1979. 19.95 (ISBN 0-918966-04-3). Image West.

Freemon, B. M., jt. ed. see Bell, D. J.

Freemon, David. Secrets of the Super Athletes: Tips for Fans & Players-Basketball. (Illus., Orig.). (gr. 7 up). 1982. pap. 1.95 (ISBN 0-440-97647-2, LFL). Dell.

Freemon, Frank R. Organic Mental Disease. LC 79-23180. (Illus.). 248p. 1981. text ed. 30.00 (ISBN 0-89335-109-1). SP Med & Sci Bks.

--Sleep Research: A Critical Review. (Illus.). 220p. 1974. 19.75x (ISBN 0-398-02540-1). C C Thomas.

Freeny, Patrick C. & Lawson, Thomas L. Radiology of the Pancreas. (Illus.). 624p. 1982. 140.00 (ISBN 0-387-90649-5). Springer-Verlag.

Freer, Carolee. Practice Dictation for Computer Shorthand: Skill Building & Transcription. (Computer Shorthand Ser.). 25p. 1984. pap. 295.00 (ISBN 0-471-80661-7). Wiley.

--Practice Dictation for Computer Shorthand: Speed Building & Transcription. (Computer Shorthand Ser.). 25p. Date not set. pap. 295.00 (ISBN 0-471-80658-7). Wiley.

Freer, Carolee, jt. auth. see Roberts, Alan.

Freer, Coburn. The Poetics of Jacobean Drama. LC 81-47599. 288p. 1982. text ed. 26.00x (ISBN 0-8018-2545-8). Johns Hopkins.

Freer, M. The Life of Marguerite D'Angouleme, Queen of Navarre, 2 vols. 1976. lib. bdg. 250.00 (ISBN 0-8490-2166-9). Gordon Pr.

Freericks, Mary & Segal, Joyce. Creative Puppetry in the Classroom. (Illus.). 148p. 1979. pap. 6.95 (ISBN 0-932720-15-3). New Plays Bks.

Freerksen, E., ed. see International Colloquium, Borstel, 1968.

Frees, Jane A. Dear Dad, Love, Jane. LC 80-68081. (Illus.). 1980. 4.95 (ISBN 0-8323-0361-5). Binford.

Frees, John Da see John, Da Free.

Freese, Arthur. Help for Your Arthritis & Rheumatism. (Orig.). 1978. pap. 2.25 (ISBN 0-451-11063-3, AE1063, Sig). NAL.

Freese, Arthur J. The Miracle of Vision. LC 76-26226. 1977. 12.45i (ISBN 0-06-011371-5, HarpT). Har-Row.

Freese, Arthur S. Help for Your Grief: Turning Emotional Loss into Growth. LC 76-44538. 1977. 9.95 (ISBN 0-8052-3640-6). Schocken.

--Managing Your Doctor: How to Get Best Possible Medical Care. LC 74-78534. 1977. pap. 2.95 (ISBN 0-8128-2342-7). Stein & Day.

--The Prime of Your Life: The Book That Makes Old Age Obsolete. LC 77-90662. Orig. Title: The End of Senility. 192p. 1981. pap. 5.95 (ISBN 0-87795-316-3). Arbor Hse.

Freese, Doris. Children's Church: A Comprehensive How-to. LC 81-22426. 128p. 1982. pap. 5.95 (ISBN 0-8024-1250-5). Moody.

--Vacation Bible School. LC 77-76179. 96p. 1977. pap. text ed. 4.95 (ISBN 0-910566-11-9); Perfect bdg. instr's. guide by Werner Graendorf 4.95 (ISBN 0-910566-27-5). Evang Tchr.

Freese, J. H., tr. see Licht, Hans.

Freese, Jan. International Data Flow. 71p. (Orig.). 1979. pap. text ed. 9.95x (ISBN 0-86238-010-3, Pub. by Chartwell Bratt England). Brookfield Pub Co.

Freese, Lee, ed. Theoretical Methods in Sociology: Seven Essays. LC 79-3998. 1980. 27.95x (ISBN 0-8229-3402-7). U of Pittsburgh Pr.

Freese, Marjorie & Duncan, Sylvia. How to Start a Consignment Shop & Make It Go. LC 84-50208. (Illus.). 112p. 1984. lib. bdg. 13.95 (ISBN 0-916317-01-3); pap. 6.95 (ISBN 0-916317-00-5). Sylvan Bks.

Freese, R. S. The Structure of Modular Lattices of Width Four with Applications to Varieties of Lattices. LC 76-49468. (Memoirs: No. 181). 91p. 1977. pap. 13.00 (ISBN 0-8218-2181-4, MEMO-181). Am Math.

Freese, R. S. & Garcia, O. C., eds. Universal Algebra & Lattice Theory. (Lecture Notes in Mathematics Ser.: Vol. 1004). 308p. 1983. pap. 17.00 (ISBN 0-387-12329-6). Springer-Verlag.

Freeston, Ewart Co & Kent, Bernard. Modelling Thames Sailing Barges. 96p. 1980. 15.00x (ISBN 0-85177-091-6, Pub. by Cornell England). State Mutual Bk.

Freestone, John & Drummond, eds. Enrico Caruso: His Recorded Legacy. LC 77-27296. (Illus.). 1978. Repr. of 1961 ed. lib. bdg. 22.50x (ISBN 0-313-20177-3, FREC). Greenwood.

Freeth, John. The Political Songster. (Folklore Ser.). 1790. 20.00 (ISBN 0-8482-3996-2). Norwood Edns.

Freeth, Zahra & Winstone, Victor. Explorers of Arabia: From the Renaissance to the Victorian Era. LC 77-15632. (Illus.). 308p. 1978. text ed. 36.00x (ISBN 0-8419-0354-9). Holmes & Meier.

Freeth, Zahra, ed. see Dickson, H. R.

Freethy, Ron. British Birds in Their Habitats. (Illus.). 224p. 1985. 25.00 (ISBN 0-88072-069-7, Pub. by Tanager). Longwood Pub Group.

--How Birds Work: A Guide to Bird Biology. (Illus.). 182p. 1982. 15.95 (ISBN 0-7137-1156-6, Pub. by Blandford Pr England). Sterling.

--How Birds Work: A Guide to Bird Biology. (Illus.). 182p. 1982. pap. 8.95 (ISBN 0-7137-1422-0, Pub. by Blandford Pr England). Sterling.

--The Making of the British Countryside. LC 80-68688. (Illus.). 192p. 1981. 24.00 (ISBN 0-7153-8012-5). David & Charles.

--The Naturalist's Guide to the British Coastline. (Illus.). 192p. 1983. 22.50 (ISBN 0-7153-8342-6). David & Charles.

Freeze, Allan, jt. ed. see Back, William R.

Freeze, Gregory L. The Parish Clergy in Nineteenth-Century Russia: Crisis, Reform, Counter-Reform. LC 82-61361. 552p. 1983. 50.00x (ISBN 0-691-05381-2). Princeton U Pr.

--The Russian Levites: Parish Clergy in the Eighteenth Century. (Russian Research Center Studies: 78). 1977. 20.00x (ISBN 0-674-78175-9). Harvard U Pr.

Freeze, Gregory L., ed. see Belliustin, I. S.

Freeze, R. A. & Back, W., eds. Physical Hydrogeology. LC 82-2976. (Benchmark Papers in Geology: Vol. 72). 431p. 1983. 48.00 (ISBN 0-87933-431-2). Van Nos Reinhold.

Freeze, R. Allan & Cherry, John A. Groundwater. (Illus.). 1979. text ed. 45.95 (ISBN 0-13-365312-9). P-H.

Freeze, R. Allan, jt. ed. see Narasimhan, T. N.

Freeze, Ray A., ed. A Fragment of an Early K'EKCHI' Vocabulary. LC 76-365636. (Monographs in Anthropology: No.2). (Illus.). iv, 70p. 1975. pap. 4.20x (ISBN 0-913134-95-3). Mus Anthro Mo.

Frege, Gottlob. The Basic Laws of Arithmetic: Exposition of the System. Furth, Montgomery, ed. & tr. (gr. 9-12). 1965. 14.00x (ISBN 0-520-00432-9). U of Cal Pr.

--The Basic Laws of Arithmetic: Exposition of the System. Furth, Montgomery, ed. (California Library Reprint Ser.: No. 116). 208p. 1982. 19.50x (ISBN 0-520-04761-3). U of Cal Pr.

--Collected Papers on Mathematics, Logic & Philosophy. McGuinness, Brian, ed. 416p. 1985. 39.95x (ISBN 0-631-12728-3). Basil Blackwell.

--Conceptual Notation & Related Articles. Bynum, Terrell W., ed. 1972. 55.00x (ISBN 0-19-824359-6). Oxford U Pr.

--Foundations of Arithmetic: A Logico-Mathematical Enquiry into the Concept of Numbers. Austin, J. L., tr. LC 68-8996. (Eng. & Ger.). 1968. 17.95 (ISBN 0-8101-0023-1); pap. 9.95 (ISBN 0-8101-0605-1). Northwestern U Pr.

--The Philosophical & Mathematical Correspondence. McGuinness, Brian, ed. Kaal, Hans, tr. LC 79-23199. 1980. lib. bdg. 31.00x (ISBN 0-226-26197-2). U of Chicago Pr.

--Posthumous Writings. Hermes, Hans, et al, eds. White, Roger & Long, Peter, trs. LC 79-10986. 1979. Repr. lib. bdg. 35.00x (ISBN 0-226-26199-9). U of Chicago Pr.

--Translations from the Philosophical Writings of Gottlob Frege. 3rd ed. Geach, Peter & Black, Max, eds. 228p. 1980. 25.00x (ISBN 0-8476-6286-1); pap. 10.95x (ISBN 0-8476-6287-X). Rowman.

Fregel, Louis E., Jr. & Fregel, Louis E. Compaq Users Handbook. LC 84-50647. 15.95 (ISBN 0-672-22037-7). Sams.

Fregert, S., et al. Patch Testing. LC 75-2387. (Illus.). 100p. 1975. pap. 18.00 (ISBN 0-387-07229-2). Springer-Verlag.

Fregert, Sigfrid. Manual of Contact Dermatitis. 1981. 16.95 (ISBN 0-8151-3282-4). Year Bk Med.

Fregly, Bert. Help Wanted: Everything You Need to Know to Get the Job You Deserve. 1980. 19.95 (ISBN 0-88280-070-1); pap. 11.95 (ISBN 0-88280-071-X). ETC Pubns.

--How to Be Self-Employed. LC 75-42017. 1977. 17.95 (ISBN 0-88280-031-0). ETC Pubns.

--How to Cast Your Own Horoscope. Baker-Carr, Sally, ed. LC 75-21892. 1976. 19.95 (ISBN 0-87949-053-5). Ashley Bks.

Fregly, M. J. & Luttge, W. G. Human Endocrinology: An Interactive Text. 366p. 1982. 27.50 (ISBN 0-444-00662-1, Biomedical Pr). Elsevier.

Fregly, Melvin & Kare, Morley. The Role of Salt in Cardiovascular Hypertension. (Nutrition Foundation Ser.). 473p. 1982. 49.50 (ISBN 0-12-267280-1). Acad Pr.

Fregosi, Claudia. Almira's Violets. LC 75-26996. (Illus.). 32p. (gr. k-3). 1976. lib. bdg. 11.88 (ISBN 0-688-84028-0). Greenwillow.

Freher, Dionysius. Freher's Analogy. Barrett, Francis, ed. (Alchemical Treatise Ser.: No. 2). 1983. pap. 1.95 (ISBN 0-916411-10-9, Pub. by Alchemical Pr). Holmes Pub.

Frehland, E. Stochastic Transport Processes in Discrete Biological Systems. (Lecture Notes in Biomathematics Ser.: Vol. 47). 169p. 1982. pap. 13.00 (ISBN 0-387-11964-7). Springer-Verlag.

Frehland, E., ed. Synergetics: From Microscopic to Macroscopic Order. (Springer Series in Synergetics: Vol. 22). (Illus.). 280p. 1984. 36.00 (ISBN 0-387-13131-0). Springer-Verlag.

Frehn, Harry R., jt. auth. see Holoviak, Stephen J.

Frehse, H. & Geissbuhler, H., eds. Pesticide Residues: A Contribution to Their Interpretation, Relevance & Legislation. (International Union of Pure & Applied Chemistry). 1979. text ed. 44.00 (ISBN 0-08-023931-5). Pergamon.

Frehse, J. & Pallaschke, D. Special Topics of Applied Mathematics: Functional Analysis, Numerical Analysis & Optimization. 248p. 1980. 59.75 (ISBN 0-444-86035-5, North-Holland). Elsevier.

Frei, Daniel. Assumptions & Perceptions in Disarmament. 321p. pap. 14.00 (UN84/0/4, UN). Unipub.

--Managing International Crisis. (Advances in Political Science: An International Ser.: Vol. 2). 1982. 25.00 (ISBN 0-8039-1849-6). Sage.

--Perceived Images: U. S. & Soviet Assumptions & Perceptions in Disarmament. LC 85-14207. 344p. 1985. text ed. 26.50x (ISBN 0-8476-7443-6). Rowman & Allanheld.

--Risks of Unintentional Nuclear War. 255p. 1982. 19.00x (ISBN 0-8002-3317-4). Intl Pubns Serv.

Frei, Daniel & Catrina, Christian. Risks of Unintentional Nuclear War. LC 82-16333. 288p. 1983. pap. text ed. 12.50 (ISBN 0-86598-106-X). Allanheld.

--Risks of Unintentional Nuclear War. 255p. 1983. pap. 19.00 (ISBN 0-86598-106-X, UN82/0/1, UN). Unipub.

--Risks of Unintentional Nuclear War. 19.00 (ISBN 0-686-84919-1, E.82.O.1). UN.

Frei, Daniel & Ruloff, Dieter. East-West Relations: Vol. 1, A Systematic Survey. LC 81-22356. 324p. 1983. 35.00 (ISBN 0-89946-136-0). Oelgeschlager.

--East-West Relations: Vol. 2, Methodology & Data. LC 81-22356. 350p. 1983. 35.00 (ISBN 0-89946-137-9). Oelgeschlager.

Frei, Daniel, ed. Definitions & Measurements of Detente: East & West Perspectives. LC 80-27960. 224p. 1981. text ed. 30.00 (ISBN 0-89946-080-1). Oelgeschlager.

Frei, Eduardo. Latin America: The Hopeful Option. Drury, John, tr. from Sp. LC 78-1358. Orig. Title: Americana Latina: Opinion y esperanza. 287p. (Orig.). 1978. pap. 7.95 (ISBN 0-88344-277-9). Orbis Bks.
--The Mandate of History & Chile's Future. Walker, Thomas W., ed. D'Escoto, Miguel, tr. from Sp. LC 77-620018. (Papers in International Studies: Latin America Ser.: No. 1). (Illus.). 1977. pap. 8.00x (ISBN 0-89680-066-0, 82-92526, Ohio U Ctr Intl). Ohio U Pr.
Frei, Emil, 3rd, jt. ed. see Holland, James F.
Frei, Ernest J. The Historical Development of the Philippine National Language. LC 77-86950. (Anthro Ser.). Repr. of 1959 ed. 16.50 (ISBN 0-404-16710-1). AMS Pr.
Frei, Hans. Lake Lucerne. (Panorama Bks.). (Illus., Fr.). 1966. 3.95 (ISBN 0-685-11286-1). French & Eur.
Frei, Hans W. The Eclipse of Biblical Narrative: A Study in Eighteenth & Nineteenth-Century Hermeneutics. LC 73-86893. 384p. 1974. pap. 9.95x (ISBN 0-300-02602-1). Yale U Pr.
Frei, R. W. & Brinkman, U. A. Analysis & Chemistry of Water Pollutants. LC 83-5556. (Current Topics in Enviromental & Toxicological Chemistry Ser.: Vol. 6). (Illus.). 304p. 1983. 49.50 (ISBN 0-677-06150-1). Gordon.
Frei, R. W., jt. auth. see Lawrence, J. F.
Frei, R. W. & Hutzinger, Otto, eds. Analytical Aspects of Mercury & Other Heavy Metals in the Environment. LC 73-88229. (Current Topics in Environmental & Toxicological Chemistry Ser.). 204p. 1975. 48.75 (ISBN 0-677-15890-4). Gordon.
Frei, R. W. & Lawrence, J. F., eds. Chemical Derivatization in Analytical Chemistry, Vol. 1: Chromatography. LC 81-5901. 356p. 1981. 49.50x (ISBN 0-306-40608-X, Plenum Pr). Plenum Pub.
--Chemical Derivization in Analytical Chemistry, Vol. 2: Separation & Continuous Flow Techniques. LC 81-5901. (Modern Analytical Chemistry Ser.). 310p. 1982. 45.00x (ISBN 0-306-40966-6, Plenum Pr). Plenum Pub.
Frei, Roland W., ed. Recent Advances in Environmental Analysis. (Current Topics in Environmental & Toxicological Chemistry Ser.: Vol.2). 362p. 1979. 80.95 (ISBN 0-677-15950-1). Gordon.
Freiberg, Arie, jt. auth. see Fox, Richard.
Freiberg, J. W. The French Press: Class, State, & Ideology. LC 80-25581. 350p. 1981. 36.95 (ISBN 0-03-058309-8). Praeger.
Freiberg, J. W., ed. Critical Sociology. 418p. 1979. 39.50x (ISBN 0-8290-0862-4). Irvington.
--Critical Sociology. 418p. pap. text ed. cancelled (ISBN 0-8290-1038-6). Irvington.
Freiberg, Karen L. Human Development: A Life-Span Approach. 2nd ed. LC 82-24736. 600p. 1983. text ed. 22.25 pub net (ISBN 0-534-01413-5). Brooks-Cole.
--Human Development: A Lifespan Approach. LC 78-14741. (Illus.). 1979. write for info. (ISBN 0-87872-177-0). Wadsworth Pub.
Freiberg, Malcolm, ed. The Generations Joined: Winthrops in America. (Massachusetts Historical Society Picture Bks.). 24p. 1977. 2.50 (ISBN 0-686-10134-0). Mass Hist Soc.
--Massachusetts Historical Society Proceedings, Vol. 95. 214p. 1984. 25.00 (ISBN 0-318-01049-6); pap. 20.00 (ISBN 0-318-01050-X). Mass Hist Soc.
--Stephen Thomas Riley: The Years of Stewardship. (Illus.). 121p. 1976. pap. 10.00 (ISBN 0-686-10136-7). Mass Hist Soc.
Freiberg, Malcolm, ed. see Knight, Sarah K.
Freiberg, Marcos A. Snakes of South America. (Illus.). 192p. 1982. 14.95 (ISBN 0-87666-912-7, PS-758). TFH Pubns.
--Turtles of South America. (Illus.). 128p. 1981. 14.95 (ISBN 0-87666-913-5, PS-757). TFH Pubns.
Freiberg, Marcos A. & Walls, Jerry G. The World of Venomous Animals. (Illus.). 192p. 1984. 19.95 (ISBN 0-87666-567-9, H-1068). TFH Pubns.
Freiberger, Nancy & Vy Thi Be. Nung Fan Slihng Vocabulary. 353p. 1976. microfiche (4) 4.73 (ISBN 0-88312-337-1). Summer Inst Ling.
Freiberger, Paul & McNeill, Dan. The Apple IIc: Your First Computer. Compute Editors, ed. (Orig.). 1985. pap. 9.95 (ISBN 0-87455-001-7). Compute Pubns.
Freiberger, Paul & Swaine, Michael. Fire in the Valley: The Making of The Personal Computer. 300p. (Orig.). 1984. pap. 9.95 (ISBN 0-07-881121-X, 121-X). Osborne-McGraw.
Freiberger, Robert H. & Kaye, Jeremy J., eds. Arthrography. (Illus.). 300p. 1979. 61.00 (ISBN 0-8385-0423-X). ACC.
Freiberger, Stephen & Chew, Paul. A Consumer's Guide to Personal Computing & Microcomputers. 208p. pap. 13.95 (5132). Hayden.
Freiberger, Walter see Alt, Franz L., et al.
Freiberger, Walter, et al, eds. Statistical Methods for the Evaluation of Computer Systems Performance. 1972. 68.00 (ISBN 0-12-266950-9). Acad Pr.
Freiberger, Waltraud & Gschwind, Brigitte B. So schreibt man Briefe besser. 128p. (Ger.). 1977. pap. 2.50 (ISBN 3-581-66301-5). Langenscheidt.
Freibert, Lucy M. & White, Barbara A., eds. Hidden Hands: An Anthology of American Women Writers, 1790 to 1870. (The Douglass Ser.). (Illus.). 400p. 1985. text ed. 30.00 (ISBN 0-317-18051-7); pap. text ed. 14.00 (ISBN 0-8135-1089-9). Rutgers U Pr.
Freiburger, Phyllis, ed. see Times Mirror Press Staff.
Freid, Allan N. & Mehr, Edwin B. Low Vision Care. LC 74-17532. 1975. 44.00 (ISBN 0-87873-016-8). Prof Press.
Freiday, Dean, ed. Barclay's Apology in Modern English. 1980. 27.00x (ISBN 0-686-87283-5, Pub. by W Sessions). State Mutual Bk.
Freidberg & Hanawalt. DNA Repair, Pt. 1A. 312p. 1981. pap. 49.75 (ISBN 0-8247-7248-2). Dekker.
Freidel, David A. Cozumel: Late Maya Settlement Patterns (Monograph) Sabloff, Jeremy A., ed. LC 83-12222. (Studies in Archaeology Ser.). 1984. 31.00 (ISBN 0-12-266980-0). Acad Pr.
Freidel, F., ed. see Acena, Albert.
Freidel, F., et al, eds. Official Papers of Presidents Roosevelt, Truman, Eisenhower, Kennedy & Johnson. (The Presidential Documents Ser.). 1980. 8710.00 (ISBN 0-89093-351-0). U Pubns Amer.
Freidel, Frank. America in the Twentieth Century. 5th, rev. ed. 1982. (KnopfC); pap. text ed. 17.00 (ISBN 0-394-32780-2). Knopf.
--Francis Lieber: Nineteenth Century Liberal. (Illus.). 11.75 (ISBN 0-8446-0632-4). Peter Smith.
--Franklin D. Roosevelt, Vol. 1: The Apprenticeship. (Illus.). 1952. 15.00 (ISBN 0-316-29304-0). Little.
--Franklin D. Roosevelt, Vol. 2: The Ordeal. (Illus.). 1954. 15.00 (ISBN 0-316-29305-9). Little.
--Franklin D. Roosevelt, Vol. 3: The Triumph. (Illus.). 1956. 15.00 (ISBN 0-316-29306-7). Little.
--Franklin D. Roosevelt, Vol. 4: Launching the New Deal. LC 52-5521. 1973. 15.00 (ISBN 0-316-29303-2); pap. 8.95 (ISBN 0-316-29302-4). Little.
--Our Country's Presidents. 9th ed. LC 66-18847. (Special Publications Ser.). (Illus.). 1973. avail. only from Natl. Geog. 6.95 (ISBN 0-87044-024-1). Natl Geog.
--Presidents of the United States. LC 81-81182. 87p. 1981. 8.00 (ISBN 0-318-11819-X). Gov Printing Office.
Freidel, Frank, jt. auth. see Minton, John D.
Freidel, Frank & Showman, Richard K., eds. Harvard Guide to American History, 2 vols. rev. ed. LC 72-81272. 1312p. 1974. 60.00x (ISBN 0-674-37560-2, Belknap Pr); pap. text ed. 15.00 one-vol. ed. (ISBN 0-674-37555-6). Harvard U Pr.
Freidel, Frank, ed. see Allen, Donald R.
Freidel, Frank, ed. see Beyer, Barry K.
Freidel, Frank, ed. see Boylan, James.
Freidel, Frank, ed. see Brye, David L.
Freidel, Frank, ed. see Carlisle, Rodney P.
Freidel, Frank, ed. see Cebula, James E.
Freidel, Frank, ed. see Chapman, Richard N.
Freidel, Frank, ed. see Christie, Jean.
Freidel, Frank, ed. see Curry, E. R.
Freidel, Frank, ed. see Davis, Polly Ann.
Freidel, Frank, ed. see Dembo, Jonathan.
Freidel, Frank, ed. see Eldot, Paula.
Freidel, Frank, ed. see Elson, Ruth Miller.
Freidel, Frank, ed. see Harry, Jeffrey.
Freidel, Frank, ed. see Hoover, Clark H.
Freidel, Frank, ed. see Jacobs, Travis B.
Freidel, Frank, ed. see Judd, Richard M.
Freidel, Frank, ed. see Keller, Richard C.
Freidel, Frank, ed. see Kesselman, Steven.
Freidel, Frank, ed. see Killigrew, John W.
Freidel, Frank, ed. see Kurtz, Micheal J.
Freidel, Frank, ed. see Lear, Linda J.
Freidel, Frank, ed. see McCreesh, Carolyn D.
Freidel, Frank, ed. see May, Dean L.
Freidel, Frank, ed. see Moley, Raymond.
Freidel, Frank, ed. see Montalto, Nicholas V.
Freidel, Frank, ed. see Mulder, Ronald A.
Freidel, Frank, ed. see Nordhauser, Norman.
Freidel, Frank, ed. see O'Sullivan, John.
Freidel, Frank, ed. see Patenaude, Lionel V.
Freidel, Frank, ed. see Prouty, Andrew M.
Freidel, Frank, ed. see Sargent, James.
Freidel, Frank, ed. see Schonbach, Morris.
Freidel, Frank, ed. see Smith, Glenn H.
Freidel, Frank, ed. see Spritzer, Doanld E.
Freidel, Frank, ed. see Stewart, Barbara M.
Freidel, Frank, ed. see Stone, David M.
Freidel, Frank, ed. see Stoneman, William E.
Freidel, Frank, ed. see Torbjorn, Sirevag.
Freidel, Frank, ed. see Tutle, Dwight W.
Freidel, Frank, ed. see Walker, Forrest A.
Freidel, Frank, ed. see Warken, Philip W.
Freidel, Frank, ed. see Weisenhunt.
Freidel, Frank, ed. see Wickens, James F.
Freidel, Frank, ed. see Wortman, Roy T.
Freidel, Frank, et al. American History: A Survey, 2 vols. 6th ed. 1975. One Vol. Ed. text ed. 27.00 (ISBN 0-394-33043-9); Vol. 1. pap. text ed. 17.00 (ISBN 0-394-33079-X); Vol. 2. pap. text ed. 17.00 (ISBN 0-394-33080-3). Knopf.
Freidel, Frank B., ed. Union Pamphlets of the Civil War, 1861-1865, 2 Vols. LC 67-17309. (The John Harvard Library). 1967. Set. 60.00x (ISBN 0-674-92130-5). Harvard U Pr.
Freiden, Rosemary, jt. auth. see Rosen, Arnold.
Freidenfelds, J. Capacity Expansion: Analysis of Simple Models with Applications. 292p. 1981. 52.25 (ISBN 0-444-00562-5, North-Holland). Elsevier.
Freidenreich, Harriet P. The Jews of Yugoslavia: A Quest for Community. LC 79-84733. (Illus.). 1979. 14.95 (ISBN 0-8276-0122-0, 439). Jewish Pubns.
Freides, Thelma K. Literature & Bibliography of the Social Sciences. LC 73-10111. (Information Sciences Ser.). 284p. 1973. 42.50 (ISBN 0-471-27790-8, Pub. by Wiley-Interscience). Wiley.
Freidheim, Elizabeth A. From Types to Theory: A Natural Method for an Unnatural Science. LC 82-17401. (Illus.). 188p. (Orig.). 1983. lib. bdg. 24.25 (ISBN 0-8191-2831-7); pap. text ed. 11.00 (ISBN 0-8191-2832-5). U Pr of Amer.
Freidheim, Robert L., ed. Managing Ocean Resources: A Primer. LC 79-53772. (Westview Special Studies in Natural Resources & Energy Management). 1979. lib. bdg. 28.00x (ISBN 0-89158-572-9). Westview.
Freidin, John. Twenty-Five Bicycle Tours in Vermont: 950 Miles of Sights, Delights & Special Events. rev. ed. LC 84-70168. (Bicycle Tours Ser.). (Illus.). 176p. 1984. pap. 7.95 (ISBN 0-942440-18-8). Backcountry Pubns.
Freidlin, M. I. & Wentzell, A. D. Random Perturbations of Dynamical Systems. (Grundlehren der Mathematischen Wissenschaften Ser.: Bd. 260). (Illus.). 340p. 1983. 58.00 (ISBN 0-387-90858-7). Springer-Verlag.
Freidlin, Mark, jt. auth. see Kirwan, Francis C.
Freidlina, R. Kh., ed. Organic Sulfur Chemistry: Ninth International Symposium on Organic Sulfur Chemistry, Riga, USSR, 9-14 June 1980. (IUPAC Symposium Ser.). (Illus.). 270p. 1981. 72.00 (ISBN 0-08-026180-9). Pergamon.
Freidman, A. J. & Donley, Carol. Einstein As Myth & Muse. (Illus.). 250p. Date not set. price not set (ISBN 0-521-26720-X). Cambridge U Pr.
Freidman, Douglas. The State & Underdevelopment in Spanish America: The Political Roots of Dependency in Peru & Argentina. (Replica Edition Ser.). 300p. 1984. softcover 22.50x (ISBN 0-86531-824-7). Westview.
Freidman, Mendel, ed. Nutritional Improvement of Food & Feed Proteins. LC 78-17278. (Advances in Experimental Medicine & Biology Ser.: Vol. 105). 894p. 1978. 95.00x (ISBN 0-306-40026-X, Plenum Pr). Plenum Pub.
Freidman, R. S., jt. auth. see Howard, L. V.
Freidman, Rita, jt. auth. see Reiss, Elayne.
Freidman, Ronald J. & Doyal, Guy T. The Hyperactive Child. 80p. pap. 4.95x (ISBN 0-317-14146-5). Interstate.
Freidmann, H. Enzymes. 1981. 75.00 (ISBN 0-87933-367-7). Van Nos Reinhold.
Freidrich, Carl J. Puerto Rico, Middle Road to Freedom. LC 74-14234. (The Puerto Rican Experience Ser.). 100p. 1975. Repr. 13.00x (ISBN 0-405-06223-0). Ayer Co Pubs.
Freidrich, Carl J., ed. see American Society for Political & Legal Philosophy.
Freidson, E. Doctoring Together: A Study of Professional Social Control. 1976. 27.50 (ISBN 0-444-99017-8, FDO/, Pub. by Elsevier). Greenwood.
Freidson, Eliot. Doctoring Together: A Study of Professional Social Control. LC 80-15513. 312p. 1980. pap. 7.95x (ISBN 0-226-26222-7, P911, Phoen). U of Chicago Pr.
--Patient's Views of Medical Practice. (Midway Reprint Ser.). 268p. 1980. pap. text ed. 10.00x (ISBN 0-226-26223-5). U of Chicago Pr.
--Profession of Medicine: A Study of the Sociology of Applied Knowledge. 1970. text ed. 28.50 scp (ISBN 0-06-042205-X, HarpC). Har-Row.
--Professional Dominance: The Social Structure of Medical Care. LC 72-116538. 1970. 26.95x (ISBN 0-202-30203-2). Aldine Pub.
Freidson, Eliot, ed. Hospital in Modern Society. LC 63-10648. (Illus.). 1963. 22.95 (ISBN 0-02-910690-7). Free Pr.
Freidson, Eliot & Lorber, Judith, eds. Medical Men & Their Work: A Sociological Reader. LC 70-140627. 494p. 1972. pap. text ed. 18.95x (ISBN 0-202-30230-X). Aldine Pub.
Freidus, Alberta J. Sumatran Contributions to the Development of Indonesian Literature, 1920-1942. (Asian Studies at Hawaii Ser.: No. 19). 76p. 1977. pap. text ed. 7.50x (ISBN 0-8248-0462-7). UH Pr.
Freienmuth Von Helms, E. German Criticism of Gustave Flaubert. LC 70-168138. (Columbia University. Germanic Studies, New Ser.: No. 7). Repr. of 1939 ed. 15.00 (ISBN 0-404-50457-4). AMS Pr.
Freier, Esther, jt. ed. see Blume, Philip.
Freier, Jerold L. Acquisition Search Programs. LC 80-26356. 32p. 1981. pap. 3.95 (ISBN 0-87576-094-5). Pilot Bks.
Freier, Rolf K. Aqueous Solutions: Data for Inorganic & Organic Compounds, 2 vols. Vol. 1, 1976. 92.00x (ISBN 3-11-001627-3); Vol. 2, 1978. 92.00x (ISBN 3-11-006537-1). De Gruyter.
Freier, S. & Eldelman, A. I., eds. Human Milk: Its Biological & Social Value. (International Congress Ser.: No. 518). 342p. 1981. 69.00 (ISBN 0-444-90183-3, Excerpta Medica). Elsevier.
Freiermuth, Donna P. Getting More from Your Commodore Plus-4. (Illus.). 160p. (Orig.). 1985. cancelled. TAB Bks.
Freiermuth, Edmond. Revitalizing Your Business: Five Steps to Successfully Turning Around Your Company. 200p. 1985. 19.95 (ISBN 0-917253-05-1). Probus Pub Co.
Freiert, jt. auth. see Coulson.
Freifeld, Karen, jt. auth. see Gross, Joy.
Freifelder, David. The DNA Molecule: Structure & Properties. LC 77-2768. (Illus.). 1978. text ed. 36.95 (ISBN 0-7167-0287-8); pap. text ed. 23.95 (ISBN 0-7167-0286-X). W H Freeman.
--Essentials of Molecular Biology. (Illus.). 350p. 1985. write for info. (ISBN 0-86720-051-0). Jones & Bartlett.
--Molecular Biology: A Comprehensive Introduction to Prokaryotes & Eukaryotes. 979p. 1983. text ed. write for info. (ISBN 0-86720-012-X). Jones & Bartlett.
--Molecular Biology & Biochemistry: Problems & Applications. LC 78-18712. (Biology Ser.). (Illus.). 1978. pap. text ed. 14.95 (ISBN 0-7167-0068-9). W H Freeman.
--Principles of Physical Chemistry with Applications to the Biological Sciences. 2nd ed. 809p. 1985. text ed. write for info. (ISBN 0-86720-046-4). Jones & Bartlett.
--Problems for Molecular Biology: With Answers & Solutions. 299p. 1983. pap. text ed. write for info. (ISBN 0-86720-013-8). Jones & Bartlett.
Freifelder, David, intro. by. Recombinant DNA: Readings from Scientific American. LC 77-29159. (Illus.). 1978. pap. text ed. 10.95 (ISBN 0-7167-0092-1). W H Freeman.
Freifelder, David M. Physical Biochemistry. 2nd ed. LC 81-19521. (Illus.). 761p. 1982. text ed. 47.95 (ISBN 0-7167-1315-2); pap. text ed. 26.95 (ISBN 0-7167-1444-2). W H Freeman.
Freifelder, Leonard R. A Decision Theoretic Approach to Insurance Ratemaking. LC 75-26414. (S. S. Huebner Foundation Monographs: No. 4). (Illus.). 141p. 1976. pap. 11.00 (ISBN 0-918930-04-9). Huebner Foun Insur.
Freifelder, Morris. Catalytic Hydrogenation in Organic Synthesis: Procedures & Commentary. LC 78-9458. 191p. 1978. 34.95 (ISBN 0-471-02945-9, Pub. by Wiley-Interscience). Wiley.
--Practical Catalytic Hydrogenation: Techniques & Applications. LC 76-123740. 1971. 42.50 (ISBN 0-471-27800-9, Pub. by Wiley-Interscience). Wiley.
Freifield, Stephen, jt. ed. see Yanick, Paul, Jr.
Freiji, I., jt. auth. see Ziadeh, Farhat J.
Freilich, Gerald & Greenleaf, Frederick P. Algebraic Methods: In Business, Economics, & the Social Sciences - a Short Course. (Mathematics Ser.). (Illus.). 311p. 1977. pap. text ed. 8.50 (ISBN 0-7167-0470-6). W H Freeman.
--Calculus: A Short Course with Applications to Business, Economics, & the Social Sciences. LC 75-37569. (Illus.). 395p. 1976. 23.95x (ISBN 0-7167-0466-8). W H Freeman.
--Calculus: A Short Course with Applications. 2nd ed. 436p. 1985. text ed. 28.95x (ISBN 0-15-505746-4, HC); instr's. manual avail. (ISBN 0-15-505748-0); solutions manual avail. (ISBN 0-15-505747-2). HarBraceJ.
Freilich, Morris, ed. The Pleasures of Anthropology. 464p. 1983. pap. 4.95 (ISBN 0-451-62240-5, Ment). NAL.
Freilich, Robert H. & Carlisle, Richard G. Section 1983, Sword & Shield: Civil Rights Violations & the Liability of Urban, State, & Local Government. LC 83-71848. 478p. 1983. 35.00 (ISBN 0-89707-110-7, 5330012). Amer Bar Assn.
Freilich, Robert H. & Levi, Peter S. Model Subdivision Regulations: Text & Commentary. 190p. 1975. 11.95. Planners Pr.
--Model Subdivision Regulations: Text & Commentary. 190p. 1975. pap. 10.95 (ISBN 0-318-13031-9); pap. 9.95 members (ISBN 0-318-13032-7). Am Plan Assn.
Freilich, Robert H. & Stuhler, Eric O., eds. The Land Use Awakening: Zoning Law in the 70's. LC 80-71122. 301p. 1980. pap. 25.00 (ISBN 0-89707-033-X, 5330010). Amer Bar Assn.
Freiligrath, Ferdinand. Poems from the German of Ferdinand Freiligrath. 59.95 (ISBN 0-8490-0848-4). Gordon Pr.
Freiling, Michael J. Understanding Data Base Management. (An Alfred Handy Guide Ser.). 63p. 1982. 3.50 (ISBN 0-88284-221-8). Alfred Pub.
Freilinger, G., et al, eds. Muscle Transplantation. (Illus.). 320p. 1981. 72.00 (ISBN 0-387-81636-4). Springer-Verlag.
Freiman & Fuller, eds. Fracture Mechanics for Ceramics, Rocks, & Concrete - STP 745. 278p. 1981. 29.00 (ISBN 0-8031-0731-5, 04-745000-30). ASTM.
Freiman & Hudson, eds. Methods for Assessing the Structural Reliability of Brittle Materials - STP 844. 226p. 1984. 39.00 (ISBN 0-8031-0265-8, 04-844000-30). ASTM.
Freiman, A., et al, eds. Festschrift zum Siebzigsten Geburtstage A. Berliner's. LC 79-7165. (Jewish Philosophy, Mysticism & History of Ideas Ser.). 1980. Repr. of 1903 ed. lib. bdg. 45.00x (ISBN 0-405-12252-7). Ayer Co Pubs.
Freiman, G. A. Foundations of a Structural Theory of Set Addition. LC 73-9804. (Translations of Mathematical Monographs Ser.: Vol. 37). 1973. 36.00 (ISBN 0-8218-1587-3, MMONO-37). Am Math.

Freiman, Grigori. It Seems I Am a Jew: A Samizdat Essay. Nathanson, Melvyn B., ed. & tr. from Russian. LC 80-404. (Science & International Affairs Ser.). 114p. 1980. 9.95 (ISBN 0-8093-0962-9). S Ill U Pr.

Freiman, I., tr. see Blok, Alexander.

Freiman, Jane S. The Art of Food Processor Cooking. 192p. 1980. pap. 8.95 (ISBN 0-8092-7004-8). Contemp Bks.

Freimuth, C. F. Self-Hypnosis. 12p. 1979. pap. 9.95 (ISBN 0-933992-07-6). Coffee Break.

Frein, J. P. Handbook of Construction Management & Organization. 704p. 4.25 (ISBN 0-318-13155-2, VNR1701). Am Soc Conc Constr.

Frein, Joseph P. Handbook of Construction Management & Organization. 2nd ed. 736p. 1980. 52.50 (ISBN 0-442-22475-3). Van Nos Reinhold.

Freind, John. History of Physick: From the Time of Galen to the Beginning of the Sixteenth Century, 2 Vols. 4th ed. Repr. of 1750 ed. Set. 75.00 (ISBN 0-404-07987-3). AMS Pr.

Freine, Sean de see De Freine, Sean.

Freinkel, Norbert, ed. Contemporary Metabolism, Vol. 1. LC 79-643531. (Illus.). 523p. 1979. 45.00x (ISBN 0-306-40127-4, Plenum Pr). Plenum Pub.

--Contemporary Metabolism, Vol. 2. LC 79-643531. (Illus.). 564p. 1982. 42.50x (ISBN 0-306-40954-2, Plenum Med. Bk.). Plenum Pub.

--The Year in Metabolism, 1977. (Illus.). 468p. (Annual). 1978. 42.50x (ISBN 0-306-32002-9, Plenum Med Bk). Plenum Pub.

Freire. Cultural Action for Freedom. (Monograph Ser.: No. 1). 1970. pap. 4.95x (ISBN 0-916690-11-3). Harvard Educ Rev.

Freire, Joaquin. The Puerto Rican Presence in the History of Cuba. (Puerto Rico Ser.). 1979. lib. bdg. 59.95 (ISBN 0-8490-2990-2). Gordon Pr.

Freire, Paulo. Education for Critical Consciousness. Ramos, Myra, tr. from Port. LC 72-12830. 180p. 1973. pap. 9.95 (ISBN 0-8164-9113-5). Continuum.

--Pedagogy in Process: The Letters to Guinea Bissau. Hunter, Carman, tr. from Portugese. LC 78-2678. 1978. 11.95 (ISBN 0-8264-0136-8). Continuum.

--Pedagogy of the Oppressed. Ramos, Myra B., tr. from Port. LC 70-110074. 1970. pap. 9.95 (ISBN 0-8264-0047-7). Continuum.

--The Politics of Education: Culture, Power, & Liberation. Macedo, Donaldo, tr. from Portuguese. LC 84-18572. (Illus.). 184p. text ed. 24.95 (ISBN 0-89789-042-6); pap. text ed. 9.95 (ISBN 0-89789-043-4). Bergin & Garvey.

Freire, Paulo, frwd. by see Giroux, Henry A.

Freireich, Emil J., et al, eds. Leukemia & Lymphoma. 368p. 1978. 52.50 (ISBN 0-8089-1166-X, 791396). Grune.

Freire-Maia, Newton & Pinheiro, Marta. Ectodermal Dysplasias: A Clinical & Genetic Study. LC 84-17183. 276p. 1984. 58.00 (ISBN 0-8451-0238-9). A R Liss.

Freire-Maia, Newton, jt. auth. see Salzano, Francisco M.

Freis, Edward see Yamori, Yukio, et al.

Freis, Edward D. & Kolata, Gina B. The High Blood Pressure Book: A Guide for Patients & Their Families. 1979. 12.95 (ISBN 0-525-12472-1, Painter-Hopkins). Dutton.

Freisem, Deborah, jt. auth. see Peacock, Nancy W.

Freiser, H., jt. auth. see Stary, J.

Freiser, Henry & Fernando, Quintus. Ionic Equilibria in Analytical Chemistry. LC 79-9746. 352p. 1979. Repr. of 1963 ed. lib. bdg. 21.50 (ISBN 0-88275-955-8). Krieger.

Freiser, Henry, ed. Ion-Selective Electrodes in Analytical Chemistry, Vol. 1. LC 78-16722. (Modern Analytical Chemistry Ser.). 453p. 1978. 65.00x (ISBN 0-306-33907-2, Plenum Pr). Plenum Pub.

--Ion-Selective Electrodes in Analytical Chemistry, Vol. 2. LC 78-16722. (Modern Analytical Chemistry Ser.). (Illus.). 302p. 1980. 49.50x (ISBN 0-306-40500-8, Plenum Pr). Plenum Pub.

Freiser, Lawrence H., jt. auth. see California Continuing Education of the Bar.

Freishtat, Brenda, jt. auth. see Siev, Ellen.

Freislich, Richard. The Last Tribal War: A History of the Bondelswart Uprising Which Took Place in Southwest Africa in 1922. 117p. 1964. 19.50x (ISBN 0-686-28314-7, F Cass Co). Biblio Dist.

Freisner, Arlyne, jt. auth. see Conley, Virginia.

Freitag, Alfred H. The Most Powerful Instruments of Economic Prediction, with Special Attention to the Stock Market. (Illus.). 165p. 1983. 87.65x (ISBN 0-86654-066-0). Inst Econ Finan.

Freitag, Mark & Woods, Anthony. Commercial Diving Reference & Operations Handbook. 414p. 1983. 41.50x (ISBN 0-471-90003-6, Pub. by Wiley-Interscience). Wiley.

Freitag, Wolfgang M. Art Books: A Basic Bibliography of Monographs on Artists. (Reference Library of the Humanities). 450p. 1985. lib. bdg. 40.00 (ISBN 0-8240-8763-1). Garland Pub.

Freitag, Wolfgang M., ed. Encyclopedie Des Arts Decoratifs et Industriels Modernes Au XXeme Siecle, 12 vols. Incl. Vol. 1. Evolution of Decorative & Industrial Art: Preface (ISBN 0-8240-2488-5); Vol. 2. Architecture (ISBN 0-8240-2489-3); Vol. 3. Architectural Ornamentation & Sculpture (ISBN 0-8240-2490-7); Vol. 4. Furniture (ISBN 0-8240-2491-5); Vol. 5. Furniture Hardware & Accessories (ISBN 0-8240-2492-3); Vol. 6. Textiles & Paper Products (ISBN 0-8240-2493-1); Vol. 7. The Art of the Book (ISBN 0-8240-2494-X); Vol. 8. Toys, Scientific & Musical Instruments, Vehicles of Transportation (ISBN 0-8240-2495-8); Vol. 9. Costume & Fashion Design (ISBN 0-8240-2496-6); Vol. 10. Stage Design, Photography & Film (ISBN 0-8240-2497-4); Vol. 11. The Environment - Street & Garden (ISBN 0-8240-2498-2); Vol. 12. The Teaching of the Decorative Arts (ISBN 0-8240-2499-0). LC 76-29204. (Illus.). Set. lib. bdg. 750.00 (ISBN 0-8240-2488-5); lib. bdg. 70.00 ea. Garland Pub.

Freitas, A. Falcao De see World Congress on Ballistocardiography & Cardiovascular Dynamics, 2nd, Oporto, 1969.

Freitas, F. Bapu. (Nehru Library for Children). (Illus.). (gr. 1-9). 1979. Pt. I. pap. 2.00 (ISBN 0-89744-173-7); Pt. II. pap. 1.50 (ISBN 0-89744-174-5). Auromere.

Freitas, William. Camoens & His Epic. 227p. 1963. pap. 4.00 (ISBN 0-912098-03-1). Cal Inst Intl St.

Freitus, Joe. The Natural World Cookbook: Complete Gourmet Meals from Wild Edibles. LC 80-51955. (Illus.). 310p. 1980. 19.95 (ISBN 0-913276-33-2). Stone Wall Pr.

--Wild Preserves: Illustrated Recipes for Over 100 Natural Jams & Jellies. LC 77-10287. (Illus.). 192p. 1977. pap. 8.95 (ISBN 0-913276-22-7). Stone Wall Pr.

Freivalds, John. The Famine Plot. 1980. pap. 2.50 (ISBN 0-8128-7036-0). Stein & Day.

--Successful Agribusiness Management. LC 84-24739. 240p. 1985. 34.95 (ISBN 0-566-00802-5). Gower Pub Co.

Freivals, Karlis. The Copper Lantern. Strahan, Bradley R., ed. (Black Buzzard Illustrated Poetry Chapbook Ser.). (Illus.). 24p. 1982. pap. 2.50 (ISBN 0-938872-01-X). Black Buzzard.

Freiwald, Leah. AppleWriter II Made Easy. 210p. (Orig.). 1985. pap. 16.95 (ISBN 0-07-881166-X, 166-X). Osborne McGraw.

Freixas, Claudio. Afro-Cuban Poetry. LC 78-57695. 1978. pap. 5.00 (ISBN 0-89729-192-1). Ediciones.

Frel, Faya C. Stamnoi: An Exhibition at the J. Paul Getty Museum. LC 80-80400. (Illus.). 38p. 1980. pap. 14.00 (ISBN 0-89236-029-1). J P Getty Mus.

Frel, Jiri. Death of a Hero. (Illus.). 80p. 1984. 16.00 (ISBN 0-89236-055-0); pap. 9.00 (ISBN 0-89236-056-9). J P Getty Mus.

--The Getty Bronze. rev. ed. LC 82-81305. (Illus.). 58p. 1982. 12.00 (ISBN 0-89236-053-4); pap. 6.00 (ISBN 0-89236-039-9). J P Getty Mus.

--Greek Portraits in the J. Paul Getty Museum. LC 81-83742. (Illus.). 76p. (Orig.). 1981. pap. text ed. 16.95 (ISBN 0-89236-032-1). J P Getty Mus.

--Roman Portraits in the Getty Museum. LC 81-50775. (Illus.). 137p. 1981. pap. 17.00 (ISBN 0-86659-004-8). SW Art Assn.

--Roman Portraits in the J. Paul Getty Museum. rev. ed. (Illus.). 137p. 1981. pap. 16.95 (ISBN 0-89236-100-X). J P Getty Mus.

Frel, Jiri, jt. auth. see True, Marion.

Frel, Jiri, ed. Greek & Roman Portraits in the J. Paul Getty Museum 1. (Occasional Papers on Antiquities: No. 2). (Illus.). 160p. 1987. pap. price not set (ISBN 0-89236-071-2). J P Getty Mus.

--Greek Vases in the J. Paul Getty Museum. (Occasional Papers on Antiquities: No. 1). (Illus.). 153p. 1983. pap. 32.50 (ISBN 0-89236-058-5). J P Getty Mus.

--Greek Vases in the J. Paul Getty Museum 2. (Occasional Papers on Antiquities: No. 3). (Illus.). 256p. 1985. pap. write for info (ISBN 0-89236-070-4). J P Getty Mus.

--The J. Paul Getty Museum Journal. (Illus.). 126p. 1975. pap. 10.00 ea. Vol. 1 (ISBN 0-89236-000-3). Vol. 2 (ISBN 0-89236-001-1). J P Getty Mus.

--The J. Paul Getty Museum Journal: No. 5. (Illus.). 182p. 1977. pap. 16.00 (ISBN 0-89236-011-9). J P Getty Mus.

Frel, Jiri, jt. auth. see Von Bothmer, Dietrich.

Freland. Getting by in Spanish. (Getting by Ser.). 1982. pap. 2.95 (ISBN 0-8120-2570-9); cassette 11.95 (ISBN 0-8120-2571-7); book & cassette 14.95 (ISBN 0-8120-7103-4). Barron.

Freligh, H. M. Studies in Revelation, 4 Vols. Schroeder, E. H., ed. 327p. 1969. pap. text ed. 2.50 ea.; Vol. 1. (ISBN 0-87509-140-7); Vol. 2. (ISBN 0-87509-141-5); Vol. 3. (ISBN 0-87509-142-3); Vol. 4. (ISBN 0-87509-143-1). Chr Pubns.

Freligh, H. M., ed. see Pardington, G. P.

Freligh, Harold M. Job. pap. 1.95 (ISBN 0-87509-097-4). Chr Pubns.

--Newborn: A Basic Handbook on Salvation for Personal or Group Study. 123p. pap. 2.95 (ISBN 0-87123-120-4). Bethany Hse.

--Say unto This Mountain. 40p. 1966. pap. 0.95 (ISBN 0-87509-128-8). Chr Pubns.

Frelinghuysen, Joseph S., jt. auth. see Kiell, Paul J.

Frem, Margie, illus. Conversation Games: Vol. III, Solutions. Rev. ed. (Illus.). 134p. (ps-6). 1981. pap. 10.00 (ISBN 0-939632-23-3). ILM.

Fremantle, Alan F. England in the Nineteenth Century, 2 vols. LC 30-6644. 1976. Repr. of 1929 ed. 58.00 (ISBN 0-527-31530-3). Kraus Repr.

Fremantle, Ann & Fremantle, Christopher. In Love with Love: One Hundred of the World's Greatest Spiritual Poems. LC 78-64360. (Spiritual Masters Ser.). 1978. pap. 2.95 (ISBN 0-8091-2136-0). Paulist Pr.

Fremantle, Anne. George Eliot. LC 72-3177. (English Literature Ser., No. 33). 1972. Repr. of 1933 ed. lib. bdg. 39.95x (ISBN 0-8383-1503-8). Haskell.

--Island of Cats. (Illus.). (gr. 1-4). 1964. 6.50 (ISBN 0-8392-3011-7). Astor-Honor.

--Loyal Enemy. 1978. Repr. of 1938 ed. lib. bdg. 20.00 (ISBN 0-8492-0859-9). R West.

Fremantle, Anne, ed. Age of Belief. facs. ed. LC 75-117793. (Essay Index Reprint Ser). 1954. 18.00 (ISBN 0-8369-1829-0). Ayer Co Pubs.

--Age of Belief: The Medieval Philosophers. (Orig.). 1955. pap. 3.95 (ISBN 0-452-00720-8, Mer). NAL.

--Latin American Literature Today. (Orig.). 1977. pap. 2.25 (ISBN 0-451-61587-5, ME1587, Ment). NAL.

Fremantle, Anne, tr. see Keller, Gottfried.

Fremantle, Anne, tr. see Schamoni, Wilhelm.

Fremantle, Arthur J. Three Months in the Southern States. LC 84-2701. (Collector's Library of the Civil War Ser.). 1984. kivar binding 26.60 (ISBN 0-8094-4454-2, Pub. by Time-Life). Silver.

--Three Months in the Southern States: April to June, 1863. LC 72-107514. Repr. of 1864 ed. 22.50x (ISBN 0-8371-3761-6, FTM&). Greenwood.

Fremantle, Christopher, jt. auth. see Fremantle, Ann.

Fremantle, Francesca & Trungpa, Chogyam, trs. from Tibetan. The Tibetan Book of the Dead: The Great Liberation Through Hearing in the Bardo. LC 74-29615. (Clear Light Ser.). (Illus.). 256p. 1975. pap. 6.95 (ISBN 0-394-73064-X). Shambhala Pubns.

Fremantle, T. F. The Book of the Rifle. (Library Classics Ser.). (Illus.). 576p. 1985. Repr. of 1901 ed. 54.00 (ISBN 0-935632-26-3). Wolfe Pub Co.

Fremgen, James M. & Liao, Shu S. The Allocation of Corporate Indirect Costs. 103p. pap. 15.95 (ISBN 0-86641-006-6). Natl Assn Accts.

Fremlin, Celia. The Hours Before Dawn. 190p. 1984. pap. 4.95 (ISBN 0-89733-101-X). Academy Chi Pubs.

--The Jealous One. 175p. 1985. pap. 4.95 (ISBN 0-89733-132-X). Academy Chi Pubs.

--Lovely Day to Die & Other Stories. LC 84-1651. (Crime Club Ser.). 192p. 1984. 11.95 (ISBN 0-385-19421-8). Doubleday.

--The Parasite Person. LC 82-45394. (Crime Club Ser.). 192p. 1982. 11.95 (ISBN 0-385-18300-3). Doubleday.

--Possession. 158p. 1985. pap. 4.95 (ISBN 0-89733-169-9). Academy Chi Pubs.

Fremlin, D. H. Consequences of Martin's Axiom. (Cambridge Tracts in Mathematics Ser.: 84). 352p. 1984. 54.50 (ISBN 0-521-25091-9). Cambridge U Pr.

--Topological Riesz Spaces & Measure Theory. LC 72-95410. 300p. 1974. 49.50 (ISBN 0-521-20170-5). Cambridge U Pr.

Fremlin, Robert. Three Friends. 64p. 1976. pap. 0.95 (ISBN 0-440-48699-8, YB). Dell.

Fremon, George & Fremon, Suzanne. Why Trade It in? LC 81-82363. 256p. 1982. pap. 3.50 (ISBN 0-87216-983-9). Jove Pubns.

--Why Trade It In? How to Keep Your Car Running Almost Indefinitely. 2nd ed. LC 76-42603. (Illus.). 176p. 1982. pap. 5.95 (ISBN 0-89709-039-X). Liberty Pub.

--Your First Car. LC 81-80572. (Illus.). 176p. 1981. pap. 5.95 (ISBN 0-89709-024-1). Liberty Pub.

Fremon, Suzanne, jt. auth. see Fremon, George.

Fremon, Suzanne, ed. Women & Men. (Reference Shelf Ser.). 1977. 8.00 (ISBN 0-8242-0607-X). Wilson.

Fremon, Suzanne, jt. ed. see Wilson, Morrow.

Fremont, Jessie B. The Story of the Guard: A Chronicle of the War. 1863. Repr. 20.00 (ISBN 0-8482-4051-0). Norwood Edns.

Fremont, John C. The Expeditions of John Charles Fremont Supplement: Proceedings of the Court Martial. Spence, Mary L. & Jackson, Donald, eds. 480p. 1973. 25.00x (ISBN 0-252-00403-5). U of Ill Pr.

--The Expeditions of John Charles Fremont Vol. 1: Travels from 1838 to 1844 & Map Portfolio. Jackson, Donald & Spence, Mary L., eds. LC 73-100374. (Illus.). 903p. 1970. 49.95 (ISBN 0-252-00086-2); map portfolio only 32.50x (ISBN 0-252-00087-0). U of Ill Pr.

--The Expeditions of John Charles Fremont Vol. 2: The Bear Flag Revolt & the Court Martial. Spence, Mary L. & Jackson, Donald, eds. (Illus.). 480p. 1973. 30.00x (ISBN 0-252-00249-0). U of Ill Pr.

--The Expeditions of John Charles Fremont Vol. 3: Travels from 1848-1854, Vol. 3. Spence, Mary L., ed. LC 73-100374. 728p. 1984. 37.50x (ISBN 0-252-00416-7). U of Ill Pr.

Fremont, Lance. The Mystery of the Cougar's Yellow Eye. (Voyager Ser.). (Orig.). 1982. pap. 3.95 (ISBN 0-8010-3506-6). Baker Bk.

Fremont, Pamela. How to Open & Run a Money-Making Travel Agency. LC 83-3517. (Wiley Series Small Business: 1-382). 224p. 1983. pap. 8.95 (ISBN 0-471-89335-8, 1-382, Pub. by Wiley Pr). Wiley.

Fremont, Robert, jt. auth. see Charosh, Paul.

Fremont, Robert, ed. Favorite Songs of the Nineties. 401p. 8.75 (ISBN 0-318-14858-7, E113). Midwest Old Settlers.

Fremont, Robert A., jt. auth. see Charosh, Paul.

Fremont, Robert A., ed. Favorite Songs of the Nineties. (Illus.). 416p. (Orig.). 1973. pap. 10.95 (ISBN 0-486-21536-9). Dover.

--Favorite Songs of the Nineties: Complete Original Sheet Music for 89 Songs. 19.00 (ISBN 0-8446-4740-3). Peter Smith.

Fremont, Robert A., jt. ed. see Charosh, Paul.

Fremont, Theodore S., et al. Informal Diagnostic Assessment of Children. (Illus.). 176p. 1977. 20.75x (ISBN 0-398-03646-2). C C Thomas.

Fremont, Trudy, jt. auth. see Fremont, Walter.

Fremont, Walter & Fremont, Trudy. Formula for Family Unity. 189p. (Orig.). 1980. pap. 3.95 (ISBN 0-89084-122-5). Bob Jones Univ Pr.

Fremont-Smith, Marion R. Foundations & Government: State & Federal Law & Supervision. LC 65-22280. 564p. 1965. 13.95x (ISBN 0-87154-278-1). Russell Sage.

--Philanthropy & the Business Corporation. LC 72-83835. 110p. 1972. pap. 4.50x (ISBN 0-87154-279-X). Russell Sage.

Fremouw, William J., jt. ed. see Golann, Stuart.

Fremouw, William J., jt. auth. see Hawkins, Raymond C.

Fremy, Pierre. Cyanophycees des Cotes d'Europe. (Memoires of the National Society of Natural Sciences & Mathematics of Cherborg Ser.). (Illus.). 1972. 30.40 (ISBN 90-6123-274-0). Lubrecht & Cramer.

Frenay, Agnes C. Understanding Medical Terminology. 6th ed. LC 77-73986. 1977. pap. text ed. 9.00 (ISBN 0-87125-038-1). Cath Health.

Frenay, Agnes C. & Mahoney, Rose M. Understanding Medical Terminology. 7th ed. LC 84-7090. (Illus.). 640p. 1984. pap. 19.50 (ISBN 0-87125-098-5). Cath Health.

Frenay, Jacques, ed. see Fleurian, Dominique de.

Frenaye, F., tr. see Bettiza, Enzo.

Frenaye, Frances, tr. see Croce, Benedetto.

Frenaye, Frances, tr. see Dem, Tidiane.

Frenaye, Frances, tr. see Deschamps, Fanny.

Frenaye, Frances, tr. see Levi, Carlo.

Frenaye, Frances, tr. see Murat, Ines.

Frenaye, Frances, tr. see Vittorini, Elio.

Frenaye, Frances, et al, trs. see Moravia, Alberto.

Frenbach, David, jt. ed. see Mackay, Louis.

French, A. The Athenian Half-Century, 478-431 B.C. French, A., tr. LC 71-145645. (Sources in Ancient History). (Illus.). 120p. 1971. pap. 15.00x (ISBN 0-424-06220-8, Pub. by Sydney U Pr). Intl Spec Bk.

French, A. L. Shakespeare & the Critics. LC 75-183221. 224p. 1972. 47.50 (ISBN 0-521-08470-9). Cambridge U Pr.

French, Mrs. A. M. Slavery in South Carolina, & the Ex-Slaves. LC 75-82051. (Illus.). Repr. of 1862 ed. 19.75x (ISBN 0-8371-1472-1, FRS&). Greenwood.

French, A. P. Vibrations & Waves. (M.I.T. Introductory Physics Ser). (Illus.). 1971. pap. text ed. 9.95x (ISBN 0-393-09936-9). Norton.

French, A. P. & Taylor, Edwin F. Introduction to Quantum Physics. (M. I. T. Introductory Physics Ser.). (Illus.). 500p. 1978. pap. text ed. 18.95x (ISBN 0-393-09106-6). Norton.

French, A. P., ed. Einstein: A Centenary Volume. LC 78-25968. (Illus.). 1979. text ed. 25.00x (ISBN 0-674-24230-0); pap. 9.95 (ISBN 0-674-24231-9). Harvard U Pr.

French, A. P., et al, eds. Niels Bohr: A Centenary Volume. (Illus.). 440p. 1985. 27.50 (ISBN 0-674-62415-7). Harvard U Pr.

French, Alfred. Czech Writers & Politics. (East European Monographs: No. 94). 435p. 1982. 35.00x (ISBN 0-914710-88-5). East Eur Quarterly.

--Disturbed Children & Their Families: Innovations in Evaluation & Treatment. LC 75-11003. text ed. 34.95 (ISBN 0-87705-263-8); pap. 14.95 (ISBN 0-87705-439-8). Human Sci Pr.

--The Growth of the Athenian Economy. LC 75-31363. 208p. 1976. Repr. of 1964 ed. lib. bdg. 19.75x (ISBN 0-8371-8506-8, FRAC). Greenwood.

French, Alfred & Berlin, Irving. Depression in Children & Adolescents. LC 79-13481. 298p. 1979. 29.95 (ISBN 0-87705-390-1). Human Sci Pr.

French, Alfred, ed. Czech Poetry: A Bilingual Antholoy, Vol. 1. (Michigan Slavic Translations Ser.: No. 2). 1979. 15.00 (ISBN 0-930042-34-4). Mich Slavic Pubns.

French, Alfred D. & Gardner, KennCorwin H., eds. Fiber Diffraction Methods. LC 80-21566. (ACS Symposium Ser.: No. 141). 1980. 49.95 (ISBN 0-8412-0589-2). Am Chemical.

French, Alice. Book of True Lovers. LC 78-94722. (Short Story Index Reprint Ser.). 1897. 18.00 (ISBN 0-8369-3101-7). Ayer Co Pubs.

--Heart of Toil. LC 70-98569. (Short Story Index Reprint Ser.). 1898. 17.00 (ISBN 0-8369-3143-2). Ayer Co Pubs.

--Knitters in the Sun. 1927. 17.25 (ISBN 0-8422-8054-5); pap. text ed. 9.50x (ISBN 0-8290-0662-1). Irvington.

--The Man of the Hour. Hardwick, Elizabeth, ed. LC 76-51666. (Rediscovered Fiction by American Women Ser.). (Illus.). 1977. Repr. of 1905 ed. lib. bdg. 30.00 (ISBN 0-405-10045-0). Ayer Co Pubs.

--Missionary Sheriff. facs. ed. LC 70-75777. (Short Story Index Reprint Ser.). 1897. 17.00 (ISBN 0-8369-3002-9). Ayer Co Pubs.

--Stories of a Western Town. 1972. lib. bdg. 22.50 (ISBN 0-8422-8055-3); pap. text ed. 8.50x (ISBN 0-8290-0673-7). Irvington.

French, Allen. General Gage's Informers: New Material upon Lexington & Concord, Benjamin Thompson As Loyalist & the Treachery of Benjamin Church, Jr. LC 68-54420. (Illus.). 1968. Repr. of 1932 ed. lib. bdg. 15.75x (ISBN 0-8371-0431-9, FRGI). Greenwood.

--Historic Concord & the Lexington Fight. 2nd ed. rev. ed. Little, David B., ed. LC 77-15933. (Illus.). 1978. 8.95 (ISBN 0-87645-098-2, Pub. by Gambit); pap. 4.95 (ISBN 0-87645-097-4). Harvard Common Pr.

--The Siege of Boston. LC 68-58326. (Illus.). 1969. Repr. of 1911 ed. 15.00 (ISBN 0-87152-052-4). Reprint.

French, Allen, ed. see MacKenzie, Frederick.

French, Anne. Susan Clegg & Her Friend Mrs. Lathrop. LC 71-94723. (Short Story Index Reprint Ser.). 1904. 17.00 (ISBN 0-8369-3102-5). Ayer Co Pubs.

--Susan Clegg & Her Neighbors' Affairs. facsimile ed. LC 70-150474. (Short Story Index Reprint Ser.). Repr. of 1906 ed. 17.00 (ISBN 0-8369-3814-3). Ayer Co Pubs.

French, Anthony P. Newtonian Mechanics. (M.I.T. Introductory Physics Ser). (Illus.). 1971. pap. text ed. 13.95x (ISBN 0-393-09970-9). Norton.

--Special Relativity. (M. I. T. Introductory Physics Ser). 1968. pap. 8.95x (ISBN 0-393-09793-5). Norton.

French, Benjamin F. Historical Collections of Louisiana, Embracing Rare & Valuable Documents Relating to the Natural, Civil, & Political History of That State, 5 vols. LC 72-14380. Repr. of 1853 ed. Set. 150.00 (ISBN 0-404-11050-9); 30.00 ea. Vol. 1 (ISBN 0-404-11051-7). Vol. 2 (ISBN 0-404-11052-5). Vol. 3 (ISBN 0-404-11053-3). Vol. 4 (ISBN 0-404-11054-1). Vol. 5 (ISBN 0-404-11055-X). AMS Pr.

--History of the Rise & Progress of the Iron Trade of the United States, 1621-1857. LC 68-55712. Repr. of 1858 ed. 25.00x (ISBN 0-678-00963-5). Kelley.

French, Benjamin F., ed. Historical Collections of Louisiana & Florida, 2 vols. LC 72-14374. Repr. of 1875 ed. Set. 55.00 (ISBN 0-404-11096-7); 27.50 ea. Vol. 1 (ISBN 0-404-11097-5). Vol. 2 (ISBN 0-404-11098-3). AMS Pr.

French, Bernada. Jewelry Craft Made Easy. (Illus.). 64p. 1976. pap. 2.00 (ISBN 0-910652-22-8). Gembooks.

French, Bernada, jt. auth. see Craw, Julia.

French, Bevan M. Meeting with the Universe: Science Discoveries from the Space Program. (NASA Ep 177 Ser.). 231p. 1981. pap. 14.00 (ISBN 0-318-11803-3). Gov Printing Office.

--Progressive Contact Metamorphism of the Biwabik Iron-Formation, Mesabi Range, Minnesota. LC 68-66592. (Bulletin: No. 45). (Illus.). 1968. 4.50x (ISBN 0-8166-0478-9). Minn Geol Survey.

French Bishops Conference, jt. auth. see West German Bishops Conference.

French, Blaire A. The Presidential Press Conference: Its History & Role in the American Political System. LC 81-40883. 54p. (Orig.). 1982. pap. text ed. 6.25 (ISBN 0-8191-2064-2). U Pr of Amer.

French, Brandon. On the Verge of Revolt: Women in American Films of the Fifties. LC 78-4294. (Ungar Film Library). 1978. 12.95x (ISBN 0-8044-2220-6); pap. 6.95 (ISBN 0-8044-6158-9). Ungar.

French, Brian. Principles of Collage. LC 78-67955. (Illus.). 1978. 10.95 (ISBN 0-87523-188-8). Emerson.

French, Brian & Butler, Anne. Practice of Collage. (Illus.). 87p. 1976. 12.50 (ISBN 0-263-05711-9). Transatlantic.

French, Bryant M. Mark Twain & the Gilded Age: The Book That Named an Era. LC 65-24438. (Illus.). 1965. 14.95 (ISBN 0-87074-053-9). SMU Press.

French, C. E., et al. Survival Strategies for Agricultural Cooperatives. 1980. text ed. 15.25x (ISBN 0-8138-0455-8). Iowa St U Pr.

French, C. S. Computer Science. 1980. 25.00x (ISBN 0-905435-13-3, Pub. by DP Pubns). State Mutual Bk.

--Computer Studies. 400p. 1982. 35.00x (ISBN 0-905435-24-9, Pub. by DP Pubns). State Mutual Bk.

French, Calvin, et al. Heart Mountains & Human Ways: Japanese Landscape & Figure Painting. LC 82-62531. (Illus.). 94p. (Orig.). 1982. pap. 14.95 (ISBN 0-295-96066-3). U of Wash Pr.

French, Calvin L. Shiba Kokan. LC 74-76104. 224p. 1974. 27.50 (ISBN 0-8348-0098-5). Weatherhill.

French, Carroll E. The Shop Committee in the United States. LC 78-641100. (Johns Hopkins University Studies in the Social Sciences, Forty-First Series, 1923: No. 2: 2). 112p. 1982. Repr. of 1923 ed. 24.50 (ISBN 0-404-61225-3). AMS Pr.

French, Charles. American Guide to U. S. Coins, 1984. (Orig.). 1983. pap. 4.95 (ISBN 0-346-12592-8). Cornerstone.

--American Guide to U. S. Coins: 1981 Edition. rev. ed. 192p. (Orig.). 1980. pap. 3.95 (ISBN 0-346-12504-9). Cornerstone.

--American Guide to U. S. Coins: 1982 Edition. (Orig.). 1981. pap. 4.95 (ISBN 0-346-12539-1). Cornerstone.

French, Charles F. American Guide to U. S. Coins, 1983. 192p. 1982. pap. 4.95 (ISBN 0-346-12573-1). Cornerstone.

--American Guide to U. S. Coins, 1985. rev. ed. 1984. pap. 4.95 (ISBN 0-317-05145-8, Fireside). S&S.

French Colonial Historical Society. Proceedings of the French Colonial Historical Society Annual Meetings, Sixth & Seventh, 1980-1981. Cooke, James J., ed. LC 76-644752. 160p. (Orig.). 1982. lib. bdg. 25.25 (ISBN 0-8191-2333-1); pap. text ed. 12.00 (ISBN 0-8191-2334-X). U Pr of Amer.

French Colonial Historical Society, 5th Meeting. Proceedings. Cooke, James J., ed. LC 80-5683. 125p. lib. bdg. 20.50 (ISBN 0-8191-1146-5); pap. text ed. 9.50 (ISBN 0-8191-1147-3). U Pr of Amer.

French, Curtis. Winning Words: Devotions for Athletes. LC 77-75467. 1983. pap. 5.95 (ISBN 0-8499-2805-2). Word Bks.

French, David & French, Elena. Working Communally: Patterns & Possibilities. LC 74-25854. 288p. 1975. 11.95x (ISBN 0-87154-291-9). Russell Sage.

French, David G. Approach to Measuring Results in Social Work. LC 70-136066. xiv, 178p. Repr. of 1952 ed. lib. bdg. 15.00x (ISBN 0-8371-5216-X, FRAM). Greenwood.

French, David N. Metallurgical Failures in Fossil Fired Boilers. LC 82-20113. 275p. 1983. 37.95x (ISBN 0-471-89841-4, Pub. by Wiley-Interscience). Wiley.

French, Derek & Saward, Heather. Dictionary of Management. 2nd ed. 450p. 1984. text ed. 41.95x (ISBN 0-566-02296-6). Gower Pub Co.

French, Dorothy K. I Don't Belong Here. LC 79-26905. (A Hiway Bk.: A High Interest-Low Reading Level Book). 104p. 1980. 8.95 (ISBN 0-664-32664-1). Westminster.

--Out of the Rough. (Sundown Fiction Ser.). 64p. 1981. 2.00 (ISBN 0-88336-707-6). New Readers.

--Pioneer Saddle Mystery. LC 75-12428. 192p. (gr. 5-10). 1975. PLB 6.19 (ISBN 0-8313-0113-9). Lantern.

French, Dwight K. National Survey of Family Growth, Cycle I: Sample Design, Estimation Procedures & Variance Estimation. Stevenson, Taloria, ed. (Series 2: No. 76). 1977. pap. text ed. 1.75 (ISBN 0-8406-0116-6). Natl Ctr Health Stats.

French, Dwight K., jt. auth. see Harris, Kenneth W.

French, E., jt. auth. see Taylour, W.

French, E. L., ed. Melbourne Studies in Education, 1961-62. LC 59-2337. 1964. 22.00x (ISBN 0-522-83604-6, Pub by Melbourne U Pr). Intl Spec Bk.

--Melbourne Studies in Education, 1963. LC 59-2337. 1964. 22.00x (ISBN 0-522-83606-2, Pub by Melbourne U Pr). Intl Spec Bk.

--Melbourne Studies in Education, 1964. LC 59-2337. 1965. 22.00x (ISBN 0-522-83605-4, Pub by Melbourne U Pr). Intl Spec Bk.

--Melbourne Studies in Education, 1965. LC 59-2337. 1966. 22.00x (ISBN 0-522-83607-0, Pub. by Melbourne U Pr). Intl Spec Bk.

--Melbourne Studies in Education, 1966. LC 59-2337. 1967. 22.00x (ISBN 0-522-83794-8, Pub by Melbourne U Pr). Intl Spec Bk.

--Melbourne Studies in Education, 1967. LC 59-2337. 1968. 22.00x (ISBN 0-522-83910-X, Pub by Melbourne U Pr). Intl Spec Bk.

--Melbourne Studies in Education, 1968-1969. LC 59-2337. 1969. 22.00x (ISBN 0-522-83937-1, Pub by Melbourne U Pr). Intl Spec Bk.

--Melbourne Studies in Education, 1970. LC 59-2337. 1970. 22.00x (ISBN 0-522-83958-4, Pub by Melbourne U Pr). Intl Spec Bk.

--Melbourne Studies in Education, 1971. LC 59-2337. 1971. 22.00x (ISBN 0-522-84003-5, Pub. by Melbourne U Pr). Intl Spec Bk.

French, Earl A. Eminent Victorian Americans. (Illus.). 1977. pap. 3.00 (ISBN 0-917482-11-5). Stowe-Day.

French, Earl A. & Royce, Diana, eds. Portraits of a Nineteenth Century Family: A Symposium on the Beecher Family. LC 76-14236. (Illus.). 1976. pap. 4.95 (ISBN 0-917482-05-0). Stowe-Day.

French, Earl A., ed. see Van Why, Joseph S.

French, Edwin O. The Two Day Wage Programs: A Primer for Operations Managers. LC 59-776. 128p. 1984. text ed. 14.95 (ISBN 0-910223-01-7). MAC Print.

French, Elena, jt. auth. see French, David.

French, Elizabeth. List of Emigrants to America from Liverpool, 1697-1707. LC 63-754. 55p. 1983. pap. 5.00 (ISBN 0-8063-0153-8). Genealog Pub.

French, Elizabeth S. Exploring the Twin Cities with Children. (Illus.). 1982. pap. 4.95 (ISBN 0-685-64394-8). Nodin Pr.

French, Fiona. Future Story. LC 83-22317. 32p. 11.95 (ISBN 0-911745-35-1). P Bedrick Bks.

French, Frances. OJT Mail Clerk Resource Materials. 2nd ed. (Gregg Office Job Training Program Ser.). (Illus.). 112p. (gr. 11-12). 1980. soft cover 6.88 (ISBN 0-07-022190-1). McGraw.

French, Frances-Jane. Abbey Theatre Series of Plays: A Bibliography. 1970. 10.95 (ISBN 0-85105-149-9). Dufour.

French, Francesca, jt. auth. see Cable, Mildred.

French, Francis G., et al. Beginning Computer Programming: BASIC. (gr. 5-9). 1983. 13.28 (ISBN 0-205-08026-X, 208026). Allyn.

French, Frank S., et al, eds. Hormonal Regulation of Spermatogenesis. LC 75-32541. (Current Topics in Molecular Endocrinology Ser.: Vol. 2). 537p. 1975. 59.50x (ISBN 0-306-34002-X, Plenum Pr). Plenum Pub.

French, Geoffrey, tr. see Dahlsgaard, Inga, et al.

French, Geoffrey, tr. see Marcussen, Ernst, et al.

French, Geoffrey, tr. see Pederson, Johannes.

French, Geoffrey, tr. see Struwe, Kamma.

French, George. Advertising: The Social & Economic Problem. LC 84-46045. (History of Advertising Ser.). 285p. 1985. lib. bdg. 30.00 (ISBN 0-8240-6739-8). Garland Pub.

French, George R. Shakespeareana Genealogica. LC 74-168139. Repr. of 1869 ed. 52.50 (ISBN 0-404-02575-7). AMS Pr.

French, Gilbert J. Life & Times of Samuel Crompton. LC 70-107527. Repr. of 1859 ed. 35.00x (ISBN 0-678-07758-4). Kelley.

French, Giles. Cattle Country of Peter French. 2nd. ed. LC 64-23094. (Illus.). 1972. pap. 6.50 (ISBN 0-8323-0280-5). Binford.

--Homesteads & Heritages: A History of Morrow County, Oregon. (Illus.). 128p. 1971. 12.50 (ISBN 0-8323-0204-X). Binford.

French, Gordon. The Battered Bastards. 1979. pap. 1.75 (ISBN 0-8439-0631-6, Leisure Bks). Dorchester Pub Co.

French Government Tourist Office. The Official Guide to the Small Country Hotels & Inns of France, 1985. 250p. (Orig.). 1985. pap. 7.95 (ISBN 2-904394-07-9, Pub. by Victoria & Albert Mus UK). Faber & Faber.

French Gov't. Tourist Office. Hotel Guide: The Country Hotel Tradition. 1985. pap. 7.95 (ISBN 2-904394-04-4). Faber & Faber.

French, H. W. Art & Artists in Connecticut. LC 70-87543. (Library of American Art Ser). 1970. Repr. of 1879 ed. lib. bdg. 22.50 (ISBN 0-306-71459-0). Da Capo.

French, Hajjar. Christiarisme en Orient. 9.00x (ISBN 0-86685-172-0). Intl Bk Ctr.

French, Hal W. & Sharma, Arvind. Religious Ferment in Modern India. 1982. 19.95x (ISBN 0-312-67134-2). St Martin.

French, Hannah D. Bookbinding in Early America: Seven Essays on Masters & Methods. 185p. 1985. avail. (ISBN 0-912296-76-3). Am Antiquarian.

French, Harold W. The Swan's Wide Waters: Ramakrishna & Western Culture. new ed. LC 74-77657. (National University Publications Ser.). 214p. 1974. 17.95x (ISBN 0-8046-9055-3, Pub by Kennikat). Assoc Faculty Pr.

French, Harriet L. Research in Florida Law. 2nd ed. LC 65-27630. 80p. 1965. 7.50 (ISBN 0-379-11653-7). Oceana.

French, Helen. Wind on the Prairies: How the West Was Really Won. (Illus.). 240p. 1982. 10.50 (ISBN 0-682-49850-5, Lochinvar). Exposition Pr FL.

French, Hollis. Jacob Hurd & His Sons, Nathaniel & Benjamin. LC 70-175722. (Architecture & Decorative Art Ser.: Vol. 39). 158p. 1972. Repr. of 1939 ed. lib. bdg. 35.00 (ISBN 0-306-70406-4). Da Capo.

--Silver Collector's Glossary & a List of Early American Silversmiths & Their Marks. LC 67-27454. (Architecture & Decorative Art Ser). 1967. lib. bdg. 19.50 (ISBN 0-306-70969-4). Da Capo.

French Institute of Petroleum, Paris, 1971, et al. Rapid Methods for the Analysis of Used Oils: Proceedings. (Illus.). 96p. 1973. text ed. 25.00x (ISBN 0-900645-10-5). Scholium Intl.

French, J. C. Himalayan Art. (Illus.). 116p. 1983. Repr. of 1931 ed. text ed. 35.00x (ISBN 0-86590-189-9). Apt Bks.

--Himalayan Art. (Illus.). 45.00 (ISBN 0-89410-507-8, Pub. by UBSPD India). Three Continents.

French, J. H. Eighteen Sixty Gazetteer of NYS. LC 82-223939. (Fr.). 1980. 25.00 (ISBN 0-932334-31-8); pap. 20.00 (ISBN 0-932334-32-6). Heart of the Lakes.

French, J. L. The Best of American Humor. 1977. Repr. of 1941 ed. lib. bdg. 12.50 (ISBN 0-8495-1601-3). Arden Lib.

--A Gallery of Old Rogues. 1977. Repr. of 1931 ed. lib. bdg. 30.00 (ISBN 0-8495-1600-5). Arden Lib.

--Lotus & Chrysanthemums: An Anthology of Chinese & Japanese Poetry. 59.95 (ISBN 0-8490-0556-6). Gordon Pr.

--Sixty Years of American Humor. 1977. Repr. of 1924 ed. lib. bdg. 30.00 (ISBN 0-8495-1602-1). Arden Lib.

French, J. Milton, ed. Life Records of John Milton, 1608-1674, 5 Vols. LC 66-20024. 1966. Repr. of 1958 ed. Set. 95.00x (ISBN 0-87752-039-9); 20.00x ea. Gordian.

French, Jack. Up the EDP Pyramid: The Complete Job Hunting Manual for Computer Professionals. LC 81-11605. 200p. (Orig.). 1981. 21.95 (ISBN 0-471-08925-7). Krieger.

French, James C. IDAM File Organizations. Stone, Harold, ed. LC 85-1066. (Computer Science: Distributed Database Systems Ser.: No. 15). 172p. 1985. 44.95 (ISBN 0-8357-1631-7). UMI Res Pr.

French, James R. Nauvoo. 305p. 1982. 12.95 (ISBN 0-934126-27-5). Randall Bk Co.

--The Outcasts. 256p. 1984. 12.95 (ISBN 0-934126-47-X). Randall Bk Co.

French, Jane, jt. auth. see French, Joel.

French, Janie P. Notable Southern Families, Vol. 6: The Doak Family. LC 74-882. (Illus.). 98p. 1974. Repr. of 1933 ed. 12.00 (ISBN 0-87152-151-2). Reprint.

French, Janine. Candidate for Love. LC 84-13581. (Starlight Romance Ser.). 192p. 1985. 11.95 (ISBN 0-385-19660-1). Doubleday.

French, Jere S. Urban Space: A Brief History of the City Square. (Illus.). 1983. pap. 21.95 (ISBN 0-8403-3109-6). Kendall Hunt.

French, Joel & French, Jane. War Beyond the Stars. LC 79-90267. 128p. 1979. pap. 4.95 (ISBN 0-89221-067-2). New Leaf.

French, John. Electrics & Electronics for Small Craft. 300p. 1980. 48.00x (ISBN 0-8464-1228-4). Beekman Pubs.

--Electrics & Electronics for Small Craft. new ed. (Illus.). 255p. 1986. write for info. (ISBN 0-229-11612-4, Pub. by Adlard Coles). Sheridan.

French, John, tr. see Aitmatov, Chingiz.

French, John C. Poe in Foreign Lands & Tongues. LC 73-1694. 1973. lib. bdg. 15.00 (ISBN 0-8414-1954-X). Folcroft.

--Problem of the Two Prologues to Chaucer's Legend of Good Women. LC 79-168140. Repr. of 1905 ed. 5.00 (ISBN 0-404-02576-5). AMS Pr.

--Problem of the Two Prologues to Chaucer's Legend of Good Women. LC 72-195907. 1905. lib. bdg. 4.95 (ISBN 0-8414-4283-5). Folcroft.

--The Problem of the Two Prologues to Chaucer's Legend of Good Women. 1976. lib. bdg. 59.95 (ISBN 0-8490-2484-6). Gordon Pr.

French, John D., ed. Frontiers in Brain Research. LC 62-19908. (Illus.). 285p. 1962. 31.00x (ISBN 0-231-02552-1). Columbia U Pr.

French, John R. P., Jr., et al. Career Change in Midlife: Stress, Social Support & Adjustment. (Illus.). 152p. (Orig.). 1983. pap. text ed. 15.00x (ISBN 0-87944-290-5). Inst Soc Res.

French, John S. Trends in Employment & Earnings for Nineteen Graduating Classes of a Teachers College: As Shown by the Record of the 1927-1936 Classes of the New Jersey State Teachers College at Newark, New Jersey. LC 79-176786. (Columbia University. Teachers College. Contributions to Education: No. 911). Repr. of 1945 ed. 22.50 (ISBN 0-404-55911-5). AMS Pr.

French, Joseph L. Great Pirate Stories, 2 vols. in 1. Repr. of 1922 ed. 35.00 (ISBN 0-89987-156-9). Darby Bks.

--Great Pirate Stories. 314p. 1985. Repr. of 1922 ed. lib. bdg. 45.00 (ISBN 0-8414-4317-3). Folcroft.

French, Joseph L., ed. Great Pirate Stories, 2 vols. in one. 1978. Repr. of 1943 ed. lib. bdg. 40.00 (ISBN 0-8495-1611-0). Arden Lib.

--Great Sea Stories. 491p. 1985. Repr. of 1943 ed. lib. bdg. 40.00 (ISBN 0-8414-6925-3). Folcroft.

--Great Sea Stories: Second Series. LC 75-122708. (Short Story Index Reprint Ser). 1925. 18.00 (ISBN 0-8369-3541-1). Ayer Co Pubs.

--Masterpieces of Mystery: Riddle Stories. 1979. Repr. of 1937 ed. lib. bdg. 20.00 (ISBN 0-8482-3957-1). Norwood Edns.

French, Joyce N. Reading & Study Skills in the Secondary School: A Sourcebook Reference. 250p. 1985. lib. bdg. 34.00 (ISBN 0-8240-8724-0). Garland Pub.

French, Julia. Education & Training for the Middle-Aged & Older Workers. 58p. 1980. 10.00 (ISBN 0-318-15736-5). Natl Inst Work.

French, Kevin. Mpanza, Sofasonke & the Political History of Soweto. 280p. 1985. pap. text ed. 16.95x (ISBN 0-86975-233-2, Pub. by Ravan Pr). Ohio U Pr.

French, L. H. Nome Nuggets. (Illus.). 64p. 1983. pap. 5.95 (ISBN 0-88240-256-0, Northern History Library). Alaska Northwest.

French, Laura. Dragon's Ransom. LC 83-91424. (Endless Quest Bks.). 160p. (gr. 5up). 1984. pap. 2.25 (ISBN 0-394-72465-8). Random.

French, Laura & Stewart, Diana. Women in Business. LC 79-13694. (Movers & Shapers Ser.). (Illus.). (gr. 4-8). 1979. PLB 13.31 (ISBN 0-8172-1377-5). Raintree Pubs.

French, Laurence, ed. Indians & Criminal Justice. LC 81-67871. 224p. 1982. text ed. 23.95x (ISBN 0-86598-063-2). Allanheld.

French, Laurence & Hornbuckle, Jim, eds. The Cherokee Perspective. 1981. 6.95 (ISBN 0-913239-16-X). Appalach Consortium.

French, Lawrence, ed. Indians & Criminal Justice. 224p. 1982. 23.95 (ISBN 0-318-02915-4). Biblio Dist.

French, Leigh, jt. auth. see Rider, Barry.

French, Loran C. Encyclopedia of Plate Varieties on U. S. Bureau-Printed Postage Stamps. LC 78-75142. (Illus.). 1979. 35.00 (ISBN 0-930412-03-6). Bureau Issues.

French, M. Conceptual Design for Engineers. 2nd ed. (Illus.). 240p. 1985. 29.50 (ISBN 0-387-15175-3). Springer-Verlag.

French, M. H. Observations on the Goat. (Animal Production & Health Papers: No. 14). 204p. 1970. pap. 15.50 (ISBN 92-5-100848-5, F303, FAO). Unipub.

French, Marilyn. Beyond Power: On Women, Men & Morals. 708p. 1985. 19.95 (ISBN 0-671-49959-9). Summit Bks.

--The Bleeding Heart. 416p. 1981. pap. 3.50 (ISBN 0-345-28896-3). Ballantine.

--The Book As World: James Joyce's Ulysses. 470p. 1976. 20.00x (ISBN 0-674-07853-5). Harvard U Pr.

--Shakespeare's Division of Experience. LC 80-23147. 384p. 1981. 15.95 (ISBN 0-671-44865-X). Summit Bks.

--Shakespeare's Division of Experience. 416p. 1983. pap. 4.50 (ISBN 0-345-30070-X). Ballantine.

--Shakespeare's Division of Experience. Date not set. 1.98 (ISBN 0-317-18853-4). S&S.

--The Women's Room. Date not set. pap. 3.50 (ISBN 0-515-06896-9). Jove Pubns.

French, Michael. Flyers. LC 82-15032. (Movie Storybooks). (Illus.). 64p. (gr. 4-7). 1983. 6.95 (ISBN 0-394-85535-3); PLB 7.99 (ISBN 0-394-95535-8). Random.

--Lifeguards Only Beyond This Point. LC 84-7660. (Pacer Bks.). 208p. (gr. 7 up). 1984. 10.95 (ISBN 0-399-21098-9). Putnam Pub Group.

--Lifeguards Only Beyond This Point. 192p. 1985. pap. 2.25 (ISBN 0-425-08408-6). Berkley Pub.

--Pursuit. LC 82-70319. 192p. (gr. 7 up). 1982. 9.95 (ISBN 0-385-28781-X). Delacorte.

--Pursuit. 192p. (YA) (gr. 9 up). 1983. pap. 2.50 (ISBN 0-440-96665-5, LFL). Dell.

--Soldier Boy. 192p. (gr. 7 up). 1986. 12.95 (ISBN 0-448-47768-8, G&D). Putnam Pub Group.

--The Throwing Season. LC 79-53598. (YA) (gr. 9-12). 1980. 8.95 (ISBN 0-440-08600-0). Delacorte.

--The Throwing Season. 224p. (YA) (gr. 9 up). 1983. pap. 2.50 (ISBN 0-440-98814-4, LFL). Dell.

French, Michael, adapted by. Indiana Jones & the Temple of Doom: The Storybook Based on the Movie. LC 84-1980. (Illus.). 64p. (gr. 3-7). 1984. 6.95 (ISBN 0-394-86387-9, BYR); PLB 7.99 (ISBN 0-394-96387-3). Random.

French, N. R., ed. Perspectives in Grassland Ecology: Results & Applications of the US-IBP Grassland Biome Study. LC 78-13971. (Ecological Studies: Vol. 32). (Illus.). 1979. 39.00 (ISBN 0-387-90384-4). Springer-Verlag.

French, P. M., jt. ed. see McCall, J. L.

French, P. M., et al, eds. Microstructural Science: Proceedings of the 7th Annual Meeting of the International Metallographic Society, 2 pts, Vol. 3. LC 73-10895. 1050p. 1975. Set. 149.00 (ISBN 0-444-00161-1). Elsevier.

French, Parker H. Overland Expedition to California. 1970. pap. 2.95 (ISBN 0-917420-03-9). Buck Hill.

French, Patrice L., ed. The Development of Meaning. 1979. pap. 14.00x (ISBN 0-89955-237-4, Pub. by Bunka Hyoron). Intl Spec Bk.

French, Patterson H. Automobile Compensation Plan. LC 68-58574. (Columbia University. Studies in the Social Sciences: No. 393). Repr. of 1933 ed. 21.00 (ISBN 0-404-51393-X). AMS Pr.

French, Paul, pseud. Lucky Starr & the Moons of Jupiter. 176p. 1984. pap. 1.95 (ISBN 0-345-31623-1, Del Rey). Ballantine.

--Lucky Starr & the Oceans of Venus. 176p. 1984. pap. 1.95 (ISBN 0-345-31563-4, Del Rey). Ballantine.

French, Paul C. We Won't Murder: Being the Story of Men Who Followed Their Conscientious Scruples & Helped Give Life to Democracy. LC 79-137541. (Peace Movement in America Ser.). 189p. 1972. Repr. of 1940 ed. lib. bdg. 13.95x (ISBN 0-89198-068-7). Ozer.

French, Peter. The Scope of Morality. 1980. 25.00x (ISBN 0-8166-0837-7); pap. 8.95x (ISBN 0-8166-0900-4). U of Minn Pr.

--Social Skills for Nursing Practice. (Illus.). 272p. 1983. pap. 17.50 (ISBN 0-7099-1009-6, Pub. by Croom Helm Ltd). Longwood Pub Group.

French, Peter & MacLure, Margaret, eds. Adult-Child Conversation: Studies in Structure & Process. 1981. 30.00 (ISBN 0-312-00515-6). St Martin.

French, Peter, et al, eds. Studies in Metaphysics. (Midwest Studies in Philosophy: Vol. 4). 1979. text ed. 29.50x (ISBN 0-8166-0887-3); pap. text ed. 12.95x (ISBN 0-8166-0888-1). U of Minn Pr.

--Foundations of Analytic Philosophy. (Midwest Studies in Philosophy: Vol. 6). 576p. 1981. 35.00 (ISBN 0-8166-1033-9); pap. 15.00 (ISBN 0-8166-1036-3). U of Minn Pr.

French, Peter A. Collective & Corporate Responsibility. 232p. 1984. 35.00x (ISBN 0-231-05836-5, King's Crown Paperbacks); pap. 16.50x (ISBN 0-231-05837-3, King's Crown Paperbacks). Columbia U Pr.

--Ethics in Government. 176p. 1983. pap. 13.95 (ISBN 0-13-290908-1). P-H.

French, Peter A. & Uehling, Theodore E., Jr., eds. Contemporary Perspectives on the History of Philosophy. (Midwest Studies in Philosophy: Vol. 8). 555p. 1983. 45.00x (ISBN 0-8166-1207-2); pap. 18.95x (ISBN 0-8166-1212-9). U of Minn Pr.

French, Peter A., jt. ed. see Fisse, Brent.

French, Peter A., et al, eds. Contemporary Perspectives in the Philosophy of Language. (Midwest Studies in Philosophy). 1979. pap. 11.95x (ISBN 0-8166-0866-0). U of Minn Pr.

--Midwest Studies in Philosophy, Vol. 9. LC 84-2349. 544p. 1984. 45.00x (ISBN 0-8166-1349-4); pap. 18.95x (ISBN 0-8166-1352-4). U of Minn Pr.

--Social & Political Philosophy. (Midwest Studies in Philosophy: Vol. 7). 600p. 1982. 45.00x (ISBN 0-8166-1130-0); pap. 18.95x (ISBN 0-8166-1129-7). U of Minn Pr.

--Studies in Epistemology. (Midwest Studies in Philosophy: Vol. 5). 1980. 35.00x (ISBN 0-8166-0944-6); pap. 15.00x (ISBN 0-8166-0947-0). U of Minn Pr.

--Studies in Ethical Theory. (Midwest Studies in Philosophy: Vol. 3). 1980. 25.00x (ISBN 0-8166-0968-3); pap. 10.95x (ISBN 0-8166-0971-3). U of Minn Pr.

French, Peter J. John Dee: The World of an Elizabethan Magus. (Illus.). 256p. 1984. pap. 12.95 (ISBN 0-7102-0385-3). Routledge & Kegan.

French Petroleum Institute Staff. Drilling Mud & Cement Slurry Rheology Manual. LC 81-85417. 108p. 1982. 29.95x (ISBN 0-87201-780-X). Gulf Pub.

French, Philip. Westerns. 2nd ed. 1977. pap. 6.95 (ISBN 0-19-519987-1, GB521, GB). Oxford U Pr.

French, Philip, ed. Three Honest Men: Edmund Wilson, F. R. Leavis, Lionel Trilling. 120p. 16.50 (ISBN 0-85635-299-3). Carcanet.

French, Philip, jt. ed. see Sissons, Michael.

French, R. A. & Hamilton, F. Ian, eds. The Socialist City: Spatial Structure & Urban Policy. LC 78-16828. 541p. 1979. 69.95x (ISBN 0-471-99689-0, Pub. by Wiley-Interscience). Wiley.

French, R. Anthony, jt. auth. see Bater, James H.

French, R. H. Open-Channel Hydraulics. 704p. 1985. 49.95 (ISBN 0-07-022134-0). McGraw.

French, R. J., jt. auth. see Carleton, A. J.

French, R. M., tr. The Way of the Pilgrim & the Pilgrim Continues His Way. 256p. pap. 7.95 (ISBN 0-86683-898-8, AY7444). Winston Pr.

French, R. M., tr. see Berdiaev, Nikolai A.

French, Ray. Coaching Rugby League. (Illus.). 80p. (Orig.). 1982. 11.95 (ISBN 0-571-11954-9); pap. 4.95 (ISBN 0-571-11955-7). Faber & Faber.

--The Rugby League Lions Australia & New Zealand Nineteen Eighty-Four. Oxley, David, intro. by. LC 84-28769. (Illus.). 160p. 1985. 21.95 (ISBN 0-571-13525-0); pap. 10.95 (ISBN 0-571-13526-9). Faber & Faber.

French, Reginald M., tr. from Rus. Way of a Pilgrim. (Illus.). 242p. 1974. (Pub. by Seabury); pap. 5.95 (ISBN 0-8164-2069-6, SP18). Winston Pr.

French, Richard. Anti-Vivisection & Medical Science in Victorian England. LC 74-2966. 436p. 1975. 47.00x (ISBN 0-691-05226-3). Princeton U Pr.

--A Guide to the Birds of Trinidad & Tobago. rev. ed. LC 76-25609. (Illus.). 1976. Repr. of 1973 ed. 25.00 (ISBN 0-915180-03-0). Harrowood Bks.

French, Richard & Beliveau, Andre. The R. C. M. P. & the Management of National Security. 77p. 1979. pap. text ed. 6.95x (ISBN 0-920380-18-2, Pub. by Inst Res Pub Canada). Brookfield Pub Co.

French, Richard E. An Estimate of Personal Wealth in Oklahoma in 1960. LC 75-630253. (University of Florida Social Sciences Monographs: No. 39). 1970. pap. 3.50 (ISBN 0-8130-0302-4). U Presses Fla.

French, Richard F., tr. see Asafiev.

French, Richard H., ed. Salinity in Watercourses & Reservoirs. 640p. 1984. text ed. 49.95 (ISBN 0-250-40616-0). Butterworth.

French, Robert. The Flyers. (Orig.). 1979. pap. 1.95 (ISBN 0-532-23157-0). Woodhill.

--Now, the Gods. 1979. pap. 1.50 (ISBN 0-532-15388-X). Woodhill.

--Road to Glory. 1979. pap. 1.50 (ISBN 0-532-15386-3). Woodhill.

--Sand of Saturn. (Orig.). 1979. pap. 1.95 (ISBN 0-532-23334-4). Woodhill.

--Them. (Orig.). 1979. pap. 1.95 (ISBN 0-532-23156-2). Woodhill.

--Vietnam: Both Sides. (Orig.). 1979. pap. 2.25 (ISBN 0-532-23177-5). Woodhill.

French, Robert D. A Chaucer Handbook. 2nd ed. LC 83-45763. Repr. of 1947 ed. 35.00 (ISBN 0-404-20100-8). AMS Pr.

--Memorial Quadrangle: Yale University. 1929. 49.50x (ISBN 0-686-83624-3). Elliots Bks.

French, Robert D., ed. Sawmill Techniques for Southeast Asia: Proceedings of 2nd Southeast Asia Sawmill Seminar, Manila, 1977, Vol. 2. LC 75-27386. (A Forest Industries Book). (Illus.). 174p. 1978. pap. 35.00 (ISBN 0-87930-105-8). Miller Freeman.

French, Robert G. Young Alec & the Magic Voice. (Children's Theatre Playscript Ser.). 1969. pap. 2.00x (ISBN 0-88020-066-9). Coach Hse.

French, Robert M. Index of Personal Names in the 1880 History of Wyoming County, New York. 40p. 1983. Repr. of 1946 ed. 7.50x (ISBN 0-932334-63-6). Heart of the Lakes.

--A Name Index for the Eighteen Seventy-Nine History of Allegany County, NY. 1978. 15.00x (ISBN 0-932334-05-9); pap. 10.00x (ISBN 0-932334-06-7). Heart of the Lakes.

French, Ron & Horvat, Michael. Parachute Movement Activities: A Complete Parachute Movement Program for Elementary Grades & Beyond. Alexander, Frank, ed. (Illus.). 82p. (Orig.). tchrs ed. 6.95 (ISBN 0-915256-13-4). Front Row.

French, Ronald & Jansma, Paul. Special Physical Education. 416p. 1982. 24.95 (ISBN 0-675-09829-7). Additional Supplements May Be Obtained From Publisher. Merrill.

French, Ruth. Dynamics of Health Care. 3rd ed. (Illus.). 1979. pap. text ed. 18.95 (ISBN 0-07-022143-X). McGraw.

--Nurse's Guide to Diagnostic Procedures. 1980. text ed. 27.00 (ISBN 0-07-022146-4); pap. text ed. 20.00 (ISBN 0-07-022147-2). McGraw.

French, S. Sequencing & Scheduling: An Introduction to the Mathematics of the Job-Shop. (Mathematics & Its Applications Ser.). 245p. pap. 37.95 (ISBN 0-470-27456-5). Halsted Pr.

French, Scott. The Big Brother Game. 240p. 1976. pap. 7.95 (ISBN 0-915914-01-8). GNU.

--The Big Brother Game. 1976. 14.00 (ISBN 0-8184-0240-7); pap. 7.95 (ISBN 0-8184-0241-5). Lyle Stuart.

--The Complete Guide to the Street Drug Game. (Illus.). 256p. 1976. 12.00 (ISBN 0-8184-0208-3); pap. 6.95 (ISBN 0-8184-0237-7). Lyle Stuart.

French, Simon, et al, eds. Multi-Objective Decision Making. 1983. 37.00 (ISBN 0-12-267080-9). Acad Pr.

French, T., et al. Mechanical Drawing. 10th ed. 576p. 1985. 27.44 (ISBN 0-07-022333-5). McGraw.

French, T. E. & Vierck, C. J. Engineering Drawing & Graphic Technology. 13th ed. 752p. 1986. text ed. price not set (ISBN 0-07-022161-8). McGraw.

French, Thomas & Fromm, Erica. Dream Interpretation. Date not set. price not set (BN#01435). Intl Univs Pr.

French, Thomas E. & Svensen, C. L. Familiar Problems in Mechanical Drawing. 1973. 9.32 (ISBN 0-07-022312-2). McGraw.

French, Thomas E. & Vierck, Charles J. Engineering Drawing & Graphic Technology. 12th ed. (Illus.). 1978. text ed. 42.95 (ISBN 0-07-022158-8). McGraw.

French, Valerie, jt. auth. see Lichtman, Allan J.

French, Walter H. & Hale, Charles B., eds. Middle English Metrical Romances, 2 vols. in 1. LC 64-18606. 1964. Repr. of 1930 ed. 32.50x (ISBN 0-8462-0494-0). Russell.

French, Warren. Frank Norris. (Twayne's United States Authors Ser.). 1962. pap. 5.95x (ISBN 0-8084-0134-3, T25, Twayne). New Coll U Pr.

--J. D. Salinger. 2nd rev. ed. (United States Author Ser.). 1976. lib. bdg. 13.50 (ISBN 0-8057-7163-8, Twayne). G K Hall.

--J. D. Salinger. (United States Authors Ser.). 1985. pap. 6.95 (ISBN 0-8057-7447-5, Twayne). G K Hall.

--John Steinbeck. 2nd ed. (United States Authors Ser.). 1975. lib. bdg. 13.50 (ISBN 0-8057-0693-3, Twayne). G K Hall.

--John Steinbeck. (United States Authors Ser.). 192p. 1984. pap. 5.95 (ISBN 0-8057-7424-6, Twayne). G K Hall.

--Season of Promise: Spring Fiction, 1968. LC 67-65993. (Literary Frontiers Ser). 53p. (Orig.). pap. 5.95 (ISBN 0-8262-0067-2). U of Mo Pr.

--Social Novel at the End of an Era. LC 66-10056. (Crosscurrents-Modern Critiques Ser.). 224p. 1966. 7.95 (ISBN 0-8093-0193-8). S Ill U Pr.

French, Warren, ed. The South & Film. LC 81-14641. (Southern Quarterly Ser.). 256p. 1981. Repr. 12.50 (ISBN 0-87805-148-1). U Pr of Miss.

French, Warren, intro. by. Twentieth Century American Literature, 1 of 7 vols. (The Great Writers Library). 668p. pap. 14.95 (ISBN 0-312-34712-X). Academy Chi Pubs.

French, Warren G., ed. American Literary Scholarship: An Annual, 1983. 496p. 1985. 37.75 (ISBN 0-8223-0640-9). Duke.

--Companion to the Grapes of Wrath. LC 77-122056. Repr. of 1963 ed. lib. bdg. 25.00x (ISBN 0-678-03156-8). Kelley.

French, Warren G. & Kidd, Walter E., eds. American Winners of the Nobel Literary Prize. LC 67-24622. Repr. of 1968 ed. 63.30 (ISBN 0-8357-9718-X, 2016218). Bks Demand UMI.

French, Wendell. The Personnel Management Process: Cases in Human Resources Administration. 5th ed. LC 81-86540. 1982. 28.95 (ISBN 0-395-31713-4); instr's manual 2.50 (ISBN 0-395-31714-2). HM.

French, Wendell I., et al. Cases in Human Administration. 2d ed. (Illus.). 1982. 14.50 (ISBN 0-395-31715-0); instr's. manual 1.00 (ISBN 0-395-31716-9). HM.

French, Wendell L. & Bell, Cecil H., Jr. Organization Development: Behavioral Science Interventions for Organization Improvement. 2nd ed. 1978. ref. o.p. 16.95 (ISBN 0-13-641688-8); pap. 16.95 (ISBN 0-13-641670-5). P-H.

--Organization Development: Behavioral Science Interventions for Organization Improvement. 3rd ed. (Illus.). 352p. 1984. pap. text ed. 20.95 (ISBN 0-13-641630-6). P-H.

French, Wendell L., et al. Understanding Human Behavior in Organizations. 768p. 1985. text ed. 30.50 scp (ISBN 0-06-042186-X, HarpC); instr's. manual avail. (ISBN 0-06-362232-7). Har-Row.

French, Wendell L., Jr., et al. Organizational Development: Theory, Practice, Research. 2nd ed. 1983. pap. 21.95 (ISBN 0-256-02689-0). Business Pubns.

French, Will. Promotional Plans in the High School. LC 72-176787. (Columbia University. Teachers College. Contributions to Education: No. 587). Repr. of 1933 ed. 22.50 (ISBN 0-404-55587-X). AMS Pr.

French, William. Further Recollections of a Western Ranchman: New Mexico 1883-1889, Vol. II. (Illus.). 1965. 20.00 (ISBN 0-87266-012-5). Argosy.

French, William, jt. auth. see Deodene, Frank.

French, William B. & Lusk, Harold F. Law of the Real Estate Business. 5th ed. 1984. 27.50 (ISBN 0-256-02853-2). Irwin.

French, William B., et al. Guide to Real Estate Licensing Examinations: For Salespersons & Brokers. 3rd ed. LC 83-23484. 367p. 1984. text ed. 27.95 (ISBN 0-471-80315-4). Wiley.

--Guide to Real Estate Licensing Examinations for Salespersons & Brokers. 4th ed. 1986. 7.95 (ISBN 0-471-82643-X). Wiley.

French, William J. & Criley, J. Michael, eds. Practical Cardiology: Ischemic & Valvular Heart Disease. (UCLA Series of Internal Medicine Today: A Comprehensive Postgraduate Library). 302p. 1982. 28.00x (ISBN 0-471-09551-6, Pub. by Wiley Med). Wiley.

French, William L. Your Handwriting & What It Means. LC 80-19831. 226p. 1980. Repr. of 1976 ed. lib. bdg. 14.95x (ISBN 0-89370-636-1). Borgo Pr.

--Your Handwriting & What It Means. (Newcastle Self-Enrichment Ser). (Illus.). 228p. 1976. pap. 4.95 (ISBN 0-87877-036-4, G-36). Newcastle Pub.

French, William P., jt. auth. see Deodene, Frank.

French, Yvonne. Mrs. Gaskell. 1979. Repr. of 1949 ed. lib. bdg. 15.00 (ISBN 0-8482-3959-8). Norwood Edns.

French-Hodges, Peter F., jt. auth. see Althaus, Catherine.

French-Lazovik, Grace. Evaluation of College Teaching: Guidelines for Summative & Formative Procedures. 1976. 0.50 (ISBN 0-317-06222-0). Assn Am Coll.

French-Lazovik, Grace, ed. Practical Approaches to Evaluating Faculty Performance. LC 81-48584. (Teaching & Learning Ser.: No. 11). 1982. 8.95x (ISBN 0-87589-925-0). Jossey-Bass.

Frend, P. M. Junior Fiction Index. 3rd ed. 1977. pap. 50.00x (ISBN 0-900092-29-7, Pub. by Hill & Son England). State Mutual Bk.

Frend, W. H. The Early Church. LC 81-43085. 1982. pap. 11.95 (ISBN 0-8006-1615-4). Fortress.

--Martyrdom & Persecution in the Early Church. (Twin Brooks Ser.). 645p. 1981. pap. 12.95 (ISBN 0-8010-3502-3). Baker Bk.

--The Rise of Christianity. LC 83-48909. (Illus.). 1042p. 1984. pap. 49.95 (ISBN 0-8006-0713-9, 1-713). Fortress.

--The Rise of the Monophysite Movement: Chapters in the History of the Church in the Fifth & Sixth Centuries. LC 72-75302. (Illus.). 400p. 1972. 74.50 (ISBN 0-521-08130-0). Cambridge U Pr.

--Saints & Sinners in the Early Church: Differing & Conflicting Traditions in the First Six Centuries. (Theology & Life Ser.: Vol. 11). 1985. pap. 8.95 (ISBN 0-89453-451-3). M Glazier.

--Town & Country in the Early Christian Centuries. 372p. 1980. 60.00x (ISBN 0-86078-055-4, Pub. by Variorum). State Mutual Bk.

Frendo, J. D., tr. from Lat. Agathias: The Histories. (Corpus Fontium Historiae Byzantinae: Vol. 2a). iv, 170p. 1975. 38.80x (ISBN 3-11-003357-7). De Gruyter.

Freneau, Philip. American Village: A Poem. Koopman, H. L. & Paltsits, V. H., eds. LC 68-57127. (Research & Source Works Ser.: No. 312). 1969. Repr. of 1906 ed. 18.50 (ISBN 0-8337-1242-X). B Franklin.

--Poems Written Between the Years 1768 & 1794. 59.95 (ISBN 0-8490-0852-2). Gordon Pr.

--Some Account of the Capture of the Ship Aurora. LC 74-140864. (Eyewitness Accounts of the American Revolution Ser.: No. 3). 1970. Repr. of 1899 ed. 10.00 (ISBN 0-405-01227-6). Ayer Co Pubs.

Freneau, Philip, jt. auth. see Brackenridge, Hugh H.

Freneau, Philip, tr. see Robin, Abbe.

Freneau, Philip M. A Collection of Poems on American Affairs & Variety of Other Subjects. LC 76-15581. 1976. Repr. of 1815 ed. lib. bdg. 60.00x (ISBN 0-8201-1174-0). Schol Facsimiles.

--Final Poems of Philip Freneau. LC 79-23056. 1980. 35.00x (ISBN 0-8201-1346-8). Schol Facsimiles.

--The Last Poems of Philip Freneau. Leary, Lewis, ed. LC 72-110270. xiii, 136p. Repr. of 1945 ed. lib. bdg. 18.75x (ISBN 0-8371-4496-5, FRLP). Greenwood.

--Letters on Various Interesting & Important Subjects. LC 43-6720. 1976. Repr. lib. bdg. 35.00x (ISBN 0-8201-1205-4). Schol Facsimiles.

--Poems Written & Published During the American Revolutionary War. Leary, Lewis, intro. by. LC 76-11754. 616p. 1976. Repr. of 1809 ed. lib. bdg. 90.00x (ISBN 0-8201-1173-2). Schol Facsimiles.

--Poems Written Between the Years 1768 & 1794. LC 76-11752. 480p. 1976. Repr. of 1795 ed. lib. bdg. 70.00x (ISBN 0-8201-1172-4). Schol Facsimiles.

--Poems, 1786 & Miscellaneous Works (1788) of Philip Freneau, 2 vols. in one. LC 74-31251. 880p. 1975. Repr. lib. bdg. 90.00x (ISBN 0-8201-1151-1). Schol Facsimiles.

--The Writings in Prose & Verse of Hezekiah Salem, Late of New England. LC 75-15901. (Illus.). 88p. 1975. lib. bdg. 25.00x (ISBN 0-8201-1156-2). Schol Facsimiles.

Frenette, Ed & Holthusen, T. Lanee, eds. Earth Sheltering: The Form of Energy & the Energy of Form: Award Winning & Selected Entries from the 1981 American Underground Space Associations Design Competition. (Illus.). 256p. 1981. 35.00 (ISBN 0-08-028052-8). Pergamon.

Freney, J. R., jt. ed. see Calbally, E. I.

Freney, J. R., jt. ed. see Ivanov, M. V.

Freney, Michael A. & Townsend, James J. The Future of Military Aviation, Vol. VI. (Significant Issues Ser.: No. 14). 51p. 1984. 8.95 (ISBN 0-89206-065-4). CSI Studies.

Freniere, H. Francis, et al, trs. see People's Court, Munich & Hitler, Adolph.

Frenkel, B. N., tr. see Babushkin, V. I., et al.

Frenkel, Jacob A., ed. Exchange Rates & International Macroeconomics. LC 83-14524. (National Bureau of Economic Research Conference Ser.). 400p. 1984. lib. bdg. 43.00x (ISBN 0-226-26249-9). U of Chicago Pr.

Frenkel, Jacob A. & Johnson, Harry G., eds. The Monetary Approach to the Balance of Payments. (Illus.). 1976. pap. 12.50 (ISBN 0-8020-6316-0). U of Toronto Pr.

Frenkel, Jacob A., jt. ed. see Dornbusch, Rudiger.

Frenkel, James R. Make More Money Writing Fiction. LC 83-15495. 240p. 1983. 12.95 (ISBN 0-668-05568-5); pap. 7.95 (ISBN 0-668-05570-7). Arco.

Frenkel, Karen A., jt. auth. see Asimov, Isaac.

Frenkel, M., jt. ed. see Arias, I. M.

Frenkel, Rene A. & McGarry, J. Denis. Carnitine Biosynthesis, Metabolism & Functions. LC 80-11971. 1980. 44.00 (ISBN 0-12-267060-4). Acad Pr.

Frenkel, Robert E. Ruderal Vegetation along Some California Roadsides. (California Library Reprint Ser.: No. 92). 1978. Repr. of 1970 ed. 21.00x (ISBN 0-520-03589-5). U of Cal Pr.

Frenkel, Stephen J. & Coolican, Alice. Unions Against Capitalism? A Sociological Comparison of the Australian Building & Metal Workers' Union. 360p. 1985. text ed. 35.00x (ISBN 0-86861-468-8); pap. 17.50x (ISBN 0-86861-476-9). Allen Unwin.

Frenkel, Stephen J., ed. Industrial Action in Australia. 184p. 1981. text ed. 24.95x (ISBN 0-86861-122-0); pap. text ed. 12.50x (ISBN 0-86861-130-1). Allen Unwin.

Frenkel-Brunswick, Else. Else Frenkel-Brunswik: Selected Papers. Heiman, Nanette & Grant, Joan, eds. LC 73-8079. (Psychological Issues Monograph: No. 31, Vol. 8, No. 3). 333p. 1974. text ed. 22.50 (ISBN 0-8236-1645-2). Intl Univs Pr.

Frenkel-Brunswik, Else, jt. auth. see Adorno, T. W.

Frenkiel, F. N. see Landsberg, H. E.

Frenkiel, Francois N. & Goodall, David W., eds. Simulation Modeling of Environmental Problems. LC 77-92369. (SCOPE Ser. (Scientific Committee on Problems of the Environment): Scope Report 9). 112p. 1978. pap. 24.95x (ISBN 0-471-99580-0, Pub. by Wiley-Interscience). Wiley.

Frensdorff, Salomon. Massora Magna. rev. ed. LC 67-11896. (Library of Biblical Studies). (Heb). 1968. 35.00x (ISBN 0-87068-052-8). Ktav.

--Ochlah W'Ochlah. 35.00x (ISBN 0-87068-194-X). Ktav.

Frenselli, Frederick J. Metropolitan Medical Center: Medical Terminology & Machine Transcription. 1985. text ed. 7.10 wkbk. (ISBN 0-538-11490-8, K49). SW Pub.

Frentz, Brand, tr. see Turchin, Valentin F.

Frentz, Henry J., jt. ed. see Chelius, Carl R.

Frentz, Herbert. California Tax Handbook: 1984 Edition. 566p. 1984. 12.50x (ISBN 0-686-89039-6, 11187-2). P-H.

Frentzel-Beyme, R., et al. Cancer Atlas of the Federal Republic of Germany: Cancer Mortality in the States of the Federal Republic of Germany, 1955-1975. (Illus.). 1979. pap. 52.00 (ISBN 0-387-09566-7). Springer-Verlag.

Frenyo, V. L., jt. auth. see Pethes, G.

Frenz, Horst & Tuck, Susan, eds. Eugene O'Neill's Critics: Voices from Abroad. LC 83-4705. 225p. 1984. 22.50x (ISBN 0-8093-1143-7). S Ill U Pr.

Frenz, Horst, jt. ed. see Hibbard, Addison.

Frenz, Horst, ed. see Nobel Foundation.

Frenz, Horst, jt. ed. see Stallknecht, Newton P.

Frenz, Horst, tr. see Hauptmann, Gerhart.

Frenz, Peter. Studien zu Traditionellen Elementen des Geschichtsdenkens und der Bildlichkeit im Werk Johann Gottfried Herders. (Mikrokosmos: Vol. 12). 283p. (Ger.). 1983. 33.70 (ISBN 3-8204-7345-9). P Lang Pubs.

Frenzel, Burkhard. Climatic Fluctuations of the Ice Age. Nairn, A. E., tr. from Ger. LC 70-170788. (Illus.). 252p. 1973. text ed. 22.50 (ISBN 0-8295-0226-2). UPB.

Frenzel, Elisabeth. Diccionario de Argumentos de la Literatura Universal. 496p. (Sp.). 1976. pap. 29.95 (ISBN 84-249-3140-8, S-29899). French & Eur.

--Diccionario De Argumentos De la Literatura Universal. 496p. (Espn.). 1976. 35.95 (ISBN 84-249-3141-6, S-50151). French & Eur.

Frenzel, G., tr. see Helwig, Jane T. & SAS Institute Inc.

Frenzel, Herbert. John Millington Synge's Work As a Contribution to Irish Folk-Lore & to the Psychology of Primitive Tribes. LC 72-191249. 1932. lib. bdg. 15.00 (ISBN 0-8414-4284-3). Folcroft.

Frenzel, Louis E. Digital Counter Handbook. 1981. pap. 10.95 (ISBN 0-672-21758-9). Sams.

Frenzel, Louis E., Jr. The Howard W. Sams Crash Course in Digital Technology. LC 82-50654. 208p. 1983. pap. 19.95 (ISBN 0-672-21845-3, 21845). Sams.

--The Howard W. Sams Crash Course in Microcomputers. 2nd ed. LC 83-60173. 328p. 1983. pap. 21.95 (ISBN 0-672-21985-9, 21985). Sams.

Frenzel, Louis E., Jr., et al. Handbook for the IBM P C. LC 83-50939. 352p. 1984. pap. 15.95 (ISBN 0-672-22004-0, 22004). Sams.

Frenzel, M. A., jt. auth. see Bradway, B. M.

Frep, Roy A. Using Tear Sheets. (Bridges for Ideas Handbook Ser.). 1963. pap. text ed. 6.00x (ISBN 0-913648-12-4). U Tex Austin Film Lib.

Frere, Edouard B. Manuel Du Bibliographe Normand, ou, Dictionnaire Bibliographique et Historique Contenant, 2 Vols. 1964. Repr. of 1860 ed. 73.00 (ISBN 0-8337-1245-4). B Franklin.

Frere, M. Hindoo Fairy Legends: (Old Deccan Days) 11.25 (ISBN 0-8446-2095-5). Peter Smith.

Frere, M., jt. auth. see Oldeman, L. R.

Frere, Mary E. Old Deccan Days. LC 78-67710. (The Folktale). Repr. of 1868 ed. 28.00 (ISBN 0-404-16087-5). AMS Pr.

Frere, Paul. Porsche 911 Story. 3rd ed. 216p. 19.95 (ISBN 0-668-06158-8). Arco.

--Sports Car & Competition Driving. LC 63-5821. 1963. 14.95 (ISBN 0-8376-0034-0). Bentley.

Frere, Paul, jt. auth. see Nye, Doug.

Frere, Paul, tr. see Boschen, Lothar & Barth, Jurgen.

Frere, R. B. Maxwell's Ghost. 1976. 17.50 (ISBN 0-575-02044-X, Pub. by Gollancz England). David & Charles.

Frere, S. S. & St. Joseph, J. K. Roman Britain from the Air. LC 82-9746. (Cambridge Air Surveys Ser.). (Illus.). 240p. 1983. 37.50 (ISBN 0-521-25088-9). Cambridge U Pr.

Frere, W. H. Antiohonale Sarisburiense, 6 Vols. 115p. 1923. text ed. 310.50 (ISBN 0-576-28701-6, Pub. by Gregg Intl Pubs England). Gregg Intl.

--The English Church in the Reigns of Elizabeth & James I: 1558-1625. 1977. lib. bdg. 59.95 (ISBN 0-8490-1773-4). Gordon Pr.

--Grauale Sarisburiense. 102p. 1894. text ed. 165.60x (ISBN 0-576-28703-2, Pub. by Gregg Intl Pubs England). Gregg Intl.

--The Use of Sarum, 2 vols. 744p. 1898. text ed. 165.60x (ISBN 0-576-99171-6, Pub. by Gregg Intl Pubs England). Gregg Intl.

Frere, Walter H. The Anaphora or Great Eucharistic Prayer: An Eirenical Study in Liturgical History. (Church Historical Society, London, New Ser.: No. 26). pap. 23.00 (ISBN 0-317-16229-2). Kraus Repr.

--English Church in the Reigns of Elizabeth & James First, 1558-1625. (History of the English Church: No. 5). Repr. of 1904 ed. 29.50 (ISBN 0-404-50755-7). AMS Pr.

--Puritan Manifestoes. 1907. 20.50 (ISBN 0-8337-4119-5). B Franklin.

Frere, Walter H., ed. The Winchester Troper, from MSS. of the Xth & XIth Centuries, with Other Documents Illustrating the Tropes in England & France. LC 70-178507. Repr. of 1894 ed. 29.50 (ISBN 0-404-56530-1). AMS Pr.

Frerichs, Wendell W. Take It to the Lord: Prayer Laments for the Afflicted. LC 81-52273. 80p. (Orig.). 1982. pap. 4.95 (ISBN 0-8066-1905-8, 10-6191). Augsburg.

Freris, A. F. The Greek Economy in the Twentieth Century. 256p. 1985. 29.95 (ISBN 0-312-34724-3). St Martin.

Freris, Andrew. The Soviet Industrial Enterprise: Theory & Practice. LC 83-40626. 192p. 1984. 22.50 (ISBN 0-312-74840-X). St Martin.

Freris, T., jt. auth. see Laithwaite, L.

Frerking, Marvin E. Crystal Oscillator Design & Temperature Compensation. 1978. 24.95 (ISBN 0-442-22459-1). Van Nos Reinhold.

Fresan, Juan. New York. (Illus.). 96p. (Orig.). 1983. pap. 7.95 (ISBN 0-87663-592-3). Universe.

Freschet, Bernice. Racoon Baby. (Illus.). 48p. (gr. 1-8). 1984. PLB 6.99 (ISBN 0-399-61149-5, Putnam). Putnam Pub Group.

Freschet, Berniece. Bernard & the Catnip Caper. (Illus.). 40p. (gr. 1-3). 1981. 9.95 (ISBN 0-684-17157-0, ScribJ). Scribner.

--Owl & the Prairie Dog. LC 69-17061. (ps-3). 1969. 3.95 (ISBN 0-684-20828-8, ScribJ). Scribner.

--Owl in the Garden. LC 84-5724. (Illus.). 32p. (ps-3). 1985. 11.75 (ISBN 0-688-04047-0); PLB 11.88 (ISBN 0-688-04048-9). Lothrop.

--The Watersnake. LC 78-31103. (Encore Edition). (Illus.). (gr. 1-3). 1979. 1.98 (ISBN 0-684-16112-5, ScribJ). Scribner.

--Wood Duck Baby. (Illus.). 48p. (gr. 1-3). 1983. pap. 6.99 (ISBN 0-399-61191-6, Putnam). Putnam Pub Group.

Freschi. Italian Opera Librettos, Vol. XVI. Brown, Howard & Weimer, Eric, eds. (Italian Opera Ser., 1640-1770). 83.00 (ISBN 0-317-20354-1). Garland Pub.

Fresco, Monte. Photographs Are My Life. (Illus.). 128p. 1983. 14.95 (ISBN 0-668-05814-5, 5814). Arco.

Fresco-Corbu, Roger. European Pipes. Riley, Noel, ed. (Antique Pocket Guides). (Illus.). 64p. (Orig.). 1982. pap. 5.95 (ISBN 0-7188-2535-7, Pub. by Lutterworth Pr UK). Seven Hills Bks.

--Vesta Boxes. (Antique Pocket Guides). (Illus.). 64p. (Orig.). 1983. pap. 5.95 (ISBN 0-7188-2582-9, Pub. by Lutterworth Pr UK). Seven Hills Bks.

Frescura, Franco. Rural Shelter in Southern Africa: A Survey of the Architecture, House Forms & Construction Methods of the Black Rural Peoples of Southern Africa. (Illus.). 208p. 1981. pap. 16.95 (ISBN 0-86975-205-7, Pub. by Ravan Pr). Ohio U Pr.

Frescura, Marina Sassu. Interferenze Lessicali: Italian-Inglese: Lexical Interference: Italian-English. 172p. (Orig., Ital. Eng.). 1984. pap. text ed. 10.00 (ISBN 0-8020-6553-8). U of Toronto Pr.

Frese, Dolores, jt. auth. see Nicholson, Lewis.

Frese, Dolores, jt. ed. see Nicholson, Lewis.

Frese, Joseph & Judd, Jacob. Business & Government. 248p. 1985. 25.00 (ISBN 0-912882-52-2). Sleepy Hollow.

Frese, Joseph R. & Judd, Jacob, eds. American Industrialization, Economic Expansion, & the Law. LC 81-4735. (The American Economic Enterprise Ser.: Vol. 3). 272p. 20.00 (ISBN 0-912882-50-6). Sleepy Hollow.

--Business Enterprise in Early New York. LC 79-9346. 224p. 1979. 17.50 (ISBN 0-912882-38-7). Sleepy Hollow.

--An Emerging Independent American Economy: Eighteen Fifteen to Eighteen Seventy-Five. LC 80-15195. 224p. 1980. text ed. 20.00 (ISBN 0-912882-40-9). Sleepy Hollow.

Frese, Michael & Sabini, John, eds. Goal Directed Behavior: The Concept of Action in Psychology. 440p. 1985. text ed. 39.95 (ISBN 0-89859-529-0). L Erlbaum Assocs.

Frese, Wolfgang, jt. auth. see Howell, Frank M.

Fresener, Patricia A., jt. ed. see Fresener, Scott O.

Fresener, Scott O. & Fresener, Patricia A., eds. How to Print T-Shirts for Fun & Profit. (Illus.). 176p. (Orig.). 1979. pap. text ed. 19.95 (ISBN 0-9603530-0-3). US Screen.

Fresenius, W & Luderwald, I., eds. Environmental Research & Protection: Inorganic Analysis. 310p. 1984. pap. 15.30 (ISBN 0-387-13469-7). Springer Verlag.

Freshman, Phil, ed. see Moorey, P. R., et al.

Freshman, Phil, ed. see Museum Staff.

Freshman, Phil, et al, eds. see Maeder, Edward, et al.

Freshman, Ron. System Design Guide, Featuring dBASE II. 183p. 1984. pap. 18.50 (ISBN 0-912677-12-0). Ashton-Tate Bks.

--Systems Development Guide Using dBASE II. 1984. 19.95 (ISBN 0-8359-7444-8). Reston.

Freshman, Samuel K. Principles of Real Estate Finance. 1980. write for info. S K Freshman.

--Principles of Real Estate Syndication. 3rd ed. LC 79-53278. (Illus.). 320p. 1980. 9.95 (ISBN 0-9600708-4-2). Law & Cap Dynamics.

--Real Estate Finance & Syndication Form Book. 1980. write for info. S K Freshman.

--Real Estate Finance & Syndication Glossary. 3rd., rev. ed. LC 79-2801. 109p. 1979. 5.95 (ISBN 0-9600708-3-4). Law & Cap Dynamics.

Freshney, Ian R., ed. Culture of Animal Cells: A Manual of Basic Technique. LC 82-24960. 310p. 1983. 49.50 (ISBN 0-8451-0223-0). A R Liss.

Freshney, R. I., jt. ed. see Thilo-Koerner, D. G.

Freshwater Biological Association, Cumbria England. Catalogue of the Library of the Freshwater Biological Association. 1979. lib. bdg. 660.00 (ISBN 0-8161-0289-9, Hall Library). G K Hall.

Fresne, Florine Du. Home Care: An Alternative to the Nursing Home. 127p. 1983. pap. 6.95 (ISBN 0-87178-030-5). Brethren.

Fresne, Jim Du see Du Fresne, Jim.

Fresne Du Cange, Charles D. Du see Du Cange, Charles D.

Fresnel, Augustin J. Oeuvres Completes, 3 vols. (Lat.). Repr. of 1866 ed. 160.00 (ISBN 0-384-16770-5). Johnson Repr.

Fresnel, Jean. Geometrie Analytique Rigide et Applications. (Progress in Mathematics Ser.: No. 18). 150p. (Fr.). 1981. text ed. 17.50x (ISBN 0-8176-3069-4). Birkhauser.

Fresno City & County Historical Society. Fresno California Illustrated. LC 80-68522. (Illus.). 192p. 1980. Repr. 13.95 (ISBN 0-914330-35-7, Pub by Pioneer Pub Co). Panorama West.

Fresnoy, Charles A. Du see Du Fresnoy, Charles A.

Fresnoy, Nicolas Lenglet Du see Lenglet Du Fresnoy, Nicolas.

Freson, Robert. The Taste of France. LC 83-6709. (Illus.). 288p. 1983. 45.00 (ISBN 0-941434-36-2). Stewart Tabori & Chang.

Fresquet, G., jt. auth. see Parramon, J. M.

Fretageot, Marie D., jt. auth. see Maclure, William.

Fretenburg, Ray. Getting Your Butterflies to Fly in Formation. LC 81-90202. 28p. 1982. 6.95 (ISBN 0-533-05099-5). Vantage.

Fretheim, Terence E. Deuteronomic History. Bailey, Lloyd R. & Furnish, Victory P., eds. 160p. (Orig.). 1983. pap. 9.95 (ISBN 0-687-10497-1). Abingdon.

--The Message of Jonah: A Theological Commentary. LC 77-72461. pap. 7.50 (ISBN 0-8066-1591-5, 10-4350). Augsburg.

--The Suffering of God: An Old Testament Perspective. Brueggemann, Walter, ed. LC 84-47921. (Overtures to Biblical Theology Ser.). 224p. 1984. pap. 10.95 (ISBN 0-8006-1538-7). Fortress.

Fretter, ed. see Zoological Society Of London - 22nd Symposium.

Fretter, V. & Graham, A. A Functional Anatomy of Invertebrates: Excluding Land Anthropods. 1976. 69.50 (ISBN 0-12-267550-9). Acad Pr.

Fretter, V. & Peake, J., eds. Pulmonates: Functional Anatomy & Physiology, Vol. 1. 1975. 64.50 (ISBN 0-12-267501-0). Acad Pr.

Fretter, Vera & Graham, Alastair. British Prosobranch Mollusks: Their Functional Anatomy & Ecology. (Illus.). xvi, 775p. 1962. 55.00x (ISBN 0-903874-12-1, Pub. by Brit Mus Nat Hist England). Sabbot-Natural Hist Bks.

Fretter, Vera & Peake, J., eds. Pulmonates: Vol. 2A, Systematics, Evolution & Ecology. 1979. 72.00 (ISBN 0-12-267502-9). Acad Pr.

--Pulmonates: Vol. 2b, Economic Malacology with Particular Reference to Achatina Fulica. 1979. 39.50 (ISBN 0-12-267541-X). Acad Pr.

Fretwell, Elbert K. Study in Educational Prognosis. LC 72-177603. (Columbia University. Teachers College. Contributions to Education: No. 99). Repr. of 1919 ed. 22.50 (ISBN 0-404-55099-1). AMS Pr.

Fretz, Bruce R. & Mills, David H. Licensing & Certification of Psychologists & Counselors: A Guide to Current Policies, Procedures, & Legislation. LC 80-8011. (Social & Behavioral Science Ser.). 1980. text ed. 21.95x (ISBN 0-87589-470-4). Jossey-Bass.

Fretz, Bruce R. & Stang, David J. Preparing for Graduate Study: Not for Seniors Only! LC 79-25328. 88p. 1980. 9.00x (ISBN 0-912704-12-8); members 7.50. Am Psychol.

Fretz, Burton, et al. Representing Older Persons: An Advocates Manual. Fried, Bruce, ed. (Orig.). 1985. pap. 30.00 (ISBN 0-932605-00-1). Natl Sen Citizens.

Fretz, Clarence Y. Story of God's People. (Christian Day School Ser). (gr. 7). pap. 5.90x (ISBN 0-87813-900-1); tchrs. guide 6.95x (ISBN 0-87813-901-X). Christian Light.

--You & Your Bible-You & Your Life. (Christian Day School Ser). (gr. 8). pap. 4.10x (ISBN 0-87813-902-8); teachrs guide 13.75x (ISBN 0-87813-903-6). Christian Light.

Fretz, Donald R. Courts & the News Media. (Ser. 810). 1977. 7.50 (ISBN 0-686-00408-6). Natl Judicial Coll.

Fretz, Sada. Going Vegetarian: A Guide for Teenagers. LC 82-14230. (Illus.). 280p. (gr. 7up). 1983. 11.50 (ISBN 0-688-01713-4). Morrow.

Fretz, Thomas A., et al. Plant Propagation Laboratory Manual. 3rd rev. ed. 1979. text ed. 13.95x (ISBN 0-8087-0668-3). Burgess.

Freuchen, Dagmar & Clifford, William. Dagmar Freuchen's Cookbook of the Seven Seas. LC 68-30504. (Illus.). 256p. 1968. 7.95 (ISBN 0-87131-016-3). M Evans.

Freuchen, Peter. Arctic Adventure. LC 74-5833. (Illus.). Repr. of 1935 ed. 32.50 (ISBN 0-404-11638-8). AMS Pr.

--Arctic Adventure: My Life in the Frozen North. 467p. 1982. Repr. of 1935 ed. lib. bdg. 35.00 (ISBN 0-89987-269-7). Darby Bks.

--Book of the Eskimos. 1972. pap. 2.95 (ISBN 0-685-49202-8, M1293, Crest). Fawcett.

--Book of the Eskimos. 1977. pap. 2.95 (ISBN 0-449-30802-2, Prem). Fawcett.

--Ivalu, the Eskimo Wife. LC 74-5834. Repr. of 1935 ed. 27.50 (ISBN 0-404-11639-6). AMS Pr.

Freud, Anna. Difficulties in the Path of Psychoanalysis: A Confrontation of Past with Present Viewpoints. LC 70-87847. (The New York Psychoanalytic Institute Freud Anniversary Lecture Ser.). 84p. 1969. text ed. 30.00 (ISBN 0-8236-1285-6). Intl Univs Pr.

--Ego & the Mechanisms of Defense. rev. ed. LC 66-30463. (Writings of Anna Freud Ser.: Vol. 2). 191p. 1967. text ed. 22.50 (ISBN 0-8236-6871-1); pap. text ed. 9.95 (ISBN 0-8236-8035-5, 26871). Intl Univs Pr.

--Indications for Child Analysis & Other Papers. LC 67-9514. (Writings of Anna Freud: Vol. 4). 706p. 1968. text ed. 50.00 (ISBN 0-8236-6873-8). Intl Univs Pr.

--Introduction to Psychoanalysis: Lectures for Child Analysts & Teachers. LC 73-16853. (Writings of Anna Freud: Vol. 1). 200p. 1974. text ed. 22.50 (ISBN 0-8236-6870-3). Intl Univs Pr.

--Introduction to the Technic of Child Analysis. LC 74-21408. (Classics in Child Development Ser). 1975. Repr. 17.00 (ISBN 0-405-06460-8). Ayer Co Pubs.

--Normality & Pathology in Childhood: Assessments of Development. LC 65-17007. (Writings of Anna Freud: Vol. 6). 273p. (Orig.). 1966. text ed. 27.50 (ISBN 0-8236-6875-4); pap. text ed. 9.95 (ISBN 0-8236-8165-3, 26875). Intl Univs Pr.
--Problems of Psychoanalytic Training, Diagnosis, & the Technique of Therapy. LC 67-9514. (Writings of Anna Freud: Vol. 7). 311p. 1971. text ed. 27.50 (ISBN 0-8236-6876-2). Intl Univs Pr.
--The Psycho-Analytical Treatment of Children. 90p. 1965. text ed. 17.50 (ISBN 0-8236-5080-4). Intl Univs Pr.
--The Psycho-Analytical Treatment of Children. LC 68-18382. xii, 98p. 17.50 (ISBN 0-8236-1960-5, BN#0196). Intl Univs Pr.
--Psychoanalysis for Teachers & Parents. Low, Barbara, tr. 1935. 8.95 (ISBN 0-87523-011-3). Emerson.
--Psychoanalysis for Teachers & Parents. Low, Barbara, tr. from Ger. 1979. pap. 1.95 (ISBN 0-393-00918-1). Norton.
--Psychoanalytic Psychology of Normal Development (1970-1980) (The Writings of Anna Freud Ser.: Vol. 8). 389p. 1981. text ed. 32.50 (ISBN 0-686-73134-4). Intl Univs Pr.
--Research at the Hampstead Child-Therapy Clinic & Other Papers. LC 67-9514. (Writings of Anna Freud Ser.: Vol. 5). 575p. 1969. text ed. 35.00 (ISBN 0-8236-6874-6). Intl Univs Pr.
Freud, Anna & Burlingham, Dorothy T. Infants Without Families: Reports on the Hampstead Nurseries. LC 72-8788. (Writings of Anna Freud: Vol. 3). 680p. 1973. text ed. 50.00 (ISBN 0-8236-6872-X). Intl Univs Pr.
--Infants Without Families: The Case Against Residential Nurseries. 128p. 1947. text ed. 15.00 (ISBN 0-8236-2640-7). Intl Univs Pr.
--War & Children. Lehrman, Philip R., ed. LC 73-7699. 191p. 1973. Repr. of 1943 ed. lib. bdg. 22.50x (ISBN 0-8371-6942-9, FRWC). Greenwood.
Freud, Anna, jt. auth. see Bergmann, Thesi.
Freud, Anna see Eissler, Ruch S., et al.
Freud, Anna, jt. auth. see Sandler, Joseph.
Freud, Anna, frwd. by. Studies in Child Psychoanalysis: Pure & Applied. LC 74-20082. (Illus.). 250p. 1975. 24.50x (ISBN 0-300-01817-7). Yale U Pr.
Freud, Arthur. All about the Parrots. LC 79-25568. (Illus.). 304p. 1984. 17.95 (ISBN 0-87605-815-2). Howell Bk.
--Of Human Sovereignty. LC 65-10993. 1965. 6.00 (ISBN 0-8022-0539-9). Philos Lib.
Freud, Ernst, et al. Sigmund Freud: His Life in Pictures & Words. Trollope, Christiane, tr. LC 78-53882. (A Helen & Kurt Wolff Bk.). (Illus.). 1978. 39.95 (ISBN 0-15-182546-7). HarBraceJ.
Freud, Ernst L., ed. see Freud, Sigmund.
Freud, G. Orthogonale Polynome. (Mathematische Eihe Ser.: No. 33). (Illus.). 294p. (Ger.). 1969. 49.95x (ISBN 0-8176-0127-9). Birkhauser.
Freud, Geza. Orthogonal Polynomials. LC 76-134028. 1971. 50.00 (ISBN 0-08-016047-6). Pergamon.
Freud, Martin. Sigmund Freud: Man & Father. 224p. 1983. 20.00 (ISBN 0-87668-722-2). Aronson.
Freud, Sigmund. Autobiographical Study. Strachey, James, ed. & tr. 1963. pap. 3.95 (ISBN 0-393-00146-6, Norton Lib.). Norton.
--The Basic Writings of Sigmund Freud. Brill, A. A., ed. & intro. by. LC 38-27462. 1938. 12.95 (ISBN 0-394-60400-8). Modern Lib.
--Beyond the Pleasure Principle. Strachey, James, ed. & tr. 96p. 1975. (Norton Lib); pap. 3.95 (ISBN 0-393-00769-3). Norton.
--Character & Culture. 1963. pap. 2.95 (ISBN 0-02-076200-3, Collier). Macmillan.
--Civilization & Its Discontents. Strachey, James, ed. & tr. 1962 14.95 (ISBN 0-393-01067-8, Norton Lib); pap. 2.95x 1963 (ISBN 0-393-09623-8). Norton.
--Civilization & Its Discontents. Strachey, James, ed. 128p. 1984. pap. 4.95 (ISBN 0-393-30158-3). Norton.
--Cocaine Papers. Byck, Robert, ed. 1975. pap. 8.95 (ISBN 0-452-00671-6, F671, Mer). NAL.
--Collected Papers of Sigmund Freud, 5 Vols. Jones, Ernest, ed. LC 61-15950. (The International Psycho-Analytic Library, Nos. 7, 8, 9, 10, 37). 1959. 36.00x ea. Vol. 1 (ISBN 0-465-01249-3). Vol. 2 (ISBN 0-465-01250-7). Vol. 3 (ISBN 0-465-01251-5). Vol. 4 (ISBN 0-465-01252-3). Vol. 5 (ISBN 0-465-01253-1). Set. 175.00x (ISBN 0-465-01248-5). Basic.
--The Complete Psychological Works: Standard Edition, 24 vols. Strachey, James, ed. & tr. from Ger. 1976. 595.00x set (ISBN 0-393-01128-3). Norton.
--Dora: An Analysis of a Case of Hysteria. 1963. pap. 2.95 (ISBN 0-02-076250-X, Collier). Macmillan.
--Dream Mechanism & Its Analysis. (Illus.). 147p. 1983. 89.95 (ISBN 0-89920-058-3). Am Inst Psych.
--Early Psychoanalytic Writings. 192p. 1985. pap. 4.95 (ISBN 0-02-076300-X, Collier). MacMillan.
--The Ego & the Id. Strachey, James, ed. Riviere, Joan, tr. (Standard ed.). 1962. pap. 2.95 (ISBN 0-393-00142-3). Norton.
--Five Lectures on Psycho-Analysis. Strachey, James, ed. 1977. 6.95 (ISBN 0-393-01133-X); pap. 3.95 (ISBN 0-393-00847-9). Norton.
--Freud: Dictionary of Psychoanalysis. Fodor, Nandor & Gaynor, Frank, eds. Repr. of 1950 ed. lib. bdg. 18.75x (ISBN 0-8371-2135-3, FRP). Greenwood.
--The Future of an Illusion. Strachey, James, ed. 1975. 10.95 (ISBN 0-393-01120-8); pap. 2.95 (ISBN 0-393-00831-2). Norton.
--General Psychological Theory. 1963. pap. 3.95 (ISBN 0-02-076350-6, Collier). Macmillan.
--General Selection from the Works of Sigmund Freud. LC 57-11436. 1957. pap. 4.95 (ISBN 0-385-09325-X, Anch). Doubleday.
--General Selections from the Works of Sigmund Freud. Rickman, John, ed. 1967. 6.95 (ISBN 0-87140-927-5). Liveright.
--Group Psychology & the Analysis of the Ego. Strachey, James, ed. & tr. 1975. 6.95 (ISBN 0-393-01117-8); pap. 2.95 (ISBN 0-393-00770-7). Norton.
--The History of the Psychoanalytic Movement. Brill, A. A., tr. (Nervous & Mental Disease Monographs: No. 25). Repr. of 1917 ed. 14.00 (ISBN 0-384-16800-0). Johnson Repr.
--The History of the Psychoanalytic Movemenf. 125p. 1985. pap. 4.95 (ISBN 0-02-076400-6, Collier). MacMillan.
--Infantile Cerebral Paralysis. Russin, Lester A., tr. LC 68-30730. 1968. 19.95x (ISBN 0-87024-094-3). U of Miami Pr.
--Inhibitions, Symptoms & Anxiety. Strachey, James, ed. Strachey, Alix, tr. 1977. 6.95 (ISBN 0-393-01166-6); pap. 3.95 (ISBN 0-393-00874-6). Norton.
--Interpretation of Dreams. Strachey, James, tr. 736p. 1980. pap. 4.95 (ISBN 0-380-01000-3, 68908-1, Discus). Avon.
--Interpretation of Dreams. Brill, A. A., tr. LC 50-6784. 6.95 (ISBN 0-394-60461-X). Modern Lib.
--The Interpretation of Dreams. 191p. 1983. Repr. of 1900 ed. lib. bdg. 21.95x (ISBN 0-686-47485-6). Buccaneer Bks.
--Introductory Lectures on Psychoanalysis: A General Introduction to Psychoanalysis. LC 77-5779. Orig. Title: General Introducton to Psychoanalysis. 1977. pap. 4.95 (ISBN 0-87140-118-5). Liveright.
--Introductory Lectures on Psychoanalysis. Strachey, James, tr. 1979. 13.98 (ISBN 0-87140-637-3). Liveright.
--Jokes & Their Relation to the Unconscious. Strachey, James, tr. (Standard ed.). 1963. pap. 4.95 (ISBN 0-393-00145-8). Norton.
--Leonardo Da Vinci: A Study in Psychosexuality. 1966. pap. 2.95 (ISBN 0-394-70132-1, V132, Vin). Random.
--Leonardo Da Vinci & a Memory of His Childhood. Strachey, James, ed. Tyson, Alan, tr. 1965. pap. 3.95 (ISBN 0-393-00149-0). Norton.
--Leonardo Da Vinci & a Memory of His Childhood. 9.95 (ISBN 0-89190-688-6, Pub. by Am Repr). Amereon Ltd.
--Letters of Sigmund Freud. Freud, Ernst L., ed. LC 74-28069. 1960. 22.50x (ISBN 0-465-03911-1). Basic.
--Moses & Monotheism. Jones, Katherine, ed. 1955. pap. 4.95 (ISBN 0-394-70014-7, V14, Vin). Random.
--New Introductory Lectures on Psychoanalysis. Strachey, James, ed. & tr. (Standard ed.). 1965. 13.97 (ISBN 0-393-01064-3); pap. 3.95 (ISBN 0-393-00743-X). Norton.
--On Aphasia. Stengel, E., tr. LC 53-13181. 105p. 1953. text ed. 25.00 (ISBN 0-8236-3740-9). Intl Univs Pr.
--On Dreams. Strachey, James, ed. 1963. pap. 2.95 (ISBN 0-393-00144-X). Norton.
--On the History of the Psychoanalytic Movement. Strachey, James, ed. Riviere, Joan, tr. (Standard ed.). 1966 10.95 (ISBN 0-393-01022-8); pap. 3.95, 1967 (ISBN 0-393-00150-4). Norton.
--Origin & Development of Psychoanalysis. 108p. 1960. pap. 3.95 (ISBN 0-89526-919-8). Regnery-Gateway.
--Origins of Psychoanalysis: Letters to Wilhelm Fliess, Drafts & Notes, 1887-1902. Bonaparte, Marie, et al, eds. Mosbacher, Eric & Strachey, James, trs. LC 54-8148. 1954. 20.00x (ISBN 0-465-05351-3); pap. 11.95x (ISBN 0-465-09711-1, TB-5076). Basic.
--Outline of Psychoanalysis. rev. ed. Strachey, James, ed. & tr. 1970. pap. 2.95 (ISBN 0-393-00151-2). Norton.
--The Physiology & Pathology of the Dream Experience. (Illus.). 101p. 1984. 97.45x (ISBN 0-89920-108-3). Am Inst Psych.
--Psychopathology of Everyday Life. Strachey, James, ed. Tyson, Alan, tr. 1971. pap. 6.95 (ISBN 0-393-00611-5). Norton.
--Question of Lay Analysis. Strachey, James, ed. & tr. (Standard ed.). 1969. pap. 3.95 (ISBN 0-393-00503-8). Norton.
--Selected Papers on Hysteria & Other Psychoneuroses. Brill, A. A., tr. (Nervous & Mental Disease Monographs: No. 4). Repr. of 1912 ed. 19.00 (ISBN 0-384-16810-8). Johnson Repr.
--Sexual Enlightenment of Children. 1963. pap. 3.95 (ISBN 0-02-076500-2, Collier). Macmillan.
--Sexuality & the Psychology of Love. 1963. pap. 2.95 (ISBN 0-02-076450-2, Collier). Macmillan.
--Studies in Parapsychology. 224p. 1985. pap. 4.95 (ISBN 0-02-076550-9, Collier). MacMillan.
--Therapy & Technique. 1963. pap. 4.95 (ISBN 0-02-076600-9, Collier). Macmillan.
--Three Case Histories. 1963. pap. 4.95 (ISBN 0-02-076650-5, Collier). Macmillan.
--Three Contributions to the Theory of Sex. Brill, A. A., tr. (Nervous & Mental Disease Monographs: Vol. 7). Repr. of 1930 ed. 19.00 (ISBN 0-384-16820-5). Johnson Repr.
--Three Contributions to the Theory of Sex. Brill, A. A., tr. from Ger. 118p. 1982. Repr. of 1925 ed. lib. bdg. 40.00 (ISBN 0-89984-211-9). Century Bookbindery.
--Three Essays on the Theory of Sexuality. Strachey, James, tr. LC 62-11202. 1982. 17.50x (ISBN 0-465-08607-1); pap. 7.95 (ISBN 0-465-09708-1, CN-5008). Basic.
--Totem & Taboo. Strachey, James, tr. 1962. pap. 3.95 (ISBN 0-393-00143-1, Norton Lib.). Norton.
--Totem & Taboo. Brill, Abraham A., tr. 1960. pap. 2.95 (ISBN 0-394-70124-0, Vin, V124). Random.
--A Young Girl's Diary. 75.00 (ISBN 0-87968-040-7). Gordon Pr.
--Zur Psychopathologie des Alltagslebens. 1968. 4.00 (ISBN 0-87497-172-1). Assoc Bk.
Freud, Sigmund & Oppenheim, D. E. Dreams in Folklore. LC 57-14990. 1958. text ed. 15.00 (ISBN 0-8236-1440-9). Intl Univs Pr.
Freudberg, Frank & Emmanuel, E. Stephen. Herpes: A Complete Guide to Relief & Reassurance. LC 82-13303. (Illus.). 160p. (Orig.). 1982. 12.95 (ISBN 0-89471-193-8); lib. bdg. 15.90 (ISBN 0-89471-187-3); pap. 6.95 (ISBN 0-89471-188-1). Running Pr.
Freudenberg, Nicholas. Not in Our Backyards! Community Action for Health & the Environment. LC 84-10524. 320p. 1984. 26.00 (ISBN 0-85345-653-4); pap. 10.00 (ISBN 0-85345-654-2). Monthly Rev.
Freudenberger, C. Dean. Food for Tomorrow. LC 83-72119. 176p. 1984. pap. 8.95 (ISBN 0-8066-2063-3, 10-2333). Augsburg.
Freudenberger, C. Dean & Minus, Paul M., Jr. A Christian Responsibility in a Hungry World. LC 75-43764. 1976. pap. 3.25 (ISBN 0-687-07567-X). Abingdon.
Freudenberger, Herbert J. & North, Gail. Situational Anxiety. 336p. 1983. pap. 8.95 (ISBN 0-88184-024-6, Publishers Group West). Carroll & Graf.
--Women's Burnout: How to Spot It, How to Reverse It, & How to Prevent It. LC 82-46035. (Illus.). 264p. 1985. 14.95 (ISBN 0-385-18803-X). Doubleday.
Freudenberger, Herbert J. & Richelson, Geraldine. Burn-Out. 224p. 1981. pap. 3.50 (ISBN 0-553-24274-1). Bantam.
Freudenberger, Herman. The Waldstein Woolen Mill. (Kress Library Publications: No. 18). (Illus.). 1963. pap. 8.95x (ISBN 0-678-09912-X, Baker Lib). Kelley.
Freudenberger, Robert, jt. auth. see Carley, Larry W.
Freudenburg, William R. & Rosa, Eugene A., eds. Public Reactions to Nuclear Power. (AAAS Selected Symposium Ser.: No. 93). 300p. 1985. 36.00x (ISBN 0-86531-708-9). Westview.
Freudenheim, Ellen. The Executive Bride: A Ten-Week Wedding Planner. 192p. 1985. pap. 7.95 (ISBN 0-553-34136-7). Bantam.
Freudenheim, Tom. American Museum Guides: Fine Arts, Vol. I. (Illus.). 192p. 1983. 16.95 (ISBN 0-02-541450-X); pap. 7.95 (ISBN 0-02-097680-1). Macmillan.
Freudenheim, Yehoshua. Government in Israel. LC 66-17246. 309p. 1967. 15.00 (ISBN 0-379-00248-5). Oceana.
Freudenstein, Ferdinand, jt. auth. see Buchsbaum, Frank.
Freudenstein, Ferdinand, jt. auth. see Stock Drive Products Staff Engineers.
Freudenthal, Elsbeth E. Flight into History: The Wright Brothers & the Air Age. 1st ed. LC 49-9110. pap. 75.00 (ISBN 0-317-10992-8, 2004787). Bks Demand UMI.
Freudenthal, Gideon. Atom & Individual in the Age of Newton: On the Genesis of the Mechanistic World View. 1985. lib. bdg. 49.00 (ISBN 90-277-1905-5, Reidel Holland). Kluwer Academic.
Freudenthal, H. Mathematics As an Educational Task. LC 72-77874. (Illus.). 680p. 1973. lib. bdg. 39.50 (ISBN 90-277-0235-7, Pub. by Reidel Holland); pap. text ed. 21.00 (ISBN 90-277-0322-1). Kluwer Academic.
Freudenthal, H., jt. auth. see Brouwer, L. E.
Freudenthal, H., ed. see Colloquium, International Union of History & Philosophy of Sciences, Utrecht, 1960.
Freudenthal, Hans. Didactical Phenomenology of Mathematical Structures. 1983. lib. bdg. 93.50 (ISBN 90-2771-535-1, Pub. by Reidel Holland). Kluwer Academic.
--Weeding & Sowing: Preface to a Science of Mathematical Education. ix, 314p. 1980. lib. bdg. 47.50 (ISBN 90-277-0789-8, Pub. by Reidel Holland); pap. 15.00 (ISBN 90-277-1072-4). Kluwer Academic.
Freudenthal, Juan R. & Katz, Jeffrey. Index to Anthologies of Latin American Literature in English Translation. 1977. lib. bdg. 20.00 (ISBN 0-8161-7861-5, Hall Reference). G K Hall.
Freudenthal, Ralph I. & Jones, Peter, eds. Polynuclear Aromatic Hydrocarbons: Chemistry, Metabolism, & Carcinogenesis. LC 75-43194. (Carcinogens: A Comprehensive Survey Ser.: Vol. 1). 465p. 1976. 69.50 (ISBN 0-89004-103-2). Raven.
Freudenthal, Ralph I., ed. see International Symposium on Analysis, Chemistry, & Biology, No. 2.
Freudiger, Ullrich D., jt. auth. see Keller, Peter D.
Freud-Loewenstein, Andrea. This Place. 544p. 1984. 14.95 (ISBN 0-86358-039-4). Routledge & Kegan.
Freuh, Alfred J. Freuh on the Theatre: Theatrical Caricatures, 1906-1962. Silverman, Maxwell, ed. LC 72-83887. (Illus.). 125p. 1972. pap. 12.00 (ISBN 0-87104-235-5). NY Pub Lib.
Freuh, Joanna. Brumas. LC 82-84279. (Illus.). 36p. (Orig.). 1983. pap. text ed. 6.95x (ISBN 0-9605550-2-1). FreshCut.
Freuler, F., et al. Cast Manual for Adults & Children. Casey, P. A., tr. from Ger. (Illus.). 1979. 25.00 (ISBN 0-387-09590-X). Springer-Verlag.
Freund, Bill. Capital & Labour in the Nigerian Tin Mines. (Ibadan History Ser.). 1981. text ed. 37.25x (ISBN 0-391-02155-9). Humanities.
--The Making of Contemporary Africa: The Development of African Society Since 1800. LC 83-48116. (Illus.). 304p. (Orig.). 1983. 25.00x (ISBN 0-253-33660-0); pap. 9.95x (ISBN 0-253-28600-X). Ind U Pr.
Freund, Deborah. Medicaid Reform: Four Studies of Case Management. 1984. 5.95 (ISBN 0-8447-3561-2). Am Enterprise.
Freund, E. Hans, jt. ed. see Mourant, John A.
Freund, E. Hans, tr. see Heidegger, Martin.
Freund, Edith. Chicago Girls. 448p. 1985. 16.95 (ISBN 0-671-50291-3, Pub. by Poseidon). S&S.
--Chicago Girls. 1985. pap. 3.95 (ISBN 0-671-55238-4). PB.
Freund, Else-Rahel. Franz Rosenweig's Philosophy of Existence. Mendes-Flohr, Paul R., tr. (Studies in Philosophy & Religion: No. 1). 1979. lib. bdg. 35.00 (ISBN 90-247-2091-5, Pub. by Martinus Nijhoff Netherlands). Kluwer Academic.
Freund, Ernst. Administrative Powers Over Persons & Property: A Comparative Survey. (Research & Source Works Ser.: No. 699). 642p. 1972. Repr. of 1928 ed. lib. bdg. 35.50 (ISBN 0-8337-4120-9). B Franklin.
--Legal Nature of Corporations. LC 71-154642. (Research & Source Works Ser.: No. 724). 1971. Repr. of 1897 ed. lib. bdg. 18.50 (ISBN 0-8337-1247-0). B Franklin.
--The Legal Nature of Corporations. 1980. lib. bdg. 49.95 (ISBN 0-8490-3106-0). Gordon Pr.
--The Police Power: Public Policy & Constitutional Rights. LC 75-17223. (Social Problems & Social Policy Ser.). 1976. Repr. of 1904 ed. 67.50x (ISBN 0-405-07493-X). Ayer Co Pubs.
--Standards of American Legislation. rev. ed. LC 65-17289. 1965. pap. 2.45x (ISBN 0-226-26271-5, P182, Phoen). U of Chicago Pr.
Freund, Ernst & Helmholz, R. H., Jr., eds. The Police Power: Public Policy & Constitutional Rights. LC 80-84868. (Historical Writings in Law & Jurisprudence Ser.: Title No. 22, Bk. 32). 918p. 1981. Repr. of 1904 ed. lib. bdg. 45.00 (ISBN 0-89941-084-7). W S Hein.
Freund, Gisele. Gisele Freund: Photographer. (Illus.). 224p. 1985. 45.00 (ISBN 0-8109-0939-1). Abrams.
--Photography & Society. Dunn, Richard, et al, trs. from Fr. LC 78-58502. Orig. Title: Photographie et Societe. (Illus.). 248p. 1982. 15.00 (ISBN 0-87923-250-1); pap. 8.95 (ISBN 0-87923-428-8). Godine.
--Photography & Society. 256p. 1981. 35.00x (ISBN 0-86092-049-6, Pub. by Fraser Bks). State Mutual Bk.
--Three Days with Joyce. Ginna, Peter St. J., tr. from French. (Illus.). 96p. 1985. 15.00 (ISBN 0-89255-096-1). Persea Bks.
Freund, James & Wieand, Kenneth. Discussion of Some Factors Affecting Labor Productivity. 1967. pap. 2.00 (ISBN 0-318-00015-6, DRA 5). Inst for Urban & Regional.
Freund, James C. Legal Ease: Fresh Insights into Lawyering. LC 84-5651. 206p. 1984. 35.00 (ISBN 0-15-004373-2, Law & Business). HarBraceJ.
Freund, Jan, jt. auth. see Freund, Raymond.
Freund, Jan L. Afghan Hound Champions, 1934-1981. (Illus.). 230p. 1985. pap. 22.95 (ISBN 0-940808-21-8). Freund Pub Co.
--Akita Champions, 1973-1981. (Illus.). 140p. 1985. pap. 22.95 (ISBN 0-940808-14-5). Freund Pub Co.
--Basenji Champions, Nineteen Hundred Forty-Five to Nineteen Hundred Eighty-One. (Illus.). 125p. 1984. pap. 22.95 (ISBN 0-940808-17-X). Freund Pub Co.
--Borzoi Champions, Nineteen Fifty-Two to Nineteen Eighty-One. (Illus.). 150p. 1984. pap. 22.95 (ISBN 0-940808-18-8). Freund Pub Co.
--Brittany Champions, Nineteen Fifty-Two to Nineteen Eighty-One. (Illus.). 240p. 1984. 26.95 (ISBN 0-940808-20-X). Freund Pub Co.
--Bull Terrier Champions, Nineteen Fifty-Two to Nineteen Eighty-One. (Illus.). 75p. 1984. pap. 22.95 (ISBN 0-940808-16-1). Freund Pub Co.

--Clumber Spaniel Champions: 1981-1982. (Illus.). 101p. 1984. pap. 19.95 (ISBN 0-940808-30-7). Freund Pub Co.

--Doberman Pinscher Champions, 1981-1982. (Illus.). 165p. 1985. pap. 19.95 (ISBN 0-940808-26-9). Freund Pub Co.

--English Springer Spaniel Champions, 1952-1981. (Illus.). 190p. 1984. pap. 22.95 (ISBN 0-940808-19-6). Freund Pub Co.

--English Toy Spaniel Champions, Nineteen Fifty-Two to Nineteen Eighty-Two. (Illus.). 95p. 1985. pap. 22.95 (ISBN 0-940808-22-6). Freund Pub Co.

--German Shepherd Champions: 1981-1982. (Illus.). 96p. 1985. pap. 19.95 (ISBN 0-940808-27-7). Freund Pub Co.

--Golden Retriever Champions, 1981. (Illus.). 190p. 1985. 22.95 (ISBN 0-940808-25-0). Freund Pub Co.

--Irish Setter Champions, Eighteen Seventy-Six to Nineteen Eighty-One. (Illus.). 280p. 1985. pap. 26.95 (ISBN 0-940808-23-4). Freund Pub Co.

--Whippet Champions: 1981-1982. (Illus.). 101p. 1984. pap. 19.95 (ISBN 0-940808-29-3). Freund Pub Co.

Freund, John, jt. auth. see Hunter, JoAnn H.

Freund, John, jt. auth. see Miller, Irwin.

Freund, John E. Modern Elementary Statistics. 6th ed. (Illus.). 576p. 1984. 31.95 (ISBN 0-13-593525-3). P-H.

--Statistics: A First Course. 3rd ed. (Illus.). 448p. 1981. text ed. 29.95 (ISBN 0-13-845958-4). P-H.

--Statistics: A First Course. 4th ed. (Illus.). 496p. 1986. text ed. 24.95 (ISBN 0-13-845975-4). P-H.

Freund, John E. & Perles, Benjamin M. Business Statistics: A First Course. (Quantitative Analysis for Business Ser.). 368p. 1974. text ed. 23.95 (ISBN 0-13-107714-7). P-H.

Freund, John E. & Walpole, Ronald E. Mathematical Statistics. 3rd ed. 1980. text ed. 36.95 (ISBN 0-13-562066-X). P-H.

Freund, John E. & Williams, Frank J. Elementary Business Statistics: The Modern Approach. 4th ed. (Illus.). 576p. 1982. text ed. 29.95 (ISBN 0-13-253120-8). P-H.

Freund, John E. & Williams, Thomas A. College Mathematics with Business Applications. 3rd ed. (Illus.). 464p. 1983. text ed. 28.95 (ISBN 0-13-146498-1). P-H.

Freund, Paul A. On Law & Justice. LC 67-29626. 1968. 15.00x (ISBN 0-674-63550-7, Belknap Pr). Harvard U Pr.

--On Understanding the Supreme Court: A Series of Lectures Delivered Under the Auspices of the Julius Rosenthal Foundation at Northwestern University, School of Law. LC 77-23550. (Illus.). vi, 130p. 1977. Repr. of 1949 ed. lib. bdg. 15.00x (ISBN 0-8371-9699-X, FROU). Greenwood.

Freund, Paul A., ed. Experimentation with Human Subjects. LC 70-107776. (Daedalus Library Ser). 1970. pap. 3.50 (ISBN 0-8076-0542-5). Braziller.

Freund, Paul A., et al. Constitutional Law: Cases & Other Problems. 4th ed. 1977. 34.00 (ISBN 0-316-29333-4); pap. 8.95 supp. (ISBN 0-316-29326-1). Little.

Freund, Peter E. The Civilized Body: Social Domination, Control & Health. LC 82-10787. 166p. 1982. text ed. 19.95x (ISBN 0-87722-285-1). Temple U Pr.

Freund, Peter G. & Goebel, C. J., eds. Quanta: Essays in Theorectical Physics Dedicated to Gregory Wentzel. LC 70-108268. pap. 107.50 (ISBN 0-317-08085-7, 2019966). Bks Demand UMI.

Freund, Philip, ed. see Rank, Otto.

Freund, R. & Minton, P. Regression Methods. (Statistics Ser.: Vol. 30). 1979. 29.75 (ISBN 0-8247-6647-4). Dekker.

Freund, Raymond & Freund, Jan. The Name Book. (Illus.). 92p. 1984. pap. 12.95 (ISBN 0-940808-31-5). Freund Pub Co.

Freund, Richard, jt. auth. see Duff, Charles.

Freund, Roberta B. Open the Book. 2nd ed. LC 66-13739. (Illus.). 184p. 1966. 15.00 (ISBN 0-8108-0107-8). Scarecrow.

Freund, Ronald. What One Person Can Do to Help Prevent Nuclear War. 2nd ed. 144p. 1983. pap. 5.95 (ISBN 0-89622-192-X). Twenty-Third.

Freund, Rudolf, et al. SAS for Linear Models: A Guide to the ANOVA & GLM Procedures. (SAS Series in Statistical Applications: Vol. 1). (Illus.). 231p. (Orig.). 1981. pap. 14.95 (ISBN 0-917382-31-5). SAS Inst.

Freund, Virginia, ed. see Strachey, William.

Freund, William C., jt. auth. see Epstein, Eugene.

Freundlich, August L. Federico Castellon: His Graphic Works, 1936-1971. (Illus.). 1979. pap. 15.00x (ISBN 0-8156-8101-1). Syracuse U Pr.

--Frank Kleinholz-the Outsider. LC 73-75849. 1969. 10.00 (ISBN 0-916224-19-8). Banyan Bks.

Freundlich, Charles I. College Vocabulary Builder. 256p. (Orig.). 1981. pap. 7.95 (ISBN 0-671-41337-6). Monarch Pr.

--Latin for the Grades, 3 Bks. (gr. 4-6). 1970. Bk. 1. pap. text ed. 5.67 (ISBN 0-87720-562-0); Bk. 2. pap. text ed. 5.67 (ISBN 0-87720-564-7); Bk. 3. pap. text ed. 5.67 (ISBN 0-87720-566-3). AMSCO Sch.

--Review Text in Latin First Year. 2nd ed. (Illus., Orig.). (gr. 7-12). 1966. pap. text ed. 7.17 (ISBN 0-87720-551-5). AMSCO Sch.

--Review Text in Latin Three & Four Years. (Orig.). (gr. 7-12). 1967. pap. text ed. 8.25 (ISBN 0-87720-558-2). AMSCO Sch.

--Review Text in Latin Two Years. (gr. 7-12). 1966. pap. text ed. 7.58 (ISBN 0-87720-555-8). AMSCO Sch.

--Workbook in Latin First Year. (Illus., Orig.). (gr. 8-11). 1963. wkbk 8.75 (ISBN 0-87720-553-1). AMSCO Sch.

--Workbook in Latin Two Years. (Illus., Orig.). (gr. 9-12). 1965. wkbk 9.17 (ISBN 0-87720-556-6). AMSCO Sch.

Freundlich, I. Pulmonary Masses, Cysts & Cavities: A Radiologic Approach. 1981. 39.95 (ISBN 0-8151-3330-8). Year Bk Med.

Freundlich, Irwin, jt. auth. see Friskin, James.

Freundlich, Irwin, ed. see Hinson, Maurice.

Freundlich, Irwin M. Diffuse Pulmonary Disease: A Radiologic Approach. LC 77-27745. (Illus.). 1979. pap. text ed. 17.95 (ISBN 0-7216-3866-X). Saunders.

--Diffuse Pulmonary Disease: A Radiologic Approach. LC 77-27745. pap. 62.30 (ISBN 0-317-26431-2, 2024987). Bks Demand UMI.

Freundlich, M. M. & Wagner, B. M., eds. Exobiology: The Search for Extraterrestrial Life. (Science & Technology Ser.: Vol. 19). (Illus.). 1969. 20.00x (ISBN 0-87703-047-2, Pub. by Am Astronaut). Univelt Inc.

Frevert. Muppet Magic. (TV & Movie Tie-ins Ser.). (Illus.). 32p. (gr. 4-12). 7.95 (ISBN 0-317-31192-1); pap. 3.95 (ISBN 0-317-31193-X). Creative Ed.

Frevert, Patricia. It's Okay to Look at Jamie. LC 81-82912. (Everyday Heroes Ser.). (Illus.). 48p. (gr. 4-8). 1982. 8.95 (ISBN 0-87191-803-X). Creative Ed.

--Patrick, Yes You Can. (Everyday Heroes Ser). (Illus.). 48p. 1983. lib. bdg. 8.95 (ISBN 0-87191-891-9). Creative Ed.

--Why Does the Weather Change? (Creative's Questions & Answer Library). (Illus.). (gr. 3-4). 1981. PLB 6.95 (ISBN 0-87191-748-3). Creative Ed.

Frevert, Patricia D. Beatrix Potter, Children's Storyteller. Redpath, Ann, ed. (People to Remember Ser.). (Illus.). 32p. (gr. 5-9). 1981. PLB 8.95 (ISBN 0-87191-801-3). Creative Ed.

--Mark Twain, an American Voice. Redpath, Ann, ed. (People to Remember Ser.). (Illus.). 32p. (gr. 5-9). 1981. PLB 8.95 (ISBN 0-87191-802-1). Creative Ed.

--Pablo Picasso, Twentieth Century Genius. Redpath, Ann, ed. (People to Remember Ser.). (Illus.). 32p. (gr. 5-9). 1981. PLB 8.95 (ISBN 0-87191-800-5). Creative Ed.

--Patty Gets Well. (Everyday Heroes Ser.). (Illus.). 48p. 1983. lib. bdg. 8.95 (ISBN 0-87191-890-0). Creative Ed.

Frevert, Patricia D. & Morse. Margaret Mead Herself. Redpath, Ann, ed. (People to Remember Ser.). (Illus.). 32p. (gr. 5-9). 1981. PLB 8.95 (ISBN 0-87191-799-8). Creative Ed.

Frevert, Richard K., jt. auth. see Schwab, Glenn O.

Frevert, W. Woerterbuch der Jaegerei. 4th ed. (Ger.). 1975. 12.00 (ISBN 3-490-05612-4, M-6990). French & Eur.

Frew, Andrew W. Frew's Daily Archive: A Calendar of Commemorations. LC 84-42612. 384p. 1984. lib. bdg. 24.95x (ISBN 0-89950-127-3). McFarland & Co.

Frew, David R. Management of Stress: Using TM at Work. LC 76-18164. 262p. 1977. 20.95x (ISBN 0-88229-254-4). Nelson-Hall.

Frew, David R., jt. auth. see Frew, Mary A.

Frew, Ivor, jt. auth. see Diamond, Charles.

Frew, James, jt. auth. see Moore, Robin.

Frew, Marian L., jt. auth. see Vermeer, Jackie.

Frew, Mary A. & Frew, David R. Comprehensive Medical Assisting: Administrative & Clinical Procedures. LC 81-9820. 756p. 1983. 24.95x (ISBN 0-8036-3858-2); wkbk. 9.95 (ISBN 0-8036-3864-7). Davis Co.

--Medical Office Administrative Procedures. LC 81-17435. (Illus.). 343p. 1983. pap. 14.95x (ISBN 0-8036-3861-2); instrs. guide avail.; wkbk. 9.95 (ISBN 0-8036-3864-7). Davis Co.

Frew, Robert. Write: A Program for Success in English Composition. (gr. 9-12). 1978. pap. text ed. 12.95x (ISBN 0-917962-45-1). Peek Pubns.

Frew, Robert, et al. Survival. 1975. pap. text ed. 12.95 (ISBN 0-917962-34-6). Peek Pubns.

--Survival-A Sequential Program for College Writing. 3rd, rev. ed. 350p. 1985. pap. 14.95x (ISBN 0-917962-50-8). Peek Pubns.

--A Writer's Guidebook. rev. ed. 270p. (Orig.). 1985. pap. text ed. 13.95x (ISBN 0-917962-85-0). Peek Pubns.

Frew, Robert M., et al. A Writer's Guidebook. 280p. (gr. 9-12). 1982. pap. text ed. 11.95x (ISBN 0-917962-69-9). Peek Pubns.

--Writer's Workshop: A Self-Paced Program for Composition Mastery. 3rd ed. 282p. 1984. paperbound wkbk. 13.95x (ISBN 0-917962-52-4). Peek Pubns.

Frew, Stephen. Street Law: Rights & Responsibilities of the EMT. 1983. text ed. 18.95 (ISBN 0-8359-7081-7). Reston.

Frewer, Ellen E., tr. see Schweinfurth, Georg A.

Frewer, Glyn. Tyto: the Odyssey of an Owl. LC 77-2769. (Illus.). (gr. 5-9). 1977. 11.25 (ISBN 0-688-41814-7); PLB 11.88 (ISBN 0-688-51814-1). Lothrop.

Frewer, Glyn see Milne, John.

Frewer, Louis B. Bibliography of Historical Writings Published in Great Britain & the Empire: Nineteen Forty to Nineteen Forty-Five. LC 74-12628. 346p. 1974. Repr. of 1947 ed. lib. bdg. 22.50x (ISBN 0-8371-7735-9, FRHW). Greenwood.

Frewin, Leslie, ed. Parnassus Near Piccadilly. 15.00 (ISBN 0-392-16445-0, SpS). Sportshelf.

Frey, jt. auth. see Kummerly.

Frey, et al. Home Tanning. facsimile ed. (Shorey Lost Arts Ser.). (Illus.). 30p. pap. 1.50 (ISBN 0-8466-6009-1, U9). Shorey.

Frey, A. J. & Dryhurst, G. Organic Electrochemistry. LC 51-5497. (Topics in Current Chemistry: Vol. 34). (Illus.). iii, 85p. 1972. pap. 22.50 (ISBN 0-387-06074-X). Springer-Verlag.

Frey, A. R. Dictionary of Numismatic Names. 1973. 22.00 (ISBN 0-685-51559-1, Pub by Spink & Son England). S J Durst.

Frey, Albert R. The Dated European Coinage Prior to 1501. updated ed. Cervin, David R., ed. LC 76-62838. (Illus.). 1978. Repr. of 1915 ed. lib. bdg. 25.00 (ISBN 0-915262-09-6). S J Durst.

--A Dictionary of Numismatic Names. pap. 30.00 (ISBN 0-384-16830-2). Johnson Repr.

--Sobriquets & Nicknames. LC 66-22671. 1966. Repr. of 1888 ed. 40.00x (ISBN 0-8103-3003-2). Gale.

--William Shakespeare & Alleged Spanish Prototypes. LC 70-169262. (Shakespeare Society of New York. Publications Ser.: No. 3). Repr. of 1886 ed. 16.00 (ISBN 0-404-54203-4). AMS Pr.

Frey, Alexander H. & Morris, Robert C., Jr. Cases & Materials on Corporations. 2nd ed. 1977. 34.00 (ISBN 0-316-29340-7). Little.

Frey, Alexander H., et al. Cases & Materials on Corporations, 1984 Supplement. LC 76-54025. 200p. 1984. pap. text ed. 9.95 (ISBN 0-316-29343-1). Little.

Frey, Alexander H., Jr. & Singmaster, David. Handbook of Cubik Math. LC 81-12525. (Illus.). 204p. 1982. text ed. 17.95x (ISBN 0-89490-060-9). Enslow Pubs.

Frey, Arthur. Cross & Swastika, the Ordeal of the German Church. McNab, J. Strathearn, tr. LC 78-63668. (Studies in Fascism: Ideology & Practice). 224p. Repr. of 1938 ed. 24.50 (ISBN 0-404-16526-5). AMS Pr.

Frey, Barbara R., jt. auth. see Noller, Ruth B.

Frey, Berta. Designing & Drafting for Handweavers. (Illus.). 240p. 1975. pap. 7.95 (ISBN 0-02-011400-1, Collier). Macmillan.

Frey, Bruno S. Democratic Economic Policy: A Theoretical Introduction. LC 83-9483. 320p. 1983. 32.50 (ISBN 0-312-19368-8). St Martin.

--International Political Economics. 250p. 1985. 34.95x (ISBN 0-85520-748-5). Basil Blackwell.

--Modern Political Economy. 166p. 1980. pap. text ed. 21.95x (ISBN 0-470-26999-5). Halsted Pr.

Frey, Carrol. Bibliography of the Writings of H. L. Mencken. LC 76-22789. 1924. lib. bdg. 10.00 (ISBN 0-8414-4227-4). Folcroft.

Frey, Charles. Shakespeare's Vast Romance: A Study of the Winter's Tale. LC 79-3063. 208p. 1980. text ed. 17.00x (ISBN 0-8262-0286-1). U of Mo Pr.

Frey, Charles H., jt. auth. see Griffith, John W.

Frey, Conrad I. Handbook For Church Officers & Boards. 1985. pap. 1.50 (ISBN 0-8100-0187-X, 15N0414). Northwest Pub.

Frey, Cynthia J., et al, eds. Public Policy Issues in Marketing. Kinnear, Thomas C. & Reece, Bonnie B. LC 79-24126. (Illus.). 160p. (Orig.). 1980. pap. 6.00 (ISBN 0-87712-202-4). U Mich Busn Div Res.

Frey, David L. The First Tetralogy Shakespeare's Scrutiny of the Tudor Myth: A Dramatic Exploration of Devine Providence. (Studies in English Literature: No. 95). 1976. text ed. 20.00x (ISBN 90-2793-185-2). Mouton.

Frey, Diane & Carlock, Jesse C. Enhancing Self Esteem. (Orig.). 1984. pap. text ed. 17.95 (ISBN 0-915202-41-7). Accel Devel.

Frey, Donald E. Tuition Tax Credits for Private Education: An Economic Analysis. (Illus.). 120p. 1983. pap. text ed. 10.50x (ISBN 0-8138-1826-5). Iowa St U Pr.

Frey, Donald G., jt. auth. see Selby, John B.

Frey, Dorothea, et al. Color Atlas of Pathogenic Fungi. (Illus.). 1979. 55.00 (ISBN 0-8151-3277-8). Year Bk Med.

Frey, G. Donald & Klobukowski, Christopher J. Nuclear Medicine Technology Examination Review Book. 2nd ed. 1980. pap. 18.00 (ISBN 0-87488-457-8). Med Exam.

Frey, G. Donald, et al. Nuclear Medicine Technology Examination Review. 3rd ed. Date not set. pap. text ed. price not set (ISBN 0-87488-654-6). Med Exam.

Frey, Gerhard, ed. Bela Juhos: Selected Papers. Foulkes, Paul, tr. LC 76-17019. (Vienna Circle Collection Ser: No. 7). 1976. lib. bdg. 55.00 (ISBN 90-277-0686-7, Pub. by Reidel Holland); pap. 28.95 (ISBN 90-277-0687-5). Kluwer Academic.

Frey, H. H., et al. Antiepileptic Drugs. (Handbook of Experimental Pharmacology Ser.: Vol. 74). (Illus.). 850p. 1985. 250.00 (ISBN 0-387-13108-6). Springer-Verlag.

Frey, Hank & Frey, Shaney. Diver Below: The Complete Guide to Skin & Scuba Diving. 1969. pap. 9.95 (ISBN 0-02-080120-3, Collier). Macmillan.

Frey, Hugo. Easy Piano Pieces. (Music for Millions Ser.: Vol. 3). 1948. pap. 7.95 (ISBN 0-8256-4003-2). Music Sales.

Frey, Iris I. Crumpets & Scones: Indecently Delicious Tea-Time Fare Around the World. (Illus.). 128p. 1982. 10.95 (ISBN 0-312-17773-9). St Martin.

--Staple It. 1979. pap. 8.95 (ISBN 0-517-53255-7). Crown.

Frey, Iris I., jt. auth. see Simmons, Amelia.

Frey, James, ed. The Governance of Intercollegiate Athletics. LC 81-83014. 224p. (Orig.). 1981. pap. text ed. 12.95 (ISBN 0-88011-004-X). Leisure Pr.

Frey, James H. Survey Research by Telephone. 208p. 1983. 24.00 (ISBN 0-8039-1996-4); pap. 12.00 (ISBN 0-8039-1997-2). Sage.

Frey, James H., jt. ed. see Johnson, Arthur T.

Frey, James N. The Last Patriot. 416p. 1984. pap. 3.50 (ISBN 0-8217-1403-1). Zebra.

Frey, James S. & Fisher, Stephen H. Israel. (World Education Ser.). (Illus.). 152p. (Orig.). 1976. pap. text ed. 6.00 (ISBN 0-910054-43-6). Am Assn Coll Registrars.

Frey, Jay J. How to Fly Floats: Seaplane Flying. (Illus.). 1972. pap. 3.00 (ISBN 0-911721-71-1, Pub. by Edo-Aire). Aviation.

Frey, Jean B. Corpus Inscriptionum Judaicarum. rev. ed. (Library of Biblical Studies). 1970. 100.00x (ISBN 0-87068-103-6). Ktav.

Frey, Jean M. Communautes Syriaques en Iran et Irak Des Origines A 1552. 382p. 1979. 70.00x (ISBN 0-686-97648-7, Pub. by Variorum). State Mutual Bk.

Frey, Jeffrey & Bhasin, Kul, eds. Microwave Integrated Circuits. 2nd ed. 1985. pap. text ed. 45.00 (ISBN 0-89006-160-2). Artech Hse.

Frey, John A. Motif Symbolism in the Disciples of Mallarme. LC 73-94193. (Catholic University of America Studies in Romance Languages & Literatures Ser: No. 55). Repr. of 1957 ed. 23.00 (ISBN 0-404-50355-1). AMS Pr.

Frey, John R., ed. see Schiller, Johann C.

Frey, John W. see Kavass, Igor I. & Sprudzs, Adolf.

Frey, Karl, et al, eds. Research in Science Education in Europe: Report of a Cooperative Study & a European Contact Workshop Organised by the Council of Europe & the Institute for Science Education, FRG (Kiel) 394p. 1977. pap. text ed. 18.50 (ISBN 90-265-0266-4, Pub. by Swets & Zeitlinger Netherlands). Hogrefe Intl.

Frey, Kenneth J., ed. Plant Breeding II. 498p. 1981. 22.95x (ISBN 0-8138-1550-9). Iowa St U Pr.

Frey, Kenneth J., ed. see Plant Breeding Symposium.

Frey, Kessler. Satsang Notes of Swami Amar Jyoti. LC 77-89524. (Illus.). 1977. 4.95 (ISBN 0-933572-01-8); pap. 2.95 (ISBN 0-933572-02-6). Truth Consciousness.

Frey, Linda & Frey, Marsha. Frederick I: The Man & His Times. 303p. 1984. 28.00x (ISBN 0-88033-058-9). East Eur Quarterly.

Frey, Linda, et al. The Gods Are Athirst: Anatole France. LC 78-31742. 1978. lib. bdg. 30.00 (ISBN 0-8482-0846-3). Norwood Edns.

Frey, Linda, et al, eds. Women in Western European History: A Select Chronological, Geographical, & Topical Bibliography from Antiquity to the French Revolution. LC 81-20300. iv, 760p. 1982. lib. bdg. 49.95 (ISBN 0-313-22858-2, FEW/). Greenwood.

--Women in Western European History: A Select Chronological, Geographical, & Topical Bibliography: The Nineteenth & Twentieth Centuries. LC 81-20300. lxvi, 1088p. 1984. lib. bdg. 55.00 (ISBN 0-313-22859-0, FRW/). Greenwood.

Frey, Louis. Analyse Ordinale Es Evangiles Synoptiques. (Mathematiques et Sciences De L'homme: No. 11). 1972. 46.50 (ISBN 0-686-21228-2); pap. 27.20x (ISBN 0-686-21229-0). Mouton.

Frey, Marsah, et al, trs. see France, Anatole.

Frey, Marsha, jt. auth. see Frey, Linda.

Frey, Nevin G. Just Feelings. 1983. 6.00 (ISBN 0-8062-2186-0). Carlton.

Frey, P. W., ed. Chess Skill in Man & Machine. 2nd ed. (Illus.). 335p. 1984. pap. 18.95 (ISBN 0-387-90815-3). Springer Verlag.

Frey, Paul R. Chemisty Problems & How to Solve Them. 8th ed. (Illus., Orig.). Date not set. pap. 7.95 (ISBN 0-06-460204-4, CO 204, COS). B&N NY.

Frey, R. & Safar, P., eds. Type & Events of Disasters: Organization in Various Disaster Situations. (Disaster Medicine Ser.: Vol. 1). (Illus.). 1980. pap. 52.00 (ISBN 0-387-09043-6). Springer-Verlag.

Frey, R. & Safer, P., eds. Resuscitation & Life Support in Disasters: Relief of Pain & Suffering in Disaster Situations. (Disaster Medicine Ser.: Vol. 2). (Illus.). 320p. 1980. pap. 55.00 (ISBN 0-387-09044-4). Springer-Verlag.

Frey, R., et al, eds. Mobile Intensive Care Units: Advanced Emergency Care Delivery Systems. (Anaesthesiology & Resuscitation: Vol. 95). 1976. pap. 31.00 (ISBN 0-387-07561-5). Springer-Verlag.

Frey, R., et al, eds. see World Congress of Anaesthesiology, 3rd, Sao Paulo, 1964.

Frey, R. G. Interests & Rights: The Case Against Animals. (Clarendon Library of Logic & Philosophy Ser.). 1980. 27.95x (ISBN 0-19-824421-5). Oxford U Pr.

--Rights, Killing & Suffering. 286p. 1983. 29.95x (ISBN 0-631-12684-8). Basil Blackwell.

--Rights, Killing & Suffering. 268p. 1985. pap. 11.95x (ISBN 0-631-14244-4). Basil Blackwell.

Frey, R. G., ed. Utility & Rights. LC 83-27327. 1984. 29.50x (ISBN 0-8166-1319-2); pap. 13.95x (ISBN 0-8166-1320-6). U of Minn Pr.

Frey, Richard L. How to Win at Contract Bridge. 1986. pap. 3.95 (ISBN 0-449-20995-4, Crest). Fawcett.

Frey, Richard L., ed. According to Hoyle. rev. ed. 1978. pap. 2.95 (ISBN 0-449-23652-8, Crest). Fawcett.

Frey, Richard L., et al, eds. New Complete Hoyle. rev. ed. LC 55-11330. 1956. 15.95 (ISBN 0-385-00126-6). Doubleday.

Frey, Robert S. & Thompson-Frey, Nancy. The Imperative of Response: The Holocaust in Human Context. 186p. 1985. lib. bdg. 21.75 (ISBN 0-8191-4633-1); pap. text ed. 10.50 (ISBN 0-8191-4634-X). U Pr of Amer.

Frey, Robert W., ed. Excursions in Southeastern Geology: Field Trip Guidebooks, 2 vols. Incl. Vol. I. Field Trips-1-13. pap. 25.00 (ISBN 0-913312-48-7); Vol. II. Field Trips-14-23. pap. 25.00 (ISBN 0-913312-49-5). (Illus., Orig.). 1980. Set. pap. 40.00 (ISBN 0-913312-50-9). Am Geol.

Frey, Roger M., jt. auth. see Kolstoe, Oliver P.

Frey, Shaney, jt. auth. see Frey, Hank.

Frey, Skip. How to Win at Dice Games. 1976. pap. 3.00 (ISBN 0-87980-325-8). Wilshire.

Frey, Stephen L. Warehouse Operations. 224p. 1983. 39.95 (ISBN 0-930206-14-2). M-A Pr.

--Warehouse Operations. 39.95 (ISBN 0-930206-14-2). Dilithium Pr.

Frey, Sylvia R. The British Soldier in America: A Social History of Military Life in the Revolutionary Period. 223p. 1981. text ed. 25.00x (ISBN 0-292-78040-0). U of Tex Pr.

Frey, T., jt. auth. see Fenyo, S.

Frey, Thomas L. & Behrens, Robert H. Lending to Agricultural Enterprises. LC 81-12874. 475p. 1981. 39.50 (ISBN 0-87267-037-6). Bankers.

Frey, Thomas L. & Klinefelter, Danny A. Coordinated Financial Statements for Agriculture. 2nd ed. pap. text ed. 14.95 (ISBN 0-930264-58-4). Century Comm.

Frey, William H. & Langseth, Muriel. Crying: The Mystery of Tears. 204p. 1985. pap. 7.95 (ISBN 0-86683-829-5, AY8450). Winston Pr.

Freyberg, Peter, jt. auth. see Osborne, Roger.

Freyberger, G. H. Abbreviations of Nuclear Power Plant Engineering. 280p. (Eng. & Ger.). 1979. 28.95 (ISBN 0-686-56591-6, M-7288, Pub. by Verlag Karl Thiemig). French & Eur.

Freyberger, H., ed. European Conference on Psychosomatic Research, 12th. (Psychotherapy & Psychosomatics: Vol. 32, No. 1-4). (Illus.). 324p. 1980. pap. 55.50 (ISBN 3-8055-3044-7). S Karger.

--Psychotherapeutic Interventions in Life-Threatening Illness. (Advances in Psychosomatic Medicine: Vol. 10). (Illus.). xviii, 206p. 1980. 40.50 (ISBN 3-8055-3066-8). S Karger.

Freyberger, H., ed. see European Conference on Psychosomatic Research, 12th, Bodo, July 1978.

Freyberger, H., ed. see European Conference on Psychosomatic Research, 9th, Vienna, April 1972.

Freyberger, H., jt. ed. see Wise, T. N.

Freycinet, Charles L. De. Souvenirs, Eighteen Seventy-Eight to Eighteen Ninety-Three. LC 73-258. (Europe 1815-1945 Ser.). 524p. 1973. Repr. of 1913 ed. lib. bdg. 65.00 (ISBN 0-306-70560-5). Da Capo.

Freyd, Max see Ludgate, Katherine E.

Freydberg, Margaret H. Winter Concert. LC 85-10955. 323p. 1985. 14.95 (ISBN 0-88150-050-X). Countryman.

Freydberg, Nicholas, jt. auth. see Gortner, Willis A.

Freyd-Wadham, H. Englisches Wirtschaftsalphabet. 6th ed. 156p. (Eng. & Ger., English Economic Terms With German Vocabulary). 1975. 9.95 (ISBN 3-87217-006-6, Pub. by Th. Grossmann). French & Eur.

Freye, Karl A. Jean's Pauls Flegeljahre. 36.00 (ISBN 0-384-16841-8); pap. 31.00 (ISBN 0-384-16840-X). Johnson Repr.

Freyer, Fred R. The Story of the July Nineteen Thirty-One Cadet Class at Brooks, March & Randolph Fields: Forty-Four Years Later. (Illus.). 100p. 1977. pap. text ed. 10.00x (ISBN 0-89126-052-8). MA-AH Pub.

Freyer, Grattan. Peadar O'Donnell. (Irish Writers Ser.). 128p. 1973. 4.50 (ISBN 0-8387-1362-9); pap. 1.95 (ISBN 0-8387-1369-6). Bucknell U Pr.

--W. B. Yeats & the Anti-Democratic Tradition. 154p. 1981. 27.50x (ISBN 0-389-20166-9, 06936). B&N Imports.

--W. B. Yeats & the Anti-Democratic Tradition. 1982. 45.00x (ISBN 0-686-99819-7, Pub. by Gill & Macmillan Ireland). State Mutual Bk.

Freyer, Grattan, ed. Bishop Stock's "Narrative" of the Year of the French: 1798. Stock, Joseph. LC 82-71112. (Illus.). 118p. 1982. 9.00 (ISBN 0-906462-07-X, Pub. by Irish Humanities Centre Ireland); pap. 5.00 (ISBN 0-906462-08-8). Dufour.

Freyer, Grattan, jt. ed. see Harris, Bernard.

Freyer, Hans. Revolution von Rechts. LC 78-63670. (Studies in Fascism: Ideology & Practice). Repr. of 1931 ed. 16.50 (ISBN 0-404-16527-3). AMS Pr.

Freyer, Tony. Harmony & Dissonance: The Swift & Erie Cases in American Federalism. (New York University School of Law Ser. in Anglo-American Legal History). 192p. 1981. 27.50x (ISBN 0-8147-2568-6). NYU Pr.

Freyer, Tony A. Forums of Order: The Federal Courts & Business in American History. Porter, Glenn, ed. LC 76-52013. (Industrial Development & the Social Fabric Ser.: No. 1). 207p. 1979. 28.50 (ISBN 0-686-74078-5). Jai Pr.

--The Little Rock Crisis: A Constitutional Interpretation. LC 83-26663. (Contributions in Legal Studies Ser.: No. 30). 192p. 1984. lib. bdg. 27.95 (ISBN 0-313-24416-2, FRL/). Greenwood.

Freyha, Anis. Dictionary of Modern Lebanese Proverbs. (Arabic & Eng.). 1974. 25.00x (ISBN 0-86685-086-4). Intl Bk Ctr.

--Dictionary of Non-Classical Vocables in Spoken Arabic. (Arabic.). 1973. 16.00x (ISBN 0-86685-098-8). Intl Bk Ctr.

Freyha, Annis. Arabic-Arabic Dictionary of the Names of Towns & Villages in Lebanon. 1974. 18.00x (ISBN 0-86685-099-6). Intl Bk Ctr.

Freyhan, F. A., ed. Lithium: Clinical & Biological Aspects. (International Pharmacopsychiatry: Vol. 5, No. 2-4). (Illus.). 192p. 1971. pap. 25.25 (ISBN 3-8055-1277-5). S Karger.

Freyhan, F. A., jt. ed. see Ban, T. A.

Freyhan, Fritz A., jt. ed. see Zubin, Joseph.

Freyhardt, H. C. Analytical Methods: High-Melting Metals. (Crystals, Growth, Properties, & Applications: Vol. 7). (Illus.). 150p. 1982. 44.00 (ISBN 0-387-11790-3). Springer-Verlag.

Freyhardt, H. C., ed. Growth & Properties. (Crystals-Growth, Properties & Applications Ser.: Vol. 2). (Illus.). 1980. 54.00 (ISBN 0-387-09697-3). Springer-Verlag.

--Organic Crystals, Germanates, Semiconductors. (Crystals, Growth, Properties & Applications: Vol. 4). (Illus.). 250p. 1980. 61.00 (ISBN 0-387-10298-1). Springer-Verlag.

--Silicon-Chemical Etching. (Crystals-Growth, Properties & Applications Ser.: Vol. 8). (Illus.). 255p. 1982. 57.00 (ISBN 0-387-11862-4). Springer-Verlag.

--Three to Five Semiconductors. (Crystals. Growth, Properties & Applications Ser.: Vol. 3). (Illus.). 180p. 1980. 45.00 (ISBN 0-387-09957-3). Springer-Verlag.

Freyhardt, H. C., et al, eds. Growth & Defect Structures. (Crystals, Growth, Properties & Applications Ser.: Vol. 10). 160p. 1984. 44.50 (ISBN 0-387-13600-2). Springer-Verlag.

Freyhofer, Horst H. The Vitalism of Hans Driesch: The Success & Decline of a Scientific Theory. (European University Studies: Series 20, Philosophy: Vol. 83). 250p. 1982. 24.20 (ISBN 3-8204-5703-8). P Lang Pubs.

Freyman, Jay M., tr. see Mahaney, William E. & Sherwin, Walter K.

Freymann & Holzer, Leslie. What's So Bad about Feeling Good. 224p. 1983. pap. 2.95 (ISBN 0-87216-997-9). Jove Pubns.

Freymann, John G. The American Health Care System: Its Genesis & Trajectory. LC 80-15512. 432p. 1980. Repr. of 1974 ed. lib. bdg. 27.50 (ISBN 0-89874-224-2). Krieger.

Freymond, Jacques. The Saar Conflict, 1945-1955. Goormaghtigh, John, frwd. by. LC 76-10856. (Case Studies of International Conflicts Ser.). (Illus.). 1976. Repr. of 1960 ed. lib. bdg. 26.00x (ISBN 0-8371-8234-4, FRSC). Greenwood.

Freyn, Hubert. Prelude to War: The Chinese Student Rebellion of 1935-1936. LC 75-39026. (China Studies: from Confucius to Mao Ser.). 122p. 1977. Repr. of 1939 ed. 17.60 (ISBN 0-88355-382-1). Hyperion Conn.

Freyne, Sean. The World of the New Testament. (New Testament Message Ser.: Vol. 2). 12.95 (ISBN 0-89453-190-5); pap. 8.95 (ISBN 0-89453-125-5). M Glazier.

Freyne, Sean & Wansbrough, Henry. Mark & Matthew. Bright, Laurence, ed. LC 71-173033. (Scripture Discussion Commentary Ser.: Pt. 7). 256p. 1971. pap. text ed. 4.50 (ISBN 0-87946-006-7). ACTA Found.

Freyre, De Matos. ABC De Puerto Rico. 1966. 8.95 (ISBN 0-87751-005-9, Pub by Troutman Press). E Torres & Sons.

Freyre, Gilberto. The Mansions & the Shanties (Sobrados E Mucambos) The Making of Modern Brazil. De Onis, Harriet, tr. from Port. LC 80-10887. (Illus.). xxxvii, 431p. 1980. Repr. of 1963 ed. lib. bdg. 42.50x (ISBN 0-313-22148-0, FRMA). Greenwood.

--New World in the Tropics: The Culture of Modern Brazil. rev. ed. LC 80-137. xii, 285p. 1980. Repr. of 1959 ed. lib. bdg. 27.50x (ISBN 0-313-22147-2, FRNW). Greenwood.

--Order & Progress: Brazil from Monarchy to Republic. Horton, Rod, tr. from Port. LC 80-11440. (Illus.). i, 422p. 1980. Repr. of 1970 ed. lib. bdg. 42.50x (ISBN 0-313-22363-7, FROP). Greenwood.

Freyre, Jorge. El Modelo Economico De Puerto Rico. LC 78-4191. (Illus.). 270p. 1979. 20.00 (ISBN 0-913480-39-8); pap. 13.00 (ISBN 0-913480-40-1). Inter Am U Pr.

Freyre, Jorge F. External & Domestic Financing in the Economic Development of Puerto Rico. 5.00 (ISBN 0-8477-2410-7); pap. 3.75 (ISBN 0-8477-2411-5). U of PR Pr.

Frey-Rohn, Liliane. From Freud to Jung. LC 73-77114. 1974. 16.00 (ISBN 0-913430-24-2). C G Jung Foun.

Freyssinet, Jacques. Le Concept De Sous-Developpement. 5th ed. (Serie Economie Du Developpement: No. 1). 1980. pap. 16.80x (ISBN 90-2797-973-1). Mouton.

Freytag, George W. Lexicon Arabico-Latinum, 4 vols. (Arabic & Lat.). 95.00x (ISBN 0-86685-124-0). Intl Bk Ctr.

Freytag, Gustav. Doctor Luther. Reimer, G. C., tr. LC 83-45642. Date not set. Repr. of 1916 ed. 27.50 (ISBN 0-404-19851-1). AMS Pr.

--Freytag's Technique of Drama. LC 11-18700. 1895. 49.00 (ISBN 0-403-00019-X). Scholarly.

--Martin Luther. LC 78-144612. Repr. of 1897 ed. 27.50 (ISBN 0-404-02577-3). AMS Pr.

--Technique of the Drama. MacEwan, Elias J., tr. LC 68-57962. 1968. Repr. of 1904 ed. 20.00 (ISBN 0-405-08534-6, Blom Pubns). Ayer Co Pubs.

--Technique of the Drama: An Exposition of Dramatic Composition & Art. McEwan, E. J., tr. 1968. Repr. of 1895 ed. 24.00 (ISBN 0-384-16851-5). Johnson Repr.

Freytag, H. The Hasselblad Way. 7th ed. (Camera Way Bks.). (Illus.). 424p. 1978. 28.95 (ISBN 0-240-50988-9). Focal Pr.

Freytag, Helen. Living in Taiwan: A Handbook for Housewives. 289p. 1980. 16.90 (ISBN 0-89955-149-1, Pub. by Mei Ya China). Intl Spec Bk.

Freytag, Justus & Ozaki, Kenji. Nominal Christianity: Studies of Church & People in Hamburg. (World Council of Churches Studies in Mission). 1970. pap. 3.50 (ISBN 0-377-82011-3). Friend Pr.

Freytag, Paul H., jt. auth. see Delong, Dwight M.

Freytet, P. & Plaziat, J. Continental Carbonate Sedimentation & Pedogenesis: Late Cretaceous & Early Tertiary of Southern France. (Contributions to Sedimentology Ser.: No. 12). (Illus.). 213p. 1982. pap. text ed. 49.60x (ISBN 3-510-57012-X). Lubrecht & Cramer.

Frey-Wettstein, M., et al. Die Bluttransfusion: Ein Vademecum. (Illus.). x, 98p. 1985. pap. 13.00 (ISBN 3-8055-4080-9). S Karger.

Frey-Wouters, Ellen. The European Community & the Third World: The Lome Convention & Its Impact. LC 79-21523. 304p. 1980. 38.95 (ISBN 0-03-055746-1). Praeger.

Frey-Wyssling, A. The Plant Cell Wall. 3rd rev. ed. 1976. 107.30 (ISBN 3-443-14009-2). Lubrecht & Cramer.

Friant, Ray J., Jr. Preparing Effective Presentations. rev. ed. LC 74-133853. 32p. 1984. pap. 3.50 (ISBN 0-87576-033-3). Pilot Bks.

Friar, John G. & Kelly, George W. Practical Spanish Grammar. 1960. pap. 4.95 (ISBN 0-385-00977-1). Doubleday.

Friar, Kimon. The Greeks. LC 83-40282. (Illus.). 144p. 1984. 24.95 (ISBN 0-385-19067-0). Doubleday.

--The Spiritual Odyssey of Nikos Kazantzakis. Stavrou, Theofanis G., intro. by. (Modern Greek History & Culture Ser.). 1979. 10.00 (ISBN 0-935476-00-8). Nostos Bks.

Friar, Kimon, tr. see Decavalles, Adonis.

Friar, Kimon, tr. see Elytis, Odysseus.

Friar, Kimon, tr. see Fostieris, Andonis.

Friar, Kimon, tr. see Kazantzakis, Nikos.

Friar, Kimon, tr. see Kindinis, Kostas.

Friar, Kimon, tr. see Ritsos, Yannis.

Friar, Kimon, tr. see Sahtouris, Miltos.

Friar, Kimon, tr. see Sinopoulos, Takis.

Friar, Kimor, tr. see Kazantzakis, Nikos.

Friar, Wayne & Davis, Percival. A Case for Creation. 3rd ed. (Illus.). 1983. pap. 6.95 (ISBN 0-8024-0176-7). Moody.

Frias-Sucre Giraud, A. Spanish-English, English-Spanish Commercial Dictionary: "The Secretary". rev. & enl. ed. (Eng. & Span.). 17.50 (ISBN 8-4261-1223-4). Heinman.

Frias-Sucre Giraud, Alejandro. Diccionario Comercial Espanol-Ingles y Ingles-Espanol. 3rd ed. 145p. (Span. & Eng.). 1977. 10.75 (ISBN 84-261-1223-4, S-14158). French & Eur.

Fribance, Austin E. Industrial Instrumentation Fundamentals. 1962. text ed. 30.95 (ISBN 0-07-022370-X). McGraw.

Friberg, Barbara, jt. ed. see Friberg, Timothy.

Friberg, Bo. The Professional Pastry Chef. LC 84-2214. (Illus.). 320p. 1984. 34.95 (ISBN 0-442-22635-7). Van Nos Reinhold.

Friberg, Ingegerd. Moving Inward: A Study of Robert Bly's Poetry. (Acta Universitatis Gothoburgensis Ser.). 1976. pap. text ed. 21.50x (ISBN 91-7346-033-8). Humanities.

Friberg, L., et al, eds. Handbook of the Toxicology of Metals. Vouk, V. 700p. 1980. 142.50 (ISBN 0-444-80075-1, Biomedical Pr). Elsevier.

Friberg, L. T., et al, eds. Cadmium & Health: A Toxicological & Epidemiological Appraisal, Vol. I. 240p. 1985. 73.00 (ISBN 0-317-19952-8). CRC Pr.

Friberg, Stig, ed. Food Emulsions. (Food Science Ser.: Vol. 5). 1976. 89.75 (ISBN 0-8247-6337-8). Dekker.

Friberg, Timothy & Friberg, Barbara, eds. Analytical Greek New Testament. 1000p. 1981. 24.95 (ISBN 0-8010-3496-5). Baker Bk.

Frich, Elisabeth. Matt Mattox Book of Jazz Dance. LC 83-4647. (Illus.). 128p. 1983. pap. 12.95 (ISBN 0-8069-7662-4). Sterling.

Frichman-McKenzie, Deborah. Great Legs in Ten Minutes a Day. (Illus.). 64p. (Orig.). (gr. 7 up). 1985. pap. 1.95 (ISBN 0-590-33763-7). Scholastic Inc.

--Sexy Legs in Twenty Days: Spot Reducing the Aerobics Way. (Illus.). 64p. 1983. 2.95 (ISBN 0-399-50780-9, Perigee). Putnam Pub Group.

--Shape Your Waist & Hips in Thirty Days: Spot Reducing the Aerobics Way. (Illus.). 64p. 1983. 2.95 (ISBN 0-399-50781-7, Perigee). Putnam Pub Group.

Frick. The Frick Collection: An Illustrated Catalogue, 9 vols. Brunet, M. & Pope, J., eds. Incl. Vol. 1. Paintings: American, British, Dutch, Flemish & German. 1968; Vol. 2. Paintings: French, Italian & Spanish. 1968. Vols. 1 & 2. 70.00x (ISBN 0-691-03859-7); Vol. 3. Sculpture: Italian. 1970; Vol. 4. Sculpture: Netherlandish, German, French & British. 1970. Vols. 3 & 4. 70.00x (ISBN 0-691-03866-X); Vols. 5 & 6. Furniture. 1982. price not set (ISBN 0-691-03867-8); Vol. 7. Porcelains, Oriental & French. 1974. 45.00x (ISBN 0-691-03811-2); Vol. 8. Limoges Painted Enamels, Oriental Rugs & English Silver. 1977. 45.00x (ISBN 0-691-03832-5); Vol. 9. Prints, Drawings & Recent Acquisitions. Date not set. price not set (ISBN 0-691-03836-8). Princeton U Pr.

Frick, C. H. Comeback Guy. LC 61-6115. (gr. 7 up). 1965. pap. 1.45 (ISBN 0-15-619450-3, VoyB). HarBraceJ.

Frick, Constance. Dramatic Criticism of George Jean Nathan. LC 70-153213. 1971. Repr. of 1943 ed. 27.50x (ISBN 0-8046-1523-3, Pub. by Kennikat). Assoc Faculty Pr.

Frick, Elizabeth. Library Research Guide to History: Illustrated Search Strategy & Sources. LC 80-83514. (Library Research Guides Ser.: No. 4). 1980. 19.50 (ISBN 0-87650-119-6); pap. 12.50 (ISBN 0-87650-123-4). Pierian.

Frick, Frank S. The City in Ancient Israel. LC 77-21984. (Society of Biblical Literature. Dissertation Ser.: No. 36). Repr. of 1977 ed. 56.30 (ISBN 0-8357-9566-7, 2017500). Bks Demand UMI.

Frick, G. William. Environmental Glossary. 2nd ed. LC 82-83908. 293p. 1982. text ed. 35.00 (ISBN 0-86587-096-9). Gov Insts.

Frick, G. William, jt. auth. see Arbuckle, J. Gorden.

Frick, G. William, ed. Environmental Glossary. 3rd ed. 336p. 1984. 38.00 (ISBN 0-86587-073-X). Gov Insts.

Frick, Grace, tr. see Yourcenar, Marguerite.

Frick, Henry C., II, jt. ed. see Nahas, Gabriel G.

Frick, J., jt. ed. see Bandhauer, K.

Frick, John W. New York's First Theatrical Center: The Rialto at Union Square. Brockett, Oscar, ed. LC 84-16255. (Theater & Dramatic Studies: No. 26). 222p. 1985. 39.95 (ISBN 0-8357-1612-0). UMI Res Pr.

Frick, P., et al, eds. Advances in Internal Medicine & Pediatrics, Vol. 49. (Illus.). 172p. 1982. 45.00 (ISBN 0-387-11444-0). Springer-Verlag.

--Advances in Internal Medicine & Pediatrics, Vol. 50. (Illus.). 190p. 1982. 46.00 (ISBN 0-387-11445-9). Springer-Verlag.

Frick, Thomas, ed. Sacred Theory of the Earth. 300p. 1985. 25.00 (ISBN 0-938190-63-6); pap. 12.95 (ISBN 0-938190-62-8). North Atlantic.

Frick, Willard B. Personality Theories: Journeys into Self: An Experiential Workbook. 1984. pap. text ed. 9.95x (ISBN 0-8077-6102-8). Tchrs Coll.

Fricke, Aaron. Reflections of a Rock Lobster: A Story About Growing up Gay. LC 81-65806. (Illus.). 120p. (Orig.). 1981. pap. 4.95 (ISBN 0-932870-09-0). Alyson Pubns.

Fricke, B., jt. auth. see Tofield, B. C.

Fricke, Charles W. Criminal Investigation & the Law. 7th ed. Payton, George T., ed. LC 74-110781. 1974. 15.00x (ISBN 0-910874-32-8). Legal Bk Co.

--Five Thousand Criminal Definitions Terms & Phrases. 5th ed. 1968. 7.00x (ISBN 0-910874-10-7). Legal Bk Co.

--Sentence & Probation, the Imposition of Penalties upon Convicted Criminals. 1960. 3.50x (ISBN 0-910874-11-5). Legal Bk Co.

Fricke, Charles W. & Payton, George T. One Thousand Police Questions & Answers. 7th ed. LC 75-32086. 1978. 8.00 (ISBN 0-910874-36-0). Legal Bk Co.

Fricke, Gerhard. Gefuehl und Schicksal Bei Heinrich V. Kleist. LC 70-149657. Repr. of 1929 ed. 19.50 (ISBN 0-404-02578-1). AMS Pr.

Fricke, Pam. Careers with an Electric Company. LC 83-26807. (Early Careers Bks.). (Illus.). 36p. (gr. 2-5). 1984. lib. bdg. 5.95 (ISBN 0-8225-0375-1). Lerner Pubns.

Fricke, Peter H., ed. Seafarer & Community. 164p. 1973. bds. 17.50x (ISBN 0-87471-197-5). Rowman.

Fricke, R. & Hartmann, F., eds. Connective Tissues-Biochemistry & Pathophysiology. LC 74-417. (Illus.). 330p. 1974. 37.00 (ISBN 0-387-06673-X). Springer-Verlag.

Fricke, Robert. Die Elliptischen Funktionen und Ihre Anwendungen, 2 Vols. LC 5-33590. 1971. Repr. of 1922 ed. Set. 95.00 (ISBN 0-384-16860-4). Johnson Repr.

Fricke, Robert & Klein, Felix. Vorlesungen Ueber Die Theorie der Automorphen Funktionen, 2 Vols. Repr. of 1912 ed. 95.00 (ISBN 0-384-16870-1). Johnson Repr.

Fricke, Robert, jt. auth. see Klein, Felix.

Fricke, Ronald. Revision of the Genus Synchiropus (Teleostei: Callionymidae) (Theses Zoologicae: Vol. 1). (Illus.). 194p. 1981. text ed. 17.50x (ISBN 3-7682-1306-4). Lubrecht & Cramer.

Fricke, Roswitha, jt. ed. see Marzona, Egidio.

Fricke, W. & Teleki, G., eds. Sun & Planetary System. 1982. 65.00 (ISBN 90-277-1429-0, Pub. by Reidel Holland). Kluwer Academic.

Frickelton, Annelise & Dierrsen, Gunther. It's Fun to Speak Danish. 1981. includes 5 cassettes 75.00 (ISBN 0-88432-092-8, DAI); listener's guide 48p; Danish-English, English-Danish Dictionary 512p. J Norton Pubs.

Fricker, E. G. God Is My Witness: The Story of the World-Famous Healer. LC 76-50557. 1977. pap. 2.75 (ISBN 0-8128-7068-9). Stein & Day.

Fricker, Francois. Einfuhrung in die Gitterpunktlehre. (Mathematical Ser.: Vol. 73). 256p. (Ger.). 1981. text ed. 51.95x (ISBN 0-8176-1236-X). Birkhauser.

Fricker, Hans-Peter. Die Musikkritischen Schriften Robert Schumanns: Versuch eines Literaturwissenschaftlichen Zugangs. (European University Studies: No. 1, Vol. 677). 286p. (Ger.). 1983. 30.00 (ISBN 3-261-03275-8). P Lang Pubs.

Fricton, et al. Differential Diagnosis of TMJ Craniofacial Pain. 1985. write for info. Ishiyaku Euro.

Frid, Tage. Tage Frid Teaches Woodworking, Bk. 3: Furniture. (Illus.). 240p. 1985. text ed. 18.95 (ISBN 0-918804-40-X, Dist. by W W Norton). Taunton.

--Tage Frid Teaches Woodworking-Joinery: Tools & Techniques. LC 78-65178. (Illus.). 224p. 1979. 17.95 (ISBN 0-918804-03-5, Dist. by W W Norton). Taunton.

--Tage Frid Teaches Woodworking: Joinery Tools & Techniques. (Illus.). 224p. 1985. text ed. 26.95 (ISBN 0-13-882218-2). P-H.

--Tage Frid Teaches Woodworking: Shaping, Veneering & Finishing. (Illus.). 224p. 1985. text ed. 26.95 (ISBN 0-13-882226-3). P-H.

--Tage Frid Teaches Woodworking-Shaping, Veneering, Finishing. LC 78-65178. (Illus.). 224p. 1981. 17.95 (ISBN 0-918804-11-6, Dist. by W W Norton). Taunton.

Friday, A. E., jt. ed. see Joysey, K. A.

Friday, Adrian & Ingram, David S., eds. The Cambridge Encyclopedia of Life Sciences. (Illus.). 432p. Date not set. pap. 39.95 (ISBN 0-521-25696-8). Cambridge U Pr.

Friday, Nancy. Forbidden Flowers. 336p. 1982. pap. 3.95 (ISBN 0-671-46266-0). PB.

--Jealousy. 1985. 19.95 (ISBN 0-688-04321-6). Morrow.

--Men in Love, Male Sexual Fantasies: The Triumph of Love over Rage. 1981. pap. 4.95 (ISBN 0-440-15903-2). Dell.

--My Mother, Myself. 480p. 1981. pap. 4.50 (ISBN 0-440-15663-7). Dell.

--My Secret Garden. 352p. 1983. pap. 3.95 (ISBN 0-671-50277-8). PB.

Friday, Paul C. & Stewart, V. Lorne, eds. Youth Crime & Juvenile Justice: International Perspectives. LC 77-7820. (Praeger Special Studies). 200p. 1977. text ed. 37.95 (ISBN 0-03-022646-5). Praeger.

Friday, Sandra K. & Hurwitz, Heidi S. The Food Sleuth Handbook. LC 81-68133. (Illus.). 288p. 1982. 15.95 (ISBN 0-689-11246-7). Atheneum.

Friday, William. How to Sell Your Product Through (Not to) Wholesalers. LC 79-90315. (Illus.). 1980. 29.50 (ISBN 0-934432-05-8). Prudential Pub Co.

--Successful Management for One to Ten Employee Businesses. LC 78-111544. (Illus.). 1979. 29.50 (ISBN 0-934432-04-X). Prudential Pub Co.

Friday, Wm. Quick Printing Encyclopedia. LC 82-144544. (Illus.). 509p. 1982. 49.50 (ISBN 0-934432-10-4). Prudential Pub Co.

Friddell, Guy. Colgate Darden: Conversations with Guy Friddell. LC 78-7026. xi, 256p. 1978. 14.95 (ISBN 0-8139-0744-6). U Pr of Va.

--We Began at Jamestown. (Illus.). 1968. 4.75 (ISBN 0-685-09020-5). Dietz.

--What Is It about Virginia? (Illus.). 1983. 10.95 (ISBN 0-685-09021-3). Dietz.

Fridegard, Jan. I, Lars Hard. Bjork, Robert E., tr. from Swedish. LC 83-1098. xvi, 105p. 1983. 14.95 (ISBN 0-8032-1963-6). U of Nebr Pr.

--Jacob's Ladder & Mercy. Bjork, Robert E., tr. from Swedish. LC 84-19626. viii, 186p. 1985. 16.95 (ISBN 0-8032-1969-5). U Of Nebr Pr.

Fridell, Squire. Acting in Television Commercials for Fun & Profit. (Illus.). 224p. 1980. 12.95 (ISBN 0-517-54108-4, Harmony); pap. 7.95 (ISBN 0-517-54071-1). Crown.

Friden, G. Studies on the Tenses of the English Verb from Chaucer to Shakespeare. (Essays & Studies on English Language & Literature: Vol. 21). pap. 19.00 (ISBN 0-317-15871-6). Kraus Repr.

Friden, Georg. James Fenimore Cooper & Ossian. 56p. 1980. Repr. of 1949 ed. lib. bdg. 10.00 (ISBN 0-8492-4627-X). R West.

Friden, George. James Fenimore Cooper & Ossian. LC 76-22512. 1949. lib. bdg. 10.00 (ISBN 0-8414-4225-8). Folcroft.

Friden, Julian & Rubin, Ira L. ECG Case Studies, Vol. 3. 1984. pap. text ed. write for info (ISBN 0-87488-217-6). Med Exam.

Fridenson, Bardon, et al, eds. see Laux, James M.

Frideres, J. Canada's Indians: Contemporary Conflicts. 1974. text ed. 11.25 (ISBN 0-13-112763-2); pap. text ed. 11.25 (ISBN 0-13-112755-1). P-H.

Frideres, James. Native People in Canada: Contemporary Conflicts. 2nd ed. LC 83-191539. viii, 344p. 1983. write for info. (ISBN 0-13-114058-2). P-H.

Fridjonsson, J. A Course in Modern Icelandic. 1978. pap. text ed. 35.00 (ISBN 0-686-46530-X). Heinman.

Fridkin, Mati, jt. ed. see Najjar, Victor A.

Fridkin, V. M. Ferroelectric Semiconductors. LC 79-14561. (Illus.). 330p. 1979. 69.50x (ISBN 0-306-10957-3, Consultants). Plenum Pub.

--Photoferroelectrics. (Ser. in Sold-State Sciences: Vol. 9). (Illus.). 1979. 40.00 (ISBN 0-387-09418-0). Springer-Verlag.

Fridkin, V. M. & Grekov, A. A., eds. Fourth Symposium on Ferroelectric Semiconductors, Rostov-on-Don, U. S. S. R., June 1981. (Ferroelectrics Ser.: Vol. 43, Nos. 3-4, & Vol. 45, Nos. 1-2). 280p. 1983. 203.50. Gordon.

Fridland, V. M. Comparative Physiology & Evolution of Vision in Invertebrates C. 1981. 30.00x (ISBN 0-686-76629-6, Pub. by Oxford & IBH India). State Mutual Bk.

--Soil Combination & Their Genesis. 1981. 60.00x (ISBN 0-686-76666-0, Pub. by Oxford & IBH India). State Mutual Bk.

Fridleifsson, Ingvar B., ed. Report of the First Meeting of the Standing Advisory Committee in Geothermal Energy Training: Pisa, Italy, Nov. 1980. 69p. 1983. pap. text ed. 8.50 (ISBN 92-808-0464-2, TUNU217, UNU). Unipub.

Fridlund, Paul. Two Fronts, a Small Town at War. 1985. 19.95 (ISBN 0-87770-326-4). Ye Galleon.

--The World of Charles Wilder: The Prosser Photographer 1870-1910. 129p. 1983. 14.95 (ISBN 0-87770-285-3). Ye Galleon.

Fridman, A. M. & Polyachenko, V. I. Physics of Gravitating Systems: Vol. 1 - Equilibrium & Stability of Gravitating Systems. Aries, A. B. & Poliakoff, I. N., trs. from Rus. (Illus.). 480p. 1984. 84.00 (ISBN 0-387-11045-3). Springer Verlag.

Fridman, A. M. & Polyachenko, V. L. Physics of Gravitating Systems: Vol. 2 - The Nonlinear Theory of Collective Processes in a Gravitating Medium: Astrophysical Application. Aries, A. B. & Poliakoff, I. N., trs. from Rus. (Illus.). 385p. 1984. 60.00 (ISBN 0-387-13103-5). Springer Verlag.

Fridman, David. Vozvrashchenie Mendelia Marantsa. 2nd ed. LC 85-61781. 150p. (Orig.). 1985. pap. price not set (ISBN 0-89830-086-X). Russica Pubs.

Fridman, Ya. B., ed. Strength & Deformation in Nonuniform Temperature Fields. LC 63-17641. 169p. 1964. 30.00x (ISBN 0-306-10688-4, Consultants). Plenum Pub.

Fridolin, Stephan, jt. auth. see Wolgemut, Michael.

Fridriksson, S. Surtsey: Evolution of Life on a Volcanic Island. LC 74-30850. 198p. 1975. 37.95x (ISBN 0-470-28000-X). Halsted Pr.

Frie, R W. & Brinkman, U. A., eds. Mutagenicity Testing & Related Analytical Techniques. (Current Topics in Environmental & Toxocological Chemistry Ser.). 330p. 1981. 60.25 (ISBN 0-677-16300-2). Gordon.

Friebel, Otto. Fulgentius, der Mythograph und Bischof. pap. 15.00 (ISBN 0-384-16880-9). Johnson Repr.

Friebert, Stuart. Dreaming of Floods: Poems. LC 72-88187. 1969. 7.95 (ISBN 0-8265-1141-4). Vanderbilt U Pr.

--Uncertain Health. LC 78-68473. 1979. 7.95 (ISBN 0-913506-08-7); pap. 3.95 (ISBN 0-913506-09-5). Woolmer-Brotherson.

--Up in Bed. LC 74-620108. (CSU Poetry Ser.: No. 1). 83p. 1974. pap. 4.95 (ISBN 0-914946-01-3). Cleveland St Univ Poetry Ctr.

Friebert, Stuart & Young, David. Longman Anthology of Poetry: Contemporary American. LC 81-15630. 1982. 17.95x (ISBN 0-582-28263-2). Longman.

Friebert, Stuart, tr. see Holub, Miroslav.

Friebert, Stuart, tr. see Krolow, Karl.

Friebert, Stuart, et al, trs. from Ger. Valuable Nail: The Selected Poems of Gunter Eich. LC 80-85332. (Field Translation Ser.: No. 5). 150p. 1981. 9.95 (ISBN 0-932440-08-8); pap. 4.95 (ISBN 0-932440-09-6). Field Translat.

Fried & Sherma. Thin Layer Chromatography. (Chromatographic Science Ser.: Vol. 17). 520p. 1982. 49.50 (ISBN 0-8247-1288-9). Dekker.

Fried, Alfred H. Handbuch der Friedensbewegung. LC 71-147449. (Library of War & Peace; Problems of the Organized Peace Movements: Selected Documents). lib. bdg. 46.00 (ISBN 0-8240-0240-7). Garland Pub.

--Restoration of Europe. (Library of War & Peace; Int'l. Organization, Arbitration & Law). lib. bdg. 46.00 (ISBN 0-8240-0344-6). Garland Pub.

Fried, Barbara. Concerto in the Key of Death. (Orig.). 1980. pap. 1.75 (ISBN 0-505-51508-3, Pub. by Tower Bks). Dorchester Pub Co.

--The Spider in the Cup: Yoknapatawpha County's Fall into the Unknowable. 1978. 3.75x (ISBN 0-674-83205-1). Harvard U Pr.

--Who's Afraid? The Phobic's Handbook. rev. ed. (Illus.). 100p. 1985. Repr. of 1972 ed. 14.95 (ISBN 0-89876-104-2). Gardner Pr.

Fried, Benjamin S., ed. Film Index of Work Measurement & Methods Engineering Subjects. 1980. 11.00 (ISBN 0-89806-027-3); members 7.00. Inst Indus Eng.

Fried, Bruce, ed. see Fretz, Burton, et al.

Fried, Bryan A., jt. auth. see Hibbard, Jack.

Fried, C., ed. Minorities: Community & Identity. (Dahlem Workshop Reports: Vol. 27). (Illus.). 430p. 1983. 27.00 (ISBN 0-387-12747-X). Springer-Verlag.

Fried, Charles. An Anatomy of Values: Problems of Personal & Social Choice. LC 78-111483. 1970. 17.50x (ISBN 0-674-03151-2). Harvard U Pr.

--Contract As Promise: A Theory of Contractual Obligation. LC 80-26548. 176p. 1982. text ed. 14.00x (ISBN 0-674-16925-5); pap. text ed. 5.95x (ISBN 0-674-16930-1). Harvard U Pr.

--Right & Wrong. 1979. 17.50x (ISBN 0-674-76905-8); pap. 6.95x (ISBN 0-674-76975-9). Harvard U Pr.

Fried, Edrita. Active-Passive. LC 78-115013. 224p. 1970. 49.50 (ISBN 0-8089-0647-X, 791400). Grune.

--Artistic Productivity & Mental Health. 188p. 1964. 18.75x (ISBN 0-398-00617-2). C C Thomas.

--The Courage to Change: From Insight to Self-Innovation. LC 79-25161. 1980. 25.00 (ISBN 0-87630-213-4). Brunner-Mazel.

--The Courage to Change: From Insight to Self-Innovation. 256p. (Orig.). 1981. pap. 7.95 (ISBN 0-394-17935-8, E786, Ever). Grove.

Fried, Edward R. & Owen, Henry, eds. The Future Role of the World Bank. LC 82-71296. (Dialogues on Public Policy Ser.). 91p. 1982. pap. 9.95 (ISBN 0-8157-2929-4). Brookings.

Fried, Edward R. & Schultze, Charles L., eds. Higher Oil Prices & the World Economy: The Adjustment Problem. LC 75-34234. pap. 75.00 (ISBN 0-317-20824-1, 2025377). Bks Demand UMI.

Fried, Edward R. & Trezise, Philip H., eds. The Future Course of U. S.-Japan Economic Relations. LC 83-62414. 100p. 1983. pap. 9.95 (ISBN 0-8157-2927-8). Brookings.

--U. S. - Canadian Economic Relations: Next Steps? (Dialogue on Public Policy Ser.). 141p. 1984. pap. 9.95 (ISBN 0-8157-2925-1). Brookings.

Fried, Edward R., et al see Pechman, Joseph A.

Fried, Elliot. Striptease. 36p. (Orig.). 1979. pap. 2.00 (ISBN 0-930090-09-8). Applezaba.

Fried, Elliot & Enriquez, Helen. The Weekend Gambler's Guide to Las Vegas. (Weekend Gambler's Ser.). (Illus.). 1980. pap. 4.95 (ISBN 0-935232-02-8). Deep River Pr.

Fried, Elliot, ed. Amorotica: A New Collection of Erotic Poetry. (Illus.). 144p. 1981. pap. 4.95 (ISBN 0-935232-04-4). Deep River Pr.

Fried, Emanuel. Dodo Bird: A Play. 72p. (Orig.). 1975. pap. 2.50 (ISBN 0-9603888-0-X). Labor Arts.

--Dodo Bird: A Play. 72p. 1975. pap. 1.95 (ISBN 0-9603888-0-X). Vanguard Bks.

--Drop Hammer. 1978. pap. 2.50 (ISBN 0-931122-05-8). West End.

--Drop Hammer: Play. 127p. (Orig.). 1977. pap. 4.50 (ISBN 0-9603888-1-8). Vanguard Bks.

--Meshugah & Other Stories. Walsh, Joy, ed. 40p. (Orig.). 1982. pap. 2.95 (ISBN 0-938838-09-1). Textile Bridge.

--Meshugah & Other Stories. 40p. (Orig.). 1982. pap. 2.95 (ISBN 0-9603888-2-6). Labor Arts.

Fried, Erich. On Pain of Seeing. Rapp, Georg, tr. LC 74-97025. (Poetry Europe Ser.: No. 11). 72p. 1969. 7.95 (ISBN 0-8040-0234-7, 82-71603, Pub. by Swallow). Ohio U Pr.

--One Hundred Poems Without a Country. Hd, Stuart, tr. from Ger. LC 80-50150. 1980. 8.95 (ISBN 0-87376-035-2). Red Dust.

Fried, Erwin, ed. see Idelchik, I. E.

Fried, Frederick. The Freida Schiff Warburg Memorial Sculpture Garden. (Illus.). 32p. pap. 0.75 (ISBN 0-87273-031-X). Bklyn Mus.

--A Pictorial History of the Carousel. (Illus.). 228p. 1983. 25.00 (ISBN 0-911572-29-5). Vestal.

Fried, Henry B. Bench Practices for Watch-Clockmakers. 1984. 9.00 (ISBN 0-317-17083-X). Am Watchmakers.

--Cavalcade of Time. 1984. 10.00 (ISBN 0-317-17084-8). Am Watchmakers.

--Repairing Quartz Watches. 1983. write for info. (ISBN 0-918845-06-8). Am Watchmakers.

--The Watch Escapement. 1984. 8.00 (ISBN 0-317-17086-4). Am Watchmakers.

--The Watch Repairer's Manual. 1984. 17.95 (ISBN 0-317-17087-2). Am Watchmakers.

Fried, Ilana. The Chemistry of Electrode Processes. 1974. 39.50 (ISBN 0-12-267650-5). Acad Pr.

Fried, Isaac. Numerical Solution of Differential Equations. (Computer Science & Applied Math Ser.). 1979. 47.50 (ISBN 0-12-267780-3). Acad Pr.

Fried, J. J. Groundwater Pollution. LC 74-29680. (Developments in Water Science: Vol. 4). 330p. 1976. 76.75 (ISBN 0-444-41316-2). Elsevier.

Fried, Jacob. Crawley: New Town. 350p. (Orig.). 1983. pap. 10.95 (ISBN 0-913244-60-0). Hapi Pr.

Fried, Jacob & Molnar, Paul. Technological & Social Change: A Transdisciplinary Model. 1979. text ed. 17.50 (ISBN 0-89433-074-8). Petrocelli.

Fried, Jacob L. Jews & Divorce. 1968. 12.50x (ISBN 0-87068-049-8). Ktav.

Fried, Jane, ed. Education for Student Development. LC 80-84302. (Student Services Ser.: No. 15). 1981. pap. text ed. 8.95x (ISBN 0-87589-863-7). Jossey-Bass.

Fried, Jerome, compiled by. The Bantam Crossword Dictionary. 1979. pap. 3.95 (ISBN 0-553-24087-0). Bantam.

Fried, Jerome, ed. see Bieler, Henry G.

Fried, Jerome, jt. ed. see Leach, Maria.

Fried, John & Edwards, John A. Organic Reactions in Steroid Chemistry, Vol. 2. LC 76-153192. 480p. 1972. 26.50. Krieger.

Fried, John H. The Guilt of the German Army. LC 75-10823. Repr. of 1942 ed. 35.00 (ISBN 0-404-14493-4). AMS Pr.

Fried, John J. Vitamin Politics. LC 83-62187. 238p. 1984. pap. 10.95 (ISBN 0-87975-222-X). Prometheus Bks.

Fried, John J. & West, John G. Trauma. LC 84-15844. 1985. 15.95 (ISBN 0-03-003267-9). HR&W.

Fried, Jonathan L. & Gettlemen, Marvin, eds. Guatemala in Rebellion: Unfinished History. (Latin America Ser.: No. 2). 368p. 1983. 17.50 (ISBN 0-394-53240-6, GP 871, GP); pap. 8.95 (ISBN 0-394-62455-6, E844, Ever). Grove.

Fried, Jonathan L., et al, eds. Guatemala in Rebellion: Unfinished History. 366p. 22.50 (ISBN 0-394-53240-6); pap. 8.95 (ISBN 0-394-62455-6). Grove.

Fried, Lawerence A. Anatomy of the Head, Neck, Face, & Jaws. 2nd ed. LC 80-16800. (Illus.). 299p. 1980. text ed. 17.50 (ISBN 0-8121-0717-9). Lea & Febiger.

Fried, Lewis & Fierst, John. Jacob A. Riis: A Reference Guide. 1977. lib. bdg. 26.00 (ISBN 0-8161-7862-3, Hall Reference). G K Hall.

Fried, Louis. Practical Data Processing Management. (Illus.). 1979. text ed. 25.95 (ISBN 0-8359-5589-3). Reston.

Fried, M. B., ed. Mark Twain on the Art of Writing. Clemens, Samuel L. LC 73-7737. 1961. lib. bdg. 10.00 (ISBN 0-8414-1968-X). Folcroft.

Fried, Marc B. Tales from the Shawangunk Mountains: A Naturalist's Musings, a Bushwhacker's Guide. LC 81-8017. (Illus.). 112p. 1981. 10.95 (ISBN 0-935272-17-8); pap. 6.95 (ISBN 0-935272-18-6). ADK Mtn Club.

Fried, Martha N. & Fried, Morton H. Transitions: Four Rituals in Eight Cultures. 1980. 14.95 (ISBN 0-393-01350-2). Norton.

--Transitions: Four Rituals in Eight Cultures. 320p. 1981. pap. 5.95 (ISBN 0-14-005847-8). Penguin.

Fried, Maurice & Broeshart, Hans. Soil-Plant System in Relation to Inorganic Nutrition. (Atomic Energy Commission Monographs). 1967. 23.50 (ISBN 0-12-268050-2). Acad Pr.

Fried, Michael. Absorption & Theatricality: Painting & Beholder in the Age of Diderot. LC 78-62843. 249p. 1980. 34.00x (ISBN 0-520-03758-8); pap. 11.50 (ISBN 0-520-04339-1, 489). U of Cal Pr.

Fried, Morton. Evolution of Political Society: An Evolutionary View. (Orig.). 1968. pap. text ed. 12.95 (ISBN 0-394-30787-9, RanC). Random.

Fried, Morton H. Fabric of Chinese Society. LC 76-75993. 1969. Repr. of 1953 ed. lib. bdg. 20.00x (ISBN 0-374-92926-2). Octagon.

Fried, Morton H., jt. auth. see Fried, Martha N.

Fried, Peter. Pregnancy & Life-Style Habits. LC 83-2650. 240p. 1983. 9.95 (ISBN 0-8253-0151-3). Beaufort Bks NY.

Fried, Peter A. & Oxorn, Harry. Smoking for Two: Cigarettes & Pregnancy. LC 80-20054. (Illus.). 1980. 10.95 (ISBN 0-02-910720-2). Free Pr.

Fried, Peter A., ed. Readings in Perception. 1974. pap. text ed. 10.95 (ISBN 0-669-89367-6). Heath.

Fried, Richard M. Men Against McCarthy. LC 75-40447. (Contemporary American History Ser.). 428p. 1976. 31.50x (ISBN 0-231-03872-0); pap. 17.00x (ISBN 0-231-08360-2). Columbia U Pr.

Fried, Robert. Introduction to Statistics. 1976. 23.95 (ISBN 0-89876-075-5). Gardner Pr.

Fried, Robert C. Planning the Eternal City: Roman Politics & Planning Since World War II. LC 72-91312. pap. 91.50 (ISBN 0-317-29583-7, 2021998). Bks Demand UMI.

Fried, Robert C. & Rabinovitz, Frances F. Comparative Urban Politics: A Performance Approach. 240p. 1980. pap. text ed. 15.95 (ISBN 0-13-154351-2). P-H.

Fried, Sherman, ed. Radioactive Waste in Geologic Storage. LC 79-9754. (ACS Symposium Ser.: No. 100). 1979. 39.95 (ISBN 0-8412-0498-5). Am Chemical.

Fried, Vilem, tr. see Macek, Josef.

Fried, Vojtech, et al. Physical Chemistry. 1977. write for info. (ISBN 0-02-339760-8, 33976). Macmillan.

Fried, W. Comparative Clinical Aspects of Sickle Cell Disease. (Chicago Sickle Cell Ser.: Vol. 2). 192p. 1982. 55.00 (ISBN 0-444-00673-7, Biomedical Pr). Elsevier.

Fried, Walter, jt. auth. see Kayton, Myron.

Fried, William & Watson, Edward B. New York in Aerial Views. (Illus.). 16.50 (ISBN 0-8446-5764-6). Peter Smith.

--New York in Aerial Views: Eighty-Six Photographs. (Illus.). 176p. (Orig.). 1981. pap. 6.50 (ISBN 0-486-24018-5). Dover.

Fried, Yehuda & Agassi, Joseph. Paranoia: A Study in Diagnosis. LC 76-21816. (Synthese Library Ser.: No. 102). 1976. lib. bdg. 29.00 (ISBN 9-0277-0705-7, Pub. by Reidel Holland); pap. 17.00 (ISBN 90-277-0705-7, Pub. by Reidel Holland). Kluwer Academic.

--Psychiatry As Medicine: Contemporary Psychotherapies. 1983. lib. bdg. 34.95 (ISBN 90-247-2837-1, Pub. by Martinus Nijhoff Netherlands). Kluwer Academic.

Frieda Carrol. Membership Applications for Clubs, Asssociations & Organizations: Samples to Duplicate & Use. 40p. 1984. pap. text ed. 6.95 (ISBN 0-318-04334-3, Pub. by F. Carrol). Prosperity & Profits.

Frieda Carrol Business Division. Freelance Writing As a Home Business: A Bibliography. 1984. pap. text ed. 3.95 (ISBN 0-318-04329-7, Pub. by F. Carrol). Prosperity & Profits.

--Sewing As a Home Business: A Bibliography. 1984. pap. text ed. 3.95 (ISBN 0-318-04350-5, Pub. by F. Carrol). Prosperity & Profits.

--Telephone Answering As a Home Business: A Bibliography. 1984. pap. text ed. 3.95 (ISBN 0-318-04353-X, Pub. by F. Carrol). Prosperity & Profits.

--Telephone Soliciting & Survey As a Home Business: A Bibliography. 1984. pap. text ed. 3.95 (ISBN 0-318-04357-2, Pub. by F. Carrol). Prosperity & Profits.

Frieda Carrol Consulting Division. Paying Office Expenses; Piggy-backing, Cooperative, Sharing, Entrepreneural Services, Bartering: A Consultants Reference. 1984. pap. text ed. 8.95 (ISBN 0-318-04335-1, Pub. by F. Carrol). Prosperity & Profits.

Frieda Carrol Research Division. Association, Club & Organization, Group Tours As a Travel Business: Bibliography Plus Workbook. 1984. pap. text ed. 4.95 (ISBN 0-318-04326-2, Pub. by F. Carrol). Prosperity & Profits.

--Catering Service: Bibliography on Breads. 1984. pap. text ed. 4.95 (ISBN 0-318-04328-9, Pub. by F. Carrol). Prosperity & Profits.

--People's Money Pages: Bibliography on Fundraising. 50p. 1984. pap. text ed. 8.95 (ISBN 0-318-04338-6, Pub. by F. Carrol). Prosperity & Profits.

Frieda Carrol Research Division Staff. Popcorn Use As Food, Crafts, Ornaments, Etc. Plus Bibliography. 1984. pap. text ed. 5.95 (ISBN 0-318-04342-4, Pub. by F. Carrol). Prosperity & Profits.

Frieda Carrol Research Project. Food Activities As a Fundraiser: A Bibliography Reference. 1984. pap. text ed. 4.95 (ISBN 0-318-04330-0, Pub. by F. Carrol). Prosperity & Profits.

--Food Business Bibliography on Donut Shops & Other Pastry Shops. 1984. pap. text ed. 4.95 (ISBN 0-318-04331-9, Pub. by F. Carrol). Prosperity & Profits.

--Magazine & Periodical References for the Entertainment Business. 1984. pap. text ed. 8.95 (ISBN 0-318-04332-7, Pub. by F. Carrol). Prosperity & Profits.

--Magazine & Periodical References for the Food Business. 1984. pap. text ed. 8.95 (ISBN 0-318-04333-5, Pub. by F. Carrol). Prosperity & Profits.

--Postage Stamp Recycling As Fundraising, Crafts & a Hobby: A Bibliography. 1984. pap. text ed. 8.95 (ISBN 0-318-04346-7, Pub. by F. Carrol). Prosperity & Profits.

Frieda Carrol Workbook Division. Calligraphy As a Home Business: A Workbook with Bibliography Reading. 1984. pap. text ed. 4.95 (ISBN 0-318-04327-0, Pub. by F. Carrol). Prosperity & Profits.

Friedan, Betty. The Feminine Mystique. 1977. pap. 4.95 (ISBN 0-440-32497-1). Dell.

--The Feminine Mystique: Twentieth Anniversary Edition. LC 83-42665. 1983. 17.50 (ISBN 0-393-01775-3). Norton.

--It Changed My Life: Writings on the Women's Movement. 416p. Repr. of 1976 ed. 7.95 (ISBN 0-393-30243-1). Norton.

--The Second Stage. 352p. 1982. pap. 6.95 (ISBN 0-671-45951-1). Summit Bks.

Friedan, Julian & Rubin, Ira. ECG Case Studies, Vol. 1. 3rd ed. 1985. pap. text ed. price not set (ISBN 0-87488-460-8). Med Exam.

Friedan, Leon, compiled by. The Law of War: A Documentary History, 2 vols. LC 72-765. 1972. Set. lib. bdg. 95.00 (ISBN 0-313-20133-1, FRLW). Greenwood.

Friedanthal, Jack & Miller, Arthur. Civil Procedure. 2nd ed. (Sum & Substance Ser.). 1979. 12.95 (ISBN 0-686-27111-4). Josephson-Kluwer Legal Educ Ctrs.

Friedberg & Hanawalt. DNA Repair, Vol. 2. 296p. 1983. 59.75 (ISBN 0-8247-1805-4). Dekker.

--DNA Repair: A Laboratory Manual of Research Procedures, Vol. 1, Pts. A & B. 424p. 1981. Pt. A. pap. 49.75 (ISBN 0-8247-7248-2); Pt. B. pap. 59.75 (ISBN 0-8247-1184-X). Dekker.

Friedberg, Ardy. Computer Freelancer's Handbook. 1984. pap. 10.95 (ISBN 0-452-25562-7, Plume). NAL.

--The Facts on File Dictionary of Fitness. 160p. 1984. 15.95 (ISBN 0-87196-809-6). Facts on File.

--How to Run Your First Marathon. 128p. 1982. pap. 6.75 (ISBN 0-671-44206-6, Fireside). S&S.

--My Greatest Day In Sports. 112p. (Orig.). (gr. 7 up). 1983. pap. 1.95 (ISBN 0-590-32388-1). Scholastic Inc.

--Reach for It. (Illus.). 96p. 1983. 7.95 (ISBN 0-671-45997-X, Fireside). S&S.

Friedberg, Ardy, jt. auth. see Mentzer, Mike.

Friedberg, Bernard, jt. ed. see Harvey, Emily D.

Friedberg, Carl, ed. see Handel, Georg F.

Friedberg, Charles K. Diseases of the Heart. 3rd ed. LC 66-12413. (Illus.). pap. 160.00 (ISBN 0-317-09685-0, 2012208). Bks Demand UMI.

Friedberg, Charles K., ed. Angina Pectoris. 1972. pap. cancelled (ISBN 0-87493-025-1, 73-026A). Am Heart.

--Myocardial Infarction. 1972. pap. 5.00 (ISBN 0-87493-027-8, 73-025A). Am Heart.

Friedberg, Erhard, jt. auth. see Crozier, Michel.

Friedberg, Errol C. DNA Repair. LC 84-18688. (Illus.). 614p. 1984. text ed. 39.95 (ISBN 0-7167-1674-7). W H Freeman.

Friedberg, Errol C., jt. auth. see Scientific American Staff.

Friedberg, Errol G. & Bridges, Bryn A. Cellular Responses to DNA Damage. LC 83-19955. (UCLA Symposia on Molecular & Cellular Biology, New Ser.: Vol. 11). 768p. 1983. 98.00 (ISBN 0-8451-2610-5). A R Liss.

Friedberg, Jack. Proofreading in the Word Processing Age. 125p. 1985. 17.95 (ISBN 0-8290-1506-X). Irvington.

Friedberg, Joan B., et al. Accept Me As I Am: Best Books of Juvenile Nonfiction on Impairments & Disabilities. 378p. 1985. 27.50 (ISBN 0-8352-1974-7). Bowker.

Friedberg, Maurice. A Decade of Euphoria: Western Literature in Post-Stalin Russia, 1954-64. LC 76-11932. pap. 92.80 (ISBN 0-317-27817-7, 2056035). Bks Demand UMI.

Friedberg, Robert. Gold Coins of the World: An Illustrated Standard Catalogue with Valuations. 5th ed. LC 80-66207. (Illus.). 484p. 1980. 29.50 (ISBN 0-87184-305-6). Coin & Curr.

--Paper Money of the United States: A Complete Illustrated Guide with Valuations. 10th ed. LC 81-65969. (Illus.). 256p. 1981. 19.50 (ISBN 0-87184-510-5). Coin & Curr.

Friedberg, Ruth C. American Art Song & American Poetry: America Comes of Age, Vol. I. LC 81-9047. 175p. 1981. 15.00 (ISBN 0-8108-1460-9). Scarecrow.

--American Art Song & American Poetry: Voices of Maturity, Vol. 2. LC 81-9047. 236p. 1984. 17.50 (ISBN 0-8108-1682-2). Scarecrow.

Friedberg, Stephen & Insel, Arnold. Introduction to Linear Algebra with Applications. (Illus.). 480p. 1986. text ed. 30.95 (ISBN 0-13-485988-X). P-H.

Friedberg, Stephen, et al. Linear Algebra. (Illus.). 1979. ref. ed. 32.95 (ISBN 0-13-537019-1). P-H.

Friedburg, Ardy. The Complete Video Cassette Recorder Book. 96p. (Orig.). 1984. pap. 3.95 (ISBN 0-523-42326-8). Pinnacle Bks.

Frieddrich Ebert Foundation, ed. Towards One World? International Responses to the Brandt Report. 1981. 33.00x (ISBN 0-85117-218-0, Pub. by M Temple Smith). State Mutual Bk.

Friede, Reinhard L. Topographic Brain Chemistry. 1966. 89.50 (ISBN 0-12-268350-1). Acad Pr.

Friedeberg-Seeley, F., tr. see Abarbanel, Judah.

Friedel, jt. auth. see Eisdorfer, C.

Friedel, Frank, ed. see Robertson, James O.

Friedel, Richard. The Movie Lover. 304p. 1983. pap. 6.95 (ISBN 0-932870-43-0). Alyson Pubns.

Friedel, Robert. Pioneer Plastic: The Making & Selling of Celluloid. LC 81-69818. (Illus.). 192p. 1983. 21.50x (ISBN 0-299-09170-8). U of Wis Pr.

Friedell, Hymer L. Radiation Protection: Concepts & Trade Offs. 7.00 (ISBN 0-686-30848-4). NCRP Pubns.

Friedemann, Marie L. Manual for Effective Community Health Nursing Practice. LC 82-20188. 288p. 1982. pap. text ed. 14.00 pub net (ISBN 0-534-01240-X). Brooks-Cole.

Frieden, B. R. Probability, Statistical Optics, & Data Analysis. (Series in Information Sciences: Vol. 10). (Illus.). 404p. 1983. 42.00 (ISBN 0-387-11769-5). Springer-Verlag.

Frieden, B. R., ed. The Computer in Optical Research: Methods & Applications. (Topics in Applied Physics: Vol. 41). (Illus.). 400p. 1980. 66.00 (ISBN 0-387-10119-5). Springer-Verlag.

Frieden, Bernard, jt. auth. see Marshall, Dale R.

Frieden, Bernard J. The Environmental Protection Hustle. (Joint Center for Urban Studies). (Illus.). 1979. 25.00x (ISBN 0-262-06068-X); pap. 6.95x (ISBN 0-262-56022-4). MIT Pr.

--The Environmental Protection Hustle. 211p. 1979. 12.50 (ISBN 0-318-12980-9); members 11.50 (ISBN 0-318-12981-7). Am Plan Assn.

--Urban-Suburban Problems. (Task Force on the Eighties Ser.). 34p. 1981. pap. 2.50 (ISBN 0-87495-038-4). Am Jewish Comm.

Frieden, Bernard J. & Kaplan, Marshall. The Politics of Neglect: Urban Aid from Model Cities to Revenue Sharing. LC 75-6792. (MIT-Harvard Joint Center for Urban Studies). 386p. 1975. 27.50x (ISBN 0-262-06061-2); pap. 7.95x (ISBN 0-262-56016-X). MIT Pr.

Frieden, Carl & Nichol, Lawrence. Protein-Protein Interactions. LC 80-29424. 403p. 1981. 71.50x (ISBN 0-471-04979-4, Pub. by Wiley-Interscience). Wiley.

Frieden, Earl, ed. Biochemistry of the Essential Ultratrace Elements. (Biochemistry of the Elements Ser.: Vol. 3). 444p. 1984. 59.50x (ISBN 0-306-41682-4, Plenum Pr). Plenum Pub.

Frieden, Earl, jt. ed. see Gilbert, Lawrence I.

Frieden, Edward H. Chemical Endocrinology. 1976. 45.00 (ISBN 0-12-268150-9). Acad Pr.

Frieden, James A. & Garrity, Paul G. Standardized Massachusetts Civil Practice Forms. write for info. Little.

Frieden, Julian & Rubin, Ira. ECG Case Studies. Vol. 1 ed. LC 77-94387. 1974. pap. 14.00 (ISBN 0-87488-003-3). Med Exam.

Frieden, Julian, jt. auth. see Rubin, Ira L.

Frieden, Ken. Genius & Monologue. LC 85-47700. 224p. 1985. text ed. 19.95x (ISBN 0-8014-1804-6). Cornell U Pr.

Frieden, Nancy M. Russian Physicians in An Era of Reform & Revolution, 1856-1905. LC 81-47128. (Illus.). 432p. 1981. 37.00x (ISBN 0-691-05335-9). Princeton U Pr.

Friedenberg, Edgar Z. Coming of Age in America: Growth & Acquiescence. Repr. of 1965 ed. text ed. cancelled (ISBN 0-8290-0034-8). Irvington.

--R. D. Laing. (Modern Masters Ser.). 128p. 1974. 9.95 (ISBN 0-670-58984-5). Viking.

--The Vanishing Adolescent. LC 85-950. xxvi, 144p. 1985. Repr. of 1959 ed. lib. bdg. 29.75x (ISBN 0-313-24920-2, FRVA). Greenwood.

Friedenberg, Edgar Z., ed. The Anti-American Generation. LC 83-4956. (Society Bks). 277p. 1971. pap. text ed. 4.95x (ISBN 0-87855-566-8). Transaction Bks.

Friedenberg, Joan & Bradley, Curtis. Bilingual Voc Ed. 53p. 1984. 5.75 (ISBN 0-318-17781-1, IN269). Natl Ctr Res Voc Ed.

--The Vocational ESL Handbook. 1984. pap. text ed. 8.95 (ISBN 0-88377-415-1). Newbury Hse.

Friedenberg, Joan E., jt. auth. see Bradley, Curtis H.

Friedenberg, Robert V., jt. auth. see Trent, Judith S.

Friedenreich, Harriet p., jt. auth. see Elazar, Daniel J.

Friedenreich, Kenneth. Christopher Marlowe: An Annotated Bibliography of Criticism since 1950. LC 79-17646. (Scarecrow Author Bibliographies Ser.: No. 43). 166p. 1979. 16.50 (ISBN 0-8108-1239-8). Scarecrow.

--Tercentenary Essays in Honor of Andrew Marvell. (Illus.). 314p. 1977. 22.50 (ISBN 0-208-01567-1, Archon). Shoe String.

Friedenreich, Kenneth, ed. Accompaninge the Players: Essays Celebrating Thomas Middleton, 1581-1980. LC 81-69121. (Studies in the Renaissance: No. 8). 248p. 1984. 37.50 (ISBN 0-404-62278-X). AMS Pr.

Friedenthal, Jack, et al. Civil Procedure, Student Edition. LC 85-3213. (Hornbook Series Student Edition). 1985. text ed. write for info. (ISBN 0-314-89166-8). West Pub.

Friedenthal, Jack H. & Singer, Michael. The Law of Evidence. LC 85-6736. (University Casebook Ser.). (Illus.). 380p. 1985. text ed. write for info. (ISBN 0-88277-229-5). Foundation Pr.

Friedenwald, Harry. Jews & Medicine & Jewish Luminaries in Medical History, 3 Vols. rev. ed. 1967. 50.00x (ISBN 0-87068-053-6). Ktav.

Friedenwald, Herbert. The Declaration of Independence: An Interpretation & an Analysis. LC 77-166325. (American Constitutional & Legal History Ser.). xii, 299p. 1974. Repr. of 1904 ed. lib. bdg. 35.00 (ISBN 0-306-70230-4). Da Capo.

Frieder, David. Algebra Simplified & Self-Taught. LC 83-2843. 144p. (Orig.). 1983. pap. 5.95 (ISBN 0-668-05797-1, 5797). Arco.

--Total Math Review for the GMAT, GRE & Other Graduate School Admission Tests. LC 81-4054. 336p. 1981. pap. 10.00 (ISBN 0-668-04981-2, 4981). Arco.

Frieder, Larry A. Commercial Banking & Holding Company Acquisitions: New Dimensions in Theory, Evaluation & Practice. Dufey, Gunter, ed. LC 80-39891. (Research for Business Decisions Ser.: No. 33). 112p. 1981. 34.95 (ISBN 0-8357-1147-1). UMI Res Pr.

--Commercial Banking & Interstate Expansion: Issues, Prospects, & Strategies. Farmer, Richard, ed. LC 84-28109. (Research for Business Decisions Ser.: No. 74). 206p. 1985. 44.95 (ISBN 0-8357-1621-X). UMI Res Pr.

Friederich, Werner P. Australia in Western Imaginative Prose Writings, 1600-1960. (Comparative Literature Studies: No. 40). xv, 279p. 1967. 22.50 (ISBN 0-8078-7040-4). U of NC Pr.

--Dante's Fame Abroad, 1350-1850. (Studies in Comparative Literature Ser.: No. 2). 582p. (Orig.). 1966. pap. 20.00 (ISBN 0-8078-7002-1). U of NC Pr.

Friederich, Werner P. & Arndt, Walter W. Challenge of Comparative Literature: And Other Addresses. De Sua, William J., ed. (Studies in Comparative Literature: No. 51). xxiii, 152p. 1970. 15.00 (ISBN 0-8078-7051-X). U of NC Pr.

Friederichsen, Kay. God's Relief for Burdens. Orig. Title: Burdens Made Light. 160p. 1974. pap. 3.95 (ISBN 0-8024-3037-6). Moody.

--God's Word Made Plain. 1958. pap. 3.95 (ISBN 0-8024-3041-4). Moody.

Friederichsen, Kay H. Las Profundas Verdades de la Biblia. Orig. Title: God's World Made Plain. 256p. (Span.). 1958. pap. 4.75 (ISBN 0-8254-1248-X). Kregel.

Friederichsen, Kay H. de see Friederichsen, Kay H.

Friederichson, Kay. God's Way Made Easy. 1984. pap. 3.95 (ISBN 0-8024-3039-2). Moody.

Friederici, Georg, tr. from Ger. Scalping in America. Repr. of 1907 ed. 7.95 (ISBN 0-8488-0034-6, Pub. by J M C & Co). Amereon Ltd.

Friederici, George. Ein Beitrag Z. Kenntnis D. Trutzwaffen D. Indonesier, Suedseevoelker U. Indianer. Repr. of 1915 ed. 15.00 (ISBN 0-384-16910-4). Johnson Repr.

Friedericy, H. J., jt. auth. see Vuyk, Beb.

Friedewald, Vincent E. Textbook of Echocardiography. LC 76-4247. pap. 62.60 (ISBN 0-317-07788-0, 2016663). Bks Demand UMI.

Friedheim, Arthur. Life & Liszt. Bullock, Theodore L., ed. LC 61-15656. (Illus.). 1961. 6.00 (ISBN 0-685-20505-3). Taplinger.

Friedheim, Robert L. The Seattle General Strike. LC 64-20487. (Illus.). 224p. 1965. 20.00x (ISBN 0-295-73927-4). U of Wash Pr.

--Understanding the Debate on Ocean Resources. (Monograph Series in World Affairs: Vol. 6, 1968-69 Ser., Bk. 3). (Orig.). 1969. 4.95 (ISBN 0-87940-020-X). Monograph Series.

Friedheim, Robert L., et al. Japan & the New Ocean Regime. 350p. 1983. softcover 32.00x (ISBN 0-86531-687-2). Westview.

Friedhoff, Arnold J., ed. Cathecholamines & Behavior. Incl. Vol. 1, Basic Neurobiology. 250p (ISBN 0-306-38411-6); Vol. 2, Neuropsychopharmacology. 238p (ISBN 0-306-38412-4). LC 75-11697. (Illus.). 1975. 27.50x ea. (Plenum Pr). Plenum Pub.

Friedhoff, Arnold J. & Chase, Thomas N., eds. Gilles de la Tourette Syndrome. (Advances in Neurology Ser.: Vol. 35). 478p. 1982. text ed. 58.00 (ISBN 0-89004-761-8). Raven.

Friedhoff, Herman, ed. Encyclopedia of the Animal World. (Illus.). 2000p. 1980. lib. bdg. 169.95x (ISBN 0-85835-427-6). M Cavendish Corp.

Friedjung, M., ed. Novae & Related Stars. (Astrophysics & Space Science Library: No. 65). 1977. lib. bdg. 39.50 (ISBN 90-277-0793-6, Pub. by Reidel Holland). Kluwer Academic.

Friedjung, M. & Viotti, R., eds. The Nature of Symbiotic Stars. 1982. 43.50 (ISBN 0-686-37436-3, Pub. by Reidel Holland). Kluwer Academic.

Friedl, Ernestine. Vasilika: A Village in Modern Greece. LC 62-14950. (Case Studies in Cultural Anthropology). (Orig.). 1962. pap. text ed. 9.95 (ISBN 0-03-011545-0, HoltC). HR&W.

--Women & Men: An Anthropologist's View. (Illus.). 148p. 1984. pap. 6.95x (ISBN 0-88133-040-X). Waveland Pr.

Friedl, Ernestine see Bishop, G. Reginald, Jr.

Friedl, Ernestine, jt. ed. see Dimen, Muriel.

Friedl, John. The Human Portrait: An Introduction to Cultural Anthropology. (Illus.). 464p. 1981. pap. text ed. 23.95 (ISBN 0-13-445353-0); pap. 11.95 (ISBN 0-13-445387-5). P-H.

Friedl, Joseph. A History of Education in McDowell County, West Virginia, 1858-1976. 1975. 10.00 (ISBN 0-87012-204-5). McClain.

Friedlaender, Ann F. & Spady, Richard H. Freight Transport Regulation: Equity, Efficiency & Competition in the Rail & Trucking Industries. 400p. 1981. 45.00x (ISBN 0-262-06072-8). MIT Pr.

Friedlaender, Ann F., jt. auth. see Due, John F.

Friedlaender, Ann F., ed. Approaches to Controlling Air Pollution. LC 77-25484. (MIT Bicentennial Ser.: Vol. 3). 1978. 45.00x (ISBN 0-262-06064-7). MIT Pr.

Friedlaender, Benedict. Renaissance des Eros Uranios. LC 75-12316. (Homosexuality: Lesbians & Gay Men in Society, History & Literature). (German.). 1975. Repr. of 1904 ed. 30.00x (ISBN 0-405-07362-3). Ayer Co Pubs.

Friedlaender, Elizabeth. Vaulting. LC 72-118228. 1979. pap. 5.95 (ISBN 0-8289-0343-3). Greene.

Friedlaender, Gary, jt. ed. see Sell, Kenneth.

Friedlaender, Jonathan S. Patterns of Human Variation: The Demography, Genetics, & Phenetics of the Bougainville Islanders. LC 74-17858. (Illus.). 288p. 1975. text ed. 25.00x (ISBN 0-674-65855-8). Harvard U Pr.

Friedlaender, Jonathan S., jt. ed. see Giles, Eugene.

Friedlaender, Marc see Adams, Charles F.

Friedlaender, Marc, et al, eds. Diary of Charles Francis Adams: June 1836-Feb 1840, Vols. 7 & 8. (The Adams Papers Series I: Diaries). 448p. 1985. text ed. 65.00x set (ISBN 0-674-20403-4, Belknap Pr). Harvard U Pr.

Friedlaender, Max. Brahms's Lieder. LC 74-24087. Repr. of 1928 ed. 22.50 (ISBN 0-404-12916-1). AMS Pr.

Friedlaender, Paul. Platon, 3 vols. Incl. Vol. 1. Seinswahrheit und Lebenswirklichkeit. 3rd rev. & enl ed. (Illus.). x, 438p. 1964 (ISBN 3-11-000137-3); Vol. 2. Die Platonischen Schriften: Erste Periode. 3rd rev. ed. vi, 358p. 1964 (ISBN 3-11-000138-1); Vol. 3. Die Platonischen Shriften: Tweite und Periode. 1975. (Ger.). 29.60x ea. De Gruyter.

--Studien zur antiken Literatur und Kunst. (Ger). 1969. 55.60x (ISBN 3-11-004049-2). De Gruyter.

Friedlaender, R. Caravaggio Studies. 1974. pap. 14.95x (ISBN 0-691-00308-4). Princeton U Pr.

Friedlaender, Walter. David to Delacroix. Goldwater, Robert, tr. LC 52-5395. (Illus.). 1952. pap. 6.95 (ISBN 0-674-19401-2). Harvard U Pr.

--Mannerism & Anti-Mannerism in Italian Painting. LC 57-8295. (Illus.). 1965. pap. 5.95 (ISBN 0-8052-0094-0). Schocken.

Friedlaender, Walter & Blunt, Anthony, eds. The Drawings of Nicolas Poussin, Catalogue Raisonne, Pt. 1: Biblical Subjects. (Warburg Institute Studies: Vol. 5, Pt. 1). Repr. of 1939 ed. 70.00 (ISBN 0-317-15011-1). Kraus Repr.

--The Drawings of Nicolas Poussin, Catalogue Raisonne, Pt. 2: History, Romance, Allegories. (Warburg Institute Studies: Vol. 5, Pt. 2). Repr. of 1949 ed. 44.00 (ISBN 0-317-15012-X). Kraus Repr.

--The Drawings of Nicolas Poussin, Catalogue Raisonne, Pt. 3: Mythological Subjects. (Warburg Institute Studies: Vol. 5, Pt. 3). Repr. of 1953 ed. 32.00 (ISBN 0-317-15013-8). Kraus Repr.

--The Drawings of Nicolas Poussin, Catalogue Raisonne, Pt. 4: Studies for the Long Gallery, the Decorative Drawings, the Illustrations to Leonardo's Treatises, the Landscape Drawings. (Warburg Institue Studies: Vol. 5, Pt. 4). 1963. 15.00 (ISBN 0-317-15015-4). Kraus Repr.

--The Drawings of Nicolas Poussin, Catalogue Raisonne, Pt. 5: Drawings after the Antique, Miscellaneous Drawings, Addenda & Corrigenda. (Warburg Institue Studies: Vol. 5, Pt. 5). 1974. 67.00 (ISBN 0-317-15018-9). Kraus Repr.

Friedland, Aaron J. Puzzles in Math & Logic: One Hundred New Recreations. (Orig.). 1971. pap. 2.50 (ISBN 0-486-22256-X). Dover.

Friedland, B. Control System Design: An Introduction to State-Space Methods. (Electrical Engineering Ser.). 512p. 1985. text ed. price not set (ISBN 0-07-022441-2). McGraw.

Friedland, B., jt. auth. see Schwarz, Ralph.

Friedland, Bea. Louise Farrenc, 1804-1875: Composer, Performer, Scholar. Buelow, George, ed. LC 80-22465. (Studies in Musicology: No. 32). 284p. 1980. 49.95 (ISBN 0-8357-1111-0). UMI Res Pr.

Friedland, Bea, ed. see Barzun, Jacques.

Friedland, Dion, et al. People Productivity in Retailing: A Manpower Development Plan. LC 80-23109. 1980. 19.95 (ISBN 0-86730-519-3). Lebhar Friedman.

Friedland, Gerald, et al. Uroradiology: An Integrated Approach, 2 vols. (Illus.). 1983. text ed. 190.00 (ISBN 0-443-08037-2). Churchill.

Friedland, Joan & Faude, Wilson. Birthplace of Democracy. LC 79-50223. (Illus.). 64p. 1979. pap. 4.95 (ISBN 0-87106-025-6). Globe Pequot.

Friedland, Joyce & Gross, Irene. Reading for Mathematics. 1984. pap. 3.25x (ISBN 0-88323-199-9, 218); tchr's. answer key 3.00x (ISBN 0-88323-142-5, 231). Richards Pub.

Friedland, Louis S. Spenser As a Fabulist. (Studies in Spenser, No. 26). 1970. pap. 40.00x (ISBN 0-8383-0031-6). Haskell.

Friedland, Louis S., ed. see Chekhov, Anton.

Friedland, Louis S., ed. see Chekhov, Anton P.

Friedland, M. L. Cases & Materials on Criminal Law & Procedure. 5th ed. LC 78-57570. 1978. lib. bdg. 60.00x (ISBN 0-8020-2308-8); text ed. 20.00x (ISBN 0-8020-2309-6). U of Toronto Pr.

Friedland, M. L., ed. Courts & Trials: A Multidisciplinary Approach. LC 75-5672. 1975. pap. 7.50 (ISBN 0-8020-6273-3). U of Toronto Pr.

Friedland, Martin L. The Trials of Israel Lipski: A True Story of a Victorian Murder in the East End of London. (Illus.). 224p. 1985. 14.95 (ISBN 0-8253-0278-1). Beaufort Bks NY.

Friedland, Mary. Earth Resources. (Science in Action Ser.). (Illus.). 48p. 1984. pap. text ed. 2.85 (ISBN 0-88102-025-7). Janus Bks.

Friedland, Mary K. Green Plants. (Science in Action Ser.). (Illus.). 48p. (gr. 9 up). 1982. pap. text ed. 2.85 (ISBN 0-915510-76-6). Janus Bks.

Friedland, Patricia A. Resources: A New York City Directory. 12p. 1984. pap. 1.50 (ISBN 0-88156-022-7). Comm Serv Soc NY.

Friedland, Robert P., ed. Selected Papers of Morris B. Bender: Memorial Volume. 464p. 1983. text ed. 58.50 (ISBN 0-89004-710-3). Raven.

Friedland, Roger. Power & Crisis in the City, Corporations, Unions & Urban Policy. LC 82-10368. 292p. 1983. 19.95 (ISBN 0-8052-3838-7). Schocken.

Friedland, Roger, jt. auth. see Alford, Robert R.

Friedland, Ronald, jt. auth. see Malatesta, Anne.

Friedland, Ronni. Breeding Macaws. (Illus.). 96p. 1984. cancelled 4.95 (ISBN 0-87666-836-8, KW-124). TFH Pubns.

--Breeding Parrots. (Illus.). 96p. 1984. cancelled 4.95 (ISBN 0-87666-811-2, KW-138). TFH Pubns.

Friedland, Ronnie & Kort, Carol, eds. The Mother's Book. 384p. 1981. 15.95 (ISBN 0-395-30527-6); pap. 9.95 (ISBN 0-395-31134-9). HM.

Friedland, Shmuel. Nonoscillation, Disconjugacy & Integral Inequalities. LC 76-25246. 1976. 13.00 (ISBN 0-8218-2176-8, MEMO-176). Am Math.

Friedland, Susan. Ribs: Over a Hundred All-American & International Recipes for Ribs & Fixings. (Harmony Particular Palate Cookbooks). pap. 5.95 (ISBN 0-517-55315-5). Crown.

Friedland, William H. Vuta Kamba: The Development of Trade Unions in Tanganyika. LC 74-81689. (Publications Ser.: No. 84). 1969. 11.95x (ISBN 0-8179-1841-8); pap. 7.95 (ISBN 0-8179-1842-6). Hoover Inst Pr.

Friedland, William H., jt. auth. see Horowitz, Irving L.

Friedland, William H. & Rosberg, Carl G., Jr., eds. African Socialism. 1964. 25.00x (ISBN 0-8047-0203-9); pap. 8.95 (ISBN 0-8047-0204-7, SP35). Stanford U Pr.

Friedland, William H., et al. Revolutionary Theory. LC 80-70921. 264p. 1982. text ed. 26.50x (ISBN 0-86598-074-8); pap. 9.50x (ISBN 0-86598-075-6). Allanheld.

--Manufacturing Green Gold: Capital, Labor, & Technology in the Lettuce Industry. (American Sociological Association Rose Monograph). (Illus.). 1981. 34.50 (ISBN 0-521-24284-3); pap. 10.95 (ISBN 0-521-28584-4). Cambridge U Pr.

Friedlander, et al. Concepts & Methods of Social Work. 2nd ed. LC 75-45164. 288p. 1976. text ed. 29.95 (ISBN 0-13-166488-3). P-H.

Friedlander, Alan L. & Cefola, Paul J., eds. Astrodynamics 1981. LC 57-43769. (Advances in the Astronautical Sciences Ser.: Vol. 46). (Illus.). 1124p. (Orig.). 1982. Pt. 1. lib. bdg. 55.00x (ISBN 0-87703-159-2, Pub. by Am Astronaut); Pt. 2. lib. bdg. 55.00x (ISBN 0-87703-161-4); Pt. 1. pap. text ed. 45.00x (ISBN 0-87703-160-6); Pt. 2. pap. text ed. 45.00x (ISBN 0-87703-162-2); Microfiche Supplement 40.00x (ISBN 0-87703-163-0). Univelt Inc.

Friedlander, Albert. Out of the Whirlwind. 1968. 10.95 (ISBN 0-8074-0043-2, 959065). UAHC.

Friedlander, Albert, jt ed. see Bronstein, Herbert.

Friedlander, Albert H., ed. Out of the Whirlwind: A Reader of Holocaust Literature. LC 75-36488. 544p. 1976. pap. 10.95 (ISBN 0-8052-0517-9). Schocken.

Friedlander, Amy, ed. see Mayo, A. D.

Friedlander, Anna F. Handbook of Photovoltaic Technologies. LC 83-49498. (Illus.). 350p. 1985. text ed. 39.00 (ISBN 0-915586-91-6). Fairmont Pr.

Friedlander, B. Z., et al, eds. Exceptional Infant: Assesment & Intervention, Vol. 3. LC 68-517. 700p. 1975. 35.00 (ISBN 0-87630-103-0). Brunner-Mazel.

Friedlander, Benjamin. Shorthand in Four Days. rev. ed. LC 52-3478. 24p. 1980. pap. 3.95 (ISBN 0-917520-02-5). Fineline.

Friedlander, C. P. The Biology of Insects. LC 76-20407. (Studies in the Biological Sciences Ser.). (Illus.). 1977. 12.50x (ISBN 0-87663-720-9). Universe.

Friedlander, Dov & Goldscheider, Calvin. The Population of Israel: Growth, Policy & Implications. LC 78-13139. 264p. 1979. 29.00x (ISBN 0-231-04572-7). Columbia U Pr.

Friedlander, E. H., tr. see Harder, T.

Friedlander, E. J. A Concise Guide to Newspaper Feature Writing. LC 81-40648. 56p. (Orig.). 1982. pap. text ed. 7.00 (ISBN 0-8191-2115-0). U Pr of Amer.

Friedlander, E. M. Etale Homotopy of Simplical Schemes. 1982. 29.00 (ISBN 0-691-08288-X); pap. 12.50 (ISBN 0-691-08317-7). Princeton U Pr.

Friedlander, E. M. & Stein, M. R., eds. Algebraic K-Theory: Proceedings. (Lecture Notes in Mathematics Ser.: Vol. 854). 517p. 1981. pap. 29.00 (ISBN 0-387-10698-7). Springer-Verlag.

Friedlander, F. G. Introduction to the Theory of Distributions. LC 82-4504. 150p. 1983. 37.50 (ISBN 0-521-24300-9); pap. 15.95 (ISBN 0-521-28591-7). Cambridge U Pr.

--The Wave Equation on a Curved Space-Time. LC 74-14435. (Cambridge Monographs on Mathematical Physics). (Illus.). 328p. 1976. 77.50 (ISBN 0-521-20567-0). Cambridge U Pr.

Friedlander, G. Shakespeare & the Jew. 59.95 (ISBN 0-8490-1032-2). Gordon Pr.

Friedlander, Gary E., et al. Osteochondral Allografts. 403p. 1983. text ed. 62.50 (ISBN 0-316-29346-6). Little.

Friedlander, Gerald. Jewish Fairy Tales & Stories. LC 78-67711. (The Folktale). (Illus.). Repr. of 1919 ed. 14.50 (ISBN 0-404-16088-3). AMS Pr.

--Jewish Sources of the Sermon on the Mount. 1976. lib. bdg. 59.95 (ISBN 0-8490-2102-2). Gordon Pr.

--Jewish Sources of the Sermon on the Mount. rev. ed. (Library of Biblical Studies). 1969. 14.95x (ISBN 0-87068-054-4). Ktav.

--Shakespeare & the Jew. LC 74-168084. Repr. of 1921 ed. 18.00 (ISBN 0-404-02579-X). AMS Pr.

Friedlander, Gerald, ed. Pirke De Rabbi Eliezer: The Chapters of Rabbi Eliezer the Great. LC 70-174366. Repr. of 1916 ed. 29.00 (ISBN 0-405-08535-4, Blom Pubns). Ayer Co Pubs.

Friedlander, Gerald, tr. from Heb. Pirke De Rabbi Eliezer (The Chapters of Rabbi Eliezer the Great) LC 80-545920. (The Judaic Studies Library: No. SPH6). 552p. 1981. pap. 12.95 (ISBN 0-87203-095-4). Hermon.

Friedlander, Gerhart, et al. Nuclear & Radiochemistry. 3rd ed. LC 81-1000. 684p. 1981. 54.95 (ISBN 0-471-28021-6, Pub. by Wiley-Interscience); pap. 31.95 (ISBN 0-471-86255-X, Pub. by Wiley-Interscience). Wiley.

Friedlander, H., jt. ed. see Schwab, George.

Friedlander, Henry & Milton, Sybil, eds. The Holocaust: Ideology, Bureaucracy & Genocide. LC 80-16913. 1981. lib. bdg. 50.00 (ISBN 0-527-63807-2). Kraus Intl.

Friedlander, Ira. The Ninety-Nine Names of Allah. (Orig.). 1978. pap. 6.50i (ISBN 0-06-090621-9, CN 621, CN). Har-Row.

Friedlander, Ira, jt. auth. see Speeth, Kathleen R.

Friedlander, Ira, ed. Submission Sayings of the Prophet Muhammad. 1977. pap. 5.95i (ISBN 0-06-090592-1, CN592, CN). Har-Row.

Friedlander, Irish & Lin, Marge. The Orient Express Chinese Cookbook: Quick & Easy Home-Style Recipes. (Creative Cooking Ser.). (Illus.). 1979. (Spec); pap. 6.95 (ISBN 0-13-642165-2, Spec). P-H.

Friedlander, Joseph S., jt. auth. see Wingate, John W.

Friedlander, Judith N. Being Indian in Hueyapan: A Study of Forced Identity in Comtemporary Mexico. LC 74-23047. (Illus.). 224p. (Orig.). 1975. pap. text ed. 10.95 (ISBN 0-312-07315-1). St Martin.

Friedlander, Kate. Psychoanalytical Approach to Juvenile Delinquency: Theory, Case Studies, Treatment. 296p. 1960. text ed. 30.00 (ISBN 0-8236-4400-6). Intl Univs Pr.

Friedlander, Lee. Lee Friedlander: Photographs. (Illus.). 108p. 30.00 (ISBN 0-686-28438-0). Haywire Pr.

Friedlander, Lee & Szarkowski, John. E. J. Bellocq: Storyville Portraits. LC 70-86413. (Illus.). 1978. 16.50 (ISBN 0-87070-250-5, 202991, Pub. by Museum of Modern Art); pap. 9.95 (ISBN 0-87070-252-1, 231134). NYGS.

Friedlander, Ludwig. Roman Life & Manners Under the Early Empire, 4 vols. Finley, Moses, ed. LC 79-4973. (Ancient Economic History Ser.). 1980. Repr. of 1913 ed. Set. lib. bdg. 160.00x (ISBN 0-405-12359-0); lib. bdg. 40.00x ea. Vol. 1 (ISBN 0-405-12360-4). Vol. 2 (ISBN 0-405-12361-2). Vol. 3 (ISBN 0-405-12486-4). Vol. 4 (ISBN 0-405-12487-2). Ayer Co Pubs.

Friedlander, M. Jewish Religion: Describing & Explaining the Philosophy & Rituals of the Jewish Faith. 35.00 (ISBN 0-87559-117-5). Shalom.

Friedlander, M., tr. see Maimonides, Moses.

Friedlander, Mark, Jr & Gurney, Gene. Handbook of Successful Franchising. 512p. 1982. pap. text ed. 14.95 (ISBN 0-442-22533-4). Van Nos Reinhold.

Friedlander, Mark P., jt. auth. see Gurney, Gene.

Friedlander, Mark P., Jr., jt. auth. see Gurney, Gene.

Friedlander, Martin, jt. ed. see Moscona, A. A.

Friedlander, Max J. From Van Eyck to Bruegel. (Illus.). 1981. 11.95x (ISBN 0-8014-9220-3, Pub. by Phaidon England). Cornell U Pr.

Friedlander, Max J. & Rosenberg, Jakob. The Paintings of Lucas Cranach. LC 77-18410. (Illus.). 600p. 1979. 125.00x (ISBN 0-8014-1061-4). Cornell U Pr.

Friedlander, Max J., et al. Die Gemalde von Lucas Cranach. (Illus.). 592p. (Ger.). 1979. 113.95x (ISBN 0-8176-0982-2). Birkhauser.

Friedlander, Melvin A. Sadat & Begin: The Domestic Politics of Peacemaking. LC 82-21826. 338p. 1983. softcover 25.00x (ISBN 0-86531-949-9). Westview.

Friedlander, Michael, tr. see Ibn Ezra.

Friedlander, Michael W. Astronomy: From Stonehenge to Quasars. (Illus.). 640p. 1985. text ed. 32.95 (ISBN 0-13-049867-X). P-H.

Friedlander, Milton, et al, eds. Simon Wiesenthal Center Annual, Vol. 2. 1985. lib. bdg. write for info. (ISBN 0-527-96489-1). Kraus Intl.

Friedlander, P. H., tr. see Harder, T.

Friedlander, Paul, ed. Plato, 3 vols. Meyerhoff, Hans, tr. Incl. Vol. 1. An Introduction. 2nd ed. 1970. 42.00x (ISBN 0-691-09812-3); pap. 12.50x (ISBN 0-691-01795-6); Vol. 2. The Dialogues, First Period. 1964; Vol. 3. The Dialogues, Second & Third Periods. 1969. 42.50x (ISBN 0-691-09814-X). (Bollingen Ser.: Vol. 59). Princeton U Pr.

Friedlander, Peter. The Emergence of a UAW Local, 1936-1939: A Study in Class & Culture. LC 74-26020. 1975. 14.95x (ISBN 0-8229-3295-4). U of Pittsburgh Pr.

Friedlander, Rena & Botein, Michael. The Process of Cable Television Franchising: A New York City Case Study. 100p. 1980. pap. 40.00 (ISBN 0-941888-08-8). Comm Media.

Friedlander, Robert A. Struggle for Supremacy: Presidential War Powers & Foreign Policy. 192p. 1985. lib. bdg. 30.00 (ISBN 0-941320-25-1). Transnatl Pubs.

--Terror-Violence: Aspects of Social Control. LC 83-19105. 332p. 1983. text ed. 32.50 (ISBN 0-379-20748-6). Oceana.

--Terrorism: Documents of International & Local Control 1977-1978, 4 vols. LC 78-26126. 1979. 180.00 set (ISBN 0-379-00690-1). Oceana.

Friedlander, Robert A., jt. ed. see Alexander, Yonah.

Friedlander, S. Introduction to the Mathematical Theory of Geophysical Fluid Dynamics. (Mathematics Studies: Vol. 41). 272p. 1980. 38.50 (ISBN 0-444-86032-0, North-Holland). Elsevier.

Friedlander, S. K. Smoke, Dust & Haze: Fundamentals of Aerosol Behavior. LC 76-26928. 317p. 1977. 46.50x (ISBN 0-471-01468-0, Pub. by Wiley Interscience). Wiley.

Friedlander, Saul. History & Psychoanalysis. Suleiman, Susan, tr. from Fr. LC 77-18524. 175p. 1978. text ed. 34.50x (ISBN 0-8419-0339-5); pap. text ed. 15.50x (ISBN 0-8419-0611-4). Holmes & Meier.

--Pius XII & the Third Reich. LC 80-12830. 238p. 1980. Repr. of 1966 ed. lib. bdg. 21.50x (ISBN 0-374-92930-0). Octagon.

--Reflections on Nazism: An Essay on Death & Kitsch. Weyr, Thomas, tr. from Fr. LC 82-48117. 160p. 1984. 13.41 (ISBN 0-06-015097-1, HarpT). Har-Row.

--When Memory Comes. 192p. 1980. pap. 3.50 (ISBN 0-380-50807-9, 60139-7, Discus). Avon.

--When Memory Comes. Lane, Helen, tr. from Fr. 192p. 1979. 9.95 (ISBN 0-374-28898-4). FS&G.

Friedlander, Saul & Hussein, Mahmoud. Arabs & Israelis: A Dialogue. Auster, Paul & Davis, Lydia, trs. from Fr. LC 75-9147. 224p. 1975. 17.50x (ISBN 0-8419-0208-9). Holmes & Meier.

Friedlander, Saul, et al, eds. Visions of Apocalypse: End or Rebirth? 272p. 1985. text ed. 28.50x (ISBN 0-8419-0673-4); pap. text ed. 15.50x (ISBN 0-8419-0755-2). Holmes & Meier.

Friedlander, W., ed. Current Reviews. LC 75-14572. (Advances in Neurology Ser.: Vol. 13). 404p. 1975. 52.50 (ISBN 0-89004-000-1). Raven.

Friedlander, Walter A. & Apte, Robert Z. Introduction to Social Welfare. 5th ed. (Illus.). 1980. text ed. 28.95 (ISBN 0-13-497032-2). P-H.

Friedlander, Walter J., ed. Current Reviews of Higher Nervous System Dysfunction. LC 74-15667. (Advances in Neurology Ser.: Vol. 7). 205p. 1975. 35.50 (ISBN 0-911216-78-2). Raven.

Friedlin, Mark. Functional Integration & Partial Differential Equations. LC 84-42874. (Annals of Mathematics Studies: No. 109). 827p. 1985. text ed. 60.00x (ISBN 0-691-08354-1); pap. text ed. 19.95x (ISBN 0-691-08362-2). Princeton U Pr.

Friedling, Sheila, ed. The Pit & the Trap: Leyb Rochman. Kohn, Moshe, tr. (Illus.). 288p. (Orig., Yiddish.). 1983. 13.95 (ISBN 0-8052-5044-1); pap. 8.95 (ISBN 0-8052-5045-X). Holocaust Pubns.

Friedman. Away We Go. (Platt & Munk Cricket Bks.). (Illus.). 24p. (ps-3). 1978. 2.50 (ISBN 0-448-46517-5, G&D). Putnam Pub Group.

--Functions of the Stomach & Intestine. 48.00 (ISBN 0-85602-048-6). Wiley.

--Fundamentals of Clinical Trials. 2nd ed. 1985. 27.50 (ISBN 0-88416-499-3). PSG Pub Co.

--Gynecologic Decision Making. 1983. 36.00. Mosby.

--Handbook of Pediatric Infections: Treatment & Concepts. write for info. Ishiyaku Euro.

--Price Theory: An Intermediate Text. 1986. text ed. price not set (ISBN 0-538-08050-7, H05). SW Pub.

Friedman, jt. auth. see Lindeman.

Friedman, jt. ed. see Beschner.

Friedman, et al. Dictionary of Real Estate Terms. 1984. 5.95 (ISBN 0-8120-2521-0). Barron.

Friedman, A. Variational Principles & Free-Boundary Problems. (Pure & Applied Mathematics Ser.). 710p. 1982. text ed. 64.95x (ISBN 0-471-86849-3, Pub. by Wiley-Interscience). Wiley.

Friedman, A., ed. see Verdon, Rene & Norman, Rachel H.

Friedman, A. P. & Granger, M. E., eds. Epidemiology & Non-Drug Treatment of Head Pain. (Research & Clinical Studies in Headache: Vol. 5). (Illus.). 1978. 26.50 (ISBN 3-8055-2803-5). S Karger.

Friedman, A. P., et al, eds. Headache Today - An Update by 21 Experts. (Research & Clinical Studies in Headache: Vol. 6). (Illus.). 1978. 27.75 (ISBN 3-8055-2924-4). S Karger.

Friedman, Ada J., ed. see Friedman, Philip.

Friedman, Aileen R., jt. auth. see Lee, Karen.

Friedman, Alan. Hermaphrodeity: The Autobiography of a Poet. 1974. pap. 2.45 (ISBN 0-380-00192-6, 16865, Bard). Avon.

Friedman, Alan H., et al. Diagnosis & Management of Uveitis: An Atlas Approach. (Illus.). 118p. 1982. lib. bdg. 98.50 (ISBN 0-683-03379-4). Williams & Wilkins.

Friedman, Alan W. Multivalence: The Moral Quality of Form in the Modern Novel. LC 78-17485. 240p. 1978. 22.50x (ISBN 0-8071-0399-3). La State U Pr.

--William Faulkner. LC 82-40274. 240p. 1985. 15.50 (ISBN 0-8044-2218-4). Ungar.

Friedman, Alan W., jt. ed. see Rossman, Charles.

Friedman, Albert B., ed. The Viking Book of Folk Ballads of the English-Speaking World. LC 56-7084. 512p. 1956. 17.95 (ISBN 0-670-74659-2). Viking.

Friedman, Alexander Z. Wellsprings of Torah. Hirschler, Gertrude, tr. from Yiddish. 584p. 1980. 14.95 (ISBN 0-910818-04-5); pap. 11.95 (ISBN 0-910818-20-7). Judaica Pr.

Friedman, Allan & Wilkins, Robert. Neurosurgical Management for the House Officer. (H. O. Series). 250p. 1984. pap. text ed. 10.95 (ISBN 0-683-03377-8). Williams & Wilkins.
Friedman, Amy, jt. auth. see Javitch, Karen.
Friedman, Amy, ed. ISBN 0-943568-01-3. 207p. (Orig.). 1983. pap. 10.00 (ISBN 0-943568-01-3). Farrah Upland.
Friedman, Andrew L. Industry & Labour: Class Struggle at Work & Monopoly Capitalism. 1977. pap. text ed. 16.75x (ISBN 0-333-23032-9). Humanities.
Friedman, Arlene, ed. see Booth, Charles & Esche, Sharon.
Friedman, Arlene, ed. see Pelletier, Nancy.
Friedman, Arlene, ed. see Wiltse, David.
Friedman, Arnold P. & Harms, Ernest. Headaches in Children. (Illus.). 160p. 1967. 16.50x (ISBN 0-398-00619-9). C C Thomas.
Friedman, Arnold P., jt. auth. see Diamond, Seymour.
Friedman, Arthur & Menon, Premachandran R. Theory & Design of Switching Circuits. LC 75-15888. (Illus.). 581p. 1975. 36.95 (ISBN 0-914894-52-8). Computer Sci.
Friedman, Arthur, ed. see Goldsmith, Oliver.
Friedman, Arthur, ed. see Wycherley, William.
Friedman, Arthur, compiled by. English Literature, Sixteen Sixty to Eighteen Hundred: A Bibliography of Modern Studies (Volume 3 1951-1956) LC 73-19999. 582p. 1974. Repr. of 1962 ed. 25.00x (ISBN 0-87752-164-6). Gordian.
Friedman, Arthur, illus. The Three Sillies. LC 80-27636. (Illus.). 32p. (gr. k-2). 1981. PLB 7.89 (ISBN 0-89375-486-2); pap. text ed. 1.95 (ISBN 0-89375-487-0). Troll Assocs.
Friedman, Arthur D. Logical Design of Digital Systems. LC 74-82932. (Illus., Solutions manual avail. only to instructors for course adoptions). 1975. text ed. 26.95 (ISBN 0-914894-50-1). Computer Sci.
Friedman, Arthur D., jt. auth. see Breuer, Melvin A.
Friedman, Audrey, jt. auth. see Zwerin, Raymond A.
Friedman, Audrey M. & Zwerin, Raymond. High Holy Day Do it Yourself Dictionary. (Illus.). 32p. (gr. k-3). 1983. pap. 5.00 (ISBN 0-8074-0162-5, 101100). UAHC.
Friedman, Avner. Differential Games. LC 73-15872. (CBMS Regional Conference Series in Mathematics: No. 18). 66p. 1974. pap. 16.00 (ISBN 0-8218-1668-3, CBMS-18). Am Math.
--Foundations of Modern Analysis. (Illus.). 250p. 1983. pap. 5.50 (ISBN 0-486-64062-0). Dover.
--Partial Differential Equations. LC 76-3513. 272p. 1976. Repr. of 1969 ed. 18.50 (ISBN 0-88275-405-X). Krieger.
--Partial Differential Equations of Parabolic Type. LC 83-12005. 364p. 1983. Repr. of 1964 ed. text ed. 21.50 (ISBN 0-89874-660-4). Krieger.
--Stochastic Differential Equations & Applications, 2 vols. (Probability & Mathematical Statistics Ser.). Vol. 1,1975. 49.50 (ISBN 0-12-268201-7); Vol. 2, 1976. 64.50 (ISBN 0-12-268202-5). Acad Pr.
Friedman, Avner & Pinsky, Mark, eds. Stochastic Analysis. 1978. 45.00 (ISBN 0-12-268380-3). Acad Pr.
Friedman, Avraham A. Haggadah Sheh Pesah. Bronstein, Harry, ed. xviii, 292p. 1974. 15.00 (ISBN 0-914787-00-4). Mutzal Me'esh Inst.
Friedman, B. Economic Stabilization Policy: Methods in Optimization. LC 73-86080. (Studies in Mathematical & Managerial Economics: Vol. 15). 375p. 1975. 64.00 (ISBN 0-444-10566-2, North-Holland). Elsevier.
Friedman, B. H. Coming Close. LC 81-71643. 224p. 1982. 11.95 (ISBN 0-914590-70-7); pap. 5.95 (ISBN 0-914590-71-5). Fiction Coll.
--Museum. LC 74-77778. 1974. 7.95 (ISBN 0-914590-02-2); pap. 3.95 (ISBN 0-914590-03-0). Fiction Coll.
--Whispers. LC 73-151219. (Fiction Ser.). 154p. 1972. 3.95 (ISBN 0-87886-021-5). Ithaca Hse.
Friedman, Barton. Adventures in the Deeps of the Mind: The Cuchulain Cycle of W. B. Yeats. LC 76-45897. (Princeton Essays in Literature Ser.). 204p. 1977. 20.00 (ISBN 0-691-06325-7). Princeton U Pr.
Friedman, Barton R. You Can't Tell the Players. (Cleveland Poets Ser.: No. 21). 46p. (Orig.). 1979. pap. 3.50 (ISBN 0-914946-17-X). Cleveland St Univ Poetry Ctr.
Friedman, Benjamin M. Corporate Capital Structures in the United States. (Illus.). 384p. 1985. lib. bdg. 48.00x (ISBN 0-226-26411-4). U of Chicago Pr.
Friedman, Benjamin M., ed. The Changing Roles of Debt & Equity in Financing U. S. Capital Formation. LC 81-16353. (National Bureau of Economic Research-Project Report). 128p. 1982. lib. bdg. 12.00x (ISBN 0-226-26340-1). U of Chicago Pr.
Friedman, Bernard. Smuts: A Reappraisal. LC 75-21835. 200p. 1976. 26.00 (ISBN 0-312-73045-4). St Martin.
Friedman, Bertha B. Foundations of the Measurement of Values: The Methodology of Location & Quantification. LC 76-176788. (Columbia University. Teachers College. Contributions to Education: No. 914). Repr. of 1946 ed. 22.50 (ISBN 0-404-55914-X). AMS Pr.
Friedman, Bill. Casino Games. (Golden Guide Ser). 160p. 1973. pap. 2.95 (ISBN 0-307-24358-3, Golden Pr). Western Pub.
Friedman, Bruce J. Let's Hear It for a Beautiful Guy. 252p. 1985. pap. 4.50 (ISBN 0-88184-138-2). Carroll & Graf.
--Let's Hear It for a Beautiful Guy: And Other Works of Short Fiction. LC 84-80787. 252p. 1984. 15.95 (ISBN 0-917657-00-4). D I Fine.
--The Lonely Guy. (McGraw-Hill Paperbacks). (Illus.). 1980. pap. 4.95 (ISBN 0-07-022438-2). McGraw.
--A Mother's Kisses. LC 85-70636. 1985. pap. 8.95 (ISBN 0-917657-39-X, Pub. by Primus Lib Contemp). D I Fine.
--Stern. 1983. 14.95 (ISBN 0-87795-554-9); pap. 6.95 (ISBN 0-87795-555-7). Arbor Hse.
--Tokyo Woes. LC 84-73518. 192p. 1985. 14.95 (ISBN 0-917657-33-0). D I Fine.
Friedman, Carol & Giddins, Gary. A Moment's Notice: Photographs of American Jazz Musicians. (Illus.). 144p. 1983. 21.95 (ISBN 0-02-872040-7). Schirmer Bks.
Friedman, Carol A. & Meade, Andre T. Reading & Writing Skills Workbook for the GED Test. LC 82-18400. (Arco's Preparation for the GED Examination Ser.). 192p. 1983. pap. 5.95 (ISBN 0-668-05540-5). Arco.
Friedman, Charles N., jt. auth. see Dollard, John D.
Friedman, Charles P. & Purcell, Elizabeth, eds. The New Biology & Medical Education: Merging the Biological, Information, & Cognitive Sciences. LC 83-80799. (Illus.). 325p. 1983. pap. 15.00 (ISBN 0-914362-40-2). J Macy Foun.
Friedman, Clarence W. Prefigurations in Meistergesang. LC 75-140020. (Catholic University of America Studies in German Ser.: No. 18). Repr. of 1943 ed. 22.00 (ISBN 0-404-50238-5). AMS Pr.
Friedman, Cyrus R., jt. ed. see Knight, Robert P.
Friedman, Dale H., jt. auth. see Neidig, Peter H.
Friedman, Daniel, jt. auth. see Valerio, Joseph M.
Friedman, Daniel, jt. ed. see McConachie, Bruce A.
Friedman, Daniel P. The Little LISPer. LC 73-91284. 58p. 1974. pap. text ed. 7.50 (ISBN 0-574-19165-8, 13-2165). SRA.
Friedman, Daniel P., jt. auth. see Filman, Robert E.
Friedman, David. The Machinery of Freedom. 240p. 1985. Repr. of 1978 ed. 11.95 (ISBN 0-317-14590-8). Cobden Pr.
Friedman, David, jt. auth. see Christy, John.
Friedman, David H. Detection of Signals by Template Matching. LC 78-79301. pap. 20.00 (ISBN 0-317-08131-4, 2003861). Bks Demand UMI.
Friedman, David L., tr. see Maitreya, Sthiramati.
Friedman, Delores L. Education Handbook for Black Families. LC 79-6537. (Illus.). 312p. 1980. 14.95 (ISBN 0-385-14881-X). Doubleday.
Friedman, Donald J. Road from Isolation: The Campaign of the American Committee for Non-Participation in Japanese Aggression, 1938-1941. LC 68-4047. (East Asian Monographs Ser: No. 25). (Orig.). 1968. pap. 11.00x (ISBN 0-674-77370-5). Harvard U Pr.
Friedman, Donna R., ed. see Bird, Roy.
Friedman, Donna R., ed. see Bronwell, Nancy.
Friedman, Donna R., ed. see Clark, Nancy.
Friedman, Donna R., ed. see Kirkman, Kay.
Friedman, Donna R., ed. see Naske, Claus M. & Rowinski, Ludwig J.
Friedman, Donna R., ed. see Walker, Carroll.
Friedman, Donna R., ed. see Woodward, Sandra K.
Friedman, E. Sharpening Laboratory Management Skills. 1978. 25.95 (ISBN 0-87489-204-X). Med Economics.
Friedman, E. A. & Neff, R. K. Pregnancy Hypertension: A Systematic Evaluation of Clinical Diagnostic Criteria. LC 76-45951. 268p. 1977. 33.00 (ISBN 0-88416-185-4). PSG Pub Co.
Friedman, E. A., ed. The John P. Merrill Festschrift: Nephrological Research Papers by Past & Present Members of the Merrill School of Nephrology. (Nephron: Vol. 22, Nos. 1-3). (Illus.). 1978. pap. 27.75 (ISBN 3-8055-2981-3). S Karger.
Friedman, Ed. The Telephone Book. Owen, Maureen & Barg, Barbara, eds. LC 79-12379. (Illus., Orig.). 1979. pap. 3.00 (ISBN 0-916382-20-6). Telephone Bks.
Friedman, Edward. Backward Toward Revolution: The Chinese Revolutionary Party. LC 73-76095. 1974. pap. 7.95x (ISBN 0-520-03279-9). U of Cal Pr.
Friedman, Edward, ed. Ascent & Decline in the World-System. (Political Economy of the World-System Annuals Ser.: Vol. 5). (Illus.). 300p. 1982. 28.00 (ISBN 0-8039-1829-1); pap. 14.00 (ISBN 0-8039-1830-5). Sage.
Friedman, Edward, jt. auth. see Virgillo, Carmelo.
Friedman, Edward H. The Unifying Concept: Approaches to the Structure of Cervantes' Comedias. LC 81-50484. 186p. 1981. 18.00x (ISBN 0-938972-00-6). Spanish Lit Pubns.
Friedman, Edwin H. Generation to Generation: Family Process in Church & Synagogue. 256p. 1985. lib. bdg. write for info. (ISBN 0-89862-059-7). Guilford Pr.
Friedman, Eli & Stillman, Richard M., eds. Internal Medicine: Review & Assessment. (Illus.). 431p. 1982. 18.95x (ISBN 0-8385-4040-6). ACC.
Friedman, Eli A., jt. auth. see Stillman, Richard M.
Friedman, Eli A., ed. Diabetic Renal-Retinal Syndrome II: Prevention & Management. 560p. 1983. 57.50 (ISBN 0-8089-1539-8, 791433). Grune.
--Strategy in Renal Failure. LC 77-11003. (Nephrology & Hypertension Ser.). 557p. 1978. 68.00 (ISBN 0-471-01597-0, Pub. by Wiley Med). Wiley.
Friedman, Eli A. & Esperance, Francis A., eds. Diabetic Renal-Retinal Syndrome, Vol. 3. LC 79-1434. 1985. price not set (ISBN 0-8089-1741-2). Grune.
Friedman, Eli A. & L'Esperance, Frances, eds. Diabetic Renal-Retinal Syndrome. (Illus.). 480p. 1980. 49.50 (ISBN 0-8089-1302-6, 791432). Grune.
Friedman, Eli A., ed. see International Society for Artificial Organs, 2nd, New York, April 18-19, 1979, et al.
Friedman, Ellen. Directory of Social Change: Women. 25.00 (ISBN 0-7045-0335-2). State Mutual Bk.
Friedman, Ellen G. Joyce Carol Oates. LC 79-4828. (Literature and Life Ser.). 1980. 16.50 (ISBN 0-8044-2221-4). Ungar.
--Joyce Carol Oates. (Literature & Life Ser.). 248p. 1984. pap. 7.95 (ISBN 0-8044-6183-X). Ungar.
--Spanish Captives in North Africa in the Early Modern Age. LC 83-47759. 320p. 1983. text ed. 27.50x (ISBN 0-299-09380-8). U of Wis Pr.
Friedman, Ellen G., jt. ed. see Smith, Raymond J.
Friedman, Emanual A., et al, eds. Uterine Physiology: Proceedings of the Brook Lodge Workshop. LC 79-332. (Illus.). 156p. 1979. text ed. 18.50 (ISBN 0-88416-263-X). PSG Pub Co.
Friedman, Emanuel, tr. see Reiffenstuhl, Gunther & Platzer, Werner.
Friedman, Emanuel A. Labor: Clinical Evaluation & Management. 2nd ed. (Illus.). 463p. 1978. 39.50 (ISBN 0-8385-5580-2). ACC.
Friedman, Emanuel A. & Beth Israel Staff. Obstetrical Decision Making. LC 82-70759. 222p. 1982. 36.00 (ISBN 0-941158-01-2, D1680-8). Mosby.
Friedman, Emanuel A., jt. auth. see Beth Israel Hospital Staff.
Friedman, Emanuel A., jt. auth. see Martius, Gerhard.
Friedman, Emanuel A., jt. auth. see Plentl, Albert A.
Friedman, Emanuel A., ed. Blood Pressure, Edema & Proteinuria in Pregnancy. LC 76-10262. (Progress in Clinical & Biological Research: Vol. 7). 296p. 1976. 39.00x (ISBN 0-8451-0007-6). A R Liss.
Friedman, Emanuel A., jt. ed. see Cohen, Wayne R.
Friedman, Emanuel A., jt. ed. see Milunsky, Aubrey.
Friedman, Emanuel B. Obstetrics. Date not set. price not set (ISBN 0-7216-3909-7). Saunders.
Friedman, Emmanuel, tr. see Kaser, Otto & Hirsch, Hans A.
Friedman, Eric, et al, eds. see Bailin, George.
Friedman, F. L. & Koffman, E. B. Problem Solving & Structured Programming in FORTRAN. 2nd ed. 1981. pap. 23.95 (ISBN 0-201-02461-6); wkbk. 7.95 (ISBN 0-201-02465-9). Addison-Wesley.
Friedman, Frank & Koffman, Elliot. Problem Solving & Structured Programming in WATFIV. LC 81-20598. (Illus.). 480p. 1982. pap. text ed. 23.95 (ISBN 0-201-10482-2). Addison-Wesley.
Friedman, Frank L., jt. auth. see Koffman, Elliot B.
Friedman, Frieda. Dot for Short. 173p. 1981. Repr. PLB 14.95x (ISBN 0-686-73781-4). Buccaneer Bks.
--Dot for Short. 168p. 1981. Repr. PLB 10.95x (ISBN 0-89967-038-5). Harmony Raine.
Friedman, G. M. & Johnson, K. G. Exercises in Sedimentology. 208p. 1982. pap. 16.95 (ISBN 0-471-87453-1). Wiley.
Friedman, G. M. & Krumbein, W., eds. Hypersaline Ecosystems. (Ecological Studies: Vol. 53). (Illus.). 500p. 1985. 98.00 (ISBN 0-387-15245-8). Springer-Verlag.
Friedman, Gary D. Primer of Epidemiology. 2nd ed. (Illus.). 1979. pap. text ed. 19.95 (ISBN 0-07-022434-X). McGraw.
Friedman, George. The Political Philosophy of the Frankfurt School. LC 80-66890. 320p. 1981. 27.50x (ISBN 0-8014-1279-X). Cornell U Pr.
--Three Years. (Private Library Collection). 1985. mini-bound 6.95 (ISBN 0-938422-22-7). SOS Pubns CA.
Friedman, Georges. Industrial Society: Emergence of the Human Problems of Automation. Stein, Leon, ed. LC 77-70497. (Work Ser.). 1977. Repr. of 1955 ed. lib. bdg. 37.50x (ISBN 0-405-10167-8). Ayer Co Pubs.
Friedman, Gerald M. & Sanders, John E. Principles of Sedimentology. LC 78-5355. 792p. 1978. text ed. 47.50 (ISBN 0-471-75245-2). Wiley.
Friedman, Gerald M., jt. ed. see Bhattacharyya, Ajit.
Friedman, Greg. It Begins with Friendship: A Fresh Approach to Prayer. 73p. (Orig.). 1984. pap. text ed. 3.95 (ISBN 0-86716-038-1). St Anthony Mess Pr.
Friedman, H., jt. ed. see Escobar, M. R.
Friedman, H. George, Jr., jt. auth. see Schreiner, Axel T.
Friedman, H. H. Diagnostic Electrocardiography & Vectorcardiography. 3rd ed. 688p. 1984. 45.00 (ISBN 0-07-022427-7). McGraw.
Friedman, H. Harold, ed. Problem-Oriented Medical Diagnosis. 3rd ed. (SPIRAL Manual Ser.). 1983. spiralbound 17.95 (ISBN 0-316-29359-8). Little.
Friedman, Hal. The Crib. 288p. (Orig.). 1984. pap. 3.50 (ISBN 0-671-52365-1). PB.
Friedman, Hank. Astrology on Your Personal Computer. 225p. 1984. pap. 9.95 (ISBN 0-89588-226-4). SYBEX.
Friedman, Harold & Schlagman, Herbert S. Corporate Counsel's Annual. 50.00 (ISBN 0-685-02520-9). Bender.
Friedman, Harold L. A Course in Statistical Mechanics. (Illus.). 272p. 1985. text ed. 54.95 (ISBN 0-13-184565-9). P-H.
--Don't Tell Mommy. 1985. pap. 3.50 (ISBN 0-671-47257-7). PB.
Friedman, Harry G. Taxation of Corporations in Massachusetts. LC 76-76678. (Columbia University. Studies in the Social Sciences: No. 74). Repr. of 1907 ed. 16.50 (ISBN 0-404-51074-4). AMS Pr.
Friedman, Henry & Meredeen, Sander. The Dynamics of Industrial Conflict: Lessons from Ford. 386p. 1980. 32.50x (ISBN 0-85664-982-1, Pub. by Croom Helm Ltd). Longwood Pub Group.
Friedman, Herb. The Complete Guide to Care & Maintenance for the IBM. (Illus.). 224p. 1986. pap. 15.95 (ISBN 0-13-160508-9). P H.
--Computer Care: The Complete Guide to Microcomputer Maintenance for Home & Office. (Illus.). 224p. 14.95 (ISBN 0-13-163833-5). P-H.
--Supercharging the IBM PC Portable. 244p. 1985. pap. 15.95 (ISBN 0-13-875790-9). P H.
--User's Guide to the IBM Portable PC. Date not set. price not set. P-H.
Friedman, Herbert. The Amazing Universe. National Geographic Society, ed. LC 74-28806. (Special Publications Ser.). (Illus.). 200p. 1975. 6.95 (ISBN 0-87044-179-5); lib. bdg. 8.50 (ISBN 0-87044-184-1). Natl Geog.
--The Cowbirds. (Illus.). 421p. 1929. photocopy ed. 36.50x (ISBN 0-398-04259-4). C C Thomas.
--Doing Your Best on the SAT. 1983. pap. text ed. 5.00x (ISBN 0-9606824-2-2). CAPP Bks.
--Sun & Earth. LC 85-14295. (Scientific American Library). (Illus.). 256p. 1985. write for info. (ISBN 0-7167-5012-0). W H Freeman.
--Understanding & Improving Behavior. rev. ed. LC 75-22951. 1980. text ed. 5.00x (ISBN 0-9606824-0-6). CAPP Bks.
Friedman, Herman, ed. Subcellular Factors Immunity. LC 79-24875. (Annals of the New York Academy of Sciences: Vol. 332). 625p. 1979. 112.00x (ISBN 0-89766-035-8). NY Acad Sci.
--Thymus Factors in Immunity. (Annals of the New York Academy of Sciences: Vol. 249). 547p. 1975. 65.00x (ISBN 0-89072-003-7). NY Acad Sci.
Friedman, Herman & Prier, James E., eds. Rubella. (Illus.). 164p. 1973. 14.75x (ISBN 0-398-02650-5). C C Thomas.
Friedman, Herman & Southam, Chester, eds. International Conference on Immunobiology of Cancer, Vol. 276. (Annals of the New York Academy of Sciences). 1976. 47.00x (ISBN 0-89072-055-X). NY Acad Sci.
Friedman, Herman, jt. ed. see Ceglowski, W. S.
Friedman, Herman, jt. ed. see Rose, Noel R.
Friedman, Herman, jt. ed. see Southam, Chester.
Friedman, Herman, et al, eds. Immunomodulation by Bacteria & Their Products. LC 81-17888. 320p. 1982. 42.50 (ISBN 0-306-40885-6, Plenum Pr). Plenum Pub.
Friedman, Howard, ed. Interpersonal Issues in Health Care. 301p. 1982. 26.50 (ISBN 0-12-268340-4). Acad Pr.
Friedman, Howard A., jt. auth. see DeGoff, Robert A.
Friedman, Howard F., jt. auth. see DiMatteo, M. Robin.
Friedman, Howard M. Securities & Commodities Enforcement: Criminal Prosecutions & Civil Injunctions. LC 79-9685. 256p. 1981. 39.50x (ISBN 0-669-03617-X). Lexington Bks.
Friedman, I. The Human Ear. Head, J. J., ed. LC 78-571217. (Carolina Biology Readers Ser.). (Illus.). 16p. (gr. 10 up). 1979. pap. 1.60 (ISBN 0-89278-273-0, 45-9673). Carolina Biological.
Friedman, I. Edward. How to Prepare for & Pass a High School Equivalency Exam. 1966. pap. 5.95 (ISBN 0-385-04537-9). Doubleday.
Friedman, Imrich & Osborn, Dennis A. Pathology of Granulomas & Neoplasms of the Nose & Paranasal Sinuses. (Illus.). 306p. 1982. 65.00 (ISBN 0-443-01410-8). Churchill.
Friedman, Ina. How My Parents Learned to Eat. LC 84-18553. (Illus.). 32p. (gr. k-3). 1984. PLB 12.95 (ISBN 0-395-35379-3). HM.
Friedman, Ina, tr. see Golan, Matti.
Friedman, Ina, tr. see Gutman, Yisrael.
Friedman, Ina, tr. see Halabi, Rafik.
Friedman, Ina, tr. see Schiff, Ze'ev & Ya'ari, Ehud.
Friedman, Ina R. Black Cop: A Biography of Tilmon O'Bryant. LC 73-20142. (Illus.). 160p. (gr. 7-11). 1974. 5.95 (ISBN 0-664-32546-7). Westminster.
Friedman, Irving. The Book of Creation. 64p. 1977. pap. 2.95 (ISBN 0-87728-289-7). Weiser.
Friedman, Irving M., jt. auth. see Viscardi, Henry, Jr.
Friedman, Irving S. British Relations with China, 1931-1939. LC 75-30056. (Institute of Pacific Relations). Repr. of 1940 ed. 21.50 (ISBN 0-404-59522-7). AMS Pr.
--British Relations with China, 1931-1939. 1972. lib. bdg. 21.50x (ISBN 0-374-92931-9). Octagon.

--World Debt Dilemma: Managing Country Risk. 352p. 1984. 45.00 (ISBN 0-318-18148-7); members 31.00 (ISBN 0-318-18149-5). Robt Morris Assocs.

Friedman, Isaiah. Germany, Turkey, & Zionism, 1897-1918. 1977. 59.00x (ISBN 0-19-822528-8). Oxford U Pr.

Friedman, Jack & Ordway, Nicholas. Income Property Appraisal & Analysis. 300p. 1981. text ed. 27.95 (ISBN 0-8359-3057-2); instr's. manual free (ISBN 0-8359-3058-0). Reston.

Friedman, Jack, ed. see Ferris, Bill.

Friedman, Jack, et al. Real Estate Appraisal. 1985. text ed. 21.95 (ISBN 0-8359-6508-2); instrs' manual avail. (ISBN 0-8359-6509-0). Reston.

Friedman, Jack P. & Baen, John S. Texas Real Estate License Examinations Guide. (Illus.). 256p. 1985. pap. 19.95 (ISBN 0-13-912494-2); pap. text ed. 14.95 (ISBN 0-317-18438-5). P-H.

Friedman, Jack P. & Harris, Jack C. Real Estate Handbook. 704p. 1984. 12.95 (ISBN 0-8120-2904-6). Barron.

Friedman, Jack P. & Pearson, Peggy. Real Estate Finance & Investment Tables. 1983. text ed. 29.95 (ISBN 0-8359-6525-2). Reston.

Friedman, Jack P., jt. auth. see Lindeman, J. Bruce.

Friedman, Jack P., jt. ed. see Blume, Marshall E.

Friedman, Jacob A. Impeachment of Governor William Sulzer. LC 68-58575. (Columbia University. Studies in the Social Sciences: No. 447). Repr. of 1939 ed. 22.50 (ISBN 0-404-51447-2). AMS Pr.

Friedman, James M. Dancer & Other Aesthetic Objects: San Francisco: Balletmonographs, 1980. LC 80-65960. xii, 144p. (Orig.). 1980. pap. 3.75 (ISBN 0-9604232-0-6). Balletmonographs.

--Dancers Are Poems. LC 83-71533. 109p. (Orig.). 1984. pap. 3.50 (ISBN 0-9604232-1-4). Balletmonographs.

Friedman, James M., jt. auth. see McMahon, Michael S.

Friedman, James T. The Divorce Handbook. updated ed. 1984. pap. 7.95 (ISBN 0-394-72327-9). Random.

--The Divorce Handbook: Your Basic Guide to Divorce. 1982. 12.50 (ISBN 0-394-52357-1). Random.

Friedman, James W. Oligopoly & the Theory of Games. (Advanced Textbooks in Economics Ser.: Vol. 8). 312p. 1977. 35.00 (ISBN 0-7204-0505-X, North-Holland). Elsevier.

--Oligopoly Theory. LC 82-22170. (Cambridge Surveys of Economic Literature Ser.). (Illus.). 272p. 1983. 37.50 (ISBN 0-521-23827-7); pap. 13.95 (ISBN 0-521-28244-6). Cambridge U Pr.

Friedman, James W. & Hoggatt, Austin C., eds. An Experiment in Non-Cooperative Oligopoly. (Research in Experimental Economics Supplement Ser.: No. 1). 216p. 1980. 32.50 (ISBN 0-89232-121-0). Jai Pr.

Friedman, Jane M. Contract Remedies in a Nutshell. LC 81-11614. (Nutshell Ser.). 323p. 1981. pap. text ed. 8.95 (ISBN 0-314-60373-5). West Pub.

Friedman, Jean E. The Revolt of the Conservative Democrats: An Essay on American Political Culture & Political Development, 1837-1844. Berkhofer, Robert, ed. LC 78-27449. (Studies in American History & Culture: No. 9). 160p. 1979. 39.95 (ISBN 0-8357-0970-1). UMI Res Pr.

Friedman, Jean E., jt. ed. see Shade, William G.

Friedman, Jeffrey B., ed. Components of the Future. 397p. 1985. pap. text ed. 35.00 (ISBN 0-940690-10-1). Soc Motion Pic & TV Engrs.

--Video Pictures of the Future. 296p. 1983. pap. text ed. 35.00 (ISBN 0-940690-07-1). Soc Motion Pic & TV Engrs.

Friedman, Jeffrey B. & Quinn, Stanley F., eds. Television Image Quality. 377p. 1984. pap. 35.00 (ISBN 0-940690-09-8). Soc Motion Pic & TV Engrs.

Friedman, Jerome. The Most Ancient Testimony: Sixteenth-Century Christian-Hebraica in the Age of Renaissance Nostalgia. LC 82-18830. x, 279p. 1983. text ed. 26.95x (ISBN 0-8214-0700-7, 82-84697). Ohio U Pr.

Friedman, Jo-Ann. Home Health Care: A Guide for Patients & Their Families. (Illus.). 1986. 22.00 (ISBN 0-393-01889-X). Norton.

Friedman, Joel W. & Strickler, George M. The Law of Employment Discrimination: Cases & Materials, Teacher's Manual. (University Casebook Ser.). 171p. 1985. pap. write for info. (ISBN 0-88277-269-4). Foundation Pr.

Friedman, Joel W. & Strickler, George M., Jr. The Law of Employment Discrimination: Cases & Materials, 1985 Supplement. (University Casebook Ser.). 175p. 1985. pap. write for info. (ISBN 0-88277-270-8). Foundation Pr.

Friedman, Joel Wm., et al. The Law of Employment Discrimination, Cases & Materials on. LC 82-21016. (University Casebook Ser.). 865p. 1982. text ed. 26.00 (ISBN 0-88277-096-9). Foundation Pr.

Friedman, John. The Monstrous Races in Medieval Art & Thought. LC 80-23181. (Illus.). 272p. 1981. text ed. 20.00x (ISBN 0-674-58652-2). Harvard U Pr.

--Urbanization, Planning, & National Development. LC 72-84049. pap. 88.00 (ISBN 0-317-07764-3, 2021901). Bks Demand UMI.

Friedman, John S., ed. First Harvest: An Institute for Policy Studies Reader, 1963-1983. LC 83-48306. 368p. 1983. 22.50 (ISBN 0-394-53501-4, GP-879); pap. 8.95 (ISBN 0-394-62491-2, E-870). Grove.

Friedman, Joseph & Weinberg, Daniel. The Economics of Housing Vouchers. (Studies in Urban Economics). 215p. 1982. 32.50 (ISBN 0-12-268360-9). Acad Pr.

Friedman, Joseph & Weinberg, Daniel H., eds. The Great Housing Experiment. (Urban Affairs Annual Review Ser.: Vol. 24). 288p. 1983. 28.00 (ISBN 0-8039-1991-3). Sage.

Friedman, Joy T. The Important Thing About. LC 80-83936. (Illus.). 96p. (gr. k-2). 1981. pap. 3.99 (ISBN 0-448-13947-2, G&D). Putnam Pub Group.

--Sounds All Around. LC 80-83935. Orig. Title: Look Around & Listen. (Illus.). 80p. (gr. k-2). 1981. PLB 10.15 (ISBN 0-448-13945-6, G&D); pap. 3.95 (ISBN 0-448-14755-6). Putnam Pub Group.

Friedman, Judi. The Eels Strange Journey. LC 75-20136. (A Let's Read & Find Out Science Bk). (Illus.). 40p. (gr. k-3). 1976. PLB 11.89 (ISBN 0-690-01007-9). Crowell Jr Bks.

--Jelly Jam, the People Preserver. rev. ed. (Illus.). 70p. (gr. 2-5). 1983. wkbk. 3.00 (ISBN 0-910812-27-6). Johnny Reads.

--Jelly Jam, the People Preserver Teaching Guide. rev. ed. (Illus.). 130p. 1984. pap. 10.00 (ISBN 0-910812-28-4). Johnny Reads.

--Puffins, Come Back! 1981. 7.95 (ISBN 0-396-07940-7). Dodd.

Friedman, Judi C. The ABC of a Summer Pond. new ed. LC 73-92631. (Illus.). (gr. k-4). 1975. 6.00 (ISBN 0-910812-14-4); pap. 3.00 (ISBN 0-910812-15-2). Johnny Reads.

Friedman, Judith & Sonnenblick, Carol. Attack Pack. 128p. (gr. 4-12). 1982. write for info. (ISBN 0-9609616-0-7). New Dir Pr.

Friedman, Judith, tr. see Reiffenstuhl, Gunther & Platzer, Werner.

Friedman, Julian R. & Sherman, Marc I. Human Rights: An International & Comparative Law Bibliography. LC 84-19300. (Bibliographies & Indexes in Law & Political Science Ser.: No. 4). xxvii, 868p. 1985. lib. bdg. 75.00 (ISBN 0-313-24767-6, FHR/). Greenwood.

Friedman, Julian R. & Wiseberg, Laurie S., eds. Teaching Human Rights. 134p. 1981. 20.00 (ISBN 0-317-34234-7). Human Rights.

Friedman, K. Crane, ed. see Rooney, John F., Jr.

Friedman, Kathi V. Legitimation of Social Rights & the Western Welfare State: A Weberian Perspective. LC 80-29600. xii, 269p. 1981. 24.50x (ISBN 0-8078-1480-6). U of NC Pr.

Friedman, Ken, jt. auth. see Rossi, Steve.

Friedman, L. Jeanne, jt. auth. see Inmon, William H.

Friedman, L. M. Government & Slum Housing: A Century of Frustrations. LC 77-74941. (American Federalism,the Urban Dimension Ser.). 1978. Repr. of 1968 ed. lib. bdg. 20.00x (ISBN 0-405-10488-X). Ayer Co Pubs.

Friedman, L. S. Microeconomic Policy Analysis. 1984. 33.95 (ISBN 0-07-022408-0). McGraw.

Friedman, Lawrance W. & Galton, Lawrence. Freedom from Backaches. 1983. pap. 3.50 (ISBN 0-671-49887-8). PB.

Friedman, Lawrence J. Gregarious Saints: Self & Community in American Abolitionism, 1830-1870. LC 81-15454. 320p. 1982. 44.50 (ISBN 0-521-24429-3); pap. 13.95 (ISBN 0-521-27015-4). Cambridge U Pr.

--Psychoanalysis. LC 68-8037. 192p. 1977. pap. 4.95 (ISBN 0-8397-6901-6). Eriksson.

--The Traveling Psychoanalyst. new ed. LC 72-180305. (Illus.). 1978. pap. 5.95 (ISBN 0-8397-8375-2). Eriksson.

Friedman, Lawrence M. American Law. LC 83-42662. 384p. 1984. 22.95 (ISBN 0-393-01890-3). Norton.

--American Law: An Introduction. 1985. pap. text ed. 14.95x (ISBN 0-393-95251-7). Norton.

--A History of American Law. 1974. pap. 14.95 (ISBN 0-671-21742-9, Touchstone Bks). S&S.

--A History of American Law. rev. ed. LC 85-10781. write for info. (ISBN 0-671-52807-6). S&S.

--Law & Society: An Introduction. 192p. 1977. pap. text ed. 13.95 (ISBN 0-13-526608-4). P-H.

--The Legal System: A Social Science Perspective. LC 74-25855. 338p. 1975. 13.50 (ISBN 0-87154-296-X). Russell Sage.

--Total Justice. LC 84-51638. 176p. 1985. text ed. 14.50x (ISBN 0-87154-297-8). Russell Sage.

--Your Time Will Come: The Law of Age Discrimination & Mandatory Retirement. LC 84-60650. (Social Research Perspectives, Occasional Reports on Current Topics). 160p. 1985. text ed. 6.95x (ISBN 0-87154-295-1). Russell Sage.

Friedman, Lawrence M. & Macaulay, Stewart. Law & the Behavioral Sciences. 2nd ed. (Contemporary Legal Education Ser.). 1075p. 1977. 25.00 (ISBN 0-672-82025-0, Bobbs-Merrill Law). Michie Co.

Friedman, Lawrence M. & Percival, Robert V. The Roots of Justice: Crime & Punishment in Alameda County, California, 1870-1910. (Studies in Legal History). xvi, 335p. 1981. 27.50x (ISBN 0-8078-1476-8). U of NC Pr.

Friedman, Lawrence M. & Scheiber, Harry N., eds. American Law & the Constitutional Order: Historical Perspectives. LC 77-16640. 544p. 1981. pap. 12.50x (ISBN 0-674-02526-1). Harvard U Pr.

--American Law & the Constitutional Order: Historical Perspectives. LC 77-16640. 1978. 27.50x (ISBN 0-674-02525-3). Harvard U Pr.

Friedman, Lawrence M., et al. Fundamentals of Clinical Trials. 2nd ed. 236p. 1981. 29.00 (ISBN 0-88416-296-6). PSG Pub Co.

Friedman, Lee M. Jewish Pioneers & Patriots. (Essay Index Reprint Ser.). Repr. of 1942 ed. 26.75 (ISBN 0-518-10146-0). Ayer Co Pubs.

--Pilgrims in a New Land. LC 78-26208. (Illus.). 1979. Repr. of 1948 ed. lib. bdg. 32.50x (ISBN 0-313-20877-8, FRPI). Greenwood.

--Zola & the Dreyfus Case. 59.95 (ISBN 0-87968-029-6). Gordon Pr.

--Zola & the Dreyfus Case. (World History Ser., No. 48). (Illus.). 1970. pap. write for info. (ISBN 0-8383-0092-8). Haskell.

Friedman, Lenemaja. Shirley Jackson. (United States Authors Ser.). 1975. lib. bdg. 13.50 (ISBN 0-8057-0402-7, Twayne). G K Hall.

Friedman, Leo R. Essential of Cross-Examination. LC 68-63003. 166p. 1968. pap. 15.00 (ISBN 0-88124-005-2, CP-30300). Cal Cont Ed Bar.

Friedman, Leon & Neuborne, Burt. Unquestioning Obedience to the President: The ACLU Case Against the Legality of the War in Vietnam. LC 76-169044. 1972. pap. 3.95x (ISBN 0-393-05470-5). Norton.

Friedman, Leon, ed. The Burger Court, Vol. 5. LC 69-13699. (Justices of the United States Supreme Court Ser.: Vol. 5). 1978. 45.00 (ISBN 0-8352-0217-8). Chelsea Hse.

--Episodes of Violence in U. S. History, 3 vols. Incl. Vol. 1. Dynamite. Adamic, Louis. LC 80-21964. 500p. Date not set (ISBN 0-87754-214-7); Vol. 2. The Dorr War. Mowry, Arthur M. LC 80-21969. 435p (ISBN 0-87754-215-5); Vol. 3. The Molly Maguires. Broehl, Wayne G., Jr. 420p. Date not set (ISBN 0-87754-216-3). LC 80-21794. (Illus.). Repr. of 1970 ed. Set. cancelled (ISBN 0-87754-133-7); cancelled. Chelsea Hse.

--United States vs. Nixon: The President Before the Supreme Court. LC 74-16403. 644p. 1980. pap. 11.95 (ISBN 0-87754-144-2). Chelsea Hse.

Friedman, Leon & Israel, Fred L., eds. The Justices of the United States Supreme Court, 1789-1978, 5 vols. LC 69-13699. 3900p. 1980. pap. 100.00 set (ISBN 0-87754-130-2). Chelsea Hse.

Friedman, Leonard, jt. ed. see Pearce, John.

Friedman, Leslie. Sex Role Stereotyping in the Mass Media: An Annotated Bibliography. LC 76-52685. (Reference Library of Social Science Ser.). 342p. 1977. lib. bdg. 42.00 (ISBN 0-8240-9865-X). Garland Pub.

Friedman, Lester D. Hollywood's Image of the Jew. LC 81-70118. (Illus.). 408p. 1982. 19.50x (ISBN 0-8044-2219-2); pap. 8.95 (ISBN 0-8044-6160-0). Ungar.

Friedman, Lionel J. Text & Iconography of Joinville's Credo. LC 58-7918. 1958. 12.00x (ISBN 0-910956-42-1). Medieval Acad.

Friedman, Lucy, jt. ed. see Barasch, Moshe.

Friedman, Lynn A., ed. On the Other Hand: New Perspectives on American Sign Language. (Language, Thought & Culture Ser.). 1977. 42.50 (ISBN 0-12-267850-8). Acad Pr.

Friedman, Lynne, jt. auth. see Heckens, Gertrude.

Friedman, M. A Beginner's Guide to Sightsinging & Musical Rudiments. 1981. pap. 19.95 (ISBN 0-13-074088-8). P-H.

--Dollars & Deficits: Inflation, Monetary Policy & the Balance of Payments. 1968. pap. 18.95 (ISBN 0-13-218289-0). P-H.

Friedman, M. & Schwartz, A. From New Deal Banking Reform to World War II in Inflation. 174p. 1980. pap. 7.95 (ISBN 0-691-00363-7). Princeton U Pr.

Friedman, M. & Schwartz, A. J. Monetary History of the United States: 1867-1960. (National Bureau of Economic Research, B.12). 1963. 63.00 (ISBN 0-691-04147-4); pap. 17.50 (ISBN 0-691-00354-8). Princeton U Pr.

Friedman, M., et al, eds. Diagnosis & Treatment of Upper Gastrointestinal Tumors. (International Congress Ser.: No. 542). 538p. 1981. 98.75 (ISBN 0-444-90189-2, Excerpta Medica). Elsevier.

Friedman, M., jt. ed. see Carter, N. L.

Friedman, M. D., jt. auth. see Byrd, P. F.

Friedman, M. H. Functions of the Stomach & Intestine: Proceedings of the Thomas (J. Earl) Memorial Symposium, 1973. LC 75-9755. pap. 119.00 (ISBN 0-317-26194-0, 2052072). Bks Demand UMI.

Friedman, M. Harold, jt. auth. see Rosenblatt, Jack.

Friedman, Marilyn M. Family Nursing: Theory & Assessment. (Illus.). 352p. 1981. pap. 17.95x (ISBN 0-8385-2532-6). ACC.

Friedman, Mark H. & Weisberg, Joseph. Temporomandibular Joint Disorders. (Illus.). 172p. 1985. pap. text ed. 48.00x (ISBN 0-86715-137-4). Quint Pub Co.

Friedman, Martha. Overcoming the Fear of Success. 208p. 1982. pap. 6.95 (ISBN 0-446-38111-X). Warner Bks.

Friedman, Martin. Martin Buber's Life & Work: The Early Years, 1878-1923. (Illus.). 480p. 1982. 29.95 (ISBN 0-525-15325-X, 02908-870). Dutton.

Friedman, Martin & Dexter, John. Hockney Paints the Stage. LC 83-5865. (Illus.). 227p. 1983. 45.00 (ISBN 0-89659-396-7). Abbeville Pr.

Friedman, Martin, et al. The Frozen Image: Scandinavian Photography. (Illus.). 208p. 35.00 (ISBN 0-89659-311-8); pap. 24.95 (ISBN 0-89659-312-6). Abbeville Pr.

Friedman, Martin B., tr. see Ginestier, Paul.

Friedman, Martin L., jt. auth. see Powell, Jane P.

Friedman, Maurice. The Confirmation of Otherness in Family, Community & Society. LC 83-5648. 320p. 1983. 18.95 (ISBN 0-8298-0651-2). Pilgrim NY.

--Contemporary Psychology: Revealing & Obscuring the Human. 200p. 1984. text ed. 19.00x (ISBN 0-8207-0166-1); pap. text ed. 10.50x (ISBN 0-8207-0168-8). Duquesne.

--The Covenant of Peace. 1983. pap. 5.00x (ISBN 0-87574-110-X, 110). Pendle Hill.

--The Healing Dialogue in Psychotherapy. LC 84-14504. 320p. 1985. 25.00 (ISBN 0-87668-730-3). Aronson.

--The Human Way. (Religion & Human Experience Ser.). 168p. 1982. 13.95 (ISBN 0-89012-025-0). Anima Pubns.

--Martin Buber: The Life of Dialogue. 3rd, rev. ed. 1976. pap. 12.00x (ISBN 0-226-26356-8). U of Chicago Pr.

--Martin Buber's Life & Work: The Later Years, 1945-1965, Vol. III. LC 83-1946. (Illus.). 493p. 1984. 32.50 (ISBN 0-525-24212-0, 03155-950). Dutton.

--Martin Buber's Life & Work: The Middle Years, 1923-1945. (Illus.). 416p. 1983. 29.95 (ISBN 0-525-24176-0, 02908-870). Dutton.

--Modern Promethean: A Dialogue with Today's Youth. LC 73-104050. (Orig.). 1969. pap. 5.00x (ISBN 0-87574-168-1). Pendle Hill.

--Problematic Rebel: Melville, Dostoievsky, Kafka, Camus. rev. ed. LC 72-101360. 1970. pap. 3.95x (ISBN 0-226-26396-7, P358, Phoen). U of Chicago Pr.

--Problematic Rebel: Melville, Dostoievsky, Kafka, Camus. rev. ed. LC 72-101360. 1970. 18.00x (ISBN 0-226-26395-9). U of Chicago Pr.

--To Deny Our Nothingness: Contemporary Images of Man with a New Preface & Appendix. LC 77-92748. 386p. 1984. pap. text ed. 14.00x (ISBN 0-226-26339-8). U of Chicago Pr.

Friedman, Maurice, ed. The Worlds of Existentialism. 1973. pap. 13.50x (ISBN 0-226-26348-7, P560, Phoen). U of Chicago Pr.

Friedman, Maurice, ed. see Buber, Martin.

Friedman, Maurice, ed. & tr. see Buber, Martin.

Friedman, Maurice, jt. ed. see Schilpp, Paul A.

Friedman, Melvin J. The Added Dimension: The Art of Mind of Flannery O'Connor. 2nd ed. LC 66-11070. xviii, 263p. 1977. pap. 9.00 (ISBN 0-8232-0711-0). Fordham.

--William Styron. LC 74-16889. 82p. 1974. 2.50 (ISBN 0-87972-071-9). Bowling Green Univ.

Friedman, Melvin J. & Clark, Beverly L. Critical Essays on Flannery O'Connor. (Critical Essays on American Literature). 1985. lib. bdg. 35.00 (ISBN 0-8161-8693-6). G K Hall.

Friedman, Melvin J., ed. Samuel Beckett Now: Critical Approaches to His Novels, Poetry, & Plays. 2nd ed. LC 74-21346. xii, 298p. 1975. pap. 3.95x (ISBN 0-226-26347-9, P602, Phoen). U of Chicago Pr.

Friedman, Melvin J. & Vickery, John B., eds. Shaken Realist: Essays in Modern Literature in Honor of Frederick J. Hoffman. LC 77-108199. xxvi, 344p. 1970. 30.00x (ISBN 0-8071-0933-9). La State U Pr.

Friedman, Melvin J., jt. ed. see Lamont, Rosette C.

Friedman, Mendel, ed. Nutritional & Toxicological Aspects of Food Safety. 596p. 1984. 79.50x (ISBN 0-306-41708-1, Plenum Pr). Plenum Pub.

--Protein Crosslinking, 2 pts. Incl. Pt. A: Biochemical & Molecular Aspects. 779p (ISBN 0-306-39087-6); Pt. B: Nutritional & Medical Consequences. 760p (ISBN 0-306-39088-4). (Advances in Experimental Medicine & Biology Ser.: Vols. 86A & 86B). 1977. 85.00x ea. (Plenum Pr). Plenum Pub.

--Protein-Metal Interactions. LC 74-13406. (Advances in Experimental Medicine & Biology Ser.: Vol. 48). 702p. 1974. 82.50x (ISBN 0-306-39048-5, Plenum Pr). Plenum Pub.

--Protein Nutritional Quality of Foods & Feeds, Pt. 1: Assay Methods-Biological, Biochemical, & Chemical. (Nutrition & Clinical Nutrition Ser.: Vol. 1). 648p. 1975. 95.00 (ISBN 0-8247-6278-9). Dekker.

--Protein Nutritional Quality of Foods & Feeds, Pt. 2: Quality Factors-Plant Breeding, Composition, Processing & Antinutrients. (Nutrition & Clinical Nutrition Ser.: Vol. 1). 1975. 95.00 (ISBN 0-8247-6282-7). Dekker.

Friedman, Meyer & Rosenman, Ray H. Type A Behavior & Your Heart. 320p. 1981. pap. 6.95 (ISBN 0-449-90059-2, Columbine). Fawcett.

--Type A Behavior & Your Heart. 1974. 16.95 (ISBN 0-394-48011-2). Knopf.

Friedman, Meyer & Ulmer, Diane. Treating Type A Behavior: And Your Heart. LC 83-47939. (Illus.). 1984. 15.95 (ISBN 0-394-52286-9). Knopf.

--Type A Behavior - Your Heart. 1985. pap. 2.95 (ISBN 0-449-23870-9, Crest). Fawcett.

Friedman, Michael. Acupressure for the Backpacker: Alternative Emergency Medical Procedures. Jacobsen, Liz, ed. (Illus.). 43p. 1983. pap. 4.95 (ISBN 0-912561-02-5). Counsel & Stress.

Friedman, Samy. Expropriation in International Law. rev. ed. Jackson, Ivor C., tr. from Fr. LC 80-26295. (The Library of World Affairs: No. 20). xv, 236p. 1981. Repr. of 1953 ed. lib. bdg. 29.75x (ISBN 0-313-20840-9, FREI). Greenwood.

Friedman, Sandor. Vascular Diseases: A Concise Guide to Diagnosis, Management, Pathogenesis, & Prevention. (Illus.). 588p. 1982. 52.00 (ISBN 0-7236-7000-5). PSG Pub Co.

Friedman, Sanford. Totempole. 416p. 1984. pap. 13.50 (ISBN 0-86547-140-1). N Point Pr.

Friedman, Sara Ann & Jacobs, David. Police! A Precinct at Work. LC 75-10137. (Illus.). 192p. (gr. 7 up). 1975. 6.95 (ISBN 0-15-263027-9, HJ). HarBraceJ.

Friedman, Sarah L. & Sigman, Marian, eds. Preterm Birth & Psychological Development. LC 80-980. (Developmental Psychology Ser.). 1980. 49.50 (ISBN 0-12-267880-X). Acad Pr.

Friedman, Saul S. Amcha: An Oral Testament of the Holocaust. LC 79-67054. 1979. pap. text ed. 17.50 (ISBN 0-8191-0867-7). U Pr of Amer.

--Land of Dust: Palestine at the Turn of the Century. LC 81-43466. (Illus.). 256p. (Orig.). 1982. lib. bdg. 26.00 (ISBN 0-8191-2403-6); pap. text ed. 13.00 (ISBN 0-8191-2404-4). U Pr of Amer.

--No Haven for the Oppressed: United States Policy Toward Jewish Refugees, 1938-1945. LC 72-2271. 315p. 1973. 15.95x (ISBN 0-8143-1474-0). Wayne St U Pr.

--The Oberammergau Passion Play: A Lance against Civilization. LC 83-17099. 256p. 1984. 22.95 (ISBN 0-8093-1153-4). S Ill U Pr.

Friedman, Scarlet & Sarah, Elizabeth. On the Problem of Men: Two Feminist Conferences. 288p. 1982. 10.95 (ISBN 0-7043-3887-4, Pub. by Quartet Bks). Herschel Gower.

Friedman, Sharon M., et al. Scientists & Journalists: Reporting Science as News. 352p. 24.95x (ISBN 0-02-910750-4). Free Pr.

Friedman, Sharon M., et al, eds. Scientists & Journalists: Reporting Science As News. (AAAS Issues in Science & Technology Ser.). 352p. 1985. 24.95x (ISBN 0-02-910750-4). Free Pr.

Friedman, Sherwood & Grossman, Jack. Filing Practice Handbook. 4th ed. (gr. 9-12). 1982. pap. 3.72 (ISBN 0-02-830900-6); tchr's guide & key 1.60 (ISBN 0-02-830910-3). Glencoe.

--Modern Clerical Practice. 4th ed. LC 74-26824. (gr. 9-12). 1975. text ed. 14.80 (ISBN 0-02-830940-5); wkbk 6.60 (ISBN 0-02-830950-2); key 3.20 (ISBN 0-02-830960-X). Glencoe.

Friedman, Sonya. Men Are Just Desserts. LC 82-61881. 256p. (Orig.). 1983. 14.50 (ISBN 0-446-51255-9); pap. 3.95 (ISBN 0-446-30338-0). Warner Bks.

--Smart Cookies Don't Crumble: A Modern Woman's Guide to Living & Loving Her Own Life. 1985. 15.95 (ISBN 0-399-13040-3). Putnam Pub Group.

Friedman, Stanford & Hoekelman, Robert. Behavioral Pediatrics: Psychological Aspects of Child Health Care. (Illus.). 448p. 1980. text ed. 21.00 (ISBN 0-07-022426-9). McGraw.

Friedman, Stephen J. & Nathan, Charles M., eds. Annual Institute on Securities Regulation, 13th. Incl. Annual Institute on Securities Regulation, 14th. Friedman, Stephen J. et al., ed. 661p. 1983. pap. text ed. 50.00 (B2-1293). LC 70-125178. 472p. 1982. text ed. 40.00 (ISBN 0-686-82490-3, B2-1293). PLI.

Friedman, Stephen J., et al. Bank Acquisitions & Takeovers, 1984. (Corporate Law & Practice Course Handbook Ser.: B4-6676). 503p. 1984. 35.00. PLI.

--Sixteenth Annual Institute on Securities Regulation. 450p. 1985. 60.00 (ISBN 0-317-27372-8, #B2-1318). PLI.

Friedman, Stephen J., et al, eds. Securities Regulation, Fifteenth Annual Institute. 565p. 1984. 50.00 (ISBN 0-317-11394-1, B2-1294). PLI.

Friedman, Stephen J. et al. see Friedman, Stephen J. & Nathan, Charles M.

Friedman, Steve. Kids Love the Apple. (Illus.). 1985. pap. 12.95 (ISBN 0-452-25645-3, Plume). NAL.

--Kids Love the Commodore 64. (Illus.). 1985. 12.95 (ISBN 0-452-25646-1, Plume). NAL.

Friedman, Susan J., jt. ed. see Skehan, Philip.

Friedman, Susan S. Psyche Reborn: The Emergence of H. D. LC 80-8378. (Illus.). 352p. 1981. 22.50x (ISBN 0-253-37826-5). Ind U Pr.

Friedman, Terry. James Gibbs. LC 84-40184. (Studies in British Art). (Illus.). 368p. 1985. 60.00x (ISBN 0-300-03172-6). Yale U pr.

Friedman, Thomas, jt. auth. see Solman, Paul.

Friedman, W. Construction Marketing & Strategic Planning. 1984. 37.95 (ISBN 0-07-022437-4). McGraw.

Friedman, W. A., jt. ed. see McVoy, K. W.

Friedman, Walter F. & Kipnees, Jerome J. Distribution Packaging. LC 75-22096. 558p. 1977. 29.50 (ISBN 0-88275-222-7). Krieger.

Friedman, Warner, jt. auth. see Gelman, Rita G.

Friedman, Wayne S., jt. auth. see Hartwell-Walker, Marie.

Friedman, William, ed. Developmental Psychology of Time. (Developmental Psychology Ser.). 1982. 36.50 (ISBN 0-12-268320-X). Acad Pr.

Friedman, William F. Advanced Military Cryptography. rev. ed. (Cryptographic Ser.). 1976. Repr. of 1941 ed. 14.80 (ISBN 0-89412-011-5). Aegean Park Pr.

--Elementary Military Cryptography. rev. ed. LC 76-53119. (Cryptographic Ser.). 1976. Repr. of 1941 ed. 14.00 (ISBN 0-89412-010-7). Aegean Park Pr.

--Elements of Cryptanalysis. LC 76-19947. (Cryptographic Ser.). 1976. pap. 16.80 (ISBN 0-89412-002-6). Aegean Park Pr.

--History of the Use of Codes. (Cryptographic Ser.). 1977. Repr. of 1928 ed. 13.80 (ISBN 0-89412-018-2). Aegean Park Pr.

--Military Cryptanalysis, 4 vols. 1980. lib. bdg. 500.00 (ISBN 0-87700-271-1). Revisionist Pr.

--Military Cryptanalysis, Pt. II. rev ed. Barker, Wayne G., ed. (Cryptographic Ser.). 161p. 1984. pap. 22.80 (ISBN 0-89412-064-6). Aegean Park Pr.

--Military Cryptanalysis, Pt. 1. 1981. pap. 20.80 (ISBN 0-89412-044-1). Aegean Park Pr.

--The Riverbank Publications, 3 vols. (Cryptographic Ser.). 1979. 18.00 ea. Vol. 1 (ISBN 0-89412-032-8). Vol. 2 (ISBN 0-89412-033-6). Vol. 3 (ISBN 0-89412-034-4). Aegean Park Pr.

--Solving German Codes in World War I. (Cryptographic Ser.). 1977. 16.80 (ISBN 0-89412-019-0). Aegean Park Pr.

Friedman, William F. & Higgins, Charles B. Pediatric Cardiac Imaging. (Illus.). 350p. 1984. 40.00 (ISBN 0-7216-1287-3). Saunders.

Friedman, William F. & Mendelsohn, Charles J. The Zimmermann Telegram of January 16, 1917 & Its Cryptographic Background. LC 76-53121. (Cryptographic Ser.). 1976. pap. 8.20 (ISBN 0-89412-009-3). Aegean Park Pr.

Friedman, William F., ed. Cryptography & Cryptanalysis Articles, 2 vols. rev. ed. (Cryptographic Ser.). 1976. Repr. of 1941 ed. Vol. 1. 16.80 (ISBN 0-89412-003-4); Vol. 2. 16.80 (ISBN 0-89412-004-2). Aegean Park Pr.

Friedman, William F., ed. see Gylden, Yves.

Friedman, William F., et al, eds. Neonatal Heart Disease. LC 73-4449. (Illus.). 386p. 1973. 70.50 (ISBN 0-8089-0802-2, 791430). Grune.

Friedman, William H. How to Do Groups. LC 84-45117. 278p. 1983. 25.00x (ISBN 0-87668-718-4). Aronson.

Friedman, Winnifred H. Boydell's Shakespeare Gallery. LC 75-23791. (Outstanding Dissertations in the Fine Arts-17th & 18th Century). (Illus.). 1976. lib. bdg. 55.00 (ISBN 0-8240-1987-3). Garland Pub.

Friedman, Wolfgang see Jessup, Philip C.

Friedman, Wolfgang & Kalmanoff, George, eds. Joint International Business Ventures. LC 61-7173. 1961. 45.00x (ISBN 0-231-02465-7). Columbia U Pr.

Friedman, Y., jt. auth. see Arazy, J.

Friedman, Yona. Toward a Scientific Architecture. Lang, Cynthia, tr. from Fr. 208p. 1975. pap. 4.95x (ISBN 0-262-56019-4). MIT Pr.

Friedman-Kien, Alvin E. & Laubenstein, Linda J., eds. AIDS: The Epidemic of Kaposi's Sarcoma & Opportunistic Infections. LC 83-25578. (Illus.). 371p. 1984. 49.50 (ISBN 0-89352-217-1). Masson Pub.

Friedmann, jt. auth. see Grossmann.

Friedmann, Arnold, et al. Interior Design: An Introduction to Architectural Interiors. 3rd ed. 536p. 1982. 31.25 (ISBN 0-444-00670-2). Elsevier.

Friedmann, Arnold, et al, eds. Environmental Design Evaluation. LC 78-24252. (Illus.). 233p. 1978. 29.50x (ISBN 0-306-40092-8, Plenum Pr). Plenum Pub.

Friedmann, Claude T. & Faguet, Robert A., eds. Extraordinary Disorders of Human Behavior. (Critical Issues in Psychiatry Ser.). 340p. 1982. text ed. 39.50 (ISBN 0-306-40875-9, Plenum Pr). Plenum Pub.

Friedmann, Eugene A., et al. The Meaning of Work & Retirement. Stein, Leon, ed. LC 77-70496. (Work Ser.). 1977. Repr. of 1954 ed. lib. bdg. 20.00x (ISBN 0-405-10166-X). Ayer Co Pubs.

Friedmann, G., et al. Emergency Roentgen Diagnosis. 1980. 21.00 (ISBN 0-8151-3281-6). Year Bk Med.

Friedmann, Georges. The Anatomy of Work: Labor, Leisure & the Implications of Automation. LC 78-6171. 1978. Repr. of 1962 ed. lib. bdg. 39.75x (ISBN 0-313-20464-0, FRAW). Greenwood.

Friedmann, Herbert. A Bestiary for St. Jerome: Animal Symbolism in European Religious Art. LC 79-607804. (Illus.). 378p. 1980. 37.50x (ISBN 0-87474-446-6). Smithsonian.

Friedmann, Hope, jt. auth. see Gribble, Mercedes.

Friedmann, J., et al. FORTRAN-IV. 2nd ed. LC 80-21709. (Self Teaching Guide Ser.: No. 1-581). 499p. 1981. pap. 14.95 (ISBN 0-471-07771-2, Pub. by Wiley Pr). Wiley.

Friedmann, John. The Good Society. 1979. 25.00x (ISBN 0-262-06070-1). MIT Pr.

--The Good Society: A Personal Account of Its Struggle with the World of Planning & a Dialectical Inquiry into the Roots of Radical Practice. 199p. 1979. pap. 6.95x (ISBN 0-262-56024-0). MIT Pr.

Friedmann, John & Weaver, Clyde. Territory & Function. 1979. 36.00x (ISBN 0-520-03928-9); pap. 7.95x (ISBN 0-520-04105-4). U of Cal Pr.

Friedmann, John & Alonso, William, eds. Regional Policy: Readings in Theory & Applications. rev. ed. 1975. 35.00x (ISBN 0-262-06057-4). MIT Pr.

Friedmann, Lawrence W. The Psychological Rehabilitation of the Amputee. (Illus.). 176p. 1978. photocopy ed. 20.75x (ISBN 0-398-03707-8). C C Thomas.

--The Surgical Rehabilitation of the Amputee. (Illus.). 576p. 1978. 54.50x (ISBN 0-398-03763-9). C C Thomas.

Friedmann, Lawrence W. & Edagawa, Naoyushi. Treatment of Disordered Function from Pain to Sexual Complaints: An Introduction to the Edagawa Method. (Illus.). 192p. 1981. 20.00x (ISBN 0-682-49665-0, University). Exposition Pr FL.

Friedmann, Paul. Anne Boleyn: A Chapter of English History, 1527-1536, 2 Vols. Repr. of 1884 ed. Set. 52.50 (ISBN 0-404-09050-8). Vol. 1. Vol. 2 (ISBN 0-404-09051-6). AMS Pr.

Friedmann, Robert. Glaubenszeugnisse Oberdeutscher Taufgesinnter, Band Zwei. (Tauferakten Kommission Ser., Vol. 12). 318p. (Ger). 9.50x (ISBN 0-8361-1186-9). Herald Pr.

--Mennonite Piety Through the Centuries. 287p. 1949. text ed. 12.95x (ISBN 0-8361-1234-2). Herald Pr.

--The Theology of Anabaptism. LC 73-7886. (Studies in Anabaptist & Mennonite History, No. 15). 176p. 1973. 9.95x (ISBN 0-8361-1194-X). Herald Pr.

Friedmann, T., jt. ed. see Ballantyne, J.

Friedmann, Theodore, ed. Gene Therapy: Fact & Fiction. LC 83-24063. 131p. (Orig.). 1983. pap. 4.95x (ISBN 0-87969-215-4). Cold Spring Harbor.

Friedmann, Thomas. Damaged Goods. LC 83-83075. 280p. (Orig.). 1984. 17.95 (ISBN 0-932966-39-X). Permanent Pr.

--Damaged Goods. LC 83-83075. 280p. 1985. pap. 10.95 (ISBN 0-932966-64-0). Permanent Pr.

--Hero - Azriel. LC 79-87896. 98p. 1979. pap. 4.00x (ISBN 0-916288-07-2). Micah Pubns.

Friedmann, Thomas & MacKillop, James. The Copy Book: Mastering Basic Grammar & Style. LC 79-27176. 288p. (Orig.). 1980. pap. text ed. 14.95 (ISBN 0-03-051026-0, HoltC); instr's. manual 19.95 (ISBN 0-03-054181-6). HR&W.

Friedmann, Wolfgang. The Future of the Oceans. 132p. 1971. pap. 5.25x (ISBN 0-8464-1194-6). Beekman Pubs.

--The Future of the Oceans. 1971. 6.95 (ISBN 0-8076-0602-2); pap. 3.95 (ISBN 0-8076-0601-4). Braziller.

Friedmann, Wolfgang, ed. Public & Private Enterprise in Mixed Economies. LC 73-12406. 410p. 1974. 42.50x (ISBN 0-231-03776-7). Columbia U Pr.

Friedmann, Wolfgang & Mates, Leo, eds. Joint Business Ventures of Yugoslav Enterprises & Foreign Firms. 192p. (Orig.). 1968. pap. 10.00x (ISBN 0-8377-0526-6). Rothman.

Friedmann, Wolfgang G. Legal Theory. 5th ed. LC 67-26509. 607p. 1967. 45.00x (ISBN 0-231-03100-9). Columbia U Pr.

Friedmann, Wolfgang G. & Garner, J. F., eds. Government Enterprise. (A Comparative Study). 351p. 1971. 31.00x (ISBN 0-231-03448-2). Columbia U Pr.

Friedmann, Wolfgang G., et al. International Financial Aid. LC 66-20494. 1966. 45.00x (ISBN 0-231-02953-5). Columbia U Pr.

Friedmann, Wolfgang G., et al, eds. Transnational Law in a Changing Society: Essays in Honor of Philip C. Jessup. LC 71-187029. 324p. 1972. 35.00x (ISBN 0-231-03619-1). Columbia U Pr.

Friedmann, Yohanan. Shaykh Ahmad Sirhindi: An Outline of His Thought & a Study of His Image in the Eyes of Posterity. 136p. 1971. 15.00x (ISBN 0-7735-0068-5). McGill-Queens U Pr.

Friedmann, Yohanan, ed. Islam in Asia: South Asia, Vol. I. LC 83-60647. 280p. 1984. 25.00 (ISBN 0-86531-635-X). Westview.

Friedric, Otto. Ring Lardner. LC 65-64769. (University of Minnesota Pamphlets on American Writers Ser.: No. 49). pap. 20.00 (ISBN 0-317-29459-8, 2055932). Bks Demand UMI.

Friedrich, et al. Experiments in Atomic Physics. (gr. 12). text ed. 6.95 (ISBN 0-7195-0467-8). Transatlantic.

Friedrich, Adolf. Afrikanische Priestertuemer. pap. 37.00 (ISBN 0-384-16920-1). Johnson Repr.

Friedrich, Carl J. The Age of the Baroque, 1610-1660. LC 83-10736. (The Rise of Modern Europe Ser.). (Illus.). xv, 367p. 1983. Repr. of 1952 ed. lib. bdg. 45.00x (ISBN 0-313-24079-5, FRAG). Greenwood.

--American Policy Toward Palestine. LC 73-147219. 1971. Repr. of 1944 ed. lib. bdg. 15.00x (ISBN 0-8371-5984-9, FRAP). Greenwood.

--Constitutional Reason of State: The Survival of the Constitutional Order. LC 57-10150. 143p. 1957. 12.50x (ISBN 0-87057-046-3). U Pr of New Eng.

--The Impact of American Constitutionalism Abroad. LC 67-25934. 122p. 1967. 7.50x (ISBN 0-8419-8712-2, Africana). Holmes & Meier.

--Inevitable Peace. Repr. of 1948 ed. lib. bdg. 15.00x (ISBN 0-8371-2397-6, FRIN). Greenwood.

--The New Image of the Common Man. LC 84-20511. xxvi, 382p. 1984. Repr. of 1950 ed. lib. bdg. 47.50x (ISBN 0-313-24243-7, FRNE). Greenwood.

--Pathology of Politics: Violence, Betrayal, Corruption, Secrecy & Propaganda. 1972. text ed. 47.50x (ISBN 0-8290-0343-6). Irvington.

--Philosophy of Law in Historical Perspective. 2nd ed. LC 57-9546. 1963. pap. 5.50x (ISBN 0-226-26466-1, P135, Phoen). U of Chicago Pr.

--Transcendent Justice: The Religious Dimensions of Constitutionalism. LC 64-20097. ix, 116p. 1964. 13.75 (ISBN 0-8223-0061-3). Duke.

Friedrich, Carl J. & Blitzer, Charles. Age of Power. (Development of Western Civilization Ser). 200p. (Orig.). (YA) (gr. 9-12). 1957. pap. 4.95x (ISBN 0-8014-9843-0). Cornell U Pr.

--The Age of Power. LC 82-2955. (The Development of Western Civilization Ser.). xiv, 200p. 1982. Repr. of 1957 ed. lib. bdg. 23.75x (ISBN 0-313-23550-3, FRAO). Greenwood.

Friedrich, Carl J., ed. see Hegel, Georg W.

Friedrich, Carl J., ed. see Kant, Immanuel.

Friedrich, Carl J., tr. see Weber, Alfred.

Friedrich, David. Crime & Justice: Perspectives from the Past. 1977. pap. text ed. 7.25 (ISBN 0-8191-0068-4). U Pr of Amer.

Friedrich, Dick & Harris, Angela. Writing for Your Reader. (Orig.). 1980. pap. 9.95 (ISBN 0-8403-2157-0). Kendall Hunt.

Friedrich, Dick, jt. ed. see Harris, Angela.

Friedrich, Eduard G., Jr. Vulvar Disease. 2nd ed. (Major Problems in Obstetrics & Gynecology Ser.: Vol. 9). (Illus.). 272p. 1983. 60.00 (ISBN 0-7216-1096-X). Saunders.

Friedrich, Ehrhard, jt. auth. see Henschel, Horst.

Friedrich, Elizabeth. The Story of God's Love. 144p. (gr. 6-9). 1985. 9.95 (ISBN 0-570-04122-8). Concordia.

Friedrich, Elizabeth & Rowland, Cherry. The Parent's Guide to Raising Twins. 320p. 1984. 13.95 (ISBN 0-312-59661-8). St Martin.

Friedrich, Engels see Marx, Karl & Engels, Friedrich.

Friedrich, Georg W., jt. auth. see Hegel, Georg.

Friedrich, Gerhard. In Pursuit of Moby Dick. 1983. pap. 5.00x (ISBN 0-87574-098-7, 098). Pendle Hill.

Friedrich, Gerhard, jt. ed. see Kittel, Gerhard.

Friedrich, Gus, et al. Classroom Communication: Context, Roles & Process. (Interpersonal Communication Ser.). (Illus.). 1976. pap. text ed. 8.95 (ISBN 0-675-08644-2). Merrill.

Friedrich, Gustav W. Education in the Eighties: Speech Communications. 176p. 1981. 17.95 (ISBN 0-8106-3166-0); pap. 11.95 (ISBN 0-8106-3165-2). NEA.

Friedrich, H. Gibt Es eine Intensive Aktionsart Im Neuenglischen. pap. 7.00 (ISBN 0-384-16930-9). Johnson Repr.

Friedrich, Hermann. Marine Biology: An Introduction to Its Problems & Results. LC 71-93028. (Biology Ser). (Illus.). 486p. 1970. 20.00x (ISBN 0-295-95011-0). U of Wash Pr.

Friedrich, Johann. William Falconer's the Shipwreck. pap. 12.00 (ISBN 0-384-16940-6). Johnson Repr.

Friedrich, Johannes. Extinct Languages. Gaynor, Frank, tr. from Ger. LC 74-139132. (Illus.). 1971. Repr. of 1957 ed. lib. bdg. 24.75x (ISBN 0-8371-5748-X, FREL). Greenwood.

--Extinct Languages. 1983. pap. 5.95 (ISBN 0-8022-0546-1). Philos Lib.

Friedrich, K. Fracture Mechanical Behavior of Short Fiber Reinforced Thermoplastic. (Progress Report of the VDI-Z: No. 18). 114p. 1984. pap. 30.00 (ISBN 0-9907000-9-7, Pub. by VDI Verlag Gmbh Dusseldorf). Heyden.

--Microstructure & Fracture of Fiber Reinforced Thermoplastic Polyethylene Terephthalate. 1982. 32.00 (ISBN 0-9961075-0-9, Pub. by VDI W Germany). Heyden.

Friedrich, K., et al. Ultra High Strength Materials. Hornbogen, E., ed. (Progress Report of the VDI-Z Ser.: No. 82). 125p. 1984. pap. 38.00 (ISBN 3-18-148205-6, Pub. by VDI Verlag Gmbh Dusseldorf). Heyden.

Friedrich, K. H. Farm Management Data Collection & Analysis: An Electronic Data Processing, Storage & Retrieval System. (Agricultural Services Bulletins: No. 34). 163p. (Eng., Fr. & Span., 2nd Printing 1980). 1977. pap. 11.75 (ISBN 92-5-100464-1, F1366, FAO). Unipub.

Friedrich, Klaus. Friction & Wear of Polymer Composites. (Progress Report of the VDI-Z Series 18: No. 15). (Illus.). 102p. 1984. pap. 32.00 (ISBN 0-9907001-1-9, Pub. by VDI Verlag Gmbh Dusseldorf). Heyden.

Friedrich, Lawrence W., ed. Nature of Physical Knowledge. 1960. 9.95 (ISBN 0-87462-420-7). Marquette.

Friedrich, Lynette K. see Hetherington, E. Mavis.

Friedrich, M., jt. ed. see Riedler, W.

Friedrich, M. H. Adoleszentenpsychosen. (Bibliotheca Psychiatrica: No. 163). (Illus.). xii, 144p. 1983. pap. 29.50 (ISBN 3-8055-3640-2). S Karger.

Friedrich, Otto. Before the Deluge. 1973. pap. 1.95 (ISBN 0-380-01044-5, 15859). Avon.

Friedrich, Otto, jt. auth. see Friedrich, Priscilla.

Friedrich, P. Supramolecular Enzymes Organization: Quarternary Structure & Beyond. (Illus.). 294p. 1985. 36.00 (ISBN 0-08-026376-3). Pergamon.

Friedrich, Paul. Agrarian Revolt in a Mexican Village. LC 77-89627. (Illus.). 1978. pap. 6.50x (ISBN 0-226-26481-5, P832). U of Chicago Pr.

Fries, Peter H. Tagmeme Sequences in the English Noun Phrase. (Publications in Linguistics & Related Fields Ser.: No. 36). 247p. 1972. pap. 5.00x (ISBN 0-88312-038-0); microfiche 3.00x (ISBN 0-88312-438-6). Summer Inst Ling.
Fries, Robert F., jt. auth. see Hughes, Paul L.
Fries, Sylvia D. Urban Idea in Colonial America. LC 77-81333. (Illus.). 236p. 1977. 29.95 (ISBN 0-87722-103-0). Temple U Pr.
Fries, U. E. From Copenhagen to Okanogan: The Autobiography of a Pioneer. 3rd ed. LC 72-89784. (Illus.). 441p. 1984. Repr. of 1949 ed. 18.95 (ISBN 0-8323-0208-2). Binford.
Fries, Yvonne & Bibin, T. The Undesirables: The Expatriation of the Tamil People of Recent Indian Origin from the Plantations in Sri Lanka. 1985. 18.50x (ISBN 0-8364-1344-X, Pub. by KP Bagchi India). South Asia Bks.
Friese, Hans. Thidrekssaga und Dietrichsepos. 27.00 (ISBN 0-384-16981-3); pap. 22.00 (ISBN 0-384-16980-5). Johnson Repr.
Friese, Ralf, tr. see Kiefer, H. & Maushart, R.
Friese, U. Erich. Aquarium Fish. (Illus.). 96p. 1980. 4.95 (ISBN 0-87666-512-1, KW-026). TFH Pubns.
--Marine Invertebrates in the Home Aquarium. (Illus.). 240p. (Orig.). 1973. 14.95 (ISBN 0-87666-793-0, PS-658). TFH Pubns.
Friese, U. Erich, tr. see Af Enehjelm, Curt.
Friese, U. Erich, tr. see Enehjelm, Curt A.
Friese, U. Erich, tr. see Nicolai, Jurgen.
Friese, U. Erich, tr. see Radtke, Georg A.
Friesel, Evyatar, ed. see Simon, Julius.
Friesel, Uwe. Tim, the Peacemaker. LC 72-145822. (Illus.). 32p. (ps-3). 8.95 (ISBN 0-87592-052-7). Scroll Pr.
Friesem, Ricky & Moushine, Naomi. Fruits of the Earth. LC 85-13488. (Illus.). 108p. 1985. pap. 8.95 (ISBN 0-915361-26-4). Adama Pubs Inc.
Friesema, H. Paul, jt. auth. see Culhane, Paul J.
Friesema, Harry P. Metropolitan Political Structure: Intergovernmental Relations & Political Integration in the Quad Cities. LC 73-147925. (Illus.). 1971. 12.00 (ISBN 0-87745-020-X). U of Iowa Pr.
Friesen, Delores. Living More with Less Study-Action Guide. 112p. (Orig.). 1981. pap. 5.95 (ISBN 0-8361-1968-1). Herald Pr.
Friesen, Duane. Moral Issues in the Control of Birth. new ed. LC 74-76587. (Illus.). 64p. 1974. pap. 1.95 (ISBN 0-87303-561-5). Faith & Life.
Friesen, Garry & Maxson, J. Robin. Decision Making & the Will of God. LC 80-24592. (Critical Concern Bks.). 1981. 12.95 (ISBN 0-930014-47-2). Multnomah.
--Decision Making & the Will of God: A Biblical Alternative to the Traditional View. LC 80-24592. (Critical Concern Ser.). 252p. 1983. pap. 8.95 (ISBN 0-88070-024-6); study guide 2.95 (ISBN 0-88070-021-1). Multnomah.
Friesen, Gerald. The Canadian Prairies: A History. LC 84-52446. (Illus.). xvi, 560p. 1985. 22.50x (ISBN 0-8032-1972-5). U of Nebr Pr.
Friesen, Gerhard K. The German Contribution to the Building of the Americas: Studies in Honor of Karl J. R. Arndt. Schatzberg, Walter, ed. LC 76-50679. pap. 106.50 (ISBN 0-317-28420-7, 2022326). Bks Demand UMI.
--The German Panoramic Novel of the Nineteenth Century. (Germanic Studies in America: Vol. 8). 232p. 1972. 33.95 (ISBN 3-261-00314-6). P Lang Pubs.
Friesen, Gerhard K. & Schatzberg, Walter, eds. The German Contribution to the Building of the Americas: Studies in Honor of Karl J. R. Arndt. LC 76-50679. 1977. 20.00x (ISBN 0-87451-133-X). Clark U Pr.
Friesen, Ivan & Frieson, Rachel. How Do You Decide? (Shalom Ser.: No. 6). 16p. pap. 0.50 (ISBN 0-8361-1975-4). Herald Pr.
Friesen, John W., ed. see Pacific Northwest Conference on Higher Education, 1978.
Friesen, John W., et al. The Teacher's Voice: A Study of Teacher Participation in Educational Decision-Making in Three Alberta Communities. LC 83-12502. (Illus.). 148p. 1983. lib. bdg. 20.00 (ISBN 0-8191-3417-1); pap. text ed. 8.75 (ISBN 0-8191-3418-X). U Pr of Amer.
Friesen, Peter H., jt. auth. see Miller, Danny.
Friesen, W., jt. auth. see Ekman, P.
Friesen, Wallace v., jt. auth. see Ekman, Paul.
Frieser, Hellmut. Photographic Information Recording. LC 75-20097. 592p. 1975. 106.95 (ISBN 0-470-28117-0). Halsted Pr.
Frieser, R. G. & Mogab, C. J., eds. Plasma Processing: Symposium on Plasma Etchins & Deposition, Proceedings. LC 81-65237. (Electrochemical Society Proceedings Ser.: Vol. 81-1). (Illus.). pap. 87.00 (ISBN 0-317-09584-6, 2051749). Bks Demand UMI.
Friesner, Arlyne. Maternity Nursing. 3rd ed. Raff, Beverly, ed. LC 77-80106. (Nursing Outline Ser.). 1982. pap. 14.50 (ISBN 0-87488-377-6). Med Exam.
Friesner, Arlyne, jt. auth. see Yura, Helen.
Friesner, Esther M. Mustapha & His Wise Dog. (Twelve Kingdoms Ser.: No. 1). 160p. 1985. pap. 2.95 (ISBN 0-380-89676-1). Avon.
Frieson, Rachel, jt. auth. see Friesen, Ivan.
Friess, Horace. Felix Adler & Ethical Culture: Memories & Studies. (Illus.). 320p. 1981. 26.00x (ISBN 0-231-05184-0). Columbia U Pr.
Friess, Horace L. & Schneider, Herbert W. Religion in Various Cultures. (Illus.). Repr. of 1932 ed. 24.00 (ISBN 0-384-16990-2). Johnson Repr.
Friess, Horace L., tr. see Schleiermacher, Friedrich E.
Friesth, E. Richard. Metrication in Manufacturing. LC 77-21838. (Illus.). 373p. 1978. 26.95 (ISBN 0-8311-1120-8). Indus Pr.
Frietzsche, Arthur H. The Monstrous Clever Young Man: The Novelist Disraeli & His Heroes. 60p. (Orig.). 1959. pap. 3.50 (ISBN 0-87421-022-4). Utah St U Pr.
--The Monstrous Clever Young Man: The Novelist Disraeli & His Heroes. 60p. 1982. Repr. of 1959 ed. lib. bdg. 10.00 (ISBN 0-8495-1735-4). Arden Lib.
Frieze, Irene H., et al. New Approaches to Social Problems: Applications of Attribution Theory. LC 79-88767. (Social & Behavioral Science Ser.). 1979. text ed. 32.95x (ISBN 0-87589-430-5). Jossey-Bass.
--Women & Sex Roles: Social Psychological Perspective. (Illus.). 1978. 16.95 (ISBN 0-393-01163-1); pap. 13.95x (ISBN 0-393-09063-9); instr's manual free (ISBN 0-393-95168-5). Norton.
Frieze, P. A., et al, eds. Marine & Offshore Safety: Proceedings of an International Conference Held at Glasgow, U. K., Sept. 7-9, 1983. (Developments in Marine Technology Ser.: Vol. 1). 612p. 1984. 129.75 (ISBN 0-444-42383-4). Elsevier.
Frigate, James B. see Barr, James, pseud.
Frigerio, ed. Recent Developments in Mass Spectrometry in Biochemistry & Medicine, Vol. 2. LC 79-19982. 502p. 1979. 65.00 (ISBN 0-306-40294-7, Plenum Pr). Plenum Pub.
Frigerio, A. & Renoz, L. Recent Developments in Chromatography & Electrophoresis. (Analytical Chemistry Symposia Ser.: Vol. 1). 358p. (Proceedings). 1979. 76.75 (ISBN 0-444-41785-0). Elsevier.
Frigerio, A., ed. Chromatography & Mass Spectrometry in Biomedical Sciences, No. 2. (Analytical Chemistry Symposia Ser.: Vol. 14). 506p. 1983. 106.50 (ISBN 0-444-42154-8). Elsevier.
--Chromatography in Biochemistry, Medicine & Environmental Research, No. 1. (Analytical Chemistry Symposia Ser.: Vol. 13). 278p. 1983. 72.50 (ISBN 0-444-42016-9, I-056-83). Elsevier.
--Recent Developments in Mass Spectrometry in Biochemistry, Medicine & Environmental Research. (Analytical Chemistry Symposia Ser.: Vol. 7). 1981. 76.75 (ISBN 0-444-42029-0). Elsevier.
--Recent Developments in Mass Spectrometry in Biochemistry, Medicine & Environmental Research: Proc. of the 8th International Symposium, Venice, June 18-19, 1983. (Analytical Chemistry Symposia Ser.: Vol. 12). 346p. 1983. 81.00 (ISBN 0-444-42055-X). Elsevier.
Frigerio, A. & Castagnoli, N., Jr., eds. Mass Spectrometry in Biochemistry & Medicine. LC 73-91164. (Monographs of the Mario Negri Institute for Pharmacological Research). 379p. 1974. 69.50 (ISBN 0-911216-53-7). Raven.
Frigerio, A. & McCamisch, M., eds. Recent Developments in Chromatography & Electrophoresis. (Analytical Chemistry Symposia Ser.: Vol. 3). 342p. 1980. 72.50 (ISBN 0-444-41871-7). Elsevier.
Frigerio, A. & McCamish, M., eds. Recent Developments in Mass Spectrometry in Biochemistry & Medicine, Vol. 6. (Analytical Chemistry Symposia Ser.: Vol. 4). 554p. 1981. 85.00 (ISBN 0-444-41870-9). Elsevier.
Frigerio, A. & Milon, H., eds. Chromatography & Mass Spectrometry in Nutrition Science & Food Safety: Proceedings of the International Symposium in Chromatography & Mass Spectrometry in Nutrition Science & Food Safety, Montreux, June 19-22, 1983. (Analytical Chemistry Symposium Ser.: No. 21). 306p. 1985. 109.25 (ISBN 0-444-42339-7, I-315-84). Elsevier.
Frigerio, A., jt. ed. see Accardi, L.
Frigerio, Alberto, ed. Recent Developments in Mass Spectrometry in Biochemistry & Medicine, Vol. 1. LC 78-1514. 670p. 1978. 89.50x (ISBN 0-306-31138-0, Plenum Pr). Plenum Pub.
Frigerio, Alberto & Ghisalberti, Emilio L., eds. Mass Spectrometry in Drug Metabolism. LC 76-53013. 544p. 1977. 65.00x (ISBN 0-306-31018-X, Plenum Pr). Plenum Pub.
Friggens, Myriam. Tales, Trails & Tommyknockers: Stories from Colorado's Past. LC 79-84876. 1979. pap. 6.95 (ISBN 0-933472-01-3). Johnson Bks.
Friggens, Paul. Gold & Grass: The Black Hills Story. LC 83-2855. (Illus.). 1983. 24.95 (ISBN 0-87108-648-4). Pruett.
Frigone, Al. School Survival Junior-Senior High: You're It-It's Up to You. McFadden, S. Michele, ed. (Illus.). 31p. (Orig.). (gr. 7-12). 1981. pap. text ed. 1.25 (ISBN 0-89262-052-8); 30 copy pack 37.50 (ISBN 0-686-78760-9). Career Pub.
Frigone, Albert. Growing Pains. McFadden, S. Michele, ed. (Illus.). (gr. 4-10). 1977. pap. text ed. 37.50 30 copy pack 1.25 ea. (ISBN 0-89262-014-5); tchrs' guide 1.25 (ISBN 0-89262-051-X). Career Pub.
Frigrjesi, T. Corticothalamic Projections & Sensorimotor Activities. 1972. 36.50 (ISBN 0-7204-7029-3). Elsevier.
Frigstad, David B. & Bravard, Wyman N. Venture Capital Proposal Package. Ramey, Emmett, ed. (Successful Business Library Ser.). 180p. 1984. 3-ring binder 37.95 (ISBN 0-916378-45-4). PSI Res.
Friguglietti, James, tr. see De Bertier de Sauvigny, G. & Pinkney, David H.
Friguglietti, James see Lefebvre, Georges.
Frigyes, A. Control & Measurement. 222p. 1980. 20.00x (ISBN 0-569-08044-4, Pub. by Collet's). State Mutual Bk.
Frigyesi, T., et al, eds. Corticothalamic Projections & Sensorimotor Activities. LC 74-181303. (Illus.). 601p. 1972. 63.00 (ISBN 0-911216-35-9). Raven.
Frigyesi, T L. Subcortical Mechanisms & Sensorimotor Activities. 293p. 1975. 110.00 (ISBN 3-456-80118-1, Pub. by Holdan Bk Ltd UK). State Mutual Bk.
Frihagen, Arvid. Offshore Tender Bidding. 180p. 1984. pap. 22.00x (ISBN 0-317-01532-X). Universitet.
Friis, Anne. Katherine Mansfield: Life & Stories. LC 74-4423. 1946. lib. bdg. 27.50 (ISBN 0-8414-4181-2). Folcroft.
Friis, E. J. American-Scandinavian Foundation 1910-1960: A Brief History. 1961. 2.95x (ISBN 0-89067-036-6). Am Scandinavian.
Friis, Erik, jt. ed. see Bayerschmidt, Carl F.
Friis, Erik J., ed. Modern Nordic Plays: Denmark. (Library of Scandinavian Literature). 1974. lib. bdg. 29.50 (ISBN 0-8290-1400-4). Irvington.
--Modern Nordic Plays: Denmark. (Library of Scandinavian Literature). 1982. pap. text ed. 10.95x (ISBN 0-8290-1161-7). Irvington.
--Modern Nordic Plays: Finland. Binham, Philip, et al, trs. from Finnish. (Library of Scandinavian Literature). 1973. lib. bdg. 29.50 (ISBN 0-8290-1403-9). Irvington.
--Modern Nordic Plays: Finland. Binham, Philip, et al, trs. from Finnish. (Library of Scandinavian Literature). 1972. pap. text ed. 10.95x (ISBN 0-8290-1162-5). Irvington.
--Modern Nordic Plays: Iceland. Boucher, Alan, et al, trs. from Icelandic. (Library of Scandinavian Literature). 1973. lib. bdg. 29.50 (ISBN 0-8290-1401-2). Irvington.
--Modern Nordic Plays: Iceland. Boucher, Alan, et al, trs. from Icelandic. (Library of Scandinavian Literature). 1982. pap. text ed. 10.95x (ISBN 0-8290-1163-3). Irvington.
--Modern Nordic Plays: Norway. Shaw, Pat, et al, trs. from Norwegian. (Library of Scandinavian Literature). 1974. lib. bdg. 29.50 (ISBN 0-8290-1402-0). Irvington.
--Modern Nordic Plays: Norway. Shaw, Pat, et al, trs. from Norwegian. (Library of Scandinavian Literature). 1982. pap. text ed. 10.95x (ISBN 0-8290-1164-1). Irvington.
Friis, Erik J., jt. ed. see Bayerschmidt, Carl F.
Friis, Erik J., ed. see Johnson, Eyvind.
Friis, Erik J., tr. see Heinesen, William.
Friis, Erik J., et al see Allardt, Erik & Andre, Nils.
Friis, Erik J., et al, eds. Five Modern Scandinavian Plays. Chorell, Walentin. Kundesen, Barbara & Morduch, Tina, trs. from Danish. LC 70-126439. (Library of Scandianvian Literature Ser.). 1971. lib. bdg. 18.25x (ISBN 0-8057-3312-4). Irvington.
--Modern Nordic Plays: Sweden. Carlson, Harry G. & Austin, Paul B., trs. from Swedish. (Library of Scandinavian Literature). 1973. Repr. lib. bdg. 29.50 (ISBN 0-8290-1404-7). Irvington.
--Modern Nordic Plays: Sweden. Carlson, Harry G. & Austin, Paul B., trs. from Swedish. (Library of Scandinavian Literature). 1982. pap. text ed. 10.95x (ISBN 0-8290-1165-X). Irvington.
Friis, Henning K., ed. Scandinavia: Between East & West. LC 78-21137. 1979. Repr. of 1950 ed. lib. bdg. 27.50x (ISBN 0-313-20864-6, FRSB). Greenwood.
Friis, Herman, ed. see Porter, Russell W.
Friis, Herman R., ed. The Pacific Basin: A History of Its Geographical Exploration. (Special Publications: No. 38). (Illus.). 457p. 1967. 10.00 (ISBN 0-318-12732-6). Am Geographical.
Friis, Leo J. Campo Aleman: The First Ten Years of Anaheim. LC 83-80593. (Illus.). 176p. 1983. 10.00 (ISBN 0-943480-55-8). Friis-Pioneer Pr.
Friis, Robert. Social Factors & Intelligence: A Bibliography, Vol. I. rev. ed. 27p. 1981. pap. 8.95 (ISBN 0-939552-00-0, 005). Human Behavior.
--Stress & Mental Health: A Bibliography, Vol. I. rev. ed. 33p. 1981. pap. 8.95 (ISBN 0-939552-02-7, 003). Human Behavior.
--Stress & Physical Health: A Bibliography, Vol. II. (Orig.). 1981. pap. 8.95 (ISBN 0-939552-04-3). Human Behavior.
--Stress & Physical Health: A Bibliography, Vol. I. rev. ed. 37p. 1981. pap. 8.95 (ISBN 0-939552-01-9, 001). Human Behavior.
--Stress & Physical Health: A Bibliography, Vol. III. 34p. (Orig.). 1984. pap. 8.95 (ISBN 0-939552-08-6). Human Behavior.
Friis, Robert, jt. auth. see Armstrong, Gail.
Friis, Robert, jt. auth. see Taff, Gail A.
Friis, Robert, ed. Stress & Substance Abuse, Vol. I. rev. ed. 34p. 1981. pap. 8.95 (ISBN 0-939552-03-5, 004). Human Behavior.
Friis-Hansen, Bent, jt. ed. see Stern, Leo.
Frijda, Nico H., ed. Otto Selz: His Contribution to Psychology. Groot, Adriaan de. (Illus.). 306p. 1981. 30.00x (ISBN 90-279-3438-X). Mouton.
Frijlinck, Wilhemina P., ed. The First Part of the Reign of King Richard the Second, or Thomas of Woodstock. LC 82-45796. (Malone Society Reprint Ser.: No. 66). Repr. of 1929 ed. 40.00 (ISBN 0-404-63066-9). AMS Pr.
Frijling-Schreuder, E. C. Children, What Are They? Understanding Child Development. Stechmann, Katherine, tr. from Dutch. LC 74-19889. 154p. 1975. text ed. 17.50 (ISBN 0-8236-0830-1); pap. text ed. 9.95 (ISBN 0-8236-8020-7, 20830). Intl Univs Pr.
Frik, W. & Goering, Ulrich. Roentgenologic Anatomy. 1980. 15.50 (ISBN 0-8151-3292-1). Year Bk Med.
Friker, Walter, jt. auth. see Many, Wesley.
Friman, Alice. Reporting from Corinth. LC 83-173208. 88p. (Orig.). 1984. pap. 6.95 (ISBN 0-935306-24-2). Barnwood Pr.
Frimann-Dahl, J. Roentgen Examinations in Acute Abdominal Diseases. 3rd ed. (Illus.). 632p. 1974. 49.50x (ISBN 0-398-02939-3). C C Thomas.
Frimer, Aryeh A., ed. Singlet Zero-Two, 4 Vols. 1985. Set. 395.00 (ISBN 0-8493-6439-6). Vol. I & II, 544 pp. Vol. III & IV, 496 pp. CRC Pr.
Frimmer, Steven. Neverland: Fabled Places & Fabulous Voyages of History & Legend. (Illus.). (gr. 7 up). 1976. 12.50 (ISBN 0-670-50625-7). Viking.
Frimmer, Susan B., jt. auth. see Savishinsky, Joel S.
Frindall, Bill & Isaacs, Victor, eds. The Wisden Book of One-Day International Cricket 1971-1985. 368p. 1985. 32.00 (ISBN 0-947766-03-0, Pub. by Gollancz England). David & Charles.
Frings, Hubert & Frings, Mable. Animal Communication. 2nd ed. LC 76-50562. 1977. pap. 6.95x (ISBN 0-8061-1393-6). U of Okla Pr.
Frings, J. W. The Occult Arts. 236p. 1981. pap. 11.00 (ISBN 0-89540-108-8, SB-108). Sun Pub.
Frings, Mable, jt. auth. see Frings, Hubert.
Frings, Manfred S., tr. see Scheler, Max.
Frings, Virginia S. Fashion: From Concept to Consumer. (Illus.). 320p. 1982. 27.95 (ISBN 0-13-306605-3). P-H.
Frink, Henry A. The New Century Speaker: For School & College. facsimile ed. LC 79-37013. (Granger Index Reprint Ser.). Repr. of 1898 ed. 21.00 (ISBN 0-8369-6312-1). Ayer Co Pubs.
Frink, Maurice. Cow Country Cavalcade: Eighty Years of the Wyoming Stock Growers Association. 243p. 1954. 7.50 (ISBN 0-912094-00-1). Old West.
--Fort Defiance & the Navajos. (Illus.). 150p. (Orig.). 1968. pap. 5.95 (ISBN 0-87108-585-2). Pruett.
Frinta, Mojmir. Genius of Robert Campin. (Studies in Art: No. 1). 1966. text ed. 26.00x (ISBN 0-686-22434-5). Mouton.
Fripiat, J., ed. Advanced Techniques for Clay Mineral Analysis. (Developments in Sedimentology Ser.: Vol. 34). 236p. 1982. 42.75 (ISBN 0-444-42002-9). Elsevier.
Fripiat, J. J., jt. ed. see Van Olphen, H.
Fripp, Edgar. Master Richard Quyny, Baliff of Stratford-Upon-Avon & Friend of William Shakespeare. 1973. Repr. of 1924 ed. 10.45 (ISBN 0-8274-0535-9). R West.
Fripp, Edgar I. Master Richard Quyny, Bailiff of Stratford-Upon-Avon & Friend of William Shakespeare. LC 74-153320. Repr. of 1924 ed. 19.00 (ISBN 0-404-02621-4). AMS Pr.
--Shakespeare Studies: Biographical & Literary. LC 72-168062. Repr. of 1930 ed. 19.00 (ISBN 0-404-07882-6). AMS Pr.
--Shakespeare's Haunts Near Stratford. LC 71-153322. Repr. of 1929 ed. 14.00 (ISBN 0-404-02622-2). AMS Pr.
--Shakespeare's Haunts Near Stratford. 1972. Repr. of 1929 ed. lib. bdg. 15.00 (ISBN 0-8414-4285-1). Folcroft.
--Shakespeare's Stratford. LC 78-153321. Repr. of 1928 ed. 12.50 (ISBN 0-404-02623-0). AMS Pr.
--Shakespeare's Stratford. facs. ed. LC 70-128886. (Select Bibliographies Reprint Ser). 1928. 18.00 (ISBN 0-8369-5506-4). Ayer Co Pubs.
Friquegnon, Marie-Louise, jt. auth. see Abelson, Raziel.
Friquegnon, Marie-Louise, jt. ed. see Abelson, Raziel.
Frisa, Heinrich. Deutsche Kulturverhaeltnisse in der Auffassung W. M. Thackerays. pap. 12.00 (ISBN 0-384-17000-5). Johnson Repr.
Frisancho, A. Roberto. Human Adaptation: A Functional Interpretation. 1981. pap. text ed. 9.95x (ISBN 0-472-08019-9). U of Mich Pr.
Frisbee, Charlotte. Music & Dance Research of the Southwestern Indians. LC 74-74663. (Detroit Studies in Music Bibliography Ser.: No. 36). 1977. 9.75 (ISBN 0-911772-86-3). Info Coord.
Frisbee, Lucy P. John F. Kennedy: America's Youngest President. LC 82-451. (Childhood of Famous Americans Ser.). (gr. 3-8). 1983. pap. 3.95 (ISBN 0-672-52737-5). Bobbs.
Frisbee-Houde, Cornelia H. Not Just Another Pretty Dress: Two Centuries of Clothing & Textiles from Cherry Hill. LC 82-81738. (Illus.). 32p. (Orig.). 1983. pap. 5.00 (ISBN 0-943366-05-4). Hist Cherry Hill.
Frisbie, Charlotte J., ed. Southwestern Indian Ritual Drama. LC 79-2308. (School of American Research Advanced Seminar Ser.). (Illus.). 384p. 1980. 30.00x (ISBN 0-8263-0521-0). U of NM Pr.

Frisbie, Charlotte J. & McAllester, David P., eds. Navajo Blessingway Singer: The Autobiography of Frank Mitchell, 1881-1967. LC 77-75661. 446p. 1978. pap. text ed. 14.95 (ISBN 0-8165-0568-3). U of Ariz Pr.

Frisbie, David A., jt. auth. see Ebel, Robert L.

Frisbie, Louise K. Florida's Fabled Inns. LC 78-56754. (Illus.). 1980. 12.95 (ISBN 0-9602960-0-X). Imperial Pub Co.

--Peace River Pioneers. LC 74-81530. (Illus.). 1974. 7.95 (ISBN 0-912458-47-X, Pub. by E A Seemann). Imperial Pub Co.

--Yesterday's Polk County. LC 75-44454. (Illus.). 1976. 7.95 (ISBN 0-912458-64-X, Pub-by E A Seemann). Imperial Pub Co.

Frisbie, R. E., ed. Guidelines for Integrated Control of Cotton Pests. (Plant Production and Protection Paper: No. 48). 187p. (Orig.). 1984. pap. 14.50 (ISBN 92-5-101430-2, F2578, FAO). Unipub.

Frisbie, W. Parker, jt. ed. see Bean, Frank D.

Frisby, D. & Sayer, D. Society. 128p. 1985. 13.95 (ISBN 0-85312-834-0, 9708, Pub. by Tavistock England); pap. 6.50 (ISBN 0-85312-852-9, 9703). Methuen Inc.

Frisby, David. The Alienated Mind. 270p. 1983. text ed. 30.45x (ISBN 0-391-02822-7, Pub. by Heinemann Ed Bks England). Humanities.

--Georg Simmel. 120p. 1984. 11.95 (ISBN 0-85312-616-X, NO. 4159); pap. 4.95 (ISBN 0-85312-617-8, NO. 4160). Methuen Inc.

--Sociological Impressionism: A Reassessment of Georg Simmel's Social Theory. xi, 210p. 1981. text ed. 45.00x (ISBN 0-435-82320-5). Gower Pub Co.

Frisby, David, tr. see Simmel, Georg.

Frisby, John. Seeing: Illusion, Brain & Mind. (Illus.). 1980. 22.50 (ISBN 0-19-217672-2). Oxford U Pr.

Frisch. Canaries. (Pet Care Ser.). 1983. pap. 3.95 (ISBN 0-8120-2614-4). Barron.

Frisch, B., jt. auth. see Bartl, R.

Frisch, Bertha & Bartl, R., eds. Bone Marrow Biopsies Updated. (Bibliotheca Haematologica Ser.: No. 50). (Illus.). viii, 132p. 1984. 41.75 (ISBN 3-8055-3863-4). S Karger.

Frisch, D. H. Arms Reduction: Program & Issues. LC 61-11253. (Twentieth Century Fund Ser.). pap. 10.00 (ISBN 0-527-02817-7). Kraus Repr.

Frisch, Ephraim. Historical Survey of Jewish Philanthropy from the Earliest Times to the Nineteenth Century. LC 79-79197. 196p. Repr. of 1924 ed. 22.50 (ISBN 0-8154-0296-1). Cooper Sq.

Frisch, H., ed. Inflation in Small Countries. (Lectures Notes in Economics & Mathematical Systems: Vol. 119). 1976. pap. 20.00 (ISBN 0-387-07624-7). Springer-Verlag.

Frisch, Harry L. & Salsburg, Z. W. Simple Dense Fluids. LC 67-23159. 1968. 81.00 (ISBN 0-12-268650-0). Acad Pr.

Frisch, Hartvig. The Constitution of the Athenians: A Philological-Historical Analysis of Pseudo-Xenofon's Treatise De Re Publica Atheniensium. facsimile ed. LC 75-13267. (History of Ideas in Ancient Greece Ser.). 1976. Repr. of 1942 ed. 20.00x (ISBN 0-405-07308-9). Ayer Co Pubs.

--Might & Right in Antiquity. "Dike" I: From Homer to the Persian Wars. facsimile ed. Martindale, C. C., tr. LC 75-13268. (History of Ideas in Ancient Greece Ser.). (Illus.). 1976. Repr. of 1949 ed. 21.00x (ISBN 0-405-07309-7). Ayer Co Pubs.

Frisch, Helmut. Schumpeterian Economics. 208p. 1983. 31.95 (ISBN 0-03-062766-4). Praeger.

--Theories of Inflation. LC 83-1871. (Cambridge Surveys of Economic Literature). 256p. 1984. 39.50 (ISBN 0-521-22470-5); pap. 13.95 (ISBN 0-521-29512-2). Cambridge U Pr.

Frisch, Hillel, jt. auth. see Sandler, Shmuel.

Frisch, Joseph C. Extension & Comprehension in Logic. LC 69-14355. 1969. 10.00 (ISBN 0-8022-2269-2). Philos Lib.

Frisch, K. C., jt. auth. see Saunders, J. H.

Frisch, K. C. & Reegen, S. L., eds. Advances in Urethane Science & Technology, Vol. 1. LC 75-150348. 209p. 1971. pap. 20.00 (ISBN 0-87762-062-8). Technomic.

--Advances in Urethane Science & Technology, Vol. 2. LC 75-150348. 268p. 1973. pap. 20.00 (ISBN 0-87762-108-X). Technomic.

--Ring-Opening Polymerization. (Kinetics & Mechanisms of Polymerization Ser: Vol. 2). 1969. 95.00 (ISBN 0-8247-1217-X). Dekker.

Frisch, K. C. & Saunders, J. H., eds. Plastic Foams, Pt.2. (Monographs on Plastics: Vol. 1). 592p. 1973. 115.00 (ISBN 0-8247-1219-6). Dekker.

Frisch, K. C., jt. ed. see Ashida, K.

Frisch, K. C., jt. ed. see Klemper, D.

Frisch, K. C., jt. ed. see Klempner, D.

Frisch, Karl Von see Von Frisch, Karl.

Frisch,.Kurt, et al, eds. Advances in Urethane Science & Technology, Vol. 8. 275p. 1981. pap. 40.00 (ISBN 0-87762-306-6). Technomic.

Frisch, Kurt C. & Reegen, S. L. Advances in Urethane Science & Technology, Vol. 5. LC 75-150348. (Illus.). 1976. pap. 30.00 (ISBN 0-87762-238-8). Technomic.

--Advances in Urethane Science & Technology, Vol. 6. LC 75-150348. (Illus.). 1978. pap. 25.00x (ISBN 0-87762-240-X). Technomic.

Frisch, Kurt C. & Klempner, Daniel, eds. Advances in Urethane Science & Technology, Vol. 9. LC 75-150348. 191p. 1984. pap. 38.50 (ISBN 0-87762-350-3). Technomic.

Frisch, Kurt C. & Reegan, S. L., eds. Advances in Urethane Science & Technology, Vol. 3. LC 75-150348. (Illus.). 200p. 1974. pap. 25.00 (ISBN 0-87762-156-X). Technomic.

Frisch, Kurt C. & Reegen, S. L., eds. Advances in Urethane Science & Technology, Vol. 4. LC 75-150348. (Illus.). 200p. 1975. pap. 30.00 (ISBN 0-87762-184-5). Technomic.

Frisch, Kurt C. & Saunders, J. H., eds. Plastic Foams, Pt.1. LC 71-157837. (Monographs on Plastics). Repr. of 1972 ed. 116.00 (ISBN 0-8357-9092-4, 2055059). Bks Demand UMI.

Frisch, Kurt C., jt. ed. see Klempner, Daniel.

Frisch, Kurt C., et al. International Progress in Urethanes, Vol. 4. LC 77-71704. 160p. 1985. pap. 35.00 (ISBN 0-87762-380-5). Technomic.

--Polyelectrolytes. LC 76-177446. (Illus.). 1976. 14.95x (ISBN 0-87762-076-8). Technomic.

Frisch, Kurt C., et al, eds. International Progress in Urethanes, Vol. 2. LC 77-71704. 173p. 1980. pap. 35.00 (ISBN 0-87762-287-6). Technomic.

--International Progress in Urethanes, Vol. 1. LC 77-71704. (Illus.). 291p. 1977. pap. 25.00x (ISBN 0-87762-216-7). Technomic.

Frisch, Max. Biedermann und Die Brandstifter. Ackermann, Paul K., ed. (gr. 10-12). 1963. pap. text ed. 11.95 (ISBN 0-395-04090-6). HM.

--Bluebeard. Skelton, Geoffrey, tr. LC 82-21250. 96p. 1983. 10.95 (ISBN 0-15-113200-3). HarBraceJ.

--Bluebeard. Skelton, Geoffrey, tr. (A Helen & Kurt Wolff Bk.). 144p. 1984. pap. 4.95 (ISBN 0-15-613198-6, Harv). HarBraceJ.

--The Firebugs. rev. ed. Bullock, Michael, tr. (A Mermaid Drama Bk.). 1985. pap. 6.95 (ISBN 0-8090-1248-0). Hill & Wang.

--Gantenbein. Bullock, Michael, tr. LC 82-48033. Orig. Title: Wilderness of Mirrors. 304p. 1982. Repr. of 1965 ed. 7.95 (ISBN 0-15-634407-6, Harv). HarBraceJ.

--Homo Faber. Bullock, Michael, tr. from Ger. LC 60-5123. 1971. pap. 4.95 (ISBN 0-15-642135-6, Harv). HarBraceJ.

--Homo Faber. Ackermann, Paul K., ed. LC 72-9379. 300p. (Orig.). 1973. pap. text ed. 13.50 (ISBN 0-395-14402-7). HM.

--I'm Not Stiller. 1958. pap. 3.95 (ISBN 0-394-70219-0, V-219, Vin). Random.

--Man in the Holocene. Skelton, Geoffrey, tr. LC 79-3351. (Helen & Kurt Wolff Bk.). (Illus.). 1981. pap. 4.95 (ISBN 0-15-656952-3, Harv). HarBraceJ.

--Man in the Holocene. Skelton, Geoffrey, tr. LC 79-3351. (A Helen & Kurt Wolff Bk.). (Illus.). 120p. 1980. 9.95 (ISBN 0-15-156931-2). HarBraceJ.

--Sketchbook, Nineteen Forty-Six to Nineteen Forty-Nine. Skelton, Geoffrey, tr. (A Helen & Kurt Wolff Bk.). 320p. pap. 8.95 (ISBN 0-15-682746-8, Harv). HarBraceJ.

--Sketchbook, Nineteen Forty-Six to Nineteen Forty-Nine. 1984. 16.75 (ISBN 0-8446-6084-1). Peter Smith.

--Sketchbook, Nineteen Sixty-Six to Nineteen Seventy-One. Skelton, Geoffrey, tr. (A Helen & Kurt Wolff Bk.). 343p. pap. 8.95 (ISBN 0-15-682747-6, Harv). HarBraceJ.

--Sketchbook, Nineteen Sixty-Six to Nineteen Seventy-One. 1984. 16.75 (ISBN 0-8446-6085-X). Peter Smith.

--Triptych. Skelton, Geoffrey, tr. LC 80-8747. (A Helen & Kurt Wolff Bk.). 128p. 1981. 7.95 (ISBN 0-15-191157-6). HarBraceJ.

Frisch, Michael H. Town into City: Springfield, Massachusetts & the Meaning of Community, 1840-1880. LC 72-178075. (Studies in Urban History). (Illus.). 464p. 1972. 20.00x (ISBN 0-674-89820-6); pap. 6.95x (ISBN 0-674-89826-5). Harvard U Pr.

Frisch, Michael H. & Walkowitz, Daniel J., eds. Working-Class America: Essays on Labor, Community, & American Society. LC 81-23971. (Working Class in American History Ser.). 336p. 1983. pap. 8.95x (ISBN 0-252-00954-1). U of Ill Pr.

Frisch, Morton J. & Stevens, Richard G., eds. American Political Thought: The Philosophic Dimension of American Statesmanship. 2nd ed. LC 83-61556. 361p. 1983. pap. text ed. 13.95 (ISBN 0-87581-293-7). Peacock Pubs.

--The Political Thought of American Statesmen: Selected Writings & Speeches. LC 72-89723. 374p. 1973. pap. text ed. 13.95 (ISBN 0-87581-142-6). Peacock Pubs.

Frisch, Nathan. Your Income Tax Organizer. 1976. pap. 4.95 (ISBN 0-517-52748-0). Crown.

Frisch, O. R., ed. Progress in Nuclear Physics, Vols. 2 & 5-9. Vol. 2. 1952. 89.00 (ISBN 0-08-013329-0); Vol. 5. 1956. 89.00 (ISBN 0-08-009043-5); Vol. 7. 1959. 89.00 (ISBN 0-08-009186-5); Vol. 8. 1960. 89.00 (ISBN 0-08-009479-1); Vol. 9. 1963. 89.00 (ISBN 0-08-010063-5). Pergamon.

Frisch, Otto R. What Little I Remember. LC 78-18096. (Illus.). 227p. 1980. pap. 13.95 (ISBN 0-521-28010-9). Cambridge U Pr.

Frisch, R. Maxima & Minima: Theory & Economic Applications. 176p. 1966. lib. bdg. 24.00 (ISBN 90-277-0093-1, Pub. by Reidel Holland). Kluwer Academic.

Frisch, Ragnar. New Methods of Measuring Marginal Utility. LC 78-15136. (Illus.). 1978. Repr. of 1932 ed. lib. bdg. 17.50x (ISBN 0-87991-863-2). Porcupine Pr.

Frisch, Robert A. ESOP for the Eighties: The Fabulous New Instrument of Corporate Finance Comes of Age. LC 81-167. 1982. 24.95 (ISBN 0-87863-003-1). Farnswth Pub.

Frisch, Shelley L., ed. see Mann, Klaus.

Frisch, Ulla. Pictures to Play with. LC 77-76468. (Illus.). (gr. 2-7). 1977. 6.95 (ISBN 0-8008-6293-7). Taplinger.

Frisch, Vern A. & Handal, Joan S. Applied Office Typewriting. 4th ed. (Illus.). (gr. 11-12). 1977. text ed. 10.32 (ISBN 0-07-022504-4). McGraw.

Frisch, Walter. Brahms & the Principle of Developing Variation. LC 82-13675. (California Studies in 19th Century Music: Vol. 2). 230p. 1984. text ed. 27.00x (ISBN 0-520-04700-1). U of Cal Pr.

Frischauer, A. S. Altspanischer Kirchenbau. (Studien zur spaetantiken Kunstgeschichte, Vol. 3). (Illus.). x, 100p. 1978. Repr. of 1930 ed. 58.80x (ISBN 3-11-005703-4). De Gruyter.

Frischauer, Paul. Beaumarchais. LC 70-113310. 1970. Repr. of 1935 ed. 21.50x (ISBN 0-8046-0993-4, Pub.by Kennikat). Assoc Faculty Pr.

Frischer, Bernard. The Sculpted Word: Epicureanism & Philosophical Recruitment in Ancient Greece. LC 81-13143. (Illus.). 340p. 1982. 32.00x (ISBN 0-520-04190-9). U of Cal Pr.

Frischer, Patricia, jt. auth. see Adams, James.

Frischknecht, F. C., jt. auth. see Keller, G. V.

Frischwasser-Ra' Anan, H. F. The Frontiers of a Nation. LC 75-6433. (The Rise of Jewish Nationalism & the Middle East Ser). 168p. 1976. Repr. of 1955 ed. 18.15 (ISBN 0-88355-320-1). Hyperion Conn.

Frisell, Wilhelm R. Human Biochemistry. (Illus.). 845p. 1982. text ed. write for info. (ISBN 0-02-339820-5). Macmillan.

Frish, S. Problems of Wave Optics. 69p. 1976. pap. 1.95 (ISBN 0-8285-0831-3, Pub. by Mir Pubs USSR). Imported Pubns.

Frishberg, Nancy J. Interpreting: An Introduction. (Illus.). 250p. (Orig.). 1985. pap. 19.95 (ISBN 0-916883-01-9). RID Pubns.

Frishkoff, Patricia A., jt. auth. see Gibson, Charles H.

Frishkoff, Paul. Financial Reporting & Changing Prices: A Review of Empirical Research. LC 82-71092. (The Financial Accounting Standards Board Research Report). 57p. (Orig.). 1982. pap. 8.00 (ISBN 0-910065-14-4). Finan Acct.

--Reporting of Summary Indicators: An Investigation of Research & Practice. LC 81-70208. (The Financial Accounting Standards Board Research Report). 74p. (Orig.). 1981. pap. 6.00 (ISBN 0-910065-13-6). Finan Acct.

Frishman, Austin M. Preparation for Pesticide Certification Examinations: Questions & Answers for Commercial Pesticide Applicators. LC 79-18406. 176p. (Orig.). 1980. pap. 10.00 (ISBN 0-668-04761-5). Arco.

Frishman, Austin M. & Schwartz, Arthur P. The Cockroach Combat Manual. LC 80-288. (Illus.). 1980. 8.95 (ISBN 0-688-03613-9). Morrow.

Frishman, William H. Clinical Pharmacology of the B-Adrenoceptor Blocking Agents. 2nd Ed. ed. (Illus.). 464p. 1984. 42.50 (ISBN 0-8385-1155-4). ACC.

Frishman, William H, jt. auth. see Packer, Milton.

Frisina, Robert, ed. Bicentennial Monograph on Hearing Impairment. LC 76-16454. 1976. softcover 3.95 (ISBN 0-88200-100-0, L9338). Alexander Graham.

Frisinger, Nellie. Jeff & Jenny & the Kidnapping. LC 78-55337. (The Jeff & Jenny Adventure Ser.). (Illus.). (gr. 2-6). 1978. pap. 2.95 (ISBN 0-89636-136-5). Accent Bks.

--Jeff & Jenny at Camp Pinecrest. (Jeff & Jenny Adventure Ser.). 128p. (Orig.). (gr. 4-6). 1984. pap. 2.95 (ISBN 0-89636-121-7). Accent Bks.

--Jeff & Jenny on the Chinchilla Ranch. LC 77-75132. (Jeff & Jenny Adventure Ser.). (Illus.). (gr. 2-6). 1977. pap. 2.95 (ISBN 0-916406-73-3). Accent Bks.

--Jeff & Jenny Winter in Alaska. LC 77-81775. (The Jeff & Jenny Adventure Ser.). (Illus.). (gr. 2-6). 1977. pap. 2.95 (ISBN 0-916406-82-2). Accent Bks.

Frisk, Donald C. Covenant Affirmations: This We Believe. 196p. (Orig.). 1981. pap. 6.95 (ISBN 0-910452-48-2). Covenant.

--New Life in Christ. 1969. pap. 2.95 (ISBN 0-910452-03-2). Covenant.

Frisk, G. A Middle English Translation de Macer Floridus of Viribus Herbarum. (Essays & Studies on English Language & Literature: Vol. 3). pap. 28.00 (ISBN 0-317-15876-7). Kraus Repr.

Frisk, Hjalmar. Griechisches Etymologisches Woerterbuch, Vol. 1. (Gr. & Ger.). 1960. 95.00 (ISBN 3-533-00652-2, M-7434, Pub. by Carl Winter). French & Eur.

--Griechisches Etymologisches Woerterbuch, Vol. 2. (Gr. & Ger.). 1960. 132.00 (ISBN 3-533-00653-0, M-7435, Pub. by Carl Winter). French & Eur.

--Griechisches Etymologisches Woerterbuch, Vol. 3. (Gr. & Ger.). 1972. 45.00 (ISBN 3-533-02203-X, M-7436, Pub. by Carl Winter). French & Eur.

Frisk, Peter D., jt. auth. see Gustafson, R. D.

Frisk, Peter D., jt. auth. see Gustafson, R. David.

Frisk, Peter D., jt. auth. see Gustafson, Roy D.

Frisken, William R. The Atmospheric Environment. LC 73-8139. pap. 20.00 (ISBN 0-317-08036-9, 2020961). Bks Demand UMI.

Frisken, William R., tr. see Aleksandrov, Yu A.

Friskey, Margaret. Birds We Know. LC 81-7745. (The New True Books). (Illus.). 48p. (gr. k-4). 1981. PLB 10.60 (ISBN 0-516-01609-1); pap. 3.95 (ISBN 0-516-41609-X). Childrens.

--Chicken Little Count-To-Ten. (Easy Reading Picture Bks.). (Illus.). 32p. (gr. k-3). 1946. PLB 10.35 (ISBN 0-516-03431-6). Childrens.

--Indian Two Feet & His Eagle Feather. LC 67-20101. (Indian Two Feet Ser.). (Illus.). 64p. (gr. k-3). 1967. PLB 10.60 (ISBN 0-516-03503-7). Childrens.

--Indian Two Feet & His Horse. (Illus.). 64p. (gr. k-3). 1959. 10.60 (ISBN 0-516-03501-0). Childrens.

--Indian Two Feet & the ABC Moose Hunt. LC 77-4467. (Indian Two Feet Ser.). (Illus.). 32p. (gr. k-2). 1977. PLB 10.60 (ISBN 0-516-03500-2). Childrens.

--Indian Two Feet & the Grizzly Bear. LC 74-7481. (Illus.). 32p. (gr. k-2). 1974. PLB 10.35 (ISBN 0-516-03508-8). Childrens.

--Indian Two Feet & the Wolf Cubs. (Illus.). 64p. (gr. k-3). 1971. PLB 10.60 (ISBN 0-516-03506-1). Childrens.

--Indian Two Feet Rides Alone. LC 80-12688. (Indian Two Feet Ser.). (Illus.). 32p. (gr. k-3). 1980. PLB 10.60 (ISBN 0-516-03523-1). Childrens.

--Seven Diving Ducks. LC 65-20889. (Easy Reading Picture Bks.). (Illus.). 32p. (gr. k-3). 1965. PLB 10.35 (ISBN 0-516-03605-X). Childrens.

--Space Shuttles. LC 81-16648. (New True Bks.). (Illus.). 48p. (gr. k-4). 1982. PLB 10.60 (ISBN 0-516-01655-5); pap. 3.95 (ISBN 0-516-41655-3). Childrens.

Friskin, James & Freundlich, Irwin. Music for the Piano: A Handbook of Concert & Teaching Material from 1580 to 1952. rev. ed. LC 72-93608. 443p. 1973. pap. 6.00 (ISBN 0-486-22918-1). Dover.

--Music for the Piano: A Handbook of Concert & Teaching Material from 1580 to 1952. 15.50 (ISBN 0-8446-5109-5). Peter Smith.

Friskney, Tom. Thirteen Lessons on I & II Thessalonians. LC 82-71253. (Bible Student Study Guide Ser.). 122p. 1982. pap. 2.95 (ISBN 0-89900-172-6). College Pr Pub.

Frison, George & Stanford, Dennis. The Agate Basin Site: A Record of the Paleoindian Occupation of the Northwestern High Plains. (Studies in Archaeology). 440p. 1982. 74.50 (ISBN 0-12-268570-9). Acad Pr.

Frison, George C. Prehistoric Hunters of the High Plains. 1978. 31.00 (ISBN 0-12-268560-1). Acad Pr.

--The Wardell Buffalo Trap Forty Eight SU Three Hundred & One: Communal Procurement in the Upper Green River Basin, Wyoming. (Anthropological Papers: No. 48). 1973. pap. 3.00x (ISBN 0-932206-46-8). U Mich Mus Anthro.

Frison, George C. & Bradley, Bruce A. Folsom Tools & Technology at the Hanson Site, Wyoming. LC 79-67812. (Illus.). 136p. 1980. 14.95x (ISBN 0-8263-0529-6). U of NM Pr.

Frison, Paul. Calendar of Change. rev., 2nd ed. (Illus.). 325p. (Orig.). 1986. pap. price not set (ISBN 0-914565-12-5). Capstan Pubns.

--Charles Wells: Pioneer-Scout-Apache Slave. 2nd, rev. ed. (Illus.). 100p. (Orig.). 1986. pap. price not set (ISBN 0-914565-09-5). Capstan Pubns.

--First White Woman in the Big Horn Basin. rev., 2nd ed. (Illus.). 125p. 1986. pap. price not set (ISBN 0-914565-10-9). Capstan Pubns.

--Grass Was Gold. rev., 2nd ed. (Illus.). 130p. 1986. pap. price not set (ISBN 0-914565-08-7). Capstan Pubns.

--Under the Ten Sleep Rim. rev., 2nd ed. (Illus.). 175p. 1986. pap. price not set (ISBN 0-914565-11-7). Capstan Pubns.

Frisoni, Gaetano. Dizionario Moderno Spagnuolo-Italiano, Italiano-Spagnuolo, 2 vols. 1865p. (Span. & Ital.). Set. 49.50x (ISBN 0-913298-51-4). S F Vanni.

Frison-Roche, Roger & Tairraz, Pierre. Montagne (Mountain) new ed. (Larousse vie, art, cite). (Illus.). 144p. (Fr.). 1975. 29.95x (ISBN 2-03-018400-4). Larousse.

Frisse, Mark, ed. see Washington University, Department of Medicine.

Frissel, M. & Van Veen, H. Simulation of Nitrogen Behaviour of Soil-Plant Systems. 300p. 1980. cloth 73.50x (ISBN 90-220-0735-9, Pub. by CAB Bks England). State Mutual Bk.

Frissel, M. J. & Reiniger, P. Simulation of Accumulation & Leaching in Soils. 124p. 1981. 70.00x (ISBN 0-686-76662-8, Pub. by Oxford & IBH India). State Mutual Bk.

--Simulation of Accumulation and Leaching in Soils. 124p. 1975. pap. 7.50 (ISBN 90-220-0530-5, PDC82, PUDOC). Unipub.

Frissel, M. J., jt. auth. see Beek, J.

Frissel, M. J., ed. Cycling of Mineral Nutrients in Agricultural Ecosystems. (Developments in Agricultural & Managed-Forest Ecology Ser.: Vol. 3). 356p. 1978. Repr. 64.00 (ISBN 0-444-41660-9). Elsevier.

Frissell, Anthony. Soprano Voice. 1971. 8.50 (ISBN 0-8283-1388-1). Branden Pub Co.

--Tenor Voice. 1971. 8.50 (ISBN 0-8283-1387-3). Branden Pub Co.

Frist, Betty. My Neighbors, the Billy Grahams. LC 83-70368. 1983. 8.95 (ISBN 0-8054-7229-0). Broadman.

Fristedt, Bert, jt. auth. see Berry, Donald A.

Fristedt, Sven L. The Wycliffe Bible, 2 vols. LC 78-63195. (Heresies of the Early Christian & Medieval Era: Second Ser.). Repr. of 1953 ed. 45.00 set (ISBN 0-404-16370-X). AMS Pr.

Frister, Robert A. Eclipse. LC 81-50764. 207p. 1982. 8.95 (ISBN 0-533-05013-8). Vantage.

Fristrom, James W. & Clegg, Michael T. Principles of Genetics. 2nd ed. LC 80-65757. (Illus.). 700p. 1986. text ed. 29.95tx (ISBN 0-913462-05-5). Chiron Pr.

Fristrup, Borge. The Greenland Ice Cap. LC 67-31985. (Illus.). 312p. 1967. 35.00x (ISBN 0-295-95209-1). U of Wash Pr.

Friswell, J. Hain. Essays on English Writers: Lord Byron, Scott, Wordsworth, Coleridge, Shelley, Keats, Landor, Barry Cornwall, Crabbe, Thomas Hood, Burns, Campbell. 1973. Repr. of 1869 ed. 35.00 (ISBN 0-8274-0654-1). R West.

--Familiar Words. 420p. 1984. Repr. of 1866 ed. lib. bdg. 50.00 (ISBN 0-89987-286-7). Darby Bks.

--Footsteps to Fame. 1887. Repr. 30.00 (ISBN 0-8274-2352-7). R West.

--Life Portraits of William Shakespeare. LC 76-168063. (Illus.). Repr. of 1864 ed. 10.00 (ISBN 0-404-02624-9). AMS Pr.

--Varia: Readings from Rare Books. 1866. Repr. 35.00 (ISBN 0-8274-3666-1). R West.

Friswell, Laura H. In the Sixties & Seventies. 1973. Repr. of 1905 ed. 45.00 (ISBN 0-8274-0655-X). R West.

--James Hain Friswell: A Memoir by His Daughter Laura Hain Friswell. 1898. Repr. 35.00 (ISBN 0-8274-2598-8). R West.

Frita, ed. see Riefenstahl, L., et al.

Fritch, Bruce E., jt. auth. see Reisman, Albert F.

Fritch, Bruce E. & Reisman, Albert F., eds. Equipment Leasing: Leveraged Leasing 1983 Supplement. 253p. 1983. pap. text ed. 40.00 (ISBN 0-686-88594-5, A5-1291). PLI.

Fritch, Elisabeeth. Golden Fires. (California Ser.: Vol. 2). 1984. pap. 3.50 (ISBN 0-8217-1309-4). Zebra.

Fritch, Elisabeth. California Book One: Passion's Trail. 1983. pap. 3.50 (ISBN 0-8217-1229-2). Zebra.

--Tides of Rapture. 1983. pap. 3.75 (ISBN 0-8217-1245-4). Zebra.

Fritch, Elizabeth. Richmond, Vol. 1: The Flame. 480p. (Orig.). 1980. pap. 2.75 (ISBN 0-89083-654-X). Zebra.

--Richmond Vol. 2: The Fire. 1980. pap. 2.75 (ISBN 0-89083-679-5). Zebra.

--Richmond Vol. 3: The Embers. 1981. pap. 2.75 (ISBN 0-89083-716-3). Zebra.

--The Sparks. (Richmond Ser.: Vol. 4). (Orig.). 1982. pap. 3.50 (ISBN 0-89083-962-X). Zebra.

Fritchie, G. Edward & Ooi, Wan H. Biology: A Laboratory Experience. 2nd ed. (Illus.). 236p. 1982. pap. text ed. 14.95x (ISBN 0-89641-082-X). American Pr.

Fritchman, June & Solomon, Karey. Living Lean off the Fat of the Land. LC 82-14932. (Illus.). 224p. (Orig.). 1983. pap. 8.95 smyth-sewn bdg. (ISBN 0-943914-03-5, Dist. by Kampmann & Co). Larson Pubns Inc.

Fritchman, Stephen. Heretic. pap. 6.95 (ISBN 0-933840-19-5). Unitarian Univ.

Friters, Gerard M. Outer Mongolia & Its International Position. LC 74-4496. 1974. Repr. of 1949 ed. lib. bdg. 24.50x (ISBN 0-374-92937-8). Octagon.

Frith, C. D., jt. auth. see Eysenck, H. J.

Frith, D. New Priorities & Developments in the Construction Market in Saudi Arabia & Iran. 206p. 1979. 209.00x (ISBN 0-86010-135-5, Pub. by Graham & Trotman England). State Mutual Bk.

Frith, David, ed. see Ibbotson, Doug & Dellor, Ralph.

Frith, Donald E. Mold Making for Ceramics. LC 84-21470. 240p. 1985. text ed. 60.00 (ISBN 0-8019-7359-7). Chilton.

Frith, Francis. Egypt & the Holy Land in Historic Photographs. White, Jon. E., selected by. 16.50 (ISBN 0-8446-5887-1). Peter Smith.

--Egypt & the Holy Land in Historic Photographs: Seventy-Seven Views. Van Haaften, Julia, ed. 112p. 1981. pap. 6.95 (ISBN 0-486-24048-7). Dover.

Frith, Greg H. Behavior Management in the Schools: A Primer for Parents. 130p. 1985. 18.75x (ISBN 0-398-05158-5). C C Thomas.

--The Role of the Special Education Paraprofessional: An Introductory Text. (Illus.). 280p. 1982. 29.75x (ISBN 0-398-04613-1). C C Thomas.

Frith, Greg H., jt. auth. see Armstrong, Steve W.

Frith, H. J. Water Fowl in Australia. 350p. 1984. 60.00x (ISBN 0-207-14472-9, Pub. by Angus & Robertson). State Mutual Bk.

--Waterfowl in Australia. (Illus.). 349p. 1967. 17.50 (ISBN 0-8248-0063-X, Eastwest Ctr). UH Pr.

Frith, H. J., jt. auth. see Hetzel, B. S.

Frith, H. J., jt. ed. see Hetzel, B. S.

Frith, Henry. Graphology. LC 80-80536. (Illus.). 128p. 1980. pap. 4.50 (ISBN 0-89345-205-X, Steinerbks). Garber Comm.

--Palmistry Secrets Revealed. pap. 3.00 (ISBN 0-87980-116-6). Wilshire.

Frith, Henry, tr. see Daryl, Philippe.

Frith, James & Andrews, Ronald. Antique Pistols Collection, 1400-1860. 25.00 (ISBN 0-87556-677-4). Saifer.

Frith, James R., ed. Measuring Spoken Language Proficiency. 69p. (Orig.). 1980. pap. text ed. 4.95 (ISBN 0-87840-188-1). Georgetown U Pr.

Frith, Mary, ed. Albendazole in Helminthiasis. (Royal Society Medicine International Congress & Symposia Ser.: No. 57). 106p. 1983. 10.00 (ISBN 0-8089-1553-3). Grune.

Frith, Michael. I'll Teach My Dog One Hundred Words. (Bright & Early Bk: No. 17). (Illus.). (ps-1). 1973. 4.95 (ISBN 0-394-82692-2, BYR); PLB 5.99 (ISBN 0-394-92692-7). Random.

--My Amazing Book of Autographs! LC 79-37407. (gr. 1-3). 1974. 4.95 (ISBN 0-394-82407-5). Beginner.

--Some of Us Walk, Some Fly, Some Swim. LC 73-158391. (Illus.). (gr. k-6). 1971. Beginner.

Frith, Nigel. The Legend of Krishna. LC 75-35449. 1976. 7.95 (ISBN 0-8052-3611-2). Schocken.

Frith Overseas Research Ltd. Agriculture in Brazil & Venezuela: Opportunities for Business. 175p. 1978. 77.00x (ISBN 0-86010-124-X, Pub. by Graham & Trotman England). State Mutual Bk.

--Winning Business in Egypt. 98p. 1978. 99.00x (ISBN 0-86010-121-5, Pub. by Graham & Trotman England). State Mutual Bk.

Frith, Owen, jt. auth. see Venning, Muriel.

Frith, Penelope. The Stick It, Stitch It & Stuff It Toybook. LC 74-32476. (Illus.). 114p. 1975. 5.95 (ISBN 0-87131-178-X). M Evans.

Frith, Simon. The Sociology of Youth. (Themes & Perspectives in Sociology Ser.). 72p. (Orig.). 1984. pap. text ed. 6.95x (ISBN 0-946183-06-6, Pub. by Causeway Pr Ltd England). Sheridan.

--Sound Effects: Youth, Leisure, & the Politics of Rock 'n' Roll. 1982. 18.00 (ISBN 0-394-50461-5); pap. 8.95 (ISBN 0-394-74811-5). Pantheon.

Frith, Stan W. The Expatriate Dilemma: How to Relocate & Compensate U. S. Employees Assigned Overseas. LC 81-2740. 192p. 1981. text ed. 19.95x (ISBN 0-88229-701-5). Nelson-Hall.

Frith, Uta & Vogel, Juliet M. Some Perceptual Prerequisites for Reading. Murray, Frank, ed. (IRA Ser. on the Development of the Reading Process). 50p. (Orig.). 1980. pap. text ed. 3.50 (ISBN 0-87207-527-3, 527). Intl Reading.

Frith, Uta, ed. Cognitive Processes in Spelling. 1983. pap. 19.00 (ISBN 0-12-268662-4). Acad Pr.

--Congnitive Processes in Spelling. LC 79-10788. 1980. 49.50 (ISBN 0-12-268660-8). Acad Pr.

Frith, William P. John Leech: His Life & Work, 2 Vols. LC 69-17491. 1969. Repr. of 1891 ed. Set. 65.00x (ISBN 0-8103-3831-9). Gale.

Frithjof, Rodi, ed. see Dilthey, Wilhelm.

Fritsch, A., et al. Infusonstherapie und Klinische Ernaehrung in der Operative Medizin. (Handbuch der Infusionstherapie und Klinischen Ernaehrung: Band 4). viii, 160p. 1985. 30.25 (ISBN 3-8055-3743-3). S Karger.

Fritsch, Charles T. Genesis. LC 59-10454. (Layman's Bible Commentary Ser: Vol. 2). 1959. pap. 4.95 (ISBN 0-8042-3062-5). John Knox.

--The Qumran Community: Its History & Scrolls. 1973. Repr. of 1956 ed. 15.00x (ISBN 0-8196-0279-5). Biblo.

Fritsch, Charles T., ed. Studies in the History of Caesarea Maritima: The Joint Expedition to Caesarea Maritima Vol. 1. LC 75-29059. (American Schools of Oriental Research, Supplement Ser.: Vol.19). 122p. 1975. text ed. 6.00x (ISBN 0-89757-319-6, Am Sch Orient Res). Eisenbrauns.

Fritsch, Felix E. Structure & Reproduction of the Algae, 2 Vols. Vol. 1. 95.00 (ISBN 0-521-05041-3); Vol. 2. 105.00 (ISBN 0-521-05042-1). Cambridge U Pr.

Fritsch, Gerhard. Between Evening & Night. Holroyd-Reece, Gitta, tr. from Ger. (Orig.). 1978. pap. 3.00 (ISBN 0-685-99434-1, Pub. by Menard Pr). Small Pr Dist.

Fritsch, Hildegard. Peter Haertlings Hoelderlin: Untersuchung zur Struktur des Romans. (American University Studies I (Germanic Languages & Literatures): Vol. 14). 154p. (Orig.). 1983. pap. text ed. 16.30 (ISBN 0-8204-0024-6). P Lang Pubs.

Fritsch, Ronald E., ed. Directory of Public & Private Programs for Emotionally Disturbed Children & Youth. LC 85-43093. 184p. 1985. 84.50 (ISBN 0-89774-199-4). Oryx Pr.

Fritsche, Joellen, jt. ed. see Bandy, Patricia.

Fritsche, Joellen, ed. see Close Up Foundation.

Fritschen, L. J. & Gay, L. W. Environmental Instrumentation. (Springer Advanced Texts in Life Sciences Ser.). (Illus.). 1979. 29.50 (ISBN 0-387-90411-5). Springer-Verlag.

Fritscher, Jack. Corporal in Charge of Taking Care of Captain O'Malley & Other Stories. 184p. 1984. pap. 10.00 (ISBN 0-917342-45-3). Gay Sunshine.

--Leather Blues. (Illus.). 96p. (Orig.). 1984. pap. 5.95 (ISBN 0-917342-49-6). Gay Sunshine.

Fritscher, John. Popular Witchcraft. 224p. 1973. 6.95 (ISBN 0-8065-0380-7). Citadel Pr.

Fritscher, John J. Popular Witchcraft. 136p. 5.00 (ISBN 0-87972-026-3). Bowling Green Univ.

Fritschi, Gerhard. Africa & Gutenberg: Exploring Oral Structures in the Modern African Novel. (European University Studies: Vol. 9). 200p. 1983. pap. 18.95 (ISBN 3-261-03322-3). P Lang Pubs.

Fritschka, E., jt. ed. see Cervos-Navarro, J.

Fritschle, Linda C. & Rudnick, Susan R. Pocket Reference to Health Disorders. (Nursing Ser.). 132p. 1983. pap. 6.95x (ISBN 0-86598-126-4). Rowman & Allanheld.

Fritschler, A. Lee. Smoking & Politics: Policy Making & the Federal Bureaucracy. 3rd ed. 208p. 1983. pap. 14.95 (ISBN 0-13-815027-3). P-H.

Fritschler, A. Lee & Ross, Bernard H. Business Regulation & Government Decision-Making. 1980. pap. text ed. 13.95 (ISBN 0-316-29362-8). Little.

--Executive's Guide to Government: How Washington Works. 1980. text ed. 19.95 (ISBN 0-316-29363-6). Little.

--How Washington Works: The Executive's Guide to Government. 200p. 1986. prof. ref. 29.95 (ISBN 0-88730-079-0); pap. 14.95 prof. ref. (ISBN 0-88730-080-4). Ballinger Pub.

Fritts, H. C. Tree Rings & Climate. 1977. 88.50 (ISBN 0-12-268450-8). Acad Pr.

Fritts, Susan R., tr. see Coleta, Anthony.

Fritts, Thomas H. New Species of Lizards of the Genus Stenocerus from Peru: (Sauria: Iguanidae) (Occasional Papers: Vol. 10). 21p. 1972. 1.25 (ISBN 0-317-04864-3). U of KS Mus Nat Hist.

Fritts, Thomas H., jt. auth. see Duellman, William E.

Fritts, William. The House. 240p. 1985. pap. 2.50 (ISBN 0-8439-2251-6, Leisure Bks). Dorchester Pub Co.

--House of Another Kind. (Orig.). 1981. pap. 2.25 (ISBN 0-505-51669-1, Pub. by Tower Bks). Dorchester Pub Co.

Fritz, Charles A. Bertrand Russell's Construction of the External World. LC 73-13400. (International Library of Psychology, Philosophy, & Scientific Method Ser.). 243p. 1974. Repr. of 1952 ed. lib. bdg. 15.00x (ISBN 0-8371-7052-4, FRBR). Greenwood.

Fritz, Chester. China Journey: A Diary of Six Months in Western Inland China, 1917. (Illus.). 218p. 1981. 14.95x (ISBN 0-295-95887-1, Pub. by Schl of Intl Studies). U of Wash Pr.

Fritz, Emanuel, compiled by. California Coast Redwood (Sequoia Sempervirens) An Annotated Bibliography to & Including 1955. LC 57-10720. xv, 267p. 1957. 15.00 (ISBN 0-8223-0376-0). Found Am Res Mgmt.

Fritz, Florence. The Unknown Story of Sanibel & Captiva. 1974. 10.00 (ISBN 0-87012-165-0). McClain.

Fritz, Foster. The Suicide Guide. LC 83-50928. (Illus.). 134p. (Orig.). 1983. pap. write for info. (ISBN 0-930179-00-5). Starry Messenger Bks.

Fritz, George J., jt. auth. see Noggle, G. Ray.

Fritz, Georgene & Smith, Nancy, eds. The Hearing Impaired Employee: An Untapped Resource. (Illus.). 140p. 1985. 19.95 (ISBN 0-88744-108-4). College-Hill.

Fritz, Hans & Dietze, Gunther, eds. Kinins III. (Advances in Experimental Medicine & Biology Ser.: Vol. 156). 1222p. 1983. 145.00x (ISBN 0-306-41167-9, Plenum Pr). Plenum Pub.

Fritz, Harry W. Montana: Land of Contrast. (Illus.). 200p. 1984. 24.95 (ISBN 0-89781-106-2). Windsor Pubns Inc.

Fritz, Harry W., jt. ed. see Myers, Rex C.

Fritz, Henry E. The Movement for Indian Assimilation, 1860 to 1890. LC 81-6650. (Illus.). 244p. 1981. Repr. of 1963 ed. lib. bdg. 23.50x (ISBN 0-313-22012-3, FRMI). Greenwood.

Fritz, Irving, ed. see Symposium on Insulin Action, Toronto, 1971.

Fritz, J., et al. Random Fields, 2 vols. (Colloquia Mathematica Ser.: Vol. 27). 1112p. 1982. Set. 170.25 (ISBN 0-444-85441-X, North-Holland). Elsevier.

Fritz, J., et al, eds. Statistical Physics & Dynamical Systems: Rigorous Results. (Progress in Physics Ser.: Vol. 10). 510p. 1985. text ed. write for info. (ISBN 0-8176-3300-6). Birkhauser.

Fritz, Jack. Small & Mini Hydropower Systems: Resource Assessment & Project Feasibility. Allen-Browne, Patricia, ed. (Illus.). 464p. 1983. 47.95 (ISBN 0-07-022470-6). McGraw.

Fritz, James, jt. auth. see Coughlin, Robert E.

Fritz, James C., jt. auth. see Titus, Harry W.

Fritz, James S. & Schenk, George H., Jr. Quantitative Analytical Chemistry. 4th ed. (Illus.). 1979. text ed. 40.00 (ISBN 0-205-06527-9, 6865275); instr's. manual avail. (ISBN 0-205-06544-9, 686544). Allyn.

Fritz, James S., et al. Local Area Networks: Selection Guidelines. (Illus.). 160p. 1985. text ed. 18.95 (ISBN 0-13-539552-6). P-H.

Fritz, Jan, ed. Clinical Sociology Review, Vol. I. 143p. (Orig.). 1982. pap. 10.50 (ISBN 0-942756-00-2). Clin Soc Assn.

Fritz, Jan M. The Clinical Sociology Handbook. Chekki, Dan A., ed. LC 82-49133. (Bibliographies in Sociology Ser.). 300p. 1985. lib. bdg. 40.00 (ISBN 0-8240-9203-1). Garland Pub.

Fritz, Jean. And Then What Happened, Paul Revere? (Illus.). 48p. (gr. 2-6). 1973. 9.95 (ISBN 0-698-20274-0, Coward); pap. 4.95 (ISBN 0-698-20541-3). Putnam Pub Group.

--Brady. (Illus.). (gr. 4-8). 1960. 7.95 (ISBN 0-698-20014-4, Coward). Putnam Pub Group.

--Brendan the Navigator. LC 78-13247. (Illus.). (gr. 2-5). 1979. 7.95 (ISBN 0-698-20473-5, Coward). Putnam Pub Group.

--The Cabin Faced West. (Illus.). (gr. 4-7). 1958. 8.95 (ISBN 0-698-20016-0, Coward). Putnam Pub Group.

--Can't You Make Them Behave, King George? (Illus.). 48p. 1982. 9.95 (ISBN 0-698-20315-1, Coward); pap. 4.95 (ISBN 0-698-20542-1). Putnam Pub Group.

--China Homecoming. (Illus.). 144p. (gr. 5 up). 1985. 12.95 (ISBN 0-399-21182-9, Putnam). Putnam Pub Group.

--The Double Life of Pocahontas. LC 83-9662. (Illus.). (gr. 4-8). 1983. 10.95 (ISBN 0-399-21016-4, Putnam). Putnam Pub Group.

--Early Thunder. (Illus.). (gr. 7-11). 1967. 9.95 (ISBN 0-698-20036-5, Coward). Putnam Pub Group.

--George Washington's Breakfast. (Illus.). (gr. 2-6). 1969. PLB 5.99 (ISBN 0-698-30099-8, Coward). Putnam Pub Group.

--George Washington's Breakfast. (Illus.). 48p. (gr. 3-8). 1984. pap. 4.95 (ISBN 0-698-20616-9, Coward). Putnam Pub Group.

--The Good Giants & The Bad Pukwudgies. (Illus.). 40p. 1982. 10.95 (ISBN 0-399-20870-4); pap. 5.95 (ISBN 0-399-20871-2). Putnam Pub Group.

--Homesick: My Own Story. (Illus.). 176p. 1982. 10.95 (ISBN 0-399-20933-6, Putnam). Putnam Pub Group.

--Homesick: My Own Story. (gr. k-6). 1984. pap. 2.95 (ISBN 0-440-43683-4, YB). Dell.

--The Man Who Loved Books. (Illus.). 48p. (gr. 7-11). 1981. 9.95 (ISBN 0-399-20715-5, Putnam). Putnam Pub Group.

--Stonewall. (Illus.). 1979. 10.95 (ISBN 0-399-20698-1, Putnam). Putnam Pub Group.

--Traitor: The Case of Benedict Arnold. (Illus.). 1981. 9.95 (ISBN 0-399-20834-8, Putnam). Putnam Pub Group.

--What's the Big Idea, Ben Franklin? (Illus.). 48p. (gr. 2-6). 1982. 9.95 (ISBN 0-698-20365-8, Coward); pap. 4.95 (ISBN 0-698-20543-X, Coward). Putnam Pub Group.

--Where Do You Think You're Going, Christopher Columbus? (Illus.). (gr. 3-7). 1980. 9.95 (ISBN 0-399-20723-6); pap. 4.95 (ISBN 0-399-20734-1). Putnam Pub Group.

--Where Was Patrick Henry on the 29th of May? (Illus.). 48p. (gr. 3-5). 1975. 9.95 (ISBN 0-698-20307-0, Coward). Putnam Pub Group.

--Where Was Patrick Henry on the 29th of May? (Illus.). (gr. 3-5). 1982. pap. 4.95 (ISBN 0-698-20544-8, Coward). Putnam Pub Group.

--Who's That Stepping on Plymouth Rock? LC 74-30593. (Illus.). 32p. (gr. 2-6). 1975. 8.95 (ISBN 0-698-20325-9, Coward). Putnam Pub Group.

--Why Don't You Get a Horse, Sam Adams? (Illus.). 48p. (gr. 2-6). 1974. 9.95 (ISBN 0-698-20292-9, Coward). Putnam Pub Group.

--Why Don't You Get a Horse, Sam Adams? (Illus.). 48p. 1982. pap. 4.95 (ISBN 0-698-20545-6, Coward). Putnam Pub Group.

--Will You Sign Here, John Hancock? LC 75-33243. (Illus.). 48p. (gr. 2-6). 1976. 9.95 (ISBN 0-698-20308-9, Coward). Putnam Pub Group.

Fritz, John, et al. Where Kings & Gods Meet: The Royal Centre at Vijayanagara India. LC 85-1117. (Illus.). 160p. 1985. 28.95x (ISBN 0-8165-0927-1). U of Ariz Pr.

Fritz, Kurt Von. Antike und moderne Tragoedie: Neun Abhandlungen. (Ger). 1962. 37.80x (ISBN 3-11-005039-0). De Gruyter.

--Griechische Geschichtsschreibung: Von Den Anfaengen Bis Thukydides, Vol. 1. (Ger). 1967. 90.00x (ISBN 3-11-005167-2). De Gruyter.

--Grundprobleme der Geschichte der antiken Wissenschaft. 759p. 1971. 55.60x (ISBN 3-11-001805-5). De Gruyter.

--Pythagorean Politics in Southern Italy. 1973. Repr. lib. bdg. 16.50x (ISBN 0-374-92939-4). Octagon.

--The Relevance of Ancient Social & Political Philosophy for Our Times: A Short Introduction to the Problem. LC 74-78098. iv, 57p. 1974. pap. 3.90x (ISBN 3-11-004859-0). De Gruyter.

--Schriften zur griechiscen und Roemischen Verfassungsgeschichte und Verfassungstheorie. 1976. 82.50x (ISBN 3-11-006567-3). De Gruyter.

Fritz, Kurt Von see Von Fritz, Kurt.

Fritz, Kurt von see Von Fritz, kurt.

Fritz, Leah. Dreamers & Dealers: An Intimate Appraisal of the Women's Movement. LC 78-73852. 350p. 1979. pap. 6.95 (ISBN 0-8070-3793-1, BP-604). Beacon Pr.

Fritz, M. Future Energy Consumption of the Third World-with Special Reference to Nuclear Power: An Individual & Comprehensive Evaluation of 156 Countries. 393p. 1981. 55.00 (ISBN 0-08-026168-X). Pergamon.

Fritz, Margot, ed. Trainer's Manual for One Day Workshop & Experimental Lab. 7.50 (ISBN 0-686-31461-1). Parents Anon.

Fritz, Martha. If the River's This High All Summer. 42p. 1974. 5.00 (ISBN 0-913219-18-5); signed 7.50 (ISBN 0-913219-19-3). Pym-Rand Pr.

Fritz, Mary. Take Nothing for the Journey: Solitude & the Non-Possessive Life. 88p. (Orig.). 1985. pap. 3.95 (ISBN 0-8091-2722-9). Paulist Pr.

Fritz, Maxine. With an Oriental Flavor. 1976. pap. 1.50 (ISBN 0-8341-0402-4). Beacon Hill.
Fritz, Michael E., et al. Cystic Fibrosis. LC 73-13832. 198p. 1973. text ed. 21.50x (ISBN 0-8422-7133-3). Irvington.
Fritz, N. Service Station Recordkeeping: A Practice Set. 1968. 13.96 (ISBN 0-07-022474-9). McGraw.
Fritz, N. & Hoffman, F. Accounting Fundamentals Text-Kit. 2nd ed. 1971. 24.60 (ISBN 0-07-022498-6). McGraw.
Fritz, N. & Wirth, R. H. Supersonic Sounds: A Business Record-Keeping Practice Set. 3rd ed. 1981. text ed. 8.88 (ISBN 0-07-022562-1). McGraw.
Fritz, Ned. Sterile Forest. (Illus.). 260p. 1983. 15.95; pap. 12.95 (ISBN 0-89015-392-2). Eakin Pubns.
Fritz, P. Handbook of Environmental Isotope Geochemistry, Vol. 2: The Terrestrial Environment, B. Date not set. write for info. (ISBN 0-444-42225-0). Elsevier.
Fritz, P. & Fontes, J. C. Handbook of Environmental Isotope Chemistry: Terrestrial Environment, Vol. 1. 546p. 1980. 93.75 (ISBN 0-444-41780-X). Elsevier.
Fritz, P., et al. Interpersonal Communication in Nursing: An Interactionist Approach. 288p. 1983. pap. 16.95 (ISBN 0-8385-4312-X). ACC.
Fritz, Patricia. Te Alabamos Senor: We Praise You O Lord. Sarre, Alicia, tr. from Span. 112p. 1984. pap. 3.95 (ISBN 0-8091-2641-9). Paulist Pr.
Fritz, Paul & Morton, Richard. Woman in the Eighteenth Century & Other Essays. (McMaster Eighteenth Century Studies). 386p. 1979. lib. bdg. 43.00 (ISBN 0-686-88536-8). Garland Pub.
Fritz, Paul & Williams, David. The Triumph of Culture: Eighteenth Century Perspectives. LC 80-80055. (McMaster 18th Century Studies). 398p. 1979. lib. bdg. 48.00 (ISBN 0-8240-4001-5). Garland Pub.
Fritz, Paul S. The English Ministers & Jacobitism Between the Rebellions of 1715 & 1745. LC 75-33706. (Illus.). 1975. 22.50x (ISBN 0-8020-5308-4). U of Toronto Pr.
Fritz, Peter. Finistere. LC 84-52840. 307p. 1985. 8.95 (ISBN 0-917615-00-X). Seeker Pr.
Fritz, Robert & Smith, Brian R. The Power of Choice. (Illus.). 21p. 1982. pap. 4.95 (ISBN 0-943290-00-7). Fainshaw Pr.
Fritz, Robert E., jt. auth. see Saib, Sabina H.
Fritz, Roger. Creating Success: A Master Plan. 224p. 1984. 15.95 (ISBN 0-8119-0701-5). Fell.
--Rate Yourself As a Manager: A Practical Workable Action Plan to Guide You to the Top. 252p. 1985. 16.95 (ISBN 0-13-753237-7); pap. 8.95 (ISBN 0-13-753229-6). P H.
Fritz, Samuel. The Journal of Father Samuel Fritz. Edmundson, George, ed. & tr. (Hakluyt Society Works Ser.: No. 2, Vol. 51). (Illus.). Repr. of 1922 ed. 42.00 (ISBN 0-317-15609-8). Kraus Repr.
Fritz, W. L., jt. auth. see Dorr, A. T.
Fritz, William J. Roadside Geology of the Yellowstone Country. (Roadside Geology Ser.). (Illus., Orig.). 1985. pap. 7.95 (ISBN 0-87842-170-X). Mountain Pr.
Fritz, William L., jt. auth. see Dorr, Robert T.
Fritze, David, ed. see Kirby, Colleen & Roberts, Laura.
Fritzell, B., et al, eds. see International Associaion of Logopedics & Phoniatrics, 18th Congress, Washington, D.C., August 1980.
Fritzhand, James. Dream Babies. 1978. pap. 2.25 (ISBN 0-380-01818-7, 35758). Avon.
--Four Sisters. LC 81-878. 512p. 1981. 14.95 (ISBN 0-688-00457-1). Morrow.
--Four Sisters. 1982. pap. 3.75 (ISBN 0-8217-1048-6). Zebra.
--The Innocent Dark. (Orig.). 1983. pap. 3.75 (ISBN 0-440-03852-9). Dell.
--Son of the Great American Novel. 1978. pap. 1.95 (ISBN 0-380-01962-0, 38448). Avon.
--Son of the Great American Novel. 5.75 (ISBN 0-8076-0591-3). Braziller.
--Starring. 1977. pap. 1.95 (ISBN 0-380-01653-2, 33118). Avon.
Fritzinger, Dennis. Tame Wilderness. 1979. wrappers 5.00 (ISBN 0-913537-11-X). Arif.
Fritzmann, Anna. Friedrich Von Logau: The Satirist. (American University Studies I (Germanic Languages & Literatures): Vol. 17). 423p. (Orig.). 1983. pap. 35.80 (ISBN 0-8204-0026-2). P Lang Pubs.
Fritzsch, H., et al, eds. Quarks, Leptons, & Beyond. (NATO ASI Series B: Physics: Vol. 122). 564p. 1985. 89.50x (ISBN 0-306-41925-4, Plenum Pr). Plenum Pub.
Fritzsch, Harald. The Creation of Matter: The Universe from Beginning to End. Steinberg, Jean, tr. from Ger. LC 83-46089. (Illus.). 307p. 1984. 19.95 (ISBN 0-465-01446-1). Basic.
--Quarks: The Stuff of Matter. LC 82-72395. (Illus.). 1983. 19.00 (ISBN 0-465-06781-6). Basic.
Fritzsche. Rabbits. (Pet Care Ser.). 80p. 1983. pap. 3.95 (ISBN 0-8120-2615-2). Barron.
Fritzsche, David J., jt. auth. see Cotter, Richard V.
Fritzsche, Gustav. William Morris' Sozialismus und Anarchistischer Kommunismus. 1967. pap. 12.00 (ISBN 0-384-17010-2). Johnson Repr.
Fritzsche, Helga. Cats. (Barron's Pet Care Ser.). (Illus.). 80p. (gr. k-12). 1982. pap. 3.95 (ISBN 0-8120-2421-4). Barron.
--Hamsters. (Barron's Pet Care Ser.). (Illus.). 80p. (gr. k-12). 1982. pap. text ed. 3.95 (ISBN 0-8120-2422-2). Barron.
Frivik, P. E., et al. Ground Freezing 1980: Selected Papers on the International Symposium on Ground Freezing, 2nd, Trondheim, June 24-26, 1980. Janbu, N. & Saetersdal, R., eds. (Developments in Geotechnical Engineering: Vol. 28). 420p. 1982. 85.00 (ISBN 0-444-42010-X). Elsevier.
Frivold, Leif. The Incarnation. 288p. 1981. pap. 19.00 (ISBN 82-00-05684-8). Universitet.
Frizen, Edwin L., ed. Christ & Caesar in Christian Missions. Coggins, Wade T. LC 79-17124. (Orig.). 1979. pap. 5.95 (ISBN 0-87808-169-0). William Carey Lib.
Frizen, Edwin L., Jr., jt. auth. see Coggins, Wade T.
Frizzell, D. D., jt. ed. see Thompson, W. Scott.
Frizzell, Dorothy B. & Andrews, Eva L., eds. Subject Index to Poetry for Children & Young People 1957-1975. LC 77-3296. xiv, 1035p. 1977. lib. bdg. 45.00x (ISBN 0-8389-0242-1). ALA.
Frizzell, Lawrence, jt. auth. see Finkel, Asher.
Frizzell, Lawrence, tr. see Thoma, Clemens.
Frizzi, Ernest. Ein Beitray Zur Ethrologie Von Bouganville und Buka. Repr. of 1914 ed. 10.00 (ISBN 0-384-17020-X). Johnson Repr.
Frizzi, Richard J., jt. auth. see Crinklaw, Frances.
Frizzle, Arnold L. Study of Some of the Influences of Regents Requirements & Examinations in French. LC 70-176789. (Columbia University. Teachers College. Contributions to Education: No. 964). Repr. of 1950 ed. 22.50 (ISBN 0-404-55964-6). AMS Pr.
Frobel, Folker, et al. The New International Division of Labour: Structural Unemployment in Industrialised Countries & Industrialisation in Developing Countries. LC 78-72087. (Studies in Modern Capitalism). (Illus.). 448p. 1982. pap. 20.95 (ISBN 0-521-28720-0). Cambridge U Pr.
--The New International Division of Labour. Burgess, P., tr. from Ger. LC 78-72087. (Studies in Modern Capitalism). (Illus.). 1980. Cambridge U Pr.
Frobenius, Leo. Voice of Africa, 2 vols. LC 68-56516. (Illus.). 1969. Repr. of 1913 ed. 73.00 (ISBN 0-405-08536-2, Blom Pubns); 37.50 ea. Vol. 1 (ISBN 0-405-08537-0). Vol. II (ISBN 0-405-08538-9). Ayer Co Pubs.
Frobenius, Leo & Fox, Douglas C. African Genesis. LC 66-29780. (Illus.). 1937. 20.00 (ISBN 0-405-08539-7, Blom Pubns). Ayer Co Pubs.
--African Genesis. 265p. 1983. pap. 8.95 (ISBN 0-913666-77-7). Turtle Isl foun.
--Prehistoric Rock Pictures in Europe & Africa. LC 74-169302. (The Museum of Modern Art Publications in Reprint from Arno Press). (Illus.). 80p. 1972. Repr. of 1937 ed. 17.00 (ISBN 0-405-01561-5). Ayer Co Pubs.
Frobieter-Mueller, Jo. Practical Stained Glass Craft. (Illus.). 144p. 1984. 22.00 (ISBN 0-88254-888-3). Hippocrene Bks.
Frocht, Max M. Photoelasticity, Vol. 2. LC 41-15564. (Illus.). pap. 130.80 (ISBN 0-317-08372-4, 2017833). Bks Demand UMI.
Frode, Diane E., jt. auth. see Ericson, Lois.
Frodesen, A. G., et al. Probability & Statistics in Particle Physics. 1979. 39.00x (ISBN 8-2000-1906-3, Dist. by Columbia U Pr). Universitet.
Frodin, D. G. Guide to Standard Floras of the World. LC 82-4501. 580p. 1985. 175.00 (ISBN 0-521-23688-6). Cambridge U Pr.
Froding, Gustaf. Poetry of Gustaf Froding. 59.95 (ISBN 0-8490-0861-1). Gordon Pr.
Frodsham, J. D., tr. see He, Li.
Frodsham, J. D., tr. see Li Ho.
Frodsham, Stanley H. Smith Wigglesworth: Apostle of Faith. 160p. 1948. pap. 1.95 (ISBN 0-88243-586-8, 02-0586). Gospel Pub.
--With Signs Following. 188p. 1946. pap. 5.95 (ISBN 0-88243-635-X, 02-0635). Gospel Pub.
Froe, A. De see De Froe, A.
Froe, Otis D. & Otyce, B. The Easy Way to Better Grades. LC 73-76959. 176p. 1959. pap. 2.95 (ISBN 0-668-03352-5). Arco.
Froeb, Herman. Ernst Koch's Prinz Rosa-Stramin: Ein Beitrag Zur Hessischen Literaturgeschichte. pap. 9.00 (ISBN 0-384-17029-3). Johnson Repr.
Froebel, Frederich. Educations of Man. Hailmann, W. N., tr. from Ger. Bd. with The Science of Education. (Contributions to the History of Psychology Pt. B, Vol. I: Psychometrics Ser.). 1978. Repr. of 1887 ed. 30.00 (ISBN 0-89093-161-5). U Pubns Amer.
Froebel, Friedrich. Education of Man. Hailmann, W. N., tr. LC 79-11037. Repr. of 1885 ed. lib. bdg. 27.50x (ISBN 0-678-08029-1). Kelley.
--Froebel Letters. Heinemann, Arnold H., ed. (Educational Ser.). 1893. Repr. 15.00 (ISBN 0-8482-3984-9). Norwood Edns.
--Mother's Songs, Games & Stores: Froebel's Mutter- und Rose-Lieder Rendered in English. LC 75-35068. (Studies in Play & Games). (Illus.). 1976. Repr. 27.50x (ISBN 0-405-07919-2). Ayer Co Pubs.
Froebel, Friedrich & Lilley, Irene M. Friedrich Froebel: A Selection from His Writings. LC 67-10990. (Cambridge Texts & Studies in Education). pap. 47.00 (ISBN 0-317-20598-6, 2024490). Bks Demand UMI.
Froehlich, A. Galois Module Structure of Algebraic Integers. (Ergebnisse der Mathematik und Ihrer Grenzgebiete 3. Folge.: Vol. 1). 262p. 1983. 34.00 (ISBN 0-387-11920-5). Springer-Verlag.
Froehlich, A., jt. auth. see Bushnell, C. J.
Froehlich, Allan F. Managing the Data Center. (Data Processing). (Illus.). 298p. 1982. 30.00 (ISBN 0-534-97942-4). Lifetime Learn.
--Managing the Data Center. 298p. 1982. 30.00 (ISBN 0-534-97942-4). Van Nos Reinhold.
--The Software Buyer's Guidebook: Strategies for Selecting Business Software. (Data Processing Ser.). 200p. 1983. 26.50 (ISBN 0-534-02702-4). Lifetime Learn.
Froehlich, John F. Companion to Cornucopia. LC 80-66879. 1980. 6.50 (ISBN 0-8233-0321-7). Golden Quill.
--A Cornucopia of Thought. 1979. 6.00 (ISBN 0-8233-0292-X). Golden Quill.
Froehlich, John P. Enjoy Yourself under This Cover. 1983. 6.50 (ISBN 0-8233-0361-6). Golden Quill.
--TRS-80 More than BASIC. LC 81-52158. 224p. 1981. pap. 10.95 (ISBN 0-672-21813-5, 21813). Sams.
Froehlich, Karlfried, ed. & tr. Biblical Interpretation in the Early Church. LC 84-47922. (Sources of Early Christian Thought Ser.). 128p. 1985. pap. 6.95 (ISBN 0-8006-1414-3, 1-1414). Fortress.
Froehlich, Margaret W. Hide Crawford Quick. LC 82-21184. 176p. (gr. 5 up). 1983. 9.95 (ISBN 0-395-33884-0). HM.
Froehlich, R. Joseph, jt. auth. see Roth, Charles E.
Froehlich, Robert. The Free Software Catalog & Directory. (Illus.). 1984. pap. 9.95 (ISBN 0-517-55448-8). Crown.
Froehlich, Ronald B. Food Additives, Student Syllabus. pap. text ed. 5.35 (ISBN 0-89420-076-3, 168008); cassette recordings 39.50 (ISBN 0-89420-205-7, 16800O). Natl Book.
Froehlich, Werner & Smith, Gudmund, eds. Psychological Processes in Cognition & Personality. LC 82-21230. (Clinical & Community Psychology Ser.). (Illus.). 284p. 1983. text ed. 47.95 (ISBN 0-89116-243-7). Hemisphere Pub.
Froehlich, Werner D., tr. see Gurwitsch, Aron.
Froehling, Lorene. Quick Meals. (Illus.). 64p. (Orig.). 1985. pap. 3.50 (ISBN 0-8249-3056-8). Ideals.
Froehlinger, Vira J., ed. Today's Hearing Impaired Child: Into the Mainstream of Education. 240p. (Orig.). 1981. pap. 12.95 (ISBN 0-88200-143-4, N6184). Alexander Graham.
Froehr, Friedrich & Orttenburger, Fritz. Introduction to Electronic Control Engineering. 220p. 1981. 49.95 (ISBN 0-471-26200-5, Pub. by Wiley-Interscience). Wiley.
Froelich, Karlfried. Biblical Interpretation in the Early Church. pap. write for info. Fortress.
Froelich, Robert E., ed. Film Reviews in Psychiatry, Psychology, & Mental Health: A Descriptive & Evaluative Listing of Educational & Instructional Films. LC 73-78294. 1974. 16.50 (ISBN 0-87650-037-8). Pierian.
Froelicher. Exercise Testing & Training. 1983. 39.95 (ISBN 0-8151-3332-4). Year Bk Med.
Froelicher, A. & Bucher, W. Calculus in Vector Spaces Without Norm. (Lecture Notes in Mathematics). (Orig.). 1966. pap. 10.70 (ISBN 0-387-03612-1). Springer-Verlag.
Froembgen, Hanns. Kemal Ataturk, a Biography. facsimile ed. Kirkness, Kenneth, tr. from Ger. LC 70-175697. (Select Bibliographies Reprint Ser). Repr. of 1935 ed. 21.00 (ISBN 0-8369-8975-9). Ayer Co Pubs.
Froes, F. H. & Eylon, D., eds. Titanium Net-Shape Technologies. 299p. 1984. 60.00 (ISBN 0-89520-482-7); members 38.00 (ISBN 0-317-37202-5); student members 19.00 (ISBN 0-317-37203-3). Metal Soc.
Froeschner, Richard C. Synopsis of the Heteropters or True Bugs of the Galapagos Islands. LC 84-600217. (Smithsonian Contributions to Zoology Ser.: No. 407). 84p. pap. 22.00 (ISBN 0-317-30173-X, 2025355). Bks Demand UMI.
Froese, Arnold & Paraskevas, Frixos, eds. Structures & Function of FC Receptors. (Receptors & Ligands in Intercellular Communication Ser.: Vol. 2). (Illus.). 312p. 1983. 49.75 (ISBN 0-8247-1814-3). Dekker.
Froese, Victor & Straw, Stanley B., eds. Research in the Language Arts. LC 80-20543. (Illus.). 336p. 1981. pap. 16.00 (ISBN 0-8391-1609-8). Pro Ed.
Froh, Alfred & King, Margaret. Games for Young People. 1943. pap. 2.25 (ISBN 0-8066-0080-2, 10-2515). Augsburg.
Froh, Riley. Wildcatter Extraordinary. 208p. 1984. 11.95 (ISBN 0-911225-03-X). Clearstream Pr.
Frohlich, A. Central Extensions, Galois Groups, & Ideal Class Groups of Numbers Fields. LC 83-19685. (Contemporary Mathematics Ser.: Vol. 24). 86p. 1983. pap. 17.00 (ISBN 0-8218-5022-9). Am Math.
Frohlich, A., ed. Algebraic Number Field: L Functions & Galois Properties. 1977. 96.00 (ISBN 0-12-268960-7). Acad Pr.
Frohlich, Edward D. Pathophysiology: Altered Regulatory Mechanisms in Disease. 3rd ed. 992p. 1983. text ed. 37.50 (ISBN 0-397-52103-0, 65-07040, Lippincott Medical). Lippincott.
--Rypins' Medical Licensure Examinations. 14th ed. 1050p. 1985. text ed. 49.00 (ISBN 0-397-50674-0, Lippincott Medical). Lippincott.
Frohlich, H. & Kremer, F., eds. Coherent Excitations in Biological Systems. (Proceedings in Life Sciences). (Illus.). 224p. 1983. 27.50 (ISBN 0-387-12540-X). Springer-Verlag.
Frohlich, Jurg. Sealing & Self-Similarity in Physics. (Progress in Physics Ser.: Vol. 7). 434p. 1983. text ed. 27.50 (ISBN 0-8176-3168-2). Birkhauser.
Frohlich, Klaus. The Emergence of Russian Constitutionalism Nineteen Hundred to Nineteen Hundred Four: The Relationship Between Social Mobilization & Political Group Formation in Pre-Revolutionary Russia. 304p. 1982. 52.50 (ISBN 90-247-2378-7, Pub. by Martinus Nijhoff Netherlands). Kluwer Academic.
Frohlich, Margaret, tr. see Richter, Gottfried.
Frohlichstein, Jack. Mathematical Fun, Games & Puzzles. (Illus., Orig.). 1962. pap. 4.50 (ISBN 0-486-20789-7). Dover.
Frohman, Daniel. Encore. LC 72-99694. (Essay Index Reprint Ser.). 1937. 24.50 (ISBN 0-8369-1466-X). Ayer Co Pubs.
Frohne, Dietrich & Pfaender, Hans J. A Colour Atlas of Poisonous Plants. Bisset, N. G., tr. from Ger. (Illus.). 292p. 1984. text ed. 58.00x (ISBN 0-7234-0839-4, Pub. by Wolfe Medical England). Sheridan.
Frohock, Fred M. Abortion: A Case Study in Law & Morals. LC 83-5614. (Contributions in Political Science Ser.: No. 102). xiii, 224p. 1983. lib. bdg. 29.95 (ISBN 0-313-23953-3, FRA/). Greenwood.
--Public Policy: Scope & Logic. LC 78-8382. 1979. 27.95 (ISBN 0-13-737932-3). P-H.
Frohock, W. M. Frank Norris. LC 68-64751. (Pamphlets on American Writers Ser: No. 68). (Orig.). 1968. pap. 1.25x (ISBN 0-8166-0482-7, MPAW68). U of Minn Pr.
--Novel of Violence in America. 5th ed. LC 57-14767. 1957. 12.95 (ISBN 0-87074-054-7). SMU Press.
--Strangers to This Ground: Cultural Diversity in Contemporary American Writing. LC 61-17183. 1961. 12.95 (ISBN 0-87074-055-5). SMU Press.
--Theodore Dreiser. (Pamphlets on American Writers Ser.: No. 102). 1972. pap. 1.25x (ISBN 0-8166-0645-5). U of Minn Pr.
Frohock, W. M., et al. Image & Theme: Studies in Modern French Fiction - Bernanos, Malraux, Sarraute, Gide, Martin Du Gard. Keane, Susan, ed. LC 79-95931. 1969. pap. 4.50x (ISBN 0-674-44395-0). Harvard U Pr.
Frohock, Wilbur. Andre Malraux. LC 74-1198. (Columbia Essays on Modern Writers Ser.: No. 71). 48p. 1974. pap. 2.50 (ISBN 0-231-03441-5). Columbia U Pr.
Frohock, Wilbur M. Andre Malraux & the Tragic Imagination. 1952. 15.00x (ISBN 0-8047-0441-4); pap. 5.95 (ISBN 0-8047-0442-2, SP42). Stanford U Pr.
--French Literature: An Approach Through Close Reading. 4th ed. 1970. 4.95 (ISBN 0-87774-000-3). Schoenhof.
--Style & Temper: Studies in French Fiction, 1925-1960. LC 67-3155. 1967. 10.00x (ISBN 0-674-85335-0). Harvard U Pr.
Frohse, Franz, et al. Atlas of Human Anatomy. 7th ed. pap. 6.95 (ISBN 0-06-460206-0, CO 206, COS). B&N NY.
--Atlas of Human Anatomy. 6th rev. & enl. ed. LC 61-15471. (Illus.). 180p. 1961. pap. text ed. 15.00x (ISBN 0-06-480289-2). B&N Imports.
Froiland, Sven G. Natural History of the Black Hills. LC 78-55071. (Illus.). pap. write for info (ISBN 0-931170-06-0); pap. 8.95. Ctr Western Studies.
Froissard, Jean. Basic Dressage. pap. 5.00 (ISBN 0-87980-219-7). Wilshire.
--Equitation. pap. 5.00 (ISBN 0-87980-188-3). Wilshire.
--Jumping: Learning & Teaching. pap. 5.00 (ISBN 0-87980-197-2). Wilshire.
Froissard, Jean & Froissard, Lilly P. The Horseman's International Book of Reference. (Illus.). 416p. 1980. 45.00 (ISBN 0-09-132400-9, NO. 0217, Pub. by Hutchinson England). Methuen Inc.
Froissard, Lilly P., jt. auth. see Froissard, Jean.
Froissart. Chronicles. Brereton, Geoffrey, tr. from Fr. (Classics Ser). 1978. pap. 5.95 (ISBN 0-14-044200-6). Penguin.
Froissart, Jean. Chronicle of Froissart, 6 Vols. Bourchier, John, tr. LC 70-168064. (Tudor Translations. First Ser.: Nos. 27-32). Repr. of 1903 ed. Set. 270.00 (ISBN 0-404-51930-X); 45.00 ea. Vol. 1 (ISBN 0-404-51931-8). Vol. 2 (ISBN 0-404-51932-6). Vol. 3 (ISBN 0-404-51933-4). Vol. 4 (ISBN 0-404-51934-2). Vol. 5 (ISBN 0-404-51935-0). Vol. 6 (ISBN 0-404-51936-9). AMS Pr.
--Here Begynneth the First Volum of Sir J. Froyssart. Bourchier, J., tr. LC 72-26004. (English Experience Ser.: No. 257). 644p. 1970. Repr. of 1523 ed. 104.00 (ISBN 90-221-0257-2). Walter J Johnson.
--Here Begynneth the Thirde & Fourthe Boke of Sir J. Froissart. LC 72-199. (English Experience Ser.: No. 250). 660p. 1970. Repr. of 1525 ed. 104.00 (ISBN 90-221-0250-5). Walter J Johnson.
--Meliador, 3 Vols. Longnon, A., ed. 1965. 125.00 (ISBN 0-384-17041-2); pap. 108.00 (ISBN 0-384-17040-4). Johnson Repr.

Froissart, Marcel, ed. Hyperbolic Equations & Waves: Battelle Seattle 1968 Recontres. LC 76-86498. (Illus.). 1970. 40.80 (ISBN 0-387-04883-9). Springer-Verlag.

Froland, Charles, et al. Helping Networks & Human Services: Creating a Partnership. (Sage Library of Social Research: Vol. 128). 180p. 1981. 24.00 (ISBN 0-8039-1625-6); pap. 12.00 (ISBN 0-8039-1626-4). Sage.

Frolander-Ulf, Monica & Lindenfeld, Frank. A New Earth: The Jamaican Sugar Worker's Cooperatives, 1975-1981. (Illus.). 240p. (Orig.). 1985. lib. bdg. 24.50 (ISBN 0-8191-4844-X); pap. text ed. 12.50 (ISBN 0-8191-4845-8). U Pr of Amer.

Frolic, B. Michael. Mao's People: Sixteen Portraits of Life in Revolutionary China. 296p. 1980. 16.50t (ISBN 0-674-54846-9); pap. 6.95 (ISBN 0-674-54845-0). Harvard U Pr.

Frolich, Edward D. Rypin's Medical Licensure Examinations. 13th ed. (Illus.). 1054p. 1981. text ed. 49.00 (ISBN 0-397-52091-3, 65-05853, Lippincott Medical). Lippincott.

Frolich, J. C., ed. Methods in Prostaglandin Research. LC 78-66346. (Advances in Prostaglandin & Thromboxane Research Ser.: Vol. 5). 256p. 1978. 42.00 (ISBN 0-89004-204-7). Raven.

Frolich, Paul. Rosa Luxemburg. 59.95 (ISBN 0-8490-0973-1). Gordon Pr.

--Rosa Luxemburg: Her Life & Work. Hoornweg, Johanna, tr. from Ger. LC 72-81776. 352p. (Orig.). 1972. pap. 6.95 (ISBN 0-85345-260-1). Monthly Rev.

Frolick, N. J. & Oppenheimer, J. Modern Political Economy. 1978. pap. 14.95 (ISBN 0-13-597120-9). P-H.

Frolick, S. J. Once There Was a President. rev. ed. LC 80-69972. (Once There Was... Ser.). 64p. (gr. 3-7). 1980. pap. 6.95 (ISBN 0-9605426-0-4). Black Star Pub.

Frolkin, V. Pulse Circuits. 390p. 1982. 9.45 (ISBN 0-8285-2467-X, Pub. by Mir Pubs USSR). Imported Pubns.

Frolkis, V. V. Aging & Life-Prolonging Processes. (Illus.). 380p. 1982. 41.50 (ISBN 0-387-81685-2). Springer-Verlag.

Frolkis, V. V. & Bezrukov, V. V. Aging of the Central Nervous System. (Interdisciplinary Topics in Gerontology: Vol. 16). (Illus.). 1979. pap. 28.25 (ISBN 3-8055-2995-3). S Karger.

Frolkis, V. V., ed. Physiology of Cell Aging. (Interdisciplinary Topics in Gerontology: Vol. 18). (Illus.). viii, 208p. 1984. 70.00 (ISBN 3-8055-3866-9). S Karger.

Frolov, A. Petrozavodsk & Kizhi: A Guide. 168p. 1984. 6.95 (ISBN 0-8285-2801-2, Pub. by Raduga Pubs USSR). Imported Pubns.

Frolov, Andrei & Frolova, Lois B. Against the Odds: A True American-Soviet Love Story. LC 83-15114. (Illus.). 250p. 1983. 14.95 (ISBN 0-914091-37-9). Chicago Review.

Frolov, I. Global Problems & the Future of Mankind. 311p. 1982. 7.95 (ISBN 0-8285-2479-3, Pub. by Progress Pubs USSR). Imported Pubns.

Frolov, Ivan, ed. Dictionary of Philosophy. LC 83-244. 464p. 1985. 8.95 (ISBN 0-7178-0604-9). Intl Pubs Co.

Frolov, Yuril P. Pavlov & His School. Dutt, C. P., tr. from Rus. LC 38-901. (Psychology Ser). 1970. Repr. of 1938 ed. 23.00 (ISBN 0-384-17060-9). Johnson Repr.

Frolova, Lois B., jt. auth. see Frolov, Andrei.

From, Franz. Perception of Other People. Maher, Brendan A. & Kvan, Erik, trs. from Dan. LC 76-138295. 179p. 1971. 24.00x (ISBN 0-231-03402-4). Columbia U Pr.

From, Lester D. & Staver, Allen E. Fundamentals of Weather: A Workbook Approach. 1979. 16.50 (ISBN 0-8403-2023-X). Kendall-Hunt.

Froman, Creel. Manuscript of Hugo Potts: An Inquiry into Meaning. LC 73-5915. 376p. 1973. 12.85x (ISBN 0-8093-0608-5). S Ill U Pr.

--The Two American Political Systems: Society, Economics, & Politics. (Illus.). 288p. 1984. pap. text ed. 17.95 (ISBN 0-13-934902-2). P-H.

Froman, Katherine. Chance to Grow. 1983. 13.95 (ISBN 0-89696-192-3). Dodd.

Froman, Lewis A., Jr. Congressmen & Their Constituencies. LC 74-15553. 127p. 1974. Repr. of 1963 ed. lib. bdg. 22.50x (ISBN 0-8371-7820-7, FRCO). Greenwood.

Froman, Robert. Angles Are Easy As Pie. LC 75-6608. (Young Math Ser.). (Illus.). 40p. (gr. k-3). 1976. PLB 11.89 (ISBN 0-690-00916-X). Crowell Jr Bks.

--A Game of Functions. LC 74-2266. (Young Math Ser.). (Illus.). 40p. (gr. k-3). 1974. PLB 10.89 (ISBN 0-690-00545-8). Crowell Jr Bks.

--The Greatest Guessing Game. LC 77-5463. (A Young Math Bk.). (Illus.). (gr. 1-3). 1978. PLB 11.89 (ISBN 0-690-01376-0). Crowell Jr Bks.

--Mushrooms & Molds. LC 71-187936. (A Let's-Read-&-Find-Out Science Book). (Illus.). (gr. k-3). 1972. PLB 11.89 (ISBN 0-690-56603-4). Crowell Jr Bks.

--Venn Diagrams. LC 75-187937. (Young Math Ser.). (Illus.). (gr. 1-5). 1972. PLB 11.89 (ISBN 0-690-85997-X). Crowell Jr Bks.

Froman, Wayne J. Merleau-Ponty: Language & the Act of Speech. LC 81-65292. 256p. 1982. 29.50 (ISBN 0-8387-5015-X). Bucknell U Pr.

Fromberg, Doris & Driscoll, Maryanne. The Successful Classroom: Management Strategies for Regular & Special Education Teachers. 1985. text ed. 22.95x (ISBN 0-8077-2778-4); pap. text ed. 15.95x (ISBN 0-8077-2771-7). Tchrs Coll.

Fromberg, Doris P. Early Childhood Education: A Perceptual Models Curriculum. LC 76-45390. pap. 67.90 (ISBN 0-317-09838-1, 2055109). Bks Demand UMI.

Fromberg, Robert & Best, Rebecca, eds. A Reader of New American Fiction. 216p. (Orig.). 1981. pap. 4.95 (ISBN 0-940096-00-5). I-Seventy-Four.

Frome, Michael. Battle for the Wilderness. (Encore Edition Ser.). 256p. 1984. Repr. of 1974 ed. softcover 20.00x (ISBN 0-86531-784-4). Westview.

--The Forest Service. (Federal Departments, Agencies, & Systems). 300p. 1984. lib. bdg. 32.00x (ISBN 0-86531-177-3). Westview.

--National Park Guide, LC 77-4075. 1984. pap. 9.95 (ISBN 0-528-84744-9). Rand.

--The National Parks. rev.. ed. (Illus.). 160p. (Orig.). 1981. pap. 9.95 (ISBN 0-528-88045-4). Rand.

--Promised Land: Adventures & Encounters in Wild America. LC 84-19074. 316p. 1985. 18.95 (ISBN 0-688-04173-6). Morrow.

--Strangers in High Places: The Story of the Great Smoky Mountains. rev. ed. LC 79-19748. 1980. lib. bdg. 18.95x (ISBN 0-87049-281-0); pap. 8.50 (ISBN 0-87049-287-X). U of Tenn Pr.

--Whose Woods These Are. LC 84-51245. (Encore Edition Ser.). 375p. 1984. Repr. of 1962 ed. pap. 35.00x (ISBN 0-86531-785-2). Westview.

Frome, Michael, ed. Issues in Wilderness Management. (A Westview Replica Edition-Softcover Ser.). 180p. 1984. pap. 18.00x (ISBN 0-86531-894-8). Westview.

Frome, Robert L. & Max, Herbert. Raising Capital: Private Placement Forms & Techniques. 723p. 1981. Annual supplements avail. 85.00 (ISBN 0-15-003987-5, H39875, Law & Business). HarBraceJ.

Froment, Diana de see De Froment, Diana.

Froment, G., jt. ed. see Delmon, B.

Froment, G. F., ed. Large Chemical Plants. (Chemical Engineering Monographs: Vol. 10). 190p. 1979. 53.25 (ISBN 0-444-41837-7). Elsevier.

Froment, Gilbert F. & Bischoff, Kenneth B. Chemical Reactor Analysis & Design. LC 78-12465. 765p. 1979. text ed. 55.50x (ISBN 0-471-02447-3). Wiley.

Froment, M. Passivity of Metals & Semiconductors: Proceedings of the Fifth International Symposium on Passivity. (Thin Films Science & Technology Ser.: Vol. 4). 1984. 125.00 (ISBN 0-444-42252-8). Elsevier.

Fromentin, Eugene. Dominique. Hoog, ed. (Bibliotheque de Cluny). pap. 6.95 (ISBN 0-685-34908-X). French & Eur.

--The Masters of Past Time: Dutch & Flemish Painting from Van Eyck to Rembrandt. (Illus.). 1981. 11.95x (ISBN 0-8014-9219-X, Pub. by Phaidon England). Cornell U Pr.

Fromer, Margaret & Fromer, Paul. A Woman's Workshop on Philippians. (Woman's Workshop Ser.). 128p. 1982. pap. 2.95 (ISBN 0-310-44771-2). Zondervan.

Fromer, Margaret & Keyes, Sharrel. Genesis I through XXV: Walking with God. rev. ed. (Fisherman Bible Studyguide Ser.). 80p. 1979. saddle-stitched 2.95 (ISBN 0-87788-297-5). Shaw Pubs.

--Genesis XXVI through L: Called by God. rev. ed. (Fisherman Bible Studyguide Ser.). 66p. 1979. pap. 2.95 saddle-stitched (ISBN 0-87788-298-3). Shaw Pubs.

--Jonah, Habakkuk, Malachi. (Fisherman Bible Studyguide Ser.). 68p. 1982. saddle-stitch 2.95 (ISBN 0-87788-432-3). Shaw Pubs.

--Let's Pray Together: Studies in Prayer. LC 74-76160. (Fisherman Bible Studyguide Ser.). 63p. 1974. saddle-stitched 2.95 (ISBN 0-87788-801-9). Shaw Pubs.

--Letters to the Thessalonians. LC 75-33441. (Fisherman Bible Studyguide Ser.). 47p. 1975. saddle-stitched 2.95 (ISBN 0-87788-489-7). Shaw Pubs.

--Letters to Timothy: Discipleship in Action. LC 74-19763. (Fisherman Bible Study Guide Ser.). 80p. 1974. saddle-stitched 2.95 (ISBN 0-87788-490-0). Shaw Pubs.

Fromer, Margaret & Nystrom, Carolyn. James: Roadmap for Down-to-Earth Christians. (Young Fisherman Bible Studyguide Ser.). (Illus.). 89p. 1982. saddle-stiched tchr's. ed. 4.95 (ISBN 0-87788-420-X); student ed. 2.95 (ISBN 0-87788-419-6). Shaw Pubs.

Fromer, Margaret, jt. auth. see Nystrom, Carolyn.

Fromer, Margot J. A.I.D.S. Acquired Immune Deficiency Syndrome. 273p. (Orig.). 1983. pap. 3.95 (ISBN 0-523-42130-3). Pinnacle Bks.

--Community Health Care & the Nursing Process. 2nd ed. LC 82-2130. (Illus.). 491p. 1983. pap. text ed. 24.95 (ISBN 0-8016-1725-1). Mosby.

--Ethical Issues in Health Care. LC 80-25058. 420p. 1981. pap. text ed. 17.95 (ISBN 0-8016-1728-6). Mosby.

--Ethical Issues in Sexuality & Reproduction. LC 82-14460. 375p. 1983. pap. text ed. 15.95 (ISBN 0-8016-1708-1). Mosby.

--Menopause. 224p. (Orig.). 1985. pap. 3.95 (ISBN 0-317-19379-1). Pinnacle Bks.

Fromer, Margot J., jt. auth. see Conn, Frances G.

Fromer, Paul, jt. auth. see Fromer, Margaret.

Fromherz, H. & King, A. English-German Chemical Terminology: An Introduction to Chemistry in English & German. 5th rev. ed. 588p. (Eng. & Ger.). 1968. 55.00 (ISBN 0-686-56603-3, M-7362, Pub. by Vlg. Chemie). French & Eur.

--Franzoesische und Deutsche Chemische Fachausdruecke. 568p. (Fr. & Ger.). 1969. 52.50 (ISBN 3-527-25094-8, M-7415, Pub. by Vlg. Chemie). French & Eur.

--French-English Chemical Terminology: An Introduction to Chemistry in French & English. 561p. (Fr. & Ger.). 1968. 52.50 (ISBN 0-686-56475-8, M-7417, Pub. by Vlg. Chemie). French & Eur.

Fromherz, Hans & King, Alexander. English-German Chemical Terminology: An Introduction to Chemistry in English & German. 5th ed. LC 68-26705. 588p. (Eng. & Ger.). 1968. 46.30x (ISBN 3-527-25093-X). VCH Pubs.

--French-English Chemical Terminology: An Introduction to Chemistry in French & English. 561p. (Fr. & Eng.). 1968. 46.30x (ISBN 3-527-25095-6). VCH Pubs.

--French-German Chemical Terminology: An Introduction to Chemistry in French & German. LC 68-54575. 588p. (Fr. & Ger.). 1969. 46.30x (ISBN 3-527-25094-8). VCH Pubs.

Fromhold, A. T. Quantum Mechanics for Applied Physics & Engineering. LC 80-19001. 1981. 34.50 (ISBN 0-12-269150-4). Acad Pr.

--Theory of Metal Oxidation, Vol. 1: Fundamentals. LC 75-23121. (Defects in Crystalline Solids: Vol. 9). (Illus.). 548p. 1976. 117.00 (ISBN 0-444-10957-9, North-Holland). Elsevier.

--Theory of Metal Oxidation Vol. 2: Space Charge. (Defects in Crystalline Solids Ser.: Vol. 12). 332p. 1980. 76.75 (ISBN 0-444-85381-2, North-Holland). Elsevier.

Froming, William J., jt. auth. see Levy, C. Michael.

Fromkin, David. The Independence of Nations. LC 81-12093. 193p. 1981. 23.95 (ISBN 0-03-059777-3); pap. 12.95 (ISBN 0-03-059778-1). Praeger.

Fromkin, Howard L., jt. auth. see Snyder, C. R.

Fromkin, Howard L. & Sherwood, John J., eds. Integrating the Organization: A Social Psychological Analysis. LC 73-21306. (Illus.). 1974. 22.50 (ISBN 0-02-910920-5). Free Pr.

Fromkin, Victoria & Rodman, Robert. An Introduction to Language. 3rd ed. LC 82-18719. 385p. 1983. pap. text ed. 18.95 (ISBN 0-03-059779-X). HR&W.

Fromkin, Victoria A., ed. Phonetic Linguistics: Essays in Honor of Peter Ladefoged. Date not set. 49.00 (ISBN 0-12-268990-9). Acad Pr.

--Speech Errors As Linguistic Evidence. LC 73-78443. (Janua Linguarum, Ser. Major: No. 77). (Illus.). 269p. 1973. text ed. 34.00x (ISBN 90-2792-668-9). Mouton.

--Tone: A Linguistic Survey. 1978. 37.50 (ISBN 0-12-267350-6). Acad Pr.

Fromm, Alan & Soames, Nicolas. Judo: The Gentle Way. (Illus.). 144p. (Orig.). 1982. pap. 10.95 (ISBN 0-7100-9025-0). Routledge & Kegan.

Fromm, David, ed. Gastrointestinal Surgery, 2 vols. (Illus.). 934p. 1985. Set. text ed. 135.00 (ISBN 0-443-08197-2). Churchill.

Fromm, Erica, jt. auth. see French, Thomas.

Fromm, Erich. Anatomy of Human Destructiveness. 576p. 1978. pap. 3.50 (ISBN 0-449-24021-5, Crest). Fawcett.

--The Art of Loving. 128p. 1974. pap. 3.80i (ISBN 0-06-080291-X, P291, PL). Har-Row.

--Art of Loving: An Enquiry into the Nature of Love. pap. 4.76i (ISBN 0-06-090001-6, CN 1, CN). Har-Row.

--Art of Loving: An Enquiry into the Nature of Love. LC 56-8750. (World Perspectives Ser.). 1956. 14.37i (ISBN 0-06-011375-8, HarpT). Har-Row.

--Beyond the Chains of Illusion. 1985. pap. 7.95 (ISBN 0-317-16272-1, Touchstone Bks). S&S.

--Escape from Freedom. 336p. 1971. pap. 4.95 (ISBN 0-380-01167-0, 69690-8, Discus). Avon.

--For the Love of Life. Kimber, Robert & Kimber, Rita, trs. 185p. 1985. 16.95 (ISBN 0-02-910930-2). Free Pr.

--The Forgotten Language. 1956. pap. 4.95 (ISBN 0-394-17483-6, E47, Ever). Grove.

--The Greatness & Limitations of Freud's Thought. LC 79-2730. 1980. 11.49i (ISBN 0-06-011389-8, HarpT). Har-Row.

--Greatness & Limitations of Freud's Thought. 1981. pap. 2.95 (ISBN 0-451-61995-1, ME1995, Ment). NAL.

--The Heart of Man: Its Genius for Good & Evil. LC 64-18053. 1980. pap. 4.33i (ISBN 0-06-090795-9, CN 795, CN). Har-Row.

--Man for Himself. 256p. 1978. pap. 2.95 (ISBN 0-449-30819-7, Prem). Fawcett.

--Man for Himself: An Inquiry into the Psychology of Ethics. 1947. 7.95 (ISBN 0-03-025530-9). HR&W.

--Marx's Concept of Man. LC 61-11935. (Milestones of Thought Ser.). xii, 263p. (With translations from Marx's Economic & Philosophical Manuscripts by T. B. Bottomore). 14.95 (ISBN 0-8044-5391-8); pap. 6.95 (ISBN 0-8044-6161-9). Ungar.

--On Disobedience & Other Essays. LC 81-2260. 144p. 1981. 9.95 (ISBN 0-8164-0500-X, Pub. by Seabury). Winston Pr.

--Psychoanalysis & Religion. (Terry Lectures Ser.). 1950. pap. 5.95 (ISBN 0-300-00089-8, Y12). Yale U Pr.

--Sane Society. 320p. 1977. pap. 2.95 (ISBN 0-449-30821-9, Prem). Fawcett.

--Sigmund Freud's Mission: An Analysis of His Personality & Influence. 11.25 (ISBN 0-8446-4544-3). Peter Smith.

--To Have or to Be? 256p. 1981. pap. 4.50 (ISBN 0-553-25437-5). Bantam.

--To Have or to Be? LC 73-130449. (World Perspectives). 1976. 13.41i (ISBN 0-06-011379-0, HarpT). Har-Row.

--The Working Class in Weimar Germany: A Psychological & Sociological Study. (Illus.). 320p. text ed. 22.50x (ISBN 0-674-95925-6). Harvard U Pr.

--You Shall Be As Gods: A Radical Interpretation of the Old Testament & Its Tradition. 1977. pap. 2.50 (ISBN 0-449-30763-8, Prem). Fawcett.

Fromm, Erich & Xirau, Ramon. Nature of Man. 1968. pap. 5.95 (ISBN 0-02-084960-5). Macmillan.

Fromm, Erich, et al. Zen Buddhism & Psychoanalysis. LC 60-5293. 1970. pap. 5.72i (ISBN 0-06-090175-6, CN175, CN). Har-Row.

Fromm, Erika & Shor, Ronald E. Hypnosis: Developments in Research & New Perspectives. 2nd ed. LC 79-89279. (Illus.). 793p. 1979. lib. bdg. 59.95x (ISBN 0-202-26085-2). Aldine Pub.

Fromm, Gary & Taubman, Paul. Policy Simulations with an Econometric Model. LC 67-30593. pap. 48.80 (ISBN 0-317-20828-4, 2025378). Bks Demand UMI.

Fromm, Gary, ed. Studies in Public Regulation. (Regulation of Economic Activity Ser.). (Illus.). 400p. 1981. 55.00x (ISBN 0-262-06074-4). MIT Pr.

Fromm, Gary & Schmalensee, eds. Studies in Public Regulation. (Regulation of Economic Activity Ser. (REA)). (Illus.). 368p. 1981. pap. text ed. 16.50x (ISBN 0-262-56028-3). MIT Pr.

Fromm, Gary, ed. see Brookings Conference on the Effects of Tax Policy on Investment.

Fromm, Georg H. Cesar Andreu Iglesias. (Norte Ser.). (Illus.). 152p. 1977. pap. 3.95 (ISBN 0-940238-06-3). Ediciones Huracan.

Fromm, Gloria G. Dorothy Richardson: A Biography. LC 77-8455. 470p. 1977. 24.95x (ISBN 0-252-00631-3). U of Ill Pr.

Fromm, H. J. Initial Rate Enzyme Kinetics. LC 75-20206. (Molecular Biology, Biochemistry, & Biophysics: Vol. 22). (Illus.). 350p. 1975. 48.00 (ISBN 0-387-07375-2). Springer-Verlag.

Fromm, Hans & Grubmueller, Klaus, eds. Konrad von Fussesbrunnen: Die Kindheit Jesu. LC 72-94025. 220p. (Ger.). 1973. 55.60x (ISBN 3-11-004140-5). De Gruyter.

Fromm, Herbert. Herbert Fromm on Jewish Music: A Composers View. LC 78-60716. 1979. 7.95 (ISBN 0-8197-0465-2). Bloch.

--Key of See: Travel Journals of a Composer. 1967. 4.00 (ISBN 0-87368-061-8). Plowshare.

Fromm, Hermann. Deutschland in der Oeffentlichen Kriegszieldiskussion Grossbritanniens 1939-1945. (European University Studies: No. 3, Vol. 167). 167p. 1982. 43.15 (ISBN 3-8204-7024-7). P Lang Pubs.

Fromm, Hieronimus, illus. The Ballad of El Cid. LC 85-40431. (Classics for Kids Ser.). (Illus.). 32p. (gr. 3 up). 1985. pap. 3.75 (ISBN 0-382-09100-0). Silver.

Fromm, M. Gerard & Smith, Bruce L. The Facilitating Environment: Clinical Applications of Winnicot's Theories. Date not set. price not set (BN#01825). Intl Univs Pr.

Fromme, Allan. The ABC of Child Care. 1982. pap. 3.95 (ISBN 0-671-46838-3). PB.

--Ability to Love. pap. 6.00 (ISBN 0-87980-000-3). Wilshire.

--The Book for Normal Neurotics. 243p. 1981. 10.95 (ISBN 0-374-11544-3). FS&G.

--The Book for Normal Neurotics. LC 81-85820. 256p. 1982. pap. 2.95 (ISBN 0-86721-139-3). Jove Pubns.

--Sixty Plus: Planning It, Living It, Loving It. 187p. 1984. 13.95 (ISBN 0-374-26556-9). FS&G.

Fromme, Marlene, et al. Cocaine: Seduction & Solution. 1984. 13.95 (ISBN 0-517-55175-6, C N Potter Bks). Crown.

Frommel, S. N. Taxation of Branches & Subsidiaries in Western Europe, Canada & the USA. 1978. pap. 34.00 (ISBN 90-200-0508-1, Pub. by Kluwer Law Netherlands). Kluwer Academic.

--Taxation of Branches & Subsidiaries in Western Europe, Canada & the USA. 121p. 1975. pap. text ed. 16.75x (ISBN 90-200-0429-8). Rothman.

Frommel, S. N. & Thompson, J. H., eds. Company Law in Europe. 680p. 1975. text ed. 45.00x (ISBN 0-8377-0530-4). Rothman.

Frommel, S. N., jt. ed. see Keeton, G. W.

Frommer. New York on Thirty Five Dollars a Day. reev. ed. (Frommer Travel Guides). (Illus.). 1984. 8.50 (ISBN 0-671-10851-4, Fireside). S&S.

Frommer, Arthur. Europe on Twenty-Five Dollars a Day, 1985-86. (Dollar-a-Day Guides Ser.). 744p. 1985. pap. 10.95 (ISBN 0-671-52473-9). Frommer-Pasmantier.

Frommer, Eva A., tr. see Aymes, Clement A.

Frommer, Eva A., tr. see Steiner, Rudolf.

Frommer, Harvery & Frommer, Myrna, eds. The Games of the Twenty-Third Olympiad: Los Angeles 1984 Commemorative Book. LC 84-80729. (Illus.). 288p. 1984. 34.94 (ISBN 0-913927-02-3); leather 49.95 (ISBN 0-913927-03-1). Intl Sport Pubns.

Frommer, Harvey. Baseball's Greatest Managers. 1985. 16.95 (ISBN 0-531-09779-X). Watts.

--Baseball's Greatest Records, Streaks & Feats. LC 82-45939. 208p. 1983. 13.95 (ISBN 0-689-11385-4). Atheneum.

--Baseball's Greatest Rivalry: The New York Yankees & Boston Red Sox. LC 83-69159. 208p. 1984. pap. 5.95 (ISBN 0-689-70666-9, 308). Atheneum.

--Baseball's Hall of Fame. (Illus.). 72p. (gr. 4-6). 1985. PLB 9.40 (ISBN 0-531-04904-3). Watts.

--Jackie Robinson. (Impact Ser.). 128p. (gr. 7-12). 1984. lib. bdg. 10.90 (ISBN 0-531-04858-6). Watts.

--New York City Baseball. LC 84-45636. 256p. 1985. pap. 8.95 (ISBN 0-689-70684-7, 324). Atheneum.

--Sports Dates: This Day in Sports. (Orig.). (gr. 5 up). 1981. pap. 2.25 (ISBN 0-448-17214-3, Pub. by Tempo). Ace Bks.

--Sports Genes. (Illus.). 160p. 1982. pap. 1.95 (ISBN 0-448-16928-2, Pub. by Tempo). Ace Bks.

--Sports Lingo: A Dictionary of the Language of Sports. LC 82-12130. 312p. 1983. pap. 7.95 (ISBN 0-689-70640-5, 289). Atheneum.

Frommer, Harvey, jt. auth. see Lieberman, Nancy.

Frommer, Herbert H. Radiology for Dental Auxiliaries. 2nd ed. LC 77-15473. (Illus.). 1978. text ed. 17.95 (ISBN 0-8016-1706-5). Mosby.

--Radiology in Dental Practice. LC 81-38411. (Illus.). 303p. 1981. text ed. 34.95 (ISBN 0-8016-1709-X). Mosby.

Frommer, Judith G. & Weitx, Margaret C. A Listener's Guide for "Elizabeth Hoche, Ingenieur". 2nd ed. (Femmes et Metiers Ser.). 10p. 1979. with tapescript to interview 12.95x, (ISBN 0-88432-082-0, F403). J Norton Pubs.

Frommer, Judith G. & Weitz, Margaret C. A Listener's Guide for "Dominique Dupuis, Directrice Commerciale". 2nd ed. (Femme et Metiers Ser.). 1979. with tapescript to interview 12.95x, (ISBN 0-88432-081-2, F403). J Norton Pubs.

--A Listener's Guide For "Josette Benoite, Femme Politique". 2nd ed. (Femme et Metiers Ser.). 12p. 1979. with transcript to interview 12.95, (ISBN 0-88432-080-4, F401). J Norton Pubs.

Frommer, Myrna, jt. ed. see Frommer, Harvery.

Fromm-Reichmann, Frieda. Principles of Intensive Psychotherapy. LC 50-9782. 1960. pap. 7.50x (ISBN 0-226-26599-4, P49, Phoen). U of Chicago Pr.

--Psychoanalysis & Psychotherapy: Selected Papers. Bullard, Dexter M., ed. LC 59-10746. 368p. 1974. pap. 9.95 (ISBN 0-226-26597-8, P580, Phoen). U of Chicago Pr.

Frompovich, Catherine. Feeding Baby Naturally from Pregnancy On. 1983. 4.95x (ISBN 0-935322-22-1). Cancer Control Soc.

Frompovich, Catherine J. Attacking Hay Fever & Winning. Koppenhaver, April M., ed. 32p. 1981. pap. 2.50 (ISBN 0-935322-15-9). C J Frompovich.

--A Child's ABC's for Nutrition Coloring Book. rev. ed. (Illus.). 32p. (ps-1). 1981. pap. text ed. 1.10 (ISBN 0-935322-17-5). C J Frompovich.

--Feeding Baby Naturally from Pregnancy on. Witt, Diana, ed. (Illus.). 104p. (Orig.). 1983. pap. 4.95 (ISBN 0-935322-22-1). C J Frompovich.

--Kids Cooking Naturally. (Illus.). 32p. (gr. 2-5). 1979. pap. 1.50 (ISBN 0-935322-04-3). C J Frompovich.

--Natural & Nutritious Cooking Course. 94p. 1982. lab manual 50.00 (ISBN 0-935322-21-3). C J Frompovich.

--Nutrition Workbook for Children. 32p. (gr. 1-5). 1978. pap. 1.60 (ISBN 0-935322-00-0). C J Frompovich.

--So You Want to Cook Naturally. 160p. 1979. pap. 2.50 (ISBN 0-935322-03-5). C J Frompovich.

--The Story How Judy Saved Her Teeth: Nutrition Made Easy. 8p. (gr. 2-3). 1982. pap. 0.59 (ISBN 0-935322-19-1). C J Frompovich.

--Understanding Body Chemistry & Hair Mineral Analysis. Koppenhaver, April M., ed. 128p. 1982. pap. text ed. 4.95 (ISBN 0-935322-18-3). C J Frompovich.

--Upgrading Decision Making. Koppenhaver, April M., ed. (Illus.). 24p. 1982. pap. text ed. 4.00 (ISBN 0-935322-16-7). C J Frompovich.

Frompovich, Catherine J. & Hay, Joanne M. Everyday Herbs for Cooking & Healing. 1980. 100 frame filmstrip, cassette, text 25.00 (ISBN 0-935322-11-6). C J Frompovich.

Frompovich, Catherine J., jt. auth. see Hoffman, Taryn.

Frompovich, Catherine J., ed. see Pack-Miller, Lisa, et al.

Fromson, S., jt. auth. see Hargreaves, David.

Fromstein, Roberta H. & Churchill, Jacqueline C. Psychosocial Intervention for Hospital Discharge Planning. (Illus.). 388p. 1982. 29.75x (ISBN 0-398-04538-0). C C Thomas.

Froncek, Thomas. Take Away One: The Amazing True Story of a Woman Forced to Kidnap Her Own Child. 368p. 1985. 15.95 (ISBN 0-312-78342-6). St Martin.

Froncek, Thomas, ed. Voices from the Wilderness: The Frontiersman's Own Story. 1983. 14.25 (ISBN 0-8446-6040-X). Peter Smith.

Frond, Bill. Better Riding. (Better Bks.). (Illus.). (gr. 7 up). 17.95x (ISBN 0-7182-0159-0, SpS). Sportshelf.

Frondizi, Risieri. Nature of the Self: A Functional Interpretation. 224p. 1971. Repr. of 1953 ed. lib. bdg. 7.00x (ISBN 0-8093-0536-4). S Ill U Pr.

--Nature of the Self: A Functional Interpretation. (Arcturus Books Paperbacks). 224p. pap. 2.45 (ISBN 0-8093-0528-3). S Ill U Pr.

--What Is Value? An Introduction to Axiology. 2nd ed. Lipp, Solomon, tr. from Sp. LC 70-128196. xi, 183p. 1971. 16.95 (ISBN 0-87548-076-4); pap. 6.95 (ISBN 0-87548-077-2). Open Court.

Froniuis, jt. auth. see Kerpel.

Fronsdal, C., et al. Selected Papers of Julian Schwinger. (Mathematical Physics & Applied Mathematics Ser.: No. 4). 1979. lib. bdg. 29.50 (ISBN 90-277-0974-2, Pub. by Reidel Holland); pap. 11.95 (ISBN 90-277-0975-0, Pub. by Reidel Holland). Kluwer Academic.

Front, Dov. Radionuclide Brain Imaging. (Illus.). 176p. 1982. 39.50 (ISBN 0-8385-8257-5). ACC.

Front, Francis. Arabic Course: A Complete MacMillan Arabic Course. 1983. 2 bks. & 4 cassettes 55.00x (ISBN 0-333-23101-5). Intl Bk Ctr.

Front, Theodore. An Antiquarian Music Dealer's Education. LC 81-159949. (Front Music Publications: No. 3). 10p. (Orig.). 1981. pap. 5.00 (ISBN 0-934082-03-0). Theodore Front.

Frontado, Jose R. Alejandro E Isabel. 96p. (Span.). 1981. pap. 2.75 (ISBN 0-311-37024-1, Edit Mundo). Casa Bautista.

Frontain, Raymond-Jean, jt. auth. see Wojcik, Jan.

Frontain, Raymond-Jean & Wojcik, Jan, eds. The David Myth in Western Literature. LC 78-69904. (Illus.). 224p. 1980. 10.95 (ISBN 0-911198-55-5). Purdue U Pr.

Fronteau, J., et al, eds. Hadronic Mechanics: Proceedings of the Institute for Basic Research, Harvard Grounds, Cambridge, MA August 2-6, 1983. 290p. 1984. pap. text ed. 70.00x (ISBN 0-911767-11-8). Hadronic Pr Inc.

--Proceedings of the Second Workshop on Hadronics Mechanics Held in Villa Olmo Centro a Volta Como, Italy Aug. 3-Aug. 6, 1984, 2 vols. 1984. Set. pap. 140.00 (ISBN 0-911767-29-0); Vol. 1, 375 pgs. pap. 70.00 (ISBN 0-317-14022-1); Vol. 2, 375 pgs. pap. 70.00 (ISBN 0-317-14023-X). Hadronic Pr Inc.

Frontera, Ann. Persistence & Change: A History of Taveta. 1978. 8.00 (ISBN 0-918456-19-3, Crossroads). African Studies Assn.

Frontera, Jose G. Neuroanatomy Laboratory Guide. pap. 6.25 (ISBN 0-8477-2310-0). U of PR Pr.

Fronterhouse, Bob D. Life in the Dead Sea. 1973. pap. 3.25 (ISBN 0-89536-131-0). CSS of Ohio.

--They Cry at Christmas. 1970. pap. 3.50 (ISBN 0-89536-237-6). CSS of Ohio.

Fronterhouse, Robert. I Want to See Jesus. 1973. 3.00 (ISBN 0-89536-108-6, 0910). CSS of Ohio.

--Ye Shall Know the Truth. 3.50 (ISBN 0-317-04099-5). CSS of Ohio.

Frontier Press Company. Lincoln Library of Essential Information, 2 vols. 43rd ed. LC 82-645884. (Illus.). (gr. 5 up). 1985. Set. 119.95 (ISBN 0-912168-12-9). Frontier Pr Co.

--Lincoln Library of Language Arts, 2 vols. 6th ed. LC 80-54173. (Illus.). 1984. Set. 67.95 (ISBN 0-912168-10-2). Frontier Pr Co.

--Lincoln Library of Sports Champions, 20 vols. 4th ed. LC 84-81800. (Illus.). 2560p. (gr. 4 up). 1985. Set. 327.50 (ISBN 0-912168-11-0). Frontier Pr Co.

Frontinus, Sextus J. Stratagems & Aqueducts. (Loeb Classical Library: No. 174). 12.50x (ISBN 0-674-99192-3). Harvard U Pr.

Fronto. Correspondence, 2 Vols. (Loeb Classical Library: No. 112-113). 12.50x ea. Vol. 1 (ISBN 0-674-99124-9). Vol. 2 (ISBN 0-674-99125-7). Harvard U Pr.

Fronto, Marcus C. M. Cornelii Frontonis Epistulae, Adnotatione Critica Instructae. LC 75-7349. (Roman History Ser.). (Illus., Latin.). 1975. Repr. 26.50x (ISBN 0-405-07070-5). Ayer Co Pubs.

Fronval, George & Dubois, Daniel. Indian Signs & Signals. Egan, E. W., tr. LC 78-57792. (Illus.). 80p. (gr. 5 up). 1978. 16.95 (ISBN 0-8069-2720-8); PLB 19.99 (ISBN 0-8069-2721-6). Sterling.

Fronza, G., ed. Mathematical Models for Planning & Controlling Air Quality: Proceedings, Vol. 17. 255p. 1982. 55.00 (ISBN 0-08-029950-4). Pergamon.

Frooks, Dorothy & Dorney, Cay. Lady Lawyer. LC 74-8881. (Illus.). 224p. 1975. 10.95 (ISBN 0-8315-0141-3). Speller.

Froomkin, Joseph. Need: A New Federal Policy for Higher Education. (Policy Paper: No. 6). viii, 88p. 1978. 4.00 (ISBN 0-318-14399-2). Inst Educ Lead.

--Needed: A New Policy for Higher Education. 96p. 1978. 5.50 (ISBN 0-318-03023-3). Inst Educ Lead.

Froomkin, Joseph, ed. The Crisis in Higher Education, No. 2. LC 83-73329. (Proceedings of the Academy of Political Science: Vol. 35). 1983. 7.95 (ISBN 0-318-01791-1). Acad Poli Sci.

Froomkin, Joseph & Jamison, Dean T., eds. Education As an Industry. LC 76-29631. (National Bureau Conference Ser.: No. 28). 496p. 1977. prof ref 30.00 (ISBN 0-88410-476-1). Ballinger Pub.

Frosch, James P., ed. Current Perspectives on Personality Disorders. LC 83-8782. (Clinical Insights Monograph). 128p. 1983. pap. 12.00x (ISBN 0-88048-013-0). Am Psychiatric.

Frosch, John. Psychodynamic Psychotherapy. Date not set. price not set (BN#5650). Intl Univs Pr.

--The Psychotic Process. LC 82-21392. xiii, 521p. 1983. text ed. 40.00 (ISBN 0-8236-5690-X). Intl Univs Pr.

Frosch, P. J., jt. auth. see Wendt, H.

Frosch, Peter J., tr. see Nasemann, Theodor.

Froschel, Merle & Sprung, Barbara, eds. Beginning Equal: A Manual about Non-Sexist Childrearing for Infants & Toddlers. Ortiz, Victoria, tr. 241p. (Orig.). 1983. pap. 10.00 (ISBN 0-9605828-4-3). Women's Action.

Froschl, Merle, et al. Including All of Us: An Early Childhood Curriculum about Disability. (Orig.). 1985. pap. text ed. 10.95 (ISBN 0-931629-00-4). Educ Equity Con.

Frossard, Andre & Pope John Paul II. Be Not Afraid! John Paul II Speaks Out on His Life, His Beliefs & His Inspiring Vision for Humanity. Foster, J. R., tr. from Fr. 252p. 1984. 13.95 (ISBN 0-312-07021-7). St Martin.

Frossard, Andre, jt. auth. see Pope John Paul II.

Frossmann, Ludwig, ed. The Metaphysical Conceptions of Henry Bergson. (Illus.). 117p. 1981. 51.45 (ISBN 0-89920-030-3). Am Inst Psych.

Frost & Frost. Magic Power of Witchcraft. 1977. 9.95 (ISBN 0-13-545376-3, Reward); pap. 4.95 (ISBN 0-13-545368-2). P-H.

Frost, A. Marine Gyro Compasses for Ships Officers. (Illus.). 145p. 1982. text ed. 21.50x (ISBN 0-85174-426-5, Pub. by Brown Son Ferguson). Sheridan.

--Practical Navigation for Second Mates. 5th ed. 281p. 1981. 25.00x (ISBN 0-85174-397-8). Sheridan.

--Principle & Practice of Navigation. 319p. 1978. 21.50x (ISBN 0-85174-310-2). Sheridan.

--The Principles & Practice of Navigation. 1981. 40.00x (ISBN 0-85174-310-2, Pub. by Nautical England). State Mutual Bk.

Frost, A. B. Bull Calf & Other Tales. LC 69-17099. (Illus.). 254p. 1970. pap. 2.50 (ISBN 0-486-22230-6). Dover.

Frost, A. John & Prechter, Robert R., Jr. Elliot Wave Principle: Key to Stock Market Profits. 4th ed. (Illus.). 190p. 1984. 21.00 (ISBN 0-932750-05-2). New Classics Lib.

Frost, Alan. Convicts & Empire: A Naval Question, 1776-1811. (Illus.). 1980. 49.95x (ISBN 0-19-554255-X). Oxford U Pr.

Frost & Sullivan. The Market for Information Security Systems in the U. S. LC 82-186344. xii, 368p. 1985. 1675.00 (ISBN 0-86621-274-4). Frost & Sullivan.

Frost, Anne. As a Tree Grows. 1985. 9.95 (ISBN 0-87949-266-X). Ashley Bks.

--Footprints in the Sand. O'Donnell, Cara, ed. 1985. 9.95 (ISBN 0-87949-265-1). Ashley Bks.

Frost, B. R. Nuclear Fuel Elements: Design-Fabrication-Performance. (International Series in Nuclear Energy). (Illus.). 244p. 1982. 39.00 (ISBN 0-08-020412-0); pap. 19.25 (ISBN 0-08-020411-2). Pergamon.

Frost, Bede. Saint John of the Cross: Doctor of Divine Love, an Introduction to His Philosophy, Theology & Spirituality. 1977. lib. bdg. 59.95 (ISBN 0-8490-2559-1). Gordon Pr.

Frost, Betty. Secrets of the Rain Forest. (Perspectives II Ser.). (Illus.). 48p. (Orig.). (gr. 7-12). 1982. pap. 2.50 (ISBN 0-87879-321-6, High Noon Books). Acad Therapy.

--Voyage of the Vagabond. (Perspective I Novel Ser.). 48p. 1982. 2.50 (ISBN 0-87879-296-1, High Noon Books). Acad Therapy.

Frost, C. Viennese Waltz. (Ballroom Dance Ser.). 1985. lib. bdg. 70.00 (ISBN 0-87700-833-7). Revisionist Pr.

Frost, Carl, et al. The Scanlon Plan for Organization Development: Identity, Participation & Equity. 197p. 1974. 15.00x (ISBN 0-87013-184-2). Mich St U Pr.

Frost, Carol. The Fearful Child, LC 82-25861. 59p. (Orig.). 1983. pap. 5.00 (ISBN 0-87886-121-1). Ithaca Hse.

--Liar's Dice. LC 78-16125. 72p. 1978. 3.50 (ISBN 0-87886-098-3). Ithaca Hse.

--The Salt Lesson. 1976. pap. 5.00 (ISBN 0-915308-09-6). Graywolf.

Frost, Carolyn O. Cataloging Nonbook Materials: Problems in Theory & Practice. Dowell, Arlene T., ed. 350p. 1983. 28.50 (ISBN 0-87287-329-3). Libs Unl.

Frost, Celestine. An Inhuman Rival. 1977. perfect bound in wrappers 3.00 (ISBN 0-685-79998-0). New Rivers Pr.

Frost, Charles. Viennese Waltz. pap. 4.00x (ISBN 0-392-16820-0, SpS). Sportshelf.

Frost, Charles & Morris, Jack. Police Intelligence Reports. LC 83-62701. (Illus.). 135p. 1983. pap. 11.95 (ISBN 0-912479-03-5). Palmer Ent.

Frost, Christopher J. Religious Melancholy or Psychological Depression: Some Issues Involved in Relating Psychology & Religion As Illustrated in a Study of Elie Wiesel. 274p. (Orig.). 1985. lib. bdg. 25.00 (ISBN 0-8191-4496-7); pap. text ed. 13.25 (ISBN 0-8191-4497-5). U Pr of Amer.

Frost, D. L. School of Shakespeare. LC 68-11283. 1968. 52.50 (ISBN 0-521-05044-8). Cambridge U Pr.

Frost, D. L., ed. Selected Plays of Thomas Middleton. LC 77-23339. (Plays by Renaissance & Restoration Dramatists Ser.). 1978. 52.50 (ISBN 0-521-21698-2); pap. 14.95 (ISBN 0-521-29236-0). Cambridge U Pr.

Frost, Darrel R., ed. Amphibian Species of the World: A Taxonomic & Geographic Reference. 750p. 1985. 85.00 (ISBN 0-942924-11-8). Assn Syst Coll.

Frost, David & Deakin, Michael. David Frost's Book of Millionaires, Multimillionaires & Really Rich People. LC 84-9498. (Illus.). 1984. 10.95 (ISBN 0-517-55444-5). Crown.

--David Frost's Book of the World's Worst Decisions. (Illus.). 1983. 12.95 (ISBN 0-517-54977-8). Crown.

--David Frosts's Book of the World's Worst Decisions. 1984. pap. 1.98 (ISBN 0-517-55331-7, Prince Paper). Crown.

Frost, David, intro. by. The Bluffer's Guides, 6 bks. Incl. Bluff Your Way in Art. Lampitt, L (517L07626); Bluff Your Way in Cinema. Wlaschin, Ken (517L0760X); Bluff Your Way in Literature. Seymoursmith, Martin; Bluff Your Way in Music. Gammond, Peter; Bluff Your Way in Opera. Coleman, Francis; Bluff Your Way in Wine. Clark, Wick. 64p. 1971. pap. 1.00 ea. Crown.

Frost, David D. Broadsides. 24p. (Orig.). 1981. pap. 4.00 (ISBN 0-932460-01-1). Summer Stream.

Frost, Dennis. Capturing Personality in Pastel: How to Create Expression & Convey Character. (Illus.). 144p. 1982. 22.50 (ISBN 0-8230-0560-7). Watson-Guptill.

Frost, Dick. The King Ranch Papers: An Unauthorized & Irreverent History of World's Largest Landowners: Kleberg Family. (Illus.). 200p. (Orig.). 1985. pap. 35.00 (ISBN 0-933883-00-5). Aquarius Rising Pr.

Frost, E. L., jt. auth. see Hoebel, Edward A.

Frost, Eleanor. Elusive Paradise, Vol. 53. (Rapture Romance Ser.). 192p. (Orig.). 1984. pap. 1.95 (ISBN 0-451-12763-3, Sig). NAL.

--A Public Affair. (Rapture Romance Ser.: No. 68). 192p. 1984. pap. 1.95 (ISBN 0-451-12872-9, Sig). NAL.

Frost, Elizabeth, jt. auth. see Shrager, David S.

Frost, Elizabeth A. Clinical Anesthesia in Neurosurgery. 544p. 1984. text ed. 49.95 (ISBN 0-409-95102-1). Butterworth.

Frost, Elizabeth A. M., ed. Recovery Room Practice. LC 84-14447. (Illus.). 448p. 1985. 29.50 (ISBN 0-86542-017-3). Blackwell Sci.

Frost, Elizabeth K. De see De Frost, Elizabeth K.

Frost, Elsa C., et al, eds. Labor & Laborers Through Mexican History. 954p. 1979. pap. 34.50x (ISBN 9-6812-0036-5). U of Ariz Pr.

Frost, Erica. Case of the Missing Chick. new ed. LC 78-18036. (Illus.). 48p. (gr. 2-4). 1979. PLB 8.59 (ISBN 0-89375-092-1); pap. 1.95 (ISBN 0-89375-008-5). Troll Assocs.

--Harold & the Dinosaur Mystery. new ed. LC 78-60123. (Illus.). 48p. (gr. 2-4). 1979. PLB 8.59 (ISBN 0-89375-088-3); pap. 1.95 (ISBN 0-89375-076-X). Troll Assocs.

--I Can Read About Ballet. LC 74-24927. (Illus.). (gr. 2-4). 1975. pap. 1.50 (ISBN 0-89375-063-8). Troll Assocs.

--I Can Read About Ghosts. LC 74-24964. (Illus.). (gr. 2-4). 1975. pap. 1.50 (ISBN 0-89375-065-4). Troll Assocs.

--I Can Read About Good Manners. LC 74-24878. (Illus.). (gr. 1-2). 1975. pap. 1.50 (ISBN 0-89375-059-X). Troll Assocs.

--Jonathan's Amazing Adventure. (Illus.). 48p. (gr. 1-3). 1986. PLB 8.59 (ISBN 0-8167-0662-X); pap. text ed. 1.95 (ISBN 0-8167-0663-8). Troll Assocs.

--A Kitten for Rosie. (Illus.). 48p. (Orig.). (gr. 1-3). 1986. PLB 8.59 (ISBN 0-8167-0650-6); pap. text ed. 1.95 (ISBN 0-8167-0651-4). Troll Assocs.

--The Littlest Pig. (Illus.). 48p. (gr. 1-3). 1986. PLB 8.59 (ISBN 0-8167-0654-9); pap. text ed. 1.95 (ISBN 0-8167-0655-7). Troll Assocs.

--Mr. Lion Goes to Lunch. (Illus.). 48p. (gr. 1-3). 1986. PLB 8.59 (ISBN 0-8167-0638-7); pap. text ed. 1.95 (ISBN 0-8167-0639-5). Troll Assocs.

--Mystery of the Midnight Visitors. new ed. LC 78-18038. (Illus.). 48p. (gr. 2-4). 1979. PLB 8.59 (ISBN 0-89375-094-8); pap. 1.95 (ISBN 0-89375-082-4). Troll Assocs.

--Mystery of the Runaway Sled. new ed. LC 78-60124. (Illus.). 48p. (gr. 2-4). 1979. PLB 8.59 (ISBN 0-89375-089-1); pap. 1.95 (ISBN 0-89375-077-8). Troll Assocs.

--The Story of Matt & Mary. (Illus.). 48p. (gr. 1-3). 1986. PLB 8.59 (ISBN 0-8167-0602-6); pap. text ed. 1.95 (ISBN 0-8167-0603-4). Troll Assocs.

Frost, Everett L. Archaeological Excavations of Fortified Sites on Taveuni, Fiji. (Social Science & Linguistics Institute Special Publications). (Illus.). 169p. 1974. pap. 8.00x (ISBN 0-8248-0266-7). UH Pr.

Frost, F. J., jt. auth. see Arnold, Channing.

Frost, Frances. Christmas in the Woods. LC 76-3835. (Illus.). 24p. (ps-3). 1976. 8.95 (ISBN 0-06-021922-X). HarpJ.

Frost, Frances M. Hemlock Wall. LC 78-144734. (Yale Series of Younger Poets: No. 27). Repr. of 1929 ed. 18.00 (ISBN 0-404-53827-4). AMS Pr.

Frost, Frank J. Greek Society. 2nd ed. 1980. pap. text ed. 8.95 (ISBN 0-669-02452-X). Heath.

--Plutarch's Themistocles: A Historical Commentary. LC 79-3208. 1980. 27.50x (ISBN 0-691-05300-6). Princeton U Pr.

Frost, Frank J., ed. Democracy & the Athenians: Aspects of Ancient Politics. LC 70-81338. (Major Issues in History Ser.). pap. 39.80 (ISBN 0-317-09303-7, 2051578). Bks Demand UMI.

Frost, Frederick H. Bridge Odds Complete: Probabilities in Contract Bridge. 2nd ed. 96p. (gr. 7 up). 1976. pap. 5.95 (ISBN 0-89412-008-5). Aegean Park Pr.

Frost, G. & Frost, Y. Witch's Grimoire of Ancient Omens, Portents, Talismans, Amulets & Charms. 1979. 14.95 (ISBN 0-13-961557-1). P-H.

Frost, Gerhard. Homing in the Presence: Meditations for Daily Living. 125p. 1978. pap. 5.95 (ISBN 0-86683-756-6). Winston Pr.

Frost, Gerhard E. Bless My Growing: For Parents, Teachers, & Others Who Learn. LC 74-77680. (Illus.). 96p. 1975. pap. 4.95 (ISBN 0-8066-1431-5, 10-0770). Augsburg.

--Blessed Is the Ordinary. (Illus.). 96p. pap. 4.95 (ISBN 0-86683-606-3). Winston Pr.

--Color of the Night: Reflections on the Book of Job. LC 77-72458. 1977. pap. 4.95 (ISBN 0-8066-1583-4, 10-1520). Augsburg.

--Kept Moments. 96p. (Orig.). 1982. pap. 5.95 (ISBN 0-86683-668-3). Winston Pr.

--A Second Look. (Orig.). 1984. pap. 6.95 (ISBN 0-86683-935-6, 8513, Pub. by Seabury). Winston Pr.

Frost, Gerhard E., ed. see Bickel, Margot & Steigert, Hermann.

Frost, Gordon. Guatemalan Mask Imagery. (Illus.). 32p. 1976. 5.00 (ISBN 0-916561-22-4). Southwest Mus.

Frost, H. Gordon. Blades & Barrels: Six Centuries of Combination Weapons. 16.95 (ISBN 0-686-11627-5); deluxe ed. 25.00 (ISBN 0-686-11628-3); presentation ed. 50.00 (ISBN 0-686-11629-1). Walloon Pr.

--The Gentlemen's Club: The Story of Prostitution in El Paso. LC 83-61186. (Illus.). 336p. 1983. 29.95 (ISBN 0-930208-15-3). Mangan Bks.

Frost, H. Gordon & Jenkins, John H. I'm Frank Hamer: The Life of a Texas Peace Officer. LC 68-31953. (Illus.). 17.50 (ISBN 0-8363-0051-3); limited ed. 150.00 (ISBN 0-685-13275-7). Jenkins.

Frost, H. J. & Ashby, M. F. Deformation-Mechanism Maps: The Plasticity & Creep of Metals & Ceramics. (Illus.). 184p. 1982. 50.00 (ISBN 0-08-029338-7); pap. 25.00 (ISBN 0-08-029337-9). Pergamon.

Frost, H. M. The Laws of Bone Structure. (Illus.). 184p. 1964. photocopy ed. 19.75x (ISBN 0-398-00623-7). C C Thomas.

Frost, H. M., jt. ed. see De Luca, Hector F.

Frost, Harold M. Bone Modeling & Skeletal Modeling Errors: Orthopaedic Lectures, Vol. 4. (Illus.). 224p. 1973. photocopy ed. 22.50x (ISBN 0-398-02667-X). C C Thomas.

--Bone Remodeling & Its Relationship to Metabolic Bone Diseases: Orthopaedic Lectures, Vol. 3. (Illus.). 226p. 1973. 22.50x (ISBN 0-398-02588-6). C C Thomas.

--An Introduction to Biomechanics. (Illus.). 160p. 1971. photocopy ed. 15.75x (ISBN 0-398-00622-9). C C Thomas.

--Orthopaedic Biomechanics: Orthopaedic Lectures, Vol. 5. (Illus.). 664p. 1973. 49.50x (ISBN 0-398-02824-9). C C Thomas.

--Orthopaedic Surgery in Spasticity: Orthopaedic Lectures, Vol. 1. (Illus.). 228p. 1972. photocopy ed. 22.75x (ISBN 0-398-02286-0). C C Thomas.

--The Physiology of Cartilaginous, Fibrous, & Bony Tissue: Orthopaedic Lectures, Vol. 2. (Illus.). 264p. 1972. photocopy ed. 32.75x (ISBN 0-398-02562-2). C C Thomas.

Frost, Holloway, jt. auth. see Green, Fitzhugh.

Frost, Holloway H. The Battle of Jutland. LC 79-6108. (Navies & Men Ser.). (Illus.). 1980. Repr. of 1964 ed. lib. bdg. 57.50x (ISBN 0-405-13037-6). Ayer Co Pubs.

Frost, J. K. The Cell in Health & Disease, Vol. 2. 2nd, rev. ed. (Monographs in Clinical Cytology). (Illus.). xii, 168p. 1985. 58.75 (ISBN 3-8055-4150-3). S Karger.

Frost, J. M. World Radio TV Handbook 1984. 600p. 1984. pap. 17.50 (ISBN 0-8230-5912-X, Billboard Bks). Watson-Guptill.

--World Radio TV Handbook, 1985. 600p. 1985. pap. 19.50 (ISBN 0-8230-5914-6). Watson-Guptill.

Frost, J. W., jt. auth. see Norman, L. D.

Frost, J. William see Weaver, Glenn.

Frost, J. William, ed. The Records & Recollections of James Jenkins. LC 83-26537. (Texts & Studies in Religion: Vol. 18). 712p. 1984. 79.95x (ISBN 0-88946-807-9). E Mellen.

Frost, Jack M. & Ratliff, Linda. My Book of Workers: Book 1. new ed. (Programmed Work Awareness Kit). 85p. (gr. 1). 1973. wkbk. 2.50 (ISBN 0-912578-18-1). Chron Guide.

--My Book of Workers: Book 2. new ed. (Programmed Work Awareness Kit). 80p. (gr. 1). 1973. wkbk. 2.50 (ISBN 0-912578-19-X). Chron Guide.

Frost, Jack M & Ratliff, Linda. Workers We Know: Teachers Manual, Level B. new ed. (Programmed Work Awareness Kit). 166p. 1973. tchrs' manual 6.50 (ISBN 0-912578-20-3). Chron Guide.

Frost, Jack M. & Taylor, Judith. Jobs Around Us: Programmed Work Awareness Kit Level A. 109p. (Orig.). 1975. Teachers Ed. 7.25 (ISBN 0-912578-23-8). Chron Guide.

--My Book of Jobs: Programmed Work Awareness Kit Level A. 94p. 1975. wkbk. 2.50 (ISBN 0-912578-25-4). Chron Guide.

Frost, Jane C. Your Future in Dental Assisting. LC 75-84955. (Careers in Depth Ser). (Illus.). 144p. (gr. 7 up). 1976. PLB 8.97 (ISBN 0-8239-0175-0). Rosen Group.

Frost, Jason. The Cutthroat. (The Warlord Ser.: No. 2). 1984. pap. 2.50 (ISBN 0-8217-1308-6). Zebra.

--The Warlord. 1983. pap. 3.50 (ISBN 0-8217-1189-X). Zebra.

--The Warlord, No. 3: Badland. 1984. pap. 2.50 (ISBN 0-8217-1437-6). Zebra.

Frost, Jens. World Radio & TV Handbook 1980. 34th ed. 1980. pap. 19.50 (ISBN 0-8230-5906-5). Watson-Guptill.

--World Radio TV Handbook 1983. 600p. 1983. pap. 17.50 (ISBN 0-8230-5910-3, Billboard Pub). Watson-Guptill.

Frost, Jerry W. The Keithian Controversy in Early Pennsylvania. 1979. lib. bdg. 32.50 (ISBN 0-8482-0847-1). Norwood Edns.

Frost, Joan. Art, Books & Children: Art Activities Based on Children's Literature. (Illus.). 98p. (gr. 1-6). 1984. Spec Lit Pr.

--Exceptional Art--Exceptional Children: Fostering Creativity & Developing Independence. (Illus.). 92p. (gr. 1-8). 1985. pap. 11.95 spiral bdg. (ISBN 0-938594-07-9). Spec Lit Pr.

Frost, Joan V. A Masque of Chameleons. 384p. 1981. pap. 2.95 (ISBN 0-449-24472-5, Crest). Fawcett.

Frost, Joan Van E. Portrait in Black. 256p. (Orig.). 1985. pap. text ed. 2.95 (ISBN 0-449-12795-8, GM). Fawcett.

Frost, Joan Van Every. Lisa. 1979. pap. 1.95 (ISBN 0-8439-0616-2, Leisure Bks). Dorchester Pub Co.

Frost, Joan van Every see Van Every Frost, Joan.

Frost, Joan VanEvery. This Fiery Promise. 1978. pap. 2.25 (ISBN 0-8439-0582-4, Leisure Bks). Dorchester Pub Co.

Frost, Joe L. & Sunderlin, Sylvia, eds. When Children Play: Proceedings of International Conference on Play & Play Environments. LC 84-20477. (Illus.). 365p. 1985. 35.00 (ISBN 0-87173-107-X); members 29.50. ACEI.

Frost, John. American Naval Biography. 1980. lib. bdg. 79.95 (ISBN 0-8490-3155-9). Gordon Pr.

--The American Speaker. LC 74-15740. (Popular Culture in America Ser.). (Illus.). 454p. 1975. Repr. 33.00x (ISBN 0-405-06375-X). Ayer Co Pubs.

--A Drop Too Many: The Revised Edition. 288p. 1982. 50.00x (ISBN 0-907675-07-7, Pub. by Buchan & Enright England). State Mutual Bk.

--Pioneer Mothers of the West; or, Daring & Heroic Deeds of American Women, Comprising Thrilling Examples of Courage, Fortitude, Devotedness & Self-Sacrifice. LC 74-3950. (Women in America Ser). (Illus.). 360p. 1974. Repr. of 1869 ed. 26.00x (ISBN 0-405-06097-1). Ayer Co Pubs.

Frost, John, jt. auth. see Wold, Tina.

Frost, John E. Maine Genealogy: A Bibliographical Guide. 1976. pap. 4.00 (ISBN 0-915592-25-8). Maine Hist.

Frost, Joseph H., jt. auth. see Lee, Daniel.

Frost, Joyce H. The Heart of Andrea. 170p. (Orig.). 1985. pap. 3.95 (ISBN 0-9614712-0-4). Wellspring Bks.

Frost, Lawrence. A Pictorial Chronology of Events in the Life of Thomas Alva Edison 1847-1931. 1985. 25.95 (ISBN 0-317-28247-6, Pub. by J M C & Co). Amereon Ltd.

Frost, Lawrence, intro. by. The Robert M. Utley: Bibliographic Checklist. 1985. pap. 4.95 (ISBN 0-8488-0004-4, Pub. by J M C & Co). Amereon Ltd.

Frost, Lawrence A. The Court Martial of General George Armstrong Custer. (Illus.). 280p. 1979. pap. 7.95 (ISBN 0-8061-1608-0). U of Okla Pr.

--Custer Album. LC 64-21319. 1964. 17.95 (ISBN 0-87564-801-0). Superior Pub.

--Custer Legends. LC 81-82502. (Illus.). 244p. 1981. 19.95 (ISBN 0-87972-180-4); pap. 9.95 (ISBN 0-87972-181-2). Bowling Green Univ.

--Custer's Seventh Cav & the Campaign of 1873. (Illus.). 250p. 1985. 42.95 (ISBN 0-89769-089-3, Dist. by Caroline Hse.). Pine Mntn.

--General Custer's Thoroughbreds: Racing, Riding, Hunting & Fighting. (Illus.). 25.50 (ISBN 0-8488-0015-X, Pub. by J M C & Co). Amereon Ltd.

--The Thomas A. Edison Album. 25.95 (ISBN 0-89190-406-9, Pub. by Am Repr). Amereon Ltd.

Frost, Lawrence A., ed. With Custer in Seventy-Four: James Calhoun's Diary of the Black Hills Expedition. LC 79-13132. (Illus.). 1979. 12.95 (ISBN 0-8425-1620-4). Brigham.

Frost, Lesley. Digging Down to China. (Illus.). 64p. (gr. 1-4). 1968. 9.95 (ISBN 0-8159-5306-2). Devin.

--Going on Two. (Illus., Orig., Poems). 1973. pap. 3.00 (ISBN 0-8159-5607-X). Devin.

--New Hampshire's Child: Derry Journals of Lesley Frost. LC 69-12099. (Illus.). 1969. 44.50x (ISBN 0-87395-043-7). State U NY Pr.

--Really, Not Really. (Illus.). 64p. (ps-3). 1966. 10.00 (ISBN 0-8159-6702-0). Devin.

Frost, M. E. see Diamond, Donald R. & McLoughlin, J. B.

Frost, Marie. Adventures with Peter Panda. (gr. k-3). 1978. pap. 1.69 (ISBN 0-87239-184-1, 42044). Standard Pub.

--Characteristics of Preschoolers. (Peter Panda Ser.). 1977. pap. 1.50 (ISBN 0-87239-143-4, 42035). Standard Pub.

--Crafts for Preschoolers. (Peter Panda Ser.). 1977. pap. 1.50 (ISBN 0-87239-144-2, 42036). Standard Pub.

--Fifty-Two Nursery Patterns. (Illus.). 48p. (Orig.). (ps-k). 1979. pap. 4.50 (ISBN 0-87239-341-0, 42046). Standard Pub.

--Fifty-Two Primary Crafts. 48p. (Orig.). 1984. pap. 2.25 (ISBN 0-87239-726-2, 2106). Standard Pub.

--Frankly Feminine: Leader's Guide. 48p. (Orig.). 1984. pap. 2.95 (ISBN 0-87239-746-7, 2970). Standard Pub.

--Fun with Peter Panda. (Illus.). (gr. k-3). 1978. pap. 1.69 (ISBN 0-87239-185-X, 42045). Standard Pub.

--Listen to Your Children. LC 80-50320. 144p. (Orig.). 1980. pap. 2.95 (ISBN 0-87239-396-8, 3000). Standard Pub.

--Listen to Your Children: Leader's Guide. 48p. (Orig.). 1984. pap. 2.95 (ISBN 0-87239-747-5, 2999). Standard Pub.

--Making the Most of Your Golden Years. LC 82-760. 96p. (Orig.). 1982. pap. 4.95 (ISBN 0-87239-550-2, 3008). Standard Pub.

--Songs for Preschoolers. (Peter Panda Ser.). 32p. 1977. pap. 1.50 (ISBN 0-87239-146-9, 42038). Standard Pub.

--Teaching Preschoolers. (Peter Panda Ser.). 32p. (Orig.). 1977. pap. 1.50 (ISBN 0-87239-147-7, 42039). Standard Pub.

--Things Happen When Women Care. LC 79-63323. 144p. (Orig.). 1979. pap. 2.95 (ISBN 0-87239-346-1, 3217). Standard Pub.

--Things Happen When Women Care: Leader's Guide. 48p. (Orig.). 1984. pap. 2.95 (ISBN 0-87239-748-3, 3218). Standard Pub.

Frost, Meigs O., jt. auth. see Wise, Frederic M.

Frost, Michael S. Taiwan's Security & United States Policy: Executive & Congressional Strategies. (Occasional Papers-Reprints Contemporary Asian Studies: No. 4). 39p. (Orig.). 1982. pap. text ed. 2.50 (ISBN 0-942182-48-0). Occasional Papers.

Frost, Miriam & Skubic, Ned. For Everything There Is a Season. (Illus.). 64p. (Orig.). 1981. pap. 7.95 (ISBN 0-86683-604-7). Winston Pr.

Frost, Miriam, jt. auth. see Hinton, Pat C.

Frost, Miriam, ed. see Emmons, Michael & Richardson, David.

Frost, Miriam, ed. see Mandel, Evelyn.

Frost, Miriam, ed. see Pilch, John J.

Frost, N. E., et al. Metal Fatigue. (Oxford Engineering Science Ser.). pap. 127.80 (ISBN 0-317-08550-6, 2051845). Bks Demand UMI.

Frost, Norman. Comparative Study of Achievement in Country & Town Schools. LC 74-176790. (Columbia University. Teachers College. Contributions to Education: No. 111). Repr. of 1921 ed. 22.50 (ISBN 0-404-55111-4). AMS Pr.

Frost, Oscott W. Joaquin Miller. (Twayne's United States Authors Ser). 1967. pap. 5.95x (ISBN 0-8084-0177-7, T119, Twayne). New Coll U Pr.

Frost, Paul, et al. Managers in Focus. 192p. 1981. text ed. 35.50x (ISBN 0-566-00468-2). Gower Pub Co.

Frost, Peter. Bakumatsu Currency Crisis. LC 79-119074. (East Asian Monographs Ser: No. 36). 1970. pap. 11.00x (ISBN 0-674-06040-7). Harvard U Pr.

--Exploring Cuzco. (Illus.). 139p. 1984. pap. 10.95 (ISBN 0-933982-05-4). Bradt Ent.

--Exploring Cuzco. 136p. 1984. pap. 10.95 (ISBN 0-933982-80-1). Bradt Ent.

Frost, Peter, jt. auth. see Cummings, L. L.

Frost, Peter J., et al. Organizational Reality: Reports from the Firing Line. 2nd ed. 1982. pap. text ed. 18.60x (ISBN 0-673-16004-1). Scott F.

--Organizational Reality: Reports from the Firing Line. 3rd ed. 1985. pap. text ed. 17.95x (ISBN 0-673-16663-5). Scott F.

Frost, Peter J., et al, eds. Organizational Culture. 420p. 1985. 29.95 (ISBN 0-8039-2459-3); pap. 14.95 (ISBN 0-8039-2460-7). Sage.

Frost, Phillip & Horwitz, Steven N. Principles of Cosmetics for the Dermatologist. LC 81-18816. (Illus.). 367p. 1982. pap. text ed. 52.95 (ISBN 0-8016-1713-8). Mosby.

Frost, R. A. Database Management Systems. 288p. 1984. 36.95 (ISBN 0-07-022564-8). McGraw.

Frost, Ralph. What Cheer? Merry Stories for All Occasions. 1977. Repr. of 1929 ed. lib. bdg. 25.00 (ISBN 0-8495-1603-X). Arden Lib.

Frost, Raymond. The Backward Society. LC 73-10735. 246p. 1973. Repr. of 1961 ed. lib. bdg. 15.00x (ISBN 0-8371-7025-7, FRBS). Greenwood.

Frost, Reuben B. & Marshall, Stanley J. Administration of PE & Athletics. 2nd ed. 480p. 1981. text ed. write for info. (ISBN 0-697-07171-5). Wm C Brown.

Frost, Richard. The Circus Villains: Poems. LC 65-24647. 55p. 1965. 5.95 (ISBN 0-8214-0010-X, 82-80117). Ohio U Pr.

--Race Against Time: Human Relations & Politics in Kenya Before Independence. (Illus.). 292p. 1978. 24.50x (ISBN 0-8476-3102-8). Rowman.

Frost, Richard H. The Mooney Case. LC 68-13222. (Illus.). 1968. 35.00x (ISBN 0-8047-0651-4). Stanford U Pr.

Frost, Robert. Collected Poems. 319p. 1983. Repr. lib. bdg. 17.95x (ISBN 0-89966-442-3). Buccaneer Bks.

--In the Clearing. LC 62-11578. 48p. (gr. 9 up). 1962. 5.95 (ISBN 0-03-031010-5). HR&W.

--North of Boston Poems. Lathem, Edward C., ed. LC 77-1401. (Illus.). 1977. 8.95 (ISBN 0-396-07440-5). Dodd.

--North of Boston, Poems. Lathem, Edward C., ed. (Illus.). 192p. 1983. pap. 5.95 (ISBN 0-396-08270-X). Dodd.

--Our Heavenly Father. LC 77-95191. 1978. pap. 3.95 (ISBN 0-88270-266-1, Pub. by Logos). Bridge Pub.

--The Poetry of Robert Frost. Lathem, Edward C., ed. 1979. pap. 9.95 (ISBN 0-03-049126-6, Owl Bks.). HR&W.

--The Poetry of Robert Frost. 1969. 17.50 (ISBN 0-03-072535-6). HR&W.

--Road Not Taken: An Introduction to Robert Frost. LC 51-9831. (Illus.). (gr. 9 up). 1951. 13.50 (ISBN 0-03-027150-9, Owl Bks.); pap. 8.95 (ISBN 0-03-000073-4). HR&W.

--Robert Frost, Farm Poultryman--The Story of Robert Frost's Career As a Breeder & Fancier of Hens. Lathem, Edward C. & Thompson, Lawrance, eds. LC 64-638. 116p. 1963. 10.00x (ISBN 0-87451-032-5). U Pr of New Eng.

--Robert Frost's Poems. enl. ed. Untermeyer, Louis, ed. 280p. 1982. pap. 4.95 (ISBN 0-671-49617-4). WSP.

--Selected Letters of Robert Frost. Thompson, L., ed. LC 64-10767. 1964. 10.00 (ISBN 0-03-043155-7). HR&W.

--Selected Poems. Graves, Robert, ed. LC 63-10970. (Rinehart Editions Ser.). 1963. pap. text ed. 12.95x (ISBN 0-03-012060-8). HR&W.

--Set My Spirit Free. LC 73-84475. 234p. 1973. pap. 4.95 (ISBN 0-88270-058-8, Pub. by Logos). Bridge Pub.

--Spring Pools. (Illus.). 64p. 1983. boxed portfolio 295.00 (ISBN 0-317-31386-X). Lime Rock Pr.

--Stopping by Woods on a Snowy Evening. LC 78-8134. (Illus.). 1978. 10.95 (ISBN 0-525-40115-6, 01063-320). Dutton.

--Stories for Lesley. Sell, Roger D., ed. LC 83-19756. (Bibliographical Society of the University of Virginia). (Illus.). 50p. 1984. 14.95x (ISBN 0-8139-0979-1). U Pr of Va.

--A Swinger of Birches: Poems of Robert Frost for Young People. LC 82-5517. (Illus.). 80p. (gr. 4 up). 1982. 17.95 (ISBN 0-916144-92-5); pap. 9.95 (ISBN 0-916144-93-3). Stemmer Hse.

--You Come Too. LC 59-12940. (Illus.). 94p. (gr. 7-9). 1959. reinforced bdg. 9.95 (ISBN 0-03-089530-8). HR&W.

Frost, Robert & Ford, Caroline. The Less Travelled Road. 1982. lib. bdg. 34.50 (ISBN 0-686-45051-5). Porter.

Frost, Robert C. Aglow with the Spirit: How to Receive the Baptism in the Holy Spirit. 1965. pap. 2.95 (ISBN 0-912106-64-6, Pub. by Logos). Bridge Pub.

--The Mystery of Life. LC 81-80616. 1981. pap. (ISBN 0-88270-512-1, Pub. by Logos). Bridge Pub.

--Overflowing Life: Everyday Living in the Spirit. rev. ed. LC 72-146696. 144p. 1973. pap. 3.95 (ISBN 0-88270-050-2, Pub. by Logos). Bridge Pub.

Frost, S. A. New Book of Dialogues. LC 72-8300. (Granger Index Reprint Ser). 1972. Repr. of 1872 ed. 18.00 (ISBN 0-8369-6387-3). Ayer Co Pubs.

Frost, S. E., Jr. Basic Teachings of the Great Philosophers. LC 62-15320. pap. 4.95 (ISBN 0-385-03007-X, C398, Dolp). Doubleday.

--The Basic Teachings of the Philosophers. 314p. 1980. Repr. of 1942 ed. lib. bdg. 25.00 (ISBN 0-89987-256-5). Darby Bks.

--Education's Own Stations: The History of Broadcast Licenses Issued to Educational Institutions. LC 71-161156. (History of Broadcasting: Radio to Television Ser). 1971. Repr. of 1937 ed. 37.50 (ISBN 0-405-03573-X). Ayer Co Pubs.

Frost, S. E., Jr., ed. The Sacred Writings of the Worlds Great Religions. 416p. 1972. pap. 6.95 (ISBN 0-07-022520-6). McGraw.

--The Sacred Writings of the World's Great Religions. 410p. 1983. Repr. of 1951 ed. lib. bdg. 40.00 (ISBN 0-89760-241-2). Telegraph Bks.

Frost, S. H., et al. Oligocene Reef-Tract Development, Southwestern Puerto Rico: Part 1 Text; Part 2, Field Guide to Reprsentative Exposures & Modern Analog. (Sedimenta IX). (Illus.). 180p. 1983. 12.00 (ISBN 0-932981-08-9). Univ Miami CSL.

Frost, S. W. Insect Life & Insect Natural History. 2nd ed. Orig. Title: General Entomology. 1959. pap. 8.50 (ISBN 0-486-20517-7). Dover.

--Insect Life & Natural History. 2nd & rev. ed. Orig. Title: General Entomology. 16.50 (ISBN 0-8446-0101-2). Peter Smith.

Frost, Sally M. Relaxation Techniques & Health Sciences: Medical Subject Analysis with Reference Bibliography. LC 85-47860. 150p. 1985. 29.95 (ISBN 0-88164-396-3); pap. 21.95 (ISBN 0-88164-397-1). ABBE Pubs Assn.

Frost, Sidney. The Whaling Question. LC 79-2491. 1979. pap. 6.95 (ISBN 0-913890-33-2). Brick Hse Pub.

Frost, Sidney W. How to Find the Right Job Fast. 112p. Date not set. pap. text ed. price not set (ISBN 0-914635-03-4). Roadrunner Pubns.

Frost, Siegmund. The Question Is the Answer. 2.00 (ISBN 0-87306-075-X). Feldheim.

Frost, Stanley. Challenge of the Klan. LC 75-94227. Repr. of 1924 ed. 15.00 (ISBN 0-404-00160-2). AMS Pr.

--Challenge of the Klan. (Illus.). Repr. of 1924 ed. cancelled (ISBN 0-8371-2192-2, FRC&, Pub. by Negro U Pr). Greenwood.

Frost, Stanley B. McGill University: For the Advancement of Learning, Vol. I: 1801-1895. (Illus.). 334p. 1980. 30.00x (ISBN 0-7735-0353-6). McGill-Queens U Pr.

--McGill University: For the Advancement of Learning, 1895-1971, Vol. 2. 512p. 1984. 49.50 (ISBN 0-7735-0422-2). McGill-Queens U Pr.

--Patriarchs & Prophets. 232p. 1963. 10.00 (ISBN 0-7735-0010-3). McGill-Queens U Pr.

--Standing & Understanding: A Re-Appraisal of the Christian Faith. LC 68-59095. pap. 46.80 (ISBN 0-317-26033-2, 2023834). Bks Demand UMI.

Frost, Stanley H. & Langenheim, Ralph L., Jr. Cenozoic Reef Biofacies: Tertiary Larger Foraminifera & Scleractinian Corals from Chiapas, Mexico. LC 72-7513. (Illus.). 388p. 1974. 50.00 (ISBN 0-87580-027-0). N Ill U Pr.

Frost, T. W. The Price Guide to Old Sheffield Plate. (Price Guide Ser.). (Illus.). 396p. 1977. 25.50 (ISBN 0-902028-07-3). Antique Collect.

Frost, Thomas. The Lives of the Conjurers. 59.95 (ISBN 0-8490-0549-3). Gordon Pr.

Frost, Thomas M. & Seng, Magnus J. Organized Crime in Chicago: Myth & Reality. LC 84-72215. 88p. 1984. pap. 4.00 (ISBN 0-911531-15-7). Loyola U Ctr Urban.

Frost, Thomas M., jt. ed. see Bensinger, Gad J.

Frost, W. A., jt. auth. see Brooks, N. R.

Frost, Wade H. The Papers of Wade Hampton Frost, M.D., a Contribution to Epidemiological Method. Rosenkrantz, Barbara G. & Maxcy, Kenneth F., eds. LC 76-40635. (Public Health in America Ser.). (Illus.). 1977. Repr. of 1941 ed. lib. bdg. 46.50x (ISBN 0-405-09826-X). Ayer Co Pubs.

Frost, Walter, ed. Heat Transfer at Low Temperatures. LC 71-186257. (International Cryogenics Monographs). (Illus.). 362p. 1975. 55.00x (ISBN 0-306-30575-5, Plenum Pr). Plenum Pub.

Frost, Walter & Moulden, T. H., eds. Handbook of Turbulence: Fundamentals & Applications, Vol. 1. LC 77-23781. (Illus.). 498p. 1977. 75.00x (ISBN 0-306-31004-X, Plenum Pr). Plenum Pub.

Frost, William. Dryden & the Art of Translation. (Yale Studies in English Ser.: No. 128). 100p. 1969. Repr. of 1955 ed. 13.00 (ISBN 0-208-00778-4, Archon). Shoe String.

Frost, William J. The Quaker Origins of Antislavery. LC 79-11744. (Illus.). 303p. 1979. lib. bdg. 25.00 (ISBN 0-8482-3961-X). Norwood Edns.

Frost, Y., jt. auth. see Frost, G.

Frostick, Michael. Aston Martin & Lagonda. 196p. 1981. 50.00x (ISBN 0-686-97069-1, Pub. by D Watson England). State Mutual Bk.

--BMW the Bavarian Motor Works. 207p. 1981. 50.00x (ISBN 0-686-97072-1, Pub. by D Watson England). State Mutual Bk.

Frostick, Michael, jt. auth. see Gill, Barrie.

Frostig, Marianne. Education for Dignity. 224p. 1976. 37.00 (ISBN 0-8089-0951-7, 791450). Grune.

Frostig, Marianne & Maslow, Phyllis. Learning Problems in the Classroom. LC 73-1578. 368p. 1973. 31.00 (ISBN 0-8089-0783-2, 791452). Grune.

Frostmann, Herbert M. International Political Terrorism & the Approaching Emergence of the Authoritarian State. (Illus.). 146p. 1981. 69.95 (ISBN 0-89266-318-9). Am Classical Coll Pr.

Frothingha, Arthur L., Jr., jt. auth. see Marquand, Allan.

Frothingham, A. W. Hispanic Glass. (Illus.). 204p. 1941. pap. 3.00 (ISBN 0-87535-052-6). Hispanic Soc.

--Prehistoric Pottery in the Collection from El Acebuchal: Site near Carmona, Province of Sevilla. (Illus.). 1953. pap. 0.60 (ISBN 0-87535-075-5). Hispanic Soc.

Frothingham, Alice W. Spanish Glass. (Illus.). 1964. 12.50 (ISBN 0-87535-127-1). Hispanic Soc.

--Tile Panels of Spain, 1500-1650. (Illus.). 1969. 30.00 (ISBN 0-87535-110-7). Hispanic Soc.

--Tile Panels of Spain, 1500-1650. (Illus.). 266p. 1969. 30.00 (ISBN 0-317-00601-0, Pub. by Hispanic Soc). Interbk Inc.

Frothingham, Jessie P. Sea Fighters from Drake to Farragut. facs. ed. LC 67-26743. (Essay Index Reprint Ser). 1902. 19.00 (ISBN 0-8369-0461-3). Ayer Co Pubs.

--Sea Fighters from Drake to Farragut. (Essay Index Reprint Ser.). Repr. of 1902 ed. lib. bdg. 16.00 (ISBN 0-8290-0838-1). Irvington.

Frothingham, O. C. Transcendentalism in New England: A History. 11.25 (ISBN 0-8446-1191-3). Peter Smith.

Frothingham, Octavius B. George Ripley. LC 75-101910. Repr. of 1883 ed. 24.50 (ISBN 0-404-02625-7). AMS Pr.

--Gerrit Smith: A Biography. LC 74-98720. Repr. of 1878 ed. 25.00x (ISBN 0-8371-2765-3, FRG&, Pub. by Negro U Pr). Greenwood.

--Transcendentalism in New England: A History. LC 59-10346. 1972. pap. 13.95x (ISBN 0-8122-1038-7, Pa. Paperbacks). U of Pa Pr.

Frothingham, Paul R. All These. facs. ed. LC 70-86752. (Essay Index Reprint Ser). 1927. 19.00 (ISBN 0-8369-1182-2). Ayer Co Pubs.

--All These. 1973. Repr. of 1927 ed. 25.00 (ISBN 0-8274-1739-X). R West.

--Confusion of Tongues. facsimile ed. LC 68-22913. (Essay Index Reprint Ser). 1917. 17.00 (ISBN 0-8369-0462-1). Ayer Co Pubs.

--Edward Everett: Orator & Statesman. LC 76-137910. (American History & Culture in the Nineteenth Century Ser). 1971. Repr. of 1925 ed. 35.00x (ISBN 0-8046-1478-4, Pub. by Kennikat). Assoc Faculty Pr.

Frothingham, Paul Revere. William Ellery Channings: His Messages from the Spirit. 1903. 10.00 (ISBN 0-8274-3708-0). R West.

Frothingham, R. Life & Times of Joseph Warren. LC 72-146148. (Era of the American Revolution Ser). 1971. Repr. of 1865 ed. lib. bdg. 59.50 (ISBN 0-306-70133-2). Da Capo.

Frothingham, Richard. History of the Siege of Boston & of the Battles of Lexington, Concord & Bunker Hill. LC 77-115680. (Era of the American Revolution Ser). 1970. Repr. of 1903 ed. lib. bdg. 49.50 (ISBN 0-306-71932-0). Da Capo.

Frothingham, Robert, ed. Songs of the Sea & Sailor's Chanteys. LC 70-99029. (Granger Index Reprint Ser). 1924. 18.00 (ISBN 0-8369-6103-X). Ayer Co Pubs.

Frothingham, Thomas E, et al. Pediatric Infectious Diseases Case Studies. 1978. 20.50 (ISBN 0-87488-048-3). Med Exam.

Frothingham, Thomas G. The American Reinforcement in the World War. facsimile ed. LC 70-152984. (Select Bibliographies Reprint Ser). Repr. of 1927 ed. 27.50 (ISBN 0-8369-5736-9). Ayer Co Pubs.

--The Naval History of the World War, 3 vols. facsimile ed. Incl. Vol. 1. Offensive Operations, 1914-15; Vol. 2. The Stress of Sea Power, 1915-16; Vol. 3. U. S. in the War, 1917-18. LC 70-165633. (Select Bibliographies Reprint Ser). Repr. of 1926 ed. 99.00 set (ISBN 0-8369-5940-X). Ayer Co Pubs.

Froud, B. Better Show Jumping. (Illus.). 96p. 1980. 9.95 (ISBN 0-7182-1440-4, Pub. by Kaye & Ward). David & Charles.

Froud, Brian. Goblins. LC 83-61236. (Illus.). 12p. (gr. 1-4). 1983. 9.95 (ISBN 0-02-735520-9). Macmillan.

Froud, Brian & Llewelyn, J. J. World of the Dark Crystal. LC 81-47572. (Illus.). 128p. 1982. 25.00 (ISBN 0-394-52168-4); pap. 14.95 (ISBN 0-394-71280-3). Knopf.

Froud, W. J. Teaching Your Horse to Jump. pap. 2.00 (ISBN 0-87980-227-8). Wilshire.

Froude, J. A. The Divorce of Catherine of Aragon. 1891. Repr. 15.00 (ISBN 0-8482-3977-6). Norwood Edns.

--The Divorce of Catherine of Aragon. 1891. 30.00 (ISBN 0-932062-60-1). Sharon Hill.

--The Life & Letters of Erasmus & the Unknown Historical Significance of the Protestant Reformation, 2 vols. (Illus.). 157p. 1984. 147.55x set (ISBN 0-89266-469-X). Am Classical Coll Pr.

Froude, J. A., tr. see Goethe, Johann W.

Froude, James A. Bunyan. Morley, John, ed. LC 68-58379. (English Men of Letters). Repr. of 1888 ed. lib. bdg 12.50 (ISBN 0-404-51711-0). AMS Pr.

--Bunyan. LC 73-11369. 1880. lib. bdg. 12.00 (ISBN 0-8414-1985-X). Folcroft.

--A Comparative Analysis of the Philosophies of Erasmus & Luther. (Illus.). 133p. 1981. Repr. of 1868 ed. 69.85 (ISBN 0-89901-038-5). Found Class Reprints.

--Divorce of Catherine of Aragon. 2nd ed. LC 68-58379. Repr. of 1891 ed. 31.50 (ISBN 0-404-02626-5). AMS Pr.

--The Earl of Beaconsfield. Repr. 25.00 (ISBN 0-8274-2214-8). R West.

--English in Ireland in the Eighteenth Century, 3 Vols. LC 70-99246. Repr. of 1881 ed. Set. 90.00 (ISBN 0-404-02640-0). AMS Pr.

--English in the West Indies, or the Bow of Ulysses. LC 74-77200. (Illus.). Repr. of 1888 ed. cancelled (ISBN 0-8371-1312-1, FRE&, Pub. by Negro U Pr). Greenwood.

--English Seamen in the Sixteenth Century. 1909. Repr. 25.00 (ISBN 0-8274-2268-7). R West.

--Froude's Life of Carlyle. Clubbe, John, ed. LC 78-19158. (Illus.). 724p. 1979. 30.00x (ISBN 0-8142-0274-8). Ohio St U Pr.

--History of England from the Fall of Wolsey to the Defeat of the Spanish Armada, 12 Vols. LC 71-91303. Repr. of 1870 ed. Set. 540.00 (ISBN 0-404-02650-8); 45.00 ea. AMS Pr.

--A History of First Forty Years of His Life, 2 vols. 1981. Repr. Set. lib. bdg. 59.00x (ISBN 0-403-00210-9). Scholarly.

--Lectures on the Council of Trent, Delivered at Oxford 1892-3. LC 68-8244. 1969. Repr. of 1901 ed. 25.00x (ISBN 0-8046-0159-3, Pub. by Kennikat). Assoc Faculty Pr.

--Letters & Memorials of Jane Welsh Carlyle. 1973. Repr. of 1883 ed. 32.00 (ISBN 0-8274-0536-7). R West.

--Life & Letters of Erasmus. LC 70-155628. Repr. of 1895 ed. 24.50 (ISBN 0-404-02627-3). AMS Pr.

--Life & Letters of Erasmus. 1903. Repr. 24.00 (ISBN 0-8274-3878-8). R West.

--Lord Beaconsfield. facsimile ed. LC 76-157333. (Select Bibliographies Reprint Ser). Repr. of 1890 ed. 19.00 (ISBN 0-8369-5793-8). Ayer Co Pubs.

--Lord Beaconsfield. 1973. Repr. of 1890 ed. 16.50 (ISBN 0-8274-1735-7). R West.

--My Relations with Carlyle: Together with a Letter from the Late Sir James Stephen, Dated Dec. 9, 1886. facsimile ed. LC 70-154150. (Select Bibliographies Reprint Ser). Repr. of 1903 ed. 12.00 (ISBN 0-8369-5766-0). Ayer Co Pubs.

--Oceana; or, England & Her Colonies. LC 72-3974. (Black Heritage Library Collection Ser.). Repr. of 1886 ed. 18.75 (ISBN 0-8369-9096-X). Ayer Co Pubs.

--The Reign of Mary Tudor. Repr. 25.00 (ISBN 0-8482-3997-0). Norwood Edns.

--Short Studies on Great Subjects. 1964. Repr. of 1906 ed. 8.95x (ISBN 0-460-00013-6, Evman). Biblio Dist.

--Short Studies on Great Subjects, 3 vols. 1878. Set. 50.00 (ISBN 0-8274-3889-3). R West.

--The Spanish Armada. 76p. 1972. pap. 1.00x (ISBN 0-87291-036-9). Coronado Pr.

--Spanish Story of the Armada & Other Essays. LC 71-144613. Repr. of 1892 ed. 24.50 (ISBN 0-404-02628-1). AMS Pr.

--Thomas Carlyle: A History of His Life in London, 2 Vols. 1971. Repr. of 1881 ed. Set. 59.00x (ISBN 0-403-00191-9). Scholarly.

--Thomas Carlyle: A History of His Life in London 1834-1881, 2 vols. 1884. 65.00 (ISBN 0-8274-3602-5). R West.

--Thomas Carlyle: The Making of an Historian & the Theory of the Hero in History, 2 vols. (Illus.). 289p. 1984. 176.50 set (ISBN 0-89266-496-7). Am Classical Coll Pr.

--Thomas Carlyle's Life in London at the End of the 19th Century, 2 vols. (Illus.). 316p. 1985. Repr. of 1909 ed. 237.50 set (ISBN 0-89901-193-4). Found Class Reprints.

--The Two Chiefs of Dunboy; or an Irish Romance of the Last Century. LC 79-8421. Repr. of 1889 ed. 44.50 (ISBN 0-404-61853-7). AMS Pr.

Froude, James A., ed. see Carlyle, Thomas.

Froula, Christine. A Guide to Ezra Pound's Selected Poems. LC 82-18776. 256p. 1983. 16.50 (ISBN 0-8112-0856-7); pap. 7.25 (ISBN 0-8112-0857-5, NDP548). New Directions.

--To Write Paradise: Style & Error in Pound's Cantos. LC 84-3649. 208p. 1985. text ed. 18.50x (ISBN 0-300-02512-2). Yale U Pr.

Froundiian-Dirair. Armenisch-Deutsches Woerterbuch. (Armenian & Ger.). 1952. 45.00 (ISBN 3-486-41021-0, Pub. by Oldenbourg). French & Eur.

Frow, Edmund & Katanka, Michael, eds. Eighteen Sixty-Eight Year of the Unions. LC 68-105638. 1968. 19.50x (ISBN 0-678-08030-5). Kelley.

Frowein, R. A., ed. Head Injuries: Tumors of the Cerebellar Region. Proceedings of the 28th Annual Meeting of the German Society of Neurosurgery, Koeln, Sept. 18-21, 1977. LC 78-15592. (Advances in Neurosurgery Ser.: Vol. 5). (Illus.). 1978. pap. 61.00 (ISBN 0-387-08964-0). Springer-Verlag.

Frowen, S. F., et al. Monetary Policy & Economic Activity in West Germany. LC 77-2403. 268p. 1977. 37.50 (ISBN 0-470-99131-3). Krieger.

Frowen, S. F., et al, eds. Monetary Policy & Economic Activity in West Germany. LC 77-2403. 268p. 1977. 69.95x (ISBN 0-470-99131-3). Halsted Pr.

Frowen, Stephen F., ed. Controlling Industrial Economies. LC 83-40071. 390p. 1984. 40.00 (ISBN 0-312-16913-2). St Martin.

Frownfelter, Donna L. Chest Physical Therapy & Pulmonary Rehabilitation. (Illus.). 1978. 29.95 (ISBN 0-8151-3296-4). Year Bk Med.

Froyen, Richard T. Macroeconomics: Theories & Policies. 2nd ed. 957p. 1985. text ed. price not set (ISBN 0-02-339410-2). Macmillan.

Froyen, Richart T. Macroeconomics: Theories & Policies. 600p. 1983. text ed. write for info. (ISBN 0-02-339780-2). Macmillan.

Frppier, Jean, jt. auth. see Chretien de Troyes.

FRS Associates. Pension Asset Management: The Corporate Decision. LC 80-69793. 1980. 8.00 (ISBN 0-910586-36-5). Finan Exec.

Frtiz, M. F. see Lepley, William M.

Frucht, Richard C. Dunarea Noastra: Romania, the Great Powers, & the Danube Question, 1914-1921. (East European Monographs: No. 113). 216p. 1982. 24.00x (ISBN 0-88033-007-4). East Eur Quarterly.

Fruchtenbaum, Arnold G. Biblical Lovemaking: A Study of the Song of Solomon. 80p. 1984. pap. 3.50 (ISBN 0-914863-03-7). Ariel Pr CA.

--Footsteps of the Messiah: A Study of the Sequence of Prophetic Events. (Illus.). 468p. 1982. 20.00 (ISBN 0-914863-02-9). Ariel Pr CA.

--Hebrew Christianity: Its Theology, History & Philosophy. Rev. ed. 142p. 1983. pap. 3.50 (ISBN 0-914863-01-0). Ariel Pr CA.

--Jesus Was a Jew. Rev. ed. LC 74-75670. 156p. 1981. pap. 2.95 (ISBN 0-914863-00-2). Ariel Pr CA.

Fruchter, Benjamin, jt. auth. see Guilford, Joy P.

Fruchtman, Bernard & Newman, Harry R. Urology Case Studies. 2nd ed. 1979. pap. 21.00 (ISBN 0-87488-017-3). Med Exam.

Fruchtman, Caroline S. Checklist of Vocal Chamber Works by Benedetto Marcello. (Detroit Studies in Music Bibliography Ser.: No. 10). 1967. pap. 2.00 (ISBN 0-911772-30-8). Info Coord.

Fruchtman, Jack. The Apocalyptical Politics of Richard Price & Joseph Priestley: A Study in Late Eighteenth Century English Republican Millennialism. LC 82-73835. (Transactions of the American Philosophical Society Ser.: Vol. 73, Pt. 4). 1983. write for info. (ISBN 0-87169-734-3). Am Philos.

Frude, Neil. The Intimate Machine: Close Encounters with Computers & Robots. LC 83-8344. 256p. 1983. 14.95 (ISBN 0-453-00450-4). NAL.

--The Intimate Machine: Close Encounters with Computers & Robots. 1984. pap. 3.95 (ISBN 0-451-62322-3, Ment). NAL.

Frude, Neil, ed. Psychological Approaches to Child Abuse. 240p. 1981. 19.50x (ISBN 0-8476-6925-4). Rowman.

Frude, Neil & Gault, Hugh, eds. Disruptive Behavior in Schools. LC 84-7237. 1984. 31.95 (ISBN 0-471-90070-2). Wiley.

Frueh, Erne & Frueh, Florence. Chicago Stained Glass. (Illus.). 160p. 1983. 19.95 (ISBN 0-8294-0435-X). Loyola.

Frueh, Florence, jt. auth. see Frueh, Erne.

Fruehan, R. J. Ladle Metallurgy Principles & Practices. 155p. 1985. 70.00 (ISBN 0-932897-01-0). Iron & Steel.

Fruehling. Relacciones Humanas. 141p. 1979. 8.44 (ISBN 0-07-022540-0). McGraw.

Fruehling, R. T. & Bouchard, S. Business Correspondence Thirty. 4th ed. 224p. 1985. price not set (ISBN 0-07-022515-X). McGraw.

Fruehling, R. T., jt. auth. see Poe, Roy W.

Fruehling, Rosemary T. & Bouchard, Sharon. Art of Writing Effective Letters. 1972. 14.95 (ISBN 0-07-022345-9). McGraw.

--Business Correspondence-Thirty. 3rd ed. Tinervia, Joseph, ed. (Illus.). 192p. (gr. 10-12). 1981. pap. text ed. 9.56 (ISBN 0-07-022513-3). McGraw.

Fruehmorgen, P. & Claasen, M. Endoscopy & Biopsy in Gastroenterology. (Illus.). 256p. 1980. pap. 19.50 (ISBN 0-387-09645-0). Springer-Verlag.

Fruge, J. C. An Acadian Pedigree. 1972. 10.00 (ISBN 0-87511-596-9). Claitors.

--Biographies of Judges of Louisiana. 1971. text ed. 12.50. Claitors.

--Fruges of Fakaitaic. 1971. pap. 10.00 (ISBN 0-87511-594-2). Claitors.

Fruhan, William E., Jr. The Fight for Competitive Advantage: A Study of the United States Domestic Trunk Air Carriers. LC 71-187108. (Illus.). 183p. 1972. 12.95x (ISBN 0-87584-097-3). Harvard Busn.

--Financial Strategy. 1979. 25.95 (ISBN 0-256-02228-3). Irwin.

Fruin, David. Data Analysis: A Basic Introduction. 1981. 25.00x (ISBN 0-317-05791-X, Pub. by Natl Inst Social Work). State Mutual Bk.

Fruin, W. Mark. Kikkoman: Company, Clan, & Community. (Harvard Studies in Business History). (Illus.). 384p. 1983. text ed. 33.00x (ISBN 0-674-50340-6). Harvard U Pr.

Fruit, John P. Mind & Art of Poe's Poetry. LC 70-85908. Repr. of 1899 ed. 17.50 (ISBN 0-404-02629-X). AMS Pr.

--The Mind & Art of Poe's Poetry. 144p. 1980. Repr. of 1899 ed. lib. bdg. 20.00 (ISBN 0-8495-1707-9). Arden Lib.

--Mind & Art of Poe's Poetry. LC 72-187170. 1899. lib. bdg. 15.00 (ISBN 0-8414-0475-5). Folcroft.

Frum, Barbara. As It Happened. 1977. 10.00 (ISBN 0-7710-3195-5). McClelland.

Fruman, Norman. Coleridge, the Damaged Archangel. LC 71-148734. 1971. 12.50 (ISBN 0-8076-0607-3). Braziller.

Frumer, Louis R. & Biskind, Elliott L. Bender's New York Evidence-CPLR. LC 62-6515. Date not set. price not set. Bender.

Frumer, Louis R., ed. Personal Injury Annual. 32.50 (ISBN 0-685-02521-7). Bender.

Frumer, Louis R., et al. Personal Injury: Actions, Defenses, Damages, 25 vols. 1957. Updates avail. looseleaf 800.00 (530); looseleaf 1983 474.50; looseleaf 1984 525.00. Bender.

Frumker, Sanford C., jt. auth. see Arnold, Norman R.

Frumkes, Lewis B. How to Raise Your I. Q. by Eating Gifted Children. 216p. 1984. pap. 6.95 (ISBN 0-07-022103-0). McGraw.

Frumkin, A. N. Surface Properties of Semiconductors. LC 63-21219. 171p. 1964. 27.50x (ISBN 0-306-10665-5, Consultants). Plenum Pub.

Frumkin, A. N. & Ershler, A. B., eds. Progress in Electrochemistry of Organic Compounds, Vol. 1. LC 77-137739. 447p. 1971. 55.00x (ISBN 0-306-39901-6, Plenum Pr). Plenum Pub.

Frumkin, Deborah S., jt. auth. see Allen, Harold.

Frumkin, Gene. Clouds & Red Earth. LC 81-9542. viii, 67p. 1982. 15.95x (ISBN 0-8040-0418-8, 82-75638, Pub. by Swallow); pap. 6.95 (ISBN 0-8040-0375-0, 82-75646, Pub. by Swallow). Ohio U Pr.

--Dostoevsky & Other Nature Poems. 1971. 5.25 (ISBN 0-941490-05-X). Solo Pr.

--Locust Cry: Poems: 1958-65. 40p. pap. 3.00 (ISBN 0-88235-018-8). San Marcos.

--Loops. (Orig.). 1980. pap. 3.00 (ISBN 0-88235-039-0). San Marcos.

--The Mystic Writing Pad. 1977. perfect bound in wrappers 2.50 (ISBN 0-88031-037-5). Invisible-Red Hill.

Frumkin, Mitch. Muscle Car Mania: An Advertising Collection 1964 to 1974. LC 81-14123. (Illus.). 176p. 1981. pap. 13.95 (ISBN 0-87938-153-1). Motorbooks Intl.

--Son of Muscle Car Mania. (Illus.). 176p. 1982. pap. 13.95 (ISBN 0-87938-154-X). Motorbooks Intl.

Frumkin, Paul, jt. auth. see Guermont, Claude.

Frumkin, V., ed. see Okudzhava, Bulat.

Frunder, H., ed. Effects & Metabolism of Insulin & Cyclic Nucleotides. (Illus.). 1978. stitched 22.00x (ISBN 0-685-87201-7). Adlers Foreign Bks.

Frungel, Frank. High Speed Pulse Technology, 4 vols. Incl. Vol. 1. Capacitor Discharges, Magneto-Hydrodynamics, X-Rays, Ultrasonics. 1965. 83.00 (ISBN 0-12-269001-X); Vol. 2. Optical Pulses, Lasers, Measuring Techniques. 1965. 77.00 (ISBN 0-12-269002-8); Vol. 3. 1976. 83.00 (ISBN 0-12-269003-6); Vol. 4. 1980. 66.00 (ISBN 0-12-269004-4). Acad Pr.

Frunzi, George L., jt. auth. see Halloran, Jack.

Frurip, David J., et al. Colonial Nails from Michilamackinac: Differentiation by Chemical & Statistical Analysis. (Archaeological Completion Report Ser.: No. 7). (Illus.). 83p. (Orig.). 1983. pap. 8.50 (ISBN 0-911872-47-7). MacKinac Island.

Frush, Charles A. A Trip from the Dalles, Oregon, to Fort Owen, Bitter Root Valley, Montana, in May & June of 1858. 15p. Date not set. pap. 3.95 (ISBN 0-87770-302-7). Ye Galleon.

Frush, James, Jr. & Eshenbach, Benson. The Retirement Residence: An Analysis of the Architecture & Management of Life-Care Housing. 116p. 1968. 11.75x (ISBN 0-398-00626-1). C C Thomas.

Frushell, Richard C. & Vondersmith, Bernard J., eds. Contemporary Thought on Edmund Spenser, with a Bibliography of Criticism of the Faerie Queene, 1900-1970. LC 74-30159. 255p. 1975. 15.00x (ISBN 0-8093-0695-6). S Ill U Pr.

Fruth, Florence K. Some Descendants of Richard Few of Chester County, Pennsylvania & Allied Lines 1682 -1976. LC 77-72866. (Illus.). 1977. 27.00 (ISBN 0-87012-274-6). F K Fruth.

Frutiger, Adrian. Type Sign Symbol. 156p. 1980. 72.50 (ISBN 0-8038-7221-6, Visual Communications). Hastings.

Frutiger, Perceval. Les Mythes de Platon: Etude Philosophique & Litteraire. facsimile ed. LC 75-13269. (History of Ideas in Ancient Greece Ser.). (Fr.). 1976. Repr. of 1930 ed. 23.50x (ISBN 0-405-07310-0). Ayer Co Pubs.

Frutkin, Susan. Aime Cesaire: Black Between Worlds. new ed. LC 73-85305. (Monographs in International Affairs). 66p. 1973. pap. text ed. 3.95 (ISBN 0-933074-21-2). AISI.

Fruton, Joseph S. A Bio-Bibliography for the History of the Biochemical Sciences Since 1800. LC 82-72158. 1982. 20.00 (ISBN 0-87169-983-4). Am Philos.

--Molecules & Life: Historical Essays on the Interplay of Chemistry & Biology. LC 72-3095. pap. 112.00 (ISBN 0-317-28456-8, 2055135). Bks Demand UMI.

Fruttero, Carl & Lucentini, Franco. The Sunday Woman. 1976. pap. 1.75 (ISBN 0-380-00865-3, 31328). Avon.

Fruzzetti, Lina M. The Gift of a Virgin: Women, Marriage & Ritual in a Bengali Society. (Illus.). 170p. 1982. 22.50 (ISBN 0-8135-0939-4). Rutgers U Pr.

Fry. Dermatology: An Illustrated Guide. (Illus.). 350p. 1984. pap. text ed. 39.95 (ISBN 0-407-00335-5). Butterworth.

--The I.R.S. Code Made Understandable. 1977. 10.00 (ISBN 0-686-17822-X). Tax Info Ctr.

Fry & Cornell. Dermatology. (Management of Common Diseasesin Family Practice Ser.). 1985. 15.00 (ISBN 0-88416-528-0). PSG Pub Co.

Fry, jt. auth. see Sanders, D. H.

Fry, et al. Illustrated Encyclopedia of Dermatology. 2nd ed. 576p. 1984. 29.95 (ISBN 0-87489-612-6). Med Economics.

Fry, Alan. The Wilderness Survival Handbook: A Practical, All-Season Guide to Short Trip Preparation & Survival Techniques for Hikers, Skiers, Backpackers, Canoeists, Travelers in Light Aircraft & Anyone Stranded in the Bush. (Illus.). 304p. 1982. 15.95 (ISBN 0-312-87951-2); pap. 8.95 (ISBN 0-312-87952-0). St Martin.

Fry, Anna M. Memories of Old Cahaba. Repr. 5.00 (ISBN 0-87397-036-5). Strode.

Fry, B. N., ed. Government Publications. 1981. 110.00 (ISBN 0-08-025216-8). Pergamon.

Fry, Barbara, et al, eds. Eastern Churches Review, Vols. I-X, 1966-1978. 2000p. 1985. pap. text ed. 80.00x (ISBN 0-89370-095-9). Borgo Pr.

Fry, Bernard M. & Hernon, Peter, eds. Government Publications: Key Papers. (Guides to Official Publications Ser.: Vol. 8). (Illus.). 684p. 1981. 110.00 (ISBN 0-08-025216-8). Pergamon.

Fry, C. George, jt. auth. see Arnold, Duane W.

Fry, C. H. The Bee-eaters. LC 84-70385. (Illus.). 320p. 1984. write for info (ISBN 0-931130-11-5). Buteo.

Fry, C. Luther. American Villagers. 1926. 10.00 (ISBN 0-8482-3964-4). Norwood Edns.

Fry, Caroline. Christ Our Example. 155p. 1976. pap. 3.95 (ISBN 0-685-53618-1). Reiner.

Fry, Carroll L. Charlotte Smith, Popular Novelist. Varma, Devendra P., ed. LC 79-8453. (Gothic Studies & Dissertations Ser.). 1980. lib. bdg. 27.50x (ISBN 0-405-12667-0). Ayer Co Pubs.

Fry, Charles R. Art Deco Interiors in Color. LC 77-75887. (Illus.). 1977. pap. 6.00 (ISBN 0-486-23527-0). Dover.

Fry, Charles R., ed. Art Deco Designs in Color. LC 75-17173. (Illus.). 48p. 1975. pap. 5.95 (ISBN 0-486-23216-6). Dover.

Fry, Charles R., ed. see Verneuil, M. P., et al.

Fry, Christine, ed. Aging in Culture & Society: Comparative Viewpoints & Strategies. (Illus.). 336p. 1980. 29.95x (ISBN 0-686-75097-7); pap. text ed. 14.95 (ISBN 0-89789-001-9). Bergin & Garvey.

--Dimensions: Age, Culture & Health. LC 80-28607. 352p. 1981. 38.95x (ISBN 0-03-052971-9). Praeger.

--Dimensions: Aging, Culture, & Health. 352p. 1981. 29.95x (ISBN 0-686-76476-5); pap. 14.95 (ISBN 0-89789-049-3). Bergin & Garvey.

Fry, Christine L., ed. Aging in Culture & Society: Comparative Viewpoints & Strategies. LC 79-13198. 336p. 1980. 36.95x (ISBN 0-03-052726-0). Praeger.

Fry, Christopher. Dark Is Light Enough. 1954. 9.95x (ISBN 0-19-500155-9). Oxford U Pr.

--Death Is a Kind of Love. (Illus.). 1979. 15.00 (ISBN 0-930954-12-2); deluxe ed. 75.00 (ISBN 0-930954-13-0). Tidal Pr.

--The Lady's Not for Burning, A Phoenix Too Frequent, & an Essay, "An Experience of Critics". 1977. pap. 6.95 (ISBN 0-19-519916-2, 507, GB). Oxford U Pr.

--Selected Plays. 368p. 1985. pap. 7.95 (ISBN 0-19-281873-2). Oxford U Pr.

--Venus Observed. 1950. 9.95x (ISBN 0-19-500395-0). Oxford U Pr.

--Yard of Sun. LC 76-121048. 1970. 9.95x (ISBN 0-19-501245-3). Oxford U Pr.

Fry, Christopher, tr. see Anouilh, Jean.

Fry, Christopher see Ibsen, Henrik.

Fry, D. B. The Nature of Religious Man. 1982. 15.95 (ISBN 0-900860-67-7, Pub. by Octagon Pr England). Ins Study Human.

Fry, Dennis B. Acoustic Phonetics: A Course of Basic Reading. (Illus.). 1976. 49.50 (ISBN 0-521-21393-2). Cambridge U Pr.

--The Physics of Speech. LC 78-56752. (Textbooks in Linguistics Ser.). (Illus.). 1979. 32.50 (ISBN 0-521-22173-0); pap. 10.95 (ISBN 0-521-29379-0). Cambridge U Pr.

Fry, Donald K. Beowulf & the Fight at Finnsburh: A Bibliography. LC 70-94760. xx, 222p. 1969. 17.50x (ISBN 0-8139-0268-1, Bibliographical Society, University of Virginia). U Pr of Va.

Fry, Donald K., compiled by. Norse Sagas Translated into English: A Bibliography. LC 79-8632. (AMS Studies in the Middle Ages: No. 3). 1980. 24.50 (ISBN 0-404-18016-7). AMS Pr.

Fry, E. A., jt. auth. see Phillimore, William P.

Fry, E. A., ed. A Calendar of Chancery Proceedings, Bills & Answers. (British Record Society Index Library Ser.: Vol. 14). pap. 19.00 (ISBN 0-317-16334-5). Kraus Repr.

Fry, E. A., ed. see British Record Society.

Fry, Earl H. Canadian Government & Politics in Comparative Perspective. 2nd ed. 286p. 1984. lib. bdg. 25.00 (ISBN 0-8191-3772-3); pap. text ed. 11.00 (ISBN 0-8191-3773-1). U Pr of Amer.

--Financial Invasion of the U. S. A. A Threat to American Society? (Illus.). 1979. 18.50 (ISBN 0-07-022591-5). McGraw.

--The Politics of International Investment. 224p. 1983. 26.50 (ISBN 0-07-022610-5). McGraw.

Fry, Earl H. & Raymond, Gregory A. The Other Western Europe: A Political Analysis of the Smaller Democracies. 2nd, rev. ed. LC 82-20707. (Studies in International & Comparative Politics: No. 14). 289p. 1983. lib. bdg. 30.00 (ISBN 0-87436-345-4); pap. text ed. 18.00 (ISBN 0-87436-346-2). Abc-Clio.

Fry, Earl H. & Radebaugh, Lee H., eds. Canada-U. S. Economic Relations on the "Conservative" Era of Mulroney & Reagan. 150p. (Orig.). 1985. pap. price not set (ISBN 0-912575-03-4). D M Kennedy Ctr Brigham.

--The Regulation of Foreign Direct Investment in Canada & the United States: Prospects & Challenges. LC 83-7693. 220p. (Orig.). 1983. pap. 14.00 (ISBN 0-912575-01-8). D M Kennedy Ctr Brigham.

Fry, Earl H., jt. ed. see Radebaugh, Lee H.

Fry, Edmund. Pantographia: Containing Accurate Copies of All the Known Alphabets in the World, Together with an English Explanation of the Peculiar Force or Power of Each Letter. LC 79-104956. 320p. 1983. lib. bdg. 49.95x (ISBN 0-89370-778-3). Borgo Pr.

Fry, Edward. Elementary Reading Instruction. 1977. 31.95 (ISBN 0-07-022585-0). McGraw.

--Reading Faster: Drillbook. 1963. text ed. 4.95x (ISBN 0-521-05046-4). Cambridge U Pr.

--Reading Instruction for Classroom & Clinic. (Illus.). 448p. 1972. text ed. 29.95 (ISBN 0-07-022604-0). McGraw.

--Skimming & Scanning: Advanced Level. (Illus.). (gr. 9 up). 1978. pap. text ed. 7.20x (ISBN 0-89061-123-8, 781). Jamestown Pubs.

Fry, Edward, jt. auth. see Sakiey, Elizabeth.

Fry, Edward A. Index of Chancery Proceedings (Reynardson's Division) Preserved in the Public Record Office A. D. 1649-1714. Vol. I: A-K. (British Record Society Index Library Ser.: Vol. 29). pap. 19.00 (ISBN 0-317-16005-2). Kraus Repr.

Fry, Edward A., ed. Abstracts of Gloucestershire Inquisitiones Post Mortem, Pt. III: Miscellaneous Series, 1-8 Charles I, 1625-1642. (British Record Society Index Library Ser.: Vol. 21). pap. 19.00 (ISBN 0-317-16000-1). Kraus Repr.

--Abstracts of Inquisitiones Post Mortem for Gloucestershire, Pt. V: 30 Edward I to 32 Edward III, 1302-1358. (British Record Society Index Library Ser.: Vol. 40). pap. 30.00 (ISBN 0-317-16021-4). Kraus Repr.

--Abstracts of Inquisitiones Post Mortem for the City of London, Pt. III: 19-45 Elizabeth, 1577-1603. (Brit. Record Soc. Index Lib. Ser.: Vol. 36). pap. 30.00 (ISBN 0-317-16014-1). Kraus Repr.

--Abstracts of Wiltshire Inquisitiones Post Mortem Returned into the Court of Chancery in the Reigns of Henry III, & Edward II: A. D. 1242-1326. (British Record Society Index Library Ser.: Vol. 37). pap. 44.00 (ISBN 0-317-16015-X). Kraus Repr.

--Calendar of Administrations in the Consistory Court of the Bishop of Chichester: 1555-1800. Bd. with Index of Wills at Canterbury, Vol. 2: Wills, 1558-1577. Ridge, C. H., ed; A Calendar of Marriage Licence Allegations, London, Vol. 2: 1660-1700. (British Record Society Index Library Ser.: Vol. 64-66). Repr. of 1940 ed. 79.00 (ISBN 0-317-16112-1). Kraus Repr.

--Calendar of Wills & Administrations in the Consistory Court of the Bishop of Worcester: 1451-1600. (British Record Society Index Library Ser.: Vol. 31). pap. 44.00 (ISBN 0-317-16006-0). Kraus Repr.

--Calendar of Wills & Administrations in the Consistory Court of the Bishop of Worcester: 1601-1652. (British Record Society Index Library Ser.: Vol. 39). pap. 19.00 (ISBN 0-317-16017-6). Kraus Repr.

--Calendar of Wills & Administrations in the Court of the Archdeacon of Taunton, Pts. I & II: Wills Only, 1537-1799. (British Record Society Index Library Ser.: Vol. 45). pap. 30.00 (ISBN 0-317-16096-6). Kraus Repr.

--A Calendar of Wills & Administrations Relating to the County of Dorset Proved in the Consistory Court (Dorsetshire Division) of the Late Diocese of Bristol: 1681-1792. (British Record Society Index Library Ser.: Vol. 22). pap. 19.00 (ISBN 0-317-16001-X). Kraus Repr.

--Calendar of Wills & Administrations Relating to the Counties of Devon & Cornwall: Proved, 1559-1779 & of Devon, 1540-1799. (British Record Society Index Library Ser.). pap. 63.00 (ISBN 0-317-16013-3). Kraus Repr.

--Calendar of Wills & Administrations Relating to the Counties of Devon & Cornwall, Proved: 1532-1800. (British Record Society Index Library Ser.: Vol. 46). pap. 30.00 (ISBN 0-317-16098-2). Kraus Repr.

--Calendar of Wills in the Consistory Court of the Bishop of Chichester: 1482-1800. (British Record Society Index Library Ser.: Vol. 49). pap. 30.00 (ISBN 0-317-16101-6). Kraus Repr.

--A Calendar of Wills Proved in the Consistory Court (City & Deanery of Bristol Division) of the Bishop of Bristol: 1572-1792. (British Record Society Index Library Ser.: Vol. 17). pap. 19.00 (ISBN 0-317-15994-1). Kraus Repr.

--Index of Chancery Proceedings (Reynardson's Division), Vol. 2: L-Z. (Brit. Record Soc. Index Lib. Ser.: Vol. 32). pap. 19.00 (ISBN 0-317-16007-9). Kraus Repr.

Fry, Edward A. & Cokayne, G. E., eds. Calendar of Marriage Licenses Issued by the Faculty Office: 1632-1714. (British Record Society Index Library Ser.: Vol. 33). pap. 30.00 (ISBN 0-317-16010-9). Kraus Repr.

Fry, Edward A. & Fry, G. S., eds. Abstracts of Wiltshire Inquisitiones Post Mortem Returned into the Court of Chancery in the Reign of King Charles I. (British Record Society Library Ser.: Vol. 23). pap. 44.00 (ISBN 0-317-16002-8). Kraus Repr.

Fry, Edward A. & Phillimore, W. P., eds. A Calendar of Wills Proved in the Consistory Court of the Bishop of Gloucester, Vol. 2: 1660-1800. (British Record Society Index Library Ser.: Vol. 34). pap. 30.00 (ISBN 0-317-16011-7). Kraus Repr.

Fry, Edward B. Barco de Vela en el Viento: Sailboat in the Wind. Gunning, Monica, tr. (Storybooks for Beginners Ser.: Bk. 4). (Illus.). 15p. (Eng. & Span.). (gr. 1). 1980. pap. 12.00 set (ISBN 0-89061-215-3, 432); pap. 3.00 ea. Jamestown Pubs.

--Barco de Vela: Sailboat. Gunning, Monica, tr. (Storybooks for Beginners Ser.: Bk. 3). (Illus.). 15p. (Eng. & Span.). (gr. 1). 1980. pap. 12.00 set (ISBN 0-89061-214-5, 432); pap. 3.00 ea. Jamestown Pubs.

--Computer Keyboarding for Children. rev. ed. (Computers & Education Ser.). (gr. 3-6). 1984. pap. text ed. 8.95x (ISBN 0-8077-2754-7). Tchrs Coll.

--Dictionary Drills. 128p. (YA) (gr. 9 up). 1980. pap. text ed. 7.20x (ISBN 0-89061-206-4, 752). Jamestown Pubs.

--The Emergency Reading Teacher's Manual. 107p. (Orig.). 1979. pap. text ed. 10.00 (ISBN 0-89061-207-2, 752S). Jamestown Pubs.

--Graphical Comprehension: How to Read & Make Graphs. (Illus.). 160p. (Orig.). (YA) (gr. 9 up). 1981. pap. text ed. 7.20x (ISBN 0-89061-240-4, 782). Jamestown Pubs.

--Ninety-Nine Phonics Charts. 1971. pap. text ed. 6.00x (ISBN 0-87673-006-3, 425). Jamestown Pubs.

--Reading Diagnosis: Informal Reading Inventories. 153p. (Orig.). 1981. pap. text ed. 20.00x (ISBN 0-89061-217-X, 754S). Jamestown Pubs.

--Reading Drills: Advanced Level. (Illus.). 192p. (gr. 9 up). 1975. pap. text ed. 7.20x (ISBN 0-89061-039-8, 751). Jamestown Pubs.

--Reading Drills: Middle Level. (Illus.). 224p. (Orig.). (gr. 4-8). 1982. pap. text ed. 7.20x (ISBN 0-89061-245-5, 750). Jamestown Pubs.

--Skimming & Scanning Middle Level. (Illus.). 160p. (Orig.). (gr. 4-8). 1982. pap. text ed. 7.20x (ISBN 0-89061-246-3, 780). Jamestown Pubs.

Fry, Edward B., et al. The Reading Teacher's Book of Lists. 195p. 1984. 17.50 (ISBN 0-13-762112-4, Busn). P-H.

Fry, Edward F. Cubism. (World of Art Ser.). (Illus.). 200p. 1985. pap. 9.95 (ISBN 0-500-20047-5). Thames Hudson.

--Sheila Isham: Recent Work. LC 81-66362. (Illus.). 1981. pap. 7.00 (ISBN 0-914782-38-X). Buffalo Acad.

Fry, Edward F. & McClintic, Miranda. David Smith: Painter, Sculpter, Draftsman. (Illus.). pap. 15.00 (ISBN 0-8076-1057-7). Braziller.

Fry, Edward F., ed. see Leger, Fernand.

Fry, Eleanor. Colorado Travel, 1846-1880. (Illus.). 20p. 1981. pap. 1.50x (ISBN 0-915617-00-5). Pueblo Co Hist Soc.

--Lake Minnequa Park. (Illus.). 20p. 1982. pap. 2.00x (ISBN 0-915617-05-6). Pueblo Co Hist Soc.

--Railroad Accidents in Colorado. (Illus.). 24p. 1982. pap. 2.00x (ISBN 0-915617-02-1). Pueblo Co Hist Soc.

--Tite Barnacle's Pueblo. (Orig.). 1986. pap. write for info. (ISBN 0-915617-12-9). Pueblo Co Hist Soc.

Fry, Elizabeth & Cresswell, Rachel L. Memoir of the Life of Elizabeth Fry: With Extracts from Her Journals & Letters, 2 vols. in one. 2nd, rev. & enl. ed. LC 70-172597. (Criminology, Law Enforcement, & Social Problems Ser.: No. 187). (Genealogical charts & with index added). 1974. Repr. of 1848 ed. 45.00x (ISBN 0-87585-187-8). Patterson Smith.

Fry, Eric, ed. Rebels & Radicals. (Illus.). 216p. 1983. text ed. 22.50x (ISBN 0-86861-285-5). Allen Unwin.

--Rebels & Radicals. (Illus.). 228p. 1985. pap. text ed. 12.50x (ISBN 0-86861-293-6). Allen Unwin.

Fry, Eric C. The Book of Knots & Ropework: Practical & Decorative. (Illus.). 176p. 1983. 4.98 (ISBN 0-517-54885-2); pap. 4.95 (ISBN 0-517-54886-0). Crown.

--Buying a House: A Guide to Finding Faults. (Illus.). 64p. 1983. 8.50 (ISBN 0-7153-8487-2). David & Charles.

Fry, F. J., ed. Ultrasound: Its Applications in Biology & Medicine, 2 vols. (Methods & Phenomena Ser.: Vol. 3). 760p. 1978. Set. 117.00 (ISBN 0-444-41641-2). Elsevier.

Fry, Fiona S. Horses. (Junior Reference Ser.). (Illus.). (gr. 6up). 1981. 8.95 (ISBN 0-7136-2114-1). Dufour.

Fry, Fiona S., jt. auth. see Fry, Peter.

Fry, Fiona S., jt. auth. see Fry, Plantagenet.

Fry, G. K. The Administrative "Revolution" in Whitehall: A Study in the Politics of Administrative Change in British Central Government since the 1950's. 218p. 1981. 25.00 (ISBN 0-7099-1010-X, Pub. by Croom Helm Ltd). Longwood Pub Group.

Fry, G. L., jt. auth. see Wratten, S. D.

Fry, G. S., jt. ed. see Fry, Edward A.

Fry, Garry L. & Ethell, Jeffrey L. Escort to Berlin: The Fourth Fighter Group in World War II. LC 79-21070. (Illus.). 336p. 1983. pap. 12.95 (ISBN 0-668-05099-3, 5099). Arco.

Fry, Gary & Berra, Kathy. YMCA Cardiac Therapy. 400p. 20.00x (ISBN 0-88035-000-8, 4206). YMCA USA.

--YMCArdiac Therapy. (Illus.). 374p. 1981. 20.00x (ISBN 0-88035-000-8). YMCA USA.

Fry, Gary F. Analysis of Prehistoric Coprolites from Utah. (University of Utah Anthropological Papers: No. 97). (Illus.). 1978. pap. text ed. 5.00x (ISBN 0-87480-142-7). U of Utah Pr.

Fry, Gary F. & Dalley, Gardiner F. The Levee Site & the Knoll Site. (University of Utah Anthropological Papers: No. 100). (Illus., Orig.). 1979. pap. 10.00x (ISBN 0-87480-153-2). U of Utah Pr.

Fry, Geoffrey. The Changing Civil Service. 144p. 1985. text ed. 20.00x (ISBN 0-04-350063-3); pap. text ed. 8.95x (ISBN 0-04-350064-1). Allen Unwin.

Fry, Geoffrey K. The Growth of Government: The Development of Ideas About the Role of the State & the Machinery & Functions of Government in Britain Since 1780. 295p. 1979. 30.00x (ISBN 0-7146-3116-7, F Cass Co). Biblio Dist.

--Statesmen in Disguise: The Changing Role of the Administrative Class of the British Home Civil Service, 1853-1966. 1969. text ed. 21.00x (ISBN 0-333-00290-3). Humanities.

Fry, George. Study of Circulation Control Systems: Public Libraries, College & University Libraries, Special Libraries. LC 61-16167. (American Library Association- Library Technology Project Ser.: No. 13). pap. 36.50 (ISBN 0-317-26364-1, 2024222). Bks Demand UMI.

--The Varnishes of the Italian Violin-Makers of the Sixteenth, Seventeenth & Eighteenth Centuries & Their Influence on Tone. (Illus.). 1977. Repr. of 1904 ed. text ed. 20.00 (ISBN 0-918624-02-9). Virtuoso.

Fry, George C. & King, James R. Islam: A Survey of the Muslim Faith. (Illus.). 204p. (Orig.). 1980. pap. 5.95 (ISBN 0-8010-3497-3). Baker Bk.

Fry, George C., et al. Great Asian Religions. 228p. 1984. pap. 9.95 (ISBN 0-8010-3511-2). Baker Bk.

Fry, George S., ed. Abstracts of Inquisitiones Post Mortem Relating to the City of London Returned into the Court of Chancery, Pt. I: Henry VII to 3 Elizabeth, 1485-1561. (British Record Society Index Library Ser.: Vol. 15). pap. 19.00 (ISBN 0-317-15992-5). Kraus Repr.

--Calendars of Wills & Administrations Relating to the County of Dorset. (British Record Society Index Library Ser.: Vol. 53). pap. 25.00 (ISBN 0-317-16107-5). Kraus Repr.

Fry, George S., jt. ed. see Phillimore, W. P.

Fry, George S. see Phillimore, W. P.

Fry, Gladys-Marie. Night Riders in Black Folk History. LC 74-34268. pap. 66.00 (ISBN 0-317-26161-4, 2024379). Bks Demand UMI.

Fry, Henry P. Modern Ku Klux Klan. LC 74-88411. Repr. of 1922 ed. 19.75x (ISBN 0-8371-1929-4, FRM, Pub. by Negro U Pr). Greenwood.

Fry, Howard T. A History of the Mountain Province. (Illus.). 284p. (Orig.). 1983. pap. 11.50 (ISBN 971-10-0036-9, Pub. by New Day Philippines). Cellar.

Fry, I. A Key to Language. 1926. 12.50 (ISBN 0-8274-2649-6). R West.

Fry, J. Beecham Manual for Family Practice. 2nd ed. 1985. lib. bdg. 40.00 (ISBN 0-85200-911-9, Pub. by MTP). Kluwer Academic.

--Present State & Future Needs in General Practice. 150p. 1983. text ed. write for info. (ISBN 0-85200-708-6, Pub. by MTP Pr England). Kluwer Academic.

Fry, J., jt. auth. see Fabb, W. E.

Fry, J., ed. The Beecham Manual for Family Practice. 300p. 1982. text ed. 29.00 (ISBN 0-85200-456-7, Pub. by MTP Pr England). Kluwer Academic.

--Common Dilemmas in Family Medicine. 1983. lib. bdg. 35.00 (ISBN 0-85200-565-2, Pub. by MTP Pr England). Kluwer Academic.

--Primary Care. 2nd ed. 530p. (Orig.). 1984. 32.00 (ISBN 0-433-10916-5, 99143014X, Pub. by Heinemann Medical). Heyden.

Fry, J., ed. see Glasspool, Michael G.

Fry, J., ed. see Ratnesar, Padnam.

Fry, J., ed. see Tatford, E. Patrick.

Fry, J., ed. see Williams, Kenneth G. & Lancaster-Smith, Michael J.

Fry, J., et al, eds. see Forgacs, Paul.

Fry, J., et al, eds. see Golding, Douglas N.

Fry, J., et al, eds. see Hood, John M.

Fry, J., et al, eds. see Martin, Anthony.

Fry, J., et al, eds. see Wharton, Christopher F.

Fry, James. Employment & Income Distribution in the African Economy. 192p. 1979. 32.00 (ISBN 0-85664-715-2, Pub. by Croom Helm Ltd). Longwood Pub Group.

Fry, James P., jt. auth. see Teorey, Toby J.

Fry, Jim, ed. see Leonard, Vincent F.

Fry, Joan & Denby-Wrightson, Kathryn. The Beginning Dressage Book: A Guide to the Basics for Horse & Rider. LC 80-16950. (Illus.). 240p. 1981. 12.95 (ISBN 0-668-04969-3, 4969). Arco.

Fry, John. Common Diseases: Their Nature, Incidence & Care. 2nd ed. LC 79-88209. 1979. text ed. 34.50 (ISBN 0-397-58256-0, 65-72572, Lippincott Medical). Lippincott.

--Common Diseases: Their Nature, Incidence & Care, 3rd ed. 437p. 1983. 35.00x (ISBN 0-942068-08-4). Bogden & Son.

--Common Diseases: Their Nature, Incidence & Care. 3rd ed. 1983. lib. bdg. 29.00 (ISBN 0-85200-454-0, Pub. by MTP Pr England). Kluwer Academic.

--Limits of the Welfare State. 240p. 1978. text ed. 37.95x (ISBN 0-566-00235-3). Gower Pub Co.

--Marcuse-Dilemma & Liberation: A Critical Analysis. 184p. 1974. pap. text ed. 10.50x (ISBN 0-391-00872-2). Humanities.

Fry, John & Hunt. The Royal College of General Practitioners: The First 25 Years. (Illus.). 350p. 1982. text ed. 29.00 (ISBN 0-85200-360-9, Pub. by MTP Pr England). Kluwer Academic.

Fry, John, jt. auth. see Geyman, John P.

Fry, John, ed. Common Dilemmas in Family Medicine. 420p. 1982. 32.00x (ISBN 0-942068-04-1). Bogden & Son.

Fry, John, et al. NHS Data Book. 1984. lib. bdg. 34.00 (ISBN 0-85200-735-3, Pub. by MTP Pr England). Kluwer Academic.

--Scientific Foundations of Family Medicine. (Illus.). 1979. 92.95 (ISBN 0-8151-3275-1). Year Bk Med.

Fry, John A. Industrial Democracy & Labour Market Policy in Sweden. 1979. 38.00 (ISBN 0-08-022462-8); pap. 18.75 (ISBN 0-08-022498-9). Pergamon.

Fry, Joseph A. Henry S. Sanford: Diplomacy & Business in 19th Century America. LC 82-8360. (History & Political Science Ser.: No. 16). (Illus.). 226p. (Orig.). 1982. pap. 9.25x (ISBN 0-87417-070-2). U of Nev Pr.

Fry, L. An Analysis of Zionism. 1982. lib. bdg. 59.00 (ISBN 0-87700-416-1). Revisionist Pr.

--Dermatology: An Illustrated Guide. 2nd ed. 164p. 1978. 75.00 (ISBN 3-456-80642-6, Pub. by Holdan Bk Ltd UK). State Mutual Bk.

--The Jews & the British Empire. 1982. lib. bdg. 59.95 (ISBN 0-87700-334-3). Revisionist Pr.

Fry, L. John. Practical Building of Methane Power Plants for Rural Energy Independence. Knox, D. Anthony, ed. LC 76-16224. (Illus.). 1974. pap. text ed. 12.00 (ISBN 0-9600984-1-0). L J Fry.

Fry, Larry. BASIC Programming for Business: A Structured Approach. LC 84-14268. 352p. 1985. pap. text ed. 20.00 (ISBN 0-8273-2245-3); instr's. guide 5.60 (ISBN 0-8273-2246-1). Delmar.

Fry, Lionel. Dermatology: An Illustrated Guide. 2nd ed. (Illus.). 1978. text ed. 19.00x (ISBN 0-906141-02-8, Pub. by Update Pubns England). Kluwer Academic.

--Dermatology An Illustrated Guide. 168p. 1978. 60.00x (ISBN 0-906141-02-8, Pub. by MTP Pr). State Mutual Bk.

--Illustrated Encyclopedia of Dermatology. 580p. 1981. text ed. 32.00 (ISBN 0-8391-1689-6). Univ Park.

Fry, Lionel & Cornell, M. Dermatology. (Management of Common Diseases in Family Practice Ser.). 1985. lib. bdg. 21.00 (ISBN 0-85200-890-2, Pub. by MTP Pr England). Kluwer Academic.

Fry, LoRheda, jt. auth. see Caperton, Thomas J.

Fry, Louis & Adams, Marsha T. The Business Microcomputer Handbook: Evaluation, Acquisition & Use. 1984. 19.45 (ISBN 0-03-071616-0). HR&W.

Fry, M. Color & Fiber. 1986. cancelled (ISBN 0-442-20055-2). Van Nos Reinhold.

Fry, Malcolm C. Discipling & Developing. (Sunday School Workers Training Course Ser.: No. 4). 1971. pap. 3.95 (ISBN 0-89265-006-0, Free Will Baptist Dept). Randall Hse.

--Discipling & Developing: Teachers Guide. 1979. pap. 1.25 (ISBN 0-89265-062-1). Randall Hse.

--Precepts for Practice. (Way of Life Ser.). 1971. pap. 3.95 (ISBN 0-89265-004-4, Free Will Baptist Dept); tchrs' guide 3.95 (ISBN 0-89265-005-2). Randall Hse.

Fry, Malcolm C. & Crowson, Milton. The Ministry of Ushering: Leader's Guide. 1980. pap. 1.50 (ISBN 0-89265-066-4). Randall Hse.

Fry, Maxwell & Drew, Jane. Tropical Architecture in the Dry & Humid Zones. 2nd ed. LC 80-20394. 264p. 1982. lib. bdg. 24.50 (ISBN 0-89874-126-2). Krieger.

Fry, Maxwell J. & Williams, Raburn M. American Money & Banking. LC 83-21619. 483p. 1984. 33.50 (ISBN 0-471-86150-2). Wiley.

Fry, Michael G. Lloyd George & Foreign Policy Volume I: The Education of a Statesman, 1890-1916. 1977. lib. bdg. 23.50x (ISBN 0-7735-0274-2). McGill-Queens U Pr.

Fry, N. The Field Description of Metamorphic Rocks. 128p. 1983. pap. 13.50x (ISBN 0-335-10037-6, Pub. by Open Univ Pr). Taylor & Francis.

Fry, N., jt. ed. see Adkinson, A. Wyle.

Fry, Norman. The Field Description of Metamorphic Rocks. (Geological Society of London Handbook Ser.: Nos. 1-572). 110p. 1984. pap. 12.95x (ISBN 0-470-27485-9, 1-572). Halsted Pr.

Fry, P. Spirits of Protest. LC 75-20832. (Cambridge Studies in Social Anthropology: No. 14). 134p. 1976. 27.95 (ISBN 0-521-21052-6). Cambridge U Pr.

Fry, P. Eileen, jt. auth. see Irvine, Betty J.

Fry, P. S., ed. Changing Conceptions of Intelligence & Intellectual Functioning: Current Theory & Research. 220p. 1985. Repr. 42.75 (ISBN 0-444-87619-7, North-Holland). Elsevier.

Fry, Patricia B., jt. auth. see Rubinstein, Ronald A.

Fry, Patricia L. The Ojai Valley: An Illustrated History. 297p. (Orig.). 1983. pap. text ed. 14.95 (ISBN 0-9612642-0-9). Matilija Pr.

Fry, Paul H. The Poet's Calling in the English Ode. LC 79-20554. 1980. 27.00x (ISBN 0-300-02400-2). Yale U Pr.

--The Reach of Criticism: Method & Perception in Literary Theory. LC 83-3535. 256p. 1983. 21.00x (ISBN 0-300-02924-1). Yale U Pr.

Fry, Peter & Fry, Fiona S. The History of Scotland. (Illus.). 248p. 1985. pap. 8.95 (ISBN 0-7448-0027-7). Routledge & Kegan.

Fry, Phillip. Blood Taxes at Harvest Time. 1978. 15.00 (ISBN 0-686-09544-8). Tax Info Ctr.

--Collecting Medical Debts, 1976. 1976. 25.00 (ISBN 0-686-15382-0). Tax Info Ctr.

--How to Collect What Others Owe You. 1976. 15.00 (ISBN 0-686-15383-9). Tax Info Ctr.

--How to Cut Your Taxes in Half by Incorporating Your Job or Business. 1978. 50.00 (ISBN 0-686-17659-6). Tax Info Ctr.

--How to Disinherit the Internal Revenue. 1978. 15.00 (ISBN 0-686-18233-2). Tax Info Ctr.

--How to Find Real Estate Bargains. 1975. 15.00 (ISBN 0-686-11156-7). Tax Info Ctr.

--Our Lady of Perpetual Deductions. 1977. 15.00 (ISBN 0-686-19031-9). Tax Info Ctr.

--Pay No More Income Taxes Without Going to Jail. new ed. 1978. 10.00 (ISBN 0-686-18232-4). Tax Info Ctr.

Fry, Plantagenet & Fry, Fiona S. The History of Scotland. 200p. 1982. 19.95x (ISBN 0-7100-9001-3). Routledge & Kegan.

Fry, Plantagenet S. The David & Charles Book of Castles. LC 80-69352. (Illus.). 496p. 1981. 24.95 (ISBN 0-7153-7976-3). David & Charles.

--Roman Britain: History & Sites. LC 83-21412. (Illus.). 560p. 1984. 37.50x (ISBN 0-389-20439-0, 08001). B&N Imports.

Fry, Richard. Scheme for a Paper Currency Together with Two Petitions Written in a Boston Gaol in 1739-1740. LC 68-57129. (Research & Source Works Ser.: No. 312). 1969. Repr. of 1908 ed. 18.50 (ISBN 0-8337-1248-9). B Franklin.

Fry, Robert E., ed. Models & Methods in Regional Exchange. (SAA Papers: No. 1). 156p. 1980. 12.00 (ISBN 0-318-17571-1); members 9.00 (ISBN 0-318-17572-X). Soc Am Arch.

Fry, Roger. Art History As an Academic Study. LC 77-1349. 1933. lib. bdg. 4.50 (ISBN 0-8414-4196-0). Folcroft.

--Vision & Design. Bullen, J. B., ed. (Oxford Paperback Books). (Illus., Orig.). 1981. pap. 12.50x (ISBN 0-19-281317-X). Oxford U Pr.

Fry, Roger, tr. see Mallarme, Stephane.

Fry, Roger E. Georgian Art, Seventeen Sixty to Eighteen Twenty: An Introductory Review of English Painting, Architecture, Sculpture During the Reign of George III. LC 76-42713. Repr. of 1929 ed. 34.50 (ISBN 0-404-15359-3). AMS Pr.

--Reflections on British Painting. LC 76-99695. (Essay Index Reprint Ser.). 1934. 20.00 (ISBN 0-8369-1350-7). Ayer Co Pubs.

--Transformations: Critical & Speculative Essays on Art. facs. ed. LC 68-14904. (Essay Index Reprint Ser). 1927. 32.00 (ISBN 0-8369-0464-8). Ayer Co Pubs.

Fry, Ronald. Work Evaluation & Adjustment: An Annotated Bibliography 1984. rev. ed. 500p. 1985. pap. write for info (ISBN 0-916671-62-3). Material Dev.

Fry, Ronald & Philen, Joyce. Bibliography on Job Placement. 62p. (Orig.). 1982. pap. 4.50x (ISBN 0-916671-32-1). Material Dev.

Fry, Ronald E., jt. auth. see Plovnick, Mark S.

Fry, Ronald R. Work Evaluation & Adjustment: An Annotated Bibliography, 1978 Supplement. 76p. (Orig.). 1979. pap. 2.50x (ISBN 0-916671-38-0). Material Dev.

--Work Evaluation & Adjustment: An Annotated Bibliography, 1947-1977. 184p. (Orig.). 1978. pap. 4.50x (ISBN 0-916671-39-9). Material Dev.

Fry, Ronald R., ed. Work Evaluation & Adjustment: An Annotated Bibliography, 1979 Supplement. 80p. (Orig.). 1980. pap. 2.50x (ISBN 0-916671-37-2). Material Dev.

Fry, Ronald R., jt. ed. see Smith, Christopher A.

Fry, Ruth T. & Hall, Joyce. Symbolic Profile. LC 76-5085. 94p. 1976. 12.95x (ISBN 0-87201-815-6). Gulf Pub.

Fry, S. A., jt. ed. see Hubner, K. F.

Fry, S. M., jt. auth. see Keates, Richard.

Fry, Sam. Gin Rummy: How to Play & Win. (Illus.). 59p. 1978. pap. 2.50 (ISBN 0-486-23630-7). Dover.

Fry, Sam, Jr., ed. see Watson, Louis H.

Fry, T. F. Computer Appreciation. 1972. 15.00 (ISBN 0-8022-2075-4). Philos Lib.

Fry, Timothy & Baker, Imogene, eds. The Rule of St. Benedict in English. 96p. (Orig.). 1982. pap. 2.25 (ISBN 0-8146-1272-5). Liturgical Pr.

Fry, Timothy, et al, eds. RB Nineteen Eighty. LC 81-1013. 627p. 1981. 24.95 (ISBN 0-8146-1211-3); pap. 17.50 (ISBN 0-8146-1220-2). Liturgical Pr.

--RB Nineteen-Eighty: The Rule of St. Benedict in Latin & English with Notes & Thematic Index. abr. ed. LC 81-12434. xii, 198p. 1981. pap. 8.95 (ISBN 0-8146-1243-1). Liturgical Pr.

Fry, Varian. War in China: America's Role in the Far East. LC 76-111741. (American Imperialism: Viewpoints of United States Foreign Policy, 1898-1941). 1970. Repr. of 1938 ed. 11.00 (ISBN 0-405-02021-X). Ayer Co Pubs.

Fry, Virginia. Exploring Biology in the Laboratory. 2nd ed. 250p. 1984. pap. 16.95x (ISBN 0-03-063373-7). SCP.

Fry, William E. Principles of Plant Disease Management. 366p. 1982. 25.50 (ISBN 0-12-269180-6). Acad Pr.

Fry, William F., Jr. Sweet Madness: A Study of Humor. LC 63-17821. (Pacific Books Paperbounds, PB-3). 1968. pap. 6.95 (ISBN 0-87015-163-0). Pacific Bks.

Fry, William H. New Hampshire As a Royal Province. LC 73-130938. (Columbia University. Studies in the Social Sciences: No. 79). Repr. of 1908 ed. 32.50 (ISBN 0-404-51079-5). AMS Pr.

Fry, William, Jr. & Allen, Melanie. Make 'em Laugh: Life Studies of Comedy Writers. LC 75-23593. 1976. 8.95 (ISBN 0-8314-0041-2). Sci & Behavior.

Fry, William R. & Hoopes, Roy. Paralegal Careers. (Illus.). 160p. (gr. 7-12). 1985. PLB 12.95 (ISBN 0-89490-105-2). Enslow Pubs.

Fryar, Maridell, jt. auth. see Thomas, David.

Fryar, Maridell, jt. auth. see Thomas, David A.

Fryatt, Norma R. Horn Book Sampler on Children's Books & Reading. LC 59-15028. 1959. 9.50 (ISBN 0-87675-030-7); pap. 6.50 (ISBN 0-87675-031-5). Horn Bk.

Fryburger, Vernon. The New World of Advertising. LC 75-21745. 1976. pap. 7.95x (ISBN 0-87251-021-2). Crain Bks.

Fryckstedt, Monica see Elizabeth, Charlotte, pseud.

Fryckstedt, Monica C. Elizabeth Gaskell's Mary Barton & Ruth: A Challenge to Christian England. (Studia Anglistica Upsaliensia Ser.: No. 43). 213p. 1982. text ed. 21.75x (Pub. by Almqvist & Wiksell Sweden). Humanities.

Fryckstedt, Olov W. In Quest of America, Study of Howell's Early Development As a Novelist. LC 76-23434. 1945. lib. bdg. 30.00 (ISBN 0-8414-4176-6). Folcroft.

Fryd, E. Anglo-Amerikansk-Dansk, Dansk-Anglo-Amerikansk Special Ordbog: English to Danish, Danish to English Dictionary. 297p. 1975. 39.95 (ISBN 0-686-92136-4, M-1276). French & Eur.

--Fransk-Dansk: Dansk-Fransk Special Ordbog. 199p. (Fr. & Danish.). 1877. 35.00 (ISBN 0-686-92211-5, M-1275). French & Eur.

--Tysk-Dansk Dansk-Tysk Special Ordbog. 175p. (Ger. & Danish.). 1974. 35.00 (ISBN 0-686-92491-6, M-1274). French & Eur.

Fryde, E. B. Humanism & Renaissance Historiography. (History Ser.: No. 21). 242p. 1986. 30.00 (ISBN 0-907628-24-9). Hambledon Press.

--The Private Library of Lorenzo de' Medici & His Sons, 1419-1510. 240p. 1985. 30.00 (ISBN 0-907628-64-8). Hambledon Press.

--Studies in Medieval Trade & Finance. 430p. 1983. 40.00 (ISBN 0-907628-10-9). Hambledon Press.

--William de la Pole, Merchant & King's Banker(1366) 175p. 1985. 27.00 (ISBN 0-907628-35-4). Hambledon Press.

Fryde, E. B., jt. ed. see Powicke, M.

Fryde, E. B., jt. ed. see Powicke, Maurice.

Fryde, Natalie. The Tyranny & Fall of Edward II: 1321-1326. LC 78-56179. 1979. 42.50 (ISBN 0-521-22201-X). Cambridge U Pr.

Fryde, Natalie, ed. List of Welsh Entries in the Memoranda Rolls: 1282-1343. 134p. 1974. text ed. 13.00x (ISBN 0-7083-0540-7, Pub. by Univ of Wales Pr England). Humanities.

Frydenger, Adrienne, jt. auth. see Frydenger, Tom.

Frydenger, Tom & Frydenger, Adrienne. The Blended Family. 240p. (Orig.). 1985. pap. 5.95 (ISBN 0-310-60861-9, Pub. by Chosen Bks). Zondervan.

Frydman, Anne, tr. see Dovlatov, Sergei.

Frydman, Maurice, tr. see Maharaj, Nisargadatta.

Frydman, Maurice, tr. see Nisargadatta Maharaj.

Frydman, Roman & Phelps, Edmund. Individual Forecasting & Aggregate Outcomes: "Rational Expectations" Examined. LC 83-10165. 256p. 1984. 39.50 (ISBN 0-521-25744-1). Cambridge U Pr.

Frye, Albert M. & Levi, Albert W. Rational Belief: An Introduction to Logic. Repr. of 1941 ed. lib. bdg. 19.75x (ISBN 0-8371-2142-6, FRRB). Greenwood.

Frye, B. L. Report Card in Nutrition: A Personalized Diet Evaluation. 122p. 1984. pap. text ed. 9.95x (ISBN 0-89787-118-9). Gorsuch Scarisbrick.

Frye, Charles. The Impact of Black Studies on the Curricula of Three Universities. 109p. 1977. pap. text ed. 11.75 (ISBN 0-8191-0223-7). U Pr of Amer.

Frye, Charles A. Towards a Philosophy of Black Studies. LC 77-90350. 1978. pap. 10.00 perfect bdg. (ISBN 0-88247-513-4). R & E Pubs.

--Values in Conflict: Blacks & the American Ambivalence Toward Violence. LC 79-5516. 1980. pap. text ed. 11.00 (ISBN 0-8191-0899-5). U Pr of Amer.

Frye, Dennis. Second Virginia Infantry. (The Virginia Regimental Histories Ser.). (Illus.). 146p. 1984. 16.45 (ISBN 0-930919-06-8). H E Howard.

Frye, Eldon C. Out of the Back Woods. 1982. 8.95 (ISBN 0-8062-1906-8). Carlton.

Frye, Fredric L. Biomedical & Surgical Aspects of Captive Reptile Husbandry. LC 81-51778. (Illus.). 456p. 40.00x (ISBN 0-935078-34-7). Veterinary Med.

--Phyllis, Phallus, Genghis Cohen & Other Creatures I Have Known. LC 84-70442. (Illus.). 152p. 1984. pap. 8.95 (ISBN 0-939674-02-5). Am Vet Pubns.

Frye, Harriet & Frye, John. North to Thule: An Imagined Narrative of the Famous "Lost" Voyage of Pytheas of Massalia of the 4th Century B.C. (Illus.). 232p. 1985. 16.95 (ISBN 0-912697-20-2). Algonquin Bks.

Frye, Jerry K. FIND: Frye's Index to Nonverbal Data. LC 80-51053. 344p. 1980. 39.95 (ISBN 0-936992-01-8); pap. 29.95 (ISBN 0-936992-02-6). U of Minn Comp Ctr.

Frye, John, jt. auth. see Frye, Harriet.

Frye, Keith. Modern Minerology. (Illus.). 336p. 1973. ref. ed. 33.95 (ISBN 0-13-595686-2). P-H.

Frye, Keith, ed. The Encyclopedia of Mineralogy. (Encylopedia of Earth Sciences Ser.: Vol. 4B). 816p. 1981. 95.00 (ISBN 0-87933-184-4). Van Nos Reinhold.

Frye, Marianne E., et al. Medical Secretary-Receptionist Simulation Project. Frazier, Lois E., ed. LC 78-78187. 1979. pap. text ed. 5.70 student manual (ISBN 0-87350-313-9); tchr's ed. 22.50 (ISBN 0-87350-316-3); forms wkbk. 16.95 (ISBN 0-87350-319-8). Milady.

Frye, Marilyn. The Politics of Reality: Essays in Feminist Theory. LC 83-2082. 176p. 1983. 18.95 (ISBN 0-89594-100-7); pap. 8.95 (ISBN 0-89594-099-X). Crossing Pr.

--Some Reflections on Separatism & Power. 1981. pap. 1.75 (ISBN 0-940302-01-2). Tea Rose Pr.

Frye, Mike, jt. auth. see Sager, Ed.

Frye, Northrop. Anatomy of Criticism. 1957. 38.50x (ISBN 0-691-06004-5); pap. 8.95x (ISBN 0-691-01298-9). Princeton U Pr.

--The Bush Garden: Essays on the Canadian Imagination. LC 71-152412. 251p. (Orig.). 1971. pap. 8.95 (ISBN 0-88784-620-3, Pub. by Hse Anansi Pr Canada). U of Toronto Pr.

--Creation & Recreation. 80p. 1980. pap. 6.50 (ISBN 0-8020-6422-1). U of Toronto Pr.

--The Critical Path: An Essay on the Social Context of Literary Criticism. LC 70-143246. (Midland Bks.: No. 158). 176p. 1971. 17.50 (ISBN 0-253-31568-9); pap. 5.95x (ISBN 0-253-20158-6). Ind U Pr.

--Divisions on a Ground: Essays on Canadian Culture. Polk, James, ed. 208p. 1982. 19.95 (ISBN 0-88784-093-0, Pub. by Hse Anansi Pr Canada). U of Toronto Pr.

--The Educated Imagination. LC 64-18815. (Midland Bks.: No. 88). 160p. 1964. pap. 5.95x (ISBN 0-253-20088-1). Ind U Pr.

--Fables of Identity: Studies in Poetic Mythology. LC 63-20974. (Orig.). 1963. pap. 5.95 (ISBN 0-15-629730-2, Harv). HarBraceJ.

--Fearful Symmetry: A Study of William Blake. 1947. pap. 9.95 (ISBN 0-691-01291-1). Princeton U Pr.

--Fools of Time: Studies in Shakespearean Tragedy. LC 67-5748. 1967. pap. 9.95 (ISBN 0-8020-6215-6). U of Toronto Pr.

--The Great Code: The Bible & Literature. LC 81-47303. 320p. 1981. 14.95 (ISBN 0-15-136902-X). HarBraceJ.

--The Great Code: The Bible in Literature. 261p. 1983. pap. 5.95 (ISBN 0-15-636480-8, Harv). HarBraceJ.

--The Myth of Deliverance: Reflections on Shakespeare's Problem Comedies. 128p. 1983. pap. 6.95 (ISBN 0-8020-6503-1). U of Toronto Pr.

--A Natural Perspective: The Development of Shakespearean Comdey & Romance. LC 65-17458. 1969. pap. 4.95 (ISBN 0-15-665414-8, Harv). HarBraceJ.

--Northrop Frye on Culture & Literature: A Collection of Review Essays. Denham, Robert D., intro. by. LC 77-12917. 1980. pap. 5.50x (ISBN 0-226-26648-6, P867, Phoen). U of Chicago Pr.

--Northrop Frye on Culture & Literature: A Collection of Review Essays. Denham, Robert D., ed. LC 77-12917. (Illus.). 1978. lib. bdg. 17.50x (ISBN 0-226-26647-8). U of Chicago Pr.

--The Return of Eden: Five Essays on Milton's Epics. 1975. 15.00x (ISBN 0-8020-1353-8). U of Toronto Pr.

--The Secular Scripture: A Study of the Structure of Romance. (Charles Eliot Norton Lectures Ser.). 192p. 1976. 15.00x (ISBN 0-674-79675-6); pap. 5.95x (ISBN 0-674-79676-4, HP 127). Harvard U Pr.

--Spiritus Mundi: Essays on Literature, Myth, & Society. LC 76-12364. 320p. 1976. 20.00x (ISBN 0-253-35432-3); pap. 7.95x (ISBN 0-253-20289-2). Ind U Pr.

--A Study of English Romanticism. LC 82-11018. viii, 180p. 1983. pap. 5.95x (ISBN 0-226-26651-6). U of Chicago Pr.

--T. S. Eliot: An Introduction. LC 80-29344. 110p. 1981. pap. 5.00x (ISBN 0-226-26649-4). U of Chicago Pr.

--The Well-Tempered Critic. LC 63-9716. (Midland Bks.: No. 77). 160p. 1963. pap. 3.95x (ISBN 0-253-20077-6). Ind U Pr.

Frye, Northrop, ed. Romanticism Reconsidered. LC 63-18020. (Essays of the English Institute). 144p. 1963. 19.50x (ISBN 0-231-02671-4); pap. 10.50x (ISBN 0-231-08589-3, 89). Columbia U Pr.

--Sound & Poetry. LC 57-11003. (Essays of the English Institute). 1957. 17.00x (ISBN 0-231-02209-3). Columbia U Pr.

Frye, Northrop, ed. see Blake, William.

Frye, Northrop see Columbia University. English Institute.

Frye, Northrop, ed. see Joint Committee of the Toronto Board of Education & the University of Toronto.

Frye, Northrop, ed. see Milton, John.

Frye, Northrop, ed. see Shakespeare, William.

Frye, Northrop, et al. Myth & Symbol: Critical Approaches & Applications. Slote, Bernice, ed. LC 63-9960. x, 197p. 1963. pap. 4.25x (ISBN 0-8032-5065-7, BB 141, Bison). U of Nebr Pr.

--The Practical Imagination: An Introduction to Poetry. 499p. 1983. pap. text ed. 6.50 scp (ISBN 0-06-042219-X, HarpC). Har-Row.

--The Practical Imagination: Stories, Poems, Plays. 1980. text ed. 11.50 scp (ISBN 0-06-040455-8, HarpC); instructor's manual avail. (ISBN 0-06-365110-6). Har-Row.

--The Harper Handbook To Literature. 608p. 1985. pap. text ed. 12.95 scp (ISBN 0-06-042217-3, HarpC). Har-Row.

Frye, Prosser H. Literary Reviews & Criticisms. facs. ed. LC 68-8462. (Essay Index Reprint Ser). 1968. Repr. of 1908 ed. 18.00 (ISBN 0-8369-0465-6). Ayer Co Pubs.

--Literary Reviews & Criticisms. LC 68-59378. 1968. Repr. of 1908 ed. 12.50x (ISBN 0-87752-040-2). Gordian.

--Romance & Tragedy: A Study of the Classic & Romantic Elements in the Great Tragedies of European Literature. LC 61-10518. (Landmark Ed.). xiv, 372p. 1980. 26.50x (ISBN 0-8032-1955-5). U of Nebr Pr.

--Visions & Chimeras. LC 66-23517. 1929. 10.00x (ISBN 0-8196-0179-9). Biblo.

Frye, Richard, jt. auth. see Knepper, William E.

Frye, Richard N. Islamic Iran & Central Asia (7th-12th Centuries) 380p. 1980. 75.00x (ISBN 0-86078-044-9, Pub. by Variorum England). State Mutual Bk.

Frye, Richard N., jt. auth. see Thomas, Lewis V.

Frye, Richard N., ed. Near East & the Great Powers. LC 77-79309. 1969. Repr. of 1951 ed. 12.50x (ISBN 0-8046-0530-0, Pub. by Kennikat). Assoc Faculty Pr.

--Sasanian Remains from Qasr-i Abu Nasr: Seals, Sealings, & Coins. LC 72-80657. (Iranian Ser: No. 1). (Illus.). 224p. 1973. 14.00x (ISBN 0-674-78960-1). Harvard U Pr.

Frye, Richard N., tr. History of Bukhara. LC 54-8493. 1954. 7.50x (ISBN 0-910956-35-9). Medieval Acad.

Frye, Roland M. Is God a Creationist? The Religious Case Against Creation Science. 256p. 1983. pap. text ed. price not set (ISBN 0-02-339560-5, Pub. by Scribner). Macmillan.

--Milton's Imagery & the Visual Arts: Iconographic Tradition in the Epic Poems. LC 77-24541. 1978. 79.00x (ISBN 0-691-06349-4). Princeton U Pr.

--The Renaissance Hamlet: Issues & Responses in 1600. LC 83-4255. (Illus.). 368p. 1984. 28.50x (ISBN 0-691-06579-9). Princeton U Pr.

--Shakespeare: The Art of the Dramatist. 288p. 1981. text ed. 12.50x (ISBN 0-04-822043-4). Allen Unwin.

--Shakespeare's Life & Times: A Pictorial Record. LC 67-11031. (Illus.). 1967. 35.00x (ISBN 0-691-06119-X); pap. 12.95 (ISBN 0-691-01318-7). Princeton U Pr.

Frye, Roland M., ed. Is God a Creationist? Religious Arguments Against Creation-Science. 256p. 1983. 15.95 (ISBN 0-684-17993-8, ScribT). Scribner.

--The Reader's Bible, A Narrative: Selections from the King James Version. LC 77-311. 638p. 1979. o.p 22.00 (ISBN 0-691-07227-2); pap. 12.50 (ISBN 0-691-01995-9). Princeton U Pr.

Frye, Russell S. Clean Water Act Permit Guidance Manual. LC 84-163163. 1984. write for info. (ISBN 0-88057-136-5). Exec Ent Inc.

Frye, Tom. Scratchin' on the Eight Ball. 351p. 1982. pap. 4.95 (ISBN 0-939644-04-5). Media Prods & Mktg.

Frye, Virginia H., jt. auth. see Long, James D.

Frye, Wendell, tr. see Stifter, Adalbert.

Frye, William E., ed. Impact of Space Exploration on Society. (Science & Technology Ser.: Vol. 8). 1966. 30.00x (ISBN 0-87703-036-7, Pub. by Am Astronaut). Univelt Inc.

Fryer. Weed Control Handbook, Vol. II. (Illus.). 1978. Vol. 2. 36.50 (ISBN 0-632-00219-0, B 1716-2, Blackwell). Mosby.

Fryer, Alan D. COBOL on Microcomputers. LC 83-51226. 8.95 (ISBN 0-672-22230-2). Sams.

Fryer, Alfred C. The Religious Thoughts of Some of Our Poets. 1911. Repr. 17.50 (ISBN 0-8274-3263-1). R West.

Fryer, Barry. Practice of Construction Management. (Illus.). 225p. 1985. pap. text ed. 20.00x (ISBN 0-00-383030-6, Pub. by Collins England). Sheridan.

Fryer, Bob, et al, eds. Law, State & Society. 234p. 1981. 31.00 (ISBN 0-7099-1004-5, Pub. by Croom Helm Ltd). Longwood Pub Group.

Fryer, Charles. A Hand in Dialogue. 128p. 1980. 17.95 (ISBN 0-227-67841-9). Attic Pr.

--A Hand in Dialogue. 128p. 1983. 17.95 (ISBN 0-227-67841-9, Pub. by J Clarke UK). Attic Pr.

Fryer, Christopher & Crane, Robert D. Jack Nicholson, Face to Face. LC 74-31265. (Illus.). 192p. 1975. 9.95 (ISBN 0-87131-175-5); pap. 5.95 (ISBN 0-87131-176-3). M Evans.

Fryer, D. W. Emerging Southeast Asia: A Study in Growth & Stagnation. 540p. 1979. 44.95 (ISBN 0-470-26298-2). Halsted Pr.

Fryer, Douglas H. & Henry, Edwin R., eds. Handbook of Applied Psychology, 2 Vols in 1. 1969. Repr. of 1950 ed. 55.00 (ISBN 0-384-17070-6). Johnson Repr.

Fryer, J. D. & Matsunaka, Shoichi. Integrated Control of Weeds. 262p. 1977. (Pub. by Japan Sci Soc Japan). Intl Spec Bk.

Fryer, J. R. The Chemical Applications of Transmission Electron Microscopy. 1979. 55.00 (ISBN 0-12-269350-7). Acad Pr.

Fryer, Jane E. The Mary Francis Sewing Book. LC 13-22543. (Illus.). 280p. 1981. Repr. of 1913 ed. lib. bdg. 38.00 (ISBN 0-940070-13-8). Doll Works.

Fryer, John. A New Account of East India & Persia, 3 vols. Crooke, William, ed. (Hakluyt Society Works Ser.: No. 2, Vols. 19, 20 & 39). (Illus.). 1909-1915. Repr. Set. 111.00 (ISBN 0-317-15688-8). Kraus Repr.

Fryer, John & Walters, Stephen. The Voyage of the Bounty Launch. ltd. ed. (Illus.). 196p. 1979. hand bound leather 192.00 (ISBN 0-904351-16-5). Genesis Pubns.

Fryer, Judith. The Faces of Eve: Women in the Nineteenth Century American Novel. LC 75-32345. (Illus.). 1976. 22.50x (ISBN 0-19-502025-1). Oxford U Pr.

--The Faces of Eve: Women in the Nineteenth Century American Novel. LC 75-32345. 1976. pap. 5.95 (ISBN 0-19-502431-1, GB 548, GB). Oxford U Pr.

--How We Hear: The Story of Hearing. LC 61-13575. (Medical Bks for Children). (Illus.). (gr. 3-9). 1961. PLB 3.95 (ISBN 0-8225-0012-4). Lerner Pubns.

Fryer, K. D., jt. auth. see Berman, Gerald.

Fryer, Lee. The Bio-Gardener's Bible. 252p. 14.95 (ISBN 0-8019-7288-4); pap. 9.95 (ISBN 0-8019-7289-2). Chilton.

Fryer, M. J. An Introduction to Linear Programming & Matrix Game Theory. LC 77-13371. 121p. 1978. pap. text ed. 14.95x (ISBN 0-470-99327-8). Halsted Pr.

Fryer, P. Staying Power. 595p. 1984. text ed. 35.50x (ISBN 0-391-03167-8). Humanities.

Fryer, Peter & Pinheiro, Patricia M. Oldest Ally: A Portrait of Salazar's Portugal. LC 81-7020. (Illus.). 280p. 1981. Repr. of 1961 ed. lib. bdg. 28.50x (ISBN 0-313-23146-X, FROA). Greenwood.

Fryer, T. B. & Miller, H. A., eds. Biotelemetry III. 1976. 49.50 (ISBN 0-12-269250-0). Acad Pr.

Fryers, Tom. The Epidemiology of Severe Intellectual Impairment: The Dynamics of Prevalence. 1984. 32.50 (ISBN 0-12-269380-9). Acad Pr.

Frykenberg, Robert. Land Tenure & Peasant in South Asia. cancelled (ISBN 0-8364-0347-9, Orient Longman). South Asia Bks.

Frykenberg, Robert E., ed. Land Control & Social Structure in Indian History. LC 69-16111. 278p. 1969. 27.50x (ISBN 0-299-05240-0). U of Wis Pr.

Fryklund, Verne C. & Kepler, Frank R. General Drafting. 4th ed. LC 78-81375. (Illus.). (gr. 9-10). 1969. text ed. 14.63 (ISBN 0-87345-095-7). McKnight.

Fryklund, Verne C. & LaBerge, Armand J. General Shop Bench Woodworking. rev. ed. (Illus.). (gr. 9-10). 1955. pap. 6.64 (ISBN 0-87345-001-9). McKnight.

--General Shop Woodworking. rev. ed. (gr. 9-10). 1972. text ed. 15.28 (ISBN 0-87345-031-0). McKnight.

Frykman, John. The Hassle Handbook. LC 84-6851. xiv, 108p. (Orig.). 1984. pap. 5.95x (ISBN 0-916147-00-2). Regent St Bks.

Fryling, Alice, jt. auth. see Fryling, Robert.

Fryling, Robert & Fryling, Alice. Handbook for Engaged Couples. LC 77-11363. 1978. pap. text ed. 2.95 (ISBN 0-87784-363-5). Inter-Varsity.

--Handbook for Married Couples. LC 84-10837. 72p. (Orig.). 1984. pap. 2.95 (ISBN 0-87784-923-4). Inter-Varsity.

Frym, Gloria. Impossible Affection. (Illus.). 1979. pap. 5.00 (ISBN 0-87922-102-X). Christopher's Bks.

Fryman, Erik, ed. see Arnold, Matthew.

Fryman, Sarah. The Measure of a Woman: Leader's Guide. (The Measure of... Ser.). 64p. 1985. pap. 3.95 (ISBN 0-8307-0988-6, 6101888). Regal.

Frymer, Berl. Jewish Horizons. LC 81-65057. 256p. 1982. 12.95 (ISBN 0-8453-4705-5). Cornwall Bks.

Frymier, Jack. Motivation & Learning in School. LC 74-83881. (Fastback Ser.: No. 43). (Orig.). 1974. pap. 0.75 (ISBN 0-87367-043-4). Phi Delta Kappa.

Frymier, Jack R. School for Tomorrow. LC 72-10647. 286p. 1973. 24.00x (ISBN 0-8211-0505-1); text ed. 21.50x 10 or more copies. McCutchan.

Fryrear, Jerry L. & Fleshman, Robert. Videotherapy in Mental Health. 352p. 1981. pap. 29.75x (ISBN 0-398-04117-2). C C Thomas.

Fryrear, Jerry L., jt. auth. see Fleshman, Bob.

Fryrear, Jerry L., jt. auth. see Krauss, David A.

Fryscak, Milan. Say It in Czech. LC 76-173447. (Orig.). 1973. pap. text ed. 2.75 (ISBN 0-486-21538-5). Dover.

Fryxell, Fritiof. Mountaineering in the Tetons: The Pioneer Period, Eighteen Ninety-Eight to Nineteen Forty. 2nd ed. Smith, Phil D., ed. LC 79-83648. (Illus.). 1978. pap. 5.95 (ISBN 0-933160-01-1). Teton Bkshop.

Fryxell, Fritiof, ed. see Matthes, Francois E.

Fryxell, Greta A., ed. Survival Strategies of the Algae. LC 82-12865. (Illus.). 176p. 1983. 34.50 (ISBN 0-521-25067-6). Cambridge U Pr.

Fryxell, Paul A. The Natural History of the Cotton Tribe. LC 78-21779. (Illus.). 264p. 1979. 19.50x (ISBN 0-89096-071-2). Tex A&M Univ Pr.

Fryxell, Roald. The Interdisciplinary Dilemma: A Case for Flexibility in Academic Thought. (Augustana College Library Occasional Papers). 16p. 1977. pap. 1.00x (ISBN 0-910182-36-1). Augustana Coll.

Fthenakis, Wassilios E., ed. see Staatsinstitut fur Fruhpadagogik.

Fthenakis, Wassilios E., et al, eds. see Staatsinstitut fur Fruhpadagogik.

Ftizsimons, Kate, compiled by. The Sometime King. (Illus.). 35.00x (ISBN 0-317-20301-0, Pub. by Minimax Bks UK). State Mutual Bk.

Fu, James S. Mythic & Comic Aspects of the Quest: Hsi Yu Chi as Seen Through Don Quixote & Huckleberry Finn. 125p. 1977. pap. 5.00x (ISBN 0-8214-0471-7, 82-93078, Pub. by Singapore U Pr). Ohio U Pr.

Fu, K. S. Applications of Pattern Recognition. 288p. 1982. 96.50 (ISBN 0-8493-5729-2). CRC Pr.

--Syntactic Methods in Pattern Recognition. (Mathematics & Science Engineering Ser.). 1974. 65.00 (ISBN 0-12-269560-7). Acad Pr.

Fu, K. S. & Yu, T. S. Statistical Pattern Classification Using Contextual Information. LC 80-40949. (Patterns Recognition & Image Processing Ser.). 191p. 1980. 63.95x (ISBN 0-471-27859-9, Research Studies Press). Wiley.

Fu, K. S., ed. Digital Pattern Recognition. 2nd ed. (Communication & Cybernetics: Vol. 10). (Illus.). 234p. 1980. pap. 36.00 (ISBN 0-387-10207-8). Springer-Verlag.

--VLSI for Pattern Recognition & Image Processing. (Springer Series in Information Sciences: Vol. 13). (Illus.). 255p. 1984. 23.00 (ISBN 0-387-13268-6). Springer-Verlag.

Fu, K. S. & Ichikawa, T., eds. Special Computer Architectures for Pattern Processing. 272p. 1981. 79.50 (ISBN 0-8493-6100-1). CRC Pr.

Fu, K. S. & Kunii, T. L., eds. Picture Engineering. (Springer Series in Information Sciences: Vol. 6). (Illus.). 320p. 1982. 33.00 (ISBN 0-387-11822-5). Springer-Verlag.

Fu, K. S. & Pavlidis, T., eds. Biomedical Pattern Recognition & Image Processing. (Dahlem Workshop Reports-Life Sciences Reseach Report Ser.: No. 15). 443p. 1979. pap. 33.80x (ISBN 0-89573-097-9). VCH Pubs.

Fu, K. S. & Tou, Julius T., eds. Learning Systems & Intelligent Robots. LC 74-11212. 452p. 1974. 65.00x (ISBN 0-306-30801-0, Plenum Pr). Plenum Pub.

Fu, K. S., jt. ed. see Chang, S. K.

Fu, King & Yu, T. S. Statistical Pattern Classification Using Contextual Information. LC 80-40949. (Electronic & Electrical Engineering Research Studies, Pattern Recognition &Image Processing Ser.: Vol. 1). pap. 50.30 (ISBN 0-317-26335-8, 2025199). Bks Demand UMI.

Fu, King Sun. Syntactic Pattern Recognition & Applications. (Advances in Computing Science & Technology Ser.). (Illus.). 640p. 1982. text ed. 52.00 (ISBN 0-13-880120-7). P-H.

Fu, King-Sun, jt. auth. see Young, Tzay Y.

Fu, King-Sun, ed. Pattern Recognition & Machine Learning. LC 77-163287. 343p. 1971. 55.00 (ISBN 0-306-30546-1, Plenum Pr). Plenum Pub.

Fu, King Sun, ed. Synactic Pattern Recognition, Applications. (Communication & Cybernetics: Vol. 14). (Illus.). 1977. 56.00 (ISBN 0-387-07841-X). Springer-Verlag.

Fu, King-Sun, jt. ed. see Zadeh.

Fu, Lo-shu. A Documentary Chronicle of Sino-Western Relations, 1644-1820, 2 vols. LC 66-18529. (Association for Asian Studies Monograph: No. 22). 792p. 1966. 29.95x (ISBN 0-8165-0151-3). U of Ariz Pr.

Fu, Pei Mei. Pei Mei's Chinese Cook Book, Vol. II. Murphy, Nancy, ed. (Illus.). 384p. 1974. 15.95 (ISBN 0-917056-09-4, Pub. by Pei Mei's Cook Inst Taiwan). Cheng & Tsui.

--Pei Mei's Chinese Cook Book, Vol. I. Murphy, Nancy, tr. from Chinese. (Illus.). 398p. 1969. 15.95 (ISBN 0-917056-08-6, Pub. by y Pei Mei's Cook Inst Taiwan). Cheng & Tsui.

--Pei Mei's Chinese Cook Book, Vol. III. Murphy, Nancy, tr. from Chinese. (Illus.). 378p. 1979. 15.95 (ISBN 0-917056-23-X, Pub. by Pei Mei's Cook Inst Taiwan). Cheng & Tsui.

Fu, Shen C. Y., et al. Traces of the Brush: Studies in Chinese Calligraphy. LC 79-24080. 1980. text ed. 67.00x (ISBN 0-300-02487-8); pap. 19.95x (ISBN 0-300-02490-8). Yale U Pr.

Fu, Tu, jt. ed. see Po, Li.

Fu, Whei-Rung. Angiography of Trauma. (Illus.). 116p. 1972. photocopy ed. 15.50x (ISBN 0-398-02287-9). C C Thomas.

Fucci, Marie. Entr'acte. Ashton, Sylvia, ed. LC 76-2304. 1977. 14.95 (ISBN 0-87949-066-7). Ashley Bks.

Fu-Chen & Byung-Nak, Song. The Saemaul Undong: The Korean Way of Rural Transformation. (Working Papers Ser.: No. 79-9). 23p. 1979. pap. 6.00 (ISBN 0-686-78258-5, CRD036, UNCRD). Unipub.

Fuchida, Mitsuo & Okumiya, Masatake. Midway: The Battle that Doomed Japan. (War Library). 224p. 1982. pap. 2.75 (ISBN 0-345-30771-2). Ballantine.

--Midway, the Battle that Doomed Japan. Kawakami, Clarke K. & Pineau, Roger, eds. (Illus.). 266p. 1955. 14.95 (ISBN 0-87021-372-5); bulk rates avail. Naval Inst Pr.

--Midway, the Battle That Doomed Japan: The Japanese Navy's Story. Kawakami, Clarke & Pineau, Roger, eds. LC 55-9027. (Illus.). 266p. 1955. 14.95 (ISBN 0-87021-372-5). Naval Inst Pr.

Fuchs, A. F. & Becker, W., eds. Progress in Oculomotor Research. (Developments in Neuroscience Ser.: Vol. 12). 686p. 1981. 123.00 (ISBN 0-444-00589-7, Biomedical Pr). Elsevier.

Fuchs, Albert. Goethe-Studien. (Kleinere Schriften zur Literatur und Geistesgeschichte). (Illus.). viii, 319p. (Ger.). 1968. 32.40x (ISBN 3-11-000239-6). De Gruyter.

Fuchs, Daniel. Saul Bellow: Vision & Revision. 350p. 1984. text ed. 35.00x (ISBN 0-8223-0503-8). Duke.

--Saul Bellow: Vision & Revision. LC 83-9061. 345p. 1985. pap. 12.95 (ISBN 0-8223-0420-1). Duke.

--Summer in Williamsburg. 380p. 1983. pap. 8.95 (ISBN 0-88184-006-8). Carroll & Graf.

Fuchs, E. & Mattson, K. Allergology & Clinical Immunology: Proceedings of the Ketotifen Workshop. (International Congress Ser.: No. 523). 58p. 1981. pap. 24.00 (ISBN 0-444-90151-5, Excerpta Medica). Elsevier.

Fuchs, Emil. Christ in Catastrophe. 1983. pap. 5.00x (ISBN 0-87574-049-9, 049). Pendle Hill.

Fuchs, Eric. Sexual Desire & Love: Origins & History of the Christian Ethic of Sexuality & Marriage. Daigle, Marsha, tr. 320p. (Fr.). 1983. pap. 15.95 (ISBN 0-8164-2467-5, Pub. by Seabury). Winston Pr.

Fuchs, Estelle & Havighurst, Robert J. To Live on This Earth: American Indian Education. rev. ed. 408p. 1983. pap. 11.95x (ISBN 0-8263-0683-7). U of NM Pr.

Fuchs, Esther. Encounters with Israeli Authors. LC 82-62086. (Illus.). 95p. 1983. pap. 7.50 (ISBN 0-916288-14-5). Micah Pubns.

Fuchs, Fritz & Klopper, Arnold, eds. Endocrinology of Pregnancy. 3rd ed. (Illus.). 306p. 1983. text ed. 44.75 (ISBN 0-06-140845-X, 14-08459, Harper Medical). Lippincott.

Fuchs, Fritz, jt. ed. see Coutinho, Elsimar M.

Fuchs, G. B. Law & Disorder: Poems & Pictures. Exner, Richard, tr. from Ger. -Eng. LC 77-85670. (German Ser: Vol. 5). 1979. 15.00 (ISBN 0-87775-118-8); pap. 6.00 (ISBN 0-87775-119-6). Unicorn Pr.

Fuchs, Gordon E. Evaluating Educational Research. LC 80-5480. 160p. 1980. pap. text ed. 8.75 (ISBN 0-8191-1104-X). U Pr of Amer.

Fuchs, H. O. & Stephens, R. I. Metal Fatigue in Engineering. LC 80-294. 1980. 45.95x (ISBN 0-471-05264-7, Pub. by Wiley-Interscience). Wiley.

Fuchs, H. P. Nomenklatur, Taxonomie & Systematik der Gattung Isoetes Linnaeus in Geschichtlicher Entwicklung. (Illus.). 1962. pap. 14.00 (ISBN 3-7682-5403-8). Lubrecht & Cramer.

Fuchs, Hans-Ulrich. Zur Lehre vom Allgemeinen Bankvertrag. (European University Studies: No. 2, Vol. 294). xxi, 212p. (Ger.). 1982. 27.90 (ISBN 3-8204-7120-0). P Lang Pubs.

Fuchs, Harald. Augustin und der Antike Friendensgedanke. LC 72-147669. (Library of War & Peace; Relig. & Ethical Positions on War). lib. bdg. 46.00 (ISBN 0-8240-0427-2). Garland Pub.

Fuchs, Henry. Selected Reprints on VLSI Technologies & Computer Graphics. 490p. 1983. 36.00 (ISBN 0-8186-0491-3). IEEE Comp Soc.

Fuchs, Jacob, tr. see Horace.

Fuchs, Jerome H. Computerized Cost Control Systems. 304p. 1976. 32.95 (ISBN 0-13-166223-6). P-H.

--Making the Most of Management Consulting Services. LC 74-6808. 224p. 1975. 15.95 (ISBN 0-8144-5371-6). AMACOM.

Fuchs, Josef. Christian Ethics in a Secular Arena. Hoose, Bernard & McNeil, Brian, trs. from Ital. & Ger. LC 84-7964. 161p. (Orig.). 1984. pap. 9.95 (ISBN 0-87840-411-2). Georgetown U Pr.

--Personal Responsibility & Christian Morality. Cleves, William, et al, trs. from Ger. LC 83-1548. 240p. (Orig.). 1983. pap. 10.95 (ISBN 0-87840-405-8). Georgetown U Pr.

Fuchs, K., et al, eds. Plateau Uplift: The Rhenish Shield-a Case History. (Illus.). 420p. 1983. 52.00 (ISBN 0-387-12577-9). Springer-Verlag.

Fuchs, L. Infinite Abelian Groups, 2 vols. (Pure & Applied Mathematics Ser.: Vol. 36). Vol. 1 1970. 59.50 (ISBN 0-12-269601-8); Vol. 2 1973. 69.50 (ISBN 0-12-269602-6). Acad Pr.

Fuchs, Lawrence H. Hawaii Pono: A Social History. 1984. pap. 5.95 (ISBN 0-15-639602-5, Harv). HarBraceJ.

--The Political Behavior of American Jews. LC 79-28711. (Illus.). 220p. 1980. Repr. of 1956 ed. lib. bdg. 24.75x (ISBN 0-313-22282-7, FUPB). Greenwood.

Fuchs, Lawrence H., et al. Should United States Immigration Policy Be Changed? 30p. 1980. 3.75 (ISBN 0-8447-2186-7). Am Enterprise.

Fuchs, Lucy. Dangerous Splendor. (YA) 1978. 8.95 (ISBN 0-685-05584-1, Avalon). Bouregy.

--Pictures of Fear. (YA) 1981. 8.95 (ISBN 0-686-73951-5, Avalon). Bouregy.

--Shadow of the Walls. 1980. 8.95 (ISBN 0-686-59800-8, Avalon). Bouregy.

--Wild Winds of Mayaland. (YA) 1978. 8.95 (ISBN 0-685-85784-0, Avalon). Bouregy.

Fuchs, M., jt. auth. see Bass, F. G.

Fuchs, Nan K. The Nutrition Detective: Treating Your Health Problems Through the Food You Eat. LC 85-4659. 220p. 1985. 16.95 (ISBN 0-87477-363-6); pap. 9.95 (ISBN 0-87477-350-4). J P Tarcher.

Fuchs, Oswald. The Psychology of Habit According to William Ockham. (Philosophy Ser). 1952. 8.00 (ISBN 0-686-11538-4). Franciscan Inst.

Fuchs, P., jt. ed. see Kohn, A.

Fuchs, P. L. & Bunnell, C. A. Carbon-Thirteen NMR Based Organic Spectral Problems. LC 78-20668. 309p. 1979. pap. text ed. 20.95 (ISBN 0-471-04907-7). Wiley.

Fuchs, Peter. African Decameron. Meister, Robert, tr. from Ger. 1964. 8.95 (ISBN 0-8392-1000-0). Astor-Honor.

Fuchs, Peter C. Epidemiology of Hospital: Associated Infections. LC 79-17036. (Illus.). 220p. 1980. text ed. 30.00 (ISBN 0-89189-072-6, 45-7-011-00). Am Soc Clinical.

Fuchs, Peter P., ed. The Music Theater of Walter Felsenstein. (Illus.). 1975. 10.95x (ISBN 0-393-02186-6). Norton.

Fuchs, R. H. Dutch Painting. (World of Art Ser.). (Illus.). 216p. 1985. pap. 9.95 (ISBN 0-500-20167-6). Thames Hudson.

Fuchs, Rachel G. Abandoned Children: Foundlings & Child Welfare in Nineteenth-Century France. LC 83-425. (European Social History Ser.). 368p. 1983. 49.50x (ISBN 0-87395-748-2); pap. 17.95x (ISBN 0-87395-750-4). State U NY Pr.

Fuchs, Roland J. Population Distribution Policies in Asia & the Pacific: Current Status & Future Prospects. LC 83-1608. (Papers of the East-West Population Institute: No. 83). vii, 40p. (Orig.). 1983. pap. text ed. 1.50 (ISBN 0-86638-008-6). E W Center HI.

Fuchs, Roland J., ed. see Anuchin, V. A.

Fuchs, Roland J., jt. ed. see Demko, George J.

Fuchs, Roland J., tr. see Demko, George J. & Fuchs, Roland J.

Fuchs, Sheldon J., ed. Complete Building Equipment Maintenance Desk Book. 450p. 1981. 49.95 (ISBN 0-13-158808-7). P-H.

Fuchs, Stephen. The Aboriginal Tribes of India. LC 76-27186. 1977. 27.50 (ISBN 0-312-00175-4). St Martin.

Fuchs, Theodore. Home-Built Lighting Equipment. 1939. spiral bdg. 6.00 (ISBN 0-573-69016-2). French.

Fuchs, Ulrich. Submicroscopy of the Arterial Vascular Wall: Observations in the State of Hypertension & Arteiosclerosis. (Experimental Pathology Ser.). (Illus.). 1977. 25.00x (ISBN 0-8002-0372-0). Intl Pubns Serv.

Fuchs, Victor. Economic Aspects of Health. LC 81-15938. (National Bureau of Economic Research-Conference Ser.). 1982. lib. bdg. 32.00x (ISBN 0-226-26785-7). U of Chicago Pr.

--Who Shall Live? LC 74-79283. 1975. 12.95x (ISBN 0-465-09185-7). Basic.

Fuchs, Victor R. Economics of the Fur Industry. LC 73-76661. (Columbia University. Studies in the Social Sciences: No. 593). Repr. of 1957 ed. 16.50 (ISBN 0-404-51593-2). AMS Pr.

--How We Live: An Economic Perspective on Americans from Birth to Death. (Illus.). 320p. 1983. 18.50 (ISBN 0-674-41225-7). Harvard U Pr.

--How We Live: An Economic Perspective on Americans from Birth to Death. 320p. 1984. pap. 7.95 (ISBN 0-674-41226-5). Harvard U Pr.

--Who Shall Live? LC 74-79283. 1983. pap. 8.25 (ISBN 0-465-09186-5). Basic.

Fuchs, Victor R. & Leveson, Irving F. Service Economy. (General Ser.: No. 87). 308p. 1968. 18.50 (ISBN 0-87014-475-8, 62, Dist. by Columbia UPr); pap. 9.00 (ISBN 0-87014-476-6). Natl Bur Econ Res.

Fuchs, Victor R., ed. Essays in the Economics of Health & Medical Care. (Human Resources & Social Institutions Ser.: No. 1). 261p. 1972. text ed. 16.00 (ISBN 0-87014-236-4, Dist. by Columbia U Pr). Natl Bur Econ Res.

--Production & Productivity in the Service Industries. (Studies in Income & Wealth Ser.: No. 34). 404p. 1969. 24.00x (ISBN 0-87014-489-8, Dist. by Columbia U Pr). Natl Bur Econ Res.

Fuchs, Viktor. Art of Singing. (Illus.). 160p. (Orig.). 1985. pap. 7.95 (ISBN 0-7145-0032-1). Riverrun NY.

Fuchs, Vivian. Of Ice & Men. 383p. 1984. 24.50 (ISBN 0-88072-057-3, Pub. by Tanager). Longwood Pub Group.

Fuchs, W. Lexikon Zur Soziologie, 2 vols. 800p. (Ger.). 1975. 12.95 (ISBN 3-499-16191-5, M-7191). French & Eur.

Fuchs, W. A., et al. Lymphography in Cancer. LC 76-84146. (Recent Results in Cancer Research: Vol. 23). 1969. 53.00 (ISBN 0-387-04685-2). Springer-Verlag.

Fuchs, W. F. Phenomenology & the Metaphysics of Presence. (Phaenomenologica Ser: No. 69). 1976. pap. 18.50 (ISBN 90-247-1822-8, Pub. by Martinus Nijhoff Netherlands). Kluwer Academic.

Fuchs, Warren, Jr. Where's the Fire? LC 85-71760. (Illus.). 180p. 1985. pap. 19.95 (ISBN 0-933341-12-1). Quinlan Pr.

Fuchs, William, as told to see Morton, Jack.

Fuchs, Yoram & Chalutz, Edo, eds. Ethylene: Biochemical, Physiological & Applied Aspects. (Advances in Agricultural Biotechnology Ser.). 1984. lib. bdg. 53.50 (ISBN 90-247-2984-X, Pub. by Martinus Nijhoff Netherlands). Kluwer Academic.

Fuchser, Larry W. Neville Chamberlain & Appeasement: A Study in the Politics of History. 256p. 1982. 18.95 (ISBN 0-393-01607-2). Norton.

Fuchshuber, Annegert. From Dinosaurs to Fossils. LC 80-28596. (Carolrhoda Start to Finish Bks.). Orig. Title: Tiere der Urwelt. (Illus.). 24p. (ps-3). 1981. PLB 5.95g (ISBN 0-87614-152-1). Carolrhoda Bks.

Fuchsman, Charles H. Peat: Industrial Chemistry & Technology. LC 79-52791. 1980. 39.50 (ISBN 0-12-264650-9). Acad Pr.

Fuchssteiner, B. & Lusky, W. Convex Cones. (Mathematics Studies: Vol. 56). 430p. 1981. 57.50 (ISBN 0-444-86290-0, North-Holland). Elsevier.

Fuchssteiner, B., jt. ed. see Bierstedt, K.

Fucik, S. & Kufner, A. Nonlinear Differential Equations. (Studies in Applied Mechanics: Vol. 2). 360p. 1980. 81.00 (ISBN 0-444-99771-7). Elsevier.

Fucik, Svatopluk. Solvability of Nonlinear Equations & Boundry Value Problems. (Mathematics & Its Applications Ser.: No. 4). 400p. 1980. 29.95 (ISBN 90-277-1077-5, Pub. by Reidel Holland). Kluwer Academic.

Fucilla, J. G. Forgotten Danteiana. LC 71-128987. (Northwestern University. Humanities Ser.: No. 5). Repr. of 1939 ed. 11.50 (ISBN 0-404-50705-0). AMS Pr.

Fucilla, Joseph G. The Teaching of Italian in the United States: A Documentary History. LC 74-17929. 304p. 1975. Repr. 19.00x (ISBN 0-405-06401-2). Ayer Co Pubs.

Fucilla, Joseph G., tr. see Metastasio, Pietro.

Fucini, Joseph J. & Fucini, Suzy. Entrepreneurs: The Men & Women Behind Famous Brand Names. (Reference Ser.). 1985. lib. bdg. 19.95 (ISBN 0-8161-8708-8); pap. 7.95 (ISBN 0-8161-8736-3). G K Hall.

Fucini, Suzy, jt. auth. see Fucini, Joseph J.

Fucito, Salvatore. Caruso & the Art of Singing. 1976. lib. bdg. 59.95 (ISBN 0-8490-1581-2). Gordon Pr.

Fuckel, K. Leopold. Symbolae Mycologicae. (Illus.). Repr. of 1877 ed. 90.00 (ISBN 0-384-17190-7). Johnson Repr.

Fuckel, L. Symbolae Mycologicae & Supplements. (Illus.). 1966. Repr. of 1877 ed. 70.00 (ISBN 3-7682-0358-1). Lubrecht & Cramer.

Fuda, George E. & Nelson, Edwin L. The Display Specialist. (Illus.). (gr. 10-12). 1976. pap. text ed. 11.80 (ISBN 0-07-022607-5). McGraw.

Fudala, Jan. Auditory Point Test. 1972. pap. 22.00x complete test package (ISBN 0-87879-081-0). Acad Therapy.

Fudala, Janet B. Tree-Bee Test of Auditory Discrimination. 1978. pap. 7.50x manual (ISBN 0-87879-196-5); flip-book 15.00x (ISBN 0-87879-197-3); form A 7.50x (ISBN 0-87879-198-1); Set Of 10. form B 7.50 (ISBN 0-87879-199-X); Set Of 10. recording forms 1 & 2 1.50x ea. Acad Therapy.

Fudell, Stanley E. How to Hold Your Job: Student Wkbk. rev. ed. 112p. 1982. wkbk. 9.00 (ISBN 0-936104-25-2, 077). Pro-Ed.

--How To Hold Your Job: Teacher's Curriculum Guide. rev. ed. 104p. 1982. tchr's ed. 19.00 (ISBN 0-936104-24-4, 076). Pro-Ed.

Fudenberg, Drew & Tirole, Jean. Dynamic Models of Oligopoly. (Fundamentals of Pure & Applied Economics Ser.: Vol. 1, Pt. 3). 80p. 1985. 16.00 (ISBN 3-7186-0279-2). Harwood Academic.

Fudenberg, H. H. & Melnick, V. L., eds. Biomedical Scientists & Public Policy. LC 78-15052. 260p. 1978. 27.50x (ISBN 0-306-40085-5, Plenum Pr). Plenum Pub.

Fudenberg, H. Hugh, ed. Biomedical Institutions, Biomedical Funding, & Public Policy. 209p. 1983. 29.50x (ISBN 0-306-41231-4, Plenum Pr). Plenum Pub.

Fudenberg, H. Hugh & Ambrogi, Fabio, eds. Immunomodulation: New Frontiers & Advances. 468p. 1984. 65.00x (ISBN 0-306-41493-7, Plenum Pr). Plenum Pub.

Fudenberg, Hugh H., et al. Basic Immunogenetics. 3rd ed. (Illus.). 1984. 29.95x (ISBN 0-19-503404-X); pap. 16.95x (ISBN 0-19-503405-8). Oxford U Pr.

Fudge, Colin, jt. ed. see Barrett, Susan.

Fudge, Don. Getting Graphic II: More Complex Algorithms. 275p. 1985. pap. 14.95 (ISBN 0-13-354952-6). P-H.

--Hi-Res Secrets. 270p. 1981. 3 ring binder 50.00 (ISBN 0-930182-21-9). Avant Garde Pub.

--Hi-Res Secrets Graphics Applications System. (Illus.). 240p. 1982. binder 50.00 (ISBN 0-930182-33-2). Avant Garde Pub.

Fudge, Edward. Christianity Without Ulcers. pap. 5.00 (ISBN 0-686-12686-6). E Fudge.

--Expository Outlines on Ephesians. 2.00 (ISBN 0-686-12688-2). E Fudge.

--Ezekiel: Prophet of Jehovah's Glory. 1.00 (ISBN 0-686-12692-0). E Fudge.

--Gold from the Gospels. pap. 2.00 (ISBN 0-686-12679-3). E Fudge.

--Preaching with Power. pap. 2.00 (ISBN 0-686-12680-7). E Fudge.

--Sermons That Demand a Decision. pap. 2.00 (ISBN 0-686-12681-5). E Fudge.

--Sermons That Strengthen. pap. 2.00 (ISBN 0-686-12682-3). E Fudge.

--Sermons to Grow on. pap. 2.00 (ISBN 0-686-12683-1). E Fudge.

--Simple Sermons That Demand a Decision. 2.00 (ISBN 0-686-12689-0). E Fudge.

--Simple Sermons That Say Something. pap. 2.00 (ISBN 0-686-12684-X). E Fudge.

--Sunday Night Sermons. pap. 2.00 (ISBN 0-686-12685-8). E Fudge.

Fudge, Edward, jt. auth. see Edwards, Bruce.

Fudge, Edward W. The Fire That Consumes: A Biblical & Historical Study of Final Punishment. 1983. 19.95 (ISBN 0-89890-018-2). Providential Pr.

Fudge, Erik C. English Word-Stress. (Illus.). 264p. 1984. text ed. 22.95 (ISBN 0-04-418004-7); pap. text ed. 11.95 (ISBN 0-04-418005-5). Allen Unwin.

Fuechtbauer, Hans. Sediments & Sedimentary Rocks 1. (Sedimentary Petrology Ser.: Pt. 2). (Illus.). 464p. 1974. lib. bdg. 36.50 (ISBN 3-510-65007-7). Lubrecht & Cramer.

Fuegi, John, ed. see International Brecht Society.

Fuegi, John, et al. Brecht: Women & Politics. (The Brecht Yearbook Ser.: Vol. 12). 368p. 1985. 28.00 (ISBN 0-8143-1788-X). Wayne St U Pr.

Fuehrer, Sr. Mary R. Study of the Relation of the Dutch Lancelot & the Flemish Perchevael Fragments to the Manuscripts of Chretien's Conte del Graal. LC 73-140025. (Catholic University Studies in German Ser.: No. 14). Repr. of 1939 ed. 23.00 (ISBN 0-404-50234-2). AMS Pr.

Fuell, A. J. see Von Wiesner, J. & Von Regel, C.

Fuellenbach, D., et al, eds. Adriamycin-Symposium. (Beitraege zur Onkologie; Contributions to Oncology: Vol. 9). (Illus.). x, 462p. 1981. pap. 33.75 (ISBN 3-8055-2966-X). S Karger.

Fuellenbach, John. Ecclesiastical Office & the Primacy of Rome: An Evaluation of Recent Theological Discussion of 1 Clement. LC 79-17574. (Studies in Christian Antiquity: Vol. 20). 278p. 1980. 26.95x (ISBN 0-8132-0551-4). Cath U Pr.

Fuelling, Daniel & Rothmaler, Audrey. Congregational Outreach & Care: A Manual for Mini-Parish Leadership. 40p. (Orig.). pap. 3.25 (ISBN 0-8066-1967-8, 10-1643). Augsburg.

Fuenllana, Miguel De. Orphenica Lyra (Seville, 1554) Jacobs, Charles, ed. (Illus.). 1978. 98.00x (ISBN 0-19-816128-X). Oxford U Pr.

Fuente, Julio De La see Malinowski, Bronislaw.

Fuente, Julio de la see Malinowski, Bronislaw & De La Fuente, Julio.

Fuente, Mario De La see De La Fuente, Mario.

Fuente, Patricia D., ed. Chicano Four: Two. (Riversedge Chapbks.). (Illus.). 96p. (Orig., Eng. & Span.). 1981. pap. 4.00 (ISBN 0-938884-03-4). RiverSedge Pr.

Fuente, Tomas De La see Cowan, Marvin W.

Fuente, Tomas de La see De La Fuente, Tomas.

Fuentes, jt. auth. see Eichborn.

Fuentes, A., jt. auth. see Eichborn, R.

Fuentes, Carlos. Aura. bilingual ed. Kemp, Lysander, tr. from Sp. LC 75-2417. 160p. 1975. 7.95 (ISBN 0-374-10701-7); pap. 6.95 (ISBN 0-374-51171-3). FS&G.

--Burnt Water. Peden, Margaret S., tr. from Span. LC 80-19148. 231p. 1980. 11.95 (ISBN 0-374-11741-1). FS&G.

--The Death of Artemio Cruz. Hileman, Sam, tr. from Span. 306p. 1964. pap. 6.95 (ISBN 0-374-50540-3). FS&G.

--Distant Relations. Peden, Margaret S., tr. from Span. LC 81-9904. 225p. 1982. 11.95 (ISBN 0-374-14082-0); pap. 7.95 (ISBN 0-374-51813-0). FS&G.

--Distant Relations. Peden, Margaret S., tr. 1983. pap. 7.95 (ISBN 0-374-51813-0). FS&G.

--The Good Conscience. Hileman, Sam, tr. from Span. 148p. 1961. pap. 6.25 (ISBN 0-374-50736-8). FS&G.
--The Hydra Head. Peden, Margaret S., tr. from Sp. LC 78-12603. 292p. 1978. 14.95 (ISBN 0-374-17397-4); pap. 9.95 (ISBN 0-374-51563-8). FS&G.
--The Old Gringo. Peden, Margaret, tr. from Spanish. 1985. 14.95 (ISBN 0-374-22578-8); 25.50 (ISBN 0-374-22428-5). FS&G.
--Terra Nostra. Peden, Margaret Sayers, tr. from Sp. 778p. 1976. 20.00 (ISBN 0-374-27327-8); pap. 13.50 (ISBN 0-374-51750-9). FS&G.
--Where the Air Is Clear. Hileman, Sam, tr. from Span. 376p. 1971. pap. 8.95 (ISBN 0-374-50919-0). FS&G.
Fuentes, Carlos, et al. Latin American Fiction Today: A Symposium. Minc, Rose S., ed. LC 79-90483. 198p. (Orig., Eng. & Span.). 1980. 9.95 (ISBN 0-935318-04-6). Edins Hispamerica.
Fuentes, Carmen. Learning the ABC's with Animals. 1984. 4.95 (ISBN 0-533-05683-7). Vantage.
Fuentes, D. & Lopez, J. A. Barrio Language Dictionary. (Span.). 1976. pap. 5.25 (ISBN 0-87505-143-X). Borden.
Fuentes, Epifanio. Knowledge Versus the College Mind. Date not set. 5.95. Vantage.
Fuentes, Ernesto F., compiled by. Nonwood Plant Fiber Pulping, Progress Report, No. 4. (TAPPI PRESS Reports). 112p. 1973. 18.95 (ISBN 0-317-36020-5, 01-01-R052). TAPPI.
Fuentes, Ernesto F., et al. Nonwood Plant Fiber Pulping: Progress Report, No. 11. (TAPPI PRESS Reports). (Illus.). 99p. 1981. pap. 38.95 (ISBN 0-89852-391-5, 01 01 R091). TAPPI.
Fuentes, Gregorio Lopez Y see Lopez y Fuentes, Gregorio.
Fuentes, Luis. La Lucha Contra el Racismo en Nuestras Escuelas: Control Comunal de las Escuelas Por las Comunidades Puertorriquenas, Negras y Chinas en la Ciudad de Nueva York. (Sp.). pap. 0.25 (ISBN 0-87348-327-8). Path Pr NY.
Fuentes, Norberto. Hemingway in Cuba. Corwin, Consuelo, tr. from Span. LC 84-2744. (Illus.). 460p. 1984. 22.50 (ISBN 0-8184-0356-X). Lyle Stuart.
Fuentes, Vilma M. Kimod & the Swan Maiden, No. 2. (Mandaya & Mansaka Tales Ser.). (Illus.). 36p. (Orig.). (gr. k-3). 1984. pap. 3.25x (ISBN 0-318-04079-4, Pub. by New Day Philippines). Cellar.
--The Monkey & the Crocodile. (Mandaya & Mansaka Tales Ser.: No. 1). (Illus.). 31p. (Orig.). (gr. k-2). 1984. pap. 3.00x (ISBN 971-10-0127-6, Pub. by New Day Philippines). Cellar.
Fuentes, Vilma M. & Edito T. De La Cruz, trs. A Treasury of Mandaya & Mansaka Folk Literature. (Illus.). 130p. (Mandaya, Mansaka.). 1980. 7.50x (ISBN 0-686-28808-4). Cellar.
Fuerboeck, Karl, jt. auth. see Tomandl, Theodor.
Fuerer-Haimendorf, Christopher V. The Naked Nagas: Head-Hunters of Assam in Peace & War. LC 76-44720. Repr. of 1946 ed. 24.50 (ISBN 0-404-15924-9). AMS Pr.
Fuerle, Richard D. The Pure Logic of Choice. 1985. 13.95 (ISBN 0-533-06401-5). Vantage.
Fuerst, Mark L., jt. auth. see Weinberg, Sanford B.
Fuerst, Norbert. Phases of Rilke. LC 72-6786. (Studies in German Literature, No. 13). 1972. Repr. of 1958 ed. lib. bdg. 43.95x (ISBN 0-8383-1663-8). Haskell.
--Victorian Age of German Literature: Eight Essays. LC 65-23845. 1965. 23.50x (ISBN 0-271-73107-9). Pa St U Pr.
Fuerst, Rene & Hume, Samuel J., eds. Twentieth Century Stage Decoration, 2 vols. in 1. LC 67-28846. (Illus.). 428p. 1968. 33.00 (ISBN 0-405-08540-0, Blom Pubns). Ayer Co Pubs.
Fuerst, Robert. Frobisher & Fuerst's Microbiology in Health & Disease. 15th ed. LC 82-42506. (Illus.). 669p. 1983. text ed. 28.95 (ISBN 0-7216-3944-5). Saunders.
--Microbiology in Health & Disease: Laboratory Manual & Workbook. 7th ed. LC 77-16985. (Illus.). 1983. pap. text ed. 12.95 (ISBN 0-7216-3945-3). Saunders.
Fuerst, W. J. Ruth, Esther, Ecclesiastes, the Song of Songs, Lamentations. LC 74-82589. (Cambridge Bible Commentary on the New English Bible, Old Testament Ser.). 250p. 1975. 32.50 (ISBN 0-521-20651-0); pap. 11.95 (ISBN 0-521-09920-X). Cambridge U Pr.
Fuerstenau, D. W., ed. see Society of Mining Engineers of AIME.
Fuerstenau, M. C. & Miller, J. D. Chemistry of Flotation. LC 84-52209. (Illus.). 177p. 1985. 22.00x (ISBN 0-89520-436-3, 436-3). Soc Mining Eng.
Fuerstenau, M. C., ed. Flotation, 2 vols. LC 76-19745. 1976. 39.00x (ISBN 0-89520-032-5). Soc Mining Eng.
Fuerstenau, Maurice C. & Palmer, R. B., eds. Gold, Silver, Uranium & Coal - Geology, Mining, Extraction, & Environment. LC 82-73914. (Illus.). 526p. 1983. pap. text ed. 40.00x (ISBN 0-89520-406-1, 406-1). Soc Mining Eng.
Fuertes, Gloria. Off the Map. Levine, Philip & Long, Ada, trs. from Span. (Poetry in Translation Ser.). 112p. 1984. 16.00x (ISBN 0-8195-5102-3); pap. 8.95 (ISBN 0-8195-6112-6). Wesleyan U Pr.
Fuess, Claude M. Calvin Coolidge: The Man from Vermont. LC 76-48974. 1977. Repr. of 1965 ed. lib. bdg. 41.25x (ISBN 0-8371-9320-6, FUCC). Greenwood.
--Creed of a Schoolmaster. LC 76-99636. (Essay Index Reprint Ser.). 1939. 18.00 (ISBN 0-8369-1608-5). Ayer Co Pubs.
--Daniel Webster, 2 Vols. 2nd ed. LC 68-8722. (American Scene Ser). (Illus.). 1968. Repr. of 1930 ed. Set. lib. bdg. 85.00 (ISBN 0-306-71186-9). Da Capo.
--Joseph B. Eastman, Servant of the People. LC 74-12881. (Illus.). 363p. 1974. Repr. of 1952 ed. lib. bdg. 21.25x (ISBN 0-8371-7769-3, FUJE). Greenwood.
--Lord Byron As a Satirist in Verse. LC 72-10825. (Studies in Byron, No. 5). 1974. lib. bdg. 39.95x (ISBN 0-8383-0554-7). Haskell.
--Rufus Choate, the Wizard of the Law. (Illus.). 278p. 1970. Repr. of 1928 ed. 19.50 (ISBN 0-208-00938-8, Archon). Shoe String.
Fuess, Claude M. & Stearns, H. C. The Little Book of Society Verse. 351p. 1980. Repr. lib. bdg. 30.00 (ISBN 0-89984-202-X). Century Bookbindery.
Fuess, Claude M., ed. Selected Essays. facsimile ed. LC 72-134078. (Essay Index Reprint Ser). Repr. of 1914 ed. 18.00 (ISBN 0-8369-2394-4). Ayer Co Pubs.
Fuess, Renate. Nicht Frage. (European University Studies: No. 1, Vol. 665). 322p. (Ger.). 1983. 38.95 (ISBN 3-8204-7415-3); 38.95 (ISBN 3-8204-7416-1). P Lang Pubs.
Fueter, Eduard. Geschichte der Neueren Historiographie. Gerhard, D. & Satler, P., eds. (Ger). 1969. Repr. of 1936 ed. 47.00 (ISBN 0-384-17210-5). Johnson Repr.
--World History, Eighteen Fifteen to Nineteen Twenty. Fay, Sidney B., tr. from Ger. LC 79-17754. (Illus.). 1980. Repr. of 1924 ed. lib. bdg. 42.50x (ISBN 0-313-22088-3, FUWH). Greenwood.
Fueter, R. Analytische Geometrie der Ebene und Des Raumes. (Mathematische Reihe Ser.: No. 2). 180p. (Ger.). 1945. 21.95x (ISBN 0-8176-0130-9). Birkhauser.
Fueyo Cuesta, Laureano. Diccionario Terminologico De Minas, Canteras y Mineralurgia. 272p. (Span.). 1973. leather 17.95 (ISBN 84-400-6971-5, S-50112). French & Eur.
Fufaev, N. A., jt. auth. see Niemark, Ju. I.
Fufuka, Karama & Fufuka, Mahiri. My Daddy Is a Cool Dude. LC 74-2883. (Illus.). 48p. (gr. 1-4). 1975. 6.95 (ISBN 0-8037-6187-2); PLB 6.89 (ISBN 0-8037-6188-0). Dial Bks Young.
Fufuka, Mahiri, jt. auth. see Fufuka, Karama.
Fugal, Peggy, ed. see Fugal, Sherman.
Fugal, Sherman. Latter-Day Laughter: A Collection of Humorous Quips, Quotes, & Anecdotes Appropriate for LDS Talks, Lessons or a Good Laugh. Fugal, Peggy, ed. LC 80-81508. 140p. 1980. 8.95 (ISBN 0-88290-141-9). Horizon Utah.
Fugard, Athol. Boesman & Lena & Other Plays. 1978. pap. 9.95 (ISBN 0-19-281242-4, GB 553, GB). Oxford U Pr.
--Dimetos & Two Early Plays. 1977. pap. 5.95 (ISBN 0-19-281210-6). Oxford U Pr.
--A Lesson from Aloes. 1981. pap. 6.95 (ISBN 0-19-281307-2). Oxford U Pr.
--A Lesson from Aloes. 1981. 9.95 (ISBN 0-394-51898-5). Random.
--Master Harold & the Boys. (Plays Ser.). 64p. 1984. pap. 4.95 (ISBN 0-14-048187-7). Penguin.
--Master Harold & the Boys. 1982. 11.95 (ISBN 0-394-52874-3). Knopf.
--Notebooks, Nineteen Sixty to Nineteen Seventy-Seven. LC 83-49025. 1984. 14.95 (ISBN 0-394-53755-6). Knopf.
--Statements: Three Plays. 1974. pap. 4.95 (ISBN 0-19-281170-3, GB564, GB). Oxford U Pr.
--Tsotsi. LC 80-5416. 168p. 1980. 8.95 (ISBN 0-394-51384-3). Random.
--Tsotsi. 1983. pap. 3.95 (ISBN 0-14-006272-6). Penguin.
Fugard, Sheila. A Revolutionary Woman. 160p. 1985. 14.95 (ISBN 0-8076-1127-1). Braziller.
Fugaro, Rocco A. A Manual of Sequential Art Activities for Classified Children & Adolescents. (Illus.). 246p. (Orig.). 1985. pap. 25.75x spiral bdg. (ISBN 0-398-05085-6). C C Thomas.
Fugate, Bryan I. Operation Barbarossa: Strategy & Tactics on the Eastern Front, 1941. (Illus.). 448p. 1984. 22.50 (ISBN 0-89141-197-6). Presidio Pr.
Fugate, Francis L. & Fugate, Roberta B. Secrets of the World's Best-Selling Writer: The Storytelling Techniques of Erle Stanley Gardner. LC 80-82544. (Illus.). 352p. 1980. 12.95 (ISBN 0-688-03701-1). Morrow.
Fugate, Howard. Cardiac Rehabilitation: The Road to a Healthy Heart. McCavitt, William E., ed. 92p. 1980. pap. 5.00 (ISBN 0-935648-06-2). Halldin Pub.
Fugate, J. Richard. What the Bible Says About Child Training. (What the Bible Says about...Ser.). (Illus.). 287p. 1980. pap. 5.95 (ISBN 0-86717-000-X). Aletheia Pubs.
Fugate, James K. Programming Tools for the IBM PC: Screen Design, Code Generator & High Memory Access. (Illus.). 272p. 1985. pap. 19.95 (ISBN 0-89303-784-2); diskette 30.00 (ISBN 0-89303-785-0). Brady Comm.
Fugate, Roberta B., jt. auth. see Fugate, Francis L.
Fugate, Stephen. Hard Summer. 224p. (Orig.). 1981. pap. 1.95 (ISBN 0-449-14389-9, GM). Fawcett.
Fugate, Stephen E. Day of the Ambushers. (Orig.). 1979. pap. 1.95 (ISBN 0-532-23158-9). Woodhill.
--Full Circle. (Orig.). 1979. pap. 1.50 (ISBN 0-532-15401-0). Woodhill.
Fugate, Wilbur. Foreign Commerce & Antitrust Laws, 2vols. 3rd ed. LC 81-83240. 973p. 1982. 110.00 set (ISBN 0-316-29535-3); Vol. 1. 57.50; Vol. 2. 57.50 (ISBN 0-316-29534-5). Little.
Fugate, Wilbur L. Foreign Commerce & the Antitrust Laws: 1984 Supplement. 1984. pap. 40.00 (ISBN 0-316-29538-8). Little.
Fugelsang, K. C., jt. auth. see Nury, F. S.
Fuger, J. & Parker, V. B. The Chemical Thrmodynamics of Actinide Elements & Compounds: Part 8, the Actinide Halides. 267p. 1984. pap. 45.00 (ISBN 92-0-149183-2, ISP424-8, IAEA). Unipub.
Fugere, A. C., jt. auth. see Goguet, Antoine Y.
Fugett, Albert F. Spokesman for the Devil. (Illus.). 165p. 1985. 14.95 (ISBN 0-9614870-0-3). Triple Seven.
Fugita, Neil. Introducing the Bible. LC 81-80874. 224p. (Orig.). 1981. pap. 4.95 (ISBN 0-8091-2392-4). Paulist Pr.
Fugitt, Eva D. He Hit Me Back First! Creative Visualization Activities for Parenting & Teaching. LC 82-83063. (Illus.). 106p. (Orig.). 1982. pap. 9.95 (ISBN 0-915190-36-2). Jalmar Pr.
Fugitt, Glenn V., jt. auth. see Johansen, Harley.
Fugitt, Jack. The Big J Handbook for Artists & Cartoonists. 1983. 19.95 (ISBN 0-533-05624-1). Vantage.
Fuglede, B. Finely Harmonic Functions. LC 72-90194. (Lecture Notes in Mathematics: Vol. 289). 188p. 1972. pap. 10.00 (ISBN 0-387-06005-7). Springer-Verlag.
Fuglesang, Andreas, ed. About Understanding: Ideas & Observations on Cross Cultural Communication. 232p. 1983. pap. text ed. 10.95 (ISBN 0-910365-01-6). Decade Media.
Fuglestad, Finn. A History of Niger, Eighteen Fifty to Nineteen Sixty. LC 83-1809. (African Studies: No. 41). 276p. 1984. 39.50 (ISBN 0-521-25268-7). Cambridge U Pr.
Fuglesten, Harlan G. Voter Turnout in North Dakota, Nineteen Fifty-Two to Nineteen Eighty-Two. (Illus.). write for info. Amer Bar Assn.
Fuglum, Per. Edward Gibbon: His View of Life & Conception of History. LC 73-16350. 1953. lib. bdg. 22.50 (ISBN 0-8414-4166-9). Folcroft.
Fuglum, Per, jt. auth. see Joyce, Michael.
Fuguitt, Glenn V., et al. Growth & Change in Rural America. LC 79-65329. (Management & Control of Growth Ser.). 101p. 1979. pap. 19.00 (ISBN 0-87420-586-7, G05); pap. 14.25 members. Urban Land.
Fuhley, Denis, pref. by see Dillon, George E.
Fuhlrott, Rolf & Dewe, Michael, eds. Library Interior Layout & Design. (IFLA Pub. Ser: 24). 145p. 1982. lib. bdg. 26.00 (ISBN 3-598-20386-1). K G Saur.
Fuhrer, Marcus J., jt. ed. see Halpern, Andrew S.
Fuhrhop, J. H., et al. Large Molecules. LC 67-11280. (Structure & Bonding Ser.: Vol. 18). (Illus.). 216p. 1974. 45.00 (ISBN 0-387-06658-6). Springer-Verlag.
Fuhrhop, Juergen & Penzlin, Gustav. Organic Synthesis. (Illus.). xi, 355p. 1983. 39.00 (ISBN 0-89573-059-6). VCH Pubs.
Fuhrman & Buck. Microcomputers for Management Decision Making. (Illus.). 400p. 1986. text ed. 26.95 (ISBN 0-13-580325-X). P-H.
Fuhrman, John. Telemanagement: How to Select & Manage Your Business Telephone System. 250p. 1985. 39.95 (ISBN 0-13-902529-4, Busn); pap. 12.95 (ISBN 0-13-902511-1). P-H.
Fuhrman, Joseph T. Tsar Alexis, His Reign & His Russia. (Russian Ser.: No. 34). 1981. 22.00 (ISBN 0-87569-040-8). Academic Intl.
Fuhrman, Joseph T; see Miliukov, Paul N.
Fuhrman, Noah. Seven Keys for Doubling Your Standard of Living (Without Increasing Your Income) 224p. 1982. pap. 6.95 (ISBN 0-02-008190-1). Macmillan.
Fuhrman, Susan, jt. auth. see Rosenthal, Alan.
Fuhrman, Susan & Rosenthal, Alan, eds. Shaping Education Policy in the States. 140p. 1981. lib. bdg. 15.00 (ISBN 0-318-03011-X); pap. 9.50 (ISBN 0-318-03625-8). Inst Educ Lead.
Fuhrmann, Babara S. & Grasha, Anthony F. A Practical Handbook for College Teachers. 315p. 1983. text ed. 25.95 (ISBN 0-316-29558-2); pap. text ed. 11.95 (ISBN 0-316-29559-0). Little.
Fuhrmann, Barbara, jt. auth. see Curwin, Richard.
Fuhrmann, Brigita. Bobbin Lace: An Illustrated Guide to Traditional & Contemporary Techniques. 160p. 1985. pap. 7.95 (ISBN 0-486-24902-6). Dover.
Fuhrmann, Ludwig. Die Belesenheit Des Jungen Byron. 119p. 1980. Repr. of 1903 ed. lib. bdg. 20.00 (ISBN 0-8414-1976-0). Folcroft.
Fuhrmann, P. A. Linear Operators & Systems: Operator Theory, Mathematical Systems Theory, Control Process. 1981. 61.95 (ISBN 0-07-022589-3). McGraw.
Fuhrmann, P. A., ed. Mathematical Theory of Networks & Systems: Proceedings of the International Symposium Beer Sheva, Israel, June 20-24,2983. (Lectures Notes in Control & Information Science Ser.: Vol. 58). x, 906p. 1984. pap. 48.00 (ISBN 0-387-13168-X). Springer-Verlag.
Fuhrmann, W. & Vogel, F. Genetic Counseling. (Heidelberg Science Library: Vol. 10). (Illus.). 160p. 1976. pap. text ed. 11.00 (ISBN 0-387-90151-5). Springer-Verlag.
--Genetic Counseling. 3rd ed. Kurth-Scherer, S., tr. from Ger. (Illus.). 188p. 1982. pap. 19.50x (ISBN 0-387-90715-7). Springer-Verlag.
Fuhs, Allen & Kingery, Marshall, eds. Instrumentation for Airbreathing Propulsion. LC 74-1603. (Illus.). 520p. 1974. 35.00 (ISBN 0-262-07058-8, PAAS34); members 19.00 (ISBN 0-317-32153-6). AIAA.
Fuhs, Pat, ed. see Nixon, Joan L.
Fuhs, Pat, ed. see Smith, Carole.
Fuis, Frank, Jr. Too Wet to Plow. 1977. 12.00 (ISBN 0-682-48844-5). Exposition Pr FL.
Fu-Jen, Li & Shu-Tse, Peng. Revolutionaries in Mao's Prisons: The Case of the Chinese Trotskyists. 1974. pap. 0.50 (ISBN 0-87348-338-3). Path Pr NY.
Fujihara, M. D, jt. auth. see Becker, C. D.
Fujii, John N., jt. auth. see Barnett, Raymond A.
Fujii, Setsuro, et al, eds. Kinins IIA: Biochemistry, Pathophysiology, & Clinical Aspects. LC 79-9079. (Advances in Experimental Medicine & Biology: Vol. 120A). 622p. 1979. 75.00x (ISBN 0-306-40196-7, Plenum Pr). Plenum Pub.
--Kinins IIB: Systemic Proteases & Cellular Function. LC 79-9079. (Advances in Experimental Medicine & Biology: Vol. 120B). 733p. 1979. 85.00x (ISBN 0-306-40197-5, Plenum Pr). Plenum Pub.
Fujii, Shinichi. Essentials of Japanese Constitutional Law. (Studies in Japanese Law & Government). 459p. 1979. Repr. of 1940 ed. 32.50 (ISBN 0-89093-213-1). U Pubns Amer.
--Tenno Seiji: Direct Imperial Rule. (Studies in Japanese History & Civilization). 415p. 1979. Repr. of 1944 ed. 30.00 (ISBN 0-89093-263-8). U Pubns Amer.
Fujii, T. & Channing, C. P. Non-Steroidal Regulations in Reproductive Biology & Medicine: Proceedings of a Satellite Symposium to the 8th International Congress of Pharmacology, Tokyo, 26-27 July 1981, Vol. 34. (Illus.). 266p. 1982. 72.00 (ISBN 0-08-027976-7, H130). Pergamon.
Fujii, T. & Sate, R., eds. Resource Allocation & Division of Space: Proceedings of an International Symposium Held at Toba Near Nagoya, Japan, 14-17, Dec. 1975. LC 77-14525. (Lecture Notes in Economics & Mathematical Systems: Vol. 147). 1977. pap. text ed. 14.00 (ISBN 0-387-08352-9). Springer-Verlag.
Fujikawa, Guyo. Millie's Secret. Duenewald, Doris, ed. (Fujikawa Board Books Ser.). (Illus.). (gr. k-3). 1978. PLB 3.50 (ISBN 0-448-14726-2, G&D). Putnam Pub Group.
--My Favorite Thing. Duenewald, Doris, ed. (Fujikawa Board Books Ser.). (Illus.). 1978. 3.50 (ISBN 0-448-14727-0, G&D). Putnam Pub Group.
Fujikawa, Gyo. Babes of the Wild. 1977. 3.50 (ISBN 0-448-12894-2, G&D). Putnam Pub Group.
--Baby Animals. (Baby's First Bks.). (Illus.). 14p. (ps). 1978. bds. 2.50 (ISBN 0-448-16281-4, G&D). Putnam Pub Group.
--Betty Bear's Birthday. (Fujikawa Board Books). (Illus.). (ps-2). 1977. 3.50 (ISBN 0-448-14369-0, G&D). Putnam Pub Group.
--Can You Count. (Fujikawa Board Bks.). 1977. 3.50 (ISBN 0-448-12893-4, G&D). Putnam Pub Group.
--Come Follow Me...to the Secret World of Elves & Fairies & Gnomes & Trolls. LC 78-22746. (Illus.). (gr. k-5). 1979. 6.95 (ISBN 0-448-16545-7, G&D). Putnam Pub Group.
--Come Out & Play. (Gyo Fujikawa Tiny Board Books). (Illus.). 14p. (ps-k). 1981. 2.25 (ISBN 0-448-15115-4, G&D). Putnam Pub Group.
--Dreamland. (Tiny Board Bks.). (Illus.). 14p. (ps). 1981. 2.25 (ISBN 0-448-15081-6, G&D). Putnam Pub Group.
--Fairy Tales. (Platt & Munk Pandabacks Ser.). (Illus.). 24p. (ps-3). 1980. 6.95 (ISBN 0-448-02814-X, G&D); pap. 1.25 (ISBN 0-448-49615-1). Putnam Pub Group.
--Fraidy Cat. LC 81-84015. (Illus.). 32p. (gr. k-3). 1982. 3.95 (ISBN 0-448-11753-3, G&D). Putnam Pub Group.
--Good Morning! (Tiny Board Bks.). (Illus.). 14p. (ps). 1981. 2.25 (ISBN 0-448-15084-0, G&D). Putnam Pub Group.
--Here I Am. (Tiny Board Bks.). (Illus.). 14p. (ps). 1981. 2.25 (ISBN 0-448-15082-4, G&D). Putnam Pub Group.
--Jenny & Jupie to the Rescue. LC 82-80870. (Checkerboard Bks.). (Illus.). 32p. (gr. k-2). 1982. 3.95 (ISBN 0-448-11754-1, G&D). Putnam Pub Group.
--Let's Eat. 1975. 3.50 (ISBN 0-448-11922-6, G&D). Putnam Pub Group.
--Let's Grow a Garden. (Fujikawa Board Books). (Illus.). (gr. k-3). 1978. 3.50 (ISBN 0-448-14613-4, G&D). Putnam Pub Group.
--Let's Play. (Fujikawa Board Bks.). 1975. 3.50 (ISBN 0-448-11958-7, G&D). Putnam Pub Group.

--The Magic Show. LC 81-80651. (Gyo Fujikawa Ser.). (Illus.). 32p. (ps-1). 1981. 3.95 (ISBN 0-448-11750-9, G&D). Putnam Pub Group.

--Me Too! LC 81-84014. (Illus.). 32p. (gr. k-3). 1982. 3.95 (ISBN 0-448-11752-5, G&D). Putnam Pub Group.

--Mother Goose. (Platt & Munk Pandabacks Ser.). (Illus.). 24p. (ps-3). 1968. pap. 5.95 (ISBN 0-448-01810-1, G&D). Putnam Pub Group.

--Mother Goose. (Gyo Fujikawa Tiny Board Books). (Illus.). 14p. (ps-k). 1981. 2.25 (ISBN 0-448-15091-3, G&D). Putnam Pub Group.

--My Animal Friend. (Gyo Fujikawa Tiny Board Books). (Illus.). 14p. (ps-k). 1981. 2.25 (ISBN 0-448-15079-4, G&D). Putnam Pub Group.

--The Night Before Christmas. (Platt & Munk Pandabacks Ser.). (Illus.). 24p. (ps-3). 1980. pap. 1.25 (ISBN 0-448-49619-4, G&D). Putnam Pub Group.

--One, Two, Three, A Counting Book. (Tiny Board Bks.). (Illus.). 14p. (ps). 1981. 2.25 (ISBN 0-448-15085-9, G&D). Putnam Pub Group.

--Our Best Friends. (Fujikawa Board Books). (Illus.). (ps-2). 1977. 3.50 (ISBN 0-448-14343-7, G&D). Putnam Pub Group.

--Puppies, Pussycats & Other Friends. 1975. 3.50 (ISBN 0-448-11920-X, G&D). Putnam Pub Group.

--Sam's All-Wrong Day. LC 82-80869. (Checkerboard Bks.). (Illus.). 32p. (Orig.). (gr. k-2). 1982. 3.95 (ISBN 0-448-11755-X, G&D). Putnam Pub Group.

--Sleepy Time. 1975. 3.50 (ISBN 0-448-11921-8, G&D). Putnam Pub Group.

--Surprise! Surprise! (Fujikawa Board Books). (Illus.). (gr. k-3). 1978. 3.50 (ISBN 0-448-14557-X, G&D). Putnam Pub Group.

--A Tiny Word Book. (Tiny Board Bks.). (Illus.). 14p. (ps). 1981. 2.25 (ISBN 0-448-15083-2, G&D). Putnam Pub Group.

--Year in, Year Out. (Tiny Board Bks.). (Illus.). 14p. (ps). 1981. 2.25 (ISBN 0-448-15080-8, G&D). Putnam Pub Group.

Fujikawa, Gyo, illus. Babies. (ps). 1963. bds. 3.95 (ISBN 0-448-03084-5, G&D). Putnam Pub Group.

--Baby Animals. (Illus.). (ps). 1963. bds. 2.50 (ISBN 0-448-03083-7, G&D). Putnam Pub Group.

--Child's Book of Poems. LC 75-86696. (Illus.). (gr. k-4). 1969. 7.95 (ISBN 0-448-01876-4, G&D). Putnam Pub Group.

--Fairy Tales & Fables. (Illus.). (gr. k-3). 1970. 6.95 (ISBN 0-448-02814-X, G&D). Putnam Pub Group.

--Gyo Fujikawa's A to Z Picture Book. LC 73-16655. (Illus.). 80p. (gr. k-3). 1974. 7.95 (ISBN 0-448-11741-X, G&D). Putnam Pub Group.

--Oh, What a Busy Day. (Illus.). 80p. (gr. k-3). 1976. 7.95 (ISBN 0-448-12511-0, G&D). Putnam Pub Group.

--Poems for Children. (Pandaback Ser.). (Illus.). 24p. (ps-3). 1980. PLB 4.99 (ISBN 0-448-13143-9, G&D); pap. 1.25 (ISBN 0-448-49616-X). Putnam Pub Group.

Fujikawa, Gyp. Shags Finds a Kitten. (Illus.). 32p. (ps-1). 1983. pap. 3.95 (ISBN 0-448-16465-5, G&D). Putnam Pub Group.

--That's Not Fair. (Illus.). 32p. (ps-2). 1983. pap. 3.95 (ISBN 0-448-16466-3, G&D). Putnam Pub Group.

Fujikawa, Yu. Japanese Medicine. LC 75-23663. (Clio Medica: 12). Orig. Title: Geschichte der Medizin in Japan. (Illus.). Repr. of 1934 ed. 15.00 (ISBN 0-404-58912-X). AMS Pr.

Fujikura, Koichiro, jt. auth. see Gresser, Julian.

Fujimaki, Maseo, jt. ed. see Whitaker, John R.

Fujimoto, Patricia. Libraries. LC 83-26252. (New True Bks.). (Illus.). 48p. (gr. k-4). 1984. lib. bdg. 10.60 (ISBN 0-516-01725-X); pap. 3.95 (ISBN 0-516-41725-8). Childrens.

Fujimoto, Yoshihide, jt. auth. see Akisada, Masayoshi.

Fujimura, Bunyu. Wet Sleeves. LC 79-90653. 156p. 1980. 7.95 (ISBN 0-912624-01-9). Nembutsu Pr.

Fujimura, Faith N., ed. Groundwater in Hawaii: A Century of Progress. 270p. 1981. text ed. 20.00x (ISBN 0-8248-0788-X, Water Resources Res Ctr). UH Pr.

Fujimura, Thomas H. The Restoration Comedy of Wit. LC 78-13942. 1978. Repr. of 1952 ed. lib. bdg. 27.50x (ISBN 0-313-21232-5, FURC). Greenwood.

Fujimura, Thomas H., ed. see Wycherley, William.

Fujino, Yukio, ed. Modern Japanese Literature in Translation: A Bibliography. LC 78-66395. 311p. 1979. 16.95x (ISBN 0-87011-339-9). Kodansha.

Fujinori, Y. Modern Analysis of Value Theory. (Lecture Notes in Economics & Mathematical Systems: Vol. 207). (Illus.). 165p. 1982. pap. 14.00 (ISBN 0-387-11949-3). Springer-Verlag.

Fujioka, Michio. Angkor Wat. LC 71-158641. (This Beautiful World Ser.: Vol. 29). (Illus.). 138p. (Orig.). 1972. pap. 4.95 (ISBN 0-87011-156-6). Kodansha.

--Japanese Residences & Gardens: A Tradition of Integration. Horton, H. Mack, tr. LC 82-48793. (Great Japanese Art Ser.). (Illus.). 48p. 1983. 18.95 (ISBN 0-87011-561-8). Kodansha.

--Kyoto Country Retreats: The Katsura & Shugakuin Palaces. LC 83-47619. (Great Japanese Art Ser.). (Illus.). 48p. 1983. 18.95 (ISBN 0-87011-602-9). Kodansha.

Fujioka, Ryoichi. Shino & Oribe Ceramics. Morse, Samuel C., tr. from Jap. LC 76-9357. (Japanese Arts Library: Vol. 1). 1977. 19.95 (ISBN 0-87011-284-8). Kodansha.

Fujisawa, Chikao. Zen & Shinto: The Story of Japanese Philosophy. LC 78-139133. 92p. Repr. of 1959 ed. lib. bdg. 15.00x (ISBN 0-8371-5749-8, FUZS). Greenwood.

Fujisawa, K., jt. ed. see Yamaguchi, N.

Fujita, H. Mathematical Theory of Sedimentation Analysis. (Physical Chemistry: Vol. 11). 1962. 75.00 (ISBN 0-12-269750-2). Acad Pr.

Fujita, H., et al, eds. Nonlinear Partial Differential Equations in Applied Science: Proceedings of the U.S.- Japan Seminar, Held in Tokyo, 1982. (Mathematics Studies: No. 81). 474p. 1984. 60.00 (ISBN 0-444-86681-7, I-128-84, North-Holland). Elsevier.

Fujita, Hiroshi. Foundations of Ultra-Centrifugal Analysis. LC 74-20899. 459p. 1975. 34.50 (ISBN 0-471-28582-X, Pub. by Wiley). Krieger.

Fujita, Hiroshi, tr. see Kurata, Michio.

Fujita, Kuniko. Black Worker's Struggles in Detroit's Auto Industry 1935-1975. LC 79-93300. 125p. 1980. 11.95 (ISBN 0-86548-010-9). R & E Pubs.

Fujita, M. Spatial Development Planning: A Dynamic Covex Programming Approach. (Studies in Regional Science & Urban Economics: Vol. 2). 336p. 1978. 66.00 (ISBN 0-444-85157-7, North-Holland). Elsevier.

Fujita, Neil S. A Crack in the Jar: What Ancient Jewish Documents Tell Us about the New Testament. 304p. (Orig.). 1986. pap. 10.95 (ISBN 0-8091-2745-8). Paulist Pr.

Fujita, S. The Ta Vai Wu Festschrift: Science of Matter. 350p. 1978. 90.25 (ISBN 0-677-13650-1). Gordon.

Fujita, S. Neil. Aim for a Job in Graphic Design & Art. Rev. ed. LC 67-14524. (Aim High Vocational Guidance Ser.). (Illus.). (gr. 7 up). 1979. PLB 8.97 (ISBN 0-8239-0480-6). Rosen Group.

Fujita, Sandra. Whatever Happened to Happily Ever After? (Uplook Ser.). 1981. pap. 0.79 (ISBN 0-8163-0378-9). Pacific Pr Pub Assn.

Fujita, Sandra R. Living with Cancer. (Outreach Ser.). 32p. 1982. pap. 0.99 (ISBN 0-8163-0482-3). Pacific Pr Pub Assn.

Fujita, Shigeji. Introduction to Non-Equilibrium Quantum Statistical Mechanics. LC 82-23209. 178p. 1983. Repr. of 1966 ed. lib. bdg. 14.50 (ISBN 0-89874-593-4). Krieger.

Fujita, Shugeji. Statistical & Thermal Physics, Pt. 1. LC 83-22250. 1985. write for info. (ISBN 0-89874-689-2). Krieger.

--Statistical & Thermal Physics, Pt. 2. 1986. write for info. (ISBN 0-89874-866-6). Krieger.

Fujita, T., jt. auth. see Tanaka, K.

Fujita, Tsuneo, et al. S.E.M. Atlas of Cells & Tissues. LC 80-85298. (Illus.). 338p. 1981. 90.00 (ISBN 0-89640-051-4). Igaku-Shoin.

Fujiwara, Hideo. Logic Testing & Design for Testability. (Series in Computer Systems). (Illus.). 304p. 1985. text ed. 35.00x (ISBN 0-262-06096-5). MIT Pr.

Fujiwara, Iwaichi. F. Kikan: Japanese Army Intelligence Operations in Southeast Asia During World War II. Yoji, Akashi, tr. from Japanese. (Illus.). 338p. (Orig.). 1983. pap. text ed. 14.50x (ISBN 0-686-45946-6, 00157). Heinemann Ed.

Fujiwara, Shizuo & Mark, Harry B., Jr., eds. Information Chemistry: Computer-Assisted Chemical Research Design. (Illus.). 386p. 1976. 65.00x (ISBN 0-86008-150-8, Pub. by Japan Sci Soc Japan). Intl Spec Bk.

Fujiwara, Yoichi. The Sentence Structure of Japanese: Viewed in the Light of Dialectology. Brannen, Noah S. & Baird, Scott J., eds. LC 73-78976. pap. 43.80 (ISBN 0-317-10167-6, 2020443). Bks Demand UMI.

Fujiwara, Yuchiku. Rikka: The Soul of Japanese Flower Arrangement. Sparnon, Norman, tr. from Japanese. (Illus.). 1976. 22.50 (ISBN 4-07-972358-X, Pub. by Shufunotomo Co Ltd Japan). C E Tuttle.

Fujiwara no Nagako. The Emperor Horikawa Diary: Sanuki no Suke Nikki. Brewster, Jennifer, tr. from Japanese. LC 77-89194. 166p. 1978. text ed. 14.00x (ISBN 0-8248-0605-0). UH Pr.

Fukai, Shinji. Ceramics of Ancient Persia. Crawford, Edna, tr. from Japanese. (Illus.). 272p. 1981. 95.00 (ISBN 0-8348-1523-0, Pub. by John Weatherhill Inc Tokyo). C E Tuttle.

--Ceramics of Ancient Persia. (Illus.). 222p. 1981. 95.00 (ISBN 0-8348-1523-0). Weatherhill.

--Persian Glass. LC 77-23736. (Illus.). 1977. 50.00 (ISBN 0-8348-1515-X). Weatherhill.

Fukasaku, Mitsusada. Philippines. LC 76-9352. (This Beautiful World Ser.: Vol. 57). (Illus., Orig.). 1976. pap. 5.25 (ISBN 0-87011-282-1). Kodansha.

Fukei, Budd. The Japanese American Story. LC 75-35578. (Illus.). 160p. 1976. 6.95 (ISBN 0-87518-048-5). Dillon.

Fu-Kiau, Kia B. The Mbongi: An African Traditional Political Institution. 98p. (Orig.). 1985. pap. 9.95 (ISBN 0-943324-14-9). Omenana.

Fukosho, K., jt. auth. see Kuronuma, K.

Fukouka, Masanobu. The One Straw Revolution. 192p. (Orig.). 1985. pap. 3.95 (ISBN 0-553-24739-5). Bantam.

Fuks, Boris A. Introduction to the Theory of Analytic Functions of Several Complex Variables. LC 63-15662. (Translations of Mathematical Monographs: Vol. 8). pap. 99.50 (ISBN 0-317-08581-6, 2012206). Bks Demand UMI.

--Special Chapters in the Theory of Analytic Functions of Several Complex Variables. LC 65-26324. (Translations of Mathematical Monographs: Vol. 14). 1965. 39.00 (ISBN 0-8218-1564-4, MMONO-14). Am Math.

Fuks, D. B. & Rokhlin, V. A. A Beginner's Course in Topology. Iacob, A., tr. from Russian. (Universitext Ser.). (Illus.). xi, 519p. 1984. pap. 32.00 (ISBN 0-387-13577-4). Springer-Verlag.

Fuks, Ladislav. The Cremator. Kandler, E. M., tr. from Czech. 176p. 1985. 14.95 (ISBN 0-7145-2808-0, Dist. by Scribner). M Boyars.

Fukuchi, Nobuo. Nimitz-The Story of Pearl Harbor from the Japanese Perspective (English-Japanese) 1975. 1.00 (ISBN 0-686-15440-1). Adm Nimitz Foun.

Fukuda, Hideichi, jt. tr. see Plutschow, Herbert.

Fukuda, Hitoshi, ed. Irrigation in the World: Comparative Development. 329p. 1976. 42.50x (ISBN 0-86008-174-5, Pub. by U of Tokyo Japan). Columbia U Pr.

Fukuda, Mitsuno, tr. see Uchinomi, Fujio.

Fukuda, Rikutaro, jt. auth. see Witt-Diamant, Ruth.

Fukuda, Ryuji. Managerial Engineering: Techniques for Improving Quality & Productivity in the Workplace. Perlstein, David, ed. Hosoyamada, Noriko, tr. from Japanese. LC 83-62993. (Illus.). 208p. (Orig.). 1983. 34.50 (ISBN 0-915299-01-1); pap. 34.50 (ISBN 0-915299-00-3). Prod Press.

Fukuda, T., jt. auth. see Ejiri, H.

Fukuda, Tadashi. Statokinetic Reflexes in Equilibrium & Movement. Okhubo, Hitoshi & Ushio, Shinya, trs. 311p. 1984. 55.00x (ISBN 0-86008-343-8, Pub. by U of Tokyo Japan). Columbia U Pr.

Fukuda, Tetsuo & Mitsuda, Hisatoshi, eds. World Issues in the Problems of Schizophrenic Psychoses. LC 79-88950. 196p. 1979. 24.50 (ISBN 0-89640-035-2). Igaku-Shoin.

Fukuda, Tetsuo, jt. ed. see Mitsuda, Hisatoshi.

Fukuda, Tsuneari, ed. Future of Japan & the Korean Peninsula. Jahng, K., tr. from Japanese. LC 78-71337. (Illus.). 1978. 14.40x (ISBN 0-930878-14-0). Hollym Intl.

Fukuda, Wayne T., jt. auth. see Montero, James P.

Fukuda, Wayne T., et al. Design Primer. (Illus.). 1979. perfect bdg. 35.00x (ISBN 0-686-24885-6). Archinform.

Fukui, Eiichir O. The Climate of Japan. LC 76-44473. (Developments in Atmospheric Science Ser.: Vol. 8). 318p. 1977. 89.50 (ISBN 0-444-99818-7). Elsevier.

Fukui, Haruhiro. Political Parties of Asia & the Pacific, 2 vols. Hughes, Colin A., et al, eds. LC 84-19252. (Historical Encyclopedia of the World's Political Parties Ser.). (Illus.). 1376p. 1985. Set. lib. bdg. 145.00 (ISBN 0-313-21350-X, FUA/). Greenwood.

Fukui, Hatsuaki, ed. Low-Noise Microwave Transistors & Amplifiers. LC 81-6994. 1981. 38.45 (ISBN 0-87942-151-7, PC01487). Inst Electrical.

Fukui, K. Theory of Orientation & Stereoselection. LC 75-25597. (Reactivity & Structure: Vol. 2). (Illus.). 120p. 1975. 27.00 (ISBN 0-387-07426-0). Springer-Verlag.

Fukui, Kenichi, ed. see Third International Congress of Quantum Chemistry, Kyoto, Japan, October 29 - Nov. 3, 1979.

Fukui, S. & Tanaka, A. Immobilized Biocatalysts-Saccharomyces Yeasts-Wastewater Treatment. (Advances in Biochemical Engineering Biotech 29 Ser.). (Illus.). 160p. 1984. 33.00 (ISBN 0-387-12860-3). Springer-Verlag.

Fukui, Saburo, jt. ed. see Chibata, Ichiro.

Fukuma, Seikan. Monshin: Hearing Faith. LC 83-60645. 150p. 1983. 7.95 (ISBN 0-912624-02-7). Nembutsu Pr.

Fukunaga, Keinosuke. Introduction to Statistical Pattern Recognition. (Electrical Science Ser.). 1972. 80.00 (ISBN 0-12-269850-9). Acad Pr.

Fukunaga, Shigeki. Contemporary Studio Glass: An International Collection. LC 82-4775. (Illus.). 240p. (Japanese.). 1982. 175.00 (ISBN 0-8348-1525-7). Weatherhill.

Fukuoka, Masanobu. The Natural Way of Farming: The Theory & Practice of Green Philosophy. LC 84-81353. (Illus.). 256p. (Orig.). 1985. pap. 13.95 (ISBN 0-87040-613-2). Japan Pubns USA.

--One Straw Revolution. LC 78-1930. 1978. 9.95 (ISBN 0-87857-220-1). Rodale Pr Inc.

Fukurai, T. Clairvoyance & Thoughtography. LC 75-7379. (Perspectives in Psychical Research Ser.). (Illus.). 1975. Repr. of 1931 ed. 21.00x (ISBN 0-405-07029-2). Ayer Co Pubs.

Fukushima, E. & Roeder, S. B. W. Experimental Pulse NMR: A Nuts & Bolts Approach. 1981. 42.95 (ISBN 0-201-10403-2). Addison-Wesley.

Fukushima, H. Index Guide to Rational Drug Therapy. 388p. 1982. 70.25 (ISBN 0-444-90273-2, Excerpta Medica). Elsevier.

Fukushima, H., et al. Index Guide to Drug Information Retrieval. 280p. 1979. 63.50 (ISBN 0-444-80139-1, Biomedical Pr). Elsevier.

Fukushima, M. Dirichlet Forms & Markov Processes. (North-Holland Mathematical Library: Vol. 23). 196p. 1980. 51.00 (ISBN 0-444-85421-5, North Holland). Elsevier.

--Functional Analysis in Markov Processes, Katata & Kyoto, Japan 1981 Proceedings. (Lecture Notes in Mathematics: Vol. 923). 307p. 1982. pap. 20.00 (ISBN 0-387-11484-X). Springer-Verlag.

Fukushima, Sho & Russell, Wrio. Men's Gymnastics. (Illus.). 224p. 1980. 25.00 (ISBN 0-571-11478-4). Faber & Faber.

Fukutake, Tadashi. Japanese Rural Society. Dore, R. P., tr. from Japanese. (Illus.). 230p. 1972. pap. 9.95x (ISBN 0-8014-9127-4, CP127). Cornell U Pr.

--The Japanese Social Structure: Its Evolution in the Modern Century. Dore, Ronald P., tr. 246p. 1986. pap. text ed. 14.50x (ISBN 0-86008-380-2, Pub. by U of Tokyo Japan). Columbia U Pr.

--Japanese Social Structure, 1870-1980. Dore, Ronald P., tr. 232p. 1982. 20.00x (ISBN 0-86008-316-0, Pub. by U of Tokyo Japan). Columbia U Pr.

--Japanese Society Today. 2nd ed. 165p. 1981. pap. 12.00x (ISBN 0-86008-291-1, Pub. by U of Tokyo Japan). Columbia U Pr.

Fukutake, Tadashi, ed. Rural Society in Japan. Japan Interpreter Staff, tr. 218p. 1980. 20.00x (ISBN 0-86008-266-0, Pub. by U of Tokyo Japan). Columbia U Pr.

Fukutake, Tadashi & Morioka, Kiyomi, eds. Sociology & Social Development in Asia: Proceedings of the Symposium. 445p. 1974. 40.00x (ISBN 0-86008-119-2, Pub. by U of Tokyo Japan). Columbia U Pr.

Fukuya, S. M. see Tolman, Edward.

Fukuyama, H., jt. ed. see Nagaoka, Y.

Fukuyama, Toshio. Heian Temples: Buodo-in & Chuson-Ji. LC 75-41337. (Heibonsha Survey of Japanese Art Ser.: Vol. 9). (Illus.). 164p. 1976. 17.50 (ISBN 0-8348-1023-9). Weatherhill.

Fukuyama, Y., et al, eds. Child Neurology: Proceedings of the Tokyo Meeting, 1981. (International Congress Ser.: Vol. 579). 420p. 1983. 93.75 (ISBN 0-444-90257-0, Excerpta Medica). Elsevier.

Fukuyama, Yoshio. The Ministry in Transition: A Case Study of Theological Education. LC 72-1395. 200p. 1973. 22.50x (ISBN 0-271-01129-7). Pa St U Pr.

Fukuzawa, Yukichi. Autobiography. Kiyooka, E., tr. from Jap. LC 66-15468. (Illus.). 407p. 1966. 37.50x (ISBN 0-231-02884-9); pap. 15.00x (ISBN 0-231-08373-4). Columbia U Pr.

Fula, Arthur N. The Golden Magnet. Lasker, Carrol, tr. from Afrikaans. LC 81-51642. 175p. 1984. 17.00 (ISBN 0-89410-291-5); pap. 7.00. Three Continents.

Fulachier, L., jt. ed. see Dumas, R.

Fulbecke, William. A Booke of Christian Ethicks or Moral Philosophie. LC 74-28856. (English Experience Ser.: No. 737). 1975. Repr. of 1587 ed. 6.00 (ISBN 90-221-0737-X). Walter J Johnson.

--The Pandectes of the Law of Nations. LC 79-84109. (English Experience Ser.: No.928). 192p. 1979. Repr. of 1602 ed. lib. bdg. 18.00 (ISBN 90-221-0928-3). Walter J Johnson.

Fulbert. The Letters & Poems of Fulbert of Chartres. Behrends, Frederick, ed. (Oxford Medieval Texts). 1976. 84.00x (ISBN 0-19-822233-5). Oxford U Pr.

Fulbright, J. William, et al. The Future of the United Nations. LC 77-70420. (Orig.). 1977. pap. 3.75 (ISBN 0-8447-2094-1). Am Enterprise.

Fulbright, Norma, et al. Young Children & Their Environments... A Readings Book Approach. 150p. 1975. pap. text ed. 6.95x (ISBN 0-8290-1389-X). Irvington.

Fulbright, Robert G. The Bible-A Special Book. (gr. 4-6). 1985. pap. 3.95 (ISBN 0-317-30995-1, 4244-17). Broadman.

--Old Testament Friends: Men of Courage. (BibLearn Ser.). (Illus.). (gr. 1-6). 1979. 5.95 (ISBN 0-8054-4251-0, 4242-51). Broadman.

Fulbrook, Julian. Administrative Justice & the Unemployed. (Studies in Labour & Social Law: Vol. 1). 356p. 1978. lib. bdg. 32.00x (ISBN 0-7201-0555-2). Mansell.

Fulbrook, Mary. Piety & Politics: Religion & the Rise of Absolutism in England, Wurttemberg & Prussia. LC 83-5316. 224p. 1984. 34.50 (ISBN 0-521-25612-7); pap. 12.95 (ISBN 0-521-27633-0). Cambridge U Pr.

Fulcanelli. Fulcanelli: Master Alchemist. Sworder, Mary, tr. from Fr. Orig. Title: Le Mystere des Cathedrales. (Illus.). 240p. 1984. pap. 12.95 (ISBN 0-914732-14-5). Bro Life Inc.

--Fulcanelli: Master Alchemist, le Mystere Des Cathedrales. 2nd ed. Sworder, Mary, tr. (Illus.). 1977. Repr. of 1971 ed. cancelled (ISBN 0-914732-06-4). Bro Life Inc.

Fulcher, A., et al. Painting & Decorating: An Information Manual. 2nd ed. (Illus.). 226p. 1981. pap. text ed. 17.25x (ISBN 0-246-11613-7, Pub. by Granada England). Brookfield Pub Co.

Fulcher, Alf, et al. Basic Building Craft Science. 164p. 1981. text ed. 14.50x (ISBN 0-246-11265-4, Pub. by Granada England). Brookfield Pub Co.

Fulcher, Claire & Grefe, Mary. Techniques for Organizational Effectiveness. 90p. 1978. 4.00 (ISBN 0-318-12415-7); members 3.00 (ISBN 0-318-12416-5). Am Assn Univ Women.

Fulcher, Derick H. Medical Care Systems: Public & Private Health Insurance in Selected Industrialised Countries. vi, 178p. (Eng., Fr. & Span.). 1974. pap. 10.00 (ISBN 92-2-101160-7, ILO3, ILO). Unipub.

Fulcher, Gordon C. Common Sense Decision-Making. LC 65-14421. pap. 22.50 (ISBN 0-317-10298-2, 2010128). Bks Demand UMI.

Fulcher, Leon C. & Ainsworth, Frank, eds. Group Care Practice with Children. 300p. (Orig.). 1985. text ed. 27.50 (ISBN 0-422-78190-8, 9630); pap. text ed. 12.95 (ISBN 0-422-78200-9, 9631). Methuen Inc.

Fulcher, Leon C., jt. ed. see Ainsworth, Frank.

Fulcher, Paul M. Foundations of English Style. 316p. 1980. Repr. of 1928 ed. lib. bdg. 25.00 (ISBN 0-89984-201-1). Century Bookbindery.

Fulcher, Walter. The Way I Heard It: Tales of the Big Bend. Miles, Elton, ed. LC 59-8126. (Illus.). 113p. 1973. Repr. of 1959 ed. pap. 5.95 (ISBN 0-292-79027-9). U of Tex Pr.

--The Way I Heard It: Tales of the Big Bend. Miles, Milton, ed. (Illus.). 113p. 1985. pap. 5.95 (ISBN 0-292-79027-9). U of Tex Pr.

Fulcher Of Chartres. A History of the Expedition to Jerusalem, 1095-1127. Fink, Sr. Harold S., ed. 1972. pap. text ed. 6.95x (ISBN 0-393-09423-5). Norton.

Fulchignoni, M., jt. ed. see Coradini, A.

Fulco, Armand J., jt. auth. see Mead, James F.

Fuld, G., jt. auth. see Fuld, M.

Fuld, George & Fuld, Melvin. Patriotic Civil War Tokens. LC 81-423. (Illus.). 80p. 1981. pap. 10.00x (ISBN 0-88000-128-3). Quarterman.

--U. S. Civil War Store Cards. rev. ed. LC 75-1785. (Illus.). 704p. 1975. 50.00x (ISBN 0-88000-135-6). Quarterman.

Fuld, George, jt. auth. see Rulau, Russ.

Fuld, James J., ed. The Book of World-Famous Libretti: The Musical Theater from 1598 to Today. (Illus.). 400p. 1984. lib. bdg. 48.00 (ISBN 0-918728-27-4). Pendragon NY.

Fuld, Leonard M. Competitive Intelligence: How to Get It, How to Use It. LC 84-19539. 720p. 1985. 24.95 (ISBN 0-471-80967-5). Wiley.

Fuld, Leonhard Felix. Police Administration: A Critical Study of Police Organizations in the United States and Abroad. LC 70-152105. (Criminology, Law Enforcement, & Social Problems Ser.: No. 141). (Illus.). 583p. (With intro. added). 1971. Repr. of 1909 ed. 18.00x (ISBN 0-87585-141-X). Patterson Smith.

Fuld, M. & Fuld, G. Guide to Civil War Store Cards. LC 82-71865. (Illus.). 1982. pap. 10.00 (ISBN 0-915262-97-5). S J Durst.

Fuld, Melvin, jt. auth. see Fuld, George.

Fulda, Michael. Oil & International Relations: Energy, Trade, Technology & Politics. Bruchey, Stuart, ed. LC 78-22681. (Energy in the American Economy Ser.). (Illus.). 1979. lib. bdg. 23.00x (ISBN 0-405-11984-4). Ayer Co Pubs.

Fulder, Stephen. About Ginseng: The Magical Herb of the East. (About Ser.). 64p. (Orig.). 1984. pap. 1.95 (ISBN 0-7225-1000-4). Thorsons Pubs.

--An End to Aging: Remedies for Life Extensions. 111p. 1983. pap. 5.95 (ISBN 0-89281-044-0). Destiny Bks.

--The Root of Being: Ginseng & the Pharmacology of Harmony. 1980. 26.00x (ISBN 0-09-142041-5, Pub. by Rider England). State Mutual Bk.

--Tao of Medicine: Ginseng, Oriental Remedies & the Pharmacology of Harmony. LC 82-1066. (Illus.). 328p. 1982. text ed. 9.95 (ISBN 0-89281-027-0). Destiny Bks.

Fulenwider, Claire K. Feminism in American Politics: A Study of Ideological Influence. LC 79-25131. 182p. 1980. 31.95 (ISBN 0-03-053461-5). Praeger.

Fulep, F. Sopianae. (Archaeologia Hungarica: Vol. 50). 391p. 1984. text ed. 57.00x (ISBN 963-05-3017-1, Pub. by Akademia Kiado Hungary). Humanities.

Fulford, M. G., jt. ed. see Cunliffe, B. W.

Fulford, Robert, jt. auth. see Murray, Joan.

Fulford, Roger. Wicked Uncles: The Father of Queen Victoria - His Brothers. facs. ed. LC 68-8461. (Essay Index Reprint Ser). 1968. Repr. of 1933 ed. 19.00 (ISBN 0-8369-0466-4). Ayer Co Pubs.

Fulgham, Barbara. Fifty Simple Ready-to-Run VIC-20 Programs. (Illus.). 176p. (Orig.). 1984. 12.95 (ISBN 0-8306-0754-4); pap. 6.95 (ISBN 0-8306-1754-X, 1754). TAB Bks.

Fulghum, David & Maitland, Terrence. South Vietnam on Trial. Manning, Robert, ed. LC 84-71522. (The Vietnam Experience Ser.: Vol. X). (Illus.). 192p. 1984. 16.95 (ISBN 0-939526-10-7). Boston Pub Co.

Fulghum, David, jt. auth. see Dougan, Clark.

Fulghum, Thomas. Tommy: The Comeback Kid. 1983. text ed. 8.95 (ISBN 0-88207-649-3). Victor Bks.

Fulginiti, Vincent A. Immunization in Clinical Practice: A Useful Guideline to Vaccines, Sera, & Immune Globulins in Clinical Practice. (Illus.). 192p. 1982. pap. text ed. 24.75 (ISBN 0-397-50539-6, 65-06869, Lippincott Medical). Lippincott.

Fulginiti, Vincent A., jt. auth. see Stiehm, E. Richard.

Fulk, Virginia N. The Reading Resource Book: Tried & True Reading Activities for Elementary Students. LC 83-83317. 224p. (Orig.). 1984. pap. text ed. 19.95 (ISBN 0-918452-68-6). Learning Pubns.

Fulke, William. Defence of the Sincere & True Translations of the Holy Scriptures into the English Tongue. Repr. of 1843 ed. 51.00 (ISBN 0-384-17230-X). Johnson Repr.

--Stapleton's Fortress Overthrown: A Rejoinder to Martiall's Reply. Repr. of 1848 ed. 31.00 (ISBN 0-384-17240-7). Johnson Repr.

Fulker, D. W., jt. auth. see Eysenck, H. J.

Fulker, Edmund N. A Model & Checklist for Administrator, Manager & Executive Career Training & Development. 1980. 2.00 (ISBN 0-87771-018-X). Grad School.

Fulker, John E. And True Deliverance Make. LC 85-80432. (Illus.). 250p. Date not set. 10.00x (ISBN 0-8338-0192-9). M Jones.

Fulker, Mary, jt. auth. see Fulker, Wilber H.

Fulker, Tina. Jukebox. LC 80-81851. 56p. 1980. pap. 3.00 (ISBN 0-9602424-4-9). Paycock Pr.

Fulker, Wilber H. & Fulker, Mary. Techniques with Tangibles: A Manual for Teaching the Blind. 84p. 1968. photocopy ed. 9.50x (ISBN 0-398-00628-8). C C Thomas.

Fulkerson, Christopher. Concerto for Harpsichord & Seven Instruments. Stover, Franklin, ed. LC 85-70263. 50p. (Orig.). 1985. pap. 11.50 (ISBN 0-931553-03-2). Comp Graphics.

Fulkerson, D. R., jt. auth. see Ford, Lester R., Jr.

Fulkerson, D. R., ed. Studies in Graph Theory, 2 pts. LC 75-24987. (MAA Studies in Mathematics: No. 11 & 12). Pt. 1, 01/1976, 199p. 16.50 (ISBN 0-88385-111-3); Pt. 2, 1976, 212p. 16.50. Math Assn.

--Studies in Graph Theory: Part II. LC 75-24987. (MAA Studies: No. 12). 212p. 1976. 16.50 (ISBN 0-88385-112-1). Math Assn.

Fulkerson, H. S. Random Recollections of Early Days in Mississippi. 1972. 10.00 (ISBN 0-87511-597-7). Claitors.

Fulkerson, Katherine. The Merchandise Buyers' Game. 1981. pap. text ed. 6.25x (ISBN 0-933836-13-9). Simtek.

Fulkerson, Paul C. How to Keep up with the Whiz Kids on the Commodore 64. (Illus.). 240p. pap. cancelled (ISBN 0-89303-501-7). Brady Comm.

Fulkerson, W. J. Hormonal Control of Lactation, Vol. 1. Horrobin, D. F., ed. (Annual Research Reviews). 1980. 18.00 (ISBN 0-88831-061-7). Eden Pr.

Fulkerson, William J. Hormonal Control of Lactation: Vol. 2. Horrobin, David F., ed. (Annual Research Reviews). 84p. 1981. 14.00 (ISBN 0-88831-087-0). Eden Pr.

Fulks, Danny G. Informal Learning in Elementary Schools. LC 78-61303. 1978. pap. text ed. 9.25 (ISBN 0-8191-0606-2). U Pr of Amer.

Fulks, Watson. Advanced Calculus: An Introduction to Analysis. 3rd ed. LC 78-5268. 731p. 1978. text ed. 42.50 (ISBN 0-471-02195-4); avail. solutions (ISBN 0-471-05125-X). Wiley.

Full, Harold. Controversy in American Education: An Anthology of Crucial Issues. 2nd ed. 448p. 1972. pap. text ed. write for info. (ISBN 0-02-339960-0, 33996). Macmillan.

Fullam, Everett L. Your Body, God's Temple. 96p. 1984. pap. 4.95 (ISBN 0-310-60851-1, Pub by Chosen Bks). Zondervan.

Fullam, Everett L. & Slosser, Bob. Living the Lord's Prayer. 144p. 1981. pap. 4.95 (ISBN 0-310-60001-4, Pub by Chosen Bks). Zondervan.

Fullan, Michael. The Meaning of Educational Change. 1982. pap. text ed. 19.95x (ISBN 0-8077-2712-1). Tchrs Coll.

Fullana Llompart, Miguel. Diccionario De L'art I Els Oficis De la Construccion. 440p. (Catalan.). 1974. 35.95 (ISBN 84-273-0372-6, S-50000). French & Eur.

Fullard, Harold & Darby, H. C. Atlas General Larousse. Reynaud-Dulaurier, Georges, ed. (Illus.). 312p. (Fr.). 1973. 88.50 (ISBN 2-03-000922-9, 997). Larousse.

Fullard, Harold, jt. auth. see Ginsberg, Norton.

Fullard, Harold, ed. see Muir, Ramsey.

Fullard, Harold, et al, eds. The Prentice-Hall University Atlas. LC 84-675201. (Illus.). 144p. 1984. 27.50 (ISBN 0-13-698259-X). P-H.

Fullarton, John. On the Regulation of Currencies. 2nd ed. LC 68-55714. Repr. of 1845 ed. 35.00x (ISBN 0-678-00571-0). Kelley.

Fullarton, John, ed. Records of the Burgh of Prestwick in the Sheriffdom of Ayr. LC 76-174286. (Maitland Club. Glasgow. Publications: No. 27). Repr. of 1834 ed. 20.00 (ISBN 0-404-52983-6). AMS Pr.

Fullenbach. European Environmental Policy East & West. 1981. text ed. 59.95 (ISBN 0-408-10689-1). Butterworth.

Fullen-Tabor. One Plus One: An Integrated Approach to Communication. 4th ed. 232p. 1984. pap. text ed. 16.95 (ISBN 0-8403-3347-1). Kendall-Hunt.

Fullenwider, Malcolm A. Hydrogen Entry & Action in Metals. (Illus.). 125p. 1983. 32.00 (ISBN 0-08-027526-5). Pergamon.

Fuller. Concise Dental Anatomy. 2nd ed. 1984. 22.50 (ISBN 0-8151-3298-0). Year Bk Med.

--New Catholic Commentary on Holy Scriptures. 1975. 49.50 (ISBN 0-442-30677-6). Van Nos Reinhold.

--Payroll Procedures. 1985. text ed. 4.15 (ISBN 0-538-11660-9, K66). SW Pub.

Fuller, jt. auth. see Von Bozzay, George D.

Fuller, jt. ed. see Brant.

Fuller, jt. ed. see Freiman.

Fuller, et al. Upright Downfall. 10.95 (ISBN 0-19-276052-1, Pub. by Oxford U Pr Childrens). Merrimack Pub Cir.

Fuller, Alvarado M. A. D. Two Thousand. LC 71-154441. (Utopian Literature Ser). (Illus.). 1971. Repr. of 1890 ed. 34.00 (ISBN 0-405-03524-1). Ayer Co Pubs.

Fuller, Andrew R. Psychology & Religion: Eight Points of View. 143p. 1977. pap. text ed. 8.75 (ISBN 0-8191-0143-5). U Pr of Amer.

Fuller, Anna. Later Pratt Portraits: Sketched in a New England Suburb. LC 79-122709. (Short Story Index Reprint Ser). (Illus.). 1911. 21.00 (ISBN 0-8369-3542-X). Ayer Co Pubs.

--Peak & Prairie. LC 75-94724. (Short Story Index Reprint Ser.). 1894. 22.00 (ISBN 0-8369-3103-3). Ayer Co Pubs.

--Pratt Portraits. LC 79-94725. (Short Story Index Reprint Ser.). 1897. 19.00 (ISBN 0-8369-3104-1). Ayer Co Pubs.

Fuller, Anne H. Buarij: Portrait of a Lebanese Muslim Village. LC 61-14633. (Middle Eastern Monographs Ser: No. 6). 1961. pap. 4.50x (ISBN 0-674-08550-7). Harvard U Pr.

Fuller, Anthony M. & Mage, Julius A. Part-Time Farming. (Rural Geography Ser.). 291p. 1980. pap. 13.80x (ISBN 0-902246-57-7, Pub. by GEO Abstracts England). State Mutual Bk.

Fuller, Arlan F., Jr., jt. auth. see Griffiths, C. Thomas.

Fuller, Arthur, jt. auth. see Perry, George S.

Fuller, Arthur B., ed. see Ossoli, Margaret F.

Fuller, Arthur B., ed. see Ossoli, Sarah M.

Fuller, B. Frank, jt. auth. see Fuller, Benjamin J.

Fuller, Barry, et al. Single-Camera Video Production Handbook: Techniques, Equipment, & Resources for Producing Quality Video Programs. (Illus.). 252p. 1982. 26.95 (ISBN 0-13-810762-9); pap. 16.95 (ISBN 0-13-810754-8). P-H.

Fuller, Benjamin A. History of Greek Philosophy, 3 vols. Set. lib. bdg. 53.50x (ISBN 0-8371-0427-0, FUGP). Greenwood.

Fuller, Benjamin J. & Fuller, B. Frank. Physician or Magician: The Myths & Realities of Patient Care. (Illus.). 1979. pap. text ed. 14.95 (ISBN 0-07-022617-2). McGraw.

Fuller, Buckminster. Operating Manual for Spaceship Earth. 13.95 (ISBN 0-89190-235-X, Pub. by Am Repr). Amereon Ltd.

Fuller, Buckminster & Dil, Anwar. Humans in Universe. (Illus.). 235p. 1983. 19.95 (ISBN 0-89925-001-7). Mouton.

Fuller, Buckminster, et al. Windfall Poems Nineteen Seventy-Seven to Nineteen Seventy-Eight: A Special Original Collection. Bush, George, ed. 1977. text ed. 5.00 (ISBN 0-9610536-0-7). Mainespring.

Fuller, C. J. The Nayars Today. LC 76-11078. (Changing Cultures Ser.). (Illus.). 1977. pap. 12.95 (ISBN 0-521-29091-0). Cambridge U Pr.

Fuller, Charlene, jt. auth. see Austin, Joan B.

Fuller, Charles. A Soldier's Play. (Mermaid Dramabook). 100p. 1982. 12.50 (ISBN 0-8090-8745-6); pap. 6.95 (ISBN 0-8090-1244-8). Hill & Wang.

Fuller, Chester. Spend Sad Sundays Singing Songs to Sassy Sisters. 1974. pap. 1.50 (ISBN 0-88378-037-2). Third World.

Fuller, Christopher J. Servants of the Goddess: The Priest of a South Indian Temple. LC 83-14369. (Cambridge Studies in Social Anthropology: No. 47). (Illus.). 240p. 1984. 39.50 (ISBN 0-521-24777-2). Cambridge U Pr.

Fuller, Claud E. Breech-Loader in the Service 1816-1917. LC 65-27415. (Illus.). 1965. 14.50 (ISBN 0-910598-03-7). Flayderman.

Fuller, Claude E. & Stewart, Richard D. Firearms of the Confederacy. LC 76-53698. 1977. Repr. of 1944 ed. 25.00x (ISBN 0-88000-103-8). Quarterman.

Fuller, Clifford. Let's Try This Way. pap. 1.00 (ISBN 0-87516-196-0). De Vorss.

Fuller, Daniel P. Gospel & Law: Contrast or Continuum? the Hermeaneutics of Dispensationalism & Covenant Theology. (Orig.). 1980. pap. 8.95 (ISBN 0-8028-1808-0). Eerdmans.

Fuller, David. Mechanical Musical Instruments As a Source for the Study of Notes Inegales. (Illus.). 20p. 1979. pap. 7.00 (ISBN 0-934276-00-5). Divisions.

Fuller, David O., ed. Counterfeit or Genuine? LC 74-82807. 1975. pap. 6.95 (ISBN 0-8254-2615-4). Kregel.

--Treasury of Evangelical Writings. LC 61-9768. 1974. pap. 8.95 (ISBN 0-8254-2613-8). Kregel.

--True or False? LC 72-93355. 1975. pap. 6.95 (ISBN 0-8254-2614-6). Kregel.

--Which Bible? 6th, rev. ed. LC 70-129737. 1975. pap. 6.95 (ISBN 0-8254-2612-X). Kregel.

Fuller, Dean. Passage. 1983. 13.95 (ISBN 0-396-08134-7). Dodd.

Fuller, Dudely D., et al. Theory & Practice of Lubrication for Engineers. 2nd ed. LC 83-27394. 682p. 1984. text ed. 64.95x (ISBN 0-471-04703-1, Pub. by Wiley-Interscience). Wiley.

Fuller, Dwain & Hutton, William, eds. Presurgical Evaluation of Eyes with Opaque Media. 240p. 1982. 46.00 (ISBN 0-8089-1470-7, 791460). Grune.

Fuller, E. G. & Hayward, E., eds. Photonuclear Reactions. (Benchmark Papers in Nuclear Physics: Vol. 2). 1976. 73.00 (ISBN 0-12-786495-4). Acad Pr.

Fuller, E. L., Jr., ed. Coal & Coal Products: Analytical Characterization Techniques. LC 82-18442. (ACS Symposium Ser.: No. 205). 326p. 1982. lib. bdg. 49.95 (ISBN 0-8412-0748-8). Am Chemical.

Fuller, Ed. Children of Divorce. (Orig.). 1981. pap. 4.50 (ISBN 0-8309-0322-4). Herald Hse.

Fuller, Edmund, ed. The Christian Idea of Education. x, 265p. 1975. Repr. of 1957 ed. 18.50 (ISBN 0-208-01470-5, Archon). Shoe String.

Fuller, Edmund, ed. see Bulfinch, Thomas.

Fuller, Edmund, ed. see Dickens, Charles.

Fuller, Edmund, ed. see Royster, Vermont.

Fuller, Elizabeth. Having Your First Baby after Thirty. LC 82-23548. 1983. 10.95 (ISBN 0-396-08154-1). Dodd.

--Having Your First Baby after Thirty: A Personal Journey from Infertility to Childbirth. 192p. 1984. pap. 7.95 (ISBN 0-396-08425-7). Dodd.

--Nima: A Sherpa in Connecticut. (Illus.). 224p. 1984. 14.95 (ISBN 0-396-08304-8). Dodd.

Fuller, Elizabeth E. Milton's Kinesthetic Vision in Paradise Lost. LC 81-65862. 320p. 1983. 37.50 (ISBN 0-8387-5027-3). Bucknell U Pr.

Fuller, Elizabeth G., jt. auth. see Swanson, Susan C.

Fuller, Ethel R. Kitchen Sonnets. 2nd ed. 1956. 4.50 (ISBN 0-8323-0142-6). Binford.

--Skylines. 1978. pap. 3.95 (ISBN 0-8323-0333-X). Binford.

Fuller, Eugene T. Priceless Possesion of a Few. 1974. 10.00 (ISBN 0-913902-41-1). Heart Am Pr.

Fuller, Francis. Vanished Dynasty Ashanti. 2nd ed. (Illus.). 241p. 1968. 32.50x (ISBN 0-7146-1663-X, F Cass Co). Biblio Dist.

Fuller, Frank. Deep Foundations. LC 80-69155. 544p. 1980. pap. 25.00x (ISBN 0-87262-256-8). Am Soc Civil Eng.

--Engineering of Pile Installations. (Illus.). 320p. 1983. 44.50 (ISBN 0-07-022618-0). McGraw.

Fuller, Frederick. The Translator's Handbook: With Special Reference to Conference Translation from French & Spanish. LC 83-22107. 160p. 1984. 12.50x (ISBN 0-271-00368-5). Pa St U Pr.

Fuller, George. Preparing for Paradise. 52p. 1985. 10.95 (ISBN 0-937310-27-1); pap. 5.95 (ISBN 0-937310-26-3). Jazz Pr.

Fuller, George & Simon, Marjorie. Adam & Eve, Etc. (Illus.). 110p. (Orig.). 1981. pap. text ed. 4.95 (ISBN 0-937310-11-5). Jazz Pr.

Fuller, George D. Behavioral Medicine, Stress Management & Biofeedback. (Orig.). 1980. pap. 225.00 (ISBN 0-686-27972-7); with sound-slide program 275.00 (ISBN 0-686-27973-5). Biofeed Pr.

--Biofeedback: Methods & Procedures in Clinical Practice. (Orig.). 1977. pap. 18.00 (ISBN 0-686-25138-5). Biofeed Pr.

--Projects in Biofeedback. (Orig.). 1980. pap. 16.95 (ISBN 0-686-27974-3). Biofeed Pr.

Fuller, George D., tr. see Braun-Blanquet, J.

Fuller, George D., jt. auth. see Jones, G. Neville.

Fuller, George W. A History of the Pacific Northwest. LC 75-41106. Repr. of 1931 ed. 32.50 (ISBN 0-404-14664-3). AMS Pr.

Fuller, George W., ed. A Bibliography of Bookplate Literature. LC 72-178635. 151p. 1971. Repr. of 1926 ed. 48.00x (ISBN 0-8103-3190-X). Gale.

Fuller Goldeen Gallery. Robert Hudson: 1983. LC 83-80400. (Illus.). 1983. pap. 8.00x (ISBN 0-9607452-2-X). Fuller Golden Gal.

Fuller, Gordon. Algebra & Trigonometry. 1971. text ed. 28.95 (ISBN 0-07-022605-9). McGraw.

--Analytic Geometry. 5th ed. LC 78-55820. 1979. text ed. 26.95 (ISBN 0-201-02414-4); ans. bk. 1.50 (ISBN 0-201-02415-2). Addison-Wesley.

--Plane Trigonometry with Tables. 5th ed. LC 77-22329. (Illus.). 1978. text ed. 29.95 (ISBN 0-07-022612-1). McGraw.

Fuller, Gordon, et al. College Algebra. 5th ed. LC 81-21779. (Mathematics Ser.). 500p. 1982. text ed. 21.50 (ISBN 0-534-01138-1). Brooks-Cole.

Fuller, Harold Q., et al. Physics: Including Human Application. 1978. text ed. 25.75 scp (ISBN 0-06-042214-9, HarpC); scp lab manual 11.50 (ISBN 0-06-042212-2); scp study guide 9.50 (ISBN 0-06-042213-0). Har-Row.

Fuller, Harry J. & Ritchie, Donald D. General Botany. 5th ed. (Illus.). 1967. pap. 5.95 (ISBN 0-06-460033-5, CO 33, COS). B&N NY.

Fuller, Harry J., et al. Plant World. 5th ed. LC 72-150106. 1972. text ed. 35.95x (ISBN 0-03-077395-4, HoltC). HR&W.

Fuller, Harry, Jr., jt. ed. see Dorfman, Ron.

Fuller, Hector. Roach & Company - Pirates & Other Stories. LC 78-113662. (Short Story Index Reprint Ser.). 1897. 17.00 (ISBN 0-8369-3391-5). Ayer Co Pubs.

Fuller, Henry B. Bertram Cope's Year. LC 78-63987. (Gay Experience Sev.). Repr. of 1919 ed. 26.00 (ISBN 0-404-61506-6). AMS Pr.

--The Chevalier of Pensieri Vani. LC 71-104457. Repr. of 1891 ed. lib. bdg. 14.00 (ISBN 0-8398-0569-1). Irvington.

Fuller, Roger & Stevenson, Olive. Policies, Programmes & Disadvantage: A Review of the Literature. (DHSS Studies in Deprivation & Disadvantage: No. 9). viii, 232p. 1983. text ed. 30.00x (ISBN 0-435-82330-2). Gower Pub Co.

Fuller, Roland & Levy, Allen. The Bassett-Lowke Story. LC 84-71044. (Illus.). 352p. 1984. 29.95 (ISBN 0-88740-008-6). Schiffer.

Fuller, Ronald. Literary Craftsmanship & Appreciation. 1973. lib. bdg. 20.00 (ISBN 0-8414-4287-8). Folcroft.

--Pilgrim: John Bunyan's Pilgrim's Progress Retold. LC 80-156. (Illus.). 48p. (gr. 5 up). 1980. 9.95 (ISBN 0-916144-44-5). Stemmer Hse.

Fuller, Roy. Collected Poems. LC 62-51612. 1962. 13.95 (ISBN 0-8023-1046-X). Dufour.

--From the Joke Shop. 64p. 1975. 10.95 (ISBN 0-233-96670-6). Dufour.

--The Individual & His Times: A Selection of the Poetry of Roy Fuller. Lee, V. J., ed. 99p. 1982. pap. 8.95 (ISBN 0-485-61008-6, Pub. by Athlone Pr Ltd). Longwood Pub Group.

--New Poems. LC 68-31827. 1968. 10.00 (ISBN 0-8023-1180-6). Dufour.

--Owls & Artificers: Oxford Lectures on Poetry. LC 70-158611. 145p. 1971. 14.95 (ISBN 0-912050-06-3). Open Court.

--Professors & Gods. LC 74-75010. 176p. 1974. 20.00 (ISBN 0-312-64785-9). St Martin.

--Souvenirs. 1980. 25.00x (ISBN 0-904388-30-1, Pub. by London Mag Edns England). State Mutual Bk.

Fuller, Roy, ed. Fellow Mortals: An Anthology of Animal Verse. (Illus.). 274p. 1984. 15.95 (ISBN 0-7121-0635-9, Pub. by Salem Hse Ltd). Merrimack Pub Cir.

Fuller, S. H. Analysis of Drum & Disk Storage Units. (Lecture Notes in Computer Science Ser.: Vol. 31). ix, 283p. 1975. pap. 19.00 (ISBN 0-387-07186-5). Springer-Verlag.

Fuller, Samuel. The Dark Page. 256p. 1983. pap. 2.95 (ISBN 0-380-62117-7, 62117-7). Avon.

Fuller, Samuel, jt. auth. see Hart, C. W.

Fuller, Samuel L. H., jt. ed. see Hart, C. W.

Fuller, Sara. The Ohio Black History Guide. 221p. 1975. 5.00 (ISBN 0-318-03184-1). Ohio Hist Soc.

Fuller, Sara S. The Paul Laurence Dunbar Collection: An Inventory to the Microfilm Edition. 40p. 1972. 1.25 (ISBN 0-318-03199-X). Ohio Hist Soc.

Fuller, Sarah. Fuller: European Musical Heritage. 352p. 1986. pap. text ed. 19.95 (ISBN 0-394-32951-1, KnopfC). Knopf.

Fuller, T., jt. auth. see Cox, S.

Fuller, Theodore, jt. auth. see Lightfoot, Paul.

Fuller, Thoams. The Church History of Britain, from the Birth of Jesus Christ Until the Year 1648, 6 Vols. 3202p. 1845. text ed. 621.00x (ISBN 0-576-78882-1, Pub. by Gregg Intl Pubs England). Gregg Intl.

Fuller, Thomas. History of the Worthies of England, 3 Vols. Nuttall, P. Austin, ed. LC 76-168071. Repr. of 1840 ed. Set. 125.00 (ISBN 0-404-02680-X). AMS Pr.

Fuller, Thomas, jt. ed. see Walten, Maximilian G.

Fuller, Tom. Settings-Dreams. LC 85-71529. 80p. (Orig.). 1985. pap. 4.45 (ISBN 0-915685-02-7). Devil Mountain Bks.

Fuller, Tony, jt. auth. see Goldman, Peter.

Fuller, Varden. Rural Worker Adjustment to Urban Life: As Assessment of the Research. LC 79-629117. (Policy Papers in Human Resources & Industrial Relations Ser.: No. 15). (Orig.). 1970. pap. text ed. 2.50x (ISBN 0-87736-115-0). U of Mich Inst Labor.

Fuller, Verna L. Four-M Classification, Pt. 1. LC 81-65748. (Illus.). 350p. 1985. 49.50 (ISBN 0-9605850-0-1); lib. bdg. 49.95 (ISBN 0-9605850-1-X). Fuller Pub.

Fuller, W. H., jt. auth. see Cope, C. B.

Fuller, W. H. & Warrick, A. W., eds. Soils in Waste Treatment & Utilization, Vols. I-II. 288p. 1984. 83.00 (ISBN 0-8493-5151-0); 71.00 (ISBN 0-8493-5152-9). CRC Pr.

Fuller, W. R. Formation & Structure of Paint Films. Federation of Societies for Coatings Technology, Educational Committee, ed. 1965. 2.50 (ISBN 0-686-95499-8). Fed Soc Coat Tech.

Fuller, Wallace H. Dust of Old Adobe. (Contemporary Poets of Dorrance Ser.). 40p. 1980. 3.50 (ISBN 0-8059-2765-4). Dorrance.

--Management of Southwestern Desert Soils. LC 74-15601. (Illus.). 195p. 1975. pap. 7.50 (ISBN 0-8165-0442-3). U of Ariz Pr.

--Soils of the Desert Southwest. LC 74-79390. (Illus.). 102p. 1975. pap. 4.95 (ISBN 0-8165-0441-5). U of Ariz Pr.

Fuller, Walter P. Saint Petersburg & Its People. LC 72-174983. (Illus.). 1972. 14.95 (ISBN 0-8200-1023-5). Great Outdoors.

Fuller, Wayne A. Introduction to Statistical Time Series. LC 76-6954. (Probability & Mathematical Statistics Ser.). 470p. 1976. 47.50x (ISBN 0-471-28715-6, Pub. by Wiley-Interscience). Wiley.

Fuller, Wayne E. The Old Country School: The Story of Rural Education in the Middle West. LC 81-16069. (Illus.). 304p. 1982. lib. bdg. 25.00x (ISBN 0-226-26882-9). U of Chicago Pr.

--The Old Country School: The Story of Rural Education in the Middle West. LC 85-8454. (Illus.). x, 302p. 1982. pap. 11.95 (ISBN 0-226-28215-5). U of Chicago Pr.

Fuller, Wayne F. The American Mail: Enlarger of the Common Life. LC 72-78254. (History of American Civilization Ser.). 390p. 1980. pap. 16.00x (ISBN 0-226-26885-3, Midway). U of Chicago Pr.

Fuller, William C. Civil-Military Conflict in Imperial Russia, 1881-1914. write for info. Amer Bar Assn.

Fuller, William C., Jr. Civil-Military Conflict in Imperial Russia, 1881-1914. LC 85-3493. (Illus.). 350p. 1985. text ed. 39.50x (ISBN 0-691-05452-5). Princeton U Pr.

Fuller-Maitland, J. A. The Consort of Music: A Study of Interpretation & Emsemble. LC 72-83279. Repr. of 1915 ed. 19.00 (ISBN 0-405-08541-9, Blom Pubns). Ayer Co Pubs.

--English Music in the Nineteenth Century. LC 76-22334. 1976. Repr. of 1902 ed. lib. bdg. 30.00 (ISBN 0-89341-019-5). Longwood Pub Group.

--English Music in the Sixth Century. 328p. 1984. pap. cancelled (ISBN 0-89341-488-3). Longwood Pub Group.

--Masters of German Music. LC 77-20818. 1977. Repr. of 1894 ed. lib. bdg. 25.00 (ISBN 0-89341-133-7). Longwood Pub Group.

Fuller-Maitland, J. A. see Hadow, William H.

Fuller-Maitland, J. A., jt. ed. see Broadwood, Lucy E.

Fuller-Maitland, J. A., ed. see Coleridge, Arthur.

Fuller-Maitland, John A. Forty Eight: Bach's Wohltemperirtes Clavier, 2 vols. LC 70-109624. (Select Bibliographies Reprint Ser). 1925. 18.00 (ISBN 0-8369-5233-2). Ayer Co Pubs.

--Robert Schumann, 1810-1856. LC 73-102841. 1970. Repr. of 1913 ed. 14.50x (ISBN 0-8046-0760-5, Pub. by Kennikat). Assoc Faculty Pr.

--Schumann's Pianoforte Works. LC 76-181159. 59p. 1927. Repr. 29.00 (ISBN 0-403-01561-8). Scholarly.

--Spell of Music: An Attempt to Analyse the Enjoyment of Music. LC 76-102239. (Select Bibliographies Reprint Ser). 1926. 15.00 (ISBN 0-8369-5124-7). Ayer Co Pubs.

Fullerton, jt. auth. see Bates.

Fullerton, Alexander. The Blooding of the Guns. LC 83-40572. 192p. 1984. 12.95 (ISBN 0-8027-0780-7). Walker & Co.

--Surface! 176p. pap. 4.95 (ISBN 0-583-12295-7, Pub. by Granada England). Academy Chi Pubs.

--The Waiting Game. 160p. 1980. pap. 3.50 (ISBN 0-583-11758-9, Pub. by Granada England). Academy Chi Pubs.

Fullerton, Brian, tr. see Holt-Jensen, Arild.

Fullerton, Clair J. Teaching Reading Comprehension: A Ten Step Program. LC 82-61478. 125p. (Orig.). 1985. pap. text ed. 12.95 (ISBN 0-88247-719-6). R & E Pubs.

Fullerton, Don, jt. ed. see King, Mervyn A.

Fullerton, Gail P. Survival in Marriage. 2nd ed. LC 76-4676. 1977. text ed. 22.95 (ISBN 0-03-089748-3, HoltC). HR&W.

Fullerton, George S. System of Metaphysics. LC 68-23290. Repr. of 1968 ed. lib. bdg. 32.00x (ISBN 0-8371-0079-8, FUSM). Greenwood.

--System of Metaphysics. 1968. Repr. of 1904 ed. 39.00x (ISBN 0-403-00125-0). Scholarly.

Fullerton, Georgiana. Ellen Middleton, a Tale, 1844. Wolff, Robert L., ed. LC 75-471. (Victorian Fiction Ser). 1975. lib. bdg. 73.00 (ISBN 0-8240-1549-5). Garland Pub.

--Grantley Manor: A Tale, 1847. Wolff, Robert L., ed. LC 75-451. (Victorian Fiction Ser.). 1975. lib. bdg. 73.00 (ISBN 0-8240-1531-2). Garland Pub.

--Mrs. Gerald's Niece: A Novel, 1869. Wolff, Robert L., ed. (Victorian Fiction Ser.). 1976. lib. bdg. 66.00 (ISBN 0-8240-1534-7). Garland Pub.

Fullerton, James H. Ice Hockey! Playing & Coaching. (Illus.). 1978. pap. 5.95 (ISBN 0-8038-3406-3). Hastings.

Fullerton, John, tr. see Vaneigem, Raoul.

Fullerton, Kemper. Essays & Sketches: Oberlin, 1904-1934. facsimile ed. LC 70-156644. (Essay Index Reprint Ser). Repr. of 1938 ed. 17.00 (ISBN 0-8369-2361-8). Ayer Co Pubs.

Fullerton, Lee. Historical Germanic Verb Morphology. (Studia Linguistica Germanica: Vol. 13). 1977. 22.00x (ISBN 3-11-006940-7). De Gruyter.

Fullerton, Peter, ed. Norman Lindsay War Cartoons: 1914-1918. (Illus.). 251p. 1983. 85.00 (ISBN 0-522-84245-3, Pub. by Melbourne U Pr Australia). Intl Spec Bk.

Fullerton, R. L. Construction Technology, Level 2, Pt. 2. (Illus.). 144p. 1982. pap. text ed. 19.95x (ISBN 0-291-39654-2). Intl Ideas.

--Construction Technology: Level 1. (Illus.). 188p. 1980. pap. text ed. 19.95x (ISBN 0-19-859520-4). Intl Ideas.

--Construction Technology: Level 2, Part 1. (Illus.). 144p. 1982. pap. 19.95x (ISBN 0-291-39653-4). Intl Ideas.

Fullerton, R. L. & Struct, M. I. Construction Technology Level 2, Pt. 1. 160p. 1981. 36.00x (ISBN 0-291-39653-4, Pub. by Tech Pr). State Mutual Bk.

--Construction Technology Level 2, Pt. 2. 160p. 1981. 36.00x (ISBN 0-291-39654-2, Pub. by Tech Pr). State Mutual Bk.

Fullerton, W. Y. Charles Spurgeon. (Golden Oldies Ser.). 288p. 1980. pap. 4.95 (ISBN 0-8024-1236-X). Moody.

Fulling, Edmund H., compiled by. Index to Botany As Recorded in the Botanical Review: Volumes 1-25, 1935-1959. Plant Names. (The Botanical Review). 1967. 12.50x (ISBN 0-89327-214-0). NY Botanical.

Fulling, Stephen, tr. see Bogolubov, Nikolai N., et al.

Fullinwider, Robert K. The Reverse Discrimination Controversy: A Moral & Legal Analysis. (Philosophy & Society Ser.). 300p. 1980. 27.50x (ISBN 0-8476-6273-X); pap. 9.95x (ISBN 0-8476-6901-7). Rowman.

Fullinwider, Robert K., ed. Conscripts & Volunteers: Military Requirements, Social Justice & the All-Volunteer Force. LC 83-3095. (Maryland Studies in Public Philosophy). 260p. 1983. text ed. 37.50x (ISBN 0-8476-7224-7); pap. text ed. 19.95x (ISBN 0-8476-7264-6). Rowman & Allanheld.

Fullinwider, S. P. Technicians of the Finite: The Rise & Decline of the Schizophrenic in American Thought, 1840-1960. LC 81-23771. (Contributions in Medical History Ser.: No. 9). ix, 253p. 1982. lib. bdg. 29.95 (ISBN 0-313-23021-8, FFI/). Greenwood.

Fullman, Everett L. Living the Lord's Prayer. (Epiphany Ser.). 128p. 1983. pap. 2.50 (ISBN 0-345-30432-2). Ballantine.

Fullman, James B. Construction Safety, Security, & Loss Prevention. LC 84-5077. (Wiley Practical Construction Guides Ser.: 1-344). 286p. 1984. text ed. 42.95x (ISBN 0-471-86821-3, Pub. by Wiley Interscience). Wiley.

Fullman, James B., jt. auth. see Shuldener, Henry L.

Fullmer, D. W. Counseling: Group Theory & System. 512p. 1982. 40.00x (ISBN 0-686-45456-1, Pub. by Careers Con England). State Mutual Bk.

Fullmer, Daniel W. Counseling: Group Theory & System. 2nd ed. LC 78-9058. 1978. 28.00x (ISBN 0-910328-12-9); pap. 17.50 (ISBN 0-910328-13-7). Carroll Pr.

Fullmer, E. L. The Slime Molds of Ohio. 1921. 1.50 (ISBN 0-86727-010-1). Ohio Bio Survey.

Fullmer, June Z. Sir Humphrey Davy's Published Works. LC 69-18029. 1969. text ed. 10.00x (ISBN 0-674-80961-0). Harvard U Pr.

Fullner, Bernd. Heinrich Heine In Deutschen Literaturgeschichten. (European University Studies Ser.: No. 1, Vol. 486). 340p. (Ger.). 1982. 38.95 (ISBN 3-8204-7016-6). P Lang Pubs.

Fullner, Norman. Airbrush Painting Art: Techniques & Projects. (Illus.). 208p. 1983. 23.95 (ISBN 0-87192-138-3, Pub. by Davis Mass). Sterling.

Fullop-Miller, Rene, ed. see Tolstoi, Lev N.

Fulmer, Robert. Planning for Presidential Succession. (Presidents Association Special Study Ser.: No. 71). 1979. pap. 20.00 (ISBN 0-8144-4072-X). AMACOM.

Fulmer, Robert M. Management & Organization. LC 78-15830. 1980. pap. 5.95 (ISBN 0-06-460176-5, CO 176, COS). B&N NY.

--The New Management. 3rd ed. 544p. 1983. text ed. write for info. (ISBN 0-02-339740-3). Macmillan.

--Practical Human Relations. rev ed. 1983. 25.95x (ISBN 0-256-02629-7). Irwin.

Fulmer, Robert M. & Franklin, Steven C. Supervision: Principles of Professional Management. 2nd ed. 1982. text ed. write for info. (ISBN 0-02-479660-3). Macmillan.

Fulmer, Robert M. & Herbert, Theodore T. Exploring the New Management. 3rd ed. 320p. 1983. text ed. write for info. (ISBN 0-02-340080-3). Macmillan.

Fulmer, Robert M., jt. auth. see Koontz, Harold.

Fulmer, Sandy. IPRA Media Guide. (Illus.). 256p. 1984. pap. 9.95 (ISBN 0-318-03395-X). Intl Rodeo.

Fulmer, William. Managing Production: The Adventure. 1984. pap. text ed. 16.43 (ISBN 0-205-08052-9, 088052); write for info. instrs' manual (ISBN 0-205-08053-7). Allyn.

Fulmer, William E. Problems in Labor Relations: Text & Cases. 1980. 29.95x (ISBN 0-256-02366-2). Irwin.

--Union Organizing: Management & Labor Conflict. LC 82-16172. 240p. 1982. 28.95 (ISBN 0-03-062603-X). Praeger.

Fulop. Alloantigen Systems of Human Leucocytes & Platelets. 1979. 32.00 (ISBN 0-9960015-2-2, Pub. by Akademiai Kaido Hungary). Heyden.

Fulop, Christina. Consumer in the Market. (Institute of Economic Affairs, Research Monographs: No. 13). pap. 2.50 technical (ISBN 0-255-69621-3). Transatlantic.

--Markets for Employment. (Institute of Economic Affairs, Research Monographs: No. 26). 1972. pap. 4.25 technical (ISBN 0-255-36021-5). Transatlantic.

Fulop, Christina & Harris, Ralph. Marketing for Central Heating. (Institute of Economic Affairs, Research Monographs: No. 4). pap. 2.50 technical (ISBN 0-255-69588-8). Transatlantic.

Fulop, T. & Roemer, M. I. International Development of Health Manpower Policy. (WHO Offset Publications: No.61). 168p. 1982. 7.50 (ISBN 92-4-170061-0). World Health.

Fulop, T., jt. auth. see Miller, G. E.

Fulop-Miller, Rene. Lenin & Ghandi. Flint, F. S. & Tait, D. F., trs. from Ger. LC 72-7057. (Select Bibliographies Reprint Ser.). 1972. Repr. of 1927 ed. 21.00 (ISBN 0-8369-6932-4). Ayer Co Pubs.

--Lenin & Ghandi. LC 79-147617. (Library of War & Peace: Non-Resistance & Non-Violence). 1972. lib. bdg. 46.00 (ISBN 0-8240-0374-8). Garland Pub.

--The Power & Secret of the Jesuits. 1930. 29.50 (ISBN 0-8414-4288-6). Folcroft.

--Rasputin the Holy Devil. 1977. Repr. of 1928 ed. lib. bdg. 30.00 (ISBN 0-8414-4308-4). Folcroft.

--Saints That Moved the World: Anthony, Augustine, Francis, Ignatius, Theresa. LC 72-13293. (Essay Index Reprint Ser.). Repr. of 1945 ed. 32.00 (ISBN 0-8369-8159-6). Ayer Co Pubs.

--Triumph Over Pain. Paul, Eden & Paul, Cedar, trs. 438p. 1983. Repr. of 1938 ed. lib. bdg. 35.00 (ISBN 0-89987-284-0). Darby Bks.

Fulop-Miller, Rene & Gregor, Joseph. Russian Theatre. x1930 ed. LC 68-21213. (Illus.). 1930. 38.50 (ISBN 0-405-08542-7, Blom Pubns). Ayer Co Pubs.

Fulop-Miller, Rene, jt. auth. see Anderson, John.

Fulpen, H. V. The Beatles: An Illustrated Diary. 176p. (Orig.). 1985. pap. 9.95 (ISBN 0-399-51123-7, Perigee). Putnam Pub Group.

Fulrath, R. M. & Pask, Joseph A., eds. Ceramic Microstructures: Their Analysis, Significance & Production. LC 74-32351. 1028p. 1976. Repr. of 1966 ed. 57.50 (ISBN 0-88275-262-6). Krieger.

Fulsher, Keith. Fishing the Thunder Creek Series. (Illus.). 100p. 1973. 7.95 (ISBN 0-88395-018-9). Freshet Pr.

Fulsher, Keith & Krom, Charles. Hair Wing Atlantic Salmon Flies. 2nd ed. Surette, Dick, ed. (Illus.). 184p. (Orig.). 1982. 25.00 (ISBN 0-9607522-0-X); pap. 15.00 (ISBN 0-686-99460-4). Fly Tyer.

Fulton. The Frontal Lobes & Human Behaviour. 30p. 1982. 50.00x (ISBN 0-85323-311-X, Pub. by LIverpool Univ England). State Mutual Bk.

Fulton, A. B. The Cytoskeleton: Cellular Architecture & Choreography. (Outline Studies in Biology). 80p. 1984. pap. text ed. 6.95 (ISBN 0-412-25510-3, 9132, Pub. by Chapman & Hall England). Methuen Inc.

Fulton, A. R. Motion Pictures: The Development of an Art. rev. ed. LC 79-6711. (Illus.). 274p. 1980. 21.95x (ISBN 0-8061-1633-1). U of Okla Pr.

Fulton, A. S. & Lings, M. Second Supplementary Catalogue of Arabic Books 1927-1957. 576p. 1960. cloth 100.00x (ISBN 0-7141-0606-2, Pub. by Brit Lib England). State Mutual Bk.

Fulton, Alice. Dance Script with Electric Ballerina. LC 83-10319. 96p. (Orig.). 1983. 16.95x (ISBN 0-8122-7901-8); pap. 8.95x (ISBN 0-8122-1155-3). U of Pa Pr.

Fulton, Alice & Hatch, Pauline. It's Here...Somewhere. 192p. (Orig.). 1985. pap. 6.95 (ISBN 0-89879-186-3, 1461). Writers Digest.

Fulton, Alice, jt. auth. see Aal, Katharyn M.

Fulton, Alvenia M. The Fasting Primer. 2nd & rev. ed. Williams, James C., ed. LC 78-60661. 1978. pap. 5.95 (ISBN 0-931564-04-2). BCA Pub.

--Vegetarian Fact or Myth - Eating to Live. 2nd & rev. ed. Williams, James C., ed. LC 78-66063. 1978. pap. 8.95 (ISBN 0-931564-03-4). BCA Pub.

Fulton, Alvenia M., ed. see Gregory, Dick.

Fulton, Chandler & Klein, Attila. Explorations in Developmental Biology. (Illus.). 1976. text ed. 32.50x (ISBN 0-674-27852-6). Harvard U Pr.

Fulton, Charles C. Modern Microcrystal Tests for Drugs: The Identification of Organic Compounds by Microcrystalloscopic Chemistry. LC 68-54599. (Illus.). pap. 121.50 (ISBN 0-317-07900-X, 2012486). Bks Demand UMI.

Fulton, David B. see Thorne, Jack, pseud.

Fulton, E. G. Vengeance, My Love. 320p. (Orig.). 1982. pap. 2.95 (ISBN 0-523-48035-0). Pinnacle Bks.

Fulton, Eleanor & Smith, Pat. Let's Slice the Ice: A Colelction of Black Children's Ring Games & Chants. (Illus.). 1978. pap. 6.00 (ISBN 0-918812-02-X). MMB Music.

Fulton, Eleanore J. & Mylin, Barbara K. An Index to the Will Books & Intestate Records of Lancaster County, Pennsylvania, 1729-1850. LC 72-10550. (Illus.). 136p. 1981. Repr. of 1936 ed. 12.50 (ISBN 0-8063-0535-5). Genealog Pub.

Fulton, George A., jt. auth. see Shapiro, Harold T.

Fulton, George G. Good Morning, Captain. (Orig.). 1978. pap. 6.95 (ISBN 0-933054-00-9). Ricwalt Pub Co.

Fulton, George P., jt. auth. see Shepro, David.

Fulton, Ginger A. When I'm a Daddy. 1985. pap. 2.95 (ISBN 0-8024-0387-5). Moody.

Fulton, Ginger Adair. When I'm a Mommy: A Little Girl's Paraphrase of Proverbs 31. (Illus.). (gr. 1-4). 1984. pap. 2.95 (ISBN 0-8024-0367-0). Moody.

Fulton, Gwen & Fulton, Gwen, illus. Did You Ever? Traditional Verse. 24p. (gr. k up). 1981. 8.95 (ISBN 0-224-01740-3, Pub. by Jonathan Cape). Merrimack Pub Cir.

Fulton, James E. & Black, Elizabeth. Dr. Fulton's Step-By-Step Program for Clearing Acne. LC 82-47522. (Illus.). 256p. 1983. 14.37i (ISBN 0-06-038020-9, HarpT). Har-Row.

Fulton, John. Beautiful Land: Palestine: Historical, Geographical & Pictorial. Davis, Moshe, ed. LC 77-70694. (America & the Holy Land Ser.). (Illus.). 1977. Repr. of 1891 ed. lib. bdg. 52.00x (ISBN 0-405-10248-8). Ayer Co Pubs.

--Memoirs of Frederick A. P. Barnard, Tenth President of Columbia College in the City of New York. 19.75 (ISBN 0-8369-7160-4, 7992). Ayer Co Pubs.

Fulton, John F. The Great Medical Bibliographers: A Study in Humanism. LC 76-30508. (The Historical Library, Yale University School of Medicine: No. 26). (Illus.). 1977. Repr. of 1951 ed. lib. bdg. 18.75 (ISBN 0-8371-9436-9, FUGM). Greenwood.

--Harvey Cushing: A Biography. Cohen, I. Bernard, ed. LC 79-7961. (Three Centuries of Science in America Ser.). (Illus.). 1980. Repr. of 1946 ed. lib. bdg. 71.50x (ISBN 0-405-12542-9). Ayer Co Pubs.

--Physiology. LC 75-23655. (Clio Medica: 5). (Illus.). Repr. of 1931 ed. 16.00 (ISBN 0-404-58905-7). AMS Pr.

--Selected Readings in the History of Physiology. 2nd ed. (Illus.). 618p. 1966. photocopy ed. 49.50x (ISBN 0-398-00630-X). C C Thomas.

--Selected Readings in the History of Physiology. 317p. 1983. lib. bdg. 85.00 (ISBN 0-89987-283-2). Darby Bks.

Fulton, John F. & Keller, Allen D. The Sign of Babinski: A Study of the Evolution of Cortical Dominance in Primates. (Illus.). 179p. 1932. photocopy ed. 16.50x (ISBN 0-398-04260-8). C C Thomas.

Fulton, John F. & Stanton, Madeline E. Michael Servetus, Humanist & Martyr. (Illus.). 98p. 1954. 45.00 (ISBN 0-317-05986-6). H Reichner.

Fulton, Junius P., jt. auth. see Keilitz, Ingo.

Fulton, Justin D. The Fight with Rome. LC 76-46077. (Anti-Movements in America). 1977. Repr. of 1889 ed. lib. bdg. 30.00x (ISBN 0-405-09950-9). Ayer Co Pubs.

Fulton, Ken. The Light-Hearted Astronomer. LC 84-6218. 128p. 1984. pap. 6.95 (ISBN 0-913135-01-1). AstroMedia Corp.

Fulton, Len. American Odyssey. (The American Dust Ser.: No.1). 1975. 7.95 (ISBN 0-913218-46-4); pap. 4.50 (ISBN 0-913218-47-2). Dustbooks.

--Dark Other Adam Dreaming. (The American Dust Ser.: No. 4). 1975. 8.95 (ISBN 0-913218-48-0); pap. 2.95 (ISBN 0-913218-49-9). Dustbooks.

--The Grassman. (Illus.). 1974. Repr. 7.95 (ISBN 0-914476-26-2). Dustbooks.

--International Directory of Little Magazines & Small Presses. 13th ed. 1977. 11.95 (ISBN 0-913218-05-7); pap. 8.95 (ISBN 0-913218-04-9). Dustbooks.

--Small Press Record of Books in Print. 5th ed. 1976. 21.95 (ISBN 0-913218-69-3). Dustbooks.

--Small Press Record of Books in Print. 6th ed. 1977. pap. 8.95 (ISBN 0-913218-03-0). Dustbooks.

Fulton, Len & Ferber, Ellen. Directory of Poetry Publishers. (Information Publications Ser.). 224p. 1985. pap. 9.95 (ISBN 0-913218-70-7). Dustbooks.

--Small Press Record of Books in Print. 14th ed. 1200p. Date not set. 29.95 (ISBN 0-913218-07-3). Dustbooks.

Fulton, Len, ed. Directory of Small Magazine - Press Editors & Publishers. 8th ed. 1977. 10.95 (ISBN 0-913218-68-5); pap. 33.00 copy (ISBN 0-686-77169-9). Dustbooks.

--International Directory of Little Magazines & Small Presses. 11th ed. 304p. 1975. 8.95 (ISBN 0-913218-16-2); pap. 5.95 (ISBN 0-913218-15-4). Dustbooks.

--International Directory of Little Magazines & Small Presses. 12th ed. 1976. 15.95 (ISBN 0-913218-12-X); pap. 19.95 (ISBN 0-913218-67-7). Dustbooks.

--Small Press Record of Books in Print, 1978. 7th ed. (Small Press Information Library). 1978. 10.95 (ISBN 0-913218-60-X). Dustbooks.

Fulton, Len & Ferber, Ellen, eds. Directory of Small Magazine - Press Editors & Publishers. 11th ed. (Dustbooks Small Press Info. Library). 250p. 1980. pap. 9.95 (ISBN 0-913218-96-0). Dustbooks.

--Directory of Small Magazine - Press Editors & Publishers. 13th ed. 1982. pap. 11.95 (ISBN 0-913218-98-7). Dustbooks.

--Directory of Small Magazine - Press Editors & Publishers. 10th ed. 1979. pap. 8.95 (ISBN 0-913218-90-1). Dustbooks.

--Directory of Small Magazine - Press Editors & Publishers. 14th ed. 200p. 1983. pap. 12.95 (ISBN 0-913218-65-0). Dustbooks.

--Directory of Small Magazine - Press Editors & Publishers: 1978-79. 9th ed. 1978. pap. 7.95 (ISBN 0-913218-62-6). Dustbooks.

--Directory of Small Magazine Press Editors & Publishers. 15th ed. 200p. 1984. pap. 13.95 (ISBN 0-913218-53-7). Dustbooks.

--Directory of Small Magazine Press Editors & Publishers. 16th ed. 1985. pap. 14.95 (ISBN 0-913218-09-X). Dustbooks.

--International Directory of Little Magazines & Small Presses. 16th ed. (Dustbooks Small Press Info. Library). 580p. 1980. 17.95 (ISBN 0-913218-94-4); pap. 13.95 (ISBN 0-913218-93-6). Dustbooks.

--International Directory of Little Magazines & Small Presses. 15th ed. 1979. 15.95 (ISBN 0-913218-88-X); pap. 11.95 (ISBN 0-913218-87-1). Dustbooks.

--International Directory of Little Magazines & Small Presses. 20th ed. 650p. 1984. 27.95 (ISBN 0-913218-52-9); pap. 18.95 (ISBN 0-913218-51-0). Dustbooks.

--International Directory of Little Magazines & Small Presses. 21st ed. 700p. 1985. 29.95 (ISBN 0-913218-45-6); pap. 19.95 (ISBN 0-913218-43-X). Dustbooks.

--International Directory of Little Magazines & Small Presses, 1978-79. 14th ed. (Small Press Information Library). 1978. 13.95 (ISBN 0-913218-58-8); pap. 10.95 (ISBN 0-913218-57-X). Dustbooks.

--International Directory of Little Magazines & Small Presses, 1982-83. 18th ed. 600p. 1982. 23.95 (ISBN 0-913218-74-X); pap. 16.95 (ISBN 0-913218-73-1). Dustbooks.

--International Directory of Little Magazines & Small Presses: 19th Annual. 600p. 1983. 25.95 (ISBN 0-913218-64-2); pap. 17.95 (ISBN 0-913218-63-4). Dustbooks.

--Small Press Record of Books in Print. 11th ed. 800p. 1982. lib. bdg. 23.95 (ISBN 0-913218-99-5). Dustbooks.

--Small Press Record of Books in Print. 9th ed. (Dustbooks Small Press Info. Library). 680p. 1980. 17.95 (ISBN 0-913218-95-2). Dustbooks.

--Small Press Record of Books in Print. 8th ed. 1979. 11.95 (ISBN 0-913218-89-8). Dustbooks.

--Small Press Record of Books in Print. 12th ed. 950p. 1983. 25.95 (ISBN 0-913218-61-8). Dustbooks.

--Small Press Record of Books in Print. 13th ed. 1000p. 1984. 27.95 (ISBN 0-913218-56-1). Dustbooks.

--Small Press Record of Books in Print, 1981-82. 10th ed. 700p. 1981. 21.95 (ISBN 0-913218-69-3). Dustbooks.

Fulton, Len & May, James B., eds. International Directory of Little Magazines & Small Presses. 10th ed. 200p. 1974. 7.95 (ISBN 0-913218-14-6); pap. 4.95 (ISBN 0-913218-13-8). Dustbooks.

Fulton, Lynn F., et al. Grant Writing Guide for Social Workers. 40p. 1972. 2.25 (ISBN 0-87506-045-5). Campus.

--Grantwriting Guide for Social Workers. 40p. 1972. pap. 2.25 (ISBN 0-87506-045-5). Campus.

Fulton, Marianne. The Wise Silence: Photographs by Paul Caponigro. (Illus.). 208p. 1983. 59.00i (ISBN 0-8212-1548-5, 948624). NYGS.

Fulton, Martin W. A Chronology of Substances of Abuse. LC 78-62253. 1978. pap. text ed. 10.00 (ISBN 0-8191-0566-X). U Pr of Amer.

Fulton, Maurice G. History of the Lincoln County War. Mullin, Robert N., ed. LC 68-13544. (Illus.). 433p. 1968. pap. 14.95 (ISBN 0-8165-0052-5). U of Ariz Pr.

Fulton, Maurice G., ed. National Ideals & Problems. facs. ed. LC 68-54346. (Essay Index Reprint Ser). 1918. 20.00 (ISBN 0-8369-0113-4). Ayer Co Pubs.

Fulton, O. & Gordon, A. Higher Education & Manpower Planning: A Comparative Study of Planned & Market Economies. 127p. 1982. 13.00 (ISBN 92-2-102973-5). Intl Labour Office.

Fulton, O., ed. Access to Higher Education. (SRHE Leverhulme: II). 202p. 1981. pap. text ed. 9.45x (Pub. by SRHE NFER). Humanities.

Fulton, Patsy F. General Office Procedures for Colleges. 1983. text ed. 11.95 wkbk. (ISBN 0-538-11940-3, K94). SW Pub.

Fulton, R. H., ed. Coffee Rust in the Americas. 120p. 1984. 18.00 (ISBN 0-89054-064-0). Am Phytopathol Soc.

Fulton, Renee J; see Bottiglia, William F.

Fulton, Richard D. Union List of Victorian Serials: A Union List of Selected Nineteenth Century British Serials Available in the U. S. & Canadian Libraries. (Reference Library of the Humanities). 758p. 1984. lib. bdg. 103.00 (ISBN 0-8240-8846-8). Garland Pub.

Fulton, Richard M., ed. The Revolution That Wasn't: A Contemporary Assessment of 1776. (National University Publication, American Studies). 1981. 22.50x (ISBN 0-8046-9259-9, Pub. by Kennikat). Assoc Faculty Pr.

Fulton, Robert. Death, Grief & Bereavement: A Bibliography, 1845-1975. Kastenbaum, Robert, ed. LC 76-19572. (Death and Dying Ser.). 1976. PLB 27.50 (ISBN 0-405-09570-8). Ayer Co Pubs.

Fulton, Robert, compiled by. A Bibliography of Death, Grief, & Bereavement II, 1975-1980. LC 81-1368. 239p. 1981. lib. bdg. 27.50x (ISBN 0-405-14212-9). Ayer Co Pubs.

Fulton, Robert, ed. Death & Dying: Challenge & Change. rev ed. LC 78-59488. (Illus.). 428p. 1981. pap. text ed. 15.00x (ISBN 0-87835-112-4). Boyd & Fraser.

Fulton, Robert I., et al, eds. Standard Selections. facsimile ed. LC 79-152150. (Granger Index Reprint Ser.). Repr. of 1907 ed. 24.00 (ISBN 0-8369-6253-2). Ayer Co Pubs.

Fulton, Robert L. Epic of the Overland: An Account of the Building of the Central & Union Pacific Railroad. LC 54-3213. 109p. 1982. lib. bdg. 44.95x (ISBN 0-89370-713-9). Borgo Pr.

Fulton, Robert L. & Trueblood, Thomas C., eds. Choice Readings. enl. & rev. ed. LC 72-5590. (Granger Index Reprint Ser.). 1972. Repr. of 1884 ed. 36.00 (ISBN 0-8369-6383-0). Ayer Co Pubs.

Fulton, Robert T. & Lloyd, Lyle L., eds. Auditory Assessment of the Difficult-to-Test. LC 71-93742. 297p. 1975. 19.95 (ISBN 0-686-74200-1). Krieger.

Fulton, Robin. Spaces Between the Stones. (Illus.). 1971. 4.50 (ISBN 0-912284-11-0); signed ltd ed 10.00 (ISBN 0-685-02578-0); pap. 2.50 (ISBN 0-912284-12-9). New Rivers Pr.

--Tree-Lines. (Illus.). 1974. signed ed. 10.00 (ISBN 0-685-46815-1); pap. 2.50 (ISBN 0-685-46816-X). New Rivers Pr.

Fulton, Robin, tr. see Gustafsson, Lars.

Fulton, Robin, tr. see Harding, Gunnar & Barkan, Stanley.

Fulton, Stanley R. & Rawlins, John C. Basic AC Circuits. Luecke, G. & Battle, C., eds. LC 80-54793. (Basic Electricity Ser.). (Illus.). 560p. 1981. 19.95 (ISBN 0-89512-041-0, LCW8168); six cassette audio course 14.95 (LCB6651). Tex Instr Inc.

--Practical Applications of AC Theory. LC 81-51518. (Illus.). 320p. (Orig.). 1981. pap. 12.00 (ISBN 0-89512-043-7, LCW8169). Tex Instr Inc.

Fulton, Sue & Buxton, Ed. Advertising Freelancers. LC 85-80109. (Illus.). 172p. 1985. pap. 15.00 (ISBN 0-917168-10-0). Executive Comm.

Fulton, Sue, ed. Handbook of Advertising & Marketing Services. annual 1984. pap. 50.00 (ISBN 0-917168-02-X). Executive Comm.

Fulton, Susan. Running An Ad Agency. LC 81-69434. 242p. 1982. pap. 20.00 (ISBN 0-917168-07-0). Executive Comm.

Fulton, Thomas W. The Sovereignity of the Sea. LC 11-7247. 1976. Repr. of 1911 ed. 44.00 (ISBN 0-527-31860-4). Kraus Repr.

Fulton, W. Intersection Theory. (Ergebnisse der Mathematik und ihrer Grenzgebiete: 3. Folge, Vol. 2). 480p. 1983. 39.00 (ISBN 0-387-12176-5). Springer-Verlag.

Fulton, William. Algebraic Curves: An Introduction to Algebraic Geometry. (Math Lecture Notes Ser.: No. 30). 1974. (Adv Bk Prog); pap. 27.95 (ISBN 0-8053-3082-8, Adv Bk Prog). Benjamin-Cummings.

--Introduction to Intersection Theory in Algebraic Geometry. LC 84-25841. (CBMS Regional Conference Series in Mathematics: Vol. 54). 82p. 1984. pap. 16.00 (ISBN 0-8218-0704-8). Am Math.

Fulton, William & MacPherson, Robert. Categorical Framework for the Study of Singular Spaces. LC 81-2246. (Memoirs Ser.: No. 243). 166p. 1981. pap. 12.00 (ISBN 0-8218-2243-8). Am Math.

Fulton, William F. The Coronary Arteries: Arteriography, Microanatomy, & Pathogenesis of Obliterative Coronary Artery Disease. (Illus.). 376p. 1965. photocopy ed. 39.75x (ISBN 0-398-00631-8). C C Thomas.

Fults, Anna C., et al. Readings in Evaluation. LC 72-79634. 1972. pap. text ed. 5.75x (ISBN 0-8134-1479-2, 1479). Interstate.

Fults, John L. Magic Squares. LC 73-23041. (Illus.). 124p. 1974. 15.95 (ISBN 0-87548-317-8); pap. 4.95 (ISBN 0-87548-198-1). Open Court.

Fultz, Jack F. Overhead: What It Is & How It Works. LC 79-57519. (Illus.). 151p. 1980. 12.00 (ISBN 0-89011-547-8). Abt Bks.

--Overhead: What It Is & How It Works. (Illus.). 160p. 1984. Repr. of 1980 ed. lib. bdg. 23.50 (ISBN 0-8191-4407-X). U Pr of Amer.

Fultz, Regina. Tower of Darkness. LC 85-90157. (Endless Quest Ser.). (Illus.). 160p. (gr. 4-6). 1985. pap. 2.25 (ISBN 0-394-74180-3). Random.

Fulves, Karl. The Children's Magic Kit: Sixteen Easy-to-Do Tricks Complete with Cardboard Cutouts. (Illus.). 32p. (Orig.). (gr. 3-6). 1981. pap. 3.50 (ISBN 0-486-24019-3). Dover.

--More Self-Working Card Tricks: 88 Fool-Proof Card Miracles for the Amateur Magician. (Magic, Legerdemain Ser.). 96p. (Orig.). (gr. 6up). 1984. pap. 3.50 (ISBN 0-486-24580-2). Dover.

--Self-Working Card Tricks: Seventy-Two Foolproof Card Miracles for the Amateur Magician. (Illus.). 113p. (Orig.). 1976. pap. 3.50 (ISBN 0-486-23334-0). Dover.

--Self-Working Mental Magic: Sixty-Seven Foolproof Mind-Reading Tricks. LC 79-50010. (Illus.). 128p. 1979. pap. 3.50 (ISBN 0-486-23806-7). Dover.

--Self Working Number Magic. (Magic Ser.). (Illus.). 128p. (Orig.). pap. 3.50 (ISBN 0-486-24391-5). Dover.

--Self-Working Paper Magic: Eighty-One Foolproof Tricks. (Magic, Legerdemain Ser.). 144p. 1985. pap. 3.50 (ISBN 0-486-24847-X). Dover.

--Self-Working Table Magic: Ninety-Seven Foolproof Tricks with Everyday Objects. (Illus.). 128p. (Orig.). 1981. pap. 3.50 (ISBN 0-486-24116-5). Dover.

Fulvio, Andrea. Roman Portraits. (Printed Sources of Western Art Ser.). (Illus.). 236p. (Latin.). 1981. pap. 30.00 slipcase (ISBN 0-915346-57-5). A Wofsy Fine Arts.

Fulweiler, Howard W. Letters from the Darkling Plain: Language & the Grounds of Knowledge in the Poetry of Arnold & Hopkins. LC 72-77839. 176p. 1972. 14.00x (ISBN 0-8262-0125-3). U of Mo Pr.

Fulwell, U. Ars Adulandi, or the Art of Flattery: A Critical Edition with a Biography of the Author. Buchanan, R., ed. (Salzburg - Elizabethan & Renaissance Studies: Vol. 109). 247p. 1984. pap. text ed. 25.50x (ISBN 0-391-03313-1, Pub. by Salzburg Austria). Humanities.

Fulwell, Ulpian. Like Will to Like. LC 72-133665. (Tudor Facsimile Texts. Old English Plays: No. 39). Repr. of 1909 ed. 49.50 (ISBN 0-404-53339-6). AMS Pr.

Fulwiler, David, jt. auth. see Evans, Derek.

Fulwiler, Kyle D. The Apple Cookbook. LC 79-12592. 108p. 1980. pap. 6.95 (ISBN 0-914718-44-4). Pacific Search.

--The Berry Cookbook. 2nd, rev. ed. 120p. 1985. pap. 6.95 (ISBN 0-914718-98-3). Pacific Search.

Fulwiler, Toby & Young, Art, eds. Language Connections: Writing & Reading Across the Curriculum. LC 82-3468. 190p. (Orig.). 1982. pap. 13.00 (ISBN 0-8141-2653-7). NCTE.

Fulwood, Robinson & Johnson, Clifford L. Hematological & Nutritional Biochemistries References Data of Persons 6 Months-74 Years of Age: United States, 1976-1980. Cox, Klaudia, tr. (Ser. 11: No. 232). 60p. 1982. pap. 1.95 (ISBN 0-8406-0267-7). Natl Ctr Health Stats.

Fulwood, Robinson, et al. Height & Weight of Adults Ages Eighteen to Seventy-Four Years by Socioeconomic & Geographic Variables: United States, 1971-74. (Ser. II: No. 224). 60p. 1981. pap. text ed. 1.95 (ISBN 0-8406-0221-9). Natl Ctr Health Stats.

Fumagalli, E. Statical & Geomechanical Models. (Illus.). xv, 182p. 1973. 62.00 (ISBN 0-387-81096-X). Springer-Verlag.

Fumagalli, M. Beonio-Brocchieri see Beonio-Brocchieri Fumagalli, M. T.

Fumagalli, Remo, et al, eds. Human Hyperlipoproteinemias: Principles & Methods. LC 73-16295. (Advances in Experimental Medicine & Biology Ser.: Vol. 38). 309p. 1973. 42.50x (ISBN 0-306-39038-8, Plenum Pr). Plenum Pub.

Fumaroli, Marc, jt. auth. see Rosenberg, Pierre.

Fumento, Rocco, ed. Forty-Second Street. (Wisconsin - Warner Bros. Screenplay Ser.). (Illus.). 220p. 1980. 17.50x (ISBN 0-299-08100-1); pap. 6.95t (ISBN 0-299-08104-4). U of Wis Pr.

Fumerton, Richard A. Metaphysical & Epistemological Problems of Perception. LC 84-11920. xiv, 211p. 1985. 19.95x (ISBN 0-8032-1966-0). U of Nebr Pr.

Fumet, ed. see Claudel, Paul.

Fumi, F. G. Physics of Semiconductors: Proceedings of the 13th International Conference, Rome, 1976. 1977. 138.50 (ISBN 0-7204-0571-8, North-Holland). Elsevier.

Fumin, Feng, et al, trs. see Moruo, Guo.

Funai, M., jt. auth. see Polhamus, J.

Funai, Mamoru. Cartoons for Kids. LC 76-44273. (Illus.). (gr. 1-4). 1977. 7.95 (ISBN 0-13-115154-1). P-H.

--Moke & Poki in the Rain Forest. LC 72-76510. (I Can Read Bk.). (Illus.). 64p. (gr. k-3). 1972. PLB 9.89 (ISBN 0-06-021927-0). HarpJ.

Funakoshi, G. Karate-Do Kyohan. 24.95x (ISBN 0-685-38447-0). Wehman.

Funakoshi, Gichin. Karate-Do-Kyohan: The Master Text. Ohshima, Tsutomu, tr. from Japanese. LC 72-90228. (Illus.). 370p. 1973. 24.95 (ISBN 0-87011-190-6). Kodansha.

--Karate-Do: My Way of Life. LC 80-84590. (Illus.). 127p. 1981. pap. 4.25 (ISBN 0-87011-463-8). Kodansha.

--Karate-Do, My Way of Life. LC 74-29563. (Illus.). 127p. 1975. 11.95 (ISBN 0-87011-241-4). Kodansha.

--Karate-Do, My Way of Life. 9.95x (ISBN 0-685-63759-X). Wehman.

Funaro, Diana. The Yestermorrow Clothes Book. (Illus.). 1976. pap. 6.95 (ISBN 0-8019-6408-3). Chilton.

Funazaki, Yasuko. Baby Owl. (Illus.). 32p. (ps). 1979. 7.95 (ISBN 0-416-30721-3, NO.0206). Methuen Inc.

Funchess, Lloyd, Jr. Tiny Shiny. 1964. 2.95 (ISBN 0-87511-052-5). Claitors.

Funchion, Michael F. Chicago's Irish Nationalists, 1881-1890. LC 76-6342. (Irish Americans Ser). 1976. 16.00 (ISBN 0-405-09337-3). Ayer Co Pubs.

Funchion, Michael F., ed. Irish American Voluntary Organizations. LC 83-6712. (Ethnic American Voluntary Organizations Ser.). xviii, 323p. 1983. lib. bdg. 45.00 (ISBN 0-313-22948-1, FIA/). Greenwood.

Funck, J. L., ed. see International Society for Artificial Organs.

Funck, R. Recent Developments in Regional Science. (Karlsruhe Papers in Regional Science). 153p. 1974. pap. 10.00x (ISBN 0-85086-034-2, NO. 2912, Pub. by Pion England). Methuen Inc.

Funck, R. & Parr, J. B., eds. The Analysis of Regional Structure: Essays in Honour of August Losch. (Karlsruhe Papers in Regional Science). 168p. 1978. pap. 13.50x (ISBN 0-85086-068-7, NO.2961, Pub. by Pion England). Methuen Inc.

Funck-Brentano, Frantz. Earliest Times. LC 77-168074. (National History of France: No. 1). Repr. of 1927 ed. 30.00 (ISBN 0-404-50791-3). AMS Pr.

--Middle Ages. LC 70-168075. (National History of France: No. 2). Repr. of 1930 ed. 30.00 (ISBN 0-404-50792-1). AMS Pr.

Funck-Brentano, Frantz, ed. National History of France. 10 Vols. in 11. LC 74-168076. Repr. of 1938 ed. Set. 330.00 (ISBN 0-404-50790-5); 30.00 ea. AMS Pr.

Funck-Brentano, Jean-Louis, jt. ed. see Blaufox, M. Donald.

Funck-Bretano. The Middle Ages. O'Neill, Elizabeth, tr. 1979. Repr. of 1926 ed. lib. bdg. 35.00 (ISBN 0-8495-1644-7). Arden Lib.

Funcken, Fred, jt. auth. see Funcken, Lilane.

Funcken, Fred, jt. auth. see Funcken, Liliane.

Funcken, Lilane & Funcken, Fred. Arms & Uniforms: The Second World War, Vol. I. (Illus.). 128p. 1984. 17.95 (ISBN 0-13-046343-4); pap. 8.95 (ISBN 0-13-046269-1). P-H.

Funcken, Liliane & Funcken, Fred. The Age of Chivalry, Pt. 2. 112p. 1981. 35.00x (ISBN 0-7063-5808-2, Pub. by Ward Lock Ed England). State Mutual Bk.

--Arms & Uniforms: The Age of Chivalry, 3 vols. 1983. 17.95 set (ISBN 0-686-84587-0). Vol. I, 102p (ISBN 0-13-046276-4). Vol. II, 109p (ISBN 0-13-046292-6). Vol. III, 104p (ISBN 0-13-046326-4). pap. 8.95 each (ISBN 0-686-84588-9); Vol. I. 17.95 (ISBN 0-13-046284-5); Vol. II. 17.95 (ISBN 0-13-046318-3). Vol. III (ISBN 0-13-046334-5). P-H.

--Arms & Uniforms: The Napoleonic Wars, Vol. I. (Illus.). 160p. (Orig.). 1984. 17.95 (ISBN 0-13-046236-5); pap. 9.95 (ISBN 0-13-046228-4). P-H.

--Arms & Uniforms: The Napoleonic Wars, Vol. II. (Illus.). 160p. 17.95 (ISBN 0-13-046251-9); pap. 9.95 (ISBN 0-13-046244-6). P-H.

--Arms & Uniforms: The Second World War, Vol. III. (Illus.). 120p. 1984. 17.95 (ISBN 0-13-046384-1); pap. 8.95 (ISBN 0-13-046376-0). P-H.

--Arms & Uniforms: The Second World War, Vol. IV. (Illus.). 120p. 1984. 17.95 (ISBN 0-13-046400-7); pap. 8.95 (ISBN 0-13-046392-2). P-H.

--The Napoleonic Wars, Vol. I. price not set. P-H.

--The Napoleonic Wars, Vol. II. price not set. P-H.

--The Second World War, Vol. I. price not set. P-H.

Fund for the Republic, Inc. Digest of the Public Record of Communism in the United States. Grob, Gerald, ed. LC 76-46078. (Anti-Movements in America). 1977. lib. bdg. 57.50x (ISBN 0-405-09951-7). Ayer Co Pubs.

Fundabunk, Lila & Davenport, Thomas. Art in Public Places in the United States. LC 75-18522. 1975. 30.00 (ISBN 0-87972-113-8). Bowling Green Univ.

Fundaburk, Emma L. The History of Economic Thought & Analysis: A Selective International Bibliography-Development of Economic Thought & Analysis, Vol. 1. LC 72-13158. 931p. 1973. lib. bdg. 30.00 (ISBN 0-8108-0580-4). Scarecrow.

--Reference Materials & Periodicals in Economics: An International List, Agriculture. LC 78-142232. 595p. 1971. 23.00 (ISBN 0-8108-0349-6). Scarecrow.

--Reference Materials & Periodicals in Economics: An International List, Major Manufacturing Industries - Automotive, Chemical, Iron & Steel, Petroleum. LC 78-142232. 778p. 1972. 25.50 (ISBN 0-8108-0453-0). Scarecrow.

Fundaburk, Emma L. & Davenport, Thomas. Art at Educational Institutions in the United States: A Handbook of Permanent, Semi-Permanent & Temporary Works of Art at Elementary & Secondary Schools, Colleges & Universities. LC 74-3187. (Illus.). 1974. 49.50 (ISBN 0-8108-0715-7). Scarecrow.

Fundaburk, Emma L. & Foreman, Mary D., eds. Sun Circles & Human Hands: The Southeastern Indians, Art & Industries. (Illus.). 12.00 (ISBN 0-910642-01-X). Fundaburk.

Fundaburk, Emma L. Art in the Environment in the United States. Foreman, Mary D. LC 75-24620. (Illus.). 224p. 12.00 (ISBN 0-910642-02-8). Fundaburk.

Fundacao Calcuste Gulbankian. Community Work & Social Change: The Report of a Study Group on Training. pap. 45.50 (ISBN 0-317-09645-1, 2005883). Bks Demand UMI.

Funderburk, Charles. Presidents & Politics: The Limits of Power. 1982. 13.00, pub net (ISBN 0-534-01086-5, 81-15444). Brooks-Cole.

Funderburk, James. Science Studies Yoga. LC 77-150857. (Illus.). 257p. (Orig.). 1977. pap. 5.95 (ISBN 0-89389-026-X). Himalayan Pubs.

Fundingsland, Ardis E. Star Journey. 1985. 4.95 (ISBN 0-533-06691-3). Vantage.

Fundora de Rodriguez Aragon, Raquel. El Canto del Viento. LC 82-62050. (Senda Poetica Ser.). 96p. (Orig.). 1983. pap. 6.95 (ISBN 0-918454-31-X). Senda Nueva.

Fundraising Committee. A. F. B. T. R. Cookbook. 2nd ed. Schultz, Olivia, ed. Repr. 7.50x (ISBN 0-686-39886-6). Assn Brain Tumor.

Fundter, J. M. Names for Dipterocarp Timbers & Trees from Asia. 252p. 1982. 42.25 (ISBN 90-220-0795-2, PDC255, Pudoc). Unipub.

Fundudis, Trian, et al, eds. Speech Retarded & Deaf Children: Their Psychological Development. LC 78-75264. 1980. 47.50 (ISBN 0-12-270150-X). Acad Pr.

Funero, Artie, jt. auth. see Traum, Artie.

Funes, Donald J. & Munson, Kenneth. Musical Involvement: A Guide to Perceptive Listening. (Illus.). 179p. (Orig.). 1975. pap. text ed. 14.95 (ISBN 0-15-564950-7, HC); boxed set of six records 24.95 (ISBN 0-15-564951-5). HarBraceJ.

Funes, Marilyn & Lazarus, Alan. Popular Careers. Piltch, Benjamin, ed. 64p. 1980. wkbk 3.50 (ISBN 0-934618-01-1). Skyview Pub.

Funesti, Orfeo. The Birthday Bird. 104p. 1972. 9.95 (ISBN 0-912282-03-7). Pulse-Finger.

Fung, Edmund S. & Mackerras, Colin. From Fear to Friendship: Australia's Policies Towards the People's Republic of China 1966-1982. LC 84-11956. 351p. 1985. text ed. 37.50x (ISBN 0-7022-1738-7). U of Queensland Pr.

Fung, K. K., tr. see Yefung, Sun.

Fung, K. T., jt. auth. see Ahamd, S. I.

Fung, Lawrence, ed. China Trade Handbook. 312p. 49.95x (ISBN 0-87196-557-7). Facts on File.

Fung, M. M., et al, eds. Hsien-tai Chung-kuo shih hsuan: 1917-1949, 2 vols. 2004p. (Chinese.). 1974. Set. 75.00x (ISBN 0-295-95425-6). U of Wash Pr.

Fung, Man-chong, tr. see Ogilvie, L. J.

Fung, R., ed. Protective Barriers for Containment of Toxic Materials. LC 80-12811. (Pollution Technology Review Ser.: No. 66). 288p. 1980. 39.00 (ISBN 0-8155-0804-2). Noyes.

--Surface Coal Mining Technology: Engineering & Environmental Aspects. LC 81-11036. (Energy Tech. Rev. 71; Pollution Tech Rev. 83). (Illus.). 380p. 1982. 45.00 (ISBN 0-8155-0866-2). Noyes.

Fung, Raymond. Households of God on China's Soil. LC 82-18974. 96p. (Orig.). 1983. pap. 5.95 (ISBN 0-88344-189-6). Orbis Bks.

Fung, Sydney S. & Lai, S. T. Twenty-Five T'ang Poets: Index to English Translations. (Renditions Bks.). (Illus.). 724p. 1984. 75.00x (ISBN 0-295-96155-4, Pub. by Chinese U Pr). U of Wash Pr.

Fung, Y., jt. ed. see Greenwood, Donald T.

Fung, Y. C. Biodynamics: Circulation. (Illus.). 355p. 1984. 33.00 (ISBN 0-387-90867-6). Springer-Verlag.

--Biomechanics: Mechanical Properties of Living Tissues. (Illus.). 400p. 1981. 34.50 (ISBN 0-387-90472-7). Springer-Verlag.

--Foundations of Solid Mechanics. 1965. ref. ed. 41.95 (ISBN 0-13-329912-0). P-H.

Fung, Yu-lan. Chuang-Tzu: A New Selected Translation with an Exposition of the Philosophy of Kuo Hsiang. lib. bdg. 79.95 (ISBN 0-87968-187-X). Krishna Pr.

Fung, Yuan-Cheng. A First Course in Continuum Mechanics. 2nd ed. (International Series in Dynamics). (Illus.). 1977. 40.95 (ISBN 0-13-318311-4). P-H.

Funge, Robert. The Lie the Lamb Knows. LC 79-65855. 1979. pap. 3.00 (ISBN 0-933180-04-7). Spoon Riv Poetry.

Fung Yuet-san. On Silk Scroll. 1985. 5.95 (ISBN 0-533-05610-1). Vantage.

Fung Yu-Lan. History of Chinese Philosophy, 2 vols. Bodde, D., tr. 1952-53. Vol. 2. 72.50 (ISBN 0-691-07115-2); pap. 19.95 (ISBN 0-691-02022-1); Vol. 1. pap. 14.95 (ISBN 0-691-02021-3). Princeton U Pr.

Fung Yu-Lang. A Short History of Chinese Philosophy. abr. ed. Bedde, Derk, ed. Orig. Title: History of Chinese Philosophy. 1966. pap. text ed. 10.95x (ISBN 0-02-910980-9). Free Pr.

Funiak, William Q. de see De Funiak, William Q. & Vaughn, Michael J.

Funigiello, Philip J. The Challenge to Urban Liberalism: Federal-City Relations During World War II. LC 78-2670. (Twentieth-Century America Ser). 296p. 1978. 23.95x (ISBN 0-87049-228-4). U of Tenn Pr.

--Toward a National Power Policy: The New Deal & the Electric Utility Industry, 1933-1941. LC 72-92695. pap. 78.50 (ISBN 0-317-28770-2, 2020622). Bks Demand UMI.

Funk & Rieber. Handbook of Welding. 380p. 1985. pap. text ed. 21.00t (ISBN 0-534-01074-1, 77F6028); write for info. (ISBN 0-534-03513-2). Breton Pubs.

Funk, A. L., compiled by. A Select Bibliography of Books on World War II: Published in the United States 1966-1975. 34p. 1975. 2.50x (ISBN 0-89126-074-9). MA-AH Pub.

Funk And Wagnalls Dictionary Staff, jt. ed. see Hayakawa, S. I.

Funk And Wagnalls Editors. Funk & Wagnall's Standard College Dictionary. new updated ed. LC 72-13007. (Funk & W Bk.). 1632p. 1977. 9.95i (ISBN 0-308-10309-2); thumb indexed 10.95i (ISBN 0-308-10310-6). T Y Crowell.

Funk, Arthur L. The Politics of Torch: The Allied Landings & the Algiers Putsch, 1942. LC 74-2020. (Illus.). viii, 322p. 1974. 25.00x (ISBN 0-7006-0123-6). U Pr of KS.

Funk, Arthur L., ed. American Committee on the History of the Second World War: Newsletter, May 1968-September 1977, No. 1-18, No. 1-18. 360p. 1978. pap. text ed. 36.00x (ISBN 0-89126-060-9). MA-AH Pub.

--Politics & Strategy in the Second World War: Germany, Great Britain, Japan, the Soviet Union & the United States. 113p. 1976. pap. text ed. 4.50x (ISBN 0-89126-024-2). MA-AH Pub.

Funk, Arthur L., compiled by. The Second World War: A Select Bibliography of Books in English since 1975. 200p. 1985. lib. bdg. 24.95 (ISBN 0-941690-15-6). Regina Bks.

Funk, B. M., jt. auth. see Schatz, A. E.

Funk, Berverley M., jt. auth. see Schatz, Anne E.

Funk, Beverley M., jt. auth. see Schatz, Anne E.

Funk, Beverly M., jt. auth. see Schatz, Anne E.

Funk, Charles E. Hog on Ice & Other Curious Expressions. LC 48-5950. (Illus.). 1948. 12.95i (ISBN 0-06-001770-8, HarpT). Har-Row.

--Hog on Ice & Other Curious Expressions. LC 84-48646. (Illus.). 224p. 1985. pap. 5.72i (ISBN 0-06-091259-6, CN 1259, CN). Har-Row.

--Thereby Hangs a Tale: Stories of Curious Word Origins. LC 50-6750. 1950. 10.95i (ISBN 0-06-001800-3, HarpT). Har-Row.

--Thereby Hangs a Tale: Stories of Curious Word Origins. LC 84-48645. 320p. 1985. pap. 7.64i (ISBN 0-06-091260-X, CN 1260, CN). Har-Row.

Funk, David A. Group Dynamic Law. LC 80-84733. xiv, 612p. 1982. 29.95 (ISBN 0-8022-2378-8). Philos Lib.

Funk, Edward R. Welding Fundamentals. 1985. text ed. write for info. (ISBN 0-534-01074-1, Breton Pubs). Wadsworth Pub.

Funk, Franz X. Van see Von Funk, Franz X.

Funk, Georg. Die Algenvegetation Des Golfes Von Neapel. (Pubbl. d. Stazione Zool. di Napoli). (Illus., Ger.). Repr. of 1927 ed. lib. bdg. 63.00 (ISBN 3-87429-142-1). Lubrecht & Cramer.

--Beitraege zur Kenntnis der Meeresalgen von Neapel, zugleich mikrophotographischer Atlas. (Pubbl. d. Stazione Zool. di Napoli). (Illus., Ger.). 1978. Repr. of 1935 ed. lib. bdg. 31.50 (ISBN 3-87429-146-4). Lubrecht & Cramer.

Funk, J. F., jt. ed. see Coffman, John S.

Funk, Jerry. Business Mathematics. 416p. 1980. pap. text ed. 24.24 (ISBN 0-205-06849-9, 1068490). Allyn.

--Business Mathematics. 656p. 1985. text ed. 18.95 (ISBN 0-675-20307-4). Additional supplements may be obtained from publisher. Merrill.

--Sportset: A Math Practice Set. 100p. pap. text ed. 9.66 (ISBN 0-205-07670-X, 177670). Allyn.

Funk, Mary & Funk, Peter. Word Power Made Simple. (Made Simple Ser.). (Illus.). 192p. 1986. pap. 4.95 (ISBN 0-385-19618-0). Doubleday.

Funk, Merle M. Shootout at Clearwater. (YA) 1979. 8.95 (ISBN 0-685-59936-1, Avalon). Bouregy.

--Wes Weatherby, Gunfighter. (YA) 1979. 8.95 (ISBN 0-685-93883-2, Avalon). Bouregy.

Funk, Nancy. Two Christmas Plays. 1984. 3.50 (ISBN 0-89536-695-9, 4872). CSS of Ohio.

Funk, Peter. It Pays to Increase Your Word Power. (gr. 11 up). pap. 3.50 (ISBN 0-553-24841-3). Bantam.

Funk, Peter, jt. auth. see Funk, Mary.

Funk, Rainer. Erich Fromm: The Courage to Be Human. 320p. 1982. 19.50 (ISBN 0-8264-0061-2). Continuum.

Funk, Robert. Challenges of Emerging Leadership: Community Based Independent Living Programs & the Disability Rights Movement. Walker, Lisa J., ed. viii, 62p. pap. 4.95 (ISBN 0-937846-94-5). Inst Educ Lead.

Funk, Robert W. A Beginning-Intermediate Grammar of Hellenistic Greek, 3 vols. 2nd, rev. ed. Incl. Vol. 1. Morphology; Vol. 2. Syntax; Vol. 3. Appendices. LC 72-88769. (Society of Biblical Literature. Sources for Biblical Studies). (Orig.). 1977. Set. pap. text ed. 19.50 (ISBN 0-89130-148-8, 06-03-02); pap. text ed. 8.95 each vol. Scholars Pr GA.

--Christopher Isherwood: A Reference Guide. 1979. lib. bdg. 27.50 (ISBN 0-8161-8072-5, Hall Reference). G K Hall.

--Jesus as Precursor. 165p. 1975. pap. 8.95 (ISBN 0-317-35699-2, 06-06-02); pap. 5.95 members (ISBN 0-317-35700-X). Scholars Pr GA.

--New Gospel Parallels, Vol. 1. LC 84-48727. (Foundations & Facets Ser.). 512p. 1985. 29.95 (ISBN 0-8006-2104-2, 1-2104). Fortress.

--Parables & Presence. LC 82-71827. 224p. 1982. 15.95 (ISBN 0-8006-0688-4, 1-688). Fortress.

Funk, Robert W., ed. Greek Grammar of the New Testament & Other Early Christian Literature. LC 61-8077. 1961. 30.00x (ISBN 0-226-27110-2). U of Chicago Pr.

--Semeia Eight: Literary Critical Studies of Biblical Texts. 131p. 1977. pap. 9.95 (ISBN 0-317-35719-0, 06-20-08); pap. 6.95 members (ISBN 0-317-35720-4). Scholars Pr GA.

Funk, Robert W., ed. see Braun, Herbert, et al.

Funk, Robert W., ed. see Bultmann, Rudolf.

Funk, Robert W., ed. see Haenchen, Ernst.

Funk, Robert W., ed. see Kasemann, Ernst, et al.

Funk, Robert W., ed. see Robinson, James M., et al.

Funk, Robert W., tr. Greek Grammar of the New Testament & Other Early Christian Literature. 28.00 (ISBN 0-310-24780-2). Zondervan.

FUnk, Robert W., tr. see Haenchen, Ernst.

Funk, Roger L., tr. see Scheler, Max.

Funk, Sandra N., ed. Conflict & Collaboration: Peaceful Solutions to the Intranursing Wars. LC 81-22319. (Illus.). 41p. (Orig.). 1981. pap. 5.00 (ISBN 0-942146-00-X). Midwest Alliance Nursing.

Funk, Sandra N., jt. ed. see Minckley, Barbara B.

Funk, V. A., ed. see Willi Henning Society, 1st Meeting.

Funk, Vicki A., jt. ed. see Platnick, Norman I.

Funk, Vicki Ann. The Systematics of Montanoa (Asteraceae-Heliantheae) (Memoirs of the New York Botanical Garden Ser.: Vol. 36). (Illus.). 1982. pap. 21.00x (ISBN 0-89327-243-4). NY Botanical.

Funk, Virginia B., jt. auth. see Linderman, Joan M.

Funk, Virginia M. Your Last Half Century May Be Better Than Your First. 2nd ed. (Consider This Ser.). (Illus.). 110p. 1984. pap. 7.95 (ISBN 0-915433-04-4). Packrat WA.

Funk, Wilfred. Six Weeks to Words of Power. (gr. 9 up). 1983. pap. 3.50 (ISBN 0-671-47761-7). PB.

Funk, Wilfred & Lewis, Norman. Thirty Days to a More Powerful Vocabulary. LC 72-94340. (Funk & W Bk.). (gr. 9-12). 1970. text ed. 12.45 (ISBN 0-308-40079-8, 430180). T Y Crowell.

Funke, Gail S., et al. Assets & Liabilities of Correctional Industries. LC 81-47679. 176p. 1981. 22.50x (ISBN 0-669-04542-X). Lexington Bks.

Funke, Gerhard, ed. Akten Des Vierten Internationalen Kant-Kongresses: Mainz 6-10, April 1974: Part III Vortraege. 1975. 23.20x (ISBN 3-11-004368-8). De Gruyter.

--Akten Des Vierten Internationalen Kant-Kongresses Mainz 6-10, April 1974: Part II, 1 & 2 Sektionen, 2 vols. xxx, 986p. (Ger.). 1974. 104.00x (ISBN 3-11-004371-8). De Gruyter.

--Akten Des Vierten Internationalen Kant-Kongresses Mainz, 6.-10. April 1974: Part I, Kant-Studien Sunderhoft, Symposien. viii, 310p. 1974. pap. 25.60x (ISBN 3-11-004369-6). De Gruyter.

Funke, Maurice. From Saint to Psychotic: The Crisis of Human Identity in the Late 18th Century. LC 83-47646. (American University Studies III: Vol. 2). 215p. (Orig.). 1983. pap. text ed. 20.55 (ISBN 0-8204-0001-7). P Lang Pubs.

Funkenstein, Daniel H. Medical Students, Medical Schools & Society During Five Eras: Factors Affecting the Career Choices of Physicians, 1958-1976. LC 77-19063. 224p. 1978. prof ref 22.00x (ISBN 0-88410-704-3). Ballinger Pub.

Funkhouser, Charles W. & Bruscemi, John N. Perspectives on Schooling for Texas Educators. 216p. 1981. pap. text ed. 12.95 (ISBN 0-8403-2436-7). Kendall-Hunt.

Funkhouser, Charles W., et al. Classroom Applications of the Curriculum: A Systems Approach. 160p. 1981. pap. text ed. 12.50 (ISBN 0-8403-2462-6). Kendall-Hunt.

Funkhouser, Erica. Natural Affinities. LC 82-74512. 68p. 1983. 12.95 (ISBN 0-914086-43-X); pap. 6.95 (ISBN 0-914086-42-1). Alicejamesbooks.

Funkhouser, G. Ray, jt. auth. see Ritti, R. Richard.

Funnell, B. M. & Riedel, W. R. Micropalaeontology of Oceans. 1971. 165.00 (ISBN 0-521-07642-0). Cambridge U Pr.

Funnell, Charles E. By the Beautiful Sea: The Rise & High Times of That Great American Resort, Atlantic City. 1983. 8.95 (ISBN 0-8135-0986-6). Rutgers U Pr.

Funston, Gwendolyn. Apricot Sky. 1985. price not set. G Funston.

Funston, Jay L., jt. ed. see Wilde, George.

Funston, John. Malay Politics in Malaysia: A Study of Umno & Pas. 1981. pap. text ed. 12.95x (ISBN 0-686-31818-8, 00116). Heinemann Ed.

Funston, Richard. Constitutional Counterrevolution. Text ed. 380p. 1977. 15.95x (ISBN 0-470-99022-8). Schenkman Bks Inc.

--A Vital National Seminar: The Role of the Supreme Court in American Political Life. LC 78-51944. 226p. 1978. pap. text ed. 9.95 (ISBN 0-87484-409-6). Mayfield Pub.

Fuoco, Frederick J. Behavioral Procedures for a Psychiatric Unit & Halfway House. (Illus.). 288p. 1985. 38.50 (ISBN 0-442-22491-5). Van Nos Reinhold.

Fuori, W., et al. Introduction to Computer Operations. 2nd ed. 1981. 23.95 (ISBN 0-13-480392-2). P-H.

Fuori, William. COBOL Programming for the IBM PC & PC XT: Vol. 1. 275p. 1984. 19.95 (ISBN 0-8359-0779-1). Reston.

--COBOL Programming for the IBM PC & PC XT: Vol. 2. 250p. 1984. 19.95 (ISBN 0-8359-0780-5). Reston.

--FORTH Programming for the IBM PC & PC XT. 224p. 19.95 (ISBN 0-8359-2099-2). Reston.

--FORTRAN 77 Programming for the IBM PC & PC XT. 224p. 1984. 19.95 (ISBN 0-8359-2096-8). Reston.

--FORTRAN 77 Programming for the IBM PC & XT. 19.95 (ISBN 0-317-12833-7). P-H.

--Pascal Programming for the IBM PC & PC XT. 1984. cancelled (ISBN 0-317-06174-7). Reston.

Fuori, William & Aufiero, Lawrence. Introduction to Information Processing. (Illus.). 512p. 1986. text ed. 26.95 (ISBN 0-13-484601-X). P-H.

Fuori, William M. Introduction to the Computer: The Tool of Business. 3rd ed. (Illus.). 720p. 1981. text ed. 24.95 (ISBN 0-13-480343-4); pap. 8.95 study guide (ISBN 0-13-480368-X). P-H.

Fuori, William M. & Gaughran, Stephen J. Structured COBOL Programming. (Illus.). 544p. 1984. pap. text ed. 25.95 (ISBN 0-13-854430-1). P-H.

Fuori, William M. & Tedesco, Dominick. Introduction to Information Processing. (Illus.). 352p. 1983. pap. text ed. 9.95 (ISBN 0-13-484634-6); text ed. 26.95 (ISBN -13-484601-X). P-H.

--Introduction to Information Processing: Study Guide. (Illus.). 80p. 1983. pap. 3.95 (ISBN 0-13-484659-1). P H.

Fuortes, M. G. see Autrum, H., et al.

Fuoss, Donald E. Blueprinting Your Coaching Career. LC 72-78962. 64p. (Orig.). 1973. pap. 2.50 (ISBN 0-87576-041-4). Pilot Bks.

--Complete Handbook of Winning Football Drills. (Illus.). 362p. 1984. 29.95x (ISBN 0-205-08071-5, 628071, Pub. by Longwood Div). Allyn.

Fuoss, Donald E. & Smith, Rowland. Effective Football Coaching: Game-Winning Techniques for Preventing Mistakes & Errors. 283p. 1980. 27.95x (ISBN 0-205-07125-2, 627125, Pub. by Longwood Div). Allyn.

Fuoss, Donald E. & Troppmann, Robert J. Creative Management Techniques in Interscholastic Athletics. LC 83-14869. 512p. 1983. Repr. lib. bdg. 27.50 (ISBN 0-89874-672-8). Krieger.
--Effective Coaching: A Psychological Approach. LC 81-7624. 348p. 1981. text ed. 26.45 (ISBN 0-471-03233-6). Wiley.
Fu Pei Mei. Chinese Cookbook, Vol. III. 1981. 20.00 (ISBN 0-911268-33-2). Heinman.
--Chinese Cookbook, Vol. I. 1969. 20.00 (ISBN 0-911268-14-6). Heinman.
--Chinese Cookbook, Vol. II. 1974. 20.00 (ISBN 0-911268-18-9). Heinman.
Fuqua, E. C., jt. auth. see Warren, Thomas B.
Fuqua, Marjorie V., jt. auth. see McCubbin, Jack H.
Fuqua, Paul. Drug Abuse: Investigation & Control. LC 77-5809. (Illus.). 1977. text ed. 27.65 (ISBN 0-07-022665-2). McGraw.
Fuqua, Paul & Wilson, Jerry. Security Investigator's Handbook. LC 78-62615. 232p. 1979. 16.95x (ISBN 0-87201-398-7). Gulf Pub.
--Terrorism: The Executive's Guide to Survival. LC 77-86461. (Illus.). 158p. 1978. 16.95x (ISBN 0-87201-821-0). Gulf Pub.
Fuqua, Robert W., jt. ed. see Greenman, James T.
Fuquay, John, jt. auth. see Bearden, H. Joe.
Furan Illustrators see Reece, Collen L.
Furay, Conal. The Grass-Roots Mind in America: The American Sense of Absolutes. LC 76-48927. 1977. pap. text ed. 6.95 (ISBN 0-531-05598-1, Dist. by M & B Fullfillment). Wiener Pub Inc.
Furay, Conal & Salevouris, Michael J. History: A Workbook of Skill Development. 1979. pap. 9.95 (ISBN 0-531-05620-1). Watts.
Furbank, P. N. E. M. Forster: A Life. LC 80-24821. (Illus.). 672p. 1981. pap. 8.95 (ISBN 0-15-628651-3, Harv). HarBraceJ.
--Samuel Butler. LC 76-43969. 1945. lib. bdg. 12.50 (ISBN 0-8414-4171-5). Folcroft.
Furbank, P. N., ed. see Dickens, Charles.
Furbank, P. N., ed. see Forster, E. M.
Furbank, P. N., jt. ed. see Grahman, Martin.
Furbank, P. N., jt. ed. see Lago, Mary.
Furbank, P. N., tr. see Svevo, Italo.
Furbank, Philip N. Samuel Butler, Eighteen Thirty-Five to Nineteen Two. 2nd ed. LC 76-131373. viii, 124p. 1971. 14.00 (ISBN 0-208-01033-5, Archon). Shoe String.
Furbee, Louanna, jt. auth. see Snively, W. D., Jr.
Furbee-Losee, Louanna. The Correct Language, Tojolabal: A Grammar with Ethnographic Notes. LC 75-25115. (American Indian Linguistics Ser.). 1976. lib. bdg. 51.00 (ISBN 0-8240-1966-0). Garland Pub.
Furber, Alan. Layout & Design for Calligraphers. LC 83-18160. (Illus.). 64p. (Orig.). 1984. pap. 4.95 (ISBN 0-317-04024-3). Taplinger.
Furber, Donald & Callahan, Anne. Erotic Love in Literature from Medieval Legend to Romantic Illusion. LC 81-52805. 216p. 1982. 15.00x (ISBN 0-87875-219-6). Whitston Pub.
Furber, E. A., ed. The Coinages of Latin America & the Caribbean. new ed. LC 74-78127. (Gleanings from the Numismatist Ser: Vol. 5). (Illus.). 385p. 1974. 30.00x (ISBN 0-88000-041-4). Quarterman.
Furber, Holden. Rival Empires of Trade in the Orient, 1600-1800. Shafer, Boyd, ed. LC 76-7337. (Europe & the World in the Age of Expansion: Vol. 2). (Illus.). 1976. 20.00x (ISBN 0-8166-0787-7); pap. 5.95x (ISBN 0-8166-0851-2). U of Minn Pr.
Furber, Holden see Burke, Edmund.
Furberg, jt. ed. see Eriksson.
Furberg, Mats. Saying & Meaning: A Main Theme in J. L. Austin's Philosophy. 299p. 1971. 20.00x (ISBN 0-87471-065-0). Rowman.
Furbush, S. A. Energy-Conservation Opportunities in the Chemical Industry. Gyftopoulos, Elias P. & Cohen, Karen C., eds. (Industrial Energy-Conservation Manuals Ser.: No. 14). (Illus.). 136p. 1982. loose-leaf 20.00x (ISBN 0-262-06081-7). MIT Pr.
Furcha, E., tr. Huldrych Zwingli Writings in Defense of the Reformed Faith: Writings in the Defense of the Reformed Faith, Vol. 1. (Pittsburgh Theological Monographs: No. 12). 1984. pap. 19.95 (ISBN 0-915138-58-1). Pickwick.
Furcha, E. J., ed. & tr. Selected Writings of Hans Denck. LC 76-7057. (Pittsburgh Original Texts & Translations Ser.: No. 1). 1976. 5.50 (ISBN 0-915138-15-8). Pickwick.
Furcha, E. J., ed. Spirit within Structure: Essays in Honor of George Jonhston on the Occasion of His Seventieth Birthday. (Pittsburgh Theological Monographs: New Ser.: No. 3). xvi, 194p. 1983. pap. 12.50 (ISBN 0-915138-53-0). Pickwick.
Furchgott, Terry. Nanda in India. (Illus.). 32p. (ps-3). 1983. 9.95 (ISBN 0-233-96860-1). Andre Deutsch.
Furchs, E. J. & Pipkin, H. Wayne, eds. Prophet, Pastor, Protestant: The Work of Huldrych Zwingli after Five Hundred Years. LC 84-14723. (Pittsburgh Theological Monographs (New Series): No. 11). (Orig.). 1984. pap. 15.00 (ISBN 0-915138-64-6). Pickwick.
Furchtgott, Ernest. Pharmacological & Biophysical Agents & Behavior. 1971. 73.50 (ISBN 0-12-269950-5). Acad Pr.
Furci, Carmelo. The Chilean Communist Party & the Road to Socialism. (Illus.). 218p. 1985. bds. 26.25x (ISBN 0-86232-236-7, Pub. by Zed Pr England). Biblio Dist.
--Chilean Communist Party & the Road to Socialism. (Illus.). 218p. 1985. pap. 10.25 (ISBN 0-86232-237-5, Pub. by Zed Pr England). Biblio Dist.
Furcolo, Foster. The New Practical Law for the Layman. LC 82-1717. 1982. pap. 6.95 (ISBN 0-87491-612-7). Acropolis.
Furcolo, Fostor. Ballots Anyone? 278p. 1982. 18.95 (ISBN 0-87073-441-5); pap. 8.95 (ISBN 0-87073-442-3). Schenkman Bks Inc.
Furda, Ivan, ed. Unconventional Sources of Dietary Fiber. LC 83-2691. (Symposium Ser.: No. 214). 315p. 1983. lib. bdg. 58.95x (ISBN 0-8412-0768-2). Am Chemical.
Furdson, Edward. The European Defense Community: A History. LC 79-21220. 1980. 27.50x (ISBN 0-312-26927-7). St Martin.
Furek, Joseph. Benediction. (Orig.). 1979. pap. 2.50 (ISBN 0-89083-505-5). Zebra.
Furen, Wang, et al. Highlights of Tibetan History. Jian, Xu, tr. (China Studies). (Illus.). 206p. (Orig.). 1984. pap. 5.95 (ISBN 0-8351-1170-9). China Bks.
Furer, Howard B. The Fuller Court, Eighteen Eighty-Eight to Nineteen Ten, 9 vols. LC 84-2873. (Supreme Court in American Life Ser.: Vol. 5). Date not set. 30.00 ea. (ISBN 0-86733-060-0); Set. 230.00x. Assoc Faculty Pr.
--The Germans in America, 1607-1970: A Chronology & Factbook. LC 72-10087. (Ethnic Chronology Ser.: No. 8). 160p. 1973. lib. bdg. 8.50 (ISBN 0-379-00506-9). Oceana.
--Harry S. Truman, 1884-1972: Chronology, Documents, Bibliographical Aids. LC 75-83749. 160p. 1970. 8.00 (ISBN 0-379-12067-4). Oceana.
--Lyndon B. Johnson 1908-1973: Chronology, Documents, Bibliographical Aids. LC 75-95015. (Presidential Chronology Ser). 154p. 1971. 8.00 (ISBN 0-379-12077-1). Oceana.
--Washington, D. C. A Chronological & Documentary History. LC 74-30371. (American Cities Chronology Ser.). 154p. 1975. 8.50 (ISBN 0-379-00611-1). Oceana.
Furer, Howard B., jt. auth. see Landevich, George J.
Furer, Howard B., ed. & compiled by. The British in America, 1578-1970: A Chronology & Factbook. LC 72-8683. (Ethnic Chronology Ser.: No. 7). 153p. 1972. 8.50 (ISBN 0-379-00507-7). Oceana.
Furer, Howard B., ed. Chicago: A Chronological & Documentary History, 1784-1970. LC 73-3078. (American Cities Chronology Ser.: No. 16). 153p. 1974. lib. bdg. 8.50 (ISBN 0-379-00609-X). Oceana.
--James A. Garfield, 1831-1881; Chester A. Arthur 1830-1886: Chronology, Documents, Bibliographical Aids. Incl. Chester A. Arthur: 1830-1886. LC 74-111214. (Oceana Presidential Chronology Ser.). 148p. 1970. 8.00 (ISBN 0-379-12065-8). Oceana.
--New York: A Chronological & Documentary History, 1524-1970. LC 74-3044. (American Cities Chronology Ser: No. 66). 153p. 1974. lib. bdg. 8.50 (ISBN 0-379-00610-3). Oceana.
Furer, Howard B., ed. & compiled by. The Scandinavians in America, Nine Hundred Eighty-Six to Nineteen Seventy: A Chronology & Fact Book. LC 72-10257. (Ethnic Chronology Ser.: No. 6). 152p. 1972. 8.50 (ISBN 0-379-00505-0). Oceana.
Furer, Howard B., jt. ed. see Lankevich, George J.
Furer, Manuel, jt. auth. see Mahler, Margaret S.
Furer-Haimendorf, Christop Von see Von Furer-Haimendorf, Christoph.
Furer-Haimendorf, Christoph. Highlanders of Arunachal Pradesh. 160p. 1982. 50.00x (ISBN 0-7069-1367-1, Pub. by Garlandfold England). State Mutual Bk.
Furer-Haimendorf, Christoph van see Von Furer-Haimendorf, Christoph.
Furer-Haimendorf, Christoph Von see Von Furer-Haimendorf, Christoph.
Furer-Haimendorf, Christoph von see Von Furer-Haimendorf, Christoph.
Furer-Haimendorf, Christoph Von, ed. Caste & Kin in Nepal, India & Ceylon: Anthropological Studies in Hindu-Buddhist Contact Zones. (Illus.). 1978. text ed. 20.50x (ISBN 0-391-01073-5). Humanities.
Furer-Haimendorf, Christoph Von, ed. see Nebesky-Wojkowitz, Rene De.
Furer-Haimendorf, Christoph Von see Von Furer-Haimendorf, Christoph.
Furer-Haimendorf, Christoph von see Von Furer-Haimendorf, Christoph.
Furer-Haimendorf, Christopher V. A Himalayan Tribe: From Cattle to Cash. 1980. 23.00x (ISBN 0-520-04074-0). U of Cal Pr.
Furer-Haimendorf, Christopher von see Von Furer-Haimendorf, Christopher.
Furer-Haimendorf, E. V. An Anthropological Bibliography of South Asia Together with a Directory of Recent Anthropological Field Work, 3 vols. Incl. Vol. 1. Up to 1954. 1958; Vol. 2. 1955-1959. 1964. pap. text ed. 78.75x (ISBN 90-2796-206-5); Vol. 3. 1960-1964. 1970. pap. 105.00x (ISBN 90-2796-302-9). pap. Mouton.
Furet, Francois. In the Workshop of History. Mandelbaum, Jonathan, tr. LC 84-2638. (Illus.). 288p. 1985. lib. bdg. 27.50x (ISBN 0-226-27336-9). U of Chicago Pr.
--Interpreting the French Revolution. Forster, Elborg, tr. LC 80-42290. 224p. 1981. 39.50 (ISBN 0-521-23574-X); pap. 11.95 (ISBN 0-521-28049-4). Cambridge U Pr.
Furet, Francois & Ozouf, Jacques. Reading & Writing: Literacy in France from Calvin to Jules Ferry. LC 82-9502. (Cambridge Studies in Oral & Literate Culture: No. 5). (Illus.). 400p. 1983. 59.50 (ISBN 0-521-22389-X); pap. 19.95 (ISBN 0-521-27402-8). Cambridge U Pr.
Furfey, P. H. see Hamel, Ignatius A.
Furfey, Paul H. Scope & Method of Sociology. LC 65-17182. 556p. Repr. of 1953 ed. 22.50 (ISBN 0-8154-0075-6). Cooper Sq.
Furfine, Sandy S. & Nowak, Nancy C. The Jewish Preschool Teachers Handbook. LC 81-67023. (Illus.). 132p. (Orig.). 1981. pap. 13.50 (ISBN 0-86705-004-7). AIRE.
Furgerson, W. F. Conserving Energy in Refrigeration. Gyftopoulos, Elias P. & Cohen, Karen C., eds. (Industrial Energy-Conservation Manuals: No. 12). 144p. 1982. loose-leaf 20.00x (ISBN 0-262-06080-9). MIT Pr.
Furgeson, Michael D. & Bohr, Paula. Living Anatomy Laboratory Manual. LC 83-43292. (Illus.). 200p. (Orig.). 1984. 12.95x (ISBN 0-940122-12-X). Multi Media Co.
Furgis, Ellen V. & Valentine, D. Eugene. Greek Cooking at Its American Best. (Illus.). spiral bdg., softcover 8.95 (ISBN 0-941968-01-4, An Everest House Book). Dodd.
Furguson, J. De Lance see Burns, Robert.
Furia, Philip. Pound's Cantos Declassified. LC 83-43227. 160p. 1984. 18.75x (ISBN 0-271-00373-1). Pa St U Pr.
Furia, Thomas E. Current Aspects of Food Colorants. LC 77-10088. 100p. (Orig.). 1977. 32.50 (ISBN 0-8493-5395-5). Krieger.
Furia, Thomas E., ed. & tr. Fenaroli's Handbook of Flavor Ingredients, 2 vols. 2nd ed. LC 72-152143. (Handbook Ser.). 1975. Vol. 1, 560p. 66.00 (ISBN 0-87819-534-3); Vol. 2, 944p. 69.00 (ISBN 0-87819-532-7). CRC Pr.
Furia, Thomas E., ed. Handbook of Food Additives, Vol. 2. 2nd ed. (Handbook Ser.). 432p. 1980. 66.00 (ISBN 0-8493-0543-8). CRC Pr.
--Handbook of Food Additives, Vol. 1. 2nd ed. LC 68-21741. (Handbook Ser.). 432p. 1979. Vol. 1. 76.50 (ISBN 0-8493-0542-X). CRC Pr.
Furio, Joanne, ed. see Raphael, Phyllis.
Furio Ceriol, Fadrique. Of Councils & Counselors, Fifteen Hundred & Seventy: An English Reworking by Thomas Blundeville of el Consejo I Consejeros Del Principe, 1559. LC 63-7083. 1963. 30.00x (ISBN 0-8201-1018-3). Schol Facsimiles.
Furioso. There Is No Death That Is Not Ennobled by So Great Cause: Anecdotes of the American Patriots 1730-1816. Cantilli, E. J. & Guernelli, J., eds. Horvath, V., tr. 80p. 1976. 9.95 (ISBN 0-686-16305-2); pap. 7.95 (ISBN 0-686-16306-0). Obranoel Pr.
Furlan, G., et al, eds. Nonconventional Energy. 750p. 1984. 75.00x (ISBN 0-306-41466-X, Plenum Pr). Plenum Pub.
--Non-Conventional Energy Sources: Proceedings of the First Latin American School & Third International Symposium, Bogota, Colombia, July 13-30, 1982. 700p. 1984. text ed. 75.00x (ISBN 9971-966-78-6, Pub. by World Sci Singapore). Taylor & Francis.
Furlan, M., jt. ed. see Beck, E. A.
Furler, Rene, jt. auth. see Thurlimann, Bruno.
Furley, David J. & Allen, R. E., eds. Studies in Pre-Socratic Philosophy, Vol. 2. (International Library of Philosophy & Scientific Method). 400p. 1975. text ed. 25.25x (ISBN 0-391-00360-7). Humanities.
Furley, David J. & Wilkie, J. S., eds. Galen: On Respiration & the Arteries, an Edition with English Translation & Commentary of De Usu Respirationis, an in Arteriis Natura Sanguis Contineatur, De Usu Pulsum, & De Causis Respirationis. LC 81-47130. 300p. 1983. 30.00x (ISBN 0-691-08286-3). Princeton U Pr.
Furley, O. W. & Watson, T. History of Education in East Africa. LC 77-23632. (Studies in East African Society & History). 1977. text ed. 21.50x (ISBN 0-88357-044-0); pap. text ed. 8.95 (ISBN 0-88357-045-9). NOK Pubs.
Furley, Peter A., et al. Geography of Biosphere. (Illus.). 1982. text ed. 99.95 (ISBN 0-408-70801-8). Butterworth.
Furley, William D. Studies in the Use of Fire in the Ancient Greek Religion. rev. ed. Connor, W. R., ed. LC 80-2650. (Monographs in Clasical Studies). (Illus.). 1981. lib. bdg. 29.00 (ISBN 0-405-14037-1). Ayer Co Pubs.
Furlong, Charles W. Let'er Buck: A Story of the Passing of the Old West. LC 77-159961. 280p. 1971. Repr. of 1921 ed. 40.00 (ISBN 0-8103-1294-8). Gale.
Furlong, Marjorie & Pill, Virginia. Edible? Incredible! Pondlife. LC 79-27779. (Illus.). 96p. 1980. lib. bdg. 11.95 (ISBN 0-87961-084-0); pap. 5.95 (ISBN 0-87961-083-2). Naturegraph.
--Wild Edible Fruits & Berries. LC 74-32015. (Illus.). 64p. 1974. 11.95 (ISBN 0-87961-033-6); pap. 5.95 (ISBN 0-87961-032-8). Naturegraph.
Furlong, Mary, jt. auth. see Kearsley, Greg.
Furlong, Mary S. & McMahon, Edward T. Consumer Law, Competencies in Law & Citizenship. 124p. 1982. pap. text ed. write for info. (ISBN 0-314-65089-X). West Pub.
--Family Law: Competencies in Law & Citizenship. (Illus.). 200p. 1983. pap. text ed. 6.95 (ISBN 0-314-77868-3). West Pub.
Furlong, Michael, jt. auth. see Nutt-Powell, Thomas E.
Furlong, Monica. Christian Uncertainties. LC 82-72129. xii, 124p. 1982. pap. 6.95 (ISBN 0-936384-06-9). Cowley Pubns.
--Contemplating Now. LC 83-70991. 128p. 1983. pap. 6.00 (ISBN 0-936384-13-1). Cowley Pubns.
--Merton: A Biography. LC 79-3588. (Illus.). 320p. 1980. 12.95i (ISBN 0-06-063079-5, HarpR). Har-Row.
--Merton: A Biography. LC 84-48218. (Illus.). 368p. 1985. pap. 8.61 (ISBN 0-06-063078-7, RD 529, HarpR). Har-Row.
--Travelling In. LC 84-71182. 130p. 1984. pap. 6.00 (ISBN 0-936384-20-4). Cowley Pubns.
Furlong, Norman. English Satire: An Anthology. 1977. Repr. of 1946 ed. lib. bdg. 25.00 (ISBN 0-8495-1604-8). Arden Lib.
Furlong, Norman, ed. English Satire: An Anthology. 1978. Repr. of 1946 ed. lib. bdg. 20.00 (ISBN 0-8482-0823-4). Norwood Edns.
Furlong, Patrick J. Indiana: An Illustrated History. 248p. 1985. 24.95 (ISBN 0-89781-152-6). Windsor Pubns Inc.
Furlong, Philip. The Old World & America. LC 82-51247. 371p. (gr. 6). 1984. pap. 12.00 (ISBN 0-89555-202-7). TAN Bks Pubs.
Furlong, R. Dulany-Furlong & Kindred Families. 1975. 25.00 (ISBN 0-87012-209-6). McClain.
Furlong, R. J., tr. see Pauwels, F.
Furlong, Stewart, jt. auth. see Wylie, Stephen.
Furlong, Stewart S., jt. auth. see Wylie, Stephen R.
Furlong, Vivian, jt. auth. see Edwards, Tony.
Furlong, William B. Shaw & Chesterton: The Metaphysical Jesters. LC 77-114616. 1970. 21.95 (ISBN 0-271-00110-0). Pa St U Pr.
Furlong, William L. & Scranton, Margaret E. The Dynamics of Foreign Policymaking: The President, the Congress & the 1977 Panama Canal Treaties. 220p. 1984. softcover 19.00x (ISBN 0-86531-804-2). Westview.
Furlong, William R. & McCandless, Byron. So Proudly We Hail: The History of the United States Flag. Langley, Harold D., ed. LC 81-607808. (Illus.). 260p. (Orig.). 1981. 25.00 (ISBN 0-87474-448-2); pap. 12.50 (ISBN 0-87474-449-0). Smithsonian.
Furlow, Elaine. Love with No Strings: The Human Touch in Christian Social Ministries. Hullum, Everett, ed. (The Human Touch Photo-Text Ser.: Volume IV). (Illus.). 1977. 6.95 (ISBN 0-937170-15-1). Home Mission.
Furlow, Elaine, et al. Light Upon the Land. (Home Mission Study). 110p. (Orig.). 1984. pap. 2.85 (ISBN 0-937170-28-3). Home Mission.
Furlow, Elaine S., jt. auth. see Rutledge, Don.
Furlow, Elaine S., ed. see Loucks, Celeste, et al.
Furlow, Elaine S., ed. see Loucks, Celeste & Hullum, Everett.
Furlow, Elaine S., ed. see Nicholas, Tim & Touchton, Ken.
Furlow, Malcolm. HO Narrow Gauge Railroad You Can Build. (Illus.). 60p. (Orig.). 1984. pap. 7.95 (ISBN 0-89024-058-2). Kalmbach.
Furman & Welcher, Frank J., eds. Standard Methods of Chemical Analysis, 5 vols. Set. 372.00 (ISBN 0-88275-253-7). Krieger.
Furman, A. L., ed. Ghost Stories. (gr. 5-8). 1964. pap. 1.95 (ISBN 0-671-43613-9). Archway.
--More Horse Stories. (gr. 5-7). 1966. pap. 1.95 (ISBN 0-671-43951-0). Archway.
Furman, Abraham L., ed. Everygirls Adventure Stories. (Illus.). (gr. 6-10). PLB 6.19 (ISBN 0-8313-0053-1). Lantern.
--Everygirls Career Stories. (Illus.). (gr. 6-10). PLB 6.19 (ISBN 0-8313-0049-3). Lantern.
--Everygirls Companion. LC 68-11184. (Everygirls Library). (gr. 5-9). 1968. PLB 6.19 (ISBN 0-685-13773-2). Lantern.
--Everygirls Detective Stories. (Illus.). (gr. 6-10). PLB 6.19 (ISBN 0-8313-0060-4). Lantern.
--More Teen-Age Ghost Stories. (gr. 6-10). 1963. PLB 6.19 (ISBN 0-8313-0052-3). Lantern.
--More Teen-Age Haunted Stories. (gr. 5-10). 1967. PLB 6.19 (ISBN 0-8313-0057-4). Lantern.
--Sports Adventures. (Young Readers Bookshelf). (Illus.). (gr. 4-7). PLB 6.19 (ISBN 0-8313-0046-9). Lantern.
--Teen-Age Detective Stories. LC 68-23983. (gr. 6-10). 1968. 4.25 (ISBN 0-8313-0044-2). Lantern.
--Teen-Age Great Rescue Stories. (gr. 6-10). PLB 6.19 (ISBN 0-8313-0050-7). Lantern.
--Teen-Age Party Time Stories. (gr. 6-10). 1966. PLB 6.19 (ISBN 0-8313-0039-6). Lantern.
--Teen-Age Secret Agent Stories. (Teen-Age Library). (gr. 5-10). PLB 6.19 (ISBN 0-8313-0042-6). Lantern.
--Teen-Age Space Adventures. 192p. 1972. PLB 6.19 (ISBN 0-8313-1595-4). Lantern.
--Teen-Age Spy Stories. (gr. 6-10). 4.25 (ISBN 0-8313-0041-8); PLB 6.19. Lantern.

Furman, D. Religion & Social Conflicts in the U. S. A. 254p. 1985. 7.95 (ISBN 0-8285-2975-2, Pub. by Progress Pubs USSR). Imported Pubns.

Furman, Deane P. & Catts, Paul E. Manual of Medical Entomology. 4th ed. LC 81-10105. (Illus.). 224p. 1982. pap. 13.95 (ISBN 0-521-29920-9). Cambridge U Pr.

Furman, Deane P. & Loomis, Edmond C. The Ticks of California (Acari Ixodida) LC 83-9265. (Bulletin of the California Insect Survey Ser.: Vol. 25). 240p. 1984. lib. bdg. 25.00x (ISBN 0-520-09685-1). U of Cal Pr.

Furman, Edna. What Nursery School Teachers Ask Us. Date not set. price not set (BN#6830). Intl Univs Pr.

Furman, Eleanor L. Retirement: You're in Charge. LC 84-3459. 176p. 1984. 24.95 (ISBN 0-03-069283-0); Feb. 1985, 176p. pap. 8.95 (ISBN 0-03-004827-3). Praeger.

Furman, Erna. A Child's Parent Dies: Studies in Childhood Bereavement. LC 73-86894. 1974. 33.00x (ISBN 0-300-01719-7); pap. 9.95x (ISBN 0-300-02645-5). Yale U Pr.

Furman, Gabriel. Antiquities of Long Island. 11.50 (ISBN 0-911660-15-1). Yankee Peddler.

Furman, Laura. The Glass House. 204p. 1980. 10.95 (ISBN 0-670-34179-7). Viking.

--The Shadow Line. LC 81-24089. 288p. 1982. 14.95 (ISBN 0-670-63764-5). Viking.

--Watch Time Fly. LC 83-47871. 170p. 1983. 14.95 (ISBN 0-670-75016-6). Viking.

Furman, N. Howell, ed. Standard Methods of Chemical Analysis: The Elements, Vol. 1. 6th ed. LC 74-23465. 1426p. 1975. Repr. of 1962 ed. 100.00 (ISBN 0-88275-254-5). Krieger.

Furman, Richard. Reaching Your Full Potential. 1985. pap. 6.95 (ISBN 0-89081-443-0). Harvest Hse.

Furman, Robert A. & Katan, Anny, eds. Therapeutic Nursery School. LC 78-75187. 329p. 1969. text ed. 27.50 (ISBN 0-8236-6500-3). Intl Univs Pr.

Furman, T. T. Approximate Methods in Engineering Design. LC 80-40891. (Mathematics in Science & Engineering Ser.). 408p. 1981. 65.00 (ISBN 0-12-269960-2). Acad Pr.

Furman, William B. Continuous Flow Analysis: Theory & Practice. (Clinical & Biochemical Analysis Ser.: Vol. 3). 1976. 59.75 (ISBN 0-8247-6320-3). Dekker.

Furmanov, D. Chapayev. 318p. 1974. 3.45 (ISBN 0-8285-0970-0, Pub. by Progress Pubs USSR). Imported Pubns.

Furmanov, Dmitry A. Chapayev. Gorchakov, O., ed. Kittell, George & Kittell, Jeanette, trs. from Rus. LC 72-90294. (Soviet Literature in English Translation Ser.). 423p. 1973. Repr. of 1935 ed. 25.00 (ISBN 0-88355-004-0). Hyperion Conn.

Furmanski, Philip, et al, eds. RNA Tumor Viruses, Oncogenes, Human Cancer & AIDS: On Frontiers of Understanding. (Developments in Oncology Ser.). 1985. lib. bdg. 49.95 (ISBN 0-89838-703-5, Pub. by Martinus Nijhoff Netherlands). Kluwer Academic.

Furmston, M. P., jt. auth. see Powell-Smith, Vincent.

Furmston, M. P & Kerridge, Roger, eds. The Effect on English Domestic Law of Membership of the European Communities & of Ratification of the European Convention on Human Rights. 1983. lib. bdg. 56.50 (ISBN 90-247-2811-8, Pub. by Martinus Nijhoff Netherlands). Kluwer Academic.

Furnas, J. C. Voyage to Windward. 478p. 1980. Repr. lib. bdg. 30.00 (ISBN 0-8492-4649-0). R West.

Furnborough, Peter, jt. auth. see Mrowicki, Linda.

Furneaux, Barbara, jt. ed. see Roberts, Brian.

Furneaux, H., intro. by see Tacitus, Cornelius.

Furneaux, Henry, et al, eds. see Tacitus.

Furneaux, Philip. The Palladium of Conscience. LC 74-122161. (Civil Liberties in American History Ser). 267p. 1974. Repr. of 1773 ed. lib. bdg. 35.00 (ISBN 0-306-71972-X). Da Capo.

Furneaux, Rupert. The Battle of Saratoga. LC 69-17940. (Illus.). 320p. 1982. pap. 9.95 (ISBN 0-8128-6125-6). Stein & Day.

--Buried Treasure. LC 79-64159. (Adventures in History Ser.). PLB 12.68 (ISBN 0-382-06298-1). Silver.

--The Money Pit Mystery. 1978. pap. 1.95 (ISBN 0-532-19173-0). Woodhill.

--The Tungus Event. 1979. pap. 1.50 (ISBN 0-8439-0619-7, Leisure Bks). Dorchester Pub Co.

Furnee, Edzard J. Die Wichtigsten Konsonantischen Erscheinungen Des Vorgriechischen Mit Einem Appendix Uber Den Vokalismus. (Janua Linguarum Ser: No. 150). 1972. pap. 51.20x (ISBN 90-2791-997-6). Mouton.

Furnell, Dennis. Health from the Hedgerow: Encyclopedia of Medicinal Plants. (Illus.). 192p. 1985. 15.95 (ISBN 0-7134-4712-5, Pub. by Batsford England). David & Charles.

Furnell, Dennis L. The Country Book of the Year. LC 79-56061. (Illus.). 192p. 1980. 22.50 (ISBN 0-7153-7878-3). David & Charles.

Furner, Mary O. Advocacy & Objectivity: A Crisis in the Professionalization of American Social Science, 1865-1905. LC 73-86403. 376p. 1975. 32.00x (ISBN 0-8131-1309-1). U Pr of Ky.

Furness, C. J. Lotus Petals: The Life & Work of Rudolf Steiner. 59.95 (ISBN 0-8490-0557-4). Gordon Pr.

Furness, Clifton J. Walt Whitman's Estimate of Shakespeare. (Studies in Whitman, No. 28). 1970. pap. 22.95x (ISBN 0-8383-0032-4). Haskell.

Furness, E. L. Introduction to Financial Economics. 1972. pap. 19.95x (ISBN 0-434-90596-8). Intl Ideas.

Furness, Eric L. Money & Credit in Developing Africa. LC 75-27161. 1976. 32.50 (ISBN 0-312-54495-2). St Martin.

--Money & Credit in Developing Africa. Livingstone, I. & Ord, H. W., eds. (Studies in the Economics of Africa). xi, 308p. 1975. pap. text ed. 12.00x (ISBN 0-435-97150-6). Heinemann Ed.

Furness, H. H., ed. see Shakespeare, William.

Furness, Helen K. Concordance to Shakespeare's Poems. LC 71-168078. Repr. of 1874 ed. 22.50 (ISBN 0-404-02645-1). AMS Pr.

Furness, Horace H., ed. see Shakespeare, William.

Furness, Mrs. Horace H. Concordance to Shakespeare's Poems: An Index to Every Word Therein Contained. LC 75-109647. (Select Bibliographies Reprint Ser). 1874. 32.00 (ISBN 0-8369-5256-1). Ayer Co Pubs.

Furness, R. S. Expressionism. (Critical Idiom Ser.). 100p. 1973. pap. 5.50 (ISBN 0-416-75670-0, 2207). Methuen Inc.

Furness, Raymond. Literary History of Germany: Literature History of Germany, Vol. 8. LC 77-10037. (The Twentieth Century, 1890-1945). 302p. 1978. text ed. 25.50x (ISBN 0-06-492310-X). B&N Imports.

--Wagner & Literature. LC 81-14391. 1982. 26.00 (ISBN 0-312-85347-5). St Martin.

Furness, S. M. Georges de la Tour, of Lorraine, 1593-1652. LC 83-45434. Repr. of 1949 ed. 55.00 (ISBN 0-404-20103-2). AMS Pr.

Furness, William H. The Home-Life of Borneo Head-Hunters: Its Festivals & Folklore. 3rd ed. LC 77-86975. 1977. Repr. of 1902 ed. 37.50 (ISBN 0-404-16711-X). AMS Pr.

Furnham. Social Behavior in Context. 1985. 17.86 (ISBN 0-205-08378-1, 798378). Allyn.

Furnham, A. & Argyle, M., eds. The Psychology of Social Situations: Selected Readings. LC 80-41189. 350p. 1981. text ed. 55.00 (ISBN 0-08-024319-3); pap. 19.50 (ISBN 0-08-023719-3). Pergamon.

Furnham, Adrian & Lewis, Alan. The Economic Mind: The Social Psychology of Economic Behavior. 352p. 1985. 35.00 (ISBN 0-312-23405-8). St Martin.

Furnish, Dorothy J. Exploring the Bible with Children. LC 74-34486. 176p. 1975. pap. 6.95 (ISBN 0-687-12426-3). Abingdon.

--Living the Bible with Children. LC 79-12297. 1979. pap. 7.75 (ISBN 0-687-22368-7). Abingdon.

Furnish, Victor P. The Moral Teaching of Paul. Rev. ed. LC 78-10633. 1985. pap. 10.95 (ISBN 0-687-27181-9). Abingdon.

--The Moral Teachings of Paul: Selected Issues. rev. ed. 144p. 1985. pap. 10.95 (ISBN 0-687-27181-9). Abingdon.

--Theology & Ethics in Paul. LC 68-17445. 1978. pap. 12.95 (ISBN 0-687-41499-7). Abingdon.

Furnish, Victor P. & Thulin, Richard L. Pentecost 3. Achtemeier, Elizabeth, et al, eds. LC 79-7377. (Proclamation 2: Aids for Interpreting the Lessons of the Church Year, Ser. A). 64p. (Orig.). 1981. pap. 3.50 (ISBN 0-8006-4098-5, 1-4098). Fortress.

Furnish, Victor P., intro. by. Corinthians II, Vol 32A. LC 83-2056. (Anchor Bible Ser.). (Illus.). 648p. 1984. 18.00 (ISBN 0-385-11199-1). Doubleday.

Furnish, Victor P., ed. see Murphy, Roland E.

Furnish, Victory P., ed. see Fretheim, Terence E.

Furniss, B. S., et al, eds. see Vogel, A. I.

Furniss, E. S. De Gaulle & the French Army: A Crisis in Civil Military Relations. (Twentieth Century Fund Ser.). Repr. of 1964 ed. 10.00 (ISBN 0-527-02818-5). Kraus Repr.

Furniss, Edgar S. Position of the Laborer in a System of Nationalism. LC 58-3121. Repr. of 1920 ed. 25.00x (ISBN 0-678-00093-X). Kelley.

Furniss, Edgar S. & Guild, Laurence R. Labor Problems: A Book of Materials for Their Study. LC 71-89733. (American Labor, from Conspiracy to Collective Bargaining, Ser. 1). 621p. 1969. Repr. of 1925 ed. 34.50 (ISBN 0-405-02122-4). Ayer Co Pubs.

Furniss, Edgar S., Jr. France, Troubled Ally. LC 74-2667. 512p. 1974. Repr. of 1960 ed. lib. bdg. 23.50x (ISBN 0-8371-7421-X, FUFR). Greenwood.

Furniss, Edgar S., Jr., ed. The Western Alliance: Its Status & Prospects. LC 65-25644. 1965. 4.75 (ISBN 0-8142-0051-6). Ohio St U Pr.

Furniss, Harry. Some Victorian Women. (Victorian Age Ser). 1923. Repr. 30.00 (ISBN 0-8482-4050-2). Norwood Edns.

Furniss, Norman & Tilton, Timothy. The Case for the Welfare State: From Social Security to Social Equality. LC 76-26414. (Midland Bks.: No. 230). 256p. 1977. 20.00x (ISBN 0-253-31322-8); pap. 8.95x (ISBN 0-253-20230-2). Ind U Pr.

Furniss, Norman F. The Mormon Conflict, 1850-1859. LC 77-5424. (Illus.). 1977. Repr. of 1960 ed. lib. bdg. 23.75x (ISBN 0-8371-9636-1, FUMC). Greenwood.

Furniss, Tim. Manned Spaceflight Log. (Illus.). 128p. 1983. 10.95 (ISBN 0-86720-631-4). Jane's Pub Inc.

--Our Future in Space. (Tomorrow's World Ser.). (Illus.). 48p. (gr. 7-9). Date not set. price not set (Pub. by Bookwright Pr). Watts.

--Space. (Modern Technology Ser.). (Illus.). 32p. (gr. 7-9). 1985. PLB 10.90 (ISBN 0-531-10087-1). Watts.

--Space Exploitation. (Today's World Ser.). (Illus.). 72p. (gr. 7-12). 1984. 14.95 (ISBN 0-7134-4265-4, Pub. by Batsford England). David & Charles.

--Space Flight: The Records. (Illus.). 176p. 1985. 14.95 (ISBN 0-85112-435-6, Pub. by Guinness Superlatives England); pap. 9.95 (ISBN 0-85112-451-8, Pub. by Guinness Superlatives England). Sterling.

Furniss, W. T. Reshaping Faculty Careers. 1981. 17.00 (ISBN 0-02-911040-8). Ace.

Furniss, W. Todd. Self-Reliant Academic. 80p. 7.50 (ISBN 0-02-910940-X). ACE.

Furnival, F. J., ed. Arthur. (EETS OS Ser.: Vol. 2). pap. 15.00 (ISBN 0-317-15832-5). Kraus Repr.

--The Book of Quinte Essence. (EETS OS Ser.: Vol. 16). pap. 15.00 (ISBN 0-317-15840-6). Kraus Repr.

--The Fifty Earliest English Wills, in the Court of Probate: 1387-1439. (EETS OS Ser.: Vol. 78). Repr. of 1882 ed. 20.00 (ISBN 0-317-15843-0). Kraus Repr.

--Political, Religious, & Love Poems. (EETRS OS Ser.: Vol. 15). Repr. of 1866 ed. 25.00 (ISBN 0-317-15837-6). Kraus Repr.

Furnival, F. J., ed. see Stubbs, Philip.

Furnivall, F. J. Adam Davy's Five Dreams about Edward 2nd. Incl. The Life of St. Alexius; Solomon's Book of Wisdom; St. Jeremies Fifteen Tokens Before Doomsday; The Lamentacion of Souls. (EETS, OS Ser.: No. 69). Repr. of 1878 ed. 10.00 (ISBN 0-527-00068-X). Kraus Repr.

--Early English Meals & Manners. 59.95 (ISBN 0-8490-0070-X). Gordon Pr.

--Hymns to the Virgin & Christ. (EETS, OS Ser.: No. 24). Repr. of 1867 ed. 12.00 (ISBN 0-527-00024-8). Kraus Repr.

--Some Three Hundred Fresh Allusions to Shakeapeare from 1594 to 1694. (New Shakespeare Soc., London, Ser. 4: No. 3). pap. 37.00 (ISBN 0-317-16182-2). Kraus Repr.

--Stacions of Rome. (EETS, OS Ser.: No. 25). Repr. of 1867 ed. 12.00 (ISBN 0-527-00025-6). Kraus Repr.

Furnivall, F. J. & Munro, John. Shakespeare's Life & Work. 1973. lib. bdg. 12.00 (ISBN 0-8414-4290-8). Folcroft.

Furnivall, F. J., ed. Andrew Boorde's Introduction of Knowledge. (EETS, ES Ser.: No. 10). Repr. of 1870 ed. 35.00 (ISBN 0-527-00224-0). Kraus Repr.

--Book of Curtesye: Caxton's Book of Curtesye. (EETS, ES Ser.: No. 3). pap. 10.00 (ISBN 0-527-00218-6). Kraus Repr.

--The Digby Plays. (EETS OS Ser.: Vol. 70). Repr. of 1896 ed. 15.00 (ISBN 0-317-15862-7). Kraus Repr.

--Digby Plays: The Digby Mysteries, Edited from the Mss. by... (New Shakespeare Soc., London, Ser.7: No. 1). pap. 13.00 (ISBN 0-317-16189-X). Kraus Repr.

--Early English Meals & Manners. (EETS, OS Ser.: No. 32). Repr. of 1868 ed. 36.00 (ISBN 0-527-00032-9). Kraus Repr.

--The Gild of St. Mary & Other Documents. (EETS, ES Ser.: No. 114). Repr. of 1920 ed. 10.00 (ISBN 0-527-00316-6). Kraus Repr.

--The Minor Poems of the Vernon MS, Pt. 2. (EETS, OS Ser.: No. 117). Repr. of 1901 ed. 55.00 (ISBN 0-527-00101-5). Kraus Repr.

--Queene Elizabethes Achademy: A Book of Precedence. (EETS, ES Ser.: No. 8). Repr. of 1869 ed. 20.00 (ISBN 0-527-00222-4). Kraus Repr.

--Tell-Trothes New Yeares Gift, & the Passionate Morrice, 1593; John Lane's Tom Tell-Trothe's Message, & His Pens Complaint, 1600; Thomas Powell's Tom of All Trades, 1631; The Glass of Godly Love (by John Rogers?), 1596. (New Shakespeare Soc., London, Ser.: Vol. 6, Nos. 2-3). pap. 52.00 (ISBN 0-317-16184-9). Kraus Repr.

--Les Trois Fils De Rois. (EETS, ES Ser.: No. 67). Repr. of 1895 ed. 43.00 (ISBN 0-527-00271-2). Kraus Repr.

Furnivall, F. J. & Clouston, W. A., eds. The Wright's Chaste Wife. (EETS, OS Ser.: Nos. 12 & 84). 1976. Repr. of 1886 ed. 15.00 (ISBN 0-527-00015-9). Kraus Repr.

Furnivall, F. J. & Gollancz, I., eds. Hoccleve's Minor Poems, Vols. I & II. (EETS OS Ser.: Vols. 61 & 73). 1892-1897. 25.00 (ISBN 0-317-15856-2). Kraus Repr.

Furnivall, F. J. & Stone, W. B., eds. Beryn: The Tale of Beryn. (EETS, ES Ser.: No. 105). Repr. of 1909 ed. 25.00 (ISBN 0-527-00307-7). Kraus Repr.

Furnivall, F. J., ed. see Chester, Eng. Diocese.

Furnivall, F. J., ed. see De Deguilleville, Guillaume.

Furnivall, F. J., ed. see Fish, Simon.

Furnivall, F. J., ed. see Giraldus.

Furnivall, F. J., ed. see Harrison, William.

Furnivall, F. J., ed. see Hoccleve, Thomas.

Furnivall, F. J., jt. ed. see Kingsley, G.

Furnivall, F. J., ed. see Lovelich, Henry.

Furnivall, F. J. see Spalding, William.

Furnivall, F. J., ed. see Thynne, Francis.

Furnivall, F. J., ed. see Vicary, Thomas.

Furnivall, F. J., jt. ed. see Viles, Edward.

Furnivall, Frederic J., ed. see Mannyng, Robert.

Furnivall, Frederick, ed. The Story of England by Robert Manning of Brunne, from Manuscripts at Lambeth Palace & the Inner Temple, 2 vols. (Rolls Ser.: No. 87). Repr. of 1887 ed. Set. 88.00 (ISBN 0-317-16810-X). Kraus Repr.

Furnivall, Frederick J. Bibliography of Robert Browning from Eighteen Thirty-Three to Eighteen Eighty-One. 3rd ed. LC 68-7488. (Bibliography & Reference Ser.: No. 212). 1968. Repr. of 1881 ed. 19.50 (ISBN 0-8337-1251-9). B Franklin.

--Early English Poems & Lives of Saints. LC 70-178574. Repr. of 1862 ed. 22.00 (ISBN 0-404-56602-2). AMS Pr.

--Love Poems & Humourous Ones: Written at the End of a Volume of Small Printed Books, A.D. 1614-1619, in the British Museum, Labelled "Various Poems". LC 76-51941. (Ballad Society, London. Publications: No. 11). Repr. of 1874 ed. 15.00 (ISBN 0-404-50825-1). AMS Pr.

Furnivall, Frederick J. & Munro, John J. Shakespeare: Life & Work. LC 77-168082. Repr. of 1908 ed. 12.50 (ISBN 0-404-02664-8). AMS Pr.

Furnivall, Frederick J., ed. Political, Religious & Love Poems. 348p. 1981. Repr. of 1866 ed. lib. bdg. 75.00 (ISBN 0-89987-276-X). Darby Bks.

--Succession of Shakespere's Works. LC 76-137318. Repr. of 1874 ed. 11.50 (ISBN 0-404-02663-X). AMS Pr.

Furnivall, Frederick J., ed. see Generides.

Furnivall, Frederick J., ed. see Laneham, Robert.

Furnivall, J., tr. see Romanov, Panteleimon S.

Furnivall, J. F. & Munro, John. The Troublesome Reign of King John: Being the Original of Shakespeare's "Life & Death of King John". LC 72-195924. 1973. Repr. of 1913 ed. lib. bdg. 15.00 (ISBN 0-8414-4291-6). Folcroft.

Furnivall, John S. Educational Progress on Training for Native Self-Rule. LC 75-30107. (Institute of Pacific Relations). Repr. of 1943 ed. 21.00 (ISBN 0-404-59524-3). AMS Pr.

--Netherlands India: A Study of Plural Economy. LC 77-86961. Repr. of 1944 ed. 39.50 (ISBN 0-404-16712-8). AMS Pr.

--Progress & Welfare in Southeast Asia: A Comparison of Colonial Policy & Practice. LC 75-30055. (Institute of Pacific Relations). Repr. of 1941 ed. 14.00 (ISBN 0-404-59525-1). AMS Pr.

--Studies in the Social & Economic Development of the Netherlands East Indies, 3 vols. in 1. LC 77-87488. Repr. of 1934 ed. 21.50 (ISBN 0-404-16712-8). AMS Pr.

Furnivall, Percey, ed. see Vicary, Thomas.

Furntratt, Ernst & Moller, Christine. Lernprinzip Erfolg, 2 pts. 235p. (Ger.). 1982. 20.55 ea. (ISBN 3-8204-5836-0). P Lang Pubs.

Furphy, Joseph. Portable Joseph Furphy. Barnes, John, ed. (Portable Australian Authors Ser.). (Illus.). xxv, 439p. 1982. text ed. 30.00 (ISBN 0-7022-1611-9); pap. 12.95 (ISBN 0-7022-1612-7). U of Queensland Pr.

Furrell, Alfred W., jt. auth. see Brewer, Bartholomew F.

Furrer, A., ed. Crystal Field Effects in Metals & Alloys. LC 76-55802. 379p. 1977. 59.50x (ISBN 0-306-31008-2, Plenum Pr). Plenum Pub.

Furrer, Dieter. Modusprobleme bei Notker: Die modalen Werte in den Nebensaetzen der Consolatio-Uebersetzung. 201p. 1971. 33.00x (ISBN 3-11-001808-X). De Gruyter.

Furrer, F. Fehlerkorrigierende Block-Codierung fuer die Datenuebertragung. (LHI Ser.: No. 36). 1981. 75.95x (ISBN 0-8176-0975-X). Birkhauser.

Furrer, P. J. Art Therapy Activities & Lesson Plans for Individuals & Groups: A Practical Guide for Teachers, Therapists, Parents & those Interested in Promoting Personal Growth in Themselves & Others. (Illus.). 144p. 1982. pap. 12.75x spiral (ISBN 0-398-04799-5). C C Thomas.

Furrer, Werner. Water Trails of Washington. rev. ed. (Illus., Orig.). 1979. pap. 5.95 (ISBN 0-913140-31-7). Signpost Bk Pub.

Furrey, Donna M. God, Where's My Daddy? 32p. (gr. 4-6). 1985. pap. 3.50 (ISBN 0-570-04130-9). Concordia.

Furrh, Mary L. & Barksdale, Jo. Hors D'oeurvres Everybody Loves. (The Quail Ridge Press Cookbook Ser.: No. 7). (Illus.). 80p. 1981. pap. 4.95 (ISBN 0-937552-11-9). Quail Ridge.

Furrow, Barry R. Malpractice in Psychotherapy. LC 79-3253. 176p. 1980. 25.00x (ISBN 0-669-03399-5). Lexington Bks.

Furrow, Melissa, ed. Selected Fifteenth Century Comic Poems. LC 83-48231. (Medieval Texts Ser.). 330p. 1985. lib. bdg. 44.00 (ISBN 0-8240-9428-X). Garland Pub.

Furse, Anna, et al, trs. see Jaget, Claude.

Furse, Chris. Elephant Island: An Antarctic Expedition. (Illus.). 1979. 27.50 (ISBN 0-904614-02-6, Pub. by Anthony Nelson Ltd, England). Buteo.

--Elephant Island: An Antarctic Expedition. 264p. 1981. 35.00x (ISBN 0-904614-02-6, Pub. by Nelson Ltd). State Mutual Bk.

Furse, Margaret L. Mysticism - Window on a World View: Introduction to Mysticism As a Pattern of Thought & Practice. LC 76-56816. Repr. of 1977 ed. 55.00 (ISBN 0-8357-9018-5, 2016384). Bks Demand UMI.

--Nothing but the Truth: What It Takes to Be Honest. LC 81-3501. 128p. 1981. 8.75 (ISBN 0-687-28130-X). Abingdon.

Furse, Margaret L., et al. The Problem of Religious Knowledge. (Rice University Studies: Vol. 60, No. 1). 129p. 1974. pap. 10.00x (ISBN 0-89263-219-4). Rice Univ.

Furst, Alan. The Caribbean Account. 1983. pap. 3.95 (ISBN 0-440-11105-6). Dell.

--Shadow Trade. 288p. 1983. 14.95 (ISBN 0-385-28884-0). Delacorte.

--Shadow Trade. 1984. pap. 3.95 (ISBN 0-440-18173-9). Dell.

Furst, Arnold. Famous Magicians of the World. 1957. pap. 3.00 (ISBN 0-87505-142-1). Borden.

--Great Magic Shows. 1968. pap. 3.00 (ISBN 0-915926-09-1). Borden.

--How to Get Publicity in Newspapers. pap. 3.95 (ISBN 0-87505-225-8). Borden.

--Post Hypnotic Instructions. pap. 5.00 (ISBN 0-87980-119-0). Wilshire.

--Rapid Induction Hypnosis & Self Hypnosis. 1982. 15.00 (ISBN 0-87505-326-2). Borden.

Furst, Arthur. Chemistry of Chelation in Cancer. 160p. 1963. 14.75x (ISBN 0-398-00633-4). C C Thomas.

Furst, Bruno. Stop Forgetting. rev. ed. Furst, Lotte & Storm, Gerrit, eds. LC 75-164727. (Illus.). 1979. pap. 9.95 (ISBN 0-385-15401-1). Doubleday.

Furst, Charles. Origins of the Mind: Mind-Brain Connections. 1979. 11.95 (ISBN 0-13-642777-4, Spec); pap. 5.95 (ISBN 0-13-642769-3, Spec). P-H.

Furst, Clara & Rockefeller, Mildred. The Effective Dance Program in Physical Education. LC 81-9494. 240p. 1982. 16.95x (ISBN 0-13-241505-4, Parker). P-H.

Furst, Clyde. Observations of Professor Maturin. LC 70-126700. Repr. of 1916 ed. 19.00 (ISBN 0-404-02665-6). AMS Pr.

Furst, Gesenius. Hebrew-English Dictionary: Hebrew & Chaldee Lexicon to the Old Testament. rev. ed. Mitchell, Edward C., ed. (Hebrew & Eng.). 47.50 (ISBN 0-87559-021-7); thumb indexed 52.50 (ISBN 0-87559-022-5). Shalom.

Furst, H., tr. see Ojetti, Ugo.

Furst, Jeffrey. The Over Twenty-Nine Health Book. LC 79-12269. (Illus.). 1979. pap. 5.95 (ISBN 0-915442-79-5, Unilaw). Donning Co.

Furst, Jeffrey, ed. Edgar Cayce's Story of Attitudes & Emotions. 1983. pap. 2.75 (ISBN 0-425-05889-1). Berkley Pub.

--Edgar Cayce's Story of Jesus. 1984. pap. 3.95 (ISBN 0-425-07701-2, Medallion). Berkley Pub.

Furst, Jill L. & Furst, Peter. North American Indian Art. (Illus.). 264p. 1984. 45.00 (ISBN 0-8478-0461-5); pap. 19.95 (ISBN 0-8478-0572-7). Rizzoli Intl.

Furst, Jill L., jt. auth. see Furst, Peter T.

Furst, Lilian R. The Contours of European Romanticism. LC 79-15141. xvi, 158p. 1980. 21.50x (ISBN 0-8032-1954-7). U of Nebr Pr.

--Counterparts: The Dynamics of Franco-German Literary Relationships, 1770-1895. LC 77-2407. 216p. 1977. text ed. 13.50x (ISBN 0-8143-1582-8). Wayne St U Pr.

--Fictions of Romantic Irony. (Harvard Studies in Comparative Literature: No. 36). 288p. 1984. text ed. 15.00x (ISBN 0-674-29935-3). Harvard U Pr.

--Romanticism. 2nd ed. (Critical Idiom Ser.). 1976. pap. 5.50x (ISBN 0-416-83920-7, NO. 2209). Methuen Inc.

Furst, Lilian R., ed. European Romanticism. 1980. 16.95x (ISBN 0-416-71870-1, NO. 2902); pap. 7.95 (ISBN 0-416-71880-9, NO. 2903). Methuen Inc.

Furst, Lillian R. & Skrine, Peter N. Naturalism. (Critical Idiom Ser.). 1971. pap. 5.50x (ISBN 0-416-65670-6, NO. 2208). Methuen Inc.

Furst, Lotte, ed. see Furst, Bruno.

Furst, M. Lawrence, jt. auth. see Morse, Donald R.

Furst, Merrick L., jt. auth. see Morse, Donald R.

Furst, P. T. Gold Before Columbus. (Illus.). 80p. 1964. 5.00 (ISBN 0-938644-16-5). Nat Hist Mus.

Furst, Peter, jt. auth. see Furst, Jill L.

Furst, Peter E. Mushrooms: Psychedelic Fungi. (Encyclopedia of Psychoactive Drugs Ser.). (Illus.). 1985. PLB 15.95x (ISBN 0-87754-767-X). Chelsea Hse.

Furst, Peter T. Hallucinogens & Culture. LC 75-25442. (Cross-Cultural Themes Ser.). (Illus.). 208p. 1976. pap. text ed. 8.95x (ISBN 0-88316-517-1). Chandler & Sharp.

Furst, Peter T. & Furst, Jill L. North American Indian Art. LC 82-40343. (Illus.). 264p. 1982. 45.00 (ISBN 0-8478-0461-5). Rizzoli Intl.

Furst, Peter T., ed. LAAG Contributions to Afro-American Ethnohistory in Latin America & the Caribbean, Vol. 1. 1976. pap. 2.75 (ISBN 0-686-36583-6). Am Anthro Assn.

Furst, Susanna & Knoll, J., eds. Opiate Receptors & the Neurochemical Correlates of Pain: Proceedings of the Third Congress of the Hungarian Pharmacological Society, Budapest, 1979. LC 80-41281. (Advances in Pharmacological Research & Practice Ser.: Vol. V). 240p. 1981. 50.00 (ISBN 0-08-026390-9). Pergamon.

Furst, Viktor. The Architecture of Sir Christopher Wren. LC 56-36662. 244p. 1956. Repr. 49.00 (ISBN 0-686-01441-3). Somerset Pub.

Furstenau, E. Dicionario de Temos Tecnicos Ingles-Portugues. 1157p. (Eng. & Port.). 1980. 95.00 (ISBN 0-686-97635-5, M-9211). French & Eur.

Furstenberg, Egon von see Von Furstenberg, Egon.

Furstenberg, Egon von see Von Furstenberg, Egon & Duhe, Camille.

Furstenberg, Frank, et al, eds. Teenage Sexuality, Pregnancy & Childbearing. 1981. 30.00x (ISBN 0-8122-7787-2); pap. 12.95x (ISBN 0-8122-1107-3). U of Pa Pr.

Furstenberg, Frank F., jt. auth. see Roth, Russell.

Furstenberg, Frank F., Jr. Unplanned Parenthood: The Social Consequences of Teenage Childbearing. LC 76-8144. 1976. 15.95 (ISBN 0-02-911010-6). Free Pr.

--Unplanned Parenthood: The Social Consequences of Teenage Childbearing. LC 76-8144. 1972. pap. text ed. 8.95 (ISBN 0-02-911030-0). Free Pr.

Furstenberg, George M. Von see Von Furstenberg, George M.

Furstenberg, George M. von see Von Furstenberg, George M.

Furstenberg, H. Recurrence in Ergodic Theory & Combinatorial Number Theory. LC 80-7518. (Rice University, Dept. of Mathematics, M. B. Porter Lectures). 228p. 1981. 27.50 (ISBN 0-691-08269-3). Princeton U Pr.

--Stationary Processes & Prediction Theory. (Annals of Mathematics Studies, Vol. 44). (Orig.). 1960. pap. 32.00x (ISBN 0-691-08041-0). Princeton U Pr.

Furstenberg-Forbes, Lynn. Hanover Heritage. 352p. 1983. pap. 2.95 (ISBN 0-523-41342-4). Pinnacle Bks.

--The Spoils of Hanover. 352p. (Orig.). 1983. pap. 3.25 (ISBN 0-523-41343-2). Pinnacle Bks.

Furtado, A. L. & Neuhold, E. J. Formal Techniques for Data Base Design. (Illus.). 115p. 1985. 24.00 (ISBN 0-387-15601-1). Springer Verlag.

Furtado, C. Economic Development of Latin America. 2nd ed. LC 74-121365. (Latin American Studies: No.8). (Illus.). 280p. 1977. 47.50 (ISBN 0-521-21197-2); pap. 12.95 (ISBN 0-521-29070-8). Cambridge U Pr.

Furtado, Celso. Accumulation & Development: The Logic of Industrial Civilization. LC 83-40058. 225p. 1983. 29.95 (ISBN 0-312-00239-4). St Martin.

--The Economic Growth of Brazil: A Survey from Colonial to Modern Times. De Aguiar, Ricardo W. & Drysdale, Eric C., trs. from Port. LC 84-10782. x, 285p. 1984. Repr. of 1968 ed. lib. bdg. 45.00x (ISBN 0-313-24448-0, FUEG). Greenwood.

--No to Recession & Unemployment: An Examination of the Brazilian Economic Crisis. 98p. 1985. pap. 5.00 (ISBN 0-8223-0537-2). Duke.

Furtado, J. I. & Mori, S. Tasek Bera: The Ecology of a Freshwater Swamp. 1982. text ed. 79.00 (ISBN 90-6193-100-2, Pub. by Junk Pubs Netherlands). Kluwer Academic.

Furtado, Joao S. Taxonomy of Amauroderma (Basidiomycetes, Polyporaceae) (Memoirs of the New York Botanical Garden: Vol. 34). (Illus.). 1981. pap. 17.50x (ISBN 0-89327-234-5). NY Botanical.

Furtado, R. D. The Oleanders. (Redbird Bk.). 1976. lib. bdg. 8.00 (ISBN 0-89253-094-4); flexible bdg. 4.00 (ISBN 0-89253-131-2). Ind-US Inc.

Furtado, R. De Loyola. Shelley: Concept of Nature. 1973. Repr. of 1958 ed. 20.00 (ISBN 0-8274-0411-5). R West.

Furtak, T., jt. auth. see Klein, M. V.

Furtak, Thomas E., jt. ed. see Chang, Richard K.

Furter, Pierre. The Planner & Lifelong Education. (Fundamentals of Educational Planning: No. 25). 68p. 1977. pap. 6.00 (ISBN 92-803-1077-1, U762, UNESCO). Unipub.

Furter, William F., ed. A Century of Chemical Engineering. LC 81-23444. 471p. 1982. text ed. 59.50 (ISBN 0-306-40895-3, Plenum Pr). Plenum Pub.

--History of Chemical Engineering: Based on a Symposium Cosponsered by the ACS Divisions of History & Industrial & Engineering Chemistry at the ACS/CSJ Chemical Congress, Honolulu, Hawaii, April 2-6, 1979. LC 80-17432. (Advances in Chemistry Ser.: No. 190). (Illus.). 435p. 1980. 41.95 (ISBN 0-8412-0512-4). Am Chemical.

Furth, Charlotte. Ting Wen-Chiang: Science & China's New Culture. LC 78-95920. (East Asian Ser: No. 42). 1970. text ed. 20.00x (ISBN 0-674-89270-4). Harvard U Pr.

Furth, Charlotte, ed. The Limits of Change: Essays on Conservative Alternatives in Republican China. LC 75-23490. (East Asian Ser.: No. 84). 448p. 1976. lib. bdg. 25.00x (ISBN 0-674-53423-9). Harvard U Pr.

Furth, David. Natural History of the Sumac Tree. (Illus.). 72p. 1985. pap. text ed. 15.00 (ISBN 0-208-02094-2, CT Academy). Shoe String.

Furth, David G. The Stink Bugs of Ohio (Hemiptera: Pentatomidae) 1974. 3.00 (ISBN 0-86727-069-1). Ohio Bio Survey.

Furth, David L. The Visionary Betrayed: Aesthetic Discontinuity in Henry James's The American Scene. (The LeBaron Russell Briggs Prize Honors Essay in English). 1980. pap. text ed. 3.95x (ISBN 0-674-94085-7). Harvard U Pr.

Furth, George, jt. auth. see Sondheim, Stephen.

Furth, H. G. The World of Grown Ups: Children's Conceptions of Society. 27.50 (ISBN 0-444-99065-8, FWO/, Pub. by Elsevier). Greenwood.

Furth, Hans G. Deafness & Learning: A Psycho-Social Approach. 140p. 1973. pap. write for info. (ISBN 0-534-00231-5). Wadsworth Pub.

--Piaget & Knowledge: Theoretical Foundations. 2nd ed. LC 80-26284. 302p. 1981. pap. 7.50x (ISBN 0-226-27420-9, Phoen.). U of Chicago Pr.

--Piaget for Teachers. (Illus.). 1970. pap. text ed. 12.95 (ISBN 0-13-674937-2). P-H.

--Thinking Without Language. LC 66-10958. 1966. 18.00 (ISBN 0-02-911000-9). Free Pr.

Furth, Hans G. & Wachs, Harry. Thinking Goes to School: Piaget's Theory in Practice with Additional Thoughts. (Illus.). 1974. pap. text ed. 8.95x (ISBN 0-19-501927-X, GB 716). Oxford U Pr.

Furth, J. Herbert, jt. auth. see Mikesell, Raymond F.

Furth, Montgomery, ed. & tr. see Frege, Gottlob.

Furth, Montgomery, ed. see Frege, Gottlob.

Furth, Montgomery, tr. see Aristotle.

Furth, R., ed. see Einstein, Albert.

Furth, Ralph Van see Conference on Mononuclear Phagocytes, Third, Noorwijk aan Zee, The Netherlands, Sept. 17-24, 1978.

Furth, Ralph van see Van Furth, Ralph.

Furthmayr, Heinz, ed. Immunochemistry of the Extracellular Matrix, 2 Vols. 208p. 1982. Vol. I, 288pp. 75.00 (ISBN 0-8493-6196-6); Vol. II, 208 pp. 59.50 (ISBN 0-8493-6197-4). CRC Pr.

Furtman, Michael J. A Boundary Waters Fishing Guide. LC 84-70248. (Illus.). 176p. 1984. 16.95 (ISBN 0-916691-01-2); pap. 8.95 (ISBN 0-916691-00-4). Birch Portage.

Furtney, Diane. It Was a Game. 24p. (Orig.). 1985. pap. 6.00 (ISBN 0-931956-20-X). Water Mark.

Furtos, Norma C. The Ostracoda of Ohio. 1933. 2.00 (ISBN 0-86727-028-4). Ohio Bio Survey.

Furttenbach, Josef. Ship Building. (Printed Sources of Western Art Ser.). (Illus.). 150p. (Ger.). 1981. pap. 45.00 slipcase (ISBN 0-915346-62-1). A Wofsy Fine Arts.

Furtwangler, A. & Urlichs, H. L. Greek & Roman Sculpture. Taylor, Horace, tr. from Ger. LC 77-23569. 1977. Repr. of 1914 ed. lib. bdg. 35.00 (ISBN 0-89341-205-8). Longwood Pub Group.

Furtwangler, Albert. The Authority of Publius: A Reading of the "Federalist" Papers. LC 83-18806. 152p. (Orig.). 1985. 19.95x (ISBN 0-8014-1643-4); pap. text ed. 7.95x. Cornell U Pr.

Furtwangler, Wilhelm. Concerning Music. L. J., Lawrence, tr. from German. LC 76-57174. (Illus.). 1977. Repr. of 1953 ed. lib. bdg. 15.00x (ISBN 0-8371-8665-X, FUCM). Greenwood.

Furtwengler, Willis J. & Konnert, William. Improving School Discipline: An Administrator's Guide. 278p. 1982. 30.95 (ISBN 0-205-07757-9, Pub. by Longwood Div). Allyn.

Furukawa, Chiyoko & Shomaker, Diana. Community Health Services for the Aged: Promotion & Maintenance. LC 81-19105. 372p. 1982. text ed. 35.95 (ISBN 0-89443-382-2). Aspen Systems.

Furukawa, Junji, jt. ed. see Vogl, Otto.

Furukawa, Naomichi, jt. ed. see Oae, Shigeru.

Furumo, Kristine M. Affiliation (To You) 1985. 5.95 (ISBN 0-8062-2302-2). Carlton.

Furuseth, Owen J. & Pierce, John T. Agricultural Land in an Urban Society. Knight, C. Gregory, ed. LC 82-18424. (Resource Publications in Geography Ser.). 89p. (Orig.). 1982. pap. 5.00 (ISBN 0-89291-149-2). Assn Am Geographers.

Furuta, Bettie L. Cookery for Lovers: Aphrodisiacs in the Kitchen. LC 84-9329. (Illus.). 235p. (Orig.). 1984. pap. 18.00x (ISBN 0-916129-00-4). Furuta.

Furuta, Soichi, tr. see Ippekiro.

Furuta, Soichi, tr. see Takamura, Kotaro.

Furuta, Tokuji. Interior Landscaping. 1982. text ed. 19.95 (ISBN 0-8359-3120-X); instr's. manual free (ISBN 0-8359-3121-8). Reston.

Furutan, A. Mother, Father, & Children: Practical Advice to Parents. 280p. pap. 6.95 (ISBN 0-85398-095-0). G Ronald Pub.

Furutan, Ali A. The Story of My Heart. (Illus.). 272p. 14.95 (ISBN 0-85398-114-0); pap. 7.50 (ISBN 0-85398-115-9). G Ronald Pub.

Furuya, Seikow Y. Japan's Foreign Exchange & Her Balance of International Payments, with Special Reference to Recent Theories of Foreign Exchange. LC 68-58576. (Columbia University. Studies in the Social Sciences: No. 299). 18.50 (ISBN 0-404-51299-2). AMS Pr.

Furvinall, F. J. & Meyer, P., eds. The Curial Made by Maystere Alain Charretier. Caxton, William, tr. (EETS OS Ser.: Vol. 54). Repr. of 1888 ed. 15.00 (ISBN 0-317-15852-X). Kraus Repr.

Fury, Carol Lee. Secrets from Sanibel: Poetry of the Islands. LC 76-9688. (Illus.). 96p. 1976. 5.95 (ISBN 0-87208-037-4); pap. 2.95 (ISBN 0-87208-035-8). Island Pr.

Fury, Kathleen, jt. auth. see CBS, Inc.

Furze-Morrish, L. The Parallel in Astrology. LC 74-15756. 1974. 7.45 (ISBN 0-914350-10-2). Vulcan Bks.

Fusaro, A. Daniel, ed. Rules of the U. S. Courts in New York. 2nd ed. LC 65-16452. 1978. 50.00 (ISBN 0-87632-070-1). Boardman.

Fusaro, Ramon M., jt. auth. see Lynch, Henry T.

Fusayama, Takao. New Concepts in Operative Dentistry. 190p. 1980. 69.00 (ISBN 0-931386-34-9). Quint Pub Co.

Fuscaldo, Anthony A., et al, eds. Laboratory Safety: Theory & Practice. LC 80-762. 1980. 48.50 (ISBN 0-12-269980-7). Acad Pr.

Fusco, Ann & Russo, Anne. Teaching Your Child to Read. (Illus.). 116p. (Orig.). 1982. pap. 12.00 (ISBN 0-9607368-0-8). Leprechaun Pr.

Fusco, Esther. Everybody Reads: A Step-by-Step Guide to Establishing a Book Division Group Program in Your School. pap. 1.00 (ISBN 0-317-06455-X). Dell.

Fusco, Luigi. The Piazza of the Decameron. Fusco, Marion & Fusco, Luigi, trs. from It. LC 76-56615. 1977. 8.95 (ISBN 0-8076-0862-9). Braziller.

Fusco, Luigi, tr. see Fusco, Luigi.

Fusco, Margie. Putting into Harbor. 1978. pap. 1.00 (ISBN 0-931122-11-2). West End.

Fusco, Marion, tr. see Fusco, Luigi.

Fusco, Peter, jt. auth. see Janson, H. W.

Fusco, Renato De see De Fusco, Renato.

Fusek, Lois, tr. from Chinese. Among the Flowers: A Translation of the Tenth-Century Anthology of Tz'u Lyrics, the Hua-Chien Chi. LC 81-12306. (Translations from the Oriental Classics Ser.). 224p. 1982. 30.00x (ISBN 0-231-04986-2); pap. 12.50x (ISBN 0-231-04987-0). Columbia U Pr.

Fuseli, Henry. The Collected English Letters of Henry Fuseli. Weinglass, David, ed. LC 81-23613. 685p. 1982. lib. bdg. 100.00 (ISBN 0-527-31894-9). Kraus Intl.

--Drawings of Fuseli. Longstreet, Stephen, ed. (Master Draughtsman Ser). treasure trove bdg. 9.95x (ISBN 0-87505-008-5); pap. 4.95 (ISBN 0-87505-161-8). Borden.

Fusfeld, Daniel R. Age of the Economist. 4th ed. 1982. pap. text ed. 10.80x (ISBN 0-673-15500-5). Scott F.

--The Age of the Economist. 5th ed. 1986. pap. text ed. 10.95x (ISBN 0-673-18211-8). Scott F.

--Economic Thought of Franklin D. Roosevelt & the Origins of the New Deal. LC 71-120205. (Columbia University Social Science Studies Ser.: No. 586). Repr. of 1956 ed. 17.50 (ISBN 0-404-51586-X). AMS Pr.

--Economics: Principles of Political Economy. 2nd ed. 1985. text ed. 27.95x (ISBN 0-673-18116-2). Scott F.

--Rise & Repression of Radical Labor, U. S. A., Eighteen Seventy Seven to Nineteen Eighteen. (Illus., Orig.). 1979. lib. bdg. 12.95 (ISBN 0-88286-050-X); pap. text ed. 2.50. C H Kerr.

Fusfeld, Daniel R. & Bates, Timothy. The Political Economy of the Urban Ghetto. LC 83-20424. (Political & Social Economy Ser.). 304p. 1984. 26.95x (ISBN 0-8093-1157-7); pap. 14.95x (ISBN 0-8093-1158-5). S Ill U Pr.

Fusfeld, Herbert I. Industrial Productivity & International Technical Cooperation. Haklisch, Carmela S., ed. (Illus.). 160p. 1982. 21.00 (ISBN 0-08-028810-3). Pergamon.

--The Technical Enterprise: Present & Future Patterns. 280p. 1986. Prof. ref. 29.95x (ISBN 0-88730-033-2). Ballinger Pub.

Fusfeld, Herbert I. & Haklisch, Carmela S., eds. Science & Technology Policy: Perspectives for the Nineteen-Eighties. LC 79-28295. (Annals of the New York Academy of Sciences: Vol. 334). 285p. 1979. 52.00x (ISBN 0-89766-037-4); pap. 42.00x (ISBN 0-89766-036-6). NY Acad Sci.

--University-Industry Research Interactions. (Technology Policy & Economic Growth Ser.). 200p. 1984. 25.00 (ISBN 0-08-030987-9). Pergamon.

Fusfeld, Herbert I. & Langlois, Richard N., eds. Current Perspectives on R & D Productivity. (The Technology Policy & Economic Growth Ser.). (Illus.). 168p. 1982. 19.50 (ISBN 0-08-028836-7, K110). Pergamon.

--Understanding R&D Productivity. 200p. 19.50 (ISBN 0-686-84787-3). Work in Amer.

Fusi, Juan P., jt. auth. see Carr, Raymond.

Fusi, Piero, jt. auth. see Fusi, Rolando.

Fusi, Rolando & Fusi, Piero. Florence: A Complete Guide for Visiting the City. (Bonechi Guides Ser.). (Illus.). 160p. 1984. pap. 9.95 (ISBN 0-88332-332-X, 8200). Larousse.

Fusilier, H. L. The Law of Agency & Real Estate. 183p. 1984. pap. text ed. 10.00 (ISBN 0-89478-109-X). U CO Busn Res Div.

Fusion Energy Foundations Staff, ed. Beam Defense: An Alternative to Nuclear Destruction. (Illus.). 176p. 1983. pap. 7.95 (ISBN 0-8168-4138-1). Aero.

Fuslier, H. L. Real Estate Law. 444p. 1977. 15.00 (ISBN 0-686-64177-9). U CO Busn Res Div.

Fuson, Benjamin. Browning & His English Predecessors in the Dramatic Monolog. LC 74-13496. 1948. lib. bdg. 10.00 (ISBN 0-8414-4240-1). Folcroft.

Fuson, Henry H. Ballads of the Kentucky Highlands. LC 77-19283. 1931. 25.00 (ISBN 0-8414-1955-8). Folcroft.

--Ballads of the Kentucky Highlands. 219p. 1980. Repr. of 1931 ed. text ed. 25.00 (ISBN 0-8492-4706-3). R West.

Fuson, Robert. Fundamental Place-Name Geography. 5th ed. 160p. 1981. pap. text ed. write for info. (ISBN 0-697-05207-9). Wm C Brown.

Fuson, Robert H. Introduction to World Geography: Regions & Cultures. LC 75-46351. 1978. pap. 10.95 (ISBN 0-8403-1413-2). Kendall-Hunt.

Fusonie, Alan & Moran, Leila, eds. Agricultural Literature: Proud Heritage - Future Promise. (Illus.). 320p. 1976. 13.50 (ISBN 0-87771-011-2); pap. 9.95 (ISBN 0-87771-010-4). Grad School.

--International Agricultural Librarianship: Continuity & Change. LC 78-67916. lib. bdg. 29.95 (ISBN 0-313-20640-6, AIA/). Greenwood.

Fuss, Abraham, ed. Studies in Jewish Jurisprudence. (Studies in Jewish Jurisprudence Ser.: Vol. 4). 320p. 1975. 14.50 (ISBN 0-87203-058-X). Hermon.

Fuss, M., jt. auth. see McFadden, D.

Fuss, M., jt. ed. see Corvilain, H.

Fuss, Paul H. Von see Von Fuss, Paul H.

Fuss, Peter, ed. see Hegel, G. W.

Fuss, Peter, ed. see Nietzsche, Friedrich.

Fuss, Peter L. The Moral Philosophy of Josiah Royce. LC 65-11590. pap. 72.00 (ISBN 0-317-08965-X, 2002965). Bks Demand UMI.

Fuss, Werner. Die Deuteronomistische Pentateuchredaktion in Exodus 3-17. (Beiheft 126 zur Zeitschrift fuer die alttestamentliche Wissenschaft). xii, 406p. 1972. 48.40x (ISBN 3-11-003854-4). De Gruyter.

Fussell, Betty. Masters of American Cookery. LC 82-40467. 424p. 1983. 18.65 (ISBN 0-8129-1062-1). Times Bks.

Fussell, C. & Quarmby, A. Study-Service: A Survey. 43p. 1974. pap. 5.00 (ISBN 0-88936-041-3, IDRC37, IDRC). Unipub.

Fussell, Edwin. Gin for Breakfast. Date not set. 8.00x (ISBN 0-89363-007-1); pap. 5.00x (ISBN 0-89363-008-X). Woolf Quarterly.

--Lucifer in Harness: American Meter, Metaphor & Diction. LC 72-4040. 224p. 1973. 22.00 (ISBN 0-691-06238-2). Princeton U Pr.

--Your Name Is You. (Poetry Series: No. 2). 1975. 8.50 (ISBN 0-89363-002-0); pap. 3.95 (ISBN 0-89363-003-9). Woolf Quarterly.

Fussell, Edwin, jt. ed. see Holmes, Charles S.

Fussell, G. E. The Classical Tradition in West European Farming. LC 77-181502. 237p. 1972. 18.50 (ISBN 0-8386-1090-0). Fairleigh Dickinson.

--Crop Nutrition: Science & Practice Before Liebig. 236p. 1971. 8.50x (ISBN 0-87291-026-1). Coronado Pr.

--English Dairy Farmer: 1500-1900. (Illus.). 357p. 1966. 27.50x (ISBN 0-7146-1309-6, F Cass Co). Biblio Dist.

--Farms, Farmers & Society. 1976. 15.00x (ISBN 0-87291-077-6). Coronado Pr.

Fussell, G. E. & Fussell, K. R. The English Country Woman: A Farmhouse Social History A.D. 1500-1900. LC 73-174864. (Illus.). Repr. of 1953 ed. 25.00 (ISBN 0-405-08543-5, Blom Pubns). Ayer Co Pubs.

Fussell, George E. English Dairy Farmer, 1500-1900. LC 67-16355. (Illus.). 1966. 29.50x (ISBN 0-678-05046-5). Kelley.

--The English Rural Labourer. LC 75-10212. 160p. 1975. Repr. of 1949 ed. lib. bdg. 15.00x (ISBN 0-8371-8178-X, FUER). Greenwood.

Fussell, J. B. & Burdick, G. R., eds. Nuclear Systems Reliability Engineering & Risk Assessment. LC 77-91478. xi, 849p. 1977. text ed. 48.00 (ISBN 0-89871-041-3). Soc Indus-Appl Math.

Fussell, K. R., jt. auth. see Fussell, G. E.

Fussell, Paul. Abroad: British Literary Traveling Between the Wars. (Illus.). 1980. 19.95 (ISBN 0-19-502767-1). Oxford U Pr.

--Abroad: British Literary Traveling Between the Wars. (Galaxy Bks.). (Illus.). 1980. pap. 6.95 (ISBN 0-19-503068-0, GB). Oxford U Pr.

--The Boy Scout Handbook & Other Observations. (Illus.). 1982. 17.95 (ISBN 0-19-503102-4). Oxford U Pr.

--The Boy Scout Handbook & Other Observations. (Illus.). 304p. 1985. pap. 7.95 (ISBN 0-19-503579-8, GB782). Oxford U Pr.

--Class. 256p. 1984. pap. 3.95 (ISBN 0-345-31816-1). Ballantine.

--Class: A Guide Through the American Status System. (Illus.). 224p. 1983. 13.95 (ISBN 0-671-44991-5). Summit Bks.

--The Great War & Modern Memory. LC 75-7352. (Illus.). 1975. pap. 8.95 (ISBN 0-19-502171-1, 483, GB). Oxford U Pr.

--The Rhetorical World of Augustan Humanism: Ethics & Imagery from Swift to Burke. LC 66-1724. pap. 80.80 (ISBN 0-317-29155-6, 2055599). Bks Demand UMI.

Fussell, Paul, ed. Siegfried Sassoon's Long Journey: Selections from the Sherston Memoirs. (Illus.). 1983. 19.95 (ISBN 0-19-503309-4). Oxford U Pr.

Fussell, Paul, Jr. Poetic Meter & Poetic Form. rev. ed. 1979. pap. text ed. 8.00 (ISBN 0-394-32120-0, RanC). Random.

Fusselle, Warner E. Scenes with the Savior. LC 84-11389. 1984. pap. 3.25 (ISBN 0-8054-1532-7). Broadman.

Fussler, Herman H. Research Libraries & Technology. 1974. 10.00x (ISBN 0-226-27558-2). U of Chicago Pr.

Fussler, Herman H. & Simon, Julian. Patterns in the Use of Books in Large Research Libraries. 2nd ed. LC 72-79916. (Chicago Studies in Library Science Ser). 1969. 11.00x (ISBN 0-226-27556-6). U of Chicago Pr.

Fussler, Herman H., ed. Function of the Library in the Modern College: Nineteenth Annual Conference of the Graduate Library School. LC 67-28464. 1954. Repr. 7.00x (ISBN 0-226-27555-8). U of Chicago Pr.

Fussler, Herman H. & Jenck, John E., eds. Management Education: Implications for Libraries & Library Schools. LC 73-92600. vi, 116p. 1974. 10.00x (ISBN 0-226-27560-4). U of Chicago Pr.

Fussner, F. Smith. The Historical Revolution: English Historical Writing & Thought 1580-1640. LC 75-40916. 1976. Repr. of 1962 ed. lib. bdg. 24.75x (ISBN 0-8371-8684-6, FUHR). Greenwood.

Fustel De Coulanges, Numa D. Le Colonat romain. Finley, Moses, ed. LC 79-4974. (Ancient Economic History Ser.). (Fr.). 1980. Repr. of 1885 ed. lib. bdg. 16.00x (ISBN 0-405-12362-0). Ayer Co Pubs.

--The Origin of Property in Land. Ashley, Margaret, tr. LC 52-45494. 153p. 1891. Repr. 22.50 (ISBN 0-8337-0803-1). B Franklin.

Fuster, Joaquin M. The Prefrontal Cortex. 232p. 1980. text ed. 36.50 (ISBN 0-89004-524-0). Raven.

Fustero, X. & Verdaguer, E. Relativistic Astrophysics & Cosmology: Proceedings of the XIV Gift International Seminar Sant Feliu de Guixols, Spain, June 27-July 1, 1983. 320p. 1984. 37.00x (ISBN 9971-966-60-3, Pub. by World Sci Singapore). Taylor & Francis.

Fuster Ortells, Joan. Diccionari Pera Ociosos. 208p. (Catalan.). 1978. pap. 6.75 (ISBN 84-297-1431-6, S-50213). French & Eur.

Fusting, Eugene M. Star-Sticks. LC 79-64888. (Illus.). 242p. (gr. 5 up). 1980. pap. text ed. 9.95 (ISBN 0-935736-27-1). Summer House.

Fuszard, Barbara. Self-Actualization for Nurses: Issue, Trends, & Strategies for Job Enrichment. 230p. 1984. 28.50 (ISBN 0-89443-871-9). Aspen Systems.

Fuszek, Rita M. Piano Music in Collections: An Index. LC 78-70023. 1982. 47.50 (ISBN 0-89990-012-7). Info Coord.

Futagawa, Shigeo. Introduction to Coin Magic. 1978. 10.00 (ISBN 0-87505-228-2); pap. 3.00 (ISBN 0-915262-37-1). Borden.

Futagawa, Yukio, jt. auth. see Rudolph, Paul.

Futagawa, Yukio, ed. & photos by see Itoh, Teiji.

Futas, Elizabeth. The Library Forms Illustrated Handbook. (Illus.). 875p. 1984. looseleaf 75.00 (ISBN 0-918212-69-3). Neal-Schuman.

Futas, Elizabeth, ed. Library Acquisition Policies & Procedures. 2nd ed. LC 82-42925. 616p. 1984. lib. bdg. 45.00 (ISBN 0-89774-024-6). Oryx Pr.

Futch, Ovid L. History of Andersonville Prison. LC 68-20413. 1968. pap. 4.50 (ISBN 0-8130-0591-4). U Presses Fla.

Futcher, Jane. Crush. 256p. 1984. pap. 2.25 (ISBN 0-380-67462-9, 67462, Flare). Avon.

--Marin-the Place, the People: Profile of a California County. (Illus.). 192p. 1985. pap. 14.95 (ISBN 0-15-657304-0, Harv). HarBraceJ.

Futcher, Jane & Conover, Robert. Marin-the Place, the People: Profile of a California County. LC 80-27986. 1981. 24.95 (ISBN 0-03-057472-2). HR&W.

Futcher, W. G. Descriptive Statistics for Introductory Measurement. (Andrews University Monographs, Studies in Education: Vol. 1). viii, 96p. 1976. text ed. 7.95 (ISBN 0-943872-50-2). Andrews Univ Pr.

Futoma, David J., et al. Analysis of Polycyclic Aromatic Hydrocarbons in Water Systems. 200p. 1981. 66.00 (ISBN 0-8493-6255-5). CRC Pr.

Futrell. Fund of Selling. 1984. 27.95 (ISBN 0-317-13118-4). Irwin.

Futrell, Charles. ABC's of Selling. 1985. pap. 18.95x (ISBN 0-256-03304-8). Irwin.

--Fundamentals of Selling. 1984. 27.95x (ISBN 0-256-03101-0). Irwin.

Futrell, Charles M. Contemporary Cases in Sales Management. LC 80-65797. 288p. 1981. pap. text ed. 15.95x (ISBN 0-03-054736-9); instr's. manual 10.00 (ISBN 0-03-054741-5). Dryden Pr.

--Sales Management. LC 80-65796. 528p. 1981. text ed. 32.95x (ISBN 0-03-049276-9); instr's. manual 10.00 (ISBN 0-03-052201-3). Dryden Pr.

Futrell, Gene A., jt. auth. see Shepherd, Geoffrey S.

Futrell, Gene A., ed. Marketing for Farmers. LC 82-70257. (Illus.). 296p. (Orig.). 1982. pap. 12.95 (ISBN 0-932250-18-1). Doane Pub.

Futrell, John C. Making an Apostolic Community of Love: The Role of the Superior According to St. Ignatius of Loyola. LC 73-139365. (Original Studies Composed in English Ser.). 239p. 1970. smyth sewn 5.00 (ISBN 0-912422-19-X); pap. 4.00 (ISBN 0-912422-08-4). Inst Jesuit.

Futrell, Mynga, jt. auth. see Geisert, Paul.

Futrell, Mynga K. & Geisert, Paul. The Well-Trained Computer: Designing Systematic Instructional Materials for the Classroom Microcomputer. LC 84-1629. (Illus.). 290p. 1984. 26.95 (ISBN 0-87778-190-7). Educ Tech Pubns.

Futrell, Robert E. United States Air Force in Korea: 1950-1953. rev. ed. LC 81-60776. 843p. 1983. 18.00 (ISBN 0-318-11837-8). Gov Printing Office.

Futrell, Robert F. Command of Observation Aviation: A Study in Control of Tactical Air Power. (USAF Historical Studies: No. 24). 51p. 1956. pap. text ed. 6.50x (ISBN 0-89126-016-1). MA-AH Pub.

--Development of AAF Base Facilities in the United States, 1939-1945. (USAF Historical Studies: No. 69). 263p. 1951. pap. text ed. 30.00x (ISBN 0-89126-129-X). MA-AH Pub.

--Development of Aeromedical Evacuation in the USAF, 1909-1960, Vol. 1. (USAF Historical Studies: No. 23). 446p. 1960. 30.00x (ISBN 0-89126-050-1). MA-AH Pub.

--Development of Aeromedical Evacuation in the USAF, 1909-1960, Vol. 2. (USAF Historical Studies: No. 23). 1960. pap. 30.00x (ISBN 0-89126-051-X). MA-AH Pub.

--Ideas, Concepts, Doctrine: A History of Basic Thinking in the United States Air Force, 1907-1964. Gilbert, James, ed. LC 79-7255. (Flight: Its First Seventy-Five Years Ser.). 1979. Repr. of 1971 ed. lib. bdg. 73.50x (ISBN 0-405-12166-0). Ayer Co Pubs.

Futrelle, Jacques. Best Thinking Machine Detective Stories. Bleiler, E. F., ed. (Orig.). 1973. pap. 4.50 (ISBN 0-486-20537-1). Dover.

--Elusive Isabel. 1976. lib. bdg. 14.95x (ISBN 0-89968-164-6). Lightyear.

--Great Cases of the Thinking Machine. Bleiler, E. F., ed. LC 76-9182. 170p. (Orig.). 1976. pap. 3.50 (ISBN 0-486-23335-9). Dover.

Futterman, J., ed. see Futterman, Marian.

Futterman, Jacob, ed. see Futterman, Marian.

Futterman, Marian. Astrology & Your Cat. Futterman, Jacob, ed. (Illus.). 1977. pap. write for info (ISBN 0-930140-01-X). Jay Pub.

--You & Your Cats Compatibility Chart. Futterman, J., ed. 1977. 2.95 (ISBN 0-930140-03-6). Jay Pub.

Futterweit, W. Polycystic Ovarian Disease. (Clinical Perspectives in Obstetrics & Gynecology Ser.). (Illus.). 155p. 1984. 49.00 (ISBN 0-387-90981-8). Springer-Verlag.

Futuko, T. R., et al. Residue Reviews, Vol. 53. Gunther, F. A., ed. (Illus.). 185p. 1974. 34.50 (ISBN 0-387-90084-5). Springer-Verlag.

Future Systems, Inc. Electronic Mail: Systems, Developments & Opportunities. (Illus.). 147p. (Orig.). 1982. pap. 385.00x (ISBN 0-940520-49-4, F114). Monegon Ltd.

--Optical Fiber Communications: Current Systems & Future Developments. (Illus.). 135p. (Orig.). 1982. pap. 450.00x (ISBN 0-940520-47-8, F116). Monegon Ltd.

--Satellite Systems of the U. S. Domestic Communications Carriers. rev. ed. (Illus.). 313p. 1983. pap. 475.00x (ISBN 0-940520-46-X, F118). Monegon Ltd.

--Teleconferencing: An Enhanced Communications Service. rev. ed. (Illus.). 207p. 1982. pap. 525.00x (ISBN 0-940520-17-6, F113). Monegon Ltd.

Futures Group. U. S. & Multilateral Diplomacy: A Handbook. LC 84-5082. 266p. 1984. lib. bdg. 40.00x (ISBN 0-379-12146-8). Oceana.

Futuyma, Douglas. Science On Trial. 1982. 16.00 (ISBN 0-394-52371-7); pap. 7.95 (ISBN 0-394-70679-X). Pantheon.

Futuyma, Douglas J. Evolutionary Biology. LC 78-27902. (Illus.). 1979. text ed. 27.50x (ISBN 0-87893-199-6). Sinauer Assoc.

Futuyma, Douglas J. & Slatkin, Montgomery, eds. Coevolution. LC 82-19496. (Illus.). 400p. 1983. text ed. 48.00x (ISBN 0-87893-228-3); pap. text ed. 27.50x (ISBN 0-87893-229-1). Sinauer Assoc.

Fuwa, K., ed. see International Conference on Atomic Spectroscopy.

Fuwa, K., et al, eds. Atomic Spectroscopy in Japan. (Journal Spectrochimica Acta Ser.: No. 36). 160p. 1981. pap. 17.50 (ISBN 0-08-028731-X). Pergamon.

Fux, Johann J. Orfeo ed Euridice. Brown, Howard M., ed. LC 76-21040. (Italian Opera 1640-1770 Ser.). 1978. lib. bdg. 77.00 (ISBN 0-8240-2618-7). Garland Pub.

--Study of Counterpoint. Mann, Alfred, ed. & tr. Orig. Title: Gradus Ad Parnassum. 1965. pap. 6.95 (ISBN 0-393-00277-2, Norton Lib). Norton.

Fuxe, K., ed. Dopaminergic Ergot Derivatives & Motor Function: Proceedings of an International Symposium, Stockholm, 1978. (Wenner-Gren Center International Symposium Series: Vol. 31). (Illus.). 1979. 89.00 (ISBN 0-08-024408-4). Pergamon.

Fuxe, K., et al. Steroid Hormone Regulation of the Brain: Proceedings of an International Symposium, 27-28 October 1980, Wenner-Gren Center, Stockholm, Sweden. (Wenner-Gren Ser.: Vol. 34). (Illus.). 428p. 1981. 88.00 (ISBN 0-08-026864-1). Pergamon.

Fuxe, K., et al, eds. Central Regulation of the Endocrine System. LC 78-27000. (Nobel Foundation Symposia Ser.). 569p. 1979. 69.50x (ISBN 0-306-40078-2, Plenum Pr). Plenum Pub.

Fuxe, Kjell, et al, eds. Central Adrenaline Neurons: Basic Aspects & Their Role in Cardiovascular Disease: Proceedings of an International Symposium 27-28 August 1979, Wenner-Gren Center, Stockholm. (Wenner-Gren Ser.: Vol. 33). (Illus.). 356p. 1980. 63.00 (ISBN 0-08-025927-8). Pergamon.

--Excitotoxins. (The Wenner-Gren International Symposium Ser.: Vol. 39). 375p. 1984. 55.00x (ISBN 0-306-41653-0, Plenum Pr). Plenum Pub.

Fuye, Allotte De La see De La Fuye, Allotte.

Fuys, David & Tischler, Rosamond. Teaching Mathematics in the Elementary School. 1979. 23.95 (ISBN 0-316-29720-8); for info. teachers manual (ISBN 0-316-29721-6). Little.

Fyans, Leslie J., ed. Achievement Motivation: Recent Trends in Theory & Research. 482p. 1980. 49.50x (ISBN 0-306-40549-0, Plenum Pr). Plenum Pub.

Fyfe, Christopher. The Bale Fillers: Western Australian Wool 1826-1916. (Illus.). 325p. 1983. 52.50x (ISBN 0-85564-224-6, Pub. by U of W Austral Pr). Intl Spec Bk.

Fyfe, E. The Real Mexico. 1976. lib. bdg. 59.95 (ISBN 0-8490-2501-X). Gordon Pr.

Fyfe, F. Marjorie, ed. see Frederick II Of Hohenstaufen.

Fyfe, H. The Illusion of National Character. 1977. lib. bdg. 59.95 (ISBN 0-8490-2035-2). Gordon Pr.

Fyfe, Henry H. Northcliffe: An Intimate Biography. LC 74-100527. (BCL Ser.: I). Repr. of 1930 ed. 26.00 (ISBN 0-404-00592-6). AMS Pr.

--Sir Arthur Pinero's Plays & Players. LC 78-6207. (Illus.). 1978. Repr. of 1930 ed. lib. bdg. 32.50x (ISBN 0-313-20391-1, FYSR). Greenwood.

Fyfe, James J. Contemporary Issues in Law Enforcement. LC 81-9144. 168p. 20.00 (ISBN 0-8039-1692-2); pap. 9.95 (ISBN 0-8039-1693-0). Sage.

--Readings on Police Use of Deadly Force. LC 81-86057. 1982. write for info. Police Found.

Fyfe, James J., ed. Police Management Today: Issues & Case Studies. LC 85-155. (Practical Management Ser.). 224p. (Orig.). 1985. pap. text ed. 19.95 (ISBN 0-317-18455-5). Intl City Mgt.

Fyfe, T. Who's Who in Dickens: A Complete Dickens Repertory in Dickens Own Words. LC 75-152551. (Studies in Dickens, No. 52). 1971. Repr. of 1913 ed. lib. bdg. 49.95x (ISBN 0-8383-1236-5). Haskell.

Fyfe, Theodore. Hellenistic Architecture: An Introductory Study. LC 74-77884. (Illus.). 216p. 1975. Repr. 20.00 (ISBN 0-89005-026-0). Ares.

Fyfe, Thomas A. Who's Who in Dickens. 352p. Repr. of 1913 ed. lib. bdg. 38.50 (ISBN 0-8495-1713-3). Arden Lib.

--Who's Who in Dickens. LC 72-190886. Repr. of 1913 ed. lib. bdg. 39.50 (ISBN 0-8414-0820-3). Folcroft.

Fyfe, Thomas A., compiled by. Who's Who in Dickens: A Complete Dickens Repertory in Dickens' Own Words. 355p. 1982. Repr. of 1912 ed. lib. bdg. 45.00 (ISBN 0-89987-278-6). Darby Bks.

Fyfe, W. S., jt. ed. see O'Connell, R. J.

Fyfe, W. S., ed. see Royal Society of London, et al.

Fyfe, W. S., et al. Fluids in the Earth's Crust: Their Significance in Metamorphic, Tectonic, & Chemical Transport Process. (Developments in Geochemistry Ser.: Vol. 1). 384p. 1978. 72.50 (ISBN 0-444-41636-6). Elsevier.

Fyfe, W. T. Edinburgh under Sir Walter Scott. 1973. Repr. of 1906 ed. 30.00 (ISBN 0-8274-0534-0). R West.

Fyffe, David E., jt. auth. see Clifton, David S., Jr.

Fyffe, Don, jt. auth. see Adams, Sexton.

Fyffe, E. W., jt. auth. see Brown, Alan C.

Fyfield, J. A. Re-Educating Chinese Anti-Communists. LC 81-84061. 1982. 22.50 (ISBN 0-312-66733-7). St Martin.

Fyhrlund, Eric. Hasington. (Orig.). 1979. pap. 1.95 (ISBN 0-532-23249-6). Woodhill.

Fyle, Clifford N., compiled by. A Krio-English Dictionary. (Krio & Eng.). 1980. text ed. 65.00x (ISBN 0-19-864409-4). Oxford U Pr.

Fyleman, Rose, ed. Pipe & Drum. LC 78-74510. (Children's Literature Reprint Ser.). (Illus.). (gr. 3-7). 1979. 15.00x (ISBN 0-8486-0010-X). Core Collection.

Fyler, John M. Chaucer & Ovid. LC 78-10369. 1979. 22.50x (ISBN 0-300-02280-8). Yale U Pr.

Fylstra, Hilary. How to Work Smarter with Personal Computer. (VisiSeries). (Illus.). 200p. (Orig.). 1983. pap. 12.95 (ISBN 0-912213-02-7). Paladin.

--How You Can Work Smarter with Personal Computers. (The Visi Ser.). 1984. pap. 12.95 (ISBN 0-912213-02-7, VisiPress). Random.

Fymat, A. L. & Zuev, V. E., eds. Remote Sensing of the Atmosphere: Inversion Methods & Applications. (Developments in Atmospheric Science Ser.: Vol. 9). 328p. 1978. 76.75 (ISBN 0-444-41748-6). Elsevier.

Fyne, Neal. The Land of the Living Dead: A Narration of the Perilous Sojourn Therein of George Cowper, Mariner, in the Year 1835. Reginald, R. & Melville, Douglas, eds. LC 77-84224. (Lost Race & Adult Fantasy Ser.). (Illus.). 1978. Repr. of 1897 ed. lib. bdg. 23.50x (ISBN 0-405-10977-6). Ayer Co Pubs.

Fynn. Mister God, This Is Anna. 192p. 1985. pap. 2.95 (ISBN 0-345-32722-5). Ballantine.

--Mister God, This Is Anna. LC 75-541. (Illus.). 192p. 1975. 7.95 (ISBN 0-03-014716-6). HR&W.

Fynn, G. W. & Powell, W. J. The Cutting & Polishing of Electro-Optic Materials. LC 78-21139. 215p. 1979. 94.95x (ISBN 0-470-26607-4). Halsted Pr.

Fynn, J. K. Asante & Its Neighbours, 1700-1807. (Legon History Ser.). xiii, 175p. 1972. 14.95 (ISBN 0-8101-0369-9); pap. 9.95x (ISBN 0-686-76949-X). Northwestern U Pr.

Fynn, John K. Asante & Its Neighbours, Seventeen Hundred to Eighteen Seven. LC 77-175917. pap. 31.80 (ISBN 0-317-29807-0, 2016707). Bks Demand UMI.

Fynn, Robert. The Lost Bone. 236p. 1984. 10.95 (ISBN 0-89697-187-2). Intl Univ Pr.

Fynne, Robert J. Montessori & Her Inspirers. 1977. lib. bdg. 59.95 (ISBN 0-8490-2277-0). Gordon Pr.

Fyodorov, Vadim. An Ordinary Magic Watch. Beveridge, N. & Mokhova, N., trs. from Rus. (Illus.). 1977. 11.95 (ISBN 0-88233-304-6); pap. 4.95 (ISBN 0-88233-305-4). Ardis Pubs.

Fyodorova, Victoria & Frankel, Haskel. The Admiral's Daughter. 1980. pap. 2.50 (ISBN 0-440-10366-5). Dell.

Fyre, H. R., jt. auth. see Minor, E. O.

Fyson. Friend Fire & the Dark Wings. 11.95 (ISBN 0-19-271467-8, Pub. by Oxford U Pr Children's). Merrimack Pub Cir.

Fyson, Bance L. Feeding the World. (Today's World Ser.). (Illus.). 72p. (gr. 7-12). 1984. 14.95 (ISBN 0-7134-4264-6, Pub. by Batsford England). David & Charles.

Fyson, J. G. Friend Fire & the Dark Wings. LC 83-670208. (Illus.). (gr. 4-7). 11.95 (ISBN 0-19-271467-8). Oxford U Pr.

Fyson, John, ed. FAO Investigates Ferro-Cement Fishing Crafts. (Illus.). 200p. (Orig.). 1974. pap. 37.25 (ISBN 0-85238-061-5, FN13, FNB). Unipub.

Fyson, Marna. Stinkerbelle the Nark: An Otter's Story. LC 75-37458. (Illus.). (YA) (gr. 7 up). 1976. 9.95 (ISBN 0-8008-7421-8). Taplinger.

Fyson, Nance L. Growing up in Edwardian Britain. LC 79-56456. (Growing up Ser.). (Illus.). 72p. (gr. 7-9). 1980. text ed. 14.95 (ISBN 0-7134-3372-8, Pub. by Batsford England). David & Charles.

--Growing Up in the Post-War Forties. (Growing Up Ser.). (Illus.). 72p. (gr. 7-12). 1985. 14.95 (ISBN 0-7134-4762-1, Pub. by Batsford England). David & Charles.

--Growing up in the Second World War. (Growing up Ser.). (Illus.). 72p. (gr. 6 up). 1981. 14.95 (ISBN 0-7134-3574-7, Pub. by Batsford England). David & Charles.

Fyson, Nance L. & Greenhill, Richard. A Family in China. LC 84-19426. (Families the World over Ser.). (Illus.). 32p. (gr. 2-5). 1985. PLB 8.95 (ISBN 0-8225-1653-5). Lerner Pubns.

Fyson, P. F. Flora of Nilgiri & Pulney Hill Tops, 3 vols. 1978. Repr. of 1915 ed. Set. 187.50 (ISBN 0-89955-266-8, Pub. by Intl Bk Dist). Intl Spec Bk.

--The Flora of the South Indian Hill Stations Ootacamund Coonoor, Kotagirl, 2 vols. (Illus.). 1339p. 1977. Set. 100.00 (ISBN 0-88065-089-3, Pub. by Messers Today & Tomorrows Printers & Publishers India). Scholarly Pubns.

Fyvie, John. Noble Dames & Notable Men of the Georgian Era. 1973. Repr. of 1910 ed. 30.00 (ISBN 0-8274-0192-2). R West.

--Some Famous Women of Wit & Beauty. (Women Ser.). 1905. 25.00 (ISBN 0-8482-3999-7). Norwood Edns.

--Some Literary Eccentrics. 1973. Repr. of 1906 ed. 30.00 (ISBN 0-8274-0193-0). R West.

--Tragedy Queens of the Georgian Era. LC 78-91503. 326p. 1909. 20.00 (ISBN 0-405-08544-3). Ayer Co Pubs.

Fyzee. Compendium of Fatimid Law. 1969. 10.00 (ISBN 0-89684-497-8). Orient Bk Dist.

Fyzee, Asaf A. Outlines of Muhammadan Law. 5th ed. 1984. pap. 13.95x (ISBN 0-19-561393-7). Oxford U Pr.

G

G. A. Ogle & Co., Pub. Biographical Sketches of the Cumberland Region of Tennessee: Memoirs & Biographical Records, an Illustrated Compendium, Pt. II. (Illus.). 291p. 1980. Repr. of 1898 ed. 22.50 (ISBN 0-89308-191-4). Southern Hist Pr.

G-Jo Institute. Arthritis Self-Health Program. 1980. pap. 4.50 (ISBN 0-916878-10-4). Falkynor Bks.

--Meditative Relaxation. 1980. pap. 4.50 (ISBN 0-916878-13-9). Falkynor Bks.

--Permanent Weight Loss Program. 1980. pap. 4.50 (ISBN 0-916878-11-2). Falkynor Bks.

--Sexual Pleasure Enhancement Program. 1980. pap. 4.50 (ISBN 0-916878-12-0). Falkynor Bks.

--Stop Smoking Soon. 1980. pap. 4.50 (ISBN 0-916878-09-0). Falkynor Bks.

G. K. Hall & Co., compiled by. Cumulated Subject Index to Psychological Abstracts, 1927-1960, 2 Vols. 1966. 745.00 (ISBN 0-8161-0570-7, Pub. byHall Library); first suppl. 1961-1965 310.00 (ISBN 0-8161-0730-0); second suppl. 1966-1968 410.00 (ISBN 0-8161-0776-9). G K Hall.

G, Laimons Juris. American Refugee Poet. 1970. pap. 4.00 (ISBN 0-9600288-0-3). Poet Papers.

--I. E. (New Years: Return of the Life Force) 1975. pap. 12.00 (ISBN 0-9600288-7-0). Poet Papers.

--A Man Without a Gun. 1983. pap. 10.00 (ISBN 0-9600288-6-2). Poet Papers.

G. V. Cast Metals for Structural & Pressure Containment Application: MPC-11. 484p. 1979. 50.00 (ISBN 0-317-33448-4, G00161); members 25.00 (ISBN 0-317-33449-2). ASME.

Gaafar, S. M., et al. Parasites, Pests & Predators. (World Animal Science Ser.: Vol. B2). Date not set. write for info. (ISBN 0-444-42175-0). Elsevier.

Gaafar, S. M., et al, eds. Pathology of Parasitic Diseases. LC 72-108014. (Illus.). 408p. 1971. 15.00 (ISBN 0-911198-28-8). Purdue U Pr.

Gaag, J. Van Der see Van Der Gaag, J. & Perlman, M.

Gaag, Jacques van der & Neenan, William B., eds. The Economics of Health Care. LC 82-3699. 444p. 1982. 46.95x (ISBN 0-03-061501-1). Praeger.

Gaal, Arlene. Ogopogo: The Million Dollar Monster. (Illus.). 128p. 1985. 6.95 (ISBN 0-88839-987-1). Hancock House.

Gaal, Lisl. Classical Galois Theory. 3rd ed. LC 73-649. viii, 248p. 1979. text ed. 11.95 (ISBN 0-8284-1268-5). Chelsea Pub.

Gaal, O., et al. Electrophoresis in the Separation of Biological Macromolecules. LC 77-28502. 422p. 1980. 103.95 (ISBN 0-471-99602-5, Pub. by Wiley-Interscience). Wiley.

Gaal, Robert A. The Diamond Dictionary. 2nd ed. (Illus.). 1977. 16.95 (ISBN 0-87311-008-0). Gemological.

Gaal, S. A. Linear Analysis & Representation Theory. LC 72-95686. (Die Grundlehren der Mathematischen Wissenschaften: Vol. 198). ix, 688p. 1973. 71.00 (ISBN 0-387-06195-9). Springer-Verlag.

Gaan, Margaret. Last Moments of a World. (Illus.). 288p. 1981. pap. 4.95 (ISBN 0-393-00066-4). Norton.

--Little Sister. 208p. 1983. 13.95 (ISBN 0-396-08096-0). Dodd.

--White Poppy: A Novel of the Opium Wars. 416p. 1985. 16.95 (ISBN 0-396-08668-3). Dodd.

Gaan, Margret. Red Barbarian: A Novel of the Opium War. 448p. 1984. 16.95 (ISBN 0-396-08296-3). Dodd.

Gaarder, A. Bruce see Bishop, G. Reginald, Jr.

Gaarder, Kenneth R. Eye Movements, Vision & Behavior: A Hierarchical Visual Information Processing Model. LC 74-14710. 156p. 1975. 14.95 (ISBN 0-470-28895-7, Pub. by Wiley). Krieger.

Gaarder, Kenneth R. & Montgomery, Penelope S. Clinical Biofeedback: A Procedural Manual for Behavioral Medicine. 2nd ed. (Illus.). 288p. 1981. pap. 26.95 (ISBN 0-683-03401-4). Williams & Wilkins.

Gaas, W., jt. auth. see Amranand, P.

Gaasch, Irene. Walk This Way Please: On Foot on the Monterey Peninsula, Carmel, Carmel Valley & Big Sur. (Illus.). 96p. (Orig.). 1984. pap. 6.95. Hummbird Pr.

Gaastra, F., jt. ed. see Blusse, L.

Gaastra, Wim, jt. auth. see Walker, John M.

Gaba, Christian. Scriptures of an African People: The Sacred Utterances of the Anlo. LC 73-85557. 189p. 1973. text ed. 14.95 (ISBN 0-88357-018-1). NOk Pubs.

Gabaccia, Donna R. From Sicily to Elizabeth Street: Housing & Social Change among Italian Immigrants, 1880-1930. LC 83-4933. (American Social History Ser.). 174p. 1984. 34.50x (ISBN 0-87395-768-7); pap. 10.95 (ISBN 0-87395-769-5). State U NY Pr.

Gabain, Marjorie, tr. see Oliver Brachfeld, F.

Gabain, Marjorie, tr. see Piaget, Jean.

Gabalac, Nancy W., jt. auth. see Ballou, Mary.

Gaballa, G. A. The Memphite Tomb: Chapel of Mose. (Modern Egyptology). 112p. 1978. text ed. 55.50x (ISBN 0-85668-088-5, Pub. by Aris & Phillips England). Humanities.

Gaballi Prat, P. Diccionario De Terminos Comerciales. 634p. (Eng. & Span.). 1963. 32.95 (ISBN 84-255-0295-0, S-31618). French & Eur.

Gabano, J. B., ed. Lithium Batteries. 1983. 79.50 (ISBN 0-12-271180-7). Acad Pr.

Gabard, E. C. & Kenney, John P. Police Writing. 106p. 1957. 9.75x (ISBN 0-398-04261-6). C C Thomas.

Gabard, E. C., jt. auth. see Bristow, Allen P.

Gabarro, J., jt. auth. see Athos, A.

Gabasov, R. & Kirillova, F. The Qualitative Theory of Optimal Processes. Casti, John L., tr. (Control & Systems Theory: Vol. 3). 1976. 110.00 (ISBN 0-8247-6545-1). Dekker.

Gabasov, R. & Kirillova, F. M., eds. Optimal Linear Systems: Methods of Functional Analysis. (Mathematical Concepts & Methods in Science & Engineering Ser.: Vol. 15). 300p. 1978. 29.50x (ISBN 0-306-40119-3, Plenum Pr). Plenum Pub.

--Singular Optimal Controls. (Mathematical Concepts & Methods in Science & Engineering Ser.: Vol. 10). (Illus.). 262p. 1978. 29.50x (ISBN 0-306-39250-X, Plenum Pr). Plenum Pub.

Gabay, Sabit, jt. ed. see Grenell, Robert.

Gabay, Sabit, et al. Metal Ions in Neurology & Psychiatry. 384p. 1985. write for info. (ISBN 0-8451-2717-9). A R Liss.

Gabb, Cecil V., jt. ed. see Sandoz, Ellis.

Gabb, M. H. & Latcham, W. E. Handbook of Laboratory Solutions. 1968. 15.00 (ISBN 0-8206-0055-5). Chem Pub.

Gabb, Michael. Creatures Great & Small. LC 79-64386. (The Question & Answer Bks.). (Illus.). (gr. 3-6). 1980. PLB 7.95 (ISBN 0-8225-1178-9). Lerner Pubns.

--Everyday Science. LC 79-64387. (The Question & Answer Bks.). (Illus.). (gr. 3-6). 1980. PLB 7.95 (ISBN 0-8225-1179-7). Lerner Pubns.

Gabba, Emilio. Republican Rome, the Army & the Allies. Cuff, P. J., tr. LC 76-14307. 1977. 43.50x (ISBN 0-520-03259-4). U of Cal Pr.

Gabbard, Fred E. Make the Eagle Mount Up. 1978. 12.00 (ISBN 0-682-48763-5). Exposition Pr FL.

Gabbard, Glen O. & Twemlow, Stuart W. With the Eyes of the Mind: An Empirical Analysis of Out-of-Body States. LC 84-15914. 286p. 1984. 26.95 (ISBN 0-03-068926-0). Praeger.

Gabbard, Lucina P. The Stoppard Plays. LC 81-52808. 184p. 1982. 18.50x (ISBN 0-87875-233-1). Whitston Pub.

Gabbard, Lucinda P. The Dream Structure of Pinter's Plays: A Psychoanalytic Approach. LC 75-26209. 296p. 1977. 24.50 (ISBN 0-8386-1848-0). Fairleigh Dickinson.

Gabbard-Alley, Anne & Porter, M. Erin. An Interpersonal Approach to Business & Professional Speech Communication. 262p. 1977. pap. text ed. 9.95x (ISBN 0-89641-001-3). American Pr.

Gabbay, Dov. Semantical Investigation in Heyting's Intuitionistic Logic. 297p. 1981. 52.50 (ISBN 90-277-1202-6, Pub. by Reidel Holland). Kluwer Academic.

Gabbay, Dov & Guenthner, Franz, eds. Handbook of Philosophical Logic: Extentions of Classical Logic, Vol. II. LC 83-4277. 1984. lib. bdg. 120.00 (ISBN 90-277-1604-8, Pub. by Reidel Holland). Kluwer Academic.

Gabbay, Dov, jt. ed. see Guenther, Franz.

Gabbay, Dov M. Investigations in Modal & Tense Logics with Applications to Problems in Philosophy & Linguistics. LC 76-17835. (Synthese Library: No. 92). 1976. lib. bdg. 50.00 (ISBN 90-277-0656-5, Pub. by Reidel Holland). Kluwer Academic.

Gabbay, Rony. Communism & Agrarian Reform in Iraq: Services for Mothers & Their Handicapped Childred. 240p. 1978. 32.00 (ISBN 0-85664-567-2, Pub. by Croom Helm). Longwood Pub Group.

Gabbay, S. M. Elementary Mathematics for Basic Chemistry & Physics. 128p. (Orig.). 1980. pap. 11.95 (ISBN 0-9604722-0-7). Basic Science Prep Ctr.

Gabbedy, J. P. Yours Is the Earth: The Life & Times of Charles Mitchell. 1972. 14.75x (ISBN 0-85564-052-9, Pub. by U of W Austral Pr). Intl Spec Bk.

Gabbiani, Giulio, ed. The Cytoskeleton in Normal & Pathologic Processes: Cell Biology. (Methods & Achievements in Experimental Pathology: Vol. 8). (Illus.). 1978. 41.75 (ISBN 3-8055-2917-1). S Karger.

--The Cytoskeleton in Normal & Pathologic Processes: Cell Physiopathology. (Methods & Achievements in Experimental Pathology: Vol. 9). (Illus.). 1978. 63.50 (ISBN 3-8055-2919-8). S Karger.

Gabbiani, Giulio, et al. Reflections on Biologic Research. LC 67-26012. (Illus.). 256p. 1967. 10.50 (ISBN 0-87527-035-2). Green.

Gabbin, Joanne V. Sterling A. Brown: Building the Black Aesthetic Tradition. LC 84-19777. (Contributions in Afro-American & African Studies Ser.: No. 86). (Illus.). 304p. 1985. lib. bdg. 35.00 (ISBN 0-313-23720-4, GSB/). Greenwood.

Gabbot, Mabel J. Have a Very Merry Christmas. LC 80-83034. 56p. (Orig.). 1981. pap. 4.50 (ISBN 0-88290-163-X, 2044). Horizon Utah.

Gabe, Joseph, et al. The Ann Scales Postcards. 1977. pap. 5.00 (ISBN 0-89439-004-X). Printed Matter.

Gabe, Julius, tr. see Harden, Maximilian.

Gabe, M. Histological Techniques. Blackith, R. E. & Kovoor, A., trs. from Fr. (Illus.). 1976. 65.80 (ISBN 0-387-90162-0). Springer-Verlag.

Gabel. Signals & Linear Systems. 3rd ed. 1986. price not set (ISBN 0-471-82513-1). Wiley.

Gabel, Creighton. Analysis of Prehistoric Economic Patterns. Spindler, George & Spindler, Louise, eds. (Studies in Anthropological Method). 88p. pap. text ed. cancelled (ISBN 0-8290-0317-7). Irvington.

--Stone Age Hunters of the Kafue: The Gwisho A Site. LC 65-22281. (Pub. by Boston U Pr). 1965. 9.50x (ISBN 0-8419-8702-5, Africana). Holmes & Meier.

Gabel, Creighton & Bennett, Norman R., eds. Reconstructing African Culture History. LC 67-25932. (Pub. by Boston U Pr). 1967. 9.50x (ISBN 0-8419-8704-1, Africana). Holmes & Meier.

Gabel, Dorothy. Introductory Science Skills. 470p. (Orig.). 1984. pap. text ed. 12.95x (ISBN 0-88133-122-8). Waveland Pr.

Gabel, Dorothy L. & Kagan, Martin H. A Summary of Research in Science Education 1978. 578p. 1980. pap. 23.95x (ISBN 0-471-08869-2, Pub. by Ronald Pr). Wiley.

Gabel, John. Beach Glass. (Cleveland Poets Ser.: No. 22). 29p. 1979. 2.50 (ISBN 0-914946-18-8). Cleveland St Univ Poetry Ctr.

Gabel, John B. & Schlam, Carl C., eds. Thomas Chaloner's in Laudem Henrici Octavi. 112p. 1979. 10.00 (ISBN 0-87291-135-7). Coronado Pr.

Gabel, Katherine, et al. The Legal Issues of Female Inmates. LC 83-110559. (Illus.). 1982. 6.00 (ISBN 0-317-04103-7). Smith Coll.

Gabel, Leona, ed. The Renaissance Reconsidered: Proceedings. LC 64-5397. (Studies in History: No. 44). 1964. pap. 10.80 (ISBN 0-87391-004-4). Smith Coll.

Gabel, Leona C. Benefit of Clergy in England in the Later Middle Ages. 1969. lib. bdg. 17.00x (ISBN 0-374-92964-5). Octagon.

--From Slavery to the Sorbonne & Beyond: The Life & Writings of Anna J. Cooper. LC 80-53219. (Smith College Studies in History: Vol. 49). (Illus.). 98p. 1982. pap. 14.40 (ISBN 0-87391-028-1). Smith Coll.

Gabel, Robert A. & Roberts, Richard A. Signals & Linear Systems. 2nd ed. LC 80-14811. 492p. 1980. text ed. 44.50 (ISBN 0-471-04958-1); solns. manual 26.00x (ISBN 0-471-09880-9). Wiley.

Gabel, Rya, tr. see Panova, V.

Gabel, Stewart & Erickson, Marilyn T. Child Development & Developmental Disabilities. (Little, Brown Ser. in Clinical Pediatrics). 1980. text ed. 32.50 (ISBN 0-316-30100-0). Little.

Gabel, Stewart, ed. Behavioral Problems of Childhood. 464p. 1981. 47.50 (ISBN 0-8089-1336-0, 791475). Grune.

Gabel, Stewart, et al. Understanding Psychological Testing in Children. 1984. write for info. (ISBN 0-471-88522-3, Pub. by Wiley Med). Wiley.

Gabel, V. P., jt. ed. see Birngruber, R.

Gabelko, Nina H. & Michaelis, John U. Reducing Adolescent Prejudice: A Handbook. 226p. pap. 15.95 (ISBN 0-686-95038-0). ADL.

--Reducing Adolescent Prejudice: A Handbook. 230p. 1981. pap. text ed. 15.95x (ISBN 0-8077-2601-X); dup. masters 17.95x (ISBN 0-8077-2639-7). Tchrs Coll.

Gabella, G. Structure of the Autonomic Nervous System. 1976. 75.00x (ISBN 0-412-13620-1, 6114, Pub. by Chapman & Hall). Methuen Inc.

Gabelman, W. H., jt. ed. see Welch, R. M.

Gabelnick, Henry L. & Litt, Mitchell. Rheology of Biological Systems. (Illus.). 320p. 1973. 24.50x (ISBN 0-398-02589-4). C C Thomas.

Gaber, Susan. Favorite Poems for Children Coloring Book. (Illus.). 48p. (Orig.). (ps-3). 1980. pap, 2.25 (ISBN 0-486-23923-3). Dover.

--Ready-to-Use Food & Drink Spot Illustrations. (Clip Art Ser.). 1981. pap. 2.95 (ISBN 0-486-24139-4). Dover.

--A Treasury of Flower Designs for Artists, Embroiderers & Craftsmen: 100 Garden Favorites. (Illus.). 80p. (Orig.). 1981. pap. 3.50 (ISBN 0-486-24096-7). Dover.

Gaber, Walter A. PC Abstracts: Abstracts & Index of Periodical Literature fo· the IBM-PC & PC Compatible User. (Reference Library of the Humanities). 400p. 1985. lib. bdg. 60.00 (ISBN 0-8240-8720-8). Garland Pub.

Gaber-Saletan, Pamela. Regional Styles In Cypriote Sculpture: The Sculpture from Idalion. Freedberg, S. J., ed. (Outstanding Dissertations in Fine Arts Ser.). (Illus.). 255p. 1985. Repr. of 1982 ed. 35.00 (ISBN 0-8240-6855-6). Garland Pub.

Gabert. Racquetball. 96p. 1984. pap. text ed. 7.95 (ISBN 0-8403-3214-9). Kendall-Hunt.

Gabert, Glen. The Public Community College: The People's University. LC 81-82469. (Fastback Ser.: No. 162). 50p. 1981. pap. 0.75 (ISBN 0-87367-162-7). Phi Delta Kappa.

Gabert, Glen, Jr. In Hoc Signo? A Brief History of Catholic Parochial Education in America. LC 72-89992. 1973. 14.95x (ISBN 0-8046-9028-6, Pub. by Kennikat). Assoc Faculty Pr.

Gabhart, D. R., jt. auth. see Gaffney, D. J.

Gabhart, Herbert C. Meeting the Challenge. 1984. 7.95 (ISBN 0-8054-5340-7, 4253-40). Broadman.

Gabin, Jane S. A Living Minstrelsy: The Poetry & Music of Sidney Lanier. viii, 182p. 1985. text ed. 15.50X (ISBN 0-86554-155-8, MUP/H145). Mercer Univ Pr.

Gabin, Sanford B. Judicial Review & the Reasonable Doubt Test. (National University Publications, Multi-Disciplinary Studies in the Law). 134p. 1980. 15.00 (ISBN 0-8046-9248-3, 9248, Pub. by Kennikat). Assoc Faculty Pr.

Gabirol, Solomon I. Fountain of Life. pap. 1.45 (ISBN 0-685-19402-7, 104, WL). Citadel Pr.

--Selected Religious Poems of Solomon Ibn Gabiro. LC 73-2210. (The Jewish People; History, Religion, Literature Ser.). Repr. of 1923 ed. 32.00 (ISBN 0-405-05274-X). Ayer Co Pubs.

Gabka, J. & Vaubel, E. Plastic Surgery: Past & Present. (Illus.). viii, 180p. 1983. 125.75 (ISBN 3-8055-3651-8). S Karger.

Gabl, F., jt. ed. see Kaiser, E.

Gable, Dan & Peterson, James A. Conditioning for Wrestling: The Iowa Way. 2nd ed. (Illus.). 160p. 1985. pap. 9.95 (ISBN 0-88011-253-0). Leisure Pr.

Gable, Fred B. Opportunities in Pharmacy Careers. LC 74-82639. (VGM Career Bks.). (Illus.). 144p. (gr. 8-12). 1974. 7.95 (ISBN 0-8442-6369-9, 6369-9); pap. 5.95 (ISBN 0-8442-6370-2, 6370-2). Natl Textbk.

Gable, John A. The Bull Moose Years: Theodore Roosevelt & the Progressive Party. (National University Publications in American Studies). 1978. 25.50x (ISBN 0-8046-9187-8, Pub. by Kennikat). Assoc Faculty Pr.

Gable, Richard W., jt. auth. see Finkle, Jason L.

Gable, Ronald. Investments & Financial Planning: The Complete Picture. 1983. text ed. 26.95 (ISBN 0-8359-3300-8). Reston.

Gabler, Hans W., ed. Chamber Music, Poems Pennyeach, & Occasional Verse: A Facsimile of Manuscripts by James Joyce, Typescripts & Proofs, Vol. 1. LC 78-10445. (James Joyce Archive Ser.). 1979. lib. bdg. 89.00 (ISBN 0-8240-2800-7). Garland Pub.

Gabler, Hans W., ed. see Joyce, James.

Gabler, James M. Wine into Words: A History & Bibliography of Wine Books in the English Language. LC 84-70446. (Illus.). 403p. 1985. 38.00 (ISBN 0-9613525-0-7). Bacchus Wine.

Gabler, MaryJean & Augustine, Lloyd. Carryover: A Maintenance Program for Language Impaired Adolescents. 103p. 1984. 3-ring binder 49.95 (ISBN 0-9610370-6-7). Thinking Pubns.

Gabler, Mel & Gabler, Norma. What Are They Teaching Our Children? 168p. 1985. 5.95 (ISBN 0-89693-362-8). Victor Bks.

Gabler, Norma, jt. auth. see Gabler, Mel.

Gabler, Ray. New England White Water River Guide. rev., 2nd ed. (Illus.). 376p. (Orig.). 1981. pap. 8.95 (ISBN 0-910146-33-0). Appalach Mtn.

Gabler, Raymond. Molecular Biophysics: An Introduction to Electrical Interactions. (Molecular Biology Ser.). 1978. 38.50 (ISBN 0-12-271350-8). Acad Pr.

Gabler, Robert E. & Sager, Robert J. Essentials of Physical Geography. 2nd ed. 1982. text ed. 36.95 (ISBN 0-03-058551-1, CBS C). SCP.

Gablik, Suzi. Has Modernism Failed? LC 83-51075. 112p. 1984. 14.95f (ISBN 0-500-23391-8). Thames Hudson.

--Has Modernism Failed? LC 83-51075. 1985. pap. 10.95 (ISBN 0-500-27385-5, Dist by Norton). Thames Hudson.

--Magritte. LC 84-51498. (World of Art Ser.). (Illus.). 228p. 1985. pap. 9.95 (ISBN 0-500-20199-4). Thames Hudson.

--Progress in Art. LC 76-62549. 192p. 1979. pap. 9.95 (ISBN 0-8478-0168-3). Rizzoli Intl.

Gabo, Naum. Gabo: Constructions, Structure, Paintings, Drawings & Engravings. LC 58-1904. 193p. 1957. Repr. 49.00 (ISBN 0-403-04073-6). Somerset Pub.

--Of Divers Arts. (Bollingen Ser. Vol. 35; A. W. Mellow Lecture Ser. No. 8). (Illus.). 1962. 32.50x (ISBN 0-691-09793-3, 224). Princeton U Pr.

Gabor, Andre. Issues in Pricing Policy. 1979. 95.00x (ISBN 0-905440-83-8, Pub. by MCB Pubns). State Mutual Bk.

--Pricing Decisions. 1980. 110.00x (ISBN 0-905440-94-3, Pub. by MCB Pubns). State Mutual Bk.

--Pricing: Principles & Practices. 1977. text ed. 36.50x (ISBN 0-435-84365-6); pap. text ed. 15.50x (ISBN 0-435-84366-4). Gower Pub Co.

Gabor, D., et al. Beyond the Age of Waste: A Report to the Club of Rome. 2nd ed. LC 80-41614. (Illus.). 265p. 1981. 48.00 (ISBN 0-08-027303-3); pap. 21.00 (ISBN 0-08-027304-1). Pergamon.

Gabor, Dennis. Innovations: Scientific, Technological & Social. 1970. pap. 3.95 (ISBN 0-19-519412-8). Oxford U Pr.

Gabor, Don. How to Start a Conversation & Make Friends. (Illus., Orig.). 1983. pap. 6.95 (ISBN 0-671-47421-9, Fireside). S&S.

Gabor, Georgia M. My Destiny: Survivor of the Holocaust. LC 81-68276. (Illus.). 319p. (Orig.). 1981. pap. 6.95 (ISBN 0-941204-00-6). Amen Pub.

Gabor, Mark. Houseboats. (Illus.). 1979. 17.95 (ISBN 0-345-27312-5); pap. 8.95 (ISBN 0-345-28117-9). Ballantine.

--The Illustrated History of Girlie Magazines: From National Police Gazette to the Present. 1984. 25.00 (ISBN 0-517-54997-2, Harmony). Crown.

--The Pin-up: A Modest History. LC 73-189116. (Illus.). 272p. 1973. pap. 6.95 (ISBN 0-87663-910-4). Universe.

Gabor, Mark, jt. auth. see Revien, Leon.

Gaboriau, Emile. File No. 113. LC 75-32793. (Literature of Mystery & Detection). 1976. Repr. of 1900 ed. 40.00x (ISBN 0-405-07871-4). Ayer Co Pubs.

--The Mystery of Orcival. 320p. 1977. Repr. of 1900 ed. lib. bdg. 14.25x (ISBN 0-89968-183-2). Lightyear.

--The Widow LeRouge. Williams, Fred & Ernst, George A., trs. from Fr. LC 75-32746. (Literature of Mystery & Detection). 1976. Repr. of 1873 ed. 17.00x (ISBN 0-405-07872-2). Ayer Co Pubs.

--The Widow LeRouge. 293p. 1980. Repr. of 1900 ed. lib. bdg. 12.50x (ISBN 0-89968-184-0). Lightyear.

Gaborit, Jean-Yves. Perfumes: The Essence & Their Bottles. LC 85-42931. (Illus.). 164p. 1985. 45.00 (ISBN 0-317-31430-0). Rizzoli Intl.

Gabow, Patricia A. Fluids & Electrolytes: Clinical Problems & Their Solutions. 1983. pap. 15.95 (ISBN 0-316-30114-0). Little.

Gabr, M. M., jt. auth. see Rao, T. S.

Gabre-Tsadick, Marta. Sheltered by the King. 128p. 1983. 7.95 (ISBN 0-310-60400-1, Pub by Chosen Bks). Zondervan.

Gabriel. The Angel Speaks Again. 1985. 7.95 (ISBN 0-533-06537-2). Vantage.

--Divine Intimacy, Vol. III. 1983. 12.95 (ISBN 0-87193-203-2). Dimension Bks.

--Divine Intimacy, Vol. II. 1983. 12.95 (ISBN 0-87193-201-6). Dimension Bks.

--Divine Intimacy, Vol. IV. 12.95 (ISBN 0-87193-204-0). Dimension Bks.

--Divine Intimacy, Vol. 1. 12.95 (ISBN 0-87193-194-X). Dimension Bks.

--Voice of the Angel. 1984. 7.95 (ISBN 0-533-05978-X). Vantage.

Gabriel, Annette M. And a Child Looked On. Date not set. 5.75 (ISBN 0-8062-2342-1). Carlton.

Gabriel, Astrik L. Skara House at the Mediaeval University of Paris. (Mediaeval Texts & Studies Ser.: No. 9). 1960. 15.95 (ISBN 0-268-00255-X). U of Notre Dame Pr.

--Student Life in Ave Maria College, Medieval Paris. (Mediaeval Studies Ser.: No. 14). (Illus.). 1955. 26.95 (ISBN 0-268-00265-7). U of Notre Dame Pr.

Gabriel, Barbra L. Biological Electron Microscopy. 240p. 1982. 36.50 (ISBN 0-442-22923-2). Van Nos Reinhold.

--Biological Scanning Electron Microscopy. 192p. 1982. 28.50 (ISBN 0-442-22922-4). Van Nos Reinhold.

Gabriel, C. J., jt. auth. see MacPherson, J. Hope.

Gabriel, Claire. Bernadette Black. 1978. pap. 1.95 (ISBN 0-532-19170-6). Woodhill.

Gabriel, Clive, jt. auth. see Shuter-Dyson, Rosamund.

Gabriel, Cynthia M., jt. auth. see Gabriel, Roger.

Gabriel, D. M., jt. auth. see Milwidsky, B. M.

Gabriel, Daniel. Sacco & Vanzetti: A Narrative Longpoem. LC 82-84445. 88p. 1984. pap. 5.00 (ISBN 0-940584-05-0). Gull Bks.

Gabriel, E. Die Langfristige Entwicklung von Spaetschizophrenien. (Bibliotheca Psychiatrica: No. 156). (Illus.). 1977. pap. 33.75 (ISBN 3-8055-2656-3). S Karger.

Gabriel, E., ed. Problems of Schizo-Affective Psychoses. (Journal Series: Psychiatria Clinica: Vol. 16, No. 2-5,). (Illus.). 240p. 1983. pap. 41.75 (ISBN 3-8055-3727-1). S Karger.

--Ueber die Beeinflussbarkeit psychiatrischer Krankheitsverlaeufe, 1980, Vol. 13, No. 3-4. (Illus.). iv, 136p. 1981. pap. 14.25 (ISBN 3-8055-2336-X). S Karger.

Gabriel, E., ed. see Donausymposium fuer Psychiatrie, 7th, Wien, 30.9.-2.10. 1976.

Gabriel, Gary. The Extra: L3. McConochie, Jean, ed. (Regents Readers Ser.). (Illus.). 68p. (gr. 7-12). 1982. pap. text ed. 2.50 (ISBN 0-88345-458-0, 20898). Regents Pub.

--Prose & Passion. (Illus.). 166p. (gr. 9-12). 1981. pap. text ed. 5.75 (ISBN 0-88345-436-X, 18838); tchr's. ed. 7.95 (ISBN 0-88345-486-6, 18839); cassettes 12.00 (ISBN 0-686-86693-2, 58840). Regents Pub.

--Whatever Happened to Sandy Fowler? McConochie, Jean, ed. (Regents Readers Ser.). 80p. (gr. 7-12). 1983. pap. text ed. 2.50 (ISBN 0-88345-498-X, 20987). Regents Pub.

Gabriel, George, tr. see Kalomiros, Alexander.

Gabriel, H. W. Twenty Steps to Power, Influence & Control Over People. 1976. 12.95 (ISBN 0-13-934976-6, Reward); pap. 4.95 (ISBN 0-13-934950-2). P-H.

Gabriel, J. W., tr. see Spies, Werner.

Gabriel, Joyce & Baldwin, Bettye. Having It All: A Practical Guide to Overcoming the Career Woman's Blues. LC 79-23283. 252p. 1979. 8.95 (ISBN 0-87131-302-2). M Evans.

Gabriel, Judy M., jt. auth. see Sack, John.

Gabriel, Leah, jt. ed. see Lyons, Deborah.

Gabriel, M. C. Poems. 8.00 (ISBN 0-89253-479-6); flexible cloth 4.00 (ISBN 0-89253-480-X). Ind-US Inc.

Gabriel, Michael. Gabriel's Friends. 1980. 25.00 (ISBN 0-917224-05-1); pap. 14.95 (ISBN 0-917224-06-X). Gregory Pubns.

--Gabriel's Friends: An A to Z Guide to Cartooning the Animal Kingdom. LC 77-95033. (Illus.). 320p. 1980. 25.00 (ISBN 0-917224-05-1); pap. 14.95 (ISBN 0-917224-06-X). Gregory Pubns.

--Micrographics 1900-1977: A Bibliography. LC 79-83891. 1978. PLB 19.00 (ISBN 0-933474-01-6). Minn Scholarly.

--Nuclear Energy & Public Safety: A Bibliography of Popular Literature, Part I. (CPL Bibliographies Ser.: No. 73). 73p. 1982. 12.00 (ISBN 0-86602-073-X). Coun Plan Librarians.

Gabriel, Michael R. & Roselle, William C. The Microform Revolution in Libraries, Vol. 3. Stueart, Robert D., ed. LC 76-5646. (Foundations in Library & Information Science Ser.). 1980. lib. bdg. 37.50 (ISBN 0-89232-008-7). Jai Pr.

Gabriel, P., jt. auth. see Demazure, M.

Gabriel, P., jt. ed. see Dlab, V.

Gabriel, P., ed. see International Conference, Ottawa, 1974.

Gabriel, Patricia. The Villagers' Book of Outstanding Homes of Miami. LC 75-31851. (Illus.). 1976. 25.00 (ISBN 0-916224-24-4). Banyan Bks.

Gabriel, Philip. The Magic of Life. (Illus.). 56p. 1984. 12.00 (ISBN 0-931494-47-8). Brunswick Pub.

Gabriel, Philip L. In the Ashes: The Story of Lebanon. LC 78-57513. 1978. cancelled (ISBN 0-87426-046-9). Whitmore.

Gabriel, Pierre & Zisman, M. Calculus of Fractions & Homotopy Theory. (Ergebnisse der Mathematik und Ihrer Grenzgebiete: Vol. 35). (Illus.). 1967. 36.00 (ISBN 0-387-03777-2). Springer-Verlag.

Gabriel, Ralph H. American Values: Continuity & Change. LC 74-24. (Contributions in American Studies: No. 15). 230p. 1974. lib. bdg. 27.50 (ISBN 0-8371-7355-8, GAV/). Greenwood.

--Lure of the Frontier. 1929. 22.50x (ISBN 0-686-83610-3). Elliots Bks.

--Religion & Learning at Yale: Church of Christ in the College & University, 1757-1957. 1958. 39.50x (ISBN 0-685-69820-3). Elliots Bks.

--Toilers of Land & Sea. 1926. 22.50x (ISBN 0-686-83829-7). Elliots Bks.

Gabriel, Ralph H. & Brown, Charles R. Christianity & Modern Thought. 11.00 (ISBN 0-8369-7217-1, 8016). Ayer Co Pubs.

Gabriel, Ralph H. see Gabriel, Ralph H.

Gabriel, Ralph H., ed. Pageant of America, 11 vols. Incl. Vol. 1. Adventurers in the Wilderness. Wissler, Clark & Skinner, Constance L. (ISBN 0-911548-56-4); Vol. 2. The Lure of the Frontier. Gabriel, Ralph H (ISBN 0-911548-57-2); Vol. 3. Toilers of Land & Sea. Gabriel, Ralph H (ISBN 0-911548-58-0); Vol. 4. The March of Commerce. Keir, Malcolm (ISBN 0-911548-59-9); Vol. 5. The Epic of Industry. Keir, Malcolm (ISBN 0-911548-60-2); Vol. 6. The Winning of Freedom. Wood, William & Gabriel, Ralph H. (ISBN 0-911548-61-0); Vol. 7. In Defense of Liberty. Wood, William & Gabriel, Ralph H.; Vol. 8. Builders of the Republic. Ogg, Frederic A; Vol. 9. Makers of a New Nation. Bassett, John S (ISBN 0-911548-64-5); Vol. 10. American Idealism. Weigle, Luther A (ISBN 0-911548-65-3); Vol. 11. The American Spirit in Letters. Williams, Stanley T (ISBN 0-911548-66-1); Vol. 12. The American Spirit in Art. Mather, Frank J., Jr., et al. (ISBN 0-911548-67-X); Vol. 13. The American Spirit in Architecture. Hamlin, Talbot F; Vol. 14. The American Stage. Coad, Oral S. & Mims, Edwin, Jr. (ISBN 0-911548-69-6); Vol. 15. Annals of American Sport. Krout, John A (ISBN 0-911548-70-X). (Illus.). 22.95 ea. US Pubs.

Gabriel, Ralph H., ed. see Royce, Sarah.

Gabriel, Richard. How to Buy Your Own House When You Don't Have Enough Money. LC 81-21182. 136p. 1982. 11.95 (ISBN 0-13-403139-3); pap. 5.95 (ISBN 0-13-403121-0). P-H.

--How to Buy Your Own House When You Don't Have Enough Money. 176p. 1983. pap. 3.95 (ISBN 0-451-12990-3, AE2990, Sig). NAL.

--Operation Peace for Galilee: The Israeli-PLO War in Lebanon. 256p. 1984. 16.95 (ISBN 0-8090-7454-0); pap. 7.95 (ISBN 0-8090-1504-8). Hill & Wang.

Gabriel, Richard, ed. Fighting Armies: Antagonists in the Middle East. LC 83-1531. (Illus.). 224p. 1983. lib. bdg. 35.00 (ISBN 0-313-23904-5, GFA/02). Greenwood.

Gabriel, Richard A. The Antagonists: A Comparative Combat Assessment of the Soviet & American Soldier. LC 83-1645. (Contributions in Military History Ser.: No. 34). (Illus.). xi, 208p. 1984. lib. bdg. 29.95 (ISBN 0-313-23127-3, GTA/). Greenwood.

--The Ethnic Factor in the Urban Polity. LC 73-10260. 1973. 22.50x (ISBN 0-8422-5125-1); pap. text ed. 9.50x (ISBN 0-8422-0344-3). Irvington.

--The Irish & Italians: Ethnics in City & Suburb. Cordasco, Francesco, ed. LC 80-857. (American Ethnic Groups Ser.). 1981. lib. bdg. 32.00x (ISBN 0-405-13420-7). Ayer Co Pubs.

--Military Incompetence: Why the American Military Doesn't Win. 224p. 1985. 16.95 (ISBN 0-317-20120-4). Hill & Wang.

--Military Incompetence: Why the American Military Doesn't Win. 224p. 1985. 16.95 (ISBN 0-8090-6928-8, Pub. by Hill & Wang). FS&G.

--The Mind of the Soviet Fighting Man: A Quantitative Survey of Soviet Soldiers, Sailors, & Airmen. LC 83-18520. xviii, 156p. 1984. lib. bdg. 35.00 (ISBN 0-313-24187-2, GMS/). Greenwood.

--The New Red Legions: A Survey Data Source Book. LC 79-24458. (Contributions in Political Science Ser.: No. 44). (Illus.). xii, 252p. 1980. lib. bdg. 40.00 (ISBN 0-313-21497-2, GAP/). Greenwood.

--The New Red Legions: An Attitudinal Portrait of the Soviet Soldier, 2 vols. LC 79-8956. (Contributions in Political Science Ser.: No. 44). (Illus.). xiv, 246p. 1980. lib. bdg. 65.00 (ISBN 0-313-21496-4, GAO/). Greenwood.

--To Serve with Honor: A Treatise on Military Ethics & the Way of the Soldier. LC 81-6254. xviii, 243p. 1982. lib. bdg. 29.95 (ISBN 0-313-22545-1, GME/). Greenwood.

Gabriel, Richard A. & Cohen, Sylvan H. The Environment: Critical Factors in Strategy Development. LC 73-13651. 1973. 32.50x (ISBN 0-8422-5131-6); pap. text ed. 8.95x (ISBN 0-8422-0355-9). Irvington.

Gabriel, Richard A. & Savage, Paul L. Crisis in Command: Mismanagement in the Army. 1978. pap. 6.95 (ISBN 0-8090-0140-3). Hill & Wang.

Gabriel, Richard A., ed. Fighting Armies: NATO & the Warsaw Pact: A Combat Assessment. LC 83-1521. (Vol. I). (Illus.). 288p. 1983. lib. bdg. 35.00 (ISBN 0-313-23903-7, GFA/01). Greenwood.

--Fighting Armies: Nonaligned, Third World & Other Ground Armies. LC 83-1534. (Illus.). xxi, 276p. 1983. lib. bdg. 35.00 (ISBN 0-313-23905-3, GFA/03). Greenwood.

Gabriel, Richard F. Complete Guide to Building a Real Estate Fortune Investing in Older Multiple Dwellings. 1975. 69.50 (ISBN 0-686-30515-9). Exec Reports.

--Insider Leverage Techniques: The Fastest Way to Build a Fortune in Real Estate. LC 80-39810. 288p. 1981. deluxe duotang binder 79.50 (ISBN 0-13-467506-1, 45). Exec Reports.

--Turnaround Selling: How to Cash in on Hidden Big-Money Opportunities in Everyday Sales Situation. 1977. 49.50 (ISBN 0-13-933176-X). Exec Reports.

Gabriel, Richard P. Performance & Evaluation of LISP Systems. (Series in Computer Systems, Research Reports & Notes). 350p. 1985. pap. text ed. 22.50x (ISBN 0-262-07093-6). MIT Pr.

Gabriel, Roger. A Patient's Guide to Dialysis & Transplantation. 175p. 1982. 10.95 (ISBN 0-85200-355-2, Pub. by MTP Pr England). Kluwer Academic.

--Postgraduate Nephrology. 3rd ed. (Illus.). 272p. 1985. pap. text ed. 17.95 (ISBN 0-407-36116-2). Butterworth.

--Renal Medicine: Concise Medical Textbook. 2nd ed. (Illus.). 288p. 1981. pap. text ed. 16.95 (ISBN 0-7216-0727-6, Bailliere-Tindall). Saunders.

Gabriel, Roger & Gabriel, Cynthia M. Medical Lists for Examinations. 295p. (Orig.). 1983. pap. text ed. 29.95 (ISBN 0-407-00233-2). Butterworth.

Gabriel, Stephen C., et al. Financing the Agricultural Sector: Future Challenges & Policy Alternatives. (Westview Special Studies in Agriculture Science & Policy). 200p. 1985. 20.00x (ISBN 0-8133-0055-X). Westview.

Gabriel, Teshome H. Third Cinema in the Third World: The Aesthetics of Liberation. Kirkpatrick, Diane, ed. LC 82-8641. (Studies in Cinema: No. 21). 160p. 1982. 39.95 (ISBN 0-8357-1359-8). UMI Res Pr.

Gabriel, Vera, jt. auth. see Schroeder, Mary N.

Gabriel, Yiannis. Freud & Society. (International Library of Group Psychotherapy & Group Process). 330p. 1983. 29.95x (ISBN 0-7100-9410-8). Routledge & Kegan.

Gabriele, Joseph. The First Days of the Dinosaurs: Text Edition. (Illus.). 32p. (Orig.). (gr. 1-3). pap. 1.95 (ISBN 0-911211-55-1, Pub. by Know & Show Bks). Penny Lane Pubns.

--The Great Age of the Dinosaurs. (Illus.). 32p. (Orig.). (gr. 1-3). 1985. pap. text ed. 1.95 (ISBN 0-911211-56-X, Pub. by Know & Show Bks). Penny Lane Pubns.

--The Last Days of the Dinosaurs: Text Editions. (Illus.). 32p. (Orig.). (gr. 1-3). 1985. pap. 1.95 (ISBN 0-911211-57-8, Pub. by Know & Show Bks). Penny Lane Pubns.

--Prehistoric Reptiles of the Sea & Air: Text Editions. 32p. (gr. 1-3). 1985. pap. 1.95 (ISBN 0-911211-58-6, Pub. by Know & Show Bks). Penny Lane Pubns.

Gabriele, Peter & Gabriele, Rosemarie. Game Techniques in Applesoft BASIC. (Illus.). 148p. 1985. pap. cancelled (ISBN 0-8159-5617-7). Devin.

Gabriele, Rosemarie, jt. auth. see Gabriele, Peter.

Gabrieli, Aldo. Dizionario dei Sinonimi e dei Contrari Analogico e Nomenclatore. 867p. (Ital.). 1983. 62.00x (ISBN 0-913298-68-9). S F Vanni.

Gabrieli, Elemer R., ed. Clinically Oriented Documentation of Laboratory Data. 1972. 65.00 (ISBN 0-12-271850-X). Acad Pr.

Gabrieli, Francesco. The Arabs: A Compact History. Attanasio, Salvator, tr. from Ital. LC 81-4226. (Illus.). viii, 215p. 1981. Repr. of 1963 ed. lib. bdg. 23.50x (ISBN 0-313-23032-3, GATA). Greenwood.

Gabrieli, Francesco, ed. Arab Historians of the Crusades. LC 68-23783. (The Islamic World Ser.). 1978. 38.50x (ISBN 0-520-03616-6). U of Cal Pr.

Gabrieli, Francesco & Costello, E. J., trs. from Ital. & Arabic. Arab Historians of the Crusades. (Cal Ser.: No. 699). 398p. 1984. pap. 9.95 (ISBN 0-520-05224-2). U of Cal Pr.

Gabrielle, Vincent. Ernest & Celestine. LC 81-6392. (Illus.). 24p. (gr. k-3). 1982. 10.25 (ISBN 0-688-00855-0); PLB 10.88 (ISBN 0-688-00856-9). Greenwillow.

--Ernest & Celestine. (ps-3). 1982. 10.75 (ISBN 0-688-00855-0); PLB 10.88 (ISBN 0-688-00856-9). Morrow.

--Ernest & Celestine's Picnic. (ps-3). 1982. 10.75 (ISBN 0-688-01250-7); PLB 10.88 (ISBN 0-688-01252-3). Morrow.

--Smile, Ernest & Celestine. (ps-3). 1982. 10.75 (ISBN 0-688-01247-7); PLB 10.88 (ISBN 0-688-01249-3). Morrow.

Gabriels, D., jt. ed. see DeBoodt, M.

Gabrielson, Ira N. Western American Alpines. LC 71-174546. (Illus.). 1972. Repr. of 1932 ed. 10.00 (ISBN 0-685-61146-9). Theophrastus.

Gabrielson, Ira N., jt. auth. see Zim, Herbert S.

Gabrielson, R. Geological Survey of Norway, No. 355, Bulletin 53. 64p. 1980. pap. 14.00x (ISBN 82-00-31391-3). Universitet.

Gabrilovich, E. Fifth Quarter. 288p. 1984. pap. 3.95 (ISBN 0-8285-2622-2, Pub. by Progress Pubs USSR). Imported Pubns.

Gabrovska, S. & Biskup, M., eds. European Guide to Social Science Information & Documentation Services. (Vienna Centre Ser.). (Illus.). 230p. 1982. 39.00 (ISBN 0-08-028927-4). Pergamon.

Gabry, G. Old Musical Instruments. (Illus.). 1978. 7.00 (ISBN 0-912728-85-X). Newbury Bks.
Gabszewicz, Anton & Freeman, Geoffrey. Bow Porcelain. (Illus.). 164p. 1985. 55.00 (ISBN 0-85331-452-7, Pub. by Lund Humphries Pubs UK). Seven Hills Bks.
Gaburo, K. Dante's Joynte. (Illus.). 12p. 1983. Repr. saddle-stitch 6.85 (ISBN 0-939044-09-9). Lingua Pr.
--Mouth-Piece. write for info. (ISBN 0-939044-08-0). Lingua Pr.
--Music in Beckett's: Play. (Paperplay Ser. Mini-Bks.: Vol. 6). 12p. 1976. saddle stitched 2.75 (ISBN 0-939044-06-4). Lingua Pr.
--Poesies. write for info. (ISBN 0-939044-07-2). Lingua Pr.
Gaburo, Kenneth. Beauty of Irrelevant Music. (Paperplay Ser. Mini-Bks.: Vol. 1). (Illus.). 22p. 1976. saddle stitched 2.75 (ISBN 0-939044-01-3). Lingua Pr.
--C---Is. (Paperplay Ser. Mini-Bks.: Vol. 2). 12p. 1976. saddle-stitched 2.75 (ISBN 0-939044-02-1). Lingua Pr.
--Concerning Commonness & Other Conceptual Dysfunctions. (Illus.). 64p. Date not set. saddle-stitched 8.75 (ISBN 0-318-03607-X). Lingua Pr.
--Extraction, Vol. 4. (Paperplay Ser. Mini-Bks.). (Illus.). 12p. 1976. saddle-stitched 2.25 (ISBN 0-939044-04-8). Lingua Pr.
--Lingua Three: In the Can: A Dialectic Mix in Three Rounds. (Illus.). 220p. Date not set. 25.98 (ISBN 0-939044-18-8). Lingua Pr.
--Murmur. (Paperplay Ser. Mini-Bks.: Vol. 3). 8p. 1976. saddle stitched 2.25 (ISBN 0-939044-03-X). Lingua Pr.
--Non-Scatological Set of Preliminary Remarks. (Paperplay Ser. Mini-Bks.: Vol. 5). 12p. 1976. saddle stitched 2.60 (ISBN 0-939044-05-6). Lingua Pr.
--Privacy One: Words Without Song. (Illus.). 48p. 1977. saddle stitched 10.00 (ISBN 0-939044-25-0). Lingua Pr.
--Privacy Two: My, My, My What a Wonderful Fall. (Illus.). 22p. 1976. saddle stitched 8.00 (ISBN 0-939044-12-9). Lingua Pr.
--Twenty Sensing (Instruction) Compositions. (Illus.). 40p. 1977. saddle stitched 7.00 (ISBN 0-939044-11-0). Lingua Pr.
--Whole Language. (Illus.). 41p. Date not set. softcover 8.75 (ISBN 0-939044-21-8). Lingua Pr.
Gaburo, Kenneth & Dunn, David. Collaboration Two: Publishing As Eco-System. (Illus.). 28p. 1983. saddle-stitch 4.75 (ISBN 0-939044-28-5). Lingua Pr.
Gaburo, Kenneth, jt. auth. see Brun, Herbert.
Gaburo, Kenneth, ed. see Lingua Press.
Gaburo, Kenneth, et al, eds. Allos: Forty-One Writings by Forty-One Writers. LC 80-80809. (Illus.). 448p. 1980. soft cover 18.95 (ISBN 0-939044-26-9). Lingua Pr.
Gaburo, Virginia. Notation. LC 77-75432. (Illus.). 176p. 1977. soft-cover 14.45 (ISBN 0-939044-16-1). Lingua Pr.
--Who Is Bruce Simonds. 44p. 1978. saddle stitched plus boxed recording 13.95 (ISBN 0-939044-22-6). Lingua Pr.
Gabutt, D. How to Budget & Control Cash. 270p. 1985. text ed. 35.50 (ISBN 0-566-02517-5). Gower Pub Co.
Gabuzda, Thomas G., jt. auth. see Erslev, Allan J.
Gaby, Alan. The Doctor's Guide to Vitamin B-6. Bresnick, Jan, ed. 272p. 1984. 15.95 (ISBN 0-87857-516-2); pap. 8.95 (ISBN 0-87857-518-9). Rodale Pr Inc.
Gaby, E. & Gaby, S. Commodore 64 Program Building Blocks. (A Byte Bk.). 256p. 1984. pap. 9.95 (ISBN 0-07-022667-6). McGraw.
--GoSubs: A Hundred Program-Building Subroutines in Timex-Sinclair BASIC. 176p. 1983. pap. 9.95 (ISBN 0-07-022677-6, BYTE Bks). McGraw.
Gaby, S., jt. auth. see Gaby, E.
Gac, Y. Le see Le Gac, Y.
Gace, Brule. Chansons De Gace Brule. Huet, Gedeon, ed. 28.00 (ISBN 0-384-17535-X); pap. 22.00 (ISBN 0-384-17530-9). Johnson Repr.
Gace Brule. Gace Bule, Trouvere Champenois. LC 80-2158. (Societe Neo-Philologique De Helsingfors Ser.: Memoires, Vol. 16). Repr. of 1951 ed. 59.50 (ISBN 0-404-19022-7). AMS Pr.
Gacek, Richard R. & Kellman, Robert M. Otolaryngology Handbook. 1985. 32.50 (ISBN 0-87527-357-2). Green.
Gach, Gary. Preparing the Ground. 48p. (Orig.). 1975. pap. text ed. 3.00 (ISBN 0-915970-02-3). Heirs Intl.
Gach, John, jt. auth. see Wozniak, Robert H.
Gach, Michael & Marco, Carolyn. ACU-Yoga: Self Help Techniques to Relieve Tension. (Illus., Orig.). 1981. pap. 12.95 (ISBN 0-87040-489-X). Japan Pubns USA.
Gach, Michael Reed see Reed-Gach, Michael.
Gache, Louis-Hippolyte. A Frenchman, a Chaplain, a Rebel: The War Letters of Pere Louis-Hippolyte Gache, S. J. Buckley, Cornelius M., tr. 282p. 1981. 8.95 (ISBN 0-8294-0376-0). Loyola.
Gack & Jahn. Herder - Lexikon Tiere. 342p. (Ger.). 1976. pap. 15.95 (ISBN 3-451-17371-9, M-7459, Pub. by Herder). French & Eur.
Gack, Christopher & Wobcke, Manfred. Israel & the Occupied Territories. (Travel Paperbacks Ser.). (Illus.). 192p. 1981. pap. 5.95 (ISBN 0-908086-22-9, Pub. by Lonely Planet Australia). Hippocrene Bks.
Gackenbach. Harry y el Terrible Quiensabeque (Harry & the Terrible Whatzit) (ps-3). pap. 1.95 (ISBN 0-590-12116-2). Scholastic Inc.
Gackenbach, Dick. Annie & the Mud Monster. LC 81-8344. (Illus.). 32p. (gr. 1-3). 1982. 11.75 (ISBN 0-688-00791-0); PLB 11.88 (ISBN 0-688-00792-9). Lothrop.
--Arabella & Mr. Crack. LC 81-15670. (Illus.). 32p. (gr. k-3). 1982. 8.95 (ISBN 0-02-735770-8). Macmillan.
--A Bag Full of Pups. LC 80-23230. (Illus.). 32p. (ps-2). 1981. 9.95 (ISBN 0-395-30081-9, Clarion). HM.
--A Bag Full of Pups. LC 80-23230. 32p. (gr. k-3). 1983. pap. 3.95 (ISBN 0-89919-179-7, Clarion). HM.
--Binky Gets a Car. (Illus.). 32p. (ps-2). 1983. 9.95 (ISBN 0-89919-144-4, Clarion). HM.
--Claude & Pepper. LC 75-25507. (Illus.). 32p. (ps-2). 1976. 7.95 (ISBN 0-395-28793-6, Clarion). HM.
--Claude the Dog. LC 74-3403. (Illus.). 32p. (ps-2). 1982. 10.95 (ISBN 0-89919-124-X, Clarion); pap. 3.60. HM.
--Claude the Dog. (gr. k-3). 1976. pap. 1.50 (ISBN 0-590-01347-5). Scholastic Inc.
--Claude the Dog. 32p. (ps-2). 1974. 10.95 (ISBN 0-395-28792-8, Clarion). HM.
--Crackle Gluck & the Sleeping Toad. LC 78-12635. (Illus.). 32p. (gr. 1-3). 1979. 7.95 (ISBN 0-395-28953-X, Clarion). HM.
--Do You Love Me? (Illus.). 48p. (gr. 1-4). 1978. pap. 1.50 (ISBN 0-440-42067-9, YB). Dell.
--Do You Love Me? LC 74-34104. (Illus.). 48p. (ps-4). 1975. 11.95 (ISBN 0-395-28794-4, Clarion). HM.
--The Dog & the Deep Dark Woods. LC 83-47694. (Illus.). 32p. (ps-3). 1984. 9.57i (ISBN 0-06-021977-7); PLB 9.89g (ISBN 0-06-021978-5). HarpJ.
--Harry & the Terrible Whatzit. LC 76-40205. (Illus.). 32p. (ps-2). 1978. 7.95 (ISBN 0-395-28795-2, Clarion). HM.
--Harry & the Terrible Whatzit. LC 76-40205. (Illus.). 32p. (ps-3). 1984. pap. 3.95 (ISBN 0-89919-223-8, Clarion). HM.
--Hattie Be Quiet, Hattie Be Good. LC 76-58697. (Early I Can Read Bk). (Illus.). 32p. (gr. 1-3). 1977. 7.64i (ISBN 0-06-021951-3); PLB 8.89 (ISBN 0-06-021952-1). HarpJ.
--Hattie Rabbit. LC 75-37018. (Early I Can Read Bk.). (Illus.). 32p. (ps-3). 1976. PLB 8.89 (ISBN 0-06-021940-8). HarpJ.
--Hattie, Tom, & the Chicken Witch. LC 79-2742. (I Can Read Bk.). (Illus.). 64p. (gr. k-3). 1980. PLB 9.89 (ISBN 0-06-021959-9). HarpJ.
--Hound & Bear. LC 76-3525. (Illus.). 32p. (ps-3). 1976. 7.95 (ISBN 0-395-28796-0, Clarion). HM.
--King Wacky. LC 83-24044. (Illus.). 32p. (ps-2). 1984. PLB 8.95 (ISBN 0-517-55265-5). Crown.
--Little Bug. (Illus.). 32p. (ps-2). 1981. 9.95 (ISBN 0-395-30080-0, Clarion). HM.
--McGoogan Moves the Mighty Rock. LC 80-8455. (Illus.). 48p. (gr. 1-4). 1981. PLB 9.89g (ISBN 0-06-021968-8). HarpJ.
--Mag the Magnificent. LC 85-2645. (Illus.). 32p. (ps-3). 1985. 12.95 (ISBN 0-89919-339-0, Clarion). HM.
--Mr. Wink & His Shadow, Ned. LC 82-47711. (Illus.). 32p. (gr. 1-4). 1983. 9.57i (ISBN 0-06-021969-6); PLB 10.89g (ISBN 0-06-021974-2). HarpJ.
--More from Hound & Bear. LC 79-4310. (Illus.). 48p. (ps-3). 1979. 7.95 (ISBN 0-395-28973-4, Clarion). HM.
--Mother Rabbit's Son Tom. LC 76-18399. (Early I Can Read Bk.). (Illus.). 32p. (gr. k-3). 1977. 7.64i (ISBN 0-06-021947-5); PLB 8.89 (ISBN 0-06-021948-3). HarpJ.
--Pepper & All the Legs. LC 78-5084. 32p. (ps-3). 1978. 7.95 (ISBN 0-395-28797-9, Clarion). HM.
--The Pig Who Saw Everything. LC 77-12741. (Illus.). 40p. 1978. 6.95 (ISBN 0-395-28798-7, Clarion). HM.
--Poppy the Panda. LC 84-4952. (Illus.). 32p. (ps-3). 1984. PLB 11.95 (ISBN 0-89919-276-9, Clarion). HM.
--What's Claude Doing? LC 83-14983. (Illus.). 32p. (ps-2). 1984. PLB 10.95 (ISBN 0-89919-224-6, Clarion). HM.
Gackenbach, Dick, retold by. & illus. The Perfect Mouse. LC 84-877. (Illus.). 32p. (ps-3). 1984. 10.95 (ISBN 0-02-736760-6). Macmillan.
--The Princess & the Pea. LC 82-17954. (Illus.). 32p. (ps-3). 1983. SBE 9.95 (ISBN 0-02-735800-3). Macmillan.
Gackenbach, Jayne, ed Sleep & Dreams: A Sourcebook. LC 84-48759. 300p. 1985. lib. bdg. 40.00 (ISBN 0-8240-8764-X). Garland Pub.
Gacula, Maximo C., Jr. & Singh, Jagbir. Statistical Methods in Food & Consumer Research. (Food Science & Technology Ser.). 1984. 79.50 (ISBN 0-12-272050-4). Acad Pr.
Gad, Carl. Johan Bojer, the Man & His Works. MacIntire, Elizabeth J., tr. 1979. Repr. of 1920 ed. lib. bdg. 30.00 (ISBN 0-8495-2001-0). Arden Lib.
--Johan Bojer, the Man & His Works. Macintire, Elizabeth J., tr. LC 73-17656. (Illus.). 260p. 1974. Repr. of 1920 ed. lib. bdg. 19.75x (ISBN 0-8371-7263-2, GAJB). Greenwood.
Gad, E. & Schall, Michaelle D. Sod. (Illus.). 58p. (Orig.). (gr. 1 up). 1983. pap. 5.50 (ISBN 0-918961-00-9). Pr Duck.
Gad, Finn. History of Greenland: Earliest Times to 1700, Vol. 1. (Illus.). 356p. 1971. 30.00x (ISBN 0-7735-0119-3). McGill-Queens U Pr.
--The History of Greenland, 1700-1782, Vol. 2. (Illus.). 350p. 1973. 35.00x (ISBN 0-7735-0156-8). McGill-Queens U Pr.
--The History of Greenland, 1782-1808, Vol. 3. 486p. 1983. 40.00x (ISBN 0-7735-0409-5). McGill-Queens U Pr.
Gadad, M. G. & Hiregoudar, H. R. Experimental Errors & Their Treatment. 220p. 1981. 20.00x (ISBN 0-86125-064-8, Pub. by Orient Longman India). State Mutual Bk.
Gadamer, Hans-Georg. Dialogue & Dialectic: Eight Hermeneutical Studies on Plato. LC 79-18887. 27.50x (ISBN 0-300-02126-7); pap. text ed. 7.95x 224pp (ISBN 0-300-02983-7). Yale U Pr.
--Essays in Philosophical Hermeneutics. LC 74-30519. (Cal Ser: No. 363). 1977. pap. 7.95 (ISBN 0-520-03475-9). U of Cal Pr.
--Hegel's Dialectic: Five Hermeneutical Studies. Smith, P. Christopher, tr. from Ger. 130p. 1982. 18.50x (ISBN 0-300-01909-2); pap. 5.95x (ISBN 0-300-02842-3, Y-418). Yale U Pr.
--Philosophical Apprenticeships. Sullivan, Robert R., tr. from German. (Studies in Contemporary German Social Thought). 205p. 1985. 17.50 (ISBN 0-262-07092-8). MIT Pr.
--Reason in the Age of Science. Lawrence, Frederick G., tr. from Ger. (Studies in Contemporary German Social Thought). 216p. 1982. 22.50x (ISBN 0-262-07085-5); pap. text ed. 7.95x (ISBN 0-262-57061-0). MIT Pr.
--Truth & Method. 516p. 1982. pap. 14.95x (ISBN 0-8264-0431-6). Continuum.
--Truth & Method. LC 75-2053. 576p. 1975. 24.50 (ISBN 0-8264-0016-7). Continuum.
--Truth & Method. (The Crossroad Paperback Ser.). 516p. 1982. pap. 16.95 (ISBN 0-8245-0431-3). Crossroad NY.
Gadave, Renne. Un Theoricien Anglais Du Droit Public Au Xvlle Siecle. Mayer, J. P., ed. LC 78-67351. (European Political Thought Ser.). (Fr.). 1979. Repr. of 1907 ed. lib. bdg. 19.00x (ISBN 0-405-11698-5). Ayer Co Pubs.
Gadbois, Robert, jt. auth. see Roberts, David.
Gadbois, Robert, jt. auth. see Sadowski, Karen.
Gadbois, Robert, jt. auth. see Woldum, Thomas.
Gadd, Bernard. Where to Go? Short Stories. 72p. (Orig.). 1983. pap. 3.45x (ISBN 0-86863-687-8, Pub. by Heinemann Pub New Zealand). Intl Spec Bk.
Gadd, C. J. History & Monuments of UR. LC 72-80145. (Illus.). Repr. of 1929 ed. 24.50 (ISBN 0-405-08545-1, Blom Pubns). Ayer Co Pubs.
--Ideas of Divide Rule in the Ancient East. (British Academy, London, Schweich Lectures on Biblical Archaeology Series, 1945). pap. 19.00 (ISBN 0-317-15910-0). Kraus Repr.
Gadd, Cyril J. The Stones of Assyria. LC 83-45767. Repr. of 1936 ed. 110.00 (ISBN 0-404-20104-0). AMS Pr.
Gadd, Edward, ed. A Dream Anonymously Dreamt. (Orig.). 1983. pap. 12.50 (ISBN 0-911623-02-7). I Klang.
Gadd, Irna & Gadd, Laurence. Arthritis Alternatives. LC 83-5642. 160p. 1985. 14.95 (ISBN 0-87196-769-3). Facts on File.
Gadd, Laurence. Deadly Beautiful: The World's Most Poisonous Animals & Plants. (Illus.). 1980. 19.95 (ISBN 0-02-542090-9). Macmillan.
Gadd, Laurence, jt. auth. see Cowan, William.
Gadd, Laurence, jt. auth. see Gadd, Irna.
Gadd, Laurence D. The Second Book of the Strange. 352p. 1981. pap. 7.95 (ISBN 0-345-29776-8). Ballantine.
Gadd, Laurence D. & World Almanac Editors. The Second Book of the Strange. LC 81-82644. (Science & the Paranormal Ser.). (Illus.). 341p. 1981. 17.95 (ISBN 0-87975-170-3). Prometheus Bks.
Gadd, May. Country Dances of Today: Book 2. 1951. pap. 0.75 (ISBN 0-917024-01-X). Country Dance & Song.
--English Country Dances of Today. 1948. pap. 0.25 (ISBN 0-917024-00-1). Country Dance & Song.
Gadd, W. L., jt. auth. see Philip, Alex J.
Gadda, Carlo E. Acquainted with Grief. Weaver, William, tr. from Ital. LC 69-12804. 244p. 1985. pap. 8.95 (ISBN 0-8076-1115-8). Braziller.
--That Awful Mess on Via Merulana. LC 65-19320. 388p. 1984. pap. 8.95 (ISBN 0-8076-1093-3). Braziller.
Gaddes, W. H. Learning Disabilities & Brain Function: A Neuropsychological Approach. (Illus.). 350p. 1980. 29.00 (ISBN 0-387-90486-7). Springer-Verlag.
--Learning Disabilities & Brain Function. 2nd ed. (Illus.). 450p. 1985. 29.90 (ISBN 0-387-96065-1). Springer-Verlag.
Gaddie, Ronald E. & Douglas, Donald. Earthworms for Ecology & Profit: Earthworms & the Ecology, Vol. II. (Illus.). 1977. pap. 6.95 (ISBN 0-916302-01-6). Bookworm Pub.
--Earthworms for Ecology & Profit: Scientific Earthworm Farming, Vol. 1. (Illus.). 192p. 1975. 9.95 (ISBN 0-916302-11-3); pap. 6.95 (ISBN 0-916302-05-9). Bookworm Pub.
Gaddis, Eugene R. Avery Memorial - The Wadsworth Atheneum: The First Modern Museum. (Illus.). 69p. 1984. pap. 5.00 (ISBN 0-918333-00-8). Wadsworth Atheneum.
Gaddis, John L. Russia, the Soviet Union, & the United States: An Interpretive History. 309p. 1978. pap. text ed. 12.50 (ISBN 0-394-34179-1, RanC). Random.
--Strategies of Containment: A Critical Appraisal of Postwar American National Security Policy. LC 81-772. 1982. 29.95x (ISBN 0-19-502944-5); pap. 10.95 (ISBN 0-19-503097-4, GB690). Oxford U Pr.
--The United States & the Origins of the Cold War, 1941-1947. LC 75-186388. (Contemporary American History Ser.). 396p. 1972. 34.00x (ISBN 0-231-03289-7); pap. 12.00x (ISBN 0-231-08302-5, 133). Columbia U Pr.
Gaddis, John L., jt. auth. see Etzold, Thomas.
Gaddis, Peggy. Desired Damnations. (Sharon Romance Ser.). 128p. (Orig.). 1981. pap. 2.25 (ISBN 0-89531-132-1, 0198-96). Sharon Pubns.
Gaddis, Robert S., jt. ed. see Coker, Lawrence T.
Gaddis, Rose M. Jack B. Yeats: Painter & Poet. (European University Studies: Series 18, Comparative Literature, Vol. 3). 51p. 1972. 15.65 (ISBN 3-261-00696-X). P Lang Pubs.
Gaddis, Temistocles. The Idea of Progress & the Bankruptcy of Progress. (Illus.). 1980. deluxe ed. 69.75 (ISBN 0-89266-264-6). Am Classical Coll Pr.
Gaddis, Thomas E. The Birdman of Alcatraz. 254p. Repr. of 1955 ed. lib. bdg. 15.95x (ISBN 0-89190-445-X, Pub. by River City Pr). Amereon Ltd.
--Unknown Men of Alcatraz. 15.95 (ISBN 0-8488-0164-4, Pub. by Amereon Hse). Amereon Ltd.
Gaddis, Thomas E. & Long, James O. Killer: A Journal of Murder. 17.95 (ISBN 0-8488-0163-6, Pub. by Amereon Hse). Amereon Ltd.
Gaddis, William. Carpenter's Gothic. 256p. 1985. 16.95 (ISBN 0-670-69793-1, E Sifton Bks). Viking.
--JR. (Contemporary American Fiction Ser.). 730p. 1985. pap. 12.95 (ISBN 0-14-008039-2). Penguin.
--The Recognitions. 1974. pap. 5.95 (ISBN 0-380-00030-X, 60921-5, Bard). Avon.
--The Recognitions. (Contemporary American Fiction Ser.). 954p. 1985. pap. 12.95 (ISBN 0-14-007768-5). Penguin.
Gaddum, John. Pharmacology. 8th ed. Mitchell, J. F. & Burgen, A. S., eds. (Illus.). 1978. 17.95x (ISBN 0-19-261307-3). Oxford U Pr.
Gaddy, C. D., et al. Behavioral Science & Human Factors in Power Plant Applications. (Illus.). 138p. 1980. spiral bdg. 30.00x (ISBN 0-87683-140-4). G P Courseware.
Gaddy, Jerr J., ed. Dust to Dust: Obituaries of the Gunfighters. (Illus.). 1977. pap. 8.95 (ISBN 0-88342-240-9). Old Army.
Gaddy, Wade E., Jr. Georgia Study Guide for Real Estate Fundamentals. 8th ed. 312p. 1981. pap. text ed. 10.95 (ISBN 0-88462-411-0, 1513-07, Real Estate Ed). Longman USA.
--Georgia Study Guide for Real Estate Fundamentals. 10th ed. 236p. 1985. pap. text ed. 10.95 (ISBN 0-88462-505-2, 1513-07, Real Estate Ed). Longman USA.
Gaddy, Wade E., Jr. & Hart, Robert E. Real Estate Fundamentals. 2nd ed. 372p. (Orig.). 1984. pap. text ed. 22.50 (ISBN 0-88462-506-0, 1513-01, Real Estate Ed). Longman USA.
Gade, D. New Dimensions in Creativity. LC 74-78396. 1974. pap. 4.00 (ISBN 0-686-14991-2, 261-08418). Home Econ Educ.
Gade, Hans. American Harbour Pilot. 3rd, rev. ed. (Illus.). 1983. 165.00 (ISBN 0-318-00242-6). Heinman.
Gade, Herman G., et al, eds. Coastal Oceanography. (NATO Conference Series IV, Marine Sciences: Vol. 11). 575p. 1983. 79.50x (ISBN 0-306-41374-4, Plenum Pr). Plenum Pub.
Gade, Richard E. Historical Survey of Anti-Semitism. pap. 5.95 (ISBN 0-8010-3747-6). Baker Bk.
Gadebusch, Hans H. Chemotherapy of Infectious Disease. LC 76-3611. (Uniscience Ser.). 1976. 39.00 (ISBN 0-8493-5105-7). CRC Pr.
--Phagocytes & Cellular Immunity. 176p. 1979. 66.00 (ISBN 0-8493-5349-1). CRC Pr.
Gademann, G. NMR-Tomography of the Normal Brain. (Illus.). 110p. 1984. 36.50 (ISBN 0-387-13233-3). Springer-Verlag.
Gaden, E. L., jt. auth. see Scott, C. D.
Gader, Bertram & Nodar, Manuel V. Apple Software for Pennies. (Orig.). 1985. pap. 10.95 (ISBN 0-446-38206-X). Warner Bks.
--Free Software for the IBM PC. 480p. (Orig.). 1984. pap. 10.95 (ISBN 0-446-38198-5). Warner Bks.
--Mac Software for Pennies. 1986. pap. 12.95 (ISBN 0-446-38285-X). Warner Bks.
Gades, Robert & Holder, Birdie H. Typewriting: A Comprehensive Program. 1979. pap. text ed. 18.95 (ISBN 0-8403-3023-5, 40302301). Kendall-Hunt.

--Typewriting: A Comprehensive Program, Working Papers. 1979. pap. text ed. 11.95 (ISBN 0-8403-2047-7). Kendall-Hunt.
Gadgil, D. R. Planning & Economic Policy in India: Enlarged & Revised Edition. 1972. 17.50x (ISBN 0-8046-8809-5, Pub. by Kennikat). Assoc Faculty Pr.
--Writings & Speeches of Professor D. R. Gadgil on Economic & Political Problems. cancelled (ISBN 0-8364-0819-5, Orient Longman). South Asia Bks.
--Writings & Speeches of Professor D. R. Gadgil on Planning & Development: 1967-71. Kamat, A. R., ed. LC 75-901569. 1974. 10.00x (ISBN 0-88386-567-X). South Asia Bks.
Gadian, David G. Nuclear Magnetic Resonance & Its Applications to Living Systems. (Illus.). 1982. 35.00x (ISBN 0-19-854627-0). Oxford U Pr.
Gadler, Steve & Adamson, Wendy. Sun Power: Facts About Solar Energy. LC 77-92290. (Real World, Crisis & Conflict Ser.). (Illus.). (gr. 5 up). 1978. PLB 6.95 (ISBN 0-8225-0643-2). Lerner Pubns.
Gadney, Alan. Busy Person's Guide to Selecting the Right Business Computer: A Visual Shortcut to Understanding & Buying, Complete with Checklists & Product Guide. (Busy Person's Computer Buying Guides Ser.). (Illus.). 304p. cancelled (ISBN 0-930828-09-7); pap. cancelled (ISBN 0-930828-08-9). Festival Pubns.
--Busy Person's Guide to Selecting the Right Personal & Home Computer: A Visual Shortcut to Understanding & Buying, Complete with Checklists & Product Guide. (Busy Person's Computer Buying Guides Ser.). (Illus.). 304p. cancelled (ISBN 0-930828-07-0); pap. cancelled (ISBN 0-930828-06-2). Festival Pubns.
--Busy Person's Guide to Selecting the Right Word Processor: A Visual Shortcut to Understanding & Buying, Complete with Checklists & Product Guide. LC 84-6076. (Busy Person's Computer Buying Guides Ser.). (Illus.). 304p. 1984. 24.95 (ISBN 0-930828-05-4); pap. 14.95 (ISBN 0-930828-04-6). Festival Pubns.
--Gadney's Guide to One Thousand Eight Hundred International Contests, Festivals & Grants in Film & Video, Photography, TV-Radio Broadcasting, Writing, Poetry, Playwriting & Journalism: Updated Address Edition. rev. ed. LC 80-66803. 610p. 1980. 22.95 (ISBN 0-930828-03-8); pap. 15.95 (ISBN 0-930828-02-X). Festival Pubns.
--Gadney's Guide to One Thousand Eight Hundred International Contests, Festivals & Grants in Film & Video, Photography, TV-Radio Broadcasting, Writing, Poetry, Playwriting & Journalism. LC 77-89041. (Orig.). 1979. 22.95 (ISBN 0-930828-01-1); pap. 15.95 (ISBN 0-930828-00-3). Festival Pubns.
--How to Enter & Win Black & White Photography Contests. 224p. 1982. 14.95 (ISBN 0-87196-571-2); pap. 6.95 (ISBN 0-87196-577-1). Facts on File.
--How to Enter & Win Clay & Glass Crafts Contests. 224p. 1983. 14.95 (ISBN 0-87196-661-1); pap. 6.95 (ISBN 0-87196-662-X). Facts on File.
--How to Enter & Win Color Photography Contests. 224p. 1982. 14.95 (ISBN 0-87196-572-0); pap. 6.95 (ISBN 0-87196-578-X). Facts on File.
--How to Enter & Win Design & Commercial Art Contests. 224p. 1982. 14.95 (ISBN 0-87196-570-4); pap. 6.95 (ISBN 0-87196-576-3). Facts on File.
--How to Enter & Win Fabric & Fiber Crafts Contests. 224p. 1983. 14.95 (ISBN 0-87196-657-3); pap. 6.95 (ISBN 0-87196-658-1). Facts on File.
--How to Enter & Win Fiction Writing Contests. 224p. 1981. 14.95 (ISBN 0-87196-519-4); pap. 6.95 (ISBN 0-87196-552-6). Facts on File.
--How to Enter & Win Film Contests. 224p. 1981. 14.95 (ISBN 0-87196-517-8); pap. 6.95 (ISBN 0-87196-524-0). Facts on File.
--How to Enter & Win Fine Arts & Sculpture Contests. 224p. 1982. 14.95 (ISBN 0-87196-573-9); pap. 6.95 (ISBN 0-87196-579-8). Facts on File.
--How to Enter & Win Jewelry & Metal Crafts Contests. 224p. 1983. 14.95 (ISBN 0-87196-659-X); pap. 6.95 (ISBN 0-87196-660-3). Facts on File.
--How to Enter & Win Non-Fiction Journalism Contests. 224p. 1981. 14.95 (ISBN 0-87196-518-6); pap. 6.95 (ISBN 0-87196-553-4). Facts on File.
--How to Enter & Win Video-Audio Contests. 1981. 14.95 (ISBN 0-87196-520-8); pap. 6.95 (ISBN 0-87196-551-8). Facts on File.
--How to Enter & Win Wood & Leather Crafts Contests. 224p. 1983. 14.95 (ISBN 0-87196-655-7); pap. 6.95 (ISBN 0-87196-656-5). Facts on File.
Gadney, Reg. Kennedy. LC 83-10802. 1983. 16.95 (ISBN 0-03-069406-X). HR&W.
GA DNR. Georgia Civil War Historical Markers. 196p. 1982. pap. 6.95 (ISBN 0-87797-066-1). Cherokee.
Gado, Frank. The Passion of Ingmar Bergman: A Biographical & Psychological Study of His Screenplays & Other Writings. 360p. Date not set. 27.75x (ISBN 0-8223-0585-2); pap. text ed. 12.75x (ISBN 0-8223-0586-0). Duke.
Gado, Frank, ed. First Person: Conversations on Writers & Writing. 159p. 1973. 9.50x (ISBN 0-912756-03-9); pap. 3.95 (ISBN 0-912756-04-7). Union Coll.
Gado, Frank, intro. by see Anderson, Sherwood.
Gadol, E. T., ed. Rationality & Sciences: A Memorial Volume for Moritz Schlick. (Illus.). 228p. 1982. 26.00 (ISBN 0-387-81721-2). Springer-Verlag.
Gadol, Joan. Leon Battista Alberti: Universal Man of the Early Renaissance. LC 72-75811. (Illus.). 1969. 20.00x (ISBN 0-226-27840-9). U of Chicago Pr.
Gadol, Joan K. Leon Battista Alberti. LC 72-75811. 1973. pap. 5.95x (ISBN 0-226-27841-7, P562, Phoen). U of Chicago Pr.
Gadon, Herman, jt. auth. see Cohen, Allan R.
Gadourek, Ivan. The Political Control of Czechoslovakia. LC 74-2841. 285p. 1974. Repr. of 1953 ed. lib. bdg. 29.75x (ISBN 0-8371-7437-6, GACZ). Greenwood.
Gadow, K. Advances in Learning & Behavioral Disabilities, Vol. 3. 1985. 47.50 (ISBN 0-89232-333-7). Jai Pr.
Gadow, Kenneth D. Children on Medication: A Primer for School Personnel. LC 79-51024. 1979. pap. text ed. 10.95 (ISBN 0-86586-012-2). Coun Exc Child.
Gadow, Kenneth D. & Bialer, Irv., eds. Advances in Learning & Behavioral Disabilities, Vol. 1. 450p. 1981. 47.50 (ISBN 0-89232-209-8). Jai Pr.
Gadow, Sally, jt. ed. see Spicker, Stuart F.
Gadow, Sandy. All about Escrow: Or How to Buy the Brooklyn Bridge & Have the Last Laugh. 2nd. ed. LC 81-65603. 183p. 1984. pap. text ed. 10.95 (ISBN 0-932956-06-8). Express.
Gadsby, Oliver, tr. see Gantschev, Ivan.
Gadsby, Oliver E., tr. see Cantieni, Benita.
Gadsby, Oliver E., tr. see Gantschev, Ivan.
Gadsby, Oliver E., tr. see Turk, Hanne.
Gadsden, S. R. & Adams, R. J. The Administration of Interlending by Microcomputer. (LIR Report 30). (Illus.). 62p. (Orig.). 1984. pap. 14.25 (ISBN 0-7123-3044-5, Pub. by British Lib). Longwood Pub Group.
Gadzuk, Marilyn W., tr. see Lionel, Frederic.
Gaebelein, Anna C. Psalms. 1939. 8.95 (ISBN 0-87213-383-4). Loizeaux.
Gaebelein, Arno C. Acts of the Apostles. rev. ed. LC 61-17224. 1965. 10.25 (ISBN 0-87213-215-3). Loizeaux.
--The Conflict of the Ages. x ed. (Illus.). 171p. pap. 5.50 (ISBN 0-9609260-1-1). Exhorters.
--The Conflict of the Ages: The Mystery of Lawlessness, Its Origin, Historic Development & Coming Defeat. XRev ed. 1983. pap. 4.95 (ISBN 0-87213-206-4). Loizeaux.
--Ezekiel. LC 72-88419. 8.95 (ISBN 0-87213-217-X). Loizeaux.
--Gaebelein's Concise Commentary on the Whole Bible. rev. ed. 1237p. 1985. Repr. of 1970 ed. 29.95 (ISBN 0-87213-209-9). Loizeaux.
--Gospel of John. rev. ed. LC 65-26586. 1965. 9.25 (ISBN 0-87213-220-X). Loizeaux.
--Gospel of Matthew. LC 61-17223. 1961. Repr. of 1910 ed. 11.95 (ISBN 0-87213-221-8). Loizeaux.
--The Prophet Daniel. LC 55-9465. 1968. pap. 5.95 (ISBN 0-8254-2701-0). Kregel.
--Revelation. LC 61-17225. 1960. 7.50 (ISBN 0-87213-223-4). Loizeaux.
Gaebelein, Frank E. The Christian, the Arts, & Truth: Regaining the Vision of Greatness. Lockerbie, D. Bruce, frwd. by. LC 85-9005. (Critical Concern Bks.). 1985. 10.95 (ISBN 0-88070-114-5). Multnomah.
--The Expositor's Bible Commentary, 5 vols. 1979. Set. 107.75 (ISBN 0-310-36568-6). Zondervan.
--Pattern of God's Truth. LC 54-6908. 1968. pap. 5.95 (ISBN 0-8024-6450-5). Moody.
Gaebelein, Frank E., ed. Expositor's Bible Commentary, Vol. 1. 1979. 22.95 (ISBN 0-310-36430-2). Zondervan.
--Expositor's Bible Commentary, Vol. 9. 464p. 1980. 19.95 (ISBN 0-310-36510-4). Zondervan.
--The Expositor's Bible Commentary, Vol. 12. 624p. 1981. 19.95 (ISBN 0-310-36540-6). Zondervan.
--Expositor's Bible Commentary: Daniel & the Minor Prophets, Vol. 7. 752p. 1985. text ed. 24.95 (ISBN 0-310-36490-6, Pub. by Regency Ref Lib). Zondervan.
--The Expositors' Bible Commentary: Matthew, Mark, Luke, Vol. 8. LC 83-11177. 1056p. (Orig.). 1984. 29.95 (ISBN 0-310-36500-7, Pub. by Regency Ref Lib). Zondervan.
--The Expositor's Bible Commentary, (Romans - Galatians, Vol. 10. 600p. 1976. 19.95 (ISBN 0-310-36520-1). Zondervan.
--The Expositor's Bible Commentary Vol. 11 (Ephesians-Philemon) 1978. 19.95 (ISBN 0-310-36530-9). Zondervan.
Gaechter, R. & Mueller, H. Plastics Additives Handbook. LC 83-62289. 320p. 1984. text ed. 59.00 (ISBN 0-02-949430-3, Pub. by Hanser International). Macmillan.
Gaeddart, Gustave R. The Birth of Kansas. LC 73-18442. (Perspectives in American History Ser.: No. 9). (Illus.). 232p. 1974. Repr. of 1940 ed. lib. bdg. 19.50x (ISBN 0-87991-335-5). Porcupine Pr.
Gaeddert, John, jt. ed. see Hartzler, Arlene.
Gaeddert, Lou Ann. Noisy Nancy Norris. LC 65-10180. (ps-1). 1971. Repr. of 1965 ed. PLB 8.95 (ISBN 0-385-04749-5). Doubleday.
Gaeddert, LouAnn. Daffodils in the Snow. LC 84-8159. 128p. (YA) (gr. 7 up). 1984. 11.95 (ISBN 0-525-44150-6, 01160-350). Dutton.
--Gustav the Gourmet Giant. LC 76-2282. (Pied Piper Book). (Illus.). (ps-3). 1979. pap. 2.25 (ISBN 0-8037-3336-4). Dial Bks Young.
--Just Like Sisters. (Illus.). 96p. (gr. 4-6). 1981. 10.25 (ISBN 0-525-32959-5, 0995-300). Dutton.
--The Kid with the Red Suspenders. LC 82-18210. (Illus.). 80p. (gr. 2-4). 1983. 9.95 (ISBN 0-525-44046-1, 0966-290). Dutton.
--Tuesday's Child, No. 26. 192p. 1985. pap. 2.25 (ISBN 0-8407-7375-7). Nelson.
--Your Former Friend, Matthew. (Illus.). 80p. (gr. 3-6). 1984. 9.95 (ISBN 0-525-44086-0, 0966-290). Dutton.
Gaede, Erwin A. Politics & Ethics: Machiavelli to Niebuhr. LC 83-19751. 168p. (Orig.). 1984. lib. bdg. 21.75 (ISBN 0-8191-3603-4); pap. text ed. 10.25 (ISBN 0-8191-3604-2). U Pr of Amer.
Gaede, Jane T. Clinical Pathology for the House Officer. (HO). (Illus.). 190p. 1982. pap. 10.95 (ISBN 0-683-03403-0). Williams & Wilkins.
Gaede, K. & Gaede, K., eds. Molecular Basis of Biological Activity, Vol. 1. 1972. 65.00 (ISBN 0-12-272850-5). Acad Pr.
Gaede, Marc, jt. auth. see Gaede, Marnie.
Gaede, Marnie & Gaede, Marc. Camera, Spade & Pen: An Inside View of Southwestern Archaeology. LC 80-23751. 160p. 1980. 29.95 (ISBN 0-8165-0663-9). U of Ariz Pr.
Gaede, S. D. Where Gods May Dwell. 168p. (Orig.). 1985. pap. 7.95 (ISBN 0-310-42971-4, Pub. by Academie Bks). Zondervan.
Gaede, Sarah, ed. see Gottlieb, Isser & Gottlieb, Irving.
Gaede, Sarah, et al. Gottlieb's Bakery: One Hundred Years of Recipes. 96p. (Orig.). 1983. pap. 8.95 (ISBN 0-939114-90-9). Gottlieb's Bakery.
Gaede, Sarah R. The Pirate's House Cookbook. (Illus.). 224p. 1982. pap. 11.95 (ISBN 0-939114-62-3). Wimmer Bks.
Gaedeke, Ralph M. & Tootelian, Dennis H. Marketing: Principles & Applications. (Illus.). 668p. 1983. text ed. 30.95 (ISBN 0-314-69649-0); tchrs.' manual avail. (ISBN 0-314-71091-4); student guide 9.95 (ISBN 0-314-71142-2). West Pub.
--Small Business Management. 2nd ed. 1985. text ed. 26.95x (ISBN 0-673-16598-1). Scott F.
Gaedeke, Ralph M., ed. Marketing in Private & Public Nonprofit Organizations: Perspectives & Illustrations. LC 76-23034. 1977. pap. text ed. 21.70x (ISBN 0-673-16509-4). Scott F.
Gaedeke, Ralph M. & Tootelian, Dennis, eds. Marketing Management. 1979. 27.10x (ISBN 0-673-16105-6). Scott F.
Gaeffke, Peter. Untersuchungen Zur Syntax Des Hindi Disputationes Rheno-Trajectinae, Vol. 2. 1967. pap. 22.00x (ISBN 0-686-21231-2). Mouton.
Gaeger, Charles De see De Gaeger, Charles.
Gaehde, Christa M., jt. auth. see Zigrosser, Carl.
Gaehde, J. E., jt. auth. see Mutherich, Florentine.
Gaehtgens, P., ed. Recent Advances in Microcirculatory Research. (Bibliotheca Anatomica Series: No. 20). (Illus.). xvi, 740p. 1981. 125.75 (ISBN 3-8055-2272-X). S Karger.
Gael, Sidney. Job Analysis: A Guide to Assessing Work Activities. LC 82-49036. (Management Ser.). 1983. text ed. 19.95x (ISBN 0-87589-564-6). Jossey-Bass.
Gaeng, Paul A. Collapse & Reorganization of the Latin Nominal Flection As Reflected in Epigraphic Sources. 24.00 (ISBN 0-916379-06-X). Scripta.
--An Inquiry into the Local Variations in Vulgar Latin As Reflected in the Vocalism of Christian Inscriptions. (Studies in the Romance Languages & Literatures: No. 77). 300p. 1968. pap. 16.50x (ISBN 0-8078-9077-4). U of NC Pr.
--Introduction to the Principles of Language. LC 83-6967. (Illus.). 254p. 1983. pap. text ed. 8.50 (ISBN 0-8191-3085-0). U Pr of Amer.
--A Study of Nominal Inflection in Latin Inscriptions: A Morpho-Syntactic Analysis. (Studies in the Romance Languages & Literatures Ser: No. 182). 229p. 1977. 15.00x (ISBN 0-8078-9182-7). U of NC Pr.
Gaenssien, R. E., jt. auth. see DeForest, P. R.
Gaenssler, Peter. Empirical Processes. Gupta, Shanti S., ed. LC 83-82637. (Institute of Mathematical Statistics Lecture Notes-Monograph Ser.: Vol. 3). x, 180p. (Orig.). 1983. pap. text ed. 20.00 (ISBN 0-940600-03-X). Inst Math.
Gaer, Joseph. Ambrose Gwinett Bierce, Bibliography & Bibliographical Data. LC 72-190384. 1974. Repr. of 1935 ed. lib. bdg. 12.00 (ISBN 0-8414-4568-0). Folcroft.
--Ambrose Gwinett Bierce: Bibliography & Dates. 1978. Repr. of 1935 ed. lib. bdg. 30.00 (ISBN 0-8495-1931-4). Arden Lib.
--Bibliography of California Literature: Fiction, Drama, & Poetry of the Gold Rush Period. LC 74-131406. (Illus.). 1970. Repr. of 1935 ed. lib. bdg. 20.50 (ISBN 0-8337-1256-X). B Franklin.
--Bibliography of California Literature: Pre-Gold Rush Period. LC 78-131407. (Bibliography & Reference Ser: No. 389). 1971. Repr. of 1935 ed. lib. bdg. 18.50 (ISBN 0-8337-1259-4). B Franklin.
--Bret Harte: Bibliography & Biographical Data. 1967. Repr. of 1935 ed. 23.50 (ISBN 0-8337-1254-3). B Franklin.
--California in Juvenile Fiction. LC 74-179390. (California Literary Research Project Monographs: No. 12). (Illus.). 62p. 1972. Repr. of 1935 ed. lib. bdg. 18.50 (ISBN 0-8337-1255-1). B Franklin.
--Frank Norris (Benjamin Franklin Norris) Bibliography & Biographical Data. LC 71-131408. 1970. Repr. of 1934 ed. 15.00 (ISBN 0-8337-1257-8). B Franklin.
--Frank Norris Bibliography & Biographical Data. LC 74-16033. 1974. Repr. of 1934 ed. lib. bdg. 17.50 (ISBN 0-8414-4566-4). Folcroft.
--How the Great Religions Began. LC 81-7764. 1981. pap. 5.95 (ISBN 0-396-08013-8). Dodd.
--Jack London: Bibliography & Biographical Data. LC 75-131409. (Bibliography & Reference Ser.: No. 383). 1971. Repr. of 1934 ed. lib. bdg. 14.00 (ISBN 0-8337-1258-6). B Franklin.
--Theatre of the Gold Rush Decade in San Francisco. LC 70-146245. (Bibliography & Reference Ser: No. 391). 1971. Repr. of 1935 ed. 17.00 (ISBN 0-8337-1261-6). B Franklin.
--What the Great Religions Believe. pap. 2.95 (ISBN 0-451-11978-9, AE1978, Sig). NAL.
Gaer, Joseph, ed. Ambrose Gwinett Bierce: A Bibliography & Biographical Data. 1935. 18.50 (ISBN 0-8337-1253-5). B Franklin.
Gaerity, Jack. Bread & Roses from Stone. facs. ed. (Shorey Lost Arts Ser.). 92p. pap. 4.95 (ISBN 0-8466-0126-5, S126). Shorey.
Gaerny, Arnold. Removable Closure of the Interdental Space. (Illus.). 196p. 1972. 38.00 (ISBN 0-931386-62-4). Quint Pub Co.
Gaertner, Georg & Krammer, Arnold. Hitler's Last Soldier in America. LC 84-40622. 1985. 17.95 (ISBN 0-8128-3007-5). Stein & Day.
Gaertner, James F. & Cooper, S. Kerry. Financial Accounting: An Introduction. (Illus.). 784p. 1985. text ed. 28.95 (ISBN 0-13-316654-6); study guide 10.95 (ISBN 0-13-316696-1). P-H.
Gaertner, K. & Hackbarth, H., eds. Research Animals & Concepts of Applicability to Clinical Medicine: Experimental Biology & Medicine, Vol. 7. (Illus.). x, 234p. 1982. pap. 63.00 (ISBN 3-8055-3492-2). S Karger.
Gaertner, W. & Wenig, A., eds. The Economics of the Shadow Economy. (Studies in Contemporary Economics: Vol. 15). xiv, 401p. 1985. pap. 29.60 (ISBN 0-387-15095-1). Springer-Verlag.
Gaertner, Wolfgang, ed. Adaptive Electronics. LC 71-189397. (Illus.). 370p. 1973. pap. 14.00x (ISBN 0-89006-013-4). Artech Hse.
Gaertringen, F. Hiller v., ed. Inscriptiones Graecae: Inscriptiones Epidauri. (Illus.). 1977. Repr. of 1929 ed. 25.00 (ISBN 0-89005-207-7). Ares.
Gaertringen, Friedrich Von see Von Gaertringen, Friedrich & Kirchner, Johannes.
Gaertringen, Friedrich Von see Kirchner, Johannes & Von Gaertringen, Friedrich.
Gaess, Roger, ed. Leaving the Bough: Fifty American Poets of the Eighties. 169p. (Orig.). 1982. 11.50 (ISBN 0-7178-0592-1); pap. 3.75 (ISBN 0-7178-0587-5). Intl Pubs Co.
Gaetan, Jasmin & Proschek, L., eds. Microanalysis & Quantification. (Methods & Achievements in Experimental Pathology: Vol. 11). (Illus.). vi, 190p. 1984. 70.00 (ISBN 3-8055-3717-4). S Karger.
Gaetschenberger, Richard. Grundzuege einer Psychologie des Zeichens, 1901. (Foundations of Semiotics: 3). 135p. 1984. 18.00x (ISBN 90-272-3273-3). Benjamins North Am.
Gaevskaya, Mariya S. Biochemistry of the Brain During the Process of Dying & Resuscitation. LC 64-17205. pap. 26.50 (ISBN 0-317-28724-9, 2020665). Bks Demand UMI.
Gafencu, Grigore. Last Days of Europe: A Diplomatic Journey in 1939. Fletcher-Allen, E., tr. (Illus.). vii, 239p. 1970. Repr. of 1948 ed. 18.50 (ISBN 0-208-00955-8, Archon). Shoe String.
--Prelude to the Russian Campaign: From the Moscow Pact (August 21st 1939) to the Opening of Hostilities in Russia (June 22nd 1941) LC 79-5207. 348p. 1981. Repr. of 1945 ed. 29.35 (ISBN 0-8305-0072-3). Hyperion Conn.
Gaff, Jerry, et al. The Cluster College. LC 77-110641. (Jossey-Bass Higher Education Ser.). Repr. of 1970 ed. 67.00 (ISBN 0-8357-9306-0, 2013940). Bks Demand UMI.
Gaff, Jerry G. General Education Today: A Critical Analysis of Controversies, Practices & Reforms. LC 82-49037. (Higher Education Ser.). 1983. text ed. 17.95x (ISBN 0-87589-560-3). Jossey-Bass.
--Toward Faculty Renewal: Advances in Faculty, Instructional, & Organizational Development. LC 75-24002. (Higher Educational Ser.). (Illus.). 1975. 19.95x (ISBN 0-87589-267-1). Jossey-Bass.
Gaff, Jerry G., jt. auth. see Klein, Thomas.
Gaff, Sally S., et al. Professional Development: A Guide to Resources. LC 77-72981. 110p. 1978. pap. 5.95 (ISBN 0-915390-11-6, Pub. by Change Mag). Transaction Pubs.
Gaffey, John D. Productivity of Labor in the Rubber Tire Manufacturing Industry. LC 68-58577. (Columbia University. Studies in the Social Sciences: No. 472). Repr. of 1940 ed. 18.50 (ISBN 0-404-51472-3). AMS Pr.
Gaffikin, Michael & Aitken, Michael, eds. The Development of Accounting Theory: Significant Contributors to Accounting Thought in the 20th Century. LC 82-82489. (Accountancy in Transition Ser.). 284p. 1982. lib. bdg. 44.00 (ISBN 0-8240-5336-2). Garland Pub.
Gaffin, Jean, ed. The Nurse & the Welfare State. 128p. 1981. 12.95 (ISBN 0-471-25713-3, Wiley Medical). Wiley.
Gaffin, Richard B. Perspectives on Pentecost. 1979. pap. 3.95 (ISBN 0-87552-269-6). Presby & Reformed.

Gaffin, Richard B., Jr., ed. Redemptive History & Biblical Interpretation: The Shorter Writings of Geerhardus Vos. 1980. 17.50 (ISBN 0-87552-270-X). Presby & Reformed.

Gaffin, Richard B., Jr., ed. see Vos, Geerhardus.

Gaffiot, Felix. Dictionnaire Abrege Latin-Francais. 1720p. (Lat. & Fr.). 1970. pap. 15.95 (ISBN 0-686-57186-X, M-6258). French & Eur.

--Dictionnaire Latin-Francais. (Lat. & Fr.). 1967. pap. 32.50 (ISBN 0-686-57187-8, M-6259). French & Eur.

Gaffney, D. J. & Gabhart, D. R. Comprehensive CPA Review, 5 Vols. 1984. Vol. 1. text ed. 1.00 (ISBN 0-07-022640-7); Vol. 2. text ed. 1.00 (ISBN 0-07-022641-5); Vol. 3. text ed. 1.00 (ISBN 0-07-022642-3); Vol. 4. text ed. 1.00 (ISBN 0-07-022643-1); Vol. 5. text ed. 1.00 (ISBN 0-07-022644-X). McGraw.

Gaffney, D. J. & Skadden, D. H. Principles of Federal Income Taxation. 1982. 32.95 (ISBN 0-07-057781-1). McGraw.

Gaffney, Dennis J., et al. Principles of Federal Income Taxation, 1984-1985. 1984-85 ed. 900p. 1984. text ed. 29.95x (ISBN 0-912503-03-3); study guide 11.95 (ISBN 0-912503-04-1). Armond-Dalton.

Gaffney, Edward M. & Moots, Philip R. Government & Campus: Federal Regulation of Religiously Affiliated Higher Education. LC 80-53164. 210p. 1981. 15.95 (ISBN 0-268-01003-X); pap. text ed. 8.95 (ISBN 0-268-01005-6). U of Notre Dame Pr.

Gaffney, Edward M., jt. auth. see Dutile, Fernand N.

Gaffney, Edward M. see McGlynn Gaffney, Edward, Jr. & Sorensen, Philip C.

Gaffney, Edward M., jt. auth. see Moots, Philip R.

Gaffney, Edward M. & Dutile, Fernand N., eds. The Federal Purse & the Rule of Law. LC 83-40116. 240p. 1986. pap. text ed. 9.95x (ISBN 0-268-00966-X, 85-09663). U of Notre Dame Pr.

Gaffney, James. Newness of Life: A Modern Introduction to Catholic Ethics. LC 79-84404. 360p. 1979. pap. 6.95 (ISBN 0-8091-2202-2). Paulist Pr.

--Sin Reconsidered. LC 82-61424. 96p. (Orig.). 1983. pap. 3.95 (ISBN 0-8091-2516-1). Paulist Pr.

Gaffney, Judith H., jt. auth. see Toye, Randall.

Gaffney, M. P. & Steen, L. A., eds. Annotated Bibliography of Expository Writing in the Mathematical Sciences. 282p. 1976. pap. 14.00 (ISBN 0-88385-422-8). Math Assn.

Gaffney, Maureen & Laybourne, Gerry B. What to Do When the Lights Go On: A Comprehensive Guide to Sixteen Millimeter Films & Related Activities for Children. (Illus.). 268p. 1981. lib. bdg. 32.50x (ISBN 0-912700-65-3); pap. 27.50x (ISBN 0-912700-69-6). Oryx Pr.

Gaffney, P. J. Fibrinolysis: Current Fundamental & Clinical Concepts. Balkuv-Ulutin, S., ed. 1978. 47.00 (ISBN 0-12-273050-X). Acad Pr.

Gaffney, Patrick. Mary's Spiritual Maternity. 4.95 (ISBN 0-910984-18-2); pap. 2.95 (ISBN 0-910984-19-0). Montfort Pubns.

Gaffney, Sean & Cashman, Seamus, eds. Proverbs & Sayings of Ireland. (Illus.). 128p. 1982. pap. 4.95 (ISBN 0-9503454-4-X, Pub. by Wolfhound Pr Media). Irish Bks Media.

Gaffney, Sean, jt. ed. see Cashman, Seamus.

Gaffney, Timothy. Jerrold Petrofsky: Biomedical Pioneer. LC 83-25268. (People of Distinction Ser.). (Illus.). 128p. (gr. 4 up). 1984. lib. bdg. 11.95 (ISBN 0-516-03201-1). Childrens.

Gaffney, Walter J., jt. auth. see Nouwen, Henri J.

Gafford, Phil E. Quo Vadis, America? LC 76-57068. 112p. 1977. 6.95 (ISBN 0-918354-01-3). Huntleigh.

Gafney, Leo & Beers, John C. Essential Math Skills. Devine, Peter, ed. 224p. 1980. pap. text ed. 7.36 (ISBN 0-07-010260-0). McGraw.

Gafney, Leo, ed. see Belstock, Alan & Smith, Gerald.

Gafney, Leo, ed. see Maher, Carolyn A., et al.

Gafni, Shlomo S. & Van der Heyden, A. The Glory of Jerusalem: An Explorer's Guide. LC 81-17053. 128p. 1982. 16.95 (ISBN 0-521-24613-X). Cambridge U Pr.

--The Glory of the Holy Land. LC 81-17054. (Illus.). 256p. 1982. 21.95 (ISBN 0-521-24612-1). Cambridge U Pr.

Gafni, Shlomo S., ed. The Glory of the New Testament. LC 83-840322. 1984. 24.50 (ISBN 0-394-53659-2, Pub. by Villard Bks). Random.

--The Glory of the Old Testament. LC 83-848323. 256p. 1984. 24.50 (ISBN 0-394-53658-4, Pub. by Villard Bks). Random.

Gafurius, Franchinus. Apologia Franchini Gafurii. (Monuments of Music & Music Literature in Facsimile, Ser. II: Vol. 96). 1979. Repr. of 1520 ed. 25.00x (ISBN 0-8450-2296-2). Broude.

--De Harmonia Musicorum Instrumentorum Opus. (Monuments of Music & Music Literature in Facsimile, Ser. II: Vol. 97). 1979. Repr. of 1518 ed. 42.50x (ISBN 0-8450-2297-0). Broude.

--Monuments of Music & Music Literature in Facsimile: Series Two Pt. 4, Vol. 96, Apologia. 1979. 25.00x (ISBN 0-8450-2296-2). Broude.

--Practica Musice. (Monuments of Music & Music Literature in Facsimile, Ser. II: Vol. 99). 1979. Repr. of 1496 ed. 42.50 (ISBN 0-8450-2299-7). Broude.

Gafurov, G. & Kim, G. F., eds. Lenin & National Liberation in the East. 468p. 1978. 8.45 (ISBN 0-8285-0399-0, Pub. by Progress Pubs Russia). Imported Pubns.

Gag, Wanda. The ABC Bunny. LC 33-27359. (Illus.). (gr. k-2). 1978. pap. 2.50 (ISBN 0-698-20465-4, Coward). Putnam Pub Group.

--ABC Bunny. (Illus.). (gr. k-2). 1933. 8.95 (ISBN 0-698-20000-4, Coward); gb 6.99 (ISBN 0-698-30000-9). Putnam Pub Group.

--The Earth Gnome. (Illus.). 48p. (gr. 1-4). 1985. 8.95 (ISBN 0-698-20618-5, Coward). Putnam Pub Group.

--The Funny Thing. (Illus.). (gr. 1-3). 1960. PLB 6.99 (ISBN 0-698-30097-1, Coward). Putnam Pub Group.

--Gone Is Gone. (Illus.). (gr. k-3). 1960. PLB 5.99 (ISBN 0-698-30179-X, Coward). Putnam Pub Group.

--Growing Pains: Diaries & Drawings from the Years 1905-17. LC 84-10557. (Borealis Bks.). (Illus.). 475p. 1984. pap. 11.95 (ISBN 0-87351-173-5). Minn Hist.

--Millions of Cats. (Illus.). (gr. k-3). 1977. 7.95 (ISBN 0-698-20091-8, Coward); pap. 2.95 (ISBN 0-698-20434-4). Putnam Pub Group.

--The Millions of Cats Day Book. (Illus.). 112p. (gr. k-2). cancelled (ISBN 0-698-20434-4, Coward); pap. cancelled (ISBN 0-698-20520-0); cancelled (ISBN 0-698-20521-9). Putnam Pub Group.

--More Tales from Grimm. 1981. pap. 5.95 (ISBN 0-698-20534-0, Coward). Putnam Pub Group.

--Nothing at All. (Illus.). (gr. 1-3). 1941. PLB 6.99 (ISBN 0-698-30264-8, Coward). Putnam Pub Group.

--Snippy & Snappy. (Illus.). (gr. 1-3). 1960. PLB 5.99 (ISBN 0-698-30319-9, Coward). Putnam Pub Group.

--Snow White & the Seven Dwarfs. (Illus.). (gr. 2-4). 1938. PLB 6.99 (ISBN 0-698-30320-2, Coward). Putnam Pub Group.

--Tales from Grimm. 1981. pap. 5.95 (ISBN 0-698-20533-2, Coward). Putnam Pub Group.

--Three Gay Tales from Grimm. (Illus.). 63p. (gr. 1-5). 1982. pap. 2.50 (ISBN 0-571-11272-2). Faber & Faber.

Gag, Wanda & Tomes, Margot. Jorinda & Joringel. (Illus., Fic). 1978. 6.95 (ISBN 0-698-20440-9, Coward). Putnam Pub Group.

--The Sorcerer's Apprentice. LC 78-23990. (Illus.). (gr. k-3). 1979. 6.95 (ISBN 0-698-20481-6, Coward). Putnam Pub Group.

Gagaev, B. M., et al. Thirteen Papers on Analysis. LC 51-5559. (Translations Ser.: No. 2, Vol. 10). 1963. Repr. of 1958 ed. 32.00 (ISBN 0-8218-1710-8, TRANS 2-10). Am Math.

Gagala, Kenneth. Economics of Minorities: A Guide to Information Sources. LC 73-17573. (Economics Information Guide Ser.: Vol. 2). 339p. 1976. 60.00x (ISBN 0-8103-1294-8). Gale.

--Union Organizing & Staying Organized. 1983. text ed. 19.95 (ISBN 0-8359-8064-2); pap. text ed. 14.95 (ISBN 0-8359-8063-4). Reston.

Gagala, Kenneth, jt. auth. see Daniels, Gene.

Gagan, David. Hopeful Travellers: Families, Land, & Social Change in Mid-Victorian Peel County, Canada West. (Ontario Historical Studies Ser.). 248p. 1981. 20.00x (ISBN 0-8020-2435-1). U of Toronto Pr.

Gagan, David P. The Denison Family of Toronto, 1792-1925. LC 72-90741. (Canadian Biographical Studies: No. 5). pap. 31.30 (ISBN 0-317-27045-1, 2023620). Bks Demand UMI.

Gagan, R. A. & Wunderlick, Ray C. The Over Forty Wellness Diet. (Illus.). 40p. 1985. pap. 2.95 (ISBN 0-318-11693-6). Consumer Info Pubns.

Gagarin, Jean X. Russian Clergy. LC 70-131035. Repr. of 1872 ed. 21.00 (ISBN 0-404-02666-4). AMS Pr.

Gagarin, Michael. Aeschylean Drama. LC 74-30520. 1976. 28.50x (ISBN 0-520-02943-7). U of Cal Pr.

--Drakon & Early Athenian Homicide Law. LC 81-2370. (Classical Monographs). 208p. 1981. text ed. 24.50x (ISBN 0-300-02627-7). Yale U Pr.

Gagarin, Yuri & Lebedev, Vladimir. Psychology & Space. (Illus.). 1970. pap. 7.95x (ISBN 0-8464-0773-6). Beekman Pubs.

Gage, Diane, jt. auth. see Gellman, Meryle.

Gage, Elsie. Your Obedient Servant. 1985. pap. 2.50 (ISBN 0-451-13913-5, Sig). NAL.

Gage, Frank W. Negro Problem in the United States, Its Rise, Development & Solution. LC 74-110111. Repr. of 1892 ed. 15.00x (ISBN 0-8371-4116-8, GNP&, Pub. by Negro U Pr). Greenwood.

Gage, Gloria. A Season for Glory. 144p. (Orig.). 1984. pap. 4.95 (ISBN 0-89636-143-8). Accent Bks.

Gage, Howard, ed. see Biomechanical & Human Factors Conference (2nd: 1967: Washington, D.C.).

Gage, Jennifer. Directory of Computerized Resources in Bilingual Education. 52p. 1982. 5.65 (ISBN 0-317-14965-2). Natl Clearinghse Bilingual Ed.

--Longitudinal Studies in Second Language Learning & Bilingual Education: A Bibliography. 39p. 1982. 3.90 (ISBN 0-317-15095-2). Natl Clearinghse Bilingual Ed.

Gage, Jennifer, jt. auth. see Stupp, Emma G.

Gage, John. Turner: Rain, Steam & Speed. LC 72-161061. (Art in Context Ser). (Illus.). 1972. 16.95 (ISBN 0-670-73289-3). Viking.

Gage, John, ed. see Goethe, Johann von.

Gage, John, ed. see Turner, J. M.

Gage, John H. The Larvae of the Coccinellidae. (Illinois Biological Monographs: Vol. 6, No. 4). pap. 8.00 (ISBN 0-384-17550-3). Johnson Repr.

Gage, John T. In the Arresting Eye: The Rhetoric of Imagism. LC 80-24893. 190p. 1981. 20.00x (ISBN 0-8071-0790-5). La State U Pr.

Gage, Joy. Lord, Can We Talk This Over? 96p. 1980. pap. 3.95 (ISBN 0-8024-4011-8). Moody.

Gage, Joy, jt. auth. see Gage, Ken.

Gage, Joy P. Broken Boundaries-Broken Lives. LC 81-66134. 1981. pap. 4.95 (ISBN 0-89636-068-7). Accent Bks.

--When Parents Cry. LC 79-56358. 160p. 1981. pap. 4.95 (ISBN 0-89636-071-7). Accent Bks.

--When Parents Cry. LC 79-56358. 1980. 7.95 (ISBN 0-89636-045-8). Accent Bks.

Gage, Julia, jt. auth. see Prince, David.

Gage, Ken & Gage, Joy. Restoring Fellowship: Judgement & Church Discipline. (Orig.). 1984. pap. 3.95 (ISBN 0-8024-4440-7). Moody.

Gage, Matilda J. Woman, Church, & State: A Historical Account of the Status of Woman Through the Christian Ages, with Reminiscenses of the Matriarchate. 2nd ed. LC 72-2602. (American Women Ser.: Images & Realities). 558p. 1972. Repr. of 1900 ed. 32.00 (ISBN 0-405-04458-5). Ayer Co Pubs.

Gage, Michael. Guide to Exposed Concrete Finishes. 161p. 18.90 (ISBN 0-318-13153-6, CCA1803). Am Soc Conc Constr.

Gage, Michael & Vandenberg, M. Hard Landscape in Concrete. LC 75-31700. 167p. 1975. 34.95x (ISBN 0-470-28913-9). Halsted Pr.

Gage, Michael & Kirkbride, Tom, eds. Design in Blockwork. 3rd ed. (Illus.). 144p. 1980. pap. 23.50x (ISBN 0-85139-162-1). Nichols Pub.

Gage, N. L. The Scientific Basis of the Art of Teaching. LC 78-6250. 1978. pap. text ed. 8.95x (ISBN 0-8077-2537-4). Tchrs Coll.

--Teacher Effectiveness & Teacher Education: The Search for a Scientific Basis. LC 71-134225. (Illus.). 1972. 14.95x (ISBN 0-87015-190-8). Pacific Bks.

Gage, N. L., ed. The Psychology of Teaching Methods: 75th Yearbook, Part 1. LC 76-16938. (National Society for the Study of Education Ser.). 1976. pap. 8.00x (ISBN 0-226-60108-0). U of Chicago Pr.

Gage, Nathaniel & Berliner, David. Educational Psychology. 3rd ed. LC 83-82704. 752p. 1983. pap. text ed. 25.95 (ISBN 0-395-32762-8); instr's manual 3.00 (ISBN 0-395-32763-6); study guide 9.95 (ISBN 0-395-32764-4). HM.

Gage, Nicholas. Eleni. 472p. 1983. 15.95 (ISBN 0-394-52093-9, RanC). Random.

--Eleni: A Savage War, a Mother's Love & Son's Revenge - A Personal Story. 640p. (Orig.). 1984. pap. 3.95 (ISBN 0-345-30122-6). Ballantine.

Gage, Patricia, jt. ed. see Fitzgerald, Hiram E.

Gage, Richard, tr. see Ikeda, Daisaku.

Gage, Richard, tr. see Itoh, Teiji.

Gage, Richard, tr. see Itoh, Tsuji.

Gage, Richard, tr. see Narazaki, M.

Gage, Richard, tr. see Omae, Kinjiro & Tachibana, Yuzuru.

Gage, Richard, tr. see Sawa, Takaaki.

Gage, Richard, tr. see Toynbee, Arnold J.

Gage, Richard, et al, trs. see Ikeda, Daisaku.

Gage, Richard L., ed. see Peccei, Aurelio & Ikeda, Daisaku.

Gage, Richard L., tr. see Ben-Dasan, Isaiah.

Gage, Richard L., tr. see Ienaga, Saburo.

Gage, Richard L., tr. see Ikeda, Daisaku.

Gage, Richard L., tr. see Ikeda, Daisaku & Inoue, Yasushi.

Gage, Richard L., tr. see Kobayashi, Takeshi.

Gage, Richard L., tr. see Mizuno, Kogen.

Gage, Richard L., tr. see Mizuno, Seiichi.

Gage, Richard L., tr. see Niwano, Nichiko.

Gage, Richard L., tr. see Niwano, Nikkyo.

Gage, Thomas. Gage's Instructions of Twenty Secondth of February, Seventeen Seventy fie to Captain Brown & Ensign D'Berniere. LC 78-140865. (Eyewitness Accounts of the American Revolution Ser., No. 3). 1970. Repr. of 1779 ed. 12.00 (ISBN 0-405-01198-9). Ayer Co Pubs.

--Thomas Gage's Travels in the New World. Thompson, J. Eric, ed. & intro. by. LC 58-6856. (The American Exploration & Travel Ser.: Vol. 58). (Illus.). 430p. (Orig.). 1985. pap. 11.95 (ISBN 0-8061-1904-7). U of Okla Pr.

Gage, Warren A. The Gospel of Genesis: Studies in Protology & Eschatology. xiii, 142p. (Orig.). 1984. pap. 8.95 (ISBN 0-931464-22-6, Pub. by Carpenter Bks). Eisenbrauns.

Gage, William & Duong Thanh Binh. Vietnamese-English Phrasebook with Useful Word List: For English Speakers. LC 75-24857. (Vietnamese Refugee Education Ser.: No. 2). 142p. (Vietnamese & Eng.). 1975. pap. 4.00 (ISBN 0-15-599012-8). Ctr Appl Ling.

Gage, William L., tr. see Lampadius, W. A.

Gage, William L., tr. see Ritter, Karl.

Gage, William W. English for Speakers of Vietnamese. (English As a Foreign Language Ser.). 366p. 1981. text & 9 cassettes 90.00x (ISBN 0-87950-617-2); cassettes separate 80.00x (ISBN 0-87950-616-4); text only 15.00x (ISBN 0-87950-310-6). Spoken Lang Serv.

Gage, William W., ed. Language in Its Social Setting. (Anthropological Society of Washington Ser.). (Illus.). 116p. 12.50x (ISBN 0-87474-460-1); pap. 6.95x (ISBN 0-87474-461-X). Smithsonian.

Gage, Wilson. The Crow & Mrs. Gaddy. LC 83-14089. (A Greenwillow Read-alone Bk.). (Illus.). 48p. (gr. 1-3). 1984. 10.25 (ISBN 0-688-02535-8); PLB 10.88 (ISBN 0-688-02536-6). Greenwillow.

--The Crow & Mrs. Gaddy. 48p. (gr. k-3). 1985. pap. 2.25 (ISBN 0-590-33643-6, Lucky Star). Scholastic Inc.

Gage, Wilson, pseud. Cully Cully & the Bear. LC 82-11715. (Illus.). 32p. (gr. k-3). 1983. 10.25 (ISBN 0-688-01767-3); PLB 10.88 (ISBN 0-688-01769-X). Greenwillow.

Gage, Wilson. Down in the Boondocks. LC 76-45380. (Greenwillow Read-Alone Bks.). (Illus.). 32p. (gr. 1-4). 1977. PLB 8.88 (ISBN 0-688-84085-X). Greenwillow.

--The Ghost of Five Owl Farm. (gr. 4-8). 1969. pap. 1.75 (ISBN 0-671-56085-9). Archway.

--Miss Osborne the Mop, No. 10. (Pickerell Ser.). (Illus.). (gr. 4-6). 1975. pap. 1.75 (ISBN 0-671-43136-6). Archway.

--Mrs. Gaddy & the Fast-Growing Vine. LC 84-18767. (A Greenwillow Read-alone Bk). (Illus.). 48p. (gr. 1-4). 1985. 10.25 (ISBN 0-688-04231-7); lib. bdg. 10.88 (ISBN 0-688-04232-5). Greenwillow.

--Mrs. Gaddy & the Ghost. LC 78-16366. (Read-Alone Bks.). (Illus.). 56p. (gr. 1-3). 1979. 8.75 (ISBN 0-688-80179-X); PLB 8.88 (ISBN 0-688-84179-1). Greenwillow.

Gagen, T. M. Topics in Finite Groups. LC 75-17116. (London Mathematical Society Lecture Note Ser.: No. 16). 80p. 1976. 13.95 (ISBN 0-521-21002-X). Cambridge U Pr.

Gager, C. S. Effects of the Rays of Radium on Plants, Vol. 4. (Memoirs of the New York Botanical Garden Ser.). 278p. 1908. 10.00 (ISBN 0-317-35496-5). NY Botanical.

Gager, C. S, tr. see DeVries, Hugo.

Gager, Delaye. French Comment on American Education. LC 79-168088. (Columbia University. Studies in Romance Philology & Literature: No. 40). Repr. of 1925 ed. 16.00 (ISBN 0-404-50640-2). AMS Pr.

Gager, John G. Kingdom & Community: The Social World of Early Christianity. 160p. 1975. pap. text ed. 14.95 (ISBN 0-13-516203-3). P-H.

--Moses in Graeco-Roman Paganism. (SBL Monograph). 8.95 (ISBN 0-89130-323-5, 06-00-16). Scholars Pr GA.

--Moses in Greco-Roman Paganism. 173p. 1972. 8.95 (ISBN 0-89130-323-5, 06-00-16); members 5.95 (ISBN 0-317-35703-4). Scholars Pr GA.

--The Origins of Anti-Semitism: Attitudes Towards Judaism in Pagan & Christian Antiquity. 1983. 24.95x (ISBN 0-19-503316-7); pap. 9.95 (ISBN 0-19-503607-7). Oxford U Pr.

Gagey, Edmond M. Ballad Opera. LC 65-16237. 1937. 20.00 (ISBN 0-405-08546-X). Ayer Co Pubs.

--San Francisco Stage: A History. Repr. of 1950 ed. lib. bdg. 19.75x (ISBN 0-8371-3927-9, GAFS). Greenwood.

Gagg, J. C. The Countryside. 9.50x (ISBN 0-392-07745-0, SpS). Sportshelf.

Gagg, M. E. Farm. (Illus.). (gr. 2). 2.50 (ISBN 0-7214-0049-3). Merry Thoughts.

--Numbers. (Illus.). (gr. 2). 2.50 (ISBN 0-7214-0052-3). Merry Thoughts.

--Puppies & Kittens. (Illus.). (gr. 2). 2.50 (ISBN 0-7214-0048-5). Merry Thoughts.

--Telling the Time. (Illus.). (gr. 2). 2.50 (ISBN 0-7214-0056-6). Merry Thoughts.

--Zoo. (Illus.). (gr. 2). 2.50 (ISBN 0-7214-0054-X). Merry Thoughts.

Gaggioli, Richard A., ed. Efficiency & Costing: Second Law Analysis of Processes. LC 83-19707. (ACS Symposium Ser.: No. 235). 460p. 1983. lib. bdg. 55.95 (ISBN 0-8412-0811-5). Am Chemical.

--Thermodynamics: Second Law Analysis. LC 80-10486. (ACS Symposium Ser.: No. 122). 1980. 34.95 (ISBN 0-8412-0541-8). Am Chemical.

Gaghen, John E. The Peanut Butter Express. 1982. 8.95 (ISBN 0-533-05316-1). Vantage.

Gagiati, Annie. Peace Where Is It? LC 73-91996. 1974. pap. 1.95 (ISBN 0-8198-0507-6). Dghtrs St Paul.

Gagini, Carlos. Redemptions: A Novel of Costa Rica. Burns, E. Bradford, tr. from Span. (Illus.). 144p. (Orig.). 1984. 14.00x (ISBN 0-916304-66-3); pap. 5.00x (ISBN 0-916304-67-1). SDSU Press.

Gagliano, Felix, jt. auth. see Baum, Edward.

Gagliano, Felix V. Communal Violence in Malaysia 1969: The Political Aftermath. LC 78-630854. (Papers in International Studies: Southeast Asia Ser.: No. 13). pap. 23.80 (ISBN 0-317-09479-3, 2005117). Bks Demand UMI.

Gagliardelli, G, jt. auth. see Ragazzini, U.

Gagliardi, Gary. How to Make Your Small Business Computer Pay off: What the First Time Business System Buyer Must Know. 285p. 1983. 15.95 (ISBN 0-534-97926-2). Van Nos Reinhold.

--How to Make Your Small Computer Pay Off: What the First-Time Business System Buyer Must Know. (Data Processing Ser.). (Illus.). 279p. 1983. 14.95 (ISBN 0-534-97926-2). Lifetime Learn.

Gagliardi, Richard L. & Valenza, Samuel W., Jr., eds. The Mathematics of the Energy Crisis. LC 78-53592. 96p. 1978. pap. 7.95 (ISBN 0-936918-01-2). Intergalactic NJ.

Gagliardi, Robert. Introduction to Communications Engineering. LC 77-18531. 508p. 1978. 49.95x (ISBN 0-471-03099-6, Pub. by Wiley-Interscience). Wiley.

Gagliardi, Robert M. Satellite Communications-An Introduction. (Engineering Ser.). (Illus.). 475p. 1984. 39.00 (ISBN 0-534-02976-0). Lifetime Learn.

Gagliardi, Robert M. & Karp, Sherman. Optical Communications. LC 75-26509. 432p. 1976. 58.50x (ISBN 0-471-28915-9, Pub. by Wiley-Interscience). Wiley.

Gagliardo, John G. Enlightened Despotism. LC 67-14301. (Europe Since 1500 Ser.). (Orig.). 1967. pap. 7.95x (ISBN 0-88295-735-X). Harlan Davidson.

--From Pariah to Patriot: The Changing Image of the German Peasant, 1770-1840. LC 72-80091. 352p. 1969. 30.00x (ISBN 0-8131-1187-0). U Pr of Ky.

--Reich & Nation: The Holy Roman Empire As Idea & Reality, 1763-1806. LC 79-2170. 384p. 1980. 25.00x (ISBN 0-253-16773-6). Ind U Pr.

Gaglione, Anthony M., jt. auth. see Artino, Ralph A.

Gagnacci-Schwicker, A. & Schwicker. International Dictionary of Metallurgy, Mineralogy, Geology & the Mining & Oil Industries. 1530p. (Eng., Fr., Ger. & Ital.). 1970. 88.00 (ISBN 3-7625-0751-1, M-7482, Pub. by Bauverlag). French & Eur.

Gagne, Cole & Caras, Tracy. Soundpieces: Interviews with American Composers. LC 81-13520. (Illus.). 436p. 1982. 25.00 (ISBN 0-8108-1474-9). Scarecrow.

Gagne, Danai A. & Thomas, Judith. Dramas in Elemental Scales: A Collection of Mini-Dramas for Voice & Orff Instruments. 1983. pap. 8.00 (ISBN 0-918812-19-4). MMB Music.

Gagne, Ellen D. The Cognitive Psychology of School Learning. 1985. text ed. 23.95 (ISBN 0-316-30165-5). Little.

Gagne, Eve E. School Behavior & School Discipline: Coping with Deviant Behavior in the Schools. LC 82-15912. 176p. 1983. lib. bdg. 23.50 (ISBN 0-8191-2748-5); pap. text ed. 11.25 (ISBN 0-8191-2749-3). U Pr of Amer.

Gagne, Robert M. Essentials of Learning for Instruction. expanded ed. LC 73-20893. 204p. 1975. pap. text ed. 15.95 (ISBN 0-03-040976-4). HR&W.

Gagne, Robert M. & Briggs, Leslie J. Principles of Instructional Design. 2nd ed. LC 78-27628. 1979. text ed. 28.95 (ISBN 0-03-040806-7, HoltC). HR&W.

Gagne, Robert M., jt. auth. see Reiser, Robert A.

Gagne, Ronald, et al. Introducing Dance in Christian Worship. (Illus.). 184p. 1984. pap. 7.95 (ISBN 0-912405-04-X). Pastoral Pr.

Gagnebin. Simone de Beauvoir ou le Refus de l'Indifference. (Collection Celebrites). 13.50 (ISBN 0-685-37194-8). French & Eur.

Gagnebin, ed. see Rousseau, Jean-Jacques.

Gagneja, Hari D., jt. auth. see Prasad, Mohan.

Gagnepain, J. J. & Meeker, Thrygve R., eds. Piezoelectricity. (Ferroelectrics Ser.: Vols. 40, Nos. 3-4; 41; & 42, Nos. 1-2). 782p. 1982. 315.00 (ISBN 0-677-16415-7). Gordon.

Gagnier, Ed. Inside Gymnastics. 5.95 (ISBN 0-8092-8875-3). Contemp Bks.

Gagnon, Andre & Gagnon, Ann. Meeting the Challenge: Library Service to Young Adults. 144p. 1985. 15.00 (ISBN 0-88802-193-3). CLA.

Gagnon, Ann, jt. auth. see Gagnon, Andre.

Gagnon, Constance. Help! for Preschoolers. (ps). 1982. 3.95 (ISBN 0-86653-061-4, GA 412). Good Apple.

Gagnon, Dennis R. Exploring the Santa Barbara Backcountry. LC 73-77044. (Illus.). 150p. (Orig.). 1981. pap. 7.95 (ISBN 0-934136-13-0). Western Tanager.

Gagnon, Francois-Marc. Paul-Emile Borduas. (Canadian Artists Ser.). 1976. pap. 5.95 ea. (Pub. by Natl Mus Canada). French ed (ISBN 0-88884-315-1). English ed (ISBN 0-88884-271-6). Nat Gal Can.

Gagnon, John. Human Sexuality in Today's World. 1977. pap. text ed. 12.95 (ISBN 0-316-30172-8). Little.

Gagnon, John H. & Greenblat, Cathy S. Life Designs. LC 77-25198. 1977. text ed. 20.00 (ISBN 0-394-33317-9, RanC); study guide o.p. 5.95 (ISBN 0-394-33331-4). Random.

Gagnon, John H. & Simon, William. Sexual Conduct: The Social Sources of Human Sexuality. 328p. 1973. text ed. 26.95x (ISBN 0-202-30261-X). Aldine Pub.

Gagnon, John H. & Smith, Barbara. Human Sexualities. 1977. pap. 17.95x (ISBN 0-673-15033-X); study guide 6.95x (ISBN 0-673-15034-8). Scott F.

Gagnon, John H. & Simon, William, eds. The Sexual Scene. rev. 2nd ed. LC 72-87668. 150p. 1973. pap. 6.95 (ISBN 0-87855-541-2); 12.95 (ISBN 0-87855-048-8). Transaction Bks.

Gagnon, Phileas. Essai de Bibliographie Canadienne, 2 vols. (French-Canadian Civilization Ser.). (Eng. & Fr.). Repr. of 1913 ed. lib. bdg. 82.00x set (ISBN 0-89197-751-1); lib. bdg. 45.00x ea. Vol. 1 (ISBN 0-697-00004-4). Vol. 2 (ISBN 0-697-00005-2). Irvington.

Gagnon, Raymond O., jt. auth. see DeLozier, James E.

Gagnor, Raymond A. & Deloger, James E. The National Ambulatory Medical Care Survey, United States, 1979 Summary: Series 13, No. 66. 55p. 1982. pap. text ed. 1.85 (ISBN 0-8406-0255-3). Natl Ctr Health Stats.

Gagola, Stephen M. Notes on Primality Testing & Factoring. (MAA Notes Ser.: Vol. 4). 34p. 1984. pap. 3.50 (ISBN 0-88385-054-0). Math Assn.

Gahagan, Judy. Interpersonal & Group Behaviour. (Essential Psychology Ser.). 1977. pap. 4.50x (ISBN 0-416-82750-0, NO. 2784). Methuen Inc.

--Social Interaction & Its Management. Herriot, Peter, ed. LC 83-15129. (New Essential Psychology Ser.). 187p. 1984. pap. 6.50x (ISBN 0-416-33780-5, NO. 4043). Methuen Inc.

Gahagan, Thomas & Lam, Conrad R. Esophageal Hiatus Hernia: Rationale & Results of Anatomic Repair. (Illus.). 208p. 1976. photocopy ed. 24.75x (ISBN 0-398-03489-3). C C Thomas.

Gahan, C. J. Coleoptera - Phytophaga - Cerambycidae. (Fauna of British India Ser.). xviii, 330p. 1974. Repr. of 1906 ed. 11.00 (ISBN 0-88065-090-7, Pub. by Messers Today & Tomorrows Printers & Publishers India). Scholarly Pubns.

Gahan, P. B., ed. Autoradiography for Biologists. 1972. 25.00 (ISBN 0-12-273250-2). Acad Pr.

Gahan, Peter B. Plant Histochemistry. (Experimental Botany: An International Series of Monographs). 1984. 41.00 (ISBN 0-12-273270-7). ACad Pr.

Gahart, Betty L. Intravenous Medications: A Handbook for Nurses & Other Allied Health Personnel. 3rd ed. LC 81-4027. 258p. 1981. pap. text ed. 16.95 (ISBN 0-8016-1719-7). Mosby.

Gaherty, Sherry, jt. ed. see Katz, William A.

Gahl, G., et al, eds. Advances in Peritoneal Dialysis. (International Congress Ser.: No. 567). 508p. 1982. 82.75 (ISBN 0-444-90232-5, Excerpta Medica). Elsevier.

Gahler, W. Grundstrukturen der Analysis, 2 vols. (Mathematische Reihe Ser.: Nos. 58 & 61). (Ger.). 1978. Vol. 1, 396p. 54.95x (ISBN 0-8176-0901-6); Vol. 2, 496p. 71.95x (ISBN 0-8176-0966-0). Birkhauser.

Gahm, Joseph, ed. see Concone, J.

Gahn, Joseph, ed. see Grieg, Edward.

Gahn, Robert. The Opelousas Country. 1973. 12.50 (ISBN 0-87511-053-3). Claitors.

Gahris, Cindi. Good Apple & Career Education. (Illus.). 144p. (gr. 3-7). 1983. wkbk. 9.95 (ISBN 0-86653-110-6, GA 463). Good Apple.

Gai, G. S., jt. ed. see Asher, Frederick.

Gaia Ltd. Staff & Myers, Norman. Gaia: An Atlas of Planet Management. LC 83-20837. (Illus.). 256p. 1984. 29.95 (ISBN 0-385-19071-9, Anchor Pr); pap. 17.95 (ISBN 0-385-19072-7, Anchor Pr). Doubleday.

Gaibi, Agostino. Armi Da Fuoco Italiane. (Illus.). 532p. (Eng. captions). 1976. 95.00 (ISBN 0-686-14973-4). Arma Pr.

Gaida, B. Electroplating Science. 254p. 1981. 75.00x (ISBN 0-85218-032-2, Pub. by Portcullio Pr). State Mutual Bk.

Gaida, Davida. Twenty Eighty-Four, Vol. 1. LC 82-62540. (Orig.). 1983. pap. 7.95 (ISBN 0-88100-022-1). Ringa Pr.

Gaidar. Cyk i Gek. (Easy Reader, A). pap. 4.25 (ISBN 0-88436-051-2, 65250). EMC.

Gaidar, A. The Deathless Trumpeter & Other Stories About Young Heroes. 165p. 1975. 3.95 (ISBN 0-8285-1130-6, Pub. by Progress Pubs. USSR). Imported Pubns.

--School. 159p. 1982. pap. 3.50 (ISBN 0-8285-2427-0, Pub. by Progress Pubs USSR). Imported Pubns.

Gaidukov, N & Elenkin, A. A. Algological Bibliography of the USSR from Beginning to 1960. (Collectanea Bibliographia Ser.: No. 3). 1976. Repr. lib. bdg. 84.00 (ISBN 3-87429-105-7). Lubrecht & Cramer.

Gaier. Lectures in Complex Approximation. 1985. text ed. 24.95 (ISBN 0-8176-3147-X). Birkhauser.

Gaier, Dieter. Vovlesungen Veber Approximation Im Komplexen. 150p. (Ger.). 1980. pap. 19.95x (ISBN 0-8176-1161-4). Birkhauser.

Gaige, Frederick H. Regionalism & National Unity in Nepal. LC 74-30520. 1975. 31.00x (ISBN 0-520-02728-0). U of Cal Pr.

Gaige, Grace, ed. Recitations for Younger Children. LC 78-74816. (Granger Poetry Library). (gr. 3-8). 1979. Repr. of 1927 ed. 19.50x (ISBN 0-89609-134-1). Granger Bk.

--Recitations, Old & New, for Boys & Girls. LC 78-73486. (Granger Poetry Library). 1979. Repr. of 1924 ed. 27.50x (ISBN 0-89609-112-0). Granger Bk.

Gail, Marzieh. Dawn over Mount Hira & Other Essays. 256p. 1976. 11.95 (ISBN 0-85398-063-2); pap. 6.95 (ISBN 0-85398-064-0). G Ronald Pub.

--Khanum: The Greatest Holy Leaf. (Illus.). 48p. 5.25 (ISBN 0-85398-112-4); pap. 2.75 (ISBN 0-85398-113-2). G Ronald Pub.

--Other People, Other Places. 288p. 13.75 (ISBN 0-85398-122-1); pap. 6.75 (ISBN 0-85398-123-X). G Ronald Pub.

--Persia & the Victorians. 1977. lib. bdg. 59.95 (ISBN 0-8490-2423-4). Gordon Pr.

--The Sheltering Branch. 101p. 1959. 6.75 (ISBN 0-87743-022-5). G Ronald Pub.

Gail, Marzieh, tr. see Abdu'l-Baha.

Gail, Marzieh, tr. see Baha'u'llah.

Gail, Marzieh, tr. see Muhammad-'Aliy-Salmani, Ustad.

Gail, Otto W. Shot into Infinity. Del Rey, Lester, ed. Currier, F., tr. from Ger. LC 75-410. (Library of Science Fiction). 1975. lib. bdg. 21.00 (ISBN 0-8240-1415-4). Garland Pub.

Gail, Richard, jt. auth. see Jleinrock, Leonard.

Gail, Robert W. Spoofledingus: Tales & Legends of. (Illus.). 64p. (Orig.). 1981. pap. 3.95 (ISBN 0-89288-026-0). Maverick.

Gail, Spangenberg, jt. auth. see Cafferty, Pastora S. J.

Gailbraith, James M. The Datax Conspiracy. LC 76-21048. 1976. 8.95 (ISBN 0-913264-25-3). Douglas-West.

Gaile, Gary L. & Willmott, Cort J. Spatial Statistics & Models. 1984. lib. bdg. 69.00 (ISBN 90-277-1618-8, Pub. by Reidel Holland). Kluwer Academic.

Gailey, A. Rural Houses of the North of Ireland. (Illus.). 350p. 1984. text ed. 48.00x (ISBN 0-85976-098-7, Pub. by John Donald Scotland). Humanities.

Gailey, Alan. Ulster Folk Ways. 2.95 (ISBN 0-913714-20-8). Legacy Bks.

Gailey, Harry A. Africa: Troubled Continent - a Problem Approach. LC 82-23342. 160p. (Orig.). 1983. pap. 6.50 (ISBN 0-89874-342-7). Krieger.

--Clifford: Imperial Proconsul. 215p. (Orig.). 1982. 22.50 (ISBN 0-86036-189-6). Krieger.

--Historical Dictionary of the Gambia. LC 75-5882. (African Historical Dictionaries Ser.: No. 4). 180p. 1975. 17.50 (ISBN 0-8108-0810-2). Scarecrow.

--A History of the Gambia. rev. ed. 256p. text ed. cancelled (ISBN 0-8290-0350-9); pap. text ed. cancelled (ISBN 0-8290-0351-7). Irvington.

--Lugard & the Abeokuta Uprising: The Demise of Egba Independence. 148p. 1982. 30.00x (ISBN 0-7146-3114-0, F Cass Co). Biblio Dist.

--Peleliu 1944. LC 83-13394. 220p. 1983. 19.95 (ISBN 0-933852-41-X). Nautical & Aviation.

--Sir Donald Cameron: Colonial Governor. LC 74-7301. (Publications Ser.: No. 139). 181p. 1974. 10.95x (ISBN 0-8179-6391-X). Hoover Inst Pr.

Gailey, Harry A., Jr. The History of Africa in Maps, No. 81444. (Illus.). 1979. pap. 6.95x (ISBN 0-87453-444-5). Denoyer.

--History of Africa Vol. 1: From Earliest Times to 1800. LC 80-15898. (Illus.). 302p. (Orig.). 1981. pap. text ed. 11.50 (ISBN 0-89874-032-0). Krieger.

--History of Africa, Vol 2: From 1800 to the Present. rev. ed. LC 80-15898. 502p. (Orig.). 1981. pap. text ed. 16.50 (ISBN 0-89874-033-9). Krieger.

Gailey, J. Benjamin, ed. Zoning & Planning Law Handbook 1985. 1985. 45.00 (ISBN 0-317-18330-3). Boardman.

Gailey, James H., Jr. Micah-Malachi. LC 59-10454. (Layman's Bible Commentary Ser: Vol. 15). 1962. pap. 4.95 (ISBN 0-8042-3075-7). John Knox.

Gailey, Kenneth D., jt. auth. see Whitten, Kenneth W.

Gaillard, A. W. & Ritter, W. Tutorials in ERP Research: Endogenous Components. (Advances in Psychology: Vol. 10). 448p. 1983. 59.75 (ISBN 0-444-86551-9, North-Holland). Elsevier.

Gaillard, B. T. So You Want to Be an Innkeeper. 1983. 8.95 (ISBN 0-533-05741-8). Vantage.

Gaillard, Bob, et al. Handbook for the Young Athlete. 1978. pap. 6.95 (ISBN 0-915950-18-9). Bull Pub.

Gaillard, Dawson. Dorothy L. Sayers. LC 80-5344. (Recognitions Ser.). 180p. 1980. 11.95 (ISBN 0-8044-2222-2); pap. 5.95 (ISBN 0-8044-6169-4). Ungar.

Gaillard, Dawson & Mosier, John. Women & Men Together: An Anthology of Short Fiction. (Illus., LC 77-078566). 1977. pap. text ed. 17.50 (ISBN 0-395-25032-3); instr's. manual 0.55 (ISBN 0-395-25033-1). HM.

Gaillard, Didier, photos by. Femmes Fatales. 1984. 22.95 (ISBN 0-394-53821-8, GP915). Grove.

Gaillard, Frye, et al. Becoming Truly Free: Three Hundred Years of Black History in the Carolinas. (Illus.). 81p. 1985. pap. 4.95 (ISBN 0-9614603-0-X). J C Smith Univ.

Gaillard, M. J. Etude Palynologique de L'Evolution Tardiet Postglaciare de la Vegetation du Moyen-Pays Romad: Suisse. (Dissertationes Botanicae Ser.: No. 77). (Illus.). 346p. 1985. lib. bdg. 42.00x (ISBN 3-7682-1396-X). Lubrecht & Cramer.

Gaillard, M. K. & Stora, R. Gauge Theories in High Energy Physics, 2 Vols. (Les Houches Summer School Proceedings Ser.: Vol. 37). 1984. Set. 231.00 (ISBN 0-444-86543-8, I-080-84, North-Holland); Vol. 1. 146.25 (ISBN 0-444-86722-8); Vol. 2. 109.75 (ISBN 0-444-86723-6). Elsevier.

Gaillard, Pieter, et al, eds. The Parathyroid Gland: Ultrastructure, Secretion, & Function. LC 65-17290. pap. 91.30 (ISBN 0-317-28099-6, 2024092). Bks Demand UMI.

Gaillard, William N. Anglo-American, American-Anglo: The Wandering Wayfarer's Wordbook. (Illus.). 57p. (Orig.). 1985. pap. 4.95 (ISBN 0-9614800-0-9). Water Lane Pub.

Gailloud, C., et al, eds. New Aspects of Vitreoretinopathology. (Modern Problems in Ophthalmology: Vol. 20). (Illus.). 1979. 118.75 (ISBN 3-8055-3038-2). S Karger.

Gaimar, Geoffrey. Anglo-Norman Metrical Chronicle of Geoffrey Gaimar. Wright, Thomas, ed. 1966. Repr. of 1850 ed. 24.00 (ISBN 0-8337-1263-2). B Franklin.

Gaimar, Geoffroy. L' Estoire des Engleis. Bell, Alexander, ed. 43.00 (ISBN 0-384-17555-4); pap. 37.00 (ISBN 0-384-17556-2). Johnson Repr.

Gain, ed. see De Tocqueville, Alexis.

Gain, D. B., ed. The Aratus Ascribed to Germanicus Caesar. (University of London Classical Studies: No. VIII). (Illus.). 146p. 1976. 65.00 (ISBN 0-485-13708-9, Pub. by Athlone Pr Ltd). Longwood Pub Group.

Gaind, Raghu N., et al, eds. Current Themes in Psychiatry, Vol. 4. LC 84-643519. 300p. 1985. text ed. 45.00 (ISBN 0-89335-221-7). SP Med & Sci Bks.

Gaind, T. & Fawzy, F., eds. Current Themes in Psychiatry, Vol. 3. 400p. 1984. 35.00 (ISBN 0-89335-187-3). SP Med & Sci Bks.

Gaine, Hugh. Journals of Hugh Gaine, Printer, 2 vols. in 1. LC 70-125694. (American Journalists Ser). 1970. Repr. of 1902 ed. 25.50 (ISBN 0-405-01671-9). Ayer Co Pubs.

Gainer, Harold, ed. Peptides in Neurobiology. LC 76-54766. (Current Topics in Neurobiology Ser.). (Illus.). 484p. 1977. 49.50x (ISBN 0-306-30978-5, Plenum Pr). Plenum Pub.

Gainer, Harold N. & Stark, Sandra L. Choice or Chance: A Guidebook to Career Planning. (Illus.). 1978. pap. text ed. 15.20 (ISBN 0-07-022672-5). McGraw.

Gainer, Lucia A. The Hidden Garden. LC 84-61580. 128p. 1985. pap. 4.95 (ISBN 0-87973-598-8, 598). Our Sunday Visitor.

Gainer, Patrick W. Folk Songs from the West Virginia Hills. LC 75-38967. 1975. 15.00 (ISBN 0-89092-001-X). Seneca Bks.

--Folk Songs from the West Virginia Hills. LC 75-38967. 236p. 1982. pap. 8.98 (ISBN 0-686-84022-4). Seneca Bks.

--Folk Songs from the West Virginia Hills. 1975. pap. 15.00. Seneca Bks.

--Witches, Ghosts & Signs, Folklore of the Southern Appalachians. LC 75-29893. 192p. 1975. 7.95 (ISBN 0-89092-006-0). Seneca Bks.

Gainer, Ruth S., jt. auth. see Cohen, Elaine P.

Gaines, Arleigh, ed. United Nations Philately, 2 vols. (Illus.). 978p. 1983. Set. 38.00x (ISBN 0-938152-03-3). R & D Pubns.

--United Nations Philately, 2 vols. (Illus.). 1000p. 1985. Set. 42.00x (ISBN 0-938152-04-1). R & D Pubns.

Gaines, Atwood D., jt. ed. see Hahn, Robert A.

Gaines, B. R., jt. ed. see Mamdani, E. H.

Gaines, Barry, jt. ed. see Cawley, A. C.

Gaines, Brian R. & Shaw, Mildred L. The Art of Computer Conversation. (Illus.). 224p. 19.95 (ISBN 0-13-047332-4). P-H.

Gaines, Charles. Stay Hungry. 256p. 1985. pap. 3.50 (ISBN 0-345-31966-4). Ballantine.

Gaines, Charles & Butler, George. Pumping Iron II: The Unprecedented Woman. (Illus.). 224p. 1984. 19.95 (ISBN 0-671-44104-3); pap. 9.95 (ISBN 0-671-44105-1). S&S.

--Pumping Iron: The Art & Sport of Bodybuilding. rev. ed. 1982. 19.95 (ISBN 0-671-41737-1); pap. 10.95 (ISBN 0-671-42688-5). S&S.

--Staying Hard. (Orig.). 1980. pap. 10.95 (ISBN 0-671-41265-5). S&S.

Gaines, Charles, jt. auth. see Arnot, Robert.

Gaines, Charles K. By the Will of Apollo. LC 76-3310. (YA) (gr. 6 up). 1976. 7.95 (ISBN 0-8265-1204-6). Vanderbilt U Pr.

--Gorgo: A Romance of Old Athens. LC 76-3311. (YA) (gr. 6 up). 1976. Repr. of 1903 ed. 7.95 (ISBN 0-8265-1203-8). Vanderbilt U Pr.

Gaines, David. Artisans Appalachia U. S. A. 1977. pap. 4.95 (ISBN 0-913239-13-5). Appalach Consortium.

--Mono Lake Guidebook. LC 81-82402. (Illus.). 120p. (Orig.). 1981. pap. 5.95 (ISBN 0-939716-00-3). Mono Lake Comm.

Gaines, David P. The World Council of Churches. 1966. 18.50 (ISBN 0-87233-816-9). Bauhan.

Gaines, Edith see McCluskey, John.

Gaines, Ernest J. The Autobiography of Miss Jane Pittman. 256p. (gr. 5 up). 1972. pap. 2.95 (ISBN 0-553-23068-9). Bantam.

--Autobiography of Miss Jane Pittman. 1971. 12.95 (ISBN 0-385-27009-7, Dial). Doubleday.

--Bloodline. 256p. 1976. pap. 6.95 (ISBN 0-393-00798-7, Norton Lib). Norton.

--Catherine Carmier. LC 80-27402. 256p. 1981. pap. 9.25 (ISBN 0-86547-022-7). N Point Pr.

--A Gathering of Old Men. LC 82-49000. 224p. 1983. 16.95 (ISBN 0-394-51468-8). Knopf.

--A Gathering of Old Men. Large Print ed. LC 83-24096. 331p. 1984. Repr. of 1983 ed. 15.95 (ISBN 0-89621-511-3). Thorndike Pr.

--A Gathering of Old Men. LC 84-40007. 224p. 1984. pap. 3.95 (ISBN 0-394-72591-3, Vin). Random.
--In My Father's House. LC 77-20357. 1978. 13.95 (ISBN 0-394-47938-6). Knopf.
--In My Father's House. 224p. 1983. pap. 4.95 (ISBN 0-393-30124-9). Norton.
--Of Love & Dust. 1979. pap. 5.95 (ISBN 0-393-00914-9). Norton.
Gaines, F. P. The Southern Plantation: A Study in the Development & the Accuracy of a Tradition. 11.25 (ISBN 0-8446-1193-X). Peter Smith.
Gaines, G. Firefighting Operations in Garden Apartments & Townhouses. 1978. pap. 15.95 (ISBN 0-87618-885-4). Fire Eng.
Gaines, George & Coleman, David. Broker Review Outline. 2nd ed. 1984. pap. 17.95 (ISBN 0-88462-469-2). Caroline Hse.
Gaines, George & Coleman, David S. Continuing Education for Real Estate Brokers & Salepersons. rev. ed. LC 84-27549. Date not set. price not set (ISBN 0-88462-522-2, Real Estate Ed). Longman USA.
Gaines, George, Jr. & Coleman, David S. Basic Real Estate Math: Explanations, Problems, Solutions. 2nd ed. 144p. (Orig.). 1983. pap. text ed. 13.95 (ISBN 0-88462-460-9, 1610-07, Real Estate Ed). Longman USA.
--Broker Review Outline. 184p. (Orig.). 1983. 17.95 (ISBN 0-88462-468-4, 1610-05, Real Estate Ed). Longman USA.
--Continuing Education for Real Estate Brokers & Salespersons. 3rd ed. LC 83-24730. 144p. 1984. pap. text ed. 8.25 (ISBN 0-88462-471-4, 1610-08, Real Estate Ed). Longman USA.
--Florida Real Estate Principles, Practices & Law. 8th ed. (Illus.). 480p. 1984. pap. text ed. 19.95 (ISBN 0-88462-474-9, 1610-01, Real Estate Ed). Longman USA.
--Real Estate Math: Explanations, Problems, Solutions. 2nd ed. 1981. pap. text ed. 10.95 (ISBN 0-88462-466-8, 1610-06, Real Estate Ed). Longman USA.
--Salesman Review Outline. 8th ed. LC 84-17915. 176p. 1984. pap. 10.95 (ISBN 0-88462-509-5, 1610-03, Real Estate Ed). Longman USA.
Gaines, George L. Insoluble Monolayers of Liquid-Gas Interfaces. LC 65-26218. (Interscience Monographs on Physical Chemistry). pap. 100.00 (ISBN 0-317-09199-9, 2006310). Bks Demand UMI.
Gaines, Helen F. Cryptanalysis: A Study of Ciphers & Their Solutions. (Illus.). 1939. pap. text ed. 4.50 (ISBN 0-486-20097-3). Dover.
Gaines, Jack. Fritz Perls: Here & Now. LC 77-90020. (Illus.). 440p. (Orig.). 1983. 18.95 (ISBN 0-9610310-0-X); pap. 12.95 (ISBN 0-9610310-1-8). Integrated Pr.
Gaines, James F. Social Structures in Moliere's Theatre. (Illus.). 293p. 1984. 22.50 (ISBN 0-8142-0358-2). Ohio St U Pr.
Gaines, James R. The Lives of the Piano. LC 82-48228. (Illus.). 215p. 1983. pap. 11.49i (ISBN 0-06-090997-8, CN 997, CN). Har-Row.
Gaines, John, jt. auth. see Epstein, Jerome.
Gaines, John S., jt. auth. see Rolle, Andrew F.
Gaines, Larry K. & Ricks, Truett A. Managing the Police Organization: Selected Readings. (Criminal Justice Ser.). (Illus.). 1978. pap. text ed. 20.95 (ISBN 0-8299-0163-9). West Pub.
Gaines, Linda, et al. TOSCA: The Total Social Cost of Coal & Nuclear Power. LC 78-26240. 144p. 1979. prof ref 29.95 (ISBN 0-88410-086-3). Ballinger Pub.
Gaines, M. & Goulding, J. Jane's Aircraft Spectaculars: Hercules. (Illus.). 1985. 12.95 (ISBN 0-7106-0324-X). Jane's Pub Inc.
Gaines, M. C., ed. Picture Stories from the Bible: The New Testament in Full-Color Comic-Strip Form. LC 80-51593. (The Comic-Book Bible Ser.: Vol. 2). (Illus.). 144p. (gr. 3-10). 1980. Repr. of 1946 ed. 7.95 (ISBN 0-934386-02-1). Scarf Pr.
--Picture Stories from the Bible: The Old Testament in Full-Color Comic-Strip Form. LC 79-66064. (Illus.). 224p. (gr. 3-10). 1979. Repr. of 1943 ed. 9.95 (ISBN 0-934386-01-3). Scarf Pr.
Gaines, Michael S., jt. auth. see McClenaghan, Leroy R.
Gaines, Pierce W. Political Works of Concealed Authorship: Relating to the United States 1789-1810. 3rd ed. LC 76-178861. xx, 226p. 1972. 18.50 (ISBN 0-208-01241-9, Archon). Shoe String.
--William Cobbett & the United States, 1792-1835: Bibliographies with Notes & Extracts. LC 79-168901. 1971. 16.50 (ISBN 0-912296-00-3, Dist. by U Pr of Va). Am Antiquarian.
Gaines, Price, ed. The Diamond Life Bulletins Policy Statistics Service, Vols. 9-12. 1550p. 1984. Set. write for info 4 binders (ISBN 0-87218-050-6). Natl Underwriter.
--Disability Income & Health Insurance: 1985 Edition. 278p. 1985. pap. 18.30 (ISBN 0-87218-041-7). Natl Underwriter.
--Life Rates & Data. 777p. 1985. pap. 17.00 (ISBN 0-87218-040-9). Natl Underwriter.
--Who Writes What, 1985. 383p. 1984. spiral bdg. 14.50 (ISBN 0-87218-039-5). Natl Underwriter.
Gaines, R. E. & Mawhin, J. L. Coincidence Degree, & Non-Linear Differential Equations. LC 76-58453. (Lecture Notes in Mathematics Ser: Vol. 568). 1977. pap. 18.00 (ISBN 0-387-08067-8). Springer-Verlag.
Gaines, Rayvond. Dreamers Are Thinkers. 1981. 5.00 (ISBN 0-682-49538-7). Exposition Pr FL.
Gaines, Richard L. Interior Plantscaping. LC 77-9350. (Illus.). 1977. 38.95 (ISBN 0-07-022678-4). McGraw.
Gaines, Steven, jt. auth. see Brown, Peter.
Gaines, Sylvia W. Data Bank Applications in Archaeology. LC 81-901. 142p. 1981. pap. 14.95x (ISBN 0-8165-0686-8). U of Ariz Pr.
Gaines, Tilford C. Techniques of Treasury Debt Management. LC 62-11849. 1962. 8.95 (ISBN 0-02-911050-5). Free Pr.
Gaines, Wesley J. African Methodism in the South: Or Twenty-Five Years of Freedom. LC 71-99379. 1969. Repr. of 1890 ed. lib. bdg. 16.00 (ISBN 0-8411-0050-0). Metro Bks.
--Negro & the White Man. LC 75-88430. Repr. of 1897 ed. cancelled (ISBN 0-8371-1889-1, GAN&, Pub. by Negro U Pr). Greenwood.
Gaines, William, ed. Sing along with Mad. 1970. pap. 1.25 (ISBN 0-451-06826-2, Y6826, Sig). NAL.
Gaines, William H., Jr. Biographical Register of Members, Virginia State Convention of 1861: First Session. LC 74-628577. 1969. pap. 1.50x (ISBN 0-88490-059-2). VA State Lib.
--Virginia History in Documents. 1621-1788. LC 73-94133. (Illus.). 1974. pap. 10.00 (ISBN 0-88490-000-2). VA State Lib.
Gaines, William M. Greasy Mad Stuff. (Illus., Orig.). 1964. pap. 0.95 (ISBN 0-451-06499-2, Q6499, Sig). NAL.
--Portable Mad. pap. 1.25 (ISBN 0-451-06742-8, Y6742, Sig). NAL.
Gaines, William M., ed. Self-Made Mad. (Illus., Orig.). pap. 1.25 (ISBN 0-451-06981-1, Y6981, Sig). NAL.
--Three-Ring Mad. (Illus., Orig.). 1964. pap. 1.25 (ISBN 0-451-06917-X, Y6917, Sig). NAL.
Gainet, J. C. Dictionnaire d'Ascetisme, 2 vols. Migne, J. P., ed. (Nouvelle Encyclopedie Theologique Ser.: Vols. 45-46). 1520p. (Fr.). Repr. of 1854 ed. lib. bdg. 192.50x (ISBN 0-89241-284-4). Caratzas.
Gainham, Sarah. A Place in the Country. 1976. pap. 1.75 (ISBN 0-380-00642-1, 27524). Avon.
Gainsborough, John A. Personal Computing & C. 200p. 1985. pap. 19.95 (ISBN 0-912677-45-7). Ashton-Tate Bks.
Gainsborough, Louis. Of Dope & Dervishes. 1980. 8.95 (ISBN 0-9603670-0-4). Rapollo Bks.
Gainsbrugh, Jonathan. Take Him to the Streets. rev. ed. LC 84-62779. 236p. 1985. pap. 6.95 (ISBN 0-910311-26-9). Huntington Hse Inc.
Gainsford. Silver Amalgam in Clinical Practice. 120p. 1976. pap. 13.00 (ISBN 0-7236-0372-3). PSG Pub Co.
Gainsford, Michael. Home Range Poultry Keeping. LC 77-85027. (Penny Pinchers Ser.). (Illus.). 1978. 4.50 (ISBN 0-7153-7552-0). David & Charles.
Gainsford, Thomas. The Rich Cabinet Furnished with Varietie of Excellent Descriptions. LC 77-38417. (English Experience Ser.: No. 458). 368p. 1972. Repr. of 1616 ed. 33.50 (ISBN 90-221-0458-3). Walter J Johnson.
--The Secretaries Study: Directions for the Inditing of Letters. LC 74-80177. (English Experience Ser.: No. 658). 1974. Repr. of 1616 ed. 14.00 (ISBN 90-221-0658-6). Walter J Johnson.
--The True Exemplary & Remarkable History of the Earle of Tirone. LC 68-54644. (English Experience Ser.: No. 25). 1968. Repr. of 1619 ed. 8.00 (ISBN 90-221-0025-1). Walter J Johnson.
Gair, Diana. Highlands Rapture. (Harlequin Romance Ser.). 1982. pap. 1.75 (ISBN 0-373-02519-X). Harlequin Bks.
--Jungle Antagonist. (Harlequin Romances Ser.). 192p. 1983. pap. 1.50 (ISBN 0-373-02530-0). Harlequin Bks.
Gair, James W. Colloquial Sinhalese Clause Structures. (Janua Linguarum, Ser. Practica: No. 83). 1970. text ed. 23.20x (ISBN 90-2790-733-1). Mouton.
Gair, R., et al. Cereal Pests & Diseases. 3rd ed. (Illus.). 260p. 1983. 19.95 (ISBN 0-85236-119-X, Pub. by Farming Pr UK). Diamond Farm Bk.
Gair, Reavley. The Children of Paul's: The Story of a Theatre Company, 1553-1608. LC 82-4185. (Illus.). 232p. 1982. 37.50 (ISBN 0-521-24360-2). Cambridge U Pr.
Gair, Reavley, ed. see Marston, John.
Gairdner, Canon W. H. T. Theories, Practices & Training Systems of a Sufi School. (Sufi Research Ser.). 1980. pap. 5.95 (ISBN 0-86304-003-9, Pub. by Octagon Pr England). Ins Study Human.
Gairdner, James. The Early Chronicles of England. 328p. 1982. Repr. lib. bdg. 50.00 (ISBN 0-8495-2133-5). Arden Lib.
--English Church in the Sixteenth Century, from the Accession of Henry Eighth to the Death of Mary, 1509-1558. LC 72-168089. (History of the English Church Ser.: No. 4). Repr. of 1902 ed. 29.50 (ISBN 0-404-50754-9). AMS Pr.
--Henry the Seventh. LC 70-112639. Repr. of 1889 ed. 11.50 (ISBN 0-404-02667-2). AMS Pr.
--Henry the Seventh. 1889. 10.00x (ISBN 0-403-00020-3). Scholarly.
--Lollardy & the Reformation in England: An Historical Survey, 4 Vols. 1965. Repr. of 1913 ed. 141.00 (ISBN 0-8337-1268-3). B Franklin.
Gairdner, James, ed. Historical Collections of a Citizen of London in the Fifteenth Century. Repr. of 1876 ed. 27.00 (ISBN 0-384-17560-0). Johnson Repr.
--Letters & Papers Illustrative of the Reigns of Richard III & Henry VII, 2 vols. (Rolls Ser.: No. 24). Repr. of 1863 ed. Set. 88.00 (ISBN 0-317-16670-0). Kraus Repr.
--Letters & Papers Illustrative to the Reigns of Richard III & Henry VII, 2 vols. LC 75-41107. Repr. of 1863 ed. Set. 72.50 (ISBN 0-404-14910-3). AMS Pr.
--Memorials of Henry VII: Bernardi Andreae Tholosatis Vita Regis Henrici Septimi; Necnon Alia Quaedam ad Eundem Regem Spectantia. (Rolls Ser.: No. 10). Repr. of 1858 ed. 60.00 (ISBN 0-317-16657-3). Kraus Repr.
--Paston Letters, 1422-1509, 6 Vols. LC 77-168090. Repr. of 1904 ed. Set. 147.00 (ISBN 0-404-02690-7); 24.50 ea. AMS Pr.
Gairdner, James, ed. see Brewer, John S.
Gairdner, James see Hues, Robert.
Gairdner, W. T., tr. see Lavelle, Louis.
Gaisberg, Frederick W. The Music Goes Round. Farkas, Andrew, ed. LC 76-29936. (Opera Biographies). (Illus.). 1977. Repr. of 1942 ed. lib. bdg. 26.50x (ISBN 0-405-09678-X). Ayer Co Pubs.
Gaiser, Gottlieb, ed. International Perspectives on James Joyce. LC 85-51201. 350p. 1985. 25.00 (ISBN 0-87875-312-5). Whitston Pub.
Gaisford, ed. Atlas of Man. LC 78-4364. (Illus.). 1978. 25.00 (ISBN 0-312-05991-4). St Martin.
Gaisser, T. K., ed. Cosmic Rays & Particle Physics - Nineteen Seventy-Eight: Bartol Conference. LC 79-50489. (AIP Conference Proceedings Ser.: No. 49). (Illus.). 1979. lib. bdg. 23.50 (ISBN 0-88318-148-7). Am Inst Physics.
Gait, Edward A. A History of Assam. 2nd rev. ed. LC 77-87078. Repr. of 1926 ed. 27.50 (ISBN 0-404-16819-1). AMS Pr.
Gait, M. J., ed. Oligonucleotide Synthesis: A Practical Approach. (Practical Approach Ser.). (Illus.). 232p. (Orig.). 1984. pap. 23.00 (ISBN 0-904147-74-6). IRL Pr.
Gaitan, Elizabeth M. From Demon Deliverance to Divine Healing. 1985. 5.95 (ISBN 0-8062-2394-4). Carlton.
Gaite, Carmen M. The Back Room. Lane, Helen R., tr. from Span. LC 83-7729. (Twentieth-Century Continental Fiction Ser.). 200p. 1983. 20.00 (ISBN 0-231-05458-0). Columbia U Pr.
Gaitens, Robert P. How to Make Big Profits Renovating Real Estate. 304p. 1982. 17.95 (ISBN 0-13-418103-4). P-H.
Gaither, Gerald H. Blacks & the Populist Revolt: Ballots & Bigotry in the "New South". LC 75-6904. (Illus.). 269p. 1977. 19.75 (ISBN 0-8173-4726-7). U of Ala Pr.
Gaither, Gloria. Decisions. 184p. 1985. pap. 6.95 (ISBN 0-8499-3015-4, 3015-4). Word Bks.
--Fully Alive! 208p. 1984. pap. 4.95 (ISBN 0-8407-5945-2). Nelson.
Gaither, Norman. Production & Operations Management: A Problem-Solving & Decision-Making Approach. 2nd ed. 784p. 1984. text ed. 36.95x (ISBN 0-03-062568-8); instr.'s solutions manual 19.95 (ISBN 0-03-062571-8); instr.'s resource manual w/transparency masters 19.95 (ISBN 0-03-062569-6). Dryden Pr.
Gaither, R. Expropriation in Mexico. 1976. lib. bdg. 59.95 (ISBN 0-8490-1797-1). Gordon Pr.
Gaito, John. Molecular Psychobiology: A Chemical Approach to Learning & Other Behavior. (Illus.). 280p. 1966. 24.50x (ISBN 0-398-00635-0). C C Thomas.
Gaito, John & Nobrega, Jose N. Introduction to Analysis of Variance Procedures. rev. ed. 250p. 1985. text ed. 22.50x (ISBN 0-8290-1349-0). Irvington.
Gaito, John, ed. Macromolecules & Behavior. LC 76-150497. 397p. 1972. 37.50x (ISBN 0-306-50025-6, Plenum Pr). Plenum Pub.
Gaitonde, P. D. Portugese Pioneers in India: Spotlight on Medicine. 1983. 27.00x (ISBN 0-8364-1052-1, Pub. by Popular Prakashan). South Asia Bks.
Gaitskell, Charles D. & Hurwitz, Al. Children & Their Art: Methods for the Elementary School. 4th ed. (Illus.). 527p. 1982. text ed. 24.95 (ISBN 0-15-507299-4, HC). HarBraceJ.
Gaitz, C. M., ed. Aging & the Brain. LC 72-77227. (Advances in Behavioral Biology Ser.: Vol. 3). 231p. 1972. 32.50x (ISBN 0-306-37903-1, Plenum Pr). Plenum Pub.
Gaitz, C. M. & Samorajski, T., eds. Aging Two Thousand: Our Health Care Destiny, Vol. 1. (Illus.). xxv, 545p. 1985. 45.00 (ISBN 0-387-96057-0). Springer-Verlag.
Gaitz, C. M., et al, eds. Aging Two Thousand: Our Health Care Destiny, Vol. 2. (Illus.). 400p. 1985. 45.00 (ISBN 0-387-96070-8). Springer-Verlag.
Gaius. The Institutes, 2 pts. Incl. Pt. 1. De Zulueta, Francis, notes by. 1946. 36.95x (ISBN 0-19-825112-2); Pt. 2. De Zulueta, Francis, commentary by. 1953. Oxford U Pr.
Gaja, Giorgio, ed. International Commercial Arbitration: Cases Under the New York Convention, 2 binders, Vol. 3. LC 78-991. (International Commercial Arbitration Ser.). 1978. write for info. looseleaf (ISBN 0-379-00599-9); Set. 200.00 (ISBN 0-686-77172-9). Oceana.
Gajate, Comandante, ed. see Gerardo, Machado.
Gajda, George. Gold Refining. 2nd rev. ed. 1980. 25.50 (ISBN 0-9608018-2-0). G Gajda.
Gajda, Patricia A. Postscript to Victory: British Policy & the German-Polish Borderlands, 1919-1925. LC 81-40634. (Illus.). 246p. (Orig.). 1982. lib. bdg. 26.00 (ISBN 0-8191-2203-3); pap. text ed. 12.25 (ISBN 0-8191-2204-1). U Pr of Amer.
Gajda, Robert, jt. auth. see Dominguez, Richard H.
Gajda, Robert J., jt. auth. see Dominguez, Richard H.
Gajdusek, D. Carleton, jt. ed. see Farquhar, Judith.
Gajdusek, Robert E. Hemingway & Joyce: A Study in Debt & Payment. LC 84-51246. 50p. (Orig.). 1984. pap. 5.00 (ISBN 0-930159-00-4). Square Circle.
--Hemingway's Paris. (Illus.). 192p. 1982. pap. 12.95 (ISBN 0-684-17785-4, ScribT). Scribner.
Gajecky, George. The Cossack Administration of the Hetmanate, 2 vols. LC 77-73708. (Sources & Documents Ser.). (Illus.). 1978. pap. 18.50x (ISBN 0-916458-02-4). Harvard Ukrainian.
Gajek, Bernhard & Wedel, Erwin. Gebrauchsliteratur-Interferenz-Kontrastivitaet Beitraege Zur Polnischen und Deutschen Literatur-und Sprachwissenschaft. (European University Studies Ser.: No. 1, Vol. 474). 390p. (Ger.). 1982. 35.25 (ISBN 3-8204-7089-1). P Lang Pubs.
Gajendra, Verna K., jt. auth. see Stenhouse, Lawrence.
Gajewski, Joseph J. Hydrocarbon Thermal Isomerizations. LC 80-70594. (Organic Chemistry Ser.). 1981. 59.50 (ISBN 0-12-273350-9). Acad Pr.
Gakenheimer, Ralph. Transportation Planning As Response to Controversy: Participation & Conflict in the Boston Case. LC 75-35905. 432p. 1975. 32.50x (ISBN 0-262-07065-0). MIT Pr.
Gakenheimer, Ralph, compiled by see Organization for Economic Cooperation & Development.
Gakov, Vladimir, ed. World's Spring. DeGaris, Roger, tr. 297p. 1981. 13.95 (ISBN 0-02-542180-8). Macmillan.
Gakwandi, Shatto A. The Novel & Contemporary Experience in Africa. LC 77-1273. 140p. 1978. text ed. 27.50x (ISBN 0-8419-0306-9, Africana); pap. text ed. 12.50x (ISBN 0-8419-0642-4). Holmes & Meier.
Gal, Allon. Brandeis of Boston. LC 79-15501. 1980. text ed. 17.50x (ISBN 0-674-08043-2). Harvard U Pr.
--Social Zionism: Theory & Issues in Contemporary Jewish Nationalism. 225p. 1973. pap. 5.50 (ISBN 0-87073-669-8). Transaction Bks.
Gal, Gedeon, ed. Guillelmi de Ockham: Scriptum in Librum Primum Sententiarum, Ordinatio, Opera Theologica, Vol. 1, Prologues et Distinctio Prima. 1967. 35.00 (ISBN 0-686-11528-7). Franciscan Inst.
Gal, Gedeon & Wood, R., eds. Guillelmi de Ockham: Quaestiones in Secundum Librum Sententiarum (Reportatio), Opera Theologica, Vol. 5. 1981. 59.00 (ISBN 0-318-00511-5). Franciscan Inst.
Gal, Hans. Franz Schubert & the Essence of Melody. 1977. 8.95 (ISBN 0-8008-2992-1, Crescendo). Taplinger.
--Johannes Brahms: His Work & Personality. Stein, Joseph, tr. from Ger. LC 76-55410. (Illus.). Repr. of 1963 ed. lib. bdg. 21.00x (ISBN 0-8371-9367-2, GABR). Greenwood.
--Schumann Orchestral Music. LC 79-52145. (BBC Music Guides Ser.). (Illus.). 64p. (Orig.). 1980. pap. 4.95 (ISBN 0-295-95696-8). U of Wash Pr.
Gal, Hans, ed. see Brahms, Johannes.
Gal, M. Le see Le Gal, M.
Gal, Susan. Language Shift: Social Determinants of Linguistic Change in Bilingual Austria. (Language, Thought & Culture Ser.). 1979. 37.50 (ISBN 0-12-273750-4). Acad Pr.
Galaburda, Albert M., jt. ed. see Geschwind, Norman.
Galagotis, Nicholas. Psychiatry in Psychoperception. 1985. 7.50 (ISBN 0-682-40215-X). Exposition Pr FL.
Galaid, Ruth C. The Health of Women. Coan, Howard, ed. 40p. 1983. pap. text ed. 1.50 (ISBN 0-8406-0274-X). Natl Ctr Health Stats.
Galambos, Andrew J. & Galambos, Suzanne J. More Lasting Than Bronze. 1982. 100.00 (ISBN 0-88078-000-2). TUSPCO.
Galambos, Edith P. Loving Hands for Jesus. (Little Learner Ser.). 24p. (gr. 2-5). 1985. 5.95 (ISBN 0-570-08951-4, 56-1543). Concordia.
Galambos, Eva C. Making Sense Out of Dollars: Economic Analysis for Local Government Decisions. 144p. 1978. 10.00 (ISBN 0-317-35160-5, 6004). Natl League Cities.
Galambos, Eva C., jt. auth. see McCarty, Marilu H.
Galambos, J. Representations of Real Numbers by Infinite Series. LC 75-44296. (Lecture Notes in Mathematics: Vol. 502). 1976. pap. 13.00 (ISBN 0-387-07547-X). Springer-Verlag.
Galambos, J. & Kotz, S. Characterizations of Probability Distributions: A Unified Approach with an Emphasis on Exponential & Related Models. (Lecture Notes in Mathematics: Vol. 675). 1978. pap. 15.00 (ISBN 0-387-08933-0). Springer-Verlag.

Galambos, Janos. The Asymptotic Theory of Extreme Order Statistics. LC 78-1916. (Probability & Mathematical Staistics Ser.). 352p. 1978. 53.50x (ISBN 0-471-02148-2, Pub. by Wiley-Interscience). Wiley.
--Introductory Probability Theory. (Statistics: Textbooks & Monographs Ser.). 256p. 1984. 25.00 (ISBN 0-8247-7179-6). Dekker.
Galambos, John T. Cirrhosis. LC 78-65970. (Illus.). 1979. text ed. 28.95 (ISBN 0-7216-3987-9). Saunders.
Galambos, John T. & Hersh, Theodore, eds. Digestive Diseases. 701p. 1983. text ed. 49.95 (ISBN 0-409-95024-6). Butterworth.
Galambos, Louis. America at Middle Age: A New History of the United States in the Twentieth Century. 176p. 1982. 14.95 (ISBN 0-07-022682-2). McGraw.
Galambos, Louis, ed. The Papers of Dwight David Eisenhower: Columbia University, 2 vols, Vols. X-XI. LC 65-27672. 1664p. 1984. Set. 60.00x (ISBN 0-8018-2720-5). Johns Hopkins.
Galambos, Louis P. & Spence, Barbara Barrow. The Public Image of Big Business in America, 1880-1940: A Quantitative Study in Social Change. LC 75-11347. (Illus.). 336p. 1975. 30.00x (ISBN 0-8018-1635-1). Johns Hopkins.
Galambos, Nancy L., jt. auth. see Lerner, Richard M.
Galambos, Suzanne J., jt. auth. see Galambos, Andrew J.
Galamian, Ivan & Green, Elizabeth. Principles of Violin Playing & Teaching. 2nd ed. (Illus.). 160p. 1985. text ed. 22.95 (ISBN 0-13-710773-0). P-H.
Galan, Cristobal. Obras Completas, Pt. 1. (Gesamtausgaben - Collected Works Ser.: No. 12). 100p. (Span. & Eng.). 1982. lib. bdg. 50.00 (ISBN 0-912024-59-3). Inst Mediaeval Mus.
Galan, E., jt. ed. see Singer, A.
Galan, F. W. Historic Structures: The Prague School Project, 1928-1946. (University of Texas Press Slavic Ser.: No. 7). 268p. 1985. text ed. 22.50x (ISBN 0-292-73032-2). U of Tex Pr.
Galan, Fernando. A Long Road. (Literacy Volunteers of America Readers Ser.). 32p. (Orig.). 1983. pap. 2.46 (ISBN 0-8428-9604-X). Cambridge Bk.
--One Summer. (Literacy Volunteers of America Readers Ser.). 32p. (Orig.). 1983. pap. 2.46 (ISBN 0-8428-9605-8). Cambridge Bk.
Galana, Laurel, jt. ed. see Covina, Gina.
Galanakis, Nita C. Personality Disorders: Medical Subject Analysis with Research Bibliography. LC 84-45649. 150p. 1985. 29.95 (ISBN 0-88164-232-0); pap. 21.95 (ISBN 0-88164-233-9). ABBE Pubs Assn.
Galan e Hildalgo, Arturo, jt. auth. see Bucksch, Herbert.
Galanin, A. D. The Theory of Thermal-Neutron Nuclear Reactors, Pt. 2. LC 58-22338. (Soviet Journal of Atomic Energy Supplement Ser.: Nos. 2-3, 1957). (Illus.). pap. 27.00 (ISBN 0-317-09426-2, 2020663). Bks Demand UMI.
Galanin, M. D., jt. auth. see Agranovitch, V. M.
Galant, Stanley P. see Nussbaum, Eliezer.
Galant, Stanley P., et al. Pediatric Allergy Case Studies. LC 80-18937. 1980. pap. 20.50 (ISBN 0-87488-195-1). Med Exam.
Galantay, Ervin Y. New Towns: Planned Towns Throughout History. LC 74-81216. (Planning & Cities Ser.). (Illus.). 192p. 1975. 15.00 (ISBN 0-8076-0766-5); pap. 5.95 (ISBN 0-8076-0767-3). Braziller.
Galante, Cosmo. The Degeneration of the Female of the Species & the Decay of the Human Society. enl. ed. (Illus.). 68p. 1973. 59.45 (ISBN 0-913314-18-8). Am Classical Coll Pr.
Galante, Lawrence. Tai Chi: The Supreme Ultimate. LC 84-50665. (Illus.). 1981. pap. 10.95 (ISBN 0-87728-497-0). Weiser.
Galante, Moses B. Kehillat Ya'acov: Commentary on the Book of Ecclesiastes, Safed 1578. 31.00 (ISBN 0-405-11953-4). Ayer Co Pubs.
Galante, Pierre. Operation Valkyrie. 1983. pap. 3.95 (ISBN 0-440-17544-5). Dell.
Galante, Susan. Tenure Dismissal. LC 84-158206. (Focus on School Law Ser.). Date not set. price not set. NJ Schl Bds.
Galanter, Eugene. Advanced Programming Handbook. LC 83-26697. (Kids & Computers Ser.). (Illus.). 192p. 1984. 14.95 (ISBN 0-399-50975-5, G&D); pap. 8.95 (ISBN 0-399-50976-3). Putnam Pub Group.
--Elementary Programming for Kids in BASIC. (Kids & Computers Ser.). (Illus.). 192p. (Orig.). 1983. 15.95 (ISBN 0-399-50938-0, G&D); pap. 7.95 (ISBN 0-399-50867-8). Putnam Pub Group.
--The Parent's Micro-Computer Handbook. LC 82-82310. (Kids & Computer Ser.). 192p. (Orig.). 1983. 14.95 (ISBN 0-399-50876-7, G&D); pap. 7.95 (ISBN 0-399-50749-3). Putnam Pub Group.
Galanter, Marc. Advances in the Psychosocial Treatment of Alcoholism. LC 84-6304. (Clinical Insights Monograph). 128p. 1984. pap. text ed. 12.00x (ISBN 0-88048-058-0, 48-058-0). Am Psychiatric.
--Biomedical Issues & Clinical Effects of Alcoholism. (Currents in Alcoholism Ser.: Vol. 5). 384p. 1979. 59.50 (ISBN 0-8089-1200-3, 793975). Grune.
--Competing Equalities: Law & the Backward Classes in India. LC 82-2017. 1984. 50.00x (ISBN 0-520-04289-1). U Pr of Cal.
Galanter, Marc, ed. Currents in Alcoholism: Psychological, Psychiatric, Sociological, Anthropological, & Epidemiological Studies, Vol. II. 506p. 1977. 65.00 (ISBN 0-8089-1008-6, 793972). Grune.
--Currents in Alcoholism: Psychological, Psychiatric, Sociological, Anthropological, & Epidemiological Topics, Vol. 4. 528p. 1978. 65.00 (ISBN 0-8089-1101-5, 793974). Grune.
--Currents in Alcoholism: Recent Advances in Research & Treatment, Vol. 8. LC 76-30552. 344p. 1981. 65.00 (ISBN 0-8089-1458-8, 793978). Grune.
--Currents in Alcoholism, Vol. 6: Treatment, Rehabilitation & Epidemiology. 400p. 1979. 54.00 (ISBN 0-8089-1201-1, 793976). Grune.
--Recent Developments in Alcholism, Vol. 2. 452p. 1984. 52.50x (ISBN 0-306-41534-8, Plenum Pr). Plenum Pub.
--Recent Developments in Alcoholism, Vol. 1. 506p. 1983. 55.00x (ISBN 0-306-41202-0, Plenum Pr). Plenum Pub.
--Recent Developments in Alcoholism, Vol. 3. 315p. 1985. 45.00x (ISBN 0-306-41852-5, Plenum Pr). Plenum Pub.
Galanti, Anthony V. & Mantell, Charles L. Polypropylene Fibers & Films. LC 65-26813. 181p. 1965. 35.00x (ISBN 0-306-30198-9, Plenum Pr). Plenum Pub.
--Polypropylene Fibers & Films. LC 65-26813. pap. 47.50 (ISBN 0-317-27902-5, 2055787). Bks Demand UMI.
Galanti, Marie. En Mouvement. 288p. 1984. 11.95 (ISBN 0-669-06367-3). Heath.
Galanti, Marie E. Lectures et Fantaisies. 1979. 13.95 (ISBN 0-395-30979-4). HM.
Galanti, Marie E., jt. auth. see Curcio, Louis L.
Galantiere, Lewis, tr. see Escholier, Raymond.
Galantiere, Lewis, tr. see Goncourt, Edmond L. & Goncourt, Jules A. De.
Galantiere, Lewis, tr. see Maritain, Jacques.
Galantiere, Lewis, tr. see Saint-Exupery, Antoine de.
Galantiere, Lewis, tr. see Saint-Exupery, Antoine De.
Galantiere, Lewis, tr. see Saint-Exupery, Antoine de.
Galarza, Ernesto. Barrio Boy. 1971. pap. 6.95 (ISBN 0-268-00441-2). U of Notre Dame Pr.
--Farm Workers & Agri-Business in California, 1947-1960. LC 76-51615. (Illus.). 1977. text ed. 24.95x (ISBN 0-268-00941-4). U of Notre Dame Pr.
--Farm Workers & Agri-Business in California, 1947-1960. LC 76-51615. 1978. pap. 9.95x (ISBN 0-268-00942-2). U of Notre Dame Pr.
--Kodachromes in Rhyme. LC 82-16140. 64p. 1983. 7.95 (ISBN 0-268-01224-5). U of Notre Dame Pr.
--Spiders in the House & Workers in the Field. LC 77-105730. (Illus.). 1970. 7.95x (ISBN 0-268-00419-6). U of Notre Dame Pr.
Galarza, Ernesto & Gallegos, Herman. Mexican Americans in the Southwest. (Illus.). 160p. pap. 4.00 (ISBN 0-686-95031-3). ADL.
Galas, Yechiel. Halacha. 192p. 1973. pap. 4.95 (ISBN 0-910818-13-4). Judaica Pr.
Galasiewicz, Z. M. Helium Four. 1971. 30.00 (ISBN 0-08-015816-1). Pergamon.
Galaskiewicz, Joseph. Social Organization of an Urban Grants Economy: A Study of Business Philanthropy & Non-Profit Organizations. Date not set. price not set (ISBN 0-12-273860-8). Acad Pr.
Galassi, J., jt. ed. see Fisketjon, G.
Galassi, John, jt. auth. see Galassi, Merna D.
Galassi, Jonathan, ed. see Montale, Eugenio.
Galassi, Jonathan, tr. see Montale, Eugenio.
Galassi, Merna D. & Galassi, John. Assert Yourself! How to Be Your Own Person. LC 76-57936. 256p. 1977. pap. 14.95 (ISBN 0-87705-299-9). Human Sci Pr.
Galassi, Peter. Before Photography. (Illus.). 1981. 22.50 (ISBN 0-87070-253-X); pap. 10.00 (ISBN 0-87070-254-8). Museum Mod Art.
Galasso, F. S. High Modulus Fibers & Composites. 126p. 1970. 45.25 (ISBN 0-677-02550-5). Gordon.
--Structure & Properties of Inorganic Solids. LC 70-104123. 1970. 50.00 (ISBN 0-08-006873-1). Pergamon.
Galasso, George J., et al, eds. Antiviral Agents & Viral Diseases of Man. 2nd ed. (Illus.). 592p. 1984. text ed. 75.00 (ISBN 0-89004-665-4). Raven.
Galatin, Malcolm & Leiter, Robert D., eds. Economics of Information. (Social Dimensions of Economics Ser.). 257p. 1981. lib. bdg. 18.00 (ISBN 0-89838-067-7). Kluwer Academic.
Galaty, Fillmore W., et al. Modern Real Estate Practice. 10th ed. LC 84-22254. (Illus.). 480p. (Orig.). 1985. pap. 29.95 (ISBN 0-88462-517-6, 1510-01, Real Estate Ed). Longman USA.
Galaty, J. G. & Aronson, D., eds. The Future of Pastoral Peoples: Proceedings of a Conference Held in Nairobi, Kenya, Aug. 4-8, 1980. 396p. 1981. pap. 25.00 (ISBN 0-88936-303-X, IDRC175, IDRC). Unipub.
Galaty, John & Bonte, Pierre. The Political Economy of African Pastoralism. 1985. 29.95 (ISBN 0-8039-2292-2). Sage.
Galaty, John & Salzman, P., eds. Change & Development in Nomadic & Pastoral Societies. (International Studies in Sociology & Social Anthropology: No. 33). 173p. 1981. pap. text ed. 24.50x (ISBN 90-04-06587-3, Pub. by E J Brill Holland). Humanities.
Galatzer, A., jt. ed. see Laron, Z.
Galavaris, George. Bread & the Liturgy: The Symbolism of Early Christian & Byzantine Bread Stamps. LC 75-98120. pap. 63.30 (ISBN 0-317-07859-3, 2015361). Bks Demand UMI.
--The Icon in the Life of the Church. (Iconography of Religions Ser.: No. 24-8). (Illus.). xv, 42p. 1981. text ed. 31.00x (ISBN 90-04-06402-8, Pub. by E J Brill Holland). Humanities.
Galaway & Hudson, Joe, eds. Perspectives on Crime Victims. LC 80-19922. (Illus.). 435p. 1980. pap. 21.95 (ISBN 0-8016-1733-2). Mosby.
Galaway, Burt, jt. auth. see Compton, Beulah.
Galaway, Burt, jt. ed. see Hudson, Joe.
Galaway, Burt, et al, eds. Community Corrections: A Reader. (Illus.). 324p. 1976. 23.50x (ISBN 0-398-03533-4). C C Thomas.
Galaway, Burton, jt. auth. see Hudson, Joe.
Galba, Marti J. de see Martorell, Joanot & De Galba, Marti J.
Galbert. The Murder of Charles the Good. Ross, James B., ed. (Medieval Academy Reprints for Teaching Ser.). 364p. 1982. pap. 9.95 (ISBN 0-8020-6479-5). U of Toronto Pr.
Galbiati, Fernando. P'eng P'ai & the Hai-Lu-Feng Soviet. LC 83-40084. 496p. 1985. 45.00x (ISBN 0-8047-1219-0). Stanford U Pr.
Galbis, Ignacio. Como el eco de un Silencio. LC 83-51277. (Senda Poetica Ser.). (Illus.). 111p. (Orig., Span.). 1984. pap. 6.95 (ISBN 0-918454-41-7). Senda Nueva.
Galbis, Ignacio R. De Mio Cid A Alfonso Reyes: Perspectivas Criticas. LC 80-53519. (Senda de Estudios y Ensayos). 139p. (Orig., Span.). 1981. pap. 9.95 (ISBN 0-918454-22-0). Senda Nueva.
--Trece Relatos Sombrios. LC 79-64142. (Senda Narrativa Ser.). (Orig., Span.). 1979. pap. 4.95 (ISBN 0-918454-14-X). Senda Nueva.
Galbraith. Basic Eye Surgery: A Manual for Surgeons in Developing Countries. (Medicine in the Tropics Ser.). (Illus.). 1979. pap. text ed. 15.00 (ISBN 0-443-01870-7). Churchill.
--A Field Guide to the Wild Flowers of South-East Australia. 39.95 (ISBN 0-00-219246-2, Collins Pub England). Greene.
Galbraith, ed. An Outline for the Young Rider. (gr. 7 up). 13.50 (ISBN 0-392-04103-0, SpS). Sportshelf.
Galbraith, Catherine A. & Mehta, Rama. India Now & Through Time. 160p. (gr. 6 up). 1980. 13.95 (ISBN 0-395-29207-7). HM.
Galbraith, D & Wilson, D. Biological Science: Principles & Patterns of Life. 3rd ed. 1978. text ed. 13.00 (ISBN 0-03-922202-0, Pub. by HR&W Canada). HR&W.
Galbraith, Den. Turbulent Taos. rev. ed. LC 83-9290. (Illus.). 48p. 1983. pap. 4.95 (ISBN 0-86534-038-2). Sunstone Pr.
Galbraith, Ian A. & Cornell, Stephen. Electronic Mail: A Revolution in Business Communications. 141p. Date not set. pap. 32.95 (ISBN 0-471-81861-5). Wiley.
Galbraith, Ian A., jt. auth. see Connell, Stephen.
Galbraith, J. K., ed. see United States National Resources Planning Board, Public Works Committee.
Galbraith, J. S. Mackinnon & East Africa, 1878-1895: A Study in the New Imperialism. LC 70-168895. (Commonwealth Ser.). (Illus.). 250p. 1972. 37.50 (ISBN 0-521-08344-3). Cambridge U Pr.
Galbraith, James D. & Galbraith, Susan S. Hartland: Change in the Heart of America. Lavey, Kathleen, ed. (Illus.). 200p. 1985. text ed. 25.00x (ISBN 0-9614844-0-3). Galbraith-Scott.
Galbraith, James M. The Money Tree: How You Can Harvest the Fruits of Free Enterprise. LC 81-71603. 176p. 1982. 12.95 (ISBN 0-942246-00-4). Benchmark Inc.
Galbraith, Jay. Designing Complex Organizations. LC 72-11887. 1973. pap. text ed. 10.50 (ISBN 0-201-02559-0). Addison-Wesley.
--Organization Design. LC 76-10421. (Illus.). 1977. text ed. 33.95 (ISBN 0-201-02558-2). Addison-Wesley.
Galbraith, Jay R. & Nathanson, Daniel A. Strategy Implementation: The Role of Structure & Process. (West Ser. in Business Policy & Planning). (Illus.). 1978. pap. text ed. 16.95 (ISBN 0-8299-0214-7). West Pub.
Galbraith, Jean. Collins Field Guide to the Wild Flowers of South-East Australia. (Illus.). 450p. 1982. 13.95x (ISBN 0-00-219246-2, Pub. by W Collins Australia). Intl Spec Bk.
Galbraith, John K. The Affluent Society. 3rd rev. ed. 1976. 15.95 (ISBN 0-395-24375-0). HM.
--Affluent Society. rev. ed. 1985. pap. 4.95 (ISBN 0-451-62394-0, ME2186, Ment). NAL.
--The Affluent Society. 4th ed. 1984. 18.95 (ISBN 0-395-36613-5). HM.
--The Age of Uncertainty. 1977. 17.95 (ISBN 0-395-24900-7); pap. 9.95 (ISBN 0-395-25947-9). HM.
--American Capitalism. pap. 3.25 (ISBN 0-395-08367-2, 18, SenEd). HM.
--American Capitalism: The Concept of Countervailing Power. LC 80-65363. 222p. 1980. 30.00 (ISBN 0-87332-178-2). M E Sharpe.
--The Anatomy of Power. 224p. 1983. 15.95 (ISBN 0-395-34400-X). HM.
--The Anatomy of Power. 1985. pap. 7.95 (ISBN 0-317-17517-3). HM.
--Annals of an Abiding Liberal. 1979. 12.95 (ISBN 0-395-27617-9). HM.
--Economic Development. LC 64-18762. 1964. 7.95x (ISBN 0-674-22701-8). Harvard U Pr.
--Economics & the Public Purpose. 1973. 18.95 (ISBN 0-395-17206-3). HM.
--Economics & the Public Purpose. 1980. pap. 3.95 (ISBN 0-451-62276-6, ME2276, Ment). NAL.
--Economics, Peace & Laughter. 1971. 7.95 (ISBN 0-395-12095-0). HM.
--Economics, Peace, & Laughter. 1981. pap. 7.95 (ISBN 0-452-00567-1, F567, Mer). NAL.
--The Great Crash, Nineteen Twenty-Nine. 50th Anniv. ed. 1979. 11.95 (ISBN 0-395-28420-1). HM.
--The Great Crash of Nineteen Twenty-Nine. 1980. pap. 3.50 (ISBN 0-380-50799-4, 63842-8, Discus). Avon.
--A Life in Our Times. 1982. pap. 8.95 (ISBN 0-345-30323-7). Ballantine.
--A Life in Our Times: Memoirs. 576p. 1981. 16.95 (ISBN 0-395-30509-8); spec. ed. 50.00 (ISBN 0-395-31135-7). HM.
--The Nature of Mass Poverty. LC 78-11839. 1979. 8.95 (ISBN 0-674-60533-0); pap. 3.95 (ISBN 0-674-60535-7). Harvard U Pr.
--The New Industrial State. 3rd, rev. ed. 1979. pap. 3.95 (ISBN 0-451-62029-1, ME2029, Ment). NAL.
--The New Industrial State. 4th ed. 480p. 1985. 19.95 (ISBN 0-395-38991-7). HM.
--The Scotch. 2nd ed. 176p. 1985. 14.95 (ISBN 0-395-39382-5). HM.
--A Theory of Price Control: The Classic Account. 1952. text ed. 7.95x (ISBN 0-674-88170-2); pap. 3.95 (ISBN 0-674-88175-3). Harvard U Pr.
--The Triumph. 1984. pap. 7.95 (ISBN 0-87795-607-3). Arbor Hse.
--The Voice of the Poor: Essays in Economic & Political Persuasion. 96p. 1983. 8.95 (ISBN 0-674-94295-7). Harvard U Pr.
Galbraith, John K. & Griffith, Luther G. Perspectives on Conservation: Essays on America's Natural Resources. Jarrett, Henry, ed. pap. 68.00 (ISBN 0-317-26465-6, 2023801). Bks Demand UMI.
Galbraith, John K., et al. National Priorities. 1969. 10.00 (ISBN 0-8183-0183-X). Pub Aff Pr.
Galbraith, John Kenneth. Annals of an Abiding Liberal. 1980. pap. 5.95 (ISBN 0-452-00544-2, F544, Mer). NAL.
--The Galbraith Reader. LC 75-19930. 1977. 12.95 (ISBN 0-87645-091-5, Pub. by Gambit). Harvard Common Pr.
--The Voice of the Poor: Essays in Economic & Political Persuasion. 96p. 1984. pap. 3.95 (ISBN 0-674-94296-5). Harvard U Pr.
Galbraith, John Kenneth & McCracken, Paul W. Reaganomics: Meaning, Means & Ends. LC 83-48640. (Charles E. Moskowitz Memorial Lecture Ser.: Vol. XXIV). 12.95 (ISBN 0-02-922890-5). Free Pr.
Galbraith, John S. Crown & Charter: The Early Years of the British South Africa Company. LC 73-93050. (Perspectives on Southern Africa Ser.). 1974. 31.00x (ISBN 0-520-02693-4). U of Cal Pr.
--The Hudson's Bay Company As an Imperial Factory. 1977. 37.50x (ISBN 0-374-92974-2). Octagon.
--Reluctant Empire: British Policy on the South African Frontier, 1834-1854. LC 77-26179. 1978. Repr. of 1963 ed. lib. bdg. 26.00x (ISBN 0-313-20087-4, GARE). Greenwood.
Galbraith, Judy. The Gifted Kids Survival Guide: (For Ages Ten & Under) LC 83-83015. (Illus.). 72p. (Orig.). (gr. k-5). 1984. pap. 6.95 (ISBN 0-915793-00-8). Free Spirit Pub Co.
--The Gifted Kids Survival Guide (for ages 11-18) LC 84-80997. (Illus.). 144p. (Orig.). (gr. 5-12). 1983. pap. 7.95 (ISBN 0-915793-01-6). Free Spirit Pub Co.
Galbraith, Judy & Schmitz, Connie C. Managing the Social & Emotional Needs of Gifted Youth: A Teacher's Survival Guide. (Illus.). 144p. (Orig.). 1985. tchr's. ed. 9.95 (ISBN 0-915793-05-9). Free Spirit Pub Co.
Galbraith, Judy, ed. see Wetherall, Charles F.
Galbraith, Kathryn O. Come Spring. LC 79-12311. 216p. (gr. 4-7). 1979. 8.95 (ISBN 0-689-50142-0, McElderry Bk). Atheneum.
--Katie Did. LC 82-3981. (Illus.). 32p. (ps-2). 1982. 9.95 (ISBN 0-689-50237-0, McElderry Bk). Atheneum.
--Something Suspicious. LC 85-4003. 168p. (gr. 3-7). 1985. 11.95 (ISBN 0-689-50322-9, McElderry Bk). Atheneum.
Galbraith, Oliver, ed. see Metcalf, Wendell O.
Galbraith, Richard. Professional Programming Techniques: Starting with the BASICs. (Illus.). 308p. 1982. 17.95 (ISBN 0-8306-2428-7); pap. 10.95 (ISBN 0-8306-0128-7, 1428). TAB Bks.
Galbraith, Robert & Boehler, Ted. Subtidal Marine Biology of California. LC 74-11235. (Illus.). 128p. (Orig.). 1974. 11.95 (ISBN 0-87961-027-1); pap. 5.95 (ISBN 0-87961-026-3). Naturegraph.
Galbraith, Robert M. Immunological In Diabetes Mellitus. 96p. 1979. 34.95 (ISBN 0-8493-5365-3). CRC Pr.
Galbraith, Ronald E. & Jones, Thomas M. Moral Reasoning: A Teaching Handbook for Adapting Kohlberg to the Classroom. (Illus.). 1976. lib. bdg. 14.95 (ISBN 0-912616-23-7); pap. 8.95 (ISBN 0-912616-22-9). Greenhaven.
Galbraith, Susan S., jt. auth. see Galbraith, James D.

Galbraith, V. H. Kings & Chroniclers: Essays in English Medieval History. (No. 4). 368p. 1982. 30.00 (ISBN 0-9506882-4-X). Hambledon Press.

Galbraith, V. H., ed. The Anonimalle Chronicle, 1333-1381. 1927. 22.00 (ISBN 0-7190-0398-9, Pub. by Manchester Univ Pr). Longwood Pub Group.

Galbraith, V. H. & Tait, James, eds. The Hereford Domesday (Circa 1160-1170) Reproduced by Collotype from Facsimile Photographs of Balliol College Ms. 350. (Pipe Roll Society, London, Ser.: No. 2, Vol. 25). Repr. of 1950 ed. 36.00 (ISBN 0-317-16412-0). Kraus Repr.

Galbraith, Vivian H. Domesday Book: Its Place in Administrative History. 1974. 34.95x (ISBN 0-19-822424-9). Oxford U Pr.

--Historical Research in Medieval England. 1977. lib. bdg. 59.95 (ISBN 0-8490-1961-3). Gordon Pr.

--The Making of Domesday Book. LC 80-2224. 1981. Repr. of 1961 ed. 36.50 (ISBN 0-404-18761-7). AMS Pr.

Galbraith, W. O. Colombia: A General Survey. 1976. lib. bdg. 59.95 (ISBN 0-8490-1643-6). Gordon Pr.

Galbreath, Edwin C. A New Extinct Emydid Turtle from the Lower Pliocene of Oklahoma. (Museum Ser.: Vol. 1, No. 16). 16p. 1948. 1.25 (ISBN 0-317-04796-5). U of Ks Mus Nat Hist.

--A New Species of Heteromyid Rodent from the Middle Oligocene of Northeast Colorado with Remarks of the Skull. (Museum Ser.: Vol. 1, No. 18). 16p. 1948. 1.25 (ISBN 0-317-04800-7). U of Ks Mus Nat Hist.

--Pliocene & Pleistocene Records of Fossil from Western Kansas & Oklahoma. (Museum Ser.: Vol. 1, no. 17). 4p. 1948. 1.25 (ISBN 0-317-04798-1). U of KS Mus Nat Hist.

Galbreath, Naomi. The Story of Passover for Children. (Illus.). 32p. (gr. k-6). pap. 2.95 (ISBN 0-8249-8084-0). Ideals.

Galchutt, Kathy, ed. see Bench, Carson E.

Galchutt, Kathy, ed. see Bench, Carson E. & Carpenter, Maryann.

Galda, Lee & Pellegrini, Anthony. Play, Language & Stories. 288p. 1986. text ed. 32.50 (ISBN 0-89391-292-1). Ablex Pub.

Galde, Dorothy. You Write the Ticket, Lord. 144p. 1983. pap. 5.95 (ISBN 0-89840-047-3). Heres Life.

Galde, Phyllis J., ed. see Stein, Diane.

Galdi, Albert P. Diagnosis & Management of Muscle Disease. LC 84-11708. (Neurologic Illness: Diagnosis & Treatment Ser.). (Illus.). 256p. 1984. text ed. 30.00 (ISBN 0-89335-205-5). SP Med & Sci Bks.

Galdier-Wilcox, Sandra & Sutton, Marilyn, eds. Understanding Death & Dying: An Interdisciplinary Approach. 3rd. ed. 428p. 1984. pap. text ed. 14.95 (ISBN 0-87484-718-4). Mayfield Pub.

Galdon, Joseph A. Typology & Seventeenth-Century Literature. (De Proprietatibus Litterarum Series: Major 28). 164p. 1975. text ed. 22.40x (ISBN 90-2793-366-9). Mouton.

Galdon, Joseph A., ed. Essays on the Philippine Novel in English. 168p. 1980. 16.00x (ISBN 0-686-28638-3); pap. 6.75x (ISBN 0-686-28639-1). Cellar.

Galdone, Joanna. The Little Girl & the Big Bear. (Illus.). 40p. (ps-3). 1980. 8.95 (ISBN 0-395-29029-5, Clarion). HM.

--The Tailypo. LC 77-23289. (ps-4). 1977. 8.95 (ISBN 0-395-28809-6, Clarion). HM.

--The Tailypo. LC 77-23289. (Illus.). 32p. (ps-3). 1984. pap. 4.95 (ISBN 0-395-30084-3, Clarion). HM.

Galdone, P., jt. auth. see Armour, Richard.

Galdone, P., illus. Hansel & Gretel. 40p. (gr. 4-6). 1982. 11.95 (ISBN 0-07-022727-6). McGraw.

Galdone, Paul. The Amazing Pig. LC 80-16990. (Illus.). 32p. (ps-3). 1981. 8.95 (ISBN 0-395-29101-1, Clarion). HM.

--Cat Goes Fiddle-i-Fee. LC 85-2686. (Illus.). (ps-2). 1985. 12.95 (ISBN 0-89919-336-6, Clarion). HM.

--Cinderella. (Illus.). (gr. k-3). 1978. 12.95 (ISBN 0-07-022684-9). McGraw.

--The Elves & the Shoemaker. LC 83-14979. (Illus.). 32p. (ps-3). 1984. PLB 11.95 (ISBN 0-89919-226-2, Clarion). HM.

--The Gingerbread Boy. (Illus.). 40p. (gr. 3). 1983. pap. 3.95 (ISBN 0-89919-163-0, Clarion). HM.

--The Greedy Old Fat Man. LC 83-2057. (Illus.). 32p. (ps-3). 1983. 10.95 (ISBN 0-89919-188-6, Clarion). HM.

--Hare & the Tortoise. (Illus.). (gr. k-3). 1962. PLB 12.95 (ISBN 0-07-022713-6). McGraw.

--Henny Penny. LC 68-24735. (Illus.). 32p. (ps-2). 1968. 12.95 (ISBN 0-395-28800-2, Clarion). HM.

--Henny Penny. LC 68-24735. (Illus.). 32p. (ps-3). 1984. pap. 4.95 (ISBN 0-89919-225-4, Clarion). HM.

--Horse, the Fox, & the Lion. LC 68-14085. (Illus.). (ps-3). 1968. 9.95 (ISBN 0-395-28802-9, Clarion). HM.

--Jack & the Beanstalk. (Illus.). 32p. (ps-3). 1982. pap. 3.45 (ISBN 0-89919-085-5, Clarion). HM.

--King of the Cats. LC 79-16659. (Illus.). 32p. (ps-3). 1980. 9.95 (ISBN 0-395-29030-9, Clarion). HM.

--King of the Cats. LC 79-16659. (Illus.). 32p. (ps-3). 1985. pap. 4.95 (ISBN 0-89919-400-1, Clarion). HM.

--The Little Red Hen. LC 72-97770. (Illus.). 32p. (ps-2). 1973. 9.95 (ISBN 0-395-28803-7, Clarion). HM.

--The Little Red Hen. (Illus.). 48p. (ps-3). 1985. pap. 4.95 (ISBN 0-89919-349-8, Clarion). HM.

--Little Tuppen. LC 67-10364. (Illus.). 32p. (ps-3). 1967. 7.95 (ISBN 0-395-28804-5, Clarion). HM.

--The Magic Porridge Pot. LC 76-3531. (Illus.). 32p. (ps-3). 1976. 7.95 (ISBN 0-395-28805-3, Clarion). HM.

--Monkey & The Crocodile. LC 78-79939. (Illus.). 32p. (ps-3). 1969. 13.95 (ISBN 0-395-28806-1, Clarion). HM.

--The Monster & the Tailor. (Illus.). 32p. (ps-3). 1982. 11.50 (ISBN 0-89919-116-9, Clarion). HM.

--Puss in Boots. LC 75-25505. (Illus.). 32p. (ps-4). 1976. 7.95 (ISBN 0-395-28808-8, Clarion). HM.

--Puss in Boots. LC 75-25505. 32p. (gr. k-3). 1983. pap. 3.95 (ISBN 0-89919-192-4, Clarion). HM.

--Rumpelstiltskin. LC 84-12741. (Illus.). 32p. (ps-3). 1985. pap. 13.95 (ISBN 0-89919-266-1, Clarion). HM.

--The Teeny-Tiny Woman. LC 84-4311. (Illus.). 32p. (ps-3). 1984. PLB 11.95 (ISBN 0-89919-270-X, Clarion). HM.

--Three Aesop Fox Fables. LC 79-133061. (Illus.). 32p. (ps-2). 1971. 10.95 (ISBN 0-395-28810-X, Clarion). HM.

--The Three Bears. (Illus.). (gr. k-3). 1973. pap. 1.95 (ISBN 0-590-11820-X). Scholastic Inc.

--The Three Bears. LC 78-158833. (Illus.). 32p. (ps-3). 1985. pap. 4.95 (ISBN 0-89919-401-X, Clarion). HM.

--The Three Billy Goats Gruff. (Illus.). 32p. (ps-3). 1981. pap. 3.45 (ISBN 0-89919-035-9, Clarion). HM.

--Three Little Pigs. LC 75-123456. (Illus.). (ps-3). 1970. 9.95 (ISBN 0-395-28813-4, Clarion). HM.

--The Three Little Pigs. LC 75-123456. (Illus.). 40p. (Orig.). (ps-3). 1984. pap. 3.95 (ISBN 0-89919-275-0, Clarion). HM.

--The Three Sillies. LC 80-22197. (Illus.). 40p. (ps-3). 1981. 9.95 (ISBN 0-395-30172-6, Clarion). HM.

--The Turtle & the Monkey. (Illus.). 32p. (ps-3). 1982. 11.95 (ISBN 0-89919-145-2, Clarion). HM.

--What's in Fox's Sack. (Illus.). 32p. (ps-1). 1982. 9.95 (ISBN 0-89919-062-6, Clarion). HM.

Galdone, Paul, jt. auth. see Titus, E.

Galdone, Paul, jt. auth. see Titus, Eve.

Galdone, Paul, retold by. & illus. The Gingerbread Boy. LC 74-11461. 40p. (ps-3). 1975. 11.95 (ISBN 0-395-28799-5, Clarion). HM.

--Hans in Luck. LC 79-16154. (Illus.). 48p. (ps-3). 1980. 5.95 (ISBN 0-8193-1011-5); PLB 5.95 (ISBN 0-8193-1012-3). Parents.

Galdone, Paul, ed. & illus. The Three Bears. LC 78-158833. (Illus.). 32p. (ps-3). 1972. 10.95 (ISBN 0-395-28811-8, Clarion). HM.

Galdone, Paul, retold by. & illus. The Three Billy Goats Gruff. LC 72-85338. (Illus.). 32p. (ps-3). 1973. 11.95 (ISBN 0-395-28812-6, Clarion). HM.

Galdone, Paul, illus. History of Mother Twaddle & the Marvelous Achievements of Her Son Jack. LC 73-9726. (Illus.). (ps-2). 1974. 7.95 (ISBN 0-395-28801-0, Clarion). HM.

--Little Red Riding Hood. LC 74-6426. (Illus.). 32p. (gr. k-3). 1974. o. p. 14.95 (ISBN 0-07-022731-4); PLB 14.95 (ISBN 0-07-022732-2). McGraw.

Galdos, B. Perez. Dona Perfecta. Serrano, Mary J., tr. 1979. Repr. of 1895 ed. lib. bdg. 30.00 (ISBN 0-8495-2005-3). Arden Lib.

Galdos, B. Perez, tr. see Lester, Helen W.

Galdos, Benita Perez see Perez Galdos, Benito.

Galdos, Benito. Gloria: Novela de Costumbres. Krappe, Alexander H., ed. (Span.). 1972. 14.50x (ISBN 0-89197-633-7); pap. text ed. 5.95x (ISBN 0-89197-514-4). Irvington.

Galdos, Benito P. Los Articulos Politicos en la Revista de Espana, 1871-1872. Dendle, Brian J. & Schraibman, Joseph, eds. xii, 159p. (Orig.). 1982. 9.75 (ISBN 0-9608168-0-1). Dendle & Schraibman.

--The Shadow. Austin, Karen O., tr. from Sp. LC 80-10549. Orig. Title: La Sombra. xiv, 58p. 1980. 10.95x (ISBN 0-8214-0553-5, 82-83467). Ohio U Pr.

--The Spendthrifts. 1978. Repr. of 1952 ed. lib. bdg. 30.00 (ISBN 0-8495-1919-5). Arden Lib.

--Tristana. (Easy Readers, Ser. B). 96p. (Span.). 1976. pap. text ed. 4.25 (ISBN 0-88436-279-5, 70269). EMC.

Galdos, Benito Perez. Miau. Gullon, Ricardo, ed. (Biblioteca De Cultura Basica Ser.). pap. 5.00 (ISBN 0-8477-0711-3). U of PR Pr.

Galdos, Benito Perez see Perez Galdos, Benito.

Galdston, Iago. Progress in Medicine. LC 76-39166. (Essay Index Reprint Ser.). 1940. 21.50 (ISBN 0-8369-2689-7). Ayer Co Pubs.

Galdston, Iago, ed. The Impact of Antibiotics on Medicine & Society. 1969. pap. text ed. 9.95 (ISBN 0-8236-8080-0, 22540). Intl Univs Pr.

--Man's Image in Medicine & Anthropology. LC 63-19871. (Institute of Social & Historical Medicine Monographs: No. 4). 525p. 1963. text ed. 40.00 (ISBN 0-8236-3120-6). Intl Univs Pr.

--Medicine & Mankind. facs. ed. LC 70-142632. (Essay Index Reprint Ser). 1936. 17.00 (ISBN 0-8369-2108-9). Ayer Co Pubs.

--Medicine & the Other Disciplines. LC 59-15725. 1960. text ed. 18.50 (ISBN 0-8236-3300-4). Intl Univs Pr.

Galdston, Iago, ed. see New York Academy Of Medicine.

Galdston, Iago, ed. see New York Academy of Medicine.

Galdston, Olive. Play with Puppets. rev. ed. (Illus.). 52p. (Orig.). 1971. pap. 1.50x (ISBN 0-686-01100-7); pap. text ed. 1.50x (ISBN 0-936426-07-1). Play Schs.

Gale, A., jt. auth. see Chapman, A.

Gale, A. G. & Johnson, E., eds. Theoretical & Applied Aspects of Eye Movement Research: Proceedings of the European Conference on Eye Movements, 2nd, Nottingham, UK, 19-23 Sept. 1983. (Advances in Psychology Ser.: Vol. 22). 566p. 1984. 68.75 (ISBN 0-444-87557-3, North Holland). Elsevier.

Gale, Adela. Harvest of Terror. 1978. pap. 1.50 (ISBN 0-8439-0529-8, Leisure Bks). Dorchester Pub Co.

Gale, Alice T., jt. auth. see Mancini, Marguerite R.

Gale, Anthony & Chapman, Antony J. Psychology & Social Problems: An Introduction to Applied Psychology. LC 83-16728. 374p. 1984. 37.95x (ISBN 0-471-90313-2, Pub. by Wiley-Interscience). Wiley.

Gale, Anthony, ed. Physiological Correlates of Human Behaviour, Vol. 1. Edwards, John A. 1983. Vol. 1. 39.50 (ISBN 0-12-273901-9); Vol. 2. 39.50 (ISBN 0-12-273902-7); Vol. 3, 1984. 49.50 (ISBN 0-12-273903-5). Acad Pr.

Gale, Barbara, jt. auth. see Wechsler, Henry.

Gale, Barry & Gale, Linda. Discover What You're Best At: The National Career Aptitude Test. (Orig.). 1982. pap. 9.95 (ISBN 0-671-41754-1). S&S.

--Discover Your High-Tech Talents. 1984. 16.95 (ISBN 0-671-49968-8); pap. 8.95 (ISBN 0-671-50740-0). S&S.

Gale, Barry G. Evolution Without Evidence: Charles Darwin & The Origin of Species. 256p. 1982. 21.95 (ISBN 0-8263-0609-8, E-31). U of NM Pr.

Gale, Bill. The Wonderful World of Walking. 319p. 5.95 (ISBN 0-318-15698-9). Natl Health Fed.

Gale, Bob, jt. auth. see Zemeckis, Robert.

Gale, Cedric. Building an Effective Vocabulary. LC 79-1496. (Orig.). 1979. pap. 5.50 (ISBN 0-8120-2041-3); answer bklet, 1 for every 25 ordered avail. (ISBN 0-8120-2167-3). Barron.

Gale, Cedric, jt. auth. see Hopper, Vincent F.

Gale, Cedric, rev. by see Fernald, James.

Gale, Christopher, et al. Cases in International Marketing. (Illus.). 448p. 1986. pap. text ed. 22.95 (ISBN 0-13-118860-7). P-H.

Gale, Clarice W., jt. auth. see Gale, Frank C.

Gale, D. & Moone, Eric. The Manipulated City. 366p. 1980. 10.95 (ISBN 0-416-60111-1, NO. 2863). Methuen Inc.

Gale, David. Theory of Linear Economic Models. 1960. 39.95 (ISBN 0-07-022728-4). McGraw.

Gale, Dennis E. Neighborhood Revitalization & the Postindustrial City: A Multinational Perspective. LC 83-47523. (The Politics of Planning Ser.). 208p. 1984. 22.00x (ISBN 0-669-06697-4). Lexington Bks.

Gale, Douglas. Money: In Disequilibrium. (Economic Handbooks). 368p. 1984. 39.50 (ISBN 0-521-26291-7); pap. 14.95 (ISBN 0-521-26917-2). Cambridge U Pr.

--Money: In Equilibrium. (Cambridge Economic Handbooks). 364p. 1982. 44.50 (ISBN 0-521-24694-6); pap. 16.95 (ISBN 0-521-28900-9). Cambridge U Pr.

Gale, E. F., et al. The Molecular Basis of Antibiotic Action. 2nd ed. LC 80-41380. 672p. 1981. 104.00 (ISBN 0-471-27915-3, Pub. by Wiley-Interscience). Wiley.

Gale, Elizabeth W. Children Together, Vol. 2. 128p. 1982. pap. 11.95 (ISBN 0-8170-0974-4). Judson.

Gale, F. & Wundersitz, J. Adelaide Aborigines. LC 82-73141. (Aboriginal Component in the Australian Economy Ser.: No. 4). 191p. 1982. pap. text ed. 19.95 (ISBN 0-909150-81-8, 1602, Pub. by ANUP Australia). Australia N U P.

Gale, Fay, ed. We Are Bosses Ourselves. (Aias Ser.: No. 41). 175p. 1983. 21.00x (ISBN 0-85575-138-X, Pub. by Australian Inst Australia); pap. text ed. 13.50x (ISBN 0-85575-139-8). Humanities.

Gale, Frank C. & Gale, Clarice W. Experiences with Plants for Young Children. LC 78-88376. (Illus.). 1975. 8.95x (ISBN 0-87015-211-4). Pacific Bks.

Gale, Frederick. Mortuary Science. (Illus.). 240p. 1960. photocopy ed. 17.75x (ISBN 0-398-04166-0). C C Thomas.

Gale, George. Theory of Science. (Illus.). 1979. text ed. 28.95 (ISBN 0-07-022680-6). McGraw.

--Upper Mississippi: Or, Historical Sketches of the Mound-Builder, the Indian Tribes, & the Progress of Civilization in the North-West. 1975. Repr. of 1867 ed. 24.00 (ISBN 0-527-03220-4). Kraus Repr.

Gale, Harold, jt. ed. see Bradbeer, Robin.

Gale, J. S. Population Genetics. LC 80-12675. (Tertiary Level Biology Ser.). 189p. 1980. 58.95x (ISBN 0-470-26970-7); pap. text ed. 34.95x (ISBN 0-470-26969-3). Halsted Pr.

Gale, Jack. How About a Career in Real Estate? 34p. (Orig.). 1979. pap. 1.95 (ISBN 0-88462-374-2, 1977-01, Real Estate Ed). Longman USA.

--The Lebanon Time-Bomb. 50p. 1982. 20.00x (ISBN 0-902030-95-7, Pub by New Park Pubns England). State Mutual Bk.

Gale, Jack L. Commercial Investment Brokerage: An Introduction with Case Studies. LC 79-67428. 296p. 1979. pap. 18.95 (ISBN 0-913652-19-9). Realtors Natl.

--Thirty Keys to Success in Real Estate. Allen, Pat, ed. LC 81-10746. 88p. (Orig.). 1981. 5.95 (ISBN 0-913652-29-6, 151). Realtors Natl.

Gale, James S., tr. see Bang, Im & Ryuk, Yi.

Gale, Janet & Marsden, Philip. Medical Diagnosis: From Student to Clinician. (Illus.). 1983. 35.00x (ISBN 0-19-261433-9). Oxford U Pr.

Gale, Janice & Gale, Stephen. Guide to Fairs, Festivals & Fun Events. 190p. 1981. pap. 6.95 (ISBN 0-686-75092-6). Banyan Bks.

--Guide to Fairs, Festivals & Fun Events. (Illus.). 190p. 1981. pap. 6.95 (ISBN 0-937928-00-3). Sightseer.

Gale, Jay. A Young Man's Guide to Sex. 1984. 14.95 (ISBN 0-03-069396-9). HR&W.

Gale, Ken & Odgers, Peter. Hotel & Catering Supervision. 288p. (Orig.). 1984. pap. 18.95x (ISBN 0-7121-0824-6). Trans-Atlantic.

Gale, Linda, jt. auth. see Gale, Barry.

Gale, R. M., ed. Philosophy of Time: A Collection of Essays. 1978. text ed. 15.50x (ISBN 0-391-00895-1); pap. text ed. 13.45x (ISBN 0-391-00896-X). Humanities.

Gale, R. P. & Opelz, Gerhard, eds. Immunobiology of Bone Marrow Transplantation, Vol. 2. (Transplantation Proceedings Ser.). 288p. 1978. 62.00 (ISBN 0-8089-1116-3, 791485). Grune.

Gale, Raymond F. Explorations into Humanness. 1977. 6.95 (ISBN 0-8158-0346-X). Chris Mass.

Gale Research Co. Library of Congress & National Union Catalogue Author Lists, 1942-1962: A Master Cummulation, 152 vols. LC 73-82135. 1969. Set. 3250.00x (ISBN 0-8103-0950-5); fiche only 1650.00x (ISBN 0-686-85981-2); U.S. vols. only 140.00x (ISBN 0-8103-0951-3). Gale.

Gale Research Company, jt. auth. see United States. Nautical Almanac Office.

Gale, Roberson G., jt. auth. see Smith, Len Young.

Gale, Robert J., jt. ed. see Lovering, David G.

Gale, Robert L. Barron's Simplified Approach to Emerson & Transcendentalism. LC 65-27505. (Orig.). (YA) 1966. pap. text ed. 1.95 (ISBN 0-8120-0246-6). Barron.

--Barron's Simplified Approach to Steinbeck's The Grapes of Wrath. LC 66-23062. (Orig.). (gr. 11 up). 1967. pap. text ed. 1.95 (ISBN 0-8120-0247-4). Barron.

--Barron's Simplified Approach to Wharton's Ethan Frome. LC 79-75837. (gr. 11 up). 1969. pap. text ed. 1.95 (ISBN 0-8120-0377-2). Barron.

--Charles Marion Russell. LC 79-53651. (Western Writers Ser.: No. 38). (Illus.). 48p. 1979. pap. 2.00x (ISBN 0-88430-062-5). Boise St Univ.

--Charles Warren Stoddard. LC 77-76320. (Western Writers Ser.: No. 30). (Illus.). 1977. pap. 2.00x (ISBN 0-88430-054-4). Boise St Univ.

--Luke Short. (United States Authors Ser.). 1981. 12.50 (ISBN 0-8057-7307-X, Twayne). G K Hall.

--Plots & Characters in the Works of Mark Twain, 2 vols. (Plots & Characters Ser.). xxiii, 191p. 1973. Set. 42.50 (ISBN 0-208-01242-7, Archon). Shoe String.

--Plots & Characters-Melville. 300p. 1972. pap. 2.95x (ISBN 0-262-57032-7). MIT Pr.

--Richard Henry Dana. LC 68-24301. (United States Authors Ser.: No. 143). 1969. lib. bdg. 13.50 (ISBN 0-8057-0184-2, Twayne). G K Hall.

--Will Henry-Clay Fisher. LC 82-71032. (Western Writer's Ser.: No. 52). (Illus., Orig.). 1982. pap. 2.00x (ISBN 0-88430-026-9). Boise St Univ.

--Will Henry-Clay Fisher (Henry W. Allen) (United States Author Ser.: No. 466). 170p. 1984. lib. bdg. 15.95 (ISBN 0-8057-7407-6, Twayne). G K Hall.

Gale, Robert P. Recent Advances in Bone Marrow Transplantation: Proceedings, Third UCLA Symposium, Park City, Utah, March 13-18, 1983. LC 83-11997. (UCLA Symposia on Molecular & Cellular Biology Ser.: Vol. 7). 932p. 1983. 98.00 (ISBN 0-8451-2606-7). A R Liss.

Gale, Robert P. & Fox, C. Fred, eds. Biology of Bone Marrow Transplantation. (ICN-UCLA Symposia on Molecular & Cellular Biology Ser.: Vol. 17). 1980. 58.50 (ISBN 0-12-273960-4). Acad Pr.

Gale, Rodney. The Natural Path to Genuine Lasting Happiness. 1976. 6.50 (ISBN 0-533-02131-6). H R Gale.

Gale, Roger W. The Americanization of Micronesia: A Study of the Consolidation of the U. S. Role in the Pacific. LC 78-68800. 1979. pap. text ed. 15.00 (ISBN 0-8191-0703-4). U Pr of Amer.

Gale, Stephen, jt. auth. see Gale, Janice.

Gale, Stephen & Olsson, Gunnar, eds. Philosophy in Geography. (Theory & Decision Library: No. 20). 1979. lib. bdg. 40.00 (ISBN 9-0277-0948-3, Pub. by Reidel Holland). Kluwer Academic.

Gale, Stephen H. Harold Pinter: An Annotated Bibliography. (Reference Publications). 1978. lib. bdg. 29.50 (ISBN 0-8161-8014-8, Hall Reference). G K Hall.

Gale, Steven H. Butter's Going up: A Critical Analysis of Harold Pinter's Work. LC 78-78833. vi, 358p. 1977. 22.50 (ISBN 0-8223-0339-6). Duke.

--Readings for Today's Writers. LC 79-21312. 1980. pap. text ed. 14.70x (ISBN 0-673-15672-9). Scott F.

--S. J. Perelman: An Annotated Bibliography. LC 84-45389. (Reference Library of the Humanities). 150p. 1985. lib. bdg. 26.00 (ISBN 0-317-18765-1). Garland Pub.

Gale, Thomas. Certaine Workes of Chirurgerie. LC 79-38108. (English Experience Ser.: No. 420). (Illus.). 200p. 1971. Repr. of 1563 ed. 74.00 (ISBN 90-221-0420-6). Walter J Johnson.

Gale, V. Several Houses. LC 74-179820. (New Poetry Ser.). Repr. of 1959 ed. 16.00 (ISBN 0-404-56020-2). AMS Pr.

Gale, Van. Job: A Mini Story in Redemption. (Orig.). 1978. pap. 3.50 (ISBN 0-89274-072-8). Harrison Hse.

Gale, Van, jt. auth. see Harrison, Buddy.

Gale, Vi. Odd Flowers & Short Eared Owls. LC 84-22886. (Illus.). slipcased ltd. ed. 35.00 (ISBN 0-915986-19-1); 20.00 (ISBN 0-915986-20-5); pap. 8.50 (ISBN 0-915986-21-3). Prescott St Pr.

Gale, Vi, ed. see Aloff, Mindy.

Gale, Vi, ed. see Cohen, Marty.

Gale, Vi, ed. see Emmons, David.

Gale, Vi, ed. see Fleming, Geranna.

Gale, Vi, ed. see Radhuber, Stanley.

Gale, Vi, ed. see Venn, George.

Gale, W. K. Ironworking. (Shire Album Ser.: No. 64). (Illus.). 32p. 1981. pap. 3.50 (ISBN 0-85263-546-X, Pub. by Shire Pubns England). Seven Hills Bks.

Gale, William. I Sat Where They Sat. pap. 2.50 (ISBN 0-686-12884-2). Schmul Pub Co.

Gale, William A., ed. Inflation: Causes, Consequents & Control. LC 81-91612. 210p. 1981. text ed. 30.00 (ISBN 0-89946-118-2). Oelgeschlager.

Gale, Zona. Miss Lulu Bett. LC 76-26895. 1976. Repr. of 1920 ed. lib. bdg. 24.75x (ISBN 0-8371-9021-5, GALB). Greenwood.

--Peace in Friendship Village. 18.00 (ISBN 0-8369-4244-2, 6055). Ayer Co Pubs.

Galeano, Eduardo. Days & Nights of Love & War. Brister, Judith, tr. from Span. LC 82-48034. 192p. 1982. 16.00 (ISBN 0-85345-620-8); pap. 8.00 (ISBN 0-85345-621-6). Monthly Rev.

--Memory of Fire: Genesis, Vol. 1. Belfrage, Cedric, tr. 289p. 1985. 18.95 (ISBN 0-318-04729-2). Pantheon.

--Open Veins of Latin America: Five Centuries of the Pillage of a Continent. Belfrage, Cedric, tr. from Span. LC 72-92036. (Illus.). 320p. 1973. pap. 8.00 (ISBN 0-85345-308-X). Monthly Rev.

Galeener, F. L., ed. see AIP International Conf., Williamsburg, 1976.

Galeev, A. A. Basic Plasma Physics I. Sudan, R. N., ed. (Handbook of Plasma Physics Ser.: Vol. 1). 730p. 1984. 163.50 (ISBN 0-444-86427-X, I-496-83, North-Holland). Elsevier.

Galeev, A. A. & Sudan, R. N., eds. Basic Plasma Physics II. (Handbook of Plasma Physics Ser.: Vol. 2). 850p. 1985. 183.50 (ISBN 0-444-86645-0, North-Holland). Elsevier.

Galef, Jack, ed. see Avery, Don.

Galef, Jack, ed. see Hooper, Patricia.

Galejs, J. Terrestrial Propagation of Long Electromagnetic Waves. 376p. 1972. 97.00 (ISBN 0-08-016710-1). Pergamon.

Galembo, Phyllis. Pale Pink. (Artists Bk.). (Illus.). 24p. (Orig.). 1983. pap. 6.00 (ISBN 0-89822-033-5). Visual Studies.

Galen. On the Natural Faculties. (Loeb Classical Library: No. 71). 12.50x (ISBN 0-674-99078-1). Harvard U Pr.

--On the Passions & Errors of the Soul. Harkins, Paul W., tr. LC 63-18104. 144p. 1964. 4.75 (ISBN 0-8142-0052-4). Ohio St U Pr.

--Three Treaties on the Nature of Science. Frede, Michael & Walzer, R., eds. 100p. 1985. lib. bdg. 15.00 (ISBN 0-915145-91-X); pap. text ed. 4.95 (ISBN 0-915145-92-8). Hackett Pub.

Galen, P. S. & Gambino, S. R. Beyond Normality: The Predictive Value & Efficiency of Medical Diagnosis. LC 75-25915. 237p. 1975. 37.50 (ISBN 0-471-29047-5, Pub. by Wiley Medical). Wiley.

Galen, Robert & Brennan, Leslie. Laboratory Diagnosis & Patient Monitoring: Clinical Chemistry. 1981. 27.95 (ISBN 0-87489-265-1). Med Economics.

Galena, J. N. Sex in Groups. 1974. pap. 1.25 (ISBN 0-685-51414-5, LB221ZK, Leisure Bks). Dorchester Pub Co.

Galeno, Joseph J. Plumbing Estimating Handbook. LC 76-57182. (Plumbing Ser.). 256p. 1976. pap. text ed. 15.00 (ISBN 0-8273-1764-6). Delmar.

Galenson, Alice. The Migration of the Cotton Textile Industry from New England to the South, 1880-1930. Bruchey, Stuart, ed. LC 84-48306. (American Economic History Ser.). 212p. 1985. lib. bdg. 30.00 (ISBN 0-8240-6654-5). Garland Pub.

--Paupa New Guinea: Selected Development Issues. 280p. 1982. 10.00 (ISBN 0-686-39670-7, RC-8201). World Bank.

Galenson, David. White Servitude in Colonial America. LC 81-7682. (Illus.). 320p. 1982. 34.50 (ISBN 0-521-23686-X). Cambridge U Pr.

--White Servitude in Colonial America: An Economic Analysis. LC 81-7682. (Illus.). 320p. 1984. pap. 9.95 (ISBN 0-521-27379-X). Cambridge U Pr.

Galenson, Eleanor, jt. auth. see Roiphe, Herman.

Galenson, Eleanor & Call, Justin D., eds. Frontiers of Infant Psychiatry. 1985 ed. LC 81-68792. Set. 75.00x (ISBN 0-465-02587-0). Basic.

--Frontiers of Infant Psychiatry, Vol. 1. LC 81-68792. 1983. 37.50x (ISBN 0-465-02585-4). Basic.

Galenson, Walter. The International Labor Organization: An American View. LC 80-52295. 372p. 1981. 27.50x (ISBN 0-299-08540-6); pap. 11.75x (ISBN 0-299-08544-9). U of Wis Pr.

--Labor Productivity in Soviet & American Industry. LC 76-49596. 1977. Repr. of 1955 ed. lib. bdg. 25.50x (ISBN 0-8371-9370-2, GALPS). Greenwood.

--Trade Union Democracy in Western Europe. LC 75-45493. 96p. 1976. Repr. of 1961 ed. lib. bdg. 22.50x (ISBN 0-8371-8752-4, GATU). Greenwood.

--The United Brotherhood of Carpenters: The First Hundred Years. (Wertheim Publications in Industrial Relations Ser.). (Illus.). 480p. 1983. text ed. 25.00x (ISBN 0-674-92196-8). Harvard U Pr.

Galenson, Walter, ed. Economic Growth & Structural Change in Taiwan: The Postwar Experience of the Republic of China. LC 78-10877. (Illus.). 512p. 1979. 39.95x (ISBN 0-8014-1157-2). Cornell U Pr.

--Foreign Trade & Investment: The Newly Industrializing Asian Countries. LC 84-40495. 512p. 1985. text ed. 30.00x (ISBN 0-299-10100-2). U of Wis Pr.

--Incomes Policy: What Can We Learn from Europe? LC 72-619695. (Pierce Ser.: No. 3). 120p. 1973. 7.50 (ISBN 0-87546-048-8). ILR Pr.

--Labor in Developing Economics. LC 76-3786. 299p. 1976. Repr. of 1962 ed. lib. bdg. 22.50x (ISBN 0-8371-8817-2, GALD). Greenwood.

Galenus. Galen's Institutio Logica. Kieffer, John S., tr. LC 64-25073. pap. 39.30 (ISBN 0-317-08964-1, 2004709). Bks Demand UMI.

Galeone, Victor. The Great Drama of Jesus: A Life of Christ for Teens. pap. 5.95 (ISBN 0-686-74586-8, 101-28). Prow Bks-Franciscan.

Galeotti, T., et al, eds. Membranes in Tumour Growth. (Developments in Cancer Research Ser.: Vol. 7). 626p. 1983. 106.50 (ISBN 0-444-80462-5, Biomedical Pr). Elsevier.

Galereia, Voennaia & Zimnego, Dvortsa. The War Gallery of the Winter Palace. 240p. 1981. 60.00x (ISBN 0-317-14332-8, Pub. by Collet's). State Mutual Bk.

Galerstein, David H. Mastering Fundamental Mathematics. (Orig.). (gr. 7). 1976. pap. text ed. 7.58 (ISBN 0-87720-226-5). AMSCO Sch.

Gales, D. V., intro. by. London Inhabitants Within the Walls, Sixteen Ninety-Five. 1966. 50.00x (ISBN 0-686-96617-1, Pub by London Rec Soc England). State Mutual Bk.

Gales, Richard L. Dwellers in Arcady: Essays in Folk-Lore. facs. ed. LC 68-8463. (Essay Index Reprint Ser). 1968. Repr. of 1931 ed. 17.00 (ISBN 0-8369-0467-2). Ayer Co Pubs.

--Studies in Arcady & Other Essays for a Country Parsonage, First Ser. LC 70-107701. (Essay Index Reprint Ser.). 1910. 24.50 (ISBN 0-8369-1502-X). Ayer Co Pubs.

--Studies in Arcady & Other Essays from a Country Parsonage, 2nd Ser. LC 70-107701. (Essay Index Reprint Ser.). 1912. 25.50 (ISBN 0-8369-1589-5). Ayer Co Pubs.

Galesloot, T. E. & Tinbergen, B. J., eds. Milk Proteins '84: Proceedings of the International Congress on Milk Proteins, Luxemburg, 7-11 May 1984. 325p. 1985. pap. 60.75 (ISBN 90-220-0860-6, PDC279, Pudoc). Unipub.

Galet, Emile J. Albert, King of the Belgians in the Great War: His Military Activities & Experiences Set Down with His Approval. 44.00 (ISBN 0-8369-7136-1, 7969). Ayer Co Pubs.

Galet, Pierre. A Practical Ampelography: Grapevine Indentification. Morton, Lucie, tr. LC 78-59631. (Illus.). 192p. 1979. 39.95x (ISBN 0-8014-1240-4). Comstock.

Galewitz, Herb, ed. see Capp, Al, et al.

Galewitz, Herb, ed. see Capp, Al & Van Buren, Raeburn.

Galewitz, Herb, ed. see Gould, Chester.

Galewitz, Herb, ed. see Hamlin, V. T.

Galfo, Armand J. Educational Research Design & Data Analysis: An Integrated Approach. (Illus.). 408p. (Orig.). 1983. lib. bdg. 31.00 (ISBN 0-8191-3392-2); pap. text ed. 17.50 (ISBN 0-8191-3393-0). U Pr of Amer.

Galford, Ellen. Moll Cutpurse: Her True History. (Illus.). 224p. 1985. 15.95 (ISBN 0-932379-05-2); pap. 7.95 (ISBN 0-932379-04-4). Firebrand Bks.

Galfridus Anglicus. Promptorium Parvulorum Sive Clericorum, Dictionarius Anglolatinus Princeps, 3 Pts. Repr. of 1865 ed. 37.00 ea. Johnson Repr.

Galfridus, Anglicus. Promptorium Parvulorum Sive Clericorum, Lexicon Anglo-Latinum Princeps, 3 Vols. LC 70-168091. (Camden Society, London. Publications, First Ser.: Nos. 25, 54, 89). (Lat.). Repr. of 1865 ed. Set. 110.00 (ISBN 0-404-50209-1); 37.00 ea. AMS Pr.

Galgan, Gerald J. The Logic of Modernity. 1982. 45.00x (ISBN 0-8147-2983-5). NYU Pr.

Galgiani, Phil. Basic Meaning in Four Parts. (Illus.). 80p. 1983. pap. 6.50 (ISBN 0-939784-05-X). CEPA Gall.

Galgoczy, Janos see Feher, Matyas & Erdy, Miklos.

Galgut, Damon. A Sinless Season. (Penguin Fiction Ser.). 1985. pap. 4.95 (ISBN 0-14-007077-X). Penguin.

Galic, C., et al, eds. Phenomenology of Unified Theories: Proceedings of the Topical Conference on Phenomenology of Unified Theories-from Standard Model to Supersymmetries, Dubrovnik, Yugoslavia May 22-28, 1983. 500p. 1984. 49.00x (ISBN 9971-966-12-3, Pub. by World Sci Singapore); pap. 21.00x (ISBN 9971-966-13-1, Pub. by World Sci Singapore). Taylor & Francis.

Galich, Alexander. Songs & Poems. Smith, Gerry, tr. from Rus. 188p. 1983. 25.00 (ISBN 0-88233-784-X). Ardis Pubs.

Galiegue, B. F. Service Management in the Retail Motor Industry in Britain. (Illus.). 160p. (Orig.). 1982. pap. 12.95 (ISBN 0-434-90650-6, Pub. by W Heinemann Ltd). David & Charles.

Galik, Marian. The Genesis of Modern Chinese Literary Criticism, 1917-1930. 349p. 1980. 21.50x (ISBN 0-8476-6081-8). Rowman.

Galil, Z., jt. ed. see Apostolico, A.

Galilea, Segundo. The Beatitudes: To Evangelize as Jesus Did. Barr, Robert R., tr. from Span. LC 83-19342. 128p. (Orig.). 1984. pap. 5.95 (ISBN 0-88344-344-9). Orbis Bks.

--Following Jesus. Phillips, Helen, tr. from Span. LC 80-24802. Orig. Title: El Seguimiento de Cristo. 128p. (Orig.). 1981. pap. 4.95 (ISBN 0-88344-136-5). Orbis Bks.

--The Future of Our Past: The Spanish Mystics Speak to Contemporary Spirituality. LC 85-71822. 96p. (Orig.). 1985. pap. 4.95 (ISBN 0-87793-296-4). Ave Maria.

Galilei, Galileo. Dialogue Concerning the Two Chief World Systems-Ptolemaic & Copernican. 2nd rev. ed. Drake, Stillman, tr. 1967. 40.00x (ISBN 0-520-00449-3); pap. 10.95x (ISBN 0-520-00450-7, CAL66). U of Cal Pr.

--Dialogues Concerning Two New Sciences. (Illus.). 1914. pap. text ed. 5.50 (ISBN 0-486-60099-8). Dover.

--Dialogues Concerning Two New Sciences. Crew, Henry & De Salvio, Alfonso, trs. (University Studies Ser.). Repr. of 1950 ed. 79.00 (ISBN 0-8357-9453-9, 2015284). Bks Demand UMI.

--Galileo Galilei: Operations of the Geometric & Military Compass. Drake, Stillman, tr. from Ital. & intro. by. LC 78-606002. (Illus.). 1978. pap. text ed. 6.95x (ISBN 0-87474-383-4). Smithsonian.

Galileo. Discoveries & Opinions of Galileo. LC 57-6305. 1957. pap. 5.50 (ISBN 0-385-09239-3, A94, Anch). Doubleday.

Galimou, K. Z., jt. auth. see Mushtari, Kh M.

Galimov, Eric M. The Biological Fractionation of Isotopes: Monograph. Vitaliano, Dorothy B., tr. 1985. 49.50 (ISBN 0-12-273970-1). Acad Pr.

Galin, D. M., et al. Sixteen Papers on Differential Equations. LC 82-20595. (AMS Translations Ser.: No. 2 vol. 118). 74.00 (ISBN 0-8218-3073-2, TRANS/2/118). Am Math.

Galin, Joseph J. Computers & the Law: A Selected Bibliography. (Public Administration Ser.: Bibliography P 1627). 1985. pap. 2.00 (ISBN 0-89028-297-8). Vance Biblios.

--Industrial Policy: A Bibliography. (Public Administration Ser.: Bibliography P 1648). 1985. pap. 2.00 (ISBN 0-89028-338-9). Vance Biblios.

--The Political Socialization of Children & Adolescents: A Bibliography. (Public Administration Ser.: Bibliography P 1653). 1985. pap. 3.00 (ISBN 0-89028-343-5). Vance Biblios.

Galina, Miguel A., jt. ed. see Acosta, Enrique V.

Galinanes, Maria T. B. De see Universidad de Puerto Rico, Centro de Investigaciones Sociales.

Galindez, Jesus de, jt. auth. see Ireland, Gordon.

Galindez, Suarez J. de see De Galindez, Suarez J.

Galindo, O. Dansk-Spansk Fagordbog. 439p. (Danish & Span.). 1979. 49.95 (ISBN 87-571-0609-6, S-39032). French & Eur.

Galindo, Sergio. La Comparsa: A Mexican Masquerade. Miller, Yvette E., ed. Brushwood, John & Brushwood, Carolyn, trs. LC 84-21826. 92p. 1984. pap. 11.50 (ISBN 0-935480-17-X). Lat Am Lit Rev Pr.

--The Precipice. Brushwood, John & Brushwood, Carolyn, trs. from Sp. (Texas Pan American Series). Orig. Title: El Bordo. (Illus.). 199p. 1969. 12.50x (ISBN 0-292-78408-2); pap. 7.95 (ISBN 0-292-76426-X). U of Tex Pr.

--Rice Powder. Patrick, Bert & Patrick, Lura L., eds. LC 78-51332. (Perivale Translation Ser: No. 5). Orig. Title: Polvos De Arroz. 43p. 1978. pap. 4.00 (ISBN 0-912288-12-4). Perivale Pr.

Galinsky, Ellen. Between Generations: The Six Stages of Parenthood. 320p. 1981. 16.95 (ISBN 0-8129-0924-0). Times Bks.

--Between Generations: The Six Stages of Parenthood. 384p. pap. 4.50 (ISBN 0-425-07566-4). Berkley Pub.

--Between Generations: The Stages of Parenthood. 384p. 1982. pap. 7.95 (ISBN 0-425-05650-3). Berkley Pub.

Galinsky, G. Karl. Ovid's Metamorphoses: An Introduction to Its Basic Aspects. LC 74-84146. 1975. 33.50x (ISBN 0-520-02848-1). U of Cal Pr.

Galinsky, Gotthard K. Aeneas, Sicily & Rome. LC 69-18059. (Princeton Monographs in Art & Archaeology: 40). pap. write for info. (2055272). Bks Demand UMI.

Galinsky, M. David, jt. auth. see Shaffer, John B.

Galipault, Joanne & Kinsman, Barbara. Solving the Computer Puzzle. Brown, Rachel, ed. (Computer Literacy Ser.). (Illus.). 64p. (gr. 1 up). 1983. pap. 6.00 (ISBN 0-88049-039-X, 7262). Milton Bradley Co.

Galis, Leon, jt. ed. see Roth, Michael D.

Galishoff, Stuart. Safeguarding the Public Health. LC 75-66. (Illus.). 191p. 1975. lib. bdg. 29.95 (ISBN 0-8371-7956-4, GPH/). Greenwood.

Galisson, R. & Coste, D., eds. Dictionnaire de Didactique des Largues. 612p. (Fr.). 1976. 22.50 (ISBN 0-686-56813-3, M-6591). French & Eur.

Galitz, Wilbert O. Handbook of Screen Format Design. LC 84-62223. 235p. (Orig.). 1985. pap. 34.50 (ISBN 0-89435-119-2, SD1192). QED Info Sci.

--Humanizing Office Automation: The Impact of Ergonomics on Productivity. LC 83-83115. 250p. 1984. pap. 34.50 (ISBN 0-89435-107-9). QED Info Sci.

--The Office Environment: Automations Impact on Tomorrow's Workplace. 1984. pap. 14.95 (ISBN 0-916875-00-8). Admin Mgmt Soc.

Galitzi, Christine A. Study of Assimilation Among the Roumanians in the United States. LC 72-76634. (Columbia University. Studies in the Social Sciences: No. 315). 1969. Repr. of 1929 ed. 21.00 (ISBN 0-404-51315-8). AMS Pr.

Galizio, Mark & Maisto, Stephen A., eds. Determinants of Substance Abuse: Biological, Psychological, & Environmental Factors. (Perspectives on Individual Differences Ser.). 454p. 1985. 42.50x (ISBN 0-306-41873-8, Plenum Pr). Plenum Pub.

Galjaard, H. Genetic Metabolic Diseases: Early Diagnosis & Prenatal Analysis. 870p. 1980. 142.75 (ISBN 0-444-80143-X, Biomedical Pr). Elsevier.

Galjaard, Hans, ed. The Future of Prenatal Diagnosis. LC 82-4484. (Illus.). 167p. 1982. text ed. 37.50 (ISBN 0-686-46474-5). Churchill.

Galkin, Alexander V., tr. see Luzikov, Valentin N.

Gall, A. Le see Le Gall, A., et al.

Gall, A. Von, ed. Der Hebraeische Pentateuch der Samaritaner, 5 pts. xciv, 440p. (Ger.). 1966. Repr. of 1918 ed. Set. 45.60x (ISBN 3-11-009258-1). De Gruyter.

Gall, C., ed. Goat Production: Breeding & Management. LC 81-66393. 1981. 80.00 (ISBN 0-12-273980-9). Acad Pr.

Gall, Dennis. Funny Judge: Milwaukee's Christ T. Seraphim. Schreiner, David & Kitchen, Denis, eds. (Illus.). 64p. 1983. pap. 6.95 (ISBN 0-87816-013-2). Kitchen Sink.

Gall, E. Mysticism Through the Ages. 59.95 (ISBN 0-8490-0697-X). Gordon Pr.

Gall, Eric P., jt. ed. see Riggs, Gail K.

Gall, Franz J. On the Functions of the Brain & Each of Its Parts, 3 vols. Lewis, W., tr. from Ger. (Contributions to the History of Psychology Ser.: Vols. XVI, XVII, & XVIII, Pt. A). 1983. Repr. of 1835 ed. 30.00 ea. U Pubns Amer.

Gall, J. C. Ancient Sedimentary Environments & the Habitats of Living Organisms: Introduction to Palaeoecology. Wallace, P., tr. from Fr. (Illus.). 230p. 1983. 26.00 (ISBN 0-387-12137-4). Springer-Verlag.

Gall, James. Astronomical Directory. 1979. pap. 8.00 (ISBN 0-88904-082-6). Gall Pubns.

--Bible Student's English-Greek Concordance & Greek-English Dictionary. (Paperback Reference Library). 376p. 1983. pap. 7.95 (ISBN 0-8010-3795-6). Baker Bk.

Gall, Joyce P. & Gall, Meredith D. Help Your Son or Daughter Study for Success: A Parent Guide. LC 85-1462. (Illus.). 43p. (Orig.). 1985. pap. 3.95 (ISBN 0-930539-02-8). M Damien Pubs.

Gall, Joyce P., jt. auth. see Gall, Meredith D.

Gall, Lorraine S. & Curby, William A. Instrumented Systems for Microbiological Analysis of Body Fluids. 192p. 1980. 56.00 (ISBN 0-8493-5681-4). CRC Pr.

Gall, Lorraine S. & Riely, Phyllis E., eds. Manual for the Determination of the Clinical Role of Anaerobic Microbiology. 96p. 1981. 42.00 (ISBN 0-8493-5935-X). CRC Pr.

Gall, Margaret & Weitz, Barbara. Write English, Bk. 1. (Speak English Ser.). (Illus.). 64p. (Orig.). 1981. pap. text ed. 4.95 (ISBN 0-88499-684-0). Inst Mod Lang.

Gall, Maryann B., ed. Baldwin's Ohio Tax Service. 1985. 115.00 (ISBN 0-8322-0123-5); combined with Ohio Tax Law & Rules 208.00 (ISBN 0-8322-0017-4). Banks-Baldwin.

Gall, Meredith, jt. auth. see Acheson, Keith.

Gall, Meredith D. Handbook for Evaluating & Selecting Curriculum Materials. 1985. pap. 19.29 (ISBN 0-205-07301-8, 237301); spiral 26.95 (ISBN 0-205-07294-1, 237294). Allyn.

Gall, Meredith D. & Gall, Joyce P. Study for Success. LC 84-14993. (Illus.). 165p. (Orig.). 1985. pap. 7.95 (ISBN 0-930539-01-X). M Damien Pubs.

Gall, Meredith D., jt. auth. see Borg, Walter S.

Gall, Meredith D., jt. auth. see Gall, Joyce P.

Gall, Sally M. Ramon Guthrie's Maximum Security Ward: An American Classic. LC 83-16836. 112p. 1984. 7.95 (ISBN 0-8262-0430-9). U of Mo Pr.

Gall, Sally M., jt. auth. see Rosenthal, M. L.

Gall, Sally M., ed. see Guthrie, Ramon.

Gall, Sandy. Behind Russian Lines: An Afghan Journal. LC 83-40334. (Illus.). 200p. 1984. 22.50 (ISBN 0-312-07260-0). St Martin.
--Don't Worry about the Money Now. 352p. 1983. 18.95 (ISBN 0-241-10959-0, Pub. by Hamish Hamilton England). David & Charles.
Gallacher, Tom. The Journeyman. 176p. 1984. 16.95 (ISBN 0-241-11265-6, Pub. by Hamish Hamilton England). David & Charles.
--Survivor. 212p. 1985. 15.95 (ISBN 0-241-11522-1, Pub. by Hamish Hamilton England). David & Charles.
Gallafent, Richard J. & Eastaway, Nigel A. Intellectual Property Law & Taxation. 1982. 89.00 (ISBN 0-686-44505-8, Pub. by Oyez Longman Pub England). State Mutual Bk.
Gallager, H. Stephen. Early Breast Cancer: Detection & Treatment. LC 75-23327. (American College of Radiology Ser.). Repr. of 1975 ed. 48.10 (ISBN 0-8357-9874-7, 2012581). Bks Demand UMI.
Gallager, H. Stephen, et al, eds. The Breast. LC 78-14811. (Illus.). 564p. 1978. text ed. 79.50 (ISBN 0-8016-1727-8). Mosby.
Gallager, Nancy E. Handlist of Arabic Medical Manuscripts at UCLA. LC 82-50985. (Aids & Research Tools in the Middle East Studies: Vol. 1). (Illus.). 44p. 1983. pap. 7.00x (ISBN 0-89003-128-2). Undena Pubns.
Gallager, Robert G. Information Theory & Reliable Communication. LC 68-26850. 588p. 1968. 54.00x (ISBN 0-471-29048-3). Wiley.
Gallagher, A. P. Coordinating Australian University Development: A Study of the Australian Universities Commission, 1959-1970. LC 82-1973. (Scholars Library). 244p. 1983. text ed. 34.50x (ISBN 0-7022-1657-7). U of Queensland Pr.
Gallagher, Arlene F. The Methods Book: Strategies for Law-Focused Education. LC 77-80622. 138p. 1977. pap. 12.95 (ISBN 0-89994-226-1). Soc Sci Ed.
Gallagher, Bernard J. & Palazzolo, Charles S. The Social World of Occupations. LC 76-41981. 1976. pap. text ed. 12.95 (ISBN 0-8403-1620-8). Kendall-Hunt.
Gallagher, Bernard J., III. Sociology of Mental Illness. (Series in Sociology). (Illus.). 1980. text ed. 25.95 (ISBN 0-13-820928-6). P-H.
Gallagher, Buell G. American Caste & the Negro College. LC 66-29471. 1966. Repr. of 1938 ed. 15.00x (ISBN 0-87752-041-0). Gordian.
Gallagher, C. A. & Watson, H. J. Quantitative Methods for Business Decisions. 1980. text ed. 35.95 (ISBN 0-07-022751-9). McGraw.
Gallagher, Catherine. The Industrial Reformation of English Fiction: Social Discourse & Narrative Form, 1832-1867. LC 84-16272. 348p. 1985. lib. bdg. 25.00X (ISBN 0-226-27932-4). U of Chicago Pr.
Gallagher, Charles A. & Maloney, George A. Embodied in Love: The Sacramental Spirituality of Sexual Intimacy. 176p. (Orig.). 1983. pap. 9.95 (ISBN 0-686-46141-X). Crossroad NY.
Gallagher, Charles C. & Helm, Eugene E., eds. Carl Philip Emanuel Bach, Six Symphonies. (The Symphony 1720-1840 Series C: Vol. 8). 1982. lib. bdg. 90.00 (ISBN 0-8240-3821-5). Garland Pub.
Gallagher, Charles F. United States & North Africa: Morocco, Algeria, & Tunisia. LC 63-20766. (American Foreign Policy Library). Repr. of 1963 ed. 55.50 (ISBN 0-8357-9182-3, 2016539). Bks Demand UMI.
Gallagher, Chuck. Call to Healing. 1983. 3.95 (ISBN 0-8215-9873-2). Sadlier.
--Hurrah for Parents. 1980. 3.95 (ISBN 0-8215-6467-6). Sadlier.
--Love Is a Couple. 1978. pap. 3.50 (ISBN 0-385-13595-5, Im). Doubleday.
--Love is a Couple. 1980. 3.95 (ISBN 0-8215-6464-1). Sadlier.
--Love Takes Greatness. 1980. 3.95 (ISBN 0-8215-6465-X). Sadlier.
--Parents Are Lovers. 1980. 3.95 (ISBN 0-8215-6466-8). Sadlier.
Gallagher, Chuck & Crilly, Oliver. Prayer, Saints, Scripture & Ourselves. LC 83-60189. 162p. (Orig.). 1983. pap. text ed. 6.95 (ISBN 0-911905-03-0). Past & Mat Rene Ctr.
Gallagher, Chuck, et al. Calling Disciples: Outlines. LC 84-60459. (Calling Disciples Ser.: Bk. 1). 64p. (Orig.). 1984. pap. text ed. 2.95 (ISBN 0-911905-23-5). Past & Mat Rene Ctr.
Gallagher, D. P. Modern Latin American Literature. 1973. pap. 3.95 (ISBN 0-19-888071-5, 400, GB). Oxford U Pr.
Gallagher, Dolores, ed. Depression in the Elderly: A Selected Bibliography. Kronauer, Margaret. LC 81-4326. (Technical Bibliographies on Aging Ser.). 58p. 1981. pap. 4.00 (ISBN 0-88474-099-4, 05756-8). Lexington Bks.
Gallagher, Dolores & Thompson, Larry W., eds. Depression in the Elderly: A Behavioral Treatment Manual. LC 81-66766. 159p. 1981. pap. 12.00 (ISBN 0-88474-125-7, 05734-7). Lexington Bks.
Gallagher, Donald & Gallagher, Idella, eds. Education of Man: The Educational Philosophy of Jacques Maritain. 1967. pap. 5.95x (ISBN 0-268-00086-7). U of Notre Dame Pr.
Gallagher, Donald, ed. see Maritain, Jacques.
Gallagher, Donald A., ed. Some Philosophers on Education: Papers Concerning the Doctrines of Augustine, Aristole, Aquinas & Dewey. 2nd ed. 1961. 6.95 (ISBN 0-87462-403-7). Marquette.
Gallagher, Donat, ed. see Waugh, Evelyn.
Gallagher, E., ed. see Royal Dublin Society.
Gallagher, Edward & Mistichelli, Judith A. Jules Verne: A Primary & Secondary Bibliography. 1980. lib. bdg. 33.50 (ISBN 0-8161-8106-3, Hall Reference). G K Hall.
Gallagher, Edward J. An Annotated Guide to Fantastic Adventures. LC 85-10988. (Starmont Reference Guides Ser.: No. 2). 192p. 1985. Repr. lib. bdg. 17.95x (ISBN 0-89370-749-X). Borgo Pr.
--A Critical Edition of the "Passion Nostre Seigneur" f rom Manuscript 1131 from the Bibliotheque Saint-Genevieve, Paris. (Studies in the Romance Languages & Literatures Ser: No. 179). 292p. 1976. pap. 15.50x (ISBN 0-8078-9179-7). U of NC Pr.
Gallagher, Edward J., jt. auth. see Feaver, Douglas A.
Gallagher, Edward J., ed. The Annotated Guide to Fantastic Adventures. LC 84-16228. (Starmont Reference Guide Ser.: Vol. 2). (Illus.). 1985. 19.95x (ISBN 0-916732-71-1); pap. text ed. 11.95 (ISBN 0-916732-70-3). Starmont Hse.
Gallagher, Eric. Christians in Ulster, Nineteen Sixty-Eight to Nineteen Eighty. 254p. 1982. 19.95x (ISBN 0-19-213237-7). Oxford U Pr.
Gallagher, Eugene V. Divine Man or Magician? Celsus & Origin on Jesus. (SBL Dissertation Ser.). 1982. pap. 13.50 (ISBN 0-89130-542-4, 06 01 64). Scholars Pr GA.
Gallagher, F. N. The Only Western Town in the East. 56p. 1980. 4.50 (ISBN 0-8059-2718-2). Dorrance.
Gallagher, Francis N. The Only Western Town in the East, Pt. II. 1982. 6.00 (ISBN 0-9608844-0-8). J R and G.
Gallagher, Frank. Days of Fear: Diary of a Hunger Strike. 117p. pap. 1.00 (ISBN 0-85342-069-6). Irish Bk Ctr.
--The Indivisible Island: The Story of the Partition of Ireland. LC 74-5772. (Illus.). 316p. 1974. Repr. of 1957 ed. lib. bdg. 22.50x (ISBN 0-8371-7515-1, GAII). Greenwood.
Gallagher, Frank & Hogan, David. The Four Glorious Years. 1971. Repr. of 1953 ed. 32.00 (ISBN 0-384-17583-X). Johnson Repr.
Gallagher, Gary w. Stephen Dodson Ramsuer: Lee's Gallant General. LC 84-13035. (Illus.). 250p. 1985. 19.95 (ISBN 0-8078-1627-2). U of NC Pr.
Gallagher, Helen, ed. The ISC Searchbook. 40p. (Orig.). 1985. pap. 5.00 (ISBN 0-942916-08-5). ISC Pubns.
Gallagher, Helen M. Robert Mills: Architect of the Washington Monument, 1781-1855. LC 74-168092. Repr. of 1935 ed. 21.00 (ISBN 0-404-02668-0). AMS Pr.
Gallagher, Hugh G. FDR's Splendid Deception. (Illus.). 256p. 1985. 16.95 (ISBN 0-396-08521-0). Dodd.
Gallagher, I. J. The Case of the Ancient Astronauts. LC 77-10822. (Great Unsolved Mysteries). (Illus.). (gr. 4-5). 1977. PLB 14.25 (ISBN 0-8172-1059-8). Raintree Pubs.
--The Case of the Ancient Astronauts. LC 77-10822. (Great Unsolved Mysteries Ser.). (Illus.). 48p. (gr. 4up). 1983. pap. 9.27 (ISBN 0-8172-2156-5). Raintree Pubs.
Gallagher, Idella, jt. ed. see Gallagher, Donald.
Gallagher, Idella, ed. see Maritain, Jacques.
Gallagher, J. A. The Decline, Revival & Fall of the British Empire. LC 82-4291. 250p. 1982. 34.50 (ISBN 0-521-24642-3). Cambridge U Pr.
Gallagher, J. J. Comparison of Brain-Injured & Non-Brain-Injured Mentally Retarded Children on Several Psychological Variables. (SRCD M). 1957. pap. 15.00 (ISBN 0-527-01570-9). Kraus Repr.
Gallagher, J. M. & Easley, J. A., eds. Knowledge & Development: Vol. 2, Piaget & Education. (Illus.). 314p. 1978. 29.50x (ISBN 0-306-40089-8, Plenum Pr). Plenum Pub.
Gallagher, J. M., jt. ed. see Overton, Willis F.
Gallagher, J. P. see Cruse, T. A.
Gallagher, J. P. & Crooker, T. W., eds. Structural Integrity Technology. (Orig.). 1979. 30.00 (ISBN 0-685-96310-1, H00144). ASME.
Gallagher, J. P., ed. see American Society of Mechanical Engineers.
Gallagher, James J. Leadership Unit: The Use of Teacher-Scholar Teams to Develop Units for the Gifted. (Illus.). 138p. 1982. pap. 12.50 tchr's ed (ISBN 0-89824-036-0). Trillium Pr.
--Teaching the Gifted Child. 2nd ed. 448p. 1985. 29.36 (ISBN 0-205-04689-4, 224689). Allyn.
Gallagher, James J. & Gowan, John C. Issues in Gifted Education. 93p. 5.50 (ISBN 0-318-16013-7, 20). NSLTIGT.
Gallagher, James J. & Nathan, Kurt C. The Trees Jobs Grow On: And How to Find the One for You. LC 80-70399. (Illus.). 80p. (Orig.). 1980. 9.95 (ISBN 0-938176-00-5). Biobehavioral Pr.
Gallagher, James J., jt. auth. see Haskins, Ron.
Gallagher, James J., jt. auth. see Kirk, Samuel A.
Gallagher, James J., ed. Application of Child Development Research to Exceptional Children. LC 75-24642. 1975. pap. text ed. 9.50 (ISBN 0-86586-003-3). Coun Exc Child.
--Gifted Children: Reaching their Potential. 440p. (Orig.). 1979. pap. 14.00 (ISBN 0-89824-012-3). Trillium Pr.
Gallagher, James J., ed. see Cox, Martha & Cox, Roger.
Gallagher, James J., jt. ed. see Haskins, Ron.
Gallagher, James J., et al. Issues in Gifted Education. 93p. 5.50 (ISBN 0-318-02136-6). NSLTIGT.
--The Status of Gifted-Talented Education: United States Survey of Needs, Practices, & Policies. 11.50 (ISBN 0-318-02207-9). NSLTIGT.
Gallagher, James J., et al, eds. Promoting the Education of the Gifted-Talented: Strategies for Advocacy. 93p. 15.25 (ISBN 0-318-02194-3). NSLTIGT.
Gallagher, James P., jt. auth. see Holleman, Thomas J.
Gallagher, Jeanette M. & Reid, D. Kim. The Learning Theory of Piaget & Inhelder. LC 83-24533. (Illus.). 276p. 1984. pap. text ed. 18.00 (ISBN 0-936104-36-8, 0491). Pro Ed.
Gallagher, Joan. With the Five Year Olds. 44p. 1969. pap. 1.95 (ISBN 0-685-46931-X). Ed Solutions.
Gallagher, John. The Basis for Christian Ethics. 256p. (Orig.). 1985. pap. 8.95 (ISBN 0-8091-2690-7). Paulist Pr.
Gallagher, John F., ed. & intro. by see Harris, Frank.
Gallagher, Joseph. Pain & the Privilege: Diary of a City Priest. LC 82-1766. 384p. 1983. pap. 7.95 (ISBN 0-385-19019-0, Im). Doubleday.
Gallagher, Joseph, ed. East African Culture History. LC 76-50927. (Foreign & Comparative Studies Program, Eastern Africa Ser.: No. 25). 93p. 1976. pap. text ed. 5.50x (ISBN 0-915984-22-9). Syracuse U Foreign Comp.
Gallagher, Joseph, et al, trs. see Camara, Helder.
Gallagher, Joseph V. Para Ser Catolico: Un Catecismo Para Hoy. new, spanish ed. 1976. pap. 1.50 (ISBN 0-8091-1939-0). Paulist Pr.
--To Be a Catholic. LC 73-137884. 96p. 1970. pap. 1.95 (ISBN 0-8091-5143-X). Paulist Pr.
Gallagher, Kathy. The I'm Sick of Carrot Sticks Cookbook. 224p. 1984. 14.95 (ISBN 0-02-542070-4). MacMillan.
Gallagher, Kathy, ed. Collection Development Manual. 1983. 15.00 (ISBN 0-317-17467-3). Wash U Med Lib.
Gallagher, Kenneth T. Philosophy of Gabriel Marcel. rev. ed. LC 62-15666. xiv, 178p. 1975. pap. 9.00 (ISBN 0-8232-0471-5). Fordham.
--The Philosophy of Knowledge. 2nd ed. LC 64-19903. xii, 307p. 1984. pap. 10.00 (ISBN 0-8232-1095-2). Fordham.
Gallagher, Lillie P. The Louisiana Keepsake, 1985. (Illus.). 128p. 1984. 10.00 (ISBN 0-9610174-7-3). Petit Press.
--Louisiana Keepsake, 1986. (Eng. & Fr.). 1985. 10.00 (ISBN 0-9610174-6-5). Petit Press.
Gallagher, M. E., ed. see Elmer, Michael.
Gallagher, Margaret. Unequal Opportunities: The Case of Women & the Media. 221p. 1981. pap. 20.75 (ISBN 92-3-101897-3, U1201, UNESCO). Unipub.
Gallagher, Mark. Day-by-Day in New York Yankee History. LC 82-83934. (Illus.). 300p. (Orig.). 1983. pap. 12.95 (ISBN 0-88011-102-X). Leisure Pr.
--Fifty Years of Yankee All-Stars. LC 83-80706. (Illus.). 192p. (Orig.). 1984. pap. 9.95 (ISBN 0-88011-161-5). Leisure Pr.
--The Yankee Encyclopedia. LC 81-86519. (Illus.). 500p. (Orig.). 1982. 39.95 (ISBN 0-88011-047-3). Leisure Pr.
Gallagher, Mary. Spend It Foolishly. 1979. pap. 2.25 (ISBN 0-380-46011-4, 46011). Avon.
Gallagher, Matthew P. The Soviet History of World War II: Myths, Memories & Realities. LC 75-32458. 1976. Repr. of 1963 ed. lib. bdg. 27.50x (ISBN 0-8371-8551-3, GASH). Greenwood.
Gallagher, Matthew P. & Spielmann, Karl F., Jr. Soviet Decision-Making for Defense: A Critique of U.S. Perspectives on the Arms Race. LC 72-170024. (Special Studies in International Politics). 112p. 1972. text ed. 22.50x (ISBN 0-275-28638-X). Irvington.
Gallagher, Maureen. The Cathedral Book. LC 82-60592. (gr. 3-6). 1983. pap. 2.95 (ISBN 0-8091-2485-8). Paulist Pr.
--God's Love for Us. (gr. 1-3). 1983. 3.95 (ISBN 0-89837-090-6, Pub. by Pflaum Pr); 3.95 (ISBN 0-89837-091-4). Peter Li.
Gallagher, Maureen, et al. Praying with Scripture Handbook. LC 82-62923. 176p. (Orig.). 1984. pap. 7.95 (ISBN 0-8091-2544-7); leader's manual with slides 22.95 (ISBN 0-8091-7751-X). Paulist Pr.
Gallagher, Michael. The Irish Labour Party in Transition, 1957-81. LC 83-62246. 326p. 1983. 25.00 (ISBN 0-7190-0866-2, Pub. by Manchester Univ Pr). Longwood Pub Group.
Gallagher, Michael & Woodcock, Martin. The Birds of Oman. (Illus.). 138p. 1981. 75.00 (ISBN 0-7043-2216-1, Pub. by Quartet England). Charles River Bks.
Gallagher, Michael & Woodcock, Martin W. The Birds of Oman. (Illus.). 288p. 1984. 75.00 (ISBN 0-7043-2216-1, Pub. by Quartet Bks); pap. 24.95 (ISBN 0-7043-3425-9, Pub. by Quartet Bks). Merrimack Pub Cir.
Gallagher, Michael, jt. auth. see Hill, L. Brooks.
Gallagher, Michael, tr. see Endo, Shusaku.
Gallagher, Michael, tr. see Nozaka, Aikyuki.
Gallagher, Nancy E. Medicine & Power in Tunisia, Seventeen Eighty to Nineteen Hundred. LC 82-22163. (Cambridge Middle East Library Ser.). 148p. 1984. 39.50 (ISBN 0-521-25124-9). Cambridge U Pr.
Gallagher, Neil. Don't Go Overseas Until You've Read This Book. LC 77-2643. 128p. 1977. pap. 3.95 (ISBN 0-87123-105-0, 210105). Bethany Hse.
--How to Save Money on Almost Everything. 4.95 (ISBN 0-87123-234-0). World Wide OR.
--The Porno Plague. LC 77-21992. (Illus.). 256p. 1977. pap. 5.95 (ISBN 0-87123-231-6, 210231). Bethany Hse.
Gallagher, Neil E. & Peregoy, Stephen M. Health in Our Lives: An Introductory Workbook. 112p. 1981. pap. text ed. 8.95 (ISBN 0-8403-2401-4). Kendall-Hunt.
Gallagher, Nora. Parlor Games. LC 79-17882. (Illus.). 1979. pap. 4.95 (ISBN 0-201-03084-5). Addison-Wesley.
Gallagher, P. B. Long Night. (Orig.). 1979. pap. 2.25 (ISBN 0-685-96934-7). Zebra.
Gallagher, Patricia. All for Love. 400p. 1981. pap. 3.50 (ISBN 0-380-77818-1, 83816-8). Avon.
--Castles in the Air. 1976. pap. 3.95 (ISBN 0-380-00570-0, 83808-7). Avon.
--Echoes & Embers. 1983. pap. 3.50 (ISBN 0-380-80929-X, 80929-X). Avon.
--The Fires of Brimstone. 1977. pap. 1.75 (ISBN 0-380-00980-3, 32573). Avon.
--Mystic Rose. 1977. pap. 3.50 (ISBN 0-380-01670-2, 82560-0). Avon.
--No Greater Love. 1979. pap. 2.50 (ISBN 0-380-44743-6, 44743-6). Avon.
--On Wings of Dreams. 416p. 1985. pap. 3.95 (ISBN 0-425-07446-3). Berkley Pub.
--Shadows of Passion. 1976. pap. 1.75 (ISBN 0-380-00928-5, 31906-3). Avon.
Gallagher, Patricia, ed. see Smithsonian Bks.
Gallagher, Patricia A. Teaching Students with Behavior Disorders: Techniques for Classroom Instruction. 300p. 1979. text ed. 21.95 (ISBN 0-89108-091-0). Love Pub Co.
Gallagher, Patrick. Paddy the Cope. 1942. 5.95 (ISBN 0-8159-6500-1). Devin.
--La Pitia: An Archaeological Series in Northwestern Venezuela. LC 75-21042. (Publications in Anthropology: No.76). 1976. pap. 12.00 (ISBN 0-913516-09-0). Yale U Anthro.
Gallagher, Patrick, ed. Logistics: Change & Synthesis. 288p. 1984. pap. 15.45 (ISBN 0-317-06629-3). Leaseway Trans Corp.
--Logistics: Contribution & Control. 282p. 1983. pap. 15.45 (ISBN 0-9610146-1-X). Leaseway Trans Corp.
Gallagher, Patrick L. The Cuban Exile. Cortes, Carlos E., ed. LC 79-6207. (Hispanics in the United States Ser.). (Illus.). 1981. lib. bdg. 25.50x (ISBN 0-405-13157-7). Ayer Co Pubs.
Gallagher, Paul F. Parametric Estimating for Executives & Estimators. 320p. 1981. 21.95 (ISBN 0-442-23997-1). Van Nos Reinhold.
Gallagher, Philip J. & Demos, George D., eds. Handbook of Counseling in Higher Education. LC 82-14484. 348p. 1983. 42.95 (ISBN 0-03-063216-1). Praeger.
Gallagher, R. H. Optimum Structural Design: Theory & Applications. LC 72-8600. (Numerical Methods in Engineering Ser.). 358p. 1973. 69.95x (ISBN 0-471-29050-5, Pub. by Wiley-Interscience). Wiley.
Gallagher, R. H. & Norrie, D. H., eds. Finite Elements in Fluids, Vol. 4. Oden, J. T. & Zienkiewicz, O. C., trs. (Numerical Methods in Engineering Ser.: 1-405). 647p. 1982. text ed. 79.95x (ISBN 0-471-10178-8). Wiley.
Gallagher, R. H., ed. see Atrek, E., et al.
Gallagher, R. H., ed. see Conference on Finite Elements Applied to Thin Shells & Curved Members (1974: University College, Cardiff, Wales).
Gallagher, R. H., jt. ed. see Desai, C. S.
Gallagher, R. H., jt. ed. see Sherphered, M.
Gallagher, R. H., et al. Finite Elements on Fluids: Finite Elements & Flow Problems, Vol. 6. Date not set. price not set (ISBN 0-471-90676-X). Wiley.
--Finite Elements in Biomechanics. LC 81-13084. (Wiley Series in Numerical Methods in Engineering). 404p. 1982. 54.95x (ISBN 0-471-09996-1, Pub. by Wiley-Interscience). Wiley.
Gallagher, R. H., jt. auth. see Atluri, S. N.
Gallagher, R. H., et al, eds. Finite Elements in Fluids, 3 vols. Incl. Vol. 1. Viscous Flow & Hydrodynamics. 290p. 1975. 79.95x (ISBN 0-471-29045-9); Vol. 2. Mathematical Foundations, Aerodynamics, & Lubrication. 287p. 1975. 79.95x (ISBN 0-471-29046-7); Vol. 3. 1978. 79.95x (ISBN 0-471-99630-0). LC 74-13573 (Pub. by Wiley-Interscience). Wiley.
--Finite Elements in Fluids, Vol. 5. (Numerical Methods in Engineering Ser.). 436p. 1984. 69.95 (ISBN 0-471-90396-5). Wiley.
Gallagher, Richard & Remsberg, Charles. Hostage Negotiation for Police: Officer Reference. 1977. 2.50 (ISBN 0-686-52997-9). MTI Tele.
Gallagher, Richard H. Finite Element Analysis: Fundamentals. (Civil Engr. & Engr. Mechanics Ser.). (Illus.). 416p. 1975. 38.95 (ISBN 0-13-317248-1). P-H.
Gallagher, Richard H., jt. auth. see McGuire, William.

Gallagher, Richard H., jt. ed. see Yamada, Yoshiaki.
Gallagher, Richard R. Collegiate Business Series: Syllabus. 1977. pap. text ed. 6.95 (ISBN 0-89420-011-9, 104021); cassette recordings 120.25 (ISBN 0-89420-135-2, 104000). Natl Book.
Gallagher, Rita. Shadowed Destiny. (Orig.). 1985. pap. 3.50 (ISBN 0-440-17969-6). Dell.
--Shadows on the Wind. (Orig.). 1982. pap. 2.95 (ISBN 0-440-18042-2). Dell.
Gallagher, Robert C. Ernie Davis: The Elmira Express, The Story of a Heisman Trophy Winner. LC 83-71997. (Illus.). 176p. 1983. 11.95 (ISBN 0-910155-03-8). Bartleby Pr.
Gallagher, Robert E. Byron's Journal of His Circumnavigation, 1764-1766. 230p. 1964. 20.00x (ISBN 0-686-79455-9, Pub. by Hakluyt Soc England). State Mutual Bk.
Gallagher, S. F., ed. Woman in Irish Legend, Life & Literature. LC 82-22792. (Irish Literary Studies: No. 14). 160p. 1983. text ed. 28.50x (ISBN 0-389-20361-0). B&N Imports.
Gallagher, Sharon & Van der Meer, Ron. Inside the Personal Computer: An Illustrated Introduction in 3 Dimensions. LC 84-6184. (Illus.). 1984. 19.95 (ISBN 0-89659-504-8). Abbeville Pr.
Gallagher, Stephen. Chimera. 320p. 1982. 13.95 (ISBN 0-312-13387-1). St Martin.
Gallagher, T. J. Simple Dielectric Liquids: Mobility, Conduction, & Breakdown. (Oxford Science Research Papers Ser). (Illus.). 1975. pap. 34.95x (ISBN 0-19-851933-8). Oxford U Pr.
Gallagher, T. J. & Pearmain, A. J. High Voltage: Measurement, Testing & Design. LC 82-20398. 245p. 1983. 39.95x (ISBN 0-471-90096-6, Pub. by Wiley-Interscience). Wiley.
Gallagher, T. James, ed. Advances in Anesthesia, Vol. 1. (Illus.). 560p. 1983. 49.95 (ISBN 0-8151-3307-3). Year Bk Med.
Gallagher, Tanya M. & Prutting, Carol A., eds. Pragmatic Assessment & Intervention Issues in Language. LC 82-17752. (Illus.). 286p. 1983. pap. 25.00 (ISBN 0-933014-78-3). College-Hill.
Gallagher, Tess. Instructions to the Double. LC 76-378309. 76p. 1975. 0. p. 12.00 (ISBN 0-915308-04-5); pap. 5.00 (ISBN 0-915308-03-7). Graywolf.
--Under Stars. LC 77-95331. 1978. 9.00 (ISBN 0-915308-19-3); pap. 5.00 (ISBN 0-915308-20-7). Graywolf.
--Willingly. LC 83-82867. 96p. 1984. 12.00 (ISBN 0-915308-45-2); pap. 6.00 (ISBN 0-915308-46-0). Graywolf.
Gallagher, Thomas. Oona O' LC 75-33938. 250p. 1976. pap. 2.95 (ISBN 0-15-671371-3, Harv). HarBraceJ.
--Paddy's Lament: Ireland 1846 to 1847; Prelude to Hatred. LC 81-48011. 352p. 1982. 14.95 (ISBN 0-15-170618-2). HarBraceJ.
Gallagher, Thomas B. Craps: How to Play & Win Like Professionals. (Illus.). 7p. 1981. pap. 5.95x (ISBN 0-938706-01-2). Casino Gam Seminars.
--Craps: How to Play & Win Like Professionals. (Illus.). 7p. 1981. pap. 3.95 (ISBN 0-938706-01-2). Fed Aviation.
--Private Pilot Written Exam Course. LC 80-70132. (Illus.). 68p. (Orig.). 1981. pap. 19.95 (ISBN 0-938706-00-4). Fed Aviation.
--Ultralight Vehicle Operation. 20p. (Orig.). 1983. pap. text ed. 4.95 (ISBN 0-938706-02-0). Fed Aviation.
Gallagher, Tom. Portugal: A Twentieth Century Interpretation. LC 82-20379. 256p. 1982. 25.00 (ISBN 0-7190-0876-X, Pub. by Manchester Univ Pr). Longwood Pub Group.
Gallagher, Tom, jt. ed. see O'Connell, James.
Gallagher, Vera. Hearing the Cry of the Poor: The Story of the St. Vincent de Paul Society. 64p. 1983. pap. 1.50 (ISBN 0-89243-174-1). Liguori Pubns.
Gallagher, Sr. Vera & Dodds, William F. Speaking Out, Fighting Back: Personal Experience of Women Who Survived Childhood Sexual Abuse in the Home. 240p. 1985. 14.95 (ISBN 0-88089-010-X). Madrona Pubs.
Gallagher, William D., ed. Selections from the Poetical Literature of the West. LC 68-29083. 1968. Repr. of 1841 ed. 40.00x (ISBN 0-8201-1019-1). Schol Facsimiles.
Gallagher, William J. Report Writing for Management. (Orig.). 1969. pap. 11.95 (ISBN 0-201-02256-7). Addison-Wesley.
--Writing the Business & Technical Report. LC 80-19781. 120p. 1980. pap. 11.95 (ISBN 0-8436-0796-3). Van Nos Reinhold.
Gallaher, Art, Jr. Plainville Fifteen Years Later. LC 61-15104. 1961. 26.00x (ISBN 0-231-02481-9). Columbia U Pr.
Gallaher, Art, Jr. & Padfield, Harlan, eds. The Dying Community. LC 79-56814. (School of American Research Advanced Seminar Ser.). 1980. 30.00x (ISBN 0-8263-0535-0). U of NM Pr.
Gallaher, Grace M. Vassar Stories. LC 71-113663. (Short Story Index Reprint Ser.). 1899. 19.00 (ISBN 0-8369-3392-3). Ayer Co Pubs.
Gallaher, John G. The Iron Marshal: A Biography of Louis N. Davout. LC 75-37956. (Illus.). 432p. 1976. 24.95x (ISBN 0-8093-0691-3). S Ill U Pr.
Gallahue, David L. Developmental Movement Exercises for Children. 397p. 1982. pap. text ed. write for info. (ISBN 0-02-340330-6). Macmillan.
--Developmental Movement Experiences for Children. LC 81-16424. 397p. 1982. pap. text ed. 24.45 (ISBN 0-471-08778-5). Wiley.
--Understanding Motor Development in Children. 455p. 1982. text ed. 25.45x (ISBN 0-471-08779-3). Wiley.
Gallahue, David L. & Meadors, William J. Let's Move: A Physical Education Program for Elementary School Teachers. 2nd ed. 1979. pap. 14.95 (ISBN 0-8403-2029-9). Kendall-Hunt.
Gallahue, David L., jt. auth. see Vannier, Maryhelen.
Gallahue, David L., et al. A Conceptual Approach to Moving & Learning. LC 75-2369. 423p. 1975. text ed. 34.45 (ISBN 0-471-29043-2). Wiley.
Gallahue, John. The Jesuit. 300p. 1984. pap. 3.95 (ISBN 0-8128-8083-8). Stein & Day.
Gallaire, H. & Minker, J., eds. Logic & Data Bases. LC 78-14032. 466p. 1978. 55.00x (ISBN 0-306-40060-X, Plenum Pr). Plenum Pub.
Gallaire, Herve, et al, eds. Advances in Data Base Theory, Vol. 1. 440p. 1981. 59.50x (ISBN 0-306-40629-2, Plenum Pr). Plenum Pub.
Gallais, Pierre. Dialectique du Recit Medieval. (Faux Titre Ser.: Band 9). 322p. (Fr.). 1982. pap. text ed. 30.50x (ISBN 90-6203-744-5, Pub. by Rodopi Holland). Humanities.
Gallais-Hamonno, Janine. Langage de Macroeconomics. 2nd ed. 312p. (Eng.-Fr.). 1973. pap. 19.95 (ISBN 0-686-57188-6, M-6260). French & Eur.
Galland, China. Women in the Wilderness. LC 80-7830. (Illus.). 256p. (Orig.). 1980. pap. 7.95i (ISBN 0-06-090817-3, CN 817, CN). Har-Row.
Galland, Frank J., ed. Dictionary of Computing: Data Communications, Hardware & Software Basics, Digital Electronics. 330p. 1982. 37.95x (ISBN 0-471-10468-X, Pub. by Wiley-Interscience); pap. 21.95x (ISBN 0-471-10469-8). Wiley.
Galland, Joseph S. Historical & Analytical Bibliography of the Literature of Cryptology. LC 75-128996. (Northwestern University. Humanities Ser.: No. 10). Repr. of 1945 ed. 29.00 (ISBN 0-404-50710-7). AMS Pr.
--Ten Favorite French Stories. (Fr.). 1985. pap. text ed. 9.95x (ISBN 0-89197-962-X). Irvington.
Galland, Rene. George Meredith & British Criticism. 120p. 1980. Repr. lib. bdg. 20.00 (ISBN 0-89987-301-4). Darby Bks.
--George Meredith & British Criticism. LC 75-35557. 1975. Repr. of 1923 ed. lib. bdg. 22.50 (ISBN 0-8414-4583-4). Folcroft.
--George Meredith, les Cinquante Premiers Annees. LC 78-145025. 1971. Repr. of 1923 ed. 18.00x (ISBN 0-403-00972-3). Scholarly.
Galland, Sarah. Peter Rabbit's Gardening Book. (Illus.). 48p. (gr. 5-9). 1984. 6.95 (ISBN 0-7232-2994-5). Warne.
Gallant, Claire B. Mediation in Special Education Disputes. LC 82-60764. 104p. (Orig.). 1982. pap. 6.95x (ISBN 0-87101-105-0). Natl Assn Soc Wkrs.
Gallant, Edward, et al. Connecticut Workers' Compensation Handbook. 384p. write for info. (ISBN 0-88063-019-1). Butterworth Legal Pubs.
Gallant, Felicia & Flanders, Rebecca. Dreamweaver. 1984. pap. 3.50 (ISBN 0-318-03626-6). Harlequin Bks.
Gallant, G. Blake & the Assimilation of Chaos. LC 78-51165. 1978. 24.00 (ISBN 0-691-06367-2). Princeton U Pr.
Gallant, Jennie. The Black Diamond. 224p. (Orig.). 1981. pap. 2.25 (ISBN 0-449-24424-5, Crest). Fawcett.
--Friends & Lovers. (Coventry Romance Ser.: No. 179). 224p. 1982. pap. 1.50 (ISBN 0-449-50280-5, Coventry). Fawcett.
--Lady Hathaway's House Party. 1980. pap. 1.75 (ISBN 0-449-50020-9, Coventry). Fawcett.
--Minuet. (Coventry Romance Ser.: No. 66). 224p. 1980. pap. 1.75 (ISBN 0-449-50097-7, Coventry). Fawcett.
--The Moonless Night. 224p. (Orig.). 1980. pap. 1.75 (ISBN 0-449-50040-3, Coventry). Fawcett.
Gallant, Marc. The Cow Book. LC 82-47816. 1983. 17.95 (ISBN 0-394-52034-3). Knopf.
--More Fun with Dick & Jane. (Fiction Ser.). 72p. (Orig.). 1985. pap. 5.95 (ISBN 0-14-007692-1). Penguin.
Gallant, Mavis. From the Fifteenth District: A Novella & Eight Short Stories. 1979. 8.95 (ISBN 0-394-50719-3). Random.
--Home Truths: Selected Canadian Stories. LC 84-45757. 330p. 1985. 17.45 (ISBN 0-394-53198-1). Random.
--Other Paris: Stories. LC 74-116951. (Short Story Index Reprint Ser). 1955. 18.00 (ISBN 0-8369-3454-7). Ayer Co Pubs.
--The Pegnitz Junction. LC 84-81627. 180p. (Orig.). 1984. pap. 6.00 (ISBN 0-915308-60-6). Graywolf.
Gallant, Peter. The Electronic Treasury Management: A Guide for Corporate & Bank Treasurers. LC 84-15376. 164p. 1985. 33.00 (ISBN 0-85941-273-3, Pub. by Woodhead-Faulkner). Longwood Pub Group.
Gallant, R. W. & Railey, J. M. Physical Properties of Hydrocarbons, Vol. 2. 2nd ed. LC 83-22604. 200p. 1984. 44.95x (ISBN 0-87201-690-0). Gulf Pub.
Gallant, Roy. Once Around the Galaxy. (Single Titles Ser.). (Illus.). 96p. (gr. 5 up). 1983. PLB 9.90 (ISBN 0-531-04681-8). Watts.
Gallant, Roy A. Fossils. (First Bks.). (Illus.). 72p. (gr. 4 up). 1985. lib. bdg. 9.40 (ISBN 0-531-04910-8). Watts.
--Ice Ages. (First Book Ser.). (Illus.). 72p. (gr. 4 up). 1985. lib. bdg. 9.40 (ISBN 0-531-04912-4). Watts.
--Lost Cities. (First Bk.). (Illus.). 72p. (gr. 4 up). 1985. lib. bdg. 9.40 (ISBN 0-531-04914-0). Watts.
--One Hundred & One Questions & Answers about the Universe. LC 84-7875. (Illus.). 96p. (gr. 1-5). 1984. 10.95 (ISBN 0-02-736750-9). Macmillan.
--Our Universe. (Illus.). 276p. 14.95 (ISBN 0-317-35141-9, 00356). Natl Geog.
Gallant, Roy A. & Sedeen, Magaret. National Geographic Picture Atlas of Our Universe. (Illus.). 276p. (gr. 6 up). 1980. lib. bdg. 16.95 (ISBN 0-87044-357-7). Natl Geog.
Gallant, T. Grady. The Friendly Dead. 1981. pap. 2.75 (ISBN 0-89083-801-1). Zebra.
--The Friendly Dead. (World at War Ser.: No. 19). 1980. pap. 2.50 (ISBN 0-89083-588-8). Zebra.
Gallapin, A. E. Aubrey Beardsley: Catalog of Drawings & Bibliographies. (Illus.). 148p. 1980. Repr. of 1945 ed. 15.00 (ISBN 0-911858-39-3). Appel.
Gallarati-Scotti, Tommaso. Life of Antonio Fogazzaro. LC 73-113311. 1970. Repr. of 1922 ed. 24.50x (ISBN 0-8046-0994-2, Pub. by Kennikat). Assoc Faculty Pr.
Gallardo, Alexander. Britain & the First Carlist War. 1980. Repr. of 1978 ed. lib. bdg. 30.00 (ISBN 0-8414-4492-7). Folcroft.
--Britain & the First Carlist War. LC 78-26910. 1978. lib. bdg. 25.00 (ISBN 0-8482-4175-4). Norwood Edns.
Gallardo, Braulio V., et al. Contabilidad De Costos I. (Span.). 1980. text ed. 12.90 (ISBN 0-538-22850-4, V85). SW Pub.
--Contabilidad De Costos II. (Span.). 1980. text ed. 12.90 (ISBN 0-538-22860-1, V86). SW Pub.
Gallardo, Jose. The Way of Biblical Justice. LC 82-83386. (Mennonite Faith Ser.: Vol. 11). 80p. (Orig.). 1983. pap. 1.50 (ISBN 0-8361-3321-8). Herald Pr.
--The Way of Biblical Justice. LC 82-83386. 80p. 1983. pap. 1.50 (ISBN 0-8361-3321-8). Herald Hse.
Gallardo, Jose M., jt. auth. see Conference, Oct. 18-21, 1970.
Gallasch, Linda. The Use of Compounds & Archaic Diction in the Works of William Morris: Anglo-Saxon Language & Literature, Vol. 60. (European University Studies: Ser. 14). 179p. 1979. pap. 20.15 (ISBN 3-261-03129-8). P Lang Pubs.
Gallati, Mary. Mary Gallati's Hostess Dinner Book. 14.50 (ISBN 0-392-07065-0, LTB). Sportshelf.
Gallati, Robert R. Introduction to Private Security. (Illus.). 352p. 1983. prof. reference 24.95 (ISBN 0-13-493403-2). P-H.
Gallati, Robert R., jt. auth. see Bottom, Norman R., Jr.
Gallatin, A. E., ed. A. E. Gallatin Collection: Museum of Living Art. (Illus.). 156p. 1954. 5.00 (ISBN 0-87633-028-6). Phila Mus Art.
Gallatin, A. E., et al. American Abstract Artists: Three Annual Yearbooks. LC 72-91381. (Contemporary Art Series). Repr. of 1939 ed. 24.00 (ISBN 0-405-00726-4). Ayer Co Pubs.
Gallatin, Albert. Considerations on the Currency & Banking System of the United States. rev. ed. LC 68-28630. 1968. Repr. of 1831 ed. lib. bdg. 15.00x (ISBN 0-8371-0438-6, GACC). Greenwood.
--Report of the Secretary of the Treasury on the Subject of Public Roads & Canals. LC 68-20392. Repr. of 1808 ed. 17.50x (ISBN 0-678-00368-8). Kelley.
--Synopsis of the Indian Tribes Within the U. S. East of the Rocky Mountains & in British & Russian Possessions in North America. LC 78-168093. Repr. of 1836 ed. 27.50 (ISBN 0-404-07127-9). AMS Pr.
Gallatin, Albert, ed. Right of the United States of America to the Northeastern Boundary Claimed by Them. facs. ed. LC 70-117876. (Select Bibliographies Reprint Ser). 1840. 32.00 (ISBN 0-8369-5329-0). Ayer Co Pubs.
Gallatin, D. B., jt. auth. see Bartlett, W. A.
Gallatin, James. The Diary of James Gallatin: Secretary to Albert Gallatin, A Great Peace Maker 1813-1827. LC 78-12126. 1979. Repr. of 1930 ed. lib. bdg. 24.75x (ISBN 0-313-21098-5, GADI). Greenwood.
Gallatin, Judith. Democracy's Children: The Development of Political Thinking in Adolescents. LC 85-60451. (Illus.). 344p. (Orig.). 1985. 39.95x (ISBN 0-933137-00-1); pap. 29.95x (ISBN 0-933137-01-X). Quod Pub Co.
Gallatin, Judith E. Abnormal Psychology. 1982. text ed. write for info. (ISBN 0-02-475510-9). Macmillan.
Gallaudet College Library, Washington, D. C. Dictionary Catalog on Deafness & the Deaf, 2 vols. 1970. Set. lib. bdg. 198.00 (ISBN 0-8161-0877-3, Hall Library). G K Hall.
Gallaudet, Edward M. Collected Writings. 600.00 (ISBN 0-87968-903-X). Gordon Pr.
--History of the College for the Deaf, 1857-1907. Fisher, Lance J. & De Lorenzo, David L., eds. LC 83-14211. xx, 288p. 1983. 17.95 (ISBN 0-913580-85-6); deluxe leatherbound 40.00 (ISBN 0-913580-89-9). Gallaudet Coll.
--Life of Thomas Hopkins Gallaudet. 75.00 (ISBN 0-8490-0537-X). Gordon Pr.
Gallaudet, John. Surrogate Soldiers. 72p. 1984. 7.95 (ISBN 0-533-06320-5). Vantage.
Gallaudet, Thomas H. Discourses. 59.95 (ISBN 0-8490-0050-5). Gordon Pr.
Gallavotti, G. The Elements of Mechanics. (Texts & Monographs in Physics). (Illus.). 528p. 1983. 48.00 (ISBN 0-387-11753-9). Springer-Verlag.
Gallawa, Robert L. On the Viability of 1300 Operation in the MX-C3 Program. 1980. 50.00 (ISBN 0-686-39231-0). Info Gatekeepers.
Gallaway, Francis. Reason, Rule & Revolt in English Classicism. 1965. lib. bdg. 23.00x (ISBN 0-374-92983-1). Octagon.
--Reason, Rule & Revolt in English Classicism. LC 65-16773. 384p. 1966. pap. 10.00x (ISBN 0-8131-0105-0). U Pr of Ky.
Gallaway, Ira. Drifted Astray: Returning the Church to Witness & Ministry. 160p. (Orig.). 1983. pap. 6.95 (ISBN 0-687-11186-2). Abingdon.
Gallaway, Marian. Constructing a Play. 380p. 1981. Repr. of 1950 ed. lib. bdg. 35.00 (ISBN 0-89984-238-0). Century Bookbindery.
Gallaz, Chrsitophe. Rose Blanche: Based on the Original Idea of Roberto Innocenti. Delessert, Etienne & Redapth, Ann, eds. Coventry, Martha, tr. from Fr. (Illus.). 32p. (gr. 3 up). 1985. 14.95 (ISBN 0-87191-994-X). Creative Ed.
Galle, Emile. Dreams into Glass. Date not set. 32.00 (ISBN 0-8446-6139-2). Peter Smith.
Galle, Fred. Azaleas. (Illus.). 600p. 1985. 65.00 (ISBN 0-88192-012-6). Timber.
Galle, Fred & Fell, Derek. All about Azaleas, Camellias & Rhododendrons. Beley, Jim, ed. LC 85-70879. (Illus.). 96p. (Orig.). 1985. pap. 5.95 (ISBN 0-89721-064-6). Ortho.
Galle, Paul L. Be Discreet. (Orig.). 1986. pap. 7.95 (ISBN 0-915175-04-5). Knights Pr.
Galle, Pierre & Masse, Roland, eds. Radionuclide Metabolism & Toxicity. (Illus.). 334p. 1982. 38.00 (ISBN 2-225-78034-X). Masson Pub.
Galle, William P., Jr., jt. auth. see Level, Dale A., Jr.
Galleani, Luigi. The End of Anarchism? 1984. lib. bdg. 79.95 (ISBN 0-87700-635-0). Revisionist Pr.
--End of Anarchism? Sartin, Max & D'Attilio, Robert, trs. from Italian. (Illus.). 83p. (Orig.). 1982. pap. 5.50 (ISBN 0-317-14866-4). Left Bank.
Gallegly, J. S., et al, eds. Essays in the Humanities. (Rice University Studies: Vol. 57, No. 1). 85p. 1971. pap. 10.00x (ISBN 0-89263-207-0). Rice Univ.
Gallego, A., ed. see International Symposium on Fosfomycin, Madrid, 1975.
Gallego, Laura. Obra Poetica. (UPREX, Poesia: No. 19). pap. 1.85 (ISBN 0-8477-0019-4). U of PR Pr.
Gallegos, jt. auth. see Eaves.
Gallegos, Frederick, jt. auth. see Dawson, Peter P.
Gallegos, Herman, jt. auth. see Galarza, Ernesto.
Gallegos, Louisa M., ed. see Crane, Barbara J.
Gallegos, Romula. Dona Barbara. Malloy, tr. 12.75 (ISBN 0-8446-1194-8). Peter Smith.
Galleli, Gene. Activity Mind-Set Guide. 1977. 1.50 (ISBN 0-914634-53-4, 7722). DOK Pubs.
Gallen, John, ed. Christians at Prayer. LC 76-22407. 1977. text ed. 14.95x (ISBN 0-268-00718-7). U of Notre Dame Pr.
--Christians at Prayer. LC 76-22407. (Liturgical Studies). 1977. pap. text ed. 5.95 (ISBN 0-268-00719-5). U of Notre Dame Pr.
Gallen, Joseph F. Cannon Law for Religious: An Explanation. LC 83-15883. 218p. (Orig.). 1983. pap. 9.95 (ISBN 0-8189-0461-5). Alba.
--Conforming Constitutions to the New Code. 58p. 1984. pap. 2.00 (ISBN 0-317-18638-8). Dghtrs St Paul.
Gallender, Carolyn N. & Gallender, Demos. Dietary Problems & Diets for the Handicapped. 224p. 1979. 16.25x (ISBN 0-398-03838-4). C C Thomas.
Gallender, Demos. Eating Handicaps: Illustrated Techniques for Feeding Disorders. (Illus.). 312p. 1979. photocopy ed. 32.50x (ISBN 0-398-03771-X). C C Thomas.
--Symbol Communication for the Severely Handicapped. (Illus.). 272p. 1980. spiral 24.75x (ISBN 0-398-04018-4). C C Thomas.
--Teaching Eating & Toileting Skills to the Multi-Handicapped in the School Setting. (Illus.). 384p. 1980. 22.75x (ISBN 0-398-03879-1). C C Thomas.
Gallender, Demos, jt. auth. see Gallender, Carolyn N.
Gallenga, Antonio C. Pearl of the Antilles. LC 79-100291. Repr. of 1873 ed. 17.50x (ISBN 0-8371-2943-5, GAA&). Greenwood.
Gallenkamp, Charles. Maya. (Art & Archeology Ser.). 448p. 1985. 22.95 (ISBN 0-670-80387-1). Viking.
Gallenkamp, Charles, jt. auth. see Meyer, Carolyn.
Gallenkamp, Charles & Johnson, Regina E., eds. Maya: Treasures of an Ancient Civilization. (Illus.). 240p. 1985. 35.00 (ISBN 0-8109-1826-9). Abrams.
Gallenstein, Edward F., ed. Chips Chats. (Illus.). 52p. ann. subscr. 5.00, with membership, bimonthly (ISBN 0-318-15942-2). Natl Wood Carver.
Galleqos, E. S. & Rennick, T. Inner Journeys: Visualization in Growth & Therapy. 160p. 1984. pap. 9.95 (ISBN 0-85500-189-5). Newcastle Pub.
Galler, Helga. Little Nerino. LC 82-183080. Orig. Title: Der Kleine Nerino. (Illus.). 28p. 1982. 8.95 (ISBN 0-907234-13-5, Pub. by Picture Bk Studio USA). Neugebauer Pr.

Galler, Janina R., ed. Nutrition & Behavior. (Human Nutrition-A Comprehensive Treatise Ser.: Vol. 5). 532p. 1984. 49.50x (ISBN 0-306-41435-X, Plenum Pr). Plenum Pub.

Galler, Meyer. Soviet Prison Camp Speech: Supplement. LC 77-89596. (Rus.). 1977. 18.00x (ISBN 0-930232-01-1). Soviet Studies.

Galler, Meyer & Marquess, Harlan E., eds. Soviet Prison Camp Speech: A Survivor's Glossary. LC 75-176411. 216p. 1972. 27.50x (ISBN 0-299-06080-2). U of Wis Pr.

Gallerstein, Gary A. Bird Owner's Home Health & Care Handbook. LC 84-9049. (Illus.). 304p. 1985. 17.95 (ISBN 0-87605-820-9). Howell Bk.

Gallery, Conor, ed. see Goldman, E. S.

Gallery, Fuller G. Robert Hudson. (Illus.). 12p. 1985. pap. write for info. (ISBN 0-9607452-4-6). Fuller Golden Gal.

Gallery, John A., ed. see Group for Environmental Education Inc.

Gallery, Tate. The Pre-Raphaelites. (Large Format Ser.). 312p. 1985. pap. 19.95 (ISBN 0-14-006993-3). Penguin.

Gallese, Liz Roman. Women Like Us: A Milestone Study Drawn from Women of the Harvard Business School Class of '75. LC 84-19095. 288p. 1985. 15.95 (ISBN 0-688-02176-X). Morrow.

Gallessich, June. The Profession & Practice of Consultation: A Handbook for Consultants, Trainers of Consultants, & Consumers of Consultation Services. LC 82-8948. (Social & Behavioral Science Ser.). 1982. text ed. 25.95x (ISBN 0-87589-527-1). Jossey Bass.

Gallet, Jeffrey H., et al. Rent Stabilization & Control Laws in N. Y. (Supplemented annually). 25.00 (ISBN 0-87526-082-9). Gould.

Gallet, Jeffry. New York Landlord & Tenant Handbook: Summary Proceedings. Gould Editorial Staff, ed. 400p. looseleaf 15.95 (ISBN 0-87526-311-9). Gould.

Gallet, L., ed. see Zola, Emile.

Gallet, Louis. The Adventures of Cyrano De Bergerac. Miller, Henry E., tr. 1898. 20.00 (ISBN 0-8274-1820-5). R West.

Galletta, Dennis F. COBOL: With an Emphasis on Program Design. (Illus.). 320p. 1985. pap. text ed. 21.95 (ISBN 0-13-139858-X). P-H.

Galletti, A., ed. & tr. The Dutch in Malabar. 1985. Repr. of 1911 ed. 50.00x (ISBN 0-8364-1340-7, Pub. by Usha). South Asia Bks.

Galletti, P. M., ed. Pharmacokinetics & Clinical Pharmacology of Beta-Blockers in Hypertension. (Cardiology: Vol. 64, Suppl. 1). (Illus.). 1979. pap. 14.25 (ISBN 3-8055-3061-7). S Karger.

Galletti, P. M., et al. Proceedings of the First International Symposium on Peizoelectricity in Biomaterials & Biomedical Devices. 318p. 1984. text ed. 85.00 (ISBN 0-677-40485-9). Gordon.

Galley, Howard, ed. The Burial of the Dead: Rite One. 1977. pap. 0.95 (ISBN 0-8164-2152-8, Pub. by Seabury). Winston Pr.

--The Burial of the Dead: Rite Two. 1977. pap. 0.95 (ISBN 0-8164-2153-6, Pub. by Seabury). Winston Pr.

--Morning & Evening Prayer. 300p. 1983. 19.95 (ISBN 0-8164-0117-9, Pub. by Seabury); leather bdg. 39.95 (ISBN 0-8164-0542-5). Winston Pr.

--The Prayer Book Office. 800p. 1980. 24.50 (ISBN 0-8164-0370-8, Pub. by Seabury). Winston Pr.

Galley, J. N. The Board & Computer Management. 185p. 1978. text ed. 29.50x (ISBN 0-220-67000-5, Pub. by Busn Bks England). Brookfield Pub Co.

Galley, John F., ed. see Southwestern Federation of Geological Societies.

Gallgher, Michael. Political Parties in the Republic of Ireland. LC 84-17161. 174p. 1985. 19.00 (ISBN 0-7190-1742-4, Pub. by Manchester Univ Pr); pap. 9.00 (ISBN 0-7190-1797-1). Longwood Pub Group.

Galli, C. & Avogaro, P., eds. Polyunsaturated Fatty Acids in Nutrition: Proceedings of a Round Table in Polyunsaturated Fatty Acids in Nutrition, Milan, Italy, April 1979. (Progress in Food & Nutrition Sciences Ser.: Vol. 4, No. 5). (Illus.). 80p. 1980. pap. 29.00 (ISBN 0-08-027362-9). Pergamon.

Galli, C., et al, eds. Dietary Lipids & Postnatal Development. LC 73-79580. (Illus.). 286p. 1973. 40.00 (ISBN 0-911216-50-2). Raven.

Galli, Claudio, et al, eds. Phospholipases & Prostaglandins. LC 77-87457. (Advances in Prostaglandin & Thromboxane Research Ser.: Vol. 3). 218p. 1978. 40.00 (ISBN 0-89004-201-2). Raven.

Galli, E., jt. auth. see Gottardi, G.

Galli, Guido, ed. Craniosynostosis. 280p. 1984. 115.00 (ISBN 0-8493-5206-1). CRC Pr.

Galli, Marcia J., jt. auth. see Jackson, Curtis E.

Galli, Mario Von see Von Galli, Mario.

Galli, Rosemary E., ed. The Political Economy of Rural Development. LC 81-1741. 282p. 1981. 44.50x (ISBN 0-87395-484-X); pap. 14.95x (ISBN 0-87395-485-8). State U NY Pr.

Galliard, J. E., tr. see Tosi, Pier F.

Galliard, T. & Mercer, E., eds. Recent Advanes in the Chemistry & Biochemistry of Plant Lipids. (Annual Proceedings of the Phytochemical Society Ser.). 1975. 67.50 (ISBN 0-12-274050-5). Acad Pr.

Galliare, Herve, et al, eds. Advances in Data Base Theory, Vol. 2. 442p. 1984. 59.50x (ISBN 0-306-41636-0, Plenum Pr). Plenum Pub.

Galliari, Gaspare. Numero Vente Quatro Invenzioni Teatrali. LC 68-21215. (Illus., It). 1969. Repr. of 1814 ed. 26.50 (ISBN 0-405-08547-8, Blom Pubns). Ayer Co Pubs.

Gallichan, Walter M. Women Under Polygamy. LC 72-9639. (Illus.). Repr. of 1914 ed. 25.00 (ISBN 0-404-57443-2). AMS Pr.

Gallichan, Walter M. & Hartley, C. G. The Story of Seville: With Three Chapters on the Artists of Seville. (Mediaeval Towns Ser.: Vol. 14). pap. 26.00 (ISBN 0-317-15220-3). Kraus Repr.

Gallick, Mary, jt. auth. see Gallick, Sarah.

Gallick, S. Lies to Live by. (Orig.). 1983. pap. 2.95 (ISBN 0-440-04786-2). Dell.

Gallick, Sara. Clothing-By-Mail Catalogue. 1982. pap. 9.95 (ISBN 0-452-25363-2, Plume). NAL.

Gallick, Sarah & Gallick, Mary. Furnish-Your-Home-by-Mail Catalogue. 1981. pap. 9.95 (ISBN 0-452-25291-1, Z5291, Plume). NAL.

Gallick, Sarah & Klein, Sardi. Our Wonderful Wedding. cancelled. Arbor Hse.

Gallick, Sarah, jt. auth. see Sequoia, Anna.

Gallico, Claudio, ed. see Verdi, Giuseppe.

Gallico, Paul. Farewell to Sport. (Autographed Sports Classics Ser.). 1981. Repr. of 1937 ed. 17.95 (ISBN 0-941372-03-0). Holtzman Pr.

--The Poseidon Adventure. 320p. (gr. 9 up). 1972. pap. 2.50 (ISBN 0-440-17006-0). Dell.

--Snow Goose. (YA) (gr. 9 up). 1941. 7.95 (ISBN 0-394-44593-7). Knopf.

--Thomasina. 256p. (gr. 5 up). 1981. pap. 2.25 (ISBN 0-380-51524-5, 59980-5, Flare). Avon.

Gallico, Paul W. Farewell to Sport. facs. ed. LC 74-128244. (Essay Index Reprint Ser). 1938. 19.50 (ISBN 0-8369-1926-2). Ayer Co Pubs.

Gallics, Paul. Beyond the Posiedon Adventure. 15.95 (ISBN 0-88411-568-2, Pub. by Aeonian Pr). Amereon Ltd.

Gallie, D. In Search of the New Working Class. LC 77-80834. (Studies in Sociology: No. 9). (Illus.). 1978. 49.50 (ISBN 0-521-21771-7); pap. 15.95 (ISBN 0-521-29275-1). Cambridge U Pr.

Gallie, Duncan. Social Inequality & Class Radicalism is France & Britain. LC 83-7535. (Illus.). 320p. 1984. 39.50 (ISBN 0-521-25764-6); pap. 14.95 (ISBN 0-521-27700-0). Cambridge U Pr.

Gallie, W. B. Peirce & Pragmatism. LC 75-25534. 247p. 1975. Repr. of 1966 ed. lib. bdg. 17.75x (ISBN 0-8371-8342-1, GAPE). Greenwood.

--Philosophers of Peace & War. LC 77-23553. 1979. pap. 9.95 (ISBN 0-521-29651-X). Cambridge U Pr.

--Philosophers of Peace & War. LC 77-23553. (Wiles Lectures Ser.: 1976). 1978. 29.95 (ISBN 0-521-21779-2). Cambridge U Pr.

Gallien, Louis E. Bases Cytologiques & Genetiques de la Sexalite, Vol. 1. (Cours & Documents de Biologie Ser.). 406p. (Fr.). 1973. 112.25 (ISBN 0-677-50540-X). Gordon.

Gallieni, Thomas M. The Unrelenting Advance of the Financial Collapse of the World. (Illus.). 121p. 1983. 86.45x (ISBN 0-86722-037-6). Inst Econ Pol.

Gallienne, Eva L., tr. see Ibsen, Henrik.

Gallienne, Eva Le see Andersen, Hans Christian.

Gallienne, Eva le see Andersen, Hans Christian.

Gallienne, Eva Le see Ewald, Carl.

Gallienne, Richard Le see Le Gallienne, Richard.

Gallier, James. Autobiography of James Gallier, Architect. LC 69-13715. (Architecture & Decorative Art Ser.). 1973. Repr. of 1864 ed. lib. bdg. 29.50 (ISBN 0-306-71247-4). Da Capo.

Galligan, D. J., ed. Essays in Legal Theory: A Collaborative Work. viii, 256p. 1985. 31.50x (ISBN 0-522-84283-6, Pub. by Melbourne Pr). Intl Spec Bk.

Galligan, Edward L. The Comic Vision in Literature. LC 83-18205. 203p. 1984. 22.50x (ISBN 0-8203-0713-0). U of Ga Pr.

Galligan, Edward L., ed. see Mencken, H. L.

Galligan, Michael. God & Evil. LC 75-36172. 96p. 1976. pap. 1.95 (ISBN 0-8091-1925-0). Paulist Pr.

Galliher, John & Cross, John. Morals Legislation Without Morality: The Case of Nevada. (Crime, Law & Deviance Ser.). 140p. 1983. 20.00 (ISBN 0-8135-0983-1); pap. 10.00 (ISBN 0-8135-1095-3). Rutgers U Pr.

Galliher, John E. Criminology: Power, Crime, & Criminal Law. McCartney, James L., ed. LC 76-47733. (Dorsey Series in Sociology). pap. 140.50 (ISBN 0-317-09072-0, 2021672). Bks Demand UMI.

Gallimore, J. G. Transverse Paraphysics: The New Science of Space, Time & Gravity Control. LC 82-50823. (Illus.). 359p. (Orig.). 1982. pap. text ed. 35.00 (ISBN 0-9603536-4-X). Tesla Bk Co.

Gallimore, Laurene, jt. auth. see Joyce, Gayle.

Gallimore, R., jt. ed. see Boggio, G.

Gallimore, Ronald & Howard, Alan, eds. Studies in a Hawaiian Community: Na Makamaka o Nanakuli. LC 79-17014. (Bernice P. Bishop Museum, Pacific Anthropological Records: No. 1). pap. 38.50 (ISBN 0-317-28837-7, 2020786). Bks Demand UMI.

Gallin, D. Intensional & Higher-Order Model Logic. (North-Holland Mathematics Studies: Vol. 19). 148p. 1976. 42.75 (ISBN 0-444-11002-X, North-Holland). Elsevier.

Gallin, Daniel. Finite Mathematics. 1984. text ed. 25.80x (ISBN 0-673-16048-3). Scott F.

Gallin, John I. & Fauci, Anthony S., eds. Acquired Immunodeficiency Syndrome (AIDS) Advannces in Host Defense Mechanisms, Vol. 5. 190p. 1985. text ed. 39.50 (ISBN 0-88167-077-4). Raven.

--Chronic Granulomatous Disease. (Advances in Host Defence Mechanisms Ser.: Vol. 3). 272p. 1983. text ed. 59.00 (ISBN 0-89004-825-8). Raven.

--Lymphoid Cells. (Advances in Host Defense Mechanisms Ser.: Vol 2). 384p. 1983. text ed. 70.50 (ISBN 0-89004-729-4). Raven.

--Mucosal Immunity. (Advances in Host Defense Mechanisms Ser.: Vol. 4). 208p. 1985. text ed. 43.50 (ISBN 0-88167-067-7). Raven.

Gallin, John I. & Quie, Paul G., eds. Leukocyte Chemotaxis: Methods, Physiology, & Clinical Implications. LC 76-58053. 442p. 1978. 62.00 (ISBN 0-89004-198-9). Raven.

Gallina, Leonard, jt. auth. see Miller, William C.

Gallinger, Herbert P., jt. ed. see Smith, Preserved.

Gallinger, Ray. Smoke Rings over the Valley. 1983. 7.95 (ISBN 0-932052-32-0). North Country.

Gallington, R. O., jt. auth. see Giachino, J. W.

Gallion, Arthur, jt. auth. see Eisner, Simon.

Gallion, Arthur B. & Eisner, Simon. The Urban Pattern, City Planning & Design. 4th ed. 528p. 1980. 14.95x (ISBN 0-442-26261-2). Van Nos Reinhold.

Gallion, Leona M. & Kavan, C. Bruce. Computer Analyzed Vocabulary-Controlled Dictation Materials for Beginning Gregg Shorthand. 2nd ed. 270p. 1981. pap. text ed. 9.50x (ISBN 0-8134-2210-8). Interstate.

Gallishaw, John. The Only Two Ways to Write a Story. 486p. 1981. Repr. of 1928 ed. lib. bdg. 40.00 (ISBN 0-8495-1964-0). Arden Lib.

--Twenty Problems of the Fiction Writer. 455p. 1983. Repr. of 1929 ed. lib. bdg. 50.00 (ISBN 0-89760-371-0). Telegraph Bks.

Gallistel, C. R. The Organization of Action: A New Synthesis. 448p. 1980. 29.95x (ISBN 0-89859-009-4). L Erlbaum Assocs.

Gallistel, C. R., jt. auth. see Gelman, Rochel.

Gallivan, G. P. Watershed. (Irish Play Ser.). pap. 3.95x (ISBN 0-912262-75-3). Proscenium.

Gallivan, Marion F. Fun for Kids: An Index to Children's Craft Books. LC 81-5649. vii, 340p. 1981. 17.00 (ISBN 0-8108-1439-0). Scarecrow.

Gallix, Francois, ed. see White, T. H.

Gallman, Robert E., ed. Recent Developments in the Study of Economic & Business History: Essays in Memory of Herman E. Krooss. LC 76-13956. (Research in Economic History: Suppl. 1). 450p. 1977. lib. bdg. 40.00 (ISBN 0-89232-035-4). Jai Pr.

Gallman, Waldemar J. Iraq under General Nuri: My Recollections of Nuri Al-Said, 1954-1958. LC 63-19559. pap. 65.30 (ISBN 0-317-19869-6, 2023105). Bks Demand UMI.

Gallo, Adrienne. F. Scott Fitzgerald. 1984. pap. cancelled (ISBN 0-8044-5976-2). Ungar.

Gallo, Angela L. Interpretation, Planetary & Age Cycles. 192p. 1978. 8.50 (ISBN 0-86690-031-4, 1117-01). Am Fed Astrologers.

Gallo, Armando. Genesis: I Know What I Like. rev. ed. LC 79-92770. (Illus.). 176p. 25.00 (ISBN 0-9604036-1-2); pap. 15.95 (ISBN 0-9604036-0-4). DIY Bks.

Gallo, Barbara G. Virginia Forms, Vol. III. 411p. 1984. 75.00 (ISBN 0-87215-766-0). Michie Co.

--Virginia Forms, Vol. IV. 382p. 1984. 75.00 (ISBN 0-87215-786-5). Michie Co.

Gallo, Barbara G., jt. auth. see Smith, George P.

Gallo, Barbara M., jt. auth. see Hudak, Carolyn M.

Gallo, D. M. & Porter, R. M., eds. Kleinian Groups & Related Topics: Proceedings, Oaxtepec, Mexico, 1981. (Lecture Notes in Mathematics: Vol. 971). 117p. 1983. pap. 11.00 (ISBN 0-387-11975-2). Springer-Verlag.

Gallo, Daniel & Kramer, Frederick. The Putnam Division. 1981. pap. 8.95 (ISBN 0-915276-29-1). Quadrant Pr.

Gallo, Donald R., ed. Confronting Writing Obstacles. 173p. (Reprinted from Fall 1977 Connecticut English Journal). 7.80 (ISBN 0-317-35259-8, 08296); members 6.00 (ISBN 0-317-35260-1). NCTE.

--Gaggle II. 64p. 1981. 5.00 (ISBN 0-8141-1821-6). NCTE.

--A Gaggle of Gimmicks. 65p. 1978. 5.00 (ISBN 0-8141-1822-4). NCTE.

--A Gaggle of Gimmicks. 65p. (Reprinted from Spring 1978 Connecticut English Journal). 5.00 (ISBN 0-8141-1822-4); members 4.00 (ISBN 0-317-35271-7). NCTE.

--The Heard Word. 144p. 1979. 6.25 (ISBN 0-8141-2060-1). NCTE.

--Reading English. 1124p. (Reprinted from Fall 1978 Connecticut English Journal). 6.30 (ISBN 0-317-35303-9, 38667); members 4.50 (ISBN 0-317-35304-7). NCTE.

--Sixteen: Short Stories by Outstanding Writers for Young Adults. LC 84-3250. 208p. (gr. 7 up). 1984. 16.95 (ISBN 0-385-29346-1). Delacorte.

--Sixteen: Short Stories by Outstanding Young Adult Writers. (gr. k-12). 1985. pap. 2.50 (ISBN 0-440-97757-6, LFL). Dell.

Gallo, Ernest A. The Poetria Nova & Its Sources in Early Rhetorical Doctrine. (De Proprietatibus Litterarum, Ser. Maior: No. 10). 1971. text ed. 26.40x (ISBN 90-2791-794-9). Mouton.

Gallo, Ezequiel. Farmers in Revolt: The Revolutions of 1893 in the Province of Santa Fe, Argentina. (Institute of Latin American Studies Monographs: No. 7). (Illus.). 97p. 1976. 35.00 (ISBN 0-485-17707-2, Pub. by Athlone Pr Ltd). Longwood Pub Group.

Gallo, F. A. Music of the Middle Ages II. (Illus.). 150p. 1985. 34.50 (ISBN 0-521-23049-7); pap. 14.95 (ISBN 0-521-28483-X). Cambridge U Pr.

Gallo, Frank J. & Campbell, Regis I. Small Residential Structures: Construction Practices & Material Take-off Estimates. LC 83-16911. 254p. 1984. 29.95 (ISBN 0-471-86914-7); 39.95 (ISBN 0-471-88359-X); student manual 12.95 (ISBN 0-471-86915-5). Wiley.

Gallo, Gary, jt. auth. see Carroll, Marilyn.

Gallo, Giovanni. The Lazy Beaver. (Illus.). 40p. (ps-3). 1983. pap. 9.95 (ISBN 0-399-20965-4, Philomel). Putnam Pub Group.

Gallo, Joseph D. & Rink, Henry W. Shaping College Writing: Paragraph & Essay. 4th ed. 166p. 1985. pap. text ed. 10.95 (ISBN 0-15-580863-X, HC); answer key avail. (ISBN 0-15-580864-8). HarBraceJ.

Gallo, Leonard, jt. auth. see Leanza, Frank.

Gallo, Michael & Kiehl, Charles. Basic Arithmetic. 1981. pap. text ed. 21.70x (ISBN 0-673-16223-0). Scott F.

--Introductory Algebra. LC 83-21825. 450p. 1984. pap. text ed. 27.95 (ISBN 0-314-78001-7); test bank avail. (ISBN 0-314-78002-5). West Pub.

Gallo, Michael A. & Nenno, Robert B. Computers in Society with BASIC & Pascal. 1985. pap. text ed. write for info. (ISBN 0-87150-852-4, 37L8700). PWS Pubs.

Gallo, Pat, ed. The Urban Experience of Italian Americans. 1977. 9.95 (ISBN 0-686-22157-5). Am Italian.

Gallo, Patrick J. Ethnic Alienation: The Italian-Americans. LC 72-9915. 254p. 1974. 24.50 (ISBN 0-8386-1244-X). Fairleigh Dickinson.

--India's Image of the International System. 101p. 1980. 13.00x (ISBN 0-89126-089-7). MA-AH Pub.

--Old Bread, New Wine: A Portrait of the Italian-Americans. LC 80-20401. 360p. 1981. 18.95 (ISBN 0-88229-146-7). Nelson-Hall.

--Swords & Plowshares: The United States & Disarmament 1898-1979. 101p. 1980. pap. text ed. 13.00x (ISBN 0-89126-090-0). MA-AH Pub.

Gallo, Philip, Jr. A Printer's Dozen. 1985. pap. write for info. (ISBN 0-931460-28-X). Bieler.

Gallo, Phillip S., Jr., jt. auth. see Linton, Marigold.

Gallo, Robert C., jt. ed. see Sarin, Prem S.

Gallo, Robert C., et al, eds. Human T-Cell Leukemia - Lymphoma Virus: The Family of Human T-Lymphotropic Retroviruses: Their Role in Malignancies & Association with AIDS. LC 84-1757. (Illus.). 375p. 1984. 55.00x (ISBN 0-87969-170-0). Cold Spring Harbor.

Gallo, Robert C., jt. ed. see Marchesi, Vincent T.

Gallo, Robert G., ed. Recent Advances in Cancer Research: Cell Biology, Molecular Biology & Tumor Virology. (Uniscience Ser.). 1977. Vol. 1, 280p. 64.95 (ISBN 0-8493-5138-3); Vol. 2, 240 Pgs. 59.95 (ISBN 0-8493-5139-1). CRC Pr.

Gallo, Robert P., jt. auth. see Turk, Frederick J.

Gallo, Rose A. F. Scott Fitzgerald. LC 76-15650. (Literature and Life Ser.). 1978. 12.95x (ISBN 0-8044-2225-7). Ungar.

--F. Scott Fitzgerald. LC 76-15650. (Literature & Life Ser.). 166p. 1984. pap. 6.95 (ISBN 0-8044-6179-1). Ungar.

Gallois, L. Les Geographes Allenmands de la Renaissance. (Illus., Fr.). 1890. pap. text ed. 21.75x (ISBN 90-6041-022-X). Humanities.

Gallon, Arthur J. Coaching: Ideas & Ideals. 2nd ed. LC 79-90061. (Illus.). 1980. text ed. 18.95 (ISBN 0-395-28693-X). HM.

Gallon, J. R., jt. ed. see Stewart, W. D.

Gallon, R. L., ed. The Psychosomatic Approach to Illness. 320p. 1982. 48.00 (ISBN 0-444-00656-7, Biomedical Pr). Elsevier.

Gallop, David, ed. Parmenides of Elea: Fragments: A Text & Translation with Introduction. (Phoenix Supplementary Ser.: Vol. 18). 160p. 1984. 20.00x (ISBN 0-8020-2443-2). U of Toronto Pr.

Gallop, David, tr. & notes by see Plato.

Gallop, Jane. The Daughter's Seduction: Feminism & Psychoanalysis. LC 81-70709. 164p. 1982. 19.95x (ISBN 0-8014-1493-8). Cornell U Pr.

--The Daughter's Seduction: Feminism & Psychoanalysis. LC 81-70709. 164p. 1984. pap. 9.95x (ISBN 0-8014-9235-1). Cornell U Pr.

--Intersections: A Reading of Sade with Bataille, Blanchot, & Klossowski. LC 80-23117. viii, 135p. 1981. 15.50x (ISBN 0-8032-2110-X). U of Nebr Pr.

--Reading Lacan. 208p. 1985. 19.95x (ISBN 0-8014-1585-3). Cornell U Pr.

Gallop, Rodney. A Book of the Basques. LC 79-174355. (Illus.). Repr. of 1930 ed. 15.00 (ISBN 0-405-08548-6, Blom Pubns). Ayer Co Pubs.

--A Book of the Basques. new ed. LC 76-137133. (Basque Bk.). (Illus.). xv, 298p. 1970. Repr. of 1930 ed. 9.00 (ISBN 0-87417-029-X). U of Nev Pr.

Gallopin, Giberte. Planning Methods & the Human Environment. (Socio-Economic Studies: No. 4). 68p. 1981. pap. 7.50 (ISBN 92-3-101894-9, U1106, UNESCO). Unipub.

Gallopoulos, Nicholas E., jt. ed. see Colucci, Joseph M.

Gallos, Philip L. Cure Cottages of Saranac Lake: Architecture & History of a Pioneer Health Resort. LC 85-8697. (Illus.). 184p. 1985. write for info. (ISBN 0-9615159-0-2). Hist Saranac.

Gallot, Mildred B. A History of Grambling State University. (Orig.). 280p. (Orig.). 1985. lib. bdg. 24.50 (ISBN 0-8191-4647-1); pap. text ed. 13.25 (ISBN 0-8191-4648-X). U Pr of Amer.

Galloway. Twelve Ways to Develop a Positive Attitude. 1975. pap. 1.95 (ISBN 0-8423-7550-3). Tyndale.

Galloway & Ball. Schools & Disruptive Pupils. LC 81-15601. 1982. pap. 10.95x (ISBN 0-582-49707-8). Longman.

Galloway, et al. Player's Manual-Paintco: A Computerized Marketing Simulation. 66p. 1985. write for info. instr's. manual for simulation (ISBN 0-02-340350-0). Macmillan.

Galloway, Albert. Illustrated Coin Dating Guide of the Eastern World. Bruce, Colin, ed. (Illus.). 134p. (Orig.). 1984. pap. 9.95 (ISBN 0-87341-046-7). Krause Pubns.

Galloway, Anne. Tovangar. 1978. 2.00 (ISBN 0-939046-25-3). Malki Mus Pr.

Galloway, Anne, jt. auth. see Saubel, Katherine S.

Galloway, B. R. The Union of England & Scotland. 300p. 1985. text ed. 38.00x (ISBN 0-85976-143-6, Pub. by Donald Scotland). Humanities.

Galloway, Bruce. Fantasy Wargaming. LC 81-48450. 224p. 1982. 14.95 (ISBN 0-8128-2862-3). Stein & Day.

--Walks in East Anglia I: Norfolk & Suffolk. (Illus.). 182p. 1981. 14.95 (ISBN 0-85115-131-0, 0-85115-135-3, Pub. by Boydell & Brewer); pap. 8.95 (ISBN 0-85115-135-3). Longwood Pub Group.

--Walks in East Anglia II: Cambridgeshire & Essex. (Illus.). 192p. 1982. 14.95 (ISBN 0-85115-163-9, Pub. by Boydell & Brewer); pap. 8.95 (ISBN 0-85115-168-X). Longwood Pub Group.

Galloway, Bruce, ed. Prejudice & Pride: Discrimination Against Gay People in Modern Britain. LC 83-11185. (Illus.). 246p. (Orig.). 1984. pap. 11.95 (ISBN 0-7100-9916-9). Routledge & Kegan.

Galloway, Charles G. Psychology for Learning & Teaching. 1976. text ed. 27.95 (ISBN 0-07-022737-3). McGraw.

Galloway, Charles M. Silent Language in the Classroom. LC 76-23912. (Fastback: No.86). (Orig.). 1976. pap. 0.75 (ISBN 0-87367-086-8). Phi Delta Kappa.

Galloway, D. Schools & Persistent Absentees. LC 84-14913. (Illus.). 200p. 1985. 30.00 (ISBN 0-08-030834-1, Pub. by Aberdeen Scotland); pap. 15.00 (ISBN 0-08-030833-3, Pub. by Aberdeen Scotland). Pergamon.

Galloway, Dale. Rebuild Your Life. 1981. pap. 4.95 (ISBN 0-8423-5323-2). Tyndale.

--You Can Win with Love. LC 76-15129. 1980. pap. 2.95 (ISBN 0-89081-233-0). Harvest Hse.

Galloway, Dale E. Dare to Discipline Yourself. 160p. 1983. pap. 5.95 (ISBN 0-8007-5129-9, Power Bks). Revell.

--Expect a Miracle. 1982. pap. 4.95 (ISBN 0-8423-0822-9). Tyndale.

--The Fine Art of Getting along with Others. 192p. 1984. 9.95 (ISBN 0-8007-1221-8). Revell.

--Una Nueva Ilusion. Ward, Rhode F., tr. 169p. (Span.). 1982. pap. 3.95 (ISBN 0-89922-158-0). Edit Caribe.

Galloway, David. The Absurd Hero in American Fiction: Updike, Styron, Bellow, Salinger. 2nd rev. ed. 281p. 1981. text ed. 22.50x (ISBN 0-292-70356-2); pap. text ed. 10.95x (ISBN 0-292-70355-4). U of Tex Pr.

--Edward Lewis Wallant. (United States Authors Ser.). 1979. lib. bdg. 14.50 (ISBN 0-8057-7250-2, Twayne). G K Hall.

--A Family Album. 1980. pap. 6.95 (ISBN 0-7145-3785-3). Riverrun NY.

--Lamaar Ransom. 250p. 1981. 11.95 (ISBN 0-7145-3686-5). Riverrun NY.

--Lamaar Ransom, Private Eye. 256p. 1987. pap. 6.95 (ISBN 0-7145-3880-9). Riverrun NY.

--Melody Jones. 1981. 9.95 (ISBN 0-7145-3807-8); pap. 4.95 (ISBN 0-7145-3733-0). Riverrun NY.

--Schools, Pupils, & Special Educational Needs. LC 84-23077. 192p. 1985. 26.00 (ISBN 0-7099-1160-2, Pub. by Croom Helm Ltd); pap. 12.00 (ISBN 0-7099-1175-0). Longwood Pub Group.

--Tamsen. 448p. 14.95 (ISBN 0-15-187992-3). HarBraceJ.

Galloway, David, ed. Elizabethan Theatre Three. (Illus.). xvi, 149p. 1973. 16.50 (ISBN 0-208-01331-8, Archon). Shoe String.

--Elizabethan Theatre Two. (Illus.). xiii, 148p. 1970. 16.50 (ISBN 0-208-01145-5, Archon). Shoe String.

--Norwich Fifteen Forty to Sixteen Forty-Two. (Records of Early English Drama Ser.). 608p. 1984. 85.00x (ISBN 0-8020-5648-2). U of Toronto Pr.

Galloway, David & Sabisch, Christian, eds. Calamus: Male Homosexuality in Twentieth Century Literature: an International Anthology. LC 81-13836. 480p. 1982. 16.50 (ISBN 0-688-00797-X). Morrow.

--Calamus: Male Homosexuality in Twentieth Century Literature: An International Anthology. 480p. 1982. pap. 9.25 (ISBN 0-688-00606-X, Quill NY). Morrow.

Galloway, David, ed. see Poe, Edgar Allan.

Galloway, David, et al. New Writers, No. 12. 1980. pap. 6.00 (ISBN 0-7145-3545-1); 12.95 (ISBN 0-7145-3542-7). Riverrun NY.

Galloway, David M. Case Studies in Classroom Management. 1978. pap. text ed. 8.95x (ISBN 0-582-48562-2). Longman.

Galloway, Dianne. Learning to Talk Word Processing. (Modern Office Ser.). (Illus.). 128p. 1984. pap. text ed. 14.95 (ISBN 0-13-595919-5). P-H.

Galloway, Eilene. Foundations of Space Law. 1986. price not set (ISBN 0-89464-005-4). Krieger.

Galloway, George B. History of the House of Representatives. 2nd, rev. ed. LC 75-35894. (Illus.). 1976. 12.45i (ISBN 0-690-01101-6). T Y Crowell.

Galloway, Gordon, ed. Collected Readings in Inorganic Chemistry, Vol. 2. 1972. 9.60 (ISBN 0-910362-00-9). Chem Educ.

Galloway, Grace G. Diary of Grace Growden Galloway: Journal Kept June 17, 1778 Through September 30, 1779. LC 71-140866. (Eyewitness Accounts of the American Revolution Ser. No. 3). 1970. Repr. of 1931 ed. 17.00 (ISBN 0-405-01191-1). Ayer Co Pubs.

Galloway, Howard P. More Clipart for Organizations. 26p. 1984. pap. 10.95 (ISBN 0-87874-018-X). Galloway.

Galloway, Howard P., jt. auth. see Bullwinkle, Alice.

Galloway, Howard P., ed. Clipart for Organizations. 25p. 1982. 9.95 (ISBN 0-87874-017-1). Galloway.

--New Dimensions in Youthwork, Vol. 1. LC 72-96322. 1973. 10.95 (ISBN 0-87874-007-4). Galloway.

--New Dimensions in Youthwork: Challenges to Youth Organizations, Vol. 2. LC 74-15245. 224p. 1974. 10.95 (ISBN 0-87874-014-7). Galloway.

Galloway, J. D. The First Transcontinental Railroad: The Central Pacific & the Union Pacific. Bruchey, Stuart, ed. LC 80-1309. (Railroads Ser.). (Illus.). 1981. Repr. of 1950 ed. lib. bdg. 35.00x (ISBN 0-405-13777-X). Ayer Co Pubs.

Galloway, J. J. A Manual of Foraminifera. 1961. Repr. of 1933 ed. 25.00 (ISBN 0-934454-60-4). Lubrecht & Cramer.

Galloway, Jeff. Galloway's Book on Running. rev. ed. Kahn, Lloyd, ed. LC 84-5585. (Illus.). 288p. (Orig.). 1984. pap. 8.95 (ISBN 0-394-72709-6). Shelter Pubns.

Galloway, John. The Gulf of Tonkin Resolution. LC 76-92556. 578p. 1970. 35.00 (ISBN 0-8386-7566-2). Fairleigh Dickinson.

--The Kennedys & Vietnam. LC 71-142548. (Interim History Ser.). (Illus.). pap. 41.00 (ISBN 0-317-09394-0, 2006283). Bks Demand UMI.

Galloway, John, ed. Criminal Justice & the Burger Court. 243p. 1978. lib. bdg. 19.95 (ISBN 0-87196-231-4). Facts on File.

--The Supreme Court & the Rights of the Accused. LC 72-80833. 460p. 1973. 19.95x (ISBN 0-87196-228-4). Facts on File.

Galloway, John D. The First Transcontinental Railroad: Central Pacific, Union Pacific. LC 83-1489. (Illus.). x, 319p. 1983. Repr. of 1950 ed. lib. bdg. 45.00x (ISBN 0-313-23851-0, GAFI). Greenwood.

Galloway, John, Jr. How to Stay Christian. 144p. 1984. pap. 8.95 (ISBN 0-8170-1038-6). Judson.

Galloway, Joseph. The Claim of the American Loyalists Reviewed & Maintained upon Incontrovertible Principles of Law & Justice. LC 72-10707. (American Revolutionary Ser.). Repr. of 1788 ed. lib. bdg. 39.00x (ISBN 0-8398-0672-8). Irvington.

--Historical & Political Reflections on the Rise & Progress of the American Rebellion. LC 8-30491. 1972. Repr. of 1780 ed. 22.00 (ISBN 0-384-17586-4). Johnson Repr.

--Letters to a Nobleman, on the Conduct of the War in the Middle Colonies. LC 72-10707. (American Revolutionary Ser.). Repr. of 1779 ed. lib. bdg. 14.50x (ISBN 0-8398-0673-6). Irvington.

--A Reply to the Observations of Lieut. Gen. Sir William Howe, on a Pamphlet, Entitled "Letters to a Nobleman". In Which His Misrepresentations Are Detected. LC 72-8751. (American Revolutionary Ser.). 1781. lib. bdg. 26.50x (ISBN 0-8398-0669-8). Irvington.

--Selected Tracts, 3 vols. LC 70-166326. (Era of the American Revolution Ser.). 1974. Set. lib. bdg. 155.00 (ISBN 0-306-70222-3). Da Capo.

Galloway, Joseph M. The Unrelated Business Income Tax. (Professional Accounting & Business Ser.). 200p. 1982. 42.00x (ISBN 0-471-09916-3, Pub. by Ronald Pr). Wiley.

Galloway, Lee. Organization & Management. LC 73-8517. (Management History Ser.: No. 40). (Illus.). 525p. 1973. Repr. of 1916 ed. 25.00 (ISBN 0-87960-045-4). Hive Pub.

Galloway, Les. The Forty Fathom Bank. 118p. (Orig.). 1984. pap. 6.00 (ISBN 0-930773-01-2). Black Heron Pr.

Galloway, Margaret A. Hospital Unit Secretary. LC 83-21347. 448p. 1984. pap. text ed. 16.95 (ISBN 0-89303-268-9). Brady Comm.

Galloway, N. R. Common Eye Diseases & Their Management. (Illus.). 290p. 1985. pap. 35.00 (ISBN 0-387-13659-2). Springer-Verlag.

--Ophthalmic Electrodiagnosis. 180p. 1981. 60.00x (ISBN 0-686-79489-3, Pub. by Lloyd-Luke England). State Mutual Bk.

Galloway, Patricia K., ed. La Salle & His Legacy: Frenchmen & Indians in the Lower Mississippi Valley. LC 82-17498. 274p. 1982. 20.00x (ISBN 0-87805-171-6). U Pr of Miss.

Galloway, Patricia K., ed. see Neitzel, Robert S.

Galloway, Patricia Kay & Rowland, Dunbar, eds. Mississippi Provincial Archives: French Dominion, 1749-1763, Vol. V. 424p. 1983. text ed. 35.00x (ISBN 0-8071-1069-8). La State U Pr.

--Mississippi Provincial Archives: French Dominion, 1729-1748, Vol. IV. LC 82-17267. 424p. 1983. text ed. 35.00x (ISBN 0-8071-1068-X). La State U Pr.

Galloway, Robert L. History of Coal Mining in Great Britain. LC 69-10851. Repr. of 1882 ed. 35.00x (ISBN 0-678-05598-X). Kelley.

Galloway, Russell. The Rich & the Poor in Supreme Court History. Aigner, Hal, ed. LC 82-62643. 200p. 1983. pap. 7.95 (ISBN 0-937572-01-2). Paradigm Pr.

Galloway, Thomas L. Recognizing Foreign Governments: The Practice of the United States. 1978. pap. 6.25 (ISBN 0-8447-3280-X). Am Enterprise.

Galloway, W. E. Catahoula Formation of the Texas Coastal Plain: Depositional Systems, Composition, Structural Development, Ground-Water Flow History, & Uranium Distribution. (Report of Investigations Ser.: RI 87). (Illus.). 59p. 1977. 3.25 (ISBN 0-686-36608-5). Bur Econ Geology.

--Terrigenous Elastic Depositional Systems. (Illus.). 420p. 1983. 41.00 (ISBN 0-387-90827-7). Springer-Verlag.

Galloway, W. E. & Brown, L. F., Jr. Depositional Systems & Shelf-Slope Relationships in Upper Pennsylvanian Rocks, North-Central Texas. (Report of Investigations Ser.: RI 75). (Illus.). 62p. 1981. Repr. of 1972 ed. 3.00 (ISBN 0-318-03182-5). Bur Econ Geology.

Galloway, W. E. & Kaiser, W. R. Catahoula Formation of the Texas Coastal Plain: Origin, Geochemical Evolution, & Characteristics of Uranium Deposits. (Report of Investigations Ser.: RI 100). (Illus.). 81p. 1980. 3.00 (ISBN 0-318-03235-X). Bur Econ Geology.

Galloway, W. E., et al. Atlas of Major Texas Oil Reservoirs. 139p. 1983. 40.00 (ISBN 0-318-03333-X). Bur Econ Geology.

--South Texas Uranium Province, Geologic Perspective. (Guidebook Ser.: GB 18). (Illus.). 81p. 1979. 3.00 (ISBN 0-686-29323-1, GB 18). Bur Econ Geology.

--Depositional Framework, Hydrostratigraphy & Uranium Mineralization of the Oakville Sandstone (Miocene), Texas Coastal Plain. (Report of Investigations Ser.: RI 113). (Illus.). 51p. 1982. 2.50 (ISBN 0-318-03245-7). Bur Econ Geology.

--Frio Formation of the Texas Gulf Coast Basin: Depositional Systems, Structural Framework, & Hydrocarbon Origin, Migration, Distribution & Exploration Potential. (Report of Investigations Ser.: RI 122). (Illus.). 78p. 1982. 4.50 (ISBN 0-318-03263-5). Bur Econ Geology.

--Depositional & Ground-Water Flow Systems in the Exploration for Uranium: Syllabus for Research Colloquium Held in Austin, 1978. (Illus.). 267p. 1979. 6.00 (ISBN 0-318-03374-7). Bur Econ Geology.

Galloway, William L. Motor Home Rental Guide. new ed. (Illus.). 110p. 1980. spiral bdg 7.95 (ISBN 0-9604230-0-1). B & G Assoc.

Gallucci, Robert L. Neither Peace Nor Honor: The Politics of American Military Policy in Viet-Nam. LC 74-24949. (Washington Center of Foreign Policy Research Studies in International Affairs: No. 24). pap. 50.00 (ISBN 0-317-20610-9, 2024151). Bks Demand UMI.

Gallucci, V. F., jt. ed. see Chapman, D. G.

Gallucci, Vincenzo, jt. ed. see Cohn, Lawrence H.

Gallun, Raymond Z. Bioblast. 240p. 1985. pap. 2.95 (ISBN 0-425-08185-0). Berkley Pub.

--Skyclimber. (Orig.). 1981. pap. 2.25 (ISBN 0-505-51682-9, Pub. by Tower Bks). Dorchester Pub Co.

Gallun, Rebecca A. & Stevenson, John W. Fundamentals of Oil & Gas Accounting. 294p. 1983. 39.95x (ISBN 0-87814-202-9, P-4314). Pennwell Bks.

Gallup, jt. auth. see Linletter.

Gallup, Alec. Phi Delta Kappa Gallup Poll of Teachers' Attitudes Toward the Public Schools. LC 84-62740. 20p. 1985. pap. 2.00 (ISBN 0-87367-793-5). Phi Delta Kappa.

Gallup, Alec M., jt. auth. see Gallup, George, Jr.

Gallup, Dick. Where I Hang My Hat. LC 70-123977. (A Full Court Rebound Bk.). 1978. 17.95 (ISBN 0-916190-26-9). Full Court NY.

--Where I Hang My Hat. 1970. 9.00 (ISBN 0-06-011398-7). Ultramarine Pub.

Gallup, Don & Gallup, Jim. Golf Courses of Colorado: A Guide to Public & Resort Courses. LC 84-70834. (Illus.). 328p. 1984. pap. 8.95 (ISBN 0-9613458-0-2). Colo Leisure.

Gallup, Donald. Ezra Pound: A Bibliography. LC 82-15995. 528p. 1983. 30.00x (ISBN 0-8139-0976-7). U Pr of Va.

--On Contemporary Bibliography: With Particular Reference to Ezra Pound. LC 73-630258. (Bibliographical Monograph: No. 4). (Illus.). 1974. Repr. of 1970 ed. 5.95 (ISBN 0-87959-047-5). U of Tex H Ransom Ctr.

Gallup, Donald, ed. The Flowers of Friendship: Letters Written to Gertrude Stein. LC 78-31881. 403p. 1979. Repr. of 1953 ed. lib. bdg. 29.00x (ISBN 0-374-92982-3). Octagon.

Gallup, Donald, ed. see O'Neill, Eugene.

Gallup, Elizabeth W. The Bi-Literal Cypher of Sir Francis Bacon. LC 76-135731. (Illus.). Repr. of 1901 ed. 24.50 (ISBN 0-404-02669-9). AMS Pr.

Gallup, George. Sophisticated Poll Watcher's Guide. new ed. LC 79-188499. 1976. 9.50x (ISBN 0-686-12114-7); pap. 4.95x (ISBN 0-686-12115-5). Princeton Opinion.

Gallup, George H. The Gallup International Public Opinion Polls, France: 1939, 1944-1975, 2 Vols. 1976. lib. bdg. 65.00 ea. Vol. 1 (ISBN 0-313-20156-0). Vol. 1 (ISBN 0-313-20157-9). Set. lib. bdg. 95.00 (ISBN 0-313-20155-2, GAINF). Greenwood.

Gallup, George H. & Rae, Saul F. Pulse of Democracy: The Public-Opinion Poll & How It Works. LC 68-55631. (Illus.). 1968. Repr. of 1940 ed. lib. bdg. 15.00x (ISBN 0-8371-0439-4, GAPD). Greenwood.

Gallup, George H., ed. The Gallup International Public Opinion Polls, Great Britain: 1937-1975, 2 vols. 1976. lib. bdg. 65.00 ea. Vol. 1 (ISBN 0-313-20153-6). Vol. 2 (ISBN 0-313-20154-4). Set. lib. bdg. 95.00 (ISBN 0-313-20152-8, GAING). Greenwood.

--The Gallup Poll: Public Opinion, Nineteen Eighty-One. LC 79-56557. 325p. 1982. lib. bdg. 49.50 (ISBN 0-8420-2200-7). Scholarly Res Inc.

--The Gallup Poll: Public Opinion, Nineteen Seventy-Nine. LC 79-56557. 325p. 1980. lib. bdg. 49.50 (ISBN 0-8420-2170-1). Scholarly Res Inc.

--The Gallup Poll: Public Opinion, 1978. LC 79-11610. 1979. lib. bdg. 49.50 (ISBN 0-8420-2159-0). Scholarly Res Inc.

--The Gallup Poll: Public Opinion, 1980. LC 79-56557. 320p. 1981. lib. bdg. 49.50 (ISBN 0-8420-2181-7). Scholarly Res Inc.

--The Gallup Poll: Public Opinion, 1982. LC 79-56557. 325p. 1983. lib. bdg. 49.50 (ISBN 0-8420-2214-7). Scholarly Res Inc.

--The Gallup Poll: Public Opinion, 1983. LC 79-56557. 300p. 1984. lib. bdg. 49.50 (ISBN 0-8420-2220-1). Scholarly Res Inc.

--The Gallup Poll: Public Opinion, 1984. LC 79-56557. 300p. 1985. 49.50 (ISBN 0-8420-2234-1). Scholarly Res Inc.

--The Gallup Poll, 1972-1977, 2 vols. new ed. LC 77-25755. 1978. text ed. 99.00x (ISBN 0-8420-2129-9). Scholarly Res Inc.

--The International Gallup Polls: Public Opinion, 1979. LC 79-3844. 350p. 1981. lib. bdg. 49.50 (ISBN 0-8420-2180-9). Scholarly Res Inc.

--The International Gallup Polls: Public Opinion, Nineteen Seventy-Eight. LC 79-3844. 1980. lib. bdg. 49.50 (ISBN 0-8420-2162-0). Scholarly Res Inc.

Gallup, George, Jr. & Gallup, Alec M. The Great American Success Story. 1985. 14.95 (ISBN 0-87094-601-3). Dow Jones-Irwin.

Gallup, George, Jr. & Procter, William. Adventures in Immortality. 1982. 12.95 (ISBN 0-07-022754-3). McGraw.

Gallup, George, Jr. & Proctor, William. Forecast Two Thousand: George Gallup Jr. Predicts the Future of America. LC 84-60481. 1984. 12.95 (ISBN 0-688-01381-3). Morrow.

Gallup, George, Jr., jt. auth. see Linkletter, Art.

Gallup, Jim, jt. auth. see Gallup, Don.

Gallup, Sarah, jt. auth. see Sharpless, Andrew.

Gallwey, Peter, ed. The Legend of St. Dismas & Other Poems. LC 83-82115. 126p. (Orig.). 1984. pap. 6.95 (ISBN 0-89870-034-5). Ignatius Pr.

Gallwey, W. Timothy. The Inner Game of Golf. 1981. 13.95 (ISBN 0-394-50534-4). Random.

--The Inner Game of Tennis. 1979. pap. 3.95 (ISBN 0-553-24755-7). Bantam.

--Inner Tennis: Playing the Game. 1976. 12.95 (ISBN 0-394-40043-7). Random.

Gallwey, W. Timothy & Kriegel, Robert. Inner Game of Skiing. 1979. pap. 3.95 (ISBN 0-553-24755-7). Bantam.

--Inner Skiing. 1977. 10.95 (ISBN 0-394-42048-9). Random.

Gallwitz, Klaus. Picasso: The Heroic Years. 232p. 1985. 65.00 (ISBN 0-89659-531-5). Abbeville Pr.

Gally, Henry. Some Consideration upon Clandestine Marriages. LC 83-48583. (Marrige, Sex & the Family in England Ser.). 265p. 1984. lib. bdg. 30.00 (ISBN 0-8240-5904-2). Garland Pub.

Gallyon, Margaret. The Early Church in Eastern England. 1979. 30.00x (ISBN 0-900963-19-0, Pub. by Terence Dalton England). State Mutual Bk.

--The Early Church in Northumbria. (Illus.). 1979. 20.00 (ISBN 0-900963-74-3, Pub. by Terence Dalton England). State Mutual Bk.
--The Early Church in Wessex & Mercia. 120p. 1981. 30.00x (ISBN 0-900963-58-1, Pub. by Terence Dalton England). State Mutual Bk.
Galm, John A. Sidney's Arcadian Poems. (Salzburg Studies in English Literature,Elizabethan & Renaissance Studies: No. 1). 229p. 1973. pap. text ed. 25.50x (ISBN 0-391-01379-3). Humanities.
Galnoor, Itzhak. Steering the Polity: Communication & Politics in Israel. (Illus.). 384p. 1982. 27.50 (ISBN 0-8039-1340-0). Sage.
Galnoor, Itzhal & Lambert, Richard D., eds. Social Information for Developing Countries. LC 72-148004. (Annals of the American Academy of Political & Social Science: No. 393). 1971. 15.00 (ISBN 0-87761-135-1); pap. 7.95 (ISBN 0-87761-134-3). Am Acad Pol Soc Sci.
Galonska, Michael L. & Center for Real Estate & Urban Economic Studies of the University of Connecticut. Connecticut Supplement for Modern Real Estate Practice. 3rd ed. LC 84-6806. 192p. (Orig.). 1984. pap. text ed. 9.95 (ISBN 0-88462-483-8, 1510-27, Real Estate Ed). Longman USA.
Galoppi-Stevens, Nanja, et al. The Best I Can Wish You. Clark, Geoffrey, ed. 60p. 1985. pap. 3.50 (ISBN 0-9604740-7-2). Ampersand RI.
Gal-Or, B. Cosmology, Physics & Philosophy. (Illus.). 522p. 1981. 34.00 (ISBN 0-387-90581-2). Springer-Verlag.
Galot, Jean. The Mystery of Christian Hope. LC 77-1222. 1977. 4.95 (ISBN 0-8189-0346-5). Alba.
--The Person of Christ. 1983. 7.50 (ISBN 0-8199-0832-0). Franciscan Herald.
--Theology of the Priesthood. Balducelli, Roger, tr. from Ital. LC 84-80017. 274p. 1985. 15.95 (ISBN 0-89870-045-0). Ignatius Pr.
Galper, Harvey, jt. auth. see Aaron, Henry J.
Galper, Jeffrey. The Politics of Social Services. 272p. 1975. pap. text ed. 19.95 (ISBN 0-13-685214-9). P-H.
--Social Work Practice: A Radical Perspective. (P-H Series Sociology & Social Work). 1980. pap. text ed. 20.95 (ISBN 0-13-819508-0). P-H.
Galper, Miriam. The Joint Custody & Co-Parenting Handbook. rev. ed. LC 80-21185. 207p. 1980. lib. bdg. 19.80 (ISBN 0-89471-116-4); pap. 8.95 (ISBN 0-89471-117-2). Running Pr.
Galperin, E. I. The Polarization Method of Seismic Studies. 1983. lib. bdg. 58.00 (ISBN 90-277-1555-6, Pub. by Reidel Holland). Kluwer Academic.
--Vertical Seismic Profiling. Hermont, A. J., tr. White, J. E., ed. 278p. 1974. 26.00 (ISBN 0-931830-06-0). Soc Exploration.
--Vertical Seismic Profiling & Its Exploration Potential. 1985. lib. bdg. 69.00 (ISBN 90-277-1450-9, Pub. by Reidel Netherlands). Kluwer Academic.
Galperin, G. Ethiopia: Population, Resources, Economy. 286p. 1981. 7.00 (ISBN 0-8285-2106-9, Pub. by Progress Pubs USSR). Imported Pubns.
Galperin, I. R. New English-Russian Dictionary, 2 vols. 1685p. (Eng. & Rus.). 1979. Set. 30.00 (ISBN 0-8285-0603-5, Pub. by Rus Lang Pubs USSR). Imported Pubns.
--New English-Russian Dictionary: Supplement. 432p. (Eng. & Rus.). 1980. 10.00 (ISBN 0-8285-1901-3, Pub. by Rus Lang Pubs USSR). Imported Pubns.
Galperine, ed. see Claudel, Paul.
Galperine, Charles, ed. Biology & the Future of Man. (Illus.). 1976. pap. 27.50x (ISBN 2-7042-0093-9, Pub. by U of Paris). Intl Spec Bk.
Galpern, A. N. The Religions of the People in Sixteenth-Century Champagne. (Historical Studies: No. 92). 1976. 19.50x (ISBN 0-674-75836-6). Harvard U Pr.
Galphin, Bruce, jt. auth. see Shavin, Norman.
Galpin, A. M. & Milligan, E. E. French Prose: An Intermediate Reader. 1965. text ed. write for info. (ISBN 0-02-340250-4). Macmillan.
Galpin, A. M., et al. Beginning Readings in Italian. 1966. text ed. write for info. (ISBN 0-02-340200-8). Macmillan.
Galpin, Frances W. A Textbook of European Musical Instruments. LC 75-36509. (Illus.). 256p. 1976. Repr. of 1956 ed. lib. bdg. 18.25x (ISBN 0-8371-8648-X, GAEM). Greenwood.
Galpin, Francis W. Music of the Sumerians. LC 78-87458. (Music Reprint Ser). 1970. Repr. of 1937 ed. lib. bdg. 25.00 (ISBN 0-306-71462-0). Da Capo.
--Music of the Sumerians & Their Immediate Successors, the Babylonians and Assyrians. LC 73-109625. (Select Bibliographies Reprint Ser). 1936. 18.00 (ISBN 0-8369-5234-0). Ayer Co Pubs.
--Music of the Sumerians & Their Immediate Successors, the Babylonians & Assyrians. Repr. of 1937 ed. lib. bdg. 22.75x (ISBN 0-8371-3928-7, GAMS). Greenwood.
--Old English Instruments of Music: Their History & Character. 3rd rev. ed. LC 74-181161. 327p. 1932. Repr. 69.00x (ISBN 0-403-01562-6). Scholarly.
--A Textbook of European Musical Instruments. 1977. lib. bdg. 59.95 (ISBN 0-8490-2737-3). Gordon Pr.
Galpin, W. F. The Grain Supply of England During the Napoleonic Period. 1973. lib. bdg. 21.50x (ISBN 0-374-92985-8). Octagon.
Galpin, W. Freeman. Pioneering for Peace: A Study of American Peace Efforts to 1846. LC 73-143429. (Peace Movement in America Ser). x, 237p. 1972. Repr. of 1933 ed. lib. bdg. 16.95x (ISBN 0-89198-069-5). Ozer.
Galpin, William F. Syracuse University History, 2 vols. Incl. Vol. 1. The Pioneer Days. (Illus.). 270p. 1952 (ISBN 0-8156-2010-1); Vol. 2. The Growing Years. (Illus.). 528p. 1960 (ISBN 0-8156-2011-X). LC 52-2118. 10.95Xea. Syracuse U Pr.
Galprin, et al. Scarred Structures of the Bile Ducts. Date not set. price not set (BN#05970). Intl Univs Pr.
Galre-Medhin, C. Collision of Altars. Rex Collings Ltd., ed. 25.00x (ISBN 0-86036-073-3, Pub. by R Collings UK). State Mutual Bk.
Galson, Sofia, frwd. by. The Organization Woman: Building a Career - An Inside Story. 192p. 1985. 16.95 (ISBN 0-89885-237-4). Human Sci Pr.
Galster, G. M. The Corregidor Affair. 1982. 8.95 (ISBN 0-533-05180-0). Vantage.
Galster, Robert. Giants of Jazz. Repr. lib. bdg. 13.25x (ISBN 0-89190-145-0, Pub. by River City Pr). Amereon Ltd.
Galston, A., et al. Life of the Green Plant. 3rd ed. 1980. 23.95 (ISBN 0-13-536326-8); pap. 20.95 (ISBN 0-13-536318-7). P-H.
Galston, Arthur. Security Syndicate Operations: Organization, Management & Accounting. enl. & rev. ed. LC 75-2634. (Wall Street & the Security Market Ser.). 1975. Repr. of 1928 ed. 21.00x (ISBN 0-405-06959-6). Ayer Co Pubs.
Galston, Arthur & Savage, Jean. Daily Life in People's China. 1975. pap. 1.65 (ISBN 0-671-48654-3). WSP.
Galston, Arthur W. Green Wisdom. (Illus.). 240p. 1983. pap. 6.95 (ISBN 0-399-50713-2, Wideview). Putnam Pub Group.
Galston, James, tr. see Walter, Bruno.
Galston, James A., tr. see Walter, Bruno.
Galston, Nina M. & Smit, Hans. International Sales: The United Nations Convention on Contracts for the International Sale of Goods. LC 84-70916. 1984. write for info. Bender.
Galston, Nina M., et al, eds. see Parker School of Foreign & Comparitive Law, Columbia University.
Galston, William A. Justice & the Human Good. LC 79-25945. 336p. 1980. lib. bdg. 25.00x (ISBN 0-226-27963-4). U of Chicago Pr.
--Kant & the Problem of History. LC 74-11620. xiv, 290p. 1975. 23.00x (ISBN 0-226-28044-6). U of Chicago Pr.
Galsworthy, Ada, tr. see De Maupassant, Guy.
Galsworthy, John. Author & Critic. LC 76-41795. 1976. lib. bdg. 10.00 (ISBN 0-8414-4411-0). Folcroft.
--Captures. LC 71-145026. 1971. Repr. of 1923 ed. 29.00x (ISBN 0-403-00973-1). Scholarly.
--Commentary. facs. ed. LC 77-134962. (Short Story Index Reprint Ser). 1911. 15.00 (ISBN 0-8369-3692-2). Ayer Co Pubs.
--Dark Flower. LC 75-145027. 1971. Repr. of 1923 ed. 39.00x (ISBN 0-403-00974-X). Scholarly.
--Ex Libris. 1979. Repr. of 1933 ed. lib. bdg. 20.00 (ISBN 0-8495-2012-6). Arden Lib.
--Five Tales. 1971. Repr. of 1918 ed. 39.00x (ISBN 0-403-00975-8). Scholarly.
--Flowering Wilderness. 15.95 (ISBN 0-89190-659-2, Pub. by Am Repr). Amereon Ltd.
--Forsyte Saga. 1933. lib. rep. ed. o.p. 25.00x (ISBN 0-684-15368-8, ScribT); pap. 12.95 (ISBN 0-684-17653-X). Scribner.
--The Forsyte Saga. 540p. 1983. Repr. lib. bdg. 32.95x (ISBN 0-89966-443-1). Buccaneer Bks.
--Fraternity. LC 72-145029. 1971. Repr. of 1923 ed. 59.00x (ISBN 0-403-00976-6). Scholarly.
--Galsworthy: Five Plays. 288p. 1984. pap. 5.95 (ISBN 0-413-54290-4, NO. 4103). Methuen Inc.
--The Inn of Tranquility: Studies & Essays. LC 72-6724. Repr. of 1912 ed. 15.00 (ISBN 0-404-10642-0). AMS Pr.
--Inn of Tranquility Studies & Essays. LC 72-131715. 1971. Repr. of 1914 ed. 14.00x (ISBN 0-403-00602-3). Scholarly.
--Jocelyn. LC 71-98836. 1971. Repr. of 1898 ed. lib. bdg. 18.75x (ISBN 0-8371-3101-4, GAJO). Greenwood.
--Jocelyn. LC 77-145030. 309p. 1898. Repr. 13.00x (ISBN 0-403-00977-4). Scholarly.
--Letters from John Galsworthy 1900-1932. Garnett, Edward, ed. LC 79-131714. 1971. 39.00 (ISBN 0-403-00601-5). Scholarly.
--Modern Comedy. 1928. 12.50 (ISBN 0-684-10197-1, ScribT). Scribner.
--Motley. 1971. Repr. of 1910 ed. 21.00 (ISBN 0-403-00978-2). Scholarly.
--Plays. 1928. 12.50 (ISBN 0-684-10198-X, ScribT). Scribner.
--The Plays of John Galsworthy. 1150p. 1980. Repr. of 1929 ed. lib. bdg. 40.00 (ISBN 0-8492-4960-0). R West.
--The Silver Spoon & the Passers by. 16.96 (ISBN 0-8488-0064-8, Pub. by Amereon Hse). Amereon Ltd.
--Strife. (Methuen Student Editions Ser.). 1984. pap. 3.95x (ISBN 0-413-54270-X, NO. 4097). Methuen Inc.
--Ten Famous Plays. LC 75-41108. (BCL Ser.: II). 1976. Repr. of 1952 ed. 41.75 (ISBN 0-404-14749-6). AMS Pr.
Galsworthy, John, et al. Spine Chillers. Eyre, A. G., ed. (Longman Simplified English Ser.). 82p. 1980. pap. 2.35x (ISBN 0-582-52672-8). Longman.
Galsworthy, Mrs. John, tr. see Maupassant, Guy De.
Galt, Alan B. Sound & Sense in the Poetry of Theodore Storm: German Language & Literature, Vol. 84. (European University Studies: Ser. 1). 130p. 1973. pap. 18.25 (ISBN 3-261-00896-2). P Lang Pubs.
Galt, Alfreda S., ed. see Burrow, Trigant.
Galt, Denham. The Bear That Had No Bump of Locality. (Illus.). 1983. 4.95 (ISBN 0-533-05290-4). Vantage.
Galt, Florella. Sandra. LC 80-22696. 142p. 1981. 8.00 (ISBN 0-938050-01-X). Shearwater.
Galt, H. S. A History of Chinese Educational Institutions, Vol. I: To the End of the Five Dynasties (A. D. 960) 1951. 25.00 (ISBN 0-686-77970-3). Heinman.
Galt, John. The Entail. Gordon, Ian A., ed. (World's Classics Ser.). 1985. pap. 7.95 (ISBN 0-19-281694-2). Oxford U Pr.
--The Life of Benjamin West. LC 60-5041. 1979. Repr. of 1820 ed. lib. bdg. 70.00x (ISBN 0-8201-1251-8). Schol Facsimiles.
--The Life of Lord Byron. LC 75-29079. 1975. Repr. of 1830 ed. lib. bdg. 50.00 (ISBN 0-8414-4540-0). Folcroft.
--The Life of Lord Byron. 372p. 1980. Repr. of 1830 ed. lib. bdg. 45.00 (ISBN 0-8492-4953-8). R West.
--The Omen. LC 79-8265. Repr. of 1825 ed. 44.50 (ISBN 0-404-61854-5). AMS Pr.
--The Provost. Gordon, Ian A., ed. (The World's Classics Ser.). 1982. pap. 4.95 (ISBN 0-19-281629-2). Oxford U Pr.
--The Provost (John M. Aiken) 358p. 1981. Repr. of 1913 ed. lib. bdg. 50.00 (ISBN 0-89760-318-4). Telegraph Bks.
--Ringan Gilhaize; or the Covenanters, 3 vols. in 2. LC 79-8266. Repr. of 1823 ed. Set. 84.50 (ISBN 0-404-61855-3). Vol. 1 (ISBN 0-404-61856-1). Vol. 2 (ISBN 0-404-61857-X). AMS Pr.
--Works, 10 vols. Meldrum, David S. & Roughead, William, eds. LC 37-3805. Repr. of 1936 ed. Set. 325.00 (ISBN 0-404-02700-8); 32.50 ea. AMS Pr.
Galt, John M. The Treatment of Insanity. LC 73-2397. (Mental Illness & Social Policy; the American Experience Ser.). Repr. of 1846 ed. 32.00 (ISBN 0-405-05205-7). Ayer Co Pubs.
Galt, Tom. Native Place: Poems. 52p. (Orig.). 1983. pap. 5.00 (ISBN 0-938050-05-2). Shearwater.
--What Is Your Anti-Nuclear Plan? 24p. 1984. pap. 1.00 (ISBN 0-938050-06-0). Shearwater.
--The World Has a Familiar Face. 85p. 1981. pap. 5.00 (ISBN 0-938050-03-6). Shearwater.
Galt, Tom, tr. see Sadaie, Fujiwara no.
Galton & Moon. Changing Schools, Changing Curriculum. 1983. pap. text ed. 12.50 (ISBN 0-06-318245-9). Har-Row.
Galton, jt. auth. see Heimlich.
Galton, Antony. The Logic of Aspect: An Axiomatic Approach. (Illus.). 1984. 29.95 (ISBN 0-19-824430-4). Oxford U Pr.
Galton, Arthur. Two Essays Upon Matthew Arnold with Some of His Letters to the Author. LC 74-16286. 1897. lib. bdg. 8.50 (ISBN 0-8414-4550-8). Folcroft.
Galton, Arthur H. Church & State in France, 1300-1907. LC 70-185939. xxiv, 290p. 1972. Repr. of 1907 ed. lib. bdg. 21.00 (ISBN 0-8337-4124-1). B Franklin.
--Urbana Scripta: Studies of Fire Living Poets & Other Essays. text ed. 13.25 (ISBN 0-8369-8160-X, 8300). Ayer Co Pubs.
Galton, D. J., jt. ed. see Belfiore, F.
Galton, Francis. English Men of Science: Their Nature & Nurture. 270p. 1970. Repr. of 1874 ed. 29.50x (ISBN 0-7146-1622-2, F Cass Co). Biblio Dist.
--Essays in Eugenics. Rosenberg, Charles, ed. LC 83-48541. (The History of Hereditarian Thought Ser.). 109p. 1985. Repr. of 1909 ed. lib. bdg. 20.00 (ISBN 0-8240-5816-X). Garland Pub.
--Finger Prints. 2nd ed. LC 63-23401. 1966. Repr. of 1892 ed. lib. bdg. 27.50 (ISBN 0-306-70910-4). Da Capo.
--Francis Galton's Art of Travel. LC 79-53734. (Illus.). 1979. 19.95 (ISBN 0-7153-5139-7). David & Charles.
--Hereditary Genius. LC 82-62300. (Classics in Psychology & Psychiatry Ser.). 390p. 1978. 20.00 (ISBN 0-86187-307-6); pap. 8.50 (ISBN 0-86187-308-4). F Pinter Pubs.
--Hereditary Genius: An Inquiry into Its Laws & Consequences. 16.50 (ISBN 0-8446-2108-0). Peter Smith.
--Inquiries into Human Faculty & Its Development. LC 72-1638. Repr. of 1907 ed. 21.50 (ISBN 0-404-08127-4). AMS Pr.
--Inquiries into Human Faculty & Its Development. 261p. 1980. Repr. lib. bdg. 20.00 (ISBN 0-89984-230-5). Century Bookbindery.
--Memories of My Life. LC 72-1639. Repr. of 1908 ed. 25.00 (ISBN 0-404-08128-2). AMS Pr.
--The Narrative of an Explorer in Tropical South Africa. LC 5-15259. 1971. Repr. of 1853 ed. 26.00 (ISBN 0-384-17590-2). Johnson Repr.
--Natural Inheritance. LC 72-1633. Repr. of 1889 ed. 22.00 (ISBN 0-404-08129-0). AMS Pr.
--Natural Inheritance. Bd. with Darwinism. (Contributions to the History of Psychology Ser., Vol. IV, Pt. D: Comparative Psychology). 1978. Repr. of 1889 ed. 30.00 (ISBN 0-89093-173-9). U Pubns Amer.
Galton, Francis see Angell, J. R., et al.
Galton, Herbert. Freedom from Illusion. 1977. 6.50x (ISBN 0-87291-087-3). Coronado Pr.
--Freedom from Illusions. 2nd, rev. ed. 200p. 1984. 12.50x (ISBN 0-87291-165-9). Coronado Pr.
Galton, Lawrence. Med Tech: The Layperson's Guide to Today's Medical Miracles. LC 84-48098. (Illus.). 356p. 1985. 19.18i (ISBN 0-06-015372-5, HarpT). Har-Row.
--One Thousand One Health Tips. 1984. 17.95 (ISBN 0-671-47689-0); pap. 7.95 (ISBN 0-671-50935-7). S&S.
--The Silent Disease: Hypertension. 1974. pap. 3.95 (ISBN 0-451-13702-7, AE2098, Sig). NAL.
--Your Child in Sports: A Complete Guide. 288p. 1980. pap. 7.95 (ISBN 0-531-09952-0). Watts.
Galton, Lawrence, jt. auth. see Barnes, Broda.
Galton, Lawrence, jt. auth. see Friedman, Lawrance W.
Galton, Lawrence, jt. auth. see Heimlich, Henry J.
Galton, Lawrence, jt. auth. see Miller, Benjamin.
Galton, Lawrence, jt. auth. see Silberstein, Warren P.
Galton, Maurice, ed. Curriculum Change. 120p. 1980. pap. text ed. 11.00x (ISBN 0-7185-1183-2, Leicester). Humanities.
Galton, Maurice & Willcocks, John, eds. Moving from the Primary Classroom. 260p. (Orig.). 1983. pap. 14.95x (ISBN 0-7100-9343-8). Routledge & Kegan.
Galton, Ray & Simpson, Alan. Hancock's Half Hour. (Entertainers Ser.). (Illus.). 136p. 1974. 8.50x (ISBN 0-7130-0087-2, Pub. by Woburn Pr England). Biblio Dist.
Galtsoff, P. S. Pearl & Hermes Reef, Hawaii, Hydrographical & Biographical Observations. (BMB). pap. 10.00 (ISBN 0-527-02213-6). Kraus Repr.
Galtsoff, Paul S., compiled by. Bibliography of Oysters & Other Marine Organisms Associated with Oyster Bottoms & Estuarine Ecology. 1972. lib. bdg. 88.50 (ISBN 0-8161-0945-1, Hall Reference). G K Hall.
Galtung, J. Peace & Social Structure. (Essays in Peace Research Ser.: Vol. 3). 1978. pap. text ed. 33.50x (ISBN 87-7241-370-0). Humanities.
--Peace & World Structure. (Essays in Peace Research Ser.: Vol. 4). 1980. pap. text ed. 82.25x (ISBN 0-391-01159-6). Humanities.
Galtung, Johan. Environment, Development, & Military Activity Towards Alternative Security Doctrines. 128p. (Orig.). 1983. 15.00x (ISBN 82-00-06360-7). Universitet.
--Global Processes & the World in the 1980s: Prolegomenon I for a Goals, Processes & Indicators of Development World Model. (Papers of the Communication Institute: No. 20). iii, 27p. (Orig.). 1982. pap. text ed. 1.00 (ISBN 0-86638-003-5). E W Center HI.
--Members of Two Worlds: A Development Study of Three Villages in Western Sicily. LC 70-114258. (Illus.). 302p. 1971. 29.00x (ISBN 0-231-03418-0). Columbia U Pr.
--Methodology & Ideology: Theory & Methods of Social Research, Vol. 1. (Orig.). 1977. pap. text ed. 22.50x (ISBN 87-7241-373-5). Humanities.
--Methodology & Ideology: Theory & Method of Social Research, Vol. 2. 1980. pap. 21.25x (ISBN 0-391-01133-2). Humanities.
--Theory & Methods of Social Research. 2nd ed. LC 67-26343. (Illus.). 534p. 1969. 37.50x (ISBN 0-231-03088-6). Columbia U Pr.
--There Are Alternatives: Four Roads to Peace & Security. LC 84-70304. (Illus.). 224p. 1984. 35.00 (ISBN 0-85124-393-2); pap. 11.95 (ISBN 0-85124-394-0). Dufour.
--The True Worlds: A Transnational Experience. LC 79-7351. (Preferred World for the 1990's Ser.). (Illus.). 469p. 1981. pap. text ed. 16.95 (ISBN 0-02-911070-X). Free Pr.
--The True Worlds: A Transnational Perspective. LC 79-7351. (Preferred Worlds for the 1990's Ser.). (Illus.). 1980. 29.95 (ISBN 0-02-911060-2). Free Pr.
Galtung, Johan, jt. ed. see Jungk, Robert.
Galtung, Johan, jt. ed. see Lederer, Katrin.
Galtung, Johan, jt. ed. see Wallensteen, Peter.
Galun, E., jt. auth. see Frankel, R.
Galun, R., jt. ed. see Obenchain, F. D.
Galun, Rachel, et al, eds. Sensory Physiology & Behavior. LC 75-14130. (Advances in Behavioral Biology Ser.: Vol. 15). 367p. 1975. 49.50x (ISBN 0-306-37915-5, Plenum Pr). Plenum Pub.
Galupkin, Esther. Kindergarten Curriculum for the Day School. 1.50 (ISBN 0-914131-39-7, C05). Torah Umesorah.
Galuppi, Baldassare. La Diavolessa. Brown, Howard M., ed. LC 76-20975. (Italian Opera 1640-1770 Ser.). 1978. lib. bdg. 83.00 (ISBN 0-8240-2643-8). Garland Pub.
--L' Olimpiade. Brown, Howard M., ed. LC 76-20965. (Italian Opera 1640-1770 Ser.). 1978. lib. bdg. 77.00 (ISBN 0-8240-2639-X). Garland Pub.
--Six Keyboard Sonatas. Serafine, Mary L., ed. 62p. 1980. pap. 7.95 (ISBN 0-8258-0059-5, 05052). Fischer Inc NY.

Galus & Guminsky, C. Metals in Mercury: Solubilities of Solids. (Solubility Data Ser.). 1986. 100.01 (ISBN 0-08-023921-8). Pergamon.

Galus, Z. Fundamentals of Electrochemical Analysis. Reynolds, G. F., tr. from Pol. LC 76-5838. (Series in Analytical Chemistry). 520p. 1976. 114.95 (ISBN 0-470-15080-7). Halsted Pr.

Galusha, David. The First Christmas. LC 81-82147. (Illus.). 32p. (ps up). 1981. wkbk. 3.95 (ISBN 0-87973-662-3, 662). Our Sunday Visitor.

Galvan, Enrique T. La Realidad Como Resultado. pap. 1.85 (ISBN 0-8477-2802-1). U of PR Pr.

Galvan, Manuel D. Manuel De Jesus Galvan's Enriquillo: The Cross & the Sword. LC 75-153323. Repr. of 1954 ed. 28.00 (ISBN 0-404-02675-3). AMS Pr.

Galvan, Robert R. Bilingualism As It Relates to Intelligence Test Scores & School Achievement among Culturally Deprived Spanish-American Children. Cordasco, Francesco, ed. LC 77-92301. (Bilingual-Bicultural Education in the U. S. Ser.). 1978. lib. bdg. 15.00x (ISBN 0-405-11083-9). Ayer Co Pubs.

Galvan, Roberto A. & Teschner, Richard V. El Diccionario del Espanol Chicano. 1977. pap. text ed. 6.95 ea. (ISBN 0-88499-146-6). Inst Mod Lang.

Galvano, Antonio. The Discoveries of the World, Unto the Year 1555. Hakluyt, Richard, tr. from Port. LC 79-26334. (English Experience Ser.: No. 112). 1969. Repr. of 1601 ed. 16.00 (ISBN 90-221-0112-6). Walter J Johnson.

Galvano, Phil. Golf Instruction. 249p. text ed. 10.95 (ISBN 0-911913-00-9). Steffen Pub Co.

--Secrets of Accurate Putting & Chipping. (Illus.). 128p. 1984. pap. 5.95 (ISBN 0-13-798018-3). P-H.

Galvao, Antonio. The Discoveries of the World from Their First Original Unto the Year 1555. Bethune, C. Drinkwater, ed. 1964. 32.00 (ISBN 0-8337-1270-5). B Franklin.

Galvao, Eduardo, jt. auth. see Wagley, Charles.

Galveston Chapter, Society for Neuroscience, Galveston, TX, Feb.-March, 1981. Proteins in the Nervous System: Structure & Function: Proceedings. Haber, Bernard, et al, eds. LC 81-20903. (Progress in Clinical and Biological Research Ser.: Vol. 79). 322p. 1982. 48.00 (ISBN 0-8451-0079-3). A R Liss.

Galveston County Genealogical Society. Ships Passenger Lists, Port of Galveston, Texas: 1846-1871. 1984. 18.50 (ISBN 0-89308-343-7). Southern Hist Pr.

Galvez, Bernardo De see De Galvez, Bernardo.

Galvez, Bernardo de see De Galvez, Bernardo.

Galvez, Manuel. Nacha Regules. 1977. lib. bdg. 59.95 (ISBN 0-8490-2330-0). Gordon Pr.

Galvin, jt. auth. see Kent.

Galvin, jt. ed. see Kent.

Galvin, Brendan. Atlantic Flyway. LC 79-3051. (Contemporary Poetry Ser.). 96p. 1980. 9.95x (ISBN 0-8203-0501-4); pap. 5.95 (ISBN 0-8203-0503-0). U of Ga Pr.

--A Birder's Dozen. LC 84-72325. 36p. (Orig.). 1984. pap. 3.50 (ISBN 0-9604740-6-4). Ampersand RI.

--The Minutes No One Owns. LC 77-73464. (Pitt Poetry Ser.). 1977. 12.95 (ISBN 0-8229-3359-4); ltd. ed 20.00x (ISBN 0-8229-3364-0); pap. 5.95 (ISBN 0-8229-5286-6). U of Pittsburgh Pr.

--No Time for Good Reasons. LC 74-4091. (Pitt Poetry Ser.). 1974. pap. 5.95 (ISBN 0-8229-5250-5). U of Pittsburgh Pr.

--Seals in the Inner Harbor. LC 85-71692. (Poetry Ser.). 1985. 14.95 (ISBN 0-88748-075-6); pap. 6.95 (ISBN 0-88748-076-4). Carnegie Mellon.

--Winter Oysters. LC 82-13367. (Contemporary Poetry Ser.). 88p. 1983. 9.95x (ISBN 0-8203-0643-6); pap. 5.95 (ISBN 0-8203-0644-4). U of Ga Pr.

Galvin, Charles O., jt. ed. see Lee, Lawrence J.

Galvin, E. Michael, ed. Potato World Handbook. 400p. 1980. perfect bdg 19.95 (ISBN 0-937358-45-2). G D L Inc.

Galvin, Elizabeth. North of the Border Recipes for South of the Border Foods. (Illus.). 154p. (Orig.). 1983. pap. text ed. 12.35 (ISBN 0-9612880-0-0). Tia Mia.

Galvin, Herman. The Yiddish Dictionary Sourcebook. 1983. 20.00x (ISBN 0-87068-715-8). Ktav.

Galvin, James. God's Mistress. LC 83-48788. (National Poetry Ser.). 64p. 1984. 12.45 (ISBN 0-06-015294-X, HarpT). Har-Row.

--God's Mistress. LC 83-48788. (Winner of the National Poetry Ser.). 64p. 1984. pap. 6.68 (ISBN 0-06-091146-8, CN). Har-Row.

Galvin, John & Allnutt, Frank, eds. Salvation for a Doomed Zoomie. LC 83-70694. 272p. 1983. 9.95 (ISBN 0-934374-01-5). Allnutt Pub.

Galvin, John P., tr. see Lohfink, Gerhard.

Galvin, Kathleen M. & Book, Cassandra. Speech-Communication. 1972. pap. text ed. 7.00 (ISBN 0-8442-5127-5). Natl Textbk.

Galvin, Kathleen M. & Brommel, Bernard J. Family Communication: Cohesion & Change. 1982. pap. text ed. 11.90x (ISBN 0-673-15380-0). Scott F.

--Family Communication: Cohesion & Change. 2nd ed. 1985. pap. text ed. 15.95x (ISBN 0-673-18174-X). Scott F.

Galvin, Kathy. Media Law: A Legal Handbook for the Working Journalist. LC 84-60496. 224p. (Orig.). 1984. pap. 14.95 (ISBN 0-917316-75-4). Nolo Pr.

Galvin, Michael E. Oilseed World Handbook. 450p. 1981. 50.00 (ISBN 0-937358-52-5). G D L Inc.

Galvin, Miles. The Organized Labor Movement in Puerto Rico. LC 77-74389. 248p. 1979. 22.50 (ISBN 0-8386-2009-4). Fairleigh Dickinson.

Galvin, Patricia, jt. auth. see Larsen, Earnest.

Galvin, Patrick. Remodeling Your Bathroom. LC 79-91444. (Popular Science Skill Bks.). (Orig.). 1980. pap. 4.95i (ISBN 0-06-090780-0, CN 780, CN). Har-Row.

Galvin, R., jt. ed. see Callaghan, N.

Galvin, R. A., jt. auth. see Paddock, J. O.

Galvin, Thomas J. Current Problems in Reference Service. LC 77-162527. (Bowker Series in Problem-Centered Approaches to Librarianship). Repr. of 1971 ed. 34.20 (ISBN 0-8357-9040-1, 2017587). Bks Demand UMI.

Galvin, Thomas J. & Lynch, Beverly P., eds. Priorities for Academic Libraries. LC 81-48572. (Higher Education Ser.: No. 39). 1982. 8.95x (ISBN 0-87589-897-1). Jossey-Bass.

Galvin, Thomas J., jt. ed. see Kent, Allen.

Galvin, Thomas J., et al, eds. Excellence in School Media Programs: Essays Honoring Elizabeth T. Fast. LC 79-26944. 238p. 1980. lib. bdg. 15.00x (ISBN 0-8389-3239-8). ALA.

Galvin, W. Randolph. Heavenly Body. 44p. 1978. pap. 2.50 (ISBN 0-88680-081-1); royalty 35.00 (ISBN 0-317-03566-5). I E Clark.

Galway, Alberic De see De Galway, Alberic.

Galway, Bonnie, tr. see Geller, Norman.

Galway, James. Flute. (A Schirmer Bk.). (Illus.). 244p. 1983. 19.95 (ISBN 0-02-871380-X); pap. 9.95 (ISBN 0-02-871400-8). Macmillan.

Galwey, Honoria. Old Irish Croonauns, & Other Tunes. LC 76-25194. 1976. Repr. of 1910 ed. lib. bdg. 15.00 (ISBN 0-8414-4520-6). Folcroft.

Galwey, P. Lane, jt. auth. see Alvey, N. G.

Galyen, Jerry & Sear, Garry. Welding: Fundamentals & Procedures. LC 83-10438. 273p. 1984. 20.95 (ISBN 0-471-06079-8); wkbk. 10.95 (ISBN 0-471-88510-X). Wiley.

Galyon, Aubrey E. The Art of Versification: Matthew of Vendome. 128p. 1980. pap. 8.50x (ISBN 0-8138-1370-0). Iowa St U Pr.

Galzigna, L., jt. ed. see Burlina, A.

Galzin, A., jt. auth. see Bourdot, H.

Gam, H. M., et al, eds. see Levett, Ada E.

Gama, Bosco Da see Phantom, D. S. & Da Gama, Bosco.

Gama, Roberto, tr. from Eng. Diccionario Biblico Arqueologico. Pfeiffer, Charles F., ed. 768p. (Span.). 1982. 32.95 (ISBN 0-311-03667-8). Casa Bautista.

Gama, Roberto, tr. see Graham, Ruth B.

Gamache, H. Eighth, Ninth & Tenth Books of Moses. 4.00x (ISBN 0-685-21888-0). Wehman.

Gamache, Henri. Candle Burning, Master Book. 2.95x (ISBN 0-685-70674-5). Wehman.

--Magic of Herbs. 3.95x (ISBN 0-685-22021-4). Wehman.

Gamache, Henry. Eighth, Ninth & Tenth Book of Moses. pap. 3.50 (ISBN 0-942272-05-6). Original Pubns.

--The Master Book of Candle Burning. pap. 3.00 (ISBN 0-942272-06-4). Original Pubns.

--The Master Key to Occult Secrets. pap. 4.95 (ISBN 0-942272-03-X). Original Pubns.

Gamache, Lawrence, ed. see Baker, Sheridan, et al.

Gamage, Arthur W. Mr. Gamage's Great Toy Bazaar 1902-1906. (Illus.). 160p. (Orig.). 1983. 35.00 (ISBN 0-8038-4745-9). Hastings.

Gamal, Adil S., ed. see Dols, Michael W.

Gamal-Eldin, E. Revision der Gattung Pulicaria (Compositae Inuleae) fuer Afrika, Makaronesien und Arabian. (Phanerogamarum Monographiae: No. 14). (Illus.). 406p. (Ger.). 1981. text ed. 35.00x (ISBN 3-7682-1294-7). Lubrecht & Cramer.

Gamal-Eldin, S., jt. auth. see Gary, J. Olmsted.

Gamal-Eldin, Saad M. Syntactic Study of Egyptian Colloquial Arabic. (Janua Linguarum, Ser. Practica: No. 34). 1967. pap. text ed. 22.00x (ISBN 90-2790-648-3). Mouton.

Gaman, P. M. & Sherrington, K. B. The Science of Food: An Introduction to Food Science, Nutrition & Microbiology. 2nd ed. (Illus.). 224p. 1981. pap. 13.75 (ISBN 0-08-025895-6). Pergamon.

Gamanovitch, Hieromonk A. Grammatika Tserkovno-Slavjanskago Jazika. 264p. 1984. pap. text ed. 9.00 (ISBN 0-317-30313-9). Holy Trinity.

Gamans, Lynda, jt. auth. see Rogers, Dorothy.

Gamarnikow, Eva, et al, eds. Gender, Class & Work. 182p. 1983. pap. text ed. 15.00x (ISBN 0-435-82337-X). Gower Pub Co.

--The Public & the Private. 180p. 1983. pap. text ed. 15.00x (ISBN 0-435-82335-3). Gower Pub Co.

Gamarnikow, Michael. Economic Reforms in Eastern Europe. LC 68-11485. 197p. 1968. 11.95x (ISBN 0-8143-1346-9). Wayne St U Pr.

Gamba, Pietro. A Narrative of Lord Byron's Last Journey to Greece. 314p. 1980. Repr. of 1945 ed. lib. bdg. 45.00 (ISBN 0-8495-2046-0). Arden Lib.

--A Narrative of Lord Byron's Last Journey to Greece. LC 75-30618. 1975. Repr. of 1825 ed. lib. bdg. 49.50 (ISBN 0-8414-4441-2). Folcroft.

Gambaccini, Paul. Paul McCartney: In His Own Words. LC 76-8068. 1983. pap. 6.95 (ISBN 0-399-41008-2, Perigee). Putnam Pub Group.

--Paul McCartney: In His Own Words. (Illus.). 112p. (Orig.). 1983. pap. 6.95 (ISBN 0-399-41008-2). Delilah Bks.

--The Rock Critic's Choice: The Top 200 Albums. (Illus.). 1978. pap. 5.95 (ISBN 0-8256-3927-1, Quick Fox). Putnam Pub Group.

Gambaccini, Peter. Bruce Springsteen. 1979. pap. 6.95 (ISBN 0-399-41015-5, Delilah). Putnam Pub Group.

--Bruce Springsteen. (Illus.). 160p. (Orig.). 1985. pap. 8.95 (ISBN 0-399-51150-4, Perigee). Putnam Pub Group.

--Getting to the Top in Photography. (Illus.). 144p. 1984. pap. 14.95 (ISBN 0-8174-3905-6, Amphoto). Watson-Guptill.

Gambari, Elio. The Global Mystery of Religious Life. new ed. (Consecration & Service Ser, No. 1). 1973. 5.00 (ISBN 0-8198-0255-7); pap. 4.00 (ISBN 0-8198-0256-5). Dghtrs St Paul.

--Unfolding the Mystery of Religious Life: Consecration & Service Ser., No. 2. 5.00 (ISBN 0-8198-0263-8); pap. 4.00 (ISBN 0-8198-0264-6). Dghtrs St Paul.

--Updating of Religious Formation. LC 75-98171. 1969. pap. 2.00 (ISBN 0-8198-0168-2). Dghtrs St Paul.

Gambaryan, P. R. How Mammals Run: Anatomical Adaptations. Hardin, H., tr. from Rus. LC 74-16190. 367p. 1974. 48.95x (ISBN 0-470-29059-5). Halsted Pr.

Gambee, Budd L., Jr. Frank Leslie & His Illustrated Newspaper. (School of Library Science Ser.). (Illus.). 86p. 1964. pap. 3.00 (ISBN 0-87506-037-4). Campus.

Gambee, Robert. Exeter Impressions. new ed. (Illus.). 206p. 1980. 14.95 (ISBN 0-8038-1961-7). Hastings.

--Manhattan Seascape. (Illus.). 256p. 1975. 15.00 (ISBN 0-8038-5043-3). Hastings.

--Nantucket Island. rev., 3rd ed. (Illus.). 192p. 1981. cancelled 15.00 (ISBN 0-8038-5077-8); pap. 10.95 cancelled (ISBN 0-8038-5078-6). Hastings.

Gambell, Ray. The Life of Sea Mammals. LC 78-56582. (Easy Reading Edition of Introduction to Nature Ser.). (Illus.). 1978. PLB 12.68 (ISBN 0-382-06186-1). Silver.

Gamberg, Herbert & Thomson, Anthony. The Illusion of Prison Reform: Corrections in Canada. LC 83-49353. (American University Studies XI (Anthropology & Sociology): Vol. 5). 167p. 1985. text ed. 21.00 (ISBN 0-8204-0093-9). P Lang Pubs.

Gambert, Steven R., ed. Contemporary Geriatric Medicine. LC 83-10978. 412p. 1983. 49.50 (ISBN 0-306-41301-9). Plenum Pub.

Gambetta, Vern. Athletics Congress' Track & Field Coaching Manual. LC 81-81394. (Illus.). 208p. (Orig.). 1981. pap. 9.95 (ISBN 0-918438-73-X). Leisure Pr.

--Track Technique Annual, 1983. (Illus.). 128p. (Orig.). 1982. pap. 8.50 (ISBN 0-911521-08-9). Tafnews.

Gambetta, Vern, ed. How Women Runners Train. (Orig.). 1980. pap. 6.50 (ISBN 0-911520-96-1). Tafnews.

Gambhirananda, tr. from Sanskrit. Sruti Gita: The Song of the Srutis. 99p. 1982. pap. 4.95x. Vedanta Pr.

Gambhirananda, Swami. History of the Ramakrishna Math & Mission. rev. ed. 344p. 1983. 11.00 (ISBN 0-87481-215-1, Pub. by Advaita Ashram India). Vedanta Pr.

--Holy Mother, Sri Sarada Devi. (Illus.). 8.95 (ISBN 0-87481-434-0). Vedanta Pr.

Gambhirananda, Swami, ed. Apostles of Ramakrishna. (Illus.). 6.95 (ISBN 0-87481-098-1). Vedanta Pr.

Gambhirananda, Swami, tr. from Sanskrit. Aitereya Upanishad. (Upanishads with Shankara's Commentary Ser.). 75p. 1980. pap. 1.25 (ISBN 0-87481-200-3). Vedanta Pr.

--Eight Upanishads, with the Commentary of Sankara, Vol. I. 408p. 1979. 8.95 (ISBN 0-87481-198-8). Vedanta Pr.

--Eight Upanishads, with the Commentary of Sankara, Vol. II. 515p. 1979. 9.95 (ISBN 0-87481-199-6). Vedanta Pr.

--Katha Upanishad. (Upanishads with Shankara's Commentary Ser.). 136p. pap. 2.95 (ISBN 0-87481-201-1). Vedanta Pr.

--Mandukya Upanishad. (Upanishads with Shankara's Commentary Ser.). 240p. 1980. pap. 3.50 (ISBN 0-87481-202-X). Vedanta Pr.

--Mundaka Upanishad with Commentary of Shankara. 100p. pap. 1.25 (ISBN 0-87481-203-8). Vedanta Pr.

--Prasna Upanishad. (Upanishads with Shankara's Commentary Ser.). 104p. 1980. pap. 1.25 (ISBN 0-686-64775-0). Vedanta Pr.

Gambhirananda, Swami, tr. see Shankara.

Gambhirananda, Swami, tr. see Shivananda, Swami.

Gambill, Edward L. Conservative Ordeal: Northern Democrats & Reconstruction, 1865 to 1869. 188p. 1981. text ed. 15.95x (ISBN 0-8138-1385-9). Iowa St U Pr.

Gambill, Henrietta. Are You Listening? LC 84-7026. (Illus.). 32p. (ps-k). 1984. lib. bdg. 7.45 (ISBN 0-89693-221-4). Dandelion Hse.

--Happy Times with the Lollipop Dragon. LC 81-86701. (Happy Day Bks.). (Illus.). 24p. (Orig.). (ps-3). 1982. pap. 1.39 (ISBN 0-87239-538-3, 3584). Standard Pub.

--How God Gives Us Chocolate. LC 82-80027. (Happy Day Bks.). (Illus.). 24p. (Orig.). (ps-3). 1982. pap. 1.39 (ISBN 0-87239-539-1, 3585). Standard Pub.

--How God Gives Us Popcorn. (Happy Days Bks.). (Illus.). 24p. (ps-2). 1984. 1.39 (ISBN 0-87239-739-4, 3709). Standard Pub.

--Self-Control. LC 82-1210. (What Does the Bible Say? Ser.). (Illus.). 32p. (gr. k-3). 1982. PLB 5.95 (ISBN 0-89565-223-4, 4941, Pub. by Childs World). Standard Pub.

--Self Control. LC 82-1201. (Values to Live By Ser.). (Illus.). (ps-3). 1982. PLB 9.95g (ISBN 0-516-06528-9). Childrens.

--Self-Control. LC 82-1201. (What is It? Ser.). 32p. (gr. k-3). 1982. PLB 7.45 (ISBN 0-89565-225-0). Childs World.

--Two by Two. (Little Happy Day Bks.). (Illus.). 24p. (ps-2). 1985. pap. 0.49 (ISBN 0-87239-936-2, 2192). Standard Pub.

Gambill, Sandra & Ashley, Clara. Mission Studies: Philippines. (Vacation Bible School Ser.). (Illus.). 32p. (Orig.). 1981. pap. 1.00 (ISBN 0-89114-105-7). Baptist Pub Hse.

Gambino, Anthony J. The Make-or-Buy Decision. 128p. pap. 15.95 (ISBN 0-86641-000-7, 80120). Natl Assn Accts.

Gambino, Anthony J. & Gartenberg, Morris. Industrial R & D Management. 132p. pap. 15.95 (ISBN 0-86641-028-7, 78109). Natl Assn Accts.

Gambino, Anthony J. & Reardon, Thomas. Financial Planning & Evaluation for the Nonprofit Organization. 170p. pap. 16.95 (ISBN 0-86641-003-1, 81125). Natl Assn Accts.

Gambino, Richard. Blood of My Blood, the Dilemma of the Italian-Americans. LC 73-11705. 360p. 1975. pap. 6.50 (ISBN 0-385-07564-2, Anch). Doubleday.

--Bread & Roses. 464p. 1982. pap. 3.50 (ISBN 0-380-59014-X, 59014-X). Avon.

Gambino, S. R., jt. auth. see Galen, P. S.

Gambitta, Richard, et al, eds. Governing Through Courts: Interdisciplinary Perspectives. (Sage Focus Editions). 300p. 1981. 28.00 (ISBN 0-8039-1719-8); pap. 14.00 (ISBN 0-8039-1720-1). Sage.

Gamble & Corley. Alabama Law of Damages. incl. latest pocket part supplement 70.95 (ISBN 0-686-90124-X); separate pocket part supplement, 1984 (for use in 1985) 16.95; separate pocket part supplement, 1984 (for use in 1985) 16.95. Harrison Co GA.

Gamble, Allan. The University of Sydney: Pen Sketches. 1982. 26.00x (ISBN 0-909798-25-7, Pub. by Sydney U Pr). Intl Spec Bk.

Gamble, Andrew. Britain in Decline: Economic Policy, Political Strategy, & the British State. LC 81-68354. 304p. 1982. 15.75 (ISBN 0-8070-4700-7). Beacon Pr.

--Britain in Decline: Economic Policy, Political Strategy, & the British State. LC 81-683554. 312p. 1983. pap. 8.95 (ISBN 0-8070-4701-5, BP649). Beacon Pr.

--An Introduction to Modern Social & Political Thought. 256p. 1981. 25.00x (ISBN 0-312-43102-3). St Martin.

Gamble, Andrew & Walkland, S. A. The British Party System & Economic Policy, 1945-1983: Studies in Adversary Politics. 1984. 29.95x (ISBN 0-19-876174-0); pap. 11.50x (ISBN 0-19-876173-2). Oxford U Pr.

Gamble, Andrew & Walton, Paul. Capitalism in Crisis: Inflation & the State. 1977. text ed. 16.50x o. p. (ISBN 0-391-00592-8); pap. text ed. 11.50x (ISBN 0-391-00593-6). Humanities.

Gamble, Clive, jt. ed. see Barker, Graeme.

Gamble, Connolly. The Continuing Education of Parish Clergy: Report of a Survey. 84p. 8.00 (ISBN 0-918983-01-0). Soc Adv Cont Ed.

Gamble, David P. A General Bibliography of the Gambia, up to 31 December, 1977. Sterling, Louise J., ed. 1979. lib. bdg. 51.00 (ISBN 0-8161-8177-2, Hall Reference). G K Hall.

Gamble, E. A. see Stanton, George M.

Gamble, E. A. see Barnes, J. C.

Gamble, Edwin, ed. see Stolzer, Thomas, et al.

Gamble, Eliza B. The God-Idea of the Ancients: Or Sex in Religion. LC 79-66997. 339p. 1981. Repr. of 1897 ed. 30.00 (ISBN 0-8305-0110-X). Hyperion Conn.

--The Sexes in Science & History. LC 75-27287. (Pioneers of the Woman's Movement Ser: an International Perspective Ser.). xii, 407p. 1976. Repr. of 1916 ed. 29.00 (ISBN 0-88355-271-X). Hyperion-Conn.

Gamble, Felton O. & Yale, Irving. Clinical Foot Roentgenology. 2nd. rev. ed. LC 74-15632. (Illus.). 448p. 1975. 31.50 (ISBN 0-88275-102-6). Krieger.

--Roentegenolia clinica del pie: Spanish Edition. LC 81-8223. 464p. 1981. 43.50 (ISBN 0-88275-864-0). Krieger.

Gamble, Geoffrey. Wikchamni Grammar. LC 77-8566. (Publications in Linguistics Ser.: Vol. 89). 1978. 17.00x (ISBN 0-520-09589-8). U of Cal Pr.

Gamble, H. Ray, jt. ed. see Stern, Norman J.

Gamble, Harry Y. The New Testament Canon: Its Making & Meaning. LC 85-4509. (Guides to Biblical Scholarship Ser.). 96p. 1985. pap. 4.50 (ISBN 0-8006-0470-9). Fortress.

Gamble, J. S. The Bambusae of British India. (Annals of the R. Bot. Garden, Calcutta Ser.: Vol. 7). (Illus.). 136p. 1978. lib. bdg. 30.00x (ISBN 0-934454-99-X). Lubrecht & Cramer.

Gamble, J. S. & Fischer, C. E. Flora of the Presidency of Madras, 3 vols. (Illus.). 2017p. 1979. Repr. of 1936 ed. lib. bdg. 150.00x (ISBN 0-934454-97-3). Lubrecht & Cramer.

Gamble, James L. Chemical Anatomy, Physiology & Pathology of Extracellular Fluid: A Lecture Syllabus. 6th ed. pap. 43.00 (ISBN 0-317-29767-8, 2017261). Bks Demand UMI.

Gamble, James L., Jr. Acid-Base Physiology: A Direct Approach. 144p. 1982. text ed. 15.00x (ISBN 0-8018-2629-2). Johns Hopkins.

Gamble, James S. The Bambusae of British India. (Illus.). Repr. of 1896 ed. 32.00 (ISBN 0-384-17605-4). Johnson Repr.

Gamble, Jay M. Steamboats on the Muskingum. (Illus.). 271p. 1971. 9.50 (ISBN 0-913423-03-3). Steamship Hist Soc.

Gamble, John. Sarsfield; or Wanderings of Youth: An Irish Tale, 3 vols. in 2. LC 79-8268. Repr. of 1814 ed. Set. 84.50 (ISBN 0-404-61859-6). Vol. 1 (ISBN 0-404-61860-X). Vol. 2 (ISBN 0-404-61861-8). AMS Pr.

--Views of Society & Manners in the North of Ireland: Letters Written in the Year 1818. LC 77-87688. 1977. Repr. of 1819 ed. 40.00 (ISBN 0-404-16487-0). AMS Pr.

Gamble, John K., compiled by. Index to Marine Treaties. (Washington Sea Grant). 438p. 1972. pap. 11.50x (ISBN 0-295-95279-2). U of Wash Pr.

Gamble, M. W. & Gamble, T. K. Introducing Mass Communication. 512p. 1986. price not set (ISBN 0-07-022770-5). McGraw.

Gamble, Maria. One Flame for Eternity. 1984. 9.95 (ISBN 0-8062-2343-X). Carlton.

Gamble, Michael & Gamble, Terri K. Communication Works. 1984. pap. text ed. 16.95 (ISBN 0-394-32804-3, RanC). Random.

--Writing & Speaking. 1983. text ed. 15.95 (ISBN 0-394-33254-7, RanC). Random.

Gamble, Michael, jt. auth. see Gamble, Teri K.

Gamble, Sidney D. Ting Hsien: A North China Rural Community. LC 68-13743. (Illus.). 1954. 32.50x (ISBN 0-8047-0630-1); pap. 8.95 (ISBN 0-8047-0632-8, SP87). Stanford U Pr.

Gamble, T. K., jt. auth. see Gamble, M. W.

Gamble, Teri K. & Gamble, Michael. Contacts: Communicating Interpersonally. 384p. 1982. text ed. 15.00 (ISBN 0-394-32558-3, RanC). Random.

Gamble, Teri K., jt. auth. see Eisenberg, Abne M.

Gamble, Terri K., jt. auth. see Gamble, Michael.

Gamble, Thomas. Savannah Duels & Duellists: 1733-1877. LC 74-2325. (Illus.). 322p. 1974. Repr. of 1923 ed. 20.00 (ISBN 0-87152-169-5). Reprint.

Gamble, Thomas, Jr. Bethesda, an Historical Sketch of Whitefield's House of Mercy in Georgia, & of the Union Society, His Associate & Successor in Philanthropy. LC 78-187383. (Illus.). 150p. 1972. Repr. of 1902 ed. 10.00 (ISBN 0-87152-078-8). Reprint.

Gamble, W. Two Irish Poets. LC 73-12449. (Goldsmith & Moore). 1948. lib. bdg. 10.00 (ISBN 0-8414-4400-5). Folcroft.

Gamble, W. L., jt. auth. see Park, R.

Gamble, William. Music Engraving & Printing: Historical & Technical Treatise. LC 72-173166. (Illus.). Repr. of 1923 ed. 27.50 (ISBN 0-405-08549-4, Blom Pubns). Ayer Co Pubs.

--Music Engraving & Printing: Historical & Technical Treatise. LC 70-155576. (Music Ser). 1971. Repr. of 1923 ed. lib. bdg. 29.50 (ISBN 0-306-70168-5). Da Capo.

Gamble, William B., ed. History of Aeronautics: A Selected List of References to Material in the New York Public Library. LC 72-137699. (New York Public Library Publications in Reprint Ser.). 1971. Repr. of 1938 ed. 24.50 (ISBN 0-405-01747-2). Ayer Co Pubs.

Gamblin, Eleanor & Morehouse, Joyce M. The Sparrow's Song. Wallace, Mary H., ed. 192p. (Orig.). 1984. pap. 5.95 (ISBN 0-912315-68-7). Word Aflame.

Gambling, Trevor. A One Year Accounting Course, 2 pts. 1969. pap. text ed. 7.00 ea.; Pt. 1. pap. text ed. (ISBN 0-08-013024-0); Pt. 2. pap. text ed. 7.00 (ISBN 0-08-013026-7). Pergamon.

--Positive Accounting: Problems & Solutions. 200p. 1984. 29.50x (ISBN 0-8448-1470-9). Crane-Russak Co.

Gamboa, Pedro S. de see De Gamboa, Pedro S.

Gamboa, Pedro Sarmiento De see Sarmiento De Gamboa, Pedro.

Gambordella, Ted. Fight for Your Life! The Secrets of Street Fighting. (Illus.). 120p. 1982. pap. 8.00 (ISBN 0-87364-251-1). Paladin Pr.

--The One Hundred Deadliest Karate Moves. (Illus.). 88p. 1981. pap. 8.00 (ISBN 0-87364-245-7). Paladin Pr.

--Tonfa Tactics: A Strategy for Total Defense. (Illus.). 144p. (Orig.). 1985. 12.00 (ISBN 0-87364-324-0). Paladin Pr.

--Weapons of the Street. (Illus.). 80p. (Orig.). 1984. pap. 8.00 (ISBN 0-87364-281-3). Paladin Pr.

Gambordella, Theodore. The Complete Book of Karate Weapons. (Illus.). 256p. 1981. 24.95 (ISBN 0-87364-206-6); pap. 14.95. Paladin Pr.

Gambrell, Mary L. Ministerial Training in Eighteenth-Century New England. (Columbia University. Studies in the Social Sciences: No. 428). Repr. of 1937 ed. 16.50 (ISBN 0-404-51428-6). AMS Pr.

Gambrill & Richey. Taking Charge of Your Social Life. 368p. 1985. write for info. (ISBN 0-534-04758-0). Wadsworth Pub.

Gambrill, Bessie L. College Achievement & Vocational Efficiency. (Columbia University. Teachers College. Contributions to Education: No. 121). Repr. of 1922 ed. 22.50 (ISBN 0-404-55121-1). AMS Pr.

Gambrill, Don & Bay, Alfred. Swimmer & Team. (Illus.). 150p. 1984. cancelled (ISBN 0-89651-707-1); pap. cancelled (ISBN 0-89651-708-X). Icarus.

Gambrill, Dorothy J. I'm Human Just Like You. (Illus.). 32p. (Orig.). 1980. 2.25 (ISBN 0-936074-02-7). AOI Corp.

Gambrill, Eileen. Casework: A Competency-Based Approach. (Illus.). 448p. 1983. 30.95 (ISBN 0-13-119446-1). P-H.

Gambrill, Eileen & Stein, Theodore J. Supervision: A Decision-Making Approach. (Vol. 35). 192p. 1983. pap. 9.95 (ISBN 0-8039-0973-X). Sage.

Gambrill, Eileen D. Behavior Modification: Handbook of Assessment, Intervention, & Evaluation. LC 76-50700. (Social Behavioral Science Ser.). (Illus.). 1977. text ed. 35.00x (ISBN 0-87589-314-7). Jossey-Bass.

Gambrill, Georgia. Genealogical Material & Local Histories in the St. Louis Public Library. 1966. first suppl., 1971 2.00 (ISBN 0-937322-01-6). St Louis Pub Lib.

Gambs, John S. Beyond Supply & Demand: A Reappraisal of Institutional Economics. LC 76-20433. 105p. 1976. Repr. of 1947 ed. lib. bdg. 15.00x (ISBN 0-8371-8993-4, GABS). Greenwood.

--John Kenneth Galbraith. (World Leaders Ser.). 1975. lib. bdg. 13.50 (ISBN 0-8057-3681-6, Twayne). G K Hall.

Gamchina, K. Dictionnaire Francais-Russe. 911p. (Fr. & Rus.). 1977. 19.95 (ISBN 0-686-92572-6, M-9066). French & Eur.

Game, Ann & Pringle, Rosemary. Gender at Work. 180p. 1983. pap. text ed. 9.95 (ISBN 0-86861-261-8). Allen Unwin.

Gamec, Hazel S. The Disappearing ABC Game Book. (Illus.). 12p. write for info. (ISBN 0-938042-02-5). Printek.

--Looking Out of the Window. (Illus.). 12p. 1980. write for info. (ISBN 0-938042-01-7). Printek.

--The Magic Pencil Counting Book. (Illus.). 12p. 1980. write for info. (ISBN 0-938042-00-9). Printek.

Gamel, Nona. Love's Secret Garden. (Candlelight Ecstasy Ser.: No. 265). 192p. (Orig.). 1984. pap. 1.95 (ISBN 0-440-15021-3). Dell.

--Tomorrow & Always. (Candlelight Ecstasy Ser.: No. 362). (Orig.). 1985. pap. 2.25 (ISBN 0-440-18987-X). Dell.

Gamelia. Sarah. 1975. pap. 3.50 (ISBN 0-913054-09-7). Poet Gal Pr.

Gamelin, T. W. Uniform Algebras & Jensen Measures. LC 78-16213. (London Mathematical Society Lecture Note Ser.: No. 32). 1979. pap. 24.95 (ISBN 0-521-22280-X). Cambridge U Pr.

Gamelin, Theodore W. Uniform Algebras. x2nd ed. LC 83-72339. 270p. text ed. 17.95 (ISBN 0-8284-0311-2). Chelsea Pub.

--Uniform Algebras & Jensen Measures. LC 78-16213. (London Mathematical Society Lecture Note Ser.: 32). pap. 42.50 (ISBN 0-317-20600-1, 2024488). Bks Demand UMI.

Gamelin, Theodore W. & Greene, Robert E. Introduction to Topology. 1983. text ed. 35.95 (ISBN 0-03-062476-2, CBS C). SCP.

Gamer, Helena M., jt. auth. see McNeill, John T.

Gamer, Robert E. The Developing Nations: A Comparative Perspective. 2nd ed. 475p. 1982. text ed. 24.29 (ISBN 0-205-07647-5, 7676476). Allyn.

--The Politics of Urban Development in Singapore. LC 78-37778. (Illus.). 304p. 1972. 39.95x (ISBN 0-8014-0708-7). Cornell U Pr.

Games Magazine Editors. The Games Magazine Big Book of Games. (Illus.). 192p. 1984. pap. 9.95 (ISBN 0-89480-806-0, 806). Workman Pub.

Gameson, A. L. Discharge of Sewage from Sea Outfalls. 140.00 (ISBN 0-08-018302-6). Pergamon.

Gamett, James & Paner, Stanley W. Nevada Post Offices: An Illustrated History. (Illus.). 1982. 30.00 (ISBN 0-913814-57-1). Nevada Pubns.

Gamette, Kent R., jt. auth. see Vontver, Louis A.

Gamewell, Mary N. The Gateway to China. Repr. of 1916 ed. 15.00 (ISBN 0-8482-4207-6). Norwood Edns.

--The Gateway to China: Pictures of Shanghai. 1916. 12.00 (ISBN 0-686-19909-X). Quaker City.

Gamez, Tana de. Yoke & the Star. 1977. pap. 1.95 (ISBN 0-8439-0475-5, Leisure Bks). Dorchester Pub Co.

Gamez, Tana De see De Gamez, Tana.

Gamillscheg, Ernst. Etymologisches Woerterbuch der Franzoesischen Sprache. 2nd ed. (Fr. & Ger.). 1969. 195.00 (ISBN 0-686-56604-1, M-7370, Pub. by Carl Winter). French & Eur.

--Romania Germanica: Sprach-und Siedlungsgeschichte der Germanen auf dem Boden des alten Roemerreiches. Incl. Vol. 1. Zu den aeltesten Beruehrungen zwischen Roemern und Germanen: Die Franken. rev. 2nd ed. (Illus.). xvi, 474p. 1970. 70.00x (ISBN 3-11-002680-5). (Ger.). De Gruyter.

Gamio, Manuel. Mexican Immigrant: His Life Story. LC 69-18778. (American Immigration Collection Ser., No. 1). (Illus.). 1969. Repr. of 1931 ed. 12.50 (ISBN 0-405-00526-1). Ayer Co Pubs.

--Mexican Immigration to the United States. LC 69-18777. (American Immigration Collection Ser., No. 1). (Illus.). 1969. Repr. of 1930 ed. 16.00 (ISBN 0-405-00525-3). Ayer Co Pubs.

--Mexican Immigration to the United States. LC 73-144233. 1971. pap. 4.50 (ISBN 0-486-22721-9). Dover.

Gamkrelidze, R. V. Principles of Optimal Control Theory. LC 77-10742. (Mathematical Concepts & Methods in Science & Engineering Ser.: Vol. 7). 185p. 1977. 32.50 (ISBN 0-306-30977-7, Plenum Pr). Plenum Pub.

Gamkrelidze, R. V., ed. Progress in Mathematics, 13 vols. Incl. Vols. 1,2,4,8 & 10. Mathematical Analysis. 1968-71. Vol. 1, 246p (ISBN 0-306-39201-1). Vol. 2 161p (ISBN 0-306-39202-X). Vol. 4, 132p (ISBN 0-306-39204-6). Vol. 8, 215p (ISBN 0-306-39208-9). Vol. 10, 109 p (ISBN 0-306-39208-9); Vols. 3, 7, 11 & 13. Probability Theory, Mathematical Statistics & Theoretical Cybernetics. 1969-72. Vol. 3, 112p (ISBN 0-306-39203-8). Vol. 7, 146p (ISBN 0-306-39207-0). Vol. 11, 120p (ISBN 0-306-39211-9). Vol. 13, 110p (ISBN 0-306-39213-5); Vol. 5. Algebra. 214p. 1969 (ISBN 0-306-39205-4); Vol. 6. Topology & Geometry. 269p. 1970 (ISBN 0-306-39206-2); Vols. 9 & 12. Alegebra & Geometry. 1971-72. Vol. 9, 253p (ISBN 0-306-39209-7). Vol. 12, 254p (ISBN 0-306-39212-7). LC 67-27902. 29.50x ea. (Plenum Pr). Plenum Pub.

--Progress in Mathematics, 4 vols. Incl. Vol. 10. Mathematical Analysis. Wood, J. S., tr. pap. 29.30 (ISBN 0-317-30355-4); Vol. 11. Probability Theory, Mathematical Statistics, & Theoretical Cybernetics. Wood, J. S., tr. pap. 33.00 (ISBN 0-317-30356-2); Vol. 12. Algebra & Geometry. Choksy, Nasli H., tr. pap. 66.00 (ISBN 0-317-30357-0); Vol. 13. Probability Theory, Mathematical Statistics & Theoretical Cybernetics. Wood, J. S., tr. pap. 29.50 (ISBN 0-317-30358-9). LC 67-27902 (2024721). Bks Demand UMI.

Gamkrelidze, R. V. & Steklov, V. A., eds. L. S. Pontryagin: Selected Works, Vol. 1. 592p. 1984. text ed. 255.00 (ISBN 2-88124-105-0). Gordon.

Gamlin, A. T., et al, eds. Mechanical Maintenance & Installation: Supplementary Training Manual. (Engineering Craftsmen: No. J21S). (Illus.). 1976. 59.95x (ISBN 0-85083-332-9). Intl Ideas.

Gamlin, Peter J & Fleming, D. R., eds. Responding to Individual Needs: A Guide for Teachers. (Learning Potential Ser.). 144p. 1985. text ed. 16.00 (ISBN 0-88937-010-9). Hogrefe Intl.

Gamm, David. Child's Play. LC 78-51069. (Illus.). 96p. (gr. 3-8). 1978. pap. 3.95 (ISBN 0-87793-150-X). Ave Maria.

Gamma, Karl. The Handbook of Skiing. LC 81-47486. (Illus.). 320p. 1981. 22.50 (ISBN 0-394-51827-6). Knopf.

Gammage, Allen Z. Basic Police Report Writing. 2nd ed. (Illus.). 344p. 1978. 29.75x (ISBN 0-398-03204-1). C C Thomas.

--Study Guide for Basic Police Report Writing. (Illus.). 288p. 1975. pap. 21.75x spiral (ISBN 0-398-03309-9). C C Thomas.

--Your Future in Law Enforcement. LC 70-88828. (Careers in Depth Ser). (gr. 7 up). 1974. PLB 8.97 (ISBN 0-8239-0178-5). Rosen Group.

Gammage, Allen Z. & Hemphill, Charles F., Jr. Basic Criminal Law. 2nd ed. 1979. text ed. 28.20 (ISBN 0-07-022756-X). McGraw.

Gammage, Allen Z. & Sachs, Stanley L. Police Unions. 204p. 1972. 29.50x (ISBN 0-398-02467-7). C C Thomas.

Gammage, Allen Z., et al. Alcoholism, Skid Row & the Police. 96p. 1972. 9.75x (ISBN 0-398-02288-7). C C Thomas.

Gammage, B. An Australian in the First World War. (Cambridge Introduction to the History of Mankind Ser.). (Illus.). 1976. pap. text ed. 4.50 (ISBN 0-521-21018-6). Cambridge U Pr.

Gammage, Philip. Children & Schooling: Issues In Childhood Socialization. (Unwin Education Bks.). 240p. 1982. pap. text ed. 12.95x (ISBN 0-04-370118-3). Allen Unwin.

Gammage, R. B. & Kaye, S. V., eds. Indoor Air & Human Health: Major Indoor Air Pollutants & Their Health Implications. (Illus.). 400p. 1985. 39.00 (ISBN 0-87371-006-1). Lewis Pubs Inc.

Gammage, R. C. History of the Chartist Movement, Eighteen Thirty-Seven to Eighteen Fifty-Four. (Illus.). 438p. 1976. pap. 10.95 (ISBN 0-85036-213-X). Dufour.

Gammage, R. G. History of the Chartist Movement, 1837-1854 & Social Oppression of the Working Classes. 465p. 1970. 32.50x (ISBN 0-7146-2687-2, F Cass Co). Biblio Dist.

Gammage, Robert G. History of the Chartist Movement Eighteen Thirty-Seven to Eighteen Fifty-Four. 2nd ed. LC 66-19691. Repr. of 1894 ed. 37.50x (ISBN 0-678-00534-6). Kelley.

Gammage, W. see Bean, C. E.

Gammans, Harold. Lincoln Names & Epithets. (Orig.). pap. 5.00 (ISBN 0-8283-1389-X). Branden Pub Co.

Gammateo, F. Di see Lacalamita, M. & Di Gammateo, F.

Gammel, John L., jt. ed. see Baker, George A., Jr.

Gammell, Alice. Polly Prindle's Book of American Patchwork Quilts. (Illus.). 260p. 1981. pap. 8.95 (ISBN 0-399-51051-6, G&D). Putnam Pub Group.

Gammell, C. J. The Branchline Age. 1977. 20.00 (ISBN 0-903485-38-9). State Mutual Bk.

--London & North Eastern Railway Branch Lines, 1945-1965. 96p. 30.00x (ISBN 0-86093-007-6, Pub. by ORPC Ltd UK). State Mutual Bk.

Gammell, Chris J. Around the Branch Lines: Great Western, Vol. 2. 96p. 30.00x (ISBN 0-86093-213-3, Pub. by ORPC Ltd UK). State Mutual Bk.

Gammell, J. L. M. S. Branch Lines, Nineteen Forty-Five to Nineteen Sixty-Five. 96p. 30.00x (ISBN 0-86093-062-9, Pub. by ORPC Ltd UK). State Mutual Bk.

Gammell, Stephen. Git along, Old Scudder. LC 82-13996. (Illus.). 32p. (gr. k-3). 1983. 11.75 (ISBN 0-688-01674-X); PLB 11.88 (ISBN 0-688-01677-4). Lothrop.

--The Story of Mr. & Mrs. Vinegar. LC 81-12347. (Illus.). 32p. (ps-3). 1982. 10.25 (ISBN 0-688-00887-9); PLB 10.88 (ISBN 0-688-00889-5). Lothrop.

--Wake Up Bear, Its Christmas. (Picture Puffins Ser.). 32p. (ps-k). 1984. pap. 3.95 (ISBN 0-14-050475-3, Puffin). Penguin.

--Wake Up, Bear...It's Christmas! LC 81-5019. (Illus.). 32p. (ps-3). 1981. 11.25 (ISBN 0-688-00692-2); PLB 11.88 (ISBN 0-688-00693-0). Lothrop.

Gammell, Stephen, tr. see McHargue, Georgess.

Gammie, John G. Daniel. (Preaching Guides Ser.). 116p. 1983. pap. 5.95 (ISBN 0-8042-3224-5). John Knox.

Gammie, John G., ed. Israelite Wisdom: Theological & Literary Essays in Honor of Samuel Terrien. LC 77-17862. 1978. pap. 18.00 (ISBN 0-89130-208-5, 00-16-03). Scholars Pr GA.

Gammie, Malcolm. Tax Strategy for Companies. 1980. 65.00x (ISBN 0-686-39496-8, Pub. by Oyez Longman Pub England). State Mutual Bk.

Gammill, Stephen L. A Programmed Introduction to Upper Gastrointestinal Radiology. 1977. pap. text ed. 19.95 (ISBN 0-316-30294-5). Little.

Gammon, Clive. A Tide of Fish. 14.50x (ISBN 0-392-06417-0, SpS). Sportshelf.

Gammon, Margaret H. Astrology & the Edgar Cayce Readings. rev. ed. 1973. pap. 3.95 (ISBN 0-87604-067-9). ARE Pr.

Gammon, Samuel R. The Presidential Campaign of Eighteen Thirty-Two. LC 78-63975. (Johns Hopkins University. Studies in the Social Sciences. Fortieth Ser. 1922: 1). Repr. of 1922 ed. 11.50 (ISBN 0-404-61220-2). AMS Pr.

--Statesman & Schemer: William, First Lord Paget, Tudor Minister. (Illus.). 296p. 1973. 22.00 (ISBN 0-208-01405-5, Archon). Shoe String.

Gammon, Samuel R., Jr. Presidential Campaign of Eighteen Thirty-Two. LC 78-96952. (Law, Politics & History Ser). 1969. Repr. of 1922 ed. lib. bdg. 25.00 (ISBN 0-306-71830-8). Da Capo.

--The Presidential Campaign of Eighteen Thirty-Two. LC 76-13176. ix, 180p. 1972. Repr. of 1922 ed. 9.00x (ISBN 0-403-00603-1). Scholarly.

Gammon, William J. A Belated Census of Earliest Settlers of Cape Girardeau County, Missouri. 70p. 6.75 (ISBN 0-915156-18-0, 18). Natl Genealogical.

Gammond, Peter. The Magic Flute. LC 79-67162. (Master Works of Opera Ser.). 15.96 (ISBN 0-382-06312-0). Silver.

--Offenbach: His Life & Times. (Life & Times Ser.). (Illus.). 192p. (YA) 1981. Repr. of 1980 ed. 12.95 (ISBN 0-87666-583-0, Z-52). Paganiniana Pubns.

--Offenbach: His Life & Times (Centenary 1980) 168p. 1981. 40.00x (ISBN 0-85936-231-0, Pub. by Midas Bks England). State Mutual Bk.

Gammond, Peter & Burnett, James. Music on Record: A Critical Guide, 4 vols. Incl. Vol. 1 & 2. Orchestral Music; Vol. 3. Chamber & Instrumental Music; Vol. 4. Opera & Vocal Music. LC 78-8183. 1978. Repr. of 1962 ed. Set. lib. bdg. 69.50x (ISBN 0-313-20514-0, GAMR). Greenwood.

Gammond, Peter & Clayton, Peter. Dictionary of Popular Music. LC 73-166229. 274p. 1961. Repr 29.00x (ISBN 0-403-01563-4). Scholarly.

Gammond, Peter & Fox, Charles. Jazz on Record: A Critical Guide. Morgan, Alun, ed. LC 78-8189. 1978. Repr. of 1960 ed. lib. bdg. 45.00x (ISBN 0-313-20513-2, GAJA). Greenwood.

Gammond, Peter & Horricks, Ray. The Music Goes Round & Round: A Cool Look at the Record Industry. 11.95 (ISBN 0-7043-2239-0, Pub. by Quartet England). Charles River Bks.

Gammond, Peter, jt. auth. see Clayton, Peter.

Gammond, Peter see Frost, David.

Gammond, Peter, ed. Duke Ellington: His Life & Music. LC 77-1927. (The Roots of Jazz Ser.). 1977. Repr. of 1958 ed. lib. bdg. 25.00 (ISBN 0-306-70874-4). Da Capo.

--An Illustrated Guide to Composers of Classical Music. LC 81-66318. (Illus.). 240p. 1981. 9.95 (ISBN 0-668-05315-1, 5315). Arco.

--An Illustrated Guide to Composers of Opera. LC 81-66319. (Illus.). 240p. 1981. 9.95 (ISBN 0-668-05317-8, 5317). Arco.

Gammons, jt. auth. see Farrugia.

Gammons, Peter. Beyond the Sixth Game. (Illus.). 280p. 1985. 15.95 (ISBN 0-395-35345-9). HM.

Gammons, Robert C., ed. see Schultes, Hermann.

Gamon, Richard Louis. The Thoughts of Thomas Robert Malthus As They Apply to the Economic Complexities of Our Present Age. (The Living Thoughts of the Great Economists Ser.). (Illus.). 127p. 1981. 77.55x (ISBN 0-918968-87-9). Inst Econ Finan.

Gamoran, Emanuel. Changing Conceptions in Jewish Education. facsimile ed. LC 74-27986. (Modern Jewish Experience Ser.). 1975. Repr. of 1924 ed. 36.50x (ISBN 0-405-06713-5). Ayer Co Pubs.

Gamoran, Mamie G. Fun Ways to Holidays. (gr. 5-9). 1951. pap. 2.00 (ISBN 0-8074-0136-6, 321400). UAHC.

Gamow, George. Mister Tompkins in Paperback. (Illus., Orig.). 1967. bds. 29.95 (ISBN 0-521-06905-X); pap. 7.95 (ISBN 0-521-09355-4). Cambridge U Pr.

--Thirty Years that Shook Physics: The Story of Quantum Theory. 240p. 1985. pap. 4.95 (ISBN 0-486-24895-X). Dover.

Gamow, George & Gritchfield, C. L. Theory of Atomic Nucleus & Nuclear Energy-Sources. LC 83-45435. Repr. of 1949 ed. 49.50 (ISBN 0-404-20105-9). AMS Pr.

Gamow, George, tr. see Khinchin, Alexander I.

Gamow, George, et al. Science in Progress, Eighth Series. facsimile ed. Baitsell, George A., ed. LC 78-37534. (Essay Index Reprint Ser). Repr. of 1953 ed. 33.00 (ISBN 0-8369-2533-5). Ayer Co Pubs.

Gampert, John, illus. Return of the Jedi. Penick, Ib, ed. LC 83-60019. (Pop-Up Bks.). (Illus.). 16p. (gr. 1-5). 1983. 5.95 (ISBN 0-394-86016-0). Random.

Gams, H. Kleine Kryptogamenflora Vol. 1 Algen. Part a.: Makroskppische Suesswasser und Luftalgen. (Illus.). 63p. (Ger.). 1969. text ed. 8.80 (ISBN 3-437-20031-3). Lubrecht & Cramer.

--Kleine Kryptogamenflora. Vol 3: Flechten. (Illus.). 244p. (Ger.). 1967. text ed. 17.60 (ISBN 3-437-20034-8). Lubrecht & Cramer.

Gams, W., jt. auth. see Schippers, B.

Gamsey, Robert. Ingathering. 1961. 4.50 (ISBN 0-87315-020-1); pap. 1.50x (ISBN 0-87315-021-X). Golden Bell.

Gamson, William A. What's News: A Game Simulation of TV News, Participant's Manual. 1984. text ed. 9.95 (ISBN 0-02-911110-2); coordinator's manual avail. (ISBN 0-02-911200-1). Free Pr.

Gamson, William A. & Modigliani, Andre. Conceptions of Social Life: A Text-Reader for Social Psychology. LC 79-89925. 1979. pap. 15.75 (ISBN 0-8191-0854-5). U Pr of Amer.

Gamson, William A., ed. SIMSOC: Simulated Society, Third Edition, Participant's Manual. 3rd ed. LC 77-84285. 1978. pap. text ed. 7.95 (ISBN 0-02-911170-6); write for info. (coordinator's manual avail.). Free Pr.

Gamson, William A., et al. Encounters with Unjust Authority. 1982. pap. 16.00x (ISBN 0-256-02746-3). Dorsey.

Gamson, Zelda F., jt. auth. see Austin, Ann E.

Gamson, Zelda F., et al. Liberating Education. LC 83-49260. (Higher Education Ser.). 1984. text ed. 16.95x (ISBN 0-87589-603-0). Jossey-Bass.

Gamst, Frederick C. Hoghead. (Case Studies in Cultural Anthropology). 128p. 1980. pap. text ed. 9.95 (ISBN 0-03-052636-1, HoltC). HR&W.

--Peasants in a Complex Society. LC 73-6554. (Basic Anthropology Units). 1974. pap. text ed. 9.95 (ISBN 0-03-091287-3, HoltC). HR&W.

--The Qemant: A Pagan-Hebraic Peasantry of Ethiopia. (Illus.). 128p. 1984. pap. text ed. 6.95x (ISBN 0-88133-047-7). Waveland Pr.

Gamst, Frederick C., ed. Studies in Cultural Anthropology. (Rice University Studies: Vol. 61, No. 2). (Illus.). 161p. 1975. pap. 10.00x (ISBN 0-89263-224-0). Rice Univ.

Gamstorp, Ingrid. Paediatric Neurology. 2nd ed. (Illus.). 416p. 1985. text ed. 59.95 (ISBN 0-407-00263-4). Butterworth.

Gamstorp, Ingrid & Sarnat, Harvey B., eds. Progressive Spinal Muscular Atrophies. (International Review of Child Neurology Ser.). (Illus.). 256p. 1984. text ed. 58.50 (ISBN 0-89004-952-1). Raven.

Gamwell, Franklin I. Beyond Preference: Liberal Theories of Independent Associations. LC 84-8523. 192p. 1985. lib. bdg. 19.00x (ISBN 0-226-28066-7). U of Chicago Pr.

Gamwell, Franklin I., jt. ed. see Cobb, John B., Jr.

Gamwell, Lynn. Cubist Criticism. Kuspit, Donald B., ed. LC 80-23812. (Studies in the Fine Arts: Criticism: No. 5). 266p. 1980. 39.95 (ISBN 0-8357-1089-0). UMI Res Pr.

Gamzatov, R. Mi Daguestan. 445p. 1974. 8.95 (ISBN 0-8285-1720-7, Pub. by Progress Pubs USSR). Imported Pubns.

--Selected Poems. dual language ed. 347p. 1974. text ed. 3.95 (ISBN 0-8285-0628-0, Pub. by Progress Pubs USSR). Imported Pubns.

Gan, Shelia, jt. ed. see Wollin, Roberta.

Ganapathy. Steam Plant Calculations Manual. LC 84-19855. 168p. 1984. 39.75 (ISBN 0-8247-7256-3). Dekker.

Ganapathy, V. Applied Heat Transfer. 667p. 1982. 55.95x (ISBN 0-87814-182-0). Pennwell Bks.

--Nomograms for Steam Generation & Utilization. LC 84-4522. 175p. 1985. 32.00 (ISBN 0-88173-000-9). Fairmont Pr.

Ganapol, B. D., ed. New Frontiers in Transport Theory: Selected Papers from the 6th Conference at U. of Ariz, Tuscon, April 1979. 122p. 1980. pap. 41.00 (ISBN 0-08-026698-3). Pergamon.

Ganaway, Loomis M. New Mexico & the Sectional Controversy 1846-1861. LC 76-8250. (Perspectives in American History Ser., No. 28). (Illus.). x, 140p. Repr. of 1944 ed. lib. bdg. 17.50x (ISBN 0-87991-352-5). Porcupine Pr.

Gancel, J. Gancel's Culinary Encyclopedia of Modern Cooking. (Illus.). 1977. text ed. 19.95 (ISBN 0-911202-06-4). Radio City.

Gan-Chaudhuri, J. Tripura: The Land & Its People. 1980. text ed. 16.25x (ISBN 0-391-01842-6). Humanities.

Ganchovski, Nedelcho. The Days of Dimitrov: As I Witnessed & Recorded Them. Maneva, Svelta, tr. 603p. 1979. 12.95 (ISBN 0-8285-2709-1, Pub. by Sofia Bulgaria). Imported Pubns.

Ganchrow, J. R., jt. ed. see Steiner, J. E.

Ganci, Dave. Hiking the Southwest: Arizona, New Mexico, & West Texas. LC 82-19418. (A Sierra Club Totebook). (Illus.). 384p. (Orig.). 1983. pap. 9.95 (ISBN 0-87156-338-X). Sierra.

Ganci, David. Desert Hiking. LC 83-51474. (Illus.). 192p. 1984. Repr. of 1979 ed. pap. 9.95 (ISBN 0-89997-036-2). Wilderness Pr.

Ganczarczyk. Activated Sludge Processes. (Pollution Engineering Ser.). 288p. 1983. 59.75 (ISBN 0-8247-1758-9). Dekker.

Gandavo P. De, Magalhaes De see De Magalhaes De Gandavo, P.

Gandelman, R. J., jt. ed. see Hoffman, L. Wladis.

Gander, Forrest, ed. see Caponegro, Mary.

Gander, Mary J. & Gardiner, Harry W. Child & Adolescent Development. 1981. text ed. 25.95 (ISBN 0-316-30322-4); tchrs'. manual free (ISBN 0-316-30319-4); study guide 8.95 (ISBN 0-316-30318-6); test bank (ISBN 0-316-30325-9). Little.

Gander, Terry. Encyclopaedia of the Modern British Army. (Illus.). 280p. 1982. 29.95 (ISBN 0-933852-33-9). Nautical & Aviation.

--Encyclopedia of the Modern Royal Air Force. (Illus.). 248p. 1985. 24.95 (ISBN 0-85059-600-9, Pub. by PSL P Stephens England). Sterling.

Gander, Terry, jt. auth. see Chamberlain, Peter.

Gander, Terry, jt. auth. see Chamberlian, Peter.

Gander, Terry see Foss, Christopher.

Gander, Terry, jt. auth. see Hogg, Ian.

Gander, W, et al, eds. Numerische Prozeduren Aus Nachlass und Lehre. Heinz Rutishauser. (International Series of Numerical Mathematics: No. 33). 127p. (Ger.). 1977. pap. 41.95x (ISBN 0-8176-0874-5). Birkhauser.

Gandert, Slade R. Protecting Your Collection: A Handbook, Survey, & Guide for the Security of Rare Books, Manuscripts, Archives & Works of Art. LC 81-7004. (Library & Archival Security Ser.: Vol. 4, Nos. 1 & 2). 144p. 1982. text ed. 19.95 (ISBN 0-917724-78-X, B78). Haworth Pr.

Gandhi, A. The Morarji Papers: Fall of the Janata Government. 314p. 1984. text ed. 16.50x (ISBN 0-391-03099-X). Humanities.

Gandhi, Indira. Eternal India. LC 80-51191. Orig. Title: Inde. (Illus.). 260p. 1980. 50.00 (ISBN 0-86565-003-9). Vendome.

--Letters to an American Friend: 1950-1984. Norman, Dorothy, ed. (A Helen & Kurt Wolff Book). (Illus.). 224p. 1985. 16.95 (ISBN 0-15-144372-6). HarBraceJ.

--The Years of Challenge: Selected Speeches of Indira Gandhi 1966-1969. rev. ed. LC 74-168325. 498p. 1973. 7.50x (ISBN 0-89684-473-0). Orient Bk Dist.

--The Years of Endeavour. 826p. 34.95 (ISBN 0-317-12343-2, Pub. by Pubns Div India). Asia Bk Corp.

Gandhi, J. S. Lawyers & Touts: A Study in the Sociology of the Legal Profession. (Studies in Sociology & Social Anthropology Ser.). 250p. 1982. text ed. 15.00x (ISBN 0-391-02661-5, Pub. by Hindustan India). Humanities.

Gandhi, K. Literature & the Evolution of Consciousness. 288p. 1984. text ed. 18.50x (ISBN 0-391-02357-8, Pub. by Allied Pubs India). Humanities.

Gandhi, Kishore. Aldous Huxley: Vedantic & Buddhistic Influences. 256p. 1980. text ed. 13.50x (ISBN 0-391-02024-2). Humanities.

Gandhi, Kishore, ed. Contemporary Relevance of Sri Aurobundo. 1973. text ed. 11.50x (ISBN 0-391-00497-2). Humanities.

Gandhi, M. K. All Men Are Brothers. (Modern Classics of Peace Ser). pap. 7.95 (ISBN 0-912018-15-1). World Without War.

--All Men Are Brothers. Kripalani, K., ed. 260p. (Orig.). 1982. pap. 5.95 (ISBN 0-934676-51-8). Greenlf Bks.

--Ashram Observances in Action. 151p. 1983. pap. 1.00 (ISBN 0-934676-36-4). Greenlf Bks.

--Autobiography. 2nd ed. 1979. pap. 6.00 (ISBN 0-685-11994-7). Heinman.

--An Autobiography or the Story of My Experiments with Truth. 2nd ed. Desai, Mahadev, tr. from Gujarati. 432p. 1983. 7.50 (ISBN 0-934676-40-2). Greenlf Bks.

--An Autobiography: Or the Story of My Experiments with Truth. 2nd ed. Desai, Mahadev, tr. from Gujarati. 432p. 1984. pap. 4.50 (ISBN 0-934676-68-2). Greenlf Bks.

--Capital & Labour. Hingorani, A. T., ed. 108p. pap. 3.00 (ISBN 0-686-87484-6). Greenlf Bks.

--Constructive Program. 40p. (Orig.). 1982. pap. 1.00 (ISBN 0-934676-59-3). Greenlf Bks.

--Delhi Diary: Daily Talks at Prayer Meetings, 1947-1948. 426p. 1982. 7.50 (ISBN 0-934676-56-9). Greenlf Bks.

--Diet & Diet Reform. Kumarappa, B., ed. 185p. (Orig.). 1983. pap. 5.50 (ISBN 0-934676-61-5). Greenlf Bks.

--Discourses on the Gita. 73p. (Orig.). 1983. pap. 1.50 (ISBN 0-934676-55-0). Greenlf Bks.

--From Yeravda Mandir. 48p. (Orig.). 1982. pap. 1.50 (ISBN 0-934676-60-7). Greenlf Bks.

--The Health Guide. LC 78-2592. 1978. 15.95 (ISBN 0-89594-005-1). Crossing Pr.

--Key to Health. Nayar, Sushila, tr. from Gujarati. 83p. (Orig.). 1982. pap. 1.50 (ISBN 0-934676-58-5). Greenlf Bks.

--Khadi, Hand-Spun Cloth. Kumarappa, B., ed. 244p. 1983. pap. 2.75 (ISBN 0-934676-39-9). Greenlf Bks.

--The Law & the Lawyers. Kher, S. B., ed. 261p. pap. 7.50 (ISBN 0-934676-57-7). Greenlf Bks.

--Letters to Mirabehn. Slade, Madeleine, ed. 367p. (Orig.). 1983. pap. 5.00 (ISBN 0-934676-53-4). Greenlf Bks.

--My Religion. Kumarappa, B., ed. 178p. (Orig.). 1983. pap. 5.00 (ISBN 0-934676-54-2). Greenlf Bks.

--The Problem of Education. Desai, J. D., ed. 327p. (Orig.). 1983. pap. 5.00 (ISBN 0-934676-62-3). Greenlf Bks.

--Sarvodaya. Agarwal, S. N., ed. 67p. 1.00 (ISBN 0-686-87485-4). Greenlf Bks.

--Satyagraha in South Africa. Desai, V. G., tr. 1980. 10.00 (ISBN 0-934676-15-1). Greenlf Bks.

--Satyagraha in South Africa. Desai, V. G., tr. from Gujarati. 1979. pap. 5.00 (ISBN 0-934676-03-8). Greenlf Bks.

--Satyagraha in South Africa. 332p. pap. 5.00 (ISBN 0-686-87443-9); 10.00 (ISBN 0-686-91571-2). Greenlf Bks.

--Socialism of My Conception. Hingorani, A. T., ed. 290p. (Orig.). 1981. pap. 4.00 (ISBN 0-934676-29-1). Greenlf Bks.

--To the Perplexed. Hingorani, A. T., ed. 236p. 1981. 8.50 (ISBN 0-934676-27-5). Greenlf Bks.

Gandhi, M. K. & Tagore, Rabindranath. Tagore-Gandhi Controversy. Prabhu, R. K., ed. 155p. (Orig.). 1983. pap. 2.00 (ISBN 0-934676-52-6). Greenlf Bks.

Gandhi, Mahatma. All Men Are Brothers: Life & Thoughts of Mahatma Gandhi As Told in His Own Words. 186p. pap. 6.95 (ISBN 0-8264-0003-5). Continuum.

--Harijan, Nineteen Thirty-Three to Nineteen Fifty-Five: A Journal of Non-Resistance, 19 vols. Cook, Blanche, et al, eds. LC 74-147621. (Garland Library of War & Peace). 1973. Set. lib. bdg. 370.00 (ISBN 0-685-38878-6); lib. bdg. 46.00 ea. Garland Pub.

--Mahatma Gandhi. Redpath, Ann, ed. (Living Philosophies Ser.). (Illus.). 32p. (gr. 9 up). 1985. lib. bdg. 8.95 (ISBN 0-88682-010-3). Creative Ed.

--Mahatma Gandhi at Work: His Own Story Continued. facsimile ed. Andrews, C. F., ed. LC 75-37343. (Select Bibliographies Reprint Ser). Repr. of 1931 ed. 23.50 (ISBN 0-8369-6690-2). Ayer Co Pubs.

--The Sayings of Mahatma Gandhi. Burgess, Peter H., ed. (Illus.). 99p. 1984. pap. 8.00 (ISBN 9971-947-65-X, Pub. by Graham Brash Singapore). Three Continents.

Gandhi, Mohandas. Gandhi on Non-Violence: Selected Texts from Gandhi's Non-Violence in Peace & War. Merton, Thomas, ed. LC 65-15672. (Orig.). 1965. pap. 4.00 (ISBN 0-8112-0097-3, NDP197). New Directions.

Gandhi, Mohandas K. Autobiography: The Story of My Experiments with Truth. (Social Sciences Ser.). 480p. 1983. pap. 6.95 (ISBN 0-486-24593-4). Dover.

--The Bhagavad Gita: An Interpretation. Parikh, Narahari D., ed. 309p. (Orig.). 1984. pap. 8.00 (ISBN 0-934676-65-8). Greenlf Bks.

--Essential Gandhi. Fischer, Louis, ed. (YA) 1963. pap. 4.95 (ISBN 0-394-71466-0, V225, Vin). Random.

--For Pacifists. Kumarappa, Bharatan, ed. 130p. (Orig.). 1981. pap. 3.00 (ISBN 0-934676-28-3). Greenlf Bks.

--Gandhi: An Autobiography. 1983. 18.95x (ISBN 0-8070-5980-3). Beacon Pr.

--Gandhi Reader: A Source Book of His Life & Writings. Jack, Homer, ed. LC 71-133812. 1970. Repr. of 1956 ed. 34.00 (ISBN 0-404-03540-X). AMS Pr.

--Gandhi's Autobiography. 1948. 8.00 (ISBN 0-8183-0223-2). Pub Aff Pr.

--Hind Swaraj, or Indian Home Rule. 110p. (Orig.). 1981. pap. 2.25 (ISBN 0-934676-25-9). Greenlf Bks.

--Man vs. Machine. Hingorani, A. T., ed. 113p. (Orig.). 1980. pap. 2.50 (ISBN 0-934676-18-6). Greenlf Bks.

--Non-Violent Resistance. Kumarappa, Bharatan, ed. LC 61-16650. 416p. (YA) 1983. pap. 8.95 (ISBN 0-8052-0017-7). Schocken.

--Nonviolence in Peace & War, 1942, 2 vols. Incl. Nonviolence in Peace & War, 1949. Ghandi, Mohandas K. LC 72-147618. (Library of War & Peace; Non-Resis. & Non-Vio.). Set. lib. bdg. 76.00 (ISBN 0-8240-0375-6); lib. bdg. 38.00 ea. Garland Pub.

--Swaraj in One Year. 2nd ed. 1921. 14.50 (ISBN 0-404-02676-1). AMS Pr.

Gandhi, Om P. Microwave Engineering & Applications. (Illus.). 543p. 1981. 66.00 (ISBN 0-08-025589-2); pap. 27.00 (ISBN 0-08-025588-4). Pergamon.

Gandhi, P. K. Rural Youth in Urban India. 1983. 26.00 (ISBN 0-8364-1062-9). South Asia Bks.

Gandhi, Rajmohan. The Rajaji Story: Warrior from the South. 1979. 12.50x (ISBN 0-8364-0562-5, Pub. by Bharathan India). South Asia Bks.

Gandhi, Ved P. Tax Burden on Indian Agriculture. LC 66-15721. (Illus.). 260p. 1966. pap. 5.00x (ISBN 0-915506-06-8). Harvard Law Intl Tax.

Gandia, Delsie M. The EEC's Generalized Scheme of Preferences & the Yaounde & Other Agreements: Benefits in Trade & Development for Less Developed Countries. LC 79-91005. 192p. 1981. text ed. 25.00x (ISBN 0-916672-47-6). Allanheld.

Gandia, Manual Z. Complete Works of Manuel Zeno Gandia, 2 vols. (Puerto Rico Ser.). 1979. Set. lib. bdg. 250.00 (ISBN 0-8490-2898-1). Gordon Pr.

Gandillac, Maurice & Jeauneau, Edouard, eds. Entretiens Sur la Renaissance Du 12e Siecle: Decades Du Centre Culturel International De Cerisy-la-Salle. (Nouvelle Ser.: No. 9). 1968. pap. 21.60x (ISBN 90-2796-020-8). Mouton.

Gandin, S. L. Planning of Meteorological Station Networks. (Technical Note Ser.: No. 11). 35p. 1970. pap. 10.00 (ISBN 0-685-02473-3, W85, WMO). Unipub.

Gandini, A. & Cheradame, H. Cationic Polymerization. (Advances in Polymer Science Ser.: Vol. 34, 35). (Illus.). 360p. 1980. 87.00 (ISBN 0-387-10049-0). Springer-Verlag.

Gandolfo, A. & Romano, J. The Nurse's Writing Handbook. 208p. 1984. pap. 14.95 (ISBN 0-8385-6997-8). ACC.

Gandolfo, G. Economic Dynamics: Methods & Models. rev. ed. (Advanced Textbooks in Economics Ser.: Vol. 16). 572p. 1980. 39.50 (ISBN 0-444-85419-3, North-Holland). Elsevier.

--Qualitative Analysis & Econometric Estimation of Continuous Time Dynamic Models. (Contributions to Economic Analysis Ser.: Vol. 136). 254p. 1981. 34.00 (ISBN 0-444-86025-8, North-Holland). Elsevier.

Gandolfo, G. & Padoan, P. C. A Disequilibrium Model of Real & Financial Accumulation in an Open Economy. (Lecture Notes in Economics & Mathematical Systems Ser.: Vol. 236). vi, 172p. 1984. pap. 14.00 (ISBN 0-387-13889-7). Springer-Verlag.

Gandolfo, Joe & Shook, Robert L. How to Make Big Money...Selling the Gandolfo Way. LC 84-47569. 192p. 1984. 14.37 (ISBN 0-06-015324-5, HarpT). Har-Row.

Gandossy, Robert P. Bad Business: The OPM Scandal & the Seduction of the Establishment. LC 85-47556. 256p. 1985. 17.95 (ISBN 0-465-00570-5). Basic.

Gandour, R. D. & Schowen, R. L., eds. Transition States of Biochemical Processes. LC 78-6659. (Illus.). 636p. 1978. 75.00x (ISBN 0-306-31092-9, Plenum Pr). Plenum Pub.

Gandrud, Pauline J. Marriage, Death & Legal Notices from Early Alabama Newspapers, 1819-1893. 618p. 1981. 42.50 (ISBN 0-89308-209-0). Southern Hist Pr.

Gandy, Charles D. & Zimmerman-Stidham, Susan. Contemporary Classics: Furniture of the Masters. LC 80-17283. (Illus.). 192p. 1982. 34.95 (ISBN 0-07-022760-8); pap. 7.95 (ISBN 0-07-022762-4). McGraw.

Gandy, D. Ross. Marx & History: From Primitive Society to the Communist Future. 201p. 1979. text ed. 14.95x (ISBN 0-292-74302-5). U of Tex Pr.

Gandy, Doreen. A New Leafing: A Journey from Grief. LC 85-70002. (Illus., Orig.). 1985. pap. 5.95 (ISBN 0-9614529-0-0). Celilo Pubns.

Gandy, Joan W. & Gandy, Thomas H. Natchez Victorian Children: Photographic Portraits, 1865-1915. LC 81-47767. (Illus.). 216p. 1981. 25.00 (ISBN 0-9606978-0-2); deluxe ed. 100.00 ltd. (ISBN 0-9606978-1-0). Myrtle Bank.

--Norman's Natchez: An Early Photographer & His Town. LC 78-15570. (Illus.). 1978. 25.00 (ISBN 0-87805-078-7). Myrtle Bank.

Gandy, Joan W., jt. ed. see Eidt, Mary B.

Gandy, John, et al, eds. Improving Social Intervention. LC 83-8713. 310p. 1983. 32.50 (ISBN 0-312-41070-0). St Martin.

Gandy, Maurice. An Uncharted Inch. 50p. (Orig.). 1982. pap. 5.00 (ISBN 0-942544-01-3). Negative Capability Pr.

Gandy, Oscar, et al, eds. see Telecommunications Policy Research Conference, Annual 10th.

Gandy, Oscar H., Jr. Beyond Agenda Setting: Information Subsidies & Public Policy. LC 82-13823. (Communication & Information Science Ser.). 1982. text ed. 32.50 (ISBN 0-89391-096-1); pap. text ed. 17.95x (ISBN 0-89391-194-1). Ablex Pub.

Gandy, R. D. & Hyland, M. Logic Colloquium 1976. (Studies in Logic: Vol. 87). 612p. 1977. 70.25 (ISBN 0-7204-0691-9, North-Holland). Elsevier.

Gandy, R. O., et al, eds. see Fenstad, J. E.

Gandy, Stanlis. Edmund Burke: A Bibliography. 1983. 54.00 (ISBN 0-8240-9244-9). Garland Pub.

Gandy, Thomas H., jt. auth. see Gandy, Joan W.

Gandy, Tillie H. Of Cabbages & Kings. 1983. 6.50 (ISBN 0-8062-2138-0). Carlton.

Gandy, Tilly H. Ears to Hear. 1984. 6.95 (ISBN 0-8062-2293-X). Carlton.

--Little Drops of Water. 1984. 7.95 (ISBN 0-8062-2312-X). Carlton.

--Ten True Tales of Reincarnation. 1984. 6.00 (ISBN 0-8062-2292-1). Carlton.

Gandz, Solomon, tr. see Maimonides, Moses.

Gane, C. & Sarson, T. Structured Systems Analysis: Tools & Techniques. 1979. 37.50 (ISBN 0-13-854547-2). P-H.

Gane, Chris & Sarson, Trish. Structured Systems Analysis: Tools & Techniques. 373p. (Orig.). 1977. 22.50 (ISBN 0-930196-00-7); pap. 15.00 (ISBN 0-686-37676-5). McDonnell Douglas.

Gane, M. Priorities in Planning. 1969. 30.00x (ISBN 0-85074-007-X, Pub. by For Lib Comm England). State Mutual Bk.

Ganeizer, G. Conozcamos la Tierra. 36p. (Span.). 1978. pap. 3.45 (ISBN 0-8285-1770-3, Pub. by Progress Pubs USSR). Imported Pubns.

Ganelius, T. H. Tauberian Reminder Theorems. (Lecture Notes in Mathematics: Vol. 232). 75p. 1971. pap. 9.00 (ISBN 0-387-05657-2). Springer-Verlag.

Ganellin, C. R. & Schwartz, J. C., eds. Frontiers in Histamine Research - A Tribute to Heinz Schild: ased on an International Symposium Held at Jouy-en-Josas (near Paris), France, 25-27 July 1984. (Illus.). 420p. 1985. 80.00 (ISBN 0-08-031989-0, Pub. by Aberdeen Scotland). Pergamon.

Ganes, Sara. Quantity in Icelandic: Production & Perception. (Untersuchungen zur Phonetik und Linquistik: No. Bd. 18). 287p. (Orig.). 1976. pap. text ed. 20.00x (ISBN 3-87118-236-2, Pub. by Helmut Buske Verlag Hamburg). Benjamins North Am.

Ganesan, A. T. & Hoch, James A., eds. Genetics & Biotechnology of Bacilli. 1984. 41.50 (ISBN 0-12-274160-9). Acad Pr.

Ganesan, A. T., et al. Molecular Cloning & Gene Regulation in Bacilli. 392p. 1982. 35.00 (ISBN 0-12-274150-1). Acad Pr.

Ganesan, Jayalakshmi, jt. auth. see Sampath, R. K.

Ganesan, K., tr. see Muhaiyaddeen, M. R.

Ganesan, R., tr. see Muhaiyaddeen, M. R.

Ganet, S. D. Luis Munoz Rivera. 1976. lib. bdg. 59.95 (ISBN 0-8490-2186-3). Gordon Pr.

Gang, T. M., jt. ed. see Lea, Kathleen.

Gangadharam, Pattisapu R. Drug Resistance in Mycobacteria. 176p. 1984. 59.00 (ISBN 0-8493-6574-0). CRC Pr.

Gangadharan, A. C. & Brown, S. J., Jr., eds. Failure Data & Failure Analysis: In Power & Processing Industries, Series Pvp-Pb-023. 109p. 1977. pap. text ed. 16.00 (ISBN 0-685-86862-1, G00123). ASME.

Gangadharan, N. Lingapurana: A Study. 1980. 22.50x (ISBN 0-8364-0618-4, Pub. by Ajanta). South Asia Bks.

Gangal, S. C., jt. ed. see Misra, K. P.

Gangarama. The Maharashta Purana: An Eighteenth Century Bengali Historical Text. Dimock, Edward C., Jr. & Gupta, Pratul C., trs. LC 64-63437. pap. 28.80 (ISBN 0-317-11006-3, 2001354). Bks Demand UMI.

Gangarosa, Louis P. Iontophoresis in Dental Practice. (Illus.). 144p. 1983. text ed. 48.00 (ISBN 0-931386-52-7). Quint Pub Co.

Gange, Susan De see Verniero, Joan.

Gangel, Elizabeth & McDaniel, Elsiebeth. You Can Reach Families Through Their Babies. 64p. 1976. pap. 2.50 (ISBN 0-88207-140-8). Victor Bks.

Gangel, Kenneth. You Can Be an Effective Sunday School Superintendent. 64p. 1981. pap. 2.50 (ISBN 0-88207-141-6). Victor Bks.

Gangel, Kenneth O. Building Leaders for Church Education. 1981. 18.95 (ISBN 0-8024-1592-X). Moody.

--The Church Education Handbook. 300p. Date not set. pap. 9.95 (ISBN 0-89693-602-3). Victor Bks.

--The Family First. pap. 3.50 (ISBN 0-88469-106-3). BMH Bks.

--Lessons in Leadership from the Bible. 1980. pap. 5.95 (ISBN 0-88469-109-8). BMH Bks.

--So You Want to Be a Leader. pap. 2.75 (ISBN 0-87509-131-8); leaders guide 2.00 (ISBN 0-87509-298-5). Chr Pubns.

--Twenty-Four Ways to Improve Your Teaching. LC 74-77453. 131p. 1974. pap. 4.50 (ISBN 0-88207-463-6). Victor Bks.

--Understanding Teaching. LC 68-24579. 96p. 1979. pap. text ed. 4.95 (ISBN 0-910566-14-3); Perfect bdg. instr's. guide 4.95 (ISBN 0-910566-26-7). Evang Tchr.

--Unwrap Your Spiritual Gifts. 120p. 1983. pap. 3.95 (ISBN 0-88207-102-5). Victor Bks.

Gangel, Kenneth O. & Benson, Warren S. Christian Education: Its History & Philosophy. 1983. 16.95 (ISBN 0-8024-3561-0). Moody.

Gangel, Kenneth O. & Grant, James M. Thus Spake Qoheleth. LC 81-71656. 160p. 1983. pap. 5.95 (ISBN 0-87509-317-5); pap. 2.95 (ISBN 0-87509-318-3). Chr Pubns.

Gangel, Kenneth O., ed. Toward a Harmony of Faith & Learning: Essays on Bible College Curriculum. 247p. 1983. pap. 13.95 (ISBN 0-912407-00-X). William Tyndale Col Pr.

Gangemi, Kenneth. Corroboree. LC 76-27241. 96p. 1977. pap. 2.95 (ISBN 0-685-56012-0). Assembling Pr.

--The Interceptor Pilot. 160p. 1981. 11.50 (ISBN 0-7145-2699-1, Dist by Scribner). M Boyars.

--The Interceptor Pilot. LC 79-56849. 160p. 1982. pap. 7.95 (ISBN 0-7145-2765-3, Dist by Scribner). M Boyars.

--OLT. LC 75-476287. 64p. 1984. pap. 5.95 (ISBN 0-7145-0660-5, Dist by Scribner). M Boyars.

--The Volcanoes from Puebla. 192p. 1979. 11.95 (ISBN 0-7145-2577-4, Dist by Scribner). M Boyars.

Gangeness, David E. & White, Roger D. Emergency Pharmacology. Bosker, Gideon, ed. LC 83-21404. 320p. 1984. pap. text ed. 19.95 (ISBN 0-89303-430-4). Brady Comm.

Gangerosa, Louis P. & Ciarlone, Alfred E. Pharmacotherapeutics in Dentistry. 512p. 1983. 35.00 (ISBN 0-8385-7842-X). ACC.

Gangiah, Kota, jt. auth. see Husain, Asghar.

Gangji, D., ed. see European Organization for Research & Treatment of Cancer.

Gangloff, Eric J., tr. & intro. by see Kinoshita Junji.

Gangloff, R. P., ed. Embrittlement by the Localized Crack Environment. LC 84-61499. (Illus.). 491p. 1984. 38.00 (ISBN 0-89520-480-0); members 24.00; student members 14.00. Metal Soc.

Gangopadhyay, Sunil. Pratidwandi. Chatterjee, Enakshi, tr. from Bengali. LC 74-900546. 1974. lib. bdg. 4.50x (ISBN 0-8364-0447-5). South Asia Bks.

Gangopadhyaya, M., tr. Nyaya: Gautama's Nyaya Sutra with Vatsyayana's Commentary. 1983. 28.50x (ISBN 0-8364-1000-9, Pub. by Indian Stud). South Asia Bks.

Gangopadhyaya, Mrinalkanti. Indian Atomosm: History & Sources. 384p. 1980. 21.00x (ISBN 0-391-02177-X). Humanities.

Gangstad, E. O. Weed Control Methods for Recreation Facility Management. 312p. 1982. 84.50 (ISBN 0-8493-5330-0). CRC Pr.

Gangstad, E. O., ed. Rights of Way Management for Weeds Control Methods. 1981. 84.50 (ISBN 0-8493-5329-7). CRC Pr.

Gangstad, Edward O. Weed Control Methods for Public Health Applications. 320p. 1980. 84.50 (ISBN 0-8493-5326-2). CRC Pr.

Gangstad, Edward O., ed. Weed Control Methods for River Basin Management. 232p. 1978. 66.00 (ISBN 0-8493-5328-9). CRC Pr.

Gangstad, John E. Great Pyramid: Signs in the Sun (Pyramid Design & Prophecy: Second Advent) LC 76-24077. (Illus.). 200p. 1976. pap. 5.95 (ISBN 0-9603374-1-5); 1980-83 supplement 3.00 (ISBN 0-9603374-2-3). Di-Tri Bks.

Gangulee, N. & Eliot, T. S. Thoughts for Meditation: A Way to Recovery from Within. 59.95 (ISBN 0-8490-1208-2). Gordon Pr.

Gangulee, N., ed. The Mind & Face of Nazi Germany: An Anthology. LC 78-63671. (Studies in Fascism: Ideology & Practice). 200p. 1979. Repr. of 1942 ed. 24.50 (ISBN 0-404-16528-1). AMS Pr.

Gangulee, N., ed. see Mazzini, Giuseppe.

Ganguli, B. N. Emma Goldman: Portrait of a Rebel Woman. 1979. 7.00x (ISBN 0-8364-0452-1). South Asia Bks.

--Indian Economic Thought: Nineteenth Century Perspectives. 1977. 7.50x (ISBN 0-8364-0419-X). South Asia Bks.

Ganguli, C. Studies in Indian Economic Problems. 1978. 11.00x (ISBN 0-8364-0242-1). South Asia Bks.

Ganguli, D. K., jt. auth. see Nomokov, V. P.

Ganguli, H. C. Human Factor Aspects of Aircraft Noise. 1972. 9.00 (ISBN 0-686-20244-9). Intl Bk Dist.

--Industrial Productivity & Motivation. 1984. 6.00x (ISBN 0-8364-1172-2, Pub. by Allied India). South Asia Bks.

--Industrial Productivity & Motivation. 1985. pap. 4.50x (ISBN 0-8364-1265-6, Pub. by Allied India). South Asia Bks.

--Structure & Processes of Organization. 1984. 14.00x (ISBN 0-8364-1163-3, Pub. by Allied India). South Asia Bks.

Ganguli, Kisari M., tr. from Sanskrit. The Mahabharata, 12 vols. 3rd ed. 1975. Set. 465.00x (ISBN 0-89684-429-3). Orient Bk Dist.

Ganguli, M. A Pilgrimage to the Nagas. 275p. 1984. text ed. 34.75x (ISBN 0-391-03154-6, Pub. by Oxford & IBH). Humanities.

Ganguly, Anil B. Fine Arts in Ancient India. 1980. 16.00x (ISBN 0-8364-0581-1, Pub. by Abhinav India). South Asia Bks.

Ganguly, Bangendu & Mira, Ganguly. Dimensions of Electoral Behaviour. 1983. 15.00x (ISBN 0-8364-0927-2, Pub. by Pearl Pub). South Asia Bks.

Ganguly, D. K. Aspects of Ancient Indian Administration. 1979. 22.50x (ISBN 0-8364-0355-X). South Asia Bks.

--History & Historians in Ancient India. 178p. 1984. text ed. 22.50x (ISBN 0-391-03250-X, Pub. by Abhinav India). Humanities.

Ganguly, D. S. Regional Economy of West Bengal: A Study in Urbanization, Growth, Potential & Optimization of Industrial Location. cancelled (ISBN 0-8364-0521-8, Orient Longman). South Asia Bks.

Ganguly, J. & Smellie, R. M., eds. Current Trends in the Biochemistry of Lipids: Proceedings. 1973. 85.00 (ISBN 0-12-274250-8). Acad Pr.

Ganguly, Shivaji, jt. ed. see Rajan, M. S.

Gani, J. The Making of Statisticians. (Illus.). 263p. 1982. 24.00 (ISBN 0-387-90684-3). Springer-Verlag.

Gani, J. & Rohatgi, V. K., eds. Contributions to Probability: A Collection of Papers Dedicated to Eugene Lukacs. LC 80-768. 1981. 55.00 (ISBN 0-12-274460-8). Acad Pr.

Gani, J., et al, eds. Progress in Statistics, 2 vols. (Colloquia Mathematica Societatis Janos Bolyai: No. 9). 912p. 1975. Set. 76.75 (ISBN 0-444-10702-9, North-Holland). Elsevier.

Ganiel, Uri, ed. Physics Teaching. 608p. 1980. pap. text ed. 35.00 (ISBN 0-86689-000-9). Balaban Intl Scie Serv.

Ganikos, Mary, ed. Counseling the Aged, with Index: A Training Syllabus for Educators. 320p. 1979. pap. text ed. 18.75 (ISBN 0-911547-27-4, 72106W34). Am Assn Coun Dev.

Ganikos, Mary, jt. ed. see Myers, Jane.

Ganikos, Mary, et al, eds. A Handbook for Conducting Workshop on the Counseling Needs of the Elderly. 47p. 1979. pap. text ed. 3.75 (ISBN 0-911547-45-2, 72137W34). Am Assn Coun Dev.

Ganikos, Mary L., ed. Counseling the Aged: A Training Syllabus for Educators, 1979. 320p. 1979. 15.75 (ISBN 0-686-36386-8, 72106W34); 18.75 (ISBN 0-911547-27-4). Am Assn Coun Dev.

Ganim, John M. Style & Consciousness in Middle English Narrative. LC 83-42559. 212p. 1983. 23.00x (ISBN 0-691-06580-2). Princeton U Pr.

Ganin, Zvi. Truman, American Jewry, & Israel, 1945-1948. 238p. 1979. text ed. 34.50x (ISBN 0-8419-0401-4); pap. 21.50 (ISBN 0-8419-0497-9). Holmes & Meier.

Ganivet, Angel. Spain: An Interpretation. LC 75-41109. 1976. Repr. of 1946 ed. 15.50 (ISBN 0-404-14755-0). AMS Pr.

Gankin, Olga H. & Fisher, Harold H. The Bolsheviks & the World War: The Origins of the Third International. 1940. 57.50x (ISBN 0-8047-0345-0). Stanford U Pr.

Ganley, Albert C., et al. After Hiroshima: America since Nineteen Forty-Five. 2nd ed. (Illus.). 356p. (Orig.). (gr. 11-12). 1985. pap. text ed. 6.25x (ISBN 0-88334-121-2). Ind Sch Pr.

Ganley, Gladys D., jt. auth. see Ganley, Oswald H.

Ganley, James P. & Roberts, Jean. Eye Conditions & Related Need for Medical Care among Persons One to Seventy-four Years, United States: Series 11, No. 228. Cox, Klaudia, ed. 60p. 1982. pap. text ed. 1.95 (ISBN 0-686-97508-1). Natl Ctr Health Stats.

Ganley, Oswald H. & Ganley, Gladys D. To Inform or to Control? The New Communications Networks. LC 81-20748. 1982. 15.95 (ISBN 0-07-022761-6). McGraw.

Ganly, John, ed. Serials for Libraries: An Annotated Guide to Continuations, Annuals, Yearbooks, Almanacs, Transactions, Proceedings, Directories, Services. 2nd ed. Sciattara, Diane. 500p. 1985. lib. bdg. 75.00 (ISBN 0-918212-85-5). Neal-Schuman.

Ganly, John V., jt. auth. see Frank, Nathalie D.

Ganmaster. Food Irradiation Now. 1982. 22.00 (ISBN 90-247-2763-4, Pub. by Martinus Nijhoff Netherlands). Kluwer Academic.

Gann, Donald, jt. ed. see Brown, J. H. U.

Gann, Ernest. High & the Mighty. LC 53-5252. 1953. 10.95 (ISBN 0-688-01786-X). Morrow.

--The High & the Mighty. 230p. 1983. Repr. lib. bdg. 16.95x (ISBN 0-89966-444-X). Buccaneer Bks.

Gann, Ernest K. The Aviator. LC 80-68543. 1981. 10.95 (ISBN 0-87795-299-X). Arbor Hse.

--The Aviator. 160p. 1984. pap. 2.95 (ISBN 0-345-32253-3). Ballantine.

--The Aviator. (General Ser.). 1981. lib. bdg. 13.95 (ISBN 0-8161-3257-7, Large Print Bks). G K Hall.

--Fate Is the Hunter. 2nd ed. 1984. pap. 9.95 (ISBN 0-671-50400-2). S&S.

--Gentlemen of Adventure. 512p. 1983. 15.95 (ISBN 0-87795-465-8). Arbor Hse.

--Gentlemen of Adventure. 1984. pap. 3.95 (ISBN 0-451-13265-3, Sig). NAL.

--A Hostage to Fortune. LC 78-54908. 1978. 16.95 (ISBN 0-394-49984-0). Knopf.

--Island in the Sky. 224p. 1981. pap. 2.50 (ISBN 0-515-05483-6). Jove Pubns.

--McCall Country Craft. 1983. pap. 14.95 (ISBN 0-515-07364-4). Chilton.

--The Magistrate. LC 81-66970. 304p. 1982. 14.50 (ISBN 0-87795-339-2). Arbor Hse.

--The Magistrate. 336p. 1984. pap. 3.95 (ISBN 0-515-07364-4). Jove Pubns.

--Masada. Orig. Title: The Antagonists. 320p. 1981. pap. 2.95 (ISBN 0-515-05443-7). Jove Pubns.

--Song of the Sirens. 256p. 1981. pap. 2.50 (ISBN 0-515-05482-8). Jove Pubns.

Gann, L. H. & Duigan, Peter. The Stability of South Africa or Why South Africa. Will Survive. 320p. 1980. 26.00. St Martin.

Gann, L. H. & Duignan, Peter. Africa South of the Sahara: The Challenge to Western Security. LC 80-82750. (Publication Ser.: No. 238). 155p. 1981. pap. 9.95x (ISBN 0-8179-7382-6). Hoover Inst Pr.

--Burden of Empire: An Appraisal of Western Colonialism in Africa South of the Sahara. LC 67-26216. (Publications Ser.: No. 69). (Illus.). 435p. 1967. pap. 6.95 (ISBN 0-8179-1692-X). Hoover Inst Pr.

--The Rulers of British Africa, 1870-1914. LC 77-92945. (Illus.). 1978. 27.50x (ISBN 0-8047-0981-5). Stanford U Pr.

--The Rulers of German Africa, 1884-1914. LC 76-54100. (Illus.). 1977. 22.50x (ISBN 0-8047-0938-6). Stanford U Pr.

--South Africa: War, Revolution, or Peace? Staar, Richard F., ed. LC 78-59131. (Publications 199 Ser.). (Illus.). 1978. pap. 6.95x (ISBN 0-8179-6992-6). Hoover Inst Pr.

--Why South Africa Will Survive. 329p. 1981. 27.50 (ISBN 0-312-87878-8). St Martin.

Gann, L. H., jt. auth. see Duignan, Peter.

Gann, L. H. & Duignan, Peter, eds. African Proconsuls: European Governors in Africa. LC 78-57054. (Illus.). 1978. 29.95 (ISBN 0-02-911190-0). Free Pr.

Gann, L. H., jt. ed. see Duignan, P.

Gann, Lewis. Guerrillas in History. LC 76-132819. (Studies Ser.: No. 28). 1971. pap. 5.95x (ISBN 0-8179-3281-X). Hoover Inst Pr.

Gann, Lewis H. The Birth of a Plural Society: The Development of Northern Rhodesia Under the British South Africa Company, 1894-1914. LC 81-18259. (Illus.). xxiii, 230p. 1982. Repr. of 1968 ed. lib. bdg. 27.50x (ISBN 0-313-23221-0, GABP). Greenwood.

Gann, Lewis H. & Duignan, Peter. White Settlers in Tropical Africa. LC 76-49445. 1977. Repr. of 1962 ed. lib. bdg. 45.00x (ISBN 0-8371-9394-X, GAWH). Greenwood.

Gann, Lewis H. & Duignan, Peter J. The Rulers of Belgian Africa: Eighteen Eighty-Four to Nineteen Fourteen. LC 79-83989. 1979. 32.00x (ISBN 0-691-05277-8). Princeton U Pr.

Gann, Lewis H. & Henriksen, Thomas H. The Struggle for Zimbabwe: Battle in the Bush. LC 81-5190. 172p. 1981. 29.95 (ISBN 0-03-059444-8). Praeger.

Gann, Lewis H., jt. auth. see Duignan, Peter.

Gann, Norma W. The Travelers' Picture Language. (Illus.). 108p. 1984. pap. 3.95 (ISBN 0-317-02658-5). Lawton Pub Co.

Gann, Pamela B., jt. auth. see Kahn, Douglas A.

Gann, Robert. Health Information for the Community. 1986. text ed. price not set (ISBN 0-566-03549-9). Gower Pub Co.

Gann, T. History of the Mayas. 1976. lib. bdg. 59.95 (ISBN 0-8490-2002-6). Gordon Pr.

Gann, Thomas. Ancient Cities & Modern Tribes: Exploration & Adventure in Maya Lands. LC 72-83086. (Illus.). Repr. of 1926 ed. 15.00 (ISBN 0-405-08550-8, Blom Pubns). Ayer Co Pubs.

--Ancient Cities & Modern Tribes: The Maya Lands. 1977. lib. bdg. 39.95 (ISBN 0-8490-1424-7). Gordon Pr.

--In an Unknown Land. facs. ed. LC 76-150182. (Select Bibliographies Reprint Ser). 1924. 27.50 (ISBN 0-8369-5695-8). Ayer Co Pubs.

--Mystery Cities of Central America. 1977. lib. bdg. 59.95 (ISBN 0-8490-2313-0). Gordon Pr.

Gann, Thomas W. Mystery Cities: Exploration & Adventure in Labaantun. LC 76-44721. (Illus.). 320p. 1977. Repr. of 1925 ed. 42.50 (ISBN 0-404-15925-7). AMS Pr.

Gann, W. D. How to Make Money Trading in Commodities, 2 vols. 310p. 1984. Set. 267.00x (ISBN 0-86654-100-4). Inst Econ Finan.

--The Reconstruction of Gann's Stocks & Commodities Wisdom from His Famous Wall Street Reports, 2 vols. (Illus.). 117p. 1983. Set. 185.75x (ISBN 0-86654-077-6). Inst Econ Finan.

Gann, William D. The Active Determination of the Buying & Selling Points in the Stock Market's Long & Short Swings. 171p. 1985. 97.85x (ISBN 0-86654-138-1). Inst Econ Finan.

--The Commodity Writings. (Illus.). 93p. 1982. 85.45x (ISBN 0-86654-036-9). Inst Econ Finan.

--How to Capture Stock Market Bargains. 167p. 1985. 127.50 (ISBN 0-86654-137-3). Inst Econ Finan.

--The Subtle Art of Choosing Early & Late Leaders in the Operations of the Stock Market. (Illus.). 167p. 1985. 185.45 (ISBN 0-86654-165-9). Inst Econ Finan.

--Successful Stock Selecting Methods. (Illus.). 159p. 1985. 177.45 (ISBN 0-86654-165-9). Inst Econ Finan.

Gann, Windell, compiled by. The Wide Margin New Testament. 1976. 8.95 (ISBN 0-88428-042-X). Parchment Pr.

Gannaway, Dave. Buying a Secondhand Boat. 104p. 1980. 15.00x (ISBN 0-245-53446-6, Pub. by Nautical England). State Mutual Bk.

--How to Be Rich & Successful, 1 Vol. LC 84-5011. 118p. (Orig.). 1984. pap. 5.95 (ISBN 0-946155-00-3). Solomon Intl.

--Winning Concepts. (Orig.). 1985. pap. write for info. Solomon Intl.

Gannes, H. Spain in Revolt. 59.95 (ISBN 0-8490-1097-7). Gordon Pr.

Gannett, Ernest. Tanker Performance & Cost: Measurement, Analysis & Management. LC 73-80638. 117p. 1969. 8.50x (ISBN 0-87033-122-1). Cornell Maritime.

Gannett, Henry. A Gazetteer of Maryland & Delaware, 2 vols. in 1. LC 75-37016. 100p. 1979. Repr. of 1904 ed. 10.00 (ISBN 0-8063-0703-X). Genealog Pub.

--A Gazetteer of Virginia & West Virginia, 2 vols. in 1. LC 74-21655. 323p. 1980. Repr. of 1904 ed. 15.00 (ISBN 0-8063-0657-2). Genealog Pub.

--A Geographic Dictionary of Connecticut & Rhode Island, 2 vols. in 1. LC 78-59123. 98p. 1978. Repr. of 1894 ed. 9.50 (ISBN 0-8063-0820-6). Genealog Pub.

--A Geographic Dictionary of Massachusetts. LC 78-59121. 126p. 1978. Repr. of 1894 ed. 12.00 (ISBN 0-8063-0818-4). Genealog Pub.

--A Geographic Dictionary of New Jersey. LC 78-59122. 131p. 1978. Repr. of 1894 ed. 12.00 (ISBN 0-8063-0819-2). Genealog Pub.

--The Origin of Certain Place Names in the United States. 2nd ed. LC 72-11709. 334p. 1977. Repr. of 1905 ed. 18.50 (ISBN 0-8063-0544-4). Genealog Pub.

--The Origin of Certain Place Names in the United States. 280p. 1978. Repr. of 1902 ed. 16.95 (ISBN 0-87928-097-2). Corner Hse.

Gannett, Henry, ed. Report of the National Conservation Commission, 3 vols. LC 72-2837. (Use & Abuse of America's Natural Resources Ser). (Illus.). 1960p. 1972. Repr. of 1909 ed. Set. 127.00, 42.00, 42.00, 43.00 (ISBN 0-405-04506-9). Vol. 1 (ISBN 0-405-04543-3). Vol. 2 (ISBN 0-405-04544-1). Vol. 3 (ISBN 0-405-04545-X). Ayer Co Pubs.

Gannett, Lewis. John Steinbeck. LC 77-10503. (American Literature Ser.: No. 49). 1979. lib. bdg. 50.00x (ISBN 0-8383-2213-1). Haskell.

Gannett, Lewis, tr. see Schacht, Hjalmar.

Gannett, Ruth S. The Dragons of Blueland. (Illus.). 96p. (gr. 1-4). pap. 1.25 (ISBN 0-440-41044-4, YB). Dell.

--Elmer & the Dragon. 96p. (Orig.). (gr. k-6). 1980. pap. 1.25 (ISBN 0-440-41761-9, Pub. by YB). Dell.

--My Father's Dragon. LC 48-6527. (Illus.). (gr. 3-7). 1948. PLB 8.99 (ISBN 0-394-91438-4, BYR). Random.

Gannett, William C. Ezra Stiles Gannett. 1875. 15.00 (ISBN 0-8414-4292-4). Folcroft.

--Ezra Stiles Gannett. LC 79-122654. 1971. Repr. of 1875 ed. 42.50x (ISBN 0-8046-1302-8, Pub. by Kennikat). Assoc Faculty Pr.

--Ezra Stiles Gannett: Unitarian Minister in Boston, 1824-1871. 1979. Repr. of 1875 ed. lib. bdg. 30.00 (ISBN 0-8492-4932-5). R West.

Gannie, Alfred. Jody. 1984. 8.95 (ISBN 0-8062-2274-3). Carlton.

Ganning, London. A Dictionary of Bad Manners. 1982. 16.95 (ISBN 0-395-32509-9); pap. 8.95 (ISBN 0-395-33012-2). HM.

Gannon, Colin A. On the Loschian Spatial Demand Curve. (Discussion Paper Ser.: No. 32). 1969. pap. 5.75 (ISBN 0-686-32201-0). Regional Sci Res Inst.

--Towards a Strategy for Conservation in a World of Technological Change. (Discussion Paper Ser.: No. 24). 1968. pap. 5.75 (ISBN 0-686-32193-6). Regional Sci Res Inst.

Gannon, Edmund C. Sub-Saharan Africa: An Introduction. 1978. pap. 15.00 (ISBN 0-930690-09-5). Coun Soc Econ.

Gannon, Francis X. Biographical Dictionary of the Left, 4 vols. Incl. Vol. 1. LC 78-113035. 624p. 1969. 8.00 (ISBN 0-88279-216-4); Vol. 2. 632p. 1971. 9.00 (ISBN 0-88279-223-7); Vol. 3. LC 76-12821. 1972. 9.00 (ISBN 0-88279-224-5); Vol. 4. LC 72-12821. 1973. 11.95 (ISBN 0-88279-226-1). 32.95 (ISBN 0-686-86876-5). Western Islands.

--Biographical Dictionary of the Left, Vol. 2. 1971. pap. 2.00 (ISBN 0-88279-108-7). Western Islands.

--Joseph D. Keenan, Labor's Ambassador in War & Peace: A Portrait of a Man & His Times. LC 85-40064. (Illus.). 230p. (Orig.). 1984. lib. bdg. 22.00 (ISBN 0-8191-3872-X, J D Keenan); pap. text ed. 12.25 (ISBN 0-8191-3873-8, J D Keenan). U Pr of Amer.

Gannon, Frank. Drugs, What They Are- How They Look- What They Do. LC 70-148361. 1971. 8.95 (ISBN 0-89388-005-1). Okpaku Communications.

Gannon, Jack. Deaf Heritage: A Narrative History of Deaf America. (Illus.). 1981. 26.95x (ISBN 0-913072-38-9); pap. 19.95x (ISBN 0-913072-39-7). Natl Assn Deaf.

Gannon, Jack R., jt. auth. see Alexander, Felicia M.

Gannon, Linda R. Menstrual Disorders & Menopause: Etiology, Maintenance & Treatment. LC 85-3629. 304p. 1985. 37.95 (ISBN 0-03-003878-2); pap. 14.95 (ISBN 0-03-063243-9). Praeger.

Gannon, Michael. Workbench Guide to Semiconductor Circuits & Projects. 256p. 1982. 17.95 (ISBN 0-13-965277-9). P-H.

Gannon, Michael V. Cross in the Sand: The Early Catholic Church in Florida, 1513-1870. LC 83-10498. 1965. pap. 12.00 (ISBN 0-8130-0776-3). U Presses Fla.

Gannon, Michael V., ed. see Fairbanks, George R.

Gannon, Paul. Monarch Notes on Huxley's Brave New World, Point Counter Point & Other Works. (Orig.). pap. 2.75 (ISBN 0-671-00714-9). Monarch Pr.

--Monarch Notes on O'Neill's Long Day's Journey into Night. (Orig.). pap. 2.95 (ISBN 0-671-00752-1). Monarch Pr.

Gannon, Philip. Korea. (World Education Ser.). (Illus.). 144p. (Orig.). 1984. pap. write for info (ISBN 0-910054-81-9). Am Assn Coll Registrars.

Gannon, Robert. Half Mile Up Without an Engine: The Essentials, the Excitement of Sailplanes Soaring. LC 81-12159. (Illus.). 198p. 1982. 18.95 (ISBN 0-13-372169-8); pap. 9.95 (ISBN 0-13-372151-5). P-H.

--How to Raise & Train an English Cocker Spaniel. pap. 2.95 (ISBN 0-87666-291-2, DS-1014). TFH Pubns.

--How to Raise & Train an Irish Setter. (Illus.). pap. 2.95 (ISBN 0-87666-319-6, DS-1024). TFH Pubns.

--Start Right with Goldfish. (Orig.). pap. 2.95 (ISBN 0-87666-081-2, M-504). TFH Pubns.

Gannon, Robert, jt. auth. see Zam, Alfred V.

Gannon, Thomas. Newport Mansions: The Gilded Age. Patrick, James B., ed. (Illus.). 88p. 1982. 20.00 (ISBN 0-940078-01-5). Foremost Pubs.

Gannon, Thomas M. & Traub, George W. The Desert & the City: An Interpretation of the History of Christian Spirituality. 338p. 1984. 8.95 (ISBN 0-8294-0452-X). Loyola.

Gannon, Timothy J. Emotional Development & Spiritual Growth. pap. 0.75 (ISBN 0-8199-0386-8, L38135). Franciscan Herald.

Gannon, Tom & Whalley, Alan. Middle Schools. (Organization in Schools Ser.). 1975. text ed. 19.50x (ISBN 0-435-80321-2). Heinemann Ed.

Ganoczy, Alexandre. An Introduction to Catholic Sacramental Theology. 1984. pap. 8.95 (ISBN 0-8091-2568-4). Paulist Pr.

Ganong, James B. Mary, We Never Knew You. 246p. (Orig.). 1982. pap. 6.50 (ISBN 0-9608620-0-5). K Pillman.

Ganong, Joan, jt. auth. see Ganong, Warren.

Ganong, Joan M. & Ganong, Warren L. Help for the Head Nurse: A Management Guide. 5th ed. LC 80-85412. (Help Series of Management Guides). (Illus.). 110p. (Orig.). 1980. pap. 12.95 (ISBN 0-933036-28-0). Ganong W L Co.

--Help for the Licensed Practical Nurse. 2nd ed. (Help Series of Management Guides). 71p. 1982. pap. 10.95 (ISBN 0-933036-11-6). Ganong W L Co.

--Help for the Unit Secretary: The Service Coordinator Concept. (Help Series of Management Guides). 64p. 1980. pap. 9.95 (ISBN 0-933036-12-4). Ganong W L Co.

--Help with Career Ladders in Nursing. (Help Series of Management Guides). 142p. 1977. pap. 14.95 (ISBN 0-933036-06-X). Ganong W L Co.

--Help with Innovative Teaching Techniques. 2nd ed. (Help Series of Management Guides). 152p. 1976. pap. 15.95 (ISBN 0-933036-08-6). Ganong W L Co.

--Help with Management by Objectives. (Help Series of Management Guides). 132p. 1975. pap. 13.95 (ISBN 0-933036-04-3). Ganong W L Co.

--Help with Managerial Leadership in Nursing: 201 Tremendous Trifles. 4th ed. (Help Series of Management Guides). 200p. 1985. pap. 19.95 (ISBN 0-933036-36-1). Ganong W L Co.

--Help with Performance Appraisal: A Results-Oriented Approach. (Help Series of Management Guides). 115p. 1981. pap. 12.75 (ISBN 0-933036-25-6). Ganong W L Co.

--Help with Primary Nursing: Accountability through the Nursing Process. 2nd ed. (Help Series of Management Guides). 90p. 1980. pap. 11.50 (ISBN 0-933036-13-2). Ganong W L Co.

--Help with Student Clinical Performance Evaluation. (Help Series of Management Guides). 90p. 1977. pap. 11.50 (ISBN 0-933036-14-0). Ganong W L Co.

--One Hundred One Exciting Exercise: Help Worksheets for Nurse Managers & Educators. (Help Series of Management Guides). 109p. 1978. pap. 10.95 (ISBN 0-933036-16-7). Ganong W L Co.

--Performance Appraisal for Productivity: The Nurse Manager's Handbook. LC 83-15676. 360p. 1983. 33.50 (ISBN 0-89443-945-6). Aspen Systems.

Ganong, W. F. & Martini, L., eds. Frontiers in Neuroendocrinology, Vol. 7. (Frontiers in Neuroendocrinology Ser.). 400p. 1982. text ed. 64.50 (ISBN 0-89004-694-8). Raven.

Ganong, W. F., jt. ed. see Martini, L.

Ganong, Warren & Ganong, Joan. Cases in Nursing Management. LC 79-2572. 360p. 1979. text ed. 38.00 (ISBN 0-89443-152-8). Aspen Systems.

--Nursing Management. 2nd ed. LC 80-10865. 350p. 1980. text ed. 27.50 (ISBN 0-89443-278-8). Aspen Systems.

Ganong, Warren L., jt. auth. see Ganong, Joan M.

Ganong, William F. Review of Medical Physiology. 12th ed. LC 85-50920. (Illus.). 583p. 1985. lexotone cover 22.50 (ISBN 0-87041-138-1). Lange.

Ganong, William F., ed. see Denys, Nicolas.

Ganong, William F., ed. see Le Clercq, Chretien.

Ganong, William F., jt. ed. see Martini, L.

Ganong, William F., jt. ed. see Martini, Luciano.

Ganos, Doreen, et al. Difficult Decisions in Medical Ethics. LC 83-19911. (Progress in Clinical & Biological Research Ser.: Vol. 139). 258p. 1983. 38.00 (ISBN 0-8451-0139-0). A R Liss.

Ganousis, Jeanette, jt. auth. see Piersma, Paul.

Gans, Alfred W. see Axelrod, Diana, et al.

Gans, C., et al. Biology of the Reptilia: Development A, Vol. 14. (Biology of the Reptilia Ser.). 704p. 1985. 60.00 (ISBN 0-471-81358-3). Wiley.

--Biology of the Reptilia: Development A, Vol. 15. (Biology of the Reptilia Ser.). 736p. 1985. 50.00 (ISBN 0-471-81204-8). Wiley.

Gans, Carl. Biomechanics: An Approach to Vertebrate Biology. LC 80-18705. 272p. 1980. pap. text ed. 6.50x (ISBN 0-472-08016-4). U of Mich Pr.

Gans, Carl & Parsons, Thomas S. A Photographic Atlas of Shark Anatomy: The Gross Morphology of Squalas Acanthias. LC 80-24528. (Illus.). 106p. 1981. spiral bnd. 8.00x (ISBN 0-226-28120-5). U of Chicago Pr.

Gans, Carl & Pough, Harvey. Biology of the Reptilia, Vol. 12. 1982. 96.50 (ISBN 0-12-274612-0). Acad Pr.

Gans, Carl, ed. Biology of the Reptiles, Vol. 9. 1979. 79.50 (ISBN 0-12-274609-0). Acad Pr.

--Biology of the Reptilia: Vol. 10, Neprology B. LC 68-9113. 1980. 66.00 (ISBN 0-12-274610-4). Acad Pr.

Gans, Carl & Gans, K. A., eds. Biology of the Reptilia: Vol. 8, Physiology B. 1979. 95.00 (ISBN 0-12-274608-2). Acad Pr.

Gans, Carl & Parson, Thomas, eds. Biology of the Reptilia: Morphology, Vol. 3. 1970. 63.50 (ISBN 0-12-274603-1). Acad Pr.

Gans, Carl & Parsons, Thomas, eds. Biology of the Reptilia: Morphology D, Vol.4. 1974. 82.50 (ISBN 0-12-274604-X). Acad Pr.

Gans, Carl & Parsons, Thomas S., eds. Biology of the Reptilia: Morphology B. Vol. 2. 1970. 62.50 (ISBN 0-12-274602-3); Vol. 5. 1976. 86.50 (ISBN 0-12-274605-8); Vol. 7. 1977. 95.00 (ISBN 0-12-274607-4). Acad Pr.

--Biology of the Reptilia, Volume 11: Morphology F. 480p. 1981. 69.50 (ISBN 0-12-274611-2). Acad Pr.

Gans, Carl & Pough, F. H., eds. Biology of the Reptilia, Vol. 13. 360p. 1983. 75.00 (ISBN 0-12-274613-9). Acad Pr.

Gans, Carl, et al. Vertebrates: A Laboratory Text. 2nd, rev. ed. Wessells, Norman K. & Center, Elizabeth M., eds. LC 81-17228. (Illus.). 288p. 1981. lab manual 14.95x (ISBN 0-86576-015-2). W Kaufmann.

Gans, David & Simon, Peter. Playing in the Band: An Oral & Visual Portrait of the Grateful Dead. LC 84-52537. (Illus.). 192p. 1985. pap. 14.95 (ISBN 0-312-61630-9). St Martin.

Gans, Eric. The End of Culture: Toward a Generative Anthropology. LC 84-16180. 1985. 35.00x (ISBN 0-520-05181-5). U of Cal Pr.

--The Origin of Language: A Formal Theory of Representation. LC 80-19653. 1981. 24.50x (ISBN 0-520-04202-6). U of Cal Pr.

Gans, Herbert, et al, eds. On the Making of Americans: Essays in Honor of David Riesman. LC 78-65118. (Illus.). 1979. 30.00x (ISBN 0-8122-7754-6). U of Pa Pr.

Gans, Herbert J. Deciding What's News: A Study of CBS Evening News, NBC Nightly News, Newsweek & Time. LC 78-53516. 1979. 12.95 (ISBN 0-394-50359-7). Pantheon.

--Deciding What's News: A Study of CBS Evening News, NBC Nightly News, Newsweek & Time. LC 79-22849. 1980. pap. 6.95 (ISBN 0-394-74354-7, Vin). Random.

--The Levittowners: Ways of Life & Politics in a New Suburban Community. (A Morningside Book). 512p. 1982. 34.00x (ISBN 0-231-05570-6); pap. 12.00x (ISBN 0-231-05571-4). Columbia U Pr.

--Popular Culture & High Culture: An Analysis & Evaluation of Taste. LC 74-79287. 1975. pap. 7.95x (ISBN 0-465-09717-0, TB-5061). Basic.

--The Urban Villagers. Rev. Expanded ed. LC 82-8577. (Illus.). 456p. 1982. pap. text ed. 8.95 (ISBN 0-02-911240-0); 17.95 (ISBN 0-02-911250-8). Free Pr.

Gans, K. A., jt. ed. see Gans, Carl.

Gans, Manfred, ed. Yeshiva Children Write Poetry: From the Heart We Sing. 6.95 (ISBN 0-914131-76-1, D43). Torah Umesorah.

Gans, Mozes Heiman. Memorbook: Pictorial History of Dutch Jewry from the Renaissance to 1940. (Illus.). 852p. 1983. 75.00 (ISBN 0-8143-1749-9). Wayne St U Pr.

Gans, Roma. Bird Talk. LC 71-132298. (A Let's-Read- and- Find-Out Science Bk). (Illus.). (gr. k-3). 1971. PLB 11.06i (ISBN 0-690-14593-4). Crowell Jr Bks.

--Birds at Night. LC 68-11062. (Crocodile Paperback Ser.). 1976. pap. 1.45 (ISBN 0-690-01257-8). Crowell Jr Bks.

--Birds Eat & Eat & Eat. LC 63-9213. (A Let's Read & Find Out Science Bk.). (Illus.). 40p. (gr. k-3). 1975. Crowell Jr Bks.

--Caves. LC 76-4881. (Let's Read & Find Out Science Book Ser.). (Illus.). (gr. k-3). 1977. PLB 11.89 (ISBN 0-690-01070-2). Crowell Jr Bks.

--Guiding Children's Reading Through Experience. LC 79-16407. 1979. pap. 7.95x (ISBN 0-8077-2569-2). Tchrs Coll.

--Hummingbirds in the Garden. LC 69-11083. (A Let's Read- & Find-Out Science Bk). (Illus.). (gr. k-3). 1969. PLB 11.89 (ISBN 0-690-42562-7). Crowell Jr Bks.

--Oil: The Buried Treasure. LC 74-7375. (A Let's-Read-&-Find-Out Science Bk). (Illus.). (gr. k-3). 1975. PLB 11.89 (ISBN 0-690-00613-6). Crowell Jr Bks.

--Rock Collecting. 2nd ed. LC 83-46170. (A Let's-Read-&-Find-Out Science Bk.). (Illus.). 32p. (gr. k-3). 1984. 11.06i (ISBN 0-690-04265-5); PLB 11.89g (ISBN 0-690-04266-3). Crowell Jr Bks.

--Study of Critical Reading Comprehension in the Intermediate Grades. (Columbia University. Teachers College. Contributions to Education: No. 811). Repr. of 1940 ed. 22.50 (ISBN 0-404-55811-9). AMS Pr.

--Water for Dinosaurs & You. LC 78-158691. (A Let's-Read-&-Find-Out Science Bk.). (Illus.). (gr. k-3). 1972. PLB 11.89 (ISBN 0-690-87027-2); pap. 2.95 (ISBN 0-690-00202-5, TYC-J). Crowell Jr Bks.

--When Birds Change Their Feathers. LC 78-20627. (Let's-Read-&-Find-Out Science Books). (Illus.). 40p. (gr. k-3). 1980. PLB 11.89 (ISBN 0-690-03948-4). Crowell Jr Bks.

Gans, Stephen. Surgical Pediatrics: Nonoperative Care. 2nd ed. 352p. 1980. 45.50 (ISBN 0-8089-1197-X, 791516). Grune.

Gans, Stephen L. Pediatric Endoscopy. 202p. 1983. 41.50 (ISBN 0-8089-1547-9, 791514). Grune.

Gansberg, Alan, jt. auth. see Gansberg, Judith.

Gansberg, Judith & Gansberg, Alan. Direct Encounters: Personal Histories of UFO Abductees. (Illus.). 1980. 11.95 (ISBN 0-8027-0639-8). Walker & Co.

Gansberg, Judith M. & Mostel, Arthur M. The Second Nine Months. 1985. pap. 3.95 (ISBN 0-671-54154-4). PB.

Gansberg, Judith M. & Mostel, Arthur P. The Second Nine Months: The Sexual & Emotional Concerns of the New Mother. LC 83-24323. 224p. (Orig.). 1984. 12.95 (ISBN 0-943392-45-4). Tribeca Comm.

Gansberger, Christine. Arabian Horse Coloring Book. 48p. 1984. pap. 2.95 (ISBN 0-8431-1013-9). Price Stern.

--Racing Car Coloring Book. 1975. pap. 2.50 (ISBN 0-8431-0225-X). Price Stern.

Gansberger, Christine, illus. Off-Road Vehicles Coloring Book. (Coloring Experience Ser). (Illus.). (gr. 3 up). 1978. pap. 2.95 (ISBN 0-8431-0468-6). Price Stern.

Ganschinietz, Linda K., ed. Decade for Decisions: 1976-1986. LC 77-82680. 1977. pap. 9.00 (ISBN 0-911754-00-8). Natl Assn Counties.

Ganser, Carl. Consumer Finance. 151p. 1982. 15.95 (ISBN 0-318-13859-X). Credit Union Natl Assn.

Gansert, Robert. Singing Energy in the Gan-Tone Method of Voice Production. Capano, Carmela, ed. LC 81-80960. 324p. 1981. 37.50 (ISBN 0-939458-00-4). Gan-Tone Pub.

Ganshof, Francois L. Etude Sur les Ministeriales En Flandre et En Lotharingie. LC 80-2029. 1981. Repr. of 1926 ed. 49.50 (ISBN 0-404-18563-0). AMS Pr.

--Feudalism. Grierson, Philip, tr. pap. 5.95xi (ISBN 0-06-131058-1, TB1058, Torch). Har-Row.

--Frankish Institutions under Charlemagne. Lyon, Bryce & Lyon, Mary, trs. LC 68-29166. 207p. 1968. 18.00x (ISBN 0-87057-108-7). U Pr of New Eng.

Gansler, Jacques S. The Defense Industry. 432p. 1980. pap. text ed. 10.95 (ISBN 0-262-57059-9). MIT Pr.

Gans-Ruedin, E. Chinese Carpets. LC 81-82719. (Illus.). 198p. 1982. 39.00 (ISBN 0-87011-485-9). Kodansha.

--Chinese Carpets. (Illus.). 39.00 (ISBN 0-87011-485-9). Apollo.

--The Great Books of Oriental Carpets. LC 83-47531. (Illus.). 180p. 1983. 28.80i (ISBN 0-06-015194-3, HarpT). Har-Row.

Gans-Ruedin, Erwin. Indian Carpets. Howard, Valerie, tr. 320p. 1984. 85.00 (ISBN 0-8478-0551-4). Rizzoli Intl.

--The Splendor of Persian Carpets. LC 78-57908. (Illus.). 552p. 1978. 100.00 (ISBN 0-8478-0179-9). Rizzoli Intl.

Ganss, G. E., frwd. by see Pousset, Edouard.

Ganss, G. E., ed. see Scutte, Joseph F.

Ganss, G. E., et al, trs. see Arrupe, Pedro.

Ganss, George E. The Jesuit Educational Tradition & Saint Louis University: Some Bearings for the University's Sesquicentennial, 1818-1968. LC 75-87922. (Illus.). 70p. 1969. 3.25 (ISBN 0-912422-02-5). Inst Jesuit.

--Saint Ignatius' Idea of a Jesuit University. 2nd ed. (Illus.). 1956. pap. 16.95 (ISBN 0-87462-437-1). Marquette.

Ganss, George E., jt. auth. see Stanley, David M.

Ganss, George E., ed. Jesuit Religious Life Today: The Principal Features of its Spirit, in Excerpts... from Official Documents. LC 77-78816. (Jesuit Primary Sources in English Translation Ser.: No. 3). 190p. 1977. pap. 3.00 (ISBN 0-912422-27-0). Inst Jesuit.

Ganss, George E., frwd. by see Arrupe, Pedro J.

Ganss, George E., ed. see Bangert, William V.

Ganss, George E., frwd. by see Clancy, Thomas H.

Ganss, George E., ed. see Clancy, Thomas H.

Ganss, George E., frwd. by see Dalmases, Candido de.

Ganss, George E., ed. see Fleming, David L.

Ganss, George E., ed. see Gruenberg, Gladys W.

Ganss, George E., ed. see Iparraguirre, Ignacio.

Ganss, George E., ed. see Mason, Sr. M. Elizabeth.

Ganss, George E., ed. see Toner, Jules J.

Ganss, George E., tr. & commentary by see Ignatius Of Loyola, St.

Gansser, Augusto. Geology of the Bhutan Himalaya. (Denkschriften der Schweizerischen Naturforschenden Gesellschaft: Vol. 96). 180p. 1983. 39.95 (ISBN 0-8176-1371-4). Birkhauser.

--Geology of the Himalayas. LC 64-8902. (De Sitter Regional Geology Ser). Repr. of 1964 ed. 85.80 (ISBN 0-8357-9898-4, 2016971). Bks Demand UMI.

Ganssler, P. & Revesz, P., eds. Empirical Distributions & Processes: Selected Papers from a Meeting at Oberwolfach, Mar. 28-Apr. 3, 1976. (Lecture Notes in Mathematics Ser.: Vol. 566). 1976. soft cover 13.00 (ISBN 0-387-08061-9). Springer-Verlag.

Ganstad, Edwin S., ed. see Olson, Adolf.

Gant, A. Mac. Destiny's Plan: The Story of a Combination Family. LC 81-90504. (Illus.). 196p. 1982. 8.95 (ISBN 0-533-05115-0). Vantage.

Gant, George. Development Administration: Meaning & Application. LC 79-3966. 356p. 1979. 24.50x (ISBN 0-299-07980-5). U of Wis Pr.

Gant, Margaret E. The Raven's Story. LC 80-105389. (Illus.). 1979. 9.95 (ISBN 0-9603138-0-X). M E Gant.

Gant, Michael S., ed. see Chase, John.

Gant, Michael S., ed. see Rowland, Leon.

Gant, Michael S., ed. see Young, John V.

Gant, Norman F. & Worley, Richard. Hypertension in Pregnancy: Concepts & Management. (Illus.). 211p. 1980. 29.95 (ISBN 0-8385-4002-3). ACC.

Gant, Roland, ed. & intro. by. Edward Thomas in the Countryside. 1977. 14.95 (ISBN 0-571-10799-0); pap. 6.95 (ISBN 0-571-11779-1). Faber & Faber.

Gant, Roland, compiled by. The Prose of Edward Thomas. 228p. 1981. Repr. of 1948 ed. lib. bdg. 25.00 (ISBN 0-89984-455-3). Century Bookbindery.

Gant, Wanda & Casale, James F., eds. Making Business Systems Effective: The Papers & Proceedings of Syntopican XIII. 500p. (Orig.). 1985. pap. text ed. 30.00 (ISBN 0-935220-13-5). Assn Info Sys.

Ganten, D. & Pfaff, D., eds. Action of Progesterone on the Brain. (Current Topics in Neuroendocrinology Ser.: Vol. 5). (Illus.). 235p. 1985. 39.00 (ISBN 0-387-13433-6). Springer-Verlag.

--Adrenal Actions on Brain. (Current Topics in Neuroendocrinology Ser.: Vol. 2). (Illus.). 180p. 1982. pap. 38.00 (ISBN 0-387-11126-3). Springer-Verlag.

--Central Cardiovascular control. (Current Topics in Neuroendocrinology Ser.: Vol. 3). (Illus.). 210p. 1983. 39.00 (ISBN 0-387-11350-9). Springer-Verlag.

--Neurobiology of Vasopressin. (Current Topics in Neuroendocrinology Ser.: Vol. 4). (Illus.). 180p. 1985. 34.50 (ISBN 0-387-11351-7). Springer-Verlag.

--Sleep: Clinical & Experimental Aspects. (Current Topics in Neuroendocrinology Ser.: Vol. 1). (Illus.). 160p. 1982. pap. 38.00 (ISBN 0-387-11125-5). Springer-Verlag.

Ganten, D., et al, eds. The Renin Angiotensin System: A Model for the Synthesis of Peptides in the Brain. (Experimental Brain Research Ser.: Supplement 4). (Illus.). 385p. 1982. pap. 47.00 (ISBN 0-387-11344-4). Springer-Verlag.

Gantenbein, James W., ed. Documentary Background of World War Two, 1931-1941. 1973. lib. bdg. 63.00x (ISBN 0-374-92988-2). Octagon.

--The Evolution of Our Latin-American Policy: A Documentary Record. LC 72-159187. xxviii, 980p. 1971. Repr. of 1950 ed. lib. bdg. 57.50x (ISBN 0-374-92987-4). Octagon.

Ganter, Grace & Yeakel, Margaret. Human Behavior & the Social Environment: A Perspective for Social Work Practice. LC 80-470. 1980. 21.00x (ISBN 0-231-04620-0). Columbia U Pr.

Gantert, Ann X., jt. auth. see Keenan, Edward P.

Gantmacher, F. Lectures in Analytical Mechanics. (Illus.). 286p. 1975. text ed. 15.00x (ISBN 0-8464-0551-2). Beekman Pubs.

Gantmacher, Felix R. Lectures on Analytical Mechanics. 2nd ed. write for info. (ISBN 0-8284-0311-2). Chelsea Pub.

--Theory of Matrices, 2 Vols. LC 59-11779. Vol. 1. 18.95 (ISBN 0-8284-0131-4); Vol. 2. 16.95 (ISBN 0-8284-0133-0). Chelsea Pub.

Ganton, Doris. Breaking & Training the Driving Horse. pap. 10.00 (ISBN 0-87980-272-3). Wilshire.

--Breaking & Training the Driving Horse. (Illus.). 80p. 10.00 (ISBN 0-318-12496-3). Am Donkey.

--Drive On. 1982. pap. 7.00 (ISBN 0-87980-393-2). Wilshire.

Gantos, Jack. Rotten Ralph. LC 75-34101. (Illus.). 48p. (gr. k-3). 1976. PLB 8.95 (ISBN 0-395-24276-2); pap. 4.50. HM.

--Rotten Ralph. (Illus.). 1980. Repr. 4.95 (ISBN 0-395-29202-6, Sandpiper). HM.

--Rotten Ralph's Rotten Christmas. LC 84-644. (Illus.). 32p. (ps-3). 1984. PLB 12.95 (ISBN 0-395-35380-7). HM.

--The Werewolf Family. (Illus.). (gr. k-3). 1980. PLB 8.95 (ISBN 0-395-28760-X). HM.

--Worse Than Rotten, Ralph. (Illus.). (gr. k-3). 1978. PLB 12.95 (ISBN 0-395-27106-1). HM.

--Worse Than Rotten, Ralph. (gr. k-3). 1982. pap. 3.95 (ISBN 0-395-32919-1). HM.

Gantschev, Ivan. The Christmas Train. LC 84-80303. (Illus.). (ps-3). 12.95 (ISBN 0-316-30346-1). Little.

--Journey of the Storks. LC 82-61835. (Illus.). 32p. (gr. k-5). 1983. 10.95 (ISBN 0-907234-27-5, Pub. by Picture Bk Studio USA). Neugebauer Pr.

--Moon Lake. Gadsby, Oliver E., tr. from Ger. Orig. Title: Der Mondsee. (Illus.). 32p. 1981. 10.95 (ISBN 0-907234-08-9, Pub. by Picture Bk Studio USA). Neugebauer Pr.

--The Moon Lake. Gadsby, Oliver, tr. from Ger. (Illus.). 32p. (gr. k up). 1985. pap. 5.95 (ISBN 0-907234-74-7, Pub. by Picture Bk Studio USA). Neugebauer Pr.

--Otto the Bear. (Illus.). 32p. (gr. k-3). 1985. 12.95 (ISBN 0-316-30348-8). Little.

--Rumprump. LC 83-25006. (Illus.). 32p. 1984. 11.95 (ISBN 0-907234-53-4, Pub. by Picture Bk Studio USA). Neugebauer Pr.

--Two Islands. Saunders, Robert, ed. LC 85-9392. (Illus.). 32p. (gr. 1 up). 1985. 11.95 (ISBN 0-88708-003-0, Pub. by Picture Bk Studio USA). Neugebauer Pr.

--The Volcano. LC 82-183395. (Illus.). 28p. 1981. 10.95 (ISBN 0-907234-03-8, Pub. by Picture Bk Studio USA). Neugebauer Pr.

Gantschev, Ivan, jt. auth. see Aoki, Hisako.

Gantt, Clarence. The Lady on My Right & Other Poems. 64p. 1982. 5.00 (ISBN 0-682-49826-2). Exposition Pr FL.

Gantt, Elisabeth, ed. Handbook of Phycological Methods. LC 78-67311. 1980. 42.50 (ISBN 0-521-22466-7). Cambridge U Pr.

Gantt, H. L. Industrial Leadership. LC 72-9507. (Management History Ser.: No. 42). (Illus.). 141p. 1973. Repr. of 1916 ed. 20.00 (ISBN 0-87960-044-6). Hive Pub.

--Organizing for Work. LC 72-9508. (Management History Ser.: No. 43). (Illus.). 118p. 1973. Repr. of 1919 ed. 20.00 (ISBN 0-87960-046-2). Hive Pub.

--Work, Wages & Profits. 2nd ed. LC 72-9509. (Management History Ser.: No. 41). (Illus.). 312p. 1973. Repr. of 1919 ed. 22.50 (ISBN 0-87960-048-9). Hive Pub.

Gantt, H. L., et al. How Scientific Management Is Applied. LC 72-9521. (Management History Ser.: No. 26). (Illus.). 128p. 1973. Repr. of 1911 ed. 17.50 (ISBN 0-87960-033-0). Hive Pub.

--Organizing for Production & Other Papers on Management, 1912-1924. (Management History Ser.: No. 71). (Illus.). 400p. 1974. Repr. of 1923 ed. 24.50 (ISBN 0-87960-102-7). Hive Pub.

Gantt, Horsley W., tr. see Luria, A. R.

Gantt, Markanne. Ready for Reading: Classroom Games for Reading Readiness. 149p. 1980. pap. 9.95 (ISBN 0-87762-285-X). Technomic.

Gantt, Michael D. & Gatza, James. Computers in Insurance. LC 80-67525. 150p. 1980. pap. 8.00 (ISBN 0-89463-029-6). Am Inst Property.

Gantt, Richard, jt. auth. see Robbins, Louise M.

Gantt, Robert B., jt. ed. see Lauffer, Richard A.

Gantt, W. Horsley. Physiological Bases of Psychiatry. (Illus.). 368p. 1958. 34.50x (ISBN 0-398-00640-7). C C Thomas.

Gantt, William A. Russian Medicine. LC 75-23669. (Clio Medica: 20). (Illus.). 1978. Repr. of 1937 ed. 19.00 (ISBN 0-404-58920-0). AMS Pr.

Gantz, Charlotte O. A Naturalist in Southern Florida. LC 74-126195. (Illus.). 1983. 12.95 (ISBN 0-87024-172-9). U of Miami Pr.

Gantz, David. The O'Hare Family Books. Incl. First Day in School (ISBN 0-517-55461-5); At the Supermarket (ISBN 0-517-55459-3); First Airplane Trip (ISBN 0-517-55458-5); Things to Do Together in the Seasons (ISBN 0-517-55460-7). (Illus.). (ps-1). 1984. bds. 3.95 ea., Paper over board with jackets. Crown.

Gantz, David, jt. auth. see Stevens, Ann.

Gantz, Jeffrey. Early Irish Myths & Sagas. (Pengiun Classic Ser.). 1982. pap. 4.95 (ISBN 0-14-044397-5). Penguin.

--Early Irish Myths & Sagas. 250p. 1985. 14.95 (ISBN 0-88029-038-2, Pub. by Dorset Pr). Hippocrene Bks.

Gantz, Jeffrey, tr. The Mabinogion. (Classic Ser.). 1976. pap. 3.95 (ISBN 0-14-044322-3). Penguin.

Gantz, Jeffrey, tr. from Welsh. Mabinogion. 400p. 1985. 16.95 (ISBN 0-88029-039-0, Pub. by Dorset Pr). Hippocrene Bks.

Gantz, Joe. Whose Child Cries: Children of Gay Parents Talk about Their Lives. LC 83-81973. 272p. 1983. 16.95 (ISBN 0-915190-40-0); pap. 8.95 (ISBN 0-915190-39-7). Jalmar Pr.

Gantz, John, jt. auth. see Rochester, Jack B.

Gantz, Nelson & Gleckman, Richard. Manual of Clinical Problems in Infectious Disease. 1979. spiral binder 16.95 (ISBN 0-316-30351-8). Little.

Ganucheau, Frank P., III, jt. auth. see Bowen, William M., IV.

Ganusovskii, Boris. Desiat' Let Za Zheleznym Zanavesom: Zapiski Zhertvy Yalty 1945-1955. LC 83-82222. Orig. Title: Ten Years Behind the Iron Curtain: Notes of a Victim of Yalta 1945-1955. (Illus.). 430p. (Rus.). pap. 16.00 (ISBN 0-88669-064-1). Globus Pubs.

Ganz, A. W. Berlioz in London. (Music Ser.). (Illus.). 222p. 1981. Repr. of 1950 ed. lib. bdg. 27.50 (ISBN 0-306-76092-4). Da Capo.

--Berlioz in London. LC 78-67015. (Encore Music Editions Ser.). (Illus.). 1979. Repr. of 1950 ed. 22.50 (ISBN 0-88355-740-1). Hyperion Conn.

Ganz, Arthur. George Bernard Shaw. LC 83-48304. (Modern Dramatists Ser.). (Illus.). 180p. 1984. 17.50 (ISBN 0-394-53502-2, GP-880); pap. 9.95 (ISBN 0-394-62492-0, E-871). Grove.

--Realms of the Self: Variations on a Theme in Modern Drama. (The Gotham Library). 256p. 1981. 27.50x (ISBN 0-8147-2979-7); pap. 13.50x (ISBN 0-8147-2980-0). NYU Pr.

Ganz, Arthur, jt. auth. see Beckson, Karl.

Ganz, Arthur, ed. Pinter: A Collection of Critical Essays. 1972. 12.95 (ISBN 0-13-676387-1, Spec). P-H.

Ganz, Charles. A Fitzgerald Medley. 1973. Repr. of 1933 ed. 30.00 (ISBN 0-8274-0403-4). R West.

Ganz, David L. Fourteen Bits. the Story of America's Bicentennial Coinage 1976: A Legal & Legislative History of 31 U.S.C. Sec. 324 D-I. LC 76-8045. (Illus., Orig.). 1978. 12.00x (ISBN 0-914478-63-X); pap. 5.00x (ISBN 0-914478-64-8). Three Continents.

--The World of Coins & Coin Collecting. (Illus.). 288p. 1985. 22.50 (ISBN 0-684-18238-6, ScribT). Scribner.

Ganz, Gabrielle. Government & Industry. 90.00x (ISBN 0-903486-34-2, Pub. by Prof Bks England). State Mutual Bk.

Ganz, Joan S. Rules: A Systematic Study. (Janua Linguarum, Ser. Minor: No. 96). (Illus.). 144p. (Orig.). 1972. pap. text ed. 13.20x (ISBN 90-2791-853-8). Mouton.

Ganz, Margaret. Elizabeth Gaskell: The Artist in Conflict. LC 68-24279. 313p. 1969. 27.50x (ISBN 0-8290-0169-7). Irvington.

Ganz, Michael & Levick, Donald. Programmed Review of Histology. (Illus.). 300p. 1985. pap. text ed. 19.50 (ISBN 0-397-50471-3, Lippincott Medical); pap. text ed. 15.75. Lippincott.

Ganz, R., jt. ed. see Muller, M. E.

Ganz, Raffael, ed. George Mikes Introduces Switzerland. (Illus.). 240p. 1977. 16.95 (ISBN 0-233-96757-5). Andre Deutsch.

Ganz, Raffael, ed. see Mikes, George.

Ganz, Rudolph, jt. auth. see Hutcheson, Ernest.

Ganz, Yaffa. Our Jerusalem. (Illus.). (gr. k-2). 1979. pap. 3.50x (ISBN 0-87441-308-7). Behrman.

Ganzel, Bill. Dust Bowl Descent. LC 83-3521. (Illus.). vi, 130p. 1984. 29.95 (ISBN 0-8032-2107-X). U of Nebr Pr.

Ganzel, Dewey. Fortune & Men's Eyes: The Career of John Payne Collier. (Illus.). 1982. 22.50x (ISBN 0-19-212231-2). Oxford U Pr.

Ganzel, Richard, jt. ed. see Francis, John G.

Ganzfried, Solomon. Code of Jewish Law: Kitzur Shulhan Arukh, 4 vols. Goldin, Hyman E., tr. (Eng. & Hebrew.). 1961. Set. 45.00 (ISBN 0-88482-412-8). Hebrew Pub.

Ganzfried, Solomon & Goldin, Hyman E. Code of Jewish Law. 626p. 1963. 17.50 (ISBN 0-88482-423-3); pap. 11.95 (ISBN 0-88482-779-8). Hebrew Pub.

Ganzglass, M. R. The Penal Code of the Somali Democratic Republic. 1950. 19.50 (ISBN 0-8135-0667-0). Brown Bk.

Ganzhorn, Jack. I've Killed Men. (Illus.). 1959. 10.50 (ISBN 0-8159-5821-8). Devin.

Gao E, jt. auth. see Cao, Xuegin.

Gaona, Francisco. Basic Spanish One, 6 vols. 1971. Set. 21.50x (ISBN 0-86589-032-3); Vol. 1, Units 1,2. 3.50x (ISBN 0-86589-033-1); Vol. 2, Units 3-4. 3.50x (ISBN 0-86589-034-X); Vol. 3, Units 5-6. 3.50x (ISBN 0-86589-035-8); Vol. 4, Units 7-8. 3.50x (ISBN 0-86589-036-6); Vol. 5, Units 9-10. 3.50x (ISBN 0-86589-037-4); Vol. 6, Unit 11-12. 3.50x (ISBN 0-86589-038-2); Student Guide I. 3.00x (ISBN 0-86589-039-0). Individual Learn.

--Basic Spanish Two, 6 vols. 1971. Set. 20.50x (ISBN 0-86589-040-4); Vol. 7, Units 13-14. 3.25x (ISBN 0-86589-041-2); Vol. 8, Units 15-16. 3.25x (ISBN 0-86589-042-0); Vol. 9, Units 17-18. 3.25x (ISBN 0-86589-043-9); Vol. 10, Units 19-20. 3.25x (ISBN 0-86589-044-7); Vol. 11, Units 21-22. 3.25x (ISBN 0-86589-045-5); Vol. 12, Units 23-24. 3.25x (ISBN 0-86589-046-3); Student Guide 2. 3.12x (ISBN 0-86589-047-1). Individual Learn.

Gaona, Victor D. & Graham, Harry L. Born to Fly: The Story of Tito Gaona. (Illus.). 132p. (Orig.). 1984. 19.95 (ISBN 0-915507-03-X); pap. 10.00 (ISBN 0-915507-04-8); boxed set 100.00 (ISBN 0-915507-04-8). Wild Rose.

Gaonkar, Ramesh. Microprocessor Architecture, Programming, & Applications with 8085-8080A. 672p. 1984. Additional supplements may be obtained from publisher. text ed. 29.95 (ISBN 0-675-20159-4). Merrill.

Gaos, Ignacio, et al. Enciclopedia Universal Juventud, 3 vols. 2290p. (Espn.). 1971. Set. 110.00 (ISBN 84-261-5705-X, S-50452). French & Eur.

Gaos, Vicente. Concierto En Mi y En Vosotros. 3.75 (ISBN 0-8477-3201-0); pap. 2.50 (ISBN 0-8477-3202-9). U of PR Pr.

GAP Committee on Adolescence. Normal Adolescence: Its Dynamics & Impact, Vol. 6. LC 62-2872. (Report: No. 68). 1968. pap. 4.00 (ISBN 0-87318-093-3, Pub. by GAP). Brunner-Mazel.

--Power & Authority in Adolescence: The Origins & Resolutions of Intergenerational Conflict, Vol. 10. LC 78-55380. (Publication: No. 101). 1978. pap. 6.50 (ISBN 0-87318-138-7, Pub. by GAP). Brunner-Mazel.

GAP Committee on Aging. Aged & Community Mental Health: A Guide to Program Development, Vol. 8. LC 72-200268. (No. 81). (Report Ser.). 1971. pap. 4.00 (ISBN 0-87318-113-1, Pub. by GAP). Brunner-Mazel.

--Psychiatry & the Aged: An Introductory Approach, Vol. 5. LC 62-2872. (Report No. 59A). 1965. pap. 2.00 (ISBN 0-87318-111-5, Pub. by GAP). Brunner-Mazel.

--The Right to Die: Decision & Decision Makers, Vol. 8. LC 64-138. (Symposium No. 12). 1973. pap. 4.00 (ISBN 0-87318-123-9, Pub. by GAP). Brunner-Mazel.

--Toward a Public Policy on Mental Health Care of the Elderly, Vol. 7. LC 62-2872. (Report No. 79). 1970. pap. 2.00 (ISBN 0-87318-110-7, Pub. by GAP). Brunner-Mazel.

GAP Committee on Child Psychiatry. The Diagnostic Process in Child Psychiatry, Vol. 3. (Report No. 38). 1957. pap. 2.00 (ISBN 0-87318-048-8, Pub. by GAP). Brunner-Mazel.

--From Diagnosis to Treatment: An Approach to Treatment Planning for the Emotionally Disturbed Child, Vol. 8. LC 73-175264. (Report No. 87). 1973. pap. 4.50 (ISBN 0-87318-121-2, Pub. by GAP). Brunner-Mazel.

--Psychopathological Disorders in Childhood: Theoretical Considerations & a Proposed Classification, Vol. 6. LC 62-2872. (Report No. 62). 1983. pap. 13.50 (ISBN 0-87630-352-1, Pub. by GAP). Brunner-Mazel.

GAP Committee on Family. Field of Family Therapy, Vol. 7. LC 62-2872. (Report No. 78). 1970. pap. 4.00 (ISBN 0-87318-107-7, Pub. by GAP). Brunner-Mazel.

GAP Committee on Governmental Agencies. Effect of the Method of Payment on Mental Health Care Practice, Vol. 9. LC 75-37988. (Report no. 95). 1975. pap. 4.00 (ISBN 0-87318-132-8, Pub. by GAP). Brunner-Mazel.

--Preventive Psychiatry in the Armed Forces: With Some Implications for Civilian Use, Vol. 4. (Report No. 47). 1960. pap. 2.00 (ISBN 0-87318-062-3, Pub. by GAP). Brunner-Mazel.

--VIP with Psychiatric Impairment, Vol. 8. LC 73-155432. (Report No. 83). 1973. pap. 2.00 (ISBN 0-87318-116-6, Pub. by GAP). Brunner-Mazel.

GAP Committee on International Relations. Psychiatrist & Public Issues, Vol. 7. LC 62-2872. (Report No. 74). 1969. pap. 2.00 (ISBN 0-87318-103-4, Pub. by GAP). Brunner-Mazel.

--Self-Involvement in the Middle East Conflict, Vol. 10. LC 78-12608. (Publication: No. 103). 1978. pap. 6.00 (ISBN 0-87318-140-9, Pub. by GAP). Brunner-Mazel.

GAP Committee on Med. Education. Education for Community Psychiatry, Vol. 6. LC 62-2872. (Report No. 64). 1967. pap. 2.00 (ISBN 0-87318-089-5, Pub. by GAP). Brunner-Mazel.

GAP Committee on Medical Education. Assessment of Sexual Function: A Guide to Interviewing, Vol. 8. LC 74-158143. (Report No. 88). 1973. pap. 4.00 (ISBN 0-87318-122-0, Pub. by GAP). Brunner-Mazel.

--The Preclinical Teaching of Psychiatry, Vol. 5. (Report: No. 54). 1962. pap. 2.00 (ISBN 0-87318-073-9, Pub. by GAP). Brunner-Mazel.

GAP Committee on Mental Health Services. Nonpsychotic Alcoholic Patient & the Mental Hospital, Vol. 7. LC 62-2872. (Report No. 70). 1968. pap. 2.00 (ISBN 0-87318-098-4, Pub. by GAP). Brunner-Mazel.

GAP Committee on Mental Retardation. Psychiatric Consultation in Mental Retardation, Vol. 10. LC 79-6358. (Publication: No. 104). 1979. pap. 4.00 (ISBN 0-87318-142-5, Pub. by GAP). Brunner-Mazel.

GAP Committee on Preventive Psychiatry. Humane Reproduction, Vol. 8. LC 73-175574. (Report No. 86). 1973. pap. 4.00 (ISBN 0-87318-120-4, Pub. by GAP). Brunner-Mazel.

--Problems of Estimating Changes in Frequency of Mental Disorders, Vol. 4. (Report No. 50). 1961. pap. 2.00 (ISBN 0-87318-067-4, Pub. by GAP). Brunner-Mazel.

GAP Committee on Psychiatry & Law. Misuse of Psychiatry in the Criminal Courts: Competency to Stand Trial, Vol. 8. LC 74-170397. (Report No. 89). 1974. pap. 7.50 (ISBN 0-87630-372-6, Pub. by GAP). Brunner-Mazel.
--Psychiatry & Sex Psychopath Legislation: The 30s to the 80s, Vol. 9. LC 77-72874. (Publications: No. 98). 1977. pap. 4.00 (ISBN 0-87318-135-2, Pub. by GAP). Brunner-Mazel.
GAP Committee on Psychiatry & Religion. Mysticism: Spiritual Quest or Psychic Disorder, Vol. 9. LC 76-45931. (Report: No. 97). 1976. pap. 4.00 (ISBN 0-87318-134-4, Pub. by GAP). Brunner-Mazel.
--The Psychic Function of Religion in Mental Illness & Health, Vol. 6. LC 62-2872. (Report: No. 67). 1968. pap. 3.00 (ISBN 0-87318-092-5, Pub. by GAP). Brunner-Mazel.
GAP Committee on Psychiatry & the Community. The Chronic Mental Patient in the Community: Vol. 10. LC 78-55381. (Publication No. 102). 1978. pap. 4.00 (ISBN 0-87318-139-5, Pub. by GAP). Brunner-Mazel.
GAP Committee on Psychiatry in Industry. What Price Compensation, Vol. 9. LC 77-80351. (Report: No. 99). 1977. pap. 5.00 (ISBN 0-87630-367-X, Pub. by GAP). Brunner-Mazel.
GAP Committee on Psychopathology. The Recruitment & Training of the Research Psychiatrist, Vol. 6. LC 62-2872. (Report No. 65). 1967. pap. 2.00 (ISBN 0-87318-090-9, Pub. by GAP). Brunner-Mazel.
GAP Committee on Public Education. Medical Practice & Psychiatry: The Impact of Changing Demands, Vol. 5. (Report No. 58). 1964. pap. 2.00 (ISBN 0-87318-077-1, Pub. by GAP). Brunner-Mazel.
GAP Committee on Social Issues. Psychiatric Aspects of School Desegregation, Vol. 3. LC 57-7606. (Report No. 37). 1957. pap. 3.00 (ISBN 0-87318-045-3, Pub. by GAP). Brunner-Mazel.
--Psychiatric Aspects of the Prevention of Nuclear War, Vol. 5. LC 64-7800. (Report No. 57). 1964. pap. 11.95 (ISBN 0-87630-396-3, Pub. by GAP). Brunner-Mazel.
GAP Committee on the College Student. Educated Woman: Prospects & Problems, Vol. 9. (Report no. 92). 1975. pap. 4.00 (ISBN 0-87318-129-8, Pub. by GAP). Brunner-Mazel.
GAP Committee on Therapeutic Care. Community Worker: A Response to Human Need, Vol. 9. LC 62-2872. (Report Ser.: No. 91). 1974. pap. 3.50 (ISBN 0-87318-128-X, Pub. by GAP). Brunner-Mazel.
GAP Committee on Therapy. Problems of Psychiatric Leadership, Vol. 8. LC 74-170958. (Report No. 90). 1974. pap. 2.00 (ISBN 0-87318-125-5, Pub. by GAP). Brunner-Mazel.
--Psychotherapy & the Dual Research Tradition, Vol. 7. LC 62-2872. (Report No. 73). 1969. pap. 2.00 (ISBN 0-87318-102-6, Pub. by GAP). Brunner-Mazel.
GAP Task Force on Recertification. Recertification: A Look at the Issues, Vol. 9. (Report: No. 96). 1976. pap. 2.50 (ISBN 0-87318-133-6, Pub. by GAP). Brunner-Mazel.
Gapany-Gapana, Vicius B. Otosclerosis: Genetics & Surgical Rehabilitation. LC 75-8545. 249p. 1975. 54.95x (ISBN 0-470-29080-3). Halsted Pr.
Gapen, D. Kaye, ed. see Library & Information Technology Association.
Gapenski, Louis J., jt. auth. see Brigham, Eugene F.
Gapinski, J. H. Macroeconomics Theory: Statics, Dynamics & Policy. 432p. 1982. 35.95x (ISBN 0-07-022765-9). McGraw.
Gapinski, James & Rockwood, Charles E., eds. Essays in Post-Keynesian Inflation. LC 79-22879. 336p. 1979. prof ref 32.50 (ISBN 0-88410-684-5). Ballinger Pub.
Gaposchkin, Sergei, tr. see Sobolev, Victor V.
Gapp, Samuel V. George Gissing, Classicist. LC 72-189876. 1936. lib. bdg. 16.50 (ISBN 0-8414-1109-3). Folcroft.
Gappa, Judith & Pearce, Janice. Sex and Gender in the Social Sciences: Reassessing the Introductory Courses. 176p. 1982. 10.00 (ISBN 0-317-36342-5). Am Sociological.
Gappa, Judith M. Part-Time Faculty: Higher Education at a Crossroads. Fife, Jonathan D., ed. LC 84-72775. (ASHE-ERIC Higher Education Research Report Ser.: No. 3, 1984). (Illus.). 125p. (Orig.). 1984. pap. 7.50 (ISBN 0-913317-12-8). Assn Study Higher Ed.
Gappa, Sylvia & Glenn, Deirdre. Room to Grow. LC 80-81681. (Learning Handbooks Ser.). 1981. pap. 6.95 (ISBN 0-8224-5875-6). Pitman Learning.
Gappert, Gary. Post-Affluent America: The Social Economy of the Future. 1978. 12.50 (ISBN 0-531-05403-9); pap. 6.95 (ISBN 0-531-05612-0). Watts.
Gappert, Gary & Knight, Richard V. Cities of the Twenty First Century. (Urban Affairs Annual Reviews: Vol. 23). (Illus.). 320p. 1982. 28.00 (ISBN 0-8039-1910-7); pap. 14.00 (ISBN 0-8039-1911-5). Sage.
Gappert, Gary, ed. The Future of Winter Cities. 300p. 1985. 28.00 (ISBN 0-317-30012-1); pap. 14.00 (ISBN 0-317-30013-X). Sage.
Gaquere, H. The Children of Fatima. (Illus.). (gr. 4-8). 2.00 (ISBN 0-8198-0217-4); pap. 1.25 (ISBN 0-8198-0218-2). Dghtrs St Paul.
Gar, Josef. Biblyografye Fun Artiklen Vegn Khurbn un Gvure. Incl. Vol. 1. LC 67-2416. (Yad Vashem-Yivo Joint Documentary Projects Bibliographical Ser.: No.). 306p. 1966. 10.00 (ISBN 0-914512-22-6); Vol. 2. (Yad Vashem-Yivo Joint Documentary Projects Bibliographical Ser.: No. 10). 338p. 1969. 15.00 (ISBN 0-914512-10-2). Yivo Inst.
Gar, Josef & Friedman, Philip. Biblyografye Fun Yidishe Bikher Vegn Khurbn un Gvure. (Yad Vashem-Yivo Joint Documentary Projects Bibliographical Ser.: No. 3). 330p. (Yiddish.). 1962. 10.00 (ISBN 0-914512-12-9, HE-65-1134). Yivo Inst.
Gara, Baljian N. see Baljian-Gara, N.
Gara, Larra & Chatfield, Charles. International War Resistance Through World War II. (The Garland Library of War & Peace). 1975. lib. bdg. 46.00 (ISBN 0-8240-0449-3). Garland Pub.
Gara, Larry. The Liberty Line: The Legend of the Underground Railroad. LC 61-6552. 216p. 1961. pap. 6.00x (ISBN 0-8131-0115-8). U Pr of Ky.
--War Resistance in Historical Perspective. 1983. pap. 5.00x (ISBN 0-87574-171-1, 171). Pendle Hill.
--Westernized Yankee: The Story of Cyrus Woodman. LC 56-14602. (Illus.). 254p. 1956. 7.50 (ISBN 0-87020-032-1). State Hist Soc Wis.
Gara, Larry, ed. While There is a Soul in Prison: 1979 Peace Calendar. 128p. spiralbound 2.50 (ISBN 0-317-36158-9, 1509). War Res League.
Gara, Laszlo. Az Ismeretlen Illyes. 2nd ed. LC 65-28178. (Hungarian). 1969. 6.00 (ISBN 0-911050-34-5). Occidental.
Gara, Otto G. & Naegeli, Bruce A. Technological Changes & the Law: A Reader. LC 79-92276. 925p. 1980. 35.00 (ISBN 0-89941-037-5). W S Hein.
Garab, Arra M. Beyond Byzantium: The Last Phase of Yeats's Career. LC 74-85148. 142p. 1969. 8.50 (ISBN 0-87580-012-2). N Ill U Pr.
Garafano, Marie, illus. The Flower Notebook: An Illustrated Journal with Space for Notes. (Illus.). 96p. 1985. lib. bdg. 12.90 (ISBN 0-89471-332-9); pap. 4.95 (ISBN 0-89471-331-0). Running Pr.
Garagiola, Joe. Baseball Is a Funny Game. 160p. 1985. pap. 2.95 (ISBN 0-553-23566-4). Bantam.
Garagon, ed. see De La Bruyere, Jean.
Garamond, Jacques N., jt. auth. see Rotzlerin, Willy.
Garan, Dominick. Against Ourselves. LC 74-8027. 1979. 9.75 (ISBN 0-685-91411-9). Philos Lib.
--The Key to the Sciences of Man. LC 74-80274. 543p. 1975. 10.00 (ISBN 0-8022-2150-5). Philos Lib.
Garas, F. K. & Armer, G. S. T., eds. Reinforced & Prestressed Microconcrete Models. (Illus.). 400p. 1981. text ed. 60.00x (ISBN 0-86095-880-9). Longman.
Garas, G. S. & Armer, F. K. Design for Dynamic Loading: The Use of Model Analysis. LC 82-7978. (Illus.). 382p. 1982. text ed. 57.00x (ISBN 0-86095-706-3). Longman.
Garas, Klara. Selected Paintings from the Old Picture Gallery. (Illus.). 1968. 25.00 (ISBN 0-8283-1116-1). Branden Pub Co.
Garate, Frances. St. Anne's Orphanage. LC 83-62395. 112p. 1984. pap. 7.50 (ISBN 0-935834-25-7). Rainbow Books.
Garattini, G., jt. ed. see Tognoni, G.
Garattini, S. & Berendes, H. W., eds. Pharmacology of Steroid Contraceptive Drugs. LC 77-6100. (Monographs of the Mario Negri Institute for Pharmacological Research). 391p. 1977. 51.00 (ISBN 0-89004-187-3). Raven.
Garattini, S. & Franchi, G., eds. Chemotherapy of Cancer Dissemination & Metastasis. LC 72-96335. (Monographs of the Mario Negri Institute for Pharmacological Research). (Illus.). 400p. 1973. 50.50 (ISBN 0-911216-46-4). Raven.
Garattini, S. & Samanin, R., eds. Central Mechanisms of Anorectic Drugs. LC 77-17749. (Monographs of the Mario Negri Institute for Pharmacological Research). 501p. 1978. 58.00 (ISBN 0-89004-219-5). Raven.
Garattini, S. & Tognoni, G., eds. Biological Markers in Mental Disorders: Proceedings of the Symposium Held in Milan, Italy, June 1983. 200p. 1984. pap. 33.00 (ISBN 0-08-031848-7). Pergamon.
Garattini, S., et al, eds. Advances in Pharmacology & Chemotherapy. Incl. Vol. 7. 1970. 80.00 (ISBN 0-12-032907-7); Vol. 8. 1971. 70.00 (ISBN 0-12-032908-5); Vol. 9. 1971. 80.00 (ISBN 0-12-032909-3); Vol. 10. 1972. 80.00 (ISBN 0-12-032910-7); Vol. 11. 1973. 80.00 (ISBN 0-12-032911-5); Vol. 14. 1977. 75.00 (ISBN 0-12-032914-X); Vol. 15. 1978. 70.00 (ISBN 0-12-032915-8) (ISBN 0-12-032982-4). 60.00 (ISBN 0-12-032981-6); Vol. 16. 1979. 60.00 (ISBN 0-12-032916-6); lib ed. 70.00. Acad Pr.
--Advances in Pharmacology & Chemotherapy, Vol. 19. 290p. 1982. 50.00 (ISBN 0-12-032919-0). Acad Pr.
--Advances in Pharmacology & Chemotherapy, Vol. 20. (Serial Publication Ser.). 1984. 45.00 (ISBN 0-12-032920-4). Acad Pr.
--Interactions Between Putative Neurotransmitters in the Brain. LC 77-83686. (Monographs of the Mario Negri Institute for Pharmacological Research). 431p. 1978. 50.50 (ISBN 0-89004-196-2). Raven.
--Benzodiazepines. LC 78-181304. (Monograph of the Mario Negri Institute for Pharmacological Research). (Illus.). 707p. 1973. 86.50 (ISBN 0-911216-25-1). Raven.
Garattini, Silvio, ed. Biological Markers in Mental Disorders. (Serono Symposia Publications Ser.). text ed. cancelled (ISBN 0-89004-391-4). Raven.
--Bone Resorption, Metastasis, & Diphosphonates. (Monographs of the Mario Negri Institute for Pharmacological Research). 225p. 1985. text ed. 39.50 (ISBN 0-88167-137-1). Raven.
Garattini, Silvio & Samanin, Rosario, eds. Anorectic Agents: Mechanisms of Action & Tolerance. (Monographs of the Mario Negri Institute for Pharmacological Research). 256p. 1981. text ed. 41.00 (ISBN 0-89004-640-9). Raven.
Garattini, Silvio, jt. ed. see De Gaetano, Giovanni.
Garattini, Silvio, et al, eds. Advances in Pharmacology & Chemotherapy, Vol. 12. (Serial Publication Ser.). 1975. 90.00 (ISBN 0-12-032912-3). Acad Pr.
--Advances in Pharmacology & Chemotherapy, Vol. 13. (Serial Publication Ser.). 1975. 85.00 (ISBN 0-12-032913-1). Acad Pr.
Garaudy, Roger. Karl Marx, Evolution of His Thought. Apotheker, Nan, tr. from French. LC 76-43305. 1976. Repr. of 1967 ed. lib. bdg. 27.50x (ISBN 0-8371-9044-4, GAKM). Greenwood.
Garavaglia, Louis A. & Worman, Charles G. Firearms of the American West, 1803-1965. LC 83-12528. (Illus.). 1984. 35.00 (ISBN 0-8263-0720-5). U of NM Pr.
Garay, L. A., jt. auth. see Dunsterville, G. C.
Garay, Ronald. Congressional Television: A Legislative History. LC 83-18563. (Contributions in Political Science Ser.: No. 111). x, 195p. 1984. lib. bdg. 27.95 (ISBN 0-313-23707-7, GAC/). Greenwood.
Garb, Forrest A. Waterflood Manual for Hewlett Packard Calculators. LC 81-20274. (Illus.). 94p. (Orig.). 1982. 21.95x (ISBN 0-87201-895-4). Gulf Pub.
Garb, Gerald. Microeconomics: Theory Applications Innovations. 342p. 1981. text ed. write for info. (ISBN 0-02-340400-0). Macmillan.
Garb, Solomon. Laboratory Tests in Common Use. 6th ed. LC 73-161127. 1976. text ed. 17.95 (ISBN 0-8261-0188-7); pap. text ed. 10.95 (ISBN 0-8261-0187-9). Springer Pub.
Garb, Solomon, jt. auth. see Gross, Steven.
Garbacz, Christopher. Economic Resources for the Elderly: Prospects for the Future. LC 83-60955. (Replica Edition Ser.). 256p. 1983. 24.00x (ISBN 0-86531-947-2). Westview.
--Industrial Polarization under Economic Integration: Latin America. (Studies in Latin American Business: No. 11). (Orig.). 1971. pap. 4.00 (ISBN 0-87755-138-3). Bureau Busn UT.
--Residential Energy Demand in the United States. (Replica Edition Ser.). 175p. 1985. pap. 20.00x (ISBN 0-86531-820-4). Westview.
Garbaczewski, P. Classical & Quantum Field Theory of Exactly Soluble Nonlinear Systems. 280p. 1984. 37.00x (ISBN 9971-966-55-7, Pub. by World Sci Singapore). Taylor & Francis.
Garbade, K. Securities Markets. (Finance Ser.). 1982. 33.95x (ISBN 0-07-022780-2). McGraw.
Garbarini, Gerald. Quiet in the Grave & Other Poems. 1976. pap. 2.00 (ISBN 0-918466-02-4). Quintessence.
Garbarini, Jean J., created by see Garrety, Martha L.
Garbarino, James. Children & Families in the Social Environment. (Modern Applications of Social Work Ser.). 1982. lib. bdg. 26.95x (ISBN 0-202-36029-6); pap. text ed. 14.95x (ISBN 0-202-36030-X). Aldine Pub.
Garbarino, James & Asp, C. Elliott. Successful Schools & Competent Students. LC 81-47704. 176p. 1981. 26.00x (ISBN 0-669-04526-8). Lexington Bks.
Garbarino, James & Gilliam, Gwen. Understanding Abusive Families. LC 79-47983. 288p. 1980. 24.50x (ISBN 0-669-03621-8); pap. 12.00x (ISBN 0-669-09782-9). Lexington Bks.
Garbarino, James & Stocking, S. Holly. Protecting Children from Abuse & Neglect: Developing & Maintaining Effective Support Systems for Families. LC 79-24239. (Social & Behavioral Science Ser.). 1980. text ed. 21.95x (ISBN 0-87589-442-9). Jossey-Bass.
Garbarino, James, jt. auth. see Whittaker, James K.
Garbarino, James, et al. Troubled Youth, Troubled Families. Whittaker, James K., ed. (Modern Applications of Social Work Ser.). (Illus.). 400p. (Orig.). 1986. lib. bdg. price not set (ISBN 0-202-36039-3); pap. price not set (ISBN 0-202-36040-7). Aldine Pub.
Garbarino, Merwyn S. Big Cypress: A Changing Seminole Community. (George & Louise Spindler - Case Studies in Cultural Anthropology Ser.). (Illus.). 137p. pap. text ed. cancelled (ISBN 0-8290-0584-6). Irvington.
Garbassi, U., jt. auth. see McCracken, D. D.
Garbaty, Thomas J. Medieval English Literature. 960p. 1983. text ed. 29.95 (ISBN 0-669-03351-0). Heath.
Garbe, D., jt. auth. see Bauer, K.
Garbe, Detlef. Buergerbeteiligung. (Democratia Experimentalis: Vol. 4). iv, 248p. (Ger.). 1982. 29.45 (ISBN 3-8204-5840-9). P Lang Pubs.
Garbe, Richard. India & Christendom: The Historical Connections Between Their Religions. Robinson, Lydia J., tr. from Ger. xi, 321p. 1959. 22.95 (ISBN 0-87548-232-5). Open Court.
Garbe, Richard, ed. see Vijnanabhiksu.
Garbedian, H. Gordon. Albert Einstein: Maker of Universes. 324p. 1981. Repr. of 1939 ed. lib. bdg. 35.00 (ISBN 0-89984-239-9). Century Bookbindery.
--Major Mysteries of Science. 306p. 1981. Repr. of 1933 ed. lib. bdg. 40.00 (ISBN 0-89984-240-2). Century Bookbindery.
Garbee, Ed & Van Dyke, Henry. Dramas De Navidad. Prince, Soledad G. & Castellon, Guillermo, trs. 1981. pap. 1.50 (ISBN 0-311-08214-9). Casa Bautista.
Garber, A. Brent & Sparks, Leroy. Learn-a-Term. LC 77-82026. 168p. 1977. pap. text ed. 19.95 (ISBN 0-912862-48-3). Aspen Systems.
Garber, A. Brent, et al. Hospital Crisis Management: A Casebook. LC 79-25691. 180p. 1979. text ed. 35.95 (ISBN 0-89443-079-3). Aspen Systems.
Garber, Aubrey. Mountain-Ese. LC 76-3278. 105p. 1976. 4.95 (ISBN 0-89227-004-7); pap. 2.95 (ISBN 0-89227-038-1). Commonwealth Pr.
Garber, Bernard J. The Old West Trail Guidebook & Scrapbook. (Illus.). 100p. 1983. soft cover 10.00 (ISBN 0-89345-952-6, Biograf Pubns). Garber Comm.
--Shards from the Heart: A Spiritual Odyssey in Twentieth Century America. LC 64-13358. 160p. 1965. 8.00 (ISBN 0-89345-004-9, Freedeeds Books). Garber Comm.
Garber, Bernard J., ed. & intro. by see Maher, Barry.
Garber, Bernard J., ed. see Miles, Thomas.
Garber, Bernard J., ed. see Steiner, Rudolf.
Garber, Brad T. Industrial Hygiene Applications of Computers. 350p. 1985. pap. text ed. 37.95 (ISBN 0-02-949340-4). Macmillan.
Garber, Clark M. Stories & Legends of the Bering Strait Eskimos. LC 74-5835. 260p. 1975. Repr. of 1940 ed. 24.50 (ISBN 0-404-11640-X). AMS Pr.
Garber, D. W. Waterwheels & Millstones: A History of Ohio Gristmills & Milling. (Illus.). 139p. 1971. pap. 4.50 (ISBN 0-318-00871-8). Ohio Hist Soc.
Garber, Edward. Genetic Pespectives in Biology & Medicine. LC 85-8454. 500p. 1985. 30.00 (ISBN 0-317-28530-0); pap. 12.00 (ISBN 0-226-28216-3). U of Chicago Pr.
Garber, Eric & Paleo, Lyn. Uranian Worlds: A Reader's Guide to Alternative Sexuality in Science Fiction & Fantasy. 1983. lib. bdg. 30.00 (ISBN 0-8161-8573-5, Hall Reference). G K Hall.
Garber, Esther P. Button Shoes. (Orig.). 1975. pap. 1.50 (ISBN 0-87178-121-2). Brethren.
--Counting My Buttons. 1979. pap. 1.95 (ISBN 0-87178-157-3). Brethren.
Garber, Eugene K. Metaphysical Tales: Stories by Eugene K. Garber. LC 80-26057. (Associated Writers Program: No. 3). 224p. 1981. text ed. 12.95 (ISBN 0-8262-0325-6). U of Mo Pr.
Garber, Frederick. The Autonomy of Self from Richardson to Huysmans. LC 81-47131. 360p. 1981. 29.00x (ISBN 0-691-06481-4). Princeton U Pr.
--Thoreau's Redemptive Imagination. LC 77-73031. (Gotham Library). 229p. 1977. pap. 30.00x (ISBN 0-8147-2965-7); pap. 15.00x (ISBN 0-8147-2966-5). NYU Pr.
--Wordsworth & the Poetry of Encounter. LC 71-157888. 207p. 1971. 16.50x (ISBN 0-252-00184-2). U of Ill Pr.
Garber, Frederick, ed. see Radcliffe, Ann.
Garber, Herbert, jt. auth. see Austin, Gilbert.
Garber, Janet. High Action Reading for Comprehension, D. Incl. Study Skills. Hansen, Merrily. pap. text ed. 2.40 (ISBN 0-87895-428-7); Vocabulary. Christensen, Barbara. pap. text ed. 2.40 (ISBN 0-87895-426-0). (Skillbooster Ser.). (gr. 4). 1979. pap. text ed. 2.40 (ISBN 0-87895-427-9). Modern Curr.
--High Action Reading for Comprehension, E. Incl. Study Skills. Hansen, Merrily. pap. text ed. 2.40 (ISBN 0-87895-531-3); Vocabulary. Christensen, Barbara. pap. text ed. 2.40 (ISBN 0-87895-529-1). (Skillbooster Ser.). (gr. 5). 1979. pap. text ed. 2.40 (ISBN 0-87895-530-5). Modern Curr.
--High Action Reading for Study Skills,F. Incl. Study Skills. Hansen, Merrily. pap. text ed. 2.40 (ISBN 0-87895-634-4); High Action Reading for Vocabulary. Christensen, Barbara. pap. text ed. 2.40 (ISBN 0-87895-632-8). (Skillbooster Ser.). (gr. 6). 1979. pap. text ed. 2.40 (ISBN 0-87895-633-6). Modern Curr.
Garber, John P. Valley of the Delaware. LC 78-83483. (Keystone State Historical Publications Ser: No. 6). (Illus.). 1969. Repr. of 1934 ed. 33.50x (ISBN 0-87198-506-3). Friedman.
Garber, Judy & Seligman, Martin E., eds. Human Helplessness: Theory & Applications. LC 79-6773. 1980. 27.50 (ISBN 0-12-275050-0). Acad Pr.
Garber, Lawrence. Sirens & Graces. 317p. 1984. 16.95 (ISBN 0-8253-0171-8). Beaufort Bks NY.
Garber, Lee O. & Benedetti, Eugene. Law & the Teacher in California. LC 66-26817. 1967. pap. text ed. 3.95x (ISBN 0-8134-0892-X, 892). Interstate.
Garber, Lee O. & Delon, Floyd G. The Law & the Teacher in Missouri. 3rd ed. xii, 156p. 1982. pap. text ed. 7.95 (ISBN 0-8134-2200-0). Interstate.

Garber, Lee O. & Edwards, Newton. School Law Casebook, 8 bks. Incl. The Public School in Our Governmental Structure. LC 71-101124. vi, 106p. 1970 (1147); The Law Relating to the Creation, Alteration, & Dissolution of School Districts. LC 62-19686. vi, 96p. 1962 (68); The Law Governing Teaching Personnel. LC 68-13439. viii, 118p. 1969 (71); The Law Governing Pupils. LC 68-13438. viii, 124p. 1969; The Law Governing School Board Members & School Board Meetings. LC 63-18443. viii, 96p. 1963. (137); Tort & Contractual Liability of School Districts & School Boards. LC 63-22405. viii, 105p. 1963. (142); The Law Governing School Property & School Building Construction. LC 64-16119. viii, 116p. 1964. (143); The Law Governing the Financing of Public Education. LC 64-18825. viii, 104p. 1964. (144). pap. text ed. 1.75x ea. Interstate.

Garber, Lee O. & Hubbard, Ben C. Law, Finance, & the Teacher in Illinois. 3rd ed. 1983. pap. 9.50x (ISBN 0-8134-2252-3). Interstate.

Garber, Lee O. & Micken, Charles M. Law & the Teacher in Pennsylvania. 3rd ed. LC 77-91732. 1978. pap. 7.95x (ISBN 0-8134-2011-3, 2011). Interstate.

Garber, Lee O. & Sales, M. Vance. The Law & the Teacher in Arkansas. 2nd ed. LC 76-5345. 196p. 1976. pap. text ed. 6.95x (ISBN 0-8134-1803-8, 1803). Interstate.

Garber, Lee O., ed. see Edwards, Newton.

Garber, Lee O., et al. Law & the Teacher in Ohio. LC 65-28321. 1966. pap. text ed. 3.95x (ISBN 0-8134-0446-0, 446). Interstate.

Garber, Lyman A. Of Men & Not of Law: The Courts are Usurping the Political Function. 1966. 6.50 (ISBN 0-8159-6400-5). Devin.

Garber, Marjorie. Coming of Age in Shakespeare. LC 80-41920. 320p. 1981. 30.00x (ISBN 0-416-30350-1, NO.2127). Methuen Inc.

Garber, Max B. & Bond, P. S. A Modern Military Dictionary: Ten Thousand Technical & Slang Terms of Military Usage. 2nd ed. LC 74-31354. 1975. Repr. of 1942 ed. 40.00x (ISBN 0-8103-4208-1). Gale.

Garber, Patty J., et al. Kinder-Fun Insect Series. rev. ed. Incl. Funny Little Ant; Ladybug, Ladybug; Fly, Fly; The Little Yellow Butterfly; The Little Mosquito; The Bad Little Cricket. (Illus.). 16p. (For partially-sighted & partially-hearing children). (ps-2). 1973. Set. pap. text ed. 16.00x (ISBN 0-89039-055-X). Ann Arbor FL.

Garber, Paul M. The Gadsden Treaty. 1959. 12.00 (ISBN 0-8446-1195-6). Peter Smith.

Garber, Randy. Built in Milwaukee: An Architectural View of the City. LC 81-70932. (Illus.). 228p. 1984. pap. 14.95 (ISBN 0-299-97015-9). U of Wis Pr.

Garber, Richard. Parents Handbook of Childhood Allergies. 208p. 1983. pap. 2.95 (ISBN 0-345-30443-8). Ballantine.

Garber, Robert. The Only Tax Book You'll Ever Need: How to Pay the Lowest Taxes Possible-Explained in Simple Terms. rev. ed. (Illus.). 1982. 4.98 (ISBN 0-517-54627-2, Harmony); pap. 5.95 (ISBN 0-517-55204-3, Harmony). Crown.

Garber, Robert A. The Only Tax Book You'll Ever Need. 1982. 4.98 (ISBN 0-517-54627-2, Harmony). Crown.

--What Executors & Administrators Should Know about Their Tax Responsibilities. LC 83-112817. (Tax-Saving Ser.). 48p. 1983. 3.00x (ISBN 0-13-952119-4, 95211-9). P-H.

Garbett, Mike & Goulding, Brian. Lancaster at War. LC 77-71044. (Illus.). 1977. text ed. 19.95 (ISBN 0-684-16468-X, ScribT). Scribner.

Garbett, Thomas. Corporate Advertising: The What, the Why, & the How. (Illus.). 224p. 1981. 39.95 (ISBN 0-07-022787-X). McGraw.

Garbicz, Adam & Klinowski, Jacek. Cinema, the Magic Vehicle: A Guide to Its Achievement, 2 vols. LC 82-10405. (Illus.). 560p. 1983. Vol. I: The Cinema Through 1949. pap. 12.50 (ISBN 0-8052-0735-X); Vol. 2: The Cinema in the Fifties. pap. 12.50 (ISBN 0-8052-0739-2). Schocken.

--Cinema, the Magic Vehicle-A Guide to Its Achievement-Journey One: The Cinema Through 1949. LC 75-2183. 551p. 1975. 27.50 (ISBN 0-8108-0801-3). Scarecrow.

--Cinema, the Magic Vehicle-A Guide to Its Achievement-Journey Two: The Cinema in the Fifties. LC 79-2183. 551p. 1979. 32.50 (ISBN 0-8108-1241-X). Scarecrow.

Garbis, et al. Federal Tax Litigation. 1984. 84.00 (ISBN 0-88712-193-4). Warren.

Garbis, M. J., et al. What the Tax Practitioner Should Know about the Supreme Court's Baggot & Sells Decisions. 36p. 1984. 2.75x (ISBN 0-317-07496-2, 95520-3). P-H.

Garbis, Marvin J. & Schwait, Allen L. Tax Refund Litigation. 264p. 1971. Incl. 1977 suppl. pap. 12.00 (ISBN 0-317-30821-1, B323); Suppl. 1977 only. pap. 2.00 (ISBN 0-317-30822-X, B324). Am Law Inst.

Garbis, Marvin J. & Struntz, Stephen C. Tax Procedure & Tax Fraud, Cases & Materials. LC 81-13080. (American Casebook Ser.). 829p. 1981. text ed. 25.95 (ISBN 0-314-61180-0). West Pub.

--Tax Procedure & Tax Fraud, 1984: Supplement to Cases & Materials. (American Casebook Ser.). 132p. 1983. pap. text ed. 4.95. (ISBN 0-314-79295-3). West Pub.

Garbo, Norman. Gaynor's Passion. 1985. 15.95 (ISBN 0-395-36081-1). HM.

--Spy. 1980. 10.95 (ISBN 0-393-01321-9). Norton.

--Spy. 288p. 1985. pap. 3.50 (ISBN 0-449-20514-2, Crest). Fawcett.

--Turner's Wife. 336p. 1984. pap. 3.50 (ISBN 0-449-20515-0, Crest). Fawcett.

--Turner's Wife: A Novel. LC 82-14221. 400p. 1983. 15.95 (ISBN 0-393-01521-1). Norton.

Garbow, B. S. Matrix Eigensystem Routines-Eispack Guide Extension. (Lecture Notes in Computer Science Ser.: Vol. 51). 1977. 25.00 (ISBN 0-387-08254-9). Springer-Verlag.

Garbuny, Max. Optical Physics. 1965. 33.00 (ISBN 0-12-275350-X). Acad Pr.

Garbus, Martin. Ready for the Defense. 304p. 1972. pap. 1.50 (ISBN 0-380-01381-9, 11403). Avon.

Garbus, Terrie, et al. Living in Washington: A Moving Experience. (Illus.). 240p. pap. 3.50 (ISBN 0-517-51851-1). Crown.

Garbutt, Cameron W. Road to the Land of R. (Illus.). 1970. pap. text ed. 1.25x (ISBN 0-8134-1208-0, 1208). Interstate.

--Road to the Land of S. (Illus.). 1969. pap. text ed. 1.25x (ISBN 0-8134-1116-5, 1116). Interstate.

--Road to the Land of TH. (Illus.). 48p. 1971. pap. text ed. 1.25x (ISBN 0-8134-1324-9, 1324). Interstate.

--What Is It? 1972. text ed. 10.95x (ISBN 0-8134-1469-5). Interstate.

Garbutt, Cameron W. & Anderson, John O. Effective Methods for Correcting Articulatory Defects. LC 78-78380. (Illus.). 218p. 1980. pap. text ed. 8.25x (ISBN 0-8134-2081-4). Interstate.

Garby, Lars & Meldon, Jerry H., eds. Respiratory Functions of Blood. LC 77-21980. (Topics in Hematology Ser.). (Illus.). 300p. 1977. 32.50x (ISBN 0-306-30998-X, Plenum Med Bk). Plenum Pub.

Garby, Lee H., jt. auth. see Smith, Edward E.

Garceau, Oliver, ed. Political Research & Political Theory. LC 68-28693. (Illus.). 1968. 17.50x (ISBN 0-674-68700-0). Harvard U Pr.

Garchik, Morton. Art Fundamentals. LC 78-10336. (Illus.). 1979. 14.95 (ISBN 0-87396-082-3). Stravon.

--Creative Visual Thinking. LC 81-66880. (Illus.). 100p. 1982. 17.50 (ISBN 0-910158-80-0). Art Dir.

Garcia. Desert Immigrants: The Mexican of El Paso, 1880-1920. LC 80-36862. (Western Americana Ser.: No. 32). (Illus.). 328p. 1981. text ed. 28.50x (ISBN 0-300-02520-3); pap. 9.95x (ISBN 0-300-02883-0, Y-433). Yale U Pr.

Garcia, jt. auth. see Cutler.

Garcia, ed. Structure, Function & Biosynthesis of Plant Cell Walls. 524p. 1984. pap. 19.00 (ISBN 0-317-12494-3). Am Soc of Plan.

Garcia, A. Dizionario Italiano-Spagnolo, Spagnolo-Italiano. 437p. (Span. & Ital.). 1980. leatherette 5.95 (ISBN 0-686-97347-X, S-31237). French & Eur.

Garcia, A. & Kielanowski, P. The Beta Decay of Hyperons. (Lecture Notes in Physics Ser.: Vol. 222). viii, 173p. 1985. pap. 10.50 (ISBN 0-387-15184-2). Springer-Verlag.

Garcia, Amador F. V. The Changing Law of International Claims, 2 vols. LC 84-42921. 953p. 1984. Set. lib. bdg. 85.00 (ISBN 0-379-20191-7). Oceana.

Garcia, Andrew. Tough Trip Through Paradise. LC 66-14758. (Illus.). 1976. pap. 3.95 (ISBN 0-89174-008-2). Comstock Edns.

Garcia, Ann O. Spirit on the Wall. LC 81-85094. 192p. (YA) 1982. 9.95 (ISBN 0-8234-0447-1). Holiday.

Garcia, Anne C. As a Greensboro Police Officer: A Humorous View. 1985. 6.75 (ISBN 0-8062-2519-X). Carlton.

Garcia, Anthony & Myers, Robert. Analogies: A Visual Approach to Writing. (Illus.). 256p. 1974. pap. text ed. 21.95 (ISBN 0-07-022825-6). McGraw.

Garcia, Antonio & Tyler, S. Lyman. The Indian Cause in the Laws of Colombia. LC 84-621750. 124p. Date not set. price not set. U of Utah Pr.

Garcia, C. B. & Zangwill, Willard I. Pathways to Solutions, Fixed Points, & Equilibria. (Computational Math Ser.). 336p. 1981. text ed. 42.95 (ISBN 0-13-653501-1). P-H.

Garcia, Carlos. Guzman, Hinde & Hannam Outstript: Being a Discovery of the Whole Art, Mystery & Antiquity of Theeves & Theeving. LC 80-2480. 1981. Repr. of 1657 ed. 49.50 (ISBN 0-404-19114-2). AMS Pr.

Garcia, Carlos, jt. auth. see Moore, W. Joan.

Garcia, Carmen I. Raffucci De see Raffucci de Garcia, Carmen I.

Garcia, Celso-Ramon & Mastroianni, Luigi, Jr. Current Therapy of Infertility, 1982-1983. 256p. 1982. text ed. 36.00 (ISBN 0-941158-02-0, D1738-3). Mosby.

Garcia, Celso-Ramon & Rosenfeld, David L. Human Fertility: The Regulation of Reproduction. LC 76-15411. (Illus.). 163p. 1977. pap. text ed. 15.00x (ISBN 0-8036-3910-4). Davis Co.

Garcia, Cindy, jt. auth. see Agnello, Virginia L.

Garcia, Cisneros F. Jose Marti y las Artes Plasticas. 1972. 9.95 (ISBN 0-88303-996-6); pap. 7.95 (ISBN 0-685-73207-X). E Torres & Sons.

Garcia, Clarita. Clarita's Cocina: Great Traditional Recipes from a Spanish Kitchen. LC 74-113069. (Illus.). 1970. 14.95 (ISBN 0-385-04657-X). Doubleday.

Garcia, Connie & Medina, Arthur. Businessman's Guide to the Caribbean. 624p. 1983. text ed. 45.00 (ISBN 0-934642-05-2); pap. 35.00 (ISBN 0-934642-08-7). Puerto Rico Almanacs.

--Guia Turistica de Puerto Rico. Rivera, Evelyn, tr. from Sp. (Illus.). 192p. (Eng.). 1983. pap. 4.95 (ISBN 0-934642-04-4). Puerto Rico Almanacs.

--The Travel Guide to Puerto Rico. (Illus.). 1980. pap. 7.95 (ISBN 0-934642-00-1). Puerto Rico Almanacs.

--The Travel Guide to Puerto Rico: 1982-83. 2nd ed. (Illus.). 340p. 1983. pap. 9.95 (ISBN 0-934642-03-6). Puerto Rico Almanacs.

Garcia, Connie, jt. auth. see Medina, Arthur.

Garcia, Darnell. Fighting Art of Tang Soo Do. LC 81-70816. (Illus.). 180p. (Orig.). 1982. pap. 7.95 (ISBN 0-86568-014-0, 350). Unique Pubns.

Garcia, David. Fairy Tales of Puerto Rico. (Children's Bks.: No. 166). (Illus.). 50p. (gr. 1-5). 1982. 9.95 (ISBN 0-934642-02-8). Puerto Rico Almanacs.

Garcia, David, jt. auth. see Ogletree, Earl J.

Garcia, Domingo. Rubik's Cube Made Simple. 32p. 1982. pap. 1.95 (ISBN 0-87523-201-9). Emerson.

Garcia, Dwight, jt. auth. see Lopez, Ivette.

Garcia, E. The Role of Theory in Linguistic Analysis: The Spanish Pronoun System. (N-H Linguistic Ser.: Vol. 19). 522p. 1975. pap. 42.75 (ISBN 0-444-10940-4, North-Holland). Elsevier.

Garcia, E. Fernandez, ed. The Book of Puerto Rico, 2 vols. 1976. lib. bdg. 250.00 (ISBN 0-87968-769-X). Gordon Pr.

Garcia, Edward & Pellegrini, Nina. Homer the Homely Hound Dog. (Illus.). 1974. 3.95 (ISBN 0-917476-02-6). Inst Rational-Emotive.

Garcia, Elizabeth. Julio. 192p. (Orig.). 1985. pap. 6.95 (ISBN 0-345-32349-1). Ballantine.

Garcia, Elvira F. A Critical Edition of Tirso de Molina's Marta la Piadosa. (Salzburg Studies in English Literature: Elizabethan & Renaissance Studies: No. 78). 1978. pap. text ed. 25.50x (ISBN 0-391-01380-7). Humanities.

Garcia, Emildo A. Indice De los Documentos y Manuscritos Delmontinos En la Biblioteca Otto G. Richter De la Universidad De Miami, Coral Gables, Florida, U.S.A. LC 79-50002. (Coleccio Cuba y Sus Jueces). 1979. pap. 4.95 (ISBN 0-89729-220-0). Ediciones.

Garcia, Emilio F. Hombres De Maiz: Unidad y Sentido a Traves De Sus Simbolos Mitologicos. LC 78-57694. 1978. pap. 8.00 (ISBN 0-89729-183-2). Ediciones.

Garcia, Enildo. Cuba: Placido, Poeta Mulato di la Emancipacion (1809-1844) LC 85-50000. (Senda de Estudios y Ensayos). (Illus.). 210p. (Orig., Span.). pap. 14.95 (ISBN 0-918454-48-4). Senda Nueva.

Garcia, Eugene E. Early Childhood Bilingualism: With Special Reference to the Mexican-American Child. (Illus.). 224p. 1983. 24.95x (ISBN 0-8263-0661-6); pap. 14.95x (ISBN 0-8263-0662-4). U of NM Pr.

Garcia, Eugene E. & Padilla, Raymond V., eds. Advances in Bilingual Education Research. LC 85-13956. 350p. 1985. 25.00x (ISBN 0-8165-0922-0). U of Ariz Pr.

Garcia, Eugene E., et al. Chicano Studies: A Multidisciplinary Approach. (Bilingual Education Ser.). 1984. text ed. 29.95x (ISBN 0-8077-2749-0). Tchrs Coll.

Garcia, Eugene N. & Spencer, Wanda. Safety for People & for Chemicals. LC 79-90457. (Illus.). 80p. (Orig.). (gr. 10-12). 1979. pap. 4.50x (ISBN 0-87881-096-X); incl. 2 tests. Mojave Bks.

Garcia, F. Chris & Hain, Paul. New Mexico Government. rev. ed. 280p. 1981. pap. 12.95x (ISBN 0-8263-0560-1). U of NM Pr.

Garcia, F. Chris, ed. La Causa Politica: A Chicano Politics Reader. LC 73-22582. 456p. 1974. text ed. 24.95 (ISBN 0-268-00542-7, 85-05422); pap. 9.95 (ISBN 0-268-00543-5, 85-05430); tchr's. guide 4.00 (ISBN 0-686-86807-2). U of Notre Dame Pr.

--Chicano Politics: Readings. LC 72-11569. 225p. 1973. text ed. 27.50x (ISBN 0-8422-5076-X); pap. text ed. 9.95x (ISBN 0-8422-0274-9). Irvington.

Garcia, F. Chris, et al. State & Local Government in New Mexico. LC 79-2189. (Illus., Orig.). (gr. 9). 1979. pap. 8.95x (ISBN 0-8263-0511-3). U of NM Pr.

Garcia, F. L. How to Analyze a Bank Statement. 7th ed. 223p. 1984. 41.50 (ISBN 0-87267-050-3). Bankers.

Garcia, F. L. & Munn, Glenn G. Encyclopedia of Banking & Finance. 8th ed. LC 83-8845. 1024p. 1983. text ed. 89.00 (ISBN 0-87267-042-2). Bankers.

Garcia, Fina, jt. auth. see Vitier, Cintio.

Garcia, Frank. How to Detect Crooked Gambling. LC 76-48201. 1977. o. p. 8.95 (ISBN 0-668-04042-4); pap. 3.95 (ISBN 0-668-04043-2). Arco.

Garcia, Frederick, ed. see Da Gama, Jose B.

Garcia, George E., jt. auth. see Sloane, Albert E.

Garcia, Gervasio L. & Quintero, A. G. Desafio y Solidaridad. LC 82-70525. (Coleccion Semilla Ser.). (Illus.). 176p. 1982. pap. 4.95 (ISBN 0-940238-54-3). Ediciones Hura.

Garcia, Gilbert N. Building American English: Oil. 1978. 4.95 (ISBN 0-88499-512-7). Inst Mod Lang.

Garcia, Gillian, jt. auth. see Cargill, Thomas.

Garcia, Gillian G., jt. auth. see Cargill, Thomas F.

Garcia, Hazel D., jt. auth. see Stevens, John D.

Garcia, Isabel, ed. Around the World with My Friends. 1985. 13.95 (ISBN 0-533-06034-6). Vantage.

Garcia, J. Puerto Rico: Equality & Freedom at Issue. LC 83-27239. (Politics in Latin America Ser.). 1984. 27.95 (ISBN 0-03-071303-X). Praeger.

Garcia, J., jt. ed. see National Association for Chicano Studies Staff.

Garcia, Jean-Claude. Financing Development in Latin America. 369p. 1980. 42.95 (ISBN 0-03-051106-2). HR&W.

Garcia, Jo, ed. Walking on the Water: Women Talk about Spirituality. Maitland, Sara. (Illus.). 224p. 1984. pap. 5.95 (ISBN 0-86068-381-8, Pub by Virago Pr). Merrimack Pub Cir.

Garcia, John D. The Moral Society. LC 75-137086. (Illus.). 325p. 1974. 8.95 (ISBN 0-87426-033-7). Whitmore.

--Psychofraud & Ethical Therapy. LC 73-92028. 200p. 1974. 6.95 (ISBN 0-87426-032-9). Whitmore.

Garcia, Jorge J., et al, eds. Philosophical Analysis in Latin America. 1984. lib. bdg. 55.00 (ISBN 90-277-1749-4, Pub. by Reidel Holland). Kluwer Academic.

Garcia, Joseph G. Jump for the Apple! The Story of Lily Pond, a Soccer-Playing Frog with Long, Long Legs. Day, Rhonda, ed. (Illus.). 28p. (gr. 4up). 1983. pap. 5.95 (ISBN 0-9612350-0-4). Goal Ent.

Garcia, Joseph R. Wayside Poems. 96p. 1982. pap. 5.00 (ISBN 0-682-49908-0). Exposition Pr FL.

Garcia, Juan R. Operation Wetback: The Mass Deportation of Mexican Undocumented Workers in 1954. LC 79-6189. (Contributions in Ethnic Studies: No. 2). (Illus.). xvii, 268p. 1980. lib. bdg. 27.50 (ISBN 0-313-21353-4, GOW/). Greenwood.

Garcia, Juana G. Panoramic History of Agriculture in Puerto Rico. (Puerto Rico Ser.). 1979. lib. bdg. 59.95 (ISBN 0-8490-2982-1). Gordon Pr.

Garcia, Lionel. Leaving Home. LC 84-72303. 240p. (Orig.). 1985. pap. 10.00 (ISBN 0-934770-42-5). Arte Publico.

Garcia, Lola. A Girlfriend at Acoma, Siyu, & an Invitation to Supper. (Illus.). 14p. (Orig.). (ps-7). 1981. pap. 3.75 (ISBN 0-915347-09-1). Pueblo Acoma Pr.

Garcia, Loretta M. Disaster Management for Nurses. Date not set. price not set. Aspen Systems.

Garcia, Luis. Beans. 1976. pap. 2.50 (ISBN 0-685-79267-6). Oyez.

--A Blue Book. 1976. pap. 2.50 (ISBN 0-685-82996-0, Pub. by Cloud Marauder). Small Pr Dist.

Garcia, Lynne S. & Ash, Lawrence R. Diagnostic Parasitology: Clinical Laboratory Manual. 2nd ed. LC 78-31497. (Illus.). 174p. 1979. pap. text ed. 16.95 (ISBN 0-8016-1741-3). Mosby.

Garcia, M., jt. ed. see National Association for Chicano Studies Staff.

Garcia, Manuel, II. A Complete Treatise on the Art of Singing, Pt. 1. Paschke, Donald V., tr. from Fr. (Music Reprint Ser.). lxi, 221p. 1983. Repr. lib. bdg. 35.00 (ISBN 0-306-76212-9). Da Capo.

--A Complete Treatise on the Art of Singing, Pt. 2. Paschke, V., tr. from Span. & pref. by. LC 74-23382. xii, 261p. 1975. Repr. of 1972 ed. lib. bdg. 29.50 (ISBN 0-306-70660-1). Da Capo.

Garcia, Marcy. The Big E: Learning Package Two: Teacher's Program. (Illus.). 192p. (Orig.). (gr. 4-7). 1983. tchrs. ed. 9.95 (ISBN 0-88499-235-7); wkbk. 2.95 (ISBN 0-88499-236-5); Set Of 10. assessment tests 9.95 (ISBN 0-88499-237-3). Inst Mod Lang.

Garcia, Margot W., jt. ed. see Daneke, Gregory A.

Garcia, Maria & Montoya, Malaguias. The Adventures of Connie & Diego: Las Aventuras De Connie y Diego. LC 78-61981. (Fifth World Tales Ser.). (Illus.). (gr. k-6). 1979. pap. text ed. 4.95 bilingual ed. (ISBN 0-89239-020-4, Imprenta De Libros Infantiles). Children's Book Pr.

Garcia, Mariano. Spanish for Law Enforcement Officers, 2 vols. 1972. Vol. 1. pap. text ed. 6.95 (ISBN 0-88499-135-0); Vol. 2. pap. text ed. 6.95 (ISBN 0-88499-137-7); instructor's guide 3.95 (ISBN 0-88499-134-2); wkbk. 1 5.95 (ISBN 0-88499-136-9); wkbk. 2 5.95 (ISBN 0-88499-138-5). Inst Mod Lang.

Garcia, Mario R. Contemporary Newspaper Design: A Structural Approach. (Illus.). 240p. 1981. text ed. 36.95 (ISBN 0-13-170381-1); pap. text ed. 20.95 (ISBN 0-13-170373-0). P-H.

--The New Adviser. 2nd. ed. (Illus.). 47p. 1978. pap. text ed. 4.50 (ISBN 0-916082-01-6). Columbia Scholastic.

Garcia, Mario R., jt. auth. see Blank, Ben.

Garcia, Mary H. & Gonzalez-Mena, Janet. The Big E: Learning Package One. Ragan, Lise B., ed. LC 75-27579. (Prog. Bk.). (gr. 1-2). 1976. tchr's program 9.95 (ISBN 0-88499-228-4); student workbook 2.95 (ISBN 0-88499-230-6); pkg. of 10 tests 9.95 (ISBN 0-88499-229-2); program package 45.00 (ISBN 0-88499-231-4). Inst Mod Lang.

Garcia, Mary J. Aerobic Dance & Fitness. (Illus.). 1978. pap. text ed. 6.95 (ISBN 0-88408-107-9). Sterling Swift.

Garcia, Max R. As Long As I Remain Alive: The Autobiography of Low-Number Survivor of Auschwitz. LC 78-65309. 1979. 10.00 (ISBN 0-916620-25-5). Portals Pr.

Garcia, Miguel. Miguel Garcia's Story. Meltzer, Albert, tr. (Illus.). 72p. (Orig.). 1982. pap. 2.50 (ISBN 0-317-14868-0). Left Bank.

Garcia, Mila, et al, eds. Filipina I: Poetry, Drama, Fiction. 160p. (Orig.). 1984. pap. 8.50x (ISBN 0-318-04080-8, Pub. by New Day Philippines). Cellar.

Garcia, Mila, et al, eds. see Women Writers in Media Now (WOMEN) Staff.

Garcia, Nasario, jt. auth. see Fernandez, Jose B.

Garcia, O. C. & Taylor, W. The Lattice of Interpretability Types of Varieties. LC 84-10997. (Memoirs of the American Mathematical Society: Vol. 305). 126p. 1984. pap. 12.00 (ISBN 0-8218-2308-6). Am Math.

Garcia, O. C., jt. ed. see Freese, R. S.

Garcia, Octavio. Otros Diaz: Memories of "Other Days"...from Mexico in Revolution to a Life of Medicine in Texas. Kimball, Virginia, ed. (Illus.). 400p. 1985. 15.95 (ISBN 0-318-03790-4). Grey Home Pr.

Garcia, Odalimira. Chicana Studies Curriculum Guide: Grades 9-12. 150p. 1978. pap. 11.00 (ISBN 0-931738-10-5). Info Systems.

Garcia, Osvaldo. Soccer for Kids. LC 78-20821. (Illus.). 1979. pap. 4.95 (ISBN 0-87701-133-8). Chronicle Bks.

Garcia, P. L., et al, eds. Differential Geometrical Methods in Mathematical Physics: Proceedings. (Lecture Notes in Mathematics: Vol. 836). 538p. 1980. 32.00 (ISBN 0-387-10275-2). Springer-Verlag.

Garcia, R., jt. auth. see Piaget, Jean.

Garcia, R. V. & Escudero, J. Drought & Man: The Nineteen Seventy-Two Case History. (Drought & Man Case Studies: Vol. 3). 1985. 40.00 (ISBN 0-08-025825-5). Pergamon.

Garcia, R. V., ed. The Roots of Catastrophe: The 1972 Case History. (The International Federation of Institutes for Advanced Studies Ser.). (Illus.). 200p. 1986. 80.00 (ISBN 0-317-30535-2, Pub by PPL). Pergamon.

Garcia, Ramon C. Metodos Estadisticos: Teoria y Practica. 1985. text ed. 18.50 (ISBN 0-538-22811-3, V811). SW Pub.

Garcia, Ramon J. & Hailstones, Thomas J. Economia Basica. (Span.). 1982. text ed. 11.00 (ISBN 0-538-22070-8, V07). SW Pub.

Garcia, Ramon J., et al. Principios y Metodos Estadisticos para Comercio y Economia (I) (Span.). 1980. text ed. 12.40 (ISBN 0-538-22810-5, V81). SW Pub.

--Principios y Metodos Estadisticos para Comercio y Economia (II) 1982. text ed. 12.40 (ISBN 0-538-22820-2, V82). SW Pub.

Garcia, Rebecca M. Rehabilitation After Myocardial Infarction. (CECN Ser.). (Illus.). 83p. 1979. 6.95x (ISBN 0-8385-8312-1). ACC.

Garcia, Reloy, jt. auth. see Sitzmann, Marion.

Garcia, Reloy & Karabatsos, James, eds. A Concordance to the Poetry of D. H. Lawrence. LC 70-120277. xvi, 523p. 1970. 32.50x (ISBN 0-8032-0768-9). U of Nebr Pr.

--A Concordance to the Short Fiction of D. H. Lawrence. LC 72-77195. xx, 474p. 1972. 29.50x (ISBN 0-8032-0807-3). U of Nebr Pr.

Garcia, Ricardo. Fostering a Pluralistic Society Through Multi-Ethnic Education. LC 78-50372. (Fastback Ser.: No. 107). 49p. 1978. pap. 0.75 (ISBN 0-87367-107-4). Phi Delta Kappa.

--Learning in Two Languages: Ensenanza Bilingue. LC 76-16879. (Fastback Ser.: No.84). 53p. (Orig.). 1976. pap. 0.75 (ISBN 0-87367-084-1). Phi Delta Kappa.

Garcia, Ricardo L. Education for Cultural Pluralism: Global Roots Stew. LC 81-80017. (Fastback Ser.: No. 159). 1981. pap. 0.75 (ISBN 0-87367-159-7). Phi Delta Kappa.

--Teaching in a Pluralistic Society: Concepts, Models, Strategies. 209p. 1981. pap. text ed. 15.95 scp (ISBN 0-06-042233-5, HarpC). Har-Row.

Garcia, Richard A., ed. The Chicanos in America, Fifteen Forty to Nineteen Seventy-Four: Chronology & Fact Book. LC 76-42300. (Ethnic Chronology Ser.: No. 26). 231p. 1977. 8.50 (ISBN 0-379-00516-6). Oceana.

Garcia, Rolando V. Nature Pleads Not Guilty: An IFIAS Report. (Illus.). 330p. 1981. 66.00 (ISBN 0-08-025823-9). Pergamon.

Garcia, Rolando V. & Escudero, Jose. Drought of Man the Nineteen Seventy-Two Case History: Vol. 2, The Constant Catastrophe-Malnutrition, Famines & Drought. (IFIAS Publications Ser.: Vol. 2). (Illus.). 304p. 1981. 50.00 (ISBN 0-08-025824-7). Pergamon.

Garcia, Rupert. Frida Kahlo: A Bibliography with Biographical Introduction. (Chicano Studies Library Publication Ser.: No. 7). (Orig.). 1983. pap. text ed. 10.00x (ISBN 0-918520-05-3). UC Chicano.

Garcia, Russ. Professional Arranger Composer, Bk. 1. 1954. 14.95 (ISBN 0-910468-05-2). Criterion Mus.

--Professional Arranger Composer, Bk. 2. LC 78-83425. 1978. 14.95 (ISBN 0-910468-06-0). Criterion Mus.

Garcia, Ryan, ed. see Read, R. B.

Garcia, S. & LeReste, L. Life Cycles, Dynamics, Exploitation & Management of Coastal Penaeid Shrimp Stocks. (Fisheries Technical Papers: No. 203). 215p. (Eng. & Fr.). 1981. pap. 16.00 (ISBN 92-5-101069-2, F2205, FAO). Unipub.

Garcia, S., jt. auth. see Troadec, J. P.

Garcia, Salvador. Las Ideas Literarias en Espana entre 1840 y 1850. LC 72-631461. (U. C. Publ. in Modern Philology: Vol. 98). Repr. of 1971 ed. 54.50 (ISBN 0-8357-9628-0, 2013797). Bks Demand UMI.

Garcia, W. Joseph. Medical Sign Language: Easily Understood Definitions of Commonly Used Medical, Dental & First Aid Terms. (Illus.). 726p. 1983. 54.50x (ISBN 0-398-04805-3); pap. 43.75x spiral (ISBN 0-398-04806-1). C C Thomas.

Garcia, Wilma. Mothers & Others: Myths of the Female in the Works of Melville, Twain & Hemingway. LC 84-47696. (American University Studies IV (English Language & Literature): Vol. 12). 190p. 1985. text ed. 23.00 (ISBN 0-8204-0127-7). P Lang Pubs.

Garcia-Amador, F. V. The Andean Legal Order: A New Community Law. LC 78-11916. 432p. 1978. lib. bdg. 32.50 (ISBN 0-379-20285-9). Oceana.

Garcia-Amador, F. V., jt. auth. see Organization of American States: General Secretariat.

Garcia-Amador, F. V., ed. see Inter-American Institute Of International Legal Studies.

Garcia-Amador, F. V., et al. Recent Codification of the Law of State Responsibility for Injuries to Aliens. LC 73-21658. 402p. 1974. lib. bdg. 30.00 (ISBN 0-379-00006-7). Oceana.

Garcia-Antezana, Jorge. Libro De Buen Amor: Concordancia Completa De los Codices De Salamanca, Toledo y Gayoso. 1100p. (Span.). 1981. microfiche 27.50x (ISBN 0-8020-0357-5). U of Toronto Pr.

Garcia-Avyens, Francisco. Quien Sabe? A Preliminary List of Chicano Reference Materials. (Bibliography & Reference Ser.: No. 11). 136p. (Orig.). 1981. pap. text ed. 6.00 (ISBN 0-89551-000-6). UCLA Chicano Stud.

Garcia-Ayvens, Francisco & Chabran, Richard, eds. Biblio-Politica: Chicano Perspectives on Library Service. LC 84-70532. (Chicano Studies Library Publication: No. 10). 284p. 1984. pap. 10.50x (ISBN 0-918520-08-8). UC Chicano.

Garcia-Barron, Carlos. Cancionero De la Hispano-Peruana De 1866. LC 79-51156. (Coleccion De Estudios Hispanicos: Hispanic Studies Collection). (Illus.). 226p. (Span.). 1980. pap. 15.00 (ISBN 0-89729-225-1). Ediciones.

Garcia-Borras, Thomas. Manual for Improving Boiler & Furnace Performance. LC 82-20124. 212p. 1983. 33.95x (ISBN 0-87201-243-3). Gulf Pub.

Garcia-Calderon, F. Latin America: Its Rise & Progress. Miall, B., tr. 1977. lib. bdg. 59.95 (ISBN 0-8490-2131-6). Gordon Pr.

Garcia Cisneros, Florencio. Santos of Puerto Rico & the Americas - Santos De Puerto Rico y las Americas. bilingual ed. LC 79-4408. 1979. pap. 9.00 (ISBN 0-87917-068-9). Ethridge.

Garcia-Cortez, Julio. Pataki: Leyendas Y Misterios De los Orishas Africanos. LC 79-54684. (Coleccion Ebano Y Canela Ser.). (Illus.). 250p. (Span.). 1980. pap. 15.00 (ISBN 0-89729-236-7). Ediciones.

Garcia de Diego, Vicenete. Diccionario de Voces Naturales. 724p. (Span.). 1968. 20.95 (ISBN 84-12031-1, S-11993). French & Eur.

Garcia de La Noceda, Joaquin. Curso de Preguntas Sobre la Teoria Atomica. LC 80-26696. 500p. 1981. pap. 7.00 (ISBN 0-8477-2326-7). U of PR Pr.

Garcia De Leon, Luis, tr. see Didactic Systems Staff.

Garcia de Palacios, Diego. Letter to the King of Spain: Being a Description of the Ancient Provinces of Guazacapan, Izalco, Cuscatlan & Chiquimula & a Description of the Ruins of Copan. Comparato, Frank E., ed. Orig. Title: Carta Dirijida al Rey de Espana. (Illus.). 72p. 1985. pap. 16.00x (ISBN 0-911437-04-5). Labyrinthos.

Garcia de Serrano, Irma, compiled by. Resoluciones de la Junta de Personal de Puerto Rico, Vols. 1, 3 & 4. LC 80-26437. (Illus., Sp.). 1980. Each. 30.00 (ISBN 0-8477-2218-X); Set. 120.00. Vol. II (ISBN 0-8477-2223-6). Vol. III. Vol. IV (ISBN 0-8477-2224-4). U of PR Pr.

Garcia-Diaz, Alberto, jt. auth. see Phillips, Don T.

Garcia Hoz, Victor. Diccionario de Pedagogia Labor, 2 vols. 3rd ed. 444p. (Span.). 1974. Set. 44.00 (ISBN 84-335-3715-6, S-12488). French & Eur.

--Diccionario Escolar Etimologico. 7th ed. 740p. (Span.). 1977. pap. 13.95 (ISBN 84-265-0123-0, S-11999). French & Eur.

--Vocabulario General de Orientacion Cientifica y Sus Estratos. 432p. (Span.). 1976. pap. 29.95 (ISBN 84-00-04273-5, S-50108). French & Eur.

Garcia Icazbalceta, Francisco Monterde see Monterde Garcia Icazbalceta, Francisco.

Garcia Icazbalceta, Joaquin. Apuntes Para un Catalogo de Escritores en Lenguas Indigenas de America. LC 77-122833. (Bibliography & Reference Ser.: No. 335). 1970. Repr. of 1866 ed. lib. bdg. 25.50 (ISBN 0-8337-1787-1). B Franklin.

--Obras de Joaquin Garcia Icazbalceta, 10 vols. LC 68-58758. (Span). 1969. Repr. of 1898 ed. Set. 225.00 (ISBN 0-8337-1798-7). B Franklin.

Garcia Lorca, F. Obras Completas. (Span). 37.50x (ISBN 0-685-20244-5). Schoenhof.

Garcia Lorca, Federico. Five Plays: Comedies & Tragicomedies. O'Connell, Richard L. & Graham-Lujan, James, trs. from Span. LC 77-4654. 1977. Repr. of 1963 ed. lib. bdg. 24.75x (ISBN 0-8371-9583-7, LOFP). Greenwood.

--The Gypsy Ballads of Garcia Lorca. Humphries, Rolfe, tr. LC 53-9826. (Poetry Paperback Ser: No. 2). 64p. 1953. 10.00x (ISBN 0-253-13670-9); pap. 4.95x (ISBN 0-253-29902-0). Ind U Pr.

--Lament for the Death of a Bullfighter: And Other Poems. Lloyd, A. L., tr. LC 76-29447. (Eng. & Span.). 1977. Repr. of 1937 ed. 13.50 (ISBN 0-404-15302-X). AMS Pr.

--Lament for the Death of a Bullfighter & Other Poems in the Original Spanish with English Translation. Lloyd, A. L., tr. from Span. LC 76-57930. 1977. Repr. of 1937 ed. lib. bdg. 18.75x (ISBN 0-8371-9322-2, GALF). Greenwood.

--Poet in New York. Belitt, Ben, tr. (Span., Eng., Span). 12.75 (ISBN 0-8446-2486-1). Peter Smith.

--Three Tragedies: Blood Wedding, Yerma, Bernarda Alba. O'Connell, Richard L. & Graham-Lujan, James, trs. from Spanish. LC 77-3056. 1977. Repr. of 1955 ed. lib. bdg. 25.00x (ISBN 0-8371-9578-0, LOTT). Greenwood.

--Tree of Song. 2nd rev. ed. Brilliant, Alan, tr. from Span. LC 70-134743. (Keepsake Ser.: Vol. 3). (Illus.). 14p. (Eng. & Span.). 1973. 10.00 (ISBN 0-87775-046-7); pap. 4.00 (ISBN 0-87775-047-5). Unicorn Pr.

Garcia Lorca, Federico see Lorca, Federico G.

Garcia Lorca, Federico see Lorca, Federico Garcia.

Garcia Lorca, Federico see Weiss, Samuel A.

Garcia Lorca, Frederico see Lorca, Federico Garcia.

Garcia-Marquez, Gabriel. The Autumn of the Patriarch. 1977. pap. 3.95 (ISBN 0-380-01774-1, 69641-X, Bard). Avon.

--The Autumn of the Patriarch. Rabassa, Gregory, tr. from Span. LC 75-30349. 288p. 1976. 13.41i (ISBN 0-06-011419-3, HarpT). Har-Row.

--Chronicle of a Death Foretold. LC 82-48884. 1983. 10.95 (ISBN 0-394-53074-8). Knopf.

--Collected Stories. Rabassa, Gregory & Bernstein, B. J., trs. from Span. LC 84-47826. 1984. 16.95i (ISBN 0-06-015364-4). Har-Row.

--Collected Stories. Rabassa, Gregory & Bernstein, S. J., trs. LC 84-47826. 320p. (Span.). 1985. pap. 6.95 (ISBN 0-06-091306-1, PL 1306, PL). Har-Row.

--In Evil Hour. 1980. pap. 2.95 (ISBN 0-380-52167-9, 64188-7, Bard). Avon.

--In Evil Hour. Rabassa, Gregory, tr. from Span. LC 74-15873. 1979. 11.49i (ISBN 0-06-011414-2, HarpT). Har-Row.

--Innocent Erendira & Other Stories. Rabassa, Gregory, tr. from Span. LC 74-15873. 1979. pap. 4.76i (ISBN 0-06-090701-0, CN 701, CN). Har-Row.

--Innocent Erendira & Other Stories. Rabassa, Gregory, tr. from Span. LC 74-15873. 1978. 11.49i (ISBN 0-06-011416-9, HarpT). Har-Row.

--Leaf Storm & Other Stories. Rabassa, Gregory, tr. from Span. LC 76-138784. 1979. pap. 4.76i (ISBN 0-06-090699-5, CN 699, CN). Har-Row.

--Leaf Storm & Other Stories. Rabassa, Gregory, tr. from Span. LC 76-138784. 192p. 1972. 10.95i (ISBN 0-06-012779-1, HarpT). Har-Row.

--No One Writes to the Colonel & Other Stories. Bernstein, J. S., tr. from Span. LC 68-15977. 1979. pap. 5.72i (ISBN 0-06-090700-2, CN 700, CN). Har-Row.

--No One Writes to the Colonel & Other Stories. LC 68-15977. 1968. 9.95i (ISBN 0-06-011417-7, HarpT). Har-Row.

--One Hundred Years of Solitude. 1971. pap. 3.95 (ISBN 0-380-01503-X, 60009-9, Bard). Avon.

--One Hundred Years of Solitude. Rabassa, Gregory, tr. LC 74-83632. 1970. 18.22i (ISBN 0-06-011418-5, HarpT). Har-Row.

Garcia-Mazas, Jose. El Poeta y la Escultura: La Espana Que Huntington Conocio. (Illus.). 1962. 2.50 (ISBN 0-87535-097-6). Hispanic Soc.

Garcia Merayo, F. Glosario De Informatica: Terminologia Ordenada Segun el Vocablo Ingles y Su Acepcion En Espanol. 290p. (Eng. & Span.). 1971. pap. 28.50 (ISBN 84-314-0001-3, S-50368). French & Eur.

Garcia Mercadal, Jose. Diccionario Lengua Espanola Forja. 24th ed. 488p. (Span.). 1977. 4.50 (ISBN 84-7105-026-9, S-50034). French & Eur.

Garcia-Molina, Hector. Performance of Update Algorithms for Replicated Data. Stone, Harold S., ed. LC 81-10454. (Computer Science Ser.: Distributed Database Systems: No. 5). 338p. 1981. 49.95 (ISBN 0-8357-1219-2). UMI Res Pr.

Garcia-Moliner, F. & Flores, F. Introduction to the Theory of Solid Surfaces. LC 78-17617. (Cambridge Monographs on Physics). (Illus.). 1979. 89.50 (ISBN 0-521-22294-X). Cambridge U Pr.

Garcia Ochoa, Maria A. La Politica Espanola en Puerto Rico Durante el Siglo XIX. LC 78-14035. 1979. 14.00 (ISBN 0-8477-0854-3); pap. 12.00 (ISBN 0-8477-0855-1). U of PR Pr.

Garcia Passalacqua, Juan M. La Alternativa Liberal: Una Vision Historica De Puerto Rico. (UPREX, Ensayo: No.27). pap. 1.85 (ISBN 0-8477-0027-5). U of PR Pr.

Garcia-Passalacqua, Juan M., jt. auth. see Heine, Jorge.

Garcia-Pelayo, R. & Testas, J. Dictionnaire moderne Larousse, francais-espagnol et espagnol-francais. (Span. & Fr.). 29.95 (ISBN 2-03-020601-6, 3773). Larousse.

Garcia-Pelayo, R., ed. Dictionnaire Moderne: Francaise-Espagnol, Espagnol-Francais. (Fr. & Span.). 35.00 (ISBN 2-03-020601-6, S-32371). French & Eur.

Garcia-Pelayo, Ramon. Diccionario Moderno Espanol-Ingles, English-Spanish. 1992p. (Span. & Eng.). 1976. 25.00 (ISBN 0-686-57189-4, M-6261). French & Eur.

--Gran Diccionario General Espanol-Ingles, English-Spanish. 930p. 1984. 24.95 (ISBN 2-03-401063-9). Larousse.

--Gran Diccionario Moderno Espanol-Ingles, English-Spanish Larousse. (Illus.). 1532p. 1984. 29.95 (ISBN 2-03-451331-2). Larousse.

Garcia-Pelayo, Ramon & Gross. Diccionario Larousse Del Espanol Moderno. (Span.). 1983. pap. 4.95 (ISBN 0-451-12352-2, Sig). NAL.

Garcia-Prada, Carlos & Wilson, William E. Tres Cuentos. 2nd ed. LC 59-4973. (Span). 1959. pap. text ed. 11.95 (ISBN 0-395-04482-0). HM.

Garcia Tous, M. R., jt. auth. see Rabassa Asenjo, Bernardo.

Garcia-Treto, Francisco O., jt. auth. see Brackenridge, R. Douglas.

Garcia-Tuduri, Mercedes. Andariega de Dios: Tiempo de exilio. LC 83-50874. (Senda Poetica Ser.). (Illus.). 73p. (Orig.). 1983. pap. 6.95 (ISBN 0-918454-39-5). Senda Nueva.

Garcia-Tuduri, Mercedes & Garcia-Tuduri, Rosaura. Ensayos Filosoficos (Sobre temas de Etica, Estetica, Metafisica, Gnoseologia y Epistemologia) LC 83-60446. (Senda de Estudios y Ensayos). 109p. (Orig.). 1983. pap. 11.95 (ISBN 0-918454-35-2). Senda Nueva.

Garcia-Tuduri, Rosaura, jt. auth. see Garcia-Tuduri, Mercedes.

Garcia y Griego, Manuel, jt. auth. see Vasquez, Carlos.

Garcia-Zamor, Jean-Claude. The Ecology of Development Administration in Jamaica, Trinidad & Tobago, & Barbados. 1977. pap. text ed. 5.00 (ISBN 0-8270-3680-9). OAS.

Garcia-Zamor, Jean-Claude, ed. Public Participation in Development Planning & Management: Cases from Africa & Asia. (A Westview Replica Ser.). 240p. 1985. pap. 22.00x (ISBN 0-86531-874-3). Westview.

Garcia-Zamor, Jean-Claude & Sutin, Stewart E., eds. Financing Development in Latin America. LC 80-194. 368p. 1980. 42.95 (ISBN 0-03-051106-2). Praeger.

Garcie, Pierre. The Rutters of the Sea: The Sailing Directions of Pierre Garcie. LC 67-17722. (Illus.). pap. 125.30 (ISBN 0-317-08232-9, 2022051). Bks Demand UMI.

Garcilaso de la Vega. The Florida of the Inca. Varner, John & Varner, Jeannette, eds. 708p. 1951. 25.00x (ISBN 0-292-73238-4); pap. 12.95 (ISBN 0-292-72434-9). U of Tex Pr.

--Royal Commentaries of the Incas, 2 vols. Markham, Clements R., ed. & tr. (Hakluyt Society, First Ser.: Nos. 41 & 45). Repr. of 1869 ed. 63.00 (ISBN 0-8337-2233-6). B Franklin.

--Royal Commentaries of the Incas & General History of Peru, 2 Vols. Livermore, Harold V., tr. from Sp. (Texas Pan American Ser.). 1622p. 1965. Set. 75.00x (ISBN 0-292-73358-5). U of Tex Pr.

Garcin, F., jt. ed. see Radouco-Thomas, C.

Garcin De Tassy, Joseph H. Histoire De la Litterature Hindouie et Hindoustanie, 3 vols. 2nd ed. (Fr). 1968. Repr. of 1871 ed. 84.00 (ISBN 0-8337-1279-9). B Franklin.

Garcke, Emile & Fells, John M. Factory Accounts, Their Principles & Practice. 4th ed. LC 75-18470. (History of Accounting Ser.). 1976. 21.00x (ISBN 0-405-07553-7). Ayer Co Pubs.

Garcy Gorman, Martha see Gorman, Martha Garcy.

Garczynska, Marie J. Tales from Russia. LC 80-52512. (The World Folktale Library). PLB 12.68 (ISBN 0-382-06597-2). Silver.

Garczynski, W., ed. Gauge Field Theories: Theoretical Studies & Computer Simulations. (Studies in High Energy Physics: Vol. 4). 800p. 1984. 67.50 (ISBN 3-7186-0121-4). Harwood Academic.

Gard, Elizabeth. The British Trade Unions. LC 82-9728. (Cambridge Introduction to the History of Mankind Topic Bk.). (Illus.). 1983. pap. 4.50 (ISBN 0-521-28225-X). Cambridge U Pr.

Gard, Grant G. Championship Selling. LC 83-19115. 188p. 1983. 14.95 (ISBN 0-13-127530-5, Busn); pap. 5.95 (ISBN 0-13-127522-4). P-H.

Gard, Michael F. EMI Control in Medical Electronics. White, Donald R., ed. LC 78-66192. (Illus.). 175p. 1979. text ed. 32.00 (ISBN 0-932263-19-4). White Consult.

Gard, Rene see Du Gard, Rene C.

Gard, Rene C. du see Du Gard, Rene C.

Gard, Richard A., ed. Buddhism. LC 61-15499. (Great Religions of Modern Man Ser). 1976. 8.95 (ISBN 0-8076-0166-7). Braziller.

Gard, Robert & Sorden, L. G. Romance of Wisconsin Place. rev. ed. LC 68-29817. 201p. 1979. pap. 4.95 (ISBN 0-686-28112-8). Milwaukee Sentinel.

Gard, Robert E. Act Nine: Plays for Youth. 110p. 1970. pap. 4.95 (ISBN 0-88361-022-1). Stanton & Lee.

--Coming Home to Wisconsin. LC 81-16563. 222p. (Orig.). 1982. pap. 9.95 (ISBN 0-88361-084-1). Stanton & Lee.

--Grassroots Theater: A Search for Regional Arts in America. LC 78-4943. 263p. 1978. Repr. of 1955 ed. lib. bdg. 27.50x (ISBN 0-313-20399-7, GAGT). Greenwood.

--The Prairie Reader. Stephens, Jim, ed. (Heartland Reader Ser.). (Illus.). 270p. 1986. 19.95 (ISBN 0-88361-097-3). Stanton & Lee.

--University Madison, USA. LC 74-146841. (Illus.). 308p. 1970. 8.95 (ISBN 0-88361-009-4). Stanton & Lee.

Gard, Robert E. & Bohrod, Aaron. Wisconsin Sketches. Lefebvre, Mark E., ed. LC 73-89027. (Illus.). 1973. 12.95 (ISBN 0-88361-026-4). Stanton & Lee.

Gard, Robert E. & Burley, Gertrude S. Community Theatre. LC 73-19113. 182p. 1975. Repr. of 1959 ed. lib. bdg. 22.50x (ISBN 0-8371-7304-3, GACT). Greenwood.

Gard, Robert E. & Sorden, L. G. Wisconsin Lore. LC 62-12168. 335p. 1971. 9.95 (ISBN 0-88361-083-3). Stanton & Lee.

Gard, Robert E., jt. auth. see Crafton, Allen.

Gard, Robert E., jt. ed. see Drummond, A. M.

Gard, Robert E., et al, eds. We Were Children Then: Ninety Wisconsin Writers, Age Sixty to Ninety-Six. LC 76-22961. 187p. 1976. pap. 9.95 (ISBN 0-88361-041-8). Stanton & Lee.

Gard, Roger Du see Du Gard, Roger M.

Gard, Roger du Martin see Martin Du Gard, Roger.

Gard, Roger Martin Du see Martin Du Gard, Roger.

Gard, Spencer A. Code of Civil Procedure 2d Annotated, 2 vols. 2nd ed. LC 79-53496. 120.00; Suppl. 1984. 15.50; Suppl. 1983. 13.50. Lawyers Co-Op.

--Florida Evidence, 2 vols. 2nd ed. LC 79-92246. 976p. 125.00; Suppl. 1984. 22.00; Suppl. 1983. 20.00. Lawyers Co-Op.

--Illinois Evidence Manual, 2 vols. 2nd ed. LC 79-83813. 1107p. 119.00; Suppl. 1984. 22.00; Suppl. 1983. 20.00. Lawyers Co-Op.

--Jones on Evidence, Civil & Criminal, 4 vols. 6th ed. LC 72-76892. 1972. Set. 224.00 (ISBN 0-686-14505-4); Suppl. 1984. 36.50; Suppl. 1983. 33.00. Lawyers Co-Op.

--Missouri Evidence, 2 vols. LC 85-50755. 1985. 129.00 (ISBN 0-318-11861-0). Lawyers Co-Op.

Gard, Wayne. Book Reviewing. 1979. Repr. of 1928 ed. lib. bdg. 20.00 (ISBN 0-8414-4622-9). Folcroft.

--The Chisholm Trail. LC 54-6204. (Illus.). 308p. (Orig.). 1984. pap. 8.95 (ISBN 0-8061-1536-X). U of Okla Pr.

--Frontier Justice. (Illus.). 324p. 1981. 22.95 (ISBN 0-8061-0194-6); pap. 9.95 (ISBN 0-8061-1755-9). U of Okla Pr.

--The Great Buffalo Hunt. LC 59-11049. (Illus.). xii, 338p. 1968. pap. 5.95 (ISBN 0-8032-5067-3, BB 390, Bison). U of Nebr Pr.

--Sam Bass. LC 36-17302. (Illus.). x, 262p. 1969. 19.95x (ISBN 0-8032-0868-5). U of Nebr Pr.

Gard, Wayne, et al. Along the Early Trails of the Southwest. LC 70-79106. (Illus.). 17.50 (ISBN 0-8363-0002-5); limited ed. 85.00 (ISBN 0-685-13269-2). Jenkins.

Garda, B. Electroplating Science. 254p. 1970. 33.00 (ISBN 0-318-12536-6); members 25.00 (ISBN 0-318-12537-4). Am Electroplate.

Gardair, J. M. Pirandello: Fantasmes et logique du double. new ed. (Collection themes et textes). 160p. (Orig., Fr.). 1972. pap. 6.75 (ISBN 2-03-035003-6, 2688). Larousse.

Gardality, Steve. Give Me Liberty. LC 81-169733. (Illus.). 1982. 12.95x (ISBN 0-9607208-0-4). Danube Inc.

Gardam, Jane. Bilgewater. LC 77-2890. 212p. (gr. 7 up). 1977. 11.75 (ISBN 0-688-80108-0). Greenwillow.

--The Hollow Land. LC 81-6620. (Illus.). 160p. (gr. 5-9). 1982. 10.25 (ISBN 0-688-00873-9). Greenwillow.

--Horse. (Julia MacRae Blackbird Bks.). (Illus.). 48p. (gr. k-3). 1982. 5.95 (ISBN 0-531-04429-7, MacRae). Watts.

Gardan, Yvon & Lucas, Michel. Interactive Graphics in CAD. 256p. (Published in England by Kogan Page). 1984. 34.95 (ISBN 0-89059-036-2, KP100, UPB). Unipub.

Gardarin, Georges & Gelenbe, Erol, eds. New Applications of Data Bases. 1984. 25.00 (ISBN 0-12-275550-2). Acad Pr.

Gardberg, C. J. & Save-Soderbergh, Torgny. Scandinavian Joint Expedition to Sudanese Nubia, Vol. 7: Late Nubian Sites, Churches & Settlementsq. (Illus.). 1970. text ed. 45.00x (ISBN 0-8419-8806-4, Africana). Holmes & Meier.

Garde, Pauline, jt. auth. see Mayer, Henry.

Garde, R. J. & Ranga-Raju, K. G. Mechanics of Sediment Transportation & Alluvial Stream Problems. 2nd ed. 1985. 34.95 (ISBN 0-470-20109-6). Halsted Pr.

Gardea, Jesus. De Alba Sombria. 151p. (Span.). 1985. pap. 7.50 (ISBN 0-910061-25-4, 1114). Ediciones Norte.

Gardel, A. Energie: Economie et Prospective. LC 79-40986. (Illus.). 1979. 88.00 (ISBN 0-08-024782-2). Pergamon.

--Energy: Economy & Prospective: A Handbook for Engineers & Economists. (Illus.). 480p. 1981. 90.00 (ISBN 0-08-025427-6). Pergamon.

Gardell, Bertil & Johansson, Gunn. Working Life: A Social Science Contribution to Work Reform. LC 80-40289. 347p. 1981. 57.95x (ISBN 0-471-27801-7, Pub. by Wiley-Interscience). Wiley.

Gardella, Peter. Innocent Ecstasy: How Christianity Gave America an Ethic of Sexual Pleasure. LC 84-27253. (Illus.). 224p. 1985. 17.95 (ISBN 0-19-503612-3). Oxford U Pr.

Garden Center of Greater Cleveland. Flowering Plant Index of Illustration & Information. 1979. lib. bdg. 210.00 (ISBN 0-8161-0301-1, Hall Library). G K Hall.

Garden Club of Lexington, Inc. Bluegrass Winners. LC 85-60214. (Illus.). 368p. 1985. 15.95 (ISBN 0-9614442-0-7). Garden Club Lex.

Garden Club of Palm Beach. The Palm Beach Cook Book. 64p. 1968. pap. 2.75 (ISBN 0-913456-64-0). Interbk Inc.

Garden Club of Savannah Book Committee, ed. Through Garden Gates. (Illus.). 28p. (Orig.). 1984. pap. 4.75 (ISBN 0-317-11351-8). Garden Club Sav.

Garden Clubs of Mississippi. Gardeners' Gourmet. 6.00 (ISBN 0-918544-87-4). Wimmer Bks.

Garden, Edward. Tchaikovsky. (The Master Musicians Ser.). (Illus.). 208p. 1973. 13.50x (ISBN 0-460-03105-8, Pub. by J. M. Dent England). Biblio Dist.

Garden, Glenn. Life B. C. (Orig.). 1980. 11.00x (ISBN 0-435-31200-6). Heinemann Ed.

Garden, Graeme. The Best Medicine. 128p. 1985. pap. 6.95 (ISBN 0-312-07709-2). St Martin.

Garden, Mary & Biancolli, Louis. Mary Garden's Story. Baxter, Annette K., ed. LC 79-8794. (Signal Lives Ser.). (Illus.). 1980. Repr. of 1951 ed. lib. bdg. 36.00x (ISBN 0-405-12840-1). Ayer Co Pubs.

Garden, Nancy. Annie on My Mind. LC 82-9189. (Illus.). 234p. (gr. 7 up). 1982. 10.95 (ISBN 0-374-30366-5); pap. 3.45 (ISBN 0-374-40413-5). FS&G.

--Devils & Demons. LC 75-44461. (Weird & Horrible Library). (gr. 6 up). 1976. 10.10i (ISBN 0-397-31666-6). Lipp Jr Bks.

--Fours Crossing. LC 80-21854. 192p. (gr. 5 up). 1981. 10.95 (ISBN 0-374-32451-4). FS&G.

--Fours Crossing. 240p. (gr. 7 up). 1982. pap. 1.95 (ISBN 0-590-32287-7). Scholastic Inc.

--The Kid's Code & Cipher Book. LC 80-10434. (Illus.). 176p. (gr. 5 up). 1981. pap. 4.95 (ISBN 0-03-059267-4). HR&W.

--The Loners. 1974. pap. 0.95 (ISBN 0-380-00104-7, 20230). Avon.

--Peace, O River. 240p. (gr. 7 up). 1985. 12.95 (ISBN 0-374-35763-3). FS&G.

--Prisoner of Vampires. LC 84-47840. (Illus.). 213p. (gr. 5 up). 1984. 12.95 (ISBN 0-374-36129-0). FS&G.

--Vampires. LC 72-13830. (gr. 7 up). 1973. pap. 2.95 (ISBN 0-397-31457-4). Lipp Jr Bks.

--Watersmeet. LC 83-11512. 202p. (gr. 5 up). 1983. 10.95 (ISBN 0-374-38244-1). FS&G.

--Witches. LC 75-12621. (Weird & Horrible Library). (Illus.). 160p. (gr. 3-5). 1975. 10.53i (ISBN 0-397-31564-3, LSC-41). Lipp Jr Bks.

Garden, R. J., ed. The Lum Hat & Other Stories: Last Tales of Violet Jacob. (Illus.). 172p. 1982. 19.00 (ISBN 0-08-028449-3); 10.00 (ISBN 0-08-028450-7). Pergamon.

Garden, Rhonda A., ed. see John, Yvonne.

Garden, William. Yacht Designs. LC 76-8772. (Illus.). 1977. 22.50 (ISBN 0-87742-066-1). Intl Marine.

Gardenas-Ruiz, Manuel, tr. see Estades, Rosa.

Gardener, Beau. The Look Again...& Again, & Again, & Again Book. LC 84-748. (Illus.). 32p. (ps-3). 1983. 11.00 (ISBN 0-688-03805-0); lib. bdg. 10.08 (ISBN 0-688-03806-9). Lothrop.

Gardener, Jeanne, jt. auth. see Smith, Betsy C.

Gardener, Leslie, ed. Mechanical Plant in Construction. (Illus.). 138p. 1979. technical 55.00 (ISBN 0-7114-4306-8). Transatlantic.

Gardener, Llyod C. The Korean War. LC 72-130383. (A New York Times Book Ser.). 1972. pap. text ed. 8.95 (ISBN 0-8129-6193-5, Dist. by M & B Fulfillment). Wiener Pub Inc.

Gardener, N. L., jt. auth. see Setchell, W. A.

Gardener, Nico, jt. auth. see Mollo, Victor.

Gardener, Nico, jt. auth. see Molo, Victor.

Gardener, Russell M. & Farkas, F. Chris, eds. Texas Celebrity Cookbook. LC 84-82018. (Illus.). 256p. 1984. 14.95 (ISBN 0-9613874-0-8). Gardner-Farkas Pr.

Gardener's Catalog People. The Gardener's Catalog, No. 2. rev. ed. (Illus.). 320p. 1983. pap. 12.95 (ISBN 0-688-01238-8, Quill NY). Morrow.

Gardenhour, Nancy D., jt. auth. see Harris, Charles M.

Gardenier. Case Studies in Risk Assessment Methods. 1985. 35.00 (ISBN 0-02-949380-3). Macmillan.

Garder, J. F. Clean Air: Law & Practice. 1976. 40.00x (ISBN 0-7219-0680-X, Pub. by Shaw & Sons). State Mutual Bk.

Gardet, L., et al. Cultures & Time. (At the Crossroads of Culture Ser.). 245p. 1976. pap. 17.25 (ISBN 92-3-101200-2, U144, UNESCO). Unipub.

Gardezi, Hassan & Rashid, Jamil, eds. Pakistan: The Roots of Dictatorship-the Political Economy of a Praetorian State. (Illus.). 412p. 1983. 35.00x (ISBN 0-86232-046-1, Pub. by Zed Pr England); pap. 12.25x (ISBN 0-86232-051-8). Biblio Dist.

Gardi, Gavin L, jt. auth. see Cook, Richard J.

Gardiakos, B., tr. see Lambros, P.

Gardiakos, S. A Catalogue of the Coins of Dalmatia et Albania, 1410-1797. (Illus.). 32p. 1970. pap. 5.00 (ISBN 0-916710-67-X). Obol Intl.

--The Coinage of Modern Greece, Crete, the Ionian Islands & Cyprus (1718-1968) (Illus.). 96p. 12.50 (ISBN 0-916710-02-5). Obol Intl.

Gardiakos, Soterios. The Coins of Cyprus, Fourteen Eighty-Nine to Fifteen Seventy-One. 2nd ed. (Illus.). 1975. pap. 5.00 (ISBN 0-916710-19-X). Obol Intl.

Gardiakos, Soterios, ed. The Coinages of Alexander the Great. (Illus.). 1007p. 1981. 295.00 (ISBN 0-916710-82-3). Obol Intl.

Gardies, Jean-Louis. Rational Grammar. Mulligan, Kevin, tr. LC 84-23002. 360p. (Fr.). 1985. 59.95x (ISBN 0-8132-0611-1). Cath U Pr.

Gardies, Jean-Louis, jt. ed. see Bulygin, Eugenio.

Gardin, J. C., et al. Archaeological Constructs. LC 78-54577. (Illus.). 1980. 42.50 (ISBN 0-521-22080-7). Cambridge U Pr.

Gardiner. Modern Algebra with Equations: A Natural Approach with Applications. (Mathematics & Its Applications Ser.). 288p. 1981. 64.95 (ISBN 0-470-27115-9). Halsted Pr.

Gardiner, jt. auth. see Hilliard.

Gardiner, A. Infinite Processes: Background to Analysis. (Illus.). 304p. 1982. 33.00 (ISBN 0-387-90605-3). Springer-Verlag.

Gardiner, A. G. The War Lords. (Wayfarer's Library). 328p. lib. bdg. 20.00 (ISBN 0-89984-232-1). Century Bookbindery.

Gardiner, A. G. & Belloc. English Essays of Today. 1936. 20.00 (ISBN 0-8482-4205-X). Norwood Edns.

Gardiner, A. H. The Kadesh Inscriptions of Ramessess II. 65p. 1975. 49.00x (ISBN 0-900416-03-3, Pub. by Griffith Inst). State Mutual Bk.

Gardiner, A. H., jt. auth. see Davies, Nina M.

Gardiner, A. W. Typewriting & Office Duplicating Processes. 7.95 (ISBN 0-8038-7084-1). Hastings.

Gardiner, Alan. Egypt of the Pharaohs: An Introduction. (Illus.). 1966. pap. 12.95 (ISBN 0-19-500267-9, 165, GB). Oxford U Pr.

--Egyptian Grammar. 3rd, rev. ed. 646p. 1978. text ed. 38.00x (ISBN 0-900416-35-1, Pub. by Aris & Phillips England). Humanities.

--The Kadesh Inscriptions of Remessess II. 59p. 1960. text ed. 11.00x (ISBN 0-900416-03-3, Pub. by Aris & Phillips England). Humanities.

--The Theory of Proper Names. (The International Library of Names Ser.). 1985. Repr. of 1954 ed. text ed. 39.50x (ISBN 0-8290-1230-3). Irvington.

Gardiner, Alan, jt. auth. see Cerny, Jaroslav.

Gardiner, Alan, ed. Ramesside Administrative Documents. 101p. 1968. Repr. of 1948 ed. text ed. 26.50x (ISBN 0-900416-40-8, Pub. by Aris & Phillips England). Humanities.

--Ramessium Papyri. (Illus.). 18p. 1955. text ed. 54.50x (ISBN 0-900416-37-8, Pub. by Aris & Phillips England). Humanities.

Gardiner, Alan H. Catalogue of the Egyptian Hieroglyphic Printing Type. 1977. pap. 6.00 (ISBN 0-89005-098-8). Ares.

--The Theory of Speech & Language. LC 79-4125. 1979. Repr. of 1951 ed. lib. bdg. 27.50x (ISBN 0-313-20987-1, GATS). Greenwood.

Gardiner, Alfred G. Many Furrows. facs. ed. LC 77-121469. (Essay Index Reprint Ser). 1924. 18.00 (ISBN 0-8369-1807-X). Ayer Co Pubs.

--Many Furrows. LC 78-108699. (Essay & General Literature Index Reprint Ser). 1970. Repr. of 1924 ed. 21.00x (ISBN 0-8046-0920-9, Pub. by Kennikat). Assoc Faculty Pr.

--Pebbles on the Shore. LC 78-108700. (Essay & General Literature Index Reprint Ser.). 1970. Repr. of 1916 ed. 24.50x (ISBN 0-8046-0921-7, Pub. by Kennikat). Assoc Faculty Pr.

--Portraits & Portents. facsimile ed. LC 79-167344. (Essay Index Reprint Ser). Repr. of 1926 ed. 23.50 (ISBN 0-8369-2499-1). Ayer Co Pubs.

--Windfalls. LC 70-105014. (Essay Index Reprint Ser.). 1920. 19.00 (ISBN 0-8369-1467-8). Ayer Co Pubs.

Gardiner, Bertha M. The French Revolution. 1883. Repr. 10.00 (ISBN 0-8482-4206-8). Norwood Edns.

Gardiner, C. F., jt. auth. see Firby, P. A.

Gardiner, C. Harvey. Naval Power in the Conquest of Mexico. Repr. of 1956 ed. lib. bdg. 15.00x (ISBN 0-8371-2457-3, GANP). Greenwood.

--Pawns in a Triangle of Hate: The Peruvian Japanese & the United States. LC 81-51278. 232p. 1981. 27.50x (ISBN 0-295-95855-3). U of Wash Pr.

--William Hickling Prescott: A Biography. (Illus.). 388p. 1969. 20.00x (ISBN 0-292-70005-9). U of Tex Pr.

Gardiner, C. Harvey, ed. Study in Dissent: The Warren-Gerry Correspondence, 1776-1792. LC 68-25557. (Illus.). 309p. 1968. 15.00x (ISBN 0-8093-0330-2). S Ill U Pr.

Gardiner, C. Harvey, ed. see Flandrau, Charles M.

Gardiner, C. Harvey, ed. see Prescott, William H.

Gardiner, C. W. Handbook of Stochastic Methods for Physics, Chemistry & the Natural Sciences. (Springer Series in Synergetics: Vol. 13). (Illus.). 450p. 1983. 45.00 (ISBN 0-387-11357-6). Springer-Verlag.

Gardiner, Clinton H. Martin Lopez. Conquistador Citizen of Mexico. LC 73-19307. 193p. 1974. Repr. of 1958 ed. lib. bdg. 15.00x (ISBN 0-8371-7322-1, GAML). Greenwood.

Gardiner, Cyril F. A First Course in Group Therapy. (Universitext Ser.). 177p. 1980. pap. 19.00 (ISBN 0-387-90545-6). Springer-Verlag.

Gardiner, Dorothy & Walker, K. Sorley. Raymond Chandler Speaking. 276p. 1984. pap. 5.95 (ISBN 0-8052-8208-4, Pub. by Allison & Busby, England). Schocken.

Gardiner, Dorothy, ed. see Chandler, Raymond.

Gardiner, Duncan B. Intonation & Music: The Semantics of Czech Prosody. LC 79-67358. (Physsardt Series in Prague Linguistics: No. 2). (Illus.). 1980. pap. 10.00 (ISBN 0-916062-04-X). Physsardt.

Gardiner, E. Norman. Athletics of the Ancient World. (Illus.). 1978. write for info. (ISBN 0-89005-257-3); pap. 12.50. Ares.

Gardiner, Edmund. Phisicall & Approved Medicines. LC 79-25834. (English Experience Ser.: No. 191). 116p. 1969. Repr. of 1611 ed. 14.00 (ISBN 90-221-0191-6). Walter J Johnson.

Gardiner, G. & Morris, A. The Price Guide to Metal Toys. (Price Guide Ser.). (Illus.). 214p. 1980. 39.50 (ISBN 0-902028-92-8). Antique Collect.

Gardiner, G., jt. auth. see Morris, A.

Gardiner, George E. La Catastrofe de Corinto. Orig. Title: The Corinthian Catastrophe. 64p. (Span.). 1976. pap. 1.95 (ISBN 0-8254-1254-4). Kregel.

--The Corinthian Catastrophe. LC 74-75106. 1975. pap. 2.25 (ISBN 0-8254-2708-8). Kregel.

--The Romance of Ruth. LC 77-79187. 1977. pap. 1.95 (ISBN 0-8254-2718-5). Kregel.

Gardiner, George H. How I Sold a Million Dollars of Real Estate in One Year. 1969. pap. 4.95 (ISBN 0-13-399790-1). P-H.

Gardiner, Gilbert, tr. see Turgenev, Ivan.

Gardiner, Gordon & Morris, Alistair. The Illustrated Encyclopedia of Metal Toys. (Illus.). 1984. 19.95 (ISBN 0-517-55399-6, Harmony). Crown.

Gardiner, Harold, ed. see Thomas A'Kempis.

Gardiner, Harold C. Mysteries' End: An Investigation of the Last Days of the Medieval Religious Stage. (Yale Studies in English Ser.: No. 103). xiv, 139p. 1967. Repr. of 1946 ed. 16.50 (ISBN 0-208-00385-1, Archon). Shoe String.

Gardiner, Harold C., ed. Great Books: A Christian Appraisal, 4 Vols. Set. 20.00 (ISBN 0-685-08819-7); Vols. 1-4. 7.50 ea. Vol. 1 (ISBN 0-8159-5610-X). Vol. 2 (ISBN 0-8159-5611-8). Vol. 3 (ISBN 0-8159-5612-6). Vol. 4 (ISBN 0-8159-5613-4). Devin.

Gardiner, Harry N. Feeling & Emotion: A History of Theories. Repr. of 1937 ed. lib. bdg. 24.75x (ISBN 0-8371-3683-0, GAFE). Greenwood.

Gardiner, Harry N., ed. Jonathan Edwards, a Retrospect. LC 75-3133. (Philosophy of America Ser.). (Illus.). 192p. 1980. Repr. of 1901 ed. 18.00 (ISBN 0-404-59142-6). AMS Pr.

Gardiner, Harry W., jt. auth. see Gander, Mary J.

Gardiner, Harvey C. Prescott & His Publishers. LC 59-5906. (Illus.). 352p. 1959. 5.95x (ISBN 0-8093-0017-6). S Ill U Pr.

Gardiner, Harvey C., ed. see Head, Francis Bond.

Gardiner, Harvey C., ed. see Holton, Isaac F.

Gardiner, Harvey C., ed. see Koster, Henry.

Gardiner, Harvey C., ed. see Merwin, Mrs. George B.

Gardiner, J. H. The Bible As English Literature. LC 78-2371. Repr. of 1906 ed. lib. bdg. 40.00 (ISBN 0-8414-4613-X). Folcroft.

--The Forms of Prose Literature. 1973. lib. bdg. 20.00 (ISBN 0-8414-4633-4). Folcroft.

Gardiner, James J. & Roberts, J. Deotis, eds. Quest for a Black Theology. LC 76-151250. 128p. 1971. 6.95 (ISBN 0-8298-0196-0). Pilgrim NY.

Gardiner, John & Mulkey, Michael, eds. Crime & Criminal Justice. 1974. pap. 8.00 (ISBN 0-918592-08-9). Policy Studies.

Gardiner, John A. The Politics of Corruption: Organized Crime in an American City. LC 79-107958. 130p. 1970. 7.50x (ISBN 0-87154-299-4). Russell Sage.

--Traffic & the Police: Variations in Law-Enforcement Policy. LC 69-18030. (Joint Center for Urban Studies Publications Ser). 1969. 14.00x (ISBN 0-674-90140-1). Harvard U Pr.

Gardiner, John A. & Lyman, Theodore R. Decisions for Sale: Corruption & Reform in Land-Use & Building Regulation. LC 78-19758. 234p. 1978. 36.95x (ISBN 0-03-044691-0). Praeger.

--Decisions for Sale: Corruption in Local Land-Use & Building Regulation. 234p. 1978. 18.95 (ISBN 0-318-12955-8); members 17.95 (ISBN 0-318-12956-6). Am Plan Assn.

--The Fraud Control Game: State Responses to Fraud & Abuse in AFDC & Medicaid Programs. LC 83-48759. (Illus.). 288p. 1984. 24.95x (ISBN 0-253-32470-X). Ind U Pr.

Gardiner, John A. & Mulkey, Michael A., eds. Crime & Criminal Justice: Issues in Public Policy Analysis. 1977. pap. 8.95x (ISBN 0-669-01059-6). Heath.

Gardiner, John H. The Bible as English Literature. 402p. 1980. Repr. of 1906 ed. lib. bdg. 42.50 (ISBN 0-8482-4191-6). Norwood Edns.

Gardiner, John M. & Kaminska, Zofia. First Experiments in Psychology. (Essential Psychology Ser.). 1975. pap. 4.50x (ISBN 0-416-81690-8, NO. 2732). Methuen Inc.

Gardiner, John R. Stone Fox. LC 79-7895. (Illus.). 96p. (gr. 2-6). 1980. 10.53i (ISBN 0-690-03983-2); PLB 10.89 (ISBN 0-690-03984-0). Crowell Jr Bks.

--Stone Fox. LC 79-7895. (Trophy Bk.). (Illus.). 96p. (gr. 2-6). 1983. pap. 2.84i (ISBN 0-06-440132-4, Trophy). HarpJ.

--Top Secret. 129p. (gr. 3-7). Date not set. 14.95 (ISBN 0-316-30368-2). Little.

Gardiner, Judith K. Craftsmanship in Context: The Development of Ben Jonson's Poetry. (Studies in English Literature Ser: No. 110). 208p. 1975. pap. text ed. 15.20x (ISBN 90-2793-191-7). Mouton.

Gardiner, Judy. Come Back Soon. LC 85-40385. 112p. (gr. 5-9). 1985. 10.95 (ISBN 0-670-80150-X). Viking.

--Miss Gathercole's Girls. 350p. 1985. 15.95 (ISBN 0-312-53455-8). St Martin.

--Who Was Sylvia? 208p. 1982. 10.95 (ISBN 0-312-87030-2). St Martin.

Gardiner, L. J. Outlines of French Literature. 1973. Repr. of 1927 ed. 20.00 (ISBN 0-8274-0194-9). R West.

Gardiner, L. J., tr. see Chretien De Troyes.

Gardiner, Leslie. Curtain Calls: Travels in Albania, Romania & Bulgaria. 206p. 1976. 20.00x (ISBN 0-7156-1026-0, Pub. by Duckworth England). Biblio Dist.

Gardiner, M. James. Program Evaluation in Church Organization. LC 77-80070. (Management Ser.). (Illus.). 1977. pap. 4.50 (ISBN 0-89305-017-2). Anna Pub.

Gardiner, Margaret. Footprints on Malekula: A Memoir of Bernard Deacon. (Illus.). 76p. 1985. 14.95 (ISBN 0-907540-45-7, Pub. by Salamander Pr). Merrimack Pub Cir.

Gardiner, Muriel. Code Name "Mary". Memoirs of an American Woman in the Austrian Underground. LC 82-20213. (Illus.). 200p. 1983. 17.50x (ISBN 0-300-02940-3). Yale U Pr.

--The Deadly Innocents: Portraits of Children Who Kill. LC 75-36379. 216p. 1985. pap. 7.95x (ISBN 0-300-03306-0). Yale U Pr.

Gardiner, Oliver C. Great Issue: Or the Three Presidential Candidates. LC 71-107475. Repr. of 1848 ed. 17.50x (ISBN 0-8371-3753-5, GGI&, Pub. by Negro U Pr). Greenwood.

Gardiner, P. A. ABC of Ophthalmology. 43p. 1979. 9.50x (ISBN 0-7279-0037-4, Pub. by British Med Assoc UK). Taylor & Francis.

Gardiner, Patrick. Nature of Historical Explanation. (Oxford Classical & Philosophical Monographs). 154p. 1952. pap. 10.95x (ISBN 0-19-824599-8). Oxford U Pr.

Gardiner, Patrick, ed. Nineteenth-Century Philosophy. LC 69-10325. 1969. pap. text ed. 14.95 (ISBN 0-02-911220-6). Free Pr.

--The Philosophy of History. (Oxford Readings in Philosophy). 1974. pap. text ed. 7.95x (ISBN 0-19-875031-5). Oxford U Pr.

--Theories of History. LC 58-6481. 1959. text ed. 19.95 (ISBN 0-02-911210-9). Free Pr.

Gardiner, Paul B. The Abysmal Failure of the German Philosophers. (Illus.). 157p. 1981. 69.75 (ISBN 0-89266-285-9). Am Classical Coll Pr.

Gardiner, Robert, ed. Conway's All the World's Fighting Ships, 1906-1921. (Illus.). 450p. 1985. 38.95 (ISBN 0-87021-907-3). Naval Inst Pr.

--Conway's All the World's Fighting Ships, 1947-1982: Part I: The Western Powers. (Illus.). 256p. 1983. 38.95 (ISBN 0-87021-918-9). Naval Inst Pr.

Gardiner, S. C. Old Church Slavonic: An Elementary Grammar. 1984. 29.95 (ISBN 0-521-23674-6). Cambridge U Pr.

Gardiner, S. R., jt. auth. see Macauley.

Gardiner, S. R., ed. see Fortescue, George M.

Gardiner, Samuel. The Thirty Years' War, 1618-1648. LC 68-25233. (British History Ser., No. 30). (Illus.). Repr. of 1903 ed. lib. bdg. 49.95x (ISBN 0-8383-0940-2). Haskell.

--What Gunpowder Plot Was. LC 68-25234. (British History Ser., No. 30). (Illus.). 1969. Repr. of 1897 ed. lib. bdg. 49.95x (ISBN 0-8383-0941-0). Haskell.

Gardiner, Samuel R. Cromwell's Place in History. LC 76-94270. (Select Bibliographies Reprint Ser). 1897. 15.00 (ISBN 0-8369-5044-5). Ayer Co Pubs.

--Cromwell's Place in History. 1897. Repr. 15.00 (ISBN 0-8482-4203-3). Norwood Edns.

--The First Two Stuarts & the Puritan Revolution: 1603-1660. 1977. Repr. of 1891 ed. lib. bdg. 25.00 (ISBN 0-8495-1911-X). Arden Lib.

--The First Two Stuarts & the Puritan Revolution, 1603-1660. 1978. Repr. of 1911 ed. lib. bdg. 20.00 (ISBN 0-8492-4925-2). R West.

--History of England, 1603-1656, 18 vols. in 3 sections. Incl. From the Accession of James First to the Outbreak of Civil War. 1603-1642, 10 vols. 265.00 (ISBN 0-404-02740-7); History of the Great Civil War. 1642-1649, 4 vols. 105.00 (ISBN 0-404-02780-6); History of the Commonwealth & Protectorate. 1649-1656, 4 vols. 105.00 (ISBN 0-404-02760-1). LC 79-168096. Repr. of 1903 ed. Set. 475.00 (ISBN 0-404-02720-2). AMS Pr.

--Oliver Cromwell. 1977. Repr. of 1909 ed. 25.00x (ISBN 0-7158-1181-9). Charles River Bks.

--Oliver Cromwell. 319p. 1980. Repr. of 1925 ed. lib. bdg. 30.00 (ISBN 0-8414-4626-1). Folcroft.

--Oliver Cromwell. 319p. 1980. Repr. of 1925 ed. lib. bdg. 30.00 (ISBN 0-8492-4954-6). R West.

--Thirty Years' War, Sixteen Eighteen to Sixteen Forty-Eight. Repr. of 1903 ed. lib. bdg. 15.00x (ISBN 0-8371-2171-X, GATY). Greenwood.

--The Thirty Years War, Sixteen Eighteen to Sixteen Fourty-Eight. LC 70-131717. 260p. 1972. Repr. of 1912 ed. 15.00x (ISBN 0-403-00604-X). Scholarly.

--The Thirty Years' War: 1618-1648. 1977. Repr. of 1891 ed. lib. bdg. 20.00 (ISBN 0-8495-1912-8). Arden Lib.

--The Thirty Years' War: 1618-1648. 1889. Repr. 25.00 (ISBN 0-8482-4223-8). Norwood Edns.

--What Gunpowder Plot Was. LC 73-131718. 1971. 9.00x (ISBN 0-403-00605-8). Scholarly.

--What the Gunpowder Plot Was. LC 76-89457. (BCL Ser.: I). Repr. of 1897 ed. 11.50 (ISBN 0-404-02677-X). AMS Pr.

Gardiner, Samuel R., ed. Documents Illustrating the Impeachment of the Duke of Buckingham in 1626. Repr. of 1889 ed. 27.00 (ISBN 0-384-17633-X). Johnson Repr.

--Documents Relating to the Proceedings Against William Prynne, in 1634 & 1637. Repr. of 1877 ed. 27.00 (ISBN 0-384-17635-6). Johnson Repr.

--Letters & Other Documents Illustrating the Relations Between England & Germany at the Commencement of the Thirty Years' War, 2 Vols. LC 70-168100. (Camden Society, London. Publications, First Ser.: Nos. 90 & 98). Repr. of 1868 ed. Set. 55.00 (ISBN 0-404-50211-3); 28.00 ea. Vol. 1 (ISBN 0-404-50190-7). Vol. 2 (ISBN 0-404-50198-2). AMS Pr.

--Letters & Other Documents Illustrating the Relations Between England & Germany at the Commencement of the Thirty Years War, 2 Vols. Vol. 90. 28.00 ea. (ISBN 0-384-17640-2); Vol. 98. pap. (ISBN 0-384-17645-3). Johnson Repr.

Gardiner, Samuel R., ed. see Great Britain Court of the Star Chamber.

Gardiner, Samuel R., ed. see Great Britain House Of Commons.

Gardiner, Samuel R., ed. see Great Britain House of Lords - 1624.

Gardiner, Samuel R., ed. see Hamilton, James.

Gardiner, Samuel R., tr. see Francisco De Jesus.

Gardiner, Sheila M. & Bennett, Terence. Cardiovascular Homeostasis: Intrarenal & Extrarenal Mechanisms. (Illus.). 1981. text ed. 37.50x (ISBN 0-19-261178-X). Oxford U Pr.

Gardiner, Stephen. The Evolution of the House. (Illus.). 302p. 1980. pap. 5.95 (ISBN 0-586-08257-3, Granada Publishing Limited). Academy Chi Pubs.

--Inside Architecture. (Illus.). 128p. 1983. 17.95 (ISBN 0-13-467381-6); pap. 8.95 (ISBN 0-13-467373-5). P-H.

--Letters of Stephen Gardiner. Muller, James A., ed. Repr. of 1933 ed. lib. bdg. 23.25x (ISBN 0-8371-4223-7, GALE). Greenwood.

--Obedience in Church & State: Three Political Tracts. Janelle, Pierre, ed. LC 68-19272. 1968. Repr. of 1930 ed. lib. bdg. 15.50x (ISBN 0-8371-0081-X, GABW). Greenwood.

Gardiner, V. & Dackombe, R. Geomorphological Field Manual. (Illus.). 272p. 1982. pap. text ed. 14.95x (ISBN 0-04-551062-8). Allen Unwin.

Gardiner, W. C. Rates & Mechanisms of Chemical Reactions. 1969. pap. 21.95 (ISBN 0-8053-3101-8). Benjamin-Cummings.

Gardiner, W. C., ed. Combustion Chemistry. (Illus.). 550p. 1984. 57.50 (ISBN 0-387-90963-X). Springer-Verlag.

Gardiner, W. Lambert. The Psychology of Teaching. LC 78-32090. 1979. pap. text ed. 16.00 pub net (ISBN 0-8185-0290-8). Brooks-Cole.

Gardiner, W. N. City on the River. 24p. (Orig.). 1985. pap. 5.00x (ISBN 0-317-27388-4). Alpine Pubns.

Garding, L. Encounter with Mathematics. LC 76-54765. 280p. 1977. 28.50 (ISBN 0-387-90229-5). Springer-Verlag.

Gardini, Maria. The Secrets of the Hand. (Illus.). 160p. 1985. pap. 12.95 (ISBN 0-02-011450-8, Collier). Macmillan.

Gardinier, David E. Historical Dictionary of Gabon. LC 81-5290. (African Historical Dictionaries Ser.: No. 30). 284p. 1981. 20.00 (ISBN 0-8108-1435-8). Scarecrow.

Gardiol, Fred. An Introduction to Microwaves. LC 83-72774. (Illus.). 400p. 1983. 50.00 (ISBN 0-89006-134-3). Artech Hse.

Gardner. Differential Oral Diagnosis of Systemic Diseases. 316p. 1970. 18.50 (ISBN 0-7236-0254-9). PSG Pub Co.

--Learning & Behavior Characteristics of Exceptional Children & Youth: A Humanistic Behavioral Approach. 1985. 32.29 (ISBN 0-205-05586-9, 225586). Allyn.

--Mishkat ul-Anwar. pap. 3.75 (ISBN 0-686-18619-2). Kazi Pubns.

--Programmed Real Estate. 1984. text ed. 11.95 (ISBN 0-538-21700-6, U70). SW Pub.

Gardner & Jewler. College Is Only the Beginning: A Student Guide to Higher Education. 352p. 1984. write for info (ISBN 0-534-04275-9). Wadsworth Pub.

Gardner & Morris. Price Guide to Metal Toys. (Illus.). 1981. 39.50 (ISBN 0-902028-92-8). Apollo.

Gardner, A. Synesius of Cyrene: Philosopher & Bishop. 1977. lib. bdg. 59.95 (ISBN 0-8490-2697-0). Gordon Pr.

Gardner, A. C. & Creelman, W. G. Navigation for School & College. 2nd ed. 263p. 1976. 18.50x (ISBN 0-85174-236-X). Sheridan.

Gardner, A. L., jt. ed. see Wilson, D. E.

Gardner, A. Ward. Good Housekeeping Dictionary of Symptoms. 256p. 1982. pap. 2.95 (ISBN 0-441-29822-2). Ace Bks.

Gardner, A. Ward, ed. Current Approaches to Occupational Health, Vol. 2. (Illus.). 416p. 1982. text ed. 41.50 (ISBN 0-7236-0618-8). PSG Pub Co.

Gardner, Adelaide. Meditation: A Practical Study. LC 68-5856. 1968. pap. 2.95 (ISBN 0-8356-0105-6, Quest). Theos Pub Hse.

Gardner, Albert C. Practical LCP: A Direct Approach to Structured Programming. (Illus.). 256p. 1982. 32.50x (ISBN 0-07-084561-1). McGraw.

Gardner, Albert T. Yankee Stonecutters. facs. ed. LC 68-58790. (Essay Index Reprint Ser). 1945. 21.00 (ISBN 0-8369-0114-2). Ayer Co Pubs.

Gardner, Alexander. Gardner's Photographic Sketch Book of the Civil War. (Illus.). 15.75 (ISBN 0-8446-0104-7). Peter Smith.

--Photographic Sketchbook of the Civil War. (Orig.). 1959. pap. 7.95 (ISBN 0-486-22731-6). Dover.

Gardner, Alfred L. The Systematics of the Genus Didelphis (Marsupialia: Didelphidae) in North & Middle America. (Special Publications: No. 4). (Illus.). 81p. (Orig.). 1973. pap. 4.00 (ISBN 0-89672-029-2). Tex Tech Pr.

Gardner, Alice. Julian, Philosopher & Emperor. LC 73-14444. (Heroes of the Nations Ser.). Repr. of 1895 ed. 30.00 (ISBN 0-404-58262-1). AMS Pr.

--Theodore of Studium, His Life & Times 759-826. 1905. 19.50 (ISBN 0-8337-1280-2). B Franklin.

Gardner, Allen H. Primer on Planning an Estate. 1981. pap. 15.95 (ISBN 0-686-84884-5). Lerner Law.

Gardner, Alvin F. Dental Examination Review Book. 6th ed. 1983. pap. text ed. 26.50 (ISBN 0-87488-429-2). Med Exam.

--Pathology of Oral Manifestations of Systematic Diseases. 1972. 34.95x (ISBN 0-02-845120-1). Hafner.

--Synopsis of Pathology for the Allied Health Professions. 480p. 1979. 48.00x (ISBN 0-398-03884-8). C C Thomas.

Gardner, Alvin F., jt. auth. see McGregor, Ian P.

Gardner, Alvin f., ed. see Joyce, Joan M.

Gardner, Alvin F., ed. see Kelsey, Charles A.

Gardner, Alvin F., ed. see Lauer, Gary.

Gardner, Alvin F., ed. see Robertson, Caroline E.

Gardner, Alvin F., ed. see Strum, Williamson B.

Gardner, Alvjn F., ed. see Lager, Eric & Zwerling, Isreal.

Gardner, Andrew. The Artist's Silkscreen Manual. (Illus.). 48p. 1984. 7.95 (ISBN 0-399-50805-8, G&D). Putnam Pub Group.

Gardner, Arthur. English Medieval Sculpture. LC 78-171421. (Illus.). 351p. 1973. Repr. of 1951 ed. 45.00 (ISBN 0-87817-110-X). Hacker.

Gardner, Augustus K. Conjugal Sins Against the Laws of Life & Health: Their Effects Upon the Father, Mother & Child. LC 73-20624. (Sex, Marriage & Society Ser.). 244p. 1974. Repr. of 1870 ed. 21.00x (ISBN 0-405-05800-4). Ayer Co Pubs.

Gardner, Averil. Angus Wilson. (English Author Ser.). 1985. lib. bdg. 15.95 (ISBN 0-8057-6891-2, Twayne). G K Hall.

Gardner, Averil, jt. auth. see Gardner, Philip.

Gardner, Beau. Guess What? LC 85-242. (Illus.). (ps-3). 1985. 13.00 (ISBN 0-688-04982-6); PLB 12.88 (ISBN 0-688-04983-4). Lothrop.

--The Turn About, Think About, Look About Book. LC 80-12885. (Illus.). 32p. (gr. k-6). 1980. 10.00 (ISBN 0-688-41969-0); PLB 10.88 (ISBN 0-688-51969-5). Lothrop.

Gardner, Benjamin F. Black. facsimile ed. LC 74-178472. (Black Heritage Library Collection). Repr. of 1933 ed. 12.00 (ISBN 0-8369-8921-X). Ayer Co Pubs.

Gardner, Bernard, jt. ed. see Alfonso, Antonio E.

Gardner, Bruce L. The Governing of Agriculture: Studies in Government & Public Policy. (Illus.). xii, 148p. 1981. pap. 9.95x (ISBN 0-7006-0215-1). U Pr of KS.

Gardner, Bruce L. & Richardson, James W., eds. Consensus & Conflict in U. S. Agriculture: Perspectives from the National Farm Summit. LC 79-7412. 292p. 1980. 17.00x (ISBN 0-89096-084-4); pap. 7.95 (ISBN 0-89096-085-2). Tex A&M Univ Pr.

Gardner, C., jt. auth. see Maycock, J. E.

Gardner, Charles. British Aircraft Corporation: A History. (Illus.). 320p. 1981. 35.00 (ISBN 0-7134-3815-0, Pub. by Batsford England). David & Charles.

--Vision & Vesture: A Study of William Blake in Modern Thought. LC 73-15646. 1916. lib. bdg. 20.00 (ISBN 0-8414-4470-6). Folcroft.

--William Blake. LC 76-118001. (Studies in Blake, No. 3). 1970. Repr. of 1919 ed. lib. bdg. 49.95x (ISBN 0-8383-1056-7). Haskell.

--William Blake: The Man. LC 79-153324. Repr. of 1919 ed. 9.00 (ISBN 0-404-07906-7). AMS Pr.

--William Blake: The Man. 1919. lib. bdg. 8.95 (ISBN 0-8414-4634-2). Folcroft.

Gardner, Charles S. Chinese Traditional Historiography. rev. ed. LC 38-13532. (Historical Monographs Ser: No. 11). 1938. 10.00x (ISBN 0-674-12550-9). Harvard U Pr.

--Union List of Selected Western Books on China in American Libraries. 2nd ed. LC 70-126771. (Bibliography & Reference Ser.: No. 345). 1970. Repr. of 1938 ed. 20.50 (ISBN 0-8337-1281-0). B Franklin.

Gardner, Clifford L. Black Caesar, Pirate. LC 80-82373. (Illus.). 96p. (gr. 4 up). 1980. 6.95 (ISBN 0-931948-09-6). Peachtree Pubs.

Gardner, Clinton C. Letters to the Third Millennium: An Experiment in East-West Communication. LC 81-12689. 272p. 1981. 12.95 (ISBN 0-912148-11-X); pap. 7.95 (ISBN 0-912148-12-8). Argo Bks.

Gardner, D., jt. ed. see Andreasen, A.

Gardner, Dame H. Religion & Literature. 1983. pap. text ed. 9.95x (ISBN 0-19-812824-X). Oxford U Pr.

Gardner, Daniel K. Chu-Hsi & the Ta-hsueh: Neo-Confucian Reflection on the Confucian Canon. (Harvard East Asian Monographs: No. 118). 300p. 1985. text ed. 20.00x (ISBN 0-674-13065-0, Pub. by Coun East Asian Stud). Harvard U Pr.

Gardner, David, jt. ed. see Thomas, Howard.

Gardner, David A. & Gardner, Marianne L. Apple BASIC Made Easy. (Illus.). 224p. 1984. text ed. 21.95 (ISBN 0-13-038928-5); pap. 15.95 (ISBN 0-13-038910-2). P-H.

--Commodore 64 BASIC Made Easy. (Illus.). 256p. 1985. text ed. 19.95 (ISBN 0-13-152067-9); pap. text ed. 14.94 (ISBN 0-13-152059-8). P-H.

--VIC-20 BASIC Made Easy. (Illus.). 256p. 1984. text ed. 19.95 (ISBN 0-13-941980-2); pap. text ed. 14.95 (ISBN 0-13-941972-1). P-H.

Gardner, David C. & Beatty, Grace J. Dissertation Proposal Guidebook: How to Prepare a Research Proposal & Get It Accepted. (Illus.). 112p. 1980. 9.50x (ISBN 0-398-04086-9); pap. 6.75x (ISBN 0-398-04087-7). C C Thomas.

--Stop Stress & Aging Now: The Methuselah Manual. LC 84-72980. (Illus.). 353p. (Orig.). 1985. pap. 12.95 (ISBN 0-9613999-9-6). ATRA.

Gardner, David C., et al. Career & Vocational Education for Mildly Learning Handicapped & Disadvantaged Youth. (Illus.). 222p. 1984. 18.75x (ISBN 0-398-04818-5). C C Thomas.

Gardner, David M. Success & Succession: Survival in the Awning Custom Products Industry. 80p. 30.00 (ISBN 0-318-01561-7, 21090). Indus Fabrics.

Gardner, David M. & Belk, Russell W., eds. A Basic Bibliography on Experimental Design in Marketing. LC 80-19563. (Bibliography Ser.: No. 37). 59p. 1980. pap. 6.00 (ISBN 0-87757-142-2). Am Mktg.

Gardner, David M. & Winter, Frederick W., eds. Proceedings of the 11th Paul D. Converse Symposium. LC 81-22920. (Illus.). 123p. (Orig.). 1982. pap. text ed. 8.00 (ISBN 0-87757-155-4). Am Mktg.

Gardner, David P. The California Oath Controversy. LC 67-16840. 1967. 28.50x (ISBN 0-520-00455-8). U of Cal Pr.

Gardner, Debbie. Survive: Don't Be a Victim. 112p. (Orig.). 1984. pap. text ed. 6.95 (ISBN 0-446-38061-X). Warner Bks.

Gardner, Deborah J., ed. New York Art Guide. 2nd ed. (Illus.). 128p. (Orig.). 1985. pap. 6.95 (ISBN 0-317-13161-3, Pub. by Art Guide Pubns England). R Silver.

Gardner, Delbert R. An Idle Singer & His Audience: A Study of William Morris's Poetric Reputation in England, 1858-1900. (Studies in English Literature: No. 92). 135p. 1975. text ed. 16.00x (ISBN 0-686-22603-8). Mouton.

Gardner, Dewey D., ed. Bibliography of Theses & Dissertations Relevant to Pharmacy Administration 1970-1974. 1976. 5.00 (ISBN 0-937526-01-0). Am Assn Coll Pharm.

Gardner, Donald, tr. see Paz, Octavio.

Gardner, Dudley. Angel with a Bushy Beard. 1980. pap. 8.95x (ISBN 0-7152-0425-4). Outlook.

Gardner, E. Saint Catherine of Siena: A Study in the Religion, Literature & History of the Fourteenth Century in Italy. 1976. lib. bdg. 59.95 (ISBN 0-8490-2557-5). Gordon Pr.

--The Story of Florence. 1976. lib. bdg. 59.95 (ISBN 0-8490-2679-2). Gordon Pr.

Gardner, E. A. Art of Greece. LC 74-84546. (Illus.). 1975. Repr. of 1925 ed. lib. bdg. 22.50 (ISBN 0-8154-0503-0). Cooper Sq.

Gardner, E. Clinton. Biblical Faith & Social Ethics. 1960. text ed. 21.50 scp (ISBN 0-06-042240-8, HarpC). Har-Row.

--The Midway Group of Texas. Bd. with The Coral Fauna of the Midway Eocene of Texas. Vaughn, T. W. & Popenoe, W. R.. (Illus.). 403p. 1933. pap. write for info. (BULL 3301). Bur Econ Geology.

Gardner, J. & Gardner, R., eds. Antiques Directory, 1985-1986: New York & Connecticut. LC 84-70342. 148p. 1985. pap. 4.95 (ISBN 0-933011-01-6). Abbotsford Pr.

Gardner, J., jt. ed. see Klopper, A.

Gardner, J. D., ed. Highway Truck Collision Analysis. 1982. 20.00 (H00237). ASME.

Gardner, J. Starkie. English Ironwork of the Seventeenth & Eighteenth Centuries. LC 69-16319. (Illus.). Repr. of 1911 ed. 33.00 (ISBN 0-405-08551-6, Blom Pubns.). Ayer Co Pubs.

Gardner, Jack & Purcell, L. Edward, eds. Suggested State Legislation, 1982. Council of State Governments. 1982. pap. 15.00 (ISBN 0-87292-022-4). Coun State Govts.

Gardner, Jack I. Gambling: A Guide to Information Sources. LC 79-23797. (Sports, Games, & Pastimes Information Guide Ser.: Vol. 8). 1980. 60.00x (ISBN 0-8103-1229-8). Gale.

Gardner, Jack L. & Purcell, L. Edward, eds. The Book of the States, 1982-83. 750p. 1982. 35.00 (ISBN 0-87292-025-9). Coun State Govts.

--State Administrative Officials: 1981-82. 288p. (Orig.). 1982. pap. 12.00 (ISBN 0-87292-021-6). Coun State Govts.

--State Elective Officials & the Legislatures 1981-82: 1981-1982. 172p. (Orig.). 1981. pap. 12.00 (ISBN 0-87292-018-6). Coun State Govts.

Gardner, James. Illustrated Soccer Dictionary for Young People. (Illus.). 125p. (gr. 4 up). 1978. pap. 2.50 (ISBN 0-13-451146-8, Pub. by Treehouse). P-H.

Gardner, James A. Legal Imperialism: American Lawyers & Foreign Aid in Latin America. 416p. 1981. 27.50x (ISBN 0-299-08130-3). U of Wis Pr.

Gardner, James B. & Purdy, J. Gerry. Computerized Running Training Programs. LC 74-110485. (Orig.). 1970. pap. 8.00 (ISBN 0-911520-00-7). Tafnews.

Gardner, James B. & Adams, George R., eds. Ordinary People & Everyday Life: Perspectives on the New Social History. 1983. text ed. 16.00 (ISBN 0-910050-66-X). AASLH Pr.

Gardner, James E. Helping Employees Develop Job Skill: A Casebook of Training Approaches. LC 76-44483. 194p. 1976. 17.50 (ISBN 0-87179-227-3). BNA.

--Safety Training for the Supervisor. 3rd ed. LC 78-52505. 1979. pap. text ed. 9.95 (ISBN 0-201-03090-X). Addison-Wesley.

--Training Interventions in Job Skill Development. LC 80-23810. (Illus.). 224p. 1981. text ed. 16.95 (ISBN 0-201-03097-7). Addison-Wesley.

--Training the New Supervisor. (Illus.). 1980. 15.95 (ISBN 0-8144-5564-6). AMACOM.

Gardner, James F. & Chapman, Michael S. Staff Development in Mental Retardation Services: A Practical Manual. LC 85-5650. 270p. (Orig.). 1985. pap. text ed. 19.95 (ISBN 0-933716-48-6, 486). P H Brookes.

Gardner, James F., et al, eds. Program Issues in Developmental Disabilities: A Resource Manual for Surveyors & Reviewers. LC 80-12555. (Illus.). 176p. (Orig.). 1980. pap. text ed. 16.95 (ISBN 0-933716-05-2, 052). P H Brookes.

Gardner, James H, ed. Technology & the Future of U. S. Industry in World Competition. (ITT Key Issues Lecture Ser.). 112p. 1985. pap. write for info. (ISBN 0-932431-03-8). White River.

Gardner, Jane, ed. see Jonson, Ben.

Gardner, Jane F., tr. see Caesar, Gaius J.

Gardner, Janette C. Annotated Bibliography of Florida Fiction, 1801-1980. LC 82-83598. 238p. 1983. limited ed 25.00x (ISBN 0-9609804-0-7). Little Bayou.

Gardner, Jeffery J. Resource Notebook on Planning. 155p. 1979. 15.00 (ISBN 0-318-16099-4). OMS.

Gardner, Jerry G. Contract Food Service-Vending. LC 73-76359. 176p. 1973. 17.95 (ISBN 0-8436-0568-5). Van Nos Reinhold.

Gardner, Johann V. Aljeksjej Theodorovich L'vov-director Imperatorskoj pridvornoj pevcheskoj kapelli i dukhovnij kompozitor. 90p. 1970. pap. 3.00 (ISBN 0-317-30387-2). Holy Trinity.

--Alliluija (Liturgijnaja), 8-mi Glasov. 1966. pap. 3.00 (ISBN 0-317-30391-0). Holy Trinity.

--Bogosluzhebncje Penije Russkoj Pravoslavnoj Tserkvi: Suschnost' Sistema I Istoria: Liturgical Chant of the Russian Orthodox Church: Its Essence, Structure & History, Vol. 1. LC 77-77086. (Illus., Orig., Rus.). 1979. text ed. 30.00 (ISBN 0-88465-008-1); pap. text ed. 25.00 (ISBN 0-686-50014-8). Holy Trinity.

--Bogosluzhebnoje Penije Russkoj Pravoslavnoj Tserkvi: Istorija, Vol. 2. LC 77-77086. (Illus.). 1981. text ed. 30.00 (ISBN 0-88465-010-3); pap. text ed. 25.00 (ISBN 0-317-30384-8). Holy Trinity.

--Bogosluzhebnoje Penije Russkoj Pravoslavnoj Tsekvi: Suschnost' Sistema I Istorija, Vol. 1. LC 77-77086. (Illus.). 1979. text ed. 30.00 (ISBN 0-88465-008-1); pap. text ed. 25.00 (ISBN 0-686-50014-8). Holy Trinity.

--Dostojino Jest', 8-mi glasov, znamennago rospjeva. 1967. pap. 3.00 (ISBN 0-317-30397-X). Holy Trinity.

Gardner, Johannes von see Von Gardner, Johann.

Gardner, John. The Art of Fiction: Notes on Craft for Young Writers. LC 83-47850. 256p. 1984. 13.95 (ISBN 0-394-50469-0). Knopf.

--The Art of Fiction: Notes on Craft for Young Writers. LC 84-40006. 256p. 1984. pap. 4.95 (ISBN 0-394-72544-1, Vin). Random.

--The Art of Living & Other Stories. LC 80-20988. (Illus.). 310p. 12.95 (ISBN 0-394-51674-5). Knopf.

--BSA Gold Star. (Super Profile). (Illus.). 56p. 1986. 9.95 (ISBN 0-85429-483-X, Pub. by G T Foulis Ltd). Interbook.

--Building Classic Small Craft. LC 76-8778. 1977. 27.50 (ISBN 0-87742-065-3). Intl Marine.

--Building Classic Small Craft, Vol. 2. LC 82-80401. (Illus.). 256p. 1984. 35.00 (ISBN 0-87742-157-9). Intl Marine.

--Chinese Politics & the Succession to Mao. (Illus.). 217p. 1982. text ed. 22.50x (ISBN 0-8419-0808-7); pap. text ed. 12.50x (ISBN 0-8419-0809-5). Holmes & Meier.

--Death & the Maiden. 1979. 9.80 (ISBN 0-89683-016-0); signed ltd. ed. 50.00 (ISBN 0-89683-017-9). New London Pr.

--Dory Book. LC 77-85409. 1978. 27.50 (ISBN 0-87742-090-4). Intl Marine.

--For Special Services. (General Ser.). 1982. lib. bdg. 13.95 (ISBN 0-8161-3477-4, Large Print Bks). G K Hall.

--For Special Services. 304p. 1985. pap. 3.50 (ISBN 0-425-05860-3). Berkley Pub.

--Frankenstein. 1979. 9.95 (ISBN 0-89683-010-1); signed ltd. ed. 60.00 (ISBN 0-89683-009-8). New London Pr.

--Freddy's Book. 1981. pap. 2.95 (ISBN 0-345-29544-7). Ballantine.

--Freddy's Book. LC 79-16681. (Illus.). 1980. 10.00 (ISBN 0-394-50920-X). Knopf.

--The Garden of Weapons. 384p. 1981. 11.95 (ISBN 0-07-022851-5). McGraw.

--Garden of Weapons. LC 83-63033. 1984. pap. 4.50 (ISBN 0-89296-097-3). Mysterious Pr.

--Icebreaker. 304p. 1985. pap. 3.50 (ISBN 0-425-06764-5). Berkley Pub.

--In the Suicide Mountains. 1980. pap. 5.95 (ISBN 0-395-29468-1). HM.

--License Renewed. (General Ser.). 1981. lib. bdg. 14.95 (ISBN 0-8161-3326-3, Large Print Bks). G K Hall.

--License Renewed. 304p. 1985. pap. 3.95 (ISBN 0-425-08633-X). Berkley Pub.

--Mickelsson's Ghosts. LC 81-48114. (Illus.). 1982. 16.95 (ISBN 0-394-50468-2). Knopf.

--Mickelsson's Ghosts. 1985. 6.95 (ISBN 0-394-72938-2, Vin). Random.

--Morale. 160p. 1980. pap. 3.45 (ISBN 0-393-00977-7). Norton.

--Nickel Mountain. 304p. 1982. pap. 3.50 (ISBN 0-345-29294-4). Ballantine.

--October Light. 1981. pap. 3.50 (ISBN 0-345-29298-7). Ballantine.

--On Becoming a Novelist. LC 82-48662. (Becoming a... Ser.). 144p. 1983. 13.41i (ISBN 0-06-014956-6, HarpT). Har-Row.

--On Becoming a Novelist. LC 82-48662. 176p. 1984. pap. 5.72 (ISBN 0-06-091126-3, CN 1126, CN). Har-Row.

--Role of Honor. (James Bond Ser.). 304p. 1984. 11.95 (ISBN 0-399-12912-X, Putnam). Putnam Pub Group.

--Role of Honor. (James Bond Ser.). 1985. lib. bdg. 15.95 (ISBN 0-8161-3850-8, Large Print Bks). G K Hall.

--Role of Honor. 304p. 1985. pap. 3.95 (ISBN 0-425-07671-7). Berkley Pub.

--Rumpelstiltskin. 1979. 9.95 (ISBN 0-89683-012-8); signed ltd. ed. 60.00 (ISBN 0-89683-011-X). New London Pr.

--The Secret Generations. 1985. 16.95 (ISBN 0-317-20680-X). Putnam Pub Group.

--The Secret Generations. 384p. 1985. 17.95 (ISBN 0-399-13037-3). Putnam Pub Group.

--The Sunlight Dialogues. 1982. pap. 4.95 (ISBN 0-345-30492-6). Ballantine.

--The Temptation Game. signed ltd. ed. 45.00 (ISBN 0-686-78138-4). New London Pr.

--Vlemk the Box-Painter. LC 79-91630. (Illus.). 1979. 15.00 (ISBN 0-935716-01-7). Lord John.

--The Werewolf Trace. (General Ser.). 1978. lib. bdg. 12.50 (ISBN 0-8161-6610-2, Large Print Bks). G K Hall.

--William Wilson. 1979. 9.95 (ISBN 0-89683-008-X); signed ltd. ed. 60.00 (ISBN 0-89683-007-1). New London Pr.

--The Wreckage of Agathon. (Obelisk Ser.). 288p. 1985. pap. 8.95 (ISBN 0-525-48180-X, 0869-260). Dutton.

Gardner, John see Carter, Judith Q.

Gardner, John, ed. Best American Short Stories Nineteen Eighty-Two. 1982. 14.95 (ISBN 0-395-32207-3). HM.

Gardner, John & Rosenberg, L. M., eds. MSS: Spring 1981. 152p. 1982. ltd. ed. 25.00 (ISBN 0-939722-12-7). Pressworks.

Gardner, John & Maier, John, trs. Gilgamesh. LC 84-47508. (Illus.). 320p. 1984. 18.95 (ISBN 0-394-53771-8). Knopf.

Gardner, John & Maier, John R., trs. Gilgamesh. 1985. pap. 9.95 (ISBN 0-394-74089-0, Vin). Random.

Gardner, John, tr. see Itaya, Kikuo.

Gardner, John, et al. In Praise of What Persists. Berg, Stephen, ed. LC 81-47651. 304p. 1984. pap. 6.68 (ISBN 0-06-091123-9, CN 1123, CN). Har-Row.

Gardner, John C. The Alliterative Morte Arthure, The Owl & the Nightingale, & Five Other Middle English Poems: In a Modernized Version with Comments on the Poems & Notes. LC 73-7728. (Arcturus Books Paperbacks). 310p. 1973. pap. 10.95 (ISBN 0-8093-0648-4). S Ill U Pr.

--Construction of Christian Poetry in Old English. LC 74-28475. (Literary Structures Ser). 159p. 1975. 8.95x (ISBN 0-8093-0705-7). S Ill U Pr.

--The Construction of the Wakefield Cycle. LC 74-5191. (Literary Structures Ser.). 173p. 1974. 8.95x (ISBN 0-8093-0668-9). S Ill U Pr.

--Grendel. 1975. pap. 2.25 (ISBN 0-345-28865-3). Ballantine.

--Grendel. (Illus.). 1971. 12.95 (ISBN 0-394-47143-1). Knopf.

--The Life & Times of Chaucer. 1977. 22.50 (ISBN 0-394-49317-6). Knopf.

--The Life & Times of Chaucer. (YA) 1978. pap. 5.95 (ISBN 0-394-72500-X, Vin). Random.

--Morte D'Arthur Notes. (Orig.). 1967. pap. 2.75 (ISBN 0-8220-0726-6). Cliffs.

--Nickel Mountain. 1973. 15.95 (ISBN 0-394-48883-0). Knopf.

--On Moral Fiction. LC 77-20409. 1978. pap. 7.95x (ISBN 0-465-05226-6, TB-5069). Basic.

--The Poetry of Chaucer. LC 76-22713. 445p. 1978. pap. 12.95x (ISBN 0-8093-0871-1). S Ill U Pr.

--Sir Gawain & the Green Knight Notes. (Orig.). 1967. pap. 2.75 (ISBN 0-8220-0515-8). Cliffs.

--The Sunlight Dialogues. 1973. pap. 1.95 (ISBN 0-345-23768-4). Ballantine.

Gardner, John F. A Book of Nature Activities. (gr. 4-8). 1967. pap. text ed. 0.50x (ISBN 0-8134-1009-6, 1009). Interstate.

--The Experience of Knowledge. 35p. 1978. pap. 1.50 (ISBN 0-913098-25-6). Myrin Institute.

--Love & the Illusion of Love. 1976. pap. 1.50 (ISBN 0-913098-12-4). Myrin Institute.

--Melville's Vision of America: A New Interpretation of Moby Dick. LC 77-80051. (Illus.). 47p. 1977. pap. 1.50 (ISBN 0-913098-07-8). Myrin Institute.

--The Poverty of a Rich Society. 32p. 1976. pap. 1.50 (ISBN 0-913098-09-4). Myrin Institute.

--The Secret of Peace & the Environmental Crisis. 40p. 1978. pap. 1.50 (ISBN 0-913098-15-9). Myrin Institute.

--Towards a Truly Public Education. 29p. 1977. pap. 1.50 (ISBN 0-913098-03-5). Myrin Institute.

Gardner, John F., ed. see Natural Science Centers Conference 1974, Nashville, Tennessee.

Gardner, John W. Excellence. rev. ed. 1984. 12.95 (ISBN 0-393-01848-2). Norton.

--Self-Renewal. rev. ed. 1981. 12.95 (ISBN 0-393-01486-X). Norton.

--Self-Renewal: The Individual & the Innovative Society. 168p. 1983. pap. 5.95 (ISBN 0-393-30112-5). Norton.

Gardner, John W. & Reese, Francesca G., eds. Quotations of Wit & Wisdom. 1980. pap. 6.95 (ISBN 0-393-00943-2). Norton.

Gardner, John W., et al. Management - Who Ever Said It Would Be Easy? The Executive's Guide for Developing the Effective Organization. 120p. (Orig.). 1983. pap. 7.95 (ISBN 0-9612352-0-9). Harper Assocs.

Gardner, Joy. Healing Yourself. 7th, rev. ed. (Illus.). 1977. pap. 4.00 (ISBN 0-9601688-1-8). Healing Yourself.

Gardner, Joyce. Basic Writing Skills with Activities & Tests. (gr. k-6). 1978. spiral bdg. 6.50 (ISBN 0-933892-00-4). Child Focus Co.

Gardner, Joyce & La Fleur, Ida. Oral Language Continuum Book. (gr. k-3). 1975. 9.00 (ISBN 0-933892-08-X). Child Focus Co.

--Psychomotor Continuum. (gr. k-2). 1977. 7.00 (ISBN 0-933892-09-8). Child Focus Co.

Gardner, Judith & Gardner, Howard. Monographs on Infancy: An Original Anthology. LC 74-21702. 316p. 1975. Repr. 23.00x (ISBN 0-405-06472-1). Ayer Co Pubs.

Gardner, Judith, jt. ed. see Gardner, Howard.

Gardner, Judith K. Readings in Developmental Psychology. 2nd ed. 1982. pap. text ed. 14.95 (ISBN 0-316-30382-8). Little.

Gardner, Judith K. & Gardner, Howard. Studies of Play: An Original Anthology. LC 74-21429. (Classics in Child Development Ser). 198p. 1975. Repr. 19.00x (ISBN 0-405-06478-0). Ayer Co Pubs.

Gardner, Judith K. & Gardner, Howard, eds. Factors Determining Intellectual Attainment: An Original Anthology. LC 74-21406. (Classics in Child Development Ser.). 204p. 1975. Repr. 19.00x (ISBN 0-405-06458-6). Ayer Co Pubs.

--First Notes by Observant Parents. LC 74-21407. (Classics in Child Development Ser). 90p. 1975. Repr. 17.00x (ISBN 0-405-06459-4). Ayer Co Pubs.

Gardner, K., jt. ed. see Lunzer, E. A.

Gardner, Katy, jt. auth. see Birke, Lynda.

Gardner, Keith, jt. auth. see McClane, A. J.

Gardner, Keith, ed. Systems & Technology for Advanced Manufacturing. 270p. 1983. 32.00 (749). SME.

Gardner, KennCorwin H., jt. ed. see French, Alfred D.

Gardner, Kenneth D., Jr., ed. Cystic Diseases of the Kidney. LC 75-31626. (Perspectives in Nephrology & Hypertension Ser.: Vol. 4). (Illus.). pap. 50.40 (ISBN 0-317-09213-8, 2015191). Bks Demand UMI.

Gardner, Kenneth D., Jr., jt. ed. see Grantham, Jared J.

Gardner, L. I. & Amacher, P., eds. Endocrine Aspects of Malnutrition: Marasmus, Kwashiorkor & Psychosocial Deprivation. LC 73-88110. 538p. 1973. 40.00 (ISBN 0-685-48386-X). Raven.

Gardner, Laurence B., jt. auth. see Sanders, Jay H.

Gardner, Leonard. Genesis: The Teacher's Guide. 1966. pap. 6.50 (ISBN 0-8381-0401-0). United Syn Bk.

Gardner, Leonard B., ed. Automated Manufacturing-STP 862. LC 85-1243. (Illus.). 255p. 1985. text ed. 38.00 (ISBN 0-8031-0422-7, 04-862000-32). ASTM.

Gardner, Leslie, jt. auth. see Bowley, Agatha H.

Gardner, Liane. Whisper in His Ear. (Orig.). 1984. pap. 3.50 (ISBN 0-671-50348-0). PB.

Gardner, Linda. The Texas Supreme Court: An Index of Selected Sources on the Court & Its Members, 1836 to 1981. (Tarlton Legal Bibliography Ser.: No. 25). 142p. 1983. pap. 15.00 (ISBN 0-935630-08-2). U of Tex Tarlton Law Lib.

Gardner, Lionel. Further Pavement Reflections. (Writers Workshop Redbird Book Ser.). 42p. 1975. 12.00 (ISBN 0-88253-544-7); pap. text ed. 4.80 (ISBN 0-88253-543-9). Ind-US Inc.

--Pavement Relections. 6.75 (ISBN 0-89253-688-8). Ind-US Inc.

Gardner, Lloyd, ed. American Foreign Policy, Present to Past: A Narrative with Readings & Documents. LC 74-2651. (Urgent Issues in American Society Ser.). 1974. 11.95 (ISBN 0-02-911310-5). Free Pr.

Gardner, Lloyd C. A Covenant with Power: America & World Order from Wilson to Reagan. 1984. 22.95 (ISBN 0-19-503357-4). Oxford U Pr.

--Economic Aspects of New Deal Diplomacy. LC 64-14507. pap. 105.30 (ISBN 0-317-09742-3, 2005473). Bks Demand UMI.

--Imperial America: American Foreign Policy since 1898. (Illus., Orig.). 1976. pap. text ed. 10.95 (ISBN 0-15-540896-8, HC). HarBraceJ.

--Safe for Democracy: The Anglo-American Response to Revolution, 1913-1923. 1984. 25.00 (ISBN 0-19-503429-5). Oxford U Pr.

--Wilson & Revolutions: 1913-1921. LC 82-45089. 160p. (Orig.). 1982. pap. text ed. 10.25 (ISBN 0-8191-2416-8). U Pr of Amer.

Gardner, Lloyd C. & O'Neill, William L. Looking Backward: A Reintroduction to American History. (Illus.). 544p. 1974. Vol. 1. pap. text ed. 26.95 (ISBN 0-07-022842-6). McGraw.

Gardner, Lynn, ed. see Wilson, Seth.

Gardner, M., ed. see Bombaugh, Charles C.

Gardner, M., et al. Atlas of Mortality from Selected Diseases in England & Wales 1968-1978. 96p. 1984. 110.00 (ISBN 0-471-90622-0). Wiley.

Gardner, M. J. & Winter, P. D. Atlas of Cancer Mortality in England & Wales, 1968-1978, Vol. 1. Taylor, C. P. & Acheson, E. D., eds. 116p. 1983. 100.00x (ISBN 0-471-90042-7, Pub. by Wiley-Medical). Wiley.

Gardner, M. Robert. Self Inquiry. (Illus.). 156p. 1983. 12.45i (ISBN 0-316-30388-7, An Atlantic Monthly Pr Bk.). Little.

Gardner, Malcolm, et al, eds. see Bockemuhl, Jochen, et al.

Gardner, Malcolm L. & Brandes, Norman S. Group Therapy for the Adolescent. LC 72-94845. (Illus.). 173p. 1984. 20.00x (ISBN 0-87668-060-0). Aronson.

Gardner, Marianne L., jt. auth. see Gardner, David A.

Gardner, Marjorie. Forbidden Reunion. (YA) 1980. 8.95 (ISBN 0-686-73926-4, Avalon). Bouregy.

--Heart Song. 1983. 8.95 (ISBN 0-317-17582-3, Avalon). Bouregy.

Gardner, Marshall B. A Journey to the Earth's Interior. large type ed. (Illus.). 1920. pap. 7.50 (ISBN 0-910122-48-2). Amherst Pr.

Gardner, Martin. Aha! Gotcha: Paradoxes to Puzzle & Delight. (Illus.). 164p. 1982. pap. text ed. 9.95 (ISBN 0-7167-1361-6); text ed. 17.95 (ISBN 0-7167-1414-0). W H Freeman.

--Aha! Insight. LC 78-51259. (Illus.). 179p. 1978. pap. text ed. 9.95 (ISBN 0-7167-1017-X). W H Freeman.

--Codes, Ciphers & Secret Writing. 96p. 1984. pap. 2.95 (ISBN 0-486-24761-9). Dover.

--Entertaining Science Experiments with Everyday Objects. Orig. Title: Science Puzzlers. (Illus.). 128p. 1981. pap. 2.50 (ISBN 0-486-24201-3). Dover.

--Entertaining Science Experiments with Everyday Objects. (Illus.). 13.50 (ISBN 0-8446-5888-X). Peter Smith.

--Fads & Fallacies. LC 57-14907. lib. bdg. 13.50x (ISBN 0-88307-102-9). Gannon.

--Fads & Fallacies in the Name of Science. 2nd ed. Orig. Title: In the Name of Science. 363p. 1957. pap. 4.95 (ISBN 0-486-20394-8). Dover.

--The Flight of Peter Fromm. LC 73-1932. 286p. 1973. pap. 6.95 (ISBN 0-913232-77-7). W Kaufmann.

--Logic Machines & Diagrams. 2nd ed. LC 82-11157. xiv, 162p. 1983. lib. bdg. 16.00x (ISBN 0-226-28243-0); pap. 5.95 (ISBN 0-226-28244-9). U of Chicago Pr.

--The Magic Numbers of Dr. Matrix. rev. ed. LC 84-43183. (Illus.). 326p. 1985. 19.95 (ISBN 0-87975-281-5); pap. 10.95 (ISBN 0-87975-282-3). Prometheus Bks.

--Martin Gardner's New Mathematical Diversions from Scientific American. LC 83-12352. (Illus.). 254p. 1984. pap. 7.95 (ISBN 0-226-28247-3). U of Chicago Pr.

--Martin Gardner's Sixth Book of Mathematical Diversions from Scientific American. LC 83-12332. (Illus.). x, 262p. 1984. pap. 7.95 (ISBN 0-226-28250-3). U of Chicago Pr.

--Mathematical Carnival. 1975. 12.95 (ISBN 0-394-49406-7). Knopf.

--Mathematical Carnival: A New Round-up of Tantalizers & Puzzles from "Scientific American". 1977. 9.95 (ISBN 0-394-49406-7, Vin); pap. 4.95 (ISBN 0-394-72349-X). Random.

--Mathematical Circus. LC 80-6135. (Illus.). 272p. 1981. pap. 4.95 (ISBN 0-394-74712-7, V-712, Vin). Random.

--Mathematical Magic Show: More Puzzles, Games, Diversions, Illusions & Other Mathematical Sleight-of-Mind from Scientific American. (Giant Ser.). (Illus.). pap. 3.95 (ISBN 0-394-72623-5, V-623, Vin). Random.

--Mathematical Puzzles. LC 61-6142. (Illus.). (gr. 7 up). 1961. 10.95 (ISBN 0-690-52360-2). Crowell Jr Bks.

--Mathematics, Magic, & Mystery. (Illus.). 176p. 1956. pap. 3.00 (ISBN 0-486-20335-2). Dover.

--Order & Surprise. LC 83-611117. (Illus.). 396p. 1983. 20.95 (ISBN 0-87975-219-X). Prometheus Bks.

--Perplexing Puzzles & Tantalizing Teasers. (Illus., Orig.). (gr. 3-6). 1971. pap. 1.50 (ISBN 0-671-41878-5). Archway.

--Puzzles from Other Worlds: Fantastical Brainteasers from Isaac Asimov's Science Fiction Magazine. 1984. pap. 5.95 (ISBN 0-394-72140-3, Vin). Random.

--The Relativity Explosion: A Lucid Account of Why Quasars, Pulsars, Black Holes & the New Atomic Clocks Are Vindicating Einstein's Revolutionary Theory. LC 76-10588. 1976. pap. 5.95 (ISBN 0-394-72104-7, Vin). Random.

--Science Fiction Puzzle Tales. (Illus.). 128p. 1981. 10.95 (C N Potter Bks). Crown.

--Science: Good, Bad & Bogus. LC 80-84405. (Science & the Paranormal Ser.). 408p. 1981. 20.95 (ISBN 0-87975-144-4). Prometheus Bks.

--Science: Good, Bad & Bogus. 432p. 1983. pap. 3.95 (ISBN 0-380-61754-4, 61754-4, Discus). Avon.

--Unexpected Hanging & Other Mathematical Diversions. 1972. pap. 6.75 (ISBN 0-671-21425-X, Fireside). S&S.

--Wheels, Life & Other Mathematical Amusements. LC 83-11592. (Illus.). 350p. 1983. text ed. 15.95 (ISBN 0-7167-1588-0); pap. 9.95 (ISBN 0-7167-1589-9). W H Freeman.

--The Whys of a Philosophical Scrivener. LC 83-4474. 484p. 1983. 22.50 (ISBN 0-688-02063-1, Quill NY); pap. 12.95 (ISBN 0-688-02064-X). Morrow.

Gardner, Martin, ed. The Annotated "Casey at the Bat". A Collection of Ballads about the Mighty Casey. 2nd ed. LC 83-24216. (Illus.). xviii, 216p. 1984. pap. 6.95 (ISBN 0-226-28263-5). U of Chicago Pr.

--Great Essays in Science. (Great American Thinkers Ser). 1970. pap. write for info. WSP.

--The Sacred Beetle & Other Great Essays in Science. LC 84-42795. 427p. 1984. 22.95 (ISBN 0-87975-257-2). Prometheus Bks.

--Scientific American Book of Mathematical Puzzles & Diversions. 1963. pap. 5.95 (ISBN 0-671-63652-9, Fireside). S&S.

--Second Scientific American Book of Mathematical Puzzles & Diversions. 1965. pap. 6.95 (ISBN 0-671-63653-7, Fireside). S&S.

Gardner, Martin, jt. ed. see Carnap, Rudolf.

Gardner, Martin, ed. see Carroll, Lewis.

Gardner, Martin, ed. see Kordemsky, Boris A.

Gardner, Martin, ed. see Loyd, Sam.

Gardner, Mary A. The Press of Latin America: A Tentative & Selected Bibliography in Spanish & Portuguese. (Institute of Latin American Studies Guides & Bibliographies Ser.: No. 4). 44p. 1973. pap. 2.00x (ISBN 0-292-76410-3). U of Tex Pr.

Gardner, Mary R. English History in Rhyme. 59.95 (ISBN 0-8490-0112-9). Gordon Pr.

Gardner, Mary S. Public Health Nursing. Rosenkrantz, Barbara G., ed. LC 76-25664. (Public Health in America Ser.). 1977. Repr. lib. bdg. 24.50x (ISBN 0-405-09819-7). Ayer Co Pubs.

Gardner, Michael, ed. see Cook, Paul J.

Gardner, Michael, ed. see Tinkham, Michael.

Gardner, Michael L. Medical Acid-Base Balance. 1978. pap. text ed. 14.50 (ISBN 0-7216-0728-4, Pub. by Bailliere-Tindall). Saunders.

Gardner, Monica M. Adam Mickiewicz: The National Poet of Poland. LC 74-135807. (Eastern Europe Collection Ser). 1970-71. Repr. of 1911 ed. 19.00 (ISBN 0-405-02749-4). Ayer Co Pubs.

Gardner, Morrison F. Test of Visual Perceptual Skills (Non-Motor) (TVPS) (Orig.). 1982. 55.00 (ISBN 0-87562-073-6). Spec Child.

Gardner, Murray B., et al. Physiological Effects of Air Pollution. 222p. 1973. text ed. 29.75x (ISBN 0-8422-7137-6). Irvington.

Gardner, N. L., jt. auth. see Setchell, W. A.

Gardner, Nancy & Gardner, Esmond, eds. Five Great Healers Speak Here. LC 82-50164. (Illus.). 138p. (Orig.). 1982. pap. 6.25 (ISBN 0-8356-0567-1, Quest). Theos Pub Hse.

Gardner, Nancy B. Fig Tree. 1965. 8.95 (ISBN 0-8392-1145-7). Astor-Honor.

Gardner, P. Catalog of Greek Coins in the British Museum-Syria. (Illus.). 1982. Repr. of 1878 ed. lib. bdg. 30.00 (ISBN 0-942666-21-6). S J Durst.

Gardner, P. S., ed. see Symposium Held by European Group for Rapid Virus Diagnosis, London, Jan. 1978.

Gardner, Paul F. Glass of Frederick Carder. 1976. 22.50 (ISBN 0-517-50440-5). Crown.

Gardner, Paul V. Frederick Carder: Portrait of a Glassmaker. LC 84-7201. (Illus.). 120p. (Orig.). 1985. pap. text ed. 25.00 (ISBN 0-87290-111-4). Corning.

--Glass. Gilchrist, Brenda, ed. LC 78-62735. (Smithsonian Illustrated Library of Antiques). (Illus.). 128p. (Orig.). 1979. 9.95 (ISBN 0-910503-25-7). Cooper-Hewitt Museum.

Gardner, Percy. History of Ancient Coinage: B. C. 700-300. LC 74-77879. (Illus.). 492p. 1975. Repr. 20.00 (ISBN 0-89005-007-4). Ares.

--New Chapters in Greek Art. LC 73-149658. (BCL Ser.: I). Repr. of 1926 ed. 29.50 (ISBN 0-404-02679-6). AMS Pr.

--Principles of Christian Art. 1977. lib. bdg. 59.95 (ISBN 0-8490-2479-X). Gordon Pr.

--Samos & Samian Coins. 1985. Repr. of 1878 ed. lib. bdg. 20.00 (ISBN 0-915262-61-4). S J Durst.

Gardner, Percy, jt. auth. see Imhoof-Blumer, F. W.

Gardner, Philip. Kingsley Amis. (English Authors Ser.). 1981. lib. bdg. 13.50 (ISBN 0-8057-6809-2, Twayne). G K Hall.

Gardner, Philip & Gardner, Averil. The God Approached: A Commentary on the Poems of William Empson. 226p. 1978. 17.50x (ISBN 0-8476-6059-1). Rowman.

Gardner, Philip, ed. E. M. Forster: The Critical Heritage. (The Critical Heritage Ser). 518p. 1973. 38.50x (ISBN 0-7100-7641-X). Routledge & Kegan.

--E. M. Forster: The Critical Heritage. (The Critical Heritage Ser.). 1984. pap. 15.00 (ISBN 0-7102-0392-6). Routledge & Kegan.

Gardner, Philip, ed. see Forster, E. M.

Gardner, Philip, et al. The BBC Micro Add-On Guide. (Illus.). 160p. (Orig.). 1985. pap. 13.95 (ISBN 0-00-383009-8, Pub. by Collins England). Sheridan.

Gardner, Philip W. The Lost Elementary Schools of Victorian England: The People's Education. LC 84-9503. 320p. 1984. 38.50 (ISBN 0-7099-1156-4, Pub. by Croom Helm Ltd). Longwood Pub Group.

Gardner, Pierce & Provine, Harriet T. Manual of Acute Bacterial Infections: Early Diagnosis & Treatment. 2nd ed. (The Spiral Manual Ser.). 448p. 1984. spiral bdg. 17.95 (ISBN 0-316-30389-5). Little.

Gardner, R., jt. ed. see Gardner, J.

Gardner, Ralph. Young, Gifted & Rich. 1984. pap. 6.95 (ISBN 0-671-47046-9, Wallaby). S&S.

Gardner, Ralph D. Horatio Alger, or the American Hero Era. 20.95 (ISBN 0-89190-222-8, Pub. by Am Repr). Amereon Ltd.

Gardner, Rene, et al. Living with the Comet & Other Stories: And Other Tails. 76p. (Orig.). 1985. pap. price not set (ISBN 0-918239-01-X). Coelacanth.

Gardner, Richard. Alternative America. 275p. 1985. pap. 19.95 (ISBN 0-933342-04-7). Resources.

--Boys & Girls Book about Divorce. LC 84-2815. (Illus.). 159p. (gr. 7 up). 1983. 15.00x (ISBN 0-87668-664-1). Aronson.

--Micro-Personal-Small Business-Home Computing Directory. 265p. 1985. pap. 29.95 (ISBN 0-933342-05-5). Resources.

--The Parents Book about Divorce. 1979. pap. 3.95 (ISBN 0-553-22984-2). Bantam.

Gardner, Richard, jt. auth. see Sartori, Giovanni.

Gardner, Richard A. The Boys & Girls Book about Divorce. (Illus.). (gr. 4 up). 1971. pap. 3.50 (ISBN 0-553-25310-7). Bantam.

--The Boys & Girls Book about One Parent Families. pap. 2.95 (ISBN 0-317-13809-X). Bantam.

--The Boys & Girls Book about Stepfamilies. pap. 2.50 (ISBN 0-317-23630-X). Bantam.

--The Boys & Girls Book about Stepfamilies. (Illus.). 180p. (gr. 3-10). 1985. pap. 2.95 (ISBN 0-933812-13-2). Creative Therapeutics.

--Child Custody Litigation: A Guide for Parents & Mental Health Professionals. 275p. 1985. 18.00 (ISBN 0-933812-12-4). Creative Therapeutics.

--Dr. Gardner's Fables for Our Times. LC 80-26098. (Illus.). 125p. (gr. k-6). 1981. 10.95 (ISBN 0-933812-06-X). Creative Therapeutics.

--Dr. Gardner's Fairy Tales for Today's Children. LC 80-16187. (Illus.). 96p. (gr. 1-6). 1978. Repr. of 1974 ed. PLB 8.25 (ISBN 0-933812-02-7). Creative Therapeutics.

--Dr. Gardner's Modern Fairy Tales. LC 76-53252. (Illus.). (ps-2). 1977. PLB 7.95 (ISBN 0-89313-002-8). G F Stickley Co.

--Dr. Gardner's Modern Fairy Tales. (Illus.). 106p. (gr. 2-6). Repr. 8.25 (ISBN 0-933812-09-4). Creative Therapeutics.

--Doctor Gardner's Stories About the Real World. 1976. pap. 1.50 (ISBN 0-380-00625-1, 29025). Avon.

--Dr. Gardner's Stories About the Real World. LC 80-16542. (Illus.). 127p. (gr. k-6). 1980. Repr. of 1972 ed. PLB 8.25 (ISBN 0-933812-04-3). Creative Therapeutics.

--Dr. Gardner's Stories About the Real World, Vol. II. LC 80-16592. (Illus.). 95p. (gr. k-6). 1983. 9.95 (ISBN 0-933812-05-1). Creative Therapeutics.

--Dorothy & the Lizard of Oz. LC 80-12787. (Illus.). 108p. (gr. 1-6). 1980. 9.95 (ISBN 0-933812-03-5). Creative Therapeutics.

--Family Evaluation in Child Custody Litigation. LC 81-22144. 343p. 1982. 19.75 (ISBN 0-933812-08-6). Creative Therapeutics.

--MBD: The Family Book About Minimal Brain Dysfunction. LC 72-96533. (Illus.). 1973. 12.50x (ISBN 0-87668-057-0). Aronson.

--The Objective Diagnosis of Minimal Brain Dysfunction. LC 79-11054. 1979. text ed. 18.75 (ISBN 0-933812-00-0). Creative Therapeutics.

--Psychotherapeutic Approaches to the Resistant Child. LC 75-5591. 384p. 1975. 25.00x (ISBN 0-87668-203-4). Aronson.

--Separation Anxiety Disorder: Psychodynamics & Psychotherapy. LC 84-26348. 180p. 1985. 15.95 (ISBN 0-933812-10-8). Creative Therapeutics.

--Therapeutic Communication with Children: The Mutual Storytelling Technique in Child Psychotherapy. LC 71-155063. 1238p. 1971. 35.00x (ISBN 0-87668-042-2). Aronson.

--Understanding Children: A Parents Guide to Child Rearing. LC 79-20004. 258p. 1979. Repr. of 1973 ed. 12.50 (ISBN 0-933812-01-9). Creative Therapeutics.

Gardner, Richard K. Library Collections: Their Origin, Selection, & Development. (Library Education Ser.). 384p. 1981. text ed. 31.95 (ISBN 0-07-022850-7). McGraw.

Gardner, Richard N. Sterling-Dollar Diplomacy in Current Perspective: The Origins & the Prospects of Our International Economic Order. LC 79-26572. 1980. 39.00x (ISBN 0-231-04944-7); pap. 15.00x (ISBN 0-231-04945-5). Columbia U Pr.

Gardner, Richard N. & Glucksmann, Andre. Sovereignty & Intervention. write for info. Trilateral Comm.

Gardner, Richard S., jt. auth. see McDonough, James L.

Gardner, Rick M. Exercises for General Psychology. 264p. (Orig.). 1980. pap. text ed. 14.95x (ISBN 0-8087-0799-X, Feffer & Simons). Burgess.

Gardner, Riley W. & Moriarty, Alice. Personality Development at Preadolescence: Explorations of Structure Formation. LC 68-16371. 356p. 1968. 22.50x (ISBN 0-295-73706-9). U of Wash Pr.

Gardner, Riley W., et al. Cognitive Control: A Study of Individual Consistencies in Cognitive Behavior. (Psychological Issues Monograph: No. 4, Vol. 1, No. 4). 85p. (Orig.). 1959. text ed. 17.50 (ISBN 0-8236-1000-4). Intl Univs Pr.

--Personality Organization in Cognitive Controls & Intellectual Abilities. (Psychological Issues Monograph: No. 8, Vol. 2, No. 4). 148p. (Orig.). 1961. text ed. 17.50 (ISBN 0-8236-4080-9). Intl Univs Pr.

Gardner, Rita & Scoging, Helen. Mega-Geomorphology. (Illus.). 1983. 42.00x (ISBN 0-19-823244-6). Oxford U Pr.

Gardner, Rita, jt. auth. see Gondie, Andrew.

Gardner, Robert. Kitchen Chemistry: Science Experiments to Do at Home. LC 82-60639. (Illus.). 128p. (gr. 5 up). 1982. lib. bdg. 9.29 (ISBN 0-671-42102-6). Messner.

--Science around the House. (Illus.). 128p. (gr. 3-7). 1985. 9.29 (ISBN 0-671-54663-5). Messner.

--Thank God It's Friday. LC 78-65836. 1978. pap. 4.95 (ISBN 0-8323-0310-0). Binford.

--This Is the Way It Works: A Collection of Machines. LC 79-7493. (Illus.). 1980. 9.95a (ISBN 0-385-14697-3). Doubleday.

--Water, the Life Sustaining Resource. LC 82-2231. 192p. (gr. 7 up). 1982. PLB 9.79 (ISBN 0-671-43655-4). Messner.

--The Whale Watchers' Guide. LC 83-17425. 170p. (YA) (gr. 7 up). 1984. lib. bdg. 10.79 (ISBN 0-671-45811-6); pap. 5.95 (ISBN 0-671-49807-X). Messner.

--The Young Athlete's Manual. (Illus.). 160p. (gr. 7 up). 1985. 9.97 (ISBN 0-671-49369-8). Messner.

Gardner, Robert E., jt. auth. see Kramer, Howard C.

Gardner, Robert K. Gardner's Guide to Atlanta. (Illus.). 78p. 1973. pap. 1.75 (ISBN 0-9600260-1-0). Collegiate Visitors.

Gardner, Robert W., jt. auth. see Palmore, James A.

Gardner, Robert W., jt. auth. see Wright, Paul.

Gardner, Robert W., jt. ed. see De Jong, Gordon F.

Gardner, Roberta. The Bed & Breakfast Guide: East Coast. 128p. 1984. pap. 9.95 (ISBN 0-671-50845-8). S&S.

Gardner, Roberta, et al. Country Inns of America: Lower New England. 1985. pap. 10.95 (ISBN 0-03-003319-5, Owl Bks). HR&W.

--Country Inns of America: Upper New England. 1985. pap. 10.95 (ISBN 0-03-003322-5, Owl Bks). HR&W.

Gardner, Roberta H. Country Inns of America: The Great Lakes. LC 81-1618. (Illus.). 96p. 1981. pap. 8.95 (ISBN 0-03-059159-7, Owl Bks.). HR&W.

Gardner, Roberta H., ed. see Andrews, Peter.

Gardner, Roberta H., tr. see Andrews, Peter.

Gardner, Rosalyn & Green, Marion. A Brief Description of Middle French Syntax. (Studies in the Romance Languages & Literatures: No. 29). xiv, 153p. 1958. pap. 9.00x (ISBN 0-8078-9029-4). U of NC Pr.

Gardner, Russell, Jr., jt. auth. see O'Neill, George W.

Gardner, Ruth. Graphology Student's Workbook. 2nd ed. (Illus.). 85p. 1975. 4.95 (ISBN 0-87542-250-0). Llewellyn Pubns.

--Judo for the Gentle Woman. LC 74-147175. (Illus.). 1971. pap. 3.25 (ISBN 0-8048-0660-8). C E Tuttle.

Gardner, Ruth, jt. auth. see Inman, Billie A.

Gardner, Sandra. Six Who Dared. LC 81-14040. (A Jem Bks.). (Illus.). 64p. (Teens reading on a 2-3rd grade level). 1981. lib. bdg. 9.29 (ISBN 0-671-43513-2). Messner.

--Street Gangs. (Single Titles Ser.). (Illus.). 128p. (YA) (gr. 7 up). PLB 8.90 (ISBN 0-531-04666-4). Watts.

Gardner, Sandra & Rosenberg, Gary. Teenage Suicide. 160p. (gr. 7 up). 1985. 9.79 (ISBN 0-671-49975-0). Messner.

Gardner, Sarah M. Quaker Idyls. LC 70-110193. (Short Story Index Reprint Ser.). 1894. 17.00 (ISBN 0-8369-3344-3). Ayer Co Pubs.

Gardner, Scott. Stop Me Before I Write More. (Illus.). 104p. (Orig.). 1984. 14.95 (ISBN 0-9614112-1-X); pap. 6.95 (ISBN 0-9614112-0-1). Draydel Pr.

Gardner, Sheldon, jt. auth. see Stevens, Gwendolyn.

Gardner, Sylvana. When Sunday Comes. LC 82-10935. 46p. 1983. 14.50 (ISBN 0-7022-1822-7); pap. 7.50 (ISBN 0-7022-1832-4). U of Queensland Pr.

Gardner, Thomas J. Criminal Evidence: Principles, Cases & Readings. (Criminal Justice Ser.). (Illus.). 1978. text ed. 25.95 (ISBN 0-8299-0148-5); instrs.' maual avail. (ISBN 0-8299-0589-8). West Pub.

--Criminal Law Principles & Cases. 3rd ed. (Illus.). 550p. 1985. text ed. 22.95 (ISBN 0-314-85237-9). West Pub.

Gardner, Thomas J. & Manian, Victor. Criminal Law. 2nd ed. (Criminal Justice Ser.). (Illus.). 500p. 1980. text ed. 26.95 (ISBN 0-8299-0320-8). West Pub.

Gardner, Thomas J. & Victor, M. Principles & Cases of the Law of Arrest, Search, & Seizure. (Illus.). 552p. 1974. pap. text ed. 28.20 (ISBN 0-07-022837-X). McGraw.

Gardner, V. R. Principles of Horticultural Production. 583p. 1966. text ed. 18.50x (ISBN 0-87013-095-1). Mich St U Pr.

Gardner, Virginia. Friend & Lover: The Life of Louise Bryant. (Illus.). 380p. 1983. 18.95 (ISBN 0-8180-0233-6). Horizon.

Gardner, Virginia, jt. ed. see Gardner, George.

Gardner, Virginia & Edwards, Myrtle S.pref. by. Cemeteries of Chester, New York. LC 77-12179. (Illus.). 142p. 1977. pap. 7.95 (ISBN 0-912526-20-3). Lib Res.

Gardner, W. H. Language, Literature, & Human Values. 1977. Repr. of 1966 ed. lib. bdg. 10.00 (ISBN 0-8482-0978-8). Norwood Edns.

--Some Thoughts on the Mayor of Casterbridge. LC 74-16131. 1930. lib. bdg. 8.00 (ISBN 0-8414-4554-0). Folcroft.

--Some Thoughts on the Mayor of Casterbridge. 52p. 1980. Repr. of 1930 ed. lib. bdg. 10.00 (ISBN 0-8492-4959-7). R West.

Gardner, W. H., ed. see Hopkins, Gerard M.

Gardner, Walter M. The British Coal-Tar Industry. Cohen, I. Bernard, ed. LC 80-2122. (Development of Science Ser.). (Illus.). 1981. lib. bdg. 40.00x (ISBN 0-405-13845-8). Ayer Co Pubs.

Gardner, Ward. New Advanced First Aid. 3rd ed. 1985. 8.50 (ISBN 0-7236-0803-2). PSG Pub Co.

Gardner, Warren H. Laryngectomee Speech & Rehabilitation. (Illus.). 260p. 1978. photocopy ed. 30.75x (ISBN 0-398-00643-1). C C Thomas.

--Left Handed Writing Instruction Manual. (Illus.). 1958. pap. text ed. 2.50x (ISBN 0-8134-0058-9, 58). Interstate.

--Text-Manual for Remedial Handwriting. 1966. pap. 2.95x (ISBN 0-8134-0847-4, 847). Interstate.

Gardner, William. Alphabet at Work. (Illus.). 140p. 1982. 14.95 (ISBN 0-312-02139-9). St Martin.

Gardner, William & Cooke, Edward I. Chemical Synonyms & Trade Names: A Dictionary & Commercial Handbook. 8th ed. LC 77-85232. 689p. 1978. 75.00x (ISBN 0-291-39678-X). Intl Pubns Serv.

Gardner, William B. The Prologues & Epilogues of John Dryden. 383p. Repr. of 1951 ed. 12.00x (ISBN 0-911858-14-8). Appel.

Gardner, William E., et al. Selected Case Studies in American History, 2 vols. new ed. (gr. 8-12). 1975. Vol. 1. pap. text ed. 9.88 (ISBN 0-205-04902-8, 7849028); Vol. 2. pap. text ed. 9.88 (ISBN 0-205-03771-2, 7837712); Tchrs.' Guide. Vol. 1. O.P. 3.64 (ISBN 0-205-02165-4, 7821654); Tchrs.' Guide. Vol. 2. O.P. 3.64 (ISBN 0-205-03772-0, 7837720). Allyn.

Gardner, William I. Children with Learning & Behavior Problems: A Behavior Management Approach. 2nd ed. 1978. text ed. 29.95 (ISBN 0-205-06067-6, 246067); pap. text ed. 25.36 (ISBN 0-205-06066-8, 246066). Allyn.

Gardner, William J. History of Jamaica: From Its Discovery by Christopher Columbus to the Year 1872. 510p. 1971. Repr. of 1909 ed. 37.50x (ISBN 0-7146-1938-8, F Cass Co). Biblio Dist.

Gardner, Wyland. Government Finance: National, State & Local. LC 77-3572. 1978. 28.95 (ISBN 0-13-360743-7). P-H.

Gardner-Loulan, JoAnn, et al. Periodo: Libro Para Chicas Sobre La Menstruacion. Schneider, Francisca M., tr. LC 82-10864. (Illus.). 104p. 1985. pap. 7.00 (ISBN 0-912078-71-5). Volcano Pr.

--Period. rev ed. LC 79-25897. (Illus.). 104p. 1981. pap. 6.00 (ISBN 0-912078-69-3). Volcano Pr.

Gardner-Thorpe, C., et al. Antiepileptic Drug Monitoring. 1977. text ed. 65.00x (ISBN 0-8464-0138-X). Beekman Pubs.

Gardocki, Gloria J. Utilization of Outpatient Care Resources. Cox, Klaudia, ed. (Special Report Ser.). 60p. 1983. pap. text ed. 1.75 (ISBN 0-8406-0271-5). Natl Ctr Health Stats.

Gardocki, Gloria J. & Pokras, Robert. Utilization of Short-Stay Hospitals by Persons with Heart Disease & Malignant Neoplasms. Shipp, Audrey, ed. (Ser. Thirteen: No. 52). 50p. 1981. pap. 1.75 (ISBN 0-8406-0214-6). Natl Ctr Health Stats.

Gardocki, Gloria J., et al. The National Ambulatory Medical Care Complement Survey: United States, 1980. Cox, Klaudia, ed. (Series 13: No. 77). 50p. 1984. pap. text ed. 1.95 (ISBN 0-8406-0292-8). Natl Ctr Health Stats.

Gardon, J. L. & Prane, J. W., eds. Non-Polluting Coatings & Coating Processes. LC 72-97719. 272p. 1973. 42.50x (ISBN 0-306-30729-4, Plenum Pr). Plenum Pub.

Gardon, John L., ed. see American Chemical Society.

Gardon, Margarita. En Jaque el Jabonero. 80p. 1982. pap. 6.00 (ISBN 0-686-37369-3). Edit Asol.

Gardos, George. Tardive Dyskinesia & Affective Disorders. LC 84-6166. (Clinical Insights Monograph). 96p. 1984. pap. text ed. 12.00x (ISBN 0-88048-060-2, 48-060-2). Am Psychiatric.

Garduk, Edith L. & Haggard, Ernest A. Immediate Effects on Patients of Psychoanalytic Interpretations. LC 79-186504. (Psychological Issues Monograph: No. 28, Vol. 7, No. 4). 86p. (Orig.). 1972. text ed. 17.50 (ISBN 0-8236-2530-3). Intl Univs Pr.

Garduno, Joseph A. Memories of the Sangre De Cristo Mountains. LC 82-71884. (Illus.). 272p. (Orig.). 1982. pap. 10.95 (ISBN 0-9608806-0-7). Assoc Pubns.

Garduno, M. Anaya see Hutchinson, C. F., et al.

Gardyne, Alexander. A Theatre of Scottish Worthies, & the Lyf, Doings & Deathe of William Elphinston, Bishop of Aberdee. Repr. of 1878 ed. 40.00 (ISBN 0-384-17655-0). Johnson Repr.

Gare, Arran, jt. ed. see Elliot, Robert.

Gare, Fran & Monica, Helen. Dr. Atkins' Diet Cook Book. 304p. 1975. pap. 3.95 (ISBN 0-553-20710-5). Bantam.

Gareau, Frederick H. Cold War, Nineteen Forty-Seven to Nineteen Sixty-Seven: A Quantitative Study. (Monograph Series in World Affairs: Vol. 6, 1968-69, Bk. 1). 78p. (Orig.). 1969. 4.95 (ISBN 0-87940-018-8). Monograph Series.

Garebian, Keith. Hugh Hood. (World Authors Ser.: No. 709). 160p. 1983. lib. bdg. 20.95 (ISBN 0-8057-6556-5, Twayne). G K Hall.

Garee, Betty. Accent on Living Buyer's Guide, 1984-85: Your Number One Source of Information on Products for the Disabled. 4th ed. 128p. 1983. pap. 10.00 (ISBN 0-915708-15-9). Cheever Pub.

--Ideas for Kids on the Go. (Orig.). 1984. pap. 6.95 (ISBN 0-915708-17-5). Cheever Pub.

Garee, Betty, ed. An Accent Guide: Going Places In Your Own Vehicle. (Illus.). 80p. (Orig.). 1982. pap. 6.50 (ISBN 0-915708-13-2). Cheever Pub.

--An ACCENT Guide to Wheelchairs & Accessories. (Illus.). 114p. 1981. pap. 7.50 (ISBN 0-915708-10-8). Cheever Pub.

--Ideas for Making Your Home Accessible. LC 79-51595. (Illus.). 1979. 6.50 (ISBN 0-915708-08-6). Cheever Pub.

--Single-Handed. (Illus.). 32p. 1978. pap. 3.50 (ISBN 0-915708-06-X). Cheever Pub.

Gareff, G. & Bassoli, F. Dizionario Italiano-Svedese, Svedese-Italiano. 442p. (Ital. & Swedish.). 1973. Leatherette 5.95 (ISBN 0-686-92541-6, M-9174). French & Eur.

Gareffa, Peter & Evory, Ann, eds. Contemporary Newsmakers 1985, 4 Vols. 1985. Set. 68.00x (ISBN 0-8103-2200-5). Gale.

Gareis, Karl. Introduction to the Science of Law: A Systematic Survey of the Law & Principles of Legal Study. Kocurek, A. & Pound, Roscoe, trs. 1977. lib. bdg. 59.95 (ISBN 0-8490-2072-7). Gordon Pr.

--Introduction to the Science of Law: Systematic Survey of the Law & Principles of Legal Study. (Modern Legal Philosophy Ser: Vol. 1). xxx, 376p. 1968. Repr. of 1911 ed. 37.50x (ISBN 0-8377-2200-4). Rothman.

Garel, Laurent, ed. see Moreau, Jean-Francois & Mazzara, Laure.

Garelick, David A., ed. see AIP Conference, Boston 1974.

Garen, Nancy. Nancy Garen's Complete Tarot Workbook: A Guide to Self-Discovery & Personal Transformation through Tarot. 176p. 1984. pap. 12.95 (ISBN 0-913425-01-X). Coltrane & Beach.

--Nancy Garen's Complete Tarot Workbook: A Guide to Self-Discovery & Personal Transformation Through Tarot. 176p. 1984. pap. 12.75. Coltrane & Beach.

Gareth Jones, E. B. Recent Advances in Aquatic Mycology. LC 74-27179. 748p. 1976. 99.95x (ISBN 0-470-29176-1). Halsted Pr.

Garett, John, jt. auth. see Calder, Julian.

Garetz, Bruce A. & Lombardi, John R. Advances in Laser Spectroscopy, Vol. I. 245p. 1982. 54.95x (ISBN 0-471-26185-8, Pub. by Wiley Heyden). Wiley.

Garetz, Bruce A. & Lombardi, John R., eds. Advances in Laser Spectroscopy, Vol. 2. 261p. 1983. 48.95x (ISBN 0-471-26281-1, Pub. by Wiley-Interscience). Wiley.

Garey, Carroll L., ed. Physical Chemistry of Pigments in Paper Coating. (TAPPI Press Books). 493p. 1977. 39.95 (ISBN 0-317-36035-3, NO. B039). TAPPI.

Garey, H. B. Historical Development of Tenses from Late Latin to Old French. (LD). 1955. pap. 16.00 (ISBN 0-527-00797-8). Kraus Repr.

Garey, Howard, jt. ed. see Perkins, Leeman L.

Garey, Jack & Morris, Charles E. Handling a Workmen's Compensation Claim. rev. ed. LC 75-10419. 164p. 1975. 25.00 (ISBN 0-938160-09-5, 6336). State Bar TX.

Garey, Laurence, tr. see Changeux, Jean-Pierre.

Garey, Michael R. & Johnson, David S. Computers & Intractability: A Guide to the Theory of NP-Completeness. LC 78-12361. (Mathematical Sciences Ser.). (Illus.). 338p. 1979. pap. text ed. 17.95 (ISBN 0-7167-1045-5). W H Freeman.

Garf, A. Life with Granny Kandiki. 16p. 1978. pap. 2.95 (ISBN 0-8285-1182-9, Pub. by Progress Pubs USSR). Imported Pubns.

Garfein, Oscar B., intro. by. Clinical Pharmacology of Cardic Antiarrhythmic Agents: Classical & Current Concepts Reevaluated. (Annals of the New York Academy of Science Ser.: Vol. 432). 323p. 1984. lib. bdg. 85.00x (ISBN 0-89766-258-X); pap. 85.00x (ISBN 0-89766-259-8). NY Acad Sci.

Garff, Michael, jt. auth. see Fichtner, Hans.

Garff, Regnal W. Handbook for New Juvenile Court Judges. 52p. 1973. 3.00 (ISBN 0-318-15766-7, T200). Natl Juv & Family Ct Judges.

Garff, Royal L. You Can Learn to Speak. 219p. 1980. pap. 2.50 (ISBN 0-87747-791-4). Deseret Bk.

Garfias, Robert. Music of One Thousand Autumns: The Togaku Style of Japanese Courtly Music. LC 75-13865. 1976. 52.50x (ISBN 0-520-01977-6). U of Cal Pr.

Garfiel, Evelyn. Service of the Heart. pap. 4.00 (ISBN 0-87980-140-9). Wilshire.

Garfield, Brian. Checkpoint Charlie. LC 81-702. 1981. 10.00 (ISBN 0-89296-054-X); ltd. ed. 30.00 (ISBN 0-89296-055-8). Mysterious Pr.

--Death Sentence. LC 75-20031. 216p. 1975. 6.95 (ISBN 0-87131-198-4). M Evans.

--Death Sentence. 1985. pap. 3.95 (ISBN 0-317-19147-0). Mysterious Pr.

--Death Wish. 1985. pap. 3.95 (ISBN 0-317-19146-2). Mysterious Pr.

--Fear in a Handful of Dust. 1985. pap. 3.95 (ISBN 0-317-19149-7). Mysterious Pr.

--The Hit. 256p. 1982. pap. 2.50 (ISBN 0-505-51838-4, Pub. by Tower Bks). Dorchester Pub Co.

--Hopscotch. 304p. 1976. pap. 1.75 (ISBN 0-449-22747-2, X2747, Crest). Fawcett.

--Hopscotch. LC 74-14536. 286p. 1975. 7.95 (ISBN 0-87131-164-X). M Evans.

--Line of Succession. 1979. pap. 1.95 (ISBN 0-449-23703-6, Crest). Fawcett.

--Necessity. LC 83-24490. 256p. 1984. 13.95 (ISBN 0-312-56258-6, Pub. by Marek). St Martin.

--Necessity. 1985. pap. 3.95 (ISBN 0-451-13511-3, Sig). NAL.

--The Romanov Succession. LC 73-91886. 420p. 1974. 8.95 (ISBN 0-87131-159-3). M Evans.

--Sliphammer. 1979. pap. 1.75 (ISBN 0-449-24215-3, Crest). Fawcett.

--Sweeney's Honor. 192p. 1980. pap. 1.95 (ISBN 0-449-24330-3, Crest). Fawcett.

--Thousand Mile War. 1975. pap. 1.95 (ISBN 0-345-24381-1). Ballantine.

--The Threepersons Hunt. LC 73-87704. 264p. 1974. 6.95 (ISBN 0-87131-140-2). M Evans.

--Tripwire. 1985. pap. 3.95 (ISBN 0-317-19148-9). Mysterious Pr.

--Valley of the Shadow. 176p. 1983. pap. 1.95 (ISBN 0-8439-2029-7, Leisure Bks). Dorchester Pub Co.

--The Vanquished. 1982. pap. 2.50 (ISBN 0-441-86044-3). Ace Bks.

Garfield, Brian, ed. The Crime of My Life: Favorite Stories by Presidents of the Mystery Writers of America. LC 83-40389. 192p. 1984. text ed. 14.95 (ISBN 0-8027-0761-0). Walker & Co.

Garfield, Charles. Peak Performance. 1985. pap. 8.95 (ISBN 0-446-37198-X). Warner Bks.

Garfield, Charles A. Psychosocial Care of the Dying Patient. (Illus.). 1978. text ed. 28.00 (ISBN 0-07-022860-4). McGraw.

Garfield, Charles A. & Bennett, Hal Z. Peak Performance: Mental Training Techniques of the World's Greatest Athletes. LC 84-71. 228p. 1984. 13.95 (ISBN 0-87477-214-1). J P Tarcher.

Garfield, Charles A., ed. Stress & Survival: The Emotional Realities of Life Threatening Illness. LC 78-31341. (Illus.). 388p. 1979. text ed. 24.95 (ISBN 0-8016-1743-X). Mosby.

Garfield, David. The Actors Studio: A Player's Place. (Illus.). 336p. 1984. 9.95 (ISBN 0-02-012310-8, Collier). Macmillan.

Garfield, E. Transliterated Dictionary of the Russian Language. LC 79-14068. (Rus.). 1979. lib. bdg. 25.00 (ISBN 0-89495-003-7); pap. 14.95 (ISBN 0-89495-011-8). ISI Pr.

Garfield, Eugene. The Awards of Science & Other Essays. (Essays of an Information Scientist Ser.: Vol. 7). 673p. 1985. 30.00 (ISBN 0-317-20208-1). ISI Pr.

--Citation Indexing. (Illus.). 274p. 1983. 24.95 (ISBN 0-89495-024-X); pap. 18.95 (ISBN 0-89495-025-8). ISI Pr.

--Essays of an Information Scientist, Vol. 6. 673p. 1984. 25.00 (ISBN 0-89495-032-0). ISI Pr.

--Essays of an Information Scientist, Vol. 1 (1962-1973). (Illus.). 544p. 1977. 25.00 (ISBN 0-89495-001-0). ISI Pr.

--Essays of an Information Scientist, Vol. 2 (1974-1976). (Illus.). 708p. 1977. 25.00 (ISBN 0-89495-002-9). ISI Pr.

--Essays of an Information Scientist, Vol. 3 (1977-1978). (Illus.). 892p. 1980. 25.00 (ISBN 0-89495-009-6). ISI Pr.

--Essays of an Information Scientist, Vol. 4 (1979-1980). (Illus.). 780p. 1981. 25.00 (ISBN 0-89495-012-6). ISI Pr.

--Essays of an Information Scientist, Vol. 5 (1981-1982). (Illus.). 849p. 1983. 25.00 (ISBN 0-89495-023-1). ISI Pr.

Garfield, Evelyn P. Julio Cortazar. LC 74-78440. (Literature and Life Ser.). 184p. 1975. 12.95 (ISBN 0-8044-2224-9). Ungar.

--Women's Voices from Latin America: Interviews with 6 Contemporary Authors. 172p. 1985. 18.95 (ISBN 0-8143-1782-0). Wayne St U Pr.

Garfield, James A. Garfield-Hinsdale Letters. Hinsdale, Mary L., ed. 1949. 24.00 (ISBN 0-527-32460-4). Kraus Repr.

--Works of James Abram Garfield, 2 Vols. facs. ed. Hinsdale, Burke A., ed. LC 73-117877. (Select Bibliographies Reprint Ser). 1882. Set. 82.50 (ISBN 0-8369-5330-4). Ayer Co Pubs.

Garfield, James B. Follow My Leader. LC 57-1611. (Illus.). 192p. (gr. 4-6). 1957. PLB 10.95 (ISBN 0-670-32332-2). Viking.

Garfield, Jay L. & Hennessey, Patricia, eds. Abortion: Moral & Legal Perspectives. LC 84-8739. 344p. 1985. lib. bdg. 30.00x (ISBN 0-87023-440-4); pap. text ed. 13.95x (ISBN 0-87023-441-2). U of Mass Pr.

Garfield, Laeh M. & Grant, Jack. Companionship in Spirit. 7.95 (ISBN 0-89087-407-7). Celestial Arts.

Garfield, Leah M. & Grant, Jack. Companions in Spirit. 192p. (Orig.). 1984. pap. 7.95 (ISBN 0-89087-407-7). Celestial Arts.

Garfield, Lee, jt. auth. see Young, Marvin.

Garfield, Leon. The Apprentices. LC 77-21770. 1978. 10.00 (ISBN 0-670-12978-X). Viking.

--Fair's Fair. LC 81-43136. (Illus.). 32p. (gr. k-3). 1983. 10.95a (ISBN 0-385-17962-6); PLB (ISBN 0-385-17963-4). Doubleday.

--Footsteps: A Novel. LC 80-65834. 192p. (gr. 7 up). 1980. 12.95 (ISBN 0-385-28294-X). Delacorte.

--The House of Cards. 304p. 1983. 12.95 (ISBN 0-312-39259-1). St Martin.

--The House of Hanover England in the Eighteenth Century. LC 75-42422. (Illus.). 128p. (gr. 6 up). 1976. 8.95 (ISBN 0-395-28904-1, Clarion). HM.

--Jack Holborn. (Illus.). (gr. 7 up). 1965. PLB 5.99 (ISBN 0-394-91323-X). Pantheon.

--Jack Holborn. (Windward Bks.). (gr. 7 up). 1965. (BYR); PLB 5.99 (ISBN 0-394-91323-X). Random.

--The King in the Garden. (Illus.). 32p. (gr. 1-3). 1985. 11.75 (ISBN 0-688-04106-X). Lothrop.

--King Nimrod's Tower. LC 81-86470. (Illus.). 32p. (ps-3). 1982. 11.75 (ISBN 0-688-01288-4). Lothrop.

--The Night of the Comet. LC 79-50670. (gr. 7 up). 1979. 8.95; PLB 8.95 (ISBN 0-385-28753-4). Delacorte.

--Shakespeare Stories. 288p. 1985. 14.95 (ISBN 0-8052-3991-X). Schocken.

--The Sound of Coaches. (Illus.). 240p. (gr. 7 up). 1985. pap. 2.95 (ISBN 0-14-030961-6, Puffin). Penguin.

Garfield, Leon & Bragg, Michael. The Writing on the Wall. LC 82-24938. (Illus.). 32p. (gr. 1-3). 1983. 10.25 (ISBN 0-688-02112-3). Lothrop.

Garfield, Nancy J. & Nelson, Richard E. Career Exploration Groups: A Facilitator's Guide. 48p. 1983. pap. 12.50 (ISBN 0-89106-022-7, 7395). Consulting Psychol.

Garfield, Patricia. Creative Dreaming. 256p. 1976. pap. 2.50 (ISBN 0-345-28468-2). Ballantine.

--Your Child's Dreams. LC 84-91042. 356p. (Orig.). 1984. pap. 3.95 (ISBN 0-345-31047-0). Ballantine.

Garfield, Paul & Lovejoy, W. Public Utility Economics. (Illus.). 1963. text ed. 31.95 (ISBN 0-13-739367-9). P-H.

Garfield Publications, ed. see Alton, Albert.

Garfield, Samuel. The Immortality of the Soul & the Perfectibility of Man. (Illus.). 1977. 45.00 (ISBN 0-89266-026-0). Am Classical Coll Pr.

--The Life of the Spirit: The Immortality of the Soul & the Perfectibility of Man. (Illus.). 1978. deluxe bdg. 41.45 (ISBN 0-930582-04-7). Gloucester Art.

Garfield, Sidney. Teeth, Teeth, Teeth. 22.50 (ISBN 0-685-07412-9). Borden.

Garfield, Sol L. Clinical Psychology: The Study of Personality & Behavior. 2nd ed. LC 83-2649. 486p. 1983. lib. bdg. 29.95x (ISBN 0-202-26094-1); pap. text ed. 18.95x (ISBN 0-202-26095-X). Aldine Pub.

Garfield, Sol. L. Psychotherapy: An Eclectic Approach. LC 79-17724. (Personality Processes Ser.). 1980. 34.95x (ISBN 0-471-04490-3, Pub. by Wiley-Interscience). Wiley.

Garfield, Sol L. & Bergin, Allen E. Handbook of Psychotherapy & Behavior Change: An Empirical Analysis. 2nd ed. LC 78-8526. 1978. text ed. 80.95x (ISBN 0-471-29178-1). Wiley.

--Handbook of Psychotherapy & Behavior Change: An Empirical Analysis. 3rd ed. 1985. 59.95 (ISBN 0-471-79995-5). Wiley.

Garfield, Viola E. & Forrest, Linn A. Wolf & the Raven: Totem Poles of Southeastern Alaska. 2nd ed. LC 49-8492. (Illus.). 161p. 1961. pap. 8.95 (ISBN 0-295-73998-3). U of Wash Pr.

Garfield, Viola E. & Wingert, Paul S. Tsimshian Indians & Their Arts. LC 68-87177. (American Ethnological Society Numbered Publications Ser: No. 18). (Illus.). 108p. 1966. pap. 4.95 (ISBN 0-295-74042-6). U of Wash Pr.

Garfinkel, jt. ed. see Abuelo.

Garfinkel, Alan. Forms of Explanation: Rethinking the Questions in Social Theory. LC 80-23341. 192p. 1981. 21.00x (ISBN 0-300-02136-4). Yale U Pr.

Garfinkel, Alan & Latorre, Guillermo. Trabajo y Vida. 1983. pap. text ed. 7.95 (ISBN 0-88377-248-5, 184 PGS.); pap. text ed. 1.95 answer key (ISBN 0-88377-249-3, 24 PGS.); cassette 12.50 (ISBN 0-88377-208-6). Newbury Hse.

Garfinkel, Alan, et al. Modismos Al Momento. LC 76-51264. 1977. pap. text ed. 7.95 (ISBN 0-88377-070-9). Newbury Hse.

Garfinkel, Barry D., jt. auth. see Golombek, Harvey.

Garfinkel, Barry H. & Practising Law Institute. Current Problems in Federal Civil Practice, 1983. LC 83-226001. (Litigation & Administration Practice Ser.: No. 234-235). 1983. 35.00. PLI.

Garfinkel, Bernard. Mao Tse-Tung. (World Leaders: Past & Present Ser.). (Illus.). 112p. 1985. lib. bdg. 15.95x (ISBN 0-87754-564-2). Chelsea Hse.

--Thatcher. (World Leaders: Past & Present Ser.). (Illus.). 112p. 1985. lib. bdg. 15.95x (ISBN 0-87754-552-9). Chelsea Hse.

Garfinkel, Bernard, jt. auth. see Siegel, Jules.

Garfinkel, Charles. Racquetball the Easy Way. LC 78-53835. (Illus., Orig.). 1978. pap. 6.95 (ISBN 0-689-70560-3). Atheneum.

Garfinkel, Charlie. Racquetball for the Serious Player. LC 81-69144. (Illus.). 160p. 1982. pap. 6.95 (ISBN 0-689-70624-3). Atheneum.

Garfinkel, Harold. Studies in Ethnomethodology. 1967. text ed. 28.95 (ISBN 0-13-858381-1). P-H.

--Studies in Ethnomethodology. (Polity Press Bk.). 304p. 1985. pap. 9.95x (ISBN 0-7456-0005-0). Basil Blackwell.

Garfinkel, Herbert. When Negroes March. LC 69-15522. (Studies in American Negro Life Ser). 1969. pap. 3.25x (ISBN 0-689-70078-4, NL13). Atheneum.

Garfinkel, Irwin. Income-Tested Transfer Programs: The Case for & Against. (Institute for Research on Proverty Monograph Ser.). 537p. 1982. 49.50 (ISBN 0-12-275880-3). Acad Pr.

Garfinkel, Irwin & Haveman, Robert H. Earnings Capacity, Poverty & Inequality. 1978. 15.50 (ISBN 0-12-275850-1). Acad Pr.

Garfinkel, Irwin, jt. auth. see Munts, Raymond.

Garfinkel, Paul E. & Garner, David M. Anorexia Nervosa: A Multidimensional Perspective. LC 82-1337. 320p. 1982. 30.00 (ISBN 0-87630-297-5). Brunner-Mazel.

Garfinkel, Paul E., jt. auth. see Garner, David M.

Garfinkel, Perry. In a Man's World: Father, Son, Brother, Friend & Other Roles Men Play. LC 85-4772. 1985. 14.95 (ISBN 0-453-00490-3). NAL.

Garfinkel, Robert & Nemhauser, George L. Integer Programming. LC 72-3881. (Decision & Control Ser.). 528p. 1972. 46.95x (ISBN 0-471-29195-1, Pub. by Wiley-Interscience). Wiley.

Garfinkle, Adam M. The Politics of the Nuclear Freeze. LC 84-6030. (Philadelphia Policy Papers). (Orig.). 1984. pap. 7.95 (ISBN 0-910191-08-5). For Policy Res.

Garfinkle, Adam M. & Wessell, Nils H., eds. Global Perspectives on Arms Control: Foreign Policy Issues. LC 83-21094. (A Foreign Policy Research Institute Ser.). 192p. 1984. text ed. 27.95 (ISBN 0-03-069658-5). Praeger.

Garforth, Francis W. Educative Democracy: John Stuart Mill on Education in Society. 1980. text ed. 29.95x (ISBN 0-19-713438-6). Oxford U Pr.

Garforth, Francis W., ed. John Locke's Of the Conduct of the Understanding. LC 66-20498. (Classics in Edcuation Ser.). 1966. pap. text ed. 4.50x (ISBN 0-8077-1398-8). Tchrs Coll.

--John Stuart Mill on Education. LC 75-115230. (Classics in Education Ser.). 1971. pap. 5.50x (ISBN 0-8077-1402-X). Tchrs Coll.

Garforth, Frank W. John Stuart Mill's Theory of Education. LC 78-31807. 269p. 1979. text ed. 28.50x (ISBN 0-06-492332-0). B&N Imports.

Garforth, John. A Day in the Life of a Victorian Policeman. (Victorian Day Ser.). 1974. pap. text ed. 5.95x (ISBN 0-04-942123-9). Allen Unwin.

Garfunkel, Zvi, ed. Mantle Flow & Plate Theory. (Benchmark Papers in Geology: No. 84). (Illus.). 416p. 1984. 59.50 (ISBN 0-442-22734-5). Van Nos Reinhold.

Garg, Ganga R. Encyclopedia of Indian Literature. 550p. 1982. text ed. 52.25x (ISBN 0-391-02779-4). Humanities.

--World Perspectives of Swami Dayananda Saraswati. 592p. 1984. text ed. 49.25x (ISBN 0-391-03078-7, Pub. by Concept India). Humanities.

Garg, H. P. Treatise on Solar Energy: Volume 1: Fundamentals of Solar Energy. LC 81-21951. 400p. 1982. 58.95x (ISBN 0-471-10180-X, Pub. by Wiley-Interscience). Wiley.

Garg, H P., et al. Solar Energy Thermal Storage. lib. bdg. 79.00 (ISBN 90-277-1930-6, Pub. by Reidel Holland). Kluwer Academic.

Garg, J., jt. auth. see Gupta, K. C.

Garg, J. B., ed. Statistical Properties of Nuclei. LC 75-182409. 665p. 1972. 75.00x (ISBN 0-306-30576-3, Plenum Pr). Plenum Pub.

Garg, Mohan L. & Kleinberg, Warren M. Clinical Training & Health Care Costs: A Basic Curriculum for Medical Education. 170p. 1985. 28.95x (ISBN 0-03-069882-0). Praeger.

Garg, Prem C. Optimal Economic Growth with Exhaustible Resources. LC 78-75019. (Outstanding Dissertations on Energy Ser.). 1979. lib. bdg. 22.00 (ISBN 0-8240-4054-6). Garland Pub.

Garg, Ramesh. Study Guide to Accompany Finance Principles. write for info. Reston.

Garg, Vijay K., jt. auth. see D'Souza, A. Frank.

Garg, Vijay K., et al. Dynamics of Railway Vehicle Systems. LC 83-21475. (Monograph). 1984. 69.50 (ISBN 0-12-275950-8). Acad Pr.

Gargan, Edward T., ed. The Intent of Toynbee's History. LC 61-10704. 1961. 5.00 (ISBN 0-8294-0029-X). Loyola.

Gargan, Edward T., ed. see Taine, Hippolyte A.

Gargan, John. Milking Your Business For All It's Worth: Tax Saving Opportunities for Small Business. (Illus.). 137p. 1982. 16.95 (ISBN 0-13-583005-2); pap. 7.95 (ISBN 0-13-582999-2). P-H.

Gargan, John J. The Complete Guide to Estate Planning. LC 78-2829. (Spectrum Reference Shelf Ser.). (Illus.). 1980. 10.95 (ISBN 0-13-159996-8, Spec). P-H.

Gargan, John J. & Coke, James G. Political Behavior & Public Issues in Ohio. LC 72-78408. 388p. 1972. 15.00x (ISBN 0-87338-124-6). Kent St U Pr.

Gargan, William & Sharma, Sue, eds. Find That Tune: An Index to Rock, Folk-Rock, Disco & Soul in Collections. LC 82-22346. 303p. 1984. lib. bdg. 42.50 (ISBN 0-918212-70-7). Neal-Schuman.

Garganigo, John F., jt. auth. see Mullen, Edward J.

Garganigs, John, jt. auth. see Mullen, Edward.

Gargano, James W. Critical Essays on John William De Forest. (Critical Essays on American Literature Ser.). 1981. 26.00 (ISBN 0-8161-8441-0, Twayne). G K Hall.

--The Masquerade Vision in Poe's Short Stories. 1977. pap. 2.50 (ISBN 0-910556-09-1). Enoch Pratt.

Gargaz, Pierre-Andre. Project of Universal & Perpetual Peace. LC 79-147424. (Library of War & Peace; Proposals for Peace: a History). lib. bdg. 46.00 (ISBN 0-8240-0216-4). Garland Pub.

Garges, Beverly L. Cry of the Lamb. (Orig.). 1982. pap. 4.50 (ISBN 0-9614041-1-6). B & S Garges.

--Everybody Knows My Name. (Orig.). 1984. pap. 4.50 (ISBN 0-9614041-0-8). B & S Garges.

Gargett, Graham. Voltaire & Protestantism. 532p. 1981. 200.00x (ISBN 0-7294-0243-6, Pub. by Voltaire Found). State Mutual Bk.

Gargiulo, Barbara. Diary of a Catechist. 88p. (Orig.). 1984. pap. 3.95 (ISBN 0-89622-213-6). Twenty-Third.

Gargiulo, Richard. Working with Parents of Exceptional Children: A Guide for Professionals. LC 84-81345. 240p. 1984. pap. text ed. 16.95 (ISBN 0-395-35767-5). HM.

Gargooian, Andrew. Urban Enterprise Zones: A Selected Review of the Literature with Annotations. (Bibliographic Ser.: No. 7). 31p. 1984. 11.50 (ISBN 0-88329-134-7). Intl Assess.

Gargrave, Ron, jt. auth. see Bunt, Sidney.

Garibaldi, Antoine, ed. Black Colleges & Universities: Challenges for the Future. LC 83-22943. 320p. 1984. 29.95x (ISBN 0-03-070302-6). Praeger.

Garibaldi, F. Rice Parboiling. (Agricultural Services Bulletins: No. 56). (Illus.). 73p. 1985. pap. 7.50 (ISBN 92-5-101400-0, F2671, FAO). Unipub.

--Rice Testing - Methods & Equipment. (Agricultural Services Bulletins: No. 18). 55p. (3rd Printing 1979). 1973. pap. 7.50 (ISBN 92-5-100739-X, F1897, FAO). Unipub.

Garibaldi, F., jt. auth. see Borasio, I.

Garibaldi, Gerald. He Gave Himself to the Sea. LC 79-21326. (Quest, Adventure, Survival Ser.). (Illus.). (gr. 4-8). 1980. PLB 14.25 (ISBN 0-8172-1561-1). Raintree Pubs.

--He Gave Himself to the Sea. LC 79-21326. (Quest, Adventure, Survival). (Illus.). 46p. (gr. 4-9). 1982. pap. 9.27 (ISBN 0-8172-2061-5). Raintree Pubs.

--Nightmare in a Sea of Mud. LC 79-22418. (Quest, Adventure, Survival). (Illus.). 46p. (gr. 4-9). 1982. pap. 9.27 (ISBN 0-8172-2066-6). Raintree Pubs.

--Nightmare in a Sea of Mud. LC 79-22418. (Quest, Adventure, Survival). (Illus.). (gr. 4-8). 1980. PLB 14.25 (ISBN 0-8172-1558-1). Raintree Pubs.

Garibaldi, Giuseppe. Manlio: Romanzo Storico Politico Contemporaneo. Campanella, Anthony P., ed. (Illus.). xx, 446p. (Ital.). 1982. 15.00x (ISBN 92-9013-002-4). Intl Inst Garibaldian.

Garibaldi, Giuseppe & Melena, Elpis. Garibaldi's Memoirs, from His Manuscript, Personal Notes & Authentic Sources. Orig. Title: Denkwurdigkeiten. (Illus.). xxvi, 226p. 1981. 12.50x (ISBN 92-9013-003-2). Intl Inst Garibaldian.

Garibyants, A. A., jt. auth. see Golubev, V. S.

Garigan, Catherine S., jt. ed. see Carter, Virginia L.

Garigue, Phillip. A Bibliographical Introduction to the Study of French Canada. LC 77-11621. 1977. Repr. of 1956 ed. lib. bdg. 19.75x (ISBN 0-8371-9807-0, GABI). Greenwood.

Garin, Eugenio. Astrology in the Renaissance. Jackson, Carolyn & Allen, June, trs. from Ital. 160p. 1983. 21.95 (ISBN 0-7100-9259-8). Routledge & Kegan.

--Italian Humanism: Philosophy & Civic Life in the Renaissance. Munz, Peter, tr. from It. LC 75-35025. 227p. 1976. Repr. of 1965 ed. lib. bdg. 19.25x (ISBN 0-8371-8578-5, GAIH). Greenwood.

--Science & Civic Life in the Italian Renaissance. Munz, Peter, tr. 11.50 (ISBN 0-8446-2110-2). Peter Smith.

Garinger, Alan K. Adult Math. Clifton, Barbarba & Tipton, Judy, eds. 290p. 1984. wkbk. 11.00 (ISBN 0-910475-25-3). KET.

--Math Handbook. Tucker, Terry, ed. 50p. 1984. wkbk. 1.50 (ISBN 0-910475-24-5). KET.

Garinger, Elmer H. The Administration of Discipline in the High School. LC 72-176795. (Columbia University. Teachers College. Contributions to Education: No. 686). Repr. of 1936 ed. 22.50 (ISBN 0-404-55686-8). AMS Pr.

Garioch, Robert. Collected Poems. 208p. pap. 8.50 (ISBN 0-85635-036-2). Carcanet.

--Complete Poetical Works. 1983. 69.00x (ISBN 0-904265-93-5, Pub. by Macdonald Pub UK). State Mutual Bk.

Garis, Howard. Uncle Wiggily's Storybook. (Illus.). 256p. (gr. 3-9). 1978. 5.95 (ISBN 0-448-40090-1, G&D). Putnam Pub Group.

Garis, Howard R. Uncle Wiggily & His Friends. (Illus.). 98p. (ps-3). 1978. 5.95 (ISBN 0-448-40504-0, G&D); PLB 3.79 (ISBN 0-448-13023-8). Putnam Pub Group.

Garis, James de see De Garis, James.

Garis, M. R. Martha Root: Lioness at the Threshold. LC 83-3913. (Illus.). 500p. 1983. 30.00 (ISBN 0-87743-184-1); pap. 16.00 (ISBN 0-87743-185-X). Baha'i.

Garitano, Rita. Rainy Day Man. LC 84-16712. 378p. 1985. 14.95 (ISBN 0-393-01949-7). Norton.

Garitee, Jerome R. The Republic's Private Navy: The American Privateering Business As Practiced by Baltimore During the War of 1812. LC 76-41487. (American Maritime Library: Vol. 8). (Illus.). 356p. 1977. 10.00 (ISBN 0-8195-5004-3); limited ed. 35.00 (ISBN 0-8195-5005-1). Mystic Seaport.

Garity, Mary, jt. auth. see Lurie, Nancy O.

Garity, Mary, ed. see Friends of the Museum, Inc.

Garity, Mary, ed. see Lurie, Nancy O.

Garity, Mary M., ed. see Henderson, Robert W. & Schwartz, Albert.

Garity, Mary M., ed. see Taylor, W. Carl.

Garlan, Edwin N. Legal Realism & Justice. xii, 161p. 1981. Repr. of 1941 ed. lib. bdg. 20.00x (ISBN 0-8377-0614-9). Rothman.

Garlan, Suares, jt. auth. see White, Timothy.

Garlan, Yvon. War in the Ancient World: A Social History. Finley, M. I., ed. Lloyd, Janet, tr. (Ancient Culture & Society Ser.). (Illus.). 200p. 1976. 7.95x (ISBN 0-393-05566-3). Norton.

Garland, A. H. Experience in the Supreme Court of the United States: With Some Reflections & Suggestions as to that Tribunal. (Illus.). 100p. 1983. Repr. of 1898 ed. lib. bdg. 20.00x (ISBN 0-8377-0618-1). Rothman.

Garland, Albert N. Infantry in Vietnam. (Vietnam Ser.: No. 1). (Illus.). 319p. 1984. Repr. of 1967 ed. 18.95 (ISBN 0-89839-065-6). Battery Pr.

--Infantry in Vietnam. 336p. 1985. pap. 3.50 (ISBN 0-515-08054-3). Jove Pubns.

Garland, Albert N., ed. A Distant Challenge: The U. S. Infantryman in Vietnam, 1967-72. (Vietnam War Ser.: No. 3). (Illus.). 372p. 1984. Repr. of 1969 ed. 19.95x (ISBN 0-89839-071-0). Battery Pr.

Garland, Andrew, et al. System 1022 User's Reference Manual. rev. ed. 500p. 1984. looseleaf 28.50X (ISBN 0-912055-09-X). Software Hse.

Garland, Blanche. Castles in the Sky. LC 84-28777. (Starlight Romance Ser.). 192p. 1985. 12.95 (ISBN 0-385-23002-8). Doubleday.

Garland, Caroline & White, Stephanie. Children & Day Nurseries. LC 80-24264. (Oxford Preschool Research Project Ser.: Vol. 4). 128p. 1980. pap. 9.50 (ISBN 0-931114-12-8). High-Scope.

Garland, Colden. Developing Competence in Teaching Reading: Instructional Modules in Reading Education. 500p. 1978. write for info. plastic comb (ISBN 0-697-06015-2). Wm C Brown.

Garland, D. & Young, P., eds. The Power to Punish: Contemporary Penalty & Social Analysis. 238p. 1983. text ed. 28.00x (ISBN 0-391-02902-9, Pub. by Heineman Ed Bks England); pap. text ed. 11.45x (ISBN 0-391-02901-0). Humanities.

Garland, D. David. Amos: A Study Guide Commentary. 96p. 1973. pap. 4.95 (ISBN 0-310-24833-7). Zondervan.

--Hosea. 128p. 1975. pap. 4.95 (ISBN 0-310-24843-4). Zondervan.

--Isaiah. (Orig.). 1968. pap. 4.95 (ISBN 0-310-24853-1). Zondervan.

--Job: A Study Guide Commentary. 160p. 1971. pap. 4.95 (ISBN 0-310-24863-9). Zondervan.

Garland, David. Punishment & Welfare: A History of Penal Strategies. 291p. 1985. text ed. write for info. (ISBN 0-566-00855-6). Gower Pub Co.

Garland, Diana R. Couples Communication & Negotiation Skills. LC 77-26981. (Workshop Models for Family Life Education Ser.). 1978. plastic comb 13.95 (ISBN 0-87304-158-5). Family Serv.

Garland, Diana S. Richmond. Working with Couples for Marriage Enrichment: A Guide to Developing, Conducting, & Evaluating Programs. LC 83-48158. (Social & Behavioral Science Ser.). 1983. text ed. 23.95x (ISBN 0-87589-573-5). Jossey-Bass.

Garland, G. D. Earth's Shape & Gravity. 1965. Pergamon.

Garland, George D. Introduction to Geophysics: Mantle, Core & Crust. 2nd ed. LC 78-54516. (Illus.). 1979. text ed. 42.95 (ISBN 0-7216-4026-5). HR&W.

Garland, Greever, jt. auth. see Reynolds, George F.

Garland, H. B. Concise Survey of German Literature. LC 78-137565. 1971. 8.95x (ISBN 0-87024-187-7). U of Miami Pr.

Garland, H. B., ed. see Kleist, H. von.

Garland, Hamlin. Boy Life on the Prairie. LC 61-16185. (Illus.). xxiv, 437p. 1961. pap. 9.95 (ISBN 0-8032-5070-3, BB 120, Bison). U of Nebr Pr.

--Boy Life on the Prairie. 389p. Date not set. Repr. of 1899 ed. lib. bdg. 35.00 (ISBN 0-89987-329-4). Darby Bks.

--The Captain of the Gray-Horse Troop. LC 73-104460. Repr. of 1902 ed. lib. bdg. 19.00 (ISBN 0-8398-0653-1). Irvington.

--Cavanagh Forest Ranger. 301p. 1984. lib. bdg. 25.00 (ISBN 0-8414-4339-4). Folcroft.

--Collected Works. Incl. Boy Life on the Prairie. 1899. Repr. 39.00x (ISBN 0-403-04596-7); Her Mountain Lover. 1901. Repr. 39.00 (ISBN 0-403-04597-5); The Captain of the Grayhorse Troop. 1902. Repr. 17.00 (ISBN 0-403-02966-X); Hesper. 1903. Repr. 39.00 (ISBN 0-403-02951-1); The Light of the Star. 1904. Repr. 29.00 (ISBN 0-403-02980-5); The Tyranny of the Dark. 1905. Repr. 29.00 (ISBN 0-403-02283-5); Witch's Gold. 1906. Repr. 29.00 (ISBN 0-686-01489-8); The Long Trail. 1907. Repr. 29.00x (ISBN 0-686-01490-1); Money Magic. 1907. Repr. 39.00x (ISBN 0-403-02988-0); The Shadow World. 1908. Repr. 29.00 (ISBN 0-403-04600-9); The Moccasin Ranch. 1909. Repr. 25.00x (ISBN 0-403-02282-7); Cavanaugh, Forest Ranger. 1910. Repr. 25.00x (ISBN 0-403-02985-6); Other Main Travelled Roads. 1910. Repr. 29.00x (ISBN 0-403-02975-9); Victor Ollnee's Disciple. 1911. Repr. 25.00x (ISBN 0-403-02970-8); The Forester's Daughter. 1914. Repr. 24.00 (ISBN 0-403-04601-7). Somerset Pub.

--Collected Works. Incl. Under the Wheel. 1890. Repr. 19.00x (ISBN 0-403-04602-5); Main Travelled Roads. 1891. Repr. 29.00 (ISBN 0-403-02981-3); A Member of the Third House. 1892. Repr. 17.00 (ISBN 0-403-04603-3); Jason Edwards. 1892. Repr. 29.00 (ISBN 0-403-04604-1); A Little Norsk. 1892. Repr. 18.00x (ISBN 0-403-04605-X); A Spoil of Office. 1892. Repr. 25.00 (ISBN 0-403-04606-8); Prairie Folks. 1899. Repr. 20.00 (ISBN 0-403-04607-6); Prairie Songs. 1893. Repr. 18.00 (ISBN 0-403-04608-4); Crumbling Idols. 1894. Repr. 14.00 (ISBN 0-403-04609-2); Rose of Dutcher's Cooly. 1895. Repr. 10.00x (ISBN 0-403-00211-7); Wayside Courtships. 1897. Repr. 16.00 (ISBN 0-403-04610-6); Ulysses S. Grant. 1898. Repr. 48.00 (ISBN 0-403-04611-4); The Spirit of Sweetwater. 1898. Repr. 18.00 (ISBN 0-403-04612-2); The Trail of the Goldseekers. 1899. Repr. 39.00 (ISBN 0-403-04613-0); The Eagle's Heart. 1900. Repr. 39.00 (ISBN 0-403-02987-2). Somerset Pub.

--Collected Works. Incl. They of the High Trails. 1916. Repr. 39.00 (ISBN 0-403-04614-9); A Son of the Middle Border. 1917. Repr. 39.00 (ISBN 0-403-02998-8); A Daughter of the Middle Border. 1921. Repr. 10.00 (ISBN 0-403-02968-6); A Pioneer Mother. 1922. Repr. 29.00 (ISBN 0-403-04615-7); The Book of the American Indian. 1923. Repr. 23.00 (ISBN 0-403-04616-5); Trail Markers of the Middle Border. 1926. Repr. 49.00 (ISBN 0-403-00984-7); The Westward March of American Settlement. 1927. Repr. 39.00 (ISBN 0-403-04617-3); Back Trailers from the Middle Border. 1928. Repr. 39.00 (ISBN 0-403-02986-4); Roadside Meetings. 1930. Repr. 39.00x (ISBN 0-403-02982-1); Companions of the Trail. 1931. Repr. 69.00 (ISBN 0-403-02978-3); My Friendly Contemporaries. 1932. Repr. 69.00 (ISBN 0-403-00982-0); Afternoon Neighbors. 1934. Repr. 69.00x (ISBN 0-403-04618-1); Iowa, O Iowa. Repr. 18.00 (ISBN 0-403-04619-X); Forty Years of Psychic Research. 1936. Repr. 25.00x (ISBN 0-403-04620-3); The Mystery of the Buried Crosses. 1939. Repr. 39.00x (ISBN 0-403-04621-1). Somerset Pub.

--Collected Works, 45 vols. 1200.00 set (ISBN 0-403-03459-0). Somerset Pub.

--A Collection. Repr. lib. bdg. write for info. Scholarly.

--The Eagle's Heart. 369p. 1984. lib. bdg. 25.00 (ISBN 0-8414-4338-6). Folcroft.

--Forty Years of Psychic Research: A Plain Narrative of Fact. LC 70-114877. (Select Bibliographies Reprint Ser). 1936. 26.50 (ISBN 0-8369-5281-2). Ayer Co Pubs.

--Hamlin Garland's Diaries. Pizer, Donald, ed. LC 68-27143. 281p. 1968. 10.00 (ISBN 0-87328-034-2). Huntington Lib.

--Her Mountain Lover. 396p. Repr. of 1900 ed. lib. bdg. 25.00 (ISBN 0-8414-4337-8). Folcroft.

--Hesper. 445p. Date not set. Repr. of 1903 ed. lib. bdg. 25.00 (ISBN 0-8414-4336-X). Folcroft.

--Iowa, O Iowa. 1979. Repr. of 1935 ed. lib. bdg. 30.00 (ISBN 0-89987-016-3). Darby Bks.

--Iowa, O Iowa. 1979. Repr. of 1935 ed. lib. bdg. 20.00 (ISBN 0-8482-4185-1). Norwood Edns.

--The Light of the Star. 278p. 1984. Repr. of 1904 ed. lib. bdg. 25.00 (ISBN 0-8414-4335-1). Folcroft.

--Main Travelled Roads. LC 79-103888. (Merrill Standard Ser.). 6.00 (ISBN 0-675-09375-9); pap. 4.00 (ISBN 0-675-09374-0). Brown Bk.

--Main Travelled Roads. 1962. pap. 3.95 (ISBN 0-451-51950-7, CE1734, Sig Classics). NAL.

--Main-Travelled Roads. 377p. Date not set. Repr. of 1891 ed. lib. bdg. 25.00 (ISBN 0-8414-4333-5). Folcroft.

--Main Travelled Roads. 377p. Date not set. Repr. of 1891 ed. lib. bdg. 35.00 (ISBN 0-89987-328-6). Darby Bks.

--A Member of the Third House. LC 68-57526. (The Muckrakers Ser.). Repr. of 1892 ed. lib. bdg. 18.50 (ISBN 0-8398-0656-6). Irvington.

--Money Magic. 355p. 1984. Repr. of 1907 ed. lib. bdg. 25.00 (ISBN 0-8414-4334-3). Folcroft.

--My Friendly Contemporaries: A Literary Log. 544p. Date not set. Repr. of 1932 ed. lib. bdg. 50.00 (ISBN 0-8414-4332-7). Folcroft.

--Other Main-Travelled Roads. 349p. 1984. Repr. of 1892 ed. lib. bdg. 40.00 (ISBN 0-8414-4329-7). Folcroft.

--Prairie Folks. new, rev. & enl. ed. LC 76-98403. Repr. of 1899 ed. 16.00 (ISBN 0-404-02684-2). AMS Pr.

--Prairie Folks. 284p. Date not set. Repr. of 1892 ed. lib. bdg. 35.00 (ISBN 0-89987-326-X). Darby Bks.

--Prairie Song & Western Story. facsimile ed. LC 73-163026. (Short Story Index Reprint Ser.). (Illus.). Repr. of 1928 ed. 20.00 (ISBN 0-8369-3940-9). Ayer Co Pubs.

--Prairie Songs, Being Chants Rhymed & Unihymed of the Level Lands of the Great West. 164p. Repr. of 1898 ed. lib. bdg. 25.00 (ISBN 0-317-16156-3). Folcroft.

--Prarie Folks: Or, Pioneer Life on the Western Praries. 1972. Repr. of 1899 ed. lib. bdg. 18.00 (ISBN 0-8422-8057-X). Irvington.

--Roadside Meetings. 474p. Repr. of 1930 ed. lib. bdg. 50.00 (ISBN 0-8414-4331-9). Folcroft.

--Rose of Dutcher's Coolly. LC 74-90103. Repr. of 1899 ed. 12.50 (ISBN 0-404-02685-0). AMS Pr.

--Rose of Dutcher's Coolly. Pizer, Donald, ed. LC 79-82509. xxxiii, 404p. 1970. pap. 5.95 (ISBN 0-8032-5071-1, BB 506, Bison). U of Nebr Pr.

--A Son of the Middle Border. LC 78-26593. xxvi, 467p. 1979. 29.95x (ISBN 0-8032-2102-9); pap. 6.95 (ISBN 0-8032-7000-3, BB 694, Bison). U of Nebr Pr.

--A Son of the Middle Border. 467p. Date not set. Repr. of 1917 ed. lib. bdg. 35.00 (ISBN 0-8414-4326-2). Folcroft.

--A Son of the Middle Border. 467p. Date not set. Repr. of 1922 ed. lib. bdg. 35.00 (ISBN 0-89987-327-8). Darby Bks.

--The Spirit of Sweetwater. 100p. 1984. Repr. of 1898 ed. lib. bdg. 25.00 (ISBN 0-8414-4327-0). Folcroft.

--A Spoil of Office. (American Studies). 1969. Repr. of 1892 ed. 26.00 (ISBN 0-384-17670-4). Johnson Repr.

--Trail-Makers of the Middle Border. (Illus.). 426p. 1984. lib. bdg. 35.00 (ISBN 0-8414-4342-4). Folcroft.

--The Trail of the Goldseeker: A Record of Travel in Prose & Verse. 264p. 1984. lib. bdg. 40.00 (ISBN 0-8414-4343-2). Folcroft.

--Victor Ollnee's Discipline. 308p. 1984. Repr. of 1911 ed. lib. bdg. 30.00 (ISBN 0-8414-4341-6). Folcroft.

--Wayside Courtships. LC 70-103509. (Short Story Index Reprint Ser.). 1897. 18.00 (ISBN 0-8369-3251-X). Ayer Co Pubs.

Garland, Hamlin, et al. Clarence A. Andrews "Christmas in the Midwest". rev. ed. (Illus.). 144p. 1984. 8.95 (ISBN 0-934582-06-8). Midwest Heritage.

Garland, Harry. Introduction to Microprocessor System Design. (Illus.). 1979. 24.95 (ISBN 0-07-022871-X); pap. 24.95 (ISBN 0-07-022870-1). McGraw.

Garland, Harry, jt. auth. see Melen, Roger.

Garland, Henry. The Berlin Novels of Theodor Fontane. 1980. 45.00x (ISBN 0-19-815765-7). Oxford U Pr.

Garland, Henry & Garland, Mary, eds. The Oxford Companion to German Literature. 1976. 39.95x (ISBN 0-19-866115-0). Oxford U Pr.

Garland, Henry B. Lessing: The Founder of Modern German Literature. LC 73-95. 1973. lib. bdg. 15.00 (ISBN 0-685-33789-8). Folcroft.

--Schiller. LC 76-39809. (Illus.). 1977. Repr. of 1949 ed. lib. bdg. 24.75x (ISBN 0-8371-9084-3, GASC). Greenwood.

Garland, Hugh. Life of John Randolph of Roanoke, 2 Vols. 11th ed. LC 68-24977. (American Biography Ser., No. 32). 1969. Repr. of 1856 ed. Set. lib. bdg. 79.95x (ISBN 0-8383-0159-2). Haskell.

Garland, Hugh A. The Life of John Randolph of Roanoke, 2 vols. in 1. 11th ed. Repr. of 1857 ed. 42.00 (ISBN 0-384-17680-1). Johnson Repr.

--The Life of John Randolph of Roanoke, 2 vols. in 1. 1981. Repr. lib. bdg. 25.00x (ISBN 0-403-00212-5). Scholarly.

Garland, J. C., ed. see Conference on the Electrical Tansport & Optical Properties of Inhomogeneous Media, 1st, Ohio State Univ., Sept. 1977.

Garland, J. D. National Electrical Code Questions & Answers, 1981. 2nd ed. 144p. (Orig.). 1981. pap. 7.95 O.P. (ISBN 0-13-609339-6). P-H.

--National Electrical Code Questions & Answers, 1984. 144p. 1985. text ed. 17.95 (ISBN 0-13-609561-5); pap. 12.95 (ISBN 0-13-609553-4). P-H.

--National Electrical Code Reference Book, 1981. 3rd ed. (Illus.). 640p. 1981. 31.95 (ISBN 0-13-609321-3). P-H.

--National Electrical Code Reference Book, 1984. 4th ed. (Illus.). 624p. 1984. text ed. 27.95 O.P. (ISBN 0-13-609546-1). P-H.

Garland, James A. The Private Stable. LC 75-44371. (Illus.). 1976. Repr. of 1903 ed. 50.00 (ISBN 0-88427-018-1). North River.

Garland, James A. & Kolodny, Ralph. The Treatment of Children Through Social Group Work: A Developmental Approach. 1980. text ed. 20.00x (ISBN 0-89182-016-7); pap. text ed. 10.00 (ISBN 0-89182-017-5). Charles River Bks.

Garland, Jim. Welcome the Traveler Home: Jim Garland's Story of the Kentucky Mountains. Ardery, Julia S., ed. LC 80-50564. 280p. 1983. 23.00 (ISBN 0-8131-1432-2). U Pr of Ky.

Garland, Joe & Sharp, Jim. Adventure: Queen of the Windjammers. LC 85-70646. (Illus.). 208p. 1984. 24.95 (ISBN 0-89272-206-1). Down East.

Garland, John. Industrial Cooperation Between Poland & the West. Farmer, Richard, ed. LC 84-28070. (Research for Business Decisions Ser: No.71). 216p. 1985. 34.95 (ISBN 0-8357-1619-8). UMI Res Pr.

Garland, John K. Chemistry of Our World. (Illus.). 768p. 1975. text ed. 19.95 (ISBN 0-02-340520-1, 34052). Macmillan.

Garland, Joseph E. Boston's Gold Coast: The North Shore 1890-1929. 1981. 19.95 (ISBN 0-316-30430-1). Little.

--Boston's North Shore: Being an Account of Life Among the Noteworthy, Fashionable, Wealthy, Eccentric & Ordinary 1823-1890. (Illus.). 1978. 19.95 (ISBN 0-316-30425-5). Little.

--Boston's North Shore, 1823-1890 & Boston's Gold Coast, 1890-1929. 1981. boxed set 40.00 (ISBN 0-316-30432-8). Little.

--Centennial History of the Boston Medical Library. (Illus.). 233p. 1975. 9.95 (ISBN 0-686-15546-7). F A Countway.

--Down to the Sea: The Fishing Schooners of Gloucester. LC 82-49340. (Illus.). 224p. 1983. 27.50 (ISBN 0-87923-470-9). Godine.

--Eastern Point, 1606-1950. 1971. 17.95 (ISBN 0-87233-019-2). Bauhan.

--The Gloucester Guide, a Retrospective Ramble. LC 72-97361. (Illus.). 1973. 2.95 (ISBN 0-930352-00-9). Nelson B Robinson.

--Guns off Gloucester. LC 75-21650. (Illus.). 1975. pap. 3.95 (ISBN 0-930352-06-8). Nelson B Robinson.

--Lone Voyager. rev. ed. LC 63-13452. (Illus.). 1978. pap. 6.95 (ISBN 0-930352-05-X). Nelson B Robinson.

--Lone Voyager: New & Revised Edition of the Life of Howard Blackburn. (Illus.). 15.00 (ISBN 0-8446-5650-X). Peter Smith.

Garland, Joseph E., ed. see Brooks, Alfred M.

Garland, Ken. Illustrated Graphics Glossary. 192p. 1981. 30.00x (ISBN 0-09-141511-X, Pub. by Barrie & Jenkins England). State Mutual Bk.

Garland, L. D., ed. see Dalton, C. W.

Garland, LaRetta & Bush, Carol. Coping Behavior. 1982. text ed. 18.95 (ISBN 0-87909-088-X); pap. text ed. 14.95 (ISBN 0-87909-089-8). Reston.

Garland, Madge. The Small Garden in the City. LC 74-76646. (Illus.). 136p. 1974. 12.50 (ISBN 0-8076-0752-5). Braziller.

Garland, Madge, jt. auth. see Black, J. Anderson.

Garland, Margaret. Terri's Dream. (Caprice Romances Ser.). 144p. (YA) (gr. 7 up). 1984. pap. 1.95 (ISBN 0-441-80104-8, Pub. by Tempo). Ace Bks.

--Winter Break. (Caprice Romance Ser.: No. 56). 160p. 1985. pap. 2.25 (ISBN 0-441-89434-8). Ace Bks.

Garland, Margret W. Songs Along the Way. Strawn, John T., ed. 48p. (Orig.). 1981. pap. write for info. (ISBN 0-943548-00-4). Strawn.

Garland, Martha M. Cambridge Before Darwin. LC 80-40327. 224p. 1980. 42.50 (ISBN 0-521-23319-4). Cambridge U Pr.

Garland, Mary. Hebbel's Prose Tragedies. LC 72-88621. (Anglica Germanica Ser.: No. 2). 364p. 1973. 64.50 (ISBN 0-521-20090-3). Cambridge U Pr.

Garland, Mary, jt. ed. see Garland, Henry.

Garland, Massimo. A Dramatic Portfolio of the Most Meaningful Paintings of the Impressionists. (Illus.). 94p. 1985. 88.95 (ISBN 0-86650-157-6). Gloucester Art.

Garland, Michael J., jt. ed. see Jonsen, Albert R.

Garland, P. B. & Crumpton, M. J., eds. The Lymphocyte Cell Surface. (Symposia Ser.: No. 45). 124p. 1981. 60.00x (ISBN 0-904498-10-7, Pub. by Biochemical England). State Mutual Bk.

Garland, P. B. & Hales, C. N., eds. Substrate Mobilization & Energy Provision in Man. (Symposia Ser.: No. 43). 228p. 1981. 32.00x (ISBN 0-904498-07-7, Pub. by Biochemical England). State Mutual Bk.

Garland, P. B. & Mathias, A. P., eds. Biochemistry of the Cell Nucleus. (Symposia Ser.: No. 42). 244p. 1981. 30.00x (ISBN 0-904498-03-4, Pub. by Biochemical England). State Mutual Bk.

Garland, P. B. & Williamson, R., eds. Biochemistry of Genetic Engineering. (Symposia Ser.: No. 44). 145p. 1981. 27.50x (ISBN 0-904498-08-5, Pub. by Biochemical England). State Mutual Bk.

Garland, Paul G. American-Brazilian Private International Law. LC 59-8602. (Bilateral Studies in Private International Law: No. 9). 125p. 1959. 15.00 (ISBN 0-379-11409-7). Oceana.

Garland, Robert. Derfflinger. 1978. pap. 1.75 (ISBN 0-532-17181-0). Woodhill.

--The Greek Way of Death. LC 85-470. (Illus.). 208p. 1985. text ed. 22.50x (ISBN 0-8014-1823-2). Cornell U Pr.

Garland, Robert R., jt. auth. see Bongiorno, Benedetto.

Garland, Rosemary, ed. My Bedtime Book of Two-Minute Stories. LC 76-96773. (Illus.). 128p. (gr. k-2). 1976. 5.95 (ISBN 0-448-01873-X, G&D). Putnam Pub Group.

Garland, Roy, ed. see Microcomputers in Primary Education, Univ. of Exeter, April 1981.

Garland, Sarah. Going Shopping. Kroupa, Melanie, ed. LC 84-71902. (Illus.). 32p. (ps-k). 1985. 6.95 (ISBN 0-87113-001-7). Atlantic Monthly.

--Having a Picnic. Kroupa, Melanie, ed. LC 84-71901. (Illus.). 32p. (ps-k). 1985. 6.95 (ISBN 0-87113-002-5). Atlantic Monthly.

--The Herb Garden. (Penguin Handbooks Ser.). 168p. 1985. pap. 12.95 (ISBN 0-14-046690-8). Penguin.

--The Herb Garden. (Penguin Handbooks Ser.). 168p. 1985. 27.50 (ISBN 0-670-36865-2). Viking.

Garland, William S. Earthquake New England: Learning to Live in a Seismic Zone. (Illus.). 64p. (Orig.). 1982. write for info. (ISBN 0-943440-00-9); pap. 6.95 (ISBN 0-686-99300-4). Home-Science.

Garlett, Marti W. Who Will Be My Teacher? The Christian Way to Stronger Schools. 256p. 1985. 12.95 (ISBN 0-8499-0471-4, 0471-4). Word Bks.

Garlick, David & Korner, P. I., eds. Frontiers in Physiological Research. 650p. Date not set. 95.00 (ISBN 0-521-26838-9). Cambridge U Pr.

Garlick, J. P., ed. Human Ecology in the Tropics. (Symposia of the Society for the Study of Human Biology Ser.: Vol. 16). 172p. 1976. cancelled (ISBN 0-85066-098-X). Taylor & Francis.

Garlick, J. P., jt. ed. see Clegg, E. J.

Garlick, Kenneth, et al, eds. see Farington, Joseph.

Garlick, Paul L. Garlick Family History. 122p. 1984. perfect bdg. 31.00 (ISBN 0-318-03873-0). Closson Pr.

Garlick, R. C., Jr. & Guidi, Angelo F. Italy & the Italians in Washington's Time. 132p. 1933. 8.50x (ISBN 0-913298-46-8). S F Vanni.

Garlick, Raymond & Mathias, Roland, eds. Anglo-Welsh Poetry Fourteen Eighty to Nineteen Eighty. LC 84-72667. (Illus.). 377p. 1985. 19.00 (ISBN 0-907476-21-X, Pub by Poetry Wales Pr UK). Dufour.

Garlick, Richard C., Jr., et al. Italy & Italians in Washington's Time. LC 74-17930. (Italian American Experience Ser.). 142p. 1975. Repr. 10.00 (ISBN 0-405-06402-0). Ayer Co Pubs.

Garliner, Daniel. Swallow Right-or Else! LC 78-75294. 110p. 1979. 9.00 (ISBN 0-87527-195-2). Green.

Garling, D. J. H., tr. see Koethe, G.

Garling, Marguerite. Human Rights Handbook. 1979. lib. bdg. 25.00 (ISBN 0-87196-403-1). Facts on File.

--The Human Rights Handbook. 300p. 1981. 15.00x (ISBN 0-333-26073-2, Pub. by Index on Censorship England). State Mutual Bk.

Garlinghouse Co. Staff, ed. Single-Level Home Plans. 2nd ed. LC 84-82406. (Illus.). 112p. 1985. pap. 2.95 (ISBN 0-938708-13-9). L F Garlinghouse Co.

--Traditional Home Plans. 2nd ed. LC 85-70893. (Illus.). 112p. 1985. pap. 2.95 (ISBN 0-938708-14-7). L F Garlinghouse Co.

Garlington, J. C. Men of the Time: Sketches of Living Notables, a Biographical Encyclopedia of Contemporaneous South Carolina Leaders. LC 74-187366. (Illus.). 471p. 1972. Repr. of 1902 ed. 25.00 (ISBN 0-87152-094-X). Reprint.

Garlington, Warren K. & Shimota, Helen E. Statistically Speaking. (Illus.). 126p. 1964. 12.75x (ISBN 0-398-00644-X). C C Thomas.

Garlington, William. Fire & Blood: A Novel. (Pioneer Paperback Ser.). 200p. (Orig.). 1984. pap. 7.95 (ISBN 0-933770-08-1). Kalimat.

Garlinski, Jazef. Poland, Soe & the Allies. 1969. 15.00 (ISBN 0-685-56062-7). Beachcomber Bks.

Garlinski, Josef. Poland in the Second World War. 400p. 1985. 25.00 (ISBN 0-87052-155-1). Hippocrene Bks.

Garlinski, Jozef. The Swift Corridor: Espionage Networks in Switzerland During World War II. (Illus.). 252p. 1981. 24.00x (ISBN 0-460-04351-X, Pub. by J. M. Dent England). Biblio Dist.

Garlits, Don. Close Calls. 175p. (Orig.). 1984. pap. 6.95 (ISBN 0-910311-19-6). Huntington Hse Inc.

Garlock, Dorothy. Annie Lash. (Orig.). 1985. pap. 3.95 (ISBN 0-445-20037-5, Pub. by Popular Lib). Warner Bks.

--Forever Victoria. 1983. pap. 3.50 (ISBN 0-515-07444-6). Jove Pubns.

--Glorious Dawn. 256p. (Orig.). 1982. pap. 2.50 (ISBN 0-449-14492-5, GM). Fawcett.

--Love & Cherish. 1982. pap. 2.50 (ISBN 0-89083-897-6). Zebra.

--A Love for All Time. (Loveswept Ser.: No. 6). 1983. pap. 1.95 (ISBN 0-553-21606-6). Bantam.

--Wild Sweet Wilderness. 400p. (Orig.). 1985. pap. 3.95 (ISBN 0-445-20011-1, Pub. by Popular Lib). Warner Bks.

Garlock, Frank. The Big Beat: A Rock Blast. 54p. 1971. pap. 1.95 (ISBN 0-89084-153-5). Bob Jones Univ Pr.

Garlock, H. B. Before We Kill & Eat You. 1.95 (ISBN 0-89985-109-6). Christ Nations.

Garlock, Jonathan, compiled by. Guide to the Local Assemblies of the Knights of Labor. LC 81-13449. (Illus.). xxvii, 268p. 1982. lib. bdg. 65.00 (ISBN 0-313-23129-X, GKL/). Greenwood.

Garlock, Ruthanne. Fire in His Bones. LC 81-80951. 1981. pap. 2.95 (ISBN 0-88270-451-6, Pub. by Logos). Bridge Pub.

Garlock, Victor P., jt. ed. see Smrtic, George R.

Garlow, James. Partners in Ministry. (Illus.). 195p. (Orig.). 1981. pap. 4.95 (ISBN 0-8341-0693-0). Beacon Hill.

Garlow, James L. LITE Manual. 1982. pap. 6.95 (ISBN 0-8341-0883-6, S-2000); Leader's Guide 14.95. Beacon Hill.

Garman, D., ed. see Rickwood, Edgell.

Garman, Douglas, tr. see Flaubert, Gustave.

Garman, E. Thomas & Eckert, Sidney W. The Consumer's World: Economic Issues & Money Management. 2nd ed. (Illus.). 1979. pap. 26.90 (ISBN 0-07-022878-7). McGraw.

Garman, Michael, jt. ed. see Fletcher, Paul.

Garman, Tom, et al. Personal Finance. LC 84-80173. 704p. 1984. text ed. 26.95 (ISBN 0-395-35663-6); instr's. manual 2.00 (ISBN 0-395-36136-2); write for info. study guide (ISBN 0-395-36102-8). HM.

Garmen, Douglas, tr. The Memoirs of Chancellor Pasquier 1767-1815. LC 68-9353. (Illus.). 292p. 1968. 24.50 (ISBN 0-8386-6981-6). Fairleigh Dickinson.

Garmendia Miangolarra, J. Ignacio de. Diccionario De Bolsa. 208p. (Span.). 1977. leatherette 14.95 (ISBN 84-368-0057-5, S-50182). French & Eur.

Garmendia y Berasategui, Ignacio de. Diccionario Maritimo Ilustrado Vasco-Castellano, Castellano-Vasco. (Vasco & Span.). 42.00x (ISBN 84-248-0047-8, S-50054). French & Eur.

Garmey, Jane. Great British Cooking: A Well Kept Secret. LC 81-40247. (Illus.). 215p. 1981. 15.50 (ISBN 0-394-50876-9). Random.

Garmey, Stephen. Gramercy Park: An Illustrated History of a New York Neighborhood. LC 84-11070. (Illus.). 192p. 1984. 19.95 (ISBN 0-917439-00-7). Balsam Pr.

Garmezy, Norman. Vulnerable & Invulnerable Children: Theory, Research, & Intervention. (Master Lectures on Developmental Psychology: Manuscript No. 1337). 7.50x (ISBN 0-912704-32-2). Am Psychol.

Garmezy, Norman, ed. Stress, Coping, & Development in Children. Rutter, Michael. (Illus.). 368p. 1983. 29.95 (ISBN 0-07-022886-8). McGraw.

Garmire, Bernard L., ed. Local Government Police Management. 2nd. rev. ed. LC 81-7174. (Municipal Management Ser.). (Illus.). 447p. 1982. text ed. 37.50 (ISBN 0-87326-024-4). Intl City Mgt.

Garmo, Charles De see De Garmo, Charles.

Garmo, Murshed. School of Heroes. (Arabic.). pap. 12.00x (ISBN 0-86685-140-2). Intl Bk Ctr.

Garmonsway, G. N. Anglo-Saxon Chronicle. Ingram, James, tr. 1978. 11.95x (ISBN 0-460-10624-4, Evman); pap. 4.95x (ISBN 0-460-11624-X, Evman). Biblio Dist.

Garmonsway, G. N., ed. Aelfric's Colloquy. rev. ed. 64p. 1978. pap. text ed. 3.75x (ISBN 0-85989-098-8, Pub. by U Exeter England). Humanities.

Garmonsway, G. N., ed. see Aelfric.

Garms, Walter I., et al. School Finance: The Economics & Politics of Public Education. (Illus.). 1978. text ed. 29.95 (ISBN 0-13-793315-0). P-H.

Garms-Homolova, et al, eds. Intergenerational Relationships. 272p. 1984. text ed. 16.80 (ISBN 0-88937-007-9). Hogrefe Intl.

Garn, Jake & Coffey, J. I. The Future of U. S. Land Based Strategic Forces. LC 80-83767. (Special Report Ser.). 80p. 1980. write for info. Inst Foreign Policy Anal.

Garn, Paul, jt. auth. see Schwenker, Robert F., Jr.

Garn, Stanley M. The Earlier Gain & Later Loss of Cortical Bone: In Nutritional Perspective. (Illus.). 168p. 1970. photycopy ed. 17.50x (ISBN 0-398-00645-8). C C Thomas.

--Human Races. 3rd ed. (Illus.). 216p. 1971. photocopy ed. 15.75x (ISBN 0-398-00646-6). C C Thomas.

--Writing the Biomedical Research Paper. 76p. 1970. pap. 9.75x spiral (ISBN 0-398-00648-2). C C Thomas.

Garn, Stanley M., ed. Readings on Race. 2nd ed. (Illus.). 324p. 1968. 24.75x (ISBN 0-398-00647-4). C C Thomas.

Garnand, Harry J. Influence of Walter Scott on Works of Balzac. LC 79-120617. 1970. Repr. lib. bdg. 16.50x (ISBN 0-374-93008-2). Octagon.

Garnaut, Ross & Clunies Ross, Anthony I. Taxation of Mineral Rents. LC 83-2088. 1983. 47.50x (ISBN 0-19-828454-3). Oxford U Pr.

Garnaut, Ross, ed. ASEAN in a Changing Pacific & World Economy. LC 79-56230. (Illus.). 557p. 1981. text ed. 15.00 (ISBN 0-7081-1302-8, 0057, Pub. by ANUP Australia). Australia N U P.

Garne, Geoffrey E. Sweet Here & Now. (Anchor Ser.). 1984. 5.95 (ISBN 0-8163-0543-9). Pacific Pr Pub Assn.

Garneau, Jean-Luc. Semantic Divergence in Anglo-French Cognates: A Synchronic Study in Contrastive Lexicography. (Edward Sapir Monograph Series in Language, Culture, & Cognition: No. 14). x, 128p. (Orig.). 1985. pap. 10.00x (ISBN 0-933104-20-0). Jupiter Pr.

Garneau, R. G. & McCawley, P. T., eds. Indonesia: Dualism, Growth & Poverty. 267p. 1981. pap. text ed. 10.00 (ISBN 0-909596-61-1, 1146, Pub. by ANUP Australia). Australia N U P.

Garnel, Donald. The Rise of Teamster Power in the West. 1971. 38.50x (ISBN 0-520-01733-1). U of Cal Pr.

Garnell, P. Guided Weapon Control Systems. 2nd ed. (Illus.). 248p. 1985. 44.00 (ISBN 0-08-025468-3). Pergamon.

Garner & Klintworth. Pathobiology of Ocular Disease, Pt. A & B. 1982. Set. 295.00. Part A, 886p (ISBN 0-8247-1295-1). Part B., 868p (ISBN 0-8247-1393-1). Dekker.

Garner, A. E., jt. auth. see Holcomb, J. D.

Garner, Alan. Alan Garner's Book of British Fairy Tales. LC 85-4586. (Illus.). 160p. 1985. 16.95 (ISBN 0-385-29425-5). Delacorte.

--Conversationally Speaking: Tested New Ways to Increase Your Personal & Social Effectiveness. 164p. (Orig.). 1981. pap. 5.95 (ISBN 0-07-022885-X). McGraw.

--Elidor. 160p. 1981. pap. 1.95 (ISBN 0-345-29042-9, Del Rey). Ballantine.

--The Owl Service. 192p. 1981. pap. 1.95 (ISBN 0-345-29044-5, Del Rey). Ballantine.

--The Red Shift. 1981. pap. 1.95 (ISBN 0-345-29858-6, Del Rey). Ballantine.

--The Weirdstone of Brinsingamen. 1981. pap. 1.95 (ISBN 0-345-29043-7, Del Rey). Ballantine.

Garner, Anita P., jt. auth. see Skeen, Patsy.

Garner, Art. Why Winners Win. 128p. 1981. 6.95 (ISBN 0-88289-267-3). Pelican.

Garner, Arthur E., et al. Curriculum for Better Schools. 368p. (Orig.). 1980. pap. 14.50 (ISBN 0-8403-2192-9). Kendall-Hunt.

Garner, Arthur G. A Long Road to Eden. (Orig.). 1979. pap. 1.95 (ISBN 0-532-23248-8). Woodhill.

Garner, Barry, jt. auth. see Yeates, Maurice.

Garner, Claud. Cornbread Aristocrat. LC 83-71547. 328p. 1983. 15.95 (ISBN 0-935304-57-6); pap. 7.95 (ISBN 0-935304-58-4). August Hse.

Garner, Clifford S. Special Techniques of Applied Kinesiology. (Illus.). viii, 55p. (Orig.). 1983. pap. 11.95 (ISBN 0-9612808-0-8). C S Garner.

Garner, Cyril W., tr. see Beckmann, Friedrich & Schmidt, Eckart.

Garner, D. R., jt. auth. see Carroll, M. E.

Garner, David M. & Garfinkel, Paul E. Handbook of Psychotherapy for Anorexia Nervosa & Bulimia. 592p. 1985. text ed. 39.50 (ISBN 0-89862-642-0). Guilford Pr.

Garner, David M., jt. auth. see Garfinkel, Paul E.

Garner, David P. & Stahl, G. Allan, eds. The Effects of Hostile Environments on Coatings & Plastics. LC 83-9230. (ACS Symposium Ser.: No. 229). 339p. 1983. lib. bdg. 47.95x (ISBN 0-8412-0798-4). Am Chemical.

Garner, Don E. Corporate Audit Costs & Staffing, 1980-1981. (Illus.). 147p. 1983. pap. text ed. 27.00 (ISBN 0-89413-106-0, 518). Inst Inter Aud.

Garner, Dwight L. Idea to Delivery: A Handbook of Oral Communication. 3rd ed. 1979. pap. write for info. (ISBN 0-534-00599-3). Wadsworth Pub.

Garner, Gerald W. The Police Meet the Press. 292p. 1984. 29.75x (ISBN 0-398-04916-5). C C Thomas.

--The Police Role in Alcohol-Related Crises. 168p. 1979. 14.75x. C C Thomas.

--Police Supervision: A Common Sense Approach. 264p. 1981. 27.50x (ISBN 0-398-04127-X). C C Thomas.

Garner, Gretchen. An Art History of Ephemera: Gretchen Garner's Catalog. (Illus.). 60p. (Orig.). 1982. pap. 15.00 (ISBN 0-9608766-0-X). Tulip Pr MN.

Garner, H. H. Psychosomatic Management of the Patient with Malignancy. 144p. 1966. 14.50x (ISBN 0-398-00651-2). C C Thomas.

Garner, Harry H. Psychotherapy & the Confrontation Problem-Solving Technique. LC 74-110426. 362p. 1971. 18.50 (ISBN 0-87527-011-5). Green.

Garner, Harry M. Chinese & Japanese Cloisonne Enamels. (Illus.). 1962. 41.50 (ISBN 0-8048-0093-6). C E Tuttle.

Garner, Sir Harry. Chinese Lacquer. (Illus.). 289p. 1979. 54.00 (ISBN 0-571-11286-2). Faber & Faber.

Garner, Helen. Monkey Grip. 1984. pap. 3.95 (ISBN 0-14-004953-3). Penguin.

Garner, Herschel W. Population Dynamics, Reproduction, & Activities of the Kangaroo Rat, Dipodomys ordii, in Western Texas. (Graduate Studies: No. 7). (Illus.). 28p. 1974. pap. 2.00 (ISBN 0-89672-014-4). Tex Tech Pr.

Garner, Howard G. Teamwork in Programs for Children & Youth: A Handbook for Administrators. (Illus.). 154p. 1982. 22.75x (ISBN 0-398-04655-7). C C Thomas.

Garner, Irene A., jt. auth. see Fearn, Leif.

Garner, J. A Name to Salute. 1982. 10.95 (ISBN 0-533-05368-4). Vantage.

Garner, J., et al. Research Studies in Elementary Mathematics. 1969. pap. 9.95x tchr's. ed. (ISBN 0-8290-1185-4). Irvington.

Garner, J. F. Planning Law in Western Europe. LC 74-30920. 353p. 1975. 38.50 (ISBN 0-444-10833-5, North-Holland). Elsevier.

--Practical Planning Law: A Handbook for Planners, Architects & Surveyors. 246p. 1981. pap. 11.50 (ISBN 0-7099-1107-6, Pub. by Croom Helm Ltd); 31.50 (ISBN 0-7099-1106-8). Longwood Pub Group.

Garner, J. F., jt. ed. see Friedmann, Wolfgang G.

Garner, J. W. Reconstruction in Mississippi. 1964. 13.25 (ISBN 0-8446-1196-4). Peter Smith.

Garner, James W. Reconstruction in Mississippi. LC 12-1798. xxx, 422p. 1968. pap. text ed. 9.95x (ISBN 0-8071-0137-0). La State U Pr.

--Studies in Government & International Law. Fairlie, John A., ed. 574p. 1972. Repr. of 1943 ed. lib. bdg. 23.00x (ISBN 0-8371-5966-0, GASG). Greenwood.

Garner, James W., tr. see Brissaud, J. B.

Garner, Jane, ed. & intro. by. The Central American Connection: Library Resources & Access. (Papers of the Seminar on the Acquisition of Latin American Library Materials: No. 28). (Orig.). 1985. pap. 35.00 (ISBN 0-317-28109-7). SALALM.

Garner, Jane, jt. ed. see De Mundo Lo, Sara.

Garner, Joe. The Commonwealth Office. LC 79-302772. 1978. text ed. 60.00x (ISBN 0-435-32355-5). Heinemann Ed.

Garner, John. The Franchise & Politics in British North America, 1755-1867. LC 76-395435. (Canadian Studies in History & Government: No. 13). pap. 67.00 (ISBN 0-317-27044-3, 2023621). Bks Demand UMI.

--How to Make & Set Nets. 1978. 25.00 (ISBN 0-685-63427-2). State Mutual Bk.

--How to Make & Set Nets: The Technology of Netting. (Illus.). 96p. 12.00 (ISBN 0-85238-031-3, FN53, FNB). Unipub.

--Modern Deep Sea Trawling Gear. 1978. 40.00 (ISBN 0-685-63436-1). State Mutual Bk.

--Modern Deep Sea Trawling Gear. 2nd ed. (Illus.). 84p. 1977. 23.75 (ISBN 0-85238-085-2, FN65, FNB). Unipub.

--Modern Inshore Fishing Gear. 1978. 40.00 (ISBN 0-685-63440-X). State Mutual Bk.

--Pelagic & Semi Pelagic Trawling Gear. 1978. 50.00x (ISBN 0-685-63446-9). State Mutual Bk.

--Pelagic & Semi-Pelagic Trawling Gear. (Illus.). 60p. 1979. 33.75 (ISBN 0-85238-088-7, FN74, FNB). Unipub.

Garner, John S. The Model Company Town: Urban Design Through Private Enterprise in Nineteenth-Century New England. LC 84-8636. (Illus.). 240p. 1985. lib. bdg. 25.00x (ISBN 0-87023-442-0). U of Mass Pr.

Garner, June B. June Brown's Guide to Let's Read. rev. ed. 56p. 1981. pap. 2.50 (ISBN 0-8143-1690-5). Wayne St U Pr.

Garner, K. C. Introduction to Control Systems Performance Measurements. 1968. 28.00 (ISBN 0-08-012499-2); pap. 11.25 (ISBN 0-08-012498-4). Pergamon.

Garner, K. C., jt. auth. see Wass, C. A.

Garner, Kathryn F. & Young, Christa G. My Prayer Diary. LC 78-17345. 1978. pap. 7.95 spiral bd (ISBN 0-8407-5657-7). Nelson.

Garner, L. E. Outline of Projective Geometry. 220p. 1981. 36.75 (ISBN 0-444-00423-8, North-Holland). Elsevier.

--Sand Resources of Texas Gulf Coast. (Report of Investigations: RI 60). (Illus.). 85p. 1967. 1.50 (ISBN 0-318-03161-2). Bur Econ Geology.

Garner, Lawrence. Dry Stone Walls. (Shire Album Ser.: No. 114). (Illus.). 32p. (Orig.). 1984. pap. 2.95 (ISBN 0-85263-666-0, Pub. by Shire Pubns England). Seven Hills Bks.

--Shropshire. (Shire County Guide Ser.: No. 7). (Orig.). 1985. pap. 4.95 (ISBN 0-85263-740-3, Pub. by Shire Pubns England). Seven Hills Bks.

Garner, Les. Stepping Stones to Women's Liberty: Feminist Ideas in the Women's Suffrage Movement, 1900-1918. LC 83-25360. 144p. 1984. 24.50 (ISBN 0-8386-3223-8). Fairleigh Dickinson.

Garner, Nathan. A Different Drummer Notes. 64p. (Orig.). 1973. pap. text ed. 3.95 (ISBN 0-8220-0389-9). Cliffs.

Garner, Patricia A. The Office Telephone: A User's Guide. (Illus.). 272p. 1984. pap. 16.95 (ISBN 0-13-631481-3). P-H.

Garner, Paul S. & Hughes, Marilyn, eds. Readings on Accounting Development: Original Anthology. new ed. LC 77-87313. (Development of Contemporary Accounting Thought Ser). 1978. lib. bdg. 34.50x (ISBN 0-405-10926-1). Ayer Co Pubs.

Garner, Philip. Philip Garner's Better Living Catalog. (Illus.). 96p. (Orig.). 1982. pap. 6.95 (ISBN 0-933328-39-7). Delilah Bks.

--Philip Garner's Utopia: Products for the Perfect World. (Illus.). 80p. (Orig.). 1984. pap. 6.95 (ISBN 0-933328-99-0). Delilah Bks.

Garner, Philip, commentary by. Rube Goldberg: A Retrospective. (Illus.). 96p. (Orig.). 1983. pap. 5.95 (ISBN 0-933328-72-9). Delilah Bks.

Garner, Philippe. Contemporary Decorative Arts: From 1940 to the Present. 224p. 1980. 29.95 (ISBN 0-87196-472-4). Facts on File.

--Emile Galle. (Illus.). 168p. 1984. 29.95 (ISBN 0-312-24416-9). St Martin.

--Twentieth Century Style & Design: Nineteen Hundred to the Present. LC 84-3706. 320p. 1985. 39.95 (ISBN 0-442-23008-7). Van Nos Reinhold.

Garner, Philippe, jt. auth. see Clarke, Bob C.

Garner, Phillipe, et al. The Amazing Bugattis: Three Generations of Craftsmen, Artists, & Designers. LC 79-54154. 1979. pap. 9.95 (ISBN 0-8120-2181-9). Barron.

Garner, R. J. & Chaudhri, S. A. The Propagation of Tropical Fruit Trees. 566p. 1982. 65.00x (ISBN 0-85198-351-0, Pub. by CAB Bks England). State Mutual Bk.

Garner, Ray. He Rescued Me. 1982. pap. 4.50 (ISBN 0-570-03628-3, 39-1074). Concordia.

Garner, Richard L. & Henderson, Donald C. Columbus & Related Family Papers, 1451-1902: An Inventory of the Boal Collection. LC 74-12303. (Penn State Studies: No. 37). 96p. 1974. pap. 5.95x (ISBN 0-271-01174-2). Pa St U Pr.

Garner, Robert, jt. auth. see Gutkoska, Joseph.

Garner, Robert H. The Way of St. Francis. 1984. 6.95 (ISBN 0-8062-1605-0). Carlton.

Garner, S. Paul. Evolution of Cost Accounting. LC 76-41238. (Accounting History Classics Ser.: Vol. 1). (Illus.). 432p. 1976. pap. 11.95 (ISBN 0-8173-8900-8). U of Ala Pr.

Garner, Sam, ed. see Scribbs, Buck.

Garner, Shirley N., et al. The Mother Tongue: Essays in Feminist Psychoanalytic Interpretation. LC 84-17560. (Illus.). 400p. 1985. text ed. 39.50x (ISBN 0-8014-1693-0); pap. text ed. 12.95x (ISBN 0-8014-9299-8). Cornell U Pr.

Garner, Stanton. Harold Frederic. (Pamphlets on American Writers Ser: No. 83). (Orig.). 1969. pap. 1.25x (ISBN 0-8166-0545-9, MPAW83). U of Minn Pr.

Garner, Stanton, ed. see Frederic, Harold.

Garner, Stanton, ed. see Lawrence, Mary.

Garner, Van H. The Broken Ring: The Destruction of the California Indians. LC 80-52892. (Illus.). 1982. 10.50 (ISBN 0-87026-057-X). Westernlore.

Garner, Wendall R. The Processing of Information & Structure. LC 73-22174. 208p. 1974. text ed. 24.95 (ISBN 0-89859-119-8). L Erlbaum Assocs.

Garner, Willa Y. & Harvey, John, Jr., eds. Chemical & Biological Controls in Forestry. LC 83-22440. (ACS Symposium Ser.: No. 238). 406p. 1984. text ed. 69.95x (ISBN 0-8412-0818-2). Am Chemical.

Garner, William R. Letters from California, 1846-1847. Craig, Donald M., ed. LC 71-124736. (Illus.). 1970. 19.95 (ISBN 0-520-01565-7). U of Cal Pr.

Garner, William V. Soviet Threat Perceptions of NATO's Eurostrategic Missiles. (The Atlantic Papers: No. 52-53). (Illus.). 204p. 1983. pap. 14.00x (ISBN 0-8476-7354-5). Rowman & Allanheld.

Garnet, Eva D. Chair Exercise Manual: An Audio-Assisted Program of Body Dynamics. LC 81-82793. (Illus.). 272p. 1982. spiral bdg. 20.00 (ISBN 0-916622-20-7). Princeton Bk Co.

--Movement Is Life: A Holistic Approach to Exercise for Older Adults. LC 81-80564. (Illus.). 168p. 1982. pap. text ed. 10.00 (ISBN 0-916622-19-3). Princeton Bk Co.

Garnet, Henry H. Past & Present Condition, & the Destiny of the Colored Race. facs. ed. LC 77-79010. (Black Heritage Library Collection Ser). 1848. 9.00 (ISBN 0-8369-8576-1). Ayer Co Pubs.

Garnet, Henry H., jt. auth. see Walker, David.

Garnet, J. Ros. Wild Flowers of Wilson's Promontory National Park. (Illus.). 1979. 7.95x (ISBN 0-85091-111-7, Pub. by Lothian). Intl Spec Bk.

Garnet, Louis. Droit et Societe dans la Grece Ancienne. Vlastos, Gregory, ed. LC 78-19346. (Morals & Law in Ancient Greece Ser.). (Fr. & Gr.). 1979. Repr. of 1955 ed. lib. bdg. 19.00x (ISBN 0-405-11543-1). Ayer Co Pubs.

Garnet, Robert W. The Telephone Enterprise: The Evolution of the Bell System's Horizontal Structure, 1876-1909. LC 84-23419. (AT&T Series in Telephone History). (Illus.). 240p. 1985. 22.50x (ISBN 0-8018-2710-8). Johns Hopkins.

Garnett, Angelica. Deceived with Kindness: A Bloomsbury Childhood. (Illus.). 192p. 1985. 14.95 (ISBN 0-15-124185-6). HarBraceJ.

Garnett, Christopher B. Kantian Philosophy of Space. LC 65-27117. 1965. Repr. of 1939 ed. 21.50x (ISBN 0-8046-0163-1, Pub. by Kennikat). Assoc Faculty Pr.

Garnett, Constance. Grand Inquisitor on the Nature of Man: Dostoevsky. 1948. pap. text ed. write for info. (ISBN 0-02-340600-3). Macmillan.

--Letters of Anton Tchekhov to His Family & Friends. 1920. 25.00 (ISBN 0-8274-2833-2). R West.

Garnett, Constance, tr. see Chekhov, Anton.

Garnett, Constance, tr. see Dostoevsky, Fyodor.

Garnett, Constance, tr. see Dostoyevsky, Fyodor.

Garnett, Constance, tr. see Goncharov, Ivan A.

Garnett, Constance, tr. see Herzen, Alexander.

Garnett, Constance, tr. see Tolstoy, Leo.

Garnett, Constance, tr. see Turgenev, Ivan.

Garnett, Constance, tr. see Turgenev, Ivan & Konovalov, S.

Garnett, Constance, tr. see Turgenev, Ivan S.

Garnett, Constance, tr. see Yarmolinsky, Avrahm.

Garnett, Constance, et al, trs. see Chekhov, Anton.

Garnett, David. First "Hippy" Revolution. 38p. 1970. 3.00 (ISBN 0-88235-053-6). San Marcos.

--Great Friends. LC 79-55596. (Illus.). 1980. 16.95 (ISBN 0-689-11039-1). Atheneum.

--Lady into Fox & a Man in the Zoo. (Illus.). 208p. 1985. pap. 6.95 (ISBN 0-7012-1923-8, Pub. by Hogarth Pr). Merrimack Pub Cir.

Garnett, David, ed. The White-Garnett Letters. LC 68-27294. 1968. 15.00 (ISBN 0-670-76257-1). Viking.

Garnett, David, ed. see Lawrence, Thomas E.

Garnett, E. Turgenev. LC 75-25925. (Studies in Russian Literature & Life, No. 100). 1974. lib. bdg. 49.95x (ISBN 0-8383-2011-2). Haskell.

Garnett, Edward. H. E. Bates. 1950. lib. bdg. 10.00 (ISBN 0-8414-4635-0). Folcroft.

--Letters from W. H. Hudson: 1901-1922. 1923. Repr. 30.00 (ISBN 0-8274-2830-8). R West.

--One Hundred Fifty-Three Letters from W. H. Hudson. 1973. Repr. of 1923 ed. lib. bdg. 25.00 (ISBN 0-8414-4636-9). Folcroft.

--Thirty Tales & Sketches. 354p. Repr. of 1929 ed. lib. bdg. 30.00 (ISBN 0-89987-325-1). Darby Bks.

--Tolstoi. LC 74-7035. (Studies in Tolstoy, No. 62). 1974. lib. bdg. 34.95x (ISBN 0-8383-1970-X). Haskell.

--Turgenev. 1979. Repr. lib. bdg. 25.00 (ISBN 0-8495-2029-0). Arden Lib.

--Turgenev. lib. bdg. 12.75 (ISBN 0-8414-4637-7). Folcroft.

Garnett, Edward, ed. see Chesterton, Gilbert K.

Garnett, Edward, ed. see Doughty, C. M.

Garnett, Edward, ed. see Doughty, Charles M.

Garnett, Edward, ed. see Galsworthy, John.

Garnett, Eugene R., jt. auth. see Rechenbach, Charles W.

Garnett, Eve. Family from One End Street. (Illus.). 222p. (gr. 4-7). 1960. 9.95 (ISBN 0-8149-0302-9). Vanguard.

Garnett, Henry. Know about the Armada. LC 66-10696. (Illus.). (gr. 7 up). 1967. 9.50 (ISBN 0-8023-1121-0). Dufour.

Garnett, James E. Selections in English Prose from Elizabeth to Victoria. Repr. of 1891 ed. 17.50 (ISBN 0-686-18789-X). Scholars Ref Lib.

Garnett, James M., ed. Selections in English Prose from Elizabeth to Victoria: 1580-1880. 1978. Repr. of 1891 ed. lib. bdg. 25.00 (ISBN 0-8495-1933-0). Arden Lib.

Garnett, John B. Bounded Analytic Functions. LC 80-81776. (Pure & Applied Mathematics Ser.). 1981. 65.00 (ISBN 0-12-276150-2). Acad Pr.

Garnett, John C. Commonsense & the Theory of International Politics. 192p. 1984. 29.50x (ISBN 0-87395-879-9); pap. 9.95x (ISBN 0-87395-880-2). State U NY Pr.

Garnett, John C., ed. The Defense of Western Europe. LC 73-88028. 250p. 1974. 22.50 (ISBN 0-312-19110-3). St Martin.

--Theories of Peace & Security: A Reader in Contemporary Strategic Thought. 1970. pap. 22.50 (ISBN 0-312-79695-1). St Martin.

Garnett, Lucy M. Balkan Home Life. LC 77-87723. (Illus.). 320p. Repr. of 1917 ed. 37.50 (ISBN 0-404-16580-X). AMS Pr.

--Mysticism & Magic in Turkey: An Account of the Religious Doctrines, Monastic Organisation & Ecstatic Powers of the Dervish Orders. LC 77-87628. (Illus.). Repr. of 1912 ed. 22.00 (ISBN 0-404-16453-6). AMS Pr.

--Turkish Life in Town & Country. LC 77-87629. Repr. of 1904 ed. 28.00 (ISBN 0-404-16454-4). AMS Pr.

--The Turkish People: Their Social Life, Religious Beliefs & Institutions & Domestic Life. LC 77-87630. (Illus.). 352p. Repr. of 1909 ed. 36.00 (ISBN 0-404-16455-2). AMS Pr.

--The Women of Turkey & Their Folk-Lore, 2 vols. LC 77-87539. Repr. of 1891 ed. 73.50 set (ISBN 0-404-16590-7). AMS Pr.

Garnett, Martha R. Samuel Butler & His Family Relations. 228p. 1980. Repr. of 1926 ed. lib. bdg. 25.00 (ISBN 0-8495-1958-6). Arden Lib.

--Samuel Butler & His Family Relations. LC 76-53551. 1976. Repr. of 1926 ed. lib. bdg. 25.00 (ISBN 0-8414-4586-9). Folcroft.

Garnett, Neva Wade. Painting French Dolls with China Painting Techniques. (Illus.). 1985. pap. 12.95 (ISBN 0-87588-245-5, 2915). Hobby Hse.

Garnett, Patricia, jt. auth. see Goodman, Morris E.

Garnett, Paul. The Inner View. 1981. 9.25 (ISBN 0-89536-478-6). CSS of Ohio.

Garnett, R. The Age of Dryden. 1977. Repr. of 1909 ed. lib. bdg. 17.50 (ISBN 0-8495-1902-0). Arden Lib.

--Essays in Librarianship & Bibliography. 1976. lib. bdg. 59.95 (ISBN 0-8490-1784-X). Gordon Pr.

--William Blake: Painter & Poet. LC 77-115857. (Studies in Blake, No. 3). 1970. Repr. of 1895 ed. lib. bdg. 27.95x (ISBN 0-8383-1074-5). Haskell.

Garnett, R, ed. see Williams, Edward E.

Garnett, R. S. Some Book-Hunting Adventures. 1973. Repr. of 1931 ed. 30.00 (ISBN 0-8274-0197-3). R West.

--Some Book-Hunting Adventures: Diversion (Shakespeare, Shelley) 1978. Repr. of 1931 ed. lib. bdg. 25.00 (ISBN 0-8495-1942-X). Arden Lib.

Garnett, R. S., ed. see Rossetti, William M.

Garnett, Richard. The Age of Dryden. facsimile ed. LC 70-164601. (Select Bibliographies Reprint Ser). Repr. of 1895 ed. 20.00 (ISBN 0-8369-5885-3). Ayer Co Pubs.

--The Age of Dryden. 1973. Repr. of 1895 ed. 17.50 (ISBN 0-8274-1280-0). R West.

--Browning's Essay on Shelley. 73p. 1980. Repr. of 1903 ed. lib. bdg. 15.00 (ISBN 0-8492-4962-7). R West.

--Brownings Essay on Shelley: Being His Introduction to the Spurious Shelley Letters. LC 73-539. 1973. lib. bdg. 6.50 (ISBN 0-8414-0968-4). Folcroft.

--Coleridge. 1978. Repr. of 1904 ed. lib. bdg. 12.50 (ISBN 0-8495-1928-4). Arden Lib.

--Coleridge. 111p. 1980. Repr. of 1904 ed. lib. bdg. 12.50 (ISBN 0-89987-307-3). Darby Bks.

--Essays in Librarianship & Bibliography. LC 79-122839. (Bibliography & Reference Ser.: No. 355). 1970. Repr. of 1899 ed. 22.50 (ISBN 0-8337-1282-9). B Franklin.

--Essays of an Ex-Librarian. LC 74-107702. (Essay Index Reprint Ser.). 1901. 20.00 (ISBN 0-8369-1503-8). Ayer Co Pubs.

--History of Italian Literature. 1973. Repr. of 1898 ed. 45.00 (ISBN 0-8274-1345-9). R West.

--Life of Emerson. LC 73-21630. (American Biography Ser., No. 32). 1974. lib. bdg. 43.95x (ISBN 0-8383-1775-8). Haskell.

--Life of John Milton. LC 77-112638. Repr. of 1890 ed. 10.00 (ISBN 0-404-02686-9). AMS Pr.

--Life of John Milton. 1890. lib. bdg. 9.75 (ISBN 0-8414-4638-5). Folcroft.

--Life of Ralph Waldo Emerson. LC 73-12352. 1972. Repr. of 1888 ed. lib. bdg. 12.50 (ISBN 0-8414-4404-8). Folcroft.

--Life of Thomas Carlyle. LC 75-30023. Repr. of 1887 ed. 21.50 (ISBN 0-404-14028-9). AMS Pr.

--Life of Thomas Carlyle. 186p. Repr. of 1887 ed. lib. bdg. 15.00 (ISBN 0-8495-1970-5). Arden Lib.

--Life of Thomas Carlyle. 1977. Repr. lib. bdg. 15.00 (ISBN 0-8495-1903-9). Arden Lib.

--Prose of Milton. 1894. Repr. 20.00 (ISBN 0-8274-3214-3). R West.

--The Twilight of the Gods. Repr. of 1903 ed. 30.00 (ISBN 0-89987-121-6). Darby Bks.

--William Blake: Painter & Poet. 1973. lib. bdg. 12.50 (ISBN 0-8414-2012-2). Folcroft.

Garnett, Richard & Gosse, Edmund W. English Literature, an Illustrated Record, 4 vols in 2. Repr. of 1935 ed. 33.00 (ISBN 0-686-02073-1). Somerset Pub.

Garnett, Richard, jt. auth. see Chesterton, G. K.

Garnett, Richard, et al, eds. The International Library of Famous Literature, 20 vols. 1977. Repr. lib. bdg. 500.00 (ISBN 0-8414-2023-8). Folcroft.
--The International Library of Famous Literature: 20 Vol. set. (Illus.). 1983. 1200.00 set (ISBN 0-89984-220-8). Century Bookbindery.
Garnett, Theodosia V. & Barbata, Jean C. A Collection of Laboratory Specimens & Diagnostic Procedures. (Quality Paperback Ser.: No. 31Q). 106p. (Orig.). 1964. pap. 1.95 (ISBN 0-8226-0310-1). Littlefield.
Garnett, William. The Extraordinary Landscape: Aerial Photographs of America. LC 82-60887. 183p. 1982. 60.00 (ISBN 0-8212-1507-8, 258628). NYGS.
Garnett, William, jt. auth. see Campbell, Lewis.
Garnham, Alan. Psycholinguistics. 300p. 1985. text ed. 35.00 (ISBN 0-416-36610-4, 9622); pap. text ed. 16.95 (ISBN 0-416-36620-1, 9623). Methuen Inc.
Garnham, Harry L. Maintaining the Spirit of Place. LC 84-26646. (Illus.). 158p. 1985. pap. 15.95 (ISBN 0-914886-29-0). PDA Pubs.
Garnham, Nicholas. Samuel Fuller. 1971. 14.95 (ISBN 0-436-09916-0, Pub. by Secker & Warburg UK). David & Charles.
Garnham, Nicholas, tr. see Mattelart, Armand, et al.
Garnham, P. C. Progress in Parasitology. (Heath Clark Lectures, 1968). (Illus.). 224p. 1971. 45.00 (ISBN 0-485-26321-1, Pub. by Athlone Pr Ltd). Longwood Pub Group.
Garnham-Wright, J. H. Building Control by Legislation: The UK Experience. LC 82-21762. (The Theory & Practice of Building Control Ser.: No. 1-667). 243p. 1983. 41.95x (ISBN 0-471-90044-3, Pub. by Wiley-Interscience). Wiley.
Garnholz, Terry & Shank, Marcia. Fun with Fables. (FunThinkers Ser.). (Illus.). 36p. (Basic Set includes: read-along book, activity book, cassete, parent's manual & box. Ensemble includes: Basic set plus 8 boxed crayons, scissors, paste & carrying case.). (gr. 1-5). 1983. pap. 8.00 Basic Set (ISBN 0-88679-028-X, EI-5624); pap. 12.00 Ensemble (ISBN 0-88679-025-5, EI-5604). Educ Insights.
--My Alphabet Sing-Along Book. (FunThinkers Ser.). (Illus.). 24p. (Basic Set includes: read-along & sing-along book, cassette, coloring book, parent's manual & box. Ensemble includes: Basic Set plus 4 boxed wipe-off crayons, 8 boxed regular crayons, 5 wipe-off cards & carrying case.). (ps-1). 1983. pap. 8.00 Basic Set (ISBN 0-88679-033-6, EI-5622); pap. 12.00 Ensemble (ISBN 0-88679-030-1, EI-5602). Educ Insights.
--My Big FunThinker ABC Coloring Book. (FunThinkers Ser.). (Illus.). 36p. (Basic Set includes: coloring book, sing-along book, cassette, parent's manual & box. Ensemble includes: Basic Set plus 5 wipe-off cards, 4 boxed wipe-off crayons, 8 boxed regular crayons & carrying case.). (ps-1). 1983. pap. 8.00 Basic Set (ISBN 0-88679-033-6, EI-5622); pap. 12.00 Ensemble (ISBN 0-88679-030-1, EI-5602). Educ Insights.
--My Big FunThinker Book of Plus 'n' Minus Games. (FunThinkers Ser.). (Illus.). 36p. (Basic Set includes: 8" x 10" activity book, 12 plastic counters, zip-lock bag, 4 drillforms, pad of paper, parent's manual & box. Ensemble includes: Basic Set plus 1 board game, 2 sets of boxed cards for game, 2 pawns, game instructions & carrying case.). (gr. k-2). 1983. pap. 8.00 Basic Set (ISBN 0-88679-005-0, EI-5625); pap. 12.00 Ensemble (ISBN 0-88679-004-2, EI-5605). Educ Insights.
--One, Two, Three What Do You See? (FunThinkers Ser.). (Illus.). 24p. (Basic Set includes: count-along book, activity book, 22 plastic counters, zip-lock bag, parent's manual & box Ensemble includes: Basic Set plus scissors, paste stick, 8 boxed regular crayons & carrying case.). (ps-1). 1983. pap. 6.00 Basic Set (ISBN 0-88679-038-7, EI-5623); pap. 10.00 Ensemble (ISBN 0-88679-035-2, EI-5603). Educ Insights.
--Ten Best-Loved Aesop's Fables for Today's Reader. (FunThinkers Ser.). (Illus.). 24p. (Basic Set includes: reading (read-along) book, cassette, activity book, parent's manual & box. Ensemble includes: Basic Set plus 8 boxed regular crayons, scissors, paste stick & carrying case.). (gr. 1-5). 1983. pap. 8.00 Basic Set (ISBN 0-88679-028-X, EI-5624); pap. 12.00 Ensemble (ISBN 0-88679-025-5, EI-5604). Educ Insights.
Garnica, Olga K. & King, Martha L., eds. Language, Children & Society: The Effect of Social Patterns on Children Learning to Communicate. new ed. (International Series in Psychobiology & Learning (Pal)). 1979. text ed. 72.00 (ISBN 0-08-023716-9). Pergamon.
Garnick, Marc & Richie, Jerome, eds. Urologic Cancer: A Multidisciplinary Approach. 270p. 1983. 35.00x (ISBN 0-306-41473-2, Plenum Pr). Plenum Pub.
Garnick, Marc B., ed. Genitourinary Cancer. (Contemporary Issues in Clinical Oncology Ser.: Vol. 5). (Illus.). 280p. 1985. text ed. 39.50 (ISBN 0-443-08350-9). Churchill.
Garnick, Marc B., jt. ed. see Rieselbach, Richard E.
Garnier. MG Sports Cars. Autocar Editors, ed. LC 78-65889. 1979. 14.95 (ISBN 0-312-50156-0). St Martin.
Garnier, ed. see D'Aubigne, Agrippa.
Garnier, Freres. Catalogue General des Ouvrages Edites Par l'Abbe Migne. LC 71-168926. 1967. Repr. of 1885 ed. 22.50 (ISBN 0-8337-2386-3). B Franklin.
Garnier, Germaine. Histoire de la Monnaie, depuis les Temps de la Plus Haute Antiquite Jusqu'au Regne de Charlemagne, 2 Vols. 1967. Repr. of 1819 ed. 44.50 (ISBN 0-8337-1285-3). B Franklin.
Garnier, H. L' Idee du Juste Prix Chez les Theologiens et Cannonistes du Moyen Age. LC 79-122228. 164p. (Fr.). 1973. Repr. of 1900 ed. lib. bdg. 20.50 (ISBN 0-8337-1286-1). B Franklin.
Garnier, J. Worship of the Dead: The Origin & Nature of Pagan Idolatry & Its Bearing Upon the Early History of Egypt & Babylonia. LC 77-85617. 1977. Repr. of 1904 ed. lib. bdg. 50.00 (ISBN 0-89341-300-3). Longwood Pub Group.
Garnier, J. C., jt. auth. see Poussin, J. C.
Garnier, Marcel & Delamare, Jean. Dictionnaire des Termes Techniques De Medecine. 19th ed. 1340p. (Fr.). 1978. 35.00 (ISBN 0-686-57190-8, M-6262). French & Eur.
Garnier, Robert. Two Tragedies: Hippolyte & Marc Antoine. Hill, Christine M. & Morrison, Mary G., eds. (Renaissance Library). 181p. (Fr.). 1975. 36.50 (ISBN 0-485-13809-3, Pub. by Athlone Pr Ltd); pap. 16.95 (ISBN 0-485-12809-8). Longwood Pub Group.
Garnier, Russell M. Annals of the British Peasantry. (Folklore Ser.). Repr. 25.00 (ISBN 0-8482-4197-5). Norwood Edns.
Garnir, H. G. Les Problemes aux Limites de la Physique Mathematique. (Mathematische Reihe Ser.: No. 23). (Illus.). 234p. (Fr.). 1958. 36.95x (ISBN 0-8176-0134-1). Birkhauser.
Garnir, H. G., ed. Boundary Value Problems for Linear Evolution-Partial Differential Equations. (NATO Advanced Study Institutes Ser. C. Math & Phys. Sciences: No. 29). 1977. lib. bdg. 55.00 (ISBN 90-277-0788-X, Pub. by Reidel Holland). Kluwer Academic.
--Singularities in Boundary Value Problems. 370p. 1982. 49.50 (ISBN 90-277-1240-9, Pub. by Reidel Holland). Kluwer Academic.
Garnir, H. G., et al. Analyse Fonctionnelle. 2nd ed. Incl. Vol. 1. Theorie Generale. 562p. 1968. 101.95 (ISBN 0-8176-0135-X); Vol. 2. Mesure et Integration dans l'Espace Euclidien. 288p. 1972. 61.95x (ISBN 0-8176-0545-2); Vol. 3. Espaces Fonctionnels Usuels. 375p. 1973. 81.95 (ISBN 0-8176-0546-0). (Mathematische Reihe Ser.: Vols. 36, 37 & 45). (Fr.). Birkhauser.
Garnir, H. G., et al, eds. Functional Analysis & Its Applications. (Lecture Notes in Mathematics: Vol. 399). xvii, 565p. 1974. pap. 28.00 (ISBN 0-387-06869-4). Springer-Verlag.
Garnsey, E. H., tr. see De Bary, Anton.
Garnsey, Gilbert. Holding Companies & Their Published Accounts Bound with Limitations of A Balance Sheet. LC 82-48364. (Accountancy in Transition Ser.). 232p. 1982. lib. bdg. 28.00 (ISBN 0-8240-5315-X). Garland Pub.
Garnsey, Leila. Wilderness Coast. 64p. 1984. 7.50 (ISBN 0-317-16204-7). Ye Galleon.
Garnsey, P. D. & Whittaker, C. R., eds. Imperialism in the Ancient World. LC 77-85699. (Cambridge Classical Studies). (Illus.). 1979. 49.50 (ISBN 0-521-21882-9). Cambridge U Pr.
Garnsey, Peter & Hopkins, Keith, eds. Trade in the Ancient Economy. LC 81-13652. 250p. 1983. text ed. 24.00x (ISBN 0-520-04803-2). U of Cal Pr.
Garnsey, Wayne. A Regents Earth Science Review. Page, Virginia, ed. (Illus.). 260p. (Orig.). (gr. 9-12). pap. text ed. 2.50 (ISBN 0-9606036-9-7). N & N Pub.
Garnsey, Wayne & Licata, Guy. A General Biology Review. (Illus.). 160p. (gr. 9-12). 1981. pap. text ed. 3.00 (ISBN 0-9606036-3-8). N & N Pub.
Garnsey, Wayne & Licota, Guy. A Regents Biology Review. (Illus.). 250p. (Orig.). 1985. pap. text ed. 2.50 (ISBN 0-9606036-6-2). N & N Pub.
Garnsey, Wayne, ed. see Moreau, Nancy.
Garnsey, Wayne, ed. see Romano, Nick.
Garny, Patricia M. Alaskan Earthquake, Nineteen Sixty-Four. (Events of Our Times Ser.: No. 11). 32p. (Orig.). (gr. 7-12). 1973. lib. bdg. 3.50 incl. catalog cards (ISBN 0-87157-712-7); pap. 1.95 vinyl laminated covers (ISBN 0-87157-212-5). SamHar Pr.
Garoche, Pierre. Dictionary of Commodities Carried by Ship. 366p. 1952. pap. 10.00x (ISBN 0-87033-019-5). Cornell Maritime.
Garofalo, James & Connelly, Kevin J. Dispute Resolution Centers in Two Parts: Major Features & Process, - Outcomes, Issues, & Future Directions. 60p. 1980. 5.00 (ISBN 0-318-15363-7). Natl Coun Crime.
Garofalo, Joe, jt. ed. see Lester, Frank K., Jr.
Garofalo, Raffaele. Criminology. Millar, Robert W., tr. LC 68-55771. (Criminology, Law Enforcement, & Social Problems Ser.: No. 71). 1968. Repr. of 1914 ed. 24.00x (ISBN 0-87585-012-X). Patterson Smith.
Garofalo, Reebee & Chapple, Steve. Rock 'n' Roll Is Here to Pay: The History & Politics of the Music Industry. LC 77-10488. 372p. 1978. 25.95x (ISBN 0-88229-395-8); pap. 13.95x (ISBN 0-88229-437-7). Nelson-Hall.
Garoian, Leon, ed. Economics of Conglomerate Growth. LC 72-628283. 132p. 1969. pap. 8.95x (ISBN 0-87071-325-6). Oreg St U Pr.
Garon, Paul. Blues & the Poetic Spirit. LC 78-2025. (Roots of Jazz Ser.). (Illus.). 1978. lib. bdg. 21.50 (ISBN 0-306-77542-5); pap. 5.95 (ISBN 0-306-80108-6). Da Capo.
--The Devil's Son-in-Law. (The Paul Oliver Blues Ser.). pap. 2.95 (ISBN 0-913714-34-8). Legacy Bks.
--Rana Mozelle: Surrealist Texts. (Illus.). 16p. 1978. pap. 2.25 (ISBN 0-941194-05-1). Black Swan Pr.
Garon, Paul, ed. The Charles H. Kerr Company Archives 1885-1985: A Century of Socialist & Labor Publishing. 64p. 1985. lib. bdg. 22.95 (ISBN 0-88286-144-1); pap. 12.95 (ISBN 0-88286-119-0). C H Kerr.
Garon, Philip A., ed. Advertising Law Anthology: 1973, Vol. I-VII. LC 73-87656. (National Law Anthology Ser.). 1973. 59.95 ea.; Vol. 1, 1973. (ISBN 0-914250-07-8). Vol.iI, 1974. Vol. III, 1975 (ISBN 0-914250-09-4). Vol. IV, 1976 (ISBN 0-914250-11-6). Vol. V, 1977-78 (ISBN 0-914250-15-9). Vol. VI, 1979 (ISBN 0-914250-18-3). Vol VII, 1980-81. text ed. 59.95 (ISBN 0-914250-22-1); complete set 344.90 (ISBN 0-914250-05-1). Intl Lib.
--Public Utilities Law Anthology, 1974, Vol. 1. LC 74-77644. (National Law Anthology Ser.). 1974. text ed. 59.95 (ISBN 0-914250-08-6). Intl Lib.
--Public Utilities Law Anthology, 1975, Vol. 2. LC 74-77644. (National Law Anthology Ser.). 1976. text ed. 59.95 (ISBN 0-914250-10-8). Intl Lib.
--Zoning Law Anthology, Vol. 1. LC 78-66283. (National Law Anthology Ser.). 1978. text ed. 59.95 (ISBN 0-914250-17-5). Intl Lib.
Garon, Philip A., ed. see Gromyko, Anatolii A.
Garon, Philip A., ed. see Sergeichuk, S.
Garonzik, Elan, ed. see Foundation Center.
Garoogian, Andrew. Robotics, Nineteen Sixty to Nineteen Eighty-Three: An Annotated Bibliography. LC 84-1763. (CompuBibs Ser.: No. 1). 119p. 1984. pap. 16.50x (ISBN 0-914791-03-6). Vantage Info.
Garoogian, Andrew & Garoogian, Rhoda, eds. Child Care Issues for Parents & Society: A Guide to Information Sources. LC 77-82800. (Social Issues & Social Problems Information Guide Ser.: Vol. 2). 1977. 60.00x (ISBN 0-8103-1314-6). Gale.
Garoogian, Rhoda. AIDS, 1981-1983: An Annotated Bibliography. LC 84-1736. (CompuBibs Ser.: No. 2). 92p. 1984. pap. 15.00x (ISBN 0-914791-05-2). Vantage Info.
Garoogian, Rhoda, jt. ed. see Garoogian, Andrew.
Garoutte, Bill. A Survey of Functional Neuroanatomy. LC 80-84809. (Illus.). 217p. 1982. pap. text ed. 9.75x (ISBN 0-930010-04-3). Jones Med.
Garoutte, Sally, ed. Uncoverings 1980. (Research Papers of American Quilt Study Group Ser.: Vol. 1). (Illus.). 76p. (Orig.). 1981. pap. 8.50x (ISBN 0-9606590-0-5). Am Quilt.
--Uncoverings 1981. (Research Papers of American Quilt Study Group Ser.: Vol. 2). (Illus.). 112p. (Orig.). 1982. pap. 9.50x (ISBN 0-9606590-1-3). Am Quilt.
--Uncoverings, 1982. (Research Papers of American Quilt Study Group: Vol. 3). (Illus.). 140p. (Orig.). 1983. pap. 10.50x (ISBN 0-9606590-2-1). Am Quilt.
--Uncoverings, 1983. (Research Papers of American Quilt Study Group Ser.: Vol. 4). (Illus.). 150p. (Orig.). 1984. pap. 12.00x (ISBN 0-9606590-3-X). Am Quilt.
--Uncoverings 1984. (Research Papers of American Quilt Study Group: Vol. 5). (Illus.). 176p. 1985. pap. 12.00 (ISBN 0-9606590-4-8). Am Quilt.
Garovoy, Marvin E., jt. ed. see Cogan, Martin G.
Garoyan, Leon & Mohn, Paul O. The Board of Directors of Cooperatives. LC 76-8631. 1976. pap. 6.00x (ISBN 0-931876-01-X, 4060). Ag & Nat Res.
Garozzo, Benito & Yallouze, Leon. The Blue Club. 172p. 1969. 9.95 (ISBN 0-571-09265-9). Faber & Faber.
GARP (Global Atmospehere Research Programme) Joint Organizing Committee. Report of the Tenth Session of the Joint Organizing Committee of GARP (Global Atmospheric Research Programme) (Orig.). 1975. pap. text ed. 25.00 (ISBN 0-685-53918-0, W333, WMO). Unipub.
GARP (Global Atmospheric Research Programme), Joint Organizing Committee, 7th Session. Report. pap. 9.00 (ISBN 0-686-93930-1, W336, WMO). Unipub.
GARP (Global Atmospheric Research Programme), Joint Organizing Committee, 6th Session. Report. pap. 5.00 (ISBN 0-686-93931-X, W337, WMO). Unipub.
GARP Tropical Experiment Board, 1st Session. Report of the GARP Experiment Board 1st Session. (GARP Special Reports: No. 4). pap. 8.00 (ISBN 0-686-93934-4, W325, WMO). Unipub.
Garpon, ed. see De La Bruyere, Jean.
Garr, Anton, ed. see Massaro, Cora.
Garr, Anton, ed. see Massaro, Cora D.
Garr, Doug. WOZ: The Prodigal Son of Silicon Valley. 160p. (Orig.). 1984. pap. 2.75 (ISBN 0-380-88484-4). Avon.
Garr, Doug, jt. auth. see Edelhart, Michael.
Garr, Robert J. Awntyrs off Arthure at the Terne Wathelyne: A Critical Edition. LC 69-16539. (Haney Foundation Ser.). 1969. 20.00x (ISBN 0-8122-7587-X). U of Pa Pr.
Garr, W. Randall. Dialect Geography of Syria-Palestine, 1000-586 B.C.E. LC 84-3639. (Illus.). 320p. 1985. text ed. 40.00 (ISBN 0-8122-7927-1). U of Pa Pr.
Garraghan, Gilbert J. A Guide to Historical Method. Delanglez, Jean, ed. LC 73-13415. 482p. 1974. Repr. of 1946 ed. lib. bdg. 31.00x (ISBN 0-8371-7132-6, GAHM). Greenwood.
--Prose Studies in Newman. 1915. Repr. 25.00 (ISBN 0-8274-3216-X). R West.
Garran, Robert R. Schubert & Schumann: Songs & Translations. 373p. 1972. Repr. of 1946 ed. 14.00x (ISBN 0-522-83999-1, Pub. by Melbourne U Pr). Intl Spec Bk.
Garrand, Victor. Augustine Laure, S.J., Missionary to the Yakimas. 1977. 7.50 (ISBN 0-87770-176-8); pap. 4.95 (ISBN 0-87770-187-3). Ye Galleon.
Garrard & Boyd. Practical Problems in Mathematics for Electricians. LC 79-56247. 1981. pap. text ed. 7.40 (ISBN 0-8273-1277-6); instructor's guide 4.20 (ISBN 0-8273-1278-4). Delmar.
Garrard, J., et al, eds. The Middle Class in Politics. 382p. 1978. text ed. 41.95x (ISBN 0-566-00225-6). Gower Pub Co.
Garrard, J. G., ed. The Eighteenth Century in Russia. (Illus.). 1973. 39.95x (ISBN 0-19-815638-3). Oxford U Pr.
Garrard, John. Leadership & Power in Victorian Towns. LC 82-62260. 256p. 1983. 25.00 (ISBN 0-7190-0897-2, Pub. by Manchester Univ Pr). Longwood Pub Group.
--Mikhail Lermontov. (World Authors Ser.). 1982. lib. bdg. 16.95 (ISBN 0-8057-6514-X, Twayne). G K Hall.
Garrard, John, ed. The Russian Novel from Pushkin to Pasternak. LC 83-1070. 320p. 1983. 31.00x (ISBN 0-300-02935-7). Yale U Pr.
Garrard, Lewis H. Wah-To-Yah & the Taos Trail. (Western Frontier Library: No. 5). 1966. pap. 6.95 (ISBN 0-8061-1016-3). U of Okla Pr.
Garrard, Mary D., jt. ed. see Broude, Norma.
Garrard, Peter J. How To Paint with Oils. 64p. 1982. pap. 6.95 (ISBN 0-89586-160-7). H P Bks.
Garratt & Hirtz. Drug Fate & Metabolism, Vol. 3. 1979. 75.00 (ISBN 0-8247-6841-8). Dekker.
Garratt, Bob, ed. see Association of Teachers of Management.
Garratt, Colin. The Last of Steam: Steam Locomotives Today. LC 76-43194. (Illus.). 128p. 1980. 20.00 (ISBN 0-8040-0754-3, 82-75786, Pub. by Swallow). Ohio U Pr.
Garratt, Geoffrey T., jt. auth. see Thompson, Edward J.
Garratt, John F. The World Encyclopedia of Model Soldiers. LC 80-84376. (Illus.). 224p. 1981. 75.00 (ISBN 0-87951-129-X). Overlook Pr.
Garratt, Sheryl, jt. auth. see Steward, Sue.
Garratty, George, jt. auth. see Petz, Lawrence D.
Garratty, George, ed. Blood Group Antigens & Disease. 145p. 1983. 22.00 (ISBN 0-914404-96-2). Am Assn Blood.
--Hemolytic Disease of the Newborn. (Illus.). 1984. text ed. 29.00 (ISBN 0-915355-05-1). Am Assn Blood.
Garraty, John. New Commonwealth, 1877-1890. (New American Nations Ser.). 1968. pap. 9.50xi (ISBN 0-06-131410-2, TB1410, Torch). Har-Row.
Garraty, John A. The American Nation: A History of the United States Since 1865, Vol. 2. 5th ed. 442p. 1983. pap. text ed. 18.50 scp (ISBN 0-06-042277-7, HarpC); instr's. manual avail. (ISBN 0-06-364687-0); scp stud rev. manual 8.50 (ISBN 0-06-044713-3). Har-Row.
--The American Nation: A History of the United States to 1877, Vol. 1. 5th ed. 459p. 1983. pap. text ed. 18.50 scp (ISBN 0-06-042274-2, HarpC); instr's manual avail. (ISBN 0-06-362367-6); scp stud rev. manual 8.95 (ISBN 0-06-044712-5). Har-Row.
--The American Nation: A History of the United States. 5th ed. 860p. 1982. text ed. 27.50 (ISBN 0-06-042275-0, HarpC); inst. manual avail. (ISBN 0-06-362367-6); inst. manual avail. (ISBN 0-06-364687-0). Har Row.
--Historical Viewpoints: Notable Articles from American Heritage, 2 Vols. 4th ed. 1983. Vol. 1, to 1877, 383. pap. text ed. 13.50 scp (ISBN 0-06-042278-5, HarpC); Vol. 2, since 1865, 400. pap. text ed. 13.50 scp (ISBN 0-06-042279-3). Har-Row.
--The Nature of Biography. Winks, Robin W., ed. LC 83-49165. (History & Historiography Ser.). 289p. 1985. lib. bdg. 30.00 (ISBN 0-8240-6363-5). Garland Pub.
--New Commonwealth: 1877-1890. Commager, Henry S. & Morris, Richard B., eds. LC 68-28198. (New American Nation Series). (Illus.). 1968. 15.00xi (ISBN 0-06-011437-1, HarpT). Har-Row.
--Right-Hand Man: The Life of George W. Perkins. LC 77-18807. 1978. Repr. of 1960 ed. lib. bdg. 34.00x (ISBN 0-313-20186-2, GARH). Greenwood.
--A Short History of the American Nation. 3rd ed. (Illus.). 577p. 1981. pap. text ed. 18.50 scp (ISBN 0-06-042271-8, HarpC); instructor's manual avail. (ISBN 0-06-362226-2). Har-Row.

--A Short History of the American Nation, 2 vols. 4th ed. 1985. To 1877, 313p. pap. text ed. 10.95 scp (ISBN 0-06-042294-7, HarpC); Since 1865, 315p. pap. text ed. 10.95 (ISBN 0-06-042295-5). Har-Row.

--A Short History of the American Nation. 4th ed. 589p. 1985. scp 17.50 (ISBN 0-06-042293-9, HarpC). Har-Row.

--Silas Wright. LC 73-120199. (Columbia University Social Science Studies Ser.: No. 552). Repr. of 1949 ed. 22.50 (ISBN 0-404-51552-5). AMS Pr.

--Unemployment in History: Economic Thought & Public Policy. LC 76-26227. 1979. 18.50i (ISBN 0-06-011457-6, CN-667, HarpT); pap. 3.95i (ISBN 0-06-090667-7). Har-Row.

--Woodrow Wilson: A Great Life in Brief. LC 76-54860. 1977. Repr. of 1956 ed. lib. bdg. 19.00x (ISBN 0-8371-9371-0, GAWW). Greenwood.

Garraty, John A. & Adams, Walter. From Main Street to the Left Bank: Students & Scholars Abroad. x, 216p. 1959. 4.00 (ISBN 0-87013-045-5). Mich St U Pr.

Garraty, John A. see Current, Richard N., et al.

Garraty, John A., ed. Quarrels That Have Shaped the Constitution. 1964. pap. 4.95xi (ISBN 0-06-131889-2, TB1889, Torch). Har-Row.

--Quarrels That Have Shaped the Constitution. 15.25 (ISBN 0-8446-5852-9). Peter Smith.

--Transformation of American Society, 1870-1890. LC 68-65043. (Documentary History of the United States Ser). vi, 266p. 1969. 19.95x (ISBN 0-87249-124-2). U of SC Pr.

Garraway, Michael O. & Evans, Robert C. Fungal Nutrition & Physiology. LC 83-23450. 401p. 1984. 44.95x (ISBN 0-471-05844-0, Pub. by Wiley-Interscience). Wiley.

Garre, Walter J. Basic Anxiety. LC 61-12621. 1962. 6.00 (ISBN 0-8022-0565-8). Philos Lib.

--The Missing Link: The Transition from Animal Instinct to Human Mind. LC 81-21084. 293p. 1982. 15.00 (ISBN 0-8022-2399-0). Philos Lib.

Garreau, Joel. The Nine Nations of North America. 448p. 1982. pap. 7.95 (ISBN 0-380-57885-9, 57885-9). Avon.

Garrelick, Renee & Bailey, William M. Concord in the Days of Strawberries & Streetcars. LC 85-50267. (Illus.). 240p. 1985. 15.00 (ISBN 0-9614575-0-3). Town Concord Mass.

Garrels, Elizabeth. Mariategui y la Argentina: Un Caso de Lentes Ajenos. LC 82-71934. 144p. (Orig., Span.). 1982. pap. 7.25 (ISBN 0-935318-08-9). Edins Hispamerica.

Garrels, Robert M. & Christ, Charles L. Solutions, Minerals & Equilibria. LC 65-12674. 1982. Repr. of 1965 ed. text ed. 25.00x (ISBN 0-87735-333-6). Freeman Cooper.

Garrels, Robert M., jt. auth. see Hunt, Cynthia A.

Garret, Maxwell R. Science-Hobby Book of Boating. rev. ed. LC 68-28032. (Science-Hobby Books). (Illus.). (gr. 5-10). 1968. PLB 4.95 (ISBN 0-8225-0554-1). Lerner Pubns.

Garret, Maxwell R. & Poulson, Mary H. Foil Fencing: Skills, Safety, Operations, & Responsibilities for the 1980s. LC 80-18426. (Illus.). 160p. 1981. text ed. 13.75x (ISBN 0-271-00273-5). Pa St U Pr.

Garret-Jones, John. Tales & Teaching of the Buddha. 1979. 18.95 (ISBN 0-04-294104-0). Allen Unwin.

Garretson. Conducting Choral Music. 5th ed. 400p. 1980. text ed. 28.57 (ISBN 0-205-07145-7, 587145). Allyn.

Garretson, Albert H., et al, eds. The Law of International Drainage Basins. LC 67-25904. 916p. 1968. 45.00 (ISBN 0-379-00320-1). Oceana.

Garretson, Lucy, jt. auth. see Selby, Henry.

Garretson, Martin S. A Short History of the American Bison. rev. facsimile ed. LC 79-169759. (Select Bibliographies Reprint Ser). Repr. of 1934 ed. 12.00 (ISBN 0-8369-5979-5). Ayer Co Pubs.

Garretson, Mervin, jt. ed. see Caccamise, Frank.

Garretson, Mervin D. Words from a Deaf Child & Other Verses. LC 84-81182. 128p. (Orig.). 1984. pap. 7.95 (ISBN 0-930805-00-3). Fragonard Pr.

Garretson, Oliver K. Relationships Between Expressed Preferences & Curricular Abilities of Ninth Grade Boys. LC 76-176976. (Columbia University. Teachers College. Contributions to Education Ser.: No. 396). Repr. of 1930 ed. 22.50 (ISBN 0-404-55396-6). AMS Pr.

Garretson, R. L. Music in Childhood Education. 2nd ed. (Illus.). 336p. 1976. ref. ed. 14.95x (ISBN 0-13-606988-6). P-H.

Garretson, Warren P. The Roughneck. 1985. 12.95 (ISBN 0-533-06568-2). Vantage.

Garrett. Tennessee Divorce, Alimony & Child Custody. 2nd ed. 62.95 (ISBN 0-686-90993-3); separate pocket part supplement, 1983 27.95 (ISBN 0-686-90994-1). Harrison Co GA.

Garrett & Hirtz. Drug Fate & Metabolism, Vol. 4. 408p. 1983. 75.00 (ISBN 0-8247-1849-6). Dekker.

--Drug Fate & Metabolism, Vol. 5. 320p. 1985. 79.50 (ISBN 0-8247-7423-X). Dekker.

Garrett, jt. auth. see Sheth.

Garrett, A. A. The History of the Society of Incorporated Accountants, 1885-1957. LC 83-49110. (Accounting History & the Development of a Profession Ser.). 360p. 1984. lib. bdg. 45.00 (ISBN 0-8240-6327-9). Garland Pub.

Garrett, Albert. British Wood Engraving of the Twentieth Century. 1980. pap. 13.00 (ISBN 0-85967-608-0). Scolar.

Garrett, Ann H., jt. ed. see Sproull, Norma.

Garrett, Anne E. & Garrett, Virginia. Pocket Handbook of Cardiac Arrhythmias: Recognition & Treatment. (Illus.). 192p. 1985. pap. text ed. 12.75 (ISBN 0-397-54530-4, Lippincott Nursing). Lippincott.

Garrett, Annette. Interviewing: Its Principles & Methods. 3rd, Rev. ed. Mangold, Margaret M. & Zaki, Elinor P., eds. LC 82-1591. 186p. 1982. 15.95 (ISBN 0-87304-195-X); pap. 8.95 (ISBN 0-87304-194-1). Family Serv.

Garrett, Arthur. The Folk of Christendom. LC 79-92433. 500p. 1981. 49.95 (ISBN 0-8022-2363-X). Philos Lib.

Garrett, Banning N. & Glaser, Bonnie S. War & Peace: The Views from Moscow & Beijing. LC 84-80320. (Policy Papers in International Affairs: No. 20). 160p. 1984. pap. 7.95x (ISBN 0-87725-520-2). U of Cal Intl St.

Garrett, Charles. Treasure Hunting Pays off! LC 76-11375. (Illus.). 92p. (Orig.). 1980. pap. 3.95 (ISBN 0-915920-37-9). Ram Pub.

Garrett, Charles, jt. auth. see Lagal, Roy.

Garrett, Charles, et al. Electronic Prospecting. Nelson, Bettye, ed. LC 76-11380. (Guidebook Ser.). (Illus.). 96p. (Orig.). 1980. pap. 4.95 (ISBN 0-915920-38-7). Ram Pub.

Garrett, Charles G. Gunslinger No. 1: The Massacre Trail. 144p. 1982. 15.00x (ISBN 0-7278-0575-4, Pub. by Severn Hse). State Mutual Bk.

--Gunslinger No. 2: The Golden Gun. 144p. 1982. 15.00x (ISBN 0-7278-0580-0, Pub. by Severn Hse). State Mutual Bk.

--Magnetic Cooling. LC 53-10474. (Harvard Monographs in Applied Science: No. 4). pap. 31.00 (ISBN 0-317-09162-X, 2001562). Bks Demand UMI.

Garrett, Charles L. Modern Metal Detectors. Deckshot, K., ed. LC 83-62839. (Illus.). 544p. (Orig.). 1985. pap. 9.95 (ISBN 0-915920-46-8, 15016). Ram Pub.

--Successful Coin Hunting. rev. ed. Nelson, Bettye, ed. LC 73-87120. (Illus.). 248p. (Orig.). 1984. pap. 7.95 (ISBN 0-915920-47-6). Ram Pub.

Garrett, Charlotte. Presences. 1977. pap. 8.00 (ISBN 0-912960-10-8). Nightowl.

Garrett, Clarke. Respectable Folly: Millenarians and the French Revolution in France and England. LC 74-24378. 252p. 1975. 24.00x (ISBN 0-8018-1618-1). Johns Hopkins.

Garrett, De Graaf, ed. Duran Duran: The Book of Words. 96p. (gr. 10 up). 1984. Perfect bound 9.95 (ISBN 0-318-03882-X). H Leonard Pub Corp.

Garrett, E. Business Ethics. 1966. pap. text ed. 16.95 (ISBN 0-13-095844-1). P-H.

Garrett, E. R., jt. ed. see Hirtz, Jean L.

Garrett, Edmund H., ed. Elizabethan Songs. LC 74-116403. (Granger Index Reprint Ser). 1895. 18.00 (ISBN 0-8369-6144-7). Ayer Co Pubs.

Garrett, Edmund H., ed. & illus. Victorian Songs. LC 78-116404. (Granger Index Reprint Ser.). 1895. 18.00 (ISBN 0-8369-6145-5). Ayer Co Pubs.

Garrett, Edward R., ed. see Hirtz, Jean L.

Garrett, Eileen J. My Life As a Search for the Meaning of Mediumship. LC 75-7380. (Perspectives in Psychical Research Ser.). 1975. Repr. of 1939 ed. 21.00x (ISBN 0-405-07030-6). Ayer Co Pubs.

Garrett, Franklin M. Atlanta & Environs: A Chronicle of Its People & Events, 2 vols. LC 54-14260. 1969. Set. 70.00 (ISBN 0-8203-0489-1). Vol. 1, 986p (ISBN 0-8203-0263-5). Vol. 2, 1080p (ISBN 0-8203-0264-3). U of Ga Pr.

--Yesterday's Atlanta. LC 74-75291. (Historic Cities Ser.: No. 8). (Illus.). 176p. 1974. 9.95 (ISBN 0-912458-35-6). E A Seemann.

--Yesterday's Atlanta. LC 74-75291. (Illus.). 1977. pap. 5.95 (ISBN 0-912458-90-9). E A Seemann.

Garrett, G. G. & Marriott, D. L., eds. Engineering Applications of Fracture Analysis: Proceedings of the First National Conference on Fracture Held in Johannesburg, South Africa, 1979. LC 80-41074. (International Ser. on the Strength & Fractures of Materials & Structures). (Illus.). 440p. 1980. 72.00 (ISBN 0-08-025437-3). Pergamon.

Garrett, Garet. Where the Money Grows. 1966. Repr. of 1911 ed. flexible cover 4.00 (ISBN 0-87034-024-7). Fraser Pub Co.

Garrett, Garet & Rothbard, Murray N. The Great Depression & New Deal Monetary Policy: Two Essays. LC 80-36791. (Cato Paper Ser.: No. 13). 131p. 1980. pap. 4.00x (ISBN 0-932790-19-4). Cato Inst.

Garrett, George. Collected Poems of George Garrett. 1984. 14.95 (ISBN 0-938626-23-X); pap. 7.95 (ISBN 0-938626-24-8). U of Ark Pr.

--Death of the Fox: A Novel about Ralegh. LC 84-18060. 744p. 1985. pap. 11.95 (ISBN 0-688-03464-0, Quill). Morrow.

--An Evening Performance. LC 85-1504. 528p. 1985. 18.95 (ISBN 0-385-19094-8). Doubleday.

--James Jones. LC 83-18665. (Album Biographies Ser.). (Illus.). 176p. 1984. 18.95 (ISBN 0-15-146049-3). HarBraceJ.

--James Jones. 1984. pap. 10.95 (ISBN 0-15-645955-8, Harv). HarBraceJ.

--Poison Pen: Or, Live Now & Pay Later. LC 83-62169. 130p. 1985. cancelled (ISBN 0-913773-06-9); cancelled (ISBN 0-913773-07-7). S Wright.

--The Succession: A Novel of Elizabeth & James. LC 74-18798. 552p. 1983. 17.95 (ISBN 0-385-02421-5). Doubleday.

--The Succession: A Novel of Elizabeth & James. LC 84-18163. 552p. 1985. Repr. of 1983 ed. 11.95 (ISBN 0-688-03915-4, Quill). Morrow.

Garrett, George, ed. Botteghe Oscure Reader. LC 73-15006. 475p. 1974. 17.50x (ISBN 0-8195-4071-4); pap. 8.95 (ISBN 0-8195-6033-2). Wesleyan U Pr.

Garrett, George, et al, eds. see Chandler, Raymond.

Garrett, George, et al, eds. see Douglas, Nathan, et al.

Garrett, George P., et al, eds. Film Scripts Four: A Hard Day's Night, The Best Man, Darling. LC 71-135273. (Orig.). 1972. Set. 27.50x (ISBN 0-89197-162-9); pap. text ed. 12.95x ea. Irvington.

--Film Scripts One: Henry V, The Big Sleep, A Streetcar Named Desire. LC 71-135273. (Orig.). 1971. pap. text ed. 27.50x set (ISBN 0-89197-163-7); pap. text ed. 12.95x ea.; avail. free instr. manual (ISBN 0-8290-0137-9). Irvington.

--Film Scripts Three: The Apartment, The Misfits, Charade. LC 71-135273. (Orig.). 1972. pap. 27.50x set (ISBN 0-89197-165-3); pap. 12.95x ea. (ISBN 0-8290-1390-3). Irvington.

--Film Scripts Two: High Noon, Twelve Angry Men, the Defiant Ones. LC 71-135273. (Orig.). 1971. pap. 27.50x set (ISBN 0-89197-165-3); pap. text ed. 12.95x ea.; avail. free instr. manual (ISBN 0-8290-0137-9). Irvington.

Garrett, George P., et al, eds. see Cunningham, John M.

Garrett, George P., et al, eds. see Miller, Arthur, et al.

Garrett, George P., et al, eds. see Owen, Alun.

Garrett, George P., et al, eds. see Raphael, Frederick.

Garrett, George P., et al, eds. see Rose, Reginald.

Garrett, George P., et al, eds. see Shakespeare, William.

Garrett, George P., et al, eds. see Stone, Peter, et al.

Garrett, George P., et al, eds. see Vidal, Gore.

Garrett, George P., et al, eds. see Wilder, Billy, et al.

Garrett, George P., et al, eds. see Williams, Tennessee.

Garrett, Gerard. The Films of David Niven. (Illus.). 256p. 1976. 14.00 (ISBN 0-8065-0557-5). Citadel Pr.

Garrett, Henry B. & Pike, Charles P., eds. Space Systems & Their Interactions with Earth's Space Environment. LC 80-15518. (Illus.). 737p. 1980. 65.00 (ISBN 0-915928-41-8, PAAS71); members 35.00 (ISBN 0-317-32194-3). AIAA.

Garrett, Henry E. Great Experiments in Psychology. 3rd ed. LC 79-24362. (Century Psychology Ser.). (Illus.). 1981. 32.50x (ISBN 0-89197-190-4); pap. text ed. 18.95x (ISBN 0-89197-776-7). Irvington.

--Statistics in Psychology & Education. LC 82-15599. xii, 491p. 1982. Repr. of 1966 ed. lib. bdg. 55.00x (ISBN 0-313-23653-4, GAST). Greenwood.

Garrett, Herbert L., jt. auth. see Edwardes, Stephen M.

Garrett, Horder W. The Sunlit Road: Readings in Verse & Prose for Every Day. 1978. Repr. of 1908 ed. lib. bdg. 20.00 (ISBN 0-8492-5242-3). R West.

Garrett, I., jt. auth. see Faktor, M. M.

Garrett, James & Levine, Edna. Rehabilitation Practices with the Physically Disabled. LC 72-13875. 569p. 1973. text ed. 42.00x (ISBN 0-231-03523-3). Columbia U Pr.

Garrett, James F. Australian Approaches to Rehabilitation in Neurotrauma & Spinal Cord Injury. (International Exchanges of Experts & Information in Rehabilitation Ser.: No. 19). 70p. write for info. (ISBN 0-939986-31-0). World Rehab Fund.

Garrett, James F., ed. Information Systems on Technical Aids for the Disabled. (International Exchange of Experts & Information in Rehabilitation Ser.: No. 17). 34p. 1982. write for info. (ISBN 0-939986-29-9). World Rehab Fund.

Garrett, James F. & Levine, Edna S., eds. Psychological Practices with the Physically Disabled. LC 62-9708. 463p. 1962. 40.00x (ISBN 0-231-02463-0). Columbia U Pr.

Garrett, James J. Antitrust Compliance: A Legal & Business Guide. LC 78-55462. 1978. text ed. 25.00 (ISBN 0-685-28859-5, B1-1254). PLI.

Garrett, James L., Jr. & Hinson, E. Glenn. Are Southern Baptists "Evangelicals"? LC 82-18870. 247p. 1983. 14.95x (ISBN 0-86554-033-0). Mercer Univ Pr.

Garrett, James L., Jr., jt. ed. see Vardaman, E. Jerry.

Garrett, Jane. The Triumphs of Providence. (Illus.). 250p. 1981. 27.95 (ISBN 0-521-23346-1). Cambridge U Pr.

Garrett, Jessie A., ed. Camp & Community: Manzanar & the Owens Valley. Larson, Ronald C. 1977. pap. 7.95 (ISBN 0-930046-00-5). CSUF Oral Hist.

Garrett, Jill. Obituaries from Tennessee Newspapers. 476p. 1980. 25.00 (ISBN 0-89308-174-4). Southern Hist Pr.

Garrett, John. Classical Dictionary of India, 2 vols. in 1. 1973. Repr. of 1873 ed. 51.50 (ISBN 0-8337-1289-6). B Franklin.

--Gothic Strains & Bourgeois Sentiments in the Novels of Mrs. Ann Radcliffe & Her Imitations. Varma, Devendra P., ed. LC 79-8454. (Gothic Studies & Dissertations Ser.). 1980. lib. bdg. 46.00x (ISBN 0-405-12668-9). Ayer Co Pubs.

--Managing the Civil Service. 1980. pap. 15.95 (ISBN 0-434-90655-7, Pub. by W Heinemann Ltd). David & Charles.

Garrett, John, jt. auth. see Auden, W. H.

Garrett, John, jt. auth. see Calder, Julian.

Garrett, John, ed. More Talking of Shakespeare. facs. ed. LC 73-128887. (Select Bibliographies Reprint Ser). 1959. 16.00 (ISBN 0-8369-5507-2). Ayer Co Pubs.

--Talking of Shakespeare. facsimile ed. LC 70-157334. (Select Bibliographies Reprint Ser). Repr. of 1954 ed. 20.00 (ISBN 0-8369-5794-6). Ayer Co Pubs.

Garrett, John, jt. ed. see Auden, W. H.

Garrett, John, tr. see Guirma, Frederic.

Garrett, John R., et al. You Don't Have to Love Each Other but... Boston Schools Pilot Project Handbook. 1975. pap. 6.50 (ISBN 0-89785-004-1). Am Inst Res.

Garrett, Julia K. Green Flag Over Texas: The Last Years of Spain in Texas. 2nd ed. LC 40-3613. (Texas Heritage Ser). (Illus.). 1969. Repr. of 1939 ed. 12.50 (ISBN 0-8363-0038-6). Jenkins.

Garrett, Karen, jt. auth. see Duster, Troy.

Garrett, Kenneth & Garrett, Wilbur. Washington, D. C. (Illus.). 1985. 16.95 (ISBN 0-318-12039-9). Skyline Press.

Garrett, Lela. Papa's Razor Strop. (Illus.). 128p. 1981. 8.00 (ISBN 0-682-49775-4). Exposition Pr FL.

Garrett, Leonard J., jt. auth. see McDonough, Adrian M.

Garrett, Leroy. The Stone-Campbell Movement. LC 80-65965. 739p. 1981. 21.95 (ISBN 0-89900-059-2). College Pr Pub.

Garrett, Lillian. Visual Design: A Problem Solving Approach. LC 75-12638. 216p. 1975. Repr. of 1967 ed. 15.50 (ISBN 0-88275-332-0). Krieger.

Garrett, M. see Mehler, Jacques & Walker, Edward.

Garrett, Malcolm, jt. auth. see De Graaf, Kaspar.

Garrett, Malcolm, jt. auth. see De Graaf, Kasper.

Garrett, Martin. Philip Massinger's Attitude to Spectacle. (Salzburg - Jacobean Drama Ser.: No. 72). 282p. 1984. pap. text ed. 25.50x (ISBN 0-391-03319-0, Pub. by Salzburg Austria). Humanities.

Garrett, Mitchell B. French Colonial Question, 1789-1791. LC 72-100292. Repr. of 1916 ed. 15.00x (ISBN 0-8371-2925-7, GAF&, Pub. by Negro U Pr). Greenwood.

--Horse & Buggy Days on Hatchet Creek. xi, 233p. 1982. pap. 7.95 (ISBN 0-8173-0120-8). U of Ala Pr.

Garrett, N., jt. ed. see Bailyn, Bernard.

Garrett, Pat. The Life of Billy the Kid. 1977. pap. 1.25 (ISBN 0-8439-0439-9, LB439, Leisure Bks). Dorchester Pub Co.

Garrett, Pat F. Authentic Life of Billy, the Kid. LC 54-10053. (Western Frontier Library: No. 3). 1967. pap. 5.95 (ISBN 0-8061-1195-X). U of Okla Pr.

Garrett, Patrick. Analog I-O Design: Acquisition, Conversion, Recovery. (Illus.). 1981. text ed. 29.95 (ISBN 0-8359-0208-0). Reston.

Garrett, Patrick H. Analog Systems for Microprocessors & Minicomputers. (Illus.). 1978. 29.95 (ISBN 0-87909-035-9). Reston.

Garrett, Paul D. St. Innocent: Apostle to America. LC 79-19634. 345p. 1979. pap. 8.95 (ISBN 0-913836-60-5). St Vladimirs.

Garrett, Peter, jt. auth. see Ginsburg, R. N.

Garrett, Peter K. The Victorian Multiplot Novel: Studies in Dialogical Form. LC 79-18658. 1980. 24.00x (ISBN 0-300-02403-7). Yale U Pr.

Garrett, Phineas, ed. Excelsior Dialogues: Comprising New & Original Material Prepared Expressly for This Work by a Corps of Able & Experienced Writers. LC 72-3005. (Granger Reprint Ser.). Repr. of 1897 ed. 14.75 (ISBN 0-8369-8240-1). Ayer Co Pubs.

--One Hundred Choice Selections, Vols. 1,2,4,5,7,18 & 31. facsimile ed. Incl. Vol. 1. 1866. 14.00 (ISBN 0-8369-6197-8); Vol. 2. 1869. 13.00 (ISBN 0-8369-6198-6); Vol. 4. 1871. 14.00 (ISBN 0-8369-6199-4); Vol. 5. 1872. 15.00 (ISBN 0-8369-6254-0); Vol. 7. 1873. 15.00 (ISBN 0-8369-6255-9); Vol. 18. 1880. 14.00 (ISBN 0-8369-6256-7); Vol. 31. 1891. 15.00 (ISBN 0-8369-6269-9). LC 78-133069. (Granger Index Reprint Ser.). Ayer Co Pubs.

Garrett, R. E. Chancery & Other Legal Proceedings. 22p. 1968. 25.00x (ISBN 0-901262-00-5, Pub. by Pinhorns UK). State Mutual Bk.

Garrett, Ramon. Hospitals: Medical Systems, Vol. 2. 1976. 17.95 (ISBN 0-442-80338-9). Van Nos Reinhold.

Garrett, Randall. Lord Darcy Investigates. 192p. (Orig.). 1983. pap. 2.75 (ISBN 0-441-49142-1). Ace Bks.

--Murder & Magic. 272p. 1982. pap. 2.75 (ISBN 0-441-54542-4). Ace Bks.

--Starship Death. 240p. 1982. pap. 2.50 (ISBN 0-8439-1074-7, Leisure Bks). Dorchester Pub Co.

--Takeoff. Freas, Polly & Freas, Kelly, eds. LC 79-9140. (Illus.). 1980. pap. 5.95 (ISBN 0-915442-84-1, Starblaze). Donning Co.

--Too Many Magicians. 352p. 1983. pap. 2.95 (ISBN 0-441-81698-3). Ace Bks.

--Too Many Magicians. 13.00 (ISBN 0-8398-2497-1, Gregg). G K Hall.

Garrett, Randall & Heydron, Vicki A. Return to Eddarta. (Gandalara Cycle Ser.: No. 6). 160p. 1985. pap. 2.75 (ISBN 0-553-24709-3). Bantam.

--The Search for Ka. 192p. 1984. pap. 2.50 (ISBN 0-553-24120-6). Bantam.

--The Steel of Raithskar. 192p. (Orig.). 1981. pap. 2.75 (ISBN 0-553-24911-8). Bantam.

--The Well of Darkness. (Gandalara Cycle Ser.: No. 4). 1983. pap. 2.75 (ISBN 0-553-24505-8). Bantam.

Garrett, Raymond. Hospitals: A Systems Approach. 224p. 1973. 21.95 (ISBN 0-442-80238-2). Van Nos Reinhold.

Garrett, Richard. P. O. W. 22.50 (ISBN 0-7153-7986-0). Hippocrene Bks.

Garrett, Roger, ed. North-South Debate Educational Implications of the Brandt Report: Educational Implications of the Brandt Report. 22.00 (ISBN 0-85633-228-3, Pub. by NFER Nelson UK). Taylor & Francis.

Garrett, Roger M., ed. Education & Development. LC 83-22982. 288p. 1984. 23.95 (ISBN 0-312-23717-0). St Martin.

Garrett, Romeo B. Famous First Facts About Negroes. LC 75-172613. 224p. 1972. 10.00 (ISBN 0-405-01987-4). Ayer Co Pubs.

Garrett, S. D. Pathogenic Root-Infecting Fungi. LC 72-10024. (Illus.). 1970. 52.50 (ISBN 0-521-07786-9). Cambridge U Pr.

--Soil Fungi & Soil Fertility: An Introduction to Soil Mycology. 2nd ed. (Illus.). 150p. 1981. 21.00 (ISBN 0-08-025507-8); pap. 9.50 (ISBN 0-08-025506-X). Pergamon.

Garrett, Sally. Until Forever. (Superromances Ser.). 1983. pap. 2.95 (ISBN 0-373-70090-3, Pub. by Worldwide). Harlequin Bks.

Garrett, Sean. The Suez Canal. Yapp, Malcolm, et al, eds. (World History Ser.). (Illus.). 32p. (gr. 10). 1980. lib. bdg. 6.95 (ISBN 0-89908-230-0); pap. text ed. 2.45 (ISBN 0-89908-205-X). Greenhaven.

Garrett, Shirley. Social Reformers in Urban China: The Chinese Y. M. C. A., Eighteen Ninety-Five to Nineteen Twenty-Six. LC 74-133218. (East Asian Ser.: No. 56). 1970. 15.00x (ISBN 0-674-81220-4). Harvard U Pr.

Garrett, Stephen A. Ideals & Reality: An Analysis of the Debate Over Viet-Nam. LC 78-59852. 1978. pap. text ed. 12.75 (ISBN 0-8191-0555-4). U Pr of Amer.

Garrett, Thomas B., ed. Vintage Station Wagon Shop Service. LC 76-57074. (Illus.). 160p. 1977. pap. 18.95 (ISBN 0-911160-85-X). Post-Era.

Garrett, Thomas M. Cases in Business Ethics. 1968. pap. text ed. 17.95 (ISBN 0-13-118703-1). P-H.

Garrett, Thomas M. & Klonoski, Richard J. Business Ethics. 2nd ed. 256p. 1986. pap. text ed. 16.95 (ISBN 0-13-095837-9). P-H.

Garrett, Thomas S. Christian Worship: An Introductory Outline. 2nd ed. 1963. 7.00x (ISBN 0-19-213210-5). Oxford U Pr.

Garrett, Virginia, jt. auth. see Garrett, Anne E.

Garrett, W. N., jt. ed. see Cole, H. H.

Garrett, Walton. Divorce, Alimony & Child Custody. 2nd, rev. ed. 423p. 1984. 62.95 (ISBN 0-317-29918-2). Harrison Co GA.

Garrett, Wilbur, jt. auth. see Garrett, Kenneth.

Garrett, William. Reminiscences of Public Men in Alabama, for Thirty Years. LC 74-34445. 816p. 1975. Repr. of 1872 ed. 32.50 (ISBN 0-87152-204-7). Reprint.

Garrett, William & Smagin, V. M. Determination of the Atmospheric Contribution of Petroleum Hydrocarbons to the Oceans. (Special Environmental Reports: No. 6). (Illus.). 27p. 1976. pap. 16.00 (ISBN 92-63-10440-9, W252, WMO). Unipub.

Garrett, William J. & Robinson, David E. Ultrasound in Clinical Obstetrics. (Illus.). 128p. 1970. photocopy ed. 19.75x (ISBN 0-398-00652-0). C C Thomas.

Garrett, William R. The Early Political Caricature in America & the History of the United States. (Illus.). 1979. 88.75 (ISBN 0-89266-164-X). Am Classical Coll Pr.

--The Early Political Caricature in America & the History of the United States. (Illus.). 161p. 1984. 77.45x (ISBN 0-89266-431-2). Am Classical Coll Pr.

--Seasons of the Family: An Introduction to Marriage & Family Life. LC 81-7240. 532p. 1982. text ed. 29.95 (ISBN 0-03-057281-9); instr's. manual 25.00 (ISBN 0-03-057282-7). HR&W.

Garrett, Willis O. Church Ushers' Manual. 64p. pap. 2.50 (ISBN 0-8007-8456-1, Spire Bks.). Revell.

Garrett, Winifred & Thornton, Mary. Canework for the Doll's House. (Illus.). 50p. 1970. 3.00 (ISBN 0-85219-597-4, Pub. by Batsford England). David & Charles.

Garrett-Price, B. A., et al. Fouling of Heat Exchangers: Characteristics, Costs, Prevention, Control, & Removal. LC 84-22689. (Illus.). 417p. 1985. 45.00 (ISBN 0-8155-1016-0). Noyes.

Garrety, Martha L. The Peabody Ducks. Garbarini, Jean J., created by. 32p. 1983. 8.95 (ISBN 0-9610374-0-7). Duck Tale Prods.

Garrey, Matthew M., et al. Gynaecology Illustrated. 2nd ed. (Illus.). 1978. pap. text ed. 21.75 (ISBN 0-443-01842-1). Churchill.

--Obstetrics Illustrated. 3rd ed. (Illus.). 550p. 1980. pap. text ed. 22.00 (ISBN 0-443-02223-2). Churchill.

Garrick, Barbara L., ed. Hematology for Medical Technologists PreTest Self-Assessment & Review. LC 78-51704. (PreTest Self-Assessment & Review Ser.). (Illus.). 1979. pap. 10.95 (ISBN 0-07-051573-5). McGraw-Pretest.

Garrick, David. Diary of David Garrick. Alexander, R. C., ed. LC 73-91901. 127p. 1928. 14.00 (ISBN 0-405-08552-4, Blom Pubns). Ayer Co Pubs.

--Journal of David Garrick Describing His Visit to France & Italy in 1763. Stone, G. W., Jr., ed. (MLA Rev. Fund Ser.: 10). 1939. pap. 10.00 (ISBN 0-527-32560-0). Kraus Repr.

--Pineapples of Finest Flavour: Or, a Selection of Sundry Unpublished Letters of the English Roscius, David Garrick. Little, David M., ed. LC 66-27076. (Illus.). 1967. Repr. of 1930 ed. 8.00x (ISBN 0-8462-0928-4). Russell.

--The Plays of David Garrick, 4 vols. Berkowitz, Gerald, ed. (Eighteenth Century English Drama Ser.). 1981. lib. bdg. 290.00 (ISBN 0-8240-3590-9). Garland Pub.

--Poetical Works of David Garrick, 2 Vols. LC 68-21214. 1968. Repr. of 1785 ed. Set. 33.00 (ISBN 0-405-08553-2); 22.00 ea. Vol. 1 (ISBN 0-405-08554-0). Vol. 2 (ISBN 0-405-08555-9). Ayer Co Pubs.

--Three Plays by David Garrick. Stein, Elizabeth P., ed. LC 67-23858. 1967. Repr. of 1926 ed. 14.00 (ISBN 0-405-08556-7). Ayer Co Pubs.

Garrick, David & Colman, George. Plays by David Garrick & George Colman the Elder. Wood, E. R., ed. LC 81-17079. (British & American Playwrights 1750-1920 Ser.). 200p. 1982. 39.50 (ISBN 0-521-23590-1); pap. 14.95 (ISBN 0-521-28057-5). Cambridge U Pr.

Garrick, Peter, jt. auth. see Hailwood, Mike.

Garrido, Charlotte M. & Walton, Lon M. Knitting Patterns for Handspun Yarns. (Illus.). 72p. 1982. pap. 5.00 (ISBN 0-933992-24-6). Coffee Break.

Garrido, J. A. Diccionario Ingles-Espanol para Medicos y Estudiantes de Medicina. 525p. (Eng. & Span.). 1979. 35.95 (ISBN 84-7193-011-0, S-34967). French & Eur.

Garrido, L., ed. Applications of Field Theory to Statistical Mechanics. (Lecture Notes in Physics Ser.: Vol. 216). viii, 352p. 1985. pap. 23.70 (ISBN 0-387-13911-7). Springer-Verlag.

--Dynamical Systems & Chaos: Proceedings, Sitges, Barcelona, Spain, 1982. (Lecture Notes in Physics: Vol. 179). 298p. 1983. pap. 20.00 (ISBN 0-387-12276-1). Springer-Verlag.

--Systems Far from Equilibrium: Sitges Conference. (Lecture Notes in Physics Ser.: Vol. 132). 403p. 1980. pap. 32.00 (ISBN 0-387-10251-5). Springer Verlag.

Garrido, L., et al, eds. Stochastic Processes in Nonequilibrium Systems: Proceedings, Sitges International School of Statistical Mechanics, June 1978, Sitges, Barcelona, Spain. (Lecture Notes in Physics: Vol. 84). 1978. pap. 25.00 (ISBN 0-387-08942-X). Springer-Verlag.

Garrido, L. A., et al, eds. The Many-Body Problem. LC 77-94344. 333p. 1969. 34.50x (ISBN 0-306-30444-9, Plenum Pr). Plenum Pub.

Garrido, L. M., et al, eds. Irreversibility in the Many-Body Problem. LC 72-87519. 470p. 1972. 65.00x (ISBN 0-306-30711-1, Plenum Pr). Plenum Pub.

Garrido, N. Index Agaricalium Chilensium with Collaboration of A. Bresinsky & C. Marticorena. (Bibliotheca Mycologica Ser.: No. 99). (Illus.). 340p. 1985. lib. bdg. 42.00x (ISBN 0-318-11864-5). Lubrecht & Cramer.

Garrido, Wilfredo, Jr. Stolia. 169p. (Orig.). 1984. pap. 6.25x (ISBN 971-10-0109-8, Pub. by New Day Philippines). Cellar.

Garrigan, Kristine O. Ruskin on Architecture: His Thought & Influence. LC 73-2045. (Illus.). 238p. 1973. 30.00x (ISBN 0-299-06460-3). U of Wis Pr.

Garrigan, Richard T., jt. ed. see Kinney, James M.

Garrigan, Timothy B. & Lopez, George A. Terrorism: A Problem of Political Violence. (CISE Learning Packages in International Studies). 40p. (Orig.). 1980. pap. text ed. 3.50x (ISBN 0-936876-36-0). Learn Res Intl Stud.

Garrigou-Lagrange, R. The Three Ways of the Spiritual Life. 1977. pap. 3.00 (ISBN 0-89555-017-2). TAN Bks Pubs.

Garrigue, Jean. Animal Hotel. LC 66-23197. 1966. 10.95x (ISBN 0-87130-006-0). Eakins.

--Chartres & Prose Poems. LC 71-152053. (Illus.). 1970. pap. 3.95 (ISBN 0-87130-008-7). Eakins.

--The Ego & the Centaur: Poems. LC 76-138236. 126p. 1972. Repr. of 1947 ed. lib. bdg. 18.75x (ISBN 0-8371-5593-2, GAEC). Greenwood.

Garrigue, Sheila. All the Children Were Sent Away. LC 75-33600. 192p. (gr. 3-5). 1976. 8.95 (ISBN 0-02-736630-8). Bradbury Pr.

--Between Friends. LC 77-90952. 176p. (gr. 4-6). 1978. 9.95 (ISBN 0-02-736620-0). Bradbury Pr.

--The Eternal Spring of Mr. Ito. LC 85-5687. 176p. (gr. 6-8). 1985. 11.95 (ISBN 0-02-737300-2). Bradbury Pr.

Garrigues, Eduardo. The Grass Rain: A Tale of Modern Africa. Lane, Helen R., tr. from Span. 288p. 1984. 17.95 (ISBN 0-02-542740-7). Macmillan.

Garrin, Stephen H. The Concept of Justice in Jakob Wassermann's Trilogy. (European University Studies, German Language & Literature: Ser. 1, Vol. 267). 107p. 1979. pap. 11.60 (ISBN 3-261-03154-9). P Lang Pubs.

Garriott, James C., jt. auth. see Lowry, W. T.

Garriott, O. K., jt. auth. see Risbeth, Henry.

Garris, Kathleen W. The Santa Casa di Loreto: Problems in Cinquecento Sculpture, 2 Vols. LC 76-23653. (Outstanding Dissertations in the Fine Arts Ser.). 1977. lib. bdg. 161.00 (ISBN 0-8240-2735-3). Garland Pub.

Garrison, A. Joseph. Solar Projects: Working Solar Devices to Cut Out & Assemble. LC 81-5130. (Illus.). 128p. (Orig.). 1981. lib. bdg. 19.80 (ISBN 0-89471-129-6); pap. 9.95 (ISBN 0-89471-130-X). Running Pr.

Garrison, Bruce & Sabljak, Mark. Sports Reporting. (Illus.). 252p. 1985. text ed. 22.50x (ISBN 0-8138-1691-2). Iowa St U Pr.

Garrison, Carolyn L., jt. auth. see Brasher, Ruth E.

Garrison, Cecil. One Thousand & One Media Ideas for the Teacher. 3rd ed. 1977. pap. text ed. 6.95x (ISBN 0-8211-0601-5). McCutchan.

--Outdoor Education: Principles & Practice. (Illus.). 256p. 1966. photocopy ed. 25.50x (ISBN 0-398-00653-9). C C Thomas.

Garrison, Charles E. On Being a Person in a World of Groups. LC 81-40113. 190p. (Orig.). 1981. pap. text ed. 10.00 (ISBN 0-8191-1693-9). U Pr of Amer.

Garrison, Chester A. A Map of Shakespeare's London. (Illus.). 8p. 1971. pap. 1.95x (ISBN 0-87071-412-0). Oreg St U Pr.

--The Vast Venture: Hardy's Epic-Drama The Dynasts. (Salzburg Studies in English Literature, Poetic Drama & Poetic Theory: No. 18). 250p. 1973. pap. text ed. 25.50x (ISBN 0-391-01381-5). Humanities.

Garrison, Christian. The Dream Eater. LC 78-55213. (Illus.). 32p. (ps-2). 1978. 10.95 (ISBN 0-02-736600-6). Bradbury Pr.

--Little Pieces of the West Wind. LC 75-887. (Illus.). 32p. (ps-3). 1978. 9.95 (ISBN 0-02-736610-3). Bradbury Pr.

Garrison, Chuck. Offshore Fishing: In Southern California & Baja. LC 80-27579. (Illus., Orig.). 1980. pap. 4.95 (ISBN 0-87701-166-4). Chronicle Bks.

Garrison, Clay, ed. see Johnson, Paul R. & Eaves, Thomas F.

Garrison, Daniel H. The Language of Virgil: An Introduction to the Poetry of the Aeneid. (Illus.). 132p. (Orig.). 1984. pap. text ed. 17.00 (ISBN 0-8204-0176-5). P Lang Pubs.

Garrison, David. Blue Oboe: A Book of Poems. vi, 43p. 1984. pap. 6.95 (ISBN 0-932269-14-1). Wyndham Hall.

Garrison, David, tr. see Aleixandre, Vicente.

Garrison, David W. Cranial Nerves: A Systems Approach. (Illus.). 156p. 1985. 20.75x (ISBN 0-398-05170-4). C C Thomas.

Garrison, Dean H. Good Lessons from Bad Examples. LC 81-68363. 1982. 3.95 (ISBN 0-8054-5186-2). Broadman.

Garrison, Dee. Apostles of Culture: The Public Librarian & American Society 1876-1920. (Illus.). 1979. 14.50 (ISBN 0-02-693850-2). Macmillan.

Garrison, Dee, ed. Rebel Pen: The Writings of Mary Heaton Vorse. (New Feminist Library). 320p. 1985. 26.50 (ISBN 0-85345-669-0); pap. 11.00 (ISBN 0-85345-670-4). Monthly Rev.

Garrison, E. B. Italian Romanesque Panel Painting. LC 75-11061. 1976. Repr. of 1949 ed. lib. bdg. 50.00 (ISBN 0-87817-180-0). Hacker.

Garrison, Eileen & Albanese, Gayle. Eucharistic Manual for Children. LC 84-60217. (Illus.). 28p. (Orig.). 1984. pap. 3.95 (ISBN 0-8192-1343-8). Morehouse.

Garrison, Ernest R. The Art & Science of Breeding Dogs. (Illus.). 145p. 1984. 67.85x (ISBN 0-89266-432-0). Am Classical Coll Pr.

Garrison, Everett & Carmichael, Hogie B. A Master's Guide to Building a Bamboo Fly Rod. 1985. pap. price not set (ISBN 0-8329-0416-3, Pub. by Winchester Pr). New Century.

Garrison, Fielding H. History of Medicine. 4th ed. LC 29-3665. (Illus.). 1960. Repr. of 1929 ed. 35.95 (ISBN 0-7216-4030-3). Saunders.

Garrison, Fielding H., jt. auth. see Wood, Casey A.

Garrison, Francis J., jt. auth. see Garrison, Wendell P.

Garrison, Gene. Wedgwood. (Illus.). 48p. 1982. 24.00 (ISBN 0-88014-061-5). Mosaic Pr OH.

Garrison, George. Westward Extension, Eighteen Forty-One to Eighteen Fifty. LC 68-24978. (American History & Americana Ser., No. 47). 1969. Repr. of 1906 ed. lib. bdg. 54.95x (ISBN 0-8383-0946-1). Haskell.

Garrison, George Pierce. Texas: A Conquest of Civilizations. LC 72-3753. (American Commonwealths: No. 15). Repr. of 1903 ed. 34.00 (ISBN 0-404-57215-4). AMS Pr.

Garrison, Guy, ed. The Changing Role of State Library Consultants. (Monograph: No. 9). 98p. 1968. 4.00x (ISBN 0-87845-031-9). U of Ill Lib Info Sci.

Garrison, James. The Darkness of God: Theology after Hiroshima. LC 83-1415. pap. 62.00 (ISBN 0-317-30139-X, 2025322). Bks Demand UMI.

--The Plutonium Culture: From Hiroshima to Harrisburg. 224p. 1981. 14.95 (ISBN 0-8264-0029-9). Continuum.

Garrison, James D. Dryden & the Tradition of Panegyric. LC 73-91676. 1975. 24.50x (ISBN 0-520-02682-9). U of Cal Pr.

Garrison, Jayne. The ABC's of Christian Mothering. 1979. 8.95 (ISBN 0-8423-0016-3). Tyndale.

Garrison, Jim. The Darkness of God: Theology after Hiroshima. 238p. 1983. pap. 8.95 (ISBN 0-8028-1956-7). Eerdmans.

Garrison, Jim & Shivpuri, Pyare. The Russian Threat: Its Myths & Realities. (Illus.). 344p. 1985. 12.95 (ISBN 0-946551-00-6, Pub. by Gateway Bks); pap. 7.95 (ISBN 0-946551-01-4). Interbook.

Garrison, Juanita B. Piedmont Garden: How to Grow by the Calendar. LC 80-23218. 1981. pap. text ed. 6.95 mechanical (ISBN 0-87249-403-9). U of SC Pr.

Garrison, Julie. Democracy in the U. S. A. (Social Studies). 24p. (gr. 6-9). 1980. wkbk. 5.00 (ISBN 0-8209-0246-2, SS-13). ESP.

Garrison, Karl C. & Force, Dewey G. The Psychology of Exceptional Children. LC 65-21809. pap. 144.30 (ISBN 0-317-09796-2, 2055144). Bks Demand UMI.

Garrison, Lemuel A. The Making of a Ranger: Forty Years with the National Parks. LC 83-10841. (Illus.). 352p. 1983. 19.95 (ISBN 0-935704-19-1); pap. 10.95 (ISBN 0-935704-18-3). Howe Brothers.

Garrison, Linda & Read, Ann K. Fitness for Every Body. LC 79-91831. (Illus.). 138p. 1980. pap. 7.95 (ISBN 0-87484-444-4). Mayfield Pub.

Garrison, Linda, et al. Fitness & Figure Control: The Creation of You. 2nd ed. LC 81-81277. (Illus.). 113p. 1981. pap. 6.95 (ISBN 0-87484-549-1). Mayfield Pub.

Garrison, Margaret F. The Firths of Cascade, Iowa. LC 78-61583. 63p. 1978. pap. 7.50 (ISBN 0-930142-04-7). Merlin Pr.

--Sagebrush Girl. 96p. 1981. 8.75 (ISBN 0-930142-05-5). Merlin Pr.

Garrison, Mark & Gleason, Abbot, eds. Shared Destiny: Fifty Years of Soviet-American Relations. LC 85-47526. 192p. 1985. 16.95 (ISBN 0-8070-0200-3). Beacon Pr.

Garrison, N. L. Status & Work of the Training Supervisor. LC 70-176797. (Columbia University. Teachers College. Contributions to Education: No. 280). Repr. of 1927 ed. 22.50 (ISBN 0-404-55280-3). AMS Pr.

Garrison, Omar. The Dictocrats: Our Unelected Rulers. 333p. 1.25 (ISBN 0-318-15647-4). Natl Health Fed.

--Encyclopedia of Prophecy. (Illus.). 1978. 10.00 (ISBN 0-8065-0559-1). Citadel Pr.

--Tantra: The Yoga of Sex. 1983. 5.98 (ISBN 0-517-54947-6); pap. 7.95. Crown.

Garrison, Omar V. Balboa: Conquistador. 1971. 8.00 (ISBN 0-8184-0011-0). Lyle Stuart.

--Encyclopedia of Prophecy. 1979. pap. text ed. 4.95 (ISBN 0-8065-0674-1). Citadel Pr.

--The Hidden Story of Scientology. 8.50 (ISBN 0-8065-0440-4). Church of Scient Info.

--Jesus Loved Them. (Illus.). 133p. 1983. 19.95 (ISBN 0-931116-06-6). Ralston-Pilot.

--Playing Dirty: The Secret War Against Beliefs. 13.95 (ISBN 0-931116-04-X). Church of Scient Info.

--Playing Dirty: The Secret War Against Beliefs. LC 80-51315. (Illus.). 288p. 1980. 10.50 (ISBN 0-931116-04-X); pap. 4.95 (ISBN 0-931116-05-8). Ralston-Pilot.

--The Secret World of Interpol. 13.95 (ISBN 0-686-74638-4). Church of Scient Info.

--The Secret World of Interpol. LC 76-24523. 1976. 8.95 (ISBN 0-931116-00-7). Ralston-Pilot.

--Secret World of Interpol. 238p. 1982. 32.00x (ISBN 0-85335-227-5, Pub. by W Maclellan Scotland). State Mutual Bk.

Garrison, Omar V., ed. Lost Gems of Secret Knowledge. 304p. 1973. 7.95 (ISBN 0-8216-0205-5). Univ Bks.

Garrison, P. Cockpit Computers & Navigation Avionics. 256p. 1982. 29.95 (ISBN 0-07-022893-0). McGraw.

Garrison, Paul. Aircraft Turbocharging. (Illus.). 144p. 1982. pap. 5.95 (ISBN 0-8306-2306-X, 2306). TAB Bks.

--All about N Gauge Model Railroading. (Illus.). 240p. (Orig.). 1982. pap. 11.95 (ISBN 0-8306-1387-0, 1387). TAB Bks.

--Autopilots, Flight Directors & Flight-Control Systems. (Illus.). 160p. (Orig.). 1985. pap. 12.95 (ISBN 0-8306-2356-6). TAB Bks.

--The Corporate Aircraft Owner's Handbook. (Illus.). 224p. 1982. 14.95 (ISBN 0-8306-9665-2); pap. 8.95 (ISBN 0-8306-2296-9, 2296). TAB Bks.

--Cross-Country Flying. (Illus.). 192p. 1980. 9.95 (ISBN 0-8306-9966-X); pap. 11.95 (ISBN 0-8306-2284-5, 2284). TAB Bks.

--Flying Without Wings: A Flight Simulation Manual. (Illus.). 144p. (Orig.). 1985. pap. 14.95 (ISBN 0-8306-2366-3, 2366). TAB Bks.

--Fun, Games & Graphics for the Apple II, IIe & IIc. (Illus.). 320p. (Orig.). 1984. 18.95 (ISBN 0-8306-0752-8, 1752); pap. 13.95 (ISBN 0-8306-1752-3). TAB Bks.

--The Illustrated Encyclopedia of General Aviation. (Modern Aviation Ser.). (Illus.). 1979. 14.95 (ISBN 0-8306-9754-3); pap. 9.95 (ISBN 0-8306-2274-8, 2274). TAB Bks.

--Investing in Oil in the Eighties. 130p. 1981. 39.95x (ISBN 0-87814-151-0). Pennwell Bks.

--Investing in Oil in the '80s: Without Spending a Fortune. 176p. 1981. 25.00 (ISBN 0-87814-151-0). Pennwell Bks.

--The Last Whole TI 99-4A Book: Programs & Possibilities. LC 83-26046. 472p. 1984. pap. 12.95 (ISBN 0-471-87920-7). Wiley.

--Lift, Thrust & Drag: A Primer of Modern Flying. (Illus.). 224p. 1982. pap. 8.95 (ISBN 0-8306-2309-4, 2309). TAB Bks.

--Night-Flying in Single-Engine Airplanes. (Illus.). 1979. 8.95 (ISBN 0-8306-9789-6); pap. 5.95 (ISBN 0-8306-2266-7, 2266). TAB Bks.

--One Hundred One Model Railroad Layouts. (Illus.). 160p. (Orig.). 1983. 17.95 (ISBN 0-8306-0514-2, 1514); pap. 11.50 (ISBN 0-8306-1514-8). TAB Bks.

--Pilot's Guide to Aviation Insurance. (Illus.). 182p. 1982. pap. 7.95 (ISBN 0-8306-2316-7, 2316). TAB Bks.

--Programming the TI-59 & HP-41 Calculators. (Illus.). 300p. (Orig.). 1982. 18.95 (ISBN 0-8306-2442-2); pap. 13.50 (ISBN 0-8306-1442-7, 1442). TAB Bks.

--Star Power: Mastering Wordstar, MailMerge, SpellStar, DataStar, SuperSort, CalcStar, InfoStar, StarIndex, CorrectStar, SarBurst, ReportStar & PlanStar. (Illus.). 320p. 1985. 24.95 (ISBN 0-8306-0742-0, 1742); pap. 16.95 (ISBN 0-8306-1742-6). TAB Bks.

--Turbo Pascal for BASIC Programmers. 250p. 1985. pap. 14.95 (ISBN 0-88022-167-4, 184). Que Corp.

Garrison, Peter. CV: Carrier Aviation. rev. ed. (Airpower Bk.). (Illus.). 112p. 1984. pap. 10.95 (ISBN 0-89141-206-9). Presidio Pr.

--Flying Airplanes: The First Hundred Hours. Parke, Robert B., ed. LC 80-7476. (Illus.). 240p. 1980. 11.95 (ISBN 0-385-14594-2). Doubleday.

--Homebuilt Airplanes: Build One Yourself & Fly Away in It. LC 79-17448. (Illus., Orig.). 1979. pap. 8.95 (ISBN 0-87701-149-4, Prism Editions). Chronicle Bks.

--Long Distance Flying. LC 80-2049. (Illus.). 1981. 14.95 (ISBN 0-385-14595-0). Doubleday.

Garrison, Philip. The Deer Paintings. 15p. (Orig.). 1969. pap. 7.50 (ISBN 0-932264-12-3). Trask Hse Bks.

--Lime Tree Notes. 1976. signed ed. 6.00 (ISBN 0-685-79234-X, Pub. by Grosseteste); pap. 2.00 (ISBN 0-686-67813-3). Small Pr Dist.

--A Woman & Certain Women. 15p. (Orig.). 1971. pap. 3.00 (ISBN 0-932264-16-6). Trask Hse Bks.

Garrison, Ray H. Managerial Accounting. 4th ed ed. 1985. 32.95x (ISBN 0-256-03261-0); study guide 11.95x (ISBN 0-256-03262-9). Business Pubns.

Garrison, Robert H., Jr. & Somer, Elizabeth. Nutrition Desk Reference. LC 82-84500. 264p. 1985. 29.95 (ISBN 0-87983-328-9). Keats.

Garrison, Robert, Jr. Lysine, Tryptophan & Other Amino Acids. Passwater, Richard A. & Mindell, Earl R., eds. (Good Health Guide Ser.). 32p. (Orig.). 1982. pap. 1.45 (ISBN 0-87983-268-1). Keats.

Garrison, Roger H. How a Writer Works. 99p. 1981. pap. text ed. 6.50 scp (ISBN 0-06-042276-9, HarpC); instructor's manual avail. (ISBN 0-06-362364-1). Har-Row.

--How a Writer Works. rev. ed. 112p. 1985. pap. text ed. 6.50 scp (ISBN 0-06-042276-9, HarpC). Har-Row.

Garrison, Ronald B. & England, Clark M. Retirement: A Time for Fulfillment. Rev. ed. 111p. 1982. pap. 9.95 (ISBN 0-9608190-1-0). Center Prof.

Garrison, Rosser W. Revision of the Genus Bnahagma of the U. S. West of the Rocky Mountains & Identification of Certain Larvae by Discriminand Analysis: Publications in Entomology. (Vol. 105). 1985. 11.00x (ISBN 0-520-09954-0). U of Cal Pr.

Garrison, Vivian, jt. ed. see Crapanzano, Vincent.

Garrison, W. L. Bondage. LC 78-72959. 1978. 5.95 (ISBN 0-933012-01-2). Coker Pub.

Garrison, Webb. Behind the Headlines. (Illus.). 192p. 1983. 12.95 (ISBN 0-8117-0817-9). Stackpole.

--Strange Facts About the Bible. (Festival Books). 1976. pap. 2.25 (ISBN 0-687-39945-9). Abingdon.

Garrison, Webb B. Codfish, Cats & Civilization. LC 77-120898. (Essay & General Literature Index Reprint Ser). 1971. Repr. of 1959 ed. 22.50x (ISBN 0-8046-1407-5, Pub. by Kennikat). Assoc Faculty Pr.

--Ogelethorpe's Folly: The Birth of Georgia. LC 82-5191. 256p. 1982. 14.95 (ISBN 0-87797-069-6). Cherokee.

Garrison, Wendell P. William Lloyd Garrison, Eighteen Hundred Five to Eighteen Seventy-Nine. LC 79-88431. 1885-1889. Repr. 63.00x (ISBN 0-8371-2479-4, GAH&). Greenwood.

Garrison, Wendell P. & Garrison, Francis J. William Lloyd Garrison, Eighteen Hundred Five to Eighteen Seventy-Nine, 4 Vols. LC 71-82191. (Anti-Slavery Crusade in America Ser). 1969. Repr. of 1885 ed. Set. 74.00 (ISBN 0-405-00629-2); 22.00 ea. Vol. 1 (ISBN 0-405-00671-3). Vol. 2 (ISBN 0-405-00672-1). Vol. 3 (ISBN 0-405-00673-X). Vol. 4 (ISBN 0-405-00674-8). Ayer Co Pubs.

Garrison, William E. & Dowd, Merle E. Handcrafting Jewelry: Designs & Techniques. LC 77-91199. 208p. 1978. pap. 6.95 (ISBN 0-8092-7529-5). Contemp Bks.

Garrison, William L. The Letters of William Lloyd Garrison, 6 vols. Incl. Vol. 1. I Will Be Heard 1822-1835. Merrill, Walter M., ed. (Illus.). 646p. 1971. 50.00x (ISBN 0-674-52660-0); Vol. 2. A House Dividing Against Itself, 1836-1840. Ruchames, Louis, ed. (Illus.). 802p. 1972. 50.00x (ISBN 0-674-52661-9); Vol. 3. No Union with Slaveholders, 1841-1849. Merrill, Walter M., ed. 1974. 45.00x (ISBN 0-674-52662-7). LC 75-133210 (Belknap Pr). Harvard U Pr.

--The Letters of William Lloyd Garrison: From Disunionism to the Brink of War, Vol. 4. Ruchames, Louis, ed. 318p. 1976. text ed. 35.00x (ISBN 0-674-52663-5, Belknap Pr). Harvard U Pr.

--The Letters of William Lloyd Garrison: To Rouse the Slumbering Land, 1868-1879, Vol. 6. Merrill, Walter M. & Ruchames, Louis, eds. 657p. 1981. text ed. 45.00x (ISBN 0-674-52666-X, Belknap Pr). Harvard U Pr.

--New Reign of Terror in the Slaveholding States, for 1859-1860. LC 76-82192. (Anti-Slavery Crusade in America Ser). 1969. Repr. of 1860 ed. 14.00 (ISBN 0-405-00631-4). Ayer Co Pubs.

--Selections from the Writings & Speeches of William Lloyd Garrison. LC 68-55886. Repr. of 1852 ed. cancelled (ISBN 0-8371-0441-6). Greenwood.

--Sonnets. LC 78-104464. Repr. of 1843 ed. lib. bdg. 14.00 (ISBN 0-8398-0658-2). Irvington.

--Thoughts on African Colonization. LC 68-28997. (American Negro: His History & Literature Ser., No. 1). (Illus.). 1968. Repr. of 1832 ed. 14.00 (ISBN 0-405-01816-9). Ayer Co Pubs.

--William Lloyd Garrison on Non-Resistance. LC 73-10286. (American History & Americana Ser., No. 47). 1973. Repr. lib. bdg. 49.95x (ISBN 0-8383-1717-0). Haskell.

--Women's Views on Guns & Self-Defense. 114p. (Orig.). 1983. pap. 5.50 (ISBN 0-911475-23-0). Second Amend.

Garrison, William L., jt. ed. see Merrill, Walter M.

Garrison, William L., et al. Letter to Louis Kossuth, Concerning Freedom & Slavery in the United States in Behalf of the American Anti-Slavery Society. LC 76-82204. (Anti-Slavery Crusade in America Ser). 1969. Repr. of 1852 ed. 9.00 (ISBN 0-405-00630-6). Ayer Co Pubs.

Garrison, William N., jt. auth. see Henrichsen, Walter A.

Garrison, Winfred E. March of Faith: The Story of Religion in America Since 1865. LC 79-138112. 1971. Repr. of 1933 ed. lib. bdg. 22.50x (ISBN 0-8371-5688-2, GAMF). Greenwood.

Garrison, Winfred E., jt. ed. see Clark, Thomas C.

Garrison, Zoe. Golden Triple Time. 448p. 1985. 15.95 (ISBN 0-453-00478-4). NAL.

Garriss, Evelyn M., jt. auth. see Browning, Iben.

Garritt, E. F. The Conception of Beauty in the Major Philosophies of the Western World, 2 vols. 337p. 1985. Set. 147.50 (ISBN 0-89266-521-1). Am Classical Coll Pr.

Garrity, Devin A., ed. Forty-Four Irish Short Stories: An Anthology of Irish Short Fiction from Yeats to Frank O'Connor. 1980. 12.95 (ISBN 0-517-34295-2). Devin.

--New Irish Poets. (Illus.). 9.50 (ISBN 0-8159-6302-5). Devin.

Garrity, John, jt. auth. see Garrity, Terry.

Garrity, Patrick J., jt. ed. see Einhorn, Robert J.

Garrity, Paul G., jt. auth. see Frieden, James A.

Garrity, Richard. Canal Boatman: My Life on Upstate Waterways. LC 77-21909. (York State Bks.). (Illus.). 240p. 1984. pap. 12.95 (ISBN 0-8156-0191-3). Syracuse U Pr.

Garrity, Terry. Total Loving by "J". 1981. pap. 2.95 (ISBN 0-671-44364-X). PB.

Garrity, Terry & Garrity, John. Story of "J". The Author of the Sensuous Woman Tells the Bitter Price of Her Crazy Success. LC 84-60479. 295p. 1984. 12.95 (ISBN 0-688-00997-2). Morrow.

Garrod, et al. Perspectives on Teaching: Learning & Development. 536p. 1984. pap. text ed. 24.95 (ISBN 0-8403-3482-6). Kendall Hunt.

Garrod, D. A. see Joint Expedition of the British School of Archaelogy in Jerusalem & the American School of Prehistoric Research, 1929-1934.

Garrod, D. J., ed. see Zoological Society of London - 29th Symposium.

Garrod, D. R. Cellular Development. 1973. pap. 6.95 (ISBN 0-412-11410-0, NO.6117, Pub. by Chapman Hall). Methuen Inc.

Garrod, David R. & Feldman, Joan D., eds. Development in the Nervous System. LC 80-42151. (British Society for Developmental Biology Symposium Ser.: No. 5). (Illus.). 350p. 1982. 95.00 (ISBN 0-521-23493-X). Cambridge U Pr.

Garrod, Dorothy A. The Upper Palaeolithic Age in Britain. LC 76-44722. Repr. of 1926 ed. 21.50 (ISBN 0-404-15926-5). AMS Pr.

Garrod, H. W. Collins. LC 73-6734. 123p. 1973. Repr. of 1928 ed. lib. bdg. 16.50x (ISBN 0-374-93011-2). Octagon.

--Keats. 157p. 1980. Repr. of 1926 ed. lib. bdg. 15.00 (ISBN 0-8495-1952-7). Arden Lib.

--The Profession of Poetry. 1978. Repr. of 1924 ed. lib. bdg. 8.50 (ISBN 0-8495-1925-X). Arden Lib.

--The Study of Good Letters. Jones, John, ed. LC 75-9845. (Illus.). 221p. 1975. Repr. of 1963 ed. lib. bdg. 18.75x (ISBN 0-8371-8119-4, GAGL). Greenwood.

--Tolstoi's Theory of Art. LC 74-13080. 1935. lib. bdg. 8.50 (ISBN 0-8414-4539-7). Folcroft.

Garrod, H. W., jt. auth. see Johnson, Lionel.

Garrod, H. W., ed. Einhard's Life of Charlemagne with Introduction & Notes. 1977. lib. bdg. 59.95 (ISBN 0-8490-1753-X). Gordon Pr.

Garrod, H. W., ed. see Horace.

Garrod, Heathcote. Poetry & the Criticism of Life. LC 76-58446. (The Charles Eliot Norton Lectures for 1929-1930). 1977. Repr. of 1931 ed. lib. bdg. 18.75x (ISBN 0-8371-9445-8, GAPO). Greenwood.

Garrod, Heathcote W. The Profession of Poetry. LC 74-16316. 1974. Repr. of 1924 ed. lib. bdg. 4.50 (ISBN 0-8414-4556-7). Folcroft.

--Profession of Poetry, & Other Lectures. facs. ed. LC 67-302142. (Essay Index Reprint Ser). 1929. 18.00 (ISBN 0-8369-0469-9). Ayer Co Pubs.

--The Study of Poetry. LC 72-196082. 1974. Repr. of 1936 ed. lib. bdg. 5.00 (ISBN 0-8414-4562-1). Folcroft.

--Wordsworth: Lectures & Essays. LC 75-28997. Repr. of 1923 ed. 12.50 (ISBN 0-404-14008-4). AMS Pr.

Garrod, Heathcote W., ed. see Keats, John.

Garrod, Herbert B. Dante, Goethe's Faust, & Other Lectures. 1913. lib. bdg. 25.00 (ISBN 0-8414-4639-3). Folcroft.

Garrod, J. W., ed. Testing for Toxicity. 365p. 1981. text ed. 37.00 (ISBN 0-85066-218-4, Pub. by Taylor & Frances England). J K Burgess.

--Testing for Toxicity. 366p. 1981. 40.00x (ISBN 0-85066-218-4). Taylor & Francis.

Garrod, L. P., et al. Antibiotic & Chemotherapy. 5th ed. (Illus.). 518p. (Orig.). 1981. text ed. 47.00 (ISBN 0-443-02143-0). Churchill.

Garrod, L. P., et al, eds. Present Diagnosis & Treatment of Septicemia. (Antibiotics & Chemotherapy: No. 21). (Illus.). 1976. 53.25 (ISBN 3-8055-2200-2). S Karger.

Garrod, S. C., jt. auth. see Sanford, A. J.

Garrod, Stan. Canada Studies Program: Activity Manual. 1st ed. Chalk, John & Yockstick, Elizabeth, eds. (Illus.). 105p. (gr. 4). 1981. Duplicate Masters 49.00 (ISBN 0-943068-27-4); Teacher's Guide 5.00 (ISBN 0-943068-26-6). Graphic Learning.

Garrone, Gabriel-Marie. Poor in Spirit: Awaiting All from God. 1978. pap. 2.95 (ISBN 0-232-51337-6). Living Flame Pr.

Garrone, R. Phylogenesis of Connective Tissue: Morphological Aspects & Biosynthesis of Sponge Intercellular Matrix. Robert, L., ed. (Frontiers of Matrix Biology: Vol. 5). (Illus.). 1978. 66.00 (ISBN 3-8055-2767-5). S Karger.

Garronsky, Serge, jt. auth. see Terry, Patricia.

Garronsky, Serge, tr. see Terry, Patricia & Garronsky, Serge.

Garrotto, Alfred J. Christ in Our Lives. (Orig.). 1980. pap. text ed. 4.95 (ISBN 0-03-056979-6). Winston Pr.

--Christians & Prayer. (Orig.). 1980. pap. text ed. 4.95 (ISBN 0-03-056981-8). Winston Pr.

--Christians Reconciling. 96p. (Orig.). 1982. pap. 4.95 (ISBN 0-86683-170-3). Winston Pr.

Garrow, David J. The FBI & Martin Luther King, Jr. 1981. 15.95 (ISBN 0-393-01509-2). Norton.

--The FBI & Martin Luther King, Jr. 1983. pap. 5.95 (ISBN 0-14-006486-9). Penguin.

--Protest at Selma: Martin Luther King, Jr. & the Voting Rights Act of 1965. LC 78-5593. (Illus.). 1978. 31.00 (ISBN 0-300-02247-6); pap. 10.95x (ISBN 0-300-02498-3). Yale U Pr.

Garry, Philip J., ed. see Arnold O. Beckman Conference in Clinical Chemical.

Garry, Stephen, tr. see Herman, Yuri.

Garry, William, et al, eds. A Checklist for Technical Skills & Other Training. (Illus.). 94p. softcover 10.00 (ISBN 0-318-13265-6, GACTP); members 7.75 (ISBN 0-318-13266-4). Am Soc Train & Devel.

Garry-McCord, Kathleen, illus. Dick Whittington. LC 80-28171. (Illus.). 32p. (gr. k-2). 1981. PLB 7.89 (ISBN 0-89375-482-X); pap. text ed. 1.95 (ISBN 0-89375-483-8). Troll Assocs.

Garsee, Lee. New Dimensions in Puppet Ministry. 1983. pap. 5.95 (ISBN 0-89137-607-0). Quality Pubns.

Garshin, M. Stories. 383p. 1982. pap. 4.00 (ISBN 0-8285-2486-6, Pub. by Progress Pubs USSR). Imported Pubns.

Garshin, V. The Frog Went Travelling. 12p. 1975. pap. 0.99 (ISBN 0-8285-1149-7, Pub. by Progress Pubs USSR). Imported Pubns.

--La Rana Viajera. (Illus.). 12p. (Span.). 1975. pap. 1.49 (ISBN 0-8285-1301-5, Pub. by Progress Pubs USSR). Imported Pubns.

Garshin, Wsewolod M. The Signal, & Other Stories. facsimile ed. Smith, Rowland, tr. from Rus. LC 77-163027. (Short Story Index Reprint Ser.). Repr. of 1915 ed. 21.00 (ISBN 0-8369-3941-7). Ayer Co Pubs.

Garside, Anne, ed. see Walters Art Gallery Trustees.

Garside, Charles, Jr. The Origins of Calvin's Theology of Music: 1536-1543. LC 78-73171. (Transactions Ser.: Vol. 69, Pt. 4). 1979. 7.00 (ISBN 0-87169-694-0). Am Philos.

--Zwingli & the Arts. (Music Ser.). xiv, 190p. 1981. Repr. of 1966 ed. lib. bdg. 25.00 (ISBN 0-306-76018-5). Da Capo.

Garside, Evelyne. China Companion: A Guide to One Hundred Cities, Resorts & Places of Interest in the People's Republic. LC 82-1403. (Illus.). 276p. 1982. 13.95 (ISBN 0-374-12198-2); pap. 7.95 (ISBN 0-374-51672-3). FS&G.

Garside, G. A. One Increasing Purpose: The Life of Henry W. Luce. 271p. 1980. 16.45 (ISBN 0-89955-150-5, Pub. by Mei Ya Pub.). Intl Spec Bk.

Garside, Patricia L., jt. auth. see Young, Ken.

Garside, R. G. The Architecture of Digital Computers. (Oxford Applied Mathematics & Computing Science Ser.). (Illus.). 1980. text ed. 74.00x (ISBN 0-19-859627-8); pap. text ed. 34.50x (ISBN 0-19-859638-3). Oxford U Pr.

Garside, Robin. Intrinsically Safe Instrumentation: A Guide. rev. & enl. ed. LC 83-12982. 224p. 1983. pap. text ed. 29.95x (ISBN 0-87664-728-X). Instru Soc.

Garside, Roger. Coming Alive: China after Mao. 1981. 12.95 (ISBN 0-07-022914-7). McGraw.

Garske, John, jt. auth. see Lynn, Steven.

Garske, John P., jt. auth. see Arkes, Hal R.

Garsoian, N. G. Paulician Heresy: A Study of the Origin & Development of Paulicianism in Armenia & the Eastern Provinces of the Byzantine Empire. (Publications in Near & Middle East Ser.: No. 6). 1967. text ed. 32.80x (ISBN 90-2790-096-5). Mouton.

Garsoian, Nina & Mathews, Thomas, eds. East of Byzantium: Syria & Armenia in the Formative Period. LC 82-9665. (Dumbarton Oaks Symposium). (Illus.). 266p. 1982. 35.00x (ISBN 0-88402-104-1). Dumbarton Oaks.

Garsoian, Nina G., ed. see Faustos of Buzand.

Garson, jt. auth. see Stewart.

Garson, Arthur, Jr. The Electrocardiogram in Infants & Children: A Systematic Approach. LC 83-1039. (Illus.). 421p. 1983. text ed. 45.00 (ISBN 0-8121-0872-8). Lea & Febiger.

Garson, Arthur, Jr., jt. ed. see Gillette, Paul C.

Garson, Arthur, Jr., et al. A Guide to Cardiac Dysrhythmias in Children. (Clinical Cardiology Monographs). 208p. 1980. 26.50 (ISBN 0-8089-1261-5, 791520). Grune.

Garson, Barbara. All the Livelong Day: The Meaning & Demeaning of Routine Work. 1977. pap. 4.95 (ISBN 0-14-004381-0). Penguin.

Garson, David. Power & Politics in the United States: A Political Economy Approach. 1977. pap. text ed. 9.95x (ISBN 0-669-92742-2). Heath.

Garson, Eugenia & Haufrecht, Herbert, eds. Laura Ingalls Wilder Songbook. LC 68-24327. (Illus.). (gr. 4 up). 1968. 16.95 (ISBN 0-06-021933-5); PLB 15.89 (ISBN 0-06-021934-3). HarpJ.

Garson, G. David. Group Theories of Politics. LC 78-134. (Sage Library of Social Research: No. 61). 216p. 1978. 24.00x (ISBN 0-8039-0518-1). Sage.

Garson, G. David & Overman, E. Samuel. Public Management Research in the U. S. LC 83-2400. 204p. 1983. 27.95 (ISBN 0-03-062159-3). Praeger.

Garson, G. David, ed. Worker Self-Management in Industry: The West European Experience. LC 77-2774. (Praeger Special Studies). 260p. 1977. 43.95 (ISBN 0-03-022406-3). Praeger.

Garson, Helen S. Truman Capote. LC 80-5336. (Literature and Life Ser.). (Illus.). 216p. 1980. 12.95 (ISBN 0-8044-2229-X); pap. 6.95 (ISBN 0-8044-6172-4). Ungar.

Garson, M. S., jt. auth. see Mitchell, A. H.

Garson, N. G. Louis Botha or John X. Merriman: The Choice of South Africa's First Prime Minister. (Commonwealth Papers: No. 12). 47p. 1969. pap. 18.95 (ISBN 0-485-17612-2, Pub. by Athlone Pr Ltd). Longwood Pub Group.

Garson, Robert A. The Democratic Party & the Politics of Sectionalism, 1941-1948. LC 73-93121. xiv, 354p. 1974. 30.00x (ISBN 0-8071-0070-6). La State U Pr.

Garst, John F., ed. see McCurry, John G.

Garst, Robert E. & Bernstein, Theodore M. Headlines & Deadlines: A Manual for Copy Editors. 4th ed. 1981. 28.00x (ISBN 0-231-04816-5); pap. 10.50x (ISBN 0-231-04817-3). Columbia U Pr.

Garstang, Donald. Giacomo Serpotta & the Stuccatori of Palermo: 1560-1790. (Studies in Architecture: Vol. XXII). (Illus.). 304p. 1984. 147.50 (ISBN 0-8390-0339-0). Abner Schram Ltd.

Garstang, John. The Hittite Empire. 1976. lib. bdg. 59.95 (ISBN 0-8490-2014-X). Gordon Pr.

--Joshua-Judges. LC 78-9518. (Kregel Limited Edition Library). 1978. 16.95 (ISBN 0-8254-2719-3). Kregel.

--Joshua Judges: The Foundations of Bible History. 1977. lib. bdg. 59.95 (ISBN 0-8490-2109-X). Gordon Pr.

--The Land of the Hittites. 1976. lib. bdg. 59.95 (ISBN 0-8490-2124-3). Gordon Pr.

Garstein, Oskar. Rome & the Counter-Reformation in Scandinavia. 630p. 1980. 40.00x (ISBN 82-00-06165-5). Universitet.

Garstin, Crosbie. High Noon. 332p. 1982. pap. 7.50 (ISBN 0-907746-11-X, Pub. by A Mott Ltd). Longwood Pub Group.

--The Owl's House. 256p. 1982. pap. 7.50 (ISBN 0-907746-07-1, Pub. by A Mott Ltd). Longwood Pub Group.

--The West Wind. 346p. 1983. pap. 7.50 (ISBN 0-907746-18-7, Pub. by A Mott Ltd). Longwood Pub Group.

Garstka, Walter U. Water Resources & the National Welfare. LC 77-74260. 1978. 32.00 (ISBN 0-918334-19-5). WRP.

Gart, Alan. Banks, Thrifts & Insurance Companies: Surviving the 1980s. 160p. 1985. 19.95. Lexington Bks.

--The Insider's Guide to the Financial Services Revolution. (Illus.). 192p. 1983. 26.50 (ISBN 0-07-022891-4). McGraw.

Garten, Edward. Tchaikovsky. (Master Musicians: No. M187). (Illus.). 1976. pap. 7.95 (ISBN 0-8226-0721-2). Littlefield.

Garten, H. F. Wagner the Dramatist. (Opera Library Ser.). (Illus.). 159p. 1978. 13.50x (ISBN 0-8476-6058-3). Rowman.

--Wagner the Dramatist. price not set. Riverrun NY.

Garten, Max. Civilized Diseases & Their Circumvention. 7.95x (ISBN 0-686-29927-2). Cancer Control Soc.

Garten, Robert L., jt. ed. see Burton, James J.

Gartenberg, Egon. Johann Strauss. (Quality Paperback Ser.). 1979. pap. 6.95 (ISBN 0-306-80098-5). Da Capo.

--Johann Strauss: The End of an Era. LC 73-12932. (Illus.). 320p. 1974. 24.95x (ISBN 0-271-01131-9). Pa St U Pr.

--Mahler: The Man & His Music. LC 77-70274. (Illus.). 1979. pap. 6.95 (ISBN 0-02-871540-3). Schirmer Bks.

--Mahler: The Man & His Music. LC 77-70274. (Illus.). 1978. 16.95 (ISBN 0-02-870840-7). Schirmer Bks.

Gartenberg, Max & Feldman, Gene, eds. The Beat Generation & the Angry Young Men. 384p. 1984. pap. 8.95 (ISBN 0-8065-0924-4). Citadel Pr.

Gartenberg, Max, jt. ed. see Feldman, Gene.

Gartenberg, Michael & Shaw, Barry. Mathematics for Financial Analysis. 240p. 1976. text ed. 28.00 (ISBN 0-08-019599-7). Pergamon.

Gartenberg, Morris, jt. auth. see Gambino, Anthony J.

Gartenhaus, Jacob. Famous Hebrew Christians. 1979. pap. 5.95 (ISBN 0-8010-3733-6). Baker Bk.

Garter, Thomas. The Most Virtuous & Godly Susanna. LC 82-45685. (Malone Society Reprint Ser.: No. 82). Repr. of 1936 ed. 40.00 (ISBN 0-404-63082-0). AMS Pr.

Garth, et al, trs. see Ovid.

Garth, Bryant. Neighborhood Law Firms for the Poor: A Comparative Study of Recent Developments in Legal Aid & in the Legal Profession. LC 80-51739. 282p. 1980. 40.00x (ISBN 90-286-0180-5). Sijthoff & Noordhoff.

Garth, Helen M. Saint Mary Magdalene in Medieval Literature. LC 78-64210. (Johns Hopkins University. Studies in the Social Sciences. Sixty-Seventh Ser. 1949: 3). Repr. of 1950 ed. 15.50 (ISBN 0-404-61315-2). AMS Pr.

Garth, Samuel. The Dispensary: With a Short Account of the Proceedings of the College of Physicians, London, in Relation to the Sick Poor (1697) & Claremont (1715) LC 74-23391. 160p. 1975. Repr. lib. bdg. 30.00x (ISBN 0-8201-1145-7). Schol Facsimiles.

Garth, Sheridan H. Pageant of the Mediterranean. rev. ed. (Illus.). 1962. 9.95 (ISBN 0-8038-5690-3). Hastings.

Garth, Will. Dr. Cyclops. 255p. Repr. 5.00 (ISBN 0-686-75374-7). Bookfinger.

--Dr. Cyclops. 155p. pap. 1.50 (ISBN 0-317-01573-7). Centaur.

Garthe, Nancy, jt. auth. see Andacht, Sandra.

Garthoff, Raymond L. Detente & Confrontation: American-Soviet Relations from Nixon to Reagan. LC 84-45855. 950p. 1985. 39.95 (ISBN 0-8157-3044-6); pap. 16.95 (ISBN 0-8157-3043-8). Brookings.

--Intelligence Assessment & Policymaking: A Case Study from the Kennedy Administration. LC 83-73220. 53p. 1984. pap. 6.95 (ISBN 0-8157-3045-4). Brookings.

--Soviet Image of Future War. 1959. 9.75 (ISBN 0-8183-0210-0). Pub Aff Pr.

--Soviet Strategy in the Nuclear Age. LC 74-10015. 283p. 1974. Repr. of 1958 ed. lib. bdg. 60.50 (ISBN 0-8371-7658-1, GASS). Greenwood.

Garthwaite, Gene R. Khans & Shahs: A Documentary Analysis of the Bakhtiyari in Iran. LC 82-19836. (Illus.). 220p. 1983. 49.50 (ISBN 0-521-24235-5). Cambridge U Pr.

Garthwite, Elloyse M., jt. auth. see Bell, Laurel.

Gartland, John J. Fundamentals of Orthopaedics. 3rd ed. LC 78-65971. (Illus.). 487p. 1979. text ed. 27.50 (ISBN 0-7216-4047-8). Saunders.

Gartland, Robert A. Cowboys & Cattle. (Stories for Young Americans Ser.). 1980. 5.95 (ISBN 0-89015-260-8). Eakin Pubns.

Gartley, Cheryle, ed. Managing Incontinence: A Guide to Living with the Loss of Urinary Control. (Illus.). 240p. 1985. 12.95 (ISBN 0-915463-13-X, Dist. by Kampmann). Jameson Bks.

Gartling, D. K., jt. ed. see Park, K. C.

Gartner. Consumer Education in the Human Services. (Pergamon Policy Studies). 1979. 30.00 (ISBN 0-08-023708-8). Pergamon.

Gartner, Alan. Public Education. (Task Force on the Eighties Ser.). 28p. 1981. pap. 2.50 (ISBN 0-87495-037-6). Am Jewish Comm.

Gartner, Alan & Riessman, Frank. How to Individualize Learning. LC 77-89842. (Fastback Ser.: No. 100). 1977. pap. 0.75 (ISBN 0-87367-100-7). Phi Delta Kappa.

--Self-Help in the Human Services. LC 77-79483. (Social & Behavioral Science Ser). 1977. text ed. 21.95x (ISBN 0-87589-338-4). Jossey-Bass.

Gartner, Alan, ed. College Programs for Paraprofessionals: A Directory of Degree-Granting Programs in the Human Services. LC 74-12066. 135p. 1975. text ed. 26.95 (ISBN 0-87705-229-8). Human Sci Pr.

Gartner, Alan & Riessman, Frank, eds. The Self-Help Revolution. (Community Psychology Ser.: Vol. 10). 304p. 1984. 29.95 (ISBN 0-89885-070-3). Human Sci Pr.

Gartner, Alan, et al, eds. After Reagan: Alternatives for the '80's. LC 83-48347. 288p. 1984. 14.90i (ISBN 0-06-015254-0, HarpT). Har-Row.

--Beyond Reagan: Alternatives for the '80's. LC 83-48347. (Social Policy Ser.). 288p. 1984. pap. 6.68i (ISBN 0-06-091100-X, CN 1100, CN). Har-Row.

--What Reagan Is Doing to Us. LC 82-47559. 307p. (Orig.). 1982. pap. 3.37i (ISBN 0-06-080596-X, P-596, PL). Har-Row.

--Public Service Employment: An Analysis of Its History, Problems & Prospects. LC 72-93186. (Special Studies in U.S. Economics, Social, & Political Issues). 1973. 59.50x (ISBN 0-275-06630-4). Irvington.

Gartner, Carol B. Rachel Carson. LC 82-40285. (Literature & Life Ser.). 175p. 1983. 12.95 (ISBN 0-8044-5425-6); pap. 6.95 (ISBN 0-8044-6177-5). Ungar.

Gartner, Chloe. Anne Bonny. 1978. pap. 1.95 (ISBN 0-89083-364-8). Zebra.

--Daughter of the Desert. 1978. pap. 2.25 (ISBN 0-89083-375-3). Zebra.

--Highland Mistress. 1981. pap. 2.95 (ISBN 0-89083-811-9). Zebra.

--Still Falls the Rain. (Orig.). 1983. pap. 3.95 (ISBN 0-440-18329-4). Dell.

Gartner Group, Inc. Staff. Top One Hundred DP Almanac, 1984. Cappelli, William S. & Ryan, Thomas A., eds. (Illus.). 497p. 1984. 295.00 (ISBN 0-317-15127-4); special library price 85.00 (ISBN 0-317-15128-2). Gartner Group.

Gartner, Leslie P. Alcohol & Pregnancy: A Retrieval Index & Bibliography of the Fetal Alcohol Syndrome. LC 84-11311. 80p. 1984. pap. text ed. 35.00x (ISBN 0-910841-03-9). Jen Hse Pub Co.

--Essentials of Oral Histology & Embryology. LC 82-90755. (Illus.). 120p. 1982. pap. text ed. 8.75 (ISBN 0-910841-00-4). Jen Hse Pub Co.

Gartner, Leslie P., jt. auth. see Hiatt, James L.

Gartner, Lloyd P., ed. Jewish Education in the United States. LC 73-112708. (Classics in Education Ser.). 1970. pap. 5.50x (ISBN 0-8077-1404-6). Tchrs Coll.

Gartner, Rosemary, jt. auth. see Archer, Dane.

Garton, George. Colt's SAA Post-War Models. 21.95 (ISBN 0-686-43083-2). Gun Room.

Garton, Janet. Jens Bjornboe: Prophet Without Honor. LC 85-25294. (Contributions to the Study of World Literature Ser.: No. 9). 192p. 1985. lib. bdg. 27.95 (ISBN 0-313-24699-8, GJE/). Greenwood.

Garton, Jean S. Who Broke the Baby? LC 79-22683. 112p. (Orig.). 1979. pap. 3.95 (ISBN 0-87123-608-7, 210608). Bethany Hse.

Garton, Joseph W. The Film Acting of John Barrymore. Jowett, Garth S., ed. LC 79-6676. (Dissertations on Film, 1980 Ser.). 1980. lib. bdg. 24.50x (ISBN 0-405-12910-6). Ayer Co Pubs.

Garton, Malinda D. Teaching the Educable Mentally Retarded: Practical Methods. 3rd ed. (Illus.). 356p. 1974. 14.75x (ISBN 0-398-00654-7). C C Thomas.

Garton, Melville. High Profile. LC 84-90065. 210p. 1984. 13.95 (ISBN 0-533-06146-6). Vantage.

Garton, Ray. Seductions. 288p. (Orig.). 1984. pap. 3.50 (ISBN 0-523-42309-8). Pinnacle Bks.

Garton, Tessa. Early Romanesque Sculpture in Apulia. LC 83-48701. (Theses from the Courtauld Institute of Art Ser.). (Illus.). 655p. 1984. lib. bdg. 90.00 (ISBN 0-8240-5978-6). Garland Pub.

Gartrell, J. W., jt. auth. see Detomasi, Don D.

Gartshore, Linda. The Machine Knitter's Dictionary. LC 83-60726. (Illus.). 192p. 1983. pap. 9.95 (ISBN 0-312-50221-4). St Martin.

Gartside, G., jt. auth. see Stewart, G. A.

Gartside, I. Model Business Letters. 3rd ed. 528p. 1981. pap. 22.95x (ISBN 0-7121-1268-5, Pub. by Macdonald & Evans England). Trans-Atlantic.

Gartside, L. English for Business Studies. 3rd ed. 416p. (Orig.). 1981. pap. text ed. 17.95 (ISBN 0-7121-0582-4). Trans-Atlantic.

--Modern Business Correspondence. 3rd ed. (Illus.). 480p. 1976. pap. 21.00x (ISBN 0-7121-1392-4, Pub. by Macdonald & Evans England). Trans-Atlantic.

Gartska, Stanley J., jt. auth. see Berney, Paul R.

Gartz, William F., et al. Saint John's Tower & Health Care Facility: An Architectural Evaluation. Moore, Gary T., ed. (Illus.). iv, 135p. 1981. 7.50 (ISBN 0-938744-20-8, R81-7). U of Wis Ctr Arch-Urban.

Garvan, Beatrice B. & Hummel, Charles F. The Pennsylvania Germans: A Celebration of Their Arts, 1683-1850. LC 82-61416. (Illus.). 200p. 1982. pap. 18.95 (ISBN 0-87633-048-0). Phila Mus Art.

Garvan, Fran J. Farmers Market Cookbook. 176p. 1982. 14.95 (ISBN 0-916782-29-8); pap. 8.95 (ISBN 0-916782-30-1). Harvard Common Pr.

Garvan, Fran J., jt. auth. see Brooks, Pat.

Garvan, Frances J. Best Restaurants Northern New England. (Best Restaurants Ser.). (Illus.). 200p. pap. cancelled (ISBN 0-89286-213-0). One Hund One Prods.

Garvan, John M. The Manobos of Mindanao. LC 77-86951. (National Academy of Sciences, Washington, D.C. Memoirs: Vol. 23). Repr. of 1931 ed. 67.50 (ISBN 0-404-16715-2). AMS Pr.

Garve, Andrew. The Ashes of Loda. 1978. pap. 1.50i (ISBN 0-06-080430-0, P 430, PL). Har-Row.

--Counterstroke. LC 78-378. 1978. 11.49i (ISBN 0-690-01748-0). T Y Crowell.

--A Hero for Leanda. 1978. pap. 1.50i (ISBN 0-06-080429-7, P 429, PL). Har-Row.

--Home to Roost. (Crime Ser). 1978. pap. 3.95 (ISBN 0-14-004741-7). Penguin.

--No Tears for Hilda. LC 75-44975. (Crime Fiction Ser). 1976. Repr. of 1950 ed. lib. bdg. 21.00 (ISBN 0-8240-2369-2). Garland Pub.

--The Riddle of Samson. 1978. pap. 1.95i (ISBN 0-06-080450-5, P 450, PL). Har-Row.

Garven, Charles. Student Journalist & Editing. Rosen, Ruth C., ed. LC 68-11055. (Student Journalist Ser). (Illus.). (gr. 7 up). 1967. PLB 8.97 (ISBN 0-8239-0117-3). Rosen Group.

Garver. At Wit's End Corner. (Illus.). pap. 1.25 (ISBN 0-686-12326-3). Christs Mission.

--Our Christian Heritage. (Illus.). 4.50 (ISBN 0-935120-00-9). Christs Mission.

--Stars in the Night. pap. 2.50 (ISBN 0-935120-01-7). Christs Mission.

--Watch Your Teaching: Home Study. pap. 4.95 (ISBN 0-935120-03-3). Christs Mission.

Garver, Bruce M. The Young Czech Party, Eighteen Seventy-Four to Nineteen Hundred One, & the Emergence of a Multi-Party System. LC 78-8584. 1978. 33.00x (ISBN 0-300-01781-2). Yale U Pr.

Garver, John B., et al. Atlas of Landforms. 3rd ed. LC 83-675974. 165p. 1984. pap. text ed. 35.95 (ISBN 0-471-87434-5). Wiley.

Garver, John J., jt. auth. see Fredrikson, Roger.

Garver, John W. China's Decision for Rapprochement With the United States, 1968-1971. (Replica Edition Ser.). 250p. 1982. softcover 23.50x (ISBN 0-86531-915-4). Westview.

Garver, Lester W., jt. auth. see Hunt, Donnell R.

Garver, Newton. Jesus, Jefferson & the Task of Friends. 1983. pap. 5.00x (ISBN 0-87574-251-3, 251). Pendle Hill.

Garver, Robert. Microwave Diode Control Devices. LC 74-82596. 1976. 42.00 (ISBN 0-89006-022-3). Artech Hse.

Garver, Susan & McGuire, Paula. Coming to North America: From Mexico, Cuba, & Puerto Rico. LC 81-65503. 224p. (YA) (gr. 7 up). 1981. 11.95 (ISBN 0-385-28160-9). Delacorte.

--Coming to North America: From Mexico, Cuba & Puerto Rico. 224p. (YA) (gr. 9-11). pap. 3.25 (ISBN 0-317-12544-3, LFL). Dell.

--From Mexico, Cuba, & Puerto Rico. (gr. 7-11). pap. 2.50 (ISBN 0-317-13311-X, LFL). Dell.

Garver, Thomas H. & Neubert, George W. Nathan Oliveira: A Survey Exhibition 1957-1983. LC 84-10550. (Illus.). 80p. 1985. pap. 14.95 (ISBN 0-918471-00-1). San Fran Mod.

Garver, Thomas H., ed. Twelve Photographers of the American Social Landscape. (Illus.). 1968. 15.00 (ISBN 0-8079-0128-8). October.

Garver, Will L. Brother of the Third Degree. LC 82-82475. (Spiritual Fiction Publications: Vol. 4). 384p. 1985. Repr. of 1927 ed. cloth 16.00 (ISBN 0-8334-0003-7, Spiritual Fiction). Garber Comm.

Garver, William L. Brother of the Third Degree. 14.95 (ISBN 0-87505-089-1). Borden.

Garvey, ed. see Corwin, Edward.

Garvey, Amy, jt. ed. see Essien-Udom, E. U.

Garvey, Amy J. Garvey & Garveyism. 1976. Repr. of 1970 ed. lib. bdg. 23.00x (ISBN 0-374-93015-5). Octagon.

Garvey, Catherine. Children's Talk. (The Developing Child Ser.). 256p. 1984. text ed. 12.50x (ISBN 0-674-11634-8); pap. 4.95 (ISBN 0-674-11635-6). Harvard U Pr.

--Play. (Developing Child Ser.). 1977. 7.95x (ISBN 0-674-67361-1); pap. 3.95 (ISBN 0-674-67363-8). Harvard U Pr.

Garvey, Catherine, jt. auth. see Feagans, Lynne.

Garvey, Chester R. The Activity of Young Children During Sleep: An Objective Study. LC 39-28089. (Illus.). x, 102p. Repr. of 1939 ed. lib. bdg. 18.75x (ISBN 0-8371-8073-2, CWGY). Greenwood.

Garvey, Daniel & Rivers, William. Broadcast Writing. LC 81-13745. 384p. 1982. pap. text ed. 18.95x (ISBN 0-582-28173-3); wkbk. 10.95x (ISBN 0-582-28171-7). Longman.

Garvey, Daniel E. & Rivers, William L. Newswriting for the Electronic Media: Principles, Examples, Applications. 272p. 1982. pap. text ed. write for info. (ISBN 0-534-01069-5). Wadsworth Pub.

Garvey, Edward B. Appalachian Hiker. LC 70-146063. (Illus.). 397p. 1971. pap. 6.00 (ISBN 0-912660-01-5). Appalachian Bks.

--Appalachian Hiker, II. rev. ed. Mallinoff, Estelle, ed. LC 70-146063. (Illus.). 1978. pap. 9.95 (ISBN 0-912660-15-5). Appalachian Bks.

Garvey, Edwin C. Process Theology & Secularization. 21p. 1972. pap. 0.75 (ISBN 0-912414-14-6). Lumen Christi.

Garvey, Eleanor M. & Wick, Peter A. Arts of the French Book, Nineteen Hundred to Nineteen Sixty-Five: Illustrated Books of the School of Paris. LC 67-16782. (Illus., Orig.). 1967. 25.00 (ISBN 0-87074-056-3); pap. 12.50 (ISBN 0-87074-057-1). SMU Press.

Garvey, Gerald. Constitutional Bricolage. LC 73-141503. 1971. 20.00 (ISBN 0-691-07539-5). Princeton U Pr.

--Strategy & the Defense Dilemma. LC 83-48737. 160p. 1984. 24.50x (ISBN 0-669-07508-6). Lexington Bks.

Garvey, Joan B. & Widmer, Mary L. Beautiful Crescent: A History of New Orleans. 2nd rev. ed. (Illus.). 249p. 1984. pap. text ed. 9.95 (ISBN 0-9612960-0-3). Garmer Pr Inc.

Garvey, John. The Ways We Are Together. 159p. 1983. 9.95 (ISBN 0-88347-153-1). Thomas More.

Garvey, John, ed. All Our Sons & Daughters. 1977. pap. 3.95 (ISBN 0-87243-074-X). Templegate.

--Modern Spirituality: An Anthology. 156p. 1985. 12.95 (ISBN 0-87243-132-0). Templegate.

Garvey, Jude. A Guide to the Transport Museums of Great Britain. (Illus.). 240p. 1983. 17.95 (ISBN 0-7207-1404-4, Pub. by Michael Joseph). Merrimack Pub Cir.

Garvey, M. A., tr. see Ranke, Leopold.

Garvey, M. A., tr. see Von Ranke, Leopold.

Garvey, Sr. M. Calixta. Syntax of the Declinable Words in the Roman de la Rose. LC 74-94208. (Catholic University in Romance Languages & Literatures Ser: No. 13). Repr. of 1936 ed. 26.00 (ISBN 0-404-50313-6). AMS Pr.

Garvey, Sr. M. Patricia, tr. see Augustine, Saint.

Garvey, Marcus. Aims & Objects of Movement for Solution of Negro Problem: A Nation of Their Own in Africa. 1924. pap. 1.50 (ISBN 0-685-20858-3). Univ Place.

--The Marcus Garvey & Universal Negro Improvement Association Papers: September 1919-August 1920, Vol. III. Hill, Robert A., ed. LC 82-13379. (Illus.). 750p. 1985. 37.50 (ISBN 0-520-05257-9). U of Cal Pr.

--Philosophy & Opinions of Marcus Garvey. Jacques-Garvey, Amy, ed. LC 69-15523. (Studies in American Negro Life Ser). 1969. pap. text ed. 8.95x (ISBN 0-689-70079-2, NL14). Atheneum.

Garvey, Margaret & Garvey, Michael, eds. The Dorothy Day Book. 9.95 (ISBN 0-87243-106-1). Templegate.

Garvey, Michael, jt. ed. see Garvey, Margaret.

Garvey, Mona. Library Displays. LC 79-86918. 88p. 1969. 14.00 (ISBN 0-8242-0395-X). Wilson.

--Library Public Relations. LC 80-17669. 160p. 1980. 18.00 (ISBN 0-8242-0651-7). Wilson.

Garvey, Robert. First Book of Jewish Holidays. (Illus.). (gr. 1-2). 1954. pap. 4.50x (ISBN 0-87068-362-4). Ktav.

Garvey, William D. Communication: The Essence of Science Facilitating Information Exchange Among Librarians, Scientists, Engineers, & Students. 1979. pap. text ed. 19.50 (ISBN 0-08-023344-9). Pergamon.

Garvi, Petr & Haimson, L. Zapiski Sotsial Demokrate, Nineteen Six-Nineteen Twenty-One. (Russian Archive Ser.: No. 1). 400p. 1982. 35.00 (ISBN 0-89250-300-9). Orient Res Partners.

Garvie, A. E. Studies in the Inner Life of Jesus. 1977. lib. bdg. 69.95 (ISBN 0-8490-2705-5). Gordon Pr.

Garvin, Andrew P. How to Win with Information or Lose Without It. Bermont, Hubert, ed. (Illus.). 175p. 1980. text ed. 19.00 (ISBN 0-930686-08-X). Bermont Bks.

Garvin, Charles & Rosenbaum, Greg. World Without Plenty. (gr. 9-12). 1975. pap. text ed. 4.00 (ISBN 0-8442-5218-2). Natl Textbk.

Garvin, Charles, et al, eds. The Work Incentive Experience. LC 77-83926. 256p. 1978. text ed. 23.50x (ISBN 0-916672-99-9). Allanheld.

Garvin, Charles D. Contemporary Group Work. (P-H Ser. in Social Work Practice). (Illus.). 304p. 1981. text ed. 26.95 (ISBN 0-13-170233-5). P-H.

Garvin, Charles D. & Seabury, Brett A. Interpersonal Practice in Social Work: Processes & Procedures. (Illus.). 416p. 1984. text ed. 27.95 (ISBN 0-13-475095-0). P-H.

Garvin, Charles D., jt. ed. see Reed, Beth G.

Garvin, David. The Economics of University Behavior. LC 80-21685. 1980. 23.50 (ISBN 0-12-276550-8). Acad Pr.

Garvin, Harry. Literature, Arts & Religion. LC 80-70270. (Bucknell Review Ser.: Vol. 26, No. 2). (Illus.). 192p. 1982. 15.00 (ISBN 0-8387-5021-4). Bucknell U Pr.

Garvin, Harry, ed. The Arts, Society & Literature. LC 83-46177. (Review Ser.: Vol. 29, No. 1). (Illus.). 200p. 1984. 15.00 (ISBN 0-8387-5080-X). Bucknell U Pr.

--Literature & History. LC 77-74403. 186p. 1977. 15.00 (ISBN 0-8387-2139-7). Bucknell U Pr.

--Rhetoric, Literature, & Interpretation. LC 83-2553. (Bucknell Review: Vol. 28, No. 2). 184p. 1983. 15.00 (ISBN 0-8387-5057-5). Bucknell U Pr.
--Romanticism, Modernism, Postmodernism: Vol. 25, No. 2. LC 79-50103. (Bucknell Review Ser.). 192p. 1980. 15.00 (ISBN 0-8387-5004-4). Bucknell U Pr.
--Science & Literature. LC 81-72026. 192p. 1983. 15.00 (ISBN 0-8387-5051-6). Bucknell U Pr.
Garvin, Harry R. Literature & Ideology. LC 81-69441. (Bucknell Review: Vol. 27, No. 1). (Illus.). 192p. 1982. 15.00 (ISBN 0-8387-5049-4). Bucknell U Pr.
--New Dimensions in the Humanities & Social Sciences. LC 76-27914. (Bucknell Review, Spring 1977). 186p. 1977. 15.00 (ISBN 0-8387-1966-X). Bucknell U Pr.
Garvin, Harry R., ed. The American Renaissance: New Dimensions. LC 82-45565. 176p. 1983. 15.00 (ISBN 0-8387-5054-0). Bucknell U Pr.
--The Arts & Their Interrelations: Bucknell Review, Fall 1978. LC 78-62038. 186p. 1979. 15.00 (ISBN 0-8387-2355-1). Bucknell U Pr.
--Makers of the Twentieth-Century Novel. LC 74-4975. 322p. 1976. 26.50 (ISBN 0-8387-1522-2). Bucknell U Pr.
--Shakespeare: Contemporary Critical Approaches: Bucknel Review, Spring 1979. LC 79-50103. 192p. 1980. 15.00 (ISBN 0-8387-2376-4). Bucknell U Pr.
--Theories of Reading, Looking, & Listening. LC 80-20475. (Bucknell Review Ser.). 192p. 1981. 15.00 (ISBN 0-8387-5007-9). Bucknell U Pr.
--Women, Literature, Criticism: Bucknell Review, Spring 1978. LC 77-95051. 177p. 1978. 15.00 (ISBN 0-8387-2230-X). Bucknell U Pr.
Garvin, Harry R. & Brady, Patrick, eds. Phenomenology, Structuralism, Semilogy, Vol. 22, No. 1. LC 75-29734. 230p. (Bucknell Review). 1975. 15.00 (ISBN 0-8387-1880-9). Bucknell U Pr.
Garvin, Harry R. & Kirkland, John D., Jr., eds. Twentieth-Century Poetry, Fiction, Theory: Bucknell Review, 1976. 231p. 15.00 (ISBN 0-8387-1934-1). Bucknell U Pr.
Garvin, John W., ed. Canadian Poets. 1926. Repr. 40.00 (ISBN 0-8274-2000-5). R West.
Garvin, Joseph N., jt. ed. see Corbett, James A.
Garvin, Katherine. The Great Tudors. 658p. 1980. Repr. of 1935 ed. lib. bdg. 50.00 (ISBN 0-8495-2049-5). Arden Lib.
--The Great Tudors. LC 74-8259. 1935. lib. bdg. 65.00 (ISBN 0-8414-4503-6). Folcroft.
Garvin, Paul L. On Linguistic Method: Selected Papers. LC 75-182468. (Janua Linguarum, Ser. Minor: No. 30). (Illus.). 199p. (Orig.). 1972. pap. text ed. 15.20x (ISBN 90-2792-005-2). Mouton.
--On Machine Translation. LC 79-182469. (Janua Linguarum Ser. Minor: No. 128). 142p. (Orig.). 1972. pap. text ed. 13.60x (ISBN 90-2792-004-4). Mouton.
--A Prague School Reader on Esthetics, Literary Structure & Style. LC 64-20583. 163p. 1964. pap. 6.95 (ISBN 0-87840-151-2). Georgetown U Pr.
Garvin, Paul L., ed. Method & Theory in Linguistics. LC 75-110950. (Janua Linguarum, Ser. Major: No. 40). 1970. text ed. 36.00x (ISBN 90-2790-722-6). Mouton.
Garvin, Paul L. & Spolsky, Bernard, eds. Computation in Linguistics: A Case Book. LC 83-12721. xii, 332p. 1983. Repr. of 1966 ed. lib. bdg. 42.50x (ISBN 0-313-24179-1, GAC0). Greenwood.
--Computation in Linguistics: A Case Book. LC 66-12755. (Indiana University Studies in the History & Theory of Linguistics). (Illus.). Repr. of 1966 ed. cancelled (ISBN 0-8357-9200-5, 2015818). Bks Demand UMI.
Garvin, Paul L., ed. see Linguistic Association of Canada & the U. S.
Garvin, Tom. The Evolution of Irish Nationalist Politics. 250p. 1981. text ed. 39.50x (ISBN 0-8419-0741-2). Holmes & Meier.
Garvin, Wilhelma C. Development of the Comic Figure in German Drama. LC 72-119091. (Studies in Comparative Literature, No. 35). 1970. Repr. of 1923 ed. lib. bdg. 22.95x (ISBN 0-8383-1087-7). Haskell.
Garvy, G. An Appraisal of the Nineteen-Fifty Census Income Data. (National Bureau of Economic Research: F.23). 1958. 43.00x (ISBN 0-691-04102-4). Princeton U Pr.
Garvy, G., ed. Appraisal of the 1950 Census Income Data. (Studies in Income & Wealth Ser.: No. 23). 460p. 1958. 40.00 (ISBN 0-691-04102-4, Dist. by Princeton U Pr). Natl Bur Econ Res.
Garvy, George. Debits & Clearing Statistics & Their Use. LC 82-15572. ix, 144p. 1982. Repr. of 1959 ed. lib. bdg. 22.50x (ISBN 0-313-23660-7, GADC). Greenwood.
--Deposit Velocity & Its Significance. LC 78-14435. (Illus.). 1978. Repr. of 1959 ed. lib. bdg. 15.75x (ISBN 0-313-21022-5, GADV). Greenwood.
--Money, Financial Flows & Credit in the Soviet Union. LC 76-58491. (National Bureau of Economic Research. Studies in International Economic Relations: No. 7). 240p. 1977. prof ref 35.00 (ISBN 0-88410-475-3). Ballinger Pub.
Garvy, Helen. Before You Shoot: A Guide to Low Budget Film Production. (Illus., Orig.). 1985. pap. text ed. 10.00 (ISBN 0-918828-06-6). Shire Pr.
--How to Fix Your Bicycle. 5th rev. ed. LC 79-93408. (Illus.). 1980. pap. 1.95 (ISBN 0-918828-05-8). Shire Pr.
--How to Fix Your BMX Bicycle. LC 79-67650. (Illus.). 64p. 1979. pap. 1.95 (ISBN 0-918828-04-X). Shire Pr.
--I Built Myself a House. rev. ed. LC 77-5597. (Illus.). 128p. 1977. pap. 2.50 (ISBN 0-918828-02-3). Shire Pr.
Garvy, John W. Homeopathy: Traditional Art & Bioelectronic Science. Liebermann, Jeremiah, ed. (Five Phase Energetics Ser.: No. 3). (Illus., Orig.). 1985. pap. 3.00 (ISBN 0-943450-04-7). Wellbeing Bks.
Garvy, John W., Jr. Five Phase Facial Diagnosis. Liebermann, Jeremiah, ed. (Five Phase Energetics Ser.: No. 3). (Illus., Orig.). 1983. pap. 3.00 (ISBN 0-943450-02-0). Wellbeing Bks.
--The Five Phases of Food: How to Begin. 2nd ed. Liebermann, Jeremiah, ed. (Five Phase Energetics Ser.: No. 1). (Illus.). 1983. pap. 3.00 (ISBN 0-943450-03-9). Wellbeing Bks.
--Introducing the Five Phases of Food: How to Begin. Liebermann, Jeremiah, ed. (Illus., Orig.). 1982. pap. 3.00 (ISBN 0-943450-00-4). Wellbeing Bks.
--The Seven Levels of Healing. Liebermann, Jeremiah, ed. (Five Phase Energetics Ser.: No. 4). (Illus.). 1985. pap. 3.00 (ISBN 0-943450-05-5). Wellbeing Bks.
--Winter Five Seasonal Cookbook. Liebermann, Jeremiah, ed. (Five Phase Cookbook Ser.: No. 1). (Illus.). 1985. pap. 6.00 (ISBN 0-943450-19-5). Wellbeing Bks.
--Yin & Yang: Two Hands Clapping. Liebermann, Jeremiah, ed. (Five Phase Energetics Ser.: No. 2). (Illus.). 1985. pap. 3.00 (ISBN 0-943450-01-2). Wellbeing Bks.
Garwick, Christine, ed. see Garwick, De C.
Garwick, De C. May This House Please Come to Order. Rev. ed. Garwick, Christine, ed. (Illus.). 81p. 1982. pap. 6.95 (ISBN 0-941656-00-4). Rieker Communications.
Garwood, Alfred N., ed. Almanac of the Fifty States: Basic Data Profiles with Comparative Tables. 468p. 1985. lib. bdg. 42.50 (ISBN 0-931845-03-3); pap. 35.00 (ISBN 0-931845-02-5). Info Pubns.
--New Jersey Economic Almanac. 300p. 1983. pap. 29.95 (ISBN 0-911273-02-6). NJ Assocs.
Garwood, Alice, jt. auth. see Brown, Gilmor.
Garwood, Darrell. Artist in Iowa, a Life of Grant Wood. LC 70-110827. (Illus.). 1971. Repr. of 1944 ed. lib. bdg. 19.75x (ISBN 0-8371-3227-4, GAAI). Greenwood.
--Under Cover: Thirty-Five Years of CIA Deception. 256p. 1985. pap. 3.95 (ISBN 0-394-62073-9, B-524, BC). Grove.
Garwood, Dave, jt. ed. see Goddard, Walter E.
Garwood, Ellen. Come to Me, Megan. 184p. Date not set. pap. text ed. 8.95 (ISBN 0-318-03653-3). Cameron Pr.
Garwood, Ellen C. Will Clayton: A Short Biography. facsimile ed. LC 73-157335. (Select Bibliographies Reprint Ser). Repr. of 1958 ed. 17.00 (ISBN 0-8369-5795-4). Ayer Co Pubs.
Garwood, Helen. Thomas Hardy: An Illustration of the Philosophy of Schopenhauer. LC 74-10776. 1911. lib. bdg. 15.00 (ISBN 0-8414-4521-4). Folcroft.
Garwood, Irving. New Studies in American Literature. 1973. Repr. of 1937 ed. 25.00 (ISBN 0-8274-0036-5). R West.
Garwood, John. The Million Peopled City: Or One Half the People of London Made Known to the Other Half. LC 84-48266. (The Rise of Urban Britain Ser.). 317p. 1985. 40.00 (ISBN 0-8240-6268-X). Garland Pub.
Garwood, Patricia, jt. auth. see Hajcak, Frank.
Garwood, S. Gray. Educating Young Handicapped Children: A Developmental Approach. 2nd ed. LC 82-20726. 563p. 1983. 32.50 (ISBN 0-89443-929-4). Aspen Systems.
Garwood, S. Gray & Fewell, Rebecca R. Educating Handicapped Infants: Issues in Development & Intervention. LC 82-16274. 549p. 1982. 31.00 (ISBN 0-89443-836-0). Aspen Systems.
Garwood, S. Gray, jt. auth. see McDavid, John W.
Garwood, William R. Catch Kid Curry! LC 81-71394. 250p. 1982. 13.95 (ISBN 0-937618-02-0). Bath St Pr.
--Kill Him, Again. LC 80-66355. 315p. 1980. 9.95 (ISBN 0-937618-00-4). Bath St Pr.
--Ringo's Tombstone. LC 81-67729. 215p. 1981. 11.95 (ISBN 0-937618-01-2). Bath St Pr.
Gary, jt. auth. see Handwerk.
Gary, A. L. & Glover, John A. Eye Color, Sex, & Children's Behavior. LC 76-3642. 186p. 1976. 19.95x (ISBN 0-88229-213-7). Nelson-Hall.
Gary, Albert L., jt. auth. see Glover, John A.
Gary, Blau, jt. ed. see Brock, Neely W.
Gary, Charles B., jt. auth. see Denlinger, Sutherland.
Gary, Charles E., ed. see Hegel, Georg W.
Gary, Charles L. Flower Fables. LC 78-13576. (Illus.). 1978. 9.95 (ISBN 0-914440-24-1). EPM Pubns.
Gary, Charles L., ed. see Music Education National Conference.
Gary Green Associates. The Philosophy & Practice of Career Education. Wood, C. L., ed. 1978. write for info. (ISBN 0-686-00891-X). Guifford-Hill.
Gary, J. H., ed. Proceedings of the Twelfth Oil Shale Symposium. 395p. 1979. 11.00 (ISBN 0-918062-08-X). Colo Sch Mines.
Gary, J. H., jt. ed. see Ruebens, John.
Gary, J. Olmsted & Gamal-Eldin, S. Cairene Egyptian Colloquial Arabic. (Descriptive Grammars Ser.). 152p. 1982. pap. 40.00 (ISBN 0-7099-3815-2, Pub by Croom Helm Ltd). Longwood Pub Group.
Gary, James H., ed. Oil Shale: Proceedings of the Seventeenth Symposium. (Illus.). 440p. 1984. pap. text ed. 25.00 (ISBN 0-918062-58-6). Colo Sch Mines.
--Oil Shale Symposium Proceedinds: 18th. (Illus.). 360p. 1985. pap. text ed. 25.00x (ISBN 0-918062-62-4). Colo Sch Mines.
--Proceedings of the Eleventh Oil Shale Symposium. (Illus.). 389p. 1978. pap. 5.00 (ISBN 0-918062-03-9). Colo Sch Mines.
--Proceedings of the Fifteenth Oil Shale Symposium. LC 82-4294. (Illus.). 597p. 1982. pap. 20.00 (ISBN 0-918062-50-0). Colo Sch Mines.
--Proceedings of the Fourteenth Oil Shale Symposium. LC 81-10238. (Illus.). 433p. 1981. pap. text ed. 15.00 (ISBN 0-918062-46-2). Colo Sch Mines.
--Proceedings of the Thirteenth Oil Shale Symposium. LC 80-18711. (Oil Shale Ser.). (Illus.). 391p. (Orig.). 1980. pap. 12.00 (ISBN 0-918062-39-X). Colo Sch Mines.
--Sixteenth Oil Shale Symposium Proceedings. (Illus.). 600p. 1983. pap. text ed. 25.00 (ISBN 0-918062-56-X). Colo Sch Mines.
Gary, Kenneth C. & Johnson, Steven D. Youth Employability: Four Awards. (Winning Monographs-1980). 134p. 1980. 8.25 (ISBN 0-318-15604-0, SN28). Natl Ctr Res Voc Ed.
Gary, Lawrence E., ed. Mental Health: A Challenge to the Black Community. 1978. text ed. 12.00 (ISBN 0-8059-2493-0). Dorrance.
Gary, Lewis E. Black Men. LC 81-9021. (Sage Focus Editions: Vol. 31). 300p. 1981. 28.00 (ISBN 0-8039-1654-X); pap. 14.00 (ISBN 0-8039-1655-8). Sage.
Gary, M., et al. Glossary of Geology. 1717p. (Eng. & Rus.). 1977. 75.00 (ISBN 0-686-92556-4, M-9113). French & Eur.
Gary, Madeleine S. Jazzbo! (Illus.). 300p. (Orig.). Date not set. pap. 8.95. New Writers Guild.
--Odes to Chili & Chili Lovers. 230p. (Orig.). Date not set. pap. 9.95 (ISBN 0-913459-06-2). New Writers Guild.
--Vignettes of the Beam in a Nigger's Eye. 126p. (Orig.). 1982. pap. 8.95 (ISBN 0-913459-00-3). New Writers Guild.
--Whispers: From Within, Vol. II. Stigler, Stephen M., ed. 150p. 1985. pap. 7.95 (ISBN 0-913459-04-6). New Writers Guild.
--Whispers: In the Wind, Vol. I. Stigler, Stephen M., ed. 150p. (Orig.). 1985. pap. 7.95 (ISBN 0-913459-03-8); Set. pap. write for info. (ISBN 0-913459-05-4). New Writers Guild.
Gary, Madeleine S., compiled by. Sophie's Choice Chili or How to Cure Your Frigidity. 96p. (Orig.). 1985. pap. 4.50 (ISBN 0-913459-02-X). New Writers Guild.
Gary, Romain. Adieu Gary Cooper. (Coll. Soleil). 13.95 (ISBN 0-685-34122-4). French & Eur.
--Au-Dela de Cette Limite Votre Ticket N'est Plus Valable. 264p. 1975. 18.50 (ISBN 0-686-55888-X). French & Eur.
--Charge d'Ame: Roman. 310p. 1977. 18.50 (ISBN 0-686-55889-8). French & Eur.
--Chien Blanc. (Coll. Soleil). 11.50 (ISBN 0-685-34123-2). French & Eur.
--Chien Blanc. 1972. 3.95 (ISBN 0-686-55890-1). French & Eur.
--Clair de Femme: Roman. 167p. 1977. 13.95 (ISBN 0-686-55891-X). French & Eur.
--The Dance of Genghis Cohn. Sykes, Camilla, tr. from Fr. LC 81-16531. 256p. 1982. pap. 5.95 (ISBN 0-8052-0693-0). Schocken.
--La Danse de Gengis Cohn. 280p. 1965. 10.95 (ISBN 0-686-55892-8). French & Eur.
--Education Europeenne. 1956. pap. 13.50 (ISBN 0-685-11154-7). French & Eur.
--Education Europeenne. 288p. 1972. 3.95 (ISBN 0-686-55893-6). French & Eur.
--Les Enchanteurs. 400p. 1973. 22.50 (ISBN 0-686-55894-4). French & Eur.
--Europa. (Coll. Soleil). 18.50 (ISBN 0-685-85705-0). French & Eur.
--Frere Ocean, 3 tomes. Incl. Tome I. Pour Sganarelle Recherche d'un Personnage et d'un Roman. 11.25 (ISBN 0-685-34125-9); Tome II. La Danse de Gengis Cohn; Tome III. La Tete Coupable. (Coll. Soleil). 11.25 ea. French & Eur.
--Gloire a Nos Illustres Pionniers. 272p. 1962. 4.95 (ISBN 0-686-55895-2). French & Eur.
--Le Grand Vestiaire. pap. 4.95 (ISBN 0-685-34126-7). French & Eur.
--Johnnie Coeur. pap. 4.95 (ISBN 0-685-34127-5). French & Eur.
--King Solomon. Wright, Barbara, tr. LC 82-48681. (Cornelia & Michael Bessie Bk.). 256p. 1983. 12.45i (ISBN 0-06-039019-0, HarpT). Har-Row.
--Lady L. (Coll. Soleil). (Fr.). 1963. 11.50 (ISBN 0-685-11285-3). French & Eur.
--Lady L. 1973. 3.95 (ISBN 0-686-55896-0). French & Eur.
Gary, Romain, pseud. The Life Before Us: Madame Rosa. price not set. New Directions.
Gary, Romain. Mangeurs D'etoiles. (Coll. Soleil). 1966. 13.95 (ISBN 0-685-11341-8). French & Eur.
--La Nuit Sera Calme. 264p. 1974. 14.95 (ISBN 0-686-55897-9). French & Eur.
--Les Oiseaux Vont Mourir au Perou: Gloire a nos Illustres Pionniers. 288p. 1975. 3.95 (ISBN 0-686-55883-9). French & Eur.
--Pour Sganarelle. 480p. 1965. 11.95 (ISBN 0-686-55884-7). French & Eur.
--Promesse De L'Aube. (Coll. Soleil). 1966. 15.95 (ISBN 0-685-11515-1). French & Eur.
--Racines du Ciel. 1956. 15.75 (ISBN 0-685-11521-6). French & Eur.
--Les Racines du Ciel. 512p. 1972. 3.95 (ISBN 0-686-55885-5). French & Eur.
--La Tete Coupable. 304p. 1968. 12.95 (ISBN 0-686-55886-3). French & Eur.
--Les Tetes de Stephanie. 438p. (Folio 946). 1977. 4.95 (ISBN 0-686-55887-1). French & Eur.
--Les Tresors de la Mer Rouge. pap. 9.50 (ISBN 0-685-34128-3). French & Eur.
--Tulipe. pap. 9.50 (ISBN 0-685-34129-1). French & Eur.
--Your Ticket Is No Longer Valid. LC 76-16695. 1977. 8.95 (ISBN 0-8076-0838-6). Braziller.
Gary, Skipper. America the Beautiful. (Social Studies). 24p. (gr. 4-5). 1979. wkbk. 5.00 (ISBN 0-8209-0238-1, SS-5). ESP.
--Basic Skills Colonies Workbook. (Basic Skills Workbooks). 32p. (gr. 4-7). 1983. 0.99 (ISBN 0-8209-0541-0, SSW-5). ESP.
--The Colonies. (Social Studies). 24p. (gr. 4-6). 1977. wkbk. 5.00 (ISBN 0-8209-0241-1, SS-8). ESP.
Garys, Walter. The Detonator. (Orig.). 1981. pap. 2.50 (ISBN 0-505-51663-2, Pub. by Tower Bks). Dorchester Pub Co.
Garza, Catarino, ed. Puerto Ricans in the U. S. LC 77-81291. 1977. 12.00 (ISBN 0-87348-552-1); pap. 2.95 (ISBN 0-87348-553-X). Path Pr NY.
Garza County Historical Society. Garza County History. 1980. 25.00 (ISBN 0-89015-266-7). Eakin Pubns.
Garza, D. & Becan-McBride, K. Phlebotomy Handbook. 464p. 1984. pap. 15.95 (ISBN 0-8385-7843-8). ACC.
Garza, Eugenio D. & Ockerman, Janet D. Adolescent Mexican American Student Attitudes of Self-Concept, Locus of Control & Family Ideology in the Lower Rio Grande Valley of Texas. LC 78-68454. 1979. perfect bdg. 9.95 (ISBN 0-88247-562-2). R & E Pubs.
Garza, Hedda, compiled by. The Watergate Investigation Index: House Judiciary Committee Hearings & Report on Impeachment. 300p. 1985. 95.00 (ISBN 0-8420-2186-8). Scholarly Res Inc.
--The Watergate Investigation Index: Senate Select Committee Hearings & Reports on Presidential Campaign Activities. LC 82-7353. 326p. 1982. lib. bdg. 95.00 (ISBN 0-8420-2175-2). Scholarly Res Inc.
Garza, Lucy M. South Texas Mexican Cookbook. 1982. 8.95 (ISBN 0-89015-344-2). Eakin Pubns.
Garza, Roberto J. Contemporary Chicano Theatre. 1975. 22.95 (ISBN 0-268-00709-8); pap. 7.95x (ISBN 0-268-00710-1). U of Notre Dame Pr.
Garza, Rodolfo, et al, eds. The Mexican American Experience: An Interdisciplinary Anthology. (Illus.). 432p. 1985. 25.00 (ISBN 0-292-75088-9); pap. 14.95 (ISBN 0-292-75083-8). U of Tex Pr.
Garza, Rodolfo de La see De la Garza, Rodolfo.
Garza Bores, Jaime. Diccionario Tecnico de Terminologia Comercial Cantable y Bancaria. (Span.). 6.95 (ISBN 0-686-56677-7, S-25235). French & Eur.
Garzanti. Encyclopedie Gegraphique. (Fr.). 1969. 25.00 (ISBN 0-686-57154-1, M-6213). French & Eur.
--Il Nuovo Dizionario Inglese-Italiano, Italiano-Inglese. 1088p. 1984. 31.95x (ISBN 0-913298-70-0). S F Vanni.
Garza-Swan, Gloria, jt. auth. see Mejias, Hugo.
Garzia, Raffaele de see De Grazia, Raffaele.
Garzilli, Enrico. Circles Without Center: Paths to the Discovery & Creation of Self in Modern Literature. LC 77-182814. 260p. 1972. 14.00x (ISBN 0-674-13165-7). Harvard U Pr.
Garzino, Salvatore J. The Rhythm Factor in Human Behavior. LC 81-81611. 1982. 8.95 (ISBN 0-87212-151-8). Libra.
Garzke, William H., Jr. & Dulin, Robert O., Jr. Battleships: Allied Battleships in World War II. (Illus.). 385p. 1980. 39.95 (ISBN 0-87021-100-5); bulk rates avail. Naval Inst Pr.
--Battleships: United States Battleships in World War 2. LC 74-29128. (Battleships Ser. Vol 1). (Illus.). 267p. 1976. 36.95 (ISBN 0-87021-099-8). Naval Inst Pr.
Garzke, William H., Jr., jt. auth. see Dulin, Robert O., Jr.
Garzke, William, Jr. & Dulin, Robert O., Jr. Battleships: Axis Battleships in World War II. 3rd ed. (Battleships Ser.: Vol. 3). (Illus.). 408p. 1985. 39.95 (ISBN 0-87021-101-3). Naval Inst Pr.
Garzon, Camilo E. Water Quality in Hydroelectric Projects: Considerations for Planning in Tropical Forest Regions. 48p. Date not set. 5.00 (ISBN 0-8213-0923-5, BK0363). World Bank.
Garzuel, Michel, jt. auth. see Van Ginneken, Wouter.
Garzya, Antonio. Storia E Interpretazione Di Testi Bizantini. 464p. 1974. 60.00x (ISBN 0-902089-63-3, Pub. by Variorum). State Mutual Bk.

Gas Chromatography Institute, 3rd Annual Buffalo, N. Y. April 4-6, 1961. Progress in Industrial Gas Chromatography: Proceedings, Vol. 1. LC 61-15520. pap. 59.80 (ISBN 0-317-10634-1, 2020700). Bks Demand UMI.
Gas Processors Suppliers Assn. Engineering Data Book: English Units 9th ed, SI Units 1st ed. 1981. 41.95 (ISBN 0-686-45985-7, P-7020). Pennwell Bks.
Gasaway, Donald C. Hearing Conservation: A Practical Manual & Guide. LC 84-16112. 318p. 1984. 34.95 (ISBN 0-214-20692-0, Busn). P-H.
Gasaway, E. B. Grey Wolf, Grey Sea. (War Library). 256p. 1983. pap. 2.75 (ISBN 0-345-30859-X). Ballantine.
Gasaway, Laura N., jt. auth. see Murphy, Maureen.
Gasaway, Laura N., et al. American Indian Legal Materials: A Union List. (American Indians at Law Ser.). 1980. text ed. 49.50 (ISBN 0-930576-31-4). E M Coleman Ent.
Gasc, Hugo. Despierta, Continente Mio. LC 78-50624. 159p. (Orig., Span.). 1978. pap. 3.50 (ISBN 0-89922-108-4). Edit Caribe.
Gascar, Pierre. Lambs of Fire. Lawrence, M., tr. LC 65-12526. 1965. 5.00 (ISBN 0-8076-0285-X). Braziller.
--Women & the Sun. Lawrence, tr. LC 76-54791. 1977. Repr. of 1964 ed. lib. bdg. 22.50x (ISBN 0-8371-9360-5, GAWS). Greenwood.
Gascoigne, Christina. Castles of Britain. (Illus.). 224p. 1980. 12.98 (ISBN 0-500-24098-1). Thames Hudson.
Gascoigne, Bamber. Quest for the Golden Hare. (Illus.). 224p. 1984. pap. 13.95 (ISBN 0-224-02116-8, Pub. by Jonathan Cape). Merrimack Pub Cir.
Gascoigne, Dinah. Yuma Dental Health Program. (Illus.). 23p. (Orig.). 1982. text ed. 9.95 (ISBN 0-9608146-5-5). Western Sun Pubns.
Gascoigne, George. Complete Works, 2 Vols. LC 68-57604. (Illus.). 1969. Repr. of 1910 ed. Set. lib. bdg. 47.50x (ISBN 0-8371-1376-8, GACW). Greenwood.
--Complete Works, 2 Vols. LC 7-42099. 1968. Repr. of 1907 ed. Set. 42.00x (ISBN 0-403-00089-0). Scholarly.
--George Gascoigne's A Hundredth Sundrie Flowres. Repr. of 1942 ed. 23.50 (ISBN 0-403-04077-9). Somerset Pub.
--Glass of Government. LC 70-133667. (Tudor Facsimile Texts. Old English Plays: No. 49). Repr. of 1914 ed. 49.50 (ISBN 0-404-53349-3). AMS Pr.
--The Posies of G. Gascoigne, Corrected & Augmented. LC 79-84110. (English Experience Ser.: No. 929). 532p. 1979. Repr. of 1575 ed. lib. bdg. 50.00 (ISBN 90-221-0929-1). Walter J Johnson.
--The Spoyle of Antwerpe Faithfully Reported by a True Englishman. LC 74-25952. (English Experience Ser.: No. 180). 52p. 1969. Repr. of 1576 ed. 8.00 (ISBN 90-221-0180-0). Walter J Johnson.
--The Steele Glas & The Complainte of Phylomene: A Critical Edition with Introduction. Wallace, William I., ed. (Salzburg Studies in English Literature, Elizabethan & Renaissance Studies: No. 24). 240p. 1975. pap. text ed. 25.50x (ISBN 0-391-01382-3). Humanities.
--The Steele Glas: Complaints of Phylomene. LC 73-6131. (English Experience Ser.: No. 597). 132p. 1973. Repr. of 1576 ed. 14.00 (ISBN 90-221-0597-0). Walter J Johnson.
--Steeleglas, Fifteen Seventy-Five & the Complaynte of Philomene Fifteen Seventy-Six. Arber, EDward, ed. 1983. pap. 12.50 (ISBN 0-87556-496-8). Saifer.
Gascoigne, George, ed. see Gilbert, Humphrey.
Gascoigne, Margaret. Discovering English Customs & Traditions. (Discovering Ser.: No. 66). 1983. pap. 3.95 (ISBN 0-85263-506-0, Pub. by Shire Pubns England). Seven Hills Bks.
--Discovering English Customs & Traditions. 3.25 (ISBN 0-913714-57-7). Legacy Bks.
Gascoigne, Robert M. A Historical Catalogue of Scientific Periodicals, 1665-1900. LC 84-48863. 200p. 1985. lib. bdg. 27.00 (ISBN 0-8240-8752-6). Garland Pub.
--A Historical Catalogue of Scientists & Scientific Books: From the Earliest Times to the Close of the 19th Century. LC 84-48013. (Reference Library of the Humanities). 1200p. 1984. lib. bdg. 150.00 (ISBN 0-8240-8959-6). Garland Pub.
Gascon, Richard. Grand Commerce et Vie Urbaine au XVIe Siecle: Lyons et ses Marchands (Environds de 1520-Environs de 1580, 2 vols. (Civilizations et Societes: No. 22). 1971. pap. 56.00x (ISBN 90-2796-967-1). Mouton.
Gascoyne, David. Collected Poems. 1982. pap. 12.95 (ISBN 0-19-211801-3). Oxford U Pr.
--Short Survey of Surrealism. (Illus.). 162p. 1971. Repr. of 1935 ed. 29.50x (ISBN 0-7146-2262-1, BHA-02262, F Cass Co). Biblio Dist.
--A Short Survey of Surrealism. (Illus.). 164p. 1982. pap. 5.95 (ISBN 0-87286-137-6). City Lights.
Gascoyne, David & Durrell, Lawrence. Paris Journal Nineteen Thirty-Seven to Nineteen Thirty-Nine. 1978. 12.00 (ISBN 0-685-99426-0, Pub. by Enitharmon). Small Pr Dist.
Gascoyne, David, et al, trs. see De Lubicz Milosz, Oscar V.
Gash, Don M., jt. ed. see Sladek, John R., Jr.
Gash, Joe. Newspaper Murders. LC 85-5423. 192p. 1985. 13.95 (ISBN 0-03-070544-4). HR&W.
--Priestly Murders. (Crime Monthly Ser.). 176p. 1985. pap. 3.95 (ISBN 0-14-008223-9). Penguin.
--Priestly Murders: A Chicago Police Mystery. 163p. 1984. 11.95 (ISBN 0-03-070543-6). HR&W.
Gash, John. Caravaggio. (Oresko-Jupiter Art Bks). (Illus.). 96p. 1981. 17.95 (ISBN 0-933516-83-5, Pub. by Oresko-Jupiter England). Hippocrene Bks.
Gash, Jonathan. Firefly Gadroon. 208p. 1985. pap. 3.50 (ISBN 0-14-008007-4). Penguin.
--Firefly Gadroon: A Lovejoy Novel of Suspense. 208p. 1984. 11.95 (ISBN 0-312-29205-8, J Kahn). St Martin.
--Gold by Gemini. (Scene of the Crime Mystery Ser.: No. 36). 1982. pap. 2.25 (ISBN 0-440-12749-1). Dell.
--The Gondola Scam. 256p. 1984. 12.95 (ISBN 0-312-33828-7, J Kahn). St Martin.
--Gondola Scam. 1985. pap. 3.50 (ISBN 0-14-007656-5). Penguin.
--The Grail Tree. (Scene of the Crime Ser.: No. 48). 288p. 1982. pap. 2.50 (ISBN 0-440-13022-0). Dell.
--The Grail Tree. LC 79-2647. 1980. 12.45i (ISBN 0-06-011462-2, HarpT). Har-Row.
--The Grail Tree. 14.95 (ISBN 0-88411-559-3, Pub. by Aeonian Pr). Amereon Ltd.
--The Judas Pair. (Scene of the Crime Mystery Ser.: No. 30). 1981. pap. 2.25 (ISBN 0-440-14354-3). Dell.
--The Judas Pair. LC 77-6889. (Harper Novel of Suspense). 1977. 12.45i (ISBN 0-06-011464-9, HarpT). Har-Row.
--Pearlhanger. 256p. 1985. 14.95 (ISBN 0-312-59970-6, J Kahn). St Martin.
--Spend Game. (Crime Monthly Ser.). 204p. 1982. pap. 3.50 (ISBN 0-14-006190-8). Penguin.
--The Vatican Rip. LC 81-14387. (A Joan Kahn Bk.). 228p. 1982. 10.95 (ISBN 0-89919-080-4). Ticknor & Fields.
--The Vatican Rip. 1983. pap. 3.50 (ISBN 0-14-006431-1). Penguin.
Gash, Karen R., jt. auth. see Lingenfelter, Richard E.
Gash, Norman. Aristocracy & People: Britain, Eighteen Fifteen to Eighteen Sixty Five in Germany. (New History of England Ser.). 375p. 1980. 20.00x (ISBN 0-674-04490-8); pap. 9.95x (ISBN 0-674-04491-6). Harvard U Pr.
--Lord Liverpool: The Life & Political Career of Robert Banks Jenkinson, Second Earl of Liverpool, 1770-1828. (Illus.). 296p. 1985. text ed. 20.00x (ISBN 0-674-53910-9). Harvard U Pr.
--Politics in the Age of Peel. 1971. pap. 2.95x (ISBN 0-393-00564-X, Norton Lib). Norton.
--Politics in the Age of Peel: A Study in the Technique of Parliamentary Representation, 1830-1850. 2nd ed. 518p. 1977. text ed. 24.00x (ISBN 0-391-00676-2). Humanities.
--Reaction & Reconstruction in English Politics, 1832 to 1852. LC 81-1813. 227p. 1981. Repr. of 1965 ed. lib. bdg. 27.50x (ISBN 0-313-22927-9, GARR). Greenwood.
Gash, Norman, ed. Age of Peel. 1969. pap. 10.95 (ISBN 0-312-01260-8). St Martin.
Gashus, O. K., jt. ed. see Gray, T. K.
Gashutz, W. Lectures on Subgroups of Sylow Type in Finite Soluble Groups. Kuhn, U., tr. (Notes on Pure Mathematics Ser.: No. 11). 100p. (Orig.). 1980. pap. text ed. 5.00 (ISBN 0-908160-22-4, 0571). Australia N U P.
Gasior, Mary A. The Four Prentices of London. LC 79-54340. (Renaissance Drama Ser.). 200p. 1982. lib. bdg. 26.00 (ISBN 0-8240-4458-4). Garland Pub.
Gasiorek, Janus M., jt. auth. see Eastop, Thomas D.
Gasiorowicz, Stephen. Elementary Particle Physics. LC 66-17637. 1966. 48.50 (ISBN 0-471-29287-7). Wiley.
--Structure of Matter: A Survey of Modern Physics. LC 78-18645. (Physics Ser.). (Illus.). 1979. text ed. 34.95 (ISBN 0-201-02511-6). Addison-Wesley.
Gasiorowicz, Stephen G. Quantum Physics. LC 73-22376. 514p. 1974. text ed. 47.95 (ISBN 0-471-29280-X). Wiley.
Gasiorowska, Xenia. The Image of Peter the Great in Russian Fiction. (Illus.). 214p. 1979. 30.00x (ISBN 0-299-07690-3). U of Wis Pr.
--Women in Soviet Fiction, 1917-1964. LC 68-16060. Repr. of 1968 ed. 57.00 (ISBN 0-8357-9781-3, 2010194). Bks Demand UMI.
Gaskell, Augusta. What Is Life? 324p. 1929. 26.75x (ISBN 0-398-04262-4). C C Thomas.
Gaskell, D. F. & Webber, B. W. The Brompton Hospital Guide to Chest Physiotherapy. 4th ed. (Illus.). 120p. 1981. pap. text ed. 12.75 (ISBN 0-632-00576-9, B-1748-0). Mosby.
Gaskell, D. R., jt. ed. see Fine, H. A.
Gaskell, David R. Metallurgical Thermodynamics. 2nd ed. (Materials Engineering Ser.). 560p. 1981. text ed. 48.00 (ISBN 0-07-022946-5). McGraw.
Gaskell, Elizabeth. Cousin Phillis & Other Tales. Easson, Angus, ed. (World's Classics Ser.). 1981. pap. 3.95 (ISBN 0-19-281554-7). Oxford U Pr.
--Cranford. 1973. pap. 2.50x (ISBN 0-460-01083-2, Evman). Biblio Dist.
--Cranford. Watson, Elizabeth, ed. (World's Classics Ser.). 1980. pap. 2.95 (ISBN 0-19-281531-8). Oxford U Pr.
--Cranford-Cousin Phillis. Keating, Peter, ed. (English Library Ser.). 1977. pap. 3.95 (ISBN 0-14-043104-7). Penguin.
--Life of Charlotte Bronte. Shelston, Alan, ed. (English Library). 1975. pap. 5.95 (ISBN 0-14-043099-7). Penguin.
--Mary Barton. 1971. 8.95x (ISBN 0-460-00598-7, Evman); pap. 2.50x (ISBN 0-460-01598-2, Evman). Biblio Dist.
--Mary Barton. Gill, Stephen, ed. (English Library Ser.). 487p. 1975. pap. 4.95 (ISBN 0-14-043053-9). Penguin.
--North & South. 1968. 9.95x (ISBN 0-460-00680-0, Evman); pap. 2.50x (ISBN 0-460-01680-6, Evman). Biblio Dist.
--North & South. Collin, Dorothy, ed. (English Library Ser). 540p. 1970. pap. 4.95 (ISBN 0-14-043055-5). Penguin.
--North & South. Easson, Angus, ed. (World's Classics Ser.). 1982. pap. 4.95 (ISBN 0-19-281595-4). Oxford U Pr.
--Ruth. 1982. pap. 4.50x (ISBN 0-460-01673-3, Evman). Biblio Dist.
--Ruth. Shelston, Alan, ed. (The World's Classics Ser.). 500p. 1985. pap. 4.95 (ISBN 0-19-281669-1). Oxford U Pr.
--Sylvia's Lovers. 1971. Repr. of 1911 ed. 12.95x (ISBN 0-460-00524-3, Evman). Biblio Dist.
--Sylvia's Lovers. Sanders, Andrew, ed. (World's Classics Ser.). 1982. pap. 7.95 (ISBN 0-19-281571-7). Oxford U Pr.
--Sylvia's Lovers. 442p. 1982. pap. text ed. 4.95x (ISBN 0-460-01524-9, Pub. by Evman England). Biblio Dist.
--Wives & Daughters. 1982. pap. 4.75x (ISBN 0-460-01110-3, Evman). Biblio Dist.
--Wives & Daughters. Smith, Frank G., ed. (English Library Ser.). 720p. 1969. pap. 4.95 (ISBN 0-14-043046-6). Penguin.
Gaskell, Elizabeth C. Cranford, & Other Tales. new facsimile ed. LC 74-150475. (Short Story Index Reprint Ser.). Repr. of 1886 ed. 24.50 (ISBN 0-8369-3815-1). Ayer Co Pubs.
--Grey Woman, & Other Tales. facsimile ed. LC 70-163028. (Short Story Index Reprint Ser.). Repr. of 1865 ed. 16.00 (ISBN 0-8369-3942-5). Ayer Co Pubs.
--Letters of Mrs. Gaskell. Chapple, John A. & Pollard, Arthur, eds. LC 67-3154. 1966. 60.00x (ISBN 0-674-52675-9). Harvard U Pr.
--Lizzie Leigh, & Other Tales. facsimile ed. LC 71-37543. (Short Story Index Reprint Ser.). Repr. of 1865 ed. 16.00 (ISBN 0-8369-4102-0). Ayer Co Pubs.
--Mary Barton. 1958. pap. 5.95 (ISBN 0-393-00245-4, Norton Lib). Norton.
--North & South. LC 70-145039. 1971. Repr. of 1914 ed. 39.00x (ISBN 0-403-00985-5). Scholarly.
--Works, 8 Vols. Ward, A. W., ed. LC 70-148782. Repr. of 1906 ed. Set. 380.00 (ISBN 0-404-07250-X); 47.50 ea. AMS Pr.
Gaskell, Jane. Atlan. 1985. pap. 3.50 (ISBN 0-88677-049-1). DAW Bks.
--The City. (Atlan Saga Ser.: No. 4). 276p. 1985. pap. 3.50 (ISBN 0-88677-085-8). DAW Bks.
--The Dragon. (Atlan Saga Ser.: No. 2). 1985. pap. 2.95 (ISBN 0-88677-021-1). DAW Bks.
--The Serpent: The Atlan Cycle, No. 1. 1985. pap. 2.95 (ISBN 0-87997-990-9). DAW Bks.
Gaskell, Mrs. Cranford. (Illus.). 297p. Date not set. Repr. of 1892 ed. lib. bdg. 30.00 (ISBN 0-89987-331-6). Darby Bks.
--The Life of Charlotte Bronte. 1947. 20.00 (ISBN 0-8274-2921-5). R West.
--Sylvia's Lovers. 440p. Date not set. Repr. of 1910 ed. lib. bdg. 30.00 (ISBN 0-89987-330-8). Darby Bks.
Gaskell, P., et al, eds. The Structure of Non-Crystalline Materials: 1982. 610p. 1983. 62.00x (ISBN 0-8002-3077-9). Taylor & Francis.
Gaskell, Peter. Artisans & Machinery. LC 68-28259. Repr. of 1836 ed. 39.50x (ISBN 0-678-05047-3). Kelley.
--Artisans & Machinery: Moral & Physical Condition of the Manufacturing Population. new ed. 399p. 1968. 42.50x (ISBN 0-7146-1395-9, F Cass Co). Biblio Dist.
--The Manufacturing Population of England. LC 73-38266. (The Evolution of Capitalism Ser.). 374p. 1972. Repr. of 1833 ed. 25.50 (ISBN 0-405-04120-9). Ayer Co Pubs.
Gaskell, Philip. Bibliography of the Foulis Press. 2nd, rev. ed. 300p. 1985. 42.50 (ISBN 0-906795-13-3). U Pr of Va.
--From Writer to Reader: Studies in Editorial Method. LC 81-8171. (Illus.). 268p. 1983. pap. 12.95x (ISBN 0-906795-25-7). U Pr of Va.
--John Baskerville: A Bibliography. rev. ed. (Illus.). xxxii, 72p. 1973. 45.00 (ISBN 0-85609-029-8). Oak Knoll.
--John Baskerville: A Bibliography. (Illus.). 72p. 40.00 (ISBN 0-87556-679-0). Saifer.
--Morvern Transformed. (Illus.). 300p. 1968. pap. 16.95 (ISBN 0-521-29797-4). Cambridge U Pr.
--A New Introduction to Bibliography. 1972. text ed. 19.95x (ISBN 0-19-818150-7). Oxford U Pr.
--Trinity College Library: The First 150 Years. LC 79-41415. (Illus.). 256p. 1981. 75.00 (ISBN 0-521-23100-0). Cambridge U Pr.
Gaskell, S. Martin. Building Control: National Legislation & the Introduction of Local By-Laws in Victorian England. 64p. (Orig.). 1983. pap. text ed. 9.75x (ISBN 0-7199-1100-1, Pub. by Bedford England). Brookfield Pub Co.
Gaskell, T. F., jt. auth. see Bates, C. C.
Gaskill, Arthur L. & Englander, David. How to Shoot a Movie & Video Story: The Technique of Pictorial Continuity. (Illus.). 128p. 1985. pap. 9.95 (ISBN 0-87100-239-6, 2239). Morgan.
Gaskill, Herbert S. Counterpoint: Libidinal Object & Subject, a Tribute to Rene A. Spitz on His 75th Birthday. LC 63-19629. pap. 52.50 (ISBN 0-317-10587-6, 2010422). Bks Demand UMI.
Gaskill, Herbert S., ed. Counterpoint: Libidinal Object & Self. LC 63-19629. x, 200p. 1985. text ed. 25.00 (ISBN 0-8236-1120-5, 01120). Intl Univs Pr.
Gaskill, Jack D. Linear Systems, Fourier Transforms & Optics. LC 78-1118. (Pure & Applied Optics Ser.). 554p. 1978. 44.50x (ISBN 0-471-29288-5, Pub. by Wiley-Interscience). Wiley.
Gaskill, P. H., ed. Eudo C. Mason: Hoelderlin & Goethe. (British & Irish Studies in German Language & Literature: Vol. 3). 168p. 1975. pap. 35.25 (ISBN 3-261-01410-5). P Lang Pubs.
Gaskill, Pamela, jt. auth. see Carroll, Robert.
Gaskin, Carol. A Day in the Life of a Racing Car Mechanic. LC 84-2430. (A Day in the Life of Ser.). (Illus.). 32p. (gr. 4-8). 1985. PLB 9.79 (ISBN 0-8167-0091-5); pap. 2.50 (ISBN 0-8167-0092-3). Troll Assocs.
--The Forbidden Towers. LC 84-16219. (The Forgotten Forest Ser.). (Illus.). 128p. (gr. 3-7). 1985. lib. bdg. 8.94 (ISBN 0-8167-0324-8); pap. text ed. 1.95 (ISBN 0-8167-0325-6). Troll Assocs.
--The Magician's Ring. LC 84-8499. (The Forgotten Forest Ser.). (Illus.). 128p. (gr. 3-7). 1985. PLB 8.94 (ISBN 0-8167-0320-5); pap. text ed. 1.95 (ISBN 0-8167-0321-3). Troll Assocs.
--Master of Mazes. LC 84-24015. (The Forgotten Forest Ser.). (Illus.). 128p. (gr. 3-7). 1985. PLB 8.94 (ISBN 0-8167-0322-1); pap. text ed. 1.95 (ISBN 0-8167-0323-X). Troll Assocs.
--The War of the Wizards. LC 84-2663. (The Forgotten Forest Ser.). (Illus.). 128p. (gr. 3-7). 1985. PLB 8.94 (ISBN 0-8167-0319-1); pap. text ed. 1.95 (ISBN 0-8167-0318-3). Troll Assocs.
Gaskin, Catherine. Edge of Glass. 1979. pap. 1.95 (ISBN 0-449-23846-6, Crest). Fawcett.
--Promises. LC 81-43631. 480p. 1982. 16.95 (ISBN 0-385-15989-7). Doubleday.
--Promises. 1983. pap. 3.95 (ISBN 0-380-65151-3, 65151). Avon.
--The Summer of the Spanish Woman. 1979. pap. 2.50 (ISBN 0-449-23809-1, Crest). Fawcett.
Gaskin, D. E. The Ecology of Whales & Dolphins. LC 82-11703. (Illus.). 434p. 1982. 25.00x (ISBN 0-435-62287-0). Heinemann Ed.
Gaskin, Ina May. Spiritual Midwifery. rev. ed. (Illus.). 1978. pap. 15.95 (ISBN 0-913990-10-8). Book Pub Co.
Gaskin, J. C. The Quest for Eternity: An Outline of the Philosophy of Religion. (Pelican Ser.). 192p. 1984. pap. 4.95 (ISBN 0-14-022538-2). Penguin.
Gaskin, John. Breathing. (Your Body Ser.). (Illus.). 32p. 1984. lib. bdg. 8.90 (ISBN 0-531-03768-1). Watts.
--Eating. (Your Body Ser.). (Illus.). 32p. (gr. 1-3). 1985. lib. bdg. 9.40 (ISBN 0-531-04632-X). Watts.
--The Heart. (Your Body Ser.). (Illus.). 32p. (gr. 1-6). 1985. PLB 9.40 (ISBN 0-317-19578-6). Watts.
--Movement. (Your Body Ser.). (Illus.). 32p. (gr. 1-3). 1985. lib. bdg. 9.40 (ISBN 0-531-04633-8). Watts.
--The Senses. (Your Body Ser.). (Illus.). 32p. (gr. 1-6). 1985. PLB 9.40 (ISBN 0-531-10051-0). Watts.
--Teeth. LC 83-50855. (Your Body Ser.). (Illus.). 32p. (gr. 2-4). 1984. PLB 9.40 (ISBN 0-531-03769-X). Watts.
Gaskin, L. J., jt. auth. see International African Institute.
Gaskin, Maxwell, ed. The Political Economy of Tolerable Survival. (Illus.). 220p. 1981. 30.00 (ISBN 0-7099-0266-2, Pub. by Croom Helm Ltd). Longwood Pub Group.
Gaskin, Stephen. Amazing Dope Tales. (Illus.). 1980. pap. 7.00 (ISBN 0-913990-29-9). Book Pub Co.
--Mind at Play. 1980. pap. 5.00 (ISBN 0-913990-24-8). Book Pub Co.
--Rendered Infamous: A Book of Political Reality. McClure, Matthew, ed. (Illus.). 224p. (Orig.). 1982. 12.00 (ISBN 0-913990-40-X); pap. 6.00 (ISBN 0-913990-32-9). Book Pub Co.
--Rendered Infamous: A Book of Political Reality. 268p. 1986. 11.95 (ISBN 0-89789-099-X). Bergin & Garvey.
Gaskin, W. D., jt. auth. see Silverthorne.
Gaskind, Bill. Perspectives on Landscape. (British Image Ser.: No. 5). 84p. 1980. pap. 10.00 (ISBN 0-7287-0168-5). Eastview.
Gaskins, Leslie F. A Primer on Dental Practice Management. 1984. pap. text ed. 15.95 (ISBN 0-8359-5669-5). Reston.
Gasner, Douglas, jt. auth. see Wagenvoord, James.
Gasow, Julia, jt. auth. see Goodall, Charles S.

Gaspar, David B. Bondmen & Rebels: A Study of Master-Slave Relations in Antigua with Implications for Colonial British America. LC 85-5222. (Studies in Atlantic History & Culture). 352p. 1985. text ed. 35.00x (ISBN 0-8018-2422-2). Johns Hopkins.
Gaspar, E. & Oncoscu, M. Radioactive Tracers in Hydrology. (Developments in Hydrology Ser.: Vol. 1). 342p. 1972. 76.75 (ISBN 0-444-40986-6). Elsevier.
Gaspar, Edmund. United States-Latin America: A Special Relationship? 1978. pap. 4.25 (ISBN 0-8447-3287-7). Am Enterprise.
Gaspar, Evelyn. The Gardener's Guide to Growing, Harvesting, & Cooking. 320p. 1985. 16.95 (ISBN 0-8038-2729-6). Hastings.
Gaspar, Max R. & Barker, Wiley F. Peripheral Arterial Disease. 3rd ed. (Major Problems in Clinical Surgery Ser.: Vol. 4). (Illus.). 528p. 1981. text ed. 44.95 (ISBN 0-7216-4054-0). Saunders.
Gaspar, Sandor. The International Trade Union Movement. 382p. 1981. 45.00x (ISBN 0-569-08699-X, Pub. by Collets). State Mutual Bk.
Gaspard, Perry A. The Baptism with the Holy Spirit. 1983. pap. 1.00 (ISBN 0-931867-02-9). Abundant Life Pubns.
--The Basic Principles of Prayer. 1984. pap. 2.00 (ISBN 0-931867-07-X). Abundant Life Pubns.
--The Different Kinds of Prayer. 88p. 1984. pap. text ed. 3.00 (ISBN 0-931867-08-8). Abundant Life Pubns.
--Freedom from Fear. 1980. pap. 2.00 (ISBN 0-931867-06-1). Abundant Life Pubns.
--The Power of God's Word. 60p. 1981. pap. 2.00 (ISBN 0-931867-05-3). Abundant Life Pubns.
--The Power of the Tongue. 1983. pap. 1.50 (ISBN 0-931867-04-5). Abundant Life Pubns.
--Redeemed from the Curse. 64p. 1983. pap. 2.00 (ISBN 0-931867-03-7). Abundant Life Pubns.
--Salvation. 1983. pap. 1.00 (ISBN 0-931867-00-2). Abundant Life Pubns.
--Water Baptism. 1983. pap. 1.00 (ISBN 0-931867-01-0). Abundant Life Pubns.
Gasparian, Rouletta & Kautzman, Doris. The Let's Write to Read Story. LC 83-61160. 80p. 1983. pap. 6.50 incl. postage & handling (ISBN 0-914059-00-9). Novel Ideas.
Gasparic, Jiri. Laboratory Handbook of Paper & Thin-Layer Chromatography. Churacek, Jaroslov, ed. LC 77-14168. 1978. 83.95x (ISBN 0-470-99298-0). Halsted Pr.
Gasparic, Jiri, jt. auth. see Vecera, Miroslov.
Gasparin, Agenor De see De Gasparin, Agenor.
Gasparini, Francesco. Il Bajazet. Brown, Howard & Wimer, Eric, eds. LC 76-21066. (Italian Opera 1640-1770 Ser.: Vol. 24). 1978. lib. bdg. 77.00 (ISBN 0-8240-2623-3). Garland Pub.
--The Practical Harmonist at the Harpsichord. Burrows, David L., ed. Stillings, Frank S., tr. from Ital. (Music Reprint Ser.: 1980). (Illus.). 1980. Repr. of 1963 ed. lib. bdg. 25.00 (ISBN 0-306-76017-7). Da Capo.
Gasparini, Graziano & Margolies, Luise. Inca Architecture. Lyon, Patricia J., tr. from Span. LC 79-3005. (Illus.). 368p. 1984. 35.00x (ISBN 0-253-30443-1). Ind U Pr.
Gasparski, Wojciech. Praxiological Studies. 1983. lib. bdg. 78.00 (ISBN 90-277-1258-1, Pub. by Reidel Holland). Kluwer Academic.
Gaspe, Philippe A. Memoires (Ottawa 1866) (Canadiana Avant 1867: No. 1). 1966. 33.20x (ISBN 90-2796-322-3). Mouton.
Gasper, Louis. The Fundamentalist Movement. (Twin Brooks Ser.). 181p. (Orig.). 1981. pap. 6.95 (ISBN 0-8010-3769-7). Baker Bk.
Gasperini, Jim. Sail with Pirates. (Time Machine Ser.: No. 4). (Illus.). 144p. (gr. 4 up). 1984. pap. 1.95 (ISBN 0-553-23808-6). Bantam.
Gasperini, Jim, jt. auth. see Byron Preiss Visual Publications Inc.
Gasperini, Richard E. Digital Experiments. (Illus.). 1976. pap. 9.95 (ISBN 0-8104-5713-X). Hayden.
Gasperini, Riechard E. Digital Troubleshooting: Practical Digital Theory & Troubleshooting Tips. 1976. pap. 11.95 (ISBN 0-8104-5708-3). Hayden.
Gasquet, Abbot, ed. see Acton, John E.
Gasquet, Amedee L. Etudes Byzantines: L'Empire Byzantin et la Monarchie Franque. 484p. 1972. Repr. of 1888 ed. lib. bdg. 30.50 (ISBN 0-8337-1291-8). B Franklin.
Gasquet, Cardinal. Monastic Life in the Middle Ages. 1979. 95.95 (ISBN 0-8490-0657-0). Gordon Pr.
Gasquet, Cardinal, ed. see Teresa, Saint.
Gasquet, Cardinal, tr. see Benedict, Saint.
Gasquet, F. A. Ancestral Prayers. 1976. 3.95 (ISBN 0-87243-068-5). Templegate.
Gasquet, Francis A. The Black Death of 1348 & 1349. 2nd ed. LC 75-23713. Repr. of 1908 ed. 24.00 (ISBN 0-404-13264-2). AMS Pr.
--English Monastic Life. fascimile ed. LC 77-157336. (Select Bibliographies Reprint Ser.). Repr. of 1904 ed. 32.00 (ISBN 0-8369-5796-2). Ayer Co Pubs.
--English Monastic Life. LC 76-118470. 1971. Repr. of 1904 ed. 27.50x (ISBN 0-8046-1219-6, Pub. by Kennikat). Assoc Faculty Pr.
--Eve of the Reformation. LC 75-118522. 1971. Repr. of 1900 ed. 33.50x (ISBN 0-8046-1144-0, Pub. by Kennikat). Assoc Faculty Pr.
--Henry the Eighth & the English Monasteries, 2 vols. LC 74-39467. (Select Bibliography Reprint Ser.). 1972. Repr. of 1888 ed. 56.75 (ISBN 0-8369-9905-3). Ayer Co Pubs.
--Henry VIII & the English Monasteries, 2 vols. (Select Bibliographies Reprint Ser.). Repr. of 1888 ed. lib. bdg. 32.00 set (ISBN 0-8290-0849-7). Irvington.
--Last Abbot of Glastonbury & Other Essays. facs. ed. LC 72-137376. (Select Bibliographies Reprint Ser). 1908. 20.00 (ISBN 0-8369-5577-3). Ayer Co Pubs.
--Monastic Life in the Middle Ages, 1792-1806. facs. ed. LC 76-137377. (Select Bibliographies Reprint Ser). 1922. 16.00 (ISBN 0-8369-5578-1). Ayer Co Pubs.
--The Old English & Other Essays. 1979. Repr. of 1897 ed. lib. bdg. 35.00 (ISBN 0-8495-2035-5). Arden Lib.
Gasquet, Francis C. Old English Bible & Other Essays. LC 68-26209. 1969. Repr. of 1897 ed. 26.50x (ISBN 0-8046-0166-6, Pub. by Kennikat). Assoc Faculty Pr.
Gasqui, J. & Goldschmidt, H. Deformations Infinitesmales des Structures Conformer Plates. (Progress in Mathematics Ser.: No. 52). (Fr.). 1984. text ed. write for info. (ISBN 0-8176-3260-3). Birkhauser.
Gass, jt. auth. see Selinker.
Gass, George H. & Kaplan, Harold M. CRC Handbook of Endocrinology. 368p. 1982. 98.00 (ISBN 0-8493-3235-4). CRC Pr.
Gass, Gertrude Z., jt. auth. see Rutledge, Aaron L.
Gass, I. G., ed. Volcanic Processes in Ore Genesis. 188p. (Orig.). 1980. pap. text ed. 46.00x (ISBN 0-900488-33-6). IMM North Am.
Gass, I. G., jt. ed. see Clifford, T. N.
Gass, I. G., et al, eds. Ophiolites & Oceanic Lithosphere. 432p. 1984. text ed. 69.95x (ISBN 0-632-01219-6). Blackwell Pubns.
Gass, J. Donald. Stereoscopic Atlas of Macular Diseases: Diagnosis & Treatment. 2nd ed. LC 76-57176. (Illus.). 412p. 1977. 77.50 (ISBN 0-8016-1754-5). Mosby.
Gass, J. G., et al, eds. Understanding the Earth: A Reader in the Earth Sciences. 384p. 1981. 35.00x (ISBN 0-686-79153-3, Pub. by Artemis England). State Mutual Bk.
Gass, Saul I. Decision Making, Models & Algorithms: A First Course. 496p. 1985. 34.95 (ISBN 0-471-80963-2). Wiley.
--Illustrated Guide to Linear Programming. 1970. 29.95 (ISBN 0-07-022960-0). McGraw.
Gass, Saul I., jt. auth. see Riley, Vera.
Gass, Saul I., ed. Operations Research: Mathematics & Models. LC 81-10849. (Proceedings of Symposia in Applied Mathematics: Vol. 25). 198p. pap. 12.00 (ISBN 0-8218-0029-9, PSAPM-25). Am Math.
Gass, Sherlock B. Criers of the Shops. facs. ed. LC 74-142633. (Essay Index Reprint Ser). 1925. 20.00 (ISBN 0-8369-2049-X). Ayer Co Pubs.
Gass, Susan & Selinker, Larry, eds. Language Transfer in Language Learning. 432p. 1983. pap. text ed. 23.95 (ISBN 0-88377-305-8). Newbury Hse.
Gass, William. Fiction & the Figures of Life. LC 78-58453. 304p. 1978. pap. 7.95 (ISBN 0-87923-254-4, Nonpareil Bk). Godine.
--In the Heart of the Heart of the Country. LC 68-11820. 1968. 10.00i (ISBN 0-06-011468-1, HarpT). Har-Row.
--Omensetter's Luck. pap. 5.95 (ISBN 0-452-25349-7, Z5349, Plume). NAL.
--On Being Blue. LC 75-43013. 96p. 1976. 6.95 (ISBN 0-87923-183-1). Godine.
--On Being Blue: A Philosophical Inquiry. LC 75-43103. 1978. pap. 6.95 (ISBN 0-87923-237-4). Godine.
--The World Within the Word. LC 79-52634. 352p. 1979. pap. 8.95 (ISBN 0-87923-298-6, Nonpareil Bks.). Godine.
Gass, William H. The Habitations of the Word: Essays. 368p. 1985. 17.95 (ISBN 0-671-52726-6). S&S.
--In the Heart of the Heart of the Country & Other Stories. LC 80-83962. 240p. 1981. pap. 7.95 (ISBN 0-87923-374-5, Nonpareil Bks). Godine.
Gassan, Arnold. A Chronology of Photography: A Critical Survey of the History of Photography As a Medium of Art. 380p. (Orig.). 1984. pap. text ed. cancelled (ISBN 0-87992-021-1). Light Impressions.
--The Color Print Book: A Survey of Contemporary Photographic Printmaking Methods for the Creative Photographer. LC 80-28859. (The Extended Photo Media Ser.: No. 3). (Illus., Orig.). 1981. pap. 9.95 (ISBN 0-87992-023-8). Light Impressions.
Gassan, Arnold H. Handbook for Contemporary Photography. 4th ed. LC 77-14576. (Illus.). 1977. 14.95 (ISBN 0-87992-009-2); pap. 8.95x (ISBN 0-87992-008-4). Light Impressions.
Gasselin, M. Edouard. Francais-Arabe Dictionary, 2 Vols. Repr. of 1974 ed. Set. 85.00x (ISBN 0-86685-344-8). Intl Bk Ctr.
Gassen, Chris, jt. auth. see Mittra, Sid.
Gassen, Hans G. & Lang, Anne, eds. Chemical & Enzymatic Synthesis of Gene Fragments: A Laboratory Manual. (Illus.). 249p. 1982. 41.10x (ISBN 0-89573-065-4). VCH Pubs.
Gassendi, Pierre. Pierre Gassendi's Institutio Logica (1658) Jones, Howard, ed. 240p. 1981. pap. text ed. 18.50x (ISBN 90-232-1817-5, Pub. by Van Gorcum Holland). Humanities.
--Selected Works. Brush, Craig B., tr. 1972. Repr. 45.00 (ISBN 0-384-17685-2). Johnson Repr.
Gasser, Doris L. Socrates, the Snowman. (Illus.). 1980. 5.00 (ISBN 0-682-49446-1). Exposition Pr FL.
Gasser, Elaine. United States: People-Questions. (People & Systems Ser). (Orig.). 1975. pap. 1.25 (ISBN 0-377-00035-3). Friend Pr.
Gasser, J. K. Composting of Agricultural & Other Wastes: Proceedings of a Seminar Organized by the Commission of the European Communities, Oxford, England, 19-22, March, 1984. 336p. 1985. 57.00 (ISBN 0-85334-357-8, Pub. by Elsevier Applied Sci England). Elsevier.
Gasser, J. K., ed. Effluents from Livestock. 1980. 76.00 (ISBN 0-85334-895-2, Pub. by Elsevier Applied Sci England). Elsevier.
--Modelling Nitrogen from Farm Wastes. (Illus.). 195p. 1979. 26.00 (ISBN 0-85334-869-3, Pub. by Elsevier Applied Sci England). Elsevier.
Gasser, Michael, jt. auth. see Rossi, Lee D.
Gasser, R. F., jt. auth. see Blechschmidt, E.
Gasser, R. P. An Introduction to Chemisorption & Catalysis by Metals. (Illus.). 1985. 29.95x (ISBN 0-19-855163-0). Oxford U Pr.
Gasser, T. & Rosenblatt, M., eds. Smoothing Techniques for Curve Estimation. (Lecture Notes in Mathematics: Vol. 757). 1979. pap. 18.00 (ISBN 0-387-09706-6). Springer-Verlag.
Gassert, Carole A. & Burrows, Susan G. Going for Heart Surgery: What You Need to Know. Hull, Nancy R., ed. (Illus.). 48p. 1985. pap. text ed. 5.00 (ISBN 0-939838-15-X). Pritchett & Hull.
Gassert, Carole A., jt. auth. see Burrows, Susan G.
Gasset, Jose Ortega Y. The Modern Theme. Cleugh, James, tr. from Span. 152p. 1981. Repr. of 1931 ed. lib. bdg. 35.00 (ISBN 0-89987-311-1). Darby Bks.
Gasset, Jose Ortega Y. see Ortega y Gasset, Jose.
Gasset, Jose Ortega Y see Ortega Y Gasset, Jose.
Gassette, Grace & Ashton, Horace. The Key. 1977. pap. 4.95 (ISBN 0-87516-229-0). De Vorss.
Gassick, Trevor Le see Barakat, Halim.
Gassick, Trevor Le see Mahfouz, Naguib.
Gassick, Trevor le see Mahfouz, Naguib.
Gassier, Pierre, ed. Life & Work of Francisco Goya. Wilson, Juliet. Lachenal, Francois, ed. (Illus.). 1971. 55.00 (ISBN 0-688-61054-4). Reynal.
Gassmann, Florian L. Amore e Psiche. Brown, Howard M. & Weimer, Eric, eds. LC 80-822. (Italian Opera Ser., 1640-1770). 354p. 1983. lib. bdg. 83.00 (ISBN 0-8240-4826-1). Garland Pub.
Gassmann, H. P. Information Computer & Communications Policies for the Eighties. 278p. 1982. 40.50 (ISBN 0-444-86327-3, North-Holland). Elsevier.
Gassmann, Robert H. Zur Syntax von Einbettungsstrukturen im Klassischen Chinesisch. (SAS-S Ser.: Vol. 6). 227p. (Ger.). 1982. 25.00 (ISBN 3-261-05002-0). P Lang Pubs.
Gassner, J. O'Neill: A Collection of Critical Essays. 1964. 12.95 (ISBN 0-13-634279-5, Spec). P-H.
Gassner, John & Nicholas, Dudley. Best Film Plays Nineteen Forty-Five. Kupelnick, Bruce S., ed. LC 76-52103. (Classics of Film Literature Ser.). 1978. lib. bdg. 39.00 (ISBN 0-8240-2876-7). Garland Pub.
Gassner, John & Nichols, Dudley. Best Film Plays, Nineteen Forty-Three to Forty-Four. LC 76-52102. (Classics of Film Literature Ser.: Vol. 11). (Illus.). 1977. Repr. of 1945 ed. lib. bdg. 39.00 (ISBN 0-8240-2875-9). Garland Pub.
--Twenty Best Film Plays, 2 vols. LC 76-52104. (Classics of Film Literature Ser.: Vol. 13). 1977. Repr. of 1943 ed. Set. lib. bdg. 69.00 ea. (ISBN 0-8240-2877-5). Garland Pub.
Gassner, John, intro. by. Best American Plays. (Third Series, 1945-1951). (Illus.). 736p. 19.95 (ISBN 0-517-50950-4). Crown.
Gassner, John, ed. & intro. by. Best American Plays: Fifth Series, 1958-1963. Incl. A Touch of the Poet; The Night of the Iguana; Who's Afraid of Virginia Woolf; The Rope Dancers; Look Homeward Angel; All the Way Home; Silent Night, Lonely Night; Two for the Seesaw; Mary, Mary; A Thousand Clowns; The Cave Dwellers; Oh, Dad, Poor Dad, Mama's Hung You in the Closet and I'm Feelin So Sad; Gideon; J. B; The Best Man; Orpheus Descending; The Dark at the Top of the Stairs. 704p. 1963. 19.95 (ISBN 0-517-50860-5). Crown.
--Best American Plays: Fourth Series, 1952-1957. Incl. I Am a Camera; Cat on a Hot Tin Roof; The Rose Tattoo; A Moon for the Misbegotten; A Hatful of Rain; Picnic; Bus Stop; Tea & Sympathy; A View from the Bridge; The Crucible; Inherit the Wind; The Caine Mutiny Court-Martial; The Fourposter; The Seven Year Itch; The Matchmaker; No Time for Sergeants; The Solid Gold Cadillac. 672p. 1958. 19.95 (ISBN 0-517-50436-7). Crown.
Gassner, John, intro. by. Best American Plays: Third Series, 1945-51. Incl. Death of a Salesman; A Streetcar Named Desire; Detective Story; The Member of the Wedding; Bell, Book & Candle; The Moon Is Blue; Mister Roberts; State of the Union; Anne of the Thousand Days; The Iceman Cometh; Come Back, Little Sheba; Billy Budd; Darkness at Noon; Summer & Smoke; All My Sons; Medea; The Autumn Garden. 736p. 1952. 19.95 (ISBN 0-517-50950-4). Crown.
Gassner, John, ed. Best American Plays: 1918-1958, Supplement. 1961. 21.95 (ISBN 0-517-50450-2). Crown.
Gassner, John, ed. & intro. by. Best Plays of the Early American Theatre: From the Beginning to 1916. 716p. 1967. 27.95 (ISBN 0-517-50949-0). Crown.
--Best Plays of the Modern American Theatre: Second Series, 1939-1946. Incl. The Glass Menagerie; The Time of Your Life; I Remember Mama; Life with Father; Born Yesterday; The Voice of the Turtle; The Male Animal; The Man Who Came to Dinner; Dream Girl; The Philadelphia Story; Arsenic & Old Lace; The Hasty Heart; Home of the Brave; Tomorrow the World; Watch on the Rhine; The Patriots; Abe Lincoln in Illinois. 768p. 1947. 23.95 (ISBN 0-517-50948-2). Crown.
Gassner, John, ed. Ideas in the Drama. LC 64-21201. (Essays of the English Institute). 1964. 18.00x (ISBN 0-231-02733-8). Columbia U Pr.
--A Treasury of the Theatre, 3 vols. Incl. Vol. 1. From Aeschylus to Ostrovsky. 1968. o.p. (ISBN 0-671-20137-9); Vol. 2. From Ibsen to Sartre (ISBN 0-671-75610-9); Vol. 3. From Wilde to Eugene Ionesco. 1951. 24.95 ea.. S&S.
--Twenty Best European Plays on the American Stage. (Best Plays Ser). (gr. 9 up). 1957. 22.50 (ISBN 0-517-50963-6). Crown.
--Twenty Best Plays of the Modern American Theatre. (Best Plays Ser). (gr. 9 up). 1939. 22.50 (ISBN 0-517-50964-4). Crown.
--Twenty-Five Best Plays of the Modern American Theatre: Early Series. (Best Plays Ser). (gr. 9 up). 1949. 16.95 (ISBN 0-517-50390-5). Crown.
Gassner, John & Barnes, Clive, eds. Best American Plays. (Sixth Ser. 1963-1967). 27.95 (ISBN 0-88411-639-5, Pub. by Aeonian Pr). Amereon Ltd.
--Best American Plays: Sixth Series, 1963-1967. 700p. (YA) 1971. 19.95 (ISBN 0-517-50951-2). Crown.
Gassner, John & Gassner, Mollie, eds. Fifteen International One-Act Plays. (Orig.). 1969. pap. 2.50 (ISBN 0-671-49110-5). WSP.
Gassner, John & Quinn, Edward, eds. Reader's Encyclopedia of World Drama. LC 69-11830. (Illus.). 1969. 17.26i (ISBN 0-690-67483-X). T Y Crowell.
Gassner, John see Columbia University. English Institute.
Gassner, Julius S., tr. see La Perouse, Comte De.
Gassner, Mollie, jt. ed. see Gassner, John.
Gasson, Harold. Firing Days: Reminiscences of a Great Western Fireman. 120p. 20.00x (ISBN 0-902888-25-0, Pub. by ORPC Ltd UK). State Mutual Bk.
--Footplate Days: More Reminiscences of a Great Western Fireman. 120p. 20.00x (ISBN 0-902888-51-X, Pub. by ORPC Ltd UK). State Mutual Bk.
--Great Western Railway Signalling Days: Final Reminiscences of a Great Western Railwayman. 140p. 20.00x (ISBN 0-86093-118-8, Pub. by ORPC Ltd UK). State Mutual Bk.
--Nostalgic Days, Further Reminiscences of a Great Western Fireman. 116p. 20.00x (ISBN 0-86093-079-3, Pub. by ORPC Ltd UK). State Mutual Bk.
Gasson, Peter C. Geometry of Spatial Forms. LC 83-12893. (Mathematics & It's Applications, Ellis Horwood Ser.). 561p. 1983. 64.95 (ISBN 0-470-20011-1); pap. 29.95x (ISBN 0-470-20009-X). Halsted Pr.
Gasson, Raphael. The Challenging Counterfeit: A Former Medium Exposes Spiritualism. 162p. 1966. pap. 1.95 (ISBN 0-912106-66-2, Pub. by Logos). Bridge Pub.
Gasson, Roy, ed. The Illustrated Edgar Allan Poe. 238p. 1981. 24.00x (ISBN 0-904041-57-3, Pub. by Jupiter England). State Mutual Bk.
--The Illustrated Mark Twain. 312p. 1981. 24.00x (ISBN 0-904041-95-6, Pub. by Jupiter England). State Mutual Bk.
--The Illustrated Oscar Wilde. 324p. 1981. 24.00x (ISBN 0-686-72292-2, Pub. by Jupiter Bks). State Mutual Bk.
--The Illustrated Robert Louis Stevenson. 264p. 1981. 24.00x (ISBN 0-904041-81-6, Pub. by Jupiter England). State Mutual Bk.
Gasster, Michael. China's Struggle to Modernize. 2nd ed. (Illus.). 256p. 1983. pap. text ed. 9.00 (ISBN 0-394-33027-7, KnopfC). Knopf.
Gast, David L., jt. auth. see Tawney, James W.
Gast, Harold, jt. auth. see Woodley, Richard.
Gast, Ira M., jt. ed. see Skinner, Charles E.
Gast, Kelly P. Paddy. LC 78-18134. (Double D Western Ser.). 1979. 7.95 (ISBN 0-385-14291-9). Doubleday.
Gast, Robert de see De Gast, Robert.
Gast, Robert De see De Gast, Robert.

Gast, Ross H. Contentious Consul: A Biography of John Coffin Jones First United States Counselor Agent at Hawaii. 1976. 10.00 (ISBN 0-87093-175-X). Dawsons.

Gast, Ross H. & Conrad, Agnes C. Don Francisco De Paula Marin: A Biography with Letters & Journal. LC 77-188980. (Illus.). 354p. 1973. 12.95x (ISBN 0-8248-0220-9). UH Pr.

Gast, Th., ed. see Conference on Vacuum Microbalance Techniques (9th: 1970: Berlin, Germany).

Gastaad Symposium, 1st International, Swiss Society for Gastroenlerology. The Liver: Quantitative Aspects of Structure & Function, Proceedings. Preisig, R. & Paumgartener, G., eds. (Illus.). 1973. 27.75 (ISBN 3-8055-1603-7). S Karger.

Gastaldi, Ugo & Klapisch, Robert, eds. Physics at LEAR with Low-Energy Cooled Antiprotons. (Ettore Majorana International Science Series, Physical Sciences: Vol. 17). 902p. 1984. 125.00x (ISBN 0-306-41384-1, Plenum Pr). Plenum Pub.

Gastang, Walter. Larval Forms & Other Zoological Verses. (Illus.). 104p. 1951. pap. 5.95 (ISBN 0-226-28423-9). U of Chicago Pr.

Gastaut, H. Dictionary of Epilepsy: Part I - Definitions. (Also avail. in French, Russian & Spanish). 1973. 8.00 (ISBN 92-4-154027-3). World Health.

--Woerterbuch der Epilepsie. (Ger.). 1975. pap. 22.50 (ISBN 3-7773-0380-1, M-7013). French & Eur.

Gastaut, Henri & Broughton, Roger. Epileptic Seizures: Clinical & Electrographic Features, Diagnosis & Treatment. (Illus.). 304p. 1972. 33.50x (ISBN 0-398-02290-9). C C Thomas.

Gastaut, Henri, et al. The Physiopathogenesis of the Epilepsies. (Illus.). 340p. 1969. photocopy ed. 36.50x (ISBN 0-398-00656-3). C C Thomas.

Gastel, A. J. Van see Van Gastel, A. J.

Gastel, Barbara. Presenting Science to the Public. (Professional Writing Ser.). (Illus.). 146p. 1983. 17.95 (ISBN 0-89495-028-2); pap. 11.95 (ISBN 0-89495-029-0). ISI Pr.

Gastel, Ruth & Mooney, Sean. Reinsurance: Fundamentals & Current Issues. 72p. (Orig.). 1983. pap. text ed. 10.00 (ISBN 0-932387-06-3). Insur Info.

Gastel, Ruth, jt. auth. see Mooney, Sean F.

Gastell, J. D. & Tiews, K. Report on Standardization of Methodology in Fish Nutrition Research: EIFAC, UNIS, ICES Working Group on Standardization of Methodology, Hamburg, Fed. Rep. of Germany, March 1979. (European Inland Fisheries Advisory Commission (EIFAC): Technical Papers: No. 36). 30p. (Eng. & Fr.). 1980. pap. 8.25 (ISBN 92-5-100918-X, F2048, FAO). Unipub.

Gasten, Ruth S., jt. auth. see Carothers, James E.

Gaster, Adrian, ed. International Authors & Writers Who's Who. 9th ed. 400p. 1982. 120.00x (ISBN 0-8103-0428-7). Gale.

--International Who's Who in Music & Musician's Directory. 9th ed. LC 73-91185. 1000p. 1980. 85.00x (ISBN 0-8103-0427-9). Gale.

Gaster, Harold. A Morning Without Clouds. 144p. 1981. 25.00x (ISBN 0-224-01964-3, Pub. by Cape England). State Mutual Bk.

--A Morning Without Clouds. 194p. 1982. 10.95 (ISBN 0-312-54833-8). St Martin.

Gaster, M. The Origin of the Kabbala. 1976. lib. bdg. 69.95 (ISBN 0-8490-2386-6). Gordon Pr.

--Roumanian Bird & Beast Stories, Rendered into English. (Folk-Lore Society, London, Monographs: Vol. 75A). pap. 35.00 (ISBN 0-317-17858-X). Kraus Repr.

--The Samaritans: History, Doctrine & Literature. 1976. lib. bdg. 134.95 (ISBN 0-8490-2563-X). Gordon Pr.

--The Samaritans: Their History, Doctrines & Literature. (British Academy, London, Schweich Lectures on Biblical Archaeology Series, 1923). pap. 28.00 (ISBN 0-317-15781-7). Kraus Repr.

Gaster, Moses. The Chronicles of Jerahmeel. rev. ed. 1971. 39.50x (ISBN 0-87068-162-1). Ktav.

--Exempla of the Rabbis. rev. ed. 1968. 35.00x (ISBN 0-87068-055-2). Ktav.

--Romanian Bird & Beast Stories. LC 78-67713. (The Folktale). Repr. of 1915 ed. 30.75 (ISBN 0-404-16089-1). AMS Pr.

--The Samaritan Oral Law & Ancient Traditions. LC 77-87609. Repr. of 1932 ed. 22.00 (ISBN 0-404-16433-1). AMS Pr.

--Studies & Texts in Folklore, Magic, Medieval Romance, Hebrew Apocrypha & Samaritan Archaeology, 3 Vols. rev. ed. 1970. Set. 45.00x (ISBN 0-87068-056-0). Ktav.

Gaster, Moses, tr. from Judeo-German. Ma'aseh Book: Book of Jewish Tales & Legends. LC 81-80356. 694p. 1981. pap. 10.95 (ISBN 0-8276-0189-1, 471). Jewish Pubns.

Gaster, Theodor H. The Dead Sea Scriptures. 2nd ed. LC 76-2840. 1976. pap. 7.95 (ISBN 0-385-08859-0, Anchor Pr). Doubleday.

--Festivals of the Jewish Year. 1962. 18.75 (ISBN 0-8446-2113-7). Peter Smith.

--Festivals of the Jewish Year: A Modern Interpretation & Guide. 1971. pap. 7.95 (ISBN 0-688-06008-0). Morrow.

--Passover, Its History & Tradition. LC 83-22678. (Illus.). 102p. 1984. Repr. of 1949 ed. lib. bdg. 22.50x (ISBN 0-313-24372-7, GAPA). Greenwood.

--Thespis: Ritual, Myth, & Drama in the Ancient Near East. 2nd rev. ed. LC 75-15735. 1975. 17.50x (ISBN 0-87752-188-3). Gordian.

Gaster, Theodor H., ed. see Frazer, James G.

Gaster, Theodore, ed. see Frazer, James.

Gaster, Theodore H. Myth, Legend & Custom in the Old Testament: A Comparative Study with Chapters from Sir James G. Frazer's Folklore in the Old Testament, 2 vols. Set. 32.00 (ISBN 0-8446-5189-3). Peter Smith.

Gasteyger, Curt. Searching for World Security. 260p. 1985. 27.50 (ISBN 0-312-70823-8). St Martin.

Gasteyger, Curt, ed. European Energy Security. 225p. 1985. 27.50 (ISBN 0-312-27064-X). St Martin.

Gastil, R. Gordon, et al. Reconnaissance Geology of the State of Baja California. LC 74-83806. (Geological Society of America Memoir Ser.: No. 140). pap. 62.00 (ISBN 0-317-29112-2, 2023734). Bks Demand UMI.

Gastil, Raymond. Cultural Regions of the United States. LC 75-8933. (Illus.). 382p. 1976. 21.00x (ISBN 0-295-95426-4). U of Wash Pr.

Gastil, Raymond D. Freedom in the World: Political Rights & Civil Liberties, 1979. LC 79-87596. (Illus.). 1979. lib. bdg. 20.00 (ISBN 0-932088-01-5). Freedom Hse.

--Freedom in the World: Political Rights & Civil Liberties, 1978. LC 78-53867. (Illus.). 1978. lib. bdg. 20.00 (ISBN 0-932088-00-7). Freedom Hse.

--Freedom in the World: Political Rights & Civil Liberties, 1981. LC 80-66430. (Illus.). 456p. 1981. lib. bdg. 35.00 (ISBN 0-313-23177-X, FR81). Greenwood.

--Freedom in the World: Political Rights & Civil Liberties, 1982. LC 80-66430. (Freedom House Annual). (Illus.). xi, 379p. 1982. lib. bdg. 35.00 (ISBN 0-313-23178-8, FR82). Greenwood.

--Freedom in the World: Political Rights & Civil Liberties 1981. 1981. 35.00. Freedom Hse.

--Freedom In the World: Political Rights & Civil Liberties 1982. (Illus.). 380p. 1982. 35.00. Freedom Hse.

--Freedom in the World: Political Rights & Civil Liberties 1983-84. LC 80-66430. x, 475p. 1984. lib. bdg. 35.00 (ISBN 0-313-23179-6, FR83). Greenwood.

--Freedom in the World: Political Rights & Civil Liberties, 1984-1985. LC 80-66430. (Freedom House Annual Ser.). (Illus.). x, 438p. 1985. lib. bdg. 35.00 (ISBN 0-313-23180-X, FR84). Greenwood.

--Social Humanities: Toward an Integrative Discipline of Science & Values. LC 76-52580. (Social & Behavioral Science Ser.). (Illus.). 1977. text ed. 25.95x (ISBN 0-87589-318-X). Jossey-Bass.

Gastil, Raymond D. & Sussman, Leonard R. Freedom in the World: Political Rights & Civil Liberties, 1980. LC 80-66430. 1980. 24.95 (ISBN 0-932088-02-3). Freedom Hse.

Gastil, Raymond D., ed. Freedom in the World: Political Rights & Civil Liberties. LC 80-50029. 331p. (Orig.). 1980. pap. 8.95 (ISBN 0-87855-852-7). Transaction Bks.

Gastineau, Clifford, ed. see Mayo Clinic Dietetic Staff, et al.

Gastineau, Clifford F., et al, eds. Fermented Food Beverages in Nutrition. (Nutrition Foundation Ser.). 1979. 70.00 (ISBN 0-12-277050-1). Acad Pr.

Gastineau, Gary L. The Stock Options Manual. 2nd ed. (Illus.). 1978. 31.50 (ISBN 0-07-022970-8). McGraw.

Gastineau, Mark. The Body You Want. LC 84-48599. (Illus.). 192p. 1985. pap. 10.53i (ISBN 0-06-091273-1, CN 1179, CN). Har-Row.

Gastinel, Francis, ed. see Musset, Alfred de.

Gastinel, Noel. Linear Numerical Analysis. LC 70-108619. 1971. 68.00 (ISBN 0-12-277150-8). Acad Pr.

Gastmann, Albert. Historical Dictionary of the French & Netherlands Antilles. LC 78-19070. (Latin American Historical Dictionaries Ser.: No. 18). 170p. 1978. lib. bdg. 17.50 (ISBN 0-8108-1153-7). Scarecrow.

Gastmans, R., jt. ed. see Basdevant, J. L.

Gaston, jt. auth. see Bender.

Gaston, A. G. Green Power: The Successful Way of A. G. Gaston. (Illus.). 1977. Repr. of 1968 ed. 8.95x (ISBN 0-916624-09-9). Troy State Univ.

--Green Power: The Successful Way of A. G. Gaston. (Illus.). 1978. pap. 2.95x (ISBN 0-916624-10-2). Troy State Univ.

Gaston, Anne M. A Study of Siva in Dance, Myth & Iconography. (Illus.). 1982. 45.00x (ISBN 0-19-561354-6). Oxford U Pr.

Gaston, Blanche P. I Like Me, Vol. I. (Continuing Ser.). (Illus.). 24p. (Orig.). (gr. k-3). 1982. 6.95x (ISBN 0-9608516-0-7); pap. 4.95x (ISBN 0-9608516-1-5). I Like Me Pubs.

--I Like Me. (Illus.). 25p. 1984. 7.95 (ISBN 0-941484-04-1). Urban Res Inst.

Gaston, C. R., ed. see Forum.

Gaston, Charles. Selections from American Poetry. Repr. of 1908 ed. 20.00 (ISBN 0-686-18788-1). Scholars Ref Lib.

Gaston, E. Thayer. Music in Therapy. (Illus.). 1968. text ed. write for info. (ISBN 0-02-340700-X, 34070). Macmillan.

Gaston, Edwin W., Jr. Conrad Richter. (Twayne's United States Authors Ser). 1965. pap. 5.95x (ISBN 0-8084-0091-6, T81, Twayne). New Coll U Pr.

Gaston, Frank J. Adjusting Executive Pay for Inflation: A Technical Exploration. (Report Ser.: No. 819). 1982. 50.00 (ISBN 0-8237-0257-X); members 10.00. Conference Bd.

Gaston, Georg. Karel Reisz. (Filmmakers Ser.). 1980. lib. bdg. 14.50 (ISBN 0-8057-9277-5, Twayne). G K Hall.

Gaston, Georg M. Jack Clayton: A Guide to References & Resources. 1981. lib. bdg. 26.00 (ISBN 0-8161-8524-7, Hall Reference). G K Hall.

--The Pursuit of Salvation: A Critical Guide to the Novels of Graham Greene. LC 84-50635. 1984. 18.50 (ISBN 0-87875-289-7). Whitston Pub.

Gaston, Herbert E. The Nonpartisan League. LC 75-316. (The Radical Tradition in America Ser.). 325p. 1975. Repr. of 1920 ed. 22.50 (ISBN 0-88355-219-1). Hyperion Conn.

Gaston, Hugh. A Complete Common-Place Book to the Holy Bible; or, a Scriptural Account of the Faith & Practices of Christians: Comprehending a Thorough Arrangement of the Various Texts of Scripture Bearing Upon the Doctrines, Duties, & C., of Revealed Religion. 1979. Repr. of 1847 ed. lib. bdg. 15.00 (ISBN 0-8482-4186-X). Norwood Edns.

Gaston, James. Planning the Air War, Four Men & Nine Days in 1941: An Inside Narrative. LC 82-600592. (Illus.). 131p. 1982. pap. 6.50 (ISBN 0-318-11814-9). Gov Printing Office.

Gaston, James C. London Poets & the American Revolution. LC 78-56499. 257p. 1979. 15.00x (ISBN 0-87875-162-9). Whitston Pub.

Gaston, Jan. Cultural Awareness Teaching Techniques. Clark, Raymond C., ed. LC 84-18007. (Pro Lingua Language Resource Handbook Ser.: No. 4). 96p. (Orig.). 1984. pap. text ed. 7.50x (ISBN 0-86647-010-7). Pro Lingua.

Gaston, Jerry. Originality & Competition in Science: A Study of the British High Energy Physics Community. LC 73-81313. 1973. 16.00x (ISBN 0-226-28429-8). U of Chicago Pr.

--The Reward System in British & American Science. LC 77-17404. (Science, Culture & Society Ser.). 204p. 1978. 40.50 (ISBN 0-471-29293-1, Pub. by Wiley-Interscience). Wiley.

Gaston, Jerry, ed. The Sociology of Science: Problems, Approaches, & Research. LC 78-70090. (Social & Behavioral Science Ser). (Illus.). 1979. text ed. 23.95x (ISBN 0-87589-397-X). Jossey-Bass.

Gaston, Jerry, jt. ed. see Merton, Robert K.

Gaston, Leroux. The Mystery of the Yellow Room: Extraordinary Adventures of Joseph Rouletabille, Reporter. LC 75-32762. (Literature of Mystery & Detection Ser.). 1976. Repr. of 1908 ed. 30.00x (ISBN 0-405-07883-8). Ayer Co Pubs.

Gaston, Margaret. Let's Light the Advent Candle. 16p. (Orig.). 1974. pap. 2.25 (ISBN 0-89536-139-6). CSS of Ohio.

Gaston, P. J. Care, Handling & Disposal of Dangerous Chemicals. rev. & enl. ed. 1970. pap. 15.00 (ISBN 0-685-11997-1). Heinman.

Gaston, Pat. The Love Arena. 400p. (Orig.). 1985. pap. 3.75 (ISBN 0-8439-2196-X, Leisure Bks). Dorchester Pub Co.

--Love to be Loved. 464p. (Orig.). 1982. pap. 3.50 (ISBN 0-8439-1141-7, Leisure Bks). Dorchester Pub Co.

Gaston, Paul M. The New South Creed: A Study in Southern Myth Making. LC 70-98640. x, 304p. 1976. pap. 7.95x (ISBN 0-8071-0256-3). La State U Pr.

--Women of Fair Hope. LC 84-103. 160p. 1984. text ed. 13.50x (ISBN 0-8203-0718-1). U of Ga Pr.

Gaston, Thomas, jt. auth. see Peacock, Frederick.

Gaston de, la Lavoissier see De La Lavoissier, Gaston.

Gastonguay, Alberte. La Jeune Franco-Americaine. (Novels by Franco-Americans in New England 1850-1940 Ser.). 65p. (Fr.). (gr. 10 up). 1980. pap. 4.50 (ISBN 0-911409-18-1). Natl Mat Dev.

Gastor, Joseph J., ed. see Adamiak, Richard.

Gastoue, Amedee. L' Art Gregorien. 3rd ed. LC 77-178576. (Fr.). Repr. of 1920 ed. 21.50 (ISBN 0-404-56607-3). AMS Pr.

--Musique et Liturgie: Le Graduel et l'Antiphonaire Romains; Histoire et Description. LC 70-178577. (Fr.). Repr. of 1913 ed. 32.50 (ISBN 0-404-56608-1). AMS Pr.

--Les Origines du chant romain: L'antiphonaire Gregorien. (Fr.). Repr. of 1907 ed. 32.50 (ISBN 0-404-56609-X). AMS Pr.

Gastrell, Francis. Notitia Cestriensis, 2 Vols. in 4. Repr. of 1850 ed. Set. 92.00 (ISBN 0-384-17700-X). Johnson Repr.

Gastroenterological Symposium, 3rd. The Sphincter of Oddi: Proceedings. Delmont, J., ed. (Illus.). 1977. 37.25 (ISBN 3-8055-2623-7). S Karger.

Gastrow, Hans & Stoeckhert, Klaus. Injection Molds: Examples for Design & Construction. LC 83-62286. 280p. 1983. text ed. 49.50 (ISBN 0-02-949440-0, Pub. by Hanser International). Macmillan.

Gastwirt, Harold P. Fraud Corruption & Holiness: The Controversy over the Supervision of Jewish Dietary Practice in New York City. LC 74-77649. 1974. 21.00x (ISBN 0-8046-9056-1, Pub. by Kennikat). Assoc Faculty Pr.

Gastwirt, Lawrence, jt. auth. see Bisio, Attilio.

Gaswirth, Marc & Whalen, Garry M. Collective Negotiations. (School Board Library Ser.). 122p. (Orig.). 1983. pap. 9.95 (ISBN 0-912337-01-X). NJ Schl Bds.

Gaszermann, Alreo. The Henry Madge Chronicles. (Illus.). 352p. 1985. 15.00 (ISBN 0-89962-485-5). Todd & Honeywell.

Gasztold, Carmen B. De see De Gasztold, Carmen B.

Gat, Dimitri. Nevsky's Demon. 304p. 1983. pap. 2.95 (ISBN 0-380-82248-2, 822482-2). Avon.

--Nevsky's Return. 240p. 1982. pap. 2.50 (ISBN 0-380-79863-8, 79863-8). Avon.

Gat, Jozzef. The Technique of Piano Playing. rev. 4th ed. Kleszky, Istvan, tr. from Hungarian. 1974. Repr. of 1964 ed. text ed. 46.00 (ISBN 0-569-00053-X). Boosey & Hawkes.

Gataker, Thomas. A Sparke Towards the Kindling of Sorrow for Zion. LC 76-57382. (English Experience Ser.: No. 800). 1977. Repr. of 1621 ed. lib. bdg. 7.00 (ISBN 90-221-0800-7). Walter J Johnson.

Gatch, Jean. School Makes Sense...Sometimes. LC 80-10281. (Books for Young Readers). 32p. 1980. 10.95 (ISBN 0-87705-494-0). Human Sci Pr.

Gatch, Milton McC. Preaching & Theology in Anglo-Saxon England: Aelfric & Wulfstan. LC 77-3277. 1979. 27.50x (ISBN 0-8020-5347-5). U of Toronto Pr.

Gatch, Milton McC. & Berkhout, Carl T., eds. Anglo-Saxon Scholarship: The First Three Centuries. 1982. lib. bdg. 26.00 (ISBN 0-8161-8321-X, Hall Reference). G K Hall.

Gatchel, R. J., et al. Behavioral Medicine & Clinical Psychology. (Handbook of Psychology & Health Ser.: Vol. 1). (Illus.). 560p. 1982. text ed. 49.95x (ISBN 0-89859-183-X). L Erlbaum Assocs.

Gatchel, Robert J. & Baum, Andrew. An Introduction to Health Psychology. 352p. 1983. pap. text ed. 17.95 (ISBN 0-394-34800-1, RanC). Random.

Gatchel, Robert J. & Mears, Frederick G. Personality: Theory, Assessment, & Research. LC 81-51856. 559p. 1982. text ed. 26.95 (ISBN 0-312-60229-4); Instr's. manual avail. St Martin.

Gatchel, Robert J., jt. auth. see Mears, Frederick G.

Gatchel, Robert J. & Price, Kenneth P., eds. Clinical Applications of Biofeedback: Appraisal & Status. LC 78-26959. (Pergamon General Psychology Ser.: Vol. 75). (Illus.). 1979. text ed. 36.00 (ISBN 0-08-022978-6); pap. text ed. 11.00 (ISBN 0-08-022977-8). Pergamon.

GATE. Report on the Field Phase of the Atlantic Tropical Experiment Operations. (GATE Report Ser.: No. 15). (Illus.). 148p. 1976. pap. 25.00 (ISBN 0-685-65022-7, W288, WMO). Unipub.

Gate, Ethel M. All the King's Trumpets. 1929. 29.50x (ISBN 0-686-51342-8). Elliots Bks.

Gatehouse, Anthony L. & Roper, Kenneth N. Film Assembly & Platemaking. (Illus.). 284p. 1980. 26.00 (ISBN 0-318-17930-X, 1506); members 13.00 (ISBN 0-318-17931-8). Graphic Arts Tech Found.

Gateley, Wilson Y., jt. auth. see Bitter, Gary G.

Gatell, Frank O. John Gorham Palfrey & the New England Conscience. LC 63-17200. 1963. 20.00x (ISBN 0-674-47700-6). Harvard U Pr.

Gatell, Frank O., jt. ed. see Weinstein, Allen.

Gatell, Frank O., et al. The Growth of American Politics: A Modern Reader. Incl. Vol. 1. Through Reconstruction. avail.; pap. 9.95x (ISBN 0-19-501545-2); Vol. 2. Since the Civil War. pap. 9.95x (ISBN 0-19-501547-9). 1972. pap. text ed. Oxford U Pr.

Gately, Geo. Here's Heathcliff. 128p. 1981. pap. 3.95 (ISBN 0-671-43089-0, Wallaby). S&S.

Gately, George. Heathcliff. (Heathcliff Cartoon Ser.: No. 1). (Illus.). 128p. (gr. 5 up). 1982. pap. 1.75 (ISBN 0-448-17335-2, Tempo). Ace Bks.

--Heathcliff, No. 1. 128p. 1984. pap. 1.95 (ISBN 0-441-32212-3). Ace Bks.

--Heathcliff & the Good Life. 128p. (Orig.). 1985. pap. 1.95 (ISBN 0-8125-6804-4, Dist. by Warner Pub Services & St. Martin). Tor Bks.

--Heathcliff at Home. 128p. (Orig.). 1985. pap. 1.95 (ISBN 0-8125-6802-8, Dist. by Warner Pub Services & St. Martin). Tor Bks.

--Heathcliff Banquet. 1982. pap. 3.95 (ISBN 0-448-12634-6). Ace Bks.

--Heathcliff Cleans House. 128p. 1985. pap. 1.95 (ISBN 0-441-32233-6). Ace Bks.

--Heathcliff Dines Out. 128p. 1985. pap. 1.95 (ISBN 0-441-32230-1). Ace Bks.

--Heathcliff Does It Again, No. 6. 128p. 1983. pap. 1.95 (ISBN 0-441-32206-9). Ace Bks.

--Heathcliff Does It Again, No. 6. 128p. 1985. pap. 1.95 (ISBN 0-441-32235-2). Ace Bks.

--Heathcliff Feast. 1982. pap. 4.95 (ISBN 0-441-32197-6). Ace Bks.

--Heathcliff First Prize! 128p. 1984. pap. 1.95 (ISBN 0-441-32221-2). Ace Bks.

--Heathcliff Gone Fishin. 128p. 1985. pap. 1.95 (ISBN 0-441-32231-X). Ace Bks.

--Heathcliff in Concert. 128p. 1983. pap. 5.95 (ISBN 0-441-32207-7). Ace Bks.

--Heathcliff: One, Two, Three, & You're Out. 128p. (Orig.). 1986. pap. 1.95 (ISBN 0-8125-6806-0, Dist. by Warner Pub Services & St. Martin). Tor Bks.

--Heathcliff Pigs Out, No. 9. 128p. 1984. pap. 2.25 (ISBN 0-441-32210-7). Ace Bks.

--Heathcliff Play by Play. 128p. 1984. pap. 4.95 (ISBN 0-441-32227-1). Ace Bks.

--Heathcliff Puzzle Sleuth, No. 3. 128p. 1982. pap. 1.75 (ISBN 0-448-16946-0). Ace Bks.

--Heathcliff Puzzlers, No. 2. (Activity Books Ser.). (Illus.). 1982. pap. 1.75 (ISBN 0-448-16830-8, Pub. by Tempo). Ace Bks.

--Heathcliff Rides Again. 128p. 1984. pap. 1.95 (ISBN 0-441-32216-6, Pub. by Tempo). Ace Bks.

--Heathcliff Round Three, No. 8. 128p. 1984. pap. 1.95 (ISBN 0-441-32209-3). Ace Bks.

--Heathcliff: Specialties, on the House. 1985. pap. 1.95 (ISBN 0-8125-6800-1). Tor Bks.

--Heathcliff Spins a Yarn. 128p. 1983. pap. 1.95 (ISBN 0-441-32204-2). Ace Bks.

--Heathcliff Spins a Yarn, No. 5. 123p. 1985. pap. 1.95 (ISBN 0-441-32223-9) (ISBN 0-317-31701-6). Ace Bks.

--Heathcliff Strikes Again, No. 7. 128p. 1983. pap. 2.25 (ISBN 0-441-32220-4). Ace Bks.

--Heathcliff Triple Threat. 128p. 1984. pap. 1.95 (ISBN 0-441-32215-8, Pub. by Charter Bks). Ace Bks.

--Heathcliff Triple Treat, No. 3. 128p. 1982. pap. 1.75 (ISBN 0-448-16945-2). Ace Bks.

--Heathcliff Wanted, No. 4. 128p. 1985. pap. 1.95 (ISBN 0-441-32211-5, Pub. by Charter Bks). Ace Bks.

--Heathcliff Working Out. 128p. 1985. pap. 4.95 (ISBN 0-441-32236-0) (ISBN 0-317-31755-5). Ace Bks.

--Heathcliff's Treasure Chest of Puzzles. (Illus.). 128p. 1982. pap. 1.75 (ISBN 0-448-16835-9, Pub. by Tempo). Ace Bks.

--Specialties on the House. (Heathcliff Ser.). 128p. (Orig.). 1985. pap. 1.95 (ISBN 0-8125-6800-1, Dist. by Pinnacle Bks, Warner Pub Services & St. Martin). Tor Bks.

--Sweet Savage Heathcliff. 128p. 1982. pap. 4.95 (ISBN 0-441-32198-4). Ace Bks.

--The World According to Heathcliff. pap. 4.95 (ISBN 0-671-50490-8). S&S.

Gately, James J. Major League Baseball: 1940-1949. 1986. pap. 5.00x (ISBN 0-916126-05-6). J J Gately.

Gatenby, Greg, ed. Whales: A Celebration. (Illus.). 252p. 1983. 49.00i (ISBN 0-316-30510-3). Little.

Gatenby, J. K. Park & Gatenby's Collection of Debts. 1981. 50.00x (ISBN 0-686-44517-1, Pub. by Oyez Longman Pub England). State Mutual Bk.

Gatenby, Rosemary. Whisper of Evil. 1982. pap. 2.50 (ISBN 0-425-04673-7). Berkley Pub.

Gater, George H. & Hiorns, F. R. The Parish of St. Martin-in-the Fields: Trafalgar Square & Neighborhood, Pt. 3. LC 70-37852. (London County Council. Survey of London: No. 20). Repr. of 1940 ed. 74.50 (ISBN 0-404-51670-X). AMS Pr.

Gater, George H. & Wheeler, E. P., eds. Parish of Saint Martin-In-the Fields: The Strand, Pt. 2. (London County Council. Survey of London: No. 18). Repr. of 1937 ed. 74.50 (ISBN 0-404-51668-8). AMS Pr.

Gaters. Die Lettische Sprache & Ihre Dialekte. 1977. 28.40x (ISBN 90-279-3126-7). Mouton.

Gates, A. I. Psychology of Reading & Spelling. LC 73-176798. (Columbia University. Teachers College. Contributions to Education: No. 129). Repr. of 1922 ed. 22.50 (ISBN 0-404-55129-7). AMS Pr.

Gates, Anita. Ninety Highest Paying Careers for the 80's. 176p. 1984. pap. 8.95 (ISBN 0-671-49869-X, Pub. by Monarch Pr). S&S.

--Ninety Most Promising Careers for the 80s. 192p. (Orig.). 1982. pap. 7.95 (ISBN 0-671-45272-X). Monarch Pr.

Gates, Anita & Klein, Shelley. Fringe Benefits: The Fifty Best Career Opportunities for Meeting Men. 1986. 16.95 (ISBN 0-917657-48-9). D I Fine.

Gates, Arnold. Nassau County in the Civil War. pap. 1.25 (ISBN 0-686-24668-3). Basin Pub.

Gates, Arnold, ed. Civil War Round Table of New York: Its History, Programs & Membership. 1976. pap. 1.25 (ISBN 0-685-73606-7). Civil War.

Gates, Arthur I. Interest & Ability in Reading. 264p. 1983. Repr. of 1931 ed. lib. bdg. 30.00 (ISBN 0-89987-323-5). Darby Bks.

Gates, Arthur I., et al. Gates-Peardon-LaClair Reading Exercises, 9 booklets. 2nd ed. Incl. Read & Remember - Book A. 64p. pap. text ed. 3.15x (ISBN 0-8077-5984-8); Read & Remember - Book B. 64p. pap. text ed. 3.15x (ISBN 0-8077-5985-6); Read & Remember - Book C. 64p. pap. text ed. 3.15x (ISBN 0-8077-5986-4); Read Beyond the Lines - Book A. 64p. pap. text ed. 3.15x (ISBN 0-8077-5987-2); Read Beyond the Lines - Book B. 64p. pap. text ed. 3.15x (ISBN 0-8077-5988-0); Read Beyond the Lines - Book C. 64p. pap. text ed. 3.15x (ISBN 0-8077-5989-9); Follow Directions - Book A. 64p. pap. text ed. 3.15x (ISBN 0-8077-5990-2); Follow Directions - Book B. 64p. pap. text ed. 3.15 (ISBN 0-8077-5991-0); Follow Directions - Book C. 64p. pap. text ed. 3.15x (ISBN 0-8077-5992-9). 1982. pap. text ed. 2.50x (ISBN 0-8077-5993-7). Tchrs Coll.

Gates, B. E. How to Represent Yourself Before the IRS. 192p. 1984. 9.95 (ISBN 0-07-022991-0). McGraw.

Gates, Brian, ed. Afro-Caribbean Religions. 1981. 40.00x (ISBN 0-686-81323-5, Pub. by Ward Lock England). State Mutual Bk.

Gates, Bronwen. Banisteriopsis & Diplopterys: Malpighiaceae. (Flora Neotropica Monograph 30). (Illus.). 238p. 1982. pap. 35.00x (ISBN 0-89327-238-8). NY Botanical.

Gates, Bruce C., et al. Chemistry of Catalytic Processes. (McGraw Hill Series in Chemical Engineering). (Illus.). 1978. text ed. 46.00 (ISBN 0-07-022987-2). McGraw.

Gates, Bruce L. Social Program Administration: The Implementation of Social Policy. (Illus.). 1980. text ed. 29.95 (ISBN 0-13-817767-8). P-H.

Gates, Bryan. How to Represent Your Client Before the IRS. 256p. 1982. 29.95 (ISBN 0-07-022993-7). McGraw.

Gates, C. M., jt. auth. see Johansen, Dorothy O.

Gates, Calvin, jt. auth. see Fleischer, Neil T.

Gates, Charles. From Cremation to Inhumation: Burial Practices at Ialysos & Kameiros during the Mid-Archaic Period, ca. 625-525 B.C. (Occasional Papers: No. 11). (Illus.). 91p. 1983. pap. 9.00x (ISBN 0-917956-39-7). UCLA Arch.

Gates, Charles M. First Century at the University of Washington, 1861-1961. LC 61-14498. (Illus.). 270p. 1961. 17.50x (ISBN 0-295-73782-4). U of Wash Pr.

Gates, Charles M., ed. Five Fur Traders of the Northwest. LC 65-63528. 296p. 1965. Repr. of 1933 ed. 7.25 (ISBN 0-87351-024-0). Minn Hist.

--Messages of the Governors of the Territory of Washington to the Legislative Assembly, 1854-1889. LC 41-52447. (Illus.). 298p. 1940. 20.00x (ISBN 0-295-95130-3, UWPSSXII). U of Wash Pr.

Gates, D. M. & Schmere, R. B., eds. Perspectives of Biophysical Ecology. LC 74-17493. (Illus.). 1975. 55.00 (ISBN 0-387-06743-4). Springer-Verlag.

Gates, David. Graphic Design Studio Procedures. rev. ed. (Illus.). 183p. 1984. 19.95 (ISBN 0-912526-30-0). Lib Res.

--Lettering for Reproduction. (Illus.). 192p. 1969. 18.50 (ISBN 0-8230-2751-1). Watson-Guptill.

--Type. 208p. 1973. 18.50 (ISBN 0-8230-5522-1). Watson-Guptill.

Gates, David A. Seasons of the Salt Marsh. LC 74-27956. 128p. 1975. 9.95 (ISBN 0-85699-121-X). Chatham Pr.

Gates, David M. Energy & Ecology. LC 84-27471. (Illus.). 300p. 1985. text ed. 40.00x (ISBN 0-87893-230-5); pap. text ed. 25.00x (ISBN 0-87893-231-3). Sinauer Assoc.

Gates, Don. I Thought I Heard a Baby Cry. 54p. 1983. pap. 4.25 (ISBN 0-940248-13-1). Guild Pr.

Gates, Doris. Blue Willow. LC 40-32435. (gr. 4-6). 1976. pap. 3.50 (ISBN 0-14-030924-1, VS30, Puffin). Penguin.

--Blue Willow. LC 68-1275. (Illus.). 176p. (gr. 4-7). 1940. 9.95 (ISBN 0-670-17557-9). Viking.

--A Fair Wind for Troy. (Greek Myths Ser.). (Illus.). (gr. 4-6). 1976. PLB 9.95 (ISBN 0-670-30505-7, Puffin). Viking.

--A Fair Wind for Troy. (Puffin Story Bks.). (Illus.). 96p. 1984. pap. 2.95 (ISBN 0-14-031718-X, Puffin). Penguin.

--A Filly for Melinda. LC 83-14617. 180p. (gr. 3-7). 1984. 11.95 (ISBN 0-670-31328-9, Viking Kestrel). Viking.

--The Golden God: Apollo. (Greek Myths Ser). (Illus.). 128p. (gr. 4-6). 1973. PLB 9.95 (ISBN 0-670-34412-5). Viking.

--The Golden God: Apollo. (Illus.). 110p. (gr. 3-7). 1983. pap. 2.95 (ISBN 0-14-031647-7, Puffin). Penguin.

--Lord of the Sky: Zeus. (Greek Myths Ser). (Illus.). 128p. (gr. 4-6). 1972. PLB 9.95 (ISBN 0-670-44051-5). Viking.

--Lord of the Sky: Zeus. (Greek Myths Ser.). (Illus.). (gr. 3-7). 1982. pap. 2.95 (ISBN 0-14-031532-2, Puffin). Penguin.

--Mightiest of Mortals: Heracles. (Greek Myths Ser.). (Illus.). 96p. (gr. 4-6). 1975. PLB 9.95 (ISBN 0-670-47556-4). Viking.

--Mightiest of Mortals: Heracles. (Puffin Story Bks.). 96p. (gr. 3-7). 1984. pap. 2.95 (ISBN 0-14-031531-4, Puffin). Penguin.

--A Morgan for Melinda. 189p. (gr. 3-7). 1982. pap. 3.95 (ISBN 0-14-031524-1, Puffin). Penguin.

--A Morgan for Melinda. LC 79-19786. (gr. 3-7). 1980. 9.95 (ISBN 0-670-48932-8). Viking.

--Two Queens of Heaven: Aphrodite & Demeter. (Greek Myths Ser). (Illus.). 96p. (gr. 4-6). 1974. PLB 9.95 (ISBN 0-670-73680-5). Viking.

--Two Queens of Heaven: Aphrodite & Demeter. (Illus.). 94p. (gr. 3-7). 1983. pap. 2.95 (ISBN 0-14-031646-9, Puffin). Penguin.

--The Warrior Goddess: Athena. (Greek Myths Ser). (Illus.). 128p. (gr. 4-6). 1972. PLB 11.95 (ISBN 0-670-74996-6). Viking.

--The Warrior Goddess: Athena. (Greek Myths Ser.). (Illus.). (gr. 3-7). 1982. pap. 2.95 (ISBN 0-14-031530-6, Puffin). Penguin.

Gates, Eleanor M. End of the Affair: The Collapse of the Anglo-French Alliance. LC 80-23585. 496p. 1981. 29.50x (ISBN 0-520-04292-1). U of Cal Pr.

Gates, Elgin. Gun Digest Book of Metallic Silhouette Shooting. LC 79-50059. (Illus.). 256p. 1979. pap. 11.95 (ISBN 0-695-81273-4). DBI.

Gates, Ernest S. Meteorology & Climatology. 4th ed. (Illus.). 1972. pap. text ed. 24.95x (ISBN 0-245-52869-5). Intl Ideas.

Gates, Frederick T. Chapters in My Life. LC 76-47956. 1977. 10.95 (ISBN 0-02-911350-4). Free Pr.

Gates, Frieda. Easy-to-Make Costumes. (Illus.). (gr. 1-3). 1981. pap. 3.95 (ISBN 0-13-222562-X, Pub. by Treehouse). P-H.

--Easy-to-Make Monster Masks & Disguises. (Illus.). (gr. 1-3). 1981. pap. 3.95 (ISBN 0-13-222794-0, Pub. by Treehouse). P-H.

--Easy-to-Make Puppets. (Illus.). (gr. 1-3). 1981. pap. 3.95 (ISBN 0-13-222596-4, Pub. by Treehouse). P-H.

--Glove, Mitten & Sock Puppets. LC 78-3068. (Illus.). (gr. k-3). 1978. 5.95 (ISBN 0-8027-6326-X); PLB 5.85 (ISBN 0-8027-6327-8). Walker & Co.

--Monsters & Ghouls: Costumes & Lore. LC 79-5385. (Illus.). 48p. (gr. 4-9). 1980. PLB 8.85 (ISBN 0-8027-6379-0). Walker & Co.

--North American Indian Masks. (Illus.). 64p. 1982. 8.95 (ISBN 0-8027-6462-2); lib. bdg. 9.85 (ISBN 0-8027-6463-0). Walker & Co.

Gates, G. E. Burmese Earthworms: An Introduction to the Systematics & Biology of Megadrile Oligochaetes with Special Reference to Southeast Asia. LC 72-83461. (Transactions Ser.: Vol. 62, Pt. 7). (Illus.). 1972. pap. 5.00 (ISBN 0-87169-627-4). Am Philos.

Gates, Gary F. Atlas of Abdominal Ultrasonography in Children. (Illus.). 1978. text ed. 35.00 (ISBN 0-443-08015-1). Churchill.

Gates, Gary P., jt. auth. see Wallace, Mike.

Gates, Geffrey. The Defence of Militarie Profession. LC 72-5996. (English Experience Ser.: No. 521). 64p. 1973. Repr. of 1579 ed. 7.00 (ISBN 90-221-0521-0). Walter J Johnson.

Gates, George A. Current Therapy in Otolaryngology: Head & Neck Surgery 1982-1983. 391p. 1982. text ed. 48.00 (ISBN 0-941158-00-4, D1770-7). Mosby.

Gates, Gilman C. Saybrook at the Mouth of the Connecticut River: The First One Hundred Years. 1935. 49.50x (ISBN 0-685-89040-6). Elliots Bks.

Gates, Grace H. The Model City of the New South: Anniston Alabama, 1872-1900. LC 77-94272. (Illus.). 320p. 1983. Repr. of 1978 ed. 12.95 (ISBN 0-87397-134-5). Strode.

Gates, Henry L., ed. see Wilson, Harriet E.

Gates, Henry L., Jr., ed. Black Literature & Literary Theory. 350p. 1984. 29.95 (ISBN 0-416-37230-9, NO. 4088); pap. 10.95 (ISBN 0-416-37240-6, NO. 4089). Methuen Inc.

Gates, Henry L., Jr., jt. ed. see Davis, Charles T.

Gates, Hilary. Directory of Library & Information Retrieval Software for Microcomputers. LC 84-24738. 59p. 1985. pap. text ed. 17.95 (ISBN 0-566-03531-6). Gower Pub Co.

Gates, Hill, jt. ed. see Ahern, Emily M.

Gates, Hubert B. Never to Rise Again. LC 82-90622. 122p. 1983. 7.95 (ISBN 0-533-05539-3). Vantage.

Gates, Janet & Jones, Charles O. Legislative Turnover. 1957. write for info. U of SD Gov Res Bur.

Gates, Jean K. Guide to the Use of Libraries & Information Sources. 5th ed. (Illus.). 288p. 1983. text ed. 21.95 (ISBN 0-07-022990-2); pap. text ed. 16.95 (ISBN 0-07-022989-9). McGraw.

Gates, John E. An Analysis of the Lexicographic Resources Used by American Biblical Scholars Today. LC 72-88670. (Society of Bibical Literature. Dissertation Ser.: No. 8). pap. 49.00 (ISBN 0-317-10146-3, 2017664). Bks Demand UMI.

Gates, John E., jt. auth. see Boatner, Maxine.

Gates, John E., jt. auth. see Boatner, Maxine T.

Gates, John K. A Touch of Nostalgia: A Glimpse of America's Past. LC 80-84010. (Illus.). 192p. (Orig.). 1980. pap. 14.95 (ISBN 0-9605168-0-8). Photographit.

Gates, John M. Schoolbooks & Krags: The United States Army in the Philippines, 1898-1902. LC 77-140917. (Contributions in Military History: No. 3). 320p. 1973. lib. bdg. 29.95 (ISBN 0-8371-5818-4, GSK/). Greenwood.

Gates, Josephine. The Live Doll's House Party. LC 6-28222. (Illus.). 102p. 1981. Repr. of 1906 ed. lib. bdg. 25.00 (ISBN 0-940070-02-2). Doll Works.

--The Live Doll's Party Days. LC 10-26376. (Illus.). 159p. 1981. Repr. of 1910 ed. lib. bdg. 25.00 (ISBN 0-940070-03-0). Doll Works.

--The Live Doll's Play Days. LC 8-25990. (Illus.). 108p. Repr. of 1908 ed. lib. bdg. 25.00 (ISBN 0-940070-04-9). Doll Works.

--The Story of Live Dolls. LC 1-24915. (Illus.). 103p. 1981. Repr. of 1901 ed. lib. bdg. 25.00 (ISBN 0-940070-05-7). Doll Works.

--The Story of the Lost Doll. LC 5-83020. (Illus.). 108p. 1981. Repr. of 1905 ed. lib. bdg. 25.00 (ISBN 0-940070-06-5). Doll Works.

--The Story of the Three Dolls. LC 5-38492. (Illus.). 148p. 1981. Repr. of 1905 ed. lib. bdg. 25.00 (ISBN 0-940070-07-3). Doll Works.

Gates, June. Basic Foods. 2nd ed. LC 80-26409. 636p. 1981. text ed. 28.95 (ISBN 0-03-049846-5, HoltC). HR&W.

Gates, Larry W. Dwelling in Scullerland. LC 85-50093. 205p. (Orig.). 1985. pap. text ed. 7.95 (ISBN 0-938232-68-1). Winston-Derek.

Gates, Lauren B., jt. auth. see Rohe, William M.

Gates, Lewis E. Studies & Appreciations. facs. ed. LC 76-134079. (Essay Index Reprint Ser). 1900. 18.00 (ISBN 0-8369-1927-0). Ayer Co Pubs.

--Three Studies in Literature: Jeffrey, Newman, Arnold. LC 72-195408. 1899. lib. bdg. 15.00 (ISBN 0-8414-4640-7). Folcroft.

Gates, Lewis E., ed. see Jeffrey, Francis.

Gates, Margaret, jt. ed. see Chapman, Jane R.

Gates, Merle E., et al. An Illustrated Guide to the Deciduous Trees of Wichita. (Illus.). 124p. (Orig.). 1983. pap. 5.95 (ISBN 0-9613426-0-9). Janus Pubns.

Gates, Merrill E. Sidney Lanier: A Paper. LC 77-14263. 1977. lib. bdg. 9.50 (ISBN 0-8414-2001-7). Folcroft.

Gates, N., jt. auth. see Innes, A. J.

Gates, Norman. A Checklist of the Letters of Richard Aldington. LC 76-21638. 186p. 1977. 9.85x (ISBN 0-8093-0781-2). S Ill U Pr.

Gates, Paul W. Fifty Million Acres. Bruchey, Stuart, ed. LC 76-56733. (Management of Public Lands in the U. S. Ser.). (Illus.). 1979. Repr. of 1954 ed. lib. bdg. 25.50x (ISBN 0-405-11332-3). Ayer Co Pubs.

--The Illinois Central Railroad & Its Colonization Work. (American Economy Ser). 1969. Repr. of 1934 ed. 26.00 (ISBN 0-384-17710-7). Johnson Repr.

--Land Policies in Kern County. 35p. 1978. pap. 2.00 (ISBN 0-943500-02-8). Kern Historical.

--The Wisconsin Pine Lands of Cornell University: A Study in Land Policy & Absentee Ownership. LC 43-14336. (Illus.). 265p. 1965. Repr. of 1943 ed. 7.50 (ISBN 0-87020-034-8). State Hist Soc Wis.

Gates, Paul W. & Swenson, Robert W. History of Public Land Law Development. Bruchey, Stuart, ed. LC 78-53547. (Management of Public Lands in the U. S. Ser.). (Illus.). 1979. Repr. of 1968 ed. lib. bdg. 55.50x (ISBN 0-405-11375-7). Ayer Co Pubs.

--History of Public Land Law Development. LC 78-21519. Repr. of 1968 ed. 45.00 (ISBN 0-89201-042-8). Zenger Pub.

Gates, Paul W. & Bruchey, Stuart, eds. The Fruits of Land Speculation: An Original Anthology. LC 78-56694. (Management of Public Lands in the U. S. Ser.). (Illus.). 1979. lib. bdg. 34.50x (ISBN 0-405-11359-5). Ayer Co Pubs.

--Public Land Policies: An Original Anthology. LC 78-56714. (Management of Public Lands in the U. S. Ser.). 1979. lib. bdg. 40.00x (ISBN 0-405-11360-9). Ayer Co Pubs.

--The Rape of the Indian Lands: An Original Anthology. LC 78-56698. (Management of Public Lands in the U. S. Ser.). 1979. lib. bdg. 23.00x (ISBN 0-405-11358-7). Ayer Co Pubs.

Gates, Paul W., et al. Four Persistent Issues: Essays on California's Land Ownership Concentration, Water Deficits, Sub-State Regionalism, & Congressional Leadership. LC 78-17964. 1978. pap. 5.75x (ISBN 0-87772-257-9). Inst Gov Stud Berk.

Gates, Ralph P. The Yellow Earth. 1983. pap. 3.00 (ISBN 0-686-40181-6). Basin Pub.

Gates, Richard. Conservation. LC 81-38482. (New True Bks.). (Illus.). 48p. (gr. k-4). 1982. PLB 10.60 (ISBN 0-516-01618-0). Childrens.

Gates, Robert A., ed. Eighteenth & Nineteenth Century American Drama. 300p. 1985. text ed. 34.50 (ISBN 0-8290-1151-X); pap. text ed. 19.95x (ISBN 0-8290-1152-8). Irvington.

Gates, Ronda, jt. auth. see Parker, Valerie.

Gates, Sam & Frankel, Mark D. Divorce in Pennsylvania. 2nd ed. (Illus.). 101p. 1983. 10.00 (ISBN 0-87387-088-3). Shumway.

Gates, Susa Y. & Widtsoe, Leah D. The Life Story of Brigham Young. facsimile ed. LC 74-164602. (Select Bibliographies Reprint Ser). Repr. of 1930 ed. 24.00 (ISBN 0-8369-5886-1). Ayer Co Pubs.

Gates, Theodore R. & Linden, Fabian. Production Costs Here & Abroad: A Comparative Study of the Experience of American Manufacturers. Bruchey, Stuart & Bruchey, Eleanor, eds. LC 76-5012. (American Business Abroad Ser.). (Illus.). 1976. 17.00x (ISBN 0-405-09280-6). Ayer Co Pubs.

Gates, Virginia E., ed. Helping Hands: The Key to Success. 3 ring notebook 20.00x (ISBN 0-88035-041-5). Human Kinetics.

Gates, Wende D. & Meckel, Gail M. Newborn Beauty. LC 79-56263. 352p. 1980. 15.95 (ISBN 0-670-57310-8). Viking.

Gates, Wende D., jt. auth. see Fox, Michael W.

Gates, William. An Outline Dictionary of Maya Glyphs. LC 77-92481. (Illus.). 1978. pap. 4.50 (ISBN 0-486-23618-8). Dover.

Gates, William, ed. see Landa, Diego De.

Gates, William E. Commentary on the Maya-Tzental Codex Perez. (Harvard University Peabody Museum of Archaeology & Ethnology Papers). pap. 15.00 (ISBN 0-527-01206-8). Kraus Repr.

Gates, Zethyl. Mariano Medina: Colorado Mountain Man. (Illus.). 1981. pap. 5.95 (ISBN 0-933472-51-X). Johnson Bks.

Gatewood, E. L. see Hull, Clark L.

Gatewood, Lael C., jt. auth. see Ackerman, Eugene.

Gatewood, Willard B. Eugene Clyde Brooks: Educator & Public Servant. LC 60-13604. pap. 73.80 (ISBN 0-317-28824-5, 2017903). Bks Demand UMI.

Gatewood, Willard B., ed. Freeman of Color: The Autobiography of Willis Augustus Hodges. LC 82-2032. (Illus.). 168p. 1982. text ed. 13.95x (ISBN 0-87049-353-1). U of Tenn Pr.

Gatewood, Willard B., Jr. Black Americans & the White Man's Burden, 1898-1903. LC 75-9945. (Blacks in the New World Ser). 363p. 1975. 22.50x (ISBN 0-252-00475-2). U of Ill Pr.

--Smoked Yankees & the Struggle for Empire: Letters from Negro Soldiers, 1898-1902. LC 78-146006. pap. 84.80 (ISBN 0-317-27556-9, 2014922). Bks Demand UMI.

Gatewood, Willard B., Jr., jt. ed. see Donovan, Timothy P.

Gatewood, Willard B., Jr., ed. see Knox, George L.

Gatfield, G. Guide to Printed Books & Manuscripts Relating to English & Foreign Heraldry & Genealogy. 59.95 (ISBN 0-8490-0269-9). Gordon Pr.

Gatfield, George. Guide to Printed Books & Manuscripts Relating to English & Foreign Heraldry & Genealogy. 1966. Repr. of 1892 ed. 45.00x (ISBN 0-8103-3121-7). Gale.

Gath, Ann. Down's Syndrome & the Family: The Early Years. 1978. 27.00 (ISBN 0-12-277450-7). Acad Pr.

Gathercole, Patricia M. Tension in Boccaccio: Boccaccio & the Fine Arts. LC 74-28151. (Romance Monographs: No. 14). 1975. 15.00x (ISBN 84-399-3503-X). Romance.

Gatherer, N. Songs & Ballads of Dundee. (Illus.). 150p. 1985. text ed. 14.25x (ISBN 0-85976-146-0, Pub. by Donald Scotland). Humanities.

Gatherer, W. A. A Study of English: Learning & Teaching the Language. (Orig.). 1980. pap. text ed. 13.50x (ISBN 0-435-10369-5). Heinemann Ed.

Gatherer, W. A. & Jeffs, R. B. Language Skills Through the Secondary Curriculum. Morgan, Michael, ed. 221p. 1980. 35.00x (ISBN 0-7157-1955-6, Pub. by H McDougall UK). State Mutual Bk.

Gatherer, W. A. & Wallace, B. Educating for Tomorrow: A Lothian Perspective. 142p. 1984. 25.00x (ISBN 0-7157-1976-9, Pub. by H McDougall UK). State Mutual Bk.

Gatherer, W. A., tr. see Buchanan, George.

Gatheru, Mugo. A Child of Two Worlds. (African Writers Ser.: No. 20). 230p. 1966. pap. text ed. 4.50x (ISBN 0-435-90020-X). Heinemann Ed.

Gathje, Curtis. The Disco Kid. LC 78-24078. (Triumph Ser.). (Illus.). (gr. 5 up). 1979. PLB 8.90 s&l (ISBN 0-531-02895-X). Watts.

Gathorne Hardy, G. Norway. LC 75-18358. 324p. 1975. Repr. of 1925 ed. lib. bdg. 18.25x (ISBN 0-8371-8325-1, GANO). Greenwood.

Gathorne-Hardy, Geoffrey M., et al, trs. see Wergeland, Henrik A.

Gathorne-Hardy, John. Operation Peeg. LC 74-8908. (gr. 2-5). 1974. 11.49i (ISBN 0-397-31594-5). Lipp Jr Bks.

Gathorne-Hardy, Jonathan. The Airship Ladyship Adventure. LC 7-54218. 1977. 11.49i (ISBN 0-397-31727-1). Lipp Jr Bks.

--The Centre of the Universe Is 18 Baedekerstrasse. 224p. 1985. 15.95 (ISBN 0-241-11492-6, Pub. by Hamish Hamilton England). David & Charles.

--Jane's Adventures In & Out of the Book. LC 80-29185. (Illus.). 192p. 1981. 13.95 (ISBN 0-87951-122-2). Overlook Pr.

Gathorne-Hardy, Robert & Williams, William P., eds. Bibliography of the Writings of Jeremy Taylor to 1700: With a Section of Tayloriana. LC 71-149932. 159p. 1971. 20.00 (ISBN 0-87580-023-8). N Ill U Pr.

Gathreaux, S. A., Jr., ed. Animal Migration, Orientation & Navigation. 1981. 55.00 (ISBN 0-12-277750-6). Acad Pr.

Gathrid, Erin, created by. A Zoo for You. LC 84-52555. (The Learning Language Ser.). (Illus.). 28p. (ps). 1985. bds. 4.95 (ISBN 0-915391-04-X, Pub. by Mad Hatter Bks). Slawson Comm.

Gathrid, Erin B., ed. see Gathrid, Jonathan.

Gathrid, Jonathan. Alphabots. Gathrid, Erin B., ed. (Illus.). 28p. (ps). bds. 4.95 (ISBN 0-915391-01-5, Pub. by Mad Hatter Bks). Slawson Comm.

Gati, Charles, ed. see Symposium on the Comparative Study of Communist Foreign Policy.

Gati, Charles, jt. ed. see Triska, Jan F.

Gati, T., et al, eds. Nutrition-Digestion-Metabolism: Proceedings of the 28th International Congress of Physiological Sciences, Budapest, 1980. LC 80-42185. (Advances in Physiological Sciences Ser.: Vol. 12). (Illus.). 400p. 1981. 55.00 (ISBN 0-08-026825-0). Pergamon.

Gati, Toby Trister, ed. The U. S., the U. N., & the Management of Global Change. (A Una-Usa Book). 392p. 1983. 40.00x (ISBN 0-686-45562-2); pap. 18.50x (ISBN 0-8147-2987-8). NYU Pr.

Gatignol, T. Theorie Cinetique des Gaz a Repartition Descrete De Vitesses. 206p. 1975. pap. 14.70 (ISBN 0-387-07156-3). Springer-Verlag.

Gatignon, Hubert, jt. auth. see Larreche, Jean-C.

Gatin, Charles Louis. Dictionnaire Aide Memoire de Botanique. 867p. (Fr.). 1924. 99.50 (ISBN 0-686-56785-4, M-6581, Pub. by Lechevalier). French & Eur.

Gatje, Charles T. & Gatje, John F. A MAP for Fractions. Marcos, Rafael, tr. (Orig., Span.). (gr. 5 up). 1981. pap. text ed. 1.95 (ISBN 0-937534-07-2). G&G Pubs.

--A Math Activity Packet for Fractions. (Orig.). 1976. pap. text ed. 1.95 (ISBN 0-937534-01-3). G&G Pubs.

Gatje, Helmut. The Qur'an & Its Exegesis: Selected Texts with Classical & Modern Muslim Interpretations. Welch, Alford T., ed. LC 74-82847. (Islamic World Ser.). 1977. 44.00x (ISBN 0-520-02833-3). U of Cal Pr.

Gatje, John F., jt. auth. see Gatje, Charles T.

Gatland & Davies. Future Cities. (World of the Future Ser.). (gr. 5-9). 1979. (Usborne-Hayes); PLB 12.95 (ISBN 0-88110-004-8); pap. 4.95 (ISBN 0-86020-239-9). EDC.

Gatland & Jeffries. Book of the Future. (World of the Future Ser.). (gr. 5-9). 1979. 12.95 (ISBN 0-86020-290-9, Usborne-Hayes). EDC.

--Robots. (World of the Future Ser.). (gr. 5-9). 1979. (Usborne-Hayes); PLB 12.95 (ISBN 0-88110-003-X); pap. 4.95 (ISBN 0-86020-241-0). EDC.

--Star Travel. (World of the Future Ser.). (gr. 5-9). 1979. (Usborne-Hayes); PLB 12.95 (ISBN 0-88110-005-6); pap. 4.95 (ISBN 0-86020-243-7). EDC.

Gatland, Bruce, jt. auth. see Fisher, Jack.

Gatland, H. B. Electronic Engineering Applications of Two Port Systems. 1976. pap. 25.00 (ISBN 0-08-019866-X). Pergamon.

Gatland, Kenneth. The Illustrated Encyclopedia of Space Technology: A Comprehensive History of Space Exploration. 288p. 1981. 24.95 (ISBN 0-517-54258-7, Harmony). Crown.

--The Young Scientist Book of Spaceflight. LC 78-17504. (Young Scientist Ser.). (gr. 4-5). 1978. text ed. 7.95 (ISBN 0-88436-526-3, 35469). EMC.

Gatland, Kenneth, jt. auth. see Jefferis, David.

Gatley, George. Heathcliff Rides Again, No. 2. 128p. 1983. pap. 1.95 (ISBN 0-441-32401-0). Ace Bks.

Gatlin, Carl. Petroleum Engineering: Drilling & Well Completion. 1960. ref. ed. 42.95 (ISBN 0-13-662155-4). P-H.

Gatlin, Lila. Eternal Marriage. 1985. 15.95 (ISBN 0-87949-252-X). Ashley Bks.

Gatlin, Lila L. Information Theory & the Living System. LC 76-187030. (Molecular Biology Ser.). (Illus.). 210p. 1972. 24.00x (ISBN 0-231-03634-5). Columbia U Pr.

Gatlin, Marilyn. Love Thoughts from Home: Messages of Light. 61p. 1983. pap. 5.50 (ISBN 0-943734-04-5). Ocean Tree Bks.

--When I Listen: A Listener's Little Book. LC 85-60794. (Illus.). 68p. 1985. pap. 5.50 (ISBN 0-317-19521-2). Ocean Tree Bks.

Gatner, jt. auth. see Fein.

Gatner, Elliott S., jt. auth. see Cordasco, Francesco.

Gatos, Harry C., ed. Properties of Elemental & Compound Semiconductors: Proceedings. LC 60-10585. (Metallurgical Society Conference Ser.: Vol. 5). pap. 88.30 (ISBN 0-317-08021-0, 2000668). Bks Demand UMI.

Gatos, Luis M. The Cat Lover's Look Book. (Odd Books for Odd Moments). (Illus.). 80p. (Orig.). 1981. pap. 4.95 cancelled (ISBN 0-938338-08-0). Winds World Pr.

Gatov, Elisabeth S. Widows in the Dark: Rescuing Your Financial Position. 127p. 1985. pap. 8.95 (ISBN 0-943004-02-0). Common Knowledge.

Gatrell. Hardy Tess Manuscripts. 1985. lib. bdg. 125.00 (ISBN 0-8240-7476-9). Garland Pub.

--Thomas Hardy Return of the Native. (Hardy Manuscripts Ser.). 1985. lib. bdg. 150.00 (ISBN 0-8240-7475-0). Garland Pub.

Gatrell, Anthony C. Distance & Space: A Geographical Perspective. (Illus.). 1983. 24.95x (ISBN 0-19-874128-6); pap. 12.95x (ISBN 0-19-874129-4). Oxford U Pr.

Gatrell, S., jt. auth. see Bareham, T.

Gatrell, Simon, ed. see Hardy, Thomas.

Gatrell, V. A., et al, eds. Crime & the Law: The Social History of Crime in Western Europe since 1500. 393p. 1984. 42.50x (ISBN 0-905118-54-5, Pub. by Salem Acad). Merrimack Pub Cir.

Gatschet, A. S. The Karankawa Indians, the Coast People of Texas. (MU PMP). 1891. 14.00 (ISBN 0-527-01184-3). Kraus Repr.

--Migration Legend of the Creek Indians with a Linguistic Historical & Ethnographic Introduction, 2 Vols. in 1. LC 5-13733. Repr. of 1888 ed. 34.00 (ISBN 0-527-32700-X). Kraus Repr.

Gatschet, Albert. Ethnographic Sketch of the Klamath Indians of Southwestern Oregon. facsimile ed. 120p. pap. 8.95 (ISBN 0-685-20313-1, S118). Shorey.

Gatschet, Albert S. Migration Legend of the Creek Indians. LC 72-83460. (Library of Aboriginal American Literature: No. 4). Repr. of 1884 ed. 30.00 (ISBN 0-404-52184-3). AMS Pr.

Gatt, Shimon, jt. ed. see Desnick, Robert J.

Gatt, Shimon, et al, eds. Enzymes of Lipid Metabolism. LC 78-866. 805p. 1978. 89.50x (ISBN 0-306-40002-2; Plenum Pr). Plenum Pub.

Gattegno, Caleb. The Adolescent & His Self. 1962. pap. 4.95 (ISBN 0-685-47811-4). Ed Solutions.

--Algebricks Exercise Workbooks 1-6. 1970. pap. 1.10 (ISBN 0-87825-001-8). Ed Solutions.

--Arithmetics. (Illus.). 28p. 1971. pap. 2.15 (ISBN 0-87825-019-0). Ed Solutions.

--Background & Principles: On Words in Color. 82p. 1962. pap. 2.15 (ISBN 0-87825-065-4). Ed Solutions.

--Book of Stories. (Illus.). 99p. 1964. pap. 2.00 (ISBN 0-87825-060-3). Ed Solutions.

--The Common Sense of Teaching Foreign Languages. (The Common Sense of Teaching Ser.). 1976. 6.95 (ISBN 0-87825-071-9). Ed Solutions.

--The Common Sense of Teaching Mathematics. (Common Sense of Teaching Ser.). (Illus.). 144p. 1974. pap. 6.95 (ISBN 0-87825-024-7). Ed Solutions.

--The Common Sense of Teaching Reading & Writing. (Common Sense of Teaching Ser.). 1985. pap. text ed. 12.95 (ISBN 0-87825-181-2). Ed Solutions.

--Eight Tales. (Illus.). 109p. 1968. pap. 3.50 (ISBN 0-87825-026-3). Ed Solutions.

--English Fidel Spelling Kit. (gr. k-12). 1978. kit 45.95 (ISBN 0-87825-139-1). Ed Solutions.

--Evolution & Memory. 1976. pap. 10.00 (ISBN 0-87825-072-7). Ed Solutions.

--An Experimental School. 1973. pap. 4.95 (ISBN 0-87825-022-0). Ed Solutions.

--Forms of Energy. (The Study of Energy. Vol. 1). 1963. 3.85 (ISBN 0-85225-682-5). Ed Solutions.

--Geoboard Geometry. 1971. pap. 1.25 (ISBN 0-87825-020-4). Ed Solutions.

--Infused Reading for French: A Microcomputer Program. (gr. k-12). 1983. incl. two 2 diskettes for Apple II 100.00 (ISBN 0-87825-185-5). Ed Solutions.

--Infused Reading for Spanish: A Microcomputer Program. (gr. k-12). 1982. incl. one diskette for Apple II 70.00 (ISBN 0-87825-183-9). Ed Solutions.

--Learning & Teaching of Foreign Languages. 45p. 1985. pap. 4.95 (ISBN 0-87825-186-3). Ed Solutions.

--Leocolor. (Orig., Span.). (gr. k-12). 1971. Word Charts. pap. 45.00 (ISBN 0-87825-094-8); Mini Word Charts & Phonic Code Charts. pap. 4.20 (ISBN 0-87825-089-1); Hojas de Trabajo. pap. 0.25 (ISBN 0-87825-088-3); Libro 1. pap. 0.45 (ISBN 0-87825-090-5); Libro 2. pap. 0.55 (ISBN 0-87825-091-3); Para Formar Palabras. pap. 2.85 (ISBN 0-87825-092-1). Ed Solutions.

--Mathematics Textbooks, 7 bks. Incl. Bk. 1. Study of Numbers up to 20. 102p. pap. text ed. 1.65 (ISBN 0-87825-011-5); Bk. 2. Study of Numbers up to 1,000. 147p. pap. text ed. 2.50 (ISBN 0-87825-012-3); Bk. 3. Applied Arithmetic. 53p. pap. text ed. 1.65 (ISBN 0-87825-013-1); Bk. 4. Fractions, Decimals, Percentages. 65p. pap. text ed. 1.65 (ISBN 0-87825-014-X); Bk. 5. Study of Numbers. 83p. pap. text ed. 1.65 (ISBN 0-87825-015-8); Bk. 6. Applied Mathematics. 104p. pap. 1.95 (ISBN 0-87825-003-4); Bk. 7. Algebra & Geometry. 92p. pap. text ed. 2.20 (ISBN 0-87825-017-4). pap. Ed Solutions.

--Mathware: A Math Workshop for Home Use Kit. 1973. 38.00 (ISBN 0-87825-010-7). Ed Solutions.

--The Mind Teaches the Brain, 3 vols. 1975. pap. 5.00 ea.; Vol. 1. pap. (ISBN 0-87825-067-0); Vol. 2. pap. (ISBN 0-685-64852-4); Vol. 3. pap. (ISBN 0-87825-069-7). Ed Solutions.

--Notes for Parents: On the Teaching of Reading. 52p. 1977. pap. 3.00 (ISBN 0-87825-021-2). Ed Solutions.

--Notes on the Gattegno Approach to Math. 31p. 1973. 1.65 (ISBN 0-87825-043-3). Ed Solutions.

--Now Johnny Can Do Arithmetic. 82p. 1971. pap. 3.50 (ISBN 0-87825-018-2). Ed Solutions.

--Of Boys & Girls. 1975. pap. 10.00 (ISBN 0-87825-030-1). Ed Solutions.

--On Being Freer. 1975. pap. 10.00 (ISBN 0-87825-070-0). Ed Solutions.

--On Death. 1978. 8.00 (ISBN 0-87825-145-6). Ed Solutions.

--On Love. 1977. 10.00 (ISBN 0-317-14966-0). Ed Solutions.

--On Spelling. 28p. 1977. pap. text ed. 3.00 (ISBN 0-87825-138-3). Ed Solutions.

--A Reading Lab Kit. 1973. 35.00 (ISBN 0-87825-009-3). Ed Solutions.

--Science of Education, 3 vols. Bd. with Facts of Awareness (ISBN 0-87825-125-1); Affectivity & Learning (ISBN 0-87825-073-5); Awareness of Awareness (ISBN 0-87825-126-X). 1977. 3.00 ea. Ed Solutions.

--The Silent Way for English. rev. ed. (Orig.). (gr. k-12). 1977. tchr's ed 6.95; Worksheets. 2.00 (ISBN 0-87825-086-7); Wall Pictures. 10.00 (ISBN 0-87825-044-1); Word Charts. 60.00 (ISBN 0-87825-133-2); Fidel Charts. 40.00 (ISBN 0-87825-134-0); Sound Color Charts. 5.00 (ISBN 0-87825-137-5); Mini Word Chart Cards. 5.25 (ISBN 0-87825-138-3); Mini Fidel Card. 1.75 (ISBN 0-87825-142-1); one thousand sentences 3.50 (ISBN 0-87825-007-7). Ed Solutions.

--The Silent Way for French. (Orig.). (gr. k-12). 1965. tchr's. ed 6.95; Hille Phrases. 2.95 (ISBN 0-87825-082-4); Trente-Six Instantanes. 2.95 (ISBN 0-87825-099-9); Huit Contes. 3.50 (ISBN 0-87825-095-6); Worksheets. 2.00 (ISBN 0-87825-083-2); Wall Pictures. 10.00 (ISBN 0-87825-052-2); Word Charts. 55.00 (ISBN 0-87825-075-1); Fidel Charts. 30.00 (ISBN 0-87825-078-6); Expanded Fidel. 5.00 (ISBN 0-87825-098-0). Ed Solutions.

--The Silent Way for Spanish. (Orig.). (gr. k-12). 1965. tchr's. ed 6.95; Mil Frases. 2.95 (ISBN 0-87825-047-6); Narraciones Breves. 2.95 (ISBN 0-87825-048-4); Ocho Cuentos. 3.50 (ISBN 0-87825-049-2); Worksheets. 2.00 (ISBN 0-87825-084-0); Wall Pictures. 10.00 (ISBN 0-87825-045-X); Word Charts. 25.00 (ISBN 0-87825-076-X); Spanish Fidel (European) 5.00 (ISBN 0-87825-079-4); Spanish Fidel (S. American) 5.00 (ISBN 0-87825-080-8). Ed Solutions.

--Teaching Foreign Languages in Schools: The Silent Way. 144p. 1972. pap. text ed. 5.95 (ISBN 0-87825-046-8). Ed Solutions.

--Towards a Visual Culture. 1971. pap. 1.65 (ISBN 0-380-01455-6, 11940, Discus). Avon.

--Towards a Visual Culture: Educating Through Television. LC 76-91461. 192p. 1969. 6.95; pap. 1.65 (ISBN 0-685-46935-2). Ed Solutions.

--The Universe of Babies: In the Beginning There Were No Words. 133p. 1973. pap. 4.95 (ISBN 0-87825-023-9). Ed Solutions.

--Visible & Tangible Math: A Microcomputer Program. 105p. (gr. k-12). 1982. incl. 12 diskettes for Apple II, tchr's. manual 25.00 (ISBN 0-87825-182-0). Ed Solutions.

--What We Owe Children. LC 72-106612. 1970. 6.95; pap. 1.65 (ISBN 0-685-64853-2). Ed Solutions.

--The White Canary: An Illustrated Tale. 31p. 1968. 6.95 (ISBN 0-85225-550-0). Ed Solutions.

--Who Cares About Health? 166p. 1979. pap. text ed. 12.50 (ISBN 0-87825-149-9). Ed Solutions.

--Words in Color. rev. ed. (Orig.). (gr. k-12). 1977. tchr's. ed. 12.95 (ISBN 0-87825-181-2); Word Charts. 100.00 (ISBN 0-87825-131-6); Phonic Code Charts. 40.00 (ISBN 0-87825-132-4); Book R-0. 0.25 (ISBN 0-87825-127-8); Book R-1. 0.65 (ISBN 0-87825-128-6); Book R-2. 1.50 (ISBN 0-87825-129-4); Book R-3. 1.50 (ISBN 0-87825-130-8); Worksheets 1-7. 3.65 (ISBN 0-87825-178-2); Worksheets 8-14. 1.65 (ISBN 0-87825-059-X). Ed Solutions.

Gattegno, Caleb & Educational Solutions' Staff. Math Mini-Tests. Incl. Primary 1. Concept-Practice Kit. 89.25 (ISBN 0-87825-162-6); Concept-Practice Kit. 57.75 (ISBN 0-87825-168-5); Extra tchrs. ed. 5.80 (ISBN 0-87825-203-7); Primary 2. Computation-Concept-Practice Kit. 99.75 (ISBN 0-87825-163-4); Concept-Practice Kit. 65.10 (ISBN 0-87825-169-3); Extra tchrs. ed. 5.80 (ISBN 0-87825-204-5); Primary 3. Computation-Concept-Practice Kit. 126.00 (ISBN 0-87825-164-2); Concept-Practice Kit. 84.00 (ISBN 0-87825-170-7); Extra tchrs. ed. 6.85 (ISBN 0-87825-205-3); Elementary. Computation-Concept-Practice Kit. 157.50 (ISBN 0-87825-165-0); Concept-Practice Kit. 105.00 (ISBN 0-87825-171-5); Extra tchrs. ed. 7.90 (ISBN 0-87825-206-1); Intermediate. Concept-Practice Kit. 126.00 (ISBN 0-87825-172-3); Extra tchrs. ed. 6.85 (ISBN 0-87825-207-X); Elementary. Computation (Remedial) Kit. 60.50 (ISBN 0-87825-200-2); Extra tchrs. ed. 4.20 (ISBN 0-87825-209-6); Intermediate. Computation (Remedial) Kit. 52.50 (ISBN 0-87825-201-0); Extra tchrs. ed. 3.15 (ISBN 0-87825-210-X); Multiplication. Computation (Remedial) Kit. 14.70 (ISBN 0-87825-202-9); Extra tchrs. ed. 2.10 (ISBN 0-87825-211-8). 1981p. (gr. k-9). Ed Solutions.

Gattegno, Caleb & Iniguez, Patricia. El Dominio de la Ortografia Espanola. 200p. (Span.). 1978. pap. text ed. 6.00 (ISBN 0-87825-146-4). Ed Solutions.

Gatten, Aileen, et al, trs. see Konishi, Jin'ichi.

Gatter, R. S. Gatter & Vallance's "Art Nouveau Jewelry", 2 vols. Set. pap. 9.00. Vol. 1 (ISBN 0-87282-071-8). Vol. 2 (ISBN 0-87282-115-3). CHB-ALF.

Gatter, Robert A. A Practical Handbook of Joint Fluid Analysis. LC 83-18704. (Illus.). 1984. text ed. 22.50 (ISBN 0-8121-0902-3). Lea & Febiger.

Gatterdam, R. W., ed. see Conference on Group Theory, University of Wisconsin-Parkside, 1972.

Gatterdam, Ronald W., jt. auth. see Fossum, Timothy V.

Gattermann, Gunter, jt. ed. see Loveday, Anthony J.

Gatti, Art. UFO: Encounters of the Fourth Kind. (Orig.). 1978. pap. 2.25 (ISBN 0-89083-336-2). Zebra.

Gatti, Daniel J., jt. auth. see Gatti, Richard M.

Gatti, David. Ready-to-Use Sale Announcements. (Dover Clip Art Pictorial Archive Ser.). (Illus.). 64p. (Orig.). 1980. pap. 2.95 (ISBN 0-486-24012-6). Dover.

Gatti, Enzo. Rich Church-Poor Church? O'Connell, Matthew, tr. from It. LC 74-77432. Orig. Title: Couli che Sa Il Dolore Dell'uomo. 138p. (Orig.). 1974. 4.95 (ISBN 0-88344-437-2). Orbis Bks.

Gatti, Florence M., jt. auth. see Cortes, Juan B.

Gatti, Guido M. Ildebrando Pizzetti. Moore, David, tr. LC 78-66891. (Encore Music Editions Ser.). (Illus.). 1979. Repr. of 1951 ed. 17.50 (ISBN 0-88355-741-X). Hyperion Conn.

Gatti, James, ed. The Limits of Government Regulation. LC 81-12858. 1981. 31.00 (ISBN 0-12-277620-8); pap. 14.50 (ISBN 0-12-277622-4). Acad Pr.

Gatti, Richard A. & Swift, M. Ataxia-Telangiectasia. 368p. 1985. write for info. (ISBN 0-8451-0309-1). A R Liss.

Gatti, Richard M. & Gatti, Daniel J. New Encyclopedic Dictionary of School Law. 312p. 1983. 32.50 (ISBN 0-13-612580-8, Parker). P-H.

Gatti-Casazza, Guilio. Memories of the Opera. (Opera Library Ser.). 1980. 19.95 (ISBN 0-7145-3518-4); pap. 9.95 (ISBN 0-7145-3665-2). Riverrun NY.

Gattiker, Irvin. Teaching Instrumental Sight Reading. LC 80-26482. 240p. cancelled 18.95 (ISBN 0-13-893156-9, Parker). P-H.

Gattin, Dana. God Is the Answer. 1984. 4.95 (ISBN 0-317-03625-4). Unity School.

Gattinger, E. Die Lyrik Lydgates. 1965. pap. 12.00 (ISBN 0-384-17720-4). Johnson Repr.

Gattinger, R., jt. ed. see McDiarmid, D. R.

Gattinoni, C. T., tr. see Jones, E. Stanley.

Gatto, John. Monarch Notes on Kesey's One Flew Over the Cuckoos Nest. 1975. pap. 3.50 (ISBN 0-671-00966-4). Monarch Pr.

Gatto, Joseph, jt. auth. see Brommer, Gerald.

Gatto, Joseph, et al. Exploring Visual Design. Brommer, Gerald F. & Horn, George F., eds. LC 78-55398. (Illus.). 1978. text ed. 16.95 (ISBN 0-87192-101-4). Davis Mass.

Gatto, Joseph A. Cities. Brommer, Gerald F. & Horn, George F., eds. LC 76-50509. (Insights to Art Ser.). (Illus.). 1977. 10.95 (ISBN 0-87192-087-5). Davis Mass.

--Color & Value: Design Elements. LC 74-82682. (Concepts of Design Ser.). (Illus.). 80p. (gr. 7up). 1974. 9.95 (ISBN 0-87192-065-4). Davis Mass.

--Emphasis: A Design Principle. LC 75-21112. (Concepts of Design Ser.). (Illus.). 80p. (gr. 7-12). 1975. 9.95 (ISBN 0-87192-075-1). Davis Mass.

Gatto, Joseph A., jt. auth. see Brommer, Gerald F.

Gatto, R., ed. Developments in High-Energy Physics: Italian Physical Society. (Course 54). 1973. 82.00 (ISBN 0-12-368854-X). Acad Pr.

--Scale & Conformal Symmetry in Hadron Physics. LC 73-4324. pap. 60.00 (ISBN 0-317-09058-5, 2011957). Bks Demand UMI.

Gatto, R. R., jt. ed. see Costa, G.

Gatton, John S., et al. The W. Hugh Peal Collection at the University of Kentucky. (The Kentucky Review Ser.: Vol. IV, No. 1). 237p. 1982. pap. text ed. 3.50 (ISBN 0-910123-00-4). U KY Lib Assocs.

Gattorna, John. Channels of Distribution. 1978. 79.00x (ISBN 0-905440-85-4, Pub. by MCB Pubns). State Mutual Bk.

--Handbook of Physical Distribution Management. 3rd ed. 576p. 1983. text ed. 56.95x (ISBN 0-566-02219-2). Gower Pub Co.

Gattorna, John, jt. auth. see Christopher, Martin.

Gatt-Rutter, J. A. Writers & Politics in Modern Italy. LC 78-18829. (Writers & Politics Ser.). 66p. 1979. 13.50x (ISBN 0-8419-0413-8); pap. text ed. 9.50x (ISBN 0-8419-0416-2). Holmes & Meier.

Gatty, A. A Key to Tennyson's "In Memoriam". LC 72-139. (Studies in Tennyson, No. 27). 1972. Repr. of 1881 ed. lib. bdg. 45.95x (ISBN 0-8383-1399-X). Haskell.

Gatty, Alfred. Key to Lord Tennyson's "In Memoriam". LC 73-13782. 1911. lib. bdg. 10.00 (ISBN 0-8414-4432-3). Folcroft.

Gatty, Harold. Finding Your Way on Land & Sea: Reading Nature's Maps. LC 82-25136. (Illus.). 272p. 1983. 8.95 (ISBN 0-8289-0502-9). Greene.

Gatty, Horatia K. Juliana Horatia Ewing & Her Books. 1979. Repr. of 1885 ed. lib. bdg. 25.00 (ISBN 0-8482-4184-3). Norwood Edns.

Gatty, Margaret, jt. auth. see Witherforce, Samuel.

Gatty, Mrs.; see Avery, Gillian.

Gatty, Oliver & Spooner, E. C. The Electrode Potential Behaviour of Corroding Metals in Aqueous Solutions. (Illus.). Repr. of 1938 ed. 40.00 (ISBN 0-384-17730-1). Johnson Repr.

Gatwood, Dwight D. Techniques for Including Musical Examples in Theses & Dissertations: A Handbook. LC 70-18258. (Illus.). 37p. (Orig.). 1970. pap. 3.95 (ISBN 0-934082-09-X, Pub. by Nashville Res Pubns TN). Theodore Front.

Gatwood, Lynn E. Devi & the Spouse Goddess: Women, Sexuality & Marriage in India. LC 85-61077. 225p. 1985. 16.00 (ISBN 0-913215-01-5). Riverdale Co.

Gatz, Konrad, et al, eds. Curtain Wall Construction. Stern, David & Winkler, Felix, trs. from Ger. LC 67-29398. (Illus.). 1965. 64.50x (ISBN 0-89197-718-X). Irvington.

Gatz, Margaret, jt. ed. see Smyer, Michael A.

Gatza, James, jt. auth. see Gantt, Michael D.

Gatza, Jim, et al. Decision Making in Administration: Text, Critical Incidents & Cases. 1979. pap. text ed. 13.95 (ISBN 0-7216-4056-7). SCP.

Gatzke, Hans W. Germany & the United States: A "Special Relationship?". (American Foreign Policy Library). (Illus.). 330p. 1980. 18.50x (ISBN 0-674-35326-9). Harvard U Pr.

--Germany's Drive to the West: (Drang Nach Weten) A Study of Germany's Western War Aims During the First World War. LC 78-6668. 1978. Repr. of 1967 ed. lib. bdg. 24.50x (ISBN 0-313-20507-8, GAGD). Greenwood.

Gatzke, Hans W., jt. auth. see Strayer, Joseph R.

Gau, George W. Determinants of Return in Real Estate Investment & the Role of Real Estate Management. (Orig.). 1983. pap. text ed. 16.95 (ISBN 0-317-02673-9). Inst Real Estate.

Gau, George W., jt. ed. see Goldberg, Michael A.

Gau, John. The Richt Vay to the Kingdome of Heuine. Mitchell, A. F., ed. Repr. of 1888 ed. 24.00 (ISBN 0-384-17750-6). Johnson Repr.

Gauba, K. L. The Assassination of Mahatma Gandhi. 1969. pap. 3.50 (ISBN 0-88253-140-9). Ind-US Inc.

--Famous & Historical Trials. (Orient Paperbacks Ser.). 186p. 1972. pap. 2.75 (ISBN 0-88253-039-9). Ind-US Inc.

Gaubatz, John. The Moot Court Book. 211p. (Orig.). 1980. pap. text ed. 14.00 (ISBN 0-672-83854-0). Michie Co.

Gaubatz, John T. & Bloom, Ira M. Estates, Trusts, & Taxes: Cases & Materials on the Wealth Transmission Process. LC 82-72902. (Analysis & Skills Ser.). 1983. write for info. Bender.

Gaube, Heinz. Iranian Cities. LC 77-25748. (Hagop Kevorkian Series on Near Eastern Art & Civilization). (Illus.). 1979. 30.00x (ISBN 0-8147-2971-1). NYU Pr.

Gauch, Hugh G. Inorganic Plant Nutrition. LC 72-76542. 488p. 1972. 49.50 (ISBN 0-87933-003-1). Van Nos Reinhold.

Gauch, Hugh G., Jr. Multivariate Analysis in Community Ecology. LC 81-9974. (Cambridge Studies in Ecology: No. 1). (Illus.). 300p. 1982. 44.50 (ISBN 0-521-23820-X); pap. 16.95 (ISBN 0-521-28240-3). Cambridge U Pr.

Gauch, Patricia L. Christina Katerina & the Box. (Illus.). 48p. 1980. pap. 2.95 (ISBN 0-698-20524-3, Coward). Putnam Pub Group.

--Fridays. (gr. 7-9). 1981. pap. 1.95 (ISBN 0-671-45356-4). Archway.

--Fridays. LC 79-17047. (gr. 7-12). 1979. 9.95 (ISBN 0-399-20703-1, Putnam). Putnam Pub Group.

--The Green of Me. 160p. (gr. 7 up). Repr. of 1978 ed. 2.25 (ISBN 0-448-47763-7). Putnam Pub Group.

--Kate Alone. 112p. (gr. 5-12). 1980. 7.95 (ISBN 0-399-20738-4, Putnam). Putnam Pub Group.

--Morelli's Game. 160p. (gr. 6 up). 1981. 9.95 (ISBN 0-399-20825-9). Putnam Pub Group.

--Morelli's Game. (gr. 7-10). 1982. pap. 2.25 (ISBN 0-671-45803-5). Archway.

--Night Talks. 160p. (gr. 5 up). 1983. pap. 10.95 (ISBN 0-399-20911-5, Putnam). Putnam Pub Group.

--Night Talks. 176p. (gr. 7-9). 1984. pap. 1.95 (ISBN 0-671-49635-2). Archway.

--This Time, Tempe Wick? LC 74-79706. (Illus.). 48p. (gr. 2-6). 1974. 6.95 (ISBN 0-698-20300-3, Coward). Putnam Pub Group.

--The Year the Summer Died. 160p. (gr. 7 up). 1985. 12.95 (ISBN 0-399-21114-4, Putnam). Putnam Pub Group.

Gauchat, Dorothy & Lyons, Arthur. All God's Children. 224p. 1985. pap. 2.50 (ISBN 0-345-31988-5). Ballantine.

Gauchhwal, B. S. Concept of Perfection in the Teachings of Kant & the Gita. 1967. 4.95 (ISBN 0-89684-186-3). Orient Bk Dist.

Gauckler, E., jt. auth. see Dejerine, Joseph J.

Gaudeamus. A Leicestershire Garland for Europa Cantat 6. 1976. 6.00 (ISBN 0-19-343615-9). Oxford U Pr.

Gaudefroy-Demombynes, Jean. Les Jugements allemands sur la musique francaise au XVIIIe siecle. LC 76-43918. (Music & Theatre in France in the 17th & 18th Centuries). Repr. of 1941 ed. 34.50 (ISBN 0-404-60159-6). AMS Pr.

Gaudefroy-Demombynes, Maurice. Muslim Institutions. LC 84-12953. 216p. 1984. Repr. of 1950 ed. lib. bdg. 35.00x (ISBN 0-313-24287-9, GAMU). Greenwood.

--Le Pelerinage a la Mekke: Etude D'histoire Religieuse. LC 77-10690. (Studies in Islamic History: No. 7). viii, 332p. 1978. Repr. of 1923 ed. lib. bdg. 27.50x (ISBN 0-87991-456-4). Porcupine Pr.

Gaudel, Andre. L' Indochine Francaise en Face du Japon. LC 73-179197. (Fr.). Repr. of 1947 ed. 19.00 (ISBN 0-404-54826-1). AMS Pr.

Gaudemet, Eugene. L' Abbe Galiani (1728-1787) et la Question du Commerce des Bles a la Fin du Regne de Louis XV. LC 72-87294. 233p. 1972. Repr. of 1899 ed. lib. bdg. 24.00 (ISBN 0-8337-1294-2). B Franklin.

Gaudemet, Jean. La Formation du Droit Canonique Medieval. 382p. 1980. 60.00x (ISBN 0-86078-056-2, Pub. by Variorum). State Mutual Bk.

Gauden, Christa. Weekend Cycling: A Selection of Fully Planned Scenic Routes for Easy Touring. 256p. (Orig.). 1984. pap. 6.95 (ISBN 0-600-20444-8, Pub. by Auto Assn-British Tourist Authority England). Merrimack Pub Cir.

Gaudet, A. John. Petits Mots Croises. (gr. 8-10). pap. text ed. 3.25x ans. key avail. (ISBN 0-88334-160-3); ans. key avail. Ind Sch Pr.

Gaudet, J. L. Organization of Inland Fisheries Administration in Europe. Rev. ed. (European inland Fisheries Advisory Commission (EIFAC): Technical Papers: No. 5). 86p. (Eng. & Fr.). 1974. pap. 7.50 (ISBN 92-5-102055-8, F1718, FAO). Unipub.

Gaudet, J. L., jt. auth. see Norling, I.

Gaudet, Marcia G. Tales from the Levee: The Folklore of St. John the Baptist Parish. (Louisiana Folklife Ser.). 116p. 1984. 10.95 (ISBN 0-940984-21-0). U of SW LA Ctr LA Studies.

Gaudet, Patricia K. The Body Beautiful. Clark, Norman L., ed. 400p. (Orig.). 1985. pap. 3.95 (ISBN 0-9614306-0-5). Five M Pubs.

Gaudiani, Claire & Herron, Carol. Strategies for Development of Foreign Language & Literature Programs. 338p. 1984. pap. 19.50x (ISBN 0-87352-124-2). Modern Lang.

Gaudiani, Claire L. The Cabaret Poetry of Theophile De Viau: Texts & Traditions. (Etudes Litteraires Francaises Ser.: No. 13). 156p. (Orig.). 1980. pap. 22.00x (ISBN 3-87808-892-2). Benjamins North Am.

Gaudier, Martin. La Borinquena: Origins & Documents on the Anthem of Puerto Rico. (Puerto Rico Ser.). 1979. lib. bdg. 59.95 (ISBN 0-8490-2875-2). Gordon Pr.

Gaudilat, Louis. Lexique Officiel des lampes Radios. 21st ed. 96p. (Fr.). 1963. pap. 12.50 (ISBN 0-686-56766-8, M-6263). French & Eur.

Gaudin, Lois S. Bibliography of Franco-Spanish Literary Relations Until the Nineteeth Century. LC 74-178937. (Institute of French Studies Publications). 71p. 1973. Repr. of 1930 ed. lib. bdg. 18.50 (ISBN 0-8337-4125-X). B Franklin.

Gaudin, Thierry. The Secret Code: The Lost & Hidden Language of the Bible, Vol. 1. LC 85-70031. 300p. (Orig.). 1985. pap. 12.95 (ISBN 0-933357-05-2). Bret Pubns.

Gaudiose, Dorothy. Prophet of the People: A Biography of Padre Pio. LC 74-7123. 1977. pap. 5.95 (ISBN 0-8189-0351-1). Alba.

Gaudon, J., ed. see Hugo, V.

Gaudon, Jean, jt. auth. see Verlaine, Paul.

Gaudon, Jean, ed. see Hugo, Victor.

Gaudreau, Carmen. Bernard et Bridget: a la cabane a sucre. (Illus.). 40p. (Fr.). (gr. k-1). 1979. pap. text ed. 1.50 (ISBN 0-911409-47-5); of 53 2x2 slides 13.25 set (ISBN 0-686-42727-0). Natl Mat Dev.

Gaudry, Albert. Essai Paleontologie Philosophique: Ouvage Faisant Echainementd Monde Animal les Temps Geologiques: Essay in Philosophical Paleontology: a Sequel to the Interconnections of the Animal World in Geologic Time. Gould, Stephen J., ed. LC 79-8331. (History of Paleontology Ser.). (Illus., Fr.). 1980. Repr. of 1896 ed. lib. bdg. 21.00x (ISBN 0-405-12712-X). Ayer Co Pubs.

Gaudry, G. I., jt. auth. see Edwards, R. E.

Gaudry, Marc, jt. ed. see Florian, Michael.

Gaudy, Anthony & Gaudy, Elizabeth. Microbiology for Environment Science Engineers. (Water Resources & Environmental Engineering Ser.). (Illus.). 704p. 1980. 45.00 (ISBN 0-07-023035-8). McGraw.

Gaudy, Elizabeth, jt. auth. see Gaudy, Anthony.

Gauer, Harold. Bury Me Not. (Orig.). 1981. pap. 2.25 (ISBN 0-505-51605-5, Pub. by Tower Bks). Dorchester Pub Co.

Gauer, Werner. Die Tongefaesse aus Dem Brunnen Unterm Stadion-Nordwall und Im Suedost-Gebiet. (Olympische Forschungen: Vol. 8). (Illus.). 254p. 1975. pap. 47.20x (ISBN 3-11-004602-4). De Gruyter.

Gaugas, Joseph M., ed. Polyamines in Biomedical Research. LC 79-40651. 474p. 1980. 109.95 (ISBN 0-471-27629-4, Pub. by Wiley-Interscience). Wiley.

Gauger, Jaclyn S. Orientation to Hearing Aids. 1978. 9.45 (ISBN 0-88200-132-9, N6362). Alexander Graham.

Gauger, Marguerite E. The Modifiability of Response to Taste Stimuli in the Preschool Child. LC 77-176799. (Columbia University. Teachers College. Contributions to Education: No. 348). Repr. of 1929 ed. 22.50 (ISBN 0-404-55348-6). AMS Pr.

Gauger, William, jt. auth. see Arthur, Lindsay G.

Gaugh, Harry. Willem de Kooning. LC 83-2787. (Modern Masters Ser.). (Illus.). 136p. 1983. 29.95 (ISBN 0-89659-332-0); pap. 16.95 (ISBN 0-89659-333-9). Abbeville Pr.

Gaugh, Harry F. The Vital Gesture: Franz Kline. 192p. 1985. 39.95 (ISBN 0-89659-571-4). Abbeville Pr.

Gaughan, Edward D. Introduction to Analysis. 2nd ed. LC 75-16601. (Contemporary Undergraduate Mathematics Ser.). 1975. text ed. 23.25 pub net (ISBN 0-8185-0172-3). Brooks-Cole.

Gaughan, Edward D. & Hall, Carl E. College Algebra & Trigonometry. LC 83-15470. (Mathematics Ser.). 550p. 1983. text ed. 22.75 pub net (ISBN 0-534-02777-6). Brooks-Cole.

Gaughan, Edward D. & Scribner, Edmund A. Introduction to Business Mathematics. LC 85-9087. 450p. 1985. 27.00 (ISBN 0-534-05238-X). Wadsworth Pub.

Gaughran, Stephen J., jt. auth. see Fuori, William M.

Gauguier, Beverly, jt. auth. see Gauquier, Anthony.

Gauguin, Paul. Drawings of Gauguin. Longstreet, Stephen, ed. (Master Draughtsman Ser). (Illus., Orig.). treasure trove bdg. 9.95x (ISBN 0-87505-009-3); pap. 4.95 (ISBN 0-87505-162-6). Borden.

--Gauguin: L'Oeuvre Grave. rev. ed. Guerin, Marcel, ed. (Illus.). 272p. (Fr.). 1980. 100.00 (ISBN 0-915346-37-0). A Wofsy Fine Arts.

--Intimate Journals. Brooks, Van W., tr. LC 8-12207. 1970. pap. 6.95 (ISBN 0-87140-216-5). Liveright.

--The Intimate Journals of Paul Gauguin. 180p. (Orig.). 1985. pap. 14.95 (ISBN 0-7103-0105-7). Routledge & Kegan.

--NOA-NOA. Theis, O. F., tr. LC 20-621. 1976. Repr. 17.50 (ISBN 0-89097-006-8). Archer Edns.

--Noa Noa. 148p. (Orig.). 1957. pap. 5.95 (ISBN 0-374-50040-1). FS&G.

--Noa Noa. Theis, O. F., tr. 1978. Repr. of 1920 ed. 25.00 (ISBN 0-8492-4913-9). R West.

--Noa Noa: The Tahitian Journal. (Fine Art Ser.). 96p. 1985. pap. 3.95 (ISBN 0-486-24859-3). Dover.

--Paul Gauguin: Letters to His Wife & Friends. Malingue, Maurice, ed. Stenning, Henry J., tr. LC 83-45768. Repr. of 1949 ed. 30.00 (ISBN 0-404-20106-7). AMS Pr.

--The Writings of a Savage. Guerin, Daniel, ed. Levieux, Eleanor, tr. 1978. 24.95 (ISBN 0-670-79173-3). Viking.

Gauhar, Altaf. Translation from the Quran. 16.95 (ISBN 0-686-18511-0). Kazi Pubns.

Gauhar, Altaf, ed. The Challenge of Islam. 393p. 1980. (Pub. by Islamic Council of Europe England); pap. 14.95 (ISBN 0-906041-03-1). Intl Spec Bk.

--Regional Integration: The Latin American Experience. 1985. pap. 28.00 (ISBN 0-317-28064-3). Westview.

--The Rich & the Poor: Development, Negotiations & Cooperation in an Assessment. 273p. 1985. pap. 12.00 (ISBN 0-8133-0292-7). Westview.

--Third World Strategy: Economic & Political Cohesion in the South. 238p. 1983. 28.95 (ISBN 0-03-069713-1); pap. 14.95 (ISBN 0-03-069712-3). Praeger.

Gaujean, Gerard, ed. see Backer, Desaix.

Gaukroger, Stephen. Explanatory Structures-Concepts of Explanation in Early Physics & Philosophy. (Harvester Studies in Philosophy Ser.: No. 6). 1978. text ed. 29.00x (ISBN 0-391-00899-4). Humanities.

Gaukroger, Stephen, ed. Descartes: Philosophy, Mathematics & Physics. (Harvester Readings in the History of Science & Philosophy Ser.: No. 1). 329p. 1980. 30.00x (ISBN 0-389-20084-0). B&N Imports.

Gaul, Henri & Millau, Christian. The Best of New York. 384p. 1982. 5.98 (ISBN 0-517-54770-8); pap. 3.98 (ISBN 0-517-54771-6). Crown.

Gauld. Differential Topology: An Introduction. (Texts & Monographs in Pure & Applied Mathematics). 312p. 1982. 39.75 (ISBN 0-8247-1709-0). Dekker.

Gauld, Alan. Mediumship & Survival. (Illus.). 288p. 1983. 18.95 (ISBN 0-434-90656-5, Pub. by W Heinemann Ltd). David & Charles.

--Mediumship & Survival: A Century of Investigations. 287p. 1984. pap. 6.95 (ISBN 0-586-08429-0, Granada England). Academy Chi Pubs.

Gauld, Alan & Cornell, A. D. Poltergeists. (Illus.). 1979. 26.95 (ISBN 0-7100-0185-1). Routledge & Kegan.

Gauld, I. D. An Introduction to the Ichneumonidae of Australia. (Illus.). 420p. 1984. pap. 80.00x (ISBN 0-565-00896-X, Pub. by Brit Mus Nat Hist England). Sabbot-Natural Hist Bks.

Gauld, I. D. & Mitchell, P. A. The Taxonomy, Distribution & Host Preferences of African Parasitic Wasps of the Subfamily Ophioninae (Hymenoptera; Inchenumonidae) 1978. 90.00x (ISBN 0-85198-409-6, Pub. by CAb Bks England). State Mutual Bk.

--The Taxonomy, Distribution & Host Preferences of Indo-Papuan Paraditic Wasps of the Subfamily Ophioninae (Hymenoptera; Ichneumonidae) 611p. 1981. 89.00 (ISBN 0-85198-482-7, Pub. by CAB Bks England). State Mutual Bk.

Gaulden, Ray. High Country Showdown. 1979. pap. 1.50 (ISBN 0-505-51438-9, Pub. by Tower Bks). Dorchester Pub Co.

--A Man Named Murdo & Rough Road to Denver. 1981. pap. 2.50 (ISBN 0-89083-771-6). Zebra.

--Shadow of the Rope. 1979. pap. 1.50 (ISBN 0-505-51439-7, Pub. by Tower Bks). Dorchester Pub Co.

--The Vengeful Men. 1979. pap. 1.75 (ISBN 0-505-51449-4, Pub. by Tower Bks). Dorchester Pub Co.

Gauldie, Enid. The Scottish Country Miller Seventeen Hundred to Nineteen Hundred: A History of Water-Powered Meal Milling in Scotland. xi, 254p. 1981. text ed. 38.00x (ISBN 0-85976-067-7, Pub. by J. Donald England). Humanities.

Gauldin, Robert. A Practical Approach to Sixteenth Century Counterpoint. (Illus.). 304p. 1985. text ed. 26.95 (ISBN 0-13-689258-2). P-H.

Gaule, Gerhart K. Preparation, Properties, & Applications. (Proceedings of the Paris International Symposium on Boron, 1964 Ser.: Vol. 2). 345p. 1966. 35.00x (ISBN 0-306-37502-8, Plenum Pr). Plenum Pub.

Gaulke, Earl H. You Can Have a Family Where Everybody Wins. LC 75-23574. 104p. 1975. pap. 3.50 (ISBN 0-570-03723-9, 12-2625). Concordia.

Gaull, G. E., ed. Biology of Brain Dysfunction. Incl. Vol. 1. 418p. 1973 (ISBN 0-306-35061-0); Vol. 2. 437p. 1974 (ISBN 0-306-35062-9); Vol. 3. 509p. 1975 (ISBN 0-306-35063-7). LC 72-80796. (Illus.). 59.50x ea. (Plenum Pr). Plenum Pub.

Gaulle, Charles De see De Gaulle, Charles.

Gaulmier, ed. see Breton, Andre.

Gault, Clare & Gault, Frank. Cartoon Book of Sports. new ed. (gr. k-3). 1977. pap. 1.50 (ISBN 0-590-04005-7). Scholastic Inc.

--The Homerun Kings. (Illus.). (gr. 2-6). 1975. pap. 1.50 (ISBN 0-590-09873-X). Scholastic Inc.

--How to Be a Good Soccer Player. (gr. 4-6). 1978. pap. 1.25 (ISBN 0-590-31562-5). Scholastic Inc.

--Norman Plays Ice Hockey. (Illus.). (gr. k-3). 1976. pap. 1.50 (ISBN 0-590-10144-7). Scholastic Inc.

--Norman Plays Second Base. (Illus.). (gr. k-3). 1974. pap. 1.50 (ISBN 0-590-03197-X). Scholastic Inc.

--Pele, the King of Soccer. (gr. 5-8). 1977. pap. 1.25 (ISBN 0-440-96944-1, LFL). Dell.

Gault, Clare, jt. auth. see **Gault, Frank.**

Gault, D. & Nagy, Thomas. Building Your First Expert Systems. 1985. pap. 29.95 incl. disk (ISBN 0-912677-53-8). Ashton-Tate Bks.

Gault, Elizabeth & Sykes, Susan. Crafts for the Disabled: A New Kind of Craft Book for People with Special Needs. LC 78-20625. (Illus.). 1979. 14.95i (ISBN 0-690-01806-1); pap. 7.95i (ISBN 0-690-01825-8, TYC-T). T Y Crowell.

Gault, Frank & Gault, Clare. How to Be a Good Baseball Player. (gr. 4-6). 1973. pap. 1.25 (ISBN 0-590-05010-9). Scholastic Inc.

--Norman Joins the Football Team. (Illus.). (gr. k-3). 1975. pap. 1.50 (ISBN 0-590-09931-0). Scholastic Inc.

Gault, Frank, jt. auth. see **Gault, Clare.**

Gault, Henri & Millau, Christian. The Best of Italy. 1984. pap. 13.95 (ISBN 0-517-55032-6). Crown.

--The Best of Los Angeles. 1984. pap. 13.95 (ISBN 0-517-55034-2). Crown.

--The Best of New York. rev. & updated ed. 1984. pap. 12.95 (ISBN 0-517-55328-7). Crown.

Gault, Hugh, jt. ed. see **Frude, Neil.**

Gault, J. W. & Pimmel, R. L. Introduction to Microcomputer-Based Digital Systems. (McGraw-Hill Series in Electronics). 1982. 42.00 (ISBN 0-07-023047-1). McGraw.

Gault, Jan, et al. Laboratory Investigations in Zoology. 176p. 1980. pap. 9.95 (ISBN 0-8403-2261-5). Kendall-Hunt.

Gault, Jan L. Free Time: Making Your Leisure Count. LC 82-24722. 146p. 1983. pap. text ed. 9.95 (ISBN 0-471-89041-3, Pub. by Wiley Pr). Wiley.

Gault, John C. Public Utility Regulation of an Exhaustible Resource: The Case of Natural Gas. LC 78-75016. (Outstanding Dissertations in Economics). 1980. lib. bdg. 37.00 (ISBN 0-8240-4051-1). Garland Pub.

Gault, Lila. The Northwest Cookbook. (Illus.). 1978. pap. 7.95 (ISBN 0-8256-3089-4, Quick Fox). Putnam Pub Group.

Gault, Lila, jt. auth. see **Weiss, Jeffrey.**

Gault, S. M. & Synge, P. M. Dictionary of Roses. 191p. 22.95 (ISBN 0-7181-0911-2, Pub. by Michael Joseph). Merrimack Pub Cir.

Gault, S. Millar & Synge, Patrick M. The Dictionary of Roses in Colour. (Illus.). 192p. 1985. pap. 14.95 (ISBN 0-7181-2182-1, Pub. by Michael Joseph). Merrimack Pub Cir.

Gault, William C. Dead Seed. 1985. 12.95 (ISBN 0-8027-5604-2). Walker & Co.

--Death in Donegal Bay. LC 83-40429. 192p. 1984. 12.95 (ISBN 0-8027-5591-7). Walker & Co.

--The Sunday Cycles. LC 79-52049. (gr. 7 up). 1979. 7.95 (ISBN 0-396-07715-3). Dodd.

--Super Bowl Bound. 1980. 7.95 (ISBN 0-396-07889-3). Dodd.

--Wild Willie, Wide Receiver. LC 74-5006. 160p. (gr. 5-7). 1974. 7.95 (ISBN 0-525-42788-0). Dutton.

Gaultier, Aloisius E. Amusing & Instructive Conversations for Children of Five Years. (Early Children's Bks). 1970. Repr. of 1800 ed. lib. bdg. 16.00 (ISBN 0-384-17760-3). Johnson Repr.

Gaultier, Andre P., jt. auth. see **Lasne, Sophie.**

Gaultier, Camille. Magic Without Apparatus. 2nd ed. Fleming, Paul, ed. Hugard, Jean, tr. from Fr. (Fleming Magic Classic Ser.: Vol. 1). (Illus.). xiv, 527p. 1980. 37.50 (ISBN 0-915926-34-2). Magic Ltd.

Gaultier, Jules De see **De Gaultier, Jules.**

Gaultney, Shirley. IOU Blues. LC 73-83921. 1974. 7.95 (ISBN 0-87949-017-9). Ashley Bks.

Gaumnitz, Jack E. The Social Security Book. 128p. 1984. 12.95 (ISBN 0-668-05958-3); pap. 6.95 (ISBN 0-668-05960-5). Arco.

Gaumnitz, Jack E., jt. auth. see **Dougall, Herbert E.**

Gaumond, J., jt. auth. see **Cote, N.**

Gaunt, Belle, jt. auth. see **Trevelyan, George.**

Gaunt, Larry D. & McDonald, Maurice E. Examining Employers' Financial Capacity to Self-Insure Under Workmen's Compensation. LC 77-17070. (Research Monograph: No. 72). 1977. pap. 15.00 (ISBN 0-88406-108-6). Ga St U Busn Pub.

Gaunt, Larry D. & Williams, Numan A. Commercial Liability Underwriting. 2nd ed. LC 82-82396. 672p. 1982. text ed. 20.00 (ISBN 0-89462-013-4). IIA.

Gaunt, Leonard. Cameras. (Photographer's Library). (Illus.). 1985. pap. cancelled (ISBN 0-240-51187-5). Focal Pr.

--Canon A Series Book. (Camera Bks.). 128p. 1983. pap. 9.95 (ISBN 0-240-51183-2). Focal Pr.

--Canon Reflex Way. 4th ed. (Camera Way Ser.). (Illus.). 500p. 1986. 29.95 (ISBN 0-240-51220-0). Focal Pr.

--Film & Paper Processing. (Photographer's Library). (Illus.). 168p. 1982. pap. 15.95 (ISBN 0-240-51110-7). Focal Pr.

--Focalguide to Lenses. 2nd ed. (Illus.). 160p. 1984. pap. cancelled (ISBN 0-240-51214-6). Focal Pr.

--Focalguide to 35mm SLR. 2nd ed. (Focalguide Ser.). (Illus.). 208p. 1984. pap. cancelled (ISBN 0-240-51213-8). Focal Pr.

--The Olympus Book. (Camera Book Ser.). 136p. 1977. pap. 9.95 (ISBN 0-240-50942-0). Focal Pr.

--Practical Exposure in Photography. LC 80-40793. (Practical Photography Ser.). (Illus.). 192p. 1981. 24.95 (ISBN 0-240-51058-5). Focal Pr.

--Praktica Book. 2nd ed. (Camera Book Ser.). 120p. 1979. pap. 9.95 (ISBN 0-240-51052-6). Focal Pr.

--Zoom & Special Lenses. LC 80-41245. (Camera Books). (Illus.). 128p. 1981. pap. 9.95 (ISBN 0-240-51069-0). Focal Pr.

Gaunt, Leonard & Petzold, Paul. The Focal Encyclopedia of Photography. Rev., enlarged ed. 1700p. 1969. desk ed. 30.95 (ISBN 0-240-50680-4). Focal Pr.

Gaunt, P. N. Three Dimensional Reconstruction in Biology. 184p. 1978. 40.00 (ISBN 0-272-79394-9, Pub by P Man Bks England). State Mutual Bk.

Gaunt, Peter. North Western Road Car Company. 128p. 40.00 (ISBN 0-86093-275-3, Pub. by ORPC Ltd UK). State Mutual Bk.

Gaunt, William. The Aesthetic Adventure. 1945. Repr. 20.00 (ISBN 0-8274-1829-9). R West.

--Arrows of Desire. 1980. Repr. of 1956 ed. lib. bdg. 30.00 (ISBN 0-8482-4192-4). Norwood Edns.

--Arrows of Desire: A Study of William Blake & His Romanistic World. LC 78-5530. Repr. of 1956 ed. lib. bdg. 30.00 (ISBN 0-8414-4484-6). Folcroft.

--A Concise History of English Painting. (Illus.). 1978. pap. 8.95 (ISBN 0-500-20016-5). Thames Hudson.

--English Painting. (The World of Art Ser.). (Illus.). 1985. pap. 9.95 (ISBN 0-500-20016-5). Thames Hudson.

--The March of the Moderns. LC 78-13860. (Illus.). 1979. Repr. of 1949 ed. 23.50 (ISBN 0-88355-795-9). Hyperion Conn.

--Marine Painting: An Historical Survey. (Illus.). 264p. 32.50 (ISBN 0-686-47009-5). Apollo.

--The Pre-Raphaelite Dream. 1943. Repr. 30.00 (ISBN 0-8274-3197-X). R West.

--The Pre-Raphaelite Dream. LC 66-14869. (Illus.). 1966. pap. 3.95 (ISBN 0-8052-0119-X). Schocken.

--Renoir. (Phaidon Color Library). (Illus.). 84p. 1983. 27.50 (ISBN 0-7148-2229-9, Pub. by Salem Hse); pap. 18.95 (ISBN 0-7148-2242-6). Merrimack Pub Cir.

--Turner. (Phaidon Color Library). (Illus.). 84p. 1983. (Pub. by Salem Hse Ltd); pap. 17.95 (ISBN 0-7148-2131-4). Merrimack Pub Cir.

--Victorian Olympus. 1953. 37.50 (ISBN 0-932062-61-X). Sharon Hill.

Gauntlett, John O., tr. see **Hall, Robert K.**

Gauquelin, Francoise. The Psychology of the Planets. 128p. (Orig.). 1982. pap. 7.95 (ISBN 0-917086-32-5). A C S Pubns Inc.

Gauquelin, Francoise, jt. auth. see **Gauquelin, Michel.**

Gauquelin, Michel. Birthtimes: A Scientific Investigation of the Secrets of Astrology. Matthews, Sarah, tr. from Fr. (Illus.). 204p. 1983. 12.95 (ISBN 0-8090-3038-1); pap. 7.95 (ISBN 0-8090-1519-6). Hill & Wang.

--The Cosmic Clocks. rev. ed. (Illus.). 192p. 1982. pap. 9.95 (ISBN 0-917086-42-2). A C S Pubns Inc.

--Cosmic Influences on Human Behavior. LC 77-28405. (Illus.). 1978. 8.95 (ISBN 0-88231-050-X). ASI Pubs Inc.

--Dreams & Illusions of Astrology. Leigh, Richard, tr. from Fr. LC 78-68134. (Science & the Paranormal Ser.). Orig. Title: Songes et Mensonges De L'astrologie. 158p. 1979. 18.95 (ISBN 0-87975-099-5). Prometheus Bks.

--How Cosmic & Atmospheric Energies Influence Your Health. pap. 8.95 (ISBN 0-943358-14-0). Aurora Press.

--Scientific Basis of Astrology: Myth or Reality. LC 68-31679. (Illus.). 1970. pap. 3.95 (ISBN 0-8128-1350-2). Stein & Day.

--Your Personality & the Planets. LC 80-5499. (Illus.). 262p. 1980. 11.95 (ISBN 0-8128-2737-6). Stein & Day.

--Your Personality & the Planets. 262p. 1984. pap. 3.50 (ISBN 0-8128-8025-0). Stein & Day.

Gauquelin, Michel & Gauquelin, Francoise. Gauquelin Book of American Charts. 384p. (Orig.). 1982. pap. 15.95 (ISBN 0-917086-33-3). A C S Pubns Inc.

Gauquier, Anthony & Gauguier, Beverly. Pilgrim Recipes. 3rd ed. 27p. 1983. pap. 3.00 (ISBN 0-9609574-0-5). A Gauquier.

Gaur, Albertine. Catalogue of Malayalam Books in the British Museum. 324p. 1981. 150.00 (ISBN 0-7141-0623-2, Pub. by Brit Lib England). State Mutual Bk.

--Catalogue of Malayalam Books in the British Museum. 324p. 1971. 67.50 (ISBN 0-7141-0623-2, Pub. by British Lib). Longwood Pub Group.

--A History of Writing. (Illus.). 224p. 1985. 25.00 (ISBN 0-684-18422-2, ScribT). Scribner.

--Indian Charters on Copper Plates in the Department of Oriental Manuscripts & Printed Books. 60p. 1981. 25.00x (ISBN 0-7141-0650-X, Pub. by Brit Lib England). State Mutual Bk.

Gaur, Ganesh. Catalogue of Panjabi Printed Books Added to the India Office Library, 1902-1964. 415p. 1975. 28.50 (ISBN 0-317-30641-3, Pub. by British Lib). Longwood Pub Group.

Gaur, Madan. Pointers in Punjab. 1985. 18.50x (ISBN 0-8364-1367-9, Pub. by Press & PR Serv). South Asia Bks.

Gaur, S. P., jt. auth. see **Tandon, V. K.**

Gaur, V. P. Mahatma Gandhi: A Study of His Message of Non-Violence. 145p. 1977. 9.95x (ISBN 0-940500-60-4, Pub. by Sterling India). Asia Bk Corp.

Gaura Purnima dasa, ed. see **Das Goswami, Satsvarupa.**

Gauri, K. K., ed. Anti-Herpes Virus Chemotherapy: Experimental & Clinical Aspects. (Advances in Ophthalmology: Vol. 38). (Illus.). 1979. 63.50 (ISBN 3-8055-2991-0). S Karger.

--Antiviral Chemotherapy: Design of Inhibitors of Viral Functions. LC 81-12858. 1981. 44.50 (ISBN 0-12-277720-4). Acad Pr.

Gaurico, Pomponio. De sculptura. (Documents of Art & Architectural History Series 2: Vol. 2). 104p. (Latin.). 1981. Repr. of 1504 ed. 25.00x (ISBN 0-89371-202-7). Broude Intl Edns.

Gauri Modi, tr. see **Svami Kripalvananda.**

Gaury, Gerald de. Traces of Travel. (Illus.). 224p. 1984. 19.95 (ISBN 0-7043-2363-X, Pub. by Quartet Bks). Merrimack Pub Cir.

Gaury, Gerald De see **De Gaury, Gerald.**

Gaury, Gerald De see **De Gaury, Gerald & Winstone, H. V.**

Gaus, Andy, tr. see **Rilke, Rainer M.**

Gaus, G. F., jt. ed. see **Benn, S. I.**

Gaus, Gerlad F. The Modern Liberal Theory of Man. LC 82-25493. 336p. 1984. 27.50x (ISBN 0-312-54083-3). St Martin.

Gaus, Hans-Joachim. Three-Phase Power & Its Measurements. (Siemens Programmed Instruction Ser.: 16). pap. 20.00 (ISBN 0-317-27745-6, 2052092). Bks Demand UMI.

Gaus, Helmut. The Function of Fiction. 1979. text ed. 17.75x (ISBN 90-6439-156-4). Humanities.

Gaus, John M. & Wolcott, Leon O. Public Administration & the Department of Agriculture. LC 75-8788. (FDR & the Era of the New Deal Ser.). 1975. Repr. of 1940 ed. lib. bdg. 65.00 (ISBN 0-306-70704-7). Da Capo.

Gaus, M. P., jt. ed. see **Hall, W. H.**

Gausden, Christa. Weekend Cycling. (Illus.). 15.75 (ISBN 0-902280-75-9, P975). Haynes Pubns.

Gausden, Christa, jt. auth. see **Crane, Nicholas.**

Gause, Christian, tr. see **Ferrero, Guglielmo.**

Gause, Don C. & Weinberg, Gerald M. Are Your Lights On? How to Figure Out What the Problem Really Is. 157p. (Orig.). 1982. text ed. 16.95 (ISBN 0-316-30522-7); pap. text ed. 7.95 (ISBN 0-316-30521-9). Little.

Gause, Frank A. & Carr, Charles C. Story of Panama. LC 75-111714. (American Imperialism: Viewpoints of United States Foreign Policy, 1898-1941). 1970. Repr. of 1912 ed. 18.00 (ISBN 0-405-02022-8). Ayer Co Pubs.

Gause, G. F. Problems of Evolution. (Connecticut Academy of Arts & Sciences Transaction: Vol. 37). 68p. 1947. pap. 10.50 (ISBN 0-208-00638-9). Shoe String.

--Search for New Antibiotics: Problems & Perspectives. 1960. 34.50x (ISBN 0-686-83732-0). Elliots Bks.

--Struggle for Existence. (Illus.). 1969. Repr. of 1934 ed. 11.95x (ISBN 0-02-845200-3). Hafner.

Gause, G. G., tr. see **Kirpichnikov, V. S.**

Gause, R. H. Church of God Polity: With Supplement. 1958. 9.95 (ISBN 0-87148-158-8). Pathway Pr.

Gause, R. Hollis. Living in the Spirit. 136p. 1980. pap. 5.25 (ISBN 0-87148-515-X). Pathway Pr.

--Revelation: God's Stamp of Sovereignty. LC 83-63383. 286p. 1983. pap. text ed. 9.95 (ISBN 0-87148-740-3). Pathway Pr.

Gausewitz, Richard. Patent Pending: Today's Inventors & Their Inventions. (Illus.). 240p. 1984. Repr. of 1983 ed. 14.95 (ISBN 0-916943-00-3). Alson Pub.

Gausewitz, Richard L. Patent Pending: Today's Inventors & Their Inventions. LC 82-9341. (Illus.). 240p. 1983. 14.95 (ISBN 0-8159-6522-2). Devin.

Gausman, Harold W. Plant Leaf Optical Properties in Visible & Near-Infrared Light. (Graduate Studies: No. 29). (Illus.). 78p. 1985. 25.00 (ISBN 0-89672-132-9); pap. 10.00 (ISBN 0-89672-131-0). Tex Tech Pr.

Gauss, Charles E. The Aesthetic Theories of French Artists, from Realism to Surrealism. LC 69-66657. (Johns Hopkins Paperbacks Ser.: No. JH-23). pap. 30.80 (ISBN 0-317-09354-1, 2007635). Bks Demand UMI.

Gauss, Christian. Selections from Rousseau. 232p. Repr. of 1920 ed. 9.00x (ISBN 0-911858-15-6). Appel.

Gauss, H. Plato's Conception of Philosophy. LC 73-21610. (Studies in Philosophy, No. 40). 1974. lib. bdg. write for info. (ISBN 0-8383-1759-6). Haskell.

Gauss, John. So, You Wanna Teach, Huh? LC 85-5301. 122p. (Orig.). 1985. lib. bdg. 16.00 (ISBN 0-8191-4629-3); pap. text ed. 4.75 (ISBN 0-8191-4630-7). U Pr of Amer.

Gauss, Karl. Briefwechsel Zwischen Carl Friedrich Gauss und W. Bolyai. 1971. Repr. of 1899 ed. 26.00 (ISBN 0-384-17765-4). Johnson Repr.

--Untersuchungen ueber Hoehere Arithmetik: including Disquisitionea Arithmeticae. 2nd ed. Maser, H., tr. LC 65-17614. 695p. (Ger.). 1981. text ed. 35.00 (ISBN 0-8284-0191-8). Chelsea Pub.

Gauss, Karl F. Disquisitiones Arithmetcae. Clarke, Arthur A., tr. LC 65-22318. pap. 124.00 (ISBN 0-317-08644-8, 2005389). Bks Demand UMI.

--General Investigations of Curved Surfaces. Hiltebeitel & Moorehead, trs. LC 65-6415. 1965. 14.00 (ISBN 0-911216-02-2). Raven.

Gauss, Kathleen M. New American Photography, Vol. I. (Illus.). 128p. 1985. 38.50x (ISBN 0-87587-126-7, Dist. by U. of New Mexico Press). LA Co Art Mus.

Gaussen, L. Divine Inspiration of the Bible. LC 75-155249. (Kregel Reprint Library). 1971. 12.95 (ISBN 0-8254-2707-X). Kregel.

Gaustad. George Berkeley in America. LC 79-64076. 1979. text ed. 24.50x (ISBN 0-300-02394-4). Yale U Pr.

Gaustad, Edwin S. Baptist Piety: The Last Will & Testimony of Obadiah Holmes. LC 79-52570. (The Baptist Tradition Ser.). 1980. lib. bdg. 17.00x (ISBN 0-405-12439-2). Ayer Co Pubs.

--Dissent in American Religion. (Chicago History of American Religion Ser.). 1973. 12.95x (ISBN 0-226-28436-0). U of Chicago Pr.

--Dissent in American Religion. LC 73-77131. xii, 184p. 1975. pap. 3.95x (ISBN 0-226-28437-9, P637, Phoen). U of Chicago Pr.

--A Documentary History of Religion in America Since 1865, Vol. 2. (Illus.). 640p. 1983. pap. 16.95 (ISBN 0-8028-1874-9). Eerdmans.

--The Great Awakening in New England. 13.75 (ISBN 0-8446-1491-2). Peter Smith.

--Religion in America: History & Historiography. LC 73-91240. (AHA Pamphlets: No. 260). 60p. 1974. pap. text ed. 1.50 (ISBN 0-87229-016-6). Am Hist Assn.

--Religious History of America. 1974. pap. 10.95 (ISBN 0-06-063093-0, RD/66, HarpR). Har-Row.

Gaustad, Edwin S., ed. Baptists: The Bible, Church Order & the Churches. original anthology ed. LC 79-52587. (The Baptist Tradition Ser.). 1980. lib. bdg. 46.00x (ISBN 0-405-12454-6). Ayer Co Pubs.

--Baptists Tradition Series, 40 bks, Vols. 1-22. (Illus.). 1980. Repr. Set. lib. bdg. 1323.00x (ISBN 0-405-12437-6). Ayer Co Pubs.

--Religion in America, 38 vols. 1969. Repr. Set. 2510.50 (ISBN 0-405-00229-7). Ayer Co Pubs.

--Religion in America: Ser. 2, 40 vols. 1972. Repr. 830.00 set (ISBN 0-405-04050-4). Ayer Co Pubs.

Gaustad, Edwin S., ed. see **Allison, William H. & Barnes, W. W.**

Gaustad, Edwin S., ed. see **Asplund, John.**

Gaustad, Edwin S., ed. see **Bacote, Samuel W.**

Gaustad, Edwin S., ed. see **Baker, J. C.**

Gaustad, Edwin S., ed. see **Baker, Robert A.**

Gaustad, Edwin S., ed. see **Bowden, Henry W.**

Gaustad, Edwin S., ed. see **Burkitt, Lemuel & Read, Jesse.**

Gaustad, Edwin S., ed. see **Clarke, John & McLoughlin, William G.**

Gaustad, Edwin S., ed. see **Dawson, Joseph M.**

Gaustad, Edwin S., ed. see **Freeman, Edward A.**

Gaustad, Edwin S., ed. see **Guild, Reuben A.**

Gaustad, Edwin S., ed. see **Howe, Claude L., Jr.**

Gaustad, Edwin S., ed. see **Jeter, Jeremiah B.**

Gaustad, Edwin S., ed. see **Knight, Richard.**

Gaustad, Edwin S., ed. see **Lambert, Byron C.**

Gaustad, Edwin S., ed. see **Lewis, James K.**

Gaustad, Edwin S., ed. see **Lumpkin, William L. & Butterfield, Lyman.**

Gaustad, Edwin S., ed. see **McBeth, H. Leon.**

Gaustad, Edwin S., ed. see **Macintosh, Douglas C.**

Gaustad, Edwin S., ed. see **McKibbens, Thomas R., Jr. & Smith, Kenneth.**

Gaustad, Edwin S., ed. see **Morris, Elias C.**

Gaustad, Edwin S., ed. see **Pitman, Walter G.**

Gaustad, Edwin S., ed. see **Powell, Adam C., Sr.**

Gaustad, Edwin S., ed. see **Purefoy, George W.**

Gaustad, Edwin S., ed. see **Robinson, H. Wheeler & Payne, Ernest A.**

Gaustad, Edwin S., ed. see **Seventh Day Baptist General Conference.**

Gaustad, Edwin S., ed. see **Smith, Elias.**

Gaustad, Edwin S., jt. ed. see **Stealey, Sydnor L.**

Gaustad, Edwin S., ed. see **Stiansen, Peder.**

Gaustad, Edwin S., ed. see **Taylor, John.**

Gaustad, Edwin S., ed. see **Tull, James E.**

Gaustad, Edwin S., jt. ed. see **Valentine, Foy D.**

Gaustad, Edwin S., ed. see **Wayland, Francis.**

Gaustad, Edwin S., ed. see **Whitsitt, William H.**

Gaustad, Edwin S., ed. see **Wood, Nathan E.**

Gaustad, John E., jt. auth. see **Zeilik, Michael.**

Gausted, Edwin S., ed. see **Jordan, Lewis G.**

Gausted, Edwins., ed. see **Dagg, John L.**

Gausten, A. K., jt. auth. see **Achenbach, J. D.**

Gaut, Gregory A., jt. auth. see **Cromett, Michael F.**

Gautam, M. R. Musical Heritage of India. 138p. 1981. text ed. 34.50x (ISBN 0-391-02237-7, Pub. by Abhinav India). Humanities.

Gautam, Om P. The Indian National Congress. 400p. 1984. text ed. 60.00x (ISBN 0-86590-388-3, Pub. by B R Pub Corp Delhi). Apt Bks.

Gautam, S. Reasons for Action. (Ajanta Series in Critical Thought II). 124p. 1983. text ed. 9.00x (Pub. by Ajanta Pubs India). Humanities.

Gautam, V. Aspects of Indian Society & Economy in the Nineteenth Century. 1972. 6.95 (ISBN 0-8426-0473-1). Orient Bk Dist.

Gautam, Vinayshil. Enterprise & Society. 1979. text ed. 9.00x (ISBN 0-391-01861-2). Humanities.

Gautama. Gautama: The Nyaya Philosophy. Junankar, N. S., tr. from Sanskrit. 1978. 25.50 (ISBN 0-89684-002-6, Pub. by Motilal Banarsidass India). Orient Bk Dist.

Gawalt, Gerald W. The Promise of Power: The Emergence of the Legal Profession in Massachusetts, 1760-1840. LC 78-57765. (Contributions in Legal Studies Ser.: No. 6). x, 254p. 1979. lib. bdg. 29.95x (ISBN 0-313-20612-0, GPP/). Greenwood.

Gawalt, Gerard W., ed. The New High Priests: Lawyers in Post-Civil War America. LC 83-18328. (Contributions in Legal Studies Ser.: No. 29). (Illus.). xiv, 214p. 1984. lib. bdg. 32.50 (ISBN 0-313-24021-3, GNH/). Greenwood.

Gawalt, Gerard W., jt. ed. see Smith, Paul H.

Gaward, Abd El. Architecture & Building Dictionary: English-French-German-Arabic. 465p. (Eng., Fr., Ger. & Arabic.). 1976. Leatherette 45.00 (ISBN 0-686-92255-7, M-9753). French & Eur.

Gawel, M., jt. auth. see Rose, Clifford F.

Gawel, Mary L., ed. see Sullivan, Harry S.

Gawle, Barbara. How to Pray: Discovering Spiritual Growth Through Prayer. (Illus.). 204p. 1984. 15.95 (ISBN 0-13-430471-3); pap. 6.95 (ISBN 0-13-430463-2). P-H.

Gawler, J. C. Dan, Pioneer Tribe of Israel. (Illus.). 40p. 1985. pap. 2.50 (ISBN 0-934666-14-8). Artisan Sales.

Gawne, Eleanor & Oerke. Dress. rev. ed. 672p. (gr. 9-12). 1975. 22.00 (ISBN 0-02-663530-5). Bennett IL.

Gawne, Eleanor J. Fabrics for Clothing. (gr. 10-12). 1973. pap. text ed. 9.72 (ISBN 0-02-666900-5). Bennett IL.

Gawne-Cain, C. E., ed. see Kafka, Franz.

Gaworski, Michael E., jt. auth. see Warming, Wanda.

Gawrecki, Drahoslay. Compact Library Shelving. LC 68-26381. (American Library Association, Library Technology Program, LTP Publications: No. 14). pap. 50.00 (ISBN 0-317-26590-3, 2024192). Bks Demand UMI.

Gawrilov, G. G. Chemical (Electroless) Nickel-Plating. 179p. 80.00x (ISBN 0-86108-048-3, Pub. by Portcullio Pr). State Mutual Bk.

Gawron, Marlene E. Busy Bodies: Finger Plays & Action Rhymes. (Illus.). (ps-1). 1981. 4.50 (ISBN 0-913545-00-7). Moonlight FL.

--Ten Little Bunnies. (Flannel Board Ser.). (Illus.). (ps-1). 1981. 3.50 (ISBN 0-913545-06-6). Moonlight FL.

Gawronski, Donald V. History: Meaning & Method. 3rd ed. 132p. 1975. pap. 7.75x (ISBN 0-673-07968-6). Scott F.

Gawronski, J. D. see Price, Jack.

Gawryn, Marvin. Reaching High: The Psychology of Spiritual Living. LC 80-24306. 200p. 1981. 11.95 (ISBN 0-938380-00-1); pap. 7.95 (ISBN 0-938380-01-X). Spiritual Renaissance Press.

Gawsworth, John. Backwaters: Excursions in the Shades. 1973. Repr. of 1932 ed. 20.00 (ISBN 0-8274-0196-5). R West.

--The Poets of Harrow School. 1934. 12.50 (ISBN 0-932062-62-8). Sharon Hill.

--The Poets of Harrow School (Byron) An Anthology. 224p. 1982. Repr. of 1934 ed. lib. bdg. 30.00 (ISBN 0-89984-007-8). Century Bookbindery.

--Ten Contemporaries, Notes Towards Their Definitive Bibliography. LC 72-192872. 1932. lib. bdg. 17.50 (ISBN 0-8414-1050-X). Folcroft.

--Ten Contemporaries, Second Series. LC 72-193506. 1933. lib. bdg. 17.50. Folcroft.

Gawthorne, J., et al, eds. Trace Element Metabolism in Man & Animals: Proceedings. 715p. 1982. 71.00 (ISBN 0-387-11058-5). Springer-Verlag.

Gawthrop, Louis C. Bureaucratic Behavior in the Executive Branch. LC 69-10568. 1969. pap. text ed. 6.95 (ISBN 0-02-911400-4). Free Pr.

--Public Sector Management, Systems, & Ethics. LC 83-48176. (Illus.). 184p. 1984. 25.00x (ISBN 0-253-34675-4). Ind U Pr.

Gawthrop, Louis C. & Gawthrop, Virginia L., eds. Public Administration Review Cumulative Index, 1940-1979. 160p. 1980. 34.50 (ISBN 0-936678-02-X). Am Soc Pub Admin.

Gawthrop, Virginia L., jt. ed. see Gawthrop, Louis C.

Gaxotte, P. Louis the Fifteenth & His Times. 69.95 (ISBN 0-8490-0558-2). Gordon Pr.

Gaxotte, Pierre. Frederick the Great. Bell, R. A., tr. from Fr. LC 75-16845. (Illus.). 420p. 1975. Repr. of 1942 ed. lib. bdg. 22.75x (ISBN 0-8371-8269-7, GAFG). Greenwood.

--The French Revolution. Phillips, Walter A., tr. 1978. Repr. of 1932 ed. lib. bdg. 40.00 (ISBN 0-8492-4911-2). R West.

Gay. Glossaire Archeologique du Moyer age et de la Renaissance, 2 tomes. (Fr.). Set. 167.00 (ISBN 0-685-34006-6). French & Eur.

Gay, A. Nolder. The View from the Closet: Essays on Gay Life & Liberation, 1973-1977. LC 78-105579. 1978. pap. 3.00x (ISBN 0-9601570-0-X). Union Park.

Gay, Carlo T. E. Xochipala: The Beginnings of Olmec Art. LC 70-187566. (Publications of the Princeton Univ. Art Museum). (Illus.). 64p. 1972. 20.00x (ISBN 0-691-03880-5). Princeton U Pr.

Gay, David. Voyage to Freedom: Story of the Pilgrim Fathers. pap. 4.95 (ISBN 0-85151-384-0). Banner of Truth.

Gay, E. Jane. With the Nez Perces: Alice Fletcher in the Field, 1889-92. Hoxie, Frederick E. & Mark, Joan T., eds. LC 80-23045. (Illus.). xxxviii, 220p. 1981. 19.95x (ISBN 0-8032-3062-1). U of Nebr Pr.

Gay, Edwin F. Facts & Factors in Economic History. LC 67-27547. Repr. of 1932 ed. 45.00x (ISBN 0-678-00309-2). Kelley.

Gay, Elizabeth K., jt. auth. see Kent, Louise A.

Gay, George. Sole Survivor. 15.00 (ISBN 0-686-31603-7). Midway Pubs.

Gay, George A., jt. auth. see Dundon, Mary L.

Gay, Gerald & Kolb, Robert. Interest Rate Futures. 1983. text ed. 28.95 O.P. (ISBN 0-8359-3114-5); pap. 19.95 (ISBN 0-8359-3113-7). Reston.

--International Finance: Concepts & Issues. LC 82-74196. 1983. pap. text ed. 22.95 (ISBN 0-8359-3135-8). Reston.

Gay, Helga C., tr. see Schalliol, Willis L.

Gay, James & Jacobs, Barbara S., eds. Competition in the Marketplace: Health Care in the 1980s, Vol. 1. (Monographs in Health Care Ser.). 128p. 1981. text ed. 14.95 (ISBN 0-89335-163-6). SP Med & Sci Bks.

--The Technolgy Explosion in Medical Science: Implications for the Health Care Industry & the Public (1981-2001) (Health Care Administration Monographs: Vol. 2). 176p. 1983. text ed. 14.95 (ISBN 0-89335-181-4). SP Med & Sci Bks.

Gay, Jean. Bibliographie des Ouvrages Relatifs a l'Afrigue et a l'Arabie. 1976. Repr. of 1958 ed. 41.00 (ISBN 0-518-19000-5). Ayer Co Pubs.

Gay, Jeanne, ed. Travel & Tourism Audiovisual Guide. 2nd ed. 1982. pap. write for info. (ISBN 0-935638-05-9). Travel & Tourism Pr.

--Travel & Tourism Bibliography & Resource Guide, 6 vols. 2nd ed. (Orig.). 1982. pap. write for info. (ISBN 0-935638-04-0). Travel & Tourism.

--Travel & Tourism Personnel Directory. 2nd ed. (Orig.). 1982. pap. cancelled (ISBN 0-935638-06-7). Travel & Tourism Pr.

Gay, John. Beggar's Opera. Griffith, Benjamin W., Jr., ed. LC 61-18353. 1962. pap. text ed. 3.95 (ISBN 0-8120-0032-3). Barron.

--The Beggar's Opera. Roberts, Edgar V., ed. LC 68-21878. (Regents Restoration Drama Ser.). xxx, 238p. 1969. 19.95x (ISBN 0-8032-0362-4); pap. 5.95x (ISBN 0-8032-5361-3, BB 269, Bison). U of Nebr Pr.

--The Beggar's Opera & Companion Pieces. Burgess, C. F., ed. LC 66-16637. (Crofts Classics Ser.). 1966. pap. text ed. 3.75x (ISBN 0-88295-037-1). Harlan Davidson.

--The Brightening Shadow. LC 80-81852. (Illus., Orig.). 1980. pap. text ed. 6.95x (ISBN 0-933662-09-2). Intercult Pr.

--Fables. 1882. 15.00 (ISBN 0-8274-2325-X). R West.

--The Plays of John Gay, 2 vols. LC 78-14747. 1978. Repr. of 1923 ed. Set. lib. bdg. 49.50 (ISBN 0-8414-2026-2). Folcroft.

--Poetical, Dramatic, & Miscellaneous Works, 6 Vols. LC 73-137415. Repr. of 1795 ed. Set. 180.00 (ISBN 0-404-02790-3); 30.00 ea. Vol. 1 (ISBN 0-404-02791-1). Vol. 2 (ISBN 0-404-02792-X). Vol. 3 (ISBN 0-404-02793-8). Vol. 4 (ISBN 0-404-02794-6). Vol. 5 (ISBN 0-404-02795-4). Vol. 6 (ISBN 0-404-02796-2). AMS Pr.

--Poetry & Prose, 2 vols. Beckwith, Charles E. & Dearing, Vinton A., eds. (Oxford English Texts Ser). 1974. Set. 69.00x (ISBN 0-19-811897-X). Oxford U Pr.

--Polly - An Opera: Being the Second Part of the Beggar's Opera. 1922. 20.00 (ISBN 0-8274-3183-X). R West.

--Red Dust on the Green Leaves. Bruner, Jerome, intro. by. LC 73-77698. (gr. 7-12). 1973. 10.50 (ISBN 0-88253-219-7, 305); pap. 6.95 (ISBN 0-933662-54-8). Intercult Pr.

--Red Dust on the Green Leaves. 256p. pap. 8.50 (ISBN 0-317-35821-9, 305); members 5.95 (ISBN 0-317-35822-7). Soc Intercult Ed Train & Res.

Gay, John & Fuller, John, eds. John Gay: Dramatic Works, 2 vols. (Oxford English Texts Ser.). (Illus.). 1983. Vol. I 95.00x (ISBN 0-19-812701-4); Vol. II 95.00x (ISBN 0-19-812320-5). Oxford U Pr.

Gay, John, jt. ed. see Lloyd, Barbara.

Gay, John, illus. The Brightening Shadow. (Illus.). 280p. 6.95 (ISBN 0-317-35806-5, 308). Soc Intercult Ed Train & Res.

Gay, John, photos by. Highgate Cemetery: Victorian Valhalla. (Illus.). 96p. 1984. pap. 11.95 (ISBN 0-88162-022-X, Pub. by Salem Hse Ltd). Merrimack Pub Cir.

Gay, John E., jt. auth. see Wantz, Molly S.

Gay, Jules. Papes Du Onzieme Siecle et la Chretiente. 2nd ed. 1970. 21.00 (ISBN 0-8337-1302-7). B Franklin.

Gay, Katherine. Acid Rain. (Impact Ser.). 96p. (gr. 7 up). 1983. PLB 9.90 (ISBN 0-531-04682-6). Watts.

Gay, Kathlyn. Cities under Stress: Can Today's City System Be Made to Work. (Impact Ser.). (Illus.). 128p. 1985. lib. bdg. 10.90 (ISBN 0-531-04926-4). Watts.

--Ergonomics: Making Products & Places Fit People. (Illus.). 128p. (gr. 6-9). 1985. PLB 11.95 (ISBN 0-89490-118-4). Enslow Pubs.

--Junkyards. LC 82-11614. (Illus.). 48p. (gr. 3-5). 1982. PLB 9.95 (ISBN 0-89490-082-X). Enslow Pubs.

Gay, Kathlyn & Barnes, Ben E. The River Flows Backward. new ed. Ashton, Sylvia, ed. LC 74-76645. 1975. 17.95 (ISBN 0-87949-027-6). Ashley Bks.

Gay, Kathlyn, jt. auth. see Gay, Martin.

Gay, L. R. Educational Evaluation & Measurement: Competencies for Analysis & Application. (Illus.). 576p. 1980. text ed. 26.95 (ISBN 0-675-08143-2). Additional supplements may be obtained from publisher. Merrill.

--Educational Research. 2nd ed. (Illus.). 464p. 1981. text ed. 27.95 (ISBN 0-675-08021-5); student guide 8.95 (ISBN 0-675-08020-7). Merrill.

Gay, L. W., jt. auth. see Fritschen, L. J.

Gay, Larry. Central Heating with Wood & Coal. LC 80-29216. (Illus.). 128p. 1981. 12.95 (ISBN 0-8289-0419-7); pap. 8.95 (ISBN 0-8289-0420-0). Greene.

--The Complete Book of Heating with Wood. LC 74-83144. 128p. 1974. pap. 5.95 (ISBN 0-88266-035-7). Garden Way Pub.

--The Complete Book of Insulating. LC 79-23945. (Illus.). 1980. 12.95 (ISBN 0-8289-0364-6); pap. 7.95 (ISBN 0-8289-0365-4). Greene.

--Heating the Home Water Supply: Wood, Coal, Solar. Griffith, Roger, ed. LC 82-24224. (Illus.). 128p. 1983. pap. 7.95 (ISBN 0-88266-311-9). Garden Way Pub.

Gay Left Collective. Homosexuality: Power & Politics. LC 80-40640. 223p. 1980. text ed. 17.95x (ISBN 0-8052-8062-6, Pub. by Allison & Busby England); pap. 7.95 (ISBN 0-8052-8061-8). Schocken.

Gay, Lettie, ed. see Rhett, Blanche S.

Gay, Marcina. The Bible Puzzle Book. 128p. (Orig.). 1984. pap. 2.25 (ISBN 0-8007-8487-1, Spire Bks). Revell.

--Bible Quizzes for Kids. 48p. (Orig.). (ps-3). 1982. pap. 1.95 (ISBN 0-87239-594-4, 3136). Standard Pub.

Gay, Martin & Gay, Kathlyn. Eating What Grows Naturally. LC 80-70278. (Illus.). 140p. 1980. pap. 5.95 (ISBN 0-89708-031-9). And Bks.

Gay, Michael. Little Boat. LC 84-42985. (Illus.). 32p. (ps-k). 1985. bds. 3.95 (ISBN 0-02-737550-1); PLB 7.95 (ISBN 0-02-737540-4). Macmillan.

--Little Plane. LC 84-42986. (Illus.). 32p. (ps-k). 1985. bds. 3.95 (ISBN 0-02-737510-2); PLB 7.95 (ISBN 0-02-737500-5). Macmillan.

Gay, Michel. The Christmas Wolf. LC 83-1441. Orig. Title: Le Loup Noel. (Illus.). 32p. (gr. k-3). 1983. PLB 10.88 (ISBN 0-688-02291-X); 10.25 (ISBN 0-688-02290-1). Greenwillow.

--Little Truck. LC 84-42983. 32p. (ps-1). 1985. PLB 7.95 (ISBN 0-02-737520-X); pap. 3.95 (ISBN 0-02-737530-7). Macmillan.

--Rabbit Express. (Illus.). 40p. (ps-3). 1985. 11.75 (ISBN 0-688-04647-9, Morrow Junior Books); PLB 10.88 (ISBN 0-688-04648-7). Morrow.

--Take Me for a Ride. LC 84-19088. (Illus.). 32p. (ps). 1985. 10.25 (ISBN 0-688-04135-3, Morrow Junior Books); PLB 10.88 (ISBN 0-688-04136-1, Morrow Junior Books). Morrow.

Gay, Nelson H., ed. see Hunt, Leigh.

Gay, Pat & PitKeathly, Jill. When I Went Home-A Study of Patients Discharged from Hospital. 90p. 1979. 25.00 (ISBN 0-900889-72-1, Pub by P Man Bks England). State Mutual Bk.

Gay, Peter. Art & Act: On Causes in History - Manet, Gropius, Mondrian. LC 75-12291. (Icon Editions). (Illus.). 320p. 1980. (HarpT); 9.95i (ISBN 0-06-430061-7). Har-Row.

--The Crystalline State. (Illus.). 1972. 20.95x (ISBN 0-02-845220-8). Hafner.

--Deism: An Anthology. 192p. (Orig.). 1968. pap. 6.95 (ISBN 0-686-47401-5). Krieger.

--The Dilemma of Democratic Socialism: Edward Bernstein's Challenge to Marx. 1979. Repr. of 1952 ed. lib. bdg. 24.50x (ISBN 0-374-93017-1). Octagon.

--Education of the Senses. LC 83-8187. (Bourgeois Experience-Victoria to Freud Ser.: Vol. 1). (Illus.). 1984. 25.00 (ISBN 0-19-503352-3). Oxford U Pr.

--The Enlightenment. rev. ed. 1985. 15.95 (ISBN 0-671-21915-4, Touchstone Bks). S&S.

--The Enlightenment: An Interpretation-the Rise of Modern Paganism, Vol. 1. 1977. pap. 9.95x (ISBN 0-393-00870-3, N870, Norton Lib). Norton.

--The Enlightenment: An Interpretation-the Science of Freedom, Vol. 2. 1977. pap. 11.95x (ISBN 0-393-00875-4, Norton Lib). Norton.

--Freud for Historians. 1985. 17.95 (ISBN 0-19-503586-0). Oxford U Pr.

--Freud, Jews & Other Germans: Masters & Victims in Modernist Culture. 1978. 22.50x (ISBN 0-19-502258-0). Oxford U Pr.

--Freud, Jews & Other Germans: Masters & Victims in Modernist Culture. LC 77-76834. 1979. pap. 9.95 (ISBN 0-19-502493-1, GB514, GB). Oxford U Pr.

--A Loss of Mastery: Puritan Historians in Colonial America. LC 67-10969. (Jefferson Memorial Lectures). 1966. 23.50x (ISBN 0-520-00456-6). U of Cal Pr.

--Party of Humanity: Essays in the French Enlightenment. 1971. pap. 6.95 (ISBN 0-393-00607-7). Norton.

--Style in History. LC 76-25490. (McGraw-Hill Paperbacks). 1976. pap. 3.95 (ISBN 0-07-023063-3). McGraw.

--Weimar Culture: The Outsider As Insider. LC 81-2046. (Illus.). xv, 205p. 1981. Repr. of 1968 ed. lib. bdg. 24.25x (ISBN 0-313-22972-4, GAWC). Greenwood.

--Weimar Culture: The Outsider As Insider. 1970. pap. 5.95xi (ISBN 0-06-131482-X, TB1482, Torch). Har-Row.

Gay, Peter & Webb, Robert. Modern Europe, Vol. 1: Modern Europe to 1815. 1973. pap. text ed. 18.50 scp (ISBN 0-06-042283-1, HarpC); instructor's manual avail. (ISBN 0-06-362249-1). Har-Row.

Gay, Peter, ed. John Locke on Education. LC 64-14307. (Classics in Education Ser.). 1964. text ed. 10.00 (ISBN 0-8077-1419-4). Tchrs Coll.

Gay, Peter & Cavanaugh, Gerald J., eds. Historians at Work, Vol. 1. LC 75-123930. 431p. 1972. text ed. 38.00x (ISBN 0-8290-0566-8). Irvington.

--Historians at Work, Vol. 4. LC 75-123930. 411p. 1975. text ed. 38.00x (ISBN 0-8290-0569-2). Irvington.

Gay, Peter & Wexler, Victor G., eds. Historians at Work, Vol. 2. LC 75-123930. 406p. 1972. text ed. 38.00x (ISBN 0-8290-0567-6). Irvington.

--Historians at Work, Vol. 3. LC 75-123930. 325p. 1975. text ed. 38.00x (ISBN 0-8290-0568-4). Irvington.

Gay, Peter, ed. see Voltaire, F. M.

Gay, Phoebe F. John Gay: His Place in the Eighteenth Century. 1973. Repr. of 1938 ed. 16.50 (ISBN 0-8274-0398-4). R West.

Gay, R., jt. auth. see Skillin, M.

Gay Rights Writer's Group Staff. It Could Happen to You: An Account of the Gay Civil Rights Campaign in Eugene, Oregon. LC 81-67972. (Illus.). 95p. 1983. 3.95 (ISBN 0-932870-25-2). Alyson Pubns.

Gay, Robert M. Emerson: A Study of the Poet As Seer. LC 80-2533. Repr. of 1928 ed. 32.75 (ISBN 0-404-19259-9). AMS Pr.

Gay Sunshine Press, compiled by. Meat: How Men Look, Act, Talk, Walk, Dress, Undress, Taste & Smell: True Homosexual Experiences from S.T.H. (Illus.). 192p. (Orig.). 1983. pap. 12.00 (ISBN 0-917342-78-X). Gay Sunshine.

Gay, Sydney H. James Madison. Morse, John T., ed. LC 70-128976. (American Statesmen: No. 12). Repr. of 1898 ed. 29.00 (ISBN 0-404-50862-6). AMS Pr.

Gay, Thomas R. & Shaffer, James D. Nineteen Eighty U. S. Census Population & Housing Characteristics, 5 vols. Incl. Bk. 1. State, SMSA, ADI, City, County Data & Indices; Bk. 2. Place Data & Indices; Bk. 3. Census Tract Data (AL-IA; Bk. 4. Census Tract Data (KS-ND; Bk. 5. Census Tract Data (OH-WY. 1000p. 1983. pap. 395.00 (ISBN 0-686-46735-3). Natl Decision.

Gay, Tim, ed. Cable Contacts Yearbook, 1983. 1982. deluxe ed. 170.00 (ISBN 0-935224-16-5). Larimi Comm.

Gay, Tim & Hurvitz, David, eds. Radio Contacts. 1982. deluxe ed. 136.00 (ISBN 0-935224-17-3). Larimi Comm.

--Television Contacts. 1982. deluxe ed. 127.00 (ISBN 0-935224-18-1). Larimi Comm.

Gay, Vernon, photos by. Discovering Pittsburgh's Sculpture. LC 82-50225. (Illus.). 462p. 1982. pap. 14.95 (ISBN 0-8229-5348-X). U of Pittsburgh Pr.

Gay, Volney P. Freud on Ritual: Reconstruction & Critique. LC 79-11385. (American Academy of Religion, Dissertation Ser.: No. 26). 1979. 14.00 (ISBN 0-89130-282-4, 010126); pap. 9.95 (ISBN 0-89130-301-4). Scholars Pr Ga.

--Reading Freud: Psychology, Neurosis, & Religion. LC 83-2917. (AAR Studies in Religion). 142p. 1983. pap. 8.25 (ISBN 0-89130-613-7, 01 00 32). Scholars Pr GA.

--Reading Jung: Science, Psychology, & Religion. LC 84-1322. (AAR-Studies in Religion). 166p. 1984. pap. 8.25 (ISBN 0-89130-675-7, 01 00 34). Scholars Pr GA.

Gay, W. B. Historical Gazetteer & Directory of Tioga County, New York - 1887. (Illus.). 848p. 1985. Repr. of 1887 ed. lib. bdg. 25.00 (ISBN 0-932334-73-3). Heart of the Lakes.

Gay, W. I., ed. Methods of Animal Experimentation, 5 vols. Vol. 1. 1965. 68.50 (ISBN 0-12-278001-9); Vol. 2. 1965. 77.50 (ISBN 0-12-278002-7); Vol. 3. 1968. 73.50 (ISBN 0-12-278003-5); Vol. 4. 1973. 67.50 (ISBN 0-12-278004-3); Vol. 5. 1974. 67.50 (ISBN 0-12-278005-1). Acad Pr.

Gay, William. Walt Whitman: His Relation to Science & Philosophy. LC 77-4051. Repr. of 1895 ed. lib. bdg. 10.00 (ISBN 0-8414-4551-6). Folcroft.

Gay, William, ed. Methods of Animal Experimentation, Vol. 6. 1981. 57.50 (ISBN 0-12-278006-X). Acad Pr.

Gay, William A., Jr., et al. Cardiothoracic Infections: Recognition, Prevention & Management of Infectious Complications Following Cardiothoracic Surgery. 55p. 1983. write for info. (ISBN 0-911741-05-4). Advanced Thera Comm.

Gaya, Harold, jt. ed. see Easmon, Charles.

Gaya, S. D. Gili see Gili Gaya, S. D.

Gayakwad, Ramakant A. OP Amps & Linear Integrated Circuit Technology. 528p. 1983. 34.95 (ISBN 0-13-637355-0). P-H.

Gayangos, Don Pascual de see De Gayangos, Don Pascual.

Gayangos, P. De see Al-Maqqari, Ahmed.

Gayangos, Pascual De see Cortes, Hernando.

Gaya-Nuno, J. A. Bibliografia Critica y Antologica De Picasso. 7.50 (ISBN 0-8477-2002-0). U of PR Pr.

Gayaree, Charles. History of Louisiana, 4 vols. 4th ed. 1974. Repr. Set. 90.00 (ISBN 0-87511-147-5). Claitors.

Gayarre, Charles. Historical Sketch of Pierre & Jean Lafitte, the Famous Smugglers of Louisiana. pap. 4.50 wrappers (ISBN 0-685-13272-2). Jenkins.

--History of Louisiana, 4 vols. 5th ed. (Illus.). 1974. Repr. 95.00 (ISBN 0-88289-041-7). Pelican.

Gay Blanc, Linda see Blanc, Linda-Gay.

Gay-Crosier, Raymond. Religious Elements in the Secular Lyrics of the Troubadours. (Studies in the Romance Languages & Literatures: No. 111). 109p. 1971. pap. 7.50x (ISBN 0-8078-9111-8). U of NC Pr.

Gay-Crosier, Raymond, ed. Albert Camus Nineteen Eighty. LC 80-22240. 330p. (Orig., Fr.). 1980. pap. 16.00 (ISBN 0-8130-0691-0). U Presses Fla.

Gaydasch, Alex. Effective Database Management. 1985. text ed. 24.95 (ISBN 0-8359-1574-3). Reston.

Gaydasch, Alexander. Principles of Electronic Data Processing Management. 300p. 1982. text ed. 26.95 (ISBN 0-8359-5604-0); instr's. manual free (ISBN 0-8359-5605-9). Reston.

Gaydon, A. G. The Spectroscopy of Flames. 2nd ed. 1974. 43.00x (ISBN 0-412-12870-5, 6120, Pub. by Chapman & Hall). Methuen Inc.

Gaydon, A. G. & Pearse, R. W. Identification of Molecular Spectra. 4th ed. 1976. 82.00 (ISBN 0-412-14350-X, NO. 6215, Pub. by Chapman & Hall). Methuen Inc.

Gaydon, A. G. & Wolfhard, H. G. Flames: Their Structure, Radiation & Temperature. 4th ed. 1979. 63.00 (ISBN 0-412-15390-4, NO. 6119, Pub. by Chapman & Hall). Methuen Inc.

Gaydos, Alice G. Please Quote Me: Selected Poems. 64p. 1980. 5.00 (ISBN 0-682-49626-X). Exposition Pr FL.

Gaydos, Janine, jt. auth. see Stoker, Richard G.

Gaydos, Michael. Eyes to Behold. LC 73-77531. 1982. pap. 4.95 (ISBN 0-89221-069-9). New Leaf.

Gaye, Phoebe F. Good Sir John. 1978. Repr. of 1930 ed. lib. bdg. 30.00 (ISBN 0-8495-1937-3). Arden Lib.

--John Gay. LC 79-39401. (Select Bibliographies Reprint Series). 1972. Repr. of 1938 ed. 21.00 (ISBN 0-8369-9906-1). Ayer Co Pubs.

Gayer, A. D., ed. Lessons of Monetary Experience: Essays in Honor of Irving Fisher. LC 70-86089. Repr. of 1937 ed. 37.50x (ISBN 0-678-00643-1). Kelley.

Gayer, Arthur D., et al. The Sugar Economy of Puerto Rico. 1976. lib. bdg. 59.95 (ISBN 0-8490-2717-9). Gordon Pr.

Gayer, R., ed. The Tectonic Evolution of the Caledonide-Appalachian Origin. (Monograph on Intedisciplinary Earth Science Research & Applications). (Orig.). 1985. pap. write for info. (ISBN 0-9904001-9-0, Pub. by Sohn Germany). Heyden.

Gayeski, Diane & Williams, David. Interactive Media. 250p. 1984. 21.95 (ISBN 0-13-469289-6); pap. 12.95 (ISBN 0-13-469131-8). P-H.

Gayeski, Diane M. Corporate & Instructional Video: Design & Production. (Illus.). 304p. 1983. 25.95 (ISBN 0-13-174243-4). P-H.

Gayford & Haskell. Clinical Oral Medicine. 2nd ed. 298p. 1979. 31.00 (ISBN 0-7236-0512-2). PSG Pub Co.

Gayford, M. L. Electroacoustics. 289p. 1971. 37.75 (ISBN 0-444-19649-8). Elsevier.

Gayle, Addison. Claude McKay: The Black Poet at War. (Broadside Critics Ser: No. 2). pap. 2.50 (ISBN 0-910296-76-6). Broadside.

--Richard Wright: Ordeal of a Native Son. 1983. 14.50 (ISBN 0-8446-6000-0). Peter Smith.

Gayle, Dennis J. The Small Developing State: Studies in International Political Economy. 200p. 1985. text ed. price not set (ISBN 0-566-05077-3). Gower Pub Co.

Gayle, Margaret. Interlude. (Superromances Ser.). 384p. 1983. pap. 2.95 (ISBN 0-373-70080-6, Pub. by Worldwide). Harlequin Bks.

Gayle, Margot & Gillon, Edmund, Jr. Cast Iron Architecture in New York. (Illus., Orig.). 1974. pap. 8.95 (ISBN 0-486-22980-7). Dover.

--Cast-Iron Architecture in New York: A Photographic Survey. (Illus.). 16.50 (ISBN 0-8446-5034-X). Peter Smith.

Gayle, Margot, pref. by. Victorian Ironwork: The Wickersham Catalogue of 1857. LC 75-22529. (The Athenaeum Library of Nineteenth Century America). (Illus.). 1977. text ed. 20.00 (ISBN 0-685-87221-1). Am Life Foun.

Gayle, Willie. Seven Seconds to Success in Selling. 1963. 14.95 (ISBN 0-13-806901-8). P-H.

--Willie Gayle's Power Selling. 1959. 12.95 (ISBN 0-13-959809-X). P-H.

Gayler, Bob. Piper Tuning Manual. (Illus.). 44p. pap. 6.95 (ISBN 0-85429-292-6, F292). Haynes Pubns.

Gayler, Robert. Private Prisoner: An Astonishing Story of Survival under the Nazis. (Illus.). 184p. 1985. 14.95 (ISBN 0-85059-724-2, Pub. by Salem Hse Ltd). Merrimack Pub Cir.

Gayler, Winston D. The Apple II Circuit Description. LC 82-61966. 240p. 1983. pap. 22.95 (ISBN 0-672-21959-X, 21959). Sams.

Gayley, C. M. English Poetry: Its Principles & Progress. 1973. Repr. of 1904 ed. 40.00 (ISBN 0-8274-0035-7). R West.

Gayley, Charles. Charles Mills Gayley Anniversary Papers. LC 67-30814. (Studies in Poetry, No. 38). 1969. Repr. of 1922 ed. lib. bdg. 54.95x (ISBN 0-8383-0715-9). Haskell.

Gayley, Charles M. The Charles Mill Gayley Anniversary Papers: 1889-1919. 1922. Repr. 11.75 (ISBN 0-8274-2042-0). R West.

--The Classic Myths in English Literature & Art. LC 77-6986. 1977. Repr. of 1911 ed. lib. bdg. 45.00 (ISBN 0-89341-163-9). Longwood Pub Group.

--Plays of Our Forefathers & Some of the Traditions Upon Which They Were Founded. LC 68-25810. (Illus.). 1968. Repr. of 1907 ed. 15.00x (ISBN 0-8196-0209-4). Biblo.

--Shakespeare & the Founders of Liberty in America. LC 77-26994. 35.00 (ISBN 0-8414-2004-1). Folcroft.

Gayley, Charles M. & Flaherty, Martin C. Poetry of the People: Comprising Poems Illustrative of the History & National Spirit of England, Scotland, Ireland, & America. 1979. Repr. of 1903 ed. lib. bdg. 20.00 (ISBN 0-8482-4183-5). Norwood Edns.

Gayley, Charles M. & Kurtz, B. P. Methods & Materials of Literary Criticism. 1920. Repr. 40.00 (ISBN 0-8274-2729-8). R West.

Gayley, Charles M. & Scott, F. N. Guide to the Literature of Aesthetics. 19.50 (ISBN 0-8337-4572-7). B Franklin.

Gayley, Charles M. & Scott, Fred N. An Introduction to the Methods & Materials of Literary Criticism: The Bases in Aesthetics & Poetics. 587p. 1982. Repr. of 1899 ed. lib. bdg. 75.00 (ISBN 0-8495-2131-9). Arden Lib.

Gayley, Charles M. & Young, Clement C. English Poetry It's Principles & Progress with Representative Masterpieces & Notes. 595p. Repr. of 1917 ed. lib. bdg. 50.00 (ISBN 0-918377-41-2). Russell Pr.

Gayley, Charles M., ed. Representative English Comedies, 4 Vols. LC 76-88240. Repr. of 1936 ed. Set. 160.00 (ISBN 0-404-01950-1); 40.00 ea. Vol. 1 (ISBN 0-404-01951-X). Vol. 2 (ISBN 0-404-01952-8). Vol. 3 (ISBN 0-404-01953-6). Vol. 4 (ISBN 0-404-01954-4). AMS Pr.

Gayley, Charles W. Francis Beaumont, Dramatist: A Portrait with Some Account of His Circle, Elizabetha & Jacobean, & of His Association with John Fletcher. 1973. Repr. of 1914 ed. 35.00 (ISBN 0-8274-0698-3). R West.

Gayley, Henry. How to Write for Development. 50p. 1981. 14.50 (ISBN 0-89964-186-5). Coun Adv & Supp Ed.

--How to Write for Development. 50p. 1981. 14.50 (ISBN 0-89964-186-5). Coun Adv & Supp Ed.

Gayley, Rano. Because of Love: My Life & Art with Meher Baba. Conlon, Ann, ed. LC 83-9845. (Illus.). 132p. 1983. 45.00 (ISBN 0-913078-45-X). Sheriar Pr.

Gaylin, W., jt. ed. see Macklin, R.

Gaylin, Wilard. Psychodynamic Understanding of Depression: The Meaning of Despair. rev. & 2nd ed. LC 84-45120. 436p. 1984. 30.00 (ISBN 0-317-15101-0). Aronson.

Gaylin, Willard. Caring. 1979. pap. 2.25 (ISBN 0-380-44693-6, 44693-6). Avon.

--Feelings. 240p. 1984. pap. 2.95 (ISBN 0-345-32493-5). Ballantine.

--Feelings: Our Vital Signs. (General Ser.). 1979. lib. bdg. 14.95 (ISBN 0-8161-6767-2, Large Print Bks). G K Hall.

--Feelings: Our Vital Signs. LC 78-2130. 1979. 10.95i (ISBN 0-06-011459-2, HarpT). Har-Row.

--The Killing of Bonnie Garland: A Question of Justice. (Illus.). 368p. 1983. pap. 6.95 (ISBN 0-14-006727-2). Penguin.

--The Rage Within: Anger in Modern Life. 320p. 1984. 16.95 (ISBN 0-671-42130-1). S&S.

Gaylin, Willard, ed. Meaning of Despair: Psychoanalytic Contributions to the Understanding of Depression. LC 68-17262. 1968. 25.00x (ISBN 0-87668-028-7). Aronson.

Gaylin, Willard & Macklin, Ruth, eds. Who Speaks for the Child? The Problems of Proxy Consent. (The Hastings Center Series in Ethics). 328p. 1982. 25.00x (ISBN 0-306-40860-0, Plenum Pr). Plenum Pub.

Gaylin, Willard, et al. Doing Good: The Limits of Benevolence. LC 77-8876. 1978. pap. 5.95 (ISBN 0-394-73372-X). Pantheon.

Gaylin, Willard, et al, eds. Violence & the Politics of Research. LC 81-15900. (The Hastings Center Series in Ethics). 272p. 1981. text ed. 25.00 (ISBN 0-306-40789-2, Plenum Pr). Plenum Pub.

Gaylor, Anne N. Abortion Is a Blessing. LC 75-24775. 140p. 1976. 4.95 (ISBN 0-88437-006-2). Psych Dimensions.

--Lead Us Not into Penn Station. 1983. 5.00 (ISBN 0-318-00995-1). Freedom Rel Found.

Gaylor, Annie L. Woe to the Women-the Bible Tells Me So. 1981. 5.95. Freedom Rel Found.

Gaylor, John. Military Badge Collecting. (Illus.). 176p. 1983. 26.50 (ISBN 0-436-37705-5, Pub. by Secker & Warburg UK). David & Charles.

Gaylord, C. N., jt. auth. see Gaylord, E. H., Jr.

Gaylord, Charles N., jt. auth. see Gaylord, Edwin H.

Gaylord, Charles N., jt. auth. see Gaylord, Edwin H., Jr.

Gaylord, Chuck. Working out Without Weights: A Gymnast's Fitness Program You Can Do at Home Without Special Equipment. LC 84-29606. (Illus.). 1985. 17.95 (ISBN 0-688-04811-0). Morrow.

Gaylord, E. H., Jr. & Gaylord, C. N. Structural Engineering Handbook. 2nd ed. 1979. 67.50 (ISBN 0-07-023123-0). McGraw.

Gaylord, E. W., jt. auth. see Hughes, G.

Gaylord, Edwin H. & Gaylord, Charles N. Design of Steel Structures. 2nd ed. (Civil Engineering Ser.). (Illus.). 640p. 1972. text ed. 46.00 (ISBN 0-07-023110-9). McGraw.

Gaylord, Edwin H., Jr. & Gaylord, Charles N. Design of Steel Bins for Storage of Bulk Solids. (Illus.). 400p. 1984. professional 70.00 (ISBN 0-13-201368-1). P-H.

Gaylord, F. R. Merchandising New & Used Trucks. 1981. 15.50. Northwood Campus Bkstore.

--Merchandising Truck Parts & Service. 1983. 17.95. Northwood Campus Bkstore.

--Organization & Management of the Truck Dealership. 1979. 15.50. Northwood Campus Bkstore.

Gaylord, Gloria L. & Ried, Glenda E. Careers in Accounting. LC 83-73709. 225p. 1984. 12.25 (ISBN 0-87094-433-9); pap. 9.95 (ISBN 0-87094-547-5). Dow Jones-Irwin.

Gaylord, Louise, jt. auth. see Abercrombie, V. T.

Gaylord, Norman. High Polymers Series, Vol. 13, Pt. 3. LC 62-15824. 318p. 1962. 32.00 (ISBN 0-686-81269-7). Krieger.

Gaylord, Norman G. Reduction with Complex Metal Hydrides. LC 55-8227. (Illus.). 1062p. 1956. text ed. 45.00 (ISBN 0-470-29436-1, Pub. by Wiley). Krieger.

Gaylord, Susan, jt. auth. see Phillips, Harry T.

Gayn, Mark. Japan Diary. LC 80-51196. 530p. 1981. pap. 9.50 (ISBN 0-8048-1369-8). C E Tuttle.

Gaynell, Catherine. Three Hundred & Sixty-Five Days of Black History. 2nd ed. (Illus.). 14p. 1983. 7.15 (ISBN 0-911249-01-X). Clover Intl.

Gaynell, Jim, jt. auth. see Cronin, Gaynell.

Gayner, Jeffrey. Namibia: The Road to Independence. 1979. pap. 15.00 (ISBN 0-930690-12-5). Coun Soc Econ.

Gaynes, Martin J., jt. auth. see Zuckman, Harvey L.

Gaynes, Norman I. Formulation of Organic Coatings. LC 67-9633. pap. 99.50 (ISBN 0-317-10671-6, 2055296). Bks Demand UMI.

Gaynor, Anne. Fate's Passion. (Orig.). 1982. pap. 3.25 (ISBN 0-8217-1022-2). Zebra.

--Rebel Rapture. 1983. pap. 3.50 (ISBN 0-8217-1136-9). Zebra.

Gaynor, Elizabeth, et al. Finland: Living Design. LC 84-42645. (Illus.). 252p. 1984. 35.00 (ISBN 0-8478-0545-X). Rizzoli Intl.

Gaynor, Frank, jt. auth. see Pei, Mario.

Gaynor, Frank, ed. New Military & Naval Dictionary. Repr. of 1951 ed. lib. bdg. 19.75x (ISBN 0-8371-2129-9, GAMN). Greenwood.

Gaynor, Frank, ed. see Freud, Sigmund.

Gaynor, Frank, jt. ed. see Pei, Mario.

Gaynor, Frank, tr. see Friedrich, Johannes.

Gaynor, Frank, tr. see Katz, David.

Gaynor, Frank, tr. see Planck, Max K.

Gaynor, John S. Life of St. Vincent Pallotti. 1980. 4.00 (ISBN 0-8198-4401-2); pap. 3.00 (ISBN 0-8198-4402-0). Dghtrs St Paul.

Gaynor, Kevin A., jt. auth. see O'Reilly, James T.

Gaynor, Stella H. Reading Comprehension Fourth Grade Measured. 100p. 1984. 29.95 (ISBN 0-913472-09-3); Apple II disc avail. Villa Pr.

Gayral, P. Les Algues des Cotes Francaises: Manche et Atlantique. (Illus.). 632p. (Orig., Fr.). 1982. pap. text ed. 28.00 (ISBN 3-87429-204-5). Lubrecht & Cramer.

Gayre Of Gayre & Nigg, Robert. The Armorial Who Is Who, 1966-1969. 3rd ed. (Illus.). 248p. 1970. 15.00 (ISBN 0-8063-0476-6). Genealog Pub.

Gaytan, C. Diccionario Mitologico. (Span.). 3.75 (ISBN 0-686-56651-3, S-25775). French & Eur.

Gaythwaite, John W. The Marine Environment & Structural Design. 236p. 1981. 26.50 (ISBN 0-442-24834-2). Van Nos Reinhold.

Gay-Tifft, Eugene, tr. see Tutein, Peter.

Gazarian-Gautier, Marie-Lise. Gabriela Mistral. 1974. 7.50 (ISBN 0-8199-0544-5). Franciscan Herald.

Gazda, George G., et al. Interpersonal Communication: A Handbook for Health Professionals. LC 82-6755. 298p. 1982. 31.50 (ISBN 0-89443-655-4). Aspen Systems.

Gazda, George M. Basic Approaches to Group Psychotherapy & Group Counseling. 3rd ed. (Illus.). 604p. 1982. 27.50x (ISBN 0-398-04652-2). C C Thomas.

--Group Counseling: A Developmental Approach. 3rd ed. 1984. text ed. 29.64 (ISBN 0-205-08142-8, 248142). Allyn.

--Innovations to Group Psychotherapy. 2nd ed. (Illus.). 344p. 1981. 16.75x (ISBN 0-398-04152-0). C C Thomas.

--Theories & Methods of Group Counseling in the Schools. 2nd ed. (Illus.). 384p. 1976. 24.75x (ISBN 0-398-03547-4). C C Thomas.

Gazda, George M. & Corsini, Raymond J. Theories of Learning: A Comparative Approach. LC 79-91101. 483p. 1980. text ed. 24.95 (ISBN 0-87581-253-8). Peacock Pubs.

Gazda, George M., jt. auth. see Catterall, Calvin D.

Gazda, George M., et al. Human Relations Development: A Manual for Educators. 3rd ed. 1983. pap. text ed. 21.00 (ISBN 0-205-08050-2, 248050); write for info. instrs' manual free (ISBN 0-205-08051-0, 248051). Allyn.

Gazdanov, Gaito. An Evening with Claire. Daynard, J., tr. 1984. 19.50 (ISBN 0-88233-934-6). Ardis Pubs.

--Vecher U Kler. (Rus.). 1979. 12.00 (ISBN 0-88233-406-9); pap. 4.50 (ISBN 0-88233-407-7). Ardis Pubs.

Gazdar, Gerald. Pragmatics: Implicature, Presupposition & Logical Form. 1979. 21.50 (ISBN 0-12-278450-2). Acad Pr.

Gazdar, Gerald & Klein, Ewan. A Bibliography of Contemporary Linguistic Research. LC 77-83358. (Library of Humanities Reference Bks.: No. 119). 445p. 1978. lib. bdg. 61.00 (ISBN 0-8240-9852-8). Garland Pub.

Gazdar, Gerald, et al. Generalized Phrase Structure Grammar. 320p. 1985. text ed. 35.00x (ISBN 0-674-34455-3); pap. text ed. 11.50x (ISBN 0-674-34456-1). Harvard U Pr.

Gaze, Harry. How to Live Forever: The Science & Practice. 205p. 1963. pap. 5.95 (ISBN 0-88697-033-4). Life Science.

Gaze, R. M. Formation of Nerve Connections. 1970. 59.50 (ISBN 0-12-278550-9). Acad Pr.

Gaze, R. M., et al, eds. Growth & the Development of Pattern: Special Issue of Journal of Embryology & Experimental Morphology, Supplement to Vol. 65. LC 81-15452. (Illus.). 324p. 1982. Cambridge U Pr.

Gazell, James A. The Future of State Court Management. (National University Pubns. Multi-Disciplinary Studies in the Law). 100p. 1977. 12.50 (ISBN 0-8046-9195-9, 9195, Pub. by Kennikat). Assoc Faculty Pr.

Gazella, Jacqueline G. Nutrition for the Childbearing Year. LC 79-64367. (Illus.). 1979. spiralbound 10.50 (ISBN 0-934104-01-8). Woodland.

Gazes. Clinical Cardiology. 2nd ed. 1983. 36.95 (ISBN 0-8151-3319-7). Year Bk Med.

Gazes, Anthimos, ed. Lexikon tes Hellenikes Glosses Tritomon: Lexicon of the Greek Language in Three Volumes, 3 vols. 2627p. (Gr.). 1980. Repr. of 1835 ed. lib. bdg. 450.00x (ISBN 0-89241-136-8). Caratzas.

Gazet, J. C. Carcinoma of the Liver, Biliary Tract & Pancreas. (Management of Malignant Disease Ser.). 200p. 1984. text ed. 29.50 (ISBN 0-7131-4333-9). E Arnold.

Gaziano, Rosalie F. Seasons & Celebrations. 144p. 1984. pap. 7.95 (ISBN 0-88289-443-9). Pelican.

Gazin, Patricia A. Castles on the Sand: An Incomplete Chronicle of the Habitations of Ancient Hermosans. (Illus.). 1977. spiral bdg., signed ltd. ed. 15.00 (ISBN 0-686-00669-0). P Gazin.

Gazit, Mordechai. The Peace Process Nineteen Sixty-Nine to Nineteen Seventy-Three: Efforts & Contacts, No. 35. (Jerusalem Papers on Peace Problems). 155p. 1983. pap. text ed. 12.00x (Pub by Magnes Israel). Humanities.

--President Kennedy's Policy toward the Arab States & Israel. 134p. (Orig.). 1983. pap. text ed. 9.95x (ISBN 0-8156-7051-6, Pub. by Shiloah Ctr Mid East & African Studies Israel). Syracuse U Pr.

Gazit, Shlomo. Risk, Glory & Rescue Operations. (Harvard Studies in International Affairs Ser.). 180p. 1982. 14.95x (ISBN 0-87674-054-9, 47); pap. 7.95x (ISBN 0-87674-079-4). U Pr of Amer.

Gazley, John G. American Opinion of German Unification, 1848-1871. LC 77-130939. (Columbia University Social Science Studies Ser.: No. 267). 1970. Repr. of 1926 ed. 10.00 (ISBN 0-404-51267-4). AMS Pr.

--The Life of Arthur Young, Seventeen Forty-One to Eighteen Twenty. (Memoirs Ser.: Vol. 97). (Illus.). 1973. 12.50 (ISBN 0-87169-097-7). Am Philos.

--The Life of Arthur Young: 1741-1820. LC 72-89402. (American Philosophical Society Memoirs Ser.: Vol. 97). pap. 160.00 (ISBN 0-317-27910-6, 2025133). Bks Demand UMI.

Gazquez, J. L., jt. ed. see Keller, J.

Gazvoda, Edward A., Jr. & Haney, William M., III. The Harvard Entrepreneurs Society's Guide to Making Money: Or the Tycoon's Handbook. 160p. 1983. pap. 6.70i (ISBN 0-316-30590-1); 6.95i. Little.

Gazzaniga, Alan B., et al. Emergency Care: Principles & Practice for the EMT-Paramedic. 2nd ed. (Illus.). 1979. 22.95 (ISBN 0-8359-1675-8); instrs'. manual avail. (ISBN 0-8359-1676-6). Reston.

Gazzaniga, Michael S. The Bisected Brain. LC 77-105426. (Neuroscience Ser.: 2). pap. 46.00 (ISBN 0-317-26218-1, 2055688). Bks Demand UMI.

--Psychology. 1980. text ed. 26.50 scp (ISBN 0-06-042286-6, HarpC); scp study guide 9.50 (ISBN 0-06-043888-6); instr's manual avail. (ISBN 0-06-362362-5). Har-Row.

--Social Brain: Discovering the Networks of the Mind. LC 85-47563. 240p. 1985. 17.95 (ISBN 0-317-20651-6). Basic.

Gazzaniga, Michael S. & Ledoux, Joseph. The Integrated Mind. LC 77-20101. (Illus.). 180p. 1978. 24.50 (ISBN 0-306-31085-6, Plenum Pr). Plenum Pub.

Gazzaniga, Michael S., ed. Handbook of Behavioral Neurobiology, Vol. 2: Neuropsychology. LC 78-21459. 586p. 1979. 55.00x (ISBN 0-306-35192-7, Plenum Pr). Plenum Pub.

--Handbook of Cognitive Neuroscience. 428p. 1984. 45.00x (ISBN 0-306-41290-X, Plenum Pr). Plenum Pub.

Gazzaniga, Michael S. & Blakemore, Colin, eds. Handbook of Psychobiology. 1975. 57.50 (ISBN 0-12-278656-4). Acad Pr.

Gazzillo, Karen W. Superheroes of Long Ago: A Teacher's Handbook. LC 82-18952. (Illus.). 176p. (Orig.). 1982. pap. 12.95 (ISBN 0-8298-0630-X). Pilgrim NY.

Gazzo, Michael see Strasberg, Lee.

Gbadamosi, Bakare & Beier, Ulli. Not Even God Is Ripe Enough. (African Writers Ser.). 1968. pap. text ed. 3.50x (ISBN 0-435-90048-X). Heinemann Ed.

Gbadamosi, T. G. The Growth of Islam Among the Yoruba: 1841-1908. (Ibadan History Ser.). (Illus.). 1978. text ed. 23.50x (ISBN 0-391-00834-X). Humanities.

Gbala, Helen. A Manual of AACR 2 Level 1 Examples. 2nd ed. Swanson, Edward, ed. 32p. 1985. pap. 12.50 (ISBN 0-936996-22-6). Soldier Creek.

Gdoutos, E. E. Problems of Mixed Mode Crack Propagation. 250p. 1984. lib. bdg. 53.00 (ISBN 90-247-3055-4, Pub. by Martinus Nijhoff Netherlands). Kluwer Academic.

Gdoutos, E. E., jt. auth. see Theocaris, P. S.

Gdowski, Charles, jt. auth. see Lachar, David.

Geach, Hugh & Szwed, Elizabeth, eds. Providing Civil Justice for Children. 240p. 1983. pap. text ed. 19.95 (ISBN 0-7131-6400-X). E Arnold.

Geach, P., ed. see Prior, Arthur N.

Geach, P. T. Logic Matters. LC 72-138286. 1972. pap. 6.95x (ISBN 0-520-03847-9, CAMPUS222). U of Cal Pr.

--Providence & Evil. LC 76-28005. 1977. 24.95 (ISBN 0-521-21477-7). Cambridge U Pr.

--Reason & Argument. LC 76-19961. 1977. pap. 6.95x (ISBN 0-520-03289-6). U of Cal Pr.

--Truth, Love, & Immortality: An Introduction to McTaggart's Philosophy. LC 78-62842. 1979. 22.00x (ISBN 0-520-03755-3). U of Cal Pr.

--The Virtues. LC 76-19627. 1977. 27.95 (ISBN 0-521-21350-9). Cambridge U Pr.

Geach, P. T., ed. see Prior, Arthur N.

Geach, Peter, ed. see Frege, Gottlob.

Geach, Peter T. Reference & Generality: An Examination of Some Medieval & Modern Theories. 3rd ed. LC 80-10977. (Contempory Philosophy Ser.). 256p. 1980. 24.95x (ISBN 0-8014-1315-X). Cornell U Pr.

Geach, Peter T., ed. see Descartes, Rene.

Geach, Peter T., tr. see Descartes, Rene.

Geagan, Daniel J. The Athenian Constitution After Sulla. LC 70-52614. (Hesperia Ser.: Supplement 12). (Illus.). 1967. pap. 12.50x (ISBN 0-87661-512-4). Am Sch Athens.

Geagea, Nilo. Mary of the Koran: A Meeting Point Between Islam & Christianism. Fares, Lawrence T., tr. LC 82-3804. 324p. 1984. 17.50 (ISBN 0-8022-2395-8). Philos Lib.

Geahigan, George, ed. Career Education in the Visual Arts: Representative Programs & Projects. 127p. 1980. 9.95 (ISBN 0-937652-13-X). Natl Art Ed.

Geake, R. Robert. Primary Tracking. rev. ed. Smith, Donald E., ed. (Michigan Tracking Program Ser.). 1975. pap. text ed. 3.25x (ISBN 0-914004-41-7). Ulrich.

Geake, R. Robert & Smith, Donald E. Visual Tracking. (Michigan Tracking Program Ser.). 1975. pap. text ed. 3.95x (ISBN 0-914004-43-3). Ulrich.

Geake, R. Robert & Smith, Judith M. Word Tracking. Smith, Donald E., ed. (Michigan Tracking Program). 1975. pap. text ed. 3.25x (ISBN 0-914004-44-1). Ulrich.

Gealt, Adelheid, ed. Domenico Tiepolo: The Punchinello Drawings. (Illus.). 196p. 1985. 85.00 (ISBN 0-8076-1132-8). Braziller.

Gealt, Adelheid M. Looking at Art. 304p. 1983. 29.95 (ISBN 0-8352-1730-2); pap. 19.95 (ISBN 0-8352-1731-0). Bowker.

Gealy, Fred D., et al. Companion to the Hymnal. 1970. 19.95 (ISBN 0-687-09259-0). Abingdon.

Geanakoplos, Deno J. Byzantium & the Renaissance: Greek Scholars in Venice: Studies in the Dissemination of Greek Learning from Byzantium to Western Europe. (Illus.). xiii, 348p. 1973. Repr. of 1962 ed. 21.00 (ISBN 0-208-01311-3, Archon). Shoe String.

--Byzantium: Church, Society, & Civilization Seen Through Contemporary Eyes. LC 83-4806. 432p. 1984. lib. bdg. 27.50x (ISBN 0-226-28460-3). U of Chicago Pr.

--Emperor Michael Palaeologus & the West, 1258-1282: A Study in Byzantine - Latin Relations. (Illus.). xii, 434p. 1973. Repr. of 1959 ed. 25.00 (ISBN 0-208-01310-5, Archon). Shoe String.

--Interaction of the "Sibling" Byzantine & Western Cultures in the Middle Ages & Italian Renaissance (330-1600) LC 74-29722. 1976. 47.00x (ISBN 0-300-01831-2). Yale U Pr.

--Western Medieval Civilization. 1979. text ed. 23.95 (ISBN 0-669-00868-0). Heath.

Geanangel, Russell A. & Wendlandt, Wesley W. Experimental Chemistry. 5th ed. 1979. 11.95 (ISBN 0-8403-2355-7). Kendall-Hunt.

Geaney, Dennis J. The Prophetic Parish: A Center for Peace & Justice. 144p. (Orig.). 1983. pap. 6.95 (ISBN 0-86683-807-4). Winston Pr.

Geaney, Dennis J. & Sokol, Dolly. Parish Celebrations: A Reflective Guide for Liturgy Planning. (Orig.). 1983. pap. 5.95 (ISBN 0-89622-190-3). Twenty-Third.

Geankoplis. Transport Processes & Unit Operations. 2nd ed. 1983. text ed. 48.97 (ISBN 0-205-07788-9, 3277887). Allyn.

Geankoplis, Christie J. Mass Transport Phenomena. LC 79-154348. 1984. Repr. of 1972 ed. 34.95 (ISBN 0-9603070-0-1). Geankoplis.

--Transport Processes: Momentum, Heat & Mass. 350p. 1983. scp 39.21 (ISBN 0-205-07787-0, 327787). Allyn.

Geankoplos, Deno J. Byzantine East & Latin West: Two Worlds of Christendom in Middle Ages & Renaissance. (Illus.). xii, 206p. 1976. Repr. of 1966 ed. 12.50 (ISBN 0-208-01615-5, Archon). Shoe String.

Gear, Bonnie. Seasons in Life. White, Mosazelle N., ed. LC 82-62324. 61p. (Orig.). 1983. pap. 5.95x (ISBN 0-936026-19-7). R&M Pub Co.

Gear, C. W. Computer Organization & Programming. 4th ed. (Computer Science Ser.). 432p. 1985. 39.95 (ISBN 0-07-023049-8). McGraw.

--Numerical Initial Value Problems in Ordinary Differential Equations. (Automatic Computation Ser). (Illus.). 1971. ref. ed. 40.00 (ISBN 0-13-626606-1). P-H.

Gear, C. William. Computer Organization & Programming. 2nd ed. (Computer Science Ser.). (Illus.). 448p. 1974. text ed. 37.95 (ISBN 0-07-023076-5). McGraw.

--Introduction to Computers, Structured Programming, & Applications. 1978. Module P: Programming & Languages. 11.95 (ISBN 0-574-21187-X, 13-4187); Module A: Applications & Algorithms In Computer Science. 11.95 (ISBN 0-574-21188-8, 13-4188); Module A: Applications & Algorithms in Science & Engineering. 11.95 (ISBN 0-574-21189-6, 13-4189); Module A: Applications & Algorithms in Business. 11.95 (ISBN 0-574-21190-X, 13-4190); Module C: Computers & Systems. 11.95 (ISBN 0-574-21191-8, 13-4191); FORTRAN & WATFIV Manual. 7.95 (ISBN 0-574-21192-6, 13-4192); Pascal Manual. 7.95 (ISBN 0-574-21193-4, 13-4193); PL/1 & PL/C Manual. 7.95 (ISBN 0-574-21194-2); Basic Manual 7.95. SRA.

--Programming in Pascal. 224p. 1983. text ed. 14.95 (ISBN 0-574-21360-0, 13-4360). SRA.

Gear, Clara E. Le see Le Gear, Clara E.

Gear, Felix B. Our Presbyterian Belief. LC 79-23421. 90p. (Orig.). 1980. pap. 6.95 (ISBN 0-8042-0676-7). John Knox.

Gear, H. S. & Deutschman, Z. Disease Control & International Travel: A Review of the International Sanitary Regulations, Vol. 10, Nos. 9-10. (Illus., Eng. Fr. & Span.). pap. 1.20 (ISBN 92-4-158001-1). World Health.

Gear, Josephine. Masters or Servants? A Study of Selected English Painters & Their Patrons of the Late 18th & Early 19th Centuries. LC 76-23619. (Outstanding Dissertations in the Fine Arts Ser.- 18th Century). (Illus.). 453p. 1977. Repr. lib. bdg. 68.00 (ISBN 0-8240-2690-X). Garland Pub.

Gear, Maria C. & Hill, Melvyn A. Working Through Narcissism: Treating Its Sado-Masochistic Structure. LC 81-65688. 512p. 1982. 30.00 (ISBN 0-87668-448-7). Aronson.

Gear, Maria C., et al. Patients & Agents: Transference & Countertransference in Psychotherapy. LC 82-24468. 340p. 1983. 27.50 (ISBN 0-87668-497-5). Aronson.

Gear, Michael, jt. auth. see Gough, Malcolm.

Gearaets, Walter J. Ocular Syndromes. 3rd ed. LC 75-6708. pap. 160.00 (ISBN 0-317-26685-3, 2056000). Bks Demand UMI.

Geare, Michael & Corby, Michael. Dracula's Diary. 1983. 10.95 (ISBN 0-8253-0143-2). Beaufort Bks NY.

Gearey, Caroline. Cowper & Mary Unwin. 30.00 (ISBN 0-8274-2109-5). R West.

Gearey, John. Goethe's "Faust". The Making of Part I. LC 80-25826. 256p. 1981. 23.50x (ISBN 0-300-02571-8). Yale U Pr.

Gearey, John, ed. see Goethe, Johann W.

Gearhart, E. A. John Updike Bibliography. 1985. 62.50 (ISBN 0-317-19967-6). Porter.

Gearhart, Elizabeth A. John Updike: A Comprehensive Bibliography with Selected Annotations. 128p. 1980. Repr. of 1978 ed. lib. bdg. 25.00 (ISBN 0-8414-4596-6). Folcroft.

--John Updike: A Comprehensive Bibliography with Selected Annotations. LC 78-11800. 1978. lib. bdg. 22.50 (ISBN 0-8482-4174-6). Norwood Edns.

Gearhart, Sally M. The Wanderground. 196p. 1984. pap. 6.95 (ISBN 0-317-03219-4). Alyson Pubns.

Gearhart, Susan W. Opportunities in Beauty Culture. (VGM Career Bks.). (Illus.). 160p. 1983. 7.95 (ISBN 0-8442-6291-9, 6291-9, Passport Bks.); pap. 5.95 (ISBN 0-8442-6292-7). Natl Textbk.

Gearhart, Suzanne. The Open Boundary of History & Fiction: A Critical Approach to the French Enlightenment. LC 84-2162. 330p. 1984. 32.50x (ISBN 0-691-06608-6). Princeton U Pr.

Gearheart, B. R. Administration of Special Education: A Guide for General Administrators & Special Educators. 228p. 1970. 14.75x (ISBN 0-398-00661-X). C C Thomas.

--Education of the Exceptional Child: History, Present Practices & Trends. (Illus.). 398p. 1983. pap. text ed. 15.25 (ISBN 0-8191-2417-6). U Pr of Amer.

Gearheart, B. R. & Wright, William S. Organization & Administration of Educational Programs for Exceptional Children. 2nd ed. (Illus.). 288p. 1979. 29.75x (ISBN 0-398-03891-0). C C Thomas.

Gearheart, Bill. Learning Disabilities: Educational Strategies. 3rd ed. LC 80-39700. (Illus.). 302p. 1981. text ed. 22.95 (ISBN 0-8016-1768-5). Mosby.

Gearheart, Bill R. Special Education for the Eighties. LC 79-20647. (Illus.). 498p. 1980. text ed. 23.95 (ISBN 0-8016-1759-6). Mosby.

--Teaching the Learning Disabled: A Combined Task Process Approach. LC 75-42478. (Illus.). 246p. 1976. 15.95 (ISBN 0-8016-1762-6). Mosby.

Gearheart, Bill R. & DeRuiter, James. Teaching Mildly & Moderately Handcapped Students. (Illus.). 384p. 1986. text ed. 26.95 (ISBN 0-13-893900-4). P-H.

Gearheart, Bill R. & Litton, Freddie W. The Trainable Retarded: A Foundations Approach. 2nd ed. LC 78-13959. (Illus.). 290p. 1979. 17.95 (ISBN 0-8016-1761-8). Mosby.

Gearheart, Bill R. & Weishahn, Mel W. The Exceptional Student in the Regular Classroom. 3rd ed. (Illus.). 416p. 1984. text ed. 22.95 (ISBN 0-8016-1756-1). Mosby.

--The Handicapped Student in the Regular Classroom. 2nd ed. LC 79-23706. 304p. 1980. text ed. 22.95 (ISBN 0-8016-1760-X). Mosby.

Gearheart, George, ed. see Hawley, Newton & Suppes, Patrick.

Gearien, James E. Methods of Drug Analysis. LC 68-25207. pap. 72.80 (20255999). Bks Demand UMI.

Gearin, Kathleen R., jt. auth. see Cleary, Edward J.

Gearing, Frederick & Sangree, Lucinda, eds. Toward a Cultural Theory of Education & Schooling. (World Anthropology Ser.). 1979. text ed. 23.20x (ISBN 90-279-7760-7). Mouton.

Gearing, P. & Brunson, E. Breaking into Print: How to Get Your Work Published. 1977. (Spec); pap. 3.45 (ISBN 0-13-081679-5, Spec). P-H.

Geary. The Complete Handbook of Home Exterior Repair & Maintenance. (Illus.). 352p. 1982. pap. 9.95 (ISBN 0-8306-1382-X, 1382). TAB Bks.

--How to Design & Build Your Own Workspace-with Plans. 384p. 1981. pap. 9.95 (ISBN 0-8306-1269-6, 1269). TAB Bks.

Geary, A. Advanced Mathematics for Technical Students. pap. 145.50 (ISBN 0-317-08483-6, 2010171). Bks Demand UMI.

Geary, C. G., ed. Aplastic Anaemia. 1979. text ed. 37.50 (ISBN 0-7216-0729-2, Pub. by Bailliere-Tindall). Saunders.

Geary, D. P., jt. auth. see Mayhall, P. D.

Geary, Dick. European Labor Protest: Eighteen Forty-Eight to Nineteen Thirty-Nine. 1981. 27.50 (ISBN 0-312-26974-9). St Martin.

Geary, Don. Build It with Plywood: Eighty-Eight Furniture Projects. (Illus.). 304p. 1983. 18.95 (ISBN 0-8306-0330-1, 1430); pap. 13.50 (ISBN 0-8306-0230-5). TAB Bks.

--The Home Brewer's Handbook. (Illus.). 240p. (Orig.). 1983. 16.95 (ISBN 0-8306-2461-9, 1461); pap. 10.25 (ISBN 0-8306-1461-3). TAB Bks.

--How to Sharpen Anything. LC 82-5955. (Illus.). 224p. (Orig.). 1983. o.p 19.95 (ISBN 0-8306-2463-5, 1463); pap. 13.95 (ISBN 0-8306-1463-X). TAB Bks.

--The Welder's Bible. (Illus.). 420p. 1980. o.p 19.95 (ISBN 0-8306-9938-4); pap. 14.95 (ISBN 0-8306-1244-0, 1244). TAB Bks.

Geary, Edward. Depredations & Massacre by the Snake River Indians. 16p. 1966. Repr. pap. 2.50 (ISBN 0-87770-049-4). Ye Galleon.

Geary, Edward A. Goodbye to Poplarhaven: Recollections of a Utah Boyhood. (Bonneville Bks.). (Illus.). 192p. 1985. pap. 8.95 (ISBN 0-87480-249-0). U of Utah Pr.

Geary, Edward J., jt. auth. see Nunn, Robert R.

Geary, Edward J., ed. Solitudes: Premieres Lectures Modernes. (Integral French Eds. Ser). (Fr). 1965. pap. text ed. 2.75x (ISBN 0-685-20247-X). Schoenhof.

Geary, Edward J., ed. see Diderot, Denis.

Geary, Frank. Land Tenure & Unemployment. LC 77-81147. Repr. of 1925 ed. 25.00x (ISBN 0-678-00509-5). Kelley.

Geary, Gerald J. The Secularization of the California Missions (1810-1846) LC 73-3572. (Catholic University of America. Studies in American Church History: No. 17). Repr. of 1934 ed. 26.00 (ISBN 0-404-57767-9). AMS Pr.

Geary, Ida. The Leaf Book: A Field Guide to Plants of Northern California. LC 78-188679. (Illus.). 388p. 1976. pap. 6.00 (ISBN 0-912908-01-7). Tamal Land.

--Plant Printing. (Illus.). 1978. pap. 3.50 (ISBN 0-912908-03-3). Tamal Land.

Geary, Leo, intro. by see Johnson, Clarence L. & Smith, Maggie.

Geary, Michael, jt. auth. see Mertens, Thomas R.

Geary, Patrick J. Furta Sacra: Thefts of Relics in the Central Middle Ages. LC 77-85538. 1978. 25.00 (ISBN 0-691-05261-1). Princeton U Pr.

Geary, R. C. & Spencer, J. E. Elements of Linear Programing Economics Application. 2nd, rev. ed. (Griffins Statistical Monograph Ser.: No. 15). 1973. pap. 13.00x (ISBN 0-02-845230-5). Hafner.

Geary, R. C., jt. auth. see Spencer, J. E.

Geary, R. C., jt. auth. see Spencer, John E.

Geary, Rosemary J., jt. auth. see Blustein, Lotte.

Geary, Steven. Fur Trapping in North America. rev. & expanded ed. LC 84-16561. (Illus.). 160p. 1985. pap. 10.95 (ISBN 0-8329-0368-X, Pub. by Winchester Pr). New Century.

Geary, T. C. Justices of the Peace & Police Magistrates in South Dakota. 1971. write for info. U of SD Gov Res Bur.

Geary, Thomas C. Law Making in South Dakota. 3rd ed. 1958. write for info. U of SD Gov Res Bur.

Geary, Thomas C. & Zuercher, Frederick W. Nineteen Seventy Ballot Propositions in South Dakota. 1970. write for info. U of SD Gov Res Bur.

Geasland, Jack, jt. auth. see Wood, Bari.

Geauque, Edwin P. The Emperor's Tea. (Illus.). 1978. 5.00 (ISBN 0-87482-095-2). Wake-Brook.

--Handbook for Collectors. rev. ed. 1983. 5.00 (ISBN 0-87482-083-9). Wake Brook.

Geauque, Pierre. Kulani & the Shama Thrush. 1982. 5.00 (ISBN 0-87482-115-0). Wake-Brook.

Geba, Bruno H. Being at Leisure-Playing at Life: A Guide to Health & Joyful Living. LC 84-82403. (Illus.). 192p. 1985. 19.95 (ISBN 0-932057-01-2); pap. 14.95 (ISBN 0-932057-00-4). Leisure Sci Sys.

Geballe, Ronald, jt. ed. see Risley, John S.

Geballe, Theodore H., jt. auth. see White, Robert M.

Gebauer, Emanuel L., jt. auth. see Cornberg, Sol.

Gebauer, Paul. Art of Cameroon. (Illus.). 395p. (Orig.). 1979. 30.00 (ISBN 0-295-96195-3, Pub. by Portland Art Museum); pap. 14.95 (ISBN 0-295-96176-7). U of Wash Pr.

Gebbers, J. O. & Burkhardt, A. Hair-Spray Induced Lung Lesion. (Illus.). 1982. 60.00 (ISBN 0-08-029788-9). Pergamon.

Gebbert, Vera. George Saint & the Dragon. (Orig.). 1979. pap. 3.95 (ISBN 0-917200-28-4). ESPress.

Gebbett, Jean R. Henslaw of Hitcham. (Illus.). 1979. 20.00 (ISBN 0-900963-76-X, Pub. by Terence Dalton England). State Mutual Bk.

Gebbie, Donald A. Reproductive Anthropology: Descent Through Woman. LC 80-42013. 321p. 1981. 54.95x (ISBN 0-471-27985-4, Pub. by Wiley-Interscience). Wiley.

Gebbie, Melinda, jt. auth. see Smith, David.

Gebelein, Bob. Re-Educating Myself: An Introduction to a New Civilization. LC 85-60221. 288p. (Orig.). 1985. pap. 9.95 (ISBN 0-9614611-0-1). Omdega Pr.

Gebelein, Charles G., ed. Polymeric Materials & Artificial Organs. LC 84-9297. (ACS Symposium Ser.: No. 256). 208p. 1984. lib. bdg. 36.95x (ISBN 0-8412-0854-9). Am Chemical.

Gebelein, Charles G. & Carraher, Charles E., Jr., eds. Bioactive Polymeric Systems: An Overview. 675p. 1985. 95.00x (ISBN 0-306-41855-X, Plenum Pr). Plenum Pub.

Gebelein, Charles G. & Koblitz, Frank K., eds. Biomedical & Dental Applications of Polymers. LC 80-29429. (Polymer Science & Technology Ser.: Vol. 14). 504p. 1981. 75.00x (ISBN 0-306-40632-2, Plenum Pr). Plenum Pub.

Gebelein, Charles G. & Williams, David J., eds. Polymers in Solar Energy Utilization. LC 83-6367. (Symposium Ser.: No. 220). 519p. 1983. lib. bdg. 59.95 (ISBN 0-8412-0776-3). Am Chemical.

Gebelein, Charles G., jt. ed. see Carraher, Charles E., Jr.

Geben, Alma. Zeppaniki: Valley of the Gentle Wind. 1984. 7.95 (ISBN 0-533-05881-3). Vantage.

Geber. Of Furnaces. Russell, Richard, tr. pap. 4.95. Alchemical Pr.

--Of the Investigation, or Search of Perfection: Or, Search of Perfection. Russell, Richard, tr. 1983. pap. 2.95 (ISBN 0-916411-08-7, Pub. by Alchemical Pr). Holmes Pub.

Geber, Beryl & Newman, Stanton. Soweto's Children: The Development of Attitudes. (European Monographs in Social Psychology: No. 20). 1980. 39.50 (ISBN 0-12-278750-1). Acad Pr.

Gebert, et al. Transformers. 2nd ed. (Illus.). 1974. 16.95 (ISBN 0-8269-1602-3). Am Technical.

Gebert, Erika, jt. auth. see Schock, Sarina.

Gebert, Gordon, ed. Health-Care. 40p. 1981. 18.25 (ISBN 0-08-028091-9). Pergamon.

Gebert, K. National Electrical Code Blueprint Reading. 9th ed. (Illus.). 1983. pap. 15.95 (ISBN 0-8269-1550-7). Am Technical.

Gebert, Kenneth L. National Electrical Code Blueprint Reading: Based on the 1984 National Electrical Code. (Based on the Nineteen Eighty Four National Electrical Code Ser.). (Illus.). 192p. 1985. pap. 15.95 (ISBN 0-317-17095-3, Pub. by Am Technical). Sterling.

--National Electrical Code Blueprint Reading. price not set. Sterling.

Geberth, V. J. Practical Aspects of Homicide Investigation: Tactics, Procedures & Forensic Techniques. (Elsevier Series in Practical Aspects of Criminal & Forensic Investigations: Vol. 1). 488p. 1982. 26.50 (ISBN 0-444-00712-1). Elsevier.

Geber the Arabian. Of Furnaces. 1984. pap. 4.95 (ISBN 0-916411-38-9, Pub. by Alchemical Pr). Holmes Pub.

Gebhard, David. Charles F. A. Voysey, Architect. LC 75-15870. (Illus.). 1975. 12.95 (ISBN 0-912158-54-9). Hennessey.

Gebhard, David & Martinson, Tom. A Guide to the Architecture of Minnesota. LC 75-36032. 1978. 17.50x (ISBN 0-8166-0773-7); pap. 10.95 (ISBN 0-8166-0775-3). U of Minn Pr.

Gebhard, David & Winter, Robert. Architecture in Los Angeles: A Compleat Guide. (Illus.). 528p. 1985. pap. 14.95 (ISBN 0-87905-087-X, Peregrine Smith). Gibbs M Smith.

Gebhard, David, ed. see Chase, John.

Gebhard, David, ed. see Hanson, A. E.

Gebhard, Elizabeth R. The Theater of Isthmia. LC 72-80813. (Illus.). pap. 33.10 (ISBN 0-317-10659-7, 2015756). Bks Demand UMI.

Gebhard, Paul H., et al. Pregnancy, Birth & Abortion. LC 75-37383. (Indiana University Institute for Sex Research Ser.). 282p. 1976. Repr. of 1958 ed. lib. bdg. 22.50x (ISBN 0-8371-8663-3, GEPB). Greenwood.

Gebhard, Ruth, jt. auth. see Davis, James A.

Gebhard, Walter. Nietzsches Totalismus: Philosophie der Natur zwischen Verklarung und Verhangnis. 398p. (Ger.). 1983. 55.20 (ISBN 3-11-008958-0). De Gruyter.

Gebhard-L'Estrange, A. H. The Tradition of Silence in Myth & Legend. 1977. lib. bdg. 59.95 (ISBN 0-8490-2755-1). Gordon Pr.

Gebhardt, Chuck. Backpacking Death Valley. 2nd ed. LC 83-81945. (Illus.). 150p. 1985. pap. 3.50. C Gebhardt.

--Inside Death Valley. rev. 3rd ed. LC 80-83123. (Illus.). 166p. 1980. pap. 5.95 (ISBN 0-9601410-1-4). C Gebhardt.

Gebhardt, Eike, ed. Science As Behavior: Sociological Approaches to the Sciences. 576p. 1982. 29.95 (ISBN 0-8264-0015-9); pap. 12.95 (ISBN 0-8264-0024-8). Continuum.

Gebhardt, Eike, jt. ed. see Arato, Andrew.

Gebhardt, M. & Neuhaus, A. Landolt-Boernstein Numerical Data & Functional Relationships in Science & Technology, New Series, Group 3: Crystal & Solid State Physics, Vol. 8, Structure Data Of Organic Compounds. Hellwege, K. H., ed. 1972. 75.60 (ISBN 0-387-05732-3). Springer-Verlag.

Gebhardt, Marie-Louise. Foolish Old Man Who Moved Mountains. LC 68-57232. (Illus., Orig.). (gr. 1-3). 1969. pap. 1.75 (ISBN 0-377-19601-0). Friend Pr.

Gebhardt, Mattie L. Meatless Recipes. LC 75-4315. (Illus.). 130p. (Orig.). 1975. pap. 2.50 (ISBN 0-8356-0304-0, Quest). Theos Pub Hse.

Gebhardt, Walter. Special Collections in German Libraries. 1977. 59.20x (ISBN 3-11-005839-1). De Gruyter.

Gebhardt, William H., jt. auth. see Edmonds, I. G.

Gebhardt-Seele, Peter A. The Computer & the Child: A Montessori Approach. LC 84-19921. 1985. 19.95 (ISBN 0-88175-013-1). Computer Sci.

Gebhart, B. Heat Transfer. 2nd ed. 1971. text ed. 40.00 (ISBN 0-07-023127-3). McGraw.

Gebhart, E. Mystics & Heretics in Italy at the End of the Middle Ages. 1977. lib. bdg. 59.95 (ISBN 0-8490-2321-1). Gordon Pr.

Gebicki, Janusz M., jt. auth. see Bielski, Benon H.

Gebler, Carlo. The Eleventh Summer. 160p. 1985. 13.95 (ISBN 0-525-24331-3, 01354-410, Pub. by W Abrahams Bk). Dutton.

Gebler, Karl Von. Galileo Galilei & the Roman Curia from Authentic Sources. Sturge, Jane, tr. LC 76-1124. 1977. Repr. of 1897 ed. lib. bdg. 28.50x (ISBN 0-915172-11-9). Richwood Pub.

Geboy, Michael J. Communication & Behavior Management in Dentistry. 186p. 1985. 16.95 (ISBN 0-683-03439-1). Williams & Wilkins.

Gebser, Jean. The Ever-Present Origin: The Foundations & Manifestations of the Aperspectiveal World. Barstad, Noel & Mickunas, Algis, trs. LC 84-2475. (Illus.). 625p. 1985. 69.95x (ISBN 0-8214-0219-6). Ohio U Pr.

Gechneioner, K. A., Jr., et al, eds. Metallurgy at High Pressures & High Temperatures: Proceedings of a Symposium, Dallas, Texas, February 25-26, 1963. LC 64-18801. (Metallurgical Society Conferences Ser.: Vol. 22). pap. 105.80 (ISBN 0-317-10359-8, 2001510). Bks Demand UMI.

Geck, Francis J. Interior Design & Decoration - an Outline. 4th ed. 272p. 1971. write for info. wire coil (ISBN 0-697-08308-X). Wm C Brown.

Geckeler, Horst, jt. auth. see Coseriu, Eugenio.

Geckinli, N. C. & Yavus, D., eds. Discrete Fourier Transformation & Its Applications to Power Spectra Estimation. (Studies in Electrical & Electronic Engineering: No. 8). 340p. 1983. 78.75 (ISBN 0-444-41713-3). Elsevier.

Geckle, George L. John Marston's Drama: Themes, Images, Sources. LC 77-89777. 224p. 1979. 23.50 (ISBN 0-8386-2157-0). Fairleigh Dickinson.

Gecseg, F. & Peak, I. Algebraic Theory of Automata. (Disquisitiones Mathematicae Hungaricae Ser.: No. 2). 326p. (Fr.). 1971. 23.50x (ISBN 0-685-27555-8). Adlers Foreign Bks.

Gecseg, F., ed. Fundamentals of Computation Theory: Proceedings. (Lecture Notes in Computer Science: Vol. 117). 471p. 1981. pap. 26.50 (ISBN 0-387-10854-8). Springer-Verlag.

Gecsei, Jan. Architecture of Videotex Systems. (Illus.). 320p. 1983. 36.95 (ISBN 0-13-044776-5). P H.

Geczi, Mike. Futures: The Anti-Inflation Investment. 1980. pap. 2.95 (ISBN 0-380-75713-3, 75713-3, Discus). Avon.

Geczy, Steven. Basic Electrical Measurements. (Illus.). 144p. 1984. pap. 19.95 (ISBN 0-13-060285-X). P-H.

Geda, Sigitas. Songs of Autumn: Bilingual Edition. Zdanys, Jonas, tr. from Lithuanian. LC 78-26139. 1979. signed ed. o.s.i. 10.00x (ISBN 0-918366-16-X); pap. 3.00 (ISBN 0-918366-11-9). Slow Loris.

Gedalge, Andre. Treatise on Fugue. Levin, A., tr. 1964. 18.00 (ISBN 0-910648-02-6). Gamut Music.

--Treatise on the Fugue. Davis, Ferdinand, tr. LC 65-11241. Repr. of 1965 ed. 110.50 (ISBN 0-8357-9744-9, 2016219). Bks Demand UMI.

Gedalia, I., et al. The Role of Fluoride in Bone Structure. LC 72-87824. 48p. 1973. 5.00 (ISBN 0-87527-103-0). Green.

Gedaliah, Robert. P. E. P.-The Productivity Effectiveness Program. 1984. pap. 2.95 (ISBN 0-03-069866-9). HR&W.

Gedalof, Robin, ed. Paper Stays Put: A Collection of Inuit Writing. (Illus.). 176p. 1980. 12.95 (ISBN 0-295-95971-1, Pub. by Hurtig Pubs). U of Wash Pr.

Gedat, Gustav-Adolf. They Built for Eternity. facsimile ed. Bainton, Roland H., tr. LC 72-167345. (Essay Index Reprint Ser). Repr. of 1953 ed. 36.00 (ISBN 0-8369-2451-7). Ayer Co Pubs.

Gedda, L. Auxology: Human Growth in Health & Disorder. Parisi, P., ed. (Serono Symposia Ser.). 1978. 52.50 (ISBN 0-12-279050-2). Acad Pr.

Gedda, Luigi. Twins in History & Science. Comparetti, Marco M., tr. (Illus.). 266p. 1961. photocopy ed. 27.75x (ISBN 0-398-00662-8). C C Thomas.

Gedda, Luigi & Brenci, Gianni. Chronogenetics: The Inheritance of Biological Time. (Illus.). 232p. 1978. 32.75x (ISBN 0-398-03641-1). C C Thomas.

Gedda, Luigi, et al. Twin Research 3, Pt. A: Twin Biology & Multiple Pregnancy. LC 81-12376. (Progress in Clinical & Biological Research Ser.: Vol. 69A). 242p. 1981. 40.00 (ISBN 0-8451-0158-7). A R Liss.

--Twin Research 3, Pt. B: Intelligence, Personality, & Development. LC 81-12376. (Progress in Clinical & Biological Research Ser.: Vol. 69B). 308p. 1981. 48.00 (ISBN 0-8451-0159-5). A R Liss.

--Twin Research 3, Pt. C: Epidemiological & Clinical Studies. LC 81-12376. (Progress in Clinical & Biological Research Ser.: Vol. 69C). 302p. 1981. 48.00 (ISBN 0-8451-0160-9). A R Liss.

Gedde, Palmer. One Plus One Equals. Kujath, Mentor, ed. 1979. pap. 4.95 (ISBN 0-8100-0103-9, 12-1712). Northwest Pub.

Gedde, Walter. A Booke of Sundry Draughtes Principally for Glasiers: Whereunto Is Annexed How to Anniel in Glas, 4 pts. LC 78-26524. (English Experience Ser.: No. 316). (Illus.). 136p. 1971. Repr. of 1616 ed. Set. 21.00 (ISBN 90-221-0316-1). Walter J Johnson.

Gedde-Dahl, Tobias. Epidermolysis Bullosa: A Clinical, Genetic & Epidemiological Study. LC 70-139446. pap. 45.00 (ISBN 0-317-28819-9, 2020511). Bks Demand UMI.

Gedder, Palmer L. Two Gether. 1983. pap. 5.95 (12N1725). Northwest Pub.

Geddes, A. M., jt. ed. see Reeves, David S.

Geddes, A. M., jt. ed. see Williams, J. D.

Geddes, Ann E. Trends in Relief Expenditures, 1910-1935. LC 74-166327. (Research Monograph Ser.: Vol. 10). 1971. Repr. of 1937 ed. lib. bdg. 19.50 (ISBN 0-306-70342-4). Da Capo.

Geddes, Anne E., jt. auth. see Cole, William M.

Geddes, Arthur. Man & Land in South Asia. 350p. 1981. text ed. 22.00x (ISBN 0-391-02474-4, Pub. by Concept India). Humanities.

Geddes, C. L. Guide to Reference Books for Islamic Studies. (American Institute of Islamic Studies: No. 9). xiv, 429p. 1985. 42.00 (ISBN 0-933017-00-6). Am Inst Islamic.

Geddes, D. M. Airways Obstruction. (Topics in Respiratory Disease Ser.). 104p. 1981. 17.95 (ISBN 0-85200-425-7, Pub. by MTP Pr England). Kluwer Academic.

Geddes, Diana. Assertive Discipline Positive Reinforcement Activities. (Illus.). 48p. 1983. wkbk 5.95 (ISBN 0-9608978-3-6). Canter & Assoc.

Geddes, Dolores. Physical Activities for Individuals with Handicapping Conditions. 2nd ed. LC 77-26228. (Illus.). 150p. 1978. pap. text ed. 11.50 (ISBN 0-8016-1793-6). Mosby.

Geddes, Elisabeth & McNeill, Moyra. Blackwork Embroidery. (Illus.). 116p. 1976. pap. 3.95 (ISBN 0-486-23245-X). Dover.

Geddes, Gary. Conrad's Later Novels. 235p. 1980. 20.00x (ISBN 0-7735-0357-9). McGill-Queens U Pr.

--War & Other Measures. (House of Anansi Poetry Ser.: No. 35). 78p. (Orig.). 1976. pap. 4.95 (ISBN 0-88784-036-1, Pub. by Hse Anansi Pr Canada). U of Toronto Pr.

Geddes, Gordon E. Welcome Joy: Death in Puritan New England. Berkhofer, Robert, ed. LC 81-1468. (Studies in American History & Culture: No. 28). 270p. 1981. 39.95 (ISBN 0-8357-1181-1). UMI Res Pr.

Geddes, James D. Ground Movements & Structures. 964p. 1981. 85.95x (ISBN 0-470-27208-2). Halsted Pr.

--Large Ground Movements & Structures. LC 78-19092. 1064p. 1978. 96.95x (ISBN 0-470-26460-8). Halsted Pr.

Geddes, Joseph A. The United Order Among the Mormons (Missouri Phase) An Unfinished Experiment in Economic Organization. LC 72-8247. Repr. of 1924 ed. 19.50 (ISBN 0-404-11001-0). AMS Pr.

Geddes, L. A. Cardiovascular Medical Devices. LC 83-16746. 392p. 1984. 47.50 (ISBN 0-471-88105-8, Pub. by Wiley-Interscience). Wiley.

Geddes, L. A. & Baker, L. E. Principles of Applied Biomedical Instrumentation. 2nd ed. LC 74-34390. (Biomedical Engineering & Health Systems Ser.). 616p. 1975. 46.95x (ISBN 0-471-29496-9, Pub. by Wiley-Interscience). Wiley.

Geddes, L. A., jt. auth. see Tacker, W. A.

Geddes, M. & Sturtridge, G. Listening Links. 1979. pap. text ed. 3.95x (ISBN 0-435-28051-1); tchrs. ed. 7.95x (ISBN 0-435-28052-X); three tapes o.p. 72.00x set (ISBN 0-435-28053-8); three cassettes 60.00x set (ISBN 0-435-28054-6). Heinemann Ed.

Geddes, Marion & Sturtridge, Gill, eds. Video in the Language Classroom. (Practical Language Teaching Ser.: No. 7). (Illus.). 192p. (Orig.). 1982. pap. text ed. 9.00x (ISBN 0-435-28971-3). Heinemann Ed.

Geddes, Marion, ed. see Nuttall, Christine.

Geddes, Marion, ed. see Wallace, Michael.

Geddes, Marion, et al. Jigsaw Listening. (Orig.). 1985. pap. text ed. 5.50x (ISBN 0-435-08112-8); Teacher's bk. 7.50x (ISBN 0-435-08113-6); cassette pack 36.00 (ISBN 0-435-08115-2). Heinemann Ed.

Geddes, Norman Bel see Bel Geddes, Norman.

Geddes, Patrick. City Development: A Study of Parks, Gardens, & Culture-Institutes. 1973. 30.00x (ISBN 0-8135-0748-0). Rutgers U Pr.

--John Ruskin: Economist. LC 73-318. 1973. Repr. of 1884 ed. lib. bdg. 10.00 (ISBN 0-8414-1337-1). Folcroft.

--John Ruskin, Economist. 1979. Repr. of 1884 ed. lib. bdg. 10.00 (ISBN 0-8492-4930-9). R West.

Geddes, Patrick & Thomson, J. Arthur. Evolution. 1979. Repr. lib. bdg. 20.00 (ISBN 0-8492-4941-4). R West.

Geddes, Patrick & Thomson, John A. The Evolution of Sex. 2nd ed. LC 72-9640. (Illus.). Repr. of 1901 ed. 25.00 (ISBN 0-404-57444-0). AMS Pr.

Geddes, Robert. Forest Edge. (Illus.). 112p. pap. 9.95 (ISBN 0-312-29877-3). St Martin.

Geddes, Robert & Clellan, Doug. The Forest Edge & Post-War Berlin. (Illus.). 128p. 1983. pap. 14.95 (ISBN 0-312-29878-1). St Martin.

Geddes, Robert N. & Mead, Daniel R. Owner's Pictorial Guide for the Care & Understanding of the Jennings Bell Slot Machine. (Illus.). 163p. (Orig.). 1980. pap. 29.95 (ISBN 0-934422-18-4). Mead Pub Corp.

--Owner's Pictorial Guide for the Care & Understanding of the Watling Bell Slot Machine. (Illus.). 148p. (Orig.). 1981. pap. 29.95 (ISBN 0-934422-04-4). Mead Pub Corp.

--Owner's Pictorial Guide for the Care & Understanding of the Mills Bell Slot Machine. 2nd ed. LC 79-88432. (Owner's Pictorial Guide Ser.). (Illus.). 179p. 1983. pap. 29.95 (ISBN 0-934422-00-1). Mead Pub Corp.

--Slot Machines on Parade. LC 79-89443. (Illus.). 200p. 1980. 39.95 (ISBN 0-934422-16-8). Mead Pub Corp.

Geddes, Sheila. The Art of Astrology: A Complete Course in the Working Techniques of Natal Astrology. (Illus.). 208p. (Orig.). 1983. pap. 9.95 (ISBN 0-85030-250-1, Pub. by Aquarian Pr England). Sterling.

Geddes, Sheila & Astrol, D. F. The Art of Astrology: A Complete Course in the Working Techniques of Natal Astrology. 208p. 1980. 40.00x (ISBN 0-85030-207-2, Pub. by Aquarian Pr England); pap. 12.95 (ISBN 0-85030-250-1, Pub. by Aquarian Pr England). State Mutual Bk.

Geddes, Virgil. Beyond Tragedy, Footnotes on the Drama. LC 77-4408. 1930. lib. bdg. 8.50 (ISBN 0-8414-4591-5). Folcroft.

--The Collected Poems of Virgil Geddes. LC 78-55723. 1978. 12.95x (ISBN 0-915032-24-4). Natl Poet Foun.

--Melodramadness of Eugene O'Neill. LC 73-7589. 1934. lib. bdg. 10.00 (ISBN 0-8414-2032-7). Folcroft.

Geddes, W. H. Tabiteuea North: Atoll Economy. LC 82-70984. (Social Change in Kiribati & Tuvalu Ser.: No. 2). (Illus.). 251p. (Orig.). 1983. pap. text ed. 12.00 (ISBN 0-909150-89-3, Pub. by Dev Stud Ctr Australia). Australia N U P.

Geddes, W. H. & Chambers, A. Islands on the Line: Team Report. LC 82-70983. (Development Studies Centre: Atoll Economy Social Change in Kiribati & Tuvalu: No. 1). 221p. 1982. pap. text ed. 17.95 (ISBN 0-909150-75-3, 1604, Pub. by ANUP Australia). Australia N U P.

Geddes, William R. The Land Dyaks of Sarawak: A Report on a Social Economic Survey of the Land Dyaks of Sarawak. LC 77-86980. Repr. of 1954 ed. 32.50 (ISBN 0-404-16716-0). AMS Pr.

--Migrants of the Mountains: The Cultural Ecology of the Blue Miao (Hmong Nyua) or Thailand. (Illus.). 1976. 35.00x (ISBN 0-19-823187-3). Oxford U Pr.

Geddie, John. The Balladists. 1896. lib. bdg. 15.00 (ISBN 0-8414-4643-1). Folcroft.

--The Home Country of R. L. Stevenson. LC 77-10929. 1977. Repr. lib. bdg. 30.00 (ISBN 0-8414-4457-9). Folcroft.

Geddie, William. Bibliography of Middle Scots Poets. (Scottish Text Society Publications Ser: No. 61). 1969. Repr. of 1912 ed. 43.00 (ISBN 0-384-17975-4). Johnson Repr.

Geddis, David, jt. auth. see Gribben, Trish.

Geden, A. S., tr. see Deussen, Paul.

Gedeon, David V., jt. auth. see Tomal, Daniel R.

Gedes, Jim. The Bright Side of Depression. (Orig.). 1985. pap. 5.95 (ISBN 0-8054-5016-5). Broadman.

Gedge, E. C. & Choksi, Mithan. Women in Modern India. LC 74-33940. (Pioneer's of the Woman's Movement Ser.). x, 161p. 1975. Repr. of 1929 ed. 16.00 (ISBN 0-88355-262-0). Hyperion-Conn.

Gedge, Pauline. Stargate. LC 81-19473. 356p. 1982. 14.95 (ISBN 0-385-27420-3, Dial). Doubleday.

--Stargate. 352p. 1984. pap. 3.95 (ISBN 0-14-006639-X). Penguin.

--The Twelfth Transforming. LC 84-47570. 544p. 1984. 16.30 (ISBN 0-06-015338-5, HarpT). Harrow.

Gedhard, David, et al. The Guide to Architecture in San Francisco & Northern California. rev. ed. LC 85-10864. (Illus.). 576p. 1985. pap. 14.95 (ISBN 0-87905-202-3). Gibbs M Smith.

Gedin, Per. Literature in the Marketplace. LC 77-76566. 208p. 1977. 12.95 (ISBN 0-87951-066-8). Overlook Pr.

Gedney, J. Tumbling & Balancing: Basic Skills & Variations. 1977. 16.95 (ISBN 0-13-932798-3). P-H.

Gedney, William J. English for Speakers of Thai. LC 58-10816. (English for Foreigners Ser.). 354p. (Eng. & Thai., Prog. Bk.). 1980. pap. 90.00x incl. 9 dual cassettes (ISBN 0-87950-613-X). Spoken Lang Serv.

Gedney, William J., ed. see Anuman, Rajadhon Phraya.

Gedo, Andras. Crisis Consciousness in Contemporary Philosophy. Genin, Salomea, tr. from German. LC 81-8338. (Studies in Marxism: Vol. 11). 289p. 1982. 19.95x (ISBN 0-930656-21-0); pap. 9.95 (ISBN 0-930656-22-9). MEP Pubns.

Gedo, John E. Advances in Clinical Psychoanalysis. (Illus.). 407p. 1981. text ed. 35.00 (ISBN 0-8236-0125-0, 00-0125). Intl Univs Pr.

--Beyond Interpretation: Toward a Revised Theory for Psychoanalysis. LC 78-13894. 280p. 1979. text ed. 27.50 (ISBN 0-8236-0499-3). Intl Univs Pr.

--Portraits of the Artist: Psychoanalysis of Creativity & Its Vicissitudes. 1983. 20.00 (ISBN 0-89862-629-3, 2629). Guilford Pr.

--Psychoanalysis & Its Discontents. LC 84-4615. 209p. 1984. 25.00 (ISBN 0-89862-639-0). Guilford Pr.

Gedo, John E. & Goldberg, Arnold. Models of the Mind: A Psychoanalytic Theory. LC 73-77132. 1976. 4.95x (ISBN 0-226-28487-5, P695, Phoen). U of Chicago Pr.

Gedo, John E. & Pollock, George H., eds. Freud: The Fusion of Science & Humanism: The Intellectual History of Psychoanalysis. LC 75-792. (Psychological Issues Monograph: No. 34-35, Vol. 9, No. 2-3). 447p. 1975. text ed. 32.50x (ISBN 0-8236-2031-X); pap. text ed. 25.00 (ISBN 0-8236-2030-1). Intl Univs Pr.

--Psychoanalysis: The Vital Issues, Vol. 1: Psychoanalysis as an Intellectualy Discipline. LC 83-26432. xiv, 436p. 32.50 (ISBN 0-8236-5385-4). Intl Univ Pr.

Gedo, John E., jt. ed. see Pollock, George H.

Gedo, Mary M. Picasso: Art As Autobiography. LC 80-11126. (Illus.). 288p. 1980. lib. bdg. 20.00x (ISBN 0-226-28482-4, PHOEN); pap. 12.50 (ISBN 0-226-28483-2). U of Chicago Pr.

--Psychoanalytic Perspectives on Art, Vol. 1. 360p. 1985. text ed. cancelled (ISBN 0-88163-007-1). L Erlbaum Assocs.

Geduld, Harry, jt. ed. see Gottesman, Ronald.

Geduld, Harry M. The Birth of the Talkies: From Edison to Jolson. LC 74-11887. 352p. 1975. 20.00x (ISBN 0-253-10743-1). Ind U Pr.

--Dr. Jekyll & Mr. Hyde: An Anthology of Commentary, Including the Text. LC 82-48271. 175p. 1983. lib. bdg. 28.00 (ISBN 0-8240-9469-7). Garland Pub.

--Filmguide to Henry V. LC 73-75788. (Filmguide Ser: No. 7). pap. 17.90 (ISBN 0-8357-9208-0, 2017622). Bks Demand UMI.

--Prince of Publishers: A Study of the Work & Career of Jacob Tonson. LC 68-64121. (Indiana University Humanities Ser.: No. 66). pap. 65.00 (ISBN 0-317-10301-6, 2005742). Bks Demand UMI.

Geduld, Harry M., jt. auth. see Gottesman, Ronald.

Geduld, Harry M., ed. Authors on Film. LC 72-75390. (Midland Bks.: No. 179). pap. 79.80 (ISBN 0-8357-9197-1, 2013005). Bks Demand UMI.

--Charlie Chaplin's Own Story. LC 84-43173. 208p. 1985. 20.00 (ISBN 0-253-11179-X). Ind U Pr.

Geduld, Harry M., ed. see Shaw, Bernard.

Gedvilas, Leo L. & Kneer, Marion E., eds. National Association for Physical Education in Higher Education Annual Conference: Proceedings, Vol. I. 195p. 1980. pap. text ed. 15.00x (ISBN 0-931250-61-7, NPR00001). Human Kinetics.

Gedye, G. R. Scientific Method in Production Management. (Illus.). 1965. 8.50x (ISBN 0-19-859802-5). Oxford U Pr.

--Works Management & Productivity. 1979. pap. 14.95 (ISBN 0-434-90658-1, Pub. by W Heinemann Ltd). David & Charles.

Gedzelman, Stanley D. The Science & Wonders of the Atmosphere. LC 79-23835. 535p. 1980. text ed. 35.00x (ISBN 0-471-02972-6); Avail. Tchr's Manual (ISBN 0-471-08013-6). Wiley.

Gee, jt. auth. see Stevens.

Gee, Audrey. Looking at Houses. (History in Focus Ser.). (Illus.). 72p. (gr. 7-12). 1983. 14.95 (ISBN 0-7134-0845-6, Batsford England). David & Charles.

Gee, Choy Y. & Choy, Dexter. Travel Industry. (Illus.). 1984. text ed. 26.50 (ISBN 0-87055-441-7). AVI.

Gee, Chuck Y. Resort Development & Management. Harless, Marjorie, ed. 1981. 34.95 (ISBN 0-86612-008-4). Educ Inst Am Hotel.

Gee, D. G. & Sturt, B. A. The Caledonide Orogen: Scandinavia & Related Areas. 110p. 1984. 186.95 (ISBN 0-471-10504-X). Wiley.

Gee, D. J., jt. auth. see Polson, Cyril J.

Gee, Donald. Concerning Spiritual Gifts. rev. ed. LC 80-83784. 144p. 1972. pap. 2.50 (ISBN 0-88243-486-1, 02-0486). Gospel Pub.

--The Fruit of the Spirit. 80p. 1975. pap. 1.25 (ISBN 0-88243-501-9, 02-0501, Radiant Bks). Gospel Pub.

--Fruitful or Barren? 90p. 1961. pap. 1.35 (ISBN 0-88243-502-7, 02-0502). Gospel Pub.

--God's Grace & Power for Today. (Charismatic Bk). 48p. 1972. pap. 0.69 (ISBN 0-88243-918-9, 02-0918). Gospel Pub.

--Is It God? (Charismatic Bks.). 30p. 1972. pap. 0.69 (ISBN 0-88243-916-2, 02-0916). Gospel Pub.

--A New Discovery. Orig. Title: Pentecost. 96p. 1932. pap. 1.00 (ISBN 0-88243-569-8, 02-0569). Gospel Pub.

--Now That You've Been Baptized in the Spirit. 176p. 1972. pap. 1.50 (ISBN 0-88243-461-6, 02-0461). Gospel Pub.

--Spiritual Gifts in the Work of the Ministry Today. 102p. 1963. pap. 1.25 (ISBN 0-88243-592-2, 02-0592). Gospel Pub.

--This Is the Way. (Radiant Bks.). Orig. Title: Studies in Guidance. 64p. 1975. pap. 0.95 (ISBN 0-88243-630-9, 02-0630). Gospel Pub.

--Toward Pentecostal Unity. Orig. Title: All with One Accord. 62p. 1961. pap. 0.60 (ISBN 0-88243-689-9, 02-0689). Gospel Pub.

--A Word to the Wise. (Radiant Bks.). Orig. Title: Proverbs for Pentecost. 80p. 1975. pap. 0.95 (ISBN 0-88243-632-5, 02-0632). Gospel Pub.

Gee, E. Gordon & Jackson, Donald W. Legal Education & Lawyer Competency. 370p. (Orig.). 1982. cancelled (ISBN 0-8425-2059-7). Brigham.

Gee, E. Gordon, jt. auth. see Bybee, Rodger W.

Gee, E. Gordon, jt. auth. see Goldstein, Stephen R.

Gee, Edward. The Divine Right & Original of the Civil Magistrate from God. LC 75-31092. Repr. of 1658 ed. 30.00 (ISBN 0-404-13510-2). AMS Pr.

Gee, Edwin A. & Tyler, Chaplin. Managing Innovation. LC 76-7056. 284p. 1976. text ed. 21.00 (ISBN 0-471-29503-5). Krieger.

Gee, Emma, ed. Counterpoint: Perspectives on Asian America. LC 76-41528. (Illus.). 1976. ltd. ed. 19.95x (ISBN 0-934052-03-4); pap. 11.95x (ISBN 0-934052-04-2). Asian Am Stud UCLA.

Gee, Erin P., jt. auth. see Hilker, Walter R.

Gee, Ernest R. Early American Sporting Books: Seventeen Thirty-Four to Eighteen Forty-Four. LC 75-167737. (American History & Americana Ser., No. 47). 1971. Repr. of 1928 ed. lib. bdg. 32.95x (ISBN 0-8383-1274-8). Haskell.

GEE (Group for Environmental Education) Process of Choice, 5 bklets. 1974. pap. 12.50x set (ISBN 0-262-57044-0); 3.00x ea. Vol. 1 (ISBN 0-262-57039-4). Vol. 2 (ISBN 0-262-57040-8). Vol. 3 (ISBN 0-262-57041-6). Vol. 4 (ISBN 0-262-57042-4). Vol. 5 (ISBN 0-262-57043-2). MIT Pr.

Gee, Harold F. Agent's Automobile Guide. 10.00 (ISBN 0-686-31026-8, 26060). Rough Notes.

--Agent's Bonding Guide. 10.00 (ISBN 0-686-31027-6, 26080). Rough Notes.

--Agent's Casualty Guide. 7.00 (ISBN 0-686-31025-X, 26100). Rough Notes.

--An Approach to Property & Casualty Insurance. 10.00 (ISBN 0-686-31028-4, 26121). Rough Notes.

Gee, Harry R. Clarinet Solos de Concours, 1897-1980: An Annotated Bibliography. LC 80-8360. 128p. 1981. 17.50x (ISBN 0-253-13577-X). Ind U Pr.

Gee, Henry. The Elizabethan Clergy & the Settlement of Religion, 1558-64. LC 83-45581. Date not set. Repr. of 1898 ed. 39.50 (ISBN 0-404-19899-6). AMS Pr.

Gee, Henry & Hardy, William J., eds. Documents Illustrative of English Church History. LC 83-45580. Date not set. Repr. of 1896 ed. 62.50 (ISBN 0-404-19898-8). AMS Pr.

Gee, J. B. L., et al, eds. Occupational Lung Disease. 296p. 1984. 48.00 (ISBN 0-89004-900-9). Raven.

Gee, J. Bernard. Occupational Lung Disease. (Contemporary Issues in Pulmonary Disease Ser.: Vol. 2). (Illus.). 272p. 1984. text ed. 32.50 (ISBN 0-443-08252-9). Churchill.

Gee, John. Hidden Pictures: Favorites by John Gee. (Illus.). 32p. (Orig.). (gr. 1-6). 1981. pap. 2.50 (ISBN 0-87534-230-2). Highlights.

--Timbertoes. (Illus.). 32p. (gr. k-2). 1967. pap. 2.50 (ISBN 0-87534-133-0). Highlights.

Gee, John, et al. Hidden Pictures for Beginners. (Illus.). 32p. (Orig.). (ps-1). 1975. pap. 2.50 (ISBN 0-87534-161-6). Highlights.

Gee, John A. Life & Works of Thomas Lupset. 1928. 28.50x (ISBN 0-685-89763-X). Elliots Bks.

--The Life & Works of Thomas Lupset. 1973. Repr. of 1928 ed. 30.00 (ISBN 0-8274-0037-3). R West.

Gee, Joshua. Trade & Navigation of Great Britain Considered: Shewing That Surest Way for a Nation to Increase in Riches, Is to Prevent the Importation of Such Foreign Commodities As May Be Rais'd at Home. LC 75-141123. (Research Library of Colonial Americana). 1971. Repr. of 1729 ed. 21.00 (ISBN 0-405-03335-4). Ayer Co Pubs.

--Trade & Navigation of Great Britain Considered. 4th ed. LC 71-97977. Repr. of 1738 ed. 27.50x (ISBN 0-678-00576-1). Kelley.

Gee, K. C. Introduction to Local Area Computer Networks. 150p. 1984. pap. 18.50 (ISBN 0-471-80036-8). Wiley.

--Introduction to Open Systems Interconnection. 61p. (Orig.). 1980. pap. 17.50x (ISBN 0-85012-250-3). Intl Pubns Serv.

--Local Area Network Gateways. 150p. 1984. pap. text ed. 12.95x (ISBN 0-471-81054-1). Wiley.

--Local Area Networks. 150p. 1982. 27.50x (ISBN 0-85012-365-8). Taylor & Francis.

--Proprietary Network Architectures. (Illus.). 258p. 1981. 110.00x (ISBN 0-85012-327-5). Intl Pubns Serv.

--Proprietary Network Architectures. 250p. 1981. pap. 109.25 (ISBN 0-471-89423-0). Wiley.

Gee, K. C., ed. see National Computing Centre.

Gee, Maggie. The Burning Book. 304p. 1984. 13.95 (ISBN 0-312-10862-1, Pub. by Marek). St Martin.

--Dying, in Other Words. LC 83-25383. 221p. 1984. 13.95 (ISBN 0-7108-0030-4); pap. 7.95 (ISBN 0-571-12527-1). Faber & Faber.

Gee, Malcolm. Dealers, Critics, & Collectors or Modern Painting: Aspects of the Parisian Art Market Between 1910 & 1930. LC 79-57508. (Outstanding Dissertations in the Fine Arts Ser.: No.5). 570p. 1982. lib. bdg. 67.00 (ISBN 0-8240-3931-9). Garland Pub.

Gee, Marguerite, ed. see Chickering, Arthur W., et al.

Gee, Marjory, ed. Captain Fraser's Voyages, 1865-1892. 224p. 1982. 30.00x (ISBN 0-540-07180-3, Pub. by Stanford Maritime England). State Mutual Bk.

Gee, Marjory, ed. see Fraser, Thomas G.

Gee, Maurice. The Half-Men of O. (Illus.). 204p. 1983. text ed. 11.95 (ISBN 0-19-558081-8, Pub. by Oxford U Pr Childrens). Merrimack Pub Cir.

--Under the Mountain. (gr. 6 up). 1984. 12.95 (ISBN 0-19-558040-0). Merrimack Pub Cir.

--The World Around the Corner. (Illus.). 72p. (gr. 3-6). 1984. 10.95 (ISBN 0-19-558061-3, Pub. by Oxford U Pr Childrens). Merrimack Pub Cir.

Gee, Ralph D., jt. auth. see Townley, Helen M.

Gee, Renie. Still More of Who Said That? 64p. 1983. 8.50 (ISBN 0-7153-8475-9). David & Charles.

--Who Said That: Omnibus Edition. 160p. 1984. 11.95 (ISBN 0-7153-8604-2). David & Charles.

Gee, Renie, ed. More of Who Said That? Quotations & Biographies of Famous People. LC 81-68498. 64p. 1982. 7.50 (ISBN 0-7153-8275-6). David & Charles.

Gee, Robyn, ed. Living in Castle Times: First Book of History. (Illus.). 24p. (gr. 3-6). 1982. 6.95 (ISBN 0-86020-622-X); lib. bdg. 11.95 (ISBN 0-88110-106-0); pap. 2.95 (ISBN 0-86020-621-1). EDC.

Gee, S., ed. Technology Transfer in Industrialized Countries. 464p. 1979. 35.00x (ISBN 90-286-0038-8). Sijthoff & Noordhoff.

Gee, S. M. Programming the Timex-Sinclair 2000. 144p. 1983. 17.95 (ISBN 0-13-729582-0); pap. 10.95 (ISBN 0-13-729574-X). P-H.

Gee, Samuel E. The Kin of Dr. Ned Gee, Lunenburg County, Virginia. LC 75-18805. (Illus.). 1975. 12.50x (ISBN 0-685-89826-1). Va Bk.

Gee, Sherman. Technology Transfer, Innovation, & International Competitiveness. LC 80-22786. 248p. 1981. 34.50x (ISBN 0-471-08468-9, Pub. by Wiley-Interscience). Wiley.

Gee, Sue, jt. auth. see Michelson, Joan.

Gee, Thomas C., jt. ed. see Criscoe, Betty L.

Geeenburg, Dan. True Adventures. 256p. (Orig.). 1985. pap. 8.95 (ISBN 0-88191-023-6). Freundlich.

Geehan, Robert, ed. see Van Til, Cornelius.

Geehr, Edward C., jt. ed. see Auerbach, Paul S.

Geehr, Richard S., ed. I Decide Who is a Jew! The Papers of Dr. Karl Lueger. LC 81-43702. (Illus.). 382p. (Orig.). 1982. PLB 30.00 (ISBN 0-8191-2493-1); pap. text ed. 16.25 (ISBN 0-8191-2494-X). U Pr of Amer.

Geekie, William J. Why Government Fails. LC 76-16320. 1977. 7.95 (ISBN 0-87212-075-9). Libra.

Geelan, Agnes. The Dakota Maverick. (Illus.). 186p. (gr. 9-12). 1983. pap. 7.95 (ISBN 0-911007-03-2). Prairie Hse.

--The Ministers' Daughters. 1982. 9.95 (ISBN 0-8062-1905-X). Carlton.

Geelhaar, Christian. Jasper Johns Working Proofs. LC 80-80499. (Illus.). 324p. (Orig.). 1980. Boxed. pap. 65.00 (ISBN 0-902825-11-9). Petersburg Pr.

--Paul Klee. (Pocket Art Ser.). 1982. pap. 4.95 (ISBN 0-8120-2186-X). Barron.

Geelhoed. Problem Management in Endocrine Surgery: Problem Oriented Approach. 1982. 30.95 (ISBN 0-8151-3412-6). Year Bk Med.

Geelhoed, E. Bruce. Charles E. Wilson & Controversy at the Pentagon, Nineteen Fifty-Three to Nineteen Fifty-Seven. LC 79-9756. (Illus.). 232p. 1979. 14.95x (ISBN 0-8143-1635-2). Wayne St U Pr.

Geelhoed, Glenn. Surgery of the Adrenal Cortex. 1985. text ed. 160.00 (ISBN 0-8391-2051-6, 21636). Univ Park.

Geelhoed, Glenn & Chernow, Bart, eds. Endocrine Aspects of Acute Illness. (Clinics in Critical Care Medicine Ser.: Vol. 5). (Illus.). 342p. 1985. text ed. 39.50 (ISBN 0-443-08309-6). Churchill.

Geels, jt. auth. see Jacobs.

Geen, Michael. Theatrical Costume & the Amateur Stage. (Illus.). (gr. 7 up). 1968. 10.00 (ISBN 0-8238-0095-4). Plays.

Geen, Russell & Donnerstein, Edward, eds. Aggression: Theoretical & Methodologic Issues. LC 82-24348. 1983. Vol. 1: Theoretical Issues. 27.50 (ISBN 0-12-278801-X); 24.50. Vol. 2: Issues in Research (ISBN 0-12-278802-8). Acad Pr.

Geen, Russell G., et al. Human Motivation: Physiological, Behavioral & Social Approaches. 1984. text ed. 34.27 (ISBN 0-205-08114-2, 798114). Allyn.

Geenen, Catharine. Quest of the Faes. (Illus.). 144p. 1985. pap. 9.95 (ISBN 0-9606240-6-6). Pearl-Win.

Geenen, Donald J. Learning Apple FORTRAN. LC 84-19936. 160p. Date not set. pap. 17.95 (ISBN 0-88175-024-7). Computer Sci.

Geer, Charles see Bitter, Gary G.

Geer, Corinne C. Southern Plantation Cookbook. 1976. 9.95 (ISBN 0-9601508-1-1). C C Geer.

Geer, D. J. Rhinestones, Periwinkles, & Evanescent Wings: Gleanings from the Heart of a Woman in Love, Vol. 1. 32p. 1983. pap. write for info. (ISBN 0-9613061-0-6). D J P Geer.

Geer, Dick. Star-Gate Diary of Discovery: A Record of Personal Insights. 76p. 1980. pap. 6.00 (ISBN 0-914794-40-X). Wisdom Garden.

--Star-Gate Symbolic System. (Illus., Orig.). 1980. 12.00 (ISBN 0-914794-38-8). Wisdom Garden.

Geer, Emily A. First Lady: The Life of Lucy Webb Hayes. LC 83-26788. (Illus.). 285p. 1984. 19.95x (ISBN 0-87338-299-4). Kent St U Pr.

Geer, Galen. Meat on the Table: Modern Small-Game Hunting. (Illus.). 216p. 1985. 14.95 (ISBN 0-87364-330-5). Paladin Pr.

Geer, J. C. Smooth Muscle Cells in Atherosclerosis. Haust, M. Daria, et al, eds. (Monographs on Atherosclerosis: Vol. 2). 1972. 24.25 (ISBN 3-8055-1377-1). S Karger.

Geer, Jack C., jt. ed. see Wissler, Robert W.

Geer, James, et al. Human Sexuality. (Illus.). 640p. 1984. text ed. 28.95 (ISBN 0-13-447516-X). P-H.

Geer, Johannes P. van de. Introduction to Multivariate Analysis for the Social Sciences. LC 71-156044. pap. 76.00 (ISBN 0-317-08696-0, 2055556). Bks Demand UMI.

Geer, Richard. Star-Gate. 1984. deluxe ed. 29.95 boxed set (ISBN 0-911167-04-8). Star-Gate.

--Star-Gate Card. 2nd ed. 1984. Boxed Set. 13.95 (ISBN 0-911167-05-6). Star-Gate.

--Star-Gate Circle Pattern. 1979. 5.95 (ISBN 0-911167-01-3). Star-Gate.

--Star-Gate Diary of Discovery. 80p. 1985. pap. 5.95 spiral wire bdg. (ISBN 0-911167-06-4). Star-Gate.

--Star-Gate Diary of Discovery: A Record of Personal Insights. 2nd ed. 80p. 1980. pap. 5.95 (ISBN 0-911167-02-1). Star-Gate.

Geer, Richard H., et al. Stargate; Keys to the Kingdom: A Complete Guide to the Stargate Insight System. (Illus.). 250p. (Orig.). 1984. pap. 7.95 (ISBN 0-911167-03-X). Star-Gate.

Geer, Russel M. On Nature Lucretuis. 1965. pap. text ed. write for info. (ISBN 0-02-341210-0). Macmillan.

Geer, Russel M., tr. see Lucretius.

Geer, Russell. Letters, Principal Doctrines, & Vatican Sayings: Epicurus. 1964. pap. text ed. write for info. (ISBN 0-02-341200-3). Macmillan.

Geer, Russell, tr. see Epicurus.

Geer, T. T. Romance of Astoria - Extracts. facs. ed. (Shorey Historical Ser.). 8p. pap. 1.95 (ISBN 0-8466-0169-9, S169). Shorey.

Geer, Thelma. Mormonism, Mama & Me. 3rd, rev. ed. LC 81-146846. (Illus.). 228p. 1983. pap. 3.95 (ISBN 0-912375-00-0). Calvary Miss Pr.

--Mormonism, Mama, & Me. 1983. pap. 4.95 (ISBN 0-87508-193-2). Chr Lit.

Geer, Thelma, ed. Mormonism, Mama & Me. 4th ed. (Illus.). 252p. 1984. pap. 4.95 (ISBN 0-912375-01-9). Calvary Miss Pr.

Geerdes, Harold P. Planning & Equipping Educational Music Facilities. LC 75-15271. (Illus.). 96p. (Orig.). 1975. pap. 8.75 (ISBN 0-940796-13-9, 1036). Music Ed Natl.

Geere, Ron. Learning to Use the VIC-20 Computer. (Learning to Use Computer Series, A Gower Read-Out Publication). 86p. (Orig.). 1982. pap. text ed. 12.00x (ISBN 0-566-03453-0). Gower Pub Co.

Geering, A. H. Das Kiefergelenk im Zahnaerztlich-Prothetischen Fall: Eine Anatomisch-radiographische Untersuchung. (Illus., Ger.). 1977. 10.25 (ISBN 3-8055-2804-3). S Karger.

Geerken, Michael & Gove, Walter. At Home & at Work: The Family's Allocation of Labor. (New Perspectives on Family Ser.). 200p. 1983. 25.00 (ISBN 0-8039-1940-9); pap. 12.50 (ISBN 0-8039-1941-7). Sage.

Geerlings, Gerald K. Wrought Iron in Architecture. 1984. 18.50 (ISBN 0-8446-6103-1). Peter Smith.

--Wrought Iron in Architecture: An Illustrated Survey. (Antiques Ser.). 202p. 1984. pap. 9.95 (ISBN 0-486-24535-7). Dover.

Geers, T. L. & Tong, P., eds. Survival of Mechanical Systems in Transient Environments. LC 79-954424. (Applied Mechanics Division Ser.: Vol. 36). 196p. 1979. 24.00 (ISBN 0-686-62963-9, G00153). ASME.

Geers, T. L., jt. ed. see Belytschko, T.

Geers, T. L., jt. ed. see Merchant, H. C.

Geertinger, Preben. Sudden Death in Infancy. (Illus.). 128p. 1968. photocopy ed. 14.50x (ISBN 0-398-00663-6). C C Thomas.

Geert Paul, Van see Van Geert, Paul.

Geertz, C. Negara: Theatre-State in 19th Century Bali. LC 80-7520. 256p. 1980. 28.50 (ISBN 0-691-05316-2); pap. 9.95 (ISBN 0-691-00778-0). Princeton U Pr.

Geertz, C., et al. Meaning & Order in Moroccan Society. LC 78-54327. (Illus.). 1979. 57.50 (ISBN 0-521-22175-7). Cambridge U Pr.

Geertz, Clifford. Agricultural Involution: The Processes of Ecological Change in Indonesia. LC 63-20356. 1963. pap. 6.95x (ISBN 0-520-00459-0, CAMPUS11). U of Cal Pr.

--Interpretation of Cultures. LC 73-81196. 1973. pap. 9.95x (ISBN 0-465-09719-7, TB-5043). Basic.

--Islam Observed: Religious Development in Morocco & Indonesia. 1971. pap. 6.00x (ISBN 0-226-28511-1, P439, Phoen). U of Chicago Pr.

--Local Knowledge: Further Essays in Interpretive Anthology. 29p. 1985. pap. 7.95 (ISBN 0-465-04159-0, CN 5130). Basic.

--Local Knowledge: Furthur Essays in Interpretive Anthropology. 292p. 1983. text ed. 18.50 (ISBN 0-465-04158-2). Basic.

--Peddlers & Princes: Social Development & Economic Change in Two Indonesian Towns. LC 62-18844. (Comparative Studies of New Nations Ser). (Illus.). 1968. pap. 3.95x (ISBN 0-226-28514-6, P318, Phoen). U of Chicago Pr.

--The Religion of Java. LC 75-18746. xvi, 396p. 1976. pap. 11.00x (ISBN 0-226-28510-3, P658, Phoen). U of Chicago Pr.

--The Social History of an Indonesian Town. LC 75-29282. (Illus.). 217p. 1975. Repr. of 1965 ed. lib. bdg. 50.00x (ISBN 0-8371-8431-2, GEIT). Greenwood.

Geertz, Clifford, jt. auth. see Geertz, Hildred.

Geertz, Hildred & Geertz, Clifford. Kinship in Bali. LC 74-11621. 1978. pap. 3.95x (ISBN 0-226-28516-2, P790, Phoen). U of Chicago Pr.

Geertz, Hildred, ed. see Raden Adjeng Kartini.

Geery. Solar Greenhouses: Underground. (Illus.). 416p. 1982. o.p 19.95 (ISBN 0-8306-0069-8); pap. 12.95 (ISBN 0-8306-1272-6, 1272). TAB Bks.

Geery, Daniel. Wasatch Trails, Vol. 2. (Illus., Orig.). 1977. pap. 2.50 (ISBN 0-915272-10-5). Wasatch Pubs.

Geeseg & Steinby. Tree Automata. 1984. 30.00 (ISBN 0-9910001-4-5, Pub. by Akademiai Kaido Hungary). Heyden.

Geesink, R. Thorner's Analytical Key to the Families of Flowering Plants. 200p. 1981. 69.00x (ISBN 0-686-45664-5, Pub. by CAB Bks England). State Mutual Bk.

Geesink, R., et al. Thonner's Analytical Key to the Families of Flowering Plants, Vol. 5. (Leiden Botanical Ser.). (Illus.). 253p. 1981. 29.50 (ISBN 90-220-0744-8, PDC225, PUDOC); pap. 19.25 (ISBN 90-220-0730-8, PDC224). Unipub.

Geesink, R., et al, eds. Thonner's Analytical Key to the Families of Flowering Plants. (Leiden Botanical Ser.: Vol. 5). 200p. 37.00 (ISBN 90-6021-461-7, Pub. by Junk Pubs Netherlands). Kluwer Academic.

Geeslin. Ballet Time. pap. 2.50 (ISBN 0-87505-269-X). Borden.

Geeslin, Campbell. The Bonner Boys. 192p. 1984. pap. 2.95 (ISBN 0-425-06470-0). Berkley Pub.

Geest, Hans van der see Van Der Geest, Bans.

Geest, Ton Van Der see Van Der Geest, Ton.

Geest, Ton Van Der see Van Der Geest, Ton, et al.

Geeting, Baxter & Geeting, Corinne. Confessions of a Tour Leader. LC 82-81127. 96p. (Orig.). 1982. pap. 4.95 (ISBN 0-88100-005-1). Natl Writers Club.

--How to Listen Assertively. LC 82-84222. 223p. 1982. pap. text ed. 8.50x (ISBN 0-671-18336-2). Intl Gen Semantics.

Geeting, Corinne, jt. auth. see Geeting, Baxter.

Geffcken, J. The Last Days of Greco-Roman Paganism. (Europe in the Middle Ages Selected Studies: Vol. 8). 344p. 1978. 74.50 (ISBN 0-444-85005-8, North-Holland). Elsevier.

Geffcken, John. Die Oracula Sibyllina. Connor, W. R., ed. LC 78-18576. (Greek Texts Commentaries Ser.). (Illus.). 1979. Repr. of 1902 ed. lib. bdg. 23.00x (ISBN 0-405-11419-2). Ayer Co Pubs.

Geffe, N., tr. see Serres, Oliver de.

Geffen, Alice. A Birdwatcher's Guide to Eastern United States. LC 77-21436. 1978. 15.95 (ISBN 0-8120-5301-X). Barron.

Geffner, A. Business Letters the Easy Way. (Easy Way Ser.). 1983. pap. 7.95 (ISBN 0-8120-2710-8). Barron.

Geffner, Anne. A Child Celebrates: The Jewish Holidays. rev 2nd ed. Stein, Charlotte M., ed. LC 79-51011. (Illus.). 60p. (Orig.). (gr. k-6). 1980. pap. 4.95 (ISBN 0-916634-08-6). Double M Pr.

Geffner, Saul & Lauren, Paul. Experimental Chemistry. 2nd ed. (gr. 10-12). 1968. pap. text ed. 8.00 (ISBN 0-87720-113-7); with wkbk. 8.92 (ISBN 0-87720-115-3). AMSCO Sch.

Geffner, Saul L. Fundamental Concepts of Modern Chemistry. (Illus.). (gr. 10-12). 1968. text ed. 11.67 (ISBN 0-87720-102-1); pap. text ed. 8.33 (ISBN 0-87720-101-3). AMSCO Sch.

Geffner, Saul L. & Kass, Gerard A. Contemporary Chemistry. (Orig.). (gr. 10-12). 1981. pap. text ed. 8.92 (ISBN 0-87720-100-5). AMSCO Sch.

Geffner, Saul L., jt. auth. see Mould, J. Albert.

Geffre, C. & Gutierrez, G., eds. Different Theologies, Common Responsibilities: Babel Or Pentecost. (Concilium Ser.: Vol.171). 128p. pap. 6.95 (ISBN 0-317-31458-0) (ISBN 0-317-31459-9). Fortress.

Geffre, C., jt. ed. see Dhavamony, M.

Geffre, Claude. The Churches of Africa. (Concilium Ser.: Vol. 106). pap. 6.95x (ISBN 0-8245-0266-3). Crossroad NY.

Geffre, Claude & Jossua, Jean-Pierre. Indifference to Religion. (Concilium 1983: Vol. 165). 128p. (Orig.). 1983. pap. 6.95 (ISBN 0-8164-2445-4, Pub. by Seabury). Winston Pr.

Geffre, Claude & Jossua, Jean-Pierre, eds. The Human, Criterion of Christian Existence? (Concilium Ser.: Vol. 155). 128p. (Orig.). 1982. pap. 6.95 (ISBN 0-8164-2386-5, Pub. by Seabury). Winston Pr.

--Monotheism. (Concilium Ser.: Vol. 177). 128p. pap. 6.95 (ISBN 0-317-31470-X, 30-30057-1902). Fortress.

--Nietzche & Christianity, Vol. 145. (Concilium 1981). 128p. (Orig.). 1981. pap. 6.95 (ISBN 0-8164-2312-1, Pub. by Seabury). Winston Pr.

--True & False Universality of Christianity. (Concilium Ser.: Vol. 135). 128p. (Orig.). 1980. pap. 5.95 (ISBN 0-8164-2277-X, Pub. by Seabury). Winston Pr.

Gefin, Laszlo K. Ideogram: History of a Poetic Method. 181p. 1982. text ed. 17.50x (ISBN 0-292-73828-5). U of Tex Pr.

Gefvert, Constance. The Confident Writer: A Norton Handbook. 1985. text ed. 12.95x (ISBN 0-393-95411-0); tchrs. ed. avail. (ISBN 0-393-95417-X); write for info. wkbk. (ISBN 0-393-95414-5); diagnostic tests avail. (ISBN 0-393-95451-X). Norton.

Gefvert, Constance, et al. Keys to American English. 396p. (Orig.). 1975. pap. text ed. 10.95 (ISBN 0-15-597858-6, HC); instructor's manual avail. (ISBN 0-15-597859-4). HarBraceJ.

Gefvert, Constance J., ed. Edward Taylor: An Annotated Bibliography, 1668-1970. LC 70-144811. (Serif Ser.: No. 19). 106p. 1971. 10.00x (ISBN 0-87338-113-0). Kent St U Pr.

Gega. Science in Elementary Education. 5th ed. 1985. pap. price not set (ISBN 0-471-82565-4). Wiley.

Gega, Peter C. Science in Elementary Education. 4th ed. LC 81-16451. 600p. 1982. text ed. 29.95 (ISBN 0-471-09678-4); tchrs. manual avail. (ISBN 0-471-09894-9). Wiley.

Gegan, Robert A. I Rejected Bypass Surgery for a Better Life. LC 81-66843. (Illus.). 300p. (Orig.). 1981. pap. 7.95 (ISBN 0-940062-01-1). Consumer Info Pubns.

--The Road to Wellness Is Paved with Pure Water. 44p. (Orig.). Date not set. pap. text ed. 2.50 (ISBN 0-318-03842-0). Consumer Info Pubns.

--The Vascular Connection. (Illus.). 220p. (Orig.). 1985. 16.95; pap. 8.95. Consumer Info Pubns.

Gegan, Robert A. & Wunderlich, Ray C. The Over Fifty Wellness Diet. (Illus.). 50p. (Orig.). 1985. write for info.; pap. write for info. Consumer Info Pubns.

Gegel, H. L., jt. ed. see Collings, E. W.

Geggus, David P. Slavery, War & Revolution: The British Occupation of Saint Dominigue, 1793-1798. (Illus.). 1982. 72.00x (ISBN 0-19-822634-9). Oxford U Pr.

Gegory, William K; see Gregory, William K.

Geguzin, Y. E. & Krivoglaz, M. A. Migration of Macroscopic Inclusions in Solids. LC 73-83894. (Studies in Soviet Science - Physical Sciences Ser.). (Illus.). 342p. 1973. 37.50x (ISBN 0-306-10889-5, Consultants). Plenum Pub.

Gehan, Edmund A., jt. auth. see Burdette, Walter J.

Gehani, Narain. ADA: An Advanced Introduction. (Software Ser.). (Illus.). 336p. 1983. pap. text ed. 22.95 (ISBN 0-13-003962-4). P-H.

--ADA: An Advanced Introduction Including Reference Manual for the Ada Programming Language. (Illus.). 672p. 1984. text ed. 32.95 (ISBN 0-13-003997-7). P-H.

--Ada: Concurrent Programming. (Illus.). 272p. 1984. pap. 26.95 (ISBN 0-13-004011-8). P-H.

--Advanced C: Food for the Educated Palate. LC 84-19851. 313p. 1984. pap. 19.95 (ISBN 0-88175-078-6). Computer Sci.

--C: An Advanced Introduction. LC 84-12145. 1984. text ed. 29.95 (ISBN 0-88175-053-0). Computer Sci.

--C for Personal Computers: IBM PC, AT&T PC 6300 & Compatibles. LC 85-5745. 300p. 1985. pap. 19.95 (ISBN 0-88175-111-1). Computer Sci.

Gehani, Narain, jt. auth. see Feuer, Alan.

Geherin, David. The American Private Eye: The Image in Fiction. (Recognitions Ser.). 180p. 1985. 14.95 (ISBN 0-8044-2243-5); pap. 7.95 (ISBN 0-8044-6184-8). Ungar.

--John D. MacDonald. LC 81-70123. (Recognitions Ser.). 200p. 1982. 13.95 (ISBN 0-8044-2232-X); pap. 6.95 (ISBN 0-8044-6173-2). Ungar.

--Sons of Sam Spade: The Private Eye Novel in the Seventies. (Recognitions Ser.). 175p. 1983. pap. 6.95 (ISBN 0-8044-6170-8). Ungar.

--Sons of Sam Spade: The Private Eye Novel in the 70s. LC 79-4823. (Recognitions Ser.). 1980. 13.95 (ISBN 0-8044-2231-1). Ungar.

Gehin, Alain. Atlas of Manipulative Techniques for the Cranium & Face. LC 85-80135. (Illus.). 269p. 1985. 34.95 (ISBN 0-939616-02-5). Eastland.

Gehl, Jurgen. Austria, Germany, & the Anschluss, Nineteen Thirty-One to Nineteen Thirty-Eight. LC 78-21293. (Illus.). 1979. Repr. of 1963 ed. lib. bdg. 24.75x (ISBN 0-313-20841-7, GEAG). Greenwood.

Gehl, Raymond H., jt. auth. see Kutash, Samuel B.

Gehlbach, Frederick R. Mountain Islands & Desert Seas: A Natural History of the U. S. - Mexican Borderlands. LC 81-40402. (Illus.). 320p. 1982. 19.95 (ISBN 0-89096-118-2). Tex A&M Univ Pr.

Gehlbach, Stephen H. Interpreting the Medical Literature: A Clinician's Guide. 256p. 1982. 12.95 (ISBN 0-669-04506-3, Collamore). Heath.

Gehle, Quentin L. The Little Brown Workbook. 2nd ed. 1983. pap. text ed. 9.95 (ISBN 0-316-28979-5); write for info tcher's manual (ISBN 0-316-28984-1); write for info anwer booklet (ISBN 0-316-28986-8). Little.

Gehle, Quentin L. & Rollo, Duncan J. The Writing Process: A Guide to College Composition. LC 76-28139. 1977. pap. text ed. 12.95 (ISBN 0-312-89495-3); instr's manual avail. St Martin.

Gehle, Walter, jt. auth. see Torklus, Detlef Von.

Gehlen, Arnold. Man in the Age of Technology. Lipscomb, Pat, tr. LC 79-23963. (European Perspectives Ser.). (Ger.). 1980. 21.00x (ISBN 0-231-04852-1). Columbia U Pr.

Gehlen, Michael P. The Politics of Coexistence: Soviet Methods & Motives. LC 79-16999. 1980. Repr. of 1967 ed. lib. bdg. 32.50x (ISBN 0-313-21290-2, GEPC). Greenwood.

Gehlen, P., et al, eds. Interatomic Potentials & Simulation of Lattice Defects. LC 72-77229. 782p. 1972. 89.50x (ISBN 0-306-30599-2, Plenum Pr). Plenum Pub.

Gehlert, Sarah. Curation in the Small Museum: Human Bones. (Miscellaneous Publications in Anthropology Ser.: No. 8). ii, 12p. 1980. pap. 0.80 (ISBN 0-913134-81-3). Mus Anthro Mo.

Gehling, Michael. The Software Source Inc. 1983. 34.95 (ISBN 0-930241-00-2). Soft Source.

Gehlke, Charles E. Emile Durkheim's Contributions to Sociological Theory. LC 74-168104. (Columbia University. Studies in the Social Sciences: No. 151). Repr. of 1915 ed. 14.00 (ISBN 0-404-51151-1). AMS Pr.

Gehlmann, John & Eisman, Philip. Say What You Mean: The Sentence, Bk 1. LC 66-19065. 1967. scp 7.64 (ISBN 0-672-73232-7). Odyssey Pr.

Gehm, F. Commodity Market Money Management. LC 82-10844. 361p. 1982. 39.95x (ISBN 0-471-09908-2, Pub. by Ronald Pr). Wiley.

Gehm, John. Bringing It Home. 304p. 1984. 14.95 (ISBN 0-914091-48-4). Chicago Review.

Gehman, Christian. Beloved Gravely: A Highly Inventive Comic Novel of Love, Friendship, & the Capacity of Dreams. 224p. 1984. 12.95 (ISBN 0-684-18233-5, ScribT). Scribner.

--Isengard & Northern Gonder. (Illus.). 48p. 1984. 10.00 (ISBN 0-915795-11-6). Iron Crown Ent Inc.

--Riders of Rohan: The Horse-Lords. (Illus.). 48p. (YA) (gr. 10-12). 1985. pap. 10.00 (ISBN 0-915795-29-9). Iron Crown Ent Inc.

Gehman, Clayton H. Children of the Conestoga. 1978. pap. 1.95 (ISBN 0-87178-133-6). Brethren.

Gehman, Edna R., jt. ed. see Gehman, Irvin G.

Gehman, Henry S., ed. The New Westminster Dictionary of the Bible. LC 69-10000. (Illus.). 106p. 1982. thumb indexed 22.95 (ISBN 0-664-21388-X). Westminster.

--The New Westminster Dictionary of the Bible. LC 69-10000. (Illus.). 106p. 1970. 19.95 (ISBN 0-664-21277-8). Westminster.

Gehman, Irvin G. & Gehman, Edna R., eds. Ancestors & Descendants of Anna Detweiler. 1967. 6.95x (ISBN 0-87813-125-6). Park View.

Gehman, Richard, jt. ed. see Condon, Eddie.

Gehman, Walt & Sumner, Lee E., Jr. Advanced Sound & Graphics in Applesoft. (Illus.). 176p. (Orig.). 1985. 12.95 (ISBN 0-8306-0892-3); pap. 12.45 (ISBN 0-8306-1892-9). TAB Bks.

Gehmlich, D. K., jt. auth. see Hammond, Seymour B.

Gehr, Marilyn. Solid Waste Management: A Selected & Annotated Bibliography, No. 1295. 1977. 7.00 (ISBN 0-686-19695-3). CPL Biblios.

Gehr, Marilyn, jt. auth. see Hallowell, Ila M.

Gehrels, T., ed. Asteroids. LC 79-19686. 1181p. 1979. 35.00x (ISBN 0-8165-0695-7). U of Ariz Pr.

--Jupiter. LC 75-36124. 1254p. 1976. 38.50x (ISBN 0-8165-0530-6). U of Ariz Pr.

--Planets, Stars & Nebulae Studied With Photopolarimetry. LC 73-86446. 1133p. 1974. 27.50x (ISBN 0-8165-0428-8). U of Ariz Pr.

Gehrels, Tom, ed. Protostars & Planets: Studies of Star Formatiand of the Origin of the Solar System. LC 78-10269. pap. 160.00 (ISBN 0-317-07759-7, 2020435). Bks Demand UMI.

Gehrels, Tom & Matthews, Mildred S., eds. Saturn. LC 84-2517. 968p. 1984. 37.50x (ISBN 0-8165-0829-1). U of Ariz Pr.

Gehret, Ellen J., et al. This Is the Way I Pass My Time. LC 84-62851. (Pennsylvania German Society Ser.: Vol. XVIII). (Illus.). 292p. 1985. 45.00 (ISBN 0-911122-48-6). Penn German Soc.

Gehret, Ellen L. Rural Pennsylvania Clothing: Being a Study of the Wearing Apparel of the German & Inhabitants in the Late 18th & Early 19th Century. Crosson, Janet G., ed. LC 73-18534. (Illus.). 309p. 1976. 29.50 (ISBN 0-87387-064-6, Liberty Cap Bks). Shumway.

Gehrig, Clyde C., jt. auth. see Biestek, Felix P.

Gehrig, Eleanor & Durso, Joe. My Luke & I. LC 75-44457. (Illus.). 224p. 1976. 11.49i (ISBN 0-690-01109-1). T Y Crowell.

Gehrig, Gail. American Civil Religion: An Assessment. LC 81-82801. (Society for the Scientific Study of Religion Monograph: Vol. 3). (Orig.). 1981. pap. 5.50 (ISBN 0-932566-02-2). Soc Sci Stud Rel.

Gehring, Charles T., ed. New York Historical Manuscripts: Dutch, Delaware Papers, (Dutch Period, Vols. XVIII-XIX. LC 73-14890. 381p. 1981. 25.00 (ISBN 0-8063-0944-X). Genealog Pub.

--New York Historical Manuscripts: Dutch, Delaware Papers, English Period, 1664-1682. LC 76-41652. (Illus.). 395p. 1977. 20.00 (ISBN 0-8063-0736-6). Genealog Pub.

--New York Historical Manuscripts: Dutch, Vols. GG, HH, & II, Land Papers. LC 73-14890. 141p. 1980. 16.50 (ISBN 0-8063-0876-1). Genealog Pub.

--New York Historical Manuscripts: Dutch. Vol. V. Council Minutes 1652-1654. LC 73-14890. 255p. 1983. 20.00 (ISBN 0-8063-1034-0). Genealog Pub.

Gehring, Donald D. Administering College & University Housing: A Legal Perspective. LC 83-7257. 1983. 9.95 (ISBN 0-912557-00-1). Coll Admin Pubns.

Gehring, Donald D., jt. auth. see Young, D. Parker.

Gehring, Donald D., ed. see Pavela, Gary.

Gehring, F. W., ed. see Jerison, M. & Gillman, L.

Gehring, F. W., ed. see Ross, K. A.

Gehring, Franz E. Mozart. facsimile ed. LC 78-37881. (Select Bibliographies Reprint Ser). Repr. of 1883 ed. 16.00 (ISBN 0-8369-6718-6). Ayer Co Pubs.

Gehring, Robert. RX for Addiction. LC 84-21986. 288p. 1985. 12.95 (ISBN 0-310-42750-9, 12738). Zondervan.

Gehring, W. J. Genetic Mosaics & Cell Differentiation. (Results & Problems in Cell Differentiation: Vol. 9). (Illus.). 1978. 51.00 (ISBN 0-387-08882-2). Springer-Verlag.

Gehring, Wes D. Charlie Chaplin: A Bio-Bibliography. LC 82-20964. (Popular Culture Bio-Bibliographies Ser.). (Illus.). 256p. 1983. lib. bdg. 35.00 (ISBN 0-313-23288-1, GEC/). Greenwood.

--Leo McCarey & the Comic Anti-Hero in American Film. Jowett, Garth S., ed. LC 79-6677. (Dissertations on Film, 1980 Ser.). 1980. lib. bdg. 24.50x (ISBN 0-405-12911-4). Ayer Co Pubs.

--W. C. Fields: A Bio-Bibliography. LC 84-4454. (Popular Culture Bio-Bibliographies Ser.). (Illus.). xv, 233p. 1984. lib. bdg. 29.95 (ISBN 0-313-23875-8, GWC/). Greenwood.

Gehringer, Edward F. Capability Architectures & Small Objects. Stone, Harold, ed. LC 82-6905. (Computer Science: Systems Programming Ser.: No. 10). 240p. 1982. 44.95 (ISBN 0-8357-1347-4). UMI Res Pr.

Gehrke, jt. ed. see Webb.

Gehrke, Dorothy. Genesis of Greed. 1983. 8.95 (ISBN 0-533-05408-7). Vantage.

Gehrke, Ralph D., tr. see Wolff, Hans W.

Gehrmann & Lester. Trigonometry. (College Outline Ser.). 1984. pap. text ed. 8.95 (ISBN 0-15-601693-1, BFP). HarBraceJ.

Gehrt, Vicky E. Lily-Fair Learns a Lesson. (Rose-Petal Place Ser.). (Illus.). 40p. (ps-3). cancelled (ISBN 0-910313-51-2). Parker Bro.

--A Matter of Music. (Rose-Petal Place Ser.). 1984. incl. cassette 7.95 (ISBN 0-910313-64-4). Parker Bro.

Gehry, Frank. Cross Currents of American Architecture. (Academy Architecture Ser.). (Illus.). 88p. 1984. pap. 14.95 (ISBN 0-312-17670-8, Pub. by Marek). St Martin.

Gehu, J. M. Documents Phytosociologiques. (Nouv. Ser.: No. 3). 1978. lib. bdg. 35.00 (ISBN 3-7682-1202-5). Lubrecht & Cramer.

Gehu, J. M., ed. Colloques Phytosociologiques: La Vegetation des Pelouses Calcaires, Vol. XI. (Illus.). 684p. 1982. lib. bdg. 63.00 (ISBN 3-7682-1425-7). Lubrecht & Cramer.

--Colloques Phytosociologiques, Strasbourg 1980: La Vegetation des Forets Alluviales, Vol. IX. (Illus.). 774p. (Eng., Ger., Fr.). 1984. lib. bdg. 70.00x (ISBN 3-7682-1383-8). Lubrecht & Cramer.

--Colloques Phytosociologiques VII: Lille 1978, le Vegetation des Sols Tourbeux. 556p. (Fr.). 1981. lib. bdg. 52.50x (ISBN 3-7682-1260-2). Lubrecht & Cramer.

--Documents Phytosociologiques. (Illus.). 521p. (Fr.). 1981. lib. bdg. 52.50x (ISBN 3-7682-1298-X). Lubrecht & Cramer.

--Documents Phytosociologiques, IV: Festschrift R. Tuexen", 2 vols. (Illus.). 1979. Set. lib. bdg. 70.00x (ISBN 3-7682-1233-5). Lubrecht & Cramer.

--La Vegetation des Pelouses Seches a Therophytes. (Colloques Phytosociologiques Ser.: No. 6). 1979. lib. bdg. 42.00 (ISBN 3-7682-1207-6). Lubrecht & Cramer.

Gehu, M. J., ed. Colloques Phytosociologiques: Les Vegetations Aquatiques et Amphibiens, Lille, 1981, Vol. X. (Illus., Fr.). 1983. lib. bdg. 52.50x (ISBN 3-7682-1383-8). Lubrecht & Cramer.

Gehweiler, John A., et al. The Radiology of Vertebral Trauma. LC 78-65376. (Monograph in Clinical Radiology: No. 16). (Illus.). 496p. 1980. text ed. 47.00 (ISBN 0-7216-4065-6). Saunders.

Geib, Margaret, jt. auth. see Dutt, Ashok K.

Geibert, Ron & Malishenko, Tucker. Early Flight, Nineteen Hundred to Nineteen Eleven: Original Photographs from the Wright Brothers Personal Collection. (Illus.). 96p. (Orig.). 1984. pap. 10.00 (ISBN 0-913428-38-8). Landfall Pr.

Geier, Alvin E. & Lamm, Nathaniel. Mathematics & Your Career. (gr. 10-12). 1978. pap. text ed. 8.42 (ISBN 0-87720-241-9). AMSCO Sch.

Geier, Clarence R. The Kimberlin Site: The Ecology of a Late Woodland Population. Wood, W. Raymond, ed. LC 75-620014. (Research Ser.: No. 12). (Illus.). 57p. (Orig.). 1975. pap. 5.00 (ISBN 0-943414-13-X). MO Arch Soc.

Geier, Frederic M., et al. Individual Differences in Emotionality, Hypothesis Formation, Vicarious Trial & Error, & Visual Discrimination Learning in Rats. LC 41-10767. (Comp. Psych. Monographs). 1941. pap. 5.00 (ISBN 0-527-24923-8). Kraus Repr.

Geier, Mary A. Cancer: What's It Doing in My Life. (Orig.). 1985. pap. 4.95 (ISBN 0-932727-05-0). Hope Pub Hse.

Geier, Woodrow A. Communion Around the Year. LC 83-72388. 64p. (Orig.). 1983. pap. 4.25 (ISBN 0-88177-002-7, DR002B). Discipleship Res.

Geierhaas, Franz G. & Hellgoth, Brigitte. The Creative Act: Paths to Realization Interviews with Fifteen Artists. LC 83-82561. (Illus.). 216p. 1984. 24.00 (ISBN 0-915169-00-2); pap. (ISBN 0-915169-00-2). Intl Print Soc.

Geiermann, Peter. The Convert's Catechism of Catholic Doctrine. 1977. pap. 2.00 (ISBN 0-89555-029-6). TAN Bks Pubs.

Geigant, Friedrich. Lexikon der Volkswirtschaft. (Ger.). 1975. 32.00 (ISBN 3-478-37050-7, M-7217). French & Eur.

Geigel, Alma S. De see Handschuh, Jeanne & Simounet de Geigel, Alma.

Geigel-Polanco, Vicente, prologue by. Indice: Mensuario de Historia, Literatura, Arte y Ciencia. facsimile ed. (Sp.). 1979. 25.00 (ISBN 0-8477-1001-7). U of PR Pr.

Geiger, Abraham. Judaism & It's History: In Two Parts. Newburgh, Charles, tr. from Ger. LC 85-9043. (Brown Classics in Judaica Ser.). 414p. 1985. pap. text ed. 17.50 (ISBN 0-8191-4491-6). U Pr of Amer.

--Nachgelassene Schriften, 5 vols. in 3. Katz, Steven, ed. LC 79-7132. (Jewish Philosophy, Mysticism & History of Ideas Ser.). 1980. Repr. of 1875 ed. Set. lib. bdg. 172.50x (ISBN 0-405-12255-1); lib. bdg. 57.50x ea. Vol. 1 (ISBN 0-405-12256-X). Vol. 2 (ISBN 0-405-12257-8). Vol. 3 (ISBN 0-405-12228-4). Ayer Co Pubs.

--Salomo Gabirol und seine Dichtungen. Katz, Steven, ed. LC 79-7130. (Jewish Philosophy, Mysticism & History of Ideas Ser.). 1980. Repr. of 1867 ed. lib. bdg. 14.00x (ISBN 0-405-12254-3). Ayer Co Pubs.

Geiger, Adolph, jt. auth. see Jackson, Eugene.

Geiger, Bernard M., ed. see Manteau-Bonamy, H. M.

Geiger, Dana F. Phaselock Loops for DC Motor Speed Control. LC 80-29578. 206p. 1981. 32.50 (ISBN 0-471-08548-0, Pub. by Wiley-Interscience). Wiley.

Geiger, Don. The Age of the Splendid Machine: Eliot, Pound, Melville, Wallace Stevens, Tolstoy. 1973. Repr. of 1961 ed. 37.50 (ISBN 0-8274-0636-3). R West.

--Dramatic Impulse in Modern Poetics. LC 67-26972. x, 166p. 1967. 17.50x (ISBN 0-8071-0506-6). La State U Pr.

Geiger, F. M., jt. auth. see Geiger, Theodore.

Geiger, Frances M., jt. auth. see Geiger, Theodore.

Geiger, G. H. & Poirier, D. R. Transport Phenomena in Metallurgy. LC 75-164648. 1973. text ed. 34.95 (ISBN 0-201-02352-0). Addison-Wesley.

Geiger, Gail. The Carafa Chapel, Renaissance Art in Rome. (Sixteenth Century Essays & Studies Ser.: Vol. V). (Illus.). 240p. 1985. smyth sewn 40.00x (ISBN 0-940474-05-0). Sixteenth Cent.

Geiger, Geoff. Decade. 16p. 1984. pap. 1.00 (ISBN 0-317-02299-7). Samisdat.

Geiger, George R. John Dewey in Perspective. LC 73-11858. 248p. 1974. Repr. of 1958 ed. lib. bdg. 22.50x (ISBN 0-8371-7094-X, GEJD). Greenwood.

--The Philosophy of Henry George. LC 75-317. (The Radical Tradition in America Ser.). 603p. 1975. Repr. of 1933 ed. 32.50 (ISBN 0-88355-220-5). Hyperion Conn.

Geiger, Gordon H., jt. auth. see Fine, H. Alan.

Geiger, H., jt. auth. see Fine, Alan H.

Geiger, H., jt. auth. see Sevruk, B.

Geiger, H. Kent. Family in Soviet Russia. LC 68-15637. (Russian Research Center Studies: No. 56). (Illus.). 1968. 22.50x (ISBN 0-674-29300-2). Harvard U Pr.

Geiger, Linda M. God Loves Me! 8 Lessons, Vol. 1. (Steps of Faith for Special Children Ser.). 1981. kit 19.95x (ISBN 0-86508-045-3); text ed. 4.95x (ISBN 0-86508-046-1). BCM Inc.

Geiger, Louis G. Higher Education in a Maturing Democracy. LC 77-2203. 1977. Repr. of 1963 ed. lib. bdg. 15.00x (ISBN 0-8371-9550-0, GEHE). Greenwood.

Geiger, Lura J. Astonish Me, Yahweh! Leader's Guide. (Illus.). 101p. (Orig.). 1984. 14.95 (ISBN 0-931055-02-4). LuraMedia.

Geiger, Lura J., et al. Astonish Me, Yahweh! (Illus.). 106p. (Orig.). 1983. wkbk. 11.95 (ISBN 0-931055-01-6). LuraMedia.

Geiger, Lura Jane. Finding Hidden Treasure: TA Groups in the Church. LC 78-71607. 1979. pap. 5.00 (ISBN 0-915190-16-8). Jalmar Pr.

Geiger, Maynard. Franciscan Missionaries in Hispanic California 1769-1848: A Biographical Dictionary. LC 74-79607. Repr. of 1969 ed. 60.50 (ISBN 0-8357-9191-2, 2015007). Bks Demand UMI.

Geiger, Maynard, ed. see Jayme, Luis.

Geiger, Maynard, tr. Letters of Alfred Robinson to the De la Guerra Family of Santa Barbara 1834-1873. 1972. 10.00 (ISBN 0-87093-162-8). Dawsons.

Geiger, Michael & Bartusch, Nancy. Alphabet in Signs: ABC's in Fingerspelling. (Illus.). 52p. 1984. pap. 5.00 (ISBN 0-317-17748-6). Modern Signs.

Geiger, Reed G. Anzin Coal Company, 1800-1833: Big Business in the Early Stages of the French Industrial Revolution. LC 74-77774. 345p. 18.00 (ISBN 0-87413-108-1). U Delaware Pr.

Geiger, Rudolf. Climate Near the Ground. 4th ed. Scripta Technica Inc, tr. LC 64-23191. 1965. 35.00x (ISBN 0-674-13500-8). Harvard U Pr.

Geiger, Theodor. Aufgaben und Stellung der Intelligenz in der Gesellschaft: The Task & Position of Intellectuals in Society. LC 74-25749. (European Sociology Ser.). 174p. 1975. Repr. 18.00x (ISBN 0-405-06504-3). Ayer Co Pubs.

--Demokratie Ohne Dogma: Democracy Without Dogma. LC 74-25752. (European Sociology Ser.). 380p. 1975. Repr. 29.00x (ISBN 0-405-06506-X). Ayer Co Pubs.

--Die Klassengesellschaft Im Schmelztiegel: Class Society in the Melting Pot. LC 74-25750. (European Sociology Ser.). 232p. 1975. Repr. 18.00x (ISBN 0-405-06505-1). Ayer Co Pubs.

--Theodor Geiger on Social Order & Mass Society. Mayntz, Renate, ed. LC 69-19157. (Heritage of Sociology Ser). 1969. pap. 2.95x (ISBN 0-226-51388-2, P333, Phoen). U of Chicago Pr.

Geiger, Theodore. Transatlantic Relations in the Prospect of an Enlarged European Community. 61p. 1970. 1.50 (ISBN 0-902594-01-X, BNZ). Inst C D Howe.

Geiger, Theodore & Geiger, F. M. Welfare & Efficiency: Their Interactions in Western Europe & Implications for International Economic Relations. (Illus.). 1979. text ed. 31.75x (ISBN 0-333-26864-4). Humanities.

Geiger, Theodore & Geiger, Frances M. Tales of Two City-States: The Development Progress of Hong Kong & Singapore. LC 73-86119. 260p. 1979. 7.00 (ISBN 0-89068-022-1). Natl Planning.

--Welfare & Efficiency: Their Interactions in Western Europe & Implications for International Economic Relations. LC 78-63434. 160p. 1978. 7.00 (ISBN 0-89068-045-0). Natl Planning.

Geiger, Walter E. Phytonymic Derivation Systems in the Romance Languages: Studies in Their Origin & Development. (Studies in the Romance Languages & Literatures: No.187). 240p. (Orig.). 1978. pap. 17.50x (ISBN 0-8078-9187-8). U of NC Pr.

Geiger, Wilhelm & Kuhn, Ernst, eds. Grundriss der iranischen Philologie, 2 vols. 1769p. 1974. Repr. of 1904 ed. 222.00x (ISBN 3-11-002491-8). De Gruyter.

Geiger, Wilhelm & Windischmann, Friedrich, eds. Zarathushtra in the Gathas & in the Greek & Roman Classics. 2nd ed. LC 74-21260. Repr. of 1899 ed. 24.50 (ISBN 0-404-12810-6). AMS Pr.

Geigle, Ray A. & Hartjens, Peter G. Setups: Representation in the United States Congress-1973. LC 75-22542. 1975. pap. 4.00 (ISBN 0-915654-10-5). Am Political.

Geijer, Agnes. A History of Textile Art: A Selective Account. (Illus.). 428p. 1982. Repr. text ed. 37.50x (ISBN 0-85667-055-3, Pub. by Sotheby Pubns England). Biblio Dist.

Geijerstam, Claes. Popular Music in Mexico. LC 75-17373. pap. 52.30 (ISBN 0-317-20583-8, 2024677). Bks Demand UMI.

Geijsbeek, John B. Ancient Double-Entry Bookkeeping. 1975. Repr. text ed. 20.00 (ISBN 0-914348-16-7). Scholars Bk.

Geijsberts, L. G., jt. auth. see Gribnau, A. A.

Geikie, Archibald. Charles Darwin As Geologist. 1977. lib. bdg. 59.95 (ISBN 0-8490-1596-0). Gordon Pr.

--Types of Scenery & Their Influence on Literature. LC 72-113335. 1970. Repr. of 1898 ed. 15.00x (ISBN 0-8046-0954-3, Pub by Kennikat). Assoc Faculty Pr.

Geikie, Roderick, et al. Dutch Barrier, Seventeen Hundred & Five to Seventeen Nineteen. LC 69-10096. 1969. Repr. of 1930 ed. lib. bdg. 22.50x (ISBN 0-8371-0082-8, GEDB). Greenwood.

Geil, Don. Like Peter. 1978. 7.95 (ISBN 0-87881-070-6). Mojave Bks.

Geil, J. Energy & Transportation: Power. 1976. pap. text ed. 8.84 (ISBN 0-13-277475-5). P-H.

Geil, J. & Johnson, S. Energy & Transportation: Industry & Careers. 1976. pap. text ed. 8.84 (ISBN 0-13-277392-9). P-H.

Geil, Lloyd H. Executive's Desk Manual of Modern Model Business Letters. 1981. 59.50 (ISBN 0-13-294090-6). Exec Reports.

Geil, Philip H. Polymer Single Crystals. LC 63-19663. (Polymer Reviews Ser: Vol. 5). 572p. 1973. Repr. of 1963 ed. text ed. 34.50 (ISBN 0-88275-088-7). Krieger.

Geimer, Reinhold, jt. ed. see Hildegard.

Gein, M., jt. ed. see Grange, Jean-Louis.

Geiogamah, Hanay, ed. New Native American Drama: Three Plays. LC 79-4733. (Illus.). 158p. 1980. 12.95 (ISBN 0-8061-1586-6); pap. 6.95 (ISBN 0-8061-1697-8). U of Okla Pr.

Geipel, John. Mame Loshn: The Making of Yiddish. (Illus.). 160p. 1982. 19.50 (ISBN 0-904526-72-0, Pub by Journeyman Pr England); pap. 9.00 (ISBN 0-904526-73-9). Flatiron Book Dist.

--The Viking Legacy: The Scandinavian Influence on the English Language. (Illus.). 225p. 1971. 15.00x (ISBN 0-87471-328-5). Rowman.

Geipel, Robert. Disaster & Reconstruction. Wagner, Philip, tr. from Ger. (Illus.). 250p. 1983. text ed. 40.00x (ISBN 0-04-904006-5); pap. text ed. 19.95x (ISBN 0-04-904007-3). Allen Unwin.

Geiringer, Hilda, tr. see Mises, Richard Von.

Geiringer, Irene, jt. auth. see Geiringer, Karl.

Geiringer, Karl. The Bach Family: Seven Generations of Creative Genius. (Music Reprint 1980 Ser.). (Illus.). 1981. Repr. of 1954 ed. lib. bdg. 45.00 (ISBN 0-306-79596-5). Da Capo.

--Brahms: His Life & Work. 3rd ed. (Music Ser.). (Illus.). xvii, 383p. 1981. lib. bdg. 42.50 (ISBN 0-306-76093-2); pap. 10.95 (ISBN 0-306-80223-6). Da Capo.

--Instruments in the History of Western Music. 3rd ed. 1978. 29.95x (ISBN 0-19-520057-8). Oxford U Pr.

--Music of the Bach Family: An Anthology. (Music Reprint Ser.). (Illus.). viii, 248p. 1980. Repr. of 1955 ed. lib. bdg. 39.50 (ISBN 0-306-79597-3). Da Capo.

Geiringer, Karl & Geiringer, Irene. Haydn: A Creative Life in Music. rev., 3rd ed. (Illus.). 416p. 1983. 24.95 (ISBN 0-520-04316-2); pap. 8.95 (ISBN 0-520-04317-0, CAL 613). U of Cal Pr.

--Johann Sebastian Bach: The Culmination of an Era. 1966. 22.50x (ISBN 0-19-500554-6). Oxford U Pr.

Geiringer, Karl, ed. see Haydn.

Geis, Darlene. Dinosaurs. (How & Why Wonder Books Ser.). (Illus., Orig.). (gr. 4-6). 1960. pap. 1.25 (ISBN 0-8431-4250-2). Wonder.

--The Gilbert & Sullivan Operas. LC 83-2582. (Illus.). 1983. 35.00 (ISBN 0-8109-0984-7). Abrams.

Geis, Darlene, ed. Walt Disney's Treasury of Children's Classics. (Illus.). 1978. 29.95 (ISBN 0-8109-0812-3). Abrams.

--Walt Disney's Treasury of Silly Symphonies. (Illus.). 224p. 1981. 29.95 (ISBN 0-8109-0813-1). Abrams.

Geis, G., jt. auth. see Binder, A.

Geis, George. Personal Financial Management with dBASE III. 250p. 1985. pap. 29.95 incl. disk (ISBN 0-912677-47-3). Ashton-Tate Bks.

Geis, George L. & Stebbins, William C. Behavior: Reflexes & Conditioned Reflexes, Pt. 1, Vol. 1. (Illus., Program bk). 1965. pap. text ed. 8.95x (ISBN 0-89197-478-4). Irvington.

Geis, George T., jt. auth. see Kuhn, Robert L.

Geis, Gilbert. Not the Law's Business: An Examination of Homosexuality, Abortion, Prostitution, Narcotics, & Gambling in the United States. LC 78-26102. 1979. pap. 4.95 (ISBN 0-8052-0621-3). Schocken.

--On White-Collar Crime. LC 81-47278. 240p. 1982. 28.00x (ISBN 0-669-04568-3). Lexington Bks.

Geis, Gilbert & Meier, Robert F. White-Collar Crime: Offenses in Business, Politics, & Professions. rev. ed. LC 76-27223. 1977. pap. text ed. 15.95 (ISBN 0-02-911600-7). Free Pr.

Geis, Gilbert, ed. see Sutherland, Edwin.

Geis, I., jt. auth. see Dickerson, R. E.

Geis, Irving, jt. auth. see Dickerson, Richard E.

Geis, Irving, jt. auth. see Huff, Darrell.

Geis, M. Christina. Georgian Court: An Estate of the Gilded Age. LC 81-65875. (Illus.). 300p. 1983. 45.00 (ISBN 0-87982-043-8). Art Alliance.

Geis, Michael L. The Language of Television Advertising. (Perspectives in Neurolinguistics, Neuropsychology & Psycholinguistics Ser.). 257p. 1982. 32.50 (ISBN 0-12-278980-6). Acad Pr.

Geisberg, Max. The German Single-Leaf Woodcut, 1500-1550, 4 vols. rev ed. Strauss, Walter, ed. LC 72-95115. (Illus.). 1974. 395.00 (ISBN 0-87817-125-8). Hacker.

Geisebrecht, Wilhel M Von see Gregorius, Saint.

Geiseman, O. A. Make Yours a Happy Marriage. 1981. pap. 3.95 (ISBN 0-570-03133-8, 12-2383). Concordia.

Geisendorfer, James. Religion in America. 175p. 1983. pap. text ed. 19.75x (ISBN 90-04-06910-0, Pub. by Magnes Press Israel). Humanities.

Geisendorfer, James V., jt. auth. see Melton, James G.

Geiser, Elizabeth & Dolin, Arnold, eds. The Business of Book Publishing. 360p. 1985. 38.75x (ISBN 0-89158-998-8). Westview.

Geiser, Karl F. Redemptioners & Indentured Servants in the Colony & Commonwealth of Pennsylvania. 1901. 75.00x (ISBN 0-686-51298-7). Elliots Bks.

Geiser, Karl F., ed. see Sombart, Werner.

Geiser, Peter, jt. auth. see Peng, Fred C.

Geiser, Robert L. The Illusion of Caring: Children in Foster Care. LC 73-6246. (Illus.). 192p. 1973. 12.95x (ISBN 0-8070-2378-7); pap. 5.95x (ISBN 0-8070-2379-5, BP490). Beacon Pr.

Geiser, Samuel W. Horticulture & Horticulturists in Early Texas. LC 46-161. 1945. pap. 4.95 (ISBN 0-87074-058-X). SMU Press.

--Naturalists of the Frontier. rev. ed. LC 48-7357. (Illus.). 1948. 12.95 (ISBN 0-87074-059-8). SMU Press.

Geisert, Arthur. Pa's Balloon & Other Pig Tales. LC 83-18552. (Illus.). 96p. (gr. k-3). 1984. 12.95 (ISBN 0-395-35381-5, 5-86480). HM.

Geisert, Paul. Genes & Populations. (EMI Programed Biology Ser). (gr. 9 up). 1967. pap. text ed. 4.50 (ISBN 0-88462-019-0, Ed Methods). Longman USA.

--Understanding the Microscope. (EMI Programed Biology Ser.). 1967. pap. text ed. 3.00 (ISBN 0-88462-018-2, Ed Methods). Longman USA.

Geisert, Paul & Futrell, Mynga. Getting Ready for the SAT. (Illus.). 224p. (Orig.). (gr. 7-12). 1983. pap. text ed. 12.00 (ISBN 0-941406-05-9). Betz Pub Co Inc.

Geisert, Paul, jt. auth. see Futrell, Mynga K.

Geisinger, David L. Kicking It: The New Way to Stop Smoking Permanently. (YA) 1980. pap. 2.50 (ISBN 0-451-13127-4, J9254, Sig). NAL.

Geiskopf, Susan. Putting It up with Honey. LC 78-59871. 224p. 1979. pap. 7.95 (ISBN 0-930356-13-6). Quicksilver Prod.

Geiskopf, Susan & Toomay, Melinda. Fast & Natural Cuisine: A Complete Guide to Easy Vegetarian & Seafood Cooking. (Illus.). 256p. 1983. pap. 8.95 (ISBN 0-930356-38-1). Quicksilver Prod.

Geisler, ed. Logistics, Vol. 1. (TIMS Studies in the Management Sciences). 184p. 24.50 (ISBN 0-318-14458-1). Inst Mgmt Sci.

Geisler, Charles C. & Popper, Frank J., eds. Land Reform, American Style. LC 83-13725. 366p. 1984. text ed. 28.00x (ISBN 0-86598-016-0). Rowman & Allanheld.

Geisler, Charles C., jt. ed. see Berardi, Gigi M.

Geisler, Linda, jt. auth. see Harvey, Andrea.

Geisler, Norm. False Gods of Our Time. (Orig.). 1985. pap. 5.95 (ISBN 0-89081-494-5). Harvest Hse.

Geisler, Norman. Ethics: Alternatives & Issues. 256p. 1971. 12.95 (ISBN 0-310-24930-9). Zondervan.

--La Etica Cristiana Del Amor. Canclini, Arnoldo, tr. from Eng. LC 77-15813. 126p. (Span.). 1977. pap. 3.50 (ISBN 0-89922-103-3). Edit Caribe.

--Inerrancy. 1980. pap. 11.95 (ISBN 0-310-39281-0). Zondervan.

Geisler, Norman L. Christian Apologetics. LC 76-24706. 464p. 1976. 14.95 (ISBN 0-8010-3704-2). Baker Bk.

--The Christian Ethic of Love. 160p. 1973. 4.95 (ISBN 0-310-24921-X). Zondervan.

--The Creator in the Court Room. 242p. 1982. pap. 5.95 (ISBN 0-317-01572-9). Mott Media.

--Decide for Yourself: How History Views the Bible. 144p. (Orig.). 1981. pap. 4.95 (ISBN 0-310-39301-9). Zondervan.

--Is Man the Measure? An Evaluation of Contemporary. 160p. (Orig.). 1982. pap. 7.95 (ISBN 0-8010-3787-5). Baker Bk.

--Miracles & Modern Thought. 208p. (Orig.). 1982. pap. 7.95 (ISBN 0-310-44681-3). Zondervan.

--Options in Contemporary Christian Ethics. LC 80-69431. 128p. (Orig.). 1981. pap. 4.95 (ISBN 0-8010-3757-3). Baker Bk.

--A Popular Survey of the Old Testament. LC 77-78578. 1977. pap. 8.95 (ISBN 0-8010-3684-4). Baker Bk.

--The Roots of Evil. (Christian Free University Curriculum Ser.). 1978. pap. 3.95 (ISBN 0-310-35751-9). Zondervan.

Geisler, Norman L. & Feinberg, Paul. Introduction to Philosophy. LC 79-54188. 1980. 14.95 (ISBN 0-8010-3735-2). Baker Bk.

Geisler, Norman L. & Nix, William E. From God to Us. 302p. (Orig.). 1974. pap. 8.95 (ISBN 0-8024-2878-9). Moody.

--General Introduction to the Bible. LC 68-18890. 1968. 19.95 (ISBN 0-8024-2915-7). Moody.

Geisler, Norman L. & Watkins, Williams D. Perspectives: Understanding & Evaluating Today's World Views. LC 84-70487. 269p. (Orig.). 1984. pap. 8.95 (ISBN 0-89840-073-2). Heres Life.

Geisler, Norman L., ed. see Augustine, Aurelius.

Geisler, Rolf. Aquarium Fish Diseases. (Illus., Orig.). 1963. pap. 3.95 (ISBN 0-87666-008-1, M-516). TFH Pubns.

Geisler, Ruth. The Christian Family Prepares for Easter. 96p. (Orig.). 1985. pap. 6.95 (ISBN 0-317-20456-4, 12-2893). Concordia.

Geisman, Ludwig, jt. ed. see Dinerman, Miriam.

Geisman, Miriam S., jt. auth. see Radics, Stephen P., Jr.

Geismar, Joan H. The Archaeology of Social Disintegration in Skunk Hollow: A Nineteenth-Century Rural Black Community. (Studies in Historical Archaeology). 230p. 1982. 27.50 (ISBN 0-12-279020-0). Acad Pr.

Geismar, Ludwig L. Family & Community Functioning: A Manual of Measurement for Social-Work Practice & Policy. 2nd, rev. ed. LC 80-17785. 317p. 1980. 16.50 (ISBN 0-8108-1332-7); pap. 9.75 (ISBN 0-8108-1341-6). Scarecrow.

--Five Hundred Fifty-Five Families: A Social Psychological Study of Young Families in Transition. LC 72-82196. 268p. 1973. 14.95 (ISBN 0-87855-044-5). Transaction Bks.

Geismar, Ludwig L. & Wood, Katherine. Family & Deliquency: Resocializing the Young Offender. LC 85-8278. Date not set. price not set (ISBN 0-89885-245-5). Human Sci Pr.

Geismar, Maxwell, ed. see Lardner, Ring.

Geison, Gerald, ed. Professions & the French State: 1700-1900. LC 83-14700. 352p. 1984. 35.00x (ISBN 0-8122-7912-3). U of Pa Pr.

Geison, Gerald L. Michael Foster & the Cambridge School of Physiology: The Scientific Enterprise in Late Victorian Society. LC 77-85539. 1978. 43.00 (ISBN 0-691-08197-2). Princeton U Pr.

Geison, Gerald L., ed. Professions & Professional Ideologies in America. LC 83-5853. x, 147p. 1983. 17.50x (ISBN 0-8078-1568-3). U of NC Pr.

Geisow, Michael J. & Barrett, Anthony N., eds. Computing in Biological Sciences. 456p. 1983. 65.00 (ISBN 0-444-80435-8, North-Holland). Elsevier.

Geiss, Imanuel. The Pan-African Movement: A History of Pan-Africanism in America, Europe & Africa. LC 74-78310. 546p. 1974. text ed. 49.50x (ISBN 0-8419-0161-9, Africana); pap. text ed. 15.95x (ISBN 0-8419-0215-1). Holmes & Meier.

Geiss, Tony, jt. auth. see Pickow, Peter.

Geiss, Tony, et al. The Sesame Street Bedtime Storybook. LC 77-93774. (Illus.). (ps-2). 1978. 5.95 (ISBN 0-394-83843-2, BYR); PLB 5.99 (ISBN 0-394-93843-7). Random.

Geissbuehler, H., et al, eds. see International Congress of Pesticide Chemistry, 4th, Zurich, 1978.

Geissbuehler, H., et al, eds. see International Congress of Pesticides Chemistry, 4th, Zurich, July 1978.

Geissbuhler, Elisabeth C., tr. see Rodin, Auguste.

Geissbuhler, H., jt. ed. see Frehse, H.

Geisse, Guillermo. Regional & Urban Development Policies: A Latin American Perspective. LC 78-103483. (Latin American Urban Research Ser.). pap. 74.50 (ISBN 0-317-29678-7, 2021904). Bks Demand UMI.

Geisser, Barbara S., et al. Neurology: Specialty Board Review. 2nd ed. 1985. pap. text ed. price not set (ISBN 0-87488-529-9). Med Exam.

Geissler, E. Kleine Enzyklopaedie Biologie. 896p. (Ger.). 1976. 28.50 (ISBN 3-87144-281-X, M-7089). French & Eur.

Geissler, E. A. & Wolff, Lise. Legal Dictionary. 200p. 1980. 45.00x (ISBN 0-686-44720-4, Pub. by Collets). State Mutual Bk.

Geissler, Eugene S., ed. Bible Prayer Book. LC 80-71052. 528p. (Orig.). 1981. pap. 4.95 (ISBN 0-87793-218-2). Ave Maria.

Geissler, Eugene S., compiled by. The Spirit Bible. LC 73-88004. 272p. 1973. pap. 2.25 (ISBN 0-87793-062-7). Ave Maria.

Geissler, H. G., et al. Psychophysical Judgement & the Process of Perception. 288p. 1983. 64.00 (ISBN 0-444-86353-2, North-Holland). Elsevier.

Geissler, H. G., et al, eds. Modern Issues in Perception. (Advances in Psychology Ser.: Vol. 11). 512p. 1984. 48.25 (ISBN 0-444-86632-9, I-118-83, North Holland). Elsevier.

Geissler, Ludwig A. Looking Beyond. LC 77-154442. (Utopian Literature Ser). 1971. Repr. of 1891 ed. 16.00 (ISBN 0-405-03525-X). Ayer Co Pubs.

Geissler, P., ed. see Bonner, C. E. B.

Geissler, P., ed. see International Association of Briologists, Taxonomic Workshop, 1979.

Geissler, Suzanne B. Jonathan Edwards to Aaron Burr, Jr. From Great Awakening to Democratic Politics. LC 81-38353. (Studies in American Religion: Vol. 1). xii, 298p. 1981. 49.95x (ISBN 0-88946-906-7). E Mellen.

Geissman, T. A. Principles of Organic Chemistry. 4th ed. LC 76-13891. (Illus.). 1035p. 1977. 38.95 (ISBN 0-7167-0177-4); tchrs. manual avail. W H Freeman.

--Workbook in Organic Chemistry: Exercises in the Properties, Behavior, & Synthesis of Organic Compounds. (Illus.). 245p. 1972. pap. text ed. 10.95x (ISBN 0-7167-0167-7). W H Freeman.

Geissman, T. A. & Crout, D. H. Organic Chemistry of Secondary Plant Metabolism. LC 71-81384. 1969. pap. 20.00 (ISBN 0-87735-201-1). Freeman Cooper.

Geissmar, Berta. Two Worlds of Music. LC 74-28326. Orig. Title: The Baton & the Jackboot. (Illus.). 327p. 1975. Repr. of 1946 ed. lib. bdg. 35.00 (ISBN 0-306-70664-4). Da Capo.

Geisst, Charles. Guide to the Financial Markets. LC 81-18514. 1982. 22.50 (ISBN 0-312-35294-8). St Martin.

Geisst, Charles, jt. auth. see Brown, Brendan.

Geisst, Charles R. Guide to the Financial Markets. LC 81-18514. 144p. 1984. pap. 10.95 (ISBN 0-312-35302-2). St Martin.

--The Political Thought of John Milton. 140p. 1984. 19.00x (ISBN 0-333-36602-6, Pub. by Salem Acad). Merrimack Pub Cir.

--Raising International Capital: International Markets & the European Institutions. 180p. 1980. 22.00x (ISBN 0-566-00282-5, 03296-4, Pub. by Saxon Hse England). Lexington Bks.

Geist, Anthony L., tr. see Guillen, Jorge.

Geist, Benjamin, ed. State Audit: Development in Public Accountability. LC 80-21772. 423p. 1981. 65.00x (ISBN 0-8419-0674-2). Holmes & Meier.

Geist, Carl. New Ways to Solve Your Refrigeration & Air Conditioning Service Problems. LC 72-87832. (Illus.). 256p. 1972. 15.95 (ISBN 0-912524-07-3). Busn News.

Geist, Chrisann S. & Calzaretta, William. Placement Handbook for Counseling Disabled Persons. (Illus.). 346p. 1982. 37.50x (ISBN 0-398-04592-5). C C Thomas.

Geist, Christopher & Nachbar, Jack. Popular Culture Reader. 3rd ed. LC 78-61077. 1983. pap. text ed. 35.00 (ISBN 0-87972-273-8); pap. 11.95 (ISBN 0-87972-274-6). Bowling Green Univ.

Geist, Harold. Bahian Adventure. 128p. 1982. 8.95 (ISBN 0-682-49868-8). Exposition Pr FL.

--The Emotional Aspects of Heart Disease. LC 76-16319. 1977. 6.95 (ISBN 0-87212-062-7). Libra.

--From Eminently Disadvantaged to Eminence. LC 78-176180. 144p. 1973. 10.50 (ISBN 0-87527-104-9). Green.

--Migraine: Psychological, Psychiatric & Physiological Aspects. LC 82-26856. 1983. text ed. 11.50 (ISBN 0-89874-601-9). Krieger.

--The Psychological Aspects of the Aging Process: With Sociological Implications. LC 68-57455. (Illus.). 196p. 1969. 12.50 (ISBN 0-87527-036-0). Green.

--The Psychological Aspects of the Aging Process with Sociological Implications. 2nd ed. LC 80-13233. 208p. 1981. text ed. 11.50 (ISBN 0-89874-073-8). Krieger.

Geist, Harold & Hawkins, C. F. Adults Going to the Hospital. LC 66-22695. (Illus.). 31p. 1966. pap. 4.10x (ISBN 0-87424-203-7); pap. 3.75x ea. 2 or more copies. Western Psych.

Geist, Harold & Manson, Morse P. Children Going to the Hospital. LC 65-28467. (Illus.). 28p. 1965. pap. 4.10x (ISBN 0-87424-202-9); pap. 3.75x ea. 2 or more copies. Western Psych.

Geist, Harold & Martinez, Cecelia. Tennis Psychology. LC 75-17651. (Illus.). 136p. 1976. 15.95 (ISBN 0-88229-120-3). Nelson-Hall.

Geist, Harry, jt. auth. see Pollack, Morris.

Geist, Harry, jt. auth. see Pollock, Morris.

Geist, Johann F. Arcades: The History of a Building Type. Smith, John H. & Newman, Jane O., trs. from Ger. (Illus.). 516p. 1982. 55.00 (ISBN 0-262-07082-0). MIT Pr.

--Arcades: The History of a Building Type. Smith, John H. & Newman, Jane O., trs. (Illus.). 516p. 1985. 17.50x (ISBN 0-262-12110-7); pap. 9.95 (ISBN 0-317-28521-1). MIT Pr.

Geist, Kenneth. Pictures Will Talk: The Life & Films of Joseph L. Mankiewicz. (Quality Paperbacks Ser.). (Illus.). 458p. 1983. pap. 9.95 (ISBN 0-306-80188-4). Da Capo.

Geist, Otto W. Archaeological Excavations at Kukulik, St. Lawrence Island, Alaska. Repr. of 1936 ed. 32.50 (ISBN 0-404-11641-8). AMS Pr.

Geist, Roland C. Bicycle People: The Nostalgic Picturial Album of the Bicycle through Art & Prose, Song & Poetry. LC 78-13567. (Illus.). 165p. 1978. 24.50 (ISBN 0-87491-273-3). Acropolis.

Geist, Sidney. Brancusi: A Study of the Sculpture. LC 82-81786. (Illus.). 235p. 1983. Repr. of 1968 ed. 40.00 (ISBN 0-87817-290-4). Hacker.

--Brancusi-The Kiss. LC 76-27502. (Icon Editions). (Illus.). 1978. (HarpT); pap. 5.95i (ISBN 0-06-430081-1, IN-81, HarpT). Har-Row.

Geist, V. Life Strategies, Human Evolution, Environmental Design: Toward a Biological Theory of Health, Vol. I. LC 78-10807. (Illus.). 1978. 39.50 (ISBN 0-387-90363-1). Springer-Verlag.

Geist, Valerius. Mountain Sheep: A Study in Behavior & Evolution. LC 77-149596. (Wildlife Behavior & Ecology Ser.). (Illus.). xvi, 384p. 1976. pap. 12.00x (ISBN 0-226-28573-1, P666, Phoen). U of Chicago Pr.

Geist, William. Toward a Safe & Sane Halloween: And Other Tales of Suburbia. LC 84-40421. 288p. 1985. 15.95 (ISBN 0-8129-1150-4). Times Bks.

Geistfeld, Annette & Juntune, Joyce. Productive Thinking. 45p. (Orig.). 1983. pap. 5.00 (ISBN 0-912773-01-4). One Hund Twenty Creat.

Geistfeld, Annette, jt. auth. see Day, Faye.

Geithman, David T., jt. auth. see Carvajal, M. J.

Geithman, David T., ed. Fiscal Policy for Industrialization & Development in Latin America. LC 74-2231. 1974. 12.50 (ISBN 0-8130-0397-0). U Presses Fla.

Geitner, F. K., jt. auth. see Bloch, H. P.

Geitner, Fred K., jt. auth. see Bloch, Heinz P.

Geitsfeld, Annette, et al. Creative Thinking Through Language Arts, 2 bks. (Illus.). 125p. 1984. pap. 12.50 ea. (ISBN 0-912773-07-3, BK. 1) (ISBN 0-912773-06-5, BK. 2). One Hund Twenty Creat.

Geiwitz, James. Psychology: Looking at Ourselves. 2nd ed. (Illus.). 1980. 25.95 (ISBN 0-316-30706-8); instr's. manual by P.S. Assocs (ISBN 0-316-30707-6); student guide by Syrdal-Lasky 8.95 (ISBN 0-316-30710-6); test bank by P. S. Assocs. avail. (ISBN 0-316-30708-4). Little.

Geiwitz, James, jt. auth. see Schaie, K. Warner.

Gejvall, Nils-Gustaf. The Fauna. LC 66-36503. (Lerna Ser: Vol. 1). (Illus.). 1969. 15.00x (ISBN 0-87661-301-6). Am Sch Athens.

Gekas, Alexandra B. & Countryman, Kathleen M. Development & Implementation of a Patient's Bill of Rights in Hospitals. LC 80-11366. 24p. 1980. pap. 10.00 (ISBN 0-87258-306-6, AHA-157164). AHPI.

Gekeler, E. Discretization Methods for Stable Initial Value Problems. (Lecture Notes in Mathematics: Vol. 1044). viii, 201p. pap. 13.00 (ISBN 0-387-12880-8). Springer-Verlag.

Gekker, Cathrine O. Practical German for the Tourist. 1976. stitched 3.00 (ISBN 0-686-00543-0). Huffman Pr.

Gekker, I. R. Interaction of Strong Electromagnetic Fields with Plasmas. Sykes, J. B. & Franklin, R. N., trs. (Oxford Studies in Physics). (Illus.). 1982. 69.00x (ISBN 0-19-851467-0). Oxford U Pr.

Gekoski, Norman. Psychological Testing: Theory, Interpretation & Practices. (Illus.). 320p. 1969. 29.75x (ISBN 0-398-00668-7). C C Thomas.

Gela, Darlene. Dinosaurs & Other Prehistoric Animals. (Illus.). 108p. (gr. 3-8). 1982. 6.95 (ISBN 0-448-02882-4, G&D). Putnam Pub Group.

Gelatt, H. B., et al. Deciding: A Leader's Guide. LC 74-186413. 45p. 1972. pap. text ed. 2.50 (ISBN 0-87447-026-9, 221603); leader's guide 6.00 (ISBN 0-87447-027-7, 221604). College Bd.

--Decisions & Outcomes: A Leader's Guide. 48p. 1973. pap. text ed. 2.50 (ISBN 0-87447-029-3, 221606); leader's guide 6.00 (ISBN 0-87447-030-7, 221608). College Bd.

Gelatt, Kirk N. Veterinary Ophthalmic Pharmacology & Therapeutics. 2d ed. (Illus.). 1978. pap. 5.00x (ISBN 0-935078-08-8). Veterinary Med.

Gelatt, Kirk N., ed. Textbook of Veterinary Opthalmology. LC 80-17291. (Illus.). 788p. 1981. text ed. 85.00 (ISBN 0-8121-0686-5). Lea & Febiger.

Gelatt, Roland. Music Makers: Some Outstanding Musical Performers of Our Day. LC 72-2334. (Music Ser.). 1972. Repr. of 1953 ed. lib. bdg. 32.50 (ISBN 0-306-70519-2). Da Capo.

Gelb, Alan. Columbus Avenue. LC 84-11739. 320p. 1984. 14.95 (ISBN 0-312-15089-X). St Martin.

--Mussolini. (Orig.). 1985. pap. price not set (ISBN 0-671-60450-3). PB.

Gelb, Alan, jt. auth. see Bradley, Keith.

Gelb, Arthur, jt. auth. see Rosenthal, A. M.

Gelb, Arthur, ed. see Analytical Sciences Corp-Technical Staff.

Gelb, Arthur, jt. ed. see Rosenthal, A. M.

Gelb, Barbara. Varnished Brass: The Decade after Serpico. LC 83-4568. 320p. 1983. 16.95 (ISBN 0-399-12871-9, Putnam). Putnam Pub Group.

Gelb, Barbara L. The Dictionary of Food & What's in It for You. 1979. pap. 3.50 (ISBN 0-345-29479-3). Ballantine.

Gelb, Bernard & Pliskin, Jeffrey. Energy Use in Mining: Patterns & Prospects. LC 79-851. 240p. 1979. prof ref 35.00 (ISBN 0-88410-088-X). Ballinger Pub.

Gelb, Bernard A. & Myers, John G. Measuring the Cost of Industrial Water Pollution Control. LC 76-45533. (Report: No. 700). (Illus.). 92p. (Orig.). 1976. pap. 30.00 (ISBN 0-8237-0134-4); pap. 10.00 member. Conference Bd.

Gelb, Betsy & Gelb, Gabriel. Marketing is Everybody's Business. 3rd ed. 1980. pap. text ed. 11.90x (ISBN 0-673-16112-9). Scott F.

Gelb, Gabriel, jt. auth. see Gelb, Betsy.

Gelb, Harold. Clinical Management of Head, Neck & TMJ Pain & Dysfunction: A Multi-Disciplinary Approach to Diagnosis & Treatment. LC 76-50148. (Illus.). 1977. text ed. 60.00 (ISBN 0-7216-4072-9). Saunders.

--Killing Pain Without Prescription. LC 79-2619. (Illus.). 1980. 14.37i (ISBN 0-06-011483-5, HarpT). Har-Row.

Gelb, Harold & Siegel, Paula M. Killing Pain without Prescription. (Illus.). 272p. 1982. pap. 5.72i (ISBN 0-06-463562-7, EH 562). B&N NY.

Gelb, Ignace J. Computer-Aided Analysis of Amorite. LC 79-84839. (Assyriological Studies Ser.: No. 21). 1980. pap. 35.00x (ISBN 0-918986-21-4). Oriental Inst.

--Glossary of Old Akkadian. (Materials for the Assyrian Dictionary Ser: No. 3). 1957. pap. text ed. 12.00x (ISBN 0-226-62307-6). U of Chicago Pr.

--Sargonic Texts in the Asmolean Museum, Oxford. LC 79-111601. (Materials for the Assyrian Dictionary Ser: No. 5). 1970. pap. 12.50x (ISBN 0-226-62309-2). U of Chicago Pr.

--Sargonic Texts in the Louvre. LC 79-111600. (Materials for the Assyrian Dictionary Ser: No. 4). 1970. pap. 11.00x (ISBN 0-226-62308-4). U of Chicago Pr.

--Study of Writing. rev. ed. LC 52-10599. (Illus.). 1963. pap. 10.00x (ISBN 0-226-28606-1, P109, Phoen). U of Chicago Pr.

Gelb, Joyce. Beyond Conflict: Black-Jewish Relations. 40p. 1980. pap. 2.00 (ISBN 0-87495-027-9). Am Jewish Comm.

Gelb, Joyce & Palley, Marian L. Women & Public Policies. LC 82-400. 208p. 1982. 21.00 (ISBN 0-691-07639-1); pap. 6.95 (ISBN 0-691-02209-7). Princeton U Pr.

Gelb, Lawrence. Your Future in Beauty Culture. rev. ed. (Careers in Depth Ser.). (Illus.). 128p. 1983. lib. bdg. 8.97 (ISBN 0-8239-0505-5). Rosen Group.

Gelb, Leslie H. & Betts, Richard K. The Irony of Vietnam: The System Worked. 1979. 26.95 (ISBN 0-8157-3072-1); pap. 9.95 (ISBN 0-8157-3071-3). Brookings.

Gelb, Michael. Body Learning: An Introduction to the Alexander Technique. 146p. 1981. 12.95 (ISBN 0-933328-03-6). Delilah Bks.

Gelb, Neil G. Using COBOL in an MP-M System. LC 82-61965. 112p. 1983. pap. 12.95 (ISBN 0-672-21936-0, 21936). Sams.

Gelb, Norman. Less than Glory. 256p. 1984. 15.95 (ISBN 0-399-12902-2, Putnam). Putnam Pub Group.

--Scramble: A Narrative History of the Battle of Britain. (Illus.). 400p. 1985. 22.95 (ISBN 0-15-179615-7). HarBraceJ.

Gelb, Saadia, jt. auth. see Criden, Yosef.

Gelb, Stephen, jt. auth. see Saul, John S.

Gelband, Henry, jt. auth. see Roberts, Nigel K.

Gelbart, S., et al, eds. see Tata Institute Studies in Mathematics Bombay 1979.

Gelbart, S. S. Weil's Representation & the Spectrum of the Metaplectic Group. (Lecture Notes in Mathematics: Vol. 530). 1976. soft cover 13.00 (ISBN 0-387-07799-5). Springer-Verlag.

Gelbart, Stephen S. Automorphic Forms & Adele Groups. (Annals of Mathematics Studies: No. 83). 280p. 1975. 26.50x (ISBN 0-691-08156-5). Princeton U Pr.

--Fourier Analysis on Matrix Space. LC 52-42839. (Memoirs: Vol. 108). 77p. 1971. pap. 9.00 (ISBN 0-8218-1808-2, MEMO-108). Am Math.

Gelbaum, B. R. Problems in Analysis. (Problem Books in Mathematics). (Illus.). 224p. 1982. 32.00 (ISBN 0-387-90692-4). Springer-Verlag.

Gelbaum, Bernard R., ed. see Pallu De La Barriere, R.

Gelber, H. G. Australian-American Alliance: Costs & Benefits. 6.75 (ISBN 0-8446-0640-5). Peter Smith.

Gelber, Jack. The Connection. 1960. 3.95 (ISBN 0-394-17222-1, E223, Ever). Grove.

Gelber, Leonard, jt. auth. see Martin, Michael.

Gelber, Leonard, jt. ed. see Martin, Michael.

Gelber, Lionel. Crisis in the West: American Leadership & the Global Balance. LC 75-857. 250p. 1975. 26.00 (ISBN 0-312-17395-4). St Martin.

Gelber, Lionel M. Rise of Anglo-American Friendship: A Study in World Politics, 1898-1906. ix, 292p. 1966. Repr. of 1938 ed. 19.50 (ISBN 0-208-00506-4, Archon). Shoe String.

Gelber, Lynne L. Instability: The Shape & Space of Claudel's Art Criticism. Kuspit, Donald B., ed. LC 80-18445. (Studies in the Fine Arts: Criticism: No. 4). 128p. 1980. 34.95 (ISBN 0-8357-1090-4). UMI Res Pr.

Gelber, S. M. Job Stands Up: Play with Music & Lyrics. (Orig.). 1975. pap. 5.00 (ISBN 0-8074-0189-7, 382660). UAHC.

Gelber, Steven M. Black Men & Businessman: The Growing Awareness of a Social Responsibility. LC 74-77654. 320p. 1974. 24.00x (ISBN 0-8046-9062-6, Pub. by Kennikat). Assoc Faculty Pr.

Gelberg. The Hare Krishna Movement. 1985. lib. bdg. 23.00 (ISBN 0-8240-8751-8). Garland Pub.

Gelberg, Steven, ed. Hare Krishna Hare Krishna: Five Distinguished Scholars in Religion Discuss the Krishna Movement in the West. LC 82-21055. (Press Eastern Philosophy & Literature Ser.). 224p. (Orig.). 1983. pap. 7.95 (ISBN 0-394-62454-8, E845, Ever). Grove.

Gelberman, Joseph. To Be Fully Alive. 89p. pap. 5.95 (ISBN 0-942494-49-0). Coleman Pub.

Gelberman, Joseph H. Haggadah: The Story of Thanksgiving. 35p. (Orig.). 1983. pap. 4.00 (ISBN 0-942494-55-5). Coleman Pub.

Gelboin, Harry & Ts'O, Paul O., eds. Polycyclic Hydrocardons & Cancer, Vol. 3. LC 78-17706. 1981. 65.00 (ISBN 0-12-279203-3). Acad Pr.

Gelboin, Harry V., ed. Polycyclic Hydrocarbons & Cancer, 2 vols. Incl. Vol. 1. Environment, Chemistry & Metabolism. 70.00 (ISBN 0-12-279201-7); Vol. 2. Molecular & Cell Biology. 1979. 70.00 (ISBN 0-12-279202-5). 1978. Acad Pr.

Gelboin, Harry V., jt. ed. see Omenn, Gilbert S.

Gelboin, Harry V., et al, eds. Genetic & Environmental Factors in Experimental & Human Cancer. 370p. 1980. 49.00x (ISBN 4-7622-0240-1, Pub. by Japan Sci Soc Japan). Intl Spec Bk.

Gelbron, Guy G. Cases on Sign Law. 1000p. 200.00 (ISBN 0-318-15614-8); members 50.00 (ISBN 0-318-15615-6). Natl Elec Sign.

Gelbuch, F. & Lopata, P. Developed Socialist Society: Basic Features & Place in History. 123p. 1980. pap. 3.95 (ISBN 0-8285-1816-5, Pub. by Progress Pubs USSR). Imported Pubns.

Geldard, F. A. Sensory Saltation: Metastability in the Perceptual World. 133p. 1975. 24.95x (ISBN 0-89859-466-9). L Erlbaum Assocs.

Geldard, Frank A. Human Senses. 2nd ed. LC 72-37432. 584p. 1972. text ed. 50.45x (ISBN 0-471-29570-1). Wiley.

--Sensory Saltation: Metastability in the Perceptual World. LC 75-22269. 133p. 1975. 10.00x (ISBN 0-470-29571-6). Halsted Pr.

Geldart, Edmund M., ed. Folklore of Modern Greece. 1976. lib. bdg. 59.95 (ISBN 0-8490-1851-X). Gordon Pr.

Geldart, L. P., jt. auth. see Sheriff, R. E.

Geldart, W. M., ed. see Aristophanes.

Geldart, William. Introduction to English Law: Elements of English Law. 9th ed. Yardley, D. C., ed. LC 83-22053. 1984. pap. 7.95x (ISBN 0-19-289171-5). Oxford U Pr.

Geldenhuys, Deon. The Diplomacy of Isolation: South African Foreign Policy Making. LC 83-40515. 295p. 1984. 25.00 (ISBN 0-312-21132-5). St Martin.

Geldenhuys, J. Norval. Commentary on Luke. (New International Commentary on the New Testament). 1951. 17.95 (ISBN 0-8028-2184-7). Eerdmans.

Gelder, Frederick van see Van Gelder, Frederick.

Gelder, George S., ed. see Epstein, Israel, et al.

Gelder, L. van, et al. Enciclopedia Juvenil Labor, 3 vols. 592p. (Espn.). 1977. Set. leatherette 54.00 (ISBN 84-335-0333-2, S-50474). French & Eur.

Gelder, Lydia Van see Van Gelder, Lydia.

Gelder, M. G., jt. ed. see Mandelbrote, B. M.

Gelder, Michael, et al. Oxford Textbook of Psychiatry. 883p. 1983. 49.00x (ISBN 0-19-261428-2); pap. 29.50x (ISBN 0-19-261294-8). Oxford U Pr.

Gelder, Nico M. Van see Jasper, Herbert H. & Van Gelder, Nico M.

Gelder, Patricia Van see Van Gelder, Patricia.

Gelder, Paul, jt. auth. see Smurthwaite, Nick.

Gelder, Roelf van see Kistemaker, Renee & Van Gelder, Roelf.

Gelder, V. Rodolphe Bresdin, 2 vols. 1976. lib. bdg. 184.00 (ISBN 90-247-1917-8, Pub. by Martinus Nijhoff Netherlands). Kluwer Academic.

Gelder, Van, jt. auth. see Reber, Ralph W.

Gelderen, Van see Van Gelderen.

Gelderman, Carol. Better Writing for Professionals: A Concise Guide. (PROCOM Ser.). 1984. pap. 9.95 (ISBN 0-673-15563-3). Scott F.

Gelderman-Curtis, C. Holland-Inside Information: The Complete Guide to Holland. 2nd ed. (Illus.). 1980. pap. 17.50 (ISBN 0-686-77971-1). Heinman.

Geldren, Gerrit van see Van Geldren, Gerrit.

Geldzahler, Henry, intro. by. Hans Hartung: Paintings, 1971-1975. LC 75-31609. (Illus.). 1975. pap. 1.50 (ISBN 0-87099-145-0). Metro Mus Art.

--Jean Arp at the Metropolitan Museum of Art. LC 72-77067. (Illus.). 1972. pap. 1.50 (ISBN 0-87099-117-5). Metro Mus Art.

Geldzahler, Henry P. Art in Transit: Subway Drawings by Keith Haring. (Illus.). 96p. 1984. pap. 12.95 (ISBN 0-517-55424-0, Harmony). Crown.

Gelee, Claude Lorrain. Drawings of Lorrain. Roethlisberger, Marcel, ed. (Master Draughtsman Ser). (Illus., Orig.). treasure trove bdg. 9.95x (ISBN 0-87505-020-4); pap. 4.95 (ISBN 0-87505-173-1). Borden.

Geleerd, Elisabeth R., ed. The Child Analyst at Work. LC 67-20281. 310p. 1967. text ed. 27.50 (ISBN 0-8236-0740-2). Intl Univs Pr.

Gelenbe, E. & Mitrani, I. Analysis & Synthesis of Computer Systems. LC 80-49992. (Computer Science and Applied Mathematical Ser.). 1980. 45.00 (ISBN 0-12-279350-1). Acad Pr.

Gelenbe, E., ed. Performance Eighty-Four: Models of Computer System Performance: Proceedings of the Anniversary Symposium of IFIP WG 7.3. on Computer Performance, 10th, Paris, France, 19-21 December, 1984. 560p. 1985. 68.00 (ISBN 0-444-87680-4, North-Holland). Elsevier.

Gelenbe, E., jt. ed. see Beilner, H.

Gelenbe, Erol, jt. ed. see Gardarin, Georges.

Gelenberg, Alan J., jt. ed. see Bassuk, Ellen L.

Gelender, Maxwell. Review Text in Chemistry. (Illus., Orig.). (gr. 10-12). 1964. pap. text ed. 7.92 (ISBN 0-87720-104-8). AMSCO Sch.

Gelenian, Ara A. Armenian-Americans of Rhode Island: Ancient Roots to Present Experiences. Conley, Patrick T., ed. (Rhode Island Ethnic Heritage Ser.). (Illus.). 37p. (Orig.). 1985. pap. 2.75 (ISBN 0-917012-73-9). RI Pubns Soc.

Gelernt, Jules. Monarch Notes on Dante's the Divine Comedy. (Orig.). pap. 3.50 (ISBN 0-671-00510-3). Monarch Pr.

Gelesnoff, Vladimir M. Paul's Epistle to the Galatians. 1977. pap. text ed. 3.00 (ISBN 0-910424-73-X). Concordant.

Geley, Gustave. Clairvoyance & Materialisation: A Record of Experiments. De Brath, Stanley, tr. LC 75-7381. (Perspectives in Psychical Research Ser.). (Illus.). 1975. Repr. of 1927 ed. 37.50x (ISBN 0-405-07031-4). Ayer Co Pubs.

Gelfand. E. T. (TV & Movie Tie-ins Ser.). (Illus.). 32p. (gr. 4-12). 1985. 7.95 (ISBN 0-317-31176-X). Creative Ed.

--Hershel Walker. (Sports Superstars Ser.). (Illus.). 32p. (gr. 3-9). 1985. 7.95 (ISBN 0-317-31195-6). Creative Ed.

--The Jeffersons. (TV & Movie Tie-ins Ser.). (Illus.). 32p. (gr. 4-12). 1985. 7.95 (ISBN 0-317-31180-8). Creative Ed.

--Magnum, P. I. (TV & Movie Tie-ins Ser.). (Illus.). 32p. (gr. 4-12). 1985. 7.95 (ISBN 0-317-31187-5). Creative Ed.

--Paul McCartney. (Rock 'n Pop Stars Ser.). (Illus.). 32p. (gr. 4-12). PLB 7.95 (ISBN 0-317-31142-5). Creative Ed.

--Wayne Gretsky. (Sports Superstars Ser.). (Illus.). 32p. (gr. 3-9). 1985. 7.95 (ISBN 0-317-31206-5). Creative Ed.

Gelfand & Walker. Ensemble Modeling. 344p. 1984. 45.00 (ISBN 0-8247-7180-X). Dekker.

Gelfand, David M., jt. auth. see Loughlin, Martin.

Gelfand, David W. Gastrointestinal Radiology: Performing & Interpreting the Fluroscopic Examinations. (Illus.). 354p. 1984. text ed. 60.00 (ISBN 0-443-08096-8). Churchill.

Gelfand, Donald. Aging: The Ethnic Factor. (Orig.). 1982. text ed. 16.95 (ISBN 0-316-30713-0); pap. 8.95 (ISBN 0-316-30714-9). Little.

Gelfand, Donald E. The Aging Network: Programs & Services. 2nd ed. (Springer Series on Adulthood & Aging: Vol. 8). 320p. 1984. 19.95 (ISBN 0-8261-3053-4). Springer Pub.

Gelfand, Donald E. & Kutzik, Alfred J., eds. Ethnicity & Aging. LC 79-14046. (Adulthood & Aging Ser.: Vol. 5). 1979. text ed. 22.95 (ISBN 0-8261-2770-3). Springer Pub.

Gelfand, Donna L. & Hartmann, Donald P. Child Behavior Analysis & Therapy. LC 74-14707. 1975. pap. text ed. 14.95 (ISBN 0-08-028053-6). Pergamon.

Gelfand, Donna M. & Hartmann, Donald P. Child Behavior Analysis & Therapy. 2nd ed. (Pergamon General Psychology Ser.: No. 50). 304p. 1984. 39.00 (ISBN 0-08-028054-4); pap. 14.95 (ISBN 0-08-028053-6). Pergamon.

Gelfand, Donna M. & Jensen, William R. Understanding Children's Behavior Disorders. 1982. text ed. 32.95 (ISBN 0-03-044211-7). HR&W.

Gelfand, Donna M. & Peterson, Lizette. Child Development & Psychopathology. 1985. 17.95 (ISBN 0-8039-2282-5); pap. 8.95 (ISBN 0-8039-2283-3). Sage.

Gelfand, Elissa D. Imagination in Confinement: Women's Writings from French Prisons. LC 83-7191. (Illus.). 264p. 1983. 19.95x (ISBN 0-8014-1543-8). Cornell U Pr.

Gelfand, Elissa D. & Hules, Virginia T. French Feminist Criticism: Women, Language, & Literature; An Annotated Bibliography. LC 82-48275. (Bibliographies of Modern Critics & Critical Schools Ser.). 300p. 1985. lib. bdg. 36.00 (ISBN 0-8240-9252-X). Garland Pub.

Gelfand, Erwin W. & Dosch, Hans-Michael, eds. Biological Basis of Immunodeficiency. 334p. 1980. text ed. 52.50 (ISBN 0-89004-361-2). Raven.

Gelfand, I. M. Representation Theory: Selected Papers. LC 82-4440. (London Mathematical Society Lecture Notes Ser. 69). 330p. 1982. pap. 34.50 (ISBN 0-521-28981-5). Cambridge U Pr.

Gelfand, I. M., jt. auth. see Vasiliev, J. M.

Gelfand, I. M., ed. Method of Coordinates, Vol. 1. (Library of School Mathematics). 1967. text ed. 10.00x (ISBN 0-262-07028-6). MIT Pr.

Gelfand, I. M., et al. Coordinate Method. (Pocket Mathematical Library). 80p. 1968. 24.50 (ISBN 0-677-20640-2). Gordon.

Gel'fand, I. M., et al. Eight Papers on Group Theory. LC 51-5559. (Translations, Ser.: No. 2, Vol. 2). 1956. 27.00 (ISBN 0-8218-1702-7, TRANS 2-2). Am Math.

Gelfand, I. M., et al. Functions & Graphs. (Pocket Mathematical Library). 110p. 1968. 24.50 (ISBN 0-677-20690-9). Gordon.

--Four Papers on Group Theory, No. 9. 231p. 1958. 35.60 (ISBN 0-8218-1709-4, UMI-2004669); pap. 30.60 (ISBN 0-317-32965-0). Am Math.

Gelfand, I. M., et al, eds. Structural-Functional Organization of Biological Systems. 448p. 1971. 27.50x (ISBN 0-262-07042-1). MIT Pr.

Gelfand, Israel M., et al. Commutative Normed Rings. LC 61-15024. 1964. 14.95 (ISBN 0-8284-0170-5). Chelsea Pub.

Gelfand, Izrail M. & Fomin, S. V. Calculus of Variations. Silverman, R., tr. (Illus.). 1963. ref. ed. 36.95 (ISBN 0-13-112292-4). P-H.

Gelfand, Lawrence E. The Inquiry. LC 75-31364. 387p. 1976. Repr. of 1963 ed. lib. bdg. 25.00x (ISBN 0-8371-8526-2, GEIN). Greenwood.

Gelfand, Lawrence E., ed. Herbert Hoover: The Great War & Its Aftermath, Nineteen Fourteen to Nineteen Twenty-Three. LC 79-10139. (Herbert Hoover Centennial Seminar Ser.). (Illus.). 254p. 1979. text ed. 20.00 (ISBN 0-87745-095-1). U of Iowa Pr.

Gelfand, Lawrence E., ed. see Holt, W. Stull.

Gelfand, M. David. Federal Constitutional Law & American Local Government. 555p. 1984. 45.00 (ISBN 0-87215-764-4). Michie Co.

Gel'fand, M. S., et al. Twelve Papers on Logic & Differential Equations. LC 51-5559. (Translations Ser.: No. 2, Vol. 29). 1963. 30.00 (ISBN 0-8218-1729-9, TRANS 2-29). Am Math.

Gelfand, Mark I. A Nation of Cities: The Federal Government & Urban America 1933-1965. (Urban Life in America Ser). 1975. 29.95x (ISBN 0-19-501941-5). Oxford U Pr.

Gelfand, S. I., et al. Learn Limits Through Problems. (Pocket Mathematical Library). 78p. 1968. 22.00 (ISBN 0-677-20720-4). Gordon.

--Sequences & Combinatorial Problems. (Pocket Mathematical Library). 92p. 1968. 24.50 (ISBN 0-677-20730-1). Gordon.

Gelfand, Toby. Professionalizing Modern Medicine: Paris Surgeons & Medical Science & Institutions in the Eighteenth Century. LC 79-8955. (Contributions in Medical History: No. 6). (Illus.). xviii, 271p. 1980. lib. bdg. 35.00 (ISBN 0-313-21488-3, GPM/). Greenwood.

Gelfano. Hearing: An Introduction to Psychological & Physiological Acoustics. 392p. 1981. 33.50 (ISBN 0-8247-1189-0). Dekker.

Gelfant, Blanche H. American City Novel. 56.50 (ISBN 0-8357-9717-1, 2016220). Bks Demand UMI.

--Women Writing in America: Voices in Collage. LC 84-40298. 290p. 1985. 20.00x (ISBN 0-87451-307-3); pap. 10.95 (ISBN 0-87451-308-1). U Pr of New Eng.

Gelfman, Judith S. Women in Television News. LC 75-33167. (Illus.). 286p. 1976. 21.50x (ISBN 0-231-03994-8). Columbia U Pr.

Gelfond, A. O. Solving Equations in Integers. 56p. 1981. pap. 2.00 (ISBN 0-8285-2053-4, Pub. by Mir Pubs USSR). Imported Pubns.

Gel'fond, A. O., et al. Twelve Papers on Number Theory & Function Theory. LC 51-5559. (Translations Ser.: No. 2, Vol. 19). 1962. 27.00 (ISBN 0-8218-1719-1, TRANS 2-19). Am Math.

Gelfond, Renee. Discover a New Beginning. LC 83-20079. (Illus.). 100p. (Orig.). 1983. pap. 6.95 (ISBN 0-914789-00-7). Serenity Hse.

Gelfond, Rhoda. Laughing Past History. (Illus., Orig.). 1976. pap. 3.50 (ISBN 0-914278-09-6). Copper Beech.

Gelin, Albert. Key Concepts of the Old Testament. Lamb, George, tr. 96p. pap. 2.45 (ISBN 0-8091-1610-3, Deus). Paulist Pr.

Gelin, Jacques B. & Miller, David W. The Federal Law of Eminent Domain. (Federal Law Library). 606p. 1982. 40.00 (ISBN 0-87215-558-7). Michie Co.

Gelin, James A. Starting Over: The Formation of the Jewish Community of Springfield, Massachusetts, 1840-1905. LC 84-23458. (Illus.). 180p. (Orig.). 1985. lib. bdg. 23.75 (ISBN 0-8191-4396-0, Inst for Massachusetts Studies); pap. text ed. 11.25 (ISBN 0-8191-4397-9). U Pr of Amer.

Gelinas, Paul. Coping with Anger. (gr. 7-12). 1979. PLB 8.97 (ISBN 0-8239-0473-3). Rosen Group.

--Coping with Loneliness. (Personal Adjustment Ser.). 144p. 1984. lib. bdg. 8.97 (ISBN 0-8239-0616-7). Rosen Group.

--Coping with Sexual Problems. (Coping with Ser.). 140p. 1981. lib. bdg. 8.97 (ISBN 0-8239-0542-X). Rosen Group.

--Coping with Weight Problems. (Personal Adjustment Ser.). 128p. 1983. PLB 8.97 (ISBN 0-8239-0598-5). Rosen Group.

--Coping with Your Emotions. rev. ed. (gr. 7-12). 1982. PLB 8.97 (ISBN 0-8239-0492-X). Rosen Group.

--Coping with Your Fears. 1986. pap. 8.97 (ISBN 0-8239-0665-5). Rosen Group.

Gelinas, Paul, jt. auth. see Gelinas, Robert.

Gelinas, Paul J., jt. auth. see Gelinas, Robert P.

Gelinas, Robert & Gelinas, Paul. Teenager Looks at Sex in Nature. LC 72-5430. (Personal Guidance, Social Adjustment Ser.). 128p. (gr. 7-12). 1978. PLB 8.97 (ISBN 0-8239-0275-7). Rosen Group.

Gelinas, Robert P. & Gelinas, Paul J. How Teenagers Can Get Good Jobs. LC 72-148142. (Personal Guidance, Social Adjustment Ser). (gr. 7 up). 1971. PLB 8.97 (ISBN 0-8239-0237-4). Rosen Group.

--Teenager & Psychology. LC 70-134901. (Personal Guidance, Social Adjustment Ser). (gr. 7 up). 1971. PLB 8.97 (ISBN 0-8239-0229-3). Rosen Group.

Geline, Robert. Trapped in the Deep. LC 79-21988. (Quest, Adventure, Survival). (Illus.). 46p. (gr. 4-9). 1982. pap. 9.27 (ISBN 0-8172-2073-9). Raintree Pubs.

--Trapped in the Deep. LC 79-21988. (Quest, Adventure, Survival). (Illus.). (gr. 4-8). 1980. PLB 14.25 (ISBN 0-8172-1559-X). Raintree Pubs.

Geline, Robert & Turner, Priscilla. Forward: Rick Barry. LC 75-42339. (Sports Profile). (Illus.). (gr. 4-11). 1976. PLB 13.31 (ISBN 0-8172-0122-X). Raintree Pubs.

Gelineau, Joseph. Psalms: A Singing Version. 256p. 1968. pap. 3.45 (ISBN 0-8091-1669-3, Deus). Paulist Pr.

Gelineau, P. Experiences in Music. 2nd ed. 1975. text ed. 34.95 (ISBN 0-07-023092-7). McGraw.

--Songs in Action. (Illus.). 320p. (Orig.). 1974. pap. text ed. 29.95 (ISBN 0-07-023071-4). McGraw.

Gelineau, Phyllis. Understanding Music Fundamentals. (Illus.). 256p. 1986. pap. text ed. 19.95 (ISBN 0-13-937004-8). P H.

Gelinier, Octave. The Enterprise Ethic. pap. 2.50 technical (ISBN 0-685-27190-0). Transatlantic.

Gelis, D. N., ed. Greek-English, English-Greek Medical Dictionary. 4th rev. ed. (Illus., Gr. & Eng.). 1978. 75.00 (ISBN 0-686-91764-2). Heinman.

Gell, Alfred. Metamorphosis of the Cassowaries: Umeda Society, Language & Ritual. (London School of Economics Monographs on Social Anthropology: No. 51). (Illus.). 366p. 1975. 45.00 (ISBN 0-485-19551-8, Pub. by Athlone Pr Ltd). Longwood Pub Group.

Gell, Heather. Music, Movement, & the Young Child. rev. ed. (Illus.). 1973. 10.50 (ISBN 0-900882-06-9). Columbia Pictures.

Gell, John. Conversational Manx. pap. 4.95 (ISBN 0-686-10838-8). British Am Bks.

Gell, Paul, commentaries by. Flowers from a Painter's Garden: The Watercolors of Paul Gell. King, Ronald, tr. (Illus.). 144p. 1983. 25.00 (ISBN 0-8109-1479-4). Abrams.

Gell, William. Reminiscences of Sir Walter Scott's Residence in Italy, 1832. 1973. Repr. of 1937 ed. 17.50 (ISBN 0-8274-0653-3). R West.

Gellar, Sheldon. Participatory Development. (Special Studies in Social, Political & Economic Development). 160p. 1986. 26.50x (ISBN 0-8133-0074-6). Westview.

--Senegal. LC 82-15946. (Nations of Contemporary Africa Ser.). 128p. 1982. lib. bdg. 22.00x (ISBN 0-89158-837-X). Westview.

Gellar, Sheldon, et al. Animation Rurale & Rural Development: The Experience of Senegal. (Special Series on Animation Rurale). 211p. (Orig.). 1980. pap. text ed. 11.05 (ISBN 0-86731-042-1). RDC Ctr Intl Stud.

Gellately, Robert. The Politics of Economic Despair: Shopkeepers & German Politics, 1890-1914. LC 74-81024. (Sage Studies in 20th Century History Ser.: Vol. 1). pap. 83.50 (ISBN 0-317-29677-9, 2021905). Bks Demand UMI.

Gellatly, Peter, ed. Beyond "1984". The Future of Library Technical Services. LC 83-17166. (Technical Services Quarterly Ser.: Vol. 1, Nos. 1/2). 265p. 1984. text ed. 24.95 (ISBN 0-86656-275-3, B275). Haworth Pr.

--The Management of Serials Automation: Current Technology & Strategies for Future Planning. LC 82-6166. (The Supplement to Serials Librarian Ser.: Vol. 6). 293p. 1982. 45.00 (ISBN 0-917724-37-2, B37); pap. 24.95 (ISBN 0-86656-310-5). Haworth Pr.

--Sex Magazines in the Library Collection: A Scholarly Study of Sex in Serials & Periodicals. LC 80-15011. (Supplement to Serials Librarian Ser.: Vol. 4). 142p. 1981. text ed. 19.95 (ISBN 0-917724-16-X, B16). Haworth Pr.

Gellen, Martin. Accessory Apartments in Single-Family Houses. 240p. 1985. text ed. 22.95x (ISBN 0-88285-105-5). Transaction Bks.

Gellens, Jay, ed. Twentieth Century Interpretations of A Farewell to Arms. (Twentieth Century Interpretations Ser). 1970. 9.95 (ISBN 0-13-303180-2, Spec). P-H.

Geller, jt. auth. see Rosenfeld.

Geller, Arthur & Geller, Deborah. Living Longer & Loving It. LC 78-5851. (Illus.). 192p. 1979. 7.95 (ISBN 0-8437-3409-4). Hammond Inc.

Geller, Bradley. Changes & Choices. LC 81-71883. 72p. (Orig.). 1982. pap. 3.75 (ISBN 0-9607566-7-1). Br-Three Pr.

Geller Communications. Hunks Postcard Book. Newman, Melissa, ed. 24p. 1984. pap. 7.95 (ISBN 0-671-50578-5). S&S.

Geller, D. & Hibbert, T. Billy Joel. (Illus.). 128p. 1985. pap. price not set (ISBN 0-07-023055-2). McGraw.

Geller, Daniel S. Domestic Factors in Foreign Policy: A Cross-Natonal Statistical Analysis. 200p. 1985. 16.95 (ISBN 0-87047-014-0); pap. 10.95 (ISBN 0-87047-015-9). Schenkman Bks Inc.

Geller, Deborah, jt. auth. see Geller, Arthur.

Geller, Dennis P., ed. see Weinberg, Gerald M.

Geller, E. P. One Hundred Selected Games. (Pergamon Russian Chess Ser.). (Illus.). 300p. 1984. 25.00 (ISBN 0-08-026914-1); pap. 15.95 (ISBN 0-08-029738-2). Pergamon.

Geller, E. Scott, et al. Preserving the Environment: New Strategies for Behavior Change. (Pergamon General Psychology Ser.: No. 102). (Illus.). 300p. 1982. 39.00 (ISBN 0-08-024615-X); pap. 12.95 (ISBN 0-08-024614-1). Pergamon.

Geller, Efim. The King's Indian Defence II: With g3 Systems. (Illus.). 128p. 1980. pap. 18.95 (ISBN 0-7134-3605-0, Pub. by Batsford England). David & Charles.

--King's Indian Defense 4E4. LC 79-56453. (Illus.). 288p. 1980. 18.95 (ISBN 0-7134-2531-8, Pub. by Batsford England). David & Charles.

--Queen's Indian Defence: Advanced Level. (Illus.). 208p. 1982. 18.95 (ISBN 0-7134-2546-6, Pub. by Batsford England). David & Charles.

Geller, Ernest. Muslim Society. LC 80-41103. (Cambridge Studies in Social Anthropology: No. 32). 267p. 1983. pap. 11.95 (ISBN 0-521-27407-9). Cambridge U Pr.

Geller, Evelyn. Forbidden Books in American Public Libraries, 1876-1939: A Study in Cultural Change. LC 83-12566. (Contributions in Librianship & Information Science Ser.: No. 46). (Illus.). xxi, 234p. 1984. lib. bdg. 29.95 (ISBN 0-313-23808-1, GFB/). Greenwood.

Geller, Evelyn, ed. Communism: End of the Monolith? (Reference Shelf Ser.: Vol. 50, No. 3). 1978. 8.00 (ISBN 0-8242-0624-X). Wilson.

--Saving America's Cities. (Reference Shelf Ser.). 1979. 8.00 (ISBN 0-8242-0631-2). Wilson.

Geller, Harriet, jt. auth. see Rosenfeld, Erwin.

Geller, Jack, jt. auth. see Lapick, Gaetan J.

Geller, L. D. Between Concord & Plymouth: The Transcendentalists & the Watsons. (Illus.). 1973. 6.00 (ISBN 0-685-42210-0). Thoreau Found.

--Pilgrim Artifacts & Genre Paintings. 1970. 0.25 (ISBN 0-940628-26-0). Pilgrim Hall.

--Sea Serpents of Coastal New England. 0.35 (ISBN 0-940628-37-6). Pilgrim Hall.

Geller, Lawrence D. & Gomes, Peter J. The Books of the Pilgrims. LC 74-30056. (Reference Library of the Humanities: No. 13). (Illus.). 100p. 1975. lib. bdg. 25.00 (ISBN 0-8240-1065-5). Garland Pub.

Geller, Leslie. Strategy Zoning: The Key to Real Estate Wealth. 352p. 1983. 24.95 (ISBN 0-13-850867-4). P-H.

Geller, Leslie M. North Cape & Other Poems. LC 82-9082. 64p. (Orig.). 1982. 10.00 (ISBN 0-942190-04-1); pap. 7.50 (ISBN 0-317-02259-8). Pubn Arts NJ.

Geller, Louis, jt. auth. see Shim, Jae K.

Geller, Max A. Advertising at the Crossroads: Federal Regulations vs. Voluntary Controls. LC 84-46044. (History of Advertising Ser.). 346p. 1985. lib. bdg. 40.00 (ISBN 0-8240-6738-X). Garland Pub.

Geller, Michael. Corpse for a Candidate. (Bud Dugan Ser.: No. 2). 1980. pap. text ed. 1.75 (ISBN 0-505-51478-8, Pub. by Tower Bks). Dorchester Pub Co.

--Disco Death Beat. (Bud Dugan Ser.: No. 3). (Orig.). 1981. pap. 1.95 (ISBN 0-505-51596-2, Pub. by Tower Bks). Dorchester Pub Co.

--The Man Who Needed Action. 1979. pap. 1.75 (ISBN 0-505-51436-2, Pub. by Tower Bks). Dorchester Pub Co.

--Mayhem on the Coney Beat. (Bud Dugan Ser.: No. 1). 1979. pap. 1.75 (ISBN 0-505-51353-6, Pub. by Tower Bks). Dorchester Pub Co.

--Red Hot & Dangerous. (Bud Dugan Ser.: No. 4). 192p. (Orig.). 1982. pap. 2.25 (ISBN 0-505-51773-6, Pub. by Tower Bks). Dorchester Pub Co.

--Thoroughbreds. 1981. pap. 2.75 (ISBN 0-8439-0901-3, Leisure Bks). Dorchester Pub Co.

--Thoroughbreds. 352p. 1984. pap. 3.50 (ISBN 0-8439-2165-X, Leisure Bks). Dorchester Pub Co.

Geller, Mona. Public School Health Programs in Thirty-Five U. S. Cities: No Standards, No Systems. (Municipal Performance Report Ser.: No. 7). 1979. pap. text ed. 5.00x (ISBN 0-916450-26-0). Coun on Municipal.

Geller, Norman. Color Me Kosher for Passover. (Illus.). 23p. (gr. 1-4). 1985. pap. 1.00 (ISBN 0-915753-06-5). N Geller Pub.

--David's Seder. (Illus.). 16p. (gr. 1-4). 1983. pap. 4.95 (ISBN 0-915753-01-4). N Geller Pub.

--The First Seven Days. (Illus.). 32p. (gr. 1-4). 1983. pap. 6.95 (ISBN 0-915753-00-6). N Geller Pub.

--I Don't Want to Visit Grandma Anymore. (Illus.). 28p. (gr. 1-4). 1984. pap. 4.95 (ISBN 0-915753-05-7). N Geller Pub.

--Talk to God, I'll Get the Message: Black Version. (Illus.). 23p. (gr. 1-4). 1985. pap. 4.95 (ISBN 0-915753-08-1). N Geller Pub.

--Talk to God, I'll Get the Message: Spanish Version. Galway, Bonnie, tr. from Eng. (Illus.). 23p. (gr. 1-4). 1985. pap. 4.95 (ISBN 0-915753-07-3). N Geller Pub.

--Talk to God...I'll Get the Message: Catholic Version. (Illus.). 23p. (gr. 1-4). 1983. pap. 4.95 (ISBN 0-915753-04-9). N Geller Pub.

--Talk to God...I'll Get the Message: Jewish Version. (Illus.). 23p. (gr. 1-4). 1983. pap. 4.95 (ISBN 0-915753-02-2). N Geller Pub.

--Talk to God...I'll Get the Message: Protestant Version. (Illus.). 23p. (gr. 1-4). 1983. pap. 4.95 (ISBN 0-915753-03-0). N Geller Pub.

Geller, Ruth. Pictures from the Past. LC 80-82075. 205p. 1980. pap. 7.95 (ISBN 0-9603008-1-3). Imp Pr.

--Seed of a Woman. LC 79-53219. 314p. (Orig.). 1979. pap. 5.95 (ISBN 0-9603008-0-5). Imp Pr.

--Triangles: A Novel. (The Feminist Ser.). 192p. (Orig.). 1984. 18.95 (ISBN 0-89594-152-X); pap. 7.95 (ISBN 0-89594-151-1). Crossing Pr.

Geller, S., ed. Solid Electrolytes. LC 77-21873. (Topics in Applied Physics: Vol. 21). (Illus.). 1977. 49.00 (ISBN 0-387-08338-3). Springer-Verlag.

Geller, Scott, jt. ed. see Feimer, Nickolaus R.

Geller, Stephen. Screenwriting. 224p. 1985. pap. 3.95 (ISBN 0-553-24110-9). Bantam.

Geller, Stephen A. Parallelism in Early Biblical Poetry. LC 78-27255. (Harvard Semitic Monographs: No. 20). 1979. 12.00 (ISBN 0-89130-275-1, 040020). Scholars Pr GA.

Geller, Stephen A., et al. A Sense of Text: The Art of Language in the Study of Biblical Literature. 113p. 1983. pap. text ed. 12.50 (ISBN 0-9602686-1-8). Dropsie Coll.

Geller, William A. Deadly Force: What We Know. (Research Contribution 1982: No. 2). 27p. pap. 2.00 (ISBN 0-317-06644-7). Am Bar Foun.

--Police Leadership in America: Crisis & Opportunity. LC 85-6284. 1985. 41.95 (ISBN 0-03-003288-1); pap. 20.95 (ISBN 0-03-003287-3). Praeger.

--Police Misconduct: Scope of the Problems & Remedies. (American Bar Foundation Research Reporter Ser.: No.23). pap. 20.00 (ISBN 0-317-30476-3, 2024819). Bks Demand UMI.

Gellerman, Robert F. The American Reed Organ. LC 73-81768. (Illus.). 14.95 (ISBN 0-911572-09-0). Vestal.

--Gellerman's International Reed Organ Atlas. LC 85-9113. (Illus.). 180p. 1985. pap. 9.95 (ISBN 0-911572-45-7, A-314). Vestal.

Gellerman, Saul. Problems & Cases for Decisions in Management. Donnelly, Paul S., ed. (Random House Business Division Ser.). 1984. pap. text ed. 12.95 (ISBN 0-394-33559-7, RanC); write for info. tchr's. ed. (ISBN 0-394-33786-7). Random.

Gellermann, William. The American Legion As Educator. LC 70-176801. (Columbia University. Teachers College. Contributions to Education: No. 743). Repr. of 1938 ed. 22.50 (ISBN 0-404-55743-0). AMS Pr.

--Martin Dies. LC 77-151620. (Civil Liberties in American History Ser.). 1972. Repr. of 1944 ed. lib. bdg. 37.50 (ISBN 0-306-70200-2). Da Capo.

Gellert, Alexander G. How to Be Your Own Phone Company. (Illus.). 96p. (Orig.). 1985. pap. 5.95 (ISBN 0-8306-1869-4, 1869). TAB Bks.

Gellert, Edward B. You're Not Too Old to Win at Tennis. LC 84-71251. (Illus.). 64p. (Orig.). 1984. pap. 6.95 (ISBN 0-9613520-0-0). C I P R A.

Gellert, Elizabeth, ed. Psychosocial Aspects of Pediatric Care. 288p. 1978. 37.00 (ISBN 0-8089-1091-4, 791535). Grune.

Gellert, Jean D. Mountain of Love. 1983. 5.95 (ISBN 0-8062-2179-8). Carlton.

Gellert, Roberta H. Public Library Decision Making: Participants, Process, & Power. 256p. 1984. write for info. (ISBN 0-208-02052-7, Archon Bks). Shoe String.

--Public Library Decision-Making: Process, Participants & Power. 256p. 1986. text ed. 27.50 (ISBN 0-208-02052-7, Lib Prof Pubns); pap. text ed. 16.50x (ISBN 0-208-02053-5). Shoe String.

Gellert, Shepard D. Nuts Come in Pairs: All You Wanted to Know about Couples Relationship & Were Afraid to Ask! Rev. ed. LC 82-74154. (Illus.). 204p. 1984. 11.95 (ISBN 0-9611122-0-4). CITE Pr.

Gellert, W. Kleine Enzyklopaedie Mathematik. 2nd ed. 837p. (Ger.). 1972. 27.50 (ISBN 3-87144-104-X, M-7090). French & Eur.

Gellert, W., et al. Kleine Enzyklopadie Mathmetik. 820p. (Ger.). 1977-78. 28.95 (ISBN 3-87144-323-9, M-7498, Pub. by Verlag Harri Deutsch). French & Eur.

Gellert, W., et al, eds. VNR Concise Encyclopedia of Mathematics. (Illus.). 816p. 1977. 22.95 (ISBN 0-442-22646-2). Van Nos Reinhold.

Gelles, D. S., ed. see AIME 113th Annual Meeting, Los Angeles, Feb. 27-29, 1984.

Gelles, Richard J. Family Violence. LC 79-14813. (Sage Library of Social Research: Vol. 84). (Illus.). 219p. 1979. 24.00 (ISBN 0-8039-1234-X); pap. 12.00 (ISBN 0-8039-1235-8). Sage.

--Sociology of the Family. 550p. 1985. 25.00 (ISBN 0-8039-2284-1). Sage.

Gelles, Richard J. & Cornell, Claire P. International Perspectives on Family Violence. LC 82-48524. 176p. 1983. 20.00x (ISBN 0-669-06199-9); pap. 12.00x (ISBN 0-669-06198-0). Lexington Bks.

--Intimate Violence in Families. LC 84-18066. 160p. 1985. 15.95 (ISBN 0-8039-2232-9); pap. 7.95 (ISBN 0-8039-2233-7). Sage.

Gelles, Richard J., jt. auth. see Straus, Murray.

Gelles, Richard J., jt. ed. see Finkelhor, David.

Gelles, Sandi. Secrets & Desires. (Candlelight Ecstasy Supreme Ser.: No. 44). 288p. (Orig.). 1984. pap. 2.50 (ISBN 0-440-17675-1). Dell.

Gellhorn, Ernest. Antitrust Law & Economics. 2nd ed. LC 80-27807. (Nutshell Ser.). 425p. 1981. pap. text ed. 8.95 (ISBN 0-8299-2117-6). West Pub.

Gellhorn, Ernest & Boyer, Barry B. Administrative Law in a Nutshell. 2nd ed. LC 81-10289. (Nutshell Ser.). 445p. 1981. pap. text ed. 8.95 (ISBN 0-314-59978-9). West Pub.

Gellhorn, Ernest & Pierce, Richard J. Regulated Industries in a Nutshell. LC 81-23126. (Nutshell Ser.). 394p. 1982. pap. text ed. 8.95 (ISBN 0-314-64561-6). West Pub.

Gellhorn, Martha. Travels with Myself & Another. 284p. 1984. pap. 9.95 (ISBN 0-907871-35-6, Pub. by Eland Bks UK). Hippocrene Bks.

--The Weather in Africa. 240p. 1981. pap. 3.50 (ISBN 0-380-55855-6, 55855-6, Bard). Avon.

Gellhorn, Martha E. Honeyed Peace: Stories. LC 70-130057. (Short Story Index Reprint Ser). 1953. 17.00 (ISBN 0-8369-3660-4). Ayer Co Pubs.

Gellhorn, Peter, tr. see Abert, Hermann.

Gellhorn, Walter. Administrative Law Problems, 1983: For Use in Conjuction with Administration Law, Cases & Comments. (University Casebook Ser.). 1983. write for info. tchr's manual (ISBN 0-88277-126-4). Foundation Pr.

--Federal Administrative Proceedings. LC 70-138237. 150p. 1972. Repr. of 1941 ed. lib. bdg. 15.00x (ISBN 0-8371-5594-0, GEFA). Greenwood.

--Individual Freedom & Governmental Restraints. LC 68-54421. (Illus.). 1968. Repr. of 1956 ed. lib. bdg. 16.00x (ISBN 0-8371-0442-4, GEIF). Greenwood.

--Ombudsmen & Others: Citizen's Protectors in Nine Countries. LC 66-23465. Repr. of 1966 ed. 88.20 (ISBN 0-8357-9171-8, 2017012). Bks Demand UMI.

--Security, Loyalty & Science. Repr. of 1950 ed. 27.00 (ISBN 0-384-18000-0). Johnson Repr.

--When Americans Complain: Governmental Grievance Procedures. LC 66-23465. (Oliver Wendell Holmes Lectures Ser: 1966). 1966. 15.00x (ISBN 0-674-95101-8). Harvard U Pr.

Gellhorn, Walter & Greenawalt, R. Kent. Sectarian College & the Public Purse: Fordham: a Case Study. LC 74-111415. 212p. 1970. 10.00 (ISBN 0-379-00456-9). Oceana.

Gellhorn, Walter, ed. The States & Subversion. LC 76-11036. vii, 454p. 1976. Repr. of 1952 ed. lib. bdg. 26.00x (ISBN 0-8371-8157-7, GESS). Greenwood.

Gellhorn, Walter, et al. Administrative Law Problems, 1983. 1983 ed. (University Casebook Ser.). 129p. 1982. pap. text ed. 24.00 (ISBN 0-88277-113-2). Foundation Pr.

Gellie, R. W., jt. auth. see IFAC Workshop, 4th, DCCS-82, Tallin, USSR, May 1982.

Gellin, G. A., jt. auth. see Maibach, H. I.

Gellin, William. Hidden from View: And Other Stories. 2nd, expanded ed. LC 83-50650. 210p. 1983. 11.95 (ISBN 0-88400-101-6). Shengold.

--Moved by Love. LC 80-52633. 272p. 1980. 10.00 (ISBN 0-88400-070-2). Shengold.

Gellinek, Christian. Hugo Grotius. (World Authors Ser.). 1983. lib. bdg. 20.95 (ISBN 0-8057-6525-5, Twayne). G K Hall.

--Hugo Grotius Drama Concordance. LC 83-70923. (Studies in German Literature, Linguistics, & Culture: Vol. 7). (Illus.). 800p. 1983. 29.50x (ISBN 0-938100-23-8). Camden Hse.

--Pax optima rerum: Friedensessais zu Grotius und Goethe, Vol. 49. LC 84-47845. (Germanic Studies in America). 155p. (German.). 1984. text ed. 18.00 (ISBN 0-8204-0147-1). P Lang Pubs.

Gellinek-Schellekens, Josepha E. The Voice of the Nightingale in Middle English Poems & Bird Debates. LC 84-47905. 191p. (Orig.). 1984. pap. text ed. 19.00 (ISBN 0-8204-0161-7). P Lang Pubs.

Gellis, Roberta. Alinor. LC 78-51278. (The Roselynde Chronicles Ser.: Bk. 2). 560p. 1983. pap. 3.95 (ISBN 0-515-07630-9). Jove Pubns.

--Alinor. (Roselynde Chronicles Ser.). 1984. lib. bdg. 13.95 (ISBN 0-8398-2861-6, Gregg). G K Hall.

--Bond of Blood. 1976. pap. 2.50 (ISBN 0-380-00713-4, 55764-2). Avon.

--Bond of Blood. 352p. 1985. pap. 3.95 (ISBN 0-515-08230-9). Jove Pubns.

--The Cornish Heiress. (The Heiress Ser.: No. 2). (Orig.). 1981. pap. 3.50 (ISBN 0-440-11515-9). Dell.

--The Dragon & the Rose. LC 80-82656. 368p. (Orig.). 1977. pap. 2.75 (ISBN 0-87216-776-3). Jove Pubns.

--The English Heiress. (Orig.). 1980. pap. 2.50 (ISBN 0-440-12141-8). Dell.

--Fire Song. (Royal Dynasty: No. 3). 384p. 1984. pap. 3.95 (ISBN 0-515-07529-9). Jove Pubns.

--Fire Song. (General Ser.). 1984. lib. bdg. 18.95 (ISBN 0-8161-3749-8, Large Print Bks). G K Hall.

--Fortune's Bride. (Orig.). 1983. pap. 3.50 (ISBN 0-440-12685-1). Dell.

--Gilliane. (Roselynde Chronicles Ser.). 1984. lib. bdg. 13.95 (ISBN 0-8398-2863-2, Gregg). G K Hall.

--Joanna. (Roselynde Chronicles Ser.). 1984. lib. bdg. 13.95 (ISBN 0-8398-2862-4, Gregg). G K Hall.

--The Kent Heiress. (Orig.). 1982. pap. 3.50 (ISBN 0-440-14537-6). Dell.

--Knight's Honor. LC 82-60687. 416p. 1983. pap. 3.50 (ISBN 0-86721-187-3). Jove Pubns.

--Rhiannon. (Roselynde Chronicles Ser.). 1984. lib. bdg. 13.95 (ISBN 0-8398-2864-0, Gregg). G K Hall.

--Roselynde. LC 77-72968. (The Roselynde Chronicles Ser.: Bk. 1). 512p. 1983. pap. 3.95 (ISBN 0-515-07629-5). Jove Pubns.

--Roselynde. (Roselynde Chronicles Ser.). 1984. lib. bdg. 13.95 (ISBN 0-8398-2860-8, Gregg). G K Hall.

--Siren Song. 400p. 1984. pap. 3.95 (ISBN 0-515-07741-0). Jove Pubns.

--The Sword & the Swan. LC 76-51629. 384p. (Orig.). 1977. pap. 2.95 (ISBN 0-86721-043-5). Jove Pubns.

--Sybelle. 416p. 1983. Jove Pubns.

--Sybelle. (Roselynde Chronicles Ser.). 1984. lib. bdg. 13.95 (ISBN 0-8398-2865-9, Gregg). G K Hall.

--A Tapestry of Dreams. 480p. 1985. pap. 6.95 (ISBN 0-425-07627-X). Berkley Pub.

--Winter Song. LC 82-80218. 400p. 1984. pap. 4.50 (ISBN 0-515-07740-2). Jove Pubns.

--A Woman's Estate. (Heiress Ser.: No. 5). 416p. (Orig.). 1984. pap. 3.95 (ISBN 0-440-19749-X). Dell.

Gellis, Sydney S. & Kagan, Benjamin M. Current Pediatric Therapy Eleven. 832p. 1984. 49.00 (ISBN 0-7216-1114-1). Saunders.

Gellis, Willard. Moon inna Baad House, 1 Vol. 73p. 1984. pap. 6.00 (ISBN 0-917455-00-2). Big Foot NY.

Gellius. Noctes Atticae. Marshall, P. K., ed. (Oxford Classical Texts Ser.). 1968. Vol. 2, Bks. 11-20. 29.50x (ISBN 0-19-814652-3). Oxford U Pr.

Gellius, Aulus. Attic Nights, 3 Vols. (Loeb Classical Library: No. 195, 200, 212). 12.50x ea. Vol. 1, Bks. 1-4 (ISBN 0-674-99215-6). Vol. 2, Bks. 6-13 (ISBN 0-674-99220-2). Vol. 3, Bks. 14-20 (ISBN 0-674-99234-2). Harvard U Pr.

Gellman, Arthur M., et al. United States Immigration for Businesses, Investors & Workers. LC 81-80685. viii, 108p. lib. bdg. 25.00 (ISBN 0-89941-098-7); pap. text ed. 15.00 (ISBN 0-89941-099-5). W S Hein.

Gellman, Barton D. Contending with Kennan: Toward a Philosophy of American Power. LC 8-4553. 192p. 1984. 21.95 (ISBN 0-03-063819-4); pap. 11.95 (ISBN 0-03-006192-X). Praeger.

Gellman, Irving P. The Sober Alcoholic: An Organizational Analysis of Alcoholics Anonymous. 1964. 14.95x (ISBN 0-8084-0279-X). New Coll U Pr.

Gellman, Irwin F. Good Neighbor Diplomacy: United States Policy in Latin America, 1933-1945. LC 79-7561. 312p. 1979. 28.50x (ISBN 0-8018-2250-5). Johns Hopkins.

Gellman, Meryle & Gage, Diane. The Confidence Quotient: Ten Steps to Conquer Self-Doubt. 128p. (Orig.). 1985. pap. 7.95 (ISBN 0-911818-91-X). World Almanac.

Gell-Mann, M. see Dal Cin, Mario, et al.

Gellner, Ernest. Legitimation of Belief. LC 74-14337. 240p. 1975. 37.50 (ISBN 0-521-20467-4). Cambridge U Pr.

--Muslim Society. LC 80-41103. (Cambridge Studies in Social Anthropology: No. 32). 280p. 1981. 49.50 (ISBN 0-521-22160-9). Cambridge U Pr.

--Nations & Nationalism. LC 83-71199. 170p. 1983. 24.50x (ISBN 0-8014-1662-0); pap. 6.95x (ISBN 0-8014-9263-7). Cornell U Pr.

--Relativism & the Social Sciences. 200p. 1985. 39.50 (ISBN 0-521-26530-4). Cambridge U Pr.

--Saints of the Atlas. LC 78-89515. (Nature of Human Society Ser). 1969. 20.00x (ISBN 0-226-28699-1). U of Chicago Pr.

--Spectacles & Predicaments: Essays in Social Theory. LC 78-67304. 1980. 47.50 (ISBN 0-521-22486-1). Cambridge U Pr.

--Words & Things: An Examination of, & an Attack on, Linguistic Philosophy. 1979. pap. 10.95 (ISBN 0-7100-0285-8). Routledge & Kegan.

Gellner, Ernest, jt. auth. see Ionescu, Ghita.

Gellner, Ernest, ed. Islamic Dilemmas: Reformers, Nationalists & Industrialization; The Southern Shore of the Mediterranean. (Religion & Society Ser.: Vol. 25). viii, 319p. 1985. 48.00x (ISBN 3-11-009763-X). Mouton.

--Soviet & Western Anthropology. LC 80-11676. 300p. 1980. 40.00x (ISBN 0-231-05120-4). Columbia U Pr.

Gellner, John & Smerek, John. The Czechs & Slovaks in Canada. LC 68-139262. pap. 52.00 (ISBN 0-317-27042-7, 2023622). Bks Demand UMI.

Gellrich, Jesse M. The Idea of the Book in the Middle Ages: Language Theory, Mythology, & Fiction. LC 84-23814. (Illus.). 296p. 1985. text ed. 27.50x (ISBN 0-8014-1722-8). Cornell U Pr.

Gelly, Dave. Lester Young. (Jazz Masters Ser.). (Illus.). 100p. 1985. 6.95 (ISBN 0-87052-010-5). Hippocrene Bks.

Gelman. Great Quarterbacks of Pro Football. (gr. 4-6). 1977. pap. 1.95 (ISBN 0-590-32564-7). Scholastic Inc.

--Lots of Boys (Follow Your Heart, No. 8. 1985. pap. 2.25 (ISBN 0-671-53158-1). Archway.

--Opening Day. (Play It Your Way Sports Bks.: No. 5). Date not set. pap. 2.25 (ISBN 0-671-53159-X). PB.

Gel'man, Anna D., et al. Complex Compounds of Transuranium Elements. LC 62-12851. 195p. 1962. 35.00x (ISBN 0-306-10516-0, Consultants). Plenum Pub.

Gelman, Harry. The Brezhnev Politburo & the Decline of Detente. 264p. 1984. 29.95x (ISBN 0-8014-1544-6); pap. 9.95x (ISBN 0-8014-9280-7). Cornell U Pr.

--Soviet Policy & Options for Advance in Latin America. LC 84-2043. Date not set. price not set. Rand Corp.

Gelman, Howard. The Films of John Garfield. (Illus.). 256p. 1975. 14.00 (ISBN 0-8065-0490-0). Citadel Pr.

--The Films of John Garfield. 1977. pap. 7.95 (ISBN 0-8065-0620-2). Citadel Pr.

Gelman, I. W. & Mazja, W. G. Abschatzung fur Differentialoperationen. 192p. (Ger.). 1981. text ed. 36.95x (ISBN 0-8176-1275-0). Birkhauser.

Gelman, Jan. Boys! Boys! Boys! (Follow Your Heart Romances Ser.). (Orig.). (gr. 5 up). 1983. pap. 1.95 (ISBN 0-671-52445-3). Archway.

--Faraway Loves. (Follow Your Heart Romance Ser.: No. 5). 128p. (Orig.). (gr. 5 up). 1984. pap. 1.95 (ISBN 0-671-47579-7). Archway.

--Summer in the Sun. (Follow Your Heart Romances Ser.). (gr. 11 up). 1983. pap. 1.95 (ISBN 0-671-46393-4). Archway.

--Summer in the Sun. 1983. pap. text ed. 1.95 (ISBN 0-671-46393-4). Pb.

--Take a Chance on Love. (Follow Your Heart Romance Ser.: No. 6). 128p. (Orig.). (gr. 5 up). 1984. pap. 1.95 (ISBN 0-671-52408-9). Archway.

Gelman, Martin I. Radiology of Orthopedic Procedures. (Saunders Monographs in Clinical Radiology: Vol. 24). (Illus.). 300p. 1984. 29.50 (ISBN 0-7216-4079-6). Saunders.

Gelman, Mitch. Can You Win the Pennant? (Play-it-Your-Way Sports Bks.). (Illus.). (gr. 9 up). 1983. pap. 2.25 (ISBN 0-671-52450-X). Archway.

--Pro Football Showdown. (Play-It-Your-Way Sports Bk.: No. 2). (Illus., Orig.). (gr. 4 up). 1983. pap. 2.25 (ISBN 0-671-46023-4). Archway.

--Super Bowl Sunday. (A Play it Your Way Sports Ser.: Bk. 4). (Orig.). (gr. 9 up). 1984. pap. 2.25 (ISBN 0-671-47578-9). Archway.

--Superbowl Sunday. (gr. 4 up). pap. 2.25 (ISBN 0-317-13577-5). Archway.

--World Series Pressure. (A Play-It-Your-Way Sports BK.: No. 3). (Illus.). 128p. (Orig.). (gr. 4 up). 1984. pap. 1.95 (ISBN 0-671-47577-0). Archway.

Gel'man, N. S., et al. Respiration & Phosphorylation of Bacteria. LC 66-26220. 238p. 1967. 32.50x (ISBN 0-306-30296-9, Plenum Pr). Plenum Pub.

--Biomembranes, Vol. 6: Bacterial Membranes & the Respiratory Chain. LC 75-4531. (Illus.). 275p. 1975. 35.00x (ISBN 0-306-39806-0, Plenum Pr). Plenum Pub.

Gelman, Rita & Seligson, Marcia. UFO Encounters. (gr. 4-6). 1978. pap. 1.50 (ISBN 0-590-05403-1). Scholastic Inc.

Gelman, Rita G. Benji at Work. (Illus.). 32p. (gr. 3-7). 1980. pap. 1.95 (ISBN 0-590-31504-8). Scholastic Inc.

--Benji Takes a Dive at Marineland. (gr. 3-7). pap. 1.95 (ISBN 0-590-31547-1). Scholastic Inc.

--Favorite Riddles, Knock-Knocks & Nonsense. (Illus.). 48p. 1980. pap. 1.95 (ISBN 0-590-31287-1). Scholastic Inc.

--Great Moments in Sports. (Illus.). 128p. (Orig.). (gr. 3-7). 1981. pap. 1.95 (ISBN 0-590-31311-8). Scholastic Inc.

--Hey, Kid! (Illus.). 32p. (gr. k-3). 1978. pap. 1.75 (ISBN 0-380-40261-0, 56812-8, Camelot). Avon.

Gelman, Rita G. & Buxbaum, Susan K. Boats That Float. LC 81-711. (Easy-Read Activity Bks.). (Illus.). 32p. (gr. 1-3). 1981. PLB 8.90 (ISBN 0-531-04305-3). Watts.

--Ouch! All About Cuts & Other Hurts. LC 76-46310. (Illus.). (gr. 1-4). 1977. 6.95 (ISBN 0-15-258839-6, HJ). HarBraceJ.

Gelman, Rita G. & Friedman, Warner. Uncle Hugh: A Fishing Story. LC 78-4918. (Illus.). (gr. k-3). 1978. 6.95 (ISBN 0-15-292789-1, HJ). HarBraceJ.

Gelman, Rita G., jt. auth. see Buxbaum, Susan K.

Gelman, Rochel & Gallistel, C. R. The Child's Understanding of Number. LC 78-5124. (Illus.). 1978. 17.50x (ISBN 0-674-11636-4). Harvard U Pr.

Gelman, Steve & Los Angeles Official Olympic Committee Staff. Official Olympic Souvenir Program. (Illus.). 324p. 1984. pap. 7.95 (ISBN 0-317-06149-6). Time-Life.

Gelman, Steve, ed. see Jordan, Henry, et al.

Gelman, Woodrow, ed. see McCay, Winsor.

Gelman, Woody, jt. ed. see Brown, Len.

Gelman, Woody, ed. see Raymond, Alex & Hammett, Dashiell.

Gelmine, Bert J., jt. auth. see Nadon, John M.

Gelong Jhampa Kelsang, see Wallace, B. Alan, pseud.

Gelperin, Alan, jt. ed. see Jacobs, Barry L.

Gelpi, Albert. The Tenth Muse: The Psyche of the American Poet. LC 74-25038. 320p. 1975. text ed. 18.50x (ISBN 0-674-87441-2). Harvard U Pr.

Gelpi, Albert, ed. Wallace Stevens: The Poetics of Modernism. (Cambridge Studies in American Literature & Culture). 182p. Date not set. price not set. (ISBN 0-521-30201-3). Cambridge U Pr.

Gelpi, Barbara, jt. ed. see Rich, Adrienne.

Gelpi, Donald L. The Divine Mother: A Trinitarian Theology of the Holy Spirit. LC 84-11921. 260p. (Orig.). 1984. lib. bdg. 24.50 (ISBN 0-8191-4034-1); pap. text ed. 12.25 (ISBN 0-8191-4035-X). U Pr of Amer.

Gelpi, Ettore. Lifelong Education & International Relations. 224p. 1985. 31.00 (ISBN 0-7099-1186-6, Pub. by Croom Helm Ltd). Longwood Pub Group.

Gelpke, R., ed. & tr. see Nizami.

Gelsema, E. S. & Kanal, L. N., eds. Pattern Recognition in Practice. 552p. 1980. 85.00 (ISBN 0-444-86115-7, North-Holland). Elsevier.

Gelsen, H., jt. auth. see Fennel, T. G.

Gelser, David, tr. see Stickelberger, E.

Gelsey, Rudi C. Imagine: A New Bible. 128p. 1982. 8.95 (ISBN 0-9608562-0-X); pap. 4.95 (ISBN 0-9608562-1-8). Good Hope Pub.

Gelsinger, Bruce E. Icelandic Enterprise: Commerce & Economy in the Middle Ages. LC 80-26116. (Illus.). 400p. 1981. text ed. 24.95 (ISBN 0-87249-405-5). U of SC Pr.

Gelso, Charles J. & Johnson, Deborah H. Explorations in Time-Limited Counseling & Therapy. (Guidance & Counseling Ser.). 300p. 1983. text ed. 25.95x (ISBN 0-8077-2726-1). Tchrs Coll.

Gelson, Sr. M. Aline. Analysis of the Realistic Elements in the Novels of Rene Bazin. LC 71-94171. (Catholic University of America Studies in Romance Languages & Literatures Ser: No. 23). Repr. of 1942 ed. 20.00 (ISBN 0-404-50323-3). AMS Pr.

Gelstein, Sylvia S. Adolescent Psychology: Medical Analysis Index with Research Bibliography. LC 85-47575. 150p. 1985. 29.95 (ISBN 0-88164-324-6); pap. 21.95 (ISBN 0-88164-325-4). ABBE Pubs Assn.

--Diagnosis of Mental Disorders: With Subject Analysis & Reference Bibliography. 150p. (Orig.). 29.95 (ISBN 0-88164-428-5); pap. 21.95 (ISBN 0-88164-429-3). ABBE Pubs Assn.

Gelstein, Sylvia Sabine. Juvenile Delinquency: Medical & Psychological Subject Analysis & Research Index with Bibliography. LC 83-71654. 154p. 1985. 29.95 (ISBN 0-88164-002-6); Softcover 21.95 (ISBN 0-88164-003-4). ABBE Pubs Assn.

Gelsthorpe, Annie L. Wings for Nurse Karen. (YA) 1978. 8.95 (ISBN 0-685-86417-0, Avalon). Bouregy.

Geltman, Eve. The Gift of Music: A New Tested Way to Progress Quickly from Rote to Reading in Music. LC 82-22149. (Illus.). 200p. 1982. 9.95 (ISBN 0-87297-053-1). Diablo.

Geltman, Sydney. Topics in Atomic Collision Theory. (Pure & Applied Physics Ser: Vol. 32). 1969. 67.50 (ISBN 0-12-279650-0). Acad Pr.

Geltner, D., jt. auth. see Moavenzadeh, F.

Geltzer, Robert L., jt. auth. see MacDonald, Duncan A.

Gelwick, Richard. Way of Discovery: An Introduction to the Thought of Michael Polanyi. 1977. pap. 4.95 (ISBN 0-19-502193-2, GB492, GB). Oxford U Pr.

Gely, Claude, ed. see Hugo, Victor.

Gelzer, David G., tr. see Cerdic Colloquium, 4th, Strasbourg, May 10-12, 1973.

Gelzer, Jay. Street of a Thousand Delights. facsimile ed. LC 75-167449. (Short Story Index Reprint Ser.). Repr. of 1921 ed. 18.00 (ISBN 0-8369-3975-1). Ayer Co Pubs.

Gelzer, Matthias. Caesar: Politician & Statesman. 368p. 1985. pap. text ed. 8.95x (ISBN 0-674-09001-2). Harvard U Pr.

Gem, T. H. Bardell Versus Pickwick: Versified & Diversified. 20.00 (ISBN 0-8274-1912-0). R West.

Gemant, Andrew. The Nature of the Genius. 216p. 1961. 18.75x (ISBN 0-398-02546-0). C C Thomas.

Gemelli, Ralph J., jt. auth. see Duffy, John C.

Gemery, H. A. & Hogendorn, J. S., eds. The Uncommon Market: Essays in the Economic History of the Atlantic Slave Trade. LC 79-294. (Studies in Social Discontinuity Ser.). 1979. 45.00 (ISBN 0-12-279850-3). Acad Pr.

Gemignami, Michael. Law & the Computer. 244p. 1981. 19.95 (ISBN 0-8436-1604-0). Van Nos Reinhold.

Gemignani, jt. auth. see Gersting.

Gemignani, Michael C. Computer Law. LC 84-82460. 1985. 67.50 (ISBN 0-318-04386-6). Lawyers Co-Op.

Geminiani, Francesco. Art of Playing on the Violin, 1751. facs. ed. Boyden, D. D., ed. 1952. 19.75 (ISBN 0-19-322200-0). Oxford U Pr.

--Treatise on Good Taste in the Art of Musick. 2nd ed. LC 68-16233. (Music Reprint Ser). 1969. Repr. of 1749 ed. lib. bdg. 19.50 (ISBN 0-306-70985-6). Da Capo.

Gemme, Leila. Monarch Notes on Mitchell's Gone with the Wind. 1975. pap. 2.50 (ISBN 0-671-00946-X). Monarch Pr.

Gemme, Leila B. Hockey Is Our Game. LC 78-12541. (Sports Primer Ser.). (Illus.). 32p. (gr. 4 up). 1979. PLB 10.60 (ISBN 0-516-03492-8). Childrens.

--The New Breed of Athlete. (Orig.). (YA) 1975. pap. 1.25 (ISBN 0-671-48150-9). WSP.

--Soccer Is Our Game. LC 79-13245. (Sports Primer Ser.). (Illus.). 32p. (gr. k-3). 1979. PLB 10.60 (ISBN 0-516-03615-7); pap. 2.95 (ISBN 0-516-43615-5). Childrens.

--T-Ball Is Our Game. LC 77-17173. (Sport Primer Ser.). (Illus.). 32p. (gr. k-3). 1978. PLB 10.60 (ISBN 0-516-03630-0). Childrens.

Gemme, Robert & Wheeler, C. C., eds. Progress in Sexology. LC 77-13011. (Perspectives in Sexuality Ser.). 634p. 1978. 42.50x (ISBN 0-306-31104-6, Plenum Pr). Plenum Pub.

Gemmell, Alan R. Developmental Plant Anatomy. (Studies in Biology: No. 15). 64p. 1969. pap. text ed. 8.95 (ISBN 0-7131-2223-4). E Arnold.

Gemmell, M. see Eckert, J., et al.

Gemmell, William. How to Pick a Perfect Growth Stock. 1975. pap. 5.00 (ISBN 0-685-49182-X). Windsor.

Gemmett, Robert J., ed. see Beckford, William.

Gemmett, Robert J., intro. by see Beckford, William.

Gemmett, Robert J., ed. see Beckford, William.

Gemmill, Anna M. Experimental Study at New York State Teachers College at Buffalo to Determine a Science Program for the Education of Elementary Classroom Teachers. LC 74-176802. (Columbia University. Teachers College. Contributions to Education: No. 715). Repr. of 1937 ed. 22.50 (ISBN 0-404-55715-5). AMS Pr.

Gemmill, Chalmers L. Physiology in Aviation. (Illus.). 124p. 1943. 14.50x (ISBN 0-398-04263-2). C C Thomas.

Gemmill, Daphne. City Air. 35p. 1975. 6.00 (ISBN 0-916450-05-8). Coun on Municipal.

Gemmill, G. T. ICCH Commodities Yearbook 1980-81. 304p. 1980. 75.00x (ISBN 0-85941-071-4, Pub. by Woodhead-Faulkner England). State Mutual Bk.

Gemmill, Helen H. E. L. The Bread Box Papers. LC 83-90063. 324p. 1983. 22.95 (ISBN 0-8059-2870-7). Dorrance.

Gemming, Elizabeth. Blow Ye Winds Westerly: The Seaports & Sailing Ships of Old New England. LC 71-158692. (Illus.). (gr. 6-9). 1972. Crowell Jr Bks.

--The Cranberry Book. LC 82-19797. (Illus.). (ps-3). 1983. 9.95 (ISBN 0-698-20568-5, Coward). Putnam Pub Group.

Gems & Mineral Magazine Staff & Cox, Jack R. A Gem Cutter's Handbook - Plastic & Gemstones. (Illus.). 20p. 1974. pap. 1.00 (ISBN 0-910652-20-1). Gembooks.

Gems & Minerals Staff, jt. auth. see Cox, Jack R.

Gems, Pam. Piaf. 1984. pap. 6.95 (ISBN 0-87910-217-9). Limelight Edns.

--Queen Christina. 80p. 1983. pap. 4.95 (ISBN 0-9508443-0-6, NO.3938). Methuen Inc.

Gen Bank-Embl. Nucleotide Sequences Nineteen Eighty-Five, Parts 1-4. (Special Supplement to Nucleic Acids Research). 2000p. (Orig.). 1985. pap. 120.00 set (ISBN 0-947946-25-X); Pt. 1. pap. 40.00 part (ISBN 0-947946-26-8). Pt. 2 (ISBN 0-947946-27-6). Pt. 3 (ISBN 0-947946-28-4). Pt. 4 (ISBN 0-947946-29-2). IRL Pr.

Genaro, Mercedes Pintor see Pintor Genaro, Mercedes.

Genasci, Gail A., jt. auth. see Wayman, Cooper H.

Genaust, Helmut. Etymologisches Woertenbuch der Botanischen Pflanzennamen. 390p. (Ger.). 1976. 62.50 (ISBN 3-7643-0755-2, M-7368, Pub. by Birkhaeuser). French & Eur.

Genaway, David C. How to Make Big Money in the Stock Market: Good Times or Bad! LC 82-12841. (Illus.). 73p. (Orig.). 1982. pap. 19.95 (ISBN 0-943970-00-8, HG4527,G46). Genaway.

--Integrated Online Library Systems: Principles, Planning & Implementation. LC 84-15406. (Professional Librarian). 151p. 1984. professional 36.50 (ISBN 0-86729-092-7, 234-BW); pap. 28.50 (ISBN 0-86729-091-9). Knowledge Indus.

Genaway, David C., ed. Conference on Integrated Online Library Systems, September 26 & 27, 1983. Columbus Ohio, Proceedings. vi, 281p. 1983. pap. 39.95 (ISBN 0-943970-02-4). Genaway.

--Conference on Integrated Online Library Systems, 1st, September 26th & 27th, 1983, Columbus, Ohio: Proceedings. 2nd, enl., rev. ed. (Orig.). 1983. pap. 39.95 (ISBN 0-317-04899-6). Genaway.

--Conference on Integrated Online Library Systems, 2nd, September 13th & 14th, 1984, Atlanta, Georgia: Proceedings. 1984. pap. 39.95 (ISBN 0-943970-04-0). Genaway.

Genazzani, A. R., et al, eds. Adrenal Androgens. 390p. 1980. text ed. 62.50 (ISBN 0-89004-488-0). Raven.

Genazzani, Andrea R., jt. ed. see Muller, Eugenio E.

Genazzani, E. & Herken, H., eds. Central Nervous System, Studies on Metabolic Regulation & Function. LC 73-13178. (Illus.). 260p. 1974. 50.00 (ISBN 0-387-06444-3). Springer-Verlag.

Genazzani, E., et al, eds. Pharmacological Modulation of Steroid Action. 312p. 1980. text ed. 46.00 (ISBN 0-89004-373-6). Raven.

Genck, Frederic H. Improving School Performance: How New School Management Techniques Can Raise Learning, Confidence & Morale. LC 82-18127. 318p. 1983. 31.95 (ISBN 0-03-062477-0). Praeger.

Genck, Fredric H. Administrative Evaluation & Compensation: Based on Performance, Vol. 2. (School Management Model Ser.). 55p. (Orig.). 1984. pap. 32.00 (ISBN 0-318-04002-6). Inst Pub Mgmt.

--Board Policy: Summary, Vol. 10. (School Management Model Ser.). 105p. (Orig.). 1984. pap. 65.00 (ISBN 0-318-04010-7). Inst Pub Mgmt.

--Financial Planning: To Control Costs, Vol. 7. (School Management Model Ser.). 35p. (Orig.). 1984. pap. 24.00 (ISBN 0-318-04007-7). Inst Pub Mgmt.

--High School Management Model, Vol. 9. (School Management Model Ser.). 120p. (Orig.). 1984. pap. 95.00 (ISBN 0-318-04009-3). Inst Pub Mgmt.

--Parent-Teacher Surveys: To Improve Confidence & Morale, Vol. 6. (School Management Model Ser.). 50p. (Orig.). 1984. pap. 28.00 (ISBN 0-318-04006-9). Inst Pub Mgmt.

--Planning & Communication: Using Information & Evaluation Positively, Vol. 4. (School Management Model Ser.). 70p. (Orig.). 1984. pap. 36.00 (ISBN 0-318-04004-2). Inst Pub Mgmt.

--The School Management Model: How-to-Do-It-Yourself Handbooks & Case Studies, 10 vols. 850p. (Orig.). 1984. Set. pap. 295.00 (ISBN 0-318-03999-0). Inst Pub Mgmt.

--The School Management Model: How-to-Do-It-Yourself Handbooks & Case Studies, 8 vols. 650p. (Orig.). 1984. Set. pap. 185.00 (ISBN 0-318-04000-X). Inst Pub Mgmt.

--The School Management Model: Overview, Vol. 1. (School Management Model Ser.). 90p. (Orig.). 1984. pap. 34.00 (ISBN 0-318-04001-8). Inst Pub Mgmt.

--Teacher Evaluation & Development: Positive & Constructive, Vol. 3. (School Management Model Ser.). 90p. (Orig.). 1984. pap. 38.00 (ISBN 0-318-04003-4). Inst Pub Mgmt.

--Teacher Merit Pay: Promises & Pitfalls, Vol. 8. (School Management Model Ser.). 30p. (Orig.). 1984. pap. 22.00 (ISBN 0-318-04008-5). Inst Pub Mgmt.

--Test Data Analysis: To Improve Student Learning & Board Support, Vol. 5. (School Management Model Ser.). 90p. (Orig.). 1984. pap. 38.00 (ISBN 0-318-04005-0). Inst Pub Mgmt.

Genck, Fredric H. & Klingenberg, Allen J. Effective Schools Through Effective Management. Seamon, Harold P., intro. by. (Illus.). 198p. (Orig.). 1978. pap. 15.00 (ISBN 0-686-36918-1). Inst Pub Mgmt.

Genco, Robert J. & Mergenhagen, Stephan E., eds. Host-Parasite Interactions in Periodontal Diseases. (Illus.). 414p. 1982. text ed. 27.00 (ISBN 0-914826-37-9). Am Soc Microbio.

Gendarme, G., tr. see Sanglerat, G., et al.

Gendel, Morgan & Levin, David. The Complete Book of Sleeping. LC 83-18066. (Illus.). 96p. 1984. pap. 3.95 (ISBN 0-943392-38-1). Tribeca Comm.

Genders, Roy. Complete Book of Herbs & Herb Growing. LC 79-93206. (Illus.). 160p. 1980. pap. 9.95 (ISBN 0-8069-3930-3). Sterling.

--Cosmetics from the Earth: A Guide to Natural Beauty. LC 85-40101. (Illus.). 208p. (Orig.). 1985. pap. 16.95 (ISBN 0-912383-20-8). Van der Marck.

--The Cottage Garden & the Old Fashioned Flowers. (Illus.). 368p. 1983. 17.95 (ISBN 0-7207-1442-7, Pub. by Michael Joseph). Merrimack Pub Cir.

--Cottage Garden Year. 1984. 40.00x (ISBN 0-317-20344-4, Pub. by Pinhorns UK). State Mutual BK.

--Encyclopaedia of Greyhound Racing. 416p. 24.95 (ISBN 0-7207-1106-1, Pub. by Michael Joseph). Merrimack Pub Cir.

--Grow Your Own Health Foods. LC 83-24223. (Illus.). 160p. 1984. pap. 6.95 (ISBN 0-8069-7834-1). Sterling.

--Growing Herbs As Aromatics. LC 77-86544. (The Living with Herbs Series: Vol. 3). (Illus.). 1977. pap. 2.50 (ISBN 0-87983-155-3). Keats.

--Mushroom Growing for Everyone. 232p. 1982. 6.95 (ISBN 0-571-11806-2). Faber & Faber.

--The Wildflower Garden. LC 76-43563. 1977. 8.95 (ISBN 0-8023-1268-3). Dufour.

Gendler, J. Ruth. The Book of Qualities. (Illus.). 112p. (Orig.). 1984. pap. 6.95 (ISBN 0-917947-00-2). Turquoise Mount.

Gendlin, Eugene. Focusing. 192p. (Orig.). 1981. pap. 3.95 (ISBN 0-553-23125-1). Bantam.

Gendlin, Eugene T. Focusing. LC 78-57406. 1978. 7.95 (ISBN 0-89696-008-0, An Everest House Book). Dodd.

Gendreau, Francis R. & Caranfa, Angelo, eds. Western Heritage: Man's Encounter with Himself & the World, a Journey for Meaning. LC 84-17268. 418p. (Orig.). 1985. lib. bdg. 28.50 (ISBN 0-8191-4251-4); pap. text ed. 13.50 (ISBN 0-8191-4252-2). U Pr of Amer.

Gendron, Bernard. Technology & the Human Condition. LC 76-28120. 1977. pap. text ed. 12.95 (ISBN 0-312-78925-4). St Martin.

Gendrop, Paul. A Guide to Architecture in Ancient Mexico. (Illus.). 1977. pap. 5.50 (ISBN 0-912434-14-7). Ocelot Pr.

Gendrop, Paul & Heyden, Doris. Pre-Columbian Architecture of Mesoamerica. LC 75-8993. (History of World Architecture Ser.). (Illus.). 340p. 1976. 50.00 (ISBN 0-8109-1018-7). Abrams.

Gendrot, Marcel, ed. Make Way for Jesus Christ. pap. 4.95 (ISBN 0-910984-52-2). Montfort Pubns.

Gendt, Rien Van see Van Gendt, Rien & Passigli, G. Garcia.

Gendusa, Sam. Building Playground Sculpture & Homes. LC 74-23019. (Illus.). pap. 7.95 (ISBN 0-9600818-1-X). Master Pr.

Gendzier, Irene L. Frantz Fanon: A Critical Study. 2nd ed. 312p. (Orig.). 1983. pap. 8.95 (ISBN 0-394-62453-X, E846, Ever). Grove.

--Managing Political Change: Social Scientists & the Third World. (WVSS in Social, Political, & Economic Development Ser.). 250p. 1984. 32.50x (ISBN 0-8133-0079-7); pap. text ed. 11.95x cancelled (ISBN 0-8133-0080-0). Westview.

--Practical Visions of Ya'qub Sanu' LC 66-28047. (Middle Eastern Monographs Ser: No. 15). 1966. pap. 4.50x (ISBN 0-674-69650-6). Harvard U Pr.

Genealogia Welforum. Eine Alte Genealogie der Welfen & des Moenchs von Weingarten. Grandaur, Georg, tr. 80p. pap. 8.00 (ISBN 0-384-14060-2). Johnson Repr.

Genealogical Association of Southwestern Michigan. Cemetery Records of Bainbridge Township in Berrien County, Michigan. 44p. 1983. 9.60 (ISBN 0-686-40546-3). Genealog Assn SW.

--Cemetery Records of Baroda Township in Berrien County, Michigan. 30p. 1983. 7.60 (ISBN 0-686-40547-1). Genealog Assn SW.

--Cemetery Records of Bertrand Township in Berrien County, Michigan. 32p. (Orig.). 1978. pap. 7.60 (ISBN 0-686-37855-5). Genealog Assn SW.

--Cemetery Records of Chikaming Township in Berrien County, Michigan. 50p. (Orig.). 1982. pap. 9.60 (ISBN 0-686-37856-3). Genealog Assn SW.

--Cemetery Records of Coloma Township in Berrien County, Michigan. 57p. (Orig.). 1983. pap. 9.60 (ISBN 0-686-37858-X). Genealog Assn SW.

--Cemetery Records of Galien Township in Berrien County, Michigan. 75p. 1984. 9.60 (ISBN 0-318-11904-8). Genealog Assn SW.

--Cemetery Records of New Buffalo Township in Berrien County, Michigan. 60p. (Orig.). 1978. pap. 9.60 (ISBN 0-686-37857-1). Genealog Assn SW.

Genealogical Association Staff of Southwestern Michigan. Cemetery Records of Lake Township in Berrien County, Michigan. 48p. 1983. pap. 9.60 (ISBN 0-318-03118-3). Genealog Assn SW.

Geneen, Harold & Moscow, Alvin. Managing. LC 84-12731. 312p. 1984. 17.95 (ISBN 0-385-17496-9). Doubleday.

Genequand, C. F. The Metaphysics of Ibn Rushd: Averroes. LC 83-15428. (Studies in Islamic Philosophy & Science). write for info. cancelled (ISBN 0-88206-059-7). Caravan Bks.

General Agreement On Tariffs And Trade. Basic Instruments & Selected Documents, Vol. 4. (Orig.). 1969. pap. 6.00 (ISBN 0-685-11718-9, G70, GATT). Unipub.

General Agreement on Tariffs & Trade. Basic Instruments & Selected Documents: 1st Through 24th Supplements. annual Incl. First. 1953. pap. 5.00 (ISBN 0-685-48339-8, G71); Second. 1954. pap. 5.00 (ISBN 0-685-48340-1, G72); Third. 1955. pap. 5.25 (ISBN 0-685-48341-X, G73); Fourth. 1956. pap. 5.00 (ISBN 0-685-48342-8, G74); Fifth. 1957. pap. 5.00 (ISBN 0-685-48343-6, G75); Sixth. 1958. pap. 5.00 (ISBN 0-685-48344-4, G76); Seventh. 1959. pap. 5.00 (ISBN 0-685-48345-2, G77); Eighth. 1960. pap. 8.50 (ISBN 0-685-48346-0, G78); Ninth. 1961. pap. 9.75 (ISBN 0-685-48347-9, G79); Tenth. 1962. pap. 9.75 (ISBN 0-685-48348-7, G80); Eleventh. 1963. pap. 8.50 (ISBN 0-685-48349-5, G81); Twelfth. 1964. pap. 8.50 (ISBN 0-685-48350-9, G82); Thirteenth. 1965. pap. 9.75 (ISBN 0-685-48351-7, G83); Fourteenth. 1966. pap. 9.75 (ISBN 0-685-48352-5, G84); Fifteenth. 1968. pap. 12.50 (ISBN 0-685-48353-3, G99); Sixteenth. 1969. pap. 12.50 (ISBN 0-685-48354-1, G85); Seventeenth. 1970. pap. 13.75 (ISBN 0-685-48355-X, G86); Eighteenth. 1972. pap. 15.75 (ISBN 0-685-48356-8, G87); Nineteenth. 1973. pap. 15.75 (ISBN 0-685-48357-6, G88); Twentieth. 1974. pap. text ed. 19.50 (ISBN 0-686-52225-7, G89); Twenty-first. 167p. 1975. pap. text ed. 19.50 (ISBN 0-685-57615-9, G90); Twenty-second. 112p. 1976. pap. text ed. 19.50 (ISBN 0-685-76007-3, G91); Twenty-third. 1977. pap. text ed. 19.50 (ISBN 0-685-59476-9, G92); Twenty-fourth. 1978. pap. text ed. 15.00 (ISBN 0-685-60672-4, G118); Twenty-Fifth. pap. 19.95 (G123, GATT); Twenty-Six. 393p. 1980. pap. 19.50 (G141, GATT); Tenty-seventh. 257p. 1981. pap. 19.50 (G149, GATT); Twenty-nineth. 235p. 1983. pap. text ed. 19.50 (ISBN 92-870-1007-2); Thirtieth. 272p. 1985. pap. 19.50 (ISBN 92-870-1010-2, G163, GATT). (Basic Instruments & Selected Documents Ser.). (Orig., Eng. & Fr.). pap. (GATT). Unipub.

--Legal Instruments Embodying the Results of the 1964-1967 Trade Conference, 5 vols. (Orig.). 1967. Set. pap. 130.00 (ISBN 0-685-11722-7, G22, GATT). Unipub.

--Third Certification Relating to Rectifications & Modifications of Schedules. (Orig., Eng. & Fr.). 1967. pap. 5.00 (ISBN 0-685-11724-3, G45, GATT). Unipub.

General Anti-Slavery Convention, London, 1843. Proceedings. Johnson, John F., ed. LC 71-83957. Repr. of 1843 ed. 27.50 (ISBN 0-8369-8525-7). Ayer Co Pubs.

General Assembly of the I.A.U., 16th, Grenoble, 1976. Proceedings. Jappel, Arnost & Muller, Edith A., eds. (Transactions of the International Astronomical Union: Vol. XVIB). 1977. lib. bdg. 66.00 (ISBN 90-277-0836-3, Pub. by Reidel Holland). Kluwer Academic.
General Assembly 14th,Brighton,1970. Transactions of the International Astronomical Union: Proceedings, Vol. 14b. De Jager, C. & Jappels, A., eds. LC 30-10103. 378p. 1971. lib. bdg. 42.00 (ISBN 90-277-0190-3, Pub. by Reidel Holland). Kluwer Academic.
General Assembly 15th,Sydney,1973 & Extraordinary General Assembly,Poland,1973. Transactions of the International Astronomical Union: Proceedings, Vol. 15b. Contopoulos, G. & Jappel, A., eds. LC 73-81827. 334p. 1974. lib. bdg. 63.00 (ISBN 90-277-0451-1, Pub. by Reidel Holland). Kluwer Academic.
General Assembly,13th,Prague,1967. Transactions of the International Astronomical Union: Proceedings, Vol. 13b. Perek, L., ed. 309p. 1968. lib. bdg. 26.00 (ISBN 90-277-0139-3, Fpub. by Reidel Holland). Kluwer Academic.
General Board of Church & Society. Third World Development: Challenge for Christians. 72p. (Subsidized). 0.10 (ISBN 0-318-16909-6, CSE2056). Bd Church & Soc.
General Conference. My Golden Key Prayer List. pap. 0.50 (ISBN 0-686-82634-5). Review & Herald.
General Conference Sabbath School Department. Sabbath School Manual. rev. ed. 1982. pap. 5.50 (ISBN 0-8127-0228-X). Review & Herald.
General Conference Youth Department. Church Heritage: A Course in Church History. pap. 2.50 (ISBN 0-686-82636-1). Review & Herald.
General Dynamics. A Guide to Radiographic Evaluation of Discontinuities in Aluminum Casting. 143p. 1973. 33.75 (ISBN 0-318-17204-6, 212). Am Soc Nondestructive.
General Electric Co. Cooking with a Food Processor. (Illus.). 1979. 10.95 (ISBN 0-394-50482-8). Random.
--General Electric Microwave Guide & Cookbook. (Illus.). 1978. 12.95 (ISBN 0-394-53151-5). Random.
General Electric Company. Components Technology & Standardization Manual, 3 vols. (Illus.). 2200p. 1981. 450.00x (ISBN 0-931690-03-X). Genium Pub.
--Data Processing Self-Study Kit. Incl. An Introduction to Electronic Data Processing. 256p. (ISBN 0-932078-38-9); An Introduction to Magnetic Discs. 98p. (ISBN 0-932078-39-7); An Introduction to Integrated Data Store. 97p. (ISBN 0-932078-40-0); Time-Sharing's BASIC Language. 250p. (ISBN 0-932078-41-9). 1970. pap. 8.50 ea. GE Tech Prom & Train.
--G-MAP Training Manual. 1970. pap. 14.95 (ISBN 0-932078-42-7). GE Tech Prom & Train.
--Modern Drafting Practices & Standards Manual. (Illus.). 940p. 1981. 140.00x (ISBN 0-931690-01-3). Genium Pub.
--SCR Manual. 6th ed. (Illus.). 656p. 1982. pap. 14.95 (ISBN 0-13-796763-2); 23.95 (ISBN 0-13-796771-3). P-H.
--Work Effectiveness. 94p. 1973. pap. 7.00 (ISBN 0-932078-01-X). GE Tech Prom & Train.
General Electric Marketing Consulting Services. Sales Situation Elements. 1973. 55.00 (ISBN 0-932078-02-8). GE Tech Prom & Train.
General Federation of Jewish Labour in Israel Executive Committee. Documents & Essays on Jewish Labour Policy in Palestine. LC 76-97280. 239p. 1975. Repr. of 1930 ed. lib. bdg. 22.50x (ISBN 0-8371-2602-9, JELP). Greenwood.
General Fisheries Council for the Mediterranean. Establishment, Structure, Functions & Activities of International Fisheries Bodies, Pt. 5. 39p. 1968. pap. 7.50 (ISBN 0-686-92808-3, F1737, FAO). Unipub.
General Foods. Cora's Country Cookbook. LC 77-77254. 1977. 2.50 (ISBN 0-87502-053-4). Benjamin Co.
General Headquarters, Ireland. Handbook for Volunteers of the Irish Republican Army. 44p. pap. 4.00 (ISBN 0-87364-074-8). Paladin Pr.
General, Manager, jt. ed. see Lockstedt, Barbara.
General Mills. Betty Crocker's International Cookbook. (Illus.). 1980. 14.95 (ISBN 0-394-50453-4). Random.
--Betty Crocker's Microwave Cookbook. LC 81-40249. (Illus.). 288p. 1981. 14.95 (ISBN 0-394-51764-4). Random.
General Mills Staff. Betty Crocker's Kitchen Secrets. (Illus.). 1983. 12.50 (ISBN 0-394-52306-7). Random.
General Strike Committee. Seattle General Strike. (Shorey Historical Ser.). 63p. pap. 6.95 (ISBN 0-8466-0227-X, S227). Shorey.
Generali, Pietro & Gossett, Philip. I Baccanti Di Roma & Excerpts From Other Operas. (Italian Opera Ser., 1810-1840). 85.00 (ISBN 0-8240-6557-3). Garland Pub.
Generides. Royal Historie of the Excellent Knight Generides. Furnivall, Frederick J., ed. LC 70-147837. (Research & Source Works Ser.: No. 727). 1971. Repr. 25.50 (ISBN 0-8337-1252-7). B Franklin.
Generoso, W., jt. ed. see Chu, E.
Generoso, W. M., et al, eds. DNA Repair & Mutagenesis in Eukaryotes. LC 80-18743. (Basic Life Sciences Ser.: Vol. 15). 470p. 1980. 55.00x (ISBN 0-306-40552-0, Plenum Pr). Plenum Pub.
Generoso, W. M., jt. ed. see Lemontt, J. F.
Generous, William T., Jr. Swords & Scales: The Development of the Uniform Code of Military Justice. LC 72-91173. 1973. 24.50x (ISBN 0-8046-9039-1, Pub by Kennikat). Assoc Faculty Pr.
Generowicz, Witold. The Train. LC 82-73216. (Illus.). 32p. (ps-3). 1983. 5.95 (ISBN 0-8037-8834-7, 0578-170). Dial Bks Young.
Genesis Project, ed. Songs for Sunshine & Rain: Genesis Project Songbook. (Illus.). 48p. (Orig.). 1981. pap. 5.95 (ISBN 0-86702-010-5). Genesis Project.
Genest, Emile. Les Belles Citations de la Litterature Francaise. 1923. Repr. 45.00 (ISBN 0-8274-1923-6). R West.
--L' Opera-Comique Connu et Inconnu: Son Histoire Depuis l'origine Jusqu'a Nos Jours. LC 80-2277. Repr. of 1925 ed. 39.50 (ISBN 0-404-18845-1). AMS Pr.
Genest, J., ed. see Clinical Research Institute of Montreal Symposium.
Genest, Jacques & Kuchel, Otto. Hypertension: Physiopathology & Treatment. 2nd ed. (Illus.). 1376p. 1983. 95.00 (ISBN 0-07-023061-7). McGraw.
Genest, John. Some Account of the English Stage from the Restoration in 1660 to 1830, 10 Vols. 1965. Repr. of 1832 ed. Set. 375.00 (ISBN 0-8337-1323-X). B Franklin.
Genest, Myles see Merluzzi, Thomas.
Genestal, Robert. La Tutelle: Etudes De Droit Prive Normand, Vol. 3. LC 80-2027. Repr. of 1930 ed. 29.00 (ISBN 0-404-18564-9). AMS Pr.
Genet, see Flanner, Janet, pseud.
Genet, Barbara. Ta-Poo-Ach Means Apple. 46p. (ps-3). 1985. cancelled (ISBN 0-86705-015-2). AIRE.
Genet, Edmond C. Memorial on the Upward Motion of Fluids. (Illus.). 7.50 (ISBN 0-8363-0069-6). Jenkins.
Genet, Jean. L' Atelier d'Alberto Giacometti. pap. 11.50 (ISBN 0-685-33950-5). French & Eur.
--Le Balcon. 1962. pap. 8.95 (ISBN 0-685-11033-8). French & Eur.
--The Balcony. Frechtman, Bernard, tr. from Fr. (Illus.). 1958. pap. 5.95 (ISBN 0-394-17214-0, E130, Ever). Grove.
--The Blacks: A Clown Show. Frechtman, Bernard, tr. from Fr. (Orig.). 1960. pap. 7.95 (ISBN 0-394-17220-5, E208, Ever). Grove.
--Bonnes. 1963. pap. 8.95 (ISBN 0-685-11051-6). French & Eur.
--Complete Poems. 1980. pap. 8.95 (ISBN 0-686-28714-2). Man-Root.
--Funeral Rites. Frechtman, Bernard, tr. from Fr. 1969. pap. 5.95 (ISBN 0-394-17163-2, B239, BC). Grove.
--Haute Surveillance. 1965. pap. 12.25 (ISBN 0-685-11229-2). French & Eur.
--Haute Surveillance. 60p. 1970. 3.95 (ISBN 0-686-56042-6). French & Eur.
--Journal Du Voleur. 1966. pap. 14.50 (ISBN 0-685-11279-9). French & Eur.
--Lettres a Roger Blin. pap. 4.95 (ISBN 0-685-33951-3). French & Eur.
--The Maids. Frechtman, Bernard, tr. from Fr. Bd. with Deathwatch. pap. 4.50 (ISBN 0-394-17390-2, E577, Ever). Grove.
--Miracle de la Rose. pap. 7.95 (ISBN 0-685-33952-1). French & Eur.
--Miracle of the Rose. Frechtman, Bernard, tr. from Fr. 1971. pap. 7.95 (ISBN 0-394-17470-4, B322, BC). Grove.
--Les Negres, Pour Jouer les Negres. pap. 11.50 (ISBN 0-685-11416-3). French & Eur.
--Notre-Dame-des-Fleurs. 1966. pap. 8.50 (ISBN 0-685-11426-0). French & Eur.
--Notre-Dame des Fleurs. 4.95 (ISBN 0-686-56043-4). French & Eur.
--Oeuvres Completes, Tome I. Incl. Saint Genet, Comedien et Martyr. Sartre, Jean-Paul. 15.95 (ISBN 0-685-36046-6). 1951-53. French & Eur.
--Oeuvres Completes, Tome II. Incl. Notre-Dame des Fleurs; Le Condamne a Mort; Miracle de la Rose; Un Chant d'Amour. 1951-53. 16.50 (ISBN 0-685-36047-4). French & Eur.
--Oeuvres Completes, Tome III. Incl. Pompes Funebres; Le Pecheur du Soquet; Querelle de Brest. 1951-53. 12.95 (ISBN 0-685-36048-2). French & Eur.
--Oeuvres Completes, Tome IV. Incl. L' Etrange Mot d'..; Ce Qui Est Reste d'un Rembrant Dechire en Petits Carres..; Le Balcon; Les Bonnes; Haute Surveillance; Lettres a Roger Blin; Comment Jouer les Bonnes; Comment jouer Le Balcon. (Coll. Soleil). 1951-53. 18.95 (ISBN 0-685-36049-0). French & Eur.
--Our Lady of the Flowers. Frechtman, Bernard, tr. from Fr. LC 61-6715. 1976. pap. 3.95 (ISBN 0-394-17903-X, B389, BC). Grove.
--Les Paravents. 288p. 1976. 14.95 (ISBN 0-686-56044-2). French & Eur.
--Poemes. pap. 5.95 (ISBN 0-685-33953-X). French & Eur.
--Querelle. Hollo, Anselm, tr. from Fr. LC 74-24898. 1975. pap. 4.95 (ISBN 0-394-17838-6, B382, BC). Grove.
--The Screens. Frechtman, Bernard, tr. from Fr. 1962. pap. 4.95 (ISBN 0-394-17245-0, E374, Ever). Grove.
--The Thief's Journal. Frechtman, Bernard, tr. from Fr. LC 64-24077. 1982. pap. 9.95 (ISBN 0-394-62437-8, E837, Ever). Grove.
--Treasures of the Night: Collected Poems of Jean Genet. Finch, Steven, tr. from Fr. (Illus.). 120p. (Orig.). 1981. 25.00x (ISBN 0-917342-75-5); pap. 6.95 (ISBN 0-917342-76-3). Gay Sunshine.
Genet, Karen A., jt. ed. see Genet, Russell M.
Genet, Malcolm, compiled by. Charles Dickens, Eighteen Hundred & Twelve to Eighteen Seventy. (Illus.). 1970. pap. 4.00 (ISBN 0-87959-009-2). U of Tex H Ransom Ctr.
Genet, Russell M. Real-Time Control with the TRS-80. LC 82-50020. 166p. 1982. pap. 14.95 (ISBN 0-672-21831-3, 21831). Sams.
Genet, Russell M., jt. auth. see Hall, Douglas S.
Genet, Russell M., jt. auth. see Trueblood, Mark.
Genet, Russell M., jt. auth. see Wolpert, Robert C.
Genet, Russell M., ed. Microcomputers in Astronomy. LC 82-84769. 253p. (Orig.). 1983. pap. 23.95 (ISBN 0-911351-03-5). Fairborn Observ.
--Solar System Photometry Handbook. LC 83-21382. (Illus.). 224p. 1983. pap. text ed. 17.95 (ISBN 0-943396-03-4). Willmann-Bell.
Genet, Russell M. & Genet, Karen A., eds. Microcomputers in Astronomy, II. 200p. (Orig.). 1984. pap. 23.95 (ISBN 0-911351-06-X). Fairborn Observ.
Genet, Russell M., jt. ed. see Wolpert, Robert C.
Genet, Russell M., jt. auth. see Hall, Douglas S.
Genetelli, Emil, jt. ed. see Cross, Frank L., Jr.
Genetski, Robert J., jt. auth. see Sprinkel, Beryl M.
Genett, Ann. Contributions of Women: Aviation. LC 74-19004. (Contributions of Women Ser.). (Illus.). (gr. 6 up). 1975. PLB 8.95 (ISBN 0-87518-089-2). Dillon.
Genette, Francis. Dictionnaire du Bricolage et du Depannage Menager. 450p. (Fr.). 1972. pap. 26.50 (ISBN 0-686-57191-6, M-6265). French & Eur.
Genette, Gerard. Figures of Literary Discourse. Sheridan, Alan, tr. (European Perspectives Ser.). 303p. 1984. 26.00x (ISBN 0-231-04984-6); pap. 11.00x (ISBN 0-231-04985-4). Columbia U Pr.
--Narrative Discourse: An Essay in Method. Lewin, Jane E., tr. from Fr. LC 79-13499. (Illus.). 288p. 1979. 27.50x (ISBN 0-8014-1099-1); pap. 8.95 (ISBN 0-8014-9259-9). Cornell U Pr.
Geneva - Conference - 1954. Nineteen Fifty-Four Geneva Conference Indo-China & Korea. LC 68-57791. Repr. of 1954 ed. lib. bdg. 20.50x (ISBN 0-8371-0652-4, GECO). Greenwood.
Geneva Institute Of International Relations. Problems of Peace, Fifth Series. facs. ed. LC 71-121470. (Essay Index Reprint Ser.). 1930. 21.00 (ISBN 0-8369-1808-8). Ayer Co Pubs.
--Problems of Peace, First Series. LC 73-105015. (Essay Index Reprint Ser.). 1927. 24.50 (ISBN 0-8369-1468-6). Ayer Co Pubs.
--Problems of Peace: Lectures. Eighth Series. facs. ed. LC 68-22914. (Essay Index Reprint Ser). 1968. Repr. of 1934 ed. 18.00 (ISBN 0-8369-0470-2). Ayer Co Pubs.
--Problems of Peace: Lectures. Second Series. facs. ed. LC 70-76899. (Essay Index Reprint Ser). 1928. 19.00 (ISBN 0-8369-0014-6). Ayer Co Pubs.
--Problems of Peace: Lectures. Third Series. facs. ed. LC 68-57317. (Essay Index Reprint Ser). 1929. 18.00 (ISBN 0-8369-0115-0). Ayer Co Pubs.
--Problems of Peace, Ninth Series. LC 70-111832. (Essay Index Reprint Ser.). 1935. 20.00 (ISBN 0-8369-1609-3). Ayer Co Pubs.
--Problems of Peace, Thirteenth Series. facs. ed. LC 68-57317. (Essay Index Reprint Ser). 1939. 18.00 (ISBN 0-8369-0042-1). Ayer Co Pubs.
--Problems of Peace, Twelfth Series. LC 74-111833. (Essay Index Reprint Ser.). 1938. 18.00 (ISBN 0-8369-1610-7). Ayer Co Pubs.
Genevro, George W., jt. auth. see Heineman, Stephen S.
Genf, September 30-October 1, 1977. Schweizerische Gesellschaft fuer Dermatologie und Venerologie: 59 Jahresversammlung, No. 59. Schuppli, R., ed. (Dermatologica: Vol. 157, No. 5). (Illus.). 1978. pap. 11.25 (ISBN 3-8055-2964-3). S Karger.
Genfan, Herb & Taetzch, Lyn. Latigo Leather. (Illus.). 160p. 1976. pap. 7.95 (ISBN 0-8230-2651-5). Watson-Guptill.
Genfan, Herb & Taetzsch, Lyn. How to Start Your Own Craft Business. (Illus.). 208p. 1974. 12.95 (ISBN 0-8230-2470-9). Watson-Guptill.
Geng, Veronica. Partners. LC 83-48812. (Illus.). 224p. 1984. 13.41i (ISBN 0-06-015295-8, HarpT). Harrow.
--Partners. LC 83-48812. (Illus.). 184p. 1985. pap. 6.95 (ISBN 0-06-091289-8, PL 1289, PL). Har-Row.
Gengerelli, J. A. see Ruckwick, Christian A.
Gengkang, Hu, et al, trs. see China Handbook Editorial Committee.
Gengle, Dean. The Netweaver's Sourcebook: A Guide to Micro Networking & Communications. LC 84-6212. 1438p. 1984. pap. 14.95 (ISBN 0-201-05208-3). Addison-Wesley.
Gen-Hua Shi, jt. auth. see Goodman, Richard.
Genicot, Leopold. La noblesse dans l'Occident medieval: Eighteen Studies in French 1952-81. 356p. 1982. 75.00x (ISBN 0-86078-111-9, Pub. by Variorum England). State Mutual Bk.
Genin, F., ed. see Marguerite D'Angouleme.
Genin, J., jt. auth. see Ginsberg, J. H.
Genin, Salomea, tr. see Gedo, Andras.
Genin, Salomea, tr. see Hoerz, Herbert, et al.
Genis, Alexandr & Vail, Peter. Sovremennaia Russkaia Proza. LC 82-18213. (Illus.). 180p. (Rus.). 1982. pap. 8.50 (ISBN 0-938920-28-6). Hermitage.
Genishi, Celia & Dyson, Anne. Language Assessment in the Early Years. Wallat, Cynthia & Green, Judith, eds. LC 84-3074. (Language & Learning for Human Service Professions). 224p. 1984. text ed. 29.50 (ISBN 0-89391-176-3); pap. text ed. 18.95 (ISBN 0-89391-246-8). Ablex Pub.
Genishi, Celia, jt. auth. see Almy, Millie.
Genji, Okubo, jt. auth. see Beckmann, George M.
Genn, E. L., jt. auth. see Genn, Robert C., Jr.
Genn, Hazel, jt. auth. see MacLean, Mavis.
Genn, Hazel, jt. ed. see Burman, Sandra.
Genn, Robert C. Illustrated Guide to Practical Solid State Circuits...with Experiments & Projects. 335p. 1983. 21.95 (ISBN 0-13-450643-X). P-H.
--Manual of Electronic Servicing Tests & Measurements. 240p. 1979. 19.95 (ISBN 0-13-553388-0, Parker). P-H.
--Practical Handbook of Solid State Troubleshooting. (Illus.). 1984. pap. 12.95 (ISBN 0-13-691295-8, Busn). P-H.
Genn, Robert C., Jr. Digital Electronics: A Workbench Guide to Circuits, Experiments & Applications. LC 81-16837. 256p. 1982. 18.95 (ISBN 0-13-214163-9); pap. 12.95 (ISBN 0-13-212530-7). P-H.
--Practical Handbook of Solid State Troubleshooting. LC 80-23897. 256p. 1981. 12.95 (ISBN 0-13-691303-2, Parker). P-H.
--Workbench Guide to Electronic Troubleshooting. 216p. 1977. 17.95 (ISBN 0-686-92088-0). P-H.
Genn, Robert C., Jr. & Genn, E. L. The Complete Microcomputer Handbook: With Tested BASIC Programs. LC 84-11485. (Illus.). 367p. 1984. plastic comb binding 23.95 (ISBN 0-13-162199-8). P-H.
Genn, Robert, Jr. Electronic Troubleshooting Handbook. 215p. 1981. pap. 8.95 (ISBN 0-13-252585-2, Reward). P-H.
Gennard, J., jt. auth. see Dunn, S.
Gennard, John. Job Security & Industrial Relations. 78p. 1979. 5.00x (ISBN 92-64-11835-7). OECD.
--Multinational Corporations & British Labour: A Review of Attitudes & Responses. (Illus.). 53p. 1972. 2.00 (ISBN 0-902594-05-2, BN6). Inst C D Howe.
Gennaro, Alphonso R., ed. see Blakiston.
Gennaro, Angelo A. De see De Gennaro, Angelo A.
Gennaro, Joseph, jt. auth. see Grillone, Lisa.
Gennaro, L. & Guzzon, F. Kirlian Photography: Research & Prospects. (Illus.). 152p. 1982. 14.95 (ISBN 0-85692-045-2, Pub. by Salem Hse Ltd). Merrimack Pub Cir.
Genne, Elizabeth & Genne, William. Church Family Camps & Conferences. LC 78-24395. 1979. pap. 2.95 (ISBN 0-8170-0818-7). Judson.
Genne, Elizabeth S. & Genne, William H. First of All Persons: A New Look at Men-Women Relationships. (Orig.). 1973. pap. 1.95 (ISBN 0-377-03041-4). Friend Pr.
Genne, William, jt. auth. see Genne, Elizabeth.
Genne, William H., jt. auth. see Genne, Elizabeth S.
Gennep, Arnold Van. Mythes et legendes d'Australie. LC 78-63231. (The Folktale). Repr. of 1906 ed. 28.00 (ISBN 0-404-16174-X). AMS Pr.
Gennep, Arnold Van see Gennep, Arnold Van.
Gennep, Arnold Van see Van Gennep, Arnold.
Gennes, J. L. de see De Gennes, J. L., et al.
Gennes, Pierre-Gilles De see De Gennes, Pierre-Gilles.
Gennesseaux, Maurice G. & Stanley, Daniel J. Neogene to Recent Displacement & Contact of Sardinian & Tunisian Margins, Central Mediterranean. LC 83-16647. (Smithsonian Contributions to the Marine Sciences Ser.: No. 23). pap. 20.00 (ISBN 0-317-29198-X, 2022254). Bks Demand UMI.
Gennings, Arthur T. Arbitration: A Practical Guide. 208p. 1984. text ed. 41.95x (ISBN 0-566-02423-3). Gower Pub Co.
Genno, Charles N. & Wetzel, Heinz, eds. The First World War in German Narrative Prose. LC 79-26625. 1980. 20.00x (ISBN 0-8020-5490-0). U of Toronto Pr.
Geno, Thomas H., ed. Foreign Language & International Studies: Toward Cooperation & Integration. LC 55-34379. 200p. 1981. pap. 7.95 (ISBN 0-915432-81-1). NE Conf Teach Foreign.
--Our Profession: Present Status & Future Directions. 1980. pap. 7.95x (ISBN 0-915432-80-3). NE Conf Teach Foreign.
Geno, Thomas H., jt. ed. see Born, Warren C.
Genoa Area Centennial Homecoming Inc. Memories of Genoa, Ohio Eighteen Sixty-Eight to Nineteen Sixty-Eight. Levee, Robert C., ed. (Illus.). 70p. (Orig.). 1968. pap. 6.40 (ISBN 0-9603006-3-5). Ottawa Co Hist.

Genot, Gerard. Elements of Narrativics, Vol. 19. (Papers in Textlinquistics). 136p. (Orig.). 1979. pap. text ed. 11.00x (ISBN 3-87118-364-4, Pub. by Helmut Buske Verlag Hamburg). Benjamins North Am.

Genoud & Inoue. Buddhist Wall Paintings of Ladakh. (Illus.). 248p. 1983. text ed. 79.95 (ISBN 2-88086-001-6, Olizane-Switzerland). Bradt Ent.

Genoud, C. & Inoue, T. Buddhist Wall-Painting of Ladakh. (Illus.). 116p. 1981. text ed. 68.45x (ISBN 2-88086-001-6, Pub. by Editions Olizane Switzerland). Humanities.

Genouvrier. Linguistique et Enseignement du Francais. 13.95 (ISBN 2-03-042171-5, 4539). Larousse.

Genouvrier, Emile, et al. Nouveau Dictionnaire des Synonymes. (Fr.). 1977. 19.95 (ISBN 0-686-57192-4, M-6266). French & Eur.

Genovese, Eugene D. From Rebellion to Revolution: Afro-American Slave Revolts in the Making of the Modern World. LC 79-17722. xxvi, 174p. 1979. 14.95 (ISBN 0-8071-0586-4). La State U Pr.

--From Rebellion to Revolution: Afro-American Slave Revolts in the Making of the Modern World. LC 80-11386. 208p. 1981. pap. 3.95 (ISBN 0-394-74485-3, Vin). Random.

--In Red & Black: Marxian Explorations in Southern & Afro-American History. 2nd ed. LC 83-25920. 496p. 1984. text ed. 24.95x (ISBN 0-87049-428-7); pap. text ed. 12.50x (ISBN 0-87049-429-5). U of Tenn Pr.

--Political Economy of Slavery: Studies in Economy & Society of the Slave South. 1967. pap. 4.95 (ISBN 0-394-70400-2, V400, Vin). Random.

--Roll, Jordan, Roll: The World the Slaves Made. 1976. pap. 10.95 (ISBN 0-394-71652-3, Vin). Random.

--World the Slaveholders Made: Two Essays in Interpretation. 1971. pap. 2.95 (ISBN 0-394-71676-0, Vin). Random.

Genovese, Eugene D. & McDonald, Forrest. Debates on American History. 64p. (Orig.). 1983. pap. text ed. 3.95 (ISBN 0-686-98000-X). Revisionary.

Genovese, Eugene D., jt. auth. see Burner, David.

Genovese, Eugene D., jt. auth. see Engerman, Stanley L.

Genovese, Eugene D., jt. auth. see Fox-Genovese, Elizabeth.

Genovese, Eugene D., jt. ed. see Miller, Elinor.

Genovese, Eugene D., ed. see Phillips, Ulrich B.

Genovese, John K. & Soap Opera Digest Editors. The Soap Opera Digest Scrapbook. (Illus.). 224p. (Orig.). 1984. pap. 6.95 (ISBN 0-8092-5385-2). Contemp Bks.

Genovese, Michael A. The Supreme Court, the Constitution, & Presidential Power. LC 80-5695. 345p. 1980. lib. bdg. 25.00 (ISBN 0-8191-1322-0); pap. text ed. 14.25 (ISBN 0-8191-1323-9). U Pr of Amer.

Genovese, Rosalie G. Families & Change: Social Needs & Public Policy. 360p. 1983 29.95; pap. 14.95 (ISBN 0-89789-045-0). Bergin & Garvey.

Genovese, Rosalie G., ed. Families & Change: Social Needs & Public Policies. 352p. 1984. 35.95 (ISBN 0-03-070636-X). Praeger.

Genovesi, Vincent J. Expectant Creativity: The Action of Hope in Christian Ethics. LC 81-43807. 172p. (Orig.). 1982. lib. bdg. 25.00 (ISBN 0-8191-2407-9); pap. text ed. 11.25 (ISBN 0-8191-2408-7). U Pr of Amer.

Genoways, Hugh H. A New Species of Spiny Pocket Mouse (Genus Liomys) from Jalisco, Mexico. (Occasional Papers: No. 5). 7p. 1971. pap. 1.25 (ISBN 0-317-05016-8). U of KS Mus Nat Hist.

--Systematics & Evolutionary Relationships of Spiny Pocket Mice, Genus Liomys. (Special Publications: No. 5). (Illus.). 368p. (Orig.). 1973. pap. 10.00 (ISBN 0-89672-030-6). Tex Tech Pr.

Gensel, Patricia G. & Andrews, Henry N. Plant Life in the Devonian. (Illus.). 396p. 1984. 29.95 (ISBN 0-03-062002-3). Praeger.

Gensemer, Robert. Intermediate Tennis. (Illus.). 224p. 1985. pap. 7.95x (ISBN 0-89582-130-3). Morton Pub.

--Tennis. 3rd ed. 1982. pap. text ed. 9.95 (ISBN 0-03-060106-1, CBS C). SCP.

Gensemer, Robert E. Humanism & Behaviorism in Physical Education. 128p. 1980. avail. (ISBN 0-8106-1488-X). NEA.

--Movement Education. 80p. 1979. pap. 5.95 (ISBN 0-8106-1823-0, 1823-0-06). NEA.

Genser, Cynthia. Taking on the Local Color. LC 76-41486. (Wesleyan Poetry Program: Vol. 85). 1977. 15.00x (ISBN 0-8195-2085-3); pap. 6.95 (ISBN 0-8195-1085-8). Wesleyan U Pr.

Genser, Cynthia K. Club Eighty-Two. (Orig.). 1979. pap. 4.50 (ISBN 0-935388-00-1). Workingmans Pr.

Gensini, Goffredo G., ed. Coronary Arteriography. 2nd ed. 1985. P.N.S. (ISBN 0-87993-225-2). Futura Pub.

Gensler, Harry J. Godel's Theorem Simplified. 88p. (Orig.). 1984. lib. bdg. 13.50 (ISBN 0-8191-3868-1); pap. text ed. 7.25 (ISBN 0-8191-3869-X). U Pr of Amer.

Gensler, Kinereth. Without Roof. LC 80-70829. 64p. (Orig.). 1981. pap. 6.95 (ISBN 0-914086-32-4). Alicejamesbooks.

Gensler, Kinereth & Nyhart, Nina. The Poetry Connection: An Anthology of Contemporary Poems with Ideas to Stimulate Children's Writing. LC 78-14926. (Orig.). 1978. pap. 7.95 (ISBN 0-915924-08-0). Tchrs & Writers Coll.

Genszler, G. William. Hay, Harmony, Hallelujah. 138p. (Orig.). 1971. pap. 5.75 (ISBN 0-89536-088-8). CSS of Ohio.

Gent, Aart Van see Hampton, Gerald M. & Van Gent, Aart.

Gent, Barbara & Sturges, Betty. The Altar Guild Book. LC 82-80469. (Illus.). 104p. (Orig.). 1982. pap. 5.50 (ISBN 0-8192-1305-5, 82-80469). Morehouse.

Gent, John, jt. auth. see Cooper, Terry.

Gent, P. F., tr. see Faustus, Johann.

Gent, Peter. The Franchise. LC 82-42804. 576p. 1983. 16.95 (ISBN 0-394-53149-3). Random.

--The Franchise. 576p. 1984. pap. 3.95 (ISBN 0-345-28299-X). Ballantine.

--North Dallas Forty. 1974. pap. 2.50 (ISBN 0-451-08906-5, E8906, Sig). NAL.

--North Dallas Forty. 304p. 1984. pap. 3.50 (ISBN 0-345-31670-3). Ballantine.

Genta, Ellen G. Dig Your Own Gold. 1976. 4.95 (ISBN 0-89036-062-6). Hawkes Pub Inc.

Genta, G. Kinetic Energy Storage. (Illus.). 1985. text ed. 84.95 (ISBN 0-408-01396-6). Butterworth.

Gentemann, Karen M., ed. Social & Political Perspectives on Energy Policy. LC 80-21963. 224p. 1981. 33.95 (ISBN 0-03-058636-4). Praeger.

Genthe, Arnold. Book of the Dance. 59.95 (ISBN 0-87968-771-1). Gordon Pr.

--Isadora Duncan. LC 79-5300. (Dance Ser.). (Illus.). 1980. Repr. of 1929 ed. lib. bdg. 27.50x (ISBN 0-8369-9306-3). Ayer Co Pubs.

Genthner, Henry & Herbert, Joseph L., Jr. Automating Zero Base Budgeting. LC 77-16518. (Illus.). 1977. text ed. 22.95 (ISBN 0-89433-050-0). Petrocelli.

Genthon, J. P. & Rottger, H. Reactor Dosimetry, 2 Vols. 1985. Set. lib. bdg. 118.00 (ISBN 90-277-2013-4, Pub. by Reidel Netherlands); Vol. I. lib. bdg. 59.00 (ISBN 90-277-2011-8); Vol. II. lib. bdg. 59.00 (ISBN 90-277-2012-6). Kluwer Academic.

Gentil, F. The Retir'd Gard'ner, 2 Vols. Hunt, John D., ed. London, George & Wise, Henry, trs. LC 79-56998. (The English Landscape Garden Ser.). 802p. 1982. Set. lib. bdg. 133.00 (ISBN 0-8240-0156-7). Garland Pub.

Gentil, Genevieve, jt. auth. see Girard, Augustin.

Gentil, Pierre Le see Le Gentil, Pierre.

Gentilcore, R. Louis & Head, C. Grant. Ontario's History in Maps. (Ontario Historical Studies Ser.). (Illus.). 304p. 1984. 160.00 (ISBN 0-8020-3415-2); Alumni Edition o. p. 400.00 (ISBN 0-8020-3402-0). U of Toronto Pr.

Gentilcore, R. Louis, ed. Ontario. (Studies in Canadian Geography). (Illus.). 1972. pap. 6.00x (ISBN 0-8020-6160-5). U of Toronto Pr.

Gentile, Anne, jt. auth. see Gentile, Richard.

Gentile, Anthony. The Judas Seed. 304p. (Orig.). 1982. pap. 2.95 (ISBN 0-440-14375-6). Dell.

Gentile, Augustine. Disability Days United States, 1975. Michael, Geraldine, ed. (Ser.10, No. 118). 1977. pap. text ed. 1.75 (ISBN 0-8406-0114-X). Natl Ctr Health Stats.

--Health Characteristics, by Geographic Region, Large Metropolitan Areas & Other Places of Residence United States - 1973-74. (Ser. 10). 1976. pap. 1.50 (ISBN 0-8406-0081-X). Natl Ctr Health Stats.

--Persons with Impaired Hearing, U. S. 1971. Knox, Kathleen, ed. LC 75-619226. (Data from the Health Interview Survey Ser 10: No. 101). 65p. 1975. pap. text ed. 1.75 (ISBN 0-8406-0048-8). Natl Ctr Health Stats.

--Physician Visits-Volume & Interval Since Last Visit: United States-1975. Stevenson, Taloria, ed. (Ser. 10: No. 128). 1978. pap. text ed. 1.75 (ISBN 0-8406-0150-6). Natl Ctr Health Stats.

Gentile, Ernest B. The Charasmatic Catechism. LC 76-22255. 1977. pap. 4.95 (ISBN 0-89221-025-7). New Leaf.

Gentile, Gennaro L. The Mouse in the Manger. LC 78-72944. (Illus.). 80p. (gr. k-4). 1978. pap. 3.95 (ISBN 0-87793-165-8). Ave Maria.

Gentile, Giovanni. Genesis & Structure of Society. Harris, H. S., tr. LC 60-8346. 228p. 1966. pap. 6.95 (ISBN 0-252-74519-1). U of Ill Pr.

--The Reform of Education. Bigongiari, Dino, tr. LC 78-63672. (Studies in Fascism: Ideology & Practice). 264p. Repr. of 1922 ed. 25.00 (ISBN 0-404-16935-X). AMS Pr.

Gentile, Lance. Using Sports for Reading & Writing Activities, 2 vols. LC 82-6322. (Illus.). 1983. Vol. I: Elementary & Middle School Years, 200p. pap. 12.50x (ISBN 0-89774-023-8); Vol. II: Middle & High School Years, 230p. pap. 12.50x (ISBN 0-89774-098-X). Oryx Pr.

Gentile, Lance M. Using Sports & Physical Education to Strengthen Reading Skills. (IRA Reading Aids Ser.). (Illus.). 90p. (Orig.). 1980. pap. text ed. 5.00 (ISBN 0-87207-225-8, 225). Intl Reading.

Gentile, Lance M. & Kamil, Michael L. Reading Research Revisited. 1983. text ed. 19.95 (ISBN 0-675-20028-8). Merrill.

Gentile, Mary C. Film Feminisms: Theory & Practice. LC 84-19780. (Contributions in Women's Studies Ser.: No. 56). ix, 182p. 1985. lib. bdg. 27.95 (ISBN 0-313-24407-3, GER/). Greenwood.

Gentile, Richard & Gentile, Anne. Retailing Strategy: How to Do It! LC 78-65369. 1978. 20.95 (ISBN 0-86730-505-3). Lebhar Friedman.

Gentile, Richard J. Influence of Structural Movement on Sedimentation During the Pennsylvanian Period in Western Missouri. LC 74-4528. 108p. 1968. 10.00x (ISBN 0-8262-7619-9). U of Mo Pr.

--Retail Advertising: A Management Approach. new ed. LC 76-7296. (Illus.). 300p. 1976. 20.95 (ISBN 0-86730-509-6). Lebhar Friedman.

Gentile, Thomas. March on Washington: August 28, 1963. (Illus.). 301p. (Orig.). 1983. pap. 6.95 (ISBN 0-9612328-0-3). New Day Pubns.

Gentili, Bruno. Theatrical Performances in the Ancient World: Hellenistic & Early Roman Theatre. (London Studies in Classical Philology: No. 2). 1978. pap. text ed. 17.75x (ISBN 0-391-01164-2). Humanities.

Gentili, G., et al. Geometry Seminar "Luigi Bianchi". (Lecture Notes in Mathematics: Vol. 1022). 177p. 1983. pap. 12.00 (ISBN 0-387-12719-4). Springer Verlag.

Gentilini, Celso, jt. auth. see Liwschitz-Garik, Michael.

Gentilini, P. & Dianzani, M. U., eds. Liver Cirrhosis. (Frontiers of Gastrointestinal Research: Vol. 8). (Illus.). vii, 280p. 1984. 63.50 (ISBN 3-8055-3724-7). S Karger.

Gentilini, P., jt. ed. see Dianzani, M. U.

Gentilini, P., ed. see International Symposium on Problems of Chronic Hepatitis, Montecatini, 1975.

Gentilini, P., et al, eds. Intrahepatic Cholestasis. LC 75-10551. 199p. 1975. 35.50 (ISBN 0-89004-049-4). Raven.

Gentilini, P., et al, eds. see International Symposium on Intrahepatic Cholestasis, 2nd, Florence, October 13-14, 1978.

Gentille, Terry. Printed Textiles: A Guide to Creative Design Fundamentals. (Illus.). 118p. 1982. 21.95 (ISBN 0-13-710657-2); pap. 12.95 (ISBN 0-13-710640-8). P-H.

Gentillet, Innocent. A Discourse Upon the Meanes of Wel Governing; Against N. Machiavell. Patericke, S., tr. LC 73-25708. (English Experience Ser.: No. 205). 374p. 1969. Repr. of 1602 ed. 62.00 (ISBN 90-221-0205-X). Walter J Johnson.

Gentilli, J., ed. Climates of Australia & New Zealand. (World Survey of Climatology Ser.: Vol. 13). 405p. 1971. 134.00 (ISBN 0-444-40827-4). Elsevier.

Gentilli, Joseph. A Geography of Climate. LC 77-10225. Repr. of 1952 ed. 13.50 (ISBN 0-404-16206-1). AMS Pr.

Gentle, E. J. & Reithmaier, L. W. Aviation-Space Dictionary. 6th ed. LC 80-67567. (Illus.). 1980. 19.95 (ISBN 0-8168-3002-9). Aero.

Gentle, Ernest, jt. auth. see Kinzey, Bert.

Gentle, Ernest, ed. see Jackson, B. R.

Gentle, Ernest, ed. see LaBarge, William H. & Holt, Robert L.

Gentle, Ernest J., ed. see Bell, Dana.

Gentle, Ernest J., ed. see Birdsall, Steve.

Gentle, Ernest J., ed. see Bridenbecker, Henry.

Gentle, Ernest J., ed. see Havener, J. K.

Gentle, Ernest J., ed. see Holder, William G.

Gentle, Ernest J., ed. see Kinsey, Bert.

Gentle, Ernest J., ed. see Kinzey, Bert.

Gentle, Ernest J., ed. see Kinzey, Bertrum.

Gentle, Ernest J., ed. see Kirschner, Edwin J.

Gentle, Ernest J., ed. see Mansir, A. Richard.

Gentle, Ernest J., ed. see Morgan, Len.

Gentle, Ernest J., ed. see Pace, Steve.

Gentle, Ernest J., ed. see Peoples, Kenneth D.

Gentle, Ernest J., ed. see Ronnberg, Erik A., Jr.

Gentle, Ernest J., ed. see Siru, William D., Jr.

Gentle, Ernest J., ed. see Toliver, Raymond F. & Constable, Trevor J.

Gentle, Ernest J., ed. see Townson, George.

Gentle, J., jt. ed. see Kennedy, W.

Gentle, Jimmie & Dauten, Dale Alan. Programmed Guide to Increasing Church Attendance. 1980. 9.00 (ISBN 0-89536-446-8). CSS of Ohio.

Gentle, Keith. Children & Art Teaching. LC 84-17615. 216p. 1985. 29.95 (ISBN 0-7099-1122-X, Pub. by Croom Helm Ltd); pap. 16.95 (ISBN 0-7099-1123-8). Longwood Pub Group.

Gentle, Lionel. Lady of Pleasure & Death. LC 84-90067. 133p. 1985. 8.95 (ISBN 0-533-06145-8). Vantage.

Gentle, Mary. Golden Witchbreed. LC 84-60458. 465p. 1984. Repr. of 1983 ed. 16.95 (ISBN 0-688-03161-7). Morrow.

--Golden Witchbreed. 1985. pap. 3.95 (ISBN 0-451-13606-3, Sig). NAL.

--A Hawk in Silver. LC 84-20145. 240p. (gr. 4 up). 1985. 10.25 (ISBN 0-688-04213-9). Lothrop.

Gentleman, David. David Gentleman's Britain. (Illus.). 224p. 1983. 27.00 (ISBN 0-396-08145-2). Dodd.

--David Gentleman's London. (Illus.). 192p. 1985. 29.95 (ISBN 0-396-08652-7). Dodd.

Gentleman, Francis. The Dramatic Censor, 2 vols. LC 78-168105. Repr. of 1770 ed. 85.00 (ISBN 0-404-02697-4). AMS Pr.

--Dramatic Censor: Or, Critical Companion, 2 Vols. LC 77-91902. 979p. 1770. Set. 44.00 (ISBN 0-405-08557-5); 22.00 ea. Vol. 1 (ISBN 0-405-08558-3). Vol. 2 (ISBN 0-405-08559-1). Ayer Co Pubs.

--A Trip to the Moon: Containing an Account of the Island of Noibla, 2 vols. in 1. Shugrue, Michael F., ed. (Flowering of the Novel, 1740-1775 Ser.: Vol. 68). 1975. lib. bdg. 61.00 (ISBN 0-8240-1167-8). Garland Pub.

Gentleman, Judith A. Mexican Oil & Dependent Development. LC 83-48896. (American University Studies X (Political Science): Vol. 2). 400p. (Orig.). 1984. text ed. 29.00 (ISBN 0-8204-0063-7). P Lang Pubs.

Gentlemen of Elvias. True Relation of the Hardships Suffered by Governor Fernando De Soto & Certain Portuguese Gentlemen During the Discovery of the Province of Florida, Now Newly Set Forth by a Gentleman of Elvias: Volume 1: Facsimile of the Original Portuguese of 1557; Volume 2: Translation & Annotations. Robertson, James A., tr. 1933. ltd. ed. 200.00x (ISBN 0-317-27605-0). Elliots Bks.

Gentles, Frederick & Steinfield, Melvin. Hangups from Way Back: Historical Myths & Canons, Vol. 1. 2nd ed. LC 74-1191. 416p. 1974. pap. text ed. 15.95 scp (ISBN 0-06-382785-9, HarpC). Har-Row.

--Hangups from Way Back: Historical Myths & Canons, Vol. 2. 2nd ed. LC 74-1191. 1974. pap. text ed. 14.50 scp (ISBN 0-06-382786-7, HarpC). Har-Row.

Gentles, Margaret. Masters of the Japanese Print: Moronobu to Utamaro. LC 74-27414. (Asia Society Ser.). (Illus.). 1979. Repr. of 1964 ed. lib. bdg. 33.00x (ISBN 0-405-06563-9). Ayer Co Pubs.

Gentner, D. & Stevens, A. L. Mental Models. 360p. 1983. text ed. 29.95x (ISBN 0-89859-242-9). L Erlbaum Assocs.

Genton, C. Y. Histopathology of the Female Genital Tract. (Illus.). 128p. 1983. pap. 14.50 (ISBN 0-387-12512-4). Springer-Verlag.

Genton, Elisabeth. Goethe Zeit: La Vie et les Opinions de Heinrich Leopold Wagner (1747-1779) (European Universtiy Studies Ser.: No. 1, Vol. 300). 516p. 1980. 52.45 (ISBN 3-8204-6541-3). P Lang Pubs.

Gentry, Alwyn H. Bignoniaceae: Crescentieae & Tourretieae, Pt. 1. LC 80-10846. (Flora Neotropica Monograph: No. 25). (Illus.). 132p. 1980. pap. 15.75x (ISBN 0-89327-222-1). NY Botanical.

Gentry, Buck. Cathouse Canyon. (The Scout Ser.: No. 14). 1984. pap. 2.50 (ISBN 0-8217-1345-0). Zebra.

--Oglala Outbreak. (The Scout Ser.: No.13). 1983. pap. 2.50 (ISBN 0-8217-1287-X). Zebra.

--The Scout, No. 1: Rowan's Raiders. 1981. pap. 2.50 (ISBN 0-89083-754-6). Zebra.

--The Scout, No. 10: Traitor's Gold. (Orig.). 1983. pap. 2.50 (ISBN 0-8217-1209-8). Zebra.

--The Scout, No. 15: Texas Tease. 240p. 1984. pap. 2.50 (ISBN 0-8217-1392-2). Zebra.

--The Scout, No. 2: Dakota Massacre. 1981. pap. 2.50 (ISBN 0-89083-794-5). Zebra.

--The Scout, No. 3. (Orig.). 1982. pap. 2.50 (ISBN 0-89083-853-4). Zebra.

--The Scout, No. 4: Cheyenne Vengeance. (Orig.). 1982. pap. 2.50 (ISBN 0-89083-969-7). Zebra.

--The Scout, No. 5: Sioux Slaughter. (Orig.). 1982. pap. 2.50 (ISBN 0-8217-1024-9). Zebra.

--The Scout, No. 6: Bandit Fury. (Orig.). 1982. pap. 2.50 (ISBN 0-8217-1075-3). Zebra.

--The Scout, No. 7: Prairie Bush. 1982. pap. 2.50 (ISBN 0-8217-1110-5). Zebra.

--The Scout, No. 8: Pawnee Rampage. 1983. pap. 2.50 (ISBN 0-8217-1161-X). Zebra.

--The Scout, No. 9: Apache Ambush. (Orig.). 1983. pap. 2.50 (ISBN 0-8217-1193-8). Zebra.

--Scout: Redskin Thrust, No. 18. 1985. pap. 2.50 (ISBN 0-8217-1592-5). Zebra.

--Yaquai Terror. (The Scout Ser.: No. 11). (Orig.). 1983. pap. 2.50 (ISBN 0-317-00700-9). Zebra.

--Yellowstone Kill. (The Scout Ser.: No. 12). 1983. pap. 2.50 (ISBN 0-8217-1254-3). Zebra.

Gentry, Celestea, ed. see Suzman, Cedric L., et al.

Gentry, Christine. When Dogs Run Wild: The Sociology of Feral Dogs & Wildlife. LC 82-17223. (Illus.). 208p. 1983. lib. bdg. 16.95X (ISBN 0-89950-062-5). McFarland & Co.

Gentry, Christine A., jt. auth. see Rourke, Margaret V.

Gentry, Curt. The Last Days of the Late, Great State of California. 1977. pap. 2.50 (ISBN 0-89174-021-X). Comstock Edns.

--Madams of San Francisco. 1977. pap. 2.25 (ISBN 0-89174-015-5). Comstock Edns.

Gentry, Curt, jt. auth. see Bugliosi, Vincent.

Gentry, Daphne S., compiled by. Virginia Land Office Inventory. rev. & enl. ed. xxx, 42p. (Orig.). 1981. pap. 5.00 (ISBN 0-88490-101-7). VA State Lib.

Gentry, Deborah, jt. auth. see Brewster, John W.

Gentry, Donald W. & O'Neill, Thomas J. Mine Investment Analysis. LC 84-51346. (Illus.). 502p. 1984. 50.00x (ISBN 0-89520-429-0, 429-0). Soc Mining Eng.

Gentry, Everett. All about Stalls & Spins. (Illus.). 144p. (Orig.). 1983. pap. 9.95 (ISBN 0-8306-2349-3, 2349). TAB Bks.

Gentry, Francis, ed. German Medieval Tales. LC 82-22050. (The German Library: Vol. 4). 320p. 1982. 19.50 (ISBN 0-8264-0272-0); pap. 8.95 (ISBN 0-8264-0273-9). Continuum.

Gentry, Francis G. & Kleinhenz, Christopher, eds. Medieval Studies in North America: Past, Present, & Future. vi, 252p. 1982. pap. 9.95x. Medieval Inst.

Gentry, George, jt. auth. see Marshall, Alfred W.

Gentry, Howard S. The Agaves of Continental North America. LC 82-6896. (Illus.). 670p. 1982. 49.50x (ISBN 0-8165-0775-9). U of Ariz Pr.

Gentry, Howard S. & Thomson, Paul H. Jojoba Handbook. 3rd ed. LC 82-83667. 168p. 1982. pap. 10.00x (ISBN 0-9602066-1-2). Bonsall Pub.

Gentry, J., jt. auth. see Johnson, G.

Gentry, John R. Immediate Effects of Interpolated Rest Periods on Learning & Performance. LC 78-176803. (Columbia University. Teachers College. Contributions to Education: No. 799). Repr. of 1940 ed. 22.50 (ISBN 0-404-55799-6). AMS Pr.

Gentry, John T. Introduction to Health Services & Community Health Systems. LC 77-78899. 1978. 24.00x (ISBN 0-8211-0612-0); text ed. 22.00x in ten or more copies. McCutchan.

Gentry, Linnell. A History & Encyclopedia of Country, Western, & Gospel Music. LC 71-166231. 1972. Repr. of 1961 ed. 59.00x (ISBN 0-403-01358-5). Scholarly.

Gentry, Matthew, ed. see Hurst, Walter E.

Gentry, Patricia. Kitchen Tools: Cooking with a Twist & a Flair. (Illus.). 200p. (Orig.). 1985. pap. 8.95 (ISBN 0-89286-257-2). One Hund One Prods.

Gentry, Pete. Rafe. 304p. (Orig.). 1982. pap. 2.95 (ISBN 0-449-12362-6, GM). Fawcett.

Gentry, Peter. King of the Golden Gate. 320p. 1981. pap. 2.95 (ISBN 0-449-14429-1). Fawcett.

--Matanza. 1979. pap. 2.25 (ISBN 0-449-14117-9, GM). Fawcett.

--Titus Gamble. 1977. pap. 1.95 (ISBN 0-449-13790-2, GM). Fawcett.

Gentry, Rodney D. Introduction to Calculus for the Biological & Life Sciences. LC 77-79470. (Illus.). 1978. text ed. 29.95 (ISBN 0-201-02477-2); avail. instr's man. o.p. 4.95; key o.p. avail. Addison-Wesley.

Gentry, Sue. Relaxation. 1982. inc. audio cassette 6.95 (ISBN 0-89486-142-5). Hazelden.

--Relaxation: A Natural High. 34p. 1.95 (ISBN 0-89486-142-5, 1411B). Hazelden.

Gentry, W. D. The Concordance Repertory of the More Characteristic Symptoms of the Materia Medica, 6 vols. 1979. Set. 300.00x (ISBN 0-686-78850-8, Pub. by Bks India England). State Mutual Bk.

Gentry, W. Doyle, ed. Handbook of Behavioral Medicine. LC 84-4566. 1984. 40.00 (ISBN 0-89862-636-6). Guilford Pr.

Gentry, W. Doyle, jt. ed. see Williams, Redford B.

Gentz, Friedrich. The French & American Revolutions Compared. Adams, John Q., tr. 1975. pap. text ed. 1.50 (ISBN 0-686-15524-6). St Thomas.

Gentz, Friedrich Von. The Origin & Principles of the American Revolution, Compared with the Origin & Principles of the French Revolution. Loss, Richard, ed. LC 77-16175. 1977. Repr. of 1800 ed. lib. bdg. 35.00x (ISBN 0-8201-1302-6). Schol Facsimiles.

Gentz, Friedrich Von & Possony, Stefan T. Three Revolutions: The French & American Revolutions Compared, & Reflections on the Russian Revolutions. Adams, John Q., tr. from German. LC 75-3866. 1976. Repr. of 1959 ed. lib. bdg. 15.00x (ISBN 0-8371-8090-2, GETR). Greenwood.

Gentz, Friedrich Von see Von Gentz, Friedrich.

Gentz, Johan, et al, eds. Perinatal Medicine. LC 83-2171. 432p. 1983. 39.95 (ISBN 0-03-063699-X). Praeger.

Gentz, William. Career Opportunities in Religion: A Guide for Lay Christians. LC 79-84206. 1979. 5.95 (ISBN 0-8015-3200-0, Hawthorn). Dutton.

Gentz, William & Roddy, Lee. Writing to Inspire. LC 82-1928. 320p. 1982. 14.95 (ISBN 0-89879-064-6). Writers Digest.

Gentz, William H. The World of Philip Potter. 1974. pap. 2.95 (ISBN 0-377-00006-X). Friend Pr.

Gentz, William H., ed. Religious Writer's Marketplace: The Definitive Sourcebook. rev. ed. LC 84-27691. 221p. 1985. pap. 17.95 (ISBN 0-89471-305-1). Running Pr.

Gentzch, W. Vectorization of Computer Programs with the Application of Computational Fluid Dynamics. (Notes on Numerical Fluid Mechanics Ser.: Vol. 7). 1984. 28.00 (ISBN 0-9904000-3-4, Pub. by Vieweg Publishing). Heyden.

Gentzler, Mason J. A Syllabus of Chinese Civilization. LC 72-197083. (Companions to Asian Studies Ser.). pap. 29.80 (ISBN 0-317-11187-6, 2015209). Bks Demand UMI.

Genua, Robert L. The Employer's Guide to Interviewing, Strategies & Tactics for Picking a Winner. (Illus.). 1979. 13.95 (ISBN 0-13-274696-4, Spec); pap. 5.95 (ISBN 0-13-274688-3, Spec). P-H.

Genung, Franklin. Stevenson's Attitude to Life. LC 73-12550. 1901. lib. bdg. 10.00 (ISBN 0-8414-4414-5). Folcroft.

Genung, J. F. Tennyson's in Memoriam. LC 76-129342. (Studies in Tennyson, No. 27). 1970. Repr. of 1883 ed. lib. bdg. 45.95x (ISBN 0-8383-1146-6). Haskell.

Genung, John F. The Idylls & the Ages. 1907. lib. bdg. 10.00 (ISBN 0-8414-4644-X). Folcroft.

--The Idylls & the Ages: A Valuation of Tennyson's Idylls of the King. 59.95 (ISBN 0-8490-0382-2). Gordon Pr.

--Rhetorical Analysis. 1897. 10.00 (ISBN 0-8274-3277-1). R West.

--Robert Louis Stevenson's Attitude to Life. 59.95 (ISBN 0-8490-0963-4). Gordon Pr.

--Tennyson's in Memoriam. LC 74-14525. 1974. Repr. of 1884 ed. lib. bdg. 20.00 (ISBN 0-8414-4545-1). Folcroft.

Genyea, Julien, jt. auth. see Callewaert, Denis M.

Genz, John L., jt. auth. see Ellison, Katherine W.

Genzel, H. see Hellwege, K. H.

Genzel, L. see Fluegge, E.

Genzlinger, Anna L. The Jessup Dimension. 164p. 1981. pap. 9.95 (ISBN 0-911306-28-5). G Barker Bks.

Genzlinger, R. Barry, et al. Straight Forward BASIC. 163p. 1984. pap. 12.95 (ISBN 0-9612704-0-3). Champlain Coll Pr.

Genzor, J., jt. ed. see Krupa, V.

Geo. A. Hormel & Company. Meat Meals in Minutes. LC 80-69809. pap. 4.95 (ISBN 0-87502-085-2). Benjamin Co.

Geo. Peabody College for Teachers. Free & Inexpensive Learning Materials. 21st biennial ed. Moore, Norman R., ed. LC 53-2471. 1983. pap. 4.95 (IP 00-9). Incentive Pubns.

Geodeke, Karl Von see Brant, Sebastian.

Geodesic Services, Inc. The Dome Scrap Book. 176p. 1981. pap. text ed. 9.95 (ISBN 0-8403-2394-8). Kendall-Hunt.

Geoffrey of Monmouth. History of the Kings of Britain. Dunn, Charles W., ed. Evans, Sebastian, tr. 1958. pap. 3.95 (ISBN 0-525-47014-X). Dutton.

Geoffrey of Auxerre. Geoffrey of Auxerre: On the Apocalypse, No. 42. Gibbons, Joseph, tr. from Latin. (Cistercian Fathers Ser.). write for info (ISBN 0-87907-642-9). Cistercian Pubns.

Geoffrey Of Monmouth. Galfredi Monumentensis Historia Britonum. Giles, John A., ed. 1966. 24.00 (ISBN 0-8337-1344-2). B Franklin.

--The History of the Kings of Britain. Thorpe, Lewis, tr. (Classic Ser). 1977. pap. 3.95 (ISBN 0-14-044170-0). Penguin.

Geoffrion, Charles A., ed. Africa: A Study Guide to Better Understanding. (African Humanities Ser.). (Orig.). 1970. pap. text ed. 2.00 (ISBN 0-941934-03-9). Indiana Africa.

Geoffrion, Leo D. & Geoffrion, Olga P. Computers & Reading Instruction. LC 83-8727. (Computers in Education). (Illus.). 224p. 1983. pap. 14.95 (ISBN 0-201-10566-7). Addison-Wesley.

Geoffrion, Leo D., compiled by. Auditory Handicaps & Reading. (Annotated Bibliography Ser.). 63p. (Orig.). 1980. pap. text ed. 2.50 (ISBN 0-87207-335-1, 335). Intl Reading.

Geoffrion, Olga P., jt. auth. see Geoffrion, Leo D.

Geoffroy, Gregory, ed. Topics in Inorganic & Organometallic Stereochemistry, Vol. 12. Elial, Ernest L. (Topics in Stereochemistry Ser.). 352p. 1981. 90.00 (ISBN 0-471-05292-2, Pub. by Wiley-Interscience). Wiley.

Geoffroy, Gregory L. & Wrighton, Mark S. Organometallic Photochemistry. LC 79-6933. 1979. 49.50 (ISBN 0-12-280050-8). Acad Pr.

Geoffroy De, La Tour-Landry see La Tour-Landry, Geoffroy de.

Geoffroy-Dechaume, Claude. Craft Jewellery. (Illus.). 144p. 1980. pap. 6.95 (ISBN 0-571-11309-5). Faber & Faber.

Geoghegan, Richard, tr. see Veniaminov, Ivan.

Geoghegan, Sheila M., ed. United States Agricultural Export Policy. (Wisconsin International Law Journal Ser.: Vol. 1 (1982)). 150p. (Orig.). 1983. pap. text ed. 8.00 (ISBN 0-933431-00-7). U Wisc Law Madison.

Geoghegan, Vincent. Reason & Eros: The Social Theory of Herbert Marcuse. 122p. 1981. pap. 5.95 (ISBN 0-86104-335-9). Pluto Pr.

Geoghegan, William E. Sail & Steam: Naval Vessels of the Confederacy. (Illus.). 160p. 1985. 50.00 (ISBN 0-87249-461-6). U of SC Pr.

Geoghgen, Richard. Aleut Language. facsimile ed. (Shorey's Indian Series). 169p. 1983. pap. 9.95 (ISBN 0-8466-0039-0, S-39). Shorey.

Geographa Staff. Road Atlas of Europe: 1985 Edition. (Geographia Maps & Atlases). (Illus.). 192p. 1985. pap. 6.95 (ISBN 0-09-219210-6, Pub. by Geo Thorn UK). Hippocrene Bks.

Geographics Editors. World Directory of Engineering Schools. 2nd ed. LC 80-66864. 1980. pap. 28.95 (ISBN 0-930722-02-7). Geographics.

Geokan, Mike. Custom Chopper Cookbook. Arman, Mike, ed. (Illus.). 104p. (Orig.). 1981. pap. text ed. 9.00 (ISBN 0-933078-05-6). M Arman.

Geological Society of America. Ten-Year Index to the Geological Society of America Bulletin, Vols. 81-90. LC 1-23380. 1980. pap. 10.00 (ISBN 0-8137-9081-6). Geol Soc.

Geometrical Topology Conference, Park City, Utah, Feb. 19-22, 1974. Geometric Topology: Proceedings. Glaser, L. C. & Rushing, T. B., eds. LC 74-34326. (Lecture Notes in Mathematics: Vol. 438). x, 459p. 1975. pap. 24.00 (ISBN 0-387-07137-7). Springer-Verlag.

Geonautics, Inc. Data Collection & Analysis Techniques for a Planned Experimental Harbor Advisory Radar (HAR) System. LC 77-135095. 123p. 1969. 19.00 (ISBN 0-403-04502-9). Scholarly.

Geophysics Research Board. Climate, Climatic Change & Water Supply. 1977. pap. 9.25 (ISBN 0-309-02625-3). Natl Acad Pr.

--Continental Scientific Drilling. 1979. pap. 5.95 (ISBN 0-309-02872-8). Natl Acad Pr.

--Continental Tectonics. (Studies in Geophysics). xii, 197p. 1980. pap. text ed. 14.95 (ISBN 0-309-02928-7). Natl Acad Pr.

--Impact of Technology on Geophysics. xii, 121p. 1979. pap. 11.75 (ISBN 0-309-02887-6). Natl Acad Pr.

Geophysics Research Board & Division Of Earth Sciences. Solid-Earth Geophysics: Survey & Outlook. 1964. pap. 5.00 (ISBN 0-309-01231-7). Natl Acad Pr.

Geophysics Research Board, National Research Council. Climate in Earth History. 1982. pap. text ed. 16.25 (ISBN 0-309-03329-2). Natl Acad Pr.

--Geophysical Predictions. LC 78-8147. (Studies in Geophysics Ser.). 1978. 14.25 (ISBN 0-309-02741-1). Natl Acad Pr.

Geophysics Research Board National Research Council. Solar Variability, Weather & Climate. 106p. 1982. pap. text ed. 11.95 (ISBN 0-309-03284-9). Natl Acad Pr.

Geophysics Study Committee. Estuaries, Geophysics, & the Environment. LC 77-82812. (Studies in Geophysics). (Illus.). 1977. pap. text ed. 9.95 (ISBN 0-309-02629-6). Natl Acad Pr.

--Upper Atmosphere & Magnetosphere. 1977. pap. 11.50 (ISBN 0-309-02633-4). Natl Acad Pr.

Geophysics Study Committee, National Research Council. Scientific Basis of Water-Resource Management. 1982. pap. text ed. 12.25 (ISBN 0-309-03244-X). Natl Acad Pr.

Georg, J. c., jt. auth. see Bagdonas, A.

Georgacarakos, George N. & Smith, Robin. Elementary Formal Logic. 1978. text ed. 32.95 (ISBN 0-07-023051-X). McGraw.

Georgakas, Dan & Surkin, Marvin. Detroit-I Do Mind Dying: A Study in Urban Revolution. LC 74-81262. 250p. 1975. pap. text ed. 9.95 (ISBN 0-312-19635-0). St Martin.

Georgakas, Dan, compiled by. Left Face: A Sourcebook of Radical Arts Organizations. rev. ed. 1984. pap. 5.00 (ISBN 0-918266-08-4). Smyrna.

Georgakas, Dan & Rubenstein, Lenny, eds. The Cineaste Interviews: The Art & Politics of the Cinema. LC 82-83804. (A Cineaste Reader Ser.). (Illus.). 416p. 1982. 25.00 (ISBN 0-941702-02-2); pap. 11.95 (ISBN 0-941702-03-0). Lake View Pr.

Georgakis, Christos, jt. ed. see Wei, James.

Georgano, G. N. The Complete Encyclopedia of Commercial Vehicles. LC 79-88062. (Illus.). 1979. 35.00 (ISBN 0-87341-024-6). Krause Pubns.

--The Complete Encyclopedia of Commercial Vehicles. 1979. 35.00. Motorbooks Intl.

--Motor Racing Camera, 1894-1916. (Illus.). 1976. 4.95 (ISBN 0-7153-7160-6). David & Charles.

Georgano, G. N., ed. The New Complete Encyclopedia of Motorcars: Eighteen Eighty-Five to the Present. (Illus.). 704p. 1982. 45.00 (ISBN 0-525-93254-2). Dutton.

Georgano, Nick. World Truck Handbook. (Jane's Handbooks). (Illus.). 335p. 1983. pap. 14.95 (ISBN 0-86720-657-8). Jane's Pub Inc.

Georgas, Demitra. Greek Settlement of the San Francisco Bay Area: Thesis. LC 76-155643. 1974. soft bdg. 9.95 (ISBN 0-88247-259-3). R & E Pubs.

Georgas, Stephen. Incorporation & Business Guide for Ontario. 6th ed. 1983. 12.95 (ISBN 0-88908-341-X). Self Counsel Pr.

George. Modern Interstitial & Intracavitary Radiation Cancer Management. LC 80-28011. (Cancer Management Ser.: Vol. 6). 128p. 1981. 42.00x (ISBN 0-89352-118-3). Masson Pub.

George & Johnson. Introductory Reading in Knowledge Representation. (Information Technology Ser.). 1984. write for info (ISBN 0-9901003-1-6, Pub. by Abacus England). Heyden.

George see Hamilton, Charles.

George, A. J., ed. see Hudson, Henry N.

George, A. S., jt. auth. see Rosser, C.

George A. Talland Memorial Conference. New Directions in Memory & Aging: Proceedings. Poon, Leonard W., et al, eds. LC 79-27548. (Illus.). 572p. 1980. text ed. 39.95x (ISBN 0-89859-035-3). L Erlbaum Assocs.

George, Abraham M. Foreign Exchange Management & the Multinational Corporation: A Manager's Guide. LC 78-19738. 298p. 1978. 38.95 (ISBN 0-03-046641-5). Praeger.

George, Abraham M. & Giddy, Ian H., eds. International Finance Handbook, 2 vols. 1983. Vol. 1. 40.00 (ISBN 0-471-81172-6); Vol. 2. 40.00 (ISBN 0-471-81174-2); Set 1832p. 80.00 (ISBN 0-471-09861-2). Wiley.

George, Alan. Resource Based Learning for School Governors. LC 84-19965. 198p. 1984. 26.50 (ISBN 0-7099-1184-X, Pub. by Croom Helm Ltd). Longwood Pub Group.

George, Alan & Liu, Joseph W. Computer Solution of Large Sparse Positive Definite. (Illus.). 256p. 1980. text ed. 41.95 (ISBN 0-13-165274-5). P-H.

George, Alan, jt. auth. see Ashman, Sandra.

George, Alan, tr. see Gilbert, Felix.

George, Albert J. The Development of French Romanticism: The Impact of the Industrial Revolution on Literature. LC 77-10903. 1977. Repr. of 1955 ed. lib. bdg. 22.50x (ISBN 0-8371-9806-2, GEDF). Greenwood.

--Lamartine & Romantic Unanimism. LC 71-168106. Repr. of 1940 ed. 18.50 (ISBN 0-404-02712-1). AMS Pr.

--Pierre-Simon Ballanche: Precursor of Romanticism. 1945. 15.00 (ISBN 0-89366-097-3). Ultramarine Pub.

George, Alex. The Banksia Book. (Illus.). 1985. 24.95 (ISBN 0-88192-050-9, Dist. by Intl Spec Bk). Timber.

--Proteaceae: Introduction to Proteaceae of Western Australia. (Illus.). 1985. 19.95 (ISBN 0-88192-051-7, Dist. by Intl Spec Bk). Timber.

George, Alexander, et al. Deterrence in American Foreign Policy: Theory & Practice. LC 74-7120. 666p. 1974. 37.50x (ISBN 0-231-03837-2); pap. 17.00x (ISBN 0-231-03838-0). Columbia U Pr.

George, Alexander L. The Chinese Communist Army in Action: The Korean War & Its Aftermath. LC 67-12659. 1967. 26.00x (ISBN 0-231-03020-7); pap. 12.00x (ISBN 0-231-08595-8). Columbia U Pr.

--Propaganda Analysis: A Study of Inferences Made from Nazi Propaganda in World War Two. LC 72-10717. (Illus.). 287p. 1973. Repr. of 1959 ed. lib. bdg. 55.00x (ISBN 0-8371-6630-6, GEPA). Greenwood.

George, Alexander L. & George, Juliette L. Woodrow Wilson & Colonel House: A Personality Study. 1956. pap. 5.00 (ISBN 0-486-21144-4). Dover.

George, Alexander L., ed. Managing U. S. Soviet Rivalry: Problems of Crisis Prevention. LC 82-16076. (Special Study in International Relations). 375p. 1983. lib. bdg. 32.00x (ISBN 0-86531-500-0); pap. text ed. 12.95x (ISBN 0-86531-501-9). Westview.

George, Andrew J., ed. The Complete Poetical Works of William Wordsworth, 10 vols. 1981. Repr. of 1919 ed. Set. lib. bdg. 400.00 (ISBN 0-89987-862-8). Darby Bks.

George, Anne, ed. see Valvano, James T.

George, Anthea, jt. auth. see Cisek, James.

George, Aurelia, jt. ed. see Anderson, Kym.

George, B. & Defoe, M., eds. Volume International Discography of the New Wave. (Illus.). 264p. (Orig.). (YA) 1980. pap. 7.95 (ISBN 0-9605778-0-7). One Ten Records.

George, B. & DeFoe, Martha, eds. International Discography of the New Wave, Vol. 2. (Illus.). 736p. 1982. pap. 12.95 (ISBN 0-7119-0050-7, Pub. by Omnibus Press). One Ten Records.

George, B. J., ed. see Hall, Jerome, et al.

George, B. James. A Practical Guide to the Comprehensive Crime Control Act of 1984. 1985. 45.00 (ISBN 0-317-29417-2, #H43864). HarBraceJ.

George, B. James, Jr. Criminal Procedure Sourcebook: Including Nineteen Seventy-Nine Supplement. LC 76-14580. 1979. Set. text ed. 60.00 (ISBN 0-686-59539-4, C6-1166); suppl. alone 25.00 (ISBN 0-686-59540-8). PLI.

George, Barbara. Bicycle Road Racing. LC 77-8096. (Superwheels & Thrill Sports Bks.). (Illus.). 36p. 1977. PLB 8.95g (ISBN 0-8225-0418-9). Lerner Pubns.

--Bicycle Track Racing. LC 77-8732. (Superwheels & Thrill Sports Bks.). (Illus.). 36p. 1977. PLB 8.95 (ISBN 0-8225-0419-7). Lerner Pubns.

George, Barbara, jt. auth. see Simes, Jack.

George, Barbara, jt. auth. see Doughty, Tom.

George, Bill. Drive-in Madness: The Jiggle Movies. Michelucci, Robert V., ed. (Illus.). 128p. 1985. pap. 14.95 (ISBN 0-911137-04-1). Imagine.

--Eroticism in the Fantasy Cinema. Michelucci, R. V., ed. (Illus.). 128p. (Orig.). 1984. write for info. (ISBN 0-911137-01-7); pap. 14.95. Imagine.

--His Story: The Life of Christ. LC 76-53630. 1977. pap. text ed. 3.95 (ISBN 0-87148-406-4). Pathway Pr.

George, C. Exercises in Integration. (Problem Bks. in Mathemetatics). (Illus.). 560p. 1984. 38.00 (ISBN 0-387-96060-0). Springer-Verlag.

George C., intro. by. Omaha Beachhead: June 6-June 13 1944. (Combat Arms Ser.: No. 8). (Illus.). 212p. 1984. Repr. of 1947 ed. 26.50x (ISBN 0-89839-076-1). Battery Pr.

George Camp Keiser Library of the Middle East Institute. Catalog of the Middle East Institute Library. 2290p. 1984. lib. bdg. 650.00 (ISBN 0-8161-0430-1, Hall Library). G K Hall.

George, Carol, ed. Remember the Ladies: New Perspectives on Women in American History. (Illus.). 256p. 1975. 14.95x (ISBN 0-8156-0110-7). Syracuse U Pr.

George, Catherine. Dream of Midsummer. (Harlequin Romances Ser.). 192p. 1983. pap. 1.75 (ISBN 0-373-02571-8). Harlequin Bks.

--Gilded Cage. (Harlequin Presents Ser.). 192p. 1983. pap. 1.95 (ISBN 0-373-10640-8). Harlequin Bks.

--Reluctant Paragon. (Harlequin Romances Ser.). 192p. 1983. pap. 1.75 (ISBN 0-373-02535-1). Harlequin Bks.

George, Charles & George, Katherine. The Protestant Mind of the English Reformation, 1570-1640. LC 77-130746. pap. 116.00 (ISBN 0-317-08472-0, 2000986). Bks Demand UMI.

George, Charles F. Topics in Clinical Pharmacology. 266p. 1980. 20.25x (ISBN 0-85313-798-6, Pub. by Kimpton England). State Mutual Bk.

George, Charles H. Revolution: European Radicals from Hus to Lenin. 1971. pap. 8.35x (ISBN 0-673-05984-7). Scott F.

George, Christopher S., ed. Candamaharosana Tantra. (American Oriental Ser.: Vol. 56). 1974. pap. 15.00x (ISBN 0-940490-56-0). Am Orient Soc.

George, Claude. Rise of British West Africa. new ed. 468p. 1968. 35.00x (ISBN 0-7146-1667-2, F Cass Co). Biblio Dist.

--Supervision in Action. 4th ed. 1985. text ed. 23.95 (ISBN 0-8359-7160-0); instr's manual avail. (ISBN 0-8359-7161-9). Reston.

George, Claude S., Jr. The History of Management Thought. 2nd ed. 256p. 1972. pap. text ed. 18.95 (ISBN 0-13-390187-4). P-H.

--Management for Business & Industry. Orig. Title: Management in Industry. 1970. text ed. 29.95 (ISBN 0-13-548578-9). P-H.

George, Conrad. Open a New Door. (Illus.). 1979. pap. 3.50 (ISBN 0-87516-374-2). De Vorss.

GEorge, D., jt. auth. see Spache.

George, D. J. Vida Maritima: Enciclopedia Ilustrada de los Animales Invertebrados del Mar. Jordana, R., ed. 288p. (Span.). 1979. 75.00 (ISBN 84-313-0624-6, S-37587). French & Eur.

George, Dan & Hirnschall, Helmut. My Spirit Soars. (Illus.). 96p. 19.95 (ISBN 0-88839-154-4). Hancock House.

George, Daniel. A Book of Anecdotes. 1957. lib. bdg. 25.00 (ISBN 0-8414-4645-8). Folcroft.

--Pick & Choose: A Gallimaufry Composed. 1979. Repr. of 1936 ed. lib. bdg. 30.00 (ISBN 0-8495-2028-2). Arden Lib.

George, David & Sharp, Roy. Marks of Maturity. 106p. 1981. pap. text ed. 2.95 (ISBN 0-88428-049-7). Parchment Pr.

George, David, jt. auth. see Olgilvie, Eric.

George, David B. & Taylor, John C., eds. Copper Smelting - An Update: Proceedings AIME Annual Meeting, Dallas, TX, 1982. (Illus.). 345p. 30.00 (ISBN 0-89520-387-1); members 20.00 (ISBN 0-317-36207-0); student members 10.00 (ISBN 0-317-36208-9). ASM.

George, David C. Layman's Bible Book Commentary: Second Corinthians, Galatians, Ephesians, Vol. 21. LC 78-74202. 1980. 5.75 (ISBN 0-8054-1191-7). Broadman.

George, David J. Common Medicines: Preliminary. 1979. pap. text ed. 8.95 (ISBN 0-317-06259-X). W H Freeman.

George, David L. Freddie Freightliner Goes to Hawaii. Murphy, Carol, ed. (Illus.). (gr. k-6). 1983. 6.50 (ISBN 0-89868-136-7); pap. 3.95 (ISBN 0-89868-137-5). ARO PUB.

--Freddie Freightliner Goes to Hollywood. Murphy, Carol, ed. (Illus.). (gr. k-6). 1982. 6.50 (ISBN 0-89868-130-8); pap. 3.95 (ISBN 0-686-91784-7). ARO Pub.

--Freddie Freightliner Goes to Kennedy Space Center. Murphy, Carol, ed. (Illus.). (gr. k-6). 1982. 5.95 (ISBN 0-89868-134-0); pap. 6.50 (ISBN 0-89868-133-2). ARO PUB.

--Freddie Freightliner Helps the Fire Department. Murphy, Carol, ed. (Illus.). (gr. k-6). 1983. 6.50 (ISBN 0-89868-134-0); pap. 3.95 (ISBN 0-89868-135-9). ARO PUB.

--Freddie Freightliner Learns to Talk. Murphy, Carol, ed. (Illus.). (gr. k-6). 1981. 6.50 (ISBN 0-89868-126-X); pap. 3.95 (ISBN 0-89868-127-8). ARO PUB.

--Freddie Freightliner Learns to Talk. (Adventures of Freddie Freightliner Ser.). (Illus.). 32p. (gr. k-3). 1983. 10.60 (ISBN 0-516-02495-7). Childrens.

--Freddie Freightliner Series. Murphy, Carol, ed. (Illus.). (gr. k-6). 35.00 set (ISBN 0-89868-124-3); pap. 23.00 set (ISBN 0-89868-125-1). ARO PUB.

--Freddie Freightliner to the Rescue. Murphy, Carol, ed. (Illus.). (gr. k-6). 1982. 6.50 (ISBN 0-89868-130-8); pap. 3.95 (ISBN 0-89868-131-6). ARO PUB.

George, David L. (Compiler) Family Book of Best Loved Poems. 1952. 15.95 (ISBN 0-385-01421-X). Doubleday.

George, Demetra. The Asteroid Goddesses. (Orig.). 1985. pap. 11.95 (ISBN 0-917086-75-9). A C S Pubns Inc.

George, Denise. The Christian As a Consumer. LC 83-26062. (Potentials: Guides for Productive Living Ser.,: Vol. 3). 114p. (Orig.). 1984. pap. 7.95 (ISBN 0-664-24518-8). Westminster.

--Dear Daughter. 1985. 6.95 (ISBN 0-8054-5663-5). Broadman.

--The Student Marriage. LC 82-72230. (Orig.). 1983. pap. 4.95 (ISBN 0-8054-6939-7, 4269-39). Broadman.

George, Denise & George, Timothy. Dear Unborn Child. LC 83-71714. 1984. pap. 4.95 (ISBN 0-8054-5658-9). Broadman.

George, Diana H. Blake & Freud. LC 80-11244. (Illus.). 288p. 1980. 24.50x (ISBN 0-8014-1286-2). Cornell U Pr.

George, Donald E. Israeli Occupation: International Law & Political Realities. 1980. 12.50 (ISBN 0-682-49439-9). Exposition Pr FL.

George, E. Madison. Which Way, Young Americans. LC 62-8187. (Orig.). 1962. pap. 2.00 (ISBN 0-87004-051-0). Caxton.

George, Emery. Holderlin's "Ars Poetica". A Part-Rigorous Analysis of Information Structure in the Late Hymns. (De Proprietatibu Litterarum Ser. Practica: No. 32). text ed. 60.80x (ISBN 90-2792-381-7). Mouton.

--Kate's Death: Poems. 1980. 8.95 (ISBN 0-88233-583-9); pap. 3.95 (ISBN 0-88233-584-7). Ardis Pubs.

--The Poetry of Miklos Radnoti: A Comparative Study. 1000p. 1986. 110.00 (ISBN 0-943828-63-5). Karz-Cohl Pub.

George, Emery, ed. Contemporary East European Poetry: An Anthology. 456p. 1983. 35.00 (ISBN 0-88233-747-5). Ardis Pubs.

George, Emery, tr. see Radnoti, Miklos.

George, Emery E., jt. ed. see Frank, Luanne T.

George, Emery E., ed. see Holderlin Bicentennial Symposium, University of Michigan, 1970.

George, Emily, ed. Martha W. Griffiths. LC 81-40922. 302p. (Orig.). 1982. lib. bdg. 27.25 (ISBN 0-8191-2347-1); pap. text ed. 13.25 (ISBN 0-8191-2348-X). U Pr of Amer.

George, Ethel T. Painting Flowers with Watercolor. LC 80-24195. (Illus.). 128p. 1985. pap. 16.95 (ISBN 0-89134-079-3). North Light Pub.

George F. Nuclear Theory, Nineteen Eighty-One: Proceedings of the Nuclear Theory Summer Workshop Institute of Theoretical Physics, Santa Barbara, CA, August 1981. xiii, 296p. 1982. 33.00x (ISBN 9971-950-06-5, Pub. by World Sci Singapore); pap. 19.00x (ISBN 9971-950-07-3, Pub. by World Sci Singapore). Taylor & Francis.

George, F. H. Artificial Intelligence: Its Philosophy & Neural Context. (Studies in Cybernetics: Vol. 9). 222p. 1985. text ed. 39.00 (ISBN 0-317-26990-9). Gordon.

--The Brain As a Computer. 2nd ed. 1973. text ed. 50.00 (ISBN 0-08-017022-6). Pergamon.

--Casino Games with the Commodore 64. (Illus.). 160p. 1984. pap. 13.95 (ISBN 0-00-383013-6, Pub. by Collins England). Sheridan.

--Computer Arithmetic. 1966. pap. 8.50 (ISBN 0-08-011463-6). Pergamon.

--Football Pools with the Commodore 64. (Illus.). 160p. 1984. pap. 13.95 (Pub. by Collins England). Sheridan.

--The Foundations of Cybernetics. 300p. 1977. text ed. 46.25x (ISBN 0-677-05340-1). Gordon.

--Horse Racing with the Commodore 64. (Illus.). 160p. (Orig.). 1985. pap. 13.95 (ISBN 0-246-12577-2, Pub. by Collins England). Sheridan.

--An Introduction to Digital Computing. 1966. pap. 7.75 (ISBN 0-08-011280-3). Pergamon.

--Machine Takeover: The Growing Threat to Human Freedom in a Computer-Controlled Society. LC 76-27722. 208p. 1977. text ed. 24.00 (ISBN 0-08-021229-8). Pergamon.

--Philosophical Foundations of Cybernetics. 1979. 28.00 (ISBN 0-9961002-6-1, Pub. by Abacus England). Heyden.

--Precision, Language & Logic. 224p. 1977. text ed. 34.00 (ISBN 0-08-019650-0). Pergamon.

--The Science of Investment. (Information Technology Ser.). 250p. 1984. 27.00 (ISBN 0-9901003-9-1, Pub. by Abacus England). Heyden.

--The Science of Philosophy. 336p. 1981. 49.95 (ISBN 0-677-05550-1). Gordon.

George, Frances V. De see Osborne, Richard H. & De George, Frances V.

George, Frank & Johnson, Les, eds. Purposive Behaviour & Teleological Explanations. (Studies in Cybernetics: Vol. 8). 334p. 1985. text ed. 64.00 (ISBN 2-88124-110-7). Gordon.

George, Frank, compiled by see Paritsis, N. C. & Stewart, D. J.

George, Frank, compiled by see Rosenberg, M. J.

George, Frank, tr. see Harand, Joseph.

George, Frank L. Standard Forgings: Collected Poems. 1978. 10.00 (ISBN 0-88233-280-5); pap. 3.50 (ISBN 0-88233-390-9). Ardis Pubs.

George, Gerald & Rights, Mollie. The Moveable Fleet: A Boatwatcher's Guide to the San Francisco Bay. Stewart, Jay, ed. LC 78-75162. (Illus.). 1979. pap. 4.95 (ISBN 0-89395-016-5). Cal Living Bks.

George, Gerald S. Biomechanics of Women's Gymnastics. 1980. text ed. 23.95 (ISBN 0-13-077461-8). P-H.

George, Harrison. I. W. W. Trial, Story of the Greatest Trial in Labor's History by One of the Defendants. LC 70-90177. (Mass Violence in America Ser.). 11.50 (ISBN 0-405-01313-2). Ayer Co Pubs.

George, Henry. Complete Works, 10 vols. LC 75-168107. Repr. of 1911 ed. Set. 325.00 (ISBN 0-404-02800-4); 32.50 ea. AMS Pr.

--Labor Question. abr. ed. Orig. Title: Condition of Labor. 47p. 1959. pap. 0.25 (ISBN 0-911312-22-6). Schalkenbach.

--Land Question: Property in Land & the Condition of Labor. 348p. 1982. 10.00 (ISBN 0-911312-59-5). Schalkenbach.

--A Perplexed Philosopher. 276p. (Avail. in Span). 1965. 3.00 (ISBN 0-911312-12-9). Schalkenbach.

--Progress & Poverty. LC 79-12191. 1979. 10.00 (ISBN 0-914016-60-1). Phoenix Pub.

--Progress & Poverty. 599p. (Avail. in Danish, Dutch, Fr., Ger., Heb., It., Korean, Span., & Swedish). 1979. centennial ed. 10.00 (ISBN 0-914016-60-1). Schalkenbach.

--Progress & Poverty. 599p. 1984. pap. 5.00 (ISBN 0-911312-58-7). Schalkenbach.

--Progress & Poverty. 220p. 1980. pap. 3.00 abridged (ISBN 0-911312-10-2). Schalkenbach.

--Protection or Free Trade. LC 80-14436. 352p. 1980. 10.00x (ISBN 0-914016-70-9). Phoenix Pub.

--Protection or Free Trade. 335p. (Avail. in Fr., Ger., Span.). 1980. 10.00 (ISBN 0-914016-70-9). Schalkenbach.

--Science of Political Economy. 545p. (Also avail. in Span.). 1981. 10.00 (ISBN 0-911312-51-X). Schalkenbach.

--Social Problems. 310p. (Avail. in Ger. Span.). 1981. 8.00 (ISBN 0-911312-17-X); pap. 3.00 (ISBN 0-911312-52-8). Schalkenbach.

George, Henry, Jr. Henry George. LC 80-27958. (American Men & Women of Letters Ser.). Orig. Title: The Life of Henry George. 640p. 1982. pap. 10.95 (ISBN 0-87754-164-7). Chelsea Hse.

--The Life of Henry George. 75.00 (ISBN 0-8490-0532-9). Gordon Pr.

--The Life of Henry George. 634p. 1960. 5.00 (ISBN 0-911312-24-2). Schalkenbach.

George, Herman, Jr. American Race Relations Theory: A Review of Four Models. 272p. lib. bdg. 25.00 (ISBN 0-8191-3813-4); pap. text ed. 13.25 (ISBN 0-8191-3814-2). U Pr of Amer.

George, Isaac. Heroes & Incidents of the Mexican War. LC 85-4693. (Sun Dance Reprints: No. 1). 296p. 1982. lib. bdg. 22.95x (ISBN 0-89370-718-X). Borgo Pr.

George, J. C. & Berger, Andrew J. Avian Myology. 1966. 74.50 (ISBN 0-12-280150-4). Acad Pr.

George, J. D., et al, eds. Underwater Photography & Television for Scientists. (Illus.). 250p. 1985. 26.95 (ISBN 0-19-854141-4). Oxford U Pr.

George, J. David & George, Jennifer. Marine Life: An Illustrated Encyclopedia of Invertebrates in the Sea. LC 79-10976. 288p. 1979. 69.95 (ISBN 0-471-05675-8, Pub. by Wiley-Interscience). Wiley.

George, James E. Law & Emergency Care. LC 80-14606. 284p. 1980. 31.95 (ISBN 0-8016-1834-7). Mosby.

George, James L., ed. Problems of Sea Power As We Approach the Twenty-First Century. LC 78-18422. 1978. 16.25 (ISBN 0-8447-2133-6); pap. 8.25 (ISBN 0-8447-2132-8). Am Enterprise.

--The U. S. Navy: Perspectives on Its Future. (WVSS in Military Affairs Ser.). 300p. 1985. pap. text ed. 19.85x (ISBN 0-8133-7052-3). Westview.

George, James L., jt. ed. see Woolley, Bruce H.

George, James N., et al, eds. Platelet Membrane Glycoproteins. 412p. 1985. 59.50x (ISBN 0-306-41857-6, Plenum Pr). Plenum Pub.

George, James Z. Political History of Slavery in the U. S. LC 77-92429. 1915. 15.00x (ISBN 0-403-00162-5). Scholarly.

--The Political History of Slavery in the United States, 2 bks. Incl. Bk. 1. The Political History of Slavery in the United States; Bk. 2. Legislative History of Reconstruction. LC 73-83944. (Black Heritage Library Collection Ser). Repr. of 1915 ed. Set. 17.00 (ISBN 0-8369-8577-X). Ayer Co Pubs.

--Political History of Slavery in the United States. LC 72-181080. Repr. of 1915 ed. 22.50x (ISBN 0-8371-1991-X, GEP). Greenwood.

George, Janet M., ed. Brunch Basket. LC 84-81269. (Illus.). 339p. 1985. 14.95 (ISBN 0-9613563-0-8). Rockford Lea.

George, Jean. Going to the Sun. LC 75-25403. 176p. (gr. 7 up). 1976. PLB 9.89 (ISBN 0-06-021942-4). HarpJ.

--My Side of the Mountain. pap. 4.95 (ISBN 0-525-45030-0). Dutton.

George, Jean C. The Cry of the Crow. LC 79-2016. 160p. (gr. 5 up). 1980. o.p 7.95 (ISBN 0-06-021956-4); PLB 10.89 (ISBN 0-06-021957-2). HarpJ.

--The Cry of the Crow. LC 79-2016. (A Trophy Bk.). 160p. (gr. 5 up). 1982. pap. 2.84i (ISBN 0-06-440131-6, Trophy). HarpJ.

--The Grizzly Bear with the Golden Ears. LC 80-7908. (Illus.). 32p. (ps-3). 1982. 10.53i (ISBN 0-06-021965-3); PLB 10.89 (ISBN 0-06-021966-1). HarpJ.

--Hook a Fish, Catch a Mountain. (gr. 4-7). 1975. 9.95 (ISBN 0-525-32155-1). Dutton.

--How to Talk to Your Animals. (Illus.). 320p. 1985. 15.95 (ISBN 0-15-142200-1). HarBraceJ.

--Julie of the Wolves. LC 72-76509. (Illus.). 176p. (gr. 7 up). 1972. 10.53i (ISBN 0-06-021943-2); PLB 11.89 (ISBN 0-06-021944-0). HarpJ.

--Julie of the Wolves. LC 72-76509. (gr. 7 up). pap. 2.50 (ISBN 0-06-440058-1, Trophy). HarpJ.

--My Side of the Mountain. (Illus.). (gr. 4-9). 1967. 10.95 (ISBN 0-525-35530-8, 01063-320). Dutton.

--One Day in the Alpine Tundra. LC 82-45590. (Illus.). 48p. (gr. 5-7). 1984. 10.53i (ISBN 0-690-04325-2); PLB 10.89g (ISBN 0-690-04326-0). Crowell Jr Bks.

--One Day in the Desert. LC 82-45924. (Illus.). 48p. (gr. 5-7). 1983. 10.53i (ISBN 0-690-04340-6); PLB 10.89g (ISBN 0-690-04341-4). Crowell Jr Bks.

--River Rats, Inc. LC 78-12318. (gr. 4-7). 1979. 8.95 (ISBN 0-525-38455-3). Dutton.

--River Rats, Inc. 128p. (gr. 7 up). 1983. pap. 1.95 (ISBN 0-590-32118-8, Vagabond). Scholastic Inc.

--The Summer of the Falcon. new ed. (gr. 5 up). 1979. pap. 2.95 (ISBN 0-06-440095-6, Trophy). HarpJ.

--The Talking Earth. LC 82-48850. 160p. (gr. 6 up). 1983. 9.57i (ISBN 0-06-021975-0); PLB 9.89g (ISBN 0-06-021976-9). HarpJ.

--Who Really Killed Cock Robin. (gr. 4-7). 1971. 8.95 (ISBN 0-525-42700-7). Dutton.

--The Wild, Wild Cookbook: A Guide for Young Wild-Food Foragers. LC 82-45187. (Illus.). 192p. (gr. 5 up). 1982. 10.53i (ISBN 0-690-04314-7); PLB 11.89g (ISBN 0-690-04315-5); pap. 4.76i (ISBN 0-690-04319-8). Crowell Jr Bks.

--The Wounded Wolf. LC 76-58711. (Illus.). (ps-3). 1978. PLB 10.89 (ISBN 0-06-021950-5). HarpJ.

George, Jennifer, jt. auth. see George, J. David.

George, John, jt. auth. see Hall, Rufus G.

George, John, jt. auth. see Holloway, Harry.

George, John A., jt. auth. see Daellenbach, Hans G.

George, John N. English Pistols & Revolvers. 1979. 20.00x (ISBN 0-87556-153-5). Saifer.

George, Jon. Day in the Forest. 16p. (gr. 3-6). 1973. pap. text ed. 5.95 (ISBN 0-87487-629-X). Birch Tree Gr.

--Day in the Jungle. 16p. (gr. 3-6). 1968. pap. text ed. 5.95 (ISBN 0-87487-630-3). Birch Tree Gr.

--Reader Parts, 2 sets. Goss, Louise, ed. (Frances Clark Library for Piano Students). (Illus.). 32p. (Orig.). (gr. k-12). pap. text ed. 5.95 pts. A & B, 1969 (ISBN 0-87487-186-7); pap. text ed. 5.95 pts. C & D, 1974 (ISBN 0-87487-187-5). Birch Tree Gr.

--Two at One Piano. Clark, Frances & Goss, Louise, eds. Incl. Bk 1. 1969. pap. text ed. 5.95 (ISBN 0-87487-141-7); Bk 2. 1972. pap. text ed. 5.95 (ISBN 0-87487-142-5); Bk 3. 1976. pap. text ed. 5.95 (ISBN 0-87487-143-3). (Frances Clark Library for Piano Students Ser.). pap. Birch Tree Gr.

George, Jon & Kraehenbuehl, David. Supplementary Solos: Levels 3 & 4. Clark, Francis & Goss, Louise, eds. (Frances Clark Library for Piano Students). 48p. (gr. k-12). 1974. pap. 7.95 (ISBN 0-87487-140-9). Birch Tree Gr.

George, Joyce. Judicial Opinion Writing Handbook. 2nd ed. LC 85-45008. 300p. 1985. lib. bdg. write for info. (ISBN 0-89941-429-X). W S Hein.

George, Judith. Do You See What I See. 160p. 1982. 9.95 (ISBN 0-399-20912-3, Putnam). Putnam Pub Group.

George, Judith S. Do You See What I See? (gr. 6 up). 1983. pap. 1.95 (ISBN 0-451-12576-2, Sig Vista). NAL.

George, Judith St. In the Shadow of the Bear. 144p. 1986. pap. 2.25 (ISBN 0-425-08442-6). Berkley Pub.

George, Judith St. see St. George, Judith.

George, Julia. Nursing Theories: The Base for Professional Nursing Practice. 2nd ed. (Illus.). 304p. 1985. pap. text ed. 15.95 (ISBN 0-13-627407-2). P-H.

George, Juliette L., jt. auth. see George, Alexander L.

George, K. D. & Shorey, John. The Allocation of Resources: Theory & Policy. (Illus.). 1978. text ed. 25.00x o. p. (ISBN 0-04-300073-8); pap. text ed. 12.50x (ISBN 0-04-300074-6). Allen Unwin.

George, Katharine, et al. The Dog Watch & Other Stories. LC 81-67685. (Illus.). 48p. (Orig.). (gr. 4-6). 1981. pap. 7.70 (ISBN 0-9607638-0-5). Cobblestone Pub.

George, Katherine, jt. auth. see George, Charles.

George, Kathleen. Rhythm in Drama. LC 79-24432. 1980. 17.95x (ISBN 0-8229-3416-7); pap. 6.95x (ISBN 0-8229-5316-1). U of Pittsburgh Pr.

George, Kay F. The Atlantic Ocean: History & Oceanography of the Bridge Between Two Worlds. 1977. lib. bdg. 69.95 (ISBN 0-8490-1462-X). Gordon Pr.

George, Kenneth D. & Joll, Caroline. Industrial Organization: Competition, Growth & Structural Change. 3rd ed. (Illus.). 336p. 1981. text ed. 35.00x (ISBN 0-04-338095-6); pap. text ed. 16.50x (ISBN 0-04-338096-4). Allen Unwin.

George, Kenneth D. & Ward, T. S. The Structure of Industry in the EEC. LC 75-319762. (University of Cambridge, Dept. of Applied Economics, Occasional Papers: 43). pap. 20.80 (ISBN 0-317-26403-6, 2024460). Bks Demand UMI.

George, Kenneth D., et al. Science Investigations for Elementary School Teachers. 1974. pap. text ed. 6.95x (ISBN 0-669-83154-9). Heath.

George, Leland E. Exactness in Bridge Bidding. 1982. 6.95 (ISBN 0-8062-1909-2). Carlton.

George, Levy, jt. auth. see Levy, Penny A.

George, Linda K. Role Transitions in Later Life. LC 79-25239. (Social Gerontology Ser.). (Orig.). 1980. pap. text ed. 9.00 pub net (ISBN 0-8185-0382-3). Brooks-Cole.

George, Linda K. & Bearon, Lucille B. Quality of Life in Older Persons: Meaning & Measurement. LC 80-13645. 238p. 1980. text ed. 24.95 (ISBN 0-87705-488-6). Human Sci Pr.

George, Llewellyn. The A to Z Horoscope Maker & Delineator. 13th, rev. ed. Bytheriver, Marylee, ed. LC 83-80177. (Illus.). 592p. (Orig.). 1984. 12.95 (ISBN 0-87542-264-0). Llewellyn Pubns.

--The New A to Z Horoscope Maker & Delineator. 14th, rev. ed. Bytheriver, Marylee, ed. LC 83-80177. (Illus.). 592p. 1985. pap. 12.95 (ISBN 0-87542-264-0, L-264). Llewellyn Pubns.

George, M. B. Basic Sailing. LC 78-184227. (Illus.). 1978. pap. 6.95 (ISBN 0-910990-03-4). Hearst Bks.

--Basic Sailing. rev. ed. (Illus.). 110p. 1984. 8.95 (ISBN 0-688-03567-1). Morrow.

George, M. Dorothy. England in Johnson's Day. LC 72-7079. (Select Bibliographies Reprint Ser.). 1972. Repr. of 1928 ed. 20.00 (ISBN 0-8369-6933-2). Ayer Co Pubs.

--England in Johnson's Day. LC 73-16145. 1928. lib. bdg. 20.00 (ISBN 0-8414-4479-X). Folcroft.

--London Life in the Eighteenth Century. 452p. 1985. pap. 8.95 (ISBN 0-89733-147-8). Academy Chi Pubs.

--London Life in the 18th Century. 452p. pap. 8.95 (ISBN 0-89733-147-8). Academy Chi Pubs.

George, Malcom F. Introduction to Christian Counseling. (Parchment Psychology Ser.). 64p. 1975. pap. 2.25 (ISBN 0-88428-038-1). Parchment Pr.

George, Margaret. One Woman's "Situation". A Study of Mary Wollstonecraft. LC 70-100381. 182p. 1970. 14.50x (ISBN 0-252-00090-0). U of Ill Pr.

--The Warped Vision: British Foreign Policy, 1933-1939. LC 83-18493. xxiii, 238p. 1983. Repr. of 1965 ed. lib. bdg. 35.00x (ISBN 0-313-24257-7, GEWV). Greenwood.

George, Margaret L. Australia & Indonesian Revolution. 236p. 1980. 27.50x (ISBN 0-522-84209-7, Pub. by Melbourne Univ Pr Australia). Intl Spec Bk.

George, Mary. Kinder Bakker. (Illus.). 167p. 1983. Set of 12. spiral 84.00 (ISBN 0-9612710-1-9, Pub. by Steketee-Van Huis). Holland Jr Welfare.

George, Mary C. Mary Bonner: Impressions of a Printmaker. LC 81-52666. (Illus.). 127p. 1982. 30.00 (ISBN 0-911536-81-7). Trinity U Pr.

George, Mary D. England in Transition: Life & Work in the 18th Century. LC 75-41110. Repr. of 1931 ed. 19.50 (ISBN 0-404-14544-2). AMS Pr.

George, Mary L. What Can I Learn? (Illus.). 128p. (Orig.). 1983. pap. 5.25 (ISBN 0-9610930-0-5). Sisters.

George, Michael. The Statue of Liberty. (Illus.). 56p. (Orig.). 1985. pap. 14.95 (ISBN 0-8109-2294-0). Abrams.

George, Michael, jt. ed. see Greenbeg, Alan.

George, Nelson. The Michael Jackson Story. 192p. (Orig.). 1984. pap. 2.95 (ISBN 0-440-15592-4). Dell.

--Top of the Charts. LC 83-8108. (Illus.). 448p. (Orig.). 1983. pap. 15.95 (ISBN 0-8329-0260-8). New Century.

George, Nelson, et al. Fresh: Hip Hop Don't Stop. 1985. write for info. (ISBN 0-394-54487-0); pap. 7.95 (ISBN 0-394-73739-3). Random.

George, Otto. Eskimo Medicine Man. LC 78-73291. (Illus.). 324p. 1979. pap. 7.95 (ISBN 0-87595-062-0). Oreg Hist Soc.

George P. Rowell & Staff. The Men Who Advertise. Asseal, Henry, ed. LC 78-299. (Century of Marketing Ser.). 1978. Repr. of 1870 ed. lib. bdg. 66.00x (ISBN 0-405-11174-6). Ayer Co Pubs.

George, Patricia L., ed. The Mood of American Youth. 72p. (Orig.). 1984. pap. 6.00 (ISBN 0-88210-155-2). Natl Assn Principals.

George, Patricia L., ed. see Maidment, Robert & Bullock, William.

George, Patricia L., ed. see Strope, John L., Jr.

George, Paul, jt. auth. see Alexander, William M.

George, Paul S. Theory & School. 106p. 1983. 5.95 (ISBN 0-318-17879-6). Natl Middle Schl.

George, Paul S. & Lawrence, Gordon D. Handbook for Middle School Teaching. 1982. pap. 15.95 (ISBN 0-673-16024-6). Scott F.

George, Peter. The Emergence of Industrial America: Strategic Factors in American Economic Growth Since 1870. LC 82-5873. 232p. 1982. 39.50x (ISBN 0-87395-578-1); pap. 12.95x (ISBN 0-87395-579-X). State U NY Pr.

--Ohio Tax Handbook 1985. price not set. P-H.

George, Peter C., jt. auth. see Dickey, Thomas S.

George, Peter J. Government Subsidies & the Construction of the Canadian Pacific Railway. Bruchey, Stuart, ed. LC 80-1284. (Railroads Ser.). (Illus.). 1981. lib. bdg. 18.00x (ISBN 0-405-13757-5). Ayer Co Pubs.

George Philip & Son Staff. Franklin Watts Atlas of North America & the World. 288p. 1984. 22.95 (ISBN 0-531-09830-3). Watts.

George Philip Group, ed. Illustrated Atlas of the World. 208p. 1981. 75.00x (ISBN 0-540-05371-6, Pub. by Philip Group England). State Mutual Bk.

George, Phyllis & Adler, Bill. The I Love America Diet. LC 82-51183. (Illus.). 192p. 1983. 11.95 (ISBN 0-688-01621-9). Morrow.

George, Pierre. Dictionnaire de la Geographie. 2nd ed. 460p. (Fr.). 1974. 47.50 (ISBN 0-686-57193-2, M-6267). French & Eur.

George, R. & Okun, R., eds. Annual Review of Pharmacology & Toxicology, Vol. 18. LC 61-5649. (Illus.). 1978. text ed. 20.00 (ISBN 0-8243-0418-7). Annual Reviews.

--Annual Review of Pharmacology & Toxicology, Vol. 19. LC 61-5649. (Illus.). 1979. text ed. 20.00 (ISBN 0-8243-0419-5). Annual Reviews.

--Annual Review of Pharmacology & Toxicology, Vol. 20. LC 61-5649. (Illus.). 1980. text ed. 20.00 (ISBN 0-8243-0420-9). Annual Reviews.

--Annual Review of Pharmacology & Toxicology, Vol. 21. LC 61-5649. (Illus.). 1981. text ed. 20.00 (ISBN 0-8243-0421-7). Annual Reviews.

--Annual Review of Pharmacology & Toxicology, Vol. 22. LC 61-5649. (Illus.). 1982. text ed. 22.00 (ISBN 0-8243-0422-5). Annual Reviews.

--Annual Review of Pharmacology & Toxicology, Vol. 23. LC 61-5649. (Illus.). 1983. text ed. 27.00 (ISBN 0-8243-0423-3). Annual Reviews.

George, R., jt. ed. see Zimmermann, E.

George, R., et al, eds. Annual Review of Pharmacology & Toxicology, Vol. 24. LC 61-5649. (Illus.). 1984. text ed. 27.00 (ISBN 0-8243-0424-1). Annual Reviews.

George, R. A., jt. auth. see Flegmann, G. W.

George, Raymond A. Vegetable Seed Production. 320p. 1985. text ed. 69.95 (ISBN 0-582-46090-5). Longman.

George, Richard R., adapted by see Dahl, Roald.

George, Richard T. de see De George, Richard T.

George, Richard T. De see De George, Richard T.

George, Rickey, jt. auth. see Dustin, Richard.

George, Rickey L. & Cristiani, Theresa S. Counseling: Theory & Practice. 2nd ed. (Illus.). 352p. 1986. text ed. 28.95 (ISBN 0-13-181298-X). P-H.

George, Rickey L. & Cristiani, Therese S. Theory, Methods, & Processes of Counseling & Psychotherapy. (Counseling & Human Development Ser.). (Illus.). 400p. 1981. 27.95 (ISBN 0-13-913905-2). P-H.

George, Robert, et al, eds. Annual Review of Pharmacology & Toxicology, Vol. 25. LC 61-5649. (Illus.). 799p. 1985. text ed. 27.00 (ISBN 0-8243-0425-X). Annual Reviews.

George, Robert E. Heirs of Tradition: Tributes of a New Zealander. LC 72-160920. (Biography Index Reprint Ser). Repr. of 1949 ed. 22.00 (ISBN 0-8369-8083-2). Ayer Co Pubs.

George, Rolf, ed. & tr. see Bolzano, Bernhard.

George, Rolf, tr. see Brentano, Franz.

George, Rolf A., tr. see Carnap, Rudolf.

George, Ronald B. & Light, Richard W., eds. Chest Medicine. (Illus.). 657p. 1982. 49.50 (ISBN 0-443-08109-3). Churchill.

George, Ronald M. California Superior Court Criminal Trial Judges' Benchbook, 1985. 995p. 1985. pap. text ed. write for info. (ISBN 0-314-94144-4). West Pub.

--California Superior Court Criminal Trial Judges' Deskbook, 1985. 987p. 1985. pap. text ed. write for info. (ISBN 0-314-94143-6). West Pub.

George, Rosemary. The Wines of Chablis. LC 84-50544. (Illus.). 1984. 29.95 (ISBN 0-85667-179-7, Pub. by P Wilson Pubs). Sotheby Pubns.

George, Roy. Targeting High-Growth Industry. 90p. (Orig.). 1983. pap. text ed. 6.00x (ISBN 0-88645-003-9, Pub. by Inst Res Pub Canada). Brookfield Pub Co.

George Sand Conference, 1st, Hofstra University. George Sand Papers: Conference Proceedings 1976. LC 79-21301. (Hofstra University Cultural & Intercultural Studies: Vol. 1). 34.50 (ISBN 0-404-61651-8). AMS Pr.

George Sand Conference, 2nd, Hofstra University, 1978. George Sand Paper: Conference Proceedings. LC 79-8844. (Hofstra University Cultural & Intercultural Studies: Vol. 2). 1981. 34.50 (ISBN 0-404-61652-6). AMS Pr.

George, Stefan. Works. LC 79-168108. (North Carolina. University. Studies in the Germanic Languages & Literature: No. 2). Repr. of 1949 ed. 34.00 (ISBN 0-404-50902-9). AMS Pr.

--The Works of Stefan George. 2nd ed. Marx, Olga & Morwitz, Ernst, trs. (Studies in the Germanic Languages & Literatures Ser.: No. 78). xxvi, 427p. 1974. 27.50 (ISBN 0-8078-8078-7). U of NC Pr.

George, Stephen. Politics & Policy in the European Community. LC 84-27315. 1985. 24.95x (ISBN 0-19-876164-3); 9.95x (ISBN 0-19-876165-1). Oxford U Pr.

George, Susan. Feeding the Few: Corporate Control of Food. 79p. 1979. pap. 4.95 (ISBN 0-89758-010-9). Inst Policy Stud.

--How the Other Half Dies: The Real Reasons for World Hunger. LC 76-52614. 328p. 1977. text ed. 15.00x (ISBN 0-916672-07-7); pap. text ed. 7.45x (ISBN 0-916672-08-5). Allanheld.

--Ill Fares the Land: Essays on Food, Hunger, & Power. LC 84-25124. 102p. 1985. pap. 5.95 (ISBN 0-89758-039-7). Inst Policy Stud.

--Warm Weather Recipes: Featuring Yogurt. 80p. 1985. 6.95 (ISBN 0-942084-13-6). LaFray Young Pub.

George, Susan & Paige, Nigel. Food for Beginners. (Illus.). 175p. pap. 4.95 (ISBN 0-906495-84-9). Inst Food & Develop.

--Food for Beginners. 12.95 (ISBN 0-906495-84-9); pap. 4.95 (ISBN 0-906495-85-7). Writers & Readers.

George, Ted. The Lives You Live As Revealed in the Heavens. LC 77-73594. 1977. 12.00 (ISBN 0-932782-00-0). Arthur Pubns.

--Uranus-Neptune-Pluto: The Spiritual Trinity. LC 79-53906. 225p. 1980. 12.00 (ISBN 0-932782-01-9). Arthur Pubns.

George, Terry, jt. auth. see Doll, John.

George, Terry, ed. The On-Your-Own Guide to Asia. rev.& 6th ed. LC 77-90889. (Illus.). 416p. (Orig.). 1983. pap. 6.95 (ISBN 0-8048-1406-6, Co-Pub by Volunteers in Asia). C E Tuttle.

George, Timothy. Theology of the Reformers. LC 82-71699. Date not set. 14.95 (ISBN 0-8054-6573-1). Broadman.

George, Timothy, jt. auth. see George, Denise.

George, Timothy F. John Robinson & the English Separatist Tradition. LC 82-14201. (National Association of Baptist Professors of Religion Dissertation Ser.: No. 1). 273p. 1982. text ed. 18.50x (ISBN 0-86554-043-8). Mercer Univ Pr.

--John Robinson & the English Separatist Tradition. (Dissertation Ser.: No. 1). 1982. pap. 18.50 (ISBN 0-86554-043-8). NABPR.

George, Uwe. In the Deserts of This Earth. Winston, Richard & Winston, Clara, trs. LC 78-23672. (Helen & Kurt Wolff Bks). (Illus.). 1979. 7.95 (ISBN 0-15-644435-6, Harv). HarBraceJ.

George, Vic & Wilding, Paul. Ideology & Social Welfare. (Radical Social Policy Ser.). 180p. 1975. pap. 6.95x (ISBN 0-7100-8290-8). Routledge & Kegan.

--Ideology & Social Welfare. 2nd ed. (Radical Social Policy Ser.). 192p. 1985. pap. 9.95 (ISBN 0-7102-0277-6). Routledge & Kegan.

--The Impact of Social Policy. (Radical Social Policy Ser.). 288p. (Orig.). 1984. pap. 14.95x (ISBN 0-7100-9670-4). Routledge & Kegan.

George, W. L. Anatole France. 1973. Repr. of 1915 ed. 15.00 (ISBN 0-8274-0399-2). R West.

--Literary Chapters. 1973. Repr. of 1918 ed. 25.00 (ISBN 0-8274-0202-3). R West.

--Novelist on Novels. LC 70-105790. 1970. Repr. of 1918 ed. 19.50x (ISBN 0-8046-0955-1, Pub. by Kennikat). Assoc Faculty Pr.

George, W. N., jt. auth. see Willis, Arthur.

George, W. N., jt. auth. see Willis, Arthur J.

George, W. R. The Making of Lloyd George. (Illus.). 184p. 1976. 17.50 (ISBN 0-208-01627-9, Archon). Shoe String.

George, Waldemar. Formes, 6 vols, Nos. 1-33. LC 70-69618. (Contemporary Art Ser). (Illus.). Repr. of 1929 ed. 230.00 (ISBN 0-405-00727-2); 44.00 ea. Vol. 1 (ISBN 0-405-00810-4). Vol. 2 (ISBN 0-405-00811-2). Vol. 3 (ISBN 0-405-00812-0). Vol. 4 (ISBN 0-405-00813-9). Vol. 5 (ISBN 0-405-00814-7). Vol. 6 (ISBN 0-405-00816-3). Ayer Co Pubs.

George Washington University. Challenges in Telecommunications & Information Handling for the New Administration. 212p. 1981. pap. text ed. 25.00x (ISBN 0-914894-30-7). Computer Sci.

George Washington University, ed. A Bibliography of American Immigration History. LC 77-3477. 1978. Repr. of 1956 ed. lib. bdg. 45.00x (ISBN 0-678-00748-9). Kelley.

George Washington University, et al. Bureaucracy at War: U. S. Performance in the Vietnam Conflict. 140p. 1985. 16.50 (ISBN 0-8133-0237-4). Westview.

George Washington University American Studies Program-Rose Bibliography Staff. Analytical Guide & Indexes to Alexander's Magazine: 1905-1909. LC 73-15076. 1974. lib. bdg. 45.00x (ISBN 0-8371-7177-6, RBALM). Greenwood.

--Analytical Guide & Indexes to the Colored American Magazine: 1900-1909, 2 vols. LC 73-15077. 1974. lib. bdg. 85.00x set (ISBN 0-8371-7176-8, RBCAM). Greenwood.

George Washington University American Studies Program-Rose Bibl. Analytical Guide & Indexes to The Crisis: 1910-1960, 3 vols. LC 73-15078. 1975. lib. bdg. 195.00x (ISBN 0-8371-7175-X, RBCRR). Greenwood.

George Washington University American Studies Program-Rose Bibliography Staff. Analytical Guide & Indexes to the Voice of the Negro: 1904-1907. LC 73-15079. 1974. lib. bdg. 65.00x (ISBN 0-8371-7174-1, RBVON). Greenwood.

George, Wesley C. The Biology of the Race Problem. 72p. 1979. pap. 2.00x (ISBN 0-911038-76-0, 132). Noontide.

George, Wilfred R. Tight Money Timing: The Impact of Interest Rates & the Federal Reserve on the Stock Market. LC 81-12131. 256p. 1982. 22.95 (ISBN 0-03-059272-0). Praeger.

George, William C., et al, eds. Educating the Gifted: Acceleration & Enrichment. LC 79-7559. (Hyman Blumberg Symposium on Research in Early Childhood Education). 256p. 1980. pap. text ed. 5.95x (ISBN 0-8018-2266-1). Johns Hopkins.

George, William C., et al, eds. see Hyman Blumberg Symposium on Research in Early Childhood Education, 1977.

George, William E. Stability & Trim for the Ship's Officer. 3rd, rev. ed. LC 82-74137. (Illus.). 359p. 1983. text ed. 15.00 (ISBN 0-87033-297-X). Cornell Maritime.

George, William H. The Scientist in Action: A Scientific Study of His Methods. LC 74-26264. (History, Philosophy & Sociology of Science Ser). 1975. Repr. 27.50x (ISBN 0-405-06592-2). Ayer Co Pubs.

George, William J., ed. see International Conference on Cyclic Nucleotide, 3rd, New Orleans, la., July 1977.

George, William R. & Marshall, Claudia E., eds. Developing New Services: Proceedings of. Symposium, October. 1983. Villanova University, Pa. LC 83-22668. 112p. (Orig.). 1984. pap. text ed. 6.00 (ISBN 0-87757-165-1). Am Mktg.

George, William R., jt. ed. see Donnelly, James H.

George, William T. Lo Que Dios Espera de Mi. LC 82-60829. 157p. (Orig.). 1983. pap. text ed. 6.95 (ISBN 0-87148-517-6). Pathway Pr.

--What God Expects of Me. LC 82-60828. 175p. (Orig.). 1982. pap. text ed. 6.95 (ISBN 0-87148-918-X). Pathway Pr.

George, Willis D. Surreptitious Entry. (Illus.). 214p. pap. 12.95x (ISBN 0-86695-006-0). Interserv Pub.

George III. Letters from George III to Lord Bute, 1756 to 1766. Sedgwick, Romney, ed. LC 81-4155. (Studies in Modern History). 277p. 1981. Repr. of 1939 ed. lib. bdg. 29.50x (ISBN 0-313-23039-0, SELG). Greenwood.

Georgel, Pierre. Drawings by Victor Hugo. (Illus.). 124p. (Orig.). 1984. pap. 5.95 (ISBN 0-901486-73-6, Pub. by Victoria & Albert Mus UK). Faber & Faber.

George Of Greece, Prince. Cretan Drama. 1959. 9.95 (ISBN 0-8315-0074-3). Speller.

Georges, Coedes. Textes d'Auteurs Grecs & Latines Relatifs a l'Extreme Orient. 1985. Repr. of 1910 ed. 20.00 (ISBN 0-89005-289-1). Ares.

Georges, Daniel E. The Geography of Crime & Violence: A Spatial & Ecological Perspective. Natoli, Salvatore, ed. LC 78-50967. (Resource Papers for College Geography Ser.). 1978. pap. text ed. 4.00 (ISBN 0-89291-128-X). Assn Am Geographers.

Georges, George C. Lagrangian & Hamiltonian Formulation of Plasma Problems. LC 70-141694. 74p. 1969. 17.50 (ISBN 0-403-04503-7). Scholarly.

Georges, Helen, tr. see Skoura, Sophia.

Georges, J. M., ed. Microscopic Aspects of Adhesion & Lubrication: Proceedings of the International Meeting of the Societe de Chimie Physique, 34th, Paris, September 14-18, 1981. (Tribology Ser.: Vol. 7). 1982. 138.50 (ISBN 0-444-42071-1). Elsevier.

Georges, Rip & Heimann, Jim. California Crazy: Roadside Vernacular Architecture. LC 79-24181. (Illus.). 144p. (Orig.). 1980. pap. 8.95 (ISBN 0-87701-171-0). Chronicle Bks.

Georges, Robert A. Greek-American Folk Beliefs & Narratives: Survivals & Living Tradition. Dorson, Richard M., ed. LC 80-727. (Folklore of the World Ser.). 1980. lib. bdg. 22.00x (ISBN 0-405-13314-6). Ayer Co Pubs.

Georges, Robert A. & Jones, Michael O. People Studying People: The Human Element in Fieldwork. LC 79-65767. 1980. 21.00x (ISBN 0-520-03989-0); pap. 5.95x (ISBN 0-520-04067-8, CAMPUS NO. 250). U of Cal Pr.

Georges, Robert A. & Stern, Stephen. American & Canadian Immigrant & Ethnic Folklore: An Annotated Bibliography. LC 80-9019. (Folklore Bibliographies Ser.). 300p. 1982. lib. bdg. 91.00 (ISBN 0-8240-9307-0). Garland Pub.

Georges, Thomas M. Business & Technical Writing Cookbook: How to Write Coherently on the Job. (Illus.). 250p. 1983. pap. 9.95 (ISBN 0-910687-00-5). Syntax Pubns.

Georges-Abeyie, Daniel E. The Criminal Justice System & Blacks. LC 84-9437. 1984. 20.00 (ISBN 0-87632-438-3). Boardman.

Georgescu, R., tr. see Popov, V. M.

Georgescu, V., jt. ed. see Dita, P.

Georgescu, Vlad. Political Ideas & the Enlightenment in the Romanian Principalities 1750-1831. (East European Monographs: No. 1). 232p. 1972. 25.00x (ISBN 0-231-02842-3). East Eur Quarterly.

Georgescu, Vlad, ed. Romania: Forty Years: 1944-1984. (The Washington Papers: Vol. XXIII, No. 115). 112p. 1985. 29.95 (ISBN 0-03-005537-7); pap. 8.95 (ISBN 0-03-005538-5). Praeger.

Georgescu-Roegen, Nicholas. Analytical Economics: Issues & Problems. LC 65-22061. (Illus.). 1966. 25.00x (ISBN 0-674-03150-4). Harvard U Pr.

--Energy & Economic Myths. LC 76-10265. 1977. pap. text ed. 14.50 (ISBN 0-08-021056-2). Pergamon.

--Entropy Law & the Economic Process. LC 78-115186. 1971. 27.50x (ISBN 0-674-25780-4); pap. 11.00x (ISBN 0-674-25781-2). Harvard U Pr.

Georgeson, B. see Petyt, George.

Georgeson, C. C. Reindeer & Caribou. facs. ed. (Shorey Historical Ser.). (Illus.). 24p. pap. 2.95 (ISBN 0-8466-0159-1, S159). Shorey.

Georget, Etienne-Jean. De la Folie: Considerations Sur Cette Maladie. LC 75-16705. (Classics in Psychiatry Ser.). (Fr.). 1976. Repr. of 1820 ed. 38.50x (ISBN 0-405-07431-X). Ayer Co Pubs.

Georgetown Law Journal Association. Crisis in Urban Government. 15.00. Anderson Pub Co.

Georgetown Law Journal Editors. Georgetown Law Journal: Media & the First Amendment in a Free Society. LC 73-81557. 248p. 1973. 15.00x (ISBN 0-87023-150-2); pap. 8.95x (ISBN 0-87023-151-0). U of Mass Pr.

Georgetown University, jt. auth. see Kilmarx, Robert A.

Georgetown University Center for Strategic & International Studies. From White House to Congress: Making the Government Work. LC 85-5701. write for info. Amer Bar Assn.

Georghiou, G. P. & Saito, Tetsuo, eds. Pest Resistance to Pesticides. 822p. 1983. 89.50x (ISBN 0-306-41246-2, Plenum Pr). Plenum Pub.
Georgi, Charlotte. The Arts & the World of Business. 2nd ed. LC 78-12103. 188p. 1979. lib. bdg. 16.00 (ISBN 0-8108-1174-X). Scarecrow.
Georgi, Charlotte & Bellanti, Robert, eds. Excellence in Library Management. (Journal of Library Administration: Vol. 6, No. 3, Fall 1985). 96p. 1985. text ed. price not set (ISBN 0-86656-478-0, B478). Haworth Pr.
Georgi, Dieter. The Opponents of Paul in Second Corinthians: A Study of Religious Propaganda in Late Antiquity. LC 84-47917. 464p. 1985. 29.95 (ISBN 0-8006-0729-5, 1-729). Fortress.
Georgi, H. Algebras in Particle Physics: From Isopin to Unified Theories. 1982. text ed. 26.95 (ISBN 0-8053-3153-0). Benjamin-Cummings.
Georgi, Howard. Weak Interactions & Modern Particle Theory. 1984. text ed. 29.95 (ISBN 0-8053-3163-8). Benjamin-Cummings.
Georgi, Jay R. Parasitology for Veterinarians. 3rd ed. LC 79-66033. (Illus.). 460p. 1980. text ed. 35.00 (ISBN 0-7216-4116-4). Saunders.
Georgia Bar Association. A Memorial of Logan Edwin Bleckley. LC 82-12459. 325p. 1982. 29.95x (ISBN 0-86554-039-X). Mercer Univ Pr.
Georgia Chapter the Society of Chartered Property & Casualty Underwriters. Municipal Risk Management. LC 79-84201. 1979. pap. text ed. 15.00 (ISBN 0-87218-301-7). Natl Underwriter.
Georgia Chapters, D. A. R. The Historical Collections Georgia Chapters, D. A. R. Old Bible Records & Land Lotteries, Vol. 4. 1969. Repr. of 1932 ed. 20.00 (ISBN 0-89308-011-X). Southern Hist Pr.
Georgia Colony. Colonial Records of the State of Georgia 1732-1782, 26 vols. in 28 pts. Candler, Allen D., ed. LC 70-138087. Repr. of 1916 ed. Set. 1820.00 (ISBN 0-404-07260-7); 65.00 ea. AMS Pr.
Georgia General Assembly. Confederate Records of the State of Georgia, 1860-1868, 6 Vols. Candler, Allen D., ed. LC 78-155622. Repr. of 1911 ed. Set. 422.50 (ISBN 0-404-07290-9); 84.50 ea. AMS Pr.
--Revolutionary Records of the State of Georgia, 1769-1784, 3 Vols. Candler, Allen D., ed. LC 72-965. Repr. of 1908 ed. Set. 225.00 (ISBN 0-404-07300-X); 75.00 ea. Vol. 1 (ISBN 0-404-07301-8). Vol. 2 (ISBN 0-404-07302-6). Vol. 3 (ISBN 0-404-07303-4). AMS Pr.
Georgia General Assembly Joint Committee to Investigate the Condition of the Georgia Penitentiary. Proceedings. facsimile ed. LC 74-3824. (Criminal Justice in America Ser.). 1974. Repr. of 1870 ed. 20.00x (ISBN 0-405-06144-7). Ayer Co Pubs.
Georgia Historical Society. The Eighteen Sixty Census of Chatham County, Georgia. 444p. 1980. 20.00 (ISBN 0-89308-124-8). Southern Hist Pr.
Georgia Hospitality & Travel Association & Smith, Susan H. Chefs' Secrets from Great Restaurants in Georgia. (Chef's Secrets Cookbooks Ser.). (Illus.). 208p. 1983. pap. 12.95 (ISBN 0-939944-06-5). Marmac Pub.
Georgia, Lowell, illus. Into the Wilderness. LC 77-93400. (Special Publications Ser. 13). (Illus.). 1978. 6.95 (ISBN 0-87044-252-X); lib. bdg. 8.50 (ISBN 0-87044-257-0). Natl Geog.
Georgia Technical Research Institute & Drucker, S. The Industrial Wood Energy Handbook. 272p. 1984. 37.50 (ISBN 0-442-22085-5). Van Nos Reinhold.
Georgia Writers' Program. Drums & Shadows: Survival Studies Among the Georgia Coastal Negroes. LC 73-3018. (Illus.). 274p. 1973. Repr. of 1940 ed. lib. bdg. 18.50x (ISBN 0-8371-6832-5, WRDS). Greenwood.
Georgiade, Nicholas G. Aesthetic Breast Surgery. (Illus.). 424p. 1983. lib. bdg. 72.00 (ISBN 0-683-03450-2). Williams & Wilkins.
--Breast Reconstruction Following Mastectomy. LC 79-15679. (Illus.). 268p. 1979. pap. text ed. 54.50 (ISBN 0-8016-1807-X). Mosby.
Georgiade, Nicholas G., jt. auth. see Sefrafin, Donald.
Georgiades, Thrasybulos. Greek Music, Verse & Dance. LC 73-4336. (Music Ser.). 157p. 1973. Repr. of 1955 ed. lib. bdg. 21.50 (ISBN 0-306-70561-3). Da Capo.
Georgiades, Thrysbulos. Music & Language: The Rise of Western Music Exemplified in Settings of the Mass. Gollner, Marie-Louise, tr. LC 82-4246. (Illus.). 150p. 1983. 29.95 (ISBN 0-521-23309-7); pap. 9.95 (ISBN 0-521-29902-0). Cambridge U Pr.
Georgiades, William D. & Clark, Donald C. Models for Individualized Instruction. LC 73-22495. text ed. 24.50x (ISBN 0-8422-5164-2). Irvington.
Georgiady, Nicholas & Romano, Louis. A Guide to an Effective Middle School. 450p. 1984. text ed. 39.50x (ISBN 0-8290-1457-8); pap. text ed. 19.95x (ISBN 0-8290-1458-6). Irvington.
Georgiady, Nicholas P. & Romano, Louis G. Focus on Censorship & the Middle School. 32p. pap. text ed. 2.50 (ISBN 0-918449-05-7). MI Middle Educ.
Georgian, Linda M. If You Really Want to do it Right: Try It the Wholistic Way. Janssen, Jacqueline, et al, eds. (Illus.). 300p. (Orig.). 1985. pap. 12.95 (ISBN 0-9611392-5-0). Georgian Intl.
Georgianna, Linda. The Solitary Self: Individuality in the Ancrene Wisse. LC 81-2190. 192p. 1981. text ed. 16.50x (ISBN 0-674-81751-6). Harvard U Pr.
Georgiev, V. St. Aliphatic Derivatives. (Survey of Drug Research in Immunologic Disease: Vol. 1). (Illus.). x, 542p. 1982. 208.75 (ISBN 3-8055-3503-1). S Karger.
--Noncondensed Aromatic Derivatives, Part II. (Survey of Drug Research in Immunologic Disease: Vol. 3). x, 582p. 1983. 208.75 (ISBN 3-8055-3687-9). S Karger.
--Noncondensed Aromatic Derivatives, Part III. (Survey of Drug Research in Immunologic Disease Series: Vol. 4). x, 334p. 1984. 123.50 (ISBN 3-8055-3799-9). S Karger.
--Noncondensed Aromatic Derivatives, Part IV. (Survey of Drug Research in Immunologic Disease: Vol. 7). x, 590p. 1985. 293.50 (ISBN 3-8055-4031-0). S Karger.
--Noncondensed Aromatic Derivatives: Pt. IV. (Survey of Drug Research in Immunologic Disease: Vol. 5). x, 606p. 1984. 208.75 (ISBN 3-8055-3856-1). S Karger.
Georgiev, V. St. see St. Georgiev, V.
Georgii, H. & Pankrath, J. Deposition of Atmospheric Pollutants. 1982. 37.00 (ISBN 90-277-1438-X, Pub. by Reidel Holland). Kluwer Academic.
Georgii, H. O. Canonical Gibbs Measures. (Lecture Notes in Mathematics: Vol. 760). 190p. 1979. pap. text ed. 16.00 (ISBN 0-387-09712-0). Springer-Verlag.
Georgii, H. W. & Jaeschke, W., eds. Chemistry of the Unpolluted & Polluted Troposphere. 1982. 63.00 (ISBN 90-277-1487-8, Pub. by Reidel Holland). Kluwer Academic.
Georgin. Comment S'Exprimer en Francais. 9.50 (ISBN 0-685-36704-5). French & Eur.
Georgin, Ch. Dictionnaire Grec-Francais. (Gr. & Fr.). pap. 14.95 (ISBN 0-686-57194-0, M-6268). French & Eur.
Georgiou, Constantine. Children & Their Literature. LC 69-10223. (Education Ser). 1969. text ed. 26.95x (ISBN 0-13-132167-6). P-H.
Georgiou, Hara & Tzedakis, Y. Excavations at Kastelli, Chania, Crete, 1976. (Occasional Papers: No. 2). (Illus.). 13p. 1978. 3.00x (ISBN 0-317-06620-X). UCLA Arch.
Georgiou, V. J. Commodore 64 Interfacing Blue Book. (Illus.). 186p. 1984. pap. 16.95 (ISBN 0-912911-01-8). Microsignal.
--VIC-20 Interfacing Blue Book. (Illus.). 104p. 1983. pap. 14.95 (ISBN 0-912911-00-X). Microsignal.
Georgiou, Vassilios J. A Parallel Pipeline Computer Architecture for Speech Processing. Stone, Harold, ed. LC 83-18133. (Computer Science: Computer Architecture & Design Ser.: No. 2). 100p. 1984. 34.95 (ISBN 0-8357-1524-8). UMI Res Pr.
Georgiyevskaya, E., jt. auth. see Barskaya, A.
Georgoff, David M. Odd-Even Retail Price Endings. LC 77-634692. 1972. pap. 5.00 (ISBN 0-87744-105-7). Mich St U Pr.
Georgopoulos, Basil S. & Cooke, Robert A. A Comparative Study of the Organization & Performance of Hospital Emergency Services. 512p. (Orig.). 1980. pap. 20.00x (ISBN 0-87944-253-0). Inst Soc Res.
Georgopoulos, Basil S., ed. Organization Research on Health Institutions. LC 72-619554. 429p. 1972. 20.00x (ISBN 0-87944-125-9). Inst Soc Res.
Georgopoulos, Chris J. Fiber Optics & Optical Isolators. Price, Edward R., ed. LC 81-52618. (Illus.). 271p. 1982. text ed. 37.00 (ISBN 0-932263-21-6). White Consult.
Georgopoulos, N., jt. ed. see Fischer, N.
Georgopoulos, S. G., jt. ed. see Dekker, J.
Georogionnis, Nicholas, ed. see Hemingway, Ernest.
Georr, Khalil. Dictionnaire Arabe Moderne Larousse. 1360p. (Arabic.). 1973. 25.00 (ISBN 0-686-56788-9, M-6584, Pub. by Larousse). French & Eur.
Geoscience Information Society. Proceedings of the Ninth Annual Meeting of the Geoscience Information Society, November 18, 1974, Miami Beach, Florida. LC 73-16672. pap. 24.80 (ISBN 0-317-30046-6, 2025048). Bks Demand UMI.
Geoscience Information Society Staff. The Future of the Journal: Proceedings, Geoscience Information Society, Meeting, 1981. Scott, M. W., ed. (Proceedings Ser.: Vol. 12). 1982. 20.00 (ISBN 0-318-02263-X). Geosci Info.
--Geological Hazards Data: Proceedings, Geoscience Information Society, Meeting, 1982. Brown, R. A., ed. (Proceedings Ser.: Vol. 13). 1983. 20.00 (ISBN 0-318-02264-8). Geosci Info.
--Proceedings of the Geoscience Information Society, Meeting, Minneapolis, 1972, Vol. 3. Phinney, H. K., ed. (Proceedings Ser.). 1973. 6.00 (ISBN 0-318-02260-5). Geosci Info.
--Retrieval of Geoscience Information: Proceedings Geoscience Information Society, Meeting, Salt Lake City, 1975. Hall, V. S., ed. (Proceedings Ser.: Vol. 6). 1976. 15.00 (ISBN 0-318-02261-3). Geosci Info.
--Roles & Responsibilities in Geoscience Information: Geoscience Information Society, Meeting, 1983. Rowell, U. H., ed. (Proceedings Ser.: Vol. 14). 1984. 20.00 (ISBN 0-318-02265-6). Geosci Info.
--Toward the Development of a Geoscience Information System: Proceedings, Geoscience Information Society, Meeting, 1971. Graves, R. W., ed. (Proceedings Ser.: Vol. 2). 1972. 3.00 (ISBN 0-318-02262-1). Geosci Info.
Geosset, Philip, ed. see Le Seur, Jean F.
Geotchius, Eugene Va n Ness see Van Ness Goetchius, Eugene.
Geothermal Resources Council, ed. Commercial Uses of Geothermal Heat. (Special Report Ser.: No. 9). (Illus.). 143p. 1980. pap. 3.50 (ISBN 0-934412-09-X). Geothermal.
--A Conference on the Commercialization of Geothermal Resources, November 28-30, 1978, San Diego, California. (Illus.). 77p. (Orig.). 1978. pap. 7.50 (ISBN 0-934412-76-6). Geothermal.
--Fractures in Geothermal Resevoirs: Presented August 27-28, Honolulu, Hawaii. (Special Report Ser.: No. 12). (Illus.). 167p. (Orig.). 1982. pap. 15.00 (ISBN 0-934412-12-X). Geothermal.
--Geothermal Potential of the Cascade Mountain Range: Exploration & Development. (Special Report Ser.: No. 10). (Illus.). 77p. (Orig.). 1981. pap. 12.00 (ISBN 0-934412-10-3). Geothermal.
--Geothermal: State of the Art. (Transactions Ser.: Vol. 1). (Illus.). 310p. 1979. Repr. of 1977 ed. 15.00 (ISBN 0-934412-51-0). Geothermal.
Geotzmann, William H. & Sloan, Kay. Looking Far North: The Harriman Expedition to Alaska, 1899. LC 82-61034. 1983. pap. 9.95 (ISBN 0-691-00591-5). Princeton U Pr.
Geoyges, Robert, ed. see International Symposium on Pulmonary Interstitium, Paris, May 1974.
Gephart, Ronald M. Revolutionary America, Seventeen Sixty-Three to Seventeen Eighty-Nine, 2 vols. LC 80-606802. 1672p. 1984. 2 vol. set 38.00. Vol. 1 (ISBN 0-8444-0359-8). Vol. 2 (ISBN 0-8444-0379-2). Lib Congress.
Gephart, William, ed. Accountability: A State, a Process, or a Product? LC 74-84288. 82p. 1975. pap. 3.50 (ISBN 0-87367-702-1). Phi Delta Kappa.
Gephart, William F. Transportation & Industrial Development in the Middle West. 1971. lib. bdg. 18.50x (ISBN 0-374-93027-9). Octagon.
Gephart, William J., ed. Accountability: A State, a Process, or a Product? 82p. 1975. 3.50 (ISBN 0-87367-702-1); members 3.00 (ISBN 0-317-35545-7). Phi Delta Kappa.
Geppert, Klaus. Die Arztliche Schweigepflicht im Strafvollzug. 40p. 1983. 8.00 (ISBN 3-11-009876-8). De Gruyter.
Gerace, P. & Mangione, S. Communication: Photography. 1976. pap. 8.84 (ISBN 0-13-153239-1). P-H.
Geraci, Philip C. Photojournalism: Making Pictures for Publication. 2nd ed. (Illus.). 1983. pap. text ed. 24.95 (ISBN 0-8403-3022-7, 40302201). Kendall-Hunt.
Geraci, Vincent J. Simultaneous Equation Models with Measurement Error. LC 79-53208. (Outstanding Dissertations in Economics Ser.). 180p. 1984. lib. bdg. 29.00 (ISBN 0-8240-4158-5). Garland Pub.
Geraci, Vincent J., jt. auth. see Burghardt, John A.
Gerada-Azzopardi, E. Malte, Joyau de la Mediterranee. (Illus., Fr.). 40.00 (ISBN 2-85518-054-6). Heinman.
Geradin, M. B. M. Fraeijs De Veubeke Memorial Volume of Selected Papers. 791p. 1980. 57.50x (ISBN 90-286-0900-8). Sijthoff & Noordhoff.
Geradin, Michel, jt. ed. see Danthine, Andre.
Geraerts. Vers une Nouvelle Philosophie Transcendantale. (Phaenomenologica Ser: No. 39). 1970. lib. bdg. 26.00 (ISBN 90-247-5024-5, Pub. by Martinus Nijhoff Netherlands). Kluwer Academic.
Geraghty, D. M., jt. ed. see Kydes, A. S.
Geraghty, John, jt. auth. see Estes, Bill.
Geraghty, Miller, Van der Leeden, & Troise. Water Atlas of the U. S. 3rd ed. LC 73-76649. 1973. 45.00 (ISBN 0-912394-03-X). Water Info.
Geraghty, Paul A. The History of Fijian Languages. LC 81-18523. (Oceanic Linguistics Special Publication Ser.: No. 19). (Illus.). 508p. 1983. pap. text ed. 25.00x (ISBN 0-8248-0802-9). UH Pr.
Geraghty, Thomas F. World Oil Co. vs. Northeast Shipbuilding, Inc. & Toiler Salvage Co. Defective Designs, Negligence. 230p. 1983. 15.00 (ISBN 0-318-11888-2); tchr's. manual 5.00 (ISBN 0-318-11889-0). Natl Inst Trial Ad.
Geraghty, Tony. Inside the SAS. (Elite Unit Ser.: No. 2). (Illus.). 249p. 1981. 17.95 (ISBN 0-89839-039-7). Battery Pr.
--Inside the SAS: 1950 to 1980. 384p. 1982. pap. 2.95 (ISBN 0-345-29749-0). Ballantine.
--This Is the SAS: A Pictorial History of the Special Air Service Regiment. LC 82-16264. (Illus.). 152p. 1983. 16.95 (ISBN 0-668-05725-4, 5725). Arco.
Gerald, Bill. Seventy-Six Ways to Make Extra Money in College. LC 83-568. 184p. (Orig.). 1983. pap. 7.95 (ISBN 0-912285-01-X). River Side Pr.
Gerald, Edward J. News of Crime: Courts & Press in Conflict. LC 83-10732. (Contributions to the Study of Mass Media & Communications Ser.: No. 1). x, 227p. 1983. lib. bdg. 29.95 (ISBN 0-313-23876-6, GNC/). Greenwood.
Gerald, Elsie F. My Emerald Life & Other Poems. 105p. (Orig.). 1983. pap. 5.95 (ISBN 0-9610096-0-8). C & E Ent Pub.
Gerald, Gregory F. Hunting the Yahoos. LC 81-69451. (Illus.). 58p. (Orig.). 1982. pap. 5.00 (ISBN 0-934996-14-8). Am Stud Pr.
Gerald, Hausman. The Day the White Whales Came to Bangor. (Illus.). 1979. pap. 3.00 (ISBN 0-89166-006-2). Cobblesmith.
Gerald, Holton, ed. see American Academy of Arts and Sciences, Boston.
Gerald, J. Edward. The British Press Under Government Economic Controls. LC 77-8442. 1977. Repr. of 1956 ed. lib. bdg. 24.75x (ISBN 0-8371-9690-6, GEBP). Greenwood.
--The Press & the Constitution, 1931-1947. 11.25 (ISBN 0-8446-0641-3). Peter Smith.
Gerald, Kevin. Reaching & Teaching Today's Youth. Wallace, Mary H., ed. 126p. 1983. pap. 4.95 (ISBN 0-912315-02-4). Word Aflame.
Gerald, M. C. & Long, J. P., eds. Instruction in Pharmacology: New Approaches & New Faces. (Health Communications & Informatics: Vol. 5, No. 1). (Illus.). 1979. pap. 8.25 (ISBN 3-8055-2992-9). S Karger.
Gerald, Mark & Eyman, William. Thinking Straight & Talking Sense: An Emotional Education Program. LC 78-71008. 1981. pap. 9.95 (ISBN 0-917476-14-X). Inst Rational-Emotive.
Gerald, Michael C. Pharmacology: An Introduction to Drugs. (Illus.). 720p. 1981. 29.95 (ISBN 0-13-662098-1). P-H.
Gerald, Michael C. & O'Bannon, Freda V. Nursing Pharmacology & Therapeutics. (Illus.). 544p. 1981. text ed. 32.95 (ISBN 0-13-627505-2). P-H.
Gerald, Michael C., jt. auth. see Eisenhauer, Laurel A.
Gerald Moore, 1899- The Schubert Song Cycles: With Thoughts on Performance. 240p. 1979. pap. 10.95 (ISBN 0-241-89165-5, Pub. by Hamish Hamilton England). David & Charles.
Geraldes, A., ed. see Meeting Held at the Gulbenkian Institute of Science, Oeiras, Portugal, Sept. 1973.
Gerald of Wales. History & Topography of Ireland. O'Meara, John, tr. 448p. 1983. pap. 5.95 (ISBN 0-14-044423-8). Penguin.
--The Journey Through Wales & the Description of Wales. Thorpe, Lewis, tr. (Penguin Classic Ser.). 1978. pap. 4.95 (ISBN 0-14-044339-8). Penguin.
Geraldson, Cornelius. An Addition to the Sea Journal of the Hollanders unto Java. LC 68-27480. (English Experience Ser.: No. 2). (Illus.). 40p. 1968. Repr. of 1598 ed. 8.00 (ISBN 90-221-0002-2). Walter J Johnson.
Geralskis-Estes, Susan. Book of Tarot. LC 80-81768. 96p. (Orig.). 1984. pap. 6.95 (ISBN 0-87100-172-1, 2172). Morgan.
Geramita & Seberry. Orthogonal Designs: Quad. Forms & Had. Matrices. (Lecture Notes in Pure & Applied Mathematics Ser.: Vol. 45). 1979. 65.00 (ISBN 0-8247-6774-8). Dekker.
Geran, O., jt. auth. see Brozovic.
Gerani, Gary. Fantastic Television. (Illus.). 1977. 14.95 (ISBN 0-517-52646-8, Harmony); pap. 8.95 (ISBN 0-517-52645-X). Crown.
Gerard, A., jt. auth. see Bigwood, E. J.
Gerard, Alain. An Outline of Food Law (Structure, Principles, Main Provisions) (Legislative Studies: No. 7). 114p. (Eng., Fr. & Span.). 1975. pap. 13.00 (ISBN 0-685-54196-7, F1020, FAO). Unipub.
Gerard, Albert S. The African Language Literatures: An Introduction to the Literary History of Sub-Saharan Africa. LC 79-3103. (Illus.). 416p. 1981. 35.00x (ISBN 0-914478-65-6); pap. 20.00x (ISBN 0-914478-66-4). Three Continents.
--Four African Literatures: Xhosa, Sotho, Zulu, Amharic. LC 74-126763. 1971. 43.75x (ISBN 0-520-01788-9). U of Cal Pr.
Gerard, Alexander. An Essay of Genius. 514p. 1975. Repr. of 1774 ed. 54.40x (ISBN 3-7705-0043-1). Adlers Foreign Bks.
--An Essay on Taste. LC 63-7081. Repr. of 1780 ed. 45.00x (ISBN 0-8201-1020-5). Schol Facsimiles.
Gerard, Alice. Please Breast Feed Your Baby. 1971. pap. 1.75 (ISBN 0-451-11605-4, AE1605, Sig). NAL.
Gerard, Auguste. Ma Mission Au Japan, 1907-1914. LC 72-168109. Repr. of 1919 ed. 29.00 (ISBN 0-404-02713-X). AMS Pr.
Gerard, B. Guadeloupe. LC 82-70580. (Illus.). 160p. 1982. 27.95 (ISBN 0-86710-022-2). Edns Vilo.
Gerard, Charles. Jazz Masters: Sonny Rollins. 1979. pap. 6.95 (ISBN 0-8256-4086-5, Amsco Music). Music Sales.
Gerard, Colin. Practical Guide to Pottery. LC 77-80602. 1978. 6.95 (ISBN 0-8120-5187-4). Barron.
Gerard, David. Charities in Britain: Conservation or Change? 187p. (Orig.). 1983. pap. text ed. 14.75x (ISBN 0-7199-1092-7, Pub. by Bedford England). Brookfield Pub Co.
Gerard, David, jt. auth. see Abrams, Mark.
Gerard, David, tr. see Masson, Andre.
Gerard, Duclois. A Romantic & Artistic Voyage Through the Monuments of Paris. 145p. 1984. 76.75 (ISBN 0-86650-108-8). Gloucester Art.
Gerard, Emily. The Land Beyond the Forest: Facts, Figures & Fancies from Transylvania, 2 vols. LC 77-87731. Repr. of 1888 ed. 56.50 set (ISBN 0-404-16530-3). AMS Pr.

Gerard, Francois C. The Future of the Church: The Theology of Renewal of Willem Adolf Visser't Hooft. LC 74-26564. (Pittsburgh Theological Monographs: No. 2). 1974. pap. 10.25 (ISBN 0-915138-01-8). Pickwick.
Gerard, Francois C., et al, trs. see Nedoncelle, Maurice.
Gerard, Gary, ed. Extractive Metallurgy of Aluminum: Proceedings. LC 63-13591. Vol. 2, Aluminum. pap. 147.30 (ISBN 0-317-10300-8, 2000688). Bks Demand UMI.
Gerard, Harold B. & Miller, Norman. School Desegregation: A Long Term Study. LC 75-28037. (Perspectives in Social Psychology Ser.). (Illus.). 323p. 1976. 35.00x (ISBN 0-306-34402-5, Plenum Pr). Plenum Pub.
Gerard, Jacqueline. La Cuisine. new ed. (Illus.). 448p. (Fr.). 1974. 12.25x (ISBN 2-03-077201-1, 3903). Larousse.
Gerard, Jariot, jt. auth. see Duras, Marguerite.
Gerard, John. Catalogus Arborum, Fructicum Ac Plantarum Tam Indigenarum Quam Exoticarum in Horto Johannis Gerardi. LC 73-6132. (English Experience Ser.: No. 598). 22p. 1973. Repr. of 1599 ed. 6.00 (ISBN 0-685-72641-X). Walter J Johnson.
--The Herbal or General History of Plants. (Illus.). xiv, 1678p. 1975. Repr. of 1633 ed. 75.00 (ISBN 0-486-23147-X). Dover.
--The Herball or General Historie of Plants, 2 vols. LC 74-80179. (English Experience Ser.: Nos. 660a-660b). 1974. Repr. of 1597 ed. Set. 214.00 (ISBN 90-221-0660-8). Walter J Johnson.
Gerard, Karen. American Survivors: Cities & Other Scenes. 352p. 1985. 22.95 (ISBN 0-15-106304-4). HarBraceJ.
Gerard, Leona B. Benchmarks II. 92p. (Orig.). pap. 6.00 (ISBN 0-317-05302-7). L B Gerard.
--Benchmarks III. (Benchmarks Ser.). 88p. (Orig.). 1983. pap. 6.00x (ISBN 0-686-89245-3). L B Gerard.
--Benchmarks IV. 83p. (Orig.). 1985. pap. 6.00 (ISBN 0-317-05303-5). L B Gerard.
--Poems Mostly about Love. 82p. 1977. pap. 6.00 (ISBN 0-317-05301-9). L B Gerard.
Gerard, Max. Dali. LC 68-28386. (Illus.). 1968. 60.00 (ISBN 0-8109-0063-7). Abrams.
Gerard, Mireille & Edwards, Pamela W. Space Station: Policy, Planning & Utilization. 30.00 (ISBN 0-915928-80-9). AIAA.
Gerard, R. & Ramis, J. P., eds. Equations Differentielles et Systemes de Pfaff Dans le Champs Complex-II. (Lecture Notes in Mathematics: Vol. 1015). 411p. 1983. pap. 20.00 (ISBN 0-387-12684-8). Springer-Verlag.
Gerard, Ralph W., ed. Food for Life. LC 52-14880. 1965. pap. 3.25x (ISBN 0-226-28790-4, P527, Phoen). U of Chicago Pr.
Gerard, Thomas. Coker's Survey of Dorsetshire. 176p. 55.00x (ISBN 0-686-75652-5, Pub. by Dorset). State Mutual Bk.
Gerard, William. Byron Restudied in His Dramas. LC 72-186959. 1886. lib. bdg. 15.00 (ISBN 0-8414-4646-6). Folcroft.
Gerarde, John. The Herball or Generall Historie of Plantes. 303p. 1984. Repr. of 1597 ed. text ed. 85.00x (ISBN 0-86590-238-0). Apt Bks.
--The Herball or Generall Historie of Plantes. 303p. 1984. Repr. of 1597 ed. text ed. 85.00x (ISBN 0-86590-238-0, Pub. by Neeraj Pub Hse New Delhi). Apt Bks.
Gerard-Gailly. Madame de Sevigny. 15.50 (ISBN 0-685-34031-7). French & Eur.
Gerardi, Michael H. & Grimm, James K. The History, Biology, Damage & Control of the Gypsy Moth. LC 72-20321. 233p. 1978. 21.50 (ISBN 0-8386-2023-X). Fairleigh Dickinson.
Gerardi, Natalie, jt. auth. see Poliakov, Leon.
Gerardin, B. Le Developpement de la Haute Volta. (Economies et Societes Series F: No. 19). 1963. pap. 26.00 (ISBN 0-317-16843-6). Kraus Repr.
Gerardin, P. Construction de Series Discretes p-Adiques. LC 75-16187. (Lecture Notes in Mathematics: Vol. 462). 180p. 1975. pap. 10.70 (ISBN 0-387-07172-5). Springer-Verlag.
Gerard-Libois, J. & Verhaegen, B., eds. Congo Nineteen Sixty-Five. Centre De Recherche et D'information Socio-Politiques. (Political Documents of a Developing Nation Ser.). 1967. 55.00x (ISBN 0-691-03012-X). Princeton U Pr.
Gerard-Libois, J. & Verhaegen, B.compiled by. Congo, Nineteen Sixty-Four: Political Documents of a Developing Nation, in French. (Centre De Recherche et d'Information Socio-Politiques Ser.). (Fr). 1966. 55.00x (ISBN 0-691-03011-1). Princeton U Pr.
Gerard-Libois, Jules. Katanga Secession. Young, Rebecca, tr. LC 66-22851. pap. 96.80 (ISBN 0-317-10956-1, 2005076). Bks Demand UMI.
Gerardo, Machado. Memorias: Ocho Anos de Lucha. Gerardo, Morales & Gajate, Comandante, eds. LC 82-84134. (Historia y Biografias Ser.). (Illus.). 224p. (Orig., Spanish.). 1982. pap. 12.95 (ISBN 0-89729-328-2). Ediciones.
Gerardo, Morales, ed. see Gerardo, Machado.
Gerard Of Cremona, tr. see Muhammad Ibn Zakariya.
Geras, Adele. Apricots at Midnight. LC 82-1728. (Illus.). 144p. (gr. 4-6). 1982. 10.95 (ISBN 0-689-30921-X). Atheneum.
--Snapshots of Paradise: Love Stories. LC 84-2934. 180p. (gr. 8 up). 1984. 11.95 (ISBN 0-689-31045-5). Atheneum.
--Voyage. LC 82-13760. 192p. (gr. 7 up). 1983. 10.95 (ISBN 0-689-30955-4). Atheneum.
Geras, Charlie, ed. see Albright, Nancy.
Geras, Norman. The Legacy of Rosa Luxemburg. 1976. 11.00 (ISBN 0-8052-7034-5, Pub. by NLB). Schocken.
--The Legacy of Rosa Luxemburg. 212p. 1984. pap. 8.95 (ISBN 0-8052-7159-7, Pub. by NLB England). Schocken.
--Marx & Human Nature: Refutation of a Legend. 96p. 1983. 17.50 (ISBN 0-8052-7181-3, Pub. by NLB England); pap. 5.50 (ISBN 0-8052-7182-1). Schocken.
Gerasimov, I. P. Geography & Ecology. 167p. 1983. 5.95 (ISBN 0-8285-2394-0, 095, Pub. by Progress Pubs USSR). Imported Pubns.
Gerasimov, I. P., ed. Global Geography-76, 12 vols. Incl. Vol. 1. Geomorphology & Paleography. pap. text ed. 25.00 (ISBN 0-08-023141-1); Vol. 2. Climatology, Hydrology, Glaciology. pap. text ed. 25.00 (ISBN 0-08-023142-X); Vol. 3. Geography of the Ocean. pap. text ed. 15.00 (ISBN 0-08-023143-8); Vol. 4. Biogeography & Soil Geography. pap. text ed. 15.00 (ISBN 0-08-023144-6); Vol. 5. General Physical Geography. pap. text ed. 15.00 (ISBN 0-08-023145-4); Vol. 6. General Economic Geography. pap. text ed. 25.00 (ISBN 0-08-023146-2); Vol. 7. Geography of Population. pap. text ed. 25.00 (ISBN 0-08-023147-0); Vol. 8. Regional Geography. pap. text ed. 25.00 (ISBN 0-08-023148-9); Vol. 9. Historical Geography. pap. text ed. 15.00 (ISBN 0-08-023149-7); Vol. 10. Geographical Education, Geographical Literature & Dissemination of Geographical Knowledge. pap. text ed. 15.00 (ISBN 0-08-023150-0); Vol. 11. General Problems of Geography & Geosystems Modelling. pap. text ed. 15.00 (ISBN 0-08-023151-9); Vol. 12. Additional Volume Including Author Index. pap. text ed. 25.00 (ISBN 0-08-023152-7). LC 78-40224. 1978. pap. text ed. 200.00 set (ISBN 0-686-67353-0). Pergamon.
--Man, Society & the Environment. 340p. 1975. 5.45 (ISBN 0-8285-0432-6, Pub. by Progress Pubs USSR). Imported Pubns.
Gerasimov, I. P., et al, eds. Natural Resources of the Soviet Union: Their Use & Renewal, English Edition. LC 74-138667. (Illus.). 349p. 1971. text ed. 38.95 (ISBN 0-7167-0248-7). W H Freeman.
Gerasimov, Ya., ed. Physical Chemistry, 2 vols. 1233p. 1974. Set. 12.40 (ISBN 0-8285-0657-4, Pub. by Mir Pubs USSR). Imported Pubns.
Gerassimov, Todor, jt. auth. see Venedikov, Ivan.
Geraty, Lawrence T., jt. auth. see Boraas, Roger S.
Geraud, G., jt. ed. see Bes, A.
Geraud, H., ed. see Guillaume De Nangis.
Geraud-Venzac, ed. see Littre.
Gerba & Goyal. Methods in Environmental Virology. 376p. 1982. 65.00 (ISBN 0-8247-1829-1). Dekker.
Gerba, Charles, jt. ed. see Bitton, Gabriel.
Gerbeaux, Jacques, et al. Pediatric Respiratory Disease. 2nd ed. LC 81-10356. 939p. 1982. 100.00 (ISBN 0-471-03456-8, Pub. by Wiley-Med). Wiley.
Gerber & Storzer. French Conversation Through Idioms. 1985. pap. 6.95 (ISBN 0-8120-2107-X). Barron.
Gerber, Aaron. Abraham: The First Hebrew. 180p. 1981. 12.50 (ISBN 0-89962-208-9). Todd & Honeywell.
--Biblical Attitudes on Human Sexuality. 176p. 1982. 15.95 (ISBN 0-89962-301-8). Todd & Honeywell.
Gerber, Adele. Goal: Carryover, an Articulation Manual & Program. LC 72-95886. (Illus.). 100p. 1973. 19.95 (ISBN 0-87722-021-2); 29 work sheets incl. Temple U Pr.
Gerber, Adele & Bryen, Diane N. Language & Learning Disabilities. LC 80-39947. (Illus.). 360p. 1981. pap. 16.00 (ISBN 0-8391-1610-1). Pro Ed.
Gerber, Adele & Goehl, Henry. Temple University Short Syntax Inventory. LC 83-18324. 1983. incl. manual, test & score sheets 34.50 (ISBN 0-8391-1972-0, 20710). Univ Park.
Gerber, Adolph. Great Russian Animal Tales. LC 73-140975. (Research & Source Works Ser.: No. 630). 1971. Repr. 19.50 (ISBN 0-8337-1325-6). B Franklin.
Gerber, Aime, jt. auth. see Heylbut, Rose.
Gerber, Albert B. The Book of Sex Lists. 1981. 12.00 (ISBN 0-8184-0320-9). Lyle Stuart.
--Sex, Pornography & Justice. (Illus.). 1965. 10.00 (ISBN 0-8184-0079-X). Lyle Stuart.
Gerber, Ann. Chicago's Classiest Cuisine. (Illus.). 304p. 1983. 25.00 (ISBN 0-914091-31-X). Chicago Review.
--Chicago's Sweet Tooth. (Illus.). 288p. 1985. 18.95 (ISBN 0-914091-77-8). Chicago Review.
Gerber, Barbara & Storzer, Gerald. French Idioms on the Way. (Illus., Fr.). 1985. pap. 4.95 (ISBN 0-8120-2108-8). Barron.
Gerber, Barbara L. & Storzer, Gerald H. Dictionary of Modern French Idioms, 2 vols. LC 76-24743. (Reference Library of the Humanities Ser.: Vol. 63). (Fr. & Eng.). 1977. Set. lib. bdg. 133.00 (ISBN 0-8240-9935-4). Garland Pub.
Gerber, Bobbie. Shelter: A Work of Ministry. 160p. 1983. pap. 8.95 (ISBN 0-8164-2622-8, Pub. by Seabury). Winston Pr.
Gerber, Carole H. Turn Your Kid into a Computer Genius. (Illus.). 250p. 1984. pap. 10.95 (ISBN 0-525-48119-2, 01063-320). Dutton.
Gerber, Dan. The Chinese Poems. (Illus.). 1978. 9.95 (ISBN 0-912090-47-2); pap. 3.95 (ISBN 0-912090-46-4). Sumac Mich.
--Departure. 1973. pap. 2.45 (ISBN 0-912090-30-8). Sumac Mich.
--Revenant. (Orig.). 1971. 4.95 (ISBN 0-912090-11-1); pap. 2.45 (ISBN 0-912090-10-3). Sumac Mich.
Gerber, David A. Black Ohio & the Color Line, 1860-1915. LC 76-27285. pap. 128.00 (ISBN 0-317-09721-0, 2021155). Bks Demand UMI.
Gerber, David A., ed. Anti-Semitism in American History. 368p. 1986. 24.95x (ISBN 0-252-01214-3). U of Ill Pr.
Gerber, Douglas E. A Bibliography of Pindar, Fifteen Thirteen to Nineteen Sixty-Six. (APA Philological Monographs). 18.00 (ISBN 0-89130-711-7, 40-00-28). Scholars Pr GA.
--A Bibliography of Pindar: 1513-1966. 160p. 1969. 18.00 (ISBN 0-8295-0161-4, 40-00-28). Scholars Pr GA.
--Pindar's Olympian I: A Commentary. (Phoenix Supplementary Volumes Ser.). 264p. 1981. 50.00x (ISBN 0-8020-5507-9). U of Toronto Pr.
Gerber, Douglas E., ed. Greek Poetry & Philosophy: Studies in Honour of Leonard Woodbury. LC 84-5578. (Homage Ser.). 352p. 1984. 32.95 (ISBN 0-89130-747-8, 00 16 08). Scholars Pr GA.
Gerber, Eduard A. & Ballato, Arthur, eds. Precision Frequency Control, Vol. 1: Acoustic Resonators & Filters. 1985. 69.50 (ISBN 0-12-280601-8). Acad Pr.
--Precision Frequency Control, Vol. 2: Oscillators & Standards. 1985. 69.50 (ISBN 0-12-280602-6). Acad Pr.
Gerber, Ellen W., et al. The American Woman in Sport. 1974. text ed. 23.95 (ISBN 0-201-02353-9). Addison-Wesley.
Gerber, Frank. The Gentle Losers. LC 79-92089. 1980. 9.95 (ISBN 0-87212-116-X). Libra.
Gerber, Frederic H., jt. auth. see Greaney, Richard B.
Gerber, Georg B. see Altman, Kurt I.
Gerber, H., ed. see International Conference on Equine Infectious Diseases, 2nd, Paris, 1969.
Gerber, H., ed. see International Conference on Equine Infectious Diseases, 3rd.
Gerber, H., ed. see Rossdale, P. D.
Gerber, Hans U. An Introduction to Mathematical Risk Theory. LC 79-89749. (S. S. Huebner Foundation Monographs: No. 8). (Illus.). 164p. 1979. pap. 15.95 (ISBN 0-918930-08-1). Huebner Foun Insur.
Gerber, Harvey. Mathematics for Elementary School Teachers. 1982. text ed. 29.95 (ISBN 0-03-058326-8, CBS C). SCP.
Gerber, Helmut E. & Davis, W. Eugene, eds. Thomas Hardy: An Annotated Bibliography of Writings about Him. LC 72-7514. (Annotated Secondary Bibliography Ser. on English Literature in Transition, 1880-1920). 841p. 1973. 25.00 (ISBN 0-87580-039-4). N Ill U Pr.
Gerber, Helmut E., jt. ed. see Davis, W. Eugene.
Gerber, Helmut E., jt. ed. see Eakin, David B.
Gerber, Helmut E., ed. see Moore, George.
Gerber, Helmut E., jt. ed. see Teets, Bruce E.
Gerber, Hermann E. & Deepak, Adarsh, eds. Aerosols & Their Climatic Effects. LC 85-1651. (Illus.). 300p. 1984. 45.00 (ISBN 0-937194-06-9). A Deepak Pub.
Gerber, Hermann E. & Hindman, Edward E., eds. Light Absorption by Aerosol Particles. LC 82-80728. (Illus.). 1982. 47.50 (ISBN 0-937194-00-X). A Deepak Pub.
Gerber, Irving. Albert Einstein: World Scientist. (American Destinty Ser. Jewish Americans). (Illus.). 1979. of 10 9.95 set (ISBN 0-87594-185-0). Book Lab.
--Arturo oscanini: Genius of Conducting. (American Destiny Ser.: Jewish Americans). (Illus.). 1979. of 10 9.95 set (ISBN 0-87594-189-3). Book Lab.
--Emma Lazarus: Poet of Liberty. (American Destiny Ser.: Jewish Americans). (Illus.). (gr. 4-12). 1979. of 10 9.95 set (ISBN 0-87594-183-4). Book Lab.
--Felisa Rincon: Woman of the Americas. (American Destiny Ser.: Puerto Ricans). (Illus.). (gr. 4-12). 1979. of ten 9.95 set (ISBN 0-87594-179-6, 4612). Book-Lab.
--George Gershwin: the Music Man. (American destiny Ser.: Jewish Americans). (Illus.). (gr. 4-12). 1979. Set of 10. 9.95 (ISBN 0-87594-184-2). Book Lab.
--Haym Solomon: Patriot of Liberty. (American Destiny Ser.: Jewish Americans). (Illus.). (gr. 4-12). 1979. of 10 9.95 set (ISBN 0-87594-182-6). Book Lab.
--Joe Dimaggio: the Yankee Clipper. (American Destiny Ser.: Italian Americans). (Illus.). (gr. 4-12). 1979. of 10 9.95 set (ISBN 0-87594-187-7). Book Lab.
--Mother Cabrini Missionary to the World. (American Destiny Ser.: Italian Americans). (Illus.). (gr. 4-12). 1979. of 10 9.95 set (ISBN 0-87594-186-9). Book Lab.
--Puerto Rico: Long Ago. (American Destiny Ser.: Puerto Rico). (Illus.). (gr. 4-12). 1978. of 10 9.95 set (ISBN 0-87594-177-X). Book-Lab.
--Ramon Betances: Father of the Poor. (American Destiny Ser.: Puerto Rico: Puerto Rico). (gr. 4-12). 1979. 9.95 set (ISBN 0-87594-180-X). Book-Lab.
--Roberto Clemente: The Pride of Puerto Rico. (American Destiny Ser.: Puerto Ricans). (gr. 4). 1978. Set of 10. 9.95 (ISBN 0-87594-178-8). Book-Lab.
Gerber, Irwin. Perspectives on Bereavement. 16.50 (ISBN 0-405-12481-3). Ayer Co Pubs.
Gerber, Irwin, et al, eds. Perspectives on Bereavement. (Thanatology Ser.). 1978. 14.50x (ISBN 0-8422-7304-2). Irvington.
Gerber, Irwin, jt. ed. see Schoenberg, Bernard.
Gerber, Israel J. The Heritage Seekers--Black Jews in Search of Identity. LC 77-2907. 1977. 9.95 (ISBN 0-8246-0214-5). Jonathan David.
Gerber, Isreal J. Job on Trial: A Book for Our Time. 217p. 1982. 14.95 (ISBN 0-318-01102-6). E P Press.
Gerber, John, jt. auth. see Blair, Walter.
Gerber, John C., ed. Twentieth Century Interpretations of The Scarlet Letter. LC 68-23438. (Twentieth Century Interpretations Series). (Orig.). 1968. 8.95 (ISBN 0-13-791582-9, Spec). P-H.
Gerber, John C., et al, eds. see Twain, Mark.
Gerber, Lane A. Married to Their Careers: Career & Family Dilemmas in Doctors' Lives. 272p. 1983. (Tavistock); pap. 9.95 (ISBN 0-422-78250-5, NO. 3812, Tavistock). Methuen Inc.
Gerber, Lane A., jt. ed. see Duffy, John C.
Gerber, Larry G. The Limits of Liberalism: Josephus Daniels, Henry Stimson, Bernard Baruch, Donald Richberg, Felix Frankfurter & the Development of the Modern American Political Economy. 425p. 1985. pap. text ed. 12.50x (ISBN 0-8147-2997-5); 42.50x (ISBN 0-8147-2985-1). NYU Pr.
Gerber, Lawrence. Hospital Restructuring: Why, When & How. LC 83-60942. 238p. 1983. text ed. 32.00 (ISBN 0-931028-36-1). Pluribus Pr.
Gerber, Leslie E. & McFadden, Margaret. Loren Eiseley. LC 82-40294. (Literature & Life Ser.). 200p. 1983. 13.95 (ISBN 0-8044-5424-8). Ungar.
Gerber, Linda, jt. auth. see Haines, Joan E.
Gerber, Linda L., jt. auth. see Haines, B. Joan.
Gerber, Lynn H., ed. Psoriatic Arthritis. 224p. 1985. 33.50 (ISBN 0-8089-1709-9, 791544). Grune.
Gerber, Margy & Pouget, Judith. Literature of the German Democratic Republic in English Translation: A Bibliography-Studies in GDR Culture & Society, a Supplementary Volume. 138p. (Orig.). 1984. lib. bdg. 22.50 (ISBN 0-8191-4025-2); pap. text ed. 9.75 (ISBN 0-8191-4026-0). U Pr of Amer.
Gerber, Margy & Cosentino, Christine, eds. Studies in GDR Culture & Society Three: Selected Papers from the Eighth International Symposium on the German Democratic Republic. Lauckner, Nancy A. & Smith, Duncan, trs. LC 83-6763. (Illus.). 270p. (Orig.). 1983. lib. bdg. 25.75 (ISBN 0-8191-3278-0); pap. text ed. 13.25 (ISBN 0-8191-3279-9). U Pr of Amer.
--Studies in GDR Culture & Society 2: Proceedings of the Seventh International Symposium on the German Democratic Republic. LC 81-43512. (Illus.). 298p. (Orig.). 1982. lib. bdg. 27.25 (ISBN 0-8191-2524-5); pap. text ed. 13.00 (ISBN 0-8191-2525-3). U Pr of Amer.
Gerber, Margy, et al, eds. Studies in GDR Culture & Society Four: Selected Papers from the Ninth New Hampshire Symposium on the German Democratic Republic. Gransow, Volker, et al, trs. 316p. (Orig.). 1984. lib. bdg. 24.75 (ISBN 0-8191-4015-5); pap. text ed. 14.50 (ISBN 0-8191-4016-3). U Pr of Amer.
--Studies in GDR Culture & Society Five: Selected Papers from the Tenth New Hampshire Symposium on the German Democratic Republic. 362p. (Orig.). 1985. lib. bdg. 24.75 (ISBN 0-8191-4767-2, Intl Symposium German Democratic Republic); pap. text ed. 15.25 (ISBN 0-8191-4768-0). U Pr of Amer.
Gerber, Margy, et al, eds. see International Symposium on the German Democratic Republic, 6th.
Gerber, Merrill J. Honeymoon. (Illinois Short Fiction Ser.). 136p. 1985. 11.95 (ISBN 0-252-01205-4). U of Ill Pr.
--I'm Kissing As Fast As I Can. 176p. 1985. pap. 2.25 (ISBN 0-449-70125-5, Juniper). Fawcett.
--Name a Star for Me. 192p. (gr. 5-9). 1983. 12.50 (ISBN 0-670-50389-4). Viking.
--Name a Star For Me. 160p. (gr. 5). 1984. pap. 2.25 (ISBN 0-451-12888-5, Sig Vista). NAL.
--Please Don't Kiss Me Now. (YA) 1982. pap. 1.95 (ISBN 0-451-11575-9, Sig Vista). NAL.
Gerber, Michael E. The E-Myth: Why Most Businesses Don't Work & What to Do about It. 200p. 1985. 14.95 (ISBN 0-88730-040-5). Ballinger Pub.
Gerber, Philip L. Robert Frost. (Twayne's United States Authors Ser). 1966. pap. 5.95x (ISBN 0-8084-0266-8, T107, Twayne). New Coll U Pr.
--Robert Frost. rev. ed. (United States Authors Ser.). 1982. lib. bdg. 12.50 (ISBN 0-8057-7348-7, Twayne). G K Hall.
--Robert Frost. rev. ed. (United States Authors Ser.: No. 107). 224p. 1984. pap. 6.95 (ISBN 0-8057-7426-2, Twayne). G K Hall.

--Theodore Dreiser. (United States Authors Ser.). 1963. lib. bdg. 13.50 (ISBN 0-8057-0212-1, Twayne). G K Hall.

--Willa Cather. (United States Authors Ser.). 1975. lib. bdg. 13.50 (ISBN 0-8057-7155-7, Twayne). G K Hall.

Gerber, Philip L., ed. Critical Essays on Robert Frost. (Critical Essays on American Literature Ser.). 1982. lib. bdg. 33.50 (ISBN 0-8161-8442-9). G K Hall.

Gerber Products Co., ed. Five Hundred Questions New Parents Ask. (Norback Bks.). (Orig.). 1982. pap. 6.95 (ISBN 0-440-52609-4, Dell Trade Pbks). Dell.

Gerber, Richard. Utopian Fantasy: A Study of English Utopian Fiction since the End of the Nineteenth Century. LC 73-12888. 1973. lib. bdg. 20.00 (ISBN 0-8414-4424-2). Folcroft.

Gerber, Richard & Birss, Robert R. High Gradient Magnetic Separation. LC 83-3586. (Electronic & Electrical Engineering Research Studies). 209p. 1983. 54.95x (ISBN 0-471-90162-8, Res Stud Pr). Wiley.

Gerber, Rudolph J. The Insanity Defense. LC 83-15904. 116p. 1984. 15.50x (ISBN 0-86733-034-1, 4034). Assoc Faculty Pr.

Gerber, S. R., jt. auth. see Sunshine, Irving.

Gerber, Samuel. Learning to Die. Dyck, Peter, tr. from Ger. LC 84-10809. 104p. (Orig.). 1984. pap. 5.95 (ISBN 0-8361-3369-2). Herald Pr.

Gerber, Samuel M., ed. Chemistry & Crime: From Sherlock Holmes to Today's Courtroom. (Other Technical Bks.). 135p. 1983. lib. bdg. 19.95 (ISBN 0-8412-0784-4). Am Chemical.

Gerber, Sanford, jt. ed. see Mencher, George T.

Gerber, Sanford E. Audiometry in Infancy. 368p. 1977. 37.00 (ISBN 0-8089-1038-8, 791545). Grune.

--Introductory Hearing Science: Physical & Psychological Concepts. LC 73-89177. (Illus.). 305p. 1974. text ed. 17.95 (ISBN 0-7216-4104-0). Saunders.

--Introductory Hearing Science: Physical & Psychological Concepts. LC 73-89177. pap. 77.80 (ISBN 0-317-26432-X, 2024988). Bks Demand UMI.

Gerber, Sanford E. & Mencher, George. The Development of Auditory Behavior. 368p. 1983. 25.50 (ISBN 0-8089-1598-3, 791546). Grune.

Gerber, Sanford E. & Mencher, George T. Auditory Dysfunction. LC 80-17347. (Illus.). 272p. 1980. text ed. 20.00 (ISBN 0-933014-60-0). College-Hill.

Gerber, Sanford E. & Mencher, George T., eds. Early Diagnosis of Hearing Loss. 384p. 1978. 34.50 (ISBN 0-8089-1153-8, 791547). Grune.

Gerber, Sanford E., jt. ed. see Mencher, George.

Gerber, Stanford N. Russkoya-Celo: The Ethnography of a Russian-American Community. LC 84-45354. (Immigrant Communities & Ethnic Minorities in the United States & Canada Ser.). 1985. 29.50 (ISBN 0-404-19407-9). AMS Pr.

Gerber, Steve & Mayerik, Val. Void Indigo. (Marvel Graphic Novel Ser.: No. 11). 4.95 (ISBN 0-87135-059-9). Marvel Comics.

Gerber, Will, et al. The Rings on Woot-Kew's Tail: Indian Legends of the Origin of the Sun, Moon & Stars. (Indian Culture Ser.). (gr. 3-9). 1973. 1.95 (ISBN 0-89992-059-4). Coun India Ed.

Gerber, William, ed. The Mind of India. LC 76-27668. (Arcturus Books Paperbacks). 288p. 1977. pap. 3.95x (ISBN 0-8093-0804-5). S Ill U Pr.

Gerberding, Keith. Why Is There Evil If God Is Good. 1984. 2.85 (ISBN 0-89536-962-1). CSS of Ohio.

Gerberding, Kieth A. How to Respond to Transcendental Meditation. (The Response Ser.). 1977. 1.75 (ISBN 0-570-07676-5, 12-2659). Concordia.

Gerberg, Mort. The Arbor House Book of Cartooning. LC 81-71666. (Illus.). 1983. 16.95 (ISBN 0-87795-372-4); pap. 8.95 (ISBN 0-87795-399-6). Arbor Hse.

--The Computer Dictionary. (Illus.). 96p. (Orig.). 1984. pap. 5.95 (ISBN 0-671-50498-3, Wallaby). S&S.

--Real Cats Don't Do Talk Shows. 96p. (Orig.). 1983. pap. 2.95 (ISBN 0-8431-0747-2). Price Stern.

--Why Did Halley's Comet Cross the Universe? And Other Spaced-Out Riddles, Jokes & Knock-Knocks. (Illus.). 32p. (Orig.). (gr. 1-4). 1985. pap. 1.95 (ISBN 0-590-33418-2). Scholastic Inc.

Gerberg, Robert J., ed. Professional Job Changing System. 13th ed. LC 81-80999. 162p. 1984. 14.95 (ISBN 0-912940-21-2). Perf Dynamics.

Gerberich, Albert H. Luther & the English Bible. LC 83-45643. Date not set. Repr. of 1933 ed. 17.50 (ISBN 0-404-19852-X). AMS Pr.

Gerbert, Joshua, ed. Textbook of Bunion Surgery. LC 80-68895. (Illus.). 356p. 1981. monograph 34.50 (ISBN 0-87993-153-1). Futura Pub.

Gerbert, Kenneth L. National Electrical Code Blueprint Reading: Based on 1981. 8th ed. LC 80-67345. pap. 50.00 (ISBN 0-317-19779-7, 2023203). Bks Demand UMI.

Gerbi, Antonello. The Dispute of the New World: The History of a Polemic, 1750-1900. Moyle, Jeremy, tr. LC 70-181396. 1973. 35.00x (ISBN 0-8229-3250-4). U of Pittsburgh Pr.

Gerbino, Mary, jt. auth. see Sanchez, Gail J.

Gerbner, et al, eds. The Analysis of Communication Content: Developments in Scientific Theories & Computer Techniques. Holsti & Krippendorff. LC 78-15413. 620p. 1978. Repr. of 1969 ed. lib. bdg. 36.00 (ISBN 0-88275-723-7). Krieger.

Gerbner, George, ed. Mass Media Policies in Changing Cultures. LC 77-2399. 1977. 40.50 (ISBN 0-471-01514-8, Pub. by Wiley-Interscience). Wiley.

Gerbner, George & Gross, Larry P., eds. Communications Technology & Social Policy: Understanding the New "Cultural Revolution". LC 73-7563. pap. 150.80 (ISBN 0-317-09559-5, 2051292). Bks Demand UMI.

Gerbner, George, et al, eds. Child Abuse: An Agenda for Action. (Illus.). 1980. pap. text ed. 13.95x (ISBN 0-19-502721-3). Oxford U Pr.

Gerbracht, Carl & Robinson, Frank E. Understanding America's Industries. (gr. 7-9). 1971. text ed. 18.64 (ISBN 0-87345-499-5). McKnight.

Gerbrands, Adrianus A. Wow-Ipits: Eight Asmat Woodcarvers of New Guinea. (Art in Its Context Field Reports: Vol. 3). (Photos). 1967. text ed. 20.80x (ISBN 0-686-22474-4). Mouton.

Gerbrands, Jan J., ed. EURASIP Directory 1983: Directory of European Signal Processing Research Institutions. LC 84-15892. 1984. lib. bdg. 59.00 (ISBN 90-277-1824-5, Pub. by Reidel Holland). Kluwer Academic.

Gerbrandt, Gary L. An Idea Book: For Acting Out & Writing Language, K-8. LC 73-93836. 68p. (Orig.). 1974. pap. 7.00 (ISBN 0-8141-2221-3). NCTE.

Gerbrandy, Pieter S. Indonesia. LC 70-179199. (Illus.). Repr. of 1950 ed. 20.00 (ISBN 0-404-54828-8). AMS Pr.

Gercan, Oktavija, jt. auth. see Brozovic, Blanka.

Gerchick, E., et al, eds. The Role of the Community Hospital in the Care of the Dying Patient & Bereaved. 250p. 1976. 37.50x (ISBN 0-8422-7278-X). Irvington.

Gerchick, Elias. The Role of the Community Hospital in the Care of the Dying Patient, & the Bereaved. 16.50 (ISBN 0-405-12506-2). Ayer Co Pubs.

Gerchow, J., jt. ed. see Hummel, K.

Gerd, Heinrich Bearbeitet von see Von Gerd Heinrich, Bearbeitet.

Gerdel, Florence & Slocum, Marianna. Vocabulario Tzeltal de Bachajon. (Vocabularios Indigenas Ser.: No. 13). 215p. (Span.). 1965. 3.00 (ISBN 0-88312-589-7). Summer Inst Ling.

Gerdeman, D. A. & Hecht, N. L. Arc Plasma Technology in Materials Science. (Applied Mineralogy: Vol. 3). (Illus.). 1972. 45.00 (ISBN 0-387-81041-2). Springer-Verlag.

Gerdes, Dick. Mario Vargas Llosa (Twas 762) (Peru) (Twayne World Authors Ser.). 232p. 1985. lib. bdg. 24.95 (ISBN 0-8057-6612-X, Twayne). G K Hall.

Gerdes, James R., ed. Personal Computing Digest, NNC 1981. LC 81-67132. (Illus.). ix, 298p. 1981. 15.00 (ISBN 0-88283-033-3). AFIPS Pr.

Gerdes, Paulus. Marx Demystifies Calculus. Lumpkin, Beatrice, tr. from Portuguese. LC 85-8988. (Studies in Marxism: Vol. 16). 136p. 1985. 19.95x (ISBN 0-930656-39-3); pap. 9.95 (ISBN 0-930656-40-7). MEP Pubns.

Gerdin, Ingela. The Unknown Balinese: Land, Labor & Inequality in Lombok. (Acta-Gothenburg Studies in Social Anthropology: No. 4). 246p. 1982. pap. text ed. 22.50x (ISBN 91-7346-108-3, Pub. by Acta-Universitas Sweden). Humanities.

Gerdine, Leigh, tr. see Keller, Hermann.

Gerding, Mildred. The Rotary Rig & Its Components: Canadian Metric Edition. 3rd ed. (Rotary Drilling Ser.: Unit I, Lesson 1). (Illus.). 1979. pap. text ed. 5.00 (ISBN 0-88698-017-8). PETEX.

Gerding, Mildred, ed. Applied Mathematics for the Petroleum Other Industries. 3rd, rev. ed. (Illus.). 274p. 1985. pap. text ed. 10.00 (ISBN 0-88698-085-2, 1.60030). PETEX.

--Fundamentals of Petroleum. 2nd ed. (Illus.). 292p. (Orig.). 1981. pap. text ed. 10.00 (ISBN 0-88698-048-8, 1.00020). PETEX.

--Helicopter Safety. rev. ed. (Rotary Drilling Ser.: Unit 5, Lesson 7). (Illus.). 37p. (Orig.). 1980. pap. text ed. 4.50 (ISBN 0-88698-075-5, 2.50710). PETEX.

--The Rotary Rig & Its Components. 3rd ed. (Rotary Drilling Ser.: Unit I, Lesson 1). (Illus.). Date not set. pap. text ed. 5.00 (ISBN 0-88698-005-4, 2.10130). PETEX.

--Well Service & Workover Profitability. (Well Servicing & Workover Ser.: Lesson 12). (Illus.). 32p. 1980. pap. text ed. 4.50 (ISBN 0-88698-068-2, 3.71220). PETEX.

Gerding, Mildred, ed. see Baker, Ron.

Gerding, Mildred, ed. see Cyrus, Cinda.

Gerding, Mildred, ed. see Grona, Nancy & Skinner, Mary L.

Gerdts, Donna B., jt. auth. see Cook, Eung-Do.

Gerdts, William, jt. auth. see Merritt, Howard.

Gerdts, William H. American Impressionism. LC 84-6365. (Illus.). 336p. 1984. 85.00 (ISBN 0-89659-451-3); Special Collector's Ed. 150.00 (ISBN 0-89659-507-2). Abbeville Pr.

--Down Garden Paths. LC 83-16335. (Illus.). 144p. 1983. 25.00 (ISBN 0-8386-3214-9). Fairleigh Dickinson.

--Painters of the Humble Truth: Masterpieces of American Still Life, 1801-1939. LC 81-11400. (Illus.). 241p. 1982. 54.95 (ISBN 0-8262-0355-8). U of Mo Pr.

Gerdts, William H. & Stebbins, Theodore E., Jr. A Man of Genius: The Art of Washington Allston, 1779-1843. LC 79-56222. (Illus.). 253p. 1980. 35.00x (ISBN 0-87846-146-9). U Pr of Va.

Gere, Anne R. Writing & Learning. 544p. 1985. text ed. write for info. (ISBN 0-02-341510-X). Macmillan.

Gere, Anne R. & Smith, Eugene. Attitudes, Language, & Change. LC 79-20099. (Orig.). 1979. pap. 6.65 (ISBN 0-8141-0217-4); pap. 5.25 members. NCTE.

Gere, Charlotte, jt. auth. see Abdy, Jane.

Gere, Edwin, Jr. Modernizing Local Government in Massachusetts: The Quest for Professionals & Reform. LC 84-13140. 208p. (Orig.). 1984. lib. bdg. 22.50 (ISBN 0-8191-4191-7); pap. text ed. 12.00 (ISBN 0-8191-4192-5). U Pr of Amer.

Gere, J., jt. auth. see Timoshenko, Stephen P.

Gere, J. A. & Pouncey, Philip. Italian Drawings: Five Artists Working in Rome, c.1550-c.1640. 176p. 1982. 395.00x (ISBN 0-7141-0783-2, Pub. by Brit Mus Pubns England). State Mutual Bk.

Gere, J. A. & Sparrow, John, eds. Geoffrey Madan's Notebooks. 1981. pap. 4.95x (ISBN 0-19-281870-8). Oxford U Pr.

Gere, J. A., ed. see Madan, Geoffrey.

Gere, James, jt. auth. see Weaver, William Jr.

Gere, James M. & Shah, Haresh C. Terra Non Firma: Understanding & Preparing for Earthquakes. 278p. 1984. pap. 11.95 (ISBN 0-7167-1497-3). W H Freeman.

Gere, John A. Drawings by Michelangelo from the British Museum. LC 79-84415. (Illus.). 111p. 1979. pap. 12.50 (ISBN 0-87598-068-6). Pierpont Morgan.

Gereboff, Joel. Rabbi Tarfon: The Tradition, the Man & Early Rabbinic Judaism. LC 78-15220. (Brown Judaic Studies: No. 7). 1979. 16.50 (ISBN 0-89130-257-3, 140007); pap. 12.00 (ISBN 0-89130-299-9). Scholars Pr GA.

Gerecke, Karl. Vademekum Technische Werte der Getreidemittelverarbeitung und Futtermitteltechnik. 160p. (Ger.). 1970. 20.00 (ISBN 3-87696-106-8, M-7133). French & Eur.

Gereffi, Gary. The Pharmaceutical Industry & Dependency in the Third World. LC 83-42560. 232p. 1983. 25.00x (ISBN 0-691-09401-2); pap. 9.95x (ISBN 0-691-02828-1). Princeton U Pr.

Gerelsegger, Heinz & Peinter, Max. Otto Wagner. (Illus.). 284p. 1985. pap. 25.00 (ISBN 0-8478-0217-5). Rizzoli Intl.

Gerencser, George A. Chloride Transport Coupling in Biological Membranes & Epithelia. 1984. 113.50 (ISBN 0-444-80522-2, I-182-84). Elsevier.

Gerend, Robert P. Partnership Power: How to Profit & Reduce Taxes Investing in Real Estate Partnerships. 232p. 1983. text ed. 16.95 (ISBN 0-8403-3161-4). Kendall-Hunt.

Geres, Paul. Prayers for Impossible Days. Hjelm, Ingalill H., tr. from Fr. LC 75-36442. 64p. 1976. pap. 2.95 (ISBN 0-8006-1214-0, 1-1214). Fortress.

Gerety, R. J., ed. Non-A, Non-B Hepatitis. LC 81-12759. 1981. 49.00 (ISBN 0-12-280680-8). Acad Pr.

Gerety, Robert J. Hepatitis B. Date not set. 79.00 (ISBN 0-12-280672-7). Acad Pr.

Gerety, Robert J., ed. Hepatitis A. LC 83-21540. 1984. 49.00 (ISBN 0-12-280670-0). Acad Pr.

Gerevas, Lawrence E. Basic Drafting Problems. 2nd ed. 240p. 1981. pap. text ed. 13.24 scp (ISBN 0-672-97866-0); tchr's. Manual scp 7.33 (ISBN 0-672-97867-9). Bobbs.

--Drafting Technology Problems. 2nd ed. 1981. pap. write for info. (ISBN 0-02-341830-3). Macmillan.

Gerez, Toni de, tr. My Song Is a Piece of Jade: Poems of Ancient Mexico in English & Spanish. LC 82-18639. (Illus.). (gr. k-3). 1984. 12.45i (ISBN 0-316-81088-6). Little.

Gerfin, Richard & Koch, Robert. Physical Geology: Student Handbook & Study Guide. 6th ed. 320p. 1982. pap. text ed. 8.95 (ISBN 0-13-669788-7). P-H.

Gergacz, John W., jt. auth. see Whitman, Douglas.

Gergel, Thomas. The Encyclopedia of New York. (The Encyclopedia of the U. S. Ser.). (Illus.). 743p. 1983. Repr. lib. bdg. 79.00x (ISBN 0-318-02798-4). Somerset Pub.

Gergely, G., ed. Ellipsometric Tables of the SIS-102 System for Mercury & Hene Laser Spectral Lines. 1971. 10.00 (ISBN 0-9960008-8-7, Pub. by Akademiai Kaido Hungary). Heyden.

Gergely, J., jt. auth. see Devenyi, T.

Gergely, J., jt. ed. see Baum, H.

Gergely, J., et al, eds. see European Immunology Meeting, 4th, Budapest, Hungary, April 12-14, 1978.

Gergely, Lajos, et al. Herpesvirus: Recent Studies, 3 vols, Vol. 3. LC 73-13558. 201p. 1974. text ed. 22.50x (ISBN 0-8422-7176-7). Irvington.

Gergely, T., jt. ed. see Domolki, B.

Gergely, T. E., ed. see IUA Symposium, College Park, Md., Aug. 7-10, 1979.

Gergely, Tibor. Busy Day, Busy People. (Illus.). (ps-1). 1973. pap. 1.95 (ISBN 0-394-82686-8). Random.

Gergely, Tibor, illus. Noah's Ark. (Illus.). 24p. (ps). 1983. 3.50 (ISBN 0-307-11482-1, 10391, Golden Bks). Western Pub.

Gergen, Joe. World Series Heroes & Goats: The Men Who Made History in America's October Classics. LC 82-611. (Random House Sports Library). (Illus.). 160p. (gr. 5-9). 1982. pap. 1.95 (ISBN 0-394-85018-1). Random.

Gergen, K. J. The Concept of Self. 1985. pap. text ed. 6.95x (ISBN 0-8290-0604-4). Irvington.

--Toward Transformation in Social Knowledge. (Springer Series in Social Psychology). (Illus.). 260p. 1982. 27.00 (ISBN 0-387-90673-8). Springer-Verlag.

Gergen, K. J., jt. auth. see Bauer, R. A.

Gergen, K. J. & Davis, K. E., eds. The Social Construction of the Person. (Springer Series in Social Psychology). (Illus.). 300p. 1985. 35.00 (ISBN 0-387-96091-0). Springer-Verlag.

Gergen, Kenneth, ed. see Lynch, Mervin D., et al.

Gergen, Kenneth J. & Gergen, Mary M. Social Psychology. 570p. 1981. text ed. 25.95 (ISBN 0-15-581562-8, HC); study guide 8.95 (ISBN 0-15-581564-4); instr's manual avail. (ISBN 0-15-581563-6). HarBraceJ.

Gergen, Kenneth J. & Gergen, Mary M., eds. Historical Social Psychology. 432p. 1984. text ed. 39.95 (ISBN 0-89859-349-2). L Erlbaum Assocs.

Gergen, Kenneth J., et al, eds. Social Exchange: Advances in Theory & Research. LC 80-18170. 324p. 1980. 29.50x (ISBN 0-306-40395-1, Plenum Pr). Plenum Pub.

Gergen, Mary M., jt. auth. see Gergen, Kenneth J.

Gergen, Mary M., jt. ed. see Gergen, Kenneth J.

Gergen, Michael & Hagen, Dolores. Computer Technology for the Handicapped. (Illus.). 253p. (Orig.). 1985. pap. text ed. 17.95 (ISBN 0-932719-00-7). Closing Gap.

Gergen, Michael J., jt. auth. see Pollack, Kenneth.

Gerger, Dawn. Tempo Word Find Puzzles, No. 6. 1982. pap. 1.50 (ISBN 0-448-05777-8, Pub. by Tempo). Ace Bks.

--Tempo Word Find Puzzles, No. 7. 1982. pap. 1.50 (ISBN 0-448-05786-7, Pub. by Tempo). Ace Bks.

Gerhard, Christian. Making Sense: Reading Comprehensive Improved Through Categorizing. LC 75-37706. (Reading Aids Ser.). 163p. 1975. pap. 8.00 (ISBN 0-87207-218-5). Intl Reading.

Gerhard, D., ed. see Fueter, Eduard.

Gerhard, Dietrich. Old Europe: A Study of Continuity, 1000-1800. LC 81-14872. (Studies in Social Discontinuity). 1981. 17.50 (ISBN 0-12-280720-0). Acad Pr.

Gerhard, Eduard, ed. Etruskische Spiegel, 5 vols. (Ger.). 1974. Repr. of 1887 ed. Set. 406.00x (ISBN 3-11-002354-7). De Gruyter.

Gerhard, Fred J., Jr. The Illinois Do-It-Yourself Divorce Kit. (Illus.). 176p. 1984. pap. 12.95 (ISBN 0-8092-5403-4). Contemp Bks.

Gerhard, George B. Monarch Notes on Warren's All the King's Men. (Orig.). pap. 3.25 (ISBN 0-671-00697-5). Monarch Pr.

Gerhard, George B., et al, eds. see Carter, Henry H.

Gerhard, H. Harris, jt. auth. see Horvitz, Leslie A.

Gerhard, Hans W. Experience with Adjustment Policies. (Occasional Papers: No. 41). 1985. pap. 7.50 (ISBN 0-317-19913-7). Intl Monetary.

Gerhard, Peter. The North Frontier of New Spain. LC 81-47917. (Illus.). 544p. 1982. 66.00 (ISBN 0-691-09394-6). Princeton U Pr.

--The Southeast Frontier of New Spain. LC 78-70295. (Illus.). 1979. 26.50x (ISBN 0-691-05273-5). Princeton U Pr.

Gerhard, R., et al. The Balanced Service System. (Illus.). 215p. 1981. pap. text ed. 15.00 (ISBN 0-318-12057-7). Responsive Syst.

Gerhardie, William. The Polyglots. 336p. 1983. Repr. of 1925 ed. 16.95 (ISBN 0-436-17385-9, Pub. by Secker & Warburg UK). David & Charles.

Gerhardsson, Birger. The Ethos of the Bible. Westerholm, Stephen, tr. from Swedish. LC 81-43077. 160p. 1981. pap. 8.95 (ISBN 0-8006-1612-X, 1-1612). Fortress.

--The Origins of the Gospel Traditions. Lund, Gene J., tr. from Swedish. LC 78-19634. 1979. 7.95 (ISBN 0-8006-0543-8, 1-543). Fortress.

Gerhardstein, Virginia B. Dickinson's American Historical Fiction. 4th ed. LC 80-23450. 328p. 1981. 20.00 (ISBN 0-8108-1362-9). Scarecrow.

Gerhardt & King. Amputations: Immediate & Early Prosthetic Management. (Illus.). 305p. 1982. text ed. 99.00 (ISBN 3-456-80766-X, Pub by Hans Huber Switzerland). J K Burgess.

Gerhardt, E. Pilzfuehrer: 245 wichtige Speise- und Giftpilze in 267 Farbfotos abgebildet un beschrieben. 2nd ed. (Illus.). 326p. 1981. pap. text ed. 8.00x (ISBN 3-405-12484-0). Lubrecht & Cramer.

Gerhardt, Elena. Recital. LC 78-181162. 1953. Repr. 19.00x (ISBN 0-403-01564-2). Scholarly.

Gerhardt, James M. The Draft & Public Policy: Issues in Military Manpower Procurement, 1945-1970. LC 70-105723. 447p. 1971. 15.00 (ISBN 0-8142-0143-1). Ohio St U Pr.

Gerhardt, Karl I. Geschichte Der Mathematik in Deutschland. Repr. of 1877 ed. 30.00 (ISBN 0-384-18150-3). Johnson Repr.

Gerhardt, Mia I. Essai d'Analyse Litteraire de la Pastorale dans les Litteratures Italienne, Espagnole et Francaise. (Romance Reprints Ser.: No. 3). (Illus.). 317p. (Fr.). 1975. pap. 29.00x (ISBN 90-6194-211-X). Benjamins North Am.

Gerhardt, Philipp, et al, eds. Manual of Methods for General Bacteriology. (Illus.). 524p. 1981. 32.00 (ISBN 0-914826-29-8); flexible bdg. 27.00 (ISBN 0-914826-30-1). Am Soc Microbio.

Gerhardt, Russe O. International SFTR Method of Measuring & Recording Joint Motion. 81p. 1975. 39.00 (ISBN 3-456-80075-4, Pub. by Holdan Bk Ltd UK). State Mutual Bk.

Gerhardt, Uta E. & Wadsworth, Michael E., eds. Stress & Stigma: Explanation & Evidence in the Sociology of Crime & Illness. LC 84-17936. 288p. 1985. 29.95 (ISBN 0-312-76606-8). St Martin.

Gerhart, Eugene C., ed. Quote It! Memorable Legal Quotations. LC 78-83771. 1969. 35.00 (ISBN 0-87632-001-9). Boardman.

Gerhart, Gail M. Black Power in South Africa: The Evolution of an Ideology. LC 75-13149. (Perspectives on Southern Africa Ser.: Vol. 19). 1978. pap. 7.95 (ISBN 0-520-03933-5, CAL423). U of Cal Pr.

Gerhart, Genevra. The Russian's World: Life & Language. (Illus.). 257p. 1974. pap. text ed. 13.95 (ISBN 0-15-577983-4, HC). HarBraceJ.

Gerhart, Mary & Russell, Allan M. Metaphoric Process: The Creation of Scientific & Religious Understanding. LC 83-15614. 217p. 1984. 16.95x (ISBN 0-912646-82-9); pap. 10.95x (ISBN 0-912646-86-1). Tex Christian.

Gerhart, Paul F. Political Activity by Public Employee Organizations at the Local Level: Threat or Promise? (Public Employee Relations Library Ser.: No. 44). pap. 6.00 (ISBN 0-87373-144-1). Intl Personnel Mgmt.

Gerhart, Philip M. & Gross, Richard J. Fundamentals of Fluid Mechanics. LC 84-9217. 1985. 39.95 (ISBN 0-201-11410-0); sol. manual 19.95 (ISBN 0-201-11411-9). Addison Wesley.

Gerhold, H. D., et al, eds. The Breeding of Pest Resistant Trees. 1966. 76.00 (ISBN 0-08-011764-3). Pergamon.

Gericault, Jean L. Gericault: Drawings & Watercolors. Berger, Klaus, ed. LC 83-45769. Repr. of 1946 ed. 49.50 (ISBN 0-404-20107-5). AMS Pr.

Gerick, David J. Water, Water Everywhere. (Illus.). 1978. 20.00 (ISBN 0-916750-75-2). Dayton Labs.

Gericke, Paul. Crucial Experiences in the Life D. L. Moody. LC 78-7570. 72p. (Orig.). 1978. pap. 3.00 (ISBN 0-914520-12-1). Insight Pr.

--Minister's Filing System. 1978. pap. 1.95 (ISBN 0-8010-3721-2). Baker Bk.

Gerig, Donald. Leadership in Crisis. LC 81-51741. 160p. 1981. pap. 4.95 (ISBN 0-8307-0797-2, 5415304). Regal.

Gerig, Reginald R. Famous Pianists & Their Technique. 3rd. ed. LC 73-18804. (Illus.). 576p. 1975. 24.95 (ISBN 0-88331-066-X). Luce.

Gerigk, Horst-Juergen. Entwurf einer Theorie des literarischen Gebildes. xii, 216p. (Ger.). 1975. 33.60 (ISBN 3-11-005876-9). De Gruyter.

Gerin, Winifred. Anne Thackeray Ritchie: A Biography. (Illus.). 1981. 32.50x (ISBN 0-19-812664-6). Oxford U Pr.

--Branwell Bronte. 338p. 1981. Repr. of 1961 ed. lib. bdg. 25.00 (ISBN 0-89760-250-1). Telegraph Bks.

--Elizabeth Gaskell. (Ser. K). (Illus.). 1976. pap. 9.95x (ISBN 0-19-281296-3). Oxford U Pr.

--Emily Bronte. 1972. pap. 8.95 (ISBN 0-19-281251-3). Oxford U Pr.

--Horatia Nelson. 1970. 21.95x (ISBN 0-19-822331-5). Oxford U Pr.

Gerin, Winifred, intro. by. The Life of Charlotte Bronte. 432p. 1982. pap. 4.95 (ISBN 0-460-01318-1, DEL 04835, Evman). Biblio Dist.

Geriner, Laura. Seven True Bear Stories. 1979. 8.95 (ISBN 0-8038-6747-6). Hastings.

Geringer, L R. Cowboy in the Wheat. LC 84-73055. 180p. (Orig.). 1985. pap. 6.90 (ISBN 0-317-13519-8). Gehry Pr.

Geringer, Laura. A Three Hat Day. LC 85-42640. (Illus.). 32p. (ps-3). 1985. 9.57i (ISBN 0-06-021988-2); PLB 9.89g (ISBN 0-06-021989-0). HarpJ.

Geringer, Lauren R. Your Own Shortcut Shorthand. LC 79-55059. (Orig.). 1980. pap. 5.95 (ISBN 0-935020-06-3). Gehry Pr.

Gerini, G. E. Researches on Ptolemy's Geography of Eastern Asia. LC 90-3098. (Illus.). 974p. 1974. 27.50x (ISBN 0-89684-449-8). Orient Bk Dist.

Gerin-Lajoie, A. Catechisme Politique Ou Elemens Du Droit Public et Constitutionnel Du Canada, Mis a la Portee Du Peuple (Montreal 1851) (Canadiana Avant 1867: No. 15). 1967. 10.40x (ISBN 90-2796-337-1). Mouton.

Gerin-Lajoie, Antoine. Catechisme Politique: Ou, Elemens Du Droit Public et Consitutionnel Du Canada, Mis a la Portee Du Peuple. Repr. of 1851 ed. 13.00 (ISBN 0-384-18165-1). Johnson Repr.

Gerisch, Robert A. The Gerisch Method of Stress-Tension Prevention. (Illus.). 92p. (Orig.). 1985. pap. 9.95 (ISBN 0-934201-01-3); audio cassette 9.95 (ISBN 0-934201-00-5). Gerisch Pub Co.

Gerischer, H. & Tovias, C. A. Advances in & Electrochemistry & Electrochemical Engineering, Vol. 13. 360p. 1984. text ed. 45.00 (ISBN 0-471-87881-2). Wiley.

Gerischer, H. & Katz, J. J., eds. Light-Induced Charge Separation in Biology & Chemistry, LSRR 12. (Dahlem Workshop Reports Ser.: L.S.R.R. No. 12). 563p. 1979. pap. 44.20x (ISBN 0-89573-081-2). VCH Pubs.

Gerischer, Heinz. Advances in Electrochemistry & Electrochemical Engineering, Vol. 12. Tobias, Charles W., ed. LC 61-15021. 361p. 1981. 56.50 (ISBN 0-471-87530-9, Pub. by Wiley-Interscience). Wiley.

Gerits, Klaus, et al. Tricks & Tips for the Commodore. Dykema, Greg, tr. 276p. (Orig., Ger.). 1984. pap. text ed. 19.95 (ISBN 0-916439-03-8). Abacus Soft.

Geritz, Albert & Laine, Amos Lee. John Rastell. (English Authors Ser.). 135p. 1983. lib. bdg. 18.95 (ISBN 0-8057-6849-1, Twayne). G K Hall.

Geritz, Albert J. John Rastell's The Pastyme of People & A New Boke of Purgatory: Critical Editions. Orgel, Stephen, ed. (The Renaissance Imagination Ser.). 28.00 (ISBN 0-317-20367-3). Garland Pub.

Gerjuoy, E., et al see Bergmann, P. G., et al.

Gerkan, Arnim Von see L'Orange, Hans P. & Von Gerkan, Arnim.

Gerke, Friedrich. Die Christlichen Sarkophage der vorkonstantinischen Zeit. (Studien Zur Spaetantiken Kunstgeschichte: Vol. 11). (Illus.). viii, 432p. 1978. Repr. of 1940 ed. 140.00x (ISBN 3-11-004999-6). De Gruyter.

Gerkin, Charles V. Crisis Experience in Modern Life: Theory & Theology for Pastoral Care. rev. ed. LC 79-892. 1979. 14.95 (ISBN 0-687-09906-4). Abingdon.

--The Living Human Document: Re-Visioning Pastoral Counseling in a Hermeneutical Mode. 224p. 1984. pap. 10.95 (ISBN 0-687-22372-5). Abingdon.

Gerkin, Pat, jt. ed. see Johnson, Eleanor.

Gerking, S. K. Estimation of Stochastic Input-Output Models. (Studies in Applied Regional Science: No. 3). 1976. pap. 16.00 (ISBN 90-207-0628-4, Pub. by Martinus Nijhoff Netherlands). Kluwer Academic.

Gerking, Shelby D., ed. Ecology of Freshwater Fish Production. LC 77-92407. 520p. 1978. 104.95x (ISBN 0-470-99362-6). Halsted Pr.

Gerl, George & Lane, George. Two Called Together. 1978. pap. text ed. 4.00 (ISBN 0-8294-0274-8); tchr's ed. 4.00 (ISBN 0-8294-0277-2). Loyola.

Gerlach, Albert A. Theory & Applications of Statistical Wave-Period Processing, 3 Vols. 1434p. 1970. 352.50 (ISBN 0-677-02510-6). Gordon.

Gerlach, Barbara. The Things That Make for Peace: Biblical Meditations. (Illus.). 64p. (Orig.). 1983. pap. 4.95 (ISBN 0-8298-0664-4). Pilgrim NY.

Gerlach, E., ed. The Physics of Selenium & Tellurium. (Springer Series in Solid State Sciences: Vol.13). (Illus.). 1979. 37.00 (ISBN 0-387-09692-2). Springer-Verlag.

Gerlach, Heather, jt. auth. see Hartson, John.

Gerlach, J., jt. auth. see Kuhlenbeck, H.

Gerlach, J., ed. see Kuhlenbeck, H.

Gerlach, Joel & Bolge, Richard. Preach the Gospel. 1982. 8.95 (ISBN 0-8100-0153-5, 15NO387). Northwest Pub.

Gerlach, John. Toward the End: Closure & Structure in the American Short Story. LC 84-2509. ix, 193p. 1985. 21.50x (ISBN 0-8173-0233-6); pap. 9.95x (ISBN 0-8173-0234-4). U of Ala Pr.

Gerlach, Larry R. Blazing Crosses in Zion: The Ku Klux Klan in Utah. (Illus.). 250p. 1982. 17.95 (ISBN 0-87421-111-5); pap. 9.95 (ISBN 0-87421-112-3). Utah St U Pr.

Gerlach, Larry R. see Weaver, Glenn.

Gerlach, Larry R., et al, eds. Legacies of the American Revolution. LC 78-5888. 242p. 1978. 11.95 (ISBN 0-87421-097-6); pap. 7.95. Utah St U Pr.

Gerlach, Luther P. & Hine, Virginia H. People, Power, Change: Movements of Social Transformation. LC 70-109434. 1970. pap. 9.63 scp (ISBN 0-672-60613-5). Bobbs.

Gerlach, Martin. Primitive & Folk Jewelry. (Illus.). 1971. pap. 7.95 (ISBN 0-486-22747-2). Dover.

--Primitive & Folk Jewelry. (Illus.). 16.75 (ISBN 0-8446-0107-1). Peter Smith.

Gerlach, Nancy, jt. auth. see DeWitt, Dave.

Gerlach, Ronald & Lamprecht, Lynn. Teaching about the Law. 354p. 1975. 15.00 (ISBN 0-87084-834-8). Anderson Pub Co.

Gerlach, Russel L. Immigrants in the Ozarks: A Study in Ethnic Geography. LC 75-4328. (University of Missouri Studies Ser.: Vol.64). (Illus.). 232p. 1976. 18.00x (ISBN 0-8262-0201-2). U of Mo Pr.

--Settlement Patterns in Missouri: A Study of Population Origins with a Wall Map. LC 84-23454. 96p. 1986. text ed. 22.00 (ISBN 0-8262-0473-2). U of Mo Pr.

Gerlach, Vernon S. An Interactive Approach to BASIC. 326p. 1983. pap. text ed. write for info. (ISBN 0-02-341500-2). Macmillan.

Gerlach, Vernon S. & Ely, Donald P. Teaching & Media: A Systematic Approach. 2nd ed. (Illus.). 1980. text ed. 32.95 (ISBN 0-13-891358-7). P-H.

Gerlach, Werner, jt. ed. see Evanoff, Philip C.

Gerlach, Wolfgang & Nirenberg, Helgard. The Genus Fusarium: A Pictorial Atlas. (Mitteilungen aus der Biologischen Bundesanstalt fuer Land-und Fortswirtschaft Berlin Dahlem: No. 209). (Illus.). 406p. pap. text ed. 42.00x (ISBN 3-489-20900-1). Parey Sci Pubs.

Gerland, Ernst. Geschichte der Physik Von Den Altesten Zeitem Bis Zum Ausgange Des Achtzehnten Jahrhunderts. Repr. of 1913 ed. 50.00 (ISBN 0-384-18180-5). Johnson Repr.

Gerle, Robert. The Art of Practising the Violin. (Illus.). 110p. 1983. pap. text ed. 10.95 (ISBN 0-85249-506-4, Pub. by Stainer & Bell England). Galaxy Music.

Gerler, Edwin, Jr. Counseling the Young Learner. (Illus.). 180p. 1982. 13.95 (ISBN 0-13-183228-X); pap. 6.95 (ISBN 0-13-183210-7). P-H.

Gerli, E. Michael, ed. Triste Deleytacion: An Anonymous Fifteenth Century Castilian Romance. LC 82-15742. 160p. (Orig., Span. & Eng.). 1983. lib. bdg. 14.95 (ISBN 0-87840-086-9). Georgetown U Pr.

Gerling, Curt. Good Enought for Grandpa. 237p. 1958. 10.00 (ISBN 0-686-09023-3). Plaza Pubs.

--Never a Dull Moment. 210p. 1974. 6.95 (ISBN 0-686-09024-1). Plaza Pubs.

Gerlinger, Lorena. The Easter Story. (Illus.). 14p. 1972. 2.75 (ISBN 0-9606712-1-8). L Gerlinger.

Gerlings, Charlotte & Ives, Suzy. Noah's Ark in Paper & Card. (Illus.). 112p. (gr. k-3). 7.95 (ISBN 0-8008-5578-7). Taplinger.

GerLings, P. G. Atlas of Histopathology of Ear Tumors. (Illus.). 168p. 1979. text ed. 37.00 (ISBN 0-8391-1435-4). Univ Park.

--Atlas of Histopathology of Ear Tumours. 168p. 1979. 90.00x (ISBN 0-686-79479-6, Pub. by Lloyd-Luke England). State Mutual Bk.

Gerlitz, Menaham. The Heavenly City. Weinbach, Sheindel, tr. from Hebrew. 1978. 6.95 (ISBN 0-87306-147-0). Feldheim.

Gerloch, M. Magnetism & Ligand-Field Analysis. LC 83-1820. (Illus.). 650p. 1984. 110.00 (ISBN 0-521-24939-2). Cambridge U Pr.

Gerlock, Amil J. & Mirfakhraee, Mansour. Essentials of Diagnostic & Interventional Angiographic Technique. (Illus.). 300p. 1984. write for info (ISBN 0-7216-1026-9). Saunders.

Gerlock, Amil J. & Sinn, Douglas P. Clinical & Radiographic Interpretation of Facial Fractures. 1981. text ed. 39.95 (ISBN 0-316-30836-6). Little.

Gerlock, Larry & Von Schmidt, Carol. Dining In Salt Lake City. 8.95 (ISBN 0-89716-139-4). Peanut Butter.

Gerloff, E. A. Organizational Theory & Design: A Strategic Approach for Management. (Management Ser.). 416p. 1985. 31.95 (ISBN 0-07-023177-X). McGraw.

Gerloff, J., jt. auth. see Krieger, W.

Gerloff, J. & Cholnoky, B. J., eds. Friedrich-Hustedt-Gedenkband: Diatomaceae 2. 1970. 87.500 (ISBN 3-7682-5431-3). Lubrecht & Cramer.

Gerloff, J., jt. ed. see Hakansson, H.

Gerloff, J., ed. see Pascher, A.

Gerloff, J., et al, eds. see Engler, A.

Gerlovich, Jack A., jt. ed. see Downs, Gary E.

Germa, Pierre. Larousse Des Citations Francaises et Etrangeres. 912p. (Fr.). 1975. 35.00 (ISBN 0-686-57195-9, M-6269). French & Eur.

Germain, ed. see De Vigny, Alfred.

Germain, Bernard F., ed. Osteoarthritis & Musculoskeletal Pain Syndromes. (Contemporary Patient Management Ser.). 1983. 33.50 (ISBN 0-87488-873-5). Med Exam.

Germain, Carel & Gitterman, Alex. The Life Model of Social Work Practice. LC 79-17816. 1980. 21.00x (ISBN 0-231-04152-7). Columbia U Pr.

Germain, Carel B. Social Work Practice in Health Care: An Ecological View. LC 83-48757. (Fields of Practice Ser.). 336p. 1984. 19.95x (ISBN 0-02-911660-0). Free Pr.

Germain, Carel B., ed. Social Work Practice: People & Environments. 336p. 1979. 31.50x (ISBN 0-231-04332-5); pap. 14.50x (ISBN 0-231-04333-3). Columbia U Pr.

Germain, Claire, ed. see Parker School of Foreign & Comparative Law.

Germain, Clarence B. Programming the IBM PC & XT: A Guide to Languages. LC 84-289. (Illus.). 352p. 1984. pap. 19.95 (ISBN 0-89303-783-4). Brady Comm.

Germain, D. Saint. The Theory & the Meaning of the Lines of the Hand with Special Emphasis on the Life & the Anticipation of One's Life Span. (Illus.). 136p. 1983. 117.85 (ISBN 0-89901-124-1). Found Class Reprints.

Germain, Edward, ed. see Crosby, Harry.

Germain, George L. Effective Coaching & Tipping. LC 74-32536. (The Effective Series Training Program for Supervisors). (Illus.). 37p. 1975. Incl. transparency masters. 3-ring binder 57.50 (ISBN 0-88061-024-7). Inst Pub GA.

--Effective Job Instruction. LC 77-77275. (The Effective Series Training Program for Supervisors). (Illus.). 38p. 1977. 3-ring binder 57.50 (ISBN 0-88061-022-0). Inst Pub GA.

--Effective Safe Behavior Reinforcement. (The Effective Series Training Program for Supervisors). (Illus.). 37p. 1975. 3-ring binder 57.50 (ISBN 0-88061-025-5). Inst Pub GA.

--Effective Safety Talk Technique. LC 74-32536. (The Effective Series Training Program for Supervisors). (Illus.). 49p. 1975. Incl. transparency masters. 3-ring binder 57.50 (ISBN 0-88061-023-9). Inst Pub GA.

--Safety Performance Management. (Illus.). 38p. Incl. transparency masters. 3-ring binder 49.50 (ISBN 0-88061-019-0). Inst Pub GA.

Germain, George L. & Kuhlman, Raymond L. The Effective Series Training Program for Supervisors, 6 manuals. 3-ring binder 345.00 (ISBN 0-88061-021-2). Inst Pub GA.

Germain, George L., jt. auth. see Bird, Frank E., Jr.

Germain, George L., jt. auth. see Clark, M. Douglas.

Germain, P. & Nayroles, B., eds. Applications of Methods of Functional Analysis to Problems in Mechanics. LC 76-5454. (Lecture Notes in Mathematics Ser: Vol. 503). 1976. pap. 27.00 (ISBN 0-387-07629-8). Springer-Verlag.

Germain, Regina, intro. by. National Recreational, Sporting & Hobby Organizations of the United States: 1986. 6th ed. LC 80-70429. 140p. 1986. pap. 30.00 (ISBN 0-910416-58-3). Columbia Bks.

Germain, Regina, jt. ed. see Colgate, Craig, Jr.

Germain, Saint. Intermediate Studies in Alchemy. new ed. LC 74-82295. (Alchemy Ser.). (Illus.). 158p. 1975. pap. 3.95 (ISBN 0-916766-01-2). Summit Univ.

Germain, Walter M. Magic Power of Your Mind. pap. 5.00 (ISBN 0-87980-093-3). Wilshire.

German American Chamber of Commerce, ed. see Forry, John I. & Theurer, Martin.

German American Chamber of Commerce, Inc., ed. see Riesenkampff, Alexander & Barron, William.

German American Chamber of Commerce, ed. see Peltzer, Martin & Treumann, Walter.

German American Chamber of Commerce, ed. see Storette, Ronald F.

German American Chamber of Commerce, ed. see Waldmann, Raymond J. & Reichelt, Rainer.

German American Chamber of Commerce, ed. see Waldmann, Raymond J. & Theurer, Martin.

German American Chamber of Commerce, ed. American Subsidiaries of German Firms: Tochtergesellschaften Deutscher Unternehmen in U. S. A. 15th ed. 250p. (Ger.). 1983. spiral bdg. 55.00 (ISBN 0-86640-009-5). German Am Chamber.

--American Subsidiaries of German Firms-Tochtergesellschaften Deutscher Unternehmen In U. S. A. 16th ed. 264p. (Ger. & Eng.). 1984. spiral bdg. 55.00 (ISBN 0-86640-017-6). German Am Chamber.

German, Andrew W. Down on T Wharf: The Boston Fisheries as Seen Through The Photographs of Henry D. Fisher. (American Maritime Library: Vol. 10). (Illus.). 160p. 1982. 20.00 (ISBN 0-913372-26-9). Mystic Seaport.

German Association of Comparative Law. Bibliograghy of German Law. Suppl. 1969-1973. 54.00x (ISBN 3-8114-0037-1). Rothman.

German, Don. Mattie's Money Tree. LC 84-11849. (Illus.). 94p. (gr. 2-4). 1984. 10.95 (ISBN 0-664-32716-8). Westminster.

German, Don & German, Joan. Make Your Own Convenience Foods: How to Make Chemical Free Foods That Are Fast, Simple & Economical. 1979. pap. 7.95 (ISBN 0-02-009630-5, Collier). Macmillan.

--Money A to Z: A Consumer's Guide to the Language of Personal Finance. 256p. 1984. 15.95 (ISBN 0-87196-836-3). Facts on File.

--Ninety Days to Financial Fitness. 160p. 1985. 15.95 (ISBN 0-02-543040-8); pap. 4.95 (ISBN 0-02-079620-X). Macmillan.

--Ninety Days to Financial Fitness. 160p. 1986. pap. 4.95 (ISBN 0-02-079620-X). MacMillan.

--The Only Money Book for the Middle Class. LC 82-14236. (Illus.). 320p. 1983. 13.95 (ISBN 0-688-01567-0). Morrow.

German, Donald R. Money & Banks. LC 78-64427. (Illus.). (gr. 2-5). 1979. 3.50 (ISBN 0-89799-125-7); pap. 1.50 (ISBN 0-89799-041-2). Dandelion Pr.

German, Donald R. & German, Joan W. Bank Employee's Marketing Handbook. 1975. 19.50 (ISBN 0-88262-085-1). Warren.

--Bank Employee's Security Handbook. 2nd ed. 233p. 1982. 37.50 (ISBN 0-88262-742-2). Warren.

--The Bank Teller's Handbook. 2nd ed. 346p. 1980. pap. 24.95 (ISBN 0-88262-528-4, 80-53403). Warren.

--How to Find a Job When Jobs Are Hard to Find. 256p. 1983. 15.95; pap. 7.95 (ISBN 0-8144-7592-2). AMACOM.

--How to Find a Job When Jobs Are Hard to Find. LC 80-69705. pap. 63.00 (ISBN 0-317-20413-0, 2023500). Bks Demand UMI.

--Tested Techniques in Bank Marketing, Vol. II. 1st ed. LC 72-4684. 42.50 (ISBN 0-88262-272-2). Warren.

German Electrical & Electronic Manufacturers Assoc., ed. Electro Buyers' Guide 1981. 1300p. (Orig.). 1981. pap. 27.50x (ISBN 0-686-79790-6). Intl Pubns Serv.

German, Gene A., jt. auth. see Leed, Theodore W.

German, Iurii P. see Herman, Yuri, pseud.

German, James. Chromosome Mutation & Neoplasia. LC 82-21697. 486p. 1983. 96.00 (ISBN 0-8451-0220-6). A R Liss.

German, James L., III, jt. ed. see Chaganti, R. S.

German, Joan, jt. auth. see German, Don.

German, Joan W. The Money Book. LC 80-25949. (Illus.). 32p. 1982. 5.95 (ISBN 0-525-66726-1). Dandelion Pr.

--What Am I? LC 78-73531. (Illus.). (ps-2). Date not set. price not set (ISBN 0-89799-163-X); pap. price not set (ISBN 0-89799-081-1). Dandelion Pr.

German, Joan W., jt. auth. see German, Donald R.

German, Kathleen M. Public Speaking: A Workbook. 1984. pap. text ed. 4.75 (ISBN 0-89917-438-8). Tichenor Pub.

German, R. M. & Lay, K. W., eds. Processing of Metal & Ceramic Powders: Proceedings. TMS-AIME Fall Meeting, Louisville, 1981. (Illus.). 337p. 45.00 (ISBN 0-89520-396-0, 219); members 30.00 (ISBN 0-317-36310-7); student members 15.00 (ISBN 0-317-36311-5). ASM.

German Science Foundation Staff, ed. Recent German Research on Problems of Parasitology, Animal Health & Animal Breeding in the Tropics & Subtropics. 135p. 1984. pap. 17.50 (ISBN 0-317-27026-5). VCH Pubs.

German Society of Metallurgy, ed. Acoustic Emission: Proceedings of the Symposium, held in Bad Nauheim, West Germany, 1979. Nicoll, A. R., tr. (Illus.). 385p. 1980. lib. bdg. 63.00 (ISBN 3-88355-030-2, Pub. by DGM Metallurgy Germany). IR Pubns.

German, Terence J. Hamann on Language & Religion. (Oxford Theological Monographs). 1981. text ed. 34.95x (ISBN 0-19-826717-7). Oxford U Pr.

German War Office. Handbook of the German Army in War, January 1917. (Illus.). 1973. Repr. of 1917 ed. 17.00x (ISBN 0-8464-0471-0). Beekman Pubs.

German, William M. Doctor's Anonymous: The Story of Laboratory Medicine. 1944. 20.00 (ISBN 0-8274-4204-1). R West.

German Workshop on Artificial Intelligence, Bad Honnef, BRD, Jan. 1981. GWAI-Eighty-One. Siekmann, Joerg H., ed. (Informatik-Fachberichte: 47). 317p. 1981. pap. 17.10 (ISBN 3-540-10859-9). Springer-Verlag.

Germane, Gayton E. Transportation Policy Issues for the 1980's. LC 82-74023. (Illus.). 512p. 1983. text ed. 25.95 (ISBN 0-201-10510-1); instrs' manual avail. Addison-Wesley.

Germane, Gayton L., ed. The Executive Course: A Handbook for Managers from America's Leading Business School. 352p. 1986. 22.95 (ISBN 0-201-11553-0). Addison-Wesley.

Germani, Gino. Authoritarianism, Fascism & National Populism. LC 77-80871. 292p. 1978. 17.95 (ISBN 0-87855-241-3); pap. 9.95 (ISBN 0-87855-642-7). Transaction Bks.

--Marginality. LC 78-62978. 148p. 1980. 5.95x (ISBN 0-87855-235-9). Transaction Bks.

--The Sociology of Modernization: Studies on Its Historical & Theoretical Aspects with Special Regard to the Latin America Case. LC 79-64855. 272p. 1981. text ed. 17.95 (ISBN 0-87855-268-5). Transaction Bk.

Germanier, R., ed. Bacterial Vaccines. 1984. 65.00 (ISBN 0-12-280880-0). Acad Pr.

Germanis, Peter, et al. Understanding Reaganomics. 64p. 1982. 4.00 (ISBN 0-317-07527-6). Heritage Found.

Germann, A. C. Police Executive Development. 112p. 1962. 12.75x (ISBN 0-398-00670-9). C C Thomas.

Germann, A. C., et al. Introduction to Law Enforcement & Criminal Justice. (Illus.). 410p. 1985. 17.50x (ISBN 0-398-05072-4). C C Thomas.

Germann, Peter. Die Soganannten Sententiae Vorronis. pap. 8.00 (ISBN 0-384-18030-2). Johnson Repr.

Germann, Richard & Arnold, Peter. Bernard Haldane Associates' Job & Career Building. LC 81-51898. 256p. 1982. pap. 6.95 (ISBN 0-89815-048-5). Ten Speed Pr.

--Bernard Haldane Associates Job & Career Building: A Step-by-Step Guide. LC 79-2620. (Illus.). 1980. 12.45i (ISBN 0-06-011486-X, HarpT). Har-Row.

Germann, Richard, et al. Working & Liking It. 176p. 1984. pap. 4.95 (ISBN 0-449-90084-3, Columbine). Fawcett.

Germann, Sheridan & Guglietti, Paul. Early Keyboard Instruments: A Bibliography of Published Works on Harpsichords, Clavichords, Early Pianos, & Related Instruments. 1981. lib. bdg. 20.00 (ISBN 0-8240-9312-7). Garland Pub.

Germano, Frank, Jr. Automatic Transaction Decomposition in a CODASYL Prototype System. Stone, Harold S., ed. LC 81-12943. (Computer Science: Distributed Database Systems Ser.: No. 6). 150p. 1981. 34.95 (ISBN 0-8357-1221-4). UMI Res Pr.

Germano, Joseph & Schmitt, Conrad. Schaum's Outline of Italian Grammar. 2nd ed. (Schaum's Outline Ser.). 288p. 1981. pap. 6.95x (ISBN 0-07-023031-5). McGraw.

Germano, William P. & Lecyn, Nancy, eds. Directory of Social & Health Agencies of New York City: 1981-1982. 576p. 1981. 50.00x (ISBN 0-231-05134-4). Columbia U Pr.

German-Reed, T. Bibliographical Notes on T. E. Lawrence's Seven Pillars of Wisdom & Revolt in the Desert. LC 76-57939. 1977. Repr. of 1928 ed. lib. bdg. 10.00 (ISBN 0-8414-4413-7). Folcroft.

Germany, jt. auth. see International Congress of Administrative Sciences.

Germany (Democratic Republic). Central Statistical Board Staff, ed. Statistical Pocket Book of the German Democratic Republic, 1981. 26th ed. LC 63-47828. (Illus.). 160p. 1981. 7.50x (ISBN 0-8002-2956-8). Intl Pubns Serv.

Germany, Lucille, jt. auth. see Sumrall, Velma.

Germar, Herb. Student Journalist & Photojournalism. LC 67-15471. (Student Journalist Ser). (gr. 7 up). 1967. PLB 8.97 (ISBN 0-8239-0125-4). Rosen Group.

Germer, Helmut. The German Novel of Education 1792-1805: A Complete Bibliography & Analysis. (Germanic Studies in America: Vol. 3). 280p. 1968. 22.45 (ISBN 3-261-00309-X). P Lang Pubs.

Germidis, Dimitri & Michalet, Charles A. International Banks & Financial Markets in Developing Countries. 94p. (Orig.). 1984. pap. 13.00x (ISBN 92-64-12635-X). OECD.

Germidis, Dimitri, ed. International Subcontracting: A New Form of Investment. (Illus.). 227p. (Orig.). 1981. pap. text ed. 13.50x (ISBN 92-64-12129-3, 41-80-08-1). OECD.

Germino, Dante. Beyond Ideology: The Revival of Political Theory. (Midway Reprint Ser.). 1976. pap. 7.00x (ISBN 0-226-28849-8). U of Chicago Pr.

--Inaugural Addresses of American Presidents: The Public Philosophy & Rhetoric. (The Presidency & the Press: Vol. VII). 56p. 1984. lib. bdg. 18.25 (ISBN 0-8191-3702-2); pap. text ed. 7.25 (ISBN 0-8191-3703-0). U Pr of Amer.

--Machiavelli to Marx: Modern Western Political Thought. LC 77-181415. 1979. 8.50x (ISBN 0-226-28850-1, P810, Phoen). U of Chicago Pr.

--Political Philosophy & the Open Society. LC 81-14312. 180p. 1982. text ed. 20.00x (ISBN 0-8071-0974-6). La State U Pr.

Germishuizen, Gerrit, ed. Transvaal Wild Flowers. 292p. 1983. 37.50 (ISBN 0-86954-108-0, Pub. by Macmillan S Africa). Intl Spec Bk.

Germogenova, O. A., tr. see Pozhela, J.

Germond, Jack W. & Witcover, Jules. Wake Us When It's Over: Presidential Politics of 1984. 448p. 1985. 17.95 (ISBN 0-02-630710-3). Macmillan.

Germond, Jack W., jt. auth. see Witcover, Jules.

Germuth, Frederick G., Jr. & Rodriguez, Eugene. Immunopathology of the Renal Glomerulus: Immune Complex Deposit & Antibasement Membrane Disease. (Illus.). 1973. 32.50 (ISBN 0-316-30839-0). Little.

Gerner, Ken. The Red Dreams. 1978. 15.00x (ISBN 0-914742-29-9); pap. 5.00 (ISBN 0-914742-29-9). Copper Canyon.

--Throwing Shadows. 80p. (Orig.). 1985. pap. 8.00 (ISBN 0-914742-87-6). Copper Canyon.

Gerner, Kristian. The Soviet Union & Central Europe in the Post-War Era: A Study in Precarious Security. 236p. 1985. 32.50 (ISBN 0-312-74905-8). St Martin.

Gernes, Sonia. The Way to St. Ives. 288p. 1982. 13.95 (ISBN 0-684-17492-8, ScribT). Scribner.

Gernet, Jacques. China & the Christian Impact: A Conflict of Cultures. LLoyd, Janet, tr. 280p. Date not set. price not set (ISBN 0-521-26681-5); pap. price not set (ISBN 0-521-31319-8). Cambridge U Pr.

--Daily Life in China on the Eve of the Mongol Invasion, 1250-1276. LC 73-110281. 1962. pap. 7.95x (ISBN 0-8047-0720-0). Stanford U Pr.

--A History of Chinese Civilisation. LC 81-10006. (Illus.). 400p. 1982. 42.50 (ISBN 0-521-24130-8). Cambridge U Pr.

--A History of Chinese Civilisation. Foster, J. R., tr. (Illus.). 800p. 1985. pap. write for info. (ISBN 0-521-31647-2). Cambridge U Pr.

Gernet, Louis. The Anthropology of Ancient Greece. Hamilton, John D. B. & Nagy, Blaise, trs. from Fr. LC 81-47598. 400p. 1981. text ed. 35.00x (ISBN 0-8018-2112-6). Johns Hopkins.

--L' Approvisionnement D'Athenes en ble au ve et au Ive Siecle. Finley, Moses, ed. LC 79-4975. (Ancient Economic History Ser.). (Fr.). 1980. Repr. of 1909 ed. lib. bdg. 14.00x (ISBN 0-405-12363-9). Ayer Co Pubs.

Gernet, N. Clever Masha. 15p. 1974. pap. 1.45 (ISBN 0-8285-1123-3, Pub. by Progress Pubs USSR). Imported Pubns.

Gernsbacher, Larry. The Suicide Syndrome. 1985. 29.95. Human Sci Pr.

Gernsback, Hugo & Fitch, Clyde. Official Radio Service Manual & Complete Directory of All Commercial Wiring Diagrams 1930. LC 85-3203. (Illus.). 352p. 1985. pap. 19.95 (ISBN 0-911572-42-2). Vestal.

Gernsback, Sidney. S. Gernsback's Nineteen Twenty-Seven Radio Encyclopedia. Orig. Title: S. Gernsback's Radio Encyclopedia. (Illus.). 172p. 1974. Repr. of 1927 ed. 14.95 (ISBN 0-914126-06-7). Vintage Radio.

Gernsheim, Alison. Victorian & Edwardian Fashion: A Photographic Survey. (Illus.). 240p. 1982. pap. 6.00 (ISBN 0-486-24205-6). Dover.

--Victorian & Edwardian Fashion: A Photographic Survey. (Illus.). 19.00 (ISBN 0-8446-5889-8). Peter Smith.

Gernsheim, Alison, jt. auth. see Gernsheim, Helmut.

Gernsheim, Alison, ed. see Coburn, Alvin L.

Gernsheim, Helmut. Incunabula of British Photography: A Bibliography of British Photographic Literature, 1839-75. (Illus.). 160p. 1984. 75.00 (ISBN 0-85967-657-9). Scolar.

--Julia Margaret Cameron: Her Life & Photographic Work. LC 73-85258. (Illus.). 204p. 1974. pap. 14.50 (ISBN 0-912334-51-7). Aperture.

--Lewis Carroll: Photographer. rev. ed. LC 68-8045. (Illus.). 1970. pap. 6.95 (ISBN 0-486-22327-2). Dover.

--Lewis Carroll: Photographer. rev. ed. (Illus.). 14.50 (ISBN 0-8446-0642-1). Peter Smith.

--The Origins of Photography. 3rd, rev. ed. LC 82-80979. (Illus.). 1983. slipcased 50.00 (ISBN 0-500-54080-2). Thames Hudson.

Gernsheim, Helmut & Fleischmann, Kaspar M. Images: The Photographs of Peter Gasser. (Illus.). 120p. 1985. 60.00. Aperture.

Gernsheim, Helmut & Gernsheim, Alison. L. J. M. Daguerre: The History of the Diorama & the Daugerreotype. LC 68-8044. (Illus.). 1969. pap. 5.95 (ISBN 0-486-22290-X). Dover.

--L. J. M. Daguerre: The History of the Diorama & the Daguerreotype. 2nd rev. ed. (Illus.). 12.50 (ISBN 0-8446-2120-X). Peter Smith.

Gernsheim, Helmut, ed. see Coburn, Alvin L.

Gernsheim, Helmut, pref. by see Jay, Bill.

Gero, George, ed. see Reich, Annie.

Gero, Ihan. Il Primo libro de' madrigali italiani et canzoni francese a due voci: Masters & Monuments of the Renaissance, Vol. 1. Bernstein, Lawrence F. & Haar, James, eds. xliv, 213p. (Ital. & Fr.). 1980. 35.00x (ISBN 0-8450-7301-X). Broude.

Gero, J. S. & Cowan, H. J. Design of Building Frames. (Illus.). 480p. 1976. 63.00 (ISBN 0-85334-644-5, Pub. by Elsevier Applied Sci England). Elsevier.

Gero, J. S., ed. Optimization in Computer-Aided Design: Proceedings of the IFIP WG 5.2. Working Conference on Optimization of Computer-Aided Design, Lyon, France, 24-26 October, 1983. 382p. 1985. 50.00 (ISBN 0-444-87690-1, North-Holland). Elsevier.

Gero, John S., ed. Computer Applications in Architecture. (Illus.). 1977. 77.75 (ISBN 0-85334-737-9, Pub. by Elsevier Applied Sci England). Elsevier.

Geroch, Robert. General Relativity from A to B. LC 77-18908. (Illus.). 1978. lib. bdg. 17.50x (ISBN 0-226-28863-3); pap. 7.95 (ISBN 0-226-28864-1). U of Chicago Pr.

--Mathematical Physics. (Chicago Lectures in Physics Ser.). 310p. 1985. lib. bdg. price not set (ISBN 0-226-28861-7); pap. text ed. price not set (ISBN 0-226-28862-5). U of Chicago Pr.

Gerogano, G. N. Racing & Sports Cars. LC 78-670084. (Source Book Ser.). (Illus.). 1973. 5.00x (ISBN 0-7063-1495-6). Intl Pubns Serv.

Gerogiannis, Nicholas, ed. see Hemingway, Ernest.

Gerok, W., jt. ed. see Bianchi, L.

Gerok, W., jt. ed. see Paumgartner, G.

Gerold, T. Histoire de la Musique des Origines a la Fin Du 14th Siecle. LC 78-162869. (Music Ser.). (Fr). 1971. Repr. of 1936 ed. lib. bdg. 55.00 (ISBN 0-306-70196-0). Da Capo.

Gerold, Theodore. Art Du Chant En France Au Dix-Septieme Siecle. (Fr). 1921. 21.00 (ISBN 0-8337-4129-2). B Franklin.

Gerold, William. College Hill: A Photographic Study of Brown University in Its Two Hundredth Year. LC 65-20874. (Illus.). 120p. 1965. 12.00 (ISBN 0-87057-089-7). U Pr of New Eng.

Gerolde, Steven. Universal Conversion Factors. LC 71-164900. 276p. 1971. 19.95x (ISBN 0-87814-005-0). Pennwell Bks.

Gerome, Jean L. A Quaderno of the Most Impressive Paintings by Gerome. (Illus.). 1980. 147.75 (ISBN 0-930582-53-5). Gloucester Art.

Geron, Frank. Beyond Valor. 352p. 1984. pap. 3.50 (ISBN 0-8217-1425-2). Zebra.

--The Geneva Transfer. 304p. 1983. pap. 3.25 (ISBN 0-8217-1268-3). Zebra.

Geronimi, Clyde. Chips Quips. LC 83-72694. (Illus.). 55p. (gr. 4 up). 1983. pap. 3.95 (ISBN 0-939126-09-5). Back Bay.

Geronimo. Geronimo's Story of His Life. (Illus.). 216p. 1973. Repr. of 1906 ed. 15.50 (ISBN 0-87928-036-0). Corner Hse.

--Geronimo's Story of His Life. Barrett, S. M., ed. LC 82-25841. (Illus.). 1983. pap. text ed. 10.95x (ISBN 0-8290-0658-3). Irvington.

Geronimo, Roger J. Incentive Economics. LC 81-90733. (Orig.). 1982. pap. 14.95x (ISBN 0-937884-06-5, Pub. by A Bennington). Hyst'ry Myst'ry.

Geronimus, Ja L. & Szego, Gabor. Two Papers on Special Functions. LC 76-30843. (Translations Ser. 2: Vol. 108). 1977. 34.00 (ISBN 0-8218-3058-9, TRANS2108). Am Math.

Geronimus, L. Ya. Orthogonal Polynomials: Estimates, Asymptotic Formulas, & Series of Polynomials Orthogonal on the Unit Circle & on an Interval. LC 60-53450. 242p. 1961. 32.50x (ISBN 0-306-10565-9, Consultants). Plenum Pub.

--Orthogonal Polynomials: Estimates, Asymptotic Formulas, & Series of Polynomials Orthogonal on the Unit Circle & on an Interval. LC 60-53450. pap. 60.50 (ISBN 0-317-28010-4, 2055801). Bks Demand UMI.

Geronld, Daniel G., ed. see Witkiewicz, Stanislaw I.

Gerostergios, Asterios. Justinian the Great: The Emperor & Saint. LC 82-82095. (Illus.). 312p. 1982. 15.95 (ISBN 0-914744-58-5); pap. 11.95 (ISBN 0-914744-59-3). Inst Byzantine.

--St. Photios the Great. LC 80-82285. (Illus.). 125p. 1980. 8.50 (ISBN 0-914744-50-X); pap. 5.50 (ISBN 0-914744-51-8). Inst Byzantine.

Gerould, Daniel. Witkacy: Stanislaw Ignacy Witkiewicz As an Imaginative Writer. LC 79-3872. (Illus.). 380p. 1981. 30.00x (ISBN 0-295-95714-X). U of Wash Pr.

Gerould, Daniel, ed. American Melodrama: Plays & Documents. LC 82-62096. 1983. 21.95 (ISBN 0-933826-20-6); pap. 8.95 (ISBN 0-933826-21-4). Performing Arts.

--Doubles, Demons & Dreamers: A Collection of International Symbolist Drama. (Orig.). 1985. 21.95 (ISBN 0-933826-77-X); pap. 9.95 (ISBN 0-933826-78-8). Performing Arts.

--Gallant & Libertine: Divertissements & Parades from Eighteenth Century France. LC 83-61194. 1983. 18.95 (ISBN 0-933826-48-6); pap. 7.95 (ISBN 0-933826-49-4). Performing Arts.

--Melodrama. LC 79-52615. (New York Literary Forum Ser.). (Illus.). 296p. (Orig.). 1980. pap. 15.00 (ISBN 0-931196-06-X). NY Lit Forum.

Gerould, Daniel, tr. see Witkiewicz, Stanislaw.

Gerould, Daniel, tr. see Witkiewicz, Stanislaw I.

Gerould, Daniel C., ed. Twentieth-Century Polish Avant-Garde Drama: Plays, Scenarios, Documents. LC 76-13659. (Illus.). 312p. 1977. 27.50x (ISBN 0-8014-0952-7). Cornell U Pr.

Gerould, G. H. Saints' Legends. 59.95 (ISBN 0-8490-0987-1). Gordon Pr.

Gerould, Gordon H. The Ballad of Tradition. LC 74-8734. 311p. 1974. Repr. of 1957 ed. 12.50x (ISBN 0-87752-165-4). Gordian.

--The Grateful Dead. LC 73-15767. 1908. lib. bdg. 27.50 (ISBN 0-8414-4472-2). Folcroft.

--The Grateful Dead. 177p. 1980. Repr. of 1908 ed. lib. bdg. 27.50 (ISBN 0-8492-4957-0). R West.

--The Grateful Dead: The History of Folk-Story. (Folk-Lore Society, London, Monographs: Vol. 60). pap. 18.00 (ISBN 0-317-17857-1). Kraus Repr.

--Saints' Legends. 1980. Repr. of 1916 ed. lib. bdg. 35.00 (ISBN 0-8414-4627-X). Folcroft.

Gerould, Gordon H., ed. Old English & Medieval Literature. LC 70-114913. (Select Bibliographies Reprint Ser). 1929. 21.50 (ISBN 0-8369-5312-6). Ayer Co Pubs.

--Old English & Medieval Literature. LC 78-95100. Repr. of 1929 ed. lib. bdg. 18.75x (ISBN 0-8371-2703-3, GEOE). Greenwood.

--Old English & Medieval Literature. LC 74-145040. 404p. 1972. Repr. of 1929 ed. 13.00x (ISBN 0-403-00989-8). Scholarly.

Gerould, Katharine F. The Aristocratic West. 1925. 15.00 (ISBN 0-8495-1965-9). Arden Lib.

--Hawaii: Scenes & Impressions. 1923. 15.00 (ISBN 0-8495-1967-5). Arden Lib.

--Modes & Morals. facsimile ed. LC 78-142634. (Essay Index Reprint Ser). Repr. of 1920 ed. 19.00 (ISBN 0-8369-2317-0). Ayer Co Pubs.

--Ringside Seats. facsimile ed. LC 71-156647. (Essay Index Reprint Ser). Repr. of 1937 ed. 18.00 (ISBN 0-8369-2318-9). Ayer Co Pubs.

--Vain Obligations. 324p. 1980. Repr. of 1915 ed. lib. bdg. 25.00 (ISBN 0-89987-306-5). Century Bookbindery.

Gerow, Edwin. A Glossary of Indian Figures of Speech. (Publications in Near & Middle East Ser. A: No. 16). 436p. 1971. text ed. 38.40x (ISBN 90-2791-759-0). Mouton.

Gerow, Edwin & Lang, Margery, eds. Studies in the Language & Culture of South Asia. LC 73-18028. (Publications on Asia of the School for International Studies: No. 23). 174p. 1974. 20.00x (ISBN 0-295-95316-0). U of Wash Pr.

Gerow, Josh R. Psychology: An Introduction. 1986. text ed. 26.95x (ISBN 0-673-18097-2). Scott F.

Gerow, Joshua R. & Lyng, R. Douglas. How to Succeed in College: A Student Guidebook. 213p. 1985. pap. 9.95 (ISBN 0-8290-0913-2). Irvington.

Gerow, Maurice, jt. auth. see Tanner, Paul.

Gerpen, Maurice Van see Van Gerpen, Maurice.

Gerrand, tr. see Allen, Robert R.

Gerrard. Prostaglandins & Blood Cell Function. (Hematology Ser.). 280p. 1985. 65.00 (ISBN 0-8247-7259-8). Dekker.

Gerrard, Anthony & Burch, J. M. Introduction to Matrix Methods in Optics. LC 72-21192. (Wiley Series in Pure & Applied Optics). pap. 92.30 (ISBN 0-317-08851-3, 2019669). Bks Demand UMI.

Gerrard, Brian, et al. Interpersonal Skills for Health Professionals. (Illus.). 272p. 1980. text ed. 19.95 O.P. (ISBN 0-8359-3138-2); pap. text ed. 14.95 (ISBN 0-8359-3136-6). Reston.

Gerrard, Brian A., jt. auth. see Gray, William A.

Gerrard, Ernest A. Elizabethan Drama & Dramatists. LC 74-184908. viii, 390p. 1972. Repr. of 1928 ed. lib. bdg. 20.00 (ISBN 0-8154-0407-7). Cooper Sq.

Gerrard, Frank. Meat Technology. 5th ed. 414p. 1981. 35.00x (ISBN 0-686-75446-8, Pub. by Northwood Bks). State Mutual Bk.

Gerrard, J. W. Food Allergy: New Perspectives. (Illus.). 328p. 1980. 28.50x (ISBN 0-398-04038-9); pap. 19.75 (ISBN 0-398-04041-9). C C Thomas.

Gerrard, Jean. Matilda Jane. LC 83-48082. (Illus.). 32p. (ps-3). 1983. 10.95 (ISBN 0-374-34865-0). FS&G.

Gerrard, Jean, jt. auth. see Gerrard, Roy.

Gerrard, John. Soils & Landforms. (Illus.). 256p. 1981. text ed. 35.00x (ISBN 0-04-551048-2); pap. text ed. 17.95x (ISBN 0-04-551049-0). Allen Unwin.

Gerrard, John W. Understanding Allergies. 88p. 1977. pap. 6.95x (ISBN 0-398-02768-4). C C Thomas.
Gerrard, Mady. Mady Gerrard's Knitwear Designs. (Illus.). 160p. (Orig.). 1983. pap. 11.95 (ISBN 0-399-50720-5, Perigee). Putnam Pub Group.
Gerrard, Michael B. The Economics of Pollution: A Bibliography, 4 pts. Incl. Pt. 1. Methods & Issues; Pt. 2. Role of Industries; Pt. 3. Effects of Pollution; Pt. 4. The Control of Pollution. (Public Administration Ser.). 1979. Pts. 1 & 2. pap. 9.50 (ISBN 0-88066-032-5, P-312, P-313); Pts. 3 & 4. pap. 9.00 (ISBN 0-88066-033-3). Vance Biblios.
Gerrard, Roy. The Favershams. LC 82-82390. (Illus.). 32p. (gr. 1 up). 1983. 10.95 (ISBN 0-374-32292-9). FS&G.
--Sir Cedric. LC 84-6111. (Illus.). 32p. (ps up). 11.95 (ISBN 0-374-36959-3). FS&G.
Gerrard, Roy & Gerrard, Jean. Matilda Jane. (Illus.). 32p. (ps-6). 1981. 11.95 (ISBN 0-575-02897-1, Pub. by Gollancz England). David & Charles.
Gerrard, W. Gas Solubilities. 92.00 (ISBN 0-08-025248-6). Pergamon.
--Hydrogen Halides in Non-Aqueous Solvents: Gas Solubilities. (Solubility Data Ser.). 1986. 100.00 (ISBN 0-08-023925-0). Pergamon.
--Organic Chemistry of Boron. 1961. 56.00 (ISBN 0-12-281250-6). Acad Pr.
--Solubility of Gases & Liquids: A Graphic Approach. LC 76-10676. (Illus.). 275p. 1976. 49.50x (ISBN 0-306-30866-5, Plenum Pr). Plenum Pub.
Gerrare, W. O. The Story of Moscow. (Mediaeval Towns Ser.: Vol. 1). pap. 26.00 (ISBN 0-317-15234-3). Kraus Repr.
Gerras, Charles, ed. Feasting on Raw Foods. (Illus.). 1980. 16.95 (ISBN 0-87857-271-6); pap. 11.95 (ISBN 0-87857-272-4). Rodale Pr Inc.
--Natural Cooking the Prevention Way. pap. 5.95 (ISBN 0-452-25260-1, Z5260, Plume). NAL.
--Rodale's Soups & Salads Cookbook & Kitchen Album. (Illus.). 288p. 1981. 15.95 (ISBN 0-87857-332-1). Rodale Pr Inc.
Gerras, Charles & Rodal Press Staff, eds. Rodale's Basic Natural Foods Cookbook. (Illus.). 912p. 1983. 21.95 (ISBN 0-87857-469-7). Rodale Pr Inc.
Gerras, Charles, ed. see Bingham, Joan & Riccio, Delores.
Gerras, Charles, ed. see Gorman, Marion.
Gerras, Charles, ed. see London, Mel.
Gerras, Charles, ed. see London, Sheryl & London, Mel.
Gerras, Charles, ed. see Minninger, Joan.
Gerras, Charlie, ed. Soups Supreme. (High Health Cookbook Ser.). (Illus.). 96p. 1983. 5.95 (ISBN 0-87857-394-1). Rodale Pr Inc.
Gerras, Charlie, ed. see Brewer, Gail S. & Greene, Janice P.
Gerras, Charlie, ed. see Powell, Barbara.
Gerrath, Jean, et al. A Plant Biology Lab Manual for a One Semester Course: Form & Function. 152p. 1982. pap. text ed. 7.95 (ISBN 0-8403-2814-1). Kendall-Hunt.
Gerraughty, Robert J. Pharmacy Examination Review Book. 8th ed. 1983. pap. text ed. 15.95 (ISBN 0-87488-421-7). Med Exam.
Gerrick, David J. About the Breast: From Folklore to Physiology. 1979. pap. text ed. 20.00 (ISBN 0-916750-00-0). Dayton Labs.
--Anatomy of the Sheep Brain: Clinical Implications. (Illus.). 1978. 20.00 (ISBN 0-916750-02-7, CX-63). Dayton Labs.
--Anatomy of the Sheep Eye: Clinical Implications. (Illus.). 1978. 20.00 (ISBN 0-916750-03-5). Dayton Labs.
--Anatomy of the Sheep Kidney: Clinical Implications. (Illus.). 1978. 20.00 (ISBN 0-916750-04-3). Dayton Labs.
--Anemia in Teens. (Illus.). 1978. 20.00 (ISBN 0-916750-05-1). Dayton Labs.
--Art & the Endocrines. (Illus.). 118p. 1981. 49.95 (ISBN 0-916750-83-3). Dayton Labs.
--Back Roads of Ohio: A Travel Guide to Back Road & Wilderness Areas in Ohio. 1974. pap. 4.95 (ISBN 0-916750-08-6). Dayton Labs.
--Chemistry of the Mind. (Illus.). 1978. 20.00 (ISBN 0-916750-16-7). Dayton Labs.
--Congenital Heart Defects. (Illus.). 1978. 20.00 (ISBN 0-916750-18-3). Dayton Labs.
--A Contribution Toward a Bibliography of Ohio Zoology. 1968. 5.00 (ISBN 0-86727-055-1). Ohio Bio Survey.
--Flatfeet: Man Adapting. (Illus.). 1978. 15.00 (ISBN 0-916750-20-5). Dayton Labs.
--Footnotes to Medicine. 172p. 1980. 13.95 (ISBN 0-916750-21-3). Dayton Labs.
--God Stories to Scare the Hell Out of You. (gr. 7 up). 1979. pap. text ed. 4.95 (ISBN 0-916750-24-8). Dayton Labs.
--Gold Prospecting in Ohio. 84p. 1980. pap. 4.95 (ISBN 0-916750-25-6). Dayton Labs.
--High Blood Pressure in Teenagers. (Illus.). 1978. 20.00 (ISBN 0-916750-27-2). Dayton Labs.
--Job Hunting in Conservation: A Guide to Job Sources in Conservation, Park Management & Ecology. 1975. pap. 11.95 (ISBN 0-916750-67-1). Dayton Labs.
--Learning Materials in Anatomy. 1978. pap. text ed. 10.00 (ISBN 0-916750-77-9). Dayton Labs.
--Mechanics of Breathing. (Illus.). 1978. 20.00 (ISBN 0-685-89666-8). Dayton Labs.
--Medical Whodunits' (gr. 7 up). 1979. pap. text ed. 5.95 (ISBN 0-916750-80-9). Dayton Labs.
--Menstrual Problems in Teenagers. 1979. pap. text ed. 20.00 (ISBN 0-685-96978-9). Dayton Labs.
--Mnemonics for Anatomy Students: A Guide to Memory Aids for the Students of Anatomy. 1975. pap. 3.45 (ISBN 0-916750-38-8). Dayton Labs.
--Murmurs in Man. (Illus.). 1978. 20.00 (ISBN 0-916750-39-6). Dayton Labs.
--Mysteries of Topical Medication. 1981. 49.95 (ISBN 0-916750-84-1). Dayton Labs.
--Ohio's Ghostly Greats: An Anthology of Ohio Ghost Stories. 1973. pap. 4.95 (ISBN 0-916750-40-X). Dayton Labs.
--Ovulation: Predicting Fertility. (Illus.). 1978. 20.00 (ISBN 0-916750-42-6). Dayton Labs.
--Pharmacogenetics. (Illus.). 1978. 20.00 (ISBN 0-916750-43-4). Dayton Labs.
--Pica. (Illus.). 1978. 20.00 (ISBN 0-916750-45-0). Dayton Labs.
--Pregnancy Testing. (Illus.). 1978. 20.00 (ISBN 0-916750-46-9). Dayton Labs.
--The Rh Problem. 1979. pap. text ed. 20.00 (ISBN 0-916750-49-3). Dayton Labs.
--Sex at the Celluar Level. (Illus.). 1978. 20.00 (ISBN 0-916750-50-7, CX-15). Dayton Labs.
--Sore Throat-The Danger Within. (Illus.). 1978. 20.00 (ISBN 0-685-89681-1). Dayton Labs.
--Sounds of the Breath. (Illus.). 1978. 20.00 (ISBN 0-916750-54-X). Dayton Labs.
--Sounds of the Heart. (Illus.). 1978. 20.00 (ISBN 0-916750-55-8). Dayton Labs.
--Sunlight: Friend or Foe. 1978. 20.00 (ISBN 0-916750-56-6). Dayton Labs.
--Surface Anatomy: Abdomen. (Illus.). 1978. 20.00 (ISBN 0-916750-57-4). Dayton Labs.
--Surface Anatomy: The Arm. (Illus.). 1978. 20.00 (ISBN 0-916750-58-2). Dayton Labs.
--Surface Anatomy: The Back. (Illus.). 1978. 20.00 (ISBN 0-916750-59-0). Dayton Labs.
--Surface Anatomy: The Head. (Illus.). 1978. 20.00 (ISBN 0-916750-60-4). Dayton Labs.
--Surface Anatomy: The Leg. 1979. 20.00 (ISBN 0-916750-61-2). Dayton Labs.
--Surface Anatomy: The Neck. (Illus.). 1978. 20.00 (ISBN 0-916750-62-0). Dayton Labs.
--Surface Anatomy: Thorax. (Illus.). 1978. 20.00 (ISBN 0-916750-63-9). Dayton Labs.
--Terror Tales for Teenagers. (gr. 5 up). 1979. pap. text ed. 4.95 (ISBN 0-916750-65-5). Dayton Labs.
--Transplants in Man. (Illus.). 1978. 20.00 (ISBN 0-916750-68-X). Dayton Labs.
--Troubles at the Metabolic Mill-Ketosis. (Illus.). 1978. 20.00 (ISBN 0-916750-70-1). Dayton Labs.
--Urinary Tract Infections: Beware. 1979. 20.00 (ISBN 0-916750-71-X). Dayton Labs.
--When Milk Is Dangerous. 1978. 20.00 (ISBN 0-916750-76-0, CX-4). Dayton Labs.
Gerrick, David J. & Dietsche, Doreen. Old Time Cures-Farmers Folklore. 104p. (Orig.). 1980. pap. 3.95 (ISBN 0-916750-41-8). Dayton Labs.
Gerrick, David J. & McDonald, Susan. Anomalies & Curiosities of Medical Practice. 114p. 1981. pap. 7.95 (ISBN 0-916750-78-7). Dayton Labs.
Gerrick, David J. & Moscovitz, Toni M. Tricks in Pediatrics. (Illus.). 1978. pap. 3.00 (ISBN 0-916750-69-8). Dayton Labs.
Gerrick, David J., jt. auth. see McDonald, Susan.
Gerrie, Brenda. Online Information Systems: Use & Operating Characteristics, Limitations & Design Alternatives. LC 83-81515. (Illus.). xii, 189p. 1983. text ed. 24.50 (ISBN 0-87815-047-1). Info Resources.
Gerringer, Arthur E. Treatise on Terrorism. 56p. 1982. 5.95 (ISBN 0-8059-2855-3). Dorrance.
Gerrish, B. A. The Old Protestantism & the New: Essays on the Reformation Heritage. LC 82-2730. 400p. 1983. lib. bdg. 38.00x (ISBN 0-226-28869-2). U of Chicago Pr.
--A Prince of the Church: Schleiermacher & the Beginnings of Modern Theology. LC 83-48924. 80p. 1984. pap. 4.95 (ISBN 0-8006-1787-8, 1-1787). Fortress.
--Tradition & the Modern World: Reformed Theology in the Nineteenth Century. LC 78-4982. 1978. lib. bdg. 20.00x (ISBN 0-226-28866-8). U of Chicago Pr.
Gerrish, Brian, ed. Reformatio Perennis: Essays on Calvin & the Reformation in Honor of Ford Lewis Battles. (Pittsburgh Theological Monograph Ser.: No. 32). 1981. pap. 16.50 (ISBN 0-915138-41-7). Pickwick.
Gerrish, H. & Dugger, W., Jr. Exploring Electricity & Electronics: Basic Fundamentals. rev. ed. LC 80-20830. (Illus.). 208p. 1981. text ed. 12.00 (ISBN 0-87006-308-1). Goodheart.
Gerrish, H. H. Electricity. 120p. 1983. 6.00 (ISBN 0-87006-412-6). Goodheart.
Gerrish, H. H. & Dugger, W. E., Jr. Transistor Electronics. LC 81-6740. 368p. 1981. 16.00 (ISBN 0-87006-394-4); wkbk. 6.00 (ISBN 0-87006-318-9). Goodheart.
Gerrish, Howard H. Technical Dictionary. rev. ed. LC 81-20005. 368p. 1982. text ed. 10.00 (ISBN 0-87006-400-2). Goodheart.
Gerrish, Howard H. & Dugger, William E., Jr. Electricity & Electronics. LC 79-6345. (Illus.). 1980. text ed. 16.00 (ISBN 0-87006-284-0); lab manual 6.00 (ISBN 0-87006-310-3). Goodheart.
Gerrits, H. A. Pheasants: Including Their Care in the Aviary. rev. ed. (Illus.). 144p. 1974. 14.95 (ISBN 0-7137-0683-X, Pub by Blandford Pr England). Sterling.
Gerritsen, Frans. Theory & Practice of Color. 1975. 40.00 (ISBN 0-442-22645-4). Van Nos Reinhold.
Gerritsen, J., et al, eds. see Bruggencate, K. T.
Gerritsen, J. K., et al, eds. Thermophysical Properties Research Literature Retrieval Guide: Supplement II, 1971-1977, 6 vols. LC 79-16324. 1979. Set. 375.00 (ISBN 0-306-67210-3, IFI Plenum). Plenum Pub.
Gerritsen, Tess. Adventure's Mistress. (Private Library Collection). 1985. mini-bound 6.95 (ISBN 0-938422-13-8). SOS Pubns CA.
Gerritsen, Theo, ed. Modern Separation of Macromolecules & Particles. LC 69-14292. (Progress in Separation & Purification Ser.: Vol. 2). (Illus.). pap. 65.50 (ISBN 0-317-09353-3, 2011958). Bks Demand UMI.
Gerritzen, L. & Van Der Put, M. Schottky Groups & Mumford Curves. (Lecture Notes in Mathematics: Vol. 817). 317p. 1980. pap. 23.00 (ISBN 0-387-10229-9). Springer-Verlag.
Gerrold, D. & Niven, L. The Flying Sorcerers. 1982. pap. 2.75 (ISBN 0-345-30494-2, Del Rey). Ballantine.
Gerrold, David. Battle for the Planet of the Apes. 10.95 (ISBN 0-89190-163-9, Pub. by Am Repr). Amereon Ltd.
--A Day for Damnation. (The War Against the Chtorr Ser.: Vol. II). 400p. 1984. 15.95 (ISBN 0-671-47553-3, Timescape); pap. 3.95 (ISBN 0-671-45121-9). PB.
--The Man Who Folded Himself. 1976. Repr. of 1973 ed. lib. bdg. 14.95 (ISBN 0-88411-191-1, Pub. by Aeonian Pr). Amereon Ltd.
--A Matter for Men: War Against the Chtorr, Vol. 1. (Science Fiction Ser.). 416p. 1984. pap. 3.95 (ISBN 0-671-45120-0). PB.
--SF Yearbook. LC 79-63463. 1979. pap. 4.95 (ISBN 0-931064-10-4). Starlog Group.
--Space Skimmer. 1976. Repr. of 1972 ed. lib. bdg. 15.95x (ISBN 0-88411-192-X, Pub. by Aeonian Pr). Amereon Ltd.
--Space Skimmer. 1981. pap. 2.50 (ISBN 0-345-29851-9, Del Rey). Ballantine.
--Trouble with Tribbles. pap. 2.75 (ISBN 0-345-31901-X). Ballantine.
--The War Against the Chtorr: Vol. 1-A Matter for Men. Date not set. 16.50 (ISBN 0-671-46493-0, Timescape); pap. 6.75 (ISBN 0-671-46494-9, Timescape). PB.
--The World of Star Trek. rev. & updated ed. (Illus.). 288p. 1984. pap. 8.95 (ISBN 0-312-94463-2). Bluejay Bks.
--Yesterday's Children. 1976. Repr. of 1972 ed. lib. bdg. 15.95x (ISBN 0-88411-193-8, Pub. by Aeonian Pr). Amereon Ltd.
Gerrold, David & Niven, Larry. The Flying Sorcerers. 1976. Repr. of 1971 ed. lib. bdg. 17.95 (ISBN 0-88411-194-6, Pub. by Aeonian Pr). Amereon Ltd.
Gerry, Chris, jt. ed. see Bromley, Ray.
Gersbach, Jo R. The Case of the Buried Money Bags. (gr. 5-8). 1978. 6.50 (ISBN 0-87881-065-X). Mojave Bks.
Gerschenkron, A. An Economic Spurt That Failed: Four Lectures in Austrian Economic History. (The Eliot Janeway Lectures on Historical Economics). 1977. 22.00x (ISBN 0-691-04216-0). Princeton U Pr.
Gerschenkron, Alexander. Continuity in History & Other Essays. LC 68-14257. 1968. 35.00x (ISBN 0-674-16800-3, Belknap Pr). Harvard U Pr.
--Continuity in History & Other Essays. LC 68-14257. pap. 139.50 (ISBN 0-317-29619-1, 2021590). Bks Demand UMI.
--Economic Backwardness in Historical Perspective: A Book of Essays. LC 62-17217. 1962. 30.00x (ISBN 0-674-22600-3, Belknap Pr). Harvard U Pr.
--Europe in the Russian Mirror. LC 76-96090. 1970. 27.95 (ISBN 0-521-07721-4). Cambridge U Pr.
Gerschenson, L. E. & Thompson, Brad E., eds. Gene Expression & Carcinogenesis in Cultured Liver. 1975. 65.00 (ISBN 0-12-281150-X). Acad Pr.
Gerschler, Malcolm C. The Clock & Watch Pronunciary. LC 82-91052. (Illus.). 256p. 1983. pap. 11.95 (ISBN 0-9609628-1-6). Wag on Wall.
Gersh, Eileen S. & Gersh, Isadore. Biology of Women. (Illus.). 324p. (Orig.). 1981. pap. text ed. 20.00 (ISBN 0-8391-1622-5). Univ Park.
Gersh, Harry. Animals Next Door: A Guide to Zoos & Aquariums of the Americas. LC 71-104745. (Orig.). 1971. pap. 5.00x (ISBN 0-8303-0088-0, Acad Edns). Fleet.
--Sacred Books of the Jews. LC 68-17320. 1972. pap. 4.95 (ISBN 0-8128-1528-9). Stein & Day.
--When a Jew Celebrates. LC 70-116678. (Jewish Values Ser). (Illus.). 256p. (gr. 5-6). 1971. pap. text ed. 6.95x (ISBN 0-87441-091-6). Behrman.
Gersh, Harry & Platzner, Robert S. Mishnah, the Oral Law. 64p. 1984. pap. 2.95 (ISBN 0-87441-390-7); tchr's 6.95 (ISBN 0-317-15397-8). Behrman.
Gersh, Harry, et al. Story of the Jew. rev. ed. LC 64-22514. (Illus.). (gr. 8-11). 1965. 5.95x (ISBN 0-87441-019-3). Behrman.
Gersh, Isadore, jt. auth. see Gersh, Eileen S.
Gersh, Isidore, ed. Submicroscopic Cytochemistry, 2vols. Incl. Vol. 1. Protein & Nucleic Acids. 1974. 73.50 (ISBN 0-12-281401-0); Vol.2. Membranes,Mitochondria, & Connective Tissue. 1974. 54.00 (ISBN 0-12-281402-9). Acad Pr.
Gersh, Marvin J. How to Raise Children at Home in Your Spare Time. rev. ed. LC 82-42524. 324p. 1983. pap. 14.95 (ISBN 0-8128-2888-7). Stein & Day.
Gersh, Marvin J. & Litt, Iris F. The Handbook of Adolescence: A Medical Guide for Parents & Teenagers. LC 77-151288. 256p. (Orig.). 1983. pap. 10.95 (ISBN 0-8128-6070-5). Stein & Day.
Gershator, David. Play Mas. 92p. (Orig.). 1981. pap. 3.00 (ISBN 0-917402-14-6). Downtown Poets.
Gershator, David, tr. see Lorca, Federico Garcia.
Gershator, Phillis. A Bibliographic Guide to the Literature of Contemporary American Poetry, 1970-1975. LC 76-41812. 1976. 16.00 (ISBN 0-8108-0977-7). Scarecrow.
--Honi & His Magic Circle. LC 79-84931. (Illus.). (gr. k-4). 1979. 6.95 (ISBN 0-8276-0167-0, 443). Jewish Pubns.
Gershefski, George W. Using Lotus 1-2-3 to Solve Your Business Problems: Planning, Budgeting, Forecasting, Capital Investment Analysis A Practical Guide to Spreadsheet Planning. LC 84-10671. 156p. 1984. pap. text ed. 21.95x (ISBN 0-8476-7346-4). Rowman & Allanheld.
Gershel, Jeffrey, jt. auth. see Crain, Ellen.
Gershen, Helen. Four Seasons Cookbook. (Illus.). 176p. (Orig.). 1983. 15.95 (ISBN 0-915572-64-8); pap. 7.95 (ISBN 0-915572-63-X). Panjandrum.
Gershenberg, Irving. Multinational Enterprises, Transfer of Managerial Know-How, Technology Choice & Employment Effects: A Case Study of Kenya. (Working Paper Ser.: No. 28). 33p. (Orig.). 1984. pap. 8.55 (ISBN 92-2-103508-5, ILO310, ILO). Unipub.
Gershenfeld, Matti, jt. auth. see Napier, Rodney.
Gershenson, Milton G., ed. New York Matrimonial Practice: Equitable Distribution After Two Years Course Handbook. LC 80-83148. 417p. 1982. pap. 35.00 (ISBN 0-686-69170-9, F4-3707). PLI.
Gershenzon, M. O. Mechta i Mysl' I. S. Turgeneva. LC 74-119760. (Brown University Slavic Reprint Ser.: No. 8). 181p. 1970. pap. 7.00x (ISBN 0-87057-124-9). U Pr of New Eng.
--Mudrost' Pushkina. 229p. (Rus.). 1984. Repr. of 1919 ed. 25.00 (ISBN 0-88233-844-7). Ardis Pubs.
Gershenzon, M. O., jt. auth. see Ivanov, V. I.
Gershenzon, Mikhail, jt. auth. see Ivanov, Viacheslav.
Gershenzon, Mikhail O. Stat'i o Pushkine. 122p. (Rus.). 1983. pap. 6.50 (ISBN 0-933884-37-0). Berkeley Slavic.
Gersher, Michael, jt. auth. see Young, Dean.
Gersher, Mike, jt. auth. see Young, Dean.
Gershevitch, Ilya, ed. The Cambridge History of Iran, Vol. 2: The Median & Achamenian Periods. (Cambridge History of Iran Ser.: No. 32). (Illus.). 964p. 1985. 95.00 (ISBN 0-521-20091-1). Cambridge U Pr.
Gershevsky, Noah D., tr. see Suslov, Sergefi P.
Gershgoren, Sid. Negative Space. 1975. 2.50 (ISBN 0-685-79484-9, Red Hill). Small Pr Dist.
Gershkoff, Ira & Trachtman, Richard. The Boston Driver's Handbook. LC 82-8692. 1982. pap. text ed. 4.95 (ISBN 0-201-11000-8). Addison-Wesley.
--The Washington Driver's Handbook: A Guide to Capital Cruising. 1984. pap. 4.95 (ISBN 0-201-11018-0, 476); counterpak of 10 47.60 (ISBN 0-201-11019-9). Addison-Wesley.
Gershman, Bennett L. Prosecutorial Misconduct. LC 84-12399. 1984. 67.50 (ISBN 0-87632-443-X). Boardman.
Gershman, Herbert S. The Surrealist Revolution in France. (Illus.). 268p. 1973. pap. 5.95 (ISBN 0-472-06188-7, AA). U of Mich Pr.
Gershom, Levi B. The Wars of the Lord: Immortality of the Soul, Vol. I: Book 1. Feldman, Seymour, tr. from Hebrew. 256p. 1984. 23.95 (ISBN 0-8276-0220-0, 605). Jewish Pubns.
Gershon, Anne A., ed. see Symposium by the New York University Medical Center & the National Foundation-March of Dimes, New York City, Mar. 1975.
Gershon, Dudley. The Power Behind Aston Martin. (Illus.). 134p. 13.50 (ISBN 0-902280-58-9, P958). Haynes Pubns.
Gershon, E. S., et al, eds. Genetic Research Strategies in Psychobiology & Psychiatry. 470p. 1981. 65.50 (ISBN 0-444-80350-5, Biomedical Pr). Elsevier.
--Genetic Research Strategies in Psychobiology & Psychiatry. (Psychobiology & Psychopathology Ser.: Vol. 1). 1981. 38.50x (ISBN 0-910286-84-1). Boxwood.
Gershon, Elliot S., et al, eds. The Impact of Biology on Modern Psychiatry. LC 76-49665. (Illus.). 288p. 1977. 39.50x (ISBN 0-306-31000-7, Plenum Pr). Plenum Pub.
Gershon, Freddie. Honey, Baby, Cookie. 1986. price not set (ISBN 0-87795-754-1). Arbor Hse.
Gershon, Karen. The Bread of Exile. 192p. 1985. 15.95 (ISBN 0-575-03599-4, Pub. by Gollancz England). David & Charles.
--Coming Back from Babylon. 1981. 20.00x (ISBN 0-575-02719-3, Pub. by Gollancz England). State Mutual Bk.
Gershon, Levi, tr. see Alon, Gedaliah.

Gershon, S., et al, eds. New Directions in Antidepressant Therapy. (Royal Society of Medicine International Congress & Symposia Ser.: No. 46). 120p. 1981. 23.00 (ISBN 0-8089-1405-7, 791549). Grune.

Gershon, Samuel & Belmaker, Robert. Management of the Acute Psychotic Patient. Date not set. price not set (ISBN 0-89004-311-6, 378). Raven.

Gershon, Samuel & Shopsin, Baron, eds. Lithium: Its Role in Psychiatric Research & Treatment. LC 72-91021. (Illus.). 369p. 1973. 35.00x (ISBN 0-306-30720-0, Plenum Pr). Plenum Pub.

Gershoni, Israel. The Emergence of Pan-Arabism in Egypt. 142p. (Orig.). 1981. pap. text ed. 9.95x (ISBN 0-8156-7050-8, Pub. by Shiloah Ctr Mid East & African Studies Israel). Syracuse U Pr.

Gershoni, Yekutiel. Black Colonialism: The Americo-Liberian Struggle for the Hinterland. (Replica Edition Ser.). 200p. 1984. softcover 19.00x (ISBN 0-86531-992-8). Westview.

Gershoy, Leo. Bertrand Barere: A Reluctant Terrorist. LC 61-11848. pap. 91.40 (ISBN 0-8357-9494-6, 2011476). Bks Demand UMI.

--The Era of the French Revolution, Seventeen Eighty-Nine to Seventeen Ninety-Nine: Ten Years that Shook the World. LC 83-22235. 190p. (Orig.). pap. 5.95 (ISBN 0-89874-718-X). Krieger.

--From Despotism to Revolution, 1763-1789. LC 83-10734. (The Rise of Modern Europe Ser.). (Illus.). xvi, 355p. 1983. Repr. of 1944 ed. lib. bdg. 45.00x (ISBN 0-313-24080-9, GEDE). Greenwood.

Gershuny, J. After Industrial Society? The Emerging Self-Service Economy. 1978. text ed. 21.25x (ISBN 0-391-00837-4); pap. text ed. 8.25x (ISBN 0-391-00847-1). Humanities.

Gershuny, Jay I. & Miles, Ian D. The New Service Economy: The Transformation of Employment in Industrialized Societies. 296p. 1983. 34.95 (ISBN 0-03-063996-4). Praeger.

Gershuny, Jonathan. Social Innovation & the Division of Labour. (The Library of Political Economy). (Illus.). 191p. 1983. 32.50 (ISBN 0-19-874131-6); pap. 12.95x (ISBN 0-19-874130-8). Oxford U Pr.

Gershuny, Theodore. Soon to Be a Major Motion Picture. LC 81-4710. 384p. 1982. pap. 8.95 (ISBN 0-03-059819-2, Owl Bks). HR&W.

Gershwin, jt. auth. see Ruben.

Gershwin, Eric & Nagy, Stephen M., eds. Evaluation & Management of Allergic & Asthmatic Disorders of Adults & Children. 320p. 1979. 26.50 (ISBN 0-8089-1206-2, 791550). Grune.

Gershwin, Ira. Lyrics on Several Occasions. rev. ed. 448p. (Orig.). 1986. 20.00 (ISBN 0-87910-050-8); pap. 11.95 (ISBN 0-87910-054-0). Limelight Edns.

Gershwin, M. E. & Merchant, B., eds. Immunologic Defects in Laboratory Animals, 2 vols. (Vol. 1 380 pp.; Vol. 2 402 pp.). 1981. Vol. 1. 45.00x (ISBN 0-306-40668-3, Plenum Pr); Vol. 2. 45.00x (ISBN 0-306-40673-X); Set. 79.50x. Plenum Pub.

Gershwin, M. Eric & Robbins, Dick L. Musculoskeletal Diseases of Children. 736p. 1983. 99.50 (ISBN 0-8089-1528-2, 791548). Grune.

Gershwin, M. Eric, ed. Bronchial Asthma: Principles of Diagnosis & Treatment. 480p. 1981. 49.50 (ISBN 0-8089-1331-X, 791551). Grune.

Gershwin, M. Eric, ed. see International Symposium of the American Society of Zoologists, Toronto, December 27-30, 1977.

Gershwin, M. Eric, et al. Nutrition & Immunity. 1985. 58.00 (ISBN 0-12-281450-9). Acad Pr.

Gerside, Roger. Coming Alive: China After Mao. 1982. pap. 4.50 (ISBN 0-451-62087-9, ME2087, Ment). NAL.

Gersman, Lana T. Dear John: A Guide to Some of the Best Seats in the City. LC 84-40086. (Illus.). 96p. 1984. pap. 2.95 (ISBN 0-943392-40-3). Tribeca Comm.

Gersmehl, Philip, et al. Physical Geography. LC 78-12212. 415p. 1980. text ed. 29.95 (ISBN 0-03-014476-0, HoltC). HR&W.

Gerson & Ter Kuile. Art & Architecture in Belgium: 1600 to 1800. (Pelican History of Art Ser.: No. 18). 1978. 50.00 (ISBN 0-670-13380-9). Viking.

Gerson, Allan. Israel, the West Bank & International Law. 285p. 1978. 35.00x (ISBN 0-7146-3091-8, F Cass Co). Biblio Dist.

Gerson, Allan, ed. Lawyers' Ethics. LC 78-62895. 315p. 1979. 17.95 (ISBN 0-87855-293-6). Transaction Bks.

Gerson, Benjamin & Anhalt, John P. High-Pressure Liquid Chromatography & Therapeutic Drug Monitoring. LC 80-16443. (Illus.). 300p. 1980. pap. text ed. 35.00 (ISBN 0-89189-077-7, 45-2-037-00). Am Soc Clinical.

Gerson, Benjamin, ed. Essentials of Therapeutic Drug Monitoring. LC 83-12873. (Illus.). 478p. 1983. text ed. 39.50 (ISBN 0-89640-088-3). Igaku-Shoin.

Gerson, Bob. Outrageous Outdoor Games. LC 83-62564. 1984. pap. 10.95 (ISBN 0-8224-5099-2). Pitman Learning.

Gerson, Corine. Son for a Day. (Illus.). 144p. (gr. 4-6). 1983. pap. 1.95 (ISBN 0-590-32771-2, Apple Paperbacks). Scholastic Inc.

Gerson, Corinne. Choices. (Orig.). 1980. pap. 1.75 (ISBN 0-505-51476-1, Pub. by Tower Bks). Dorchester Pub Co.

--The Closed Circle. 144p. (Orig.). (gr. 4-6). 1981. pap. 1.95 (ISBN 0-590-31792-X, Apple Paperbacks). Scholastic Inc.

--Good Dog, Bad Dog. LC 83-2635. (Illus.). 32p. (gr. k-3). 1983. 9.95 (ISBN 0-689-30986-4). Atheneum.

--How I Put My Mother Through College. LC 80-21681. 144p. (gr. 4-8). 1981. PLB 10.95 (ISBN 0-689-30810-8). Atheneum.

--Oh, Brother! LC 81-8052. 132p. (gr. 3-7). 1982. PLB 11.95 (ISBN 0-689-30878-7). Atheneum.

--Passing Through. 208p. (YA) (gr. 8 up). pap. 1.95 (ISBN 0-440-96958-1, LFL). Dell.

--Son for a Day. LC 79-22613. (Illus.). 140p. (gr. 3-7). 1980. 10.95 (ISBN 0-689-30742-X). Atheneum.

--Tread Softly. LC 78-72199. (gr. 4-7). 1979. 7.95 (ISBN 0-8037-9058-9). Dial Bks Young.

Gerson, Cyrelle K. More Than Dispensing. LC 80-65958. 120p. 1980. 24.00 (ISBN 0-917330-31-5). Am Pharm Assn.

Gerson, Cyrelle K. & Beavers, Eleanor, eds. Rational Geriatric Drug Therapy: An Interdisciplinary Approach, 2 vols. 1979. pap. text ed. 25.00 (ISBN 0-917330-43-9). Am Pharm Assn.

Gerson, G., ed. Intensive Care. 2nd ed. 200p. 1984. 23.00 (ISBN 0-433-11611-0, 991430077, Pub. by Heinemann Medical). Heyden.

Gerson, Jack. The Back of the Tiger: A Novel. 1985. 14.95 (ISBN 0-8253-0261-7). Beaufort Bks NY.

--The Whitehall Sanction. 320p. 1985. pap. 3.50 (ISBN 0-8125-0364-3, Dist. by Pinnacle Bks, Warner Pub Services & St. Martin). Tor Bks.

Gerson, Jacob J. Horatio Nelson Lay & Sino-British Relations, 1854-1864. LC 71-188976. (East Asian Monographs Ser: No. 47). 1972. 11.00x (ISBN 0-674-40625-7). Harvard U Pr.

Gerson, Joannes. The Ad Deum Vadit of Jean Gerson. Repr. of 1917 ed. 12.00 (ISBN 0-384-18210-0). Johnson Repr.

Gerson, Joel & Madry, Bobbi R. Standard Textbook for Professional Estheticians. Rubinstein, Israel, ed. (Illus.). 1983. 21.35 (ISBN 0-87350-147-0); pap. 19.05 (ISBN 0-87350-090-3). Milady.

Gerson, Joseph, ed. see New England Regional Office of the American Friends Service Committee.

Gerson, Kathleen. Hard Choices: How Women Decide about Work, Career, & Motherhood. LC 84-8602. 350p. 1985. 19.95 (ISBN 0-520-05171-8). U of Cal Pr.

Gerson, L. P., tr. see Aristotle.

Gerson, Lennard D. The Secret Police in Lenin's Russia. LC 75-44707. 368p. 1976. 19.95 (ISBN 0-87722-085-9). Temple U Pr.

Gerson, Lennard D., ed. Lenin & the Twentieth Century: A Bertram D. Wolfe Retrospective. (Publication Ser.: No. 293). xvii, 216p. 1984. lib. bdg. 27.95 (ISBN 0-8179-7931-X); pap. 7.95 (ISBN 0-8179-7932-8). Hoover Inst Pr.

Gerson, Louis L. John Foster Dulles. LC 67-24039. (American Secretaries of State & Their Diplomacy New Ser. 1925-1961: Vol. 17). 1967. 23.00 (ISBN 0-8154-0077-2). Cooper Sq.

--Woodrow Wilson & the Rebirth of Poland, 1914-1920: A Study in the Influence on American Policy of Minority Groups of Foreign Origin. LC 74-179575. xi, 166p. 1972. Repr. of 1953 ed. 16.00 (ISBN 0-208-01229-X, Archon). Shoe String.

Gerson, M. S., jt. auth. see Appleyard, Donald.

Gerson, Max. Cancer Therapy Fifty Cases Reviewed. 9.95 (ISBN 0-939236-00-1). Cancer Control Soc.

--A Cancer Therapy: Results of Fifty Cases. 3rd ed. 432p. 9.95 (ISBN 0-317-16366-3). World Wide Or.

Gerson, Noel. The Swamp Fox, Francis Marion. 1980. pap. 2.25 (ISBN 0-89176-001-6, 6001). Mockingbird Bks.

Gerson, Noel B. Jefferson Square. LC 68-14054. 512p. 1968. 6.95 (ISBN 0-87131-011-2). M Evans.

--Statue in Search of a Pedestal: A Biography of the Marquis de Lafayette. 15.95 (ISBN 0-88411-640-9, Pub. by Aeonian Pr). Amereon Ltd.

--The Swamp Fox, Francis Marion. 17.95 (ISBN 0-88411-642-5, Pub. by Aeonian Pr). Amereon Ltd.

Gerson, Noll B. Clear for Action: A Biographical Novel about David Farragut. 15.95 (ISBN 0-88411-641-7, Pub. by Aeonian Pr). Amereon Ltd.

Gerson, Richard F. The Right Vitamins: A Guide to over One Hundred Fifty Common Health Problems & the Vitamins & Minerals That Can Help. (Illus.). 144p. (Orig.). 1984. pap. 7.95 (ISBN 0-8092-5405-0). Contemp Bks.

Gerson, Robert A. Music in Philadelphia. LC 76-95121. Repr. of 1940 ed. lib. bdg. 19.25x (ISBN 0-8371-3930-9, GEMP). Greenwood.

Gerson, Simon W. After Fifty Years: Revisiting the Soviet Union. LC 78-53200. (Illus.). 1978. pap. 0.60 (ISBN 0-916972-03-8). NWR Pubns.

--Pete: The Story of Peter V. Cacchione, New York's First Communist Councilman. LC 76-29039. 215p. 1976. 10.00 (ISBN 0-7178-0482-8); pap. 3.50 (ISBN 0-7178-0473-9). Intl Pubs Co.

Gerson, Stanley, tr. see Bjorkstein, Ingmar.

Gerson, Sylvia P., jt. auth. see Covert, Mildred L.

Gerson, Trina. Holiday Crafts. 80p. (ps-7). 1983. pap. text ed. write for info. (ISBN 0-9605878-1-0). Anirt Pr.

--Holiday Songs. 84p. (ps-7). 1984. pap. text ed. write for info. (ISBN 0-9605878-2-9). Anirt Pr.

--Poetic Shapes. 52p. (ps-7). 1981. pap. text ed. 2.95 (ISBN 0-9605878-0-2). Anirt Pr.

Gersoni-Edelman, Diane. Work-Wise: Learning about the World of Work from Books--Critical Guide to Book Selection & Usage. LC 79-11920. (Selection Guide Ser.: No. 3). 258p. 1980. 22.95 (ISBN 0-87436-264-4). Neal-Schuman.

Gersov, A. S. Finnish-Danish-Finnish Dictionary: Suomi-Tanska-Suomi. 315p. (Finnish & Danish.). 1976. pap. 14.95 (ISBN 951-0-07507-8, M-9648). French & Eur.

Gersovitz, Mark, jt. auth. see Eaton, Jonathan.

Gersovitz, Mark, ed. Selected Economic Writings of W. Arthur Lewis. (Selected Economic Writings Ser.). 832p. 1983. 75.00X (ISBN 0-686-82268-4). NYU Pr.

Gersovitz, Mark, et al, eds. The Theory & Experience of Economic Development: Essays in Honor of Sir W. Arthur Lewis. 416p. 1982. text ed. 37.50x (ISBN 0-04-330323-4). Allen Unwin.

Gerspach, M. Coptic Textile Designs. 1975. pap. 3.00 (ISBN 0-486-22849-5). Dover.

--Coptic Textile Designs. (Illus.). 10.25 (ISBN 0-8446-5190-7). Peter Smith.

Gerstein, B. C. & Dybowski, C. R. Transient Techniques in NMR of Solids: An Introduction to Theory & Practice. Date not set. price not set (ISBN 0-12-281180-1). Acad Pr.

Gerstein, Dean R., jt. auth. see Olson, Steve.

Gerstein, Dean R., ed. Towards the Prevention of Alcohol Problems: Government, Business, & Community Action. 192p. 1984. pap. text ed. 14.95 (ISBN 0-309-03485-X). Natl Acad Pr.

Gerstein, Dean R., jt. ed. see Levison, Peter K.

Gerstein, Harold, ed. Techniques in Clinical Endodontics. (Illus.). 416p. 1983. 39.50 (ISBN 0-7216-4087-7). Saunders.

Gerstein, Linda. Nikolai Strakhov. LC 79-139720. (Russian Research Center Studies: No. 65). 1971. 15.00x (ISBN 0-674-62475-0). Harvard U Pr.

Gerstein, Marvin. Beat Me, Whip Me, Make Me Write Bad Checks. Johnston, William L., ed. (Chapbooks: No. 10). 35p. 1982. pap. 3.00 (ISBN 0-932884-09-1). Red Herring.

Gerstein, Mordicai. Arnold of the Ducks. LC 82-47735. (Illus.). 64p. (gr. k-3). 1983. 11.06i (ISBN 0-06-022002-3); PLB 11.89g (ISBN 0-06-022003-1). HarpJ.

--Arnold of the Ducks. LC 82-47735. (Trophy Picture Bk.). (Illus.). 64p. (gr. k-3). 1985. pap. 3.80i (ISBN 0-06-443080-4, Trophy). HarpJ.

--Follow Me! LC 82-14116. (Illus.). 32p. (gr. k-3). 1983. 10.25 (ISBN 0-688-01855-6); PLB 10.88 (ISBN 0-688-01856-4). Morrow.

--Roll Over! LC 83-18884. (Illus.). 32p. (ps-1). 1984. 5.95 (ISBN 0-517-55209-4). Crown.

--The Room. LC 83-47709. (Illus.). 32p. (ps-3). 1984. 9.57i (ISBN 0-06-021998-X); PLB 9.89g (ISBN 0-06-021999-8). HarpJ.

--William, Where Are You? (A Fold-Out Bk.). (Illus.). 32p. (ps-1). 1985. 6.95 (ISBN 0-517-55644-8). Crown.

Gerstein, Mordicai, tr. see Levy, Elizabeth.

Gerstel, Naomi & Gross, Harriet. Commuter Marriage: A Study of Work & Family. 228p. 1984. text ed. 17.50 (ISBN 0-89862-076-7). Guilford Pr.

Gerstell, Richard. The Steel Trap in North America: The Illustrated Story of Its Design, Production, & the Use with Furbearing & Predatory Animals, from Its Colorful Past to the Present Controversy. Senko, Peggy, ed. (Illus.). 384p. 1985. 44.95 (ISBN 0-8117-1698-8). Stackpole.

Gerstell, Vivian S. Silversmiths of Lancaster, Pennsylvania 1730-1850. LC 72-86855. (Illus.). 160p. 1972. 9.50 (ISBN 0-915010-17-8). Sutter House.

Gersten, Leon, jt. auth. see Traiger, Arthur.

Gersten, Martin, jt. auth. see Koplin, Richard S.

Gersten, Robert. Spirit of Ole Brant Lake. 1985. 8.95 (ISBN 0-533-06602-6). Vantage.

Gersten, S. M. Topology of the Automorphism: Group of a Free Group. (London Mathematical Society Lecture Note Ser.: No. 102). 200p. Date not set. pap. price not set. (ISBN 0-521-31523-9). Cambridge U Pr.

Gerstenberg, Alice. The Pot Boiler. 24p. 1983. pap. 1.25x (ISBN 0-88680-206-7). I E Clark.

Gerstenberg, Heinrich W. Von. Vermischte Schriften, 3 vols. 1262p. Repr. of 1815 ed. 180.00 (ISBN 0-384-18220-8). Johnson Repr.

Gerstenberger, Donna. The Complex Configuration: Modern Verse Drama. (Salzburg Studies in English Literature, Poetic Drama & Poetic Theory: No. 5). 178p. 1973. pap. text ed. 25.50x (ISBN 0-391-01383-1). Humanities.

--Iris Murdoch. LC 74-126290. (Irish Writers Ser.). 85p. 1975. 4.50 (ISBN 0-8387-7774-0); pap. 1.95 (ISBN 0-8387-7731-7). Bucknell U Pr.

--Richard Hugo. LC 82-74093. (Western Writers Ser.: No. 59). (Illus., Orig.). 1983. pap. 2.00x (ISBN 0-88430-033-1). Boise St Univ.

Gerstenberger, Donna & Hendrick, George. Fourth Directory of Periodicals: Publishing Articles in English & American Literature & Language. LC 74-21506. 234p. 1974. 18.95x (ISBN 0-8040-0675-X, 82-73732, Pub. by Swallow); (Pub. by Swallow). Ohio U Pr.

Gerstenberger, Donna, ed. see Alexander, Harriet S.

Gerstenberger, Erhard S. & Schrage, Wolfang. Suffering. Steely, John E., tr. LC 79-20499. (Biblical Encounters Ser.). Orig. Title: Leiden. 1980. pap. 10.95 (ISBN 0-687-40574-2). Abingdon.

Gerstenberger, Erhard S. & Schrage, Wolfgang. Woman & Man: Biblical Encounter Ser. Stott, Douglas W., tr. from Ger. LC 81-10898. 256p. (Orig.). 1982. pap. 10.95 (ISBN 0-687-45920-6). Abingdon.

Gerstenblith, Patty. The Levant at the Beginning of the Middle Bronze Age. (American Schools of Oriental Research Dissertation Ser.: No. 5). 1983. text ed. 15.00x (ISBN 0-89757-105-3, Pub. by Am Sch Orient Res). Eisenbrauns.

Gerstenbrand, F., et al. Neuroimaging. (Illus.). 327p. 1985. pap. 49.00 (ISBN 3-437109-41-3, Pub. by Gustav Fisher Verlag). VCH Pubs.

Gerstenbrand, F., et al, eds. Clinical Experiences with Budipine in Parkinson Therapy. (Illus.). 260p. 1985. pap. 26.50 (ISBN 0-387-13764-5). Springer-Verlag.

Gerstenfeld, Arthur. Technological Innovation: Government-Industry Cooperation. LC 78-14800. 277p. 1979. 42.50x (ISBN 0-471-03647-1, Pub. by Wiley-Interscience). Wiley.

Gerstenfeld, Arthur, ed. Science Policy Perspectives U. S. A.: The U. S. & Japan (Symposium) LC 82-18159. 1982. 37.50 (ISBN 0-12-281280-8). Acad Pr.

Gerstenfeld, Sheldon L. The Bird Care Book. (Illus.). 224p. 1981. o. p. 11.95 (ISBN 0-201-03908-7); pap. 7.95 (ISBN 0-201-03909-5). Addison-Wesley.

--Taking Care of Your Cat. LC 79-2338. (Illus.). 1979. o. p. 11.95 (ISBN 0-201-03058-6); pap. 7.95 (ISBN 0-201-03059-4). Addison-Wesley.

--Taking Care of Your Dog. LC 79-2339. (Illus.). 1979. o. p. 11.95 (ISBN 0-201-03060-8); pap. 7.95 (ISBN 0-201-03061-6). Addison-Wesley.

Gerstenzang, Adolph. Alphabet Shorthand in Fifteen Days. 64p. pap. 5.95 (ISBN 0-399-51173-3, Perigee). Putnam Pub Group.

Gerstenzang, Sharon D. Cook with Me Sugar Free: Favorite Sweets, Snacks, & Desserts for Children... & Grown-Ups, Too! (Illus.). 192p. 1983. 9.95 (ISBN 0-671-46472-8, Fireside). S&S.

Gerster, Georg. Sahara, Desert of Destiny. facs. ed. Thomson, Stewart, tr. LC 70-133521. (Select Bibliographies Repint Ser). 1960. 21.50 (ISBN 0-8369-5553-6). Ayer Co Pubs.

Gerster, Patrick & Cords, Nicholas. Myth in American History. 1977. pap. text ed. write for info. (ISBN 0-02-473290-7). Macmillan.

Gerster, Patrick, jt. auth. see Cords, Nicholas.

Gersting & Gemignani. Intro to Computer Literacy. 700p. 1986. pap. price not set (ISBN 0-02-341530-4). Macmillan.

Gersting, J. L., jt. auth. see Alton, E. V.

Gersting, Judith L. Mathematical Structures for Computer Science. LC 82-2550. (Illus.). 432p. 1982. text ed. 28.95 (ISBN 0-7167-1305-5); solutions manual avail. W H Freeman.

Gersting, Judith L. & Kuczkowski. Yes-No, Stop-Go: Some Patterns in Mathematic Logic. LC 76-46376. (Young Math Ser.). (Illus.). (gr. k-3). 1977. PLB 11.89 (ISBN 0-690-01130-X). Crowell Jr Bks.

Gersting, Judith L., jt. auth. see Kuczkowski, Joseph E.

Gerstinger, Heinz. Lope de Vega & Spanish Drama. Rosenbaum, Samuel, tr. from Ger. LC 72-90812. (Literature and Life Ser.). (Illus.). 1974. 12.95 (ISBN 0-8044-2227-3). Ungar.

--Pedro Calderon De la Barca. Peters, Diana S., tr. (Literature and Life Ser.). (Illus.). 12.95 (ISBN 0-8044-2226-5). Ungar.

Gerstle, C. Andrew. Circles of Fantasy: Convention in the Plays of Chikamatsu. (Harvard East Asian Monographs: No. 116). 312p. 1984. text ed. 25.00x (ISBN 0-674-13171-1). Harvard U Pr.

Gerstle, Donna & Raitt, Helen. Tonga Pictorial... a Tapestry of Pride... Kupesi 'o Tonga.. LC 74-75535. (Illus.). 100p. (Orig., Eng. & Tongan.). 1974. pap. 5.95 (ISBN 0-914488-02-3). Rand-Tofua.

Gerstle, Susan L., jt. auth. see Buttaci, Sal St. John.

Gerstle, Susan L., jt. auth. see Buttaci, Salvatore St. John.

Gerstle, Susan L., jt. auth. see St. John Buttaci, Sal.

Gerstle, Susan L., jt. ed. see Buttaci, Sal S.

Gerstle, Susan L., jt. ed. see Buttaci, Salvatore S.

Gerstle, Susan L., jt. ed. see Buttaci, Salvatore St. John.

Gerstle, Susan L., jt. ed. see St. John Buttaci, Salvatore.

Gerstler, Amy. The True Bride. 95p. (Orig.). 1985. letter press 15.00 (ISBN 0-932499-03-1); pap. 8.00 (ISBN 0-932499-04-X). Lapis Pr.

--White Marriage & Recovery. (Tadbooks Ser.). 24p. 1984. pap. 4.00 (ISBN 0-89807-104-6); signed & numbered o.p. 10.50 (ISBN 0-89807-105-4). Illuminati.

Gerstner, John. Bible Inerrancy Primer. 1981. pap. 2.95 (ISBN 0-88469-144-6). BMH Bks.

--Predestination Primer. 1981. pap. 2.95 (ISBN 0-88469-145-4). BMH Bks.

--Reconciliation Primer. 1981. pap. 2.95 (ISBN 0-88469-143-8). BMH Bks.

Gerstner, John H. A Primer on Dispensationalism. 1982. pap. 1.75 (ISBN 0-87552-273-4). Presby & Reformed.

--A Primer on Free Will. 1982. pap. 1.50 (ISBN 0-87552-272-6). Presby & Reformed.

--A Primer on Justification. 32p. 1983. pap. 1.50 (ISBN 0-87552-276-9). Presby & Reformed.

--A Primer on the Atonement. 32p. 1984. pap. 1.50 (ISBN 0-87552-278-5). Presby & Reformed.

--A Primer on the Deity of Christ. 40p. 1984. pap. 1.75 (ISBN 0-87552-277-7). Presby & Reformed.

--The Problem of Pleasure. 1983. pap. 1.50 (ISBN 0-87552-275-0). Presby & Reformed.

--Teachings of Jehovah's Witnesses. pap. 1.75 (ISBN 0-8010-3718-2). Baker Bk.
--Teachings of Mormonism. pap. 1.95 (ISBN 0-8010-3719-0). Baker Bk.
--Teachings of Seventh-Day Adventism. pap. 1.75 (ISBN 0-8010-3720-4). Baker Bk.
--Theology of the Major Sects. (Twin Brooks Ser). 1960. pap. 6.95 (ISBN 0-8010-3656-9). Baker Bk.
Gerstner, Karl. The Spirit of Color: The Art of Karl Gerstner. Stierlin, Henri, ed. (Illus.). 220p. 1981. 45.00 (ISBN 0-262-07084-7). MIT Pr.
Gerstner-Hirzel, Arthur. Economy of Action & the Word in Shakespeare's Plays. LC 70-168111. Repr. of 1957 ed. 5.40 (ISBN 0-404-02715-6). AMS Pr.
--Economy of Action & the Word in Shakespeare's Plays. 1957. Repr. 8.50 (ISBN 0-8274-2218-0). R West.
Gerston, Larry N. Making Public Policy: From Conflict to Resolution. 1983. pap. text ed. 14.10x (ISBN 0-673-15644-3). Scott F.
Gerston, Rich. Just Open the Door: A Complete Guide to Experiencing Environmental Education. 2nd ed. (Illus.). 112p. 1983. pap. text ed. 9.75x (ISBN 0-8134-2249-3). Interstate.
Gerstung, Estella, ed. see Clark, Barbara R.
Gersuni, G. V., ed. Sensory Processes at the Neuronal & Behavioral Levels. 1971. 73.50 (ISBN 0-12-281350-2). Acad Pr.
Gersuny, Carl. Work Hazards & Industrial Conflict. LC 80-51506. (Illus.). 178p. 1981. 16.00x (ISBN 0-87451-189-5). U Pr of New Eng.
Gersuny, Carl, jt. auth. see Poggie, John J.
Gersuny, Carl, et al. Some Effects of Technological Change on New England Fishermen. (Marine Technical Report Ser.: No. 42). 1975. pap. 1.00 (ISBN 0-938412-14-0). URI MAS.
Gerszi, Terez, et al. From Leonardo to Van Gogh: Master Drawings from Budapest. LC 84-22370. (Illus.). 224p. (Orig.). 1985. pap. 22.95 (ISBN 0-86559-064-8). Art Inst Chi.
Gert, Bernard, jt. auth. see Culver, Charles M.
Gert, Bernard, jt. auth. see Fessenden-Raden, June.
Gert, Bernard, ed. Man & Citizen: Thomas Hobbes De Homine. Wood, Charles T., tr. 1972. pap. text ed. 6.45x (ISBN 0-391-00849-8). Humanities.
Gert, Bernard, ed. see Hobbes, Thomas.
Gerteiny, Alfred G. Historical Dictionary of Mauritania. LC 81-5291. (African Historical Dictionaries Ser.: No. 31). 116p. 1981. 17.50 (ISBN 0-8108-1433-1). Scarecrow.
Gerteis, Louis S. From Contraband to Freedman: Federal Policy Toward Southern Blacks, 1861-1865. LC 72-801. (Contributions in American History Ser.: No. 29). 255p. 1973. lib. bdg. 29.95 (ISBN 0-8371-6372-2, GFC/). Greenwood.
Gertel, Elliot, jt. auth. see Siegel, Seymour.
Gerth, Dawn M., ed. see Arnold, Lee E., Jr.
Gerth, Dawn M., ed. see McIntyre, Alice.
Gerth, Hans & Mills, C. Wright. Character & Social Structure: The Psychology of Social Institutions. LC 53-12721. pap. 4.95 (ISBN 0-15-616759-X, Harv). HarBraceJ.
Gerth, Hans H., ed. see Weber, Max.
Gerth, Hans H., tr. see Weber, Max.
Gerth, Vel. Tendril. (Illus.). 1983. pap. 2.00 (ISBN 0-942648-04-8). Vardaman Pr.
Gertiz, Albert J., ed. see Rastell, John.
Gertler. Essays on the Macroeco Method. (Outstanding Dissertations Economy Ser.: No. II). 1985. PLB 34.00 (ISBN 0-8240-4162-3). Garland Pub.
Gertler, Edward. Maryland & Delaware Canoe Trails. 2nd ed. (Illus.). 221p. 1983. pap. 8.95 (ISBN 0-9605908-1-1). Seneca Pr MD.
Gertler, L. O., ed. Planning the Canadian Environment. LC 68-57715. pap. 77.80 (ISBN 0-317-30431-3, 2024930). Bks Demand UMI.
Gertler, T. Elbowing the Seducer. 323p. 1984. 16.95 (ISBN 0-394-52254-0). Random.
--Elbowing the Seducer. (Contemporary American Fiction Ser.). 320p. 1985. pap. 5.95 (ISBN 0-14-007792-8). Penguin.
Gertman, Paul M., jt. auth. see Blum, John.
Gertman, Paul M., jt. auth. see Egdahl, Richard H.
Gertman, Paul M., jt. ed. see Egdahl, Richard H.
Gertner, Michael H. The Morphology of the Modern French Verb. (Janua Linguarum Ser. Practica: No. 204). 1973. pap. 23.20x (ISBN 90-2792-504-6). Mouton.
Gertner, Richard. International Motion Picture Almanac, Vol. 28. 649p. 1983. 47.00 (ISBN 0-900610-29-8). Quigley Pub Co.
--International Motion Picture Almanac, Vol. 45. 715p. 1974. 17.00 (ISBN 0-900610-10-7). Quigley Pub Co.
--International Motion Picture Almanac, Vol. 46. 704p. 1975. 19.00 (ISBN 0-900610-12-3). Quigley Pub Co.
--International Motion Picture Almanac, Vol. 47. 770p. 1976. 24.00 (ISBN 0-317-20174-3). Quigley Pub Co.
--International Motion Picture Almanac, Vol. 48. 754p. 1977. 26.00 (ISBN 0-317-20175-1). Quigley Pub Co.
--International Motion Picture Almanac, Vol. 49. 730p. 1978. 30.00 (ISBN 0-900610-18-2). Quigley Pub Co.
--International Motion Picture Almanac, Vol. 51. 709p. 1980. 35.00 (ISBN 0-317-20176-X). Quigley Pub Co.
--International Motion Picture Almanac, Vol. 52. 718p. 1981. 38.00 (ISBN 0-900610-24-7). Quigley Pub Co.
--International Motion Picture Almanac, Vol. 52. 714p. 1982. 42.00 (ISBN 0-900610-26-3). Quigley Pub Co.
--International Motion Picture Almanac, Vol. 54. 702p. 1983. 47.00 (ISBN 0-317-20184-0). Quigley Pub Co.
--International Motion Picture Almanac, Vol. 55. 705p. 1984. 50.00 (ISBN 0-900610-30-1). Quigley Pub Co.
--International Television Almanac, Vol. 18. 678p. 15.00 (ISBN 0-900610-09-3). Quigley Pub Co.
--International Television Almanac, Vol. 20. 640p. 1975. 19.00 (ISBN 0-900610-13-1). Quigley Pub Co.
--International Television Almanac, Vol. 21. 708p. 1976. 24.00 (ISBN 0-900610-15-8). Quigley Pub Co.
--International Television Almanac, Vol. 22. 681p. 1977. 26.00 (ISBN 0-900610-17-4). Quigley Pub Co.
--International Television Almanac, Vol. 23. 652p. 1978. 30.00 (ISBN 0-900610-19-0). Quigley Pub Co.
--International Television Almanac, Vol. 24. 679p. 1979. 33.00 (ISBN 0-900610-21-2). Quigley Pub Co.
--International Television Almanac, Vol. 25. 649p. 1980. 35.00 (ISBN 0-900610-23-9). Quigley Pub Co.
--International Television Almanac, Vol. 26. 650p. 1981. 38.00 (ISBN 0-317-20183-2). Quigley Pub Co.
--International Television Almanac, Vol. 27. 653p. 1982. 42.00 (ISBN 0-900610-27-1). Quigley Pub Co.
--International Television Almanac, Vol. 29. 689p. 1984. 50.00 (ISBN 0-900610-31-X). Quigley Pub Co.
--Internbational Motion Picture Almanac, Vol. 50. 742p. 1979. 33.00 (ISBN 0-900610-20-4). Quigley Pub Co.
Gertner, Richard, ed. International Motion Picture Almanac, 1984, Vol. 56. 714p. 1985. 50.00 (ISBN 0-900610-32-8). Quigley Pub Co.
--International Television Almanac 1984, Vol. 30. 678p. 1985. 50.00 (ISBN 0-900610-33-6). Quigley Pub Co.
Gertsbakh, I. B. Models of Preventive Maintenance. (Studies in Mathematical & Managerial Economics: Vol. 23). 1977. 57.50 (ISBN 0-7204-0465-7, North-Holland). Elsevier.
Gertsbakh, I. B. & Kordonskiy, K. B. Models of Failure. (Engineering Science Library). (Illus.). 1969. pap. 20.00 (ISBN 0-387-04569-4). Springer-Verlag.
Gertsch, Alfred. Der Steigende Ruhm Miltons. Repr. of 1927 ed. 54.00 (ISBN 0-384-18230-5). Johnson Repr.
Gertsch, W. J., ed. see Comstock, John H.
Gertsch, Willis J. American Spiders. 2nd ed. 320p. 1979. 36.50 (ISBN 0-442-22649-7). Van Nos Reinhold.
Gertz. Construction, Mechanics' & Materialmen's Liens. (The Law in South Carolina Ser.). 24.95 (ISBN 0-686-90981-X). Harrison Co GA.
Gertz, Elmer. For the First Hours of Tomorrow: The New Illinois Bill of Rights. LC 72-76865. (Studies in Illinois Constitution Making). 187p. 1972. pap. 10.00x (ISBN 0-252-00274-1). U of Ill Pr.
--The Odyssey of a Barbarian: The Biography of George Sylvester Viereck. LC 78-24801. 305p. 1979. 19.95 (ISBN 0-87975-108-8). Prometheus Bks.
Gertz, Elmer & Pisciotte, Joe. Charter for a New Age: An Inside View of the Sixth Illinois Constitutional Convention. LC 80-10837. (Studies in Illinois Constitution Making Ser.). 392p. 1980. 15.00x (ISBN 0-252-00820-0). U of Ill Pr.
Gertz, Elmer, jt. auth. see Tobin, A. I.
Gertz, Elmer & Lewis, Felice F., eds. Henry Miller: Years of Trial & Triumph, 1962-1964: The Correspondence of Henry Miller & Elmer Gertz. LC 78-3547. (Illus.). 361p. 1978. 19.95x (ISBN 0-8093-0860-6). S Ill U Pr.
Gertz, Elmer, et al. A Guide to Estate Planning. LC 82-10790. 191p. (Orig.). 1983. pap. 9.95 (ISBN 0-8093-1103-8). S Ill U Pr.
--Quest for a Constitution: A Man Who Wouldn't Quit-A Political Biography of Samuel Witwer of Illinois. LC 84-13226. 1984. 20.00 (ISBN 0-8191-4208-5). U Pr of Amer.
Gertz, Ernest, et al. Michigan Tax Practice & Procedure. LC 83-81081. 1984. write for info. U MI Law CLE.
Gertz, Jim, jt. auth. see Hauff, Steve.
Gertz, Steven M., ed. see ASTM Committee D-19 on Water.
Gertzel, Cherry. Party & Locality in Northern Uganda, 1945-1962. (Commonwealth Papers: No. 16). (Illus.). 100p. 1974. pap. 22.50 (ISBN 0-485-17616-5, Pub. by Athlone Pr Ltd). Longwood Pub Group.
Gertzel, Cherry J. The Politics of Independent Kenya, 1963-8. LC 73-124293. pap. 48.00 (ISBN 0-317-11320-8, 2015296). Bks Demand UMI.
Gertzel, Cheryl, et al, eds. The Dynamics of the One-Party State in Zambia. LC 83-25535. (Illus.). 262p. 1984. 35.00 (ISBN 0-7190-1069-1, Pub. by Manchester Univ Pr). Longwood Pub Group.
Gertzog, Irwin N. Congressional Women: Their Recruitment, Treatment & Behavior. LC 84-4714. (Women & Politics Ser.). 304p. 1984. 29.95x (ISBN 0-03-063058-4). Praeger.
Gert zur Heide, Karl. Deep South Piano. (The Paul Oliver Blues Ser.). pap. 2.95 (ISBN 0-913714-32-1). Legacy Bks.
Gerulaitis, Leonardas V. Printing & Publishing in Fifteenth Century Venice. 204p. 1976. 25.00x (ISBN 0-8389-0126-3). ALA.
Geruson, Richard T. & McGrath, Dennis. Cities & Urbanization. LC 76-17251. 233p. 1977. text ed. 13.95 (ISBN 0-275-23440-1, HoltC). HR&W.
Gerutis, Albertas, et al. Lithuania: Seven Hundred Years. 6th ed. Budreckis, Algirdas, tr. LC 75-80057. 1969. 16.00 (ISBN 0-87141-028-1). Manyland.
Gervais, David. Flaubert & Henry James: A Study in Contrasts. 240p. 1978. text ed. 29.50x (ISBN 0-06-492375-4). B&N Imports.
Gervais, Gilbert. Daily Prayer Poems & Words of Wisdom. 1984. 5.95 (ISBN 0-533-05772-8). Vantage.
Gervais, J. L. & Jacob, M., eds. Non-Linear & Collective Phenomena in Quantum Physics. vii, 514p. 1983. 60.00x (ISBN 9971-950-64-2, Pub. by World Sci Singapore); pap. 28.00x (ISBN 9971-950-65-0, Pub. by World Sci Singapore). Taylor & Francis.
Gervais, Marcel, ed. Journey: A Home & Group Bible Study Program. (Illus.). Set. 60.00; Old Testament, Set 20 Bklts. 30.00 (ISBN 0-8091-9279-9); New Testament Set, 20 Bklts. 30.00 (ISBN 0-8091-9280-2); bklt. 1.50 ea. Paulist Pr.
Gervais, Robert L. & Dittburner, Delos A. What Do You Do When...? A Handbook for Classroom Discipline Problems with Practical & Positive Solutions. 178p. (Orig.). 1985. lib. bdg. 21.75 (ISBN 0-8191-4810-5); pap. text ed. 10.25 (ISBN 0-8191-4811-3). U Pr of Amer.
Gervaise, Claude see Expert, Henry.
Gervase. Historical Works, the Chronicle of the Reigns of Stephen, Henry II & Richard I, 2 vols. Stubbs, William, ed. (Rolls Ser.: No. 73). Repr. of 1879 ed. Set. 120.00 (ISBN 0-317-16796-0). Kraus Repr.
Gervase, Charles J., jt. auth. see Dreher, Barbara B.
Gervasi, Frank H. Big Government: The Meaning & Purpose of the Hoover Commission Report. LC 81-13351. xii, 366p. 1982. Repr. of 1949 ed. lib. bdg. 36.00x (ISBN 0-313-23111-7, GEBG). Greenwood.
Gervasi, Tom. America's War Machine: The Pursuit of Global Dominance. LC 84-48245. (Arsenal of Democracy Ser.: No. III). 352p. 1985. 29.95 (ISBN 0-394-54102-2). Grove.
--America's War Machine: The Pursuit of Global Dominance. LC 84-48245. (Arsenal of Democracy Ser.: No. III). 352p. 1985. pap. 14.95 (ISBN 0-394-62247-2, E-945, Ever). Grove.
--Arsenal of Democracy II: American Military Power in the 1980s & the Origins of the New Cold War. rev. ed. LC 80-993. (Illus.). 272p. (Orig.). 1981. pap. 12.95 (ISBN 0-394-17662-6, E760, Ever). Grove.
--The Myth of Soviet Military Supremacy. 1985. cancelled (ISBN 0-393-01776-1). Norton.
Gervasutti, Giusto. Gervasutti's Climbs. LC 78-70839. 202p. 1979. pap. 7.95 (ISBN 0-916890-67-8). Mountaineers.
Gerven, Lieven Van see Van Gerven, Lieven.
Gerver, D. & Sinaiko, H. W., eds. Language Interpretation & Communication. LC 78-15195. (NATO Conference Series III: Human Factors, Vol. 6). 437p. 1978. 45.00x (ISBN 0-306-40051-0, Plenum Pr). Plenum Pub.
Gerver, Elisabeth. Computers & Adult Learning. 128p. 1984. 34.00x (ISBN 0-335-10577-7, Pub. by Open Univ Pr); pap. 13.00x (ISBN 0-335-10423-1, Pub. by Open Univ Pr). Taylor & Francis.
Gerver, Jane. Raggedy Ann & Andy & the Haunted Doll House. LC 81-18016. 1982. 4.95 (ISBN 0-672-52720-0). Bobbs.
Gerver, Jane, ed. see Hudson, Eleanor.
Gerver, Jane E. Peter Rabbit's Sniffy Adventure. LC 83-62606. (Sniffy Bks.). (Illus.). 24p. (gr. k-2). 1984. 3.95 (ISBN 0-394-86352-6, BYR). Random.
--Three Cheers for Kneesaa! An Ewok Adventure. LC 83-62250. (Ewok Mini-Storybooks). (Illus.). 32p. (ps-3). 1983. pap. 1.25 (ISBN 0-394-86354-2, BYR). Random.
Gervers, Michael, ed. The Cartulary of the Knights of St. John of Jerusalem in England. (Records of Social & Economic History Ser.). 1982. 195.00x (ISBN 0-19-725996-0). Oxford U Pr.
Gervinus, Georg G. Shakespeare Commentaries. Bunnett, Fanny E., tr. LC 74-168112. Repr. of 1877 ed. 37.50 (ISBN 0-404-02716-4). AMS Pr.
Gerwick, Ben C. & Woolery, John C. Construction & Engineering Marketing for Major Project Services. LC 82-8383. (Practical Construction Guides Ser.). 419p. 1983. 51.95 (ISBN 0-471-09886-8, Pub. by Wiley-Interscience). Wiley.
Gerwick, Ben C., Jr. & Peters, V. P., eds. Russian-English Dictionary of Prestressed Concrete & Concrete Construction. 120p. (Rus. & Eng.). 1966. 38.50 (ISBN 0-677-00260-2). Gordon.
Gerwick, Ben C., Jr., et al, eds. Arctic Engineering for the Twenty-First Century. (Proceedings of the First Spilhaus Symposium Ser.). 240p. 1985. text ed. 30.00 (ISBN 0-933957-00-9). Marine Tech Soc.
Gerwig, Anne M. Barron's How to Prepare for the College Board Achievement Tests - Latin. LC 64-23527. (gr. 11-12). 1965. pap. 6.95 (ISBN 0-8120-0125-7). Barron.
Gerwig, George W. Art of the Short Shory. LC 72-194099. 1909. lib. bdg. 10.00 (ISBN 0-8414-1059-3). Folcroft.
Gerwig, H. George. Shakespeare's Ideals of Womanhood. 59.95 (ISBN 0-8490-1042-X). Gordon Pr.
Gerwig, Norma A., jt. auth. see King, Virginia G.
Gerwin, Donald. Budgeting Public Funds: The Decision Process in an Urban School District. LC 69-17326. 184p. 1969. 29.50x (ISBN 0-299-05270-2). U of Wis Pr.
--Budgeting Public Funds: The Decision Process in an Urban School District. LC 69-17326. pap. 46.00 (ISBN 0-317-29007-X, 2023726). Bks Demand UMI.
--The Employment of Teachers. LC 73-20854. 1974. 26.00x (ISBN 0-8211-0610-4); pap. text ed. 23.25x 10 or more copies. McCutchan.
Gerwin, K. S. & Glorig, A. Detection of Hearing Loss & Ear Disease in Children. (Illus.). 208p. 1974. 16.75x (ISBN 0-398-03175-4). C C Thomas.
Gerwin, Kenneth S., jt. auth. see Glorig, Aram.
Gerwitz, J. L., ed. Attachment & Dependency. LC 72-6913. 251p. 1972. 10.95 (ISBN 0-470-29709-3). Halsted Pr.
Gery, Jacques. Characoids of the World. (Illus.). 1978. 29.95 (ISBN 0-87666-458-3, H-961). TFH Pubns.
Gery, John. Charlemagne: A Song of Gestures. 65p. 1983. pap. 5.95 (ISBN 0-935684-05-0). Plumbers Ink Bks.
Gerzon, Mark. A Choice of Heroes: The Changing Faces of American Manhood. 1984. 13.95 (ISBN 0-395-32208-1); pap. 6.95 (ISBN 0-395-36143-5). HM.
Gerzon, Mark F., jt. ed. see Hiatt, Thomas A.
Gesau, Frans A. M. Alting Von see Alting von Gesau, Frans A. & Pelkmans, Jacques.
Gesau, Frans A. von Gesau see Alting von Gesau, Frans A. & Pelkmans, Jacques.
Gesch, Roy. To Love & to Cherish. 1985. 4.95 (ISBN 0-570-04214-3, 15-2174). Concordia.
Gesch, Roy C. Confirmed in Christ. 1983. pap. 1.95 (ISBN 0-570-03911-8, 12-2852). Concordia.
Gesch, Roy G. Help, I'm in College. LC 70-77282. 1969. pap. 3.50 (ISBN 0-570-03100-1, 12-2663). Concordia.
Gescheider, George A. Psychophysics: Method & Theory. 177p. 1976. text ed. 14.95 (ISBN 0-89859-120-1). L Erlbaum Assocs.
--Psychophysics: Method, Theory, & Application. 2nd ed. 304p. 1984. text ed. 24.95 (ISBN 0-89859-375-1). L Erlbaum Assocs.
Gescheidt, Alfred & Bradley, Josephine. City Cat. Burke, Thomas F., ed. (Illus.). 64p. (Orig.). Date not set. pap. 7.95 (ISBN 0-87654-060-4). Pomegranate Calif.
Geschiere, Peter. Village Communities & the Authority of the State: Changing Relations in Maka Villages Since 1900. Rev., Abr. ed. (Monographs from the African Studies Centre). 300p. 1983. Repr. of 1978 ed. 49.95x (ISBN 0-7103-0015-8, Kegan Paul). Routledge & Kegan.
Geschiere, Peter & Binsbergen, Wim M., eds. Old Modes of Production & Capitalist Encroachment. (Monographs from the African Studies Centre, Leiden). 400p. 1985. 49.95x (ISBN 0-7103-0089-1). Routledge & Kegan.
Geschwender, Arlyne. Real Estate Principles & Practices: A Contemporary Approach. 280p. (Orig.). 1983. pap. text ed. 18.95 (ISBN 0-89787-907-4). Gorsuch Scarisbrick.
Geschwender, J. A. Class, Race & Worker Insurgency. LC 76-62581. (American Sociological Association Rose Monograph Ser.). (Illus.). 1977. 32.50 (ISBN 0-521-21584-6). Cambridge U Pr.
Geschwind, N., ed. Boston Studies in the Philosophy of Science, Vol. 16: Selected Papers on Language & the Brain. LC 75-8602. (Synthese Library: No. 68). 549p. 1974. 66.00 (ISBN 90-277-0262-4, Pub. by Reidel Holland); pap. 18.95 (ISBN 90-277-0263-2). Kluwer Academic.
Geschwind, Norman & Galaburda, Albert M., eds. Cerebral Dominance: The Biological Foundations. (Illus.). 240p. 1984. text ed. 27.50x (ISBN 0-674-10658-X). Harvard U Pr.
Geschwind, S., ed. Electron Paramagnetic Resonance. LC 77-186261. 584p. 1972. 65.00x (ISBN 0-306-30580-1, Plenum Pr). Plenum Pub.
Gese, Hartmut. Essays on Biblical Theology. Crim, Keith R., tr. LC 81-65658. 256p. (Orig.). 1981. pap. 13.50 (ISBN 0-8066-1894-9, 10-2087). Augsburg.

Gesell, Arnold, et al. Biographies of Child Development: The Mental Growth Careers of Eight-Four Infants & Children. LC 74-21409. (Classsics in Child Development Ser). (Illus.). 350p. 1975. Repr. 31.00x (ISBN 0-405-06461-6). Ayer Co Pubs.

--Infant & Child in the Culture of Today: The Guidance of Development in Home & Nursery School. rev. ed. LC 73-4083. (Illus.). 432p. 1974. 18.22i (ISBN 0-06-011506-8, HarpT). Har-Row.

--Youth: Years from Ten to Sixteen. 1956. 17.26i (ISBN 0-06-011510-6, HarpT). Har-Row.

Gesell, Arnold L. The Embryology of Behavior: The Beginnings of the Human Mind. LC 72-138113. (Illus.). 289p. 1972. Repr. of 1945 ed. lib. bdg. 22.50x (ISBN 0-8371-5689-0, GEEB). Greenwood.

--Infant Development: The Embryology of Early Human Behavior. LC 73-142858. (Illus.). 108p. 1972. Repr. of 1952 ed. lib. bdg. 24.75x (ISBN 0-8371-5957-1, GEID). Greenwood.

--Mental Growth of the Pre-School Child. 1968. Repr. of 1925 ed. 59.00x (ISBN 0-403-00127-7). Scholarly.

--Studies in Child Development. LC 76-138114. (Illus.). 224p. 1972. Repr. of 1948 ed. lib. bdg. 29.75x (ISBN 0-8371-5690-4, GECD). Greenwood.

Gesell, Arnold L. & Gesell, Beatrice C. The Normal Child & Primary Education. 342p. 1981. Repr. of 1912 ed. lib. bdg. 40.00 (ISBN 0-89984-241-0). Century Bookbindery.

Gesell, Arnold L. & Thompson, Helen. Infant Behavior: Its Genesis & Growth. LC 71-95101. Repr. of 1934 ed. lib. bdg. 24.75x (ISBN 0-8371-2704-1, GEIB). Greenwood.

Gesell, Beatrice C., jt. auth. see Gesell, Arnold L.

Gesell, Laurence E. The Administration of Public Airports. LC 81-67998. (Illus.). 312p. (Orig.). 1981. 19.75 (ISBN 0-9606874-0-8). Coast Aire.

Gesell, Silvio. Collected Writings. 600.00 (ISBN 0-87968-904-8). Gordon Pr.

Gesell, Thomas F., et al, eds. Natural Radiation Environment III: Proceedings, 2 vols. LC 80-607130. (DOE Symposium Ser.). 1789p. 1980. Set. pap. 52.75 (ISBN 0-87079-129-X, CONF-780422); microfiche 4.50 (ISBN 0-87079-458-2, CONF-780422). DOE.

Gesellschaft Fuer Biologische Chemie, 21st Colloquium, Mossbach-Baden, 1970. Mammalian Reproduction: Proceedings. Gibian, H. & Plotz, J., eds. LC 77-140558. (Illus.). 1970. 46.00 (ISBN 0-387-05066-3). Springer-Verlag.

Gesellschaft Fuer Biologische Chemie, 24th, Mossbach-Baden, 1973. Regulation of Transcription & Translation in Eukaryotes: Proceedings. Bautz, E., ed. (Illus.). 300p. 1973. 52.00 (ISBN 0-387-06472-9). Springer-Verlag.

Gesellschaft fuer Informatik: 3 Jahrestagung, Hamburg 1973. Lecture Notes in Computer Science, Vol. 1. Bauer, W., ed. xi, 508p. 1973. pap. 21.00 (ISBN 0-387-06473-7). Springer Verlag.

Gesellschaft fur Geschichte des Weines e.V., et al, eds. Bibliographie zur Geschichte des Weines, 1 Vol., 3 Supplements. 1161p. (Ger.). 1984. Supp. 1. 15.00 (ISBN 3-598-10387-5); Supp. 2. 28.00 (ISBN 3-598-10389-1); Supp. 3. 30.00 (ISBN 3-598-10507-X); Main Vol. lib. bdg. 40.00 (ISBN 3-598-10388-3). K G Saur.

Gesellschaft fur Information und Dokumentation Staff, ed. Dictionary of Reprography: German with Definitions in English, French, & Spanish. 353p. 1982. lib. bdg. 20.00 (ISBN 3-598-10444-8). K G Saur.

Gesellschaft fur Information und Dokumentation Editors. Forschungs-und Entwicklungsprojekte in Informationwissenschaft und-praxis. (Informationsdienste 3: Vol. 8). 360p. (Ger.). 1985. lib. bdg. 16.00 (ISBN 3-598-20828-6). K G Saur.

Gesellschaft fur Information und Dokumentation, ed. Internationale Iud-Gremien. (Informationsdienste). 200p. 1985. lib. bdg. 22.50 (ISBN 3-598-20829-4). K G Saur.

--Verzeichnis deutscher Datenbanken, Datenbankbetreiber und Informationsvermittlungsstellen. (Informationsdienste). 450p. 1985. lib. bdg. 30.00 (ISBN 3-598-10582-7). K G Saur.

Gesellschaft zur Forderung der Wissenschaft des Judentums. Festschrift Siebzigsten Geburtstage Jakob Guttmanns. Katz, Steven, ed. LC 79-7155. (Jewish Philosophy, Mysticism & History of Ideas Ser.). 1980. Repr. of 1915 ed. lib. bdg. 25.50x (ISBN 0-405-12253-5). Ayer Co Pubs.

Gesenius, Wilhelm. Hebrew & Chaldee Lexicon: Keyed to Strong's Exhaustive Concordance. Tregelles, Samuel P., tr. (Hebrew & Chaldee.). kivar 24.95 (ISBN 0-8010-3801-4); pap. 19.95 (ISBN 0-8010-3736-0). Baker Bk.

Gesenius, William. Hebrew & Chaldee Lexicon, Tregelles Translation. (Hebrew & Chaldee.). 1949. 12.95 (ISBN 0-8028-8029-0). Eerdmans.

--Hebrew & English Lexicon to the Old Testament. 2nd ed. Brown, Francis, et al, eds. Robinson, Edward, tr. (Hebrew & Eng.). 1959. Repr. of 1907 ed. 34.95x (ISBN 0-19-864301-2). Oxford U Pr.

Gesensway, Daniel B., ed. Psychoanalytic Psychiatry for Lawyers. 393p. 1982. 40.00 (ISBN 0-686-40804-7, B403). Am Law Inst.

Geshe, Dhargyey, jt. auth. see Geshe, Rabten.

Geshe, Rabten & Geshe, Dhargyey. Advice from a Spiritual Friend. rev. ed. Beresford, Brian, ed. & tr. from Tibetan. (A Wisdom Basic Book, Orange Ser.). (Illus.). 160p. 1984. pap. 8.95 (ISBN 0-86171-017-7, Wisdom Pubns). Great Traditions.

Geshe Wangyal, tr. see Lo-dro of Drepung.

Geshner, John, jt. auth. see Kovac, Alexander.

Gesick, Lorraine, ed. Centers, Symbols, & Hierarchies: Essays on the Classical States of Southeast Asia. LC 83-50993. (Yale Univ. Southeast East Asia Monograph: No. 26). 241p. 1983. pap. 14.00 (ISBN 0-938692-04-6). Yale U SE Asia.

Geske, Terry G., jt. ed. see McMahon, Walter W.

Gesler, Wilbert. Health Care in Developing Countries. 1984. 5.00 (ISBN 0-89291-182-4). Assn Am Geographers.

Gesner, Abraham. Practical Treatise on Coal, Petroleum & Other Distilled Oils. 2nd ed. Gesner, George W., ed. LC 67-29511. Repr. of 1865 ed. 25.00x (ISBN 0-678-00440-4). Kelley.

Gesner, Carol. Shakespeare & the Greek Romance: A Study of Origins. LC 70-11509. 232p. 1970. 21.00x (ISBN 0-8131-1220-6). U Pr of Ky.

Gesner, Clark. You're a Good Man, Charlie Brown. 1980. pap. 1.95 (ISBN 0-449-20556-8, Crest). Fawcett.

Gesner, Conrad. Curious Woodcuts of Fanciful & Real Beasts. Gillon, Edmund V., Jr., ed. (Pictorial Archives Ser). Orig. Title: Selection of 16th & 17th-Century Woodcuts from Gesner & Topsell's Natural Histories. (Illus., Orig.). 1971. pap. 5.95 (ISBN 0-486-22701-4). Dover.

--The Newe lewell of Health. LC 73-171759. (English Experience Ser.: No. 381). 540p. 1971. Repr. of 1576 ed. 51.00 (ISBN 90-221-0381-1). Walter J Johnson.

--The Treasure of Euonymus: Conteyninge the Hid Secretes of Nature. Morwyng, P., tr. LC 63-6477. (English Experience Ser.: No. 97). 408p. 1969. Repr. of 1559 ed. 45.00 (ISBN 90-221-0097-9). Walter J Johnson.

Gesner, G., ed. Anthology of American Poetry. (Avenel Home Library). 720p. 1983. 7.98 (ISBN 0-517-38558-9, Avenel); jacketed ed. 7.98 (ISBN 0-517-38557-0). Outlet Bk Co.

Gesner, George W., ed. see Gesner, Abraham.

Gesner, Konrad. Beast & Animals in Decorative Woodcuts of the Renaissance. Grafton, Carol B., ed. (Illus.). 64p. (Orig.). 1983. pap. 3.95 (ISBN 0-486-24430-X). Dover.

Gess, Denise. Good Deeds. LC 83-14985. 1984. 12.95 (ISBN 0-517-55194-2). Crown.

Gess, Diane, ed. see Rothstein, Evelyn.

Gess, Diane, jt. auth. see Rothstein, Evelyn.

Gessa, G. L. & Corsini, G. U., eds. Apomorphine & Other Dopaminomimetics: Basic Pharmacology. 344p. 1981. text ed. 53.50 (ISBN 0-89004-667-0). Raven.

Gessa, G. L., jt. ed. see Costa, E.

Gessa, G. L., jt. ed. see Di Chiara, G.

Gessa, G. L., jt. ed. see Sandler, M.

Gessa, Gian L., jt. ed. see Corsini, Giovanni U.

Gessaman, James A. Ecological Energetics of Homeotherms. LC 72-80316. 155p. 1973. pap. 7.50 (ISBN 0-87421-053-4). Utah St U Pr.

Gessard, M. F., ed. see De Valois, Marguerite.

Gessel, Van C., tr. see Endo, Shusaku.

Gessel, Van C., tr. see Shusaku Endo.

Gessel, Van G., intro. by. The Showa Anthology: Modern Japanese Short Stories, 2 Vols. LC 85-40070. 230p. 1985. 17.95 ea. Vol. 1 (ISBN 0-87011-739-4). Vol. 2 (ISBN 0-87011-747-5). Kodansha.

Gessert, Robert & Hehir, J. Bryan. The New Nuclear Debate. LC 76-3357. (Special Studies Ser.). (Orig.). 1976. pap. 2.00t (ISBN 0-87641-215-0). Coun Rel & Intl.

Gessford, John E. Modern Information Systems: Designed for Decision Support. LC 78-74684. 1980. text ed. 29.95 (ISBN 0-201-03099-3). Addison-Wesley.

--The Use of Reservoir Water for Hydroelectric Power Generation. Bruchey, Stuart, ed. LC 78-22684. (Energy in the American Economy Ser.). (Illus.). 1979. lib. bdg. 12.00x (ISBN 0-405-11987-9). Ayer Co Pubs.

Gessinger, G. H. Powder Metallurgy of Superalloys. (Monographs in Materials). 330p. 1984. text ed. 69.95 (ISBN 0-408-11033-3). Butterworth.

Gessler, U., jt. ed. see Seybold, D.

Gessner, Lynne. Edge of Darkness. LC 79-4859. 1979. 8.95 (ISBN 0-8027-6367-7). Walker & Co.

Gessner, Robert. Massacre: A Survey of Today's American Indian. LC 72-38831. (Civil Liberties in American History Ser). 418p. 1972. Repr. of 1931 ed. lib. bdg. 45.00 (ISBN 0-306-70445-5). Da Capo.

Gessner, Robert A. Manufacturing Information Systems: Implementation Planning. LC 84-7408. 221p. 1984. text ed. 31.95x (ISBN 0-471-80843-1, Wiley-Interscience). Wiley.

--Master Production Schedule Planning. 1985. 33.50 (ISBN 0-471-82658-8). Wiley.

Gessow, Alfred & Myers, Garry C., Jr. Aerodynamics of the Helicopter. LC 67-26126. 1967. 28.00 (ISBN 0-8044-4275-4). Ungar.

Gesswein, Armin R. With One Accord in One Place. 93p. (Orig.). 1978. pap. 1.75 (ISBN 0-87509-161-X). Chr Pubns.

Gest, Alexander P. Engineering. LC 63-10287. (Our Debt to Greece & Rome Ser). Repr. of 1930 ed. 17.50 (ISBN 0-8154-0078-0). Cooper Sq.

Gest, Howard, ed. see Symposium, Bloomington, Oct., 1970.

Gest, J. M. The Lawyer in Literature. 59.95 (ISBN 0-8490-0490-X). Gordon Pr.

Gest, John M. The Law & Lawyers of Honore De Balzac. 1911. 30.00 (ISBN 0-8274-2808-1). R West.

--The Lawyer in Literature (Dickens, Scott, Balzac) 1913. 35.00 (ISBN 0-89984-231-3). Century Bookbindery.

--Old Yellow Book Source of Robert Browning's the Ring & the Book. LC 78-92953. (Studies in Browning, No. 4). 1924. lib. bdg. 58.95x (ISBN 0-8383-1058-3). Haskell.

Geste, Justin. Complete Book of Outrageous & Atrocious Practical Jokes. LC 85-4451. (Illus.). 144p. 1985. pap. 5.95 (ISBN 0-385-23044-3, Dolp). Doubleday.

Geston, Mark S. The Siege of Wonder. LC 75-36624. 180p. 1976. 12.50 (ISBN 0-385-11359-5). Ultramarine Pub.

Gestwicki, Ronald. Santa Claus: The Tooth Fairy & Other Stories - A Child's Introduction to Religion. Ashton, Sylvia, ed. LC 77-80276. 1977. 14.95 (ISBN 0-87949-108-6). Ashley Bks.

Gesualda Of The Holy Spirit, Sr. Saint Theresa, the Little Flower. (Illus.). 1960. 4.95 (ISBN 0-8198-0142-9); pap. 3.95. Dghtrs St Paul.

Gesunius, William. Gesenius' Hebrew Grammar. 2nd ed. Kautzsch, E. & Cowley, A. E., eds. 1910. 27.50x (ISBN 0-19-815406-2). Oxford U Pr.

Getchell, Bud. Physical Fitness: A Way of Life. 3rd ed. LC 62-17654. 258p. 1983. pap. 16.45 (ISBN 0-471-09635-0). Wiley.

Getchell, Bud & Anderson, Wayne. Being Fit: A Personal Guide. 312p. 1982. pap. text ed. 9.95x (ISBN 0-471-86353-X, Pub. by Wiley Pr). Wiley.

Getchell, Charles, tr. see Salin, Pascal.

Getchell, David R., et al, eds. Mariner's Catalog, Vol. 2. LC 73-88647. 1974. pap. 2.00 (ISBN 0-87742-046-7). Intl Marine.

Getches, David H. Water Law in a Nutshell. LC 84-3675. (Nutshell Ser.). 439p. 1984. pap. text ed. 11.95 (ISBN 0-314-81281-4). West Pub.

Getches, David H., et al. Federal Indian Law Cases & Materials. LC 79-3906. (American Casebook Ser.). 600p. 1979. text ed. 24.95 (ISBN 0-8299-2027-7); 1983 supplement 7.95 (ISBN 0-314-71765-X). West Pub.

Gethen, Ann. Let's Have Tea in Britain. 1984. 9.95 (ISBN 0-8062-2307-3). Carlton.

Gethers, Judith. The Fabulous Gourmet Food Processor Cookbook. 384p. (Orig.). 1981. pap. 7.95 (ISBN 0-345-29586-2). Ballantine.

--Italian Country Cooking: For the American Kitchen. LC 83-50865. (Illus.). 1984. 17.95 (ISBN 0-394-53355-0, Pub. by Villard Bks). Random.

Gethers, Judith & Lefft, Elizabeth. The World-Famous Ratner's Meatless Cookbook. 192p. 1983. pap. 2.95 (ISBN 0-345-30348-2). Ballantine.

Gethers, Martha. Dimensions. 54p. 1984. pap. 5.00 (ISBN 0-9612296-2-4). Williams Com.

Gethers, Peter, ed. see Simon, Roger L.

Gethin, David. Point of Honor: An Espionage Thriller. 188p. 1985. 12.95 (ISBN 0-684-18291-2, ScribT). Scribner.

--Wyatt. 192p. 1983. 12.95 (ISBN 0-312-89517-8, J Kahn). St Martin.

--Wyatt & the Moresby Legacy. 180p. 1984. 13.95 (ISBN 0-312-89520-8, J Kahn). St Martin.

Gething, Judith. Sex Discrimination & the Law in Hawaii: A Guide to Your Legal Rights. LC 78-10636. 122p. 1979. pap. 3.95 (ISBN 0-8248-0620-4). UH Pr.

Gething, Mary J., ed. Protein Transport & Secretion. (Current Communications in Molecular Biology Ser.). 220p. (Orig.). 1985. pap. 30.00 (ISBN 0-87969-183-2). Cold Spring Harbor.

Gething, Michael J. & Peacock, Lindsay T. RAF Air Power Today. (Warbirds Illustrated Ser.: No.25). (Illus.). 1984. pap. 9.95 (ISBN 0-85368-634-3, Arms & Armour Pr). Sterling.

Gething, Mike. F-15 Eagle. (Illus.). 11.95 (ISBN 0-668-05902-8). Arco.

Gething, P. J. D. Radio Direction Finding. (IEE Electromagnetic-Waves Ser.: No. 4). 253p. 1978. 53.00 (ISBN 0-901223-71-9, EW004). Inst Elect Eng.

Gething, Richard. Calligraphotechnia, or, the Art of Faire Writing. LC 73-6134. (English Experience Ser.: No. 599). 1973. Repr. of 1619 ed. 14.00 (ISBN 90-221-0599-7). Walter J Johnson.

Gething, Thomas W. Aspects of Meaning in Thai Nominals: A Study in Structural Semantics. (Janua Linguarum, Ser. Practica: No. 141). (Illus.). 104p. (Orig.). 1972. pap. text ed. 16.80x (ISBN 90-2792-339-6). Mouton.

Gethyn-Jones, Eric. George Thorpe & the Berkeley Company. 296p. 1982. text ed. 18.50x (ISBN 0-904387-83-6, Pub. by Alan Sutton England). Humanities.

Getis, A. & Boots, B. Models of Spatial Processes. LC 75-17118. (Cambridge Geographical Studies Ser.: No.8). 1978. 42.50 (ISBN 0-521-20983-8). Cambridge U Pr.

Getis, Arthur. Models of Spatial Processes: An Approach to the Study of Point, Line & Area Patterns. LC 75-17118. (Cambridge Geographical Studies: No. 8). pap. 53.50 (ISBN 0-317-26406-0, 2024462). Bks Demand UMI.

Getis, Arthur & Getis, Judith. Human Geography. 512p. 1985. text ed. write for info. (ISBN 0-02-341580-0). Macmillan.

Getis, Arthur, et al. Geography. 1981. text ed. write for info. (ISBN 0-02-341550-9); student study guide 6.95 (ISBN 0-02-431580-X). Macmillan.

Getis, Judith, jt. auth. see Getis, Arthur.

Getlein, Frank. John Safer. LC 82-90372. (Illus.). 1982. 50.00 (ISBN 0-89674-008-0). J J Binns.

--Mary Cassatt: Paintings & Prints. LC 80-66523. (Illus.). 156p. 1980. 25.00 (ISBN 0-89659-181-6); pap. 16.95 (ISBN 0-89659-155-7). Abbeville Pr.

--Twenty-Five Impressionist Masterpieces. (Illus.). 64p. 1981. 12.95 (ISBN 0-8109-2247-9). Abrams.

Getlein, Frank & Harrison, Helen A. Jimmy Ernst: A Survey, 1942-1983. LC 85-70639. (Illus.). 48p. (Orig.). 1985. write for info. (ISBN 0-933793-01-4). Guild Hall.

Getman, Frederick H. The Life of Ira Remsen. Cohen, I. Bernard, ed. LC 79-7962. (Three Centuries of Science in America Ser.). (Illus.). 1980. Repr. of 1940 ed. lib. bdg. 16.00x (ISBN 0-405-12543-7). Ayer Co Pubs.

Getman, Jack, et al, eds. see New York State Bar Association.

Getman, Julius, et al see Labor Law Group.

Getman, Julius G. & Blackburn, John D. Labor Relations: Law, Practice & Policy. 2nd ed. LC 82-21042. 749p. 1982. text ed. 22.00 (ISBN 0-88277-102-7); pap. text ed. write for info. (ISBN 0-88277-165-5). Foundation Pr.

Getman, Julius G., et al. Union Representation Elections: Law & Reality. LC 78-13271. 218p. 1976. 9.95x (ISBN 0-87154-302-8). Russell Sage.

--Discrimination in Employment. 4th ed. 870p. 1979. 26.00 (ISBN 0-87179-306-7); Supplement, available separately. 5.00 (ISBN 0-87179-397-0). BNA.

Getmused, Allison. Alice's Adventuricks: Adventures in Wonderland, Part 1. (Limericklets (Limerick Booklets): No. 48). (Illus.). 16p. (Orig.). (gr. 6-7). 1984. pap. 1.00x (ISBN 0-938338-60-9). Winds World Pr.

--Alice's Adventuricks: Adventures in Wonderland, Part 2. (Limericklets (Limerick Booklets): No. 49). (Illus.). 16p. (Orig.). (gr. 6-7). 1984. pap. 1.00 (ISBN 0-938338-61-7). Winds World Pr.

--Alice's Adventuricks: Adventures in Wonderland, Part 3. (Limericklets (Limerick Booklets): No. 50). (Illus.). 16p. (Orig.). (gr. 6-7). 1984. pap. 1.00x (ISBN 0-938338-62-5). Winds World Pr.

Getoor, R. K. Markov Processes: Ray Processes & Right Processes, Vol. 440. (Lecture Notes in Mathematics Ser). v, 118p. 1975. pap. 13.00 (ISBN 0-387-07140-7). Springer-Verlag.

Getrev, I. E. Modelling the Bipolar Transistor. (Computer-Aided Design of Electronic Circuits: Vol. 1). 270p. 1978. 70.25 (ISBN 0-444-41722-2). Elsevier.

Getscher, Marks. James McNeil Whitstler. 1985. lib. bdg. 49.00 (ISBN 0-8240-9000-4). Garland Pub.

Getschmann. You Don't Know Me but... A Collection of Prize-Winning Recipes. pap. 8.95 (ISBN 0-87505-081-6). Borden.

Getsinger, John. Luis. LC 75-17658. (Illus.). 48p. (Eng. & Span.). (gr. 3-7). 1976. 7.50 (ISBN 0-88468-004-5). Ethridge.

Getsslain, Dom. The Cuckold-Blooded Killer. (Murders in Miniature Ser.: No. 3). (Illus.). 16p. (Orig.). 1984. pap. 1.00x (ISBN 0-938338-80-3). Winds World Pr.

Gette, Bernard Le see Le Gette, Bernard.

Gettel, James. The Fundamental Reform of Philosophy. 54p. 1984. 3.95 (ISBN 0-89697-183-X). Intl Univ Pr.

Gettel, Ronald. Twice Burned. LC 82-61792. 192p. (Orig.). 1983. 12.95 (ISBN 0-8027-5485-6). Walker & Co.

Gettens, Rutherford J. The Freer Chinese Bronzes, Vol. 2. (Oriental Studies No. 7). (Illus.). 1969. 30.00 (ISBN 0-934686-11-4). Freer.

Gettens, Rutherford J. & Stout, George L. Painting Materials: A Short Encyclopedia. (Illus.). 1965. pap. 5.00 (ISBN 0-486-21597-0). Dover.

Gettens, Rutherford J., compiled by. Abstracts of Technical Studies in Art & Archeology, 1943-1952. (Occasional Papers Ser: Vol. 2, No. 2). 1955. pap. 6.00 (ISBN 0-934686-04-1). Freer.

Gettens, Rutherford J., et al. Two Early Chinese Bronze Weapons with Meteoritic Iron Blades. (Occasional Papers Ser: Vol. 4, No. 1). (Illus.). 1971. pap. 5.00 (ISBN 0-934686-08-4). Freer.

Getter, Charles D., jt. auth. see Snedaker, Samuel C.

Gettings, Fred. Dictionary of Astrology. 320p. 1985. 28.50 (ISBN 0-7100-9672-0); pap. 21.95 (ISBN 0-7102-0650-X). Routledge & Kegan.

--Dictionary of Occult, Hermetic & Alchemical Sigils. 1981. 40.00 (ISBN 0-7100-0095-2). Routledge & Kegan.

--How to Interpret Dreams, Omens & Fortune Telling Signs. pap. 3.00 (ISBN 0-87980-399-1). Wilshire.

--Palmistry Made Easy. pap. 5.00 (ISBN 0-87980-114-X). Wilshire.

Gettins, W. J. & Wyn-Jones, E., eds. Techniques & Applications of Fast Reactions in Solution. (Nato Advanced Study Institutes Series: Math & Physical Sciences: No. C50). 1979. lib. bdg. 58.00 (ISBN 90-277-1022-8, Pub. by Reidel Holland). Kluwer Academic.

Gettis, Alan. Sun-Faced Haiku Moon-Faced Haiku. 32p. 1983. 10.00 (ISBN 0-318-01006-2); pap. 3.50 (ISBN 0-318-01007-0). High Coo Pr.

--Snowed In. 20p. 1978. 7.00 (ISBN 0-913719-34-X); pap. 2.00 (ISBN 0-913719-33-1). High-Coo Pr.

--Sun Faced-Moon Faced Haiku, 2 Vols. 64p. 1982. Set. text ed. 10.00 (ISBN 0-913719-22-6); Vol. 1, 32 pp. pap. 3.50 ea. (ISBN 0-913719-20-X). Vol. 2, 32 pp (ISBN 0-913719-21-8). High-Coo Pr.

Gettleman, Barry, jt. auth. see Prager, Audrey.

Gettleman, Marvin, ed. The Johns Hopkins University Seminary of History & Politics, 1877-1912: The Records of an American Educational Institution. Date not set. 80.00 (ISBN 0-8240-8645-7). Garland Pub.

Gettleman, Marvin, et al, eds. El Salvador: Central America in the New Cold War. LC 81-82119. (Illus.). 320p. (Orig.). 1981. pap. 7.95 (ISBN 0-394-17956-0, E792, Ever). Grove.

Gettleman, Marvin E. The Dorr Rebellion: A Study in American Radicalism: 1833-1849. LC 79-1205. 288p. 1980. Repr. of 1973 ed. lib. bdg. 13.50 (ISBN 0-88275-894-2). Krieger.

--An Elusive Presence: The Discovery of John H. Finley & His America. LC 79-891. (Illus.). 354p. 1979. 24.95x (ISBN 0-88229-312-5). Nelson-Hall.

Gettleman, Marvin E., ed. The Johns Hopkins University Seminary of History & Politics, 1877-1912. Date not set. 80.00 (ISBN 0-8240-8648-1). Garland Pub.

--The Johns Hopkins University Seminary of History & Politics, 1877-1912: The Records of an American Educational Institution. 80.00 (ISBN 0-8240-8646-5). Garland Pub.

--The Johns Hopkins University Seminary of History & Politics, 1877-1912: The Records of an American Educational Institution. 80.00 (ISBN 0-8240-8649-X). Garland Pub.

--The Johns Hopkins University Seminary of History & Politics, 1877-1912. (The Records of an American Educational Institution Ser.). 80.00 (ISBN 0-8240-8647-3). Garland Pub.

Gettleman, Marvin E. & Franklin, Jane, eds. Vietnam & America: A Documented History. LC 84-48110. 448p. 1985. 22.50 (ISBN 0-394-54134-0, GP-937). Grove.

--Vietnam & America: A Documented History. 1985. 29.50 (ISBN 0-394-62277-4, E-949, Ever); pap. 11.95 (ISBN 0-394-62277-4). Grove.

Gettleman, Marvin E., et al, eds. El Salvador: Central America in the New Cold War. 412p. pap. 9.95 (ISBN 0-394-17956-0). Grove.

Gettlemen, Marvin, jt. ed. see Fried, Jonathan L.

Gettmann, Royal A., ed. George Gissing & H. G. Wells: Their Friendship & Correspondence. 285p. 1983. Repr. of 1961 ed. lib. bdg. 40.00 (ISBN 0-89760-373-7). Telegraph Bks.

Gettrust, K. V., et al. Applied Nursing Diagnosis: Guides for Comprehensive Care Planning. 208p. Date not set. 13.95 (ISBN 0-471-81697-3). Wiley.

Getty, Alice. The Gods of Northern Buddhism. LC 62-15617. (Illus.). 1962. 39.50 (ISBN 0-8048-1129-6). C E Tuttle.

Getty, Cathleen & Humphreys, Winnifred. Understanding the Family: Stress & Change in American Family Life. (Illus.). 548p. 1981. pap. 22.95 (ISBN 0-8385-9265-1); o. p. 21.95x (ISBN 0-8385-9266-X). ACC.

Getty, David J. & Howard, James H., Jr., eds. Auditory & Visual Pattern Recognition. LC 81-7750. 240p. 1981. 29.95x (ISBN 0-89859-087-6). L Erlbaum Assocs.

Getty, Harry T. Interethnic Relationships in the Community of Tucson. Cortes, Carlos E., ed. LC 76-1259. (Chicano Heritage Ser.). (Illus.). 1976. 23.50x (ISBN 0-405-09503-1). Ayer Co Pubs.

Getty, Ian A. & Lussier, Antoine S., eds. As Long as the Sun Shines & Water Flows: A Reader in Canadian Native Studies. (The Nakoda Institute Occasional Papers Ser.). 384p. 1983. 29.95 (ISBN 0-7748-0181-6, Pub. by U of BC); pap. 12.50 (ISBN 0-7748-0184-0). Intl Spec Bk.

Getty, J. Arch. Origins of the Great Purges: The Soviet Communist Party Reconsidered, 1933-1938. (Soviet & East European Studies). 320p. 1985. 34.50 (ISBN 0-521-25921-5). Cambridge U Pr.

Getty, J. Paul. How to Be a Successful Executive. 192p. 1984. pap. 2.95 (ISBN 0-515-07912-X). Jove Pubns.

--How to Be Rich. LC 65-27098. 224p. 1984. pap. 3.50 (ISBN 0-515-08307-0). Jove Pubns.

Getty, Mary A. Philippians & Philemon. (New Testament Message Ser.: Vol. 14). 8.95 (ISBN 0-89453-202-2); pap. 4.95 (ISBN 0-89453-137-9). M Glazier.

Getty, Mary A. & Karris, Robert J. First Corinthians, Second Corinthians, No. 7. (Collegeville Bible Commentary Ser.). 128p. 1983. pap. 2.50 (ISBN 0-8146-1307-1). Liturgical Pr.

Getty, Norris M., jt. auth. see DeVeau, Frederic J.

Getty, R. J., ed. see Lucan.

Getty, Robert. Atlas for Applied Veterinary Anatomy. 2nd ed. LC 65-7104. pap. 94.30 (ISBN 0-317-29447-4, 2055944). Bks Demand UMI.

--Sisson & Grossman's-The Anatomy of the Domestic Animal, 2 vols. 5th ed. LC 78-81821. (Illus.). 2110p. 1975. Vol. 1. text ed. 49.00 (ISBN 0-7216-4102-4); Vol. 2. text ed. 44.00 (ISBN 0-7216-4107-5). Saunders.

Gettys, Joseph M. How to Study Acts. 219p. 1976. pap. 3.75x (ISBN 0-87921-028-1). Attic Pr.

--How to Study Ephesians. rev. ed. 64p. 1976. pap. 3.50x (ISBN 0-87921-056-7). Attic Pr.

--How to Study I Corinthians. 128p. 1968. pap. 3.75x (ISBN 0-8042-3532-5). Attic Pr.

--How to Study John. 153p. 1960. pap. 3.75x (ISBN 0-8042-3568-6). Attic Pr.

--How to Study Luke. rev. ed. 153p. 1975. pap. 3.75x (ISBN 0-87921-027-3). Attic Pr.

--How to Study Philippians, Colossians, & Philemon. 87p. 1964. pap. text ed. 3.75x (ISBN 0-8042-3472-8). Attic Pr.

--How to Study the Revelation. rev. ed. 117p. 1973. pap. 3.50x (ISBN 0-87921-029-X). Attic Pr.

--Surveying the Historical Books. 164p. 1963. pap. 3.00x (ISBN 0-8042-3664-X). Attic Pr.

--Surveying the Pentateuch. 147p. 1962. pap. 3.25x (ISBN 0-8042-3676-3). Attic Pr.

Getz & Feigert. The Politics & Process of American Government. 1985. 30.00 (ISBN 0-205-06862-6, 766862). Allyn.

Getz, Arthur. Humphrey, the Dancing Pig. LC 79-20616. (Illus.). (ps-3). 1980. PLB 9.89 (ISBN 0-8037-4497-8). Dial Bks Young.

Getz, C. W., ed. The Wild Blue Yonder: Songs of the Air Force, 2 vols, Vol. 1. LC 81-52998. (Illus.). 312p. 1981. 15.95x (ISBN 0-941196-00-3). Redwood Pr.

Getz, D. & Hakala, William T., eds. American-Swedish Handbook. 9th rev. ed. 140p. 1982. pap. 9.45 (ISBN 0-9609620-0-X). Swedish Council.

Getz, Donald J. & McGraw, Lora. Vision Training for Better Learning. 1981. spiral bound 15.95 (ISBN 0-87804-430-2). Mafex.

Getz, Gene. A Estatura de Uma Mulher. Batista, Jaoa, ed. Ferreira, Ruth V., tr. 144p. (Port.). 1981. pap. 1.60 (ISBN 0-8297-1075-2). Life Pubs Intl.

--Joshua: Defeat to Victory. LC 78-53358. 176p. 1979. pap. 5.95 (ISBN 0-8307-0643-7, 5410509). Regal.

--Loving One Another. LC 79-63450. 143p. 1979. pap. 4.95 (ISBN 0-88207-786-4). Victor Bks.

--Praying for One Another. 132p. 1982. pap. 4.50 (ISBN 0-88207-351-6). Victor Bks.

--Serving One Another. 156p. 1984. pap. 4.95 (ISBN 0-88207-612-4). Victor Bks.

Getz, Gene A. Abraham: Trials & Triumphs. LC 76-24038. 160p. 1976. pap. 5.95 (ISBN 0-8307-0446-9, 5404509). Regal.

--Believing God When You Are Tempted to Doubt: The Measure of a Christian; Studies in James I. 160p. pap. 5.95 (ISBN 0-8307-1021-3, 5418416). Regal.

--Building up One Another. LC 76-19918. 120p. 1976. pap. 4.50 (ISBN 0-88207-744-9). Victor Bks.

--Doing Your Part When You'd Rather Let God Do It All: The Measure of a Christian Based on James 2-5. LC 84-17749. 1985. pap. 5.95 (ISBN 0-8307-1002-7, 5418395). Regal.

--Encouraging One Another. 1981. pap. 4.95 (ISBN 0-88207-256-0). Victor Bks.

--Joseph: From Prison to Palace. LC 82-18571. 1983. pap. 5.95 (ISBN 0-8307-0870-7, 5417907). Regal.

--Looking up When You Feel Down: Based on Ephesians 1-3. LC 85-2041. 158p. 1985. pap. 5.95 (ISBN 0-8307-1028-0, 5418463). Regal.

--The Measure of a Christian: Studies in James 1. LC 83-4440. (The Measure of...Ser.). 160p. 1983. pap. 5.95 (ISBN 0-8307-0881-2, 5417930). Regal.

--The Measure of a Christian: Studies in Philippians. LC 83-3002. (The Measure of...Ser.). 182p. 1983. pap. 5.95 (ISBN 0-8307-0883-9, 5417939). Regal.

--The Measure of a Christian: Studies in Titus. LC 83-2939. (A Measure of...Ser.). 200p. 1983. pap. 5.95 (ISBN 0-8307-0882-0, 5417935). Regal.

--Measure of a Church. LC 75-17160. (Orig.). 1975. pap. 3.50 (ISBN 0-8307-0398-5, 5014700). Regal.

--Measure of a Family. LC 76-46872. (Orig.). 1977. pap. 3.95 (ISBN 0-8307-0445-0, 5015006). Regal.

--Measure of a Man: A Practical Guide to Christian Maturity. LC 74-175983. 224p. (Orig.). 1974. pap. 4.95 (ISBN 0-8307-0291-1, 5012104). Regal.

--The Measure of a Marriage. LC 78-53356. 144p. 1980. pap. 3.50 (ISBN 0-8307-0638-0, 5017203). Regal.

--The Measure of a Marriage Workbook. 96p. 1980. lab manual 5.95 (ISBN 0-8307-0756-5, 5202701). Regal.

--The Measure of a Woman. LC 77-74533. (Orig.). 1977. pap. 3.50 (ISBN 0-8307-0537-6, 5016118). Regal.

--The Measure of a Woman. LC 77-74533. (The Measure of... Ser.). 1984. pap. 4.95 (ISBN 0-8307-0981-9, 5418320). Regal.

--Moses: Moments of Glory, Feet of Clay. LC 75-23519. 160p. (Orig.). 1976. pap. 4.95 (ISBN 0-8307-0400-0, 5403200). Regal.

--Nehemiah: A Man of Prayer & Persistence. LC 80-53102. 1981. pap. 5.95 (ISBN 0-8307-0778-6, 5414500). Regal.

--Refinemos la Perspectiva. Serrano, Guillermo, tr. 364p. (Span.). 1982. pap. 7.25 (ISBN 0-89922-156-4). Edit Caribe.

--Sharpening the Focus of the Church. 360p. 1984. pap. 7.95 (ISBN 0-89693-393-8). Victor Bks.

--When the Pressure's On: Take a Lesson from Elijah. LC 83-21119. (Take a Lesson from... Ser.). 1984. pap. 5.95 (ISBN 0-8307-0923-1, 5418100). Regal.

--When You Feel Like a Failure: Take a Lesson from David. rev. ed. LC 77-99282. (Take a Lesson from...Ser.). 160p. 1984. pap. 5.95 (ISBN 0-8307-0977-0, 5418319). Regal.

Getz, Gene A., jt. auth. see Zuck, Roy B.

Getz, George. Business Law. 5th ed. (gr. 9-12). 1977. text ed. 15.40 (ISBN 0-02-831100-0); wkbk. 5.60 (ISBN 0-02-831110-8); tchr's. manual, tests & key 6.60 (ISBN 0-02-831120-5). Glencoe.

Getz, Jerome L., tr. see Nelson, Alvar.

Getz, Lorine M. Flannery O'Connor: Her Life, Library & Book Reviews. LC 80-82800. (Studies in Women & Religion: Vol. 5). 237p. 1980. 49.95x (ISBN 0-88946-997-0). E Mellen.

--Nature & Grace in Flannery O'Connor's Fiction. LC 82-22458. (Studies in Art & Religious Interpretation: Vol. 2). 192p. 1982. 39.95x (ISBN 0-88946-550-9). E Mellen.

Getz, Lowell & Stasiowski, Frank. Financial Management for the Design Professional: Handbook for Architects, Engineers & Interior Designers. (Illus.). 192p. 1984. 32.50 (ISBN 0-8230-7179-0, Whitney Lib). Watson-Guptill.

Getz, Malcolm. Public Libraries: An Economic View. LC 80-10651. 208p. 1980. text ed. 21.00x (ISBN 0-8018-2395-1). Johns Hopkins.

Getz, Malcolm, jt. auth. see Watson, Donald S.

Getz, Mike. Baseball's Three Thousand-Hit Men. 1982. 7.95 (ISBN 0-9608076-0-8). Gemmeg Pr.

--The Mets Trivia Book. LC 84-47517. (Illus.). 144p. (Orig.). 1984. pap. 6.95 (ISBN 0-88011-225-5). Leisure Pr.

Getz, Steven. Environment & the Deaf Child. 188p. 1956. 18.50x (ISBN 0-398-04264-0). C C Thomas.

Getz, W. M., ed. Mathematical Modelling in Biology & Ecology: Proceedings of a Symposium Held at the CSIR, Pretoria, July 1979. (Lecture Notes in Biomathematics Ser.: Vol. 33). viii, 355p. 1980. pap. 28.00 (ISBN 3-540-09735-X). Springer-Verlag.

Getz, William L. & Allen, David B. Brief Counseling with Suicidal Persons. LC 80-8375. 288p. 1982. 24.50x (ISBN 0-669-04090-8). Lexington Bks.

Getzel, George & Mellor, M. Joanna, eds. Gerontological Social Work Practice in the Community. LC 85-2767. (Journal of Gerontological Social Work Ser.: Vol. 8, Nos. 3 & 4). 296p. 1985. text ed. 24.95 (ISBN 0-86656-145-5, B145); pap. 16.95 (ISBN 0-86656-256-7). Haworth Pr.

Getzel, George S. Group Work with Kin & Friends Caring for the Elderly. 1982. pap. 1.50. Comm Serv Soc NY.

--Helping Elderly Couples in Crisis. 1982. pap. 1.50 (ISBN 0-318-00913-7). Comm Serv Soc NY.

Getzel, George S., jt. auth. see Mellor, Joanna.

Getzel, George S. & Mellor, M. Joanna, eds. Gerontological Social Work Practice in Long-Term Care. LC 82-21371. (Journal of Gerontological Social Work Ser.: Vol. 5, Nos. 1-2). 191p. 1983. text ed. 24.95 (ISBN 0-86656-146-3, B146). Haworth Pr.

Getzels, Jacob W. & Csikszentmihalyi, Mihaly. The Creative Vision: A Longitudinal Study of Problem Finding in Art. LC 76-16862. 293p. 1976. 41.50x (ISBN 0-471-01486-9, Pub. by Wiley-Interscience). Wiley.

Getzels, Jacob W., et al. Educational Administration As a Social Process: Theory, Research, Practice. 1968. text ed. 36.95 scp (ISBN 0-06-041161-9, HarpC). Har-Row.

Getzels, Judith & Thurow, Charles, eds. Rural & Small Town Planning. 350p. 1980. 4.95 (ISBN 0-318-13075-0). Am Plan Assn.

Getzels, Judith, et al, eds. Rural & Small Town Planning. LC 79-93345. (Illus.). 326p. (Orig.). 1980. pap. 14.95 (ISBN 0-918286-19-0). Planners Pr.

Getzels, Judith N. & Elliott, Peter. Private Planning for the Public Interest: A Study of Approaches to Urban Problem Solving by Nonprofit Organizations. 156p. 1975. pap. 10.95 (ISBN 0-318-13062-9); pap. 8.95 members (ISBN 0-318-13063-7). Am Plan Assn.

Getzels, Judith N., jt. auth. see Hapgood, Karen E.

Getzler, Israel. Martov: Political Biography of a Russian Social Democrat. 1967. 44.50 (ISBN 0-521-05073-1). Cambridge U Pr.

--Neither Toleration nor Favour: The Australian Chapter of Jewish Emancipation. 153p. 1970. 19.50x (ISBN 0-522-83961-4, Pub. by Melbourne U Pr). Intl Spec Bk.

Getzoff, Ann & McClenahan, Carolyn. Stepkids: A Survival Guide for Teenagers in Stepfamilies. LC 83-21779. 192p. 1984. 13.95 (ISBN 0-8027-0757-2). Walker & Co.

--Stepkids: A Survival Guide for Teenagers in Stepfamilies...& for Stepparents Doubtful of Their Own Survival. 171p. (YA) 1985. pap. 8.95 (ISBN 0-8027-7236-6). Walker & Co.

Getz-Preziosi, P., tr. see Thimme, Jurgen.

Getz-Preziosi, Pat. Early Cycladic Sculpture: An Introduction. (Illus.). 110p. 1985. pap. 16.95 (ISBN 0-89236-101-8). J P Getty Mus.

--Sculptors of the Cyclades: Individual & Tradition in the Third Millennium B.C. (Illus.). 1985. text ed. 75.00x (ISBN 0-472-10067-X). U of Mich Pr.

Geuder, Patricia, et al, eds. They Really Taught Us How to Write. LC 74-16760. 140p. 1974. pap. 7.00 (ISBN 0-8141-5422-0). NCTE.

Geue, Chester H. & Geue, Ethel H. A New Land Beckoned: German Immigration to Texas, 1844-1847. LC 81-86307. (Illus.). 178p. 1982. Repr. of 1972 ed. 18.50 (ISBN 0-8063-0981-4). Genealog Pub.

Geue, Ethel H. New Homes In a New Land: German Immigration to Texas, 1847-1861. LC 81-86306. (Illus.). 166p. 1982. Repr. of 1970 ed. 18.50 (ISBN 0-8063-0980-6). Genealog Pub.

Geue, Ethel H., jt. auth. see Geue, Chester H.

Geursen, R. G., jt. ed. see Seiler, F. R.

Geurts, Reiner. Hair Colour in the Horse. Dent, Anthony, tr. from Dutch. (Illus.). pap. 9.95 (ISBN 0-85131-290-X, BL189). J A Allen.

Geus, J. W., jt. ed. see Bootsma, G. A.

Geus, Leonard F. de see Bibb, Benjamin O.

Geuseau, Frans Alting von see Alting von Geuseau, Frans A.

Geuss, R. The Idea of a Critical Theory: Habermas & the Frankfurt School. LC 80-422474. (Modern European Philosophy Ser.). 140p. 1981. 27.95 (ISBN 0-521-24072-7); pap. 8.95 (ISBN 0-521-28422-8). Cambridge U Pr.

Geutary, Helene & Casanova, Patrice. Skin Deep. (Illus.). 1984. 24.95 (ISBN 0-394-53812-9, GP 911). Grove.

Geuther, Maria, tr. see Swedish Academy of Engineering.

Geva, Tamara. Split Seconds: A Remembrance. LC 83-27509. 368p. 1984. pap. 8.95 (ISBN 0-87910-006-0). Limelight Edns.

Gevaert, F. A., ed. see Gretry, Andre.

Gevarter, William B. Artificial Intelligence, An Overview: Combined Compilation of Volumes 5A, 5B, 5C of Robotics. LC 83-73202. (Artificial Intelligence Applications Ser.). 244p. 1984. lib. bdg. 49.00x (ISBN 0-89934-225-6, BT916). Business Technology Bks.

--Artificial Intelligence, An Overview, Pt. A. The Core Ingredients. LC 83-73201. (Robotics & Artifical Intelligence Applications Ser.: Vol. 5A). 76p. 1984. pap. 19.50x (ISBN 0-89934-194-2, BT013). Business Technology Bks.

--Artificial Intelligence, An Overview, Part B. Fundamental Application Areas. LC 83-73201. (Robotics & Artificial Intelligence Applications Ser.: Vol. 5B). 110p. pap. 24.50x (ISBN 0-89934-196-9, BT014, BT145, Pub. by Business-Technology Bks). Business Technology Bks.

--Artificial Intelligence, An Overview, Part C: Basic Topics. LC 83-73201. (Robotics & Artificial Intelligence Applications Ser.: Vol. 5C). 56p. pap. 19.50x (ISBN 0-89934-198-5, BT015, Pub. by Business-Technology Bks). Business Technology Bks.

--Artificial Intelligence & Robotics: Five Overviews (Robotics, Expert Systems, Computer Vision, Computer-Based Natural Language Processing & Artificial Inteligence) LC 84-70998. (Robotics & Artificial Intelligence Applications Ser.: Vols. 1-5C). 696p. 1984. lib. bdg. 99.50x (ISBN 0-89934-227-2, BT918). Business Technology Bks.

--Artificial Intelligence, Expert Systems, Computer Vision, & Natural Language Processing. LC 84-6014. (Illus.). 226p. 1984. 36.00 (ISBN 0-8155-0994-4). Noyes.

--Computer-Based Natural Language Processing: An Overview. LC 83-70570. (Robotics & Artificial Intelligence Applications Ser.: Vol. 4). 75p. 1984. pap. 19.50x (ISBN 0-89934-182-9, BT-004). Business Technology Bks.

--Computer Vision: An Overview. LC 83-70569. (Robotics & Artificial Intelligence Applications Ser.: Vol. 3). 175p. 1984. pap. 34.50x (ISBN 0-89934-180-2, BT-003). Business Technology Bks.

--Expert Systems: An Overview. LC 83-70568. (Robotics & Artificial Intelligence Applications Ser.: Vol. 2). 80p. 1984. pap. 19.50x (ISBN 0-89934-178-0, BT-002). Business Technology Bks.

--Intelligent Machines: An Introductory Perspective of Artificial Intelligence & Robotics. LC 84-22326. (Illus.). 240p. 1985. text ed. 33.95 (ISBN 0-13-468810-4). P-H.

--Robotics: An Overview. LC 83-70567. (Robotics & Artificial Intelligence Applications Ser.: Vol. 1). 110p. 1984. pap. 24.50x (ISBN 0-89934-176-4, BT-001). Business Technology Bks.

Gevarter, William B., ed. Robotics & Artificial Intelligence: Four Overviews, Vols. 1-4 in 1 combined ed. Incl. Robotics: An Overview; Expert Systems: An Overview; Computer Vision: An Overview; Computer-Based Natural Language Processing: An Overview. LC 83-70571. (Robotics & Artificial Intelligence Applications Ser.). 1984. lib. bdg. 85.00x (ISBN 0-89934-184-5, BT905). Business Technology Bks.

Gever, John, et al. The Eleventh Hour: Energy, Agriculture, & the U. S. Economy. 320p. 1985. prof. ref. 34.95 (ISBN 0-88730-074-X); pap. 14.95 prof. ref. (ISBN 0-88730-075-8). Ballinger Pub.

Gever, Larry, et al, eds. Nursing Drug Handbook 1985. 880p. 1984. 19.95 (ISBN 0-916730-86-7). Springhouse Corp.

Gever, Larry N., et al, eds. Drugs. 2nd ed. LC 84-1333. (Nurse's Reference Library Ser.). (Illus.). 1984. text ed. 23.95 (ISBN 0-916730-87-5). Springhouse Corp.

Gevirtz, Don. The New Entrepreneurs: Innovation in American Business. (Nonfiction Ser.). 320p. 1985. pap. 6.95 (ISBN 0-14-007973-4). Penguin.

Gevirtz, Don L. & Kotkin, Joel. Business Plan for America: An Entrepreneur's Manifesto. LC 83-2114. 288p. 1984. 15.95 (ISBN 0-399-12844-1, Putnam). Putnam Pub Group.

Gevirtz, Eliezer. The Mystery of the Missing Pushke. (Illus.). 200p. (gr. 5-7). 1982. 7.95 (ISBN 0-87306-291-4). Feldheim.

Gevitz, Norman. The D. O.'s: Osteopathic Medicine in America. LC 82-47978. 200p. 1982. text ed. 18.50x (ISBN 0-8018-2777-9). Johns Hopkins.

Gewecke, Cliff. Day-by-Day in Dodgers History. LC 82-83940. (Illus.). 300p. (Orig.). 1984. pap. 12.95 (ISBN 0-88011-108-9). Leisure Pr.

Gewehr, Wesley M. Rise of Nationalism in the Balkans, 1800-1930. xi, 137p. 1967. Repr. of 1931 ed. 16.00 (ISBN 0-208-00507-2, Archon). Shoe String.

Gewertz, Deborah B. Sepik River Societies: A Historical of the Chambri & Their Neighbors. LC 82-48902. 266p. 1983. text ed. 27.50x (ISBN 0-300-02872-5). Yale U Pr.

Gewirth, Alan. Human Rights: Essays on Justification & Applications. LC 81-21933. 384p. 1983. lib. bdg. 35.00x (ISBN 0-226-28877-3); pap. 12.00x (ISBN 0-226-28878-1). U of Chicago Pr.

--Marsilius of Padua, 2 vols. in one. Mayer, J. P., ed. LC 78-67352. (European Political Thought Ser.). 1979. Repr. of 1956 ed. Set. lib. bdg. 62.00x (ISBN 0-405-11699-3). Ayer Co Pubs.

--Political Philosophy. 1965. write for info. (ISBN 0-02-341670-X, 34167). Macmillan.

--Reason & Morality. LC 77-13911. 1978. pap. text ed. 9.95x (ISBN 0-226-28876-5). U of Chicago Pr.

Gewirth, Alan, tr. see Marsilius Of Padua.

Gewirtz, Allan & Quintas, Louis V., eds. International Conference on Combinatorial Mathematics, Second. (Annals of the New York Academy of Sciences: Vol. 319). 602p. (Orig.). 1979. pap. 112.00x (ISBN 0-89766-010-2). NY Acad Sci.

Gewirtz, Arthur. Restoration Adaptations of Early 17th Century Comedies. LC 82-15937. 214p. 1983. lib. bdg. 26.00 (ISBN 0-8191-2722-1); pap. text ed. 12.25 (ISBN 0-8191-2723-X). U Pr of Amer.

Gewirtz, Herman. Essentials of Physics. rev. ed. LC 67-30941. (gr. 9-12). 1974. pap. text ed. 7.95 (ISBN 0-8120-0278-4). Barron.

--How to Prepare for the College Board Achievement Test - Physics. 3rd ed. LC 79-9283. (gr. 11-12). 1980. Barron.

Gewirtz, Herman, ed. Barron's Regents Exams & Answers Physics. rev. ed. LC 56-39359. 250p. (gr. 10-12). 1982. pap. text ed. 4.50 (ISBN 0-8120-3167-9). Barron.

Gewirtz, J. L. Three Determinants of Attention-Seeking in Young Children. (Society for Research in Child Development). 1954. pap. 14.00 (ISBN 0-527-01561-X). Kraus Repr.

Gewirtz, Jacob L., jt. auth. see Kurtines, William M.

Gewurz, Elias. Hidden Treasures of the Ancient Qabalah. 1922. 4.50 (ISBN 0-911662-31-6). Yoga.

--Mysteries of the Qabalah. 1922. 4.50 (ISBN 0-911662-32-4). Yoga.

Gey, H. F., et al. Structure & Chemistry of the Aging Heart. 238p. 1974. text ed. 24.00x (ISBN 0-8422-7168-6). Irvington.

Gey, K F. & La Carlson. Metabolic Effects of Nicotinic Acid & its Derivatives. 1251p. 495.00 (ISBN 3-456-00384-6, Pub. by Holdan Bk Ltd UK). State Mutual Bk.

Geyer, Alan. The Idea of Disarmament, Rethinking the Unthinkable. 256p. 1982. 17.95 (ISBN 0-87178-397-5); pap. 11.95 (ISBN 0-87178-396-7). Brethren.

--Idea of Disarmament, Rethinking the Unthinkable. 256p. 1985. 11.95. Brethren.

Geyer, Celesta see Dimples, Dolly, pseud.

Geyer, Dick. Wreck Diving: A Guide for Sport Divers. LC 82-10575. (New Century Aquatics Ser.). (Illus.). 1982. pap. 7.95 (ISBN 0-8329-0131-8). New Century.

Geyer, Felix R. & Schweitzer, David, eds. Alienation: Problems of Meaning, Theory, & Method. 288p. 1981. 28.00x (ISBN 0-7100-0835-X). Routledge & Kegan.

Geyer, Georgie A. Buying the Night Flight. 1985. pap. 4.95 (ISBN 0-440-32770-9, LE). Dell.

--Buying the Night Flight: The Autobiography of a Woman Foreign Correspondent. (Radcliffe Biography Ser.). 320p. 1983. 16.95 (ISBN 0-385-28081-5, Sey Lawr). Delacorte.

Geyer, Georgie Anne. The Young Russians. LC 74-23874. 1975. 12.95 (ISBN 0-88280-021-3). ETC Pubns.

Geyer, Grant B., jt. auth. see Bollens, John C.

Geyer, James, jt. auth. see Wilson, Robert M.

Geyer, James R. & Matanzo, Jane B. Programmed Reading Diagnosis for Teachers: With Prescriptive References. new ed. (Elementary Education Ser). (Orig.). 1977. pap. text ed. 10.95 (ISBN 0-675-08456-3); 4 audio tapes 35.00 (ISBN 0-675-08457-1). Merrill.

Geyer, Nancy. Frailties. 1986. 17.95 (ISBN 0-316-30892-7). Little.

Geyer, Paul, ed. Itinera Hierosolymitana, Saeculi 3-8. (Corpus Scriptorum Ecclesiasticorum Latinorum Ser: Vol. 39). Repr. of 1898 ed. 40.00 (ISBN 0-384-18270-4). Johnson Repr.

Geyer, R. A. Submersibles & Their Use in Oceanography & Ocean Engineering. (Elsevier Oceanography Ser.: Vol. 17). 384p. 1977. 78.75 (ISBN 0-444-41545-9). Elsevier.

Geyer, R. A., ed. Marine Environmental Pollution, Vol. 1: Hydrocarbons. (Oceanography Ser.: Vol. 27A). 592p. 1981. 110.75 (ISBN 0-444-41847-4). Elsevier.

--Marine Environmental Pollution, Vol. 2: Dumping & Mining. (Oceanography Ser.: Vol. 27B). 574p. 1981. 110.75 (ISBN 0-444-41855-5). Elsevier.

Geyer, R. A., ed. see Slotnick, M. M.

Geyer, R. F. & Zouwen, J. van der, eds. Dependence & Inequality: A Systems Approach to the Problems of Mexico & Other Developing Countries. (Systems Science & World Order Library: Innovations in Systems Science). (Illus.). 336p. 1982. 39.00 (ISBN 0-08-027952-X). Pergamon.

--Sociocybernetics, Vols. 1 & 2. 1978. Vol. 1. pap. 17.00 (ISBN 90-207-0854-6, Pub. by Martinus Nijhoff Netherlands); Vol. 2. pap. 17.00 (ISBN 90-207-0855-4). Kluwer Academic.

Geyer, Richard A., ed. CRC Handbook of Geophysical Exploration at Sea. 464p. 1983. 86.50 (ISBN 0-8493-0222-6). CRC Pr.

Geyer, William, jt. ed. see Huseboe, Arthur R.

Geyikdagi, Mehmet Y. Risk Trends of U. S. Multinational & Domestic Firms. 172p. 1983. 29.95 (ISBN 0-03-061924-6). Praeger.

Geyikdaqi, Mehmet Y. Political Parties in Turkey: The Role of Islam. LC 83-24470. 177p. 1984. 25.95 (ISBN 0-03-063824-0). Praeger.

Geyl, P, et al. The Pattern of the Past: Can We Determine It. LC 68-23291. 126p. 1949. Repr. lib. bdg. 15.00x (ISBN 0-8371-0083-6, GEPP). Greenwood.

Geyl, Pieter. Encounters in History. 11.50 (ISBN 0-8446-2125-0). Peter Smith.

--The Revolt of the Netherlands Fifteen Fifty-Five to Sixteen Hundred & Nine. 2nd ed. LC 79-53235. (Illus.). 1980. text ed. 26.50x (ISBN 0-06-492382-7); pap. text ed. 9.95x (ISBN 0-06-492383-5). B&N Imports.

--Use & Abuse of History. vi, 97p. 1970. Repr. of 1955 ed. 16.50 (ISBN 0-208-00827-6, Archon). Shoe String.

--Use & Abuse of History. 1955. 14.50x (ISBN 0-686-83843-2). Elliots Bks.

Geyman, John. Family Practice: Foundations of Changing Health Care. 2nd ed. 384p. 1985. write for info. (ISBN 0-8385-2538-5). ACC.

Geyman, John P. & Fry, John. Family Practice: An International Perspective in Developed Countries. 192p. 1983. 29.95 (ISBN 0-8385-2541-5). ACC.

Geyser, O. & Coetzer, P. W. Bibliographies on South African Political History: General Sources on South African Political History Since 1902, Vol. 2. 1979. lib. bdg. 68.00 (ISBN 0-8161-8245-0, Hall Reference). G K Hall.

Geysson, Bernard. Soulages. (QLP Ser.). (Illus.). 96p. 1980. 9.95 (ISBN 0-517-54105-X). Crown.

Geytenbeek, Brian & Geytenbeek, Helen. Gidabal Grammar & Dictionary. (AIAS Linguistics Ser.: No. 17). (Orig.). 1971. pap. text ed. 11.00x (ISBN 0-85575-019-7). Humanities.

Geytenbeek, Helen, jt. auth. see Geytenbeek, Brian.

Gezi, Kal & Bradford, Ann. The Mystery at Misty Falls. LC 80-15708. (Mystery Ser.). (Illus.). 32p. (gr. k-4). 1980. PLB 7.45 (ISBN 0-89565-147-5). Childs World.

--The Mystery in the Secret Club House. LC 78-6418. (Mystery Ser.). (Illus.). (gr. k-3). 1978. PLB 7.45 (ISBN 0-89565-027-4). Childs World.

--The Mystery of the Blind Writer. LC 80-12395. (Mystery Ser.). (Illus.). 32p. (gr. k-4). 1980. PLB 7.45 (ISBN 0-89565-145-9). Childs World.

--The Mystery of the Live Ghosts. LC 78-8142. (Mystery Ser.). (Illus.). (gr. k-3). 1978. PLB 7.45 (ISBN 0-89565-026-6). Childs World.

--The Mystery of the Missing Raccoon. LC 78-6455. (Mystery Ser.). (Illus.). (gr. k-3). 1978. PLB 7.45 (ISBN 0-89565-025-8). Childs World.

--The Mystery of the Square Footprints. LC 80-10437. (Mystery Ser.). (Illus.). 32p. (gr. k-4). 1980. PLB 7.45 (ISBN 0-89565-144-0). Childs World.

Gezi, Kal, jt. auth. see Bradford, Ann.

GFD, jt. ed. see Dokumentationsring Padagogik.

Gfollner, S. Adelheid. John Masefield's Stellung Zum Religion. (SSEL Poetic Drama Ser.: No. 47). (Orig.). 1979. pap. text ed. 25.50x (ISBN 0-391-01613-X). Humanities.

Ghabbour, I., jt. ed. see Kassas, M.

Ghadar, Fariborz & Stobaugh, Robert. The Petroleum Industry in Oil-Importing Developing Countries. LC 81-48556. 240p. 1983. 28.00x (ISBN 0-669-05419-4). Lexington Bks.

Ghadar, Kobrin & Ghadar, Moran. Managing International Political Risk: Strateges & Techniques. 183p. 1983. pap. 25.00 (ISBN 0-939296-05-5). Bond Pub Co.

Ghadar, Moran, jt. auth. see Ghadar, Kobrin.

Ghadially, F. N. Diagnostic Electron Microscopy of Tumors. LC 79-42839. 1980. text ed. 119.95 (ISBN 0-407-00156-5). Butterworth.

Ghadially, Feroze N. Diagnostic Electron Microscopy of Tumours. 2nd ed. 484p. 1985. text ed. 99.95 (ISBN 0-407-00299-5). Butterworth.

--Diagnostic Ultrastructural Pathology. (Illus.). 120p. (Orig.). 1984. pap. text ed. 19.95 (ISBN 0-407-00356-8). Butterworth.

--Fine Structure of Synovial Joints. (Illus.). 348p. 1983. text ed. 119.95. Butterworth.

--Ultrastructural Pathology of the Cell & Matrix. 2nd ed. 752p. 1982. text ed. 199.95 (ISBN 0-407-00166-2). Butterworth.

Ghadimi, Hossein. Total Parenteral Nutrition: Premises & Promises. LC 74-17152. (Wiley Clinical Pediatrics, Maternal & Child Health Ser.). Repr. of 1975 ed. 160.00 (ISBN 0-8357-9994-8, 2015192). Bks Demand UMI.

Ghahremani, G. G., jt. ed. see Meyers, M. A.

Ghai, C. L. A Textbook of Practical Physiology. xiii, 239p. 1984. pap. text ed. 15.95x (ISBN 0-7069-2592-0, Pub. by Vikas India). Advent NY.

Ghai, D. P., et al. The Basic-Needs Approach to Development: Some Issues Regarding Concepts & Methodology. 113p. 1980. pap. 8.55 (ISBN 92-2-101801-6, ILO69, ILO). Unipub.

Ghai, Dharam & Godfrey, Martin. Planning for Basic Needs in Kenya: Performance, Policies & Prospects. vii, 166p. (3rd Impression, 1981). 1979. pap. 11.50 (ISBN 92-2-102171-8, ILO153, ILO). Unipub.

Ghai, Dharam, jt. auth. see Khan, Azizur R.

Ghai, Dharam, jt. ed. see Court, David.

Ghai, Dharam, ed. see International Labour Office Staff.

Ghai, Dharam, et al. Planning for Basic Needs in Kenya: Performance, Policies & Prospects. International Labour Office, Geneva, ed. (Illus.). 166p. (Orig.). 1981. pap. 11.40 (ISBN 9-22-102171-8). Intl Labour Office.

Ghai, Dharam, et al, eds. Agrarian Systems & Rural Development. LC 79-16547. 375p. 1980. text ed. 44.50x (ISBN 0-8419-0541-X). Holmes & Meier.

Ghai, O. P. & Kumar, Narendra. International Publishing Today: Problems & Prospects. 237p. 1984. text ed. 25.00x (ISBN 0-86590-273-9, Pub. by Bookmans Club India). Apt Bks.

Ghai, S. K., ed. see Powell, James N.

Ghai, Y., ed. Studies of Law in Social Change & Development: Law in the Political Economy of Public Enterprise-African Perspectives. 15.00 (ISBN 0-686-35892-9); pap. 10.00 (ISBN 0-686-37198-4). Intl Ctr Law.

Ghai, Y. & Luckham, R., eds. The Political Economy of Law: A Third World Reader. write for info. Intl Ctr Law.

Ghai, Yash, jt. auth. see Ramanadham, V. V.

Ghai, Yash, ed. Law in the Political Economy of Public Enterprise: African Perspectives. (Studies of Law in Social Change & Development: No. 1). 351p. 1983. text ed. 39.50x (ISBN 0-8419-9746-2, Africana). Holmes & Meier.

--Studies of Law in Social Change & Development: Law in the Political Economy of Public Enterprise. 15.00 (ISBN 0-686-35905-4); pap. 10.00 (ISBN 0-686-37208-5). Intl Ctr Law.

Ghairian, A. In Search of Nirvana, a New Perspective on Alcohol & Drug Dependency. 96p. 1985. 6.95 (ISBN 0-85398-208-2); pap. 3.50 (ISBN 0-85398-209-0). G Ronald Pub.

Ghalem, Ali. A Wife for My Son. Kaziolas, G., tr. Orig. Title: Une Femme Pour Mon Fils. 212p. (Orig.). 1984. pap. 5.95 (ISBN 0-916650-17-0). Banner Pr NY.

Ghali, A. Circular Storage Tanks & Silos. LC 79-12406. 210p. 1979. 37.00x (ISBN 0-419-11500-5, NO.6121, Pub. by E & FN Spon England). Methuen Inc.

Ghali, A. & Neville, A. M. Structural Analysis: A Unified Classical & Matrix Approach. 2nd ed. 1978. pap. 29.95x (ISBN 0-412-14990-7, 6122, Pub. by Chapman & Hall). Methuen Inc.

Ghali, Mirrit B. The Policy of Tomorrow. El Faruqi, Ismail R., tr. LC 54-837. viii, 139p. 1971. pap. 3.50x (ISBN 0-87950-263-0). Spoken Lang Serv.

Ghali, Moheb, ed. Tourism & Regional Growth. (Studies in Applied Regional Science: No. 11). 1977. pap. 16.00 (ISBN 90-207-0716-7, Pub. by Martinus Nijhoff Netherlands). Kluwer Academic.

Ghalib, Asadullah. Ghalib, Seventeen Ninety-Seven to Eighteen Sixty-Nine: Life & Letters, Vol. 1. Russell, Ralph & Islam, Khurshidul, eds. 1969. 25.00x (ISBN 0-674-35435-4). Harvard U Pr.

Ghalib, Mirza A. Whispers of the Angel (Nawa-E-Sarosh) (Illus.). 56p. 1969. 3.00 (ISBN 0-88253-384-3). Ind-US Inc.

Ghalib, Miza A. Ghazels of Ghalib: Versions from the Urdu. Ahmad, Aliiaz, ed. LC 76-173987. pap. 51.00 (ISBN 0-317-09874-8, 2022715). Bks Demand UMI.

Ghalsasi, L. P., et al. Topics in Organic Chemistry, Vol. I. 1981. 30.00x (ISBN 0-86125-416-3, Pub. by Orient Longman India). State Mutual Bk.

--Topics in Organic Chemistry, Vol. II. 1981. 30.00x (ISBN 0-86125-677-8, Pub. by Orient Longman India). State Mutual Bk.

Ghanadian, R., ed. Endocrinology of Prostatic Tumours. (Illus.). 300p. 1982. text ed. 55.00 (ISBN 0-85200-416-8, Pub. by MTP Pr England). Kluwer Academic.

Ghanananda, Swami & Steward-Wallace, John, eds. Women Saints of East & West. LC 79-65731. 1979. pap. 6.95 (ISBN 0-87481-036-1). Vedanta Pr.

Ghanayem, Ishaq I. & Voth, Alden H. The Kissinger Legacy: American Middle East Policy. LC 83-24512. (Illus.). 192p. 1984. 24.95 (ISBN 0-03-069752-2). Praeger.

Ghandhi, Sorab K. Semiconductor Power Devices: Physics of Operation & Fabrication Technology. LC 77-8019. 1977. 45.95x (ISBN 0-471-02999-8, Pub by Wiley-Interscience). Wiley.

--Theory & Practice of Microelectronics. LC 68-28501. (Illus.). 1968. 50.95x (ISBN 0-471-29718-6, Pub. by Wiley-Interscience). Wiley.

--Theory & Practice of Microelectronics. LC 83-19994. 504p. 1984. Repr. of 1968 ed. 47.50 (ISBN 0-89874-702-3). Krieger.

--VLSI Fabrication Principles: Silicon & Gallium Arsenide. LC 82-10842. 665p. 1983. 56.50 (ISBN 0-471-86833-7, Pub. by Wiley-Interscience). Wiley.

Ghandi, Mohandas K; see Gandhi, Mohandas K.

Ghandour, Mounir. Arabic Conversation. pap. 5.00x (ISBN 0-86685-041-4); book & two cassettes 30.00 (ISBN 0-686-70463-0). Intl Bk Ctr.

--Learn Arabic Reading & Writing I. pap. 50.00x incl. 2hr. VHS videocassette (ISBN 0-86685-040-6); book & 2 cassettes 30.00 (ISBN 0-686-96752-6). Intl Bk Ctr.

Ghandour, N., et al, trs. see Bayes, Ronald H.

Ghanem, Fathy. The Man Who Lost His Shadow. Stewart, Desmond, tr. from Arabic. 352p. (Orig.). 1981. 14.00x (ISBN 0-89410-206-0); pap. 8.00x (ISBN 0-89410-207-9). Three Continents.

--The Man Who Lost His Shadow. Stewart, Desmond, tr. (African Writers Ser.: No. 223). 352p. 1980. pap. text ed. 6.50x (ISBN 0-435-90223-7). Heinemann Ed.

Ghani, M. A. & Mugaffar, N. Relations between the Parasitic Predator Complex & the Host-Plants of Coccids in Pakistan. 60p. 1974. 39.00x (ISBN 0-85198-288-3, Pub. by CAB Bks England). State Mutual Bk.

Ghani, M. A. & Cheema, M. A., eds. Biology, Ecology & Behaviour of Principal Natural Enemies of Major Insect Pests of Forest Trees in Pakistan. 100p. 1973. 49.00x (ISBN 0-85198-283-2, Pub. by CAB Bks England). State Mutual Bk.

Ghani, M. A., jt. ed. see Rao, V. P.

Ghanoonparvar, M. R. Persian Cuisine: Regional & Modern Foods, Bk. 2. LC 82-61268. (Illus., Orig.). 1984. pap. 12.95 (ISBN 0-939214-23-7). Mazda Pubs.

--Prophets of Doom: Literature as a Socio-Political Phenomenon in Modern Iran. LC 84-17304. 242p. 1985. lib. bdg. 23.50 (ISBN 0-8191-4292-1); pap. text ed. 12.00 (ISBN 0-8191-4293-X). U Pr of Amer.

Ghanoonparvar, Mohammad R. Persian Cuisine: Traditional Foods, Bk. 1. LC 82-61281. (Illus.). 250p. (Orig.). 1982. write for info. (ISBN 0-939214-11-3); pap. 12.95 (ISBN 0-939214-10-5). Mazda Pubs.

Ghanoonparvar, Mohammad R. & Givehchian, Fatemeh. Persian for Beginners. (Illus.). 112p. (YA) 1985. text ed. 12.00 (ISBN 0-939214-26-1). Mazda Pubs.

Ghanoonparvar, Mohammad R., tr. see Azaad, Meyer.

Ghanoonparvar, Mohammed R., tr. see Banisadr, Abolhassan.

Ghantus, Elias T. Arab Industrial Integration: A Strategy for Development. (Illus.). 240p. 1982. 36.50 (ISBN 0-7099-1117-3, Pub. by Croom Helm Ltd). Longwood Pub Group.

Gharaibeh, Fawzi. Economics of the West Bank & Gaza Strip. (Replica Edition). 152p. 1985. pap. 18.50x (ISBN 0-8133-7011-6). Westview.

Gharatchedaghi, Cyrus. Distribution of Land in Varamin: An Opening Phase of the Agrarian Reform in Iran. 179p. 1967. 20.00x (ISBN 3-8100-0087-6). Intl Pubns Serv.

Ghareeb, Edmund. The Kurdish Question in Iraq. LC 81-8897. (Contemporary Issues in the Middle East Ser.). (Illus.). 240p. 1981. 22.00x (ISBN 0-8156-0164-6); pap. 12.95x (ISBN 0-8156-2286-4). Syracuse U Pr.

Ghareeb, Edmund, ed. Split Vision: Arab Portrayal in the American Media. LC 77-90775. 171p. 1977. pap. 8.00 (ISBN 0-934484-11-2). Inst Mid East & North Africa.

--Split Vision: The Portrayal of Arabs in the American Media. rev & exp. ed. LC 83-71909. 397p. 1983. 12.95 (ISBN 0-943182-00-X); pap. 6.95 (ISBN 0-943182-01-8). Am-Arab Affairs.

Gharib, Georges, jt. ed. see Berselli, Costante.

Ghasemy, A. Asghar, tr. see Shariati, Ali.

Ghasemy, Ali A., tr. see Shariati, Ali.

Ghatak, A. K., jt. auth. see Sodha, M. S.

Ghatak, A. K., jt. auth. see Thyagarajan, K.

Ghatak, A. K. & Thyagarajan, K, eds. Contemporary Optics. LC 77-21571. (Optical Physics & Engineering Ser). (Illus.). 380p. 1978. 45.00x (ISBN 0-306-31029-5, Plenum Pr). Plenum Pub.

Ghatak, Subrata. Monetary Economics in Developing Countries. 1981. 26.00 (ISBN 0-312-54418-9). St Martin.

--Technology Transfer to Developing Countries, Vol. 27. Altman, Edward I. & Walter, Ingo, eds. LC 80-82478. (Contemporary Studies in Economic & Financial Analysis). 200p. 1981. 34.50 (ISBN 0-89232-160-1). Jai Pr.

Ghatak, Subrata & Ingersent, Kenneth A. Agriculture & Economic Development. LC 83-49200. (Studies in Development). 392p. 1984. text ed. 28.50x (ISBN 0-8018-3225-X); pap. text ed. 12.95X (ISBN 0-8018-3226-8). Johns Hopkins.

Ghattas, Emile. Inventory Management in Lebanon. 1977. 15.00x (ISBN 0-8156-6047-2, Am U Beirut). Syracuse U Pr.

Ghattas, Nabih. Dictionary of Economics, Business, & Finance in English & Arabic with Arabic Glossary. 30.00x (ISBN 0-86685-271-9). Intl Bk Ctr.

Ghauri, M. S. The Morphology & Taxonomy of Male Scale Insects (Homoptera: Coccoidea) (Illus.). vii, 221p. 1962. 24.50x (ISBN 0-565-00580-4, Pub. by British Mus Nat Hist England). Sabbot-Natural Hist Bks.

Ghausi, M. & Laker, K. Modern Filter Design: Active RC & Switched Capacitor. 1981. 41.95 (ISBN 0-13-594663-8). P-H.

Ghazi, A. Mercy for the Mankind, Vol. II. 1981. 4.00 (ISBN 0-686-97848-X). Kazi Pubns.

--Messenger of Allah, Vol. I. 1981. 3.50 (ISBN 0-686-97850-1). Kazi Pubns.

--Messenger of Allah, Vol. II. 1981. 4.50 (ISBN 0-686-97851-X). Kazi Pubns.

--Our Prophet, Vol. II. 1981. 2.50 (ISBN 0-686-97846-3). Kazi Pubns.

Ghazi, A & Watson, R. T., eds. Intercomparison of Stratospheric-Mesospheric Data: Proceedings of the Topical Meeting of the COSPAR Interdisciplinary Scientific Commission A (Meeting A1) of the COSPAR 25th Plenary Meeting, Graz, Austria, 25 June-7 July 1984. (Illus.). 148p. 1985. pap. 49.50 (ISBN 0-08-032734-6, Pub. by PPL). Pergamon.

Ghazi, A, jt. ed. see Zerefos, C S.

Ghazi, R. World of Islam: Coloring Book. pap. 2.50 (ISBN 0-686-83562-X). Kazi Pubns.

Ghazzala, Ali. Oil & the Political Failure of the Arab World: Its Economic & Historical Meaning. (Illus.). 127p. 1983. 99.85x (ISBN 0-86722-052-X). Inst Econ Pol.

Ghazzali, Ahmad. Sawanih: Inspiration from the World of Pure Spirits. Pourjavady, Nasrollah, tr. (The Ancient Persian Treatise on Love Ser.). 132p. 1985. 29.95 (ISBN 0-7103-0091-3, Kegan Paul International). Routledge & Kegan.

Ghazzali, Al. Ethical Philosophy. 1970. 12.00x (ISBN 0-87902-162-4). Orientalia.

--Mysteries of Worship in Islam: The Book of the Ihya' on Worship Translated with Commentary & Introduction. Calverley, E. E., tr. pap. 10.00 (ISBN 0-87902-200-0). Orientalia.

Ghearailt, Terry M., abridged by see Kickham, Charles J.

Ghebali, Victor-Yves, ed. see Carnegie Endowment for International Peace.

Ghedini, Francesco. Northern Italian Cooking. 224p. 1984. pap. 9.95 (ISBN 0-525-48129-X, 0966-290). Dutton.

Ghedini, Silvano. Software for Photometric Astronomy. LC 82-8574. (Illus.). 224p. 1982. pap. text ed. 26.95 (ISBN 0-943396-00-X). Willmann-Bell.

Gheerbrant, Alain, jt. auth. see Chevalier, Jean.

Ghelardi, Robert, jt. auth. see Dahm, Charles.

Ghelderode, Michel De. L' Ecole des Bouffons. 96p. 1953. 4.95 (ISBN 0-686-56045-0). French & Eur.

--Ghelderode: Seven Plays, Vol. 1. Incl. Chronicles of Hell; Barabbas; The Women at the Tomb; Pantagleize; The Blind Men; Three Actors & Their Drama; Lord Halewyn. (Mermaid Dramabook Ser.). 304p. (Orig.). 1960. pap. 4.95 (ISBN 0-8090-0719-3). Hill & Wang.

--Sortileges. 279p. 1966. 4.95 (ISBN 0-686-56046-9). French & Eur.

--Theatre, 5 vols. 328p. 1952-70. Vol. 1. 12.95 (ISBN 0-686-56047-7); Vols. 2 & 3. 16.95 ea.; Vol. 4. 8.95 (ISBN 0-686-56048-5); Vol. 5. 10.95 (ISBN 0-686-56049-3). French & Eur.

Ghelev, Paul, ed. see Jackson, Mildred & Teague, Terri.

Ghelis, Charis & Yon, Jeannine. Protein Folding. (Molecular Biology Ser.). 556p. 1982. 74.50 (ISBN 0-12-281520-3). Acad Pr.

Ghent, Dorothy Van see Van Ghent, Dorothy.

Ghent, W. J. The Reds Bring Reaction. 1977. lib. bdg. 59.95 (ISBN 0-8490-2505-2). Gordon Pr.

Ghent, William J. Road to Oregon. LC 77-111787. (BCL Ser.: I). (Illus.). Repr. of 1929 ed. 22.00 (ISBN 0-404-02717-2). AMS Pr.

--Road to Oregon: A Chronicle of the Great Emigrant Trail. (Illus.). 1971. Repr. of 1929 ed. 19.00x (ISBN 0-403-00987-1). Scholarly.

Gheorghe, A. Processing & Synthesis of Hydrogeological Data. 1978. 43.00 (ISBN 0-9961002-7-X, Pub. by Abacus England). Heyden.

Gheorghe, Adrian. Applied Systems Engineering. 342p. 1982. text ed. 48.95x (ISBN 0-471-09997-X, Pub.by Wiley-Interscience). Wiley.

Gheorghiu, A. & Dragomir, V. Geometry of Structural Forms. (Illus.). 319p. 1978. 44.50 (ISBN 0-85334-683-6, Pub. by Elsevier Applied Sci England). Elsevier.

Gherardelli, F., ed. Invariant Theory. (Lecture Notes in Mathematics Ser.: Vol.996). 159p. 1983. pap. 12.00 (ISBN 0-387-12319-9). Springer Verlag.

Gherlach, Luther P. & Hine, Virginia H. People, Power, Change. 1970. pap. text ed. write for info. (ISBN 0-02-341620-3). Macmillan.

Gherman, E. M. Stress & the Bottom Line: A Guide to Personal Well-Being & Corporate Health. 352p. 1981. 16.95 (ISBN 0-8144-5696-0). AMACOM.

Ghersini, G., jt. ed. see Braun, T.

Ghertman, Michel & Allen, Margaret. An Introduction to the Multinationals. LC 83-22919. 150p. 1984. 25.00 (ISBN 0-312-43304-2). St Martin.

Ghey, G., jt. auth. see Barber, N. F.

Ghez, Gilbert R. & Becker, Gary S. The Allocation of Time & Goods over the Life Cycle. (Studies in Human Behavior & Social Institutions: No. 6). 204p. 1975. 12.50 (ISBN 0-87014-514-2, Dist. by Columbia U Pr). Natl Bur Econ Res.

Ghezzi, Bert. The Angry Christian: How to Control & Use Your Anger. (Living As a Christian Ser.). 108p. (Orig.). 1980. pap. 2.95 (ISBN 0-89283-086-7). Servant.

--Facing Your Feelings: How to Get Your Emotions to Work for You. (Living as a Christian Ser.). 112p. 1983. pap. 2.95 (ISBN 0-89283-133-2). Servant.

--Getting Free: How Christians Can Overcome the Flesh & Conquer Persistent Personal Problems. (Living As a Christian Ser.). 112p. 1982. pap. 2.95 (ISBN 0-89283-117-0). Servant.

Ghezzi, Bert & Kinzer, Mark. Emotions As Resources: A Biblical & Pastoral Perspective. 110p. 1983. pap. 6.95 (ISBN 0-89283-158-8). Servant.

Ghezzi, Carlo & Jazayeri, Mehdi. Programming Language Concepts. LC 81-16032. 327p. 1982. text ed. 33.50 (ISBN 0-471-08755-6). Wiley.

Ghezzo, Marta A. Solfege, Ear Training, Rhythm, Dictation, & Music Theory: A Comprehensive Course. LC 78-16047. 272p. 1980. 21.75 (ISBN 0-8173-6403-X). U of Ala Pr.

Ghia, K. & Ghia, U., eds. Advances in Grid Generation. (FED Ser.: Vol. 5). 219p. 1983. pap. text ed. 40.00 (ISBN 0-317-02550-3, G00222). ASME.

Ghia, K. N., et al, eds. see American Society of Mechanical Engineers.

Ghia, U., jt. ed. see Ghia, K.

Ghiardi, James & Kircher, John. Punitive Damages: 1981-1983, 2 vols. LC 81-10088. 95.00; Suppl., 1982. 20.00; Suppl., 1983. 25.00. Callaghan.

Ghidalia, Vic & Elwood, Roger. Venus Factor. 1977. pap. 1.25 (ISBN 0-532-12475-8). Woodhill.

Ghidalia, Vic, ed. Feast of Fear. 1977. pap. 1.50 (ISBN 0-532-15245-X). Woodhill.

--Nightmare Garden. 1976. pap. 1.25 (ISBN 0-532-12411-1). Woodhill.

Ghidini, Gustavo. Consumer Legislation in Italy. 1980. 42.50 (ISBN 0-442-30426-9). Van Nos Reinhold.

Ghiglieri, Michael P. The Chimpanzees of the Kibale Forest: A Field Study of Ecology & Social Structure. LC 83-10115. (Illus.). 272p. 1983. 35.00x (ISBN 0-231-05594-3). Columbia U Pr.

Ghiglione, Loren, ed. The Buying & Selling of America's Newspapers. 200p. 1984. 21.95x (ISBN 0-89730-109-9). R J Berg & Co.

--Gentlemen of the Press. 435p. 1984. 24.95x (ISBN 0-89730-110-2). R J Berg & Co.

--Improving Newswriting. 138p. (Orig.). 1982. pap. 4.95 (ISBN 0-943086-01-9). Am Soc News.

Ghikas, Mary, ed. Authority Control: The Key to Tomorrow's Catalog. 208p. 1982. lib. bdg. 32.50 (ISBN 0-912700-85-8). Oryx Pr.

Ghil, M., et al, eds. Turbulence & Predictability in Geophysical Fluid Dynamics & Climate Dynamics: Proceedings of the International School of Physics, Enrico Fermi Course LXXXVIII, Varenna, Italy, 14 June-24 June, 1983. (Enrico Fermi Ser.: Vol. 88). 464p. 1985. 79.75 (ISBN 0-444-86936-0, North-Holland). Elsevier.

Ghilchik, Margaret, jt. auth. see Price, Leonard.

Ghildyal. Soilphysics Theory & Practice. 1985. 39.95 (ISBN 0-470-20125-8). Wiley.

Ghiocel, D. & Lungu, D. Wind, Snow & Temperature Effects on Structures Based on Probability. 1975. 44.00 (ISBN 0-9961003-7-7, Pub. by Abacus England). Heyden.

Ghione, F., jt. ed. see Ciliberto, C.

Ghiotti, et al. Dictionnaire Italien-Francais, Francais-Italien de la Langue d'Aujourd'hui. (Fr. & Ital.). 1976. 27.50 (ISBN 0-686-57196-7, M-6270). French & Eur.

Ghiotti, C., ed. Il Nuovissimo Ghiotti: Vocabolario Italiano-Francese, Francese-Italiano. 2390p. (Fr. & Ital.). 1980. 58.00x (ISBN 0-913298-74-3). S F Vanni.

Ghiradella, Robert V. Fragments. 64p. (Orig.). 1980. pap. 3.95 (ISBN 0-918222-20-6). Apple-Wood.

Ghirardelli, B. & Holme, T. Viaggio a Roma. (Illus.). 1975. pap. text ed. 4.95x (ISBN 0-582-36209-1). Longman.

Ghirardi, G. C., jt. auth. see Fonda, L.

Ghirardo, Diane, tr. see Rossi, Aldo.

Ghisalberti, Emilio L., jt. ed. see Frigerio, Alberto.

Ghiselin, Brewster. Windrose. (University of Utah Press Poetry Ser.). 252p. 1980. 19.95 (ISBN 0-87480-167-2). U of Utah Pr.

Ghiselin, Brewster, ed. Creative Process. pap. 3.95 (ISBN 0-451-62329-0, ME2329, Ment). NAL.

--The Creative Process: A Symposium. 1985. 7.95 (ISBN 0-520-05453-9, CAL 735). U of Cal Pr.

Ghiselin, Michael. The Triumph of the Darwinian Method. LC 84-4491. x, 288p. 1984. pap. 9.95x (ISBN 0-226-29024-7). U of Chicago Pr.

Ghiselin, Michael T. The Economy of Nature & the Evolution of Sex. LC 73-78554. 1974. 36.50x (ISBN 0-520-02474-5). U of Cal Pr.

Ghiselli, Edwin E. & Brown, Clarence W. Personnel & Industrial Psychology. 2nd ed. LC 54-10632. (McGraw-Hill Series in Psychology). pap. 126.00 (ISBN 0-317-08272-8, 2003754). Bks Demand UMI.

Ghiselli, Edwin E., jt. auth. see Brown, Clarence W.

Ghiselli, Edwin E., et al. Measurement Theory for the Behavioral Sciences. LC 80-27069. (Psychology Ser.). (Illus.). 494p. 1981. text ed. 36.95 (ISBN 0-7167-1048-X); pap. 23.95 (ISBN 0-7167-1252-0). W H Freeman.

Ghista, D. Biomechanics of Medical Devices. LC 80-15480. (Biomedical Engineering & Instrumentation Ser.: Vol. 7). 1981. 99.75 (ISBN 0-8247-6848-5). Dekker.

Ghista, D. N. Osteoarthromechanics. 1982. 58.00 (ISBN 0-07-023168-0). McGraw.

--Spinal Cord Injury Medical Engineering. (Illus.). 560p. 1986. 54.75x (ISBN 0-398-05167-4). C C Thomas.

Ghista, D. N., ed. Applied Physiological Mechanics. (Biomedical Engineering & Computation Ser.: Vol. 1). 936p. 1980. text ed. 164.25 (ISBN 3-7186-0013-7). Harwood Academic.

--Foundations of Noninvasive Cardiovascular Diagnostic Processes. (Advances in Cardiovascular Physics: Vol. 4). (Illus.). 1980. 48.75 (ISBN 3-8055-2923-6). S Karger.

Ghista, D. N. & Roaf, R., eds. Orthopaedic Mechanics: Procedures & Devices. 1979. 59.00 (ISBN 0-12-281650-1). Acad Pr.

Ghista, D. N. & Yang, W. J., eds. Cardiovascular Engineering. (Advances in Cardiovascular Physics: Pt. I-IV). (Illus.). xxxxviii, 960p. 1983. 184.75 (ISBN 3-8055-3613-5). S Karger.

--Cardiovascular Engineering, Part I: Modelling. (Advances in Cardiovascular Physics: Vol. 5). (Illus.). xiv, 230p. 1983. 61.00 (ISBN 3-8055-3609-7). S Karger.

--Cardiovascular Engineering, Part II: Monitoring. (Advances in Cardiovascular Physics: Vol. 5). (Illus.). viii, 280p. 1983. 61.00 (ISBN 3-8055-3610-0). S Karger.

--Cardiovascular Engineering, Part III: Diagnosis. (Advances in Cardiovascular Physics: Vol. 5). (Illus.). x, 158p. 1983. 48.75 (ISBN 3-8055-3611-9). S Karger.

--Cardiovascular Engineering: Protheses, Assist & Artificial Organs, Pt. IV. (Advances in Cardiovascular Physics: Vol. 5). (Illus.). viii, 292p. 1983. 61.00 (ISBN 3-8055-3612-7). S Karger.

Ghista, D. N., et al, eds. Theoretical Foundations of Cardiovascular Processes. (Advances in Cardiovascular Physics: Vol. 1). (Illus.). 1978. 41.75 (ISBN 3-8055-2850-7). S Karger.

--Blood: Rheology, Hemolysis, Gas & Surface Interactions. (Advances in Cardiovascular Physics: Vol. 3). (Illus.). 1979. 41.75 (ISBN 3-8055-2852-3). S Karger.

--Cardiograms: Theory & Applications. (Advances in Cardiovascular Physics: Vol. 2). (Illus.). 1979. 11.50 (ISBN 3-8055-2851-5). S Karger.

Ghista, Dhanjoo N., ed. Human Body Dynamics: Impact, Occupational & Athletic Aspects. (Oxford Medical Engineering Ser.). (Illus.). 1982. 69.00x (ISBN 0-19-857548-3). Oxford U Pr.

Ghista, Dhanjoo N. & Roaf, R., eds. Orthopaedic Mechanics, Procedures & Devices. LC 77-93201. 1981. Vol. II August, 1981. 83.50 (ISBN 0-12-281602-1); Vol. III, January 1982. 66.00 (ISBN 0-12-281603-X). Acad Pr.

Ghizzetti, A. & Ossicini, A. Quadrature Formulae. 1970. 43.50 (ISBN 0-12-281750-8). Acad Pr.

--Quadrature Formulae. (International Series of Numerical Mathematics: No. 13). 192p. 1970. 37.95x (ISBN 0-8176-0530-4). Birkhauser.

Ghlonti, L. & Djavakhishvili, A. Settlements of the Kuro-Araxes Culture. (Occasional Papers on the Near East: Vol. 21). (Illus.). 42p. 1984. 10.00 (ISBN 0-317-12238-X). Undena Pubns.

Ghodes, Clarence, ed. see Emerson, Ralph Waldo.

Gholson, Barry. The Cognitive-Developmental Basis of Human Learning: Studies in Hypothesis Testing. LC 80-307. (Developmental Psychology Ser.). 1980. 29.50 (ISBN 0-12-282350-8). Acad Pr.

Gholson, J. Barry & Rosenthal, Ted R. L. Applications of Cognitive-Developmental Theory. LC 83-21462. (Developmental Psychology Series). 1984. 45.00 (ISBN 0-12-282320-6). Acad Pr.

Gholson, Ronald E. & Buser, Robert L. Cocurricular Activity Programs in Secondary Schools. 24p. 1983. pap. 4.00 (ISBN 0-88210-145-5). Natl Assn Principals.

Gholston, H. D., jt. auth. see Wohlauer, Gabriele E.

Gholston, Homer N. The Koiec Corollary. (Orig.). 1979. pap. 1.95 (ISBN 0-532-23253-4). Woodhill.

Ghonaimy, M. A., et al. see IFAC Conference, Cairo, Egypt, Nov. 1977.

Ghori, Karmatullah K. China Doll. 180p. 1984. pap. 3.95 (ISBN 0-8351-1524-0). China Bks.

Ghorpade, Kumar D., jt. auth. see Mathis, Wayne N.

Ghorpade, M. Y. Sunlight & Shadows. (Illus.). 128p. 1983. 24.00 (ISBN 0-575-03283-9, Gollancz England). David & Charles.

Ghosal, A., et al. Examples & Exercises in Operations Research. (Studies in Operations Research Ser.). 272p. 1975. 56.75 (ISBN 0-677-03910-7). Gordon.

Ghosal, Amitava. Applied Cybernetics: Its Relevance to Operations Research. (Studies in Operations Research Ser.). 176p. 1978. 38.50 (ISBN 0-677-05410-6). Gordon.

Ghose, Ajit K., ed. Agrarian Reform in Contemporary Developing Countries. LC 83-13703. 384p. 1983. 35.00 (ISBN 0-312-01445-7). St Martin.

Ghose, Aurobindo. Guidance from Sri Aurobindo: Letters to a Young Disciple. Doshi, Nagin, ed. 285p. 1974. 6.00 (ISBN 0-89071-205-0). Matagiri.

--The Immortal Fire. Jhunjhuniwala, Shyam S., ed. 216p. (Orig.). 1974. pap. 4.50 (ISBN 0-89071-209-3). Matagiri.

Ghose, Jogendra C., ed. see Rammohun Roy, R.

Ghose, Kalyani, tr. see Sircar, Badal.

Ghose, M. Selected Poems. 8.00 (ISBN 0-89253-546-6); flexible cloth 4.00 (ISBN 0-89253-547-4). Ind-US Inc.

Ghose, Prabodh C. Shakespeare's Mingled Drama. 1966. Repr. 20.00 (ISBN 0-8274-3381-6). R West.

Ghose, Prema, ed. see Ballard, John.

Ghose, Rabindra N. EMP Environment & System Hardness Design. LC 83-51067. (Illus.). 250p. 1984. text ed. 42.00 (ISBN 0-932263-16-X). White Consult.

Ghose, S. Changing India. 1978. 12.50 (ISBN 0-89684-550-8). Orient Bk Dist.

Ghose, S. N. Dante Gabriel Rossetti & Contemporary Criticism. LC 74-13023. 1929. lib. bdg. 20.00 (ISBN 0-8414-4537-0). Folcroft.

Ghose, Sankar. Indian National Congress: Its History & Heritage. LC 76-900644. 1976. 8.00x (ISBN 0-88386-776-1). South Asia Bks.

--Leaders of Modern India. 454p. 1980. 29.95x (ISBN 0-940500-31-0). Asia Bk Corp.

Ghose, Sisirkumar. The Later Poems of Tagore. LC 74-27426. 304p. 1975. Repr. of 1961 ed. lib. bdg. 22.50x (ISBN 0-8371-7902-5, GHPT). Greenwood.

--The Mystic As a Force for Change. rev. ed. LC 80-53954. 144p. 1980. pap. 4.75 (ISBN 0-8356-0547-7, Quest). Theos Pub Hse.

Ghose, Sri A. Selections from Sri Aurobindo's Savitri. Aldridge, Mary, ed. (Illus.). 253p. 1975. pap. 3.75 (ISBN 0-89071-214-X). Matagiri.

Ghose, T. K., et al. Immobilized Enzymes I. (Advances in Biochemical Engineering Ser.: Vol. 10). (Illus.). 1978. 43.00 (ISBN 0-387-08975-6). Springer-Verlag.

Ghose, T. K., et al, eds. Mass Transfer & Process Control. LC 72-152360. (Advances in Biochemical Engineering Ser.: Vol. 13). (Illus.). 1979. 57.00 (ISBN 0-387-09468-7). Springer-Verlag.

--Advances in Biochemical Engineering, Vol. 3. LC 73-152360. (Illus.). 250p. 1974. 49.00 (ISBN 0-387-06546-6). Springer-Verlag.

--Advances in Biochemical Engineering, Vol. 5. LC 72-152360. 1977. 35.00 (ISBN 0-387-08074-0). Springer-Verlag.

Ghose, Zulfikar. The Beautiful Empire. LC 83-19495. (Tusk Bks.). 384p. 1984. 22.50 (ISBN 0-87951-959-2); pap. 7.95 (ISBN 0-87951-960-6). Overlook Pr.

--A Different World. LC 84-42674. 318p. 1985. 15.95 (ISBN 0-87951-982-7). Overlook Pr.

--Don Bueno. 243p. 1984. 16.95 (ISBN 0-03-069398-5). HR&W.

--The Fiction of Reality. 146p. 1984. 29.00 (ISBN 0-333-29093-3, Pub. by Salem Acad). Merrimack Pub Cir.

--Hamlet, Prufrock & Language. 1978. 15.95x (ISBN 0-312-35723-0). St Martin.

--The Incredible Brazilian. LC 83-42920. (Tusk Bks.). 320p. 22.50 (ISBN 0-87951-200-8); pap. 7.95 (ISBN 0-87951-195-8). Overlook Pr.

--Jets from Orange. LC 67-28020. (Pakistani-Fr, Eng). 1967. 11.95 (ISBN 0-8023-1128-8). Dufour.

--A Memory of Asia: New & Selected Poems. Taylor, R. D. & Sheppard, Ann, eds. 82p. (Orig.). 1984. 14.95 (ISBN 0-931604-18-4); pap. 8.95 (ISBN 0-931604-19-2). Curbstone Pub NY TX.

--A New History of Torments. 1982. 16.50 (ISBN 0-03-061949-1). HR&W.

Ghosh. China Nuclear & Political Strategy. 1975. 16.50 (ISBN 0-89684-499-4). Orient Bk Dist.

Ghosh, A. Chanakya. (Illus.). (gr. 1-8). 1979. pap. 3.00 (ISBN 0-89744-152-4). Auromere.

--The City in Early Historical India. (Illus.). 98p. 1973. 6.50x (ISBN 0-89684-377-7). Orient Bk Dist.

--Income Distribution & the Structure of Production. 240p. 1984. text ed. 24.50x (ISBN 0-391-03103-1, Pub. by Aberdeen U Scotland). Humanities.

--The Koran & the Kafir: Islam & the Infidel. (Illus.). 190p. 1983. pap. 5.95 (ISBN 0-9611614-0-X). Ghosh A.

--The Koran & the Kafir: Islam & the Infidel. rev., 2nd ed. (Illus.). 200p. (Orig.). 1983. pap. 7.35 (ISBN 0-9611614-1-8). Ghosh A.

--Legends from Indian History. (Illus.). (gr. 1-8). 1979. pap. 3.00 (ISBN 0-89744-157-5); 4.50. Auromere.

--Planning, Programming & Input-Output Models: Selected Papers on Indian Planning. LC 68-29327. (University of Cambridge Dept. of Applied Economics Monographs: No. 15). pap. 43.80 (ISBN 0-317-29405-9, 2055839). Bks Demand UMI.
--Programming & Interregional Input-Output Analysis: An Application to the Problem of Industrial Location in India. LC 72-76092. (University of Cambridge, Dept. of Applied Economics, Monograph: 22). pap. 28.00 (ISBN 0-317-26405-2, 2024461). Bks Demand UMI.
Ghosh, A. & Chakraborty, D. Contribution to National & Regional Planning Problems. 174p. 1983. 49.00x (ISBN 0-317-20267-7, Pub. by K P Bagchi & Co India). State Mutual Bk.
Ghosh, A. B. Price Trends & Policies in India. 1974. 10.50x (ISBN 0-686-20291-0). Intl Bk Dist.
Ghosh, Arabinda. Competition & Diversification in the United States Petroleum Industry. LC 84-24932. (Illus.). 176p. 1985. lib. bdg. 35.00 (ISBN 0-89930-064-2, GHC/, Quorum). Greenwood.
--OPEC, the Petroleum Industry, & United States Energy Policy. LC 82-13245. (Illus.). 206p. 1983. lib. bdg. 35.00 (ISBN 0-89930-010-3, GOU/, Quorum). Greenwood.
Ghosh, Avijit, jt. auth. see Craig, C. Samuel.
Ghosh, Avijit & Craig, Samuel, eds. The Relationship of Advertising Expenditures to Sales: An Anthology of Classic Articles. LC 84-46070. (History of Advertising Ser.). 400p. 1985. lib. bdg. 50.00 (ISBN 0-8240-6764-9). Garland Pub.
Ghosh, B. N. Principles of Economic Science. 1983. text ed. 18.95x (ISBN 0-686-45575-4, Pub. by Vikas India). Advent NY.
--Scientific Method & Social Research. 254p. 1984. (Sterling Pubs India); pap. text ed. 12.95x (ISBN 0-86590-723-4). Apt Bks.
Ghosh, B. N. & Ghosh, Roma. A Textbook of Deductive Logic. (Illus.). ix, 134p. 1984. text ed. 18.95x (ISBN 0-7069-2482-7, Pub. by Vikas India). Advent NY.
Ghosh, Bijan K., ed. Organization of Prokaryotic Cell Membrane, Vols. I & II. 1981. Vol. I, 272p. 86.00 (ISBN 0-8493-5653-9); Vol. II, 224p. 86.00 (ISBN 0-8493-5654-7). CRC Pr.
Ghosh, D. N. Banking Policy in India: An Evaluation. 1979. 19.00x (ISBN 0-8364-0526-9). South Asia Bks.
Ghosh, Jajneshwar. A Study of Yoga. 2nd rev. ed. 1977. 16.95 (ISBN 0-89684-014-X, Pub. by Motilal Banarsidass India); pap. 12.50 (ISBN 0-89684-015-8). Orient Bk Dist.
Ghosh, Jyotish C. Bengali Literature. LC 78-3657. (BCL Ser.: II). Repr. of 1948 ed. 18.50 (ISBN 0-404-14545-0). AMS Pr.
--Bengali Literature. 198p. 1976. Repr. of 1948 ed. 11.50x (ISBN 0-87471-827-9). Rowman.
Ghosh, K. Plannning India's Future. 1978. 15.00x (ISBN 0-88386-906-3). South Asia Bks.
Ghosh, M. K. Life Beyond Death. 271p. 1984. text ed. 41.50x (ISBN 0-391-03302-6, Pub. by Cosmo India). Humanities.
Ghosh, Moni. Our Struggle: A Short History of Trade Union Movement in Tisco Industry at Jamshedpur. LC 74-900968. 278p. 1973. 10.00x (ISBN 0-88386-514-9). South Asia Bks.
Ghosh, Niva. Freud & Adler on Man & Society. 1983. 11.50x (ISBN 0-8364-0962-0, Pub. by Mukhopadhyay India). South Asia Bks.
Ghosh, P. C. Mahatma Gandhi As I Saw Him. 280p. 27.00x (ISBN 0-686-78837-0, Pub. by Bks India England). State Mutual Bk.
Ghosh, P. K. Introduction to Photoelectron Spectroscopy. LC 82-17374. (Chemical Analysis: A Series of Monographs on Analytical Chemisty & Its Applications). 377p. 1983. 58.95x (ISBN 0-471-06427-0, Pub. by Wiley-Interscience). Wiley.
--Mathematical Analysis: Differential Calculus, Vol. I. (A Modern Approach Ser.: Vol. 1). 484p. 1981. 30.00x (ISBN 0-86125-528-3, Pub. by Orient Longman India). State Mutual Bk.
--Mathematical Analysis: Integral Calculus (A Modern Approach) 356p. 1981. 30.00x (ISBN 0-86125-647-6, Pub. by Orient Longman India). State Mutual Bk.
Ghosh, Prabodh C. Poetry & Religion As Drama. 1979. Repr. of 1965 ed. lib. bdg. 25.00 (ISBN 0-8492-4940-6). R West.
Ghosh, Pradip K., ed. Developing Africa: A Modernization Perspective. LC 83-26672. (International Development Resource Bks.: No. 20). (Illus.). viii, 435p. 1984. lib. bdg. 45.00 (ISBN 0-313-24156-2, GAF/). Greenwood.
--Developing Latin America: A Modernization Perspective. LC 83-26671. (International Development Resource Bks.: No. 19). (Illus.). x, 416p. 1984. lib. bdg. 45.00 (ISBN 0-313-24155-4, GLA/). Greenwood.
--Developing South Asia: A Modernization Perspective. LC 83-26600. (International Development Resource Bks.: No. 18). xv, 582p. 1984. lib. bdg. 55.00 (ISBN 0-313-24154-6, GSA/). Greenwood.
--Development Cooperation & Third World Development. LC 83-26679. (International Development Resource Bks.: No. 15). xv, 497p. 1984. lib. bdg. 49.95 (ISBN 0-313-24151-1, GCO/). Greenwood.
--Development Policy & Planning: A Third World Perspective. LC 83-26492. (International Development Resource Bks.: No. 8). (Illus.). xvii, 626p. 1984. lib. bdg. 55.00 (ISBN 0-313-24144-9, GDP/). Greenwood.
--Disarmament & Development: A Global Perspective. LC 83-26683. (International Development Resource Bks.: No. 17). (Illus.). xv, 447p. 1984. lib. bdg. 45.00 (ISBN 0-313-24153-8, GDS/). Greenwood.
--Economic Integration & Third World Development. LC 83-26686. (International Development Resource Bks.: No. 12). xvii, 407p. 1984. lib. bdg. 45.00 (ISBN 0-313-24148-1, GEI/). Greenwood.
--Economic Policy & Planning in Third World Development. LC 83-26493. (International Development Resource Bks.: No. 7). xix, 711p. 1984. lib. bdg. 59.95 (ISBN 0-313-24143-0, GHO/). Greenwood.
--Energy Policy & Third World Development. LC 83-22742. (International Development Research Bks.: No. 4). (Illus.). xvii, 392p. 1984. lib. bdg. 45.00 (ISBN 0-313-24140-6, GEN/). Greenwood.
--Foreign Aid & Third World Development. LC 83-26450. (International Development Resource Bks.: No. 10). xv, 365p. 1984. lib. bdg. 45.00 (ISBN 0-313-24146-5, GFO/). Greenwood.
--Health, Food, & Nutrition in Third World Development. LC 83-26504. (International Development Resource Bks.: No. 6). (Illus.). xviii, 617p. 1984. 55.00 (ISBN 0-313-24142-2, GHF/). Greenwood.
--Industrialization & Development: A Third World Perspective. LC 83-1228. (International Development Resource Bks.: No. 1). (Illus.). xvi, 552p. 1984. lib. bdg. 45.00 (ISBN 0-313-24137-6, GIN/). Greenwood.
--International Trade & Third World Development. LC 83-27457. (International Development Resource Bks.: No. 16). (Illus.). xvi, 569p. 1984. lib. bdg. 49.95 (ISBN 0-313-24152-X, GTR/). Greenwood.
--Multi-National Corporations & Third World Development. LC 83-26680. (International Development Resource Bks.: No. 11). (Illus.). xv, 473p. 1984. lib. bdg. 35.00 (ISBN 0-313-24147-3, GMN/). Greenwood.
--New International Economic Order: A Third World Perspective. LC 83-26484. (International Development Resource Bks.: No. 9). (Illus.). xvi, 561p. 1984. lib. bdg. 49.95 (ISBN 0-313-24145-7, GNI/). Greenwood.
--Population, Environment & Resources, & Third World Development. LC 83-26430. (International Development Resource Bks.: No. 5). (Illus.). xx, 634p. 1984. lib. bdg. 55.00 (ISBN 0-313-24141-4, GPL/). Greenwood.
--Technology Policy & Development: A Third World Perspective. LC 83-22771. (International Development Resource Bks.: No. 3). (Illus.). xv, 593p. 1984. lib. bdg. 49.95 (ISBN 0-313-24139-2, GTE/). Greenwood.
--Third World Development: A Basic Needs Approach. LC 83-26681. (International Development Resource Bks.: No. 13). (Illus.). xv, 436p. 1984. lib. bdg. 45.00 (ISBN 0-313-24149-X, GTW/). Greenwood.
--Urban Development in the Third World. LC 83-22859. (International Development Resource Bks.: No. 2). (Illus.). xviv, 546p. 1984. lib. bdg. 45.00 (ISBN 0-313-24138-4, GUD/). Greenwood.
Ghosh, Pradip K. & Morrison, Denton E., eds. Appropriate Technology in Third World Development. LC 83-26682. xiv, 494p. 1984. lib. bdg. 49.95 (ISBN 0-313-24150-3, GAT/). Greenwood.
Ghosh, R. Aesthetic Theory & Art. (Ajanta's Series on Aesthetics: No. 1). 152p. 1979. pap. text ed. 7.50 (ISBN 0-391-03179-1, Pub by Ajanta Pubns India). Humanities.
Ghosh, Ratna, jt. ed. see Kurian, George.
Ghosh, Roma, jt. auth. see Ghosh, B. N.
Ghosh, S. K. The Outcry of Police Brutality. 1984. 8.75x (ISBN 0-8364-1110-2, Pub. by Ashish). South Asia Bks.
--Police in Ferment. 140p. 1981. 17.95 (ISBN 0-317-12335-1, Pub. by Lights & Life Pubs India). Asia Bk Corp.
--Women in a Changing Society. 1985. 18.50x (ISBN 0-8364-1313-X, Pub. by Ashish). South Asia Bks.
Ghosh, S. L., tr. see Basu, Manoje.
Ghosh, S. N., ed. Advances in Cement Technology: Critical Reviews & Case Studies on Manufacturing, Quality Control, Optimization & Use. (Illus.). 775p. 1982. 110.00 (ISBN 0-08-028670-4). Pergamon.
Ghosh, S. P. Hindu Religious Art & Architecture. (Illus.). 148p. 1983. text ed. 30.00x (ISBN 0-86590-124-4). Apt Bks.
Ghosh, Sachindra L., tr. see Basu, Manoje.
Ghosh, Sadhan K. My English Journey. 12.00 (ISBN 0-89253-670-5). Ind-US Inc.
Ghosh, Sakti P., ed. see National Computer Conference, 1978.
Ghosh, Sakti P., et al, eds. Data Base File Organization: Theory & Applications of Consecutive Retrieval Property (Symposium) Kambayashi, Y. & Lipski, W. (Notes & Reports in Computer & Science Applied Mathematics Ser.). 1983. 21.50 (ISBN 0-12-281860-1). Acad Pr.
Ghosh, Samir K., ed. Man, Language & Society: Contributions to the Sociology of Language. (Janua Linguarum, Ser. Minor: No. 109). 1972. pap. text ed. 20.80x (ISBN 90-2792-120-2). Mouton.
Ghosh, Sananda L. Mejda: The Family & the Early Life of Paramahansa Yogananda. LC 80-54206. (Illus.). 330p. 1980. 8.50 (ISBN 0-87612-265-9). Self Realization.
Ghosh, Sanjib K. Analytical Photogrammetry. LC 79-1063. (Illus.). 1979. 33.00 (ISBN 0-08-023883-1). Pergamon.
Ghosh, Sucheta. The Role of India in the Emergence of Bangladesh. 1984. 18.50x (ISBN 0-8364-0780-6). South Asia Bks.
Ghosh, Suresh C. Dalhousie in India: 1848-1856. LC 75-904110. 1975. 9.50x (ISBN 0-88386-577-7). South Asia Bks.
Ghosha, Jogesachandra. Hindu Woman of India. 140p. 1983. text ed. 15.95x (ISBN 0-86590-153-8). Apt Bks.
Ghosha, R. C. Brief Survey of Ancient Sanskrit Literature. 1977. 12.00x (ISBN 0-686-22660-7). Intl Bk Dist.
Ghoshal, Baladas. Indonesian Politics, Nineteen Fifty-Five to Fifty-Nine: The Emergence of Guided Democracy. 1983. 18.00x (ISBN 0-8364-0990-6, Pub. by KP Bagchi India). South Asia Bks.
Ghoshal, Nani G., et al. The Venous Drainage of the Domestic Animal. (Illus.). 268p. 1981. text ed. 20.00 (ISBN 0-7216-4117-2). Saunders.
Ghoshal, Sarat C., ed. The Sacred Books of the Jainas (Bibliotheca Jainica, 11 vols. Repr. of 1940 ed. 324.00 (ISBN 0-404-19549-0). AMS Pr.
Ghoshal, Sarat C., ed. & commentary by see Manikyanandi.
Ghoshel, Nani G., et al. The Venous Drainage of the Domestic Animals. LC 80-53898. pap. 69.50 (ISBN 0-317-26433-8, 2024989). Bks Demand UMI.
Ghossein, Mirene, jt. ed. see Boullata, Kamal.
Ghougassian, Joseph P. Gordon W. Allport's Ontopsychology of the Person. LC 70-171470. 1972. 8.75 (ISBN 0-8022-2069-X). Philos Lib.
--Kahlil Gibran: Wings of Thought. 1973. pap. 2.95 (ISBN 0-8065-0387-4). Citadel Pr.
--Kahlil Gibran: Wings of Thought. (Illus.). 235p. 1973. 7.50 (ISBN 0-685-30347-0). Philos Lib.
--Toward Women: A Study of the Origins of Western Attitudes Through Greco-Roman Philosophy. LC 77-92325. 1977. pap. 3.95x (ISBN 0-930994-01-9). Lukas & Sons.
Ghuman, Paul A. The Cultural Context of Thinking: A Comparative Study of Punjabi & English Boys. 136p. 1975. 11.00x (ISBN 0-85633-078-7, Pub. by NFER Nelson UK). Taylor & Francis.
Ghurayyib, Rose. Al-Tawahhujwal-Uful. 290p. (Orig., Arabic.). 1978. 14.00x (ISBN 0-89410-151-X); pap. 8.00 (ISBN 0-89410-152-8). Three Continents.
Ghurbal, Muhammad S. The Beginnings of the Egyptian Question & the Rise of Mehemet Ali. LC 74-15089. Repr. of 1928 ed. 24.50 (ISBN 0-404-12139-X). AMS Pr.
Ghurye, Charlotte W. The Movement Toward a New Social & Political Consciousness in Postwar German Prose. (European University Studies, German Language & Literature: Ser. 1, Vol. 45). 128p. 1971. pap. 18.25 (ISBN 3-261-00044-9). P Lang Pubs.
--The Writer & Society: Studies in the Fiction of Guenter Grass & Heinrich Boll. (European University Studies, German Language & Literature: Ser. 1, Vol. 139). 76p. 1976. pap. 11.75 (ISBN 3-261-01861-5). P Lang Pubs.
Ghurye, G. S. Gods & Men. 1962. 39.50x (ISBN 0-317-27474-0). Elliots Bks.
--The Scheduled Tribes of India. LC 79-66430. (Social Science Classics Ser.). 399p. 1980. text ed. 29.95 (ISBN 0-87855-308-8); pap. 7.95 (ISBN 0-87855-692-3). Transaction Bks.
--Vedic India. 1979. 46.00 (ISBN 0-89684-061-1, Pub. by Motilal Banarsidass India). Orient Bk Dist.
Ghurye, Govind S. Whither India? LC 74-901838. 431p. 1974. 26.00x (ISBN 0-89684-467-6). Orient Bk Dist.
Ghyka, Matila. The Geometry of Art & Life. 2nd ed. LC 77-78586. 1978. pap. 3.50 (ISBN 0-486-23542-4). Dover.
GI Conference on Theoretical Computer Science, 3rd, Darmstadt, Mar. 1977. Theoretical Computer Science. Tzschach, H. & Waldschmidt, K. G., eds. (Lecture Notes in Computer Science: Vol. 48). 1977. soft cover 25.00 (ISBN 3-540-08138-0). Springer-Verlag.
GI Conference, 2nd, Karlsruhe, May 20-23, 1975. Automata Theory & Formal Languages. Brakhage, H., ed. (Lecture Notes in Computer Science: Vol. 33). viii, 292p. 1975. pap. 18.00 (ISBN 0-387-07407-4). Springer-Verlag.
Giacaglia, G. E., ed. see COSPAR-IAU-IUTAM Symposium, Sao Paulo, Brazil, June 19-21, 1974.
Giacaglia, G. E., ed. see Symposium, University of Sao Paulo, 1969.
Giacconi & Ruffini, R. Physics & Astrophysics of Neutron Stars & Black Holes: Proceedings. (Enrico Fermi Summer School Ser.: Vol. 65). 876p. 1980. pap. 57.50 (ISBN 0-444-85446-0, North-Holland). Elsevier.
Giacconi, Mirella, jt. auth. see Caglioti, Luciano.
Giacconi, Mirella, tr. see Rigutti, Mario.
Giacconi, R. & Gursky, H., eds. X-Ray Astronomy. LC 74-79569. (Astrophysics & Space Science Library: No. 43). 450p. 1974. lib. bdg. 76.00 (ISBN 90-277-0295-0, Pub. by Reidel Holland); pap. 34.00 (ISBN 90-277-0387-6). Kluwer Academic.
Giacconi, Riccardo. X-Ray Astronomy. 1981. 44.50 (ISBN 90-277-1261-1, Pub. by Reidel Holland). Kluwer Academic.
Giacconi, Riccardo, jt. auth. see Tucker, Wallace.
Giacconi, Richard & Setti, Giancarlo, eds. X-Ray Astronomy. (NATO Advanced Study Institutes Series, C. Mathematical & Physical Sciences: No. 60). 400p. 1980. lib. bdg. 47.50 (ISBN 90-277-1156-9, Pub. by Reidel Holland). Kluwer Academic.
Giachery, Ugo. Shoghi Effendi: Recollections. (Illus.). 248p. 1973. 14.95 (ISBN 0-85398-050-0, 331-065). G Ronald Pub.
Giachino, J. W. Arc Welding. (Illus.). 1977. pap. text ed. 7.95 (ISBN 0-8269-3083-2). Am Technical.
Giachino, J. W. & Beukema, H. J. Engineering Technical Drafting. 4th ed. (Illus.). 730p. 1978. 24.00 (ISBN 0-8269-1154-4). Am Technical.
--Everyday Sketching & Drafting. 2nd ed. (Illus.). 172p. 1973. pap. 9.95 (ISBN 0-8269-1162-5). Am Technical.
--Freehand Sketching. 2nd ed. (Illus.). 116p. 1973. pap. 7.95 (ISBN 0-8269-1022-X). Am Technical.
--Print Reading for Welders. 2nd ed. 1978. 11.95 (ISBN 0-8269-3022-0). Am Technical.
Giachino, J. W. & Gallington, R. O. Course Construction in Industrial Arts, Vocational & Technical Education. 4th ed. 1977. text ed. 18.95 (ISBN 0-8269-4065-X). Am Technical.
Giachino, J. W., et al. Welding Technology. 2nd ed. (Illus.). 1973. 18.95 (ISBN 0-8269-3063-8). Am Technical.
Giachino, Joseph W. Gas Welding. LC 76-51152. (Illus.). pap. 24.00 (ISBN 0-317-11070-5, 2015730). Bks Demand UMI.
Giachino, Joseph W. & Beukema, Henry J. Drafting Technology. 2nd ed. LC 64-12817. (Illus.). pap. 116.00 (ISBN 0-317-10628-7, 2011278). Bks Demand UMI.
--Engineering Drafting Problems. LC 73-75065. (Illus.). pap. 26.00 (ISBN 0-317-10654-6, 2012977). Bks Demand UMI.
Giachino, Joseph W. & Weeks, W. Welding Skills. (Illus.). 432p. 1985. 19.95 (ISBN 0-8269-3001-8, Dist. by Sterling). Am Technical.
Giachino, Joseph W., et al. Welding Skills & Practices. LC 77-123471. pap. 108.00 (ISBN 0-317-10910-3, 2012979). Bks Demand UMI.
Giacobini, Ezio, et al, eds. The Aging Brain: Cellular & Molecular Mechanism of Aging in the Nervous System. (Aging Ser.: Vol. 20). 304p. 1982. text ed. 48.50 (ISBN 0-89004-802-9). Raven.
--Tissue Culture in Neurobiology. 530p. 1980. text ed. 74.50 (ISBN 0-89004-461-9). Raven.
Giacoletto, L. J. Electronics Designer's Handbook. 2nd ed. 1977. 86.50 (ISBN 0-07-023149-4). McGraw.
Giacomelli, Mario. Mario Giacomelli. Alinder, James, ed. LC 83-81265. (Untitled Ser.: No.32). (Illus.). 1983. pap. 16.00 (ISBN 0-933286-34-1). Friends Photography.
Giacomini, Afton. Trophy Winning Facet Cuts. Cox, Jack R., ed. (Illus.). 32p. 1974. pap. text ed. 2.50 (ISBN 0-910652-19-8). Gembooks.
Giacomini, Edward D. & California Continuing Education of the Bar. Financing California Businesses. LC 76-19641. 1976. 65.00 (ISBN 0-88124-041-9). Cal Cont Ed Bar.
Giacomini, Edward D., et al. Advising California Employers. LC 81-65536. (Illus.). xiv, 635p. 1981. 70.00 (ISBN 0-88124-078-8). Cal Cont Ed Bar.
Giacomino, Don E. Accounting Two - Accounting for Management Decision-Making. 169p. 1981. 14.95 (ISBN 0-318-13857-3). Credit Union Natl Assn.
Giacomo, Giuseppe & Illica, Luigi, eds. La Boheme. (Metropolitan Opera Classics Library). 224p. 1983. 17.45i (ISBN 0-316-56838-4); pap. 9.70i (ISBN 0-316-56839-2). Little.
Giacomo, James Di see Di Giacomo, James.
Giacomo, M., jt. auth. see Dubois, J.
Giacomo, P., jt. auth. see Ferro Milone, A.
Giacomo Da Lentino. Poetry of Giacomo Da Lentino. (Harvard Studies in Romance Languages). 1915. 18.00 (ISBN 0-527-01099-5). Kraus Repr.
Giaconni, Mirella, tr. see Bellone, Enrico.
Giaconni, R., ed. see International Astronomical Union Symposium, 55, Madrid, May 11-13, 1972.
Giaconni, Ricardo, tr. see Bellone, Enrico.
Giacosa, Giorgio. Uomo e Cavallo Sulla Moneta Greca. 1973. 37.50 (ISBN 0-318-03945-1). Numismatic Fine Arts.
Giacovazzo, Carmelo. Direct Methods in Crystallography. 1980. 70.00 (ISBN 0-12-282450-4). Acad Pr.
Giaever, John. White Desert: The Official Account of the Norwegian-British-Swedish Antarctic Expedition. Huggard, E. M., tr. LC 69-10097. (Illus.). 1969. Repr. of 1954 ed. lib. bdg. 16.00x (ISBN 0-8371-1318-0, GIWD). Greenwood.
Gia-Fu Feng, ed. see Chuang Tsu.
Gia-Fu Feng, ed. see Lao Tsu.
Giallombardo, Rose. Juvenile Delinquency: A Book of Readings. 4th ed. LC 81-6927. 591p. 1982. pap. text ed. 17.50 (ISBN 0-471-08344-5). Wiley.

--The Social World of Imprisoned Girls. LC 80-22340. 328p. 1981. Repr. of 1974 ed. text ed. 22.50 (ISBN 0-89874-285-4). Krieger.

--Society of Women: A Study of a Women's Prison. LC 66-14132. 244p. 1966. pap. text ed. 18.95x (ISBN 0-471-29729-1). Wiley.

Giallombardo, Rose, ed. Contemporary Social Issues: A Reader. LC 74-32306. (Illus.). pap. 155.80 (ISBN 0-317-09399-1, 2055104). Bks Demand UMI.

Giamatti, A. Bartlett. Earthly Paradise & the Renaissance Epic. 1966. pap. 11.95 (ISBN 0-691-01292-X). Princeton U Pr.

--Exile & Change in Renaissance Literature. LC 83-12561. 184p. 1984. 15.95x (ISBN 0-300-03074-6). Yale U Pr.

--Western Literature, 3 vols. Incl. Vol. 1. The Ancient World. Von Staden, Heinrich, ed. 550p. pap. (ISBN 0-15-595276-5); Vol. 2. The Middle Ages, Renaissance, Enlightenment. Hollander, Robert, ed. 550p. pap. (ISBN 0-15-595277-3); Vol. 3. The Modern World. Brooks, Peter, ed. 552p. pap. (ISBN 0-15-595278-1). 1971. 12.95 ea. (HC); instructor's manual avail. (ISBN 0-15-595279-X, HC). HarBraceJ.

Giamatti, Valentine. Minimum of Italian Grammar & Answer Key. 1964. pap. 6.50x (ISBN 0-913298-13-1). S F Vanni.

Giammati, A. Bartlett, ed. Dante in America: The First Two Centuries. LC 83-2350. (Medieval & Renaissance Texts & Studies: Vol. 23). 430p. 1983. 20.00 (ISBN 0-86698-059-8). Medieval & Renaissance NY.

Giammattei, Helen, jt. auth. see Davis, Mary K.

Giammattei, Victor M. & Anderson, Jamie G. Training Programs & Careers in Animal Health Technology & Veterinary Nursing in North America. LC 84-73071. (Illus.). 146p. 1985. pap. 12.00 (ISBN 0-916280-01-2). Dillon-Tyler Pubs.

Giammattei, Victor M. & Reichert, N. Greer. Art of a Vanished Race: The Mimbres Classic Black-on-White. LC 75-28600. (Illus.). 96p. 1975. pap. 6.95 (ISBN 0-916280-00-4). Dillon-Tyler Pubs.

Giammatteo, Dolores M., jt. auth. see Giammatteo, Michael C.

Giammatteo, Michael C. Beyond Relevancy: A Book for Teachers of the Future. (Illus.). 1973. pap. 6.00 (ISBN 0-918428-09-2). Sylvan Inst.

--The Box, the Amoeba, & the Egg: The Flow to Self-Discovery. (Illus.). 1974. pap. 4.00 (ISBN 0-918428-07-6). Sylvan Inst.

--Circles of Life. (Illus., Orig.). 1973. pap. 4.00 (ISBN 0-918428-01-7). Sylvan Inst.

--Hear It Straight: The I.A.I. Process...to Help Us Communicate. (Illus.). 1974. pap. 4.00 (ISBN 0-918428-06-8). Sylvan Inst.

--Insights About Your Outsides. (Illus.). 1974. pap. 4.00 (ISBN 0-918428-00-9). Sylvan Inst.

--The Intimidators. (Illus., Orig.). pap. 4.00 (ISBN 0-918428-03-3). Sylvan Inst.

--Myths Away, or Myths Are a Way. (Illus., Orig.). 1973. pap. 4.00 (ISBN 0-918428-04-1). Sylvan Inst.

--The Power Seekers. (Illus., Orig.). 1973. pap. 4.00 (ISBN 0-918428-02-5). Sylvan Inst.

--Rings Around Your Mind: How to Program Your Mind to Control Stress, Fear, & Self-Destructive Behavior Patterns. (Illus.). 1976. pap. text ed. 6.00 (ISBN 0-918428-08-4). Sylvan Inst.

--The Thin Fine Line. (Illus., Orig.). 1975. pap. 4.00 (ISBN 0-918428-05-X). Sylvan Inst.

Giammatteo, Michael C. & Giammatteo, Dolores M. Executive Well-Being, Stress & Administrators. 72p. (Orig.). 1980. pap. text ed. 6.00 (ISBN 0-88210-104-8). Natl Assn Principals.

Giammatteo, Michael C., ed. The Transescence: The Child in the Middle. 73p. 1980. pap. text ed. 5.00 (ISBN 0-918428-11-4). Sylvan Inst.

Giammatteo, Michael C., et al. Forces on Leadership. 80p. 1981. pap. 6.00 (ISBN 0-88210-116-1). Natl Assn Principals.

Giammatteo, Mike & Mattox, Phil. Paths of Life. (Illus.). 1977. 4.00 (ISBN 0-918428-10-6). Sylvan Inst.

Giammatti, Victor M. Raising Small Meat Animals. LC 75-21050. 1976. 18.50 (ISBN 0-8134-1741-4); text ed. 13.95x. Interstate.

Giampa, Janice. Pasta Fantasia. (Illus.). 128p. 1983. pap. 9.95 (ISBN 0-933614-22-5). Peregrine Pr.

Giampalmi, Joe. Complete Book of Linebacker Play. LC 83-13437. 156p. 1983. 15.95 (ISBN 0-13-157511-2, Busn). P-H.

Giampetruzzi, Louis. Contemporary Accordian. 1981. pap. 7.95 (ISBN 0-8256-0240-8, Oak). Music Sales.

Gianakaris, C. J. Julius Caesar. LC 83-48273. 350p. 1985. lib. bdg. 47.00 (ISBN 0-8240-9072-1). Garland Pub.

Gianakaris, C. J., jt. ed. see Davidson, Clifford.

Gianakos, Larry J. Television Drama Programming: A Comprehensive Chronicle, 1975-1980. LC 81-5319. 471p. 1981. 27.50 (ISBN 0-8108-1438-2). Scarecrow.

--Television Drama Series Programming: A Comprehensive Chronicle, 1947-1959. LC 80-17023. 581p. 1980. 35.00 (ISBN 0-8108-1330-0). Scarecrow.

--Television Drama Series Programming: A Comprehensive Chronicle, 1959-1975. LC 78-650. 806p. 1978. 37.50 (ISBN 0-8108-1116-2). Scarecrow.

--Television Drama Series Programming: A Comprehensive Chronicle, 1980-1982. LC 83-3388. 686p. 1983. 45.00 (ISBN 0-8108-1626-1). Scarecrow.

Gianakos, Perry E., ed. see Ade, George.

Gianakoulis, Theodore. The Land & People of Greece. rev. ed. LC 75-37745. (Portraits of the Nations Ser.). (Illus.). (gr. 6 up). 1972. 9.89 (ISBN 0-397-31523-6). Lipp Jr Bks.

Gianaris, Nicholas V. Economic Development: Thought & Problems. 1978. 14.95 (ISBN 0-8158-0355-9). Chris Mass.

--The Economics of the Balkan Countries: Albania, Bulgaria, Greece, Romania, Turkey, & Yugoslavia. LC 81-10748. 204p. 1982. 31.95x (ISBN 0-03-060232-7). Praeger.

--Greece & Yugoslavia: An Economic Comparision. LC 83-27010. 272p. 1984. 34.95 (ISBN 0-03-071466-4). Praeger.

Gianatsis, Jim. Design & Tuning for Motorcross. LC 80-28239. (Illus.). 96p. (Orig.). 1981. pap. 10.95 (ISBN 0-87938-129-9). Motorbooks Intl.

Gianburco, Carolyn, ed. see Rosand, Ellen.

Giancana, Antoinette & Renner, Thomas C. Mafia Princess: Growing Up in Sam Giancana's Family. LC 83-63294. (Illus.). 448p. 1984. 15.95 (ISBN 0-688-02620-6). Morrow.

--Mafia Princess: Growing Up in Sam Giancana's Family. 408p. 1985. pap. 3.95 (ISBN 0-380-69849-8). Avon.

Gian-Carlo Rota, jt. auth. see Birkhoff, Garrett.

Giancoli, Douglas C. General Physics. (Illus.). 976p. 1984. text ed. 42.95 (ISBN 0-13-350884-6). P-H.

--General Physics, Vol. II. LC 84-8432. (Illus.). 480p. 1984. text ed. 25.95 (ISBN 0-13-350992-3). P-H.

--General Physics, Vol. I. (Illus.). 480p. 1984. text ed. 25.95 (ISBN 0-13-350984-2). P-H.

--The Ideas of Physics. 2nd ed. (Illus.). 528p. 1978. text ed. 23.95 (ISBN 0-15-540559-4, HC); instructor's manual avail. (ISBN 0-15-540560-8). HarBraceJ.

--Physics: Principles with Applications. 2nd ed. (Illus.). 864p. 1985. text ed. 35.95 (ISBN 0-13-672627-5); study guide by Joseph Boyle 12.95 (ISBN 0-13-672635-6). P-H.

Gianelli, Domenic W. The Story of My Life. LC 83-90940. 1984. 8.95 (ISBN 0-533-05948-8). Vantage.

Giangrande, Carole. The Nuclear North: The People, the Regions & the Arms Race. 232p. (Orig.). 1983. pap. 9.95 (ISBN 0-88784-136-8, Pub. by Hse Anansi Pr Canada). U of Toronto Pr.

Giangrande, G., ed. Corolla Londiniensis, Vol. 2. 214p. 1982. pap. text ed. 28.25x (ISBN 90-70265-35-4, Pub. by Gieben Holland). Humanities.

Giangrande, Giuseppe, ed. Corolla Londiniensis. (London Studies in Classical Philology: No. 8). 177p. 1981. text ed. 28.25x (ISBN 9-070265-63-X, Pub. by Gieben Holland). Humanities.

Giangrande, Lawrence. The Use of "Spoudaiogeloion" in Greek & Roman Literature. LC 78-182466. (Studies in Classical Lit. Ser.: Vol. 6). 1972. pap. text ed. 11.20x (ISBN 0-686-22637-2). Mouton.

Giangrasso, et al. Basic Mathematics: A Problem Solving Approach. (Illus.). 448p. (Orig.). 1983. pap. text ed. 14.95 (ISBN 0-8403-3129-0). Kendall-Hunt.

Giangreco, C. Joseph & Giangreco, Marianne R. Education of the Hearing Impaired. (Illus.). 204p. 1976. pap. 15.50x (ISBN 0-398-00673-3). C C Thomas.

Giangreco, Marianne R. Canoe Country Poems. 44p. 1981. 4.95 (ISBN 0-935054-05-7). Webb-Newcomb.

Giangreco, Marianne R., jt. auth. see Giangreco, C. Joseph.

Giannakopoulos, G. & Siarenos, E. Greek-English, English-Greek Dictinary of the 20th Century, 2 Vols. 1984. Set. 50.00 (ISBN 0-317-26246-7, Pub. by P Efstathiadis & Sons Greece). Greek-English 650 P. English-Greek 700 P. Heinman.

Giannasi, David E. The Flavonoid Systematics of the Genus Dahlia: Compositae. LC 66-6394. (Memoirs of the New York Botanical Garden: Vol. 26, No. 2). (Illus.). 1975. pap. 12.00x (ISBN 0-89327-019-9). NY Botanical.

Giannella, Donald A., ed. Religion & the Public Order: An Annual Review of Church & State & of Religion, Law, & Society. LC 64-17164. pap. 72.00 (ISBN 0-317-20699-0, 2024114). Bks Demand UMI.

Giannella, M., jt. auth. see Melchiorre, C.

Giannelli, F. Human Chromosomes DNA Synthesis. Beckman, L. & Hauge, M., eds. (Monographs in Human Genetics: Vol. 5). 1970. 20.00 (ISBN 3-8055-0448-9). S Karger.

Giannelli, F., jt. auth. see Adinolfi, Matteo.

Giannelli, Paul C. Giannelli, Ohio Evidence Manual. (Baldwin's Ohio Practice Ser.). 696p. 1982. Annual cum. supp. 85.00 (ISBN 0-8322-0026-3). Banks-Baldwin.

Giannelli, Paul C., jt. auth. see Kurtz, William A.

Giannelli, Paul C., ed. Ohio Rules of Evidence Handbook. 296p. 1980. pap. 28.50 (ISBN 0-8322-0051-4). Banks-Baldwin.

Giannetti, Louis. Masters of the American Cinema. 255p. 1981. text ed. 24.95 (ISBN 0-13-560110-X); pap. text ed. 20.95 (ISBN 0-13-560102-9). P-H.

--Understanding Movies. 3rd ed. (Illus.). 512p. 1982. pap. 18.95 (ISBN 0-13-936310-6). P-H.

Giannetti, Louis & Eyman, Scott. Flashback: A Brief History of Film. (Illus.). 480p. 1986. pap. text ed. 19.95 (ISBN 0-13-322223-3). P-H.

Giannetti, Louis D. Godard & Others: Essays on Film Form. LC 73-2893. (Illus.). 184p. 1975. 20.00 (ISBN 0-8386-1291-1). Fairleigh Dickinson.

Giannini, A. James. The Biological Foundations of Clinical Psychiatry. 1985. pap. text ed. price not set (ISBN 0-87488-449-7). Med Exam.

--Psychiatric, Psychogenic, & Somatopsychic Disorders Handbook. 1978. pap. 17.95 (ISBN 0-87488-596-5). Med Exam.

Giannini, A. James & Slaby, Andrew E. Handbook of Overdose & Detoxification Emergencies. 1982. pap. text ed. 16.95 (ISBN 0-87488-182-X). Med Exam.

Giannini, Allan V. The Best Guide to Allergy. (Appleton Consumer Health Guides Ser.). (Illus.). 134p. 1981. 15.95 (ISBN 0-8385-0645-3); pap. 9.95 (ISBN 0-8385-0644-5). ACC.

Giannini, David. Stem. 1982. 3.00 (ISBN 0-934834-29-6). White Pine.

Giannini, Vera, tr. see Silvan, Matthew.

Gianniny, Omer A., Jr., jt. auth. see Vaughan, Joseph L.

Giannitrapani, D. The Electrophysiology of Intellectual Functions. (Illus.). xvi, 248p. 1985. 70.00 (ISBN 3-8055-3878-2). S Karger.

Giannitrapani, Duilio. The Electrophysiology of Intellectual Functions. 248p. 1985. 98.25. Transaction Bks.

Giannone, Richard. Music in Willa Cather's Fiction. LC 67-10664. pap. 66.50 (ISBN 0-317-09853-5, 2022556). Bks Demand UMI.

Giannoni, Carlo B. Conventionalism in Logic: A Study in the Linguistic Foundation of Logical Reasoning. (Janua Linguarum, Ser. Major: No. 46). 157p. 1971. text ed. 17.60x (ISBN 0-686-22486-8). Mouton.

Giannotti, John B. & Smith, Richard W. Treasury Management: A Practitioners Handbook. 508p. 1981. 64.50 (ISBN 0-471-08062-4). Wiley.

--Treasury Management Practioners' Handbook: A Practical Approach to Treasury Management in the Multinational Corporation. LC 8-1523. 536p. 1981. 64.50x (Pub. by Wiley Interscience). Wiley.

Giannoulas, Ted & Strasberg, Andy. The Famous Chicken Baseball Quiz Book. LC 84-50261. (Illus.). 128p. (Orig.). 1984. pap. 4.95 (ISBN 0-915391-00-7). Slawson Comm.

Gianos, Mary P., ed. Introduction to Modern Greek Literature. LC 67-30722. 1969. text ed. 29.50x (ISBN 0-8057-3125-3); pap. text ed. 16.50x (ISBN 0-89197-801-1). Irvington.

Gianos, Phillip L. Political Behavior: Metaphors & Models of American Politics. LC 81-83361. 246p. 1982. pap. 8.95x (ISBN 0-913530-26-3). Palisades Pub.

Gianotti, Charles R. The New Testament & the Mishnah. 1983. pap. 3.50 (ISBN 0-8010-3791-3). Baker Bk.

Gianotti, J. G., jt. ed. see Griffin, O. M.

Gianpietri, Peter. The Successful Rules of Artistic Composition. (Illus.). 154p. 1983. 79.75x (ISBN 0-86650-080-4). Gloucester Art.

Gianquinta, Mariano. Multiple Integrals in the Calculus of Variations & Nonlinear Elliptic Systems. LC 82-24072. (Annals of Mathematics Studies: No. 105). 313p. 1983. 35.00x (ISBN 0-691-08330-4); pap. text ed. 16.50x (ISBN 0-691-08331-2). Princeton U Pr.

Giansiracusa, David F. & Kantrowitz, Fred G. Rheumatic & Metabolic Bone Diseases in the Elderly. LC 79-57515. (Illus.). 240p. 1981. 25.95 (ISBN 0-669-03630-7, Collamore). Heath.

Giantssod, Lemuel. Gulliver's Travelimericks II: A Voyage to Brobdingnag Pt. I. (Limericklets Ser.). (Illus.). 1984. pap. cancelled (ISBN 0-938338-56-0). Winds World Pr.

Giantssod, Lemul. Gulliver's Travelimericks III: A Voyage to Brobdingnag Pt. II. (Limericklets Ser.). (Illus.). 1984. pap. cancelled (ISBN 0-938338-57-9). Winds World Pr.

Gianturco. Allessandro Stradella. (Italian Cantata in the 17th Century Ser.). 1985. text ed. 60.00 (ISBN 0-8240-8883-2). Garland Pub.

Gianturco, Carolyn, ed. Carlo Capellini, Vol. 16. (The Italian Cantana in the 17th Century Ser.). 60.00 (ISBN 0-8240-8890-5). Garland Pub.

Gianturco, Carolyn, ed. see Biagi, Gabriella.

Gianturco, Carolyn, ed. see Lindgren, Lowwell.

Gianturco, Carolyn, ed. see Massenkeil, Gunther.

Gianturco, Daniel T. & Smith, Harmon L. The Promiscuous Teenager. (Illus.). 128p. 1974. 12.75x (ISBN 0-398-03117-7). C C Thomas.

Gianturco, F. The Transfer of Molecular Energies by Collision: Recent Quantum Treatments. (Lecture Notes in Chemistry: Vol. 11). (Illus.). 327p. 1979. pap. 25.00 (ISBN 0-387-09701-5). Springer-Verlag.

Gianturco, F. A. & Stefani, G., eds. Wavefunctions & Mechanisms from Electron Scattering Processes. (Lecture Notes in Chemistry Ser.: Vol. 35). ix, 279p. 1984. 19.70 (ISBN 0-387-13347-X). Springer-Verlag.

Gianturco, Franco A., ed. Atomic & Molecular Collision Theory. LC 81-15362. (NATO ASI Series B, Physics: Vol. 71). 525p. 1982. 75.00x (ISBN 0-306-40807-4, Plenum Pr). Plenum Pub.

Giantvalley, Scott. Walt Whitman, Eighteen Thirty-Eight to Nineteen Thirty-Nine: A Reference Guide. 1981. lib. bdg. 52.00 (ISBN 0-8161-7856-9, Hall Reference). G K Hall.

Gianuario, Annibale, jt. auth. see Anfuso, Nella.

Gianutsos, Rosamond, jt. ed. see Ebihara, May.

Giap, Vo Nguyen. How We Won the War. LC 76-5629. (Illus.). 64p. 1976. pap. 4.00 (ISBN 0-916894-01-0). Recon Pubns.

--The Military Art of People's War: Selected Writings of General Vo Nguyen Giap. Stetler, Russell, ed. LC 75-105317. pap. 63.90 (ISBN 0-317-11270-8, 2019254). Bks Demand UMI.

Giaquinta, Guglielmo. Tomorrow's Priests. Apostolic Oblates Of Stanton Calif, tr. LC 70-114408. 1970. pap. 0.95 (ISBN 0-8198-0164-X). Dghtrs St Paul.

Giarchi, George G. Between McAlpine & Polaris: A Social Inscape Study. 256p. (Orig.). 1984. pap. 25.00x (ISBN 0-7100-9435-3). Routledge & Kegan.

Giardina, Anthony. Men with Debts. LC 83-47958. 280p. 1984. 13.95 (ISBN 0-394-52834-4). Knopf.

Giardina, Denise. Good King Harry. LC 83-48823. 448p. 1984. 15.86 (ISBN 0-06-015277-X, HarpT). Har-Row.

Giardinelli, Mempo. El Cielo con las Manos. 173p. (Span.). 1981. pap. 8.00 (ISBN 0-910061-04-1, 1105). Ediciones Norte.

--Vidas Ejemplares. 141p. (Span.). 1982. pap. 7.00 (ISBN 0-910061-11-4, 1110). Ediciones Norte.

Giaretto, Henry. Intergrated Treatment of Child Sexual Abuse. LC 81-86712. 25.00 (ISBN 0-8314-0061-7). Sci & Behavior.

Giarini, O. Cycles, Value & Employment: Response to the Economic Crisis. (Illus.). 90p. 1984. 22.00 (ISBN 0-08-031284-5); pap. 10.50 (ISBN 0-08-031283-7). Pergamon.

Giarini, Orio. Dialogue on Wealth & Welfare: An Alternative View of World Capital Formation, a Report to the Club of Rome. (Illus.). 368p. 1980. pap. 24.00 (ISBN 0-08-026087-X). Pergamon.

Giarini, Orio & Louberge, Henri. The Diminishing Returns of Technology: An Essay on the Crisis in Economic Growth. 1978. pap. text ed. 8.50 (ISBN 0-08-023337-6). Pergamon.

Giarrantani, Frank. Regional & Interregional Input-Output Analysis: An Annotated Bibliography. LC 75-45868. 1976. 6.00 (ISBN 0-89092-008-7). West Va U Pr.

Giarrantani, Frank, jt. auth. see Miernyk, William H.

Giarratani, Frank, jt. auth. see Hoover, Edgar M.

Giarratano, Joseph. Foundations of Computer Technology. Incl. Modern Computer Concepts. Giarratano, Joseph. 272p. pap. 22.95 (ISBN 0-672-21815-1, 21815); Set of 2 vols. pap. 39.95 (ISBN 0-672-21816-X, 21816). 240p. 1983. pap. 22.95 (ISBN 0-672-21814-3, 21814). Sams.

Giarratano, Joseph C. BASIC: Advanced Concepts, 4 vols. LC 82-50018. 214p. 1982. pap. 22.95 (ISBN 0-672-21942-5, 21942); Vols. 3 & 4. 39.95 (21943-3); Vols. 1-4. 69.95 (22045-8). Sams.

--BASIC: Fundamental Concepts. LC 82-50017. 198p. 1982. pap. 22.95 (ISBN 0-672-21941-7, 21941). Sams.

--Commodore 64 BASIC Guide. Starnes, C., ed. 200p. 1984. pap. 14.95 (ISBN 0-913847-01-1). Computext Inc.

Gibaldi & Perrier. Pharmacokinetics. (Drugs & the Pharmaceutical Sciences Ser.). 432p. 1982. 34.50 (ISBN 0-8247-1042-8). Dekker.

Gibaldi, Joseph & Achtert, Walter S. A Guide to Professional Organizations for Teachers of Language & Literature. vii, 62p. 1978. pap. 5.00x (ISBN 0-87352-125-0, W325). Modern Lang.

--MLA Handbook for Writers of Research Papers. 2nd ed. 222p. 1984. pap. text ed. 7.95x (ISBN 0-87352-132-3). Modern Lang.

Gibaldi, Joseph, jt. auth. see Achtert, Walter S.

Gibaldi, Joseph, jt. auth. see Clements, Robert J.

Gibaldi, Joseph, ed. Approaches to Teaching Chaucer's Canterbury Tales. LC 80-22909. (Approaches to Teaching Masterpieces of World Literature Ser.: No. 1). xvi, 175p. (Orig.). 1980. 25.00x (ISBN 0-87352-476-4); pap. 12.50x (ISBN 0-87352-475-6). Modern Lang.

--Introduction to Scholarship in Modern Languages & Literatures. LC 81-1254. xi, 143p. 1981. 19.00x (ISBN 0-87352-092-0, T150C); pap. 9.50 (ISBN 0-87352-093-9, T150P). Modern Lang.

Gibaldi, Joseph & Mirollo, James V., eds. The Teaching Apprentice Program in Language & Literature. LC 81-1159. (Options for Teaching Ser.: No. 4). ix, 133p. (Orig.). 1981. pap. 11.00x (ISBN 0-87352-303-2, J203). Modern Lang.

Gibaldi, Joseph, ed. see Barricelli, Jean-Pierre, et al.

Gibaldi, M. Handbook of Clinical Pharmacokinetics. 1181p. 1983. text ed. 98.00 (ISBN 0-683-10004-1). Williams & Wilkins.

Gibaldi, Milo. Biopharmaceutics & Clinical Pharmacokinetics. 3rd ed. LC 83-13593. (Illus.). 330p. 1984. text ed. 22.50 (ISBN 0-8121-0896-5). Lea & Febiger.

--Biopharmaceutics & Clinical Pharmacokinetics. 2nd ed. Lea & Febiger.

Gibat. The Lore of Still Building. Rev. ed. 188p. 1980. pap. 5.00 (ISBN 0-686-92658-7). Rutan Pub.

Gibat, jt. auth. see Howard.

Gibb, Allan & Webb, Terry. Policy Issues in Small Business Research. 224p. 1980. text ed. 37.95x (ISBN 0-566-00312-0). Gower Pub Co.
Gibb, Andrew. Glasgow: The Making of a City. (Illus.). 197p. 1983. 25.25 (ISBN 0-7099-0161-5, Pub. by Croom Helm Ltd); pap. 11.95 (ISBN 0-7099-1169-6). Longwood Pub Group.
Gibb, C. C. More Than Enough. 83p. pap. 4.95 (ISBN 0-88172-071-2). Believers Bkshelf.
Gibb, Christopher. Richard the Lionheart & the Crusades. (Life & Times Ser.). (Illus.). 64p. (gr. 7-9). 1985. price not set (Pub. by Bookwright Pr). Watts.
Gibb, D. M., jt. auth. see Studd, John.
Gibb, Elias. Ottoman Literature. 59.95 (ISBN 0-8490-0781-X). Gordon Pr.
Gibb, George, ed. see Lam, Roger.
Gibb, George S. The Whitesmiths of Taunton: A History of Reed & Barton, 1824-1943. LC 75-41755. (Companies & Men: Business Enterprises in America). (Illus.). 242p. 1976. Repr. of 1943 ed. 46.50x (ISBN 0-405-08071-9). Ayer Co Pubs.
Gibb, George S., jt. auth. see Hidy, Ralph W.
Gibb, George S., jt. auth. see Wall, Bennett H.
Gibb, H. A. Modern Trends in Islam. LC 76-159188. xiii, 141p. 1971. Repr. of 1947 ed. lib. bdg. 18.50x (ISBN 0-374-93046-5). Octagon.
--The Travels of IBN Battuta, A.D. 1325-1354, 2 vols. in one, Vols. 110, 117. Defremery, C. & Sanguimetti, B. R., trs. from Arabic. (Hakluyt Society Works Series II). (Illus.). 1962. 72.00 (ISBN 0-317-15075-8). Kraus Repr.
Gibb, H. A. & Kramers, J. H., eds. Shorter Encyclopedia of Islam. (Illus.). 678p. 1957. 85.00x (ISBN 0-8014-0150-X). Cornell U Pr.
Gibb, H. A., tr. see Ibn Al-Qalanisi.
Gibb, H. A., et al see Lewis, B., et al.
Gibb, H. A. R., ed. see Defremery, C. & Sanguinetti, B. R.
Gibb, Hamilton A. Arab Conquests in Central Asia. LC 75-11477. (BCL Ser.: I). Repr. of 1923 ed. 16.00 (ISBN 0-404-02718-0). AMS Pr.
--Mohammedanism: An Historical Survey. 2nd ed. 1953. pap. 5.95x (ISBN 0-19-500245-8, 90). Oxford U Pr.
--Studies on the Civilization of Islam. Shaw, Stanford J. & Polk, William R., eds. LC 81-47987. 369p. 1982. pap. 11.95x (ISBN 0-691-00786-1). Princeton U Pr.
Gibb, Hamilton A., ed. Whither Islam? A Survey of Modern Movements in the Moslem World. LC 73-180338. Repr. of 1932 ed. 27.00 (ISBN 0-404-56263-9). AMS Pr.
Gibb, Henry & Gibb, Laurie. Ski Touring with Kids: A Guide to Winter Activities with Children. LC 81-15748. (Illus.). 200p. (Orig.). 1982. pap. 8.95 (ISBN 0-87108-596-8). Pruett.
Gibb, J. M., ed. Venture Capital Markets for the Regeneration of Industry: Proceedings of the 4th Symposium on the Financing & Innovation, Held by the Commission of the European Communities, Luxembourg 23-25, Nov., 1983. 348p. 1984. 35.25 (ISBN 0-444-87567-0). Elsevier.
Gibb, Jack R. Trust: A New View of Personal & Organizational Development. 1978. 15.00 (ISBN 0-89615-006-2); pap. 8.95. Omicron Pr.
Gibb, James. The Book of Sherborne. 1981. 40.00x (ISBN 0-86023-081-3, Pub. by Barracuda England). State Mutual Bk.
Gibb, John & Montgomery, William. The Confessions of Augustine. 2nd ed. LC 78-66639. (Ancient Philosophy Ser.). 554p. 1982. lib. bdg. 67.00 (ISBN 0-8240-9597-9). Garland Pub.
Gibb, John, ed. see Augustine.
Gibb, Laurie, jt. auth. see Gibb, Henry.
Gibb, Robert. The Names of the Earth in Summer. (Stone Country Poetry Ser.: No. 14). (Illus.). 64p. (Orig.). 1983. pap. 6.00x (ISBN 0-930020-13-8). Stone Country.
--The Winter House: Poems. LC 83-16841. (Breakthrough Ser.: No. 43). 80p. 1984. pap. 6.95 (ISBN 0-8262-0437-6). U of MO Pr.
Gibb, Robin, et al. Bee Gees: The Biography. Leaf, David, ed. LC 78-74097. (Illus.). 1979. 6.95 (ISBN 0-440-04072-8). Delilah Bks.
Gibb, Sandra, jt. auth. see Fredericksson, Jaye.
Gibb, Terence C. Principles of Mossbauer Spectroscopy. 254p. 1976. 43.00x (ISBN 0-412-13960-X, NO. 6123, Pub. by Chapman & Hall England); pap. 19.95x (ISBN 0-412-23060-7, NO. 6586, Pub. by Chapman & Hall England). Methuen Inc.
Gibb, Thomas R., Jr., ed. Analytical Methods in Oceanography. new ed. LC 75-41463. (Advances in Chemistry Ser.: No. 147). 1975. 39.95 (ISBN 0-8412-0245-1). Am Chemical.
Gibbany, Etta M. Star Beams. 24p. 1958. pap. 1.50 (ISBN 0-88053-323-4, S-304). Macoy Pub.
Gibbard, Graham S., et al, eds. Analysis of Groups: Contributions to Theory, Research & Practice. LC 73-10941. (Social & Behavioral Science Ser.). 1973. 23.95x (ISBN 0-87589-205-1). Jossey-Bass.
Gibbes, Bessie, jt. auth. see Holloway, Cheatham.
Gibbes, Phoebe. The Life & Adventures of Mr. Francis Clive, 1764, 2 vols. in 1. LC 75-1172. (Novel in England, 1700-1775 Ser). 1975. lib. bdg. 61.00 (ISBN 0-8240-1168-6). Garland Pub.
Gibbes, Robert W. Documentary History of the American Revolution, 3 vols. LC 73-134701. 1972. Repr. of 1853 ed. 16.50 ea. Vol. 1 (ISBN 0-87152-106-7). Vol. 2 (ISBN 0-87152-107-5). Vol. 3 (ISBN 0-87152-108-3). Set. 49.50 (ISBN 0-87152-301-9). Reprint.
Gibbes, Robert W., ed. Documentary History of the American Revolution, Consisting of Letters & Papers Relating to the Contest for Liberty Chiefly in South Carolina. LC 78-140873. (Eyewitness Accounts of the American Revolution Ser., No. 3). 1970. Repr. of 1853 ed. 52.00 (ISBN 0-405-01192-X). Ayer Co Pubs.
Gibbin, Edward. The Decline & Fall of the Roman Empire, One-Volume Abridgement. Saunders, Dero A., ed. (Penguin English Library). 704p. 1983. pap. 6.95 (ISBN 0-14-043189-6). Penguin.
Gibbins, H. De B. English Social Reformers. 1978. Repr. of 1892 ed. lib. bdg. 20.00 (ISBN 0-8492-1045-3). R West.
Gibbins, Neil L., et al. Law of Free Public Education in West Virginia: A Handbook for School Personnel, Board Members & Students. LC 77-88649. 1978. pap. 4.95x (ISBN 0-8134-2000-8, 2000). Interstate.
Gibble, Kenneth L. The Feast of Enemies. 1984. 3.00 (ISBN 0-89536-671-1). CSS of Ohio.
--Mr. Songman: The Slim Whitman Story. 160p. (Orig.). 1982. 9.95 (ISBN 0-87178-587-0). Brethren.
--The Preacher as Jacob: A Paradigm for Pulpit Ministry. 144p. (Orig.). 1985. pap. 8.95 (ISBN 0-8164-2633-3, AY8587, Pub. by Seabury). Winston Pr.
--Yeast, Salt & Secret Agents. 1979. pap. 4.95 (ISBN 0-87178-968-X). Brethren.
Gibbney, H. J. Eurobodalla: History of the Moruya District. (Illus.). 206p. 1981. 15.00 (ISBN 0-908120-35-4, Pub. by Lib Australian Hist). Australia N U P.
Gibbon. Kittens. 2.98 (ISBN 0-517-27548-1). Outlet Bk Co.
Gibbon, D. L. Aeration of Activated Sludge in Sewage Treatment. LC 74-8138. 126p. 1975. text ed. 28.00 (ISBN 0-08-018156-2). Pergamon.
Gibbon, Dafydd. Perspectives of Intonation Analysis: Forum Linguisticum, Vol. 9. 309p. 1976. pap. 33.95 (ISBN 3-261-01734-1). P Lang Pubs.
Gibbon, Dafydd & Richter, Helmut, eds. Intonation, Accent & Rhythm: Studies in Discourse Phonology. LC 84-3212. (Research in Text Theory Ser.: Vol. 8). 350p. 1984. 59.20x (ISBN 3-11-009832-6). De Gruyter.
Gibbon, David. Holland: A Picture Book to Remember Her By. (Illus.). 3.98 (ISBN 0-517-28857-5). Outlet Bk Co.
Gibbon, David, jt. auth. see Bartlett, Jane.
Gibbon, Edward. Autobiography. (World's Classics Ser., No. 139). 16.95 (ISBN 0-19-250139-9). Oxford U Pr.
--Decline & Fall of the Roman Empire, 6 vols. 1978. Repr. of 1910 ed. 9.95x ea. (Evman). Vol. 1 (ISBN 0-460-00434-4). Vol. 2 (ISBN 0-460-00435-2). Vol. 3 (ISBN 0-460-00436-0). Vol. 4 (ISBN 0-460-00474-3). Vol. 5 (ISBN 0-460-00475-1). Vol. 6 (ISBN 0-460-00476-X). Biblio Dist.
--The Decline & Fall of the Roman Empire, 3 Vols. LC 32-28173. 1932. 8.95 ea.; Vol. 1. (ISBN 0-394-60401-6); Vol. 2. (ISBN 0-394-60402-4); Vol. 3. (ISBN 0-394-60403-2). Modern Lib.
--The Decline & Fall of the Roman Empire. Bourne, Frank C., abridged by. 735p. pap. 4.25 (ISBN 0-440-31879-3, LE). Dell.
--History of Christianity. LC 79-169227. (Atheist Viewpoint Ser.). (Illus.). 912p. 1972. Repr. of 1883 ed. 51.00 (ISBN 0-405-03796-1). Ayer Co Pubs.
--History of Christianity. 59.95 (ISBN 0-8490-0319-9). Gordon Pr.
--The History of the Decline & Fall of the Roman Empire, 7 vols. Bury, John B., ed. LC 78-168113. (Illus.). Repr. of 1914 ed. Set. 300.00 (ISBN 0-404-02820-9). AMS Pr.
--Mahomet & the Political Theory of the Arab Empire, 2 vols. (Illus.). 328p. 1984. Repr. of 1901 ed. 217.85 set (ISBN 0-89901-181-0). Found Class Reprints.
--Memoirs of My Life. Radice, Betty, intro. by. (English Library). 224p. 1984. pap. 4.95 (ISBN 0-14-043217-5). Penguin.
--The Memoirs of the Life of Edward Gibbon. Hill, George B., ed. 1900. 40.00 (ISBN 0-8274-2706-9). R West.
--Miscellaneous Works, 5 vols. Sheffield, John, ed. LC 76-171363. (Illus.). Repr. of 1814 ed. 48.00 ea. Vol. 1 (ISBN 0-404-02831-4). Vol. 1 (ISBN 0-404-02832-2). Vol. 3 (ISBN 0-404-02833-0). Vol. 4 (ISBN 0-404-02834-9). Vol. 5 (ISBN 0-404-02835-7). Set. 240.00 (ISBN 0-404-02830-6). AMS Pr.
--Private Letters of Edward Gibbon, 2 Vols. Prothero, Rowland E., ed. LC 71-151596. Repr. of 1896 ed. Set. 75.00 (ISBN 0-404-02751-2). AMS Pr.
Gibbon, Guy. Anthropological Archaeology. LC 84-4321. 432p. 1984. 29.50 (ISBN 0-317-05136-9). Columbia U Pr.
Gibbon, Guy & Spencer, Robert F., eds. Prairie Archaeology: Papers in Honor of David A. Baerreis. (University of Minnesota, Publications in Anthropology: No. 3). 170p. 1983. pap. 9.50 (ISBN 0-911599-02-9). Dept Anthro U Minn.
Gibbon, Guy E. The Mississippian Occupation of the Red Wing Area: Microfiche Edition. (Minnesota Prehistoric Archaeology Ser.: No. 13). 394p. 1979. 12.50x (ISBN 0-87351-137-9). Minn Hist.
--The Sheffield Site: An Oneota Site on the St. Croix River. LC 73-6715. (Minnesota Prehistoric Archaeology Ser., No. 10). (Illus.). 62p. 1973. pap. 4.00x (ISBN 0-87351-079-8). Minn Hist.
Gibbon, Guy E. & Spencer, Robert F., eds. Oneota Studies. (University of Minnesota, Publications in Anthropology Ser.: No. 1). 122p. 1983. pap. 7.50 (ISBN 0-911599-00-2). Dept Anthro U Minn.
Gibbon, John. Personal Recollections of the Civil War. 1978. Repr. 25.00 (ISBN 0-89029-042-3). Pr of Morningside.
Gibbon, John, compiled by. Artillerist's Manual. LC 74-84270. Repr. of 1860 ed. lib. bdg. 32.50x (ISBN 0-8371-5007-8, GIAM). Greenwood.
Gibbon, John & Allan, Lorraine, eds. Timing & Time Perception. (Annals of The New York Academy of Sciences Ser.: Vol. 423). 654p. 1984. lib. bdg. 144.00x (ISBN 0-89766-240-7); pap. 144.00x (ISBN 0-89766-241-5). NY Acad Sci.
Gibbon, John M. Canadian Folk Songs (Old & New) LC 74-26593. 1927. lib. bdg. 12.50 (ISBN 0-8414-4579-6). Folcroft.
--Melody & the Lyric: From Chaucer to Cavaliers. LC 65-15882. (Studies in Poetry, No. 38). 1969. Repr. lib. bdg. write for info. (ISBN 0-8383-0555-5). Haskell.
Gibbon, Lardner, jt. auth. see Henderson, William L.
Gibbon, Lewis G. A Scots Quair: A Trilogy of Sunset Song, Cloud Howe, & Grey Granite. LC 77-75288. 496p. 1982. pap. 9.95 (ISBN 0-8052-0710-4). Schocken.
Gibbon, M., ed. see AE.
Gibbon, Monk. Mount Ida. 478p. 1984. pap. 11.95 (ISBN 0-905473-99-X, Pub. by Wolfhound Pr Ireland). Irish Bks Media.
--The Pupil: A Memory of Love. 128p. 1981. 9.95 (ISBN 0-905473-68-X, Pub. by Wolfhound Pr Ireland). Irish Bks Media.
--Red Shoes Ballet & the Tales of Hoffman, Vol. 14. Kupelnick, Bruce S., ed. LC 76-52106. (Classics of Film Literature Ser.). 1978. lib. bdg. 47.00 (ISBN 0-8240-2878-3). Garland Pub.
Gibbon, Perceval. Vrouw Grobelaar & Her Leading Cases. facs. ed. LC 73-142263. (Short Story Index Reprint Ser). 1906. 18.00 (ISBN 0-8369-3747-3). Ayer Co Pubs.
Gibboney, Jan D., tr. see Management Sciences for Health, et al.
Gibbons & Dysken, eds. Statistical & Methodological Advances in Psychiatric Research. 184p. 1983. 29.95 (ISBN 0-89335-186-5). SP Med & Sci Bks.
Gibbons, Alan. Algorithmic Graph Theory. 250p. 1985. 47.50 (ISBN 0-521-24659-8); pap. 17.95 (ISBN 0-521-28881-9). Cambridge U Pr.
Gibbons, Alice. The People Time Forgot. LC 81-9466. 324p. 1981. pap. 6.95 (ISBN 0-8024-8692-4). Moody.
Gibbons, Andy & Nelson, Jeanne D. Shhh Is a Four Letter Word! Laughs for Library Lovers. LC 83-62296. 120p. (Orig.). 1984. pap. text ed. 9.95 (ISBN 0-88247-702-1). R & E Pubs.
Gibbons, Arnold. Information, Ideology & Communication: The New Nations' Perspectives on an Intellectual Revolution. 232p. (Orig.). 1985. lib. bdg. 23.50 (ISBN 0-8191-4509-2); pap. text ed. 11.75 (ISBN 0-8191-4510-6). U Pr of Amer.
Gibbons, Barbara. Calories Don't Count if You Eat Standing up! 96p. 1984. pap. 3.95 (ISBN 0-8092-5366-6). Contemp Bks.
--The International Slim Gourmet Cookbook. LC 78-2136. 1978. 16.30i (ISBN 0-06-011507-6, HarpT). Har-Row.
--Lean Cuisine. LC 79-1663. (Illus.). 1980. pap. 7.64i (ISBN 0-06-090737-1, CN). Har-Row.
--The Slim Gourmet Cookbook. LC 75-23883. 416p. 1976. 17.26 (ISBN 0-06-011517-3, HarpT). Har-Row.
--Slim Gourmet Sweets & Treats. LC 82-47737. 320p. 1982. 14.37i (ISBN 0-06-015057-2, HarpT). Har-Row.
--The Year-Round Turkey Cookbook: A Guide to Delicious, Nutritious Dining with Today's Versatile Turkey. (Illus., Orig.). 1979. pap. 6.95 (ISBN 0-07-023161-3). McGraw.
Gibbons, Barbara & Consumer Guide Editors. Diet Watchers Cookbook. LC 77-90867. (Illus.). 1978. 12.95i (ISBN 0-06-011509-2, HarpT); pap. 7.95i (ISBN 0-06-011508-4, TD-305, HarpT). Har-Row.
--Lean Cuisine. LC 79-1663. (Illus.). 1980. 13.41i (ISBN 0-06-011498-3, HarpT). Har-Row.
Gibbons, Bob. How Flowers Work: A Guide to Plant Biology. (Illus.). 160p. 1984. 15.95 (ISBN 0-7137-1278-3, Pub. by Blandford Pr England). Sterling.
Gibbons, Boyd. Wye Island. 1979. pap. 5.95 (ISBN 0-14-005230-5). Penguin.
--Wye Island: Outsiders, Insiders & Resistance to Change. LC 76-47399. (Resources for the Future Ser.). (Illus.). 248p. 1977. 20.95x (ISBN 0-8018-1936-9). Johns Hopkins.
--Wye Island: Outsiders, Insiders, & Resistance to Change. 248p. 1977. 20.95 (ISBN 0-8018-1936-9). Resources Future.
Gibbons, Brian. Growplan Gardening Guide. (Illus.). 180p. 1979. 8.95 (ISBN 0-7153-7697-7). David & Charles.
--Jacobean City Comedy. 2nd ed. 1981. pap. 13.95x (ISBN 0-416-73460-X, NO. 2040). Methuen Inc.
Gibbons, Brian, ed. see Congreve, Lillian.
Gibbons, Brian, ed. see Tourneur, Cyril.
Gibbons, Cromwell. Republic, U.S.A. 1965. 10.00 (ISBN 0-8159-6709-8). Devin.
Gibbons, D. E. Applied Hypnosis & Hyperempiria. LC 79-20879. 227p. 1979. 24.50x (ISBN 0-306-40271-8, Plenum Pr). Plenum Pub.
Gibbons, D. J., jt. auth. see Ehrenberg, W.
Gibbons, David & De Koninck, Rodolphe. Agricultural Modernization, Poverty & Inequality. 256p. 1979. text ed. 41.95x (ISBN 0-566-00331-7). Gower Pub Co.
Gibbons, Don. The Criminological Enterprise: Theories & Perspectives. (P-H Series in Sociology). 1979. pap. text ed. 18.95 (ISBN 0-13-193615-8). P-H.
Gibbons, Don C. Changing the Lawbreaker: The Treatment of Delinquents & Criminals. LC 81-65008. 330p. 1980. pap. text ed. 8.95x (ISBN 0-86598-017-9). Allanheld.
--Changing the Lawbreaker: The Treatment of Delinquents & Criminals. 330p. 1980. 8.95 (ISBN 0-318-02917-0). Biblio Dist.
--Delinquent Behavior. 3rd ed. (Illus.). 1981. text ed. 26.95 (ISBN 0-13-197962-0). P-H.
--Society, Crime, & Criminal Behavior. 4th ed. (Illus.). 576p. 1982. text ed. 29.95 (ISBN 0-13-820118-8). P-H.
Gibbons, Don C. & Krohn, Marvin D. Delinquent Behavior. 4th ed. (Illus.). 368p. 1986. text ed. 26.95 (ISBN 0-13-197989-2). P-H.
Gibbons, Emma & Jessup, George. Figure Control for Fun & Fitness. (Illus.). 1979. pap. text ed. 4.95 (ISBN 0-8403-1959-2, 40195902). Kendall-Hunt.
Gibbons, Euell. Stalking the Wild Asparagus. 1970. pap. 6.95 field guide ed. (ISBN 0-679-50223-8). McKay.
Gibbons, Euell & Gibbons, Joe. Feast on a Diabetic Diet. rev. ed. 336p. 1978. pap. 2.95 (ISBN 0-449-23853-9, Crest). Fawcett.
Gibbons, Faye. Mighty Close to Heaven. 192p. (gr. 5-9). 1985. PLB 10.25 (ISBN 0-688-04147-7, Morrow Junior Books). Morrow.
--Some Glad Morning. LC 81-22549. 240p. (gr. 4-6). 1982. 12.25 (ISBN 0-688-01068-7). Morrow.
Gibbons, Felton. Catalogue of Italian Drawings in the Art Museum, Princeton University, 2 vols. LC 76-3252. (Illus.). 1977. Set. text ed. 115.00x (ISBN 0-691-03888-0). Princeton U Pr.
--Dosso & Battista Dossi: Court Painters at Ferrara. LC 68-11441. (Monographs in Art & Archaeology: No. 39). (Illus.). 1968. 69.00 (ISBN 0-691-03850-3). Princeton U Pr.
Gibbons, Floyd. The Red Knight of Germany: The Story of Baron Von Richthofen, Germany's Great War Bird. Gilbert, James, ed. LC 79-7256. (Flight: Its First Seventy-Five Years Ser.). (Illus.). 1979. Repr. of 1927 ed. lib. bdg. 28.50x (ISBN 0-405-12167-9). Ayer Co Pubs.
Gibbons, Floyd P. The Red Napoleon: A Novel. LC 75-26975. (Lost American Fiction Ser.). 494p. 1976. Repr. of 1929 ed. 9.85 (ISBN 0-8093-0764-2). S Ill U Pr.
Gibbons, Francis. Joseph F. Smith. LC 84-70071. (Illus.). 1984. 10.95 (ISBN 0-87747-988-7). Deseret Bk.
Gibbons, Francis M. Brigham Young, Modern Moses, Prophet of God. LC 81-7766. 286p. 1981. 8.95 (ISBN 0-87747-858-9). Deseret Bk.
--Heber J. Grant: Man of Steel, Prophet of God. LC 79-11649. 252p. 1979. 8.95 (ISBN 0-87747-755-8). Deseret Bk.
--Joseph Smith: Martyr-Prophet of God. LC 77-2019. 1977. 7.95 (ISBN 0-87747-637-3). Deseret Bk.
--Lorenzo Snow: Spiritual Giant, Prophet of God. LC 82-83648. (Illus.). 247p. 1982. 8.95 (ISBN 0-87747-936-4). Deseret Bk.
Gibbons, G. F., et al. Biochemistry of Cholesterol. 370p. 1982. 102.25 (ISBN 0-444-80348-3, Biomedical Pr). Elsevier.
Gibbons, G. W., et al, eds. The Very Early Universe. LC 83-7330. (Illus.). 500p. 1983. 52.50 (ISBN 0-521-25349-7). Cambridge U Pr.
--The Very Early Universe. 480p. 1985. 24.95 (ISBN 0-521-31677-4). Cambridge U Pr.
Gibbons, Gail. Boat Book. LC 82-15851. (Illus.). 32p. (ps-3). 1983. reinforced binding 12.95 (ISBN 0-8234-0478-1). Holiday.
--Check It Out. LC 85-5414. (Illus.). 32p. (gr. 4-8). 1985. 12.95 (ISBN 0-15-216400-6, HJ). HarBraceJ.
--Check it Out! The Book about Libraries. LC 85-5414. (Illus.). 32p. (gr. 4-8). 1985. pap. 12.95 (ISBN 0-15-216400-6). HarBraceJ.
--Christmas Time. LC 82-1038. (Illus.). 32p. (ps-3). 1982. Reinforced bdg. 12.95 (ISBN 0-8234-0453-6). Holiday.
--Christmas Time. (Illus.). 32p. (gr. k-3). 1985. pap. 5.95 (ISBN 0-8234-0575-3). Holiday.
--Clocks & How They Go. LC 78-22498. (Illus.). (gr. k-4). 1979. 10.53i (ISBN 0-690-03973-5); PLB 10.89 (ISBN 0-690-03974-3). Crowell Jr Bks.
--Department Store. LC 83-45053. (Illus.). 32p. (gr. k-4). 1984. 10.53i (ISBN 0-690-04366-X); PLB 10.89g (ISBN 0-690-04367-8). Crowell Jr Bks.
--Fill It Up! LC 84-45345. (Illus.). 32p. (gr. k-4). 1985. 9.57i (ISBN 0-690-04439-9); PLB 9.89g (ISBN 0-690-04440-2). Crowell Jr Bks.

--Fire! Fire! LC 83-46162. (Illus.). 40p. (gr. k-4). 1984. 9.57i (ISBN 0-690-04417-8); PLB 9.89g (ISBN 0-690-04416-X). Crowell Jr Bks.
--Halloween. LC 84-519. (Illus.). 32p. (ps-3). 1984. reinforced bdg. 12.95 (ISBN 0-8234-0524-9); pap. 5.95 (ISBN 0-8234-0577-X). Holiday.
--Lights! Camera! Action!: How a Movie Is Made. LC 85-47536. (Illus.). 32p. (gr. 1-4). 1985. 9.57i (ISBN 0-690-04476-3); PLB 9.89g (ISBN 0-690-04477-1). Crowell Jr Bks.
--Locks & Keys. LC 79-7825. (Illus.). 32p. (gr. 1-4). 1980. 10.10i (ISBN 0-690-04058-X); PLB 9.89 (ISBN 0-690-04059-8). Crowell Jr Bks.
--The Magnificent Morris Mouse Clubhouse. (Easy-Read Story Bks.). (Illus.). 32p. (gr. k-3). 1981. lib. bdg. 8.60 (ISBN 0-531-04302-9). Watts.
--The Milk Makers. LC 84-20081. (Illus.). 32p. (gr. k-3). 1985. 12.95 (ISBN 0-02-736640-5). Macmillan.
--The Missing Maple Syrup Sap Mystery: Or How Maple Syrup Is Made. LC 79-14437. (Illus.). (gr. 1-3). 1979. 8.95 (ISBN 0-7232-6167-9). Warne.
--New Road! LC 82-45917. (Illus.). 32p. (gr. k-4). 1983. 10.53i (ISBN 0-690-04342-2); PLB 10.89g (ISBN 0-690-04343-0). Crowell Jr Bks.
--Paper, Paper Everywhere. LC 82-3109. (Illus.). 32p. (ps-3). 1983. 10.95 (ISBN 0-15-259488-4, HJ). HarBraceJ.
--Playgrounds. LC 84-19285. (Illus.). 32p. (ps-2). 1985. reinforced bdg. 12.95 (ISBN 0-8234-0553-2). Holiday.
--The Post Office Book. LC 81-43888. (Illus.). 32p. (gr. k-3). 1982. 9.13i (ISBN 0-690-04198-5); PLB 9.89 (ISBN 0-690-04199-3). Crowell Jr Bks.
--The Seasons of Arnold's Apple Tree. LC 84-4484. (Illus.). 32p. (ps-3). 1984. 13.95 (ISBN 0-15-271246-1, HJ). HarBraceJ.
--Sun Up, Sun Down. LC 82-23420. (Illus.). 32p. (gr. 1-3). 1983. 13.95 (ISBN 0-15-282781-1, HJ). HarBraceJ.
--Thanksgiving Day. LC 83-175. (Illus.). 32p. (gr. k-3). 1983. reinforced bdg. 12.95 (ISBN 0-8234-0489-7). Holiday.
--Thanksgiving Day. (Illus.). (gr. k-3). 1984. incl. cassette 19.95 (ISBN 0-941078-63-9); pap. 12.95 incl. cassette (ISBN 0-941078-61-2); pap. 27.95 4 bks., cassette & guide (ISBN 0-941078-62-0); sound filmstrip 22.95 (ISBN 0-941078-60-4). Live Oak Media.
--Thanksgiving Day. LC 83-175. (Illus.). (gr. k-3). 1985. pap. 5.95 (ISBN 0-8234-0576-1). Holiday.
--Things to Make & Do for Halloween. LC 75-19396. (Things to Make & Do Ser.). (Illus.). 48p. (gr. k-2). 1976. PLB 8.90 (ISBN 0-531-01103-8). Watts.
--Tool Book. LC 81-13386. (Illus.). 32p. (ps-3). 1982. reinforced bdg. 12.95 (ISBN 0-8234-0444-7). Holiday.
--Trucks. LC 81-43039. (Illus.). 32p. (ps-2). 1981. 10.53i (ISBN 0-690-04118-7); PLB 10.89 (ISBN 0-690-04119-5). Crowell Jr Bks.
--Trucks. LC 81-43039. (Trophy Picture Bk.). (Illus.). 32p. (ps-1). 1985. pap. 2.84i (ISBN 0-06-443069-3, Trophy). HarpJ.
--Tunnels. LC 83-18589. (Illus.). 32p. (ps-2). 1984. reinforced bdg 12.95 (ISBN 0-8234-0507-9). Holiday.
--Valentine's Day. (Illus.). 32p. (ps-3). 1986. reinforced 12.95 (ISBN 0-8234-0572-9). Holiday.
Gibbons, H. A. France & Ourselves. 59.95 (ISBN 0-8490-0189-7). Gordon Pr.
Gibbons, Herbert A. Foundation of the Ottoman Empire. 379p. 1968. Repr. of 1916 ed. 35.00x (ISBN 0-7146-1984-1, F Cass Co). Biblio Dist.
--John Wanamaker, 2 Vols. LC 70-137911. (American History & Culture in the Nineteenth Century Ser.). 1971. Repr. of 1926 ed. Set. 72.50x (ISBN 0-8046-1479-2, Pub. by Kennikat). Assoc Faculty Pr.
Gibbons, Ian, jt. auth. see Topping, Anne L.
Gibbons, Irene R., tr. see Mechanicus, Philip.
Gibbons, J. D., jt. auth. see Pratt, J.
Gibbons, J. F., et al, eds. Laser & Electron Beam Solid Interactions & Materials Processing. (Materials Research Society Proceedings: Vol. 1). 630p. 1981. 90.00 (ISBN 0-444-00595-1, North-Holland). Elsevier.
Gibbons, J. Whitfield & Sharitz, Rebecca R., eds. Thermal Ecology: Proceedings. LC 74-600136. (AEC Symposium Ser.). 687p. 1974. 25.25 (CONF-730505); microfiche 4.50 (ISBN 0-87079-225-3, CONF-730505). DOE.
Gibbons, J. Whitfield, jt. ed. see Thorp, James H.
Gibbons, James C. A Retrospect of Fifty Years, 2 vols. in 1. LC 79-38447. (Religion in America, Ser. 2). 720p. 1972. Repr. of 1916 ed. 47.50 (ISBN 0-405-04066-0). Ayer Co Pubs.
Gibbons, James E. Appraising in a Changing Economy: Collected Writings of James E. Gibbons. 274p. 1982. 15.00 (ISBN 0-911780-58-0). Am Inst Real Estate Appraisers.
Gibbons, James S. Banks of New York, Their Dealers, the Clearing House, & the Panic of 1857. LC 68-28631. (Illus.). 1968. Repr. of 1859 ed. lib. bdg. 26.00x (ISBN 0-8371-0084-4, GIBN). Greenwood.
--Public Debt of the United States. LC 78-129033. (Research & Source Works Ser.: No. 525). 1970. Repr. of 1867 ed. lib. bdg. 19.00 (ISBN 0-8337-1328-0). B Franklin.
Gibbons, Jean D. Nonparametric Methods for Quantitative Analysis. 2nd. ed. LC 84-73390. (American Sciences Press Series in Mathematical & Management Sciences Ser.: Vol. 2). 1985. 34.50 (ISBN 0-935950-09-5). Am Sciences Pr.
Gibbons, Jean D., et al. Selecting & Ordering Populations: A New Statistical Methodology. LC 77-3700. (Probability & Mathematical Statistics). 569p. 1977. 55.50x (ISBN 0-471-02670-0, Pub. by Wiley-Interscience). Wiley.
Gibbons, Joe, jt. auth. see Gibbons, Euell.
Gibbons, John. Road to Nazareth: Through Palestine Today. LC 77-180339. Repr. of 1936 ed. 26.00 (ISBN 0-404-56264-7). AMS Pr.
Gibbons, John, jt. auth. see Fraser, Edward.
Gibbons, John, jt. auth. see Smith, Douglas.
Gibbons, John H. & Chandler, W. U. Energy: The Conservation Revolution. LC 80-28431. 275p. 1981. 25.00x (ISBN 0-306-40670-5, Plenum Pr). Plenum Pub.
Gibbons, John T., jt. auth. see Smith, Douglas C.
Gibbons, Joseph, tr. see Geoffrey of Auxerre.
Gibbons, Joseph C. Whatever Happened to Friday? & Other Questions Catholics Ask. LC 79-91275. (Orig.). 1980. pap. 2.95 (ISBN 0-8091-2278-2). Paulist Pr.
Gibbons, Julie. My Secret Place. (Illus.). 20p. (Orig.). (gr. 1-4). 1975. pap. 3.50 (ISBN 0-911336-61-3). Sci of Mind.
--There Is Only One Me. 20p. (gr. 1-4). 1974. pap. 3.50 (ISBN 0-911336-56-7). Sci of Mind.
Gibbons, Kristin L., jt. auth. see Scott, Kenneth.
Gibbons, Lois O., ed. see Bainton, Roland H.
Gibbons, Maurice. The New Secondary Education: A Phi Delta Kappa Task Force Proposal. 199p. 1976. 6.50 (ISBN 0-87367-763-3); members 5.50 (ISBN 0-317-35573-2); pap. 5.00 (ISBN 0-87367-762-5); pap. 4.00 members (ISBN 0-317-35574-0). Phi Delta Kappa.
--The New Secondary Education: A Phi Delta Kappa Task Force Report. LC 75-26386. (Orig.). 1976. pap. 5.00 (ISBN 0-87367-762-5). Phi Delta Kappa.
Gibbons, Michael & Gummett, Philip, eds. Science, Technology & Society Today. LC 83-20639. 192p. 1984. 16.00 (ISBN 0-7190-1090-X, Pub. by Manchester Univ Pr); pap. 7.50 (ISBN 0-7190-0878-6). Longwood Pub Group.
Gibbons, Phebe H. Pennsylvania Dutch. rev ed. LC 77-134378. Repr. of 1882 ed. 29.00 (ISBN 0-404-08426-5). AMS Pr.
Gibbons, Philip, tr. see Prishvin, Mikhail M.
Gibbons, R., ed. A Window on Poland. 128p. 1983. pap. 4.00 (ISBN 0-317-36708-0). Kosciuszko.
Gibbons, Reginald, ed. TQ Twenty: Twenty Years of Triquarterly. (Illus.). 28.00 (ISBN 0-916366-31-6). Pushcart Pr.
Gibbons, Reginald, jt. ed. see Graff, Gerald.
Gibbons, Reginald, tr. see Cernuda, Luis.
Gibbons, Reginald, tr. see Guillen, Jorge.
Gibbons, Robert. Yellow & Black. (Illus.). 24p. 1980. 25.00 (ISBN 0-939622-09-2); pap. 6.00 (ISBN 0-686-29010-0). Four Zoas Night Ltd.
Gibbons, Robert & Ashford, Bob. Himalayan Kingdoms: Nepal, Sikkim, & Bhutan. (Illus.). 250p. 1983. 17.50 (ISBN 0-88254-802-6). Hippocrene Bks.
Gibbons, Robert C. Woldman's Engineering Alloys. 6th ed. 1979. 92.00 (ISBN 0-87170-086-7). ASM.
Gibbons, Robert J., ed. Dimensions of Corporate Strategy: Selected Readings. LC 83-82105. (Orig.). 1983. pap. text ed. 24.00 (ISBN 0-89462-016-9). IIA.
--Research Philosophy & Techniques: Selected Readings. LC 82-84587. 244p. (Orig.). 1983. pap. text ed. 15.00 (ISBN 0-89462-015-0). IIA.
Gibbons, Robert J., et al. Premium Auditing Applications, 2 vols. LC 81-80774. 681p. 1981. Vol. 1. pap. 18.00; Vol. 2. pap. 18.00. IIA.
Gibbons, Robert J., et al, eds. Principles of Premium Auditing, 2 vols. LC 81-80774. 668p. 1981. Vol. 1. pap. 14.00 (ISBN 0-89462-009-6, PA 91); Vol. 2. pap. 14.00 (ISBN 0-89462-010-X). IIA.
Gibbons, S. R. & Morican, P. World War One. (Modern Times Ser.). (Illus.). 144p. (Orig.). (gr. 9-12). 1965. pap. text ed. 4.75 (ISBN 0-582-20421-6). Longman.
Gibbons, Sheila, jt. auth. see Beasley, Maurine.
Gibbons, Sherry, et al. Evenings of Joy & Inspiration for Parish Leaders. LC 83-62197. 64p. (Orig.). 1983. pap. text ed. 2.95 (ISBN 0-911905-08-1). Past & Mat Rene Ctr.
Gibbons, Stella. Cold Comfort Farm. 1977. pap. 3.95 (ISBN 0-14-000140-9). Penguin.
--Cold Comfort Farm. Date not set. 12.75 (ISBN 0-8446-6148-1). Peter Smith.
Gibbons, Thomas. The Exhibition: Scenes from the Life of John Merrick. 1980. pap. 1.85x (ISBN 0-686-68848-1). Dramatists Play.
Gibbons, Tom. Rooms in the Darwin Hotel: Studies in English Literary Criticism & Ideas 1880-1920. LC 73-83715. 174p. 1973. 15.00x (ISBN 0-85564-072-3, Pub. by U of W Austral Pr). Intl Spec Bk.
Gibbons, Whit. Their Blood Runs Cold: Adventures with Reptiles & Amphibians. LC 82-17395. (Illus.). 158p. (Orig.). 1983. pap. 9.95 (ISBN 0-8173-0133-X). U of Ala Pr.
Gibbons, William E., jt. auth. see Hibbard, Lester T.
Gibbons, William F. Those Black Diamond Men. LC 74-22785. (The Labor Movement in Fiction & Non-Fiction). Repr. of 1902 ed. 27.50 (ISBN 0-404-58431-4). AMS Pr.
Gibbs. Understanding Cats. (Animal World Ser.). (gr. 3-6). 1981. 7.95 (ISBN 0-86020-207-0, Usborne-Hayes); PLB 12.95 (ISBN 0-88110-088-9); pap. 4.95 (ISBN 0-86020-185-6). EDC.
Gibbs & Kramer. Islam: A Shorter Encylopaedia. (Arabic.). 1974. 75.00x (ISBN 0-317-20257-X). Intl Bk Ctr.
Gibbs, A. C., ed. Middle English Romances. (York Medieval Texts). 1966. 11.95 (ISBN 0-8101-0101-7). Northwestern U Pr.
Gibbs, A. J. & Harrison, B. D. Plant Virology: The Principles. LC 76-1924. 292p. 1979. 37.95x (ISBN 0-470-26637-6). Halsted Pr.
Gibbs, A. M. THe Art & Mind of Shaw. LC 82-19158. 260p. 1983. 23.95x (ISBN 0-312-04992-7). St Martin.
Gibbs, A. P. Christian Baptism. 1982. pap. 4.50 (ISBN 0-937396-62-1). Walterick Pubs.
--The Lord's Supper. pap. 5.00 (ISBN 0-937396-25-7). Walterick Pubs.
--The Preacher & His Preaching. 16.95 (ISBN 0-937396-31-1); pap. 10.95 (ISBN 0-937396-30-3). Walterick Pubs.
--Scriptural Principles of Gathering. pap. 1.95 (ISBN 0-937396-37-0). Walterick Pubs.
--Through the Scriptures. pap. 5.95 (ISBN 0-937396-45-1). Walterick Pubs.
--Worship: The Christian's Highest Occupation. pap. 5.95 (ISBN 0-937396-57-5). Walterick Pubs.
--Your Quiet Time. 16p. 1981. pap. 1.25 (ISBN 0-89107-244-6). Good News.
Gibbs, A. R. & Seal, R. M. Atlas of Pulmonary Pathology. (Illus.). 135p. 1982. text ed. 52.00 (ISBN 0-397-58283-8, 65-73117, Lippincott Medical). Lippincott.
Gibbs, Alan G., tr. see Plesner, A. I.
Gibbs, Angela, tr. see Kallberg, Sture.
Gibbs, Barbara. Green Pharmacy. 384p. 1983. 40.00x (ISBN 0-906908-64-7, Pub. by A Hilger). State Mutual Bk.
Gibbs, Charles H., jt. ed. see Lundeen, Harry C.
Gibbs, Donald A. Subject & Author Index to Chinese Literature Monthly. (Sinology Ser.). 173p. 1978. pap. text ed. 5.95 (ISBN 0-88710-135-6). Far Eastern Pubns.
Gibbs, Donald A., et al. Bibliography of Studies & Translations of Modern Chinese Literature Nineteen Eighteen to Nineteen Forty-Two. (East Asian Monographs: No. 61). 400p. 1975. 25.00x (ISBN 0-674-07111-5). Harvard U Pr.
Gibbs, Dudley & Greenhalgh, Marilyn E. Biotechnology, Chemical Feedstocks & Energy Utilization. LC 83-62199. 184p. 1983. 22.50 (ISBN 0-86187-346-7). F Pinter Pubs.
Gibbs, E., jt. auth. see Gibbs, M.
Gibbs, E. Paul, ed. Virus Diseases of Food Animals: A World Geography of Epidemiology & Control, Vol. 1. LC 81-521. (International Perspectives Ser.). 1982. 59.50 (ISBN 0-12-282201-3). Acad Pr.
--Virus Diseases of Food Animals: A World Geography of Epidemiology & Control, Vol. 2. LC 81-66681. (Disease Monographs). 1982. 73.50 (ISBN 0-12-282202-1). Acad Pr.
Gibbs, Eddie. I Believe in Church Growth. 1982. pap. 9.95 (ISBN 0-8028-1921-4). Eerdmans.
Gibbs, Ellen & Gibbs, Mary. The Bible References of John Ruskin. 310p. 1973. Repr. of 1898 ed. 20.00 (ISBN 0-8274-0652-5). R West.
Gibbs, Emily, jt. ed. see Swank, Jerold.
Gibbs, Emily A. & Perry, Jim, eds. Forty Computer Games from Kilobaud Microcomputing. 148p. 1980. 7.95 (ISBN 0-88006-023-9, BK1381). Green Pub Inc.
--Some of the Best from Kilobaud Microcomputing. 223p. 1980. 10.95 (BK7311). Green Pub Inc.
Gibbs, Errol A. & Lindo, Marjorie G. The Dilemma of Our Society: A Proposal for Moral Maturity. (Illus.). 311p. 1980. 15.00 (ISBN 0-682-49650-2). Exposition Pr FL.
Gibbs, Frederic A., jt. auth. see Boshes, Louis D.
Gibbs, G. Ian. Dictionary of Gaming, Modelling & Simulation. LC 78-59784. pap. 43.50 (ISBN 0-317-11019-5, 2021906). Bks Demand UMI.
Gibbs, G. W. & Pintus, P. Health & Safety in the Canadian Mining Industry. 249p. (Orig.). 1978. pap. text ed. 16.00x (ISBN 0-88757-003-8, Pub. by Ctr Resource Stud Canada). Brookfield Pub Co.
Gibbs, George. Alphabetical Vocabularies of the Clallam & Lumni. LC 75-168115. (Library of American Linguistics: No. 11). Repr. of 1863 ed. 28.50 (ISBN 0-404-50991-6). AMS Pr.
--Alphabetical Vocabulary of the Chinook Language. LC 72-168141. (Library of American Linguistics: No. 13). (Chinook.). Repr. of 1863 ed. 28.50 (ISBN 0-404-50993-2). AMS Pr.
--Dictionary of the Chinook Jargon, or Trade Languages of Oregon. LC 76-168142. (Library of American Linguistics: No. 12). (Chinook.). Repr. of 1863 ed. 28.50 (ISBN 0-404-50992-4). AMS Pr.
--Dictionary of the Nisqually Indian Language of Western Washington. (Shorey Indian Ser.). 82p. Repr. of 1877 ed. pap. 9.95 (ISBN 0-8466-4022-8, I22). Shorey.
--Indian Tribes of Washington Territory. 56p. 1978. 7.50 (ISBN 0-87770-206-3); pap. 4.95 (ISBN 0-87770-050-8). Ye Galleon.
--Memoirs of the Administrations of Washington & John Adams, 2 Vols. 1971. Repr. of 1846 ed. lib. bdg. 60.00 (ISBN 0-8337-1331-0). B Franklin.
Gibbs, George, et al. Languages of the Tribes of the Extreme Northwest, Alaska, the Aleutians & Adjacent Territories. (Shorey Indian Ser.). (Illus.). 56p. pap. 4.95 (ISBN 0-8466-4019-8, I19). Shorey.
--Tribes of the Extreme Northwest, Alaska, the Aleutians & Adjacent Territories. (Illus.). 156p. pap. 9.95 (ISBN 0-8466-4018-X, I18). Shorey.
--Tribes of Western Washington & Northwest Oregon. 204p. pap. 16.95 (ISBN 0-8466-4020-1, I20). Shorey.
Gibbs, George W. New Zealand Butterflies. (Illus.). 208p. 1983. 45.00 (ISBN 0-00-216955-X, Pub. by W Collins New Zealand). Intl Spec Bk.
Gibbs, Gerald. Complete Guide to Credit & Loans. 224p. (Orig.). 1982. pap. 2.95 (ISBN 0-87216-931-6). Jove Pubns.
Gibbs, Gloria & Clark, Nicolette. Finders Keepers. 1978. pap. 1.95 (ISBN 0-532-19169-2). Woodhill.
Gibbs, Graham. Learning to Study. 88p. 1981. 29.00x (ISBN 0-86082-246-X, Pub. by Natl Ext England). State Mutual Bk.
--Teaching Students to Learn. 111p. 1981. (Pub. by Open Univ Pr); pap. 14.00x (ISBN 0-335-10033-3). Taylor & Francis.
Gibbs, Greg. Willowby's World of Unicorns "Activity Book". (Willowby's World Ser.). 14p. (Orig.). (gr. 2-6). 1984. pap. 2.00x (ISBN 0-910349-03-7). Cloud Ten.
Gibbs, H. G. & Richards, T. H., eds. Stress, Vibration & Noise Analysis in Vehicles. (Illus.). 485p. 1975. 68.50 (ISBN 0-85334-642-9, Pub. by Elsevier Applied Sci England). Elsevier.
Gibbs, J. P. Norms, Deviance & Social Control. 29.95 (ISBN 0-444-01551-5, GND/, Pub. by Elsevier). Greenwood.
Gibbs, J. Willard. Elementary Principles in Statistical Mechanics. LC 80-84972. 224p. 1981. 22.00 (ISBN 0-918024-19-6); pap. text ed. 12.00 (ISBN 0-918024-20-X). Ox Bow.
--Scientific Papers, 2 vols. Set. 21.50 (ISBN 0-8446-2127-7). Peter Smith.
Gibbs, Jack P. Crime, Punishment, & Deterrence. LC 75-17662. 272p. 1975. 22.50 (ISBN 0-444-99016-X, GCR/, Pub. by Elsevier). Greenwood.
Gibbs, Jack P. & Martin, Walter T. Status Integration & Suicide: A Sociological Study. LC 64-3173. (Illus.). 1964. 8.00 (ISBN 0-87114-009-8). U of Oreg Bks.
Gibbs, Jack P., ed. Social Control: Views from the Social Sciences. (Sage Focus Editions: Vol. 51). (Illus.). 288p. 1982. 28.00 (ISBN 0-8039-0615-3); pap. 14.00 (ISBN 0-8039-0616-1). Sage.
Gibbs, James. Book of Architecture. LC 68-17153. (Illus.). 1968. Repr. of 1728 ed. 66.00 (ISBN 0-405-08560-5, Blom Pubns). Ayer Co Pubs.
Gibbs, James, ed. Critical Perspectives on Wole Soyinka. LC 79-89931. (Critical Perspectives Ser.). (Illus.). 274p. (Orig.). 1980. 24.00 (ISBN 0-914478-49-4); pap. 14.00 (ISBN 0-914478-50-8). Three Continents.
Gibbs, James, ed. see Banda, Innocent O., et al.
Gibbs, James A. Oregon's Salty Coast. LC 78-11899. (Illus.). 1978. 10.95 (ISBN 0-87564-222-5). Superior Pub.
--Pacific Graveyard. 3rd enl. ed. LC 64-21182. (Illus.). 1973. pap. 7.95 (ISBN 0-8323-0225-2); map 2.00 (ISBN 0-8323-0050-0). Binford.
--Sentinels of the North Pacific. (Illus.). 1955. 8.95 (ISBN 0-8323-0011-X). Binford.
--Shipwrecks of the Pacific Coast. 2nd rev. & enl. ed. LC 57-13208. (Illus.). 1971. pap. 7.95 (ISBN 0-8323-0391-7). Binford.
--Shipwrecks Off Juan De Fuca. LC 68-28924. (Illus.). 1968. 8.95 (ISBN 0-8323-0012-8); map 2.00 (ISBN 0-8323-0051-9). Binford.
--Tillamook Light: A True Account of Oregon's Tillamook Rock Lighthouse. LC 79-65015. (Illus.). 1979. pap. 5.95 (ISBN 0-8323-0334-8). Binford.
Gibbs, James L., ed. Peoples of Africa. abridged ed. LC 77-28105. 1978. text ed. 14.95 (ISBN 0-03-039371-X, HoltC). HR&W.
Gibbs, James W. Dixie Clockmakers. (Illus.). 191p. 1979. 19.95 (ISBN 0-88289-059-X). Pelican.
--Pennsylvania Clocks & Watches: Antique Timepieces & Their Makers. LC 83-62539. (Illus.). 320p. 1984. 39.50 (ISBN 0-271-00367-7). Pa St U Pr.
Gibbs, Jim. Disaster Log of Ships. encore ed. LC 78-155334. (Illus.). 1971. 9.95 (ISBN 0-87564-208-X). Superior Pub.
--Maritime Memories of Puget Sound. LC 76-18150. (Illus.). 1976. 17.95 (ISBN 0-87564-219-5). Superior Pub.
Gibbs, Joan, jt. ed. see Brown, Julian.
Gibbs, John & McGee, Robert W. Let Accounting Help You Manage: A Managerial Accounting Primer. 257p. 1981. 17.95 (ISBN 0-13-531319-8); pap. 8.95 (ISBN 0-13-531301-5). P-H.
Gibbs, John A. Unit Steel Band. 1978. 7.50 (ISBN 0-682-48775-9). Exposition Pr FL.
Gibbs, John C. & Widaman, Keith F. Social Intelligence: Measuring the Development of Sociomoral Reflection. 272p. 1982. text ed. 35.00 (ISBN 0-13-815910-6). P-H.
Gibbs, Katherine. Travelin' Woman. (Orig.). 1980. pap. 1.95 (ISBN 0-8439-0728-2, Leisure Bks). Dorchester Pub Co.

Gibbs, Katherine L. Portrait of the Artist As a Young Man Notes. (Orig.). 1964. pap. 3.25 (ISBN 0-8220-1057-7). Cliffs.
Gibbs, Kenneth T. Business Architectural Imagery in America: 1870-1930. Foster, Stephen C., ed. LC 84-2743. (Architecture & Urban Design Ser.: No. 10). 210p. 1985. 39.95 (ISBN 0-8357-1575-2). UMI Res Pr.
Gibbs, Lee & Stevenson, Taylor. Myth & the Crisis of Historical Consciousness. LC 75-33049. (American Academy of Religion. Section Papers). 1975. pap. 9.95 (ISBN 0-89130-053-8, 010915). Scholars Pr GA.
Gibbs, Lee W., tr. see Ames, William.
Gibbs, Lewis. The Admirable Lady Mary. 1949. Repr. 25.00 (ISBN 0-8274-1816-7). R West.
Gibbs, Lewis, pseud. Sheridan. LC 75-103189. 1970. Repr. of 1947 ed. 23.50x (ISBN 0-8046-0826-1, Pub. by Kennikat). Assoc Faculty Pr.
Gibbs, Lewis. Sheridan. 1973. Repr. of 1947 ed. 13.00 (ISBN 0-8274-0400-X). R West.
Gibbs, Lois Marie. Love Canal: My Story. LC 81-14508. 174p. 1982. 12.95x (ISBN 0-87395-587-0); pap. 8.95x 321 0-87395-588-9. State U NY Pr.
Gibbs, M. Christians with Secular Power. LC 80-8048. (Laity Exchange). 144p. (Orig.). 1981. pap. 5.95 (ISBN 0-8006-1389-9, 1-1389). Fortress.
Gibbs, M. & Gibbs, E. The Bible References of John Ruskin. 59.95 (ISBN 0-87968-729-0). Gordon Pr.
Gibbs, M., ed. Structure & Function of Chloroplasts. LC 79-130575. (Illus.). 1971. 38.00 (ISBN 0-387-05258-5). Springer-Verlag.
Gibbs, M. & Latzko, E., eds. Photosynthesis Two: Photosynthetic Carbon Metabolism & Related Processes. (Encyclopedia of Plant Physiology, New Ser.: Vol. 6). (Illus.). 1979. 118.00 (ISBN 0-387-09288-9). Springer-Verlag.
Gibbs, M. E. & Mark, R. F. Inhibition of Memory Formation. LC 73-82140. 564p. 1973. 55.00x (ISBN 0-306-30750-2, Plenum Pr). Plenum Pub.
Gibbs, Marcia G., jt. ed. see Gibbs, Richard W.
Gibbs, Margaret. Leader Dogs for the Blind. LC 82-4612. (Illus.). 252p. 1982. 16.95 (ISBN 0-87714-095-2); pap. 11.95 (ISBN 0-87714-094-4). Denlingers.
--Saints Beyond the White Cliffs: Stories of English Saints. facs. ed. LC 75-148211. (Biography Index Reprint Ser.). (Illus.). 1947. 20.00 (ISBN 0-8369-8058-1). Ayer Co Pubs.
Gibbs, Margaret S., jt. ed. see Lachenmeyer, Juliana R.
Gibbs, Margaret S., et al, eds. Community Psychology: Theoretical & Empirical Approaches. 1980. text ed. 25.95 (ISBN 0-89876-056-9). Gardner Pr.
Gibbs, Marion & Lang, J. Bishops & Reform: 1215-1272. 216p. 1962. 26.00x (ISBN 0-7146-1476-9, F Cass Co). Biblio Dist.
Gibbs, Marion E., tr. see Von Eschenbach, Wolfram.
Gibbs, Mark, ed. see Mouw, Richard J.
Gibbs, Martin, jt. ed. see Ting, Irwin P.
Gibbs, Mary, jt. auth. see Gibbs, Ellen.
Gibbs, Mary A. A Most Romantic City. (General Ser.). 1978. lib. bdg. 10.95 (ISBN 0-8161-6583-1, Large Print Bks). G K Hall.
--Renegade Girl. 224p. 1981. pap. 1.95 (ISBN 0-449-50198-1, Crest). Fawcett.
--The Tulip Tree. 1979. pap. 1.75 (ISBN 0-449-50000-4, Coventry). Fawcett.
Gibbs, Mary Ann. Kitty. (Coventry Romance Ser.: No. 198). 192p. 1982. pap. 1.50 (ISBN 0-449-50301-1, Coventry). Fawcett.
Gibbs, Mifflin W. Shadow & Light: An Autobiography. LC 68-28998. (American Negro: His History & Literature Ser., No. 1). 1968. Repr. of 1902 ed. 16.00 (ISBN 0-405-01817-7). Ayer Co Pubs.
Gibbs, Peter. Rumblings. (Theatrescripts Ser.). 48p. 1985. pap. 4.95 (ISBN 0-413-59650-8, 9682). Methuen Inc.
Gibbs, Philip H., ed. Bridging the Atlantic. facs. ed. LC 78-128245. (Essay Index Reprint Ser). 1943. 16.75 (ISBN 0-8369-1928-9). Ayer Co Pubs.
Gibbs, Polly. Play Tunes: A Supplement to "Singing & Playing". 1971. 2.00x (ISBN 0-19-385156-3). Oxford U Pr.
Gibbs, R. Darnley. Chemotaxonomy of Flowering Plants, 4 vols. (Illus.). 2500p. 1974. 150.00x set (ISBN 0-7735-0098-7). McGill-Queens U Pr.
Gibbs, R. J. & Shaw, R. P., eds. Transport Processes in Lakes & Oceans. LC 77-11099. (Marine Science Ser.: Vol. 7). 296p. 1977. 49.50x (ISBN 0-306-35507-8, Plenum Pr). Plenum Pub.
Gibbs, Rafe. Beckoning the Bold. LC 76-16212. 266p. 1976. 6.95 (ISBN 0-89301-031-6). U Pr of Idaho.
Gibbs, Richard. Rubber Tires on Your Bike. (Origins Ser.). (gr. 4-6). 1984. PLB 8.90 (ISBN 0-531-04693-1). Watts.
--Women Prime Ministers. LC 81-86273. (In Profile Ser.). PLB 12.68 (ISBN 0-382-06638-3). Silver.
Gibbs, Richard C., jt. auth. see Costello, Maurice J.
Gibbs, Richard W. & Gibbs, Marcia G., eds. Family History Is Fun. 1978. 24.95 (ISBN 0-932924-00-X). Gibbs Pub OH.
Gibbs, Ronald, jt. auth. see Sweet, Richard L.
Gibbs, Ronald J., ed. Suspended Solids in Water. LC 74-19329. (Marine Science Ser.: Vol. 4). 320p. 1974. 55.00x (ISBN 0-306-35504-3, Plenum Pr). Plenum Pub.
Gibbs, Ronald K., jt. auth. see Taylor, Paul A.
Gibbs, Ronald S. & Weinstein, Alan J. Antibiotic Therapy in Obstetrics & Gynecology. LC 80-23095. 228p. Date not set. pap. 23.50 (ISBN 0-471-06003-8). Krieger.
Gibbs, Russell. Exercises for the Elderly. 152p. 1981. 15.00x (ISBN 0-906908-53-1, Pub. by Norman England). State Mutual Bk.
Gibbs, Sharon, jt. auth. see National Museum of American History Ser.
Gibbs, Stephen, jt. auth. see Miles, Edward.
Gibbs, Sunny, ed. see Hashagen, Werner R.
Gibbs, T. Kongi's Harvest: Study Aid. Rex Collings Ltd., ed. 20.00x (ISBN 0-317-20270-7, Pub. by R Collings UK). State Mutual Bk.
Gibbs, Tam, tr. see Men-Ching, Cheng.
Gibbs, Terry R. & Popolato, Alphonse, eds. LASL Explosive Property Data. (Los Alamos Scientific Laboratory Series on Dynamic Material Properties). 1980. 42.50x (ISBN 0-520-04012-0). U of Cal Pr.
Gibbs, Thomas E., jt. auth. see Meredith, Jack R.
Gibbs, Tony. Advanced Sailing. LC 74-83575. (Illus.). 1978. 8.95 (ISBN 0-312-00630-6); pap. 6.95 (ISBN 0-312-00631-4). St Martin.
--The Coastal Cruiser. (Illus.). 1981. 24.95 (ISBN 0-393-03267-1). Norton.
--Cruising in a Nutshell: The Art & Science of Enjoyable Coastwise Voyaging in Small Auxiliary Yachts. LC 83-42664. (Illus.). 285p. 1984. 19.95 (ISBN 0-393-03289-2). Norton.
--Practical Sailing. new ed. LC 70-172014. (Illus.). 1977. pap. 6.95 (ISBN 0-910990-37-9). Hearst Bks.
Gibbs, Tony & Sports Illustrated Editors. Sports Illustrated Power Boating. LC 72-13277. 1973. pap. 2.95i (ISBN 0-397-00972-0, LP81). Har-Row.
Gibby, Robert G., jt. auth. see Hutt, Max L.
Gibeau, Dawn. What Will I Be Living. (Infinity Ser.: No. 4). 1972. text ed. 2.50 (ISBN 0-03-004041-8, 233); tchr's. guide by Joan Uselmann 1.15 (ISBN 0-03-004046-9, 234). Winston Pr.
Gibeault, Victor A. Turfgrass Water Conservation. LC 85-70730. (Illus.). 184p. 1985. pap. 10.00 (ISBN 0-931876-69-9, 21405). Ag & Nat Res.
Gibellini, Rosino, ed. Frontiers of Theology in Latin America. Drury, John, tr. from Ital. LC 78-9147. Orig. Title: La nuova frontiera della Teologia in Latina America. 333p. (Orig.). 1979. pap. 10.95 (ISBN 0-88344-144-6). Orbis Bks.
Giber, J., et al, eds. Defect Complexes in Semiconductor Structures: Proceedings, Metrafuered, Hungary, 1982. (Lecture Notes in Physics: Vol. 175). 308p. 1983. pap. 20.00 (ISBN 0-387-11986-8). Springer-Verlag.
Gibert, Buch & Jose Y Palleja, J. De. Enciclopedia Universal De Perros, 2 vols. 1176p. (Espn.). 1977. Set. 120.00 (ISBN 84-255-0480-5, S-50538). French & Eur.
Gibert, Creighton E. The Works of Girolamo Savoldo: The 1955 Dissertation, with a Review of Research, 1955-1985. Freedberg, S. J., ed. (Outstanding Dissertations in Fine Arts Ser.). (Illus.). 690p. 1985. Repr. of 1955 ed. 70.00 (ISBN 0-8240-6856-4). Garland Pub.
Gibert, James, ed. see Lewis, Cecil.
Gibert, Stephen P. Soviet Images of America. LC 76-28569. 167p. 1977. pap. 9.95x (ISBN 0-8448-1075-4). Crane-Russak Co.
Gibian, George. Tolstoy & Shakespeare. LC 74-11281. 1957. lib. bdg. 8.50 (ISBN 0-8414-4529-X). Folcroft.
Gibian, George, ed. The Achievements of Vladimir Nabokov: Essays, Studies, Reminiscences & Stories. Parker, Stephen J. 256p. (Orig.). 1984. pap. text ed. 6.95 (ISBN 0-86731-079-0). RDC Ctr Intl Stud.
Gibian, George, ed. see Dostoevsky, Fyodor.
Gibian, George, ed. see Gogol, Nikolai V.
Gibian, George, ed. see Gogol, Nikoli V.
Gibian, George, ed. see Tolstoy, Leo.
Gibian, H., ed. see Gesellschaft Fuer Biologische Chemie, 21st Colloquium, Mossbach-Baden, 1970.
Gibilisco, Joseph A., jt. auth. see Stafne, Edward C.
Gibilisco, Stan. Basic Transistor Course. 2nd ed. (Illus.). 288p. 1984. 19.95 (ISBN 0-8306-0105-8, 1605); pap. 13.50 (ISBN 0-8306-0605-X). TAB Bks.
--Black Holes, Quasars & Other Mysteries of the Universe. (Illus.). 208p. 1984. pap. 13.50 (ISBN 0-8306-1525-3, 1525). TAB Bks.
--Comets, Meteors & Asteroids: How They Affect Earth. (Illus.). 208p. (Orig.). 1985. pap. 12.95 (ISBN 0-8306-1905-4, 1905). TAB Bks.
--Encyclopedia of Electronics. LC 84-16437. (Illus.). 1024p. 1984. 60.00 (ISBN 0-8306-2000-1, 2000). TAB Bks.
--Understanding Einstein's Theories of Relativity: Man's New Perspective on the Cosmos. (Illus.). 208p. (Orig.). 1983. o.p 18.95 (ISBN 0-8306-0505-3); pap. 11.50 (ISBN 0-8306-1505-9, 1505). TAB Bks.
--Violent Weather: Hurricanes, Tornadoes & Storms. LC 84-8873. (Illus.). 176p. (Orig.). 1984. pap. text ed. 13.95 (ISBN 0-8306-1805-8, 1805). TAB Bks.
Gibilisco, Stan, jt. auth. see Turner, Rufus P.
Giblett, Eloise R. Genetic Markers in Human Blood. (Illus.). 1969. 25.25 (ISBN 0-632-05290-2, B 1814-2, Blackwell). Mosby.
Giblin, James. The Skyscraper Book. LC 81-43038. (Illus.). 96p. (gr. 3-6). 1981. 10.53 (ISBN 0-690-04154-3); PLB 9.89 (ISBN 0-690-04155-1). Crowell Jr Bks.
Giblin, James & Ferguson, Dale. The Scarecrow Book. (Illus.). (gr. 2-4). 1980. 1.98 (ISBN 0-517-53862-8). Crown.
Giblin, James C. Chimney Sweeps. LC 81-43878. (Illus.). 64p. (gr. 4-8). 1982. 11.06i (ISBN 0-690-04192-6); PLB 11.89g (ISBN 0-690-04193-4). Crowell Jr Bks.
--Fireworks, Picnics, & Flags: The Story of the Fourth of July Symbols. LC 82-9612. (Illus.). 96p. (gr. 3-6). 1983. 11.95 (ISBN 0-89919-146-0, Clarion); pap. 4.95 (ISBN 0-89919-174-6). HM.
--The Truth about Santa Claus. LC 85-47541. (Illus.). 96p. (gr. 3-7). 1985. 11.06i (ISBN 0-690-04483-6); PLB 11.89g (ISBN 0-690-04484-4). Crowell Jr Bks.
Giblin, L. T. How to Have Confidence & Power in Dealing with People. 1956. 16.95 (ISBN 0-13-410688-1, Parker). P-H.
Giblin, P. J. Graphs, Surfaces & Homology: An Introduction to Algebraic Topology. 2nd ed. 1981. pap. 16.95 (ISBN 0-412-23900-0, NO. 6610, Pub. by Chapman & Hall). Methuen Inc.
Giblon, Shirley T., jt. auth. see Narrol, Harvey G.
Gibney, Frank. Five Gentlemen of Japan: The Portrait of a Nation's Character. LC 74-781480. 1973. pap. 7.95 (ISBN 0-8048-1108-3). C E Tuttle.
--Japan: The Fragile Superpower. rev. ed. 1985. pap. 8.95 (ISBN 0-452-00776-3, F707, Mer). NAL.
--Miracle by Design: The Real Reasons Behind Japan's Economic Success. 256p. 1982. 15.50 (ISBN 0-8129-1024-9). Times Bks.
--The Operators. LC 75-32546. 284p. 1976. Repr. of 1960 ed. lib. bdg. 18.00x (ISBN 0-8371-8492-4, GIOP). Greenwood.
Gibney, Michael J., jt. ed. see Kritchevsky, David.
Gibney, R. F. Container Lines: The Strategy Game. 1985. 150.00 (ISBN 0-907432-84-0). Lloyds London Pr.
Giboire, Clive, ed. see Van Nimmen, Jane.
Gibor, Aharon, intro. by. Conditions for Life: Readings from Scientific American. LC 76-22196. (Illus.). 256p. 1976. text ed. 23.95 (ISBN 0-7167-0480-3); pap. text ed. 11.95 (ISBN 0-7167-0479-X). W H Freeman.
Gibran, Kahlil. Broken Wings. Ferris, Anthony R., tr. 1965. pap. 2.95 (ISBN 0-8065-0190-1, 190). Citadel Pr.
--Earth Gods. (Illus.). 1931. 10.95 (ISBN 0-394-40344-4). Knopf.
--Forerunner. (Illus.). 1920. 9.95 (ISBN 0-394-40350-9). Knopf.
--Garden of the Prophet. (Illus.). 1933. 9.95 (ISBN 0-394-40352-5). Knopf.
--Jesus the Son of Man. (Illus.). 1928. 14.95 (ISBN 0-394-43124-3). Knopf.
--Kahlil Gibran: A Self-Portrait. Ferris, Anthony R., tr. 1967. pap. 3.95 (ISBN 0-8065-0108-1, 241). Citadel Pr.
--Lazarus & His Beloved. 64p. 1973. 5.95 (ISBN 0-8464-1165-2). Beekman Pubs.
--Madman. (Illus.). 1918. 8.95 (ISBN 0-394-40382-7). Knopf.
--Mirrors of the Soul. 1972. pap. 3.95 (ISBN 0-8065-0270-3). Citadel Pr.
--Nymphs of the Valley. (Illus.). 1948. 8.95 (ISBN 0-394-43883-3). Knopf.
--The Procession. 1972. pap. 3.95 (ISBN 0-8065-0274-6). Citadel Pr.
--Prophet. (Illus.). (YA) 1923. 7.95 (ISBN 0-394-40428-9); deluxe ed. 13.95 holiday boxed ed. (ISBN 0-394-40426-2); pocket ed. 7.95 (ISBN 0-394-40427-0). Knopf.
--Prophet: Regular. 7.95 (ISBN 0-394-40428-9). Random.
--Prose Poems. (Illus.). 1947. 7.95 (ISBN 0-394-40434-3). Knopf.
--Sand & Foam. (Illus.). 1926. 9.95 (ISBN 0-394-44369-1). Knopf.
--A Second Treasury of Kahlil Gibran. 7.95 (ISBN 0-8065-0230-4); pap. 5.95 (ISBN 0-8065-0411-0). Citadel Pr.
--Secrets of the Heart. Ferris, Anthony R., tr. from Arabic. 1978. pap. 5.95 (ISBN 0-8065-0062-X). Citadel Pr.
--Spirits Rebellious. Wolf, Martin L., ed. Ferris, Anthony R., tr. from Arabic. 128p. 1973. pap. 3.95 (ISBN 0-8065-0364-5). Citadel Pr.
--Spirits Rebellious. (Illus.). 1948. 7.95 (ISBN 0-394-44668-2). Knopf.
--Spiritual Sayings of Kahlil Gibran. Ferris, Anthony R., tr. 1965. pap. 3.95 (ISBN 0-8065-0041-7, 197). Citadel Pr.
--Tear & a Smile. (Illus.). 1950. 9.95 (ISBN 0-394-44804-9). Knopf.
--Tears & Laughter. 96p. 1984. pap. 3.95 (ISBN 0-8065-0903-1). Citadel Pr.
--Third Treasury of Kahlil Gibran. LC 73-90950. 484p. 1974. 9.95 (ISBN 0-8065-0403-X). Citadel Pr.
--A Third Treasury of Kahlil Gibran. Sherfan, Andrew D., ed. 1978. pap. 5.95 (ISBN 0-8065-0648-2). Citadel Pr.
--Thoughts & Meditations. Ferris, Anthony R., tr. 128p. 1984. pap. 3.95 (ISBN 0-8065-0916-3, 240). Citadel Pr.
--Treasury of Kahlil Gibran. 7.95 (ISBN 0-8065-0260-6). Citadel Pr.
--A Treasury of Kahlil Gibran. Wolf, Martin L., ed. Ferris, Anthony R, tr. from Arabic. 448p. 1974. pap. 6.95 (ISBN 0-8065-0410-2). Citadel Pr.
--Voice of the Master. 1963. pap. 3.95 (ISBN 0-8065-0022-0, 150). Citadel Pr.
--Wanderer. (Illus.). 1932. 10.95 (ISBN 0-394-45094-9). Knopf.
Gibrill, Hashim. Class & Class Struggle in Africa. Omenana Collective, ed. (Etudes et Analyses Marxistes en Afrique Ser.). 30p. (Orig.). 1983. pap. text ed. 3.00 (ISBN 0-943324-07-6). Omenana.
Gibson. Anchor Daily Devotional. 1983. 8.95 (ISBN 0-88207-336-2). Victor Bks.
--Microbial Degradation of Organic Compounds. (Microbiology Ser.). 520p. 1984. 89.75 (ISBN 0-8247-7102-8). Dekker.
--Walking the Maine Coast. (Illus.). 1977. pap. 4.50 (ISBN 0-89272-028-X). Down East.
Gibson & Mitchell. Introduction to Counseling & Guidance. 2nd ed. 747p. 1986. text ed. 22.50 write for info. (ISBN 0-02-341800-1). Macmillan.
Gibson & Roberson. British Bus Fleets No. 7 Midlands. pap. 4.00x (ISBN 0-392-08748-0, SpS). Sportshelf.
Gibson, A., ed. Controlled Fusion & Plasma Physics: Invited Papers from the Eleventh European Conference of the European Physical Society Plasma Physics Division, 5-9 September 1983, Aachen, Federal Republic of Germany. 276p. 1984. pap. 24.00 (ISBN 0-08-030286-6). Pergamon.
Gibson, A. Barbara, et al. Death Education: A Concern for the Living. LC 81-86311. (Fastback Ser.: No. 173). 50p. (Orig.). 1982. pap. 0.75 (ISBN 0-87367-173-2). Phi Delta Kappa.
Gibson, A. E. Processing of Polymer Composite Materials. 1986. price not set (ISBN 0-08-027617-2); pap. price not set (ISBN 0-08-027616-4). Pergamon.
Gibson, A. H. & Newton, W. E., eds. Current Perspective in Nitrogen Fixation. 534p. 1981. 90.00 (ISBN 0-444-80291-6, Biomedical Pr). Elsevier.
Gibson, A. M. Political Crime. facs. ed. LC 69-16851. (Select Bibliographies Reprint Ser). 1885. 21.50 (ISBN 0-8369-5007-0). Ayer Co Pubs.
Gibson, Agnes C., tr. see Grunwedel, Albert.
Gibson, Alan G. Eight Years in Kaffraria, 1882-1890. LC 79-82052. (Illus.). Repr. of 1891 ed. cancelled (ISBN 0-8371-1573-6, GIK&, Pub. by Negro U Pr). Greenwood.
Gibson, Arrell. The American Indian: Prehistory to the Present. 618p. 1980. pap. text ed. 14.95 (ISBN 0-669-04493-8). Heath.
--The Oklahoma Story. LC 77-18608. (Illus.). 1978. 14.95 (ISBN 0-8061-1461-4). U of Okla Pr.
--West in the Life of the Nation. 1976. 21.95x (ISBN 0-669-61515-3). Heath.
Gibson, Arrell M. The Chickasaws. (Civilization of the American Indian Ser.: Vol. 109). (Illus.). 320p. 1971. pap. 10.95 (ISBN 0-8061-1042-2). U of Okla Pr.
--The Encyclopedia of Missouri. (The Encyclopedia of the U. S. Ser.). (Illus.). 600p. 1985. Repr. lib. bdg. 79.00x (ISBN 0-403-09982-X). Somerset Pub.
--The History of Oklahoma. LC 83-40325. (Illus.). 300p. 1984. 14.95x (ISBN 0-8061-1883-0). U of Okla Pr.
--Life & Death of Colonel Albert Jennings Fountain. LC 65-11229. (Illus.). 1975. pap. 8.95 (ISBN 0-8061-1231-X). U of Okla Pr.
--Oklahoma: A History of Five Centuries. 2nd ed. LC 81-40284. (Illus.). 320p. 1981. Repr. 19.95 (ISBN 0-8061-1758-3). U of Okla Pr.
--The Santa Fe & Taos Colonies: Age of the Muses, 1900-1942. LC 82-40452. (Illus.). 328p. 1983. 24.95 (ISBN 0-8061-1835-0). U of Okla Pr.
--Wilderness Bonanza: The Tri-State Mining District of Missouri, Kansas & Oklahoma. LC 77-177335. (Illus.). 350p. 1972. 19.95 (ISBN 0-8061-0990-4); pap. 9.95 (ISBN 0-8061-1033-3). U of Okla Pr.
Gibson, Arrell M., ed. see Dale, Edward E.
Gibson, Arrell M., ed. see Kipling, Rudyard.
Gibson, Arthur. Biblical Semantic Logic. 1981. 32.50 (ISBN 0-312-07796-3). St Martin.
--The Silence of God: Creative Response to the Films of Ingmar Bergman. LC 81-18754. 171p. 1978. soft cover 9.95x (ISBN 0-88946-951-2). E Mellen.
Gibson, Arthur, tr. see Fabro, Cornelio.
Gibson, Arthur, et al. Truth in Advertising. LC 72-7241. 45p. 1984. Repr. of 1972 ed. 19.95x (ISBN 0-88946-912-1). E Mellen.
Gibson, Arthur C., jt. auth. see Brown, James H.
Gibson, Arthur H. Artists of Early Michigan: A Biographical Dictionary of Artists Native to or Active in Michigan 1701-1900. LC 74-32480. (Illus.). 216p. 1975. text ed. 9.95x (ISBN 0-8143-1528-3). Wayne St U Pr.
Gibson, Barbara G. Personal Computers in Business: An Introduction & Buyers Guide. (Illus., Orig.). 1982. pap. 2.95 (ISBN 0-9609780-0-3). Apple Comp.
Gibson, Betty S. Pride of the Golden Bear. 656p. 1981. text ed. 25.00 (ISBN 0-8403-2397-2). Kendall-Hunt.
Gibson, Boyce. Religion of Dostoevsky. 214p. 6.95 (ISBN 0-664-20989-0). Brown Bk.

Gibson, Byron H. Word Power: A Short Guide to Vocabulary & Spelling. rev. ed. 1975. pap. 4.00 (ISBN 0-912112-22-0). Everett-Edwards.

Gibson, C., ed. Selected Plays of Philip Massinger. LC 77-80835. (Plays by Renaissance & Restoration Dramatists Ser.). 1978. 49.50 (ISBN 0-521-21728-8); pap. 13.95x (ISBN 0-521-29243-3). Cambridge U Pr.

Gibson, C. D. Drawings. 1978. Repr. of 1894 ed. lib. bdg. 50.00 (ISBN 0-8492-0986-2). R West.

Gibson, C. G. Singular Points of Smooth Mappings. (Research Notes in Mathematics Ser.: No. 25). 239p. 1979. pap. text ed. 23.95 (ISBN 0-273-08410-0). Pitman Pub MA.

Gibson, C. G. & Wirthmuller, K. Topological Stability of Smooth Mappings. (Lecture Notes in Mathematics: Vol. 552). 1976. soft cover 13.00 (ISBN 0-387-07997-1). Springer-Verlag.

Gibson, Carol, ed. The Facts on File Dictionary of Mathematics. 224p. 1981. 14.95 (ISBN 0-87196-512-7). Facts on File.

Gibson, Catherine, ed. see Monroe City County Fine Arts Council.

Gibson, Cecil. History of British Dinkytoys 1934-1964. (Illus.). 1966. pap. 11.95 (ISBN 0-87938-008-X, Pub. by Mikansue & Modeller's World England). Motorbooks Intl.

Gibson, Charles. The Aztecs Under Spanish Rule: A History of the Indians of the Valley of Mexico, 1519-1810. (Illus.). 1964. 45.00x (ISBN 0-8047-0196-2); pap. 15.95x (ISBN 0-8047-0912-2). Stanford U Pr.

--Inca Concept of Sovereignty & the Spanish Administration in Peru. LC 69-19004. Repr. of 1948 ed. lib. bdg. 15.75x (ISBN 0-8371-1021-1, TLGI). Greenwood.

--Spain in America. (New American Nation Ser.). 1968. pap. 4.95xi (ISBN 0-06-133077-9, TB3077, Torch). Har-Row.

--Spain in America. LC 66-21705. (New American Nation Ser.). (Illus.). 1966. 16.30xi (ISBN 0-06-011520-3, HarpT). Har-Row.

--Tlaxcala in the Sixteenth Century. (Illus.). 1952. 25.00x (ISBN 0-8047-0615-8). Stanford U Pr.

Gibson, Charles, jt. auth. see Kubler, George.

Gibson, Charles, jt. ed. see Peckham, Howard.

Gibson, Charles D. Boca Grande: A Series of Historical Essays. LC 82-90197. (Illus.). 250p. (Orig.). 1982. pap. text ed. 12.95 (ISBN 0-9608996-0-X). C D Gibson.

--Gibson Girl & Her America. Gillon, Edmund V., ed. LC 68-28065. (Illus., Orig.). 1969. pap. 5.95 (ISBN 0-486-21986-0). Dover.

--Pictures of People. 1978. Repr. of 1894 ed. lib. bdg. 50.00 (ISBN 0-8492-0985-4). R West.

Gibson, Charles Dana. The Ordeal of Convoy Ny 119. LC 73-83176. (Illus.). 178p. 1973. 10.00 (ISBN 0-913344-15-X). South St Sea Mus.

Gibson, Charles E. Handbook of Knots & Splices: & Other Work with Hempen & Wire Rope. (Illus.). (gr. 7 up). 9.95 (ISBN 0-87523-146-2). Emerson.

Gibson, Charles H. & Frishkoff, Patricia A. Cases in Financial Reporting. 2nd ed. LC 84-26150. 448p. 1985. pap. text ed. write for info. (ISBN 0-534-04500-6). Kent Pub Co.

--Financial Statement Analysis. 2nd ed. LC 82-21155. 544p. 1982. text ed. write for info. (ISBN 0-534-01344-9). Kent Pub Co.

Gibson, Charles R. Heroes of the Scientific World. facs. ed. LC 79-117794. (Essay Index Reprint Ser.). 1913. 21.50 (ISBN 0-8369-1653-0). Ayer Co Pubs.

Gibson, Colin, ed. see Massinger, Philip.

Gibson, Cyrus F. Managing Organizational Behavior. 1980. 27.95x (ISBN 0-256-02237-2). Irwin.

Gibson, Cyrus F., jt. auth. see Lucas, Henry.

Gibson, D. Down's Syndrome: The Psychology of Mongolism. LC 77-87381. 1979. 52.50 (ISBN 0-521-21914-0). Cambridge U Pr.

Gibson, D. M. First Aid Homoeopathy in Accidents & Ailments. 1982. pap. 5.95x (ISBN 0-685-76564-4, Pub. by British Homoeopathy Assoc.). Formur Intl.

Gibson, Dauhrice & McFatter, Janiece. Computations Handbook: Preparation for the College Level Academic Skills Test. (Illus.). 480p. 1985. pap. text ed. 15.95 (ISBN 0-13-322421-X). P-H.

Gibson, David & Brown, Roy I. Managing the Severely Retarded: A Sampler. (Illus.). 500p. 1976. 32.75x (ISBN 0-398-03513-X). C C Thomas.

Gibson, David M., jt. ed. see Hjellming, Robert M.

Gibson, David W., jt. auth. see Meyer, Carl F.

Gibson, Dee, et al. Songs to Brighten Your Day: For Teachers of Young Children. (Orig.). 1984. pap. 6.95 (ISBN 0-916123-00-6); audio tape & Bk package 9.95 (ISBN 0-916123-01-4). Ed Graphics Pr.

Gibson, Dennis, ed. see Bande, Alexandre.

Gibson, Dennis L. Live, Grow & Be Free: A Guide to Self-Parenting. LC 82-82412. 136p. 1982. pap. 5.95 (ISBN 0-89840-030-9). Here's Life.

Gibson, Diane & Kaplan, Kathy. Short-Term Treatment in Occupational Therapy. LC 84-9115. (Occupational Therapy in Mental Health Ser.: Vol. 4, No. 3). 114p. 1984. 19.95 (ISBN 0-86656-342-3). Haworth Pr.

Gibson, Diane, ed. Occupational Therapy with Borderline Patients. LC 83-13008. (Occupational Therapy in Mental Health Ser.: Vol. 3, No. 3). 91p. 1983. text ed. 19.95 (ISBN 0-86656-262-1, B262). Haworth Pr.

Gibson, Diane, jt. ed. see Ellsworth, Paul D.

Gibson, Donald, ed. A Parson in the Vale of White Horse: George Woodward's Letters from East Hendred, 1753-61. 192p. 1982. pap. text ed. 8.75x (ISBN 0-86299-025-4, Pub. by Alan Sutton England). Humanities.

Gibson, Donald B. The Politics of Literary Expression: A Study of Major Black Writers. LC 80-27284. (Contributions in Afro-American & African Studies: No. 63). 240p. 1981. lib. bdg. 29.95 (ISBN 0-313-21271-6, GPE/). Greenwood.

Gibson, Donald B., ed. Modern Black Poets: A Collection of Critical Essays. 1973. 12.95 (ISBN 0-13-588392-X, Spec). P-H.

Gibson, Donald B., jt. ed. see Anselment, Carol.

Gibson, Donald M., ed. Australia & America-Are We the Same? Proceedings on a Seminar on Multinationals, Law, Unions, & Women's Rights. LC 77-83706. 1977. pap. 5.95 (ISBN 0-909162-06-9). Australiana.

Gibson, Dot. Boarding House Reach. 192p. 1981. pap. 7.95 (ISBN 0-941162-00-1). D Gibson.

--Cookbook Organizer. (Orig.). 1982. pap. 5.95 (ISBN 0-941162-01-X). D Gibson.

--Golden Isles Cuisine. 256p. 1978. pap. 9.95 (ISBN 0-918544-19-X). D Gibson.

Gibson, Duane, ed. A Citizen's Guide to Community Development. 48p. 1980. pap. 3.75 (ISBN 0-87866-164-6). Petersons Guides.

Gibson, Duncan. Energy Graphics. (Illus.). 144p. 1983. 21.95 (ISBN 0-13-277624-3). P-H.

Gibson, Duncan L., ed. Energy Graphics. World Eagle Editors. 88p. (Orig.). 1982. pap. text ed. 9.95 (ISBN 0-9608014-0-5). World Eagle.

Gibson, E. Principles of Perceptual Learning & Development. 1969. 36.00 (ISBN 0-13-709618-6). P-H.

Gibson, E. Burr, jt. auth. see Breivik, Patricia S.

Gibson, E. J., ed. Developments in Building Maintenance, Vol. 1. (Illus.). 260p. 1979. 33.50 (ISBN 0-85334-801-4, Pub. by Elsevier Applied Sci England). Elsevier.

Gibson, E. Lawrence. Get off My Ship: Ensign Berg vs. the U.S. Navy. 1978. pap. 4.95 (ISBN 0-380-40071-5, 40071-5). Avon.

Gibson, Edgar C. The Book of Job. 266p. 1983. lib. bdg. 10.00 (ISBN 0-86524-170-8, 1801). Klock & Klock.

Gibson, Edmund. Codex Juris Ecclesiastici Anglicani, 2 Vols. 1761. text ed. 372.60x (ISBN 0-318-12111-5, Pub. by Gregg Intl Pubs England). Gregg Intl.

Gibson, Edwin W. Collected Stories & Essays. 1982. 8.95 (ISBN 0-533-05429-X). Vantage.

Gibson, Eleanor J. & Levin, Harry. The Psychology of Reading. 1975. pap. 12.50x (ISBN 0-262-57052-1). MIT Pr.

Gibson, Elizabeth. The Water Is Wide. LC 83-12327. 272p. 1984. 11.95 (ISBN 0-310-31820-3, 12327). Zondervan.

Gibson, Elsie. Honest Prayer. LC 80-39570. 120p. (Orig.). 1981. pap. 7.95 (ISBN 0-664-24348-7). Westminster.

Gibson, Eva. Colleen. 150p. (Orig.). 1985. pap. 2.95 (ISBN 0-87123-809-8). Bethany Hse.

--Melissa. 137p. (Orig.). 1982. pap. 2.95 (ISBN 0-87123-575-7, 200575). Bethany Hse.

--Michelle. LC 83-72409. 176p. 1984. pap. 2.95 (ISBN 0-87123-405-X, 200405). Bethany Hse.

--Sara (Springflower) 144p. (Orig.). (gr. 8-12). 1984. pap. 2.95 (ISBN 0-87123-598-6). Bethany Hse.

Gibson, Evan K. C. S. Lewis, Spinner of Tales: A Guide to His Fiction. LC 80-19754. pap. 73.50 (ISBN 0-317-30140-3, 2025323). Bks Demand UMI.

Gibson, Florence, jt. auth. see Gibson, George.

Gibson, Florence E. Attitudes of the New York Irish Toward State & National Affairs, 1848-1892. (Columbia University. Studies in the Social Sciences: No. 563). Repr. of 1951 ed. 24.50 (ISBN 0-404-51563-0). AMS Pr.

Gibson, Francis. Gibby: The Memoirs 0f a Horsey Man. 1978. pap. 5.95 (ISBN 0-85131-277-2, NL51). J A Allen.

Gibson, Frank, jt. auth. see Golembiewski, Robert T.

Gibson, Frank, et al. Real Estate Law. LC 82-22998. 620p. 1983. text ed. 29.50 (ISBN 0-88462-454-4, 1560-01, Real Estate Ed). Longman USA.

Gibson, Frank F., jt. auth. see Dunfee, Thomas W.

Gibson, Frank K. & Prather, James E. Management of Program Evaluation. LC 84-7521. 1984. softbound 7.95 (ISBN 0-89854-101-8). U of GA Inst Govt.

Gibson, Frederick W. Queen's University, Vol II, 1917-1961: To Serve & Yet Be Free. 512p. 1983. 49.50x (ISBN 0-7735-0376-5). McGill-Queens U Pr.

Gibson, G. & Skett, P. Introduction to Drug Metabolism. 350p. 1985. text ed. 49.95 (ISBN 0-412-26390-4, 9643, Pub by Chapman & Hall); pap. text ed. 25.00 (ISBN 0-412-26400-5, 9644, Pub. by Chapman & Hall). Methuen Inc.

Gibson, G. & Skett, Paul. Introduction to Drug Metabolism. 350p. 1985. 49.95x (ISBN 0-412-26390-4, Pub. by Chapman & Hall); pap. 25.00x (ISBN 0-412-26400-5). Methuen Inc.

Gibson, G. G. & Ioannides, C., eds. Safety Evaluation of Nitrosatable Drugs & Chemicals. (Illus.). 275p. 1981. text ed. 39.50 (ISBN 0-85066-212-5, Pub. by Taylor & Francis England). J K Burgess.

Gibson, G. G. & Walker, R., eds. Food Toxicology: Proceedings of the International Symposium on Food Toxicology, Guildford, U. K., July 1983. 400p. 1985. 72.00 (ISBN 0-85066-272-9, Pub. by Falmer Pr). Taylor & Francis.

Gibson, G. J. Clinical Tests of Respiratory Function. 348p. 1984. pap. text ed. 24.50 (ISBN 0-88167-006-5). Raven.

Gibson, G. L., jt. auth. see Cooke, E. M.

Gibson, George. Captain Incognito. 224p. 1980. 12.00x (ISBN 0-245-53040-1, Pub. by Nautical England). State Mutual Bk.

Gibson, George & Gibson, Florence. Marriages of Monmouth County, New Jersey, 1795-1843. LC 81-80887. 143p. 1981. pap. 10.00 (ISBN 0-8063-0938-5). Genealog Pub.

Gibson, George, ed. Canberra. new ed. 1979. text ed. 4.25 (ISBN 0-7081-1296-X, Pub. by ANUP Australia). Australia N U P.

Gibson, George M. Story of the Christian Year. LC 71-142635. (Essay Index Reprint Ser.). (Illus.). Repr. of 1945 ed. 25.00 (ISBN 0-8369-2770-2). Ayer Co Pubs.

Gibson, Gerald D., jt. auth. see Gray, Michael H.

Gibson, Gerald O. & Gray, Michael H., eds. A Bibliography of Discographies: Volume I Classical Music, 1925-1975. LC 77-22661. 1977. 25.00 (ISBN 0-8352-1023-5). Bowker.

Gibson, Gerald W. Mastering Organic Chemistry: A Problem Solving Approach. LC 77-78569. 1979. pap. text ed. 18.95 (ISBN 0-7216-4111-3, CBS C). SCP.

Gibson, Glenn A. & Gibson, Mary L. Understanding & Selecting Small Business Computers. (Illus.). 400p. 1986. text ed. 28.95 (ISBN 0-13-937046-3). P-H.

Gibson, Glenn A. & Liu, Yu-Cheng. Microcomputers for Engineers & Scientists. (Illus.). 1980. text ed. 38.95 (ISBN 0-13-580886-3). P-H.

Gibson, Glenn A. & Young, James R. Introduction to Programming Using FORTRAN 77. (Illus.). 480p. 1982. pap. text ed. 22.95 (ISBN 0-13-493551-9). P-H.

Gibson, Glenn A., jt. auth. see Liu, Yu-Cheng.

Gibson, Gordon, ed. see Estermann, Carlos.

Gibson, Gordon, et al, eds. International Symposium on Immunotoxicology. 1984. 36.00 (ISBN 0-12-282180-7). Acad Pr.

Gibson, Gordon D., ed. see Estermann, Carlos.

Gibson, Graeme. Eleven Canadian Novelists. LC 72-91503. (Illus.). 324p. 1973. pap. 9.95 (ISBN 0-88784-615-7, Pub. by Hse Anansi Pr Canada). U of Toronto Pr.

--Perpetual Motion. LC 83-9772. 283p. 1983. 12.95 (ISBN 0-312-60132-8). St Martin.

Gibson, Guadalupe, ed. Our Kingdom Stands on Brittle Glass. 1983. pap. text ed. 11.95x (ISBN 0-87101-119-0). Natl Assn Soc Wkrs.

Gibson, Guy. Enemy Coast Ahead. LC 78-169417. (Literature & History of Aviation Ser). 1972. Repr. of 1946 ed. 19.00 (ISBN 0-405-03762-7). Ayer Co Pubs.

Gibson, H., jt. auth. see Hoover, Herbert C.

Gibson, H. B. Hans Eysenck: The Man & His Work. 275p. 1981. text ed. 26.50x (ISBN 0-7206-0566-0, Pub. by Peter Owen England). Humanities.

--Hypnosis: Its Nature & Therapeutic Uses. LC 77-92821. 1980. pap. 4.95 (ISBN 0-8008-4043-7). Taplinger.

Gibson, Harry, jt. auth. see Rademacher, Robert.

Gibson, Hugh, ed. see Ciano, Galeazzo.

Gibson, Ian. Assassination of Federico Garcia Lorca. 268p. 1983. pap. 5.95 (ISBN 0-14-006473-7). Penguin.

--The English Vice: Beating, Sex & Shame in Victorian England. LC 83-49421. 384p. 1984. cancelled (ISBN 0-394-53877-3, GP923); pap. cancelled (ISBN 0-394-62186-7, E 937). Grove.

Gibson Inc. The Banjo. Repr. of 1927 ed. 6.00 (ISBN 0-686-21419-6). Mih.

Gibson, J., jt. auth. see Grainger, L.

Gibson, J. A. Diseases of Forest Trees Widely Planted as Exotics in the Tropics & Southern Hemisphere, Part 1. 1975. 30.00x (ISBN 0-85074-036-3, Pub. by for Lib Comm England). State Mutual Bk.

--Diseases of Forest Trees Widely Planted as Exotics in the Tropics & Southern Hemisphere, Part 2. 1978. 30.00x (ISBN 0-85074-028-2, Pub. by For Lib Comm England). State Mutual Bk.

Gibson, J. B. Histological Typing of Tumors of the Liver, Biliary Tract & Pancreas. (World Health Organization: International Histological Classification of Tumours Ser.: No. 20). (Illus.). 1978. text ed. 42.00 (ISBN 92-4-176020-6, 70-1-020-20); text & slides 128.50 (ISBN 0-89189-121-8, 70-1-020-00). Am Soc Clinical.

Gibson, J. B. & Oakeshoff, J. G., eds. Genetic Studies of Drosophila Populations. 267p. (Orig.). 1981. pap. text ed. 10.00 (ISBN 0-686-30658-9, 0069, Pub. by ANUP Australia). Australia N U P.

Gibson, J. C., jt. ed. see Foakes, R. A.

Gibson, J. E. Computing in Structural Engineering. (Illus.). xv, 290p. 1975. 52.00 (ISBN 0-85334-614-3, Pub. by Elsevier Applied Sci England). Elsevier.

--Designing the New City: A Systematic Approach. LC 76-44899. (Systems Engineering & Analysis Ser.). 288p. 1977. 46.95x (ISBN 0-471-29752-6, Pub. by Wiley-Interscience). Wiley.

--Thin Shells: Computing & Theory. (International Series in Structure & Solid Body Mechanics). (Illus.). 1980. 47.00 (ISBN 0-08-023275-2); pap. 18.00 (ISBN 0-08-024204-9). Pergamon.

Gibson, J. E., jt. auth. see LaConte, P.

Gibson, J. J. see Lepley, William M.

Gibson, J. M. & Dawson, L. R., eds. Layered Structures Epitaxy & Interfaces, Vol. 37. LC 85-3077. 1985. text ed. 50.00 (ISBN 0-931837-02-2). Materials Res.

Gibson, J. Paul. Shakespeare's Use of the Supernatural. LC 79-144615. Repr. of 1908 ed. 15.00 (ISBN 0-404-02719-9). AMS Pr.

Gibson, J. R. Electronic Logic Circuits. (Illus.). 114p. 1981. text ed. 25.70 (ISBN 0-205-07603-3, 207603). Allyn.

--Electronic Logic Circuits. 2nd ed. 135p. 1983. pap. text ed. 13.95 (ISBN 0-7131-3407-0). E Arnold.

Gibson, J. S. A Simplified Guide to Bishops' Transcripts & Marriage Licenses, Their Location & Indexes in England, Wales, & Ireland. LC 82-82482. 33p. 1984. pap. 4.00 (ISBN 0-8063-0995-4). Genealog Pub.

--A Simplified Guide to Probate Jurisdictions: Where to Look for Wills in Great Britain & Ireland. LC 82-82481. (Illus.). 72p. 1982. pap. 5.00 (ISBN 0-8063-0994-6). Genealog Pub.

Gibson, J. Sullivan, jt. auth. see Batten, J. W.

Gibson, J. Tyrone. Medication Law & Behavior. LC 75-36008. 429p. 1976. 25.50 (ISBN 0-471-29760-7). Krieger.

Gibson, J. W. & Crogman, W. H. Progress of a Race: Or, Remarkable Advancement of the American Negro. facs. ed. LC 79-81118. (Black Heritage Library Collection Ser). 1902. 31.25 (ISBN 0-8369-8578-8). Ayer Co Pubs.

Gibson, James. Locke's Theory of Knowledge & Its Historical Relations. LC 18-10164. pap. 88.00 (ISBN 0-317-08834-3, 2050743). Bks Demand UMI.

Gibson, James, compiled by. The Burns Calendar. LC 70-144555. (Illus.). Repr. of 1874 ed. 11.50 (ISBN 0-404-08513-X). AMS Pr.

Gibson, James, ed. & intro. by see Hardy, Thomas.

Gibson, James, ed. see Hardy, Thomas.

Gibson, James E. Dr. Bodo Otto & the Medical Background of the American Revolution. (Illus.). 342p. 1937. 34.50x (ISBN 0-398-04265-9). C C Thomas.

Gibson, James E., ed. Formaldehyde Toxicity. LC 82-6189. (Chemical Industry Institute of Toxicology Ser.). (Illus.). 312p. 1983. text ed. 59.95 (ISBN 0-89116-275-5). Hemisphere Pub.

Gibson, James J. The Ecological Approach to Visual Perception. LC 78-69585. (Illus.). 1979. text ed. 39.95 (ISBN 0-395-27049-9). HM.

--The Perception of the Visual World. LC 74-17588. (Illus.). 235p. 1974. Repr. of 1950 ed. lib. bdg. 22.50x (ISBN 0-8371-7836-3, GIVW). Greenwood.

--The Senses Considered as Perceptual Systems. LC 83-1716. (Illus.). xiv, 335p. 1983. Repr. of 1966 ed. lib. bdg. 55.00x (ISBN 0-313-23961-4, GISE). Greenwood.

--The Senses Considered as Perceptual Systems. (Illus.). 336p. 1983. pap. text ed. 15.95x (ISBN 0-88133-062-0). Waveland Pr.

Gibson, James L. & Bingham, Richard D. Civil Liberties & Nazis: The Skokie Free-Speech Controversy. LC 84-26320. 240p. 1985. 34.95x (ISBN 0-03-001634-7). Praeger.

Gibson, James L., et al. Organizations: Behavior, Structure, Processes. 5th ed. 1985. 29.95x (ISBN 0-256-03265-3). Business Pubns.

--Organizations Closeup: A Book of Readings. 5th ed. 1985. pap. 15.95 (ISBN 0-256-03266-1). Business Pubns.

Gibson, James R. Farming the Frontier: The Agricultural Opening of the Oregon Country, 1786-1846. (Illus.). 288p. 1985. 25.00 (ISBN 0-295-96297-6). U of Wash Pr.

--Feeding the Russian Fur Trade: Provisionment of the Okhotsk Seaboard & the Kamchatka Peninsula, 1639-1856. LC 79-81319. (Illus.). 358p. 1969. 27.50x (ISBN 0-299-05230-3). U of Wis Pr.

--How to Make More in Music: A Freelance Guide. 128p. (Orig.). 1984. pap. 9.95 (ISBN 0-915849-00-3). Workbks Pr.

--Imperial Russia in Frontier America: The Changing Geography of Supply of Russian America, 1784-1867. (The Andrew H. Clark Series in the Historical Geography of North America). (Illus.). 1976. pap. text ed. 9.95x (ISBN 0-19-501875-3). Oxford U Pr.

Gibson, James R. & Shur, L. A., eds. Russian California, 1812-41. 1980. 60.00x (ISBN 0-686-79474-5, Pub. by Hakluyt Soc England). State Mutual Bk.

Gibson, James W. & Cornwell, Clifton. Creative Speech Communication. 1978. pap. text ed. write for info. (ISBN 0-02-341720-X). Macmillan.

Gibson, James Y. Story of the Zulus. rev. ed. LC 72-109326. Repr. of 1911 ed. 25.00x (ISBN 0-8371-3592-3, GIZ&, Pub. by Negro U Pr). Greenwood.

Gibson, Jamie. Four B Goes Wild. (Illus.). 160p. 1984. pap. 2.25 (ISBN 0-671-50984-5). Archway.

Gibson, Jane, jt. auth. see Padzensky, Herbert R.

Gibson, Janice. Psychology for the Classroom. 2nd ed. (Illus.). 640p. 1981. pap. text ed. 28.95 (ISBN 0-13-733352-8); student study guide 12.95 (ISBN 0-13-733386-2). P-H.
Gibson, Janice T. Discipline Is Not a Dirty Word. LC 83-1010. 176p. 1983. 13.95 (ISBN 0-86616-027-2); pap. 7.95 (ISBN 0-86616-023-X). Greene.
--Living: Human Development Through the Lifespan. 560p. 1983. text ed. 23.95 (ISBN 0-394-34912-1, RanC); 5.95 (ISBN 0-394-34914-8). Random.
Gibson, Jean. Basic Christian Training. (Believer's Bible Lessons Ser.). 1980. pap. 5.95 (ISBN 0-937396-06-0). Walterick Pubs.
--Intermediate Christian Training. 1981. pap. 6.95 (ISBN 0-937396-60-5). Walterick Pubs.
--Survey in Basic Christianity. (Believer's Bible Lessons Ser.). 1979. pap. 4.95 (ISBN 0-937396-41-9). Walterick Pubs.
Gibson, Jeremy S. Wills & Where to Find Them (in Great Britain) LC 74-2775. (Illus.). 210p. 1974. 15.00 (ISBN 0-8063-0619-X). Genealog Pub.
Gibson, Jerry D. & Melsa, James L. Introduction to Nonparametric Detection with Applications. (Mathematics in Science & Engineering Ser.). 1975. 70.00 (ISBN 0-12-282150-5). Acad Pr.
Gibson, Joan. Open the Window! Healing Ideas for the Lonely & Depressed. 128p. 1985. pap. 6.95 (ISBN 0-946551-17-0, Pub. by Gateway Bks). Interbook.
Gibson, John. The Book of Hu & the Book of Tyana. LC 84-19096. (Illus.). 136p. 1984. 15.00 (ISBN 0-8022-2449-0). Philos Lib.
--Common Symptoms Described for Nurses. 2nd ed. (Blackwell Scientific Pubns.). (Illus.). 200p. 1978. 6.75 (ISBN 0-632-00442-8, B 1825-8). Mosby.
--Fifty Hikes in Maine: Day Hikes & Backpacking Trips from the Coast to Katahdin. 2nd, rev. ed. LC 82-25276. (Fifty Hikes Ser.). (Illus.). 192p. (Orig.). 1983. pap. 8.95 (ISBN 0-942440-13-7). Backcountry Pubns.
--Modern Physiology & Anatomy for Nurses. 2nd ed. (Illus.). 352p. 1981. pap. text ed. 17.95 (ISBN 0-632-00795-8, B 1832-0). Mosby.
--Reminiscences of Sir Walter Scott. Repr. of 1871 ed. lib. bdg. 8.50 (ISBN 0-8414-4647-4). Folcroft.
Gibson, John C. Great Western Locomotive Design: A Critical Appreciation. (Illus.). 160p. 1984. 19.95 (ISBN 0-7153-8606-9). David & Charles.
--Textbook of Syrian Semitic Inscriptions: Aramaic Inscriptions, Including Inscriptions in the Dialect of Zenjirli, Vol. 2. (Illus.). 1975. 39.95x (ISBN 0-19-813186-0). Oxford U Pr.
--Textbook of Syrian Semitic Inscriptions: Vol. 3 Phonecian Inscriptions, Including Inscriptions in the Mixed Dialect of Arslan Tash. (Illus.). 1982. 39.50x (ISBN 0-19-813199-2). Oxford U Pr.
Gibson, John C. L. Genesis, Vol. 1 chs. 1-11. LC 81-7477. (Daily Study Bible-Old Testament Ser.). 224p. 1981. 12.95 (ISBN 0-664-21801-6); pap. 6.95 (ISBN 0-664-24568-4). Westminster.
--Genesis, Vol. 2, chs. 12-50. LC 81-7477. (Daily Study Bible-Old Testament Ser.). 336p. 1982. 12.95 (ISBN 0-664-21804-0); pap. 7.95 (ISBN 0-664-24571-4). Westminster.
--Textbook of Syrian Semitic Inscription: Vol. 1, Hebrew & Moabite Inscriptions. 1971. text ed. 25.95x (ISBN 0-19-813159-3). Oxford U Pr.
Gibson, John E. Managing Research & Development. LC 81-2033. 367p. 1981. 48.95x (ISBN 0-471-08799-8, Pub. by Wiley-Interscience). Wiley.
Gibson, John M., jt. auth. see Green, Richard L.
Gibson, John M., ed. see Doyle, Arthur Conan.
Gibson, John S. Deacon Brodie Father to Jekyll & Hyde. (Illus.). 158p. 1977. 11.50x (ISBN 0-87471-879-1). Rowman.
--The United States International Visitor Program: Strengthening the Community Organization. 108p. 1979. 1.00 (ISBN 0-318-15385-8). Natl Coun Intl Visitors.
Gibson, Jon. Melody III, Book II. pap. 10.00 (ISBN 0-89439-003-1). Printed Matter.
Gibson, Joyce & Hance, Eleanor. You Can Teach Juniors & Middlers. 64p. 1981. pap. 2.50 (ISBN 0-88207-145-9). Victor Bks.
Gibson, Karen. The Annapolis Diet. 304p. 1984. 13.95 (ISBN 0-312-03842-9). St Martin.
Gibson, Katharine. Goldsmith of Florence: A Book of Great Craftsmen. facs. ed. LC 67-30215. (Essay Index Reprint Ser). 1929. 31.00 (ISBN 0-8369-0473-7). Ayer Co Pubs.
Gibson, Katherine. The Tall Book of Bible Stories. LC 57-10952. (Tall Bks.). (Illus.). 128p. (gr. k-3). 1980. 5.95 (ISBN 0-06-021935-1); PLB 7.89 (ISBN 0-06-021936-X). HarpJ.
Gibson, Katherine W., et al. On Our Own. 224p. 1982. pap. 2.50 (ISBN 0-380-60269-5, 60269-5). Avon.
Gibson, Keiko M. Stir Up the Precipitable World. 1985. 8.00 (ISBN 0-934834-69-5). White Pine.
Gibson, Kerr, jt. auth. see Quirin, G. David.
Gibson, Kristi, jt. ed. see Rohmann, Gloria.
Gibson, L., jt. auth. see Alexander, John W.
Gibson, Lay J. & Renteria, Alfonso C., eds. The U. S. & Mexico: Borderland Development & the National Economies. (Replica Edition Ser.). 300p. 1985. pap. 25.00x (ISBN 0-86531-870-0). Westview.
Gibson, Litzka R. How to Read Palms. LC 77-2290. 1977. pap. 4.95. Fell.
Gibson, M. & Biggs, R. D., eds. Seals & Sealing in the Ancient Near East. LC 76-44923. (Bibliotheca Mesopotamica Ser: Vol. 6). 160p. 1977. pap. 29.00x (ISBN 0-89003-022-7); cloth & microfiche 39.00. Undena Pubns.
Gibson, M. A., jt. auth. see Gibson, S.
Gibson, McGuire. Excavations at Nippur. LC 75-9054. (Oriental Institute Communications Ser.: No. 22). 1976. pap. 15.00x (ISBN 0-226-62339-4). U of Chicago Pr.
Gibson, McGuire, jt. ed. see Downing, Theodore E.
Gibson, McGuire, et al. Excavations at Nippur: Twelfth Season. LC 78-59117. (Oriental Institute Communications Ser.: No. 23). (Illus.). 1978. pap. 22.00x (ISBN 0-918986-22-2). Oriental Inst.
Gibson, McGuire, et al, eds. Uch Tepe I, Tell Razuk, Tell Ahmed al-Mughir, Tell Ajamat. Thuesen, Ingolf & Sanders, John C. (The Chicago-Copenhagen Expedition to the Hamrin Ser.). (Illus.). xi, 198p. 1981. pap. 25.00x (ISBN 0-918986-34-6). Oriental Inst.
Gibson, Margaret. The Butterfly Ward. LC 79-678155. 135p. 1980. 10.95 (ISBN 0-8149-0834-9). Vanguard.
--Considering Her Condition. 120p. 1981. 8.95 (ISBN 0-8149-0855-1). Vanguard.
--Lanfranc of Bec. 1978. 45.00x (ISBN 0-19-822462-1). Oxford U Pr.
--Long Walks in the Afternoon: Poems. LC 82-275. 72p. 1982. text ed. 13.95x (ISBN 0-8071-1017-5); pap. 5.95 (ISBN 0-8071-1018-3). La State U Pr.
--Signs: Poems. LC 78-11961. viii, 64p. 1979. 13.95x (ISBN 0-8071-0493-0); pap. 4.95 (ISBN 0-8071-0494-9). La State U Pr.
Gibson, Margaret, jt. auth. see Hunt, R. W.
Gibson, Margaret, ed. Boethius: His Life, Thought & Influence. (Illus.). 478p. 1982. text ed. 48.00x (ISBN 0-631-11141-7). Biblio Dist.
Gibson, Margaret & McCann, Richard, eds. Landscape & Distance: Contemporary Poets from Virginia. LC 75-2350. 120p. 1975. 5.75x (ISBN 0-8139-0622-9); pap. 4.95x (ISBN 0-8139-0656-3). U Pr of Va.
Gibson, Margaret, ed. see Lanfranc.
Gibson, Margaret I. The Roots of Russian Through Chekhov: A Study in Word-Formation. LC 81-43705. 236p. (Orig.). 1982. lib. bdg. 25.50 (ISBN 0-8191-2681-0); pap. text ed. 12.25 (ISBN 0-8191-2682-9). U Pr of Amer.
Gibson, Margaret W. Emma Smith: Elect Lady. LC 54-7910. 1954. pap. 8.00 (ISBN 0-8309-0256-2). Herald Hse.
Gibson, Marsha. Passion's Treasure. 352p. (Orig.). 1982. pap. 3.25 (ISBN 0-505-51805-8, Pub. by Tower Bks). Dorchester Pub Co.
Gibson, Martin L. Editing in the Electronic Era. 2nd ed. 1984. text ed. 24.95x (ISBN 0-8138-0965-7). Iowa St U Pr.
Gibson, Mary. Workers' Rights. LC 83-17788. (Philosophy & Society Ser.). 166p. 1983. 23.50x (ISBN 0-8476-6756-1); pap. 7.95x (ISBN 0-8476-7351-0). Rowman & Allanheld.
Gibson, Mary, ed. To Breathe Freely: Risk, Consent, & Air. (Maryland Studies in Public Philosophy). 220p. 1985. 35.00x (ISBN 0-8476-7416-9). Rowman & Allanheld.
Gibson, Mary J. & Heath, Angela, eds. International Survey of Periodicals in Gerontology. 2nd ed. LC 82-152919. 92p. (Orig.). 1982. pap. text ed. 10.00 (ISBN 0-910473-02-1). Intl Fed Ageing.
Gibson, Mary Jo. Older Women Around the World. 75p. 1985. pap. 5.00 (ISBN 0-910473-15-3). Intl Fed Ageing.
Gibson, Mary L., jt. auth. see Gibson, Glenn A.
Gibson, Michael. Gods, Men & Monsters from the Greek Myths. LC 81-14542. (World Mythologies Ser.). (Illus.). 156p. 1982. 15.95 (ISBN 0-8052-3793-3). Schocken.
--Growing Roses. (Illus.). 200p. 1984. 18.95 (ISBN 0-917304-92-6). Timber.
--The Vikings. LC 77-86712. (Peoples of the Past Ser.). (Illus.). 61p. (gr. 4 up). 1977. PLB 13.72 (ISBN 0-382-06122-5). Silver.
--The Vikings. (Peoples of the Past Ser.). 80p. (gr. 4 up). 1985. pap. 5.75 (ISBN 0-382-06912-9). Silver.
Gibson, Michael & Box, Sue. Discovering Ancient Mysteries. (Full Color Fact Books). (Illus.). 32p. (gr. 4-12). 1981. PLB 7.95 (ISBN 0-8219-0015-3, 35549). EMC.
Gibson, Michael & Pike, Trisha. All about Knights. (Full Color Fact Bks.). (Illus.). 32p. (gr. 4-12). 1982. PLB 7.95 (ISBN 0-8219-0016-1, 35547). EMC.
Gibson, Michael J., ed. see Doyle, Arthur Conan.
Gibson, Michael S. & Langstaff, Michael J. An Introduction to Urban Renewal. (The Built Environment Ser.). (Illus.). 384p. 1984. pap. 11.95 (ISBN 0-09-147501-5, Pub. by Hutchinson Educ). Longwood Pub Group.
Gibson, Miles. The Sandman. 192p. 1985. 12.95 (ISBN 0-312-69912-3, Pub. by Marek). St Martin.
Gibson, Miles E. Agricultural Aviation. 100p. (Orig.). 1974. pap. 9.95 (ISBN 0-942306-02-3). Diversified Pub Co.
--Agricultural Pilot & Chemicals. (Illus.). 75p. (Orig.). 1974. pap. 9.95 (ISBN 0-942306-05-8). Diversified Pub Co.
--All about Crop Dusting. 95p. (Orig.). 1968. pap. 9.95 (ISBN 0-942306-01-5). Diversified Pub Co.
--A Million Dollar Aviator. 109p. (Orig.). 1976. pap. text ed. 9.95 (ISBN 0-942306-04-X). Diversified Pub Co.
--So You Think You Want to Be a Crop-Duster. rev. ed. (Illus.). 140p. 1978. pap. 9.95 (ISBN 0-942306-00-7). Diversified Pub Co.
Gibson, Morgan. The Great Brook Book. (Illus.). 80p. 1981. 25.00 (ISBN 0-939622-18-1); pap. 7.00 (ISBN 0-939622-17-3). Four Zoas Night.
Gibson, Morgan, tr. Tantric Poems of Kukai. 1985. 5.00 (ISBN 0-934834-67-9). White Pine.
Gibson, Morris. One Man's Medicine. 218p. 1983. 12.95 (ISBN 0-8253-0122-X). Beaufort Bks NY.
--A View of the Mountains. LC 83-29728. 224p. 1984. 13.95 (ISBN 0-8253-0186-6). Beaufort Bks NY.
--A View of the Mountains. 256p. 1985. pap. 2.95 (ISBN 0-449-20704-8, Crest). Fawcett.
Gibson, Nevin. Golf's Greatest Shots by the World's Greatest Players. 160p. 1981. 9.95 (ISBN 0-89962-218-6). Todd & Honeywell.
Gibson, Norman R. The Case for International Money. Wilkins, Mira, ed. LC 78-3913. (International Finance Ser.). 1978. lib. bdg. 24.50x (ISBN 0-405-11217-3). Ayer Co Pubs.
Gibson, Otis. The Chinese in America. Daniels, Roger, ed. LC 78-54816. (Asian Experience in North America Ser.). 1979. Repr. of 1877 ed. lib. bdg. 26.50x (ISBN 0-405-11272-6). Ayer Co Pubs.
Gibson, Price. Quality Circles: An Approach to Productivity Improvement. (Studies in Productivity: Highlights of the Literature Ser.: Vol. 26). 79p. 1982. pap. 35.00 (ISBN 0-08-029507-X). Work in Amer.
--Quality Circles: One Approach to Productivity Improvement. (Work in America Institute Studies in Productivity). 1982. 35.00 (ISBN 0-08-029507-X). Pergamon.
Gibson, R., compiled by. Modern French Poets on Poetry. LC 78-73241. 1979. 39.50 (ISBN 0-521-05078-2). Cambridge U Pr.
Gibson, R. W. Disclosure by Australian Companies. (Illus.). 354p. 1971. 25.00x (ISBN 0-522-83996-7, Pub. by Melbourne U Pr). Intl Spec Bk.
Gibson, Ralph. Days at Sea. LC 74-13171. 72p. 1974. pap. 12.95 (ISBN 0-912810-15-7). Lustrum Pr.
--Deja-Vu: Second in the Black Trilogy. LC 72-96851. 52p. 1972. 12.95 (ISBN 0-912810-06-8). Lustrum Pr.
--The Somnambulist. 2nd ed. LC 73-88292. (Illus.). 48p. 1973. 12.95 (ISBN 0-912810-09-2). Lustrum Pr.
--Syntax. LC 82-83708. (Illus.). 80p. 1983. 24.95 (ISBN 0-912810-39-4). Lustrum Pr.
Gibson, Ralph, et al, eds. Contact: Theory. LC 80-7809. (Illus.). 176p. 1982. 35.00 (ISBN 0-912810-30-0); pap. 17.95 (ISBN 0-912810-31-9). Lustrum Pr.
Gibson, Ray. British Nemerteans. LC 81-18193. (Synopses of the British Fauna Ser.: No. 24). 200p. 1982. 37.50 (ISBN 0-521-24619-9). Cambridge U Pr.
--Nemerteans. (Illus.). 1972. text ed. 11.00x (ISBN 0-09-111990-1, Hutchinson U Lib); pap. text ed. 6.00x (ISBN 0-09-111991-X, Hutchinson U Lib). Humanities.
Gibson, Raymond W. Forever in Debt. (Orig.). 1980. pap. text ed. 5.75 (ISBN 0-89536-461-1). CSS of Ohio.
Gibson, Rex. Teacher-Parent Communication: One School & Its Practice. 1981. 15.00x (ISBN 0-686-45451-0, Pub. by Cambridge Inst Ed England). State Mutual Bk.
Gibson, Richard. African Liberation Movements: Contemporary Struggles Against White Minority Rule. (Illus.). 1972. pap. 4.95 (ISBN 0-19-501617-3, GB). Oxford U Pr.
Gibson, Robert. Career Development in the Elementary School. LC 75-179456. 1972. pap. text ed. 10.95x (ISBN 0-675-09161-6). Merrill.
Gibson, Robert L. & Mitchell, Marianne. An Introduction to Guidance. (Illus.). 1981. text ed. write for info. (ISBN 0-02-341730-7). Macmillan.
Gibson, Robert L., et al. Development & Management of Counseling Programs & Guidance Services. 448p. 1983. text ed. write for info. (ISBN 0-02-341770-6). Macmillan.
Gibson, Robert S., jt. auth. see Suratt, Paul M.
Gibson, Robert W., Jr. & Kunkel, Barbara K. Japanese Scientific & Technical Literature: A Subject Guide. LC 80-39693. (Illus.). xv, 560p. 1981. lib. bdg. 75.00 (ISBN 0-313-22929-5, GJS/). Greenwood.
Gibson, Robert W., Jr., ed. The Special Library Role in Networks: Proceedings of a Conference. 296p. 1980. pap. 10.50 (ISBN 0-87111-279-5). SLA.
Gibson, Robert W., Jr., ed. see Special Libraries Association.
Gibson, Roger F. The Philosophy of W. V. Quine: An Expository Essay. LC 81-16338. 1982. 22.00 (ISBN 0-8130-0707-0). U Presses Fla.
Gibson, Ronald. Jefferson Davis & the Confederacy: Chronology-Documents-Bibliographical Aids. LC 77-10189. (Presidential Chronology Ser.). 205p. 1977. 15.00 (ISBN 0-379-12095-X). Oceana.
--Name & Subject Index to the Presidential Chronology Series: From George Washington to Gerald Ford. LC 77-21512. (Presidential Chronology Ser.). 141p. 1977. 15.00 (ISBN 0-379-12094-1). Oceana.
Gibson, Roxie C. Do Ragweeds Bloom? LC 84-51429. 104p. 1984. 6.95 (ISBN 0-938232-56-8). Winston-Derek.
--Hey, God! Hurry! LC 82-60193. (Illus.). 52p. (gr. 3-5). 1982. 3.95 (ISBN 0-938232-08-8, 32534). Winston-Derek.
--Hey, God! Listen! LC 82-60195. (Illus.). 68p. (gr. 3-5). 1982. 3.95 (ISBN 0-938232-06-1, 32466). Winston-Derek.
--Hey, God! What Is America? LC 81-71025. (Illus.). 52p. (gr. 3-5). 1982. 3.95 (ISBN 0-938232-05-3, 32795). Winston-Derek.
--Hey, God! What is Christmas. LC 82-60192. (Illus.). 64p. (gr. 3-5). 3.95 (ISBN 0-938232-09-6, 32752). Winston-Derek.
--Hey, God! Where are You? LC 82-60194. (Illus.). 64p. (gr. 3-5). 1982. 3.95 (ISBN 0-938232-07-X, 32485). Winston-Derek.
Gibson, Ruth E. In Search of Young Parents. 120p. (Orig.). 1984. pap. 4.95 (ISBN 0-8341-0911-5). Beacon Hill.
Gibson, S. & Gibson, M. A. An Index to Rawlinson's Collections (Circa 1700-1750) for a New Edition of "Anthenae Oxonienses". Bd. with A Bibliography of Thomas Heywood. Clark, A. M. Repr. of 1925 ed. (Oxford Bibliographical Society Ser.: Vol. 1, Pt. 2). pap. 13.00 (ISBN 0-317-17860-1). Kraus Repr.
Gibson, S. & Hindle, C. J. Philip Bliss (Seventeen Eighty-Seven to Eighteen Fifty-Seven) Editor & Bibliographer. (Oxford Bibliography Society Ser.: Vol. 3, Pt. 2). pap. 13.00. Kraus Repr.
Gibson, S. & Holdsworth, William. Charles Viner's General Abridgement of Law & Equity. Bd. with A Bibliography of Izaack Walton's Lives. Butt, J. E. Repr. of 1930 ed; Supplementary Note to "A Bibliography of the Works of Samuel Daniel". Sellers, H. Repr. (Oxford Bibliography Society Ser.: Vol. 2, Pt. 4). pap. 13.00 (ISBN 0-317-17862-8). Kraus Repr.
Gibson, S., ed. A Bibliography of the Works of Thomas Fuller. (Oxford Bibliography Society Ser.: Vol. 4, Pt. 1). pap. 13.00 (ISBN 0-317-15211-4). Kraus Repr.
Gibson, Sam. Expressions: The Real Truths. 1982. 4.95 (ISBN 0-8062-1787-1). Carlton.
Gibson, Sandra. Beyond the Mind. (Orig.). 1981. pap. 2.50 (ISBN 0-505-51665-9, Pub. by Tower Bks). Dorchester Pub Co.
Gibson, Scott L., jt. auth. see Castel, Albert.
Gibson, Sheila, jt. auth. see Jarvis, Peter.
Gibson, Shirley. I Am Watching. LC 73-75842. (House of Anansi Poetry Ser.: No. 26). 58p. 1973. 2.00 (ISBN 0-88784-126-0, Pub. by Hse Anansi Pr Canada); pap. 3.95 (ISBN 0-88784-026-4). U of Toronto Pr.
Gibson, Stephen E., jt. ed. see Cohen, Kalman J.
Gibson, Stephen W. Amateur Radio License Guide. 1981. 24.95 (ISBN 0-8359-0214-5); pap. 14.95 (ISBN 0-8359-0213-7). Reston.
Gibson, T. E. Veterinary Anthelmintic Medication. 272p. 1975. 60.00x (ISBN 0-85198-311-1, Pub. by CAB Bks England). State Mutual Bk.
Gibson, T. E., ed. Weather & Parasitic Animal Disease. (Technical Note Ser.: No. 159). 174p. 1978. pap. 30.00 (ISBN 92-63-10497-2, W410, WMO). Unipub.
Gibson, Thomas. The Facts About Speculation. 1965. Repr. of 1923 ed. flexible cover 8.00 (ISBN 0-87034-014-X). Fraser Pub Co.
--Sacrifice & Sharing in the Philippine Highlands: Religion & Society among the Buid of Mindoro. (London School of Economics Monographs on Social Anthropology: No. 58). (Illus.). 1986. 49.50 (ISBN 0-485-48242-8, Pub. by Athlone Pr Ltd). Longwood Pub Group.
Gibson, Tom. The Royal College of Physicians & Surgeons of Glasgow. 1983. 90.00x (ISBN 0-86334-013-X, Pub. by Macdonald Pub UK). State Mutual Bk.
--A Soldier of India. LC 81-52952. 288p. 1982. 11.95 (ISBN 0-312-74245-2). St Martin.
Gibson, Tony. Resources & the Teacher. (Illus.). 160p. 1975. 12.95x (ISBN 0-8464-0792-2). Beekman Pubs.
Gibson, Ulric P. & Singer, Rexford D. Water Well Manual: A Practical Guide for Locating & Constructing Wells for Individual & Small Community Water Supplies. LC 71-153696. (Illus.). 156p. 1971. pap. 13.00 (ISBN 0-912722-00-2). Prem Press.
Gibson, W. Paris During the Commune. LC 75-1245. (World History Ser., No. 48). 1974. lib. bdg. 49.95x (ISBN 0-8383-1776-6). Haskell.
Gibson, W., jt. auth. see Curtis, Charles H.
Gibson, W., ed. see Howells, William D.
Gibson, W. C., jt. auth. see Eccles, Sir J. C.
Gibson, W. H., Sr. History of the United Brothers of Friendship, & Sisters of the Mysterious Ten, 2 pts. Incl. Pt. 1. A Negro Order; Pt. 2. Semi-centennial of the Public Career of W. H. Gibson, Sr., from the Year 1847 to 1897. LC 72-157367. (Black Heritage Library Collection Ser). Repr. of 1897 ed. 18.75 (ISBN 0-8369-8805-1). Ayer Co Pubs.
Gibson, W. L., Jr., et al, eds. Methods for Land Economics Research. LC 66-19269. xviii, 242p. 1967. pap. 3.95x (ISBN 0-8032-5225-0, BB 352, Bison). U of Nebr Pr.

Gibson, W. M. & Pollard, B. R. Symmetry Principles in Elementary Particle Physics. LC 74-31796. (Cambridge Monographs on Physics). (Illus.). 395p. 1980. 85.00 (ISBN 0-521-20787-8); pap. 29.95 (ISBN 0-521-29964-0). Cambridge U Pr.
Gibson, W. Martin. The Physics of Nuclear Reactions. LC 79-40063. (Illus.). 288p. 1980. 53.00 (ISBN 0-08-023078-4); pap. 18.50 (ISBN 0-08-023077-6). Pergamon.
Gibson, Walker. Come As You Are. 1958. 5.95 (ISBN 0-8038-1106-3). Hastings.
--Persona: A Style Study for Readers & Writers. 1969. pap. text ed. 5.50 (ISBN 0-394-30198-6, RanC). Random.
--Tough, Sweet & Stuffy: An Essay on Modern American Prose Styles. LC 84-6520. xii, 179p. 1984. Repr. of 1966 ed. lib. bdg. 25.00x (ISBN 0-313-24449-9, GITS). Greenwood.
Gibson, Walker, jt. auth. see Kierzek, John M.
Gibson, Walter. Black Americans: Biological Facts & Fancies. 1983. 7.95 (ISBN 0-533-05522-9). Vantage.
--Dunninger's Secrets. LC 73-76823. 220p. 1974. 7.95 (ISBN 0-8184-0166-4). Lyle Stuart.
--Houdini on Magic. 3.00x (ISBN 0-685-21975-5). Wehman.
--How to Win at Backgammon. (Illus.). 166p. pap. 4.95 (ISBN 0-399-50815-5, G&D). Putnam Pub Group.
--Magic for All Ages. pap. 4.00 (ISBN 0-87980-389-4). Wilshire.
--The Master Magicians. (Illus.). 224p. 1984. pap. 6.95 (ISBN 0-8065-0921-X). Citadel Pr.
--Pinochle Is the Name of the Game. (Illus.). 144p. (Orig.). 1975. pap. 1.25i (ISBN 0-06-465019-7, PBN-5019). Har-Row.
--Poker Is the Name of the Game. (Illus.). 144p. (Orig.). 1975. pap. 1.25i (ISBN 0-06-465018-9, PBN-5018). Har-Row.
--The Shadow & the Golden Master. LC 83-63032. (The Shadow Ser.). 1984. 14.95 (ISBN 0-89296-073-6); ltd. ed. 45.00 (ISBN 0-89296-074-4). Mysterious Pr.
Gibson, Walter, ed. see Houdini, Harry.
Gibson, Walter B. Fell's Official Guide to Knots & How to Tie Them. rev. ed. (Illus.). 160p. 1985. 12.95 (ISBN 0-8119-0689-2). Fell.
--Houdini's Escapes & Magic. LC 75-30523. (Funk & W Bk.). (Illus.). 656p. 1976. 12.50i (ISBN 0-308-10220-7); (TYC-T). T Y Crowell.
--Hoyle's Modern Encyclopedia of Card Games, Rules of All the Basic Games & Popular Variations. LC 73-163085. 408p. 1974. pap. 8.95 (ISBN 0-385-07680-0, Dolp). Doubleday.
--Key to Hypnotism. pap. 1.50 (ISBN 0-87497-077-6). Assoc Bk.
--New Magician's Manual. LC 73-87046. (Illus.). 144p. 1975. pap. 5.95 (ISBN 0-486-23113-5). Dover.
--The New Magician's Manual: Tricks & Routines with Instructions for Expert Performances by the Amateur. (Illus.). 13.00 (ISBN 0-8446-5191-5). Peter Smith.
--Popular Card Tricks. pap. 3.50 (ISBN 0-87505-249-5). Borden.
--Popular Card Tricks. (Illus.). 47p. 1981. pap. 3.50 (ISBN 0-915926-05-9). Magic Ltd.
--Professional Magic for Amateurs. (Illus.). 225p. 1974. pap. 4.00 (ISBN 0-486-23012-0). Dover.
--Professional Magic for Amateurs. (Illus.). 9.75 (ISBN 0-8446-5035-8). Peter Smith.
Gibson, Walter B., jt. auth. see Young, Morris N.
Gibson, Walter M. & Teitelbaum, Henry H., eds. Ion-Solid Interactions Nineteen Eighty, 3 vols. 1652p. 195.00 (ISBN 0-85296-457-9, IN002). Inst Elect Eng.
Gibson, Walter S. Bruegel. (World of Art Ser.). (Illus.). 216p. 1985. pap. 9.95 (ISBN 0-500-20156-0). Thames Hudson.
--Hieronymous Bosch. (World of Art Ser.). (Illus.). 180p. 1985. pap. 9.95f (ISBN 0-500-20134-X). Thames Hudson.
--Hieronymus Bosch: An Annotated Bibliography. 211p. 1983. lib. bdg. 37.50 (ISBN 0-8161-8347-3, Hall Reference). G K Hall.
--The Paintings of Cornelis Engebrechtsz. LC 76-23620. (Outstanding Dissertations in the Fine Arts - 16th Century). (Illus.). 1977. Repr. of 1969 ed. lib. bdg. 68.00 (ISBN 0-8240-2691-8). Garland Pub.
Gibson, Weldon B. SRI: The Founding Years. 1980. 22.50x (ISBN 0-913232-80-7). Pub Serv Ctr.
Gibson, Wilfrid. Collected Poems, 1905-1925. LC 71-145042. 1971. Repr. of 1933 ed. 70.00x (ISBN 0-403-00988-X). Scholarly.
Gibson, William. Burning Chrome. 1986. price not set (ISBN 0-87795-780-0). Arbor Hse.
--The Cobweb. LC 79-50932. 1979. pap. 6.95 (ISBN 0-689-70590-5, 251). Atheneum.
--Count Zero. 224p. 1986. 15.95 (ISBN 0-87795-769-X). Arbor Hse.
--The Distancers. 1986. price not set (ISBN 0-87795-689-8). Arbor Hse.
--Family Life & Morality: Studies in Black & White. LC 79-57076. 116p. 1980. pap. text ed. 9.25 (ISBN 0-8191-0969-X). U Pr of Amer.
--Mass for the Dead. LC 67-25481. 1968. pap. 6.95 (ISBN 0-689-70542-5, 226). Atheneum.
--The Miracle Worker. (gr. 6-9). pap. 2.95 (ISBN 0-553-24778-6). Bantam.
--Miracle Worker. (YA) 1957. 10.95 (ISBN 0-394-40630-3). Knopf.
--Monday after the Miracle. LC 83-45070. 160p. 1983. pap. 9.95 (ISBN 0-689-11396-X). Atheneum.
--Neuromancer. Carr, Terry, ed. 288p. 1984. pap. 2.95 (ISBN 0-441-56956-0, Pub. by Ace Science Fiction). Ace Bks.
--The Seesaw Log: A Chronicle of the Stage Production with the Text of Two for the Seesaw. 288p. 1984. pap. 7.95 (ISBN 0-87910-008-7). Limelight Edns.
--Shakespeare's Game. LC 77-15912. 1978. 10.95 (ISBN 0-689-10877-X); pap. 5.95 (ISBN 0-689-70573-5, 241). Atheneum.
Gibson, William, tr. see Ramon y Cajal, Santiago.
Gibson, William C. Creative Minds in Medicine: Scientific, Humanistic, & Cultural Contributions by Physicians. (Illus.). 256p. 1963. 22.75x (ISBN 0-398-00676-8). C C Thomas.
--Young Endeavour: Contributions to Science by Medical Students of the Past Four Centuries. (Illus.). 312p. 1958. photocopy ed. 27.50x (ISBN 0-398-00677-6). C C Thomas.
Gibson, William C., jt. auth. see Craigie, E. Horne.
Gibson, William C., compiled by. Excitement & Fascination of Science, Vol. 1. 1965. text ed. 6.50 (ISBN 0-8243-1602-9). Annual Reviews.
--The Excitement & Fascination of Science, Vol. 2. LC 65-29005. 1978. text ed. 12.00 (ISBN 0-8243-2601-6); pap. text ed. 10.00 (ISBN 0-8243-2602-4). Annual Reviews.
Gibson, William M. Theodore Roosevelt Among the Humorists: W. D. Howells, Mark Twain, & Mr. Dooley. LC 79-17592. (John C. Hodges Lecture Ser.). 96p. 1980. 8.95x (ISBN 0-87049-263-2). U of Tenn Pr.
--William D. Howells. (Pamphlets on American Writers Ser: No. 63). (Orig.). 1967. pap. 1.25 (ISBN 0-8166-0436-3, MPAW63). U of Minn Pr.
Gibson, William M. & Arms, George. A Bibliography of William Dean Howells. 182p. 1980. Repr. of 1948 ed. lib. bdg. 17.50 (ISBN 0-8495-1951-9). Arden Lib.
Gibson, William M. & Arms, George A. Bibliography of William Dean Howells. 1971. Repr. of 1948 ed. lib. bdg. 17.50 (ISBN 0-8414-4648-2). Folcroft.
Gibson, William M. & Arms, George, eds. Bibliography of William Dean Howells. LC 71-137708. (New York Public Library Publications in Reprint Ser). 1971. Repr. of 1948 ed. 17.50 (ISBN 0-405-01743-X). Ayer Co Pubs.
Gibson, William M. & Lohmann, Christoph K., eds. Selected Letters of W. D. Howells: Vol. 6, 1912-1920. (Critical Editions of American Literature Ser.). 270p. 1983. lib. bdg. 36.50 (ISBN 0-8057-8532-9, Twayne). G K Hall.
Gibson, William M., ed. see Clemens, Samuel L.
Gibson, William M., ed. see Crane, Stephen.
Gibson, William M., ed. see Twain, Mark.
Gibson, Williams E. A Covenant Group for Lifestyle Assessment. 111p. 3.75 (ISBN 0-317-32267-2). Alternatives.
Gibson-Cowan, tr. see Ivanov, Vsevolod V.
Gibson Craig, James T. Papers Relative to the Marriage of King James the Sixth of Scotland with the Princess Anna of Denmark. LC 70-168143. (Bannatyne Club, Edinburgh. Publications: No. 26). Repr. of 1828 ed. 27.50 (ISBN 0-404-52732-9). AMS Pr.
Gibson-Jarvie, Robert. The City of London: A Financial & Commercial History. (Illus.). 128p. 1979. 14.50 (ISBN 0-85941-090-0). Woodhead-Faulkner.
--The London Metal Exchange: A Commodity Market. 208p. 1981. 40.00x (ISBN 0-85941-042-0, Pub. by Woodhead-Faulkner England). State Mutual Bk.
--The London Metal Exchange: A Commodity Market. 256p. 1983. 25.00 (ISBN 0-89397-173-1). Nichols Pub.
Gick, Georg J. & Swinger, Marlys. Shepherd's Pipe Songs from the Holy Night: A Christmas Cantata for Children's Voices or Youth Choir. Choral ed. LC 71-85805. (Illus.). 64p. 1969. pap. 2.50 choral ed. (ISBN 0-87486-011-3); cassette 4.95 (ISBN 0-686-66331-4). Plough.
Gick, James E. African Violets from Mother Nature. (Illus.). 1978. pap. 2.50 (ISBN 0-918170-30-3, HP-505, Future Crafts Today). Gick.
--Cactus & Succulents from Mother Nature. (Illus.). 1977. pap. 2.50 (ISBN 0-918170-27-3, HP-503, Future Crafts Today). Gick.
--Ferns from Mother Nature. (Future Crafts Today Ser.). (Illus.). 1977. pap. 2.50 (ISBN 0-918170-25-7, HP-501). Gick.
--Patterns for Stained Glass. (Illus.). 1977. pap. 3.00 (ISBN 0-918170-24-9). Gick.
Gidal, Nachum T. Land of Promise: Photographs of Palestine from 1850 to 1948. LC 85-40037. (Illus.). 152p. 1985. 35.00 (ISBN 0-912383-14-3). Van der Marck.
Gidal, Peter. Understanding Beckett: A Study of Monologue & Gesture in the Works of Samuel Beckett. 246p. 1985. 27.50 (ISBN 0-312-83080-7). St Martin.
Gidal, Sonja. My Village in Portugal. (Illus.). (gr. 4-8). 1972. PLB 5.69 (ISBN 0-394-92128-3). Pantheon.
Gidal, Sonia & Gidal, Tim. My Village in Switzerland. (Illus.). (gr. 5-6). 1961. PLB 5.69 (ISBN 0-394-91918-1). Pantheon.
Gidal, Tim, jt. auth. see Gidal, Sonia.
Gidbeau, Kenneth W., jt. auth. see Miller, George H.
Gidcomb, Johnny & Barron, Emily. How to Play the Guitar. LC 72-128458. (Illus.). 1970. pap. 4.95 (ISBN 0-87695-102-7). Aurora Pubs.
Giddan, Jane J. & Giddan, Norman S. Teaching Language with Pictures. (Illus.). 232p. 1984. 24.75x (ISBN 0-398-04972-6). C C Thomas.
Giddan, Norman S. Journey of Youth. 1985. pap. text ed. 13.95 (ISBN 0-915744-36-8). Character Res.
Giddan, Norman S. & Austin, Michael J. Peer Counseling & Self-Help Groups on Campus. (Illus.). 202p. 1982. 19.75x (ISBN 0-398-04724-3). C C Thomas.
Giddan, Norman S., jt. auth. see Giddan, Jane J.
Giddens, A., jt. ed. see Stanworth, P.
Giddens, Anthony. Capitalism & Modern Social Theory: An Analysis of the Writings of Marx, Durkheim & Max Weber. LC 70-161291. 1971. 44.50 (ISBN 0-521-08293-5); pap. 12.95x (ISBN 0-521-09785-1). Cambridge U Pr.
--Central Problems in Social Theory: Action, Structure & Contradiction in Social Analysis. LC 79-64667. 1979. 31.00x (ISBN 0-520-03972-6); Campus No. 241. pap. 9.95x (ISBN 0-520-03975-0). U of Cal Pr.
--The Constitution of Society: Outline of the Theory of Structuration. LC 84-40290. 417p. 1984. 35.00 (ISBN 0-520-05292-7). U of Cal Pr.
--A Contemporary Critique of Historical Materialism. LC 81-+009. 250p. 1981. 27.50x (ISBN 0-520-04535-1, CAL 288); pap. 10.95x (ISBN 0-520-04490-8). U of Cal Pr.
--The National State & Violence. 1985. 35.00 (ISBN 0-520-05635-3). U of Cal Pr.
--Politics & Sociology in the Thought of Max Weber. (Studies in Sociology). 64p. 1972. pap. 6.00x (ISBN 0-333-13436-2). Humanities.
--Profiles & Critiques in Social Theory. 230p. 1983. 24.50x (ISBN 0-520-04933-0); pap. 8.95x (ISBN 0-520-04964-0). U of Cal Pr.
--Sociology: A Brief but Critical Introduction. 182p. 1982. pap. text ed. 10.95 (ISBN 0-15-505554-2, HC). HarBraceJ.
--Studies in Social & Political Theory. LC 77-74568. 1977. 15.00x (ISBN 0-465-08270-X). Basic.
Giddens, Anthony, ed. Positivism & Sociology. 1974. pap. text ed. 14.50x (ISBN 0-435-82341-8). Gower Pub Co.
--Sociology of Suicide: A Reader. 424p. 1971. 32.50x (ISBN 0-7146-2591-4, F Cass Co). Biblio Dist.
Giddens, Anthony & Held, David, eds. Classes, Power & Conflict: Classical & Contemporary Debates. LC 81-43382. 640p. 1982. 43.50x (ISBN 0-520-04489-4); pap. 14.95x (ISBN 0-520-04627-7, CAMPUS 290). U of Cal Pr.
Giddens, Anthony & Mackenzie, Gavin, eds. Social Class & the Divison of Labour. LC 82-4275. (Illus.). 374p. 1982. 39.50 (ISBN 0-521-24597-4); pap. 13.95 (ISBN 0-521-28809-6). Cambridge U Pr.
Giddens, Anthony, ed. see Durkheim, Emile.
Giddens, Anthony, jt. ed. see Stanworth, Philip.
Giddens, E. Lynn. Eternal Inspirations: A True Story on Adoption. 120p. 1983. pap. 4.50 (ISBN 0-9612334-0-0). Amberly Pubns.
--Faces of Adoption. 102p. (Orig.). 1983. pap. 5.50 (ISBN 0-9612334-1-9). Amberly Pubns.
Giddens, J. E. & Todd, R. L., eds. Microbial-Plant Interactions. 68p. 1984. 11.00 (ISBN 0-89118-078-8). Am Soc Agron.
Giddens, Paul H. The Birth of the Oil Industry. LC 72-2839. (Use & Abuse of America's Natural Resources Ser.). (Illus.). 292p. 1972. Repr. of 1938 ed. 23.50 (ISBN 0-405-04507-7). Ayer Co Pubs.
--Early Petroleum Industry: Pt. One Birth of the Oil Industry, Pt. Two Sources & Bibliography. LC 73-18385. (Perspectives in American History Ser.: No. 10). (Illus.). 418p. 1974. Repr. of 1938 ed. lib. bdg. 27.50x (ISBN 0-87991-325-8). Porcupine Pr.
--Standard Oil Company (Indiana) Oil Pioneer of the Middle West. LC 75-41757. (Companies & Men: Business Enterprises in America). (Illus.). 1976. Repr. of 1955 ed. 64.00x (ISBN 0-405-08073-5). Ayer Co Pubs.
Gidding, Franklin H. The Principles of Sociology. 1911. 25.00 (ISBN 0-8482-4216-5). Norwood Edns.
--The Principles of Sociology. 1911. 25.00 (ISBN 0-686-17698-7). Quality Lib.
Gidding, J. Calvin, et al, eds. Advances in Chromatography, Vol. 16. 1978. 65.00 (ISBN 0-8247-6659-8). Dekker.
Gidding, Joshua. The Old Girl. LC 79-26850. 264p. 1980. pap. 5.95 (ISBN 0-03-057998-8). HR&W.
Giddings. Advances in Chromatography, Vol. 19. 336p. 1981. 65.00 (ISBN 0-8247-1246-3). Dekker.
--Advances in Chromatography, Vol. 20. 304p. 1982. 65.00 (ISBN 0-8247-1868-2). Dekker.
--Advances in Chromatography, Vol. 21. (Illus.). 360p. 1983. 65.00 (ISBN 0-8247-1679-5). Dekker.
--Advances in Chromatography, Vol. 22. 288p. 1983. 65.00 (ISBN 0-8247-7049-8). Dekker.
--Advances in Chromatography, Vol. 23. 272p. 1984. 65.00 (ISBN 0-8247-7075-7). Dekker.
--Advances in Chromatography, Vol. 24. 328p. 1984. 65.00 (ISBN 0-8247-7253-9). Dekker.
Giddings, et al. Advances in Chromatography, Vol. 18. 1980. 65.00 (ISBN 0-8247-6960-0). Dekker.
--Advances in Chromatography, Vol. 17. 1979. 65.00 (ISBN 0-8247-6902-3). Dekker.
Giddings, Al, jt. auth. see Earle, Sylvia.
Giddings, Franklin H. Democracy & Empire: With Studies of Their Psychological, Economic & Moral Foundations. LC 72-5745. (Select Bibliographies Reprint Ser.). 1972. Repr. of 1900 ed. 23.50 (ISBN 0-8369-6908-1). Ayer Co Pubs.
--The Principles of Sociology: An Analysis of the Phenomena of Association & of Social Organization. (American Studies). 1970. Repr. of 1926 ed. 32.00 (ISBN 0-384-18430-8). Johnson Repr.
--The Scientific Study of Human Society. LC 73-14155. (Perspectives in Social Inquiry Ser.). 264p. 1974. Repr. 13.00x (ISBN 0-405-05501-3). Ayer Co Pubs.
Giddings, J. C. Dynamics of Chromatography, Pt. 1: Principles & Theory. LC 65-24914. (Chromatographic Science Ser.: Vol. 1). Repr. of 1965 ed. 83.80 (ISBN 0-8357-9081-9, 2017687). Bks Demand UMI.
Giddings, J. Calvin. Chemistry, Man, & Environmental Change: An Integrated Approach. (Illus.). 450p. 1973. text ed. 25.30 scp (ISBN 0-06-382790-5, HarpC). Har-Row.
Giddings, J. Calvin & Keller, R. A., eds. Advances in Chromatography, Vol. 10. 256p. 1974. 65.00 (ISBN 0-8247-1238-2). Dekker.
--Advances in Chromatography, Vol. 11. 232p. 1974. 65.00 (ISBN 0-8247-6173-1). Dekker.
Giddings, J. Calvin & Keller, Roy A., eds. Advances in Chromatography, Vol. 3. LC 65-27435. Repr. of 1966 ed. 54.80 (ISBN 0-8357-9079-7, 2055065). Bks Demand UMI.
--Advances in Chromatography, Vol. 7. 1968. 65.00 (ISBN 0-8247-1237-4). Dekker.
--Advances in Chromatography, Vol. 8. 1969. 65.00 (ISBN 0-8247-1240-4). Dekker.
--Advances in Chromatography, Vol. 9. 1970. 65.00 (ISBN 0-8247-1241-2). Dekker.
Giddings, J. Calvin, et al, eds. Advances in Chromatography, Vol. 12. 296p. 1975. 65.00 (ISBN 0-8247-6206-1). Dekker.
--Advances in Chromatography, Vol. 15. 1977. 65.00 (ISBN 0-8247-6500-1). Dekker.
--Advances in Chromatography, Vol. 14. 1976. 65.00 (ISBN 0-8247-6436-6). Dekker.
Giddings, J. L. The Archeology of Cape Denbigh. LC 63-10231. (Illus.). 347p. 1964. 30.00x (ISBN 0-87057-080-3). U Pr of New Eng.
Giddings, J. Louis. Ancient Men of the Arctic. LC 84-21999. 444p. (Orig.). 1985. pap. 12.95 (ISBN 0-295-96045-0). U of Wash Pr.
Giddings, John A., jt. ed. see Greenspan, Kalman.
Giddings, John C. & Keller, R. A., eds. Advances in Chromatography, 2 vols. LC 65-27435. Vol. 2. pap. 100.00 (ISBN 0-317-10426-8, 2055072); Vol. 13. pap. 61.00 (ISBN 0-317-10427-6). Bks Demand UMI.
--Advances in Chromatography, Vol. 5. LC 65-27435. pap. 84.00 (ISBN 0-317-08523-9, 2055064). Bks Demand UMI.
Giddings, John C. & Keller, Roy A., eds. Advances in Chromatography, 3 Vols. LC 65-27435. Vol. 1, 1965. pap. 102.00 (ISBN 0-317-11191-4, 2017688); Vol. 4, 1967. pap. 98.50 (ISBN 0-317-11192-2); Vol. 6, 1968. pap. 89.80 (ISBN 0-317-11193-0). Bks Demand UMI.
Giddings, Joshua R. Exiles of Florida. Thompson, Arthur W., intro. by. LC 64-19159. (Floridiana Facsimile & Reprint Ser). (Illus.). 1964. Repr. of 1858 ed. 10.75 (ISBN 0-8130-0085-8). U Presses Fla.
--Exiles of Florida - or, the Crimes Committed by Our Government Against the Maroons Who Fled from South Carolina & Other Slave States Seeking Protection Under Spanish Laws. LC 70-82193. (Anti-Slavery Crusade in America Ser). 1969. Repr. of 1858 ed. 15.00 (ISBN 0-405-00632-2). Ayer Co Pubs.
--Speeches in Congress. LC 68-55887. Repr. of 1853 ed. 22.00x (ISBN 0-8371-0444-0, GIS&, Pub. by Negro U Pr). Greenwood.
Giddings, L. E., jt. auth. see Mani, M. S.
Giddings, Paula. When & Where I Enter: The Impact of Black Women on Race & Sex in America. LC 84-60089. 403p. 1984. 15.95 (ISBN 0-688-01943-9). Morrow.
--When & Where I Enter: The Impact of Black Women on Race & Sex in America. LC 85-47761. 408p. 1985. pap. 7.95 (ISBN 0-553-34225-8). Bantam.
Giddings, Robert & Holland, Elizabeth. J. R. R. Tolkien: The Shores of the Middle-Earth. LC 82-6759. 289p. 1982. lib. bdg. 24.00 (ISBN 0-89093-472-X, Aletheia Bks). U Pubns Amer.
Giddings, Robert, ed. The Changing World of Charles Dickens. LC 83-3769. (Critical Studies). 240p. 1983. text ed. 27.50x (ISBN 0-389-20372-6). B&N Imports.
--J. R. R. Tolkien: This Far Land. LC 83-6347. (Critical Studies). 206p. 1984. text ed. 27.50x (ISBN 0-389-20374-2). B&N Imports.
--Mark Twain: A Sumptuous Variety. (Critical Studies). 256p. 1985. 27.50x (ISBN 0-389-20541-9, 08103). B&N Imports.
Giddings, Robert, ed. see Keats, John.

Giddings, Ruth W. Yaqui Myths & Legends. LC 60-63129. (Illus.). 180p. 1968. pap. 6.50 (ISBN 0-8165-0467-9). U of Ariz Pr.

Giddins, Gary. Rhythm-A-Ning: Jazz Tradition & Innovation in the '80s. 320p. 1985. 17.95 (ISBN 0-19-503558-5). Oxford U Pr.

--Riding on a Blue Note: Jazz & American Pop. 1981. 19.95x (ISBN 0-19-502835-X). Oxford U Pr.

--Riding on a Blue Note: Jazz & American Pop. 1981. pap. 9.95 (ISBN 0-19-503213-6, GB 713, GB). Oxford U Pr.

Giddins, Gary, jt. auth. see Friedman, Carol.

Giddy, Ian H., jt. ed. see George, Abraham M.

Gide, Andre. Ainsi Soit-Il ou les Jeux Sont Faits: Essai. pap. 4.50 (ISBN 0-685-34134-8). French & Eur.

--Amyntas. 224p. 1926. 4.95 (ISBN 0-686-56060-4). French & Eur.

--Anthologie de la Poesie Francaise. 1954. 36.95 (ISBN 0-686-56061-2). French & Eur.

--L' Arbitraire. pap. 6.95 (ISBN 0-685-34135-6). French & Eur.

--Cahiers. 412p. 1970. 15.95 (ISBN 0-686-56062-0). French & Eur.

--Les Cahiers et les Poesies d'Andre Walter. 224p. 1952. 4.95 (ISBN 0-686-56063-9). French & Eur.

--Caves Du Vatican. 1956. 18.95 (ISBN 0-685-11068-0). French & Eur.

--Les Caves du Vatican. (Folio 34). 1972. 3.95 (ISBN 0-686-56064-7). French & Eur.

--Correspondance avec Andre Rouveyre (1909-1951) 14.95 (ISBN 0-685-34139-9). French & Eur.

--Correspondance avec Andre Suares (1908-1920) 4.95 (ISBN 0-685-34140-2). French & Eur.

--Correspondance avec Arnold Bennett, Vingt Ans d'Amitie Litteraire (1911-1931, 2 tomes. (Textes Litter. Franc.). Set. 15.90 (ISBN 0-685-34136-4). French & Eur.

--Correspondance avec Francis Jammes (1893-1938) 8.95 (ISBN 0-685-34138-0). French & Eur.

--Correspondance avec Francois Mauriac (1912-1951) 15.75 (ISBN 0-685-34137-2). French & Eur.

--Correspondance avec Paul Valery (1890-1942) 29.95 (ISBN 0-685-34142-9). French & Eur.

--Correspondance avec Roger Martin du Gard (1913-1951, 2 tomes. Set. 39.95 (ISBN 0-685-34141-0). French & Eur.

--Corydon. 1978. lib. bdg. 20.00x (ISBN 0-374-93051-1). Octagon.

--Corydon: Essai. pap. 11.95 (ISBN 0-685-34143-7). French & Eur.

--The Counterfeiters. 448p. 1973. pap. 4.95 (ISBN 0-394-71842-9, Vin). Random.

--Dostoevsky. 211p. 1981. Repr. of 1925 ed. lib. bdg. 25.00 (ISBN 0-89760-319-2). Telegraph Bks.

--Dostoievesky. (Coll. Idees). pap. 3.95 (ISBN 0-685-34144-5). French & Eur.

--L' Ecole des Femmes: Avec Robert, Genevieve, le Promethee Mal Enchaine. 299p. 1970. 18.95 (ISBN 0-686-56068-X). French & Eur.

--Ecole des Femmes: Nouvelles. 1961. pap. 4.95 (ISBN 0-685-11152-0). French & Eur.

--Les Faux-Monnayeurs. 364p. (Folio 879). 1972. 4.95 (ISBN 0-686-56069-8). French & Eur.

--Les Faux-Monnayeurs. (Documentation thematique). (Illus., Fr.). pap. 2.95 (ISBN 0-685-13918-2, 110). Larousse.

--Faux-Monnayeurs: Rompin. 1956. 11.50 (ISBN 0-685-11181-4). French & Eur.

--Feuillets d'Automne. pap. 7.50 (ISBN 0-685-34145-3). French & Eur.

--Immoralist. Howard, Richard, tr. LC 70-98648. 1970. pap. 3.95 (ISBN 0-394-70008-2, V8, Vin). Random.

--The Immoralist. Howard, Richard, tr. LC 83-42856. 171p. 7.95 (ISBN 0-394-60500-4). Modern Lib.

--Immoraliste. 1958. 9.50 (ISBN 0-685-11245-4). French & Eur.

--L' Immoraliste. 192p. 1972. 3.95 (ISBN 0-686-56051-5). French & Eur.

--Immoraliste. Marks, Elaine & Tedeschi, Richard, eds. 1963. text ed. write for info. (ISBN 0-02-342210-6). Macmillan.

--Incidences: Essai. pap. 6.95 (ISBN 0-685-34146-1). French & Eur.

--Interviews Imaginaires. pap. 3.95 (ISBN 0-685-34147-X). French & Eur.

--Isabelle. Pell, Elsie, ed. (Fr). 1947. text ed. 8.95x (ISBN 0-89197-249-8); pap. text ed. 2.50x (ISBN 0-89197-805-4). Irvington.

--Isabelle: Roman. (Fr). 1960. pap. 3.95 (ISBN 0-685-11259-4). French & Eur.

--Journal, 2 tomes. Incl. Tome I. (1889-1939) 39.95 (ISBN 0-685-36051-2); Tome II. (1939-1949), Souvenirs. 42.95 (ISBN 0-685-36052-0). (Bibl. de la Pleiade). (Fr.). 1939-54. French & Eur.

--Journal des Faux-Monnayeurs: Essai. pap. 9.50 (ISBN 0-685-34150-X). French & Eur.

--Journal Nineteen Forty-Two to Nineteen Forty-Nine. (Fr.). pap. 7.95 (ISBN 0-685-34149-6). French & Eur.

--Journal, Nineteen Thirty-Nine to Nineteen Forty-Two. (Fr.). pap. 6.95 (ISBN 0-685-34148-8). French & Eur.

--Lafcadio's Adventures. Bussy, Dorothy, tr. from Fr. LC 79-24000. 1980. Repr. of 1925 ed. lib. bdg. 12.50x (ISBN 0-8376-0452-4). Bentley.

--Lafcadio's Adventures. 1925. pap. 2.95 (ISBN 0-394-70096-1, V96, Vin). Random.

--Litterature Engagee: Essai. pap. 6.95 (ISBN 0-685-34151-8). French & Eur.

--The Living Thoughts of Montaigne. 1979. Repr. of 1939 ed. lib. bdg. 17.50 (ISBN 0-8495-2017-7). Arden Lib.

--Notes on Chopin. Frechtman, Bernard, tr. from Fr. LC 78-3640. 1978. Repr. of 1949 ed. lib. bdg. 22.50x (ISBN 0-313-20371-7, GINC). Greenwood.

--Les Nourritures Terrestres et les Nouvelles Nourritures: Poesies. (Coll. Soleil). 1960. 11.95 (ISBN 0-685-11427-9). French & Eur.

--Les Nouvelles Nourritures. 256p. 1972. 3.95 (ISBN 0-686-56052-3). French & Eur.

--Oscar Wilde. pap. 6.95 (ISBN 0-685-34152-6). French & Eur.

--Oscar Wilde: A Study. Gordon, L., tr. 69.95 (ISBN 0-87968-229-9). Gordon Pr.

--Paludes. pap. 6.95 (ISBN 0-685-23909-8). French & Eur.

--Paludes. 160p. 1973. 3.95 (ISBN 0-686-56053-1). French & Eur.

--Porte Etroite. 1960. 11.50 (ISBN 0-685-11503-8). French & Eur.

--La Porte Etroite. 192p. 1972. 3.95 (ISBN 0-686-56054-X). French & Eur.

--Pretextes et Nouveaux Pretextes. 12.95 (ISBN 0-685-34153-4). French & Eur.

--Le Promethee Mal Enchaine: Nouvelles. pap. 7.95 (ISBN 0-685-34154-2). French & Eur.

--Retouches a mon Retour de l'U.R.S.S. 128p. 1937. 4.95 (ISBN 0-686-56055-8). French & Eur.

--Le Retour de l'Enfant Prodigue: Recit. pap. 7.95 (ISBN 0-685-34155-0). French & Eur.

--Retour De l'URSS. Incl. Retouches a Mon Retour de l'URSS. pap. 5.25 (ISBN 0-685-34156-9). French & Eur.

--Le Retour du Tchad. pap. 5.50 (ISBN 0-685-34157-7). French & Eur.

--Return from the U. S. S. R. & Afterthoughts on My Return. Howard, Richard, tr. 192p. Date not set. 15.95 (ISBN 0-374-24950-4). FS&G.

--Romans, Recits Et Soties: Oeuvres Lyriques. (Bibl. de la Pleiade). 1959. 42.95 (ISBN 0-685-11539-9). French & Eur.

--Saul. pap. 3.95 (ISBN 0-685-23910-1, 2586). French & Eur.

--The School for Wives-Robert-Genevieve or the Unfinished Confidence. Bussy, Dorothy, tr. from Fr. LC 79-23993. 1980. Repr. of 1929 ed. lib. bdg. 12.50x (ISBN 0-8376-0454-0). Bentley.

--Self-portraits, the Gide-Valery Letters, 1890-1942. Mallet, Robert, ed. Guicharnaud, June, tr. LC 65-25125. pap. 86.50 (ISBN 0-317-26503-2, 2024041). Bks Demand UMI.

--La Sequestree de Poitiers. 145p. 1977. 3.95 (ISBN 0-686-56056-6). French & Eur.

--Si le Grain ne Meurt: Memoires. (Coll. Soleil). 1966. 12.95 (ISBN 0-685-11561-5). French & Eur.

--Si le Gran ne Meurt: Memoires. (Coll. Folio). pap. 4.50 (ISBN 0-685-34158-5). French & Eur.

--Souvenirs de la Cour d'Assises. 120p. 1914. 3.95 (ISBN 0-686-56057-4). French & Eur.

--Strait Is the Gate. Bussy, Dorothy, tr. from Fr. LC 79-23999. Orig. Title: La Porte Etroite. 1980. Repr. of 1924 ed. lib. bdg. 12.50x (ISBN 0-8376-0453-2). Bentley.

--Strait Is the Gate. Bussy, Dorothy, tr. 1956. pap. 2.45 (ISBN 0-394-70027-9, V27, Vin). Random.

--La Symphonie Pastorale. 1972. 3.95 (ISBN 0-686-56058-2). French & Eur.

--Symphonie Pastorale. O'Brien, Justin & Shackleton, M., eds. 1954. pap. text ed. 5.95 (ISBN 0-669-27383-X). Heath.

--Symphonie Pastorale: Roman. (Coll. Soleil). 1953. pap. 7.95 (ISBN 0-685-11579-8). French and Eur.

--Theatre. Incl. Saul; Le Roi Candaule; Oedipe; Persephone; Le Treizieme Arbre. 8.25 (ISBN 0-685-34161-5). French & Eur.

--Thesee. 116p. 1946. 3.95 (ISBN 0-686-56059-0). French & Eur.

--Two Legends: Oedipus & Theseus. Russell, John, tr. 1958. pap. 2.95 (ISBN 0-394-70066-X, V66, Vin). Random.

--Two Symphonies. 1977. pap. 3.95 (ISBN 0-394-72454-2, Vin). Random.

--Voyage au Congo. pap. 5.95 (ISBN 0-685-34159-3). French & Eur.

--Le Voyage d'Urien: Nouvelles. pap. 4.95 (ISBN 0-685-34160-7). French & Eur.

Gide, Andre & Barrault, Jean-Louis. The Trial: A Dramatization Based on Kafka's Novel. LC 63-18574. (Illus.). (YA) (gr. 9 up). 1963. pap. 3.95 (ISBN 0-8052-0053-3). Schocken.

Gide, Andre & Gosse, Edmund. The Correspondence of Andre Gide & Edmund Gosse: 1904-1928. Brugmans, Linette F., ed. LC 77-22619. (New York University. Studies in Romance Languages & Literature: No. 2). 1977. Repr. of 1959 ed. lib. bdg. 22.50x (ISBN 0-8371-9736-8, GICO). Greenwood.

Gide, Andre & Mauriac, Francois. Correspondance, Andre Gide-Francois Mauriac, 1912-1950. 280p. 1971. 11.95 (ISBN 0-686-56066-3). French & Eur.

Gide, Andre, et al. Correspondance 1897-1944, 2 vols, Vol. 1. 1976. 75.00 (ISBN 0-686-56067-1). French & Eur.

--Correspondance 1891-1938. 351p. 1975. 35.00 (ISBN 0-686-56065-5). French & Eur.

Gide, Andre P. Dostoevsky. LC 78-14443. 1979. Repr. of 1961 ed. lib. bdg. 22.50x (ISBN 0-313-21178-7, GIDO). Greenwood.

Gide, C., jt. auth. see Fourier, C.

Gide, Charles. Communist & Co-Operative Colonies. Row, Ernest F., tr. LC 72-2939. Repr. of 1930 ed. 19.50 (ISBN 0-404-10705-2). AMS Pr.

--Consumer's Cooperative Societies. LC 73-154045. (World History Ser., No. 48). 1971. Repr. of 1921 ed. lib. bdg. 51.95x (ISBN 0-8383-1276-4). Haskell.

--Principles of Political Economy. Row, Ernest F., tr. from Fr. LC 78-126685. Repr. of 1924 ed. 18.50 (ISBN 0-404-02739-3). AMS Pr.

Gideon, D. N. & American Gas Association Pipeline Research Committee. Earth Current Effects on Buried Pipelines: Analysis of Observations of Telluric Gradients & Their Effects. 77p. pap. 10.00 (ISBN 0-318-12600-1, L30570). Am Gas Assn.

Gideon, D. N., et al. Comparison of Dispersion from LNG Spills over Land & Water & LNG Dispersion in Weather. 104p. 1974. pap. 5.00 (ISBN 0-318-12595-1, M19877). Am Gas Assn.

--Earth Current Effects on Buried Pipelines: Analysis of Ohio & Vancouver Field Tests. 54p. 1968. pap. 2.50 (ISBN 0-318-12599-4, L30510). Am Gas Assn.

Gideon, Virtus E. Luke: A Study Guide Commentary. (Orig.). 1967. pap. 4.95 (ISBN 0-310-24973-2). Zondervan.

Gideon, Virtus E., jt. auth. see Vaughan, Curtis.

Gideonse, Hendrik D. In Search of More Effective Service: Inquiry as a Guiding Image for Educational Reform in America. xvii, 144p. 1983. pap. 5.95 perfect bd. (ISBN 0-915645-00-9). Univ Cinn Coll Ed.

Gidio, Sandra de see De Gidio, Sandra.

Gidley, Charles. The Raging of the Sea. 548p. 1984. 18.95 (ISBN 0-233-97647-7). Andre Deutsch.

--The Raging of the Sea. LC 84-40460. 543p. 1985. 17.95 (ISBN 0-670-80374-X). Viking.

Gidley, J. A., jt. auth. see Elwell, W. T.

Gidley, James W. Paleocene Primates of the Fort Union, with Discussion of Relationships of Eocene Primates. Bd. with The Fort Union of the Crazy Mountain Field, Montana, & Its Mammalian Faunas. Simpson, George G. Repr. of 1937 ed. LC 78-72717. 42.50 (ISBN 0-404-18292-5). AMS Pr.

Gidley, M. Kopet: A Documentary Narrative of Chief Joseph's Last Years. LC 80-54428. (Illus.). 126p. 1981. 25.00x (ISBN 0-295-95794-8). U of Wash Pr.

--With One Sky above Us: Life on an American Indian Reservation at the Turn of the Century. LC 84-22088. (Illus.). 160p. (Orig.). pap. 9.95 (ISBN 0-295-96164-3). U of Wash Pr.

Gidley, Mick, ed. The Vanishing Race: Selections from Edward S. Curtis' the North American Indian. LC 76-23476. (Illus.). 1977. 9.95 (ISBN 0-8008-7945-7). Taplinger.

Gidlost, Menelaus. Mytholimericks IV: The Trojan War. (Limericklets Ser.: No. 38). (Illus.). 1983. pap. 1.00 (ISBN 0-938338-48-X). Winds World Pr.

Gidlow, Elsa. Ask No Man Pardon: The Philosophical Significance of Being Lesbian. 1976. 2.00 (ISBN 0-9606568-1-2). Druid Heights.

--Elsa, I Come with My Songs: The Autobiography of Elsa Gidlow. LC 84-29288. (Illus.). 425p. (Orig.). 1985. pap. 10.95x (ISBN 0-912932-12-0). Booklegger Pr.

--Makings for Meditation. (Illus.). 1973. 2.00 (ISBN 0-9606568-0-4). Druid Heights.

--Sapphic Songs Eighteen to Eighty. (Illus.). 1982. 5.95 (ISBN 0-9606568-4-7). Druid Heights.

Gidmark, Jill B. Melville Sea Dictionary: A Glossed Concordance & Analysis of the Sea Language in Melville's Nautical Novels. LC 82-6122. xiii, 534p. 1982. lib. bdg. 49.95 (ISBN 0-313-23330-6, GMD/). Greenwood.

Gidney, James B., jt. auth. see Pieper, Thomas.

Gidney, James B., jt. auth. see Weeks, Philip.

Gidney, James B., ed. see Heald, Edward T.

Gidney, James B., tr. see Romains, Jules.

Gido, Jack. An Introduction to Project Planning. 1974. pap. 6.75 (ISBN 0-932078-48-6). GE Tech Prom & Train.

--An Introduction to Project Planning. LC 84-4960. 168p. 1984. Repr. of 1974 ed. 10.00 (ISBN 0-9613322-0-4). Project Plan.

--Introduction to Project Planning. 168p. (Orig.). 1984. pap. text ed. 12.00 (ISBN 0-8311-1160-7). Indus Pr.

--Project Management Software Directory. 120p. 1985. pap. 21.95 (ISBN 0-8311-1163-1). Indus Pr.

Gidwani, N. N., jt. auth. see Roy, Ashim K.

Gidwani, N. N., ed. Comparative Librarianship. 1973. 10.50 (ISBN 0-686-20202-3). Intl Bk Dist.

Gidwani, N. W., jt. auth. see Roy, Ashim K.

Giebelhaus, August W. Business & Government in the Oil Industry: A Case Study of Sun Oil, 1876 to 1945, Vol. 5. Porter, Glenn, ed. LC 77-7795. (Industrial Development & the Social Fabric Monographs). 425p. (Orig.). 1980. lib. bdg. 40.00 (ISBN 0-89232-089-3). Jai Pr.

Gieben, Servus, ed. see Grosseteste, Robert.

Gieber, Gale, jt. auth. see Cordell, Frank.

Gieber, Robert L. An English-French Glossary of Educational Terminology. LC 80-5652. 212p. (Eng. & Fr.). 1980. lib. bdg. 23.00 (ISBN 0-8191-1344-1); pap. text ed. 11.75 (ISBN 0-8191-1345-X). U Pr of Amer.

Giebisch, G., ed. Transport Across Multi-Membrane Systems. (Membrane Transport in Biology: Vol. 3). (Illus.). 1978. 99.00 (ISBN 0-387-08596-3). Springer-Verlag.

--Transport Organs. (Membrane Transport in Biology Ser.: Vol. 4, Pt. A & B). (Illus.). 1979. 183.00 (ISBN 0-387-08895-4). Springer-Verlag.

Giebisch, Gerhard, jt. ed. see Seldin, Donald W.

Giebisch, Gerhard H., jt. ed. see Hoffman, Joseph F.

Gieck, Kurt. Engineering Formulas. 4th ed. 260p. 1983. 18.95 (ISBN 0-07-023219-9). McGraw.

Giedion, S. Congres International D'Architecture Moderne (C.I.A.M.), 6th: Bridgewater (England), 1947, A Decade of New Architecture 1937-1947. Repr. 54.00 (ISBN 0-317-15328-5). Kraus Repr.

Giedion, Siegfried. Mechanization Takes Command. (Illus.). 1969. pap. 13.95 (ISBN 0-393-00489-9, Norton Lib). Norton.

Giedion, Sigfried. Architecture & the Phenomena of Transition: The Three Space Conceptions in Architecture. LC 71-95921. (Illus.). pap. 79.50 (ISBN 0-317-10591-4, 2021592). Bks Demand UMI.

--The Beginnings of Architecture: The Eternal Present, a Contribution on Constancy & Change, Vol. 2. LC 80-8733. (The A. W. Mellon Lectures in the Fine Arts, No. 6, 1957, Bolligen Ser.: XXXV: 6,11). (Illus.). 604p. 1981. 65.00x (ISBN 0-691-09945-6); pap. 19.95 (ISBN 0-691-01835-9). Princeton U Pr.

--Space, Time & Architecture: The Growth of a New Tradition. 5th rev. & enl. ed. LC 67-17310. (Charles Eliot Norton Lectures Ser: 1938-1939). (Illus.). lvi, 897p. 35.00 (ISBN 0-674-83040-7). Harvard U Pr.

Giedion-Welcker, Carola, compiled by. In Memoriam James Joyce. LC 75-13347. 1975. Repr. of 1941 ed. lib. bdg. 10.00 (ISBN 0-8414-4543-5). Folcroft.

Giedion-Welcker, Carols, compiled By. In Memoriam James Joyce. 55p. 1980. Repr. of 1914 ed. lib. bdg. 10.00 (ISBN 0-8495-2043-6). Arden Lib.

Giedymin, Jerzy. Science & Convention: Essays on the Origin & Significance of the Conventionalist Philosophy of Science. (Foundations & Philosophy of Science & Technology Ser.). 260p. 1981. 33.00 (ISBN 0-08-025790-9). Pergamon.

Giedymin, Jerzy, ed. see Ajdukiewicz, Kazimierz.

Giefer, Gerald J. Sources of Information in Water Resources. LC 75-20953. 312p. 1976. 30.00 (ISBN 0-912394-15-3). Water Info.

Giefer, Gerald J. & Todd, David K. Water Publications of State Agencies, 2 vols. LC 72-75672. 1976. Set. 49.50 (ISBN 0-912394-04-8). Water Info.

Giefer, Gerald J. & Todd, David K., eds. Water Publications of State Agencies - First Supplement. LC 72-75672. 1976. 28.00 (ISBN 0-912394-17-X). Water Info.

Giegerich, Heinz J. Metrical Phonology & Phonological Structure: German & English. (Cambridge Studies in Linguistics). (Illus.). 350p. Date not set. 49.50 (ISBN 0-521-26626-2). Cambridge U Pr.

Giegerich, W. & Trier, W., eds. Glass Machines: Construction & Operation of Machines for the Forming of Hot Glass. Kreidl, Norbert J., tr. LC 68-56941. (Illus.). 1969. 56.00 (ISBN 0-387-04493-0). Springer-Verlag.

Giegold, William C. Practical Management Skills for Engineers & Scientists. (Engineering Ser.). (Illus.). 430p. 1982. 27.50. Lifetime Learn.

Giegold, William C. & Grindle, Crosby R. In Training: A Practical Guide to Management Development. (Management Development Ser.). 225p. 1983. 25.00x (ISBN 0-534-02705-9). Lifetime Learn.

Giehman, I. I. & Skorohod, A. V. Controlled Stochastic Processes. LC 79-4107. 1979. 43.00 (ISBN 0-387-90410-7). Springer-Verlag.

--The Theory of Stochastic Processes III. (Grundlehren der Mathematischen Wissenschften: Vol. 232). 1979. 65.50 (ISBN 0-387-90375-5). Springer-Verlag.

Giele, Janet Z. Women & the Future: Changing Sex Roles in Modern America. LC 77-2472. 1979. pap. text ed. 14.95 (ISBN 0-02-911690-2). Free Pr.

--Women & the Future: Changing Sex Roles in Modern America. LC 77-2472. 1978. 14.95 (ISBN 0-02-911700-3). Free Pr.

--Women in the Middle Years: Current Knowledge & Directions for Research & Policy. (Wiley Series on Personality Processes). 344p. 1981. 39.50x (ISBN 0-471-09611-3, Pub. by Wiley-Interscience). Wiley.

Giele, Janet Z. & Smock, Audrey C. Woman: Roles & Status in Eight Countries. LC 76-39950. 443p. 1977. 36.50x (ISBN 0-471-01504-0, Pub. by Wiley-Interscience). Wiley.

Gielen, M., jt. auth. see Brocas, J.

Gielgud, Adam, ed. Memoirs of Prince Adam Czartoryski & His Correspondence with Alexander I. LC 78-135808. (Eastern Europe Collection Ser). 1970. Repr. of 1888 ed. 40.00 (ISBN 0-405-02750-8). Ayer Co Pubs.

Gielgud, John. An Actor in His Time. (Illus.). 1982. pap. 4.95 (ISBN 0-14-005636-X). Penguin.

--Ages of Man. LC 78-74196. 96p. 1979. pap. 1.95 (ISBN 0-89845-009-8, TTC200); bk & 2 cassette pkg. 17.96 (ISBN 0-89845-011-X, CP200). Caedmon.
--Stage Directions. LC 78-23580. 1979. Repr. of 1963 ed. lib. bdg. 24.75x (ISBN 0-313-21035-7, GISD). Greenwood.
--Stage Directions. 1979. pap. 8.95 (ISBN 0-87830-568-8). Theatre Arts.
Gielgud, John, ed. see Chekhov, Anton.
Gielnik, S. J. & Gossling, W. F., eds. Input, Output & Marketing: Proceedings of the 1977 London Conference & the 1979 Toledo Ohio Workshop. (I.-O.P.C. Conference Ser.: No. 4). (Illus.). 1980. 50.00x (ISBN 0-904870-14-6, Pub. by Input-Output England). Kelley.
Gielow, Fred C., Jr. Laughter, Love, & a Barbershop Song. LC 80-65128. 1980. 9.75 (ISBN 0-9603938-0-3). Gielow.
Gier, Nicholas F. Wittgenstein & Phenomenology. LC 80-26980. (Ser. in Philosphy). 260p. 1981. 49.50x (ISBN 0-87395-518-8); pap. 15.95x (ISBN 0-87395-519-6). State U NY Pr.
Gierach, John. Fly Fishing the High Country. LC 84-4805. (Illus.). 108p. 1984. pap. 7.50 (ISBN 0-87108-662-X). Pruett.
Giere, Ronald, jt. ed. see Asquith, Peter D.
Giere, Ronald N. Understanding Scientific Reasoning. 2nd ed. LC 83-22562. 1984. pap. text ed. 19.95 (ISBN 0-03-063068-1, HoltC). HR&W.
Giere, Ronald N. & Westfall, Richard S., eds. Foundations of Scientific Method: The Nineteenth Century. LC 72-79910. pap. 59.70 (ISBN 0-8357-9213-7, 2055202). Bks Demand UMI.
Giergielewicz, Mieczyslaw, ed. Polish Civilization - Essays & Studies. 304p. 1979. 16.00 (ISBN 0-8147-2972-X). Polish Inst Art & Sci.
Giergielewicz, Mieczyslaw & Krzyzanowski, Ludwik, eds. Polish Civilization: Essays & Studies. LC 78-52747. 1979. 35.00x (ISBN 0-8147-2972-X). NYU Pr.
Giering, Edward J. B-17 Bomber Crew Diary. 1985. pap. 10.00x (ISBN 0-89745-069-8). Sunflower U Pr.
Gierloff-Emden, Hans G. Mexico: Eine Landeskunde. (Illus.). 634p. 1970. 61.60x (ISBN 3-11-002708-9). De Gruyter.
Gierman, James, ed. see Kubota, Takayuki.
Giertz, Bo. The Hammer of God. Nelson, Clifford A., tr. from Swedish. LC 60-8902. 344p. 1973. pap. 8.50 (ISBN 0-8066-1310-6, 10-2940). Augsburg.
Gierut, Casimir F. Taxpayers Message to Congress: Repeal the Federal Reserve Bank's Pandora's Box of Criminal Acts. 288p. 9.25 (ISBN 0-318-17465-0). Natl Comm Repeal.
Gieryn, Thomas F., ed. see Merton, Robert K.
Gierz, G. Bundles of Topological Vector Spaces & Their Duality. (Lecture Notes in Mathematics: Vol. 955). 296p. 1982. pap. 16.00 (ISBN 0-387-11610-9). Springer-Verlag.
Gierz, G., et al. A Compendium of Continuous Lattices. 380p. 1980. 24.00 (ISBN 0-387-10111-X). Springer-Verlag.
Gies, Frances. Joan of Arc: The Legend & the Reality. LC 80-7900. (Illus.). 256p. 1981. 14.95i (ISBN 0-690-01942-4, HarpT). Har-Row.
--The Knight in History. LC 84-47571. (Illus.). 192p. 1984. 16.30 (ISBN 0-06-015339-3, HarpT). Har-Row.
Gies, Frances & Gies, Joseph. Life in a Medieval City. LC 74-13058. (Illus.). 288p. 1981. pap. 5.72i (ISBN 0-06-090880-7, CN 880, CN). Har-Row.
--Women in the Middle Ages. LC 77-25832. (Illus.). 1978. 10.95i (ISBN 0-690-01724-3). T Y Crowell.
Gies, Frances, jt. auth. see Gies, Joseph.
Gies, Joseph & Gies, Frances. Life in a Medieval Castle. LC 74-13058. (Illus.). 1979. pap. 5.72i (ISBN 0-06-090674-X, CN 674, CN). Har-Row.
--Women in the Middle Ages. 264p. 1980. pap. 4.76 (ISBN 0-06-464037-X, BN 4037, BN). B&N NY.
Gies, Joseph, jt. auth. see Gies, Frances.
Gies, Thomas G. & Sichel, Werner, eds. Deregulation: Appraisal before the Fact. (Michigan Business Studies: Vol. 2, No. 4). (Illus.). 189p. 1982. 10.00 (ISBN 0-87712-222-9). U Mich Busn Div Res.
Gies, Thomas G., jt. ed. see Sichel, Werner.
Gies, Tom, et al. Inflation in Wholesale Distribution: Management Policies for Survival & Success. 108p. 40.00 (ISBN 0-318-15137-5); NAW commodity line association members 36.00 (ISBN 0-318-15138-3); NAW members 32.00 (ISBN 0-318-15139-1). Natl Assn Wholesale Dists.
Giesbrecht, Martin. Wealth of People. LC 73-19520. 159p. 1977. 9.95x (ISBN 0-913232-11-4); pap. 5.95 (ISBN 0-913232-99-8). W Kaufmann.
Giese, A. C., ed. Photophysiology. Incl. Vol. 1. General Principles - Action of Light on Plants. 1964. 67.50 (ISBN 0-12-282601-9); Vol. 2. Action of Light on Animals & Microorganisms, Photobiochemical Mechanisms, Bioluminescence. 1964. 67.50 (ISBN 0-12-282602-7); Vols. 3 & 4. Current Topics. 1968; Vols. 5-7. Current Topics in Photobiology & Photochemistry. Vol. 5, 1970. 64.50 (ISBN 0-12-282605-1); Vol. 6, 1971. 67.50 (ISBN 0-12-282606-X); Vol. 7, 1972. 67.50 (ISBN 0-12-282607-8); Vol. 8. 1973. 67.50 (ISBN 0-12-282608-6). Acad Pr.
Giese, Arthur C. Blepharisma: The Biology of a Light-Sensitive Protozoan. LC 73-190525. (Illus.). xii, 370p. 1973. 27.50x (ISBN 0-8047-0817-7). Stanford U Pr.
--Living with Our Sun's Ultraviolet Rays. LC 75-44225. (Illus.). 198p. 1976. 25.00x (ISBN 0-306-30883-5, Plenum Pr). Plenum Pub.
Giese, Arthur C. & Pearse, John S., eds. Reproduction of Marine Invertebrates: Acoelomate & Psuedocollomate Metazoans, Vol. 1. 1974. 78.00 (ISBN 0-12-282501-2). Acad Pr.
--Reproduction of Marine Invertebrates: Molluscs: Pelecypods & Lesser Classes, Vol. 5. LC 72-84365. 1979. 70.00 (ISBN 0-12-282505-5). Acad Pr.
Giese, Elizabeth A. & Currat, Nancy. Alpha Books to Color Presents St. Louis. (Alpha Books to Color Ser.: No. 1). (Illus.). 30p. (gr. k-10). 1982. pap. 2.95 (ISBN 0-912507-00-4). Three Star Ent.
Giese, Elizabeth A., et al. Alpha Books to Color Presents Kansas City. (Alpha Books to Color: No. 2). (Illus.). 30p. (gr. k-5). 1983. pap. cancelled (ISBN 0-912507-02-0). Three Star Ent.
Giese, Frank. Artus Desire, Priest & Pamphleteer of the Sixteenth Century. (Studies in the Romance Languages & Literatures: No. 136). 190p. 1973. pap. 10.50x (ISBN 0-8078-9136-3). U of NC Pr.
Giese, Frank S. & Wilder, Warren F. French Lyric Poetry: An Anthology. LC 64-7849. 1965. pap. 7.87 scp (ISBN 0-672-63038-9). Odyssey Pr.
--French Lyric Poetry: An Anthology. 117p. 1965. pap. text ed. write for info. (ISBN 0-02-342500-8). Macmillan.
Giese, J. W., jt. auth. see Anderson, Hershel M.
Giese, Lester J. Budget Builder I for Community Associations. LC 82-90784. 63p. 1982. 21.95 (ISBN 0-910049-01-7). Condo Mgmt.
--Condominium, Homeowner & Cooperative Community Associations-Information Resource. 40p. (Orig.). 1984. pap. text ed. 13.95 (ISBN 0-910049-03-3). Condo Mgmt.
--Condominium Reserve Builder. 1983. pap. text ed. 32.50 (ISBN 0-910049-02-5). Condo Mgmt.
Giese, Lester J. & Kuehn, Robert W. Model Business Policies for Community Associations. LC 82-72000. 79p. 1982. 29.95 (ISBN 0-910049-00-9). Condo Mgmt.
Giese, Lucretia & Luckey, Laura C. Selections from the M. & M. Karolik Collection of American Painting, 1815-1865. (Illus.). 1976. pap. 2.95 (ISBN 0-87846-180-9). Mus Fine Arts Boston.
Giese, P., et al, eds. Explosion Seismology in Central Europe: Data & Results. 1976. 86.20 (ISBN 0-387-07764-2). Springer-Verlag.
Giese, Pearse. Reproduction of Marine Invertebrates: Entoprocts: Lesser Callomates. 1975. Vol. 2. 80.50. Acad Pr.
Giese, Vincent J. You Got It All: A Personal Account of a White Priest in a Chicago Ghetto. LC 79-92505. (Illus.). 252p. 1980. pap. 5.95 (ISBN 0-87973-526-0, 526). Our Sunday Visitor.
--Youth for Peace: A Handbook for Young Christian Peacemakers. LC 84-60751. 120p. 1984. pap. 5.95 (ISBN 0-87973-596-1, 596). Our Sunday Visitor.
Giese, William & Klammer, Thomas. Intermediate Accounting: A Flow Approach. (Illus.). 1008p. 1984. text ed. 38.95 (ISBN 0-13-469735-9); study guide 17.95. P-H.
Giese, William F. Sainte-Beuve: A Literary Portrait. LC 76-137054. (University of Wisconsin Studies, Language & Literature: No. 31). 368p. 1974. Repr. of 1931 ed. lib. bdg. 24.75x (ISBN 0-8371-5515-0, GISB). Greenwood.
--Victor Hugo: The Man & the Poet. Repr. 30.00 (ISBN 0-8274-3671-8). R West.
Giesea, Roberta, jt. auth. see Coletti, Mina S.
Giesea, Roberta K., jt. auth. see Coletti, Mina S.
Giesecke, et al. Engineering Graphics: With Computer Graphics. 3rd ed. 888p. 1985. text ed. write for info. (ISBN 0-02-342650-0). Macmillan.
--Technical Drawing: With Computer Graphics. 7th ed. 872p. 1985. text ed. write for info. (ISBN 0-02-342690-X). Macmillan.
Giesecke, Albert A. American Commercial Legislation Before 1789. 1970. Repr. of 1910 ed. text ed. 20.50 (ISBN 0-8337-1333-7). B Franklin.
Giesecke, F. H., et al. Technical Drawing Problems. 6th ed. (Series I). 1981. pap. text ed. write for info. (ISBN 0-02-342740-X). Macmillan.
Giesecke, Frederick E., et al. Engineering Graphics. 3rd ed. (Illus.). 928p. 1981. text ed. write for info. (ISBN 0-02-342620-9, 34272). Macmillan.
--Technical Drawing. 7th ed. (Illus.). 1980. text ed. write for info. (ISBN 0-02-342610-1). Macmillan.
--Technical Drawing. 8th ed. 780p. 1986. 29.00 (ISBN 0-02-342600-4). Macmillan.
Giesecke, Minnie. The Genesis of Hand Preference. LC 78-72795. Repr. of 1936 ed. 18.00 (ISBN 0-686-63637-6). AMS Pr.
--Genesis of Hand Preference. (SRCD M). 1936. 15.00 (ISBN 0-527-01490-7). Kraus Repr.
Giesecke, William B., jt. auth. see Speegle, Roger.
Gieseker, D. Module of Curves. (Tata Institute Lectures on Mathematics). 99p. 1983. pap. 9.00 (ISBN 0-387-11953-1). Springer-Verlag.
Gieseking, Audrey, jt. auth. see Joseph, Marjory.
Gieseking, Hal. The Complete Handbook for Travelers. 1984. pap. 7.95 (ISBN 0-671-53271-5, Wallaby). PB.
Gieseking, J. E., ed. Soil Components, Vol. Two: Inorganic Components. (Illus.). 770p. 1974. 102.00 (ISBN 0-387-06862-7). Springer-Verlag.
Gieseking, Walter & Leimar, Karl. Piano Technique. 12.50 (ISBN 0-8446-4546-X). Peter Smith.
Gieseking, Walter & Leimer, Karl. Piano Technique. (Illus.). 140p. pap. 2.95 (ISBN 0-486-22867-3). Dover.
Gieselman, Robert D., ed. Readings in Business Communication. 1982. pap. 8.80x (ISBN 0-87563-223-8). Stipes.
Giesen, Rosemary, jt. auth. see Caveny, Sylvia.
Giesen, Rosemary, jt. auth. see Thompson, Brenda.
Giesey, Ralph. If Not, Not: The Oath of the Aragonese & the Legendary Laws of the Sobrarbe. LC 67-21023. 1968. 29.00 (ISBN 0-691-05128-3). Princeton U Pr.
Giesinger, Adam. From Catherine to Khrushchev. LC 75-312926. (Illus.). 443p. 1981. 13.00 (ISBN 0-914222-05-8). Am Hist Soc Ger.
Giesinger, Adam, ed. see Keller, Conrad.
Gieske, Millard. Minnesota Farmer-Laborism: The Third Party Alternative. LC 79-1115. (Illus.). 1979. 15.00 (ISBN 0-8166-0890-3). U of Minn Pr.
Giess, E. A., et al, eds. Electronic Packaging Materials Science, Vol. 40. LC 85-4849. 1985. text ed. 36.00 (ISBN 0-931837-05-7). Materials Res.
Giessen, B. C., ed. Developments in the Structural Chemistry of Alloy Phases. LC 77-94080. 288p. 1969. 32.50x (ISBN 0-306-30428-7, Plenum Pr). Plenum Pub.
Giessen, B. C., jt. ed. see Chang, Leroy L.
Giessen, B. C., jt. ed. see Kear, B. H.
Giessen, Bill C., jt. ed. see Grant, Nicholas J.
Giessen, Hans van der see Walsh, Patricia M. & Van Der Giessen, Hans.
Giesser, Barbara, jt. auth. see Scheinberg, Labe C.
Giessler, Phillip B. Referred by Luke, M.D. 1976. pap. 1.80 (ISBN 0-89536-204-X). CSS of Ohio.
Giesy, John P., ed. Microcosms in Ecological Research: Proceedings. LC 80-23472. (DOE Symposium Ser.). 1110p. 1980. pap. 36.50 (CONF-781101); microfiche 4.50 (ISBN 0-87079-454-X, CONF-781101). DOE.
Giet, Franz. Zur Tonitat Nordchinesischer Mundarten. Repr. of 1950 ed. 46.00 (ISBN 0-384-18465-0). Johnson Repr.
Gietzen, Jean J. A People Set Apart. 1983. pap. 6.95 (ISBN 0-89390-047-8). Resource Pubns.
Giff, Patricia. Today Was a Terrible Day. LC 84-19623. 32p. (ps-3). 1980. 10.95 (ISBN 0-670-71830-0). Viking.
--Watch Out Ronald Morgan. (gr. 1-3). 1985. 9.95 (ISBN 0-670-80433-9). Viking.
Giff, Patricia G. Next Year I'll Be Special. LC 79-19174. 32p. (gr. k-3). 1980. 7.95 (ISBN 0-525-35810-2). Dutton.
Giff, Patricia R. The Almost Awful Play. LC 83-17101. (Illus.). 32p. (gr. 1-3). 1984. 9.95 (ISBN 0-670-11458-8, Viking Kestrel). Viking.
--The Almost Awful Play. LC 84-17922. (Illus.). 32p. (ps-3). 1985. pap. 3.95 (ISBN 0-14-050530-X). Penguin.
--The Beast in Ms. Rooney's Room. (The Kids of the Polk Street School Ser.: No. 1). 80p. (Orig.). (gr. 1-4). 1984. pap. 2.25 (ISBN 0-440-40485-1, YB). Dell.
--The Candy Corn Contest. (The Kids of the Polk Street School Ser.: No. 3). 80p. (Orig.). (ps-6). 1984. pap. 2.25 (ISBN 0-440-41072-X, YB). Dell.
--December Secrets. (The Kids of the Polk Street School Ser.: No. 4). (Illus.). 80p. (gr. k-6). pap. 2.25 (ISBN 0-440-41795-3, YB). Dell.
--Fish Face. (The Kids of the Polk Street School Ser.: No. 2). 80p. (Orig.). (gr. 1-4). 1984. pap. 2.25 (ISBN 0-440-42557-3, YB). Dell.
--Fourth Grade Celebrity. LC 79-50678. (Illus.). (gr. 4-6). 1979. 8.95 (ISBN 0-440-02725-X); PLB 8.89 (ISBN 0-440-02726-8). Delacorte.
--The Fourth Grade Celebrity. 128p. (gr. k-6). 1981. pap. 2.25 (ISBN 0-440-42676-6, YB). Dell.
--Fourth Grade Celebrity. (Illus.). 128p. (gr. 4-6). 1984. 8.95 (ISBN 0-385-28308-3). Delacorte.
--The Gift of the Pirate Queen. LC 82-70310. (Illus.). 160p. (gr. 4-8). 1982. 9.95 (ISBN 0-440-02970-8); PLB 9.89 (ISBN 0-440-02972-4). Delacorte.
--The Gift of the Pirate Queen. (Illus.). 160p. (gr. 4-8). 1983. pap. 2.25 (ISBN 0-440-43046-1, YB). Dell.
--The Gift of the Pirate Queen. LC 82-70310. (Illus.). 160p. (gr. 4-6). 1982. 11.95 (ISBN 0-385-28338-5); PLB 11.95 (ISBN 0-385-28339-3). Delacorte.
--The Girl Who Knew It All. LC 79-50677. (Illus.). (gr. 4-6). 1979. 6.95 (ISBN 0-440-03137-0); PLB 6.89 (ISBN 0-440-03139-9). Delacorte.
--The Girl Who Knew It All. 128p. (gr. k-6). 1981. pap. 2.25 (ISBN 0-440-42855-6, YB). Dell.
--The Girl Who Knew It All. (Illus.). (gr. 4-6). 1984. 6.95 (ISBN 0-385-28362-8); PLB 6.95 (ISBN 0-385-28363-6). Delacorte.
--Have You Seen Hyacinth Macaw? 128p. (gr. 4-8). 1982. pap. 1.75 (ISBN 0-440-43450-5, YB). Dell.
--Have You Seen Hyacinth Macaw? (Illus.). (gr. 4-6). 1984. 11.95 (ISBN 0-385-28389-X); PLB 11.95 (ISBN 0-385-28390-3). Delacorte.
--Have You Seen Hyacinth Macaw: A Mystery. LC 80-68729. (Illus.). 128p. (gr. 4-7). 1981. 9.95 (ISBN 0-440-03467-1); PLB 9.89 (ISBN 0-440-03472-8). Delacorte.
--In the Dinosaur's Paw. (The Kids of the Polk Street School Ser.: No. 5). (Illus.). 80p. (gr. k-6). 1985. pap. 2.25 (ISBN 0-440-44150-1, YB). Dell.
--Lazy Lions, Lucky Lambs. (The Kids of the Polk Street School Ser.: No. 7). (Illus.). 80p. (gr. k-6). 1985. pap. 2.25 (ISBN 0-440-44640-6, YB). Dell.
--Left-Handed Shortstop. (Illus.). 128p. (gr. k-6). 1981. pap. 1.75 (ISBN 0-440-44672-4, YB). Dell.
--Left-Handed Shortstop. (Illus.). (gr. 4-6). 1984. 9.95 (ISBN 0-385-28533-7); PLB 9.95 (ISBN 0-385-28534-5). Delacorte.
--Left-Handed Shortstop: A Novel. LC 80-65835. (Illus.). 128p. (gr. 4-6). 1980. 11.95 (ISBN 0-440-04553-3); PLB 11.95 (ISBN 0-385-28534-5). Delacorte.
--Loretta P. Sweeny, Where are You? (Illus.). 144p. (gr. 4-8). 1984. pap. 2.25 (ISBN 0-440-44926-X, YB). Dell.
--Purple Climbing Days. (The Kids of the Polk Street School Ser.: No. 9). (Illus.). 80p. (gr. 5 up). 1984. pap. 2.25 (ISBN 0-440-47309-8, YB). Dell.
--Rat Teeth. LC 83-16601. (Illus.). 144p. (gr. 4-6). 1984. 12.95 (ISBN 0-385-29339-9); PLB 12.95 (ISBN 0-385-29309-7). Delacorte.
--Rat Teeth. (gr. k-6). 1985. pap. 2.50 (ISBN 0-440-47457-4, YB). Dell.
--Say "Cheese", No. 10. (The Kids of the Polk Street School Ser.). (Illus.). (gr. 6-9). 1985. pap. 2.25 (ISBN 0-440-47639-9, YB). Dell.
--Snaggle Doodles. (The Kids of the Polk Street School Ser.: No. 8). 80p. (gr. 1-4). pap. 2.25 (ISBN 0-440-48068-X, YB). Dell.
--Suspect. (Illus.). 80p. (gr. 7 up). 1982. 8.95 (ISBN 0-525-45108-0, 0869-260, Skinny Bk). Dutton.
--Today Was a Terrible Day. (Pucture Puffin Ser.). (Illus.). 32p. 1984. pap. 3.95 (ISBN 0-14-050453-2, Puffin). Penguin.
--Today Was a Terrible Day. (Illus.). (gr. k-3). 1984. incl. cassette 19.95 (ISBN 0-941078-50-7); pap. 12.95 incl. cassette (ISBN 0-941078-48-5); pap. 27.95 4 bks, cassette, & guide (ISBN 0-941078-49-3); sound fimlstrip 22.95 (ISBN 0-941078-47-7). Live Oak Media.
--The Valentine Star. (The Kids of the Polk Street School Ser.: No. 6). (Illus.). 80p. (Orig.). (gr. k-6). 1985. pap. 2.25 (ISBN 0-440-49204-1, YB). Dell.
--The Winter Worm Business. (Illus.). 144p. (gr. 4-7). 1983. pap. 1.95 (ISBN 0-440-49259-9, YB). Dell.
--The Winter Worm Business. (Illus.). (gr. 4-6). 1984. 8.95 (ISBN 0-385-29152-3); PLB 8.95 (ISBN 0-385-29154-X). Delacorte.
--The Winter Worm Business: A Novel. LC 81-65490. 128p. (gr. 4-6). 1981. 11.95 (ISBN 0-385-29152-3); PLB 8.89 (ISBN 0-440-09547-6). Delacorte.
Giff, Patricia R. & Kramer, Anthony. Loretta P. Sweeny, Where Are You? LC 83-5164. (Illus.). 144p. (gr. 4-6). 1983. 11.95 (ISBN 0-385-29298-8); PLB 11.95 (ISBN 0-385-29299-6). Delacorte.
Giffard, C. Anthony, jt. auth. see Hachten, William.
Giffen, Naomi M. The Roles of Men & Women in Eskimo Culture. LC 74-5837. Repr. of 1930 ed. 14.00 (ISBN 0-404-11642-6). AMS Pr.
Giffen, Robert. Economic Inquiries & Studies, 2 Vols. (The Development of Industrial Society Ser.). 942p. 1971. Repr. of 1904 ed. 65.00x (ISBN 0-7165-1758-2, BBA 03545, Pub. by Irish Academic Pr). Biblio Dist.
--Essays in Finance. LC 82-48183. (Gold, Money, Inflation & Deflation Ser.). 479p. 1982. lib. bdg. 61.00 (ISBN 0-8240-5235-8). Garland Pub.
--Growth of Capital. LC 67-29505. Repr. of 1889 ed. 22.50x (ISBN 0-678-00664-4). Kelley.
--Stock Exchange Securities. LC 68-9574. Repr. of 1877 ed. 22.50x (ISBN 0-678-00423-4). Kelley.
Giffen, Walter C. Queueing: Basic Theory & Application. LC 76-44996. (Grid Industrial Engineering Ser.). Repr. of 1978 ed. 92.50 (ISBN 0-8357-9144-0, 2015244). Bks Demand UMI.
Giffin, James M., jt. auth. see Carlson, Delbert G.
Giffin, James M., jt. auth. see Strang, Paul D.
Giffin, Kim & Barnes, Richard. Trust of Self & Others. (Interpersonal Communication Ser.). (Illus.). 96p. 1976. pap. text ed. 8.95 (ISBN 0-675-08647-7). Merrill.
Giffin, Kim & Patton, Bobby R. Basic Readings in Interpersonal Communication: Theory & Application. 2nd ed. (Auer Ser.). 272p. 1976. pap. text ed. 12.20 scp (ISBN 0-06-042329-3, HarpC). Har-Row.
--Fundamentals of Interpersonal Communication. 2nd ed. (Auer Ser.). 263p. 1976. text ed. 19.50 scp (ISBN 0-06-042315-3, HarpC); instructor's manual avail. (ISBN 0-06-362351-X). Har-Row.
Giffin, Kim, jt. auth. see Duldt, Bonnie W.
Giffin, Kim, jt. auth. see Patton, Bobby R.
Giffin, Mary E. Studies on Chaucer & His Audience. LC 74-18083. 1974. Repr. of 1956 ed. lib. bdg. 27.50 (ISBN 0-8414-4570-2). Folcroft.
Giffin, Paul A. Seasons Come Spring. 1979. 5.00 (ISBN 0-682-49491-7). Exposition Pr FL.
Giffin, Rodney & Giffin, Sara. In the Catacombs of Rome. 1982. pap. 3.00 (ISBN 0-89536-524-3). CSS of Ohio.
Giffin, Sara. Home at Last. 1984. 7.95 (ISBN 0-89536-958-3). CSS of Ohio.
Giffin, Sara, jt. auth. see Giffin, Rodney.
Giffin, Vernon O. Veil & More Folklore of the Eastern Shore. 1983. 5.50 (ISBN 0-9610674-0-3). McClain.

Giffin, Walter C. Transform Techniques for Probability Modeling. (Operation Research Industrial Engineering Ser.). 1975. 59.50 (ISBN 0-12-282750-3). Acad Pr.

Gifford & McWilliam. Buildings of Scotland. 1985. 25.00 (ISBN 0-14-071068-X). Penguin.

Gifford, jt. auth. see Barrett.

Gifford, Barry. Beautiful Phantoms: Selected Poems, 1968-1980. 100p. (Orig.). 1981. pap. 5.00 (ISBN 0-939180-00-6). Tombouctou.

--Horse Hauling Timber Out of Hokkaido Forest. (Illus.). 1979. pap. 4.95 (ISBN 0-87922-126-7). Christopher's Bks.

--Kerouac's Town. rev. ed. LC 76-50838. (Modern Authors Monograph Ser.: No. 2). (Illus.). 75p. 1977. pap. 3.50 (ISBN 0-916870-07-3). Creative Arts Bk.

--Landscape with Traveler: The Pillow Book of Francis Reeves. 1982. pap. 6.25 (ISBN 0-03-060604-7, Owl Bks). HR&W.

--Letters to Proust. 1976. 1.50 (ISBN 0-934834-05-9). White Pine.

--The Neighborhood of Baseball: A Personal History of the Chicago Cubs. LC 84-80171. (Illus.). 205p. 1985. pap. 7.95 (ISBN 0-916870-83-9, A Donald S. Ellis Book). Creative Arts Bk.

--Persimmons, Poems for Paintings. 1977. bound in wrappers 3.50 (ISBN 0-685-22219-5, Pub. by Shaman Drum Pr). Small Pr Dist.

--Port Tropique. LC 80-15440. 200p. 1980. pap. 5.95 (ISBN 0-916870-31-6, Black Lizard Bks). Creative Arts Bk.

--Port Tropique. LC 80-15440. (Black Lizard Fiction Ser.). 200p. 1980. 9.95 (ISBN 0-916870-32-4). Creative Arts Bk.

--Port Tropique. (A Black Lizard Bk.). 200p. pap. 5.95 (ISBN 0-916870-31-6). Creative Arts Bk.

--A Quinzaine in Return for a Portrait of Mary Sun. 1977. pap. 2.50 (ISBN 0-935388-04-4). Workingmans Pr.

--An Unfortunate Woman. LC 83-82560. 185p. (Orig.). 1984. 14.95 (ISBN 0-916870-73-1, Donald S. Ellis); pap. 7.95 (ISBN 0-916870-74-X). Creative Arts Bk.

Gifford, Barry & Lee, Lawrence. Jack's Book: An Oral Biography of Jack Kerouac. 1979. pap. 5.95 (ISBN 0-14-005269-0). Penguin.

Gifford, Barry, jt. auth. see Lee, Lawrence.

Gifford, Barry, ed. As Ever: The Collected Correspondence of Allen Ginsberg & Neal Cassady. LC 77-82182. 275p. 1977. 15.00 (ISBN 0-916870-09-X); pap. 5.95 (ISBN 0-916870-08-1). Creative Arts Bk.

Gifford, Barry, ed. see Curtis, Edward S.

Gifford, Barry, tr. see Jammes, Francis.

Gifford, Charles S. & Fluitt, John L. Test-Taking Made Easier. 1981. text ed. 2.40 (ISBN 0-8134-2194-2). Interstate.

Gifford, Courtney D. Directory of U. S. Labor Organizations: 1984-85 Edition. 86p. 1984. pap. text ed. 15.00 (ISBN 0-87179-457-8). BNA.

Gifford, Courtney D. & Hobgood, William P. Directory of U. S. Labor Arbitrators. 460p. 1985. 40.00 (ISBN 0-87179-494-2). BNA.

Gifford, Courtney D., ed. Directory of U. S. Labor Organizations: 1982-83 Edition. 139p. 1982. pap. text ed. 15.00 (ISBN 0-686-84387-8). BNA.

Gifford, Daniel J. & Raskind, Leo J. Federal Antitrust Law Cases & Materials. LC 83-10638. (American Casebook Ser.). 694p. 1983. text ed. 22.95 (ISBN 0-314-73463-5). West Pub.

--Federal Antitrust Law, Cases & Materials, 1985 Supplement. (American Casebook Ser.). 63p. 1984. 2.95 (ISBN 0-314-87392-9). West Pub.

Gifford, Daphne, jt. ed. see Mellows, W. T.

Gifford, Denis. The British Comic Catalogue, 1874-1974. LC 75-35486. 210p. 1976. lib. bdg. 35.00 (ISBN 0-8371-8649-8, GCC/). Greenwood.

--The British Film Catalogue, 1895-1970: A Guide to Entertainment Films. LC 82-49222. (Cinema Classics Ser.). 900p. 1985. lib. bdg. 125.00 (ISBN 0-8240-5760-0). Garland Pub.

--The Great Cartoon Stars. 128p. 1981. 24.00x (ISBN 0-904041-34-4, Pub. by Jupiter England). State Mutual Bk.

Gifford, Dennis. The Golden Age of Radio: British Radio, an Illustrated Companion. (Illus.). 288p. 1985. 32.00 (ISBN 0-7134-4234-4, Pub. by Batsford England). David & Charles.

Gifford, Derek. A Practical Handbook for Radiologists & Radiographers. 632p. 1984. text ed. 32.00 (ISBN 0-471-90172-5, Pub by Wiley Med). Wiley.

Gifford, Don. Joyce Annotated: Notes for Dubliners & Portrait of the Artist as a Young Man. 2nd ed. LC 80-29448. (Illus.). 310p. 1982. 29.50x (ISBN 0-520-04189-5); pap. 9.95 (ISBN 0-520-04610-2, CAL 542). U of Cal Pr.

Gifford, Douglas. Warriors, Gods & Spirits from Central & South American Mythology. (World Mythologies Ser.). (Illus.). 132p. 1983. 15.95 (ISBN 0-8052-3857-3). Schocken.

Gifford, Douglas, ed. Scottish Short Stories, 1800-1900. pap. 11.95 (ISBN 0-7145-0657-5). Riverrun NY.

Gifford, E. H., jt. auth. see Andrews, Samuel J.

Gifford, E. W. Tongan Myths & Tales. (BMB). Repr. of 1924 ed. 25.00 (ISBN 0-527-02111-3, BMB, NO. 8). Kraus Repr.

--Tongan Place Names. (BMB). Repr. of 1923 ed. 31.00 (ISBN 0-527-02109-1, BMB, NO. 6). Kraus Repr.

--Tongan Society. (BMB). Repr. of 1929 ed. 64.00 (ISBN 0-527-02167-9, BMB, NO. 6). Kraus Repr.

Gifford, E. W., jt. auth. see Barrett, S. A.

Gifford, E. W., jt. auth. see Kroeber, Alfred L.

Gifford, Edward. Archaeological Excavations in Yap. LC 60-63050. (University of California, Anthropological Records: Vol. 18, No. 2). pap. 20.00 (ISBN 0-317-29122-X, 2021316). Bks Demand UMI.

Gifford, Edward W. & Shutler, Dick. Archaeological Excavations in New Caledonia. LC 56-4866. (University of California, Anthropological Records: Vol. 18, No. 1). pap. 38.00 (ISBN 0-317-29127-0, 2021315). Bks Demand UMI.

Gifford, Edward W & Block, Gwendoline H.compiled by. California Indian Nights Entertainment. LC 76-43713. Repr. of 1930 ed. 32.50 (ISBN 0-404-15546-4). AMS Pr.

Gifford, Ernest M., jt. auth. see Foster, Adriance S.

Gifford, Ernest M., jt. ed. see Rost, Thomas L.

Gifford, F. Tape: a Radio News Handbook. (Communication Arts Bks.). 1977. 13.50 (ISBN 0-8038-7161-9). Hastings.

Gifford, Frank & Mangel, Charles. Gifford on Courage. LC 76-21862. 320p. 1976. 9.95 (ISBN 0-87131-223-9). M Evans.

Gifford, Frederick L. The Early History of the Village of Clifton Springs. LC 84-50920. (Village History Ser.). (Illus.). 64p. (Orig.). 1984. pap. 3.00 (ISBN 0-9613464-0-X). Gifford F L.

Gifford, George. A Discourse of the Subtill Practises of Devilles by Witches & Sorcerers. LC 77-6745. (English Experience Ser.: No. 871). 1977. Repr. of 1587 ed. lib. bdg. 8.00 (ISBN 90-221-0871-6). Walter J Johnson.

--A Plaine Declaration That Our Brownists Be Full Donatists. LC 74-80180. (English Experience Ser.: No. 661). 1974. Repr. of 1590 ed. 14.00 (ISBN 90-221-0661-6). Walter J Johnson.

Gifford, George E., ed. Dear Jeffie: Being the Letters from Jeffries Wyman to His Son Jeffries Wyman, Jr. LC 78-58830. (gr. 6 up). 1978. 15.00 (ISBN 0-87365-796-9). Peabody Harvard.

--Psychoanalysis, Psychotherapy, & the New Engand Medical Scene, 1894-1944. 1978. 40.00 (ISBN 0-88202-169-9). Watson Pub Intl.

Gifford, George E., Jr. Cecil County, Maryland, 1608-1850. LC 74-84769. (Illus.). 241p. 1974. 7.50 (ISBN 0-686-11977-0). G E Gifford Memorial.

Gifford, George E., Jr., ed. Physician Signers of the Declaration of Independence. (Illus.). 1976. 14.95 (ISBN 0-88202-159-1). Watson Pub Intl.

Gifford, Griselda. Because of Blunder. (Illus.). 1977. 12.50 (ISBN 0-575-02310-4, Pub. by Gollancz England). David & Charles.

--Mirabelle's Secret. (Illus.). 1976. 9.95 (ISBN 0-575-02091-1, Pub. by Gollancz England). David & Charles.

Gifford, Henry. Pasternak: A Critical Study. LC 76-9735. (Major European Authors Ser.). (Illus.). 1977. 42.50 (ISBN 0-521-21288-X). Cambridge U Pr.

--Pasternak: A Critical Study. LC 76-9735. (Major European Authors Ser.). 280p. 1981. pap. 17.95 (ISBN 0-521-28677-8). Cambridge U Pr.

--Tolstoy. (Past Masters Ser.). 1982. 12.95x (ISBN 0-19-287544-2); pap. 3.95 (ISBN 0-317-04410-9). Oxford U Pr.

Gifford, Henry, jt. auth. see Tomlinson, Charles.

Gifford, Henry, ed. see Tolstoy, Leo.

Gifford, J. Daniel. The Automotive Security System Design Handbook. (Illus.). 240p. (Orig.). 1985. 18.95 (ISBN 0-8306-0734-X, 1734); pap. 12.95 (ISBN 0-8306-1734-5). TAB Bks.

Gifford, James C. Archaeological Explorations in Caves of the Point of Pines Region, Arizona. LC 79-9180. (Anthropological Papers: No. 36). 218p. 1980. pap. 8.95x (ISBN 0-8165-0360-5). U of Ariz Pr.

--Prehistoric Pottery Analysis & the Ceramics of Barton Ramie in the Belize Valley. LC 75-40772. (Peabody Museum Memoirs: Vol. 18). 1976. pap. 17.50x (ISBN 0-87365-691-1). Peabody Harvard.

Gifford, James C. & Smith, Watson. Gray Corrugated Pottery from Awatovi. LC 78-50909. (Peabody Museum Papers: Vol. 69). 1978. pap. 20.00 (ISBN 0-87365-194-4). Peabody Harvard.

Gifford, James F., ed. Undergraduate Medical Education & the Elective System: Experience with the Duke Curriculum, 1966-75. LC 77-84615. pap. 64.30 (ISBN 0-317-26746-9, 2023383). Bks Demand UMI.

Gifford, Sr. James F. The Evolution of a Medical Center: A History of Medicine at Duke University to 1941. LC 73-185464. xi, 299p. 1972. 21.00 (ISBN 0-8223-0290-X). Duke.

Gifford, Jessica L. Judicial Notice in Arizona. 81p. 1978. 6.30 (ISBN 0-910039-05-4). Az Law Inst.

Gifford, John A., jt. ed. see Rapp, George.

Gifford, N. L. When in Rome: An Introduction to Relativism & Knowledge. LC 82-10374. (SUNY Series in Philosophy). 159p. 1983. 32.50x (ISBN 0-87395-667-2); pap. 8.95x (ISBN 0-87395-668-0). State U NY Pr.

Gifford, Prosser, ed. France & Britain in Africa: Imperial Rivalry & Colonial Rule. 1972. 77.00x (ISBN 0-300-01289-6). Yale U Pr.

--The National Interests of the United States in Foreign Policy: Seven Discussions at the Wilson Center December 1980 - February 1981. LC 81-40792. 204p. (Orig.). 1981. lib. bdg. 15.50 (ISBN 0-8191-1786-2); pap. text ed. 8.50 (ISBN 0-8191-1787-0). U Pr of Amer.

--The Treaty of Paris (1738) in a Changing States System: Papers from a Conference January 26-27, 1984. LC 85-9139. 218p. (Orig.). 1985. lib. bdg. 29.75 (ISBN 0-8191-4752-4, Pub. by Woodrow Wilson Intl. Ctr.); pap. text ed. 18.50 (ISBN 0-8191-4753-2). U Pr of Amer.

Gifford, Prosser & Louis, Roger W., eds. Britain & Germany in Africa: Imperial Rivalry & Colonial Rule. LC 67-24500. pap. 160.00 (ISBN 0-317-11347-X, 2006158). Bks Demand UMI.

Gifford, Prosser & Louis, William R., eds. The Transfer of Power in Africa: Decolonization, 1940-1960. LC 81-1931. 704p. 1982. text ed. 38.00x (ISBN 0-300-02568-8). Yale U Pr.

Gifford, R. W., jt. auth. see Manger, W. M.

Gifford, Roger & Millington, R. J. Energetics of Agriculture & Food Production: With Special Emphasis on the Australian Situation. (Bulletin Ser.: No. 288). 29p. (2nd Printing 1977). 1975. pap. 6.00 (ISBN 0-643-00147-6, C042, CSIRO). Unipub.

Gifford, Roger M. Energetics of Agriculture & Food Production. (Illus.). 29p. 1977. pap. 2.25x (ISBN 0-643-00147-6, Pub. by CSIRO). Intl Spec Bk.

Gifford, Terry, jt. auth. see Roberts, Neil.

Gifford, Thomas. Benchwarmer Bob. LC 74-13550. (Illus.). 128p. (Orig.). 1974. pap. 10.00 (ISBN 0-685-50666-5). Piper.

--The Cavanaugh Quest. 1977. pap. 2.50 (ISBN 0-345-29065-8). Ballantine.

--The Glendower Legacy. 1979. pap. 2.50 (ISBN 0-671-82678-6). PB.

--Hollywood Gothic. 1980. pap. 2.50 (ISBN 0-345-29009-7). Ballantine.

--The Wind Chill Factor. 384p. 1985. pap. 3.50 (ISBN 0-345-32336-X). Ballantine.

Gifford, Virginia S., compiled by. Music for Oboe, Oboe D'Amore, & English Horn: A Bibliography of Materials at the Library of Congress. LC 83-8517. (Music Reference Collection: No. 1). xli, 431p. 1983. lib. bdg. 49.95 (ISBN 0-313-23762-X, GMO/). Greenwood.

Gifford, W. The Works of Ben Jonson, 9 vols. 1979. Repr. of 1875 ed. Set. lib. bdg. 300.00 (ISBN 0-8495-2004-5). Arden Lib.

Gifford, William, ed. Anti-Jacobin; or, Weekly Examiner. Nos. 1-36, 1 vol. LC 68-57996. 1797-1798. lib. bdg. 74.50 (ISBN 0-404-19501-6). Incl. vols. 1-12. AMS Pr.

Gifford, William, ed. see Massinger, Philip.

Gifford, William, tr. see Juvenal.

Gifford, William C. & Owens, Elisabeth A. International Aspects of U. S. Income Taxation: Cases & Materials, Vol. II, Pt. 3. LC 80-18605. 760p. (Orig.). 1982. pap. text ed. 25.00x (ISBN 0-915506-26-2). Harvard Law Intl Tax.

Gifford, William C. & Streng, William P. International Tax Planning. 2nd ed. 1979. 45.00 (ISBN 0-87179-271-0). Tax Mgmt.

Gifford, William C., Jr. & Streng, William P. International Tax Planning. 2nd ed. LC 74-76783. 746p. 1979. text ed. 45.00 (ISBN 0-87179-271-0). BNA.

Gifford, William, Jr., tr. see Juvenal.

Giffords, Gloria. Mexican Folk Retablos: Masterpieces on Tin. LC 72-92107. (Illus.). 160p. 1974. 35.00 (ISBN 0-8165-0322-2). U of Ariz Pr.

Gifft, Helen, et al. Nutrition, Behavior & Change. LC 79-170033. 1972. ref. ed. 25.95 (ISBN 0-13-627836-1). P-H.

Gifis, Steven H. Dictionary of Legal Terms: A Simplified Guide to the Language of Law. LC 83-2726. 511p. 1983. pap. 5.95 (ISBN 0-8120-2013-8). Barron.

--Law Dictionary. rev. ed. LC 74-18126. 240p. 1975. pap. 4.95 pocket-sized (ISBN 0-8120-0543-0). Barron.

--Law Dictionary. 2nd ed. LC 84-6474. 1984. 8.95 (ISBN 0-8120-2085-5). Barron.

Gifkins, R. C., ed. Strength of Metals & Alloys (ICSMA 6) Proceedings of the 6th International Conference, Melbourne, Australia, August 16-20, 1982, 3 Vols. LC 82-9851. (International Series on the Strength & Fracture of Materials & Structures). 1200p. 1982. 240.00 (ISBN 0-08-029325-5). Pergamon.

Gifted Children Newsletter Staff & Alvino, James. Parents Guide to Raising a Gifted Child: Recognizing & Devolpment of Your Child's Potential. 1984. 19.95 (ISBN 0-316-03727-3). Little.

Gifter, Mordechai. The Philosophy & Structure of the Middos Program. (Annual Fryer Memorial Lecture Ser.). 0.50 (ISBN 0-914131-48-6, I31). Torah Umesorah.

Gigante, Marcello. Nomes Basileus. Vlastos, Gregory, ed. LC 78-19351. (Morals & Law in Ancient Greece Ser.). 1979. Repr. of 1956 ed. lib. bdg. 23.00x (ISBN 0-405-11544-X). Ayer Co Pubs.

Gigase, P. L. & Van Marck, E. E., eds. From Parasitic Infection to Parasitic Disease. (Contributions to Microbiology & Immunology Series: Vol. 7). (Illus.). x, 270p. 1982. 76.25 (ISBN 3-8055-3543-0). S Karger.

Gigch, John P. van see Van Gigch, John P.

Gigch, John P. Van see Van Gigch, John P. & Hill, Richard E.

Gigh, Van. Metamodels & Metasystems. 1984. 33.00 (ISBN 0-9901003-7-5, Pub. by Abacus England). Heyden.

Gigi Coe. Present Value. LC 79-90491. (Illus.). 1980. pap. 5.95 (ISBN 0-913890-35-9). Brick Hse Pub.

Gigihara, Y., jt. ed. see Yoshida, H.

Gigli, Beniamino. The Memoirs of Beniamino Gigli. Farkas, Andrew, ed. Silone, Darina, tr. LC 76-29937. (Opera Biographies). (Illus.). 1977. Repr. of 1957 ed. lib. bdg. 24.50x (ISBN 0-405-09679-8). Ayer Co Pubs.

Gigli, I. N., et al, eds. Immunodermatology. (Illus.). 195p. 1983. pap. 21.00 (ISBN 0-387-11738-5). Springer-Verlag.

Gigliesi, Primerose & Friend, Robert, trs. from Chinese. The Effendi & the Pregnant Pot. (Illus.). 88p. (Orig.). 1982. pap. 2.50 (ISBN 0-8351-1027-3). China Bks.

Giglio, Giovanni. Triumph of Barabbas. Mosbacher, E., tr. LC 74-180401. Repr. of 1937 ed. 29.00 (ISBN 0-404-56125-X). AMS Pr.

Giglio, James M. H. M. Daugherty & the Politics of Expediency. LC 78-17106. 300p. 1978. 20.00x (ISBN 0-87338-215-3). Kent St U Pr.

Giglio, James N. & Thielen, Greg G. Truman in Cartoon & Caricature. (Illus.). 166p. 1984. 14.95 (ISBN 0-8138-1806-0). Iowa St U Pr.

Gigliolo, Pier P., ed. Language & Social Context. (Education Ser). 1972. pap. 5.95 (ISBN 0-14-080244-4). Penguin.

Gigliotti, Richard & Jackson, Ronald. Security Design for Maximum Protection. 480p. 1984. text ed. 34.95 (ISBN 0-409-95119-6). Butterworth.

Gignac, Francis T. An Introductory New Testament Greek Course. 4.20 (ISBN 0-8294-0223-3). Loyola.

Gignguay, Michel. Dictionnaire d'Informatique: Francais-Anglais. 152p. (Fr.-Eng.). 1976. pap. 32.50 (ISBN 0-686-57197-5, M-6272). French & Eur.

Gigon, Olof. Studien zur antiken Philosophie. Graeser, Andreas, ed. 1972. 54.80x (ISBN 3-11-003928-1). De Gruyter.

Gigoryau, L., et al. Fundamentals of Soviet State Law. 1971. 16.00x (ISBN 0-8464-0440-0). Beekman Pubs.

Gigout, Eugene, ed. see Sacchini, Antonio.

Gihman, I. I. & Skorohod, A. V. Stochastic Differential Equations. Wickwire, K., tr. from Rus. LC 72-86885. (Ergebnisse der Mathematik und Ihrer Grenzgebiete: Vol. 72). viii, 354p. 1972. 56.00 (ISBN 0-387-05946-6). Springer-Verlag.

--The Theory of Stochastic Processes I. (Grundlehren der Mathematischen Wissenschaften: Vol. 210). 570p. 1974. 71.00 (ISBN 0-387-06573-3). Springer-Verlag.

Gihman, L. I. & Skorohod, A. V. The Theory of Stochastic Processes II. (Die Grunglehren der Mathematischen Wissenschaften Ser.: Vol. 218). 441p. 1975. 68.00 (ISBN 0-387-07247-0). Springer-Verlag.

Gihon, John H. Geary & Kansas. facsimile ed. LC 74-165634. (Select Bibliographies Reprint Ser). Repr. of 1857 ed. 22.00 (ISBN 0-8369-5943-4). Ayer Co Pubs.

Gijlstra, D. J. Legal Issues of European Integration. 118p. 1984. 24.00 (ISBN 90-654-4172-7). Kluwer Academic.

--Legal Issues of European Integration, 1982. 1983. lib. bdg. 18.00 (ISBN 90-654-4140-9, Pub. by Kluwer Law & Taxation). Kluwer Academic.

--Legal Issues of European Integration 1982-1983. 1984. lib. bdg. 24.00 (ISBN 0-318-01660-5, Pub. by Kluwer Law Netherlands). Kluwer Academic.

--Legal Issues of European Integration, 1984. 1984. pap. text ed. 28.50 (ISBN 90-654-4205-7, Pub. by Kluwer Law Netherlands). Kluwer Academic.

Gijlstra, D. J. & Bronkhorst, H. J. Leading Cases & Materials on the Agricultural Policy of the EEC. 250p. 1983. 22.00 (ISBN 90-654-4070-4, Pub. by KLuwer Law Netherlands). Kluwer Academic.

Gijlstra, D. J. & Murphy, D. F. Leading Cases & Materials on the Competition Law in the European Economic Community. 2nd, rev., enl. & updated ed. 1979. pap. 26.00 (ISBN 90-268-1094-6, Pub. by Kluwer Law Netherlands). Kluwer Academic.

Gijlstra, D. J. & Murphy, F. Leading Cases & Materials on the Competition Law of the ERC: 1984-85. pap. text ed. 32.00 (ISBN 90-6544-111-5, Pub. by Kluwer Law Netherlands). Kluwer Academic.

Gijlstra, D. J. & Schermers, H. G. Leading Cases on th Law of the European Communities. 4th ed. 582p. 1982. 28.00 (ISBN 90-654-4068-2, Pub. by Kluwer Law Netherlands). Kluwer Academic.

Gijlstra, D. J., ed. Legal Issues of European Integration. (Law Review of the Europa Institute of the University of Amsterdam: Vol. 1977). 1978. pap. 10.00 (ISBN 90-268-0964-6, Pub. by Kluwer Law Netherlands). Kluwer Academic.

Gijlstra, D. J. & Baardman, Bob, eds. Competition Law in Western Europe & the U. S. A, Vols. A & B. 280.00 (ISBN 0-686-40940-X, Pub. by Kluwer Law Netherlands). Kluwer Academic.

Gijlstra, D. J. & Schermers, H. G., eds. Legal Issues of European Integration. (Law Review of the Europa Instituut (University of Amsterdam) Ser.: No. 1). 124p. 1974. 18.00 (ISBN 90-268-0738-4, Pub. by Kluwer Law Netherlands). Kluwer Academic.

--Legal Issues of European Integration. (Law Review of the Europa Instituut (University of Amsterdam) Ser.: No.2). 148p. 1974. 22.00 (ISBN 90-268-0774-0, Pub. by Kluwer Law Netherlands). Kluwer Academic.

--Legal Issues of European Integration. (Law Review of the Europa Instituut (University of Amsterdam) Ser.: No. 1). 158p. 1975. 22.00 (ISBN 90-268-0795-3, Pub. by Kluwer Law Netherlands). Kluwer Academic.

--Legal Issues of European Integration. (Law Review of the Europa Instituut (University of Amsterdam) Ser.: No. 1). 134p. 1976. 20.00 (ISBN 90-268-0905-0, Pub. by Kluwer Law, Netherlands). Kluwer Academic.

--Legal Issues of European Integration. (Law Review of the Europa Instituut (University of Amsterdam) Ser.: No. 2). 106p. 1976. pap. 16.00 (Pub. by Kluwer Law Netherlands). Kluwer Academic.

--Legal Issues of European Integration. (Law Review of the Europa Instituut (University of Amsterdam) Ser.: No. 1). 134p. 20.00 (ISBN 90-268-0960-3, Pub. by Kluwer Law Netherlands). Kluwer Academic.

--Legal Issues of European Integration. (Law Review of the Europa Instituut (University of Amsterdam) Ser.: No. 2). 76p. 1977. 12.00 (ISBN 90-268-0964-6, Pub. by Kluwer Law Netherlands). Kluwer Academic.

--Legal Issues of European Integration. (Law Review of the Europa Instituut (University of Amsterdam) Ser.: No. 1). 98p. 1977. 16.00 (ISBN 90-268-1028-8, Pub. by Kluwer Law Netherlands). Kluwer Academic.

--Legal Issues of European Integration. (Law Review of the Europa Instituut (Univeristy of Amsterdam) Ser.: No. 2). 120p. 1978. 18.00 (ISBN 90-268-1079-2, Pub. by Kluwer Law Netherlands). Kluwer Academic.

--Legal Issues of European Integration. (Law Review of the Europa Instituut (University of Amsterdam) Ser.: No. 1). 144p. 1979. pap. 20.00 (ISBN 90-268-1070-9, Pub. by Kluwer Law Netherlands). Kluwer Academic.

--Legal Issues of European Integration. (Law Review of the Europa Instituut (Univeristy of Amsterdam) Ser.: No. 2). 120p. 1979. 19.00 (ISBN 90-268-1178-0, Pub. by Kluwer Law Netherlands). Kluwer Academic.

--Legal Issues of European Integration: Law Review of the Europa Instituut (University of Amsterdam) Ser. 124p. Biennial. write for info. (Pub. by Kluwer Law Netherlands). Kluwer Academic.

--Legal Issues of European Integration: Law Review of the European Instituut (University of Amsterdam) Ser. (No. 2). 160p. 1975. pap. 22.00 (ISBN 90-268-0848-8, Pub. by Kluwer Law Netherlands). Kluwer Academic.

Gijlstra, D. J., et al. Leading Cases & Materials on the Law of the European Communities. 3rd., rev. & expanded ed. 1979. pap. 26.00 (ISBN 90-268-1095-4, Pub. by Kluwer Law Netherlands). Kluwer Academic.

Gijlstra, D. J., et al, eds. Leading Cases & Materials on the Law of the European Communities. 1975. pap. 17.00 (ISBN 90-268-0806-2, Pub. by Kluwer Law Netherlands). Kluwer Academic.

--Legal Issues of European Integration. 120p. 1980. pap. 18.50 (ISBN 90-268-1079-2, Pub. by Kluwer Law Netherlands). Kluwer Academic.

--Legal Issues of European Integration, Vol. 1. 1979. pap. 24.00 (ISBN 90-268-1070-9, Pub. by Kluwer Law Netherlands). Kluwer Academic.

Gijlstra-Lauwaars, et al. Legal Issues of European Integration 1983-1: Law Review of the University of Amsterdam. 1984. pap. text ed. 22.00 (ISBN 90-654-4161-1, Pub. by Kluwer Law Netherlands). Kluwer Academic.

Gijstra, D. J. & Volker, E. L. Materials on the Law of the European Communities, 1983. 550p. 1983. pap. 32.00 (ISBN 90-65-44069-0). Kluwer Academic.

Gik, Y., jt. auth. see Karpov, A.

Gikey, Langdon. Creationism on Trial: Evolution & God at Little Rock. 240p. 1985. pap. 9.95 (ISBN 0-86683-780-9). Winston Pr.

Gikow, Louise. Boober Fraggle's Celery Souffle. LC 84-6858. (Illus.). (ps-2). 1984. 5.95 (ISBN 0-03-000722-4). HR&W.

--Boober Fraggle's Ghosts. (Illus.). 48p. (gr. 1-4). 1985. 5.95 (ISBN 0-03-004549-5). HR&W.

--Follow That Fraggle. LC 85-5479. (Illus.). 32p. (gr. k-2). 1985. 4.95 (ISBN 0-03-004558-4). HR&W.

--Goldilocks: Baby Piggy's Dream. LC 84-22348. (Picturebacks Ser.). (Illus.). 32p. (ps-3). 1985. pap. 1.95 (ISBN 0-394-87223-1, BYR). Random.

--The Last Days of Fraggle Rock. LC 85-5425. 48p. (gr. 1-4). 1985. 6.95 (ISBN 0-03-004548-7). HR&W.

--The Legend of the Doozer Who Didn't. LC 84-6623. (Fraggle Rock Bks.). (Illus.). (ps-2). 1984. 5.95 (ISBN 0-03-000717-8); pap. 1.95 (ISBN 0-03-004563-0). HR&W.

--The Muppet Babies at the Circus. LC 84-61436. (Sniffy Bks.). (Illus.). 24p. (ps-k). 1985. pap. 4.95 (ISBN 0-394-87105-7, BYR). Random.

--Sprocket's Christmas Tale. LC 84-6526. (Fraggle Rock Bks.). (Illus.). (gr. 1-4). 1984. 7.95 (ISBN 0-03-000708-9). HR&W.

--What's A Fraggle? (Illus.). 1984. 5.70 (ISBN 0-03-071086-3); pap. 1.95 (ISBN 0-03-071889-9). HR&W.

Gil, Alexander. The New Starr of the North, Shining Upon the King of Sweden. LC 76-57383. (English Experience Ser.: No. 801). 1977. Repr. of 1632 ed. lib. bdg. 7.00 (ISBN 90-221-0801-5). Walter J Johnson.

Gil, Ann G. Wilson Worm. 1983. 4.95 (ISBN 0-533-05737-X). Vantage.

Gil, Carlos B. Life in Provincial Mexico: National & Regional History As Seen from Mascota, Jalisco, 1867-1972. LC 82-620031. (Latin American Studies: Vol. 53). 1983. text ed. 20.00x (ISBN 0-87903-053-4). UCLA Lat Am Ctr.

Gil, David. Unravelling Social Policy. 180p. 1982. 15.95x (ISBN 0-87073-458-X); pap. 9.95 (ISBN 0-87073-459-8). Schenkman Bks Inc.

Gil, David G. Beyond the Jungle: Essays on Human Possibilities, Social Alternatives, & Radical Practice. 1979. lib. bdg. 15.00 (ISBN 0-8161-9004-6, Univ Bks). G K Hall.

--The Challenge of Social Equality: Essays on Social Policy, Social Development, & Political Practice. 230p. 1977. text ed. 9.95 (ISBN 0-87073-603-5). Schenkman Bks Inc.

--Violence Against Children: Physical Child Abuse in the United States. LC 77-130809. (Commonwealth Fund Publications Ser). (Illus.). 1970. 12.00x (ISBN 0-674-93941-7); pap. 5.95 (ISBN 0-674-93942-5). Harvard U Pr.

Gil, David G., ed. Child Abuse & Violence. LC 77-91865. 1979. 32.50 (ISBN 0-404-16044-1); pap. 11.95 (ISBN 0-404-16045-X). AMS Pr.

Gil, David G. & Gil, Eva A., eds. Toward Social & Economic Justice. 256p. lib. bdg. 18.95 (ISBN 0-87047-009-4); pap. text ed. 10.95 (ISBN 0-87047-008-6). Schenkman Bks Inc.

Gil, Eliana. Outgrowing the Pain: A Book for & about Adults Abused As Children. 2nd ed. LC 83-82956. (Illus.). 100p. (Orig.). 1984. lib. bdg. 6.95 stitch bdg. (ISBN 0-9613205-0-8). Launch Pr.

Gil, Eva A., jt. ed. see Gil, David G.

Gil, Federico, et al, eds. Chile at the Turning Point: Lessons of the Socialist Years, 1970-1973. LC 79-10311. 488p. 1979. text ed. 26.95 (ISBN 0-915980-88-6). ISHI PA.

Gil, Federico G. Latin American-United States Relations. 339p. 1971. pap. text ed. 11.95 (ISBN 0-15-550195-X, HC). HarBraceJ.

Gil, L. Suarez, ed. Diccionario Tecnico Maritimo: Ingles-Espanol, Espanol-Ingles. 708p. (Eng. & Span.). 1980. pap. 75.00 (ISBN 84-205-0772-5, S-32729). French & Eur.

Gil, Lourdes. Neumas. LC 77-79956. (Senda Poetica Ser.). (Illus., Orig., Span.). 1977. pap. 3.95 (ISBN 0-918454-01-8). Senda Nueva.

--Vencido el Fuego de la especie. SLUSA, ed. LC 83-60004. (Poetry Ser.). (Illus.). 90p. (Orig., Span.). 1983. pap. 4.00 (ISBN 0-9606758-5-X). SLUSA.

Gilabert, Frank, jt. auth. see Arnstein, William E.

Gilad, Benny & Loeb, Peter. The Stat Tutor. 300p. 1983. pap. text ed. 16.95 (ISBN 0-394-32964-3, RanC). Random.

Gilam, Abraham. The Emancipation of the Jews in England. Stansky, Peter & Hume, Leslie, eds. LC 81-48359. (Modern British History Ser.). 193p. 1982. lib. bdg. 31.00 (ISBN 0-8240-5155-6). Garland Pub.

Gilandas, Alex, et al. Handbook of Neuropsychological Assessment. 304p. 1984. 45.00 (ISBN 0-8089-1645-9, 791553). Grune.

Gilandas, Alex J., et al. Handbook of Neuropsychological Assessment. 303p. 1984. 45.00 (ISBN 0-8089-1645-9). Acad Pr.

Gilardi, Gerald L. Glucose Nonfermenting Gramnegative Bacteria in Clinical Microbiology. 256p. 1978. 76.00 (ISBN 0-8493-5331-9). CRC Pr.

Gilat, Gideon, et al see Alder, B., et al.

Gilb, Corinne L. Hidden Hierarchies: The Professions & Government. LC 76-22. 307p. 1976. Repr. of 1966 ed. lib. bdg. 20.00x (ISBN 0-8371-8751-6, GIHH). Greenwood.

Gilb, Tom. Software Metrics. (Illus.). 282p. (Orig.). 1982. pap. text ed. 29.95 (ISBN 0-86238-034-0, Pub. by Chartwell-Bratt England). Brookfield Pub Co.

Gilb, Tom & Weinberg, Gerald M. Humanized Input: Techniques for Reliable Keyed Input. LC 83-62495. 283p. 1977. pap. 24.95 (ISBN 0-89435-073-0). QED Info Sci.

Gilbar, Anne. The Lunch Box Book. (Orig.). 1984. 3.95 (ISBN 0-671-50069-4). S&S.

Gilbar, Steven. Good Books: A Book Lover's Companion. LC 82-5554. 464p. 1982. 20.00 (ISBN 0-89919-127-4); pap. 9.95 (ISBN 0-89919-132-0). Ticknor & Fields.

Gilbarg, D. & Trudinger, N. S. Elliptic Partial Differential Equations of Second Order. 2nd ed. (Grundlehren der mathematischen Wissenschaften. A Series of Comprehensive Studies in Mathematics: Band 224). 530p. 1983. 48.00 (ISBN 0-387-13025-X). Springer Verlag.

Gilbart, Helen. Pathways: A Guide to Reading & Study Skills. LC 81-81701. (Illus.). 400p. 1982. pap. text ed. 12.95 (ISBN 0-395-31717-7); instr's. manual 1.00 (ISBN 0-395-31718-5). HM.

Gilbart, Helen & Howland, Joseph W. Getting Ready for the College Level Academic Skills Test. 2nd ed. Hackworth, Robert D., ed. (Illus.). 180p. 1984. pap. text ed. 8.95x (ISBN 0-943202-13-2). H & H Pub.

Gilbart, James W. History of Banking in America. LC. 67-17491. Repr. of 1837 ed. 27.50x (ISBN 0-678-00242-8). Kelley.

--History, Principles, & Practice of Banking, 2 Vols. rev. ed. LC 68-28632. 1968. Repr. of 1882 ed. Set. lib. bdg. 45.00x (ISBN 0-8371-0445-9, GIHP). Greenwood.

Gilberg, Richard L. Pumpkin Cookbook. LC 83-90765. (Illus.). 124p. (Orig.). 1983. pap. 6.95 (ISBN 0-936402-01-6). Gilmar Pr.

Gilberg, Trond, jt. auth. see Simon, Jeffrey.

Gilbersleeve, Thomas R. Successful Data Processing System Analysis. 2nd ed. (Illus.). 384p. 1985. text ed. 30.95 (ISBN 0-13-860495-9). P-H.

Gilberstad, Harold & Duker, Jan. A Handbook of Clinical & Acturial MMPI Interpretations. pap. text ed. cancelled (ISBN 0-8290-0628-1). Irvington.

Gilberstadt, Harold & Duker, Jan. A Handbook for Clinical & Actuarial MMPI Interpretation. LC 81-40902. 144p. 1982. pap. text ed. 9.25 (ISBN 0-8191-2257-2). U Pr of Amer.

Gilbert. Gilbert of Hoyland: Treasties, Epistles, & Sermons. Braceland, Lawrence C., tr. (Fathers Ser.: No. 34). 1981. 12.95 (ISBN 0-317-02699-2). Cistercian Pubns.

--Making & Managing Policy: Formulation, Analysis, Evaluation. (Public Administration & Public Policy Ser.). 432p. 1984. 35.00 (ISBN 0-8247-7168-0). Dekker.

--Potential Fulfilled - What Saved Them, Vol. 2. 4.50 (ISBN 0-86690-106-X). Am Fed Astrologers.

Gilbert & Gilbert. Algebra & Trigonometry. 1986. text ed. write for info (ISBN 0-534-06120-6). Wadsworth Pub.

--College Trigonometry. 1985. write for info (ISBN 0-534-03647-3). Wadsworth Pub.

Gilbert & Sullivan. The Authentic Gilbert & Sullivan Songbook: 92 Unabridged Selections from All 14 Operas. Binney, M. & Lavender, P., eds. 18.50 (ISBN 0-8446-5576-7). Peter Smith.

--The Complete Plays of Gilbert & Sullivan. 19.95 (ISBN 0-8488-0051-6, Pub by Amereon Hse). Amereon Ltd.

--The Pirates of Penzance. Botsford, Ward, adapted by. LC 81-5173. (Illus.). 48p. (gr. 5 up). 1981. 8.95 (ISBN 0-394-84993-0); PLB 9.99 (ISBN 0-394-94993-5). Random.

Gilbert, jt. auth. see Martin.

Gilbert, et al. College Algebra. 2nd ed. 1985. text ed. write for info (ISBN 0-534-05298-3). Wadsworth Pub.

Gilbert, A., jt. auth. see Bryce-Smith, D.

Gilbert, A., jt. auth. see Cundall, R. B.

Gilbert, A. H. Dante's Conception of Justice. 59.95 (ISBN 0-87968-995-1). Gordon Pr.

--A Geographical Dictionary of Milton. 59.95 (ISBN 0-8490-0216-8). Gordon Pr.

Gilbert, A. J. Literary Language from Chaucer to Johnson. LC 79-53434. 224p. 1979. text ed. 28.50x (ISBN 0-06-492403-3). B&N Imports.

Gilbert, Alan. Development Planning & Spatial Structure. LC 75-30804. 207p. 1976. 44.95x (ISBN 0-471-29904-9, Pub. by Wiley-Interscience). Wiley.

--Marx's Politics: Communists & Citizens. 320p. 1981. 27.50x (ISBN 0-8135-0903-3). Rutgers U Pr.

Gilbert, Alan & Gugler, Josef. Cities, Poverty & Development: Urbanization in the Third World. (Illus.). 272p. 1982. pap. 12.95 (ISBN 0-19-874084-0). Oxford U Pr.

Gilbert, Alan & Healey, Patsy. The Political Economy of Land: The State & Urban Development in Venezuela. 200p. 1985. text ed. write for info. (ISBN 0-566-05007-2). Gower Pub Co.

Gilbert, Alan & Ward, Peter M. Housing; The State & the Poor: Policy & Practice in Three Latin American Cities. (Illus.). 352p. 1985. write for info. (ISBN 0-521-26299-2). Cambridge U Pr.

Gilbert, Alan & Hardoy, Jorge E., eds. Urbanization in Contemporary Latin America: Critical Approaches to the Analysis of Urban Issues. LC 81-21876. (Illus.). 286p. 1982. 57.95 (ISBN 0-471-10183-4). Wiley.

Gilbert, Alan H., ed. & tr. see Machiavelli, Niccolo.

Gilbert, Allan H. Dante & His Comedy. LC 63-17157. (Gotham Library). pap. 41.30 (ISBN 0-8357-9477-6, 2010348). Bks Demand UMI.

--Dante's Conception of Justice. LC 76-166199. (BCL Ser.: I). Repr. of 1925 ed. 15.00 (ISBN 0-404-02757-1). AMS Pr.

--A Geographical Dictionary of Milton. 1979. Repr. of 1919 ed. lib. bdg. 35.00 (ISBN 0-8495-2014-2). Arden Lib.

--Literary Criticism: Plato to Dryden. 1978. Repr. of 1940 ed. lib. bdg. 35.00 (ISBN 0-8492-0999-4). R West.

--Principles & Practice of Criticism: Hamlet, the Merry Wives, Othello. LC 77-168145. Repr. of 1959 ed. 15.00 (ISBN 0-404-02758-X). AMS Pr.

--Symbolic Persons in the Masques of Ben Jonson. LC 79-85910. (BCL Ser.: I). Repr. of 1948 ed. 23.00 (ISBN 0-404-02759-8). AMS Pr.

Gilbert, Allan H., ed. & tr. Dante Alighieri, Inferno: The Italian Text with Translation & Notes. LC 68-54577. xlvi, 373p. 1969. 25.00 (ISBN 0-8233-0066-8). Duke.

Gilbert, Allan H., ed. Literary Criticism: Plato to Dryden. LC 61-12266. (Waynebooks Ser: No. 1). 713p. 1962. pap. 8.95 (ISBN 0-8143-1160-1). Wayne St U Pr.

Gilbert, Amos. A Sketch of the Life of Thomas Skidmore. (Young America Ser.: No. 2). 64p. lib. bdg. 14.95 (ISBN 0-88286-061-5); pap. 3.95 (ISBN 0-88286-060-7). C H Kerr.

Gilbert, Amy M. Executive Agreements & Treaties, Nineteen Forty-Six to Nineteen Seventy-Three. 1973. 10.00 (ISBN 0-9600690-1-1). Irwinton.

--Executive Agreements & Treaties, Nineteen Forty-Six to Nineteen Seventy-Three: Framework of the Foreign Policy of the Period. 1973. 10.00 (ISBN 0-9600690-1-1). Thomas-Newell.

Gilbert, Anna. The Leavetaking. (General Ser.). 1981. lib. bdg. 13.95 (ISBN 0-8161-3203-8, Large Print Bks). G K Hall.

--The Long Shadow. 1985. 15.95 (ISBN 0-312-49667-2). St Martin.

--Miss Bede is Staying. 320p. 1983. 12.95 (ISBN 0-312-53471-X). St Martin.

Gilbert, Anne G. Teaching the Three R's Through Movement Experiences. LC 76-19465. 1977. pap. 9.95x (ISBN 0-8087-0751-5). Burgess.

Gilbert, Ariadne. More Than Conquerors. facs. ed. LC 68-58791. (Essay Index Reprint Ser). 1914. 23.75 (ISBN 0-8369-1036-2). Ayer Co Pubs.

Gilbert, Arthur. The Passover Seder. (Illus.). 1965. pap. 2.95x (ISBN 0-87068-504-X). Ktav.

--Your Neighbor Worships. 31p. 1.50 (ISBN 0-686-74968-5). ADL.

Gilbert, Arthur & Tarcov, Oscar. Your Neighbor Celebrates. 38p. 0.75 (ISBN 0-686-74967-7). ADL.

--Your Neighbor Celebrates. 6.00x (ISBN 0-87068-364-0, Pub. by Friendly Hse). Ktav.

Gilbert, B. The Trailblazers. LC 73-76268. (Old West Ser). (Illus.). (gr. 7 up). 1973. 17.27 (ISBN 0-8094-1459-7, Pub. by Time-Life). Silver.

Gilbert, B., jt. auth. see Hayes, E.

Gilbert, B., ed. see Mastermar, C. F.

Gilbert, B. Miles. Mammalian Osteology. rev. ed. LC 80-84455. (Illus.). 428p. (Orig.). 1980. pap. 25.00 (ISBN 0-9611174-0-0). Bone Bks.

Gilbert, B. Miles & Martin, Larry D. Avian Osteology. LC 81-90059. (Illus.). 252p. (Orig.). 1981. pap. 20.00 (ISBN 0-9611174-1-9). Bone Bks.

Gilbert, Benjamin F. & Bauer, K. Jack, eds. Ports in the West. (Illus.). 98p. 1982. pap. text ed. 9.95x (ISBN 0-89745-022-1). Sunflower U Pr.

Gilbert, Bentley B. Britain Since Nineteen Eighteen. 2nd ed. 1980. 23.50 (ISBN 0-312-09876-6). St Martin.

Gilbert, Bil. Chulo: A Year among the Coatimundis. LC 83-18299. (Illus.). 297p. 1984. pap. 9.50 (ISBN 0-8165-0842-9). U of Ariz Pr.

--In God's Countries. LC 83-23384. xviii, 203p. 1984. 14.95 (ISBN 0-8032-2117-7). U of Nebr Pr.

--The Trailblazers. (The Old West Ser.). (Illus.). 1973. 14.95 (ISBN 0-8094-1458-9). Time-Life.

--Westering Man: The Life of Joseph Walker. LC 82-69128. 352p. 1983. 17.95 (ISBN 0-689-11241-6). Atheneum.

--Westering Man: The Life of Joseph Walker. LC 84-22055. 352p. (Orig.). 1985. pap. 9.95 (ISBN 0-8061-1934-9). U of Okla Pr.

Gilbert, Bill. This City, This Man: The Cookingham Era in Kansas City. LC 78-13401. (Illus.). 1978. 16.00 (ISBN 0-87326-021-X). Intl City Mgt.

Gilbert, Blair L. Patter Chatter. pap. 2.00 (ISBN 0-87505-245-2). Borden.

Gilbert, Bob & Theroux, Gary. The Top Ten: Nineteen Fifty-Six to Present. LC 82-10478. (Illus.). 320p. 1982. pap. 12.95 (ISBN 0-671-43215-X, Fireside). S&S.

Gilbert, Bruce. Remembering. LC 80-54370. 96p. 1981. 4.95 (ISBN 0-87159-139-1). Unity School.

Gilbert, Brynn. Love's Bold Embrace. 1979. pap. 2.25 (ISBN 0-505-51402-8, Pub. by Tower Bks). Dorchester Pub Co.

Gilbert, C. Italian Art: Fourteen Hundred to Fifteen Hundred. 1980. pap. 18.95 (ISBN 0-13-507947-0). P-H.

Gilbert, C. H., Jr. Raymond Berry's Complete Guide for Pass Receivers. LC 82-3427. 179p. 1982. pap. 5.95 (ISBN 0-13-752949-X, Reward). P-H.

Gilbert, C. H., Jr., jt. auth. see Berry, Raymond.

Gilbert, C. Hampton. Here Lies Duffy Baker. 1978. 8.00 (ISBN 0-682-49047-4). Exposition Pr FL.

Gilbert, C. M. The Ozine Conquest. 1981. pap. 1.75 (ISBN 0-8439-0891-2, Leisure Bks). Dorchester Pub Co.

Gilbert, C. M. & Christensen, M. N. Physical Geology Laboratory Course. 2nd ed. 1967. 21.95 (ISBN 0-07-023206-7). McGraw.

Gilbert, Carolyn A. Communicative Performance of Literature. (Illus.). 1977. pap. write for info. (ISBN 0-02-342900-3). Macmillan.

Gilbert, Carter R. see Pritchard, Peter C.

Gilbert, Celia. Bonfire. LC 82-74513. 72p. 1983. 12.95 (ISBN 0-914086-45-6); pap. 6.95 (ISBN 0-914086-44-8). Alicejamesbooks.

--Queen of Darkness. LC 76-54855. 1977. 9.95 (ISBN 0-670-58395-2). Viking.
Gilbert, Charles. American Financing of World War I. LC 73-79060. (Contributions in Economics & Economic History: No. 1). (Illus.). 1970. lib. bdg. 29.95 (ISBN 0-8371-1496-9, GIA/). Greenwood.
Gilbert, Charles, jt. auth. see Kroоss, Herman E.
Gilbert, Charles, ed. see Kogl, Sandy.
Gilbert, Charles B. & Harris, Ada V. Poems by Grades: Grammar, Vol. 2. facs. ed. LC 78-149103. (Granger Index Reprint Ser). 1907. 23.50 (ISBN 0-8369-6228-1). Ayer Co Pubs.
--Poems by Grades: Primary, Vol. 1. facs. ed. LC 74-149102. (Granger Index Reprint Ser). 1907. 21.00 (ISBN 0-8369-6227-3). Ayer Co Pubs.
Gilbert, Charles E. Governing the Suburbs. LC 67-13024. 1974. pap. 94.50 (ISBN 0-317-09636-2, 2005743). Bks Demand UMI.
Gilbert, Charles E., ed. Implementing Governmental Change, Vol. 466. LC 82-63181. (The Annals of the American Academy of Political & Social Science). 256p. 1983. 15.00 (ISBN 0-8039-1983-2); pap. 7.95 (ISBN 0-8039-1984-0). Sage.
Gilbert, Chester G. & Pogue, Joseph E. Energy Resources of the United States: A Field for Reconstruction. 1980. lib. bdg. 59.95 (ISBN 0-8490-3112-5). Gordon Pr.
--Petroleum: A Resource Interpretation. 1980. lib. bdg. 49.95 (ISBN 0-8490-3109-5). Gordon Pr.
Gilbert, Chris. The ABC's of 1-2-3. 225p. 1984. pap. 14.95 (ISBN 0-89588-168-3). SYBEX.
Gilbert, Christine B., jt. ed. see Gillespie, John T.
Gilbert, Christopher. Across the Mutual Landscape. LC 83-83009. 92p. 1984. 14.00 (ISBN 0-915308-48-7); pap. 6.00 (ISBN 0-915308-49-5). Graywolf.
Gilbert, Claire. Nerval's Double: A Structural Study. LC 79-4593. (Romance Monographs: No. 34). 199p. 1979. 19.00x (ISBN 84-499-2818-4). Romance.
Gilbert, Clinton W. Mirrors of Washington. facsimile ed. LC 79-156649. (Essay Index Reprint Ser). Repr. of 1921 ed. 21.50 (ISBN 0-8369-2363-4). Ayer Co Pubs.
--The Mirrors of Washington. LC 79-156649. (Essay Index Reprint Ser.). (Illus.). 256p. Repr. of 1921 ed. lib. bdg. 18.50x (ISBN 0-8290-0477-7). Irvington.
Gilbert, Colleen B. A Bibliography of the Works of Dorothy L. Sayers. 263p. 1978. 24.00 (ISBN 0-208-01755-0, Archon). Shoe String.
Gilbert, Creighton. Change in Piero Della Francesca. LC 62-19124. (Illus.). 5.00 (ISBN 0-685-71754-2). J J Augustin.
Gilbert, Creighton, ed. Renaissance Art. LC 70-92848. (Icon Editions). (Illus.). 270p. 1973. pap. 7.95xi (ISBN 0-06-430033-1, IN-33, HarpT). Har-Row.
Gilbert, Creighton, tr. from It. The Complete Poems & Selected Letters of Michelangelo. LC 79-87767. 1980. 30.00x (ISBN 0-691-03925-9); pap. 9.95x (ISBN 0-691-00324-6). Princeton U Pr.
Gilbert, D. L. Natural Resources & Public Relations. 2nd ed. LC 76-143896. 320p. 1975. 8.00 (ISBN 0-933564-03-1). Wildlife Soc.
Gilbert, Daniel L., ed. Oxygen & Living Processes: An Interdisciplinary Approach. (Topics in Environmental Physiology & Medicine Ser.). (Illus.). 401p. 1981. 69.00 (ISBN 0-387-90554-5). Springer Verlag.
Gilbert, Dave. Walkers Guide to Harpers Ferry, West Virginia. LC 82-63068. (Illus.). 80p. 1983. pap. 4.95 (ISBN 0-933126-28-X). Pictorial Hist.
Gilbert, Dave T. Where Industry Failed: Water-Powered Mills at Harpers Ferry, W. Va. LC 84-60831. (Illus.). 92p. 1984. pap. 6.95 (ISBN 0-933126-49-2). Pictorial Hist.
Gilbert, David. Some Ancient Christmas Carols with the Tunes to Which They Were Formally Sung in the West of England. LC 72-6976. 1972. lib. bdg. 12.50 (ISBN 0-88305-249-0). Norwood Edns.
Gilbert, David N. & Sanford, Jay P., eds. Infectious Diseases: Current Topics, Vol. 1. 272p. 1979. 28.50 (ISBN 0-8089-1162-7, 791552). Grune.
Gilbert, De Witt, ed. The Future of the Fishing Industry of the United States. (University of Washington Publications in Fisheries Ser.: No. 4). (Illus.). 346p. 1968. pap. 20.00x (ISBN 0-295-95204-0). U of Wash Pr.
Gilbert, Dennis & Kahl, Joseph A. American Class Structure: A New Synthesis. 1982. pap. 18.00x (ISBN 0-256-02678-5). Dorsey.
Gilbert, Dennis, et al. Microcomputers: A Review of Federal Agency Experiences. (National Bureau of Standards Special Publication 500-102. Computer Science & Technology Ser.). 146p. (Orig.). 1983. pap. 5.50 (ISBN 0-318-11739-8). Gov Printing Office.
Gilbert, Dennis A., jt. auth. see Weber, Paul J.
Gilbert, Donald. Jellyfish Bones the Humor of Zen. Angilly, Richard, ed. (Illus.). 168p. (Orig.). 1980. pap. 7.95x (ISBN 0-931290-25-2). Blue Dragon.
Gilbert, Donald D. How to Be Safe in an Unsafe World. 1984. 13.95. Horizon Utah.
Gilbert, Doris W. Breaking the Word Barrier. LC 77-173596. (Illus.). 240p. 1972. pap. text ed. 15.95 (ISBN 0-13-081661-2). P-H.
--Power & Speed in Reading. 1956. text ed. 15.95 (ISBN 0-13-685040-5). P-H.
--Study in Depth. (Orig.). 1966. pap. text ed. 18.95 (ISBN 0-13-858902-X). P-H.
--Turning Point in Reading. (Illus.). 1969. pap. text ed. 15.95 (ISBN 0-13-933085-2). P-H.
Gilbert, Doris W. & Forte, M. Cecile. Breaking the Reading Barrier. 2nd ed. (Illus.). 336p. 1984. pap. text ed. 16.95 (ISBN 0-13-081456-3). P-H.
Gilbert, Dorothy. Can I Make One: A Craft Book for the Pre-School Child. (Illus.). (ps). 1970. 11.95 (ISBN 0-571-09303-5). Transatlantic.
Gilbert, Douglas. American Vaudeville, Its Life & Times. 428p. 6.75 (ISBN 0-318-14830-7, E112). Midwest Old Settlers.
--Lost Chords: The Diverting Story of American Popular Songs. LC 74-139203. 1971. Repr. of 1942 ed. lib. bdg. 23.50 (ISBN 0-8154-0370-4). Cooper Sq.
Gilbert, Douglas & Kilby, Clyde S. C. S. Lewis: Images of His World. LC 73-8697. pap. 48.00 (ISBN 0-317-30141-1, 2025324). Bks Demand UMI.
Gilbert, Douglas, jt. auth. see Fazio, James R.
Gilbert, Douglas L., ed. see Wildlife Management Institute.
Gilbert, Eddie. Sex to Sexty: 30 Different. (Illus.). 1964. pap. 2.95x ea. Wehman.
Gilbert, Edith. All about Parties. LC 68-8522. 1968. 6.95 (ISBN 0-9600786-0-6). Jet'iquette.
--The Complete Wedding Planner. 256p. 1984. pap. 7.95 (ISBN 0-446-37322-2). Warner Bks.
--Let's Set the Table with Edith Gilbert. LC 75-309635. (Illus.). 37p. (Orig.). 1973. 8.95 (ISBN 0-9600786-1-4). Jet'iquette.
Gilbert, Edmund W. Exploration of Western America, Eighteen Hundred to Eighteen Fifty. LC 65-26291. (Illus.). 1966. Repr. of 1933 ed. 23.50 (ISBN 0-8154-0079-9). Cooper Sq.
Gilbert, Edna. A Way with Words: On Creative Writing. 95p. 1968. pap. 3.25 (ISBN 0-85225-533-0). Ed Solutions.
Gilbert, Edward M., Jr., jt. auth. see Miller, Constance O.
Gilbert, Edwin. A Season in Monte Carlo. LC 75-40512. 1976. 8.95 (ISBN 0-87795-131-4). Arbor Hse.
Gilbert, Elizabeth R. Fairs & Festivals: A Smithsonian Guide to Celebrations in Maryland, Virginia, & Washington, D.C. LC 82-600152. (Illus.). 160p. 1982. pap. 4.50 (ISBN 0-87474-473-3). Smithsonian.
Gilbert, Elliot. Monarch Notes on Keats' Poetry. (Orig.). pap. 2.50 (ISBN 0-671-00785-8). Monarch Pr.
--Monarch Notes on Thackeray's Vanity Fair & Henry Esmond. (Orig.). pap. 2.75 (ISBN 0-671-00727-0). Monarch Pr.
Gilbert, Enid F. & Huntington, Robert W. An Introduction to Pathology. (Illus.). pap. text ed. 13.95x (ISBN 0-19-502253-X). Oxford U Pr.
Gilbert, Eugene, jt. auth. see Pourade, Richard F.
Gilbert, Everett E. Sulfonation & Related Reactions. Olah, George A., ed. LC 76-52491. 542p. 1977. Repr. of 1965 ed. lib. bdg. 32.50 (ISBN 0-88275-528-5). Krieger.
Gilbert, Felix. End of the European Era: Eighteen Ninety to the Present. 3rd ed. (History of Modern Europe Ser.). 1984. pap. text ed. 10.95x (ISBN 0-393-95440-4). Norton.
--End of the European Era, 1890 to the Present. 2nd ed. (Illus.). 1979. 24.95x (ISBN 0-393-05690-2). Norton.
--History: Choice & Commitment. 1977. 32.50x (ISBN 0-674-39656-1, Belknap Pr). Harvard U Pr.
--Machiavelli & Guicciardini: Politics & History in Sixteenth-Century Florence. 368p. 1984. pap. 8.95 (ISBN 0-393-30123-0). Norton.
--The Pope, His Banker & Venice. LC 80-13062. (Illus.). 167p. 1980. text ed. 12.50x (ISBN 0-674-68975-5). Harvard U Pr.
--To the Farewell Address: Ideas of Early American Foreign Policy. 1961. pap. 7.95x (ISBN 0-691-00574-5). Princeton U Pr.
Gilbert, Felix, ed. Hilter Directs His War. George, Alan, tr. xxxiii, 185p. 1982. Repr. of 1950 ed. lib. bdg. 20.00 (ISBN 0-374-93062-7). Octagon.
--The Historical Essays of Otto Hintze. 1975. 35.00x (ISBN 0-19-501819-2). Oxford U Pr.
--Historical Studies Today. LC 70-163367. 480p. 1972. pap. 10.95x (ISBN 0-393-09402-2). Norton.
--The Norton History of Modern Europe, 7 vols. Incl. Vol. 1. The Foundations of Early Modern Europe, 1460-1559. Rice, Eugene F., Jr. pap. 5.95x (ISBN 0-393-09898-2); Vol. 2. The Age of Religious Wars, 1559-1689. Dunn, Richard S. 7.95x (ISBN 0-393-09021-3); Vol. 3. Kings & Philosophies, 1689-1789. Krieger, Leonard. 9.95x (ISBN 0-393-09905-9); Vol. 4. Age of Revolution, 1789-1850. Breunig, Charles. 7.95x (ISBN 0-393-09143-0); Vol. 5. Age of Nationalism, 1850-1890. Rich, Norman. 6.95x (ISBN 0-393-09183-X); Vol. 6. End of European Era, 1890 to Present. Gilbert, Felix; Eighteenth Century Europe, 1715-1789. Woloch, Isser. 6.95x (ISBN 0-393-95214-2). 1979. Norton.
Gilbert, Felix, jt. ed. see Craig, Gordon A.
Gilbert, Felix, ed. see Robertson, William.
Gilbert, Fontelle, ed. Minorities & Community Colleges. 1979. pap. 7.50 (ISBN 0-87117-092-2). Am Assn Comm Jr Coll.
Gilbert, Francis S. Hoverflies. (Naturalists Handbooks: No. 5). (Illus.). 96p. Date not set. price not set (ISBN 0-521-25766-2). Cambridge U Pr.
Gilbert, G. G., ed. Pidgin & Creole Languages. LC 79-15866. 320p. 1980. 39.50 (ISBN 0-521-22789-5). Cambridge U Pr.
Gilbert, G. K. Glaciers & Glaciation, Vol. 3. (Harriman Alaska Expedition 1899 Ser.). 1910. 41.00 (ISBN 0-527-38163-2). Kraus Repr.
Gilbert, G. M. The Psychology of Dictatorship: Based on an Examination of the Leaders of Nazi Germany. LC 79-15335. (Illus.). 1979. Repr. of 1950 ed. lib. bdg. 22.50x (ISBN 0-313-21975-3, GIPD). Greenwood.
Gilbert, G. N. & Mulkay, Michael. Opening Pandora's Box: A Sociological Analysis of Scientists' Discourse. LC 83-5338. 1984. 37.50 (ISBN 0-521-25418-3); pap. 12.95 (ISBN 0-521-27430-3). Cambridge U Pr.
Gilbert, G. Nigel. Modelling Society: An Introduction to Loglinear Analysis for Social Researchers. (Contemporary Social Research Ser.). 1981. text ed. 28.50x (ISBN 0-04-312009-1); pap. text ed. 12.50x (ISBN 0-04-312010-5). Allen Unwin.
Gilbert, G. Nigel & Heath, Christian. Social Actions & Artificial Intelligence. 206p. 1985. text ed. 27.00x (ISBN 0-566-00768-1). Gower Pub Co.
Gilbert, G. Nigel & Abell, Peter, eds. Accounts & Action: Surrey Conferences on Sociological Theory & Methods. 190p. 1983. text ed. 33.50x (ISBN 0-566-00620-0). Gower Pub Co.
Gilbert, Gail, tr. see Briusov, Valery.
Gilbert, Gary & Koehler, Donald. Applied Finite Mathematics. (Illus.). 560p. 1984. 31.95 (ISBN 0-07-023222-9). McGraw.
Gilbert, Geoffrey M., et al. Accounting & Auditing for Employee Benefit Plans: Annual Supplement. 1978. 78.00 (ISBN 0-88262-217-X, 78-56016). Warren.
Gilbert, George. Captain Cook's Final Voyage: The Journal of Midshipman George Gilbert. Holmes, Christine, ed. (Illus.). 158p. 1982. text ed. 20.00x (ISBN 0-8248-0787-1). UH Pr.
--Collecting Photographica: The Images & Equipment of the First Hundred Years of Photography. (Illus.). 1980. pap. 4.95 (ISBN 0-8015-1409-6, Hawthorn). Dutton.
--Complete Photography Careers Handbook: How to Find the Right Photographic Career. (Illus.). 256p. 1982. 15.95 (ISBN 0-525-93238-0, 01549-460); pap. 7.95 (ISBN 0-525-93237-2, 0772-230). Dutton.
--Photography: The Early Years, a Historical Guide for Collectors. LC 78-20163. (Illus.). 181p. 1980. 21.10i (ISBN 0-06-011497-5, HarpT). Har-Row.
--The Sixty Dramatic Illustrations in Full Colours of the Cathedral Cities of England. (A Promotion of the Arts Library). (Illus.). 99p. 1983. 297.85 (ISBN 0-86650-046-4). Gloucester Art.
Gilbert, Glen A. Air Traffic Control: The Uncrowded Sky. LC 73-6005. (Illus.). 160p. 1973. 19.95x (ISBN 0-87474-140-8). Smithsonian.
Gilbert, Glenn G. Linguistic Atlas of Texas German. 156p. 1972. 125.00x (ISBN 0-292-70088-1). U of Tex Pr.
Gilbert, Glenn G., ed. The German Language in America: A Symposium. 231p. 1971. 15.95x (ISBN 0-292-70149-7). U of Tex Pr.
--Texas Studies in Bilingualism. (Studia Linguistica Germanica, No. 3). 1970. 48.40x (ISBN 3-11-002691-0). De Gruyter.
Gilbert, Glenn G. & Ornstein, Jacob, eds. Problems in Applied Educational Sociolinguistics: Readings on Language & Culture Problems of United States Ethnic Groups. (Janua Linguarum, Series Minor: No. 162). 1978. pap. text ed. 13.40x (ISBN 90-279-7726-7). Mouton.
Gilbert, Gorman & Samuels, Robert E. The Taxicab: An Urban Transportation Survivor. LC 82-2726. (Illus.). xiv, 200p. 1982. 19.95x (ISBN 0-8078-1528-4). U of NC Pr.
Gilbert, Grove K. Report of the Geology of the Henry Mountains: U.S. Geographical & Geological Survey of the Rocky Mounntain Region. Albritton, Claude C., Jr., ed. LC 77-6519. (History of Geology Ser.). (Illus.). 1978. Repr. of 1877 ed. lib. bdg. 21.00x (ISBN 0-405-10441-3). Ayer Co Pubs.
Gilbert, Harold L., ed. A Manual for Classroom Teachers: How to Recognize & Help Children with Mental & Emotional Disorders. (Illus.). 194p. 1969. pap. text ed. 8.95x (ISBN 0-8422-0003-7). Irvington.
Gilbert, Harry M. & Larky, Arthur I. Practical Pascal. 1984. 14.95 (ISBN 0-538-10400-7, J40). SW Pub.
Gilbert, Harvey A. Modern Radiation Oncology: Classic Literature & Current Management, Vol. II. (Illus.). 672p. 1984. text ed. 62.75 (ISBN 0-06-140911-1, 14-09119, Harper Medical). Lippincott.
Gilbert, Helen, et al, eds. see La Lande, Michael.
Gilbert, Henry. Stories of Great Writers. 1973. Repr. of 1914 ed. 8.50 (ISBN 0-8274-0733-5). R West.
Gilbert, Herbert. Only a Child. 32p. 1983. 5.95 (ISBN 0-89962-289-5). Todd & Honeywell.
Gilbert, Herman C. The Negotiations: A Novel of Tomorrow. 315p. 14.95 (ISBN 0-910671-00-1). Chicago Review.
Gilbert, Humphrey. A Discourse of a Discovery for a New Passage to Cataia. Gascoigne, George, ed. LC 68-54645. (English Experience Ser.: No. 72). 88p. 1968. Repr. of 1576 ed. 11.50 (ISBN 90-221-0072-3). Walter J Johnson.
Gilbert, J., ed. Analysis of Food Contaminants. (Illus.). 400p. 1984. 74.00 (ISBN 0-85334-255-5, I-168-84, Pub. by Elsevier Applied Sci England). Elsevier.
Gilbert, J. K. & Fjallbrant, Nancy. Making Library Research Results Pay. 1981. 90.00 (ISBN 0-686-79294-7, Pub. by MCB Pubns). State Mutual Bk.
Gilbert, J. R., jt. auth. see Beynon, J. H.
Gilbert, Jack. Monolithos: Poems Nineteen Sixty-Two & Nineteen Eighty-Two. LC 83-83011. 93p. 1984. pap. 6.00 (ISBN 0-915308-42-8). Graywolf.
--Monolithos: Poems 1962 & 1982. LC 81-48135. 112p. 1982. 11.50 (ISBN 0-394-52386-5). Knopf.
--Views of Jeopardy. LC 72-144762. (Yale Series of Younger Poets: No. 58). Repr. of 1962 ed. 18.00 (ISBN 0-404-53858-4). AMS Pr.
Gilbert, Jack G. Edmund Waller. (English Authors Ser.: No. 266). 1979. lib. bdg. 15.95 (ISBN 0-8057-6763-0, Twayne). G K Hall.
--Jonathan Swift: Romantic & Cynic Moralist. LC 72-6768. (English Literature Ser., No. 33). 1972. Repr. of 1966 ed. lib. bdg. 39.95x (ISBN 0-8383-1649-2). Haskell.
Gilbert, Jacqueline. A House Called Bellevigne. (Harlequin Presents). 192p. 1983. pap. 1.95 (ISBN 0-373-10600-9). Harlequin Bks.
--Scorpio Summer. (Harlequin Romances Ser.). (Orig.). 1980. pap. 1.25 (ISBN 0-373-02308-1). Harlequin Bks.
--The Trodden Paths. (Harlequin Romances Ser.). 192p. 1982. pap. 1.50 (ISBN 0-373-02492-4). Harlequin Bks.
Gilbert, James. Another Chance. LC 81-14245. 1981. pap. text ed. 8.00 (ISBN 0-394-32220-7, KnopfC). Knopf.
--Another Chance: Postwar America, 1945-1968. Wilson, R. Jackson, frwd. by. LC 81-8916. 307p. 1981. 29.95 (ISBN 0-87722-224-X). Temple U Pr.
Gilbert, James, ed. The Books of Miles, Westland & Bristol Aircraft: An Original Anthology, 3 vols. in 1. LC 79-7281. (Flight: Its First Seventy-Five Years Ser.). (Illus.). 1979. lib. bdg. 58.00x (ISBN 0-405-12190-3). Ayer Co Pubs.
--Flight: Its First Seventy-Five Years, 57 bks, Vols. 1-12. (Illus.). 1979. Set. lib. bdg. 2238.50x (ISBN 0-405-12146-6). Ayer Co Pubs.
--Literature & History of Aviation Ser, 35 bks. 1972. Repr. Set. 953.00 (ISBN 0-405-03789-9). Ayer Co Pubs.
Gilbert, James, ed. see Antique Airplane Association.
Gilbert, James, ed. see Archibald, Norman.
Gilbert, James, ed. see Bridgeman, William & Hazard, Jacqueline.
Gilbert, James, jt. ed. see Caidin, Martin.
Gilbert, James, ed. see Caproni, Gianni.
Gilbert, James, ed. see Carter, Kit C. & Mueller, Robert.
Gilbert, James, ed. see Chichester, Francis C.
Gilbert, James, ed. see Clouston, A. E.
Gilbert, James, ed. see Cochran, Jacqueline & Odlum, Floyd.
Gilbert, James, ed. see Coppens de Houthulst, Willy.
Gilbert, James, ed. see Craven, Wesley F. & Cate, James L.
Gilbert, James, ed. see Dollfus, Charles & Bouche, Henri.
Gilbert, James, ed. see Dornbusch, Charles E. & Paszek, Lawrence J.
Gilbert, James, ed. see Duke, Neville & Lanchbery, Edward.
Gilbert, James, ed. see Earhart, Amelia.
Gilbert, James, ed. see Eckener, Hugo.
Gilbert, James, ed. see Everest, Frank K., Jr.
Gilbert, James, ed. see Farre, Henry.
Gilbert, James, ed. see Foulois, Benjamin D. & Glines, Carroll V.
Gilbert, James, ed. see Fraser, Chelsea.
Gilbert, James, ed. see Futrell, Robert F.
Gilbert, James, ed. see Gibbons, Floyd.
Gilbert, James, ed. see Glines, Carroll V., Jr.
Gilbert, James, ed. see Green, William & Cross, Roy.
Gilbert, James, ed. see Green, William & Pollinger, Gerald.
Gilbert, James, ed. see Grinnell-Milne, Duncan, et al.
Gilbert, James, jt. ed. see Gurney, Gene.
Gilbert, James, ed. see Hall, Bert & Niles, John J.
Gilbert, James, ed. see Hall, James N.
Gilbert, James, ed. see Hansell, Haywood S., Jr.
Gilbert, James, ed. see Hartney, Harold E.
Gilbert, James, ed. see Haydon, Frederick S.
Gilbert, James, ed. see Historical Office of the Army Air Force.
Gilbert, James, ed. see Lay, Beirne, Jr. & Bartlett, Sy.
Gilbert, James, ed. see Lockheed Aircraft Corporation.
Gilbert, James, ed. see Luukkanen, Eino.
Gilbert, James, ed. see Mansfield, Harold.
Gilbert, James, jt. ed. see Maurer, Maurer.
Gilbert, James, ed. see Miller, Francis T.
Gilbert, James, ed. see Momyer, William W.
Gilbert, James, ed. see Moore, Byron.
Gilbert, James, ed. see Nordhoff, Charles & Hall, James N.
Gilbert, James, ed. see Osur, Alan M.

Gilbert, James, ed. see Rosenberry, C. R.

Gilbert, James, ed. see Royal Aeronautical Society.

Gilbert, James, jt. ed. see Stewart, James T.

Gilbert, James, ed. see Stout, William B.

Gilbert, James, ed. see U. S. Air Force.

Gilbert, James, ed. see Verdon-Roe, Alliott.

Gilbert, James, ed. see Vigilant.

Gilbert, James, ed. see Wykeham, Peter.

Gilbert, James B. Work Without Salvation: America's Intellectual & Industrial Alienation, 1880-1910. LC 74-2249. 256p. 1977. 24.00x (ISBN 0-8018-1954-7). Johns Hopkins.

Gilbert, James H. Trade & Currency in Early Oregon. LC 77-168145. (Columbia University. Studies in the Social Sciences: No. 68). Repr. of 1907 ed. 16.50 (ISBN 0-404-51068-X). AMS Pr.

Gilbert, James N. Criminal Investigation. (Public Service Technology Ser.). 496p. 1980. text ed. 25.95 (ISBN 0-675-08186-6). Merrill.

--Criminal Investigation. 2nd ed. 512p. Date not set. text ed. 25.95 (ISBN 0-675-20358-9). Additional supplements maybe obtained fron publisher. Merrill.

Gilbert, Jane. Efforts at Intermunicipal Cooperation for Solid Waste Disposal: Why They Fail. (Discussion Paper Ser.: No. 68). 1973. pap. 4.50 (ISBN 0-686-32234-7). Regional Sci Res Inst.

Gilbert, Janet P., jt. auth. see Beal, Mary R.

Gilbert, Jayne, jt. auth. see Rose, Jim.

Gilbert, Jim, ed. see Durand, Dawn.

Gilbert, Jim, ed. see Jeffrey, Kevin & Jeffrey, Nan.

Gilbert, Jim, ed. see Palley, Reese.

Gilbert, Jimmie, jt. auth. see Gilbert, Linda.

Gilbert, Jimmie, et al. College Algebra. (Illus.). 496p. 1981. text ed. 29.95 (ISBN 0-13-141804-1). P-H.

Gilbert, John. Dinosaurs Discovered. LC 80-82756. (Illus.). 96p. 1981. 8.95 (ISBN 0-88332-252-8, 8174). Larousse.

--The Gardening Encyclopedia. (Illus.). 189p. 1985. 14.95 (ISBN 0-85613-732-4, Pub. by Salem Hse Ltd). Merrimack Pub Cir.

Gilbert, John, jt. auth. see Foreman, Martin.

Gilbert, John see Hills, Philip.

Gilbert, John, intro. by. Complete Works of Oscar Wilde. 956p. 1985. 14.95 (ISBN 0-600-39372-0, Pub. by Hamlyn Pub Group England). Hippocrene Bks.

Gilbert, John, ed. see Shakespeare, William.

Gilbert, John H., ed. Speech & Cortical Functioning. (Based upon a symposium). 1972. 47.50 (ISBN 0-12-282850-X). Acad Pr.

Gilbert, John M. Hunting Reserves & Hunting in Medieval Scotland. 1980. text ed. 52.50x (ISBN 0-85976-030-8). Humanities.

Gilbert, John R. Pastor As Shepherd of the School Community. 52p. 1983. 4.00 (ISBN 0-318-00788-6). Natl Cath Educ.

Gilbert, John T. Detention, Liberation & Marriage of Maria Clementine Stuart. 220p. 1969. text ed. 25.00x (Pub. by Irish Academic Pr Ireland). Biblio Dist.

--Documents Relating to Ireland, 1795-1804. 282p. 1969. Repr. of 1893 ed. text ed. 30.00x (ISBN 0-7165-0048-5, BBA 02164, Pub. by Irish Academic Pr. Ireland). Biblio Dist.

--A Jacobite Narrative of the War in Ireland, 1688-1691. 358p. 1969. Repr. of 1892 ed. text ed. 25.00x (ISBN 0-7165-0050-7, BBA 02165, Pub. by Irish Academic Pr. Ireland). Biblio Dist.

Gilbert, John T., ed. Chartularies of St. Mary's Abbey, Dublin, Preserved in the Bodleian Library: Annals of Ireland, 2 vols. (Rolls Ser.: No. 80). Repr. of 1884 ed. Set. 120.00 (ISBN 0-317-16803-7). Kraus Repr.

--Historic & Municipal Documents, Ireland, 1172-1320, from the Archives of the City of Dublin. (Rolls Ser.: No. 53). Repr. of 1870 ed. 60.00 (ISBN 0-317-16701-4). Kraus Repr.

--History of the Irish Confederation & the War in Ireland, 1641-1649, Containing a Narrative of Affairs of Ireland, 7 vols. LC 72-144616. Repr. of 1891 ed. Set. 350.00 (ISBN 0-404-02840-3); 50.00 ea. AMS Pr.

--Register of the Abbey of St. Thomas, Dublin. (Rolls Ser.: No. 94). Repr. of 1889 ed. 44.00 (ISBN 0-317-16817-7). Kraus Repr.

--Technical Environmental Guidelines for Offshore Oil & Gas Development. 330p. 1983. 46.95x (ISBN 0-87814-208-8, P-4317). Pennwell Bks.

Gilbert, John T. E., ed. Environmental Planning Guidelines for Offshore Oil & Gas Development. (Illus.). 64p. 1982. pap. text ed. 6.00x (ISBN 0-8248-0792-8, Eastwest Ctr). UH Pr.

Gilbert, Joseph. Interpreting Psychological Test Data: Associating Personality & Behavior with Response to the Bender-Gestalt, Human Figure Drawing Weschler Adult Intellegence Scale, & the Rorschach Ink Blot Tests: Vol. II, Behavioral Attribute Antecedent. 224p. 1980. text ed. 19.95 (ISBN 0-442-25324-9). Van Nos Reinhold.

Gilbert, Karen D. Picture Indexing for Local History Materials. new ed. LC 73-91411. (Illus.). 36p. 1974. pap. text ed. 3.45 (ISBN 0-912526-12-2). Lib Res.

Gilbert, Karen E., jt. auth. see Cullen, Francis T.

Gilbert, Katharine. Aesthetic Studies: Architecture & Poetry. LC 79-124762. Repr. of 1952 ed. 15.00 (ISBN 0-404-02765-2). AMS Pr.

Gilbert, Katharine & Kuhn, Helmut. A History of Esthetics. rev. ed. LC 76-163548. 613p. 1972. Repr. of 1954 ed. lib. bdg. 33.75x (ISBN 0-8371-6207-6, GIHE). Greenwood.

Gilbert, Kathleen. Blackbird in the Sumac: Selected Poems by Kathleen Gilbert. (Illus.). 15p. (Orig.). 1984. pap. 2.50 (ISBN 0-915913-01-1). Violetta Bks.

--Minor Arcana, Poetry & Prose. (Illus.). 18p. (Orig.). 1985. pap. 2.50 (ISBN 0-915913-03-8). Violetta Bks.

--A Poet's Guide to Freelance Selling. (Illus.). 27p. 1983. pap. 2.75 (ISBN 0-915913-00-3). Violetta Bks.

Gilbert, Kathleen, et al. My Dear Most Editorial Sir: The Collected Letters of Violetta La Chance to Editors & Others. (Illus.). 30p. (Orig.). 1984. pap. 2.50 (ISBN 0-915913-02-X). Violetta Bks.

Gilbert, Kay, jt. auth. see Tolman, Newton F.

Gilbert, Keith G., et al, eds. Aero-Optical Phenomena. LC 81-20490. (Illus.). 412p. 1982. 55.00 (ISBN 0-915928-60-4, PAAS80); members 35.00 (ISBN 0-317-32118-8). AIAA.

Gilbert, Ken. Mountain Trace, Book II. LC 80-80065. 240p. 1983. 14.95 (ISBN 0-934750-20-3); pap. 9.45 (ISBN 0-934750-19-X). Jalamap.

Gilbert, Kenneth. Alaskan Poker Stories. (Shorey Historical Ser.). (Illus.). 48p. Shorey.

Gilbert, Kenneth, ed. Mountain Trace. (Illus.). 337p. 1980. 12.00 (ISBN 0-686-96759-3). Jalamap.

Gilbert, Kenneth G. Mountain Trace. 1980. 12.00 (ISBN 0-87012-376-9). McClain.

Gilbert, Kent S., jt. auth. see Watabe, Masakazu.

Gilbert, Kevin. People Are Legends. (Paperback Poets Ser.). 1979. 12.95x (ISBN 0-7022-1238-5); pap. 8.95x (ISBN 0-7022-1239-3). U of Queensland Pr.

Gilbert, L. C. see Ruckwick, Christian A.

Gilbert, L. I., ed. Juvenile Hormones. LC 76-21097. 582p. 1976. 65.00x (ISBN 0-306-30959-9, Plenum Pr). Plenum Pub.

Gilbert, LaBritta. I Can Do It! I Can Do It! One Hundred Thirty-Five Successful Independent Learning Activities. (Illus.). 167p. (Orig.). 1984. pap. 12.95 (ISBN 0-87659-107-1, 10002). Gryphon Hse.

Gilbert, Larry L., ed. see Pacific Northwest Conference on Higher Education, 1976.

Gilbert, Lawerence E. & Raven, Peter H, eds. Coevolution of Animals & Plants. rev. ed. (Illus.). 277p. 1980. pap. 9.95x (ISBN 0-292-71056-9). U of Tex Pr.

Gilbert, Lawrence I. & Frieden, Earl, eds. Metamorphosis: A Problem in Developmental Biology. rev. 2nd ed. LC 81-17691. 598p. 1981. 49.50x (ISBN 0-306-40692-6, Plenum Pr). Plenum Pub.

Gilbert, Lela, jt. auth. see Ezell, Lee.

Gilbert, Linda & Gilbert, Jimmie. Elements of Modern Algebra. 352p. 1983. pap. text ed. write for info (ISBN 0-87150-458-8, 2830, Prindle). PWS Pubs.

--Intermediate Algebra. (Illus.). 512p. 1983. text ed. 26.95 (ISBN 0-13-469536-4). P-H.

Gilbert, Llsa. Survivors: And Other New York Poems. 32p. (Orig.). 1985. pap. 4.00 (ISBN 0-934776-05-9). Bard Pr.

Gilbert, Lucia, et al. Men in Dual-Career Families: Present Realities & Future Prospects. 208p. 1985. text ed. 22.50 (ISBN 0-89859-560-6). L Erlbaum Assocs.

Gilbert, Lucy & Webster, Paula. Bound by Love: The Sweet Trap of Daughterhood. LC 81-65760. 200p. 1983. pap. 8.95 (ISBN 0-8070-6711-3, BP 658). Beacon Pr.

Gilbert, Lynn & Moore, Gaylen. Particular Passions: Talks with Women Who Have Shaped Our Times. (Illus.). 352p. 1981. 19.95 (ISBN 0-517-54371-0, C N Potter Bks). Crown.

Gilbert, M. Lloyd George. 1968. 8.95 (ISBN 0-13-353961-X, Spec); pap. 1.95. P-H.

Gilbert, M. S. Biography of the Unborn. 2nd ed. 1963. 14.95x (ISBN 0-02-845260-7). Hafner.

Gilbert, M. S., jt. auth. see Pettersson, H.

Gilbert, Marie. The Song & the Seed. (Illus.). 1983. 10.00 (ISBN 0-940580-27-6); pap. 5.00 (ISBN 0-940580-28-4). Green River.

Gilbert, Marilyn. Clear Writing: A Business Guide. LC 82-16043. (Self-Teaching Guides Ser.). 286p. 1983. pap. text ed. 9.95 (ISBN 0-471-86755-1, Pub. by Wiley Pr). Wiley.

Gilbert, Marilyn B., jt. auth. see Gilbert, Thomas F.

Gilbert, Martin. Atlas of American History. (Historical Atlases Ser.). 112p. 1985. Repr. 17.95 (ISBN 0-88029-016-1, Pub. by Dorset Pr). Hippocrene Bks.

--Atlas of British History. (Historical Atlas Ser.). (Illus.). 118p. 1985. Repr. of 1968 ed. 17.95 (ISBN 0-88029-017-X, Pub. by Dorset Pr). Hippocrene Bks.

--Auschwitz & the Allies. (Illus.). 368p. 1982. pap. 8.50 (ISBN 0-03-057058-1). HR&W.

--Churchill's Political Philosophy. (Thank-Offering to Britain Lectures Ser., 1980). 1981. 26.95x (ISBN 0-19-726005-5). Oxford U Pr.

--Churchill's Political Philosophy. 119p. 1981. 40.00x (Pub. by Brit Acad England). State Mutual Bk.

--Exile & Return: The Struggle for a Jewish Homeland. (Illus.). 364p. 1978. 12.95 (ISBN 0-397-01249-7). Brown Bk.

--The Final Journey: The Fate of the Jews in Nazi Europe. (Illus.). 1980. 12.50 (ISBN 0-8317-3325-X, Mayflower Bks). Smith Pubs.

--The Holocaust. 64p. 1979. pap. 5.95 (ISBN 0-8090-1389-4). Hill & Wang.

--The Holocaust: The History of the Jews of Europe During the Second World War. LC 85-5523. (Illus.). 488p. 1985. 19.95 (ISBN 0-03-062416-9). HR&W.

--Jerusalem: Rebirth of City. 1985. 25.00 (ISBN 0-670-80789-3, E Sifton Bks). Viking.

--The Jews of Hope. (Nonfiction Ser.). 272p. 1985. price not set. Penguin.

--The Jews of Hope: The Plight of Soviet Jewry Today. LC 84-40461. (Illus.). 237p. 1985. 15.95 (ISBN 0-670-80377-4, E. Sifton Bks). Viking.

--The Macmillan Atlas of the Holocaust. LC 81-675599. (Illus.). 256p. 1982. 18.99x (ISBN 0-02-543380-6). Macmillan.

--Macmillan Atlas of the Holocaust. (Quality Paperbacks Ser.). (Illus.). 256p. 1984. pap. 13.95 (ISBN 0-306-80218-X). Da Capo.

--Winston Churchill: The Wilderness Years. LC 82-9279. (Illus.). 1982. 16.95 (ISBN 0-395-31869-6). HM.

--Winston S. Churchill, 3 pts, Companion Vol. 4. Incl. Pt. 1. January 1917-June 1919 (ISBN 0-395-24585-0); Pt. 2. July 1919-March 1921. 40.00 (ISBN 0-395-24584-2); Pt. 3. April 1921-November 1922. 40.00 (ISBN 0-395-24587-7). 1978. Set. 120.00 (ISBN 0-395-26055-8). HM.

--Winston S. Churchill: Companion Vol. III, 2 parts. 1973. 80.00 (ISBN 0-395-16974-7); Part 1. July 1914-April 1915 40.00 (ISBN 0-395-14754-9); Part 2. May 1915-December 1916 40.00 (ISBN 0-395-14755-7). HM.

--Winston S. Churchill: Companion Vol. V, Part One, The Exchequer Years 1922-1929. 1981. 95.00 (ISBN 0-395-27778-7). HM.

--Winston S. Churchill: Companion Vol. V, Part Two, The Wilderness Years 1929-1935. 1981. 95.00 (ISBN 0-395-27779-5). HM.

--Winston S. Churchill: Finest Hour, Nineteen Thirty-Nine to Nineteen Forty-One, Vol. 6. LC 66-12065. (Illus.). 1308p. 1983. 40.00 (ISBN 0-395-34402-6). HM.

--Winston S. Churchill: The Prophet of Truth, 1929-1939, Vol. 5. 1977. 40.00 (ISBN 0-395-25104-4). HM.

--Winston S. Churchill, Vol. III: The Challenge of War, 1914-1916. 1971. 40.00 (ISBN 0-395-13153-7). HM.

--Winston S. Churchill: Vol. V: Pt. 3, The Coming of War 1936-1939. 1983. 95.00 (ISBN 0-395-33076-9). HM.

--Winston S. Churchill, 1916-1922, Vol 4. LC 66-12065. (The Stricken World Ser.). 992p. 1975. 40.00 (ISBN 0-395-20436-4). HM.

Gilbert, Marvin. God, Me, & Thee. (Discovery Bk.). 1980. 1.50 (ISBN 0-88243-841-7, 02-0841); tchr's ed 3.95 (ISBN 0-88243-331-8, 02-0331). Gospel Pub.

Gilbert, Mary. Das Gesprach in Fontanes Gesellschaftsromanen. (Ger). 18.00; pap. 13.00 (ISBN 0-384-18483-9). Johnson Repr.

Gilbert, Mercedes. Aunt Sara's Wooden God. LC 76-144617. Repr. of 1938 ed. 21.50 (ISBN 0-404-00161-0). AMS Pr.

Gilbert, Michael. The Black Seraphim. LC 83-48020. 256p. 1984. 13.41i (ISBN 0-06-015220-6, HarpT). Har-Row.

--The Black Seraphim. (Crime Monthly Ser.). 224p. 1985. pap. 3.50 (ISBN 0-14-007563-1). Penguin.

--The Empty House. (Penguin Crime Monthly Ser.). 1980. pap. 2.95 (ISBN 0-14-005142-2). Penguin.

--End-Game. 247p. 1982. 12.98i (ISBN 0-06-014976-0, HarpT). Har-Row.

--End-Game. 256p. 1983. pap. 2.95 (ISBN 0-14-006749-3). Penguin.

--The Killing of Katie Steelstock. LC 79-3409. (A Harper Novel of Suspense Ser.). 304p. 1980. 10.95i (ISBN 0-06-011494-0, HarpT). Har-Row.

--The Killing of Katie Steelstock. 304p. 1981. pap. 3.95 (ISBN 0-14-005838-9). Penguin.

--The Long Journey Home. LC 84-48600. 224p. 1985. 14.37 (ISBN 0-06-015430-6, HarpT). Har-Row.

--Mr. Calder & Mr. Behrens. 256p. 1983. pap. 2.95 (ISBN 0-14-006637-3). Penguin.

--The Night of the Twelfth. (Crime Ser). 1978. pap. 2.95 (ISBN 0-14-004615-1). Penguin.

--Smallbone Deceased. 208p. 1974. pap. 3.95 (ISBN 0-14-003810-8). Penguin.

Gilbert, Michael, ed. see Hare, Cyril.

Gilbert, Michael A. How to Win an Argument. 1979. pap. 4.95 (ISBN 0-07-023215-6). McGraw.

--Office Party. 1984. pap. 3.50 (ISBN 0-671-53228-6). PB.

--Yellow Angel. (Orig.). 1985. pap. 3.50 (ISBN 0-671-54425-X). PB.

Gilbert, Michael F. The Oxford Book of Legal Anecdotes. Date not set. price not set (ISBN 0-19-214112-0). Oxford U Pr.

Gilbert, Milton. Currency Depreciation & Monetary Policy. Wilkins, Mira, ed. LC 78-3914. (International Finance Ser.). (Illus.). 1978. Repr. of 1939 ed. lib. bdg. 17.00x (ISBN 0-405-11218-1). Ayer Co Pubs.

--Export Prices & Export Cartels. LC 72-136379. Repr. of 1940 ed. 23.00 (ISBN 0-404-02766-0). AMS Pr.

--Quest for World Monetary Order: Gold-Dollar System & Its Aftermath. LC 80-17865. 255p. 1980. 37.95x (ISBN 0-471-07998-7, Pub. by Wiley-Interscience). Wiley.

Gilbert, Milton & Kravis, Irving B. An International Comparison of National Products & the Purchasing of Currencies. LC 82-48303. (The World Economy Ser.). 203p. 1983. lib. bdg. 28.00 (ISBN 0-8240-5358-3). Garland Pub.

Gilbert, Minnie. Sunrise Song. 96p. 1984. 8.95 (ISBN 0-89015-468-6). Eakin Pubns.

Gilbert, Miriam. Glory Be: The Career of a Young Hair Stylist. (Illus.). (gr. 6-9). 1967. PLB 6.95 (ISBN 0-8038-2608-7). Hastings.

--Rosie: The Oldest Horse in St. Augustine. LC 67-30409. (Illus., Eng., Fr. & Spain.). (gr. k-6). 1974. pap. 1.95 (ISBN 0-87208-007-2). Island Pr.

--Science-Hobby Book of Aquariums. rev. ed. LC 67-17406. (Science Hobby Bks). (Illus.). (gr. 5-10). 1968. PLB 4.95 (ISBN 0-8225-0551-7). Lerner Pubns.

--Science-Hobby Book of Shell Collecting. rev. ed. LC 67-17404. (Science Hobby Bks). (gr. 5-10). 1968. PLB 4.95 (ISBN 0-8225-0557-6). Lerner Pubns.

Gilbert, Miriam, jt. auth. see Carlsen, G. R.

Gilbert, Miriam, jt. auth. see Guy, May.

Gilbert, Miriam, jt. auth. see Warner, Marie P.

Gilbert, Miriam A., jt. tr. see Klaus, Carl H.

Gilbert, Mitchell. An Owner's Manual for the Human Being. 1980. pap. 4.95 (ISBN 0-87728-496-2). Weiser.

Gilbert, N. & Specht, H. Planning for Social Welfare: Issues, Models & Tasks. 1977. text ed. 28.95 (ISBN 0-13-679555-2). P-H.

Gilbert, Nan. Unchosen. (gr. 7 up). 1963. PLB 11.89 (ISBN 0-06-021971-8). HarpJ.

Gilbert, Neil. Capitalism & the Welfare State: Dilemmas of Social Benevolence. LC 83-42872. 1983. 18.00x (ISBN 0-300-03112-2). Yale U Pr.

--Capitalism & the Welfare State: Dilemmas of Social Benevolence. LC 83-42872. 1985. pap. 5.95x (ISBN 0-300-03477-6, Y-542). Yale U Pr.

--Clients or Constituents: Community Action in the War on Poverty. LC 74-110627. (Jossey-Bass Behavioral Science Ser.). Repr. of 1970 ed. 39.60 (ISBN 0-8357-9305-2, 2013922). Bks Demand UMI.

Gilbert, Neil & Specht, Harry. Dimensions of Social Welfare Policy. (Illus.). 208p. 1974. 31.95 (ISBN 0-13-214486-7). P-H.

--Dynamics of Community Planning. LC 77-22182. 216p. 1977. prof ref 25.00 (ISBN 0-88410-362-5). Ballinger Pub.

--Handbook of the Social Services. (Illus.). 704p. 1981. text ed. 47.00 (ISBN 0-13-381806-3). P-H.

Gilbert, Neil, ed. see Adams, Paul.

Gilbert, Neil, ed. see Jaffe, Eliezer D.

Gilbert, Neil, et al. An Introduction to Social Work Practice. (P-H Ser. in Social Work Practice). (Illus.). 1980. text ed. 27.95 (ISBN 0-13-479105-3). P-H.

Gilbert, Norma. The Joy of Chicken. 2nd ed. 1977. pap. 2.95 (ISBN 0-89596-217-9, Argent Bks). Merit Pubns.

--Statistics. 2nd ed. 1981. text ed. 32.95 (ISBN 0-03-058091-9, CBS C); instr's manual 9.95 (ISBN 0-03-058093-5). SCP.

Gilbert, O. & Whittaker, R. The Historical Meaning of Savonarola as a Religious, Moral & Political Prophet & the Progress of the Reformation in Italy. 189p. 1985. 88.45 (ISBN 0-89266-514-9). Am Classical Coll Pr.

Gilbert, O. E., jt. auth. see Roeder, D.

Gilbert, Pamela. Compendium of the Biographical Literature on Deceased Entomologists. (Illus.). 1977. 70.00x (ISBN 0-565-00786-6, Pub. by Brit Mus Nat Hist). Sabbot-Natural Hist Bks.

Gilbert, Pamela, ed. Entomology: A Guide to Information Services. 288p. 1983. 29.00x (ISBN 0-7201-1680-5). Mansell.

Gilbert, Paul. Depression: From Psychology to Brain State. 256p. 1984. text ed. 29.95 (ISBN 0-86377-007-X). L Erlbaum Assocs.

Gilbert, Philip. Software Design & Development. 608p. 1983. text ed. 33.95 (ISBN 0-574-21430-5, 13-4430); instr's. guide avail. (ISBN 0-574-21431-3, 13-4431). SRA.

Gilbert, R. Pierre et les Cambrioleurs. (Illus., Fr.). (gr. 7-9). 1969. pap. 7.95 (ISBN 0-312-61075-0). St Martin.

Gilbert, R. & Weinacht, R. Function Theoretic Methods in Differential Equations. (Research Notes in Mathematics Ser.: No. 8). (Orig.). 1976. pap. text ed. 27.95 (ISBN 0-273-00306-2). Pitman Pub MA.

Gilbert, R., jt. auth. see Llewellyn, J. A.

Gilbert, R. A. The Golden Dawn: Twilight of the Magicians. 128p. 1983. pap. 7.95 (ISBN 0-85030-278-1). Newcastle Pub.

Gilbert, Dr. R., jt. auth. see Llewellyn, Dr. J. A.

Gilbert, R. J. & Lovelock, D. W., eds. Microbial Aspects of the Deterioration of Materials. (Society of Applied Bacteriology Technical Ser.). 1975. 39.00 (ISBN 0-12-282950-6). Acad Pr.

Gilbert, R. J., jt. ed. see Baillie, A.

Gilbert, R. P. Constructive Methods for Elliptic Equations. LC 73-21280. (Lectures Notes in Mathematics: Vol. 365). vii, 397p. 1974. pap. 18.00 (ISBN 0-387-06690-X). Springer-Verlag.
--Function Theoretic Methods in Partial Differential Equations. (Mathematics in Science & Engineering Ser: Vol. 54). 1969. 75.00 (ISBN 0-12-283050-4). Acad Pr.
Gilbert, R. P., jt. ed. see Colton, D. L.
Gilbert, Ralph J., jt. auth. see Hall, R. D.
Gilbert, Richard. Caffeine: The Most Popular Stimulant. (Encyclopedia of Psychoactive Drugs Ser.). (Illus.). 1985. PLB 15.95x (ISBN 0-87754-756-4). Chelsea Hse.
--Mountaineering for All. (Illus.). 136p. 1981. 19.95 (ISBN 0-7134-3350-7, Pub. by Batsford England). David & Charles.
--Nicotine: An Old-Fashioned Addiction. (Encyclopedia of Psychoactive Drugs Ser.). (Illus.). 1985. lib. bdg. 15.95x (ISBN 0-87754-751-3). Chelsea Hse.
--The Prophetic Imperative. 1980. pap. 6.75 (ISBN 0-933840-16-0). Unitarian Univ.
Gilbert, Richard A., et al. Attorney's Guide to Pension & Profit-Sharing Plans. 3rd ed. 1985. 120.00 (ISBN 0-88124-130-X). Cal Cont Ed Bar.
Gilbert, Richard P. & Moylan, Charles E. Maryland Criminal Law: Practice & Procedure. 792p. PLB 50.00 (ISBN 0-87215-618-4). Michie Co.
Gilbert, Rita, jt. auth. see McCarter, William.
Gilbert, Rob. The Impotent Image: Reflections of Ideology in the Secondary School Curriculum. LC 84-13517. 250p. 1984. 33.00x (ISBN 1-85000-010-7, Pub. by Falmer Pr); pap. 20.00 (ISBN 0-317-12584-2, Pub. by Falmer Pr). Taylor & Francis.
Gilbert, Robert. Business Practice Set: SAAL Manufacturing Limited Financial Operating Budget. 64p. 1981. pap. text ed. 7.95 (ISBN 0-8403-2346-8). Kendall-Hunt.
Gilbert, Robert I., Jr. & Mielke, James H. The Analysis of Prehistoric Diets. (Studies in Archaeology). 1984. 65.00 (ISBN 0-12-283260-4). Acad Pr.
Gilbert, Robert P. & Buchanan, James. First-Order Elliptic Systems: A Functional Theoretic Approach. 1983. 49.50 (ISBN 0-12-283280-9). Acad Pr.
Gilbert, Robert P. & Newton, Roger G. Analytic Methods in Mathematical Physics. 590p. 1970. 112.25 (ISBN 0-677-13560-2). Gordon.
Gilbert, Robert P., ed. Plane Ellipticity & Related Problems. LC 82-11562. (Contemporary Mathematics Ser.: Vol. 11). 256p. 1982. 22.00 (ISBN 0-8218-5012-1, CONM/11). Am Math.
Gilbert, Rodney V. The Unequal Treaties: China & the Foreigner. (Studies in Chinese History & Civilzation). 248p. 1977. Repr. of 1929 ed. 19.50 (ISBN 0-89093-075-9). U Pubns Amer.
Gilbert, Ronald R. & Peters, J. Douglas. Social Security Disability Claims, Vol. 1. LC 79-92367. 1983. 014 87.50; Suppl. 1984. 28.00. Lawyers Co-Op.
Gilbert, Rose, jt. auth. see Smith, Lauren.
Gilbert, Rose B. & McMillan, Patricia H. Decorating Country-Style: The Look & How to Have It. LC 78-68324. (Illus.). 1980. 17.95 (ISBN 0-385-14086-X). Doubleday.
Gilbert, Rudolph. Four Living Poets. LC 73-18191. Repr. of 1944 ed. lib. bdg. 7.50 (ISBN 0-8414-4495-1). Folcroft.
--Shine Perishing Republic. LC 65-15883. (Studies in Poetry, No. 38). 1969. Repr. of 1936 ed. lib. bdg. 75.00x (ISBN 0-8383-0556-3). Haskell.
Gilbert, Russell W. Bilder und Gedanke: Poems. LC 74-26228. (Penn. German Ser.: Vol. 9). 1975. 12.50 (ISBN 0-911122-31-1). Penn German Soc.
Gilbert, S. M. Monarch Notes on Woolf's Mrs. Dalloway & to the Lighthouse. (Orgi). pap. 2.75 (ISBN 0-671-00883-8). Monarch Pr.
Gilbert, Sandra. In the Fourth World: Poems. LC 78-11144. 80p. 1979. pap. 5.95 (ISBN 0-8173-8527-4). U of Ala Pr.
--Monarch Notes on Forster's Passage to India & Howards End. (Orig.). pap. 2.95 (ISBN 0-671-00712-2). Monarch Pr.
--Monarch Notes on Lawrence's Sons & Lovers & Other Works. (Orig.). pap. 3.25 (ISBN 0-671-00716-5). Monarch Pr.
--Monarch Notes on Shakespeare's Twelfth Night. (Orig.). pap. 2.95 (ISBN 0-671-00645-2). Monarch Pr.
--Monarch Notes on Yeats' Poetry. (Orig.). pap. 4.50 (ISBN 0-671-00738-6). Monarch Pr.
Gilbert, Sandra & Gubar, Susan, eds. Norton Anthology of Literature by Women: The Tradition in English. 1985. pap. text ed. 19.95x (ISBN 0-393-95391-2); tchr's. ed. avail. (ISBN 0-393-95394-7); 28.95 (ISBN 0-393-01940-3). Norton.
Gilbert, Sandra M. Acts of Attention: The Poems of D. H. Lawrence. 341p. 1972. 27.50x (ISBN 0-8014-0731-1). Cornell U Pr.
--Emily's Bread: Poems. (Illus.). 112p. 1984. 15.95 (ISBN 0-393-01849-0); pap. 6.95 (ISBN 0-393-30150-8). Norton.
--The Summer Kitchen. Hazzard, Barbara. LC 83-81453. (Illus.). 48p. (Orig.). 1983. pap. 8.50 (ISBN 0-940592-14-2). Heyeck Pr.
Gilbert, Sandra M. & Gubar, Susan. The Madwoman in the Attic: A Study of Women & the Literary Imagination in the Nineteenth Century. LC 78-20792. (Illus.). 733p. 1979. pap. 16.95 (ISBN 0-300-02596-3). Yale U Pr.
Gilbert, Sandra M. & Gubar, Susan, eds. Shakespeare's Sisters: Feminist Essays on Women Poets. LC 78-9510. (Midland Bks.: No. 263). 368p. 1979. 25.00x (ISBN 0-253-11258-3); pap. 12.95x (ISBN 0-253-20263-9). Ind U Pr.
Gilbert, Sara. By Yourself. LC 82-13962. (Illus.). 80p. (gr. 3-6). 1983. PLB 10.88 (ISBN 0-688-01688-X); pap. 7.50 (ISBN 0-688-01687-1). Lothrop.
--How to Live with a Single Parent. (gr. 7 up). 1982. PLB 11.88 (ISBN 0-688-00633-7); pap. 6.50 (ISBN 0-688-00587-X). Lothrop.
--How to Take Tests. LC 83-7115. 160p. (gr. 5up). 1983. 10.25 (ISBN 0-688-02469-6); pap. 7.50 (ISBN 0-688-02470-X). Morrow.
--Trouble at Home. LC 81-1385. 192p. (gr. 7 up). 1981. 11.25 (ISBN 0-688-41995-X); PLB 11.88 (ISBN 0-688-51995-4). Lothrop.
--Using Your Head: The Many Ways of Being Smart. LC 84-9736. (Illus.). 128p. (gr. 5-9). 1984. 9.95 (ISBN 0-02-736720-7). Macmillan.
--Using Your Head: The Many Ways of Being Smart. (gr. 5-9). 9.95 (ISBN 0-317-13422-1). Macmillan.
--What Happens in Therapy. LC 82-15233. 144p. (gr. 6 up). 1982. PLB 10.88 (ISBN 0-688-01458-5); pap. 6.00 (ISBN 0-688-01459-3). Lothrop.
--You Are What You Eat: A Common-Sense Guide to the Modern American Diet. LC 76-39806. 160p. (gr. 5 up). 1977. 10.95 (ISBN 0-02-736020-2, 73602). Macmillan.
Gilbert, Scott F. Developmental Biology. LC 84-10658. (Illus.). 600p. 1985. text ed. 33.95x (ISBN 0-87893-246-1). Sinauer Assoc.
Gilbert, Skeet. Fundamentals of Profitable Stamp Investing. (Illus.). 1967. pap. 2.00 (ISBN 0-685-19958-4). S Gilbert.
Gilbert, Stephen G. Atlas of General Zoology. LC 65-25236. 1965. pap. text ed. 11.95x (ISBN 0-8087-0709-4). Burgess.
--Pictorial Anatomy of the Cat. rev. ed. LC 67-21200. (Illus.). 128p. 1975. pap. 8.95x (ISBN 0-295-95454-X). U of Wash Pr.
--Pictorial Anatomy of the Dogfish. LC 74-152331. (Illus.). 66p. (Orig.). 1973. pap. text ed. 7.95x (ISBN 0-295-95148-6). U of Wash Pr.
--Pictorial Anatomy of the Fetal Pig. 2nd, rev. ed. LC 63-10797. (Illus.). 96p. 1966. pap. 7.95x (ISBN 0-295-73877-4). U of Wash Pr.
--Pictorial Anatomy of the Frog. LC 65-14843. (Illus.). 71p. 1965. pap. 7.95x (ISBN 0-295-73878-2). U of Wash Pr.
--Pictorial Anatomy of the Necturus. LC 78-152332. (Illus.). 54p. (Orig.). 1973. pap. text ed. 7.95x (ISBN 0-295-95149-4). U of Wash Pr.
Gilbert, Steven E., jt. auth. see Forte, Allan.
Gilbert, Stuart. James Joyce's "Ulysses". 1955. pap. 4.95 (ISBN 0-394-70013-9, V13, Vin). Random.
Gilbert, Stuart see Joyce, James.
Gilbert, Stuart, tr. see Camus, Albert.
Gilbert, Stuart, tr. see De Tocqueville, Alexis.
Gilbert, Stuart, tr. see Dujardin, Edouard.
Gilbert, Stuart, tr. see Malraux, Andre.
Gilbert, Stuart, tr. see Picon, Gaetan.
Gilbert, Stuart, tr. see Saint-Exupery, Antoine De.
Gilbert, Stuart, tr. see Saint-Exupery, Antoine de.
Gilbert, Stuart, tr. see Saint-Exupery, Saint Antoine De.
Gilbert, Stuart, tr. see Simenon, Georges.
Gilbert, Thomas. Voyage from New South Wales to Canton in the Year Seventeen Eighty-Eight. (Illus.). 85p. 1968. Repr. of 1789 ed. 25.00 (ISBN 0-8398-0659-0). Parnassus Imprints.
Gilbert, Thomas F. Human Competence: Engineering Worthy Performance. LC 77-26700. 1978. 37.50 (ISBN 0-07-023217-2). McGraw.
Gilbert, Thomas F. & Gilbert, Marilyn B. Thinking Metric. 2nd ed. LC 77-20190. (Self-Teaching Guide Ser.). 141p. 1978. pap. text ed. 6.95 (ISBN 0-471-03427-4, Pub. by Wiley Pr). Wiley.
Gilbert, V. F. & Tatla, D. S., eds. Women Studies: A Bibliography of Dissertations 1870-1982. 450p. 1985. 75.00x (ISBN 0-631-13714-9). Basil Blackwell.
Gilbert, Victor F. & Tatla, Darshan S. Immigrants, Minorities & Race Relations. 188p. 1984. 37.00 (ISBN 0-7201-1691-0). Wilson.
Gilbert, Victor F., compiled by. Labour & Social History Theses. 200p. 1982. 32.00 (ISBN 0-7201-1647-3). Mansell.
Gilbert, W. S. Additional Adventures of Messrs. Box & Cox: A Continuation of the Dramatic History of Box & Cox. MacPhail, Ralph, Jr., ed. Bd. with Penelope Anne. Burnand, F. C. LC 75-304933. (Illus.). 74p. 1974. pap. 10.00 (ISBN 0-9601580-0-6). Parenthesis Pr.
--Bab Ballads. Ellis, James, ed. LC 77-102668. 1970. 22.50x (ISBN 0-674-05800-3, Belknap Pr); pap. 9.95 (ISBN 0-674-05801-1). Harvard U Pr.
--Foggerty's Fairy, & Other Tales. 1980. Repr. of 1890 ed. lib. bdg. 35.00 (ISBN 0-89341-484-0). Longwood Pub Group.
--The Mikado. (Facsimile Classics Ser.). (Illus.). 1979. 5.95 (ISBN 0-8317-6000-1, Mayflower Bks). Smith Pubs.
--The Savoy Operas. 900p. Date not set. 19.95 (ISBN 0-88029-043-9, Pub. by Dorset Pr). Hippocrene Bks.
--Yeomen of the Guard. (Facsimile Classics Ser.). (Illus.). 1979. Repr. of 1929 ed. 5.95 (ISBN 0-8317-9940-4, Mayflower Bks). Smith Pubs.
Gilbert, W. S. & Sullivan, Arthur. The Complete Plays of Gilbert & Sullivan. (Illus.). 640p. 1976. pap. 12.95 (ISBN 0-393-00828-2, Norton Lib). Norton.
Gilbert, Wilfred C., ed. see U. S. Library of Congress Legislative Reference Service.
Gilbert, William H. The Eastern Cherokees. LC 76-43714. (BAE. Anthropological Papers: No. 23). Repr. of 1943 ed. 27.50 (ISBN 0-404-15547-2). AMS Pr.
Gilbert, William J. Modern Algebra with Applications. LC 76-22756. 348p. 1976. 38.50x (ISBN 0-471-29891-3, Pub by Wiley-Interscience). Wiley.
Gilbert, William S. Plays by W. S. Gilbert. Rowell, George, ed. LC 81-12248. (British & American Playwrights 1750-1920 Ser.). (Illus.). 250p. 1982. 39.50 (ISBN 0-521-23589-8); pap. 10.95 (ISBN 0-521-28056-7). Cambridge U Pr.
Gilbert, William S. & Sullivan, Arthur S. The Authentic Gilbert & Sullivan Songbook: 92 Unabridged Selections from All 14 Operas, Reproduced from Early Vocal Scores. Spero, James, ed. LC 76-55953. (Illus.). 1978. pap. 10.95 (ISBN 0-486-23482-7). Dover.
Gilbert, Wyatt G. A Geological Guide to Mount McKinley National Park. Pistrang, Marvin, ed. (Illus.). 52p. (Orig.). 1979. pap. 5.00 (ISBN 0-9602876-0-4). Alaska Natural.
Gilbert, Zack. My Own Hallelujahs. 1971. pap. 1.50 (ISBN 0-88378-016-X). Third World.
Gilbert, Zoe. Fruit Growing in Southern Africa. 1980. 32.00x (ISBN 0-686-69982-3, Pub. by Bailey & Swinton South Africa). State Mutual Bk.
Gilbert-Carter, H., tr. see Raunkiaer, Christen.
Gilbertie, Sal. Herb Gardening at Its Best. LC 77-23678. 1978. pap. 8.95, 1980 (ISBN 0-689-70595-6, 255). Atheneum.
--Home Gardening at Its Best: Productive Ways to Grow Your Own Fresh Vegetables. Sheehan, Lawrence, ed. LC 76-11549. (Illus.). 1977. 12.95 (ISBN 0-689-10742-0); pap. 5.95 (ISBN 0-689-70563-8). Atheneum.
Gilbert Of Hoyland. Gilbert of Hoyland: Sermons on the Song of Songs, 1. Braceland, Lawrence C., tr. from Latin. LC 77-23026. (Fathers Ser.: No. 14). 1978. 15.95 (ISBN 0-87907-414-0). Cistercian Pubns.
--Gilbert of Hoyland, Sermons on the Song of Songs, II. (Fathers Ser.: No. 20). 1979. 8.95 (ISBN 0-87907-420-5). Cistercian Pubns.
--Gilbert of Hoyland: Sermons on the Song of Songs, III. Braceland, Lawrence C., tr. (Fathers Ser.: No. 26). 1979. 8.95 (ISBN 0-87907-426-4). Cistercian Pubns.
Gilbert-Rolfe, Jeremy. Immanence & Contradiction: Essays on the Artistic Device. (Illus.). 150p. (Orig.). 1985. pap. 14.95 (ISBN 0-915570-21-1). Oolp Pr.
Gilbertson, A. A. Intravenous Technique & Therapy. (Illus.). 158p. 1984. pap. 13.50x (ISBN 0-433-11620-X, Pub. by W Heinemann Med Bks). Sheridan Med Bks.
Gilbertson, Alan D. Developing the Rehabilitation Facility Personnel Manual. 65p. (Orig.). 1981. pap. 7.75x (ISBN 0-916671-12-7). Material Dev.
Gilbertson, Alan D., ed. Contract Bidding for Rehabilitation Facilities. (Illus.). 98p. (Orig.). 1980. pap. 7.75x (ISBN 0-916671-23-2). Material Dev.
Gilbertson, Catherine. Harriet Beecher Stowe. 330p. 1982. Repr. of 1937 ed. lib. bdg. 40.00 (ISBN 0-89987-316-2). Darby Bks.
Gilbertson, David, et al. Practical Ecology for Geography & Biology: Survey, Mapping & Data Analysis. (Illus.). 350p. (Orig.). 1985. pap. 11.95 (ISBN 0-09-162651-X, Pub. by Hutchinson Educ). Longwood Pub Group.
Gilbertson, Irvy. More Practical Puppet Plays. LC 80-65306. 64p. (Orig.). (gr. 1-5). 1980. pap. 2.50 (ISBN 0-88243-747-X, 02-0747). Gospel Pub.
--Practical Puppet Plays. LC 77-75600. 64p. 1977. pap. text ed. 2.50 (ISBN 0-88243-746-1, 02-0746). Gospel Pub.
--Puppet Plays for Missionettes. LC 82-82483. 64p. (Orig.). 1982. pap. 2.95 saddlestitched (ISBN 0-88243-736-4, 02-0736). Gospel Pub.
Gilbertson, Merrill T. Way It Was in Bible Times. LC 59-10759. (Illus.). 1959. pap. 5.50 (ISBN 0-8066-1442-0, 10-7000). Augsburg.
Gilbertson, R. L., jt. auth. see Lindsey, J. P.
Gilbertson, Robert L. Fungi That Decay Ponderosa Pine. LC 74-77206. 197p. 1974. pap. 14.95x (ISBN 0-8165-0361-3). U of Ariz Pr.
Gilbey, J. F. Secret Fighting Arts of World. 10.95x (ISBN 0-685-63779-4). Wehman.
Gilbey, John F. Secret Fighting Arts of the World. LC 63-7910. (Illus.). 1963. bds. 9.75 (ISBN 0-8048-0515-6). C E Tuttle.
--Way of a Warrior. (Illus.). 150p. 1983. 20.00 (ISBN 0-938190-03-2). North Atlantic.
--Way of a Warrior. (Illus.). 150p. 1985. pap. 8.95 (ISBN 0-938190-04-0). North Atlantic.
Gilbey, Quintin. Fun Was My Living. 14.50 (ISBN 0-392-00259-0, LTB). Sportshelf.
Gilbey, Walter. Hounds in Old Days. 2nd ed. (Illus.). 192p. 1979. 10.95 (ISBN 0-904558-35-5). Saiga.
--Sport in the Olden Time. 117p. 1975. 13.50 (ISBN 0-904558-04-5). Saiga.
Gilbo, Anna-Carolyn. I Hate You! Love, Don: The Autobiography of a Teacher. LC 85-50515. (Illus.). 72p. (Orig.). 1985. pap. 5.95 (ISBN 0-933741-00-6). Lexis Pr.
Gilbo, Patrick F. The American Red Cross the First Century: A Pictorial History. LC 80-8204. (Illus.). 256p. 1981. 25.00i (ISBN 0-06-011461-4, HarpT). Har-Row.
Gilboa, Amir. Light of Lost Suns. Kaufman, Shirley, tr. from Heb. LC 78-61062. (Persea Ser. of Poetry in Translation). 1979. 10.00 (ISBN 0-89255-037-6); pap. 4.95 (ISBN 0-89255-038-4). Persea Bks.
Gilboa, Yehoshua A. A Language Silenced: Hebrew Culture in the Soviet Union. LC 80-70920. 320p. 1982. 25.00 (ISBN 0-8386-3072-3). Fairleigh Dickerson.
Gilborn, Alice, jt. auth. see Gilborn, Craig.
Gilborn, Craig. Durant: The Fortunes & Woodland Camps of a Family in the Adirondacks. (Illus.). 170p. 1981. 19.95 (ISBN 0-686-75331-3). Adirondack Mus.
--Rustic Furniture in America: The Adirondack Museum's Guide To. (Illus.). 336p. cancelled (ISBN 0-932052-36-3). North Country.
Gilborn, Craig & Gilborn, Alice. Museum of the Adirondacks. (Illus.). 64p. 1984. pap. 3.50 (ISBN 0-910020-36-1). Adirondack Mus.
Gilborn, Craig, et al. A. F. Tait: Artist in the Adirondacks. (Illus.). 75p. 1974. pap. 2.00 (ISBN 0-686-74843-3). Adirondack Mus.
Gilboy, Elizabeth L. Wages in Eighteenth Century England. LC 79-81457. 1969. Repr. of 1934 ed. 11.00x (ISBN 0-8462-1362-1). Russell.
Gilboy, Robert C. Spell It Fast! The Quick Way to Spell the 25,000 Most Misspelled Words Using Sixty Stimulating Word Lists. LC 81-1146. 286p. 1981. pap. 5.95 (ISBN 0-87491-071-4). Acropolis.
Gilbreath, jt. auth. see Van Matre.
Gilbreath, Alice. The Continental Shelf: An Underwater Frontier. (Ocean World Science Library). (Illus.). (gr. 5 up). 1985. PLB 10.95 (ISBN 0-87518-301-8). Dillon.
--The Great Barrier Reef. (Ocean World Science Library). (Illus.). (gr. 5 up). 1985. PLB 10.95 (ISBN 0-87518-300-X). Dillon.
--The Ring of Fire. (Ocean World Science Library). (Illus.). (gr. 5 up). 1985. PLB 10.95 (ISBN 0-87518-302-6). Dillon.
--River in the Ocean: The Story of the Gulf Stream. (Ocean World Science Library). (Illus.). 96p. (gr. 5 up). 1985. PLB 10.95 (ISBN 0-87518-297-6). Dillon.
--Slab, Coil, & Pinch: A Beginners Pottery Book. (Illus.). (gr. 3-7). 1977. 10.00 (ISBN 0-688-22105-X); PLB 8.16 (ISBN 0-688-32105-4). Morrow.
Gilbreath, Kent. Red Capitalism: An Analysis of the Navajo Economy. LC 72-12547. pap. 39.30 (ISBN 0-317-29296-X, 2055512). Bks Demand UMI.
Gilbreath, Kent, ed. Business & the Environment: Toward Common Ground. 2nd ed. LC 84-5867. 533p. (Orig.). 1984. pap. 12.95 (ISBN 0-89164-081-9). Conservation Foun.
Gilbreath, Robert. Managing Construction Contracts: Operational Controls for Commerical Risks. (Construction Management & Engineering Ser.: 1-102). 281p. 1983. text ed. 34.95x (ISBN 0-471-87635-6, Pub. by Wiley-Interscience). Wiley.
Gilbreth, Frank & Carey, Ernestine G. Belles on Their Toes. 240p. 1984. pap. 2.50 (ISBN 0-553-23916-3). Bantam.
Gilbreth, Frank B. Bricklaying System. LC 74-14805. (Management History Ser.: No. 31). 325p. 1974. Repr. of 1909 ed. 24.00 (ISBN 0-87960-034-9). Hive Pub.
--Concrete System. (Management History Ser.: No. 70). (Illus.). 182p. 1974. Repr. of 1908 ed. 24.00 (ISBN 0-87960-106-X). Hive Pub.
--Field System. LC 73-1168. (Management History Ser.: No. 30). (Illus.). 194p. 1973. Repr. of 1908 ed. 18.50 (ISBN 0-87960-027-6). Hive Pub.
--Motion Study. LC 72-89986. (Management History Ser.: No. 14). (Illus.). xxiii, 139p. 1972. Repr. of 1911 ed. 18.50 (ISBN 0-87960-016-0). Hive Pub.
Gilbreth, Frank B. & Carey, Ernestine G. Cheaper by the Dozen. rev. ed. LC 63-20411. (Illus.). 1963. 15.34i (ISBN 0-690-18632-0). T Y Crowell.
Gilbreth, Frank B. & Gilbreth, Lillian M. Fatigue Study. LC 73-1155. (Management History Ser.: No. 29). (Illus.). viii, 167p. 1973. Repr. of 1916 ed. 17.50 (ISBN 0-87960-028-4). Hive Pub.
Gilbreth, Frank B., jt. auth. see Taylor, Frederick W.
Gilbreth, Frank B., et al. Scientific Management Course. LC 79-92317. (Management History Ser.: No. 77). 180p. 1975. Repr. of 1912 ed. 22.50 (ISBN 0-87960-114-0). Hive Pub.
Gilbreth, Frank B., Jr. & Carey, Ernestine G. Belles on Their Toes. LC 50-13907. (Illus.). 1950. 8.95i (ISBN 0-690-13023-6). T Y Crowell.
--Cheaper by the Dozen. 188p. Repr. of 1948 ed. lib. bdg. 15.95 (ISBN 0-88411-289-6, Pub. by Aeonian Pr). Amereon Ltd.
Gilbreth, Frank B., Jr. & Carey, Ernestine. Cheaper by the Dozen. (gr. 6 up). pap. 2.95 (ISBN 0-553-25018-3). Bantam.

Gilbreth, Frank B., Jr. & Carey, Ernestine G. Cheaper by the Dozen. (General Ser.). 1984. lib. bdg. 14.95 (ISBN 0-8161-3736-6, Large Print Bks); pap. 9.95 (ISBN 0-8161-3773-0, Large Print Bks). G K Hall.
Gilbreth, Lillian M. The Psychology of Management. LC 72-9514. (Management History Ser.: No. 22). ix, 344p. 1973. Repr. of 1914 ed. 22.50 (ISBN 0-87960-026-8). Hive Pub.
Gilbreth, Lillian M., jt. auth. see Gilbreth, Frank B.
Gilbreth, Terry, jt. auth. see Saffell, David C.
Gilbreth, Terry J. Governing Geothermal Steam: Intergovernmental Relations & Energy Policy. Bruchey, Stuart, ed. LC 78-22685. (Energy in the American Economy Ser.). 1979. lib. bdg. 25.50x (ISBN 0-405-11988-7). Ayer Co Pubs.
Gilbride, Colleen, ed. see Paffrath, Jim & Cangialosi, Karen.
Gilburne, Miles R. & Johnson, Ronald L., eds. The Computer Law Annual 1985. 1985. 60.00 (ISBN 0-317-29409-1, #H44038). HarBraceJ.
Gilby, Thomas. Poetic Experience. LC 77-15970. 1934. lib. bdg. 16.50 (ISBN 0-8414-4438-2). Folcroft.
--Poetic Experience. 114p. 1980. Repr. of 1934 ed. lib. bdg. 20.00 (ISBN 0-8492-4976-7). R West.
Gilby, Thomas, ed. see Aquinas, Saint Thomas.
Gilby, Thomas, ed. see Aquinas, Thomas.
Gilby, Thomas, ed. see St. Thomas Aquinas.
Gilcher, Edwin, ed. Bibliography of George Moore. LC 72-125334. 274p. 1970. 20.00 (ISBN 0-87580-017-3). N Ill U Pr.
Gilchrest, Barbara A. Skin & Aging Processes. 160p. 1983. 64.00 (ISBN 0-8493-5472-2). CRC Pr.
Gilchrist. Muppets: Light On Your Feet, No. 2. 1.95 (ISBN 0-317-31789-X). Tor Bks.
--Muppets: Short, Green & Handsome, No. 1. 1.95 (ISBN 0-317-31788-1). Tor Bks.
Gilchrist, A. Life of William Etty. 824p. write for info. (ISBN 0-7158-1358-7, Pub. by EP Pub England). State Mutual Bk.
Gilchrist, Agnes A. William Strickland-Architect & Engineer 1788-1854. enl. ed. LC 69-13714. (Architecture & Decorative Art Ser.). (Illus.). 1969. Repr. of 1950 ed. lib. bdg. 32.50 (ISBN 0-306-71235-0). Da Capo.
Gilchrist, Alan B., jt. auth. see D Auria, John M.
Gilchrist, Alexander. The Life of William Blake. Todd, Ruthven, ed. (Illus.). 432p. 1982. pap. text ed. 8.95x (ISBN 0-460-01971-6, Pub. by Evman England). Biblio Dist.
--Life of William Blake: With Selections from His Poems & Other Writings, 2 vols. enl. ed. (Illus.). 993p. 1969. Set. 50.00x (ISBN 0-87753-017-3). Phaeton.
Gilchrist, Andrew. Russian Professor. 224p. 1985. pap. 2.95 (ISBN 0-931773-22-9). Critics Choice Paper.
Gilchrist, Anne. Anne Gilchrist: Her Life & Writings. 2nd ed. Gilchrist, Herbert H., ed. LC 74-148783. Repr. of 1887 ed. 27.00 (ISBN 0-404-02767-9). AMS Pr.
--Mary Lamb. LC 78-148784. Repr. of 1883 ed. 25.00 (ISBN 0-404-07348-4). AMS Pr.
Gilchrist, Anne, jt. auth. see Whitman, Walt.
Gilchrist, Brad & Gilchrist, Guy. Muppets, No. 4: Chickens Are People Too. 128p. (Orig.). 1985. pap. 1.95 (ISBN 0-8125-7369-2, Dist. by Warner Pub Services & St. Martin). Tor Bks.
--Muppets, No. 5: Together Again. 128p. (Orig.). 1986. pap. 1.95 (ISBN 0-8125-7371-4, Dist. by Warner Pub Services & St. Martin). Tor Bks.
Gilchrist, Brad, jt. auth. see Gilchrist, Guy.
Gilchrist, Brenda, ed. Pottery. LC 78-62727. (Smithsonian Illustrated Library of Antiques). (Illus.). 128p. (Orig.). 1981. 9.95 (ISBN 0-910503-32-X). Cooper-Hewitt Museum.
Gilchrist, Brenda, ed. see Bishop, Robert & Coblentz, Patricia.
Gilchrist, Brenda, ed. see Cavallo, Adolph S.
Gilchrist, Brenda, ed. see Denny, Walter B.
Gilchrist, Brenda, ed. see Gardner, Paul V.
Gilchrist, Brenda, ed. see Karshan, Donald.
Gilchrist, Brenda, ed. see Ketchum, William C., Jr.
Gilchrist, Brenda, ed. see McNab, Jessie.
Gilchrist, Brenda, ed. see Mastai, Marie-Louise.
Gilchrist, Brenda, ed. see Patterson, Jerry E.
Gilchrist, Brenda, ed. see Shaffer, Douglas H.
Gilchrist, Bruce, jt. ed. see Leininger, Joseph E.
Gilchrist, Cheery. Finding Out about Nineteen Thirties Britain. (Finding Out About Ser.). (Illus.). 64p. (gr. 7-12). 1984. 12.95 (ISBN 0-7134-4352-9, Pub. by Batsford England). David & Charles.
Gilchrist, Cherry. Astrology. (History in Focus Ser.). (Illus.). 72p. (YA) (gr. 7-10). 1982. bds. 14.95 (ISBN 0-7134-3543-7, Pub. by Batsford England). David & Charles.
--Finding Out about Life in Britain in World War One. (Finding Out about Ser.). (Illus.). 48p. (gr. 7-12). 1985. 12.50 (ISBN 0-7134-4817-2, Pub. by Batsford England). David & Charles.
--People at Work: Nineteen Thirty to the Nineteen Eighty's. (Illus.). 72p. (gr. 7-12). 1983. 14.95 (ISBN 0-7134-1366-2, Pub. by Batsford England). David & Charles.
--A Visit to the Library. (Information Bks.). 4.95 (ISBN 0-317-30683-9); pap. 1.95 (ISBN 0-317-30684-7). Cambridge U Pr.
Gilchrist, Christopher. How to Plan Your Life Insurance. 2nd ed. 192p. 1985. 13.50 (ISBN 0-85941-300-4, Pub. by Woodhead-Faulkner); pap. 5.95 (ISBN 0-85941-301-2). Longwood Pub Group.
--Unit Trusts: What Every Investor Should Know. 3rd ed. 111p. (Orig.). 1982. 17.50 (ISBN 0-85941-209-1). Woodhead-Faulkner.
Gilchrist, Ellen. The Annunciation. 1983. 14.45i (ISBN 0-316-31302-5). Little.
--In the Land of Dreamy Dreams. 1985. 14.45 (ISBN 0-316-31304-1); pap. 6.70 (ISBN 0-316-31306-8). Little.
--Victory over Japan. 1985. 7.95 (ISBN 0-316-31309-2). Little.
--Victory over Japan: A Book of Stories. 256p. 1984. 15.45i (ISBN 0-316-31303-3). Little.
Gilchrist, Francis G. Survey of Embryology. 1968. text ed. 51.95 (ISBN 0-07-023208-3). McGraw.
Gilchrist, Guy & Gilchrist, Brad. Froggy Mountain Breakdown. (Muppets Ser.: No. 3). 128p. (Orig.). 1985. pap. 1.95 (ISBN 0-8125-7367-6, Dist. by Pinnacle Bks, Warner Pub Services & St. Martin). Tor Bks.
--Jim Henson's Muppets: Moving Right Along! 1984. pap. 4.95 (ISBN 0-317-14026-4, Fireside). S&S.
--Light on Our Feet. (Muppets Ser.: No. 2). 128p. (Orig.). 1984. pap. 1.95 (ISBN 0-8125-7365-X, 57365-X). Tor Bks.
--Moving Right Along: The Muppets Strip. 1984. pap. 4.95 (Fireside Bks). S&S.
--Muppets: Froggy Mountain Breakdown, No. 3. 1985. 1.95 (ISBN 0-8125-7367-6). Tor Bks.
--Short, Green & Handsome. (Muppets Ser.: No. 1). 128p. (Orig.). 1984. pap. 1.95 (ISBN 0-8125-7363-3). Tor Bks.
Gilchrist, Guy, jt. auth. see Gilchrist, Brad.
Gilchrist, Herbert H., ed. see Gilchrist, Anne.
Gilchrist, J. D. Extraction Metallurgy. 2nd ed. 1979. pap. 18.75 (ISBN 0-08-021712-5). Pergamon.
--Fuel, Furnaces & Refractories. 2nd ed. 1977. text ed. 37.00 (ISBN 0-08-020430-9); pap. text ed. 12.75 (ISBN 0-08-020429-5). Pergamon.
Gilchrist, Jack. Hidden Profits in Stamping: A Creative Materials Management Guide. LC 77-2145. 128p. 1977. 21.50 (ISBN 0-8436-0818-8). Van Nos Reinhold.
Gilchrist, Janet, jt. auth. see Richardson, R. L.
Gilchrist, Joelyn & Wood, Jacqueline. The Campus Survival Cookbook. (Illus.). 160p. 1973. pap. 5.95 (ISBN 0-688-05030-1, Quill NY). Morrow.
Gilchrist, Joelyn S., jt. auth. see Wood, Jacqueline.
Gilchrist, John, jt. auth. see McDowell, Josh.
Gilchrist, John A., jt. auth. see Griggs, Gary B.
Gilchrist, Lawson J. The World's Best Epigrams. 231p. 1980. Repr. of 1924 ed. lib. bdg. 30.00 (ISBN 0-8495-3327-9). Arden Lib.
Gilchrist, Lewayne D., jt. auth. see Schinke, Steven P.
Gilchrist, M. R., tr. see Calvin, Jean.
Gilchrist, Margaret. The Psychology of Creativity. (The Second Century in Australian Education Ser.: Vol. 4). 102p. 1972. pap. 7.50x (ISBN 0-522-84024-8, Pub. by Melbourne U Pr). Intl Spec Bk.
Gilchrist, Mrs. Mary Lamb. 1883. 25.00 (ISBN 0-932062-63-6). Sharon Hill.
Gilchrist, Octavius. Examination of the Charges Maintained by Messrs. Malone, Chalmers & Others, of Ben Jonson's Enmity - Towards Shakespeare. LC 70-168146. Repr. of 1808 ed. 11.50 (ISBN 0-404-02768-7). AMS Pr.
Gilchrist, Peter. Fight That Ticket in Ontario. 4th ed. 111p. 1980. 3.95 (ISBN 0-88908-326-6). Self Counsel Pr.
--Small Claims Court Guide for Ontario. 4th ed. 127p. 1979. 4.95 (ISBN 0-88908-322-3). Self Counsel Pr.
Gilchrist, Peter S. My Amateur World. (Illus.). 200p. 1975. text ed. 10.00 (ISBN 0-917122-01-1). Gilchem Corp.
--Someday I'll Travel. LC 80-85057. (Illus.). 200p. 1980. text ed. 20.00 (ISBN 0-917122-02-X). Gilchem Corp.
Gilchrist, R., ed. GLIM 82: Proceedings of the International Conference on Generalized Linear Models, 1982. (Lecture Notes in Statistics: Vol. 14). (Illus.). 188p. 1982. pap. 14.00 (ISBN 0-387-90777-7). Springer-Verlag.
Gilchrist, R. M. The Stone Dragon & Other Tragic Romances. LC 82-49096. (Degeneration & Regeneration Ser.). 216p. 1984. lib. bdg. 30.00 (ISBN 0-8240-5554-3). Garland Pub.
Gilchrist, Robert S. & Roberts, Bernice R. Curriculum Development: A Humanized Systems Approach. LC 72-93705. 1974. pap. 4.95 (ISBN 0-8224-1687-5). Pitman Learning.
Gilchrist, Rupert. Dragonard Blood. 1977. 11.95 (ISBN 0-285-62283-8, Pub. by Souvenir Pr). Intl Spec Bk.
--The House at Three O'Clock. (Slaves Without Masters Ser.: Vol. 1). 232p. 1983. 13.95 (ISBN 0-285-62516-0, Pub. by Souvenir Pr). Intl Spec Bk.
--Master of Dragonard Hill. 1977. 10.95 (ISBN 0-285-62223-4, Pub. by Souvenir Pr). Intl Spec Bk.
Gilchrist, T. L. & Rees, C. W. Carbenes, Nitrenes, & Arynes. 131p. 1969. pap. 12.50x (ISBN 0-306-50026-4, Plenum Pr). Plenum Pub.
Gilchrist, T. L. & Storr, R. C. Organic Reactions & Orbital Symmetry. 2nd ed. LC 78-54578. (Cambridge Texts in Chemistry & Biochemistry Ser.). (Illus.). 1979. 75.00 (ISBN 0-521-22014-9); pap. 24.95 (ISBN 0-521-29336-7). Cambridge U Pr.
Gilchrist, Theo E. Halfway up the Mountain. LC 77-29020. (Illus.). (gr. k-2). 1978. 8.89 (ISBN 0-397-31805-7). Lipp Jr Bks.
Gilchrist, W. Statistical Modelling. 300p. 1985. 29.95 (ISBN 0-471-90380-9). Wiley.
Gilchrist, W. & Murray, W. J., eds. Press in the French Revolution. LC 77-150256. 1971. 47.50x (ISBN 0-89197-596-9). Irvington.
Gild, David C. Mayor of Casterbridge Notes. (Orig.). 1966. pap. 2.75 (ISBN 0-8220-0816-5). Cliffs.
Gildart, R. C. Montana's Missouri River. (Montana Geographic Ser.). (Illus.). 104p. (Orig.). 1984. 13.95 (ISBN 0-938314-10-6). MT Mag.
Gildart, R. C. & Wassink, Jan. Montana Wildlife. (Montana Geographic Ser.: No. 3). (Illus.). 128p. 1982. pap. 12.95 (ISBN 0-938314-04-1). MT Mag.
Gildas. De Excidio Brittaniae. Giles, J. A., tr. from Lat. pap. 6.95 (ISBN 0-686-25501-1). British Am Bks.
--Gildas: The Ruin of Britain & Other Works. Winterbottom, Michael, ed. 162p. 1978. 16.00x (ISBN 0-8476-6079-6). Rowman.
Gildea, Joan H., jt. auth. see Zimmerman, Sol S.
Gildea, Joseph, ed. see Gregory the Great.
Gildea, Sr. Marianna. Expressions of Religious Thought & Feeling in the Chansons De Geste. LC 75-94172. (Catholic University of America Studies in Romance Languages & Literatures Ser: No. 25). 1969. Repr. of 1943 ed. 30.00 (ISBN 0-404-50325-X). AMS Pr.
Gildea, Ray, Jr. Arsenic & Old Lead: A Layman's Guide to Pollution & Conservation. LC 74-17509. 1975. pap. 2.00 (ISBN 0-87805-065-5). U Pr of Miss.
Gildea, Robert. Education in Provincial France, 1800-1914: A Study of Three Departments. (Illus.). 1983. 55.00x (ISBN 0-19-821941-5). Oxford U Pr.
Gildea, Robert L. Meeting the Media. 1983. 25.00 (ISBN 0-318-04489-7, MTMD). Bank MKTG Assn.
Gildenberg, ed. see International Symposium on Radiofrequency Lesion Making Procedures, Chicago, Nov. 19, 1976.
Gildenberg, P. L. The Chronic Pain Patient. DeVaul, R. A., ed. (Pain & Headache Ser.: Vol. 7). (Illus.). viii, 148p. 1984. 27.00 (ISBN 3-8055-3911-8). S Karger.
Gildenberg, P. L., ed. Safety & Clinical Efficacy of Implanted Neuroaugmentive Devices. (Applied Neurophysiology: Vol. 40, Nos. 2-4). (Illus.). 1978. pap. 24.75 (ISBN 3-8055-2925-2). S Karger.
--Symposium of the International Society for Research in Stereoencephalotomy, 7th, Sao Paulo, June 24, 1977. (Advances in Stereoencephalotomy: Vol. 8). (Illus.). 1978. pap. 41.75 (ISBN 3-8055-2946-5). S Karger.
Gildenberg, P. L. & Long, D. M., eds. Seminar on Spinal Cord Stimulation for the Control of Pain & other Neurological Disorders. (Journal-Applied Neurophysiology: Vol. 44, No. 4). (Illus.). vi, 84p. 1982. pap. 21.00 (ISBN 3-8055-3531-7). S Karger.
Gildenberg, P. L, ed. see International Symposium on Stereoencephalotomy Research, 6th, Tokyo, October 1973.
Gildenberg, P. L., et al, eds. Neural Prosthesis & Neurostimulation. (Applied Neurophysiology: Vol. 45, No. 1-2). (Illus.). iv, 208p. 1981. pap. 33.25 (ISBN 3-8055-3500-7). S Karger.
Gildenberg, P. L., et al, eds. see World Society for Stereotactic & Functional Neurosurgery, 8th Meeting, Zurich, July 1981 & European Society for Stereotactic & Functional Neurosurgery, 5th Meeting, Zurich, July, 1981.
Gildenberg, Ph. L., ed. Proceedings of the Third International Meeting on Spinal Cord Stimulation. (Illus.). 176p. 1981. pap. 44.75 (ISBN 3-8055-3462-0). S Karger.
Gildenberg, Ph. L., ed. see Annual Meeting of the Japanese Society for Stereotactic & Functional Neurosurgery, 15th, Maebashi, October 1976.
Gildenberg, Philip L., jt. ed. see Grossman, Robert G.
Gilder, Cornelia B. Preservation for Profit: Ten Case Studies in Commercial Rehabilitation. (Illus.). 27p. (Orig.). 1980. pap. 3.00 (ISBN 0-942000-02-1). Pres League NYS.
Gilder, Eric & Port, June G. The Dictionary of Composers & Their Music: Every Listener's Companion. 432p. 1978. 15.00 (ISBN 0-87196-318-3). Facts on File.
Gilder, George. The Spirit of Enterprise. 1984. 17.95 (ISBN 0-671-45482-X). S&S.
--Visible Man. LC 77-20411. 1978. 12.50 (ISBN 0-465-09041-9). Basic.
--Wealth & Poverty. LC 80-50556. 1981. 19.95 (ISBN 0-465-09105-9). Basic.
Gilder, J. B., jt. auth. see Gilder, J. L.
Gilder, J. L. & Gilder, J. B. Authors at Home. 1973. Repr. of 1888 ed. 25.00 (ISBN 0-8274-0732-7). R West.
Gilder, Jamison, ed. Modernizing State Policies: Community Colleges & Lifelong Education. (Orig.). 1981. pap. 7.50 (ISBN 0-87117-107-4). Am Assn Comm Jr Coll.
--Policies for Lifelong Education. 1979. pap. 5.00 (ISBN 0-87117-091-4). Am Assn Comm Jr Coll.
Gilder, Joseph B., ed. American Idea. LC 74-109139. (Granger Index Reprint Ser.). 1902. 18.00 (ISBN 0-8369-6123-4). Ayer Co Pubs.
Gilder, Jules. More Telephone Accessories You Can Build. 129p. 1981. 6.50 (ISBN 0-686-98104-9). Telecom Lib.
--One Hundred & Ten IC Timer Projects. 1979. pap. 6.95 (ISBN 0-8104-5688-5). Hayden.
--Telephone Accessories You Can Build. (Illus.). 1976. pap. 7.25 (ISBN 0-8104-5748-2). Hayden.
Gilder, Jules H. Apple IIc & IIe Assembly Language. 220p. 1985. pap. 18.95 (ISBN 0-412-01121-2, 9667). Methuen Inc.
--BASIC Computer Programs in Science & Engineering. 256p. 1980. pap. 10.95 (ISBN 0-8104-0761-2); 2 apple disks 39.95 incl. Hayden.
--IBM Programs in Science & Engineering. 256p. pap. 16.95 (6356). Hayden.
--Telephone Accessories You Can Build. 84p. 1976. 7.25 (ISBN 0-686-98103-0). Telecom Lib.
Gilder, Jules H. & Barrus, J. Scott. Pascal Programs in Science & Engineering. 2nd ed. 384p. pap. 18.95 (6265). Hayden.
Gilder, Richard W. Letters of Richard Watson Gilder. 26.25 (ISBN 0-8369-7137-X, 7970). Ayer Co Pubs.
Gilder, Rosamond. Enter the Actress. facs. ed. LC 74-134081. (Essay Index Reprint Ser.). 1931. 24.50 (ISBN 0-8369-2158-5). Ayer Co Pubs.
--Enter the Actress: The First Women in the Theatre. (Illus.). 1959. pap. write for info. (ISBN 0-87830-502-5). Theatre Arts.
--John Gielgud's Hamlet: a Record of Performance. facsimile ed. LC 79-148882. (Select Bibliographies Reprint Ser). Repr. of 1937 ed. 18.00 (ISBN 0-8369-5675-3). Ayer Co Pubs.
Gilder, Rosamond & Freedley, George. Theatre Collections in Libraries & Museums, an International Handbook. (Library of Literature, Drama & Criticism). 1970. Repr. of 1936 ed. 18.00 (ISBN 0-384-18487-1). Johnson Repr.
Gilder, Rosamond, tr. see Calve, Emma.
Gilder, William H. Ice-Pack & Tundra: An Account of the Search for the Jeanette & a Sledge Journey Through Siberia. LC 74-5838. Repr. of 1883 ed. 24.00 (ISBN 0-404-11643-4). AMS Pr.
--Schwatka's Search: Sledging in the Arctic in Quest of the Franklin Records. LC 74-5839. Repr. of 1881 ed. 24.00 (ISBN 0-404-11644-2). AMS Pr.
Gilderbloom, John & Keating, Dennis. An Evaluation of Rent Control in Orange. 110p. 1983. 50.00 (ISBN 0-686-46771-X). Foun Natl Prog.
Gilderbloom, John I., et al, eds. Rent Control: A Source Book. 2nd ed. LC 80-70624. 320p. 1981. 11.95 (ISBN 0-938806-01-7). Foun Natl Prog.
Gilderhus, Mark T. Diplomacy & Revolution: U. S. - Mexican Relations Under Wilson & Carranza. LC 76-26388. 159p. 1977. 14.95x (ISBN 0-8165-0630-2); pap. 5.95x (ISBN 0-8165-0561-6). U of Ariz Pr.
Gildersleeve, B. L. The Creed of the Old South. 59.95 (ISBN 0-87968-961-7). Gordon Pr.
Gildersleeve, Basil L. Essays & Studies. (American Studies). 1968. Repr. of 1890 ed. 35.00 (ISBN 0-384-18501-0). Johnson Repr.
--Syntax of Classical Greek from Homer to Demosthenes: First Part-The Syntax of the Simple Sentence Embracing the Doctrine of the Moods & TENSES, Second Part-The Syntax of Simple Sentence Continued Embracing the Doctrine of the Article. x, 332p. 1980. Repr. of 1867 ed. 38.00x (ISBN 0-317-19840-8, Pub. by Boumas Boekhuis Netherlands). Benjamins North AM.
Gildersleeve, Basil L. & Lodge, G. Latin Grammar. 3rd ed. 1895. 19.95 (ISBN 0-312-47355-9). St Martin.
Gildersleeve, Basil L., ed. see Persius.
Gildersleeve, Basil L., ed. see Pindarus.
Gildersleeve, T. R., jt. auth. see Laden, Hyman N.
Gildersleeve, Thomas. Data Processing Project Management. 330p. 1974. 19.95 (ISBN 0-442-25309-5); pap. 18.95 (ISBN 0-442-22824-4). Van Nos Reinhold.
Gildersleeve, Thomas R. Organizing & Documenting Data Processing Information. 1977. pap. text ed. 10.95x (ISBN 0-8104-5739-3). Hayden.
Gildersleeve, Thomas R. & Reynolds, Dean W. Data Processing Project Management. 2nd ed. (Illus.). 224p. 1985. 29.95 (ISBN 0-442-22851-1). Van Nos Reinhold.
Gildersleeve, Virginia C. Government Regulation of the Elizabethan Drama. LC 75-7238. 259p. 1975. Repr. of 1961 ed. lib. bdg. 18.75x (ISBN 0-8371-8097-X, GIGR). Greenwood.
--Many a Good Crusade. LC 79-8795. (Signal Lives Ser.). (Illus.). 1980. Repr. of 1954 ed. lib. bdg. 46.00x (ISBN 0-405-12841-X). Ayer Co Pubs.
Gildin, Hilail. Rousseau's Social Contract: The Design of the Argument. LC 82-20148. 240p. 1983. lib. bdg. 22.50x (ISBN 0-226-29368-8); pap. 7.95 (ISBN 0-226-29369-6). U of Chicago Pr.
Gildner, Gary. Blue Like the Heavens: New & Selected Poems. LC 83-19746. (Pitt Poetry Ser.). 155p. 1984. 14.95x (ISBN 0-8229-3490-6); pap. 6.95 (ISBN 0-8229-5358-7). U of Pittsburgh Pr.
--The Crush. 175p. 1983. 11.50 (ISBN 0-88001-032-0). Ecco Pr.

--Digging for Indians. LC 77-158183. (Pitt Poetry Ser.). 1971. 12.95 (ISBN 0-8229-3230-X); pap. 5.95 (ISBN 0-8229-5224-6). U of Pittsburgh Pr.
--First Practice. LC 72-78533. (Pitt Poetry Ser). 1969. 12.95 (ISBN 0-8229-3179-6); pap. 5.95 (ISBN 0-8229-5208-4). U of Pittsburgh Pr.
--Letters from Vicksburg. LC 75-43072. (Illus.). 1976. 10.00 (ISBN 0-87775-096-3); pap. 4.00 (ISBN 0-87775-097-1). Unicorn Pr.
--Nails. LC 74-17528. (Pitt Poetry Ser.). 1975. 12.95 (ISBN 0-8229-3293-8); pap. 5.95 (ISBN 0-8229-5257-2). U of Pittsburgh Pr.
--The Runner. LC 77-14692. (Pitt Poetry Ser.). 1978. ltd. ed. o.p. 20.00x (ISBN 0-8229-3361-6); pap. 5.95 (ISBN 0-8229-5291-2). U of Pittsburgh Pr.
Gildner, Gary & Gildner, Judith, eds. Out of This World: Poems from the Hawkeye State. 1975. 5.50 (ISBN 0-8138-1255-0). Iowa St U Pr.
Gildner, Judith, jt. ed. see Gildner, Gary.
Gildon, Charles. The Deist's Manual; or a Rational Enquiry into the Christian Religion. Wellek, Rene, ed. LC 75-11220. (British Philosophers & Theologians of the 17th & 18th Centuries: Vol. 23). 1976. Repr. of 1705 ed. lib. bdg. 51.00 (ISBN 0-8240-1774-9). Garland Pub.
--Life of Mr. Thomas Betterton: The Late Eminent Tragedian, (18th Century Shakespeare, Vol. 4. 279p. 1970. Repr. of 1710 ed. 27.50x (ISBN 0-7146-2517-5, F Cass Co). Biblio Dist.
--The Plays of Charles Gildon. Backscheider, Paula R., ed. LC 78-66609. (Eighteenth-Century English Drama Ser.: Vol. 17). 1979. lib. bdg. 73.00 (ISBN 0-8240-3591-7). Garland Pub.
Gildon, Charles see Dennis, John.
Gildrie, Richard P. Salem, Massachusetts, Sixteen Twenty-Six to Sixteen Eighty-Three: A Covenant Community. LC 74-20841. (Illus.). 187p. 1975. 17.50x (ISBN 0-8139-0532-X). U Pr of Va.
Gildzen, Alex. A Year Book. 150p. (Orig.). 1975. pap. 3.00 (ISBN 0-913028-27-4). North Atlantic.
Gile, Lehand H. Soils & Stratigraphy of Dunes along a Segment of Farm Road, 1731 Bailey County, Texas. 78p. 1981. 3.00 (ISBN 0-318-17667-X, 81-2). Intl Ctr Arid & Semi-Arid.
Gilead, Zerubavel & Krook, Dorothea. Gideon's Spring. 1985. 19.95 (ISBN 0-89919-308-0). Ticknor & Fields.
Gileadi, Avraham. The Apocalyptic Book of Isaiah. Gileadi, Avraham, tr. 206p. (Hebrew.). 1982. 9.95 (ISBN 0-910511-00-4). Hebraeus Pr.
Gileadi, Eliezer, ed. Electrosorption. LC 67-15143. 221p. 1967. 35.00x (ISBN 0-306-30283-7, Plenum Pr). Plenum Pub.
Giler, S., jt. auth. see Kaplan, I.
Giles. Cardiomyopathy. 1986. price not set (ISBN 0-88416-464-0). PSG Pub Co.
Giles, A. B. & Wood, D. H. Oakwood Salt Dome, East Texas: Geologic Framework, Growth History, & Hydrocarbon Production. (Geological Circular Ser.: GC 83-1). (Illus.). 55p. 1983. 2.50 (ISBN 0-318-03156-6). Bur Econ Geology.
Giles, A. D., jt. auth. see Snelling, E. C.
Giles, Anne E. Merwan: Stories of Meher Baba for Children. LC 80-53858. (Illus.). 96p. (Orig.). (gr. 3-7). 1980. pap. 4.95 (ISBN 0-913078-41-7). Sheriar Pr.
Giles, Barbara, jt. auth. see Giles, Carl.
Giles, Carl. Journalism: Dateline, the World. LC 73-76364. 160p. (YA) (gr. 9-12). 1973. PLB 8.95 (ISBN 0-8239-0269-2); student's wkbk. 1.00 (ISBN 0-8239-0271-4). Rosen Group.
Giles, Carl & Giles, Barbara. Buyer's Guide to Component TV. (Illus.). 224p. (Orig.). 1985. 19.95 (ISBN 0-8306-0881-8, 1881); pap. 12.95 (ISBN 0-8306-1881-3). TAB Bks.
--Glue It! (Illus.). 112p. (Orig.). 1984. 14.95 (ISBN 0-8306-0201-1); pap. 8.95 (ISBN 0-8306-1801-5, 1801). TAB Bks.
--Steel Homes. (Illus.). 320p. (Orig.). 1984. 21.95 (ISBN 0-8306-0641-6, 1641); pap. 15.50 (ISBN 0-8306-1641-1). TAB Bks.
--Ventilation: Your Secret Key to an Energy-Efficient Home. (Illus.). 160p. (Orig.). 1984. 15.95 (ISBN 0-8306-0681-5, 1681); pap. 8.95 (ISBN 0-8306-1681-0). TAB Bks.
Giles, Edward, ed. Documents Illustrating Papal Authority, A.D. 96-454. LC 78-59023. 1979. Repr. of 1952 ed. 28.00 (ISBN 0-88355-696-0). Hyperion Conn.
Giles, Eugene & Friedlaender, Jonathan S., eds. The Measures of Man: Methodologies in Biological Anthropology. LC 76-28638. (Peabody Museum Press Ser.). (Illus.). 1976. cloth 40.00x (ISBN 0-87365-800-0); pap. 25.00x (ISBN 0-87365-782-9). Peabody Harvard.
Giles, Eugene V., jt. auth. see Atkinson, M. Jourdan.
Giles, F. A. Herbaceous Perennials. (Illus.). 1980. text ed. 21.95 (ISBN 0-8359-2822-5). Reston.
Giles, Floyd, jt. auth. see Turgeon, A. J.
Giles, Floyd A., jt. auth. see Keith, Rebecca M.
Giles, G. B. Marketing. 4th ed. 236p. 1983. pap. text ed. 13.95x (ISBN 0-7121-2804-2). Trans-Atlantic.
Giles, G. R., jt. ed. see Cushieri, A.
Giles, Geoffrey J. Students & National Socialism in Germany. LC 85-42686. (Illus.). 384p. 1985. text ed. 47.50x (ISBN 0-691-05453-3). Princeton U Pr.
Giles, H. A. China & the Manchus. lib. bdg. 79.95 (ISBN 0-87968-519-0). Krishna Pr.
--Confucianism & Its Rivals. lib. bdg. 79.95 (ISBN 0-87968-520-4). Krishna Pr.
--The Religions of Ancient China. 59.95 (ISBN 0-8490-0941-3). Gordon Pr.
Giles, H. A., tr. see Fa-hsien, Fl.
Giles, H. H. & McCutchen, S. P. Exploring the Curriculum. Zechiel, A. N., ed. 362p. 1981. Repr. of 1942 ed. lib. bdg. 30.00 (ISBN 0-89760-317-6). Telegraph Bks.
Giles, Haywood D. Out of My Tree. LC 81-82694. 276p. 1982. 15.95 (ISBN 0-8022-2396-6). Philos Lib.
Giles, Henry. Illustrations of Genius (Cervantes, Wordsworth, Burns, De Quincey) 1854. Repr. 35.00 (ISBN 0-8274-2555-4). R West.
--Illustrations of Genius, in Some of Its Relations to Culture & Society. 1979. Repr. of 1854 ed. lib. bdg. 35.00 (ISBN 0-8414-4599-0). Folcroft.
--Illustrations of Genius: In Some of Its Relations to Culture & Society. 15.75 (ISBN 0-8369-7254-6, 8053). Ayer Co Pubs.
Giles, Henry & Giles, Janice H. Harbin's Ridge. 14.95 (ISBN 0-88411-643-3, Pub. by Aeonian Pr). Amereon Ltd.
Giles, Herbert. Chuang-Tzu: Taoist Philosopher & Chinese Mystic. 1961. 14.95 (ISBN 0-04-299002-5). Allen Unwin.
--A History of Chinese Literature. 1973. Repr. of 1923 ed. 40.00 (ISBN 0-8274-0731-9). R West.
Giles, Herbert A. China & the Chinese. 1902. 25.00 (ISBN 0-686-19903-0). Quaker City.
--The Civilization of China. 1911. Repr. 20.00 (ISBN 0-8274-2064-1). R West.
--The Classical History of Chinese Literature, 3 vols. 455p. 1985. Set. 187.45 (ISBN 0-86650-147-9). Gloucester Art.
--Confucianism & Its Rivals. LC 77-27155. (Hibbert Lectures: 1914). Repr. of 1915 ed. 24.50 (ISBN 0-404-60416-1). AMS Pr.
--A Glossary of Reference on Subjects Connected with the Far East. 328p. 1978. Repr. 11.50 (ISBN 0-89684-134-0, Pub. by Cosmo Pubns India). Orient Bk Dist.
--A Glossary of Reference on Subjects Connected with the Far East. 3rd ed. 328p. 1974. Repr. of 1900 ed. 16.50x (ISBN 0-87471-510-5). Rowman.
--The Growth & Glories of Chinese Literature, 2 vols. 1985. Set. 197.75 (ISBN 0-89266-533-5). Am Classical Coll Pr.
--Religions of Ancient China. LC 79-95067. (Select Bibliographies Reprint Ser). 1905. 17.00 (ISBN 0-8369-5069-0). Ayer Co Pubs.
--Religions of Ancient China. LC 76-20524. 1976. Repr. of 1905 ed. lib. bdg. 17.00 (ISBN 0-8414-4518-4). Folcroft.
Giles, Herbert A., tr. from Chinese. Chuang Tzu. (Unwin Paperbacks Ser.). 336p. (Orig.). 1980. pap. 7.50 (ISBN 0-04-299009-2). Allen Unwin.
Giles, Herbert A., tr. see Chuang Tzu.
Giles, Herbert G. A History of Chinese Literature. LC 73-77576. 1973. pap. 5.95 (ISBN 0-8048-1097-4). C E Tuttle.
Giles, Howard. Language & Social Psychology. (Illus.). 272p. 1979. text ed. 27.00 (ISBN 0-8391-1356-0). Univ Park.
Giles, Howard & Powesland, Peter. Speech Style & Social Evaluation. (European Monographs in Social Psychology Ser.). 1975. 39.00 (ISBN 0-12-283750-9). Acad Pr.
Giles, Howard & Robinson, W. Peter. Language: Social Psychological Perspectives: Selected Papers from the First International Conference on Social Psychology & Language Held at the University of Bristol, England, July 1979. Smith, Philip M., ed. LC 80-40714. 450p. 1980. 72.00 (ISBN 0-08-024696-6). Pergamon.
Giles, Howard & Saint-Jacques, Bernard. Language & Ethnic Relations: Language & Ethnic Interaction Section of the Sociolinguistics Program of the 9th World Congress of Sociology. LC 79-40709. (Illus.). 1979. 39.00 (ISBN 0-08-023720-7). Pergamon.
Giles, Howard, jt. auth. see Ryan, Ellen B.
Giles, Howard & St. Clair, R. N., eds. Recent Advances in Language, Communication & Social Psychology. 256p. 1985. text ed. 34.95 (ISBN 0-86377-000-2). L Erlbaum Assocs.
Giles, Howard, jt. ed. see St. Clair, Robert N.
Giles, Howard, jt. ed. see Scherer, Klaus R.
Giles, Howard, jt. ed. see Turner, John G.
Giles, J. A. Memorials of King Alfred. 1863. 45.00 (ISBN 0-8274-2711-5). R West.
Giles, J. A., ed. Six Old English Chronicles. LC 68-57866. (Bohn's Antiquarian Library Ser). Repr. of 1848 ed. 27.50 (ISBN 0-404-50010-2). AMS Pr.
Giles, J. A., ed. see Alan Of Tewkesbury.
Giles, J. A., ed. see Alfred The Great.
Giles, J. A., ed. see Ascham, Roger.
Giles, J. A., ed. see William Of Malmesbury.
Giles, J. A., tr. see Gildas.
Giles, J. A., tr. see Nennius.
Giles, J. A., tr. see Paris, Matthew.
Giles, J. A., tr. see Roger Of Wendover.
Giles, J. E. Bases Biblicas De la Etica. 1979. Repr. of 1977 ed. 4.25 (ISBN 0-311-46028-3). Casa Bautista.
Giles, J. R. Convex Analysis with Application in the Differentiation of Convex Functions. (Research Notes in Mathematics Ser.: No. 58). 170p. (Orig.). 1982. pap. text ed. 22.95 (ISBN 0-273-08537-9). Pitman Pub MA.
Giles, James E. Esto Creemos los Bautistas. 111p. 1981. pap. 2.50 (ISBN 0-311-09091-5). Casa Bautista.
--Medical Ethics: A Patient-Centered Approach. 224p. 1983. 18.95 (ISBN 0-87073-314-1); pap. 11.95 (ISBN 0-87073-315-X). Schenkman Bks Inc.
--Pastoral Care & Counselling. pap. text ed. 10.95 (ISBN 0-311-72535-X). Casa Bautista.
--La Psicologia y el Ministerio Cristiano. 384p. 1982. Repr. of 1978 ed. 3.20 (ISBN 0-311-42059-1). Casa Bautista.
Giles, James R. Claude McKay. LC 76-10154. (United States Authors Ser.: No. 271). 1976. lib. bdg. 12.50 (ISBN 0-8057-7171-9, Twayne). G K Hall.
--Irwin Shaw. (United States Authors Ser.). 1983. lib. bdg. 14.50 (ISBN 0-8057-7382-7, Twayne). G K Hall.
--James Jones. (United States Authors Ser.). 1981. lib. bdg. 13.50 (ISBN 0-8057-7293-6, Twayne). G K Hall.
Giles, Janet H. The Enduring Hills. 1984. lib. bdg. 17.50 (ISBN 0-8161-3648-3, Large Print Bks). G K Hall.
Giles, Janice H. The Believers. 1976. pap. 1.75 (ISBN 0-380-00666-9, 29322). Avon.
--Forty Acres & No Mule. 1967. 7.95 (ISBN 0-395-07736-2). HM.
--The Great Adventure. 1976. pap. 1.75 (ISBN 0-380-00727-4, 30007). Avon.
--Johnny Osage. 1977. pap. 1.75 (ISBN 0-380-01810-1, 35667). Avon.
--The Kinta Years. 1973. 7.95 (ISBN 0-395-14011-0). HM.
--The Land Beyond the Mountain. 17.95 (ISBN 0-88411-644-1, Pub. by Aeonian Pr.). Amereon Ltd.
--The Land Beyond the Mountains. new ed. LC 58-9062. 308p. 1974. 15.95 (ISBN 0-910220-62-X). Berg.
--The Plum Thicket. (General Ser.). 1984. lib. bdg. 17.95 (ISBN 0-8161-3647-5, Large Print Bks). G K Hall.
--Shady Grove. LC 78-12454. 260p. 1978. Repr. of 1968 ed. 16.00 (ISBN 0-89783-002-4). Larlin Corp.
--Voyage to Santa Fe. 1977. pap. 1.75 (ISBN 0-380-00965-X, 32417-2). Avon.
--Wellspring. LC 75-15989. 272p. 1975. 8.95 (ISBN 0-395-20731-2). HM.
Giles, Janice H., jt. auth. see Giles, Henry.
Giles, John A. Scriptores Rerum Gestarum Willelmi Conquestoris. 1966. 24.00 (ISBN 0-8337-1348-5). B Franklin.
Giles, John A., ed. Benedicti Abbatis Petriburgensis De Vita et Miraculis S. Thomae Cantuar. Repr. of 1850 ed. 24.00 (ISBN 0-8337-1341-8). B Franklin.
--Chronicon Angliae Petriburgense. 1966. Repr. of 1845 ed. 24.00 (ISBN 0-8337-1342-6). B Franklin.
--Memorials of King Alfred, Being Essays on the History & Antiquities of England During the 9th Century, the Age of King Alfred. (Research & Source Works Ser: No. 287). 1969. Repr. of 1863 ed. 26.00 (ISBN 0-8337-1346-9). B Franklin.
--Revolte Du Conte De Warwick Contre le Roi Edward 4e. (Fr). 1849. 24.00 (ISBN 0-8337-1347-7). B Franklin.
--Vita Quorundum Anglo-Saxonum: Original Lives of Anglo-Saxons Who Lived Before the Conquest. 1966. Repr. of 1854 ed. 24.00 (ISBN 0-8337-1349-3). B Franklin.
Giles, John A., ed. see Baker, Geoffrey.
Giles, John A., ed. see Bede the Venerable.
Giles, John A., ed. see Geoffrey Of Monmouth.
Giles, John A., tr. see De Lion, Gwoffrey, et al.
Giles, Katherine. A Share of Earth & Glory. 528p. 1982. pap. 3.50 (ISBN 0-515-04756-2). Jove Pubns.
Giles, Ken & Smith, Clive. Match Fishing Our Way. 1978. 13.50 (ISBN 0-7153-7692-6). David & Charles.
Giles, Kenneth. Death among the Stars. (Walker British Paperback Mysteries Ser.). 192p. 1985. pap. 2.95 (ISBN 0-8027-3112-0). Walker & Co.
--Death & Mr. Prettyman. 1984. pap. 2.95 (ISBN 0-8027-3086-8). Walker & Co.
--Death Cracks a Bottle. 1985. pap. 2.95 (ISBN 0-8027-3119-8). Walker & Co.
--A File on Death. 1985. pap. 2.95 (ISBN 0-8027-3103-1). Walker & Co.
--Murder Pluperfect. 1984. pap. 2.95 (ISBN 0-8027-3094-9). Walker & Co.
--Some Beasts No More. (Walker British Paperback Mysteries Ser.). 1985. pap. 2.95 (ISBN 0-8027-3144-9). Walker & Co.
Giles, Kenneth, jt. ed. see Bourne, Geoffrey.
Giles, Kenneth L. & Sen, S. K., eds. Plant Cell Culture in Crop Improvement. (Basic Life Sciences Ser.: Vol. 22). 514p. 1982. 65.00x (ISBN 0-306-41160-1, Plenum Pr). Plenum Pub.
Giles, Lancelot. Siege of the Peking Legations: A Diary. 1970. 18.50x (ISBN 0-85564-041-3, Pub. by U of W Austral Pr). Intl Spec Bk.
Giles, Lionel, tr. from Chinese. A Gallery of Chinese Immortals: Selected Biographies Translated from Chinese Sources. LC 75-36229. Repr. of 1948 ed. 10.50 (ISBN 0-404-14478-0). AMS Pr.
Giles, Lionel, jt. tr. see Johnston, Charles.
Giles, Lionel, tr. see Mencius.
Giles, Llewellyn I. Songs from My Father's Pockets. (Illus.). 64p. 1983. pap. 4.50 perf. bound (ISBN 0-937724-01-7). Shadow Pr.
Giles, Lucille. Color Me Brown. rev. ed. (Illus.). 47p. (gr. k-6). 1974. pap. 3.00 (ISBN 0-87485-017-7). Johnson Chi.
Giles, M. A., tr. see Fa-hsien, Fl.
Giles, Marsha J. & Conway, Joyce E. Beat the Supermarket Blues & Eat Well Too: Grocery Shopping to Save Dollars. (Illus.). 139p. (Orig.). 1984. pap. 9.95 (ISBN 0-916739-00-7). Purpose Bks.
Giles, Mary. Francisco de Osuna: The Third Spiritual Alphabet, Vol 1. (Classics of Western Spirtuality Ser.). 1982. 16.95 (ISBN 0-8091-0266-8); pap. 11.95 (ISBN 0-8091-2145-X). Paulist Pr.
Giles, Mary E. The Feminist Mystic & Other Essays on Women & Spirituality. 208p. 1982. pap. 8.95 (ISBN 0-8245-0432-1). Crossroad NY.
Giles, Molly. Rough Translations: Stories. LC 84-16363. 135p. 1985. 13.95 (ISBN 0-8203-0744-0). U of Ga Pr.
Giles, Raymond. Dark Master. 224p. 1978. pap. 2.50 (ISBN 0-449-13622-1, GM). Fawcett.
--Hellcat of Sabrehill. 384p. (Orig.). 1983. pap. 3.50 (ISBN 0-449-12382-0, GM). Fawcett.
--Rebels of Sabrehill. 1977. pap. 2.75 (ISBN 0-449-13695-7, GM). Fawcett.
--Rogue Black. 208p. 1978. pap. 2.25 (ISBN 0-449-13809-7, GM). Fawcett.
--Sabrehill. 1978. pap. 2.50 (ISBN 0-449-13956-5, GM). Fawcett.
--Slaves of Sabrehill. 1978. pap. 2.95 (ISBN 0-449-13970-0, GM). Fawcett.
--Storm over Sabrehill. 1978. pap. 2.95 (ISBN 0-449-14018-0, GM). Fawcett.
Giles, Robert, jt. auth. see Wells, Larry.
Giles, Robert H., Jr. Wildlife Management. LC 78-15700. (Animal Science Ser.). (Illus.). 416p. 1978. text ed. 29.95 (ISBN 0-7167-0082-4). W H Freeman.
Giles, Robert L. Layout of E. H. V. Substations. LC 73-132285. (Institution of Electrical Engineers, IEE Monograph Ser.: No. 5). pap. 59.30 (ISBN 0-317-08132-2, 2004345). Bks Demand UMI.
Giles, Ronald V. Fluid Mechanics & Hydraulics. (Schaum's Outline Ser). (Orig.). 1962. pap. 9.95 (ISBN 0-07-023234-2). McGraw.
Giles, Thomas, jt. auth. see McMullin, Rian.
Giles, Tony & Stansfeld, Malcolm. The Farmer As Manager. (Illus., Orig.). 1980. text ed. 25.00x (ISBN 0-04-658228-2); pap. text ed. 10.50x (ISBN 0-04-658229-0). Allen Unwin.
Giles, Yvonne, jt. auth. see Stover, Patricia.
Giles Of Rome. Giles of Rome: Errores Philosophorum. Riedl, John C., tr. 1944. 7.95 (ISBN 0-87462-429-0); price not set med phil texts. Marquette.
--Giles of Rome: Theorems on Existence & Essence. Murray, Michael V., tr. (Medieval Philosophical Texts in Translation: No. 7). 1953. pap. 7.95 (ISBN 0-87462-207-7). Marquette.
Giles-Sims, Jean. Wife Battering: A Systems Theory Approach. (Perspectives on Marriage & the Family Ser.). 197p. 1983. 17.50 (ISBN 0-89862-075-9, 2075). Guilford Pr.
Gilev, Vladimir P. My Dear Fifteen Dollars, Not for the World Would I Part with You. LC 85-71311. 148p. (Orig.). 1985. pap. 10.95 (ISBN 0-931494-73-7). Brunswick Pub.
Gilfillan, George. Modern Literature & Literary Men, Being a Second Gallery of Literary Portraits. 376p. 1984. Repr. of 1849 ed. lib. bdg. 85.00 (ISBN 0-89760-256-0). Telegraph Bks.
--The Poetical Works of Johnson, Parnell, Gray & Smollett. 254p. 1981. Repr. of 1855 ed. lib. bdg. 40.00 (ISBN 0-89760-318-4). Telegraph Bks.
Gilfillan, Harriet W. I Went to Pit College. LC 74-25389. (The Labor Movement in Fiction & Non-Fiction Ser.). Repr. of 1934 ed. 21.50 (ISBN 0-404-58494-2). AMS Pr.
Gilfillan, Merrill. Light Years: Selected Early Works, 1969-1972. LC 76-58864. (Selected Works Ser.: No. 1). 1977. pap. 4.95 (ISBN 0-912652-30-6, Dynamite Books). Blue Wind.
--To Creature. LC 75-9973. 40p. 1975. pap. 3.95 (ISBN 0-912652-12-8). Blue Wind.
Gilfillan, Robert. Poems & Songs. 4th ed. LC 79-144465. Repr. of 1851 ed. 16.00 (ISBN 0-404-08556-3). AMS Pr.
Gilfillan, S. C. Sociology of Invention. 1970. pap. 4.95x (ISBN 0-262-57020-3). MIT Pr.
Gilfillian, George, ed. see Beattie, James.
Gilfond, Henry. Countries of the Sahara. LC 80-2269. (First Bks.). (Illus.). (gr. 4 up). 1981. PLB 8.90 (ISBN 0-531-04271-5). Watts.
--The Exective Branch of the U. S. Government. LC 80-25729. (First Books About Washington Ser.). (gr. 4 up). 1981. PLB 8.90 (ISBN 0-531-04251-0). Watts.
--Favorite Short Stories. (gr. 5 up). 4.50 (ISBN 0-8027-6023-6). Walker & Co.
--Gambia Ghana Libia. LC 80-23043. (First Bks.). (gr. 4 up). 1981. PLB 8.90 (ISBN 0-531-04274-X). Watts.
--Heroines of America. LC 74-118207. (Heroes of Ser.). (Illus.). (gr. 7-12). 1970. 7.95 (ISBN 0-8303-0105-4). Fleet.

Gill, Jack C., et al. Competency in College Mathematics. 3rd ed. LC 84-147965. (Illus.). 514p. (Orig.). 1983. pap. text ed. 19.95x (ISBN 0-943202-09-4). H & H Pub.

Gill, Jean. Images of My Self: Meditation & Self-Exploration Through the Imagery of the Gospels. 128p. 1982. pap. 3.95 (ISBN 0-8091-2463-7). Paulist Pr.

--Unless You Become Like a Child: The Role of the Inner Child in Our Spiritual Journey. 96p. (Orig.). 1985. pap. 4.95 (ISBN 0-8091-2717-2). Paulist Pr.

Gill, Jerry H. Essays on Kierkegaard. LC 72-88030. pap. 52.00 (ISBN 0-317-08954-4, 2003458). Bks Demand UMI.

--Faith in Dialogue: A Christian Apologetic. 160p. 1985. 12.95 (ISBN 0-8499-0495-1, 0495-1). Word Bks.

--Metaphilosophy: An Introduction. LC 82-40230. (Orig.). 1982. pap. text ed. 7.50 (ISBN 0-8191-2650-0). U Pr of Amer.

--On Knowing God. LC 81-10481. 174p. 1981. pap. 9.95 (ISBN 0-664-24380-0). Westminster.

--Philosophy & Religion: Some Contemporary Perspectives. LC 68-54894. pap. 95.50 (ISBN 0-317-08950-1, 2003459). Bks Demand UMI.

--Toward Theology. LC 82-45009. 130p. (Orig.). 1982. PLB 21.50 (ISBN 0-8191-2429-X); pap. text ed. 9.00 (ISBN 0-8191-2430-3). U Pr of Amer.

--Wittgenstein & Metaphor. LC 80-5690. 246p. 1981. lib. bdg. 21.25 (ISBN 0-8191-1600-9); pap. text ed. 12.00 (ISBN 0-8191-1601-7). U Pr of Amer.

Gill, John. Cause of God & Truth. (Giant Summit Ser.). 336p. 1981. pap. 7.95 (ISBN 0-8010-3761-1). Baker Bk.

--Country Pleasures. LC 75-28398. (Selected Poets Ser.). 80p. (Orig.). 1975. 13.95 (ISBN 0-912278-60-9); pap. 6.95 (ISBN 0-912278-61-7). Crossing Pr.

--From the Diary of Peter Doyle: And Other Poems. LC 81-12770. 80p. 1982. 10.95 (ISBN 0-934184-13-5); pap. 4.50 (ISBN 0-934184-14-3). Alembic Pr.

--Reminiscenses of Four Years as a Private Soldier in the Confederate Army. 1983. Repr. of 1904 ed. 16.95 (ISBN 0-89201-108-4). Zenger Pub.

--The Tenant. 160p. 1985. 14.95 (ISBN 0-89733-142-7); pap. 3.95 (ISBN 0-89733-141-9). Academy Chi Pubs.

Gill, John, ed. For the Love of Cats: A Collection of Drawings with Writings Selected from Prose & Poetry. (Illus.). 128p. (Orig.). 1985. 15.95 (ISBN 0-89594-185-6); pap. 7.95 (ISBN 0-89594-174-0). Crossing Pr.

--New American & Canadian Poetry. 280p. 1971. pap. 7.95 (ISBN 0-8070-6409-2). Crossing Pr.

--Notices of the Jews & Their Country by the Classic Writers of Antiquity. LC 70-97281. (Judaica Ser). 180p. 1972. Repr. of 1872 ed. lib. bdg. 22.50x (ISBN 0-8371-2603-7, GINJ). Greenwood.

Gill, John & Gill, Elaine G., eds. The Proverb Book: Wit & Wisdom of the Ages. 144p. 12.95 (ISBN 0-89594-092-2); pap. 3.95 (ISBN 0-89594-093-0). Crossing Pr.

Gill, John H., ed. & afterword by see Stein, Gertrude.

Gill, John L. Design & Analysis of Experiments in the Animal & Medical Sciences, Vol. 1. (Illus.). 1978. text ed. 18.50x (ISBN 0-8138-0020-X). Iowa St U Pr.

--Design & Analysis of Experiments in the Animal & Medical Sciences, Vol. 2. (Illus.). 1978. text ed. 16.95x (ISBN 0-8138-0060-9). Iowa St U Pr.

--Design & Analysis of Experiments in the Animal & Medical Sciences, Vol. 3. (Illus.). 1978. pap. text ed. 9.95x (ISBN 0-8138-0110-9). Iowa St U Pr.

Gill, Joseph. Byzantium & the Papacy, Eleven Ninety-Eight to Fourteen Hundred. 1979. 32.00x (ISBN 0-8135-0864-9). Rutgers U Pr.

--The Council of Florence. LC 78-63345. (The Crusades & Military Orders: Second Ser.). (Illus.). 480p. Repr. of 1959 ed. 37.50 (ISBN 0-404-17016-1). AMS Pr.

Gill, Joseph B. The Great Pyramid Speaks to You. LC 82-9142. 147p. 1984. 13.95 (ISBN 0-8022-2405-9). Philos Lib.

Gill, Joseph L. Personalized Stress Management: A Manual for Everyday Life & Work. LC 82-90115. (Illus.). 175p. 1983. 14.95 (ISBN 0-910819-00-9); pap. 9.95 (ISBN 0-910819-01-7). Counsel & Consult.

Gill, Joseph O. Gill's Index to Journals, Articles, & Books Relating to Gems & Jewelry. 1978. 5.00 (ISBN 0-87311-009-9). Gemological.

Gill, K. F., jt. auth. see Schwarzenbach, J.

Gill, Kathleen D., ed. ERISA: The Law & the Code. 426p. 1985. pap. text ed. 25.00 (ISBN 0-87179-465-9). BNA.

Gill, Kathleen R. Snow on the Sea. 128p. (gr. 4-8). 1982. 7.95 (ISBN 0-89962-254-2). Todd & Honeywell.

Gill, Kay, ed. Government Research Directory: Supplement. 3rd ed. 150p. 1985. pap. 200.00x (ISBN 0-317-19641-3). Gale.

Gill, Kay, jt. ed. see Kruzas, Anthony T.

Gill, L. T., jt. auth. see Graham, Robin L.

Gill, Lafayette B. Non-Ferrous Extractive Metallurgy. LC 79-28696. 346p. 1980. 55.50x (ISBN 0-471-05980-3, Pub. by Wiley-Interscience). Wiley.

Gill, Lindy, jt. auth. see Maltby, Arthur.

Gill, M. S. Himalayan Wonderland: Travels in Lahaul-Spiti. (Illus.). 1979. 11.95x (ISBN 0-7069-0820-1, Pub. by Vikas India). Advent NY.

--Himalayan Wonderland: Travels in Lahul-Spiti. (Illus.). 1974. 7.50x (ISBN 0-7069-0820-1). Intl Bk Dist.

Gill, Manohar S. Agriculture Cooperatives: A Case Study of Punjab. viii, 560p. 1984. text ed. 45.00x (ISBN 0-7069-2371-5, Pub. by Vikas India). Advent NY.

--Folk Tales of Lahaul. 1977. 9.00x (ISBN 0-7069-0522-9). Intl Bk Dist.

Gill, Margaret A. Tunbridge Ware. (Shire Album Ser.: No. 130). (Orig.). 1985. pap. 3.50 (ISBN 0-85263-712-8, Pub. by Shire Pubns England). Seven Hills Bks.

Gill, Margaret B. The Miracle of Love. 48p. 1985. 6.95 (ISBN 0-89962-438-3). Todd & Honeywell.

Gill, Marilyn, jt. auth. see Hacikyan, A. Jack.

Gill, Merton M. Analysis of Transference: Theory & Technique, Vol. 1. LC 81-23654. (Psychological Issues Series: Monograph No. 53). 200p. 1981. text ed. 25.00 (ISBN 0-8236-0139-0). Intl Univs Pr.

--Topography & Systems in Psychoanalytic Theory. LC 59-9821. (Psychological Issues Monograph: No. 10, Vol. 3, No. 2). 179p. (Orig.). 1963. text ed. 20.00 (ISBN 0-8236-6560-7); pap. text ed. 17.50 (ISBN 0-8236-6580-1). Intl Univs Pr.

Gill, Merton M. & Brenman, Margaret. Hypnosis & Related States: Psychoanalytic Studies in Regression. LC 59-9821. 276p. 1959. text ed. 32.50 (ISBN 0-8236-2400-5). Intl Univs Pr.

Gill, Merton M. & Hoffman, Irwin Z. Analysis of Transference, Vol. 2: Studies of Seven Audio-Recorded Psychoanalytic Sessions. LC 81-23654. (Psychological Issues Ser.: Monograph No. 54). 240p. 1982. 25.00 (ISBN 0-8236-0140-4). Intl Univs Pr.

Gill, Merton M., jt. auth. see Brenman, Margaret.

Gill, Merton M., jt. auth. see Pribram, Karl H.

Gill, Merton M. & Holzman, Philip S., eds. Psychology Versus Metapsychology: Psychoanalytic Essays in Memory of George S. Klein. LC 75-23354. (Psychological Issues Monograph: No. 36, Vol. 9, No. 4). 376p. 1975. text ed. 30.00 (ISBN 0-8236-5586-5); pap. text ed. 25.00 (ISBN 0-8236-5585-7). Intl Univs Pr.

Gill, N. T. & Vear, K. C. Agricultural Botany 1: Dicotyledonous Crops. 3rd ed. (Illus.). 268p. 1980. 45.00x (ISBN 0-7156-1250-6, BPA-03456, Pub. by Duckworth England). Biblio Dist.

--Agricultural Botany 2: Monocotyledonous Crops. 3rd ed. (Illus.). 259p. 1980. 45.00x (ISBN 0-7156-1251-4, BPA-03457, Pub. by Duckworth England). Biblio Dist.

Gill, Nancy. Using Cereal Boxes. (Illus.). 13p. (gr. 4-6). 1980. pap. 5.95 (ISBN 0-933358-73-3). Enrich.

--Vocabulary Boosters I. (gr. 4-6). 1985. pap. 5.95 (ISBN 0-8224-7280-5). Pitman Learning.

--Vocabulary Boosters II. (gr. 4-6). 1985. pap. 5.95 (ISBN 0-8224-7281-3). Pitman Learning.

Gill, Nancy G. Parents' Guide to School Selection: San Mateo-Santa Clara County Edition. (Illus.). 146p. (Orig.). 1985. pap. 10.95 (ISBN 0-9613846-0-3). Haskala Pr.

Gill, Owen. Whitegate: An Approved School in Transition. 150p. 1974. 39.00x (ISBN 0-85323-452-3, Pub. by Liverpool Univ England). State Mutual Bk.

Gill, Patricia J., jt. auth. see Wohlking, Wallace.

Gill, Peter. Microcomputer Assisted Learning in the Primary School. (Ward Lock Educational Ser.). 29.00x (ISBN 0-7062-4241-6, Pub. by Ward Lock Educational). State Mutual Bk.

--Sleeper's Den. 1984. pap. 4.95 (ISBN 0-7145-0718-0). Riverrun NY.

--Small Change & Kick for Touch: Two Plays. 128p. 1985. (Dist. by Scribner); pap. 8.95 (ISBN 0-7145-2826-9). M Boyars.

Gill, Peter E. Moral Judgments of Violence Among Irish & Swedish Adolescents. (Goteborg Studies in Educational Sciences: No. 32). (Orig.). 1980. pap. text ed. 19.50x (ISBN 91-7346-076-1). Humanities.

Gill, Phillida. The Lost Ears. (Illus.). 32p. (ps-k). 1981. lib. bdg. 8.90 (ISBN 0-531-04065-8). Watts.

Gill, Phillip S., jt. ed. see Johnson, Julian F.

Gill, Pratap S. Dismantling Democracy: Memoirs of An Indian Politician. 1984. 22.50x (ISBN 0-8364-1143-9, Pub. by Lancer India). South Asia Bks.

Gill, Pritam S. Concepts of Sikhism. 183p. 1979. 10.00x (ISBN 0-89684-379-3). Orient Bk Dist.

Gill, R. D. Gamma-Ray Angular Correlations. 1975. 44.00 (ISBN 0-12-283850-5). Acad Pr.

Gill, R. M. Carbon Fibres in Composite Materials. (Illus.). 207p. 1972. 22.50x (ISBN 0-8448-0642-0). Crane-Russak Co.

Gill, R. W. & Dadd, M. J., eds. Proceedings of the Fourth Meeting of the World Federation for Ultrasound in Medicine & Biology. (Illus.). 500p. 1985. 100.00 (ISBN 0-08-032792-3, Pub. by P P A). Pergamon.

Gill, Raj. Jo Bole: A Novel on Punjab Today. 1985. 12.00x (ISBN 0-8364-1302-4, Pub. by Vanity). South Asia Bks.

--The Torch-Bearer: A Novel. (Vikas Library of Modern Indian Writing: No. 19). 239p. 1983. text ed. 30.00 (ISBN 0-7069-2209-3, Pub. by Vikas India). Advent NY.

Gill, Richard. Economics: A Text with Readings. 3rd ed. LC 77-16814. (Illus.). 1978. text ed. 29.30x (ISBN 0-673-16166-8). Scott F.

--Economics & the Public Interest. 4th ed. 1980. pap. 15.80x (ISBN 0-673-16160-9). Scott F.

--Happy Rural Seat: The English Country House & the Literary Imagination. LC 72-75192. (Illus.). Repr. of 1972 ed. 81.30 (ISBN 0-8357-9254-4, 2016959). Bks Demand UMI.

Gill, Richard, ed. Plasma Physics & Nuclear Fusion Research. LC 80-2770. 1981. 66.50 (ISBN 0-12-283860-2). Acad Pr.

Gill, Richard, et al. Singing Saying Dancing Playing: Level One. 1984. pap. 32.00 incl. 6 cassettes, Book (ISBN 0-918812-25-9). MMB Music.

Gill, Richard T. Economic Development: Past & Present. 3rd ed. (Illus.). 160p. 1973. pap. 16.95 (ISBN 0-13-223362-2). P-H.

--Economics & the Private Interest: An Introduction to Microeconomics. 2nd ed. LC 75-22754. 288p. 1976. pap. text ed. 18.40x (ISBN 0-673-16161-7); student guide 8.95x (ISBN 0-673-16159-5). Scott F.

Gill, Robert. VNR Manual of Rendering with Pen & Ink. 2nd ed. 1984. pap. 18.95 (ISBN 0-317-12940-6). Van Nos Reinhold.

Gill, Robert W. Basic Perspective. (Illus.). 1980. pap. 4.95f (ISBN 0-500-27043-0). Thames Hudson.

--Creative Perspective. (Illus.). 1980. pap. 6.95 (ISBN 0-500-27056-2). Thames Hudson.

Gill, Roger, jt. ed. see Alexander, Peter.

Gill, Roma, ed. As You Like It. (Oxford School Shakespeare Ser.). (Illus.). 144p. (Orig.). (gr. 9-12). 1984. pap. 6.95 (ISBN 0-19-831934-7, Pub. by Oxford U Pr Childrens). Merrimack Pub Cir.

--Henry IV, Part I. (Oxford School Shakespeare Ser.). (Illus.). 144p. (Orig.). (gr. 9-12). 1984. pap. 6.95 (ISBN 0-19-831948-7, Pub. by Oxford U Pr Childrens). Merrimack Pub Cir.

--Julius Caesar. (Oxford School Shakespeare Ser.). (Illus.). 144p. (Orig.). (gr. 9-12). 1984. pap. 6.95 (ISBN 0-19-831935-5, Pub. by Oxford U Pr Childrens). Merrimack Pub Cir.

--Macbeth. (Oxford School Shakespeare Ser.). (Illus.). 144p. (Orig.). (gr. 9-12). 1984. pap. 6.95 (ISBN 0-19-831933-9, Pub. by Oxford U Pr Childrens). Merrimack Pub Cir.

--The Merchant of Venice. (Oxford School Shakespeare Ser.). (Illus.). 144p. (gr. 9-12). 1984. pap. 6.95 (ISBN 0-19-831936-3, Pub. by Oxford U Pr Childrens). Merrimack Pub Cir.

--A Midsummer Night's Dream. (Oxford School Shakespeare Ser.). (Illus.). 144p. (Orig.). (gr. 9-12). 1984. pap. 6.95 (ISBN 0-19-831938-X, Pub. by Oxford U Pr Childrens). Merrimack Pub Cir.

--Romeo & Juliet. (Oxford School Shakespeare Ser.). (Illus.). 144p. (Orig.). (gr. 9-12). 1984. pap. 6.95 (ISBN 0-19-831937-1, Pub. by Oxford U Pr Childrens). Merrimack Pub Cir.

Gill, Roma, ed. see Marlowe, Christopher.

Gill, Roma, ed. see Middleton, Thomas.

Gill, Roma, ed. see Tourneur, Cyril.

Gill, Rowland, ed. see Sandifer, Kevin, et al.

Gill, Rowland P., ed. Public Relations Are an Asset for Archives & Museums. (No. 6). 32p. (Orig.). 1985. pap. text ed. 5.00 (ISBN 0-910653-12-7, 8101-L). Archival Servs.

Gill, Rowland P., ed. see Carter, Kenneth.

Gill, Rowland P., ed. see Larkin, Stacy & Hughes, Jeff.

Gill, Rowland P., ed. see Sandifer, Kevin.

Gill, Rowland P., ed. see Sandifer, Kevin W.

Gill, S. S. Political Economy of Indo-Soviet Relations. 1984. 24.00x (ISBN 0-8364-1144-7, Pub. by Ramesh'n India). South Asia Bks.

Gill, Sam. Beyond the "Primitive". Religions of Nonliterate Peoples. (Illus.). 200p. 1982. pap. 13.95 (ISBN 0-13-076034-X). P-H.

--Native American Religions. 208p. 1981. pap. text ed. write for info. (ISBN 0-534-00973-5). Wadsworth Pub.

--Native American Traditions. 200p. 1983. pap. text ed. write for info. (ISBN 0-534-01374-0). Wadsworth Pub.

Gill, Sam D. Sacred Words: A Study of Navajo Religion & Prayer. LC 80-659. (Contributions in Intercultural & Comparative Studies: No. 4). (Illus.). xxvi, 257p. 1981. lib. bdg. 29.95 (ISBN 0-313-22165-0, GSW/). Greenwood.

Gill, Shelley R. Kiana's Iditarod. (Illus.). 60p. (Orig.). (gr. k-6). 1984. pap. 8.95 (ISBN 0-934007-00-4). Paws Four Pub.

Gill, Stephen, ed. The Salisbury Plain Poems of William Wordsworth. LC 74-4865. (Wordsworth Ser). (Illus.). 352p. 1975. 42.50x (ISBN 0-8014-0892-X). Cornell U Pr.

Gill, Stephen & Kermode, Frank, eds. William Wordsworth. (The Oxford Authors Ser.). 1984. 29.95x (ISBN 0-19-254175-7); pap. 9.95 (ISBN 0-19-281333-1). Oxford U Pr.

Gill, Stephen, ed. see Dickens, Charles.

Gill, Stephen, ed. see Gaskell, Elizabeth.

Gill, Stephen, ed. see Trollope, Anthony.

Gill, Susan, jt. auth. see Cate, Phillip D.

Gill, Suzanne L. File Management & Information Retrieval Systems: A Manual for Managers & Technicians. LC 80-22785. (Illus.). 193p. 1981. lib. bdg. 18.50 (ISBN 0-87287-229-7). Libs Unl.

--Library Automation: An Introduction for Library Technicians. 175p. (Orig.). pap. text ed. cancelled (ISBN 0-87287-400-1). Libs Unl.

Gill, Tarlochan S. Asoka: A Historical Play. 80p. 1984. text ed. 8.95x (ISBN 0-86590-179-1). Apt Bks.

Gill, Thomas J., III, jt. ed. see Wegmann, Thomas C.

Gill, W. J. The Pilgrim Fathers. Reeves, Marjorie, ed. (Then & There Ser.). (Illus.). 79p. (Orig.). (gr. 7-12). pap. text ed. 3.75 (ISBN 0-582-20395-3). Longman.

Gill, Wendy, tr. see European Syndicate of Soccer Experts.

Gill, Wesley F. Uncommon Valor: A Game-by-Game History of the Army-Navy Football Rivalry. (Illus.). 304p. 1985. pap. 12.95 (ISBN 0-88011-245-X). Leisure Pr.

Gill, William A. Morgann's Essay on the Dramatic Character of Sir John Falstaff. LC 73-1883. 1912. lib. bdg. 15.00 (ISBN 0-8414-2003-3). Folcroft.

Gill, William A., ed. see Morgann, Maurice.

Gill, William H. Always a Commander: The Reminiscences of Major General William H. Gill. (Illus.). 124p. 1974. pap. 7.50x (ISBN 0-89839-077-X). Battery Pr.

Gill, William W. Myths & Songs from the South Pacific. Dorson, Richard M., ed. LC 77-70596. (International Folklore Ser.). 1977. Repr. of 1876 ed. lib. bdg. 25.50x (ISBN 0-405-10095-7). Ayer Co Pubs.

Gillam, A. J. Simple Chess Tactics. (Chess Player). (Illus.). 128p. 1984. pap. 4.95 (ISBN 0-88254-903-0). Hippocrene Bks.

Gillam, Alan. The Principles & Practice of Selling. 160p. (Orig.). 1982. pap. 14.95 (ISBN 0-434-90661-1, Pub. by W Heinemann Ltd). David & Charles.

Gillam, Tony. Simple Checkmates. 1978. pap. 6.95 (ISBN 0-7134-1482-0, Pub. by Batsford England). David & Charles.

--Simple Chess Tactics. 1978. pap. 6.95 (ISBN 0-7134-1480-4, Pub. by Batsford England). David & Charles.

--Starting Chess. 1978. pap. 7.95 (ISBN 0-7134-1478-2, Pub. by Batsford England). David & Charles.

Gillam, W. S., ed. see Deming, H. G.

Gillan, Garth, jt. auth. see Lemert, Charles C.

Gillan, Maria. Flowers from the Tree of Night. LC 81-18087. 64p. (Orig.). 1981. pap. 5.00 (ISBN 0-941608-00-X). Chantry Pr.

Gillan, Patricia & Gillan, Richard. Sex Therapy Today. LC 77-78402. 1977. pap. 4.95 (ISBN 0-394-17024-5, E702, Ever). Grove.

--Sex Therapy Today. 234p. 1976. 25.00x (ISBN 0-7291-0045-6, Pub. by Open Bks England). State Mutual Bk.

Gillan, Richard, jt. auth. see Gillan, Patricia.

Gilland. Next Seventy Years. 1979. 17.00 (ISBN 0-9961002-3-7, Pub. by Abacus England). Heyden.

Gillanders, John. Pipe & Tube Bending Manual. LC 84-631. 220p. 1984. 24.95x (ISBN 0-87201-493-2). Gulf Pub.

Gillard, David. The Struggle for Asia, Eighteen Twenty Eight to Nineteen Fourteen. 1978. text ed. 31.50x (ISBN 0-8419-7000-9). Holmes & Meier.

Gillard, David, ed. British Documents on Foreign Affairs: Reports & Papers from the Foreign Office Confidential Print, 20 vols. (The Near & Middle East, 1856-1914 Ser.). 1985. Set. 1400.00x (ISBN 0-89093-602-1). U Pubns Amer.

Gillard, John T. The Catholic Church & the Negro. (Basic Afro-American Reprint Library). 1969. Repr. of 1929 ed. 19.00 (ISBN 0-384-18550-9). Johnson Repr.

Gillard, Quentin. Incomes & Accessibility: Metropolitan Labor Force Participation, Commuting, Income Differentials in the United States, 1960-1970. (Research Papers Ser: No. 175). 1977. 10.00 (ISBN 0-89065-082-9). U Chicago Dept Geog.

Gillard, William H. & Tooke, Thomas R. The Niagara Escarpment: From Tobermory to Niagara Falls. LC 73-84434. (Illus.). 1974. pap. 6.00 (ISBN 0-8020-6214-8). U of Toronto Pr.

Gillaspie, Beulah V. Consumer Questions & Their Significance. LC 71-176804. (Columbia University. Teachers College. Contributions to Education: No. 947). Repr. of 1949 ed. 22.50 (ISBN 0-404-55947-6). AMS Pr.

Gillaspie, Jon A., ed. Catalogue of Music in Bath Reference Library. 1985. lib. bdg. 500.00 text (ISBN 0-86291-370-5). K G Saur.

Gillbe, G. V., jt. ed. see Moore, J. R.

Gillberg, Christopher, jt. auth. see Coleman, Mary.

Gille, Bertrand. Histoire des Techniques. (Historique Ser.). 1680p. 67.50 (ISBN 0-686-56463-4). French & Eur.

Gille, J. C. & Kuhn, P. M. The International Radiometersonde Intercomparison Programme: 1970-71. (Technical Note Ser.: No. 128). (Illus.). xiv, 128p. 1973. pap. 20.00 (ISBN 0-685-39018-7, W135, WMO). Unipub.

Gille, Michelline. Cote d'Azur. (Bonechi Guides Ser.). (Illus.). 128p. 1984. text ed. 14.95 (ISBN 88-7009-073-6, 8267). Larousse.

Gilleard, Chris & Watt, Glenda. Coping with Aging Parents. 1983. 30.00x (ISBN 0-86334-019-9, Pub. by Macdonald Pub UK); pap. 20.00x (ISBN 0-86334-000-8). State Mutual Bk.

Gillelan, G. Howard. The Complete Book of the Bow & Arrow. rev., 3rd ed. LC 76-30484. (Illus.). 330p. 1981. pap. 11.95 (ISBN 0-8117-2118-3). Stackpole.

Gilleland, Brady B., ed. see Petronius.

Gilleland, Martha J. Basic Experiments for General, Organic, & Biological Chemistry. new ed. 226p. 1982. 13.95 (ISBN 0-314-63239-5). West Pub.

--Introduction to General, Organic & Biological Chemistry. (Illus.). 832p. 1982. text ed. 31.95 (ISBN 0-314-63173-9). West Pub.

Gillemot, L. F. Material Testing Laboratories. (Engineering Laboratories Ser.: No. 1). 38p. 1970. pap. 5.00 (ISBN 92-3-100826-9, U373, UNESCO). Unipub.

Gillen, Cornelius. Metamorphic Geology: An Introduction to Tectonic & Metamorphic Processes. (Special Topics in Geology Ser.). (Illus.). 160p. (Orig.). 1982. text ed. 25.00x (ISBN 0-04-551057-1); pap. text ed. 9.95x (ISBN 0-04-551058-X). Allen Unwin.

Gillen, F. J., jt. auth. see Spencer, Baldwin.

Gillen, Garth. From Sign to Symbol. 153p. 1982. text ed. 28.00x (ISBN 0-391-02593-7, Pub. by Harvester England). Humanities.

Gillen, Lucy. Comme une Hirondelle Au Printemps. (Harlequin Romantique). 192p. 1983. pap. 1.95 (ISBN 0-373-41212-6). Harlequin Bks.

--Doctor Toby, That Man Next Door & My Beautiful Heathen. (Harlequin Romances (3-in-1) Ser.). 576p. 1983. pap. 3.95 (ISBN 0-373-20079-X). Harlequin Bks.

--Un Etrangere au si Joli Nom. (Harlequin Romantique Ser.). 192p. 1983. pap. 1.95 (ISBN 0-373-41224-X). Harlequin Bks.

--Sweet Kate, A Time Remembered: Dangerous Stranger. (Harlequin Romances Ser.). 576p. 1982. pap. 3.50 (ISBN 0-373-20060-9). Harlequin Bks.

Gillen, Stephen E., jt. auth. see Combs, Richard.

Gillen, William J., jt. auth. see Cicchetti, Charles J.

Gillenson, M. L. Database: The Fundamentals. 1985. 34.95 (ISBN 0-471-80702-8). Wiley.

Gillenson, Mark L. & Goldberg, Robert. Strategic Planning Systems Analysis, & Database Design: The Continuous Flow Approach. LC 83-10212. 228p. 1984. 32.50x (ISBN 0-471-89066-9, Pub. by Wiley-Interscience). Wiley.

Gillenwater, Jay Y., ed. Year Book of Urology, 1981. 1981. 44.95 (ISBN 0-8151-3471-1). Year Bk Med.

--Year Book of Urology 1983. 1983. 44.95 (ISBN 0-8151-3473-8). Year Bk Med.

--Year Book of Urology, 1984. 1984. 44.95 (ISBN 0-8151-3474-6). Year Bk Med.

Gillenwater, Jay Y. & Howards, Stuart S., eds. Year Book of Urology, 1982. 1982. 44.95 (ISBN 0-8151-3472-X). Year Bk Med.

Gillenwater, Susan & Dennis, Virginia. Extra Cash for Women. LC 82-2679. 312p. (Orig.). 1982. pap. 8.95 (ISBN 0-89879-061-1). Writers Digest.

Gilleo, Alma. Air Travel from the Beginning. LC 77-24134. (From the Beginning Ser.). (Illus.). (gr. 1-4). 1977. PLB 6.50 (ISBN 0-89565-002-9); pap. 2.75 (ISBN 0-686-77017-X). Childs World.

--Communications from the Beginning. LC 77-24211. (From the Beginning Ser.). (Illus.). (gr. 1-4). 1977. PLB 6.50 (ISBN 0-89565-003-7); pap. 2.75 (ISBN 0-89565-129-7). Childs World.

--The Easter Basket Mystery. (Holiday Tales). (Illus., Books & cassettes sold as 10 book set only). (primer). incl. cassette 22.00 (ISBN 0-89290-011-3). Soc for Visual.

--Land Travel from the Beginning. LC 77-24068. (From the Beginning Ser.). (Illus.). (gr. 1-4). 1977. PLB 6.50 (ISBN 0-89565-000-2); pap. 2.75 (ISBN 0-89565-128-9). Childs World.

--Learning About Monsters. LC 81-38481. (Learning About Ser.). (Illus.). 48p. (gr. 2-6). 1982. lib. bdg. 11.00 (ISBN 0-516-06535-1). Childrens.

--The Mystery of the Missing Valentines. (Holiday Tales). (Illus., Books & cassettes sold as 10 book set only). (ps). 1977. incl. cassette 22.00 (ISBN 0-89290-010-5). Soc for Visual.

--Prince Charles, Growing up in Buckingham Palace. LC 78-18938. (Illus.). (gr. k-4). 1978. PLB 6.95 (ISBN 0-89565-029-0). Childs World.

--Water Travel from the Beginning. LC 77-22822. (From the Beginning Ser.). (Illus.). (gr. 1-4). 1977. PLB 6.50 (ISBN 0-89565-001-0). Childs World.

Gilleo, Alma, ed. The Elves & the Shoemaker. LC 65-2642. (Holiday Tales). (Illus.). (ps). 1977. pap. 22.00 10 bks. & 1 casette (ISBN 0-89290-013-X). Soc for Visual.

--The Four Servants. LC 74-734828. (Fairy Tales of the Brothers Grimm Cassette Bks Ser.). (Illus.). 16p. 1976. pap. 22.00 incl. 10 bks. & one cassette (ISBN 0-89290-009-1). Soc for Visual.

--The Golden Buttons. LC 74-734827. (Fairy Tales of the Brothers Grimm Cassette Bks). (Illus.). 16p. (ps). 1976. pap. 22.00 10 bks. & one cassette (ISBN 0-89290-008-3); cassette incl. (ISBN 0-685-70098-4). Soc for Visual.

--The Goose-Girl, 10 bks. & one cassette. LC 74-734823. (Fairy Tales of the Brothers Grimm Cassette-Bks). (Illus.). 16p. (ps). 1976. Set. 22.00 (ISBN 0-89290-005-9). Soc for Visual.

--Hans Clodhopper, 10bks. & one cassette. LC 76-730154. (Hans Christian Andersen Cassette Bks). (Illus.). 1976. Set. 22.00 (ISBN 0-89290-002-4). Soc for Visual.

--King Grisly-Beard, 10 bks. & one cassette. LC 74-734822. (Fairy Tales of the Brothers Grimm Cassette Bks). (Illus.). 16p. (ps). 1976. 10 bks. & one cassette 22.00 (ISBN 0-89290-004-0). Soc for Visual.

--The Little Mermaid, 10 bks. LC 76-730155. (Hans Christian Andersen Cassette Bks). (Illus.). 1976. 22.00 (ISBN 0-89290-003-2); cassette incl. (ISBN 0-685-70093-3). Soc for Visual.

--The Water of Life, 10 bks. & one cassette. LC 74-734825. (Fairy Tales of the Brothers Grimm Cassette Bks). (Illus.). 1976. Set. 22.00 (ISBN 0-89290-006-7). Soc for Visual.

--The Wild Swans, 10 bks. & one cassette. LC 76-730152. (Hans Christian Andersen Cassette Bks). (Illus.). 1976. Set. 22.00 (ISBN 0-89290-000-8); cassette incl. (ISBN 0-685-70090-9). Soc for Visual.

Gilleo, Alma, ed. see Cook, Emilie C.

Giller, Henri, jt. auth. see Morris, Allison.

Giller, Henri, jt. auth. see Rutter, Micheal.

Giller, Norman. The Book of Tennis Lists. LC 85-40399. 224p. 1985. 15.00 (ISBN 0-8128-3063-6). Stein & Day.

--L. A. Eighty-Four. (Illus.). 192p. 1983. pap. 7.95 (ISBN 0-03-063818-6). HR&W.

--The Nineteen Eighty-Four Olympic Handbook. (Illus.). 206p. 1984. pap. 7.95 (ISBN 0-317-06147-X). HR&W.

--The Olympics Handbook, 1984. LC 83-17168. (Illus.). 208p. 1984. pap. 7.95 (ISBN 0-03-063818-6). HR&W.

Giller, Norman M. An Adventure in Architecture. 248p. 1977. text ed. 12.50x (ISBN 0-930558-01-4). Virgo Pr.

Giller, P. S. Community Structure & the Niche. (Outline Studies in Ecology). 186p. 1984. pap. text ed. 11.95 (ISBN 0-412-25110-8, NO. 9033, Pub. by Chapman & Hall). Methuen Inc.

Gillerman, Dorothy. The Cloture of Notre-Dame & Its Role in the 14th Century Choir Program. LC 76-23623. (Outstanding Dissertations in the Fine Arts - 2nd Series - Medieval). (Illus.). 292p. 1977. Repr. of 1973 ed. lib. bdg. 69.00 (ISBN 0-8240-2693-4). Garland Pub.

Gillers, Stephen & Dorsen, Norman. Regulation of Lawyers: Problems of Law & Ethics. LC 84-52487. 1985. text ed. 28.00 (ISBN 0-316-31380-7). Little.

Gillers, Stephen, ed. Looking at Law School: A Student Guide from the Society of American Law Teachers. LC 84-9897. (Orig.). 1977. pap. 8.95 (ISBN 0-452-00709-7, Mer). NAL.

--Looking at Law School: A Student Guide from the Society of American Law Teachers. LC 76-53301. 1977. 9.95 (ISBN 0-8008-4966-3). Taplinger.

Gilles, Albert S. Comanche Days. LC 74-77543. pap. 36.00 (ISBN 0-317-20112-3, 2023179). Bks Demand UMI.

Gilles, Anthony E. Fundamentalism: What Every Catholic Needs to Know. 72p. (Orig.). 1985. pap. text ed. 3.75 (ISBN 0-86716-043-8). St Anthony Mess Pr.

--People of the Book: The Story Behind the Old Testament. (Illus.). 178p. (Orig.). 1983. pap. text ed. 5.95 (ISBN 0-86716-026-8). St Anthony Mess Pr.

--People of the Creed: The Story Behind the Early Church. (The People Ser.: Vol. 3). (Orig.). 1985. pap. text ed. 5.95 (ISBN 0-86716-046-2). St Anthony Mess Pr.

--The People of the Way: The Story Behind the New Testament. (Illus.). 142p. (Orig.). 1984. pap. 5.95 (ISBN 0-86716-036-5). St Anthony Mess Pr.

Gilles, Floyd H., et al. Developing Human Brain: Growth & Epidemiologic Neuropathology. (Illus.). 360p. 1983. 54.50 (ISBN 0-7236-7017-X). PSG Pub Co.

Gilles, G., jt. auth. see Romagnesi, H.

Gilles, H. M., jt. auth. see Peters, W.

Gilles, Jean, ed. How to Run Your House. LC 72-97091. 1973. 7.95 (ISBN 0-89795-007-0). Farm Journal.

Gilles, Maria V. Byrons Dramen. (European University Studies: No. 14, Vol. 103). 151p. (Ger.). 1982. 17.90 (ISBN 3-8204-5818-2). P Lang Pubs.

Gilles, R. Mechanisms of Osmoregulation in Animals: Maintenance of Cell Volume. LC 78-4608. 667p. 1979. 144.95x (ISBN 0-471-99648-3, Pub. by Wiley-Interscience). Wiley.

Gilles, R. & Balthazart, J., eds. Neurobiology. (Proceedings in Life Sciences Ser.). (Illus.). 430p. 1985. 69.50 (ISBN 0-387-15480-9). Springer-Verlag.

Gilles, R., ed. see European Society for Comparative Physiology & Biochemistry, 1st Conference, Liege, Belgium, 1979.

Gilles, R., jt. ed. see Gilles-Baillien, M.

Gilles, Tim. Engine Mechanics: Diagnosis & Repair. (Illus.). 350p. Date not set. pap. text ed. write for info. (ISBN 0-534-04842-0, 77F6065). Breton Pubs.

Gilles-Baillien, M. & Gilles, R., eds. Intestinal Transport: Fundamental & Comparative Aspects. (Proceedings in Life Sciences Ser.). (Illus.). 210p. 1983. 44.50 (ISBN 0-387-12430-6). Springer-Verlag.

Gillespie. Practical Narcotics Investigation. Date not set. price not set (ISBN 0-444-00873-X). Elsevier.

Gillespie, A., ed. Technological Change & Regional Development. (Pion London Papers in Regional Science Ser.: No. 12). (Illus.). 171p. 1984. pap. 14.00x (ISBN 0-85086-107-1, NO. 5072). Methuen Inc.

Gillespie, A. R., jt. auth. see Siegal, B. S.

Gillespie, Abraham L. The Syntactic Revolution. Milazzo, Richard, ed. LC 75-22994. (Illus.). 190p. 1981. pap. 12.95 (ISBN 0-915570-05-X). Oolp Pr.

Gillespie, Allesia M. A Manual of Fluorometric & Spectrophotometric Experiments. 146p. 1985. pap. text ed. 25.00 (ISBN 2-88124-005-4). Gordon.

Gillespie, Angus K. Folklorist of the Coal Fields: George Korson's Life & Work. LC 79-25839. (Illus.). 1980. 22.50 (ISBN 0-271-00255-7). Pa St U Pr.

Gillespie, Anna, jt. auth. see Gillespie, John.

Gillespie, Bryan. Independent Study & Research in Literature. LC 75-2175. 1975. 3.50 (ISBN 0-912112-07-7). Everett-Edwards.

Gillespie, Cecil. Accounting Systems: Procedures & Methods. 3rd ed. (Illus.). 720p. 1971. ref. ed. 37.95 (ISBN 0-13-001933-X). P-H.

Gillespie, Charles A. Cone 04-Low Fire Pottery. 2nd. Ed ed. (Illus.). 72p. 1983. pap. 9.95 (ISBN 0-9609974-1-5). C A Gillespie.

Gillespie, Charles B. A Miner's Sunday, 1849. Jones, William R., ed. (Illus.). 18p. 1976. pap. 1.00 (ISBN 0-89646-005-3). Outbooks.

Gillespie, Clark. Your Pregnancy Month by Month. rev. ed. LC 81-47789. (Illus.). 240p. 1982. 13.41i (ISBN 0-06-014933-7, HarpT). Har-Row.

--Your Pregnancy Month by Month. LC 84-48601. (Illus.). 256p. 1985. 14.37 (ISBN 0-06-181310-9, HarpT). Har-Row.

--Your Pregnancy Month by Month. LC 84-48601. (Illus.). 256p. 1985. pap. 8.61i (ISBN 0-06-091257-X, CN). Har-Row.

Gillespie, Cloie. People... for God Sake. 1982. 7.95 (ISBN 0-533-05232-7). Vantage.

Gillespie, D. H., jt. auth. see Strayer, D. R.

Gillespie, Daniel T. A Quantum Mechanics Primer: An Elementary Introduction to the Formal Theory of Non-Relativistic Quantum Mechanics. LC 74-3107. 137p. (Orig.). 1973. pap. text ed. 21.95x (ISBN 0-470-29912-6). Halsted Pr.

Gillespie, David, et al. Organizational Response to Changing Community Systems. LC 76-25890. (Illus.). 88p. 1976. pap. 4.50x (ISBN 0-87338-196-3, Pub. by Comp. Adm. Research Inst.). Kent St U Pr.

Gillespie, Dizzy & Fraser, Al. To Be or Not to Bop: Memoirs. LC 77-76237. (Illus.). 1979. 17.95 (ISBN 0-385-12052-4). Doubleday.

--To Be or Not to Bop: Memoirs of Dizzy Gillespie. (Quality Paperbacks Ser.). (Illus.). 574p. 1985. pap. 12.95 (ISBN 0-306-80236-8). Da Capo.

Gillespie, Elgy. The Country Life Picture Book of Ireland. (Illus.). 1982. 19.95 (ISBN 0-393-01627-7). Norton.

Gillespie, Elgy, ed. The Liberties of Dublin: Its History, People & Future. (Illus.). 1973. 15.95 (ISBN 0-905140-25-7). Irish Bk Ctr.

Gillespie, Esther see Clark, Thomas C.

Gillespie, Esther A., jt. auth. see Clark, Thomas C.

Gillespie, Esther A., jt. ed. see Clark, Thomas C.

Gillespie, Frances E. Labor & Politics in England: 1850-1867. 1967. lib. bdg. 20.00x (ISBN 0-374-93078-3). Octagon.

Gillespie, George H., jt. ed. see Meyerhoff, Roland.

Gillespie, Gerald. German Baroque Poetry. LC 74-110363. (World Authors Ser.). 1971. lib. bdg. 15.95x (ISBN 0-8057-2360-9). Irvington.

Gillespie, Gerald E. Daniel Casper von Lohenstein's Historical Tragedies. LC 65-18733. 193p. 1966. 6.25 (ISBN 0-8142-0053-2). Ohio St U Pr.

Gillespie, Glenn. Michigan Criminal Law & Procedure: 1978-1983, 5 vols. LC 78-888. 360.00 (ISBN 0-317-12080-8). Callaghan.

Gillespie, Iain E. & Thomson, T. J. Gastroenterology: An Integrated Course. 3rd ed. (Illus.). 320p. 1983. pap. text ed. 17.00 (ISBN 0-443-02342-5). Churchill.

Gillespie, J. H., jt. auth. see Appel, M. J.

Gillespie, James. Modern Livestock & Poultry Production. 2nd ed. LC 79-50918. (Illus.). 662p. 1983. text ed. 26.80 (ISBN 0-8273-2200-3); instr's guide 5.25 (ISBN 0-8273-2201-1). Delmar.

Gillespie, James E. The Influence of Oversea Expansion on England to 1700. 1972. lib. bdg. 24.00x (ISBN 0-374-93079-1). Octagon.

Gillespie, James E., Jr. The Reed Trio: An Annotated Bibliography of Original Published Works. LC 74-174729. (Detroit Studies in Music Bibliography Ser.: No. 20). 1971. pap. 2.00 (ISBN 0-911772-42-1). Info Coord.

--Solos for Unaccompanied Clarinet: An Annotated Bibliography. LC 73-87277. (Detroit Studies in Music Bibliography Ser.: No. 28). 1973. 5.00 (ISBN 0-911772-58-8); pap. 2.00 (ISBN 0-89990-010-0). Info Coord.

Gillespie, James H. & Timoney, John F. Hagan & Bruner's Infectious Diseases of Domestic Animals. 7th rev. ed. LC 80-15937. (Illus.). 912p. 1981. 49.50x (ISBN 0-8014-1333-8). Cornell U Pr.

Gillespie, Jane. Ladysmead. LC 82-16773. 176p. 1982. 9.95 (ISBN 0-312-46433-9). St Martin.

--Ladysmead. (Nightingale Paperbacks Ser.). 1984. pap. 9.95 (ISBN 0-8161-3744-7, Large Print Bks). G K Hall.

--Teverton Hall. 224p. 1984. 11.95 (ISBN 0-312-79371-5). St Martin.

Gillespie, Jane Baldwin. Making Melody. LC 83-22461. 1983. pap. 4.95 (ISBN 0-87233-073-7). Bauhan.

Gillespie, Janet. Joyful Noise. LC 79-123931. 1971. 11.95i (ISBN 0-06-011532-7, HarpT). Har-Row.

Gillespie, Joan. Algeria, Rebellion & Revolution. LC 75-25487. (Illus.). 208p. 1976. Repr. of 1960 ed. lib. bdg. 19.75x (ISBN 0-8371-8425-8, GIAL). Greenwood.

Gillespie, John. Five Centuries of Keyboard Music. (Illus.). xii, 463p. 1972. pap. 7.95 (ISBN 0-486-22855-X). Dover.

Gillespie, John & Gillespie, Anna. A Bibliography of Nineteenth-Century American Piano Music: With Location Sources & Composer Biography-Index. LC 84-8993. (Music Reference Collection Ser.: No. 2). xiii, 358p. 1984. lib. bdg. 39.95 (ISBN 0-313-24097-3, GNP/). Greenwood.

Gillespie, John & Spirt, Diana L. The Young Phenomenon: Paperbacks in Our Schools. LC 72-2653. (ALA Studies in Librarianship: No. 3). pap. 38.00 (ISBN 0-317-26350-1, 2024228). Bks Demand UMI.

Gillespie, John, ed. Japan: Annual Volume of the Council on National Literatures, 1983. Walker, Janet & Clark, Richard C. LC 77-126039. (Review of National Literatures Ser.). 1984. pap. 20.00 (ISBN 0-918680-23-9). Griffon Hse.

--Nineteenth-Century American Piano Music. LC 77-90383. 1978. pap. 10.95 (ISBN 0-486-23602-1). Dover.

--Nineteenth-Century European Piano Music. 343p. 1977. pap. 9.50 (ISBN 0-486-23447-9). Dover.

--Nineteenth-Century European Piano Music: Unfamiliar Master Works. 15.00 (ISBN 0-8446-5577-5). Peter Smith.

Gillespie, John T. The Elementary School Paperback Collection. LC 85-11215. 256p. 1985. pap. text ed. 17.50x (ISBN 0-8389-0419-X). ALA.

--The Junior High School Paperback Collection. LC 85-11248. 185p. 1985. pap. text ed. 17.50x (ISBN 0-8389-0420-3). ALA.

--Model School District Media Program: Montgomery County as a Case Study. LC 77-5022. 216p. 1977. pap. text ed. 12.00x (ISBN 0-8389-3192-8). ALA.

--Paperback Books for Young People: An Annotated Guide to Publishers & Distributors. 2nd ed. LC 77-21627. 232p. 1977. pap. 12.00x (ISBN 0-8389-0248-0). ALA.

--Paperback Books for Young People: An Annotated Guide to Publishers & Distributors. 2nd ed. pap. 10.00 tchr's. ed. (ISBN 0-317-06456-8). Dell.

--Paperback Books for Young People: An Annotated Guide to Publishers & Distributors. 2nd ed. LC 77-21627. pap. 57.80 (ISBN 0-317-26563-6, 2023950). Bks Demand UMI.

--Paperback Books for Young People: An Annotated Guide to Publishers & Distributors. 2nd ed. 232p. 1977. pap. 10.00 (ISBN 0-8389-0248-0). Assn Library Serv.

Gillespie, John T. & Lembo, Diana L. Juniorplots: A Book Talk Manual for Teachers & Librarians. LC 67-18146. 222p. 1967. 15.95 (ISBN 0-8352-0063-9). Bowker.

Gillespie, John T. & Spirt, Diana L. Administering a School Library Media Center. rev. ed. 381p. 1983. 34.95 (ISBN 0-8352-1514-8). Bowker.

--Creating a School Media Program. LC 77-164032. (Illus.). pap. 61.50 (ISBN 0-8357-9039-8, 2013305). Bks Demand UMI.

Gillespie, John T. & Gilbert, Christine B., eds. Best Books for Children: Pre-School Through the Middle Grades. 3rd ed. 600p. 1985. 34.50 (ISBN 0-8352-2131-8). Bowker.

Gillespie, Joseph E., jt. auth. see Fabreau, Donald F.

Gillespie, Judith A. & Zinnes, Dina A., eds. Missing Elements in Political Inquiry: Logic & Levels of Analysis. (Sage Focus Editions). 264p. 1982. 24.00 (ISBN 0-8039-1802-X); pap. 12.00 (ISBN 0-8039-1803-8). Sage.

Gillespie, Judith A., jt. ed. see Heater, Derek.

Gillespie, K. & Hecht, J. C. Casebook in Retail Business Management: Applications & Cases. 3rd ed. 128p. 1983. 8.80 (ISBN 0-07-023229-6). McGraw.

Gillespie, K., jt. auth. see Wingate, I.

Gillespie, Karen & Hecht, Joseph C. Retail Business Management. 3rd, rev. ed. LC 82-21700. (Illus.). 480p. 1983. text ed. 24.30 (ISBN 0-07-023228-8). McGraw.

Gillespie, Karen R. Creative Supervision. 399p. 1981. pap. text ed. 16.95 (ISBN 0-15-515822-8, HC); instr's. manual avail. (ISBN 0-15-515823-6). HarBraceJ.

Gillespie, Kate. The Tripartite Relationship: Government, Foreign Investors & Local Investors During Egypt's Economic Opening. LC 83-21221. 236p. 1984. 28.95 (ISBN 0-03-069559-7). Praeger.

Gillespie, L., ed. The Young Engineer: An Annotated Bibliography 1890-1978. 104p. 9.00 (ISBN 0-318-12198-0, EC47). Accred Bd Eng & Tech.

Gillespie, L. Kay. Cancer Quackery: The Label of Quack & Its Relationship to Deviant Behavior. LC 78-68453. 1979. perfect bdg. 9.95 (ISBN 0-88247-563-0). R & E Pubs.

Gillespie, La Roux K., et al. James Hughes: Biography of a Western Pioneer. 239p. 1983. 40.00 (ISBN 0-912017-00-7); pap. 30.00 (ISBN 0-912017-01-5). Fam Hist & Gen.
Gillespie, LaRoux K. Deburring Technology for Improved Manufacturing. LC 81-51202. (Illus.). 646p. 1981. text ed. 27.50 (ISBN 0-87263-068-4). SME.
--Ireton, Oklahoma. 75p. 1985. pap. 15.00 (ISBN 0-912017-04-X). Fam Hist & Gen.
--The Iretons of Kansas & Oklahoma. 350p. 1985. 40.00 (ISBN 0-912017-02-3); pap. 30.00 (ISBN 0-912017-03-1). Fam Hist & Gen.
Gillespie, LaRoux K., ed. Advances in Deburring. LC 78-57204. (Illus.). 1978. text ed. 17.95x (ISBN 0-87263-044-7). SME.
--Deburring Capabilities & Limitations. LC 76-47179. (Illus.). text ed. 15.95 (ISBN 0-87263-038-2). SME.
Gillespie, Lori, jt. auth. see Truett, Carol.
Gillespie, Mabel. Where the Birds Are. LC 76-55062. (Illus., Orig.). 1976. pap. 4.95 (ISBN 0-932384-03-X). Tashmoo.
Gillespie, Marcia, et al, eds. But Thinking Makes It So: Conformity & Deviance in Social Problems. LC 76-41779. 208p. 1977. pap. text ed. 6.95x (ISBN 0-8422-5250-9). Irvington.
Gillespie, Mary L. Coordination of Services: Hospital to Home. 19p. 1980. 4.95 (ISBN 0-88737-157-4, 21-1818). Natl League Nurse.
Gillespie, Michael. Hegel, Heidegger & the Ground of History. LC 84-2472. (Illus.). 1984. lib. bdg. 22.00x (ISBN 0-226-29376-9). U of Chicago Pr.
Gillespie, Michael P. Inverted Volumes Improperly Arranged: James Joyce & His Trieste Library. Litz, Walton, ed. LC 83-5736. (Studies in Modern Literature: No. 10). 134p. 1983. 34.95 (ISBN 0-8357-1415-2). UMI Res Pr.
Gillespie, Neal C. Charles Darwin & the Problems of Creation. LC 79-11231. 1982. pap. 7.50x (ISBN 0-226-29375-0). U of Chicago Pr.
--Charles Darwin & the Problems of Creation. LC 79-11231. 1979. lib. bdg. 16.50x (ISBN 0-226-29374-2). U of Chicago Pr.
Gillespie, Patricia. Teaching Reading to the Special Needs Child: An Ecological Approach. (Special Education Ser.). 1979. text ed. 25.95 (ISBN 0-675-08274-9). Merrill.
Gillespie, Patti P. & Cameron, Kenneth M. Western Theatre: Revolution & Revival. (Illus.). 608p. 1984. text ed. write for info. (ISBN 0-02-343050-8). Macmillan.
Gillespie, Patti P., jt. auth. see Cameron, Kenneth M.
Gillespie, Paul, ed. Foxfire Seven. LC 80-2962. (Illus.). 512p. 1982. 19.95 (ISBN 0-385-15243-4, Anchor Pr); pap. 9.95 (ISBN 0-385-15244-2). Doubleday.
Gillespie, Richard. Soldiers of Peron: Argentina's Montoneros. 1982. 29.95x (ISBN 0-19-821131-7). Oxford U Pr.
Gillespie, Robert. Cryptopic Crosswords. 145p. 1983. 12.95 (ISBN 0-13-194738-9); pap. 4.95 (ISBN 0-13-194720-6). P-H.
--Daily Crosswords, No. 1, No. 1. 128p. 1981. pap. 1.75 (ISBN 0-441-13541-2). Ace Bks.
--The Man Chain. LC 79-12276. 75p. 1979. 4.00 (ISBN 0-87886-102-5). Ithaca Hse.
Gillespie, Robert, ed. The Daily Crosswords, No. 7. 128p. (Orig.). (gr. 8 up). 1982. pap. 1.95 (ISBN 0-441-13546-3, Tempo). Ace Bks.
Gillespie, Robert, jt. ed. see Kostuik, J. P.
Gillespie, Robert B. Heads You Lose. 224p. 1985. 14.95 (ISBN 0-396-08549-0). Dodd.
--Print-Out. 224p. 1983. 11.95 (ISBN 0-396-08100-2). Dodd.
Gillespie, Robert H., ed. Adhesives for Wood: Research, Applications, & Needs. LC 84-14780. 250p. 1985. 36.00 (ISBN 0-8155-0997-9). Noyes.
Gillespie, Robert W., jt. auth. see Levin, Harry L.
Gillespie, Sheena & Stanley, Linda. Someone Like Me: Images for Writing. 5th ed. 1984. pap. text ed. 11.95 (ISBN 0-316-31368-8); manual avail. (ISBN 0-316-31369-6). Little.
Gillespie, Sheena, et al. The Writer's Craft: A Process Reader. 1985. pap. text ed. 11.95x (ISBN 0-673-18173-1). Scott F.
Gillespie, Susan, tr. see Putz, Helmut.
Gillespie, Thomas, jt. auth. see Lang, Larry.
Gillespie, W. A., jt. auth. see Slade, N.
Gillespie, W. Irwin. In Search of Robin Hood: The Effect of Federal Budgetary Policies During the 1970s on the Distribution of Income in Canada. 66p. 1978. 4.00 (ISBN 0-88806-034-3, HIP2). Inst C D Howe.
Gillespie, W. Jay, jt. auth. see Cantu, Robert C.
Gillespie, Wilma & Redford, Jeannette. Health Occupations Education: A Review of the Literature. 189p. 1980. 11.00 (ISBN 0-318-15482-X, IN216). Natl Ctr Res Voc Ed.
Gillespie-Addison, A. D., tr. see Leonhard, Blumenthal Von.
Gillespy, Rosalynne H. Space Wars. LC 78-730966. 1978. pap. text ed. 245.00 (ISBN 0-89290-111-X, CM-31). Soc for Visual.
Gillet, Charles R., tr. see Krueger, Gustav.
Gillet, Henri. Design Motifs of the Decorative Twenties in Color. (Pictorial Archive Ser.). 32p. 1985. pap. 4.50 (ISBN 0-486-24803-8). Dover.
Gillet, Jean W. & Temple, Charles. Understanding Reading Problems: Assessment & Instruction. 1982. text ed. 24.95 (ISBN 0-316-31352-1); tchrs' manual avail. (ISBN 0-316-31354-8). Little.
Gillet, Jean W., jt. auth. see Temple, Charles.
Gillet, Lev. The Burning Bush. 1975. pap. 2.95 (ISBN 0-87243-063-4). Templegate.
--In Thy Presence. LC 77-1040. 144p. 1977. pap. 2.95 (ISBN 0-913836-34-6). St Vladimirs.
--On the Invocation of the Name of Jesus. 1985. pap. 4.95 (ISBN 0-87243-133-9). Templegate.
Gillet, Louis. Claybook for James Joyce. Markow-Totevy, Georges, tr. 135p. 1981. Repr. of 1958 ed. lib. bdg. 25.00 (ISBN 0-8495-1969-1). Arden Lib.
Gillet, Louis, jt. auth. see Rolland, Romain.
Gillet, Marcel. Les Charbonnages Du Nord De la France Au XIXe Siecle. (Industrie et Artisanat: No. 8). (Illus.). 1973. pap. 36.00x (ISBN 90-2797-260-5). Mouton.
Gillet, Pamela. Auditory Processes. LC 74-80092. 1974. pap. 5.00x (ISBN 0-87879-094-2). Acad Therapy.
--Of Work & Worth: Career Ed. for Exceptional Children & Youth. LC 80-84931. 340p. 1981. text ed. 19.95x (ISBN 0-913420-90-5). Olympus Pub Co.
Gillet, Ransom H. Democracy in the United States. facs. ed. LC 75-126234. (Select Bibliographies Reprint Ser). 1868. 23.50 (ISBN 0-8369-5460-2). Ayer Co Pubs.
Gillet, S. E., ed. see De Carvajal, M.
Gillet, V., jt. ed. see DeWitt, C.
Gillet, V., jt. auth. see Danos, M.
Gilleto, Sebastian B. The Changing Tide. (Fictional Ser.). 246p. 1981. Leatherette cover 4.00 (ISBN 0-686-36143-1). Intl Print.
Gillett, Billy E. Methods of Operations Research. (Illus.). 1976. text ed. 45.00 (ISBN 0-07-023245-8). McGraw.
Gillett, Charles R. Burned Books: Neglected Chapters in British History & Literature, 2 vols. LC 74-12951. (Illus.). 1975. Repr. of 1932 ed. lib. bdg. 47.50x (ISBN 0-8371-7778-2, GIBB). Greenwood.
Gillett, Charlie. The Sound of the City: Rise of Rock and Roll. rev. ed. LC 84-42671. 528p. 1984. pap. 7.95 (ISBN 0-394-72638-3). Pantheon.
Gillett, E. Investment in the Environment: Recent Housing, Planning & Transport Policies in Scotland. 160p. 1983. 19.80 (ISBN 0-08-030367-6); pap. 11.70 (ISBN 0-08-030363-3). Pergamon.
Gillett, E. H. Historical Patterns of Destruction of Ancient Cities & Empires. (Illus.). 139p. 1982. Repr. of 1867 ed. 79.85 (ISBN 0-89901-039-3). Found Class Reprints.
Gillett, Edward & MacMahon, Kenneth A., eds. A History of Hull. (Illus.). 1980. 49.95x (ISBN 0-19-713436-X). Oxford U Pr.
Gillett, Eric. Poets of Our Time. 1977. Repr. of 1932 ed. 15.00 (ISBN 0-89984-186-4). Century Bookbindery.
Gillett, Eric, jt. auth. see Entwistle, William J.
Gillett, Ezra H. The Life & Times of John Huss: The Bohemian Reformation of the Fifteenth Century, 2 vols. LC 77-85271. Repr. of 1863 ed. Set. 94.50 (ISBN 0-404-16150-2). AMS Pr.
Gillett, James B. Six Years with the Texas Rangers, 1875 to 1881. Quaife, Milo M., ed. LC 76-4495. (Illus.). xxxvi, 279p. 1976. 22.50x (ISBN 0-8032-0889-8); pap. 5.95 (ISBN 0-8032-5844-5, BB 624, Bison). U of Nebr Pr.
Gillett, K. & Yaldwyn, J. Australian Seashores in Colour. LC 77-109409. (Illus.). 1970. 5.00 (ISBN 0-8048-0861-9). C E Tuttle.
Gillett, Margaret. We Walked Very Warily: A History of Women at McGill. (Illus.). 496p. 1981. 18.95 (ISBN 0-920792-08-1). Eden Pr.
Gillett, Margaret & Laska, John A. Foundation Studies in Education: Justifications & New Directions: A Source Book. LC 73-7899. 430p. 1973. 16.00 (ISBN 0-8108-0671-1). Scarecrow.
Gillett, Margaret & Sibbald, Kay, eds. A Fair Shake: Autobiographical Essays by McGill Women. 425p. (Orig.). 1984. pap. 16.95 (ISBN 0-920792-31-6). Eden Pr.
Gillett, Marnie, jt. auth. see Druckrey, Timothy.
Gillett, Mary. Bugles at the Border. LC 68-25853. (Illus.). (gr. 6 up). 1968. PLB 7.95 (ISBN 0-910244-50-2). Blair.
Gillett, Philip. Calculus & Analytic Geometry. 928p. 1981. text ed. 34.95 (ISBN 0-669-00641-6); solutions guide, vol. 1 8.95 (ISBN 0-669-00642-4); solutions guide vol. 2 8.95 (ISBN 0-669-03212-3); solutions guide vol. 3 8.95 (ISBN 0-669-03213-1); selected study & solutions guide 9.95 (ISBN 0-669-05170-5); linear algebra suppl. 2.95 (ISBN 0-669-05142-X); revised problem sets 2.95 (ISBN 0-669-06334-7). Heath.
--Calculus & Analytic Geometry. 2nd ed. 992p. text ed. 35.95 (ISBN 0-669-06059-3). Heath.
Gillett, Richard W. The Human Enterprise: A Christian Perspective on Work. LC 85-50675. 100p. (Orig.). 1985. pap. write for info. (ISBN 0-934134-34-0). Leaven Pr.
Gillett, W. B. & Moon, J. E. Solar Collectors: Test Methods & Design Guidelines. 1985. lib. bdg. 39.50 (ISBN 90-277-2052-5, Pub. by Reidel Netherlands). Kluwer Academic.
Gillett, Will D. & Pollack, Seymour V. Introduction to Engineered Software. 450p. 1982. pap. text ed. 30.95 (ISBN 0-03-056902-8, HoltC). HR&W.
Gillette, A. S. & Gillette, Michael. Stage Scenery: Its Construction & Rigging. 3rd ed. 448p. 1981. text ed. 23.50 scp (ISBN 0-06-042332-3, HarpC). Har-Row.
Gillette, Arthur L. Beyond the Nonformal Fashion: Towards Educational Revolution in Tanzania. 312p. (Orig.). 1977. pap. text ed. 6.00 (ISBN 0-932288-47-2). Ctr Intl Ed U of MA.
Gillette, Clayton P. Law of Municipal Finance. write for info. Little.
Gillette, Cynthia, et al. Small Farmer Credit: Cultural & Social Factors Affecting Small Farmer Participation in Formal Credit Programs & the Political Economy of Distributing Agricultural Credit & Benefits. (Occasional Paper Ser.: No. 3). 57p. (Orig.). 1973. pap. text ed. 4.85 (ISBN 0-86731-016-2). RDC Ctr Intl Stud.
Gillette, David D. Walkers: Prehistoric Animals of the Southwest. (Illus.). 32p. (gr. 1-6). 1984. pap. 2.95 (ISBN 0-89013-176-7). Museum NM Pr.
Gillette, Ed. Balboa Park: A Pictorial Guide. (Illus.). 128p. (Orig.). 1984. pap. 5.95 (ISBN 0-9613638-1-9). Photo Graphics.
Gillette, Elizabeth R., ed. Action for Wilderness. LC 79-189967. (Battlebook Ser.). 224p. (Orig.). 1972. pap. 2.25 (ISBN 0-87156-062-3). Sierra.
Gillette, F. L., jt. auth. see Ziemann, Hugo.
Gillette, Frank, ed. Between Paradigms: The Mood & Its Purpose. (Social Change Ser.). 208p. 1973. 46.25 (ISBN 0-677-15060-1). Gordon.
Gillette, George W. Man's Search for Truth. (Illus.). 1976. pap. 14.95 (ISBN 0-87516-224-X). De Vorss.
Gillette, Harriet E. Systems of Therapy in Cerebral Palsy. (Illus.). 96p. 1974. 13.75x (ISBN 0-398-00680-6). C C Thomas.
Gillette, Howard, Jr., jt. ed. see Cutler, William W., 3rd.
Gillette, J. Michael. Designing with Light: An Introduction to Stage Lighting. LC 78-51945. (Illus.). 195p. 1978. pap. text ed. 10.95 (ISBN 0-87484-420-7). Mayfield Pub.
Gillette, J. R. & Mitchell, J. R., eds. Concepts in Biochemical Pharmacology, Part 3: Pharmacokinetics. (Handbook of Experimental Pharmacology Ser.: Vol. 28). (Illus.). xxxiii, 480p. 1975. 147.00 (ISBN 0-387-07001-X). Springer-Verlag.
Gillette, Jackman. Psoriasis: The Story of a Man Who Helped Himself. LC 80-81893. 1980. pap. 6.95 (ISBN 0-8180-2101-2). Horizon.
Gillette, James R., et al, eds. Microsomes & Drug Oxidations: Proceedings. 1969. 65.00 (ISBN 0-12-283650-2). Acad Pr.
Gillette, John. Coat Pocket Bird Book. McKee, Russell, ed. (Illus.). 160p. 1984. pap. 9.95 (ISBN 0-941912-05-1). TwoPeninsula Pr.
--Coat Pocket Bird Book. LC 83-62005. 160p. 1984. pap. 9.95 (ISBN 0-317-27286-1). Mich Nat Res.
Gillette, John M. Constructive Rural Sociology. 1913. 15.00 (ISBN 0-8482-4201-7). Norwood Edns.
Gillette, King C. The Human Drift. LC 76-27838. 200p. 1976. Repr. of 1894 ed. lib. bdg. 35.00x (ISBN 0-8201-1276-3). Schol Facsimiles.
Gillette, Louise. Glorious Treasure. (Tapestry Ser.: No. 013). (Orig.). 1984. pap. 2.95 (ISBN 0-671-52343-0). PB.
Gillette, Michael. The Cortes Letter. 240p. 1983. pap. 2.75 (ISBN 0-380-83881-8, 83881-8). Avon.
Gillette, Michael, jt. auth. see Gillette, A. S.
Gillette, Ned & Dostal, John. Cross-Country Skiing. 2nd ed. LC 79-19415. (Illus.). 240p. 1983. pap. 9.95 (ISBN 0-89886-079-2). Mountaineers.
--Cross-Country Skiing. 256p. 1984. pap. 3.95 (ISBN 0-553-23875-2). Bantam.
Gillette, Ned & Reynolds, Jan. Everest Grand Circle: A Climbing & Skiing Adventure through Nepal & Tibet. (Illus.). 264p. 1985. 22.50 (ISBN 0-89886-111-X). Mountaineers.
Gillette, Paul. California Red Wine Book. (Wine Library: Vol. 1). (Illus.). 1984. pap. 6.95 (ISBN 0-913290-76-9). Camaro Pub.
--California White Wine Book. (Wine Library: Vol. 2). (Illus.). 1984. pap. 6.95 (ISBN 0-913290-77-7). Camaro Pub.
--The Chinese Godfather. 416p. (Orig.). 1980. pap. 2.75 (ISBN 0-449-14344-9, GM). Fawcett.
--Three Hundred Five East. LC 72-94017. 1977. 9.50 (ISBN 0-87795-082-2). Arbor Hse.
--Unusual Sex Behavior & Practices. (Orig.). 1974. pap. 1.50 (ISBN 0-87067-453-6, BH453). Holloway.
Gillette, Paul, jt. auth. see Jandt, Fred E.
Gillette, Paul C. & Garson, Arthur, Jr., eds. Pediatric Cardiac Dysrhythmias. (Clinical Cardiology Monographs). 496p. 1981. 56.00 (ISBN 0-8089-1332-8, 791554). Grune.
Gillette, Paul J. Grushenka. (Orig.). 1966. pap. 1.95 (ISBN 0-87067-610-5, BH610). Holloway.
Gillette, R. M., jt. auth. see Dupre, M. J.
Gillette, Ronald. Hardware & Variety. 84p. (Orig.). 1984. pap. 6.00 (ISBN 0-942582-07-1). Erie St Pr.
Gillette, William. Retreat from Reconstruction: 1869 to 1879. LC 79-12450. 1980. text ed. 32.50x (ISBN 0-8071-0569-4); pap. 8.95x (ISBN 0-8071-1006-X). La State U Pr.
--The Right to Vote: Politics & the Passage of the Fifteenth Amendment. LC 74-94492. (Studies in Historical & Political Science: Eighty-Third Series (1965)). 192p. 1965. 18.50x (ISBN 0-8018-0218-0); pap. 5.95x (ISBN 0-8018-1090-6). Johns Hopkins.
--The Right to Vote: Politics & the Passage of the 15th Amendment. LC 78-64243. (Johns Hopkins University. Studies in the Social Sciences. Eighty-Third Ser. 1965: 1). Repr. of 1965 ed. 18.50 (ISBN 0-404-61348-9). AMS Pr.
Gillette, William H. Plays by William Hooker Gillette. Cullen, Rosemary & Wilmeth, Don B., eds. LC 82-14692. (British & American Playwrights Ser.: 1750 - 1920). (Illus.). 250p. 1983. 39.50 (ISBN 0-521-24089-1); pap. 13.95 (ISBN 0-521-28431-7). Cambridge U Pr.
Gilletz, Norene. The Pleasures of Your Food Processor. 368p. 1984. pap. 9.95 (ISBN 0-446-37952-2). Warner Bks.
Gilley, Jeanne M., et al. Early Childhood: Development & Education. LC 78-73823. 1980. pap. 14.80 (ISBN 0-8273-1579-1); instructor's guide 4.80 (ISBN 0-8273-1580-5). Delmar.
Gilley, Leonard. Hippopotamus & Flowers. 1968. pap. 1.50 (ISBN 0-686-14910-6). Goliards Pr.
Gilley, Mickey. Mickey Gilley's Texas Cookbook. Newman, Melissa, ed. 160p. (Orig.). 1984. pap. 8.95 (ISBN 0-671-50487-8, Fireside). S&S.
Gilley, Robert. God's Plan for the World, New Testament Survey. (International Correspondence Program Ser.). 169p. (Orig.). 1984. pap. 6.95 (ISBN 0-87148-362-9). Pathway Pr.
Gillham, Anabel. Friends & Lovers for Life. 1982. pap. 5.95 (ISBN 0-8423-0931-4). Tyndale.
Gillham, Bill. The Early Words Picture Book. (Illus.). (ps-k). 1983. 7.95 (ISBN 0-698-20583-9, Coward). Putnam Pub Group.
--The Early Words Picture Book. 32p. (ps). 1985. pap. 3.95 (ISBN 0-698-20621-5, Coward). Putnam Pub Group.
--First Words Language Programme. (Illus.). 1979. text ed. 15.95x (ISBN 0-04-371059-X); pap. 6.75 (ISBN 0-04-371060-3). Allen Unwin.
--The First Words Language Programme. (Illus.). 96p. 1980. pap. text ed. 13.95 (ISBN 0-04-371060-3). Univ Park.
--The First Words Picture Book. LC 81-12452. (Illus.). 32p. (gr. 1-5). 1982. 7.95 (ISBN 0-698-20560-X, Coward); pap. 3.95 (ISBN 0-698-20605-3). Putnam Pub Group.
--Home Before Long. (Illus.). 112p. (gr. 3-7). 1984. 9.95 (ISBN 0-233-97561-6). Andre Deutsch.
--My Brother Barry. (Illus.). 96p. (gr. 2-7). 1982. 9.95 (ISBN 0-233-97358-3). Andre Deutsch.
--A Place to Hide. (Illus.). 112p. (gr. 2-6). 1983. 9.95 (ISBN 0-233-97496-2). Andre Deutsch.
--The Rich Kid. LC 85-71252. (Illus.). 112p. (gr. 3-7). 1985. 9.95 (ISBN 0-233-97684-1). Andre Deutsch.
--Two Words Together: A First Sentences Language Programme. 64p. 1983. text ed. 19.50x (ISBN 0-04-371091-3); pap. text ed. 8.95x (ISBN 0-04-371092-1). Allen Unwin.
--What Happens Next? (Illus.). 32p. (ps-k). 1985. 7.95 (ISBN 0-399-21255-8, Putnam). Putnam Pub Group.
Gillham, Bill & Hulme, Susan. Let's Look for Colors. LC 83-24047. (Let's Look Bks.). (Illus.). 24p. (ps-1). 1984. 4.95 (ISBN 0-698-20612-6, Coward). Putnam Pub Group.
--Let's Look for Numbers. LC 83-24066. (Let's Look Bks.). (Illus.). 24p. (ps-1). 1984. 4.95 (ISBN 0-698-20613-4, Putnam). Putnam Pub Group.
--Let's Look for Opposites. LC 83-24065. (Let's Look Bks.). (Illus.). 24p. (ps-1). 1984. 4.95 (ISBN 0-698-20614-2, Putnam). Putnam Pub Group.
--Let's Look for Shapes. LC 83-25177. (Let's Look Bks.). (Illus.). 24p. (ps-1). 1984. 4.95 (ISBN 0-698-20615-0, Putnam). Putnam Pub Group.
Gillham, Bill, ed. Problem Behaviour in the Secondary School: A Systems Approach. 195p. 1981. 26.00 (ISBN 0-7099-0129-1, Pub. by Croom Helm Ltd); pap. 9.75 (ISBN 0-7099-1102-5). Longwood Pub Group.
--Reconstructing Educational Psychology. 198p. 1978. 25.00 (ISBN 0-85664-631-8, Pub. by Croom Helm Ltd); pap. 11.50 (ISBN 0-85664-667-9). Longwood Pub Group.
Gillham, D. G. Keats-Poems of Eighteen Twenty. 224p. 1969. pap. text ed. 14.95x (ISBN 0-7121-0141-1, Pub. by Macdonald & Evans England). Trans-Atlantic.
Gillham, David G. William Blake. LC 72-80296. (British Authors Ser). (Illus.). 224p. 1973. 37.50 (ISBN 0-521-08680-9); pap. 10.95 (ISBN 0-521-09735-5). Cambridge U Pr.
Gillham, E. H. & Hope, M. A. Birds of the North Kent Marshes. 1981. 26.00x (ISBN 0-905540-43-3, Pub. by Hollewell Pubns). State Mutual Bk.
Gillham, John K., jt. ed. see Riew, C. Keith.
Gillham, Mary. A Naturalist in New Zealand. 16.50x (ISBN 0-392-14176-0, SpS). Sportshelf.
Gillham, Nicholas W. Organelle Heredity. LC 75-43195. 618p. 1978. 77.00 (ISBN 0-89004-102-4). Raven.
Gillham, Roger. An Enthusiast's Guide to Scalextric Cars & Equipment of Past & Present. (Illus.). 135p. 10.95 (ISBN 0-85429-286-1, F286). Haynes Pubns.
Gillham, W. E., jt. ed. see Howarth, C. I.

Gillhoff, Gerd, tr. see Kierkegaard, Soren.

Gilli, Angelo C. Modern Organizations of Vocational Education. 1976. 24.95x (ISBN 0-271-01223-4, 76-1883). Pa St U Pr.

Gilli, Angelo C., Sr. Education for Work. 1979. pap. text ed. 13.95 (ISBN 0-89669-051-2). Collegium Bk Pubs.

--Electrical Principles for Electronics. rev ed. LC 77-4676. (Illus.). 1977. text ed. 32.00 (ISBN 0-07-023293-8). McGraw.

Gilli, P. V., jt. auth. see Beckmann, G.

Gilliam, Ann, ed. Voices for the Earth: A Treasury of the Sierra Club Bulletin. LC 79-530. (Illus.). 592p. 1979. 19.95 (ISBN 0-87156-254-5). Sierra.

Gilliam, Brenda, jt. auth. see Setliff, Gail.

Gilliam, Camp. Myths & Modern Education. LC 74-24849. viii, 108p. 1975. pap. text ed. 3.50x (ISBN 0-8134-1701-5, 1701). Interstate.

Gilliam, Dona & McCaskill, Mizzy. Tinwhistle for Beginners. (Illus.). 45p. (Orig.). (gr. 3-6). 1981. pap. 3.00 (ISBN 0-9604626-1-9). Twos Co Music.

--The Whistler's Pocket Companion. (Illus.). 128p. (Orig.). 1981. pap. 6.00 (ISBN 0-9604626-0-0). Twos Co Music.

Gilliam, E. W. Seventy Ninety-One: A Tale of San Domingo. facsimile ed. LC 70-37591. (Black Heritage Library Collection). Repr. of 1890 ed. 17.25 (ISBN 0-8369-8967-8). Ayer Co Pubs.

Gilliam, George H. Business Entities. LC 82-243174. (A Virginia Law Practice System). 1983. 75.00 (ISBN 0-87215-509-9). Michie Co.

Gilliam, George H., jt. auth. see Humphrey, Dudley.

Gilliam, Gwen, jt. auth. see Garbarino, James.

Gilliam, Harold. Weather of the San Francisco Bay Region. (California Natural History Guides: No. 6). (Illus., Orig.). 1962. pap. 3.95 (ISBN 0-520-00469-8). U of Cal Pr.

Gilliam, James E. Autism: Diagnosis, Instruction, Management, & Research. (Illus.). 332p. 1981. 26.75x (ISBN 0-398-04072-9). C C Thomas.

Gilliam, Laurence, ed. B. B. C. Features. Repr. of 1950 ed. 25.00 (ISBN 0-8492-9950-0). R West.

Gilliam, Marita H., ed. see Fails Management Institute.

Gilliam, Olive. Living Through the Twentieth Century. 4.95 (ISBN 0-533-00341-5). Vantage.

--Qumran & History: The Place of the Teachers in Religion. 3.95 (ISBN 0-533-01167-1). Vantage.

Gilliam, Olive K. Witness the Power of Woman. 6.95 (ISBN 0-533-04372-7). Vantage.

Gilliam, Olivia L., jt. ed. see Morey, Sylvester M.

Gilliam, Pat, jt. auth. see Kurtz, Jerry.

Gilliam, Reginald E., Jr. Black Political Development: An Advocacy Analysis. LC 73-88999. 1974. 26.50x (ISBN 0-8046-7089-7, Pub. by Kennikat). Assoc Faculty Pr.

Gilliam, Terry & Cowel, Lucinda. Animations of Mortality. LC 78-60982. (Illus.). 1978. pap. 9.95 (ISBN 0-413-39380-1, NO.0066). Methuen Inc.

Gillianti, Simone. Rick Springfield. (Illus.). 64p. (gr. 4 up). 1984. PLB 8.29 (ISBN 0-671-53103-4). Messner.

--Rick Springfield. 1984. pap. 2.95 (ISBN 0-671-53102-6). Wanderer Bks.

Gilliar, W. G., tr. see Dvorak, J., et al.

Gilliar, Wolfgang, ed. see Dvorak, Jiri, et al.

Gilliar, Wolfgang, tr. see Gustavson, Rolf.

Gilliard, Charles. A History of Switzerland. LC 78-17481. (Illus.). 1978. Repr. of 1955 ed. lib. bdg. 15.00x (ISBN 0-313-20529-9, GIHS). Greenwood.

Gilliard, E. Thomas. Living Birds of the World. LC 58-10729. (Illus.). 1958. 9.95 (ISBN 0-385-06871-9). Doubleday.

Gilliard, Frank D., tr. see Bengtson, Hermann.

Gilliard, Pierre. Thirteen Years at the Russian Court a Personal Record of the Last Years & Death of the Czar Nicholas Second & His Family. LC 75-115539. (Russia Observed, Series I). 1970. Repr. of 1921 ed. 18.00 (ISBN 0-405-03029-0). Ayer Co Pubs.

Gilliat, Mary. Designing Rooms for Children. 128p. 1985. 15.45i (ISBN 0-316-31378-5). Little.

Gilliat-Smith, E. The Story of Brussels. (Mediaeval Towns Ser.: Vol. 25). pap. 35.00 (ISBN 0-317-15223-8). Kraus Repr.

Gilliat-Smith, Ernest. The Story of Bruges. 1976. lib. bdg. 59.95 (ISBN 0-8490-2676-8). Gordon Pr.

Gilliatt, Mary. The Complete Book of Home Design. (Illus.). 348p. 1984. 24.50i (ISBN 0-316-31371-8). Little.

--The Decorating Book. 1981. 39.95 (ISBN 0-394-51098-4). Pantheon.

--Decorating on the Cheap. LC 82-40499. (Illus.). 153p. 1984. 22.50 (ISBN 0-89480-353-0, 353); pap. 12.95 (ISBN 0-89480-354-9, 354). Workman Pub.

--Mary Gilliatt's Mix-&-Match Decorating Book. LC 83-42811. (Illus.). 1984. spiral bd. 18.45 (ISBN 0-394-42128-0). Pantheon.

Gilliatt, Penelope. Jacques Tati. (Entertainers Ser.). (Illus.). 96p. 1976. 11.50x (ISBN 0-7130-0145-3, Pub. by Woburn Pr England). Biblio Dist.

--Mortal Matters. LC 83-2090. 176p. 1983. 13.95 (ISBN 0-698-11245-8, Coward). Putnam Pub Group.

--Nobody's Business. LC 77-186943. 192p. 1972. 10.00 (ISBN 0-670-51497-7). Viking.

--They Sleep Without Dreaming. 224p. 1985. 14.95 (ISBN 0-396-08493-1). Dodd.

Gilliatt, R. W. & Asbury, A. K., eds. BIMR Neurology 4: Peripheral Nerve Disorders. 320p. 1984. text ed. 39.95 (ISBN 0-407-02297-X). Butterworth.

Gillibrand, P. & Maddock, V., eds. The Manager & His Words: An Introduction to the Vocabulary of Business English Studies. (English for Specific Purposes Ser.). 96p. 1982. 7.95 (ISBN 0-08-028637-2). Pergamon.

Gillie, Angelo C. Principles of Post-Secondary Vocational Education. LC 73-87883. 1974. text ed. 22.95 (ISBN 0-675-08866-6). Merrill.

Gillie, Angelo C. & Pratt, Arden L. Marine Technology Programs: Where We Are & Where We're Going. LC 78-28301. pap. 20.00 (ISBN 0-317-10859-X, 2020570). Bks Demand UMI.

Gillie, C. Movements in English Literature, 1900-1940. LC 74-16993. 200p. 1975. 39.50 (ISBN 0-521-20655-3); pap. 10.95 (ISBN 0-521-09922-6). Cambridge U Pr.

Gillie, Christopher. Character in English Literature. 1965. text ed. 10.50x (ISBN 0-7011-0715-4). Humanities.

--Preface to Jane Austen. 2nd ed. (Preface Books). (Illus.). 191p. 1985. pap. text ed. 8.95 (ISBN 0-582-35481-1). Longman.

Gillie, Christopher, ed. Companion to British Literature. (Illus.). 880p. 1980. Repr. of 1972 ed. 54.00x (ISBN 0-8103-2022-3). Gale.

Gillie, D. R., ed. see Pilsudski, Jozef.

Gillie, F. B. An Approach to Town Planning. (Publications of the Institute of Social Studies Paperback Ser.: No. 3). 164p. 1971. pap. text ed. 8.80x (ISBN 90-2791-760-4). Mouton.

--Basic Thinking in Regional Planning. (Publications of the Institute of Social Studies Major: No. 14). 1967. text ed. 9.60x (ISBN 90-2790-111-2). Mouton.

Gillie, Oliver & Mercer, Derrick. The Complete Book of Body Maintenance. (Illus.). 1980. pap. 9.95 (ISBN 0-393-00941-6). Norton.

Gillies, Dee A. Nursing Management: Systems Approach. (Illus.). 487p. 1982. 19.95 (ISBN 0-7216-4135-0). Saunders.

Gillies, Dee A. & Alyn, Irene B. Patient Assessment & Management by the Nurse Practitioner. LC 75-28793. (Illus.). 320p. 1976. text ed. 13.95 (ISBN 0-7216-4133-4). Saunders.

--Saunders Tests for Self-Evaluation of Nursing Competence. 3rd. ed. 1980. text ed. 17.95 (ISBN 0-7216-4157-1). Saunders.

Gillies, Emily. Creative Dramatics for All Children. Markun, Patricia M. & Cohen, Monroe D., eds. LC 72-97349. (Illus.). 64p. 1976. Repr. of 1973 ed. 4.00x (ISBN 0-87173-020-0). ACEI.

Gillies, George & Gillies, Harriet. Scriptural Outline of the Baptism of the Holy Spirit. 32p. 1972. pap. 1.50 (ISBN 0-88368-062-9). Whitaker Hse.

Gillies, Harold & Millard, D. Ralph, Jr. Principles & Art of Plastic Surgery, 2 Vols. 690p. 1966. Vol. 1. 87.50 (ISBN 0-316-31376-9); Vol. 2. 87.50 (ISBN 0-316-31377-7). Little.

Gillies, Harriet, jt. auth. see Gillies, George.

Gillies, James. Where Business Fails. 172p. 1981. pap. text ed. 9.95x (ISBN 0-920380-53-0, Pub. by Inst Res Pub Canada). Brookfield Pub Co.

Gillies, Jean. Patterns for Applique & Pieced Work & Ways to Use Them. LC 82-12020. (Illus.). 136p. 1982. 13.95 (ISBN 0-385-18135-3). Doubleday.

--Stitch Something Special: More Than Forty Things To Make from Scraps. 144p. 1985. 16.95 (ISBN 0-385-23173-3). Doubleday.

Gillies, Jerry. Men on Women. 240p. 1984. 15.95 (ISBN 0-396-08281-5). Dodd.

--Moneylove. 208p. 1979. pap. 3.50 (ISBN 0-446-32231-8). Warner Bks.

--Moneylove: How to Get the Money You Deserve for Whatever You Want. LC 78-166653. 168p. 1978. 7.95 (ISBN 0-87131-274-3). M Evans.

Gillies, John. A Guide to Caring for & Coping with Aging Parents. LC 81-1138. 1981. pap. 5.95 (ISBN 0-8407-5772-7). Nelson.

--A Guide to Compassionate Care of the Aging. 224p. 1985. pap. 7.95 (ISBN 0-8407-5427-2). Nelson.

--Historical Collections of Accounts. 582p. 1981. Repr. of 1754 ed. 24.95x (ISBN 0-85151-325-5). Banner of Truth.

--The Soviet Union: The World's Largest Country. (Discovering Our Heritage Ser.). (Illus.). 176p. (gr. 5 up). 1985. PLB 10.95 (ISBN 0-87518-290-9). Dillon.

Gillies, John, jt. auth. see Price, Walter K.

Gillies, John W. Principles of Pictorial Photography. LC 72-9201. (The Literature of Photography Ser.). Repr. of 1923 ed. 20.00 (ISBN 0-405-04910-2). Ayer Co Pubs.

Gillies, M. T. Compressed Food Bars. LC 74-82949. (Food Technology Review Ser: No. 18). 116p. 1975. 12.00 (ISBN 0-8155-0547-7). Noyes.

--Nonwoven Materials-Recent Developments. LC 79-5445. (Chemical Technology Review: No. 141). (Illus.). 372p. 1980. 45.00 (ISBN 0-8155-0776-3). Noyes.

Gillies, M. T., ed. C-One-Based Chemicals from Hydrogen & Carbon Monoxide. LC 82-3444. (Chemical Technology Rev.: No. 209). (Illus.). 379p. 1982. 47.00 (ISBN 0-8155-0901-4). Noyes.

--Chemical Additives for Fuels: Developments Since 1978. LC 81-18939. (Chemical Technology Review: No. 203, Energy Technology Review: No. 76). (Illus.). 308p. 1982. 48.00 (ISBN 0-8155-0886-7). Noyes.

--Coatings Technology Annual-First Edition. 354p. 1978. 40.00 (ISBN 0-8155-0705-4). Noyes.

--Potable Water from Wastewater. LC 81-1886. (Pollution Technology Review: No. 76). (Illus.). 305p. 1981. 42.00 (ISBN 0-8155-0845-X). Noyes.

--Powder Coatings: Recent Developments. LC 80-26426. (Chemical Tech. Rev.: 183). (Illus.). 326p. 1981. 48.00 (ISBN 0-8155-0836-0). Noyes.

--Solventless & High Solids Industrial Finishes: Recent Developments. LC 80-21553. (Chemical Technology Review: No. 179). (Illus.). 342p. 1981. 48.00 (ISBN 0-8155-0828-X). Noyes.

--Stabilizers for Synthetic Resins: Recent Developments. LC 81-16758. (Chemical Technology Review: No. 199). (Illus.). 356p. 1982. 54.00 (ISBN 0-8155-0872-7). Noyes.

--Water-Based Industrial Finishes: Recent Developments. LC 80-17520. (Chemical Technology Review Ser.: No. 167). 435p. 1980. 48.00 (ISBN 0-8155-0812-3). Noyes.

Gillies, R. F. Lecture Notes on Medical Microbiology. 2nd ed. (Illus.). 1978. softcover 13.00 (ISBN 0-632-00062-7, B1826-6, Blackwell). Mosby.

Gillies, R. R. Gillies & Dodds Bacteriology Illustrated. 5th ed. LC 82-23595. (Illus.). 224p. (Orig.). 1984. pap. text ed. 28.00 (ISBN 0-443-02809-5). Churchill.

Gillies, Robert P. Memoirs of a Literary Veteran: Including Sketches & Anecdotes of the Most Distinguished Literary Characters from 1794-1849, 3 Vols. LC 71-148785. Repr. of 1851 ed. Set. 72.50 (ISBN 0-404-07650-5). Vol. 1 (ISBN 0-404-07651-3). Vol. 2 (ISBN 0-404-07652-1). Vol. 3 (ISBN 0-404-07653-X). AMS Pr.

--Recollections of Sir Walter Scott, Bart. LC 73-8885. Repr. of 1837 ed. lib. bdg. 25.00 (ISBN 0-8414-2040-8). Folcroft.

Gilliespie, John T., ed. More Juniorplots: A Guide for Teachers & Librarians. LC 77-8786. 1977. 15.95 (ISBN 0-8352-1002-2). Bowker.

Gilligan, C., et al. Business Decision Making. 197p. 1983. text ed. 30.00x (ISBN 0-86003-518-2, Pub. by Allan England); pap. text ed. 15.25x. Humanities.

Gilligan, Carol. In a Different Voice: Psychological Theory & Women's Development. LC 81-13478. 240p. 1982. 15.00 (ISBN 0-674-44543-0). Harvard U Pr.

--In a Different Voice: Psychological Theory & Women's Development. 192p. 1983. pap. 5.95 (ISBN 0-674-44544-9). Harvard U Pr.

Gilligan, Francis J. Morality of the Color Line. LC 71-94478. Repr. of 1928 ed. cancelled (ISBN 0-8371-2353-4, GIM&, Pub. by Negro U Pr). Greenwood.

Gilligan, Lawrence & Nenno, Robert. Intermediate Algebra for College Students. 2nd ed. 567p. 1984. pap. text ed. 20.95 (ISBN 0-669-05696-0). Heath.

Gilligan, Lawrence & Nenno, Robert B. Basic Algebra: A Semi-Programmed Approach. LC 76-12810. (Illus.). 1977. pap. text ed. 21.70x (ISBN 0-673-16221-4). student solution manual 8.25 (ISBN 0-673-16222-2). Scott F.

--College Algebra. 1981. text ed. 25.55x (ISBN 0-673-16229-X). Scott F.

--College Algebra & Trigonometry: Precalculus Math. 1981. text ed. 25.55 (ISBN 0-673-16230-3). Scott F.

--Finite Mathematics: An Elementary Approach. 2nd ed. 1979. text ed. 23.80x (ISBN 0-673-16235-4). Scott F.

Gilligan, Lawrence, jt. auth. see Taylor, Claudia.

Gilligan, Shannon. Mona Is Missing. 64p. (Orig.). 1984. pap. 1.95 (ISBN 0-553-15283-1). Bantam.

--The Mystery of Ura Senke. (Choose Your Own Adventure Ser.: No. 44). 128p. (Orig.). (gr. 5). 1985. pap. 1.95 (ISBN 0-553-24892-8). Bantam.

--The Search for Champ. (Skylark Choose Your Own Adventure: No. 14). 50p. 1983. pap. 1.95 (ISBN 0-553-15227-0). Bantam.

--The Three Wishes. (Skylark Choose Your Own Adventure Ser.: No. 15). 64p. (Orig.). (gr. 1-3). 1984. pap. text ed. 1.95 (ISBN 0-553-15241-6, Skylark). Bantam.

Gilligan, Sonia C. The Heterosexuals Are Coming: The Fusion Strategy. LC 70-152827. (Illus.). 195p. (Orig.). 1972. pap. 4.50 (ISBN 0-685-24669-8, F&B 100). Fusion Groups.

Gilliland, A. R. & Jordan, R. H. Educational Measurements & the Classroom Teacher. 269p. 1983. Repr. of 1924 ed. lib. bdg. 30.00 (ISBN 0-89987-349-9). Darby Bks.

Gilliland, Alexis. Long Shot for Rosinante. 192p. 1981. pap. 2.25 (ISBN 0-345-29854-3, Del Rey). Ballantine.

Gilliland, Alexis A. The End of the Empire. 176p. 1983. pap. 2.25 (ISBN 0-345-31334-8, Del Rey). Ballantine.

--The Pirates of Rosinante. 224p. (Orig.). 1982. pap. 2.50 (ISBN 0-345-30659-7, Del Rey). Ballantine.

--Revolution from Rosinante. 192p. (Orig.). 1981. pap. 2.25 (ISBN 0-345-29265-0, Del Rey). Ballantine.

Gilliland, Bruce. The River Kingdom. 1985. 12.95 (ISBN 0-533-06338-8). Vantage.

Gilliland, Burl E., et al. Theories & Strategies in Counseling & Psychotherapy. (Illus.). 384p. 1984. text ed. 26.95 (ISBN 0-13-913574-X). P-H.

Gilliland, Dean S. Pauline Theology & Mission Practice. 304p. 1983. pap. 12.95 (ISBN 0-8010-3788-3). Baker Bk.

Gilliland, Dolores S. Selected Women of the Scriptures of Stamina & Courage. (Illus.). 1978. pap. 3.95 (ISBN 0-931446-02-3). Honor Bks.

Gilliland, Glaphre. When the Pieces Don't Fit... God Makes the Difference. 176p. 1984. pap. 5.95 (ISBN 0-310-45341-0). Zondervan.

Gilliland, H. Indian Children's Books. 1980. write for info. (ISBN 0-89992-502-2); pap. 7.95 (ISBN 0-89992-503-0). Coun India Ed.

--Readability Formula. 1980. 00.15 (ISBN 0-89992-508-1). Coun India Ed.

Gilliland, Hap. Bill Red Coyote Is a Nut. (Beginning Reading for All Ages Ser.). 1981. 1.95 (ISBN 0-89992-101-9). Coun India Ed.

--Broken Ice. (Indian Culture Ser.). (gr. 1-8). 1972. 1.95 (ISBN 0-89992-024-1). Coun India Ed.

--Chant of the Red Man. (Indian Culture Ser.). (Illus.). 1976. 3.95 (ISBN 0-89992-048-9). Coun India Ed.

--Coyote's Pow-Wow. (Indian Culture Ser.). (gr. 1-6). 1972. 1.95 (ISBN 0-89992-022-5). Coun India Ed.

--No One Like a Brother. (Indian Culture Ser.). (gr. 4-12). 1970. 1.95 (ISBN 0-89992-003-9). Coun India Ed.

--We Live on an Indian Reservation. (Beginning Reading for All Ages Ser.). 1981. 1.95 (ISBN 0-89992-100-0). Coun India Ed.

Gilliland, Hap, jt. auth. see Shows, Harry B.

Gilliland, Hap, ed. see Dygert, Janice.

Gilliland, Jean. The Fourteenth Day Conspiracy. LC 80-51212. 224p. 1980. pap. 6.95 (ISBN 0-934616-09-4). Valkyrie Pub Hse.

Gilliland, Ken. Trucking: A Truck Driver's Workbook. McFadden, S. Michele, ed. LC 79-90760. 1984. pap. text ed. 19.50x (ISBN 0-89262-029-3). Career Pub.

--Trucking: Instructor's Guide. McFadden, S. Michele, ed. 1982. pap. text ed. 50.00 (ISBN 0-89262-030-7). Career Pub.

Gilliland, Ken & Millard, J. Trucking: A Truck Driver's Training Handbook. McFadden, S. Michele, ed. LC 79-90760. (Illus.). 434p. 1981. lib. bdg. 29.50x (ISBN 0-89262-057-9). Career Pub.

Gilliland, Ken, et al. Trucking: A Truck Driver's Training Handbook. LC 79-90760. (Illus.). 434p. (Orig.). 1981. pap. text ed. 24.50x (ISBN 0-89262-025-0). Career Pub.

Gilliland, Marion S. The Material Culture of Key Marco, Florida. LC 75-15798. 1975. 15.00 (ISBN 0-8130-0362-8). U Presses Fla.

Gilliland, Mary. Gathering Fire. LC 82-13022. 65p. 1982. pap. 5.00 (ISBN 0-87886-119-X). Ithaca Hse.

Gilliland, Mary E. Frisco: A Colorful Colorado Community. LC 84-71449. (Illus.). 144p. (Orig.). 1984. 12.00 (ISBN 0-9603624-3-6). Alpenrose Pr.

--Summit: A Gold Rush History of Summit County, Colorado. LC 80-65781. (Illus.). 336p. (Orig.). 1980. text ed. 18.95 (ISBN 0-9603624-1-X); pap. text ed. 12.00 (ISBN 0-9603624-0-1). Alpenrose Pr.

--The Summit Hiker. LC 83-71361. (Illus.). 97p. (Orig.). 1983. pap. text ed. 8.95 (ISBN 0-9603624-2-8). Alpenrose Pr.

Gilliland, Ray & Kovach, Tom. The Dark Side of the Moon. (Indian Culture Ser.). 32p. (gr. 1-4). 1984. 6.95 (ISBN 0-89992-386-0); pap. 2.45 (ISBN 0-89992-086-1). Coun India Ed.

Gilliland, Robert M., jt. auth. see White, Robert.

Gillim, Marion H. Incidence of Excess Profits Taxation. LC 68-58579. (Columbia University. Studies in the Social Sciences: No. 514). Repr. of 1945 ed. 17.50 (ISBN 0-404-51514-2). AMS Pr.

Gillin, Donald G. Warlord: Yen Hsi-Shan in Shansi Province, 1911-1949. 1966. 38.00x (ISBN 0-691-03067-7). Princeton U Pr.

Gillin, John. Archaeological Investigations in Central Utah. (HU PMP). pap. 15.00 (ISBN 0-527-01243-2). Kraus Repr.

--Barama River Caribs of British Guiana. (HU BMB). 1936. 31.00 (ISBN 0-527-01233-5). Kraus Repr.

Gillin, John L. Criminology & Penology. 3rd ed. LC 71-138238. (Illus.). 615p. 1972. Repr. of 1945 ed. lib. bdg. 46.00x (ISBN 0-8371-5595-9, GICP). Greenwood.

--Criminology & Penology. 1926. 20.00 (ISBN 0-8482-4202-5). Norwood Edns.

--The Dunkers: A Sociological Interpretation. LC 72-8248. Repr. of 1906 ed. 20.00 (ISBN 0-404-11002-9). AMS Pr.

--Taming the Criminal: Adventures in Penology. LC 69-14927. (Criminology, Law Enforcement, & Social Problems Ser.: No. 71). (Illus.). 1969. Repr. of 1931 ed. 15.00x (ISBN 0-87585-071-5). Patterson Smith.

Gillin, John P. Moche: A Peruvian Coastal Community. LC 75-11858. (Illus.). 166p. 1973. Repr. of 1947 ed. lib. bdg. 22.00x (ISBN 0-8371-5075-2, SMID). Greenwood.

Gilling, Cynthia M., jt. auth. see Nash, D. F.

Gilling, Dick & Brightwell, Robin. The Human Brain. LC 82-15467. (Illus.). 192p. 1983. 15.95 (ISBN 0-87196-710-3). Facts on File.

Gillingham, Bryan. The Polyphonic Sequence in Wolfenbuttel 677. (Wissenschaftliche Abhandlungen - Musicological Studies Ser.: No. 35). 80p. 1982. lib. bdg. 30.00 (ISBN 0-931902-14-2). Inst Mediaeval Mus.

--Saint-Martial Mehrstimmigkeit: Polyphony. (Wissenschaftliche Abhandlungen-Musicological Studies: Vol. 44). 240p. (Eng. & Ger.). 1983. lib. bdg. 38.00 (ISBN 0-931902-38-X). Inst Mediaeval Mus.

Gillingham, E. Leonard. Dealing with Conflict. LC 81-20662. 144p. 1982. 8.75 (ISBN 0-687-10329-0). Abingdon.

Gillingham, F. J. Advances in Stereotactic & Functional Neurosurgery Four: Proceedings. (Acta Neurochirurgica Supplementum: Vol. 30). (Illus.). 444p. 1981. pap. 35.00 (ISBN 0-387-90501-4). Springer-Verlag.

Gillingham, F. J. & Hitchcock, E. R., eds. Advances in Stereotezctic & Functional Neurosurgery: Proceedings. LC 77-22266. (Acta Neurochirurgica: Supplementum 24). (Illus.). 1977. 81.50 (ISBN 0-387-81422-1). Springer-Verlag.

Gillingham, F. J., et al, eds. Stereotactic Treatment of Epilepsy. LC 76-25838. 1976. pap. 82.60 (ISBN 0-387-81374-8). Springer-Verlag.

Gillingham, J., et al. Advances in Sterotactic & Functional Neurosurgery. (Acta Neurochinurgica Ser.: Suppl. 21). (Illus.). 280p. 1974. pap. 75.60 (ISBN 0-387-81212-1). Springer-Verlag.

Gillingham, John. The Angevin Empire. Clanchy, M. T., ed. (Foundations of Medieval History Ser.). 120p. 1984. text ed. 19.50x (ISBN 0-8419-1011-1); pap. 13.50x (ISBN 0-8419-1012-X). Holmes & Meier.

--Industry & Politics in the Third Reich: Ruhr, Hitler, & Europe. 160p. 1985. 20.00x (ISBN 0-231-06260-5). Columbia U Pr.

--The Life & Times of Richard I. (Kings & Queens of England Ser.). (Illus.). 224p. 1973. text ed. 17.50x (ISBN 0-297-99572-3, GWN 04662, Pub. by Weidenfeld & Nicolson England). Biblio Dist.

--The Wars of the Roses: Peace & Conflict in Fifteenth-Century England. 278p. 1982. text ed. 22.50x (ISBN 0-8071-1005-1). La State U Pr.

Gillingham, John & Holt, J. C., eds. War & Government in the Middle Ages: Essays in Honour of J. O. Prestwich. LC 84-423. (Illus.). 210p. 1984. 45.00x (ISBN 0-389-20475-7, 08037). B&N Imports.

Gillingham, John, tr. see Mayer, Hans E.

Gillingham, Peter N., jt. auth. see Schumacher, E. F.

Gillings & Douglass. Biostats: A Primer for Health Care Professionals. (Illus.). 275p. 1985. pap. 19.50 (ISBN 0-932137-02-4). Cavco Pubns.

Gillings, Dennis, jt. auth. see Hadler, Nortin M.

Gillings, Richard. Mathematics in the Time of the Pharaohs. (Illus.). 298p. 1982. pap. 6.00 (ISBN 0-486-24315-X). Dover.

Gillington, Alice E. Old Christmas Carols of the Southern Counties. LC 76-25121. 1976. Repr. of 1910 ed. lib. bdg. 17.50 (ISBN 0-8414-4534-6). Folcroft.

--Songs of the Open Road. (Folklore Ser). 15.00 (ISBN 0-8482-4221-1). Norwood Edns.

Gillington, M. C. A Day with Lord Byron. 1973. 10.00 (ISBN 0-8274-0650-9). R West.

--A Day with William Morris. Repr. 10.00 (ISBN 0-8274-2155-9). R West.

Gillingwater, D., jt. ed. see Button, K. J.

Gillis, Carroll. As the Stars in Number. 144p. 1981. 7.50 (ISBN 0-682-49792-4). Exposition Pr FL.

Gillis, Christina M. The Paradox of Privacy: Epistolary Form in Clarissa. LC 83-25903. (University of Florida Humanities Monographs: No. 54). viii, 167p. (Orig.). 1984. pap. 12.00 (ISBN 0-8130-0761-5). U Presses Fla.

Gillis, Daniel. Furtwangler & America. (Illus.). 1970. 5.00 (ISBN 0-87141-031-1). Manyland.

--Furtwangler & America. LC 75-125028. (Illus.). 148p. 1980. Repr. of 1971 ed. 7.95 (ISBN 0-87867-079-3). Ramparts.

--Vita. LC 79-52906. 111p. 1979. pap. 5.00 (ISBN 0-87867-072-6). Ramparts.

Gillis, Everett A. Capsuled in Summer. (Illus.). 64p. (Orig.). 1985. pap. 9.95 (ISBN 0-938328-03-4). Pisces Pr TX.

--Far Beyond Distance. 64p. 1981. 9.95 (ISBN 0-938328-01-8). Pisces Pr TX.

--Goldie. (Illus.). 64p. (Orig.). (gr. 3-7). 1982. pap. 8.00 (ISBN 0-938328-02-6). Pisces Pr TX.

--South by West: A Galaxy of Southwestern & Western Scenes & Portraits. 48p. (Orig.). 1981. pap. 5.00 (ISBN 0-938328-00-X). Pisces Pr TX.

--The Waste Land As Grail Romance: Eliot's Use of the Medieval Grail Legends. (Graduate Studies: No. 6). 26p. 1974. pap. 2.00 (ISBN 0-89672-013-6). Tex Tech Pr.

Gillis, F. J., jt. auth. see Stone, Ruth M.

Gillis, Frank J., ed. see Collins, Lee.

Gillis, Frederick. Moonbeams for Ellen. 1983. 5.95 (ISBN 0-533-05439-7). Vantage.

Gillis, Gerald L. Bent, but Not Broken. (Orig.). Date not set. pap. price not set (ISBN 0-87844-065-8). Sandlapper Pub Co.

Gillis, J. A. Hawaiian Incident. facs. ed. LC 77-117878. (Select Bibliographies Reprint Ser). 1897. 14.00 (ISBN 0-8369-5331-2). Ayer Co Pubs.

Gillis, Jack. The Car Book 1984. (A Tilden Press Bk.). (Illus.). 143p. 1984. pap. 7.95 (ISBN 0-525-48089-7, 0772-230). Dutton.

--The Car Book, 1985. LC 84-48328. (Illus.). 144p. 1985. 17.26i (ISBN 0-06-015412-8, HarpT). Harper Row.

--The Car Book, 1985. LC 84-48328. (Illus.). 144p. 1985. pap. 8.61i (ISBN 0-06-464097-3, BN). Harper Row.

Gillis, James C., jt. auth. see Wood, David E.

Gillis, James M. Collected Writings. 600.00 (ISBN 0-87968-905-6). Gordon Pr.

--False Prophets. LC 77-93339. (Essay Index Reprint Ser.). 1925. 18.00 (ISBN 0-8369-1351-5). Ayer Co Pubs.

--False Prophets. 1929. Repr. 25.00 (ISBN 0-8274-2330-6). R West.

Gillis, John. Social Influence in Psychotherapy. 59p. 1979. pap. 4.95 (ISBN 0-932930-08-5). Pilgrimage Inc.

Gillis, John R. The Development of European Society Seventeen Seventy to Eighteen Seventy. LC 82-20234. (Illus.). 316p. 1983. pap. text ed. 13.25 (ISBN 0-8191-2898-8). U Pr of Amer.

--For Better, for Worse: British Marriages, 1600 to the Present. (Illus.). 393p. 1985. 29.95 (ISBN 0-317-28538-6). Oxford U Pr.

--Prussian Bureaucracy in Crisis, 1840-1860: Origins of an Administrative Ethos. LC 70-130826. 1971. 22.50x (ISBN 0-8047-0756-1). Stanford U Pr.

--Youth & History: Tradition & Change in European Age Relations, 1770 to Present. rev. ed. LC 81-7919. (Studies in Social Discontinuity). 1981. 12.95 (ISBN 0-12-785264-6). Acad Pr.

Gillis, John S. Too Tall, Too Small. LC 82-9233. 1982. 12.95 (ISBN 0-918296-15-3). Inst Personality & Ability.

Gillis, Joseph, jt. auth. see Burr, Keith.

Gillis, M. Arthur. Microcomputers in Financial Institutions. LC 84-73254. 1985. 25.00 (ISBN 0-87094-580-7). Dow Jones-Irwin.

Gillis, M. F., jt. ed. see Phillips, R. D.

Gillis, Malcolm, ed. see Musgrave, Richard A.

Gillis, Malcolm, et al. Taxation & Mining: Nonfuel Minerals in Bolivia & Other Countries. LC 77-23806. 384p. 1978. prof ref 50.00 (ISBN 0-88410-458-3). Ballinger Pub.

--Economics of Development. 650p. 1983. text ed. 23.95x (ISBN 0-393-95253-3). Norton.

Gillis, Phyllis. Entrepreneurial Mothers. LC 82-42685. 384p. 1984. 16.95 (ISBN 0-89256-248-X); pap. 10.95 (ISBN 0-89256-256-0). Rawson Assocs.

Gillis, R. A. & Kent, K. M., eds. Importance of the Nervous System in the Initiation & Treatment of Cardiac Arrhythmias. (Cardiology: Vol. 61, No. 1). (Illus.). 1976. 18.00 (ISBN 3-8055-2437-4). S Karger.

Gillis, Ruth J. Children's Books for Times of Stress: An Annotated Bibliography. LC 76-48517. pap. 86.30 (ISBN 0-317-10361-X, 2055194). Bks Demand UMI.

Gillis, S. Malcolm, ed. Tax & Investment Policies for Hard Minerals: Public & Multinational Enterprise in Indonesia. Beals, Ralph E. LC 70-23352. 320p. 1980. prof ref 35.00 (ISBN 0-88410-488-5). Ballinger Pub.

Gillis, Steven & Inman, F. P., eds. Contemporary Topics in Molecular Immunology, Vol. 10: The Interleukins. 316p. 1985. 42.50x (ISBN 0-306-41776-6, Plenum Pr). Plenum Pub.

Gillis, William, ed. see Durrenmatt, Friedrich.

Gillis, William R. Gold Rush Days with Mark Twain. LC 71-93533. (Illus.). Repr. of 1930 ed. 12.50 (ISBN 0-404-02774-1). AMS Pr.

--Gold Rush Days with Mark Twain. LC 77-131719. 1971. 11.00 (ISBN 0-403-00606-6). Scholarly.

Gillison, A. N. & Anderson, D. J. Vegetation Classification in Australia. LC 81-68097. 229p. 1981. text ed. 13.50 (ISBN 0-7081-1309-5, 1077, Pub. by ANUP Australia). Australia N U P.

Gillison, A. N. & Anderson, D. J., eds. Vegetation Classification in Australia. 229p. 1983. (Pub. by CSIRO Australia). Intl Spec Bk.

--Vegetation Classification in Australia. 229p. 1981. 55.00x (ISBN 0-7081-1309-5, Pub. by CSIRO Australia). State Mutual Bk.

Gillispie, Charles C. Edge of Objectivity: An Essay in the History of Scientific Ideas. 1960. pap. 12.95 (ISBN 0-691-02350-6). Princeton U Pr.

--Genesis & Geology: A Study in the Relations of Scientific Thought, Natural Theology & Social Opinion in Great Britain, 1790-1850. LC 51-10449. (Historical Monographs Ser: No. 58). 1951. 20.00x (ISBN 0-674-34480-4). Harvard U Pr.

--Lazare Carnot Savant. LC 78-132238. 1971. 45.00 (ISBN 0-691-08082-8). Princeton U Pr.

--The Montgolfier Brothers & the Invention of Aviation, 1783-1784: With a Word on the Importance of Ballooning for the Science of Heat & for the Art of Building Railroads. LC 82-61363. (Illus.). 272p. 1983. 35.00 (ISBN 0-691-08321-5). Princeton U Pr.

--Science & Polity in France at the End of the Old Regime. LC 80-7521. (Illus.). 472p. 1980. 57.50x (ISBN 0-691-08233-2). Princeton U Pr.

Gillispie, Charles C., ed. Dictionary of Scientific Biography, Supple. I, Vol. 15. LC 69-18090. 1978. 55.00 (ISBN 0-684-14779-3, ScribR). Scribner.

--Dictionary of Scientific Biography: Compact Edition, 8 vols. LC 69-18090. 1970-1980. Set. text ed. 750.00 (ISBN 0-684-16962-2, ScribR); text ed. 80.00 ea. Scribner.

Gillispie, Charles C., ed. see Diderot, Denis.

Gillissen, G. & Theurer, K. E., eds. New Aspects in Physiological Antitumor Substances. (Illus.). x, 228p. 1985. pap. 17.25 (ISBN 3-8055-4002-7). S Karger.

Gillman, Gavin P., jt. auth. see Uehara, Goro.

Gillman, James. Life of S. T. Coleridge. LC 72-187489. 1838. lib. bdg. 25.00 (ISBN 0-8414-0562-X). Folcroft.

Gillman, K. & Newson, M. D. Soil Pipes & Pipeflow. (Bgrg Research Monography Ser.). 1980. pap. 9.90x (ISBN 0-686-27388-5, Pub. by GEO Abstracts England). State Mutual Bk.

Gillman, L., jt. auth. see Jerison, M.

Gillman, Leni, jt. auth. see Gillman, Peter.

Gillman, Leonard & McDowell, Robert. Calculus. 1973. pap. 14.95x (ISBN 0-393-09350-6). Norton.

Gillman, Leonard & McDowell, Robert H. Calculus. 2nd ed. (Illus.). 1978. text ed. 39.95x (ISBN 0-393-09051-5); solutions manual 7.95x (ISBN 0-393-09054-X). Norton.

Gillman, Neil. Gabriel Marcel on Religious Knowledge. LC 80-5061. 315p. 1980. text ed. 25.25 (ISBN 0-8191-1034-5); pap. text ed. 14.00 (ISBN 0-8191-1035-3). U Pr of Amer.

Gillman, Peter & Gillman, Leni. Collar the Lot: How Britain Interned & Expelled Its Wartime Refugees. (Illus.). 228p. 1981. 17.95 (ISBN 0-7043-2244-7, Pub. by Quartet England). Charles River Bks.

--Collar the Lot: How Britain Interned & Expelled Its Wartime Refugees. (Illus.). 344p. pap. 12.95 (ISBN 0-7043-3408-9, Pub. by Quartet Bks). Merrimack Pub Cir.

Gillman, Richard. Too Much Alone. 2nd ed. LC 75-179831. (New Poetry Series). Repr. of 1965 ed. 16.00 (ISBN 0-404-56031-8). AMS Pr.

Gillmar, Stanley, jt. auth. see Green, Mary.

Gillmer, Richard S. Death of a Business: The Red Wing Pottery. LC 68-25961. (Illus.). 1968. 10.00 (ISBN 0-87018-021-5). Ross.

Gillmer, Thomas & Johnson, Bruce. Introduction Naval Architecture. LC 81-85439. (Illus.). 400p. 1982. text ed. 23.95x (ISBN 0-87021-318-0). Naval Inst Pr.

--Introduction to Naval Architecture. (Illus.). 400p. 1982. 23.95 (ISBN 0-87021-318-0); bulk rates avail. Naval Inst Pr.

Gillmer, Thomas C. Modern Ship Design. 2nd ed. LC 74-25031. (Illus.). 355p. 1975. text ed. 18.95x (ISBN 0-87021-388-1). Naval Inst Pr.

Gillmor, C. Stewart. Coulomb & the Evolution of Physics & Engineering in Eighteenth Century France. LC 79-155006. (Illus.). 1971. 34.50x (ISBN 0-691-08095-X). Princeton U Pr.

Gillmor, Donald M. Free Press & Fair Trial. 1966. 12.00 (ISBN 0-8183-0170-8). Pub Aff Pr.

Gillmor, Donald M. & Barron, Jerome A. Mass Communication Law: Cases & Comment. 4th ed. 1100p. 1984. text ed. 33.95 (ISBN 0-314-78005-X). West Pub.

--Mass Communications Law, Cases & Comment. 3rd ed. LC 79-15306. (American Casebook Ser.). 1008p. 1979. text ed. 19.95 (ISBN 0-8299-2050-1). West Pub.

Gillmor, Frances. Flute of the Smoking Mirror: A Portrait of Nezahualcoyotl - Poet-King. (Illus.). 197p. 1983. Repr. of 1949 ed. 9.95 (ISBN 0-87480-225-3). U of Utah Pr.

--The King Danced in the Marketplace. LC 63-11970. (Illus.). 1978. pap. 14.95 (ISBN 0-87480-148-6). U of Utah Pr.

Gillmor, Frances & Wetherill, Louisa W. Traders to the Navajos: The Story of the Wetherills of Kayenta. LC 52-9210. 1965. pap. 6.95 (ISBN 0-8263-0040-5). U of NM Pr.

Gillmore, Inez H. Angel Island. Reginald, R. & Melville, Douglas, eds. LC 77-84229. (Lost Race & Adult Fantasy Ser.). (Illus.). 1978. Repr. of 1914 ed. lib. bdg. 33.00x (ISBN 0-405-10979-2). Ayer Co Pubs.

Gillmore, Parker. Days & Nights by the Desert. LC 72-3982. (Black Heritage Library Collection Ser.). Repr. of 1888 ed. 22.50 (ISBN 0-8369-9097-8). Ayer Co Pubs.

Gillock, William L. Fanfare. 16p. (gr. 4-12). 1957. pap. text ed. 5.95 (ISBN 0-87487-632-X). Birch Tree Gr.

--Lyric Preludes. 32p. (gr. 4-12). 1958. pap. text ed. 5.95 (ISBN 0-87487-649-4). Birch Tree Gr.

Gillon, Adam. Eternal Solitary: A Study of Joseph Conrad. LC 60-14919. 191p. 1960. text ed. 19.50x (ISBN 0-8290-0171-9). Irvington.

--Joseph Conrad. (English Author Ser.). 1982. lib. bdg. 13.50 (ISBN 0-8057-6820-3, Twayne). G K Hall.

--Joseph Conrad. (English Authors Ser.). 232p. 1984. pap. 6.95 (ISBN 0-8057-6889-0, Twayne). G K Hall.

Gillon, Edmond V. A New England Town in Early Photographs: 149 Illus. of Southbridge, Massachusetts,1878-1930. 12.00 (ISBN 0-8446-5491-4). Peter Smith.

Gillon, Edmond V., Jr. Decorative Frames & Borders: 396 Examples from the Renaissance to the Present Day. 13.50 (ISBN 0-8446-4744-6). Peter Smith.

Gillon, Edmund, Jr. & Lancaster, Clay. Victorian Houses: A Treasury of Lesser-Known Examples. (Illus.). 14.75 (ISBN 0-8446-5110-9). Peter Smith.

Gillon, Edmund, Jr., jt. auth. see Gayle, Margot.

Gillon, Edmund V. Art Nouveau: An Anthology of Design & Illustration from the Studio. LC 73-82624. (Illus.). 13.50 (ISBN 0-8446-0644-8). Peter Smith.

--Cut & Assemble Early New England Village. (Illus.). pap. 3.95 (ISBN 0-486-23536-X). Dover.

--Early New England Gravestone Rubbings. (Illus.). 15.25 (ISBN 0-8446-2129-3). Peter Smith.

--New York Then & Now: 83 Manhattan Sites Photographed in the Past & Present. 11.50 (ISBN 0-8446-5524-4). Peter Smith.

Gillon, Edmund V., jt. auth. see Sanders, Ronald.

Gillon, Edmund V., ed. Cartouches & Decorative Small Frames: 396 Examples from the Renaissance to Art Deco. (Illus.). 9.25 (ISBN 0-8446-5192-3). Peter Smith.

--A New England Town in Early Photographs: Illustrations of Southbridge, Massachusetts 1878 - 1930. LC 75-463. (Illus.). 176p. (Orig.). 1976. pap. 6.50 (ISBN 0-486-23286-7). Dover.

Gillon, Edmund V., ed. see Gibson, Charles D.

Gillon, Edmund V., Jr. Art Nouveau: An Anthology. (Illus., Orig.). 1969. pap. 3.95 (ISBN 0-486-22388-4). Dover.

--Cartouches & Decorative Small Frames: 396 Examples from the Renaissance to Art Deco. LC 74-15173. (Pictorial Archive Ser). (Illus.). 128p. 1975. pap. 4.50 (ISBN 0-486-23122-4). Dover.

--Decorative Frames & Borders: 396 Examples from the Renaissance to the Present Day. LC 72-96186. (Illus.). 224p. (Orig.). 1973. pap. 6.00 (ISBN 0-486-22928-9). Dover.

--Early Illustrations & Views of American Architecture. (Illus.). 1971. pap. 11.95 (ISBN 0-486-22750-2). Dover.

--Early Illustrations & Views of American Architecture. (Illus.). 18.00 (ISBN 0-8446-0112-8). Peter Smith.

--Early New England Gravestone Rubbings. (Illus., Orig.). 1966. pap. 7.95 (ISBN 0-486-21380-3). Dover.

--Geometric Design & Ornament. abr. ed. Orig. Title: Ornament. (Illus.). 1970. pap. 3.95 (ISBN 0-486-22526-7). Dover.

--Geometric Design & Ornament: 374 Illustrations for Artists & Designers. 11.75 (ISBN 0-8446-4547-8). Peter Smith.

--Middle Ages: Dover Coloring Book. (gr. 2-6). pap. 2.50 (ISBN 0-486-22743-X). Dover.

--Pennsylvania Dutch Farm: To Cut Out & Assemble. (Encore Edition). (Orig.). 1979. pap. 2.49 (ISBN 0-684-17368-9). Scribner.

--Pictorial Calligraphy & Ornamentation. (Illus.). 96p. (Orig.). 1972. pap. 4.00 (ISBN 0-486-22788-X). Dover.

--Picture Sourcebook for Collage & Decoupage. LC 74-82206. (Illus.). 144p. (Orig.). 1974. pap. 6.50 (ISBN 0-486-23095-3). Dover.

--South Street: A Photographic Guide to New York City's Historic Seaport. 11.25 (ISBN 0-8446-5578-3). Peter Smith.

--Victorian Stencils for Design & Decoration. LC 68-26054. (Illus., Orig.). 1968. pap. 4.50 (ISBN 0-486-21995-X). Dover.

--Victorian Stencils for Design & Decoration. LC 68-26054. 1968. lib. bdg. 15.00x (ISBN 0-88307-604-7). Gannon.

Gillon, Edmund V., Jr. & Lancaster, Clay. Victorian Houses: A Treasury of Lesser-Known Examples. (Illus.). 128p. (Orig.). 1973. pap. 6.95 (ISBN 0-486-22966-1). Dover.

Gillon, Edmund V., Jr., jt. auth. see Spero, James.

Gillon, Edmund V., Jr., ed. see Gesner, Conrad.

Gillon, Jack. Le Menu Gastronomique: An Interpretation of Nouvelle Cuisine. (Illus.). 168p. 1983. 12.50 (ISBN 0-904265-60-9, Pub. by Salem Hse Ltd). Merrimack Pub Cir.

Gillon, Philip. Israelis & Palestinians: Co-Existence Or...The Credo of Elie Eliachar. (Illus.). 182p. 1978. pap. 12.00 (ISBN 0-86036-078-4, Pub. by R Collings UK). Three Continents.

Gillon, Werner. A Short History of African Art. 1985. 21.95 (ISBN 0-8160-0139-1). Facts on File.

Gillooly, William B. Literature Search: Document Retrieval in the Behavioral Sciences. (Illus., Orig.). 1969. pap. text ed. 1.25 (ISBN 0-685-16734-8). Mariner Pr.

Gillot, Cedric. Entomology. LC 79-21675. 747p. 1980. 55.00x (ISBN 0-306-40366-8, Plenum Pr); pap. text ed. 25.00 (ISBN 0-306-40514-8, Plenum Pr). Plenum Pub.

Gillot, Edward, tr. see Pouillon, Fernand.

Gillott, C. A., jt. auth. see Sawyer, John G.

Gillow, Joseph. Literary & Biographical History; or Bibliographical Dictionary of English Catholics from the Breach with Rome, in 1534, to the Present Time, 5 Vols. 1962. Repr. of 1892 ed. 205.00 (ISBN 0-8337-1356-6). B Franklin.

Gillpatrick, W. The Man Who Likes Mexico. 1976. lib. bdg. 59.95 (ISBN 0-8490-2201-0). Gordon Pr.

Gillquist, Peter E. Let's Quit Fighting About the Holy Spirit. 160p. 1974. pap. 4.95 (ISBN 0-310-25001-3). Zondervan.

--Love Is Now. new ed. 1970. 4.95 (ISBN 0-310-36941-X). Zondervan.

Gillray, James. Works of James Gillray. LC 68-21201. (Illus.). 1968. Repr. of 1851 ed. 50.00 (ISBN 0-405-08562-1, Blom Pubns). Ayer Co Pubs.

Gillson, Margery. Developing a High School Chemistry Course Adapted to the Differentiated Needs of Boys & Girls. LC 75-176805. (Columbia University. Teachers College. Contributions to Education Ser.: No. 709). Repr. of 1937 ed. 22.50 (ISBN 0-404-55709-0). AMS Pr.

Gilluly, James, et al. Principles of Geology. 4th ed. LC 74-23076. (Geology Ser.). (Illus.). 527p. 1975. text ed. 30.95 (ISBN 0-7167-0269-X). W H Freeman.

Gillum, Donald R. Industrial Level Measurement. (Instructional Resource Package). (Illus.). 115p. 1984. pap. text ed. 29.95 student guide (ISBN 0-87664-761-1); instr's. guide 10.00 (ISBN 0-87664-762-X). Instru Soc.

Gillum, Gary P., jt. auth. see Dahlin, Therrin C.

Gillum, Gary P., compiled by. Of All Things! A Nibley Quote Book. 192p. 1982. 10.95 (ISBN 0-941214-03-6). Signature Bks.

Gillum, Nickol, ed. Marketing Handbook. 1985. pap. write for info. (ISBN 0-915355-22-1). Am Assn Blood.

Gillum, Perry. The Christian Life. (Whole Man Whole World Bible Lessons Ser.). 151p. (Orig.). 1983. pap. 3.95 (ISBN 0-934942-46-3, 2418). White Wing Pub.

--History of Christianity. (Whole Man Whole World Bible Lessons Ser.). 140p. (Orig.). 1984. pap. 3.95 (ISBN 0-934942-48-X); text ed. 2.95 (ISBN 0-934942-49-8); tchr's. ed. 2.95 (ISBN 0-934942-47-1). White Wing Pub.

Gilly, Adolfo. Inside the Cuban Revolution. Gutierrez, Felix, tr. LC 74-1780. 83p. 1975. Repr. of 1964 ed. lib. bdg. 15.00x (ISBN 0-8371-7399-X, GICR). Greenwood.

--The Mexican Revolution. 336p. 1983. 25.00 (ISBN 0-8052-7144-9, Pub. by NLB England); pap. 11.50 (ISBN 0-8052-7145-7). Schocken.

Gilman. The Blind Side. (Edge Ser.: No. 44). 192p. (Orig.). 1984. pap. 2.25 (ISBN 0-523-42042-0). Pinnacle Bks.

--Times Past. (Apache Ser.: No. 25). 208p. (Orig.). 1983. pap. 2.25 (ISBN 0-523-41676-8). Pinnacle Bks.

Gilman, Albert, ed. see Shakespeare, William.

Gilman, Alfred G., et al, eds. Goodman & Gilman's The Pharmacological Basis of Therapeutics. 6th ed. 1980. text ed. write for info. (ISBN 0-02-344720-6). Macmillan.

Gilman, Antonio. A Later Prehistory of Tangier, Morocco. LC 75-20595. (American School of Prehistoric Research Bulletins: No. 29). (Illus.). 1975. pap. 9.25x (ISBN 0-87365-531-1). Peabody Harvard.

Gilman, Antonio & Thornes, John B. Land-Use & Prehistory in South-East Spain. (London Research Series in Geography: No. 8). (Illus.). 256p. 1984. text ed. 35.00x (ISBN 0-04-913022-6). Allen Unwin.

Gilman, Arthur. Library of Religious Poetry. 59.95 (ISBN 0-8490-0521-3). Gordon Pr.

--Rome. 1885. Repr. 15.00 (ISBN 0-8482-4219-X). Norwood Edns.

--The Story of Rome: From the Earliest Times to the End of the Republic. 1827. 30.00 (ISBN 0-8274-3951-2). R West.

Gilman, Arthur, jt. auth. see Church, Alfred J.

Gilman, Arthur, ed. Cambridge Seventeen Seventy-Six with the Diary of Dorothy Dudley. LC 79-120869. (American Bicentennial Ser). 1970. Repr. of 1875 ed. 22.50x (ISBN 0-8046-1262-5, Pub. by Kennikat). Assoc Faculty Pr.

Gilman, Beatrice I. Sculpture of the 16th-18th Centuries in the Collection of the Hispanic Society of America. (Illus.). 360p. 1930. 6.00 (ISBN 0-317-00627-4, Pub. by Hispanic Soc). Interbk Inc.

--Sculpture of 13th-15th Centuries in the Collection of the Hispanic Society of America. (Illus.). 360p. 1930. 5.00 (ISBN 0-317-00626-6, Pub. by Hispanic Soc). Interbk Inc.

Gilman, Benjamin I. Hopi Songs. LC 76-17498. (A Journal of American Ethnology & Archaeology: Vol. 5). Repr. of 1908 ed. 35.00 (ISBN 0-404-58045-9). AMS Pr.

Gilman, Benjamin I., jt. auth. see Fewkes, Jessie W.

Gilman, Caroline. The Poetry of Travelling in the United States. LC 71-104465. 1977. Repr. of 1838 ed. lib. bdg. 16.00 (ISBN 0-8398-0660-4). Irvington.

Gilman, Carolyn. Where Two Worlds Meet: The Great Lakes Fur Trade. LC 82-2089. (Museum Exhibit Ser.: No. 2). (Illus.). 148p. (Orig.). 1982. pap. 18.95 (ISBN 0-87351-156-5). Minn Hist.

Gilman, Chandler. Legends of a Log Cabin. LC 75-104466. Repr. of 1835 ed. lib. bdg. 15.50 (ISBN 0-8398-0661-2). Irvington.

Gilman, Charlotte. Women & Economics. 75.00 (ISBN 0-87968-282-5). Gordon Pr.

Gilman, Charlotte & Stetson, Perkins. The Man-Made World: Or, Our Androcentric Culture. 1971. Repr. of 1911 ed. 22.00 (ISBN 0-384-18560-6). Johnson Repr.

Gilman, Charlotte P. Herland: A Lost Feminist Utopian Novel. LC 78-20418. 1979. 8.95 (ISBN 0-394-50388-0); pap. 3.95 (ISBN 0-394-73665-6). Pantheon.

--His Religion & Hers: A Study of the Faith of Our Fathers & the Work of Our Mothers. LC 75-29509. (Pioneers of the Woman's Movement: An International Perspective Ser.). xi, 300p. 1976. Repr. of 1923 ed. 26.50 (ISBN 0-88355-377-5). Hyperion-Conn.

--The Living of Charlotte Perkins Gilman: An Autobiography. LC 72-2604. (American Women Ser: Images & Realities). (Illus.). 386p. 1972. Repr. of 1935 ed. 24.50 (ISBN 0-405-04459-3). Ayer Co Pubs.

--Women & Economics: A Study of the Economic Relation Between Men & Women As a Factor in Social Evolution. Degler, Carl N., ed. 18.50 (ISBN 0-8446-2130-7). Peter Smith.

--Women & Economics: The Economic Factor Between Men & Women As a Factor in Social Evolution. Degler, Carl, ed. 1970. pap. 7.95xi (ISBN 0-06-133073-6, TB3073, Torch). Har-Row.

--The Yellow Wallpaper. 64p. 1973. pap. 3.95 (ISBN 0-912670-09-6). Feminist Pr.

Gilman, Daniel C. James Monroe. Morse, John T., Jr., ed. LC 73-128966. (American Statesmen: No. 14). Repr. of 1898 ed. 27.00 (ISBN 0-404-50864-2). AMS Pr.

--The Launching of a University. 1972. Repr. of 1906 ed. 21.50 (ISBN 0-8422-8059-6). Irvington.

--The Life of James Dwight, Dana, Scientific Explorer, Mineralogist, Geologist, Zoologist, Professor in Yale University. 19.00 (ISBN 0-8369-7138-8, 7971). Ayer Co Pubs.

--University Problems in the United States. LC 75-89182. (American Education: Its Men, Institutions & Ideas, Ser. 1). 1969. Repr. of 1898 ed. 15.00 (ISBN 0-405-01419-8). Ayer Co Pubs.

--University Problems in the United States. 1972. Repr. of 1898 ed. lib. bdg. 12.00 (ISBN 0-8422-8058-8). Irvington.

--University Problems in the United States. 1971. Repr. 32.00 (ISBN 0-384-18562-2). Johnson Repr.

Gilman, Dorothy. Amazing Mrs. Pollifax. Date not set. pap. 2.95 (ISBN 0-449-20912-1, Crest). Fawcett.

--The Clairvoyant Countess. 224p. 1978. pap. 1.95 (ISBN 0-449-23561-0, Crest). Fawcett.

--Elusive Mrs. Pollifax. LC 76-144266. 1971. 8.95 (ISBN 0-385-09463-9). Doubleday.

--Elusive Mrs. Pollifax. 1985. pap. 2.95 (ISBN 0-449-20855-9, Crest). Fawcett.

--Maze in the Heart of the Castle. LC 82-45198. 240p. (gr. 8 up). 1983. 12.95 (ISBN 0-385-17817-4). Doubleday.

--Mrs. Pollifax & the Hong Kong Buddha. LC 85-4335. 192p. 1985. 14.95 (ISBN 0-385-19959-7). Doubleday.

--Mrs. Pollifax on Safari. 1978. pap. 1.95 (ISBN 0-449-23414-2, Crest). Fawcett.

--Mrs. Pollifax on the China Station. LC 82-45972. (Illus.). 192p. 1983. 12.95 (ISBN 0-385-14525-X). Doubleday.

--A Nun in the Closet. 1979. pap. 1.95 (ISBN 0-449-23632-3, Crest). Fawcett.

--A Palm for Mrs. Polifax. 192p. 1985. pap. 2.95 (ISBN 0-449-20864-8, Crest). Fawcett.

--A Palm for Mrs. Pollifax. LC 72-89947. 240p. 1973. 5.95 (ISBN 0-385-09134-6). Doubleday.

--A Palm for Mrs. Pollifax. 1984. pap. 2.40 (ISBN 0-449-23446-0, Crest). Fawcett.

--The Tightrope Walker. 224p. 1980. pap. 1.95 (ISBN 0-449-24305-2, Crest). Fawcett.

--The Tightrope Walker. (General Ser.). 1980. lib. bdg. 12.95 (ISBN 0-8161-3026-4, Large Print Bks). G K Hall.

--Unexpected Mrs Pollifax. 1985. pap. 2.95 (ISBN 0-449-20828-1, Crest). Fawcett.

--The Unexpected Mrs. Pollifax. (Nightingale Paperbacks Ser.). 342p. 1984. pap. 9.95 (ISBN 0-8161-3368-9, Large Print Bks). G K Hall.

--The Unexpected Mrs. Pollifax. 1986. pap. 2.95 (ISBN 0-449-20674-2, Crest). Fawcett.

Gilman, Dugan. Upstate. LC 79-142724. (Wesleyan Poetry Program: Vol. 55). 1971. 15.00x (ISBN 0-8195-2055-1); pap. 6.95 (ISBN 0-8195-1055-6). Wesleyan U Pr.

Gilman, Ernest B. The Curious Perspective: Literary & Pictorial Wit in the Seventeenth Century. LC 78-6075. (Illus.). 1978. Yale U Pr.

Gilman, George. Death Drive. (Edge Ser.: No. 27). 1980. pap. 1.75 (ISBN 0-523-41309-2, Dist. by Independent News Co.). Pinnacle Bks.

--Steele's War: The Preacher. (Steele Ser.: No. 26). 192p. (Orig.). 1984. pap. 2.50 (ISBN 0-523-41917-1). Pinnacle Bks.

Gilman, George C. Edge: Towering Nightmare, No. 30. 1980. pap. 1.75 (ISBN 0-523-41312-2). Pinnacle Bks.

Gilman, George G. Apache Death. (Edge Ser. No. 3). 1981. pap. 1.95 (ISBN 0-523-41769-1). Pinnacle Bks.

--Apache Death. (Edge Ser.: No. 3). 160p. 1984. pap. 2.50 (ISBN 0-523-42343-8). Pinnacle Bks.

--Arapaho Revenge. (Edge Ser.: No. 43). 192p. 1983. pap. 2.25 (ISBN 0-523-42041-2). Pinnacle Bks.

--Ashes & Dust. (Edge Ser.: No. 19). (Orig.). 1981. pap. 1.75 (ISBN 0-523-41297-5). Pinnacle Bks.

--Black As Death. (The Undertaker Ser.: No. 1). 192p. (Orig.). 1985. pap. 2.50 (ISBN 0-317-19679-0). Pinnacle Bks.

--Black Vengeance. (Edge Ser.: No. 10). 1981. pap. 1.95 (ISBN 0-523-41771-3). Pinnacle Bks.

--Bloody Summer. (Edge Ser.: No. 9). 192p. 1981. pap. 1.75 (ISBN 0-523-41287-8). Pinnacle Bks.

--Bloody Sunrise. (Edge Ser.: No. 42). 192p. 1983. pap. 2.25 (ISBN 0-523-42021-8). Pinnacle Bks.

--California Kill. (Edge Ser., No. 7). 1981. pap. 1.75 (ISBN 0-523-41285-1). Pinnacle Bks.

--Death Deal. (Edge Ser.: No. 35). 160p. 1981. pap. 1.95 (ISBN 0-523-41776-4). Pinnacle Bks.

--Death Trail. (Steele: No. 12). 1978. pap. 1.50 (ISBN 0-523-40378-X). Pinnacle Bks.

--Death's Bounty. (Edge Ser.: No. 12). 1974. pap. 1.75 (ISBN 0-523-41290-8). Pinnacle Bks.

--Echoes of War. (The Edge Ser.: No. 23). 1978. pap. 1.50 (ISBN 0-523-40485-9). Pinnacle Bks.

--Edge. (Edge Ser., No. 5). 160p. 1981. pap. 1.95 (ISBN 0-523-41836-1). Pinnacle Bks.

--Edge: California Killing, No. 7. 128p. 1982. 15.00x (ISBN 0-7278-0570-3, Pub. by Severn Hse). State Mutual Bk.

--Edge Meets Steele: Matching Pair. 208p. (Orig.). 1982. pap. 2.25 (ISBN 0-523-41894-9). Pinnacle Bks.

--Edge: Montana Melodrama, No. 40. 192p. (Orig.). 1982. pap. 2.25 (ISBN 0-523-41451-X). Pinnacle Bks.

--Edge: The Blue, the Grey, & the Red, No. 6. 128p. 1982. 15.00x (ISBN 0-7278-0565-7, Pub. by Severn Hse). State Mutual Bk.

--Edge: Town on Trial, No. 36. 160p. 1981. pap. 1.95 (ISBN 0-523-41799-3). Pinnacle Bks.

--Eve of Evil. (Edge Ser.: No. 28). 1978. pap. 1.50 (ISBN 0-523-40204-X, Dist. by Independent News Co.). Pinnacle Bks.

--The Final Shot. (Edge Ser.: No. 16). 160p. (Orig.). 1981. pap. 1.75 (ISBN 0-523-41294-0). Pinnacle Bks.

--Fort Despair. (Steele Ser.: No. 23). 192p. 1983. pap. 1.95 (ISBN 0-523-41914-7). Pinnacle Bks.

--Frightened Gun, No. Thirty Two. (Edge Ser.). (Orig.). 1980. pap. 1.75 (ISBN 0-523-41314-9). Pinnacle Bks.

--The Guilty Ones. (Edge Ser.: No. 31). 1982. pap. 1.95 (ISBN 0-523-42037-4). Pinnacle Bks.

--The Hated. (Edge Ser.: No. 13). 160p. 1978. pap. 1.50 (ISBN 0-523-40462-X). Pinnacle Bks.

--Hell's Seven. (Edge Ser.: No. 8). 160p. 1981. pap. 1.75 (ISBN 0-523-41286-X). Pinnacle Bks.

--The House on the Range. (Edge Ser.: No. 45). 192p. (Orig.). 1984. pap. 2.25 (ISBN 0-523-42227-X). Pinnacle Bks.

--Killer's Breed. (Edge Ser., No. 4). 192p. 1982. pap. 1.95 (ISBN 0-523-42032-3). Pinnacle Bks.

--The Killing Claim. (Edge Ser.: No. 41). 192p. 1982. pap. 2.25 (ISBN 0-523-41924-4). Pinnacle Bks.

--The Living, the Dying & the Dead. (Edge Ser.: No. 29). 1981. pap. 1.95 (ISBN 0-523-41775-6). Pinnacle Bks.

--The Loner. (Edge Ser.: No. 1). 144p. 1981. pap. 1.75 (ISBN 0-523-41279-7). Pinnacle Bks.

--Massacre Mission. (Edge Ser.: No. 38). 160p. 1981. pap. 1.95 (ISBN 0-523-41449-8). Pinnacle Bks.

--The Moving Cage. (Edge Ser.: No. 47). 192p. (Orig.). 1984. pap. 2.50 (ISBN 0-523-42266-0). Pinnacle Bks.

--Paradise Loses. (Edge Ser.: No. 15). 160p. 1981. pap. 1.75 (ISBN 0-523-41293-2). Pinnacle Bks.

--The Prisoners. (Edge Ser.: No. 39). 192p. 1982. pap. 1.95 (ISBN 0-523-41450-1). Pinnacle Bks.

--Red Fury. (Edge Ser.: No. 33). 160p. 1982. pap. 1.95 (ISBN 0-523-42033-1). Pinnacle Bks.

--Red River. (Edge Ser.: No. 6). 192p. 1981. pap. 1.95 (ISBN 0-523-41770-5). Pinnacle Bks.

--Revenge Ride. (Edge Ser.: No. 49). 192p. (Orig.). 1985. pap. 2.50 (ISBN 0-523-42268-7). Pinnacle Bks.

--Rhapsody in Red. (Edge Ser.: No. 21). 1982. pap. 1.95 (ISBN 0-523-41454-4). Pinnacle Bks.

--A Ride in the Sun. (Edge Ser.: No. 34). 160p. 1982. pap. 1.95 (ISBN 0-523-41987-2). Pinnacle Bks.

--Satan's Daughters. (Steele Ser.: No. 17). 160p. 1980. pap. 1.50 (ISBN 0-523-40527-8). Pinnacle Bks.

--Savage Dawn. (Edge Ser.: No. 26). 1981. pap. 1.95 (ISBN 0-523-41837-X). Pinnacle Bks.

--School for Slaughter. (Edge Ser.: No. 48). 192p. (Orig.). 1985. pap. 2.50 (ISBN 0-523-42267-9). Pinnacle Bks.

--Sioux Uprising. (Edge Ser.: No. 11). 1980. pap. 1.75 (ISBN 0-523-41289-4). Pinnacle Bks.

--Slaughter Road. (Edge Ser.: No. 22). 160p. 1982. pap. 1.95 (ISBN 0-523-42029-3). Pinnacle Bks.

--Slaughterday. (Edge Ser: No. 24). 1981. pap. 1.75 (ISBN 0-523-41302-5). Pinnacle Bks.

--Steele: The Big Game, No. 22. 192p. (Orig.). 1982. pap. 1.95 (ISBN 0-523-41455-2). Pinnacle Bks.

--Steele: The Tarnished Star, No. 19. 160p. 1981. pap. 1.75 (ISBN 0-523-41452-8). Pinnacle Bks.

--Sullivan's Law. (Edge Ser.: No. 20). 1981. pap. 1.95 (ISBN 0-523-41774-8). Pinnacle Bks.

--Ten Grand. (Edge Ser.: No. 2). 144p. 1982. pap. 2.50 (ISBN 0-523-42322-5). Pinnacle Bks.

--Ten Tombstones. (Edge Ser.: No. 18). 192p. 1981. pap. 1.95 (ISBN 0-523-41773-X). Pinnacle Bks.

--Tiger's Gold. (Edge Ser.: No. 14). 192p. 1975. pap. 1.95 (ISBN 0-523-41772-1). Pinnacle Bks.

--Two of a Kind. 160p. 1982. pap. 2.25 (ISBN 0-523-42031-5). Pinnacle Bks.

--Vengeance at Ventura. (Edge Ser.: No. 37). 160p. 1981. pap. 1.95 (ISBN 0-523-41448-X). Pinnacle Bks.

--Vengeance Valley. (Edge Ser.: No. 17). 160p. (Orig.). 1981. pap. 1.95 (ISBN 0-523-41838-8). Pinnacle Bks.

--Violence Trail. (The Edge Ser.: No. 25). 1981. pap. 1.95 (ISBN 0-523-41802-7). Pinnacle Bks.

--Wagons East. (Steele Ser.: No. 21). 192p. 1982. pap. 1.95 (ISBN 0-523-41454-4). Wiley.

--Wanted for Murder. (Steele Ser.: No. 20). 192p. 1982. pap. 1.95 (ISBN 0-523-41453-6). Pinnacle Bks.

Gilman, George S. Killer's Breed. (Edge Ser.: No. 4). 1984. pap. 2.50 (ISBN 0-523-42349-7). Pinnacle Bks.

Gilman, Glenn. Human Relations in the Industrial Southeast. LC 74-7609. (Illus.). 327p. 1974. Repr. of 1956 ed. lib. bdg. 19.50x (ISBN 0-8371-7589-5, GIHU). Greenwood.

Gilman, H. Organic Syntheses Collective Volumes: Vols. 1-9, Vol. 1. 580p. 1941. 42.95 (ISBN 0-471-30030-6, Pub. by Wiley-Interscience). Wiley.

Gilman, Irene P., jt. ed. see Fleming, Jane L.

Gilman, J. D. & Clive, John. KG 200. (General Ser.). 1978. lib. bdg. 14.95 (ISBN 0-8161-6591-2, Large Print Bks). G K Hall.

Gilman, J. J., jt. ed. see Drucker, Daniel C.

Gilman, John, jt. auth. see Heide, Robert.

Gilman, John J. Art & Science of Growing Crystals. LC 63-11432. (Science & Technology of Materials Ser.). 493p. 1963. 72.95x (ISBN 0-471-30177-9, Pub. by Wiley-Interscience). Wiley.

Gilman, Joseph C. A Manual of Soil Fungi. facsimile ed. (Illus.). 1957. pap. 17.50x (ISBN 0-8138-2320-X). Iowa St U Pr.

Gilman, Julia M. William Wells & Maconaquah, White Rose of the Miamis. LC 85-60341. 327p. (Orig.). 1985. pap. 10.95 (ISBN 0-9614890-2-2). Jewel Pub Co.

Gilman, Kenneth & Public Management Institute Staff. Computers for Nonprofits. LC 81-80946. 1981. 3 ring binder 49.00x (ISBN 0-916664-32-5). Public Management.

Gilman, Lawrence. Aspects of Modern Opera: Estimates & Inquiries. LC 68-25288. (Studies in Music, No. 42). 1969. Repr. of 1909 ed. lib. bdg. 46.95x (ISBN 0-8383-0302-1). Haskell.

--Edward MacDowell. 59.95 (ISBN 0-8490-0096-3). Gordon Pr.

--Edward MacDowell: A Study. 2nd ed. LC 67-27455. (Music Ser). 1969. Repr. of 1908 ed. lib. bdg. 22.50 (ISBN 0-306-70979-1). Da Capo.

--Music of To-Morrow & Other Studies. facs. ed. LC 71-128246. (Essay Index Reprint Ser). 1907. 14.00 (ISBN 0-8369-1830-4). Ayer Co Pubs.

--Music of To-Morrow & Other Studies. LC 73-153249. (Essay & General Literature Index Reprint Ser). 1971. Repr. of 1907 ed. 19.50x (ISBN 0-8046-1502-0, Pub. by Kennikat). Assoc Faculty Pr.

--Nature in Music, & Other Studies in the Tone Poetry of Today. facs. ed. LC 67-22096. (Essay Index Reprint Ser). 1914. 15.00 (ISBN 0-8369-0475-3). Ayer Co Pubs.

--Phases of Modern Music. facs. ed. LC 68-22915. (Essay Index Reprint Ser). 1904. 15.00 (ISBN 0-8369-0476-1). Ayer Co Pubs.

--Phrases of Modern Music. 59.95 (ISBN 0-8490-0832-8). Gordon Pr.

--Toscanini & Great Music. 12.25 (ISBN 0-8369-7253-8, 8052). Ayer Co Pubs.

--Wagner's Operas. LC 71-181163. 268p. 1937. Repr. 39.00x (ISBN 0-403-01565-0). Scholarly.

Gilman, Leonard & Rose, Allen J. APL: An Interactive Approach. 3rd ed. LC 83-14716. 366p. 1983. pap. 26.45x (ISBN 0-471-09304-1). Wiley.

Gilman, Lois. The Adoption Resource Book. LC 84-47622. 240p. (Orig.). 1984. pap. 6.95i (ISBN 0-06-091160-3, CN1160, CN). Har-Row.

--The Adoption Resource Book: A Comprehensive Guide to All the Things You Need to Know & Ought to Know about Creating an Adoptive Family. LC 84-47622. (Illus.). 240p. (Orig.). 1984. 16.30i (ISBN 0-06-015340-7, HarpT). Har-Row.

Gilman, Margaret. Baudelaire the Critic. 1971. Repr. of 1943 ed. lib. bdg. 20.00x (ISBN 0-374-93088-0). Octagon.

Gilman, Margaret, ed. Foreign Language Tests & Techniques. 136p. 1956. pap. 7.95x (ISBN 0-915432-56-0). NE Conf Teach Foreign.

Gilman, Margaret C., jt. auth. see Gilman, Stanwood.

Gilman, Marilyn. Diary of a Woman Doctor. 1981. pap. 2.75 (ISBN 0-89083-718-X). Zebra.

--Doctor's Hospital. (Orig.). 1983. pap. 2.95 (ISBN 0-8217-1206-3). Zebra.

--Doctors' Wives. 1983. pap. 2.95 (ISBN 0-8217-1256-X). Zebra.

Gilman, Marion B. & Gilman, Richard. Desserts & Pastries: A Professional Primer. LC 84-2384. (Illus.). 256p. 1984. 24.95 (ISBN 0-442-22763-9). Van Nos Reinhold.

Gilman, Martin G. The Financing of Foreign Direct Investment. 200p. 1981. 26.00 (ISBN 0-312-28982-0). St Martin.

Gilman, Mary L., ed. Acronyms, Initialisms, & Other Abbreviations. 24p. 1982. pap. 4.00 (ISBN 0-318-01727-X). Natl Shorthand Rptr.

--Glossaries. 109p. 1983. pap. 9.00 (ISBN 0-318-01722-9). Natl Shorthand Rptr.

Gilman, Mary L., compiled by. Three Thousand Sound-Alikes & Look Alikes. 60p. 1983. pap. 6.00 (ISBN 0-318-01718-0). Natl Shorthand Rptr.

Gilman, Nicholas P. Profit Sharing Between Employer & Employee: A Study in the Evolution of the Wages System. facsimile ed. LC 78-165635. (Select Bibliographies Reprint Ser). Repr. of 1889 ed. 26.50 (ISBN 0-8369-5944-2). Ayer Co Pubs.

--Socialism & the American Spirit. facsimile ed. LC 70-150183. (Select Bibliographies Reprint Ser). Repr. of 1893 ed. 23.50 (ISBN 0-8369-5696-6). Ayer Co Pubs.

Gilman, Rhoda R. & Holmquist, June D., eds. Selections from "Minnesota History". A Fiftieth Anniversary Anthology. (Illus.). 369p. (Twenty-eight articles by noted authors). 1979. Repr. 8.95 (ISBN 0-87351-025-9). Minn Hist.

Gilman, Rhoda R., ed. see Porter, Rufus.

Gilman, Rhoda R., et al. Red River Trails: Oxcart Routes Between St. Paul & the Selkirk Settlement, 1820-1870. LC 78-11045. (Illus.). 104p. 1979. pap. 7.95 (ISBN 0-87351-133-6). Minn Hist.

Gilman, Richard. Decadence: The Strange Life of an Epithet. 192p. 1979. 8.95 (ISBN 0-374-13567-3); pap. 4.95 (ISBN 0-374-51553-0). FS&G.

--The Making of Modern Drama. LC 74-1171. 292p. 1974. pap. 4.50 (ISBN 0-374-51148-9). FS&G.

Gilman, Richard, jt. auth. see Gilman, Marion B.

Gilman, Richard, jt. ed. see Bentley, Eric.

Gilman, Richard M. Behind World Revolution: The Strange Career of Nesta H. Webster, Vol. 1. LC 82-90685. (Illus.). 128p. 1982. pap. 7.95 (ISBN 0-910087-00-8). Insight Bks.

Gilman, Robert C. The Warlock of Rhada. 176p. 1985. pap. 2.75 (ISBN 0-441-87310-3). Ace Bks.

Gilman, Ronald L. Tennessee Corporations: Tennessee Practice Systems Library Selection. LC 79-91162. looseleaf bdg. 87.50; Suppl. 1984. 22.00; Suppl. 1983. 20.00. Lawyers Co-Op.

Gilman, Samuel. Memoirs of a New England Village Choir. (Music Reprint Ser.). 150p. 1983. Repr. of 1829 ed. lib. bdg. 27.50 (ISBN 0-306-76175-0). Da Capo.

Gilman, Sander. On Blackness without Blacks: Essays on the Image of the Black in Germany. 200p. 1982. lib. bdg. 26.00 (ISBN 0-8161-9026-7, Univ Bks). G K Hall.

Gilman, Sander L. Difference & Pathology: Stereotypes of Sexuality, Race, & Madness. LC 85-7809. (Illus.). 304p. 1985. 34.95x (ISBN 0-8014-1785-6); pap. 12.95x (ISBN 0-8014-9332-3). Cornell U Pr.

--Jewish Self-Hatred: Anti-Semitism & the Hidden Language of the Jews. LC 85-45050. 464p. 1985. text ed. 28.50x (ISBN 0-8018-3276-4). Johns Hopkins.

--Nietzschean Parody. 1982. 40.00x (ISBN 3-416-01092-2, Pub. by Bouvier Verlag Ger). State Mutual Bk.

--Nietzschean Parody: An Introduction to Reading Nietzsche. (Studien zur Germanistik, Anglistik und Komparatistik: Vol. 38). xi, 136p. (Orig.). 1976. pap. 14.00x (ISBN 3-416-01092-2, Pub. by Bouvier Verlag W Germany). Benjamins North Am.

--Seeing the Insane. LC 81-10193. 241p. 1982. 39.95x (ISBN 0-471-86722-5, Pub. by Ronald Pr). Wiley.

--Seeing the Insane. 241p. 1985. pap. 18.95 (ISBN 0-471-82457-7). Wiley.

--Seeing the Insane: A Cultural History of Psychiatric Illustration. LC 81-10193. (Illus.). 500p. 1981. 45.00 (ISBN 0-87630-233-9); pap. 25.00. Brunner-Mazel.

Gilman, Sander L., ed. Introducing Psychoanalytic Theory. LC 82-9477. 280p. 1982. pap. 17.50 (ISBN 0-87630-312-2). Brunner-Mazel.

Gilman, Sander L., ed. see Agricola, Johannes.

Gilman, Sander L., jt. ed. see Chamberlin, Edward J.

Gilman, Sander L., ed. see Diamond, Hugh W.

Gilman, Sharlene see Mallis, Jackie.

Gilman, Sid & Winans-Newman, Sarah. Manter & Gatz's Essentials of Clinical Neuroanatomy & Neurophysiology. 6th ed. LC 81-17437. (Essential of Medical Education Ser.). (Illus.). 218p. 1982. pap. 13.95x (ISBN 0-8036-4155-9). Davis Co.

Gilman, Sid, et al, eds. Disorders of the Cerebellum. LC 80-23393. (Contemporary Neurology Ser.: No. 21). (Illus.). 415p. 1981. text ed. 45.00x (ISBN 0-8036-4150-8). Davis Co.

Gilman, Sidney. The Competitive Dynamics of Container Shipping. 152p. 1983. text ed. 56.95x (ISBN 0-566-00573-5). Gower Pub Co.

Gilman, Stanley F., ed. Solar Energy Heat Pump Systems for Heating & Cooling Buildings. new ed. (Illus.). 1966. pap. 15.00x (ISBN 0-271-00506-8). Pa St U Pr.

Gilman, Stanley H., jt. auth. see Newton, Alwin B.

Gilman, Stanwood & Gilman, Margaret C. Land of the Kennebec. 1966. 12.00 (ISBN 0-8283-1112-9). Branden Pub Co.

Gilman, Stephen. Accounting Concepts of Profit. LC 82-48365. (Accountancy in Transition Ser.). 656p. 1982. lib. bdg. 72.00 (ISBN 0-8240-5316-8). Garland Pub.

--The Art of La Celestina. LC 76-49053. 1977. Repr. of 1956 ed. lib. bdg. 24.75x (ISBN 0-8371-9349-4, GILC). Greenwood.

--Galdos & the Art of the European Novel, Eighteen Sixty-Seven to Eighteen Eighty-Seven. LC 80-8550. 416p. 1981. 38.00 (ISBN 0-691-06456-3). Princeton U Pr.

Gilman, Stephen, ed. see Castro, Americo.

Gilman, W. H. see Emerson, Ralph Waldo.

Gilman, W. H., et al see Emerson, Ralph Waldo.

Gilman, Wilbur E. Milton's Rhetoric, Studies in His Defense of Liberty. LC 76-25152. 1939. lib. bdg. 7.25 (ISBN 0-8414-4435-8). Folcroft.

Gilman, Wilbur E., ed. Milton's Rhetoric: Studies in His Defence of Liberty. LC 74-93243. 1970. Repr. of 1939 ed. 10.00x (ISBN 0-87753-018-1). Phaeton.

Gilman, William H. see Emerson, Ralph Waldo.

Gilman, William H., ed. see Emerson, Ralph Waldo.

Gilmartin, Brian G. The Gilmartin Report. 1978. 12.95 (ISBN 0-8065-0641-5). Citadel Pr.

Gilmartin, Jean. The Bromeliaceae of Ecuador. (Monographiae Phanerogamarum Ser.: No. 5). (Illus.). 1972. 42.00 (ISBN 3-7682-0725-0). Lubrecht & Cramer.

Gilmartin, Kevin J. & Rossi, Robert J., eds. Monitoring Educational Outcomes & Public Attitudes. LC 82-1034. (Illus.). 224p. 1982. 29.95x (ISBN 0-89885-054-1). Human Sci Pr.

Gilmartin, Kevin J., et al. Social Indicators: An Annotated Bibliography of Current Literature. LC 78-67062. (Library of Social Science). 137p. 1979. lib. bdg. 28.00 (ISBN 0-8240-9755-6). Garland Pub.

Gilmartin, Kevin J., jt. auth. see Rossi, Robert J.

Gilmartin, Richard J., ed. see Struzzo, John A., et al.

Gilmartin, Thelma. What Happens to Me When I Fish the Sea & a Fish Catches Me. LC 76-12929. (Illus.). 36p. (Orig.). (gr. 1-3). 1976. pap. 2.95 (ISBN 0-89317-009-7). Windward Pub.

Gilmer, Ann. Love in the Sun. (YA) 1978. 8.95 (ISBN 0-685-53390-5, Avalon). Bouregy.

--Nurse at Breakwater Hotel. 1982. 8.95 (ISBN 0-686-84730-X, Avalon). Bouregy.

Gilmer, B. V. Applied Psychology: Adjustments in Living & Work. 2nd ed. (Illus.). 464p. 1974. text ed. 30.95 (ISBN 0-07-023210-5). McGraw.

Gilmer, B. V & Deci, Edward L. Industrial & Organizational Psychology. 4th ed. (M-H Series in Psychology). (Illus.). 1976. text ed. 32.95 (ISBN 0-07-023289-X). McGraw.

Gilmer, B. Von Haller. Psicologia General. (Span.). 1975. 13.30 (ISBN 0-06-313150-1, IntlDept). Har-Row.

Gilmer, Elizabeth M. see Dix, Dorothy, pseud.

Gilmer, Harry. The If-You Form an Israelite Law. LC 75-23136. (Society of Biblical Literature. Dissertation Ser.: No. 15). Repr. of 1975 ed. 36.80 (ISBN 0-8357-9572-1, 2017518). Bks Demand UMI.

Gilmer, J. Edward. Salvation in a Town at the Edge of Hell. 1984. 8.95 (ISBN 0-533-05871-6). Vantage.

Gilmer, J. Lance. Hell Has No Exit. (Orig.). 1976. pap. 2.25 (ISBN 0-87067-043-3, BH043). Holloway.

--Hell Is Forever. (Orig.). 1977. pap. 2.25 (ISBN 0-87067-039-5, BH039). Holloway.

--The Last Touchdown. (Orig.). 1978. pap. 2.25 (ISBN 0-87067-040-9, BH040). Holloway.

Gilmer, J. R., ed. Commercial Utilization of Space. (Advances in the Astronautical Sciences Ser.: Vol. 23). 1968. 60.00x (ISBN 0-87703-026-X, Pub. by Am Astronaut). Univelt Inc.

Gilmer, Robert. Commutative Semigroup Rings. LC 83-51596. (Chicago Lectures in Mathematics Ser.). xii, 380p. 1984. lib. bdg. 30.00x (ISBN 0-226-29391-2); pap. 12.00x (ISBN 0-226-29392-0). U of Chicago Pr.

Gilmer, Wesley. Cochran's Law Lexicon. 5th ed. LC 72-95860. 429p. 1973. Repr. text ed. 9.50 (ISBN 0-87084-148-3). Anderson Pub Co.

--The Law Dictionary. LC 72-95860. 429p. 1973. pap. text ed. 7.50 (ISBN 0-87084-149-1). Anderson Pub Co.

--Legal Research, Writing & Advocacy. 462p. 1978. 16.00. Anderson Pub Co.

Gilmer, Wesley, Jr. Anderson's Manual for Notaries Public. 5th ed. 901p. 1976. pap. 12.50 (ISBN 0-87084-039-8). Anderson Pub Co.

--The Law Dictionary. Rev. ed. 1986. 15.00 (ISBN 0-684-18429-X, ScribT); pap. 7.95 (ISBN 0-684-18385-4). Scribner.

Gilmore. Aging, a Challenge to Science & Social Policy, Vol. 2: Medicine & Social Science. (Illus.). 1981. text ed. 68.50x (ISBN 0-19-261255-7). Oxford U Pr.

Gilmore, Al-Tony, ed. Revisiting Blassingame's "The Slave Community". The Scholar's Respond. LC 77-84765. (Contributions in Afro-American & African Studies: No. 37). 1978. lib. bdg. 27.50 (ISBN 0-8371-9879-8, GJB/). Greenwood.

Gilmore, Albert F. East & West of Jordon. Davis, Moshe, ed. LC 77-70695. (America & the Holy Land Ser.). (Illus.). 1977. Repr. of 1929 ed. lib. bdg. 20.00x (ISBN 0-405-10249-6). Ayer Co Pubs.

Gilmore, Alden S. & Rich, Thomas A. Mental Retardation: A Programmed Manual for Volunteer Workers. (Illus.). 152p. 1973. 9.75x (ISBN 0-398-00681-4). C C Thomas.

Gilmore, Anne, jt. ed. see Taylor, Rex.

Gilmore, Charles M. Beginner's Guide to Microprocessors. 2nd ed. (Illus.). 224p. 1984. 14.95 (ISBN 0-8306-0695-5, 1695); pap. 9.95 (ISBN 0-8306-1695-0). TAB Bks.

--Instruments & Measurements. Schuler, Charles A., ed. (Basic Skills in Electricity & Electronics Ser.). (Illus.). 192p. (gr. 11-12). 1980. pap. text ed. 18.08 (ISBN 0-07-023297-0). McGraw.

--Introduction to Microprocessors. LC 80-26115. (Basic Skills in Electricity & Electronics). 320p. 1981. 21.52 (ISBN 0-07-023304-7). McGraw.

Gilmore, Charles W. Fossil Lizards of North America. (Illus.). 201p. Repr. 24.95 (ISBN 0-318-17269-0); institutions 22.45 (ISBN 0-318-17270-4); 10 or more 14.97 ea. Riverside Mus.

Gilmore, Christopher C. The Bad Room. 256p. 1983. pap. 2.95 (ISBN 0-380-82669-0, 82669-0). Avon.

Gilmore City History Book Committee Staff. Iowa's Limestone Capital Gilmore City Centennial, 1883-1983. 368p. 1983. write for info. (ISBN 0-89279-053-9). Gilmore City.

Gilmore, D. E., ed. see Crouse, William H. & Anglin, Donald L.

Gilmore, D. E., ed. see Feirer, John L.

Gilmore, D. E., ed. see Schulz, Erich J.

Gilmore, David B. The Essence & the Vocation of Man. (Illus.). 123p. 1980. deluxe ed. 57.50 (ISBN 0-89920-009-5). Am Inst Psych.

Gilmore, David D. The People of the Plain: Class & Community in Lower Andalusia. LC 79-20048. 1980. 29.00x (ISBN 0-231-04754-1). Columbia U Pr.

Gilmore, Desmond. Environmental Factors in Mammal Reproduction. (Illus.). 340p. 1981. text ed. 53.50 (ISBN 0-8391-1656-X). Univ Park.

Gilmore, Donald R. Developing the "Little" Economies: A Survey of Area Development Programs in the United States. (Illus.). 160p. 1960. 3.00 (ISBN 0-317-33985-0, 210). Comm Econ Dev.

Gilmore, Elaine & MacDonald, Lachlan, eds. The Collector's Book of Doll Poems. (Illus.). 1982. 12.95 (ISBN 0-914598-37-6). Padre Prods.

Gilmore, Ellen M., jt. auth. see Massachusetts Parole Board.

Gilmore, Eunice & Gilmore, John. Give Your Child a Future. 230p. 1982. 16.95 (ISBN 0-13-356964-0); pap. 7.95 (ISBN 0-13-356956-X). P-H.

Gilmore, Eunice C., jt. auth. see Gilmore, J. V.

Gilmore, G. Don. Angels, Angels, Everywhere. LC 81-8525. 180p. 1981. 11.95 (ISBN 0-8298-0477-3); pap. 6.95 (ISBN 0-8298-0479-X). Pilgrim NY.

--No Matter How Dark, the Valley: The Power of Faith in Times of Need. LC 81-48208. 141p. 1982. pap. 7.64i (ISBN 0-06-063121-X, RD-391, HarpR). Har-Row.

Gilmore, Gene. Editing Exercises. 112p. 1974. pap. 7.50x (ISBN 0-87835-071-3). Boyd & Fraser.

--Modern Newspaper Editing. 3rd ed. 400p. 1982. text ed. 20.00x (ISBN 0-87835-127-2). Boyd & Fraser.

Gilmore, Gene & Root, Robert. Editing in Brief. 2nd ed. LC 75-40871. 1977. pap. text ed. 11.25x (ISBN 0-87835-062-4). Boyd & Fraser.

Gilmore, Gene, ed. High School Journalism Today. 2nd ed. LC 76-17155. (Illus.). 128p. 1976. pap. text ed. 3.95x (ISBN 0-8134-1818-6, 1818). Interstate.

Gilmore, Grant. Ages of American Law. 1977. 21.00x (ISBN 0-300-01951-3); pap. 6.95x (ISBN 0-300-02352-9). Yale U Pr.

--The Death of Contract. LC 73-15149. (Law Forum Ser: No. 8). 162p. 1976. pap. 4.95x (ISBN 0-8142-0267-5). Ohio St U Pr.

--Security Interests in Personal Property, 2 Vols. 1508p. 1965. 100.00 (ISBN 0-316-31374-2). Little.

Gilmore, Grant, jt. auth. see Kessler, Friedrich.

Gilmore, H. B. Ask Me If I Care. 192p. (Orig.). 1985. pap. 2.25 (ISBN 0-449-70073-9, Juniper). Fawcett.

Gilmore, H. B., adapted by see Stevenson, Jocelyn.

Gilmore, H. William, et al. Operative Dentistry. 4th ed. LC 81-19017. (Illus.). 379p. 1982. text ed. 35.95 (ISBN 0-8016-1823-1). Mosby.

Gilmore, Hilary. Irish Art Heritage From Two Thousand B.C. (Illus.). 96p. 1983. 15.00 (ISBN 0-86278-042-X, Pub. by O'Brien Pr Ireland); pap. 8.95 (ISBN 0-86278-043-8, Pub. by O'Brien Pr Ireland). Irish Bks Media.

Gilmore, Horace H. Model Planes for Beginners. rev. ed. LC 57-10991. (Illus.). (gr. 5 up). 1957. PLB 8.89 (ISBN 0-06-021991-2). HarpJ.

--Model Rockets for Beginners. LC 61-8522. (Illus.). (gr. 5 up). 1961. PLB 8.89 (ISBN 0-06-022005-8). HarpJ.

Gilmore, J. Herbert. They Chose to Live: The Racial Agony of an American Church. LC 72-75577. pap. 51.50 (ISBN 0-317-07872-0, 2012911). Bks Demand UMI.

Gilmore, J. V. & Gilmore, Eunice C. Give Your Child a Future. 320p. 6.95 (ISBN 0-317-36057-4). T Jefferson Res Ctr.

Gilmore, James. My Southern Friends by Edmund Kirke. LC 72-101143. (Southern Literature & History: No. 65). Repr. of 1863 ed. lib. bdg. 38.95x (ISBN 0-8383-1218-7). Haskell.

Gilmore, James & Kirke, Edmund. Among the Pines: Or, South in Secession-Time. LC 79-101142. (American Literature Ser., No. 49). 1972. Repr. of 1862 ed. lib. bdg. 38.95x (ISBN 0-8383-1219-5). Haskell.

Gilmore, James R. Among the Pines: Or, South in Secession-Time. facs. ed. LC 78-89436. (Black Heritage Library Collection Ser). 1862. 18.00 (ISBN 0-8369-8579-6). Ayer Co Pubs.

--Down in Tennessee & Back by Way of Richmond. facs. ed. LC 76-157368. (Black Heritage Library Collection Ser). 1864. 18.75 (ISBN 0-8369-8806-X). Ayer Co Pubs.

--Down in Tennessee, Back by Way of Richmond. LC 76-107515. Repr. of 1864 ed. 19.75x (ISBN 0-8371-3762-4, GDT&, Pub. by Negro U Pr). Greenwood.

--My Southern Friends. facs. ed. LC 78-83964. (Black Heritage Library Collection Ser.). 1863. 18.00 (ISBN 0-8369-8580-X). Ayer Co Pubs.

Gilmore, Jane, jt. auth. see Gilmore, Robert.

Gilmore, Janet C. The Catalog of Boat Catalogs. (Illus.). 176p. 1983. pap. 9.95 (ISBN 0-916076-63-6). Writing.

Gilmore, Jeanne, jt. auth. see Gilmore, Robert.

Gilmore, John, jt. auth. see Gilmore, Eunice.

Gilmore, Louis. For Sale by Owner. 1974. 6.95 (ISBN 0-671-21690-2, Fireside). S&S.

--For Sale by Owner. 1979. pap. 6.95 (ISBN 0-671-25120-1, Fireside). S&S.

Gilmore, Maeve, ed. see Peake, Mervyn.

Gilmore, Melvin. Notes on the Gynecology & Obstetrics of the Arikara Tribe of Indians, Vol. 14, No. 1. 1980. pap. 2.50 (ISBN 0-686-69103-2). Acoma Bks.

Gilmore, Melvin R. Prairie Smoke. LC 78-168148. (Illus.). Repr. of 1929 ed. 18.00 (ISBN 0-404-02776-8). AMS Pr.

--Uses of Plants by the Indians of the Missouri River Region. LC 77-89833. (Illus.). xviii, 149p. 1977. 13.95x (ISBN 0-8032-0935-5); pap. 5.95 (ISBN 0-8032-5872-0, BB 644, Bison). U of Nebr Pr.

Gilmore, Michael T. American Romanticism & the Marketplace. LC 84-23936. 192p. 1985. lib. bdg. 19.95x (ISBN 0-226-29395-5). U of Chicago Pr.

--Middle Way: Puritanism & Ideology in American Romantic Fiction. 1977. 22.50x (ISBN 0-8135-0837-1). Rutgers U Pr.

Gilmore, Michael T. & Sack, Allen. Eighty-Eight Passages to Develop Reading Comprehension. 3rd ed. 168p. 1984. pap. text ed. 7.95 (ISBN 0-89026-800-2); tchr's. ed. 9.95 (ISBN 0-89026-802-9); tchr's. manual for wkbk. 4.95 (ISBN 0-89026-804-5); software manual with ten diskettes, bks. & tchr's. guide 6.95 (ISBN 0-89026-805-3). College Skills.

Gilmore, Myron P. The World of Humanism, Fourteen Fifty-Three to Fifteen Seventeen. LC 83-10718. (The Rise of Modern Europe Ser.). (Illus.). xv, 326p. 1983. Repr. of 1952 ed. lib. bdg. 45.00x (ISBN 0-313-24081-7, GIWO). Greenwood.

Gilmore, Norbert & Wainberg, Mark A. Viral Mechanisms of Immunosuppression. LC 85-5788. (Progress in Leukocyte Biology Ser.: Vol. 1). 302p. 1985. 44.00 (ISBN 0-8451-4100-7). A R Liss.

Gilmore, Norman, ed. see Knauff, Thomas L.

Gilmore, Norman, ed. see Knauff, Thomas L.

Gilmore, Perry & Glatthorn, Allan A. Children In & Out of School. (Language & Ethnography Ser.: No. 2). 300p. 1982. 29.95x (ISBN 0-15-599073-X); pap. 19.95x (ISBN 0-15-599074-8). Ctr Appl Ling.

Gilmore, Richard. A Poor Harvest: The Clash of Policies & Interests in the Grain Trade. LC 81-19309. (Professional Studies). (Illus.). 320p. 1982. 25.00x (ISBN 0-582-28193-8). Longman.

Gilmore, Robert. Catastrophe Theory for Scientists & Engineers. LC 80-22154. 666p. 1981. 58.95x (ISBN 0-471-05064-4, Pub. by Wiley-Interscience). Wiley.

--Lie Groups, Lie Algebras & Some of Their Applications. LC 73-10030. 587p. 1974. 56.95x (ISBN 0-471-30179-5, Pub. by Wiley-Interscience). Wiley.

Gilmore, Robert & Gilmore, Jane. Chantez La Louisiane. 25p. (Fr.). 1983. pap. 9.95 (ISBN 0-88289-424-2). Pelican.

Gilmore, Robert & Gilmore, Jeanne. Chantez Encore. 63p. (French.). 1983. pap. 9.95 (ISBN 0-88289-425-0). Pelican.

Gilmore, Robert C., ed. New Hampshire Literature: A Sampler. LC 81-51608. (Illus.). 352p. 1981. 25.00x (ISBN 0-87451-210-7); pap. 11.95 (ISBN 0-87451-211-5). U Pr of New Eng.

Gilmore, Robert K. Ozark Baptizings, Hangings, & Other Diversions: Theatrical Folkways of Rural Missouri, 1885-1910. LC 83-40324. (Illus.). 296p. 1984. 14.95 (ISBN 0-8061-1854-7). U of Okla Pr.

Gilmore, Susan. What Goes on at a Radio Station? LC 83-18906. (Photo Bks.). (Illus.). 40p. (gr. 1-5). 1984. PLB 8.95g (ISBN 0-87614-223-4). Carolrhoda Bks.

Gilmore, Susan K. The Counselor-in-Training. (Illus.). 1973. 23.95 (ISBN 0-13-183293-X). P-H.

Gilmore, Susan K. & Fraleigh, Patrick W. Communication at Work. LC 80-69467. (Illus.). 150p. (Orig.). 1980. 6.95 (ISBN 0-938070-00-2). Friendly Oregon.

Gilmore, Theopolis L. & Kwasa, Shadrack O. Swahili Phrase Book. LC 63-12918. pap. 4.95 (ISBN 0-8044-6176-7). Ungar.

Gilmore, Thomas B., ed. Early Eighteenth-Century Essays on Taste. LC 78-161932. 370p. 1972. 55.00x (ISBN 0-8201-1092-2). Schol Facsimiles.

Gilmore, William C. The Grenada Intervention: Analysis & Documentation. LC 84-9649. Date not set. price not set (ISBN 0-7201-1723-2). Mansell.

Gilmore, William J. Elementary Literacy on the Eve of the Industrial Revolution: Trends in Rural New England, 1760-1830. 91p. pap. 5.95 (ISBN 0-912296-57-7). U Pr of Va.

Gilmour, B., jt. auth. see Haynes, J. H.

Gilmour, D. Biochemistry of Insects. 1961. 56.50 (ISBN 0-12-284050-X). Acad Pr.

Gilmour, David. Lebanon: The Fractured Country. (Illus.). 256p. 1984. pap. 8.95 (ISBN 0-312-47739-2). St Martin.

--The Transformation of Spain: From Franco to the Constitutional Monarchy. 336p. 1985. 19.95 (ISBN 0-318-04755-1). Merrimack Pub Cir.

Gilmour, Garth, jt. auth. see Lydiard, Arthur.

Gilmour, H. B. So Long, Daddy. LC 82-22417. 384p. 1983. 14.95 (ISBN 0-937858-13-7). Newmarket.

--So Long Daddy. 352p. 1985. pap. 3.50 (ISBN 0-425-07512-5). Berkley Pub.

--Why Wembley Couldn't Sleep. (Illus.). 32p. (gr. k-2). 1985. 4.95 (ISBN 0-03-004557-6). HR&W.

Gilmour, Ian. Britain Can Work. 272p. 1983. 34.95x (ISBN 0-85520-571-7). Basil Blackwell.

Gilmour, James, jt. ed. see Cordell, Arthur J.

Gilmour, M. B., jt. auth. see Haynes, J. H.

Gilmour, Oswald W. With Freedom to Singapore. LC 70-79200. Repr. of 1950 ed. 19.50 (ISBN 0-404-54829-6). AMS Pr.

Gilmour, Pat. Artists at Curiven. (Illus.). 167p. 16.95 (ISBN 0-905005-80-5, Pub. by Salem Hse Ltd); pap. 10.95 (ISBN 0-905005-75-9, Pub. by Salem Hse Ltd). Merrimack Pub Cir.

--Artists in Print: An Introduction to Prints & Printmaking. LC 83-61268. (Illus.). 144p. 1984. pap. 16.95 (ISBN 0-88186-500-1). Parkwest Pubns.

--Kelpra Studio: The Rose & Chris Prater Gift. (Illus.). 112p. pap. 9.95 (ISBN 0-905005-67-8, Pub. by Salem Hse Ltd). Merrimack Pub Cir.

--Ken Tyler, Master Printer: And the American Printmaking Renaissance. (Illus.). 160p. 1986. 25.00 (ISBN 0-933920-16-4). Hudson Hills.

Gilmour, Pat, ed. Artists at Curwen. (Tate Gallery Art Ser). (Illus.). 1977. pap. 22.95 (ISBN 0-8120-0934-7). Barron.

Gilmour, Peter. Physical Distribution Management in Australia. 1974. 95.00x (ISBN 0-7015-1793-X, Pub. by MCB Pubns). State Mutual Bk.

--Praying Together. LC 77-91623. (Illus.). 1978. pap. 1.95 (ISBN 0-88489-097-X); leader's manual 1.00 (ISBN 0-88489-120-8). St Mary's.

Gilmour, Peter & Lansbury, Russell D. Marginal Manager: The Changing Role of Supervisors in Australia. (Illus.). 179p. 1985. text ed. 30.00x (ISBN 0-7022-1686-0). U of Queensland Pr.

Gilmour, Peter & Miller, Jeffrey. Perspectives in Materials Management: A Case Study. 1979. 80.00x (ISBN 0-86176-003-4, Pub. by MCB Pubns). State Mutual Bk.

Gilmour, Peter, jt. auth. see Love, Thomas J.

Gilmour, Peter, jt. auth. see Rados, David L.

Gilmour, R. Business Systems Handbook: Analysis, Designs & Documentation Standards. 1979. 33.95 (ISBN 0-13-107755-4). P-H.

Gilmour, R., jt. ed. see Duck, S.

Gilmour, Robin. The Idea of the Gentleman in the Victorian Novel. 208p. 1981. text ed. 19.50x (ISBN 0-04-800005-1). Allen Unwin.

Gilmour, Robin, ed. The Development of Social Psychology. 1980. 55.00 (ISBN 0-12-284080-1); pap. 27.50 (ISBN 0-12-284082-8). Acad Pr.

Gilmour, Robin & Duck, Steve, eds. The Emerging Field of Personal Relationships. 336p. 1985. text ed. 32.50 (ISBN 0-89859-547-9). L Erlbaum Assocs.

Gilmour, Robin, ed. see Trollope, Anthony.

Gilmour, Stephen C. Index to a History of Madison, the Capitol of Wisconsin: Including the Four Lakes Country. 30p. (Orig.). 1985. pap. 4.00 (ISBN 0-910255-45-8). Wisconsin Gen.

Gilmour, W. Weir. Famous Scots. 104p. 1982. 20.00x (ISBN 0-85335-231-3, Pub. by W Maclellan Scotland). State Mutual Bk.

Gilmour-Bryson, Anne, ed. Computer Applications to Medieval Studies. LC 84-4519. (Studies in Medieval Culture: No. XVII). vi, 194p. 1984. 16.95 (ISBN 0-918720-25-7); pap. 9.95 (ISBN 0-918720-18-4). Medieval Inst.

Gilmovsky, Norman. My Life, My Destiny. LC 82-46083. (Illus.). 320p. 1984. 22.50 (ISBN 0-317-02674-7). Cornwall Bks.

Gilmurray, John & Riddell, Roger. The Struggle for Health. 60p. 1979. 1.50 (ISBN 0-317-36669-6); more than 10 copies 1.00 ea. Africa Fund.

Giloi, W. K. Principles of Continuous System Simulation. (Illus.). 1976. pap. 19.50x (ISBN 3-5190-2336-9). Adlers Foreign Bks.

Giloi, W. K. & Shriver, B. D., eds. Methodologies for Computer System Design: Proceedings of the IFIP WG 10.1 Working Conference on Methodologies for Computer System Design, Lille, France, 15-17 September, 1983. 344p. 1985. 55.75 (ISBN 0-444-87687-1, North-Holland). Elsevier.

Giloi, W. K., jt. ed. see Berg, H. K.

Giloi, Wolfgang K. Interactive Computer Graphics: Data Structures, Algorithms, Languages. (Illus.). 1978. ref. ed. 34.95 (ISBN 0-13-469189-X). P-H.

Gilot, Francoise. The Fugitive Eye. (Illus.). 1975. 7.00x (ISBN 0-89363-024-1); pap. 4.00x (ISBN 0-89363-022-5). Woolf Quarterly.

--Interface: The Painter & the Mask. LC 83-61745. Orig. Title: Le Regard et Son Masque. (Illus.). 200p. 1983. 18.95 (ISBN 0-912201-02-9); pap. 9.95 (ISBN 0-912201-03-7). Cal State Pr.

Gilot, Francoise & Lake, Carlton. Life with Picasso. 384p. 1981. pap. 4.50 (ISBN 0-380-55475-5, 55475-5, Discus). Avon.

Gilot, Michel, jt. auth. see Sgard, Jean.

Giloth, Barbara E., jt. auth. see Kernaghan, Salvinija G.

Gilow, Betty & Tickle, Phyllis. It's No Fun to Be Sick by Paula & Her Friends. (Illus.). 1976. 3.95 (ISBN 0-918518-02-4). St Luke TN.

Gilpatric, Guy. Brownstone Front. facsimile ed. LC 75-37544. (Short Story Index Reprint Ser.). Repr. of 1934 ed. 16.00 (ISBN 0-8369-4103-9). Ayer Co Pubs.

Gilpatrick, Delbert H. Jeffersonian Democracy in North Carolina, 1789-1816. 1967. lib. bdg. 19.50x (ISBN 0-374-93098-8). Octagon.

Gilpatrick, Gil. Allagash: The Story of Maine's Legendary Wilderness Waterway. (Illus.). 240p. 1983. 14.95 (ISBN 0-89933-044-4). DeLorme Pub.

--Building a Strip Canoe. rev. ed. (Illus.). 128p. (Orig.). 1985. pap. 9.95 (ISBN 0-89933-026-6). DeLorme Pub.

--The Canoe Guide's Handbook: How to Plan & Guide a Trip for 2-12 People. (Illus.). 160p. (Orig.). 1981. pap. 7.95 (ISBN 0-89933-011-8). DeLorme Pub.

Gilpatrick, Lottie, et al, trs. see Twitchell, Paul.

Gilpin, A. & Williams, A. Dictionary of Energy Technology. 416p. 1982. 49.95 (ISBN 0-408-01108-4). Butterworth.

Gilpin, Alan. Air Pollution. 2nd ed. (Austriailan Environment Ser.). (Illus.). 1978. pap. 9.95x (ISBN 0-7022-1178-8). U of Queensland Pr.

--Dictionary of Economic Terms. 1970. pap. 6.00 (ISBN 0-8022-2037-1). Philos Lib.

--Dictionary of Environmental Terms. 191p. 1976. 14.95x (ISBN 0-7022-1010-2); pap. 8.95x (ISBN 0-7022-1011-0). U of Queensland Pr.

--Environmental Policy in Australia. (Australian Environment Ser.: No. 8). (Illus.). 380p. 1981. text ed. 36.25x (ISBN 0-7022-1366-7); pap. text ed. 21.75x (ISBN 0-7022-1367-5). U of Queensland Pr.

Gilpin, Alan & Hartmann, Hanns. Air Pollution & Energy in Australia: Economic & Policy Implications. LC 81-17355. (East-West Environment & Policy Institute Research Report Ser.: No. 6). v, 63p. (Orig.). 1981. pap. text ed. 3.00 (ISBN 0-86638-028-0). E W Center HI.

Gilpin, Alec R. Territory of Michigan, 1805-1837. 230p. 1970. 8.00 (ISBN 0-87013-155-9). Mich St U Pr.

--War of Eighteen-Twelve in the Old Northwest. (Illus.). vii, 286p. 1958. 6.50 (ISBN 0-87013-032-3). Mich St U Pr.

Gilpin, Arthur. Nature Photography. (Countryside Leisure Ser.). (Illus.). 1978. 9.95 (ISBN 0-7158-0614-9). Charles River Bks.

Gilpin, Doris C., jt. ed. see Anthony, James E.

Gilpin, Geoff. Ada: A Guided Tour & Tutorial. 352p. 1985. 22.95 (ISBN 0-13-004045-2); pap. 16.95 (ISBN 0-13-003914-4). P-H.

Gilpin, George H. The Strategy of Joy: An Essay on the Poetry of Samuel Taylor Coleridge. (Salzburg Studies in English Literature, Romantic Reassessment: No.3). 1972. pap. text ed. 25.50x (ISBN 0-391-01384-X). Humanities.

Gilpin, John F. Edmonton: Gateway to the North. (Illus.). 320p. 1984. 29.95 (ISBN 0-89781-094-5). Windsor Pubns Inc.

Gilpin, Laura. The Enduring Navaho. (Illus.). 277p. 1968. 37.50 (ISBN 0-292-78378-7). U of Tex Pr.

--Indian Arts Fund Collection. (Illus.). 1970. 3.50 (ISBN 0-89013-042-6). Museum NM Pr.

Gilpin, Michael. Group Selection in Predator-Prey Communities. (Monographs in Population Biology: No. 9). 120p. 1974. 19.00 (ISBN 0-691-08157-3); pap. 8.95 (ISBN 0-691-08161-1). Princeton U Pr.

Gilpin, R. Biblical Demonology: A Treatise on Satan's Temptations. 1982. lib. bdg. 20.00 (ISBN 0-86524-093-0, 9805). Klock & Klock.

Gilpin, Robert. War & Change in World Politics. LC 81-2885. (Illus.). 192p. 1981. 24.95 (ISBN 0-521-24018-2). Cambridge U Pr.

--War & Change in World Politics. LC 81-2885. (Illus.). 288p. 1983. pap. 10.95 (ISBN 0-521-27376-5). Cambridge U Pr.

Gilpin, Robert G., Jr. American Scientists & Nuclear Weapons Policy. 1962. 35.00x (ISBN 0-691-07501-8). Princeton U Pr.

--France in the Age of the Scientific State. LC 68-14442. (Center of International Studies Ser.). 1968. 46.00 (ISBN 0-691-05619-6). Princeton U Pr.

--U. S. Power & the Multinational Corporation: The Political Economy of Direct Foreign Investment. LC 75-7265. 1975. 16.95x (ISBN 0-465-08951-8). Basic.

Gilpin, W. Clark. The Millenarian Piety of Roger Williams. LC 78-20786. 1979. lib. bdg. 19.00x (ISBN 0-226-29397-1). U of Chicago Pr.

Gilpin, William. Mission of the North American People. 2nd ed. LC 68-16234. (American Scene Ser.). (Illus.). 218p. 1974. Repr. of 1874 ed. lib. bdg. 32.50 (ISBN 0-306-71013-7). Da Capo.

--Observations on the Western Parts of England Relative to Picturesque Beauty. 412p. 1984. Repr. of 1798 ed. 49.00x (ISBN 0-85546-182-9, Pub. by Richmond Pub England). State Mutual Bk.

--Observations Relative Chiefly to Picturesque Beauty on the Highland of Scotland. 562p. 1984. Repr. of 1789 ed. 69.00x (ISBN 0-317-07142-4, Pub. by Richmond Pub England). State Mutual Bk.

--Observations Relative Chiefly to Picturesque Beauty on the Mountains & Lakes of Cumberland & Westmoreland. 626p. 1984. Repr. of 1786 ed. 75.00x (ISBN 0-85546-179-9, Pub. by Richmond Pub England). State Mutual Bk.

--Remarks on Forest Scenery & Other Woodland Views Illustrated by the Scenes of New Forest in Hampshire. 746p. 1984. Repr. of 1791 ed. 82.00 (ISBN 0-85546-181-0, Pub. by Richmond Pub England). State Mutual Bk.

Gilreath, Charles L. Computer Literature Searching: Research Strategies & Databases. 180p. 1984. softcover 22.00x (ISBN 0-86531-526-4). Westview.

Gilreath, Esmarch S. Experimental Procedures in Elementary Qualitative Analysis. 1968. text ed. 20.95 (ISBN 0-07-023213-X). McGraw.

Gilreath, Kenneth J., jt. auth. see Cushenbery, Donald C.

Gil-Robles, Jose M. Diccionario de Terminos Electorales y Parlamentarios. 268p. (Span.). 1977. pap. 15.25 (ISBN 84-306-3039-2, S-50001). French & Eur.

Gilroy & Swan. Building Networks: Cooperation As a Strategy for Success in a Changing World. 280p. 1984. pap. text ed. 12.95 (ISBN 0-8403-3254-8). Kendall-Hunt.

Gilroy, A. B., ed. see Swaroop, S.

Gilroy, Curtis L. Army Manpower Economics. (WVSS Ser.). 300p. 1985. pap. text ed. 25.00x (ISBN 0-8133-0190-4). Westview.

Gilroy, John & Holliday, Patti. Basic Neurology. 1982. pap. text ed. write for info. (ISBN 0-02-343690-5). Macmillan.

Gilroy, John & Meyer, John S. Medical Neurology. 3rd ed. (Illus.). 1979. text ed. write for info. (ISBN 0-02-343640-9). Macmillan.

Gilroy, John, jt. auth. see Holt, Ted.

Gilroy, Pamela J. Kids in Motion. 60p. (Orig.). 1985. pap. text ed. 11.95 (ISBN 0-88450-923-0, 7227-B). Communication Skill.

Gilroy, Thomas P. & Russo, Anthony C. Bargaining Unit Issues: Problems Criteria, Tactics. (Public Employee Relations Library Ser.: No. 43). pap. 10.00 (ISBN 0-87373-143-3). Intl Personnel Mgmt.

Gilsbach, J. M. Intraoperative Doppler Sonography in Neurosurgery. (Illus.). 120p. 1983. pap. 16.50 (ISBN 0-387-81768-9). Springer-Verlag.

Gilsdorf, Helen M., ed. Modern Liturgy Index. 2nd ed. 1984. pap. 6.95 (ISBN 0-89390-040-0). Resource Pubns.

Gilsenan, Michael. Saint & Sufi in Modern Egypt: An Essay in the Sociology of Religion. (Monographs in Social Anthropology). (Illus.). 1973. 34.00x (ISBN 0-19-823181-4). Oxford U Pr.

Gilsenan, Nancy P., jt. auth. see Tallman, Shirley B.

Gilsinan, James F. Doing Justice: How the System Works - As Seen by the Participants. 251p. 1982. 13.95 (ISBN 0-13-217315-8); pap. 5.95 (ISBN 0-13-217307-7). P-H.

Gilson, Christopher & Berkman, Harold W. Advertising: Concepts & Strategies. 596p. 1980. text ed. 29.00 (ISBN 0-394-32265-7, RanC). Random.

Gilson, Christopher & Schiffman, Leon. Principles of Marketing. 608p. Date not set. text ed. 19.95 (ISBN 0-394-32839-6, RanB); write for info. (ISBN 0-394-34293-3). Random.

Gilson, Christopher, jt. auth. see Berkman, Harold W.

Gilson, Christopher, et al. Consumer Revenge: How to Handle Greedy Landlords, Shoddy Sellers, Crooked Contractors & Other Consumer Frustrations. 352p. 1983. pap. 6.95 (ISBN 0-399-50709-4, Perigee). Putnam Pub Group.

--Marketing Basics. (Illus.). 500p. Date not set. text ed. 25.95 (ISBN 0-394-33976-2, RanC); Student Course Mastery Guide 8.95 (ISBN 0-394-33925-8, RanC). Random.

Gilson, David, ed. A Bibliography of Jane Austen. (Soho Bibliographies Ser.). (Illus.). 1982. 110.00x (ISBN 0-19-818173-6). Oxford U Pr.

Gilson, Etienne. The Christian Philosophy of St. Augustine. xii, 398p. 1983. Repr. of 1960 ed. lib. bdg. 35.00 (ISBN 0-88254-873-5). Octagon.

--The Christian Philosophy of St. Thomas Aquinas. x, 502p. 1983. Repr. of 1956 ed. lib. bdg. 45.00 (ISBN 0-88254-874-3). Octagon.

--Dante & Philosophy. Moore, David, tr. 12.75 (ISBN 0-8446-0645-6). Peter Smith.

--From Aristotle to Darwin & Back Again: A Journey in Final Causality, Species & Evolution. Lyon, John, tr. from Fr. LC 83-40114. 240p. 1984. text ed. 22.95x (ISBN 0-268-00967-8, 85-09671). U of Notre Dame Pr.

--God & Philosophy. (Powell Lectures Ser.). 1941. pap. 6.95x (ISBN 0-300-00097-9, Y8). Yale U Pr.

--Heloise & Abelard. 1960. pap. 7.95 (ISBN 0-472-06038-4, 38, AA). U of Mich Pr.

--History of Philosophy & Philosophical Education. (Aquinas Lecture). 1947. 7.95 (ISBN 0-87462-112-7). Marquette.

--Index Scolastico-Cartesien. 1964. Repr. of 1913 ed. 28.50 (ISBN 0-8337-1357-4). B Franklin.

--The Philosophy of St. Bonaventure. 1965. 7.50 (ISBN 0-8199-0526-7). Franciscan Herald.

--Philosophy of St. Thomas Aquinas. LC 72-190713. 1924. lib. bdg. 20.00 (ISBN 0-8414-0825-4). Folcroft.

--The Unity of Philosophical Experience. 352p. 1982. pap. 15.00 (ISBN 0-87061-075-9). Chr Classics.

--Wisdom & Love in Saint Thomas Aguinas. (Aquinas Lecture). 1951. 7.95 (ISBN 0-87462-116-X). Marquette.

Gilson, Etienne H. Elements of Christian Philosophy. LC 78-10231. 1978. Repr. of 1960 ed. lib. bdg. 35.00 (ISBN 0-313-20734-8, GIEL). Greenwood.

--The Philosophy of St. Thomas Aquinas. facsimile ed. Elrington, G. A., ed. Bullough, Edward, tr. from Fr. LC 70-157337. (Select Bibliographies Reprint Ser). Repr. of 1937 ed. 26.50 (ISBN 0-8369-5797-0). Ayer Co Pubs.

Gilson, George. Concrete Flatwork Manual. 160p. (Orig.). 1982. pap. 7.75 (ISBN 0-910460-93-0). Craftsman.

Gilson, Goodwin W. & Palmer, Rose. Speedwriting Medical Dictation Course. 266p. 1960. text ed. 24.80 scp (ISBN 0-672-96153-9); scp tchr's manual 7.33 (ISBN 0-672-96154-7); scp cassette tapes 232.92 (ISBN 0-672-97884-9). Bobbs.

Gilson, Goodwin W. & Platt, Naomi. Letter Perfect: The Accurate Secretary. 336p. 1985. pap. 8.95 (ISBN 0-668-06114-6). Arco.

Gilson, Jamie. Can't Catch Me, I'm the Gingerbread Man. LC 80-39748. 160p. (gr. 5-9). 1981. 11.25 (ISBN 0-688-00435-0); PLB 11.88 (ISBN 0-688-00436-9). Lothrop.

--Can't Catch Me, I'm the Gingerbread Man. (gr. 5-7). 1982. pap. 1.95 (ISBN 0-671-44835-8). Archway.

--Dial Leroi Rupert, DJ. (Illus.). (gr. 4-6). 1981. pap. 1.75 (ISBN 0-671-56099-9). Archway.

--Dial Leroi Rupert, DJ. LC 79-4662. (Illus.). (gr. 4 up). 1979. 10.00 (ISBN 0-688-41888-0); PLB 10.88 (ISBN 0-688-51888-5). Lothrop.

--Do Bananas Chew Gum. 1981. pap. 1.95 (ISBN 0-671-42690-7). Archway.

--Do Bananas Chew Gum? LC 80-11414. 160p. (gr. 5-9). 1980. 10.00 (ISBN 0-688-41960-7); PLB 10.88 (ISBN 0-688-51960-1). Lothrop.

--Four-B Goes Wild. LC 83-948. (Illus.). 160p. (gr. 4-6). 1983. 10.25 (ISBN 0-688-02236-7). Lothrop.

--Harvey, the Beer Can King. LC 78-1807. (Illus.). 128p. (gr. 4-6). 1983. 10.25 (ISBN 0-688-02382-7). Lothrop.

--Harvey the Beer Can King. (gr. 2-6). 1985. pap. 2.25 (ISBN 0-671-50985-3). PB.

--Hello, My Name Is Scrambled Eggs. LC 84-10075. (Illus.). 160p. (gr. 4-6). 1985. 10.25 (ISBN 0-688-04095-0). Lothrop.

--Thirteen Ways to Sink a Sub. (Illus.). (gr. 3-7). 1982. 11.75 (ISBN 0-688-01304-X). Lothrop.

--Thirteen Ways to Sink a Sub. (Illus.). 128p. (gr. 3-6). 1983. pap. 1.95. Archway.

Gilson, Mary B. What's Past Is Prologue. Baxter, Annette K., ed. LC 79-8793. (Signal Lives Ser.). 1980. Repr. of 1940 ed. lib. bdg. 32.50x (ISBN 0-405-12842-8). Ayer Co Pubs.

Gilson, Roy R. In the Morning Glow. LC 72-94726. (Short Story Index Reprint Ser.). 1902. 17.00 (ISBN 0-8369-3105-X). Ayer Co Pubs.

Gilson, Thomas. The New England Farm. 1984. 12.95 (ISBN 0-9612556-0-9). Countryman.

--The New England Farm. LC 83-51095. (Illus.). 64p. (Orig.). 1983. pap. 12.95 (ISBN 0-9612556-0-9). Wickwire Pr.

Gilstad, June R. Thinking & Reading in High School: An Introductory Guide to Instructional Thinking & Reading. 47p. (Orig.). (gr. 9-12). 1981. pap. text ed. 4.50x (ISBN 0-939132-00-1). Bluejay Pr IN.

Gilston, Samuel & Swit, David, eds. FDA Compilation of Case Studies of Drug Recalls. 1976. pap. 7.50 ea. 1-5 copies (ISBN 0-914176-09-9); pap. 7.25 ea. 6-15 copies; pap. 6.95 ea. 16-25 copies; pap. 6.75 ea. 26 or more copies. Wash Busn Info.

Gilstrap, Frank. How to Do Your Own Texas Divorce for Under Fifty Dollars. 7th ed. 80p. 1983. pap. 7.95 (ISBN 0-938356-00-3). How-to Pr.

Gilstrap, Marie, jt. auth. see Nester, Eugene.

Gilstrap, Robert, jt. auth. see Dzama, Mary Ann.

Gilstrap, Robert, jt. ed. see Beyer, Barry K.

Gilsvik, Bob. The Complete Book of Trapping. (Illus.). 172p. (gr. 7). Repr. of 1976 ed. 9.95 (ISBN 0-8019-6444-X); lib. bdg. 9.95. A R Harding Pub.

--The Guide to Good Cheap Hunting. LC 77-8759. (Illus.). 1979. pap. 5.95 (ISBN 0-8128-6031-4). Stein & Day.

Giltay, J. W. Bow Instruments: Their Form & Construction. LC 75-181164. 129p. 1923. Repr. 39.00x (ISBN 0-403-01566-9). Scholarly.

Giltner, Fern M., ed. Women's Issues in Religious Education. 1985. pap. 12.95 (ISBN 0-89135-051-9). Religious Educ.

Gilula, Norton B., ed. Membrane-Membrane Interactions. (Society of General Physiologists Ser.: Vol. 34). 230p. 1980. text ed. 42.00 (ISBN 0-89004-377-9). Raven.

GilYepes, Jose A. The Challenge of Venezuelan Democracy. 275p. 1981. 29.95 (ISBN 0-87855-401-7). Transaction Bks.

Gilzean, Elizabeth. Something to Do at Home. 14.50 (ISBN 0-392-12847-0, SpS). Sportshelf.

Giman, Lawrence J. Making the Most of Your Money: Your Personal Guide to Successful Financial Planning. LC 84-25954. 528p. 1985. 24.95 (ISBN 0-03-003892-8). HR&W.

Gimarc, Benjamin M. Molecular Structure & Bonding: The Qualitative Molecular Orbital Theory. 1979. 23.00 (ISBN 0-12-284150-6). Acad Pr.

Gimbel, Henning. Work Simplification in Danish Public Libraries: The Report of the Work Simplification Committee of the Danish Library Association. LC 69-15862. (American Library Associaton- Library Technology Program Ser.: No. 15). pap. 72.30 (ISBN 0-317-26345-5, 2024227). Bks Demand UMI.

Gimbel, Joan. Surrender Mountain. 192p. 1985. 13.95 (ISBN 0-8027-0854-4). Walker & Co.

Gimbel, John. The American Occupation of Germany: Politics & the Military, 1945-1949. LC 68-26778. 1968. 27.50x (ISBN 0-8047-0667-0). Stanford U Pr.

--A German Community Under American Occupation. 1961. 20.00x (ISBN 0-8047-0061-3). Stanford U Pr.

--The Origins of the Marshall Plan. LC 75-39334. xiv, 344p. 1976. 27.50x (ISBN 0-8047-0903-3). Stanford U Pr.

Gimbel, Theo. Healing Through Colour. 108p. 1980. 23.95x (ISBN 0-8464-1017-6). Beekman Pubs.

--Healing Through Colour. 1980. 18.95x (ISBN 0-85207-146-9, Pub. by Daniel Co England). State Mutual Bk.

Gimbel, Wendy. Edith Wharton: Orphancy & Survival. LC 84-13443. (Landmark Dissertations in Women's Studies). 186p. 1984. 29.95x (ISBN 0-03-070707-2). Praeger.

Gimblett, Barbara Kirshenblatt see Kirshenblatt-Gimblett, Barbara.

Gimblett, F. & Hood, K. Chemistry, Physics & Technology of Macromolecular Inorganic Compounds & Materials, Pt. 1. 1969. 27.00 (ISBN 0-686-92699-4). Elsevier.

--Chemistry, Physics & Technology of Macromolecular Inorganic Compounds & Materials, Pt. 2. 1970. 27.00 (ISBN 0-686-92697-8). Elsevier.

Gimbutas, Marija. Bronze Age Cultures in Central & Eastern Europe. 1965. text ed. 88.00x (ISBN 90-2790-998-9). Mouton.

--Goddesses & Gods of Old Europe, 7000 to 3500 B.C. Myths, Legends, & Cult Images. 1982. pap. 14.95 (ISBN 0-520-04655-2). U of Cal Pr.

Gimbutas, Marija, ed. Neolithic Macedonia. LC 76-18606. (Monumenta Archaeologica Ser). (Illus.). 1976. 28.00 (ISBN 0-685-79156-4). U of S Cal Pr.

Gimello, Robert M. & Gregory, Peter N., eds. Studies in Ch'an & Hua-Yen. (Studies in East Asian Buddhism: No. 1). 402p. 1983. pap. text ed. 14.95x (ISBN 0-8248-0835-5). UH Pr.

Gimenez, J. P. Caribbean Echoes. 1977. lib. bdg. 59.95 (ISBN 0-8490-1575-8). Gordon Pr.

Gimenez, Juan. A Matter of Time. Metz, Bernd, ed. (Illus.). 64p. (Orig., Span.). 1985. pap. 8.95 (ISBN 0-87416-012-X). Catalan Communs.

Gimenez, P., ed. Muscular Exercise in Chronic Lung Disease: Proceedings of Meeting on Factors Limiting Exercise, Nancy, France, 13-15 Sept. 1978. LC 79-40806. (Special Issue of the Bulletin Europeen De Physiopathologie Respiratoire). (Illus.). 1980. 62.00 (ISBN 0-08-024930-2). Pergamon.

Gimenez Sales, Miguel. Diccionario Espanol-Frances, Espagnol-Francais. 736p. (Span. & Fr.). 1975. pap. 3.95 (ISBN 84-02-04265-1, S-50394). French & Eur.

Gimeno, E. Diccionario Lexicon Frances-Espanol, Espanol-Frances. 384p. (Fr. & Span.). 1975. leatherette 3.75 (ISBN 84-303-0099-6, S-31393). French & Eur.

Gimeno, Jose B. Education in Latin America & the Caribbean - Trends & Prospects, 1970-2000: Regional Conference of Ministers of Education & Those Responsible for Economic Planning of Member States in Latin America & the Caribbean, Organized by UNESCO, Mexico City, 1979. (Illus.). 190p. 1983. pap. text ed. 17.00 (ISBN 92-3-101908-2, U1304, UNESCO). Unipub.

Gimeno, Jose B. & Ibanez, M. The Education of Primary & Secondary School Teachers. (Studies on the Evaluation of Qualifications at the Higher Education Level). (Illus.). 271p. 1981. pap. 22.50 (ISBN 92-3-101750-0, U1142, UNESCO). Unipub.

Gimferrer, Pere. Max Ernst. LC 83-61926. (Illus.). 128p. 1984. 14.95 (ISBN 0-8478-0523-9). Rizzoli Intl.

Gimignano, Folgore Da San see Da San Gimignano, Folgore.

Gimlette, John D. Malay Poisons & Charm Cures. 2nd ed. LC 77-87027. Repr. of 1923 ed. 22.00 (ISBN 0-404-16821-3). AMS Pr.

--Malay Poisons & Charm Cures. 3rd ed. (Oxford in Asia Paperbacks Ser.). 1981. pap. 13.95x (ISBN 0-19-638150-9). Oxford U Pr.

Gimmestad, Ben. Legion Fifty. 10.00 (ISBN 0-87018-022-3). Ross.

Gimmestad, Nancy, jt. ed. see Rivlin, Asher E.

Gimmestad, Victor E. Joseph Hergesheimer. (United States Authors Ser.: No. 473). 1984. lib. bdg. 17.95 (ISBN 0-8057-7414-9, Twayne). G K Hall.

Gimmestad, Nancy, jt. auth. see Rivlin, Asher E.

Gimmy, Arthur E. Tennis Clubs & Racquet Sport Projects: A Guide to Appraisal, Market Analysis, Development & Financing. 94p. 1978. 15.00 (ISBN 0-911780-45-9). Am Inst Real Estate Appraisers.

Gimondo, Angelo. Italian First Year. (gr. 8-11). 1978. wkbk. 9.17 (ISBN 0-87720-593-0). AMSCO Sch.

--Italian First Year. (Orig.). (gr. 7-12). 1975. pap. text ed. 7.83 (ISBN 0-87720-590-6). AMSCO Sch.

Gimpel, Jean. The Cathedral Builders. LC 82-48042. (Illus.). 128p. 22.50 (ISBN 0-394-52893-X, GP 859). Grove.

--The Cathedral Builders. Waugh, Teresa, tr. LC 84-47572. (Illus.). 192p. 1984. pap. 8.61i (ISBN 0-06-091158-1, CN 1158, CN). Har-Row.

--The Medieval Machine: The Industrial Revolution of the Middle Ages. 1977. pap. 6.95 (ISBN 0-14-004514-7). Penguin.

Gimpel, Max & Agress, Hyman. A Thanksgiving Celebration. 1976. pap. 1.45 (ISBN 0-87029-127-0, 20155-8). Abbey.

Gimpel, Scott E., jt. auth. see Tondo, Clovis L.

Gimpl, Caroline A. The Correspondant & the Founding of the French Third Republic. LC 74-5773. 239p. 1974. Repr. of 1959 ed. lib. bdg. 22.50x (ISBN 0-8371-7517-8, GITR). Greenwood.

Gimsing, N. J. Cable Supported Bridges: Concepts & Design. 400p. 1983. 74.95 (ISBN 0-471-90130-X). Wiley.

Gimson, A. C. An Introduction to the Pronunciation of English. 3rd ed. 352p. 1980. 32.00x (ISBN 0-686-69895-9, Pub. by Arnold Pubs England). State Mutual Bk.

Gimson, Gary. Arab Shipping, 1985. 1984. 195.00 (ISBN 0-905597-18-4, Pub. by Seatrade). State Mutual Bk.

Gimson, Gary, ed. Arab Shipping, 1985. 1984. 220.00 (ISBN 0-905597-14-1, Pub. by Seatrade). State Mutual Bk.

Gin, Maggie. Regional Cooking of China. rev. ed. LC 84-5269. (Illus.). 192p. 1984. pap. 7.95 (ISBN 0-89286-242-4). One Hund One Prods.

Gin, Margaret. One-Pot Meals. LC 76-41173. (Illus.). 1976. pap. 6.95 (ISBN 0-89286-100-2). One Hund One Prods.

--Tomatoes. LC 77-3481. (The Edible Garden Ser.). (Illus.). 1977. pap. 2.50 (ISBN 0-89286-111-8). One Hund One Prods.

Ginalski, William, jt. auth. see DeBanks, Henward M.

Ginat, Joseph. Women in Muslim Rural Society. LC 79-66432. 259p. 1981. 29.95 (ISBN 0-87855-342-8). Transaction Bk.

Ginch, Bill, jt. auth. see Miranda, Fred.

Ginch, William & Miranda, Alfred, Jr. TV Trivia. (Orig.). 1984. pap. 3.50 (ISBN 0-345-32005-0). Ballantine.

Gindele, Egon, ed. Bibliographie Zur Geschichte und Theologie Des Augustiner Eremiten Ordens Bis Zum Beginn der Reformation. (Spaetmittelalter und Reformation: Texte und Untersuchungen, Vol. 1). 1977. text ed. 74.00x (ISBN 3-11-004949-X). De Gruyter.

Gindely, Anton. History of the Thirty Years War, 2 vols. facsimile ed. Brook, Andrew T., tr. LC 71-37882. (Select Bibliographies Reprint Ser). Repr. of 1885 ed. Set. 92.50 (ISBN 0-8369-6719-4). Ayer Co Pubs.

--History of the Thirty Years' War, Vol. II. Brook, Andrew T., tr. LC 71-37882. (Illus.). 456p. Repr. of 1885 ed. lib. bdg. 44.00 (ISBN 0-8290-0497-1). Irvington.

--History of the Thirty Years' War, Vol. I. Brook, Andrew T., tr. LC 71-37882. (Illus.). 456p. Repr. of 1885 ed. lib. bdg. 44.00 (ISBN 0-8290-0496-3). Irvington.

Ginder, Geri, jt. auth. see Blevin, Margo.

Ginders, James A. A Guide to Napkin Folding. 1980. pap. 10.95 (ISBN 0-8436-2140-0). Van Nos Reinhold.

Gindes, B. New Concepts in Hypnosis. 4.00x (ISBN 0-685-22059-1). Wehman.

Gindes, Bernard C. New Concepts of Hypnosis. pap. 5.00 (ISBN 0-87980-108-5). Wilshire.

Gindick, Jon. Country & Blues Harmonica for the Musically Hopeless. (Illus.). 128p. 1984. pap. 12.95 (ISBN 0-932592-08-2). Klutz Pr.

--The Natural Blues & Country Western Harmonica. (Illus.). 130p. 1978. pap. 5.95 (ISBN 0-930948-01-7). Cross Harp.

--The Natural Blues & Country Western Harmonica. 2nd ed. LC 77-83727. (Illus.). 1978. 5.95 (ISBN 0-930948-01-7). J Gindick.

--The Natural Blues & Country Western Harmonica. (Illus.). 128p. pap. 5.95 (ISBN 0-8256-9923-1). Music Sales.

--Rock n' Blues Harmonica. 2nd ed. (Illus.). 1982. 6.95 (ISBN 0-930948-02-5). J Gindick.

--Rock N' Blues Harmonica: Stories, Lessons & Record Index. (Illus.). 224p. 1983. pap. 6.95 (ISBN 0-930948-02-5). Cross Harp.

Gindin, James. The English Climate: An Excursion into a Biography of John Galsworthy. LC 79-98060. (Illus.). 1979. lib. bdg. 12.00x (ISBN 0-472-08349-X, 08349). U of Mich Pr.

--Postwar British Fiction. LC 76-6558. 246p. 1976. Repr. of 1962 ed. lib. bdg. 25.00x (ISBN 0-8371-8800-8, GIPB). Greenwood.

Gindin, James, ed. see Hardy, Thomas.

Gine, Evarist, jt. auth. see Araujo, Aloisio.

Ginell, R. Association Theory: The Phases of Matter & Their Transformations. (Studies in Physical & Theoretical Chemistry: Vol. 1). 224p. 1979. 47.00 (ISBN 0-444-41753-2). Elsevier.

Giner, Salvador & Archer, Margaret S., eds. Contemporary Europe: Social Structures & Cultural Patterns. (International Library of Sociology). 1978. 29.95x (ISBN 0-7100-8790-X). Routledge & Kegan.

Ginestet, Bernard. Margaux. (Illus.). 192p. 1985. 19.95 (ISBN 0-03-006014-1). HR&W.

--Saint-Julien. 192p. 1985. 19.95 (ISBN 0-03-006017-6). HR&W.

Ginestier, Paul. The Poet & the Machine. Friedman, Martin B., tr. 1961. pap. 6.95x (ISBN 0-8084-0248-X). New Coll U Pr.

Ginet, C. Knowledge, Perception, & Memory. LC 75-8602. (Philosophical Studies: No. 5). 207p. 1975. 39.50 (ISBN 90-277-0574-7, Pub. by Reidel Holland). Kluwer Academic.

Ginet, Carl & Shoemaker, Sydney, eds. Knowledge & Mind: Philosophical Essays. 1982. 32.50x (ISBN 0-19-503148-2). Oxford U Pr.

Ginet, Margaret W. Sing! Sing! Sing! 5.95 (ISBN 0-685-82604-X). R & E Pubs.

Ginever, C. A., tr. see Riedl, Frederick.

Gingell, Julia R., ed. Aphorisms from the Writings of Herbert Spencer. 170p. 1981. Repr. of 1984 ed. lib. bdg. 35.00 (ISBN 0-8495-0065-6). Arden Lib.

Gingell, Lesley. The ABC's of the Open Classroom. new ed. LC 72-12723. (Illus.). 288p. 1973. 12.95 (ISBN 0-88280-004-3). ETC Pubns.

Gingell, Rika. Cooking on the Move: Stove-Top Baking, Cooking in Yachts, Campers, Trailers & Other Small Places. LC 82-19057. 192p. 1984. pap. 7.95 (ISBN 0-88427-052-1, Dist. by Dodd, Mead). North River.

Gingell, Susan. E. J. Pratt on His Life & Poetry. (Collected Works of E. J. Pratt Ser.). 267p. 1984. pap. 12.95 (ISBN 0-8020-6567-8). U of Toronto Pr.

Ginger, Ann, ed. The International Juridical Association Bulletin 1932-1942, 3 vols. (Franklin D. Roosevelt & the Era of the New Deal Ser.). 1232p. 1982. Repr. lib. bdg. 195.00 (ISBN 0-306-79176-5); lib. bdg. 70.00. Da Capo.

Ginger, Ann F. Jury Selection in Civil & Criminal Trials, 2 vols. LC 84-7200. 1984. Set. 150.00 (ISBN 0-915544-14-8). Lawpress Ca.

--The Law, the Supreme Court, & the People's Right. rev. ed. LC 76-43260. 1977. pap. text ed. 7.95 (ISBN 0-8120-5274-9). Barron.

Ginger, Ann F. & Meiklejohn Civil Liberties Institute Staff. The Pentagon Papers Case Collection: Annotated Procedural Guide & Index. new ed. LC 75-14531. 200p. 1975. pap. 10.00x (ISBN 0-913876-07-0). Meiklejohn Civ Lib.

Ginger, Ann F., ed. Angela Davis Case Collection: Annotated Procedural Guide & Index. LC 74-75744. 1974. 5.00x (ISBN 0-913876-05-4). Meiklejohn Civ Lib.

--Angela Davis Case Collection Annotated Procedural Guide & Index. LC 74-75744. 162p. 1974. pap. 17.50 (ISBN 0-379-00161-6). Oceana.

--Human Rights Docket U.S. 1979. LC 79-4334. 1979. pap. 35.00 (ISBN 0-913876-11-9). Meiklejohn Civ Lib.

--The Pentagon Papers Trial: Index-Catalog. LC 75-14531. 208p. 1975. pap. 17.50 (ISBN 0-379-00314-7). Oceana.

Ginger, Ann F., ed. see Brown, Cynthia S.

Ginger, Ann Fagan & Christiano, David, eds. The Cold War Against Labor. 650p. (Orig.). 1985. write for info. Meiklejohn Civ Lib.

Ginger, Ray. Age of Excess: The United States from Eighteen Seventy-Seven to Nineteen Fourteen. 2nd ed. (Illus.). 416p. 1975. pap. text ed. write for info. (ISBN 0-02-343700-6, 34370). Macmillan.

--Eugene V. Debs: A Biography. Orig. Title: Bending Cross. 1962. pap. 5.95 (ISBN 0-02-003310-9, Collier). Macmillan.

--Six Days or Forever? Tennessee vs. John Thomas Scopes. 1974. pap. 8.95 (ISBN 0-19-519784-4, GB416, GB). Oxford U Pr.

Gingerich, Duane & F & S Press Book, eds. Medical Product Liability: A Comprehensive Guide & Sourcebook. 464p. 1981. prof ref. 74.50x. Ballinger Pub.

Gingerich, Duane, jt. ed. see Research Group.

Gingerich, Irving. Contrapuntal Ear Training: Aural Excercises. 127p. 1982. pap. 5.00 (ISBN 0-686-46778-7). Fitzsimons.

Gingerich, Martin E. W. H. Auden: A Reference Guide. 1977. lib. bdg. 20.00 (ISBN 0-8161-7889-5, Hall Reference). G K Hall.

Gingerich, Melvin. The Christian & Revolution. LC 68-12028. (Conrad Grebel Lecture, No. 12). 1968. 8.95 (ISBN 0-8361-1573-2). Herald Pr.

--The Christian & Revolution. LC 68-12028. 256p. 1968. 8.95 (ISBN 0-8361-1573-2). Herald Hse.

Gingerich, Orland. The Amish of Canada. LC 72-94800. 248p. 1978. pap. 4.95 (ISBN 0-8361-1856-1). Herald Pr.

Gingerich, Owen & Welther, Barbara L. Planetary, Lunar & Solar Positions, 1650-1805. LC 83-1805. (Memoirs: Vol. 59S). 1983. 20.00 (ISBN 0-87169-590-1). Am Philos.

Gingerich, Owen, ed. Astrophysics & Twentieth Century Astronomy to 1950, Vol. 4, Pt. A. LC 83-10164. (General History of Astronomy Ser.). 206p. 1984. 29.95 (ISBN 0-521-24256-8). Cambridge U Pr.

--The Nature of Scientific Discovery. LC 74-18374. (Illus.). 616p. 1975. 25.00x (ISBN 0-87474-148-3). Smithsonian.

--Theory & Observations of Normal Stellar Atmospheres: Proceedings of the Third Harvard-Smithsonian Conference on Stellar Atmosphere. 1970. 40.00x (ISBN 0-262-07035-9). MIT Pr.

Gingerich, Owen, jt. ed. see Lang, Kenneth R.

Gingerich, Owen, intro. by. New Frontiers in Astronomy: Readings from Scientific American. LC 75-8902. (Illus.). 369p. 1975. text ed. 23.95 (ISBN 0-7167-0520-6); pap. text ed. 11.95 (ISBN 0-7167-0519-2). W H Freeman.

Gingerich, Solomon F. Essays in the Romantic Poets. LC 70-75994. 1969. Repr. of 1924 ed. lib. bdg. 19.50x (ISBN 0-374-93117-8). Octagon.

--Wordsworth. LC 72-196436. 1908. lib. bdg. 15.00 (ISBN 0-8414-4651-2). Folcroft.

Gingery, David J. Charcoal Foundry. rev. ed. 80p. (Orig.). 1983. pap. 6.95 (ISBN 0-9604330-8-2). D J Gingery.

--Designing & Building the Sheet Metal Brake, Bk. 7. LC 80-66142. (Build Your Own Metal Working Shop from Scrap Ser.). (Illus.). 52p. (Orig.). 1980. pap. 6.95 (ISBN 0-9604330-6-6). D J Gingery.

--The Dividing Head & Deluxe Accessories. LC 80-66142. (Build Your Own Metal Working Shop from Scrap Ser.: Bk. 6). (Illus.). 160p. (Orig.). 1982. pap. 8.95 (ISBN 0-9604330-5-8). D J Gingery.

--The Drill Press. LC 80-66142. (Build Your Own Metal Working Shop from Scrap Ser.: Bk. 5). (Illus.). 128p. (Orig.). 1982. pap. 7.95 (ISBN 0-9604330-4-X). D J Gingery.

--Lil Bertha-Compact Electric Furnace. 1984. pap. 7.95 (ISBN 0-917914-16-3). Lindsay Pubns.

--The Metal Lathe. LC 80-66142. (Build Your Own Metal Working Shop from Scrap Ser.: Bk. 2). (Illus.). 128p. (Orig.). 1980. pap. 7.95 (ISBN 0-9604330-1-5). D J Gingery.

--The Metal Shaper. LC 80-66142. (Build Your Own Metal Working Shop from Scrap: Bk. 3). (Illus.). 144p. (Orig.). 1980. pap. 7.95 (ISBN 0-9604330-2-3). D J Gingery.

--The Milling Machine. LC 80-66142. (Build Your Own Metal Working Shop from Scrap Ser.: Bk. 4). (Illus.). 160p. (Orig.). 1981. pap. 7.95 (ISBN 0-9604330-3-1). D J Gingery.

Ginglend, David R. & Carlson, Bernice W. Ready to Work? Development of Occupational Skills, Attitudes, & Behaviors with Mentally Retarded Persons. LC 76-58841. Repr. of 1977 ed. 39.80 (ISBN 0-8357-9023-1, 2016397). Bks Demand UMI.

Ginglend, David R. & Stiles, Winifred E. Music Activities for Retarded Children. (Illus., Orig.). 1965. pap. 13.95 (ISBN 0-687-27309-9). Abingdon.

Gingles, Bertie C. The Cunningham Family. (Illus.). 431p. Repr. of 1957 ed. 24.95 (ISBN 0-913383-02-3). McClanahan Pub.

Gingold, Alfred. Items from Our Catalog. 80p. 1982. pap. 4.95 (ISBN 0-380-81695-4, 81695). Avon.

--More Items from Our Catalog. 80p. 1984. pap. 5.95 (ISBN 0-380-84657-8, 84657). Avon.

Gingold, Alfred, jt. auth. see Buskin, John.

Gingold, Diane J. The George Verdak Collection: Eras of the Dance. LC 76-72823. (Illus.). 1976. pap. 6.50 (ISBN 0-89280-004-6). Montgomery Mus.

Gingold, Diane J., jt. auth. see Montgomery Museum of Fine Arts.

Gingold, Diane J., ed. Anne Goldthwaite: Eighteen Sixty-Nine to Nineteen Forty-Four. LC 77-74790. (Illus.). 1977. pap. 5.00 (ISBN 0-89280-006-2). Montgomery Mus.

--Master Prints from the Fifteenth Through Eighteenth Centuries. LC 77-84545. (Illus.). 1977. pap. 9.00 (ISBN 0-89280-007-0). Montgomery Mus.

--Venetian Drawings from the Collection of Janos Scholz. LC 76-307. (Illus.). 128p. (Orig.). 1976. pap. 6.00 (ISBN 0-685-66417-1). Montgomery Mus.

Gingold, Diane J., ed. see Montgomery Museum of Fine Arts.

Gingold, Kurt, tr. from Rus. Soviet Urethane Technology, Vol. 1. (Soviet Progress in Polyurethanes Ser.). Orig. Title: Intez I Fiziko-Khimiia Polimerov, No. 7. (Illus., Orig.). 1972. pap. 19.00 (ISBN 0-87762-069-5). Technomic.

Gingold, Yenny N., jt. auth. see Golbert, Albert S.

Gingras, Angele D. Best in Congressional Humor: From Busing to Bugging. LC 72-12394. (Illus.). 168p. 1973. o. p. 6.50 (ISBN 0-87491-344-6); pap. 4.95 (ISBN 0-87491-345-4). Acropolis.

Gingras, Gustave. Feet Was I to the Lame. LC 78-318484. 1980. 9.95 (ISBN 0-285-64837-3, Pub. by Souvenir Pr). Intl Spec Bk.

Gingras, Louie & Rainboldt, Jo. Coyote & Kootenai. (gr. 2-6). 1977. 1.95 (ISBN 0-89992-067-5). Coun India Ed.

Gingras, Rosario C., ed. Second-Language Acquisition & Foreign Language Teaching. 107p. 1978. pap. 8.50x (ISBN 0-15-599075-6). Ctr Appl Ling.
Gingrich, F. Wilbur. Shorter Lexicon of the Greek New Testament. 2nd ed. 256p. 1983. 20.00 (ISBN 0-310-25030-7). Zondervan.
Gingrich, F. Wilbur, rev. by see Danker, Frederick W.
Gingrich, Harold W. Electrical Machinery, Transformers, & Control. (Illus.). 1978. ref. 29.95 (ISBN 0-13-247320-8). P-H.
Gingrich, Newt. America: A Blueprint for the Future. Date not set. pap. 6.95 (ISBN 0-671-55902-8). PB.
Gingrich, Newt, et al. Window of Opportunity: A Blueprint for the Future. 1984. 14.95 (ISBN 0-312-93922-1). St Martin.
Gingrich, Raymond E. Fellowship with the Word of Life: Studies in I, II, III John. pap. 4.95 (ISBN 0-88469-042-3). BMH Bks.
Gingrich, Wilbur F. & Danker, Frederick W. Greek-English Lexicon of the New Testament. rev 2nd. ed. 1979. 42.50 (ISBN 0-310-20570-0). Zondervan.
Ginguay, M. Dictionnaire d'Informatique: Anglais-Francais. 172p. (Eng. & Fr.). 1977. pap. 27.50 (ISBN 0-686-57299-8, F-137100). French & Eur.
Ginguay, Michael. Diccionario de Informatica. 184p. (Span.). 1972. pap. 23.50 (ISBN 84-311-0004-4, S-50130). French & Eur.
Ginguay, Michel & Lauret, Annette. Lexique d'Informatique. 244p. (Fr.). 1973. pap. 32.50 (ISBN 0-686-57198-3, M-6273). French & Eur.
Gingyera-Pinycwa, G. A. Apolo Milton Obote & His Times. LC 73-91414. (Studies in East African Society & History). (Illus.). 1977. text ed. 21.50x (ISBN 0-88357-034-3); pap. text ed. 7.95x (ISBN 0-88357-035-1). NOK Pubs.
Gini, Corraco & Royal Institute of International Affairs. Report on the Problem of Raw Materials & Foodstuffs. Bd. with Raw Materials & Colonies. LC 82-48298. (The World Economy Ser.). 325p. 1982. lib. bdg. 39.00 (ISBN 0-8240-5353-2). Garland Pub.
Giniger, Ken S., compiled by. Compact Treasury of Inspiration. 320p. (Orig.). 1983. pap. 3.50 (ISBN 0-515-07442-X). Jove Pubns.
Gink, K. Hungary Towns & Countryside. 12.00 (ISBN 0-912729-12-0). Newbury Bks.
Ginn, James R. Fables for Small Fry. 1984. 4.95 (ISBN 0-533-06064-8). Vantage.
Ginn, Peter L. Introduction to Process Control & Digital Minicomputers. LC 82-6036. 292p. 1982. 29.95x (ISBN 0-87201-180-1). Gulf Pub.
Ginn, Robert J. The College Graduate's Career Guide. 256p. 1982. pap. 5.95 (ISBN 0-684-17852-4, ScribT). Scribner.
Ginn, Roman. Adventure in Spiritual Direction: A Prophetic Pattern. (Orig.). 1979. pap. 2.95 (ISBN 0-914544-27-6). Living Flame Pr.
--The Conversion of Samson. LC 82-24073. 1983. pap. 3.50 (ISBN 0-932506-21-6). St Bedes Pubns.
--Jonah: The Spirituality of a Reluctant Prophet. (Orig.). pap. 2.95 (ISBN 0-914544-21-7). Living Flame Pr.
Ginna, Peter St. J., tr. see Freund, Gisele.
Ginneken, J. K. van see Van Ginneken, J. K. & Muller, A. S.
Ginneken, Wouter Van see International Labour Office Staff.
Ginneken, Wouter van see Van Ginneken, Wouter & Garzuel, Michel.
Ginneken, Wouter van & Park, Jong-goo, eds. Generating Internationally Comparable Income Distribution Estimates. (World Employment Programme). (Illus.). 176p. 1985. pap. 14.25 (ISBN 92-2-103666-9, ILO348, ILO). Unipub.
Ginneken, Wouter van see Van Ginneken, Wouter & Baron, Christopher.
Ginnett, Elsie, jt. auth. see Storm, Margaret.
Ginns, Patsy M. Rough Weather Makes Good Timber: Carolinians Recall. LC 76-20765. (Illus.). xiv, 189p. 1977. 14.95 (ISBN 0-8078-1288-9); pap. 8.95 (ISBN 0-8078-4071-8). U of NC Pr.
--Snowbird Gravy & Dishpan Pie: Mountain People Recall. LC 81-16296. (Illus.). xiv, 209p. 1982. 12.95 (ISBN 0-8078-1516-0). U of NC Pr.
Gino, Carol. The Nurse's Story. 1983. pap. 3.95 (ISBN 0-553-23667-9). Bantam.
--The Place of Hope. 368p. Date not set. 15.95 (ISBN 0-671-49499-6, Linden). S&S.
--Rusty's Story. 1985. pap. price not set. Bantam.
Ginor, Fanny. Socio-Economic Disparities in Israel. 313p. 1979. 24.95 (ISBN 0-87855-332-0); pap. 9.95 (ISBN 965-216-000-8). Transaction Bks.
Ginorio, Carmen, jt. auth. see Cabanillas, Berta.
Ginott, Haim. Between Parent & Child. 1969. pap. 3.50 (ISBN 0-380-00821-1, 69468-9). Avon.
--Between Parent & Teenager. 1971. pap. 3.50 (ISBN 0-380-00820-3, 69476-X). Avon.
Ginott, Haim G. Teacher & Child. Markel, Robert, ed. LC 70-182448. 323p. 1972. 14.95 (ISBN 0-02-543340-7). Macmillan.
Ginott, Hainor G. Teacher & Child. 1975. pap. 3.95 (ISBN 0-380-00323-6, 70008-5). Avon.
Gins, et al. Reading for Mastery & Enrichment. 208p. 1984. pap. text ed. 14.95 (ISBN 0-8403-3525-3). Kendall-Hunt.
Gins, Madeline. What the President Will Say & Do!! 160p. (Orig.). 1984. 14.95 (ISBN 0-930794-93-1); pap. 7.95 (ISBN 0-930794-92-3). Station Hill Pr.
Gins, Madeline H., jt. auth. see Arakawa.
Ginsberg, Allen. Collected Poems: 1947-1980. LC 84-47573. (Illus.). 672p. 1984. 26.44i (ISBN 0-06-015341-5, HarpT). Har-Row.
--Composed on the Tongue. Allen, Donald, ed. LC 79-21115. 160p. 1980. pap. 6.95 (ISBN 0-912516-29-1). Grey Fox.
--Empty Mirror: Early Poems. (Orig.). 1961. pap. 3.50 (ISBN 0-87091-030-2). Corinth Bks.
--The Fall of America: Poems of These States, 1965-1971. LC 72-84228. (Pocket Poets Ser.: No. 30). 190p. 1972. pap. 4.95 (ISBN 0-87286-063-9). City Lights.
--First Blues: Rags, Ballads & Harmonium Songs Nineteen Seventy-One to Nineteen Seventy-Four. LC 75-23082. 1975. 17.95 (ISBN 0-916190-04-8); pap. 6.00 (ISBN 0-916190-05-6). Full Court NY.
--The Gates of Wrath: Rhymed Poems, 1948-1952. LC 72-76541. 66p. (Orig.). 1973. pap. 3.00 (ISBN 0-912516-01-1). Grey Fox.
--Gay Sunshine Interview. LC 74-75457. 64p. 1974. pap. 1.95 (ISBN 0-912516-05-4). Grey Fox.
--Howl & Other Poems. LC 56-8587. (Pocket Poets Ser.: No. 4). (Orig.). 1956. pap. 2.95 (ISBN 0-87286-017-5). City Lights.
--Indian Journals. LC 73-13934. 1970. 6.50 (ISBN 0-87286-145-7); pap. 3.00 (ISBN 0-87286-018-3). City Lights.
--Iron Horse. LC 73-93941. 1974. pap. 3.00 (ISBN 0-87286-077-9). City Lights.
--Journals: Early Fifties Early Sixties. Ball, Gordon, ed. & intro. by. LC 76-54581. (Illus.). 1977. pap. 6.95 (ISBN 0-394-17034-2, E704, Ever). Grove.
--Kaddish & Other Poems: Nineteen Fifty-Eight to Nineteen Sixty. LC 60-14775. (Pocket Poets Ser.: No. 14). (Orig.). 1961. pap. 3.95 (ISBN 0-87286-019-1). City Lights.
--Mind Breaths: Poems, 1972-1977. LC 77-541. (Pocket Poets Ser.: No. 35). 1978. pap. 4.95 (ISBN 0-87286-092-2). City Lights.
--Mostly Sitting Haiku. 2nd rev., exp. ed. (Xtras Ser.: No. 6). 36p. (Orig.). 1983. pap. 2.50 (ISBN 0-89120-014-2). From Here.
--Planet News: Poems, 1961-1964. LC 68-25477. (Pocket Poet Ser.: No. 23). (Orig.). 1968. pap. 3.50 (ISBN 0-87286-020-5). City Lights.
--Plutonian Ode & Other Poems, 1977-1980. LC 81-7657. (Pockets Poets Ser.: No. 40). 80p. 1981. 10.95 (ISBN 0-87286-126-0); pap. 4.95 (ISBN 0-87286-125-2). City Lights.
--Reality Sandwiches: Poems, 1953-1960. LC 63-12219. (Pocket Poets Ser.: No. 18). (Orig.). 1963. pap. 4.95 (ISBN 0-87286-021-3). City Lights.
--Sad Dust Glories: Poems Work Summer in Woods 1974. 2nd ed. 1975. saddlestitched in wrappers 2.50 (ISBN 0-935388-01-X). Workingmans Pr.
--Scenes along the Road. Charters, Ann, compiled by. (Illus.). 56p. (Orig.). 1985. pap. 7.95 (ISBN 0-87286-168-6). City Lights.
--The Visions of the Great Rememberer. LC 74-77758. (Haystack Bks.). (Illus.). 72p. 1974. pap. 3.50 (ISBN 0-913142-03-4). Mulch Pr.
Ginsberg, Allen & Orlovsky, Peter. Straight Hearts' Delight: Love Poems & Selected Letters. Leyland, Winston, ed. (Illus.). 240p. 1980. 20.00 (ISBN 0-917342-64-X, Gay Sunshine); pap. 8.95 (ISBN 0-917342-65-8). Gay Sunshine.
Ginsberg, Allen, jt. auth. see Burroughs, William.
Ginsberg, Allen, et al. Nuke Chronicles. Gosciak, Josh & Kenny, Maurice, eds. (Contact II Chapbook: No. 1). (Illus.). 32p. (Orig.). 1980. pap. 3.00 (ISBN 0-936556-00-5). Contact Two.
--Madeira & Toasts for Basil Bunting's 75th Birthday. Williams, Jonathan, ed. (Illus.). 1977. pap. 10.00 (ISBN 0-912330-28-7). Jargon Soc.
Ginsberg, Ben. The Sibling Rivalry Monster. (Illus.). 48p. (Orig.). (gr. 3-5). 1985. pap. 12.95 (ISBN 0-89594-184-8). Crossing Pr.
Ginsberg, Benjamin. The Consequences of Consent: Elections, Citizen Control & Popular Acquiescence. 1982. pap. text ed. 11.95 (ISBN 0-394-34929-6, RanC). Random.
Ginsberg, Benjamin, jt. auth. see Lowi, Theodore J.
Ginsberg, Elaine. Virginia Woolf: Centennial Papers. Gottlieb, Laura Moss, ed. LC 82-50826. 350p. 1984. 25.00x (ISBN 0-87875-242-0). Whitston Pub.
Ginsberg, H. L., et al, trs. Five Megilloth & the Book of Jonah. LC 69-19043. (Illus.). 135p. (Eng. & Heb.). 1969. 7.50 (ISBN 0-8276-0045-3, 166). Jewish Pubns.
Ginsberg, Harold, jt. auth. see Dulbecco, Renato.
Ginsberg, Harold S., ed. The Adenoviruses. (The Viruses Ser.). 590p. 1984. 85.00x (ISBN 0-306-41592-5, Plenum Pr). Plenum Pub.
Ginsberg, Harold S. & Vogel, Henry J., eds. Transfer & Expression of Eukaryotic Genes. (P & S Biomedical Symposia Ser.). 1984. 65.00 (ISBN 0-12-284650-8). Acad Pr.
Ginsberg, Irving W. Fundamentals of Electro-Optical Remote Sensing. (Orig.). 1986. write for info. (ISBN 0-89464-003-8). Krieger.
Ginsberg, J. H. & Genin, J. Statistics. 432p. 1984. 37.50 (ISBN 0-471-06494-7). Wiley.
--Statistics & Dynamics. 2nd ed. 925p. 45.50 (ISBN 0-471-09745-4). Wiley.
Ginsberg, Jekuthiel, jt. auth. see Smith, David E.
Ginsberg, Jerry H. & Glenin, Joseph. Dynamics. 2nd ed. 608p. 1984. text ed. 37.50 (ISBN 0-471-06495-5). Wiley.
Ginsberg, Judith. Tradition & Theme in the "Annals" of Tacitus. rev. ed. Connor, W. R., ed. LC 80-2651. (Monographs in Classical Studies). 1981. lib. bdg. 20.00 (ISBN 0-405-14038-X). Ayer Co Pubs.
Ginsberg, Leon H. The Practice of Social Work in Public Welfare. LC 82-71888. 1983. 18.95 (ISBN 0-02-911760-7). Free Pr.
--Social Work in Public Welfare. 1983. 18.95 (ISBN 0-317-30546-8). Free Pr.
Ginsberg, Leon H., jt. auth. see Harbert, Anita S.
Ginsberg, Lev. Tartini: His Life & Times. Axelrod, Herbert R., ed. Levin, I., tr. from Rus. (Illus.). 384p. 1981. 29.95 (ISBN 0-87666-590-3, Z-58). Paganiniana Pubns.
Ginsberg, Louis H. The Israelian Heritage of Judaism. 15.00x (ISBN 0-87334-013-2). Ktav.
Ginsberg, Merle. Boy George. (Illus.). 192p. (Orig.). 1984. pap. 2.95 (ISBN 0-440-10761-X). Dell.
Ginsberg, Mirra. Good Morning, Chick. (Illus.). (ps-3). pap. 2.50 (ISBN 0-590-31952-3). Scholastic Inc.
Ginsberg, Mitchell I. Current Issues in Title XX Programs. 51p. 5.00 (ISBN 0-317-35039-0, 5611); 5-20 copies 4.00 ea.; 21 or more copies 3.50 ea. Natl Conf Soc Welfare.
--The Future Relationship Between Publicly Funded Social Services & Income Support Programs. 71p. 5.00 (ISBN 0-317-35043-9, 5610); 5-20 copies 4.00 ea.; 21 or more 3.50 ea. Natl Conf Soc Welfare.
Ginsberg, Morris. The Idea of Progress: A Revaluation. LC 77-138239. 82p. 1972. Repr. of 1953 ed. lib. bdg. 15.00x (ISBN 0-8371-5596-7, GIIP). Greenwood.
Ginsberg, Morris, ed. Law & Opinion in England in the Twentieth Century. LC 74-7537. 407p. 1974. Repr. of 1959 ed. lib. bdg. 21.25x (ISBN 0-8371-7576-3, GILO). Greenwood.
Ginsberg, Norton & Fullard, Harold. The Aldine University Atlas. 1969. pap. text ed. 9.75x (ISBN 0-673-05995-2). Scott F.
Ginsberg, Philip M., jt. auth. see Seidel, Andrew D.
Ginsberg, R. N., et al. Geology of Calcareous Algae: Notes for a Short Course. (Sedimenta I). (Illus.). 70p. (Orig.). 1972. 6.00 (ISBN 0-932981-01-1). Univ Miami CSL.
Ginsberg, Ralph B. Anomie & Aspirations: A Reinterpretation of Durkheim's Theory. Zuckerman, Harriet & Merton, Robert K., eds. LC 79-8999. (Dissertations on Sociology Ser.). 1980. lib. bdg. 30.50x (ISBN 0-405-12969-6). Ayer Co Pubs.
Ginsberg, Ralph B., ed. see American Academy of Political & Social Science, Annual Meeting, 83rd.
Ginsberg, Ralph B., jt. ed. see Rejda, George E.
Ginsberg, Ralph B., jt. ed. see Richardson, John, Jr.
Ginsberg, Ralph B., jt. ed. see Roof, Wade C.
Ginsberg, Robert. Welcome to Philosophy! A Handbook for Students. LC 76-29222. 1982. 8.00x (ISBN 0-87735-521-5); pap. 4.95x (ISBN 0-87735-522-3). Freeman Cooper.
Ginsberg, Seymour, et al. Studies in Abstract Families of Languages. LC 52-42839. (Memoirs: No. 87). 51p. 1983. pap. 9.00 (ISBN 0-8218-1287-4, MEMO-87). Am Math.
Ginsberg, Sigmund G. Managememt: An Executive Perspective. LC 81-66815. (Business Ser.). 400p. text ed. 23.00 (ISBN 0-936328-07-X). Dame Inc.
Ginsberg, Stephen P. Guide to an Effective Out-Patient Ophthalmic Surgery Center. LC 84-51524. 272p. 1985. 39.50 (ISBN 0-943432-33-2). Slack Inc.
Ginsberg, Victor see Colowick, Sidney P. & Kaplan, Nathan O.
Ginsberg, Warren. The Cast of Character: The Representation of Personality in Ancient & Medieval Literature. 208p. 1983. 27.50x (ISBN 0-8020-5596-6). U of Toronto Pr.
Ginsborg, Paul. Daniele Manin & the Venetian Revolution of 1848-49. LC 78-56180. (Illus.). 1979. 47.50 (ISBN 0-521-22077-7). Cambridge U Pr.
Ginsbourg, Sam. The Diary of a Young English Teacher. (China Spotlight Ser.). 131p. 1984. pap. 3.95 (ISBN 0-8351-1432-5). China Bks.
--My First Sixty Years in China. (Illus.). 373p. 1982. pap. text ed. 5.95 (ISBN 0-8351-1109-1). China Bks.
Ginsburg. Cases & Materials on Equal Employment. 4th ed. 863p. 1980. 50.00 (ISBN 0-318-03079-9). GWU Natl Law.
--Cases & Materials on Federal Labor Standards Act. 2nd ed. 502p. 1976. 30.00 (ISBN 0-318-03080-2). GWU Natl Law.
Ginsburg, A. David. Clinical Reasoning in Patient Care. 224p. 1980. pap. text ed. 17.50x (ISBN 0-06-140915-4, 14-09150, Harper Medical). Lippincott.
Ginsburg, Christian D. Introduction to the Massoretico Critical Edition of the Hebrew Bible. rev. ed. 1966. 79.50x (ISBN 0-87068-060-9). Ktav.
Ginsburg, David. Propellanes: Structure & Reactions. (Monographs in Modern Chemistry: Vol. 7). 272p. 1975. 81.20x (ISBN 3-527-25602-4). VCH Pubs.
Ginsburg, David C. Coheleth & Song of Songs, with a Commentary Historical & Critical, 2 Vols. in 1. rev. ed. (Library of Biblical Studies Ser). 1970. 59.50x (ISBN 0-87068-059-5). Ktav.
Ginsburg, Douglas H. Regulation of Broadcasting: Law & Policy Towards Radio, Television & Cable Communications. LC 78-11973. (American Casebook Ser.). 741p. 1978. text ed. 24.95 (ISBN 0-8299-2017-X). West Pub.
Ginsburg, Douglas H. & Director, Mark D. Regulation of Broadcasting: 1983 Supplement. (American Casebook Ser.). 182p. 1983. pap. text ed. 5.50 (ISBN 0-314-75957-3). West Pub.
Ginsburg, G. P. Emerging Strategies in Social Psychological Research. LC 78-18506. 319p. 1979. 53.95x (ISBN 0-471-99690-4, Pub. by Wiley-Interscience). Wiley.
Ginsburg, Gerry, et al, eds. Discovery Strategies in the Psychology of Action, Vol. 35. (European Monographs in Social Psychology). Date not set. price not set (ISBN 0-12-284760-1). Acad Pr.
Ginsburg, Harvey, jt. auth. see McCoy, Ingeborg.
Ginsburg, Helen. Full Employment & Public Policy: The United States & Sweden. LC 76-55536. 256p. 1983. 25.00x (ISBN 0-669-01318-8). Lexington Bks.
Ginsburg, Helen, ed. Poverty, Economics, & Society. LC 80-6115. 361p. 1981. lib. bdg. 25.75 (ISBN 0-8191-1385-9); pap. text ed. 14.00 (ISBN 0-8191-1386-7). U Pr of Amer.
Ginsburg, Herbert. Children's Arithmetic: How They Learn It & How You Teach It. LC 76-47212. (Illus.). 208p. 1983. pap. text ed. 16.00 (ISBN 0-936104-29-5, 0377). Pro Ed.
Ginsburg, Herbert & Opper, Sylvia. Piaget's Theory of Intellectual Development. 2nd ed. (Illus.). 1979. pap. 16.95 (ISBN 0-13-675132-6). P-H.
Ginsburg, Herbert, ed. The Development of Mathematical Thinking. (Developmental Psychology Ser.). 424p. 1982. 44.00 (ISBN 0-12-284780-6). Acad Pr.
Ginsburg, Janet H., jt. auth. see Elman, Natalie M.
Ginsburg, Jekuthiel, jt. auth. see Smith, David E.
Ginsburg, L. Vieuxtemps. Axelrod, Herbert R., ed. Levin, I., tr. from Russ. (Illus.). 190p. 1984. 19.95 (ISBN 0-86622-018-6, Z-87). Paganiniana Pubns.
Ginsburg, Lev. History of the Violoncello. Axelrod, Herbert R., ed. Tchistyakova, Tanya, tr. (Illus.). 392p. 1983. 30.00 (ISBN 0-87666-597-0, Z-72). Paganiniana Pubns.
--Ysaye. Axelrod, Herbert R., ed. (Illus.). 576p. 1980. 25.00 (ISBN 0-87666-620-9, Z-31). Paganiniana Pubns.
Ginsburg, Madeleine. Fashion Illustration. (The Victoria & Albert Museum Introductions to Decorative Arts Ser.). (Illus.). 48p. 1982. 9.95 (ISBN 0-88045-002-9). Stemmer Hse.
--Victorian Dress in Photographs. (Illus.). 192p. 1983. text ed. 42.50x (ISBN 0-8419-0838-9). Holmes & Meier.
Ginsburg, Madeleine, intro. by. An Age of Elegance. (Illus., Orig.). 1985. pap. 9.95 (ISBN 0-948107-11-1, Pub. by Victoria & Albert Mus UK). Faber & Faber.
Ginsburg, Mirra. Across the Stream. LC 81-20306. (Illus.). 24p. (ps-1). 1982. 10.75 (ISBN 0-688-01204-3); PLB 10.88 (ISBN 0-688-01206-X). Greenwillow.
--The Chick & the Duckling. Suteyev, V., tr. LC 74-188773. 32p. (ps-1). 1972. 12.95 (ISBN 0-02-735940-9). Macmillan.
--Good Morning, Chick. LC 80-11352. (Illus.). 32p. (ps). 1980. 11.75 (ISBN 0-688-80284-2); PLB 11.88 (ISBN 0-688-84284-4). Greenwillow.
--How the Sun Was Brought Back to the Sky: Adapted from a Slovenian Folk Tale. LC 74-19060. (Illus.). 32p. (ps-2). 1975. 8.95 (ISBN 0-02-735750-3). Macmillan.
--Little Rystu. LC 76-30485. (Illus.). 32p. (gr. k-3). 1978. PLB 11.88 (ISBN 0-688-84097-3). Greenwillow.
--The Magic Stove. LC 82-12523. (Illus.). (gr. 2-4). 1983. 11.95 (ISBN 0-698-20566-9, Coward). Putnam Pub Group.
--The Night It Rained Pancakes. LC 79-16137. (Greenwillow Read-Alone Bks.). (Illus.). 56p. (gr. k-3). 1980. 8.75 (ISBN 0-688-80241-9); PLB 8.88 (ISBN 0-688-84241-0). Greenwillow.
--The Sun's Asleep Behind the Hill. LC 81-6615. (Illus.). 32p. (ps-1). 1982. 11.25 (ISBN 0-688-00824-0); PLB 11.88 (ISBN 0-688-00825-9). Greenwillow.
--The Twelve Clever Brothers & Other Fools. LC 79-2409. (Illus.). (gr. 3-6). 1979. PLB 10.89 (ISBN 0-397-31862-6). Lipp Jr Bks.
--Two Greedy Bears: Adapted from a Hungarian Folk Tale. LC 76-8819. (Illus.). 32p. (ps-2). 1976. 9.95 (ISBN 0-02-736450-X, 73645). Macmillan.
--Where Does the Sun Go at Night? LC 79-16151. (Illus.). 32p. (gr. k-3). 1980. 10.95 (ISBN 0-688-80245-1); PLB 10.88 (ISBN 0-688-84245-3). Greenwillow.
Ginsburg, Mirra, ed. & tr. see Zamyatin, Yevgeny.
Ginsburg, Mirra, tr. Last Door to Aiya: A Selection of the Best New Science Fiction from the Soviet Union. LC 68-16347. (YA) 1968. 10.95 (ISBN 0-87599-135-1). S G Phillips.
Ginsburg, Mirra, tr. see Alexandrova, Vera.
Ginsburg, Mirra, tr. see Bulgakov, Mikhail.
Ginsburg, Mirra, tr. see Dostoyevsky, Fyodor.
Ginsburg, Mirra, tr. see Obukhova, Lydia.
Ginsburg, Mirra, tr. see Zamyatin, Yevgeny.

Ginsburg, Norman. Class, Capital & Social Policy. (Critical Texts in Social Work & the Welfare State). 1979. text ed. 26.50x (ISBN 0-333-21581-8). Humanities.

Ginsburg, Norton, jt. auth. see Borgese, Elizabeth M.

Ginsburg, Norton, ed. Essays on Geography & Economic Development. LC 60-2105. (Research Papers Ser.: No. 62). 196p. 1960. pap. 10.00 (ISBN 0-89065-003-9). U Chicago Dept Geog.

Ginsburg, Norton & Lalor, Bernard A., eds. China: The Eighties Era. 375p. 1984. 28.50x (ISBN 0-86531-668-6). Westview.

Ginsburg, Norton, jt. ed. see Borgese, Elisabeth M.

Ginsburg, Norton, jt. ed. see Borgese, Elizabeth M.

Ginsburg, Norton, jt. ed. see Leung, C. K.

Ginsburg, Paul B., jt. auth. see Frech, H. E.

Ginsburg, R. N. & Garrett, Peter. Seminar on Organism-Sediment Interrelations 1968. (Bermuda Biological Station Special Pubn.: No. 2). (Illus.). ii, 154p. 1969. pap. 7.00 (ISBN 0-917642-02-3). Bermuda Bio.

Ginsburg, R. N., jt. auth. see James, N. P.

Ginsburg, R. N., ed. Tidal Deposits: A Case Book of Recent Examples & Fossil Counterparts. LC 75-28228. (Illus.). xiii, 421p. 1975. 52.00 (ISBN 0-387-06823-6). Springer-Verlag.

Ginsburg, R. N., et al. South Florida Carbonate Sediments. (Sedimenta II). (Illus.). 71p. (Orig.). 1972. pap. 6.00 (ISBN 0-932981-02-X). Univ Miami CSL.

Ginsburg, Robert N. & Stanley, Steven M. Seminar on Organism-Sediment Interrelationships, 1969. (Bermuda Biological Station Special Pubn.: No. 6). (Illus.). iv, 110p. 1970. pap. 6.00 (ISBN 0-917642-06-6). Bermuda Bio.

Ginsburg, Robert N., ed. Evolving Concepts in Sedimentology. LC 72-4016. (The John Hopkins University Studies in Geology: No. 21). pap. 51.00 (ISBN 0-317-28475-4, 2020737). Bks Demand UMI.

Ginsburg, Robert N., ed. see Liddell, W. D. & Ohlhorst, S. L.

Ginsburg, Ruth B. Selective Survey of English Language Studies on Scandinavian Law. vi, 53p. (Orig.). 1970. pap. text ed. 4.50x (ISBN 0-8377-0600-9). Rothman.

Ginsburg, Ruth R., et al. Nueva Vista. (gr. 7-12). 1978. text ed. 19.40 (ISBN 0-205-05878-7, 4258789); 6.36Wkbk (ISBN 0-205-03662-7, 4236629). Allyn.

--Vista Hispanica. (gr. 9-12). 1978. text ed. 19.40 (ISBN 0-205-05875-2, 4258754); tchr's ed. 5.96 (ISBN 0-205-05877-9, 4258770). Allyn.

Ginsburg, S. Algebraic & Automata-Theoretic Properties of Formal Languages. LC 73-86082. (Fundamental Studies in Computer Science: Vol. 2). 313p. 1975. 64.00 (ISBN 0-444-10586-7, North-Holland). Elsevier.

--Stochastic Models of Migration. Date not set. price not set. Elsevier.

Ginsburg, S. G., jt. auth. see Karol, N. H.

Ginsburg, Sigmund G. Management: An Executive Perspective. 1983. text ed. 28.95 (ISBN 0-8359-4207-4). Reston.

--Ropes for Management Success: Climb Higher, Faster. 176p. 1984. 15.95 (ISBN 0-13-783135-8); pap. 7.95 (ISBN 0-13-783127-7). P-H.

Ginsburg, Victor. Biology of Carbohydrates, Vol. 1. LC 80-20758. 336p. 1981. 70.95 (ISBN 0-471-03905-5, Pub. by Wiley-Interscience). Wiley.

Ginsburg, Victor & Robbins, Phillips W. Biology of Carbohydrates, Vol. 2. (Biology of Carbohydrates Ser.: 1-504). 342p. 1984. 80.00 (ISBN 0-471-03906-3, Pub. by Wiley-Interscience). Wiley.

Ginsburg, Victor, jt. ed. see Colowick, S.

Ginsburg, Victor see Colowick, Sidney P. & Kaplan, Nathan O.

Ginsburgh, V. A. & Waelbroeck, J. L. Activity Analysis & General Equilibrium Modelling. (Contributions to Economic Analysis Ser.: Vol. 125). 374p. 1981. 61.75 (ISBN 0-444-86011-8, North-Holland). Elsevier.

Ginsburgs. The Legal Framework of Trade. 1976. pap. 24.00 (ISBN 90-247-1850-3, Pub. by Martinus Nijhoff Netherlands). Kluwer Academic.

Ginsburgs, George. Calendar of Diplomatic Affairs, Democratic People's Republic of Korea, 1945-1975. Kim, Roy U., ed. LC 77-71677. 275p. 1977. lib. bdg. 25.00 (ISBN 0-379-20354-5). Oceana.

--The Citizenship Law of the U. S. S. R. 1984. lib. bdg. 75.00 (ISBN 90-247-2863-0, Pub. by Martinus Nijhoff Netherlands). Kluwer Academic.

Ginsburgs, George, jt. auth. see Slusser, Robert M.

Ginsburgs, George K. & Kim, Roy U. Calendar of Diplomatic Affairs Democratic People's Republic of Korea 1945-1975. 1977. 27.50 (ISBN 0-918542-00-6). Symposia Pr.

Ginsbury, Norman, tr. see Ibsen, Henrik.

Ginstling, A. M., jt. auth. see Budnikov, P. P.

Ginswick, Jules, ed. Labour & the Poor in England & Wales 1849-1851, 3 vols. Incl. Vol. I. Lancashire; Cheshire; Yorkshire. (Illus.). 316p. 30.00x (ISBN 0-7146-2907-3); pap. 12.50x (ISBN 0-7146-4038-7); Vol. 2. Northumberland & Durham; Staffordshire, The Midlands. (Illus.). 228p. 30.00x (ISBN 0-7146-2960-X); pap. 12.50x (ISBN 0-7146-4039-5); Vol. 3. South Wales, North Wales. (Illus.). 264p. 30.00x (ISBN 0-7146-2961-8); pap. 12.50x (ISBN 0-7146-4040-9). (Illus.). 1983. pap. (F Cass Co). Biblio Dist.

Ginter, Jay J., jt. ed. see Rettig, R. Bruce.

Ginter, Joe. I Wanted to Be Famous. (Illus.). 1981. pap. 5.00 (ISBN 0-682-49806-8). Exposition Pr FL.

Ginter, Peter M. & Rucks, Andrew C. Basic Decision Making on the Microcomputer. 475p. 1985. pap. text ed. 23.95 (ISBN 0-394-33928-2, RanC). Random.

Ginter, Steve. Chance Vought F7U Cutlass. (Naval Fighter Ser.: No. 6). 106p. 1982. pap. 13.95. Naval Fighters.

--Chance Vought F7U Cutlass. (Naval Fighter Ser.: No. 6). 106p. 1982. pap. 13.95 (ISBN 0-942612-06-X). Aviation.

--North American T-Twenty-Eight Trojan. (Naval Fighters Ser.: No. 5). (Illus.). 66p. 1981. pap. 8.95 (ISBN 0-942612-05-1). Aviation.

--North American T-28 Trojan. (Naval Fighters Ser.: No. 5). (Illus.). pap. 8.95 (ISBN 0-942612-05-1). Naval Fighters.

Ginter, Steve & Picciani, Ron. North American FJ-1 Fury. (Naval Fighter Ser.: No. 7). (Illus.). 1983. pap. 5.50 (ISBN 0-942612-07-8). Aviation.

Ginter, Steve, ed. see Koehnen, Richard.

Ginter, Steve J. North American FJ-2 Fury. (Naval Fighters Ser.: No. 10). (Illus.). 46p. (Orig.). pap. 8.95 (ISBN 0-942612-10-8). Aviation.

Ginter, Steven J. Grumman HU-16 Albatross. (Naval Fighters Ser.: No. 11). (Illus.). 74p. (Orig.). pap. 14.95 (ISBN 0-942612-11-6). Aviation.

--Lockheed C-121 Constellation. (Naval Fighters Ser.). (Illus.). 78p. (Orig.). 1983. pap. 13.95 (ISBN 0-942612-08-6). Aviation.

--McDonnell FH-1 Phantom. (Naval Fighters Ser.: No. 3). (Illus.). 30p. (Orig.). 1981. pap. 4.25 (ISBN 0-942612-03-5). Aviation.

--McDonnell F2H Banshee. (Naval Fighters Ser.: No. 2). (Illus.). 78p. (Orig.). 1980. pap. 7.95 (ISBN 0-942612-02-7). Aviation.

--McDonnell F3H Demon. (Naval Fighters Ser.: No. 12). (Illus.). 1985. pap. 19.95 (ISBN 0-942612-12-4). Naval Fighters.

--Naval Fighters Chance: Vought F7U Cutlass. (Naval Fighters Ser.: No. 6). (Illus.). 106p. 1982. pap. 13.95 (ISBN 0-942612-06-X). Naval Fighters.

Ginter, Val. Manhattan Trivia. LC 85-60455. (Illus.). 180p. (Orig.). 1985. pap. 7.95 (ISBN 0-933341-05-9). Quinlan Pr.

Ginther, John R. But You Look So Well! LC 77-26009. 163p. 1978. 17.95 (ISBN 0-88229-399-0). Nelson-Hall.

Ginther, K. & Benedek, W., eds. New Perspectives & Conceptions of International Law: An Afro-American Dialogue. (Oesterreichische Zeitschrift fuer Oeffentliches Recht und Voeikerrecht: Supp. 6). 240p. 1983. pap. 18.30 (ISBN 0-387-81780-8). Springer-Verlag.

Gintis, Herbert, jt. auth. see Bowles, Samuel.

Ginzberg, Asher see Ha-am, Achad, pseud.

Ginzberg, Eli. American Jews: The Building of a Voluntary Community. (Texts & Studies Hebrew). 1980. 15.00 (ISBN 0-911934-06-5). Am Jewish Hist Soc.

--American Medicine: The Power Shift. 168p. 1985. text ed. 32.50x (ISBN 0-8476-7439-8). Rowman & Allanheld.

--Effecting Change in Large Organizations. LC 57-13484. 155p. 1957. 21.50x (ISBN 0-231-02249-2). Columbia U Pr.

--Good Jobs, Bad Jobs, No Jobs. LC 79-10706. 1979. 16.50x (ISBN 0-674-35710-8). Harvard U Pr.

--Health Manpower & Health Policy. LC 78-62203. (Conservation of Human Resources Ser.: No. 10). 244p. 1978. text ed. 21.00x (ISBN 0-916672-19-0). Allanheld.

--Human Resources: The Wealth of a Nation. LC 73-9263. 183p. 1973. Repr. of 1958 ed. lib. bdg. 15.00x (ISBN 0-8371-6999-2, GIHR). Greenwood.

--The Ineffective Soldier: The Lost Divisions. LC 75-29042. (Illus.). 225p. 1975. Repr. of 1959 ed. lib. bdg. 15.00x (ISBN 0-8371-8467-3, GIIT). Greenwood.

--The Limits of Health Reform. LC 77-75244. 1977. 12.50x (ISBN 0-465-04117-5). Basic.

--The Manpower Connection: Education & Work. 288p. 1975. 17.50x (ISBN 0-674-54810-8). Harvard U Pr.

--The Negro Potential. LC 56-9606. 144p. 1956. pap. 11.00x (ISBN 0-231-08546-X). Columbia U Pr.

--School-Work Nexus: Transition of Youth from School to Work. LC 80-82882. (Foundation Monograph Ser.). 84p. (Orig.). 1981. pap. 5.00 (ISBN 0-87367-425-1). Phi Delta Kappa.

--Talent & Performance. LC 64-7534. 265p. 1964. 29.00x (ISBN 0-231-02766-4). Columbia U Pr.

--Understanding Human Resources. 1984. 25.00 (ISBN 0-89011-602-4). Abt Bks.

--Urban Health Services: The Case of New York. LC 70-134987. 250p. 1970. 30.00x (ISBN 0-231-03515-2). Columbia U Pr.

Ginzberg, Eli & Berman, H. American Worker in the Twentieth Century. LC 63-10647. 1963. 17.00 (ISBN 0-02-911730-5). Free Pr.

Ginzberg, Eli & Conservation of Human Resources Staff. Manpower Strategy for the Metropolis. LC 68-27290. 321p. 1968. 29.00x (ISBN 0-231-03161-0). Columbia U Pr.

Ginzberg, Eli & Ostow, Miriam. The Coming Physician Surplus: In Search of a Public Policy. LC 84-4894. (Conservation of Human Resources Ser.: Vol. 23). 144p. 1984. 31.95x (ISBN 0-8476-7364-2); Tables incl. Rowman & Allanheld.

--Men, Money & Medicine. LC 79-101134. 291p. 1969. 26.00x (ISBN 0-231-03366-4). Columbia U Pr.

Ginzberg, Eli & Vojta, George. Beyond Human Scale: Large Corporation at Risk. LC 84-45317. 192p. 1985. 16.95 (ISBN 0-465-00658-2). Basic.

Ginzberg, Eli & Yohalem, Alice M. Educated American Women: Life-Styles & Self-Portraits. LC 66-28964. 198p. 1966. 28.00x (ISBN 0-231-03027-4); pap. 12.00x (ISBN 0-231-03604-3). Columbia U Pr.

Ginzberg, Eli, ed. Employing the Unemployed. LC 79-5352. 250p. 1980. 15.00x (ISBN 0-465-01957-9). Basic.

--Jobs for Americans. 1976. 9.95 (ISBN 0-13-510024-0); pap. 4.50 (ISBN 0-13-510016-X). Am Assembly.

--Jobs for Americans. (The American Assembly Ser.). 1976. pap. 4.50 (Spec). P-H.

--The U. S. Health Care System: A Look to the 1990s. (Conservation of Human Resources Ser.: Vol. 26). 150p. 1985. 36.50x (ISBN 0-8476-7468-1). Rowman & Allanheld.

--Values & Ideals of American Youth. LC 72-6798. (Essay Index Reprint Ser). 1972. Repr. of 1961 ed. 24.50 (ISBN 0-8369-7252-X). Ayer Co Pubs.

Ginzberg, Eli & Yohalem, Alice M., eds. Corporate Lib: Women's Challenge to Management. LC 72-12371. (Policy Studies in Employment & Welfare,: No. 17). (Illus.). 163p. 1973. 14.50x (ISBN 0-8018-1475-8). Johns Hopkins.

Ginzberg, Eli, jt. ed. see Conservation of Human Resources Project Staff.

Ginzberg, Eli, et al. Democratic Values & the Rights of Management. LC 63-20227. 217p. 1963. 31.00x (ISBN 0-231-02664-1). Columbia U Pr.

--The Ineffective Soldier: Breakdown & Recovery. LC 75-29042. (Illus.). 284p. 1975. Repr. of 1959 ed. lib. bdg. 16.50x (ISBN 0-8371-8468-1, GIIU). Greenwood.

--The Ineffective Soldier: Patterns of Performance. LC 75-29042. (Illus.). 340p. 1975. Repr. of 1959 ed. lib. bdg. 18.50x (ISBN 0-8371-8469-X, GIIV). Greenwood.

--The Middle-Class Negro in the White Man's World. LC 67-26364. 1967. 27.50x (ISBN 0-231-03096-7); pap. 12.00x (ISBN 0-231-08596-6). Columbia U Pr.

--Optimistic Tradition & American Youth. LC 62-19173. 160p. 1962. 22.50x (ISBN 0-231-02601-3). Columbia U Pr.

--The Negro Potential. LC 80-17250. (Illus.). xvi, 144p. 1980. Repr. of 1963 ed. lib. bdg. 22.50x (ISBN 0-313-22389-0, GINP). Greenwood.

--Home Health Care: Its Role in the Changing Health Services Market. LC 84-3468. (Conservation of Human Resources Ser.: No. 18). (Illus.). 196p. 1984. text ed. 29.50x (ISBN 0-916672-65-4). Rowman & Allanheld.

--Occupational Choice: An Approach to a General Theory. LC 51-10961. pap. 71.80 (ISBN 0-317-26823-6, 2023484). Bks Demand UMI.

--Work Decisions in the Nineteen Eighties. 137p. 1981. 24.95 (ISBN 0-86569-094-4). Auburn Hse.

--Local Health Policy in Action: The Municipal Health Services Program. (Conservation of Human Resources Ser.: Vol. 24). 160p. 1985. 28.50x (ISBN 0-8476-7425-8). Rowman & Allanheld.

Ginzberg, L. & Davidson, I. Genizah Studies in Memory of Solomon Schechter, 3 vols. Incl. Vol. 1. Midrash & Haggadah. Ginzberg, L. 1969. Repr. of 1928 ed. 17.50 (ISBN 0-87203-015-6); Vol. 2. Geonic & Early Karaitic Halakah. Ginzberg, L. Repr. of 1929 ed. 17.50 (ISBN 0-87203-016-4); Vol. 3. Liturgical & Secular Poetry. Davidson, I. Repr. of 1928 ed. 15.00 (ISBN 0-87203-017-2). LC 73-76172. Set. 45.00 (ISBN 0-87203-093-8). Hermon.

Ginzberg, Lev R. & Golenberg, Edward. Lectures in Theoretical Population Biology. (Illus.). 352p. 1985. pap. text ed. 18.95 (ISBN 0-13-528043-5). P-H.

Ginzberg, Louis. Commentary on the Palestinian Talmud, 4 vols. Set. 100.00 set (ISBN 0-87068-150-8). Ktav.

--Legends of the Bible. LC 56-9915. 620p. 1956. 14.95 (ISBN 0-8276-0036-4, 168). Jewish Pubns.

--Legends of the Jews, 7 Vols. LC 76-58650. 1956. Set. 80.00 (ISBN 0-8276-0148-4); 11.95 ea. Vol. 1 (172). Vol. 2 (173). Vol. 3 (174). Vol. 4 (175). Vol. 5 (176). Vol. 6 (177). Vol. 7 (178). Jewish Pubns.

--Of Jewish Law & Lore. LC 55-6707. (Temple Bks). 1970. pap. 5.95 (ISBN 0-689-70231-0, T12). Atheneum.

--Students Scholars & Saints. LC 85-9089. (Brown Classics in Judaica Ser.). 312p. 1985. pap. text ed. 12.75 (ISBN 0-8191-4490-8). U Pr of Amer.

Ginzberg, M. J. & Reitman, W., eds. Decision Support Systems. 200p. 1982. 36.25 (ISBN 0-444-86472-5, North-Holland). Elsevier.

Ginzberg, Michael, ed. see Anderson, Niels B., et al.

Ginzberg, Michael, ed. see Ariav, Gadi & Clifford, James.

Ginzberg, Michael, ed. see Reitman, Walter.

Ginzberg, V. L. Theoretical Physics & Astrophysics. Haar, D. Ter, tr. (International Series in Natural Philosophy: Vol. 99). (Illus.). 1979. pap. 37.00 (ISBN 0-08-023066-0). Pergamon.

Ginzburg. Le Voci Della Sera. Bullock, ed. (Italian Texts Ser.). 158p. (Ital.). 1982. pap. text ed. 5.95 (ISBN 0-7190-0857-3, Pub. by Manchester Univ Pr). Longwood Pub Group.

Ginzburg, A. I., ed. see Moscow, Vsesoiuznyi Nauchno-issledovatel'skii Institut Mineral'nogo Syr'ia.

Ginzburg, Abraham. Algebraic Theory of Automata. LC 68-23492. (ACM Monograph Ser.). 1968. 50.00 (ISBN 0-12-285050-5). Acad Pr.

Ginzburg, Carlo. The Cheese & the Worms. Tedeschi, John & Tedeschi, Anne, trs. (Illus.). 1982. pap. 6.95 (ISBN 0-14-006046-4). Penguin.

--The Cheese & the Worms: The Cosmos of a Sixteenth Century Miller. Tedeschi, John & Tedeschi, Anne, trs. from Ital. LC 79-3654. Orig. Title: Il Formaggio e i vermi: Il cosmo di un mugnaio del 1500. 208p. 1980. text ed. 18.50x (ISBN 0-8018-2336-6). Johns Hopkins.

--The English of Piero. (Illus.). 176p. Date not set. 16.95 (ISBN 0-8052-7253-4, Pub. by Verso England). Schocken.

--The Night Battles. Tedeschi, John & Tedeschi, Anne, trs. LC 83-48061. 232p. 1984. 18.50x (ISBN 0-8018-2605-5). Johns Hopkins.

--The Night Battles: Witchcraft & Agrarian Cults in the Sixteenth & Seventeenth Centuries. Tedeschi, John & Tedeschi, Anne, trs. (Penguin Nonfiction Ser.). 240p. 1985. pap. 8.95 (ISBN 0-14-007688-3). Penguin.

Ginzburg, Carlo, ed. I Costituti Di Don Pietro Manelfi. LC 72-3473. (Corpus Reformatorum Italicorum & Biblioteca Ser.). (Illus.). 101p. 1970. pap. 10.00 (ISBN 0-87580-510-8). N Ill U Pr.

Ginzburg, Eugenia. Within the Whirlwind. Boland, Ian, tr. LC 80-8748. (Helen & Kurt Wolff Bk.). 1981. 17.50 (ISBN 0-15-197517-5). HarBraceJ.

Ginzburg, Eugenia S. Journey into the Whirlwind. Stevenson, Paul & Hayward, Max, trs. from Rus. LC 74-16406. (Illus.). 418p. 1975. pap. 8.95 (ISBN 0-15-646509-4, Harv). HarBraceJ.

Ginzburg, Evgeniia. Krutoi Marshrut. LC 84-732266. (Kniga Pervaia Ser.: Pt. 1). 440p. (Russ.). 1985. 17.00 (ISBN 0-911971-06-8). Effect Pub.

--Krutoi Marshrut: Journey into the Whirlwind. LC 84-73266. (Kniga Vtoraia Ser.: Pt. 2). 352p. 1985. 16.00 (ISBN 0-911971-07-6). Effect Pub.

Ginzburg, L. R. Theory of Natural Selection & Population Growth. 1983. text ed. 25.95 (ISBN 0-8053-3180-8). Benjamin-Cummings.

Ginzburg, Moisei. Style & Epoch. Senkevitch, Anatole, Jr., tr. from Rus. (Oppositions Bks.). (Illus.). 200p. 1982. 30.00 (ISBN 0-262-07088-X). MIT Pr.

Ginzburg, Natalia. All Our Yesterdays. Davidson, Angus, tr. from Italian. 300p. 1985. 14.95 (ISBN 0-85635-593-3, Dist. by Harper & Row). Carcanet.

--Family Sayings. Low, D. M., tr. from Ital. 220p. 14.95 (ISBN 0-85635-504-6). Carcanet.

--The Little Virtues. Davis, Dick, tr. from Ital. 110p. 1985. 14.95 (ISBN 0-85635-553-4). Carcanet.

--No Way. 1976. pap. 1.75 (ISBN 0-380-00838-6, 31054-6, Bard). Avon.

--Ti Ho Sposato per Allegria. (Easy Readers, Ser. A). 48p. (Ital.). 1976. pap. text ed. 3.25 (ISBN 0-88436-228-0, 55252). EMC.

Ginzburg, V. Key Problems of Physics & Astrophysics. 167p. 1978. 4.45 (ISBN 0-8285-0789-9, Pub. by Mir Pubs USSR). Imported Pubns.

Ginzburg, V., jt. auth. see Agranovich, V. M.

Ginzburg, V. L. Physics & Astrophysics: A Selection of Key Problems. Glebov, O. & Ter Haar, G., trs. 144p. 1985. 23.50 (ISBN 0-08-026498-0); pap. 12.50 (ISBN 0-08-026499-9). Pergamon.

--Propagation of Electromagnetic Waves in Plasma. (Russian Monographs & Texts on the Physical Science Ser.). 846p. 1962. 135.25 (ISBN 0-677-20080-3). Gordon.

--Propagation of Electromagnetic Waves in Plasmas. 2nd rev. ed. 1971. 72.00 (ISBN 0-08-015569-3). Pergamon.

Ginzburg, V. L. & Lebedev, P. N. Waynflete Lectures on Physics: Selected Topics in Contemporary Physics & Astrophysics. Haar, D. ter, tr. LC 82-24619. (International Series in Natural Philosophy: Vol. 106). (Illus.). 133p. 1983. 25.00 (ISBN 0-08-029147-3). Pergamon.

Ginzburg, V. L. & Kirzhnits, D. A., eds. High-Temperature Superconductivity. Agyei, A. K., tr. from Russian. LC 82-5295. 364p. 1982. 59.50x (ISBN 0-306-10970-0, AACR2, Consultants). Plenum Pub.

Ginzburg, Vitalii L. The Astrophysics of Cosmic Rays. 2nd., Rev. & Supplemented ed. Hardin, Ron, ed. LC 73-606893. (U. S. National Aeronautics & Space Administration. NASA Technical Translation Ser.: TT F-561). pap. 20.00 (ISBN 0-317-09306-1, 2003731). Bks Demand UMI.

Ginzburg, Vitaly L. Elementary Processes for Cosmic Ray Astrophysics. (Topics in Astrophysics & Space Physics Ser.). 140p. 1969. 45.25 (ISBN 0-677-01980-7). Gordon.

--Origin of Cosmic Rays. (Topics in Astrophyscis & Space Physics Ser.). 70p. 1969. 23.25 (ISBN 0-677-01970-X). Gordon.

Giobbi, Edward. Italian Family Cooking. 1978. pap. 6.95 (ISBN 0-394-72564-6, Vin). Random.

Giobbi, Edward & Wolff, Richard. Eat Right, Eat Well: The Italian Way. Jones, Judith B., ed. LC 84-47893. (Illus.). 1985. 19.95 (ISBN 0-394-53071-3). Knopf.

Gioeli, Richard. Cancer is Good for You. (Illus.). 1981. pap. text ed. 3.95 (ISBN 0-933278-11-X). Twen Fir Cent.

Gioello & Berke. Fashion Production Terms. LC 78-62289. (The Language of Fashion Ser.). (Illus.). 1979. lib. bdg. 25.00 (ISBN 0-87005-200-4). Fairchild.

Gioello, Debbie A. Fairchild's Designer: Stylist Handbook, 2 vols. (Illus.). 1979. Vol. 1. (ISBN 0-87005-332-9); Vol. 2. (ISBN 0-87005-333-7); Set. 35.00 (ISBN 0-686-76815-9); tracing pad 7.95 (ISBN 0-87005-334-5). Fairchild.

--Profiling Fabrics: Properties, Performance, & Construction Techniques. (Language of Fashion Ser.). (Illus.). 325p. 1981. text ed. 27.50 (ISBN 0-87005-259-4). Fairchild.

--Understanding Fabrics: From Fiber to Finished Cloth. (Language of Fashion Ser.). (Illus.). 350p. 1982. text ed. 30.00 (ISBN 0-87005-377-9). Fairchild.

Gioello, Debbie A. & Berke, Beverly. Figure Types & Size Ranges. LC 78-20736. (Language of Fashion Ser.). (Illus.). 1979. 12.50 (ISBN 0-87005-291-8). Fairchild.

Gioffre, Marisa. Starstruck. 144p. (Orig.). (gr. 5-8). 1985. pap. 2.25 (ISBN 0-590-33797-1, Apple Paperbacks). Scholastic Inc.

Gioia, A. A. & Goldsmith, D. L., eds. The Theory of Arithmetic Functions. (Lecture Notes in Mathematics: Vol. 251). 287p. 1972. pap. 13.00 (ISBN 0-387-05723-4). Springer-Verlag.

Gioiella, E. & Bevil, C. Nursing Care of the Aging Client. 592p. 1984. 34.95 (ISBN 0-8385-7014-3). ACC.

Giok Po Oey. Checklist of Vietnamese Holdings of the Wason Collection, Cornell University Libraries, As of June 1971. 337p. 1971. 6.50 (ISBN 0-87727-084-8, DP 84). Cornell SE Asia.

Giolas, Thomas G. Hearing-Handicapped Adults. (Illus.). 240p. 1982. 26.95 (ISBN 0-13-384693-8). P-H.

Giolas, Thomas G. & Randolph, Kenneth. Basic Audiometry: Including Impedance Measurement. LC 76-7113. (Cliffs Speech & Hearing Ser.). (Illus.). 1977. pap. text ed. 4.95 (ISBN 0-8220-1813-6). Cliffs.

Gionanni, Cosimo & De Medici, Lorenzo. The Political Philosophy of the Great De Medici As Revealed by Their Correspondence, 2 vols. (Illus.). 1985. Set. 227.50 (ISBN 0-86722-106-2). Inst Econ Pol.

Gioncu, Victor. Thin Reinforced Concrete Shells: Special Analysis Problems. LC 78-10388. 500p. 1979. 78.95x (ISBN 0-471-99735-8, Pub. by Wiley-Interscience). Wiley.

Giongo, G. M., jt. ed. see Graziani, M.

Giono. Oeuvres Romanesques Completes: Angelo, Mort d'un Personnage, Le Hussard sur le Toit, Le Bonheur fou, Vol. 4. 1744p. 47.95 (ISBN 0-686-56514-2). French & Eur.

--Oeuvres Romanesques Completes: Pour Saluer Melville, L'Eau Vive, Un Roi sans Divertissement, Noe, Fragments d'un Paradis, Vol. 3. 1604p. 49.95 (ISBN 0-686-56513-4). French & Eur.

Giono, Jean. Accompagnes de la Flute. (Illus.). 148p. 1959. 125.00 (ISBN 0-686-53947-8). French & Eur.

--Les Ames Fortes. 384p. (Folio 249). 1972. 4.50 (ISBN 0-686-53948-6). French & Eur.

--Ames Fortes. 1958. pap. 8.50 (ISBN 0-685-10993-3). French and Eur.

--Angelo: Roman. (Coll. Soleil). 10.50 (ISBN 0-685-34165-8). French & Eur.

--Batailles dans la Montagne. 368p. 1937. 5.95 (ISBN 0-686-53949-4). French & Eur.

--Blue Boy. Clarke, Katherine A., tr. from Fr. LC 81-4371. 256p. 1981. pap. 9.50 (ISBN 0-86547-037-5). N Point Pr.

--Bonheur Fou: Roman. 1957. 14.50 (ISBN 0-685-11050-8). French & Eur.

--Le Chant du Monde. 320p. 1976. 4.50 (ISBN 0-686-53950-8). French & Eur.

--Chant Du Monde: Roman. (Coll. Soleil). 1963. 14.50 (ISBN 0-685-11074-5). French & Eur.

--Le Cheval Fou. 80p. 1974. 4.50 (ISBN 0-686-53951-6). French & Eur.

--La Chute des Anges, un Deluge le Coeur Chef. 8.95 (ISBN 0-686-53952-4). French & Eur.

--Colline. 192p. 1960. 3.95 (ISBN 0-686-53953-2). French & Eur.

--Colline. deluxe ed. 45.40 (ISBN 0-685-34172-0). French & Eur.

--Colline: Roman. (Coll. Soleil). 1960. 11.50 (ISBN 0-685-11091-5). French and Eur.

--Un De Baumugne. (Coll. Soleil). 1957. 12.25 (ISBN 0-685-11608-5). French & Eur.

--Un De Baumugnes. 256p. 1957. 3.95 (ISBN 0-686-53955-9). French & Eur.

--Un De Baumugnes: Livre des Conduite du Metteur en Scene (Indications et Dialogues) (Illus.). 172p. 1961. 30.00 (ISBN 0-686-53954-0). French & Eur.

--Le Desastre de Pavie. 408p. 1963. 29.95 (ISBN 0-686-53956-7). French & Eur.

--Le Deserteur. 3.95 (ISBN 0-686-53957-5). French & Eur.

--Le Deserteur et Autres Recits. 288p. 1973. 17.50 (ISBN 0-686-53958-3). French & Eur.

--Deux Cavaliers de l'Orage. (Coll. Soleil). 13.50 (ISBN 0-685-34166-6). French & Eur.

--Deux Cavaliers De l'Orage. 288p. 1972. 3.95 (ISBN 0-686-53959-1). French & Eur.

--Domitien: Avec Joseph a Dothan. 296p. 1959. 4.95 (ISBN 0-686-53960-5). French & Eur.

--L' Eau Vive: L'Oiseau Bague, Vol. 2. 288p. 1973. 3.95 (ISBN 0-686-53962-1). French & Eur.

--L' Eau Vive: Rondeurs des Jours, Vol. 1. 1973. 3.95 (ISBN 0-686-53961-3). French & Eur.

--Ecrits Pacifistes. 310p. 1978. 4.95 (ISBN 0-686-53963-X). French & Eur.

--Ennemonde. 14.95 (ISBN 0-7206-2801-6). Dufour.

--Ennemonde et Autres Caracteres. 1973. 3.95 (ISBN 0-686-53964-8). French & Eur.

--Ennemonde et Autres Caracteres: Roman. (Coll. Soleil). 13.50 (ISBN 0-685-34167-4). French & Eur.

--Faust Au Village: Nouvelles. 156p. 1977. 15.95 (ISBN 0-686-53965-6). French & Eur.

--Le Grand Troupeau. 1972. 3.95 (ISBN 0-686-53966-4). French & Eur.

--Grand Troupeau: Roman. 1964. 8.50 (ISBN 0-685-11221-7). French & Eur.

--Grands Chemins. (Coll. Soleil). 1964. 14.95 (ISBN 0-685-11222-5). French & Eur.

--Les Grands Chemins. 1973. 3.95 (ISBN 0-686-53967-2). French & Eur.

--Harvest. Fluchere, Henri & Myers, Geoffrey, trs. from Fr. (Giono Novels Ser.). 192p. (Orig.). 1984. pap. 9.00 (ISBN 0-86547-124-X). N Point Pr.

--Une Histoire D'Amour. (Illus.). 60p. 1969. 25.00 (ISBN 0-686-53968-0). French & Eur.

--Horseman on the Roof. Griffin, Jonathan, tr. from Fr. 432p. 1982. pap. 12.50 (ISBN 0-86547-060-X). N Point Pr.

--Le Hussard sur le Toit. 512p. 1972. 4.95 (ISBN 0-686-53970-2). French & Eur.

--Le Hussard sur le Toit: Roman. (Coll. Soleil Ser.). 14.50 (ISBN 0-685-34168-2). French & Eur.

--L' Iris de Suse. 320p. 1974. 3.95 (ISBN 0-686-53971-0). French & Eur.

--L' Iris de Suse: Roman. (Coll. Soleil). 12.50 (ISBN 0-685-34169-0). French & Eur.

--Jean le Bleu. 288p. 1974. 3.95 (ISBN 0-686-53972-9). French & Eur.

--Jean le Bleu: Nouvelles. (Coll. Soleil). 13.25 (ISBN 0-685-34170-4). French & Eur.

--Joy of Man's Desiring. Clarke, Katherine A., tr. from Fr. LC 80-14932. 472p. 1980. pap. 12.50 (ISBN 0-86547-015-4). N Point Pr.

--Man Who Planted Hope & Grew Happiness. pap. 2.00 (ISBN 0-685-11658-1). Friends Nature.

--The Man Who Planted Trees. LC 85-9925. (Illus.). 56p. 1985. 13.50 (ISBN 0-930031-02-4). Chelsea Green Pub.

--La Mission. (Illus.). 1971. 12.50 (ISBN 0-686-53973-7). French & Eur.

--Mort d'un Personnage. 256p. 1949. 9.95 (ISBN 0-686-53974-5). French & Eur.

--Le Moulin de Pologne. 1972. 3.95 (ISBN 0-686-53975-3). French & Eur.

--Naissance de L'Odyssee. 240p. 1938. 8.95 (ISBN 0-686-53976-1). French & Eur.

--Noe: Chroniques. 384p. 1973. 3.95 (ISBN 0-686-53977-X). French & Eur.

--Notes sur l'Affaire Dominici. 160p. 1955. 3.95 (ISBN 0-686-53978-8). French & Eur.

--Oeuvres Romanesques, Tome I. Incl. Naissance de l'Odyssee; Colline; Un de Beaumugnes; Regain; Solitude de la Pitie; Le Grand Troupeau. (Bibliotheque de la Pleiade). 41.50 (ISBN 0-685-34163-1). French & Eur.

--Oeuvres Romanesques, Tome II. Incl. Jean le Bleu; Le Chant de la Montagne; Que Ma Joie Demeure; Batailles dans la Montagne. (Bibliotheque de la Pleiade). 41.50 (ISBN 0-685-34164-X). French & Eur.

--Le Poids du Ciei. 319p. 1971. 4.95 (ISBN 0-686-53981-8). French & Eur.

--Pour Saluer Melville. 184p. 1941. 5.95 (ISBN 0-686-53982-6). French & Eur.

--Precisions. 5.95 (ISBN 0-686-53983-4). French & Eur.

--Provence. deluxe ed. 57.75 (ISBN 0-685-34173-9). French & Eur.

--Que Ma Joie Demeure. (Coll. Soleil). 1959. 18.50 (ISBN 0-685-11519-4). French & Eur.

--Que Ma Joie Demeure. 512p. 1959. 3.95 (ISBN 0-686-53984-2). French & Eur.

--Que Ma Joie Demeure. (Nouveaux Classiques Larousse). (Illus., Fr.). pap. 2.95 (ISBN 0-685-14063-6, 111). Larousse.

--Que Ma Vie Demeure. 12.95 (ISBN 0-686-53985-0). French & Eur.

--Recherche de la Purete. deluxe ed. 1750.00 (ISBN 0-685-34174-7). French & Eur.

--Recits de la Demi-brigade. (Coll. Soleil). 15.75 (ISBN 0-685-34171-2). French & Eur.

--Regain. 192p. 1958. 3.95 (ISBN 0-686-53986-9). French & Eur.

--Regain: Roman. (Coll. Soleil). (Fr). 1958. 13.25 (ISBN 0-685-11524-0). French & Eur.

--Un Roi sans Divertissement. 256p. 1972. 3.95 (ISBN 0-686-53987-7). French & Eur.

--Le Serpent d'Etoiles. 192p. 1962. 3.95 (ISBN 0-686-53989-3). French & Eur.

--Solitude de la Pitie. 1973. 3.95 (ISBN 0-686-53990-7). French & Eur.

--The Song of the World. Fluchere, Henri & Myers, Geoffrey, trs. from Fr. LC 80-28523. 320p. 1981. pap. 11.00 (ISBN 0-86547-038-3). N Point Pr.

--The Straw Man. Johnson, Phyllis, tr. LC 82-73715. 472p. 1982. pap. 14.00 (ISBN 0-86547-071-5). N Point Pr.

--Les Terrasses de l'Ille d'Elbe. 192p. 1976. 12.50 (ISBN 0-686-53991-5). French & Eur.

--Theatre. 368p. 1943. 5.95 (ISBN 0-686-53992-3). French & Eur.

--To the Slaughterhouse. 14.95 (ISBN 0-7206-3602-7). Dufour.

--Triomphe de la Vie. 296p. 1942. 8.95 (ISBN 0-686-53993-1). French & Eur.

--Voyage en Italie. 264p. 1954. 7.95 (ISBN 0-686-53994-X). French & Eur.

--Les Vraies Richesses. 240p. 1936. 11.95 (ISBN 0-686-53995-8). French & Eur.

--Yves Brayer. (Coll. Art Moderne). deluxe ed. 55.25 (ISBN 0-685-34175-5). French & Eur.

Giono, Jean & Allioux, Alain. Hortense ou l'Eau Vive. 9.95 (ISBN 0-686-53969-9). French & Eur.

Giono, Jean, et al. Rome. 1958. 32.50 (ISBN 0-686-53988-5). French & Eur.

--Oeuvres Romanesques Completes. 1733p. 1977. 49.95 (ISBN 0-686-53980-X). French & Eur.

Giordan, Alma R. Torch-Bearer & Other Poems. LC 72-87813. 79p. 1972. 4.00 (ISBN 0-8233-0180-X). Golden Quill.

Giordani, Igino. Diary of Fire. 127p. (Orig.). 1982. pap. 3.95 (ISBN 0-911782-41-9). New City.

--Mary of Nazareth. (Orig.). 1965. 6.00 (ISBN 0-8198-0092-9); pap. 5.00 (ISBN 0-8198-0093-7). Dghtrs St Paul.

--Saint Catherine of Siena. 1981. 8.00 (ISBN 0-8198-0493-2); pap. 7.00 (ISBN 0-8198-6809-4). Dghtrs St Paul.

--St. Paul Apostle & Martyr. (Obelisk Ser.). 1961. 8.00 (ISBN 0-8198-0138-0); pap. 7.00 (ISBN 0-8198-0139-9). Dghtrs St Paul.

--Social Message of Jesus. 1977. 4.50 (ISBN 0-8198-0467-3); pap. 3.50 (ISBN 0-8198-0468-1). Dghtrs St Paul.

--Social Message of the Early Church Fathers. 1977. 3.95 (ISBN 0-8198-0469-X); pap. 2.95 (ISBN 0-8198-0470-3). Dghtrs St Paul.

Giordano, jt. auth. see Schneck.

Giordano, Al. Basic Business Machine Calculations: A Complete Course. 2nd ed. (Illus.). 1978. pap. 22.95x ref. ed. (ISBN 0-13-057315-9). P-H.

--Business Mathematics-Electronic Calculation. (Illus.). 304p. 1981. text ed. 25.95 (ISBN 0-13-105163-6); pap. text ed. 21.95 (ISBN 0-13-105155-5). P-H.

Giordano, Al & Maxwell, G. W. College Business Mathematics. (Illus.). 1977. pap. text ed. 22.95 (ISBN 0-13-142018-6). P-H.

Giordano, Albert G. Concise Dictionary of Business Terminology. 464p. 1981. text ed. 14.95 (ISBN 0-13-166553-7, Spec); pap. text ed. 5.95 (ISBN 0-13-166546-4). P-H.

Giordano, Arthur A. & Hsu, Frank M. Least Square Estimation with Applications to Digital Signal Processing. 416p. 1985. 44.90 (ISBN 0-471-87857-X, Pub. by Wiley-Interscience). Wiley.

Giordano, Carmelo, ed. Sorbents & Their Clinical Applications. 1980. 67.50 (ISBN 0-12-285250-8). Acad Pr.

Giordano, Frank. Texas Wines & Wineries. Lubeck, Scott, ed. (Illus.). 171p. 1984. 19.95 (ISBN 0-932012-86-8). Texas Month Pr.

Giordano, Frank R., Jr. I'd Have My Life Unbe: Thomas Hardy's Self-Destructive Characters. LC 83-1230. (Illus.). xx, 208p. 1984. text ed. 18.75x (ISBN 0-8173-0174-7). U of Ala Pr.

Giordano, Gerard. Teaching Writing to Learning Disabled Students. LC 83-25753. 158p. 1984. spiralbound 30.95 (ISBN 0-89443-580-9). Aspen Systems.

Giordano, Grace P., jt. auth. see Giordano, Joseph.

Giordano, Joseph & Giordano, Grace P. The Ethno-Cultural Factor in Mental Health: A Literature Review & Bibliography. 56p. 1977. pap. 2.25 (ISBN 0-87495-007-4). Am Jewish Comm.

Giorgetti, Pietro, jt. auth. see Norman, Jill.

Giorgi, A., ed. Journal of Phenomenological Psychology. (JPP Ser.: Vol. 13-1). 150p. 1982. pap. text ed. 9.00x. Humanities.

--Journal of Phenomenological Psychology. (JPP Ser.: Vol. 13-2). 226p. 1982. pap. text ed. 9.00x. Humanities.

--Journal of Phenomenological Psychology. (JPP Spring 1984 Ser.: Vol. 15-1). 106p. 1984. pap. text ed. 10.50x (ISBN 0-317-13890-1). Humanities.

--Journal of Phenomenological Psychology: Fall 1983. 269p. 1983. text ed. 9.00x. Humanities.

--Journal of Phenomenological Psychology: Fall 1980, Vol. VII, No. 2. 118p. 1980. pap. text ed. 9.00x. Humanities.

--Journal of Phenomenological Psychology: Spring 1983, 14-1. (JPP 14-1). 123p. 1983. pap. text ed. 9.00x. Humanities.

Giorgi, A., et al, eds. Duquesne Studies in Phenomenological Psychology, Vol. 3. 1979. pap. text ed. 9.50x (ISBN 0-8207-0137-8). Duquesne.

--Duquesne Studies in Phenomenological Psychology, Vol. 4. 300p. 1983. pap. 11.00x (ISBN 0-8207-0164-5). Duquesne.

Giorgi, Amadeo, ed. Journal of Phenomenological Psychology: Fall 1977, Vol. 8, No. 1. 1978. pap. text ed. 9.00x (ISBN 0-391-01223-1). Humanities.

Giorgi, Amedeo. Phenomenology & Psychological Research. 250p. 1985. pap. text ed. 13.00x (ISBN 0-8207-0174-2). Duquesne.

--Psychology As a Human Science: A Phenomenologically Based Approach. 1970. pap. text ed. 12.20 (ISBN 0-06-042304-8, HarpC). Harrow.

Giorgi, Amedeo, ed. Journal of Phenomenological Psychology: Spring 1978, Vol. 8, No. 2. 1978. pap. text ed. 9.00x (ISBN 0-391-01242-8). Humanities.

Giorgi, Amedeo, et al. Duquesne Studies in Phenomenological Psychology, Vol. 1. xiv, 398p. 1973. pap. text ed. 5.00x (ISBN 0-391-00280-5). Humanities.

Giorgi, Amedeo, et al, eds. Journal of Phenomenological Psychology: Studies in the Science of Human Experience & Behavior, Vols. 1-7. (Biannual pub.). 1970. Vols.1-6. pap. 5.00 each issue; Vol. 7. pap. 9.00x each issue. Humanities.

Giorgi, Louis P. Windows of St. Justin Martyr. LC 80-67119. (Illus.). 136p. 1982. 25.00 (ISBN 0-87982-034-9). Art Alliance.

Giorgi, Rubina. Figure Di Nessuno. LC 75-4966. 131p. 1976. pap. 7.95 (ISBN 0-915570-02-5). Oolp Pr.

Giorgi, Valerie D. Colver-Culver Family Genealogy. (Illus.). 700p. 1984. text ed. 35.00 (ISBN 0-9614222-0-3). Giorgi.

Giorno, John. Balling Buddah. pap. 3.50x (ISBN 0-686-73476-9). Kulchur Foun.

Giorno, John, et al. Manifestos. (Great Bear Pamphlets: No. 18). 1967. pap. 3.50 (ISBN 0-89366-073-6). Ultramarine Pub.

Giorno, Ralph C. Immunohistology & Histochemistry of the Lymphoid System. (Illus.). 180p. 1984. 28.50x (ISBN 0-398-04898-3). C C Thomas.

Gioscia, Victor. TimeForms. 198p. 1974. 48.75 (ISBN 0-677-04850-5). Gordon.

Gioseffi, Daniela. Eggs in the Lake. (New Poets of America Ser.: No. 5). 1979. 10.00 (ISBN 0-918526-13-2); pap. 5.00 (ISBN 0-918526-14-0). Boa Edns.

Giovacchini, Peter. Treatment of Primitive Mental Status. LC 78-74990. 536p. 1978. 30.00x (ISBN 0-87668-347-2). Aronson.

--The Urge to Die. 1983. pap. 5.95 (ISBN 0-14-006314-5). Penguin.

Giovacchini, Peter, ed. Tactics & Techniques in Psychoanalytic Therapy: Countertransference, Vol. 2. LC 75-144143. 484p. 1975. 25.00 (ISBN 0-87668-202-6). Aronson.

Giovacchini, Peter & Boyer, L. Bryce, eds. Technical Factors in the Treatment of the Severely Disturbed Patient. LC 81-20587. 568p. 1982. 30.00 (ISBN 0-87668-630-7). Aronson.

Giovacchini, Peter, jt. ed. see Feinstein, Sherman C.

Giovacchini, Peter L. Character Disorders & Adaptive Mechanisms. Rev. ed. LC 83-11957. 552p. 1984. 35.00 (ISBN 0-87668-641-2). Aronson.

--A Clinician's Guide to Reading Freud. LC 82-14891. 251p. 1982. 25.00 (ISBN 0-87668-484-3). Aronson.

--Psychoanalysis of Character Disorders. LC 73-17742. 356p. 1975. 25.00x (ISBN 0-87668-119-4). Aronson.

Giovacchini, Peter L., jt. auth. see Feinstein, Sherman C.

Giovacchini, Peter L., jt. ed. see Feinstein, Sherman C.

Giovachinni, Peter & Boyer, Bryce L. Psychoanalytic Treatment of Schizophrenic Borderline & Characterological Disorders. LC 80-66352. 422p. 1980. 30.00 (ISBN 0-87668-408-8). Aronson.

Giovanella, Beppino, jt. auth. see Fogh, Jorgen.

Giovanella, Beppino, jt. ed. see Fogh, Jorgen.

Giovanelli, M., ed. see October 1976.

Giovanelli, Ronald. Secrets of the Sun. 196p. 1984. 19.95 (ISBN 0-521-25521-X). Cambridge U Pr.

Giovannelli, G., et al, eds. Hypertension in Children & Adolescents. 364p. 1981. text ed. 57.00 (ISBN 0-89004-523-2). Raven.

Giovannetti. Max. LC 76-50008. (Illus.). 96p. (ps-12). 1977. 6.95 (ISBN 0-689-50082-3, McElderry Bk). Atheneum.

Giovannetti, Alberto. The Italians of America. (Orig.). 1979. pap. 2.50 (ISBN 0-532-25001-X). Woodhill.

--Requiem for a Spy. LC 79-8926. 288p. 1983. 14.95 (ISBN 0-385-15612-X). Doubleday.

Giovannetti, S., ed. see International Congress, 6th, Florence, June 1975.

Giovannetti, S., ed. see International Symposium on Unilateral Renal Function Studies, 1st, Montecatini Terme, May 1977, et al.

Giovanni, Facini & Gossett, Philip. Il Barone Di Dolsheim & Excerpts From His Early Operas. (Italian Opera Ser., 1810-1840). 85.00 (ISBN 0-8240-6578-6). Garland Pub.

Giovanni, Gentile. Education & the Concept of Culture. (Illus.). 251p. 1984. 88.75 (ISBN 0-89266-485-1). Am Classical Coll Pr.

Giovanni, George Di see Di Giovanni, George & Harris, H. S.

Giovanni, Nikki. Black Feeling, Black Talk. rev. ed. 3rd ed. 1970. pap. 2.50 (ISBN 0-910296-07-3). Broadside.

--Black Feeling, Black Talk-Black Judgement. 1970. pap. 4.95 (ISBN 0-688-25294-X). Morrow.

--Black Judgement. 1968. pap. 2.50 (ISBN 0-910296-31-6). Broadside.

--Cotton Candy on a Rainy Day. LC 78-16897. 1978. pap. 4.50 (ISBN 0-688-08365-X). Morrow.

--Ego Tripping & Other Poems for Young Readers. LC 73-81745. (Illus.). 48p. (gr. 2-7). 1974. 8.50 (ISBN 0-88208-020-2); pap. 5.95 (ISBN 0-88208-019-9). Lawrence Hill.

--Gemini: An Extended Autobiographical Statement on My First Twenty-Five Years of Being a Black Poet. 1976. pap. 3.95 (ISBN 0-14-004264-4). Penguin.

--My House. LC 72-116. 96p. 1972. pap. 4.95 (ISBN 0-688-05021-2). Morrow.

--Recreation. 4.50 (ISBN 0-685-24800-3); pap. 3.00 (ISBN 0-910296-44-8); tape 5.00 (ISBN 0-685-24801-1). Broadside.

--Spin a Soft Black Song. LC 76-163572. (Illus.). 54p. (gr. 2 up). 1971. 7.95 (ISBN 0-8090-8795-2). Hill & Wang.

--Spin a Soft Black Song. Rev. ed. (Illus.). 64p. 1985. 8.95 (ISBN 0-8090-8796-0). Hill & Wang.

--Spin a Soft Black Song. LC 84-19287. (Illus.). 57p. (ps up). 1985. 8.95. FS&G.

--Those Who Ride the Night Winds. LC 82-20811. 121p. 1983. 9.95 (ISBN 0-688-01906-4). Morrow.

--Those Who Ride the Night Winds. 64p. (Orig.). 1984. pap. 4.95 (ISBN 0-688-02653-2, Quill NY). Morrow.

--Vacation Time: Poems for Children. LC 79-91643. (Illus.). 32p. 1981. 5.95 (ISBN 0-688-03657-0); pap. 4.95 (ISBN 0-688-00507-1). Morrow.

--The Women & the Men. LC 75-16237. 1979. pap. 5.95 (ISBN 0-688-07947-4). Morrow.

Giovanni, Nikki & Walker, Margaret. A Poetic Equation: Conversations Between Nikki Giovanni & Margaret Walker. LC 73-85494. (Illus.). 135p. 1974. 9.95 (ISBN 0-88258-003-5). Howard U Pr.

Giovanni, Norman Di see Borges, Jorge L.

Giovanni, Norman T. see Costantini, Humberto.

Giovanni, Norman T. Di see Borges, Jorge L.

Giovanni, Norman T. di see Borges, Jorge L.

Giovannini, G. Ezra Pound & Dante. LC 74-7249. (Studies in Dante, No. 9). 1974. lib. bdg. 39.95x (ISBN 0-8383-1952-1). Haskell.

Giovannitti, Arturo. The Collected Poems of Arturo Giovannitti. LC 74-17931. (Italian American Experience Ser). 240p. 1975. Repr. 18.00x (ISBN 0-405-06403-9). Ayer Co Pubs.

--The Walker & Other Poems. (Poets of Revolt Ser.: No. 3). 64p. 1985. 13.95 (ISBN 0-88286-175-1); pap. 3.95 (ISBN 0-88286-150-6). C H Kerr.

Giovannoni, Jeanne M. & Becerra, Rosina. Defining Child Abuse. LC 79-7180. (Illus.). 1982. 24.95 (ISBN 0-02-911750-X); pap. 14.95 (ISBN 0-02-911780-1). Free Pr.

Giovannoni, Jeanne M., jt. auth. see Billingsley, Andrew.

Giovannoni, Jeanne M., et al. Child Abuse & Neglect: An Examination from the Perspective of Child Development Knowledge. LC 77-90387. 1978. pap. 11.95 perfect bdg. (ISBN 0-88247-514-2). R & E Pubs.

Giovanoni, Richard & Warren, Roger G. Mosby's Fundamentals of Animal Health Technology: Principles of Pharmacology. (Illus.). 243p. pap. text ed. 17.95 (ISBN 0-8016-5402-5). Mosby.

Giovio, Paolo. The Worthy Tract of Paulus Iovius. Daniel, Samuel, tr. LC 76-13497. 300p. 1976. Repr. of 1585 ed. lib. bdg. 50.00x (ISBN 0-8201-1272-0). Schol Facsimiles.

Gipatric, Guy. The Canmy Mr. Glencannon. 13.95 (ISBN 0-88411-574-7, Pub. by Aeonian Pr). Amereon Ltd.

Gipe, George. The Great American Sports Book. LC 78-4707. (Illus.). 1978. 15.95 (ISBN 0-385-13091-0). Doubleday.

--Gremlins. 278p. 1984. pap. 2.95 (ISBN 0-380-86561-0, 86561-0). Avon.

--Gremlins. (Illus.). 77p. (gr. 3-7). pap. 2.95 (ISBN 0-380-89003-8). Avon.

--The Last Time When. 1981. pap. 8.95 (ISBN 0-345-30391-1, World Almanac). Newspaper Ent.

Gipe, Paul. Wind Energy: How to Use It. 416p. 1983. pap. 16.95 (ISBN 0-8117-2273-2). Stackpole.

Gippius, Vasily V. Gogol. Maguire, R., tr. 1981. 22.50 (ISBN 0-88233-612-6). Ardis Pubs.

--Gogol. LC 63-7522. (Brown University Slavic Reprint Ser.: No. 1). 245p. (Rus). 1963. pap. 10.00x (ISBN 0-87057-069-2). U Pr of New Eng.

Gippius, Zinaida. Pis'ma K Berberovoi I Khodasevichu. Sheikholeslami, Erika F., ed. (Rus.). 1978. pap. 3.00 (ISBN 0-88233-298-8). Ardis Pubs.

Gippius, Zinaida N. Selected Works of Zinaida Hippius. Pachmuss, Temira, ed. LC 72-188447. pap. 81.80 (ISBN 0-317-29016-9, 2020253). Bks Demand UMI.

Gipps, Caroline & Goldstein, Harvey. Monitoring Children: An Evaluation of the Assessment of Performance Unit. xi, 196p. 1983. 30.00x (ISBN 0-435-80345-X). Heinemann Ed.

Gipps, Caroline, et al. Testing Children: Standardized Testing in Local Education Authorities & Schools. iv, 188p. 1984. text ed. 30.00x (ISBN 0-435-82323-X). Heinemann Ed.

Gips, James, jt. auth. see Stiny, George.

Gipson, Fred. Cowhand: The True Story of a Working Cowboy. LC 77-89509. 232p. 1977. Repr. of 1948 ed. 10.95 (ISBN 0-89096-040-2). Tex A&M Univ Pr.

--Curly & the Wild Boar. LC 77-25644. (Illus.). (gr. 5 up). 1979. 8.64i (ISBN 0-06-022014-7); PLB 9.89 (ISBN 0-06-022015-5). HarpJ.

--Curly & the Wild Boar. LC 77-25644. (Illus.). 96p. (gr. 5 up). 1980. pap. 1.95 (ISBN 0-06-440116-2, Trophy). HarpJ.

--Hound-Dog Man. LC 49-7116. 1966. (HarpT); text ed. 9.89i (ISBN 0-06-011541-6). Har-Row.

--Hound-Dog Man. LC 80-10995. viii, 247p. 1980. pap. 4.95 (ISBN 0-8032-7005-4, BB 748, Bison). U of Nebr Pr.

--Little Arliss. LC 77-17643. (Illus.). 1978. 8.64i (ISBN 0-06-022008-2); PLB 9.89 (ISBN 0-06-022009-0). HarpJ.

--Little Arliss. LC 77-17643. (Illus.). 96p. (gr. 5 up). 1980. pap. 1.95 (ISBN 0-06-440108-1, Trophy). HarpJ.

--Old Yeller. LC 56-8780. (Illus.). 1956. 12.45i (ISBN 0-06-011545-9, HarpT); lib. bdg. 12.89i (ISBN 0-06-011546-7). Har-Row.

--Old Yeller. 1964. pap. 3.37i (ISBN 0-06-080002-X, P2, PL). Har-Row.

--Savage Sam. LC 62-7948. (Illus.). 1962. (HarpT); PLB 12.89i (ISBN 0-06-011561-0). Har-Row.

--Savage Sam. (gr. 1-5). 1976. pap. 2.84i (ISBN 0-06-080377-0, P377, PL). Har-Row.

Gipson, Fred, jt. auth. see Langford, J. O.

Gipson, James. Winning the Investment Game. 192p. 1984. 17.95 (ISBN 0-07-023292-X). McGraw.

Gipson, John D., jt. auth. see Barnett, Joe R.

Gipson, Lawrence H. The British Empire Before the American Revolution, 15 vols. Incl. Vol. 2. The British Isles & the American Colonies: The Southern Plantations, 1748-1754. rev. ed. 1960. 15.00 (ISBN 0-394-41782-8); Vol. 3. The British Isles & the American Colonies: The Northern Plantations, 1748-1754. rev. ed. 1960. 15.00 (ISBN 0-394-41783-6); Vol. 4. Zones of International Friction: North America, South of the Great Lakes Region, 1748-1754. 15.00 (ISBN 0-394-45340-9); Vol. 4. Zones of International Friction: The Great Lakes Frontier, Canada, the West Indies, India, 1748-1754014vol. 5. 15.00 (ISBN 0-394-45341-7); Vol. 6. The Great War for the Empire: The Years of Defeat, 1754-1757. 15.00 (ISBN 0-394-42718-1); Vol. 7. The Great War for the Empire: The Victorious Years, 1758-1760. 15.00 (ISBN 0-394-45057-4); Vol. 8. The Great War for the Empire: The Culmination, 1760-1763. 15.00 (ISBN 0-394-42719-X); Vol. 9. The Triumphant Empire. 1956. 15.00 (ISBN 0-394-44963-0); Vol. 11. The Triumphant Empire: The Rumbling of the Coming Storm, 1766-1770. 1965. 15.00 (ISBN 0-394-41791-7); Vol. 12. The Triumphant Empire: Britain Sails into the Storm, 1770-1776. 1965. 15.00 (ISBN 0-394-41795-X); Vol. 13. The Triumphant Empire: The Empire Beyond the Storm, 1770-1776. 1967. 15.00 (ISBN 0-394-41797-6); Vol. 14. A Bibliographical Guide to the History of the British Empire, 1748-1776. 1968. 15.00 (ISBN 0-394-41686-4). Vols. 2-7, 9, 11-15. 15.00 ea. Knopf.

--The Coming of the Revolution: 1763-1775. (New American Nation Ser). 1954. 16.95i (ISBN 0-06-011575-0, HarpT). Har-Row.

Gipson, Leland F. How to Use the Tremendous Power of Creative Prayer. LC 80-85276. 114p. (Orig.). 1981. pap. 2.95 (ISBN 0-9605014-0-1). Levada.

Gipson, Morrell. Favorite Nursery Tales. (Illus.). 32p. 1983. 9.95 (ISBN 0-385-17960-X); PLB write for info (ISBN 0-385-17961-8). Doubleday.

--Rip Van Winkle. LC 83-20624. (Illus.). 32p. (ps-3). 1984. 10.95 (ISBN 0-385-18757-2); PLB 10.95 (ISBN 0-385-18758-0). Doubleday.

Gipson, R. McCandless. The Life of Emma Thursby. (Music Reprint Ser.). 1980. Repr. of 1940 ed. lib. bdg. 35.00 (ISBN 0-306-76016-9). Da Capo.

Gipson, Richard M. The Life of Emma Thursby, Eighteen Forty-Five to Nineteen Thirty-One. LC 40-29867. (Illus.). 470p. 1940. 8.00x (ISBN 0-685-73912-0, New York Historical Soc.). U Pr of Va.

Gipson, Thelma H. Entanglements of Life. 1982. 5.95 (ISBN 0-533-05086-3). Vantage.

Giquel, Prosper. A Journal of the Chinese Civil War 1864. Leibo, Steven A., ed. Weston, Debbie, tr. LC 84-16136. 184p. 1985. text ed. 20.00x (ISBN 0-8248-0985-8). UH Pr.

Giradet, Edward. Afghanistan: The Soviet War. LC 84-17960. 256p. 1985. 19.95 (ISBN 0-312-00923-2). St Martin.

Giradot, N. J. Myth & Meaning in Early Taoism: The Theme of Chaos. Date not set. 36.00 (ISBN 0-317-18508-X). U of Cal Pr.

Giradoux, Jean. Carnet des Dardanelles. 23.75 (ISBN 0-685-34178-X). French & Eur.

--Combat Avec l'Ange. pap. 9.95 (ISBN 0-685-33907-6). French & Eur.

--De Pleins Pourvoirs a sans Pouvoirs. pap. 5.95 (ISBN 0-685-33909-2). French & Eur.

--Elpenor. pap. 7.95 (ISBN 0-685-33911-4). French & Eur.

--Le Film de Bethanie. (Texte de Les Anges du Peche). pap. 6.50 (ISBN 0-685-33912-2). French & Eur.

--Les Gracques. pap. 6.50 (ISBN 0-685-33915-7). French & Eur.

--Visitations. (Coll. Le Fleuron). pap. 7.95 (ISBN 0-685-33932-7). French & Eur.

Giragosian, N. Successful Product & Business Development. 1978. 59.75 (ISBN 0-8247-6770-5). Dekker.

Giragosian, Paul A., jt. auth. see Lord, Norman W.

Giraldi Cinthio. Giraldi Cinthio on Romances. Snuggs, Henry L., tr. LC 68-12971. 216p. 1968. 20.00x (ISBN 0-8131-1158-7). U Pr of Ky.

Giraldo, G. & Beth, E. Role of Viruses in Human Cancer, Vol. 2. 1984. 75.00 (ISBN 0-444-80584-2, I-201-84). Elsevier.

Giraldo, G. & Beth, E., eds. Role of Viruses in Human Cancer. 292p. 1980. 60.00 (ISBN 0-444-00440-8, Biomedical Pr). Elsevier.

Giraldo, G. & Beth, Elke, eds. Epidemic of Acquired Immune Deficiency Syndrome (AIDS) & Kaposi's Sarcoma. (Antibiotics & Chemotherapy Ser.: Vol. 32). (Illus.). viii, 164p. 1984. 55.00 (ISBN 3-8055-3876-6). S Karger.

Giraldo, G., et al, eds. From Oncogenes to Tumor Antigens. 270p. 1985. 66.75 (ISBN 0-444-80672-5). Elsevier.

Giraldo, Z. I. Public Policy & the Family: Wives & Mothers in the Labor Force. LC 80-7692. 240p. 1980. 26.00x (ISBN 0-669-03762-1). Lexington Bks.

Giraldo, Z. I., ed. Women in American Law, Vol. 2: From the New Deal to the Present. (Illus.). 350p. 1985. text ed. 47.50x (ISBN 0-8419-0920-2); pap. text ed. 22.50x (ISBN 0-8419-0921-0). Holmes & Meier.

Giraldus. Cambrensis Historical Works. Wright, Thomas, ed. LC 68-55551. (Bohn's Antiquarian Library Ser). Repr. of 1863 ed. 35.00 (ISBN 0-404-50015-3). AMS Pr.

--The English Conquest of Ireland. Furnivall, F. J., ed. (EETS, OS Ser.: No. 107). Repr. of 1896 ed. 40.00 (ISBN 0-527-00111-2). Kraus Repr.

--English Conquest of Ireland, A.D. 1166-1185. LC 68-25237. (British History Ser., No. 30). 1969. Repr. of 1896 ed. lib. bdg. 49.95x (ISBN 0-8383-0947-X). Haskell.

Giralestone, Gathrone R. The Care & Cure of Crippled Children. Phillips, William R. & Rosenberg, Janet, eds. LC 79-6900. (Physically Handicapped in Society Ser.). (Illus.). 1980. Repr. of 1924 ed. lib. bdg. 12.00x (ISBN 0-405-13111-9). Ayer Co Pubs.

Giralt-Miracle, Daniel. New Interiors, No. 1. 246p. 1982. (Pub. by Editorial Blume Spain). Intl Spec Bk.

Girard, Albert. Commerce Francais a Seville Et Cadiz Au Temps De Habsbourg, 3 pts. in 1. 1967. Repr. of 1932 ed. 36.50 (ISBN 0-8337-1358-2). B Franklin.

Girard, Augustin & Gentil, Genevieve. Cultural Development: Experiences & Policies. 2nd ed. 189p. 1984. pap. 26.25 (ISBN 92-3-102020-X, U1374, UNESCO). Unipub.

Girard, Charles. United States Exploring Expedition During the Years 1838, 1839, 1840, 1841, 1842 Under the Command of Charles Wilkes, U.S.N. Herpetology, 2 vols, Vol. 20. Srling, Keir B., ed. LC 77-81095. (Biologists & Their World Ser.). (Illus.). 1978. Repr. of 1858 ed. lib. bdg. 50.00x (ISBN 0-405-10678-5). Ayer Co Pubs.

Girard, Denis. Dictionnaire Francais-Anglais et Anglais-Francais. 1464p. (Fr.-Eng.). 1972. 27.50 (ISBN 0-686-57300-5, M-6274). French & Eur.

Girard, Denis, et al, eds. Cassell's French Dictionary. LC 77-7669. (Fr. & Eng.). 1977. thumb indexed 21.95 (ISBN 0-02-522620-7); standard 19.95 (ISBN 0-02-522610-X); 9.95 (ISBN 0-02-522670-3). Macmillan.

Girard, F., ed. see Dotzauer, J. J.

Girard, Hazel. A Giant Walked among Them. LC 77-81432. (Half Tall Tales of Paul Bunyan). (Illus.). 1977. 8.00. M Jones.

Girard, Hazel B. & Girard, Marvin E. Rail Fences & Roosters: Poems & Almost Poems. LC 78-4802. 96p. 1978. 6.00 (ISBN 0-8233-0276-8). Golden Quill.

Girard, Jacques, photos by. Versailles Gardens: Sculpture & Mythology. (Illus.). 304p. 1985. 50.00 (ISBN 0-86565-052-7). Vendome.

Girard, James P. Changing All Those Changes. Young, Al, ed. LC 76-11428. 1976. pap. 3.95 (ISBN 0-918412-01-3). Yardbird Wing.

Girard, Joe. How to Sell Yourself. 1984. pap. 7.95 (ISBN 0-446-37772-4). Warner Bks.

Girard, Joe & Brown, Stanley H. How to Sell Anything to Anybody. 240p. 1979. pap. 3.95 (ISBN 0-446-32516-3); pap. 6.95 (ISBN 0-446-38232-9). Warner Bks.

Girard, Linda. You Were Born on Your Very First Birthday. Tucker, Kathy, ed. LC 84-17220. (Concept Bks). (Illus.). 32p. (ps-3). 1983. PLB 10.75 (ISBN 0-8075-9455-5). A Whitman.

Girard, Linda W. Earth, Sea & Sky: The Work of Edmond Halley. (Biography Ser.). (Illus.). 64p. (gr. 3 up). 1985. 9.75 (ISBN 0-8075-1868-9). A Whitman.

--My Body Is Private. Tucker, Kathleen, ed. (Illus.). 32p. (gr. k-3). 1984. PLB 10.25 (ISBN 0-8075-5320-4). A Whitman.

--Who is a Stranger & What Should I Do? Levine, Abby, ed. LC 84-17313. (Concept Bks.). (Illus.). 32p. (gr. 2-6). 1985. PLB 10.25 (ISBN 0-8075-9014-2). A Whitman.

Girard, Louis J. Advanced Techniques in Ophthalmic Microsurgery: Corneal Surgery, Vol. II. LC 78-31773. (Illus.). 305p. 1980. text ed. 94.50 (ISBN 0-8016-1835-5). Mosby.

--Advanced Techniques in Ophthalmic Micro Surgery: Ultrasonic Fragmentation for Intraocular Surgery, Vol. 1. LC 78-20733. (Illus.). 286p. 1979. text ed. 94.50 (ISBN 0-8016-1837-1). Mosby.

Girard, Marcel, ed. see Zola, Emile.

Girard, Marvin E. Makin' Circles with a Rope. LC 84-62882. (Illus.). 160p. (YA) Date not set. 12.00 (ISBN 0-8338-0191-0). M Jones.

--These, My Singing Words: A Collection of Poems. LC 76-1233. 119p. 1976. 6.00 (ISBN 0-8233-0240-7). Golden Quill.

Girard, Marvin E., jt. auth. see Girard, Hazel B.

Girard, Pat. Flying Machines. LC 79-28842. (Machine World Ser.). (Illus.). (gr. 2-4). 1980. PLB 14.65 (ISBN 0-8172-1333-3). Raintree Pubs.

Girard, Paul F. A Short History of Roman Law: Being the First Part of His "Manuel Elementaire De Droit Romain.". Lefrox, A. H. & Cameron, J. H., trs. LC 79-1603. 1981. Repr. of 1906 ed. 20.35 (ISBN 0-88355-906-4). Hyperion Conn.

Girard, R. M. Texas Rocks & Minerals: An Amateur's Guide. (Illus.). 109p. 1964. Repr. 2.50 (ISBN 0-686-29314-2, GB 6). Bur Econ Geology.

Girard, Raphael. Esotericism of the Popol Vuh. LC 78-74712. (Illus.). 1979. 14.00 (ISBN 0-911500-13-8); pap. 8.50 (ISBN 0-911500-14-6). Theos U Pr.

Girard, Rene. Deceit, Desire & the Novel: Self & Other in Literary Structure. Freccero, Yvonne, tr. from Fr. LC 65-28582. 305p. 1966. pap. 8.95x (ISBN 0-8018-1830-3). Johns Hopkins.

--To Double Business Bound: Essays on Literature, Mimesis, & Anthropology. LC 78-8418. pap. 62.30 (ISBN 0-317-20488-2, 2022995). Bks Demand UMI.

--Violence & the Sacred. Gregory, Patrick, tr. LC 77-4539. 1977. pap. 8.95 (ISBN 0-8018-2218-1). Johns Hopkins.

Girard, Rene, ed. Proust: A Collection of Critical Essays. LC 77-9577. 1977. Repr. of 1962 ed. lib. bdg. 24.75x (ISBN 0-8371-9710-4, GIPR). Greenwood.

Girard, Robert C. Brethren, Hang Loose. 1972. pap. 6.95 (ISBN 0-310-25041-2). Zondervan.

Girard, Sharon. Funeral Music & Customs in Venezuela. LC 79-28501. (Special Studies: No. 22). 96p. 1980. pap. text ed. 8.95 (ISBN 0-87918-050-1). ASU Lat Am St.

Girard, Victor. Proto-Takanan Phonology. LC 76-631856. (U. C. Publ. in Linguistics: Vol. 70). Repr. of 1971 ed. 41.70 (ISBN 0-8357-9638-8, 2015097). Bks Demand UMI.

Girard, Weldon. How to Make Big Money Selling Commercial & Industrial Property. 1977. 24.95 (ISBN 0-13-417956-0, Busn). P-H.

Girard De Rousillon. Poeme Bourguignon du XIVe Siecle. LC 72-1634. (Yale Romanic Studies: No. 16). (Fr.). Repr. of 1939 ed. 42.00 (ISBN 0-404-53216-0). AMS Pr.

Girardet, Fredy. The Cuisine of Fredy Girardet. Hill, Judith & Hill, Michael, trs. LC 84-6700. 1984. 17.95 (ISBN 0-688-03950-2). Morrow.

Girardet, P., ed. Research & Methodology in General Pediatrics: A Swiss Experience. (Journal: Paediatrician: Vol. 9, Nos. 5-6). (Illus.). 128p. 1981. pap. 30.00 (ISBN 3-8055-2661-X). S Karger.

Girardier, Lucien & Stock, Michael J., eds. Mammalian Thermogenesis. LC 83-1929. (Illus.). 359p. 1983. 80.00 (ISBN 0-412-23550-1, NO. 6822, Pub. by Chapman & Hall). Methuen Inc.

Girardin, Emile De see Blanqui, Jerome A. & De Girardin, Emile.

Girardin, R. L. Essay on Landscape: On the Means of Improving & Embellishing the Country Round Our Habitations, Bound with a Tour to Ermenonville. Hunt, John D., ed. LC 79-56979. (The English Landscape Garden Ser.). 326p. 1982. lib. bdg. 53.00 (ISBN 0-8240-0171-0). Garland Pub.

Girardot, N. J. Myth & Meaning in Early Taoism: The Themes of Chaos (hun-tun) LC 81-21964. (Hermeneutics Ser.). (Illus.). 430p. 1983. 34.00 (ISBN 0-520-04330-8). U of Cal Pr.

Girardot, Norman J. & Ricketts, Mac L., eds. Imagination & Meaning: The Scholarly & Literary Worlds of Mircea Eliade. 240p. 1982. pap. 9.95 (ISBN 0-8164-2371-7, Pub. by Seabury). Winston Pr.

Girardot, R. G., et al, eds. New Directions In International Law: Essays in Honour of Wolfgang Abendroth. 592p. 1982. 75.00 (ISBN 0-317-07423-7). Transnatl Pubs.

Giraud. Eugene Fromentin. pap. 7.95 (ISBN 0-685-34909-8). French & Eur.

--Manuel de Bibliographie Litteraire pour les XVIe, XVIIe, XVIIIe Siecles Francais (1921-1935, 2 tomes. 15.50 ea.; Set. 35.75 (ISBN 0-685-35966-2). French & Eur.

Giraud, A. & Petit, M. Ionospheric Techniques & Phenomena. (Geophysics & Astrophysics Monographs: No. 13). 1978. 45.00 (ISBN 90-277-0499-6, Pub. by Reidel Holland); pap. write for info. (ISBN 90-277-0500-3, Pub. by Reidel Holland). Kluwer Academic.

Giraud, J. & Pamart, J. Riverain. Les Nouveaux mots dans le vent. 271p. (Fr.). 1974. pap. 11.95 (ISBN 2-03-070334-6, 2717). Larousse.

Giraud, Marcel. A History of French Louisiana, Vol. 1: The Reign of Louis XIV, 1698-1715. LC 71-18156. (Illus.). 398p. 1974. 32.50x (ISBN 0-8071-0247-4). La State U Pr.

Giraud, Raymond. Unheroic Hero in the Novels of Stendahl, Balzac & Flaubert. 1969. lib. bdg. 19.00x (ISBN 0-374-93154-2). Octagon.

Giraud, Victor, jt. auth. see Chateaubriand, Rene de.

Giraud, Yves, ed. La Vie Theatrale dans les Provinces du Midi. (Etudes Litteraires Francaises Ser.: No. 6). 264p. (Orig.). 1980. pap. 21.00x (ISBN 3-87808-885-X). Benjamins North Am.

Giraudeau, A. & Gore, Francis. Dictionnaire Francais-Tibetain (Tibet Oriental) 310p. (Fr. & Tibetian.). 1956. 49.95 (ISBN 0-686-57301-3, M-6275). French & Eur.

Giraudoux, Jean. Adorable Clio. 224p. 1939. 8.95 (ISBN 0-686-53996-6). French & Eur.

--Adventures de Jerome Bardini. 190p. 1964. 7.95 (ISBN 0-686-53999-0). French & Eur.

--Amphitryon Thirty Eight. 1967. pap. 9.95 (ISBN 0-685-10998-4). French & Eur.

--Amphitryon Thirty Eight. 192p. 1967. 3.95 (ISBN 0-686-53997-4). French & Eur.

--Apollon De Bellac. 1962. pap. 7.95 (ISBN 0-685-11010-9). French & Eur.

--L' Apollon de Bellac: Avec: L'Impromptu de Paris. 160p. 1975. 3.95 (ISBN 0-686-53998-2). French & Eur.

--Aventures De Jerome Bardini. 1964. pap. 3.95 (ISBN 0-685-11022-2). French & Eur.

--Bella: Collection Diamant. 1959. 11.95 (ISBN 0-685-11040-0). French & Eur.

--Choix des Elues. pap. 7.95 (ISBN 0-685-33906-8). French & Eur.

--Les Cinq Tentations de la Fontaine. 303p. 1958. 7.95 (ISBN 0-686-54000-X). French & Eur.

--Les Contes d'un Matin. pap. 4.50 (ISBN 0-685-33908-4). French & Eur.

--L' Ecole des Indifferents. pap. 7.95 (ISBN 0-685-33910-6). French & Eur.

--Eglantine. 232p. 1927. 7.95 (ISBN 0-686-54001-8). French & Eur.

--Electra. 192p. 1963. 3.95 (ISBN 0-686-54002-6). French & Eur.

--Electre. 1963. pap. 8.50 (ISBN 0-685-11156-3). French & Eur.

--Electre. Patty, James S., ed. LC 65-19222. (Fr.). 1982. pap. text ed. 12.95x (ISBN 0-89197-138-6). Irvington.

--Folle de Chaillot. 1960. pap. 7.90 (ISBN 0-685-11194-6). French & Eur.

--La Folle de Chaillot. 160p. 1968. 3.95 (ISBN 0-686-54003-4). French & Eur.

--La Francaise et la France. pap. 4.95 (ISBN 0-685-33913-0). French & Eur.

--La France Sentimentale. pap. 7.95 (ISBN 0-685-33914-9). French & Eur.

--Giraudoux: Four Plays, Vol. 1. Incl. Ondine; The Enchanted; The Madwoman of Chaillot; The Apollo of Bellac. (Mermaid Dramabook Ser.). 255p. (Orig.). 1958. pap. 6.25 (ISBN 0-8090-0712-6). Hill & Wang.

--Giraudoux: Three Plays, Vol. 2. La Farge, Phyllis & Judd, Peter H., trs. from Fr. Incl. Siegfried; Amphitryon 38; Electra. (Mermaid Dramabooks Ser.). 247p. (Orig.). 1964. pap. 6.95 (ISBN 0-8090-0731-2). Hill & Wang.

--Guerre De Troie N'Aura Pas Lieu. 1963. pap. 7.95 (ISBN 0-685-11227-6). French & Eur.

--La Guerre de Troie n'Aura pas Lieu. 186p. 1963. 3.95 (ISBN 0-686-54004-2). French & Eur.

--La Guerre de Troie n'aura pas lieu. (Classiques Larousse). (Illus., Fr.). pap. 1.95 (ISBN 0-685-13933-6, 113). Larousse.

--L' Impromptu de Paris. pap. 7.95 (ISBN 0-685-33916-5). French & Eur.

--Intermezzo. 1964. pap. 7.95 (ISBN 0-685-11254-3). French & Eur.

--Intermezzo. 192p. 1964. 3.95 (ISBN 0-686-54005-0). French & Eur.

--Intermezzo. Reilly, John H., ed. LC 67-14570. (Fr.). 1967. pap. text ed. 12.95x (ISBN 0-89197-232-3). Irvington.

--Judith. pap. 8.95 (ISBN 0-685-33917-3). French & Eur.

--Juliette au Pays des Hommes. pap. 8.95 (ISBN 0-685-33918-1). French & Eur.

--Litterature. (Coll. Idees). 1967. pap. 3.95 (ISBN 0-685-33919-X). French & Eur.

--La Menteuse: Roman. (Coll. Diamant). 13.50 (ISBN 0-685-33920-3). French & Eur.

--Oeuvres Litteraires Diverses; Prose Narrative; Critique. 85.00 (ISBN 0-685-34177-1). French & Eur.

--Ondine. pap. 8.50 (ISBN 0-685-33921-1). French & Eur.

--Ondine. 288p. 1953. 7.95 (ISBN 0-686-54007-7); pap. 3.95 (ISBN 0-686-54008-5). French & Eur.

--Or dans la Nuit: Chroniques et Prefaces Litteraires 1910-1943. 11.50 (ISBN 0-685-33922-X). French & Eur.

--Plins pouvoirs. pap. 5.95 (ISBN 0-685-33923-8). French & Eur.

--Portugal. Bd. with Combat Avec l'Image. pap. 7.50 (ISBN 0-685-33924-6). French & Eur.

--Pour Lucrece. pap. 11.50 (ISBN 0-685-33925-4). French & Eur.

--Un Prince. 4.95 (ISBN 0-686-54009-3). French & Eur.

--Provinciales. (Coll. Diamant). 12.95 (ISBN 0-685-23908-X). French & Eur.

--Provinciales. 7.95 (ISBN 0-686-54010-7); pap. 3.95 (ISBN 0-686-54011-5). French & Eur.

--Racine. LC 77-24244. 1938. lib. bdg. 9.50 (ISBN 0-8414-4604-0). Folcroft.

--Racine. 1980. Repr. of 1938 ed. lib. bdg. 10.00 (ISBN 0-8492-4948-1). R West.

--Siegfried. pap. 8.50 (ISBN 0-685-33926-2). French & Eur.

--Siegfried et le Limousin. 1956. pap. 7.95 (ISBN 0-685-11563-1). French & Eur.

--Simon le Pathetique. pap. 7.95 (ISBN 0-685-33927-0). French & Eur.

--Sodome et Gomorrhe. pap. 5.95 (ISBN 0-685-33928-9). French & Eur.

--Souvenir de Deux Existences. 1975. 6.95 (ISBN 0-686-54012-3). French & Eur.

--Le Sport. 76p. 1977. 6.95 (ISBN 0-686-54013-1). French & Eur.

--Supplement au Voyage de Cook. pap. 7.95 (ISBN 0-685-33929-7). French & Eur.

--Suzanne et le Pacifique. pap. 7.95 (ISBN 0-685-33930-0). French & Eur.

--Tessa. pap. 7.95 (ISBN 0-685-33931-9). French & Eur.

--Theatre, Tome III. Incl. Electre; Supplement au Voyage de Cook; L' Impromptu de Paris; Cantique des Cantiques; Ondine. 1958-59. 17.95 (ISBN 0-685-35877-1). French & Eur.

--Theatre, Tome I. Incl. Siegfried; Fin de Siegfried; Amphitryon 38; Judith. 1958-59. 17.95 (ISBN 0-685-36050-4). French & Eur.

--Theatre, Tome II. Incl. Intermezzo; Tessa; La Guerre de Troie n'Aura pas Lieu. 1958-59. 17.95 (ISBN 0-685-36053-9). French & Eur.

--Theatre: Avec: Sodome et Gommorrhe, L'Appollon de Bellac, La Folle de Chaillot, Pour Lucrece, Vol. 4. 340p. 1959. 17.95 (ISBN 0-686-54014-X). French & Eur.

Giraudoux, Jean & Body, Jacques. Lettres. 290p. 1975. 35.00 (ISBN 0-686-54006-9). French & Eur.

Giraudoux, Jean see Weiss, Samuel A.

Girault, C. & Reisig, W., eds. Application & Theory of Petri Nets-Strassbourg 1980 & Bad Honneff 1981: Proceedings. (Informatik-Fachberichte: Vol. 52). 337p. 1982. pap. 16.70 (ISBN 0-387-11189-1). Springer-Verlag.

Girault, Maurice. Stochastic Processes. (Econometrics & Operations Research: Vol. 3). (Illus.). 1966. 22.50 (ISBN 0-387-03629-6). Springer-Verlag.

Girault, Rene, jt. auth. see Bouvier, Jean.

Girault, V. & Raviart, P. A. Finite Element Approximation of the Navier-Stokes Equations. rev. ed. (Lecture Notes in Mathematics Ser.: Vol. 749). 202p. 1979. pap. 17.00 (ISBN 0-387-09557-8). Springer-Verlag.

Girdano, Daniel, jt. auth. see Everly, George.

Girdano, Daniel A. Better Late Than Never: How Men Can Avoid a Midlife Fitness Crisis. (Illus.). 256p. 1981. 12.95t (ISBN 0-13-074773-4, Spec); pap. 5.95b (ISBN 0-13-074765-3). P-H.

--Occupational Health Promotion: A Practical Guide to Program Development. 251p. 1986. text ed. price not set (ISBN 0-02-343730-8). Macmillan.

Girdano, Daniel A. & Dusek-Girgano, Dorothy. Drug Education: Content & Methods. 3rd ed. (Illus.). 352p. 1980. text ed. 14.95 (ISBN 0-394-34876-1, RanC). Random.

Girdano, Daniel A. & Everly, George S. Controlling Stress & Tensison: A Holistic Approach. 2nd ed. (Illus.). 256p. 1986. pap. text ed. 15.95 (ISBN 0-13-172123-2). P-H.

Girdano, Daniel A. & Everly, George S., Jr. Controlling Stress & Tension: A Holistic Approach. (Illus.). 1979. 18.95 (ISBN 0-13-172114-3); pap. 8.95 (ISBN 0-13-172106-2). P-H.

Girdano, Daniel A., et al. Experiencing Health. (Illus.). 576p. 1985. pap. text ed. 21.95 (ISBN 0-13-294455-3). P-H.

Girdharry, Arnold R. Marriage for Sale: Three One-Act Plays. 1985. 6.95 (ISBN 0-8062-2324-3). Carlton.

Girdler, Allan. Corvette, A Piece of the Action: A Complete Anthology of Corvettes. (Automobile Quarterly Library). (Illus.). 1978. simulated leather 38.95 (ISBN 0-525-08649-8). Dutton.

--Customizing Your Van. 2nd, rev. ed. Caiati, Carl, rev. by. (Illus.). 256p. 1983. 16.95 (ISBN 0-8306-0212-7); pap. 10.95 (ISBN 0-8306-0112-0, 212). TAB Bks.

Girdlestone, Cuthbert. Mozart & His Piano Concertos. Orig. Title: Mozart's Piano Concertos,Il. 1952. pap. 8.50 (ISBN 0-486-21271-8). Dover.

Girdlestone, Cuthbert M. Mozart & His Piano Concertos. LC 52-3317. pap. 127.80 (ISBN 0-317-10059-9, 2004793). Bks Demand UMI.

Girdlestone, Robert B. Synonyms of the Old Testament. 1948. pap. 5.95 (ISBN 0-8028-1548-0). Eerdmans.

--Synonyms of the Old Testament: Numerically Coded to Strong's Exhaustive Concordance. White, Donald R., ed. 400p. 1983. deluxe ed. 22.95 (ISBN 0-8010-3798-0); pap. 17.95 kivar bdg. (ISBN 0-8010-3789-1). Baker Bk.

Girdwood, Ronald H. Clinical Pharmacology. 25th ed. (Illus.). 610p. 1984. pap. write for info. (ISBN 0-7216-0952-X, Pub. by Bailliere-Tindall). Saunders.

Girdwood, Ronald H., ed. Clinical Pharmacology. 24th ed. 1980. pap. text ed. 29.95 (ISBN 0-7216-0730-6, Pub. by Bailliere-Tindall). Saunders.

Gire, Ken, Jr. The Christmas Duck. (Sower Ser.). (Illus.). 133p. 1983. pap. 5.95 (ISBN 0-88062-112-5). Mott Media.

Girgis, Makram. Neural Substrates of Limbic Epilepsy. (Illus.). 200p. 1981. 42.50 (ISBN 0-87527-238-X). Green.

Girgis, Makrim. The Dementias. (Illus.). 350p. 1985. 42.50 (ISBN 0-87527-350-5). Green.

Girgis, Maurice. Industrial Progress in Small Oil-Exporting Countries: The Prospect for Kuwait. 195p. 1984. 30.00x (ISBN 0-86531-596-5). Westview.

Girgis, Samir. The Predominance of the Islamic Tradition of Leadership in Egypt During Bonaparte's Expedition, Vol. 47. (European University Studies-History & Allied Studies: No. 3). 138p. 1975. 18.25 (ISBN 3-261-01528-4). P Lang Pubs.

Girgus, J. S., jt. auth. see Coren, S.

Girgus, Joan S., jt. auth. see Coren, Stanley.

Girgus, Sam B. The American Self: Myth, Ideology, & Popular Culture. 1982. pap. 9.95x (ISBN 0-8263-0646-2). U of NM Pr.

--The Law of the Heart: Individualism & the Modern Self in American Literature. 192p. 1979. text ed. 13.50x (ISBN 0-292-74622-9). U of Tex Pr.

--The New Covenant: Jewish Writers & the American Idea. LC 83-12458. xiii, 220p. 1984. 19.95 (ISBN 0-8078-1577-2). U of NC Pr.

Giri, N. C., jt. auth. see Das, M. N.

Giri, V. V. My Life & Times, Vol. 1. 1976. 15.00x (ISBN 0-89684-436-6). Orient Bk Dist.

--My Life & Times, Vol 1. LC 76-904158. 1976. 14.00x (ISBN 0-333-90133-9). South Asia Bks.

Giriappa, S. & Vivekananda, M. Agricultural Development of India. 1985. 12.50x (ISBN 0-8364-1306-7, Pub. by Ashish). South Asia Bks.

Girifalco, L. A. & Welch, D. O. Point Defects & Diffusion in Strained Metals. 180p. (Orig.). 1967. 57.75 (ISBN 0-677-01400-7). Gordon.

Girija, Khanna. Indian Women Today. 1979. 12.50x (ISBN 0-7069-0679-9). South Asia Bks.

Girindranath Mukhopadhyaya. The Surgical Instruments of the Hindus, 2 vols. LC 75-23714. Repr. of 1914 ed. 47.50 set (ISBN 0-404-13340-1). AMS Pr.

Girion, Barbara. The Chicken Bone Wish. (Illus.). 160p. (gr. 4-6). 1982. pap. 2.25 (ISBN 0-590-33927-3, Apple Paperbacks). Scholastic Inc.

--A Handful of Stars. 176p. (gr. 7 up). 1981. 11.95 (ISBN 0-684-17167-8, ScribJ). Scribner.

--A Handful of Stars. 192p. (YA) (gr. 7 up). 1983. pap. 2.25 (ISBN 0-440-93642-X, LFL). Dell.

--In the Middle of a Rainbow. LC 83-3300. 208p. (gr. 7 up). 1983. 12.95 (ISBN 0-684-17885-0, ScribJ). Scribner.

--In the Middle of a Rainbow. (Pacer Bks.). 1984. pap. 2.25 (ISBN 0-399-21080-6). Putnam Pub Group.

--Joshua, the Czar, & the Chicken Bone Wish. LC 78-15012. (Illus.). (gr. 4-6). 1978. 10.95 (ISBN 0-684-15929-5, ScribJ). Scribner.

--Like Everybody Else. 176p. (gr. 5 up). 1982. pap. 1.95 (ISBN 0-440-44872-7, YB). Dell.

--Like Everybody Else. LC 80-21850. 192p. (gr. 6-8). 1980. 9.95 (ISBN 0-684-16715-8, ScribJ). Scribner.

--Misty & Me. 176p. (gr. 4-6). pap. 2.25 (ISBN 0-590-33748-3, Apple Paperbacks). Scholastic Inc.

--Misty & Me. LC 79-15925. (gr. 4-6). 1979. 11.95 (ISBN 0-684-16227-X, ScribJ). Scribner.

--A Tangle of Roots. 192p. (gr. 7 up). 1979. 9.95 (ISBN 0-684-16074-9, ScribJ). Scribner.

--A Tangle of Roots. 160p. (Orig.). (gr. 5 up). 1985. pap. 2.25 (ISBN 0-448-47747-5). Putnam Pub Group.

--A Very Brief Season. (gr. 7 up). 1984. 11.95 (ISBN 0-684-18088-X, ScribJ). Scribner.

--A Very Brief Season. 160p. 1985. pap. 2.25 (ISBN 0-425-08417-5, Pub. by Berkley-Pacer). Berkley Pub.

Girl Scouts of the U. S. A. Brownies' Own Songbook. 48p. (gr. 1-3). 1968. pap. 2.25 (ISBN 0-88441-351-9, 23-130). GS.

--From Dreams to Reality: Adventures in Careers. (From Dreams to Reality Ser.). 64p. (gr. 7-12). 1978. pap. 2.25 (ISBN 0-88441-319-5, 20-810). GS.

--Girl Scout Badges & Signs. (Illus.). 208p. (gr. 4-6). 1980. pap. text ed. 3.00 (ISBN 0-88441-326-8, 20-711). GS.

--Mundos a Explorar: Guia para Lideres de Brownie y Junior Girl Scouts. 104p. (Span.). (gr. 1-6). 1981. pap. 2.50 (ISBN 0-88441-332-2, 20-709). GS.

--Mundos a Explorar: Manual Para las Brownie y las Junior Girl Scouts. 293p. (Orig., Span.). (gr. 1-6). 1981. pap. 3.75 (ISBN 0-88441-331-4, 20-708). GS.

--Worlds to Explore Brownie & Junior Leaders Guide. (Illus.). 1981. pap. 2.50 (ISBN 0-88441-318-7, 20-702). GS.

--Worlds to Explore Handbook for Brownie & Junior Girl Scouts. (Illus.). 392p. (gr. 1-6). 1977. pap. text ed. 3.75 (ISBN 0-88441-316-0, 20-700). GS.

Girl Scouts of the United States of America. Handbook for Camp Directors & Administrators. 56p. 1967. 0.25 (ISBN 0-88441-108-7, 19-425). GS.

Girl Scouts of the U.S. Daisy Low of the Girl Scouts: The Story of Juliette Gordon Low, Founder of the Girl Scouts of United States of America. rev. ed. (YA) 1975. pap. 0.35 (ISBN 0-88441-134-6, 19-991). GS.

Girl Scouts of the USA. Be An EQ Traveler. (gr. 1-8). 1971. pap. write for info. (ISBN 0-88441-122-2, 19-966). GS.

Girl Scouts of the U.S.A. Careers to Explore for Brownie & Junior Girl Scouts. 80p. (Orig.). (gr. 6-12). 1979. 3.25 (ISBN 0-88441-324-1, 20-813). GS.

Girl Scouts of the USA. Cooking Out-of-Doors: For Juniors, Brownies, Cadettes, Seniors & Leaders. (Illus.). 224p. (gr. 1-12). 1960. spiral bdg. 5.00 (ISBN 0-88441-128-1, 19-984). GS.

--A Council Guide to Eco-Action. 24p. (gr. 9 up). 1970. pap. 0.50 (ISBN 0-88441-013-7, 19-939). GS.

--Exploring the Hand Arts: For Juniors, Cadettes, Seniors, & Leaders. 112p. (gr. 4-12). 1955. pap. 2.95 (ISBN 0-88441-140-0, 19-994). GS.

--Feeding a Crowd. 50p. (gr. 4-12). 1973. pap. 0.35 (ISBN 0-88441-125-7, 19-977); pap. 1.00 pack of 6. GS.

Girl Scouts of the U.S.A. From Dreams to Reality: Career Cards. (From Dreams to Reality Ser.). (gr. 7-12). 1978. pap. 2.25 (ISBN 0-88441-320-9, 20-811). GS.

--Girl Scout Badges & Signs: Leaders Guide. 88p. 1980. pap. text ed. 2.50 (ISBN 0-88441-327-6, 20-712). GS.

--Girl Scout Pocket Songbook: For Juniors, Cadettes, Seniors, & Leaders. 56p. (gr. 5-12). 1972. pap. 0.60 (ISBN 0-88441-306-3, 20-192). GS.

Girl Scouts of the USA. The Great Cookie Caper or, How to Discover the World, Starting with a Cookie or Anything Else. (Illus.). 20p. (Minimum order 10). (gr. 1-3). 1973. 0.50 (ISBN 0-88441-138-9, 26-250). GS.

--Helping Leaders Help Girls Grow. 1972. boxed kit 4.00 (ISBN 0-88441-252-0, 19-978). GS.

Girl Scouts of the U.S.A. Let's Make It Happen! (GS Catalogue: No. 20-815). 72p. (YA) (gr. 9-12). 3.00 (ISBN 0-88441-322-5). GS.

--Moreabouts for Brownie Girl Scout Leaders. (Illus.). 96p. 1980. pap. text ed. 3.50 (ISBN 0-88441-328-4, 20-703). GS.

--Outdoor Education in Girl Scouting. (Illus.). 172p. 1984. pap. text ed. 6.00 (ISBN 0-88441-454-X, 26-217). GS.

Girl Scouts of the USA. Planning Trips with Girl Scouts: A Guide for Leaders. rev. ed. 24p. (gr. 1-8). 1982. pap. 2.50 (ISBN 0-88441-142-7, 19-998). GS.

--Safety-Wise: For Girls (Grade 7-12) & Adults Who Work Directly with Girls. rev. ed. 1982. pap. 1.25 (ISBN 0-88441-428-0, 26-203). GS.

--Sing Together: A Girl Scout Songbook. (Illus.). 192p. (gr. 1-12). 1973. 5.00 (ISBN 0-88441-309-8, 20-206). GS.

--Skip to My Lou: For Brownies, Juniors, Cadettes, Seniors & Leaders. 32p. (gr. 1-8). 1958. pap. 1.25 (ISBN 0-88441-307-1, 20-199). GS.

Girl Scouts of the U.S.A. Training about Girl Scouting. 72p. 1978. pap. 4.00 (ISBN 0-88441-431-0, 26-180). GS.

--Wide World of Girl Guiding & Girl Scouting. (Illus.). 88p. (gr. 1-6). 1980. pap. text ed. 3.95 (ISBN 0-88441-143-5, 19-713). GS.

--Wide World of Girl Guiding & Girl Scouting: Leaders Guide. 24p. pap. text ed. 1.75 (ISBN 0-88441-144-3, 19-714). GS.

Girl Scouts of the U.S.A., Our Chalet Committee of Wagggs. Our Chalet Songbook. 2nd ed. 94p. (Lat., Fr., Turkish, Ital., Ger., Gr. & Finnish.). 1978. 2.00 (ISBN 0-88441-364-0, 23-929); in 7 languages avail. GS.

Girl Scouts of the USA Staff. Games for Girl Scouts. rev. ed. 96p. (gr. 1-12). 1969. pap. 2.50 (ISBN 0-88441-310-1, 20-630). GS.

Girl Scouts of the U.S.A. Staff. You Make the Difference: Cadette & Senior Girl Scout Leader's Guide. 40p. (Orig.). 1980. pap. text ed. 2.50 (ISBN 0-88441-330-6, 20-705). GS.

--You Make the Difference: Handbook for Cadette & Senior Girl Scouts. (Illus.). 72p. (Orig.). (YA) (gr. 7-12). 1980. pap. text ed. 3.25 (ISBN 0-88441-329-2, 20-704). GS.

Girling, J. S. America & the Third World. (Illus.). 1980. 26.95x (ISBN 0-7100-0318-8). Routledge & Kegan.

Girling, John L. Thailand: Society & Politics. LC 80-69822. (Politics & International Relations of Southeast Asia Ser.). 320p. 1981. 29.95x (ISBN 0-8014-1130-0). Cornell U Pr.

--Thailand: Society & Politics. LC 80-69822. 312p. (Orig.). 1985. pap. text ed. 9.95x (ISBN 0-8014-9328-5). Cornell U Pr.

Girling, Richard. The Forest on the Hill. LC 81-69973. 288p. 1982. 13.95 (ISBN 0-670-39187-5). Viking.

Girling, Robert H. Multinational Institutions & the Third World. LC 84-18131. 232p. 1985. 35.95 (ISBN 0-03-001003-9); pap. 14.95 (ISBN 0-03-001004-7). Praeger.

Girls of Lady Eden's School, London. Just How Stories. (Illus.). 23p. (ps-3). 1981. 9.95 (ISBN 0-224-01713-6, Pub. by Jonathan Cape). Merrimack Pub Cir.

Girma-Selassie, Asfaw see Asfaw, Girma-Selassie, et al.

Girnau, G. & Haack, A. Tunnelling Research. pap. 22.00 (ISBN 0-08-029952-0). Pergamon.

Girod, Gordon H. The Deeper Faith: An Exposition of the Canons of Dort. 1978. pap. 1.95 (ISBN 0-8010-3725-5). Baker Bk.
--Words & Wonders of the Cross. (Pocket Pulpit Library). 1979. pap. 2.95 (ISBN 0-8010-3741-7). Baker Bk.
Girod, Roger, et al, eds. Social Policy in Western Europe & the U. S. A., Nineteen Fifty to Nineteen Eighty: An Assessment. LC 84-17747. 128p. 1985. 25.00 (ISBN 0-312-73376-3). St Martin.
Girodet, J. Dictionnaire du Bon Francais. 896p. (Fr.). 1981. lib. bdg. 37.50 (ISBN 2-04-010580-8, M-9362). French & Eur.
Girodias, Maurice, ed. The Olympia Reader. LC 65-14205. (Illus.). 704p. 1980. pap. 5.95 (ISBN 0-394-17648-0, B437, BC). Grove.
Girodo, Michel. Shy? (gr. 10 up). 1981. pap. 2.95 (ISBN 0-671-43061-0). PB.
Girola, Renata, tr. see Pareto, Vilfredo.
Girolami, Anne-Marie, jt. auth. see Martineau, Richard.
Girolamo, Costanzo Di see Di Girolamo, Costanzo.
Gironda, Vince & Kennedy, Robert. Unleashing the Wild Physique: Ultimate Bodybuilding for Men & Women. LC 84-8451. (Illus.). 192p. 1984. 16.95 (ISBN 0-8069-4180-4); pap. 9.95 (ISBN 0-8069-7888-0). Sterling.
Girosky, Michael B., jt. auth. see Grolle, Carl G.
Girouard, Blanche M. World Is for the Young: & Other Stories. facsimile ed. LC 70-167450. (Short Story Index Reprint Ser.). Repr. of 1935 ed. 18.00 (ISBN 0-8369-3976-X). Ayer Co Pubs.
Girouard, Mark. Alfred Waterhouse & the Natural History Museum. (Illus.). 64p. 1981. pap. 4.50x (ISBN 0-565-00831-5, Pub. by Brit Mus Nat Hist England). Sabbot-Natural Hist Bks.
--Alfred Waterhouse & the Natural History Museum. LC 80-53742. (Illus.). 1981. 18.50x (ISBN 0-300-02578-5). Yale U Pr.
--Cities & People: A Social & Architectural History. LC 85-40461. 416p. 1985. 29.95 (ISBN 0-300-03502-0). Yale U Pr.
--Life in the English Country House. 1980. pap. 12.95 (ISBN 0-14-005406-5). Penguin.
--Life in the English Country House: A Social & Architectural History. LC 78-9088. (Illus.). 1978. 38.50x (ISBN 0-300-02273-5). Yale U Pr.
--The Return to Camelot: Chivalry & the English Gentleman. LC 81-51343. (Illus.). 320p. 1981. 42.00x (ISBN 0-300-02739-7). Yale U Pr.
--The Return to Camelot: Chivalry & the English Gentleman. LC 81-51343. (Illus.). 320p. 1985. pap. 12.95 (ISBN 0-300-03473-3, Y-549). Yale U Pr.
--Robert Smythson & the Elizabethan Country House. LC 83-50004. (Illus.). 328p. 1983. 40.00x (ISBN 0-300-03134-3). Yale U Pr.
--Robert Smythson & the Elizabethan Country House. LC 83-50004. (Illus.). 336p. 1985. pap. 13.95x (ISBN 0-300-02389-8, Y-548). Yale U Pr.
--Sweetness & Light: The 'Queen Anne' Movement, 1860-1900. (Illus.). 1977. 55.00x (ISBN 0-19-817330-X). Oxford U Pr.
--Sweetness & Light: The "Queen Anne" Movement, 1860-1900. LC 77-30113. (Illus.). 272p. 1984. pap. text ed. 16.95x (ISBN 0-300-03068-1, Y-491). Yale U Pr.
--Victorian Country House. LC 79-64077. 1979. 50.00x (ISBN 0-300-02390-1). Yale U Pr.
--The Victorian Country House. rev. & enl. ed. LC 79-64077. (Illus.). 448p. 1985. pap. 16.95 (ISBN 0-300-03472-5, Y-547). Yale U Pr.
--Victorian Pubs. LC 83-51291. (Illus.). 232p. 1984. text ed. 36.00 (ISBN 0-300-03199-8); pap. 16.95 (ISBN 0-300-03201-3, Y-492). Yale U Pr.
Giroud, Antoine. The Nutrition of the Embryo. (Illus.). 136p. 1970. photocopy ed. 16.75x (ISBN 0-398-00684-9). C C Thomas.
Giroud, Francoise. An Honorable Woman: Marie Curie-Sklodowska. Davis, Lydia, tr. from Fr. 350p. 1985. text ed. 32.50 (ISBN 0-8419-0977-6); pap. 13.95 (ISBN 0-8419-0978-4). Holmes & Meier.
Giroud, J. P., jt. ed. see Willoughby, D. A.
Giroux, E. X. A Death for a Dancer: A Robert Forsythe Mystery. 192p. 1985. 12.95 (ISBN 0-312-18868-4). St Martin.
--A Death for a Darling. 192p. 1985. 13.95 (ISBN 0-312-18607-X). St Martin.
--A Death for Adonis. 160p. 1984. 11.95 (ISBN 0-312-18610-X). St Martin.
--A Death for Adonis. 160p. 1986. pap. 2.95 (ISBN 0-345-32889-2). Ballantine.
Giroux, Gary & Rose, Peter S. Financial Forecasting in Banking: Methods & Applications. Dufey, Gunter, ed. LC 80-29141. (Research for Business Decisions Ser.: No. 37). 196p. 1981. 39.95 (ISBN 0-8357-1156-0); pap. 14.95 (ISBN 0-8357-1505-1). UMI Res Pr.
Giroux, Henry. Ideology, Culture & the Process of Schooling. 184p. 1981. write for info. (ISBN 0-905273-19-2, Pub. by Falmer Pr). Taylor & Francis.
Giroux, Henry & Purpel, David. The Hidden Curriculum & Moral Education: Deception or Discovery? LC 82-62034. 448p. 1983. 26.00x (ISBN 0-8211-1519-7); text ed. 23.25x. McCutchan.
Giroux, Henry A. Ideology, Culture & the Process of Schooling. 168p. 1981. 24.95 (ISBN 0-87722-228-2). Temple U Pr.
--Ideology, Culture, & the Process of Schooling. 250p. 1984. pap. 9.95 (ISBN 0-87722-370-X). Temple U Pr.
--Theory & Resistance in Education: A Pedagogy for the Opposition. Freire, Paulo, frwd. by. 304p. 1983. text ed. 27.95 (ISBN 0-89789-031-0); pap. 12.95 (ISBN 0-89789-032-9). Bergin & Garvey.
Giroux, Henry A., jt. auth. see Aronowitz, Stanley.
Giroux, Henry A., et al, eds. Curriculum & Instruction: Alternatives in Education. LC 80-84142. 1981. 26.00x (ISBN 0-8211-0615-5); text ed. 23.25x 10 or more copies. McCutchan.
Giroux, James A. Drawing a Conclusion: Advanced Level. Spargo, Edward, ed. (Comprehension Skills Ser). (Illus.). 64p. (gr. 9 up). 1974. pap. text ed. 4.00x (ISBN 0-89061-015-0, CB-4A). Jamestown Pubs.
Giroux, James A. & Twining, James E. Making a Judgment: Advanced Level. Spargo, Edward, ed. (Comprehension Skills Ser.). (Illus.). 64p. (gr. 9 up). 1978. pap. text ed. 4.00x (ISBN 0-89061-013-4, CB-2A). Jamestown Pubs.
Giroux, James A. & Williston, Glenn R. Appreciation of Literary Forms: Advanced Level. Spargo, Edward, ed. (Comprehension Skills Ser.). (Illus.). 64p. (gr. 9 up). 1974. pap. text ed. 4.00x (ISBN 0-89061-018-5, CB-7A). Jamestown Pubs.
--Isolating Details & Recalling Specific Facts. Spargo, Edward, ed. (Comprehension Skills Ser.). (Illus.). 64p. 1978. Middle Level gr. 6-8. pap. text ed. 4.00x (ISBN 0-89061-072-X, CB-9M); Advanced Level gr. 9 up. pap. text ed. 4.00x (ISBN 0-89061-020-7, CB-9A). Jamestown Pubs.
--Making an Inference: Advanced Level. Spargo, Edward, ed. (Comprehension Skills Ser.). (Illus.). 64p. (gr. 9 up). 1978. pap. text ed. 4.00x (ISBN 0-89061-016-9, CB-5A). Jamestown Pubs.
--Recognizing Tone: Advanced Level. Spargo, Edward, ed. (Comprehension Skills Ser.). (Illus.). 64p. (gr. 9 up). 1974. pap. text ed. 4.00x (ISBN 0-89061-017-7, CB-6A). Jamestown Pubs.
--Retaining Concepts & Organizing Facts: Advanced Level. Spargo, Edward, ed. (Comprehension Skills Ser). (Illus.). 64p. (gr. 9 up). 1974. pap. text ed. 4.00x (ISBN 0-89061-019-3, CB-8A). Jamestown Pubs.
--Understanding Characters: Advanced Level. Spargo, Edward, ed. (Comprehension Skills Ser.). (Illus.). 64p. (gr. 9 up). 1974. pap. text ed. 4.00x (ISBN 0-89061-014-2, CB-3A). Jamestown Pubs.
--Understanding the Main Idea: Advanced Level. Spargo, Edward, ed. (Comprehension Skills Ser). (Illus.). 64p. (gr. 9 up). 1974. pap. text ed. 4.00x (ISBN 0-89061-012-6, CB-1). Jamestown Pubs.
Giroux, Leo, Jr. The Rishi: A Novel. 372p. 1985. 16.95 (ISBN 0-87131-463-0). M Evans.
Giroux, Paul L. God's Plan for the Human Race. 1980. 5.00 (ISBN 0-682-49270-1). Exposition Pr FL.
Giroux, Robert. The Book Known as Q: A Consideration of Shakespeare's Sonnets. LC 81-69149. (Illus.). 256p. 1982. 17.95 (ISBN 0-689-11260-2). Atheneum.
--The Book Known As Q: A Consideration of Shakespeare's Sonnets. LC 83-5737. 352p. pap. 7.95 (ISBN 0-394-71728-7, Vin). Random.
Giroux, Robert, ed. see Bishop, Elizabeth.
Giroux, Roy, ed. see Pietrofesa, John, et al.
Giroux, Roy F. & Biggs, Donald A., eds. College Student Development Revisited: Programs, Issues & Practices. rev. ed. 364p. 1979. 9.75 (ISBN 0-911547-18-5, 72104W34); members 7.25. Am Assn Coun Dev.
Giroux, S., jt. auth. see Maurais, J.
Girsanov, I. V. Lectures on Mathematical Theory of Extremum Problems. Louvish, D., tr. from Rus. LC 72-80360. (Lecture Notes in Economics & Mathematical Systems: Vol. 67). (Illus.). 139p. 1972. pap. 11.00 (ISBN 0-387-05857-5). Springer-Verlag.
Girshick, M. A., jt. auth. see Blackwell, David A.
Girshin, Mark. Ubiystvo Emigranta. LC 83-159. 145p. (Rus.). 1983. pap. 7.00 (ISBN 0-938920-29-4). Hermitage.
Girth, Marjorie. Bankruptcy Options for the Consumer Debtor. 177p. 1981. 30.00 (ISBN 0-686-74819-0, A1-1281). PLI.
Girtin, Thomas. Nothing but the Best. 1960. 8.95 (ISBN 0-8392-1078-7). Astor-Honor.
Giruad, Jean & Charlier, Jean-Michel. The Man with the Silver Star. (Lt. Blueberry Ser.). (Illus.). 48p. pap. 4.95 (ISBN 2-205-06578-5). Dargaud Pub.
Girvan, Norman. Corporate Imperialism: Conflict & Expropriation. Transnational Corporations & Economic Nationalism in the Third World. LC 78-11411. 241p. 1978. pap. 5.95 (ISBN 0-85345-472-8). Monthly Rev.
Girvan, Ritchie. Finnsburuh. (English Literature Ser.). 22.95 (ISBN 0-8383-0035-9). Haskell.
Girvin, E. A. Phineas F. Bresse: A Prince in Israel. Dayton, Donald W., ed. (The Higher Christian Life Ser.). 464p. 55.00 (ISBN 0-8240-6407-0). Garland Pub.
Giry, Arthur. Manuel De Diplomatique. 1965. Repr. of 1894 ed. 55.00 (ISBN 0-8337-1360-4). B Franklin.
Girzaitis, Loretta. Listening: A Response Ability. LC 72-77722. (Illus.). 1972. pap. 3.25 (ISBN 0-88489-047-3). St Marys.
--Listening: A Response-Ability. LC 72-77722. 1977. pap. 3.95x (ISBN 0-8358-0355-4). Upper Room.
Girzone, Joseph F. Gloria. 53p. (gr. 7 up). 1982. 5.00 (ISBN 0-911519-01-7). Richelieu Court.
--Joshua. 320p. 1983. 12.00 (ISBN 0-911519-03-3). Richelieu Court.
--Joshua II. 320p. 1985. 12.00 (ISBN 0-911519-08-4). Richelieu Court.
--Kara: The Lonely Falcon. (Illus.). 52p. (YA) 1985. Repr. of 1979 ed. 5.50 (ISBN 0-911519-05-X). Richelieu Court.
--Who Will Teach Me? 61p. 1982. 5.00 (ISBN 0-911519-00-9). Richelieu Court.
Gisbert, jt. auth. see De Toro, M.
Gisbert, M. Toro de see De Toro Gisbert, M.
Gisborne, Maria & Williams, Edward E. Maria Gisborne & Edward Williams, Shelley's Friends: Their Journal & Letters. 14.50x (ISBN 0-8061-0232-2). U of Okla Pr.
Giscard, Valerie. Passion's Pleasure. (Orig.). 1982. pap. 3.50 (ISBN 0-8217-1034-6). Zebra.
--Rapture's Embrace. 1984. pap. 2.50 (ISBN 0-8217-1376-0). Zebra.
Giscard d'Estaing, Valerie-Anne. The World Almanac Book of Inventions. (Illus.). 384p. 1985. pap. 9.95 (ISBN 0-345-32661-X). World Almanac.
Giscombe, C. S. Postcards. LC 77-13756. 57p. 1977. 3.50 (ISBN 0-87886-089-4). Ithaca Hse.
Gise, Jean & Hovey, Carla. Metrics All Around. (gr. 1-6). 1976. pap. 6.50 (ISBN 0-918932-35-1). Activity Resources.
Gisell, Paul. Anatole France & His Circle. Repr. of 1922 ed. 25.00 (ISBN 0-8274-3786-2). R West.
Gisevius, Hans B. To the Bitter End. Winston, Richard & Winston, Clara, trs. from Ger. LC 74-29633. 632p. 1975. Repr. of 1947 ed. lib. bdg. 31.25x (ISBN 0-8371-7983-1, GIBE). Greenwood.
Gish, Arthur. Beyond the Rat Race. 192p. 1.45 (ISBN 0-317-32266-4). Alternatives.
Gish, Arthur G. Beyond the Rat Race. rev. ed. LC 73-9336. 208p. 1973. pap. 5.95 (ISBN 0-8361-1985-1). Herald Pr.
--Living in Christian Community. LC 79-11848. 384p. 1979. 9.95 (ISBN 0-8361-1887-1). Herald Pr.
--Living in Christian Community. LC 79-11848. 384p. 1979. pap. 9.95 (ISBN 0-8361-1887-1). Herald Hse.
Gish, Duane T. Dinosaurs: Those Terrible Lizards. LC 77-89152. (Illus.). 1977. 7.95. Master Bks.
--Evolution? The Fossils Say No! 3rd ed. LC 79-52441. (Illus.). pap. 4.95 (ISBN 0-89051-057-1). Master Bks.
--Speculations & Experiments Related to the Origin of Life: A Critique. (ICR Technical Monograph: No. 1). (Illus.). 41p. 1972. pap. 5.95 (ISBN 0-89051-010-5). Master Bks.
--Up with Creation! Acts, Facts, Impacts, Vol. 3. LC 78-55612. (Illus.). 1978. pap. 6.95 (ISBN 0-89051-048-2). Master Bks.
Gish, Duane T. & Wilson, Clifford. Manipulating Life: Where Does It Stop? LC 81-64588. 1981. 9.95 (ISBN 0-89051-071-7, Pub. by Master Bks). Master Bks.
Gish, Duane T., jt. auth. see Morris, Henry M.
Gish, Duane T., ed. see Bliss, Richard.
Gish, Lillian & Pinchot, Ann. Lillian Gish: The Movies, Mr. Griffith & Me. (Illus.). 388p. 1983. pap. 9.95 (ISBN 0-13-536482-5). P-H.
Gish, Mark F. Pretty Things. 1983. 8.95 (ISBN 0-533-05150-9). Vantage.
Gish, Nancy K. Hugh MacDiarmid: The Man & His Work. 248p. 1984. 29.75 (ISBN 0-333-29473-4, Pub. by Salem Hse Ltd). Merrimack Pub Cir.
--Time in the Poetry of T. S. Eliot: A Study in Structure & Theme. 160p. 1981. 29.50x (ISBN 0-389-20192-8, 06957). B&N Imports.
Gish, Noel. Long Island Studies Program: Activity Manual. Yockstick, Elizabeth, ed. (Illus.). 111p. (gr. 4). 1981. Duplicate Masters 49.00 (ISBN 0-943068-10-X). Graphic Learning.
Gish, Noel J. Long Island Studies Program: Work-A-Text. Yockstick, Elizabeth, ed. (Illus.). 111p. (Orig.). 1981. wkbk. 3.50 (ISBN 0-943068-00-2); Teacher's Guide 5.00 (ISBN 0-943068-09-6). Graphic Learning.
Gish, O., ed. Crisis in the Public Sector--Challenge to the Public Health: American Public Health Association 1980 Meeting in Detroit, Michigan, USA. 48p. 1982. pap. 16.50 (ISBN 0-08-028948-7). Pergamon.
Gish, Oscar. Doctor Migration & World Health. 151p. 1971. pap. text ed. 6.75x (ISBN 0-7135-1611-9, Pub. by Bedford England). Brookfield Pub Co.
Gish, Oscar & Feller, L. Lee. Planning Pharmaceuticals for Primary Health Care: The Supply & Utilization of Drugs in the Third World. 138p. 1979. 5.00x (ISBN 0-87553-127-X, 066). Am Pub Health.
Gish, Robert. Hamlin Garland: The Far West. LC 76-45134. (Western Writers Ser.: No. 24). 1976. pap. 2.00x (ISBN 0-88430-023-4). Boise St Univ.
--Paul Horgan: Yankee Plainsman, No. 459. LC 83-12611. (United States Authors Ser.). 143p. 1983. lib. bdg. 16.95 (ISBN 0-8057-7399-1, Twayne). G K Hall.
Gishford, Anthony, tr. see Von Bulow, Hans & Strauss, Richard.
Gisler, Galen R. & Friel, Eileen D. Index of Galaxy Spectra. (Astronomy & Astrophysics Ser.: Vol. 10). 200p. 1979. 38.00x (ISBN 0-912918-19-5, 0919). Pachart Pub Hse.
Gisler, Margaret, jt. auth. see Eberts, Marjorie.
Gisolfi, A. M. & Coleman, C. Classical Italian Songs. 1955. 12.50x (ISBN 0-913298-64-6). S F Vanni.
Gispen, W. H. The Bible Student's Commentary: Exodus. (The Bible Student's Commentary). 352p. 1982. 15.95 (ISBN 0-310-43970-1). Zondervan.
--Brain Phosphoproteins: Characterization & Function: Proceedings of a Workshop at the State University of Utrecht, Sept. 1981. (Progress in Brain Research Ser.: Vol. 56). 454p. 1982. 89.25 (ISBN 0-444-80412-9, Biomedical Pr). Elsevier.
Gispen, W. H. & Traber, J., eds. Aging of the Brain. (Developments in Neurology Ser.: Vol. 7). 318p. 1984. 67.50 (ISBN 0-444-80546-X, I-008-84, Biomedical Pr). Elsevier.
Gissel, Sven & Jutikkala, E. Desertion & Land Colonization in the Nordic Countries, 1300-1600. (Scandinavian Research Project on Deserted Farms & Villages Ser.: Vol. 11). 304p. 1982. text ed. 13.50x (ISBN 91-22-00431-9, Pub. by Almqvist & Wiksell Sweden). Humanities.
Gisselquist, David. Oil Prices & Trade Deficits: U. S. Conflicts with Japan & West Germany. LC 79-20632. (Praeger Special Studies). 158p. 1980. 37.95 (ISBN 0-03-052381-8). Praeger.
--The Political Economics of International Bank Lending. LC 81-8636. 272p. 1981. 37.95 (ISBN 0-03-059377-8). Praeger.
Gisser, David G., jt. auth. see Carlson, A. Bruce.
Gisser, Micha. Intermediate Price Theory: Analysis, Issues & Applications. (Illus.). 672p. 1981. text ed. 31.95 (ISBN 0-07-023312-8). McGraw.
Gissing, Algernon, ed. see Gissing, George R.
Gissing, Ellen. Some Personal Recollections of George Gissing. 1929. lib. bdg. 8.50 (ISBN 0-8414-4652-0). Folcroft.
Gissing, Ellen, ed. see Gissing, George R.
Gissing, George. Autobiographical Notes. 59.95 (ISBN 0-87968-682-0). Gordon Pr.
--Born in Exile. Coustillas, Pierre, ed. (Society & the Victorians Ser.). 1978. text ed. 22.75x (ISBN 0-85527-872-2). Humanities.
--Born in Exile: A Novel, 3 Vols. in 1. LC 68-54266. Repr. of 1892 ed. 37.50 (ISBN 0-404-02786-5). AMS Pr.
--Charles Dickens. LC 73-21711. (Studies in Dickens, No. 52). 1974. lib. bdg. 43.95x (ISBN 0-8383-1774-X). Haskell.
--Critical Studies of Works of Charles Dickens. LC 65-26454. (Studies in Fiction, No. 34). 1969. Repr. of 1924 ed. lib. bdg. write for info. (ISBN 0-8383-0557-1). Haskell.
--Crown of Life. LC 72-80635. Repr. of 1899 ed. 24.50 (ISBN 0-404-02814-4). AMS Pr.
--Demos. 1983. pap. 8.95 (ISBN 0-901759-20-1, NO. 3876). Methuen Inc.
--Demos: A Story of English Socialism. LC 75-148786. Repr. of 1892 ed. 15.00 (ISBN 0-404-02778-4). AMS Pr.
--Denzil Quarrier. LC 79-80634. Repr. of 1892 ed. 18.50 (ISBN 0-404-02787-3). AMS Pr.
--The Emancipated. Coustillas, Pierre, ed. LC 77-80328. 469p. 1978. 22.50 (ISBN 0-8386-2171-6). Fairleigh Dickinson.
--Emanicipated: A Novel, 3 Vols. in 1. LC 74-75983. Repr. of 1890 ed. 30.00 (ISBN 0-404-02785-7). AMS Pr.
--Eve's Ransom. LC 74-87055. Repr. of 1895 ed. 18.50 (ISBN 0-404-02798-9). AMS Pr.
--Eve's Ransom. 125p. 1980. pap. 3.95 (ISBN 0-486-24016-9). Dover.
--The House of Cobwebs. 300p. 1980. Repr. of 1914 ed. lib. bdg. 25.00 (ISBN 0-89760-315-X). Telegraph Bks.
--Human Odds & Ends. Fletcher, Ian & Stokes, John, eds. LC 76-20076. (Decadent Consciousness Ser.). 1978. lib. bdg. 46.00 (ISBN 0-8240-2759-0). Garland Pub.
--In the Year of Jubilee. LC 75-80633. Repr. of 1894 ed. 21.50 (ISBN 0-404-02797-0). AMS Pr.
--In the Year of Jubilee. (Illus.). 416p. 1982. pap. 6.50 (ISBN 0-486-24251-X). Dover.
--Letters of George Gissing to Members of His Family. LC 77-130257. (English Literature Ser., No. 33). 1970. Repr. of 1927 ed. lib. bdg. 58.95x (ISBN 0-8383-1158-X). Haskell.
--A Life's Morning, 3 Vols. in 1. LC 76-75985. Repr. of 1888 ed. 30.00 (ISBN 0-404-02779-2). AMS Pr.
--A Life's Morning. 1947. 25.00 (ISBN 0-8274-2944-4). R West.
--A Life's Morning. Coustillas, Pierre, ed. 408p. (Orig.). 1985. pap. 8.95 (ISBN 0-416-01091-1, NO. 9282). Methuen Inc.
--Nether World. 1975. pap. 8.95x (ISBN 0-460-00362-3, Evman). Biblio Dist.
--The Nether World. Goode, John, ed. 469p. 24.50 (ISBN 0-8386-1543-0). Fairleigh Dickinson.
--The Nether World. 412p. 1982. pap. text ed. 6.95x (ISBN 0-460-01362-9, Pub. by Evman England). Biblio Dist.
--The Nether World. 1983. pap. 7.95 (ISBN 0-7108-0319-2, NO. 3877). Methuen Inc.
--New Grub Street. Bergonzi, Bernard, ed. (English Library). 1976. pap. 4.95 (ISBN 0-14-043032-6). Penguin.

--New Grub Street. Date not set. pap. 8.95 (ISBN 0-394-60525-X). Modern Lib.

--Odd Women, 3 Vols. in 1. LC 70-75986. Repr. of 1893 ed. 30.00 (ISBN 0-404-02788-1). AMS Pr.

--Odd Women. 1971. pap. 3.25 (ISBN 0-393-00610-7). Norton.

--The Odd Women. 1978. Repr. lib. bdg. 30.00 (ISBN 0-8492-4921-X). R West.

--The Odd Women. 1983. pap. 3.95 (ISBN 0-452-00645-7, Mer). NAL.

--Our Friend the Charlatan. LC 78-80631. Repr. of 1901 ed. 18.50 (ISBN 0-404-02815-2). AMS Pr.

--Paying Guest. LC 68-54267. Repr. of 1895 ed. 16.00 (ISBN 0-404-02799-7). AMS Pr.

--The Private Papers of Henry Ryecroft. 1914. 35.00 (ISBN 0-8495-6263-5). Arden Lib.

--The Private Papers of Henry Ryecroft. 1978. Repr. of 1914 ed. lib. bdg. 30.00 (ISBN 0-8492-4920-1). R West.

--The Private Papers of Henry Ryecroft. 1983. pap. 8.95 (ISBN 0-7108-0323-0, NO. 3878). Methuen Inc.

--Short Stories of Today & Yesterday. 1929. 25.00 (ISBN 0-8274-3408-1). R West.

--Sleeping Fires. LC 83-12402. iv, 101p. 1983. pap. 4.95 (ISBN 0-8032-7011-9, BB 852, Bison). U of Nebr Pr.

--Thyrza: A Tale, 3 Vols. in 1. LC 72-75984. Repr. of 1893 ed. 30.00 (ISBN 0-404-02789-X). AMS Pr.

--Thyrza: A Tale. Korg, Jacob, ed. 495p. 24.50 (ISBN 0-8386-1544-9). Fairleigh Dickinson.

--Thyrza: A Tale. King, Jacob, ed. 528p. (Orig.). 1985. pap. 7.95 (NO. 9280). Methuen Inc.

--Town Traveller. LC 68-54268. Repr. of 1898 ed. 18.00 (ISBN 0-404-02813-6). AMS Pr.

--The Town Traveller. 247p. 1980. Repr. of 1927 ed. lib. bdg. 25.00 (ISBN 0-89984-231-3). Century Bookbindery.

--The Town Traveller. 1979. Repr. of 1898 ed. lib. bdg. 30.00 (ISBN 0-8492-4931-7). R West.

--The Town Traveller. 279p. 1981. Repr. of 1798 ed. lib. bdg. 20.00 (ISBN 0-89760-320-6). Telegraph Bks.

--The Town Traveller. Coustillas, Pierre, ed. 324p. 1981. text ed. 21.50x (ISBN 0-85527-902-8, Pub. by Harvester England). Humanities.

--Unclassed. LC 68-54269. Repr. of 1896 ed. 15.00 (ISBN 0-404-02811-X). AMS Pr.

--The Unclassed. 1983. pap. 10.95 (ISBN 0-686-47743-X, NO. 3879). Methuen Inc.

--Veranilda: A Romance. LC 68-54270. Repr. of 1904 ed. 15.00 (ISBN 0-404-02816-0). AMS Pr.

--Whirlpool. LC 71-80632. Repr. of 1897 ed. 18.00 (ISBN 0-404-02812-8). AMS Pr.

--The Whirlpool. Parinder, Patrick, ed. LC 77-80329. 467p. 24.50 (ISBN 0-8386-2172-4). Fairleigh Dickinson.

--The Whirlpool. 464p. (Orig.). 1984. pap. 7.95 (ISBN 0-7012-1910-6). Merrimack Pub Cir.

--The Whirlpool. Parrinder, Patrick, ed. 496p. (Orig.). 1985. pap. 7.95 (ISBN 0-416-01081-4, NO. 9281). Methuen Inc.

--Will Warburton: A Romance of Real Life. LC 71-98635. Repr. of 1905 ed. 10.00 (ISBN 0-404-02817-9). AMS Pr.

--Workers in the Dawn, 3 Vols. in 1. LC 68-59358. Repr. of 1880 ed. 55.00 (ISBN 0-404-02777-6). AMS Pr.

--Workers in the Dawn. Coustillas, Pierre, ed. 920p. (Orig.). 1985. pap. 8.95 (ISBN 0-416-01101-2, NO. 9283). Methuen Inc.

Gissing, George R. Charles Dickens: A Critical Study. LC 75-145043. 324p. 1972. Repr. of 1898 ed. 39.00 (ISBN 0-403-00480-2). Scholarly.

--House of Cobwebs. facsimile ed. LC 77-160932. (Short Story Index Reprint Ser.). Repr. of 1906 ed. 20.00 (ISBN 0-8369-3911-5). Ayer Co Pubs.

--Immortal Dickens. LC 26-1214. 1969. Repr. of 1925 ed. 16.00 (ISBN 0-527-33700-5). Kraus Repr.

--The Letters of George Gissing to Eduard Bertz: 1887-1903. Young, Arthur C., ed. LC 80-12936. xl, 337p. 1980. Repr. of 1961 ed. lib. bdg. 37.50x (ISBN 0-313-22454-4, GILE). Greenwood.

--Letters of George Gissing to Members of His Family. 1927. 21.00 (ISBN 0-403-00480-2). Scholarly.

--Letters to Members of His Family. Gissing, Algernon & Gissing, Ellen, eds. LC 26-1214. Repr. of 1927 ed. 26.00 (ISBN 0-527-33720-X). Kraus Repr.

--Victim of Circumstances, & Other Stories. facsimile ed. LC 73-169551. (Short Story Index Reprint Ser.). Repr. of 1927 ed. 17.00 (ISBN 0-8369-4013-X). Ayer Co Pubs.

Gisslen, W. Professional Banking. 346p. 1985. 26.95 (ISBN 0-471-88668-8); Trade Ed. 28.95 (ISBN 0-471-81444-X). Wiley.

Gisslen, Wayne. Professional Cooking. LC 82-2610. 680p. 1983. 29.95 (ISBN 0-471-86758-6); text ed. 34.95 (ISBN 0-471-08248-1); tchr's. manual avail. (ISBN 0-471-89521-0). Wiley.

Gist, Jerre W., jt. auth. see Welch, Michael W.

Gist, Margaret A. Love & War in the Middle English Romances. LC 78-63499. Repr. of 1947 ed. 30.00 (ISBN 0-404-17147-8). AMS Pr.

Gist, N. P. & Fava, S. F. Urban Society. 6th ed. 1974. text ed. 24.75 scp (ISBN 0-690-00493-1, HarpC). Har-Row.

Gitanjali. Poems of Gitanjali. 128p. 1982. (Oriel); pap. 9.95 (ISBN 0-85362-202-7). Routledge & Kegan.

Gitchel, Sam & Foster, Lorri. Let's Talk about...S E X: A Read & Discuss Guide for People 9 to 12 & Their Parents. (Illus.). 59p. (gr. 4-7). 1983. pap. 4.95 (ISBN 0-9610122-0-X). Plan Par Fresno.

Gitchel, Sam, jt. auth. see Foster, Lorri.

Giteau, Cecile. Dictionnaire des Arts du Spectacle: Theatre, Cinema, Cirque, Danse, Radio... 456p. (Fr., Eng. & Ger.). 1970. 52.50 (ISBN 0-686-57302-1, M-6276). French & Eur.

Gitelman, Howard M. Workingmen of Waltham: Mobility in American Urban Industrial Development, 1850-1890. LC 74-6822. (Illus.). 208p. 1974. 19.50x (ISBN 0-8018-1570-3). Johns Hopkins.

Gitelman, Morton, jt. auth. see Wright, Robert R.

Gitelman, Zvi. Becoming Israelis: Political Resocialization of Soviet & American Immigrants. LC 82-634. (Israeli Studies). 384p. 1982. 28.95x (ISBN 0-03-061374-4). Praeger.

Gitelman, Zvi Y. Jewish Nationality & Soviet Politics: The Jewish Sections of the CPSU, 1917-1930. LC 77-154996. (Research Institute on Communist Affairs Ser.). 488p. 1972. 50.00 (ISBN 0-691-07542-5). Princeton U Pr.

Gitelson, Alan, jt. ed. see Dubnick, Mel.

Gitelson, Alan R., et al. American Political Parties: Stability & Change. LC 83-81461. 432p. 1984. text ed. 19.95 (ISBN 0-395-34360-7); instr's. manual 2.00 (ISBN 0-395-34361-5). HM.

Gitelson, Maxwell. Psychoanalysis: Science & Profession. LC 72-8789. xiv, 439p. 40.00 (ISBN 0-8236-5255-6). Intl Univs Pr.

Gitelson, Susan A., jt. ed. see Curtis, Michael.

Gitenstein, Judy. Summer Camp. (Skylark Choose Your Own Adventure Ser.: No. 18). (gr. 2-4). 1984. pap. 1.95 (ISBN 0-553-15262-9, Skylark). Bantam.

Githens, John, tr. see Halbritter, Kurt.

Githens, Thomas S. Drug Plants of Africa. (African Handbooks Ser.: Vol. 8). 125p. 1949. 6.75x (ISBN 0-686-24086-3). Univ Mus of U.

Githens, Thomas S. & Wood, Carroll E. Jr. Food Resources of Africa. (African Handbooks Ser.: Vol. 3). (Illus.). 105p. 1943. 7.50x (ISBN 0-686-24087-1). Univ Mus of U PA.

Gitin, David. City Air. LC 73-91971. 52p. 1974. 5.95 (ISBN 0-87886-042-8); pap. 2.95 (ISBN 0-87886-041-X). Ithaca Hse.

--Guitar Against the Wall. 60p. 1972. 6.00 (ISBN 0-915572-08-7). Panjandrum.

--Legwork. 1977. signed 15.00 (ISBN 0-685-88995-5); in wrappers 3.00 (ISBN 0-685-88996-3). Oyez.

--This Once: New & Selected Poems, 1965-1978. LC 79-1108. (The Selected Works Ser.: No. 3). 1979. 17.95 (ISBN 0-912652-48-9); signed & numbered 29.95x (ISBN 0-912652-50-0); pap. 7.95 (ISBN 0-912652-49-7). Blue Wind.

Gitin, Maria. Little Movies. LC 75-302547. 59p. 1975. 3.50 (ISBN 0-87886-051-7). Ithaca Hse.

--The Melting Pot. LC 77-15580. (Illus.). 1977. 15.95 (ISBN 0-912278-94-3); pap. 6.95 (ISBN 0-912278-95-1). Crossing Pr.

--Night Shift. LC 77-21969. (Orig.). 1978. pap. 5.95 (ISBN 0-912652-37-3, Dynamite Bks). Blue Wind.

Gitisetan, Dariush. Iran: Politics & Government under the Pahlavis; An Annotated Bibliography. LC 84-23587. 214p. 1985. 15.00 (ISBN 0-8108-1770-5). Scarecrow.

Gitler, Carlos, jt. ed. see Estrada, Sergio.

Gitler, Ira. Jazz Masters of the Forties. (Roots of Jazz Ser.). 290p. 1982. lib. bdg. 25.00 (ISBN 0-306-76155-6); pap. 8.95 (ISBN 0-306-80224-4). Da Capo.

--Jazz Masters of the Forties. (Quality Paperbacks Ser.). (Illus.). 300p. 1984. pap. 8.95 (ISBN 0-306-80224-4). Da Capo.

--Swing to Bop: An Oral History of Jazz in the 1940s. 352p. 1985. 19.95 (ISBN 0-19-503664-6). Oxford U Pr.

Gitler, Ira, jt. auth. see Feather, Leonard.

Gitlin. Inside Prime Time. Date not set. pap. 8.95 (ISBN 0-394-73787-3). Pantheon.

Gitlin, Richard A. Bankruptcy Code & Real Estate Lenders: Troubled Real Estate Loans & Documentation. LC 82-62770. (Real Estate Law & Practice Course Handbook Ser.: No. 225). 158p. 1983. 35.00. PLI.

Gitlin, Todd. Inside Prime Time. LC 83-42818. 352p. 1983. 16.45 (ISBN 0-394-53308-9). Pantheon.

--The Whole World Is Watching: Mass Media in the Making & Unmaking of the New Left. LC 78-68835. 1980. 14.95 (ISBN 0-520-03889-4); pap. 7.95 (ISBN 0-520-04024-4, CAL 454). U of Cal Pr.

Gitlitz, David, tr. see Calderon de la Barca, Pedro.

Gitlitz, David M., tr. from Span. Francisco de Quevado: Songs of Love & Death & in between. 298p. 1980. 15.00x (ISBN 0-87291-145-4). Coronado Pr.

Gitlitz, James P. New York Uncontested Divorces & Annulments. 200p. 25.00 (ISBN 0-87526-258-9). Gould.

--Uncontested Divorces & Annulments in New York. 2nd ed. 175p. (Supplemented annually). text ed. 25.00. Gould.

Gitlitz, Jonah, intro. by. Fact Book on Direct Marketing: Nineteen Eighty-Five Statistical Update. 8th, rev. ed. (Illus.). 303p. 1985. pap. 79.95 (ISBN 0-933641-00-1); pap. 49.95 member (ISBN 0-317-18926-3). Direct Mktng Assn.

Gitlow, Abraham L. Economics of the Mount Hagen Tribes, New Guinea. LC 48-6051. (American Ethnological Society Monographs: No. 12). (Illus.). 124p. 1947. 15.00x (ISBN 0-295-74071-X). U of Wash Pr.

Gitlow, Benjamin. I Confess. LC 72-1243. (Select Bibliography Reprint Ser.). 1972. Repr. of 1940 ed. 29.00 (ISBN 0-8369-6825-5). Ayer Co Pubs.

--I Confess. LC 75-318. (The Radical Tradition in America). 619p. 1975. Repr. of 1940 ed. 35.75 (ISBN 0-88355-221-3). Hyperion Conn.

--Whole of Their Lives. (Americanist Classics Ser.). 1965. pap. 1.00 pocketsize (ISBN 0-88279-014-5). Western Islands.

--Whole of Their Lives: Communism in America - a Personal History & Intimate Portrayal of Its Leaders. LC 78-179726. (Biography Index Reprint Ser.). Repr. of 1948 ed. 22.50 (ISBN 0-8369-8094-8). Ayer Co Pubs.

Gitlow, Howard S. Stat City: Understanding Statistics through Realistic Applications. 1982. pap. 15.25x (ISBN 0-256-02654-8). Irwin.

Gitlow, Stanley E. & Peyser, Herbert. Alcoholism: A Practical Treatment Guide. 304p. 1980. 24.50 (ISBN 0-318-15286-X). Natl Coun Alcoholism.

Gitlow, Stanley E. & Peyser, Herbert, eds. Alcoholism: A Practical Treatment Guide. 304p. 1980. 39.50 (ISBN 0-8089-1227-5, 791555). Grune.

Gitman, et al. Business World. 2nd ed. 1986. pap. price not set (ISBN 0-471-82305-8). Wiley.

Gitman, L. & Woodford-Williams, E., eds. Research, Training & Practice in Clinical Medicine of Aging. (Interdisciplinary Topics in Gerontology: Vol. 5). 1970. 15.00 (ISBN 3-8055-0505-1). S Karger.

Gitman, L. J. & Robana, A. Portstrat: A Portfolio Strategy Simulation. 232p. 1982. pap. 22.95 (ISBN 0-471-08416-6). Wiley.

Gitman, Larry & Moses, Edward A. Financial Management: Cases. 1978. text ed. 25.95 (ISBN 0-8299-0167-1); instr's. manual avail. (ISBN 0-8299-0480-8). West Pub.

Gitman, Lawrence J. Fundamentos De Administracion Financiera. Herrera, Jesus V. & Mei Mei Alicia Chu Polido, eds. Restrepo, Carlos S., tr. from Eng. (Span.). 1978. text ed. 18.30 (ISBN 0-06-313160-9, Pub. by HarLA Mexico). Har-Row.

--Personal Finance. 3rd ed. 750p. 1984. text ed. 30.95x (ISBN 0-03-068911-2); instr's. manual 20.00 (ISBN 0-03-068912-0). Dryden Pr.

--Principles of Managerial Finance. 3rd ed. 800p. 1982. text ed. 30.50 scp (ISBN 0-06-042334-X, HarpC); scp study guide 12.95 (ISBN 0-06-042333-1); instr's manual and test bank avail. (ISBN 0-06-362363-3); transparency master avail. Har-Row.

--Principles of Managerial Finance. 4th ed. 800p. 1985. text ed. 30.50 scp (ISBN 0-06-042357-9, HarpC); instr's. manual avail. (ISBN 0-06-362376-5); trans. master avail. (ISBN 0-06-362377-3); test bank avail. (ISBN 0-06-362234-3). Har-Row.

Gitman, Lawrence J. & Joehnk, Michael D. Fundamentals of Investing. 2nd ed. 782p. 1984. text ed. 27.50 scp (ISBN 0-06-042355-2, HarpC); scp instr's. manual 8.50 (ISBN 0-06-362373-0); scp study guide 12.95 (ISBN 0-06-042356-0). Har-Row.

Gitman, Lawrence J. & McDaniel, Carl. Student Study Guide to Accompany Business World. 229p. 1983. pap. 12.95 (ISBN 0-471-86390-4). Wiley.

--Workbook for Slide Lecture Program to Accompany Business World. 290p. 1983. pap. 16.00 (ISBN 0-471-88708-0). Wiley.

Gitman, Lawrence J. & Moses, Edward A. Financial Management Cases. 2nd ed. (Illus.). 450p. 1984. text ed. 30.95 (ISBN 0-314-78008-4); write for info. instr's. manual (ISBN 0-314-78010-6). West Pub.

Gitman, Lawrence J., et al. Managerial Finance: Theory & Practice. LC 84-15647. 1025p. 1984. text ed. 32.50 scp (ISBN 0-06-042336-6, HarpC). Har-Row.

Gitman, Lawrence J., Jr., ed. Business World. McDaniel, Carl. LC 82-17577. 662p. 1983. 26.95 (ISBN 0-471-08165-5); tchr's. manual avail. (ISBN 0-471-87095-1). Wiley.

Gitman, Leo. Endocrines & Aging. (Illus.). 320p. 1967. photocopy ed. 27.50x (ISBN 0-398-00685-7). C C Thomas.

Gitnick, Gary. Gastroenterology. (Medical Outline Ser.). 1984. pap. text ed. write for info (ISBN 0-87488-172-2). Med Exam.

--Handbook of Gastrointestinal Emergencies. 1982. pap. text ed. 28.95 (ISBN 0-87488-057-2). Med Exam.

Gitnick, Gary, ed. Controversies in Gastroenterology. (Illus.). 296p. 1984. text ed. 30.00 (ISBN 0-443-08236-7). Churchill.

Gitnick, Gary L. Gastroenterology. LC 82-23686. (Internal Medicine Today: A Comprehensive Postgraduate Library: A Comprehensive Postgraduate Library). 425p. 1983. 35.00 (ISBN 0-471-09566-4, Pub. by Wiley Med). Wiley.

Gitsch, E. & Reinold, E., eds. Jahrestagung der Bayerischen Gesellschaft fuer Geburtshilfe und der Oesterreichischen Gesellschaft fuer Gynaekologie und Geburtshilfe, Muenchen, Juni 1981. (Gynaekologische Rundschau Journal: Vol. 21, Suppl. 2). (Illus.). vii, 234p. 1981. pap. 22.25 (ISBN 3-8055-3478-7). S Karger.

--Jahrestagung der Bayerischen Gesellschaft fuer Geburtshilfe und Frauenheilkunde und der Oesterreichischen Gesellschaft fuer Gynaekologie und Geburtshilfe, Velden am Woerthersee, Juni 1983. (Journal: Gynaekologische Rundschau: Vol. 23, Suppl. 3). (Illus.). viii, 244p. 1984. pap. 23.50 (ISBN 3-8055-3802-2). S Karger.

--Jahrestagung der Oesterreichischen Gesellschaft fuer Gynaekologie und Geburtshilfe, Bad Ischl, Juni 1982. (Journal: Gynaekologische Rundschau: Vol. 22, Supplement 1). (Illus.). vi, 190p. 1982. 21.50 (ISBN 3-8055-3625-9). S Karger.

--Jahrestagung der Oesterreichischen Gesellschaft fuer Gynaekologie und Mitterndorf, Juni 1984. (Illus.). vi, 190p. 1985. pap. 23.50 (ISBN 3-8055-4013-2). S Karger.

Gitsch, E., ed. see Janisch, H., et al.

Gitsch, Eduard & Palmrich, Adolf. Gynecological Operative Anatomy: The Simple & Radical Hysterectomy Atlas. (Illus.). 1977. 84.00x (ISBN 3-11-006691-2). De Gruyter.

Gittell, Marilyn, et al. School Boards & School Policy: An Evaluation of Decentralization in New York City. LC 72-92475. (Special Studies in U. S. Social, Political & Economic Issues Ser.). (Illus.). 1973. text ed. 24.00x (ISBN 0-89197-929-8); pap. text ed. 12.50x (ISBN 0-89197-930-1). Irvington.

--Local Control in Education: Three Demonstration School Districts in New York City. LC 73-185779. (Special Studies in U.S. Economic, Social & Political Issues). 1972. 24.50x (ISBN 0-89197-827-5); pap. text ed. 12.50x (ISBN 0-89197-828-3). Irvington.

--Limits to Citizen Participation: The Decline of Community Organizations. LC 80-15950. (Sage Library of Social Research: Vol. 109). (Illus.). 280p. 1980. 28.00 (ISBN 0-8039-1478-4). Sage.

Gittelman, Martin, ed. Strategic Intervention for Hyperactive Children. LC 81-14407. 244p. 1981. 27.50 (ISBN 0-87332-202-9). M E Sharpe.

Gittelman, Philip, jt. auth. see Krefetz, Gerald.

Gittelman-Klein, Rachel. Recent Advances in Child Psychopharmacology. LC 76-15118. 272p. 1975. text ed. 26.95 (ISBN 0-87705-260-3). Human Sci Pr.

Gittelsohn, Alan, et al. Annotated Bibliography of Cause-of-Death Validation Studies: 1958-1979. 60p. 1981. pap. text ed. 1.95 (ISBN 0-8406-0236-7). Natl Ctr Health Stats.

Gittelsohn, Roland B. The Extra Dimension. 228p. 1983. pap. 7.95 (ISBN 0-8074-0170-6, 168500). UAHC.

--Love, Sex & Marriage: A Jewish View. (Illus.). (gr. 10-12). 1980. pap. 7.95x (ISBN 0-8074-0046-7, 142683). UAHC.

--Wings of the Morning: Little Lower than the Angels. rev. ed. (Illus.). (gr. 10). 1969. text ed. 7.00 (ISBN 0-8074-0194-3, 161850). wkbk. 2.25 (ISBN 0-8074-0196-X, 161852). UAHC.

Gittelson, Bernard. Biorhythm: A Personal Science. rev. ed. 1984. pap. 3.95 (ISBN 0-446-32276-8). Warner Bks.

Gittelson, Celia. Saving Grace. LC 81-47520. 224p. 1981. 10.95 (ISBN 0-394-51776-8). Knopf.

Gittelson, Natalie. Dominus: A Woman Looks at Men's Lives. 304p. 1978. 10.00 (ISBN 0-374-14177-0). FS&G.

Gitter, A. George & Grunin, Robert, eds. Communication: A Guide to Information Sources. LC 79-54692. (Psychology Information Guide Ser.: Vol. 3). 1980. 60.00x (ISBN 0-8103-1443-6). Gale.

Gitter, Kurt A. & Fisher, Pat. Japenese Fan Paintings From Western Collection. LC 84-19097. 136p. 1985. 24.95 (ISBN 0-295-96282-8). U of Wash Pr.

Gitter, Lena L. Montessori Approach to Special Education: An Equipment, Teaching & Feedback Manual. LC 75-171955. 1971. pap. 9.95 (ISBN 0-685-90520-9). Mafex.

Gitter, Samuel, ed. Algebraic Topology, Symposium in Honor of Jose Adem: Proceedings. LC 82-13812. (Contemporary Mathematics Ser.: Vol. 12). 372p. 1982. pap. 24.00 (ISBN 0-8218-5010-5, CONM-12). Am Math.

Gitterman, Alex, jt. auth. see Germain, Carel.

Gitterman, Alex see Shulman, Lawrence.

Gitterman, John, tr. see Oppenheimer, Franz.

Gitterman, John M., tr. see Oppenheimer, Franz.

Gitterman, M. & Halpern, V., eds. Qualitative Analysis of Physical Problems. LC 80-767. 1981. 27.00 (ISBN 0-12-285150-1). Acad Pr.

Gittinger, J. Price. Compounding & Discounting Tables for Project Analysis: With a Guide to Their Applications. 2nd, rev. ed. LC 84-49364. 1984. pap. text ed. 10.95x (ISBN 0-8018-2409-5). Johns Hopkins.

--Economic Analysis of Agricultural Projects. 2nd ed. LC 82-15262. (World Bank Ser.). 525p. 1982. text ed. 37.50x (ISBN 0-8018-2912-7); pap. text ed. 14.95x (ISBN 0-8018-2913-5). Johns Hopkins.

--North American Agriculture in a New World. (Illus.). 85p. 1970. 2.00 (ISBN 0-88806-089-0, CAC30). Inst C D Howe.

Gittinger, John W., Jr. Ophthalmology: A Clinical Introduction. 267p. 1984. pap. text ed. 18.95 (ISBN 0-316-31470-6). Little.

Gittinger, Mattiebelle. Master Dyers to the World: Technique & Trade in Early Indian Dyed Cotton Textiles. McEuen, Caroline K., ed. (Illus.). 208p. 1982. pap. 20.00 (ISBN 0-87405-020-0). Textile Mus.

--Splendid Symbols: Textiles & Tradition in Indonesia. LC 79-50373. (Illus.). 240p. (Orig.). 1979. pap. 20.00 (ISBN 0-87405-011-1). Textile Mus.

Gittings, Clare. Death, Burial & the Individual in Early Modern England. 224p. 1984. 34.50 (ISBN 0-7099-1167-X, Pub. by Croom Helm Ltd). Longwood Pub Group.

Gittings, Elisa. Shape Books. (Illus., Orig.). (gr. k-3). 1974. pap. 3.95 (ISBN 0-918932-40-8). Activity Resources.

Gittings, James A. Bread, Meat & Raisins after the Dance. LC 77-83883. 1977. 7.00 (ISBN 0-89430-006-7). Palos Verdes.

Gittings, John. The Role of the Chinese Army. LC 80-28560. xix, 331p. 1981. Repr. of 1967 ed. lib. bdg. 32.50x (ISBN 0-313-22879-5, GIRC). Greenwood.

--Role of the Chinese Army. (Royal Institute of International Affairs Ser.). 1967. 19.95x (ISBN 0-19-500160-5). Oxford U Pr.

Gittings, R., jt. auth. see Manton, Jo.

Gittings, Robert. Collected Poems. 1976. pap. text ed. 16.00x (ISBN 0-435-14359-X). Heinemann Ed.

--John Keats: The Living Year Twenty-One September Eighteen Eighteen to Twenty-One September Eighteen Nineteen. LC 78-6098. (Illus.). 247p. 1978. Repr. of 1968 ed. lib. bdg. 24.75x (ISBN 0-313-20390-3, GIJK). Greenwood.

--The Mask of Keats. 174p. 1979. Repr. lib. bdg. 25.00 (ISBN 0-89987-303-0). Darby Bks.

--The Nature of Biography. LC 78-3136. (The Jessie & John Danz Lecture Ser.). 1978. 10.00x (ISBN 0-295-95604-6); pap. 4.95x (ISBN 0-295-96046-9). U of Wash Pr.

--People, Places, Personal. 64p. 1985. pap. 8.95 (ISBN 0-436-17980-6, Pub. by Secker & Warburg). David & Charles.

--Shakespeare's Rival. LC 76-3689. (Illus.). 138p. 1976. Repr. of 1960 ed. lib. bdg. 24.75x (ISBN 0-8371-8814-8, GISR). Greenwood.

Gittings, Robert & Manton, Jo. Dorothy Wordsworth. (Illus.). 1985. 17.95 (ISBN 0-19-818519-7). Oxford U Pr.

--The Second Mrs. Hardy. LC 79-63567. (Illus.). 1979. 14.95x (ISBN 0-295-95668-2). U of Wash Pr.

Gittings, Robert, ed. Selected Poems & Letters of Keats. (The Poetry Bookshelf). 1966. pap. text ed. 4.00x (ISBN 0-435-15045-6). Heinemann Ed.

Gittings, Robert, ed. see Keats, John.

Gittings, Robert, jt. ed. see Reeves, James.

Gittins, jt. auth. see Bergman.

Gittins, A. R., jt. ed. see Stark, R. W.

Gittins, Anne. Tales from the South Pacific Islands. LC 76-5411. (Illus.). 96p. (gr. 3 up). 1977. 4.95 (ISBN 0-916144-02-X). Stemmer Hse.

Gittins, Diana. Fair Sex: Family Size & Structure in Britain, 1930-39. LC 81-21248. 256p. 1982. 27.50x (ISBN 0-312-27962-0). St Martin.

--Fair Sex: Family Size & Structure 1900-39. 256p. 1982. cased 50.00x (ISBN 0-686-44685-2, Pub. by Hutchinson); pap. 30.00x (ISBN 0-686-44686-0). State Mutual Bk.

Gittins, H. Leigh. Pocatello Portrait: The Early Years, Eighteen Seventy-Eight to Nineteen Twenty-Eight. LC 82-50896. (Illus.). 224p. 1983. 19.95 (ISBN 0-89301-089-8). U Pr of Idaho.

Gittins, L., ed. see International Conference on the Hydraulic Transport of Solids in Pipes.

Gittins, Lavinia. Wear in Slurry Pipelines. (BHRA Information Ser.). (Illus.). 173p. (Orig.). 1980. pap. 41.00x (ISBN 0-906085-45-4). BHRA Fluid.

Gittins, Mark J., jt. auth. see Home, R. W.

Gittins, R. Canonical Analysis. (Biomathematics Ser.: Vol. 12). (Illus.). 320p. 1984. 45.00 (ISBN 0-387-13617-7). Springer-Verlag.

Gittleman, Edwin. Jones Very: The Effective Years, 1833-1840. LC 67-16202. 436p. 1967. 34.00x (ISBN 0-231-03043-6). Columbia U Pr.

Gittleman, Ron. Christmas for Classical Guitar. 1980. pap. 5.95 (ISBN 0-8256-9981-9). Music Sales.

Gittleman, Sol. Frank Wedekind. LC 68-28489. 1980. Repr. 11.95 (ISBN 0-8044-2233-8). Ungar.

--From Shtetl to Suburbia: The Family in Jewish Literary Imagination. LC 78-53646. 1978. 12.95x (ISBN 0-8070-6364-9, BP-591); pap. 5.95 (ISBN 0-8070-6365-7). Beacon Pr.

--Sholom Aleichem: A Non-Critical Introduction. (De Proprietatibus Litterarum Ser. Didactica: No. 3). 1974. pap. text ed. 13.60x (ISBN 90-2792-606-9). Mouton.

Gittler, Joseph. Jewish Life in the United States. 208p. 1981. 25.00x (ISBN 0-8147-2982-7). NYU Pr.

Gittler, Josephine. Standards Relating to Juvenile Probation Function: Intake & Predisposition Investigative Services. LC 77-3257. (IJA-ABA Juvenile Justice Standards Project Ser.). 208p. 1980. prof ref 22.50 (ISBN 0-88410-248-3); pap. 12.50 (ISBN 0-88410-828-7). Ballinger Pub.

Gittleson, Celia. Saving Grace. (Fiction Ser.). 256p. 1985. pap. 3.95 (ISBN 0-14-007789-8). Penguin.

Gittleson, Stephen & Pirisino, Jim. Filing System for Apple Writer: Minute Manual for WPL. 200p. 1985. bk. & software disk 99.95 (ISBN 0-913131-11-3). Minuteware.

Gittner, Louis. Listen Listen Listen. Farish, Starr, ed. 320p. (Orig.). 1980. pap. 8.95 (ISBN 0-9605492-0-X). Touch Heart.

--There Is a Rainbow. (Illus.). 65p. (Orig.). 1981. pap. 5.95 (ISBN 0-9605492-1-8). Touch Heart.

--Words from the Source. Steiger, Brad, ed. 168p. 1975. 8.95 (ISBN 0-13-963348-0). Touch Heart.

Gittus, J. Cavities & Cracks in Creep & Fatigue. 1981. 61.00 (ISBN 0-85334-965-7, Pub. by Elsevier Applied Sci England). Elsevier.

--Creep, Viscoelasticity & Creep Fracture in Solids. (Illus.). 725p. 1975. 92.50 (ISBN 0-85334-597-X, Pub. by Elsevier Applied Sci England). Elsevier.

--Irradiation Effects in Crystalline Solids. (Illus.). 523p. 1978. 81.50 (ISBN 0-85334-778-6, Pub. by Elsevier Applied Sci England). Elsevier.

Gittus, John H., ed. Water Reactor Fuel Element Performance: Computer Modeling. (Illus.). 728p. 1983. 192.50 (ISBN 0-85334-217-2, I-171-83, Pub. by Elsevier Applied Sci England). Elsevier.

Gitzelmann, Richard, jt. ed. see Cockburn, Forrester.

Gitzen, Walter, ed. Alumina as a Ceramic Material. 16.00 (ISBN 0-916094-46-4). Am Ceramic.

Giuberti, F. Materials for a Study on Twelfth Century Scholasticism. (History of Logic Ser.: Vol. II). 158p. 1982. 32.50x (Pub. by Bibliopolis Italy); pap. text ed. 18.45x (ISBN 88-7088-056-7). Humanities.

Giudice, G. The Sea Urchin Embryo: A Developmental Biological System. (Illus.). 260p. 1985. 49.00 (ISBN 0-387-15353-5). Springer-Verlag.

Giudice, Giovanni. Developmental Biology of the Sea Urchin Embryo. 1973. 76.50 (ISBN 0-12-285750-X). Acad Pr.

Giudice, Luisa Del, ed. Western Jerusalem: University of California Studies on Tasso. LC 84-20560. (Italian Literary Studies). 150p. (Orig.). 1985. pap. 12.95 (ISBN 0-915570-22-X). Oolp Pr.

Giuffey, George R. see Dryden, John.

Giuliana, Emilio R., ed. Two-Dimensional Real-Time Ultrasonic Imaging of the Heart. 1985. lib. bdg. 92.50 (ISBN 0-89838-671-3, Pub. by Martinus Nijhoff Netherlands). Kluwer Academic.

Giuliani. Heart Disease. 1985. 75.00 (ISBN 0-8151-3495-9). Year Bk Med.

Giuliani, George, jt. auth. see Minge, M. Ronald.

Giuliani, George A., jt. auth. see Bowman, Thomas F.

Giuliani, Peter A. & Watts, Duane E. Financial Management of Law Firms. 114p. pap. 25.00 (ISBN 0-89707-063-1). Chicago Review.

--Management Controls & Reporting. 61p. pap. 25.00 (ISBN 0-89707-064-X). Chicago Review.

Giuliano, Francis A., ed. Introduction to Oil & Gas Technology. 2nd ed. (Short Course Handbooks). (Illus.). 194p. 1981. text ed. 32.00 (ISBN 0-934634-48-3); pap. text ed. 24.00. Intl Human Res.

Giuliano, Mariani, ed. Pathophysiology of Plasma Protein Metabolism. 416p. 1985. 59.50x (ISBN 0-306-41771-5, Plenum Pr). Plenum Pub.

Giuliano, Vincent. Into the Information Age, a Perspective for Federal Action on Information. 142p. 1979. 9.00 (ISBN 0-317-36993-8). ALA.

Giuliano, Vincent, et al. Into the Information Age: A Perspective for Federal Action on Information. 142p. 1979. pap. text ed. 9.00x (ISBN 0-8389-0283-9). ALA.

Giuliano, William, ed. see Vallejo, Antonio B.

Giumarra, Nancy, ed. see Curran, June.

Giurescu, Anca. Les Mots Composés Dans les Langues Romanes. (Janua Linguarum, Series Practica: No. 228). 172p. (Fr.). 1976. pap. text ed. 21.60x (ISBN 90-2793-481-9). Mouton.

Giurgea, Corneliu E. Fundamentals to a Pharmacology of the Mind. (Illus.). 472p. 1981. 37.75x (ISBN 0-398-04130-X). C C Thomas.

Giurgola, Aldo & Mitchell, Ehrman. Mitchell-Giurgola Architects. LC 83-42909. (Illus.). 288p. 1984. pap. 29.95 (ISBN 0-8478-0495-X). Rizzoli Intl.

Giuseffi, Mary S. Too Much Rain: An Abortion Journal. (Illus.). 36p. (Orig.). 1984. pap. 4.00 (ISBN 0-9613645-0-5). Giuseffi-Crum Ent.

Giuseppi, Montague S. Naturalization of Foreign Protestants in the American & West Indian Colonies, Etc. LC 64-19759. 196p. 1979. Repr. of 1921 ed. 14.00 (ISBN 0-8063-0157-0). Genealog Pub.

Giusti, P., jt. auth. see Ciardelli, F.

Giusti, P., jt. ed. see Chiellini, E.

Giusti-Lanham, Hedy. Cooking for Company. 256p. 1983. pap. 9.95 (ISBN 0-8120-2699-3). Barron.

Giusti-Lanham, Hedy & Dodi, Andrea. The Cuisine of Venice. LC 78-8539. 1978. 19.95 (ISBN 0-8120-5138-6). Barron.

Giustiniani, Sebastiano. Four Years at the Court of Henry VIII, 2 Vols. Brown, Rawdon, tr. from It. LC 75-133813. Repr. of 1854 ed. 62.50 (ISBN 0-404-02836-5). AMS Pr.

Givans, Cheryl. The Winter of My Loneliness. 1984. 5.75 (ISBN 0-8062-2145-3). Carlton.

Givant, Steven, jt. ed. see McKenzie, Ralph.

Givargizov, E. I., ed. Growth of Crystals, Vol. 13. 380p. 1985. 65.00x (ISBN 0-306-18113-4, Consultants). Plenum Pub.

Givehchian, Fatemeh, jt. auth. see Ghanoonparvar, Mohammad R.

Givel, J. C. & Saegesser, F., eds. Colo-Proctology. (Illus.). 190p. 1984. pap. 21.50 (ISBN 0-387-12557-4). Springer-Verlag.

Given, Barbara A. & Simmons, Sandra J. Gastroenterology in Clinical Nursing. 3rd ed. LC 79-13048. (Illus.). 1979. pap. text ed. 19.95 (ISBN 0-8016-1855-X). Mosby.

--Gastroenterology in Clinical Nursing. 4th ed. LC 83-6777. (Illus.). 512p. 1983. pap. text ed. 21.95 (ISBN 0-8016-1869-X). Mosby.

Given, Bruce, et al. Tire Tracks & Tread Marks, 3 vols. LC 77-78931. 88p. 1977. 10.95x (ISBN 0-87201-869-5). Gulf Pub.

Given, Dave F. The Dave Given Rock 'n' Roll Star's Handbook. 1980. 15.00 (ISBN 0-682-49577-8, Banner). Exposition Pr FL.

Given, Effie G., jt. auth. see Steinmetz, Libby.

Given, James Buchanan. Society & Homicide in Thirteenth-Century England. LC 76-23372. 1977. 22.50x (ISBN 0-8047-0939-4). Stanford U Pr.

Given, P. H. & Cohen, A. D., eds. Interdisciplinary Studies of Peat & Coal Origins. LC 77-71662. (Microform Publication: No. 7). (Illus.). 1977. 4.00 (ISBN 0-8137-6007-0). Geol Soc.

Given, Welker. Further Study of Shakespeare's Othello. LC 72-16926. (Shakespeare Society of New York. Publications: No. 11). Repr. of 1899 ed. 22.00 (ISBN 0-404-54211-5). AMS Pr.

Givens. Adolescence in Females. (Gynecologic Endocrinology Ser.: Vol. 8). 1985. 75.00 (ISBN 0-8151-3532-7). Year Bk Med.

--Hormone Secreting Pituitary Tumors. 1982. 70.00 (ISBN 0-8151-3530-0). Year Bk Med.

Givens, Bettye. Red Headed Tree. 67p. 1985. 10.00 (ISBN 0-911051-22-8). Plain View.

Givens, Bill. Flying with Loran C. (Illus.). 208p. (Orig.). 1985. pap. 15.95 (ISBN 0-8306-2370-1). TAB Bks.

Givens, David. Love Signals. 224p. pap. 3.95 (ISBN 0-523-42431-0). Pinnacle Bks.

Givens, David B. Love Signals: How to Attract a Mate. 1983. 12.95 (ISBN 0-517-55037-7). Crown.

Givens, Douglas R. An Analysis of Navajo Temporality. 1977. pap. text ed. 8.00 (ISBN 0-8191-0213-X). U Pr of Amer.

Givens, Ellen M., jt. auth. see Ehrlich, Ruth A.

Givens, J. R. The Hypothalmus in Health & Disease. 1984. 65.00 (ISBN 0-8151-3531-9). Year Bk Med.

Givens, J. R., jt. ed. see Flamigni, C.

Givens, James R. Clinical Use of Sex Steroids. 1980. 55.00 (ISBN 0-8151-3528-9). Year Bk Med.

--Endocrine Causes of Menstrual Disorders. (Illus.). 1978. 55.00 (ISBN 0-8151-3526-2). Year Bk Med.

--Endocrinology of Pregnancy. 1981. 59.00 (ISBN 0-8151-3529-7). Year Bk Med.

Givens, James R., et al, eds. The Infertile Female: Proceedings of the Annual Symposium of Gynecological Endocrinology, Univ. of Tennessee. (Illus.). 1979. 55.00 (ISBN 0-8151-3527-0). Year Bk Med.

Givens, Janet E. Just Two Wings. LC 83-2710. (Illus.). 32p. (ps-2). 1984. PLB 8.95 (ISBN 0-689-31001-3). Atheneum.

--Something Wonderful Happened. LC 81-10780. (Illus.). 32p. (ps-2). 1982. PLB 8.95 (ISBN 0-689-30904-X). Atheneum.

Givens, Richard A. Advocacy: The Art of Pleading a Cause. LC 79-26332. (Trial Practice Ser.). xxi, 417p. 1980. (Shepard); pap. 22.00 (ISBN 0-07-023356-X). McGraw.

--Advocacy: The Art of Pleading a Cause. (Trial Publications). 417p. 1980. write for info. (Pub. By Shepards-McGraw). McGraw.

--Antitrust: An Economic Approach. 1983. 55.00 (ISBN 0-318-12029-1). NY Law Pub.

--Legal Strategies for Industrial Innovations. 580p. 1983. 75.00 (ISBN 0-07-023331-4). McGraw.

--Legal Strategies for Industrial Innovation. (Commercial Law Publications). 777p. 1982. write for info. (Pub. By Shepards-McGraw). McGraw.

Given-Wilson, C. & Curteis, A. The Royal Bastards of Medieval England. (Illus.). 200p. 1984. 25.00x (ISBN 0-7102-0025-0). Routledge & Kegan.

Given-Wilson, Chris, jt. auth. see Butler, Lionel.

Givern, Howard, tr. see Navarre, Yves.

Givet, Jacques. The Anti-Zionist Complex. Abel, Evelyn, tr. from Fr. LC 81-16693. 192p. 1982. 11.95 (ISBN 0-89961-019-6). SBS Pub.

Givey, David W. The Social Thought of Thomas Merton. 1983. 9.50 (ISBN 0-8199-0859-2). Franciscan Herald.

Givierge, Marcel. Course in Cryptography. (Cryptographic Ser.). 1978. 20.80 (ISBN 0-89412-028-X). Aegean Park Pr.

Givler, R. C. see Franz, Shepherd I.

Givner, Joan. Katherine Anne Porter: A Life. 572p. 1984. 10.95 (ISBN 0-671-50586-6, Touchstone Bks). S&S.

--Katherine Anne Porter: Converstions. (Literary Conversations Ser.). 1986. 17.95 (ISBN 0-87805-266-6); pap. 9.95 (ISBN 0-87805-267-4). U Pr of Miss.

--Tentacles of Unreason. LC 84-24154. (Illinois Short Fiction Ser.). 144p. 1985. 11.95 (ISBN 0-252-01203-8). U of Ill Pr.

Givoiset, Mariette, tr. see Campinchi, R., et al.

Givon, T. Syntax: A Functional-Typological Introduction, Vol. 1. LC 84-6195. 440p. 1984. 49.00x (ISBN 0-915027-07-0); pap. text ed. 30.00 (ISBN 0-915027-08-9). Benjamins North Am.

Givon, T., ed. Topic Continuity in Discourse: A Quantitative Cross-Language Study. (Typological Studies in Language: 3). 492p. 1983. 50.00x (ISBN 90-272-2867-1); pap. 30.00 (ISBN 90-272-2863-9). Benjamins North Am.

Givon, Talmy. On Understanding Grammar. (Perspectives in Neurolinguistics & Psycholinguistics Ser.). 1979. 39.50 (ISBN 0-12-285450-0). Acad Pr.

Givone, Donald O. & Roesser, Robert P. Microprocessors-Microcomputers: An Introduction. (Illus.). 480p. 1980. text ed. 40.00 (ISBN 0-07-023326-8). McGraw.

Givoni, B. Man, Climate & Architecture. 2nd ed. 1976. (Pub. by Elsevier Applied Sci England); pap. 35.25 (ISBN 0-85334-108-7). Elsevier.

Givry, Grillot De. Witchcraft, Magic & Alchemy. (Illus.). 15.25 (ISBN 0-8446-0113-6). Peter Smith.

Giwojna, Peter. Marine Hermit Crabs. (Illus.). 1978. pap. 7.95 (ISBN 0-87666-471-0, PS-752). TFH Pubns.

Giza, Joanne & Black, Catherine F. Great Baltimore Houses. LC 81-85673. (Illus.). 88p. (Orig.). 1982. pap. 9.95 (ISBN 0-940776-01-4). Maclay Assoc.

Gizelis, Gregory. Narrative Rhetorical Devices of Persuasion in the Greek Community of Philadelphia. Dorson, Richard M., ed. LC 80-728. (Folklore of the World Ser.). 1980. lib. bdg. 28.50x (ISBN 0-405-13315-4). Ayer Co Pubs.

Gizzi, Michael. Avis or the Replete Birdman. (Burning Deck Poetry Ser.). 1979. 15.00 (ISBN 0-930900-67-7); pap. 4.00 (ISBN 0-930900-68-5). Burning Deck.

--Species of Intoxication. (Burning Deck Poetry Ser.). 68p. 1983. 15.00 (ISBN 0-930901-10-X); pap. 4.00 (ISBN 0-930901-11-8). Burning Deck.

Gjelle, S, et al. Geological Survey of Norway. (No. 343, Bulletin 48). pap. 16.00x (ISBN 82-00-31377-8, Dist. by Columbia U Pr.). Universitet.

Gjelsness, Rudolph H. The American Book in Mexico. (School of Library Science Ser.). (Illus.). 92p. 1957. pap. 3.00 (ISBN 0-87506-038-2). Campus.

Gjelsvik, Atle. The Theory of Thin Walled Bars. LC 80-26501. 248p. 1981. 42.95x (ISBN 0-471-08594-4, Pub. by Wiley-Interscience). Wiley.

Gjelsvik, Tore. Norwegian Resistance, Nineteen Forty to Nineteen Forty-Five: Nineteen Forty to Nineteen Forty-Five. 1979. 25.00x (ISBN 0-7735-0507-5). McGill-Queens U Pr.

--Results from Norwegian Antarctic Research, 1974-1977. (Norsk Polarinstitutt Skrifter: Vol. 169). (Illus.). 117p. 1980. pap. 9.00x (ISBN 8-2903-0703-9). Universitet.

Gjelton, Tom. Schooling in Isolated Communities. 100p. 5.00 (ISBN 0-318-13440-3). Assn Exper Ed.

Gjerde, Jon. From Peasants to Farmers: The Migration from Balestrand, Norway, to the Upper Middle West. (Interdisciplinary Perspectives on Modern History Ser.). (Illus.). 272p. 1985. 32.50 (ISBN 0-521-26068-X). Cambridge U Pr.

Gjerset, Knut. History of the Norwegian People. LC 79-101272. (Illus.). Repr. of 1932 ed. 57.50 (ISBN 0-404-02818-7). AMS Pr.

--Norwegian Sailors on the Great Lakes. Scott, Franklyn D., ed. LC 78-15207. (Scandinavians in America Ser.). (Illus.). 1979. Repr. of 1928 ed. lib. bdg. 19.00x (ISBN 0-405-11636-5). Ayer Co Pubs.

Gjerstad, Einar. Ages & Days in Cyprus. (Studies in Mediterranean Archaeology, Pocketbooks: No. 12). 174p. 1980. pap. text ed. 23.50x (ISBN 91-85058-97-1, Pub. by Paul Astroms Sweden). Humanities.

Gjerstad, Ole, jt. auth. see Ya-Otto, John.

Gjersvik, Maryanne. Green Fun. LC 74-75042. 1975. pap. 6.95 (ISBN 0-85699-104-X). Chatham Pr.

Gjertsen, Derek. Classics of Science: A Study of Twelve Enduring Scientific Works. LC 83-27539. 384p. 1984. text ed. 24.95x (ISBN 0-936508-09-4); pap. text ed. 15.95x (ISBN 0-936508-12-4). Barber Pr.

Gjesdahl, Maurice S., jt. auth. see Niebel, Benjamin W.

Gjessing, Egil, jt. ed. see Christman, Russell F.

Gjessing, Lieve. Contribution to the Somatology of Periodic Catatonia. Marshall, H., tr. 1976. text ed. 89.00 (ISBN 0-08-015650-9). Pergamon.

Gjetset, Knut. Norwegian Sailors in American Waters. Scott, Franklyn D., ed. LC 78-15186. (Scandinavians in American Ser.). (Illus.). 1979. Repr. of 1933 ed. lib. bdg. 23.00x (ISBN 0-405-11637-3). Ayer Co Pubs.

Gjorgov, A. N. Barrier Contraception & Breast Cancer. (Contributions to Gynecology & Obstetrics: Vol. 8). (Illus.). 1980. soft cover 21.00 (ISBN 3-8055-0330-X). S Karger.

G. J. Van, Der Plaats see Van Der Plaats, G. J.

GJW Government Relations & Stephenson, Peter, eds. Handbook of World Development: The Guide to the Brandt Report. LC 81-48090. 177p. 1982. 11.50x (ISBN 0-8419-0779-X); pap. 4.95x (ISBN 0-8419-0778-1). Holmes & Meier.

Glaab, Charles N. & Brown, A. Theodore. A History of Urban America. 3rd ed. 1983. pap. text ed. write for info. (ISBN 0-02-344120-8, 34411). Macmillan.

Glaab, Charles N. & Larsen, Lawrence H. Factories in the Valley: Neenah-Menasha 1870-1915. LC 69-63012. (Illus.). 294p. 1969. 10.00 (ISBN 0-87020-106-9). State Hist Soc Wis.

Glab, Edward, Jr., ed. Latin American Culture Studies: Information & Materials for Teaching about Latin America. 3rd ed. (Latin American Culture Studies Project Ser.). xi, 466p. 1981. pap. text ed. 9.95x (ISBN 0-86728-001-8). U TX Inst Lat Am Stud.

Glaberman, Martin. The Grievance: Poems from the Shop Floor. (Singlejack Little Bks.). 31p. (Orig.). 1980. pap. 0.95 (ISBN 0-917300-12-2). SingleJack Bks.

--Wartime Strikes. (Illus., Orig.). 1980. pap. 6.00 (ISBN 0-935590-11-0). Bewick Edns.

Glacel, Barbara P. Regional Transit Authorities: A Policy Analysis of Massachusetts. 300p. 1983. 38.95 (ISBN 0-03-063003-7). Praeger.

Glacken, Clarence J. The Great Loochoo: A Study of Okinawan Village Life. LC 73-6394. (Illus.). 324p. 1973. Repr. of 1955 ed. lib. bdg. 19.00x (ISBN 0-8371-6897-X, GLGL). Greenwood.

--Traces on the Rhodian Shore: Nature & Culture in Western Thought from Ancient Times to the End of the Eighteenth Century. LC 67-10970. 1967. pap. 13.95x (ISBN 0-520-03216-0, CAMPUS 170). U of Cal Pr.

Glackens, Ira. Did Molly Pitcher Say That? The Men & Women Who Made American History: The First 300 Years. (Illus.). 350p. 1984. 20.00 (ISBN 0-8180-0828-8). Horizon.

--A Measure of Sliding Sand. LC 76-18450. 1977. 8.95 (ISBN 0-8397-5740-9). Eriksson.

--William Glackens & "The Eight". The Artist Who Freed American Art. LC 57-8771. (Illus.). 320p. 1983. 20.00 (ISBN 0-8180-0139-9); pap. text ed. 9.95 (ISBN 0-8180-0138-0). Horizon.

Glackin, James. Elements of Explosives Production. 60p. 1976. pap. 5.00 (ISBN 0-87364-083-7). Paladin Pr.

Glad, Donald D. & Glad, Virginia B. Interpersonality Synopsis. 1963. 4.95 (ISBN 0-87212-006-6). Libra.

Glad, John & Weissbort, Daniel, eds. Russian Poetry: The Modern Period. LC 78-8650. (Iowa Translations Ser.). 424p. 1978. text ed. 25.00x (ISBN 0-87745-083-8); pap. 12.50 (ISBN 0-87745-084-6). U of Iowa Pr.

Glad, John, tr. see Alexeyeva, Ludmilla.

Glad, John, tr. see Klyuev, Nikolai.

Glad, John, tr. see Shalamov, Varlam.

Glad, Virginia B., jt. auth. see Glad, Donald D.

Gladden, E. N. Civil Services of the United Kingdom: 1885-1970. (Illus.). 289p. 1967. 27.50x (ISBN 0-7146-1066-6, F Cass Co). Biblio Dist.

--History of Public Administration, 2 vols. 1972. 75.00x set (ISBN 0-7146-1310-X, F Cass Co). Biblio Dist.

--Local Corporational & International Administration: A Student's Guide to Public Administration. (Illus.). 229p. 1972. pap. text ed. 14.95x (ISBN 0-8464-1264-0). Beekman Pubs.

Gladden, Lee & Gladden, Vivianne C. Heirs of the Gods: A Space Age Interpretation of the Bible. LC 78-53852. (Illus.). 324p. Repr. of 1979 ed. 15.95 (ISBN 0-686-37960-8). Bel-Air.

Gladden, Lee, jt. auth. see Williams, Margaret.

Gladden, M. H., jt. auth. see Boyd, I. A.

Gladden, Vivianne C., jt. auth. see Gladden, Lee.

Gladden, Washington. Applied Christianity: Moral Aspects of Social Questions. LC 75-17224. (Social Problems & Social Policy Ser.). 1976. Repr. of 1886 ed. 24.50x (ISBN 0-405-07494-8). Ayer Co Pubs.

--Being a Christian. LC 72-4168. (Select Bibliographies Reprint Ser.). 1972. Repr. of 1876 ed. 14.00 (ISBN 0-8369-6880-8). Ayer Co Pubs.

--Ruling Ideas of the Present Age. 1971. Repr. of 1895 ed. 23.00 (ISBN 0-384-18865-6). Johnson Repr.

--Tools & the Man: Property & Industry Under the Christian Law. LC 75-353. (The Radical Tradition in America Ser). 308p. 1975. Repr. of 1893 ed. 21.50 (ISBN 0-88355-222-1). Hyperion Conn.

--Who Wrote the Bible? A Book for the People. LC 72-5435. (Select Bibliographies Reprint Ser.). 1972. Repr. of 1891 ed. 22.00 (ISBN 0-8369-6909-X). Ayer Co Pubs.

--Witnesses of the Light. facs. ed. LC 77-84307. (Essay Index Reprint Ser). 1903. 17.75 (ISBN 0-8369-1081-8). Ayer Co Pubs.

Gladden, Washington T. Working People & Their Employers. LC 75-89734. (American Labor: From Conspiracy to Collective Bargaining Ser., No. 1). 1969. Repr. of 1876 ed. 15.00 (ISBN 0-405-02123-2). Ayer Co Pubs.

Gladding, W. J. A Group of Theatrical Caricatures Being Twelve Plates. LC 73-130095. (Dunlap Soc. N.S. 4). (Illus.). 1970. Repr. of 1897 ed. lib. bdg. 16.50 (ISBN 0-8337-1362-0). B Franklin.

Glade, Carol C. Carol's Perils. 1985. 5.75 (ISBN 0-8062-2230-1). Carlton.

Glade, John, ed. see Samson, Richard W.

Glade, John J., ed. see Whimbey, Arthur.

Glade, Merton. Days of Wine & Murder. 170p. 1985. pap. 3.95 (ISBN 0-946626-06-5, Pub. by Dedalus Bks England). Hippocrene Bks.

Glade, Philip R., jt. ed. see Bloom, Barry R.

Glade, Phyllis J., ed. see Sherwood, Keith.

Glade, William P. & Baldwin, Emily. Social Studies: Economics, International Relations, & Political Science. (Latin American Curriculum Units for Junior & Community Colleges Ser.). v, 85p. (Orig.). 1981. pap. text ed. 4.95x (ISBN 0-86728-005-0). U TX Inst Lat Am Stud.

Glade, William P. & Ross, Stanley R., eds. Criticas constructivas del sistema politico mexicano. (Encuesta Politica Mexico: No. 2). 254p. (Eng. & Span.). 1973. pap. 7.95x (ISBN 0-292-71012-7). U of Tex Pr.

Glade, William P., Jr. & Anderson, Charles W. Political Economy of Mexico: Two Studies. LC 63-10531. 256p. 1963. pap. 7.95x (ISBN 0-299-02894-1). U of Wis Pr.

Glader, Eugene. Amateurism & Athletics. 1978. pap. text ed. 14.95 (ISBN 0-918438-13-6). Leisure Pr.

Glades County Commissioners. Glades County, Florida History. Wright, Betty, ed. LC 82-61321. (A Pioneer Heritage Presentation Ser.). 208p. 1983. pap. 10.00 (ISBN 0-935834-09-5). Rainbow Books.

Gladfelter, Bruce G. Meseta & Campina Landforms in Central Spain. LC 75-133028. (Research Papers Ser.: No. 130). (Illus., Orig.). 1971. pap. 10.00 (ISBN 0-89065-037-3, 130). U Chicago Dept Geog.

Gladfelter, Irl A. Dental Evidence: A Handbook for Police. (Illus.). 208p. 1975. photocopy ed. 25.00x (ISBN 0-398-03323-4). C C Thomas.

Gladilin, Anatolii. Bol'Shoi Begovoi Den' 220p. (Rus.). 1983. 22.50 (ISBN 0-88233-834-X). Ardis Pubs.

--FSSR (Frantsuzskaia Sovetskaia Sotsialisticheskaia Respublika) LC 84-73267. 160p. (Russ.). 1985. 10.00 (ISBN 0-911971-08-4). Effect Pub.

Gladilin, Anatoly. Kakim Ia Byl Togda. 200p. (Rus.). 1985. 25.00 (ISBN 0-87501-001-6). Ardis Pubs.

--The Making & Unmaking of a Soviet Writer. Lapeza, David, tr. from Rus. LC 78-74199. 1979. 12.50 (ISBN 0-88233-354-2); pap. 3.50 (ISBN 0-88233-355-0). Ardis Pubs.

Gladish, Fred, jt. auth. see Zuckerman, Lawrence.

Gladish, Richard R. Bishop William Henry Benade: Founder & Reformer. (Illus.). 400p. 1983. 15.00 (ISBN 0-910557-07-1). Acad New Church.

Gladkii, A. Formal Grammars & Languages. (Fundamental Studies in Computer Science: Vol. 7). Date not set. 58.75 (ISBN 0-7204-0497-5, North-Holland). Elsevier.

Gladkij, Aleksej V. & Mel'cuk, Igor A. Elements of Mathematical Linguistics. LC 81-38391. (Janua Linguarum Series Maior: No. 110). xxii, 247p. 1983. 43.60x (ISBN 90-279-3118-6). Mouton.

Gladkov, F. Cemento. 383p. 1983. 8.95 (ISBN 0-317-05067-2, Pub by Raduga Pubs USSR). Imported Pubns.

Gladkov, F. V. Cement: A Novel. Arthur, A. S. & Ashleigh, C., trs. LC 60-13978. pap. 9.95 (ISBN 0-8044-6178-3). Ungar.

Gladkov, Fedor V. Restless Youth. Parker, R. & Scott, V., trs. from Rus. LC 75-39000. (Soviet Literature in English Translation Ser.). (Illus.). 265p. 1976. Repr. of 1958 ed. 21.00 (ISBN 0-88355-403-8). Hyperion-Conn.

Gladkov, K. The Atom from A to Z. Zimmerman, Michael, tr. from Russian. 263p. 1971. 9.95x (ISBN 0-8464-0160-6). Beekman Pubs.

--The Powerhouse of the Atom. (Illus.). 303p. 1972. 14.95x (ISBN 0-8464-0741-8). Beekman Pubs.

--Powerhouse of the Atom. 1980. 15.00x (ISBN 0-89875-003-2, Pub. by U Pr Pacific). Intl Spec Bk.

Gladman, Donna. It's Sunday Night Again? Zapel, Arthur L., ed. LC 79-84726. (Illus.). 1979. pap. text ed. 4.95 (ISBN 0-916260-04-6). Meriwether Pub.

Gladney, Marion G., jt. auth. see Hayes, Helen.

Gladson, Deek. The Midas Manual: A Guide to Independent Avocations. (Illus.). 96p. (Orig.). 1981. 8.00 (ISBN 0-89316-624-3); pap. 5.00 (ISBN 0-89316-623-5). Exanimo Pr.

--The Miser's Manual: A Guide to Profitable Self-Employment. (Illus.). 96p. (Orig.). 1981. 8.00 (ISBN 0-89316-625-1); pap. 5.00 (ISBN 0-686-71584-5). Exanimo Pr.

--The Owkhooter's Manual: The Poor Man's Guide to Financial Independence, Vol. I. 48p. (Orig.). 1984. pap. 5.00 (ISBN 0-89316-633-2). Exanimo Pr.

Gladson, Jerry. Who Said Life Is Fair? Wheeler, Gerald, ed. 128p. 1985. pap. 6.95 (ISBN 0-8280-0242-8). Review & Herald.

Gladstein, Gerald, ed. see Rogers, Carl & Skinner, B. F.

Gladstein, Mimi R. The Ayn Rand Companion. LC 84-540. (Illus.). xii, 130p. 1984. lib. bdg. 25.00 (ISBN 0-313-22079-4, GAR/). Greenwood.

Gladstone. Vocabulaire De Medecine & Des Sciences Connexes Anglais-Francais-Anglais. (Eng. & Fr.). 21.95 (ISBN 0-685-36682-0). French & Eur.

Gladstone, et al. The Contractor's Exam Book. 3rd ed. 250p. 1985. pap. 27.95 (ISBN 0-930644-07-7). Engineers Pr.

Gladstone, Alan, jt. ed. see Windmuller, John P.

Gladstone, Arthur A. & Kirkness, Elizabeth. Beyond the Scalpel: Reflections of a Vermont Surgeon. LC 79-91350. (Illus.). 136p. (Orig.). 1979. pap. 6.95 (ISBN 0-933050-04-6). New Eng Pr VT.

Gladstone, Bernard. Complete Guide to Furniture Finishing & Refinishing. 1981. (Fireside); pap. 8.95 (ISBN 0-671-25604-1). S&S.

--Hints & Tips for the Handyperson. Orig. Title: Hints & Tips for the Handyman. 152p. 1975. pap. 1.95 (ISBN 0-346-12173-6). Cornerstone.

--The New York Times Complete Manual of Home Repair. LC 75-13756. 1980. 15.95 (ISBN 0-8129-0873-2). Times Bks.

--The Simon & Schuster Complete Guide to Home Repair & Maintenance. LC 83-20409. 431p. 1984. 24.95 (ISBN 0-671-25601-7). S&S.

Gladstone, Bernard & Bottomley, Tom, eds. Boatkeeper: The Boatowner's Manual to Maintenance, Repair, & Construction. LC 84-80492. (Illus.). 288p. 1984. 17.95 (ISBN 0-688-03565-5). Morrow.

Gladstone, Diana. Training Your Horse or Pony. 160p. 1985. 12.50 (ISBN 0-947647-43-0, Pub. by Fanciers Supplies). Longwood Pub Group.

Gladstone, F. J. Voluntary Action in a Changing World. 137p. 1979. pap. text ed. 9.75x (ISBN 0-7199-1033-1, Pub. by Bedford England). Brookfield Pub Co.

Gladstone, Frances. Anne's Youth. LC 83-40459. 128p. 1984. 13.95 (ISBN 0-8052-3890-5). Schocken.

Gladstone, Francis. Charity, Law & Social Justice. 211p. (Orig.). 1982. pap. text ed. 12.50 Brit. pds. (ISBN 0-7199-1084-6, Pub. by Bedford England). Brookfield Pub Co.

--The Politics of Planning. 1977. 15.00 (ISBN 0-85117-106-0). Transatlantic.

Gladstone, John. Air Conditioning & Mechanical Trades: Preparing for the Contractor's License Examination. LC 74-18258. (Illus.). 425p. 1980. pap. 19.95 (ISBN 0-930644-04-2). Engineers Pr.

--Air Conditioning Journeyman's Exam Book. 90p. 1984. 12.95 (ISBN 0-930644-08-5). Engineers Pr.

--Air Conditioning Testing-Adjusting-Balancing: A Field Practice Manual. 2nd ed. 160p. 1981. 21.95 (ISBN 0-442-22714-0). Van Nos Reinhold.

--Journeyman General Mechanical Examination: An Illustrated Review. (Illus.). 189p. 16.95 (ISBN 0-930644-03-4). Engineers Pr.

Gladstone, John & Perpich, George. Florida Air Conditioning Contractor's Handbook. 2nd ed. LC 83-81755. 385p. 1983. 21.95 (ISBN 0-930644-05-0). Engineers Pr.

Gladstone, John, ed. Short-Cut Building Code Excerpts: South Florida Building Code 1984 Mechanical Section & Contractors Code of Dade County Chapter 10. 62p. 1984. 9.75 (ISBN 0-930644-09-3). Engineers Pr.

Gladstone, Meredith. Small Needlepoint Treasures: A Complete How-to Workbook for Making Quick Needlepoint Gifts. LC 78-23750. (Illus.). 1979. pap. 6.95 (ISBN 0-688-08388-9). Morrow.

Gladstone, Nancy & Brand, Jeffry. My Day Care Book. (Illus., Orig.). (ps). 1984. pap. 3.95 (ISBN 0-87659-110-1). Gryphon Hse.

Gladstone, Penelope. Travels of Alexine. (Illus.). 1971. 12.50 (ISBN 0-7195-2044-4). Transatlantic.

Gladstone, Ralph see Euripides.

Gladstone, Ralph, tr. see Jarry, Alfred.

Gladstone, Robert M., jt. auth. see Wilburn, Michael D.

Gladstone, T. H. The Englishman in Kansas; or, Squatter Life & Border Warfare. LC 74-155700. lxvi, 328p. 1971. 26.95x (ISBN 0-8032-0800-6); pap. 6.95x (ISBN 0-8032-5742-2, BB 536, Bison). U of Nebr Pr.

Gladstone, W. E. Archaic Greece & the East. LC 77-94879. 1978. Repr. of 1892 ed. lib. bdg. 15.00 (ISBN 0-89341-177-9). Longwood Pub Group.

--An Enquiry into the Time & Place of Homer. 1876. Repr. 30.00 (ISBN 0-8274-2278-4). R West.

--Speeches & Public Addresses, 2 Vols. in 1. Hutton, A. & Cohen, H., eds. LC 11-34472. Repr. of 1894 ed. Set. 48.00 (ISBN 0-527-33950-4). Kraus Repr.

--Studies on Homer & the Homeric Age, 3 vols. LC 77-94580. 1978. Repr. of 1858 ed. lib. bdg. 75.00 (ISBN 0-89341-176-0). Longwood Pub Group.

Gladstone, W. J. Dictionnaire Anglais-Francais des Sciences Medicales et Paramedicales. 1154p. (Fr.). 1978. 95.00 (ISBN 0-686-56787-0, M-6583, Pub. by Maloine). French & Eur.

--Dictionnaire Anglais-Francais des Sciences Medicales et Paramedicales. (Eng. & Fr.). 1978. 99.95 (ISBN 0-686-57303-X, M-6277). French & Eur.

Gladstone, William. Preparation for the ACT. 352p. (Orig.). 1985. pap. 8.95 (ISBN 0-671-50220-4, Dist by S&S). Monarch Pr.

Gladstone, William E. Arthur Henry Hallam. LC 73-15672. 1898. lib. bdg. 8.50 (ISBN 0-8414-4454-4). Folcroft.

--The Gladstone Diaries: January 1869-June 1871, Vol. 7. Matthew, H. C., ed. (Illus.). 1982. 79.00x. Oxford U Pr.

--The Gladstone Diaries: July 1871-December 1874, Vol. 8. Matthew, H. C., ed. (Illus.). 1982. 79.00x (ISBN 0-19-822639-X). Oxford U Pr.

--The Gladstone Diaries: Volumes V & VI, 1844-1868, Vol. 4 & 5. Matthew, H. C., ed. (Gladstone Diaries Ser.). (Illus.). 1978. 149.00x set (ISBN 0-19-822445-1). Oxford U Pr.

--Gladstone Diaries: 1825-1839, Vols. 1 & 2. Foot, M. R., ed. 1968. 115.00x (ISBN 0-19-821370-0). Oxford U Pr.

--The Gladstone Diaries: 1840-1854, Vols. 3 & 4. Foot, M. R. & Foot, M. R., eds. (Illus.). 1975. Set. 129.00x (ISBN 0-19-822425-7). Oxford U Pr.

--Gleanings of Past Years, 1843-1878: And Later Gleanings, 8 Vols. LC 72-148788. Repr. of 1897 ed. Set. 250.00 (ISBN 0-404-08850-3). AMS Pr.

--Later Gleanings. LC 72-8478. (Essay Index Reprint Ser.). 1972. Repr. of 1897 ed. 24.50 (ISBN 0-8369-7314-3). Ayer Co Pubs.

Gladtke, E., et al. Pharmacokinetics. Wilkinson, P. J., tr. from Ger. (Illus.). 1979. pap. 19.50 (ISBN 0-387-09183-1). Springer-Verlag.

Gladue, E. Ted, Jr. China's Perception of Global Politics. LC 82-13572. 258p. 1983. lib. bdg. 26.75 (ISBN 0-8191-2700-0); pap. text ed. 13.00 (ISBN 0-8191-2701-9). U Pr of Amer.

Gladue, Ted E., Jr. China's Perceptions of Global Issues: Series in Political Science. 1981. write for info. (ISBN 0-8046-9286-6, Pub. by Kennikat). Assoc Faculty Pr.

Gladwell, G. M. Contact Problems in the Classical Theory of Elasticity. (Mechanics of Elastic & Viscoelastic Solids Ser.). 716p. 1980. 60.00x (ISBN 9-0286-0440-5); pap. 35.00x (ISBN 9-0286-0760-9). Sijthoff & Noordhoff.

Gladwell, I. & Wait, R., eds. A Survey of Numerical Methods for Partial Differential Equations. (Illus.). 1979. 49.50x (ISBN 0-19-853351-9). Oxford U Pr.

Gladwell, R. & Sayers, D. K., eds. Computational Techniques for Ordinary Differential Equations. LC 79-42626. (IMA & ITS Applications Conference Ser.). 1980. 33.00 (ISBN 0-12-285780-1). Acad Pr.

Gladwin, David. Victorian & Edwardian Canals. 1976. 19.95 (ISBN 0-7134-3061-3, Pub. by Batsford England). David & Charles.

Gladwin, Harold, et al. Excavations at Snaketown: Material Culture. LC 65-23304. 305p. 1965. 19.95x (ISBN 0-8165-0031-2). U of Ariz Pr.

Gladwin, Harold S. Excavations at Casa Grande, Arizona. (Illus.). 30p. 1970. Repr. of 1928 ed. 5.00 (ISBN 0-916561-19-4). Southwest Mus.

Gladwin, Mary F. Channel Island Hopping. (Island Hopping Travel Bks.). (Illus.). 240p. (Orig.). 1984. pap. 12.95 (ISBN 0-7221-3816-4, Pub. by Gentry Bks UK). Hippocrene Bks.

Gladwin, Thomas. East Is a Big Bird: Navigation & Logic on Puluwat Atoll. LC 75-95922. 1970. pap. 6.95x (ISBN 0-674-22426-4). Harvard U Pr.

Gladwin, Thomas & Saidin, Ahmad. Slaves of the White Myth: The Psychology of Neocolonialism. LC 80-14939. 1981. text ed. 13.00x (ISBN 0-391-01936-8). Humanities.

Gladwin, Thomas N. Environment, Planning & the Multinational Corporation. Altman, Edward I. & Walter, Ingo, eds. LC 76-10400. (Contemporary Studies in Economic & Financial Analysis: Vol. 8). 350p. 1977. lib. bdg. 36.50 (ISBN 0-89232-014-1). Jai Pr.

Gladwin, Thomas N. & Walter, Ingo. Multinationals Under Fire: Lessons in the Management of Conflict. LC 79-21741. 689p. 1980. 47.95x (ISBN 0-471-01969-0, Pub. by Wiley-Interscience). Wiley.

Gladwyn, Hubert. Halfway to Nineteen Eighty-Four. LC 66-27476. 89p. 1966. 14.00x (ISBN 0-231-02991-8). Columbia U Pr.

Gladwyn, Hubert M. Europe after De Gaulle. Crozier, Brian, ed. LC 70-86972. (World Realities Ser). (Orig.). 1969. 4.95 (ISBN 0-8008-2520-9). Taplinger.

Glaenzer, Richard, tr. see Grenard, Fernand.

Glaenzer, Richard B. Literary Snapshots. 1920. Repr. 15.00 (ISBN 0-8274-2960-6). R West.

Glaeser, et al. Invitation to Fly. 2nd ed. 640p. 1985. write for info. (ISBN 0-534-04800-5). Wadsworth Pub.

Glaeser, B., ed. Ecodevelopment: Concepts, Projects, Strategies. (Illus.). 300p. 1984. 49.50 (ISBN 0-08-028936-3, 2300/3). Pergamon.

Glaeser, Bernhard. Ecodevelopment in Tanzania: An Empirical Contribution on Needs, Self-Sufficiency & Environmentally-Sound Agriculture on Peasant Farms. Antal, David, tr. LC 83-23736. xx, 229p. 1984. 25.20x (ISBN 3-11-009719-2). Mouton.

Glaeser, Ludwig. Mies Van der Rohe: Furniture & Drawings. LC 76-24509. (Illus.). 1977. pap. 6.95 (ISBN 0-87070-555-5). Museum Mod Art.

Glaeser, P. S., ed. Data for Science & Technology: Proceedings of the International CODATA Conference, Eighth, Jachranka, Poland, 4-7 Oct., 1982. 350p. 1983. 49.00 (ISBN 0-444-86668-X, I-460-83, North Holland). Elsevier.

--Data for Science & Technology: Proceedings of the 7th International CODATA Conference, Kyoto, Japan, 8-11 October 1980. (Illus.). 638p. 1981. 165.00 (ISBN 0-08-026201-5); pap. 46.00 (ISBN 0-08-026203-1). Pergamon.

Glaeser, W. A., ed. see American Society for Metals.

Glaeser, W. A., et al, eds. Wear of Materials. Incl. Wear of Materials, 1979. Ludema, K. C. et al., ed. 685p. 1979. 60.00 (H00143); Wear of Materials. Ludema, K. C., ed. 1983. pap. text ed. 85.00 (H00254). 585p. 1977. pap. text ed. 50.00 (ISBN 0-685-81976-0, H00100). ASME.

Glaeser, Werner. What Am I Bid? LC 82-13862. 1984. 10.95 (ISBN 0-87949-217-1). Ashley Bks.

Glaesner, Kay M. Miracle of Christmas. (Orig.). 1982. pap. 2.50 (ISBN 0-937172-39-1). JLJ Pubs.

Glaessner, Martin. The Dawn of Animal Life: A Biohistorical Study. LC 83-5188. (Cambridge Earth Science Ser.). 256p. 1985. 49.50 (ISBN 0-521-23507-3); pap. 19.95 (ISBN 0-521-31216-7). Cambridge U Pr.

Glagolev, A. N. Motility & Taxis in Prokaryotes. (Physicochemical Biology Reviews Supplement Ser.: Soviet Scientific Reviews, Sect. B, Vol. 4). 310p. 1984. text ed. 126.00 (ISBN 3-7186-0160-5). Harwood Academic.
Glahe, F., ed. Adam Smith & the Wealth of Nations, 1776-1976: Bicentennial Essays. LC 77-91609. 1978. pap. 8.95x (ISBN 0-87081-082-0). Colo Assoc.
Glahe, F. R., jt. ed. see Dowling, M.
Glahe, Fred R. Macroeconomics: Theory & Policy. 3rd ed. (Illus.). 516p. 1985. text ed. 27.95x (ISBN 0-15-551268-4, HC); student wkbk. avail. (ISBN 0-15-551271-4). HarBraceJ.
Glahe, Fred R. & Lee, Dwight R. Microeconomics: Theory & Applications. 558p. 1981. text ed. 23.95 (ISBN 0-15-558623-8, HC); student wkbk. 8.95 (ISBN 0-15-558625-4); instr's manual avail. (ISBN 0-15-558624-6). HarBraceJ.
Glahe, Fred. R., ed. Collected Papers of Kenneth E. Boulding, Vol. 1. LC 77-135288. 1971. 19.50x (ISBN 0-87081-011-1). Colo Assoc.
Glahe, Fred R., ed. Collected Papers of Kenneth E. Boulding, Vol. 2. LC 77-135288. 1971. 19.50x (ISBN 0-87081-012-X). Colo Assoc.
Glaiser, Stephen & Mulley, Corinne. Public Control of the British Bus Industry. 146p. 1983. text ed. 33.00x (ISBN 0-566-00560-3). Gower Pub Co.
Glaister, Geoffrey. Glaister's Glossary of the Book: Terms Used in Paper-Making, Printing, Bookbinding, & Publishing. LC 76-47975. 1979. 75.00 (ISBN 0-520-03364-7). U of Cal Pr.
Glaister, Stephen. Fundamentals of Transport Economics. 1981. 27.50x (ISBN 0-312-31152-4). St Martin.
--Mathematical Models for Economists. 3rd ed. 216p. 1984. pap. 12.95x (ISBN 0-631-13712-2). Basil Blackwell.
Glamann, Kristof. Dutch Asiatic Trade Sixteen Twenty to Seventeen Forty. 2nd ed. xiv, 334p. 1981. 39.50 (ISBN 90-247-9050-6, Pub. by Martinus Nijhoff Netherlands). Kluwer Academic.
Glamour Magazine Editors. Glamour Beauty Book. rev. ed. 1972. pap. 1.95 (ISBN 0-686-66667-4, Fireside). S&S.
Glamour Magazine Editors, jt. auth. see Morrison, Maggie.
Glampson, Ann, et al. A Guide to the Assessment of Community Needs & Resources. 1975. 25.00x (ISBN 0-317-05790-1, Pub. by Natl Inst Social Work). State Mutual Bk.
Glancy, Eileen. James Dickey: The Critic As Poet. LC 70-155723. 1971. 7.50x (ISBN 0-87875-011-8). Whitston Pub.
Glancy, Ruth F. Dicken's Christmas Books, Christmas Stories & Other Short Fiction: An Annotated Bibliography. DeVries, Duane, ed. LC 83-49323. (Dickens Bibliography Ser.). 1985. lib. bdg. 78.00 (ISBN 0-8240-8988-X). Garland Pub.
Glander-Bandyk, jt. auth. see Droge.
Glandon, Virginia E. Arthur Griffith & the Advanced-Nationalist Press: Ireland, 1900-1922. LC 83-48755. (American University Studies IX (History): Vol. 2). 339p. 1985. text ed. 33.00 (ISBN 0-8204-0041-6). P Lang Pubs.
Glanfield, P. Applied Cook-Freezing. (Illus.). 203p. 1980. 33.50 (ISBN 0-85334-888-X, Pub. by Elsevier Applied Sci England). Elsevier.
Glang, R., jt. auth. see Maissel, L.
Glanmor, Williams, ed. Early Modern Glamorgan. (Glamorgan County History Ser.). 717p. 1974. text ed. 31.50x (ISBN 0-317-06372-3, Pub. by Univ of Wales Pr England). Humanities.
Glansdorff, P., ed. see CISM (International Center for Mechanical Sciences), Dept. of Mechanics of Solids.
Glantz, Micheal H. & Thompson, J. Dana, eds. Resource Management & Environmental Uncertainty: Lessons from Coastal Upwelling Fisheries. LC 80-16645. (Advances in Environmental Science & Technology Ser.). 491p. 1981. 77.50x (ISBN 0-471-05984-6, Pub. by Wiley-Interscience). Wiley.
Glantz, P. O., et al, eds. Oral Interfacial Reactions of Bone, Soft Tissue & Saliva. (Illus.). 150p. 1985. pap. text ed. 40.00 (ISBN 0-947946-41-1). IRL Pr.
Glantz, Stanton A. Mathematics for Biomedical Applications. LC 77-20320. 1979. 24.50x (ISBN 0-520-03599-2). U of Cal Pr.
--Primer of Biostatistics. (Illus.). 384p. 1981. pap. text ed. 13.95 (ISBN 0-07-023370-5). McGraw.
Glanvill, A. B. & Denton, E. N. Injection-Mould Design Fundamentals. (Illus.). 1965. 27.95 (ISBN 0-8311-1033-3). Indus Pr.
Glanvill, John & Martin, Henry. The Copies of Two Speeches in Parliament, the One by John Glanvill, Esquire, the Other by Sir Henry Martin, Knight. LC 74-28858. (English Experience Ser.: No. 739). 1975. Repr. of 1628 ed. 3.50 (ISBN 90-221-0739-6). Walter J Johnson.
Glanvill, John, et al, trs. see Le Bovier De Fontenelle, Bernard.
Glanvill, Joseph. Essays on Several Important Subjects in Philosophy & Religion. Repr. of 1676 ed. 32.00 (ISBN 0-384-18880-X). Johnson Repr.
--Plus Ultra. LC 58-9452. 1978. Repr. of 1668 ed. 35.00x (ISBN 0-8201-1243-7). Schol Facsimiles.
--Saducismus Triumphatus: Or, Full & Plain Evidence Concerning Witches & Apparitions. LC 66-60009. 1966. Repr. of 1689 ed. 75.00x (ISBN 0-8201-1021-3). Schol Facsimiles.
--Scepsis Scientifica: Or Confest Ignorance, the Way to Science, 2 vols. in 1. Wellek, Rene, ed. LC 75-11222. (British Philosophers & Theologians of the 17th & 18th Centuries Ser.). 330p. 1978. lib. bdg. 51.00 (ISBN 0-8240-1776-5). Garland Pub.
--Two Choice & Useful Treatises: The One, One Lux Orientalis,...the Other, A Discourse of Truth by the Late Reverend Dr. Rust. Wellek, Rene, ed. LC 75-11223. (British Philosophers & Theologians of the 17th & 18th Centuries Ser.). 532p. 1978. lib. bdg. 51.00 (ISBN 0-8240-1777-3). Garland Pub.
Glanville, Brian. The History of the World Cup. (Illus.). 288p. 1984. pap. 10.95 (ISBN 0-571-13245-6). Faber & Faber.
Glanville, James L. Italy's Relations with England, 1896-1905. LC 78-64153. (Johns Hopkins University. Studies in the Social Sciences. Fifty-Second Ser. 1934: 1). Repr. of 1934 ed. 18.50 (ISBN 0-404-61263-6). AMS Pr.
Glanville, Sir John. Voyage to Cadiz in 1625. Grosart, A. B., ed. Repr. of 1883 ed. 27.00 (ISBN 0-384-18890-7). Johnson Repr.
Glanville, Joseph. Some Discourse, Sermons & Remains. Wellek, Rene, ed. LC 75-11221. (British Philosophers & Theologians of the 17th & 18th Centuries Ser.). 1979. lib. bdg. 51.00 (ISBN 0-8240-1775-7). Garland Pub.
Glanville, Ranulph de. Translation of Glanville: (A Treatise on the Laws & Customs of the Kingdom of England) Beames, John, tr. from Latin. xl, 362p. 1980. Repr. of 1812 ed. lib. bdg. 30.00x (ISBN 0-8377-0313-1). Rothman.
Glanville, Stephen R. The Legacy of Egypt. LC 76-44448. (Illus.). 1976. Repr. of 1942 ed. lib. bdg. 34.00x (ISBN 0-8371-9092-4, GLLE). Greenwood.
Glanz, Dawn. How the West Was Drawn: American Art & the Settling of the Frontier. Seidel, Linda, ed. LC 81-16218. (Studies in the Fine Arts: Iconography: No. 6). 218p. 1982. 39.95 (ISBN 0-8357-1276-1). UMI Res Pr.
Glanz, Rudolf. Aspects of the Social, Political, & Economic History of the Jews in America. 1984. 25.00x (ISBN 0-87068-463-9). Ktav.
--The German Jewish Women, Vol. 2. 25.00x (ISBN 0-87068-462-0). Ktav.
--The Jewish Female in America: Two Female Generations, 1820-1929, Vol. 1. 25.00x (ISBN 0-87068-461-2). Ktav.
Glanz, Rudolph. German Jew in America: An Annotated Bibliography Including Books, Pamphlets & Articles of Special Interest. 1969. 39.50x (ISBN 0-87068-061-7). Ktav.
Glanzman, George S. Deuteronomy. Pt. 1. pap. 1.00 (ISBN 0-8091-5028-X); Pt. 2. pap. 1.00 (ISBN 0-8091-5029-8). Paulist Pr.
Glaphre. Talking with God. (Woman's Workshop Ser.). 160p. (Orig.). 1985. pap. 3.95 (ISBN 0-310-45341-0, Pub. by Lamplight). Zondervan.
Glapthorne, Henry. The Hollander: A Comedy Written Sixteen Thirty-Five. LC 79-84112. (English Experience Ser.: No.931). 76p. 1979. Repr. of 1640 ed. lib. bdg. 9.50 (ISBN 90-221-0931-3). Walter J Johnson.
--The Lady Mother. LC 82-45709. (Malone Society Reprint Ser.: No. 109). Repr. of 1958 ed. 40.00 (ISBN 0-404-63108-8). AMS Pr.
Glare, G. P., ed. Oxford Latin Dictionary: Fasicle 3, Gorgonia-Libero. (Lat.). 1973. pap. 49.50x (ISBN 0-19-864217-2). Oxford U Pr.
Glare, P. G., ed. Oxford Latin Dictionary, (Lat.). 1971. pap. 49.50x (ISBN 0-19-864216-4). Oxford U Pr.
--Oxford Latin Dictionary. 1982. 145.00x (ISBN 0-19-864224-5). Oxford U Pr.
--Oxford Latin Dictionary, Fascicle 5. (Lat.). 1976. pap. 49.50x (ISBN 0-19-864218-0). Oxford U Pr.
--Oxford Latin Dictionary: Fascicle 1, a-Calcitro. (Lat.). 1968. pap. 49.50x (ISBN 0-19-864209-1). Oxford U Pr.
--Oxford Latin Dictionary: Fascicle 2, Calcitro-Demitto. (Lat.). 1969. pap. 49.50x (ISBN 0-19-864215-6). Oxford U Pr.
--Oxford Latin Dictionary: Fascicle 7. (Orig., Lat.). 1980. pap. 49.50x (ISBN 0-19-864220-2). Oxford U Pr.
--Oxford Latin Dictionary: Fascicle 8. (Lat.). 1982. pap. 48.00x (ISBN 0-19-864221-0). Oxford U Pr.
Glaros, Alan G., jt. auth. see Coleman, James C.
Glas, Norbert. Conception, Birth & Early Childhood. 153p. 1983. pap. 8.95 (ISBN 0-910142-54-8). Anthroposophic.
Glas, Werner. The Waldorf School Approach to History. Rev. ed. 102p. 1981. pap. 6.95 (ISBN 0-88010-004-4). Anthroposophic.
Glas, Werner, ed. see Asten, Dietrich V.
Glasby, G. P., ed. Marine Manganese Deposits. LC 76-48895. (Oceanography Ser.: Vol. 15). 494p. 1977. 85.00 (ISBN 0-444-41524-6). Elsevier.
Glasby, J. Encyclopedia of the Alkaloids, Vol. 4. 408p. 1983. 75.00x (ISBN 0-306-41217-9, Plenum Pr). Plenum Pub.
Glasby, J. S. Encyclopedia of the Alkaloids, 2 Vols. LC 75-17753. 1423p. 1975. Set. 145.00x (ISBN 0-306-30845-2, Plenum Pr). Plenum Pub.
--Encyclopedia of the Alkaloids, Vol. 3. LC 75-17753. 527p. 1977. 85.00x (ISBN 0-306-31026-0, Plenum Pr). Plenum Pub.
Glasby, John S. Boundaries of the Universe. LC 76-162638. (Illus.). 1972. 18.50x (ISBN 0-674-08015-7). Harvard U Pr.
--Enciclopedia de Antibioticos. 700p. (Espn.). 1978. pap. 53.95 (ISBN 84-7288-027-3, S-50564). French & Eur.
--Encyclopedia of Antibiotics. 2nd ed. LC 78-13356. 467p. 1979. 114.95 (ISBN 0-471-99722-6, Pub. by Wiley-Interscience). Wiley.
--Encyclopedia of the Terpenoids. LC 81-19866. 2324p. 1982. 567.00 (ISBN 0-471-27986-2, Pub by Wiley-Interscience). Wiley.
Glasco, Gordon. The Days of Eternity. LC 81-43615. (Illus.). 480p. 1983. 15.95 (ISBN 0-385-17085-8). Doubleday.
--The Days of Eternity. Grey, Linda, ed. 464p. 1984. pap. text ed. 3.95 (ISBN 0-553-24360-8). Bantam.
Glasco, Laurence A. Ethnicity & Social Structure: Irish, Germans & Native-Born of Buffalo, N.Y., 1850-1860. Cordasco, Francesco, ed. LC 80-859. (American Ethnic Groups Ser.). 1981. lib. bdg. 38.50x (ISBN 0-405-13422-3). Ayer Co Pubs.
Glascock, Scot, jt. auth. see Brown, Carol.
Glascock, Scott, jt. auth. see Brown, Carol.
Glascoff, Donald G. & Practising Law Institute. New Directions for the Thrift Industry. LC 83-62449. (Commercial Law & Practice Course Handbook Ser.: No. 310). (Illus.). 880p. 1983. 35.00. PLI.
Glase, Jon C. Tested Studies for Laboratory Teaching: Proceedings of the Second Workshop-Conference of the Association of Biology-Laboratory Education (ABLE) LC 81-81747. 288p. 1981. text ed. 19.95 (ISBN 0-8403-2471-5). Kendall-Hunt.
Glase, Jon C., ed. Tested Studies for Laboratory Teaching: Proceedings of the First Workshop of the Association for Biology Laboratory Education. LC 80-82832. 288p. 1980. text ed. 19.95 (ISBN 0-8403-2271-2). Kendall-Hunt.
Glasemen, Steven. Comparative Studies in Software Acquisition: Management Organization Versus the Development Process. LC 81-48559. (Computer Science Ser.). (Illus.). 144p. 1982. 22.00x (ISBN 0-669-05422-4). Lexington Bks.
Glasenapp, C. F., jt. auth. see Ellis, William A.
Glaser & Lompscher. Cognitive & Motivational Aspects of Instruction. 190p. 1983. 47.00 (ISBN 0-444-86351-6, I-109-82, North-Holland). Elsevier.
Glaser & Stematsky. Human Herpes Virus Infections: Clinical Aspects. (Infectious Diseases & Antimicrobial Agents Ser.: Vol. 2). 272p. 1982. 45.00 (ISBN 0-8247-1536-5). Dekker.
Glaser, Anton. History of Binary & Other Nondecimal Numeration. rev. ed. LC 81-51176. (Illus.). 218p. 1981. ltd. ed. 28.00x (ISBN 0-938228-00-5). Tomash Pubs.
--Neater by the Meter: An American Guide to the Metric System. LC 73-88193. (Illus.). 112p. (Orig.). 1974. pap. 3.50 (ISBN 0-9600324-4-4). A Glaser.
Glaser, Barbara, jt. auth. see Kirschenbaum, Howard.
Glaser, Barney, jt. auth. see Strauss, Anselm.
Glaser, Barney G. Experts Versus Laymen: A Study of the Patsy and the Subcontractor. 172p. 1976. Repr. text ed. 12.95 (ISBN 0-87855-217-0). Transaction Bks.
--Organizational Scientists: Their Professional Careers. LC 68-25515. 1964. 22.50x (ISBN 0-672-51186-X); pap. text ed. 9.95x (ISBN 0-89197-872-0). Irvington.
Glaser, Barney G. & Strauss, Anselm L. Awareness of Dying. LC 65-12454. 1965. lib. bdg. 26.95x (ISBN 0-202-30001-3). Aldine Pub.
--Discovery of Grounded Theory: Strategies for Qualitative Research. LC 66-28314. 281p. 1967. pap. text ed. 14.95x (ISBN 0-202-30260-1). Aldine Pub.
--Time for Dying. LC 67-17601. 285p. 1968. 26.95x (ISBN 0-202-30027-7). Aldine Pub.
Glaser, Bonnie S., jt. auth. see Garrett, Banning N.
Glaser, Byron, jt. auth. see Neumeier, Marty.
Glaser, Daniel, jt. ed. see Carter, Robert.
Glaser, Dianne. The Case of the Missing Six. LC 77-16443. (Illus.). 160p. (gr. 4-6). 1978. 6.95 (ISBN 0-8234-0318-1). Holiday.
--The Diary of Trilby Frost. LC 75-37080. 192p. (gr. 6 up). 1976. 9.95 (ISBN 0-8234-0277-0). Holiday.
--Summer Secrets. LC 77-3820. 128p. (gr. 7 up). 1977. 5.95 (ISBN 0-8234-0305-X). Holiday.
Glaser, Edward M. Experiment in the Development of Critical Thinking. LC 79-176806. (Columbia University. Teachers College. Contributions to Education: No. 843). Repr. of 1941 ed. 22.50 (ISBN 0-404-55843-7). AMS Pr.
Glaser, Edward M., jt. auth. see Greenberg, Paul D.
Glaser, Edward M., et al. Putting Knowledge to Use: Facilitating the Diffusion of Knowledge & the Implementation of Planned Change. LC 83-11281. (Social & Behavioral Science Ser.). 1983. text ed. 35.00x (ISBN 0-87589-572-7). Jossey-Bass.
Glaser, Elton. Relics. 51p. 1984. 15.00x (ISBN 0-8195-2118-3); pap. 6.95 (ISBN 0-8195-1119-6). Wesleyan U Pr.
Glaser, Frederick B., jt. ed. see Smart, Reginald G.
Glaser, G. Temporal Lobe Psychomotor Seizures. write for info. (ISBN 0-443-08000-3). Churchill.
Glaser, G. H., et al, eds. Antiepileptic Drugs: Mechanisms of Action. (Advances In Neurology: Vol. 27). 750p. 1980. text ed. 97.00 (ISBN 0-89004-251-9). Raven.
Glaser, Gilbert H., jt. auth. see Matthews, W. B.
Glaser, Hermann, ed. The German Mind of the Nineteenth Century: A Literary & Historical Anthology. 416p. 1981. 17.50 (ISBN 0-8264-0041-8); pap. 8.95 (ISBN 0-8264-0044-2). Continuum.
Glaser, Hy. How to Write Lyrics That Make Sense & Dollars. 1977. 9.95 (ISBN 0-682-48764-3, Banner). Exposition Pr FL.
Glaser, Jerome. Allergy in Childhood. (Illus.). 556p. 1956. photocopy ed. 55.75x (ISBN 0-398-05134-8). C C Thomas.
Glaser, Joel S., jt. auth. see Trobe, Jonathan D.
Glaser, John W. Caring for the Special Child. LC 84-82551. 97p. (Orig.). 1985. pap. 6.95 (ISBN 0-934134-14-6). Leaven Pr.
Glaser, Joseph, jt. auth. see Flynn, James.
Glaser, Kurt. Learning Difficulties: Causes & Psychological Implications - A Guide for Professionals. (Illus.). 112p. 1974. 11.25x (ISBN 0-398-03157-6). C C Thomas.
Glaser, Kurt, tr. see Meyer, L. F. & Nassau, Erich.
Glaser, L. C., ed. see Geometrical Topology Conference, Park City, Utah, Feb. 19-22, 1974.
Glaser, Lance A. & Dobberpuhl, Daniel W. The Design & Analysis of VLSI Circuits. 556p. 1985. text ed. 39.95 (ISBN 0-201-12580-3); write for info. solution manual (ISBN 0-201-12581-1). Addison-Wesley.
Glaser, Luis, jt. ed. see Frazier, William A.
Glaser, Lynn, ed. Indians or Jews? An Introduction...to a Reprint of Manasseh Ben Israel's "the Hope of Israel". LC 72-96513. 1973. Repr. of 1650 ed. 24.50 (ISBN 0-8337-5536-6). B Franklin.
Glaser, Matt & Grappelli, Stephane. Jazz Violin. 1981. pap. 9.95 (ISBN 0-8256-0194-0, Oak). Music Sales.
Glaser, Michael. Does Anyone Know Where a Hermit Crab Goes? LC 82-84341. (Illus.). 32p. (Orig.). (ps-3). 1983. pap. 3.95 (ISBN 0-911635-00-9). Knickerbocker.
--Driftwood. LC 85-50601. (Illus.). 32p. (ps-3). 1985. pap. 3.95 (ISBN 0-911635-01-7). Knickerbocker.
Glaser, Milton. Milton Glaser: Graphic Design. LC 73-79228. (Illus.). 240p. 1973. 85.00 (ISBN 0-87951-013-7); pap. 30.00 (ISBN 0-87951-188-5). Overlook Pr.
Glaser, Milton & Folon, Jean-Michel. The Conversation. (Illus.). 1984. 12.95 (ISBN 0-517-55218-3, Harmony). Crown.
Glaser, Milton, ed. see Beard, James, et al.
Glaser, Milton, tr. see Hecht, Anthony & Hollander, John.
Glaser, Nina. Outside of Time: Sixty Photographs. LC 84-10960. (Illus.). 88p. 1984. 27.95 (ISBN 0-916965-05-8); pap. 17.95 (ISBN 0-916965-04-X); signed limited ed. 50.00 (ISBN 0-916965-06-6). Beaux-Arts Pr.
Glaser, Peter E. & Walker, Raymond F. Thermal Imaging Techniques. LC 64-19979. 280p. 1964. 32.50x (ISBN 0-306-30172-5, Plenum Pr). Plenum Pub.
Glaser, Peter E., jt. ed. see Salisbury, John W.
Glaser, R., ed. Advances in Instructional Psychology, Vol. 1. 320p. 1978. 29.95x (ISBN 0-89859-422-7). L Erlbaum Assocs.
--Advances in Instructional Psychology, Vol. 2. 368p. 1982. 29.95x (ISBN 0-89859-176-7). L Erlbaum Assocs.
--Research & Development & School Change. 128p. 1978. 14.95 (ISBN 0-89859-449-9). L Erlbaum Assocs.
Glaser, Robert. Adaptive Education: Individual Diversity & Learning. LC 76-56081. (Principles of Educational Psychology Ser.). 1977. pap. text ed. 6.95 (ISBN 0-03-015291-7, HoltC). HR&W.
Glaser, Robert, jt. auth. see Pellegrino, James W.
Glaser, Robert, ed. Nature of Reinforcement. 1971. 53.50 (ISBN 0-12-286250-3). Acad Pr.
Glaser, Rollin. Retail Personnel Management. LC 77-79342. 1977. 19.95 (ISBN 0-86730-506-1). Lebhar Friedman.
Glaser, Rollin O. All Quiet on the Western Front Notes. (Orig.). 1965. pap. 2.50 (ISBN 0-8220-0155-1). Cliffs.
Glaser, Victoria. Training for Musicianship. 17.95x (ISBN 0-8008-7829-9, Crescendo). Taplinger.
Glaser, William A. The Brain Drain: Emigration & Return. LC 77-30576. (UNITAR Studies). 1978. pap. text ed. 24.00 (ISBN 0-08-022415-6). Pergamon.
--Health Insurance Bargaining: Foreign Lessons for Americans. 1978. text ed. 25.95 (ISBN 0-89876-058-5). Gardner Pr.
--Pretrial Discovery & the Adversary System. LC 68-54410. 300p. 1968. 10.00x (ISBN 0-87154-305-2). Russell Sage.
Glaser, William A., jt. ed. see McPhee, William N.
Glaserfeld, Ernst von, jt. auth. see Steffe, Leslie P.
Glaser-Wohrer, Evelyn. An Analysis of John Barth's Weltanschauung: His View of Life & Literature. (Salzburg Studies in English Literature: No. 5). 1977. pap. text ed. 31.75x (ISBN 0-391-01385-8). Humanities.

Glasgal, Ralph. Techniques in Data Communications. 200p. 1983. text ed. 39.00 (ISBN 0-89006-122-X). Artech Hse.

Glasgo, Philip W. Valuation of Savings & Loan Associations. Dufey, Gunter, ed. LC 81-14825. (Research for Business Decisions Ser.: No. 47). 140p. 1981. 39.95 (ISBN 0-8357-1269-9). UMI Res Pr.

Glasgoleva, Galina, tr. see Vishneva-Sarafanova, N.

Glasgow. Index to a Private Collection of Notices Entitled Memorabilia of the City of Glasgow. (Maitland Club, Glasgow. Publications: No. 39). 1836. 10.00 (ISBN 0-404-53013-3). AMS Pr.

Glasgow City Corporation Staff. Municipal Glasgow: Its Evolution & Enterprises. Lees, Lynn H. & Lees, Andrew, eds. LC 84-48289. (The Rise of Urban Britain Ser.). 1985. Repr. of 1914 ed. lib. bdg. 50.00 (ISBN 0-8240-6291-4). Garland Pub.

Glasgow, David. Watch & Clock Making. (Illus.). 1977. Repr. of 1885 ed. 25.00 (ISBN 0-7158-1215-7). Charles River Bks.

Glasgow, Douglas G. The Black Underclass: Poverty, Unemployment, & Entrapment of Ghetto Youth. LC 79-28310. (Social & Behavioral Science Ser.). 1980. text ed. 21.95x (ISBN 0-87589-392-9). Jossey-Bass.

--The Black Underclass: Poverty, Unemployment & Entrapment of Ghetto Youth. LC 80-54227. 1981. pap. 5.95 (ISBN 0-394-74725-9, V-725, Vin). Random.

Glasgow, Ellen. Barren Ground. (American Century Ser.). 409p. 1957. pap. 9.95 (ISBN 0-8090-0014-8). Hill & Wang.

--Barren Ground. 11.75 (ISBN 0-8446-4019-0). Peter Smith.

--Barren Ground. 516p. 1985. pap. 8.95 (ISBN 0-15-610685-X, Harv). HarBraceJ.

--Barren Ground. 20.95 (ISBN 0-88411-645-X, Pub by. Aeonian Pr). Amereon Ltd.

--The Battle-Ground. 512p. Repr. of 1902 ed. lib. bdg. 25.00 (ISBN 0-918377-30-7). Russell Pr.

--The Deliverance: A Romance of the Virginia Tobacco Fields. 534p. Repr. of 1904 ed. lib. bdg. 30.00 (ISBN 0-918377-31-5). Russell Pr.

--The Descendant. 276p. Repr. of 1900 ed. lib. bdg. 20.00 (ISBN 0-918377-34-X). Russell Pr.

--The Freeman & Other Poems. 56p. 1973. pap. 4.85 (ISBN 0-910120-00-5). Americanist.

--The Freeman & Other Poems. LC 75-41112. Repr. of 1902 ed. 11.50 (ISBN 0-404-14780-1). AMS Pr.

--In This Our Life. 302p. 1981. Repr. of 1941 ed. lib. bdg. write for info (ISBN 0-89190-152-3, Pub. by River City Pr). Amereon Ltd.

--The Miller of Old Church. 432p. Repr. of 1911 ed. lib. bdg. 25.00 (ISBN 0-918377-29-3). Russell Pr.

--The Romantic Comedians. 346p. Repr. of 1926 ed. lib. bdg. 20.00 (ISBN 0-918377-33-1). Russell Pr.

--The Sheltered Life. 395p. Repr. of 1932 ed. lib. bdg. 20.00 (ISBN 0-918377-32-3). Russell Pr.

--The Sheltered Life. 408p. 1985. pap. 8.95 (ISBN 0-15-681690-3, Harv). HarBraceJ.

--The Sheltered Life. 17.95 (ISBN 0-88411-646-8, Pub. by Aeonian Pr). Amereon Ltd.

--They Stooped to Folly: A Comedy of Morals. 351p. Repr. of 1929 ed. lib. bdg. 20.00 (ISBN 0-918377-38-2). Russell Pr.

--Veil of Iron. 462p. Repr. lib. bdg. 25.00 (ISBN 0-918377-37-4). Russell Pr.

--Vein of Iron. pap. 7.95 (ISBN 0-15-693476-0, Harv). HarBraceJ.

--The Voice of the People. Repr. lib. bdg. 22.95 (ISBN 0-89190-151-5, Pub. by River City Pr). Amereon Ltd.

--The Voice of the People. Godshalk, W. L., ed. (Masterworks of Literature Ser.). 1972. 10.95 (ISBN 0-8084-0030-4); pap. 7.95x (ISBN 0-8084-0031-2). New Coll U Pr.

--The Voice of the People. LC 71-96882. 444p. Repr. of 1900 ed. lib. bdg. 18.50 (ISBN 0-8398-0662-0). Irvington.

--The Voice of the People. Troth, Henry, tr. 444p. Repr. of 1902 ed. lib. bdg. 30.00 (ISBN 0-918377-36-6). Russell Pr.

--The Wheel of Life. 474p. Repr. of 1906 ed. lib. bdg. 25.00 (ISBN 0-918377-35-8). Russell Pr.

Glasgow, Ellen A. Certain Measure: An Interpretation of Prose Fiction. 1943. 17.00 (ISBN 0-527-34000-6). Kraus Repr.

--The Deliverance: A Romance of the Virginia Tobacco Fields. 21.75 (ISBN 0-8369-7161-2, 7993). Ayer Co Pubs.

--The Descendant. Hardwick, Elizabeth, ed. LC 76-51667. (Recovered Fiction by American Women Ser). 1977. Repr. of 1926 ed. lib. bdg. 26.00x (ISBN 0-405-10046-9). Ayer Co Pubs.

Glasgow, Ellen Anderson Gholson. The Romantic Comedians. Hardwick, Elizabeth, ed. LC 76-51668. (Rediscovered Fiction by American Women). 1977. Repr. of 1926 ed. lib. bdg. 30.00 (ISBN 0-405-10047-7). Ayer Co Pubs.

Glasgow, Eric, jt. auth. see Walton, James.

Glasgow, George. Continental Statesmen. LC 70-110903. 1970. Repr. of 1930 ed. 23.50x (ISBN 0-8046-0886-5, Pub. by Kennikat). Assoc Faculty Pr.

--From Dawes to Locarno. LC 72-7101. (Select Bibliographies Reprint Ser.). 1972. Repr. of 1925 ed. 21.50 (ISBN 0-8369-6935-9). Ayer Co Pubs.

--Minoans. LC 70-101042. 1969. Repr. of 1923 ed. 15.00x (ISBN 0-8046-0708-7, Pub. by Kennikat). Assoc Faculty Pr.

Glasgow, Janis, ed. George Sand: Collected Essays. LC 83-50327. 375p. 1985. 30.00x (ISBN 0-87875-300-1). Whitston Pub.

Glasgow University Media Group. Bad News, Vol. 1. 326p. 1976. pap. 17.95x (ISBN 0-7100-0792-2). Routledge & Kegan.

--More Bad News, Vol. 2. (Illus.). 1980. pap. 18.95x (ISBN 0-7100-9328-4). Routledge & Kegan.

Glasgow University Media Group Members. Really Bad News. 14.95 (ISBN 0-86316-051-4); pap. 6.95 (ISBN 0-906495-44-X). Writers & Readers.

Glashagel, Char, jt. ed. see Glashagel, Jerry.

Glashagel, Jerry & Glashagel, Char, eds. Valuing Families. 54p. 1977. pap. 5.00x (ISBN 0-88035-060-1). Human Kinetics.

--Valuing Families. 54p. 5.00x (ISBN 0-88035-060-1, 496). YMCA USA.

Glashagel, Jerry, et al. Digging in Camp Director's Handbook. pap. 7.00x (ISBN 0-88035-025-3). Human Kinetics.

--Digging In Camp Counselor's Handbook. 56p. 1976. pap. 12.00x (ISBN 0-88035-022-9). Human KInetics.

Glashan, Roy, compiled by. American Governors & Gubernatorial Elections, 1775-1978: A Statistical Compilation. LC 79-15021. 1979. lib. bdg. 45.00x (ISBN 0-930466-17-9). Meckler Pub.

Glasheen, Adaline. A Third Census of Finnegans Wake. LC 75-3770. 1977. 32.50x (ISBN 0-520-02980-1). U of Cal Pr.

Glashoff, K. & Gustafson, S. A. Linear Optimization & Approximation: An Introduction to the Theoretical Analysis & Numerical Treatment of Semi-Infinite Programs. (Applied Mathematical Science Ser.: Vol. 45). (Illus.). 197p. 1983. pap. 21.50 (ISBN 0-387-90857-9). Springer-Verlag.

Glashow & Goldstein, Mahler. Shoot the Works: How to Shoot It, How to Sell It. (Illus.). 96p. 14.95 (ISBN 0-87165-058-4, Amphoto). Watson-Guptill.

Glashow, Sheldon, jt. ed. see Frampton, Paul.

Glasier, Philip. Falconry & Hawking. (Illus.). 312p. 1979. 29.50 (ISBN 0-8231-2020-1). Branford.

Glasiher, J. Meteorological Observations at Jerusalem. 1982. 20.00x (ISBN 0-686-45727-7, Pub. by Palestine Explo England). State Mutual Bk.

Glaskov, I. B., jt. auth. see Estrin, Y. B.

Glaskow, Wasili G. History of the Cossacks. LC 67-31332. (Photos). 1968. 9.95 (ISBN 0-8315-0035-2). Speller.

Glaskowsky, N. A., jt. auth. see Wiesner, D. A.

Glaskowsky, Nicholas A., jt. auth. see Wiesner, Donald A.

Glasman, Ronald M., jt. ed. see Vidich, Arthur J.

Glasnapp, Douglas & Poggio, John. Essentials of Statistical Analysis for the Behavioral Sciences. 624p. 1985. text ed. 26.95 (ISBN 0-675-20369-4). Additional supplements maybe obtained from publisher. Merrill.

Glasner, David. Politics, Prices & Petroleum: The Political Economy of Energy. LC 84-19134. (Illus.). 300p. 1985. pap. 12.95 (ISBN 0-88410-954-2). PIPPR.

--Politics, Prices & Petroleum: The Political Economy of Energy. (Pacific Institute in Public Policy Research Ser.). 352p. 1985. professional reference 35.00x (ISBN 0-88410-953-4); pap. write for info. (ISBN 0-88410-954-2). Ballinger Pub.

Glasner, Lynne & Thypin, Marilyn. American Government & Its Citizens. (Government Ser. Wkbk.). (Illus.). 64p. (gr. 7-12). 1984. Set, incl. 2 texts, 1 wkbk., & 1 teacher's guide. 15.85 (ISBN 0-941342-11-5, 1043); Set, incl. 2 texts, teacher's guide, & wkbk. pap. 3.95 (ISBN 0-941342-13-1). Entry Pub.

--American Government: How It Works. (Government Ser.). (Illus.). 96p. (Orig.). (gr. 7-12). 1984. Bk. 1, Set, incl. texts, wkbk., & tchs' guide. 15.85 (ISBN 0-941342-09-3, 1041); pap. text ed. 4.95 2 texts, wkbk, & TG (ISBN 0-941342-13-1). Entry Pub.

--Teacher's Guide to the Government Series. 32p. (gr. 7-12). 1984. Set, incl.2 texts, 1 wkbk., & 1 tchr's. guide. 15.85; tchr's. guide 2.00 (ISBN 0-941342-12-3). Entry Pub.

Glasner, Lynne & Thypin, Marylin. We the People of the United States. (Government Ser.: Bk. 2). (Illus.). 96p. (Orig.). (gr. 7-12). 1984. Set, incl. 2 texts, 1 wkbk., & 1 tchr's. guide. 15.85 (ISBN 0-941342-13-1, 1042); Bk. 2. pap. text ed. 4.95 (ISBN 0-941342-10-7). Entry Pub.

Glasner, Lynne, jt. auth. see Thypin, Marilyn.

Glasner, M. S. Proximal Flows. (Lecture Notes in Mathematics: Vol. 517). 1976. pap. 13.00 (ISBN 0-387-07689-1). Springer-Verlag.

Glasner, Peter E., jt. ed. see Black, Alan W.

Glasofer, Seymour, jt. auth. see Loring, Murray.

Glasofer, Seymour & Mandelker, Lester, eds. Veterinarian's Treasury of Practice Tips II. 144p. 22.50 (ISBN 0-935078-14-2). Veterinary Med.

Glasoleva, Fania, et al, trs. see Losin, V.

Glaspell, Susan. Ambrose Holt & Family. 315p. Repr. of 1931 ed. lib. bdg. 25.00x (ISBN 0-89984-650-5). Century Bookbindery.

--Brook Evans. 312p. Repr. of 1928 ed. lib. bdg. 20.00 (ISBN 0-89984-651-3). Century Bookbindery.

--Plays. LC 83-48837. Repr. of 1920 ed. 29.50 (ISBN 0-404-20108-3). AMS Pr.

--The Visioning: A Novel. 464p. Repr. of 1911 ed. lib. bdg. 30.00 (ISBN 0-89984-652-1). Century Bookbindery.

Glaspie, Catherine. Jessica Strange. 48p. (Orig.). 1984. pap. 4.95 (ISBN 0-89962-391-3). Todd & Honeywell.

Glasrud, Bruce & Smith, Alan. Race Relations in British North America, 1607-1783. LC 81-18824. 368p. 1982. 24.95x (ISBN 0-88229-388-5). Nelson-Hall.

Glass, A. M. Ordered Permutation Groups. LC 81-16996. (London Mathematical Society Lecture Note Ser.: No. 55). (Illus.). 250p. 1982. pap. 27.95 (ISBN 0-521-24190-1). Cambridge U Pr.

Glass, Al, jt. auth. see Glass, Mary E.

Glass, Alastair M., jt. auth. see Lines, Malcom E.

Glass, Alexander J., ed. see American Society for Testing & Materials.

Glass, Amee & Hackett, Dorothy. Ngaanyatjarra Texts. rev. ed. (AIAS New Ser.: No. 16). 144p. 1979. pap. text ed. 10.25x (ISBN 0-391-01683-0). Humanities.

--Pitjantjatjara Grammar: A Tagmemic View of the Ngaanyatjara (Warburton Ranges) Dialect. (AIAS Linguistics Ser.: No. 13). (Illus., Orig.). 1970. pap. text ed. 8.75x (ISBN 0-85575-000-6). Humanities.

Glass, Andrew. Jackson Makes His Move. LC 81-15957. (Illus.). 48p. (gr. 1-4). 1982. 9.95 (ISBN 0-7232-6207-1). Warne.

--My Brother Tries to Make Me Laugh. LC 83-14989. (Illus.). 32p. (ps-1). 1984. 11.50 (ISBN 0-688-02257-X); PLB 10.51 (ISBN 0-688-02259-6). Lothrop.

Glass, Aronld L., et al. Cognition. 2nd ed. 522p. Date not set. text ed. 19.95 (ISBN 0-394-35057-X, RanC). Random.

Glass, Bentley. Progress or Catastrophe: The Nature of Biological Science & Its Impact on Human Society. Anshen, Ruth N., ed. 160p. 1985. 29.95 (ISBN 0-03-001747-5); pap. 9.95 (ISBN 0-03-001748-3). Praeger.

Glass, Bentley see Avery, G. S., Jr.

Glass, Bentley, ed. see Symposium on Light & Life, 1960.

Glass, Bentley, et al, eds. Forerunners of Darwin, 1745-1859. LC 59-9978. (Illus.). 479p. pap. 10.95x (ISBN 0-8018-0222-9). Johns Hopkins.

Glass, Bill & McEachern, James E. Plan to Win. 160p. 1984. 8.95 (ISBN 0-8499-0431-5, 0431-5). Word Bks.

Glass, Billy P. Introduction to Planetary Geology. LC 81-17057. (Planetary Science Ser.: No. 2). (Illus.). 1982. 32.50 (ISBN 0-521-23579-0); pap. cancelled (ISBN 0-521-28052-4). Cambridge U Pr.

Glass, Carol see Merluzzi, Thomas.

Glass, Carter. An Adventure in Constructive Finance. facsimile ed. LC 75-2635. (Wall Street & the Security Markets Ser.). 1975. Repr. of 1927 ed. 35.50x (ISBN 0-405-06960-X). Ayer Co Pubs.

Glass, Carter M. Linear Systems with Applications & Discrete Analysis. LC 75-40282. (Illus.). 550p. 1976. text ed. 37.95 (ISBN 0-8299-0081-0). West Pub.

Glass, Charles & Foster, Robert. Cacti & Succulents for the Amateur. (Illus.). 72p. 1980. pap. 4.95 (ISBN 0-7137-0834-4, Pub. by Blandford Pr England). Sterling.

Glass, D. V. & Taylor, P. A. Population & Emigration in Nineteenth Century Britain. (Government & Society in 19th. Century Britain Ser.). 132p. 1976. 20.00x (ISBN 0-7165-2219-5, BBA 02037, Pub. by Irish Academic Pr Ireland). Biblio Dist.

Glass, D. V., ed. Introduction to Malthus. 205p. 1966. 24.00x (ISBN 0-7146-1579-X, F Cass Co). Biblio Dist.

Glass, David C. & Singer, Jerome E. Urban Stress: Experiments on Noise & Social Stressors. LC 78-182640. (Social Psychology Ser.). 1972. 33.50 (ISBN 0-12-286050-0). Acad Pr.

Glass, David C., ed. Environmental Influences. LC 68-56103. (Illus.). 316p. 1969. 13.00x (ISBN 0-87470-012-4). Rockefeller.

--Genetics. LC 68-24635. (Illus.). 270p. 1968. 13.00x (ISBN 0-87470-008-6). Rockefeller.

--Neurophysiology & Emotion. LC 67-31389. (Illus.). 256p. 1967. 13.00x (ISBN 0-87470-006-X). Rockefeller.

Glass, David V. Population Policies & Movements in Europe. LC 67-19728. Repr. of 1940 ed. 35.00x (ISBN 0-678-05049-X). Kelley.

Glass, Dick & Crow, Ron. The CET Exam Book. (Illus.). 210p. (Orig.). 1984. 14.95 (ISBN 0-8306-0670-X); pap. 9.95 (ISBN 0-8306-1670-5, 1670). TAB Bks.

Glass, Dorothy F. Italian Romanesque Sculpture: An Annotated Bibliography. 1983. lib. bdg. 49.00 (ISBN 0-8161-8331-7, Hall Reference). G K Hall.

Glass, Elliot & Arcario, Paul. Speak Freely: Conversational American English. 346p. 1985. pap. text ed. 10.95 (ISBN 0-15-583171-2, HC). HarBraceJ.

Glass, Elliot, et al. Everyday Spanish: A Basic Textbook. 2nd ed. 1984. pap. text ed. 16.95 (ISBN 0-89529-155-X). Avery Pub.

Glass, Elliot S. El Politico Honesto. 157p. (Orig.). 1981. 10.00x (ISBN 0-916304-49-3). SDSU Press.

Glass, Esther E. Larry & Kathy. LC 64-10186. (Illus.). 136p. (gr. 5-8). 1964. 4.95 (ISBN 0-8361-1384-5). Herald Pr.

Glass, Frank W. The Fertilizing Seed: Wagner's Concept of the Poetic Intent. Buelow, George, ed. LC 82-21813. (Studies in Musicology: No. 63). 336p. 1983. 44.95 (ISBN 0-8357-1396-2). UMI Res Pr.

Glass, Fred J. Jewelry Craft. 70p. 1971. pap. 2.95 (ISBN 0-915462-01-X). Paragraph Pr.

--Metal Craft. (Illus.). 70p. 1971. pap. 2.95 (ISBN 0-915462-04-4). Paragraph Pr.

--Paper Craft. (Illus.). 76p. 1971. pap. 2.95 (ISBN 0-915462-05-2). Paragraph Pr.

--Pewter Craft. (Illus.). 65p. 1971. pap. 2.95 (ISBN 0-915462-03-6). Paragraph Pr.

--Stencil Craft. (Illus.). 64p. 1971. pap. 2.95 (ISBN 0-915462-02-8). Paragraph Pr.

Glass, G. Bank: EDV von A-Z. 96p. (Ger. & Eng., Bank - Data Processing A-Z). 1977. 9.95 (ISBN 3-7819-1090-3, M-7303, Pub. by Knapp). French & Eur.

Glass, Gene V. Design & Analysis of Time-Series Experiments. Willson, Victor L. & Gottman, John M., eds. LC 74-84779. (Illus.). 200p. 1975. text ed. 19.50x (ISBN 0-87081-063-4). Colo Assoc.

Glass, Gene V. & Hopkins, Kenneth D. Statistical Methods in Education & Psychology. 2nd ed. (Illus.). 608p. 1984. text ed. 33.95 (ISBN 0-13-844944-9). P-H.

Glass, Gene V., jt. auth. see Hopkins, Kenneth D.

Glass, Gene V., ed. Evaluation Studies Review Annual, Vol. 1. LC 76-15865. (Illus.). 1976. 40.00 (ISBN 0-8039-0704-4). Sage.

Glass, Gene V., et al. School Class Size: Research & Policy. (Illus.). 176p. 1982. 22.50 (ISBN 0-8039-1805-4). Sage.

--Meta-Analysis in Social Research. LC 81-5673. (Illus.). 272p. 1981. 25.00 (ISBN 0-8039-1633-7). Sage.

Glass, George. Competitive Judo: Throwing Techniques & Weight Control. (Illus.). 96p. (Orig.). 1977. pap. 3.95 (ISBN 0-571-10915-2). Faber & Faber.

Glass, George B., ed. Gastrointestinal Hormones. (Comprehensive Endocrinology Ser.). 1028p. 1980. text ed. 127.50 (ISBN 0-89004-395-7). Raven.

--Progress in Gastroenterology, Vols. I-II. LC 68-11924. (Illus.). 1968. Vol. 1, 1968 528pps. 117.00 (ISBN 0-8089-0149-4, 791561); Vol. II, 1970 544pps. 99.50 (ISBN 0-8089-0150-8, 7915-62). Grune.

--Progress in Gastroenterology, Vol. III. 1072p. 1977. 139.00 (ISBN 0-8089-1025-6, 791563). Grune.

Glass, George B. & Sherlock, Paul, eds. Progress in Gastroenterology. (Vol. 4). 624p. 1983. 89.50 (ISBN 0-8089-1555-X, 791564). Grune.

Glass, H. Bentley, ed. The Roving Naturalists: Travel Letters of Theodosius Dobzhansky. LC 79-55229. (Memoirs Ser.: Vol. 139). 1980. pap. 10.00 (ISBN 0-87169-139-6). Am Philos.

Glass, Henry A. Story of the Psalters. LC 72-1635. Repr. of 1888 ed. 18.50 (ISBN 0-404-08308-0). AMS Pr.

Glass, Hiram B. Science & Ethical Values. LC 81-13170. ix, 101p. 1981. Repr. of 1965 ed. lib. bdg. 22.50x (ISBN 0-313-23141-9, GLSE). Greenwood.

--Science & Liberal Education. LC 60-8285. (Davis Washington Mitchell Lectures). pap. 31.80 (ISBN 0-317-09391-6, 2003383). Bks Demand UMI.

Glass, Isabel. Bedside Manners. (Orig.). 1980. pap. 2.50 (ISBN 0-449-14310-4, GM). Fawcett.

--Fifth Avenue Store Only. 288p. 1975. pap. 1.50 (ISBN 0-532-15160-7). Woodhill.

Glass, J. Colin. Introduction to Mathematical Methods in Economics. 352p. 1980. text ed. 38.95 (ISBN 0-07-084116-0). McGraw.

Glass, James M. Delusion: Internal Dimensions of Political Life. LC 84-16193. (Illus.). 272p. 1985. 22.50 (ISBN 0-226-29797-7). U of Chicago Pr.

Glass, Jesse, Jr. Enoch. (WEP Poetry Ser.: No. 5). 16p. 1982. pap. 2.00 (ISBN 0-917976-11-8). White Ewe.

Glass, Joanna M. Canadian Gothic & American Modern. 1977. pap. 3.35x (ISBN 0-685-80038-5). Dramatists Play.

--Woman Wanted. 256p. 1985. 14.95 (ISBN 0-312-88644-6). St Martin.

Glass, John B. see Wauchope, Robert.

Glass, Justine. Witchcraft-the Sixth Sense. pap. 5.00 (ISBN 0-87980-174-3). Wilshire.

Glass, Lillian & Liebmann-Smith, Richard. How to Deprogram Your Valley Girl. LC 82-21964. (Illus.). 64p. (Orig.). 1982. pap. 2.95 (ISBN 0-89480-239-9). Workman Pub.

Glass, Malcolm. Bone Love. LC 78-14337. (University of Central Florida Contemporary Poetry Ser.). viii, 68p. 1978. 8.95 (ISBN 0-8130-0616-3). U Presses Fla.

Glass, Marion & Atchison, Evelyn. Integrated Studies in Patient Care. LC 76-46127. 1978. pap. text ed. 16.00 (ISBN 0-8273-1608-9); instructor's guide 4.10 (ISBN 0-8273-1609-7). Delmar.

--Integrated Studies in Patient Care. 1978. 19.95 (ISBN 0-442-22699-3). Van Nos Reinhold.

Glass, Marjorie. Antiques, the Best of the Best. (Illus.). 176p. 1983. 19.95 (ISBN 0-913765-01-5); pap. 14.95 (ISBN 0-913765-03-1). Krantz Co.

Glass, Mary E. Nevada's Turbulent Fifties: Decade of Political & Economic Change. LC 80-25651. (Nevada Studies in History & Political Science: No. 15). (Illus.). ix, 137p. (Orig.). 1981. pap. 5.75x (ISBN 0-87417-062-1). U of Nev Pr.

--Silver & Politics in Nevada: 1892-1902. LC 72-92547. (Lancehead Ser). (Illus.). xi, 242p. 1970. 5.50 (ISBN 0-87417-026-5). U of Nev Pr.

Glass, Mary E. & Glass, Al. Touring Nevada: A Historic & Scenic Guide. (Illus.). 253p. (Orig.). 1983. pap. 7.95 (ISBN 0-87417-074-5). U of Nev Pr.

Glass, Montagu. Potash & Perlmutter: Their Co-Partnership Ventures & Adventures. facsimile ed. LC 74-27988. (Modern Jewish Experience Ser.). (Illus.). 1975. Repr. of 1909 ed. 35.50x (ISBN 0-405-06715-1). Ayer Co Pubs.

Glass, Mrs. Quintard. Cemetery Inscriptions from Dyer County, Tennessee. 240p. 1978. 15.00 (ISBN 0-89308-095-0). Southern Hist Pr.

Glass, Norman, tr. see De Nerval, Gerard.

Glass, P. V. Population Policies & Movements in Europe. 490p. 1967. 37.50x (ISBN 0-7146-1580-3, F Cass Co). Biblio Dist.

Glass, Paul & Singer, Louis. Singing Soldiers: A History of the Civil War in Song. LC 75-14127. (Quality Paperback Ser.). Orig. Title: The Spirit of the Sixties. (Illus.). xx, 300p. 1975. pap. 6.95 (ISBN 0-306-80021-7). Da Capo.

Glass, Philip, jt. auth. see DeJong, Constance.

Glass, R., jt. auth. see Nicholls, J.

Glass, Raymond M., et al. Teaching Exceptional Students in the Regular Classroom. 1982. text ed. 24.95 (ISBN 0-316-14060-0); tchrs' manual avail. (ISBN 0-316-14061-9). Little.

Glass, Robert. Real-Time Software. (Illus.). 464p. 1984. text ed. 26.95 (ISBN 0-13-767103-2). P-H.

Glass, Robert E. Gene Function: E. Coli & Its Heritable Elements. LC 81-69893. (Illus.). 480p. 1982. 42.50x (ISBN 0-520-04619-6); pap. 20.00 (ISBN 0-520-04654-4, CAMPUS 297). U of Cal Pr.

Glass, Robert H. & Ericsson, Ronald J. Getting Pregnant in the Nineteen Eighties: New Advances in Infertility Treatment & Sex Preselection. (Illus.). 128p. 1982. 10.95 (ISBN 0-520-04828-8). U of Cal Pr.

Glass, Robert L. Computing Catastrophes. 1983. 11.00 (ISBN 0-686-35783-3). Computing Trends.

--Modern Programming Practices: A Report from Industry. (Illus.). 304p. 1982. text ed. 34.95 (ISBN 0-13-597294-9). P-H.

--The Power of Peonage. 1979. 9.00 (ISBN 0-686-23742-0). Computing Trends.

--The Second Coming: More Computing Projects Which Failed. 1980. 9.00 (ISBN 0-686-26939-X). Computing Trends.

--Software Reliability Guidebook. (Illus.). 1979. text ed. 32.95 (ISBN 0-13-821785-8). P-H.

--Software Soliloquies. 1981. 10.00 (ISBN 0-686-31797-1). Computing Trends.

--The Universal Elixir & Other Computing Projects which Failed. 1977. 9.00 (ISBN 0-686-23609-2). Computing Trends.

Glass, Robert L. & Noiseux, Ronald A. Software Maintenance Guidebook. (Illus.). 208p. 1981. text ed. 34.95 (ISBN 0-13-821728-9). P-H.

Glass, Ruth & Pollins, Harold. London's Newcomers: The West Indian Migrants. LC 61-16042. (Illus.). 1961. 18.50x (ISBN 0-674-53850-1). Harvard U Pr.

Glass, Stuart. A Divorce Dictionary: A Book for You & Your Children. (Illus.). 80p. (gr. 7 up). 1980. 7.95 (ISBN 0-316-31581-8). Little.

Glass, Thomas E., ed. Crisis in Urban Schools. LC 73-4330. 1973. 39.00x (ISBN 0-8422-5095-6); pap. text ed. 8.50x (ISBN 0-8422-0298-6). Irvington.

Glass, Thomas E., et al. Community Control in Education: A Study in Power Transition. LC 77-74529. 118p. 1978. 14.85 (ISBN 0-87812-157-9, 3450). Pendell Pub.

Glass, Thomas G., Jr. Management of Poisonous Snakebite. (Illus.). 182p. (Orig.). 1976. pap. text ed. 20.00 (ISBN 0-9614759-1-9). Glass Pub Co.

--Snakebite First Aid. (Illus.). 41p. 1981. pap. 5.00 (ISBN 0-9614759-0-0). Glass Pub Co.

Glassberg, Andrew D. Representation & Urban Community. 200p. 1981. 24.50x (ISBN 0-8448-1408-3). Crane-Russak Co.

Glassberg, Bert Y. Barron's Teen-Age Sex Counselor. rev. ed. LC 65-20276. (Orig.). (gr. 7-12). 1970. pap. text ed. 1.50 (ISBN 0-8120-0167-2). Barron.

Glassbrenner, Alfred, jt. auth. see Lau, Charley.

Glassbrook, D. W., jt. auth. see Arotsky, J.

Glassburner, Bruce, ed. The Economy of Indonesia: Selected Readings. LC 77-127777. (Illus.). 448p. 1971. 39.95x (ISBN 0-8014-0600-5). Cornell U Pr.

Glassco, John. Memoirs of Montparnasse. 1970. 8.95x (ISBN 0-19-540202-2). Oxford U Pr.

Glasscock, C. B. Then Came Oil. LC 75-6474. (History & Politics of Oil Ser.). (Illus.). 349p. 1976. Repr. of 1938 ed. 23.50 (ISBN 0-88355-292-2). Hyperion Conn.

Glasscock, Michael. The Real Estate Investing Profit Guide: How to Successfully Finance, Purchase, & Manage Income Property. (Illus.). 276p. 1982. 19.95 (ISBN 0-13-763136-7); pap. 11.95 (ISBN 0-13-763128-6). P-H.

Glasscock, Michael E., jt. auth. see Shambaugh, George E.

Glasscock, Paula, jt. auth. see Weber, Sally.

Glasscoe, Marion. The Medieval Mystical Tradition in England. 191p. 1984. 25.00 (ISBN 0-85991-160-8, Pub. by Boydell & Brewer). Longwood Pub Group.

Glasscoe, Marion, ed. The Medieval Mystical Tradition in England. 249p. 1980. pap. 14.50x (ISBN 0-686-86100-0, Pub. by U Exeter, England). Humanities.

--Revelation of Love. 111p. 1976. pap. text ed. 4.50x (ISBN 0-85989-061-9, Pub. by U Exeter England). Humanities.

Glasscote, Raymond M., et al. The Uses of Psychiatry in Smaller General Hospitals. LC 82-22719. 144p. 1983. pap. 12.00x (ISBN 0-89042-108-0, 42-108-0). Am Psychiatric.

Glasse, Hannah. The Art of Cookery Made Plain & easy. 227p. 1983. text ed. 40.00 (ISBN 0-907325-17-3); text ed. 60.00 quarter leather. U pr of Va.

Glasse, James D. Profession: Minister. LC 68-17447. Repr. of 1968 ed. 33.50 (ISBN 0-8357-9021-5, 2011670). Bks Demand UMI.

--Putting It Together in the Parish. LC 71-185548. 1972. 7.75 (ISBN 0-687-34932-X). Abingdon.

Glasse, Robert M. Huli of Papua: A Cognatic Descent System. (Cahiers de l'Homme, Nouvelle Ser.: No. 8). (Illus., Orig.). 1968. pap. text ed. 15.60x (ISBN 90-2796-067-4). Mouton.

Glasser, Ala. Synthetic Feelings & Popular Culture. LC 78-24017. 1979. 14.95 (ISBN 0-87949-132-9). Ashley Bks.

Glasser, Alan. Research & Development Management. (Illus.). 384p. 1982. 32.95 (ISBN 0-13-774091-3). P-H.

Glasser, Allen J. & Zimmerman, Irla L. Clinical Interpretation of the Wechsler Intelligence Scale for Children. LC 67-11952. (Illus.). 160p. 1967. pap. 19.00 (ISBN 0-8089-0151-6, 791575). Grune.

Glasser, Arthur F. & McGavran, Donald A. Contemporary Theologies of Mission. 320p. (Orig.). 1983. pap. 12.95 (ISBN 0-8010-3790-5). Baker Bk.

Glasser, Carrie. Wage Differentials. LC 77-76638. (Columbia University Studies in the Social Sciences: No. 476). (Illus.). 1969. Repr. of 1940 ed. 16.50 (ISBN 0-404-51476-6). AMS Pr.

Glasser, Diane, jt. auth. see Pollack, Cecelia.

Glasser, Hannelore. Artist's Contracts of the Early Renaissance. LC 76-23624. (Outstanding Dissertations in the Fine Arts - 2nd Series - 15th Century). (Illus.). 1977. Repr. of 1965 ed. lib. bdg. 68.00 (ISBN 0-8240-2694-2). Garland Pub.

Glasser, Joseph. Fundamentals of Applied Industrial Management. (Illus.). 20.00 (ISBN 0-8283-1542-6). Branden Pub Co.

Glasser, Lawrence M., tr. see Solodovnikov, A. S.

Glasser, Mark, et al. Explorations in National Cinemas. Lawton, Ben & Staiger, Janet, eds. (Film Studies Annual, 1977: Pt. 1). (Illus.). vi, 160p. (Orig.). 1977. pap. 7.50 (ISBN 0-913178-52-7). Redgrave Pub Co.

Glasser, Morton & Pelto, Gretel H. Medical Merry-Go-Round: A Plea for Reasonable Medicine. (Illus.). vii, 167p. (Orig.). 1980. pap. 9.95 (ISBN 0-913178-54-3). Redgrave Pub Co.

Glasser, Naomi, ed. What Are You Doing? LC 80-7586. 340p. 1982. pap. 6.68i (ISBN 0-06-090947-1, CN 947, CN). Har-Row.

Glasser, Otto. Doctor W. C. Rontgen. 2nd ed. (Illus.). 192p. 1972. 20.25x (ISBN 0-398-02196-1). C C Thomas.

Glasser, Paul H. & Mayadas, Nazneen. Group Workers at Work: Theory & Practice in the Eighties. 450p. 1985. 32.50x (ISBN 0-86598-160-4). Rowman & Allanheld.

Glasser, Paul H., et al, eds. Individual Change Through Small Groups. LC 73-14113. (Illus.). 1974. 18.00 (ISBN 0-02-911810-7); pap. text ed. 18.95 (ISBN 0-02-911800-X). Free Pr.

Glasser, Perry. Suspicious Origins. 1983. 6.00 (ISBN 0-89823-049-7). New Rivers Pr.

Glasser, Ralph. The Net & the Quest: Patterns of Community & How They Can Survive Progress. LC 77-81678. 1978. 15.00x (ISBN 0-87663-726-8, Pica Pr). Universe.

Glasser, Ronald J. Another War, Another Peace. 256p. 1985. 14.95 (ISBN 0-671-50767-2). Summit Bks.

--Three Hundred Sixty-Five Days. LC 77-156599. 1971. O.P. 6.95 (ISBN 0-8076-0615-4); pap. 7.95 (ISBN 0-8076-0995-1). Braziller.

--Ward 402. LC 73-79048. 1973. Braziller.

Glasser, S., jt. ed. see Balin, H.

Glasser, Selma. Prize-Winning Recipes. 1984. 9.95 (ISBN 0-531-09829-X). Watts.

Glasser, Stanley R. & Bullock, David W., eds. Cellular & Molecular Aspects of Implantation. LC 80-20471. 518p. 1981. 65.00x (ISBN 0-306-40581-4, Plenum Pr). Plenum Pub.

Glasser, Stephen P. & Clark, Pamela I. The Clinical Approach to Exercise Testing. (Illus.). 251p. 1980. pap. text ed. 27.50 (ISBN 0-06-140942-1, 14-09424, Harper Medical). Lippincott.

Glasser, Stephen P., ed. Noncardiac Surgery in the Cardiac Patient: Management & Assessment. LC 82-82381. (Illus.). 416p. 1983. 49.50 (ISBN 0-87993-183-3). Futura Pub.

Glasser, William. Identity Society. 320p. 1975. pap. 7.21i (ISBN 0-06-090446-1, CN446, CN). Har-Row.

--Mental Health or Mental Illness. LC 60-15216. (Illus.). 1961. 7.95i (ISBN 0-06-002010-5, HarpT). Har-Row.

--Mental Health or Mental Illness: Psychiatry for Practical Action. 1983. pap. 4.76i (ISBN 0-06-091092-5, CN1092, CN). Har-Row.

--Positive Addiction. LC 75-15305. (Illus.). 176p. 1976. 12.45i (ISBN 0-06-011558-0, HarpT). Har-Row.

--Positive Addiction. LC 84-48643. 176p. 1985. pap. 5.72i (ISBN 0-317-15384-6, CN 1243, CN). Har-Row.

--Reality Therapy. LC 65-14672. 1965. 11.49i (ISBN 0-06-002040-7, HarpT). Har-Row.

--Reality Therapy: A New Approach to Psychiatry. 1975. pap. 6.25i (ISBN 0-06-090414-3, CN414, CN). Har-Row.

--Reality Therapy: A New Approach to Psychiatry. 1975. pap. 3.80i (ISBN 0-06-080348-7, P348, PL). Har-Row.

--Schools Without Failure. 320p. 1975. pap. 6.95i (ISBN 0-06-090421-6, CN421, CN). Har-Row.

--Schools Without Failure. LC 68-28199. 1969. 9.95i (ISBN 0-06-002011-3, HarpT). Har-Row.

--Schools Without Failure. 256p. 1975. pap. 3.37i (ISBN 0-06-080349-5, P349, PL). Har-Row.

--Take Effective Control of Your Life. LC 84-47574. 256p. 1984. 14.37i (ISBN 0-06-015342-3, HarpT). Har-Row.

--Take Effective Control of Your Life. LC 84-47574. 288p. 1985. pap. 6.95 (ISBN 0-06-091292-8, PL 1292, PL). Har-Row.

Glasser, William & Powers, William T. Stations of the Mind: New Directions for Reality Therapy. LC 80-8205. (Illus.). 288p. 1981. 14.37i (ISBN 0-06-011478-9, HarpT). Har-Row.

Glassey, Lionel K. Politics & the Appointment of Justices of the Peace: 1675-1720. (Historical Monographs). 1979. 32.50x (ISBN 0-19-821875-3). Oxford U Pr.

Glassey, Stanley C. Groundwork of Criticism: Judging Poetry. LC 73-7455. 175p. 1974. Repr. of 1947 ed. lib. bdg. 18.75x (ISBN 0-8371-6934-8, GLGC). Greenwood.

Glassford, Robert G. Application of a Theory of Games to the Transitional Eskimo Culture. LC 75-35070. (Studies in Play & Games). 1976. 23.50x (ISBN 0-405-07920-6). Ayer Co Pubs.

Glassgold, A. E., ed. see Nebula to Honor Henry Draper, Dec. 4-5, 1981.

Glassgold, Peter, ed. & tr. Hwaet! A Little Old English Anthology of American Modernist Poetry. 88p. (Orig., Translation from Modern Eng. into Old Eng.). 1985. pap. 6.95 (ISBN 0-940650-42-8). Sun & Moon MD.

Glassgold, Peter, ed. Living Space: Poems of the Dutch "Fiftiers". LC 79-15580. 1979. 7.95 (ISBN 0-8112-0746-3); pap. 4.95 (ISBN 0-8112-0747-1, NDP493). New Directions.

Glassgold, Peter, jt. ed. see Laughlin, J.

Glassie, Henry. All Silver & No Brass: An Irish Christmas Mumming. 1983. 8.95 (ISBN 0-8122-1139-1). U of Pa Pr.

--Folk Housing in Middle Virginia: A Structural Analysis of Historic Artifacts. LC 75-11653. (Illus.). 1975. 19.95x (ISBN 0-87049-173-3); pap. 9.50x (ISBN 0-87049-268-3). U of Tenn Pr.

--Irish Folk History: Texts from the North. LC 81-43516. (Illus.). 160p. (Orig.). 1982. 17.50x (ISBN 0-8122-7825-9); pap. 8.95x (ISBN 0-8122-1123-5). U of Pa Pr.

--Passing the Time in Ballymenone: Culture & History of an Ulster Community. LC 81-43515. (American Folklore Society Ser.). (Illus.). 832p. 1982. 35.00x (ISBN 0-8122-7823-2). U of Pa Pr.

--Pattern in the Material Folk Culture of the Eastern United States. rev. ed. LC 75-160630. (Amercian Folklore Society Ser.). (Illus.). 1971. 22.50x (ISBN 0-8122-7569-1); pap. 9.95x (ISBN 0-8122-1013-1, Pa Paperbks). U of Pa Pr.

Glassie, Henry, jt. auth. see Leach, MacEdward.

Glassie, Henry, ed. Irish Folktales. 338p. 1985. 19.95 (ISBN 0-318-12056-9). Pantheon.

Glassie, Henry, et al. Folksongs & Their Makers. 179p. 1971. pap. 5.00 (ISBN 0-87972-006-9). Bowling Green Univ.

Glassie, Henry H., jt. auth. see Cosentino, Andrew J.

Glassley, Ray. Indian Wars of the Pacific Northwest. 2nd ed. LC 72-77590. (Illus.). 274p. 1972. 9.50 (ISBN 0-8323-0014-4). Binford.

Glassman, Alan M. The Challenge of Management: A Behavioral Orientation. LC 77-16095. 304p. 1978. pap. text ed. 24.45 (ISBN 0-471-02767-7). Wiley.

Glassman, Alan M. & Cummings, Thomas G. Industrial Relations. 1985. text ed. 25.95 (ISBN 0-673-16007-6); instr's. manual incl. Scott F.

Glassman, Alex, ed. Printing Fundamentals. 1983. write for info (ISBN 0-89852-045-2). TAPPI.

Glassman, Alfred. Universal Atlas of Central Massachusetts & Metropolitan Worcester. Glassman, Michail, ed. (Illus.). 96p. (Orig.). 1984. pap. 7.95 (ISBN 0-932427-00-6). Univ Pub MA.

Glassman, Armand B. & Umlas, Joel, eds. Cryopreservation of Tissues & Solid Organs for Transplantation. 112p. 1983. 21.00 (ISBN 0-914404-87-3). Am Assn Blood.

Glassman, Barbara. Maui Art & Creative People. Cain, Priscilla, ed. (The Maui Network Directory Ser.). (Illus.). 32p. (Orig.). 1985. 8.95 (ISBN 0-9614443-0-4). B Glassman.

Glassman, Bernard. Anti-Semitic Stereotypes Without Jews: Images of the Jews in England, 1290-1700. LC 75-16391. 218p. 1975. 13.95 (ISBN 0-8143-1545-3). Wayne St U Pr.

Glassman, Bernard T., jt. auth. see Maezumi, Hakuyu T.

Glassman, Bernard T., jt. ed. see Maezumi, Hakuyu T.

Glassman, Bruce. The Crash of Twenty-Nine & the New Deal. LC 85-40172. (Turning Points in American History Ser.). (Illus.). 64p. (gr. 5 up). 1985. 13.96 (ISBN 0-382-06978-1). Silver.

--The Crash of Twenty Nine & the New Deal. LC 85-40172. (Turning Points in American History Ser.). (Illus.). 64p. (gr. 5 up). 1985. pap. 5.95. Silver.

Glassman, Bruce, jt. auth. see McNear, Robert.

Glassman, Craig. Off the Wall. (Illus.). 277p. 1980. 12.95 (ISBN 0-8119-0410-5, Pegasus Rex). Fell.

Glassman, Don. Writers' & Artists' Rights. LC 77-95457. (Illus.). pap. 4.25 (ISBN 0-931536-01-4). Writers Pr.

Glassman, Elizabeth. Reading Prints: A Selection of 16th to Early 19th-Century Prints from the Menil Collection. LC 81-83964. (Menil Foundation Ser.). (Illus.). 124p. 1985. pap. 7.50x (ISBN 0-939594-01-3). Menil Found.

Glassman, Elizabeth, jt. auth. see Davidson, Kathryn.

Glassman, Eugene H. The Translation Debate. LC 80-29286. 128p. (Orig.). 1981. pap. 4.25 (ISBN 0-87784-467-4). Inter Varsity.

Glassman, Henry S. Lead the Way, Rangers - Fifth Ranger Bn. (Illus.). 104p. 1980. pap. 6.95 (ISBN 0-934588-03-1). Ranger Assocs.

Glassman, J. Driver Education & Traffic Safety. 2nd ed. 1976. pap. text ed. 10.64 (ISBN 0-13-220582-3); student guide 9.12 (ISBN 0-13-220566-1). P-H.

Glassman, Jon D. Arms for the Arabs: The Soviet Union & War in the Middle East. LC 75-29254. (Illus.). 254p. 1976. 24.00x (ISBN 0-8018-1747-1). Johns Hopkins.

Glassman, Judith. The Cancer Survivors: And How They Did It. LC 82-23448. 432p. 1983. 18.95 (ISBN 0-385-27673-7, Dial). Doubleday.

Glassman, Lenore & Jackson, Yvette. You Ain't Lived Til You Grow Old. (Illus.). 104p. (Orig.). 1980. pap. 4.95 (ISBN 0-918464-44-7). Lyco Pub.

Glassman, Michail, ed. Universal Atlas of Metropolitan Boston & Eastern Massachusetts. 18th ed. (Illus.). 208p. 1985. pap. 11.50 (ISBN 0-932427-01-4). Univ Pub MA.

Glassman, Michail, ed. see Glassman, Alfred.

Glassman, Paul. Belize Guide. LC 82-62939. 112p. (Orig.). 1983. pap. 11.95x (ISBN 0-930016-03-3). Passport Pr.

--Costa Rica. LC 84-60704. (Illus.). 192p. 1984. pap. 12.95x (ISBN 0-930016-04-1). Passport Pr.

--Guatemala Guide. LC 77-74034. (Orig.). 1978. pap. 15.95x (ISBN 0-930016-00-9). Passport Pr.

--Lake Atitlan & Chichicastenahgo, the Complete Guide. 345p. 1978. 3.50 (ISBN 0-318-14570-7). Intl Guatemala.

--Lake Atitlan & Chichicastenango: The Complete Guide. LC 76-364141. 1976. 3.50 (ISBN 0-930016-01-7). Passport Pr.

Glassman, Peter. J. S. Mill: The Evolution of a Genius. LC 84-16286. 240p. 18.00. U Presses Fla.

Glassman, Peter J. Language & Being: Joseph Conrad & the Literature of Personality. LC 75-29092. 286p. 1976. 26.00x (ISBN 0-231-03999-9). Columbia U Pr.

Glassman, Ronald M. & Murvar, Vatro, eds. Max Weber's Political Sociology: A Pessimistic Vision of a Rationalized World. LC 83-1678. (Contributions in Sociology Ser.: No. 45). (Illus.). viii, 295p. 1984. lib. bdg. 35.00 (ISBN 0-313-23642-9, GMW/). Greenwood.

Glassman, Ronald M., jt. ed. see Antonio, Robert J.

Glassman, S. F. Flora of Ponape. (BMB). Repr. of 1952 ed. 19.00 (ISBN 0-527-02317-5). Kraus Repr.

Glassman, Samuel. Epic of Survival: The Story of Anti-Semitism. LC 80-69018. 400p. 20.00x (ISBN 0-8197-0481-4). Bloch.

Glassman, Sidney. A Guide to Residential Management. 2nd. ed. 260p. 1978. pap. 16.00 (ISBN 0-86718-053-6). Natl Assn Home.

Glassmann, S. F. A Revision of B. E. Dahlgren's Index of American Palms. (Phaneroga Marum Mongraphiae: No. 6). 1972. 42.00 (ISBN 3-7682-0765-X). Lubrecht & Cramer.

Glassmire, Carol G. Price Guide to the Collector's Encyclopedia of Cloth Dolls. 48p. 1985. pap. 4.95 (ISBN 0-87069-384-0). Wallace-Homestead.

--Price Guide to the Twentieth Century Dolls Series. rev. ed. 224p. 1983. pap. 9.95 (ISBN 0-87069-379-4). Wallace-Homestead.

Glassner, Andrew S. Computer Graphics User's Guide. LC 83-50378. 240p. 1984. pap. 19.95 (ISBN 0-672-22064-4, 22064). Sams.

Glassner, Barry. Essential Interactionism: On the Intelligibility of Prejudice. (International Library of Sociology). (Illus.). 1980. 22.95x (ISBN 0-7100-0381-1). Routledge & Kegan.

Glassner, Barry, jt. auth. see Moreno, Jonathan D.

Glassner, Barry, jt. auth. see Sylvan, David.

Glassner, Jean-Jacques, jt. auth. see Cassin, Elena.

Glassner, Lester & Harris, Brownie. Dime Store Days. 128p. 1981. 25.00 (ISBN 0-670-27279-5, Studio). Viking.

Glassner, Martin, jt. ed. see Papadakis, Nikos.

Glassner, Martin I. Bibliography on Land-Locked States. LC 80-51737. 60p. 1980. 20.00x (ISBN 90-286-0290-9). Sijthoff & Noordhodf.

--Transit Problems of Three Asian Land-Locked Countries: Afghanistan, Nepal & Laos. (Occasional Papers-Reprints Series in Contemporary Asian Studies: No. 4-1983 (57)). 52p. (Orig.). 1983. pap. text ed. 3.00 (ISBN 0-942182-56-1). U MD Law.

Glassner, Martin I. & Deblij, Harm J. Systematic Political Geography. 3rd ed. LC 79-26750. 537p. 1980. text ed. 39.00 (ISBN 0-471-05228-0). Wiley.

Glassner, Martin I., ed. Global Resources: Challenges of Interdependence. 718p. 1983. 43.95 (ISBN 0-03-068782-9); pap. 23.95 (ISBN 0-03-068783-7). Praeger.

Glassner, Martin I., ed. see Foreign Policy Association.

Glassock, Richard J. Current Therapy in Nephrology & Hypertention 1984-1985. 400p. 1984. casebound 44.00 (ISBN 0-317-01541-9). Mosby.

Glasson, B. C. EDP System Development Guidelines. LC 83-72639. 268p. 1984. pap. 24.95 (ISBN 0-89435-072-2). QED Info Sci.

Glasson, John. An Introduction to Regional Planning. 2nd ed. (The Built Environment Ser.). (Illus.). 422p. 1984. pap. 8.95 (ISBN 0-09-133751-8, Pub. by Hutchinson Educ). Longwood Pub Group.

Glasson, T. Francis. Moses in the Fourth Gospel. LC 63-5666. (Studies in Biblical Theology: No. 40). 1963. pap. 10.00x (ISBN 0-8401-3040-6). A R Allenson.

Glasson, Thomas F., ed. Revelation of John. (Cambridge Bible Commentary on the New English Bible, New Testament Ser.). (Orig.). 1965. 16.95 (ISBN 0-521-04208-9); pap. 8.95x (ISBN 0-521-09256-6). Cambridge U Pr.

Glasson, William H. History of Military Pension Legislation in the United States. LC 68-56656. (Columbia University, Studies in the Social Sciences Ser.: No. 32). Repr. of 1900 ed. 16.50 (ISBN 0-404-51032-9). AMS Pr.

Glasspool, John. Boats of the Longshoremen. 136p. 1980. 18.00x (ISBN 0-245-53111-4, Pub. by Nautical England). State Mutual Bk.

Glasspool, Michael. Eyes: Their Problems & Treatments. LC 83-19651. (Illus.). 128p. (Orig.). 1984. 12.95 (ISBN 0-668-05636-3); pap. 7.95 (ISBN 0-668-05642-8). Arco.

Glasspool, Michael G. Atlas of Ophthalmology. LC 82-51029. (Illus.). 128p. 1982. text ed. 50.00 (ISBN 0-8391-1779-5, 19852). Univ Park.

--Problems in Ophthalmology. Fry, J. & Williams, K., eds. LC 81-68115. (Problems in Practice Ser.: Vol. 6). (Illus.). 141p. 1982. text ed. 20.00x (ISBN 0-8036-4158-3). Davis Co.

Glasspool, Susan, tr. see Berti, Luciano.

Glasstone, R. Better Ballet. (Illus.). 96p. 1980. 9.95 (ISBN 0-7182-1453-6, Pub. by Kaye & Ward). David & Charles.

Glasstone, Richard. Better Ballet. LC 78-55577. (Illus.). 1979. 8.95 (ISBN 0-498-02307-9); pap. 4.95 (ISBN 0-498-02308-7). A S Barnes.

--Better Ballet. (Better Bks). (Illus.). (gr. 7 up). 17.95x (ISBN 0-7182-1453-6, SpS). Sportshelf.

Glasstone, Samuel. Energy Deskbook. 464p. 1983. 29.95 (ISBN 0-442-22928-3). Van Nos Reinhold.

--Energy Deskbook: DOE Technical Information Center. LC 82-12853. 463p. 1982. pap. 12.50 (ISBN 0-87079-468-X, DOE-1R-5114-1); microfiche 4.50 (ISBN 0-87079-469-8). DOE.

--Sourcebook on Atomic Energy. 3rd ed. LC 79-1206. 892p. 1979. Repr. of 1967 ed. lib. bdg. 49.50 (ISBN 0-88275-898-5). Krieger.

--Thermodynamics for Chemists. LC 72-189791. 528p. 1972. Repr. of 1947 ed. 31.50 (ISBN 0-88275-021-6). Krieger.

Glasstone, Samuel & AEC Technical Information Center. Public Safety & Underground Nuclear Detonations. 276p. 1971. 23.50 (ISBN 0-87079-315-2, TID-25708). DOE.

Glasstone, Samuel & Jordan, Walter H. Nuclear Power & Its Environmental Effects. LC 80-67303. (Illus.). 400p. 1980. 25.95 (ISBN 0-89448-022-7, 690005); pap. 17.95 (ISBN 0-89448-024-3, 690006). Am Nuclear Soc.

Glasstone, Samuel & Lovberg, Ralph H. Controlled Thermonuclear Reactions: An Introduction to Theory & Experiment. LC 75-11911. 540p. 1975. Repr. of 1960 ed. 32.50 (ISBN 0-88275-326-6). Krieger.

Glasstone, Samuel & Sesonske, Alexander. Nuclear Reactor Engineering. 3rd ed. 800p. 1980. 42.50 (ISBN 0-442-20057-9). Van Nos Reinhold.

Glasstone, Samuel, jt. auth. see Bell, George I.

Glasstone, Victor. The London Coliseum. (Theatre in Focus Ser.). (Illus.). 55p. (Orig.). 1980. pap. text ed. 55.00x incl. slides (ISBN 0-85964-065-5). Chadwyck-Healey.

--Victorian & Edwardian Theatres: An Architectural & Social Survey. (Illus.). 192p. 1975. 17.50x (ISBN 0-674-93591-8). Harvard U Pr.

Glastonbury, Bryan. Homeless Near a Thousand Homes: A Study of Homeless Families in South Wales & the West of England. 1971. 32.00x (ISBN 0-317-05817-7, Pub. by Natl Inst Social Work). State Mutual Bk.

Glasunov, I. S. & Dowd, J. E. Kaunas Rotterdam Intervention Study: Behavioural & Operational Components of Health Intervention Programmes. 322p. 1982. pap. 58.75 (ISBN 0-444-80386-6, Biomedical Pr). Elsevier.

Glatfelter, Charles H. Pastors & People: German & Lutheran Reformed Churches in the Pennsylvania Field, 1717-1793, Vol. II, The History. LC 80-83400. (Penn. German Ser.: Vol. 15). (Illus.). 25.00 (ISBN 0-911122-44-3). Penn German Soc.

--Pastors & People: German Lutheran & Reformed Churches in the Pennsylvania Field, 1717-1793. LC 80-83400. (Penn. German Ser.: Vol. 13). (Illus.). 1979. 30.00 (ISBN 0-911122-40-0). Penn German Soc.

Glathe, Alfred B. Hume's Theory of the Passions & of Morals: A Study of Books 2 & 3 of the Treatise. (Publications in Philosophy Ser: Vol. 24). Repr. of 1950 ed. 24.00 (ISBN 0-384-18905-9). Johnson Repr.

Glathorn, Allan A. & Shields, Carmel R. Differentiated Supervision for Catholic Schools. 72p. 1983. 4.75 (ISBN 0-318-00781-9). Natl Cath Educ.

Glatstein, jt. auth. see Bleehan.

Glatstein, Jacob. Selected Poems of Jacob Glatstein. Whitman, Ruth, tr. 1973. 7.50 (ISBN 0-8079-0176-8); pap. 2.95 (ISBN 0-8079-0175-X). October.

Glatstein, Jacob, et al. Anthology of Holocaust Literature. LC 68-19609. (Temple Bks). 1972. pap. text ed. 6.95x (ISBN 0-689-70343-0, T23). Atheneum.

Glatt, E., jt. ed. see Shelly, M. W.

Glatt, M. M. & Marks, J., eds. The Dependence Phenomenon. 300p. 1982. 42.00x (ISBN 0-942068-03-3). Bogden & Son.

--The Dependence Phenomenon. 1983. lib. bdg. 36.00 (ISBN 0-85200-487-7, Pub. by MTP Pr England). Kluwer Academic.

Glatt, Max. Alcoholic & the Help He Needs. LC 73-16957. 194p. 1974. 7.95 (ISBN 0-8008-0165-2). Taplinger.

Glattbach, Jack. Media & the Developing World: Pluralism or Polarization? (Seven Springs Studies). 36p. 1982. pap. 3.00 (ISBN 0-943006-08-2). Seven Springs.

Glatter, Otto & Kratky, H. C., eds. Small Angle X-Ray Scattering. 1982. 70.00 (ISBN 0-12-286280-5). Acad Pr.

Glatter, Ron, jt. auth. see Piper, David W.

Glatthaar, Joseph T. The March to the Sea & Beyond: Sherman's Troops in the Savannah & Carolina Campaigns. (American Social Experience Ser.). 352p. 1985. 27.95x (ISBN 0-8147-3001-9). NYU Pr.

Glatthorn, Allan A. Differentiated Supervision. LC 83-73347. 100p. 1984. pap. text ed. 8.50 (ISBN 0-87120-124-0, 611-84326). Assn Supervision.

--Guide for Developing an English Curriculum for the Eighties. 143p. 1980. pap. 7.80 (ISBN 0-8141-1922-0). NCTE.

--Writing for Success. 1985. pap. 7.95 (ISBN 0-673-15915-9). Scott F.

--Writing in the Schools: Improvement Through Effective Leadership. 96p. (Orig.). 1981. pap. 8.00 (ISBN 0-88210-128-5). Natl Assn Principals.

Glatthorn, Allan A. & Adams, Herbert R. Listening Your Way to Management Success. 128p. 1984. pap. 7.95 (ISBN 0-673-15802-0). Scott F.

Glatthorn, Allan A., jt. auth. see Gilmore, Perry.

Glattke, Theodore J. Short-Latency Auditory Evoked Potentials. (Illus.). 160p. 1983. pap. 18.00 (ISBN 0-8391-1715-9, 14710). Univ Park.

Glatzer, H. & Hogan, T. On the Move with the NEC PC 8200. 256p. pap. 14.95 cancelled (ISBN 0-89303-736-2). Brady Comm.

Glatzer, Hal. The Birds of Babel-Satellites for a Human World. LC 83-50167. 240p. 1983. pap. text ed. 12.95 (ISBN 0-672-22033-4). Sams.

--How to Use Zenith Heath Computers. 1984. 19.95 (ISBN 0-318-01742-3). S-A Design Bks.

--Introduction to Word Processing. LC 81-84004. (Illus.). 205p. 1981. pap. 8.95 (ISBN 0-89588-076-8, W101). SYBEX.

GLatzer, Hal & Hogan, Thom. NEC PC 8201 User's Guide. 1984. cancelled (ISBN 0-89303-696-X). Brady Comm.

Glatzer, N. N., ed. see Kafka, Franz.

Glatzer, Nahum. The Judaic Tradition. 352p. 1982. pap. text ed. 9.95x (ISBN 0-87441-344-3). Behrman.

Glatzer, Nahum, ed. see Buber, Martin.

Glatzer, Nahum N. The Dimensions of Job: A Study & Selected Readings. LC 69-11936. 320p. 1973. pap. 7.70 (ISBN 0-8052-0378-8). Schocken.

--Franz Rosenzweig: His Life & Thought. 2nd ed. LC 53-656. 1962. pap. 8.95 (ISBN 0-8052-0021-5). Schocken.

--The Loves of Franz Kafka. (Illus.). 128p. 1985. 12.95 (ISBN 0-8052-4001-2). Schocken.

Glatzer, Nahum N., ed. Hammer on the Rock: A Midrash Reader. LC 62-18155. 1962. pap. 4.95 (ISBN 0-8052-0032-0). Schocken.

--Language of Faith: A Selection from the Most Expressive Jewish Prayers. LC 65-14823. 1974. Eng. Language ed. 4.95 (ISBN 0-8052-3559-0). Schocken.

--Modern Jewish Thought: A Source Reader. LC 76-9139. 1976. pap. 7.50 (ISBN 0-8052-0542-X). Schocken.

--Passover Haggadah: Including Readings on the Holocaust, with English Translation, Introduction & Commentary. 3rd ed. LC 69-10846. (Illus., Bilingual ed). 1979. pap. 3.95 (ISBN 0-8052-0624-8). Schocken.

Glatzer, Nahum N., ed. see Agnon, Y.

Glatzer, Nahum N., ed. see Buber, Martin.

Glatzer, Nahum N., ed. see Kafka, Franz.

Glatzer, Nahum N., ed. see Schurer, Emil.

Glatzer, Paula. The Complaint of the Poet: The Parnassus Plays. (Salzburg Studies in English Literature: Elizabethan & Renaissance Studies: No. 60). 1977. pap. text ed. 25.50x (ISBN 0-391-01386-6). Humanities.

Glatzer, Wolfgang, jt. auth. see Ballerstedt, Elke.

Glatzle, Mary & Fiore, Evelyn. Muggable Mary. 1982. pap. 2.75 (ISBN 0-425-05042-4). Berkley Pub.

Glau, Gregory R. Business Graphics for the Macintosh. 250p. 1985. pap. 19.95 (ISBN 0-87094-693-5). Dow Jones-Irwin.

--Business Power for Your Apple. 288p. 1984. 32.50 (ISBN 0-442-22779-5). Van Nos Reinhold.

Glau, Gregory R., et al. Annotated BASIC: A New Technique for Neophytes, Vol. 1. McCarthy, Nan & Crocker, Chris, eds. 160p. (Orig.). 1981. pap. 10.95 (ISBN 0-88006-028-X, BK 7384). Green Pub Inc.

Glauber, Helen M., ed. see Glauber, I. Peter.

Glauber, I. Peter. Stuttering: A Psychoanalytic Understanding. Glauber, Helen M., ed. LC 82-8125. 208p. 1983. 24.95 (ISBN 0-89885-154-8). Human Sci Pr.

Glauber, R. J., ed. Quantum Optics. (Italian Physical Society: Course 42). 1970. 105.00 (ISBN 0-12-368842-6). Acad Pr.

Glauberman, G. Factorization in Local Subgroups of Finite Groups. LC 77-13373. (Conference Board of the Mathematical Sciences Ser.: No. 33). 74p. 1977. pap. 13.00 (ISBN 0-8218-1683-7, CBMS33). Am Math.

Glauert, jt. auth. see Kelsey.

Glauert, A. Fixation, Dehydration & Embedding of Biological Specimens. (Practical Methods in Electron Microscopy Ser.: Vol. 3, No. 1). 1975. pap. 18.00 (ISBN 0-444-10666-9, Biomedical Pr). Elsevier.

Glauert, A. M. Practical Methods in Electron Microscopy, Vols. 1-8. Vol. 1, 1972. 87.25 (ISBN 0-444-10404-6, Biomedical Pr); Vol. 2, 1974. 76.75 (ISBN 0-444-10644-8); Vol. 3, 1975. 76.75 (ISBN 0-444-10665-0); Vol. 4, 1975. 38.50 (ISBN 0-444-10807-6); Vol. 5, 1977. 103.00 (ISBN 0-7204-0605-6); Vol. 6, 1978. 91.50 (ISBN 0-7204-0636-6); Vol. 7, 1979. 70.25 (ISBN 0-7204-0665-X); Vol. 8, 1980. 70.25 (ISBN 0-444-80166-9). Elsevier.

Glauert, H. The Elements of Aerofoil & Airscrew Theory. LC 82-22233. (Science Classics). 232p. 1983. pap. 15.95 (ISBN 0-521-27494-X). Cambridge U Pr.

Glauert, Michael, jt. auth. see Kelsey, Hugh.

Glaumann, Hans, et al, eds. Plasma Protein Secretion by the Liver. 1984. 75.00 (ISBN 0-12-286180-9). Acad Pr.

Glauning, Otto, ed. see Lydgate, John.

Glaus, Marlene. From Thoughts to Words. 1965. pap. text ed. 6.00 (ISBN 0-8141-1817-8). NCTE.

Glauser, E. C., tr. see Kollbrunner, C. F. & Basler, K.

Glauser, Frederick L., ed. Signs & Symptoms in Pulmonary Medicine. (Illus.). 242p. 1983. text ed. 28.75 (ISBN 0-397-50544-2, 65-06943, Lippincott Medical). Lippincott.

Glauser, M., ed. see European Organization for Research & Treatment of Cancer (E.O.R.T.C.) International Antimicrobial Therapy Project Group, Lausanne, 1978.

Glautier, M. W. & Underdown, B. Accounting Theory & Practice. (Illus.). 1977. pap. text ed. 18.95x (ISBN 0-8464-0108-8). Beekman Pubs.

Glaves-Smith, J. R., jt. auth. see Melly, George.

Glavin, John P. Behavioral Strategies for Classroom Management. LC 73-86934. 160p. 1974. pap. 10.95x (ISBN 0-675-08873-9). Merrill.

--Ferment in Special Education. LC 74-12133. 250p. 1974. 34.50x (ISBN 0-8422-5197-9). Irvington.

Glavin, John P., ed. Major Issues in Special Education. 1973. 29.50x (ISBN 0-8422-5109-X). Irvington.

--Perceptual - Motor Training for Handicapped Children. 246p. 1975. pap. text ed. 14.95x (ISBN 0-8422-0518-7). Irvington.

Glavin, Mary, tr. see Mellot, Michel.

Glawischnig, Dieter, jt. auth. see Koerner, Friedrich.

Glawischnig, H., jt. auth. see Ryssel, H.

Glawischnig, H., jt. ed. see Ryssell, H.

Glay, M. Le see Maximillian.

Glaysher, Frederick, ed. see Hayden, Robert.

Glaze, Andrew. A Masque of Surgery. 1974. saddlestitched in wrappers 1.60 (ISBN 0-685-78977-2, Pub. by Menard Pr). Small Pr Dist.

Glaze, Anita J. Art & Death in a Senufo Village. LC 79-2174. (Illus.). 288p. 1981. 27.50x (ISBN 0-253-17107-5). Ind U Pr.

Glaze, Bert T., jt. auth. see Coons, Alvin E.

Glaze, Bob, photos by. Portrait of Chicago. LC 81-81322. (Portrait of America Ser.). (Illus.). 80p. (Orig., Text by Les Krantz). 1981. pap. 6.95 (ISBN 0-912856-70-X). Graphic Arts Ctr.

Glaze, Jack A., tr. see Francisco, Clyde T.

Glaze, Linda S. Critical Analysis of Valle-Inclan's Ruedo Iberico. LC 84-81669. (Hispanic Studies Collection). 206p. (Orig.). 1985. pap. 12.95 (ISBN 0-89729-357-6). Ediciones.

Glaze, R. E., Jr. No Easy Salvation. LC 66-10708. 72p. 1984. pap. 4.00 (ISBN 0-914520-06-7). Insight Pr.

Glazebrook, G. P., ed. see Hargrave, James.

Glazebrook, James, tr. see Valiron, George.

Glazebrook, Philip. Journey to Kars. LC 84-45094. 320p. 1984. 12.95 (ISBN 0-689-11504-0). Atheneum.

--Journey to Kars: A Modern Traveller in the Ottoman Lands. (Illus.). 256p. 1985. pap. 7.95 (ISBN 0-03-005607-1, Owl Bks.). HR&W.

Glazebrook, Richard, ed. A Dictionary of Applied Physics, 5 vols. Set. 120.00 (ISBN 0-8446-1199-9); 24.00 ea. Peter Smith.

Glazener, E. R., jt. auth. see Groneman, Chris H.

Glazer, A. M., jt. auth. see Burns, Gerald.

Glazer, A. N., et al, eds. Chemical Modification of Proteins. LC 74-84210. (Laboratory Techniques in Biochemistry & Molecular Biology: Vol. 4, Pt. 1). 205p. 1975. pap. 17.50 (ISBN 0-444-10811-4, North-Holland). Elsevier.

Glazer, Alan S. & Jaenicke, Henry J. A Framework for Evaluating an Internal Audit Function. (Illus.). 1980. pap. text ed. 16.00 (ISBN 0-89413-082-X). Inst Inter Aud.

Glazer, Amihai. Managing Money with Your Commodore 64. (Illus.). 144p. 1985. pap. 14.95 (ISBN 0-13-550641-7). P-H.

--Managing Money with Your IBM PC. (Illus.). 208p. 1985. pap. 16.95 (ISBN 0-13-550658-1). P-H.

--Managing Money with Your VIC-20. LC 84-18233. (P-H Personal Computing Ser.). (Illus.). 180p. 1985. pap. text ed. 13.95 (ISBN 0-13-550682-4). P-H.

Glazer, Edward, jt. ed. see Pyle, Ian.

Glazer, Howard I., jt. ed. see Fensterheim, Herbert.

Glazer, Joan & Williams, Gurney, III. Introduction to Children's Literature. (Illus.). 736p. 1979. 28.95 (ISBN 0-07-023380-2). McGraw.

Glazer, Joan I. Literature for Early Childhood. (Illus.). 240p. 1981. pap. text ed. 14.50 (ISBN 0-675-08039-8). Merrill.

Glazer, Joe, jt. auth. see Fowke, Edith.

Glazer, Mark, jt. auth. see Bohannan, Paul.

Glazer, Myra, ed. Burning Air & a Clear Mind: Contemporary Israeli Women Poets. LC 80-22487. (Illus.). xxviii, 135p. 1981. 17.95x (ISBN 0-8214-0572-1, 82-83657); pap. 8.95 (ISBN 0-8214-0617-5, 82-83665). Ohio U Pr.

Glazer, Myra, ed. see Wilkerson, Gerri.

Glazer, Myron. The Research Adventure: Promise & Problems of Field Work. 1972. pap. text ed. 9.00 (ISBN 0-394-31709-2, RanC). Random.

Glazer, Nathan. American Judaism. rev. ed. LC 57-8574. (Chicago History of American Civilization Ser). 1972. 12.50x (ISBN 0-226-29839-6); pap. 7.50 (ISBN 0-226-29841-8, CHAC7). U of Chicago Pr.

--Ethnic Dilemmas, 1964-1982. 384p. 1983. 20.00 (ISBN 0-674-26852-0). Harvard U Pr.

--Ethnic Dilemmas: 1964-1982. 272p. 1985. pap. 8.95 (ISBN 0-674-26853-9). Harvard U Pr.

--Mediating Structures & Welfare. 250p. cancelled (ISBN 0-88410-823-6). Ballinger Pub.

--The Public Interest on Crime & Punishment. LC 83-25861. 1984. 26.00 (ISBN 0-89011-589-3). Abt Bks.

--The Social Basis of American Communism. LC 74-4658. 244p. 1974. Repr. of 1961 ed. lib. bdg. 15.00x (ISBN 0-8371-7476-7, GLAC). Greenwood.

Glazer, Nathan & Moynihan, Daniel P. Beyond the Melting Pot: The Negroes, Puerto Ricans, Jews, Italians, & Irish of New York City. 2nd ed. 1970. pap. 9.95x (ISBN 0-262-57022-X). MIT Pr.

Glazer, Nathan & Ueda, Reed. Ethnic Groups in History Textbooks. LC 82-24267. 80p. 1983. pap. 5.00 (ISBN 0-89633-064-8). Ethics & Public Policy.

Glazer, Nathan, jt. auth. see Riesman, David.

Glazer, Nathan, intro. by. Clamor at the Gates: The New American Immigration. 350p. 1985. 25.95 (ISBN 0-917616-70-7); pap. 10.95 (ISBN 0-917616-69-3). ICS Pr.

Glazer, Nathan, ed. The Public Interest on Crime & Punishment. 294p. 1984. lib. bdg. 28.00 (ISBN 0-8191-4138-0); pap. text ed. 12.00 (ISBN 0-8191-4139-9). U Pr of Amer.

--The Public Interest on Education. 1984. 26.00 (ISBN 0-89011-590-7). Abt Bks.

--The Public Interest on Education. (Illus.). 280p. 1984. lib. bdg. 28.00 (ISBN 0-8191-4140-2); pap. text ed. 12.00 (ISBN 0-8191-4141-0). U Pr of Amer.

Glazer, Nathan & Moynihan, Daniel P., eds. Ethnicity: Theory & Experience. LC 74-21230. 512p. 1975. 25.00x (ISBN 0-674-26855-5); pap. 8.95x (ISBN 0-674-26856-3). Harvard U Pr.

Glazer, Nathan, jt. ed. see Gorham, William.

Glazer, Nathan, et al, eds. Ethnic Pluralism & Public Policy: Achieving Equality in the United States & Britain. LC 83-16283. 320p. 1984. 27.50x (ISBN 0-669-07345-8). Lexington Bks.

Glazer, Nona Y. & Waehrer, Helen Y. Woman in a Man-Made World. 2nd ed. 1977. pap. 18.95 (ISBN 0-395-30607-8). HM.

Glazer, Robin K. Letting Go. (Illus.). 320p. 1983. 17.95 (ISBN 0-8065-0833-7); pap. 9.95 (ISBN 0-8065-0844-2). Citadel Pr.

Glazer, Sidney, tr. see Abu Khaldun Sati Al Husri.

Glazer, Tom. Do Your Ears Hang Low? LC 78-20072. (Illus.). 96p. (gr. 1-3). 1980. 12.95 (ISBN 0-385-12602-6); PLB (ISBN 0-385-12603-4). Doubleday.

--Eye Winker, Tom Tinker, Chin Chopper. LC 72-97497. (Illus.). (ps-3). 1978. 10.95 (ISBN 0-385-08200-2); pap. 3.95 (ISBN 0-385-13344-8, Zephyr). Doubleday.

--Eye Winker, Tom Tinker, Chin Chopper: A Collection of Musical Finger Plays. LC 72-97497. (Illus.). 64p. (gr. 1-7). 1973. 10.95 (ISBN 0-385-08200-2); PLB 10.95 (ISBN 0-385-09453-1). Doubleday.

--Music for Ones & Twos: Songs & Games for the Very Young Child. LC 82-45199. (Illus.). 96p. (ps). 1983. pap. 7.95 (ISBN 0-385-14252-8). Doubleday.

Glazer, Tom, ed. Tom Glazer's Treasury of Songs for Children. (Illus.). 9.95 (ISBN 0-686-74302-4). J R Pubns.

Glazerson, Matityahu. Death & Beyond. Lederman, S. & Lederman, L., eds. 13p. (Orig.). 1981. pap. 0.99 (ISBN 0-686-85950-2). Feldheim.

Glazier, Ira & H, Michael. The Famine Immigrants: Lists of Irish Immigrants Arriving at the Port of New York, 1846-1851. LC 83-80078. 638p. 1985. Vol. V: 10/1849-05/1950. 45.00x (ISBN 0-8063-1123-1). Genealog Pub.

Glazier, Ira A. & Tepper, Michael H., eds. The Famine Immigrants: Lists of Irish Immigrants Arriving at the Port of New York, 1846-1851, Vol. 1 - January, 1846 to June, 1847. LC 83-80078. 841p. 1983. 45.00 (ISBN 0-8063-1024-3). Genealog Pub.

--The Famine Immigrants: Lists of Irish Immigrants Arriving at the Port of New York, 1846-1851, Vol. II-July 1847-June 1848. LC 83-80078. 722p. 1983. 45.00 (ISBN 0-8063-1045-6). Genealog Pub.

--The Famine Immigrants: Lists of Irish Immigrants Arriving at the Port of New York, 1846-1851, Vol. III-July 1848-March 1849. LC 83-80078. 695p. 1984. 45.00 (ISBN 0-8063-1056-1). Genealog Pub.

--The Famine Immigrants: Lists of Irish Immigrants Arriving at the Port of New York, 1846-1851, Vol. IV - April 1849 - September 1849. LC 83-80078. 814p. 1984. 45.00 (ISBN 0-8063-1084-7). Genealog Pub.

Glazier, Kenneth M. Africa South of the Sahara: A Select & Annotated Bibliography, 1964-1968. LC 77-88767. (Bibliographical Ser.: No. 42). 1969. 7.95x (ISBN 0-8179-2421-3); pap. 4.95 (ISBN 0-8179-2422-1). Hoover Inst Pr.

Glazier, Loss P., ed. see Arguelles, Ivan.

Glazier, Lyle. Stills from a Moving Picture. (Paunch Ser.: No. 39). 1974. pap. 4.00 (ISBN 0-9602478-3-1). Paunch.

Glazier, Richard. A Manual of Historic Ornament: Treating Upon the Evolution, Tradition & Development of Architecture & the Applied Arts. 5th ed. LC 70-163174. (Tower Bks.). (Illus.). vi, 183p. 1972. Repr. of 1933 ed. 50.00x (ISBN 0-8103-3937-4). Gale.

--A Manual of Historic Ornaments. 4th ed. 192p. 1983. pap. 7.95 (ISBN 0-442-22999-2). Van Nos Reinhold.

Glazier, Stephan D., ed. Caribbean Ethnicity Revisited. (Ethnic Groups Ser.). 166p. 1985. pap. text ed. 25.00 (ISBN 0-677-06615-5). Gordon.

Glazier, Stephen. Lost Provinces. 1981. pap. 5.95 (ISBN 0-380-77255-8, 77255-8). Avon.

Glazier, Stephen D. Marchin' the Pilgrims Home: Leadership & Decision-Making in an Afro-Caribbean Faith. LC 82-24179. (Contributions to the Study of Religion Ser.: No. 10). (Illus.). xx, 165p. 1983. lib. bdg. 29.95 (ISBN 0-313-23464-7, GPI/). Greenwood.

Glazier, Stephen D., ed. Perspectives on Pentecostalism: Case Studies from the Caribbean & Latin America. LC 80-7815. 207p. 1980. lib. bdg. 22.75 (ISBN 0-8191-1071-X); pap. text ed. 12.00 (ISBN 0-8191-1072-8). U Pr of Amer.

Glazier, Teresa F. The Least You Should Know about English Basic Writing Skills: Form C. 2nd ed. LC 83-10695. 286p. 1984. pap. text ed. 15.95 (ISBN 0-03-063153-X, HoltC). HR&W.

--The Least You Should Know about English: Basic Writing Skills, Form B. 2nd ed. 1983. pap. text ed. 15.95 (ISBN 0-03-061698-0). HR&W.

Glazman, I. M., jt. auth. see Akhiezer, N. I.

Glazman, I. M., jt. auth. see Akhiezer, N. I.

Glazov, V. M. & Vigdorovich, V. N. Microhardness of Metals & Semiconductors. LC 70-128504. 226p. 1971. 35.00x (ISBN 0-306-10848-8, Consultants). Plenum Pub.

Glazov, V. M., et al. Liquid Semiconductors. LC 68-31237. (Monographs in Semiconductor Physics: Vol. 2). 362p. 1969. 39.50x (ISBN 0-306-30358-2, Plenum Pr). Plenum Pub.

Glazunov, I. Telegrams from Nicaragua. 64p. 1984. pap. 12.95 (ISBN 0-8285-2835-7, Pub. by Novosti Pr USSR). Imported Pubns.

Glazunov, Ilya. Art Books from the U.S.S.R. 268p. 1981. 75.00x (ISBN 0-569-08519-5, Pub. by Collet's). State Mutual Bk.

Glazunov, Il'ya. Moscow Planeta. 268p. 1978. 150.00x (Pub. by Collet's). State Mutual Bk.

Glazunov, Ilya, jt. auth. see Vysotsky, Sergei.

Glazyrin, V., et al. Soviet Employee's Rights in Law. 208p. 1978. 3.45 (ISBN 0-8285-0343-5, Pub. by Progress Pubs USSR). Imported Pubns.

Glazzard, Peggy. Learning Activities & Teaching Ideas for the Special Child in the Regular Classroom. (Illus.). 368p. 1982. pap. text ed. 17.95 (ISBN 0-13-527093-6). P-H.

Gleadow, R. F. Chapter One - Engraved-Roller Printing. 75.00x (ISBN 0-686-98193-6, Pub. by Soc Dyers & Colour). State Mutual Bk.

Gleadow, Rupert. Magic & Divination. (Illus.). 1977. Repr. of 1941 ed. 25.00x (ISBN 0-7158-1148-7). Charles River Bks.

--Magic & Divination. (Illus.). 308p. 1976. Repr. of 1941 ed. 17.50x (ISBN 0-87471-808-2). Rowman.

Gleadow, Rupert, tr. see De Lubicz, Isha S.

Gleanbard East Echo, compiled by. Teenagers Themselves. LC 85-13530. (Illus.). 256p. (gr. 9-12). 1985. pap. 9.95 (ISBN 0-915361-33-7). Adama Pubs Inc.

Gleanings Staff. Five Hundred Answers. 1975. pap. text ed. 1.50 (ISBN 0-686-20933-8). A I Root.

--Honey Plants Manual. 1977. pap. text ed. 2.50 (ISBN 0-686-20934-6). A I Root.

--Starting Right with Bees. (Illus.). 1976. pap. text ed. 1.50 (ISBN 0-686-20935-4). A I Root.

Glease, Hannah. The Magic Tree & the Curious Badger. (Magic Tree Bks.). (Illus.). 32p. (gr. 2-4). pap. 3.95 (ISBN 0-317-31289-8). Creative Ed.

--The Magic Tree & the Flyaway Birds. (Magic Tree Bks.). (Illus.). 32p. (gr. 2-4). pap. 3.95 (ISBN 0-317-31292-8). Creative Ed.

--The Magic Tree & the Missing Acorn. (Magic Tree Bks.). (Illus.). 32p. (gr. 2-4). pap. 3.95 (ISBN 0-317-31290-1). Creative Ed.

--The Magic Tree in Winter. (Magic Tree Bks.). (Illus.). 32p. (gr. 2-4). pap. 3.95 (ISBN 0-317-31291-X). Creative Ed.

Gleasner, Bill & Gleasner, Diana. Big Island Traveler's Guide. (Illus.). 1978. pap. 4.00 (ISBN 0-932596-05-3, Pub. by Oriental). Intl Spec Bk.

--Hawaiian Gardens: Photographed on Kauai. LC 77-73322. (Illus.). 1978. pap. 4.00 (ISBN 0-932596-01-0, Pub. by Oriental). Intl Spec Bk.

--Kauai: Traveler's Guide. (Illus.). 1978. pap. 4.00 (ISBN 0-932596-03-7, Pub. by Oriental). Intl Spec Bk.

--Maui: Traveler's Guide. (Illus.). 69p. (Orig.). 1978. pap. 4.00 (ISBN 0-932596-08-8, Pub. by Oriental). Intl Spec Bk.

--Oahu: Traveler's Guide. (Illus.). 65p. (Orig.). 1978. pap. 4.00 (ISBN 0-932596-04-5, Pub. by Oriental). Intl Spec Bk.

Gleasner, Diana. Breakthrough: Women in Science. LC 83-1177. (Breakthrough Ser.). (Illus.). (gr. 6 up). 1983. 12.95 (ISBN 0-8027-6501-7). Walker & Co.

--Breakthrough: Women in Writing. (Breakthrough Ser.). (Illus.). 192p. (gr. 5 up). 1980. 9.95 (ISBN 0-8027-6384-7). Walker & Co.

--Charlotte: Touch of Gold. LC 83-48036. (Illus.). 88p. 1983. 25.00 (ISBN 0-914788-74-4). East Woods.

--Dynamite. (Inventions that Changed our Lives). (Illus.). 64p. (gr. 4-6). 1982. 7.95 (ISBN 0-8027-6466-5); lib. bdg. 8.85 (ISBN 0-8027-6467-3). Walker & Co.

--The Movies. (Inventions That Changed Our Lives Ser.). (Illus.). (gr. 4-6). 1983. 7.95 (ISBN 0-8027-6482-7); lib. bdg. 8.85 (ISBN 0-8027-6483-5). Walker & Co.

Gleasner, Diana, jt. auth. see Gleasner, Bill.

Gleasner, Diana C. Illustrated Swimming, Diving & Surfing Dictionary for Young People. (Illus.). (gr. 4 up). pap. 2.50 (ISBN 0-13-451195-6). P-H.

--Windsurfing. (Illus.). 64p. (Orig.). 1985. pap. 7.95 (ISBN 0-934802-24-6). ICS Bks.

Gleasner, Diane. Plaid Mouse. (Illus.). (ps-3). plastic bdg. 1.75 (ISBN 0-8198-0123-2); pap. 1.00 (ISBN 0-8198-0124-0). Dghtrs St Paul.

Gleason, A. M., et al, eds. The William Lowell Putnam Mathematical Competition: Problems & Solutions - 1938-1964. LC 80-80493. 652p. 1980. 35.00 (ISBN 0-88385-428-7). Math Assn.

Gleason, Abbot, jt. ed. see Garrison, Mark.

Gleason, Abbott. European & Muscovite: Ivan Kireevsky & the Origins of Slavophilism. LC 71-172324. (Russian Research Center Studies: No. 68). (Illus.). 421p. 1972. 20.00x (ISBN 0-674-26924-1). Harvard U Pr.

--Young Russia: The Genesis of Russian Radicalism in the 1860s. LC 82-23875. xiv, 438p. 1983. pap. 12.00x (ISBN 0-226-29961-9). U of Chicago Pr.

Gleason, Abbott, et al, eds. Bolshevik Culture: Experiment & Order in the Russian Revolution. LC 84-48253. (Illus.). 352p. 1985. 27.50x (ISBN 0-253-31206-X). Ind U Pr.

Gleason, Andrew M. Elementary Course in Probability for the Cryptanalyst. (Orig.). pap. 24.80 (ISBN 0-89412-072-7). Aegean Park Pr.

Gleason, Arthur. Inside the British. 1978. Repr. of 1917 ed. lib. bdg. 25.00 (ISBN 0-8495-1936-5). Arden Lib.

--What the Workers Want: A Study of British Labor. (English Workers & the Coming of the Welfare State Ser., 1918-1945). 518p. 1985. lib. bdg. 60.00 (ISBN 0-8240-7612-5). Garland Pub.

Gleason, Arthur, jt. auth. see Kellogg, Paul U.

Gleason, David K. Over Boston: Aerial Photographs. (Illus.). 144p. 1985. Repr. of 1983 ed. 34.95 (ISBN 0-8071-1283-6). La State U Pr.

--Over New Orleans: Aerial Photographs. (Illus.). 144p. 1983. 29.95 (ISBN 0-9612038-0-3). D K Gleason.

--Over New Orleans: Aerial Photographs. (Illus.). 144p. 1985. Repr. of 1983 ed. 29.95 (ISBN 0-8071-1288-7). La State U Pr.

--Plantation Homes of Louisiana & the Natchez Area. LC 82-7723. (Illus.). 134p. 1982. 29.95 (ISBN 0-8071-1058-2). La State U Pr.

Gleason, David K., photos by. Over Boston: Aerial Photographs. (Illus.). 144p. 1985. 29.95 (ISBN 0-9612038-3-8). D K Gleason.

Gleason, Elisabeth G. Reform Thought in Sixteenth Century Italy. Massey, James A., ed. LC 81-5648. (American Academy of Religion Texts & Translations Ser.). 1981. pap. text ed. 10.95 (ISBN 0-89130-498-3, 01-02-04). Scholars Pr GA.

Gleason, G. Essentials of FORTRAN. LC 72-90224. 1973. pap. text ed. 14.95 (ISBN 0-03-091400-0, HoltC). HR&W.

Gleason, G., jt. auth. see Eisenbud, M.

Gleason, G. H. Introduction a la linguistique. (Sciences humaines et sociales). (Fr). pap. 20.95 (ISBN 2-03-070351-6, 3652). Larousse.

Gleason, G. R. Better Judo. rev. ed. (Better Sport Bk.). (Illus.). 96p. 1981. Repr. of 1978 ed. text ed. 17.95x (ISBN 0-7182-0485-9, SpS). Sportshelf.

Gleason, Gary M., jt. auth. see Horn, L. Wayne.

Gleason, Gary N. & Horn, Lister W. Structured COBOL. LC 78-31566. (Illus.). 1979. pap. 16.95x (ISBN 0-87835-079-9). Boyd & Fraser.

Gleason, Gayle, photos by. The New York Restaurant Datebook 1986. 120p. Date not set. cancelled (ISBN 0-943998-09-3). Prince St ED.

Gleason, H. A. New Britton & Brown Illustrated Flora of the Northeastern United States & Adjacent Canada, 3 Vols. rev. ed. (Illus.). 1975. Set. 115.00x (ISBN 0-02-845300-X). Hafner.

Gleason, Harold & Becker, Warren. Chamber Music: Haydn to Bartok. 2nd ed. (Music Literature Outlines: Ser. V). 1980. pap. text ed. 12.75 (ISBN 0-89917-267-9, Frangipani Press). TIS Inc.

--Early American Music. 2nd ed. LC 80-53731. (Music Literature Outlines Ser. III). 1981. pap. text ed. 13.75 (ISBN 0-89917-265-2, Frangipani Pr). TIS Inc.

--Examples of Music Before Fourteen Hundred. 2nd ed. 1986. pap. text ed. write for info (ISBN 0-89917-035-8, Frangipani Press). TIS Inc.

--Music in the Baroque. 3rd ed. LC 79-66417. (Music Literature Outlines: Ser. II). 1979. pap. 13.75 (ISBN 0-89917-016-1, Frangipani Pr). TIS Inc.

--Music in the Middle Ages & Renaissance. 3rd ed. (Music Literature Outlines: Ser. I). 1981. pap. text ed. 13.75 (ISBN 0-89917-034-X, Frangipani Pr). TIS Inc.

--Twentieth Century American Composers. 2nd ed. LC 80-53732. (Music Literature Outlines: Series IV). 1980. 13.75 (ISBN 0-89917-266-0, Frangipani Press). TIS Inc.

Gleason, Harole. Methods of Organ Playing. 6th ed. 1979. 27.95 (ISBN 0-13-579466-8). P-H.

Gleason, Henry A. & Cronquist, Arthur. Manual of Vascular Plants. 810p. 1963. text ed. write for info. (ISBN 0-87150-760-9, Pub. by Willard Grant Pr). PWS Pubs.

--Natural Geography of Plants. LC 64-15448. (Illus.). 420p. (gr. 9 up). 1964. 55.00x (ISBN 0-231-02668-4). Columbia U Pr.

Gleason, Herbert P., jt. auth. see Butler, Robert N.

Gleason, Herbert P., ed. Getting Better: A Report on Health Care from the Salzbug Seminar. LC 80-23486. 150p. 1980. text ed. 30.00 (ISBN 0-89946-053-4). Oelgeschlager.

Gleason, John H. The Genesis of Russophobia in Great Britain. LC 70-159189. ix, 314p. 1971. Repr. of 1950 ed. lib. bdg. 21.50x (ISBN 0-374-93156-9). Octagon.

Gleason, John J., Jr. Consciousness & the Ultimate. LC 80-21397. 192p. (Orig.). 1981. pap. 7.75 (ISBN 0-687-09470-4). Abingdon.

Gleason, John M. see Alexander, Yonah.

Gleason, Joseph, jt. auth. see Cleary, Joseph.

Gleason, Judith I. This Africa: Novels by West Africans in English & French. (Northwestern University African Studies Ser.: No. 14). 1965. 14.95x (ISBN 0-8101-0103-3). Northwestern U Pr.

Gleason, Katherine F. The Dramatic Art of Robert Browning. LC 76-40070. 1927. lib. bdg. 15.00 (ISBN 0-8414-4431-5). Folcroft.

Gleason, M. Present Company. 1978. 5.00 (ISBN 0-8233-0278-4). Golden Quill.

Gleason, Madeleine. Selected Poems. LC 73-186603. (Living Poets' Library Ser). pap. 2.50 (ISBN 0-686-02574-1). Dragons Teeth.

Gleason, Madeline. Here Comes Everybody: New & Selected Poems. LC 75-37508. (Illus.). 52p. (Orig.). 1976. pap. 4.50 (ISBN 0-915572-16-8). Panjandrum.

Gleason, Marian. All Our Yesterdays. 1960. 2.50 (ISBN 0-8233-0029-3). Golden Quill.

--Bystanding. 1982. 5.50 (ISBN 0-8233-0354-3). Golden Quill.

Gleason, Michael W. Belief & Technique. LC 80-83173. 1981. 8.95 (ISBN 0-87212-146-1). Libra.

Gleason, Norma. Cryptograms & Spygrams. 128p. (Orig.). 1981. pap. 3.50 (ISBN 0-486-24036-3). Dover.

Gleason, Norma C. & Orloff, Chet. Portland's Public Art: A Guide & History. (Illus.). 82p. (Orig.). 1984. pap. text ed. 4.95 (ISBN 0-87595-059-0). Oreg Hist Soc.

Gleason, Philip. Conservative Reformers: German-American Catholics & the Social Order. 1968. 22.95x (ISBN 0-268-00061-1). U of Notre Dame Pr.

Gleason, Philip, ed. Contemporary Catholicism in the United States. 1969. 21.95x (ISBN 0-268-00306-8). U of Notre Dame Pr.

Gleason, Robert J. Icebound in the Siberian Arctic. LC 77-1320. (Illus.). 1977. pap. 4.95 (ISBN 0-88240-067-3). Alaska Northwest.

Gleason, Ronne R. Poetica Erotica. Lewanski, Bob, ed. (Illus.). 167p. (Orig.). 1985. 3.50 (ISBN 0-9608030-1-7). Taoist Pubs.

Gleason, S. Everett, jt. auth. see Langer, William L.

Gleason, Walter. Essentials of Business Math. 496p. 1982. pap. text ed. write for info. (ISBN 0-87150-350-6, 2752, Prindle). PWS Pubs.

--Statistics: A First Course. 416p. 1981. text ed. write for info. (ISBN 0-534-00909-3). Wadsworth Pub.

Gleason, Walter, tr. see Fonvizin, Dennis.

Gleason, Walter J. Moral Idealists, Bureaucracy, & Catherine the Great. 261p. 1981. 25.00x (ISBN 0-8135-0917-3). Rutgers U Pr.

Gleave, J. A. Moulds & Casts for Orthopaedic & Prosthetic Appliances. (Illus.). 192p. 1972. 21.50x (ISBN 0-398-02293-3). C C Thomas.

Gleave, M. B., jt. ed. see Clark, B. D.

Gleaves, Edwin S. & Tucker, John M., eds. Reference Services & Library Education: Essays in Honor of Frances Neel Cheney. LC 81-48266. 320p. 1982. 31.50x (ISBN 0-669-05320-1). Lexington Bks.

Gleaves, R. Modula Two for Pascal Programmers. (Books on Professional Computing). (Illus.). 155p. 1984. pap. 16.95 (ISBN 0-387-96051-1). Springer-Verlag.

Gleazer, Edmund J., Jr. The Community College: Values, Vision & Vitality. 1980. pap. 6.50 (ISBN 0-87117-097-3); pap. 8.00 0-87117-097-3. Am Assn Comm J Coll.

Gleazer, Edmund J., Jr., ed. The Community College: Values, Vision & Vitality. 190p. (Orig.). 1980. pap. 8.00 (ISBN 0-87117-097-3). Am Assn Comm Jr Coll.

Gleazer, Edmund J., Jr., et al. The Foreign Student in United States Community & the Junior Colleges. LC 77-93769. 86p. 1978. pap. 5.00 (ISBN 0-87447-047-1, 237328). College Bd.

Gleba, Y. Y. & Sytnik, K. M. Protoplast Fusion: Genetic Engineering in Higher Plants. (Monographs on Theoretical & Applied Genetics: Vol. 8). (Illus.). 245p. 1984. 55.00 (ISBN 0-387-13284-8). Springer-Verlag.

Glebov, I. A. & Komarsky, E. G. Synchronous Generators in Electrophysical Installations. Skrebtsov, G. P., tr. from Rus. LC 81-48563. (Illus.). 208p. 1982. 31.00x (ISBN 0-669-05434-8). Lexington Bks.

Glebov, O., tr. see Ginzburg, V. L.

Glebov, oles, tr. see Danin, D.

Gleckman, Richard, jt. auth. see Gantz, Nelson.

Gleckner, Robert & Enscoe, Gerald, eds. Romanticism: Points of View. 2nd ed. LC 75-4682. (Waynebks Ser: No. 40). 352p. 1975. pap. text ed. 5.95x (ISBN 0-8143-1543-7). Wayne St U Pr.

Gleckner, Robert F. Blake & Spenser. LC 85-45. (Illus.). 384p. 1985. text ed. 29.50x (ISBN 0-8018-2521-0). Johns Hopkins.

--Blake's Prelude: "Poetical Sketches". LC 82-47976. 216p. 1983. text ed. 18.50x (ISBN 0-8018-2850-3). Johns Hopkins.

--Byron & the Ruins of Paradise. LC 80-11656. (Illus.). xxiv, 365p. 1980. Repr. of 1967 ed. lib. bdg. 37.50x (ISBN 0-313-22421-8, GLBR). Greenwood.

Gleckner, Robert F., jt. auth. see DuBuque, Jean H.

Gleckner, Robert F., intro. by see Byron, George G.

Gledhill, Alan. Pakistan: The Development of Its Laws & Constitution. LC 80-20180. (The British Commonwealth, the Development of Its Laws & Constitutions Ser.: Vol. 8). x, 263p. 1980. Repr. of 1957 ed. lib. bdg. 32.50x (ISBN 0-313-20842-5, GLPA). Greenwood.

--Republic of India, Development of Its Laws & Constitution. LC 77-98761. xii, 309p. Repr. of 1951 ed. lib. bdg. 15.75x (ISBN 0-8371-2813-7, GLRI). Greenwood.

Gledhill, D. The Names of Plants. 150p. Date not set. price not set (ISBN 0-521-30549-7); pap. price not set (ISBN 0-521-31562-X). Cambridge U Pr.

Gledhill, T., et al. A Key to British Freshwater Crustacea: Malacostraca. 1976. 20.00x (ISBN 0-900386-24-X, Pub. by Freshwater Bio). State Mutual Bk.

Gledhill, V. X. Discovering Computers. 1981. 16.95 (ISBN 0-574-28214-9, 11-401111); instr's guide avail. (11-401102); specimen set avail. (11-4011100). SRA.

--Discovering Computers. write for info. McGraw.

Glees, Anthony. Exile Politics During the Second World War: The German Social Democrats in Britain. (Oxford Historical Monographs). (Illus.). 1982. 39.95x (ISBN 0-19-821893-1). Oxford U Pr.

Glees, P., jt. ed. see Voth, D.

Gleeson & Colvin. Words Most Often Misspelled & Mispronounced. 1984. pap. 3.50 (ISBN 0-671-53154-9). PB.

Gleeson, Bill. Backroad Wineries of California. LC 84-28520. (Illus.). 128p. (Orig.). 1985. pap. 7.95 (ISBN 0-87701-318-7). Chronicle Bks.

--Small Hotels of California. LC 83-27306. (Orig.). 1984. pap. 7.95 (ISBN 0-87701-293-8). Chronicle Bks.

Gleeson, D., jt. ed. see Whittany, G.

Gleeson, Denis, ed. Identity & Structure. 212p. 1979. 20.00x (ISBN 0-905484-01-0, Pub. by Nafferton England); pap. 15.00x (ISBN 0-905484-06-1). State Mutual Bk.

--Youth Training & the Search for Work: A Study of Young People in Crisis. (Routledge Education Bks.). 200p. (Orig.). 1983. pap. 19.95x (ISBN 0-7100-9513-9). Routledge & Kegan.

Gleeson, Geof. All about Judo. (EP Sports Ser.). (Illus.). 1975. 6.95 (ISBN 0-7158-0590-8). Charles River Bks.

--Judo Inside Out. (Illus.). 156p. 1983. 12.95 (ISBN 0-86019-100-1, Pub. by Lepus England). Sterling.

Gleeson, Geoff. All about Judo. (Illus.). 144p. 1985. pap. 7.95 (ISBN 0-7136-2572-4, Pub. by A & C Black). Sterling.

Gleeson, Geraldine A. Health Interview Survey Procedure 1957-1974. Stevenson, Taloria, ed. LC 74-32057. (Programs & Collected Procedures Ser. 2: No. 11). 55p. 1975. pap. text ed. 1.15 (ISBN 0-8406-0037-2). Natl Ctr Health Stats.

Gleeson, John R., III. Sportscape. LC 84-52105. (Illus.). 176p. (Orig.). 1984. pap. 12.95 (ISBN 0-912661-04-6). Woodsong Graph.

Glegg, Gordon L. Design of Design. LC 69-12432. (Cambridge Engineering Pubns.). (Illus.). 1969. 19.95 (ISBN 0-521-07447-9). Cambridge U Pr.

--The Development of Design. 120p. 1981. 21.95 (ISBN 0-521-23794-7). Cambridge U Pr.

--Making & Interpreting Mechanical Drawings. (Illus.). 1971. 8.95 (ISBN 0-521-09680-4). Cambridge U Pr.

--The Science of Design. (Illus.). 112p. 1973. 18.95 (ISBN 0-521-20327-9). Cambridge U Pr.

--The Selection of Design. LC 72-80591. (Illus.). 96p. 1972. Cambridge U Pr.

Gleghorn, B. E., jt. ed. see Datta, V. N.

Glehn, M. E. Von see Hiller, Ferdinand.

Gleich, C. C. Von see Charbon, Marie.

Gleich, G. J., ed. see Symposium of the Collegium Internationale Allergologicum, 12th, New Orleans, La., September 1978.

Gleichen, Count. With the Camel Corps up the Nile. (Illus.). 1976. Repr. 25.00 (ISBN 0-7158-1108-8). Charles River Bks.

Gleicher, Jules. The Accidental Revolutionary: Essays on the Political Teaching of Jean-Paul Sartre. LC 82-20067. 216p. (Orig.). 1983. lib. bdg. 21.50 (ISBN 0-8191-2835-X); pap. text ed. 8.75 (ISBN 0-8191-2836-8). U Pr of Amer.

Gleicher, Norbert. Reproductive Immunology. LC 81-11812. (Progress in Clinical & Biological Research Ser.: Vol. 70). 510p. 1981. 86.00 (ISBN 0-8451-0070-X). A R Liss.

Gleicher, Norbert, ed. Principles of Medical Therapy in Pregnancy. 1320p. 1985. 125.00x (ISBN 0-306-41845-2, Plenum Pr). Plenum Pub.

Gleicher, Norbert, jt. ed. see Elkayam, Uri.

Gleicher, Norbert, et al. Fertility: A Guide for the Couple with Infertility Problems. 130p. 1985. text ed. 14.95 (ISBN 0-8290-1526-4). Irvington.

Gleig, G. R. The Life of Sir Walter Scott. LC 73-7579. 1871. lib. bdg. 17.50 (ISBN 0-8414-2034-3). Folcroft.

Gleijeses, Piero. The Dominican Crisis: The Nineteen Sixty-Five Constitutional Revolt & American Intervention. Lipson, Lawrence, tr. LC 72-29253. 480p. 1979. text ed. 38.50x (ISBN 0-8018-2025-1). Johns Hopkins.

Gleim, Irvin N. Auditing & EDP. 712p. 1983. pap. 24.95x (ISBN 0-911238-48-4). B of A.

--CIA Examination Review, 2 vols. 2nd ed. LC 84-71646. 1456p. 1984. Vol. I, Outlines & Study Guides, 768pp. pap. text ed. 19.95 (ISBN 0-917537-10-6); Vol. II, Problems & Solutions, 688pp. pap. text ed. 19.95 (ISBN 0-917537-11-4); Set. pap. text ed. 39.90 (ISBN 0-917537-12-2). Accounting.

--Managerial Accounting. 672p. 1983. pap. 24.95x (ISBN 0-911238-47-6). B of A.

--Private Pilot: FAA Written Exam. 2nd ed. LC 84-71033. 288p. (Orig.). 1984. pap. text ed. 9.95 (ISBN 0-917539-01-X). Aviation Pubns.

--Private Pilot Handbook. LC 82-70245. 1296p. (Orig.). 1982. 27.95 (ISBN 0-917539-00-1). Aviation Pubns.

Gleim, Irvin N. & Campbell, Terry L. Managerial Accounting Objective Questions & Explanations. LC 84-70971. 672p. (Orig.). 1984. pap. text ed. 14.95 (ISBN 0-917537-03-3). Accounting.

Gleim, Irvin N. & Collins, William A. Financial Accounting: Objective Questions & Explanations. 768p. 1983. pap. 24.95x (ISBN 0-911238-29-8). B of A.

--Financial Accounting: Objective Questions & Explanations. 2nd ed. LC 84-72592. 734p. 1985. pap. text ed. 14.95 (ISBN 0-917537-14-9). Accounting.

Gleim, Irvin N. & Delancy, Patrick R. CPA Examination Review, 2 vols. 12th ed. 1985. Vol. 1, Outlines & Study Guide. pap. 32.95 (ISBN 0-471-81951-4); Vol. 2, Problems & Solutions. pap. write for info. (ISBN 0-471-81949-2); Set. pap. 65.90 (ISBN 0-471-81988-3). Wiley.

--Directory of Accounting & Auditing Pronouncement as of July 1, 1984. (CPA Examination Review Ser). 48p. 1984. pap. 8.45 (ISBN 0-471-82019-9). Wiley.

--Updating Supplemental of January, 1985. (CPA Examination Review Ser.). 1985. pap. price not set (ISBN 0-471-82196-9). Wiley.

Gleim, Irvin N. & Delaney, Patrick R. CPA Examination Review: Vol. 1 - Outlines & Study Guides. 11th ed. LC 84-15268. (CPA Examination Review Ser.: 1-645). 1253p. 1984. pap. 31.95x (ISBN 0-471-80083-X); non-saleable tchr's manual avail. (ISBN 0-471-80084-8); Vols. I & II Set. 63.90 (ISBN 0-471-80081-3). Wiley.

--CPA Examination Review: Vol. 2 - Problems & Solutions. 11th ed. (CPA Examination Review Ser.: 1-645). 1103p. 1984. pap. 31.95x (ISBN 0-471-80082-1); non-saleable tchr.'s manual avail. (ISBN 0-471-80084-8); Set. 63.90 (ISBN 0-471-80081-3). Wiley.

Gleim, Irvin N. & Hillison, William A. Auditing & EDP Objective Questions & Explanations. LC 83-70105. 752p. (Orig.). 1983. pap. text ed. 14.95 (ISBN 0-917537-07-6). Accounting.

Gleim, Irvin N., jt. auth. see Delaney, Patrick R.

Gleim, Irvin N., et al. Federal Tax Objective Questions & Explanations. 2nd ed. LC 84-72591. 704p. 1985. pap. text ed. 14.95 (ISBN 0-917537-13-0). Accounting.

--Federal Tax: Objective Questions & Explanations. 688p. 1983. pap. 24.95x (ISBN 0-911238-32-8). B of A.

--Business Law: Objective Questions & Explanations. 672p. 1983. pap. 24.95x (ISBN 0-911238-46-8). B of A.

--Business Law Objective Questions & Explanations. LC 82-72901. 672p. (Orig.). 1982. pap. text ed. 14.95 (ISBN 0-917537-04-1). Accounting.

Gleim, Irwin N. CMA Examination Review, 2 vols. 2nd ed. 1984. pap. 49.95 set (ISBN 0-911238-99-9, Acct Pubns). B of A.

Gleiss, Alfred & Hirsch, Martin. Common Market Cartel Law. 3rd ed. Orig. Title: Kommentar zum EWG-Kartellrecht. 796p. 1981. 95.00 (ISBN 0-87179-320-2). BNA.

Gleit, J., jt. auth. see Eckstein, J.

Gleit, Joyce, jt. auth. see Eckstein, Joan.

Gleiter, Jan & Thompson, Kathleen. Daniel Boone. LC 84-9816. (Raintree Stories (Clippers) Ser.). (Illus.). (gr. k-4). 1984. PLB 14.25 (ISBN 0-8172-2120-4); PLB 27.99 incl. cassette (ISBN 0-8172-2242-1); pap. 9.27g (ISBN 0-8172-2263-4); pap. 23.95g incl. cassette (ISBN 0-8172-2273-1); cassette 14.00. Raintree Pubs.

--Paul Bunyan & Babe the Blue Ox. LC 84-9786. (Raintree Stories Clippers Ser.). (Illus.). (gr. k-4). 1984. PLB 14.25 (ISBN 0-8172-2119-0); PLB 27.99 incl. cassette (ISBN 0-8172-2241-3); pap. 9.27g (ISBN 0-317-13174-5); pap. 23.95 incl. cassette (ISBN 0-8172-2272-3); cassette 14.00. Raintree Pubs.

--Pocahontas. LC 84-9819. (Raintree Stories Clippers Ser.). (Illus.). (gr. k-4). 1984. PLB 14.25 (ISBN 0-8172-2118-2); PLB 27.99 incl. cassette (ISBN 0-8172-2240-5); pap. 9.27g (ISBN 0-8172-2261-8); pap. 23.95g (ISBN 0-8172-2271-5); cassette 14.00. Raintree Pubs.

Gleiter, Jan, retold by. The Legend of Sleepy Hollow. LC 84-9931. (Raintree Stories Clippers Ser.). (Illus.). (gr. k-4). 1984. PLB 14.25 (ISBN 0-8172-2117-4); PLB 27.99 incl. cassette (ISBN 0-8172-2239-1); pap. 9.27g (ISBN 0-8172-2260-X); pap. 23.95g incl. cassette (ISBN 0-8172-2270-7); cassette 14.00. Raintree Pubs.

Gleitman, Henry. Basic Psychology. 500p. 1982. text ed. 25.95x (ISBN 0-393-95254-1); write for info. instr's manual; study guide 10.95x (ISBN 0-393-95261-4); write for info. test item file. Norton.

--Psychology. (Illus.). 1981. 27.95x (ISBN 0-393-95102-2); study guide 10.95x (ISBN 0-393-95110-3); instr's. manual avail. (ISBN 0-393-95105-7). Norton.

--Psychology. 2nd ed. 1986. text ed. price not set (ISBN 0-393-95378-5); (ISBN 0-393-95384-X); price not set study guide (ISBN 0-393-95381-5); price not set test item file (ISBN 0-393-95387-4). price not set transparencies. Norton.

Gleitman, Henry, jt. auth. see Gleitman, Lila.

Gleitman, Lila & Gleitman, Henry. Phrase & Paraphrase: Some Innovative Uses of Language. (Illus.). 1971. 14.95x (ISBN 0-393-04333-9). Norton.

Gleitman, Lila, jt. auth. see Landau, Barbara.

Gleitman, Lila R., jt. ed. see Wanner, Eric.

Glejser, H., ed. Quantitative Studies of International Economic Relations. 282p. 1976. 44.75 (ISBN 0-444-10902-1, North-Holland). Elsevier.

Glekel, Jeffrey. Business Crimes: A Guide For Corporate & Defense Counsel. 440p. 1982. text ed. 50.00 (ISBN 0-686-97902-8, C3-1172). PLI.

Gleland, Hardman F. Our Prehistoric Ancestors. 1928. 17.50 (ISBN 0-8482-4213-0). Norwood Edns.

Glemare, M., jt. auth. see Cabioch, L.

Glembotskii, V. A., et al. Flotation. LC 63-21692. (Illus.). 1963. 37.00x (ISBN 0-911184-07-4). Primary.

Glen, E. S., ed. see International Continence Society Conference, 5th, Glasgow, Sept. 4-6, 1976.

Glen, Frederick. The Social Psychology of Organizations. (Essential Psychology Ser.). 1976. pap. 4.50x (ISBN 0-416-84050-7, 2735). Methuen Inc.

Glen, Heather. Vision & Disenchantment: Blake's Songs & Wordsworth's Lyrical Ballads. LC 82-9565. 350p. 1983. 49.50 (ISBN 0-521-25084-6); pap. 17.50 (ISBN 0-521-27198-3). Cambridge U Pr.

Glen, Irma, ed. Religious Science Hymnal. 3rd ed. 225p. 1982. Repr. of 1956 ed. 8.00 (ISBN 0-87516-489-7). De Vorss.

Glen, Jan, jt. auth. see Glen, Simon.

Glen, John. Early Scottish Melodies. LC 77-144557. (Illus.). Repr. of 1900 ed. 22.00 (ISBN 0-404-08649-7). AMS Pr.

Glen, Robert. Urban Workers in the Industrial Revolution. LC 83-43002. 256p. 1984. 30.00 (ISBN 0-312-83472-1). St Martin.

Glen, Simon & Glen, Jan. Sahara Handbook: Algeria, Lybia, Egypt, Niger, Mali. Rev. 2nd ed. (Illus.). 316p. (Orig.). 1984. pap. 19.95 (ISBN 0-903909-10-3, Roger Lascelles). Bradt Ent.

Glen, Thomas L. Rubens & the Counter Reformation: Studies in His Religious Paintings Between 1609 & 1620. LC 76-23621. (Outstanding Dissertations in the Fine Arts Ser.). 1977. lib. bdg. 68.00 (ISBN 0-8240-2692-6). Garland Pub.

Glen, William. Continental Drift & Plate Tectonics. (Physics & Physical Science Ser.). 192p. 1975. pap. text ed. 12.95 (ISBN 0-675-08799-6). Merrill.

--The Road to Jaramillo: Critical Years of the Revolution in Earth Science. LC 80-51647. (Illus.). xvi, 459p. 1982. 40.00x (ISBN 0-8047-1119-4). Stanford U Pr.

Glenbard East Echo, compiled by. The Teenagers Themselves. LC 83-26568. (Illus.). 271p. 1984. 16.95 (ISBN 0-915361-04-3, Dist. by Watts). Adama Pubs Inc.

Glenbow Historical Library, Glenbow-Alberta Institute. Catalogue of the Glenbow Historical Library. 1973. Four Vols. lib. bdg. 400.00 (ISBN 0-8161-0994-X, Hall Library). G K Hall.

Glencorss, A., jt. auth. see Cottan, G. B.

Glencross, R. M., ed. Calendar of Wills, Administrations & Accounts Relating to the Counties of Cornwall & Devon in the Connotorial Archdiaconal Court of Cornwall: Pt. 1, 1569-1699. (British Record Society Index Library Ser.: Vol. 56). pap. 35.00 (ISBN 0-317-16341-8). Kraus Repr.

Glenday, Graham & Jenkins, Glenn P. Worker Adjustment to Liberalized Trade: Costs & Assistance Policies. (Working Paper: No. 426). i, 86p. 1980. 5.00 (ISBN 0-686-36212-8, WP-0426). World Bank.

Glendening, Frank S. Business Interruption Insurance: What Is Covered. LC 79-92558. 245p. 1980. pap. text ed. 20.00 (ISBN 0-87218-304-1). Natl Underwriter.

Glendening, P. J. Teach Yourself Icelandic. (Teach Yourself Ser.). pap. 4.95 (ISBN 0-679-10181-0). McKay.

Glendening, Parris N. & Reeves, Mavis M. Pragmatic Federalism: An Intergovernmental View of American Government. 2nd ed. LC 83-62328. (Illus.). 1984. pap. 12.95 (ISBN 0-913530-36-0). Palisades Pub.

Glendenning, Frank, ed. Educational Gerontology: International Perspectives. 240p. 1985. 25.00 (ISBN 0-312-23756-1). St Martin.

Glendenning, G. William & Holtom, Robert B. Personal Lines Underwriting. 2nd ed. LC 77-81989. 582p. 1982. text ed. 20.00 (ISBN 0-89462-003-7). IIA.

Glendenning, Norman R. Direct Nuclear Reactions: Monograph. LC 82-24365. 392p. 1983. 65.00 (ISBN 0-12-286320-8). Acad Pr.

Glendinning, Carline. Unshared Care: Parents & Their Disabled Children. (International Library of Social Policy). 370p. (Orig.). 1983. pap. 14.95x (ISBN 0-7100-9468-X). Routledge & Kegan.

Glendinning, Eric H. English in Mechanical Engineering. (English in Focus Ser). 1974. pap. text ed. 9.95x (ISBN 0-19-437512-9); tchr's ed. 12.00x (ISBN 0-19-437501-3). Oxford U Pr.

Glendinning, Nigel. Goya & His Critics. LC 76-49697. 1977. Yale U Pr.

Glendinning, O. N., tr. see Baroja, Julio C.

Glendinning, Ralph. Death Match. 336p. 1985. pap. 3.95 (ISBN 0-515-08225-2). Jove Pubns.

--The Ultimate Game. 1981. 13.95 (ISBN 0-671-42016-X, Wyndham Bks). S&S.

--The Ultimate Game. 1985. pap. 3.95 (ISBN 0-515-08425-5). Jove Pubns.

Glendinning, Richard & Glendinning, Sally. Gargantua: The Mighty Gorilla. LC 73-21644. (Famous Animal Stories Ser.). (Illus.). 48p. (gr. 2-5). 1974. PLB 7.68 (ISBN 0-8116-4855-9). Garrard.

--Stubby: Brave Soldier Dog. LC 78-4575. (Famous Animal Stories Ser.). (Illus.). (gr. 2-5). 1978. PLB 7.68 (ISBN 0-8116-4864-8). Garrard.

Glendinning, Sally. Doll: Bottle-Nosed Dolphin. LC 80-13660. (Young Animal Adventures Ser.). 40p. (gr. 2). 1980. PLB 7.98 (ISBN 0-8116-7501-7). Garrard.

--Jimmy & Joe Find a Ghost. LC 79-82107. (Jimmy & Joe Ser.). (Illus.). (gr. k-3). 1969. PLB 7.98 (ISBN 0-8116-4701-3). Garrard.

--Jimmy & Joe Fly a Kite. LC 77-120461. (Jimmy & Joe Ser.). (Illus.). (gr. k-3). 1970. PLB 7.98 (ISBN 0-8116-4704-8). Garrard.

--Jimmy & Joe Get a Hens' Surprise. LC 74-97163. (Jimmy & Joe Ser.). (Illus.). (gr. k-3). 1970. PLB 7.98 (ISBN 0-8116-4702-1). Garrard.

--Jimmy & Joe Go to the Fair. LC 72-158356. (Jimmy & Joe Ser.). (Illus.). (gr. k-3). 1971. PLB 7.98 (ISBN 0-8116-4706-4). Garrard.

--Jimmy & Joe Have a Real Thanksgiving. LC 74-1184. (Jimmy & Joe Ser.). (Illus.). 40p. (gr. k-3). 1974. PLB 7.98 (ISBN 0-8116-4709-9). Garrard.

--Jimmy & Joe Look for a Bear. LC 71-102909. (Jimmy & Joe Ser.). (Illus.). (gr. k-3). 1970. PLB 7.98 (ISBN 0-8116-4703-X). Garrard.

--Jimmy & Joe Meet a Halloween Witch. LC 74-132036. (Jimmy & Joe Ser.). (Illus.). (gr. k-3). 1971. PLB 7.98 (ISBN 0-8116-4705-6). Garrard.

--Jimmy & Joe Save a Christmas Deer. LC 72-7835. (Jimmy & Joe Ser.). (Illus.). 40p. (gr. k-3). 1973. PLB 7.98 (ISBN 0-8116-4708-0). Garrard.

--Jimmy & Joe See a Monster. LC 74-190544. (Jimmy & Joe Ser.). (Illus.). 40p. (gr. k-3). 1972. PLB 7.98 (ISBN 0-8116-4707-2). Garrard.

--Little Blue & Rusty: Red Kangaroos. LC 80-13935. (Young Animal Adventures Ser.). 40p. (gr. 2). 1980. PLB 7.98 (ISBN 0-8116-7502-5). Garrard.

--Pen: Emperor Penguin. LC 80-13212. (Young Animal Adventures Ser.). 40p. (gr. 2). 1980. PLB 7.98 (ISBN 0-8116-7500-9). Garrard.

--Queen Victoria: English Empress. LC 71-116038. (Century Biographies Ser.). (Illus.). (gr. 6). 1971. PLB 4.47 (ISBN 0-8116-4750-1). Garrard.

Glendinning, Sally, jt. auth. see Glendinning, Richard.

Glendinning, Victoria. Edith Sitwell: A Unicorn among Lions. LC 80-2721. (Illus.). 384p. 1981. 17.95 (ISBN 0-394-50439-9). Knopf.

--Elizabeth Bowen. 1979. pap. 3.50 (ISBN 0-380-44354-6, Discus). Avon.

--Vita: A Bibliography of Vita Sackville-West. LC 84-62075. (Illus.). 464p. 1985. pap. 9.95 (ISBN 0-688-04111-6, Quill). Morrow.

--Vita: The Life of Vita Sackville-West. LC 83-47961. (Illus.). 426p. 1983. 17.95 (ISBN 0-394-52023-8). Knopf.

Glendon, Barbara. Corporate Responsibility: Case Studies & Empowerment Strategies. 48p. (Orig.). 1985. pap. 2.50 (ISBN 0-89622-229-2); tchr's. guide 1.50 (ISBN 0-89622-237-3). Twenty Third.

Glendon, Mary A., et al. Comparative Legal Traditions in a Nutshell. LC 82-2022. (Nutshell Ser.). 402p. 1982. pap. text ed. 9.95 (ISBN 0-314-65175-6). West Pub.

--Comparative Legal Traditions: Text, Materials & Cases on the Civil Law, Common Law & Socialist Law Traditions with Special Reference to French, West German, English & Soviet Law. (American Casebook Ser.). 1190p. 1985. text ed. 32.95 (ISBN 0-314-91764-0). West Pub.

Glendower, Christopher. American History at the Beginning of the Century Through Its Most Significant Political & Social Caricatures. (Illus.). 177p. 1985. 89.95 (ISBN 0-89920-123-7). Am Inst Psych.

Glenesk, Neil, jt. auth. see Houston, Joseph.

Glenin, Joseph, jt. auth. see Ginsberg, Jerry H.

Glenisson, ed. L' Amour dans les Romans de Francois Mauriac. 21.95 (ISBN 0-685-34310-3). French & Eur.

Glenisson, Jean & Keul, Michael, eds. International Bibliography of Historical Sciences, Vol. 49, 1980. 406p. 1984. lib. bdg. 57.00 (ISBN 3-598-20404-3). K G Saur.

Glenisson, Jean, et al, eds. International Bibliography of Historical Sciences, Vol. 50, 1981. (International Bibliography of Historical Sciences Ser.). 1985. lib. bdg. 57.00 (ISBN 3-598-20405-1). K G Saur.

Glenister, S. H. Stories of Great Craftsmen. facs. ed. LC 75-128247. (Essay Index Reprint Ser). 1939. 19.00 (ISBN 0-8369-1831-2). Ayer Co Pubs.

Glenn. How to Prove Astrology. 5.00 (ISBN 0-86690-005-5). Am Fed Astrologers.

--The Study of Entrepreneurship. (Management Ser.). Date not set. price not set (ISBN 0-471-82522-0). Wiley.

Glenn, Alfred A. Taking Your Faith to Work. (Orig.). 1980. pap. 4.95 (ISBN 0-8010-3748-4). Baker Bk.

Glenn, Andrea. Kansas in Color: Photographs Selected by Kansas Magazine. LC 82-60564. (Illus.). 128p. 1982. 14.95 (ISBN 0-7006-0229-1). U Pr of KS.

Glenn, Armon. The Way It Was on River Road. 188p. 1980. 10.95 (ISBN 0-914378-65-1). Countryman.

Glenn, Barbara H., jt. ed. see Franta, Gregory E.

Glenn, Barbara H., ed. see International Solar Energy Society, American Section, Annual Meeting, Philadelphia, 1981.

Glenn, Constance, ed. Kathe Kollwitz-Jake Zeitlin: Jake Zetlin Bookshop & Gallery 1937; the Art Museum & Galleries, California State University, Long Beach-1979. (Illus.). 64p. (Orig.). 1979. pap. 12.50 (ISBN 0-936270-14-4). Art Mus Gall.

Glenn, Constance W. Jim Dine Drawings. (Illus.). 224p. 1985. 60.00 (ISBN 0-8109-0824-7). Abrams.

--Roy Lichtenstein Ceramic Sculpture. (Illus.). 64p. (Orig.). 1977. pap. 20.00 (ISBN 0-936270-05-5). Art Mus Gall.
Glenn, Constance W. & Rice, Leland. Frances Benjamin Johnston: Women of Class & Station. (Illus.). 96p. (Orig.). 1979. pap. 12.50 (ISBN 0-936270-12-8). Art Mus Gall.
Glenn, Constance W., ed. Centric Two: Barbara Kasten Installation-Photographs. (Illus.). 8p. 1982. pap. 8.50. Art Mus Gall.
--Figurative Sculpture: Ten Artists-Two Decades. (Illus.). 48p. 1984. 12.50 (ISBN 0-936270-21-7). Art Mus Gall.
--Renate Ponsold - Robert Motherwell: Apropos Robinson Jeffers. (Illus.). 50p. 1980. pap. 45.00 (ISBN 0-936270-18-7). Art Mus Gall.
Glenn, Deirdre, jt. auth. see Gappa, Sylvia.
Glenn, Donna, jt. auth. see Becker, Sarah.
Glenn, Edmund S. Man & Mankind: Conflict & Communication Between Cultures. LC 81-3474. (Communication & Information Science Ser.). 300p. 1981. 39.50 (ISBN 0-89391-068-6). Ablex Pub.
Glenn, Edward. Cook's Inlet Exploring Expedition. (Shorey Historical Ser.). 14p. pap. 2.75 (ISBN 0-8466-0044-7, S44). Shorey.
Glenn, Elizabeth. Taste of Love. (Harlequin American Romance Ser.). 256p. 1983. pap. 2.25 (ISBN 0-373-16036-4). Harlequin Bks.
--What Love Endures. (Superromances Ser.). 384p. 1983. pap. 2.95 (ISBN 0-373-70067-9, Pub. by Worldwide). Harlequin Bks.
Glenn, Ethel C., et al. Your Voice & Articulation. 320p. 1984. pap. text ed. write for info. (ISBN 0-02-344070-8). Macmillan.
Glenn, Garrard. Army & the Law. LC 72-168168. Repr. of 1943 ed. 18.00 (ISBN 0-404-02819-5). AMS Pr.
Glenn, Gary A. & Glenn, Peggy. Don't Get Burned: A Family Fire-Safety Guide. LC 82-6872. (Illus.). 210p. (Orig.). 1982. lib. bdg. 10.95 (ISBN 0-936930-81-0); pap. 7.95. Aames-Allen.
--Don't Get Burned! A Family Fire Safety Guide. 1982. 7.95 (ISBN 0-318-04699-7). Phoenix Soc.
Glenn, Harold. Automechanics. rev. ed. (gr. 9-12). 1976. text ed. 21.28 (ISBN 0-02-662380-3); wkbk & ans. sheets 6.64 (ISBN 0-02-662390-0); tchr's. guide free. Bennett IL.
Glenn, Harold T. Exploring Power Mechanics. (Illus.). (gr. 7-12). 1973. 15.96 (ISBN 0-02-663660-3); prog. wkbk. 5.32 (ISBN 0-02-663670-0). Bennett IL.
--Glenn's Capri. 1975. pap. 7.75 (ISBN 0-8092-8165-1). Contemp Bks.
--Glenn's Firebird Tune-up & Repair Guide. new ed. LC 73-20678. (Glenn's Automotive Ser.). (Illus.). 336p. 1974. 7.75 (ISBN 0-8092-8437-5). Contemp Bks.
Glenn, Harold T., jt. auth. see Coles, Clarence W.
Glenn, Howard J., ed. Biologic Applications of Radiotracers. 224p. 1982. 66.50 (ISBN 0-8493-6009-9). CRC Pr.
Glenn, J. SI Units for Nursing. 1981. pap. text ed. 4.95 (ISBN 0-06-318180-0, Pub. by Har-Row Ltd England). Har-Row.
Glenn, J. A. Children Learn to Measure. 1980. text ed. 15.70 (ISBN 0-06-318155-X, IntlDept); pap. text ed. 7.80 (ISBN 0-06-318156-8). Har-Row.
--Teaching Primary Mathematics: Strategy & Evaluation. 1977. text ed. 9.50 (ISBN 0-06-318071-5, IntlDept); pap. text ed. 7.50 (ISBN 0-06-318072-3, IntlDept). Har-Row.
--The Third R: Towards a Numerate Society. 1978. (IntlDept); pap. text ed. 6.60 (ISBN 0-06-318076-6, IntlDept). Har-Row.
Glenn, J. A. & Littler, G. H., eds. A Dictionary of Mathematics. LC 83-25739. (Illus.). 240p. 1984. 18.95x (ISBN 0-389-20451-X, 08011). B&N Imports.
Glenn, James F., ed. Urologic Surgery. 3nd ed. (Illus.). 1168p. 1983. text ed. 125.00 (ISBN 0-06-140922-7, 14-09234, Harper Medical). Lippincott.
Glenn, James L. My Work Among the Florida Seminoles. Kersey, Harry A., Jr., ed. LC 81-19794. (Illus.). xiii, 121p. 1982. 12.00 (ISBN 0-8130-0717-8). U Presses Fla.
Glenn, James R. Ethics in Decision Making. LC 85-12025. (The Wiley Series in Management). Date not set. 18.95 (ISBN 0-471-82244-2). Wiley.
Glenn, Jeannette Y. Astrology - Psychology Reference Manual. LC 76-26803. 1982. text ed. 16.95 (ISBN 0-914350-15-3). Vulcan Bks.
Glenn, Jessie M. Neuter Plural in Latin Iambic & Trochaic Verse. (LD). 1939. pap. 16.00 (ISBN 0-527-00776-5). Kraus Repr.
Glenn, Jim. Programmed Poker. 160p. 1981. 9.95 (ISBN 0-8317-7152-6, Rutledge Pr). Smith Pubs.
Glenn, Jim, jt. auth. see McMillin, John.
Glenn, John. Children Learning Geometry. 1979. text ed. 15.50 (ISBN 0-06-318118-5, IntlDept); pap. text ed. 7.80 (ISBN 0-06-318119-3). Har-Row.
Glenn, John S., jt. auth. see Coffey, Rosalie L.
Glenn, Jules, jt. ed. see Kanzer, Mark.
Glenn, June B. Are You Prepared to Be Alone? 6.75 (ISBN 0-8062-2268-9). Carlton.
Glenn, Kathleen M. Azorin (Jose Martinez Ruiz) (World Authors Ser.). 1981. lib. bdg. 15.95 (ISBN 0-8057-6446-1, Twayne). G K Hall.
Glenn, Linda, jt. auth. see Wolfensberger, Wolf.
Glenn, Lois. Charles W. S. Williams: A Checklist. LC 75-17277. (Serif Series: No. 33). 128p. 1976. 12.00x (ISBN 0-87338-179-3). Kent St U Pr.
Glenn, Lowell M., jt. auth. see Mangum, Garth L.
Glenn, Mark D. & Weiner, Richard D. Electroconvulsive Therapy: A Programmed Text. (Illus.). 180p. 1985. text ed. 23.50 (ISBN 0-88048-205-2, 48-205-2). Am Psychiatric.
Glenn, Mel. Class Dismissed! High School Poems. (YA) 1982. 11.95 (ISBN 0-89919-075-8). HM.
--One Order to Go. LC 84-5018. 192p. (gr. 7 up). 1984. PLB 11.95 (ISBN 0-89919-257-2, Clarion). HM.
Glenn, Menachem. Jewish Tales & Legends. 441p. 1929. 6.95 (ISBN 0-88482-857-3). Hebrew Pub.
Glenn, Michael. On Diagnosis: A Systemic Approach. LC 84-7095. 224p. 1984. 20.00 (ISBN 0-87630-361-0). Brunner-Mazel.
--Trouble on the Hill: And Other Stories. LC 79-88413. 156p. (Orig.). 1979. pap. 4.95 (ISBN 0-930720-61-X). Lake View Pr.
Glenn, Myra C. Campaigns Against Corporal Punishment: Prisoners, Sailors, Women & Children in Antebellum America. (American Social History Ser.). 240p. 1984. 34.50x (ISBN 0-87395-812-8); pap. 10.95x (ISBN 0-87395-813-6). State U NY Pr.
Glenn, Norval D. Cohort Analysis. LC 77-75942. (University Papers: Quantitative Applications in the Social Sciences, No. 5). 72p. 1977. 5.00 (ISBN 0-8039-0794-X). Sage.
Glenn, Paul J. Apologetics. LC 80-51330. 303p. 1980. pap. 6.00 (ISBN 0-89555-157-8). TAN Bks Pubs.
--Tour of the Summa. LC 78-66307. 1978. pap. 12.50 (ISBN 0-89555-081-4). TAN Bks Pubs.
Glenn, Peggy. How to Start & Run a Successful Home Typing Business. 3rd ed. LC 83-3879. 179p. 1983. 14.95 (ISBN 0-936930-82-9). Aames-Allen.
--How to Start & Run a Successful Home Typing Business. 4th ed. 179p. 1984. pap. 14.95 (ISBN 0-317-31514-5). Aames-Allen.
--Kerosene Heaters: A Consumer's Review. LC 84-276. (Illus.). 88p. (Orig.). 1984. lib. bdg. 6.95 casebound (ISBN 0-936930-56-X); pap. 3.75 (ISBN 0-936930-57-8). Aames-Allen.
--Publicity for Books & Authors: A Do-It-Yourself Handbook for Small Publishing Firms & Enterprising Authors. LC 84-28288. (Illus.). 180p. 1985. 16.95 (ISBN 0-936930-92-6); pap. 12.95 (ISBN 0-936930-91-8). Aames-Allen.
--Word Processing Profits at Home. rev. ed. LC 83-15479. 220p. 1984. 19.95 (ISBN 0-936930-90-X); pap. 14.95 (ISBN 0-936930-84-5). Aames-Allen.
Glenn, Peggy, jt. auth. see Glenn, Gary A.
Glenn, Peter, ed. National Radio Publicity Directory-Fall 84. 270p. 1985. 150.00 (ISBN 0-317-07189-0). Peter Glenn.
Glenn, Peter & Brill, Chip, eds. Madison Avenue Handbook, 1984. 26th ed. 400p. 1984. pap. 25.00 (ISBN 0-87314-013-3). Peter Glenn.
Glenn, Robert B., et al, eds. Language & Culture: A Book of Readings. 1974. pap. 5.95 (ISBN 0-918616-07-7). Northern Mich.
Glenn, Robin D. Legal Issues Affecting Licensing of TV Program Material in the European Economic Community. 49p. 1983. 7.50 (ISBN 0-318-03977-X). Intl Law Inst.
Glenn, Ronald. Lanu, a Son of Samoa. 267p. 1982. pap. 6.95 (ISBN 0-943270-00-6). Mountain View.
Glenn, Ronald E. & Blinn, James E. Mobile Hydraulic Testing. LC 79-107426. (Illus.). pap. 84.00 (ISBN 0-317-10998-7, 2004564). Bks Demand UMI.
Glenn, Thomas A. Merion in the Welsh Tract with Sketches of the Townships of Haverford & Radnor. lib. bdg. 100.00 (ISBN 0-8492-4903-1). R West.
Glenn, William, et al, eds. Thoracic & Cardiovascular Surgery. 4th ed. (Illus.). 1695p. 1983. 150.00 (ISBN 0-8385-8956-1). ACC.
Glenn, William E., jt. auth. see Conrad, William R., Jr.
Glenn, William V., Jr., et al. Multiplanar CT Of The Spine. (Illus.). 544p. 1984. text ed. 125.00 (ISBN 0-8391-1910-0, 20230). Univ Park.
Glenn, William W. Between North & South: A Maryland Journalist Views the Civil War. Marks, Bayly E. & Schatz, Mark N., eds. LC 74-4981. 430p. 1976. 32.50 (ISBN 0-8386-1581-3). Fairleigh Dickinson.
Glennan, Thomas K. The Management of Demonstration Programs in the Department of Health & Human Service. LC 85-9398. 1985. 10.00 (ISBN 0-8330-0649-5). Rand Corp.
Glenner, G. G. Amyloid & Amyloidosis: Proceedings. (International Congress Ser.: No. 497). 630p. 1980. 119.25 (ISBN 0-444-90124-8, Excerpta Medica). Elsevier.
Glenner, Richard A. The Dental Office: A Pictorial History. LC 83-63457. (Illus.). 152p. 1984. pap. 9.95 (ISBN 0-933126-42-5). Pictorial Hist.
Glennerster, Howard. Paying for Welfare. 224p. 1985. 39.95x (ISBN 0-631-13971-0); pap. 14.95x (ISBN 0-631-13972-9). Basil Blackwell.
Glennerster, Howard, et al. Planning for Priority Groups. (Illus.). 200p. 1984. 34.95x (ISBN 0-85520-575-X). Basil Blackwell.
Glennie, Alexander. Sermons Preached on Plantations to Congregations of Negroes. facsimile ed. LC 75-161260. (Black Heritage Library Collection). Repr. of 1844 ed. 16.25 (ISBN 0-8369-8819-1). Ayer Co Pubs.
Glennie, Colin. Village Water Supply in the Decade: Lessons From Field Experience. LC 82-23749. 152p. 1983. 31.95x (ISBN 0-471-10525-2, Pub. by Wiley-Interscience). Wiley.
Glennie, K. W., ed. Introduction to the Petroleum Geology of the North Sea. 236p. 1984. pap. text ed. 31.00x (ISBN 0-632-01268-4, Pub. by Blackwell Sci UK). Blackwell Pubns.
Glennon, Betty. Comprehension Two. Reynolds, Patti, ed. (Golden Step Ahead Workbooks). (Illus.). 36p. (gr. 2-3). 1984. 1.95 (ISBN 0-307-23553-X, Golden Bks). Western Pub.
--Math Enrichment. Reynolds, Patti, ed. (Golden Step Ahead Workbooks). (Illus.). 36p. (gr. 2-3). 1984. 1.95 (ISBN 0-307-23549-1, Golden Bks). Western Pub.
--Sentence Building Two. Reynolds, Patti, ed. (Golden Step Ahead Workbks.). (Illus.). 36p. 1984. 1.95 (ISBN 0-307-23552-1, Golden Bks). Western Pub.
Glennon, Canon J. Your Healing Is Within You. LC 80-82616. 1980. pap. 4.95 (ISBN 0-88270-457-5, Pub. by Logos). Bridge Pub.
Glennon, James. Making Friends with Opera. pap. 6.50x (ISBN 0-392-13769-0, ABC). Sportshelf.
--Making Friends with Piano Music. pap. 6.50x (ISBN 0-392-13738-0, ABC). Sportshelf.
Glennon, Jim. How Can I Find Healing. LC 84-73039. 1985. pap. 3.50 (ISBN 0-88270-580-6). Bridge Pub.
Glennon, Michael, jt. auth. see Ehrenhalt, Alan.
Glennon, Michael J & Franck, Thomas M. United States Foreign Relations Law, Documents & Sources, 5 vols. Incl. Vol. 1. Executive Agreements. 1200p.; Vol. 2. Treaties. 1200p. (ISBN 0-379-20356-1); Vol. 3. The War Power. 1200p. (ISBN 0-379-20357-X); Vol. 4. International Economic Regulation.; Vol. 5. Cases. (ISBN 0-379-20359-6). LC 80-18165. 1981-1984. 40.00 ea. (ISBN 0-379-20355-3); Set. 200.00. Oceana.
Glennon, Robert J. The Iconoclast As Reformer: Jerome Frank's Impact on American Law. LC 84-17504. 256p. 1985. text ed. 24.95x (ISBN 0-8014-1565-9). Cornell U Pr.
Glennon, Vincent J. & Callahan, Leroy G. Elementary School Mathematics: A Guide to Current Research. LC 75-29896. 200p. 1975. pap. 6.25 (ISBN 0-87120-076-7). NCTM.
Glennon, Vincent J., ed. The Mathematical Education of Exceptional Children & Youth: An Interdisciplinary Approach. LC 80-29518. (Illus.). 408p. 1981. 19.50 (ISBN 0-87353-171-X). NCTM.
Glennon, William. The Adventures of Harlequin. (Children's Theatre Playscript Ser.). 1968. pap. 2.25x (ISBN 0-88020-007-3). Coach Hse.
--Aladdin. (Children's Theatre Playscript Ser.). 1956. pap. 2.25x (ISBN 0-88020-009-X). Coach Hse.
--Ali Baba & the Magic Cave. (Children's Theatre Playscript Ser.). 1969. pap. 2.25x (ISBN 0-88020-010-3). Coach Hse.
--Alice in Wonderland. (Children's Theatre Playscript Ser.). 1967. pap. 2.25x (ISBN 0-88020-011-1). Coach Hse.
--Beauty & the Beast. (Children's Theatre Playscript Ser.). 1966. pap. 2.25x (ISBN 0-88020-012-X). Coach Hse.
--Cinderella. (Children's Theatre Playscript Ser.). 1969. pap. 2.25x (ISBN 0-88020-013-8). Coach Hse.
--Hansel & Gretel. (Children's Theatre Playscript Ser.). 1966. pap. 2.25x (ISBN 0-88020-014-6). Coach Hse.
--Jack & the Beanstalk. (Children's Theatre Playscript Ser.). 1969. pap. 2.25x (ISBN 0-88020-015-4). Coach Hse.
--My Friend, the Fox. (Children's Theatre Playscript Ser.). 1968. pap. 2.25x (ISBN 0-88020-016-2). Coach Hse.
--The Pied Piper. (Children's Theatre Playscript Ser.). 1968. pap. 2.25x (ISBN 0-88020-017-0). Coach Hse.
Glenny, Lyman A., ed. Funding Higher Education: A Six Nation Analysis. LC 79-4557. 256p. 1979. 39.95 (ISBN 0-03-049616-0). Praeger.
Glenny, Lyman A., et al. Presidents Confront Reality: From Edifice Complex to University Without Walls. LC 75-24014. (Higher Education Ser. & the Carnegie Council Ser.). (Illus.). 272p. 1975. 21.95x (ISBN 0-87589-272-8). Jossey-Bass.
Glenny, Michael, tr. see Aksyonov, Vassily.
Glenny, Michael, tr. see Kaminskaya, Dina.
Glenny, Michael, tr. see Lakshin, Vladimir.
Glenny, Michael, tr. see Schoeck, Helmut.
Glenny, Michael, tr. see Solzhenitsyn, Alexander.
Glenny, Michael, tr. see Trifonov, Yuri.
Glenny, Tamara, tr. see Aleshkovsky, Yuz.
Glentop. Apple Pascal Programming. Date not set. price not set. Hayden.
Glentop & Honeytold. Commodore 64 BASIC Programming. 1984. incl. disk 29.95 (ISBN 0-317-06577-7, 7630). Hayden.
Glenwick, David & Jason, Leonard, eds. Behavorial Community Psychology: Progress & Prospects. LC 79-21457. 1980. 39.95x (ISBN 0-03-052111-4). Praeger.
Glenz, Wolfgang W., ed. The Plastics Industry in Western Europe. 158p. 1984. 19.95. Macmillan.
Glerum, Richard Z. & Blake, Donna J. Vocational Decision Workbook. 1977. 4.50x (ISBN 0-910328-14-5); guide o.p. 2.50. Carroll Pr.
Glery, Val, jt. auth. see Budd, Brian.
Gles, Margaret. Come Play Hide & Seek. LC 73-20376. (Easy Venture Ser.). (Illus.). 32p. (gr. k-2). 1975. PLB 7.47 (ISBN 0-8116-6053-2). Garrard.
Gleseking, Hal. Bed & Breakfast: North America. 250p. 1985. pap. 7.95 (ISBN 0-671-53271-5). Frommer-Pasmantier.
Gleser, Goldine C., jt. auth. see Gottschalk, Louis A.
Gleser, Goldine C., et al. Prolonged Psychological Effects of a Disaster: A Study of Buffalo Creek. (Personality & Psychopathology Ser.). 1981. 27.50 (ISBN 0-12-286260-0). Acad Pr.
Gleser, Goldine G., jt. auth. see Ihilevich, David.
Gleser, S. I., et al. The Diatoms of the USSR, Fossil & Recent, Vol. 1. (Illus.). 403p. 1979. Repr. of 1974 ed. lib. bdg. 79.20 (ISBN 3-87429-168-5). Lubrecht & Cramer.
Glesnes-Anderson, Valerie, jt. auth. see Pena, Jesus J.
Gless, Darryl J. Measure for Measure, the Law & the Convent. LC 79-83990. 1979. 29.00 (ISBN 0-691-06403-2). Princeton U Pr.
Glessing, Robert J. The Underground Press in America. LC 84-6521. (Illus.). xvi, 207p. 1984. Repr. of 1970 ed. lib. bdg. 29.75x (ISBN 0-313-24450-2, GLUP). Greenwood.
Glew, G., ed. Advances in Catering Technology. (Illus.). 450p. 1980. 96.25 (ISBN 0-85334-844-8, Pub. by Elsevier Applied Sci England). Elsevier.
--Catering Equipment & Systems Design. (Illus.). 480p. 1977. 70.50 (ISBN 0-85334-730-1, Pub. by Elsevier Applied Sci England). Elsevier.
Glew, Robert H. & Peters, Stephen P., eds. Practical Enzymology of the Sphingolipidoses. LC 77-15819. (Laboratory & Research Methods in Biology & Medicine: Vol. 1). 322p. 1977. 47.00 (ISBN 0-8451-1650-9). A R Liss.
Gleye, Paul H. The Architecture of Los Angeles. (Illus.). 240p. 1983. 35.00 (ISBN 0-86558-004-9). LA Lib Architecture.
Gleysteen, Jan. Mennonite Tourguide to Western Europe. LC 84-683. 340p. (Orig.). 1984. pap. 12.95 (ISBN 0-8361-3360-9). Herald Pr.
--Symphony in Steam. LC 66-17851. (Illus.). 1972. 7.50 (ISBN 0-9600578-1-1). Trogon Pubns.
Glezen, G. W., jt. auth. see Taylor, D. H.
Glezen, G. William, jt. auth. see Taylor, Donald H.
Glezer, Aleksandr. Polden' I Polnoch' LC 83-63004. (Russica Poetry Ser.: No. 7). 120p. (Russian.). 1985. 15.00 (ISBN 0-89830-087-8); pap. 7.95 (ISBN 0-89830-076-2). Russica Pubs.
Glezer, Leon. Tariff Politics: Australian Policy-Making 1960-1980. 360p. 1982. 35.00x (ISBN 0-522-84190-2, Pub. by Melbourne U Pr). Intl Spec Bk.
Glezerman, G. Classes & Nations. 271p. 1979. pap. 2.45 (ISBN 0-8285-0218-8, Pub. by Progress Pubs USSR). Imported Pubns.
Glezerman, M. & Jecht, E. W., eds. Varicocele & Male Infertility, II. (Illus.). 135p. 1984. pap. 17.00 (ISBN 0-387-12985-5). Springer Verlag.
Glezerman, M., et al. Algebraic Topology. (Translations, Ser.: No. 1, Vol. 7). 1962. 24.00 (ISBN 0-8218-1607-1, TRANS 1-7). Am Math.
GLH, ed. see Balahura, Robert.
Gliauda, Jurgis. Simas. 1971. 5.00 (ISBN 0-87141-042-7). Manyland.
--Sonata of Icarus. Sealey, Raphael, tr. (Illus.). 1968. 5.00 (ISBN 0-87141-024-9). Manyland.
Glib, Tom. Critical-Factor Communication & Control. LC 84-61514. (Illus.). pap. cancelled (ISBN 0-89435-122-2, CF 1222). QED Info Sci.
Glick. Fundamentals of Human Lymphoid Cell Culture. 176p. 1980. 35.00 (ISBN 0-8247-6988-0). Dekker.
Glick, Allen. Winters Coming, Winters Gone. 368p. 1985. 15.95 (ISBN 0-523-42550-3). Pinnacle Bks.
Glick, Bert. Ancient Alibi. 1978. 2.50 (ISBN 0-931020-11-5). Crosscut Saw.
--Cookie Aura: Poems. 3rd ed. 1977. pap. 2.50 (ISBN 0-931020-07-7). Crosscut Saw.
--Earthquake Weather. 1980. pap. 3.00 (ISBN 0-931020-17-4). Crosscut Saw.
--Joyous Entry: Selected Poems 1974-82. 56p. (Orig.). 1982. pap. 3.00 (ISBN 0-931020-20-4). Crosscut Saw.
--Low Threshold. 1979. pap. 2.50 (ISBN 0-931020-12-3). Crosscut Saw.
--Primal Ripe. (Illus.). 56p. (Orig.). 1981. pap. 3.00 (ISBN 0-931020-19-0). Crosscut Saw.
--Raku Eyes. 1977. pap. 2.50 (ISBN 0-931020-09-3). Crosscut Saw.
Glick, Carl. Shake Hands with the Dragon. LC 75-162513. 334p. 1971. Repr. of 1941 ed. 43.00x (ISBN 0-8103-3765-7). Gale.
Glick, Carl, jt. auth. see McCleery, Albert.
Glick, Clarence E. Sojourners & Settlers: Chinese Migrants in Hawaii. LC 80-13799. 421p. 1980. text ed. 20.00x (ISBN 0-8248-0707-3). UH Pr.
Glick, D. Methods of Biochemical Analysis, Vol. 31. 480p. 1985. 64.95 (ISBN 0-471-82177-2). Wiley.
Glick, D., ed. see Holmes, K. C. & Blow, D. M.

Glick, David. Methods of Biochemical Analysis, Vol. 27. (Methods of Biochemical Analysis Ser.). 537p. 1981. 62.50 (ISBN 0-471-06503-X, Pub. by Wiley-Interscience). Wiley.
--Methods of Biochemical Analysis, Vol. 28. LC 54-7232. 430p. 1982. 58.50 (ISBN 0-471-08370-4, Pub. by Wiley-Interscience). Wiley.
--Methods of Biochemical Analysis, Vol. 29. 507p. 1983. text ed. 64.50 (ISBN 0-471-86283-5, 2-180, Pub. by Wiley-Interscience). Wiley.
--Methods of Biochemical Analysis, Vol. 30. (Methods of Biochemical Analysis Ser.: No. 2180). 377p. 1984. 49.50 (ISBN 0-471-80276-X, Pub. by Wiley-Interscience). Wiley.
Glick, David, ed. Methods of Biochemical Analysis. LC 54-7273. 435p. (Pub. by Wiley Interscience); Vol. 26, 1980. 59.50 (ISBN 0-471-04798-8). Wiley.
--Methods of Biochemical Analysis, Vol. 4. LC 54-7232. 372p. 1957. 31.50 (ISBN -470-30525-8). Krieger.
--Methods of Biochemical Analysis, Vol. 6. LC 54-7232. 368p. 1958. 33.00 (ISBN -470-30591-6). Krieger.
--Methods of Biochemical Analysis, Vol. 8. LC 54-7232. 410p. 1960. 33.50 (ISBN -470-30657-2). Krieger.
--Methods of Biochemical Analysis, Vol. 11. 442p. (Orig.). 1963. 35.00 (ISBN 0-470-30738-2). Krieger.
--Methods of Biochemical Analysis, Vol. 12. 499p. (Orig.). 1964. 35.00 (ISBN 0-470-30742-0). Krieger.
--Methods of Biochemical Analysis, Vol. 16. 446p. (Orig.). 1968. 35.00 (ISBN 0-470-30750-1). Krieger.
--Methods of Biochemical Analysis, Vols. 14, 15, 17-19. Vol. 14, 1966, 562p. 35.00 (ISBN 0-470-30747-1); Vol. 15, 1967, 531p. 35.00 (ISBN 0-470-30749-8); Vol. 17, 1969, 428p. 35.00 (ISBN 0-470-30752-8); Vol. 18, 1969, 416p. 35.00 (ISBN 0-471-30753-X); Vol. 19, 1971, 632p. 35.00 (ISBN 0-471-30754-8, Pub. by Wiley). Krieger.
--Methods of Biochemical Analysis, Vol. 20. 572p. (Orig.). 1973. 35.00 (ISBN 0-471-30755-6). Krieger.
--Methods of Biochemical Analysis, Vol. 23. LC 54-7232. 356p. 1976. 35.00 (ISBN 0-471-01413-3). Krieger.
--Methods of Biochemical Analysis: Analysis of Biogenic Amines & Their Related Enzymes. LC 54-7232. 358p. (Orig.). 1971. Supplemental Ed. 35.00 (ISBN 0-471-30420-4). Krieger.
--Methods of Biochemical Analysis: Analysis of Biochemical Amines & Their Related Enzymes, Vol. 24. LC 54-7232. 512p. 1977. 35.00 (ISBN -471-02764-2). Krieger.
Glick, David & Rosenbaum, R., eds. Techniques of Biochemical & Biophysical Morphology, Vol. 3. LC 72-153. 214p. 1977. 27.50 (ISBN 0-471-02219-5, Pub. by Wiley). Krieger.
Glick, David M. Biochemistry Review. 7th ed. LC 80-19927. (Basic Science Review Bks.). 1980. pap. 12.75. Med Exam.
--Medical Examination Review: Biochemistry. 8th ed. 1983. pap. text ed. 12.75. Med Exam.
Glick, David M., ed. Biochemistry Review. 6th ed. (Basic Science Review Bks.). 1975. spiral bdg. 12.75 (ISBN 0-87488-202-8). Med Exam.
Glick, Edward B. The Triangular Connection: America, Israel & American Jews. 160p. 1982. text ed. 8.50x (ISBN 0-04-353008-7). Allen Unwin.
Glick, Ferne P. & Pellman, Donald R. Breaking Silence: A Family Grows with Deafness. LC 82-6067. 208p. (Orig.). 1982. 10.95 (ISBN 0-8361-1999-1); pap. 6.95 (ISBN 0-8361-3300-5). Herald Pr.
Glick, H., jt. ed. see Atkins, B.
Glick, Henry R. Courts, Politics & Justice. (Illus.). 320p. 1982. pap. text ed. 18.95 (ISBN 0-07-023490-6). McGraw.
Glick, Ira, et al. Family Therapy & Research: An Annotated Bibliography. 2nd ed. 308p. 1981. 45.50 (ISBN 0-8089-1431-6, 791588). Grune.
Glick, Ira D. & Kessler, David, eds. Marital & Family Therapy: An Introductory Text. 2nd ed. 380p. 1980. 35.50 (ISBN 0-8089-1232-1, 791590). Grune.
Glick, Ira O., et al. The First Year of Bereavement. LC 74-12499. 311p. 1974. 34.95 (ISBN 0-471-30421-2, Pub. by Wiley-Interscience). Wiley.
Glick, Joel, jt. auth. see Lorusso, Julia.
Glick, Joseph. The Development of Social Understanding. 288p. 1978. 28.95 (ISBN 0-89876-054-2). Gardner Pr.
Glick, Joseph & Clarke-Stewart, K. Alison, eds. The Development of Social Understanding. LC 77-25044. (Studies in Social & Cognitive Development: Vol. I). 288p. 1978. 19.95x (ISBN 0-470-99367-7). Halsted Pr.
Glick, Leonard & Hebding, Daniel E. Introduction to Social Problems. LC 78-67953. 536p. 1980. text ed. 17.95 (ISBN 0-394-34836-2, RanC). Random.
Glick, Leonard, jt. auth. see Hebding, Daniel E.
Glick, Leslie A. Multilateral Trade Negotiations: World Trade after the Tokyo Round. LC 80-70919. 440p. 1984. text ed. 49.95x (ISBN 0-86598-036-5). Rowman & Allanheld.
--Trading with Saudi Arabia: A Guide to the Shipping, Trade, Investment & Tax Laws of Saudi Arabia. LC 79-55002. 620p. 1980. text ed. 57.50x (ISBN 0-916672-43-3). Allanheld.
Glick, Paul C. American Families. LC 73-84751. (Census Monograph). (Illus.). xiv, 240p. 1976. Repr. of 1957 ed. 18.00x (ISBN 0-8462-1743-0). Russell.
Glick, Paul C., jt. auth. see Carter, Hugh.
Glick, Rush G. & Newsom, Robert S. Fraud Investigation: Fundamentals for Police. (Illus.). 358p. 1974. 25.75x (ISBN 0-398-03070-7). C C Thomas.
Glick, Ruth & Buckholtz, Eileen. Doom Stalker. (Micro Adventure Ser.: No. 7). 128p. (Orig.). (gr. 6 up). 1985. pap. 1.95 (ISBN 0-590-33382-8). Scholastic Inc.
--Mindbenders. (Micro Adventure Ser.). 128p. (Orig.). (gr. 7 up). 1984. pap. 1.95 (ISBN 0-590-33169-8). Scholastic Inc.
--Mission of the Secret Spy Squad. (Twistaplot Ser.: No. 10). (Illus.). 112p. (Orig.). (gr. 7 up). 1984. pap. 1.95 (ISBN 0-590-32867-0). Scholastic Inc.
Glick, Ruth, jt. auth. see Buckholtz, Eileen.
Glick, Stanley D. Cerebral Lateralization in Nonhuman Species. (Behavioral Biology Ser.). Date not set. 49.50 (ISBN 0-12-286480-8). Acad Pr.
Glick, Thomas, compiled by. Darwinism in Texas. LC 72-185614. (Illus.). 38p. 1972. 7.00 (ISBN 0-87959-032-7). U of Tex H Ransom Ctr.
Glick, Thomas F. Irrigation & Society in Medieval Valencia. LC 79-95923. (Illus.). 1970. 25.00x (ISBN 0-674-46675-6, Belknap Pr). Harvard U Pr.
--Islamic & Christian Spain in the Early Middle Ages: Comparative Perspectives on Social & Cultural Formation. LC 78-70296. 1978. 39.50 (ISBN 0-691-05274-3). Princeton U Pr.
--The Old World Background of the Irrigation System of San Antonio, Texas. (Southwestern Studies Ser.: No. 35). 1972. pap. 3.00 (ISBN 0-87404-142-2). Tex Western.
Glick, Thomas F., ed. see Herrera, Emilio.
Glick, Thomas H. The Process of Neurologic Care in Medical Practice. (Illus.). 392p. 1984. text ed. 25.00x (ISBN 0-674-71080-0). Harvard U Pr.
Glick, Wendell. The Recognition of Henry David Thoreau: Selected Criticism since 1848. LC 69-15845. pap. 100.50 (ISBN 0-317-29154-8, 2055608). Bks Demand UMI.
Glick, Wendell, ed. Great Short Stories of Henry David Thoreau. LC 82-47560. (Great Short Works Ser.). 352p. (Orig.). 1982. pap. 3.80i (ISBN 0-06-080598-6, P 598, PL). Har-Row.
Glick, Wendell see Thoreau, Henry D.
Glicken, Morley D., ed. Toward Effective Social Work Practice. LC 74-6248. 300p. 1974. text ed. 34.50x (ISBN 0-8422-5171-5); pap. text ed. 8.50x (ISBN 0-8422-0401-6). Irvington.
Glickfeld, Madelyn, ed. Antiquated Subdivisions: Beyond Lot Mergers & Vested Rights. (Monograph: No. 85-1). (Illus.). 170p. 1985. pap. text ed. 15.00 (ISBN 0-318-04681-4). Lincoln Inst Land.
Glickman. Supervision of Instruction: A Developmental Approach. 1985. 31.44 (ISBN 0-205-08468-0, 238468). Allyn.
Glickman, Albert S. & Brown, Zenia H. Changing Schedules at Work: Patterns & Implications. 104p. 1974. pap. 6.95 (ISBN 0-911558-04-7). W E Upjohn.
Glickman, Albert S., jt. auth. see Sheppard, David I.
Glickman, Albert S., ed. The Changing Composition of the Work-Force: Implications for Future Research & Its Application. LC 82-615. 200p. 1982. 29.50x (ISBN 0-306-40995-X, Plenum Pr). Plenum Pub.
Glickman, Albert S., et al. Top Management Development & Succession: An Exploratory Study. 94p. 1968. 2.00 (ISBN 0-317-33997-4, 227). Comm Econ Dev.
Glickman, Beatrice M. & Springer, Nesha B. Who Cares for the Baby? Choices in Child Care. LC 77-75293. 1979. pap. 4.95 (ISBN 0-8052-0625-6). Schocken.
--Who Cares for the Baby? Choices in Child Care. LC 77-75293. 1978. 9.95 (ISBN 0-8052-3667-8). Schocken.
Glickman, Carl. Developmental Supervision: Alternative Practices for Helping Teachers Improve Instruction. 65p. 1981. 5.00 (ISBN 0-317-33679-7, 611-81234). Assn Supervision.
Glickman, Carl D., jt. auth. see Wolfgang, Charles H.
Glickman, Esther. Child Placement Through Clinically Oriented Casework. LC 56-10783. 448p. 1957. 30.00x (ISBN 0-231-02127-5). Columbia U Pr.
Glickman, Florence J. Seventeen & in Between. 3.95 (ISBN 0-686-10139-1). Wagon & Star.
Glickman, Franklin S. & Shalita, Alan R. A Handbook of Dermatology. 1985. 37.50 (ISBN 0-87527-360-2). Green.
Glickman, Gene & Glickman, Toby. The New York Red Pages: A Radical Tourist Guide. 176p. 1984. 29.95 (ISBN 0-03-069786-7); pap. 9.95 (ISBN 0-03-069784-0). Praeger.
Glickman, Gladys. Franchising. 100.00 (ISBN 0-685-02522-5). Bender.
--Franchising, 4 vols, Vols. 15, 15A, 15B, 15C. (Business Organizations Ser.). 1969. Updates avail. looseleaf 300.00 (ISBN 0-317-09705-9, 314); looseleaf 1983 174.50; looseleaf 1984 205.00. Bender.
Glickman, Hal. The Musical Commodore 64. 176p. (Orig., Music Arranged by Laura Goodfriend). (gr. 4-12). 1984. pap. 14.95 (ISBN 0-88190-425-2, BO425). Datamost.
Glickman, Irving, et al. Periodontal Disease: Immunological Factors, I. LC 72-10934. (Illus.). 220p. 1973. text ed. 29.50x (ISBN 0-8422-7061-2). Irvington.
Glickman, L., ed. Psychiatric Consultation in the General Hospital. (Experimental & Clinical Psychiatry Ser.: Vol. 3). 1980. 37.50 (ISBN 0-8247-6880-9). Dekker.
Glickman, Linda. Inpatient Utilization of Short-Stay Hospitals by Diagnosis: United States, 1975. Stevenson, Taloria, ed. (Ser. 13: No. 35). 1978. pap. 1.75 (ISBN 0-8406-0123-9). Natl Ctr Health Stats.
Glickman, Maurice. From Crime to Rehabilitation. 228p. 1983. text ed. 35.40x (ISBN 0-566-00539-5). Gower Pub Co.
Glickman, Norman, jt. auth. see Adams, F. Gerard.
Glickman, Norman J. An Area-Stratified Regional Econometric Model. (Discussion Paper Ser.: No. 58). 1972. pap. 4.50 (ISBN 0-686-32225-8). Regional Sci Res Inst.
--Cities & the International Division of Labor. (Working Paper Ser.: No. 31). 37p. 1984. 5.00 (ISBN 0-318-11681-2). LBJ Sch Pub Aff.
--An Econometric Forecasting Model for the Philadelphia Region. (Discussion Paper Ser.: No. 39). 1970. pap. 5.75 (ISBN 0-686-32208-8). Regional Sci Res Inst.
--Economic Policy & the Cities: In Search of Reagan's "Real" Urban Policy. (Working Paper Ser.: No. 26). 38p. 1984. 5.00 (ISBN 0-318-01668-0). LBJ Sch Public Affairs.
--The Growth & Management of the Japanese Urban System. (Studies in Urban Economics Ser.). 1979. 41.50 (ISBN 0-12-286950-8). Acad Pr.
Glickman, Norman J. & Tani, Akihiko. Economic & Regional Policy in Postwar Japan. (Working Paper Ser.: No. 27). 48p. 1984. 5.00 (ISBN 0-318-01667-2). LBJ Sch Public Affairs.
Glickman, Norman J. & Wilson, Robert H. The Economic Context of Urban Policy. (Working Paper Ser.: No. 28). 47p. 1984. 5.00 (ISBN 0-318-01666-4). LBJ Sch Public Affairs.
Glickman, Norman J., ed. Econometric Analysis of Regional Systems: Explorations in Model Building & Policy Analysis. (Studies in Urban Economics Ser.). 1977. 38.50 (ISBN 0-12-286550-2). Acad Pr.
Glickman, Robert J., ed. Poetry of Julian Del Casal: A Critical Edition, 3 vols. Incl. Vol. 1. 1976. 15.00 (ISBN 0-8130-0540-X); pap. 6.50 (ISBN 0-8130-0572-8); Vol. 2. 1978. 20.00 (ISBN 0-8130-0596-5); Vol. 3. 1977. 17.50 (ISBN 0-8130-0576-0). LC 76-22800. U Presses Fla.
Glickman, Rose L. Russian Factory Women: Workplace & Society, 1880-1914. LC 83-6968. 250p. 1984. lib. bdg. 22.50x (ISBN 0-520-04810-5). U of Cal Pr.
Glickman, S. Craig. A Song for Lovers. LC 75-21454. 204p. (Orig.). 1976. pap. 5.95 (ISBN 0-87784-768-1). Inter-Varsity.
Glickman, Toby, jt. auth. see Glickman, Gene.
Glickman, William G. Winners on the Tennis Court. 48p. (gr. 6 up). 1979. pap. 1.25 (ISBN 0-380-43307-9, 43307-9, Camelot). Avon.
Glicksberg, Abraham. Educational Values in the Shulchan Aruch. LC 84-50678. 144p. 1984. 10.00 (ISBN 0-88400-105-9). Shengold.
Glicksberg, Abraham A. Come Back, Jewish Youth, Come Back Home. LC 83-60003. 1983. pap. 3.95 (ISBN 0-88400-094-X). Shengold.
Glicksberg, Charles. The Literature of Nihilism. 354p. 1975. 32.50 (ISBN 0-8387-1520-6). Bucknell U Pr.
Glicksberg, Charles I. Creative Writing. 604p. 1961. pap. 3.95 (ISBN 0-87532-169-0). Hendricks House.
--Literature & Religion: A Study in Conflict. LC 77-23753. 1977. Repr. of 1960 ed. lib. bdg. 22.50x (ISBN 0-8371-9753-8, GLLR). Greenwood.
--The Literature of Commitment. LC 75-5148. 467p. 1976. 35.00 (ISBN 0-8387-1685-7). Bucknell U Pr.
--Modern Literary Perspectivism. LC 79-125979. 1970. 9.95 (ISBN 0-87074-061-X). SMU Press.
--Self in Modern Literature. LC 63-18887. 1963. 22.75x (ISBN 0-271-73101-X). Pa St U Pr.
--Tragic Vision in Twentieth-Century Literature. LC 63-8904. (Crosscurrents-Modern Critiques Ser.). 205p. 1963. 7.95 (ISBN 0-8093-0091-5). S Ill U Pr.
--Writing the Short Story. 302p. 1953. pap. 3.95 (ISBN 0-87532-167-4). Hendricks House.
Glicksberg, Charles I., ed. American Literary Criticism: Nineteen Hundred to Nineteen Fifty. 584p. 1969. 9.45 (ISBN 0-87532-064-3). Hendricks House.
Glicksburg, Joy B. Crosswords for Language Arts. (gr. 1-5). 1985. pap. 5.95 (ISBN 0-8224-2353-7). Pitman Learning.
Glicksman, Arvin S., jt. auth. see Slaby, Andrew E.
Glicksman, Hal. The Musical Atari. (Musical Ser.). 160p. (gr. 4-12). 1984. pap. 14.95 (ISBN 0-88190-345-0). Datamost.
Glicksman, Hal & Simon, Kent. Games Ataris Play. (Illus.). 224p. 1983. pap. text ed. 14.95 (ISBN 0-88190-118-0, BO118). Datamost.
Glicksman, Hal, et al. Everything You Need to Know to Do Your Taxes with SuperCalc. LC 84-16254. (Woodbury Computer Bk.). 224p. (Orig.). 1985. cancelled; pap. 12.95 (ISBN 0-8069-7932-1). Sterling.
Glicksman, M. Gum Technology in the Food Industry. (Food Science & Technology Ser). 1969. 85.00 (ISBN 0-12-286350-X). Acad Pr.
Glicksman, M. E., ed. see Metallurgical Society of AIME Staff.
Glicksman, Martin. Food Hydrocolloids. 232p. 1982. 65.00 (ISBN 0-8493-6041-2). CRC Pr.
--Food Hydrocolloids, Vol. II. 208p. 1983. 72.00 (ISBN 0-8493-6042-0). CRC Pr.
Glickson. Bleomycin: Chemistry & Clinical Applications. write for info. (ISBN 0-8247-1289-7). Dekker.
Glickson, J. D., et al. Vasopressin, I: Chemical & Clinical Aspects. 204p. 1974. 24.50x (ISBN 0-8422-7123-6). Irvington.
Glickstein, Barbra. Bulletin Board Extravaganzas. (gr. k-8). 1981. 6.95 (ISBN 0-86653-002-9, GA229). Good Apple.
Glickstein, Cyrus, jt. auth. see Ewen, Sol J.
Glidden, Hope H. The Storyteller As Humanist: The Serees of Guillaume Bouchet. LC 80-70809. (French Forum Monographs: No. 25). 183p. (Orig.). 1981. pap. 12.50x (ISBN 0-917058-24-0). French Forum.
Glidden, Ralph. Exploring the Yellowstone High Country: A History of the Cooke City Area. 2nd & rev. ed. (Illus.). 120p. pap. 5.95 (ISBN 0-9608876-0-1). Cooke City.
Gliddon, George R., jt. auth. see Nott, J. C.
Glide, Salmoneus T. Mytholimericks VI: Jason & the Golden Fleece. (Limericklets Ser.: No. 40). (Illus.). 1983. pap. 1.00 (ISBN 0-938338-50-1). Winds World Pr.
Glidewell, John. The Social Context of Learning & Development. 239p. 1977. 28.95 (ISBN 0-89876-055-0). Gardner Pr.
Glidewell, John C., ed. The Social Context of Learning & Development. LC 76-8867. 239p. 1977. 18.95x (ISBN 0-470-15078-5). Halsted Pr.
Gliese, W., et al, eds. see I.A.U Symposium No. 61, Perth, Western Australia, 13-17 August, 1973.
Gliglois. Gliglois. (Harvard Studies in Romance Languages). 1932. 18.00 (ISBN 0-527-01106-1). Kraus Repr.
Gligoric, S. & Sokolov, V. The Sicilian Defence, Bk. 1. 1972. pap. 9.90 (ISBN 0-08-017276-8). Pergamon.
Gligoric, Svetozar. Play the Nimzo-Indian Defense. (Pergamon Chess Ser.). (Illus.). 175p. 1985. 19.95 (ISBN 0-08-026928-1); pap. 11.95 (ISBN 0-08-026927-3). Pergamon.
Gliklikh, Y. E., jt. ed. see Borisovich, Y. G.
Glim, Jo Ann, ed. Lights! Camera! Action, Vol. 2. (How to Make Cable TV Work for You). 1985. write for info. (ISBN 0-9609790-1-8). Direct Market.
Glimcher, Arnold, et al. Jean Dubuffet: Simulacres. Pace Gallery, ed. LC 78-106008. (Illus.). 45p. (Orig.). 1969. pap. text ed. 5.00 (ISBN 0-938608-25-8). Pace Gallery Pubns.
Glimcher, Arnold B., jt. auth. see Vitz, Paul C.
Glimm, jt. auth. see Jaffee.
Glimm, J. & Jaffe, A. Quantum Physics: A Functional Integral Point of View. (Illus.). 416p. 1981. 28.00 (ISBN 0-387-90551-0); pap. 19.50 (ISBN 0-387-90562-6). Springer-Verlag.
Glimm, James & Lax, Peter D. Decay of Solutions of Systems of Nonlinear Hyperbolic Conservation Laws. LC 52-42839. (Memoirs Ser.: Vol. 101). 112p. 1970. pap. text ed. 9.00 (ISBN 0-8218-1801-5, MEMO-101). Am Math.
Glimm, James Y. Flatlanders & Ridgerunners: Folktales from the Mountains of Northern Pennsylvania. LC 82-10895. (Illus.). 240p. 1983. 11.95 (ISBN 0-8229-3471-X); pap. 5.95 (ISBN 0-8229-5345-5). U of Pittsburgh Pr.
Glimn-Lacy, Janice & Kaufman, Peter B. Botany Illustrated. 1984. pap. 19.45 (ISBN 0-442-22969-0). Van Nos Reinhold.
Gliner, Bob. Beyond Coping. 273p. (Orig.). 1982. pap. 5.95x (ISBN 0-910029-01-6). Dell.
--Godzilla Meets Master Charge. 228p. (Orig.). 1982. pap. 4.95x (ISBN 0-910029-00-8). Advocate Hse.
Gliner, Erast, tr. see Braginsky, V. B., et al.
Glines, Carroll V., jt. auth. see Foulois, Benjamin D.
Glines, Carroll V., Jr. The Compact History of the United States Air Force. Gilbert, James, ed. LC 79-7258. (Flight: Its First Seventy-Five Years Ser.). (Illus.). 1979. lib. bdg. 34.50x (ISBN 0-405-12169-5). Ayer Co Pubs.
--Doolittle's Tokyo Raiders. Gilbert, James, ed. LC 79-7259. (Flight: Its First Seventy-Five Years Ser.). (Illus.). 1979. Repr. of 1964 ed. lib. bdg. 20.00x (ISBN 0-405-12170-9). Ayer Co Pubs.
--The Saga of the Air Mail. Gilbert, James, ed. LC 79-2192. (Flight: Its First Seventy-Five Years Ser.). (Illus.). 1979. Repr. of 1968 ed. lib. bdg. 19.00x (ISBN 0-405-12213-6). Ayer Co Pubs.
Glines, Edna L. A Turtle on Her Toe. LC 83-17870. (Illus.). 66p. 1984. 9.95 (ISBN 0-9612160-0-X). Tumbleweed Pub Co.

Glinka, Mikhail I. Memoirs. Mudge, Richard B., tr. from Rus. LC 79-27875. (Illus.). xi, 264p. 1980. Repr. of 1963 ed. lib. bdg. 27.50x (ISBN 0-313-22331-9, GLME). Greenwood.

Glinka, N. General Chemistry. Sobolev, D., tr. (Russian Monographs). (Illus.). 694p. 1965. 92.50 (ISBN 0-677-20560-0). Gordon.

--Problems in General Chemistry. 256p. 1973. 18.00x (ISBN 0-8464-1121-0). Beekman Pubs.

Glinka, N. L. General Chemistry, 2 vols. 768p. 1981. 16.50 set (ISBN 0-8285-2119-0, Pub. by Mir Pubs USSR). Imported Pubns.

--Problems & Exercises in General Chemistry. 288p. 1981. 7.95 (ISBN 0-8285-2407-6, Pub. by Mir Pubs USSR). Imported Pubns.

Glinkov, G. M., jt. auth. see Glinkov, M. A.

Glinkov, M. A. & Glinkov, G. M. A General Theory of Furnaces. 1980. 8.45 (ISBN 0-8285-1799-1, Pub. by Mir Pubs USSR). Imported Pubns.

Glinski, J. & Stephiewski, W., eds. Soil Aeration & Its Role for Plants. 288p. 1985. 72.00 (ISBN 0-8493-5250-9). CRC Pr.

Glinsky, Vladimir. Confessionary Questions: A Preparation for the Sacrament of Penitence with Text of the Office. pap. 0.25 (ISBN 0-686-05391-5). Eastern Orthodox.

Glinz, W. Chest Trauma: Diagnosis & Management. (Illus.). 310p. 1981. 59.59 (ISBN 0-387-10409-7). Springer-Verlag.

Glinz, Werner. Diagnostic & Operative Arthroscopy of the Knee Joint. Spati-Tuchschmid, Edith, tr. (Illus.). 130p. 1980. text ed. 59.00 (ISBN 3-456-80943-3, Pub. by Hans Huber Switzerland). J K Burgess.

Gliozzo, Charles A. Bibliography of Ecclesiastical History of the French Revolution. LC 73-154506. (Bibliographia Tripotamopolitana: No. 6). 1972. 8.00x (ISBN 0-931222-05-2). C E Barbour.

--Bibliography of Ecclesiastical History of the French Revolution. LC 73-154506. 1972. 8.00 (ISBN 0-931222-05-2). Pitts Theolog.

Glismann, H. H. & Weiss, F. D. On the Political Economy of Protection in Germany. (Working Paper: No. 427). 30p. 1980. pap. 3.00 (ISBN 0-686-39768-1, WP-0427). World Bank.

Glissant, Edouard. Monsieur Toussaint: A Play. Foster, Joseph G. & Franklin, Barbara A., trs. from Fr. LC 82-51665. (Illus.). 1982. 16.00x (ISBN 0-89410-128-5); pap. 8.00x (ISBN 0-89410-129-3). Three Continents.

Glisson, Jerry & Taylor, Jack R. The Church in a Storm. LC 82-74208. (Orig.). 1983. pap. 5.95 (ISBN 0-8054-5522-1). Broadman.

Glisson, T. H. Introduction to System Analysis. 704p. 1985. 45.95 (ISBN 0-07-023391-8). McGraw.

Glist, Virginia J. Lend an Ear: A Skills Approach to Effective Listening. (Market Builder Library Selection Ser.). 112p. (Orig.). 1983. pap. 6.95 (ISBN 0-912169-01-X). R & R Newkirk.

Glittenberg, Jody, jt. auth. see Deyoung, Carol.

Glitz, Maurice L., jt. auth. see Borror, Donald.

Gloag, John. Victorian Comfort: A Social History of Design 1830-1900. (Illus.). 268p. 1980. Repr. 25.00 (ISBN 0-7153-6329-8). David & Charles.

--Victorian Taste. (Illus.). 168p. 1980. Repr. 28.00 (ISBN 0-7153-5739-5). David & Charles.

Gloag, Julian. Blood for Blood. 302p. 1985. 15.95 (ISBN 0-03-006012-5). HR&W.

--Lost & Found. 1983. pap. 2.95 (ISBN 0-671-44292-9). PB.

Gloag, P. J. & Delitzsch, F. The Messiahship of Christ. 628p. 1983. lib. bdg. 23.50 Smythe Sewn (ISBN 0-86524-146-5, 9514). Klock & Klock.

Gloag, Paton J. A Critical & Exegetical Commentary on the Acts of the Apostles, 2 vols. 1979. 29.95 (ISBN 0-86524-006-X, 4402). Klock & Klock.

Gloaguen, Philippe & Josse, Pierre, eds. Hip Pocket Guide to Mexico, Belize, Guatemala & the French Antilles. (Collier World Traveler Ser.). (Illus.). 192p. 1985. pap. 6.95 (ISBN 0-02-097020-X, Collier). Macmillan.

--Hip Pocket Guide to Northern & Central Europe. (Collier World Traveler Ser.). (Illus.). 192p. 1985. pap. 6.95 (ISBN 0-02-097030-7, Collier). Macmillan.

Gloaguen, Philippe, et al, eds. Hip Pocket Guide to Greece & Yugoslavia. (Collier World Traveler Ser.). (Illus.). 192p. 1985. pap. 6.95 (ISBN 0-02-097040-4, Collier). Macmillan.

Glob, P. V. The Bog People: Iron-Age Man Preserved. Bruce-Mitford, R. L., tr. LC 69-20391. (Illus.). 200p. 1969. 27.50 (ISBN 0-8014-0492-4). Cornell U Pr.

--The Mound People: Danish Bronze-Age Man Preserved. Bulman, Joan, tr. from Danish. LC 73-2602. (Illus.). 180p. 1974. 27.50 (ISBN 0-8014-0800-8). Cornell U Pr.

Global Engineering Documents. The Commercial Guide to Government Packaging, Vol. 2. 1st ed. Eary, David K., ed. 635p. 1985. Looseleaf 219.04 (ISBN 0-912702-30-3). Global Eng.

--Qualified Products List & Sources. 64th ed. 344p. 1985. lib. bdg. 57.50 (ISBN 0-912702-28-1). Global Eng.

Global Interdependence Center Staff, jt. ed. see McClellan, Joel.

Global Tropospheric Chemistry Panel, National Research Council. Global Tropospheric Chemistry: A Plan for Action. 208p. 1984. pap. 20.95 (ISBN 0-309-03481-7). Natl Acad Pr.

Globe, Alexander. Peter Stent. (Illus.). 350p. 1985. 60.00 (ISBN 0-7748-0221-9). U BC Pr.

Globe, Leah A., jt. auth. see Eisenberg, A.

Globe, Leah A., jt. auth. see Eisenberg, Azriel.

Globerman, S., jt. auth. see Daly, D. J.

Globerman, Steven. Cultural Regulation in Canada. 114p. 1983. pap. text ed. 11.95x (ISBN 0-920380-81-6, Pub. by Inst Res Pub Canada). Brookfield Pub Co.

--U. S. Ownership of Firms in Canada: Issues & Policy Approaches. LC 79-51649. (Canadian-U. S. Prospect Ser.). 104p. 1979. 5.00 (ISBN 0-88806-052-1, CUSP3). Natl Planning.

Globerson, Amiela, jt. ed. see Feldman, Michael.

Globerson, Arye. Higher Education & Employment: A Case Study of Israel. LC 78-60131. (Praeger Special Studies). 189p. 1979. 38.95 (ISBN 0-03-046226-6). Praeger.

Globerson, S. Performance Criteria & Incentive Systems. (Advances in Industrial Engineering Ser.: No. 1). 250p. 1985. 59.95 (ISBN 0-444-42427-X). Elsevier.

Globus, Gordon, et al, eds. Consciousness & the Brain: A Scientific & Philosophical Inquiry. LC 75-44478. (Illus.). 378p. 1976. 39.50x (ISBN 0-306-30878-9, Plenum Pr). Plenum Pub.

Glock, Charles & Bellah, Robert N., eds. The New Religious Consciousness. 391p. 29.50 (ISBN 0-686-95181-6); pap. 6.95 (ISBN 0-686-99471-X). ADL.

Glock, Charles Y. & Stark, Rodney. Christian Beliefs & Anti-Semitism. LC 78-31750. (Univ. of California Five-Year Study of Anti-Semitism). 1979. Repr. of 1966 ed. lib. bdg. 24.75x (ISBN 0-313-20969-3, GLCB). Greenwood.

--Northern California Church Member Study, 1963. LC 79-63206. 1979. codebk. write for info. (ISBN 0-89138-980-6). ICPSR.

Glock, Charles Y., jt. auth. see Quinley, Harold E.

Glock, Charles Y., jt. auth. see Stark, Rodney.

Glock, Charles Y., ed. Survey Research in the Social Sciences. LC 67-25911. 544p. 1967. 10.00x (ISBN 0-87154-331-1). Russell Sage.

Glock, Charles Y. & Bellah, Robert N., eds. The New Religious Consciousness. LC 75-17295. 1976. 31.00x (ISBN 0-520-03083-4); pap. 6.95 (ISBN 0-520-03472-4). U of Cal Pr.

Glock, Charles Y., et al. Adolescent Prejudice. 260p. text ed. 18.95x (ISBN 0-8290-0751-2); pap. text ed. 6.95x (ISBN 0-8290-0281-2). Irvington.

Glock, Charles Y., jt. auth. see Apostle, Richard A.

Glock, Marvin & Bender, David. Probe. 3rd ed. (No. 174). 384p. 1984. Additional supplements may be obtained from publisher. pap. text ed. 14.95 (ISBN 0-675-20146-2); tapes, Discount given for multiple sets 125.00 (ISBN 0-675-20114-4). Merrill.

Glock, Marvin D. & Bender, David. Probe. abridged ed. (Communication Skills Ser.). 1978. pap. text ed. 10.95x (ISBN 0-675-08373-7); 1 set 80.00 (ISBN 0-675-08372-9). Merrill.

Glock, Marvin D. & Bender, David S. Probe: College Developmental Reading. 2nd ed. 1980. text ed. 14.50 (ISBN 0-675-08144-0, C57). Additional supplements may be obtained from publisher. Merrill.

Glock, Oriel, jt. auth. see Branford, Susan.

Glock, Waldo S. Eighteenth Century English Literary Studies: A Bibliography. LC 83-20057. 1984. 52.50 (ISBN 0-8108-1658-X). Scarecrow.

Glock, Waldo S., jt. auth. see Agerter, Sharlene R.

Glocker, Theodore W. The Government of American Trade Unions. LC 78-63944. (Johns Hopkins University. Studies in the Social Sciences. Thirty-First Ser. 1913: No. 2). Repr. of 1913 ed. 24.50 (ISBN 0-404-61193-1). AMS Pr.

--Government of American Trade Unions. LC 75-156412. (American Labor Ser., No. 2). 1971. Repr. of 1913 ed. 15.00 (ISBN 0-405-02920-9). Ayer Co Pubs.

Glockling, Frank. Chemistry of Germanium. 1969. 44.00 (ISBN 0-12-286450-6). Acad Pr.

Glockner, H., ed. see Hegel, Georg W.

Glodny-Wiercziuski, Dorothea, ed. see Hollonuis, Ludwig.

Glodowski, R. J., ed. Through-Thickness Tension Testing of Steel- STP 794. LC 82-72887. 152p. 1983. text ed. 21.00 (ISBN 0-8031-0232-1, 04-794000-02). ASTM.

Gloeckle, W. The Quantum Mechanical Few-Body Problem. (Texts & Monographs in Physics). (Illus.). 220p. 1983. 32.00 (ISBN 0-387-12587-6). Springer-Verlag.

Gloeckner, Carolyn. Fernando Valenzuela. Schroeder, Howard, ed. (Sports Closeups Ser.). (Illus.). 48p. (gr. 5-6). 1985. PLB 9.95 (ISBN 0-89686-256-9). Crestwood Hse.

--Joe Theismann. Schroeder, Howard, ed. (Sports Closeups Ser.). (Illus.). 48p. (gr. 5-6). 1985. PLB 9.95 (ISBN 0-89686-250-X). Crestwood Hse.

--Marvelous Marvin Hagler. Schroeder, Howard, ed. (Sports Closeups Ser.). (Illus.). 48p. (gr. 5-6). 1985. PLB 9.95 (ISBN 0-89686-257-7). Crestwood Hse.

--Sugar Ray Leonard. Schroeder, Howard, ed. (Sports Closeups Ser.). (Illus.). 48p. (gr. 5-6). 1985. PLB 9.95 (ISBN 0-89686-253-4). Crestwood Hse.

Gloeden, Wilhelm von see Von Gloeden, Wilhelm.

Gloess, Paul Y. Understanding LISP. (Handy Guide). 64p. (Orig.). 1983. pap. 3.50 (ISBN 0-88284-219-6). Alfred Pub.

Glogan, Joseph. Sportsmans Book of U. S. Records. (Illus.). 96p. (Orig.). 1980. pap. text ed. 4.95 (ISBN 0-937328-00-6). NY Outdoor Guide.

--Sportsmans Book of U. S. Records. 3rd ed. (Illus.). 144p. 1982. pap. text ed. 4.95 (ISBN 0-937328-02-2). NY Outdoor Guide.

--Sportsmans Book of U. S. Records. 4th ed. (Illus.). 168p. 1983. pap. text ed. 4.95 (ISBN 0-937328-03-0, Dist. by Caroline House, Inc.). NY Outdoor Guide.

--Sportsmans Book of U.S. Records. 2nd ed. (Illus.). 122p. 1981. pap. text ed. 4.95 (ISBN 0-937328-01-4). NY Outdoor Guide.

--Sportsman's Book of U.S. Records. 5th ed. (Illus.). 104p. pap. text ed. 3.95 (ISBN 0-937328-04-9). NY Outdoor Guide.

Gloge, Detlef. Optical Fiber Technology. LC 75-23777. 1976. 36.35 (ISBN 0-87942-062-6, PC0588). Inst Electrical.

Glogowski, Maryruth P., jt. ed. see Provan, Jill.

Glombiewski, jt. auth. see Cohen.

Gloor, B. & Bruckner, R., eds. Rehabilitation of the Visually Disabled & the Blind at Different Ages. (Illus.). 164p. 1980. pap. text ed. 19.50 (ISBN 3-456-80790-2, Pub. by Hans Huber Switzerland). J K Burgess.

Gloor, Robert, ed. Medicine, the Community & Health. LC 81-51720. 145p. 1981. 14.50 (ISBN 0-913590-79-7). Slack Inc.

Glorfeld, Louis E., et al. A Concise Guide for Writers. 6th ed. LC 83-22828. 227p. 1980. pap. text ed. 11.95 (ISBN 0-03-062628-5, HoltC). HR&W.

Glorig, A., jt. auth. see Gerwin, K. S.

Glorig, Aram & Gerwin, Kenneth S. Otitis Media: Proceedings. (Illus.). 328p. 1972. photocopy ed. 32.75x (ISBN 0-398-02294-1). C C Thomas.

Glorig, Aram, ed. Audiometry: Principles & Practices. LC 77-10869. 286p. 1977. lib. bdg. 18.00 (ISBN 0-88275-604-4). Krieger.

Glorioso, Robert M. & Colon-Osorio, Fernando C. Engineering Intelligent Systems: Concepts, Theory, & Application. 2nd ed. (Illus.). 472p. 1980. 29.00 (ISBN 0-932376-06-1, EY-AX011-DP). Digital Pr.

Glorioso, Robert M. & Hill, F. S., Jr. Introduction to Engineering. (Illus.). 448p. 1975. ref. ed. 27.95x. P-H.

Glos, George E. Comparative Law. xxxv, 787p. 1979. 35.00x (ISBN 0-8377-0610-6). Rothman.

Gloss, August. The Genius of the German Lyric. 1976. lib. bdg. 59.95 (ISBN 0-8490-1879-X). Gordon Pr.

Gloss, David S. & Wardle, Miriam G. Introduction To Safety Engineering. LC 83-16751. 612p. 1984. 55.00 (ISBN 0-471-87667-4, Wiley-Interscience). Wiley.

Glossbrenner, Alfred. The Complete Handbook of Personal Computer Communications: Everything You Need to Know to Go Online with the World. 352p. 1983. pap. 14.95 (ISBN 0-312-15718-5). St Martin.

--The Complete Handbook of Personal Computer Communications: Everything You Need to Go Online with the World. rev., enl. ed. (Illus.). 480p. 1985. pap. 14.95 (ISBN 0-312-15760-6). St Martin.

--Going Online: Communications of the DEC Rainbow. (DECbooks). 325p. 1984. 21.00 (ISBN 0-932376-73-8, EY-00035-DP). Digital Pr.

--How to Buy Software: The Master Guide to Picking the Right Program. LC 83-21175. 600p. 1984. pap. 14.95 (ISBN 0-312-39551-5). St Martin.

--How to Get Free Software: The Master Guide to Free Programs for Every Brand of Personal Home Computer. LC 84-31284. 432p. 1984. 14.95 (ISBN 0-312-39563-9). St Martin.

--Personal Computer Communications for the DEC Rainbow. (DECbooks). write for info. Digital Pr.

Glossbrenner, Alfred, jt. auth. see Costello, Patty.

Glossbrenner, Alfred, jt. auth. see Lau, Charley.

Glossinger, John. You Are Born to Victory. 115p. 1981. pap. 3.95 (ISBN 0-87516-445-5). De Vorss.

Glossman, Hartmut, et al. Functional & Structural Nature of Biomembranes: I. LC 73-1290. (Illus.). 184p. 1972. text ed. 24.00x (ISBN 0-8422-7044-2). Irvington.

Glossner, O. Commercial Arbitration in the Federal Republic of Germany. 1984. lib. bdg. 34.00 (ISBN 90-654-4185-9, Pub. by Kluwer Law Netherlands). Kluwer Academic.

Glossop, R. H. Method Study & the Furniture Industry. LC 75-112711. 1970. 25.00 (ISBN 0-08-015653-3). Pergamon.

Glossop, Ronald J. Confronting War: An Examination of Humanity's Most Pressing Problem. LC 82-23950. 304p. 1983. 19.95x (ISBN 0-89950-073-0). McFarland & Co.

Gloster, Hugh M. Negro Voices in American Fiction. LC 65-17895. 1965. Repr. of 1948 ed. 17.00x (ISBN 0-8462-0577-7). Russell.

Gloster, Jesse E. Minority Economic, Political & Social Development. LC 78-62738. 1978. pap. text ed. 21.00 (ISBN 0-8191-0593-7). U Pr of Amer.

--North Carolina Mutual Life Insurance Company: Its Historical Development & Current Operations. LC 75-41758. (Companies & Men: Business Enterprises in America). (Illus.). 1976. 34.50x (ISBN 0-405-08074-3). Ayer Co Pubs.

GLottheil, Richard J., ed. Oriental-Literature, 4 Vols. 1985. Repr. of 1900 ed. Set. lib. bdg. 200.00 (ISBN 0-89760-260-9). Vols. 1 & 2: The Literature of Persia, Vol 1: 410 p., Vol 2: 296 p. Vol 3: The Literature of India, 467 p. Vol. 4: The Literature of China, 451 p. Telegraph Bks.

Glotz, Gustave. L'Ordalie Dans la Grece Primitive. Vlastos, Gregory, ed. LC 78-19352. (Morals & Law in Ancient Greece Ser.). 1979. Repr. of 1904 ed. lib. bdg. 12.00x (ISBN 0-405-11545-8). Ayer Co Pubs.

--La Solidarite de la Famille Dan le Droit Criminel en Grece. LC 72-7891. (Greek History Ser.). (Fr.). Repr. of 1904 ed. 43.00 (ISBN 0-405-04787-8). Ayer Co Pubs.

Glotzer, Arline. Monarch's Complete Guide to Law Schools. (Illus.). 192p. (Orig.). 1981. pap. 6.95 (ISBN 0-671-09192-1). Monarch Pr.

Glotzer, Arline & Sheiman, Bruce. Lovejoy's Guide to Graduate Business Schools. (Orig.). 1983. pap. 14.95 (ISBN 0-671-44884-6). Monarch Pr.

Glotzer, Barry M. The Computer Concepts Coloring Book. (Illus.). 128p. (Orig.). 1985. pap. 8.61i (ISBN 0-06-460308-3, COS 308). B&N NY.

Glotzer, David. Occasions of Grace: Poems by David Glotzer. (Illus.). 1978. bound 75.00 (ISBN 0-685-27834-4); deluxe ed. 110.00 signed (ISBN 0-685-27835-2). Heron Pr.

Glotzer, Judith A., jt. ed. see Nestor, Joanne P.

Gloucester Art Press Editors, ed. A Portfolio of Dramatic & Romantic Illustrations in Full Colours of the Great Railroads of the Past. (Illus.). 87p. 1985. 165.50 (ISBN 0-86650-166-5). Gloucester Art.

Gloucester, Richard & Hobhouse, Hermione. Oxford & Cambridge. (Illus.). 184p. 1980. 8.98 (ISBN 0-500-34081-1). Thames Hudson.

Gloucester 350th Anniversary Celebration, Inc. Gloucester 350th Anniversary Program. 1973. 1.00 (ISBN 0-930352-04-1). Nelson B Robinson.

Gloudemans, Robert J. Property Tax Limits. (Research & Information Ser.). 55p. 1978. 11.50 (ISBN 0-88329-030-8). Intl Assess.

--Use-Value Farmland Assessments: Theory, Practice & Impact. LC 74-83299. (Studies in Property Taxation). 73p. 1974. pap. 14.00 (ISBN 0-88329-050-2). Intl Assess.

Glovach, Linda. The Little Witch's Birthday Book. (gr. 1-4). 1981. 7.95 (ISBN 0-13-537977-6). P-H.

--The Little Witch's Birthday Book. (Illus.). 48p. 1984. pap. 4.95 (ISBN 0-13-538125-8). P-H.

--Little Witch's Black Magic Book of Disguises. (gr. 1-4). 1973. (Pub. by Treehouse); pap. 3.95 (ISBN 0-13-537944-X). P-H.

--Little Witch's Black Magic Book of Games. (gr. 1-4). 1974. 7.95 (ISBN 0-13-537928-8). P-H.

--Little Witch's Black Magic Cookbook. (Illus.). (gr. 1-4). 1972. pap. 3.95 (ISBN 0-13-537936-9, Pub. by Treehouse). P-H.

--Little Witch's Carnival Books. (Illus.). 48p. (gr. 1-4). 1982. 7.95 (ISBN 0-13-538074-X). P-H.

--The Little Witch's Cat Book. (Illus.). 48p. (gr. 2-5). 1985. pap. 9.95 (ISBN 0-13-537697-1). P-H.

--The Little Witch's Christmas Book. (Illus.). 48p. (gr. 1-4). 1982. pap. 4.95 (ISBN 0-13-538090-1, Pub. by Treehouse). P-H.

--Little Witch's Halloween Book. LC 75-11713. (Illus.). (gr. 1-4). 1975. 7.95 (ISBN 0-13-537985-7). P-H.

--The Little Witch's Halloween Book. (Illus.). 32p. (gr. 1-4). 1983. pap. 4.95 (ISBN 0-13-538116-9, Pub. by Treehouse Bks). P-H.

--The Little Witch's Spring Holiday Book. LC 82-21466. (Illus.). 48p. (ps-4). 1983. 8.95 (ISBN 0-13-538108-8). P-H.

--The Little Witch's Thanksgiving Book. (Illus.). (gr. 1-4). 1981. pap. 2.50 (ISBN 0-13-538009-X, Pub. by Treehouse). P-H.

--The Little Witch's Thanksgiving Book. LC 76-9847. (Illus.). 48p. (gr. 1-4). 1976. PLB 7.95 (ISBN 0-13-537993-8). P-H.

--The Little Witch's Valentine Book. (Illus.). 48p. 1984. 8.95 (ISBN 0-13-538026-X). P-H.

Glovach, Linda & Glovach, Linda. The Little Witch's Dinosaur Book. (Illus.). 48p. (gr. 1-4). 1984. 9.95 (ISBN 0-13-537739-0). P-H.

Glover, A., ed. see Beaumont, Francis & Fletcher, John.

Glover, Al. Paradise Valley. 1975. 4.00 ea. Bellevue Pr.

--A Trio in G. (Illus.). 92p. (Orig.). 1971. pap. 3.00 (ISBN 0-686-05063-0). Frontier Press Calif.

Glover, B. History of Six Spanish Verbs Meaning to Take, Seize, Grasp. LC 70-114578. (Janua Linguarum, Ser. Practica: No. 109). (Orig.). 1971. pap. text ed. 9.60x (ISBN 0-686-22394-2). Mouton.

Glover, B. & Schuder, P. The Competitive Runner's Handbook: The Complete Training Program for All Distance Running. 467p. 1983. 16.95 (ISBN 0-670-23365-X). Viking.

Glover, Beulah. Narratives of Collecton County. LC 84-1993. (Illus.). 160p. 1984. pap. 16.50 (ISBN 0-87152-397-3). Reprint.

Glover, Bob & Schuder, Pete. The Competitive Runner's Handbook: The Complete Training Program for All Distance Running. 467p. (Orig.). 1983. pap. 7.95 (ISBN 0-14-046565-0). Penguin.

Glover, Bob & Shepard, Jack. The Runner's Handbook: A Complete Fitness Guide for Men & Women on the Run. (Handbook Ser). 1978. pap. 6.95 (ISBN 0-14-046325-9). Penguin.

Glover, Bob & Shepherd, Jack. The Runner's Handbook. 192p. 1985. pap. 7.95 (ISBN 0-14-046713-0). Penguin.

--The Runner's Handbook: A Complete Fitness Guide for Men & Women on the Run. (Illus.). 1978. 14.95 (ISBN 0-670-61087-9). Viking.

--The Runner's Handbook Training Diary. (Handbooks Ser.). 1978. pap. 4.95 (ISBN 0-14-046373-9). Penguin.

Glover, Bob & Weisenfeld, Murry. The Injured Runner's Training Guide: The Coach's & Doctor's for Preventing Running Through, & Coming Back from Injury. (Handbooks Ser.). 208p. 1985. pap. 6.95 (ISBN 0-14-046641-X). Penguin.

Glover, Charles C. History of the Gentleman on Horseback. (Illus.). 95p. 1982. pap. 4.95 (ISBN 0-87770-266-7). Ye Galleon.

Glover, D. M. Genetic Engineering. (Outline Studies in Biology). 79p. 1980. pap. 6.95 (ISBN 0-412-16170-2, NO. 6394, Pub. by Chapman & Hall). Methuen Inc.

Glover, D. M., ed. DNA Cloning, 2 vols, Vols. 1 & 2. (Practical Approach Ser.). (Illus.). 250p. (Orig.). 1985. Vol. 1. pap. text ed. 25.00 ea. (ISBN 0-947946-18-7). Vol. 2 (ISBN 0-947946-19-5). IRL Pr.

Glover, David. The Lost Village. 192p. 1984. 11.95 (ISBN 0-312-49902-7). St Martin.

--The Sociology of the Mass Media. (Themes & Perspectives in Sociology Ser.). 80p. (Orig.). 1984. pap. text ed. 6.95 (ISBN 0-946183-05-8, Pub. by Causeway Pr Ltd England). Sheridan.

Glover, David & Strawbridge, Sheelagh. The Sociology of Knowledge. (Themes & Perspectives in Sociology Ser.). 80p. (Orig.). 1985. pap. text ed. 6.95x (ISBN 0-946183-10-4, Pub. by Causeway Pr Ltd England). Sheridan.

Glover, David M. Gene Cloning: The Mechanics of DNA Manipulation. 1985. 29.95 (ISBN 0-412-26600-8, NO. 9338, Pub. by Chapman & Hall); pap. 11.95 (ISBN 0-412-25430-1, NO. 9161, Pub. by Chapman & Hall). Methuen Inc.

Glover, Dennis. Hot Water Sailor & Landlubber Ho. (Illus.). 248p. 1982. 16.95x (ISBN 0-00-216985-1, Pub. by W Collins New Zealand). Intl Spec Bk.

Glover, Dennis W. & Glover, Margaret M. Respiratory Therapy: Basics for Nursing & the Allied Health Professions. LC 78-6500. (Illus.). 222p. 1978. pap. 13.95 (ISBN 0-8016-1863-0). Mosby.

Glover, Donald, ed. American Academy of Advertising Annual Meeting, Proceedings. 1984. pap. 15.00 (ISBN 0-931030-07-2). Am Acad Advert.

Glover, Donald E. C. S. Lewis: The Art of Enchantment. LC 80-21421. xii, 235p. 1981. 18.95x (ISBN 0-8214-0566-7, 82-83574); pap. 9.00x (ISBN 0-8214-0609-4, 82-83582). Ohio U Pr.

Glover, Edward. The Birth of the Ego. LC 68-19217. 1968. text ed. 15.00 (ISBN 0-8236-0520-5). Intl Univs Pr.

--On the Early Development of Mind: Selected Papers on Psychoanalysis, Vol. 1. 483p. 1956. text ed. 40.00 (ISBN 0-8236-3760-3); pap. text ed. 11.95 (ISBN 0-8236-8169-6, 023760). Intl Univs Pr.

--The Roots of Crime: Selected Papers on Psychoanalysis, Vol. 2. 1960. text ed. 27.50 (ISBN 0-8236-5860-0); pap. text ed. 10.95 (ISBN 0-8236-8270-6, 025860). Intl Univs Pr.

--Technique of Psychoanalysis. rev. ed. 404p. 1968. text ed. 35.00 (ISBN 0-8236-6400-7). Intl Univs Pr.

Glover, Elizabeth. The Gold & Silver Wyre-Drawers. (Illus.). 91p. 1979. 47.50x (ISBN 0-8476-3144-3). Rowman.

--The Gold & Silver Wyre-Drawers. 1979. 65.00x (ISBN 0-686-97113-2, Pub. by Phillimore England). State Mutual Bk.

Glover, Fred. A Fresh Look at Heuristic Principles for Integer Progamming. 1977. 2.50 (ISBN 0-686-64187-6). U CO Busn Res Div.

Glover, Fred & Mevert, Peter. Direct Benders Custs for Fixed Charge Problems by a Primal Compactification. 1975. 2.50 (ISBN 0-686-64195-7). U CO Busn Res Div.

Glover, Fred & Mulvey, John M. Network-Related Scheduling Models for Problems with Quasi-Adjacency & Block Adjacency Structures. 1976. 2.50 (ISBN 0-686-64194-9). U CO Busn Res Div.

Glover, Fred & Rogozinski, Jacques. Resort Development: A Network-Related Model for Optimizing Sites & Visits. 1980. 2.50 (ISBN 0-686-64184-1). U CO Busn Res Div.

Glover, Fred, jt. auth. see Freed, Ned.

Glover, Fred, et al. Selecting Subsets of Maximum Diversity. 1977. 2.50 (ISBN 0-686-64186-8). U CO Busn Res Div.

--Improved Computer-Based Planning Techniques. 1977. 2.50 (ISBN 0-686-64189-2). U CO Busn Res Div.

Glover, G. French Steam Locomotives, 1840-1950. 96p. 1974. 35.00x (ISBN 0-85992-011-9, Pub. by B Rose Pub). State Mutual Bk.

Glover, Horace S., tr. see Menne, A.

Glover, J. A., jt. auth. see Dixon, D. N.

Glover, J. C. B., ed. The Philosophy of Mind. (Oxford Readings in Philosophy). 1977. pap. text ed. 8.95x (ISBN 0-19-875038-2). Oxford U Pr.

Glover, J. Garrett. The Cubist Theatre. Foster, Stephen, ed. LC 83-3631. (Studies in the Fine Arts: The Avant Garde: No. 38). 172p. 1983. 39.95 (ISBN 0-8357-1439-X). UMI Res Pr.

Glover, J. Littleton, Jr. & Anderson, William E. Collections: A Georgia Law Practice System. (Law Practice Systems Ser.). 370p. 1984. looseleaf 75.00 (ISBN 0-87215-759-8, 69825). Michie Co.

Glover, J. N. Laws of the Turks & Caicos Islands, 3 vols., only vols. 4,6,7 available. rev. ed. 1970-80. 147.50 set (ISBN 0-379-12700-8). Oceana.

Glover, Jack. Bobbed Wire V Bible. rev. ed. ltd. ed. 20.00 (ISBN 0-685-83426-3); pap. 7.95 (ISBN 0-685-83427-1). Cow Puddle.

--Glovers Illustrated Letters. (Illus.). limited ed. 20.00 (ISBN 0-685-83428-X); pap. 7.95 (ISBN 0-685-83429-8). Cow Puddle.

Glover, James W. & Carver, Henry C. Tables of Compound Interest Functions & Logarithms of Compound Interest Functions. 1921. 3.00x (ISBN 0-685-21808-2). Wahr.

Glover, James W. & U. S. Dept. of Commerce, Bureau of the Census. United States Life Tables: 1890, 1901, 1910, & 1901-1910. LC 75-37267. (Demography Ser.). (Illus.). 1976. Repr. of 1921 ed. 46.50x (ISBN 0-405-07997-4). Ayer Co Pubs.

Glover, Jane. Cavalli. LC 77-23638. (Illus.). 1978. 26.00 (ISBN 0-312-12546-1). St Martin.

Glover, Janice. Lighter Side of the Library. LC 74-75520. 128p. 1974. 4.95 (ISBN 0-88492-003-8). W S Sullwold.

Glover, Jean. Human Sexuality in Nursing Care. LC 84-19881. 160p. (Orig.). 1984. pap. 11.95 (ISBN 0-7099-1141-6, Pub. by Croom Held Ltd). Longwood Pub Group.

Glover, Jesse. Bruce Lee's Non-Classical Gung Fu. 130p. 1978. pap. 10.95 (ISBN 0-9602328-1-8). Glover Pubns.

--Bruce Lee's Non-Classical Gung-Fu, Bk. II. 65p. 1980. pap. 10.95 (ISBN 0-9602328-2-6). Glover Pubns.

Glover, Jesse R. Bruce Lee's Non-Classical Stickinghands. Hart, Edward C., ed. (Illus.). 200p. 1982. 20.00 (ISBN 0-9602328-3-4). Glover Pubns.

Glover, John. London's Railways Today. LC 80-70293. (Illus.). 96p. 1981. 17.50 (ISBN 0-7153-8070-2). David & Charles.

Glover, John, ed. Peter of Ickham: Le Livere de Reis de Brittanie e le Livere de Reis de Engleterre (From Brutus to 1274, with Two Continuations & a Translation) Repr. of 1865 ed. 44.00 (ISBN 0-317-16689-1). Kraus Repr.

Glover, John A. Becoming a More Creative Person. (Illus.). 256p. 1980. (Spec); pap. 5.95 (ISBN 0-13-072124-7). P-H.

--A Parent's Guide to Intelligence Testing: How to Help Your Child's Intellectual Development. LC 78-25991. 288p. 1979. 23.95x (ISBN 0-88229-423-7); pap. 11.95 (ISBN 0-88229-670-1). Nelson-Hall.

Glover, John A. & Bruning, Roger H. Educational Psychology: Principles & Applications. 1982. pap. text ed. 24.95 (ISBN 0-316-31766-7); for info. tchr's Manual (ISBN 0-316-31765-9); for info. Avail. Test Bank (ISBN 0-316-31764-0). Little.

Glover, John A. & Gary, Albert L. Behavior Modification: An Empirical Approach to Self-Control. LC 79-88. 208p. 1979. 18.95x (ISBN 0-88229-298-6). Nelson-Hall.

--Mainstreaming Exceptional Children. (Orig.). 1976. pap. 3.95 (ISBN 0-910286-49-3). Boxwood.

Glover, John A., jt. auth. see Gary, A. L.

Glover, John A., et al. Teaching: Why Not Try Psychology? (Orig.). 1979. pap. text ed. 8.95 (ISBN 0-8403-1772-7). Kendall-Hunt.

Glover, John D. Public Loans to Private Business. Bruchey, Stuart & Carosso, Vincent P., eds. LC 78-18961. (Small Business Enterprise in America Ser.). (Illus.). 1979. lib. bdg. 37.00x (ISBN 0-405-11465-6). Ayer Co Pubs.

Glover, John D., et al. The Administrator: Cases on Human Aspects in Management. 5th ed. 1973. text ed. 27.95x (ISBN 0-256-00170-7). Irwin.

Glover, John H., ed. see Muller, Herbert W.

Glover, Jonathan. Causing Death & Saving Lives. 1977. pap. 4.95 (ISBN 0-14-022003-8, Pelican). Penguin.

--What Sort of People Should There Be? 192p. 1984. pap. 5.95 (ISBN 0-14-022224-3, Pelican). Penguin.

Glover, Judith. Batsford Colour Book of Kent. (Illus.). 64p. 1976. 11.95 (ISBN 0-7134-4783-4, Pub. by Batsford England). David & Charles.

--Batsford Colour Book of Sussex. (Illus.). 64p. 1980. pap. 7.95 (ISBN 0-7134-3275-6, Pub. by Batsford England). David & Charles.

--Drink Your Own Garden. (Illus.). 112p. 1981. Repr. of 1979 ed. 15.95 (ISBN 0-7134-1347-6, Pub. by Batsford England). David & Charles.

--Sisters & Brothers. 288p. 1984. 12.95 (ISBN 0-312-72747-X). St Martin.

--The Stallion Man. LC 82-17049. 256p. 1983. 13.95 (ISBN 0-312-75542-2). St Martin.

Glover, Margaret M., jt. auth. see Glover, Dennis W.

Glover, Michael. The Fight for the Channel Ports. (Illus.). 256p. 1985. cancelled (ISBN 0-436-18210-6, Pub. by Secker & Warburg UK). David & Charles.

--The Fight for the Channel Ports: Calais to Brest 1940, A Study in Confusion. (Illus.). 269p. 1985. 25.00 (ISBN 0-8133-0300-1). Westview.

--The Napoleonic Wars: An Illustrated History 1792-1815. (Illus.). 240p. 1982. pap. 14.95 (ISBN 0-88254-710-0). Hippocrene Bks.

Glover, Michael C., jt. auth. see Askari, Hossein.

Glover, P., jt. auth. see Staveley, H.

Glover, Peggy D. Library Services for the Woman in the Middle. (Orig.). 1985. lib. bdg. 20.00 (ISBN 0-208-02070-5, Lib Prof Pubns); pap. text ed. 14.50 (ISBN 0-208-02073-X, Lib Prof Pubns). Shoe String.

Glover, R. H. Major Societal Changes in U. S. (1933-44 & 1945-75) Contextual Mapping. 1977. 2.00 (ISBN 0-87447-057-9, 251714). College Bd.

Glover, R. S., ed. The Bristol Channel & Severn Estuary. 48p. 1984. pap. 6.00 (ISBN 0-08-031423-6). Pergamon.

Glover, Randy & Talmey, Paul. Improved Modeling & Solution of Practical Management Science Problems Through Netforms: Inventory Systems, Pt. 1. 1977. 2.50 (ISBN 0-686-64188-4). U CO Busn Res Div.

Glover, Rhoda, et al. Plantagenet "Rich & Beautiful...". A History of the Shire of Plantagenet, Western Australia. 429p. 1980. 21.00x (ISBN 0-85564-175-4, Pub. by U of West Australia Pr Australia). Intl Spec Bk.

Glover, Richard G. Peninsular Preparation: The Reform of the British Army, 1795-1809. LC 63-25938. pap. 80.80 (ISBN 0-317-08279-5, 2051444). Bks Demand UMI.

Glover, Robert, jt. auth. see Grubb, Norton.

Glover, Robert, et al. Stepping Up: Placing Minority Women into Managerial & Professional Jobs. 1979. softcover 4.95x (ISBN 0-913420-83-2). Olympus Pub Co.

Glover, Robert E. Transient Ground Water Hydraulics. 1978. 21.00 (ISBN 0-918334-24-1). WRP.

Glover, S. L. Origin & Occurrance of Gem Stones in Washington. (Shorey Prospecting Ser.). 32p. 1975. pap. 2.95 (ISBN 0-8466-0001-3). Shorey.

Glover, S. W. & Hopwood, D. A., eds. Genetics As a Tool in Microbiology. (Society for General Microbiology Symposium: No. 31). (Illus.). 450p. 1981. text ed. 75.00 (ISBN 0-521-23748-3). Cambridge U Pr.

Glover, Sheldon L. Preliminary Report on Petroleum & Natural Gas in Washington. (Report of Investigations Ser.: No. 4). (Illus.). 24p. 1936. 0.25 (ISBN 0-686-34727-7). Geologic Pubns.

Glover, Stephen L., ed. see Eliason, Robert E.

Glover, Stephen L., ed. see Naylor, Tom L.

Glover, Susanne & Grewe, Georgeann. Bone up on Book Reports. (gr. 3-8). 1981. 5.95 (ISBN 0-86653-001-0, GA228). Good Apple.

Glover, Susanne, et al. A Bulletin Board Book for All Seasons. (gr. k-6). 1980. 5.95 (ISBN 0-916456-79-X, GA 160). Good Apple.

Glover, Suzanne & Grewe, Georgeann. Holiday Happenings. (Bulletin Boards Ser.). (gr. 1-4). 1982. pap. 8.95 (ISBN 0-88160-046-6). Learning Wks.

--Math Magic. (Bulletin Boards Ser.). (gr. 3-6). 1982. pap. 8.95 (ISBN 0-88160-047-4). Learning Wks.

Glover, T. R. The Challenge of the Greek & Other Essays. (Illus.). 241p. 1981. Repr. of 1942 ed. lib. bdg. 35.00 (ISBN 0-8495-1973-X). Arden Lib.

--Herodotus. LC 70-100515. (BCL Ser.: I). Repr. of 1924 ed. 16.00 (ISBN 0-404-02828-4). AMS Pr.

--Jesus in the Experience of Men. LC 78-23617. 1921. 27.00 (ISBN 0-8414-4616-4). Folcroft.

--The Jesus of History. LC 78-25986. 27.50 (ISBN 0-8414-4488-9). Folcroft.

--Poets & Puritans. 1979. Repr. of 1915 ed. lib. bdg. 30.00 (ISBN 0-8414-4629-6). Folcroft.

--Poets & Puritans. 1973. Repr. of 1915 ed. 20.00 (ISBN 0-8274-1572-9). R West.

Glover, Terrot R. The Ancient World: A Beginning. LC 79-11456. 1980. Repr. of 1944 ed. lib. bdg. 32.50x (ISBN 0-313-21459-X, GLAW). Greenwood.

--Challenge of the Greek: And Other Essays. LC 75-39171. (Essay Index Reprint Ser.). Repr. of 1942 ed. 20.00 (ISBN 0-8369-2690-0). Ayer Co Pubs.

--The Conflicts of Religion in the Early Roman Empire. LC 74-20182. vii, 358p. 1975. Repr. of 1909 ed. lib. bdg. 32.50 (ISBN 0-8154-0510-3). Cooper Sq.

--From Pericles to Philip. 17.25 (ISBN 0-317-28501-7, 7817). Ayer Co Pubs.

--Greek Byways. (Illus.). 319p. 1981. Repr. of 1932 ed. lib. bdg. 45.00 (ISBN 0-8495-1976-4). Arden Lib.

--Greek Byways. LC 74-101043. 1969. Repr. of 1932 ed. 24.50x (ISBN 0-8046-0709-5, Pub. by Kennikat). Assoc Faculty Pr.

--Herodotus. LC 70-99661. (Select Bibliographies Reprint Ser.). 1924. 19.50 (ISBN 0-8369-5090-9). Ayer Co Pubs.

--Life & Letters in the Fourth Century. LC 68-10923. 1968. Repr. of 1901 ed. 11.00x (ISBN 0-8462-1065-7). Russell.

--Springs of Hellas. LC 74-122878. (Essay & General Literature Index Reprint Ser). 1971. Repr. of 1945 ed. 21.00x (ISBN 0-8046-1333-8, Pub. by Kennikat). Assoc Faculty Pr.

Glover, Tony. Blues Harp. (Illus., Orig.). 1973. pap. 6.95 (ISBN 0-8256-0018-9, 000018, Oak). Music Sales.

--Blues Harp Songbook. (Illus.). pap. 8.95 with recordiing (ISBN 0-8256-0157-6, Oak). Music Sales.

--Rock Harp. 1981. pap. 7.95 (ISBN 0-8256-0230-0, Oak). Music Sales.

Glover, Vernon J., jt. auth. see Wilson, Spencer.

Glover, Waldo. Mister Glover's Groton. LC 78-9592. (Illus.). 1978. 13.95x (ISBN 0-914016-53-9). Phoenix Pub.

Glover, Warren. Sememic & Grammatical Structures in Gurung. (SIL Linguistics & Related Fields Ser: No. 49). 232p. 1974. 8.75x (ISBN 0-88312-059-3); microfiche 3.00x (ISBN 0-88312-459-9). Summer Inst Ling.

Glover, William R. Huna: The Ancient Religion of Positive Thinking. (Orig.). 1979. pap. text ed. 5.00 (ISBN 0-910764-05-0). Huna Res Inc.

Glover, Willis B. Biblical Origins of Modern Secular Culture. LC 84-14868. xx, 300p. 1984. 23.95 (ISBN 0-86554-138-8, MUP-H129). Mercer Univ Pr.

Gloversmith, Frank. Class, Culture & Social Change: A Reconsideration of the 1930's. 1980. text ed. 43.00x (ISBN 0-391-01739-X). Humanities.

Gloversmith, Frank, ed. The Theory of Reading. LC 84-280. 264p. 1984. 27.50x (ISBN 0-389-20467-6, 08028). B&N Imports.

Glowa, John R. Inhalants: Glue, Gas & Sniff. (Encyclopedia of Psychoactive Drugs Ser.). (Illus.). 1985. PLB 15.95x (ISBN 0-87754-758-0). Chelsea Hse.

Glowacki, Janusz. Give Us This Day. Brodzinski, Konrad, tr. from Polish. 1984. 10.95 (ISBN 0-312-32741-2). St Martin.

Glowacki, Joseph W. Photography Foundations: The Student Photojournalist. (Illus.). 72p. (gr. 9-12). pap. text ed. 5.95 (ISBN 0-916084-11-6). Columbia Scholastic.

Glower, D. D. & Saline, E. L., eds. A Response to Advancing Technologies: Repositioning Engineering Education to Serve America's Future. 50p. 1982. 4.00 (ISBN 0-317-36390-5). Am Soc Ag Eng.

Glowinski & Lions, eds. Computing Methods in Applied Sciences & Engineering. 724p. 1980. 70.25 (ISBN 0-444-86008-8, North-Holland). Elsevier.

Glowinski, R. Numerical Methods for Nonlinear Variational Problems. (Springer Series in Computational Physics). (Illus.). 475p. 1984. 64.00 (ISBN 0-387-12434-9). Springer-Verlag.

Glowinski, R. & Lions, J. L. Computing Methods in Applied Sciences & Engineering, VI. 1984. 74.00 (ISBN 0-444-87597-2). Elsevier.

Glowinski, R., jt. auth. see Fortin, M.

Glowinski, R. & Lions, J. L., eds. Computing Methods in Applied Sciences & Engineering: Proceedings of the Fifth International Symposium, Versailles, France, December 14-18, 1981, Vol. 5. 626p. 1982. 95.00 (ISBN 0-444-86450-4, I-321-82, North-Holland). Elsevier.

Glowinski, R., ed. see International Symposium, 3rd, December 5-9, 1977.

Glowinski, R., et al. Numerical Analysis of Variational Inequations. (Studies in Mathematics & Its Applications: Vol. 8). 776p. 1981. 95.75 (ISBN 0-444-86199-8, North-Holland). Elsevier.

--Energy Methods in Finite Element Analysis. LC 78-13642. (Numerical Methods in Engineering Ser.). 361p. 1979. 82.95x (ISBN 0-471-99723-4, Pub. by Wiley-Interscience). Wiley.

Glowinski, R., et al, eds. Computing Methods in Applied Sciences & Engineering. (Lecture Notes in Economics & Mathematical Systems Ser.: Vol. 134). 1976. soft cover 23.00 (ISBN 0-387-07990-4). Springer-Verlag.

--Computing Methods in Applied Sciences. (Lecture Notes in Physics Ser.: Vol. 58). (Eng. & Fr.). 1976. soft cover 23.00 (ISBN 0-387-08003-1). Springer-Verlag.

Gloxhuber, C. Anionic Surfactants, Vol. 10: Biochemistry, Toxicology, Dermatology. (Surfactant Ser.: Vol. 10). 472p. 75.00 (ISBN 0-8247-6946-5). Dekker.

Gloy, Karen. Die Kantische Theorie der Naturwissenschaft. 1976. 32.00x (ISBN 3-11-006569-X). De Gruyter.

Gloyna, E. F. Waste Stabilization Ponds. (Monographs Ser: No. 60). 175p. 1971. pap. 8.00 (ISBN 92-4-140060-9, 1444). World Health.

Gloyna, E. F. & Ledbetter, J. O. Principles of Radiological Health. (Environmental Health Engineering Textbk Ser: Vol. 1). 1969. 34.25 (ISBN 0-8247-1250-1). Dekker.

Glubb, Faris. Zionist Relations with Nazi Germany. LC 79-90569. 6.00 (ISBN 0-911026-11-8). New World Press NY.

Glubb, John. The Changing Scenes of Life: An Autobiography. (Illus.). 272p. 1983. 24.95 (ISBN 0-7043-2329-X, Pub. by Quartet Bks). Merrimack Pub Cir.

--Short History of the Arab Peoples. LC 69-16907. 1970. pap. 12.95 (ISBN 0-8128-1351-0). Stein & Day.

Glubb, John, jt. auth. see Churchill, Winston S.

Glubb, John B. The Story of the Arab Legion. LC 76-7060. (The Middle East in the 20th Century Ser.). 1976. Repr. of 1948 ed. lib. bdg. 42.50 (ISBN 0-306-70763-2). Da Capo.
--War in the Desert: An R. A. F. Frontier Campaign. LC 80-1929. Repr. of 1961 ed. 38.00 (ISBN 0-404-18964-4). AMS Pr.
--The Way of Love. LC 75-44945. 1976. 7.95x (ISBN 0-916624-00-5); pap. 2.95x (ISBN 0-916624-01-3). Troy State Univ.
Glubetich, Dave. Double Your Money in Real Estate Every Two Years. Moretz, Judy, ed. LC 80-142122. (Illus.). 232p. 1980. 13.95 (ISBN 0-9601530-4-7, Dist by Har-Row). Impact Pub.
--How to Grow a Moneytree. 2nd ed. Wigginton, Dave, ed. LC 81-80569. 137p. 1981. pap. 8.95 (ISBN 0-9601530-0-4, Dist. by Har-Row). Impact Pub.
--The Monopoly Game. 4th ed. Wigginton, Dave, ed. LC 75-20848. 1979. pap. 8.95 (ISBN 0-9601530-2-0, Dist. by Har-Row). Impact Pub.
--Real Estate Turnaround Formulas. Bennett, Barbara, ed. 1985. pap. 49.00 (ISBN 0-930187-00-8). Impact Pub.
Glubok, Shirley. Art & Archaeology. LC 65-11448. (Illus.). (gr. 3-7). o.p 6.95 (ISBN 0-06-022040-6); PLB 11.89 (ISBN 0-06-022041-4). HarpJ.
--Art of Colonial America. LC 77-102964. (Art of America Ser.). (Illus.). 48p. (gr. 4-8). 1970. 10.95 (ISBN 0-02-736070-9). Macmillan.
--The Art of Egypt Under the Pharaohs. LC 79-23336. (Illus.). 48p. (gr. 4 up). 1980. 10.95 (ISBN 0-02-736470-4). Macmillan.
--The Art of the Comic Strip. LC 78-24342. (Art of America Ser.). (Illus.). 52p. (gr. 4 up). 1979. 12.95 (ISBN 0-02-736500-X). Macmillan.
--The Art of the New American Nation. LC 76-160073. (Art of America Ser.). (Illus.). 48p. (gr. 4 up). 1972. 10.95 (ISBN 0-02-736140-3). Macmillan.
--Art of the North American Indian. LC 64-11829. (Illus.). (gr. 2-6). 1964. HarpJ.
--The Art of the Southeastern Indians. LC 77-20850. (Illus.). (gr. 4 up). 1978. 10.95 (ISBN 0-02-736480-1, 73648). Macmillan.
--The Art of the Spanish in the United States & Puerto Rico. LC 75-185218. (Art of America Ser.). (Illus.). 48p. (gr. 4up). 1972. 10.95 (ISBN 0-02-736130-6). Macmillan.
--The Art of the Woodland Indians. LC 76-12434. (Art of America Ser.). (Illus.). 48p. (gr. 4 up). 1976. 10.95 (ISBN 0-02-736440-2, 73644). Macmillan.
--Dolls' Houses: Life in Miniature. LC 77-25663. (Illus.). 104p. (gr. 5 up). 1984. 14.90i (ISBN 0-06-022016-3); PLB 14.89g (ISBN 0-06-022017-1). HarpJ.
--Doll's Houses: Life in Miniature. (Illus.). (gr. 5 up). 1984. 14.90 (ISBN 0-06-022016-3). Har-Row.
--Knights in Armor. LC 69-10208. (Illus.). (gr. 3-7). 1969. HarpJ.
Glubok, Shirley & Tamarin, Alfred. The Mummy of Ramose. LC 76-21392. (Illus.). 1978. 9.57i (ISBN 0-06-022039-2); PLB 11.89 (ISBN 0-06-022042-2). HarpJ.
--Olympic Games in Ancient Greece. LC 74-25408. (Illus.). 120p. (gr. 5-9). 1976. PLB 11.89 (ISBN 0-06-022048-1). HarpJ.
--Olympic Games in Ancient Greece. LC 75-25408. (A Trophy Bk.). (Illus.). 128p. (gr. 5-9). 1984. pap. 4.95i (ISBN 0-06-440137-5, Trophy). HarpJ.
Glubok, Shirley, ed. Discovering Tut-Ankh-Amen's Tomb. LC 68-12069. (Illus.). 144p. (gr. 5 up). 1968. 14.95 (ISBN 0-02-736030-X). Macmillan.
Glubokovsky, N. N. Blagovjestije Khristikanskoj Slavi v Apokalipsisje. 116p. 1966. pap. 5.00 (ISBN 0-317-29139-4). Holy Trinity.
Gluck, Barbara R. Beckett & Joyce: Friendship & Fiction. LC 76-50290. 225p. 1979. 22.50 (ISBN 0-8387-2060-9). Bucknell U Pr.
Gluck, Carol. Japan's Modern Myths: Ideology in the Late Meiji Period. LC 85-600. (Studies of the East Asian Institute, Columbia University). (Illus.). 440p. 1985. text ed. 37.00x (ISBN 0-691-05449-5). Princeton U Pr.
Gluck, Cellin & Takeda, Yasushi, eds. You Mean to Say You Still Don't Know Who We Are? Seven Kabuki Plays. Unno, Mitsuko, tr. from Japanese. 260p. 1976. pap. 7.95 (ISBN 4-89360-033-8, Pub. by Personally Oriented Ltd. SoPA). C E Tuttle.
Gluck, Elsie. John Mitchell, Miner: Labor's Bargain with the Gilded Age. LC 72-158853. Repr. of 1929 ed. 14.50 (ISBN 0-404-02829-2). AMS Pr.
Gluck, Felix, ed. Modern Publicity, Vol. 48. 1979. 42.50 (ISBN 0-02-857800-7). Macmillan.
Gluck, Florence W., ed. see Hawes, Stephen.
Gluck, Harold. Avoiding Travel Rip-Offs & Other Tips for Travelers. LC 79-9841. 24p. 1979. pap. 2.50 (ISBN 0-87576-079-1). Pilot Bks.
Gluck, Herb, jt. auth. see Lewis, Jerry.
Gluck, Herb, jt. auth. see Mantle, Mickey.
Gluck, J. K., jt. auth. see Henry, C. D.
Gluck, Jay & Gluck, Sami. A Survey of Persian Handicraft. (Survey of Persian Art Ser.). (Illus.). 416p. 1977. 125.00 (ISBN 4-89360-024-9, Pub. by Personally Oriented Ltd.SoPA (Ashiya, Japan)). C E Tuttle.
Gluck, Jay, ed. Ukiyo: Stories of "The Floating World" of Postwar Japan. LC 63-21851. 1964. 8.95 (ISBN 0-8149-0108-5). Vanguard.
Gluck, Jay, ed. see Pope, Arthur U.
Gluck, Louis, ed. Intrauterine Asphyxia & the Developing Fetal Brain. (Illus.). 1977. 62.95 (ISBN 0-8151-3711-7). Year Bk Med.
--Modern Perinatal Medicine. (Illus.). 550p. 1975. 61.50 (ISBN 0-8151-3714-1). Year Bk Med.
Gluck, Louise. Descending Figure. LC 80-223. (American Poetry Ser.: Vol. 20). 48p. (Orig.). 1981. pap. 5.95 (ISBN 0-912946-72-5). Ecco Pr.
--Firstborn. LC 81-5454. (American Poetry Ser.). 53p. 1983. pap. 5.95 (ISBN 0-912946-93-8). Ecco Pr.
--The House on Marshland. LC 74-21764. (The American Poetry Ser: Vol. 5). 64p. 1976. pap. 4.95 (ISBN 0-912946-19-9). Ecco Pr.
--The Triumph of Achilles, No. 32. Halpern, Daniel, ed. (American Poetry Ser.). 64p. 1985. 13.50 (ISBN 0-88001-081-9). Ecco Pr.
Gluck, Mary. Georg Lukacs & His Generation, Nineteen Hundred to Nineteen Eighteen. (Illus.). 320p. 1985. text ed. 25.00x (ISBN 0-674-34865-6). Harvard U Pr.
Gluck, Myke. Mechanics for Gymnastics Coaching: Tools for Skill Analysis. (Illus.). 176p. 1982. 29.75x (ISBN 0-398-04559-3). C C Thomas.
Gluck, Peter R. & Meister, Richard J. Cities in Transition: Social Change & Institutional Responses in Urban Development. LC 79-12217. 1979. pap. text ed. 8.95x (ISBN 0-317-30662-6). Wiener Pub Inc.
Gluck, Robert. Andy. 1973. 4.00 (ISBN 0-915572-05-2). Panjandrum.
--Elements of a Coffee Service: A Book of Stories. LC 82-20143. (Writing 41 Ser.). 106p. (Orig.). 1983. pap. 5.95 (ISBN 0-87704-058-3). Four Seasons Foun.
--Jack the Modernist. 185p. 1985. pap. 7.95 (ISBN 0-933322-27-5). Sea Horse.
Gluck, Robert & Boone, Bruce, trs. from Fr. La Fontaine. LC 81-90653. (Illus.). 72p. 1981. pap. 5.00 (ISBN 0-9607630-0-7). Black Star.
Gluck, Sami, jt. auth. see Gluck, Jay.
Gluck, Sherna, ed. From Parlor to Prison: Five American Suffragists Talk About Their Lives. LC 76-43975. 1976. Repr. lib. bdg. 20.00x (ISBN 0-374-93161-5). Octagon.
--From Parlor to Prison: Five American Suffragists Talk about Their Lives. 320p. 1985. pap. 10.00 (ISBN 0-85345-676-3). Monthly Rev.
Gluckel. The Memoirs of Gluckel of Hameln. Lowenthal, Marvin, tr. from Ger. LC 77-75290. 1977. pap. 7.95 (ISBN 0-8052-0572-1). Schocken.
Gluckin, Doreen & Edelhart, Michael. The Body at Thirty. 288p. 1983. pap. 3.50 (ISBN 0-425-06070-5). Berkley Pub.
--The Body at Thirty: A Woman Doctor Talks to Women. LC 82-2527. (Illus.). 240p. 1982. 12.95 (ISBN 0-87131-371-5). M Evans.
Gluckman, Jack L. Medical Management of the Ear, Nose & Throat. (Illus.). 350p. Date not set. price not set (ISBN 0-7216-4153-9). Saunders.
Gluckman, Max. Custom & Conflict in Africa. 173p. 1969. pap. 9.95x (ISBN 0-06-480325-2). B&N Imports.
--Politics, Law & Ritual in Tribal Society. (Illus.). 376p. 1965. pap. 12.95x (ISBN 0-631-08750-8). Basil Blackwell.
Gluckman, Max, ed. see Forde, Daryll, et al.
Gluckman, P. D. & Johnston, J. M., eds. Respiratory Control & Lung Development in the Fetus & Newborn. (Reproductive & Perinatal Medicine Ser.: No. III). 1985. 50.00 (ISBN 0-916859-12-6). Perinatology.
Glucksberg, Harold & Singer, Jack W. Cancer Care: A Personal Guide. LC 79-16930. 1980. 27.50X (ISBN 0-8018-2255-6). Johns Hopkins.
--Cancer Care: A Personal Guide. 448p. pap. 12.95 (ISBN 0-684-17784-6, ScribT). Scribner.
Glucksberg, Sam & Danks, Joseph H. Experimental Psycholinguistics: An Introduction. 233p. 1975. text ed. 14.95 (ISBN 0-89859-147-3). L Erlbaum Assocs.
Glucksman, Myron L., jt. auth. see Cantor, Morton B.
Glucksman, Paul H., ed. World-Wide German Dictionary. (Ger.). 1978. pap. 2.50 (ISBN 0-449-30850-2, Prem). Fawcett.
Glucksmann, A. Sex Determination & Sexual Dimorphism in Mammals. 174p. 1978. pap. cancelled (ISBN 0-85109-790-1). Taylor & Francis.
--Sexual Dimorphism in Human & Mammalian Biology & Pathology. LC 80-42373. 374p. 1981. 55.00 (ISBN 0-12-286960-5). Acad Pr.
Glucksmann, Alfred & Smith, M. I. Sex Determination & Sexual Dimorphism in Mammals. LC 78-63273. (Wykeham Science Ser.: No. 54). 174p. 1979. pap. 13.50x (ISBN 0-8448-1370-2). Crane-Russak Co.
Glucksmann, Andre. The Master Thinkers. Pearce, Brian, tr. from Fr. LC 78-20164. 1980. 16.95i (ISBN 0-06-011639-0, HarpT). Har-Row.
Glucksmann, Andre, jt. auth. see Gardner, Richard N.
Glueck, jt. auth. see Ivancevich.
Glueck, Bernard. Studies in Forensic Psychiatry. LC 16-20410. (Criminal Science Monograph: No. 2). 1968. Repr. of 1915 ed. 16.00 (ISBN 0-527-34112-6). Kraus Repr.
--Studies in Forensic Psychiatry. 269p. 1983. Repr. of 1916 ed. lib. bdg. 85.00 (ISBN 0-8495-2141-6). Arden Lib.
Glueck, Bernard, tr. see Schilder, Paul.
Glueck, E., jt. auth. see Glueck, S.
Glueck, Eleanor, jt. auth. see Glueck, S.
Glueck, Eleanor, jt. auth. see Glueck, Sheldon.
Glueck, Eleanor T., jt. auth. see Glueck, Sheldon.
Glueck, Eleanor T., jt. auth. see Glueck, Sheldon S.
Glueck, Eleanor T., jt. ed. see Glueck, Sheldon S.
Glueck, Nelson. Hesed in the Bible. 1968. 12.50x (ISBN 0-87820-104-1, Pub. by Hebrew Union). Ktav.
--The Other Side of the Jordan. 260p. 1970. pap. text ed. 10.00x (ISBN 0-89757-000-6, Am Sch Orient Res). Eisenbrauns.
Glueck, S. & Glueck, E. Of Delinquency & Crime: A Panorama of Years of Search & Research. 384p. 1974. 40.75x (ISBN 0-398-02989-X). C C Thomas.
Glueck, S. & Glueck, Eleanor. Five Hundred Delinquent Women. Repr. of 1934 ed. 29.00 (ISBN 0-527-34080-4). Kraus Repr.
Glueck, S., ed. Roscoe Pound & Criminal Justice. LC 65-18283. 272p. 1965. 12.50 (ISBN 0-379-00200-0). Oceana.
Glueck, Sheldon. Continental Police Practice: In the Formative Years. 88p. 1974. 9.75x (ISBN 0-398-02880-X). C C Thomas.
Glueck, Sheldon & Glueck, Eleanor. After Conduct of Discharged Offenders. (Cambridge Studies in Criminology: Vol. 5). pap. 13.00 (ISBN 0-317-17877-6). Kraus Repr.
--Family Environment & Delinquency. (International Library of Sociology & Social Reconstruction Ser.). xi, 328p. 1982. Repr. of 1962 ed. lib. bdg. 35.00x (ISBN 0-8377-0616-5). Rothman.
--Toward a Typology of Juvenile Offenders: Implications for Therapy & Prevention. LC 71-115014. 200p. 1970. 43.50 (ISBN 0-8089-0648-8, 791600). Grune.
Glueck, Sheldon & Glueck, Eleanor T. Delinquents & Nondelinquents in Perspective. LC 68-25609. 1968. 17.50x (ISBN 0-674-19600-7). Harvard U Pr.
Glueck, Sheldon, ed. Probation & Criminal Justice: Essays in Honor of Herbert C. Parsons. facsimile ed. LC 74-3825. (Criminal Justice in America Ser.). 1974. Repr. of 1933 ed. 25.50x (ISBN 0-405-06145-5). Ayer Co Pubs.
Glueck, Sheldon S. Crime & Correction. 1952. 24.00 (ISBN 0-527-34064-2). Kraus Repr.
--Mental Disorder & the Criminal Law. 1925. 29.00 (ISBN 0-527-34092-8). Kraus Repr.
--Nuremberg Trial & Aggressive War. 1946. 15.00 (ISBN 0-527-34096-0). Kraus Repr.
--War Criminals: Their Prosecution & Punishment. 1944. 20.00 (ISBN 0-527-34116-9). Kraus Repr.
Glueck, Sheldon S. & Glueck, Eleanor T. After-Conduct of Discharged Offenders. 1945. 15.00 (ISBN 0-527-34060-X). Kraus Repr.
--Criminal Careers in Retrospect. 1943. 22.00 (ISBN 0-527-34072-3). Kraus Repr.
--Five Hundred Criminal Careers. 1930. 17.00 (ISBN 0-527-34076-6). Kraus Repr.
--Juvenile Delinquents Grown up. 1940. 23.00 (ISBN 0-527-34084-7). Kraus Repr.
--Later Criminal Careers. 1937. 17.00 (ISBN 0-527-34088-X). Kraus Repr.
--One Thousand Juvenile Delinquents. 1934. 23.00 (ISBN 0-527-34100-2). Kraus Repr.
--Physique & Delinquency. 1956. 34.00 (ISBN 0-527-34104-5). Kraus Repr.
Glueck, Sheldon S. & Glueck, Eleanor T., eds. Preventing Crime, a Symposium. 1936. 30.00 (ISBN 0-527-34108-8). Kraus Repr.
Glueck, William & Snyder, Neil. Readings in Business Policy & Strategy from Business Week. 2nd ed. (Management Ser.). (Illus.). 336p. 1982. 17.50x (ISBN 0-07-059540-2). McGraw.
Glueck, William, jt. auth. see Stevens, George E.
Glueck, William F. Management Essentials. 312p. 1979. 21.95x (ISBN 0-03-045416-6); instr's. manual 10.00 (ISBN 0-03-045501-4). Dryden Pr.
Glueck, William F., jt. auth. see Bedeian, Arthur G.
Glueck, William F., jt. auth. see Ivancevich, John M.
Glueck, William F., jt. auth. see Mikovich, George T.
Glueck, William F., ed. Personnel: A Book of Readings. 1979. pap. 15.25x (ISBN 0-256-02078-7). Business Pubns.
Glueck, William F. & Stevens, George E., eds. Cases & Exercises in Personnel Human Resources Management. 3rd. ed. 1983. pap. 16.95 (ISBN 0-256-02430-8). Business Pubns.
Glueckman, A. J., jt. auth. see Natale, Richard.
Gluesing, Debra & Gluesing, Laura. More Recipes: From Minnesota with Love, Vol. II. 260p. (Orig.). 1985. pap. 4.50 comb bd. (ISBN 0-913703-09-5). New Boundary Design.
Gluesing, Laura, jt. auth. see Gluesing, Debra.
Gluhbegovic, Nedzad & Williams, Terence H. The Human Brain: A Photographic Guide. (Illus.). 176p. 1980. text ed. 36.75 (ISBN 0-06-140945-6, 14-09457, Harper Medical). Lippincott.
Glumstele, Adonis. Mytholimericks VII: The Aeneid. (Limerickets Ser.: No. 41). (Illus.). 1983. pap. 1.00 (ISBN 0-938338-51-X). Winds World Pr.
Glunt, James D., jt. ed. see Phillips, Ulrich B.
Glunt, Ruth R. Lighthouses & Legends of the Hudson River. LC 74-84583. (Illus.). 154p. 1975. 10.95 (ISBN 0-912526-14-9). Lib Res.
Glunz, Hans. Britannien und Bibeltext. Repr. of 1930 ed. 16.00 (ISBN 0-384-18950-4). Johnson Repr.
--Die Lateinische Vorlage der Westsaechsischen Evangelienversion. pap. 8.00 (ISBN 0-384-18955-5). Johnson Repr.
--Shakespeare und Morus. Repr. of 1938 ed. 20.00 (ISBN 0-384-18960-1). Johnson Repr.
--Verwendung des Konjunktivs im Altenglischen. Repr. of 1929 ed. 12.00 (ISBN 0-384-18965-2). Johnson Repr.
Glusberg, Jorge, ed. UIA International Exhibition of Architecture, Cairo 1985. (Academy Architecture Ser.). (Illus.). 88p. 1985. pap. 14.95 (ISBN 0-312-82780-6). St Martin.
Gluschke, Wolfgang, et al. Copper, the Next Fifteen Years: A United Nations Study. 1978. lib. bdg. 21.00 (ISBN 90-277-0898-3, Pub. by Reidel Holland); pap. 8.95 (ISBN 90-277-0899-1, Pub. by Reidel Holland). Kluwer Academic.
Glusker, David L. & Misner, Peter L. Words for Your Wedding, the Wedding Service Book. LC 83-80796. 186p. (Orig.). 1983. pap. 7.95 (ISBN 0-912769-00-9); looseleaf 14.95 (ISBN 0-912769-01-7). L Tapley.
Glusker, Irwin, ed. A Southern Album: Recollections of Some People & Places & Times Gone By. LC 75-12416. (Illus.). 168p. 1975. 38.41i (ISBN 0-8487-0399-5). Oxmoor Hse.
Glusker, Irwin, ed. see Abbott, Shirley.
Glusker, Jenny, jt. ed. see McLachlan, Dan.
Glusker, Jenny P. & Trueblood, Kenneth N. Crystal Structure Analysis: A Primer. 2nd ed. (Illus.). 320p. 1985. text ed. 37.50x (ISBN 0-19-503531-3); pap. 18.95x (ISBN 0-19-503543-7). Oxford U Pr.
Glusker, Jenny P., ed. Structural Crystallography in Chemistry & Biology. LC 80-13858. (Benchmark Papers in Physical Chemistry & Chemical Physics: Vol. 4). 421p. 1981. 50.00 (ISBN 0-87933-368-5). Van Nos Reinhold.
Gluski, J. Proverbs: English, French, German, Italian, Spanish, Russian. 448p. 1971. 51.00 (ISBN 0-444-40904-1). Elsevier.
Glustrom, Simon. Language of Judaism. rev. ed. 1973. pap. 8.95x (ISBN 0-87068-224-5). Ktav.
--When Your Child Asks: A Handbook for Jewish Parent. LC 56-8037. 1970. pap. text ed. cancelled (ISBN 0-8197-0267-6). Bloch.
Glut, D. F. The Dinosaur Dictionary. (Fascinating World of Dinosaurs Ser.). (Illus.). 1985. pap. 5.98 (ISBN 0-517-45589-7). Outlet Bk Co.
Glut, Donald. Frankenstein Lives Again. LC 80-23272. (Illus.). 1981. pap. 4.95 (ISBN 0-89865-081-X). Donning Co.
Glut, Donald F. Classic Movie Monsters. LC 77-16014. (Illus.). 1978. 22.50 (ISBN 0-8108-1049-2). Scarecrow.
--The Dinosaur Scrapbook. 1980. 19.95 (ISBN 0-8065-0671-7). Citadel Pr.
--The Dinosaur Scrapbook. 320p. 1982. pap. 9.95 (ISBN 0-8065-0816-7). Citadel Pr.
--The Dracula Book. LC 75-4917. (Illus.). 410p. 1975. 21.00 (ISBN 0-8108-0804-8). Scarecrow.
--The Empire Strikes Back. 1980. pap. 2.25 (ISBN 0-345-28392-9, Del Rey). Ballantine.
--The Frankenstein Catalog. LC 81-6026. (Illus.). 540p. 1984. lib. bdg. 29.95x (ISBN 0-89950-029-3). McFarland & Co.
--The Frankenstein Legend: A Tribute to Mary Shelley & Boris Karloff. LC 73-944. (Illus.). 398p. 1973. 21.00 (ISBN 0-8108-0589-8). Scarecrow.
--The New Dinosaur Dictionary. (Illus.). 256p. 1982. 19.95 (ISBN 0-8065-0782-9). Citadel Pr.
--The New Dinosaur Dictionary. (Illus.). 288p. 1984. pap. 12.95 (ISBN 0-8065-0918-X). Citadel PR.
Glutman, Bill. Field Generals: Anderson, Montana, Theismann, White. 192p. 1982. pap. 2.25 (ISBN 0-448-13773-9). Ace Bks.
Gluyas, Constance. Rogue's Mistress. (Orig.). 1977. pap. 2.95 (ISBN 0-451-11099-4, AE1099, Sig). NAL.
Gluzman, Yakov, ed. Eukaryotic Transcription: The Role of Cis-and Trans-Acting Elements in Initiation. (Current Communications in Molecular Biology Ser.). 206p. (Orig.). 1985. pap. 30.00 (ISBN 0-87969-186-7). Cold Spring Harbor.
--Eukaryotic Viral Vectors. LC 82-4216. 221p. 44.00x (ISBN 0-87969-153-0). Cold Spring Harbor.
Gluzman, Yakov & Shenk, Thomas, eds. Enhancers & Eukaryotic Gene Expression. (Current Communications in Molecular Biology Ser.). 218p. 1983. pap. text ed. 27.00x (ISBN 0-87969-161-1). COld Spring Harbor.
Glyde, John. Life of Edward Fitz-Gerald. LC 70-148790. Repr. of 1900 ed. 15.00 (ISBN 0-404-08823-6). AMS Pr.
--Life of Edward Fitz-Gerald. 1973. Repr. of 1900 ed. 25.00 (ISBN 0-8274-1382-3). R West.
Glymour, Clark. Theory & Evidence. LC 79-3209. 352p. 1980. 38.00x (ISBN 0-691-07240-X); pap. 15.00x LPE (ISBN 0-691-10077-2). Princeton U Pr.
Glymour, Clark, jt. ed. see Stalker, Douglas.
Glymph, Thavolia & Kushma, John J., eds. Essays on the Postbellum Southern Economy. LC 84-40564. (Walter Prescott Webb Memorial Lectures Ser.: No. 18). 128p. 1985. text ed. 17.50x (ISBN 0-89096-227-8). Tex A&M Univ Pr.
Glyn, Anthony. Companion Guide to Paris. (Illus.). 352p. 1985. pap. 10.95 (ISBN 0-13-154410-1). P-H.

Glyn, Elinor. The Great Moment. (Barbara Cartland's Library of Love: Vol. 14). 214p. 1980. 12.95x (ISBN 0-7156-1474-6, Pub. by Duckworth England). Biblio Dist.

--His Hour. (Barbara Cartland's Library of Love: Vol. 2). 182p. 1979. 12.95x (ISBN 0-7156-1378-2, Pub. by Duckworth England). Biblio Dist.

--Man & Maid. (Barbara Cartland's Library of Love: Vol. 10). 182p. 1979. 12.95x (ISBN 0-7156-1386-3, Pub. by Duckworth England). Biblio Dist.

--The Reason Why. (Barbara Cartland's Library of Love: Vol. 6). 246p. 1979. 12.95x (ISBN 0-7156-1382-0, Pub. by Duckworth England). Biblio Dist.

--The Sequence. (Barbara Cartland's Library of Love: Vol. 17). 213p. 1980. 12.95x (ISBN 0-7156-1477-0, Pub. by Duckworth England). Biblio Dist.

--Six Days. (Barbara Cartland's Library of Love: Vol. 12). 213p. 1980. 12.95x (ISBN 0-7156-1471-1, Pub. by Duckworth England). Biblio Dist.

--The Vicissitudes of Evangeline. (Barbara Cartland's Library of Love: Vol. 8). 182p. 1979. 12.95x (ISBN 0-7156-1385-5, Pub. by Duckworth England). Biblio Dist.

Glyn, Margaret H. Elizabethan Virginal Music & Its Composers. LC 77-75230. 1977. Repr. of 1934 ed. lib. bdg. 20.00 (ISBN 0-89341-086-1). Longwood Pub Group.

Glyn, Robert. Aspects of Welsh History. 345p. 1969. text ed. 16.75x (ISBN 0-900768-22-3, Pub. by Univ of Wales Pr England). Humanities.

Glyn, Williams. The Desert & the Dream. 230p. 1975. text ed. 17.50x (ISBN 0-7083-0579-2, Pub. by Univ of Wales Pr England). Humanities.

Glyn-Jones, Kenneth, ed. see Barker, Edmund S.

Glynn, J. A., jt. auth. see Stewart, E. W.

Glynn, James A. Writing Across the Curriculum Using Sociological Concepts. 64p. 1983. wkbk. 4.95 (ISBN 0-9603180-2-X). Fairway Hse.

Glynn, James A., jt. auth. see Stewart, Elbert W.

Glynn, Jeanette. The Grandfather. 1984. pap. 7.50 (ISBN 0-939296-11-X). Bond Pub Co.

Glynn, Joseph. Construction of Cranes & Machinery, Circa 1850. (Illus.). 12.50 (ISBN 0-87556-102-0). Saifer.

--The Eternal Mystic: St. Teresa of Avila, the First Woman Doctor of the Church. 271p. 1982. 7.95 (ISBN 0-533-05407-9). Vantage.

Glynn, L. E. & Steward, M. W. Immunochemistry: An Advanced Textbook. LC 77-1630. 628p. 1977. 149.95x (ISBN 0-471-99508-8, Pub. by Wiley-Interscience). Wiley.

--Structure & Function of Antibodies. 306p. 1981. 19.95 (ISBN 0-471-27917-X, Pub. by Wiley-Interscience). Wiley.

Glynn, L. E., ed. Tissue Repair & Regeneration. (Handbook of Inflammation: Vol. 3). 598p. 1981. 128.50 (ISBN 0-444-80278-9, Biomedical Pr). Elsevier.

Glynn, L. E. & Schlumberger, H. D., eds. Experimental Models of Chronic Inflammatory Diseases. 1977. 49.00 (ISBN 0-387-08095-3). Springer-Verlag.

Glynn, L. E. & Steward, M. W., eds. Antibody Production. LC 80-41378. 231p. 1981. 19.95 (ISBN 0-471-27916-1, Pub. by Wiley-Interscience). Wiley.

--Immunochemistry: An Advanced Textbook. LC 77-1630. pap. text ed. 159.50 (ISBN 0-317-28975-6, 2052064). Bks Demand UMI.

Glynn, Maryanne C. Student Guide to the Registered Nurse (R.N.) Examination. Tarlow, David M., ed. (Illus.). 1981. pap. 12.95 (ISBN 0-931572-03-7). Datar Pub.

Glynn, Peter W. & Wellington, Gerard M. Corals & Coral Reefs of the Galapagos Islands. LC 82-25161. (Illus.). 1984. lib. bdg. 45.00x (ISBN 0-520-04713-3). U of Cal Pr.

Glynn, Peter W., jt. auth. see Robertson, D. Ross.

Glynn, Prudence. Skin to Skin: Eroticism in Dress. LC 82-81091. (Illus.). 1982. 22.50 (ISBN 0-19-520391-7). Oxford U Pr.

Glynn, Ruth, jt. auth. see Burn, Lucilla.

Glynn, Sean. Government Policy & Agricultural Development. 1977. pap. 13.50x (ISBN 0-85564-077-4, Pub. by U of W Austral Pr). Intl Spec Bk.

Glynn, Thomas. The Building. Lish, Godon, ed. LC 85-40226. 416p. 1986. 17.95 (ISBN 0-394-54582-6). Knopf.

--Temporary Sanity. LC 76-4765. 1976. 8.95 (ISBN 0-914590-28-6); pap. 3.95 (ISBN 0-914590-29-4). Fiction Coll.

Glynne-Jones, Marjorie. Music: Schooling in the Middle Years. (Basic Books in Education Ser.). 176p. 1974. 16.00 (ISBN 0-208-01390-3). Shoe String.

Glyph. Glyph, I. LC 76-47370. pap. 55.50 (ISBN 0-317-20658-3, 2024141). Bks Demand UMI.

Glysson, E. A., et al, eds. Innovations in the Water & Wastewater Fields. (Illus.). 240p. 1984. text ed. 34.95 (ISBN 0-250-40645-4). Butterworth.

GMA Research Corporation. Beef Usage Attitudes & Opportunities in Foodservice & Customer Markets. Adolf, Mary M., ed. (Illus.). 250p. (Orig.). 1984. pap. 185.00 (ISBN 0-88700-003-7). Natl Live Stock.

Gmehling, et al, eds. Vapor-Liquid Equilibrium Data Collection Tables & Diagrams of Data for Binary & Multicomponent Mixtures up to Moderate Pressures; Constants of Correlation Equations for Computer Use: Part 2b: Organic Hydroxy Compounds: Alcohols & Phenols. LC 79-670289. (Dechema Chemistry Data Ser.: Vol. 1). 1978. text ed. 103.50x (ISBN 3-921567-12-2, Pub. by Dechema Germany). Scholium Intl.

Gmehling, J. & Onken, U. Vapor-Liquid Equilibrium Data Collection: Aqueous Organic Systems, Vol. I, Pt. I. rev. ed. Behrens, D. & Eckermann, R., eds. (Dechema Chemistry Data Ser.). 698p. 1981. text ed. 120.00x (ISBN 3-921567-01-7, Pub. by Dechema Germany). Scholium Intl.

--Vapor-Liquid Equilibrium Data Collection Part 2d, Organic Hydroxy Compounds: Alcohols & Phenols (Supplement 2) (Dechema Chemistry Data Ser.: Vol. I). (Illus.). 800p. 1982. 117.50x (ISBN 0-686-43226-6, Pub. by Dechema Germany). Scholium Intl.

--Vapor-Liquid Equilibrium Data Collection Part 5 Carboxylic Acids, Anhydrides, Esters. (Vol. I). (Illus.). 715p. 1982. 122.00x (ISBN 0-686-43231-2, Pub. by Dechema Germany). Scholium Intl.

--Vapor-Liquid Equilibrium Data Collection Tables & Diagrams of Data for Binary & Multicomponent Mixtures up to Moderate Pressures; Constants of Correlation Equations for Computer Use: Part 2a: Organic Hydroxy Compounds: Alcohols, No. 1. LC 79-670289. (Dechema Chemistry Data Ser.). 1978. text ed. 110.00x (ISBN 3-921567-09-2). Scholium Intl.

--Vapor-Liquid Equilibrium Data Collection Tables & Diagrams of Data for Binary & Multicomponent Mixtures up to Moderate Organic Hydroxy Compounds: Alcohols & Phenols, Vol. I, Pt. 2b. (Dechema Chemistry Data Ser.). 1979. text ed. 103.50x (ISBN 3-921567-01-7). Scholium Intl.

--Vapor-Liquid Equilibrium Data Collection: Volume I, Part 1A - Supplement 1 to Aqueous Organic Systems. 1981. lib. bdg. 127.50x (ISBN 3-921-56733-5, Pub. by Dechema Germany). Scholium Intl.

--Vapor-Liquid Equilibrium Data Collection: Volume I, Part 2C-Organic Hydroxy Compounds: Alcohols (Supplement 1) (Dechema Chemistry Data Ser.). (Illus.). 698p. 1982. lib. bdg. 105.00x (ISBN 3-921-56729-7). Scholium Intl.

Gmehling, J., et al. Aromatic Hydrocarbons: Vol. I, Pt. 7, Vapor-Liquid Equilibrium Data Collection. Behrens, D. & Eckermann, R., eds. (Dechema Chemistry Data Ser.). 564p. 1980. text ed. 110.00x (ISBN 3-9215-6723-8, Pub. by Dechema Germany). Scholium Intl.

--Vapor-Liquid Equilibrium Data Collection: Aldehydes, Ketones, Ethers, Vol. 1, Parts 3 & 4. Behrens, Dieter & Eckermann, Reiner, eds. LC 79-670289. (Dechema Chemistry Ser.). (Illus.). 1979. lib. bdg. 115.00x (ISBN 3-921-56714-9, Pub by Dechema Germany). Scholium Intl.

Gmelch, George. The Irish Tinkers: The Urbanization of an Itinerant People. 2nd ed. (Illus.). 212p. 1985. pap. text ed. 7.95x (ISBN 0-88133-158-9). Waveland Pr.

Gmelch, George & Kroup, Ben. To Shorten the Road: Folktales From Ireland's Travelling People. (Illus.). 189p. 1978. 10.95 (ISBN 0-905140-37-0, Pub. by O'Brien Pr Ireland); pap. 6.95 (ISBN 0-86278-002-0). Irish Bks Media.

Gmelch, Sharon. Tinkers & Travellers: Ireland's Nomads. (Illus.). 144p. 1975. 14.95 (ISBN 0-905140-69-9, Pub. by O'Brien Pr Ireland); pap. 9.95 (ISBN 0-905140-66-4). Irish Bks Media.

Gmelch, Sharon, ed. Irish Life. 256p. 1979. 18.95 (ISBN 0-905140-46-X, Pub. by O'Brien Pr Ireland); pap. 11.95 (ISBN 0-86278-003-9). Irish Bks Media.

Gmelch, Walter H. Beyond Stress to Effective Management. LC 82-2577. 251p. 1982. pap. text ed. 9.95 (ISBN 0-471-09659-8); leader's guide 5.00 (ISBN 0-471-80382-0). Wiley.

--Relieving Stress Set. (Wiley Self-Teaching Guide Ser.). 1983. pap. 18.90 (ISBN 0-471-88661-0, Wiley Press). Wiley.

Gmelch, Walter H. & Miskin, Val D. Productivity Teams: Beyond Quality Circles. LC 84-2386. (Wiley Professional Development Programs Ser.: 1-389). 304p. 1984. text ed. 55.95x (ISBN 0-471-89072-3); leader's guide 1.00 (ISBN 0-471-82474-7). Wiley.

Gmur, B. Making Health Decisions. 2nd ed. 1975. 21.28 (ISBN 0-13-547927-4); workbook 7.96 (ISBN 0-13-547943-6). P-H.

Gnade, Michael. People in My Camera. 1978. text ed. 14.95 (ISBN 0-8038-5876-0, Pub. by Fountain). Morgan.

--People in My Camera. (Illus.). 200p. 1984. 14.95 (ISBN 0-85242-632-1, 3632). Morgan.

--Perfect Nude Photography. 200p. 19.95 (ISBN 0-85242-768-9, 54768, Pub. by Fountain). Morgan.

Gnaegy, Charles. A Promise of Summer. (Orig.). 1979. pap. 2.25 (ISBN 0-532-22172-9). Woodhill.

Gnagey, William J. Motivating Classroom Discipline. 148p. 1981. pap. text ed. write for info. (ISBN 0-02-344140-2). Macmillan.

Gnagey, William J., ed. see Karmel, Marilyn O. & Karmel, Louis J.

Gnaiger, E. & Forstner, H., eds. Polarographic Oxygen Sensors: Aquatic & Physiological Applications. (Illus.). 370p. 1983. 52.00 (ISBN 0-387-11654-0). Springer-Verlag.

Gnam, Rene. The Business of Direct Mail. Clifton, Barbara, ed. 250p. 1984. wkbk. 26.00 (ISBN 0-910475-23-7). KET.

Gnanadesikan, Ram, ed. Statistical Data Analysis: Proceedings of Symposia in Applied Mathematics, Vol. 28. LC 82-24308. (Proceedings of Symposia in Applied Mathematics: Vol. 28). 142p. 1983. pap. 17.00 (ISBN 0-8218-0040-X). Am Math.

Gnanadesikan, Ramanathan. Methods for Statistical Data Analysis of Multivariate Observations. LC 76-14994. (Probability & Mathematical Statics Ser.). 311p. 1977. 38.50x (ISBN 0-471-30845-5, Pub. by Wiley-Interscience). Wiley.

Gnaneswarananda, Swami. Yoga for Beginners. Gupta, Mallika C., ed. LC 74-29557. 200p. 1975. pap. 4.95 (ISBN 0-9600826-1-1). Vivekananda.

Gnann, Pearl R. & Lebay, Mrs. Charles. Georgia Salzburgers & Allied Families. 1979. Repr. of 1956 ed. 27.50 (ISBN 0-89308-012-8). Southern Hist Pr.

Gnap, John L. & Flaster, Nancy. Easy Sleep. 1978. 8.95 (ISBN 0-8128-2435-0). Stein & Day.

Gnaphaeus, Gulielmus. The Comedy of Acolastus. Carver, P. L., ed. (EETS, OS Ser.: No. 202). Repr. of 1937 ed. 20.00 (ISBN 0-527-00202-X). Kraus Repr.

Gnauck, A. H., jt. auth. see Straskraba, M.

Gnecchi, R., et al. Coin Types of Imperial Rome. 1977. 15.00 (ISBN 0-89005-225-5). Ares.

Gnedenko, B. The Theory of Probability. 392p. 1978. 8.45 (ISBN 0-8285-0748-1, Pub. by Mir Pubs USSR). Imported Pubns.

Gnedenko, B. V. Theory of Probability. Yankovsky, George, tr. from Russian. 392p. 1969. 17.00x (ISBN 0-8464-0922-4). Beekman Pubs.

--The Theory of Probability & the Elements of Statistics. 5th ed. Seckler, Bernard, tr. from Rus. LC 61-13496. 529p. 1985. pap. text ed. 9.95 (ISBN 0-8284-1132-8, 132). Chelsea Pub.

Gnedenko, B. V. & Puri, M. L., eds. Nonparametric Statistical Inference, 2 Vols. (Colloquia Mathematica Societatis Janos Bolyai Ser.: Vol. 32). 910p. 1983. 144.75 (ISBN 0-444-86196-3, I-095-83, North Holland). Elsevier.

Gnedenko, Boris V. & Khinchin, Alexander Y. Elementary Introduction to the Theory of Probability. 5th ed. Boron, Leon F., tr. 1961. pap. text ed. 4.50 (ISBN 0-486-60155-2). Dover.

Gneist, Rudolph. The History of the English Constitution, 2 vols. Ashworth, Philip A., tr. from Ger. 1980. Repr. of 1886 ed. Set. lib. bdg. 75.00x (ISBN 0-8377-0613-0). Rothman.

Gneuss, Helmut, jt. ed. see Lapidge, Michael.

Gnielinski, Stefan Von see Von Gnielinski, Stefan.

Gnilka, Joachim & Mussner, Franz. The Epistle to the Phillipians & the Epistle to the Colossians. McKenzie, John L., ed. LC 81-605. (New Testament for Spiritual Reading Ser.). 180p. 1981. pap. 4.95 (ISBN 0-8245-0126-8). Crossroad NY.

Gnirk, P. F., jt. auth. see Lindblom, U. E.

Gnirss, Christa & Dettweiler, Hans, eds. International Bibliography of Reprints. 2334p. Set. lib. bdg. 250.00 (ISBN 0-317-11844-7). Vol. 1-3: Bks & Serials (ISBN 3-7940-3433-3) (ISBN 3-598-03434-2). Vol. 2: Periodicals, Newspapers, Annuals, Conference Reports, Etc. K G Saur.

Gnosis, Inc. Learning LISP. 192p. 1983. 21.95 (ISBN 0-13-527821-X); disk 14.95 (ISBN 0-13-527813-9); book & disk 29.95 (ISBN 0-13-527839-2). P-H.

Gnugnoli, Guiliano, jt. auth. see Maisel, Herbert.

Gnuse, Robert. Authority of the Bible, Theories of Inspiration Revelation & the Canon of Scripture. (Theological Inquirers Ser.). 240p. (Orig.). 1985. pap. 6.95 (ISBN 0-8091-2692-3). Paulist Pr.

--You Shall Not Steal: Community & Property in the Biblical Tradition. LC 85-4810. 176p. (Orig.). 1985. pap. 9.95 (ISBN 0-88344-799-1). Orbis Bks.

Gnuse, Robert K. The Dream Theophany of Samuel: Its Structure in Relation to Ancient Near Eastern Dreams & its Theological Significance. 278p. (Orig.). 1984. lib. bdg. 27.25 (ISBN 0-8191-3716-2); pap. text ed. 14.25 (ISBN 0-8191-3717-0). U Pr of Amer.

Gnuva, Paul. Vox--Enciclopedia Cultural, Tomo 6: Pueblos. 210p. (Espn.). 1977. leatherette 29.95 (ISBN 84-7153-493-2, S-50503). French & Eur.

Go, K. G., et al, eds. Recent Progress in the Study & Therapy of Brain Edema. 722p. 1984. 95.00x (ISBN 0-306-41471-6, Plenum Pr). Plenum Pub.

Go, Shizuko. Requiem. LC 84-48698. 120p. 1985. 14.95 (ISBN 0-87011-716-5, Dist. by Har-Row). Kodansha.

Goacher, Brian & Reid, Margaret I. School Reports to Parents. 208p. 1984. 16.00x (ISBN 0-7005-0643-8, Pub. by NFER Nelson UK). Taylor & Francis.

Goacher, Denis. If Hell, Hellas. LC 82-82067. 60p. (Orig.). 1982. pap. 4.95 (ISBN 0-915032-22-8). Natl Poet Foun.

--Logbook. 1972. signed 6.00 (ISBN 0-685-78946-2, Pub. by Grosseteste); sewn in wrappers 3.00 (ISBN 0-685-78947-0). Small Pr Dist.

--Transversions. 1973. signed 4.00 (ISBN 0-685-78940-3, Pub. by Grosseteste); sewn in wrappers 2.00 (ISBN 0-685-78941-1). Small Pr Dist.

Goad, Caroline. Horace in the English Literature of 18th Century. LC 67-30804. (Studies in Comparative Literature, No. 35). 1969. Repr. of 1918 ed. lib. bdg. 95.00x (ISBN 0-8383-0701-9). Haskell.

Goad, Harold E. Franciscan Italy. 1979. Repr. of 1926 ed. lib. bdg. 40.00 (ISBN 0-8495-2034-7). Arden Lib.

Goad, K. J. & Halsey, D. H. Ammunition, Grenades & Mines. LC 81-23411. (Brassey's Battlefield Weapons Systems & Technology: Vol. 3). 160p. 1982. 35.00 (ISBN 0-08-028326-8, T120); pap. 17.50 (ISBN 0-08-028327-6). Pergamon.

Goad, L. H., ed. Preparing Teachers for Lifelong Education. (Advances in Lifelong Education Ser.: Vol. 8). (Illus.). 200p. 1984. 28.00 (ISBN 0-08-026786-6); pap. 12.50 (ISBN 0-08-026787-4). Pergamon.

Goad, Marcine H., jt. auth. see Crane, Ruth.

Goad, Nancy A., jt. auth. see Wakefield, James A.

Goad, Tom W. Delivering Effective Training. LC 82-50125. 183p. 1982. pap. 18.50 (ISBN 0-88390-173-0). Univ Assocs.

Goadby, Edwin. The England of Shakespeare. LC 76-168169. Repr. of 1881 ed. 16.00 (ISBN 0-404-02839-X). AMS Pr.

Goadby, J. Jackson. The Best Society & Other Lectures. 1898. Repr. 20.00 (ISBN 0-8274-1928-7). R West.

Goadby, Robert, tr. see Cervantes Saavedra, Miguel De.

Goaman. Mysteries & Marvels of Animal World. (Mysteries & Marvels Ser.). (Illus.). 32p. (gr. 6up). 1984. 7.95 (ISBN 0-86020-752-8); PLB 12.95 (ISBN 0-88110-168-0); pap. 4.95 (ISBN 0-86020-751-X). EDC.

Goaman, Karen, ed. see Hill.

Goanatilake, Susantha. Crippled Minds: An Exploration into Colonial Culture! 1982. 39.00x (ISBN 0-686-94059-8, Pub. by Garlandfold England). State Mutual Bk.

Goar, Maria St. see Steiner, Rudolf.

Goar, Maria St., tr. see Steiner, Rudolf.

Goas, Guy. Modern English Prose. 260p. 1983. lib. bdg. 20.00 (ISBN 0-8495-0614-X). Arden Lib.

Goater, B. The Butterflies & Moths of Hampshire & the Isle of Wight. 453p. 1974. 35.00x (ISBN 0-317-07037-1, Pub. by EW Classey UK). State Mutual Bk.

Goates, J. Rex, et al. General Chemistry: Theory & Description. 788p. 1981. text ed. 28.95 (ISBN 0-15-529535-7, HC); solutions manual avail. (ISBN 0-15-529536-5). HarBraceJ.

Goatsend, Slim. Thor's Goats & Other Crazy Ways to Ride Around. (Odd Books for Odd Moments Ser.). (Illus.). 72p. (Orig.). 1982. pap. 3.95cancelled (ISBN 0-938338-07-2). Winds World Pr.

Goaz, Paul W. & White, Stuart C. Oral Radiology: Principles & Interpretation. LC 81-18802. (Illus.). 695p. 1982. text ed. 36.95 (ISBN 0-8016-1886-X). Mosby.

Goaz, Paul W., jt. auth. see Wood, Norman K.

Gob, Albert & Zauner, Renate. Speaking of: Backaches. Humphreys, Martha, tr. from Ger. LC 78-72877. (Medical Adviser Ser.). (Illus.). 128p. 1979. pap. 3.95 (ISBN 0-8326-2233-8, 7451). Delair.

Gobat, Samuel. Journal of Three Years' Residence in Abyssinia. LC 72-78576. Repr. of 1851 ed. 25.00x (ISBN 0-8371-1416-0, GOA&, Pub. by Negro U Pr). Greenwood.

Gobb, Mario. Political, Economic, & Labor in Spain. LC 81-52617. (Multinational Industrial Relations Ser.: No. 10a). 134p. pap. 18.00 (ISBN 0-89546-034-3). Indus Res Unit-Wharton.

Gobbel, A. Roger & Huber, Phillip C. Creative Designs with Children at Worship. LC 80-82225. 96p. (Orig.). 1981. pap. 5.95 (ISBN 0-8042-1526-X). John Knox.

Gobbel, A. Roger, et al. Helping Youth Interpret the Bible: A Teaching Resource. LC 84-3916. 204p. 1984. pap. 9.95 (ISBN 0-8042-1580-4). John Knox.

Gobbell, Phyllis C. Like a Promise. LC 83-71490. 1983. 8.95 (ISBN 0-8054-7319-X). Broadman.

Gobbi, Tito. My Life. LC 79-7784. (Illus.). 240p. 1980. 14.95 (ISBN 0-385-15627-8). Doubleday.

--Tito Gobbi on His World of Italian Opera. (Illus.). 266p. 1984. 17.95 (ISBN 0-531-09767-6). Watts.

Gobble, William & Harwood, Bruce M. North Carolina Real Estate. 2nd ed. LC 83-19047. (Illus.). xviii, 650p. 1984. 24.95 (ISBN 0-8359-4952-4). Reston.

Gobel, F., tr. see Schuh, Fred.

Gobel, Heinrich. Tapestries of the Lowlands. West, Robert, tr. LC 73-79046. (Illus.). 1974. Repr. of 1924 ed. lib. bdg. 75.00 (ISBN 0-87817-132-0). Hacker.

Gobel, R., et al, eds. Abelian Groups & Modules. (CISM International Centre for Mechanical Sciences Ser.: Vol. 287). (Illus.). xii, 531p. pap. 40.60 (ISBN 0-387-81847-2). Springer-Verlag.

Gobelain, Alfred. American, Chinese & Foreign Pottery in Some of the Leading Museums of the United States. (Illus.). 129p. 1984. 89.85x (ISBN 0-86650-111-8). Gloucester Art.

Gobello, Jose. Diccionario Lunfardo Ilustrado. (Span.). 55.00 (ISBN 0-686-56669-6, S-33076). French & Eur.

Gober, Dom. Black Cop. (Black Cop Ser.: No. 1). (Orig.). 1974. pap. 2.25 (ISBN 0-87067-097-2, BH097). Holloway.

Gober, James W. Come Go with Me. 176p. 1982. 8.95 (ISBN 0-89962-271-2). Todd & Honeywell.

Gober, Lasley F. The Christmas Lover's Handbook. LC 85-13450. (Illus.). 256p. 1985. pap. 12.95 (ISBN 0-932620-53-1). Betterway Pubns.

Goberna, M. Regina. Our Father Saint Benedict. Green, Maurus, tr. from Catalan. (Illus.). 128p. (Orig.). 1983. pap. 4.95 (ISBN 0-911782-45-1). New City.

Gobert, D. L. Red & the Black Notes. (Orig.). 1967. pap. 2.95 (ISBN 0-8220-1111-5). Cliffs.

Gobert, David, jt. auth. see Oudot, Simone.

Gobert, E., jt. auth. see Oxley, T.

Gobert, James J. & Cohen, Neil P. Rights of Prisoners. (Individual Rights Publications). 500p. 1981. write for info. (Pub. By Shepards-McGraw). McGraw.

Gobert, James J., jt. auth. see Cohen, Neil P.

Gobert, James J., jt. auth. see Shepard's & McGraw-Hill.

Gobetz, Giles E. Adjustment & Assimilation of Slovenian Refugees. Cordasco, Francesco, ed. LC 80-860. (American Ethnic Groups Ser.). 1981. lib. bdg. 22.00x (ISBN 0-405-13423-1). Ayer Co Pubs.

Gobineau, A. de. The Moral & Intellectual Diversity of Races. Rosenberg, Charles, ed. LC 83-48534. (The History of Hereditarian Thought Ser.). 512p. 1984. Repr. of 1856 ed. lib. bdg. 60.00 (ISBN 0-317-14533-9). Garland Pub.

Gobineau, Arthur. The Renaissance, Savonarola - Cesare - Borgia -Julius II - Leo X - Michael Angelo. Levy, Oscar, ed. 349p. 1981. Repr. of 1903 ed. lib. bdg. 50.00 (ISBN 0-89984-235-6). Century Bookbindery.

Gobineau, Arthur De see De Gobineau, Arthur.

Gobineau, Conte D. Romances of the East. LC 73-6282. (The Middle East Ser.). Repr. of 1878 ed. 24.50 (ISBN 0-405-05340-1). Ayer Co Pubs.

Gobineau, Joseph A. Golden Flower. facsimile ed. Redman, B. R., tr. LC 68-54347. (Essay Index Reprint Ser). 1924. 15.00 (ISBN 0-8369-0477-X). Ayer Co Pubs.

Gobineau, Marceline. Stephanie the Emperor's Agent. 1977. pap. 1.75 (ISBN 0-380-01822-5, 36129). Avon.

Goble, Danney. Progressive Oklahoma: The Making of a New Kind of State. LC 79-4734. (Illus.). 1980. 15.95 (ISBN 0-8061-1510-6). U of Okla Pr.

Goble, Danny, jt. auth. see Scales, James R.

Goble, Dorothy, jt. auth. see Goble, Paul.

Goble, Ermina S., ed. see Calasibetta, Charlotte M.

Goble, Frank. Excellence in Leadership. LC 72-79880. (Illus.). 1978. pap. 5.95 (ISBN 0-916054-84-5). Green Hill.

--Excellence in Leadership. 223p. 1972. pap. 6.95 (ISBN 0-916054-51-9). T Jefferson Res Ctr.

Goble, Frank & Brooks, B. David. The Case for Character Education. 170p. (Orig.). 1983. pap. 7.95 (ISBN 0-89803-129-X, Dist. by Kampmann). Green Hill.

Goble, Frank G. Beyond Failure: How to Cure a Neurotic Society. LC 77-77328. 218p. 1977. pap. 4.95 (ISBN 0-916054-51-9). T Jefferson Res Ctr.

--A Third Force: The Psychology of Abraham Maslow. 1984. pap. 3.95 (ISBN 0-671-50983-7). PB.

Goble, Frank G. & Brooks, B. David. The Case for Character Education. LC 83-70068. 180p. 1983. pap. 7.95 (ISBN 0-938308-09-2). T Jefferson Res Ctr.

Goble, N. M. & Porter, J. F. The Changing Role of the Teacher. 16.00x (ISBN 0-85633-131-7, Pub. by NFER Nelson UK). Taylor & Francis.

Goble, Neil. Asimov Analyzed. LC 73-169988. 1972. 5.95 (ISBN 0-88358-113-2). Mirage Pr.

Goble, Paul. Buffalo Woman. LC 83-15704. (Illus.). 32p. (gr. kup). 1984. PLB 12.95 (ISBN 0-02-737720-2). Bradbury Pr.

--The Gift of the Sacred Dog. LC 80-15843. (Illus.). 32p. (ps-3). 1984. pap. 3.95 (ISBN 0-02-043280-1). Bradbury Pr.

--The Girl Who Loved Wild Horses. LC 77-20500. (Illus.). 32p. (gr. k-3). 1978. 11.95 (ISBN 0-02-736570-0). Bradbury Pr.

--The Great Race of the Birds & Animals. LC 85-4202. (Illus.). 32p. (ps-2). 1985. PLB 12.95 (ISBN 0-02-736950-1). Bradbury Pr.

--Star Boy. LC 82-20599. (Illus.). 32p. (gr. k up). 1983. 12.95 (ISBN 0-02-722660-3). Bradbury Pr.

Goble, Paul & Goble, Dorothy. The Friendly Wolf. LC 74-77664. (Illus.). 32p. (ps-2). 1975. 9.95 (ISBN 0-02-736540-9). Bradbury Pr.

--Lone Bull's Horse Raid. LC 73-76546. (Illus.). 64p. (gr. 4-6). 1973. 11.95 (ISBN 0-02-736580-8). Bradbury Pr.

Goble, Phillip. The Rabbi from Tarsus. 112p. 1981. pap. 4.95 (ISBN 0-8423-5124-8). Tyndale.

--The Rabbi from Tarsus. 1981. pap. 11.50 incl. cassette (ISBN 0-8423-5122-1). Tyndale.

Goble, Phillip E. Everything You Need to Grow a Messianic Synagogue. LC 74-28017. (Orig.). 1974. pap. 3.95 (ISBN 0-87808-421-5). William Carey Lib.

Goble, Phillip E., ed. Everything You Need to Grow a Messianic Yeshiva. LC 81-1032. 312p. (Orig.). 1981. pap. 10.95 (ISBN 0-87808-181-X). William Carey Lib.

Goble, Robert & Goble, Wendy. Cogeneration: A Campus Option? 63p. 17.50 (ISBN 0-317-33652-5); members 12.50 (ISBN 0-317-33653-3). Assn Phys Plant Admin.

Goble, Warwick, illus. The Fairy Book. LC 79-14514. (Facsimile Classics Ser.). (Illus.). 1979. Repr. of 1923 ed. 8.95 (ISBN 0-8317-3163-X, Mayflower Bks). Smith Pubs.

Goble, Wendy, jt. auth. see Goble, Robert.

Goblet, Y. M. Twilight of Treaties. LC 70-110930. 1970. Repr. of 1936 ed. 24.50x (ISBN 0-8046-0913-6, Pub by Kennikat). Assoc Faculty Pr.

Goblet D'Alviella, Eugene F. Lectures on the Origin & Growth of the Conception of God as Illustrated by Anthropology & History. Wicksteed, P. H., tr. LC 77-27163. (Hibbert Lectures: 1887). Repr. of 1892 ed. 26.50 (ISBN 0-404-60409-9). AMS Pr.

--The Migration of Symbols. Birdwood, G., ed. LC 76-154638. (Illus.). 277p. 1972. Repr. of 1894 ed. 21.00 (ISBN 0-8337-0762-0). B Franklin.

Gobran, Alfonse. Beginning Algebra. 3rd ed. 400p. 1982. text ed. write for info. (ISBN 0-87150-349-2, 2741, Prindle). PWS Pubs.

--Intermediate Algebra. 2nd ed. 1979. text ed. write for info. (ISBN 0-87150-230-5, PWS 1841, Prindle). PWS Pubs.

--Intermediate Algebra. 3rd ed. 528p. 1983. text ed. write for info (ISBN 0-87150-363-8, 2791, Prindle). PWS Pubs.

Gobry, Ivan, jt. auth. see Pascal, Blaise.

Goby, Marshall J., ed. Alcoholism: Treatment & Recovery. LC 83-15214. 300p. pap. 29.00 (ISBN 0-87125-089-6). Cath Health.

Goc, Michael. The Bud Norton Story. (Illus.). 168p. 1982. pap. 12.95 (ISBN 0-939398-02-8). Fox River.

Gocek, Matilda A. Benedict Arnold: A Reader's Guide & Bibliography. LC 73-77233. 28p. 1973. pap. 3.45 (ISBN 0-912526-04-1). Lib Res.

--Love Is a Challenge. LC 78-12327. (Keepers of the Light Ser.). (Illus.). 72p. 1978. pap. 3.95 (ISBN 0-912526-22-X). Lib Res.

--Orange County, New York: A Reader's Guide & Bibliography. LC 73-77313. 60p. 1973. pap. 3.45 (ISBN 0-912526-05-X). Lib Res.

--The Tuxedo Park Library: Social Aspects of Growth, 1901-1940. LC 68-58969. (Illus.). 1968. 10.95 (ISBN 0-912526-00-9). Lib Res.

Gochberg. Stage of Dreams: The Dramatic Art of Alfred de Musset (1828-1834) (Hist. des Idees et Crit. Litt.). 26.50 (ISBN 0-685-34954-3). French & Eur.

Gochberg, Herbert S., jt. ed. see Switzer, Richard.

Gochet, Paul. Outline of a Nominalist Theory of Propositions: An Essay in the Theory of Meaning & in the Philosophy of Logic. Jackson, Margareth & Dale, Anthony, trs. from Fr. (Synthese Library: No. 98). 204p. 1980. lib. bdg. 39.50 (ISBN 9-0277-1031-7, Pub. by Reidel Holland). Kluwer Academic.

Gochnour, Elizabeth. Gochnour Idiom Screening Test (GIST) 6p. 1977. pap. text ed. 4.90x (ISBN 0-8134-1970-0, 1970). Interstate.

Gochnour, Elizabeth A. Everything They Didn't Teach You: A Practical Handbook for Speech & Language Clinicians. LC 77-75921. 86p. 1977. pap. text ed. 3.25x (ISBN 0-8134-1957-3, 1957). Interstate.

Gochnour, Elizabeth A. & Smith, Theresa B. The Language of Life. 2nd ed. (Illus.). 406p. 1981. pap. text ed. 8.25x (ISBN 0-8134-2162-4, 2162). Interstate.

Gochros, Harvey L. & Fischer, Joel. Treat Yourself to a Better Sex Life. (Illus.). 1980. 16.95 (ISBN 0-13-930685-4, Spec); pap. 7.95 (ISBN 0-13-930677-3). P-H.

Gochros, Harvey L., jt. auth. see Fischer, Joel.

Gochros, Harvey L., jt. auth. see Shore, David A.

Gochros, Harvey L., et al. Helping the Sexually Oppressed. (Illus.). 416p. 1986. text ed. 29.95 (ISBN 0-13-386129-5). P-H.

Gochros, Jean S. What to Say after You Clear Your Throat. LC 79-16042. (Orig.). 1980. pap. 7.95 (ISBN 0-916630-18-8). Pr Pacifica.

Gocke, David J., jt. auth. see Krugman, Saul.

Gocke, Michael E., jt. auth. see Schafer, Eldon L.

Gockel, H. Cross & Common Man. 1980. 5.95 (ISBN 0-8100-0119-5, 12N1716). Northwest Pub.

Gockel, Heinz. Individualisiertes Sprechen: Lichtenbergs Bemerkungen im Zusammenhang von Erkenntnistheorie und Sprachkritik. Quellen und Forschungen zur Sprach-und Kulturgeschichte der Germanischen, Voelker N. F. 52. viii, 218p. (Ger.). 1973. 28.40x (ISBN 3-11-003991-5). De Gruyter.

Gockel, Herman W. Answer to Anxiety. 1965. pap. 4.95 (ISBN 0-570-03704-2, 12-2254). Concordia.

--Daily Walk with God. 1982. 15.95 (ISBN 0-570-03298-9, 15-2171); pap. 10.95 (ISBN 0-570-03855-3, 12YY2810). Concordia.

--Give Your Life a Lift. 1983. pap. 5.50 (ISBN 0-570-03891-X, 12-2973). Concordia.

--My Hand in His. rev. ed. LC 60-15577. 1975. pap. 6.50 (ISBN 0-570-03232-6, 12-2613). Concordia.

--What Jesus Means to Me. 1956. 4.95 (ISBN 0-570-03021-8, 6-1008). Concordia.

Gockel, Herman W. & Saleska, Edward J., eds. Child's Garden of Prayer. (Illus.). (gr. k-2). 1981. pap. 1.50 (ISBN 0-570-03412-4, 56-1016). Concordia.

Goczolowa, jt. auth. see Rudzka.

Goda, Sidney. Articulation Therapy & Consonant Drill Book. LC 74-93566. 174p. 1970. 30.50 (ISBN 0-8089-0649-6, 791615). Grune.

Goda, Toshimi. Random Seas & Design of Maritime Structures. 320p. 1985. 37.50x (ISBN 0-86008-369-1, Pub. by U of Tokyo Japan). Columbia U Pr.

Godaert, F. La Lettre D'Affaires: Initiation. 142p. (Fr.). 1977. pap. 14.95 (ISBN 0-686-92538-6, M-9014). French & Eur.

Godaert, P. La Lettre D'Affaires. Le Courrier Quotidien. 161p. (Fr.). 1980. pap. 14.95 (ISBN 0-686-97424-7, M-9021). French & Eur.

Godana, Bonaya. Africa's Shared Water Resources: Legal & Institutional Aspects of the Nile, Niger & Senegal River Systems. LC 85-8370. 250p. 1985. lib. bdg. 25.00x (ISBN 0-931477-44-1). Lynne Rienner.

Godard, Francis, jt. auth. see Castells, Manuel.

Godard, Jean-Luc. Alphaville. (Lorrimer Classic Screenplay Ser.). (Illus.). o. s. i. 10.95 (ISBN 0-8044-2236-2); pap. 6.95 (ISBN 0-8044-6214-3). Ungar.

--Le Petit Soldat. (Lorrimer Classic Screenplay Ser.). (Illus.). 10.95 (ISBN 0-8044-2237-0); pap. 6.95 (ISBN 0-8044-6215-1). Ungar.

--Pierrot le Fou. (Lorrimer Classic Screenplay Ser.). (Illus.). 10.95 (ISBN 0-8044-2238-9); pap. 6.95 (ISBN 0-8044-6216-X). Ungar.

--Weekend; Wind from the East. (Lorrimer Classic Screenplay Ser.). (Illus.). 12.95 (ISBN 0-8044-2235-4); pap. 8.95 (ISBN 0-8044-6217-8). Ungar.

--A Woman Is a Woman; a Married Woman; Two or Three Things That I Know About Her. (Lorrimer Classic Screenplay Ser.). (Illus.). o. s. i. 12.95 (ISBN 0-8044-2239-7); pap. 8.95 (ISBN 0-8044-6218-6). Ungar.

Godard, Jerry C. Mental Forms Creating: William Blake Anticipates Freud, Jung, & Rank. (Illus.). 186p. (Orig.). 1985. lib. bdg. 22.75 (ISBN 0-8191-4831-8); pap. text ed. 11.00 (ISBN 0-8191-4832-6). U Pr of Amer.

Godart, O., jt. ed. see Heller, M.

Goday, Dale. Dressing Thin. 1980. 6.95 (ISBN 0-671-25471-5, 25471, Fireside). S&S.

Goday, Dale & Cochran, Molly. Dressing Thin: How to Look up to 35 Pounds Thinner Without Losing an Ounce. 128p. 1981. pap. 6.95 (ISBN 0-671-43826-3, Fireside). S&S.

Godber, George. The Health Service: Past, Present & Future. (Heath Clark Lectures, 1973). 48p. 1975. 18.95 (ISBN 0-485-26324-6, Pub. by Athlone Pr Ltd). Longwood Pub Group.

Godber, Joyce. The Story of Bedford. 160p. 1982. 35.00x (ISBN 0-900804-24-6, Pub. by White Crescent England). State Mutual Bk.

Godbey, Allen H. Lost Tribes: A Myth. rev. ed. (Library of Biblical Studies). 1970. 45.00x (ISBN 0-87068-102-8). Ktav.

Godbey, Geoffrey. Leisure in Your Life: An Exploration. Rev. ed. (Illus.). 304p. 18.95 (ISBN 0-317-30657-X). Venture Pub PA.

Godbey, Geoffrey, et al. Triples: A New Tennis Game. (Illus.). 22p. (Orig.). 1980. pap. 2.98x (ISBN 0-910251-01-0). Venture Pub PA.

Godbey, Geoffrey C. Leisure in Your Life: An Exploration. 1981. pap. text ed. 17.95 (ISBN 0-03-057673-3, HoltC); instr's manual 19.95 (ISBN 0-03-058258-X). HR&W.

Godbey, Marty. Dining in Historic Kentucky: A Restaurant Guide with Recipes. LC 85-61512. (Illus.). 224p. 1985. 12.95 (ISBN 0-913383-04-X). McClanahan Pub.

Godbey, W. B. Six Tracts by W. B. Godbey. Faupel, David W., ed. (The Higher Christian Life Ser.). 479p. 1985. 60.00 (ISBN 0-8240-6420-8). Garland Pub.

Godbillon, C. Dynamical Systems on Surfaces. (Univeritext Ser.). (Illus.). 201p. 1983. pap. 21.00 (ISBN 0-387-11645-1). Springer-Verlag.

Godbold, E. Stanley & Woody, Robert H. Christopher Gadsden & the American Revolution. LC 82-6915. (Illus.). 314p. 1983. text ed. 24.95x (ISBN 0-87049-362-0); pap. text ed. 12.95x (ISBN 0-87049-363-9). U of Tenn Pr.

Godbold, E. Stanly, Jr. Ellen Glasgow & the Woman Within. LC 71-165068. (Illus.). xiv, 322p. 1972. 30.00x (ISBN 0-8071-0040-4). La State U Pr.

Godbolt, Jim. A History of Jazz in Britain, Nineteen Nineteen to Nineteen Fifty. (Illus.). 306p. 1985. 24.95 (ISBN 0-7043-2452-0, Pub. by Quartet Bks). Merrimack Pub Cir.

Godbolt, S., jt. ed. see Morton, L. T.

Godby, Joyce G. The Gift of Peace. 128p. 1984. 7.95 (ISBN 0-89962-378-6). Todd & Honeywell.

--God Makes the Difference. (Contemporary Poets of Dorrance Ser.). 128p. 1981. 6.95 (ISBN 0-8059-2764-6). Dorrance.

Goddard. Information Sources in Geographical Science. (Butterworths Guides to Information Sources Ser.). 1983. text ed. write for info. (ISBN 0-408-10690-5). Butterworth.

--On the Trail of the UCC. 1981. pap. 8.95 (ISBN 0-8298-0353-X). Pilgrim NY.

Goddard, jt. auth. see Parish.

Goddard, A. J., ed. see International Seminar, Imperial College of Science & Technology, UK & Williams.

Goddard, Alice L. David, My Jewish Friend. (gr. 3-6). 1968. pap. 1.95 (ISBN 0-377-07701-1). Friend Pr.

Goddard, Anthea. The Vienna Pursuit. 1977. pap. 1.50 (ISBN 0-505-51131-2, Pub. by Tower Bks). Dorchester Pub Co.

Goddard, Arthur, ed. Harry Elmer Barnes, Learned Crusader: The New History in Action. LC 68-57017. (Illus.). 1968. 29.95 (ISBN 0-87926-002-5). R Myles.

Goddard, Carrie L., jt. auth. see Burkholder, Ruth C.

Goddard, Carrie Lou. Isn't It a Wonder! LC 75-15664. (Illus.). (gr. k-3). 1976. 8.75 (ISBN 0-687-19715-5). Abingdon.

Goddard, Chris. Jazz Away from Home. (Roots of Jazz Ser.). (Illus.). 319p. 1985. Repr. of 1979 ed. lib. bdg. 35.00 (ISBN 0-306-76270-6). Da Capo.

Goddard, Donald, jt. auth. see Pointer, Larry.

Goddard, Dwight. The Buddha's Golden Path. 2nd rev. ed. LC 78-72435. Repr. of 1931 ed. 27.00 (ISBN 0-404-17296-2). AMS Pr.

--The Buddha's Golden Path. 214p. 1981. pap. 9.00 (ISBN 0-89540-074-X, SB-074). Sun Pub.

Goddard, Dwight, ed. see Lankavatara-Sutra.

Goddard, E., tr. see Steiner, Rudolf.

Goddard, E. D. & Vincent, B., eds. Polymer Adsorption & Dispersion Stability. LC 83-25787. (ACS Symposium Ser.: No. 240). 477p. 1984. lib. bdg. 79.95 (ISBN 0-8412-0820-4). Am Chemical.

Goddard, E. H., jt. auth. see Dartnell, G. E.

Goddard, E. H., ed. see Hatzfeld, Jean.

Goddard, E. R. Women's Costume in French Texts of the 11th & 12th Centuries. 1973. Repr. of 1927 ed. 24.00 (ISBN 0-384-19040-5). Johnson Repr.

Goddard, Frederick O. Two-Sector Model of Economic Growth with Technological Progress. LC 75-625421. (University of Florida Social Sciences Monographs: No. 36). 1969. pap. 3.50 (ISBN 0-8130-0270-2). U Presses Fla.

Goddard, Frederick W. & James, Eric J. The Elements of Physical Chemistry. LC 67-105999. pap. 135.00 (ISBN 0-317-09843-8, 2004943). Bks Demand UMI.

Goddard, H. A. Principles of Administration Applied to Nursing Service. (Monograph Ser.: No. 41). (Also avail. in French & Spanish). 1958. 4.80 (ISBN 92-4-140041-2). World Health.

Goddard, H. C. Studies in New England Transcendentalism. 1978. Repr. of 1960 ed. lib. bdg. 30.00 (ISBN 0-8492-4906-6). R West.

Goddard, Harold C. Blake's Fourfold Vision. LC 56-7354. (Orig.). 1956. pap. 5.00x (ISBN 0-87574-086-3). Pendle Hill.

--Chaucer's Legend of Good Women. 107p. 1980. Repr. of 1908 ed. lib. bdg. 20.00 (ISBN 0-8495-1959-4). Arden Lib.

--Chaucer's Legend of Good Women. LC 75-29077. 1975. lib. bdg. 17.50 (ISBN 0-8414-4449-8). Folcroft.

--Meaning of Shakespeare. LC 51-2288. 1951. 33.00x (ISBN 0-226-30040-4). U of Chicago Pr.

--Meaning of Shakespeare, 2 vols. LC 51-2288. 1960. Vol. 1. pap. 11.00x (ISBN 0-226-30041-2, P50, Phoen); Vol. 2. pap. 8.50x (ISBN 0-226-30042-0, P51). U of Chicago Pr.

--Studies in New England Transcendentalism. 1960. text ed. 15.50x (ISBN 0-391-00599-5). Humanities.

Goddard, Henry H. Feeble-Mindedness. LC 76-39391. (Select Bibliographies Reprint Series). 1972. Repr. of 1914 ed. 44.25 (ISBN 0-8369-9907-X). Ayer Co Pubs.

--Feeble-Mindedness: Its Causes & Consequences. LC 73-2401. (Mental Illness & Social Policy; the American Experience Ser.). Repr. of 1926 ed. 43.00 (ISBN 0-405-05207-3). Ayer Co Pubs.

--How to Rear Children in the Atomic Age. (Illus.). 3.00 (ISBN 0-910748-04-7). Hopkins.

--Human Efficiency & Levels of Intelligence. Rosenberg, Charles, ed. LC 83-48542. (The History of Hereditarian Thought Ser.). 128p. 1985. lib. bdg. 20.00 (ISBN 0-8240-5817-8). Garland Pub.

--The Kallikak Family: A Study in the Heredity of Feeble-Mindedness. LC 73-2966. (Classics in Psychology Ser.). Repr. of 1931 ed. 13.00 (ISBN 0-405-05139-5). Ayer Co Pubs.

Goddard, Ives. Delaware Verbal Morphology: A Descriptive & Comparative Study. Hankamer, Jorge, ed. LC 78-66556. (Outstanding Dissertations in Linguistics Ser.). 1985. 32.00 (ISBN 0-8240-9685-1). Garland Pub.

Goddard, J. B. see Diamond, Donald R. & McLoughlin, J. B.

Goddard, J. B., ed. Industrial Innovation & Regional Economic Development. 120p. 1980. pap. 17.25 (ISBN 0-08-026102-7). Pergamon.

Goddard, J. B. & Champion, A. G., eds. The Urban & Regional Transformation of Britain. 1983. pap. 15.95x (ISBN 0-416-30900-3, NO. 3924). Methuen Inc.

Goddard, John, jt. auth. see Clarke, Brian.

Goddard, John, ed. Leisure, Recreation & Tourism. (Journal of Regional Studies: No. 15). (Illus.). 96p. 1981. pap. 17.00 (ISBN 0-08-028945-2). Pergamon.

Goddard, K. Crime Scene Investigation. 1977. 19.95 (ISBN 0-87909-172-X); solns. manual avail. (ISBN 0-87909-165-7). Reston.

Goddard, Ken. The Alchemist. 416p. (Orig.). 1985. lib. bdg. 14.95 (ISBN 0-553-05057-5). Bantam.

Goddard, Kenneth. Balefire. 1984. pap. 3.95 (ISBN 0-553-24029-3). Bantam.

Goddard, Kenneth, jt. auth. see Cope, Jeff.

Goddard, L. & Routley, R. The Logic of Significance & Context, Vol. 1. LC 73-8025. 641p. 1973. 58.95x (ISBN 0-470-30865-6). Halsted Pr.

Goddard, Leonard. Philosophical Problems. 1977. pap. 6.00x (ISBN 0-7073-0136-X, Pub. by Scottish Academic Pr Scotland). Columbia U Pr.

Goddard, M. & Butler, M., eds. Viruses & Wastewater Treatment: Proceedings of International Symposium Held at the University of Surrey, Guilford, 15-17 September 1980. (Illus.). 316p. 1981. 66.00 (ISBN 0-08-026401-8). Pergamon.

Goddard, Madeleine V., tr. see Donoso Cortes, Juan.

Goddard Memorial Symposium, Twelfth. Skylab & Pioneer Report. Bolger, Philip H. & Richards, Paul B., eds. (Science & Technology Ser: Vol. 36). (Illus.). 160p. 1975. lib. bdg. 20.00x (ISBN 0-87703-071-5, Pub. by Am Astronaut). Univelt Inc.

Goddard Memorial Symposium - Washington D.C. - 1961. Space Age in Fiscal Year 2001. Konecci, E., et al, eds. (Science & Technology Ser.: Vol. 10). 1967. 35.00x (ISBN 0-87703-038-3, Pub. by Am Astronaut). Univelt Inc.

Goddard Memorial Symposium, 14th. Satellite Communications in the Next Decade: Proceedings. Jaffe, Leonard, ed. (Science & Technology: Vol. 44). (Illus.). 1977. 20.00x (ISBN 0-87703-088-X, Pub. by Am Astronaut). Univelt Inc.

Goddard Memorial Symposium, 15th. Export of Aerospace Technology. Tross, Carl H., ed. (Science & Technology: Vol. 46). 1978. lib. bdg. 20.00x (ISBN 0-87703-093-6). Univelt Inc.

Goddard Memorial Symposium, 3rd, Washington D. C., 1965. Scientific Experiments for Manned Orbital Flight: Proceedings. Badgley, P. C., ed. (Science & Technology Ser.: Vol. 4). 1965. 30.00x (ISBN 0-87703-032-4, Pub. by Am Astronaut). Univelt Inc.

Goddard Memorial Symposium - 5th - 1967. Voyage to the Planets. (Science & Technology Ser.: Vol. 16). 20.00x (ISBN 0-87703-044-8, Pub. by Am Astronaut). Univelt Inc.

Goddard Memorial Symposium- 7th - Washington D. C. - 1969. Reducing Cost of Space Transportation. (Science & Technology Ser.: Vol. 21). (Illus.). 1969. 25.00x (ISBN 0-87703-049-9, Pub. by Am Astronaut). Univelt Inc.

Goddard, Murray. How to Be Your Own Architect. (Illus.). 1977. 11.95 (ISBN 0-8306-7988-X); pap. 8.95 (ISBN 0-8306-6988-4, 988). TAB Bks.

Goddard, Neville, jt. auth. see Gross, Darwin.

Goddard, P. E. Morphology of the Hupa Language. (CU PAAE). Repr. of 1905 ed. 51.00 (ISBN 0-527-01359-5). Kraus Repr.

Goddard, P. E., jt. auth. see Kew, Della.

Goddard, Peter. David Bowie: Out of the Cool. (Illus.). 128p. 1983. pap. 9.95 (ISBN 0-8253-0181-5). Beaufort Bks NY.

--Genesis: Peter Gabriel, Phil Collins & Beyond. (Illus.). 128p. 1984. pap. 9.95 (ISBN 0-8253-0243-9). Beaufort Bks NY.

--The Police Chronicles. (Illus.). 128p. 1984. pap. 9.95 (ISBN 0-8253-0192-0). Beaufort Bks NY.

--The Rolling Stones: The Last Tour. LC 82-4572. (Illus.). 128p. 1982. pap. 9.95 (ISBN 0-8253-0118-1). Beaufort Bks NY.

--Springsteen: The Boss, Live. (Illus.). 128p. Date not set. pap. 9.95 (ISBN 0-8253-0258-7). Beaufort Bks NY.

--Van Halen. (Illus.). 128p. 1984. pap. 9.95 (ISBN 0-8253-0242-0). Beaufort Bks NY.

--The Who: The Last Tour. (Illus.). 128p. 1983. pap. 9.95 (ISBN 0-8253-0137-8). Beaufort Bks NY.

Goddard, Peter, jt. auth. see Kamin, Philip.

Goddard, Pliny E. Indians of the Northwest Coast. 2nd ed. LC 72-81191. (Handbook Ser.: No. 10). (Illus.). 175p. 1972. Repr. of 1934 ed. lib. bdg. 25.00 (ISBN 0-8154-0428-X). Cooper Sq.

--Indians of the Southwest. LC 74-20181. (Illus.). 205p. 1975. Repr. of 1931 ed. lib. bdg. 25.00 (ISBN 0-8154-0511-1). Cooper Sq.

--Indians of the Southwest. LC 76-41766. (Beautiful Rio Grande Classics Ser.). (Illus.). 248p. 1976. Repr. of 1913 ed. lib. bdg. 17.50 (ISBN 0-87380-113-X). Rio Grande.

--Myths & Tales from the San Carlos Apache. LC 76-43715. (AMNH. Anthropological Pap.: Vol. 29, Pt. 1). Repr. of 1918 ed. 16.50 (ISBN 0-404-15548-0). AMS Pr.

--Navajo Texts. LC 76-44071. (AMNH. Anthropological Papers: Vol. 34, Pt. 1). Repr. of 1933 ed. 16.00 (ISBN 0-404-15775-0). AMS Pr.

Goddard, Ruth. Porfirio Salinas. LC 75-20743. (Illus.). 1975. cloth 35.00 (ISBN 0-914872-04-4, Pub. by Rock House Pr). Austin Pr.

Goddard, Ruth & Dobie, J. Frank. Ralph Ogden & the Seven Mustangs. LC 73-15099. 8.50 (ISBN 0-8363-0082-3). Jenkins.

Goddard, Samuel A. Letters on the American Rebellion: 1860 to 1865. LC 73-179521. (Select Bibliographies Reprint Ser.). Repr. of 1870 ed. 32.00 (ISBN 0-8369-6650-3). Ayer Co Pubs.

Goddard, Scott, ed. see Von Bulow, Hans.

Goddard, Stephen, ed. A Guide to Information Sources in the Geographical Sciences. (Illus.). 288p. 1983. text ed. 27.50x (ISBN 0-389-20403-X, 07287). B&N Imports.

Goddard, Thomas A. Handbook of Sierra Leone. LC 78-92744. Repr. of 1925 ed. 21.50x (ISBN 0-8371-2175-2, GSL&, Pub. by Negro U Pr). Greenwood.

Goddard, Walter E. & Garwood, Dave, eds. Master Production Scheduling Reprints. 183p. 1977. pap. 13.50 (ISBN 0-935406-26-3). Am Prod & Inventory.

Godden, E. & Malnic, J. Rock Paintings of Aboriginal Australia. (Illus.). 1982. 50.50x (ISBN 0-589-50323-5, Pub by Reed Australia). Humanities.

Godden, G., ed. Staffordshire Porcelain. LC 83-175803. (Illus.). 500p. 1983. text ed. 135.50x (ISBN 0-246-11494-0, Pub. by Granada England). Humanities.

Godden, G. A. British Porcelain: An Illustrated Guide. (Illus.). 451p. 1974. 40.00 (ISBN 0-214-66851-7, Pub. by Barrie & Jenkins England). Seven Hills Bks.

--Lowestoff Porcelains. (Illus.). 1985. 62.50 (ISBN 0-907462-64-2). Antique Collect.

--Ridgeway Porcelains. (Illus.). 1985. 59.50 (ISBN 0-907462-65-0). Antique Collect.

Godden, G. M. Henry Fielding: A Memoir. LC 74-3417. 1978. Repr. of 1909 ed. lib. bdg. 50.00 (ISBN 0-8414-4500-1). Folcroft.

Godden, Geoffrey. Caughly & Worcester Porcelains, 1775-1800. (Illus.). 336p. 1981. 69.50 (ISBN 0-907462-01-4). Antique Collect.

--Coalport & Coalbrookdale Porcelains. (Illus.). 310p. 1981. 69.50 (ISBN 0-907462-02-2). Antique Collect.

--Godden's Guide to English Porcelain. (Illus.). 286p. 1980. text ed. 32.00x (ISBN 0-246-11002-3). Humanities.

--Godden's Guide to English Porcelain. (Illus.). 286p. 1983. 29.95 (ISBN 0-246-11002-3, Pub. by Salem Hse Ltd). Merrimack Pub Cir.

--Oriental Export Market Porcelain & Its Influence on European Wares. (Illus.). 384p. 1980. text ed. 65.50x (ISBN 0-246-11057-0). Humanities.

--Oriental Export Porcelain & Its Influence on European Wares. (Illus.). 1979. 69.95x (ISBN 0-8464-0052-9). Beekman Pubs.

Godden, Geoffrey A. British Porcelain: An Illustrated Guide. (Illus.). 464p. 39.00 (ISBN 0-214-66851-7, NO.0221, Pub. by Barrie & Jenkins England). Methuen Inc.

--British Pottery: An Illustrated Guide. (Illus.). 416p. 1983. 50.00 (ISBN 0-8390-0317-X). Abner Schram Ltd.

--British Pottery, An Illustrated Guide. (Illus.). 452p. 1980. 40.00 (ISBN 0-214-20034-5, Pub. by Hutchinson Pub UK). Seven Hills Bks.

--Chamberlain Worcester Porcelain: 1788-1852. (Illus.). 384p. 1982. 100.00 (ISBN 0-8390-0295-5). Abner Schram Ltd.

--Chamberlain-Worcester Porcelain, 1788-1852. (Illus.). 375p. 1982. 140.00 (ISBN 0-09-145860-9, Pub. by Hutchinson Pub UK). Seven Hills Bks.

--Encyclopedia of British Pottery & Porcelain Marks. LC 64-22014. (Illus.). 765p. 1983. 35.00 (ISBN 0-916838-91-9). Schiffer.

--Encyclopedia of British Pottery & Porcelian Marks. 765p. 1984. 35.00 (ISBN 0-257-65782-7, Pub. By Hutchinson Pub UK). Seven Hills Bks.

--Godden's Guide to Mason's China & the Ironstone Wares. (Illus.). 316p. 1980. 44.50 (ISBN 0-902028-86-3). Antique Collect.

--Godden's Guide to Mason's China & The Ironstone Waras. (Illus.). 1980. 44.50 (ISBN 0-902028-86-3). Apollo.

--The Handbook of British Pottery & Porcelain Marks. (Illus.). 193p. 1983. pap. 11.50 (ISBN 0-214-20192-9, Pub. by Hutchinson Pub UK). Seven Hills Bks.

--An Illustrated Encyclopedia of British Pottery & Porcelain. 2nd ed. 416p. 1981. 110.00x (ISBN 0-214-20692-0, Pub. by Barrie & Jenkins England). State Mutual Bk.

--Illustrated Encyclopedia of British Pottery & Porcelain. 360p. 1980. 40.00 (ISBN 0-214-20692-0, Pub. by Hutchinson Pub UK). Seven Hills Bks.

--Minton Pottery & Porcelain of the First Period, 1793-1850. (Illus.). 168p. 1968. 50.00 (ISBN 0-257-66717-2, Pub. by Barrie & Jenkins England). Seven Hills Bks.

Godden, Gertrude M. Henry Fielding: A Memoir. 326p. 1980. Repr. of 1909 ed. lib. bdg. 40.00 (ISBN 0-8495-2125-4). Arden Lib.

--Mussolini: The Birth of the New Democracy. 1977. lib. bdg. 59.95 (ISBN 0-8490-2309-2). Gordon Pr.

--Mussolini: The Birth of the New Democracy. 1979. lib. bdg. 69.95 (ISBN 0-87700-300-9). Revisionist Pr.

Godden, Hilkka. Timber Reader. 1984. pap. 20.00x (ISBN 0-86237-003-5, Pub. by Selecteditions). State Mutual Bk.

Godden, Irene P. Library Technical Services: Operations & Management. (Library & Information Sciences Series). 1984. 32.00 (ISBN 0-12-287040-9). Acad Pr.

Godden, Irene P., compiled by. Collection Development & Acquisitions, 1970-80: An Annotated Critical Bibliography. LC 81-18530. 146p. 1982. 15.00 (ISBN 0-8108-1499-4). Scarecrow.

Godden, J., ed. Harrier: Ski-Jump to Victory. (Brassey Bks.). (Illus.). 160p. 1983. 18.00 (ISBN 0-08-031166-0); pap. 9.00 (ISBN 0-08-031167-9). Pergamon.

Godden, J. A. Godden's Guide to English Porcelains. 1975. 39.95x (ISBN 0-686-73980-9). Beekman Pubs.

Godden, Jean H. Carter: The Will to Win. (Illus.). 64p. hand bound 24.00 (ISBN 0-88014-024-0). Mosaic Pr OH.

--Hasty Put-Ins. (Illus.). 64p. 1982. 20.00 (ISBN 0-88014-038-0). Mosaic Pr OH.

Godden, John O., ed. Cancer in Childhood. LC 73-15003. 249p. 1974. 32.50x (ISBN 0-306-30763-4, Plenum Pr). Plenum Pub.

--Cancer in Childhood. LC 73-15003. pap. 64.80 (ISBN 0-317-30343-0, 2024715). Bks Demand UMI.

Godden, John O., ed. see Symposium, Roswell Park Memorial Institute, Buffalo, Sept. 1974.

Godden, Jon & Godden, Rumer. Shiva's Pigeons: An Experience of India. (Illus.). 384p. 1972. 25.00 (ISBN 0-670-64055-7, Studio). Viking.

Godden, Malcolm, ed. see Aelfric.

Godden, Rumer. The Battle of Villa Fiorita. 1980. pap. 1.50 (ISBN 0-380-00310-4, 23259-6). Avon.

--Breakfast with the Mikolides. 16.95 (ISBN 0-88411-647-6, Pub. by Aeonian Pr). Amereon Ltd.

--Breakfast with the Nikolides. 1975. pap. 1.50 (ISBN 0-380-00536-0, 24489). Avon.

--China Court. 288p. 1982. pap. 7.50 (ISBN 0-907746-16-0, Pub. by A Mott Ltd). Longwood Pub Group.

--The Dark Horse. LC 81-10352. 216p. 1982. 11.95 (ISBN 0-670-25664-1). Viking.

--The Diddakoi. LC 76-184788. 160p. 1972. 9.95 (ISBN 0-670-27220-5). Viking.

--The Doll's House. (Puffin Story Books). 1976. pap. 3.50 (ISBN 0-14-030942-X, Puffin). Penguin.

--The Dragon of Og. LC 81-2620. (Illus.). 64p. (gr. 4-6). 1981. 9.95 (ISBN 0-670-28168-9). Viking.

--Five for Sorrow, Ten for Joy. 256p. 1981. pap. 2.75 (ISBN 0-449-24372-9, Crest). Fawcett.

--Five for Sorrow, Ten for Joy. 1979. 10.95 (ISBN 0-670-31701-2). Viking.

--Four Dolls. LC 83-14157. (Illus.). 144p. (gr. 4-6). 1984. reinforced 11.75 (ISBN 0-688-02801-2). Greenwillow.

--Gulbadan: Portrait of a Rose Princess at the Mughal Court. LC 80-51752. (Illus.). 160p. 1981. 14.95 (ISBN 0-670-35756-1, Studio). Viking.

--Hans Christian Andersen. 1955. 30.00 (ISBN 0-8274-2466-3). R West.

--A Kindle of Kittens. LC 78-15931. (Illus.). (gr. k-3). 1979. 8.95 (ISBN 0-670-41301-1). Viking.

--Mr. McFadden's Hallowe'en. 128p. (gr. 4-6). 1975. 10.95 (ISBN 0-670-49271-X). Viking.

--The Mousewife. LC 82-2617. (Illus.). 40p. (gr. 2-5). 1982. 9.95 (ISBN 0-670-49180-2). Viking.

--The River. 16.95 (ISBN 0-88411-648-4, Pub. by Aeonian Pr). Amereon Ltd.

--The Rocking Horse Secret. LC 77-25480. (Illus.). (gr. 3-7). 1978. 11.50 (ISBN 0-670-60243-4). Viking.

--The Tale of the Tales: The Beatrix Potter Ballet. LC 79-166292. (Illus.). 208p. 1971. 21.95 (ISBN 0-7232-1421-2). Warne.

--Thursday's Children. 256p. 1984. 15.95 (ISBN 0-670-71196-9). Viking.

--The Valiant Chatti-Maker. LC 83-7000. (Illus.). 64p. (gr. 3-7). 1983. 9.95 (ISBN 0-670-74236-8, Viking Kestrel). Viking.

Godden, Rumer & Cooney, Barbara. The Story of Holly & Ivy. (Illus.). 32p. (ps-5). 1985. 12.95 (ISBN 0-670-80622-6). Viking.

Godden, Rumer, jt. auth. see Godden, Jon.

Godden, Rumer, tr. see De Gasztold, Carmen B.

Goddu, A. The Physics of William of Ockham. (Studies und Texte zur Geistesgeschichte des Mittelalters: No. 16). 310p. 1984. text ed. 39.25x (ISBN 90-04-06912-7, Pub. by E J Brill). Humanities.

Gode, Alexander. French at Sight. LC 62-17089. (gr. 9-12). text ed. 7.50 (ISBN 0-8044-0182-9); pap. 3.45 (ISBN 0-8044-6181-3). Ungar.

--Natural Science in German Romanticism. LC 70-168170. (Columbia University. Germanic Studies, New Ser.: No. 11). Repr. of 1941 ed. 19.00 (ISBN 0-404-50461-2). AMS Pr.

Gode, Alexander, jt. auth. see Stillman, Clark.

Gode, Alexander & Ungar, Frederick, eds. Anthology of German Poetry Through the Nineteenth Century. 2nd rev. ed. LC 73-163479. (Ger. & Eng.). 1963. 14.50 (ISBN 0-8044-2242-7); pap. 5.95 (ISBN 0-8044-6241-0). Ungar.

Gode, Alexander, tr. see Kraus, Karl.

Gode, Alexander, tr. see Petersen, Carol.

Godechot. Les Institutions De la France Sous la Revolution et l'Empire. 42.95 (ISBN 0-685-36097-0). French & Eur.

Godechot, Jacques. The Counter Revolution: Doctrine & Action, 1789-1804. Attanasio, Salvator, tr. from Fr. LC 70-159820. 416p. 1981. pap. 10.95 (ISBN 0-691-00788-8). Princeton U Pr.

Godecker, Sr. Mary H. Angelus Silesius' Personality. LC 76-140023. (Catholic University Studies in German Ser.: No. 10). 1970. Repr. of 1938 ed. 18.00 (ISBN 0-404-50230-X). AMS Pr.

Godefroy, Frederic. Lexique de l'ancien Francais. 544p. (Fr.). 1976. 39.95 (ISBN 0-686-57305-6, M-6282). French & Eur.

Godefroy, Vincent. The Dramatic Genius of Verdi, Vol. 2. LC 75-13981. 1978. 12.95 (ISBN 0-312-21946-6). St Martin.

Godel. Cost Estimating of Energy Conservation Systems. 1986. cancelled (ISBN 0-442-26362-7). Van Nos Reinhold.

Godel, Jules B. Guide to Information Sources in the Construction Industry. LC 73-78673. pap. 32.00 (ISBN 0-317-10840-9, 2005795). Bks Demand UMI.

--Sources of Construction Information: An Annotated Guide to Reports, Books, Periodicals, Standards, and Codes. LC 77-4671. 673p. 1977. 40.00 (ISBN 0-8108-1030-1). Scarecrow.

Godel, Kurt. Consistency of the Continuum Hypothesis. (Annals of Mathematics Studies, Vol. 3). (Orig.). 1940. pap. 14.95x (ISBN 0-691-07927-7). Princeton U Pr.

Godelier, M. Perspectives in Marxist Anthropology. Brain, R., tr. LC 76-11081. (Studies in Social Anthropology: No. 18). (Illus.). 1977. pap. 12.95 (ISBN 0-521-29098-8). Cambridge U Pr.

Godelier, Maurice. Un Domaine Conteste: L'anthropologie Economique Recueil De Textes. (Textes De Sciences Sociales: No. 5). 1974. pap. 14.00x (ISBN 90-2797-308-3). Mouton.

--The Making of Great Men: Male Domination & Power Among the New Guinea Baruya. (Cambridge Studies in Social Anthropology: No. 55). (Illus.). 272p. Date not set. price not set (ISBN 0-521-25917-7); pap. price not set (ISBN 0-521-31212-4). Cambridge U Pr.

--Rationality & Irrationality in Economics. Pearce, Brian, tr. from Fr. LC 72-92033. 336p. (Eng.). 1975. pap. 7.50 (ISBN 0-85345-349-7). Monthly Rev.

Godement, R. & Jacquet, H. Zeta-Functions of Simple Algebras. LC 72-76391. (Lecture Notes in Mathematics: Vol. 260). 197p. 1972. pap. 10.00 (ISBN 0-387-05797-8). Springer-Verlag.

Goden, D. Pest Slugs & Snails: Biology & Control. Gruber, S., tr. from Ger. (Illus.). 470p. 1983. 75.00 (ISBN 0-387-11894-2). Springer-Verlag.

Godes, Mark. Dear Bobby Simpson. LC 84-15001. 144p. (Orig.). 1984. pap. 4.95 (ISBN 0-440-51737-0, Dell Trade Pbks). Dell.

Godet, Frederic. Studies in Paul's Epistles. LC 84-7138. 1984. 11.95 (ISBN 0-8254-2723-1). Kregel.

Godet, Frederic L. Commentary on Luke. 3rd ed. LC 81-18614. (Kregel Reprint Library). 576p. 1981. Repr. of 1887 ed. 19.95 (ISBN 0-8254-2720-7). Kregel.

--Commentary on Romans. LC 77-79189. (Kregel Reprint Library). 1977. 19.95 (ISBN 0-8254-2715-0). Kregel.

--Studies in the New Testament. LC 84-7137. 398p. 1984. 12.95 (ISBN 0-8254-2722-3). Kregel.

--Studies in the Old Testament. LC 84-7143. 408p. 1984. Repr. of 1899 ed. text ed. 11.95 (ISBN 0-8254-2721-5). Kregel.

Godet, Michel. The Crisis in Forecasting & the Emergence of the "Prospective" Approach: With Case Studies in Energy & Air Transport. LC 78-10548. (Pergamon Policy Studies). 1979. 19.50 (ISBN 0-08-022487-3). Pergamon.

Godey, John. Fatal Beauty. LC 84-3068. 312p. 1984. 14.95 (ISBN 0-689-11481-8). Atheneum.

--Fatal Beauty. 1985. pap. 3.95 (ISBN 0-446-32908-8). Warner Bks.

--The Taking of Pelham One, Two, Three. 17.95 (ISBN 0-88411-649-2, Pub. by Aeonian Pr). Amereon Ltd.

--The Taking of Pelham 1-2-3. 1982. pap. 3.50 (ISBN 0-686-85862-X). Dell.

Godey's Lady's Book & Peterson's Magazine. Victorian Alphabets, Monograms & Names for Needle Workers. LC 74-79939. 128p. 1974. pap. 3.95 (ISBN 0-486-23072-4). Dover.

--Victorian Needlepoint Designs. LC 74-24489. (Illus.). 48p. 1975. pap. 2.25 (ISBN 0-486-23163-1). Dover.

Godfraind, K. & Meyer, P., eds. Cell Membrane in Function & Dysfunction of Vascular Tissue, 1981. (Argenteuil Symposia Ser.: Vol. 5). 278p. 1981. 80.50 (ISBN 0-444-80316-5, Biomedical Pr). Elsevier.

Godfraind, T. & Albertini, A., eds. Calcium Modulators: Proceedings of the International Symposium on Calcium Modulators, Venice, June 17-18, 1982. (Giovanni Lorenzini Foundation Ser.: Vol. 15). 380p. 1983. 68.00 (ISBN 0-444-80464-1, Biomedical Pr). Elsevier.

Godfraind, T., et al, eds. Calcium Entry Blockers in Cardiovascular & Cerebral Dysfunctions. 330p. 1984. lib. bdg. 55.00 (ISBN 0-89838-658-6, Pub. by Martinus Nijhoff Netherlands). Kluwer Academic.

Godfraind, Theophile, et al, eds. Calcium Entry Blockers & Tissue Protection. 276p. text ed. 46.50 (ISBN 0-89004-719-7). Raven.

Godfray, Hugh. An Elementary Treatise on the Lunar Theory. Cohen, I. Bernard, ed. LC 80-2125. (Development of Science Ser.). (Illus.). 1981. lib. bdg. 12.00x (ISBN 0-405-13847-4). Ayer Co Pubs.

Godfrey. Custer's Last Battle, 1876. (Illus.). 44p. 1976. pap. 3.95 (ISBN 0-89646-000-2). Outbooks.

--What Darwin Began. 1985. 14.29 (ISBN 0-205-08379-X, 678379). Allyn.

Godfrey & Chang. The Telidon Book. 1982. text ed. 39.95 (ISBN 0-8359-7548-7). Reston.

Godfrey, A. I. Quantitative Methods for Managers. 1977. pap. text ed. 19.95x (ISBN 0-7131-3349-X). Intl Ideas.

Godfrey, Audrey M., jt. auth. see Godfrey, Kenneth W.

Godfrey, Charles & Feldman, Michael. The Ageless Exercise Plan: A Complete Guide to Fitness after Fifty. (Illus.). 96p. 1985. pap. 8.95 (ISBN 0-07-023629-1). McGraw.

Godfrey, Charles & Price, E. A. Arithmetic. pap. 121.30 (ISBN 0-317-08560-3, 2051353). Bks Demand UMI.

Godfrey, Charles & Siddons, A. W. Four-Figure Tables. text ed. 3.50x (ISBN 0-521-05097-9). Cambridge U Pr.

Godfrey, D. Modern Technical Communication. 300p. 1983. 12.95 (ISBN 0-07-548071-9). McGraw.

Godfrey, Darren O. Stories for Killing Time. 48p. 1985. 6.95 (ISBN 0-89962-484-7). Todd & Honeywell.

Godfrey, Dave & Parkhill, Douglas. Gutenberg Two: The New Electronics & Social Change. 2nd rev. ed. 224p. 1980. 10.95 (ISBN 0-686-98075-1). Telecom Lib.

Godfrey, David & Sterling, Sharon. The Elements of CAL. 1983. text ed. 22.95 (ISBN 0-8359-1701-0); pap. text ed. 17.95 (ISBN 0-8359-1700-2). Reston.

Godfrey, Edward S. see Carroll, John M.

Godfrey, Elbert D. Unforgettable Sounds. (The Mental Therapy Ser.). 128p. 1981. 6.50 (ISBN 0-89962-030-2). Todd & Honeywell.

Godfrey, Eleanor P. & Fiedler, Fred E. Boards, Management, & Company Success. (Illus.). 134p. pap. text ed. 3.00x (ISBN 0-8134-0491-6, 491). Interstate.

Godfrey, Eleanor S. The Development of English Glassmaking, 1560-1640. LC 75-19021. xii, 288p. 1976. 25.00 (ISBN 0-8078-1256-0). U of NC Pr.

Godfrey, Elizabeth. English Children in the Olden Time. 1978. Repr. of 1907 ed. lib. bdg. 35.00 (ISBN 0-8482-4171-1). Norwood Edns.

--English Children in the Olden Time. 336p. 1980. Repr. of 1910 ed. 18.50 (ISBN 0-87928-104-9). Corner Hse.

--Yosemite Indians. (Illus.). 36p. 1977. pap. 2.50 (ISBN 0-939666-21-9). Yosemite Natl Hist.

Godfrey, F. M. Italian Architecture. 340p. 1971. 39.00x (ISBN 0-85458-290-8, Pub. by Academy Editions England). State Mutual Bk.

Godfrey, G. Bernard, tr. see Hart, F., et al.

Godfrey, Howard. Handbook on Tax-Exempt Organizations. LC 83-4537. 423p. 1983. 39.95 (ISBN 0-13-382127-7, Busn). P-H.

Godfrey, John. Dabble: Selected Poems, 1966-1980. 96p. (Orig.). 1982. 17.95 (ISBN 0-916190-12-9); pap. 6.00 (ISBN 0-916190-13-7). Full Court NY.

--Twelve Hundred & Four-the Unholy Crusade. (Illus.). 1980. 39.95x (ISBN 0-19-215834-1). Oxford U Pr.

--Where the Weather Suits My Clothes. Elmslie, Kenward, ed. 32p. 1985. pap. 6.00 (ISBN 0-915990-25-3). Z Pr.

Godfrey, John M. Monetary Expansion in the Confederacy. LC 77-14775. (Dissertations in American Economic History Ser.). 1978. 17.00 (ISBN 0-405-11034-0). Ayer Co Pubs.

Godfrey, Keith. Compartmental Models & their Application. 1983. 55.00 (ISBN 0-12-286970-2). Acad Pr.

Godfrey, Kenneth W. & Godfrey, Audrey M. Women's Voices. LC 82-5006. (Illus.). 448p. 1982. pap. 9.95 (ISBN 0-87747-909-7). Deseret Bk.

Godfrey, Laurie R., ed. Scientists Confront Creationism. 352p. 1984. pap. 7.95 (ISBN 0-393-30154-0). Norton.

Godfrey, Leslie. The Planned Vegetable Garden. 224p. 1979. 30.00x (ISBN 0-460-04401-X, Pub. by J M Dent England). State Mutual Bk.

Godfrey, M. D. Machine Independent Organic Software Tools. 2nd ed. 1983. 30.00 (ISBN 0-12-286982-6). Acad Pr.

Godfrey, Marie H. Early Settlers of Barbour Co., Ala, Vols. 1 & 2. 376p. 1979. 25.00 (ISBN 0-89308-160-4). Southern Hist Pr.

Godfrey, Martin, jt. auth. see Bienefeld, Manfred.

Godfrey, Martin, jt. auth. see Ghai, Dharam.

Godfrey, Martyn. The Beast. rev. ed. (Encounters Ser.). 96p. 1985. pap. 3.95 (ISBN 0-8219-0164-8, 35355); wkbk. 1.20 (ISBN 0-8219-0165-6, 35714). EMC.

--Spin Out. (Encounters Sre.). 96p. 1985. pap. text ed. 3.95 (ISBN 0-8219-0166-4, 35356); wkbk 1.20 (ISBN 0-8219-0167-2, 35715). EMC.

Godfrey, Michael A. A Sierra Club Naturalist's Guide to the Piedmont of Eastern North America. LC 79-22328. (Naturalists Guide Ser.). (Illus.). 432p. 1980. 19.95 (ISBN 0-87156-268-5); pap. 9.95 (ISBN 0-87156-269-3). Sierra.

--Winter Birds of the Carolinas & Nearby States. LC 76-56988. (Illus.). 1977. 10.00 (ISBN 0-910244-94-4). Blair.

Godfrey, Robert C. Session Plans. Langdon, Danny G., ed. LC 77-25427. (Instructional Design Library). (Illus.). 96p. 1978. 19.95 (ISBN 0-87778-120-6). Educ Tech Pubns.

Godfrey, Robert K. & Wooten, Jean W. Aquatic & Wetland Plants of Southeastern United States: Dicotyledons. LC 80-16452. (Illus.). 944p. 1981. lib. bdg. 45.00x (ISBN 0-8203-0532-4). U of Ga Pr.

--Aquatic & Wetland Plants of Southeastern United States: Monocotyledons. LC 76-28924. 736p. 1979. 40.00x (ISBN 0-8203-0420-4). U of Ga Pr.

Godfrey, Robert K., jt. auth. see Kurz, Herman.

Godfrey, Robert S. Building Construction Cost Data, 1984. 42nd ed. LC 55-20084. 420p. 1983. pap. 32.25 (ISBN 0-911950-63-X); pap. 25.75 members. Natl Assn Home.

--Means Man-Hour Standards. 1st ed. 576p. 1983. text ed. 89.95 (ISBN 0-911950-60-5). R S Means.

--Repair & Remodeling Cost Data 1984. 5th ed. LC 80-644930. 374p. 1984. pap. 35.75 (ISBN 0-911950-65-6); pap. 27.00 members. Natl Assn Home.

--Residential Light Commercial Cost Data: 1984. 3rd ed. 410p. 1984. pap. 33.25 (ISBN 0-911950-64-8). Natl Assn Home.

Godfrey, Robert S., ed. see R. S. Means Co. Staff.

Godfrey, Sima. Yale French Studies: The Anxiety of Anticipation. (No. 66). 1984. pap. 11.95x (ISBN 0-300-03180-7). Yale U Pr.

Godfrey, Sima N., tr. see Pleynet, Marcelin.

Godfrey, Smith. The English Companion: An Idiosyncratic Guide to England & Englishness from A to Z. LC 84-16036. 256p. 1985. 15.95 (ISBN 0-517-55584-0, C N Potter). Crown.

Godfrey, T. & Reichelt, J. Industrial Enzymology. 1982. 85.00x (ISBN 0-943818-00-1, Nature Pr). Groves Dict Music.

Godfrey, Thomas, ed. Murder for Christmas. LC 82-60904. (Illus.). 480p. 1982. 19.95 (ISBN 0-89296-057-4); ltd. ed. 35.00 (ISBN 0-89296-058-2). Mysterious Pr.

Godfrey, Vincent. The Man Who Broke a Thousand Chains. LC 67-23365. (Illus.). 1968. 12.50 (ISBN 0-87491-303-9). Acropolis.

Godfrey, W. Earl. Birds of Canada. Crosby, John A., tr. (Illus.). 1966. 27.50 (ISBN 0-660-00126-8, 56282-4, Pub. by Natl Mus Canada). Nat Gal Can.

Godfrey, W. H., ed. The Parish of Chelsea, Part 4: The Royal Hospital, Chelsea. LC 71-138271. (London County Council. Survey of London: No. 11). Repr. of 1927 ed. 74.50 (ISBN 0-404-51661-0). AMS Pr.

Godfrey, W. Robert & Boyd, Jesse L., III, eds. Through Christ's Word: A Festschrift for Philip E. Hughes. 272p. (Orig.). Date not set. pap. 10.95 (ISBN 0-87552-274-2). Presby & Reformed.

Godfrey, Walter H., ed. Parish of Chelsea, Pt. 1. LC 71-138271. (London County Council. Survey of London: No. 2). Repr. of 1909 ed. 74.50 (ISBN 0-404-51652-1). AMS Pr.

--The Parish of St. Pancras, Part 4: King's Cross Neighbourhood. LC 76-37851. (London County Council. Survey of London: No. 24). Repr. of 1952 ed. 74.50 (ISBN 0-404-51674-2). AMS Pr.

Godfrey, William G. Pursuit of Profit & Preferment in Colonial North America: John Bradstreet's Quest. 346p. 1982. text ed. 23.45x (ISBN 0-88920-108-0, Pub. by Wilfrid Laurier U Pr). Humanities.

Godfriaux, Bruce L., ed. Power Plant Waste Heat Utilization in Aquaculture. LC 78-73590. 288p. 1979. text ed. 38.00 (ISBN 0-916672-24-7). Allanheld.

Godi, Art. Creative Listing Handbook. LC 80-23493. (Illus.). 267p. (Orig.). 1981. 14.95 (ISBN 0-913652-24-5, 124). Realtors Natl.

Godin. The Analysis of Tides. 292p. 1982. 70.00x (ISBN 0-85323-441-8, Pub. by Liverpool Univ England). State Mutual Bk.

Godin, Alfred. Wild Mammals of New England. (Illus.). 208p. 1985. pap. 8.95 (ISBN 0-89933-012-6). Globe Pequot.

Godin, Alfred J. Wild Mammals of New England. LC 77-4785. (Illus.). 320p. 1977. 28.50 (ISBN 0-8018-1964-4). Johns Hopkins.

Godin, Andre. The Psychology of Religious Vocations: Problems of the Religious Life. Wauck, LeRoy A., ed. LC 82-24708. 136p. (Orig.). 1983. lib. bdg. 21.50 (ISBN 0-8191-3007-9); pap. text ed. 9.25 (ISBN 0-8191-3008-7). U Pr of Amer.

--Psycological Dynamics of Religious Experience. Turton, Mary, tr. from Fr. Orig. Title: Psychologie des Experiences Religieuses. 240p. 1985. pap. 13.95 (ISBN 0-89135-039-X). Religious Educ.

Godine, David R. The Well Made Book. (Illus.). 48p. Date not set. 6.95 (ISBN 0-87923-481-4). Godine.

Godine, David R., jt. auth. see Dubus, Andre.

Goding, James W. Monoclonal Antibodies. 1984. 24.50 (ISBN 0-12-287020-4). Acad Pr.

Godish, Thaddeus. Air Quality: Concepts, Issues, & Practice. (Illus.). 400p. 1985. 39.95 (ISBN 0-87371-019-3). Lewis Pubs Inc.

Godiwalla, Yezdi H. Strategic Management: Broadening Business Policy. LC 82-22483. 320p. 1983. 39.95 (ISBN 0-03-059388-3). Praeger.

Godiwalla, Yezdi M., et al. Corporate Strategy & Functional Management. LC 79-65182. 160p. 1979. 29.95x (ISBN 0-03-049781-7). Praeger.

Godkin, E. L. Unforeseen Tendencies of Democracy. 1976. lib. bdg. 59.95 (ISBN 0-8490-2784-5). Gordon Pr.

Godkin, Edwin L. Life & Letters of Edwin Lawrence Godkin, 2 vols. Ogden, Rollo, ed. LC 70-137055. 1972. Repr. of 1907 ed. lib. bdg. 32.50x (ISBN 0-8371-5516-9, GOLL). Greenwood.

--Reflections & Comments, Eighteen Sixty-Five to Eighteen Ninety-Five. 15.00 (ISBN 0-8369-7315-1, 8108). Ayer Co Pubs.

--Unforeseen Tendencies of Democracy. facsimile ed. LC 76-37153. (Essay Index Reprint Ser). Repr. of 1898 ed. 20.00 (ISBN 0-8369-2500-9). Ayer Co Pubs.

Godkin, James. Land War in Ireland. LC 72-102605. (Irish Culture & History Ser). 1970. Repr. of 1870 ed. 42.50x (ISBN 0-8046-0782-6, Pub. by Kennikat). Assoc Faculty Pr.

Godlas, Alan, tr. see Nurbakhsh, Javad.

Godlewski, Nancy, ed. see Muntzing, L. Manning.

Godley, A. D. Reliquiae, 2 vols. Fletcher, C. R., ed. 1973. Repr. of 1926 ed. 75.00 (ISBN 0-8274-0201-5). R West.

Godley, A. D., ed. see Moore, Thomas.

Godley, Michael R. The Mandarin-Capitalists from Nanyang: Overseas Chinese Enterprise in the Modernisation of China 1893-1911. (Cambridge Studies in Chinese History, Literature & Institutions Ser.). (Illus.). 288p. 1981. 52.50 (ISBN 0-521-23626-6). Cambridge U Pr.

Godley, Wynne & Cripps, Francis. Macroeconomics. (Masterguides Ser.). 1983. 19.95 (ISBN 0-19-215358-7). Oxford U Pr.

Godlington, Doug, jt. auth. see Heller, Mark.

Godlington, Douglas. Tackle Ski-ing. pap. 8.95x (ISBN 0-09-117721-9, SpS). Sportshelf.

Godlovitch, et al. Animals, Men & Morals. 1974. pap. 2.95 (ISBN 0-394-17825-4, E625, Ever). Grove.

Godman & Marquis, eds. Paediatric Cardiology Vol. 2: Heart Disease in the Neonate. (Illus.). 1979. text ed. 57.50 (ISBN 0-443-01921-5). Churchill.

Godman, A. & Payne, E. M. F. Longman Dictionary of Scientific Usage. (Illus.). 1979. pap. text ed. 15.95x (ISBN 0-582-52587-X). Longman.

Godman, Arthur. Barnes & Noble Thesaurus of Chemistry. (Illus.). 256p. (gr. 11 up). 1983. 13.41i (ISBN 0-06-015175-7); pap. 6.68i (ISBN 0-06-463578-3, EH 578). B&N NY.

--Barnes & Noble Thesaurus of Computer Science: The Principles of Computer Science Explained & Illustrated. LC 83-48348. (Illus.). 256p. 1984. 13.41i (ISBN 0-06-015270-2); pap. 6.68i (ISBN 0-06-463594-5). Har-Row.

--Barnes & Noble Thesaurus of Science. (Illus.). 256p. (gr. 11 up). 1983. 13.41i (ISBN 0-06-015176-5, EH 580); pap. 6.68i (ISBN 0-06-463580-5, EH 580). B&N NY.

--The Color-Coded Guide to Microcomputers. LC 83-47884. (Illus.). 256p. 1983. 9.95i (ISBN 0-06-463590-2, EH 590). B&N NY.

--The Color-Coded Guide to Microcomputers. 1984. pap. 9.57 (ISBN 0-06-463590-2). Har-Row.

--Illustrated Dictionary of Chemistry in English with English-Arabic & Arabic-English Glossaries. 1982. 12.00x (ISBN 0-86685-352-9). Intl Bk Ctr.

--Illustrated Dictionary of Science in English with English-Arabic & Arabic-English Glossaries. 1982. 12.00x (ISBN 0-86685-354-5). Intl Bk Ctr.

--Longman Illustrated Dictionary of Chemistry. (Illustrated Dictionaries Ser.). (Illus.). 256p. 1982. text ed. 7.95x (ISBN 0-582-55550-7). Longman.

Godman, David, ed. Be As You Are: The Teachings of Sri Ramana Maharshi. 256p. 1985. pap. 8.95 (ISBN 1-85063-006-2, Ark Paperbacks). Routledge & Kegan.

Godman, F. Ducane, ed. see Maudslay, A. P.

Godman, Henry. Supreme Commander. Dudley, Cliff, ed. LC 80-80658. 128p. 1980. pap. 3.95 (ISBN 0-89221-076-1). New Leaf.

Godman, John D. American Natural History: Mastogogy & Rambles of a Naturalist, Part No. 1, 3 vols. in one. LC 73-17821. (Natural Sciences in America Ser.). (Illus.). 1079p. 1974. Repr. 74.00x (ISBN 0-405-05737-7). Ayer Co Pubs.

Godman, Peter, ed. Alcuin: The Bishops, Kings, & Saints of York. (Medieval Texts Ser.). 1982. 74.00x (ISBN 0-19-822262-9). Oxford U Pr.

--Poetry of the Carolingian Renaissance. LC 84-40699. (Illus.). 384p. 1985. 39.50x (ISBN 0-8061-1939-X). U of Okla Pr.

Godman, Stanley, tr. see Badt, Kurt.

Godman, Stanley, tr. see Blume, Friedrich.

Godman, Stanley, tr. see Jaspers, Karl.

Godnick, Newton E., jt. auth. see Tepper, Bette.

Godoli, Ezio, jt. auth. see Borsi, Franco.

Godolphin, F. R., ed. & intro. by. Great Classical Myths. LC 64-10293. 7.95 (ISBN 0-394-60417-2). Modern Lib.

Godon, Lesley. A Country Herbal. (Illus.). 9.98 (ISBN 0-8317-4446-4). Smith Pubs.

Godoretzky, N. T. The Humiliated Christ in Modern Russian Thought. 59.95 (ISBN 0-8490-0376-8). Gordon Pr.

Godow, Annette G. Human Sexuality. LC 81-14031. (Illus.). 669p. 1982. text ed. 18.95 (ISBN 0-8016-1861-4). Mosby.

Godown, Marian & Rawchuck, Alberta. Yesterday's Ft. Myers. LC 75-559. (Historic Cities Ser.: No. 15). (Illus.). 1975. 7.95 (ISBN 0-912458-49-6). E A Seemann.

Godoy, Horacio H., jt. auth. see Lagos, Gustavo.

Godoy, Jose F. Porfirio Diaz. 1976. lib. bdg. 59.95 (ISBN 0-8490-0880-8). Gordon Pr.

Godoy, R., jt. ed. see Ferraro, R.

Godschalk, David R. & Brower, David J. Constitutional Issues of Growth Management. LC 78-71241. 476p. 1979. pap. 20.95 (ISBN 0-918286-16-6). Planners Pr.

--Constitutional Issues of Growth Management. rev. ed. 476p. 1979. pap. 18.95 (ISBN 0-318-12953-1); pap. 16.95 members (ISBN 0-318-12954-X). Am Plan Assn.

Godschalk, David R., ed. Planning in America: Learning from Turbulence. 240p. 1974. pap. 10.00 (ISBN 0-318-13052-1); pap. 8.00 members (ISBN 0-318-13053-X). Am Plan Assn.

Godsey, John D. Preface to Bonhoeffer: The Man & Two of His Shorter Writings. LC 79-7378. 80p. 1979. pap. 3.50 (ISBN 0-8006-1367-8, 1-1367). Fortress.

Godsey, John D., jt. ed. see Kelly, Geffrey B.

Godshald, William, ed. see Robinson, Randal F.

Godshalk, Fred I., et al. Measurement of Writing Ability. LC 66-15921. (Research Monograph: No. 6). 92p. 1966. pap. 6.50 (ISBN 0-87447-060-9, 251700). College Bd.

Godshalk, W. L. The Marlovian World Picture. (Studies in English Literature: No. 93). 224p. 1974. pap. text ed. 32.00x (ISBN 90-2793-252-2). Mouton.

Godshalk, W. L., ed. see Glasgow, Ellen.

Godshalk, William, ed. see Halio, Jay L. & Millard, Barbara C.

Godshalk, William, ed. see Harvey, Nancy L. & Carey, Anna K.

Godshalk, William, ed. see Hinchcliffe, Judith.

Godshalk, William, ed. see Jacobs, Henry.

Godshalk, William L. In Quest of Cabell. (James Branch Cabell Ser.). 1975. lib. bdg. 69.95 (ISBN 0-87700-217-7). Revisionist Pr.

--Patterning in Shakespearean Drama: Essays in Criticism. LC 72-94504. (De Proprietatibus Litterarum, Ser. Practica: No. 69). 199p. 1973. pap. text ed. 27.20x (ISBN 90-2792-472-4). Mouton.

Godshalk, William L., ed. Twelfth Night: An Annotated Bibliography. 1984. lib. bdg. 20.00 (ISBN 0-8240-9324-0). Garland Pub.

Godshalk, William L., ed. see Forker, et al.

Godshalk, William L., ed. see Hinchcliffe, Judith.

Godshall, C. David. Prayers in Dialogue: Series C. 1972. 5.75 (ISBN 0-89536-189-2). CSS of Ohio.

Godshall, David C. Prayers in Dialogue B: (Con-Luth) 1984. 6.50 (ISBN 0-89536-692-4, 4869). CSS of Ohio.

Godson. Thirty-Five Years of NATO. 1984. 15.95 (ISBN 0-317-30929-3). Dodd.

Godson, Joseph, jt. ed. see Schapiro, Leonard.

Godson, Roy. American Labor & European Politics: The AFL As a Transnational Force. LC 76-491. 230p. 1976. 17.50x (ISBN 0-8448-0919-5); pap. 9.95x (ISBN 0-8448-0920-9). Crane-Russak Co.

--The Kremlin & Labor: A Study in National Security Policy. LC 77-85317. (Strategy Paper Ser.: No. 32). 79p. 1977. 9.95x (ISBN 0-8448-1274-9); pap. 3.25x (ISBN 0-8448-1225-0). Crane-Russak Co.

--Labor in Soviet Global Strategy. LC 83-27116. (NSIC Strategy Paper Ser.: No. 40). (Illus.). 120p. 1984. pap. 6.95x (ISBN 0-8448-1472-5). Crane-Russak Co.

Godson, Roy & Haseler, Stephen. Eurocommunism: Implications for East & West. LC 78-15475. 1979. 22.50x (ISBN 0-312-26720-7); pap. 8.95 (ISBN 0-312-26721-5). St Martin.

Godson, Roy, jt. auth. see Lefever, Ernest W.

Godson, Roy, ed. Analysis & Estimates. (Intelligence Requirements for the 1980's: Vol. 2). 224p. 1980. pap. 7.50 (ISBN 0-87855-827-6). Transaction Bks.

--Clandestine Collection. (Intelligence Requirements for the Nineteen Eighties Ser.: Vol. 5). 225p. 1982. pap. 8.50 (ISBN 0-87855-831-4). Transaction Bks.

--Counterintelligence. (Intelligence Requirements for the Nineteen Eighties Ser.: Vol. 3). 384p. 1981. pap. 7.95 (ISBN 0-87855-829-2). Transaction Bks.

--Covert Action. (Intelligence Requirements for the Nineteen Eighties Ser.: Vol. 4). 200p. 1981. pap. 7.50 (ISBN 0-87855-830-6). Transaction Bks.

--Elements of Intelligence, Vol. I. rev. ed. (Intelligence Requirements for the 1980's: Vol. VI). 150p. 1983. pap. 6.00 (ISBN 0-87855-954-X). Transaction Bks.

--Intelligence Requirements for the 1980's: Intelligence & Policy. 1985. 14.95x (ISBN 0-669-10901-0); pap. text ed. price not set (ISBN 0-669-11134-1). Lexington Bks.

Godson, Roy S., jt. auth. see Shultz, Richard H., Jr.

Godson, Susan H. Viking of Assault: Admiral John Leslie Hall, Jr., & Amphibious Warfare. LC 81-43489. (Illus.). 250p. (Orig.). 1982. lib. bdg. 26.00 (ISBN 0-8191-2159-2); pap. text ed. 12.00 (ISBN 0-8191-2160-6). U Pr of Amer.

Godson, V. see Diamond, Donald R. & McLoughlin, J. B.

Godson, W. L., jt. auth. see Iribarne, J. V.

Godstein, Sidney M., jt. auth. see Corning Museum of Glass.

Godstow Nunnery. The English Register of Godstow Nunnery, Pt. 1. Clark, A., ed. (EETS, OS Ser.: No. 129). Repr. of 1905 ed. 29.00 (ISBN 0-527-00124-4). Kraus Repr.

--The English Register of Godstow Nunnery, Pts. 2 & 3. Clark, A., ed. (EETS, OS Ser.: No. 130). Repr. of 1911 ed. Set. 36.00 (ISBN 0-527-00125-2). Kraus Repr.

Godwin, A. H. Gilbert & Sullivan: A Critical Appreciation of the Savoy Operas. LC 68-26216. 1969. Repr. of 1926 ed. 22.50x (ISBN 0-8046-0170-4, Pub. by Kennikat). Assoc Faculty Pr.

--Gilbert & Sullivan: A Critical Approach to the Savoy Operas. 1926. 20.00 (ISBN 0-8274-2408-6). R West.

Godwin, Benjamin. Lectures on Slavery. LC 74-79808. Repr. of 1836 ed. cancelled (ISBN 0-8371-4591-0, GOL&, Pub. by Negro U Pr). Greenwood.
Godwin, Christine, jt. auth. see Schneller, Gertrude.
Godwin, David. Godwin's Practical Encyclopedia of Cabalistic Magick. 2nd, rev. & expanded ed. Weschcke, Carl L., ed. (Sourcebook Ser.). 500p. 1981. pap. 15.00 (ISBN 0-87542-292-6, L-292). Llewellyn Pubns.
Godwin, David J., et al. Computed Tomography of the Chest. (Illus.). 492p. 1984. text ed. 65.00 (ISBN 0-397-50591-4, 65-07560, Lippincott Medical). Lippincott.
Godwin, Edward & Godwin, Stephani. Warrior Bard: The Life of William Morris. LC 70-103190. 1970. Repr. of 1947 ed. 19.50x (ISBN 0-8046-0827-X, Pub. by Kennikat). Assoc Faculty Pr.
--Warrior Bird: The Life of William Morris. 1978. Repr. of 1947 ed. lib. bdg. 25.00 (ISBN 0-8495-1938-1). Arden Lib.
Godwin, Edward & Godwin, Stepheni. Warrior Bard: The Life of William Morris. 176p. 1980. Repr. lib. bdg. 25.00 (ISBN 0-8492-4955-4). R West.
Godwin, Elizabeth. The Passion & the Rage. 1980. pap. 1.95 (ISBN 0-449-14320-1, GM). Fawcett.
Godwin, Fay & Purves, Peter. Tess: The Story of a Guide Dog. (Illus.). 128p. 1981. 11.95 (ISBN 0-575-02959-5, Pub. by Gollancz England). David & Charles.
Godwin, Fay, photos by. Land. Fowles, John, ed. LC 85-50112. 1985. 35.00 (ISBN 0-316-29114-5); signed, numbered ltd. ed. 100.00 (ISBN 0-316-31825-6). Little.
Godwin, Francis. The Man in the Moon or a Discourse of a Voyage Thither by D. Gonsales. Mabon, E., tr. LC 77-38188. (English Experience Ser.: No. 459). 136p. 1972. Repr. of 1638 ed. 20.00 (ISBN 90-221-0459-1). Walter J Johnson.
Godwin, Frank. Connie. Blackbeard, Bill, ed. LC 76-53041. 1977. 15.95 (ISBN 0-88355-637-5); pap. 6.95 (ISBN 0-88355-636-7). Hyperion Conn.
Godwin, G. Conversations with George Moore. LC 73-21564. (English Literature Ser., No. 33). 1974. lib. bdg. 49.95x (ISBN 0-8383-1811-8). Haskell.
Godwin, Gail. Dream Children. 256p. 1983. pap. 3.50 (ISBN 0-380-62406-0, 62406-0, Bard). Avon.
--The Finishing School. 336p. 1985. 16.95 (ISBN 0-670-31494-3). Viking.
--Glass People. 224p. 1979. pap. 3.50 (ISBN 0-446-30568-5). Warner Bks.
--Mr. Bedford & the Muses. LC 83-47870. 240p. 1983. 14.95 (ISBN 0-670-49235-3). Viking.
--Mr. Bedford & the Muses. (General Ser.). 1984. lib. bdg. 15.95 (ISBN 0-8161-3673-4, Large Print Bks). G K Hall.
--Mr. Bedford & the Muses. 240p. (Orig.). 1984. pap. 3.95 (ISBN 0-380-69377-1). Avon.
--A Mother & Two Daughters. LC 81-65286. 576p. 1982. 16.95 (ISBN 0-670-49021-0). Viking.
--A Mother & Two Daughters. 608p. 1983. pap. 3.95 (ISBN 0-380-61598-3, 61598-3). Avon.
--The Odd Woman. 432p. 1983. pap. 3.95 (ISBN 0-446-30569-3, 305693). Warner Bks.
--The Odd Woman. (Contemporary American Fiction Ser.). 432p. 1985. pap. 6.95 (ISBN 0-14-008221-2). Penguin.
--The Perfectionists. 224p. 1985. pap. 5.95 (ISBN 0-317-19382-1). Penguin.
--Violet Clay. 368p. 1979. pap. 3.95 (ISBN 0-446-30567-7). Warner Bks.
Godwin, Gail & Ravenel, Shannon, eds. The Best American Short Stories, 1985. Duel ed. 320p. 1985. 14.95 (ISBN 0-395-36450-7); pap. 8.95 (ISBN 0-395-39058-3). HM.
Godwin, George. The Great Mystics. LC 74-2430. (St. Paul, Plotinus, St. Augustine, St. Francis, St. Teresa, Martin Luther, Jacob Boehme, George Fox, Emanuel Swedenborg, William Blake). 1945. lib. bdg. 22.50 (ISBN 0-8414-4499-4). Folcroft.
--London Shadows: A Glance at the "Homes" of the Thousands. LC 84-48273. (The Rise of Urban Britain Ser.). 79p. 1985. 20.00 (ISBN 0-8240-6275-2). Garland Pub.
Godwin, H. J. Inequalities on Distribution Functions. (Griffin's Statistical Monograph: No. 16). 96p. 1964. pap. 10.95x (ISBN 0-85264-043-9). Lubrecht & Cramer.
Godwin, Harry. The Archives of the Peat Bogs. (Illus.). 1981. 65.00 (ISBN 0-521-23784-X). Cambridge U Pr.
--Fenland: Its Ancient Past & Uncertain Future. LC 77-8824. (Illus.). 1978. 37.50 (ISBN 0-521-21768-7). Cambridge U Pr.
--History of the British Flora: A Factual Basis for Phytogeography. 2nd ed. (Cambridge Science Classics Ser.). 551p. 1984. pap. 34.50 (ISBN 0-521-26941-5). Cambridge U Pr.
Godwin, Johnnie C. Layman's Bible Book Commentary: Mark, Vol. 16. LC 78-54774. 1979. 5.75 (ISBN 0-8054-1186-0). Broadman.
Godwin, Joscelyn. Cosmic Music: Keys for the Musical Interpretation of Reality. 260p. 1985. pap. 9.95 (ISBN 0-89281-070-X). Inner Tradit.
--Mystery Religions: In the Ancient World. LC 81-47423. (Illus.). 180p. (Orig.). 1981. pap. 9.57i (ISBN 0-06-063140-6, CN4020, HarpR). Har-Row.
Godwin, Joscelyn, ed. see Scarlatti, Allessandro.
Godwin, Joscelyn, tr. see Guenon, Rene.
Godwin, Lamond, jt. auth. see Marshall, F. Ray.
Godwin, Nadine. Complete Guide to Travel Agency Automation. LC 81-83505. (Travel Management Library). (Illus.). 160p. 1982. 12.95 (ISBN 0-916032-13-2). Merton Hse.
Godwin, Pacho. Beloved Exile. LC 83-45995. 432p. (Orig.). 1984. pap. 6.95 (ISBN 0-553-34101-4). Bantam.
Godwin, Parke. The Fire When It Comes. LC 82-45108. (Science Fiction Ser.). 192p. 1984. 11.95 (ISBN 0-385-18171-X). Doubleday.
--A New Study of the Sonnets of Shakespeare. LC 78-168172. Repr. of 1900 ed. 21.50 (ISBN 0-404-02848-9). AMS Pr.
--A Popular View of the Doctrines of Charles Fourier. 2nd ed. LC 72-2951. Repr. of 1844 ed. 10.00 (ISBN 0-404-10716-8). AMS Pr.
--A Popular View of the Doctrines of Charles Fourier. Bd. with Democracy, Constructive & Pacific. 55p. LC 77-187451. (The American Utopian Adventure Ser.). 175p. 1973. Repr. of 1844 ed. lib. bdg. 19.50x (ISBN 0-87991-006-2). Porcupine Pr.
Godwin, Parke, jt. auth. see Kaye, Marvin.
Godwin, Paul H. The Chinese Defense Establishment: Continuity & Change in the 1980s. LC 83-5834. (Special Studies on East Asia). 198p. 1983. softcover 25.00x (ISBN 0-86531-568-X). Westview.
Godwin, Paul S. Armed Forces of the People's Republic of China. 245p. 1999. lib. bdg. 25.00 (ISBN 0-8133-0086-X). Westview.
Godwin, R. Kenneth, jt. auth. see Miller, Warren B.
Godwin, Shiri. Christian Social Thought in India, 1962-77. (Orig.). 1983. pap. 6.00 (ISBN 0-8364-0988-4, Pub. by Christian Lit Soc India). South Asia Bks.
Godwin, Stephani, jt. auth. see Godwin, Edward.
Godwin, Stephen R. & Peterson, George E. Guide to Assessing Capital Stock Condition, Vol. 2. Hatry, Harry P., ed. LC 84-7437. (Guides to Managing Urban Capital Ser.). 32p. (Orig.). 1984. pap. text ed. 10.00x (ISBN 0-87766-337-8). Urban Inst.
Godwin, Stepheni, jt. auth. see Godwin, Edward.
Godwin, William. The Adventures of Caleb Williams. LC 80-2481. Repr. of 1926 ed. 49.50 (ISBN 0-404-19115-0). AMS Pr.
--The Adventures of Caleb Williams, or, Things As They Are. LC 67-71435. 1966. 7.95 (ISBN 0-304-91758-3). Dufour.
--Caleb Williams. McCracken, David, ed. 1977. pap. 8.95 (ISBN 0-393-00861-4, N861, Norton Lib). Norton.
--Caleb Williams. McCracken, David, ed. (Oxford English Novels Ser). 1970. 9.95x (ISBN 0-19-255331-3). Oxford U Pr.
--Cloudesley: A Tale, 3 vols. in 1. LC 79-8270. Repr. of 1830 ed. 44.50 (ISBN 0-404-61863-4). AMS Pr.
--De la Justice Politique. Pollin, Burton R., ed. Constant, Benjamin, tr. LC 72-6661. 1972. 49.50x (ISBN 0-87395-175-1). State U NY Pr.
--Deloraine, 3 vols. in 2. LC 79-8271. Repr. of 1833 ed. Set. 84.50 (ISBN 0-404-61867-7). AMS Pr.
--Elopement of Percy Bysshe Shelley & Mary Wollenstonecraft. LC 77-1972. 1911. lib. bdg. 12.50 (ISBN 0-8414-4300-9). Folcroft.
--Enquirer. LC 65-26365. Repr. of 1797 ed. 37.50x (ISBN 0-678-00129-4). Kelley.
--Enquiry Concerning Political Justice. 59.95 (ISBN 0-8490-0121-8). Gordon Pr.
--Enquiry Concerning Political Justice. abr. ed. Carter, K. Codell, ed. 1971. pap. 9.95x (ISBN 0-19-871019-4). Oxford U Pr.
--Enquiry Concerning Political Justice. Kramnick, Isaac, ed. (Classics Ser.). 828p. 1986. pap. 6.95 (ISBN 0-14-040030-3, Pelican). Penguin.
--Essays. LC 77-23245. 1977. Repr. of 1873 ed. lib. bdg. 35.00 (ISBN 0-8414-4502-8). Folcroft.
--Essays. 293p. 1980. Repr. of 1873 ed. lib. bdg. 35.00 (ISBN 0-8492-4974-0). R West.
--Fleetwood, or, the New Man of Feeling. LC 72-162889. (Bentley's Standard Novels: No. 22). Repr. of 1832 ed. 25.00 (ISBN 0-404-54422-3). AMS Pr.
--Fleetwood: or, The New Man of Feeling, 3 vols. Paulson, Ronald, ed. LC 78-60852. (Novel 1720-1805 Ser.: Vol. 14). 1979. Set. lib. bdg. 112.00 (ISBN 0-8240-3663-8). Garland Pub.
--Four Early Pamphlets, 1783-1784. LC 66-10082. 1966. 50.00x (ISBN 0-8201-1022-1). Schol Facsimiles.
--Godwin's Political Justice: A Reprint of the Essay on Property. 1890. 29.00 (ISBN 0-403-00021-1). Scholarly.
--Life of Geoffrey Chaucer, 4 vols. LC 71-168173. Repr. of 1804 ed. Set. 145.00 (ISBN 0-404-02850-0). AMS Pr.
--Lives of the Necromancers. lib. bdg. 69.95 (ISBN 0-87968-281-7). Gordon Pr.
--Mandeville: A Tale of the Seventeenth Century in England, 3 vols. in 2. LC 79-8272. Repr. of 1817 ed. Set. 84.50 (ISBN 0-404-61871-5). Vol. 1 (ISBN 0-404-61872-3). Vol. 2 (ISBN 0-404-61873-1). AMS Pr.
--Mandeville: A Tale of the Seventeenth Century in England, 3 vols. Repr. of 1817 ed. Set. lib. bdg. 400.00 (ISBN 0-89984-199-6). Century Bookbindery.
--Memoirs of Mary Wollstonecraft. 1973. lib. bdg. 75.00 (ISBN 0-87968-022-9). Gordon Pr.
--Memoirs of Mary Wollstonecraft. LC 72-92965. (English Biography Ser., No. 31). 1969. Repr. of 1927 ed. lib. bdg. 49.95x (ISBN 0-8383-0975-5). Haskell.
--Memoirs of the Author of a Vindication of the Rights of Woman. (The Feminist Controversy in England, 1788-1810 Ser.). 1974. lib. bdg. 61.00 (ISBN 0-8240-0861-8). Garland Pub.
--Of Population. LC 63-23523. Repr. of 1820 ed. 45.00x (ISBN 0-678-00030-1). Kelley.
--The Pantheon: or, Ancient History of the Gods of Greece & Rome. Feldman, Burton & Richardson, Robert D., eds. LC 78-60886. (Myth & Romanticism Ser.). 1984. lib. bdg. 80.00 (ISBN 0-8240-3560-7). Garland Pub.
--Political Justice. 59.95 (ISBN 0-8490-0873-5). Gordon Pr.
--St. Leon: A Tale of the Sixteenth Century. LC 74-162884. (Illus.). Repr. of 1835 ed. 32.50 (ISBN 0-404-54405-3). AMS Pr.
--St. Leon: A Tale of the Sixteenth Century. LC 70-131318. (Gothic Novels Ser). 1971. Repr. of 1831 ed. 46.50 (ISBN 0-405-00802-3). Ayer Co Pubs.
--St. Leon: A Tale of the Sixteenth Century, 4 vols. (The Feminist Controversy in England, 1788-1810 Ser.). 1974. Set. lib. bdg. 242.00 (ISBN 0-8240-0862-6). Garland Pub.
--Thoughts on Man, His Nature, Productions, & Discoveries. LC 68-55719. Repr. of 1831 ed. 37.50x (ISBN 0-678-00442-0). Kelley.
--Uncollected Writings 1785-1822. LC 68-24208. (Illus.). 1968. 60.00x (ISBN 0-8201-1023-X). Schol Facsimiles.
Godwin-Austen, H. N., jt. auth. see Blandford, W. T.
Godwin-Austen, Robert, jt. auth. see Forbes, Edward.
Godwin-Jones, Robert, tr. from Ger. Tales of Courtship by Jeremias Gotthelf. LC 84-48102. (American University Studies I (Germanic Languages & Literature): Vol. 35). 241p. 1984. text ed. 28.00 (ISBN 0-8204-0177-3). P Lang Pubs.
Gody, Dale & Ross, Monique. How to Dress Rich. 128p. 1983. pap. 6.95 (ISBN 0-671-45334-3, Fireside). S&S.
Godzich, Wlad, tr. see Todorov, Tzvetan.
Goe, Vernon, jt. auth. see Labbe, John T.
Goebbels, Joseph. Communism with the Mask Off: The Jewish Origin of Communism. 1982. lib. bdg. 59.95 (ISBN 0-87700-406-4). Revisionist Pr.
--Goebbels Diaries, Nineteen Forty-Two to Nineteen Forty-Three. Lochner, Louis P., tr. LC 74-108391. Repr. of 1948 ed. lib. bdg. 45.00 (ISBN 0-8371-3815-9, GODI). Greenwood.
--My Part in Germany's Fight. 1984. lib. bdg. 79.95 (ISBN 0-87700-614-8). Revisionist Pr.
Goebel, jt. auth. see Banas.
Goebel, C. J., jt. ed. see Freund, Peter G.
Goebel, Dorothy B. & Goebel, Julius. Generals in the White House. facsimile ed. LC 78-134082. (Essay Index Reprint Ser). Repr. of 1945 ed. 18.00 (ISBN 0-8369-2501-7). Ayer Co Pubs.
Goebel, Heinz & Mueller, Traudel. DU & ICH: 00920690xtspraktisches Handbuch fuer Deutsch als Zweitsprache im Kin dergarten. 288p. 1983. 18.00 (ISBN 3-468-49990-6); Medienvorlagen 18.50 (ISBN 3-468-49991-4); Liederheft 3.50 (ISBN 3-468-49992-2). Langenscheidt.
Goebel, Jane O. Speechcraft. (Illus.). 1967. pap. text ed. 1.25x (ISBN 0-8134-0946-2, 946). Interstate.
--Speechlore. (Illus.). 66p. (gr. 5-8). 1964. pap. text ed. 1.25x (ISBN 0-8134-0170-4, 170). Interstate.
Goebel, Julius. Equality of States: A Study in the History of Law. LC 73-109921. Repr. of 1923 ed. 12.50 (ISBN 0-404-02849-7). AMS Pr.
--Felony & Misdemeanor: A Study in the History of Criminal Law. (Middle Ages Ser.). 488p. 1976. pap. 11.95x (ISBN 0-8122-1087-5, Pa Paperbacks). U of Pa Pr.
--The Struggle for the Falkland Islands: A Study in Legal & Diplomatic History. 512p. 1982. text ed. 38.00x (ISBN 0-300-02943-8); pap. text ed. 11.95x (ISBN 0-300-02945-4, Y-445). Yale U Pr.
Goebel, Julius & Naughton, T. Raymond. Law Enforcement in Colonial New York. LC 71-108239. (Criminology, Law Enforcement, & Social Problems Ser.: No. 122). 1970. Repr. of 1944 ed. 35.00x (ISBN 0-87585-122-3). Patterson Smith.
Goebel, Julius, jt. auth. see Goebel, Dorothy B.
Goebel, Julius, Jr. History of the Supreme Court, Vol. 1: Antecedents & Beginnings to 1800. Roberts, Ray, ed. 1971. 60.00 (ISBN 0-02-541350-3). Macmillan.
Goebel, Julius, Jr. & Smith, Joseph H., eds. The Law Practice of Alexander Hamilton, Vol. 1. LC 64-13900. 1964. 80.00x (ISBN 0-231-08944-9). Columbia U Pr.
--The Law Practice of Alexander Hamilton, Vol. 2. 1969. 80.00x (ISBN 0-231-08945-7). Columbia U Pr.
--The Law Practice of Alexander Hamilton, Vol. 3. 1980. 80.00x (ISBN 0-231-08946-5). Columbia U Pr.
--The Law Practice of Alexander Hamilton, Vol. 4. 1980. 80.00x (ISBN 0-231-08930-9). Columbia U Pr.
--The Law Practice of Alexander Hamilton, Vol. 5. 1981. 80.00x (ISBN 0-231-08929-5). Columbia U Pr.
Goebel, Julius L. Recognition Policy of the United States. LC 68-56657. (Columbia University Studies in the Social Sciences: No. 158). Repr. of 1915 ed. 19.50 (ISBN 0-404-51158-9). AMS Pr.
Goebel, K. Organopgraphy of Plants, Especially of the Archegoniatae & Spermatophyta, 2 Vols. Balfour, Issac B., tr. from Ger. (Illus.). 977p. 1969. Repr. of 1905 ed. lib. bdg. 35.00 (ISBN 0-02-845320-4). Lubrecht & Cramer.
Goebel, Otto. Deutsche Rohstoffwirtschaft Im Weltkrieg Einschliesslich des Hindenburg-Programms. (Wirtschafts-Und Sozialgeschichte des Weltkrieges (Deutsche Serie)). (Ger.). 1930. 75.00x (ISBN 0-317-27434-1). Elliots Bks.
Goebel, Patrice, ed. see Molnar, Paul J.
Goebel, Paul R. & Miller, Norman G. Handbook of Mortgage Mathematics & Financial Tables. (Illus.). 416p. 1981. 25.95 (ISBN 0-13-380410-0); pap. 13.95 (ISBN 0-686-71764-3). P-H.
Goebel, Paul R., jt. auth. see Miller, Norman G.
Goebel, R. & Walker, E., eds. Abelian Group Theory: Proceedings. (Lecture Notes in Mathematics Ser.: Vol. 874). 447p. 1981. pap. 27.00 (ISBN 0-387-10855-6). Springer-Verlag.
Goebel, R., et al, eds. Abelian Group Theory. (Lecture Notes in Mathematics Ser.: Vol. 1006). 771p. 1983. 32.00 (ISBN 0-387-12335-0). Springer-Verlag.
Goebel, Sylvia & Martin, Rosemary. Mattel Dolls: The 60's. 210p. (Orig.). 1979. pap. 9.95 (ISBN 0-9607128-0-1). Pixie Pr AZ.
Goebel, Ulrich, jt. auth. see McDonald, William C.
Goebel, Ulrich, et al. Johann Wolfgang von Goethe: One Hundred & Fifty Years of Continuing Vitality. LC 84-50028. (Proceedings of the Comparative Literature Symposium: Vol. 15). 232p. 1984. pap. 50.00 (ISBN 0-89672-117-5). Tex Tech Pr.
Goebel, W., ed. Genetic Approaches to Microbial Pathogenicity. (Current Topics in Microbiology & Immunology Ser.: Vol. 118). (Illus.). 310p. 1985. 59.00 (ISBN 0-387-15597-X). Springer-Verlag.
Goebell, H., ed. European Pancreatic Club: EPC 14th Meeting, Essen, Sept.-Oct. 1982, Abstracts. (Journal: Digestion: Vol. 25, No. 1). 80p. 1982. pap. 24.75 (ISBN 3-8055-3633-X). S Karger.
Goebell, H., jt. ed. see Kasper, W.
Goecke, C., ed. Actual Standing in EPH Gestosis: Proceedings of the Meeting of the Society for the Study of Pathophysiology of Pregnancy-Organization Gestosis, 16th, Aachen, 15-18 June, 1984. (International Congress Ser.: No. 657). 504p. 1985. 94.50 (ISBN 0-444-80656-3, Excerpta Medica). Elsevier.
Goedecke. Dictionary of Electrical Engineering, Telecommunications & Electronics: English-German-French, Vol. 3. 1967. 39.00 (ISBN 0-9913001-1-4, Pub. by O Brandstetter WG). Heyden.
--Dictionary of Electrical Engineering, Telecommunications & Electronics: French-English-German, Vol. 2. 1966. 34.00 (ISBN 0-9913001-0-6, Pub. by O Brandstetter WG). Heyden.
Goedecke, D. W. Dictionary of Materials Testing, 3 vols. 1979. 169.00 (ISBN 0-9961073-1-2, Pub. by VDI W Germany). Heyden.
Goedecke, W. Woerterbuch der Elektrotechnik, Fernmeldetechnik und Elektonik, Vol. 1. (Ger., Eng. & Fr., Dictionary of Electrical Engineering, Telecommunication Engineering & Electronics). 1966-68. 56.00 (ISBN 3-87097-013-8, M-7018). French & Eur.
--Woerterbuch der Elektrotechnik, Fernmeldetechnik und Elektronik, Vol. 2. (Fr., Eng. & Ger., Dictionary of Electrical Engineering, Telecommuunications Engineering & Electronics). 1966-68. 56.00 (ISBN 3-87097-014-6, M-7019). French & Eur.
Goedert, Jeanne E. Generalizing From the Experimental Housing Allowance Program: An Assessment of Site Characteristics. write for info. Urban Inst.
Goedert, Jeanne E. & Goodman, John L., Jr. Indicators of the Quality of U. S. Housing. 55p. 1977. pap. 10.00x (ISBN 0-87766-204-5, 20200). Urban Inst.
Goedhard, W. J., ed. see World Congress on Ballistocardiography & Cardiovascular Dynamics, 4th, Amsterdam, April 14-16, 1975.
Goedhart, C., ed. Jelle Zijlstra, a Central Banker's View. 1985. lib. bdg. 32.90 (ISBN 90-247-3184-4, Pub. by Martinus Nijhoff Netherlands). Kluwer Academic.
Goedicke, Hans. Near Eastern Studies: In Honor of William Foxwell Albright. LC 70-142817. 504p. 1971. 40.00x (ISBN 0-8018-1235-6). Johns Hopkins.
--The Protocol of Neferyt. LC 76-47371. (Near East Studies). 216p. 1977. text ed. 19.50x (ISBN 0-8018-1905-9). Johns Hopkins.
--Re-used Blocks from the Pyramid of Amenemhet I at Lisht. LC 75-159406. (Illus.). 1972. 20.00 (ISBN 0-87099-107-8). Metro Mus Art.
--The Report about the Dispute of a Man with His Ba: Papyrus Berlin 3024. LC 70-131472. pap. 64.00 (ISBN 0-317-09898-5, 2002277). Bks Demand UMI.
--Studies in the Hekanakhte Papers. (Illus.). 154p. (Orig.). 1984. pap. text ed. 24.00 (ISBN 0-9613805-0-0). Halgo Inc.

Goedicke, Hans, ed. Perspectives on the Battle of Kadesh. (Illus.). 216p. (Orig.). pap. write for info. (ISBN 0-9613805-1-9). Halgo Inc.

Goedicke, Hans & Roberts, J. J., eds. Unity & Diversity: Essays in the History, Literature, & Religion of the Ancient Near East. LC 74-24376. (Johns Hopkins University Near Eastern Studies). pap. 60.00 (ISBN 0-317-11301-1, 2016572). Bks Demand UMI.

Goedicke, Patricia. Crossing the Same River. LC 79-18809. 64p. 1980. lib. bdg. 8.50x (ISBN 0-87023-287-8); pap. 4.50 (ISBN 0-87023-288-6). U of Mass Pr.

--The Dog That Was Barking Yesterday. (Orig.). 1979. pap. 5.00 (ISBN 0-89924-022-4). Lynx Hse.

--For the Four Corners. LC 76-365687. 60p. 1976. 3.50 (ISBN 0-87886-074-6). Ithaca Hse.

--The Trail that Turns on Itself. LC 78-7551. 81p. 1978. 3.50 (ISBN 0-87886-094-0). Ithaca Hse.

--The Wind of Our Going. 120p. (Orig.). 1985. pap. 8.00 (ISBN 0-914742-84-1). Copper Canyon.

Goedsche, C. R. Sag's Auf Deutsch: A First Book for German Conversation. (Illus., Ger.). (gr. 10 up). 1979. pap. text ed. 6.95x (ISBN 0-8290-0026-7). Irvington.

Goedsche, Charlotte, tr. see Stanzel, F. K.

Goedsche, Curt R., jt. auth. see Spann, Meno.

Goeghan, Jim, et al. Best One-Act Plays from Los Angeles: Actors' Theatre-Los Angeles Theatre Centre. Kierland, Joseph S., ed. (Illus.). 144p. (Orig.). 1985. 16.95 (ISBN 0-915572-79-6); pap. 7.95 (ISBN 0-915572-78-8). Panjandrum.

Goehl, Henry, jt. auth. see Gerber, Adele.

Goehle, Donna G. Decision Making in Multinational Corporations. Dufey, Gunter, ed. LC 80-23596. (Research for Business Decisions: No. 18). 242p. 1980. 39.95 (ISBN 0-8357-1102-1). UMI Res Pr.

Goehler, Erich. Lexikon des Nebenstrafrechts. 2nd ed. (Ger.). 1977. pap. 44.00 (ISBN 3-406-01806-8, M-7245). French & Eur.

Goehlert, Robert. City & Regional Planning: A Bibliography of Journal Literature 1945-1975. (Public Administration Ser.: P 124). 1978. pap. 5.50 (ISBN 0-88066-009-0). Vance Biblios.

--Concepts of Political & Social Authority: A Selected Bibliography. (Public Administration Ser.: Bibliography P 1655). 1985. pap. 2.25 (ISBN 0-89028-345-1). Vance Biblios.

--Congress & Law-Making: Researching the Legislative Process. LC 79-11554. 168p. 1979. pap. text ed. 13.50 (ISBN 0-87436-335-7). ABC-Clio.

--Guide to Soviet Politics. (Public Administration Ser.: Bibliography P-955). 1982. pap. 7.50 (ISBN 0-88066-151-8). Vance Biblios.

--John Stuart Mill: A Bibliography. (Public Administration Ser.: Bibliography P-932). 1982. pap. 13.50 (ISBN 0-88066-147-X). Vance Biblios.

--Local Government: A Selected Bibliography of Journal Literature. (Public Administration Ser.: P 177). 1979. pap. 6.50 (ISBN 0-88066-015-5). Vance Biblios.

--Municipal Government: A Selected Bibliography of Journal Literature. (Public Administration Ser.: P 176). 1979. pap. 7.50 (ISBN 0-88066-014-7). Vance Biblios.

--Political & Social Advertising: A Selected Bibliography. (Public Administration Ser.: Bibliography P 1654). 1985. pap. 2.00 (ISBN 0-89028-344-3). Vance Biblios.

--Political Science Research Guide. (Public Administration Ser.: Bibliography P-956). 1982. pap. 20.00 (ISBN 0-88066-152-6). Vance Biblios.

--Reference Tools in Political Science. (Public Administration Ser.: Bibliography: P 255). 1979. pap. 6.50 (ISBN 0-88066-023-6). Vance Biblios.

--The Welfare State & Welfare Economics: A Bibliography. (Public Administration Ser.: Bibliography P-874). 1981. pap. 7.50 (ISBN 0-88066-129-1). Vance Biblios.

--The Writings of Kenneth Boulding: A Bibliography. (Public Administration Ser.: Bibliography P-901). 56p. 1982. pap. 8.25 (ISBN 0-88066-139-9). Vance Biblios.

Goehlert, Robert & Herczeg, Claire. Anarchism: A Bibliography. (Public Administration Ser.: Bibliography P-902). 122p. 1982. pap. 16.00 (ISBN 0-88066-140-2). Vance Biblios.

Goehlert, Robert & Hoffmeister, Elizabeth R. The CIA: A Bibliography. (Public Administration Ser.: Bibliography P-498). 79p. 1980. pap. 8.50 (ISBN 0-88066-070-8). Vance Biblios.

Goehlert, Robert & Martin, Fenton. The Parliament of Great Britain: A Bibliography. LC 82-47920. (Special Series in Libraries & Librarianship). 240p. 1983. 28.00x (ISBN 0-669-05700-2). Lexington Bks.

Goehlert, Robert & Sayre, John. The United States Congress. 320p. 1981. text ed. 50.00 (ISBN 0-02-911900-6). Free Pr.

Goehlert, Robert U. Policy Studies on Judicial Processes: A Selected Bibliography. LC 83-139385. (Public Administration Ser.: P-1153). 12p. 1983. 2.00 (ISBN 0-88066-403-7). Vance Biblios.

--Policy Studies on Local Affairs: A Selected Bibliography. LC 83-137274. (Public Administration Ser.: P-1150). 12p. 1983. 2.00 (ISBN 0-88066-400-2). Vance Biblios.

--Studies on Food Policy: A Selected Bibliography. LC 82-235340. (Public Administration Series-Bibliography: P-1091). 8p. 1983. 2.00 (ISBN 0-88066-281-6). Vance Biblios.

Goehlert, Robert U. & Martin, Fenton S. Policy Analysis & Management: A Bibliography. 398p. 1984. lib. bdg. 55.00 (ISBN 0-87436-387-X). ABC-Clio.

--The Presidency: A Research Guide. 300p. 1984. lib. bdg. 28.50 (ISBN 0-87436-373-X). ABC-Clio.

Goehlert, Robert U. & Musto, Frederick W. State Legislatures: A Bibliography. 229p. 1985. lib. bdg. 35.00 (ISBN 0-87436-422-1). ABC-Clio.

Goehner, Patricia A., jt. auth. see Archer, Sarah E.

Goehri Ethridge, Myrna L. Fearing No Evil: One Woman's Life of Tragedy & Victory. (Illus.). 108p. (Orig.). 1984. pap. 5.95 (ISBN 0-941018-12-1). Martin Pr CA.

Goehring, Eleanor E. Tennessee Folk Culture: An Annotated Bibliography. LC 81-16036. (Illus.). 152p. 1982. text ed. 16.50x (ISBN 0-87049-344-2). U of Tenn Pr.

Goehring, Harvey J., Jr. Statistical Methods in Education. LC 80-84066. (Illus.). viii, 337p. 1981. text ed. 27.50 (ISBN 0-87815-033-1). Info Resources.

Goehring, Keith. Has Judicial Reorganization Increased the Cost of South Dakota's Judicial System. 1984. write for info. U of SD Gov Res Bur.

Goehringer, Alfred E., Jr. Drop a Dime on Your Kid: A Parent's Guide to Drug Abuse. 1977. pap. 1.50 (ISBN 0-9601704-1-3). Goehringer & Sons.

Goeke, John C. Factors Related to the Alienation of the Male Married Offender. LC 79-65261. 130p. 1980. 10.95 (ISBN 0-86548-011-7). R & E Pubs.

Goeke, K. & Reinhard, P. G. Time Dependent Hartree-Fock & Beyond, Bad Honnef, FRG, 1982 Proceedings. (Lecture Notes in Physics: Vol. 171). 426p. 1982. pap. 23.00 (ISBN 0-387-11950-7). Springer-Verlag.

Goekoop, V. The Logic of Invariable Concomitance in the Tattvacintamani: Gangesa's Amunitinirupana & Vyaptivada. 162p. 1967. lib. bdg. 24.00 (ISBN 90-277-0024-9, Pub. by Reidel Holland). Kluwer Academic.

Goel, Aruna. Indian Philosphy: Naya Vaisesika & Modern Science. 1984. text ed. 25.00x (ISBN 0-86590-279-8, Sterling Pubs India). Apt Bks.

Goel, D. P. & Mittal, S. P. Revision in Chemistry, No. I. (Illus.). vi, 91p. (Orig.). 1983. pap. text ed. 5.95x (ISBN 0-86131-378-X, Pub. by Orient Longman Ltd India). Apt Bks.

Goel, L. Public Personnel Administration. (Illus.). 364p. 1984. pap. text ed. 12.95 (ISBN 0-86590-534-7, Pub. by Sterling Pubs India). Apt Bks.

Goel, M. L., jt. auth. see Milbrath, Lester W.

Goel, M. K., jt. auth. see Haran, S. Hari.

Goel, N. S., et al. On the Volterra & Other Nonlinear Models of Interacting Populations. (Reviews of Modern Physics Monographs). 1971. 39.00 (ISBN 0-12-287450-1). Acad Pr.

Goel, Narendra & Richter-Dyn, Nira. Stochastic Models in Biology. 1974. 47.50 (ISBN 0-12-287460-9). Acad Pr.

Goel, S. L. International Civil Service. xx, 420p. 1984. text ed. 35.00x (ISBN 0-86590-225-9, Pub. by Sterling Pubs India). Apt Bks.

--Public Health Administration. xiii, 472p. 1984. text ed. 50.00x (ISBN 0-86590-527-4, Pub. by Sterling Pubs India). Apt Bks.

Goeldner, C. R. The Airline Skier: 1977-78. 77p. 1978. 15.00 (ISBN 0-89478-045-X). U CO Busn Res Div.

--The Aspen Skier: 1977-78. 80p. 1978. 15.00 (ISBN 0-89478-043-3). U CO Busn Res Div.

--The Colorado Skier. 92p. 1978. 25.00 (ISBN 0-89478-044-1). U CO Busn Res Div.

--How to Conduct a Skier Survey. 67p. 1983. pap. text ed. 25.00 (ISBN 0-89478-101-4). U Co Busn Res Div.

--The Vail Skier: (1977-78 Season) 106p. 1978. 15.00 (ISBN 0-686-64156-6). U CO Busn Res Div.

Goeldner, C. R. & Buchman, Tom. NSAA Economic Analysis of North American Ski Areas: 1981-82 Season. 136p. 1982. pap. text ed. 40.00 (ISBN 0-89478-073-5). U Co Busn Res Div.

Goeldner, C. R. & Courteney, Sally. Colorado Ski & Winter Recreation Statistics, 1977: (1976-77 Season) 124p. 1977. 20.00 (ISBN 0-89478-036-0). U CO Busn Res Div.

Goeldner, C. R. & Dicke, Karen. Colorado Ski & Winter Recreation Statistics, 1978: (1977-78 Season) 117p. 1978. 20.00 (ISBN 0-89478-048-4). U CO Busn Res Div.

--Colorado Ski Industry Characteristics & Finanicial Analysis, 1982. 71p. 1982. pap. text ed. 25.00 (ISBN 0-89478-070-0). U CO Busn Res Div.

--NSAA Economic Analysis of North American Ski Areas: (1973-74) 122p. 1974. 25.00 (ISBN 0-686-64147-7). U CO Busn Res Div.

Goeldner, C. R. & Duea, K. P. NSAA Economic Analysis of North American Ski Areas: 1983-84 Season. 140p. 1984. pap. 50.00 (ISBN 0-89478-081-6). U CO Busn Res Div.

Goeldner, C. R. & Duea, Karen. Colorado Ski Industry Characteristics & Financial Analysis: 1981-82 Season. 89p. 1983. pap. text ed. 25.00 (ISBN 0-89478-075-1). U Co Busn Res Div.

--Colorado Ski Industry Characteristics & Financial Analysis: 1983-84 Season. 95p. 1985. pap. text ed. 25.00 (ISBN 0-89478-083-2). U CO Busn Res Div.

--Colorado Ski Industry Characteristics & Financial Analysis,1982-83 Season. 93p. 1983. pap. text ed. 25.00 (ISBN 0-89478-107-3). U Co Busn Res Div.

--Travel Trends in the United States & Canada. 262p. 1984. pap. text ed. 45.00 (ISBN 0-89478-078-6). U Co Busn Res Div.

Goeldner, C. R. & Farwell, Ted. NSAA Economic Analysis of North American Ski Areas: (1978-79 Season) 148p. 1979. 30.00 (ISBN 0-686-64143-4). U CO Busn Res Div.

--NSAA Economic Analysis of North American Ski Areas: (1977-78) 140p. 1978. 30.00 (ISBN 0-686-64144-2). U CO Busn Res Div.

--NSAA Economic Analysis of North American Ski Areas: (1975-76) 116p. 1976. 25.00 (ISBN 0-686-64145-0). U CO Busn Res Div.

--NSAA Economic Analysis of North American Ski Areas: (1974-75) 124p. 1975. 25.00 (ISBN 0-686-64146-9). U CO Busn Res Div.

--NSAA Economic Analysis of North American Ski Areas: 1980-81 Season. 1981. pap. text ed. 40.00 (ISBN 0-89478-058-1). U CO Busn Res Div.

--NSAA Economic Analysis of North American Ski Areas (79-80 Season) 1979-80 Season. 139p. 1980. 35.00 (ISBN 0-89478-054-9). U CO Busn Res Div.

Goeldner, C. R. & Fellhauer, Cheryl. The Aspen Summer Visitor. 97p. 1976. 10.00 (ISBN 0-89478-028-X). U CO Busn Res Div.

--Colorado Ski & Winter Recreation Statistics, 1976: (1975-76 Season) 123p. 1977. 10.00 (ISBN 0-89478-030-1). U CO Busn Res Div.

Goeldner, C. R. & Fergesen, J. E. Aspen In-Room Survey, 1983: 1982-83 Season. 109p. 1983. 25.00. U CO Busn Res Div.

Goeldner, C. R. & Gortmaker, Gwen. The Aspen Design Conference Visitor. 56p. 1976. 10.00 (ISBN 0-89478-029-8). U CO Busn Res Div.

Goeldner, C. R. & Harrington, Jack. Aspen In Room Survey: 1978-79. 173p. pap. 25.00 (ISBN 0-89478-104-9). U CO Busn Res Div.

--Vail Peak Day Survey. 130p. 25.00 (ISBN 0-686-64155-8). U CO Busn Res Div.

Goeldner, C. R. & Manire, James. What's Published about Colorado. 1985. 25.00 (ISBN 0-89478-079-4). U CO Busn Res Div.

Goeldner, C. R. & Phillips, Nicola. The Vail Skier: (1976-77 Season) 80p. 1977. 10.00 (ISBN 0-686-64157-4). U CO Busn Res Div.

Goeldner, C. R. & Sletta, Yvonne. The Breckenridge Skier. 97p. 1975. 10.00 (ISBN 0-89478-021-2). U CO Busn Res Div.

Goeldner, C. R., jt. auth. see Dicke, Karen.

Goeldner, C. R., jt. auth. see McIntosh, R. W.

Goeldner, C. R., et al. What's Published about Colorado. 139p. 1978. 15.00 (ISBN 0-686-64142-6). U CO Busn Res Div.

--NSAA Economic Analysis of North American Ski Areas: 1982-83 Season. 137p. 1983. pap. text ed. 45.00 (ISBN 0-89478-106-5). U Co Busn Res DIv.

--The Vail Skier: (1975-76 Season) 121p. 1976. 10.00 (ISBN 0-686-64158-2). U CO Busn Res Div.

Goeldner, Charles R. & Duea, Karen. Colorado Ski & Winter Recreation Statistics, 1982. 129p. 1983. pap. text ed. 25.00 (ISBN 0-89478-074-3). U Co Busn Res Div.

Goeldner, Charles R., jt. auth. see McIntosh, Robert W.

Goeldner, Paul, compiled by. Texas Catalog. LC 75-28599. (Historic American Building Survey Ser.). (Illus.). 247p. 1975. pap. 5.00 (ISBN 0-911536-62-0). Trinity U Pr.

Goeler, Eberhard von see Von Goeler, Eberhard & Weinstein, Roy.

Goelet, Francis. The Voyages & Travels of Francis Goelet, Seventeen Fourty-Six to Seventeen Fifty-Eight. Scott, Kenneth, ed. (Illus.). 20.00 (ISBN 0-8398-0663-9). Parnassus Imprints.

Goell, Yohai. Bibliography of Modern Hebrew Literature in English Translation. 132p. 1968. casebound 14.95x (ISBN 0-87855-187-5). Transaction Bks.

Goeller, Carl. Writing & Selling Greeting Cards. 1980. 10.95 (ISBN 0-87116-124-9). Writer.

--Writing to Communicate. 1975. pap. 3.50 (ISBN 0-451-62222-7, ME2222, Ment). NAL.

Goeller, L. F., Jr. Design Background for Telephone Switching, Vol. IX. 1978. 10.75 (ISBN 0-686-98065-4). Telecom Lib.

Goeller, Lee & Goldstone, Gerald. The Business Communications Review Manual of PBXs. 2nd ed. 350p. 1982. 145.00 (ISBN 0-686-98056-5). Telecom Lib.

Goellnicht, Donald C. The Poet-Physician: Keats & Medical Science. LC 83-47618. 304p. 1984. 26.95x (ISBN 0-8229-3807-3). U of Pittsburgh Pr.

Goelman, Hillel, et al, eds. Awakening to Literacy. LC 84-727. 256p. 1984. pap. 15.00x (ISBN 0-435-08207-8). Heinemann Ed.

Goeltz, Judith. Jet Stress: What It Is & How to Cope with It; a Traveler's Guide for Dealing with the Physical Stress of Flying. LC 79-89366. 304p. 1981. 11.95 (ISBN 0-86664-000-2). Tony Pr-Ent.

Goeltz, Judith & Lazenby, Patricia. The Beginner's Natural Food Cookbook. new ed. 192p. (Orig.). 1975. pap. 5.95 (ISBN 0-89036-048-0). Hawkes Pub Inc.

Goeltz, Judy. The Beginner's Natural Food Guide & Cookbook. 232p. 5.95 (ISBN 0-318-15638-5). Natl Health Fed.

Goelzer, Daniel L., jt. auth. see Law & Business Inc. Staff.

Goen, C. C. Broken Churches, Broken Nation: Denominational Schism & the Coming of the American Civil War. 208p. 1985. 17.50 (ISBN 0-86554-166-3, MUP-H156); pap. 13.50 (ISBN 0-86554-187-6, MUP-P17). Mercer Univ Pr.

Goen, C. C., ed. see Chandler, Douglas R.

Goen, C. C., ed. see Edwards, Jonathan.

Goen, Tex, Jr. Smile... or I'll Kick Your Bed! LC 80-20223. (Illus.). 192p. 1981. 12.95 (ISBN 0-393-01433-9). Norton.

Goenner, M. E. Mary-Verse of the Teutonic Knights. LC 72-140022. (Catholic University of America Studies in German: No. 19). Repr. of 1943 ed. 20.00 (ISBN 0-404-50239-3). AMS Pr.

Goepfert, Paul. Chiasma. (Illus.). 96p. 1980. pap. 4.50 (ISBN 0-915572-39-7). Panjandrum.

Goepp, Charles, tr. see Auerbach, Berthold.

Goepper, Roger & Whitfield, Roderick. Treasures from Korea: Art Through 5000 Years. (Illus.). 265p. (Orig.). 1984. 40.00x (ISBN 0-253-36050-1); pap. 20.00x (ISBN 0-253-28860-6). Ind U Pr.

Goerch, Carl. Ocracoke. (Illus.). 1984. pap. 6.95 (ISBN 0-89587-031-2). Blair.

Goerge, Diana Hume & Nelson, Malcolm A. Epitaph & Icon: A Field Guide to the Old Burying Grounds of Cape Cod, Martha's Vineyard & Nantucket. (Illus.). 128p. (Orig.). 1983. 12.95 (ISBN 0-940160-21-8); pap. 19.95 (ISBN 0-940160-17-X). Parnassus Imprints.

Goergen, Don. The Sexual Celibate. 272p. 1975. 5.00 (ISBN 0-8164-0268-X, Pub. by Seabury). Winston Pr.

Goering, Carroll E. Engine & Tractor Power. 1985. text ed. 40.50 (ISBN 0-534-05814-0, 77F6068). Breton Pubs.

Goering, Gladys V. Women in Search of Mission. LC 80-66787. (Illus.). 136p. 1980. pap. 3.95 (ISBN 0-87303-062-1). Faith & Life.

Goering, H. W. Political Testament of Hermann Goering. Blood-Ryan, H. W., tr. LC 71-180403. Repr. of 1939 ed. 26.00 (ISBN 0-404-56127-6). AMS Pr.

Goering, Hermann. Germany Reborn. 1977. lib. bdg. 59.95 (ISBN 0-8490-1888-9). Gordon Pr.

--Germany Reborn. Whisker, James, tr. viii, 67p. 1983. pap. 4.00 (ISBN 0-939482-09-6). Noontide.

--Goering's Last Letter to His Accuser, Prosecuter, Judge & Hangman: Winston Churchill. 1982. lib. bdg. 59.95 (ISBN 0-87700-396-3). Revisionist Pr.

Goering, John M., jt. ed. see Kalachek, Edward.

Goering, Max. Francesco Guardi. LC 83-45770. Repr. of 1944 ed. 37.50 (ISBN 0-404-20109-1). AMS Pr.

Goering, Oswald H., jt. auth. see Van der Smissen, Betty.

Goering, T. James. Agricultural Land Settlement. (World Bank Issues Paper). 73p. 1978. pap. 5.00 (ISBN 0-686-36061-3, PP-7801). World Bank.

Goering, Theodore J. & D'Silva, Emmanuel H. Natural Rubber. (Illus.). 66p. (Orig.). 1982. pap. text ed. 5.00 (ISBN 0-8213-0045-8). World Bank.

Goering, Ulrich, jt. auth. see Frik, W.

Goerlich, Robert F., ed. see Goerlich, Shirley B.

Goerlich, Shirley B. Genealogy: A Practical Research Guide. Goerlich, Robert F., ed. LC 84-60815. (Illus.). 1984. 20.00 (ISBN 0-317-19324-4). RSG Pub.

Goerling, T. James. Tropical Root Crops & Rural Development. (Working Paper: No. 324). 85p. 1979. 5.00 (ISBN 0-686-36081-8, WP-0324). World Bank.

Goerlitz. Handlexikon Zur Politikwissenschaft, 2 vols. 530p. (Ger.). 1973. pap. 9.50 (ISBN 3-499-16169-9, M-7438, Pub. by Rowohlt). French & Eur.

--Handlexikon Zur Rechtswissenschaft, 2 vols. 544p. (Ger.). 1974. 9.50 (ISBN 3-499-16179-6, M-7439, Pub. by Rowohlt). French & Eur.

Goerlitz, Walter, ed. History of the German General Staff. (Encore Edition Ser.). 530p. 1985. 35.00x (ISBN 0-8133-0195-5). Westview.

Goerner, E. A., ed. Democracy in Crisis: New Challenges to Constitutional Democracy in the Atlantic Area. (International Studies Ser.). 1971. text ed. 12.95x (ISBN 0-268-00451-X). U of Notre Dame Pr.

Goerner, H. Cornell. All Nations in God's Purpose. LC 78-50360. 1979. pap. 4.95 (ISBN 0-8054-6312-7). Broadman.

Goerner, Lee, ed. see Allende, Isabel.

Goerner, Lee, ed. see Berger, John J.

Goerner, Lee, ed. see Tallent, Elizabeth.

Goerner, Lee, ed. see Thomson, David.

Goertler, H., ed. see International Congress of Applied Mechanics, 11th, Munich, 1964.

Goertler, H., ed. see International Union of Theoretical & Applied Mechanics Symposium, Freiberg 1957.

Goertz, Donald C. Select Epigrams of Martial. LC 74-127795. 128p. 1971. 5.95 (ISBN 0-8216-0150-4). Univ Bks.

Goertz, Hans J. Profiles of Radical Reformers. 228p. 1982. pap. 9.95x (ISBN 0-8361-1250-4). Herald Pr.

Goertz, Hans-Jurgen, ed. Umstrittenes Taufertum 1525-1975. 1975. 22.50x (ISBN 0-8361-1128-1). Herald Pr.

Goertzel, Mildred G., jt. auth. see Goertzel, Victor.
Goertzel, Mildred G., et al. Three Hundred Eminent Personalities: A Psychosocial Analysis of the Famous. LC 78-1149. (Social & Behavioral Science & Higher Education Ser.). 1978. text ed. 35.00x (ISBN 0-87589-370-8). Jossey-Bass.
Goertzel, Victor & Goertzel, Mildred G. Cradles of Eminence. 1978. pap. 5.95 (ISBN 0-316-31846-9). Little.
Goertzen, Anna R. Mama Nlundi-Our Adopted Mother. 1982. 8.95 (ISBN 0-533-05023-5). Vantage.
Goes. Das Brandopfer. (Easy Readers, C). pap. 4.25 (ISBN 0-88436-057-1, 45274). EMC.
Goes, Albrecht. Loffelchen: Eine Erzahlung. Schweitzer, Christoph E., ed. LC 68-13150. (Orig., Ger.). 1968. pap. text ed. 2.50x (ISBN 0-89197-280-3). Irvington.
Goes, F., ed. see International Society for Ultrasonic Diagnosis in Ophthalmology, Ghent, May 1973.
Goesch, Keith, jt. auth. see Mauriac, Francois.
Goeschel, Joachim. Strukturelle und instrumentalphonetische Untersuchungen zur gesprochenen Sprache. LC 72-76054. (Studia Linguistica Germanica Vol. 9). (Illus.). 1973. 40.40x (ISBN 3-11-003624-X). De Gruyter.
Goeschen, Sammlung, jt. ed. see Maurer, Friedrich.
Goessel, M. Nonlinear Time-Discrete Systems: A General Approach by Nonlinear Superposition. (Lecture Notes in Control & Information Science: Vol. 41). 112p. 1982. pap. 10.00 (ISBN 0-387-11914-0). Springer-Verlag.
Goetchius, Eugene V. & Price, Charles P. The Gifts of God. LC 84-60627. 128p. (Orig.). 1984. pap. 4.95 (ISBN 0-8192-1349-7). Morehouse.
Goethals, Eric J., ed. Cabonic Polymerization & Related Processes. 1984. 35.00 (ISBN 0-12-287470-6). Acad Pr.
--Polymeric Amines & Ammonium Salts: International Symposium on Polymeric Amines & Ammonium Salts, Ghent, Belgium, 24-26 September 1979. LC 80-40324. (IUPAC Symposium Ser). 424p. 1980. 115.00 (ISBN 0-08-023941-2). Pergamon.
Goethals, George R., jt. auth. see Worchel, Stephen.
Goethals, George W. & Klos, Dennis S., eds. Experiencing Youth: First-Person Accounts. 2nd ed. 1976. pap. 14.95 (ISBN 0-316-31851-5). Little.
Goethals, Gregor. The TV Ritual: Worship at the Video Altar. LC 80-66072. (Illus.). 180p. 1982. pap. 7.25 (ISBN 0-8070-3223-9, BP 625, Pub. by Ariadne Bks.). Beacon Pr.
Goethals, Gregor T. The TV Ritual: Worship at the Video Alter. pap. 11.95 (ISBN 0-8070-3223-9, BPA 625). Beacon Pr.
Goethe. Romans: Les Souffrances du jeune Werther, Les Affinites Electives, Wilhelm Meister. 1424p. 39.95 (ISBN 0-686-56515-0). French & Eur.
--Selected Poems. Swales, Martin, ed. (Clarendon German Ser.). 1975. pap. 8.95x (ISBN 0-19-832468-5). Oxford U Pr.
--The Sorrows of Young Werther, the New Melusina, Novelle. (Rinehart Editions). 1949. pap. text ed. 10.95 (ISBN 0-03-008900-X, HoltC). HR&W.
--Theatre Complet. 1376p. write for info. French & Eur.
--Torquato Tasso. Prudhoe, J., tr. from Ger. (Classics of Drama in English Translation). 1979. pap. 6.50 (ISBN 0-7190-0720-8, Pub. by Manchester Univ Pr). Longwood Pub Group.
Goethe see Hedge, F. H. & Noa, L.
Goethe, et al. German Poetry from Seventeen Fifty to Nineteen Hundred. Browning, Robert M., tr. from Ger. LC 83-23980. (German Library: Vol. 39). 320p. 1984. 19.50x (ISBN 0-8264-0282-8); pap. 9.95 (ISBN 0-8264-0283-6). Continuum.
Goethe, J. W. The Metamorphosis of Plants. 56p. 3.50 (ISBN 0-938250-03-5). Bio-Dynamic Farm.
Goethe, J. W. von. Wilhelm Meister, Vol. 1: The Years of Apprenticeship, Bks. 1-3. Waidson, H. M., tr. from Ger. 1982. pap. 7.95 (ISBN 0-7145-3924-4); 11.95 (ISBN 0-7145-3675-X). Riverrun NY.
--Wilhelm Meister, Vol. 2: The Years of Apprenticeship, Bks. 4-6. Waidson, H. M., tr. from Ger. 1982. pap. 7.95 (ISBN 0-7145-3926-0); 11.95 (ISBN 0-7145-3699-7). Riverrun NY.
--Wilhelm Meister, Vol. 3: The Years of Apprenticeship, Bks. 7 & 8. Waidson, H. M., tr. from Ger. 1982. pap. 7.95 (ISBN 0-7145-3928-7); 11.95 (ISBN 0-7145-3702-0). Riverrun NY.
--Wilhelm Meister, Vol. 4: The Years of Travel, Bk. 1. Waidson, H. M., tr. from Ger. 1982. 11.95 (ISBN 0-7145-3827-2); pap. 7.95 (ISBN 0-7145-3930-9). Riverrun NY.
--Wilhelm Meister, Vol. 5: The Years of Travel, Bk. 2. Waidson, H. M., tr. from Ger. 1982. 11.95 (ISBN 0-7145-3838-8); pap. 7.95 (ISBN 0-7145-3932-5). Riverrun NY.
--Wilhelm Meister, Vol. 6: The Years of Travel, Bk. 3. Waidson, H. M., tr. from Ger. 1982. 11.95 (ISBN 0-7145-3840-X); pap. 7.95 (ISBN 0-7145-3934-1). Riverrun NY.
Goethe, J. W. Von see Von Goethe, J. W.
Goethe, J. W. Von see Von Goethe, J. W. & Steiner, Rudolf.
Goethe, Johann V. Theory of Colours. new ed. Eastlake, C. L., tr. (Illus.). 428p. 1967. 35.00x (ISBN 0-7146-1107-7, F Cass Co). Biblio Dist.
Goethe, Johann von. Goethe on Art. Gage, John, ed. LC 79-65774. (Illus.). 256p. 1980. 25.00 (ISBN 0-520-03995-5); pap. 7.95 (ISBN 0-520-03996-3). U of Cal Pr.
Goethe, Johann von Wolfgang see Von Goethe, Johann W.
Goethe, Johann W. Dr. Faust: An Art Book, 2 vols. (Illus.). 237p. 1984. Repr. of 1908 ed. Set. 217.55x (ISBN 0-89901-161-6). Found Class Reprints.
--Egmont. Waidson, H. M., ed. (German Text Ser.). 146p. 1974. pap. 9.95x (ISBN 0-631-01670-8). Basil Blackwell.
--Egmont: A Play. Passage, Charles E., tr. LC 79-5051. 1980. pap. 4.95 (ISBN 0-8044-6185-6). Ungar.
--Egmont: A Play. Passage, Charles E., tr. from Ger. 110p. 1985. pap. 5.95 (ISBN 0-8044-6185-6). Ungar.
--Elective Affinities. LC 75-40993. 305p. 1976. Repr. of 1963 ed. lib. bdg. 24.75x (ISBN 0-8371-8709-5, VAGEA). Greenwood.
--Elective Affinities. (Penguin Classic Ser.). 1978. pap. 4.95 (ISBN 0-14-044242-1). Penguin.
--Elective Affinities. Mayer, Elizabeth & Bogan, Louise, trs. LC 63-18317. 305p. pap. 5.95 (ISBN 0-89526-956-2). Regnery-Gateway.
--Elective Affinities. Froude, J. A. & Boylan, R. D., trs. LC 63-20159. pap. 4.95x (ISBN 0-8044-6186-4). Ungar.
--Essays on Art & Literature. Gearey, John, ed. Von Nardroff, Ernest & Von Nardroff, Ellen, trs. from Ger. (Gothe in English Ser.). (Illus.). 270p. 1985. 29.95 (ISBN 3-518-03058-2). Suhrkamp.
--The Eternal Feminine: Selected Poems of Goethe. Ungar, Frederick, ed. LC 76-15651. 192p. 1980. 14.50 (ISBN 0-8044-2256-7). Ungar.
--Faust, Pt. 1. Prudhoe, J., tr. from Ger. (Classics of Drama in English Translation Ser.). 1974. pap. 6.50 (ISBN 0-7190-0570-1, Pub. by Manchester Univ Pr). Longwood Pub Group.
--Goethe's Autobiography. 1949. 15.00 (ISBN 0-8183-0224-0). Pub Aff Pr.
--Goethe's "Faust". LC 61-5971. (Anchor Literary Library). pap. 7.95 (ISBN 0-385-03114-9, Anch). Doubleday.
--Goethe's "Faust". Fairley, Barker, tr. LC 74-151823. (Illus.). 1970. pap. 6.00 (ISBN 0-8020-6153-2). U of Toronto Pr.
--Goethe's Plays. Passage, Charles E., tr. from German. LC 79-4834. 1980. 30.00 (ISBN 0-8044-2258-3). Ungar.
--Goethe's Theory of Colours. lib. bdg. 79.95 (ISBN 0-87968-196-9). Gordon Pr.
--Goethe's World View: Presented in His Reflections & Maxims. Ungar, Frederick, ed. Norden, Heinz, tr. LC 63-18513. pap. 4.50 (ISBN 0-8044-6192-9). Ungar.
--Gotz Von Berlichingen. Passage, Charles E., tr. LC 65-16623. (Orig.). pap. 4.75 (ISBN 0-8044-6187-2). Ungar.
--Hermann & Dorothea. Coogan, Daniel, tr. LC 66-21737. (Bilingual). pap. 3.95 (ISBN 0-8044-6188-0). Ungar.
--Iphigenia in Tauris. Passage, Charles E., tr. 7.00 (ISBN 0-8044-2253-2); pap. 4.95 (ISBN 0-8044-6189-9). Ungar.
--Die Leiden Des Jungen Werthers. 2nd ed. Stahl, E. L., ed. (German Text Ser.). 336p. 1972. pap. 9.95x (ISBN 0-631-01900-6). Basil Blackwell.
--Novels & Tales. Boylar, R. D., ed. & tr. 1890. 45.00 (ISBN 0-8274-3052-3). R West.
--Novels & Tales of Goethe. 1976. lib. bdg. 69.95 (ISBN 0-8490-2360-2). Gordon Pr.
--The Poems of Goethe. 75.00 (ISBN 0-87968-151-9). Gordon Pr.
--The Poems of Goethe. Bowring, E. A., et al, trs. (Translated in the original metres). 1882. 45.00 (ISBN 0-8274-3155-4). R West.
--The Soothsayings of Bakis: Goethe's Tragi-Comic Observations on Life, Time, & History. Jantz, Harold, ed. LC 66-25527. pap. 24.00 (ISBN 0-317-08237-X, 2003864). Bks Demand UMI.
--Sufferings of Young Werther. Morgan, Bayard Q., tr. LC 63-21612. pap. 4.95x (ISBN 0-8044-6190-2). Ungar.
--Theory of Colours. 1970. pap. 9.95 (ISBN 0-262-57021-1). MIT Pr.
--Torquato Tasso. Passage, Charles E., tr. LC 65-28701. pap. 3.95 (ISBN 0-8044-6191-0). Ungar.
Goethe, Johann W., jt. auth. see Nerval, Gerard de.
Goethe, Johann W. see Von Goethe, Johann W.
Goethe, Johann W. von. The Autobiography of Johann Wolfgang von Goethe. Vol. I. pap. 15.00 (ISBN 0-226-30057-9, Phoen); Vol. II. pap. 15.00 (ISBN 0-226-30058-7, P603). U of Chicago Pr.
--Faust. Hamlin, Cyrus, ed. Arndt, Walter, tr. from Ger. (Critical Edition Ser). 24p. 1976. pap. text ed. 10.95x (ISBN 0-393-09208-9). Norton.
--Faust, Pts. 1 & 2. abr. ed. MacNiece, Louis, tr. 1960. pap. 6.95 (ISBN 0-19-500410-8). Oxford U Pr.
--Faust: Pt. I. MacIntyre, C. F., tr. LC 51-1865. 1957. pap. 4.95 (ISBN 0-8112-0056-6, NDP70). New Directions.
--Goethe, the Lyricist. 2nd, rev. ed. LC 78-31302. (BCL Ser.: No. I). Repr. of 1955 ed. 27.00 (ISBN 0-404-50916-9). AMS Pr.
--Johann Wolfgang Von Goethe's Roman Elegies & Venetian Epigrams. Lind, L. R., tr. from Ger. LC 74-7172. xii, 228p. 1974. 22.50x (ISBN 0-7006-0125-2). U Pr of KS.
Goethe, Johann W. Von see Von Goethe, Johann W.
Goethe, Johann W von see Von Goethe, Johann W.
Goethe, Johann W. Von see Von Goethe, Johann W.
Goethe, Johann W. von see Von Goethe, Johann W.
Goethe, Johann W. Von see Von Goethe, Johann W.
Goethe, Johann W. von see Von Goethe, Johann W.
Goethe, Johann W. Von see Von Goethe, Johann W.
Goethe, Johann Wolfgang Von. The Autobiography of Johann Wolfgang Von Goethe. Oxenford, John, tr. from Ger. 1975. Vol. II. 15.00 (ISBN 0-226-30056-0). U of Chicago Pr.
Goethe, Katharina E. Goethe's Mother. LC 73-37695. (Women of Letters Ser.). Repr. of 1880 ed. 27.50 (ISBN 0-404-56752-5). AMS Pr.
Goethe, Meredyth. Why Nurnberg? (Illus.). 256p. 1981. text ed. 12.95 (ISBN 0-9606714-0-4). Goethe Pubs.
Goethe, W. H., et al, eds. Handbook of Nautical Medicine. (Illus.). 570p. 1984. text ed. 65.00 (ISBN 0-387-12956-1). Springer-Verlag.
Goethe, W. J. The Sorrows of the Young Werther. (Illus.). 131p. 1984. 55.75 (ISBN 0-89266-481-9). Am Classical Coll Pr.
Goethert, Reinhard, jt. auth. see Caminos, Horacio.
Goetinck, Jean F. Essai sur le Role des Allemands dans le "Dicctionnaire Historique et Critique". (Etudes Litteraires Francaises Ser.: No. 22). 121p. (Orig., Fr.). 1982. pap. 19.00x (ISBN 3-87808-960-0). Benjamins North Am.
Goetnick, Paul F., jt. ed. see Kelley, Robert O.
Goetsch, Charles. Phonology of the Low German Deeds in the Oldest Registy at Riga, Latvia. (LM). 1934. pap. 16.00 (ISBN 0-527-00819-2). Kraus Repr.
Goetsch, Charles C. Essays on Simeon E. Baldwin. LC 80-54505. 290p. (Orig.). 1981. pap. text ed. 12.00 (ISBN 0-939328-01-1). U Conn Sch Law.
Goetsch, David. Cad-Cam Workbook. 1983. text ed. 4.95 wkbk. (ISBN 0-538-33320-0, IE32). SW Pub.
Goetsch, David L. Drafting & Drawing for Structural Systems. 368p. 1982. 21.95 (ISBN 0-442-22996-8); pap. 7.95 (ISBN 0-442-22996-8). Van Nos Reinhold.
--Introduction to Computer-Aided Drafting. (Illus.). 272p. 1983. text ed. 26.95 (ISBN 0-13-479287-4). P-H.
--Structural Drafting. (Drafting Ser.). (Illus.). 355p. (Orig.). 1982. pap. text ed. 18.80 (ISBN 0-8273-1930-4); instr's. guide 4.20 (ISBN 0-8273-1931-2). Delmar.
Goetsch, H. B. Parental Income & College Opportunities. LC 72-176807. (Columbia University. Teachers College. Contributions to Education: No. 795). Repr. of 1940 ed. 22.50 (ISBN 0-404-55795-3). AMS Pr.
Goetsch, H. W. How to Prepare & Use Marketing Plans for Profit. LC 79-91046. 1979. pap. text ed. 20.00 (ISBN 0-686-63539-6). Am Mktg.
Goetsch, Hal W. How to Prepare & Use Marketing Plans for Profit. LC 79-91046. (Illus.). 50p. 1979. saddle stitch, softcover 24.95x (ISBN 0-686-32847-7). Marketing for Profit.
Goetschalckx, J. & Rolling, L. Lexicography in the Electronic Age. 276p. 1982. 38.50 (ISBN 0-444-86404-0, North-Holland). Elsevier.
Goetschius, E. V., tr. see Kaiser, Otto & Kummel, Werner G.
Goetschius, Percy. Counterpoint Applied in the Invention, Fugue & Other Polyphonic Forms. LC 75-109734. (Illus.). 318p. 1975. Repr. of 1902 ed. lib. bdg. 22.50x (ISBN 0-8371-4224-5, GOCO). Greenwood.
--Homophonic Forms of Musical Composition. LC 70-122594. Repr. of 1898 ed. 20.00 (ISBN 0-404-02853-5). AMS Pr.
--Lessons in Music Form. LC 79-109735. Repr. of 1904 ed. lib. bdg. 19.75x (ISBN 0-8371-4225-3, GOMF). Greenwood.
--Structure of Music. LC 72-109736. Repr. of 1934 ed. lib. bdg. 22.00x (ISBN 0-8371-4226-1, GOSM). Greenwood.
--The Theory & Practice of Tone-Relations. LC 72-109968. 187p. 1973. Repr. of 1931 ed. lib. bdg. 21.50x (ISBN 0-8371-6182-7, GOTR). Greenwood.
Goette, John A. Jade Lore. 2nd ed. LC 76-21489. (Illus.). 1976. 26.50 (ISBN 0-89344-009-4). Ars Ceramica.
Goettelmann, Paul A. The Baptistry of Frejus: A Restoration Based on the Architectural & Historical Evidence. (Illus.). 75p. 1984. Repr. of 1933 ed. 25.00x (ISBN 0-939738-23-6). Zubal Inc.
Goetti, Ernst. Die Gotischen Bewegungsverben: Ein Beitrag Zur Erforschung Des Gotischen Wortschatzes Mit Einem Ausblick Auf Wulfilas Uebersetzungstechnik. LC 73-88296. (Ger.). 1974. 42.40x (ISBN 3-11-004331-9). De Gruyter.
Goettinger, H., ed. Diagnostik und Therapie des Prostatakarzinoms. (Beitraege zur Urologie: Vol. 1). 1979. soft cover 14.25 (ISBN 3-8055-0294-X). S Karger.
Goettsch, Scherrie & Weinberg, Steve. Terrace Hill: The Story of a House & the People Who Touched It. (Illus.). 120p. 1978. 9.95 (ISBN 0-87069-243-7). Wallace-Homestead.
Goettsche, Ron & Fogg, Bob. Down to Earth: The Jason Journal. LC 83-17971. 250p. (Orig.). 1984. pap. 6.95x (ISBN 0-915223-11-2). Synergy Pubs.
Goettsche, Ron, jt. auth. see Fogg, Bob.
Goetz, Charles J. Law & Economics Cases & Materials. LC 83-21787. (American Casebook Ser.). 547p. 1983. pap. text ed. 21.95 (ISBN 0-314-76541-7). West Pub.
Goetz, Christopher G. Neurotoxins in Clinical Practice. LC 85-2107. (Neurologic Illness: Diagnosis & Treatment Ser.). 400p. 1985. text ed. 55.00 (ISBN 0-89335-224-1). SP Med & Sci Bks.
Goetz, Delia. Deserts. (Illus.). (gr. 3-7). 1956. PLB 10.88 (ISBN 0-688-31232-2). Morrow.
Goetz, Delia, jt. tr. see Recinos, Adrian.
Goetz, Delia see Recinos, Adrian & Goetz, Delia.
Goetz, Delia, jt. tr. see Recinos, Adrian.
Goetz, Elizabeth M., jt. auth. see Allen, K. Eileen.
Goetz, Elizabeth M. & Allen, K. Eileen, eds. Early Childhood Education: Special Environmental, Policy & Legal Considerations. LC 83-9950. 354p. 1983. 32.00 (ISBN 0-89443-879-4). Aspen Systems.
Goetz, Helga. The Inuit Print ('Estampe Inuit) (Illus.). 1980. 24.95x (ISBN 0-660-50278-X, 56393-6, Pub. by Natl Mus Canada); pap. 17.95 (ISBN 0-660-00082-2, 56392-8, Pub. by Natl Mus Canada). U of Chicago Pr.
Goetz, Hilde, ed. see International Symposium, First, Berlin, Nov. 1972.
Goetz, Joan. El Amor y la Juventud. Montero, Lidia D., tr. from Eng. (Illus.). 96p. 1981. pap. 2.20 (ISBN 0-311-46058-5). Casa Bautista.
Goetz, Joseph. Mirrors of God. 1984. pap. 4.95 (ISBN 0-86716-031-4). St Anthony Mess Pr.
Goetz, Judith P. & Le Compte, Margaret D. Ethnology & Qualitative Design in Educational Research. 1984. 32.00 (ISBN 0-12-287480-3). Acad Pr.
Goetz, M. H. & Stur, O. B., eds. Paediatric Respiratory Disease. (Progress in Respiration Research: Vol. 17). (Illus.). x, 306p. 1982. 81.00 (ISBN 3-8055-2658-X). S Karger.
Goetz, Sr. Mary P. Concept of Nobility in German Didactic Literature of the Thirteenth Century. LC 79-140021. (Catholic University Studies in German Ser.: No. 5). Repr. of 1935 ed. 21.00 (ISBN 0-404-50225-3). AMS Pr.
Goetz, W. Werner Krauss. 1976. lib. bdg. 59.95 (ISBN 0-8490-2814-0). Gordon Pr.
Goetzberger, A. & Zerbst, M., eds. Solid State Devices Nineteen Eighty-Two: ESSDERC-SSSDT Meeting at Munich, 13-16 September 1982. (Illus.). 201p. 1983. 46.00x (ISBN 3-87664-072-5). VCH Pubs.
Goetze, Albrecht. Kizzuwatna & the Problem of Hittite Geography. LC 78-63566. (Yale Oriental Ser. Researches: 22). Repr. of 1940 ed. 22.50 (ISBN 0-404-60322-X). AMS Pr.
--Old Babylonian Omen Texts. LC 79-3537. (Yale Oriental Series: Babylonian Texts: No. 10). (Illus.). 176p. Repr. of 1966 ed. 37.50 (ISBN 0-404-60265-7). AMS Pr.
--Old Babylonian Omen Texts. 1947. 36.50x (ISBN 0-686-83651-0). Elliots Bks.
Goetze, Alfred. Fruehneuhochdeutsches Glossar. 7th ed. (Kleine Texte, No. 101). (Ger.). 1971. Repr. of 1967 ed. bds. 7.90x (ISBN 3-11-003527-8). De Gruyter.
Goetze, Bernard A. Security in Europe: A Crisis of Confidence. LC 84-16008. 240p. 1984. 33.95 (ISBN 0-03-001089-6). Praeger.
Goetze, H. Form & Line: An Introduction to Photographic Design & Derivatives. (Photo Tips Ser.). (Illus.). 96p. (Orig.). 1980. pap. 4.95 (ISBN 0-85242-703-4, Argus Bks England). Morgan.
Goetze, Hans. Photographing with Four Hundred ASA. (Photo Tips Ser.). (Illus.). 96p. (Orig.). 1982. pap. 4.95 (ISBN 0-85242-748-4, Argus Bks England). Morgan.
Goetze, Mary. The Cat Came Back: And Other American Folksongs Arranged for Two- & Three-Part Children's Voices & Orff Instruments. 1984. pap. 6.00 (ISBN 0-918812-35-6). MMB Music.
--Sing We Noel. 1984. write for info. (ISBN 0-918812-42-9). MMB Music.
Goetze, Rolf. Building Neighborhood Confidence: A Humanistic Strategy for Urban Housing. LC 76-7469. 128p. 1976. prof ref. 20.00 (ISBN 0-88410-442-7). Ballinger Pub.
--Rescuing the American Dream: Public Policies & the Crisis in Housing. LC 82-18748. 150p. 1983. text ed. 24.50x (ISBN 0-8419-0855-9); pap. text ed. 14.50x (ISBN 0-8419-0862-1). Holmes & Meier.
--Understanding Neighborhood Change: The Role of Expectations in Urban Revitilization. LC 79-2539. 192p. 1979. prof ref 29.95 (ISBN 0-88410-493-1). Ballinger Pub.
Goetzl, Edward J. & Kay, A. B., eds. Current Perspectives in Allergy. LC 82-9494. (Contemporary Issues in Clinical Immunology & Allergy Ser.: Vol. 1). (Illus.). 185p. 1982. pap. text ed. 19.50 (ISBN 0-443-02503-7). Churchill.
Goetzman, Robert. James Anthony Froude: A Bibliography of Studies. LC 75-24080. (Reference Library of the Humanities: Vol. 27). 1977. lib. bdg. 28.00 (ISBN 0-8240-9985-0). Garland Pub.

Goetzmann, William. When the Eagle Screamed: The Romantic Horizon in American Diplomacy, 1800-1860. 138p. 1966. pap. text ed. 10.95 (ISBN 0-394-34180-5, RanC). Random.

Goetzmann, William H. Army Exploration in the American West, 1803-1863. LC 79-14764. (Illus.). xx, 489p. 1979. 31.50x (ISBN 0-8032-2103-7); pap. 9.95 (ISBN 0-8032-7003-8, BB 716, Bison). U of Nebr Pr.

--Exploration & Empire: The Explorer & the Scientist in the Winning of the American West. (Illus.). 1978. pap. 13.95x (ISBN 0-393-00881-9, N881, Norton Lib). Norton.

Goetzmann, William H. & Porter, Joseph C. The West As Romantic Horizon. LC 81-12424. (Illus.). 128p. 1981. 34.50 (ISBN 0-936364-04-1); pap. 18.95 (ISBN 0-936364-05-X). U of Nebr Pr.

Goetzmann, William H., et al. The West As Romantic Horizon. LC 81-12424. 128p. (Orig.). 1981. 34.95 (ISBN 0-936364-04-1); pap. 17.95 (ISBN 0-936364-05-X). Joslyn Art.

Goetz-Stankiewicz, Marketa. The Silenced Theatre: Czech Playwrights Without a Stage. LC 79-13423. 1979. 30.00x (ISBN 0-8020-5426-9). U of Toronto Pr.

Goetz-Stankiewicz, Marketa, ed. DramaContemporary: Czechoslovakia. (DramaContemporary Ser.). 222p. (Orig.). 1985. 21.95 (ISBN 0-933826-75-3); pap. 9.95 (ISBN 0-933826-76-1). Performing Arts.

Goeurot, John. The Regiment (Sic) of Life, Newly Corrected & Enlarged. LC 76-57385. (English Experience Ser.: No. 802). 1977. Repr. of 1546 ed. lib. bdg. 28.00 (ISBN 90-221-0802-3). Walter J Johnson.

Goez, Eric & Sanders, William. Apple Almanac. (Illus.). 1984. pap. 19.95 (ISBN 0-8359-0096-7). Reston.

Goez, Eric & Sanders, William B. Apple Almanac. 240p. 1983. pap. 19.95 (ISBN 0-88190-109-1, BO109). Datamost.

Goff, Beatrice L. Symbols of Ancient Egypt in the Late Period (21st Dynasty) (Religion & Society Ser.). 1979. text ed. 62.40x (ISBN 90-279-7622-8). Mouton.

Goff, Beth. Where Is Daddy? The Story of a Divorce. LC 69-14608. (Illus.). 32p. (ps-k). 1969. 8.95 (ISBN 0-8070-2388-4); pap. 3.95 (ISBN 0-8070-2305-1, BP 694). Beacon Pr.

Goff, Charles W. Legg-Calve-Perthes Syndrome: And Related Osteochondroses of Youth. (Illus.). 344p. 1954. photocopy ed. 29.75x (ISBN 0-398-04267-5). C C Thomas.

Goff, Colin, ed. see Sutherland, Edwin.

Goff, Eris. Four Winds & Seven Seas. 1985. 6.50 (ISBN 0-8062-2469-X). Carlton.

--Sword Against The Wind. 1983. 5.75 (ISBN 0-8062-2013-9). Carlton.

Goff, Frederick R. The Delights of a Rare Book Librarian. 1975. 3.00 (ISBN 0-89073-001-6). Boston Public Lib.

--Early Printing in Georgetown (Potomak) 1789-1800. 28p. 1958. pap. 3.00x (ISBN 0-912296-24-0, Dist. by U Pr of Va). Am Antiquarian.

--Incunabula in American Libraries: A Supplement to the Third Census of Fifteenth-Century Books Recorded in North American Collections. 104p. 1972. 10.00 (ISBN 0-686-31068-3). Biblio Soc Am.

--Incunabula in American Libraries: A Supplement to the Third Census of Fifteenth-Century Books Recorded in North American Collections (1964) LC 72-76024. xii, 104p. 1972. 10.00x (ISBN 0-8139-0939-2, Bibliographical Society of America). U Pr of Va.

--Incunabula in American Libraries: A Third Census of 15th Century Books Recorded in North American Collections. LC 72-10463. 1973. 90.00 (ISBN 0-527-34200-9). Kraus Intl.

--The Permanence of Johann Gutenberg. LC 78-89558. (Bibliographical Monograph: No. 3). 1974. Repr. of 1970 ed. 5.95 (ISBN 0-87959-048-3). U of Tex H Ransom Ctr.

Goff, Georgeanna, jt. auth. see Guth, Phyllis.

Goff, Gretchen. Bulimia: The Binge-Eating & Purging Syndrome. 16p. 1983. pap. 0.70 (ISBN 0-89486-204-9). Hazelden.

Goff, Guillermo. El Matrimonio y la Familia en la Vida Christiana. 240p. (Span.). 1985. pap. 7.00 (ISBN 0-311-46097-6). Casa Bautista.

Goff, H. N. Other Fools & Their Doings. facsimile ed. LC 70-38651. (Black Heritage Library Collection). Repr. of 1880 ed. 17.50 (ISBN 0-8369-9009-9). Ayer Co Pubs.

Goff, Harry. Inventions Wanted! LC 79-56695. (Illus.). 160p. (Orig.). 1980. pap. 5.95 (ISBN 0-914960-24-5). Academy Bks.

Goff, Harry, jt. auth. see Murphy, John D.

Goff, Jacques Le see Le Goff, Jacques.

Goff, Jacques Le see Le Goff, Jacques, et al.

Goff, James & Goff, Margaret. In Every Person Who Hopes... (Orig.). 1980. pap. 3.75 (ISBN 0-377-00096-5). Friend Pr.

Goff, John H. Placenames of Georgia: Essays of John H. Goff. Utley, Francis L. & Hemperley, Marion R., eds. LC 73-83366. (Illus.). 536p. 1975. 20.00 (ISBN 0-8203-0342-9). U of Ga Pr.

Goff, John S. George W. P. Hunt & His Arizona. LC 72-78585. (Illus.). 320p. 12.00 (ISBN 0-87026-038-3). Westernlore.

Goff, Kenneth. Brainwashing. 1979. pap. 2.50 (ISBN 0-911038-27-2). Noontide.

Goff, Kenneth, ed. Brain-Washing. 64p. 1983. pap. 2.50 (ISBN 0-941380-03-3). Emissary Pubns.

Goff, Lynda J., ed. Algal Symbiosis: A Continuum of Interaction Strategies. LC 83-7275. (Illus.). 224p. 1984. 42.50 (ISBN 0-521-25541-4). Cambridge u Pr.

Goff, Margaret, jt. auth. see Goff, James.

Goff, Martin. Victorian & Edwardian Surrey. 1972. 19.95 (ISBN 0-7134-0123-0, Pub. by Batsford England). David & Charles.

Goff, Martyn. The Royal Pavilion Brighton. (Folio Miniature Ser.). 48p. 1976. 4.95 (ISBN 0-7181-1477-9, Pub. by Michael Joseph). Merrimack Pub Cir.

--Short Guide to Long Play. 12.50 (ISBN 0-392-04571-0, LTB). Sportshelf.

Goff, Neil M. Federal Income Taxation of Corporate Liquidations. (Taxation Publications). 1200p. 1984. write for info. (Pub. By Shepards-McGraw). McGraw.

Goff, Paul E. Nature, Children & You. LC 81-18911. vi, 144p. 1982. 14.95 (ISBN 0-8214-0607-8, 82-83939); pap. 6.95 (ISBN 0-8214-0679-5, 82-84423). Ohio U Pr.

Goff, Regina M. Problems & Emotional Difficulties of Negro Children As Studied in Selected Communities & Attributed by Parents - Children to the Fact That They Are Negro. LC 76-476808. (Columbia University. Teachers College. Contributions to Education: No. 960). Repr. of 1949 ed. 22.50 (ISBN 0-404-55960-3). AMS Pr.

Goff, Richard, et al. The Twentieth Century: A Brief Global History. rev., 2nd ed. 425p. 1986. pap. text ed. 19.95 (ISBN 0-394-35464-8, KnopfC). Knopf.

--The Twentieth Century: A Brief Global History. 425p. 1983. pap. text ed. 13.95 (ISBN 0-394-34181-3, RanC). Random.

Goff, Richard D. Confederate Supply. LC 68-57274. (Duke Historical Publication Ser.). pap. 54.60 (ISBN 0-317-08166-7, 2017904). Bks Demand UMI.

Goff, Stanley, et al. Brothers: Black Soldiers in Nam. 240p. 1985. pap. 3.50 (ISBN 0-425-07590-7). Berkley Pub.

--Brothers: Black Soldiers in Nam. (Illus.). 232p. 1982. 14.95 (ISBN 0-89141-139-9). Presidio Pr.

Goff, T. J. Le see Le Goff, T. J.

Goff, Thomas. The Raging Turke, or Baiazet the Second, 2 vols. Bd. with The Courageous Turke, or Amvrath the Third. Goff, Thomas. Repr. of 1968 ed. LC 82045727. (Malone Society Reprint Ser.: No. 128). Set. 80.00 (ISBN 0-404-63128-2). AMS Pr.

Goffart, Walter. Barbarians & Romans, A.D. Four Hundred Eighteen to Five Hundred Eighty-Four: The Techniques of Accomodation. LC 80-7522. 240p. 1980. 35.00x (ISBN 0-691-05303-0). Princeton U Pr.

Goffart, Walter, tr. see Erdmann, Carl.

Goffart, Walter A. Le Mans Forgeries: A Chapter from the History of Church Property in the Ninth Century. LC 66-18246. (Historical Studies: No. 76). 1966. 25.00x (ISBN 0-674-51875-6). Harvard U Pr.

Goffe, Thomas. The Courageous Turk. O'Malley, Susan G. & Orgel, Stephen, eds. LC 78-66772. (Renaissance Drama Ser.). 1979. lib. bdg. 40.00 (ISBN 0-8240-9737-8). Garland Pub.

Goffe, Toni. Toby's Animal Rescue Service. (Illus.). 48p. (ps-3). 1982. 8.50 (ISBN 0-241-10580-3, Pub. by Hamish Hamilton England). David & Charles.

Goffee, Robert, jt. auth. see Scase, Richard.

Goffen, William. Court Officer, Senior Court Officer, Court Clerk. 6th ed. LC 83-9980. 240p. 1983. pap. 9.00 (ISBN 0-668-05615-0, 5615). Arco.

Goffer, Zvi. Archaeological Chemistry: A Sourcebook on the Applications of Chemistry to Archaeology, Vol. 55. LC 79-1425. (Chemical Analysis, Analytical Chemistry & Its Applications Ser.). 376p. 1980. 56.50x (ISBN 0-471-05156-X, Pub. by Wiley-Interscience). Wiley.

Goffi, Carlos. Tournament Tough: A Guide to Junior Championship Tennis. (Illus.). 192p. 1985. 13.95 (ISBN 0-03-071598-9). HR&W.

Goffin, J. L., jt. auth. see Buckley, A. G.

Goffin, J. L. & Rousseau, J. M., eds. Applications. (Mathematical Programming Studies: Vol. 20). 218p. 1982. 27.75 (ISBN 0-444-86478-4, I-341-82, North-Holland). Elsevier.

Goffin, Peter. Art & Science of Stage Management. 1953. 10.00 (ISBN 0-8022-0602-6). Philos Lib.

Goffin, R. J. The Testamentary Executor in England & Elsewhere. Helmholz, R. H. & Reams, Bernard D., Jr., eds. LC 80-84960. (Historical Writings in Law & Jurisprudence Ser.: No. 26, Bk. 40). 154p. 1981. Repr. of 1901 ed. lib. bdg. 32.50 (ISBN 0-89941-092-8). W S Hein.

Goffin, Robert. Horn of Plenty: The Story of Louis Armstrong. LC 77-8050. (Roots of Jazz). 1977. Repr. of 1947 ed. lib. bdg. 29.50 (ISBN 0-306-77430-5). Da Capo.

--Horn of Plenty; the Story of Louis Armstrong. Bezou, James F., tr. LC 78-4838. 304p. 1978. lib. bdg. 24.25x (ISBN 0-313-20398-9, GOHP). Greenwood.

--Jazz: From the Congo to the Metropolitan. Schaap, Walter & Feather, Leonard G., trs. from Fr. LC 74-23384. (Roots of Jazz Ser). xii, 254p. 1975. Repr. of 1944 ed. lib. bdg. 25.00 (ISBN 0-306-70680-6). Da Capo.

Goffinet, Donald R., jt. auth. see Portlock, Carol S.

Gofflot, L. V. Theatre Au College Du Moyen Age a Nos Jours, Avec Bibliographie Et Appendices. 1907. 23.50 (ISBN 0-8337-1365-5). B Franklin.

Goffman, Casper & Pedrick, George. First Course in Functional Analysis. 2nd ed. LC 82-74164. 242p. 1983. text ed. 15.95 (ISBN 0-8284-0319-8). Chelsea Pub.

Goffman, Erving. Asylums: Essays on the Social Situation of Mental Patients & Other Inmates. LC 61-13812. pap. 6.95 (ISBN 0-385-00016-2, A277, Anch). Doubleday.

--Behavior in Public Places: Notes on Social Organization of Gatherings. LC 80-19005. viii, 248p. 1980. Repr. of 1963 ed. lib. bdg. 24.75x (ISBN 0-313-22390-4, GOBP). Greenwood.

--Behavior in Public Places: Notes on the Social Organization of Gatherings. LC 62-11850. 1966. 17.00 (ISBN 0-02-911930-8); pap. 9.95x (ISBN 0-02-911940-5). Free Pr.

--Encounters: Two Studies in the Sociology of Interaction. LC 61-16844. (Orig.). 1961. pap. 7.20 scp (ISBN 0-672-60818-9). Bobbs.

--Encounters: Two Studies in the Sociology of Interaction. 1961. pap. text ed. write for info. (ISBN 0-02-344560-2). Macmillan.

--Forms of Talk. (Conduct & Communication Ser.). 335p. 1981. 32.00x (ISBN 0-8122-7790-2); pap. 10.95 (ISBN 0-8122-1112-X). U of Pa Pr.

--Frame Analysis: An Essay on the Organization of Experience. LC 74-4644. 1974. 25.00x (ISBN 0-674-31656-8). Harvard U Pr.

--Gender Advertisements. (Illus., Orig.). 1979. pap. 9.57i (ISBN 0-06-090633-2, CN 633, CN). Har-Row.

--Gender Advertisements. LC 78-23351. (Illus.). 1979. 15.00x (ISBN 0-674-34191-0). Harvard U Pr.

--Interaction Ritual: Essays in Face-to-Face Behavior. 1982. pap. 4.95 (ISBN 0-394-70631-5). Pantheon.

--Presentation of Self in Everyday Life. LC 59-9138. 1959. pap. 4.95 (ISBN 0-385-09402-7, A174, Anch). Doubleday.

--The Presentation of Self in Everyday Life. LC 72-97587. 276p. 1973. Repr. of 1959 ed. 22.50 (ISBN 0-87951-014-5). Overlook Pr.

--Relations in Public. 390p. 1972. pap. 7.95xi (ISBN 0-06-131957-0, TB 1957, Torch). Har-Row.

--Strategic Interaction. LC 74-92857. (Conduct & Communication Ser). 1970. 9.95x (ISBN 0-8122-7607-8); (Pa Paperbks). U of Pa Pr.

Goffman, I. J., ed. Federal Taxation: As a Instrument of Social & Economic Policy: A Symposium. LC 72-5017. (Symposia on Law & Society Ser.). 104p. 1972. Repr. of 1968 ed. lib. bdg. 19.50 (ISBN 0-306-70501-X). Da Capo.

Goffman, Irving. Stigma: Notes on the Management of Spoiled Identity. (Orig.). 1963. pap. 4.95 (ISBN 0-13-846626-2, Spec). P-H.

Goffman, Jerry M. Batterers Anonymous: Self-Help Counseling for Men Who Batter. LC 84-73081. 75p. 1984. pap. 9.95 (ISBN 0-9612754-0-5). Batterers Anon.

Goffman, William & Warren, Kenneth. Scientific Information Systems & the Principle of Selectivity. LC 80-49. 202p. 1980. 31.95 (ISBN 0-03-056081-0). Praeger.

Goffstein, M. B. An Artist. LC 79-2663. (Illus.). 32p. 1980. 11.49i (ISBN 0-06-022012-0); PLB 9.89 (ISBN 0-06-022013-9). HarpJ.

--An Artists Album. LC 85-42612. (A Charlotte Zolotow Bk.). (Illus.). 48p. (ps up). 1985. 11.49i (ISBN 0-06-021994-7); PLB 11.89g (ISBN 0-06-021995-5). HarpJ.

--Brookie & Her Lamb. rev. ed. LC 67-26372. (Illus.). 32p. (ps-3). 1981. 6.95 (ISBN 0-374-30990-6). FS&G.

--Daisy Summerfields Style. 1979. pap. 1.25 (ISBN 0-440-91744-1). Dell.

--Family Scrapbook. LC 78-51435. (Illus.). 48p. (ps up). 1978. 7.95 (ISBN 0-374-32269-4). FS&G.

--Fish for Supper. LC 75-27598. (Illus.). 32p. (gr. k-2). 1976. PLB 5.89 (ISBN 0-8037-2572-8). Dial Bks Young.

--Goldie the Dollmaker. LC 79-85369. (Illus.). 55p. (ps up). 1969. 7.95 (ISBN 0-374-32739-4); pap. 3.45 (ISBN 0-374-42740-2). FS&G.

--Laughing Latkes. LC 81-68932. (Illus.). 32p. (ps up). 1980. 6.95 (ISBN 0-374-34364-0). FS&G.

--Little Schubert. LC 72-79889. (Illus.). 48p. (gr. 2 up). 1985. 10.95 (ISBN 0-87923-540-3); pap. 5.95 (ISBN 0-87923-508-X). Godine.

--Lives of the Artists. LC 81-68932. (Illus.). 48p. (ps-3). 1981. 8.95 (ISBN 0-374-34628-3). FS&G.

--Me & My Captain. LC 74-6699. (Illus.). 32p. (ps up). 1974. 6.95 (ISBN 0-374-34901-0). FS&G.

--My Crazy Sister. LC 76-2286. (Illus.). (gr. k-3). 1976. 5.95 (ISBN 0-8037-6198-8). Dial Bks Young.

--My Editor. (Illus.). 32p. 1985. 5.95 (ISBN 0-374-21691-6). FS&G.

--My Noah's Ark. LC 77-25666. (Illus.). 1978. 9.57i (ISBN 0-06-022022-8). HarpJ.

--Natural History. LC 79-7318. (Illus.). 32p. (ps-3). 1979. 8.95 (ISBN 0-374-35498-7). FS&G.

--Neighbors. LC 78-19491. (Illus.). 1979. 9.57i (ISBN 0-685-91758-4). HarpJ.

--Sleepy People. rev. ed. LC 66-10723. (Illus.). (ps-2). 1979. 6.95 (ISBN 0-374-37030-3). FS&G.

--Two Piano Tuners. LC 71-106399. (Illus.). 72p. (ps-3). 1971. 7.95 (ISBN 0-374-38019-8). FS&G.

--The Underside of the Leaf. LC 75-188252. 160p. (gr. 7 up). 1972. 10.95 (ISBN 0-374-38031-7). FS&G.

--A Writer. LC 83-49488. (Charlotte Zolotow Bk.). (Illus.). 32p. (ps up). 1984. 11.89i (ISBN 0-06-022142-9); PLB 11.89g (ISBN 0-06-022143-7). HarpJ.

Gofman, I. Alexander Golvin. 192p. 1981. 60.00x (ISBN 0-317-14214-3, Pub. by Collet's). State Mutual Bk.

Gofman, John W. An Irreverent, Illustrated View of Nuclear Power: "Irrevy"; from Blunderland to Seabrook IV. LC 78-73212. 1979. pap. 3.95 (ISBN 0-932682-00-6). Comm Nuclear Respon.

--Radiation & Human Health: A Comprehensive Investigation of the Evidence Relating Low-Level Radiation to Cancer & Other Diseases. LC 80-26484. (Illus.). 928p. 1981. 29.95 (ISBN 0-87156-275-8). Sierra.

Gofman, John W. & O'Connor, Egan. X-Rays: Health Effects of Common Exams. LC 84-23527. (Illus.). 456p. 1985. 25.00 (ISBN 0-87156-838-1). Sierra.

Gofman, John W. & Tamplin, Arthur R. Poisoned Power: The Case Against Nuclear Power Before & After Three Mile Island. LC 79-16781. 1979. pap. 5.95 (ISBN 0-87857-288-0). Comm Nuclear Respon.

Gofman, John W. see Lawrence, John H. & Hamilton, J. G.

Goforth, Allene, ed. Energy & Agriculture: A Classified Title List to the Microfiche Collection. 116p. 1981. pap. text ed. 25.00 (ISBN 0-667-00666-4). Microfilming Corp.

--Food & Nutrition: A Bibliographic Guide to the Microform Collection. 96p. 1981. pap. text ed. 50.00 (ISBN 0-667-00591-9). Microfilming Corp.

--Rehabilitation & Handicapped Literature, 1950-1978: A Bibliographic Guide to the Microfiche Collection. 409p. 1981. 50.00 (ISBN 0-667-00614-1). Microfilming Corp.

Goforth, Rosalind. Goforth of China. 384p. 1969. pap. 4.95 (ISBN 0-87123-181-6, 200181). Bethany Hse.

Gogan, Robert. Engineering Triumphs: L3. McConochie, Jean, ed. (Regents Readers Ser.). (gr. 7-12). pap. text ed. 2.25 (ISBN 0-88345-496-3, 20913). Regents Pub.

--Natural Wonders, Level 1. McConochie, Jean, ed. (Regents Readers Ser). 52p. (gr. 7-12). 1982. pap. text ed. 2.75 (ISBN 0-88345-451-3, 20709). Regents Pub.

Gogarty, Oliver. Elbow Room. 48p. 1971. Repr. of 1939 ed. 12.50x (ISBN 0-7165-1388-9, BBA 02053, Pub. by Cuala Press Ireland). Biblio Dist.

--An Offering of Swans. 40p. 1971. Repr. of 1923 ed. 12.50x (ISBN 0-7165-1360-9, BBA 02054, Pub. by Cuala Press Ireland). Biblio Dist.

--Wild Apples I. 44p. 1971. Repr. of 1930 ed. 12.50x (ISBN 0-7165-1371-4, BBA 02056, Pub. by Cuala Press Ireland). Biblio Dist.

--Wild Apples II. 52p. 1971. Repr. of 1928 ed. 12.50x (ISBN 0-7165-1406-0, BBA 02055, Pub. by Cuala Press Ireland). Biblio Dist.

Gogarty, Oliver S. As I Was Going Down Sackville Street. LC 75-41113. Repr. of 1937 ed. 24.50 (ISBN 0-404-14715-1). AMS Pr.

--As I Was Going Down Sackville Street. LC 37-4752. 1967. pap. 2.25 (ISBN 0-15-609004-X, Harv). HarBraceJ.

--Collected Poems. 12.00 (ISBN 0-8159-5204-X). Devin.

--It Isn't This Time of Year at All: an Unpremeditated Biography. LC 78-108392. Repr. of 1954 ed. lib. bdg. 18.75x (ISBN 0-8371-3814-0, GOTY). Greenwood.

Gogarty, Paul. Snap Box. 1972. 6.00 (ISBN 0-685-29884-1, Pub. by Trigram Pr); signed ed. 12.00 (ISBN 0-685-29885-X); pap. 3.50 (ISBN 0-685-29886-8). Small Pr Dist.

Goggans, Sadie. Units of Work & Centers of Interest in the Organization of the Elementary School Curriculum. LC 70-176809. (Columbia University. Teachers College. Contributions to Education: No. 803). Repr. of 1940 ed. 22.50 (ISBN 0-404-55803-8). AMS Pr.

Goggin, Jim. Turk Murphy Just for the Record: A Discography with Photos, Sketches, Interviews & a Complete Index. LC 82-62235. (Illus.). 360p. 1983. 20.00 (ISBN 0-916870-57-X); pap. text ed. 12.95 o. p. (ISBN 0-916870-58-8). Creative Arts Bk.

Goggin, John M. Spanish Majolica in the New World: Types of the Sixteenth to Eighteenth Centuries. LC 68-24636. (Publications in Anthropology: No. 72). 1968. pap. 12.00 (ISBN 0-913516-05-8). Yale U Anthro.

Gogh, Anna Van see Van Gogh, Anna.

Gogh, Anna Van see Van Gogh, Anna & Anderson, Jack.

Gogh, Vincent Van see Van Gogh, Vincent.

Gogna, Ruth M. Hollywood Nineteen Eighty Crossword Puzzle. 80p. (Orig.). (gr. 7 up). pap. 9.95 (ISBN 0-931290-36-8). Alchemy Bks.

Gogniat, Maurice. Indian & Wild West Toys You Can Make. LC 79-91392. (Illus.). 64p. (gr. 4-12). 1980. pap. 4.95 (ISBN 0-8069-8892-4). Sterling.
Gogol. Oeuvres Completes. 2080p. 46.95 (ISBN 0-686-56516-9). French & Eur.
Gogol, John M. Native American Words. (Poetry Chapbook Ser.). 1.50 (ISBN 0-686-24988-7). Mr Cogito Pr.
Gogol, John M. & Davies, Robert A. Columbus Names the Flowers: Mr. Cogito's 12th Year Poetry Anthology. (Illus.). 104p. (Orig.). 1985. pap. 6.95 (ISBN 0-932191-04-5). Mr Cogito Pr.
Gogol, N. Nikolai Gogol: A Selection. 396p. 1980. 11.00 (ISBN 0-8285-1831-9, Pub. by Progress Pubs USSR). Imported Pubns.
--Nikolai Gogol: A Selection. (Vol. 2). 397p. 1981. 11.00 (ISBN 0-8285-2383-5, Pub. by Progress Pubs USSR). Imported Pubns.
Gogol, N. V. Nevskii Pvospekt. Kirilloff, A., ed. (Library of Russian Classics). 84p. (Rus.). pap. text ed. 9.95x (ISBN 0-904679-07-1). Basil Blackwell.
--The Overcoat. Forsyth, James, ed. (Library of Russian Classics). 142p. pap. text ed. 9.95x (ISBN 0-631-14392-0). Basil Blackwell.
--Revizor. Harrison, W, ed. (Library of Russian Classics). 215p. pap. text ed. 9.95x (ISBN 0-631-13864-1). Basil Blackwell.
--The Tale of How Ivan Ivanovich Quarrelled with Ivan Nikiforovich: Quarrel of Two Ivans. Pitcher, H, ed. (Library of Russian Classics). 142p. pap. text ed. 9.95x (ISBN 0-900186-25-9). Basil Blackwell.
--Taras Bul'ba. Holttum, V. E, ed. (Library of Russian Classics). 286p. pap. text ed. 9.95x (ISBN 0-900186-34-8). Basil Blackwell.
Gogol, Nicolai. Dead Souls. 16.95 (ISBN 0-89190-261-9, Pub. by Am Repr). Amereon Ltd.
--The Overcoat. 64p. (Orig.). 1981. pap. 4.50 (ISBN 0-904526-27-5, Pub. by Journeyman Pr England). Flatiron Book Dist.
--Taras Bulba. Repr. lib. bdg. 10.95 (ISBN 0-88411-138-5, Pub. by Aeonian Pr). Amereon Ltd.
Gogol, Nicolai V. The Overcoat, & Other Tales of Good & Evil. Magarshack, David, tr. from Rus. LC 79-17318. 1979. Repr. of 1965 ed. lib. bdg. 12.50x (ISBN 0-8376-0442-7). Bentley.
Gogol, Nikolai. Arabesques. Tulloch, Alexander, tr. from Rus. 1982. 27.50 (ISBN 0-88233-435-2); pap. 6.00 (ISBN 0-88233-436-0). Ardis Pubs.
--The Complete Tales of Nikolai Gogol, 2 vols. Kent, Leonard, ed. LC 84-16221. (Illus.). xlii, 647p. 1985. Vol. I. pap. 9.95 (ISBN 0-226-30068-4); Vol. II. pap. 9.95 (ISBN 0-226-30069-2). U of Chicago Pr.
--Dead Souls. (Classics Ser). (gr. 11 up). pap. 1.95 (ISBN 0-8049-0122-8, CL-122). Airmont.
--Dead Souls. MacAndrew, Andrew, tr. 1961. pap. 2.95 (ISBN 0-451-51866-7, CE1866, Sig Classics). NAL.
--Dead Souls. Magarshack, David, tr. (Classics Ser.). (Orig.). 1961. pap. 3.95 (ISBN 0-14-044113-1). Penguin.
--Diary of a Madman. Wilks, R., tr. from Rus. (Classics Ser). 1973. pap. 2.95 (ISBN 0-14-044273-1). Penguin.
--Diary of a Madman & Other Stories. MacAndrew, Andrew, tr. 1961. pap. 2.50 (ISBN 0-451-51824-1, CE1824, Sig Classics). NAL.
--Government Inspector. Campbell, D. J., tr. from Rus. 1981. pap. text ed. 5.00x (ISBN 0-435-20963-9). Heinemann Ed.
--The Government Inspector. Mitchell, Adrian, tr. (Theatrescripts Ser.). 48p. 1985. pap. 5.50 (ISBN 0-413-58470-4, 9482). Methuen Inc.
--The Government Inspector. Raby, Peter, ed. Igateiff, Leonid, tr. LC 73-187162. (Minnesota Drama Editions: No. 7). pap. 32.00 (ISBN 0-317-28151-8, 2055872). Bks Demand UMI.
--The Inspector General. Popkin, Henry, ed. MacAndrew, Andrew, tr. 1976. pap. 0.95 (ISBN 0-380-00585-9, 28878, Bard). Avon.
--Meditations on the Divine Liturgy. 58p. (Orig.). 1985. pap. 3.00 (ISBN 0-317-30300-7). Holy Trinity.
--Razmishljenije o Bozhestvennoj Liturgii. 48p. pap. 2.00 (ISBN 0-317-29135-1). Holy Trinity.
--Selected Passages from Correspondence with Friends. Zeldin, Jesse, tr. LC 69-14661. 1969. 14.95x (ISBN 0-8265-1126-0). Vanderbilt U Pr.
--Taras Bulba y Novelas de Petersburgo. 358p. (Span.). 1979. 7.95 (ISBN 0-8285-1729-0, Pub. by Progress Pubs USSR). Imported Pubns.
Gogol, Nikolai V. Dead Souls. Reavey, George, tr. from Rus. 1971. pap. 9.95 (ISBN 0-393-00600-X, Norton Lib). Norton.
--Dead Souls. Gibian, George, ed. 1985. 29.95x (ISBN 0-393-01736-2). Norton.
--The Mantle & Other Stories. facsimile ed. Field, Claud, tr. from Rus. LC 77-152940. (Short Story Index Reprint Ser.). Repr. of 1916 ed. 15.00 (ISBN 0-8369-3799-6). Ayer Co Pubs.
--Overcoat & Other Tales of Good & Evil. 1965. pap. 4.95 (ISBN 0-393-00304-3, Norton Lib). Norton.
--St. John's Eve & Other Stories. facsimile ed. Hapgood, Isabelf., tr. from Rus. LC 70-152941. (Short Story Index Reprint Ser.). (From Evenings at the Farm - St. Petersburg Stories). Repr. of 1886 ed. 17.00 (ISBN 0-8369-3800-3). Ayer Co Pubs.
Gogol, Nikolay. The Theater of Nikolay Gogol. Ehre, Milton & Gottschalk, Fruma, trs. LC 79-23745. xxvi, 206p. 1980. lib. bdg. 18.50x (ISBN 0-226-30064-1); pap. 5.95x (ISBN 0-226-30066-8). U of Chicago Pr.
Gogol, Nikolay V. Taras Bulba. 1977. pap. 1.95x (ISBN 0-460-01740-3, Evman). Biblio Dist.
Gogol, Nikoli V. Dead Souls. Gibian, George, ed. (Critical Editions Ser.). 1985. pap. text ed. write for info. (ISBN 0-393-95292-4). Norton.
Gogolak, Pete. Kicking the Football Soccer Style. Siegener, Ray, ed. 1972. pap. 1.25 (ISBN 0-689-70406-2, A-43, Aladdin). Atheneum.
Gogos, Costas G., jt. auth. see Tadmor, Zehev.
Gogotov, L. N., et al. Microbial Activities. (Advances in Biochemical Engineering-Biotechnology Ser.: Vol. 28). (Illus.). 200p. 1983. 35.50 (ISBN 0-387-12791-7). Springer-Verlag.
Gogou, Katerina. Three Clicks Left. Hirschman, Jack, tr. from Greek. LC 82-63186. (Literature Ser.: No. 2). 64p. 1983. pap. 4.50 (ISBN 0-941842-01-0). Night Horn Books.
Goguel, Catherine M. & Viatte, Francoise. Roman Drawings of the Sixteenth Century from the Musee Du Louvre, Paris. Carini, Anselmo & McCullagh, Suzanne Folds, trs. LC 79-90234. (Illus.). 166p. (Orig.). 1979. pap. 9.95 (ISBN 0-86559-036-2). Art Inst Chi.
Goguel, Francois, jt. auth. see Einaudi, Mario.
Goguel, Jean. Geologie, 2 vols. (Methodique Ser.). 53.95 ea. French & Eur.
--Geophysique. (Methodique Ser.). 1336p. 53.95 (ISBN 0-686-56430-8). French & Eur.
--Tectonics. Thalmann, H. E., tr. LC 62-7477. (Geology Ser.). (Illus.). 384p. 1962. 38.95 (ISBN 0-7167-0217-7). W H Freeman.
Goguel, Maurice. The Life of Jesus. Wyon, Olive, tr. LC 75-41114. Repr. of 1933 ed. 32.50 (ISBN 0-404-14546-9). AMS Pr.
Goguet, Antoine Y. & Fugere, A. C. The Origin of Laws, Arts, & Sciences & Their Progress Among the Most Ancient Nations, 3 vols. LC 72-1630. (Illus.). Repr. of 1761 ed. 110.00 set (ISBN 0-404-08230-0). AMS Pr.
Goh. Economics of Modernization. 1978. 14.00x (ISBN 0-685-50300-3). State Mutual Bk.
Goh, Austin. Breaking Power of Wing Chun Kung Fu. 1984. 25.00 (ISBN 0-901764-64-7, Pub. by P H Crompton Ltd UK). State Mutual Bk.
Goh, B. S. Management & Analysis of Biological Populations. (Developments in Agricultural & Managed-Forest Ecology Ser.: Vol. 8). 288p. 1980. 76.75 (ISBN 0-444-41793-1). Elsevier.
Goh, P. S. Eyewitness. (Writing in Asia Ser.). 1976. pap. text ed. 5.50x (ISBN 0-686-60352-4, 00224). Heinemann Ed.
Gohagan, John K. Quantitative Analysis for Public Policy. (Quantitative Methods for Management Ser.). (Illus.). 1980. text ed. 34.95x (ISBN 0-07-023570-8). McGraw.
Gohagan, John K., et al. Early Detection of Breast Cancer: Risk, Detection Protocols, & Therapeutic Implications. LC 81-17884. 224p. 1982. 38.95x (ISBN 0-03-059389-1). Praeger.
Gohberg, I. & Goldberg, S. Basic Operator Theory. 304p. 1981. 14.95x (ISBN 3-7643-3028-7). Birkhauser.
Gohberg, I. & Kal, M., eds. Topics in Functional Analysis: Essays Dedicated to M. G. Krein on the Occasion of His 70th. Birthday. (Adv. in Mathematics Supplementary Studies: Vol. 3). 1978. 90.00 (ISBN 0-12-287150-2). Acad Pr.
Gohberg, I., et al. Matrix Polynomials. (Computer Science & Applied Mathematics Ser.). 1982. 55.00 (ISBN 0-12-287160-X). Acad Pr.
--Matrices & Indefinite Scalar Products. (Operator Theory Ser.: Vol. 8). 302p. 1983. text ed. 39.95 (ISBN 3-7643-1527-X). Birkhauser.
Gohberg, I. C. & Fel'dman, I. A. Convolution Equations & Projection Methods for Their Solution. LC 73-22275. (Translations of Mathematical Monographs: Vol. 41). 262p. 1974. 56.00 (ISBN 0-8218-1591-1, MMONO-41). Am Math.
Gohberg, I. C. & Krein, M. G. Introduction to the Theory of Linear Nonselfadjoint Operators. LC 67-22348. (Translations of Mathematical Monographs: Vol. 18). 378p. pap. 36.00 (ISBN 0-8218-1568-7, MMONO-18). Am Math.
--Theory & Applications of Volterra Operators in Hilbert Space. LC 71-120134. (Translations of Mathematical Monographs: Vol. 24). 1970. 64.00 (ISBN 0-8218-1574-1, MMONO-24). Am Math.
Gohberg, I. Z. & Feldman, I. A. Faltungsgleichungen und Projektionsverfahren Zu Ihrer Losung. Prossdorf, S., ed. (Mathematische Reihe Ser.: No. 49). 288p. (Ger.). 1974. 39.95x (ISBN 0-8176-0722-6). Birkhauser.
Gohberg, Israel, et al. Einfuehrung in die Theorie der Eindimensionalen Singularen Integraloperatoren. (Mathematische Reihe: No. 63). (Illus.). 379p. (Ger.). 1979. 68.95x (ISBN 0-8176-1020-0). Birkhauser.
Gohdes, Clarence. American Literature in Nineteenth Century England. LC 63-9473. (Arcturus Books Paperbacks). 202p. 1963. pap. 1.65 (ISBN 0-8093-0086-9). S Ill U Pr.
--Periodicals of American Transcendentalism. LC 77-136380. Repr. of 1931 ed. 16.00 (ISBN 0-404-02854-3). AMS Pr.
--Scuppernong: North Carolina's Grape & Its Wines. LC 81-9873. (Illus.). 125p. 1982. 14.95 (ISBN 0-8223-0460-0). Duke.
Gohdes, Clarence, ed. American Short Stories Series: 1832-1936, 83 vols. Set. 1000.00 (ISBN 0-8290-0751-2). Irvington.
Gohdes, Clarence & Marovitz, Sanford E., eds. Bibliographical Guide to the Study of the Literature of the U.S.A. 5th, rev. ed. LC 84-1677. 300p. 1984. lib. bdg. 29.75 (ISBN 0-8223-0592-5). Duke.
Gohdes, Clarence see Anderson, Charles R.
Gohdes, Clarence, ed. see Rossetti, William M.
Gohdes, Clarence, ed. see Whitman, Walt.
Gohdes, Clarence L. Hunting in the Old South: Original Narratives of the Hunters. LC 67-13895. (Southern Literary Studies Ser.). pap. 49.00 (ISBN 0-317-28747-8, 2051645). Bks Demand UMI.
--Periodicals of American Transcendentalism. LC 76-107803. (Select Bibliographies Reprint Ser). 1931. 19.00 (ISBN 0-8369-5206-5). Ayer Co Pubs.
Gohdes, Clarence L., ed. Essays on American Literature, in Honor of Jay B. Hubbell. LC 67-25597. pap. 90.00 (ISBN 0-317-26748-5, 2023385). Bks Demand UMI.
--Literature & Theater of the States & Regions of the United States: An Historical Bibliography. LC 66-30584. pap. 72.00 (ISBN 0-317-26749-3, 2023386). Bks Demand UMI.
Goheen, John D. & Mothershead, John L., eds. Collected Papers of Clarence Irving Lewis. LC 73-97913. 1970. 32.50x (ISBN 0-8047-0717-0). Stanford U Pr.
Goheen, Peter G. Victorian Toronto, 1850-1900: Pattern & Process of Growth. LC 76-137736. (Research Papers: No. 127). 278p. 1970. pap. 10.00 (ISBN 0-89065-034-9). U Chicago Dept Geog.
Goheen, Robert F. Human Nature of a University. 1969. 16.50 (ISBN 0-691-09348-2). Princeton U Pr.
Gohier, Urbain D. Antimilitarisme et la Paix. LC 76-147548. (Library of War & Peace; Control & Limitation of Arms). lib. bdg. 46.00 (ISBN 0-8240-0329-2). Garland Pub.
Gohlke, Annetee, ed. Peanut Butter Favorites. LC 83-61904. 64p. 1983. pap. 3.95 (ISBN 0-89821-053-4). Reiman Assocs.
Gohlke, Annette. Ground Beef Round-up. LC 79-56741. (Illus.). 96p. (Orig.). 1979. pap. 3.95 (ISBN 0-89821-032-1). Reiman Assocs.
Gohlke, Annette, ed. Appealing Appetizers. LC 82-83968. 64p. 1982. pap. 3.95 (ISBN 0-89821-044-5). Reiman Assocs.
--Appealing Apple Recipes. LC 78-64516. 72p. 1978. pap. 3.95 (ISBN 0-89821-026-7). Reiman Assocs.
--Award Winning Recipes. 72p. 1978. pap. 3.95 (ISBN 0-89821-023-2). Reiman Assocs.
--Bar Cookie Bonanza. LC 82-60453. 68p. 1982. pap. 3.95 (ISBN 0-89821-044-5). Reiman Assocs.
--Cakes Aplenty. 72p. 1975. pap. 3.95 (ISBN 0-89821-008-9). Reiman Assocs.
--Chicken Country Style. LC 81-85696. 84p. 1982. pap. 3.95 (ISBN 0-89821-040-2). Reiman Assocs.
--Cookie Jar Cookbook. 72p. 1976. pap. 3.95 (ISBN 0-89821-016-X). Reiman Assocs.
--Country Squash. LC 83-61948. 64p. 1983. pap. 3.95 (ISBN 0-89821-054-2). Reiman Assocs.
--Egg Recipes by the Dozen. LC 83-63229. 66p. 1984. pap. 3.95 (ISBN 0-89821-057-7). Reiman Assocs.
--Harvest of Honey. LC 83-63230. 66p. 1984. pap. 3.95 (ISBN 0-89821-058-5). Reiman Assocs.
--Hearty Helpings. LC 83-63231. 64p. 1984. pap. 3.95 (ISBN 0-89821-059-3). Reiman Assocs.
--Homemade Breads. 64p. 1977. pap. 3.95 (ISBN 0-89821-019-4). Reiman Assocs.
--Microwave Magic. 88p. 1977. pap. 3.95 (ISBN 0-89821-020-8). Reiman Assocs.
--Microwave Magic II. LC 82-62678. 64p. 1982. pap. 3.95 (ISBN 0-89821-049-6). Reiman Assocs.
--Microwave Treats. LC 81-84087. 64p. 1981. pap. 3.95 (ISBN 0-89821-038-0). Reiman Assocs.
--My Oh My Country Pies. LC 83-60923. 64p. 1983. pap. 3.95 (ISBN 0-89821-051-8). Reiman Assocs.
--Palate Pleasing Pork. LC 83-63080. 64p. 1983. pap. 3.95 (ISBN 0-89821-056-9). Reiman Assocs.
--Pasta, Please. LC 82-50005. 68p. 1982. pap. 3.95 (ISBN 0-89821-042-9). Reiman Assocs.
--Pies Aplenty. 64p. 1975. pap. 3.95 (ISBN 0-89821-007-0). Reiman Assocs.
--Sweets 'n' Treats. (Illus.). 68p. (Orig.). 1980. pap. 3.95 (ISBN 0-89821-034-8). Reiman Assocs.
--Vegetable Bounty. 60p. 1975. pap. 3.95 (ISBN 0-89821-009-7). Reiman Assocs.
Gohlke, Annette, ed. see Kronschnabel, Darlene.
Gohlke, Madelon S. The Normal Heart. LC 81-8379. (Minnesota Voices Project Ser.: No. 4). (Illus.). 78p. 1981. pap. 3.00 (ISBN 0-89823-027-6). New Rivers Pr.
Gohlke, Mary & Jennings, Max. I'll Take Tomorrow: The Story of a Courageous Woman Who Dared to Subject Herself to a Medical Experiment; The First Successful Heart-Lung Transplant. Heffernen, Maureen, ed. LC 84-28803. 204p. 12.95 (ISBN 0-87131-458-4). M Evans.
Gohlman, William E., tr. from see Sina, Ibn.
Gohman, Fred. Mystery at Indian Island. (Illus.). (gr. 6-10). 1953. PLB 6.19 (ISBN 0-8313-0062-0). Lantern.
--Spider Webb Mysteries. LC 68-23985. (Illus.). (gr. 5-10). 1969. PLB 6.19 (ISBN 0-8313-0063-9). Lantern.
Gohmann, John W. Air & Rail Labor Relations: A Judicial History of the Railway Labor Act. 1979. pap. text ed. 17.95 (ISBN 0-8403-1966-5, 40196601). Kendall-Hunt.
--Arbitration & Representation: Applications in Air & Rail Labor Relations. LC 80-84183. 228p. 1981. text ed. 25.50 (ISBN 0-8403-2335-2). Kendall-Hunt.
Gohn, Jack. Kingsley Amis: A Checklist. LC 75-44709. (Serif Series: No. 34). 248p. 1976. 14.00x (ISBN 0-87338-182-3). Kent St U Pr.
Gohn, Jack B., ed. see Benoit, Emile.
Goh Poh Seng. If We Dream Too Long. (Writing in Asia Ser.). 1972. text ed. 7.00x (ISBN 0-686-60439-3, 00225). Heinemann Ed.
--The Immolation. (Writing in Asia Ser.). 1977. pap. text ed. 5.50x (ISBN 0-686-60440-7, 00226). Heinemann Ed.
Gohrbandt, Erwin, et al, eds. Handbuch der Plastischen Chirurgie, 2 vols. Incl. Vol. 1. Allgemeine Plastische Chirurgie, 2 pts. 1972. of 2 344.00x set (ISBN 3-11-004365-3); Vol. 2. Spezielle Plastische Chirurgie, 4 pts. 1973. 1138.00x set of 4 (ISBN 3-110046-49-0). (Ger.). De Gruyter.
Gohre, Paul. Three Months in a Workshop: A Practical Study. LC 74-38277. (Evolution of Capitalism Ser.). 236p. 1972. Repr. of 1895 ed. 25.50 (ISBN 0-405-04121-7). Ayer Co Pubs.
Gohring, jt. ed. see Caldwell, D. K.
Goicocchea, Ambrose, et al. Multiobjective Decision Analysis with Engineering & Business Applications. 519p. 1982. text ed. 44.95 (ISBN 0-471-06401-7). Wiley.
Goicoecha, Jose M. Elementary Spanish: A First Year College Textbook. 121p. 1969. pap. text ed. 6.95x (ISBN 0-8290-1093-9). Irvington.
Goicoechea, David, ed. The Great Year of Zarathustra, 1881-1981. LC 83-14732. 384p. 1984. lib. bdg. 27.00 (ISBN 0-8191-3497-X); pap. text ed. 15.25 (ISBN 0-8191-3498-8). U Pr of Amer.
Goil, N. K., ed. Asian Social Science Bibliography with Annotations & Abstracts, 1966. 490p. 1971. 18.50 (ISBN 0-379-00303-1). Oceana.
Goilo, E. R. Hablemos Papiamento. 1974. pap. text ed. 10.00x (ISBN 0-686-10805-1). Intl Learn Syst.
--Papiamentu Textbook. 4th ed. pap. 12.50 (ISBN 0-685-58559-X). Heinman.
--Papiamentu Textbook. 6th ed. 1976. pap. 10.00x (ISBN 0-686-10806-X). Intl Learn Syst.
Goin, Coleman J. & Goin, Olive B. Man & the Natural World: An Introduction to Life Science. 2nd ed. (Illus.). 672p. 1975. text ed. write for info. (ISBN 0-02-344240-9, 34424). Macmillan.
Goin, Coleman J., et al. Introduction to Herpetology. 3rd ed. LC 77-13554. (Illus.). 378p. 1978. text ed. 26.95 (ISBN 0-7167-0020-4). W H Freeman.
Goin, Kenn, ed. see Bloom, Frances & Bloom, Deborah.
Goin, Kenn, ed. see Swinburne, Laurence & Bank, Stanley.
Goin, Kenneth, jt. ed. see Cross, Lee.
Goin, Kenneth L., jt. auth. see Pope, Alan.
Goin, Olive B., jt. auth. see Goin, Coleman J.
Goines, Brenda. Medical Record Policies & Procedures. (Illus.). 160p. 1985. text ed. 24.95 (ISBN 0-89303-656-0). Brady Comm.
Goines, David L. A Constructed Roman Alphabet. LC 80-83954. (Illus.). 192p. 1982. 50.00 (ISBN 0-87923-375-3); ltd. ed. 150.00 (ISBN 0-87923-376-1). Godine.
Goines, Donald. Black Gangster. rev. ed. 288p. (Orig.). 1983. pap. 2.45 (ISBN 0-87067-263-0, BH263). Holloway.
--Black Girl Lost. (Orig.). 1973. pap. 2.25 (ISBN 0-87067-042-5, BH042). Holloway.
--Crime Partners. (Orig.). 1974. pap. 2.25 (ISBN 0-87067-029-8, BH029). Holloway.
--Cry Revenge! (Orig.). 1974. pap. 2.25 (ISBN 0-87067-069-7, BH069). Holloway.
--Daddy Cool. (Orig.). 1974. pap. 2.25 (ISBN 0-87067-041-7, BH041). Holloway.
--Death List. (Orig.). 1974. pap. 2.25 (ISBN 0-87067-070-0, BH070). Holloway.
--Dopefiend. (Orig.). 1971. pap. 2.25 (ISBN 0-87067-044-1, BH044). Holloway.
--Eldorado Red. (Orig.). pap. 2.25 (ISBN 0-87067-067-0, BH067). Holloway.
--Inner City Hoodlum. 224p. (Orig.). 1975. pap. 2.25 (ISBN 0-87067-033-6, BH033). Holloway.
--Kenyatta's Escape. (Orig.). 1974. pap. 2.25 (ISBN 0-87067-071-9, BH071). Holloway.
--Kenyatta's Last Hit. 224p. (Orig.). 1975. pap. 2.25 (ISBN 0-87067-024-7, BH024). Holloway.
--Never Die Alone. (Orig.). 1974. pap. 2.25 (ISBN 0-87067-018-2, BH018). Holloway.
--Street Players. 192p. (Orig.). 1973. pap. 2.25 (ISBN 0-87067-034-4, BH034). Holloway.
--Swamp Man. (Orig.). 1974. pap. 2.25 (ISBN 0-87067-026-3, BH026). Holloway.
--White Man's Justice: Black Man's Grief. 224p. (Orig.). 1973. pap. 2.25 (ISBN 0-87067-027-1, BH027). Holloway.
--Whoreson. (Orig.). 1971. pap. 2.25 (ISBN 0-87067-046-8, BH046). Holloway.

Going, Allen J. Bourbon Democracy in Alabama, 1874-1890. LC 71-141279. (Illus.). 256p. 1972. Repr. of 1951 ed. lib. bdg. 15.00x (ISBN 0-8371-5876-1, GOBD). Greenwood.
Going, Charles B. David Wilmot, Free Soiler: A Biography of the Great Advocate of the Wilmot Proviso. 1966. 16.50 (ISBN 0-8446-1200-6). Peter Smith.
--Principles of Industrial Engineering. LC 77-17900. (Management History Ser.: No. 45). 177p. Repr. of 1911 ed. 18.50 (ISBN 0-87960-049-7). Hive Pub.
Going, William T. Scanty Plot of Ground: Studies in the Victorian Sonney. (Studies in English Literature: No. 106). 1976. text ed. 17.60x (ISBN 90-2793-015-5). Mouton.
Goings, L. F., jt. auth. see Billiet, W. E.
Goings, Leslie F. Automotive Air Conditioning. LC 73-84847. pap. 49.00 (ISBN 0-317-10803-4, 2015779). Bks Demand UMI.
Goins, C., ed. see Pouler, Wilfred B.
Goins, Charles R. & Morris, John W. Oklahoma Homes: Past & Present. LC 80-5239. (Illus.). 288p. 1981. 32.50 (ISBN 0-8061-1668-4). U of Okla Pr.
Goins, John E. Pocketknives-Markings, Manufacturers & Dealers. 2nd ed. LC 82-83511. (Illus.). 280p. (Orig.). 1982. pap. 8.95 (ISBN 0-940362-06-6). Knife World.
Goins, W. C. & Sheffield, Riley. Blowout Prevention. 2nd ed. LC 70-101145. (Practical Drilling Technology Ser.: Vol. 1). 336p. 1983. 39.95x (ISBN 0-87201-073-2). Gulf Pub.
Goione, Pellegrino W., jt. ed. see Paul, Raymond.
Goirand, Roger, jt. auth. see Cohen, Jean P.
Goist, Park D. From Main Street to State Street: Town, City, & Community in America. (National University Publications Interdisciplinary Urban Ser.). 1977. 17.95x (ISBN 0-8046-9185-1, Pub. by Kennikat). Assoc Faculty Pr.
Goist, R. C. Bicycle People. 1982. 79.00 (ISBN 0-686-45835-4, Pub. by Selpress England). State Mutual Bk.
Goitein, H. Primitive Ordeal & Modern Law. xvii, 302p. 1980. Repr. of 1923 ed. lib. bdg. 32.50x (ISBN 0-8377-0612-2). Rothman.
Goitein, S. D. Jews & Arabs: Their Contacts Through the Ages. 3rd ed. LC 74-9141. 271p. 1974. pap. 6.95 (ISBN 0-8052-0464-4). Schocken.
--A Mediterranean Society: The Jewish Communities of the Arab World As Portrayed in the Documents of the Cairo Geniza. Bd. with Vol. I. Economic Foundations. 1968. 40.00x (ISBN 0-520-00484-1); Vol. 2. The Community. 1971. 46.50x (ISBN 0-520-01867-2); Vol. 3. The Family. 1978. 46.50x (ISBN 0-520-03265-9). LC 67-22430. (Near Eastern Center, UCLA). U of Cal Pr.
--A Mediterranean Society: The Jewish Communities of the Arab World As Portrayed in the Documents of the Cairo Geniza-Vol. IV, Daily Life. LC 67-22430. (Illus.). 600p. 1983. text ed. 38.50x (ISBN 0-520-04869-5). U of Cal Pr.
Goitein, S. D., ed. Religion in a Religious Age. 10.00x (ISBN 0-87068-268-7, Pub. by an Academic Inst). Ktav.
Goitia, Fernando, jt. auth. see Wolf, Reinhart.
Gojmerac, Walter L. Bees, Beekeeping, Honey & Pollination. (Illus.). 1980. lib. bdg. 19.50 (ISBN 0-87055-342-9). AVI.
Gokak, V. K. An Integral View of Poetry: An Indian Perspective. LC 75-908960. 1975. 11.00x (ISBN 0-88386-726-5). South Asia Bks.
--Poetic Approach to Language with Special Reference to the History of English. LC 76-26145. 1952. lib. bdg. 27.50 (ISBN 0-8414-4526-5). Folcroft.
Gokak, Vinayak K. Narahari: Prophet of India. 298p. 1972. pap. 7.95 (ISBN 0-317-20882-9). CSA Pr.
--Sri Aurobindo-Seer & Poet. LC 73-900907. 185p. 1974. 8.00x (ISBN 0-89684-454-4). Orient Bk Dist.
Gokalp, Ziya. Turkish Nationalism & Western Civilization: Selected Essays of Ziya Gokalp. Berkes, Niyazi, ed. & tr. from Turkish. LC 81-13235. 336p. 1982. Repr. of 1959 ed. lib. bdg. 27.50x (ISBN 0-313-23196-6, GOTN). Greenwood.
Gokay, Nancy H. Sugarbush: Making Maple Syrup. LC 80-17582. (Illus.). 32p. (Orig.). (gr. 3-4). 1980. pap. 2.50 (ISBN 0-910726-95-7). Hillsdale Educ.
Gokcen, N. A. Thermodynamics. LC 75-332953. 460p. 1975. text ed. 29.90x (ISBN 0-918910-01-3). Techscience Inc.
Gokcen, N. A., jt. auth. see Martin, L. R.
Gokcen, Nev A., ed. Chemical Metallurgy - A Tribute to Carl Wagner: Proceedings. AIME Annual Meeting, Chicago, 1981. (Illus.). 506p. 50.00 (ISBN 0-89520-382-0); members 30.00 (ISBN 0-317-36234-8); student members 16.00 (ISBN 0-317-36235-6). ASM.
Gokel, G. W. & Korzeniowski, S. H. Macrocyclic Polyether Syntheses. (Reactivity & Structure Ser.: Vol. 13). (Illus.). 410p. 1982. 120.00 (ISBN 0-387-11317-7). Springer-Verlag.
Gokel, G. W., jt. auth. see Durst, H. D.
Gokel, G. W., jt. auth. see Weber, W. P.
Gokel, George W., jt. auth. see Durst, H. Dupont.
Gokey, Francis X. The Terminology for the Devil & Evil Spirits in the Apostolic Fathers. LC 79-8100. 224p. Repr. of 1961 ed. 29.00 (ISBN 0-404-18412-X). AMS Pr.
Gokhale, B. G. Bharatavarsha: A Political & Cultural History of India. 360p. 1982. text ed. 22.00x (ISBN 0-391-02792-1, 41075, Pub. by Sterling Publishers). Humanities.
--Surat in the Seventeenth Century: A Study in Urban History of Pre-Modern India. (Scandinavian Inst. of Asian Studies: No. 28). 1977. pap. text ed. 13.00x (ISBN 0-7007-0099-4). Humanities.
Gokhale, Balkrishna G. Buddhism & Asoka. LC 78-72443. Repr. of 1948 ed. 41.50 (ISBN 0-404-17298-9). AMS Pr.
Gokhale, D. V. & Kullback, S. The Information in Contingency Tables. (Statistics Ser.: Vol. 23). 1978. 55.00 (ISBN 0-8247-6698-9). Dekker.
Gokhale, Namita. Paro: Dreams of Passion. 160p. 1985. 12.95 (ISBN 0-7011-2770-8, Pub. by Chatto & Windus-Hogarth Pr). Merrimack Pub Cir.
Gokhale, Narayan R. Hailstorms & Hailstone Growth. LC 75-19480. 550p. 1976. 49.50x (ISBN 0-87395-313-4). State U NY Pr.
Gokhale, V. V., ed. see Vidyakara.
Gokhberg, Izrail T., jt. auth. see Boltyanskii, Vladimir G.
Gokhfeld, D. A. & Cherniavsky, O. F. Limit Analysis of Structures at Thermal Cycling. (Mechanics of Plastic Solids Ser.: No. 4). 576p. 1980. 110.00x (ISBN 90-286-0455-3). Sijthoff & Noordhoff.
Gokhman, D., tr. see Bogoyavlensky, O. I.
Golab, Caroline. Immigrant Destinations. LC 77-81334. 256p. 1978. 34.95 (ISBN 0-87722-109-X). Temple U Pr.
Golab, Stanislaw, ed. Tensor Calculus. 371p. 1974. 85.00 (ISBN 0-444-41124-0). Elsevier.
Golan. Structure Sheaves: Lecture Notes in Pure & Applied Mathematics, Vol. 56. 1980. 37.50 (ISBN 0-8247-1178-5). Dekker.
Golan, Galia. The Czechoslovak Reform Movement: Communism in Crisis, 1962-1968. LC 76-163059. (Soviet & East European Studies Ser.). pap. 89.30 (ISBN 0-317-29445-8, 2055942). Bks Demand UMI.
--Reform Rule in Czechoslovakia: The Dubcek Era, 1968-1969. LC 72-83587. pap. 83.80 (ISBN 0-317-26401-X, 2024458). Bks Demand UMI.
--The Soviet Union & the Palestine Liberation Organization: An Uneasy Alliance. LC 80-18760. 304p. 1980. 34.95 (ISBN 0-03-057319-X). Praeger.
Golan, Jonathan S. Decomposition & Dimension in Module Catagories, Vol. 33. (Lecture Notes in Pure & Applied Math Ser.). 1977. 45.00 (ISBN 0-8247-6643-1). Dekker.
--Localization of Noncommutative Rings. (Pure & Applied Mathematics Ser.: Vol. 30). 352p. 1975. 55.00 (ISBN 0-8247-6198-7). Dekker.
Golan, Matti. Shimon Peres: A Biography. Friedman, Ina, tr. LC 82-7354. (Illus.). 275p. (Hebrew.). 1982. 25.00 (ISBN 0-312-71736-9). St Martin.
Golan, Michael & Whitson, Curtis H. Well Performance. (Illus.). 1986. text ed. price not set (ISBN 0-934634-75-0). Intl Human Res.
Golan, N. Passing Through Transition. 352p. 1981. text ed. 21.95 (ISBN 0-02-912070-5). Free Pr.
Golan, Naomi. Passing Through Transitions: A Guide for Practioners. LC 83-70837. 1983. 10.95x (ISBN 0-02-912080-2). Free Pr.
--The Perilous Bridge: Helping Clients Through Mid-Life Transitions. 256p. 1986. 22.95x (ISBN 0-02-912090-X). Free Pr.
--The Perilous Bridge: Helping Clients Through Mid-Life Transitions. 256p. 1985. 22.95x (ISBN 0-02-912090-X). Free Pr.
--Treatment in Crisis Situations. LC 77-85350. (Treatment Approaches in the Human Services Ser., Gen. Ed. Francis J. Turner). 1978. text ed. 18.95 (ISBN 0-02-912060-8). Free Pr.
Golan, Romy, jt. auth. see Silver, Kenneth.
Goland, Martin. Normal & Abnormal Growth of the Prostate. (Illus.). 964p. 1975. 62.00x (ISBN 0-398-03299-8). C C Thomas.
Golann, Cecil P. Mission on a Mountain: The Story of Abraham & Isaac. LC 73-7498. (Foreign Lands Ser.). (Illus.). 32p. (gr. k-5). 1975. PLB 5.95 (ISBN 0-8225-0363-8). Lerner Pubns.
Golann, Stuart & Eisdorfer, Carl, eds. Handbook of Community Mental Health. 2nd ed. (Illus.). Date not set. price not setx (ISBN 0-8290-0085-2). Irvington.
Golann, Stuart & Fremouw, William J., eds. The Right to Treatment for Mental Patients. 320p. 1976. 27.95x (ISBN 0-8290-0863-2). Irvington.
Golann, Stuart, et al. The Bethlehem Diaries: Student - Mental Patient Encounters. LC 74-12420. 240p. 1985. text ed. 24.50x (ISBN 0-8290-0241-3); pap. text ed. 12.95x (ISBN 0-8290-0242-1). Irvington.
Golant, Stephen M. A Place to Grow Old: The Meaning of Environment in Old Age. LC 84-5042. (Columbia Studies of Social Gerontology & Aging). 432p. 1984. 40.00x (ISBN 0-231-04840-8). Columbia U Pr.
--The Residential Location & Spatial Behaviour of the Elderly: A Canadian Example. LC 72-77307. (Research Papers: No. 143). (Orig.). 1972. pap. 10.00 (ISBN 0-89065-050-0). U Chicago Dept Geog.
Golant, Susan K., jt. auth. see Ludington-Hoe, Susan.
Golant, V. E., et al. Fundamentals of Plasma Physics. LC 79-19650. (Plasma Physics Ser.). 405p. 1980. 85.50x (ISBN 0-471-04593-4, Pub. by Wiley-Interscience). Wiley.
Golanty, Eric & Harris, Barbara. Marriage & the Family. LC 81-82013. (Illus.). 480p. 1982. text ed. 24.95 (ISBN 0-395-28721-9); instr's. manual 1.00 (ISBN 0-395-28722-7). HM.
Golanty, Eric, jt. auth. see Edlin, Gordon.
Golany, Gideon. Earth-Sheltered Habitat: History, Architecture & Urban Design. 192p. 1982. 21.95 (ISBN 0-442-22992-5); 14.95 (ISBN 0-442-22993-3). Van Nos Reinhold.
--New Towns Planning & Development: A World-Wide Bibliography. LC 72-93819. (Urban Land Institute, ULI Research Report: 20). pap. 64.00 (ISBN 0-317-20029-1, 2023237). Bks Demand UMI.
Golany, Gideon, ed. Arid Zone Settlement Planning: The Israeli Experience. (Pergamon Policy Studies). 1979. 63.00 (ISBN 0-08-023378-3). Pergamon.
--Desert Planning. 192p. 1982. 110.00 (ISBN 0-89397-119-7). Nichols Pub.
--Housing in Arid Lands: Design & Planning. LC 80-41108. 257p. 1980. 133.95x (ISBN 0-470-27055-1). Halsted Pr.
--Urban Planning for Arid Zones: American Experiences & Directions. LC 77-10472. pap. 66.80 (ISBN 0-317-28052-X, 2055775). Bks Demand UMI.
Golany, Gideon & Walden, Daniel, eds. The Contemporary New Communities Movement in the United States. LC 74-13861. (Illus.). 168p. 1974. 12.50x (ISBN 0-252-00434-5). U of Ill Pr.
Golany, Gideon S. Design for Arid Regions. 400p. 1982. text ed. 36.95 (ISBN 0-442-22924-0). Van Nos Reinhold.
Golas, Thaddeus. The Lazy Man's Guide to Enlightenment. 96p. 1980. pap. 2.95 (ISBN 0-553-23961-9). Bantam.
--The Lazy Man's Guide to Enlightenment. 80p. 1972. pap. 2.00 (ISBN 0-916108-01-5). Seed Center.
Golaszewski, Jean M. & Kornbluh, Joyce L. Women Workers View: Their Learning. (Program on Women & Work Ser.). 82p. 1983. pap. 4.00 (ISBN 0-87736-347-1). U of Mich Inst Labor.
Golay, Frank H. & Hauswedell, Marianne H. An Annotated Guide to Philippine Serials. (Data Papers: No. 101). 1976. pap. 5.00 (ISBN 0-87727-101-1, DP 101). Cornell SE Asia.
Golay, Frank H., ed. The United States & the Philippines. LC 66-22802. 1966. pap. 1.95 (ISBN 0-936904-06-2). Am Assembly.
Golay, Frank H. & Lush, Peggy, eds. Directory of the Cornell Southeast Asia Program: 1951-1976. 88p. 1976. 3.00 (ISBN 0-87727-103-8, DP 103). Cornell SE Asia.
Golay, Keith J. Learning Patterns & Temperament Styles: A Systematic Guide to Maximizing Student Achievement. LC 82-62144. 109p. (Orig.). 1982. pap. text ed. 8.95 (ISBN 0-9610076-0-5). Manas Sys.
Golay, M. Introduction to Astronomical Photometry. Thornley, G. J., tr. from Fr. LC 73-91430. (Astrophysics & Space Science Library: No. 41). 1974. lib. bdg. 63.00 (ISBN 90-277-0428-7, Pub. by Reidel Holland). Kluwer Academic.
Golb, Norman & Pritsak, Omeljan. Khazarian Hebrew Documents of the Tenth Century. 152p. 1982. 39.50x (ISBN 0-8014-1221-8). Cornell U Pr.
Golbarth, Albert. I Am a Sonnet. (Sansfolio Ser.: No. 4). 28p. (Orig.). 1980. pap. 2.00x (ISBN 0-913282-22-7). Seven Woods Pr.
Golberg, Leon, ed. Carcinogenesis Testing of Chemicals. LC 74-11693. (Uniscience Ser.). 144p. 1974. 55.00 (ISBN 0-8493-5085-9). CRC Pr.
--Structure Activity Correlation as a Predictive Tool in Toxicology: Fundamentals, Methods, & Applications. LC 82-3007. (Chemical Industry Institute of Toxicology Ser.). (Illus.). 330p. 1983. text ed. 59.50 (ISBN 0-89116-276-3). Hemisphere Pub.
Golberg, Michael A. An Introduction to Probability Theory with Statistical Applications. (Mathematical Concepts in Science & Engineering Ser.: Vol. 29). 674p. 1984. 69.50x (ISBN 0-306-41645-X, Pub. by Plenum Pr). Plenum Pub.
Golbert, Albert S. & Gingold, Yenny N. Latin American Laws & Institutions. LC 81-12189. 592p. 1982. 44.95 (ISBN 0-03-060233-5). Praeger.
Golbitz, Frances G., jt. auth. see Golos, Natalie.
Golbitz, Pat, jt. auth. see Schoen, Elin.
Golbitz, Pat, ed. see Adams, Jane.
Golbitz, Pat, ed. see Bass, Ronald.
Golbitz, Pat, ed. see Bateson, Mary C.
Golbitz, Pat, ed. see Bessell, Harold.
Golbitz, Pat, ed. see Blanchard, Kenneth & Johnson, Spencer.
Golbitz, Pat, ed. see Blanchard, Kenneth & Lorber, Robert.
Golbitz, Pat, ed. see Blanchard, Kenneth & Zigarmi, Drea.
Golbitz, Pat, ed. see Brata, Sasthi.
Golbitz, Pat, ed. see Follett, Ken.
Golbitz, Pat, ed. see Hartz, Peter F.
Golbitz, Pat, ed. see Holleran, Andrew.
Golbitz, Pat, ed. see Horwitz, Merle H.
Golbitz, Pat, ed. see Hungry Wolf, Adolf & Hungry Wolf, Beverly.
Golbitz, Pat, ed. see Hyman, B. D.
Golbitz, Pat, ed. see Johnson, Spencer & Wilson, Larry.
Golbitz, Pat, ed. see Leigh, Wendy.
Golbitz, Pat, ed. see Lloyd, Sarah.
Golbitz, Pat, ed. see Lueth, Shirley.
Golbitz, Pat, ed. see Mayer, Gloria G.
Golbitz, Pat, ed. see Meade, Marion.
Golbitz, Pat, ed. see O'Toole, Patricia.
Golbitz, Pat, ed. see Pinckney, Callan & Batson, Sallie.
Golbitz, Pat, ed. see Rumsey, Tim.
Golbitz, Pat, ed. see Sanger, Sirgay & Kelly, John.
Golbitz, Pat, ed. see Sedgwick, John.
Golbitz, Pat, ed. see Shore, Sammy.
Golbitz, Pat, ed. see Stewart, Fred M.
Golbitz, Pat, ed. see Terrill, Ross.
Golbitz, Pat, ed. see Tweedie, Jill.
Golbitz, Pat, ed. see Viscott, David.
Golbitz, Pat, ed. see Weber, Eric.
Golbitz, Pat, ed. see Weisinger, Hendrie D.
Golblatt, Margaret A. Legal Looseleaf Services: A Computer-Based Approach. Date not set. price not set. Am Assn Law Libs.
Golbus, Mitchell S., ed. see Annual Birth Defects Conference, San Francisco, Ca., 1978.
Golby, J. M. & Purdue, G. W. The Civilisation of the Crowd: Popular Culture in England, 1750-1900. 250p. 1985. 20.00x (ISBN 0-8052-3988-X). Schocken.
Gold. Biography of Judge John Appleton. 1985. write for info. Oceana.
Gold, Annalee. How to Sell Fashion. 2nd ed. LC 78-51903. (Illus.). 1978. 12.50 (ISBN 0-87005-201-2). Fairchild.
--Seventy-Five Years of Fashion. LC 74-24531. (Illus.). 1975. 10.00 (ISBN 0-87005-144-X). Fairchild.
Gold, Arthur & Fizdale, Robert. The Gold & Fizdale Cookbook: Food for Good Living. LC 83-19255. 416p. 1984. 19.45 (ISBN 0-394-50414-3). Random.
--Misia. LC 79-2223. (Illus.). 1980. 16.95 (ISBN 0-394-48710-9). Knopf.
--Misia: The Life of Misia Sert. LC 80-27340. (Illus.). 340p. 1981. Repr. 12.95 (ISBN 0-688-00391-5, Quill NY). Morrow.
Gold, Artie. Some of the Cat Poems. (Illus.). 1978. pap. 2.00 (ISBN 0-916696-08-1). Cross Country.
Gold, Avie. Hoshanos. (Art Scroll Mesorah Ser.). 160p. 1980. 11.95 (ISBN 0-89906-162-1); pap. 8.95 (ISBN 0-89906-163-X). Mesorah Pubns.
Gold, Avner. The Dream. Reinman, Y. Y., ed. (Ruach Ami Ser.: No. 2). (Illus.). 112p. (gr. 7-11). 1983. pap. 4.95 (ISBN 0-935063-01-3). CIS Comm.
--The Impostor. Reinman, Y. Y., ed. (Ruach Ami Ser.: No. 5). 192p. 1985. 9.95 (ISBN 0-935063-14-5); pap. 7.95 (ISBN 0-935063-13-7). CIS Comm.
--The Promised Child. Reinman, Y. Y., ed. (Ruach Ami Ser.: No.1). (Illus.). 128p. (gr. 7-11). 1985. 7.95 (ISBN 0-935063-10-2); pap. 5.95 (ISBN 0-935063-00-5). CIS Comm.
--Twilight. Reinman, Y. Y., ed. (Ruach Ami Ser.: No. 4). (Illus.). 128p. (gr. 7-11). 1985. 7.95 (ISBN 0-935063-11-0); pap. 5.95 (ISBN 0-935063-03-X). CIS Comm.
--The Year of the Sword. Reinman, Y. Y., ed. (Ruach Ami Ser.: No. 3). (Illus.). 112p. 1984. pap. 4.95 (ISBN 0-935063-02-1). CIS Comm.
Gold, B. Brown. The Organization of Afferents from the Brain Stem Nuclei to the Cerebellar Cortex in the Cat. (Advances in Anatomy, Embryology & Cell Biology: Vol. 62). (Illus.). 100p. 1980. pap. 32.00 (ISBN 0-387-09960-3). Springer-Verlag.
Gold, Barbara K., ed. Literary & Artistic Patronage in Ancient Rome. (Illus.). 207p. 1982. text ed. 27.50x (ISBN 0-292-74631-8). U of Tex Pr.
Gold, Barry A. & Miles, Matthew B. Whose School Is It Anyway? Parent-Teacher Conflict Over an Innovative School. LC 81-8562. 416p. 1981. 39.95 (ISBN 0-03-059674-2). Praeger.
Gold, Bela. Productivity, Technology, & Capital Economic Analysis, Managerial Strategies, & Government Policies. LC 79-4749. 352p. 1979. 31.50x (ISBN 0-669-02957-2). Lexington Bks.
--Wartime Economic Planning in Agriculture. LC 68-58580. (Columbia University. Studies in the Social Sciences: No. 551). Repr. of 1949 ed. 34.50 (ISBN 0-404-51551-7). AMS Pr.
Gold, Bela, ed. Technological Change: Economics, Management & Environment. LC 74-17112. 1975. 33.00 (ISBN 0-08-018012-4). Pergamon.
Gold, Bela, et al. Evaluating Technological Innovations: Methods, Expectations, & Findings. LC 79-4749. 384p. 1980. 35.50x (ISBN 0-669-03638-2). Lexington Bks.
Gold, Bela, et al, eds. Technological Progress & Industrial Leadership: The Growth of the U. S. Steel Industry, 1900-1965. LC 83-48756. 832p. 1984. 60.00x (ISBN 0-669-07535-3). Lexington Bks.
Gold, Bernard & Magarian, Judith A. Famous People in American History. (gr. 3-8). 1979. 6.50 (ISBN 0-918932-59-9). Activity Resources.
Gold, Bernard & Rader, Charles M. Digital Processing of Signals. LC 82-14072. 282p. 1983. Repr. of 1969 ed. lib. bdg. 19.50 (ISBN 0-89874-548-9). Krieger.
Gold, Bernard, jt. auth. see Rabiner, Lawrence R.
Gold, Carol S. Solid Gold Customer Relations: A Professional Resource Guide. 122p. 1983. 10.95 (ISBN 0-13-822338-6); pap. 5.95 (ISBN 0-13-822320-3). P-H.
Gold, Charles, jt. auth. see Wolfman, Peri.

Gold, Charlotte & Mackenzie, Susan, eds. Wide World of Arbitration: An Anthology. 211p. 27.50 (ISBN 0-318-12391-6); members 20.00 (ISBN 0-318-12392-4). Am Arbitration.

Gold, Clotilde, jt. auth. see Vasquez, James A.

Gold, David T. Fire Brigade Training Manual: Emergency Forces Training for Work Environments. Carwile, Ruth, ed. LC 82-82125. (Illus.). 236p. 1982. pap. text ed. 17.00 (ISBN 0-87765-224-4, SPP-73); training manual 21.50 (SPP-73M). Natl Fire Prot.

Gold, Don. Bellevue. 448p. 1983. pap. 3.95 (ISBN 0-440-10473-4). Dell.

--The Intermediate Two Bids in Bridge: A Modern Alternative for Standard American Bidders. (Illus.). 1981. 7.95 (ISBN 0-682-49579-4). Exposition Pr FL.

Gold, Doris B. Honey in the Lion: Collected Poems. LC 78-73259. 1979. pap. 3.00 (ISBN 0-9602036-1-3). Biblio NY.

Gold, E. J. The Human Biological Machine As a Transformational Apparatus. Lourie, Iven, pref. by. LC 85-60946. 176p. (Orig.). 1985. pap. 12.50 (ISBN 0-89556-046-1). IDHHB.

--Lazy Man's Guide to Death & Dying. LC 83-82409. 1983. pap. 8.95 (ISBN 0-89556-041-0). IDHHB.

--New American Book of the Dead. LC 81-82579. (Illus.). 1981. pap. 9.95 (ISBN 0-89556-029-1). IDHHB.

--Shakti. (Illus.). 1973. pap. 4.95 (ISBN 0-89556-005-4). IDHHB.

Gold, Eddie & Ahrens, Art. The Golden Era Cubs: Eighteen Seventy-Six to Nineteen Forty. LC 84-60184. 180p. 1985. 12.95 (ISBN 0-931028-66-3). Pluribus Pr.

Gold, Eddie, jt. auth. see Ahrens, Art.

Gold, Edgar. Maritime Transport: The Evolution of International Marine Policy & Shipping Law. LC 80-8641. (Illus.). 448p. 1981. 40.00x (ISBN 0-669-04338-9). Lexington Bks.

Gold, Edward. Owl. (SCOP Ser.: No. VII). 1983. pap. 4.50 (ISBN 0-930526-06-6). SCOP Pubns.

Gold, Ellen B. The Changing Risk of Disease in Women: An Epidemiologic Approach. LC 81-48270. 352p. 1983. 35.00 (ISBN 0-669-05319-8, Collamore). Heath.

Gold, Elliot M. & Singletary, Shirley A. Definitive Buyer's Guide to Teleconferencing Products & Services. 157p. 1983. softcover 40.00 (ISBN 0-07-600004-4). McGraw.

Gold, Erma & Stambler, Helen. The Around the World Jewish Cookbook. (Illus.). 1964. 8.95x (ISBN 0-87068-378-0). Ktav.

Gold, F., tr. see Bichat, Marie F.

Gold, F., tr. see Bichat, Xavier.

Gold, Faye & Grandfield, Raymond J. Business & Office Careers. (Illus.). 220p. (gr. 7-12). 1975. pap. 5.50 (ISBN 0-87005-148-2). Fairchild.

--Distribution & Distributive Careers. (Distributive Career Ser., Bk. 1). (Illus.). 100p. (gr. 7-12). 1972. wkbk. 3.50 (ISBN 0-87005-112-1). Fairchild.

--Working for a Wholesaler. (Distributive Career Ser., Bk. 4). (Illus.). 128p. (gr. 7 up). 1973. text ed. 3.50 (ISBN 0-87005-119-9). Fairchild.

--Working in a Service Industry. (Distributive Career Ser., Bk. 3). (Illus.). 128p. (gr. 10-12). 1973. pap. text ed. 3.50 (ISBN 0-87005-117-2). Fairchild.

--Working in a Store. (Distributive Career Ser., Bk. 2). (Illus.). 96p. (gr. 9-12). 1972. pap. 3.50 (ISBN 0-87005-114-8). Fairchild.

--Working in the Transportation Industry. (Distributive Career Ser., Bk. 5). (Illus.). 128p. (gr. 9-12). 1974. wkbk 3.50 (ISBN 0-87005-121-0). Fairchild.

Gold, Faye & Kushins, Milton. Modern Supermarket Operations. 3rd ed. (Illus.). 260p. 1981. text ed. 18.50 (ISBN 0-87005-263-2); instructor's guide 2.50 (ISBN 0-87005-366-3). Fairchild.

Gold, Gerald. Gandhi: A Pictorical Biography. LC 82-22478. (Illus.). 192p. 1983. 16.95 (ISBN 0-937858-27-7); pap. 9.95 (ISBN 0-937858-20-X). Newmarket.

--Modern Commodity Futures Trading. LC 75-5442. 14.95 (ISBN 0-910418-01-2). Commodity Res.

Gold, Gerald L. Saint Pascal: Changing Leadership & Social Organization in a Quebec Town. (Illus.). 215p. 1985. pap. text ed. 7.95x (ISBN 0-88133-164-3). Waveland Pr.

Gold, H., jt. auth. see Calmon, C.

Gold, Harris, jt. auth. see Probstein, Ronald F.

Gold, Harry. The Sociology of Urban Life. (Illus.). 416p. 1982. 27.95 (ISBN 0-13-821371-2). P-H.

Gold, Harvey J. Mathematical Modeling of Biological Systems: An Introductory Guidebook. LC 77-8193. 357p. 1977. 43.50x (ISBN 0-471-02092-3, Pub. by Wiley-Interscience). Wiley.

Gold, Herbert. Biafra Goodbye. (Orig.). 1970. pap. 4.25 (ISBN 0-685-04864-0). Twowindows Pr.

--Family. 224p. 1983. pap. 2.75 (ISBN 0-523-41887-6). Pinnacle Bks.

--Family: A Novel in the Form of a Memoir. LC 81-66964. 1981. 11.95 (ISBN 0-87795-332-5). Arbor Hse.

--Fathers. 1983. 16.95 (ISBN 0-87795-549-2); pap. 8.95 (ISBN 0-87795-550-6). Arbor Hse.

--Mister White Eyes. 241p. 1984. 15.95 (ISBN 0-87795-636-7). Arbor Hse.

--True Love. LC 82-72063. 1982. 14.50 (ISBN 0-87795-425-9). Arbor Hse.

--Waiting for Cordelia. LC 76-29231. 1977. 8.95 (ISBN 0-87795-154-3). Arbor Hse.

--A Walk on the West Side: California on the Brink. LC 80-70216. 208p. 1981. 12.95 (ISBN 0-87795-305-8); pap. 5.95 (ISBN 0-87795-322-8). Arbor Hse.

Gold, Herbert & Asher, Don. Stories of Misbegotten Love & Angel on My Shoulder & Other Stories. (Capra Back-to-Back Bks.). 128p. (Orig.). 1985. pap. 7.50 (ISBN 0-88496-234-2). Capra Pr.

Gold, Herbert & Stevenson, David L., eds. Stories of Modern America. 1969. pap. 12.95 (ISBN 0-312-76230-5). St Martin.

Gold, Jay J. & Josimovich, John B. Gynecologic Endocrinology. 3rd ed. (Illus.). 918p. 1980. 82.00 (ISBN 0-06-140954-5, 09549, Harper Medical). Lippincott.

Gold, Jerome. The Negligence of Death. 179p. (Orig.). 1984. pap. 7.95 (ISBN 0-930773-00-4). Black Heron Pr.

Gold, Joel A. Principles of Psychological Research. 248p. 1984. 17.00x (ISBN 0-256-02858-3). Dorsey.

Gold, Joel J., ed. see Johnson, Samuel.

Gold, John. Valued Environments. Burgess, Jacquelin, ed. (Illus.). 1982. text ed. 35.00x (ISBN 0-04-710001-X). Allen Unwin.

Gold, John, jt. ed. see Burgess, Jacquelin.

Gold, John R. An Introduction to Behavioural Geography. 1980. 39.95x (ISBN 0-19-823233-0); pap. 12.95x (ISBN 0-19-823234-9). Oxford U Pr.

Gold, Joseph. Fund Agreement in the Courts, 2 vols. 1982. Set. 20.00; Vol. 1, xv, 159p 1962. 3.50 (ISBN 0-939934-03-5); Vol. 2, ix, 499p 1982. 17.50 (ISBN 0-939934-17-5). Intl Monetary.

--Legal & Institutional Aspects of the International Monetary System: Selected Essays. Evensen, Jane B. & Oh, Jai K., eds. xx, 633p. 1979. 17.50 (ISBN 0-939934-13-2). Intl Monetary Fund.

--Legal & Institutional Aspects of the International Monetary System: Selected Essays, Vol. II. xviii, 947p. 1984. 40.00 (ISBN 0-939934-34-5). Intl Monetary.

--Legal & Institutional Aspects of the International Monetary System: Selected Essays. Evensen, Jane B. & Oh, Jai K., eds. LC 79-10168. pap. 160.00 (ISBN 0-317-28776-1, 2020605). Bks Demand UMI.

--Legal & Institutional Aspects of the International Monetary System: Selected Essays, Vol. 2. xviii, 947p. 1984. 40.00 (ISBN 0-317-19911-0). Intl Monetary.

--Legal & Institutional Aspects of the International Monetary System: Selected Essays, Vol. 2. LC 79-10168. pap. 160.00 (ISBN 0-317-26162-2, 2024271). Bks Demand UMI.

--The Multilateral System of Payments: Keynes, Convertibility, & the International Monetary Fund's Articles of Agreement. (Occasional Papers: No. 6). 31p. 1981. pap. 5.00 (ISBN 0-317-04007-3). Intl Monetary.

--The Stature of Dickens: A Centenary Bibliography. LC 70-151368. pap. 69.00 (ISBN 0-317-27040-0, 2023625). Bks Demand UMI.

Gold, Joyce. From Windmills to the World Trade Center: A Walking Guide to Lower Manhattan. (Illus.). 96p. (Orig.). 1983. pap. 2.75 (ISBN 0-686-38105-X). Old Warren.

Gold, Judith H., ed. The Psychiatric Implications of Menstruation. (Progress in Psychiatry Ser.). 128p. 1985. text ed. 15.95x (ISBN 0-88048-093-9, 48-093-9). Am Psychiatric.

Gold, K. D. The Great American Office Poster. (Illus.). 240p. (Orig.). 1984. pap. 9.95 (ISBN 0-9613576-0-6). Poky Nose Pr.

Gold, Leonard, tr. see Shaham, Nathan.

Gold, Lloyd. A Grave Undertaking. 65p. 1976. pap. 3.35x (ISBN 0-685-73010-7). Dramatists Play.

Gold, Louise, jt. auth. see Kane, Kay.

Gold, Marc. Marc Gold: "Did I Say That?". Articles & Commentary on the Try Another Way System. LC 80-51793. (Illus.). 347p. 1980. pap. text ed. 18.95 (ISBN 0-87822-219-7, 2197). Res Press.

--Try Another Way Training Manual. LC 80-52142. 114p. (Orig.). 1980. pap. 8.95 (ISBN 0-87822-222-7, 2227). Res Press.

Gold, Mark S. Eight Hundred-Cocaine. 64p. 1984. pap. 2.95 (ISBN 0-553-34094-8). Bantam.

Gold, Mark S. & Lydiard, R. Bruce, eds. Advances in Psychopharmacology: Predicting & Improving Treatment Response. 344p. 1984. 90.00 (ISBN 0-8493-5680-6). CRC Pr.

Gold, Martin & Mann, David W. Expelled to a Friendlier Place: A Study of Effective Alternative Schools. (Illus.). 192p. 1984. text ed. 12.95x (ISBN 0-472-08046-6). U of Mich Pr.

Gold, Martin E. Law & Social Change: A Study of Land Reform in Sri Lanka. 272p. 1984. pap. text ed. 11.95x (ISBN 0-8290-1576-0). Irvington.

Gold, Mary. Holding On - A Woman & Farm: Shenandoah Valley 1920's-1930's, Letters of Mary Gold. Woodrich, Mary Neville, ed. LC 85-51145. (Illus.). 184p. (Orig.). 1985. pap. 6.95 (ISBN 0-9614789-0-X). Treehouse Pr.

Gold, Mary C. Teaching Reading in the Social Studies: A Global Approach for K-5. rev. ed. (Illus.). 106p. (Orig.). (gr. k-5). 1983. pap. 14.95 (ISBN 0-943804-29-9). U of Denver Teach.

Gold, Maxine, ed. see Benedict, Helen, et al.

Gold, Michael. Jews Without Money. pap. 1.75 (ISBN 0-380-01309-6, 29520-2, Bard). Avon.

--Jews Without Money. 312p. 1984. pap. 7.95 (ISBN 0-88184-026-2). Carroll & Graf.

--One-Hundred-Twenty Million. facsimile ed. LC 77-178438. (Short Story Index Reprint Ser.). Repr. of 1929 ed. 14.50 (ISBN 0-8369-4039-3). Ayer Co Pubs.

Gold, Michael E. Dialogue on Comparable Worth. LC 83-8508. 120p. (Orig.). 1983. 14.00 (ISBN 0-87546-098-4); pap. 7.50 (ISBN 0-87546-099-2). ILR Pr.

Gold, Milton J. Education of the Gifted-Talented. (Perspective Through a Retrospective Ser.: Vol. 6). 508p. 18.95 (ISBN 0-318-02199-4). NSLTIGT.

Gold, Ned. Eight Who Wrestled Death. LC 79-23215. (Quest, Adventure, Survival). (Illus.). (gr. 4-8). 1980. PLB 14.25 (ISBN 0-8172-1554-9). Raintree Pubs.

--Eight Who Wrestled Death. LC 79-23215. (Quest, Adventure, Survival). (Illus.). 46p. (gr. 4-9). 1982. pap. 9.27 (ISBN 0-8172-2056-9). Raintree Pubs.

Gold, Penny S. The Lady & the Virgin: Image, Attitude & Experience in Twelfth-Century France. LC 84-23701. (Women in Culture & Society Ser.). (Illus.). 228p. 1985. lib. bdg. 20.00x (ISBN 0-226-30087-0). U of Chicago Pr.

Gold, Peter. Tibetan Reflections. (Illus.). 112p. (Orig.). 1984. pap. 11.95 (ISBN 0-86171-022-3, Wisdom Pubns). Great Traditions.

Gold, Peter A. Wham Bham & Thank You, Captain. 1984. 11.95 (ISBN 0-533-05790-6). Vantage.

Gold, Philip. Military Claim. 188p. 1985. 17.95 (ISBN 0-913729-05-1). Paragon Hse.

Gold, Phyllis. Please Don't Say Hello: Living with Childhood Autism. LC 74-13185. (Illus.). 48p. (gr. 6-10). 1975. 10.95 (ISBN 0-87705-211-5). Human Sci Pr.

Gold, R., jt. auth. see Bassett, L.

Gold, Raymond L. Ranching, Mining, & the Human Impact of Natural Resources Development. (Illus.). 200p. 1984. 24.95 (ISBN 0-88738-025-5). Transaction Bks.

Gold, Richard, jt. auth. see Arndt, Rolf.

Gold, Richard H., jt. ed. see Bassett, Lawrence W.

Gold, Robert. Point of Departure. (gr. 7-12). 1981. pap. 2.25 (LE). Dell.

Gold, Robert, jt. auth. see Duncan, David.

Gold, Robert, ed. Stepping Stones. 320p. (Orig.). (YA) (gr. 7 up). 1981. pap. 2.75 (ISBN 0-440-98269-3, LE). Dell.

--Stepping Stones: Seventeen Powerful Stories of Growing Up. 320p. (YA) (gr. 7 up). pap. 2.75 (ISBN 0-440-98269-3, LFL). Dell.

Gold, Robert L. Borderland Empires in Transition: The Triple-Nation Transfer of Florida. LC 69-11515. (Illus.). 288p. 1969. 10.00x (ISBN 0-8093-0368-X). S Ill U Pr.

Gold, Robert S. Jazz Talk. (The Roots of Jazz Ser.). xii, 329p. 1982. Repr. of 1975 ed. lib. bdg. 25.00 (ISBN 0-306-76155-6). Da Capo.

Gold, Robert S., ed. Point of Departure: Nineteen Stories of Youth & Discovery. 192p. (Orig.). (gr. 7 up). 1961. pap. 2.50 (ISBN 0-440-96983-2, LFL). Dell.

Gold, Ronald G., jt. auth. see Turner, Richard W.

Gold, Ruth, jt. auth. see Siegel, Ernest.

Gold, S. M. Recreation Planning & Design. 1980. 43.50 (ISBN 0-07-023644-5). McGraw.

Gold, Steven. State Fiscal Indicators. (Legislative Finance Paper Ser.). 107p. 1982. 20.00 (ISBN 0-317-36350-6). Natl Conf State Legis.

--State Urban Enterprise Zones: A Policy Overview. (Legislative Finance Paper Ser.). 54p. 6.25 (ISBN 0-317-36346-8). Natl Conf State Legis.

Gold, Steven C., ed. see Institute of Labor & Industrial Relations.

Gold, Steven D. State & Local Fiscal Relations in the Early 1980s. LC 83-12562. (Changing Domestic Priorities Ser.). 90p. (Orig.). 1983. pap. 9.95x (ISBN 0-87766-351-3). Urban Inst.

Gold, Sylvia. A Selection of Isadora Duncan Dances: The Schubert Selection, Written in Sutton Dance Writing. Sutton, Valerie, ed. 100p. (Orig.). 1984. write for info. (ISBN 0-914336-20-7). Ctr Sutton Movement.

--A Selection of Isadora Duncan Dances: Written in Sutton Dance Writing. (Illus.). 100p. 1984. 30.00 (ISBN 0-914336-20-7). Ctr Sutton Movement.

Gold, V. Advances in Physical Organic Chemistry, Vol. 19. (Serial Publication). 1983. 69.50 (ISBN 0-12-033519-0). Acad Pr.

Gold, V., ed. Advances in Physical Organic Chemistry. Incl. Vol. 11. 1975. 70.00 (ISBN 0-12-033511-5); Vol. 12. 1975. 65.00 (ISBN 0-12-033512-3); Vol. 13. 1976. 80.00 (ISBN 0-12-033513-1); Vol. 14. 1977. 70.00 (ISBN 0-12-033514-X). (Serial Publication). Acad Pr.

--Advances in Physical Organic Chemistry, Vol. 16. 1979. 60.00 (ISBN 0-12-033516-6). Acad Pr.

--Advances in Physical Organic Chemistry, Vol. 20. LC 62-22125. (Serial Publication Ser.). 1984. 50.00 (ISBN 0-12-033520-4). Acad Pr.

Gold, V. & Bethell, D., eds. Advances in Physical Organic Chemistry, Vol. 15. 1978. 65.00 (ISBN 0-12-033515-8). Acad Pr.

--Advances in Physical Organic Chemistry, Vol. 18. (Serial Publication Ser.). 1982. 70.00 (ISBN 0-12-033518-2). Acad Pr.

--Advances in Physical Organic Chemistry, Vol. 21. (Serial Publication Ser.). Date not set. 51.50 (ISBN 0-12-033521-2). Acad Pr.

Gold, Veronica, jt. auth. see Mandell, Colleen J.

Gold, Victor, ed. Advances in Physical Organic Chemistry. Incl. Vol. 1. 1963. 80.00 (ISBN 0-12-033501-8); Vol. 2. 1964. 60.00 (ISBN 0-12-033502-6); Vol. 3. 1965. 55.00 (ISBN 0-12-033503-4); Vol. 4. 1966. 70.00 (ISBN 0-12-033504-2); Vol. 5. 1967. 75.00 (ISBN 0-12-033505-0); Vol. 6. 1968. 70.00 (ISBN 0-12-033506-9); Vol. 7. 1969. 70.00 (ISBN 0-12-033507-7); Vol. 8. 1970. 80.00 (ISBN 0-12-033508-5); Vol. 9. 1972. 60.00 (ISBN 0-12-033509-3); Vol. 10. 1973. 50.00 (ISBN 0-12-033510-7). Acad Pr.

Gold, Winifred A., jt. auth. see Bash, Deborah M.

Gold, Yuthas-Smith. Reading & Other College Survival Skills. 2nd ed. 1982. pap. text ed. 13.95 (ISBN 0-8403-2735-8, 40273501). Kendall-Hunt.

Gol'danskii, V. I. Mossbauer Effect & Its Applications in Chemistry. LC 64-21682. 119p. 1964. 32.50x (ISBN 0-306-10677-9, Consultants). Plenum Pub.

Gol'danskii, V. I. & Polikanov, S. M. The Transuranium Elements. LC 73-83895. (Illus.). 161p. 1973. 35.00x (ISBN 0-306-10901-8, Consultants). Plenum Pub.

Goldanskii, V. I., jt. auth. see Fluck, E.

Goldanskii, V. I. & Herber, R. H., eds. Chemical Applications of Mossbauer Spectroscopy. LC 68-18671. (Illus.). 1968. 95.00 (ISBN 0-12-287350-5). Acad Pr.

Goldaper, Sam & Pincus, Arthur. How to Talk Basketball. LC 83-20977. (Illus.). 144p. (Orig.). 1983. pap. 7.95 (ISBN 0-934878-38-2). Dembner Bks.

Goldaras, Jose L., et al. Tres Goldaras En la Poesia Del Siglo XX. LC 80-7043. (Coleccion Espejo de Paciencia). (Illus.). 143p. (Orig., Span.). 1981. pap. 7.95 (ISBN 0-89729-280-4). Ediciones.

Goldaras, Jose R. Ser Algo: E. U.-Cuba-Puerto Rico(Federalismo: Union Para la Defensa Para la Union. LC 79-53923. 1979. pap. 7.00 (ISBN 0-89729-201-4). Ediciones.

Golday, Adrienne. The Rose & the Pickle. (Illus.). 7.95 (ISBN 0-930509-00-5). Wisdom Bk Pubs.

Goldbach, John & Ross, Michael J. Politics, Parties & Power. LC 79-47991. 382p. 1980. 15.95x (ISBN 0-913530-20-4); pap. 10.95x (ISBN 0-913530-21-2). Palisades Pub.

Goldbarth, Albert. Albert's Horoscope Almanac. 1985. pap. price not set (ISBN 0-931460-27-1). Bieler.

--Coprolites. 1973. 5.00 (ISBN 0-685-37297-9); pap. 2.50 (ISBN 0-685-37298-7). New Rivers Pr.

--Curve Overlapping Narratives. 1977. saddlestitched in wrappers 1.25 (ISBN 0-685-84037-9). New Rivers Pr.

--Different Fleshes: A Novel-Poem. 1979. text ed. 7.95 (ISBN 0-934888-00-0); pap. 4.95 (ISBN 0-934888-01-9). Hobart & Wm Smith.

--Eurekas. LC 80-28023. (Raccoon Bks.). 24p. 1981. pap. 3.95 (ISBN 0-918518-21-0). St Luke TN.

--Faith. LC 81-82536. (Illus.). 108p. 1981. pap. 4.00 (ISBN 0-89823-030-6). New Rivers Pr.

--Keeping. LC 75-320301. 50p. 1975. 3.50 (ISBN 0-87886-053-3). Ithaca Hse.

--Opticks. LC 73-90124. 72p. 1974. 5.95 (ISBN 0-913282-02-2); signed ltd. ed. 40.00 (ISBN 0-913282-04-9); pap. 3.75 (ISBN 0-913282-03-0). Seven Woods Pr.

--Original Light: New & Selected Poems, 1973-1983. 140p. 1983. 12.95 (ISBN 0-86538-031-7); pap. 7.95 (ISBN 0-86538-032-5). Ontario Rev NJ.

--Who Gathered & Whispered Behind Me. 64p. (Orig.). 1980. pap. 4.25 (ISBN 0-934332-27-4). L'Epervier Pr.

Goldbeck, David. Designing the Convenient Kitchen. (Illus.). 100p. (Orig.). 1985. pap. 12.95x (ISBN 0-9606138-1-1). Ceres Pr.

Goldbeck, David, jt. auth. see Goldbeck, Nikki.

Goldbeck, Nikki. As You Eat So Your Baby Grows: A Guide to Nutrition in Pregnancy. (Illus.). 24p. 1978. pap. 1.45 (ISBN 0-9606138-9-7). Ceres Pr.

--Cooking What Comes Naturally. rev. ed. (Illus.). 192p. 1981. pap. 4.95 (ISBN 0-9606138-0-3). Ceres Pr.

--How to Cope with Menstrual Problems: A Wholistic Approach. Passwater, Richard A. & Mindell, Earl R., eds. (Good Health Guide Ser.). 32p. (Orig.). 1983. pap. 1.45 (ISBN 0-87983-300-9). Keats.

Goldbeck, Nikki & Goldbeck, David. The Dieter's Companion: A Guide to Nutritional Self-Sufficiency. 1977. pap. 2.95 (ISBN 0-451-11685-2, AE1685, Sig). NAL.

--The Good Breakfast Book. (Illus.). 199p. 1984. pap. 5.95 (ISBN 0-9606138-2-X). Ceres Pr.

--Nikki & David Goldbeck's American Wholefoods Cuisine: Over 1300 Meatless Wholesome Recipes from Short Order to Gourmet. 1983. pap. 8.95 (ISBN 0-452-25582-1, Plume). NAL.

--Nikki & David Goldbeck's American Wholefoods Cuisine: Over 1300 Meatless Wholesome Recipes from Short Order to Gourmet. 1983. 17.95 (ISBN 0-453-00434-2). NAL.

--The Supermarket Handbook. expanded ed. 1976. pap. 3.95 (ISBN 0-451-13352-8, Sig). NAL.

--The Supermarket Handbook: Access to Whole Foods. 1974. pap. 5.95 (ISBN 0-452-25323-3, Z5323, Plume). NAL.

Goldbeck, W. B. A Business Perspective on Industry & Health Care. LC 77-7982. (Springer Series on Industry & Health Care: Vol. 2). 1978. pap. 18.00 (ISBN 0-387-90298-8). Springer-Verlag.

--Industry's Voice in Health Policy. (Springer Series on Industry & Health Care: Vol. 7). 1979. pap. 18.00 (ISBN 0-387-90429-8). Springer-Verlag.

Goldbecker, William & Hart, Ernest H. This Is the German Shepherd. (Illus.). 296p. 12.95 (ISBN 0-87666-298-X, PS-614). TFH Pubns.

Goldberg & Braslow. Better Speech Can Be Fun: F Book; L Book; R Book; S Book; & TH Book. 1973. text ed. 1.50 ea. Expression.

Goldberg, jt. auth. see Schwarz.

Goldberg, A. & Rimington, C. Diseases of Porphyrin Metabolism. (Illus.). 248p. 1962. photocopy ed. 22.50x (ISBN 0-398-00689-X). C C Thomas.

Goldberg, A. A. & Parsons, D. G., eds. Modern Concepts in Nitrate Delivery Systems. (Royal Society of Medicine International Congress & Symposium Ser.). 196p. 1983. 17.00 (ISBN 0-8089-1588-6, 791618). Grune.

Goldberg, A. J., jt. ed. see Swain, M. C.

Goldberg, A. S., ed. see International Powder Technology & Bulk Solids Conference Staff.

Goldberg, A. S., ed. see International Powder Technology & Bulk Solids Exhibition & Conference (1973: Harrogate, Eng.) Staff.

Goldberg, Alan. Solar Flames, Being the First Radius of the Poem. (Orig.). 1984. pap. 4.00 (ISBN 0-916939-01-4). Red Leopard.

Goldberg, Alan J., ed. Hospital Departmental Profiles. LC 82-6250. 140p. (Orig.). 1982. pap. 25.00 (ISBN 0-939450-13-5, 133120). AHPI.

Goldberg, Alan J. & Massachusetts Hospital Association, eds. Hospital Departmental Profiles. 140p. 1982. 25.00 (ISBN 0-939450-13-5, C-133120); members 20.00 (ISBN 0-317-36946-6). Am Hospital.

Goldberg, Alan M., ed. Acute Toxicity Testing. (Alternative Methods in Toxicology Ser.). 304p. 1984. text ed. 45.00 (ISBN 0-913113-03-4). M Liebert.

--In Vitro Toxicology. (Alternative Methods in Toxicology Ser.). 500p. 1985. text ed. 67.00 (ISBN 0-913113-05-0). M Liebert.

--Product Safety Evaluation. (Alternative Methods in Toxicology Ser.). 376p. 1983. text ed. 49.50 (ISBN 0-913113-00-X). M Liebert.

Goldberg, Alan M. & Hanin, Israel, eds. Biology of Cholinergic Function. LC 74-14473. 730p. 1976. 69.50 (ISBN 0-911216-98-7). Raven.

Goldberg, Alan M., jt. ed. see Hanin, Israel.

Goldberg, Alfred. Design Guide to the 1985 Uniform Building Code. (Illus., Orig.). 1985. pap. 39.00 (ISBN 0-9614808-0-7). GRDA Pubns.

Goldberg, Alfred, ed. History of the United States Air Force 1907-1957. LC 71-169418. (Literature & History of Aviation Ser). 1971. Repr. of 1957 ed. 46.50 (ISBN 0-405-03763-5). Ayer Co Pubs.

Goldberg, Alvin & Pegels, C. Carl. Quality Circles in Health Care Facilities. 192p. 1984. 26.50. Aspen Systems.

Goldberg, Alvin H., jt. auth. see Rust, Art, Jr.

Goldberg, Anatol. Ilya Ehrenberg: Writing, Politics & the Art of Survival. 320p. 1984. 17.95 (ISBN 0-670-39354-1). Viking.

Goldberg, Arnold, jt. auth. see Gedo, John E.

Goldberg, Arnold, ed. Advances in Self Psychology. LC 80-13918. 554p. 1980. text ed. 35.00 (ISBN 0-8236-0098-X, 00-098). Intl Univs Pr.

--The Future of Psychoanalysis: Essays in Honor of Heinz Kohut. LC 83-251. (Illus.). xx, 514p. 1983. text ed. 45.00X (ISBN 0-8236-2105-7). Intl Univs Pr.

Goldberg, Arnold, ed. see Kohut, Heinz.

Goldberg, Arnold, jt. ed. see Stepansky, Paul E.

Goldberg, Arnold I. Progress in Self-Psychology, Vol. 1. 294p. 1985. text ed. write for info. (ISBN 0-89862-300-6). Guilford Pr.

Goldberg, Arnold I. & Kohut, H., eds. Psychology of the Self: A Casebook. LC 77-92188. 460p. 1978. text ed. 40.00 (ISBN 0-8236-5582-2). Intl Univs Pr.

Goldberg, Arthur J. Equal Justice: The Warren Era in the Supreme Court. LC 72-167921. (Julius Rosenthal Memorial Lecture Ser.: 1971). Repr. of 1971 ed. 32.00 (ISBN 0-8357-9456-3, 2014553). Bks Demand UMI.

Goldberg, Arthur J., jt. auth. see Caradon.

Goldberg, Audrey G. Body Massage for the Beauty Therapist. (Illus.). 1972. pap. 11.50 (ISBN 0-434-90669-7, Pub. by W Heinemann Ltd). David & Charles.

--Care of the Skin. (Illus.). 1975. pap. 13.95 (ISBN 0-434-90672-7, Pub. by W Heinemann Ltd). David & Charles.

Goldberg, B., ed. Solar Radiation Measurements in Developing Countries. 135p. 1983. pap. 23.00 (ISBN 0-08-030547-4). Pergamon.

Goldberg, B. B., jt. auth. see Rose, Joseph L.

Goldberg, B. Z. The Sacred Fire. 285p. 1974. pap. 3.95 (ISBN 0-8065-0456-0). Citadel Pr.

--Sacred Fire. (Illus.). 1958. 7.50 (ISBN 0-8216-0146-6). Univ Bks.

Goldberg, Barry & Wells, Peter N. Ultrasonics in Clinical Diagnosis. 3rd ed. (Illus.). 1983. pap. 35.00 (ISBN 0-443-02141-4). Churchill.

Goldberg, Barry B. Abdominal Ultrasonography. 2nd ed. LC 84-2257. 528p. 1984. 55.00x (ISBN 0-471-08569-3, Pub. by Wiley Med). Wiley.

--Ultrasound in Cancer. (Clinics in Diagnostic Ultrasound Ser.: Vol. 6). (Illus.). 224p. 1980. 26.00 (ISBN 0-443-08144-1). Churchill.

Goldberg, Barry B., et al. Diagnostic Uses of Ultrasound. LC 75-8779. (Illus.). 480p. 1975. 75.00 (ISBN 0-8089-0879-0, 791627). Grune.

Goldberg, Barth H. Valuation of Divorce Assets. LC 84-20804. 689p. 1984. text ed. 80.00 (ISBN 0-314-87659-6). West Pub.

Goldberg, Ben Z. The Jewish Problem in the Soviet Union: Analysis & Solution. LC 82-15842. (Illus.). x, 374p. 1982. Repr. of 1961 ed. lib. bdg. 45.00x (ISBN 0-313-23692-5, GOJE). Greenwood.

Goldberg, Benjamin. The Mirror & Man. LC 85-718. 264p. 1985. text ed. 20.00 (ISBN 0-8139-1064-1). U Pr of Va.

Goldberg, Bernard, ed. Communication Channels: Characterization & Behavior. LC 75-23596. 1976. 21.80 (ISBN 0-87942-058-8, PP00638). Inst Electrical.

Goldberg, Betty S. Chinese Kosher Cooking. LC 83-5178. (Illus.). 330p. 1984. 14.95 (ISBN 0-8246-0292-7). Jonathan David.

Goldberg, Bruce. Past Lives, Future Lives: Accounts of Regression & Progression Through Hypnosis. LC 83-8748. 1982. lib. bdg. 16.95x (ISBN 0-89370-659-0). Borgo Pr.

--Past Lives, Future Lives: Accounts of Regression & Progression Through Hypnosis. 1982. pap. 6.95 (ISBN 0-87877-059-3). Newcastle Pub.

Goldberg, Carl. In Defense of Narcissism: The Creative Self in Search of Meaning. 224p. 1980. text ed. 25.95x (ISBN 0-89876-005-4). Gardner Pr.

Goldberg, Carl & Goldberg, Merle C. The Human Circle: An Existential Approach to the New Group Therapies. LC 73-75523. 271p. 1973. 22.95x (ISBN 0-911012-67-2). Nelson-Hall.

Goldberg, Carole E. Public Law Two-Eighty. 60p. 1975. pap. 5.00 (ISBN 0-935626-19-0). U Cal AISC.

Goldberg, Charles H., et al. Pascal. (Programming Language Ser.). (Illus.). 1984. pap. text ed. 23.75 (ISBN 0-87835-139-6); instr's. manual 8.00 (ISBN 0-87835-142-6). Boyd & Fraser.

Goldberg, D. M. & Werner, M., eds. Selected Topics in Clinical Enzymology: Proceedings of the Third International Congress of Clinical Enzymology, Salzburg, Austria, September 6-9, 1981. 362p. 1983. 64.00 (ISBN 3-11-009688-9). De Gruyter.

Goldberg, D. M., jt. ed. see Werner, M.

Goldberg, Daniel C., ed. Contemporary Marriage: Special Issues in Couples Therapy. (Dorsey Professional Bks.). 1985. 45.00 (ISBN 0-256-03484-2). Dorsey.

Goldberg, David & Huxley, Peter. Mental Illness in the Community. 1980. 11.95x (ISBN 0-422-76740-9, NO. 2038, Pub. by Tavistock). Methuen Inc.

--Mental Illness in the Community: The Pathway to Psychiatric Care. 191p. 1981. 11.95 (ISBN 0-422-76740-9, NO. 2038). Methuen Inc.

Goldberg, David, et al. PL-1 & PL-C Workbook. (Illus.). 176p. 1984. pap. 8.95 (ISBN 0-13-677618-3). P-H.

Goldberg, David E., jt. auth. see Dillard, Clyde R.

Goldberg, David M. Clinical Biochemistry Reviews, Vol. 3. (Clinical Biochemistry Reviews Ser.). 477p. 1982. 48.00x (ISBN 0-471-09868-X, Pub. by Wiley Med). Wiley.

--Mortages & Foreclosure. 2nd ed. 105p. 1983. pap. 5.95 (ISBN 0-88908-580-3). Self Counsel Pr.

Goldberg, David M., ed. Annual Review of Clinical Biochemistry, Vol. 1. LC 80-15463. 379p. 1980. 44.00x (ISBN 0-471-04036-3, Pub. by Wiley Med); Vol. 2. 48.00x (ISBN 0-471-08297-X). Wiley.

Goldberg, David M. & Werner, Mario, eds. Progress in Clinical Enzymology. LC 80-80965. (Illus.). 304p. 1980. 54.50x (ISBN 0-89352-091-8). Masson Pub.

--Progress in Clinical Enzymology, Vol. 2. 300p. 1983. 74.50 (ISBN 0-89352-206-6). Masson Pub.

Goldberg, Dick. Careers Without Reschooling: A Survival Guide to the Job Hunt for Liberal Arts Graduates. 262p. 1985. pap. 10.95 (ISBN 0-8264-0355-7). Continuum.

Goldberg, E. D. Black Carbon in the Environment: Properties, Distribution & Health Effects. (Environmental Science & Technology Ser.). 192p. 1985. 15.00 (ISBN 0-471-81979-4). Wiley.

Goldberg, E. D., ed. Atmospheric Chemistry, Berlin, 1982. (Dahlem Workshop Reports, Physical & Chemical: Vol. 4). (Illus.). 400p. 1982. 25.00 (ISBN 0-387-11651-6). Springer-Verlag.

--The Nature of Seawater, PCRR 1. (Dahlem Workshop Reports Physical & Chemical Sci. Rsch. Rept. Ser.: No. 1). (Illus.). 719p. 1975. pap. 70.60x (ISBN 0-89573-083-9). VCH Pubs.

Goldberg, E. G. A Guide to Marine Pollution. 178p. 1972. 48.75 (ISBN 0-677-12500-3). Gordon.

Goldberg, E. Maltilda & Connelly, Naomi. The Effectiveness of Social Care for the Elderly. 264p. 1983. text ed. 30.00x (ISBN 0-435-83353-7). Gower Pub Co.

Goldberg, E. Matilda. Helping the Aged: A Field Experiment in Social Work. 1970. 32.00x (ISBN 0-317-05818-5, Pub. by Natl Inst Social Work). State Mutual Bk.

Goldberg, E. Matilda & Warburton, R. William. Ends & Means in Social Work. (National Institute Social Services Library: No. 35). (Illus., Orig.). 1980. text ed. 24.95x (ISBN 0-04-360053-0); pap. text ed. 11.50x (ISBN 0-04-360054-9). Allen Unwin.

--Ends & Means in Social Work: The Development & Outcome of a Case Review System for Social Workers. 1979. 32.00x (ISBN 0-317-05819-3, Pub. by Natl Inst Social Work). State Mutual Bk.

Goldberg, E. Matilda, et al. Problems, Tasks & Outcomes: The Evaluation of Task-Centered Casework in Three Settings. (National Institute Social Services Library: No. 47). 320p. 1985. text ed. 37.50x (ISBN 0-04-361053-6). Allen Unwin.

Goldberg, E. P. & Nakajima, A. Biomedical Polymers: Polymeric Materials & Pharmaceuticals for Biomedical Use. LC 80-17691. 1980. 43.50 (ISBN 0-12-287580-X). Acad Pr.

Goldberg, Edward D. The Health of the Oceans. 172p. (Orig.). 1976. pap. 10.50 (ISBN 92-3-101356-4, U281, UNESCO). Unipub.

Goldberg, Edward D., ed. North Sea Science: Papers Presented at the NATO Science Committee Conference, November 1971. (Illus.). 420p. 1973. 40.00x (ISBN 0-262-07056-1). MIT Pr.

--The Sea: Marine Chemistry. LC 62-18366. (Ideas & Observations on Progress in the Study of the Seas Ser.: Vol. 5). 895p. 1974. 94.95x (ISBN 0-471-31090-5, Pub. by Wiley-Interscience). Wiley.

Goldberg, Edward D., et al, eds. The Sea: Marine Modeling. LC 62-18366. (Ideas & Observations on Progress in the Study on the Seas Ser.: Vol. 6). 1048p. 1977. 100.00x (ISBN 0-471-31091-3, Pub. by Wiley-Interscience). Wiley.

Goldberg, Edward L. Patterns in Late Medici Art Patronage. LC 83-42561. (Illus.). 456p. 1984. 50.00x (ISBN 0-691-04019-2). Princeton U Pr.

Goldberg, Enid. Moving Fast on the Slow Track: Strategies for Career Success. 224p. 1986. pap. 9.95 (ISBN 0-673-18087-5). Scott F.

Goldberg, Eugene P. Targeted Drugs. (Polymers in Biology & Medicine Ser.). 288p. 1983. 63.50 (ISBN 0-471-04884-4, Pub. by Wiley-Interscience). Wiley.

Goldberg, Gale, jt. auth. see Middleman, R.

Goldberg, Gary, jt. auth. see Johner, Martin.

Goldberg, George. A Lawyer's Guide to Commercial Arbitration. 2nd ed. LC 83-71295. (Illus.). 167p. 1983. 40.00 (ISBN 0-8318-0443-2, B443). Am Law Inst.

--A Lawyer's Guide to Commercial Arbitration. 162p. 1977. pap. 10.00 (ISBN 0-317-32235-4, B246). Am Law Inst.

--Reconsecrating America. 160p. 1984. 9.95 (ISBN 0-8028-3607-0). Eerdmans.

Goldberg, Gerald J. Heart Payments. LC 81-65285. 312p. 1982. 14.95 (ISBN 0-670-36466-5). Viking.

Goldberg, Gertrude S. & Johnson, Harriet C. Government Money for Everyday People. 2nd ed. 1984. pap. 12.50 (ISBN 0-536-04593-3). Adelphi Univ.

Goldberg, H. Greentown's Youth: Disadvantaged Youth in a Development Town in Israel. 160p. 1984. pap. text ed. 12.00x (ISBN 90-232-2048-X, Pub. by Van Gorcum Holland). Humanities.

Goldberg, H., jt. auth. see DiMascio, A.

Goldberg, H., ed. Ethnic Groups-Special Topics: Vol. 1, Ethnic Groups in Israeli Society. 67.25 (ISBN 0-677-40065-9). Gordon.

Goldberg, H. E. Cave Dwellers & Citrus Growers. LC 70-174260. (Illus.). 200p. 1972. pap. 34.50 (ISBN 0-521-08431-8). Cambridge U Pr.

Goldberg, H. F., jt. auth. see Lynn, T. S.

Goldberg, Harold. Advanced Commodity Spread Trading. 1985. 65.00 (ISBN 0-318-04663-6). Windsor.

--Extending the Limits of Reliability Theory. LC 81-4534. 263p. 1981. 42.95 (ISBN 0-471-07799-2, Pub. by Wiley Interscience). Wiley.

--The Inflation Profit Formula. 1984. pap. 50.00 (ISBN 0-318-04662-8). Windsor.

Goldberg, Harriet. Jardin de Nobles Donzellas by Fray Martin de Cordoba. (Studies in the Romance Languages & Literatures: No. 137). 310p. 1974. pap. 16.50x (ISBN 0-8078-9137-1). U of NC Pr.

Goldberg, Harriet L. Child Offenders: A Study in Diagnosis & Treatment. LC 69-14928. (Criminology, Law Enforcement, & Social Problems Ser.: No. 75). 1969. Repr. of 1948 ed. 15.00x (ISBN 0-87585-075-8). Patterson Smith.

Goldberg, Harry & Culbertson, Ron. A Slice of the Apple. 1983. 12.95 (ISBN 0-317-04728-0). Hayden.

Goldberg, Harry F., jt. auth. see Lynn, Theodore S.

Goldberg, Harvey E., ed. & tr. from Hebrew. The Book of Mordechai: A Study of the Jews of Libya - Selections from the Highid Mordechai of Mordechai Hakohen. LC 80-11470. 238p. 1980. text ed. 22.00 (ISBN 0-89727-005-3). ISHI PA.

Goldberg, Henry, jt. auth. see Moss, Albert.

Goldberg, Henry, jt. ed. see Moss, Albert.

Goldberg, Herb. The Hazards of Being Male: Surviving the Myth of Masculine Privilege. 1977. pap. 3.50 (ISBN 0-451-13731-0, Sig). NAL.

--The New Male-Female Relationship. LC 82-20886. 320p. 1983. 14.95 (ISBN 0-688-01877-7). Morrow.

--The New Male-Female Relationship. 1984. pap. 3.95 (ISBN 0-451-13047-2, Sig). NAL.

--The New Male: From Self-Destruction to Self-Care. 1980. pap. 2.95 (ISBN 0-451-09339-9, E9339, Sig). NAL.

Goldberg, Herb, jt. auth. see Bach, George.

Goldberg, Herman, et al. Dyslexia: Interdisciplinary Approaches to Reading Disabilities. 217p. 1983. 23.00 (ISBN 0-8089-1484-7, 791628). Grune.

Goldberg, Herman K. & Schiffman, Gilbert B. Learning Disabilities: An Interdisciplinary Approach. 1982. cancelled (791628). Grune.

Goldberg, Hillel. Israel Salanter: Text, Structure, Idea. 1982. 25.00x (ISBN 0-87068-709-3). Ktav.

--Wherever I Go, I Go to Jerusalem. 240p. 1985. 12.95 (ISBN 0-940646-09-9); pap. 8.95 (ISBN 0-940646-10-2). Rossel Bks.

Goldberg, Howard S. & Scadron, Michael D. Physics of Stellar Evolution & Cosmology. 405p. 1982. 59.50 (ISBN 0-677-05540-4). Gordon.

Goldberg, Hyman J. & Ripa, Louis W. Oral Hygiene in Oral Health. (Illus.). 408p. 1977. photocopy ed. 44.50x (ISBN 0-398-03590-3). C C Thomas.

Goldberg, I. Single Cell Protein. (Biotechnology Monographs: Vol. 1). (Illus.). 260p. 1985. 49.50 (ISBN 0-387-15308-X). Springer-Verlag.

Goldberg, I., tr. see De Gourmont, Remy.

Goldberg, I. A. & Gordon, R. A. How to Read Newspaper Stock Transactions. 56p. 1969. pap. 12.95 (ISBN 0-677-40145-0). Gordon.

Goldberg, I. A. & Gordon, R. S. Introduction to Methods for Buying & Selling Stock. 110p. 1969. 24.50. Gordon.

Goldberg, I. Ignacy. Selected Bibliography of Special Education. LC 67-19388. (Orig.). 1967. pap. 3.95x (ISBN 0-8077-1434-8). Tchrs Coll.

Goldberg, I. Ignacy, jt. auth. see Lippman, Leopold.

Goldberg, Isaac. Brazilian Literature. LC 78-58257. (Essay Index in Reprint Ser.). 1978. 24.50x (ISBN 0-8486-3019-X). Core Collection.

--Brazilian Literature. 69.95 (ISBN 0-87968-197-7). Gordon Pr.

--The Drama of Transition: Native & Exotic Playcraft. (Illus.). 487p. 1982. Repr. of 1922 ed. lib. bdg. 35.00 (ISBN 0-89984-246-1). Century Bookbindery.

--George Gershwin: A Study in American Music. LC 58-11627. (Illus.). 1958. pap. 5.95 (ISBN 0-8044-6195-3). Ungar.

--Major Noah. LC 74-39475. (Select Bibliographies Reprint Ser.). 1972. Repr. of 1936 ed. 18.75 (ISBN 0-8369-9908-8). Ayer Co Pubs.

--Man Mencken: A Biographical & Critical Survey. LC 68-54271. Repr. of 1925 ed. 27.00 (ISBN 0-404-02857-8). AMS Pr.

--Queen of Hearts: The Passionate Pilgrimage of Lola Montez. LC 75-91505. 308p. 1936. 18.00 (ISBN 0-405-08563-X). Ayer Co Pubs.

--Sir William Gilbert. 59.95 (ISBN 0-8490-2610-5). Gordon Pr.

--Story of Gilbert & Sullivan. LC 76-113194. Repr. of 1928 ed. 20.00 (ISBN 0-404-02858-6). AMS Pr.

--Story of Gilbert & Sullivan. 59.95 (ISBN 0-8490-1134-5). Gordon Pr.

--Studies in Spanish-American Literature. 59.95 (ISBN 0-8490-1149-3). Gordon Pr.

--Theatre of George Jean Nathan. LC 68-54272. (BCL Ser.: I). Repr. of 1926 ed. 21.50 (ISBN 0-404-02859-4). AMS Pr.

--Tin Pan Alley. LC 60-63364. (Illus.). 1961. pap. 5.95 (ISBN 0-8044-6196-1). Ungar.

--Wonder of Words: An Introduction to Language for Every Man. LC 74-164294. 1971. Repr. of 1938 ed. 46.00x (ISBN 0-8103-3777-0). Gale.

Goldberg, Isaac, jt. auth. see Witmark, Isidore.

Goldberg, Isaac, ed. Mexican Poetry: An Anthology. 1977. lib. bdg. 59.95 (ISBN 0-8490-2238-X). Gordon Pr.

--Six Plays of the Yiddish Theatre. 1977. lib. bdg. 59.95 (ISBN 0-8490-2611-3). Gordon Pr.

Goldberg, Isaac, ed. see Andreyev, L. N.

Goldberg, Isaac, ed. see Artzibashev, Michael.

Goldberg, Isaac, ed. & tr. see Assis, Joaquim M.

Goldberg, Isaac, ed. see Babel, Isaac.

Goldberg, Isaac, ed. see Chekhov, Anton.

Goldberg, Isaac, ed. & tr. see Dolores, Carmen.

Goldberg, Isaac, ed. see Gorki, Maxim.

Goldberg, Isaac, ed. & tr. see Medeiros, E. Albuquerque.

Goldberg, Isaac, ed. & tr. see Netto, Coelho.

Goldberg, Isaac, tr. Modern Russian Classics. Incl. Silence. Andreyev, Leonid; White Dog. Sologub, Fyodor; Father. Chekhov, Anton; Her Lover. Gorki, Maxim; Letter. Babel, Isaac. pap. 3.00 (ISBN 0-8283-1450-0, IPL). Branden Pub Co.

Goldberg, Isaac, tr. see Blanco Fombona, Rufino.

Goldberg, Isaac, tr. see Deassis, Machado J. & Neto, C.

Goldberg, Isaac, tr. see Marroquin, Lorenzo.

Goldberg, Isaac, tr. see Pinski, David.

Goldberg, Isaac, tr. see Pinsky, David.

Goldberg, Isaac, tr. see Verga, Giovanni, et al.

Goldberg, Israel. Israel: A History of the Jewish People. LC 72-162629. 715p. 1949. Repr. lib. bdg. 29.50x (ISBN 0-8371-6196-7, GOIS). Greenwood.

Goldberg, Issac. Studies in Spanish-American Literature. LC 67-27600. 1968. Repr. of 1920 ed. 23.50 (ISBN 0-8046-0171-2, Pub. by Kennikat). Assoc Faculty Pr.

Goldberg, Issac, ed. Brazilian Tales. pap. 4.00 (ISBN 0-8283-1426-8, IPL). Branden Pub Co.

Goldberg, Ivan K., jt. auth. see Kutscher, Austin H.

Goldberg, Rosamond W. Occupational Diseases in Relation to Compensation & Health Insurance. LC 68-58581. (Columbia University. Studies in the Social Sciences: No. 345). Repr. of 1931 ed. 22.50 (ISBN 0-404-51345-X). AMS Pr.
Goldberg, Rosamond W., jt. auth. see Goldberg, Jacob A.
Goldberg, Roselee. Performance: Live Art Nineteen Hundred & Nine to the Present. LC 78-6780. (Illus.). 1979. pap. 6.95 (ISBN 0-8109-2181-2). Abrams.
Goldberg, Rube. Bobo Baxter: An Original Compilation, First Collection of the Complete Daily Strip, Which Ran from 1927 to 1928. Blackbeard, Bill, ed. LC 76-53042. (Classics of American Comic Strips Ser.). (Illus.). 1977. 18.75 (ISBN 0-88355-639-1); pap. 10.00 (ISBN 0-88355-638-3). Hyperion Conn.
Goldberg, S., jt. auth. see Gohberg, I.
Goldberg, S. L. An Essay on King Lear. LC 73-84318. 212p. 1974. 37.50 (ISBN 0-521-20200-0); pap. 11.95 (ISBN 0-521-09831-9). Cambridge U Pr.
Goldberg, Sally. Growing with Games: Making Your Own Educational Games. 1985. pap. 12.95 (ISBN 0-472-06364-2). U of Mich Pr.
--Teaching with Toys: Making Your Own Educational Toys. 96p. 1981. pap. 8.95 (ISBN 0-472-06334-0). U of Mich Pr.
Goldberg, Samuel. Army Training of Illiterates in World War Two. LC 74-176810. (Columbia University. Teachers College. Contributions to Education: No. 966). Repr. of 1951 ed. 22.50 (ISBN 0-404-55966-2). AMS Pr.
--Probability in Social Science. (Mathematical Modelling & Applications Ser.: Vol. 1). 144p. 1983. text ed. 18.95x (ISBN 0-8176-3089-9). Birkhauser.
Goldberg, Samuel, jt. auth. see Bishop, Richard.
Goldberg, Samuel A. Sales of Real Property. 605p. 1971. 35.00 (ISBN 0-317-30765-7, B253). Am Law Inst.
--Sales of Real Property. 605p. 1971. 35.00 (ISBN 0-317-32258-3, B253). Am Law Inst.
Goldberg, Samuel I. Curvature & Homology. (Illus.). xviii, 315p. pap. 6.50 (ISBN 0-486-64314-X). Dover.
Goldberg, Sander M. The Making of Menander's Comedy. LC 80-5322. 1980. 23.50x (ISBN 0-520-04250-6). U of Cal Pr.
Goldberg, Seymour. Pension Disputes & Settlements, Supplement No. 3. LC 78-59106. pap. 82.70 (ISBN 0-8357-9482-2, 2016185). Bks Demand UMI.
--Unbounded Linear Operators: Theory & Applications. (Mathematics Ser.). 199p. 1985. pap. 6.00 (ISBN 0-486-64830-3). Dover.
Goldberg, Sheldon, ed. Coronary Artery Spasm & Thrombosis. LC 83-1850. (Cardiovascular Clinics Ser.: Vol. 14: No. 1). (Illus.). 223p. 1983. text ed. 40.00x (ISBN 0-8036-4161-3). Davis Co.
Goldberg, Stanley. Understanding Relativity: Origin & Impact of a Scientific Revolution. LC 83-22368. 494p. 1984. 24.95 (ISBN 0-8176-3150-X). Birkhauser.
Goldberg, Stanley J., et al. Pediatric & Adolescent Echocardiography: A Handbook. 2nd ed. (Illus.). 480p. 1980. 51.50 (ISBN 0-8151-3720-6). Year Bk Med.
--Doppler Echocardiography. LC 84-12245. (Illus.). 178p. 1985. text ed. 30.00 (ISBN 0-8121-0951-1). Lea & Febiger.
Goldberg, Stephen. Clinical Anatomy Made Ridiculously Simple. (Illus.). 175p. 1984. pap. text ed. 14.95 (ISBN 0-940780-02-X). Medmaster.
--Clinical Neuroanatomy Made Ridiculously Simple. (Illus.). 89p. (Orig.). 1983. pap. text ed. 9.95 (ISBN 0-940780-00-3). MedMaster.
--The Four Minute Neurologic Exam. (Illus.). 58p. (Orig.). 1984. pap. text ed. 6.95 (ISBN 0-940780-05-4). MedMaster.
--Neuroanatomica Clinica Hecha Ridiculamente Simple. 89p. (Orig., Span.). 1985. pap. text ed. 9.95 (ISBN 0-940780-03-8). Medmaster.
--Ophthalmology Made Ridiculously Simple. (Illus.). 84p. (Orig.). 1984. pap. text ed. 9.50 (ISBN 0-940780-01-1). MedMaster.
Goldberg, Steve. Graphiti (Four Quadrants) (gr. 5-9). 1976. pap. 3.50 (ISBN 0-918932-64-5). Activity Resources.
--Graphiti (One Quadrant) (gr. 2-4). 1976. pap. 3.50 (ISBN 0-918932-24-6). Activity Resources.
--Pholdit. (gr. 3 up). 1972. 4.25 (ISBN 0-918932-67-X). Activity Resources.
Goldberg, Steve, et al. Dispute Resolution. LC 85-50081. 1985. text ed. price not set (ISBN 0-316-31928-7). Little.
Goldberg, Steven H. The First Trial (Where Do I Sit? What Do I Say?) LC 82-2653. (Nutshell Ser.). 396p. 1982. pap. text ed. 8.95 (ISBN 0-314-65588-3). West Pub.
Goldberg, Steven R. & Stolerman, Ian P. Behavioral Analysis of Drug Dependence. Date not set. price not set (ISBN 0-12-287140-5). Acad Pr.
Goldberg, Steven S. New York University 2ND Annual Institute on State & Local Taxation & Conference on Property Taxation. 1984. Updates avail. looseleaf, 2nd annual institute 65.00, (489); looseleaf 1984 60.00. Bender.
--N.Y.U. Annual Conference on Taxation of Investments. 1984. looseleaf, 1st annual conference 65.00 (487). Bender.
--Special Education Law: A Guide for Parents, Advocates, & Educators. (Critical Topics in Law & Society). 244p. 1982. 24.50x (ISBN 0-306-40848-1, Plenum Pr). Plenum Pub.
Goldberg, Susan & DiVitto, Barbara A. Born Too Soon: Pre-term Birth & Early Development. LC 82-18381. (Illus.). 201p. 1983. text ed. 19.95 (ISBN 0-7167-1445-0); pap. text ed. 8.95 (ISBN 0-7167-1446-9). W H Freeman.
Goldberg, V. V., jt. auth. see Akivis, M. A.
Goldberg, Walter H. Mergers: Motives, Modes, Methods. 350p. 1983. 32.50 (ISBN 0-89397-155-3). Nichols Pub.
Goldberg, Walter H., ed. Ailing Steel: The Transatlantic Quarrel. LC 83-40527. 400p. 1986. 37.50 (ISBN 0-312-01502-X). St Martin.
--Governments & Multinationals: The Policy of Control vs. Autonomy. LC 82-3591. 352p. 1983. 35.00 (ISBN 0-89946-145-X). Oelgeschlager.
Goldberg, Yaffa G. A Gift of Challahs. Zakutinsky, R., ed. (Illus.). 32p. (Orig.). (gr. k-6). 1981. pap. 3.95 (ISBN 0-911643-00-1). Aura Pub.
Goldberg-Bartura, Maurie, tr. see Oz, Amos.
Goldberger, A. S., jt. ed. see Aigner, D. J.
Goldberger, Alan S. Sports Officiating: A Legal Guide. LC 82-83925. (Illus.). 176p. (Orig.). 1984. pap. 9.95t (ISBN 0-88011-092-9). Leisure Pr.
Goldberger, Anthony M. Variability in Continuation School Populations: A Study of the Significance of Differences in the Proportions of Child Workers. LC 70-178803. (Columbia University. Teachers College. Contributions to Education: No. 454). Repr. of 1931 ed. 22.50 (ISBN 0-404-55454-7). AMS Pr.
Goldberger, Arthur & Duncan, Otis D., eds. Structural Equation Models in the Social Sciences. LC 72-7701. (Quantitative Studies in Social Relations Ser.). 1973. 39.50 (ISBN 0-12-785270-0). Acad Pr.
Goldberger, Arthur S. Econometric Theory. LC 64-10370. (Wiley Publication in Applied Statistics). pap. 102.50 (ISBN 0-317-26262-9, 2055712). Bks Demand UMI.
Goldberger, Ary L. Myocardial Infarction: Electrocardiographic Differential Diagnosis. 2nd ed. LC 78-31981. (Illus.). 278p. 1979. text ed. 34.95 (ISBN 0-8016-1860-6). Mosby.
Goldberger, Ary L. & Goldberger, Emanuel. Clinical Electrocardiography: A Simplified Approach. 2nd ed. LC 80-27024. (Illus.). 305p. 1981. text ed. 22.95 (ISBN 0-8016-1865-7). Mosby.
Goldberger, David. Folk Song Book, 2 vols, Vols. I-II. (CMP Piano Library). 1963. Vol. I. pap. 3.50 (ISBN 0-8256-4100-4); Vol. II. pap. 3.50 (ISBN 0-8256-4102-0). Music Sales.
Goldberger, David, jt. auth. see Zeitlin, Poldi.
Goldberger, Emanuel. How Physicians Think: An Analysis of Medical Diagnosis & Treatment. (Illus.). 200p. 1965. 19.75x (ISBN 0-398-00690-3). C C Thomas.
--A Primer of Water, Electrolyte & Acid-Base Syndromes. 6th ed. LC 79-16693. (Illus.). 472p. 1980. text ed. 18.50 (ISBN 0-8121-0685-7). Lea & Febiger.
--Textbook of Clinical Cardiology. LC 81-38350. (Illus.). 1069p. 1982. text ed. 37.95 (ISBN 0-8016-1864-9). Mosby.
Goldberger, Emanuel & Wheat, Myron W., Jr. Treatment of Cardiac Emergencies. 3rd ed. LC 81-14155. (Illus.). 416p. 1982. pap. text ed. 29.95 (ISBN 0-8016-1857-6). Mosby.
Goldberger, Emanuel, jt. auth. see Goldberger, Ary L.
Goldberger, Iefke. The Catch. 1982. pap. 4.95 (ISBN 0-913370-15-0, Sol Press). Wisconsin Bks.
--The Weeping Crab. 36p. (Orig.). 1984. pap. 4.95 (ISBN 0-913370-16-9, Sol Press). Wisconsin Bks.
Goldberger, Jeanne M. For Parents of a Tongue Thruster. 2p. 1975. pap. text ed. 0.25x (ISBN 0-8134-1700-7, 1700); pap. text ed. 3.00 25 copies; pap. text ed. 10.00 100 copies. Interstate.
--Tongue Thrust Correction. 4th ed. LC 77-90374. 100p. 1978. pap. 4.95x (ISBN 0-8134-2006-7, 2006). Interstate.
Goldberger, Leo, ed. Psychoanalysis & Contemporary Science, Vol. 3. 1974. text ed. 35.00 (ISBN 0-8236-5143-6). Intl Univs Pr.
Goldberger, Leo & Breznitz, Shlomo, eds. Handbook of Stress: Theoretical & Clinical Aspects. 804p. 1982. 49.95 (ISBN 0-02-912030-6). Free Pr.
Goldberger, M. L. Collision Theory. rev ed. LC 75-15669. 930p. 1975. Repr. of 1964 ed. 52.50 (ISBN 0-88275-313-4). Krieger.
Goldberger, Paul. The City Observed - New York: A Guide to the Architecture of Manhattan. LC 78-21795. (Illus.). 1979. 15.00 (ISBN 0-394-50450-X). Random.
--The City Observed-New York: A Guide to the Architecture of Manhattan. LC 78-21797. (Illus.). 1979. pap. 8.95 (ISBN 0-394-72916-1, Vin). Random.
--A Monograph of the Works of McKim, Mead & White 1879-1915. (Quality Paperbacks Ser.). 405p. 1985. pap. 24.50 (ISBN 0-306-80240-6). Da Capo.
--On the Rise. LC 83-45116. (Illus.). 352p. 1983. 19.95 (ISBN 0-8129-1088-5). Times Bks.
--On the Rise: Architecture & Design in a Postmodern Age. 352p. 1985. pap. 8.95 (ISBN 0-14-007632-8). Penguin.
--The Skyscraper. LC 81-47480. (Illus.). 224p. 1983. pap. 12.95 (ISBN 0-394-71586-1). Knopf.
Goldberger, Paul, jt. auth. see Leich, Jean F.
Goldberger, Robert F., ed. Biological Regulation & Development, Vol. 1: Gene Expression. LC 78-21893. 576p. 1978. 55.00x (ISBN 0-306-40098-7, Plenum Pr). Plenum Pub.
--Biological Regulation & Development, Vol. 2: Molecular Organization & Cell Function. LC 78-21893. 636p. 1980. 59.50x (ISBN 0-306-40486-9, Plenum Pr). Plenum Pub.
Goldberger, Robert F. & Yamamoto, Keith, eds. Biological Regulation & Development, Vol. 3B. (Hormone Action Ser.). 326p. 1984. 42.50x (ISBN 0-306-41442-2, Plenum Pr). Plenum Pub.
--Biological Regulation & Development, Vol. 3A: Hormone Action. LC 82-8941. 360p. 1982. 45.00x (ISBN 0-306-40925-9, Plenum Pr). Plenum Pub.
Goldbert, Miriam & Werle, Martha, eds. Psychological Foundations of Education: Readings. 350p. 1974. text ed. 34.50x (ISBN 0-8422-5187-1). Irvington.
Goldblat, J. Agreements for Arms Control: A Critical Survey. 388p. 1982. 41.00x (ISBN 0-85066-229-X). Taylor & Francis.
Goldblat, Josef. Arms Control Agreements: A Handbook. LC 83-2167. 346p. 1983. 15.95x (ISBN 0-03-063709-0). Praeger.
Goldblatt, Burt. Burt Goldblatt's Jazz Gallery One. Schlamm, Rhoda, ed. LC 82-61418. (Illus.). 200p. 1982. pap. 18.95 (ISBN 0-910945-00-4). Newbold Pub.
Goldblatt, David. Neuroscience & Clinical Neurology Review. LC 78-8560. (Arco Medical Review Ser.). (Illus.). 1979. pap. text ed. 10.00x (ISBN 0-668-03370-3). Arco.
--Neuroscience & Clinical Neurology Review. 224p. 1979. pap. 13.95 (ISBN 0-668-03370-3). ACC.
Goldblatt, Harold, tr. see Halbwachs, Maurice.
Goldblatt, Harvey, jt. ed. see Picchio, Riccardo.
Goldblatt, Howard, jt. auth. see Yaffe, Byron.
Goldblatt, Howard, tr. from Chinese. Chinese Literature for the Nineteen Eighties: The Fourth Congress of Writers & Artists. LC 82-744. 195p. 1982. 35.00 (ISBN 0-87332-208-8). M E Sharpe.
Goldblatt, Howard, tr. see Chen, Jo-hsi.
Goldblatt, Howard, tr. see Hsiao Hung.
Goldblatt, Howard, tr. see Hwang, Chun-ming.
Goldblatt, Howard, tr. see Jiang, Yang.
Goldblatt, Howard, tr. see Xiao Hong.
Goldblatt, R. Axiomatising the Logic of Computer Programming. (Lecture Notes in Computer Science Ser.: Vol. 130). 304p. 1982. pap. 20.00 (ISBN 0-387-11210-3). Springer-Verlag.
--Topoi: The Categorial Analysis of Logic. (Studies in Logic & the Foundations of Mathematics Ser.: Vol. 98). 1980. 69.25 (ISBN 0-444-85207-7, North Holland). Elsevier.
Goldblith, S. A., et al, eds. Freeze Drying & Advanced Food Technology. 1975. 95.00 (ISBN 0-12-288450-7). Acad Pr.
Goldblith, Samuel A. & Decareau, Robert V. An Annotated Bibliography on Microwaves: Their Properties, Production, & Application to Food Processing. 1973. 32.50x (ISBN 0-262-07049-9). MIT Pr.
Goldblum, N., et al, eds. Rift Valley Fever. (Contributions to Epidemiology & Biostatistics: Vol. 3). (Illus.). xii, 196p. 1981. pap. 35.50 (ISBN 3-8055-1770-X). S Karger.
Goldblum, Nathan, jt. ed. see Pullman, Bernard.
Goldbratt, Howard, tr. see Hong, Xiao.
Goldbrunner, Josef. Cure of Mind, Cure of Soul: Depth Psychology & Pastoral Care. 1962. pap. 2.50x (ISBN 0-268-00067-0). U of Notre Dame Pr.
--Individuation: A Study of the Depth Psychology of Carl Gustav Jung. 1964. pap. 1.25x (ISBN 0-268-00131-6). U of Notre Dame Pr.
--Realization: The Anthropology of Pastoral Care. 1966. 18.95 (ISBN 0-268-00227-4). U of Notre Dame Pr.
Goldbrunner, Josef, ed. New Catechetical Methods. (Contemporary Catechetics Ser.). (Orig.). 1965. 5.95 (ISBN 0-268-00189-8); pap. 1.25x (ISBN 0-268-00390-4). U of Notre Dame Pr.
Goldburg, Arnold, jt. auth. see Pao, Yih-Ho.
Goldburger. The Heroic Life According to Andre Malraux & Earlier Advocates of Human Grandeur: The Heroic Life According to Andre Malraux & Earlier Advocates of Human Randeur. (Bibliotheque des Lettres Modernes). 17.50 (ISBN 0-685-34273-5). French & Eur.
Goldchmidt, H. J. Interstitial Alloys. LC 67-31095. pap. 159.80 (ISBN 0-317-28021-X, 2055797). Bks Demand UMI.
Golde, David W. & Marks, Paul A. Normal & Neoplastic Hematopoiesis. LC 83-19604. (UCLA Symposia on Molecular & Cellular Biology Ser.: Vol. 9). 614p. 1983. 96.00 (ISBN 0-8451-2608-3). A R Liss.
Golde, David W., ed. Hematopoiesis. (Methods in Hematology Ser.: Vol. 11). (Illus.). 358p. 1984. text ed. 55.00 (ISBN 0-443-08286-3). Churchill.
Golde, David W., et al, eds. Hematopoietic Cell Differentiation. (ICN-UCLA Symposia on Molecular Biology, 1978 Ser.: Vol. 10). 1978. 55.00 (ISBN 0-12-287750-0). Acad Pr.
Golde, Peggy, jt. ed. see Shimkin, Demitri B.
Golde, Roger A. Muddling Through: The Art of Properly Unbusinesslike Management. LC 76-888. 1976. 13.95 (ISBN 0-8144-5411-9). AMACOM.
--Muddling Through: The Art of Properly Unbusinesslike Management. LC 76-888. 185p. 1979. pap. 5.95 (ISBN 0-8144-7523-X). Am Mgmt Assns.
--What You Say Is What You Get. 1979. 9.95 (ISBN 0-8015-8530-9, Hawthorn). Dutton.
Golde, Takaku. Hematopoietic Stem Cells. (Hematology Ser.). 480p. 1985. 69.75 (ISBN 0-8247-7224-5). Dekker.
Goldemberg, Isaac. The Fragmented Life of Don Jacobo Lerner. Picciotto, Robert S., tr. LC 76-15056. 192p. 8.95 (ISBN 0-89255-002-3). Persea Bks.
--The Fragmented Life of Don Jacobo Lerner. Picciotto, Robert, tr. 186p. (Span.). 1985. pap. 8.95 (ISBN 0-89255-003-1). Persea Bks.
--Hombre de Paso, Just Passing Through. Unger, David & Goldemberg, Isaac, trs. 81p. (Orig., Span. & Eng.). 1981. pap. 7.00 (ISBN 0-910061-07-6). Ediciones Norte.
--Play by Play. St Martin, Hardie, tr. 180p. (Span.). 1985. 13.95 (ISBN 0-89255-092-9). Persea Bks.
Goldemberg, Isaac, tr. see Goldemberg, Isaac.
Goldemberg, Issac. Tiempo al Tiempo. 172p. (Span.). 1983. pap. 8.50 (ISBN 0-910061-18-1, 1111). Ediciones Norte.
--La Vida a Plazos de Don Jacobo Lerner. 274p. (Span.). 1980. pap. 8.50 (ISBN 0-910061-00-9, 1101). Ediciones Norte.
Goldemberg, Rose L. All about Jewelry: The One Indispensable Guide for Buyers, Wearers, Lovers & Investors. LC 82-72057. (Illus.). 1983. 15.95 (ISBN 0-87795-419-4, Pub. by Priam); pap. 6.95 (ISBN 0-87795-453-4). Arbor Hse.
Golden, Abner. The Kidney. 2nd ed. LC 76-30733. 222p. 1977. 19.50 (ISBN 0-686-74090-4). Krieger.
Golden, Abner & Powell, Deborah E. Understanding Human Disease. 2nd ed. 700p. 1985. 26.95 (ISBN 0-683-03724-2). Williams & Wilkins.
Golden, Archie S., et al. The Art of Teaching Primary Care. (Springer Series on Medical Education: Vol. 4). 1981. text ed. 34.50 (ISBN 0-8261-2960-9). Springer Pub.
Golden, Arthur see Whitman, Walt.
Golden, B. L. & Bodin, L. D. International Workshop on Current & Future Directions in the Routing & Scheduling of Vehicles & Crews: Proceedings. 139p. 1981. pap. 19.95 (ISBN 0-471-09897-3, Pub. by Wiley-Interscience). Wiley.
Golden, Ben R., jt. auth. see Rhyne, Pamela J.
Golden, Bruce. The Beach Boys: Southern California Pastoral. LC 76-5902. (The Woodstock Popular Music of Today Ser.: Vol. 1). 64p. (Orig.). 1976. lib. bdg. 14.95x (ISBN 0-89370-102-5). Borgo Pr.
Golden, Bruce, tr. see Campinchi, R., et al.
Golden, Bruce L., et al. Statistics & Optimization: The Interface American Sciences Press. LC 84-72719. (American Sciences Press Series in Mathematical & Management Sciences: Vol. 11). 1984. 49.75 (ISBN 0-935950-08-7). Am Sciences Pr.
Golden, C. J. Diagnosis & Rehabilitation in Clinical Neuropsychology. 2nd ed. (Illus.). 336p. 1981. 24.75x (ISBN 0-398-04438-4). C C Thomas.
Golden, Charles. Current Topics in Rehabilitation Psychology. 256p. 1984. 32.00 (ISBN 0-8089-1641-6, 791624). Grune.
Golden, Charles, et al, eds. Applied Techniques in Behavioral Medicine. 464p. 1981. 39.50 (ISBN 0-8089-1404-9, 791622). Grune.
Golden, Charles A., et al. Interpretation of the Halstead-Reitan Neuropsychological Test Battery: A Casebook Approach. (Illus.). 401p. 1980. 39.50 (ISBN 0-8089-1298-4, 791621). Grune.
Golden, Charles J. Clinical Interpretation of Objective Psychological Tests. 272p. 1979. 20.00 (ISBN 0-8089-1163-5, 791620). Grune.
Golden, Charles J. & Anderson, Sandra. Learning Disabilities & Brain Dysfunction: An Introduction for Educators & Parents. (Illus.). 176p. 1979. 14.00x (ISBN 0-398-03861-9). C C Thomas.
Golden, Charles J. & Vicente, Peter J. Foundations of Clinical Neuropsychology. 520p. 1983. 49.50x (ISBN 0-306-41286-1, Plenum Pr). Plenum Pub.
Golden, Charles J., et al. Item Interpretation of the Luria-Nebraska Neuropsychological Battery. LC 81-16393. xii, 243p. 1982. 25.00x (ISBN 0-8032-2105-3). U of Nebr Pr.
Golden, Charles J., et al, eds. Clinical Neuropsychology: Interface with Neurological & Psychiatric Disorders. 1983. 26.00 (ISBN 0-8089-1541-X, 791623). Grune.
Golden, Clinton S. & Ruttenberg, Harold J. The Dynamics of Industrial Democracy. LC 72-2372. (FDR & the Era of the New Deal Ser.). 388p. 1973. Repr. of 1942 ed. lib. bdg. 42.50 (ISBN 0-306-70472-2). Da Capo.
Golden, Edward J. The Art & Science of Real Estate Investment Analysis. 300p. 1980. leatherette bdg. 24.95 (ISBN 0-9604532-0-2). Adv Prof Seminars.
Golden, Eithne, tr. see Ostria Gutierrez, Alberto.
Golden, Evelyn. Glimpses. (Living Poets' Library Ser.). 1983. pap. 3.50 (ISBN 0-686-84154-9). Dragons Teeth.
Golden, Ferol, jt. auth. see Golden, Liza.
Golden, Frederic. Colonies in Space: The Next Giant Step. LC 76-46784. (Illus.). (gr. 7 up). 1977. 8.95 (ISBN 0-15-219400-2, HJ). HarBraceJ.
--Quasars, Pulsars, & Black Holes: A Scientific Detective Story. LC 75-37646. (Illus.). 128p. 1976. 9.95 (ISBN 0-684-14501-4, ScribT). Scribner.

--The Trembling Earth: Probing & Predicting Quakes. LC 83-3262. (Illus.). 192p. (gr. 7 up). 1983. 13.95 (ISBN 0-684-17884-2, ScribJ). Scribner.

Golden, Gale, jt. auth. see Gotwald, William.

Golden, Gary. Survey Research Methods. 69p. 1982. 15.00 (ISBN 0-317-37024-3); members 10.00 (ISBN 0-317-37025-1). ALA.

Golden, Hal. The Grant Seekers: The Foundation Fund Raising Manual. LC 76-13235. 194p. 1976. lib. bdg. 17.00 (ISBN 0-379-00685-5). Oceana.

Golden, Hal & Hanson, Kitty. Techniques of Working with the Working Press. LC 62-11972. 232p. 1962. 10.00 (ISBN 0-379-00056-3). Oceana.

Golden, Harry. Only in America. LC 72-9917. 317p. 1973. Repr. of 1950 ed. lib. bdg. 29.50x (ISBN 0-8371-6607-1, PIOS). Greenwood.

--Only in America. 18.95 (ISBN 0-8488-0080-X, Pub. by Amereon Hse). Amereon Ltd.

Golden, Herbert. Studies in Honor of Samuel Montifiore Waxman. LC 68-59217. 263p. 1969. text ed. 19.50x (ISBN 0-8419-8715-7). Holmes & Meier.

Golden, Hilda. Urbanization & Cities: A Historical & Comparitive Perspective on Our Urbanizing World. 560p. 1981. text ed. 19.95 (ISBN 0-669-03175-5). Heath.

Golden, Irwin B., jt. auth. see Stuart, Charles E.

Golden, James L., et al. The Rhetoric of Western Thought. 3rd ed. 1982. pap. text ed. 14.95 (ISBN 0-8403-2916-4, 40291601). Kendall Hunt.

Golden, James R. The Dynamics of Change in NATO: A Burden Sharing Perspective. LC 83-19185. (Washington Papers: No. 96). 256p. 1983. 28.95x (ISBN 0-03-069562-7). Praeger.

--Investment Behavior by United States Railroads: 1870-1914. LC 75-2582. (Dissertations in American Economic History Ser.). (Illus.). 1975. 28.00x (ISBN 0-405-07202-3). Ayer Co Pubs.

Golden, James R., et al, eds. Conventional Deterrence in NATO: Alternatives for European Defense. 256p. 1984. 27.00x (ISBN 0-669-07397-0). Lexington Bks.

Golden, Joseph. Help! Guide to Seeking, Selecting & Surviving an Arts Consultant. 56p. 6.50 (ISBN 0-317-36771-4). Am Council Arts.

--Olympus on Main Street: A Process for Planning a Community Arts Facility. LC 80-16479. 248p. 1980. 12.95x (ISBN 0-8156-0156-5). Syracuse U Pr.

--On the Dotted Line: The Anatomy of a Contract. 77p. pap. 6.50 (ISBN 0-317-36357-3, NO. 415). Am Council Arts.

Golden, Larry B., jt. auth. see Cull, John G.

Golden, Lawrence G. & Zimmerrian, Donald. Effective Retailing. 1980. 27.50 (ISBN 0-395-30609-4); Instr's. manual 3.00 (ISBN 0-395-30610-8). HM.

Golden, Lawrence J. Equitable Distribution of Property. LC 83-14900. (Family Law Ser.). 377p. 1984. 70.00 (ISBN 0-07-051911-0, Shepards-McGraw). McGraw.

Golden, Leon & Hardison, O. B., Jr. Aristotle's Poetics: A Translation & Commentary for Students of Literature. LC 81-14829. 1981. pap. 10.50 (ISBN 0-8130-0720-8). U Presses Fla.

Golden, Leon, ed. Transformations in Literature & Film: Selected Papers from the Sixth Annual Florida State University Conference on Literature & Film. LC 82-20195. 114p. 1982. pap. 8.00 (ISBN 0-8130-0744-5). U Presses Fla.

Golden, Liza & Golden, Ferol. Recipes from Arizona with Love. (Orig.). 1985. pap. 4.25 comb bd. (ISBN 0-913703-10-9). New Boundary Design.

Golden, M. Patricia, ed. The Research Experience. LC 75-17321. 1976. pap. text ed. 15.95 (ISBN 0-87581-188-4). Peacock Pubs.

Golden, Mary. The Friendship Quilt Book. LC 84-51788. (Illus.). 152p. (Orig.). 1985. pap. 14.95 (ISBN 0-89909-062-1). Yankee Bks.

Golden, Michael. The Design of Reality: An Essay Concerning Human Fulfillment. 187p. 1984. text ed. 12.95 (ISBN 0-9613722-7-3). Pleiades Pub.

Golden, Morris. Fielding's Moral Psychology. LC 66-28115. 192p. 1966. 15.00x (ISBN 0-87023-022-0). U of Mass Pr.

--In Search of Stability. 1960. pap. 6.95x (ISBN 0-8084-0163-7). New Coll U Pr.

--The Self Observed: Swift, Johnson, Wordsworth. LC 70-179137. 199p. 1972. 17.50x (ISBN 0-8018-1289-5). Johns Hopkins.

Golden, N., retold by see Gruelle, Johnny.

Golden, Neil. Analysis of the Tax Reform Act of 1984, Enacted July 18, 1984. LC 84-216060. Date not set. price not set. Bender.

Golden, Renny & Collins, Shelia. Struggle Is a Name for Hope. (Worker Writer Ser.: No. 3). 48p. (Orig.). 1982. pap. 3.00 (ISBN 0-931122-24-4). West End.

Golden, Richard M. The Godly Rebellion: Parisian Cures & the Religious Fronde, 1652-1662. LC 80-25282. xi, 221p. 1981. 22.50x (ISBN 0-8078-1466-0). U of NC Pr.

Golden, Robert & Cox, Sarah. Down the Road: Unemployment & the Fight for the Right to Work. 124p. 8.95 (ISBN 0-904613-43-7); pap. 2.95 (ISBN 0-904613-35-6). Writers & Readers.

Golden, Robert & Sullivan, Mary C. Flannery O'Connor & Caroline Gordon: A Reference Guide. 1977. lib. bdg. 28.50 (ISBN 0-8161-7845-3, Hall Reference). G K Hall.

Golden, Ruth I. Improving Patterns of Language Usage. LC 60-7261. 211p. 1960. 6.95x (ISBN 0-8143-1124-5). Wayne St U Pr.

Golden, S. Frederick Goddard Tuckerman. (Twayne's United States Authors Ser.). 1966. pap. 5.95x (ISBN 0-8084-0138-6, T104, Twayne). New Coll U Pr.

Golden, Samuel A. Frederick Goddard Tuckerman. LC 66-17065. (United States Authors Ser.). 1966. lib. bdg. 7.95 (ISBN 0-89197-764-3); pap. text ed. 3.25x (ISBN 0-89197-997-2). Irvington.

Golden, Sandy. Driving the Drunk Off the Road: A Handbook for Action. LC 83-8982. 178p. 1984. pap. 6.95 (ISBN 0-87491-744-1). Acropolis.

--Driving the Drunk off the Road: A Handbook for Action. LC 83-8982. 192p. 1983. pap. 7.95 (ISBN 0-914757-01-6). Quince Mill Bks.

Golden, Sean, jt. auth. see Fallon, Peter.

Golden, Sean & Fallon, Peter, eds. Soft Day: A Miscellany of Contemporary Irish Writing. LC 78-63298. 1979. text ed. 7.95 (ISBN 0-268-01694-1). U of Notre Dame Pr.

Golden, Sherry. Good Tastes: The Sherry Golden Cookbook. Nicholas, Nancy, ed. LC 84-48656. (Illus.). 320p. 1985. 22.95 (ISBN 0-394-53181-7); pap. 12.95 (ISBN 0-394-73857-8). Knopf.

Golden Square Service Ltd., ed. The Successful Franchise: A Working Strategy. 144p. 1985. text ed. 29.50x (ISBN 0-566-02584-1). Gower Pub Co.

Golden, Ursula. Penny Links: A Novel. 156p. 1981. pap. 8.95 (ISBN 0-416-00891-7, NO. 0213). Methuen Inc.

Golden, William. A Brief History of the English Drama. 1975. Repr. of 1890 ed. 25.00 (ISBN 0-8274-4118-5). R West.

--A Brief History of the English Drama from the Earliest to the Latest TImes. 1978. Repr. of 1890 ed. lib. bdg. 25.00 (ISBN 0-8495-1941-1). Arden Lib.

Golden, William T., et al, eds. Science Advice to the President. LC 79-28743. (Pergamon Policy Studies). 268p. 1980. 55.00 (ISBN 0-08-025963-4). Pergamon.

Goldenber, Norman S., et al, eds. see Casenotes Publishing Company Inc.

Goldenberg, Carl T. Read English, Bk. 4. (Speak English Ser.). (Illus.). 80p. (Orig.). 1983. pap. text ed. 4.95 (ISBN 0-88499-678-6). Inst Mod Lang.

--Write English, Bk. 5. (Speak English Ser.). (Illus.). 64p. (Orig.). 1983. pap. text ed. 4.95 (ISBN 0-88499-688-3). Inst Mod Lang.

Goldenberg, E. Paul. Special Technology for Special Children. LC 79-11565. (Illus.). 200p. 1979. pap. 15.00 (ISBN 0-8391-1441-9). Pro Ed.

Goldenberg, Edie & Traugott, Michael. Campaigning for Congress. LC 84-1840. 207p. 1984. pap. 9.95 (ISBN 0-87187-283-8). Congr Quarterly.

Goldenberg, Gideon, jt. ed. see Kister, M. J.

Goldenberg, Herbert. Contemporary Clinical Psychology. 2nd ed. LC 82-12784. (Psychology Ser.). 480p. 1982. text ed. 22.00 pub net (ISBN 0-534-01239-6). Brooks-Cole.

Goldenberg, Herbert, jt. auth. see Goldenberg, Irene.

Goldenberg, I. Ira. Oppression & Social Intervention: The Human Condition & the Problem of Change. LC 78-6869. (Illus.). 208p. 1978. 19.95x (ISBN 0-88229-349-4); pap. 11.95x (ISBN 0-88229-601-9). Nelson-Hall.

Goldenberg, Irene & Goldenberg, Herbert. Family Therapy: An Overview. 2nd ed. LC 84-21387. (Psychology Ser.). 354p. 1985. text ed. 17.75 pub net (ISBN 0-534-04686-X). Brooks-Cole.

--A Family Therapy Workbook. 2nd ed. 1985. pap. text ed. 7.50 pub net (ISBN 0-534-04687-8). Brooks-Cole.

Goldenberg, Joseph A. Shipbuilding in Colonial America. LC 74-32136. xiii, 306p. 1976. 15.00x (ISBN 0-8139-0588-5, Mariners Museum). U Pr of Va.

Goldenberg, Leon. Housing for the Elderly: New Trends in Europe. 1981. lib. bdg. 42.00 (ISBN 0-8240-7139-5). Garland Pub.

Goldenberg, Naomi R. Changing of the Gods: Feminism & the End of Traditional Religions. LC 78-19602. 1979. pap. 7.95 (ISBN 0-8070-1111-8, BP600). Beacon Pr.

Goldenberg, Norman, et al, eds. see Casenotes Publishing Co. Staff.

Goldenberg, Norman, et al, eds. see Casenotes Publishing Company Inc.

Goldenberg, Norman S. & Breyer, Stephen G. Casenote Legal Briefs-Administrative Law: Adaptable to Courses Utilizing Breyer & Stewart's Casebook on Administrative Law & Regulatory Policy. LC 85-104149. write for info. Casenotes Pub.

Goldenberg, Norman S. & Mueller, Addison. Casenote Legal Briefs-Contracts: Adaptable to Courses Utilizing Mueller, Rosett & Lopez, Casebook on Contract Law & Its Application. LC 84-245648. (Illus.). 138p. Date not set. price not set. Casenotes Pub.

Goldenberg, Norman S., ed. see Casenotes Publishing Company Inc.

Goldenberg, Norman S., et al. Casenote Legal Briefs-Torts: Adaptable to Courses Utilizing Epstein, Gregory, & Kalven's Casebook on Torts. LC 85-119303. write for info. Casenotes Pub.

--Casenote Legal Briefs-Taxation: Adaptable to Courses utilizing Bittker & Clark's Casebook on Estate & Gift Taxation. LC 85-146571. 66p. Date not set. price not set. Casenotes Pub.

--Casenote Legal Briefs-Torts: Adaptable to Courses Utilizing Franklin & Rabin's Casebook on Tort Law & Alternatives. LC 84-252051. 89p. write for info. Amer Bar Assn.

Goldenberg, Norman S., et al, eds. see Casebooks Publishing Company Inc.

Goldenberg, Norman S., et al, eds. see Casenote Publishing Company Inc.

Goldenberg, Norman S., et al, eds. see Casenotes Publishig Company Inc. Staff.

Goldenberg, Norman S., et al, eds. see Casenotes Publishing Co., Inc. Staff.

Goldenberg, Norman S., et al, eds. see Casenotes Publishing Company Inc.

Goldenberg, Norman S, et al, eds. see Casenotes Publishing Company Inc.

Goldenberg, Norman S., et al, eds. see Casenotes Publishing Company Inc.

Goldenberg, Norman S., et al, eds. see Casenotes Publishing Company, Inc.

Goldenberg, Norman S., et al, eds. see Casenotes Publishing Company Inc.

Goldenberg, Norman s., et al, eds. see Casenotes Publishing Company Inc.

Goldenberg, Norman S., et al, eds. see Casenotes Publishing Company Inc.

Goldenberg, Norman S., et al, eds. see Casenotes Publishing Company Inc. Staff.

Goldenberg, Robert. The Sabbath-Law of R. Meir. LC 78-14370. (Brown University. Brown Judaic Studies: No. 6). 1978. pap. 9.00 (ISBN 0-89130-249-2, 140006). Scholars Pr GA.

Goldenberg, Samuel, ed. Local Impacts of the Law of the Sea. (Washington Sea Grant). 141p. 1973. pap. 7.50x (ISBN 0-295-95312-8). U of Wash Pr.

Goldenberg, Sheldon, jt. ed. see Brannigan, Augustine.

Goldenberg, Shirley, jt. auth. see Finkelman, Jacob.

Goldenberg, Susan. Canadian Pacific: Portrait of a Conglomerate. (Illus.). 320p. 1983. 24.95x (ISBN 0-87196-904-1). Facts on File.

--The Thomson Empire. 272p. 1985. 16.95 (ISBN 0-8253-0259-5). Beaufort Bks NY.

--Trading: Inside the World's Leading Stock Exchanges. (Illus.). 352p. 1986. 24.95 (ISBN 0-15-191005-7). HarBraceJ.

Goldenbergy, Norman S., jt. auth. see Krause, Harry D.

Gol'denblat, I. & Nikolaenko, N. A. Calculations of Thermal Stresses in Nuclear Reactors. LC 64-13143. 78p. 1964. 25.00x (ISBN 0-306-10671-X, Consultants). Plenum Pub.

Goldenman, Gretta, ed. see Rifas, Leonard.

Goldensohn, Lorrie. Dreamwork. (Porch Chapbook Ser.: No. 4). (Illus.). 1980. pap. 3.00 (ISBN 0-932968-16-3); signed & numbered ed. 5.00 (ISBN 0-686-60168-8). Porch Pubns.

--The Tether. LC 82-21685. 65p. pap. 4.95 (ISBN 0-934332-39-8). L'Epervier Pr.

Goldenson, Robert M., ed. Longman Dictionary of Psychology & Psychiatry. LC 83-13591. (Walter D. Glanze Bk.). 800p. 1983. 39.95 (ISBN 0-582-28257-8). Longman.

Goldenson, Robert M., et al. Disability & Rehabilitation Handbook. (Illus.). 1978. text ed. 39.95 (ISBN 0-07-023658-5). McGraw.

Goldenson, Suzanne. Vintage Places: A Connoisseur's Guide to North American Wineries & Vineyards. LC 85-8775. (Illus.). 272p. (Orig.). 1985. 14.95 (ISBN 0-915590-76-X); pap. 8.95 (ISBN 0-915590-71-9). Main Street.

Goldenstern, Maurice. How to Become a Successful International Financier & Make a Fortune Out of It. (Illus.). 148p. 1982. 71.85x (ISBN 0-86654-023-7). Inst Econ Finan.

Goldenthal, Allan B. The Teenage Employment Guide. Rev. ed. (Illus.). 208p. (Orig.). (gr. 9-12). 1983. pap. 9.95 (ISBN 0-671-43542-6). Monarch Pr.

--Think Chinese, Speak Chinese. (Illus.). (gr. 10-12). 1978. price not set; pap. text ed. 14.95 (ISBN 0-88345-358-4, 18602); cassettes 45.00 (ISBN 0-686-67814-1, 58687). Regents Pub.

Goldenweiser, Alexander. History, Psychology & Culture. 13.25 (ISBN 0-8446-0647-2). Peter Smith.

--Totemism. 59.95 (ISBN 0-8490-1223-6). Gordon Pr.

Goldenweiser, Alexander, jt. auth. see Ogburn, William F.

Goldenweiser, Alexander A. Anthropology: An Introduction to Primative Culture. LC 37-7979. 1971. Repr. of 1937 ed. 36.00 (ISBN 0-384-19090-1). Johnson Repr.

Goldenweiser, E. A. American Monetary Policy. LC 82-48207. (Gold, Money, Inflation & Deflation Ser.). 407p. 1982. lib. bdg. 50.00 (ISBN 0-8240-5236-6). Garland Pub.

Golden-Wolfe, Malka. Malka - A Total Celebration (A Survival Manual) LC 80-53000. (Illus., Orig.). 1980. pap. 9.95 (ISBN 0-937946-00-1). Univ Goddess.

Golder, Diane. The Newspaper & You: A Reading Skills Workbook. (Orig.). (gr. 9). 1980. wkbk. 7.67 (ISBN 0-87720-300-8). AMSCO Sch.

Golder, F. A. Bering's Voyages, 2 Vols. 1968. lib. bdg. 37.50x (ISBN 0-374-93173-9). Octagon.

--Guide to Materials for American History in Russian Archives, 2 Vols. 1917-1937. Set. 24.00 (ISBN 0-527-00694-7). Kraus Repr.

Golder, F. A., ed. see Platonov, Sergei F.

Golder, Frank A. Documents of Russian History, 1914-1917. 1964. 13.25 (ISBN 0-8446-1201-4). Peter Smith.

Goldfarb, Alan S., et al. Organic Chemicals Manufacturing Hazards. LC 81-65889. 430p. 1981. text ed. 59.95 (ISBN 0-250-40409-5). Butterworth.

Goldfarb, Alvin, jt. auth. see Wilson, Edwin.

Goldfarb, Clare R., jt. auth. see Goldfarb, Russell M.

Goldfarb, Jeffrey C. On Cultural Freedom: An Exploration of Public Life in Poland & America. LC 82-8325. (Chicago Original Paperbacks). 216p. 1983. lib. bdg. 25.00x (ISBN 0-226-30099-4); pap. text ed. 12.50x (ISBN 0-226-30100-1). U of Chicago Pr.

Goldfarb, Johanna & Tibbetts, Edith. Breastfeeding Handbook: A Practical Reference for Physicians, Nurses & Other Health Professionals. LC 72-20601. (Illus.). 256p. 1980. 16.95x (ISBN 0-89490-030-7). Enslow Pubs.

Goldfarb, Lori A., et al. Tapping the Wellsprings: A Problem-Solving Guide for Families with Disabled & Chronically Ill Members. (Orig.). 1985. pap. text ed. price not set. (ISBN 0-933716-55-9, 559). P-H Brookes.

Goldfarb, Mace. Fighters, Refugees, Immigrants: A Story of the Hmong. LC 82-4370. (Illus.). 48p. (gr. 4 up). 1982. lib. bdg. 9.95g (ISBN 0-87614-197-1). Carolrhoda Bks.

Goldfarb, Robert S., ed. Contemporary Studies in Labor Economics & Industrial Relations. 1984. 40.00 (ISBN 0-89232-346-9). Jai Pr.

Goldfarb, Ronald & Raymond, James. Clear Understandings: A Guide to Legal Writing. 174p. 1983. pap. 8.95 (ISBN 0-394-70634-X). Random.

Goldfarb, Ronald L. The Contempt Power. LC 63-20342. 366p. 1963. 29.00x (ISBN 0-231-02654-4). Columbia U Pr.

--Migrant Farm Workers: A Caste of Despair. (Illus.). 232p. 1981. 19.95 (ISBN 0-8138-1790-0). Iowa St U Pr.

Goldfarb, Russell M. Sexual Repression & Victorian Literature. LC 70-101685. 222p. 1970. 20.00 (ISBN 0-8387-7619-1). Bucknell U Pr.

Goldfarb, Russell M. & Goldfarb, Clare R. Spiritualism & Nineteenth-Century Letters. LC 76-19841. 492p. 1978. 20.00 (ISBN 0-8386-2025-6). Fairleigh Dickinson.

Goldfarb, Sally. Inside the Law Schools: A Guide by Students for Students. 3rd, rev. ed. 336p. 1983. pap. 9.95 (ISBN 0-525-48059-5, 0966-290). Dutton.

Goldfarb, Sally, jt. auth. see Barrett, Joan.

Goldfarb, Theodore, jt. auth. see Swartz, Clifford.

Goldfarb, W. Growth & Change of Schizophrenic Children: A Longitudinal Study. LC 74-13824. 271p. 1974. 15.00 (ISBN 0-470-31102-9). Krieger.

Goldfarb, Warren D., ed. see Herbrand, Jacques.

Goldfarb, William. An Investigation of Reaction Time in Older Adults & Its Relationship to Certain Observed Mental Test Patterns. LC 78-176811. (Columbia University. Teachers College. Contributions to Education: No. 831). Repr. of 1941 ed. 22.50 (ISBN 0-404-55831-3). AMS Pr.

--Water Law. LC 84-9597. 300p. 1984. text ed. 34.95 (ISBN 0-250-40627-6). Butterworth.

Goldfarb, William, et al. A Time to Heal. LC 69-17281. 148p. 1969. text ed. 17.50 (ISBN 0-8236-6550-X). Intl Univs Pr.

--Psychotic Children Grown Up: A Prospective Follow-Up Study in Adolescence & Adulthood. LC 77-93594. (Special Issue of Issues in Child Mental Health). 96p. 1978. pap. 9.95 (ISBN 0-87705-331-6). Human Sci Pr.

Goldfeder, Cheryl & Goldfeder, James. The Girl Who Wouldn't Talk. 1974. pap. 3.50 (ISBN 0-913072-17-6). Natl Assn Deaf.

Goldfeder, James, jt. auth. see Goldfeder, Cheryl.

Goldfein, Alan. Heads: A Metafictional History of Western Civilization 1762-1975. 1973. pap. 2.45 (ISBN 0-688-05177-4). Morrow.

Goldfeld, L., ed. see Rademacher, H.

Goldfeld, Stephen M. & Chandler, Lester V. The Economics of Money & Banking. 8th ed. 628p. 1981. text ed. 30.50 scp (ISBN 0-06-041236-4, HarpC); write for info. instr's. manual avail. (ISBN 0-06-361167-8). Har-Row.

Goldfield, Bina. The Efemcipated English Handbook. (Illus.). 121p. (Orig.). 1983. pap. 5.95 (ISBN 0-317-04140-1). Westover Pr.

Goldfield, David R. Cotton Fields & Skyscrapers: Southern City & Region, 1607 to 1980. LC 82-6582. (Illus.). 232p. 1982. text ed. 22.50x (ISBN 0-8071-1029-9). La State U Pr.

--Urban Growth in the Age of Sectionalism: Virginia 1847-1861. LC 77-3514. 1977. 27.50x (ISBN 0-8071-0269-5). La State U Pr.

Goldfield, David R. & Brownell, Blaine A. Urban America: From Downtown to No Town. LC 78-69562. (Illus.). 1979. pap. text ed. 18.95 (ISBN 0-395-27397-8). HM.

Goldfield, David R., jt. ed. see Brownell, Blaine A.

Goldfield, Lea N. An Inquiry into the Authenticity of Moses Maimonides' Treatise on Resurrection. 1985. text ed. 19.95x (ISBN 0-88125-088-0). Ktav.

Goldfield, Norbert & Goldsmith, Seth B. Financial Mangement of Ambulatory Care. 250p. 1984. 28.95 (ISBN 0-87189-077-1). Aspen Systems.

Goldfield, Randy J. Implementing Word Processing. 1983. 24.95 (ISBN 0-02-912100-0). Free Pr.

Goldfield Stock Exchange, Goldfield, Nevada. Goldfield Stock Exchange: The Constitution & by Laws. pap. 7.50 (ISBN 0-686-10844-2). British Am Bks.

Goldfinger, Stephen E., jt. ed. see Johnson, G. Timothy.

Goldfischer, Dan & Heffernan, Melissa. Ride Guide for North Jersey & Beyond. LC 85-50728. (Illus.). 102p. (Orig.). 1985. pap. 5.95 (ISBN 0-933855-00-1). White Meadow.

Goldfrank, David, ed. The Monastic Rule of Losif Volotsky. 1983. pap. 14.95 (ISBN 0-87907-936-3). Cistercian Pubns.

Goldfrank, Esther S. Changing Configurations in the Social Organization of a Blackfoot Tribe During the Reserve Period. Bd. with Observations on Northern Blackfoot Kinship. Hanks, L. M., Jr. & Richardson, Jane. (Illus.). 37p. LC 46-1392. (American Ethnological Society Monographs: Nos. 8-9). (Illus.). 81p. 1945. 15.00x (ISBN 0-295-74067-1). U of Wash Pr.

--Social & Ceremonial Organization of Cochiti. LC 28-11444. (American Anthro. Association Memoirs). 1927. 14.00 (ISBN 0-527-00532-0). Kraus Repr.

Goldfrank, J., jt. ed. see Humez, N.

Goldfrank, Lewis & Kirstein, Robert. Toxologic Emergencies. 2nd ed. 224p. 1981. pap. 18.50 (ISBN 0-8385-8965-0). ACC.

Goldfrank, Lewis, jt. ed. see Flomenbaum, Neal.

Goldfrank, Lewis, et al. Goldfrank's Toxicologic Emergencies. 3rd ed. 704p. 1985. price not set (ISBN 0-8385-8972-3). ACC.

Goldfrank, Lewis R. & Kirstein, Robert, eds. Toxicologic Emergencies: A Comprehensive Handbook in Problem Solving. 2nd ed. (Illus.). 447p. 1982. 45.00 (ISBN 0-8385-8965-0). ACC.

Goldfried, M. R. & Davison, G. C. Clinical Behavior Therapy. LC 75-25665. 1976. text ed. 32.95 (ISBN 0-03-008151-3, HoltC). HR&W.

Goldfried, Marvin R., ed. Converging Themes in Psychotherapy: Trends in Psychodynamic Humanistic & Behavioral Practice. 416p. 1982. text ed. 26.95 (ISBN 0-8261-3620-6). Springer Pub.

Goldgar, Bertrand A. The Curse of Party: Swift's Relations with Addison & Steele. LC 76-12357. 1976. Repr. of 1961 ed. lib. bdg. 25.00 (ISBN 0-8414-4546-X). Folcroft.

--The Curse of the Party: Swift's Relations with Addison and Steele. 1979. Repr. of 1961 ed. lib. bdg. 32.50 (ISBN 0-8495-2031-2). Arden Lib.

--Walpole & the Wits: The Relation of Politics to Literature, 1722-1742. LC 76-6809. viii, 256p. 1976. 19.50x (ISBN 0-8032-0893-6). U of Nebr Pr.

Goldgar, Bertrand A., ed. see Pope, Alexander.

Goldhaber, Dale. Lifespan Human Development. Date not set. text ed. price not set (ISBN 0-12-288460-4). Acad Pr.

Goldhaber, Gerald. Organizational Communication. 3rd ed. 528p. 1983. text ed. write for info. (ISBN 0-697-04219-7); instrs.' manual avail. (ISBN 0-697-04220-0). Wm C Brown.

Goldhaber, Gerald, et al. Information Strategies. Voigt, Mel, ed. LC 79-756. (Communication & Information Science Ser.). 368p. 1984. text ed. 35.00 (ISBN 0-89391-151-8). Ablex Pub.

Goldhaber, Gerald M. & Rogers, Donald P. Auditing Organizational Communication Systems: The ICA Communication Audit. 1979. text ed. 55.00 (ISBN 0-8403-2027-2). Kendall-Hunt.

Goldhaber, Gerald M., jt. auth. see Zannes, Estelle.

Goldhaber, Jacob K. & Ehrlich, Gertrude. Algebra. LC 78-9889. 430p. 1980. Repr. of 1970 ed. lib. bdg. 23.50 (ISBN 0-88275-765-2). Krieger.

Goldhaber, Nat & Denniston, Denise. TM: An Alphabetical Guide to the Transcendental Meditation Program. (Illus.). 1976. pap. 3.95 (ISBN 0-345-24096-0). Ballantine.

Goldhaber, Stanley, et al. Construction Management: Principles & Practices. LC 76-58397. (Construction Management & Engineering Ser.). 312p. 1977. 49.95x (ISBN 0-471-44270-4, Pub. by Wiley-Interscience). Wiley.

Goldhagen, Nancy P. Parole Crociate Per Gli Studenti. (Illus.). 48p. (Ital.). 1983. pap. 3.95 (ISBN 0-8442-8021-6, 8021-6, Passport Bks). Natl Textbk.

Goldhahn, W. E., jt. auth. see Merrem, G.

Goldhamer, Herbert. The Adviser. 196p. 1978. 30.25 (ISBN 0-444-99040-2). Elsevier.

--The Foreign Powers in Latin America. LC 77-173754. (A Rand Corporation Research Study). 296p. 1972. 35.00 (ISBN 0-691-05646-3). Princeton U Pr.

--The Soviet Soldier: Soviet Military Management at the Troop Level. LC 74-26727. 360p. 1975. 22.50x (ISBN 0-8448-0615-3); pap. 14.50x (ISBN 0-8448-0652-8). Crane-Russak Co.

Goldhamer, Herbert & Marshall, Andrew W. Psychosis & Civilization. Grob, Gerald N., ed. LC 78-22560. (Historical Issues in Mental Health Ser.). (Illus.). 1979. Repr. of 1953 ed. lib. bdg. 14.00x (ISBN 0-405-11914-3). Ayer Co Pubs.

Goldhammer, Arthur, tr. see Bachelard, Gaston.

Goldhammer, Arthur, tr. see Badie, Bertrand & Birnbaum, Pierre.

Goldhammer, Arthur, tr. see Birnbaum, Pierre.

Goldhammer, Arthur, tr. see Bourricaud, Francis.

Goldhammer, Arthur, tr. see Castel, Francoise & Castel, Robert.

Goldhammer, Arthur, tr. see Clement, Catherine.

Goldhammer, Arthur, tr. see Crozier, Michel & Friedberg, Erhard.

Goldhammer, Arthur, tr. see Delaporte, Francois.

Goldhammer, Arthur, tr. see Dockes, Pierre.

Goldhammer, Arthur, tr. see Duby, Georges.

Goldhammer, Arthur, tr. see Le Goff, Jacques.

Goldhammer, Arthur, tr. see Mousnier, Roland E.

Goldhammer, Arthur, tr. see Raeff, Marc.

Goldhammer, Arthur, tr. see Rodinson, Maxime.

Goldhammer, Arthur, tr. see Schnapper, Dominique.

Goldhammer, Arthur, tr. see Starobinski, Jean.

Goldhammer, Arthur, tr. see Yourcenar, Marguerite.

Goldhammer, Robert, et al. Clinical Supervision. 2nd ed. LC 79-25334. 216p. 1980. text ed. 30.95 (ISBN 0-03-046571-0, HoltC). HR&W.

Goldhar, J., jt. ed. see Dean, B.

Goldhill, Simon. Language, Sexuality, Narrative: The Oresteia. 320p. 1985. 59.50 (ISBN 0-521-26535-5). Cambridge U Pr.

Goldhor, Herbert. An Introduction to Scientific Research in Librarianship. LC 79-631732. (Monograph: No. 12). 201p. 1972. 5.00x (ISBN 0-87845-036-X). U of Ill Lib Info Sci.

Goldhor, Herbert, ed. Education for Librarianship: The Design of the Curriculum of Library Schools. LC 78-633332. (Monograph: No. 11). 195p. 1971. 5.00x (ISBN 0-87845-033-5). U of Ill Lib Info Sci.

Goldhurst, Richard, jt. auth. see Wilson, Kenneth D.

Goldich, Samuel S., et al. Precambrian Geology & Geochronology of Minnesota. LC 61-8016. (Bulletin: No. 41). (Illus.). 1961. 4.00x (ISBN 0-8166-0224-7). Minn Geol Survey.

Goldie, I., ed. Surgery in Rheumatoid Arthritis. (Reconstruction Surgery & Traumatology: Vol. 18). (Illus.). vi, 214p. 1981. 47.00 (ISBN 3-8055-1445-X). S Karger.

Goldie, James H., jt. ed. see Bruchovsky, Nicholas.

Goldie, W., jt. auth. see Reid, F. H.

Goldie, W., jt. ed. see Reid, F. H.

Goldin, A. & Hawking, F., eds. Advances in Chemotherapy, 3 vols. Incl. Vol. 1. 1964. 85.00 (ISBN 0-12-009101-1); Vol. 2. Goldin, A., et al, eds. 1965. 85.00 (ISBN 0-12-009102-X); Vol. 3. 1968. 85.00 (ISBN 0-12-009103-8). Acad Pr.

Goldin, Albert. Your Guide to Care of the Heart. LC 83-61170. 128p. 1984. 10.95 (ISBN 0-89313-035-4). G F Stickley Co.

Goldin, Alice, jt. auth. see Eichenbaum, Sharon.

Goldin, Amy. Manny Farber. LC 78-58402. 72p. (Orig.). 1978. pap. 9.00x (ISBN 0-934418-01-2). La Jolla Mus Contemp Art.

Goldin, Augusta. Bottom of the Sea. LC 66-10194. (A Let's-Read-&-Find-Out Science Bk). (Illus.). (ps-3). 1967. Crowell Jr Bks.

--Ducks Don't Get Wet. LC 65-11647. (Crocodile Paperback Ser.). (Illus.). (gr. k-3). 1965. pap. 1.45 (ISBN 0-690-01258-6). Crowell Jr Bks.

--Ducks Don't Get Wet. LC 65-11647. (A Let's-Read-&-Find-Out Science Bk). (Illus.). (gr. k-3). PLB 11.89 (ISBN 0-690-24668-4). Crowell Jr Bks.

--Geothermal Energy: A Hot Prospect. LC 80-8800. (Illus.). (gr. 7 up). 1981. 11.95 (ISBN 0-15-230662-5, HJ). HarBraceJ.

--Oceans of Energy: Reservoir of Power for the Future. LC 79-3767. (Illus.). 114p. (gr. 7 up). 8.95 (ISBN 0-15-257688-6, HJ). HarBraceJ.

--The Shape of Water. LC 77-12850. 64p. (gr. 1-3). 1979. PLB 7.95 (ISBN 0-385-02385-5). Doubleday.

--Spider Silk. LC 64-18164. (Crocodile Paperback Ser.). 1976. pap. 1.45 (ISBN 0-690-01262-4). Crowell Jr Bks.

--Spider Silk. LC 64-18164. (A Let's-Read-&-Find-Out Science Bk). (Illus.). (gr. k-3). 1964. PLB 11.89 (ISBN 0-690-76075-2). Crowell Jr Bks.

--Straight Hair, Curly Hair. LC 66-12669. (A Let's Read & Find out Science Bk). (Illus.). (gr. k-3). 1966. PLB 11.89 (ISBN 0-690-77921-6). Crowell Jr Bks.

--Straight Hair, Curly Hair. LC 66-12669. (Crocodile Paperbacks Ser.). (Illus.). 33p. (gr. k-3). 1972. pap. 3.95 (ISBN 0-690-77928-3). Crowell Jr BKs.

--Water: Too Much, Too Little, Too Polluted. LC 82-48760. (Illus.). 224p. (gr. 7 up). 1983. 12.95 (ISBN 0-15-294819-8, HJ). HarBraceJ.

Goldin, Barbara. The Citizenship Handbook. 128p. (Orig.). 1983. pap. 6.95 (ISBN 0-671-45331-9). Monarch Pr.

Goldin, Claudia D. Urban Slavery in the American South, 1820-1860: A Quantitative History. LC 75-20887. (Illus.). 1976. lib. bdg. 16.00x (ISBN 0-226-30104-4). U of Chicago Pr.

Goldin, Edwin. Waves & Photons: An Introduction to Quantum Optics. LC 82-10991. (Pure & Applied Optics Ser.). 211p. 1982. 29.95x (ISBN 0-471-08592-8, Pub. by Wiley-Interscience). Wiley.

Goldin, Frederick, ed. & tr. Lyrics of the Troubadours & Trouveres: An Anthology & a History. 16.00 (ISBN 0-8446-5036-6). Peter Smith.

Goldin, Frederick, tr. The Song of Roland. 1978. pap. 5.95x (ISBN 0-393-09008-6). Norton.

Goldin, Gerald A. & McClintok, Edwin C., eds. Task Variables in Mathematical Problem Solving. (Problem Solving Ser.). 495p. 1984. pap. text ed. 16.95 (ISBN 0-89168-056-X). L Erlbaum Assocs.

Goldin, Grace. Come Under the Wings: A Midrash on Ruth. 2nd ed. LC 79-91327. 85p. 1980. pap. 4.95 (ISBN 0-8276-0171-9, 451). Jewish Pubns.

Goldin, Hyman. The Yiddish Teacher. rev. ed. 144p. 1977. pap. 5.95 (ISBN 0-88482-687-2). Hebrew Pub.

Goldin, Hyman E. Illustrated Bible Stories. 256p. 1930. 5.95 (ISBN 0-88482-585-X). Hebrew Pub.

--Jew & His Duties. 246p. 1953. pap. 6.95 (ISBN 0-88482-429-2). Hebrew Pub.

--Magic Ring. 249p. 1941. 6.00 (ISBN 0-88482-731-3). Hebrew Pub.

--Three Kings. 144p. 1929. 4.95 (ISBN 0-88482-737-2). Hebrew Pub.

Goldin, Hyman E., jt. auth. see Ganzfried, Solomon.

Goldin, Hyman E., tr. see Ganzfried, Solomon.

Goldin, Judah. The Living Talmud. 1957. pap. 3.95 (ISBN 0-451-62344-4, Ment). NAL.

Goldin, Marshall D. Intensive Care of the Surgical Patient. 1981. 51.95 (ISBN 0-8151-3732-X). Year Bk Med.

Goldin, Stephen. And Not Make Dreams Your Master. 224p. (Orig.). 1981. pap. 2.25 (ISBN 0-449-14410-0, GM). Fawcett.

--Assault on the Gods. 192p. 1981. pap. 2.25 (ISBN 0-449-24455-5, Crest). Fawcett.

--Assault on the Gods. LC 76-56498. 181p. 1977. 9.95 (ISBN 0-385-12269-1). Authors Co-op.

--The Eternity Brigade. 256p. (Orig.). 1982. pap. 2.50 (ISBN 0-449-14336-8, GM). Fawcett.

--Mindflight. 1978. pap. 1.75 (ISBN 0-449-13980-8, GM). Fawcett.

--A World Called Solitude. 224p. 1982. pap. 2.25 (ISBN 0-449-24486-5, Crest). Fawcett.

Goldin, Stephen & Sky, Kathleen. Business of Being a Writer. 313p. (Orig.). 1985. pap. 8.95 (ISBN 0-88184-206-0). Carroll & Graf.

Goldin, Stephen, jt. auth. see Smith, E. E.

Goldina, Marina, tr. see Gorchakov, Nikolai.

Goldina, Miriam, tr. see Gorchakov, Nikolai M.

Goldine, James H., jt. ed. see Bruchovsky, Nicholas.

Golding. Synopsis of Rheumatic Disease. 4th ed. 314p. 1982. 24.50 (ISBN 0-7236-0627-7). PSG Pub Co.

Golding, A., tr. see Seneca, Lucius Annaeus.

Golding, Alfred S. Classicistic Acting: Two Centuries of a Performance Tradition at the Amsterdam Schouwberg to Which Is Appended an Annotated Translation of the "Lessons on the Principles of Gesticulation & Mimic Expression" of Johannes Jelgerhuis, Rz. LC 83-21833. (Illus.). 644p. 1984. lib. bdg. 39.50 (ISBN 0-8191-3680-8). U Pr of Amer.

Golding, Alfred S., tr. see Lang, Franz.

Golding, Amy T. Miniature Travellers. (Illus.). 1959. 3.50 (ISBN 0-8338-0025-6). M Jones.

Golding, Arthur, tr. see Ovidius Naso, Publius.

Golding, Brage, jt. ed. see Fleury, Paul A.

Golding, Charles W. What It Takes to Get to the Top...& Stay There. LC 82-24035. 208p. 1983. 13.95 (ISBN 0-399-12817-4, Putnam). Putnam Pub Group.

Golding, Claud. Great Names in History, 356 B. C. to A. D. 1910. facs. ed. LC 68-29206. (Essay Index Reprint Ser). 1968. Repr. of 1935 ed. 20.00 (ISBN 0-8369-0479-6). Ayer Co Pubs.

Golding, Claude. The Throne of Britain. 1979. Repr. lib. bdg. 30.00 (ISBN 0-8495-2040-1). Arden Lib.

Golding, D. H. Project Planning & Control. 1978. 85.00x (ISBN 0-85012-198-1). Intl Pubns Serv.

Golding, D. N & Barrett, J. The Practical Treatment of Backache & Sciatica. 1984. lib. bdg. 26.75 (ISBN 0-85200-773-6, Pub. by MTP Pr England). Kluwer Academic.

Golding, David, et al. Power, Control & Bureaucracy. 1978. 90.00x (ISBN 0-86176-013-1, Pub. by MCB Pubns). State Mutual Bk.

Golding, Douglas N. Problems in Arthritis & Rheumatism. Fry, J., et al, eds. LC 81-68109. (Problems in Practice Ser.: Vol. 4). (Illus.). 160p. 1982. text ed. 20.00x (ISBN 0-8036-4168-0). Davis Co.

--Tutorials in Clinical Rheumatology. 160p. pap. text ed. cancelled (ISBN 0-272-79611-5). Pitman Pub MA.

Golding, E. W. The Generation of Electricity by Wind Power. Rev. ed. 1976. 25.00x (ISBN 0-419-11070-4, NO. 6127, Pub. by E & FN Spon). Methuen Inc.

Golding, G. F. Records & Songs of Saxon Times. LC 73-4818. 1973. lib. bdg. 17.50 (ISBN 0-8414-2025-4). Folcroft.

Golding, J., et al, eds. Access to Law: The Second Seminar on Australian Lawyers & Social Change. 336p. (Orig.). 1980. pap. text ed. 12.95 (ISBN 0-7081-1305-2, 0581). Australia N U P.

Golding, J. F., jt. auth. see Mangan, G. L.

Golding, Jean & Macfarlane, Aidan. Cot Deaths. 208p. 1981. 45.00x (ISBN 0-7291-0198-3, Pub. by Open Bks England); pap. 29.00x (ISBN 0-7291-0193-2). State Mutual Bk.

Golding, Jean, et al. Sudden Infant Death: Patterns, Puzzles, & Problems. 1985. 25.00x (ISBN 0-295-96302-6). U of Wash Pr.

Golding, John. Fernand Leger: The Mechanic. (Masterpieces in the National Gallery Ser.). 1976. pap. 3.95 (ISBN 0-88884-308-9, Pub. by Natl Mus Canada). Nat Gal Can.

Golding, John & Elderfield, John. The Drawings of Henri Matisse. LC 84-50423. (Illus.). 1985. 29.95f (ISBN 0-500-23401-9). Thames Hudson.

Golding, John, jt. auth. see Paz, Octavio.

Golding, John, jt. auth. see Penrose, Roland.

Golding, Lawrence, et al, eds. Y's Way to Physical Fitness. Rev. ed. (Illus.). 172p. 1982. 24.95x (ISBN 0-88035-002-4). YMCA USA.

Golding, Leila P. Sherri. 150p. (Orig.). 1985. pap. 2.95 (ISBN 0-87123-861-6). Bethany Hse.

Golding, Louis. In the Steps of Moses the Conqueror. 1978. Repr. lib. bdg. 27.50 (ISBN 0-8492-0996-X). R West.

--James Joyce. LC 72-196435. 1933. lib. bdg. 28.50 (ISBN 0-8414-4654-7). Folcroft.

Golding, Louis T. An Elizabethan Puritan. Repr. of 1937 ed. 25.00 (ISBN 0-686-19887-5). Ridgeway Bks.

--An Elizabethan Puritan: Arthur Golding. facsimile ed. LC 71-165636. (Select Bibliographies Reprint Ser). Repr. of 1937 ed. 24.50 (ISBN 0-8369-5945-0). Ayer Co Pubs.

Golding, Martin P. Legal Reasoning. 228p. 1984. text ed. 15.00 (ISBN 0-394-33575-9, KnopfC); pap. text ed. 7.00 (ISBN 0-394-33191-5). Knopf.

--Philosophy of Law. (Foundation of Philosophy Ser.). 176p. 1975. pap. text ed. 13.95 (ISBN 0-13-664128-8). P-H.

Golding, Martin P., ed. Nature of Law. 1966. 17.00 (ISBN 0-394-30213-3, RanC). Random.

Golding, Morton J. Bitter Winds. 352p. 1984. pap. 3.50 (ISBN 0-515-07865-4). Jove Pubns.

Golding, P. Alcoholism: Analysis of a World Wide Problem. 560p. 1983. lib. bdg. 70.00 (ISBN 0-85200-713-2, Pub. by MTP Pr Netherlands). Kluwer Academic.

Golding, P., ed. Alcoholism: A Modern Perspective. (Illus.). 539p. 1982. 49.50x (ISBN 0-942068-00-9). Bogden & Son.

Golding, Peter & Elliot, Philip. Making the News. LC 78-41006. (Illus.). 241p. 1980. text ed. 35.00x (ISBN 0-582-50460-0). Longman.

Golding, Stephen L., jt. auth. see Roesch, Ronald.

Golding, Steve & Kormann, Chris. The Home Accountant Desk Reference. Date not set. pap. write for info (ISBN 0-912003-48-0). Bk Co.

Golding, William. The Brass Butterfly. 80p. 1969. pap. 4.95 (ISBN 0-571-09073-7). Faber & Faber.

--Darkness Visible. 265p. 1979. 14.95 (ISBN 0-374-13502-9). FS&G.

--Darkness Visible. 276p. 1985. pap. 5.95 (ISBN 0-15-623931-0, Harv). HarBraceJ.

--An Egyptian Journal. (Illus.). 240p. (Orig.). 1985. 19.95 (ISBN 0-571-13593-5). Faber & Faber.

--Free Fall. LC 60-5431. (YA) (gr. 9-12). 1962. pap. 3.95 (ISBN 0-15-633468-2, Harv). HarBraceJ.

--The Inheritors. 224p. 1981. pap. 3.95 (ISBN 0-671-53139-5). WSP.

--Lord of the Flies. (gr. 9 up). 1962. 16.95 (ISBN 0-698-10219-3, Coward). Putnam Pub Group.

--Lord of the Flies. 13.95 (ISBN 0-88411-695-6, Pub. by Aeonian Pr). Amereon Ltd.

--A Moving Target. 202p. 1982. 14.95 (ISBN 0-374-21573-1); pap. 7.95 (ISBN 0-374-51850-5). FS&G.

--The Paper Men. 191p. 1984. 15.95 (ISBN 0-374-22980-5). FS&G.

--The Paper Men. LC 84-27984. 204p. 1985. pap. 5.95 (ISBN 0-15-670800-0, Harv). HarBraceJ.

--Pincher Martin. LC 57-10059. Orig. Title: Two Deaths of Christopher Martin. 1968. pap. 3.95 (ISBN 0-15-671833-2, Harv). HarBraceJ.

--The Pyramid. LC 67-19198. 192p. 1981. pap. 3.95 (ISBN 0-15-674703-0, Harv). HarBraceJ.

--Rites of Passage. 278p. 1980. 14.95 (ISBN 0-374-25086-3). FS&G.

--The Scorpion God: Three Short Novels. 1984. pap. 3.95 (ISBN 0-15-679658-9, Harv). HarBraceJ.

Golding, William G. The Hot Gates & Other Occasional Pieces. LC 66-12363. pap. 3.95 (ISBN 0-15-642180-1, Harv). HarBraceJ.

--The Inheritors. LC 62-16724. 1963. pap. 3.95 (ISBN 0-15-644379-1, Harv). HarBraceJ.

--The Spire. LC 63-15314. 1965. pap. 3.95 (ISBN 0-15-684741-8, Harv). HarBraceJ.

Golding, William R. Idiolects in Dickens: The Major Techniques & Chronological Development. LC 84-17783. 192p. 1985. 22.50 (ISBN 0-312-40481-6). St Martin.

Goldingay, John. Old Testament Commentary Survey. 2nd ed. Hubbard, Robert & Branson, Mark L., eds. 66p. 1981. pap. 2.95 (ISBN 0-8308-5499-1). Inter-Varsity.

--Treasure in Earthen Vessels: Jeremiah & the Servant of the Lord. 144p. (Orig.). 1982. pap. text ed. 8.95 cancelled (ISBN 0-85364-338-5). Attic Pr.

Goldinge, Arthur, tr. see Caesar, Caius Julius.

Goldinger, Milton, jt. auth. see Burr, John.

Goldini. Theatre: La Locandiera, Le Valet de deux Maitres, La Trilogie de la Villegiature. 1584p. 41.50 (ISBN 0-686-56517-7). French & Eur.

Goldish, Dorothy M. Basic Mathematics for Beginning Chemistry. 3rd ed. 1982. pap. 10.95x (ISBN 0-02-344430-4). Macmillan.

Goldkamp, John S. Two Classes of Accused: A Study of Bail & Detention in America. LC 79-13042. (Illus.). 288p. 1979. prof ref 27.50 (ISBN 0-88410-802-3). Ballinger Pub.

Goldkamp, John S. & Gottfredson, Michael R. Policy Guidelines for Bail: An Experiment in Court Reform. LC 84-26798. 307p. 1985. 34.95 (ISBN 0-87722-381-5). Temple U Pr.

Goldknopf, David. The Life of the Novel. LC 72-75512. 256p. 1972. 19.00x (ISBN 0-226-30142-7). U of Chicago Pr.

--The Life of the Novel. LC 72-75512. x, 218p. 1974. pap. 2.95x (ISBN 0-226-30143-5, P591, Phoen). U of Chicago Pr.

Goldkuhl, G., jt. auth. see Sundburg, M.

Goldlat, jt. auth. see SIPRI Staff.

Goldmacher, I. Selling Microcomputers & Software. 256p. 1985. 15.95 (ISBN 0-07-023661-5). McGraw.

Goldman. Occupational Hazards in Dentistry. 1984. 29.50 (ISBN 0-8151-3755-9). Year Bk Med.

Goldman, jt. auth. see Yardley.

Goldman, A. S. & Slattery, T. B. Maintainability: A Major Element of System Effectiveness. 2nd ed. LC 76-40242. 298p. 1977. Repr. of 1967 ed. 18.50 (ISBN 0-88275-292-8). Krieger.

Goldman, Abe, jt. ed. see Brylawski, E. Fulton.

Goldman, Abram F., tr. see Graef, Martin, et al.

Goldman, Alan. Public Communication: Perception, Criticism, Performance. LC 80-24016. 1983. lib. bdg. 29.50 (ISBN 0-89874-244-7). Krieger.

--Unveiling the Self: Frontiers in Human Communication. 1979. pap. text ed. 17.95 (ISBN 0-8403-2072-8). Kendall-Hunt.

Goldman, Alan H. Justice & Reverse Discrimination. LC 78-63595. 1979. 29.00 (ISBN 0-691-07233-7); pap. 8.50 (ISBN 0-691-02003-5). Princeton U Pr.

--The Moral Foundations of Professional Ethics. LC 80-11696. (Philosophy & Society Ser.). 305p. 1980. 26.50x (ISBN 0-8476-6274-8); pap. 9.95x (ISBN 0-8476-6285-3). Rowman.

Goldman, Albert. Elvis. LC 81-8130. (Illus.). 598p. 1981. 14.95 (ISBN 0-07-023657-7). McGraw.

--Elvis. 736p. 1982. pap. 3.95 (ISBN 0-380-60350-0, 60350-0). Avon.

--Grass Roots: Marijuana in America Today. LC 77-11806. (Illus.). 1979. 12.95i (ISBN 0-06-011554-8, HarpT). Har-Row.

--The Mine & the Mint: Sources for the Writings of Thomas DeQuincey. LC 65-13063. 224p. 1965. 5.95 (ISBN 0-8093-0187-3). S Ill U Pr.

Goldman, Albert, ed. see Wagner, Richard.

Goldman, Alex J. Child's Dictionary of Jewish Symbols. (Illus.). (gr. 1-4). 5.00 (ISBN 0-685-09470-7). Feldheim.

--The Eternal Books Retold. LC 82-9030. 384p. pap. 12.95 (ISBN 0-8298-0625-3). Pilgrim NY.

--A Handbook for the Jewish Family: Understanding & Enjoying the Sabbath & Other Holidays. LC 58-12938. (Illus.). 1983. pap. 14.95 (ISBN 0-8197-0085-1). Bloch.

--Judaism Confronts Contemporary Issues. LC 78-54570. 1979. 12.95 (ISBN 0-88400-056-7). Shengold.

Goldman, Allen M. & Wolf, Stuart A., eds. Percolation, Localization, & Superconductivity. (NATO ASI Series B: Physics: Vol. 109). 472p. 1984. 79.50x (ISBN 0-306-41713-8, Plenum Pr). Plenum Pub.

Goldman, Alvin L. Labor Law & Industrial Relations in the U. S. A. 376p. 1984. pap. text ed. 25.00 (ISBN 0-87179-444-6). BNA.

--Labor Law & Industrial Relations in the United States of America. 2nd ed. LC 84-951. Date not set. price not set (ISBN 0-87179-444-6, Pub. by Kluwer Law Netherlands). Kluwer Academic.

Goldman, Alvin L. see Labor Law Group.

Goldman, Amy B., ed. Procedures in Skeletal Radiology. 720p. 1984. 99.50 (ISBN 0-8089-1655-6, 7916-41). Grune.

Goldman, Amy Beth & Dines, David M., eds. Shoulder Arthrography. (Radiology Library). 1982. text ed. 45.00 (ISBN 0-316-31931-7). Little.

Goldman, Ann, jt. auth. see Lissauer, Tom.

Goldman, B. Lex Mercatoria. 1984. pap. 10.00 (ISBN 90-6544-194-8, Pub. by Kluwer Law Netherlands). Kluwer Academic.

Goldman, Beate. Letters to a Stranger. LC 81-50429. (VI Ser.). 50p. (Orig.). 1981. pap. text ed. 4.00 (ISBN 0-931846-18-8). Wash Writers Pub.

Goldman, Bernard. Reading & Writing in the Arts: A Handbook. rev. ed. LC 77-27856. 172p. 1978. text ed. 10.95x (ISBN 0-8143-1604-2); pap. text ed. 5.95 (ISBN 0-8143-1605-0). Wayne St U Pr.

Goldman, Bernard S., jt. ed. see Adelman, Allan G.

Goldman, Bert A. Directory of Unpublished Experimental Mental Measures, Vol. 1. Saunders, John, ed. LC 73-17342. 223p. 1974. text ed. 26.95 (ISBN 0-87705-130-5). Human Sci Pr.

--Directory of Unpublished Experimental Mental Measures: 1971-1972, Vol. 2. Busch, John C., pref. by. LC 73-17342. 518p. 1978. 34.95 (ISBN 0-87705-300-6). Human Sci Pr.

Goldman, Bert A., ed. Directory of Unpublished Experimental Mental Measures: Vol. 4, 1975-1976. 1983. 39.95 (ISBN 0-89885-100-9). Human Sci Pr.

Goldman, Bert A. & Busch, John C., eds. Directory of Unpublished Experimental Mental Measures: Vol. 3, 1973-74. LC 73-17342. 448p. 1982. 39.95 (ISBN 0-89885-095-9). Human Sci Pr.

Goldman, Berthold. European Commercial Law. 1973. 32.50 (ISBN 0-685-40617-2). Bender.

Goldman, Bob, et al. Death in the Locker Room: Steroids & Sports. (Illus.). 456p. 1984. 19.95 (ISBN 0-89651-155-3). Icarus.

Goldman, Bobby. Aces Scientific. LC 80-123418. 169p. 1978. pap. 6.95 (ISBN 0-939460-03-3). M Hardy.

--Winners & Losers at the Bridge Table. 103p. 1979. pap. 3.95 (ISBN 0-939460-05-X). M Hardy.

Goldman, Bruce, et al. Your Check Is in the Mail. rev. ed. 432p. 1984. pap. 7.95 (ISBN 0-446-37926-3). Warner Bks.

Goldman, Burt, jt. auth. see Sehested, Ove H.

Goldman, Carl A. Help!... There's a Computer in the Office! (Illus., Orig.). 1979. 8.95 (ISBN 0-933670-00-1). Rising Star.

Goldman, Charles & Horne, Alexander. Limnology. (Illus.). 633p. 1982. text ed. 39.95 (ISBN 0-07-023651-8). McGraw.

Goldman, Charles R. Freshwater Crayfish V. (Illus.). 1983. lib. bdg. 35.00 (ISBN 0-87055-438-7). AVI.

Goldman, Charles R., ed. Primary Productivity in Aquatic Environments. 1966. 33.50x (ISBN 0-520-01425-1). U of Cal Pr.

Goldman, Charles R., et al, eds. Environmental Quality & Water Development. LC 72-83739. (Illus.). 510p. 1973. 46.95 (ISBN 0-7167-0256-8). W H Freeman.

Goldman, Charlotte. Good Grooming. (Illus.). 1981. pap. text ed. 135.00 (ISBN 0-89290-184-5, A643-SATC). Soc for Visual.

Goldman, Charlotte & Pozzi-Johnson, David. Daily Living Skills. LC 79-73907. (Illus.). 1979. pap. text ed. 135.00 (ISBN 0-89290-151-9, A584-SATC). Soc for Visual.

Goldman, David. Presidential Losers. LC 75-103678. (Pull Ahead Books Ser.). (Illus.). (gr. 5-11). 1970. PLB 4.95 (ISBN 0-8225-0457-X). Lerner Pubns.

Goldman, David, et al. Narcotrafico, S. A. 2nd ed. Lozano, Salvador, et al, trs. from Eng. (Illus.). 478p. (Span.). 1985. pap. 10.00 (ISBN 0-933488-39-4). New Benjamin.

Goldman, David E., jt. ed. see Adelman, William J., Jr.

Goldman, Deborah, jt. auth. see Rosenbloom, David H.

Goldman, E. S. Going Back to Sea. new ed. Gallery, Conor, ed. 1977. 5.95 (ISBN 0-918760-01-1); pap. 2.95 (ISBN 0-918760-00-3). Hearne Bks.

Goldman, Edward A., ed. Jews in a Free Society: Challenges & Opportunities. 12.50x (ISBN 0-87820-112-2). Ktav.

Goldman, Edwin F., ed. see Arban, Jean B.

Goldman, Elizabeth & Farnan, Nancy J. Developing Writers in Grades 7-12. 294p. (gr. 7-12). 1985. 39.80 (ISBN 0-940444-23-2). Kabyn.

Goldman, Elizabeth, jt. auth. see Fearn, Leif.

Goldman, Elizabeth, jt. auth. see McCabe, Robert E.

Goldman, Emma. Anarchism & Other Essays. (Illus.). 1970. pap. 4.50 (ISBN 0-486-22484-8). Dover.

--Anarchism, & Other Essays. 69.95 (ISBN 0-87968-621-9). Gordon Pr.

--Living My Life. LC 71-111090. Repr. of 1934 ed. 32.50 (ISBN 0-404-02860-8). AMS Pr.

--Living My Life, 2 Vols. LC 73-109546. (Civil Liberties in American History Ser.). 1976. Repr. of 1931 ed. Set. lib. bdg. 95.00 (ISBN 0-306-71900-2). Da Capo.

--Living My Life. (Illus.). 1930. pap. 6.50 ea.; Vol. 1. pap. (ISBN 0-486-22543-7); Vol. 2. pap. (ISBN 0-486-22544-5). Dover.

--Living My Life. abr. ed. Drinnon, Richard & Drinnon, Anna M., eds. 1977. pap. 9.95 (ISBN 0-452-00669-4, F669, Mer). NAL.

--Living My Life, 2 Vols. Set. 28.50 (ISBN 0-8446-0648-0). Peter Smith.

--Living My Life: The Autobiography of Emma Goldman. LC 82-19199. (Illus.). 1056p. (Orig.). 1982. pap. 11.95 (ISBN 0-87905-096-9, Peregrine Smith). Gibbs M Smith.

--My Disillusionment in Russia. 13.75 (ISBN 0-8446-0115-2). Peter Smith.

--Place of the Individual in Society. 16p. 1984. Repr. of 1939 ed. 2.00 (ISBN 0-930439-05-8). Cobden Pr.

--The Psychology of Political Violence. 59.95 (ISBN 0-87968-160-8). Gordon Pr.

--The Social Significance of the Modern Drama. 69.95 (ISBN 0-8490-1067-5). Gordon Pr.

--Traffic in Women & Other Essays on Feminism. Shulman, Alix K., ed. (Illus., Orig.). 1971. pap. 3.00 (ISBN 0-87810-001-6). Times Change.

--The White Slave Traffic. 69.95 (ISBN 0-8490-1292-9). Gordon Pr.

Goldman, Emma & Berkman, Alexander. Mother Earth Anthology. 1000.00 (ISBN 0-87968-420-8). Gordon Pr.

--Mother Earth Anthology, 6 vols. 1976. lib. bdg. 1000.00 (ISBN 0-8490-2287-8). Gordon Pr.

Goldman, Eric. Rendezvous with Destiny: A History of Modern American Reform. 1978. pap. 3.95 (ISBN 0-394-72538-7, Vin). Random.

Goldman, Eric A. Visions, Images & Dreams: Yiddish Film Past & Present. Kirkpatrick, Diane, ed. LC 83-15565. (Studies in Cinema: No. 24). 242p. 1983. 39.95 (ISBN 0-8357-1515-9). UMI Res Pr.

Goldman, Eric F. Charles J. Bonaparte, Patrician Reformer: His Early Career. LC 78-64190. (Johns Hopkins University. Studies in the Social Sciences. Sixty-First Ser. 1943: 2). Repr. of 1943 ed. 17.50 (ISBN 0-404-61297-0). AMS Pr.

--The Crucial Decade: America, Nineteen Forty-Five to Nineteen Fifty-Five. LC 81-13399. ix, 298p. 1982. Repr. of 1956 ed. lib. bdg. 27.50x (ISBN 0-313-23147-8, GOCD). Greenwood.

--Crucial Decade & After: America 1945-1960. (YA) 1961. pap. 3.95 (ISBN 0-394-70183-6, V183, Vin). Random.

--John Bach McMaster, American Historian. LC 73-154664. 1971. Repr. of 1943 ed. lib. bdg. 17.00x (ISBN 0-374-93179-8). Octagon.

Goldman, Eric F., ed. Historiography & Urbanization: Essays in American History in Honor of W. S. Holt. LC 67-27601. 1968. Repr. of 1941 ed. 21.50x (ISBN 0-8046-0172-0, Pub. by Kennikat). Assoc Faculty Pr.

Goldman, Errol, jt. auth. see Billings, Rolland G.

Goldman, Etan & Stewart, Brian. A Light in the Darkness. 119p. (Orig.). 1982. 2.25 (ISBN 0-942334-00-0). Reignbow.

Goldman, Ethel. I Like Fruit. LC 68-56699. (Nature Bks for Young Readers). (Illus.). (gr. k-5). 1969. PLB 5.95 (ISBN 0-8225-0270-4). Lerner Pubns.

Goldman, F. The Arts in Higher Adult Education: A Second Review of Programs. 1967. 2.50 (ISBN 0-87060-021-4, REP 117). Syracuse U Cont Ed.

Goldman, George & Milman, Donald S. Addiction: Theory & Treatment: New Approaches to an Old Problem. 288p. (Orig.). 1980. text ed. 20.95 (ISBN 0-8403-2183-X). Kendall-Hunt.

Goldman, George, jt. ed. see Milman, Donald.

Goldman, George D. & Milman, Donald S. Psychoanalytic Psychotherapy. LC 77-79454. 176p. 1978. pap. text ed. 11.95 (ISBN 0-394-34766-8, RanC). Random.

Goldman, George D., jt. auth. see Milman, Donald S.

Goldman, George D. & Milman, Donald S., eds. Modern Woman: Her Psychology & Sexuality. 296p. 1969. 19.75x (ISBN 0-398-00693-8). C C Thomas.

Goldman, George D. & Stricker, George, eds. Practical Problems of a Private Psychotherapy Practice. LC 81-12684. 286p. 1982. 25.00 (ISBN 0-87668-483-5). Aronson.

Goldman, George D., jt. ed. see Milman, Donald S.

Goldman, Gerald, jt. auth. see Shepard, Morris A.

Goldman, H. & Marder, M. Physicians' Guide to Diseases of the Oral Cavity. 1981. 39.50 (ISBN 0-87489-240-6). Med Economics.

Goldman, Hannah G., jt. auth. see Dreier, William A.

Goldman, Harold. Emma Paterson: She Led Women into a Man's World. 127p. 1973. 12.95x (ISBN 0-8464-0372-2). Beekman Pubs.

Goldman, Harold, jt. auth. see Seigel, David.

Goldman, Harold L. Student Resource & Activity Manual to Accompany Koontz & Fulmer's a Practical Introduction to Business. 3rd ed. 1981. pap. 9.95x (ISBN 0-256-02510-X). Irwin.

Goldman, Henry M. & Cohen, D. Walter. Periodontal Therapy. 6th ed. LC 79-13055. (Illus.). 1218p. 1979. 49.95 (ISBN 0-8016-1875-4). Mosby.

Goldman, Henry M. & Isenberg, Gerald. An Atlas of the Surgical Management of Periodontal Disease. (Illus.). 232p. 1982. 68.00 (ISBN 0-931386-41-1). Quint Pub Co.

Goldman, Hersh. Step by Step to Jerusalem. 45p. 1978. pap. 2.95 (ISBN 0-88482-760-7). Hebrew Pub.

Goldman, Howard, jt. auth. see Tessler, Richard.

Goldman, Howard H., ed. Review of General Psychiatry. LC 84-82084. 696p. 1984. lexotone cover 24.00 (ISBN 0-87041-300-7). Lange.

Goldman, I. David, ed. Proceedings of the Second Workshop on Folyl & Antifolyl Polyglumates. LC 85-3531. 416p. 1985. 45.00 (ISBN 0-03-002033-6). Praeger.

Goldman, I. David, et al, eds. Folyl & Antifolyl Polyglutamates. (Advances in Experimental Medicine & Biology Ser.: Vol. 163). 420p. 1983. 55.00x (ISBN 0-306-41262-4, Plenum Pr). Plenum Pub.

Goldman, Irving. Ancient Polynesian Society. LC 74-116028. 1970. 30.00x (ISBN 0-226-30114-1). U of Chicago Pr.

--The Cubeo: Indians of the Northwest Amazon. LC 79-13079. 305p. 1979. pap. 8.95x (ISBN 0-252-00770-0). U of Ill Pr.

Goldman, J., ed. Health Care Technology Evaluation. (Lecture Notes in Medical Informatics: Vol. 6). 1979. pap. 17.00 (ISBN 0-387-09561-6). Springer-Verlag.

Goldman, J. M. & Lowenthal, R. M., eds. Leucocytes: Separation Collection & Transfusion. 1976. 79.50 (ISBN 0-12-288550-3). Acad Pr.

Goldman, Jacquelin. Becoming a Psychotherapist. (Illus.). 140p. 1976. 15.75x (ISBN 0-398-03497-4). C C Thomas.

Goldman, Jacquelin, et al. Psychological Methods of Child Assessment. LC 83-20889. 384p. 1984. 30.00 (ISBN 0-87630-348-3). Brunner-Mazel.

Goldman, James. Lion in Winter. 1966. 9.95 (ISBN 0-394-40615-X). Random.

--The Lion in Winter. 124p. 1983. pap. 4.95 (ISBN 0-14-048174-5). Penguin.

--Lion in Winter. 11.95 (ISBN 0-88411-652-2, Pub. by Aeonian Pr). Amereon Ltd.

Goldman, James & Sondheim, Stephen. Follies. 1971. 10.50 (ISBN 0-394-47362-0). Random.

Goldman, Jane & Kennedy, Laetitia. The New York Urban Athlete: Sports, Fitness & Fun in the Big Apple. (Illus.). 288p. 1983. 9.95 (ISBN 0-671-46323-3). Frommer-Pasmantier.

Goldman, Jane, et al. The New York Athlete: Sports, Fitness & Fun in the Big Apple. 1983. pap. 8.95 (ISBN 0-686-45252-6). S&S.

Goldman, Jean, ed. The Art Institute of Chicago Centennial Lectures. (Museum Studies: No. 10). (Illus.). 370p. 1983. pap. 35.00 (ISBN 0-8092-5979-6). Art Inst Chi.

Goldman, Jeanine, et al. Perspectives de France: Workbook. (Illus.). 224p. 1982. 10.95 (ISBN 0-13-660530-3). P-H.

Goldman, Jerome M., jt. auth. see Reinis, Stanislav.

Goldman, John M. & Priesler, Harvey, eds. BIMR Hematology 2: Leukemias. (Illus.). 320p. 1984. text ed. 59.95 (ISBN 0-407-02336-4). Butterworth.

Goldman, Jordan. Public Relations in the Marketing Mix. LC 83-71076. 224p. 1985. pap. 14.95 (ISBN 0-87251-084-0). Crain Bks.

Goldman, Joshua & Zolotow, Nina. System 1032 Host Language Interface User's Guide. rev. ed. (Illus.). 126p. 1985. looseleaf 21.50x (ISBN 0-912055-11-1). Software Hse.

Goldman, Joshua, jt. auth. see Zolotow, Nina.

Goldman, Judith. American Prints: Process & Proofs. LC 81-47244. (Icon Editions Ser.). (Illus.). 176p. 1979. 24.04i (ISBN 0-06-433261-6, HarpT). Har-Row.

--American Prints: Process & Proofs. LC 81-47244. (Icon Editions Ser.). (Illus.). 176p. 1982. pap. 15.34i (ISBN 0-06-430116-8, IN-116, HarpT). Har-Row.

--James Rosenquist. (Nonfiction Ser.). (Illus.). 160p. 1985. 45.00 (ISBN 0-670-80589-0). Viking.

Goldman, Juliette, jt. auth. see Goldman, Ronald.

Goldman, Katie. In the Wings. LC 82-70200. 176p. (gr. 6 up). 1982. 10.95 (ISBN 0-8037-3968-0). Dial Bks Young.

--Pay As You Exit. (YA) 1985. 12.95 (ISBN 0-8037-0191-8). Dial Bks Young.

Goldman, L., ed. The Biomedical Laser: Technology & Clinical Applications. (Illus.). 350p. 1981. 42.00 (ISBN 0-387-90571-5). Springer-Verlag.

Goldman, L. H. Saul Bellow's Moral Vision: A Critical Study of the Jewish Experience. 1983. text ed. 29.50x (ISBN 0-8290-1056-4); pap. text ed. 16.95x (ISBN 0-8290-1535-3). Irvington.

Goldman, Larry L., jt. auth. see Aranyi, Laszlo.

Goldman, Laurel. Sounding the Territory. LC 81-12409. 320p. 1982. 13.50 (ISBN 0-394-51935-3). Knopf.

--Sounding the Territory. (YA) (gr. 7-12). 1983. pap. 3.50 (ISBN 0-440-38176-2, LE). Dell.

Goldman, Laurence. Talk Never Dies: The Language of Huli Disputes. LC 83-18294. 352p. 1984. 49.95x (ISBN 0-422-78210-6, NO. 4009). Methuen Inc.

Goldman, Leo. Using Tests in Counseling. LC 77-151115. (Orig.). 1971. text ed. 23.80x (ISBN 0-673-16456-X, Appleton-Century-Crofts). Scott F.

Goldman, Leo, ed. Research Methods for Counselors: Practical Approaches in Field Settings. LC 77-10950. (Counseling & Human Development Ser.). 439p. 1978. text ed. 34.95x (ISBN 0-471-02339-6). Wiley.

Goldman, Leon. Applications of the Laser. LC 82-7834. 332p. 1982. Repr. of 1973 ed. lib. bdg. 49.95 (ISBN 0-89874-481-4). Krieger.

--Biomedical Aspects of the Laser. (Illus.). 1981. 42.00 (ISBN 0-387-90571-5). Springer-Verlag.

--Conference on the Laser, Third, Vol. 267. (Annals of the New York Academy of Sciences). 481p. 1976. 57.00x (ISBN 0-89072-021-5). NY Acad Sci.

--Introduction to Modern Phototherapy. (Illus.). 144p. 1978. 19.25x (ISBN 0-398-03716-7). C C Thomas.

--Laser Cancer Research. (Recent Results in Cancer Research: Vol. 4). (Illus.). 1966. 15.00 (ISBN 0-387-03643-1). Springer-Verlag.

Goldman, Leon & Rockwell, James R., Jr. Lasers in Medicine. LC 77-163181. (Illus.). 394p. 1971. 92.50 (ISBN 0-677-02430-4). Gordon.

Goldman, Leon, et al. Laboratory Diagnosis in Dermatology. LC 70-176170. 300p. 1985. 37.50 (ISBN 0-87527-149-9). Green.

Goldman, Louis. Turkey, a Week in Samil's World. LC 75-169983. (Face to Face Books Ser.). (Illus.). 48p. (gr. k-2). 1973. 8.95 (ISBN 0-02-736230-2, CCPr). Macmillan.

Goldman, M. A Guide to the X-Ray Department. 100p. 1978. pap. 10.50 (ISBN 0-7236-0493-2). PSG Pub Co.

Goldman, M., jt. auth. see Abragam, A.

Goldman, Marcus S. Sir Philip Sidney & the Arcadia. 1934. lib. bdg. 15.00 (ISBN 0-8414-4655-5). Folcroft.

Goldman, Margaret F. My A, B, C, D, E Thinking, Feeling & Doing Book. LC 83-90397. (Illus.). 48p. (ps up). 11.95 (ISBN 0-914237-00-4). L & M Bks.

Goldman, Marion S. Gold Diggers & Silver Miners: Prostitution & Social Life on the Comstock Lode. (Women & Culture Ser.). 256p. 1981. text ed. 18.50x (ISBN 0-472-09332-0); pap. text ed. 9.50x (ISBN 0-472-06332-4). U of Mich Pr.

Goldman, Marion S. & Rabow, Jerome. Studies in Psychoanalytic Sociology: A Text & Reader. LC 83-86. 1985. text ed. write for info. (ISBN 0-89874-608-6). Krieger.

Goldman, Mark. High Hopes: The Rise & Decline of Buffalo, New York. LC 82-19629. (Illus.). 352p. 1983. 44.50x (ISBN 0-87395-734-2); pap. 14.95x (ISBN 0-87395-735-0). State U NY Pr.

--The Reader's Art: Virginia Woolf As Literary Critic. (Depropriatibus Litterarum Ser.: No. 19). 1976. pap. text ed. 17.60x (ISBN 90-2793-275-1). Mouton.

Goldman, Marshall. Enigma of Soviet Petroleum: Half Empty or Half Full? (Illus.). 216p. (Orig.). 1980. text ed. 19.95x (ISBN 0-04-333015-0); pap. text ed. 8.95x (ISBN 0-04-333016-9). Allen Unwin.

Goldman, Marshall I. Environmental Pollution in the Soviet Union: The Spoils of Progress. 1975. pap. 4.95 (ISBN 0-262-57029-7). MIT Pr.

--The U. S. S. R. in Crisis: The Failure of an Economic System. 1983. 15.00 (ISBN 0-393-01715-X); pap. 4.95x (ISBN 0-393-95336-X). Norton.

Goldman, Martin. The Demon in the Aether: The Story of James Clerk Maxwell, the Father of Modern Science. 320p. 1983. 30.00 (ISBN 0-9960042-2-X, Pub. by A Hilger England). Heyden.

Goldman, Marvin & Bustad, Leo K., eds. Biomedical Implications of Radiostrontium Exposure: Proceedings. LC 72-600049. (AEC Symposium Ser.). 411p. 1972. pap. 18.25 (ISBN 0-87079-152-4, CONF-710201); microfiche 4.50 (ISBN 0-87079-153-2, CONF-710201). DOE.

Goldman, Mayer C. The Public Defender: A Necessary Factor in the Administration of Justice. facsimile ed. LC 74-3826. (Criminal Justice in America Ser.). 1974. Repr. of 1917 ed. 15.00x (ISBN 0-405-06146-3). Ayer Co Pubs.

Goldman, Meredith & Lissauer, T. Human Body. (Young Scientist Ser.). (Illus.). 32p. (gr. 6 up). 1983. 7.95 (ISBN 0-86020-748-X); lib. bdg. 12.95 (ISBN 0-88110-150-8); pap. 4.95 (ISBN 0-86020-747-1). EDC.

Goldman, Merle. China's Intellectuals. LC 81-2945. 320p. 1981. text ed. 20.00x (ISBN 0-674-11970-3). Harvard U Pr.

--Literary Dissent in Communist China. LC 67-17311. 1971. pap. text ed. 3.75x (ISBN 0-689-70260-4, 168). Atheneum.

Goldman, Merle, ed. Modern Chinese Literature in the May Fourth Era. (East Asian Ser.: Vol. 89). 1977. 25.00x (ISBN 0-674-57910-0, Social Science Research Council). Harvard U Pr.

--Modern Chinese Literature in the May Fourth Era. (East Asian Studies: No. 89). 480p. 1985. pap. text ed. 9.95x (ISBN 0-674-57911-9). Harvard U Pr.

Goldman, Merle R. Literary Dissent in Communist China. LC 67-17311. (East Asian Ser.: No. 29). 1967. 20.00x (ISBN 0-674-53625-8). Harvard U Pr.

Goldman, Mervin J. Principles of Clinical Electrocardiography. 11th ed. LC 62-13252. (Illus.). 438p. 1982. lexotone cover 15.00 (ISBN 0-87041-082-2). Lange.

Goldman, Mervin J., jt. auth. see Goldschlager, Nora.

Goldman, Michael. Acting & Action in Shakespearean Tragedy. LC 84-17745. 164p. 1985. text ed. 20.00x (ISBN 0-691-06630-2). Princeton U Pr.

Goldman, Morris. Fluorescent Antibody Methods. LC 68-14660. 1968. 55.00 (ISBN 0-12-289050-7). Acad Pr.

Goldman, Myer & Cope, David. A Radiographic Index. 7th ed. (Illus.). 112p. 1982. pap. text ed. 10.00 (ISBN 0-7236-0660-9). PSG Pub Co.

Goldman, Nancy L. Female Soldiers--Combatants or Noncombatants? Historical & Contemporary Perspectives. LC 81-13318. (Contributions in Women's Studies: No. 33). (Illus.). xix, 307p. 1982. lib. bdg. 35.00 (ISBN 0-313-23117-6, GFS/). Greenwood.

Goldman, Nancy L. & Segal, David R., eds. The Social Psychology of Military Service, Vol. VI. (War, Revolution & Peacekeeping Ser.). 303p. 1976. 28.00 (ISBN 0-8039-0598-X); pap. 14.00 (ISBN 0-8039-0599-8). Seven Locks Pr.

Goldman, Nathan C. Space Commerce: Free Enterprise on the High Frontier. LC 84-16761. 208p. 1985. 25.00 ea. (ISBN 0-88730-003-0). Ballinger Pub.

Goldman, Norma & Nyenhuis, Jacob E. Latin Via Ovid: A First Course. 2nd ed. LC 77-22501. (Illus.). 524p. 1982. 17.95x (ISBN 0-8143-1732-4). Wayne St U Pr.

Goldman, Norma & Szymanski, Ladislas. English Grammar for Students of Latin. Morton, Jacqueline, ed. 200p. 1983. pap. 6.00x (ISBN 0-934034-03-6). Olivia & Hill.

Goldman, Peter & Fuller, Tony. Charlie Company: What Vietnam Did to Us. LC 82-14375. (Illus.). 384p. 1983. 15.95 (ISBN 0-688-01549-2). Morrow.

--Charlie Company: What Vietnam Did to Us. 1984. pap. 3.95 (ISBN 0-317-05475-9). Ballantine.

--The Quest for the Presidency. LC 85-47615. (Illus.). 320p. 1985. 16.95 (ISBN 0-553-05100-8). Bantam.

Goldman, Peter L. The Death & Life of Malcolm X. 2nd ed. LC 79-18105. 438p. 1979. pap. 8.95x (ISBN 0-252-00774-3). U of Ill Pr.

Goldman, R. D., et al, eds. Cell Motility. LC 76-17144. (Cold Spring Harbor Conferences on Cell Proliferation Ser.: Vol. 3). (Illus.). 1404p. 1976. 3 bk. set 133.00 (ISBN 0-87969-117-4). Cold Spring Harbor.

Goldman, Ralph M. Arms Control & Peacekeeping. 301p. 1982. pap. text ed. 11.00 (ISBN 0-394-32886-8, RanC). Random.

--Contemporary Perspectives on Politics. LC 76-3602. 454p. 1976. Repr. of 1972 ed. text ed. 14.95 (ISBN 0-87855-148-4). Transaction Bks.

--Search for Consensus: The Story of the Democratic Party. LC 79-1207. 417p. 1979. 34.95 (ISBN 0-87722-152-9). Temple U Pr.

Goldman, Ralph M., ed. Transnational Parties: Organizing the World's Precincts. LC 83-12369. (Illus.). 374p. 1983. lib. bdg. 27.75 (ISBN 0-8191-3400-7); pap. text ed. 15.00 (ISBN 0-8191-3401-5). U Pr of Amer.

Goldman, Richard, jt. auth. see Wallat, Cynthia.

Goldman, Richard, et al. Looking at Children: Field Experiences in Child Study. Peck, Johanne & Lehane, Stephen, eds. LC 76-15127. 1976. pap. text ed. 14.95 (ISBN 0-89334-001-4). Humanics Ltd.

Goldman, Richard F. Richard Franko Goldman: Selected Essays & Reviews, 1948-1968. Klotzman, Dorothy, ed. LC 79-56152. (I. S. A. M. Monographs: No. 13). 262p. 1980. pap. 10.00 (ISBN 0-914678-13-2). Inst Am Music.

--The Wind Band, Its Literature & Technique. LC 73-16627. (Illus.). 286p. 1974. Repr. of 1961 ed. lib. bdg. 25.00x (ISBN 0-8371-7200-4, GOWB). Greenwood.

Goldman, Richard F., ed. Landmarks of Early American Music 1760-1800. LC 72-1631. Repr. of 1943 ed. 24.50 (ISBN 0-404-08309-9). AMS Pr.

Goldman, Richard M., jt. auth. see Champagne, David W.

Goldman, Robert & Weinberg, Joel. Statistics: An Introduction. (Illus.). 672p. 1985. text ed. 31.95 (ISBN 0-13-845918-5). P-H.

Goldman, Robert P. God's Priests & Warriors: The Bhrgus of the Mahabharata. LC 76-41255. (Studies in Oriental Culture). 195p. 1977. 21.50x (ISBN 0-231-03941-7). Columbia U Pr.

Goldman, Robert P., tr. see Ramayana.

Goldman, Ron. Design of An Interactive Manipulator Programming Environment. Stone, Harold, ed. LC 84-28091. (Computer Science; Artificial Intelligence Ser.: No. 16). 158p. 1985. 44.95 (ISBN 0-8357-1616-3). UMI Res Pr.

Goldman, Ronald. Readiness for Religion. 1970. pap. 4.95 (ISBN 0-8164-2060-2, SP70, Pub. by Seabury). Winston Pr.

--Religious Thinking from Childhood to Adolescence. 1964. Repr. text ed. 23.75x (ISBN 0-7100-1459-7). Humanities.

--Religious Thinking from Childhood to Adolescence. 1968. pap. text ed. 6.95 (ISBN 0-8164-2061-0, SP53, Pub. by Seabury). Winston Pr.

Goldman, Ronald & Goldman, Juliette. Children's Sexual Thinking: A Comparative Study of Children Aged 5 to 15 in Australia, North America, Britain & Sweden. 368p. 1982. 26.95x (ISBN 0-7100-0883-X). Routledge & Kegan.

Goldman, Sheldon. Constitutional Law & Supreme Court Decision Making: Cases & Essays. 800p. 1982. text ed. 28.50 scp (ISBN 0-06-042379-X, HarpC). Har-Row.

Goldman, Sheldon & Jahnige, Thomas P. The Federal Courts As a Political System. 2nd ed. (American Political Ser.). 305p. 1976. pap. text ed. 12.20 scp (ISBN 0-06-042382-X, HarpC). Har-Row.

--The Federal Courts As a Political System. 3rd ed. 263p. 1985. pap. text ed. 10.95 scp (ISBN 0-06-042376-5, HarpC). Har-Row.

Goldman, Sheldon & Sarat, Austin, eds. American Court Systems: Readings in Judicial Process & Behavior. LC 78-19160. (Illus.). 648p. 1978. text ed. 32.95 (ISBN 0-7167-0061-1); pap. text ed. 17.95 (ISBN 0-7167-0060-3). W H Freeman.

Goldman, Sherman, ed. see Kushi, Michio.

Goldman, Shifra M. Contemporary Mexican Painting in a Time of Change. LC 80-17107. (Texas Pan American Ser.). (Illus.). 255p. 1981. text ed. 32.50x (ISBN 0-292-71061-5). U of Tex Pr.

Goldman, Shifra M. & Ybarra-Frausto, Tomas, eds. Arte Chicano: A Comprehensive Annotated Bibliography of Chicano Art, 1965-1981. (Chicano Studies Library Publications: No. 11). (Illus.). 190p. 1985. pap. text ed. 25.00x (ISBN 0-918520-09-6). UC Chicano.

Goldman, Solomon. The Jew & the Universe. LC 73-2200. (The Jewish People; History, Religion, Literature Ser.). Repr. of 1936 ed. 23.50 (ISBN 0-405-05265-0). Ayer Co Pubs.

Goldman, Susan. Cousins Are Special. Rubin, Caroline, ed. LC 75-11924. (Self-Starter Bks). (Illus.). (ps-2). 1978. PLB 9.25 (ISBN 0-8075-1317-2). A Whitman.

--Grandma Is Somebody Special. Rubin, Caroline, ed. LC 76-18980. (Self-Starter Bks.). (Illus.). 32p. (ps-1). 1976. PLB 9.25 (ISBN 0-8075-3034-4). A Whitman.

Goldman, T. & Neito, M. M., eds. Proceedings of Nineteen Eighty-Four Meeting of the Division of Particles & Fields, American Physical Society. 600p. 1985. 67.00 (ISBN 0-317-27180-6). Taylor & Francis.

Goldman, T., et al. Intense Medium Energy Sources of Strangeness: AIP Conference Proceedings No. 102, UC, Santa Cruz, 1983. (Subseries on Particles & Fields: No. 31). 1983. lib. bdg. 32.75 (ISBN 0-88318-201-7). Am Inst Physics.

Goldman, Vivien. Bob Marley: Soul Rebel-Natural Mystic. (Illus.). 96p. 1981. pap. 6.95 (ISBN 0-312-08727-6). St Martin.

Goldman, W. Darryl. Stand in the Door. LC 80-65309. 176p. 1980. pap. 2.95 (ISBN 0-88243-599-X, 02-0599). Gospel Pub.

Goldman, William. Adventures in the Screen Trade: A Personal View of Hollywood & Screenwriting. LC 82-17602. 432p. (Orig.). 1983. 17.50 (ISBN 0-446-51273-7); pap. 8.95 (ISBN 0-446-37625-6). Warner Bks.

--Boys & Girls Together. 704p. 1984. pap. 3.95 (ISBN 0-446-32124-9). Warner Bks.

--The Color of Light. 352p. 1984. 17.50 (ISBN 0-446-51274-5). Warner Bks.

--The Color of Light. 400p. 1985. pap. 3.95 (ISBN 0-446-32587-2). Warner Bks.

--Control. 352p. 1982. 14.95 (ISBN 0-385-28162-5). Delacorte.

--Control. 1983. pap. 3.95 (ISBN 0-440-11464-0). Dell.

--Heat. LC 84-40656. 256p. 1985. 17.50 (ISBN 0-446-51275-3). Warner Bks.

--Marathon Man. 272p. 1975. pap. 3.95 (ISBN 0-440-15502-9). Dell.

--Marathon Man. 15.95 (ISBN 0-88411-653-0, Pub. by Aeonian Pr). Amereon Ltd.

--The Princess Bride. 1984. pap. 3.50 (ISBN 0-345-31532-4). Ballantine.

--The Season: A Candid Look at Broadway. Rev. ed. LC 84-4409. 448p. 1984. pap. 8.95 (ISBN 0-87910-023-0). Limelight Edns.

--The Silent Gondoliers, By S. Morgenstern. 128p. 1985. pap. 3.50 (ISBN 0-345-32583-4, Pub. by Del Rey). Ballantine.

Goldman-Morrison. Psychodrama: Experience & Process. 144p. 1984. pap. text ed. 12.95 (ISBN 0-8403-3322-6). Kendall-Hunt.

Goldmann, Freda H., jt. auth. see Liverwright, A. A.

Goldmann, Kjell. Is My Enemy's Enemy My Friend's Friend? 110p. (Orig.). 1979. pap. text ed. 10.50x (ISBN 0-317-02802-2, Pub. by Chartwell-Bratt England). Brookfield Pub Co.

Goldmann, Kjell & Sjostedt, Gunnar, eds. Power, Capabilities, Interdependence: Problems in the Study of International Influence. LC 77-84076. (Sage Modern Politics Ser.: Vol. 3). (Illus.). 300p. 1979. 28.00 (ISBN 0-8039-9884-8); pap. 14.00 (ISBN 0-8039-9885-6). Sage.

Goldmann, Kjell, et al. Democracy & Foreign Policy. 300p. 1985. text ed. price not set (ISBN 0-566-05012-9). Gower Pub Co.

Goldmann, Lucien. Cultural Creation in Modern Society. Grahl, Bart, tr. from Fr. LC 75-46394. 150p. 1976. 14.50 (ISBN 0-914386-08-5); pap. 5.50 (ISBN 0-914386-09-3). Telos Pr.

--Essays on Method in the Sociology of Literature. Boelhower, William Q., tr. from Fr. LC 79-89567. 1980. lib. bdg. 14.00 (ISBN 0-914386-19-0); pap. 5.50 (ISBN 0-914386-20-4). Telos Pr.

--Hidden God. Thody, Philip, tr. (International Library of Philosophy & Scientific Method Ser.). 1976. text ed. 24.00x (ISBN 0-7100-3621-3). Humanities.

--Lukacs & Heidegger: Towards a New Philosophy. Boelhower, William Q., tr. pap. 8.95 (ISBN 0-7100-8794-2). Routledge & Kegan.

--The Philosophy of the Enlightenment: The Burgess & the Enlightenment. Maas, Henry, tr. from Fr. 1973. 17.50x (ISBN 0-262-07060-X). MIT Pr.

--Racine. Hamilton, Alastair, tr. from French. (Orig.). 1981. pap. 4.95 (ISBN 0-906495-77-6). Writers & Readers.

--Toward a Sociology of the Novel. 1975. pap. 12.95x (ISBN 0-422-76350-0, NO. 3448, Pub. by Tavistock). Methuen Inc.

Goldmann, Peter. Seatrade U. S. Yearbook 1985. 1985. 300.00x (ISBN 0-905597-15-X, Pub. by Seatrade). State Mutual Bk.

Goldmann, Robert B. A Work Experiment: Six Americans in a Swedish Plant. LC 75-45049. 48p. 1976. pap. 3.50 (ISBN 0-916584-00-3). Ford Found.

Goldmann, Robert B. & Wilson, A. J., eds. From Independence to Statehood: Managing Ethnic Conflict in Six African & Asian States. LC 83-6663. 300p. 1984. 27.50 (ISBN 0-312-30723-3). St Martin.

Goldmark, Josephine. Pilgrims of Forty-Eight. facsimile ed. LC 74-27989. (Modern Jewish Experience Ser.). (Illus.). 1975. Repr. of 1930 ed. 29.00x (ISBN 0-405-06716-X). Ayer Co Pubs.

Goldmark, Josephine & Hopkins, Mary D. Comparison of an Eight-Hour Plant & a Ten-Hour Plant: U. S. Public Health Bulletin, No. 106. Stein, Leon, ed. LC 77-70495. (Work Ser.). 1977. Repr. of 1920 ed. lib. bdg. 20.00x (ISBN 0-405-10168-6). Ayer Co Pubs.

Goldmark, Josephine, jt. auth. see Brandeis, Louis D.

Goldmark, Josephine C. Impatient Crusader: Florence Kelley's Life Story. LC 76-23383. 217p. 1976. Repr. of 1953 ed. lib. bdg. 22.50x (ISBN 0-8371-9011-8, GOIM). Greenwood.

Goldmark, Pauline & Hopkins, Mary, eds. The Gypsy Trail: An Anthology for Campers, 2 vols. LC 78-74817. (Granger Poetry Library). 1979. 29.75x ea.; Vol. 1. (ISBN 0-89609-135-X); Vol. 2. (ISBN 0-89609-136-8). Granger Bk.

Goldmark, Pauline & Hopkins, Marycompiled by. The Gypsy Trail: An Anthology for Campers. rev. & enl. ed. LC 72-460. (Granger Index Reprint Ser.). Repr. of 1914 ed. 21.00 (ISBN 0-8369-6364-4). Ayer Co Pubs.

Goldmeier, Erich. The Memory Trace: Its Formation & Its Fate. (Illus.). 288p. 1982. text ed. 29.95x (ISBN 0-89859-172-4). L Erlbaum Assocs.

--Similarity in Visually Perceived Forms. LC 72-83230. (Psychological Issues Monograph: No. 29, Vol. 8, No. 1). 135p. 1972. text ed. 17.50 (ISBN 0-8236-6077-X). Intl Univs Pr.

Goldner, F. H., jt. auth. see MacRae, D.

Goldner, George R. Niccolo & Piero Lamberti. LC 77-94697. (Outstanding Dissertations in the Fine Arts Ser.). 1978. lib. bdg. 58.00 (ISBN 0-8240-3229-2). Garland Pub.

Goldner, Kathryn & Vogel, Carole G. Why Mount St. Helens Blew Its Top. LC 81-12482. (Illus.). 80p. (gr. 5 up). 1981. PLB 9.95 (ISBN 0-87518-219-4). Dillon.

Goldner, Kathryn A. & Vogel, Carol G. The Dangers of Strangers. (Illus.). (gr. 5-8). 1983. 10.95 (ISBN 0-686-89162-7). Dillon.

Goldner, Marian see Grandma, Marian, pseud.

Goldner, Nancy. The Stravinsky Festival. LC 73-84996. (Illus.). 304p. 1973. 15.00x (ISBN 0-87130-037-0). Eakins.

Goldner, Paul, jt. auth. see DeVault, Mary.

Goldner, Paul, et al. The Texas Instruments Home Computer. cancelled 12.95 (ISBN 0-89303-888-1). Brady Comm.

Goldoni, et al. La Cecchina Ossia la Buona Figiuola, la Clemenza, di Tito, Leonida in Tegea Didone Abbandonata, Don Chisciotte in Sierra Morona. LC 76-20993. (Italian Opera Ser. 1640 to 1770: No. II). 400p. 1983. lib. bdg. 83.00 (ISBN 0-8240-4819-9). Garland Pub.

Goldoni, Carlo. The Comedies of Goldoni. Zimmern, Helen, ed. & intro. by. Incl. A Curious Mishap; The Beneficant Bear; The Fan; The Spendthrift Miser. LC 76-48424. (Library of World Literature Ser.). 1978. Repr. of 1892 ed. 21.45 (ISBN 0-88355-544-1). Hyperion Conn.

--The Comic Theatre: A Comedy in Three Acts. Miller, John W., tr. LC 69-14867. xxii, 94p. 1969. 9.95x (ISBN 0-8032-0056-0). U of Nebr Pr.

--Four Comedies. Davies, Frederick, tr. from Ital. 336p. 1968. pap. 5.95 (ISBN 0-14-044204-9). Penguin.

--Liar. Davies, Frederick H., tr. (Orig.). 1963. pap. 3.50x (ISBN 0-87830-531-9). Theatre Arts.

--Memoirs of Carlo Goldoni. Drake, William A., ed. Black, John, tr. from Fr. LC 76-8013. 1976. Repr. of 1926 ed. lib. bdg. 32.50x (ISBN 0-8371-8871-7, GOME). Greenwood.

--Memoirs of Carlo Goldoni. 1926. 35.00 (ISBN 0-932062-64-4). Sharon Hill.

--Servant of Two Masters. Davies, Frederick H., tr. (Orig.). 1961. pap. 3.50x (ISBN 0-87830-537-8). Theatre Arts.

--Three Comedies: Mine Hostess, the Boors, & the Fan. Bax, Clifford & Rawson, I. M., trs. from Italian. LC 79-4666. 1979. Repr. of 1961 ed. lib. bdg. 27.50x (ISBN 0-313-21259-7, GOTC). Greenwood.

Goldoni, Carlo see Brown, Howard M.

Goldoni, Carolo. Campiello: A Venetian Comedy. Graham-Jones, Susanna, tr. from Ital. Bryden, Bill. (National Theatre Plays Ser.). viii, 64p. (Orig.). 1976. pap. text ed. 5.50x (ISBN 0-435-23359-9). Heinemann Ed.

Goldovsky, Boris. Good Afternoon, Ladies & Gentlemen! Intermission Scripts from the Met Broadcasts. LC 83-49338. (Illus.). 192p. 1984. 15.95 (ISBN 0-253-32588-9); cassette 7.95 (ISBN 0-253-32587-0); bk. & cassette 22.50 (ISBN 0-253-32589-7). Ind U Pr.

Goldovsky, Boris & Cate, Curtis. My Road to Opera: The Recollections of Boris Goldsovsky As Told to Curtis Cate. 1979. 15.00 (ISBN 0-395-27760-4). HM.

Goldovsky, Boris & Peltz, Mary E. Accents on Opera: A Series of Brief Essays Stressing Known & Little Known Facts & Facets of a Familiar Art. facsimile ed. LC 77-156651. (Essay Index Reprint Ser). Repr. of 1953 ed. 25.00 (ISBN 0-8369-2398-7). Ayer Co Pubs.

Goldovsky, Boris & Schoep, Arthur. Bringing Soprano Arias to Life. 1973. pap. text ed. 13.50 (ISBN 0-02-870540-8). Schirmer Bks.

Goldovsky, Boris & Wolf, Thomas. Touring Opera: A Manual for Small Companies. Fox, Leland, ed. LC 75-26252. (National Opera Association Monograph Ser.: No. 3). (Illus.). 113p. (Orig.). 1975. pap. 7.50 (ISBN 0-938178-01-6). Natl Opera Assn.

Goldowsky, Barbara. Ferry to Nirvana. LC 83-80372. 64p. 1983. pap. write for info. (ISBN 0-88100-031-0). Natl Writ Pr.

Goldowsky, Siebert. Usher Parsons, M. D. Physician & Surgeon of Providence. 1985. write for info. F A Countway.

Goldratt, Eliyahu M. & Cox, Jeff. The Goal: Excellence in Manufacturing. 262p. (Orig.). 1985. pap. 9.95 (ISBN 0-88427-060-2). North River.

Goldreich, Esther, jt. auth. see Goldreich, Gloria.
Goldreich, Gloria. Four Days. 352p. 1983. pap. 3.50 (ISBN 0-449-20091-4, Crest). Fawcett.
--Leah Children. 369p. 1985. 16.95 (ISBN 0-02-544450-6). Macmillan.
--Leah's Journey. 448p. 1985. pap. 3.95 (ISBN 0-425-07795-0). Berkley Pub.
--This Burning Harvest. 400p. 1983. pap. 3.50 (ISBN 0-425-06078-0). Berkley Pub.
Goldreich, Gloria & Goldreich, Esther. What Can She Be? a Legislator. (What Can She Be? Ser). (Illus.). (gr. 1-5). 1978. 11.25 (ISBN 0-688-41865-1); PLB 11.88 (ISBN 0-688-51865-6). Lothrop.
Goldreich, Gloria, ed. A Treasury of Jewish Literature: From Biblical Times to Today. LC 81-6967. 256p. (gr. 5 up). 1982. 13.45 (ISBN 0-03-053831-9). HR&W.
Goldring, D. James Elroy Flecker. 188p. 1980. Repr. of 1922 ed. lib. bdg. 25.00 (ISBN 0-89984-226-7). Century Bookbindery.
Goldring, David & Middlekamp, J. Neal. The Camp Health Manual. 171p. 1984. 14.95 (ISBN 0-87603-072-X). Am Camping.
Goldring, Douglas. Gone Abroad: A Story of Travel, Chiefly in Italy & the Balearic Isles. 1925. 25.00 (ISBN 0-89984-013-2). Century Bookbindery.
--James Elroy Flecker. 1922. 25.00 (ISBN 0-8274-2596-1). R West.
--The Nineteen Twenties. LC 75-28131. 1975. Repr. of 1945 ed. lib. bdg. 30.00 (ISBN 0-8414-4548-6). Folcroft.
--Reputations. LC 68-16294. 1968. Repr. of 1920 ed. 21.00x (ISBN 0-8046-0174-7, Pub. by Kennikat). Assoc Faculty Pr.
--South Lodge. LC 77-18261. 1977. lib. bdg. 25.00 (ISBN 0-8414-4600-8). Folcroft.
Goldring, Elizabeth, jt. ed. see Piene, Otto.
Goldring, Elizabeth O. Laser Treatment. Barnes, Jane, ed. 85p. 1983. pap. write for info (ISBN 0-940054-01-9). Blue Giant Pr.
Goldring, Gvirol & Kalish, Rafael. Hyperfine Interactions of Excited Nuclei, 4 vols. LC 78-127883. (Illus.). 1378p. 1971. Set. 377.75 (ISBN 0-677-14600-0); 106.50 ea. Vol. 1, 386p (ISBN 0-677-15120-9). Vol. 2, 400p (ISBN 0-677-15130-6). Vol. 3, 280p (ISBN 0-677-15140-3). Vol. 4, 396p (ISBN 0-677-15150-0). Gordon.
Goldring, Judith. Quick Response Therapy: A Time Limited Treatment Approach. LC 80-11362. 142p. 1980. 18.95 (ISBN 0-87705-499-1). Human Sci Pr.
Goldring, Mark. Computers & Crafts: A Practical Guide. 120p. 7.95 (ISBN 0-9614141-0-3). Am Council Arts.
Goldring, Maude. Charlotte Bronte, the Woman. LC 76-26960. 1976. Repr. of 1915 ed. lib. bdg. 20.00 (ISBN 0-8414-4536-2). Folcroft.
Goldring, Patrick. Britain by Train. 208p. 1983. pap. 5.95 (ISBN 0-600-20669-6, Pub. by Auto Assn-British Tourist Authority England). Merrimack Pub Cir.
Goldring, Sidney, jt. auth. see O'Leary, James L.
Goldring, William, jt. ed. see Chasis, Herbert.
Goldring, Winifred. Handbook of Paleontology for Beginners & Amateurs: The Fossils, Pt. 1. (Illus.). 394p. 1960. Repr. 6.75 (ISBN 0-87710-363-1). Paleo Res.
Goldrisk, James. The King's Ships Were at Sea: The War in the North Sea, August 1914 to February 1915. (Illus.). 320p. 1984. 23.95 (ISBN 0-87021-334-2). Naval Inst Pr.
Goldron, Romain. Minstrels & Masters: The Triumph of Polyphony. LC 68-1789. 1968. Volume 3 4.95 (ISBN 0-385-02342-1). Doubleday.
Goldsack, S. J. Ada for Specification: Possibilities & Limitations. (Ada Companion Ser.). (Illus.). 280p. 1985. 37.50 (ISBN 0-521-30853-4). Cambridge U Pr.
Goldsberry, Steven. Maui the Demigod: An Epic Novel of Mythical Hawaii. (Illus.). 400p. 1985. 18.95 (ISBN 0-671-47788-9, Pub. by Poseidon). S&S.
Goldsborough, Edmund K. Ole Mars An' Ole Miss. facsimile ed. LC 74-37592. (Black Heritage Library Collection). Repr. of 1900 ed. 22.00 (ISBN 0-8369-8968-6). Ayer Co Pubs.
Goldsborough, J. Carter. Only Forty Miles of Pavement. (Illus.). 260p. 1984. 16.95 (ISBN 0-89015-477-5). Eakin Pubns.
Goldsborough, Jennifer F. Eighteenth & Nineteenth Century Maryland Silver in the Collection of the Baltimore Museum of Art. Harper, Ann B., ed. LC 75-15344. (Illus.). 1975. pap. 14.50 (ISBN 0-912298-37-5). Baltimore Mus.
--Silver in Maryland. LC 83-62171. (Illus.). 330p. (Orig.). 1983. pap. 30.00 (ISBN 0-938420-27-5). Md Hist.
Goldsborough, June. What's in the Woods? LC 76-10271. (Illus.). 32p. 1976. pap. 2.95 (ISBN 0-13-955047-X). P H.
Goldsborough, June, jt. auth. see Foster, John.
Goldsborough, June, illus. The Dandelion Mother Goose. LC 78-72131. (Illus.). (gr. k-3). 1979. 6.75 (ISBN 0-89799-097-8); pap. 3.50 (ISBN 0-89799-052-8). Dandelion Pr.
--Stories to Grow On. (Illus.). 64p. (ps-3). 6.95 (ISBN 0-528-82420-1). Rand.
Goldsborough, W. W. The Maryland Line in the Confederate Army: 1861-1865. 412p. 1984. Repr. of 1900 ed. 35.00 (ISBN 0-317-26001-4). Butternut Pr.
Goldsbrough, et al. Analog Electronics for Microcomputer Systems. LC 83-61062. 440p. 1983. pap. 19.95 (ISBN 0-672-21821-6, 21821). Sams.
Goldsbrough, Paul. Technibook IV: Microprocessor Interfacing with the 8255 PPI Chip with Experiments. Blacksburg Group, ed. LC 79-63864. (Technibook Ser.). pap. text ed. 8.50 (ISBN 0-89704-006-6). E & L Instru.
Goldsby, Arthur R., jt. ed. see Albright, Lyle F.
Goldsby, Richard A. Cells & Energy. 2nd ed. 1977. pap. text ed. write for info. (ISBN 0-02-344300-6, 34430). Macmillan.
--Race & Races. 2nd ed. 1977. write for info. (ISBN 0-02-344310-3, 34431). Macmillan.
Goldscheider, C., jt. auth. see Jianou, Ionel.
Goldscheider, Calvin. Jewish Continuity & Change: Emerging Patterns in America. LC 84-48746. (Jewish Political & Social Studies). (Illus.). 256p. 1985. 24.95 (ISBN 0-253-33157-9). Ind U Pr.
Goldscheider, Calvin & Zuckerman, Alan S. The Transformation of the Jews. LC 84-198. (Chicago Studies in the History of Judaism). 308p. 1985. 24.95 (ISBN 0-226-30147-8). U of Chicago Pr.
Goldscheider, Calvin, jt. auth. see Friedlander, Dov.
Goldscheider, Calvin, jt. auth. see Goldstein, Sidney.
Goldscheider, Calvin, jt. auth. see Kobrin, Frances E.
Goldscheider, Calvin, ed. Urban Migrants in Developing Nations: Patterns & Problems of Adjustment. LC 83-10372. (Replica Edition Ser.). 288p. 1983. softcover 24.00x (ISBN 0-86531-974-X). Westview.
Goldscheider, Cecile. Homage to Rodin. (Illus.). 108p. 8.95 (ISBN 0-686-74779-8). Bklyn Mus.
Goldscheider, Ludwig. Art Without Epoch: Works of Distant Times Which Still Appeal to Modern Taste. LC 76-42710. Repr. of 1937 ed. 34.00 (ISBN 0-404-15361-5). AMS Pr.
--Etruscan Sculpture. LC 76-42712. Repr. of 1941 ed. 54.00 (ISBN 0-404-15362-3). AMS Pr.
--Roman Portraits. LC 76-42709. Repr. of 1940 ed. 28.50 (ISBN 0-404-15363-1). AMS Pr.
Goldscheider, Ludwig, ed. Rodin Sculptures. (Illus.). 196p. 1985. 24.95 (ISBN 0-7148-1946-8, Pub. by Phaidon Pr England). Hippocrene Bks.
Goldscheider, Robert. Eckstrom's Licensing in Foreign & Domestic Operations: Forms, 3 vols. LC 58-13380. 1978-79. Annual revisions avail. looseleaf 225.00 (ISBN 0-87632-075-2). Boardman.
Goldscheider, Robert & Arnold, Tom. The Law & Business of Licensing: Licensing in the 1980's. 2nd ed. LC 82-161484. 1983. 195.00 (ISBN 0-87632-136-8). Boardman.
Goldscheider, Robert & De Haas, Michel, eds. Arbitration & the Licensing Process. LC 81-6111. 1981. 85.00 (ISBN 0-87632-341-7). Boardman.
Goldschieder, Ludwig. Towards Modern Art: Or, King Solomon's Picture Book. LC 52-9478. 1952. Repr. 39.00x (ISBN 0-403-08924-7). Somerset Pub.
Goldschlager, jt. auth. see Wharton.
Goldschlager, Nora & Goldman, Mervin J. Electrocardiography: Essentials of Interpretation. LC 84-81105. (Illus.). 236p. 1984. lexotone cover 13.00 (ISBN 0-87041-290-6). Lange.
Goldschlager, Nora, jt. auth. see Jacobson, Lester.
Goldschlager, Nora F., jt. auth. see Wharton, J. Marcus.
Goldschmid, Harvey J., et al, eds. Industrial Concentration: The New Learning. 1974. pap. 11.95 (ISBN 0-316-31941-4). Little.
Goldschmidt, jt. auth. see Lion, Daisy.
Goldschmidt, Arthur, Jr. A Concise History of the Middle East. 2nd rev. ed. 450p. 1983. lib. bdg. 32.00x (ISBN 0-86531-598-1); pap. text ed. 12.50x (ISBN 0-86531-599-X). Westview.
Goldschmidt, Bertrand. The Atomic Complex: A Worldwide Political History of Nuclear Energy. LC 82-70371. Orig. Title: Le Complexe Atomique. 520p. 1982. 31.00 (ISBN 0-89448-550-4, 690007); pap. 24.00 (ISBN 0-89448-551-2, 690008). Am Nuclear Soc.
Goldschmidt, David M. Lectures on Character Theory. LC 80-81648. (Mathematics Lecture Ser.: No. 8). 245p. 1980. text ed. 18.00 (ISBN 0-914098-17-9). Publish or Perish.
Goldschmidt, Dietrich, ed. see Nitsch, Wolfgang.
Goldschmidt, E. P. Hieronymus Muenzer & Seine Bibliothek. (Warburg Institute Studies: Vol. 4). Repr. of 1938 ed. 32.00 (ISBN 0-317-15440-0). Kraus Repr.
--Medieval Texts & Their First Appearance in Print. LC 68-54232. 1969. Repr. of 1943 ed. 10.00x (ISBN 0-8196-0226-4). Biblo.
Goldschmidt, H., jt. auth. see Gasqui, J.
Goldschmidt, H., ed. Physical Modalities in Dermatologic Therapy: Radiotherapy, Electrosurgery, Phototherapy, Cryosurgery. 1978. 57.00 (ISBN 0-387-90267-8). Springer-Verlag.
Goldschmidt, H., tr. see Braun-Falco, O. & Lukacs, S.
Goldschmidt, H. J. Interstitial Alloys. LC 67-31095. 632p. 1968. 89.50x (ISBN 0-306-30646-8, Plenum Pr). Plenum Pub.
Goldschmidt, Louise A. Diary of a Childhood. LC 84-50329. (Illus.). 64p. 1984. 18.00 (ISBN 0-88400-104-0). Shengold.
Goldschmidt, Lucien & Naef, Weston J. The Truthful Lens. 241p. 1980. 125.00 (ISBN 0-8139-1036-6). Grolier Club.
Goldschmidt, Richard. The Material Basis of Evolution. rev. ed. LC 81-15969. (Silliman Milestones in Science Ser.). 482p. 1982. text ed. 45.00x (ISBN 0-300-02822-9); pap. 13.95x (ISBN 0-300-02823-7, Y-427). Yale U Pr.
Goldschmidt, Richard B. Golden Age of Zoology. LC 56-7347. Orig. Title: Portraits from Memory: Recollections of a Zoologist. (Illus.). 191p. 1966. pap. 6.95x (ISBN 0-295-74043-4, WP19). U of Wash Pr.
Goldschmidt, Victor W., jt. ed. see Uram, Earl M.
Goldschmidt, W. R., ed. The Uses of Anthropology. 1979. pap. 7.50 (ISBN 0-686-36569-0). Am Anthro Assn.
Goldschmidt, Walter. As You Sow: Three Studies in the Social Consequences of Agribusiness. LC 77-84435. 560p. 1978. 16.50x (ISBN 0-916672-10-7); pap. text ed. 7.95x (ISBN 0-916672-11-5). Allanheld.
--Culture & Behavior of the Sebei: A Study in Continuity & Adaptation. LC 74-82848. 1976. 46.00x (ISBN 0-520-02828-7). U of Cal Pr.
--Kambuya's Cattle: The Legacy of an African Herdsman. LC 68-31589. 1968. 30.00x (ISBN 0-520-01472-3). U of Cal Pr.
--Sebei Law. LC 67-15561. 1967. 31.00x (ISBN 0-520-00489-2). U of Cal Pr.
Goldschmidt, Walter, ed. see Alkire, William.
Goldschmidt, Walter, ed. see Sutlive, Vinson H., Jr.
Goldschmidt, Werner & Rodriguez-Novas, Jose. American-Argentine Private International Law. LC 66-17537. 118p. 1967. 15.00 (ISBN 0-379-11415-1). Oceana.
Goldschmidt, Y. & Admon, K. Profit Measurement During Inflation: Accounting, Economic & Financial Aspects. LC 77-4500. (Operations Managment Ser.). 328p. 1977. 51.95x (ISBN 0-471-01983-6, Pub. by Wiley-Interscience). Wiley.
Goldschmidt, Yaaqov, jt. auth. see Shashua, Leon.
Goldschmidt, Yaaqov, et al. The Impact of Inflation on Financial Activity in Business: With Applications to the U. S. Farming Sector. LC 85-14196. 175p. 1985. 35.00x (ISBN 0-8476-7427-4). Rowman & Allanheld.
Goldschmidt-Clermont, Luisella. Unpaid Work in the Household. (Women, Work & Development Ser.: No. 1). 137p. 1983. pap. 10.00 (ISBN 92-2-103085-7, ILO207, ILO). Unipub.
--Unpaid Work in the Household: A Review of Economic Evaluation Methods. (Women, Work & Development: No. 1). xi, 137p. 1983. 11.50 (ISBN 92-2-103085-7). Intl Labour Office.
Goldschmiedt, Henry. Practical Formulas for Hobby or Profit. (Illus.). 1973. 17.00 (ISBN 0-8206-0235-3). Chem Pub.
Goldschneider, Robert. Technology Management Handbook 1984. 1984. 47.50 (ISBN 0-87632-334-4). Boardman.
Goldsheider, Calvin. Rural Migration in Developing Nations: Comparative Studies of Korea, Sri Lanka, & Mali. (Replica Edition Ser.). 275p. 1984. pap. 25.00x (ISBN 0-86531-832-8). Westview.
Goldshore, Lewis P., jt. auth. see Institute for Continuing Legal Education N. J.
Goldsmid, Charles A., ed. Introductory Sociology: A Set of Syllabi. 209p. 1977. 8.50 (ISBN 0-317-33279-1). Am Sociological.
Goldsmid, Edmund M. Complete Catalogue of All the Publications of the Elsevier Presses at Leyden, Amsterdam, the Hague & Utrecht. 35.00 (ISBN 0-685-47534-4). Milford Hse.
Goldsmid, H. J. Thermoelectric Refrigeration. LC 64-7761. 240p. 1964. 45.00x (ISBN 0-306-30178-4, Plenum Pr). Plenum Pub.
Goldsmid, H. J., ed. Problems in Solid State Physics. 1968. 32.00x (ISBN 0-85086-000-8, NO. 2940, Pub. by Pion England). Methuen Inc.
Goldsmid, H. J., et al, eds. see Tsidil'Kovskii, I. M.
Goldsmid, Paula. Did You Ever. (Illus.). 30p. (Orig.). (ps-k). 1971. pap. 3.00 (ISBN 0-914996-01-0). Lollipop Power.
Goldsmith see Balderston, Katherine C.
Goldsmith, Alice, jt. auth. see Lansing, Adrienne.
Goldsmith, Arnold L. American Literary Criticism: Vol. III, 1905-1965. (United States Author Ser.). 1979. lib. bdg. 16.50 (ISBN 0-8057-7265-0, Twayne). G K Hall.
--The Golem Remembered 1909-1980: Variations of a Jewish Legend. LC 81-74580. (Illus.). 181p. 1981. 15.95 (ISBN 0-8143-1683-2). Wayne St U Pr.
Goldsmith, Arthur A. & Blustain, Harvey S. Local Organization & Participation in Integrated Rural Development in Jamaica. (Special Series on Rural Local Organization: No. 3). (Illus.). 140p. (Orig.). 1980. pap. text ed. 8.95 (ISBN 0-86731-030-8). RDC Ctr Intl Stud.
Goldsmith, B., jt. auth. see Goldsmith, F. B.
Goldsmith, B., jt. auth. see Warren, A.
Goldsmith, Barbara. Little Gloria: Happy at Last. 1981. pap. 5.95 (ISBN 0-440-15120-1). Dell.
--Little Gloria...Happy at Last. LC 79-3483. (Illus.). 1980. 15.95 (ISBN 0-394-42836-6). Knopf.
--The Straw Man. 1981. pap. 2.75 (ISBN 0-345-29423-8). Ballantine.
--The Straw Man. 272p. 1975. 7.95 (ISBN 0-374-27090-2). FS&G.
Goldsmith, C. CPAs Who Sell: How to Bring in New Business. 192p. 1985. 24.95 (ISBN 0-07-023671-2). McGraw.
Goldsmith, C. C., ed. Linear Algebra & Geometry (Draft Edition) LC 71-142241. (School Mathematics Project Ser., Further Mathematics). 1971. text ed. 9.95 (ISBN 0-521-08030-4). Cambridge U Pr.
Goldsmith, D., jt. auth. see Wagoner, R.
Goldsmith, D. L., jt. ed. see Gioia, A. A.
Goldsmith, Donald. The Evolving Universe: An Introduction to Astronomy. 2nd ed. 1984. text ed. 31.95 (ISBN 0-8053-3331-2); instr's manual 5.95 (ISBN 0-8053-3334-7). Benjamin-Cummings.
--Nemesis: The Sun's Companion Star & Other Theories of Mass Extinction. (Illus.). 192p. 1985. 15.95 (ISBN 0-8027-0872-2). Walker & Co.
--The Quest for Extraterrestrial Life: A Book of Readings. LC 79-57423. (Illus.). 308p. 1980. 20.00x (ISBN 0-935702-08-3); pap. text ed. 13.50x (ISBN 0-935702-02-4). Univ Sci Bks.
Goldsmith, Donald & Levy, Donald. From the Black Hole to the Infinite Universe. LC 73-86412. (Illus.). 300p. 1974. pap. text ed. 17.00x (ISBN 0-8162-3323-3). Holden-Day.
Goldsmith, Donald, jt. auth. see Owen, Tobias.
Goldsmith, Donald, ed. Scientists Confront Velikovsky. (Illus.). 192p. 1977. 19.95x (ISBN 0-8014-0961-6). Cornell U Pr.
--Scientists Confront Velikovsky. 1979. pap. 3.95 (ISBN 0-393-00928-9). Norton.
Goldsmith, E. I., ed. see Conference on Experimental Medicine & Surgery in Primates, 2nd, New York, 1969.
Goldsmith, E. I., ed. see Conference on Experimental Medicine & Surgery in Primates, 3rd, Lyon, June 1972.
Goldsmith, E. L., jt. auth. see Seddon, J.
Goldsmith, Earl A. Counseling with Confidence. 155p. 1984. pap. 5.95 (ISBN 0-916945-01-4). V I Pr.
Goldsmith, Elizabeth. God Can Be Trusted. 1974. pap. 3.95 (ISBN 0-903843-85-4). OMF Bks.
Goldsmith, Elizabeth E. Ancient Pagan Symbols. (Illus.). Repr. of 1929 ed. 10.00 (ISBN 0-404-02861-6). AMS Pr.
--Ancient Pagan Symbols. LC 68-18025. (Illus.). xxxix, 220p. 1976. Repr. of 1929 ed. 30.00x (ISBN 0-8103-4140-9). Gale.
Goldsmith, Emanuel S. Architects of Yiddishism at the Beginning of the Twentieth Century: A Study in Jewish Cultural History. LC 73-2894. 309p. 1976. 27.50 (ISBN 0-8386-1384-5). Fairleigh Dickinson.
Goldsmith, Emanuel S. & Scult, Mel, eds. Dynamic Judaism: The Essential Writings of Mordecai M. Kaplan. 256p. (Orig.). 1985. text ed. 22.00x (ISBN 0-8052-3997-9); pap. 12.95 (ISBN 0-8052-0786-4). Schocken.
Goldsmith, Evelyn. Research into Illustration: An Approach & a Review. (Illus.). 272p. 1984. 39.50 (ISBN 0-521-25674-7); pap. 16.95 cancelled (ISBN 0-521-27640-3). Cambridge U Pr.
Goldsmith, F. B. & Goldsmith, B. Conservation in Perspective. 474p. 1983. 53.95 (ISBN 0-471-10321-7). Wiley.
Goldsmith, Frank & Kerr, Lorin E. Occupational Safety & Health: The Prevention & Control of Work-Related Hazards. LC 81-20034. 320p. 1982. 29.95x (ISBN 0-89885-092-4). Human Sci Pr.
Goldsmith, Gail. Ballad of Patty Hearst. LC 77-94319. (Illus.). 1978. 8.50 (ISBN 0-9601560-1-1). Forsyth Gall.
Goldsmith, Gary, jt. auth. see Mackenzie, Kent.
Goldsmith, Harold F., jt. auth. see Lee, Everett S.
Goldsmith, Henry A., jt. auth. see Rosen, Milton J.
Goldsmith, Henry A., jt. ed. see Rosen, Milton J.
Goldsmith, Howard. Toto the Timid Turtle. LC 80-15096. 32p. 1980. 10.95 (ISBN 0-87705-525-4). Human Sci Pr.
--The Twiddle Twins' Haunted House. LC 85-7794. (Illus.). 40p. (ps-2). 1985. 8.95 (ISBN 0-89845-370-4); lib. bdg. 9.45 (ISBN 0-89845-371-2). Caedmon.
--What Makes a Grumble Smile? LC 76-25210. (Imagination Ser.). (Illus.). (gr. 1-5). 1977. lib. bdg. 7.47 (ISBN 0-8116-4403-0). Garrard.
Goldsmith, Howard R. How to Make a Fortune in Import-Export. 1981. text ed. 18.95 (ISBN 0-8359-2962-0, Reward Edn); pap. text ed. 10.95 (ISBN 0-8359-2961-2). Reston.
Goldsmith, Ilse. Anatomy for Children. LC 64-15111. (Illus.). 96p. (gr. 4 up). 1964. 8.95 (ISBN 0-8069-3000-4); PLB 10.99 (ISBN 0-8069-3001-2). Sterling.
--Human Anatomy for Children. (Illus.). (gr. 5-8). 1969. pap. 2.50 (ISBN 0-486-22355-8). Dover.
Goldsmith, Jay P. & Karotkin, Edward H. Assisted Ventilation of the Neonate. LC 80-53489. (Illus.). 390p. 1981. text ed. 42.00 (ISBN 0-7216-4154-7). Saunders.
Goldsmith, Jeff C. Can Hospitals Survive? LC 81-67969. 250p. 1981. 27.50 (ISBN 0-87094-248-4). Dow Jones-Irwin.
Goldsmith, Joe. How to Hand Raise Baby Birds. (Illus.). 16p. (Orig.). 1983. pap. text ed. 3.95 (ISBN 0-910335-00-1). Avian Pubns.
Goldsmith, Joel. Beyond Words & Thoughts. 6.00 (ISBN 0-8216-0041-9). Univ Bks.
--Conscious Union with God. 6.00 (ISBN 0-8216-0050-8). Univ Bks.
--The Master Speaks. 192p. 1984. pap. 5.95 (ISBN 0-8065-0912-0). Citadel Pr.

Goldsmith, Joel S. The Altitude of Prayer. Sinkler, Lorainne, ed. LC 74-25082. 160p. 1975. 9.57i (ISBN 0-06-063171-6, HarpR). Har-Row.

--Art of Meditation. LC 56-13258. 1957. 11.49i (ISBN 0-06-063150-3, HarpR). Har-Row.

--Art of Spiritual Healing. LC 59-14532. 1959. 11.49i (ISBN 0-06-063170-8, HarpR). Har-Row.

--Awakening Mystical Consciousness. Sinkler, Lorraine, ed. LC 79-3601. 176p. 1980. 9.95i (ISBN 0-06-063174-0, HarpR). Har-Row.

--Beyond Words & Thoughts. 200p. 1974. pap. 4.95 (ISBN 0-8065-0447-1). Citadel Pr.

--Conscious Union with God. 1977. pap. text ed. 5.95 (ISBN 0-8065-0578-8). Citadel Pr.

--Consciousness Is What I Am. Sinkler, Lorraine, ed. LC 76-9967. 160p. 1976. 9.57i (ISBN 0-06-063173-2, HarpR). Har-Row.

--The Contemplative Life. 212p. 1976. pap. 5.95 (ISBN 0-8065-0523-0). Citadel Pr.

--I Am the Vine. 1972. pap. 1.00 (ISBN 0-87516-138-3). De Vorss.

--The Infinite Way. pap. 5.95 (ISBN 0-87516-309-2). De Vorss.

--Infinite Way Letters. 1954. pap. 3.95 (ISBN 0-87516-137-5). De Vorss.

--Joel Goldsmith's Gift of Love. LC 82-11891. 96p. 1983. 8.61i (ISBN 0-686-92026-0, HarpR). Har-Row.

--The Letters. 299p. 1980. pap. 5.95 (ISBN 0-87516-386-6). De Vorss.

--Living Between Two Worlds. LC 73-18679. 1974. 8.95i (ISBN 0-06-063191-0, HarpR). Har-Row.

--Living Now. Sinkler, Lorraine, ed. 192p. 1984. pap. 5.95 (ISBN 0-8065-0911-2). Citadel Pr.

--Living the Infinite Way. rev. ed. LC 61-9646. 1961. 10.53i (ISBN 0-06-063190-2, HarpR). Har-Row.

--Love & Gratitude. 1972. pap. 1.75 (ISBN 0-87516-139-1). De Vorss.

--Man Was Not Born to Cry. 1984. pap. 5.95 (ISBN 0-8065-0915-5). Citadel Pr.

--The Mystical I. Sinkler, Lorraine, ed. LC 73-149745. 1971. 9.57i (ISBN 0-06-063195-3, HarpR). Har-Row.

--Our Spiritual Resources. LC 78-16010. 192p. 1983. pap. 6.68 (ISBN 0-06-063212-7, RD 478, HarpR). Har-Row.

--Parenthesis in Eternity. LC 64-10368. 1963. 14.90i (ISBN 0-06-063230-5, HarpR). Har-Row.

--Practicing the Presence. LC 58-7474. 1958. 10.53i (ISBN 0-06-063250-X, HarpR). Har-Row.

--Realization of Oneness: The Practice of Spiritual Healing. 200p. 1974. pap. 5.95 (ISBN 0-8065-0453-6). Citadel Pr.

--Secret of the Twenty-Third Psalm. 1972. pap. 1.00 (ISBN 0-87516-140-5). De Vorss.

--Spiritual Interpretation of Scripture. pap. 5.95 (ISBN 0-87516-310-6). De Vorss.

--Thunder of Silence. LC 61-7340. 1961. 00272731x 11.49 (ISBN 0-06-063270-4, HarpR). Har-Row.

--Truth. 1972. pap. 1.00 (ISBN 0-87516-141-3). De Vorss.

--The World Is New. LC 62-7953. 1978. 8.95i (ISBN 0-06-063291-7, HarpR). Har-Row.

Goldsmith, John A. Autosegmental Phonology. Hankamer, Jorge, ed. LC 78-67735. (Outstanding Dissertations in Linguistics Ser.). 1985. 26.00 (ISBN 0-8240-9673-8). Garland Pub.

Goldsmith, John R., ed. Environmental Epidemiology. 272p. 1985. 83.50 (ISBN 0-8493-5468-4). CRC Pr.

Goldsmith, Judith. Chidbirth Wisdom: From the World's Oldest Societies. (Illus.). 320p. 1985. pap. 9.95 (ISBN 0-312-92095-4). Congdon & Weed.

--Childbirth Wisdom: From the World's Oldest Societies. 320p. 1984. 18.95 (ISBN 0-312-92094-6). Congdon & Weed.

Goldsmith, Lawrence C. Watercolor Bold & Free. (Illus.). 160p. 1980. 22.50 (ISBN 0-8230-5654-6). Watson-Guptill.

Goldsmith, Lee S., jt. ed. see Bertolet, Mary M.

Goldsmith, Lisa A., jt. ed. see Bellak, Leopold.

Goldsmith, Lowell A., jt. auth. see Lazarus, Geralds.

Goldsmith, Lowell A., ed. Biochemistry & Physiology of the Skin, 2 vols. (Illus.). 1983. Set. 150.00x (ISBN 0-19-261253-0). Oxford U Pr.

Goldsmith, Lynn. The Police. (Illus.). 112p. 1983. pap. 9.95 (ISBN 0-312-61995-2). St Martin.

Goldsmith, M. Leviticus-Deuteronomy. (Bible Study Commentary Ser.). 126p. 1980. pap. 4.50 (ISBN 0-87508-151-7). Chr Lit.

Goldsmith, M., jt. ed. see Bollinger, L. E.

Goldsmith, M. M. Hobbes's Science of Politics. LC 66-18860. 1966. 26.00x (ISBN 0-231-02803-2); pap. 13.00x (ISBN 0-231-02804-0). Columbia U Pr.

--Private Vices, Public Benefits: Bernard Mandeville's Social & Political Thought. (Ideas in Context Ser.). 220p. Date not set. price not set. (ISBN 0-521-30036-3). Cambridge U Pr.

Goldsmith, Margaret. Christina of Sweden: A Psychological Biography. 1977. Repr. of 1935 ed. lib. bdg. 25.00 (ISBN 0-8492-1041-0). R West.

--Florence Nightingale: The Woman & the Legend. 320p. Repr. of 1937 ed. lib. bdg. 45.00 (ISBN 0-918377-64-1). Russell Pr.

--Madame De Stael. 1973. Repr. of 1938 ed. 25.00 (ISBN 0-8274-0401-8). R West.

--Seven Women Against the World. LC 75-21989. (Pioneers of the Woman's Movement Ser.). (Illus.). ix, 236p. 1976. Repr. of 1894 ed. 21.00 (ISBN 0-88355-316-3). Hyperion-Conn.

Goldsmith, Margaret & Voigt, Frederick. Hindenberg. LC 72-1289. (Select Bibliography Reprint Ser.). 1972. Repr. of 1930 ed. 18.00 (ISBN 0-8369-6826-3). Ayer Co Pubs.

Goldsmith, Margaret E. The Figure of Piers Plowman. (Piers Plowman Studies: No. 2). 127p. 1981. text ed. 30.00 (ISBN 0-85991-077-6, BAB-04621, Pub. by Boydell & Brewer). Longwood Pub Group.

Goldsmith, Margaret L., tr. see Feiler, Arthur.

Goldsmith, Margot, jt. auth. see Wolfe, Maxine G.

Goldsmith, Martin. Islam & Christian Witness. LC 83-6112. 160p. 1983. pap. 4.95 (ISBN 0-87784-809-2). Inter-Varsity.

Goldsmith, Maurice. Frederic Joliot-Curie. 1976. 19.95x (ISBN 0-8464-0426-5). Beekman Pubs.

--Frederic Joliot-Curie. 1976. text ed. 16.25x (ISBN 0-85315-342-6). Humanities.

--Young Scientists Companion. (Illus.). (gr. 9 up). 14.50x (ISBN 0-392-02027-0, SpS). Sportshelf.

Goldsmith, Maurice & Shaw, Edwin. Europe's Giant Accelerator. 288p. 1977. 33.00x (ISBN 0-85066-121-8). Taylor & Francis.

Goldsmith, Maurice, ed. see International Symposium on Science & Technology for Development, Singapore, 1979.

Goldsmith, Maurice, et al, eds. Einstein: The First Hundred Years. (Illus.). 188p. 1980. 23.00 (ISBN 0-08-025019-X). Pergamon.

Goldsmith, Melissa. Winter Sign. 1985. 5.95 (ISBN 0-533-06606-9). Vantage.

Goldsmith, Michael, jt. auth. see Younger, Irving.

Goldsmith, Michael, et al. Today's Father: A Guide to Understanding, Enjoying & Making Things for the Growing Family. (Winston Family Handbooks). 96p. (Orig.). 1984. pap. 9.95 (ISBN 0-86683-849-X, AY8494). Winston Pr.

Goldsmith, Oliver. The Bee & Other Essays: Together with the Life of Nash. 416p. 1981. Repr. of 1914 ed. lib. bdg. 40.00 (ISBN 0-89984-243-7). Century Bookbindery.

--The Belles Letters Series, the English Drama. 283p. 1980. Repr. of 1905 ed. lib. bdg. 30.00 (ISBN 0-89987-324-3). Century Bookbindery.

--Citizen of the World & the Bee. 1970. Repr. of 1934 ed. 7.95x (ISBN 0-460-00902-8, Pub. by Evman England). Biblio Dist.

--Complete Poetical Works. Repr. of 1911 ed. 49.00x (ISBN 0-403-08925-5). Somerset Pub.

--Edwin & Angelina. facsimile ed 1765. wrappers 2.00 (ISBN 0-911132-08-2). Phila Free Lib.

--Essays on Goldsmith by Scott, Macaulay & Thackeray, & Selections from His Writings. Repr. of 1946 ed. 25.00x (ISBN 0-403-04056-6). Somerset Pub.

--The Good Natur'd Man & She Stoops to Conquer. Baker, George P., ed. 1979. Repr. of 1905 ed. lib. bdg. 25.00 (ISBN 0-8495-2003-7). Arden Lib.

--The Good Natur'd Man & She Stoops to Conquer. 285p. 1982. Repr. of 1903 ed. lib. bdg. 30.00 (ISBN 0-8495-2127-0). Arden Lib.

--The Miscellaneous Works, 7 vols. 1791. Set. 250.00 (ISBN 0-686-17752-5). Ridgeway Bks.

--New Essays. Crane, Ronald S., ed. LC 68-57605. Repr. of 1927 ed. lib. bdg. 18.75x (ISBN 0-8371-0447-5, GONE). Greenwood.

--A Prospect of Society. Dobell, Bertram, ed. 1978. Repr. of 1902 ed. lib. bdg. 17.50 (ISBN 0-8482-4162-2). Norwood Edns.

--She Stoops to Conquer. Hopper, Vincent F. & Lahey, Gerald B., eds. (Illus.). (gr. 9 up). 1958. pap. text ed. 3.95 (ISBN 0-8120-0158-3). Barron.

--She Stoops to Conquer. Balderston, Katherine G., ed. LC 51-6755. (Crofts Classics Ser.). 1951. pap. text ed. 3.75x (ISBN 0-88295-039-8). Harlan Davidson.

--She Stoops to Conquer. Lavin, J. A., ed. (New Mermaids Ser.). 1980. pap. 6.95x (ISBN 0-393-90046-0). Norton.

--She Stoops to Conquer. Shefter, Harry, ed. (Illus.). (YA) 1984. pap. 2.95 (ISBN 0-671-50998-5, Re). PB.

--She Stoops to Conquer. Shefter, Harry, ed. (Enriched Classics Edition Ser.). 176p. pap. 2.95 (ISBN 0-671-50998-5). WSP.

--Vicar of Wakefield. (Classics Ser). (YA) (gr. 10 up). 1964. pap. 1.25 (ISBN 0-8049-0052-3, CL-52). Airmont.

--The Vicar of Wakefield. 304p. 1982. Repr. lib. bdg. 30.00 (ISBN 0-8495-2126-2). Arden Lib.

--Vicar of Wakefield. 1976. 12.95x (ISBN 0-460-00295-3, Evman); pap. 4.50x (ISBN 0-460-01295-9, Evman). Biblio Dist.

--The Vicar of Wakefield. (Reader's Request Ser.). 1980. lib. bdg. 10.95 (ISBN 0-8161-3072-8, Large Print Bks). G K Hall.

--Vicar of Wakefield. pap. 1.95 (ISBN 0-451-51723-7, CE1723, Sig Classics). NAL.

--The Vicar of Wakefield. Friedman, Arthur, ed. (Oxford English Novels Ser.). 1974. 19.95x (ISBN 0-19-255345-3). Oxford U Pr.

--The Vicar of Wakefield. 304p. 1980. Repr. of 1906 ed. lib. bdg. 25.00 (ISBN 0-8492-4950-3). R West.

--The Vicar of Wakefield. 1982. Repr. lib. bdg. 19.95x (ISBN 0-89966-373-7). Buccaneer Bks.

--Vicar of Wakefield. 1982. pap. 2.50 (ISBN 0-14-043159-4). Penguin.

--The Vicar of Wakefield. Friedman, Arthur, ed. (World's Classics Ser.). 1981. pap. 2.50 (ISBN 0-686-95061-5). Oxford U Pr.

Goldsmith, Oliver, tr. see Marteilhe, Jean.

Goldsmith, Ollie. Some Thoughts That Seem Important. (Illus.). 1983. 9.90 (ISBN 0-911843-00-0). Myriad.

Goldsmith, P., ed. Tropospheric Chemistry with Emphasis on Sulphur & Nitrogen Cycles & the Chemistry of Clouds & Precipitation: A Selection of Papers from the Fifth International Conference of the Commission on Atmospheric Chemistry & Global Pollution. (Illus.). 467p. 1985. 91.00 (ISBN 0-08-031448-1, Pub. by P P L). Pergamon.

Goldsmith, Peter, jt. ed. see Davies, Owen.

Goldsmith, R. W., et al. Studies in the National Balance Sheet of the United States, 2 vols. (National Bureau of Economic Research: Nos. 1-11). 1963-64. Vol. 1. 40.00x (ISBN 0-691-04179-2); Vol. 2. 40.00x (ISBN 0-691-04180-6); 72.00x set (ISBN 0-685-47791-6). Princeton U Pr.

Goldsmith, Raymond W. Comparative National Balance Sheets: A Study of Twenty Countries, 1688-1978. LC 84-16277. (Illus.). 376p. 1985. lib. bdg. 49.00x (ISBN 0-226-30153-2). U of Chicago Pr.

--The Financial Development of India. LC 82-7094. 264p. 1983. text ed. 38.00x (ISBN 0-300-02030-9). Yale U Pr.

--The Financial Development of India, Japan, & the United States. LC 82-8541. 136p. 1983. text ed. 15.00x (ISBN 0-300-02934-9). Yale U Pr.

--The Financial Development of Japan. LC 82-8378. 256p. 1983. text ed. 33.00x (ISBN 0-300-02933-0). Yale U Pr.

--Financial Intermediaries in the American Economy since 1900. LC 75-19713. (National Bureau of Economic Research Ser.). (Illus.). 1975. Repr. 33.00x (ISBN 0-405-07593-6). Ayer Co Pubs.

--The National Balance of the United States, 1953 to 1980. LC 82-2746. (National Bureau of Economic Research Monograph). 1982. lib. bdg. 30.00x (ISBN 0-226-30152-4). U of Chicago Pr.

--The National Wealth of the United States in the Postwar Period. LC 75-19714. (National Bureau of Economic Research Ser.). (Illus.). 1975. Repr. 34.50x (ISBN 0-405-07594-4). Ayer Co Pubs.

--Study of Saving in the United States, 3 Vols. LC 69-13910. 1955-1956. Repr. Set. lib. bdg. 114.00x (ISBN 0-8371-0998-1, GOSS). Greenwood.

Goldsmith, Raymond W., ed. Institutional Investors & Corporate Stock - A Background Study. (Studies in Capital Formation & Financing Ser.: No. 13). 480p. 1973. text ed. 29.00 (ISBN 0-87014-237-2, Dist. by Columbia U Pr). Natl Bur Econ Res.

Goldsmith, Raymond W., et al. Studies in the National Balance Sheet of the United States, 2 Vols. (Studies in Capital Formation & Financing Ser.: No. 11). 1963. Set. 70.00 (ISBN 0-691-04180-6, Dist. by Princeton U Pr); Vol. 1. 38.50 (ISBN 0-686-66494-9); Vol. 2. 38.50 (ISBN 0-686-66495-7). Natl Bur Econ Res.

Goldsmith, Robert H. Nutrition & Learning. LC 80-82680. (Fastback Ser.: No. 147). 1980. pap. 0.75 (ISBN 0-87367-147-3). Phi Delta Kappa.

--World & National Food & Nutrition Problems: A Selected Bibliography. (Public Administration Ser.: P-1336). 151p. 1983. pap. 18.75 (ISBN 0-88066-766-4). Vance Biblios.

Goldsmith, Ruth M. Phoebe Takes Charge. LC 82-13955. 240p. (gr. 5-9). 1983. 11.95 (ISBN 0-689-50266-4, McElderry Bk). Atheneum.

Goldsmith, S. J. Twenty Twentieth Century Jews. LC 70-101827. (Biography Index Reprint Ser). 1962. 20.00 (ISBN 0-8369-8000-X). Ayer Co Pubs.

Goldsmith, Scott. Analyzing Economic Impact in Alaska. (ISER Report Ser.: No. 52). (Illus.). 74p. 1981. pap. 5.00 (ISBN 0-88353-029-5). U Alaska Inst Res.

Goldsmith, Selwyn. Designing for the Disabled. (Illus.). 1977. 70.00 (ISBN 0-900630-50-7, Pub. by RIBA). Intl Spec Bk.

Goldsmith, Seth. Health Care Management: A Contemporary Perspective. LC 80-25645. 263p. 1981. text ed. 29.50 (ISBN 0-89443-336-9). Aspen Systems.

Goldsmith, Seth B. Ambulatory Care: Theory & Practice. LC 77-10315. 135p. 1978. 26.50 (ISBN 0-912862-46-7). Aspen Systems.

--Theory Z Hospital Management: Lessons from Japan. LC 83-15574. 149p. 1983. 25.00 (ISBN 0-89443-949-9). Aspen Systems.

Goldsmith, Seth B., jt. auth. see Goldfield, Norbert.

Goldsmith, Sharon. Human Sexuality: The Family Source Book. 1985. 16.95 (ISBN 0-8016-1887-8). Mosby.

Goldsmith, Steven. The Trance State: How People Change. 140p. 1985. text ed. 16.95x (ISBN 0-8290-1465-9). Irvington.

Goldsmith, Sue. A-B-C, 1-2-3. (Illus.). 80p. (ps-2). 1984. pap. text ed. 5.95 (ISBN 0-86530-024-0). Incentive Pubns.

Goldsmith, Ulrich, et al, eds. Hypatia: Essays in Classics, Comparative Literature, & Philosophy. 1985. 25.00x (ISBN 0-87081-156-8). Colo Assoc.

Goldsmith, Ulrich K. Stefan George. LC 78-110601. (Columbia Essays on Modern Writers Ser.). 48p. 1970. pap. 2.50 (ISBN 0-231-03204-8). Columbia U Pr.

Goldsmith, Ulrich K., ed. see Weigand, Hermann J.

Goldsmith, V. F., jt. auth. see Allison, A. F.

Goldsmith, W. B., Jr. BASIC Programs for Home Financial Management. 314p. 1981. 18.95 (ISBN 0-13-066522-3); pap. 12.95 (ISBN 0-13-066514-2). P-H.

Goldsmith, Walter & Clutterbuck, David. The Winning Streak. 1985. 19.95 (ISBN 0-394-54485-4). Random.

Goldsmith, William. Psychiatric Drugs for the Non-Medical Mental Health Worker. (Illus.). 188p. 1977. 19.75x (ISBN 0-398-03635-7). C C Thomas.

Goldsmith, William W., jt. ed. see Clavel, Pierre.

Goldspink, D. F., ed. The Development & Specialisation of Skeletal Muscle. (Society for Experimental Biology Seminar Ser.: No. 7). (Illus.). 200p. 1981. 54.50 (ISBN 0-521-23317-8); pap. 23.95 (ISBN 0-521-29907-1). Cambridge U Pr.

Goldspink, G., ed. Differentiation & Growth of Cells in Vertebrate Tissues. 1974. 45.00x (ISBN 0-412-11390-2, NO.6128, Pub. by Chapman & Hall). Methuen Inc.

Goldstein. Advances in Prenatal Medicine. 1979. 34.95 (ISBN 0-8151-3763-X, YBMP). Year Bk Med.

--Ausgewahlte Schriften: Selected Papers. (Phaenomenologica Ser: No. 43). 1971. lib. bdg. 53.00 (ISBN 90-247-5047-4, Pub. by Martinus Nijhoff Netherlands). Kluwer Academic.

Goldstein & Buckley. The Screw Reader. 12.50 (ISBN 0-8184-0073-0). Lyle Stuart.

Goldstein, et al. Contemporary Collection. 48p. (gr. 3-12). 1974. pap. text ed. 7.95 (ISBN 0-87487-627-3). Birch Tree Gr.

Goldstein, A., jt. auth. see Goldstein, J.

Goldstein, A. P. Structured Learning Therapy: Toward a Psychotherapy for the Poor. 1973. 50.00 (ISBN 0-12-288750-6). Acad Pr.

Goldstein, A. P. & Kanfer, Frederick H., eds. Maximizing Treatment Gains: Transfer Enhancement in Psychotherapy. LC 78-31265. 1979. 43.50 (ISBN 0-12-288050-1). Acad Pr.

Goldstein, A. S. Business Tranfers: An Accountant's & Attorney's Guide. 49.95 (ISBN 0-471-81285-4). Wiley.

Goldstein, Abraham S. The Insanity Defense. LC 79-26323. 289p. 1980. Repr. of 1967 ed. lib. bdg. 39.75x (ISBN 0-313-22202-9, GOID). Greenwood.

--The Passive Judiciary: Prosecutorial Discretion & the Guilty Plea. LC 81-11749. 114p. 1981. text ed. 14.95x (ISBN 0-8071-0856-1). La State U Pr.

Goldstein, Aileen. Neurological Critical Care. (Critical Care in Nursing Ser.: 1-677). (Illus.). 167p. (Orig.). 1984. pap. text ed. 15.00x (ISBN 0-471-88798-6). Wiley.

Goldstein, Al., frwd. by. The Classic Book of Dirty Jokes Anecdota Americana. 1981. 3.98 (ISBN 0-517-33636-7, Bell). Outlet Bk Co.

Goldstein, Alan & Foa, Edna B. Handbook of Behavioral Interventions. LC 79-16950. (Personality Processes Ser.). 1980. 50.95x (ISBN 0-471-01789-2, Pub. by Wiley-Interscience). Wiley.

Goldstein, Alan, ed. ALA Worldwide Directory & Fact Book, 1984-85. Rev. ed. Orig. Title: ALA Convention Sovenir Program. (Illus.). 228p. 1984. pap. text ed. 35.00 (ISBN 0-915959-00-3). Am Logistics Assn.

Goldstein, Alan J., jt. auth. see Chambless, Dianne L.

Goldstein, Albert, ed. Quality Assurance in Diagnostic Ultrasound. 66p. 10.00 (ISBN 0-318-12815-2, 329). Am Inst Ultrasound.

Goldstein, Alice, jt. auth. see Goldstein, Sidney.

Goldstein, Allan, jt. ed. see Bergsma, Daniel.

Goldstein, Allan, jt. ed. see Fefer, Alexander.

Goldstein, Allan L., ed. Thymic Hormones & Lymphokines: Basic Chemistry & Clinical Applications. (GWUMC Department of Biochemistry Annual Spring Symposia Ser.). 684p. 1984. 75.00x (ISBN 0-306-41649-2, Plenum Pr). Plenum Pub.

Goldstein, Allan L., jt. ed. see Bergsma, Daniel.

Goldstein, Alvin H. The Unquiet Death of Julius & Ethel Rosenberg. LC 75-8336. (Illus.). 96p. 1975. 8.95 (ISBN 0-88208-052-0). Lawrence Hill.

Goldstein, Amy J. & Granade, Charles, eds. Graduate Programs in Engineering & Applied Sciences 1986. 20th ed. (Peterson's Annual Guides to Graduate Study Ser.). 900p. (Orig.). pap. 24.95 (ISBN 0-87866-346-0). Petersons Guides.

--Graduate Programs in the Physical Sciences & Mathematics 1986. 20th ed. (Annual Guides to Graduate Study Ser.). 650p. (Orig.). 1985. pap. 22.95 (ISBN 0-87866-345-2). Petersons Guides.

Goldstein, Amy J. & Ready, Barbara C., eds. Graduate Programs in the Biological, Agricultural, & Health Sciences 1986. 20th ed. (Annual Guides to Graduate Study Ser.). 2050p. (Orig.). 1985. pap. 28.95 (ISBN 0-87866-344-4). Petersons Guides.

Goldstein, Amy J., jt. ed. see Conley, Diane.

Goldstein, Andrew & Wikler, Madeline. My Very Own Jewish Home. LC 83-4357. (Illus.). 40p. (ps-4). 1979. pap. 4.95 (ISBN 0-930494-08-3). Kar Ben.

Goldstein, Arnold P. Prescriptions for Child Mental Health & Education. 1978. pap. text ed. 13.00 (ISBN 0-08-022249-8). Pergamon.

--Psychological Skill Training: The Structured Learning Technique. LC 81-5861. (PGPS Ser.: No. 99). (Illus.). 235p. 1981. 27.00 (ISBN 0-08-026321-6). Pergamon.

--Psychotherapeutic Attraction. LC 79-119598. 260p. 1971. 18.25 (ISBN 0-08-016398-X). Pergamon.

Goldstein, Arnold P. & Michaels, Gerald Y. Empathy: Development, Training & Consequence. 304p. 1985. text ed. 29.95 (ISBN 0-89859-538-X). L Erlbaum Assocs.

Goldstein, Arnold P. & Sorcher, Melvin. Changing Supervisor Behavior. LC 73-10059. 1975. pap. text ed. 8.25 (ISBN 0-08-017769-7). Pergamon.

Goldstein, Arnold P. & Stein, Norman. Prescriptive Psychotherapies. LC 75-5620. 1976. pap. text ed. 16.00 (ISBN 0-08-019505-9). Pergamon.

Goldstein, Arnold P., jt. auth. see Miron, Murray S.

Goldstein, Arnold P. & Segall, Marshall H., eds. Aggression in Global Perspective. (Pergamon General Psychology Ser.: No. 115). (Illus.). 475p. 1983. 49.50 (ISBN 0-08-026346-1). Pergamon.

Goldstein, Arnold P., jt. ed. see Apter, Steven J.

Goldstein, Arnold P., jt. ed. see Kanfer, Frederick H.

Goldstein, Arnold P., et al. School Violence. (Illus.). 272p. 1984. text ed. 27.95 (ISBN 0-13-794545-0). P-H.

--In Response to Aggression: Methods of Control & Prosocial Alternatives. rev. ed. (Pergamon General Psychology Ser.: No. 98). (Illus.). 576p. 1981. 52.00 (ISBN 0-08-025580-9); pap. 18.25 (ISBN 0-08-025579-5). Pergamon.

--Police Crisis Intervention. LC 76-48283. (Pergamon General Psychology Ser.: Vol. 80). 175p. 1979. 26.00 (ISBN 0-08-023873-4); pap. 8.75 (ISBN 0-08-023874-2). Pergamon.

--Applying Structured Learning Therapy. LC 76-16518. 1977. text ed. 33.00 (ISBN 0-08-021109-7); pap. text ed. 16.50 (ISBN 0-08-021108-9). Pergamon.

--Skillstreaming the Adolescent: A Structured Learning Approach to Teaching Prosocial Skills. LC 79-66179. (Illus.). 232p. (Orig.). 1979. pap. text ed. 12.95 (ISBN 0-87822-205-7, 2057). Res Press.

Goldstein, Arnold P., et al, eds. Police & the Elderly. LC 78-27400. (Pergamon General Psychology Ser.: Vol. 78). 1979. pap. 8.50 (ISBN 0-08-023893-9). Pergamon.

Goldstein, Arnold S. Basic Book of Business Agreements. LC 82-84448. 1983. loose-leaf 49.95 (ISBN 0-913864-83-8). Enterprise Del.

--Case Problems in Community Pharmacy Management. LC 73-102703. Repr. of 1970 ed. 22.50 (ISBN 0-8357-9397-4, 2014544). Bks Demand UMI.

--Complete Guide to Buying & Selling a Business. LC 82-24769. (Wiley Series Small Business Management). 273p. 1983. 24.95x (ISBN 0-471-87091-9, Pub by Ronald Pr). Wiley.

--The Complete Guide to Buying & Selling a Business. LC 84-6792. 288p. 1984. pap. 9.95 (ISBN 0-452-25622-4, Plume). NAL.

--EMS & the Law: A Legal Handbook for EMS Personnel. LC 83-2560. (Illus.). 192p. 1983. 19.95 (ISBN 0-89303-423-1); pap. 12.95 (ISBN 0-89303-422-3). Brady Comm.

--Getting Paid: Building Your Powerful Credit & Collection Strategy. LC 83-16704. (Wiley Series on Small Business Management: 1-471). 274p. 1984. 24.95 (ISBN 0-471-88989-X, Pub. by Ronald Pr). Wiley.

--Handbook of Turnaround Strategies. Date not set. 49.95 (ISBN 0-913864-92-7). Enterprise Del.

--Own Your Own: The No-Cash Down Business Guide. LC 82-22973. 208p. 1983. 19.95 (ISBN 0-13-647487-X); pap. 6.95 (ISBN 0-13-647479-9). P-H.

--The Small Business Legal Problem-Solver. 240p. 1983. 24.95 (ISBN 0-8436-0890-0); pap. cancelled. Van Nos Reinhold.

--Starting on a Shoestring: Building A Business Without a Bank Roll. LC 83-23379. (Small Business Management Ser.: 1-471). 286p. 1984. 12.95 (ISBN 0-471-88439-1, Ronald Pr); pap. 12.95. Wiley.

--Strategies & Techniques for Saving the Financially-Distressed Small Business. LC 75-43922. 48p. 1976. pap. 3.95 (ISBN 0-87576-054-6). Pilot Bks.

Goldstein, Arthur, jt. auth. see Paperno, Lloyd J.

Goldstein, Arthur P. & Rosenbaum, Alan. Aggress-Less: How to Turn Anger & Aggression into Positive Action. (Illus.). 130p. 1982. 12.95 (ISBN 0-13-018747-X); pap. 5.95 (ISBN 0-13-018739-9). P-H.

Goldstein, Avram. Flying Out of Danger: A Pilot's Guide to Safety. 140p. 1984. pap. 6.50 (ISBN 0-317-14776-5). Aviation.

--IFR Principles & Practice. (Illus.). 1978. pap. 6.50 (ISBN 0-911720-93-6). Aviation.

Goldstein, Avram, ed. The Opiate Narcotics: Neurochemical Mechanisms of Analgesia & Dependence. 270p. 1976. text ed. 29.00 (ISBN 0-08-019869-4). Pergamon.

Goldstein, Avram, et al. Principles of Drug Action: The Basis of Pharmacology. 2nd ed. LC 73-15871. 834p. 1974. 52.00x (ISBN 0-471-31260-6, Pub. by Wiley-Medical). Wiley.

Goldstein, B. R. The Astronomy of Levi Ben Gerson, 1288-1344. (Studies in the History of Mathematics & Physical Science: Vol. 11). (Illus.). 300p. 1985. 68.00 (ISBN 0-387-96132-1). Springer-Verlag.

Goldstein, Barbara, jt. auth. see McCoy, Esther.

Goldstein, Barbara, ed. see Annual Conference of the Royal Institute of British Architects, U. of Hull, 14-17 July, 1976.

Goldstein, Bernard & Goldstein, Estelle T. Toy Soldiers. (Illus.). 48p. 1982. 24.00 (ISBN 0-88014-047-X). Mosaic Pr OH.

Goldstein, Bernard & Oldham, Jack. Children & Work: A Study of Socialization. LC 78-62894. 200p. 1979. text ed. 12.95 (ISBN 0-87855-285-5). Transaction Bks.

Goldstein, Bernard D., jt. ed. see Laskin, Sidney.

Goldstein, Bernard R. The Astronomical Tables of Levi Ben Gerson. (Connecticut Academy of Arts & Sciences Transaction Ser.: No. 45). 285p. 1974. 25.00 (ISBN 0-208-01425-X, Archon). Shoe String.

Goldstein, Bernard R., ed. Ibn al-Muthannea's Commentary on the Astronomical Tables of al-Khwearizmei: Two Hebrew Versions. LC 67-13434. (Yale Studies in the History of Science & Medicine Ser.: No. 2). (Illus.). pap. 105.00 (ISBN 0-317-09378-9, 2016770). Bks Demand UMI.

Goldstein, Bernice & Tamura, Kyoko. Japan & America: A Comparative Study in Language & Culture. LC 74-81653. 1975. 7.50 (ISBN 0-8048-1109-1). C E Tuttle.

Goldstein, Catherine, jt. auth. see Kohl, Sam.

Goldstein, Catherine, jt. ed. see Bertin, Marie-Jose.

Goldstein, Charles. Bunker. Malkin, Esther, tr. from Fr. LC 74-116978. (Temple Bks). 1973. pap. 3.95 (ISBN 0-689-70347-3, T27). Atheneum.

Goldstein, D. M., jt. auth. see Prange, G. W.

Goldstein, D. M., ed. see Prange, G. W.

Goldstein, Darra. A la Russe: A Cook Book of Russian Hospitality. 320p. 1983. 16.95 (ISBN 0-394-53018-7). Random.

Goldstein, Darra, tr. see Teffi, Nadezhda.

Goldstein, David. The Ashkenazi Haggadah. (Illus.). 140p. 1985. 75.00 (ISBN 0-8109-1819-6). Abrams.

--Hebrew Incunables in the British Isles: A Preliminary Census. (Illus.). 50p. (Orig.). 1985. pap. 14.25 (ISBN 0-7123-0047-3, Pub. by British Lib). Longwood Pub Group.

--Hebrew Manuscript Painting. (Illus.). 80p. (Orig.). 1985. pap. 7.50 (ISBN 0-7123-0054-6, Pub. by British Lib). Longwood Pub Group.

Goldstein, David, ed. see Weiss, Joseph.

Goldstein, David, tr. The Jewish Poets of Spain. (Classics Ser.). 224p. 1983. pap. 5.95 (ISBN 0-14-044250-2). Penguin.

Goldstein, David I. Dostoyevsky & the Jews. (University of Texas Press Slavic Ser.: No. 3). 256p. 1981. 20.00x (ISBN 0-292-71528-5). U of Tex Pr.

Goldstein, Diane, jt. auth. see Wilkinson, William.

Goldstein, Donald P. Gestational Trophoblastic Disease. LC 74-12910. (Major Problems in Obstetrics & Gynecology Ser.: Vol. XIV). (Illus.). 225p. 1982. text ed. 48.00 (ISBN 0-7216-4147-4). Saunders.

Goldstein, Donald P., jt. auth. see Emans, S. Jean.

Goldstein, Dora B. Pharmacology of Alcohol. (Illus.). 1983. text ed. 24.95x (ISBN 0-19-503111-3); pap. text ed. 16.95x (ISBN 0-19-503112-1). Oxford U Pr.

Goldstein, Doris. Trial of Faith: Religion & Politics in Tocqueville's Thought. 144p. 1975. 21.00 (ISBN 0-444-99001-1). Elsevier.

Goldstein, Doris M., ed. Bioethics: A Guide to Information Sources. (The Health Affairs Information Guide Ser.: Vol. 8). 375p. 1982. 60.00x (ISBN 0-8103-1502-5). Gale.

Goldstein, E. Bruce. Sensation & Perception. 2nd ed. 481p. 1984. text ed. write for info. (ISBN 0-534-03035-1). Wadsworth Pub.

Goldstein, Eda G. Ego Psychology & Social Work Practice. LC 83-48027. (Treatment Approaches in the Human Services Ser.). 368p. 1983. 17.95x (ISBN 0-02-911920-0). Free Pr.

Goldstein, Edward. Selective Audio-Visual Instruction for Mentally Retarded Pupils. (Illus.). 116p. 1964. 12.50x (ISBN 0-398-00697-0). C C Thomas.

Goldstein, Eleanor C., ed. Aging, Vol. 1 (incl. 1979-1980 Supplements) (Social Issues Resources Ser.). 1981. 70.00 (ISBN 0-89777-020-X). Soc Issues.

--Aging, Vol. 2 (incl. 1981-1983 Supplements) 1984. 56.00 (ISBN 0-89777-052-8). Soc Issues.

--Alcohol, Vol. 1 (incl. 1975-1976 Supplements) (Social Issues Resources Ser.). 1977. 70.00 (ISBN 0-89777-006-4). Soc Issues.

--Alcohol, Vol. 2 (incl. 1977-1981 Supplements) (Social Issues Resources Ser.). 1982. 70.00 (ISBN 0-89777-038-2). Soc Issues.

--Alcohol: Incl. 1982-1984 Supplements, Vol. 3. 1983. 42.00 (ISBN 0-89777-070-6). Soc Issues.

--Communication, Vol. 1 (incl. 1978-1979 Supplements) (Social Issues Resources Ser.). 1980. 70.00 (ISBN 0-89777-019-6). Soc Issues.

--Communication, Vol. 2 (incl. 1980-1984 Supplements) 1984. 70.00 (ISBN 0-89777-051-X). Soc Issues.

--Consumerism, Vol. 1 (incl. 1980 & 1981 Supplements) (Social Issues Resources Ser.). 1982. 70.00 (ISBN 0-89777-025-0). Soc Issues.

--Consumerism, Vol. 2 (incl. 1982-1984 Supplements) 1984. 42.00 (ISBN 0-89777-057-9). Soc Issues.

--Corrections, Vol. 1 (incl. 1976-1977 Supplements) (Social Issues Resources Ser.). 1977. 70.00 (ISBN 0-89777-011-0). Soc Issues.

--Corrections, Vol. 2 (incl. 1978-1982 Supplements) (Social Issues Resources Ser.). 1983. 70.00 (ISBN 0-89777-043-9). Soc Issues.

--Corrections, Vol. 3 (incl. 1983-1984 Supplement) (Social Issues Resources Ser.). 1984. 28.00 (ISBN 0-89777-075-7). Soc Issues.

--Crime, Vol. 1 (incl. 1976-1977 Supplements) (Social Issues Resources Ser.). 1978. 70.00 (ISBN 0-89777-010-2). Soc Issues.

--Crime, Vol. 2 (incl. 1978-1982 Supplements) (Social Issues Resources Ser.). 1983. 70.00 (ISBN 0-89777-042-0). Soc Issues.

--Crime, Vol. 3 (incl. 1983-1984 Supplement) (Social Issues Resources Ser.). 1984. 28.00 (ISBN 0-89777-074-9). Soc Issues.

--Death & Dying, Vol. 1 (incl. 1980 & 1981 Supplement) (Social Issues Resources Ser.). 1982. 70.00 (ISBN 0-89777-027-7). Soc Issues.

--Death & Dying: Incl. 1982-1983 Supplements, Vol. 2. 1984. 42.00 (ISBN 0-89777-059-5). Soc Issues.

--Defense, Vol. 1 (incl. 1980 & 1981 Supplement) (Social Issues Resources Ser.). 1982. 70.00 (ISBN 0-89777-024-2). Soc Issues.

--Defense: Incl. 1982-1984 Supplements, Vol. 2. 1983. 42.00 (ISBN 0-89777-056-0). Soc Issues.

--Drugs, Vol. 1 (incl. 1973 & 1974 Supplements) (Social Issues Resources Ser.). 1975. 70.00 (ISBN 0-89777-002-1). Soc Issues.

--Drugs, Vol. 2 (incl. 1975-1979 Supplements) (Social Issues Resources Ser.). 1980. 70.00 (ISBN 0-89777-034-X). Soc Issues.

--Drugs, Vol. 3 (incl. 1980-1984 Supplements) (Social Issues Resources Ser.). 1984. 70.00 (ISBN 0-89777-066-8). Soc Issues.

--Energy, Vol. 1 (incl. 1973 & 1974 Supplements) (Social Issues Resources Ser.). 1976. 70.00 (ISBN 0-89777-003-X). Soc Issues.

--Energy, Vol. 2 (incl. 1975-1979 Supplements) (Social Issues Resources Ser.). 1980. 70.00 (ISBN 0-89777-035-8). Soc Issues.

--Energy, Vol. 3 (incl. 1980-1984 Supplements) (Social Issues Resources Ser.). 1984. 70.00 (ISBN 0-89777-067-6). Soc Issues.

--Ethics, Vol. 1 (incl. 1980 & 1981 Supplement) (Social Issues Resources Ser.). 1982. 70.00 (ISBN 0-89777-026-9). Soc Issues.

--Ethics, Vol. 2 (Incl. 1982-1984 Supplements) 1984. 42.00 (ISBN 0-89777-058-7). Soc Issues.

--Ethnic Groups, Vol. 1 (incl. 1978-1979 Supplements) (Social Issues Resources Ser.). 1980. 70.00 (ISBN 0-89777-016-1). Soc Issues.

--Ethnic Groups, Vol. 2 (incl. 1980-1984 Supplements) (Social Issues Resources Ser.). 1984. 70.00 (ISBN 0-89777-048-X). Soc Issues.

--Family, Vol. 1 (incl. 1976-1977 Supplements) (Social Issues Resources Ser.). 1978. 70.00 (ISBN 0-89777-009-9). Soc Issues.

--Family, Vol. 2 (incl. 1978-1982 Supplements) (Social Issues Resources Ser.). 1983. 70.00 (ISBN 0-89777-041-2). Soc Issues.

--Family, Vol. 3 (incl. 1983-1984 Supplement) (Social Issues Resources Ser.). 1984. 28.00 (ISBN 0-89777-073-0). Soc Issues.

--Food, Vol. 1 (incl. 1975-1976 Supplements) (Social Issues Resources Ser.). 1977. 70.00 (ISBN 0-89777-004-8). Soc Issues.

--Food, Vol. 2 (incl. 1977-1981 Supplements) (Social Issues Resources Ser.). 1982. 70.00 (ISBN 0-89777-036-6). Soc Issues.

--Food, Vol. 3 (Incl. 1982-1984 Supplements) 1984. 42.00 (ISBN 0-89777-068-4). Soc Issues.

--Habitat, Vol. 1 (incl. 1978-1979 Supplements) (Social Issues Resources Ser.). 1980. 70.00 (ISBN 0-89777-017-X). Soc Issues.

--Habitat, Vol. 2 (incl. 1980-1984 Supplements) (Social Issues Resources Ser.). 1983. 70.00 (ISBN 0-89777-049-8). Soc Issues.

--Health, Vol. 1 (incl. 1977-1978 Supplements) (Social Issues Resources Ser.). 1979. 70.00 (ISBN 0-89777-013-7). Soc Issues.

--Health, Vol. 2 (incl. 1979-1983 Supplements) (Social Issues Resources Ser.). 1984. 70.00 (ISBN 0-89777-045-5). Soc Issues.

--Human Rights, Vol. 1(incl. 1981-1982 supplements) (Social Issues Resources Ser.). 1983. 70.00 (ISBN 0-89777-029-3). Soc Issues.

--Human Rights, Vol. 2 (incl. 1983-1984 Supplement) (Social Issues Resources Ser.). 1984. 28.00 (ISBN 0-89777-061-7). Soc Issues.

--Mental Health, Vol. 1 (incl. 1977-1978 Supplements) (Social Issues Resources Ser.). 1979. 70.00 (ISBN 0-89777-014-5). Soc Issues.

--Mental Health, Vol. 2 (incl. 1979-1983 Supplements) (Social Issues Resources Ser.). 1984. 70.00 (ISBN 0-89777-046-3). Soc Issues.

--Money, Vol. 1 (incl. 1975-1976 Supplements) (Social Issues Resources Ser.). 1977. 70.00 (ISBN 0-89777-007-2). Soc Issues.

--Money, Vol. 2 (incl. 1977-1981 Supplements) (Social Issues Resources Ser.). 1982. 70.00 (ISBN 0-89777-039-0). Soc Issues.

--Money, Vol. 3 (Incl. 1982-1984 Supplements) 1984. 42.00 (ISBN 0-89777-071-4). Soc Issues.

--Pollution, Vol. 1 (incl. 1973 & 1974 Supp.) (Social Issues Resources Ser.). 1975. 70.00 (ISBN 0-89777-000-5). Soc Issues.

--Pollution, Vol. 2 (incl. 1975-1979 Supplements) (Social Issues Resources Ser.). 1980. 70.00 (ISBN 0-89777-032-3). Soc Issues.

--Pollution, Vol. 3 (incl. 1980-1984 Supplements) (Social Issues Resources Ser.). 1984. 70.00 (ISBN 0-89777-064-1). Soc Issues.

--Population, Vol. 1 (incl. 1973 & 1974 Supplements) (Social Issues Resources Ser.). 1976. 70.00 (ISBN 0-89777-001-3). Soc Issues.

--Population, Vol. 2 (incl. 1975-1979 Supplements) (Social Issues Resources Ser.). 1980. 70.00 (ISBN 0-89777-033-1). Soc Issues.

--Population, Vol. 3 (incl. 1980-1984 Supplements) (Social Issues Resources Ser.). 1984. 70.00 (ISBN 0-89777-065-X). Soc Issues.

--Privacy, Vol. 1 (incl. 1976-1977 Supplements) (Social Issues Resources Ser.). 1978. 70.00 (ISBN 0-89777-008-0). Soc Issues.

--Privacy, Vol. 2 (incl. 1978-1982 Supplements) (Social Issues Resources Ser.). 1983. 70.00 (ISBN 0-89777-040-4). Soc Issues.

--Religion, Vol. 1 (incl. 1979-1980 Supplements) (Social Issues Resources Ser.). 1981. 70.00 (ISBN 0-89777-021-8). Soc Issues.

--Religion, Vol. 2 (incl. 1981-1984 Supplements) 1982. 56.00 (ISBN 0-89777-053-6). Soc Issues.

--School, Vol. 1 (incl. 1977-1978 Supplements) (Social Issues Resources Ser.). 1979. 70.00 (ISBN 0-89777-015-3). Soc Issues.

--School, Vol. 2 (incl. 1979-1983 Supplements) (Social Issues Resources Ser.). 1984. 70.00 (ISBN 0-89777-047-1). Soc Issues.

--Sexuality, Vol. 1(incl. 1981 & 1982 Supplements) (Social Issues Resources Ser.). 1983. 70.00 (ISBN 0-89777-030-7). Soc Issues.

--Sports, Vol. 1 (incl. 1979-1980 Supplements) (Social Issues Resources Ser.). 1981. 70.00 (ISBN 0-89777-023-4). Soc Issues.

--Sports, Vol. 2 (incl. 1981-1984 Supplements) 1984. 56.00 (ISBN 0-89777-055-2). Soc Issues.

--Technology, Vol. 1(incl. 1981 & 1982 Supplements) (Social Issues Resources Ser.). 1983. 70.00 (ISBN 0-89777-028-5). Soc Issues.

--Third World, Vol. 1(incl. 1981 & 1982 Supplements) (Social Issues Resources Ser.). 1983. 70.00 (ISBN 0-89777-031-5). Soc Issues.

--Transportation, Vol. 1 (incl. 1978-1979 Supplements) (Social Issues Resources Ser.). 1980. 70.00 (ISBN 0-89777-018-8). Soc Issues.

--Transportation, Vol. 2 (incl. 1980-1984 Supplements) (Social Issues Resources Ser.). 1984. 70.00 (ISBN 0-89777-050-1). Soc Issues.

--Women, Vol. 1 (incl. 1977-1978 Supplements) (Social Issues Resources Ser.). 1979. 70.00 (ISBN 0-89777-012-9). Soc Issues.

--Women, Vol. 2 (incl. 1979-1983 Supplements) (Social Issues Resources Ser.). 1984. 70.00 (ISBN 0-89777-044-7). Soc Issues.

--Work, Vol. 1 (incl. 1975-1976 Supplements) (Social Issues Resources Ser.). 1977. 70.00 (ISBN 0-89777-005-6). Soc Issues.

--Work, Vol. 2 (incl. 1977-1981 Supplements) (Social Issues Resources Ser.). 1982. 70.00 (ISBN 0-89777-037-4). Soc Issues.

--Work, Vol. 3 (Incl. 1982-1984 Supplements) 1984. 42.00 (ISBN 0-89777-069-2). Soc Issues.

--Youth, Vol. 1 (incl. 1979-1980 Supplements) (Social Issues Resources Ser.). 1981. 70.00 (ISBN 0-89777-022-6). Soc Issues.

--Youth, Vol. 2 (incl. 1981-1984 Supplements) 1984. 56.00 (ISBN 0-89777-054-4). Soc Issues.

Goldstein, Elliot, et al. Air Pollution & the Politics of Control. 182p. 1973. text ed. 23.50x (ISBN 0-8422-7136-8). Irvington.

Goldstein, Eric A., ed. An Assessment of New York City's Transportation Service & Its Impact on Business & Health. 132p. 1977. 5.00 (ISBN 0-318-15828-0). Natl Resources Defense Coun.

Goldstein, Ernest. Edward Hicks: The Peaceable Kingdom. (Let's Get Lost in a Painting Ser.). (Illus.). 1983. 9.95 (ISBN 0-8116-1001-2). NAL.

--Emanuel Leutze: Washington Crossing the Delaware. (Let's Get Lost in a Painting). (Illus.). 1983. 9.95 (ISBN 0-8116-1002-0). NAL.

--Grant Wood: American Gothic. (Let's Get Lost in a Painting Ser.). 52p. 1984. 9.95. NAL.

--Winslow Homer: The Gulf Stream. (Let's Get Lost in a Painting Ser.). (Illus.). 1983. 9.95 (ISBN 0-8116-1000-4). NAL.

Goldstein, Ernest, jt. auth. see Rosenberg, Bernard.

Goldstein, Ernest, jt. auth. see Saunders, Robert.

Goldstein, Estelle T., jt. auth. see Goldstein, Bernard.

Goldstein, Frances. Children's Treasure Hunt Travel Guide to Britain. LC 78-71424. (Illus.). 1979. pap. 6.95 (ISBN 0-933334-00-1, Dist. by Hippocrene). Paper Tiger Pap.

--Children's Treasure Hunt Travel Guide to Italy. LC 79-67280. (Illus., Orig.). (gr. k-12). 1980. pap. 6.95 (ISBN 0-933334-01-X, Dist. by Hippocrene). Paper Tiger Pap.

--Children's Treasure Hunt Travel to Belgium & France. LC 80-85012. (Children's Treasure Hunt Travel Guide Ser.). (Illus.). 230p. (Orig.). (gr. k-12). 1981. pap. 6.95 (ISBN 0-933334-02-8, Dist. by Hippocrene). Paper Tiger Pap.

Goldstein, Fred & Goldstein, Stan. Prime-Time Television: Prime-Time Shows from Milton Berle to "Falcon Crest". 12.98 (ISBN 0-517-55071-7). Crown.

Goldstein, Frederic. Physical Geology Laboratory Manual. 1976. spiral bdg. 8.95 (ISBN 0-88252-049-0). Paladin Hse.

Goldstein, Gary & Sternberg, Alex. From Kata to Competition: The Complete Karate Handbook. LC 81-15040. (Illus.). 208p. 1982. 14.95 (ISBN 0-668-05241-4, 5241). Arco.

Goldstein, Gary, jt. auth. see Sternberg, Alex.
Goldstein, Gerald. A Clinician's Guide to Research Design. LC 79-18818. 288p. 1981. text ed. 24.95x (ISBN 0-88229-340-0). Nelson-Hall.
Goldstein, Gerald & Ruthven, Leslie. Rehabilitation of the Brain-Damaged Adult. (Applied Clinical Psychology Ser.). 280p. 1983. 27.50x (ISBN 0-306-40498-2). Plenum Pub.
Goldstein, Gerald, ed. Advances in Clinical Neuropsychology, Vol. 1. 198p. 1984. 29.50x (ISBN 0-306-41502-X, Plenum Pr). Plenum Pub.
Goldstein, Gerald & Hersen, Michel, eds. Handbook of Psychological Assessment. LC 84-3092. (Pergamon General Pyschology Ser.: No. 131). 500p. 1984. 60.00 (ISBN 0-08-029401-4). Pergamon.
Goldstein, Gerald & Neuringer, Charles, eds. Empirical Studies of Alcoholism. LC 76-17285. 288p. 1976. prof ref 22.00x (ISBN 0-88410-127-4). Ballinger Pub.
Goldstein, Gerald, jt. ed. see Tarter, Ralph E.
Goldstein, Gersham & Bittker, Boris I., eds. Index to Federal Tax Articles. 1982. 245.00 (ISBN 0-88262-018-5). Warren.
Goldstein, Gideon & Mackay, Ian R. Human Thymus. LC 75-102173. 320p. 1970. 12.00 (ISBN 0-87527-012-3). Green.
Goldstein, Gil. The Jazz Composer's Companion. (Illus.). 144p. pap. 12.95 (ISBN 0-8256-4207-8). Music Sales.
Goldstein, H. Reading & Listening Comprehension at Various Controlled Rates. LC 71-176812. (Columbia University. Teachers College, Contributions to Education Ser.: No. 821). Repr. of 1940 ed. 22.50 (ISBN 0-404-55821-6). AMS Pr.
--Readings in Family Therapy. 1969. pap. text ed. 9.95x (ISBN 0-8290-1184-6). Irvington.
Goldstein, Harold. Training & Education By Industry. 80p. 1980. 15.00 (ISBN 0-318-15753-5). Natl Inst Work.
Goldstein, Harold, ed. The Changing Environment for Library Services in the Metropolitan Area. (Allerton Park Institute Ser.: No. 12). 158p. 1966. pap. 4.00x (ISBN 0-87845-007-6). U of Ill Lib Info Sci.
Goldstein, Harold M. & Horowitz, Morris A. Health Personnel: Meeting the Explosive Demand for Medical Care. LC 76-55042. 128p. 1977. 31.50 (ISBN 0-912862-36-X). Aspen Systems.
--Utilization of Health Personnel: A Five Hospital Study. LC 78-12011. 180p. 1979. text ed. 31.00 (ISBN 0-89443-080-7). Aspen Systems.
Goldstein, Harriet I. & Goldstein, Vetta. Art in Everyday Life. 4th ed. (Illus.). 1954. text ed. write for info. (ISBN 0-02-344480-0, 34448). Macmillan.
Goldstein, Harris A., jt. auth. see Starr, Bernard D.
Goldstein, Harris K. Research Standards & Methods for Social Workers. rev. ed. LC 70-84001. 1980. pap. 12.50x (ISBN 0-87655-551-2). Collage Inc.
Goldstein, Harvey. The Design & Analysis of Longitudinal Studies: Their Role in the Measurment of Change. 1979. 35.00 (ISBN 0-12-289580-0). Acad Pr.
Goldstein, Harvey, jt. auth. see Gipps, Caroline.
Goldstein, Harvey, jt. auth. see Levy, Philip.
Goldstein, Harvey A. One Hundred & Twenty-Two Minutes a Month to Greater Profits. LC 84-82281. 176p. 1985. 18.95 (ISBN 0-931349-00-1); pap. 11.95 (ISBN 0-931349-01-X). Granville Pubns.
Goldstein, Helen, jt. auth. see Goldstein, Shelly.
Goldstein, Helen H. Kid's Cuisine. Bolch, Judy, ed. LC 83-60306. (Illus.). 64p. (Orig.). (gr. k-7). 1983. pap. 5.95 (ISBN 0-935400-09-5). News & Observer.
Goldstein, Henry, jt. auth. see Lautman, Kay P.
Goldstein, Herb, compiled by. A Compendium of Land Trust Documents. 1976. pap. 3.00 (ISBN 0-686-84741-5). Comm Serv.
Goldstein, Herbert. Fundamental Aspects of Reactor Shielding. Repr. of 1959 ed. 28.00 (ISBN 0-384-19100-2). Johnson Repr.
Goldstein, Herbert & Goldstein, Marjorie T. The Reasoning Ability of Mildly Retarded Learners. LC 80-65500. 80p. (Orig.). 1980. pap. 6.00 (ISBN 0-86586-102-1). Coun Exc Child.
Goldstein, Herman. Policing a Free Society. LC 76-13589. 1977. pap. 14.95 prof ref (ISBN 0-88410-784-1). Ballinger Pub.
Goldstein, Howard. Creative Change: A Cognitive-Humanistic Approach to Social Work Practice. 280p. 1984. pap. 14.95 (ISBN 0-422-78650-0, NO. 9169, Pub. by Tavistock England). Methuen Inc.
--Social Learning & Change: A Cognitive Approach to Human Services. LC 80-23446. 516p. 1981. 19.95x (ISBN 0-87249-402-0). U of SC Pr.
--Social Learning & Change: A Cognitive Approach to Human Services. 514p. 1984. pap. 14.95 (ISBN 0-422-79120-2, NO. 9168). Methuen Inc.
--Social Work Practice: A Unitary Approach. LC 73-4687. 1973. Repr. text ed. 14.95x (ISBN 0-87249-285-0). U of SC Pr.
Goldstein, Howard, jt. auth. see Stark, James.
Goldstein, Imre, tr. see Biro, Yvette.
Goldstein, Inge, jt. auth. see Goldstein, Martin.
Goldstein, Inge F., jt. auth. see Goldstein, Martin.
Goldstein, Irving & Lane, Fred. Goldstein Trial Technique: Nineteen Sixty-Nine to Nineteen Eighty-Four, 3 vols. 2nd ed. LC 84-23915. Set. 200.00 (ISBN 0-317-12038-7); Suppl., 1982. 60.00; Suppl., 1983. 69.00. Callaghan.
Goldstein, Irving S. Organic Chemicals from Biomass. 320p. 1981. 92.00 (ISBN 0-8493-5531-1). CRC Pr.
Goldstein, Irving S., ed. Wood Technology: Chemical Aspects. LC 77-2368. (ACS Symposium Ser.: No. 43). 1977. 34.95 (ISBN 0-8412-0373-3). Am Chemical.
Goldstein, Irwin J. & Etzler, Marilynn E. Chemical Taxonomy, Molecular Biology, & Function of Plant Lectins. LC 83-19937. (Progress in Clinical & Biological Research Ser.: Vol 138). 314p. 1983. 38.00 (ISBN 0-8451-0138-2). A R Liss.
Goldstein, Irwin J., ed. Carbohydrate-Protein Interaction. LC 78-25788. (ACS Symposium Ser.: No. 88). 1979. 26.95 (ISBN 0-8412-0466-7). Am Chemical.
Goldstein, Irwin L. Training in Organizations: Needs, Assessments, Development, & Evaluation. 2nd ed. 275p. 1985. pap. 11.00 (ISBN 0-534-05604-0). Brooks-Cole.
--Training: Program Development & Evaluation. LC 74-82036. (Behavioral Science in Industry Ser). 1974. pap. text ed. 7.25 pub net (ISBN 0-8185-0132-4). Brooks-Cole.
Goldstein, Israel. My World as a Jew, Vol. 1. LC 82-42721. (Illus.). 352p. 1984. 27.50 (ISBN 0-8453-4765-9). Cornwall Bks.
--My World as a Jew, Vol. 2. LC 82-42621. (Illus.). 416p. 1984. 27.50 (ISBN 0-8453-4780-2). Cornwall Bks.
--Toward a Solution. facs. ed. LC 79-128248. (Essay Index Reprint Ser). 1940. 21.00 (ISBN 0-8369-1877-0). Ayer Co Pubs.
Goldstein, J. Migration & Rural Development: Research Directions on Interrelations. (Economic & Social Development Papers: No. 8). 69p. (Eng., Fr. & Span.). 1979. pap. 7.50 (ISBN 92-5-100817-5, F1868, FAO). Unipub.
Goldstein, J. & Goldstein, A. Crime, Law & Society. LC 77-136009. 1971. pap. text ed. 14.95 (ISBN 0-02-912260-0). Free Pr.
Goldstein, J. A., ed. see Ford Foundation Program Tulane University, Jan. to May, 1947.
Goldstein, J. H., ed. Sports, Games, & Play: Social & Psychological Viewpoints. 480p. 1979. 39.95 (ISBN 0-89859-467-7). L Erlbaum Assocs.
--Sports Violence. (Springer Series in Social Psychology). (Illus.). 250p. 1983. 26.00 (ISBN 0-387-90828-5). Springer-Verlag.
Goldstein, J. H., jt. ed. see McGhee, P. E.
Goldstein, J. I., jt. ed. see Marder, A. R.
Goldstein, Jack. Triumph Over Disease: By Fasting & Natural Diet. 245p. 1.95 (ISBN 0-318-15691-1). Natl Health Fed.
Goldstein, Jeffrey H. Aggression & Crimes of Violence. Lana, Robert & Rosnow, Ralph, eds. (Reconstruction of Society Ser). (Illus.). 1975. 19.95x (ISBN 0-19-501935-0); pap. 6.95x (ISBN 0-19-501936-9). Oxford U Pr.
--Social Psychology. LC 78-64447. 1980. 22.25i (ISBN 0-12-287050-6); instr's manual 10.00i (ISBN 0-12-287052-2). Acad Pr.
Goldstein, Jeffrey H., ed. Reporting Science: The Case of Aggression. 140p. 1985. text ed. 16.50 (ISBN 0-89859-608-4); pap. 8.95 (ISBN 0-89859-671-8). L Erlbaum Assocs.
Goldstein, Jeffrey H. & McGhee, Paul E., eds. The Psychology of Humor: Theoretical Perspectives & Empirical Issues. 1972. 43.50 (ISBN 0-12-288950-9). Acad Pr.
Goldstein, Jeri, ed. see Williams, Robin & Williams, Linda.
Goldstein, Jerome. How to Start a Family Business & Make It Work. LC 84-3995. 168p. 1984. 9.95 (ISBN 0-87131-435-5). M Evans.
--In Business for Yourself: A Guide to Starting a Small Business & Running It Your Way. (Illus.). 208p. 1982. 12.95 (ISBN 0-684-17436-7, ScribT). Scribner.
--Recycling: How to Re-Use Wastes in Home, Industry & Society. LC 78-20983. (Illus.). 1979. 14.95x (ISBN 0-8052-3706-2). Schocken.
Goldstein, Jerome A. Semigroups of Linear Operators & Applications. (Mathematical Monographs). 356p. 1985. 42.50x (ISBN 0-19-503540-2). Oxford U Pr.
Goldstein, Joan. Environmental Decision Making in Rural Locales: The Pine Barrens. LC 81-5208. 186p. 1981. 29.95 (ISBN 0-03-059604-1). Praeger.
--The Politics of Offshore Oil. LC 82-7697. 208p. 1982. 25.95 (ISBN 0-03-059813-3). Praeger.
Goldstein, Joel. Kentucky Government & Politics. 300p. (Orig.). 1984. pap. text ed. 10.95x (ISBN 0-89917-421-3). Tichenor Pub.
Goldstein, Joel H. The Effects of the Adoption of Woman Suffrage: Sex Differences in Voting Behavior Illinois 1914-1921. LC 84-18282. (Landmark Dissertations in Women's Studies). 270p. 1984. 29.95x (ISBN 0-03-064187-X). Praeger.
Goldstein, Joel K. The Modern American Vice Presidency: The Transformation of a Political Institution. LC 81-47918. 360p. 1981. 31.00x (ISBN 0-691-07636-7); pap. 10.95 (ISBN 0-691-02208-9). Princeton U Pr.
Goldstein, Jon H. Competition for Wetlands in the Midwest: An Economic Analysis. LC 74-149240. pap. 29.80 (ISBN 0-317-26460-5, 2023796). Bks Demand UMI.
Goldstein, Jonathan. Philadelphia & the China Trade, Sixteen Eighty-Two to Eighteen Forty-Six: Commercial, Cultural, & Attitudinal Effects. LC 77-1638. (Illus.). 1978. 17.75x (ISBN 0-271-00512-2). Pa St U Pr.
Goldstein, Jonathan A. II Maccabees: A New Translation with Introduction & Commentary, Vol. 41-A. LC 82-45200. (Anchor Bible Ser.). (Illus.). 624p. 1983. 18.00 (ISBN 0-385-04864-5). Doubleday.
--The Letters of Demosthenes. LC 67-19652. 320p. 1968. 29.00x (ISBN 0-231-03017-7). Columbia U Pr.
Goldstein, Jonathan A., tr. & intro. by. Maccabees One. LC 75-32719. (Anchor Bible Ser.: Vol. 41). (Illus.). 18.00 (ISBN 0-385-08533-8, Anchor Pr). Doubleday.
Goldstein, Jone R., jt. auth. see Couture, Barbara.
Goldstein, Joseph. The Experience of Insight: A Simple & Direct Guide to Buddhist Meditation. LC 82-42682. 185p. (Orig.). 1983. pap. 7.95 (ISBN 0-87773-226-4). Shambhala Pubns.
Goldstein, Joseph & Katz, J. Family & the Law. LC 65-10189. 1965. text ed. 24.75 (ISBN 0-02-912280-5). Free Pr.
Goldstein, Joseph, et al. Beyond the Best Interests of the Child. 1984 ed. pap. 9.95x (ISBN 0-317-30589-1). Free Pr.
--Criminal Law: Theory & Process. 2nd ed. LC 73-22533. (Illus.). 1974. text ed. 50.00 (ISBN 0-02-912310-0). Free Pr.
--Before the Best Interests of the Child. LC 79-64249. 1980. 16.95 (ISBN 0-02-912220-1); pap. 4.95 (ISBN 0-02-912210-4). Free Pr.
--In the Best Interest of the Child. 192p. 1985. 16.03x (ISBN 0-02-912180-9); pap. 9.95x (ISBN 0-02-912380-1). Free Pr.
--In the Best Interests of the Child. 192p. 15.95 (ISBN 0-02-912180-9); pap. 8.95 (ISBN 0-02-912380-1). Free Pr.
--In the Best Intrests of the Child. 192p. 1985. 15.95 (ISBN 0-02-912180-9); pap. 8.95 (ISBN 0-02-912380-1). Free Pr.
--The My Lai Massacre & Its Cover-up: Beyond the Reach of Law? LC 75-38298. 1976. 17.00 (ISBN 0-02-912230-9). Free Pr.
Goldstein, Joseph, jt. auth. see Becker, Loftus E.
Goldstein, Joseph I. & Yakowitz, Harvey, eds. Practical Scanning Electron Microscopy: Electron & Ion Microprobe Analysis. LC 74-34162. (Illus.). 582p. 1975. 49.50 (ISBN 0-306-30820-7, Plenum Pr). Plenum Pub.
Goldstein, Joseph I., et al. Scanning Electron Microscopy & X-Ray Microanalysis: A Text for Biologists, Materials Scientists & Geologists. 688p. 1981. 32.50x (ISBN 0-306-40768-X, Plenum Pr). Plenum Pub.
Goldstein, Karen A., jt. auth. see Coughlin, Robert E.
Goldstein, Karen J., ed. Annual Abstracts of Speech, Voice, Language & Hearing. 1979. text ed. 15.95 (ISBN 0-316-31948-1). Little.
Goldstein, Kenneth M. & Blackman, Sheldon. Cognitive Style: Five Approaches & Relevant Research. LC 78-1378. 1978. 36.95 (ISBN 0-471-31275-4, Pub. by Wiley-Interscience). Wiley.
Goldstein, Kenneth S. A Guide for Field Workers in Folklore. LC 64-24801. xx, 199p. 35.00x (ISBN 0-8103-5000-9); pap. 20.00x (ISBN 0-8103-5041-6). Gale.
Goldstein, Kenneth S., ed. see Brewster, Paul G.
Goldstein, Kenneth S., ed. see Fowke, Edith.
Goldstein, Kenneth S., ed. see Hudson, Arthur P.
Goldstein, Kenneth S., ed. see Jackson, George P.
Goldstein, Kenneth S., ed. see Morris, Alton C.
Goldstein, Kurt. A Kurt Goldstein Reader: The Shaping of Neuropsychology. Rieber, R. W., ed. LC 78-22720. 32.50 (ISBN 0-404-60868-X). AMS Pr.
--Language & Language Disturbances. LC 48-11852. (Illus.). 386p. 1953. 56.00 (ISBN 0-8089-0156-7, 791650). Grune.
Goldstein, L., jt. auth. see Adams, W.
Goldstein, L. & Prescott, David, eds. Cell Biology: A Comprehensive Treatise, 4 vols. Incl. Vol. 1. 1978. 65.00 (ISBN 0-12-289501-0); Vol. 2. The Structure & Replication of Genetic Material. 1979. 65.00 (ISBN 0-12-289502-9). LC 78-10457. Acad Pr.
Goldstein, Larry, jt. auth. see Graff, Lois.
Goldstein, Larry, et al. Brief Calculus & Its Applications. 3rd ed. (Illus.). 448p. 1984. 32.95 (ISBN 0-13-111898-6). P-H.
--Calculus & Its Applications. 3rd ed. (Illus.). 656p. 31.95 (ISBN 0-13-111880-3). P-H.
Goldstein, Larry J. Abstract Algebra: A First Course. LC 72-12790. (Illus.). 1973. 33.95x (ISBN 0-13-000851-6). P-H.
--The Adam Home Computer: An Introduction to SmartBASIC & Applications. (Illus.). 240p. 1985. pap. 7.95 (ISBN 0-89303-296-4). Brady Comm.
--Advanced BASIC & Beyond for the IBM PC. LC 83-15725. (Illus.). 384p. 1983. pap. text ed. 19.95 (ISBN 0-89303-324-3); bk. & diskette 49.95 (ISBN 0-89303-325-1); diskette 30.00 (ISBN 0-89303-326-X). Brady Comm.
--Computers & Their Applications. (Illus.). 672p. 1986. text ed. 26.95 (ISBN 0-13-163544-1). P-H.
--Getting Started with Your Hyperion. cancelled 17.95 (ISBN 0-89303-487-8). Brady Comm.
--The Graphics Generator: Business & Technical Graphics for the IBM Personal Computer. (Illus.). 155p. 1982. 95.00 (ISBN 0-89303-266-2); diskettes o.p. 95.00 (ISBN 0-89303-495-9). Brady Comm.
--IBM PCjr: Introduction to BASIC Programming & Applications. (Illus.). 384p. 1984. pap. 14.95 (ISBN 0-89303-539-4); diskette 20.00 (ISBN 0-89303-537-8); cancelled 34.95 (ISBN 0-89303-545-9). Brady Comm.
--TRS-80 Models III & IV: Programming & Applications. (Illus.). 320p. 1984. 15.95 (ISBN 0-89303-903-9). Brady Comm.
Goldstein, Larry J. & Goldstein, Martin. IBM Personal Computer: An Introduction to Operating System, BASIC Programming & Applications. rev. ed. LC 83-11780. (Illus.). 400p. 1983. 18.95 (ISBN 0-89303-530-0); diskette 25.00 (ISBN 0-89303-526-2); bk. & diskette 43.95 (ISBN 0-89303-527-0). Brady Comm.
Goldstein, Larry J. & Mosher, F. Commodore 64 BASIC Programming & Applications. LC 83-25705. (Illus.). 320p. 1984. 15.95 (ISBN 0-89303-381-2). Brady Comm.
Goldstein, Larry J. & Rensin, Joseph K. Compaq Portable Computer User's Guide. LC 83-17140. (Illus.). 400p. 1983. pap. 18.95 (ISBN 0-89303-389-8). Brady Comm.
Goldstein, Larry J. & Schneider, David. Finite Mathematics & Its Applications. 2nd ed. (Illus.). 528p. 1984. 31.95 (ISBN 0-13-317313-5). P-H.
--Microsoft BASIC for the Macintosh. (Illus.). 576p. 1984. pap. 21.95 (ISBN 0-89303-662-5). Brady Comm.
Goldstein, Larry J., jt. auth. see Graff, Lois.
Goldstein, Larry J., jt. auth. see Rensin, Joseph K.
Goldstein, Larry Joel & Nunnally, Charles. Zenith-Heath Personal Computer: An Introduction to the Operating System, BASIC Programming & Applications. cancelled 15.95 (ISBN 0-318-01430-0). Brady Comm.
Goldstein, Laurence. The Flying Machine & Modern Literature. LC 84-48043. (Illus.). 288p. 1985. 27.50 (ISBN 0-253-32218-9). Ind U Pr.
--Ruins & Empire: The Evolution of a Theme in Augustan & Romantic Literature. LC 76-50889. pap. 71.50 (ISBN 0-317-26643-8, 2025438). Bks Demand UMI.
Goldstein, Laurence, jt. ed. see Lewis, David L.
Goldstein, Lee. Communes, Law & Commonsense: A Legal Manual for Communities. LC 74-77447. (Illus.). 1974. pap. 3.35 (ISBN 0-9603468-0-5). New Community.
Goldstein, Leon. Introduction to Comparative Physiology. LC 76-26009. 1977. text ed. 31.95 (ISBN 0-03-012411-5, HoltC). HR&W.
Goldstein, Leon J., jt. auth. see Dawidowicz, Lucy S.
Goldstein, Leonard. George Chapman: Aspects of Decadence in Early 17th Century Drama, 2 vols. (Salzburg Studies in English Literature, Jacobean Drama Studies Ser.: No. 31). 440p. 1975. Set. pap. text ed. 50.75x (ISBN 0-391-01387-4). Humanities.
Goldstein, Leslie F. The Constitutional Rights of Women: Cases in Law & Social Change. 1979. pap. text ed. 17.95x (ISBN 0-582-28063-X). Longman.
Goldstein, Lester & Precott, David M., eds. Cell Biology: Vol III, a Comprehensive Treatise, Gene Expression: the Production of RNAs. LC 80-10715. 1980. 80.00 (ISBN 0-12-289503-7). Acad Pr.
Goldstein, Lester & Prescott, David N., eds. Cell Biology: Vol. IV, a Comprehensive Treatise, Gene Expression: Translation & the Behavior of Proteins. 1980. 65.00 (ISBN 0-12-289504-5). Acad Pr.
Goldstein, Lewis P., jt. auth. see Salmon, Shirley.
Goldstein, Lisa. The Dream Years. LC 85-7458. 192p. 1985. 14.95 (ISBN 0-553-05090-7). Bantam.
--The Red Magician. (Orig.). 1983. pap. 2.50 (ISBN 0-671-49907-6, Timescape). PB.
Goldstein, Lou & Softsync, Inc. Commodore LOGO from A to Z: The Complete Book of the LOGO Language. 256p. pap. cancelled (ISBN 0-89303-465-7). Brady Comm.
Goldstein, Lou & Softsync Inc. How to Build Programs for Your Commodore 64. (Illus.). 300p. 12.95 (ISBN 0-317-12842-6). P-H.
Goldstein, Lou, jt. auth. see Softsyn Staff.
Goldstein, Louis A. & Dickerson, Robert C. Atlas of Orthopaedic Surgery. 2nd ed. LC 80-25987. (Illus.). 646p. 1981. text ed. 119.95 (ISBN 0-8016-1884-3). Mosby.
--Atlas of Orthopaedic Surgery, Vols. 1 & 2. LC 74-12842. (Illus.). 1039p. 1974. 150.00 set (ISBN 0-8016-1883-5). Mosby.
Goldstein, Lynn, ed. see Kolkmeyer, Alexandra.
Goldstein, Lynn, rev. by see Ritzenthaler, Robert E.
Goldstein, Lynne, jt. auth. see Buikstra, Jane E.
Goldstein, Lynne G. Mississippian Mortuary Practices. LC 82-101139. (Scientific Papers Ser.: No. 4). (Illus.). 196p. 1980. pap. 9.00 (ISBN 0-942118-08-1). Ctr Amer Arche.
Goldstein, M. & Dillon, W. R. Discrete Discriminant Analysis. 190p. 1978. 34.50x (ISBN 0-471-04167-X, Pub. by Wiley-Interscience). Wiley.
Goldstein, Mahler, jt. auth. see Glashow.
Goldstein, Malcolm. George S. Kaufman: His Life, His Theater. (Illus.). 1979. 29.95x (ISBN 0-19-502623-3). Oxford U Pr.
--The Political Stage: American Drama & Theater of the Great Depression. (Illus.). 1974. 29.95x (ISBN 0-19-501745-5). Oxford U Pr.

--Pope & the Augustan Stage. LC 72-1632. (Stanford University. Stanford Studies in Language & Literature: No. 17). Repr. of 1958 ed. 20.00 (ISBN 0-404-51827-3). AMS Pr.

Goldstein, Malcolm, ed. see Rowe, Nicholas.

Goldstein, Malcolm L. The Art of Thornton Wilder. LC 65-10239. xii, 179p. 1965. pap. 4.25x (ISBN 0-8032-5074-6, BB 308, Bison). U of Nebr Pr.

Goldstein, Marc & Feldberg, Michael. The Vasectomy Book: A Complete Guide to Decision Making. LC 81-1023. (Illus.). 192p. (Orig.). 1983. pap. 5.95 (ISBN 0-87477-274-5). J P Tarcher.

Goldstein, Marjorie T., jt. auth. see Goldstein, Herbert.

Goldstein, Mark S., jt. auth. see Blum, James D.

Goldstein, Mark S., ed. see American Institute of Certified Public Accountants.

Goldstein, Martin & Goldstein, Inge. The Experience of Science: An Interdisciplinary Approach. 424p. 1984. 22.50x (ISBN 0-306-41538-0, Plenum Pr). Plenum Pub.

--How We Know: An Exploration of the Scientific Process. LC 80-39869. (Da Capo Quality Paperbacks Ser.). (Illus.). 376p. 1981. pap. 8.95 (ISBN 0-306-80140-X). Da Capo.

Goldstein, Martin & Goldstein, Inge F. How We Know: An Exploration of the Scientific Process. LC 77-20510. (Illus.). 375p. 1978. 18.95x (ISBN 0-306-31069-4, Plenum Pr). Plenum Pub.

Goldstein, Martin, jt. auth. see Goldstein, Larry J.

Goldstein, Martin & Simha, Robert, eds. The Glass Transition & the Nature of the Glassy State, Vol. 279. (Annals of the New York Academy of Sciences). 246p. 1976. 28.00x (ISBN 0-89072-053-3). NY Acad Sci.

Goldstein, Martin E. American Policy Toward Laos. LC 72-416. (Illus.). 347p. 1973. 25.00 (ISBN 0-8386-1131-1). Fairleigh Dickinson.

--America's Foreign Policy: Drift or Decision. LC 84-20221. (Illus.). 556p. (Orig.). 1984. pap. text ed. 14.95x (ISBN 0-8420-2209-0). Scholarly Res Inc.

Goldstein, Marty & Waldman, Stu. Black Book: 1985. (Illus.). 1200p. 1985. 90.00 (ISBN 0-916098-18-4). Creat Black Bk.

--Creative Black Book Portfolio Edition: 1985. (Illus.). 825p. 1985. 55.00 (ISBN 0-916098-17-6). Creat Black Bk.

--Creative Black Book: 1985, 2 vols. (Illus.). 1200p. 1985. Set. 90.00 (ISBN 0-916098-16-8). Creat Black Bk.

Goldstein, Marty & Waldman, Stuart. Black Book: 1986. (Illus.). 1300p. 1986. 95.00 (ISBN 0-916098-22-2). Creat Black Bk.

--Creative Black Book Portfolio Edition Europe: 1985. (Illus.). 825p. 1985. 55.00 (ISBN 0-916098-19-2). Creat Black Bk.

--Creative Black Book Portfolio Edition: 1986. (Illus.). 1000p. 1986. 60.00 (ISBN 0-916098-21-4). Creat Black Bk.

--Creative Black Book: 1986, 2 vols. (Illus.). 1300p. 1986. 95.00. Creat Black Bk.

Goldstein, Matthew, jt. auth. see Dillon, William R.

Goldstein, Max, jt. auth. see Roberts, Allen.

Goldstein, Melvyn C. English-Tibetan Dictionary of Modern Tibetan. LC 83-18119. 600p. 1984. lib. bdg. 45.00 (ISBN 0-520-05157-2). U of Cal Pr.

Goldstein, Menek, et al, eds. Ergot Compounds & Brain Function: Neuroendocrine & Neuropsychiatric Aspects. Calne, D. & Lieberman, A. (Advances in Biochemical Psychopharmacology Ser.: Vol. 23). 441p. 1980. text ed. 64.50 (ISBN 0-89004-450-3). Raven.

Goldstein, Michael J., jt. auth. see Baker, Bruce L.

Goldstein, Michael J., ed. The Experience of Anxiety: A Casebook. 2nd ed. Palmer, James O. 1975. pap. text ed. 9.95x (ISBN 0-19-501921-0). Oxford U Pr.

Goldstein, Michael J., et al. Abnormal Psychology: Experiences, Origins, & Interventions. (Illus.). 622p. 1980. text ed. 28.95 (ISBN 0-316-31955-4); instr's manual avail. (ISBN 0-316-31956-2). Little.

--Pornography & Sexual Deviance. LC 72-97753. 1973. 29.50x (ISBN 0-520-02406-0); pap. 2.45 (ISBN 0-520-02619-5). U of Cal Pr.

Goldstein, Michael L. Election 'Eighty-Four Curriculum Guide. 36p. (Orig.). 1984. pap. text ed. 12.00 (ISBN 0-930331-00-1). Pub Aff Res.

Goldstein, Milton. The Magnificent West: Yosemite. LC 72-85054. 224p. 1976. 35.00 (ISBN 0-385-03296-X). Doubleday.

Goldstein, Morris. Have Flexible Exchange Rates Handicapped Macroeconomic Policy? LC 80-16268. (Special Papers in International Economics: No. 14). pap. 22.00 (ISBN 0-317-27144-X, 2024750). Bks Demand UMI.

Goldstein, Morris & Khan, Mohsin. Effects of Slowdown in Industrial Countries on Growth in Non-Oil Developing Countries. (Occasional Papers: No. 12). 42p. 1982. pap. 5.00 (ISBN 0-317-04012-X). Intl Monetary.

Goldstein, Murray, et al, eds. Cerebrovascular Disorders & Stroke. LC 78-62496. (Advances in Neurology Ser.: Vol. 25). 420p. 1979. text ed. 59.50 (ISBN 0-89004-294-2). Raven.

Goldstein, Nathan. The Art of Responsive Drawing. 3rd ed. (Illus.). 384p. 1984. 30.95 (ISBN 0-13-047746-X); pap. 25.95 (ISBN 0-13-047738-9). P-H.

--A Drawing Handbook: Themes, Tools, & Techniques. (Illus.). 256p. 1986. pap. text ed. 17.95 (ISBN 0-13-219312-4). P-H.

--Figure Drawing: The Structure, Anatomy, & Expressive Design of Human Form. (Illus.). 330p. 1981. text ed. 27.95; pap. text ed. 25.95 (ISBN 0-13-314435-6). P-H.

--One Hundred American & European Drawings: A Portfolio. 116p. 1982. portfolio 24.95 (ISBN 0-13-634691-X). P-H.

--Painting: Visual & Technical Fundamentals. LC 78-15907. 1979. 26.95 (ISBN 0-13-647800-X). P-H.

Goldstein, Nettie & Warner, Norma. How Hip Are You, Bk 1. (Hip Reader Program). (Illus.). (gr. 5-12). 1977. 2.95 (ISBN 0-87594-160-5); wkbk 3.75 (ISBN 0-686-85723-2). Book-Lab.

Goldstein, Norm & Associated Press. Frank Sinatra: Ol' Blue Eyes. 1982. pap. 8.95 (ISBN 0-03-061921-1, Owl Bks). HR&W.

Goldstein, Norman N. & Free, Michael J. Foundations of Physiological Instrumentation: A Source Book with Experiments. (Illus.). 400p. 1979. photocopy ed. 45.75x (ISBN 0-398-03795-7). C C Thomas.

Goldstein, Patti, jt. auth. see Kritsick, Stephen.

Goldstein, Paul. Copyright, Patent, Trademark & Related State Doctrines: Cases & Materials on the Law of Intellectual Property. 2nd ed. LC 81-3201. (University Casebook Ser.). 955p. 1981. text ed. 25.00 (ISBN 0-88277-029-2). Foundation Pr.

--Copyright, Patent, Trademark & Related State Doctrines: Cases & Materials on the Law of Intellectual Property. 2nd ed. (University Casebook Ser.). 183p. 1982. pap. text ed. write for info. tchrs. manual (ISBN 0-88277-105-1). Foundation Pr.

--Copyright, Patent, Trademark & Related State Doctrines: Cases & Materials on the Law of Intellectual Property, 1985 Statute Supplement. 2nd ed. (Universtiy Casebook Ser.). 252p. 1985. pap. write for info. (ISBN 0-88277-259-7). Foundation Pr.

--Copyright, Patent, Trademark & Related State Doctrines: Cases & Materials on the Law of Intellectual Property, 1985 Case Supplement. 2nd ed. (Unversity Casebook Ser.). 197p. 1985. pap. write for info. (ISBN 0-88277-260-0). Foundation Pr.

--Real Estate Transactions. 2nd ed. (University Casebook Ser.). 1985. write for info (ISBN 0-88277-248-1). Foundation Pr.

--Real Estate Transactions: Cases & Materials on Land Transfer, Development & Finance. LC 80-11638. (University Casebook Ser.). 812p. 1980. text ed. 23.00 (ISBN 0-88277-005-5). Foundation Pr.

--Real Estate Transactions: Cases & Materials on Land Transfer, Development & Finance; Statute, Form & Problem Supplement. 2nd ed. (University Casebook Ser.). 164p. pap. write for info. (ISBN 0-88277-264-3). Foundation Pr.

--Real Property. LC 84-5919. (University Casebook Ser.). 1362p. 1984. text ed. 30.00 (ISBN 0-88277-170-1). Foundation Pr.

--Real Property, Teacher's Guide. (University Casebook Ser.). 415p. 1984. write for info (ISBN 0-88277-218-X). Foundation Pr.

Goldstein, Paul J. Prostitution & Drugs. LC 78-24766. 208p. 1979. 26.00x (ISBN 0-669-02833-9). Lexington Bks.

Goldstein, Paula & Bibliowicz, Meryl. Birdseye Word Skills: Nouns & Adjectives. (Mastery Masters Ser.). (gr. 4-6). 1982. pap. 5.95 (ISBN 0-8224-0711-6). Pitman Learning.

--Birdseye Word Skills: Verbs & Adverbs. (Mastery Masters Ser.). (gr. 4-6). 1982. pap. 5.95 (ISBN 0-8224-0712-4). Pitman Learning.

Goldstein, Philip. Genetics Is Easy. rev. ed. (Illus.). (gr. 9 up). 8.05 (ISBN 0-8313-1539-3). Lantern.

Goldstein, Philip, jt. auth. see Caverly, Philip W.

Goldstein, Phyllis J. How to Start a Successful, Money-Making "Business" while Attending College. (Illus.). 48p. (Orig.). 1982. pap. 6.95 (ISBN 0-910481-00-8). Money-Maker.

Goldstein, R., jt. ed. see Nordhaus, W. D.

Goldstein, R. J. Diseases of Aquarium Fishes. (Illus.). pap. 7.95 (ISBN 0-87666-795-7, PS-201). TFH Pubns.

--Introduction to Cichlids. 1970. pap. 9.95 (ISBN 0-87666-788-4, PS-662). TFH Pubns.

Goldstein, R. J., et al. Heat Transfer in Energy Conservation. (Bk. No. H00106). 136p. 1977. 18.00 (ISBN 0-685-46848-8). ASME.

Goldstein, Rebecca. The Mind-Body Problem. 1983. 13.95 (ISBN 0-394-52474-8). Random.

--The Mind-Body Problem. 304p. (gr. 5 up). pap. 4.50 (ISBN 0-440-35651-2, LE). Dell.

Goldstein, Richard & Sachs, Stephen, eds. Applied Poverty Research. (Orig.). 1982. pap. 8.00 (ISBN 0-918592-52-6). Policy Studies.

Goldstein, Richard & Sachs, Stephen M., eds. Applied Poverty Research. LC 83-16126. 316p. 1984. 25.00x (ISBN 0-86598-137-X). Rowman & Allanheld.

Goldstein, Richard J., ed. Fluid Mechanics Measurements. LC 83-4292. (Illus.). 630p. 1983. text ed. 55.00 (ISBN 0-89116-244-5). Hemisphere Pub.

Goldstein, Robert C. Database: Technology & Management. 352p. 1985. 28.95 (ISBN 0-471-88737-4). Wiley.

Goldstein, Robert J. Cichlids of the World. (Illus.). 382p. 1973. 29.95 (ISBN 0-87666-032-4, H-945). TFH Pubns.

--Political Repression in Modern America. 1978. lib. bdg. 25.00 (ISBN 0-8161-8253-1, Univ Bks). G K Hall.

--Political Repression in Modern America: 1870 to the Present. 2nd ed. 704p. 1985. pap. text ed. 13.95x (ISBN 0-87047-013-2); 22.50 (ISBN 0-87047-012-4). Schenkman Bks Inc.

--Political Repression in Nineteenth Century Europe. LC 83-10541. 416p. 1983. 28.50x (ISBN 0-389-20419-6, 07305). B&N Imports.

Goldstein, Roberta B. Cry Before Dawn. LC 74-15523. 80p. 1974. 5.00 (ISBN 0-8233-0216-4). Golden Quill.

--Fling Jeweled Pebbles. 1963. 2.75 (ISBN 0-8233-0030-7). Golden Quill.

--Memories That Burn & Bless. LC 84-90360. 80p. 1984. 6.50 (ISBN 0-8233-0385-3). Golden Quill.

--Wood Burns Red. 1966. 3.00 (ISBN 0-8233-0031-5). Golden Quill.

Goldstein, Ronald. Change Your Smile. (Illus.). 300p. 1984. 23.95 (ISBN 0-86715-144-7). Quint Pub Co.

Goldstein, Rose. Time to Pray. LC 72-91792. 7.95 (ISBN 0-87677-141-X). Hartmore.

Goldstein, Rose B. Songs to Share. (Illus.). 64p. (Eng. & Heb.). (ps-5). 2.95x (ISBN 0-8381-0720-6, 10-720). United Syn Bk.

Goldstein, Ruby. Third Man in the Ring: As Told to Frank Graham. LC 77-138622. (Illus.). 216p. Repr. of 1959 ed. lib. bdg. 15.00x (ISBN 0-8371-5734-X, GOTM). Greenwood.

Goldstein, Ruth M. & Zornow, Edith. Movies for Kids: A Guide for Parents & Teachers on the Entertainment Film for Children. rev. ed. LC 79-6149. (Illus.). 300p. 1980. 15.95 (ISBN 0-8044-2267-2); pap. 7.95 (ISBN 0-8044-6194-5). Ungar.

--The Screen Image of Youth: Movies about Children & Adolescents. LC 80-14053. (Illus.). xxi, 363p. 1980. 22.00 (ISBN 0-8108-1316-5). Scarecrow.

Goldstein, Sam. Animalimericks: Book I-Wild Cats. (Limericklets (Limerick Booklets Ser.): No. 2). (Illus.). 16p. (Orig.). 1982. pap. 1.00 (ISBN 0-938338-10-2). Winds World Pr.

--Animalimericks: Book II Primates. (Limericklets (Limerick Booklets) Ser.: No. 3). (Illus.). 16p. 1982. pap. 1.00 (ISBN 0-938338-11-0). Winds World Pr.

--Animalimericks: Book III: The Weasel Tribe. (Limericklets Ser.: No. 4). (Illus.). 16p. (Orig.). 1982. pap. 1.00 (ISBN 0-938338-17-X). Winds World Pr.

--Animalimericks: Book IV: Equidae. (Limericklets Ser.: No. 5). (Illus.). 16p. (Orig.). 1982. pap. 1.00 (ISBN 0-938338-15-3). Winds World Pr.

--Animalimericks: Book V: Extinct Reptiles. (Limericklets Ser.: No. 8). (Illus.). 16p. (Orig.). 1982. pap. 1.00 (ISBN 0-938338-16-1). Winds World Pr.

--The Birdicide of Cock Robin, & Other Murderous Words Ending in Cide. (Weirdictionaries Ser.). (Illus.). 68p. (Orig.). 1982. pap. 3.95 cancelled (ISBN 0-938338-04-8). Winds World Pr.

--Herculimericks. (Limericklets: No. 18). (Illus.). 1983. pap. 1.00 (ISBN 0-938338-29-3). Winds World Pr.

--Herculimericks III. (Limericklets: No. 43). (Illus.). 1983. pap. 1.00 (ISBN 0-938338-53-6). Winds World Pr.

--More Printer's Limericks. (Limericklets Ser.: No. 7). (Illus.). 16p. 1982. pap. 1.00 (ISBN 0-938338-19-6). Winds World Pr.

--A Printer's Limericks. (Limericklet Ser.). (Illus.). 16p. 1982. pap. 1.00 (ISBN 0-938338-18-8). Winds World Pr.

--What Are You Afraid of? An Illustrated Dictionary of Fearful Words Ending in Phobia. (Weirdictionaries Ser.). (Illus.). 72p. (Orig.). 1982. pap. 3.95 cancelled (ISBN 0-938338-05-6). Winds World Pr.

Goldstein, Sanford. Gaijin Aesthetics. (W.N.J Ser.: No. 17). 1983. 10.00; signed ed. o.p. 20.00; pap. 6.00. Juniper Pr WI.

Goldstein, Sanford, tr. see Ishikawa, Takuboku.

Goldstein, Sanford, tr. see Mori, Ogai.

Goldstein, Sanford, tr. see Soseki, Natsume.

Goldstein, Sanford, tr. see Takeda, Taijun.

Goldstein, Shelly & Goldstein, Helen. The Index to Coca-Cola Collectibles. pap. 8.95 (ISBN 0-936118-04-0). Wallace-Homestead.

Goldstein, Sid. The Spirit of Cooking: Behind the Scenes with Northern California's Best Chefs. Harlib, Leslie & Goldstein, Suzanne, eds. LC 84-48114. (Illus.). 120p. (Orig.). 1984. pap. 8.95 (ISBN 0-917887-01-8). Land Plenty Prods.

Goldstein, Sidney. Lectures on Fluid Mechanics. LC 60-12712. (Lectures in Applied Mathematics Ser.: Vol. 2A). xvi, 311p. 1982. pap. 42.00 (ISBN 0-8218-0048-5, LAM-2-1). Am Math.

Goldstein, Sidney & Goldscheider, Calvin. Jewish Americans: Three Generations in a Jewish Community. (Brown Classics in Judaica Ser.). (Illus.). 294p. 1985. pap. text ed. 13.25 (ISBN 0-8191-4721-4). U Pr of Amer.

Goldstein, Sidney & Goldstein, Alice. Surveys of Migration in Developing Countries: A Methodological Review. LC 81-4285. (Papers of the East-West Population Institute: No. 71). v, 120p. (Orig.). 1981. pap. text ed. 2.50 (ISBN 0-86638-021-3). E W Center HI.

Goldstein, Sidney, jt. auth. see Mayer, Kurt B.

Goldstein, Sidney & Sly, David, eds. Basic Data Needed for the Study of Urbanization. (Working Papers: No. 1). 100p. 1975. 10.00 (ISBN 0-685-93697-X, ORD1, ORDINA). Unipub.

--The Measurement of Urbanization & Projection of Urban Population. (Working Papers: No. 2). 224p. 1975. pap. 15.00 (ISBN 0-685-93699-6, ORD4, ORDINA). Unipub.

--Patterns of Urbanization: Comparative Country Studies, 2 vols. 750p. 1976. Set. 60.00 (ISBN 0-685-93700-3, ORD6, ORDINA). Unipub.

Goldstein, Sidney M. Pre-Roman & Early Roman Glass in the Corning Museum of Glass. LC 78-70440. (Catalog Ser.). (Illus.). 312p. 1979. 40.00 (ISBN 0-87290-067-3). Corning.

Goldstein, Sidney M., et al. Cameo Glass: Masterpieces from 2000 Years of Glassmaking. LC 82-70395. (Illus.). 144p. (Orig.). 1982. pap. text ed. 15.00 (ISBN 0-87290-105-X). Corning.

Goldstein, Sol. Divorced Parenting: How to Make It Work. 232p. 1984. pap. 8.95 (ISBN 0-525-48124-9, 0869-260, Obelisk). Dutton.

Goldstein, Sonja & Solnit, Albert J. Divorce & Your Child: Practical Suggestions for Parents. LC 83-51297. 160p. 1984. 17.50x (ISBN 0-300-02810-5). Yale U Pr.

--Divorce & Your Child: Practical Suggestions for Parents. LC 83-51297. 160p. 1985. pap. 5.95 (ISBN 0-300-03414-8, Y-535). Yale U Pr.

Goldstein, Stan, jt. auth. see Goldstein, Fred.

Goldstein, Stanley L., jt. auth. see Bullough, Robert V., Jr.

Goldstein, Stephen R. & Gee, E. Gordon. Law & Public Education: Cases & Materials. 2nd ed. (Contemporary Legal Education Ser.). 1059p. 1981. text ed. 25.00 (ISBN 0-672-84199-1). Michie Co.

Goldstein, Stephen R., jt. auth. see Buss, William G.

Goldstein, Steven. China Briefing, 1984. 126p. 1985. 22.00 (ISBN 0-8133-0222-6); pap. 12.50 (ISBN 0-8133-0223-4). Westview.

Goldstein, Steven M. & Sears, Kathrin. The People's Republic of China: A Basic Handbook. 4th ed. (Illus.). 160p. (Orig.). 1984. pap. 7.50x (ISBN 0-936876-17-4). Learn Res Intl Stud.

Goldstein, Sue. The Second Underground Shopper. 384p. 1984. pap. 6.95 (ISBN 0-317-14497-9). Andrews McMeel Parker.

--The Underground Shoppers Guide to Off-Price Shopping. 528p. (Orig.). 1984. pap. 3.95 (ISBN 0-446-32531-7). Warner Bks.

Goldstein, Susan B. & Sies, Luther F. The Communication Contract. (Illus.). 384p. 1974. 38.50x. C C Thomas.

Goldstein, Suzanne, ed. see Goldstein, Sid.

Goldstein, Sydney, ed. Modern Developments in Fluid Dynamics, 2 Vols. (Illus.). 1938. pap. text ed. 8.50 ea.; Vol. 1. pap. text ed. (ISBN 0-486-61357-7); Vol. 2. pap. text ed. (ISBN 0-486-61358-5). Dover.

Goldstein, Thomas. Dawn of Modern Science: From the Arabs to Leonardo Da Vinci. 1980. 12.95 (ISBN 0-395-26298-4). HM.

--Dawn of Modern Science: From the Arabs to Leonardo da Vinci. 1982. pap. 7.95 (ISBN 0-395-32132-8). HM.

Goldstein, Toby. Frozen Fire: The Story of the Cars. (Illus.). 128p. (Orig.). 1985. pap. 7.95 (ISBN 0-8092-5257-0). Contemp Bks.

Goldstein, Tom. The News at Any Cost: How Journalists Compromise Their Ethics to Shape the News. 252p. 1985. 18.95 (ISBN 0-671-49960-2). S&S.

Goldstein, Vetta, jt. auth. see Goldstein, Harriet I.

Goldstein, Wallace L. Teaching English As a Second Language: An Annotated Bibliography. LC 75-17987. (Reference Library of the Humanities Ser.: Vol. 23). 218p. 1975. lib. bdg. 41.00 (ISBN 0-8240-9991-5). Garland Pub.

--Teaching English as a Second Language: An Annotaed Bibliography, Vol. 2. LC 83-48197. 334p. 1983. lib. bdg. 41.00 (ISBN 0-8240-9097-7). Garland Pub.

Goldstein, Waller, ed. Planning, Politics, & the Public Interest. LC 78-1720. 202p. 1978. 22.50x (ISBN 0-231-04538-7). Columbia U Pr.

Goldstein, Walter. Dilemma of British Defense: The Imbalance Between Commitments & Resources. LC 66-63556. 98p. (Orig.). 1966. pap. 1.50 (ISBN 0-8142-0054-0). Ohio St U Pr.

Goldstein, William. Controversial Issues in Our Schools. LC 80-82679. (Fastback Ser.: No. 146). 1980. pap. 0.75 (ISBN 0-87367-146-5). Phi Delta Kappa.

--An Introduction to Borderline Conditions & Their Therapy. 235p. 1985. 25.00 (ISBN 0-87668-905-5). Aronson.

--Selling School Budgets in Hard Times. LC 84-61201. (Fastback Ser.: No. 215). 50p. 1984. pap. 0.75 (ISBN 0-87367-215-1). Phi Delta Kappa.

--Supervision Made Simple. LC 82-60800. (Fastback Ser.: No. 180). 50p. 1982. pap. 0.75 (ISBN 0-87367-180-5). Phi Delta Kappa.

Goldstein, William & DeVita, Joseph. Successful School Commmunications: A Manual & Guide for Administrators. (Illus.). 1977. 19.50x (ISBN 0-13-872036-3, Parker). P-H.

Goldstein-Jackson, Kevin. The Dictionary of Essential Quotations. LC 83-2815. 188p. 1983. text ed. 26.50x (ISBN 0-389-20393-9). B&N Imports.

--Things to Make with Everyday Objects. LC 79-22045. (Illus.). 152p. (gr. 3-7). 1980. PLB 8.95 (ISBN 0-689-30743-8). Atheneum.

Goldstein-Jackson, Kevin, compiled by. The Dictionary of Essential Quotations. 188p. 1984. pap. 6.95 (ISBN 0-8226-0389-6, Helix Bks). Rowman & Allanheld.

Goldstein-Jackson, Kevin, et al. Experiments with Everyday Objects: Science Activities for Children, Parents & Teachers. LC 77-13232. (Illus.). 1978. 13.95 (ISBN 0-13-295287-4, Spec); (Spec). P-H.

Goldstene, Paul N. The Collapse of Liberal Empire: Science & Revolution in the Twentieth Century. LC 76-27367. 1977. 18.50x (ISBN 0-300-02029-5). Yale U Pr.

--The Collapse of Liberal Empire: Science & the Revolution in the Twentieth Century. (Political Science Ser.). 160p. 1980. pap. 7.95 (ISBN 0-88316-540-6). Chandler & Sharp.

Goldstick, David T. & Janik, Carolyn. The Complete Guide to Co-ops & Condominiums. LC 82-22513. 240p. 1983. 7.95 (ISBN 0-452-25400-0, Plume). NAL.

Goldstine, Daniel. The Dance-Away Lover. 1978. pap. 2.50 (ISBN 0-345-29763-6). Ballantine.

Goldstine, Dora, ed. Expanding Horizons in Medical Social Work. LC 54-11423. 1955. 17.50x (ISBN 0-226-30164-8). U. of Chicago Pr.

--Readings in the Theory & Practice of Medical Social Work. LC 54-8906. (Midway Reprint Ser). 345p. 1974. pap. 12.50x (ISBN 0-226-30162-1). U of Chicago Pr.

Goldstine, H. H. A History of Numerical Analysis from the 16th to the 19th Century. LC 77-5029. (Studies in the History of Mathematics & Physical Sciences: Vol. 2). (Illus.). 1977. pap. text ed. 39.50 (ISBN 0-387-90277-5). Springer-Verlag.

--A History of the Calculus of Variations from the Seventeenth Through the Nineteenth Century. (Studies in the History of Mathematics & Physical Sciences: Vol. 5). (Illus.). 410p. 1980. 59.00 (ISBN 0-387-90521-9). Springer-Verlag.

Goldstine, Herman H. The Computer from Pascal to Von Neumann. LC 70-173755. (Illus.). 400p. 1980. 37.00x (ISBN 0-691-08104-2); pap. 9.95x (ISBN 0-691-02367-0). Princeton U Pr.

--New & Full Moons One Thousand & One B. C. to A. D. Sixteen Fifty One. LC 72-89401. (Memoirs Ser.: Vol. 94). 1973. 10.00 (ISBN 0-87169-094-2). Am Philos.

Goldston, Angela, jt. auth. see Graham, Richard.

Goldston, Eli. The Quantification of Concern: Some Aspects of Social Accounting. LC 72-75528. (Benjamin Fairless Memorial Lectures Ser.). 75p. 1972. 12.00x (ISBN 0-231-03675-2). Columbia U Pr.

Goldston, Richard T., et al. Practitioners Laboratory. 178p. 1983. lab manual 15.00x (ISBN 0-935078-27-4). Veterinary Med.

Goldston, Robert. Great Depression. (Illus.). 1978. pap. 2.25 (ISBN 0-449-30834-0, Prem). Fawcett.

--The Life & Death of Nazi Germany. 1978. pap. 2.25 (ISBN 0-449-30830-8, Prem). Fawcett.

--Next Year in Jerusalem. 1979. pap. 1.95 (ISBN 0-449-24103-3, Crest). Fawcett.

--The Road Between the Wars: Nineteen Eighteen to Nineteen Forty-One. 256p. 1980. pap. 1.95 (ISBN 0-449-24294-3, Crest). Fawcett.

--The Road Between the Wars: 1918-1941. LC 78-51330. (Illus.). (gr. 7 up). 1978. 8.95 (ISBN 0-8037-7467-2). Dial Bks Young.

--The Russian Revolution. 1977. pap. 2.25 (ISBN 0-449-30845-6, Q760, Prem). Fawcett.

--Sinister Touches: The Secret War Against Hitler. LC 81-65853. 176p. (gr. 7 up). 1982. 11.95 (ISBN 0-8037-7903-8, 01160-350). Dial Bks Young.

--The Sword of the Prophet. 224p. 1981. pap. 2.50 (ISBN 0-449-24393-1, Crest). Fawcett.

--The Sword of the Prophet: A History of the Arab World from the Time of Mohammed to the Present Day. (Illus.). 1979. 11.95 (ISBN 0-8037-8372-8). Dial Bks Young.

Goldston, Will. Exclusive Magical Secrets. LC 76-27457. (Illus.). 506p. 1977. pap. 6.95 (ISBN 0-486-23432-0). Dover.

Goldstone, A. H. Examination Haematology. (Illus.). 206p. 1978. pap. 10.00 (ISBN 0-7216-4192-X). Saunders.

Goldstone, Adrian & Sweetser, Wesley D. A Bibliography of Arthur Machen. LC 72-6469. (English Literature Ser., No. 33). 180p. 1972. Repr. of 1965 ed. lib. bdg. 49.95x (ISBN 0-8383-1614-X). Haskell.

Goldstone, Bette P. Lessons to Be Learned: A Study of Late Eighteenth-Century English Didactic Children's Literature. LC 84-47785. (American University Studies XIV (Education): Vol. 7). 240p. 1985. text ed. 26.50 (ISBN 0-8204-0140-4). P Lang Pubs.

Goldstone, Gerald, jt. auth. see Goeller, Lee.

Goldstone, Harmon H. & Dalrymple, Martha. History Preserved: A Guide to New York City Landmarks & Historic Districts. LC 76-9142. (Illus.). 1976. pap. 9.95 (ISBN 0-8052-0544-6). Schocken.

Goldstone, Herbert. Coping with Vulnerability: The Achievement of John Osborne. 274p. (Orig.). 1982. lib. bdg. 25.50 (ISBN 0-8191-2617-9); pap. text ed. 12.25 (ISBN 0-8191-2618-7). U Pr of Amer.

Goldstone, Jerry. Decision Making in Vascular Surgery. 220p. 1984. text ed. 39.50 (ISBN 0-8016-1889-4, D1889-4). Mosby.

Goldstone, Leonard A. Statistics in the Management of Nursing Services. 288p. 1980. 50.00 (ISBN 0-272-79598-4, Pub by P.Man Bks England). State Mutual Bk.

--Understanding Medical Statistics. (Illus.). 181p. (Orig.). 1983. pap. 15.50x (ISBN 0-433-12402-4, Pub by W Heinemann Med Bks). Sheridan Med Bks.

--Understanding Medical Statistics. x, 181p. (Orig.). 1984. pap. 20.00 (ISBN 0-433-12402-4, Pub. by Heinman Med Bkk). Heinman.

Goldstone, Richard & Lass, A., eds. Mentor Book of Short Plays. pap. 3.95 (ISBN 0-451-62215-4, ME2215, Ment). NAL.

Goldstone, Richard A. Contexts of the Drama. LC 68-13092. (Illus.). 1968. text ed. 28.95 (ISBN 0-07-023662-3). McGraw.

Goldstone, Richard H. & Anderson, Gary, eds. Thornton Wilder: A Bibliographical Checklist of Work by & about Thornton Wilder. LC 79-6273. (AMS Studies in Modern Literature: No. 7). 120p. 1982. 29.50 (ISBN 0-404-18046-9). AMS Pr.

Goldstraw, Irma E. Derek Walcott: An Annotated Bibliography of His Works, 1944-1980. Davis, Charles T. & Louis-Gates, Henry, eds. LC 80-9049. (Reference Library of the Humanities). 192p. 1983. lib. bdg. 43.00 (ISBN 0-8240-9321-6). Garland Pub.

--Derek Walcott, the Primary Sources: An Annotated Bibliography of the Published Works, 1944-1980. 1981. lib. bdg. 43.00 (ISBN 0-8240-9321-6). Garland Pub.

Goldstrich, Joe D. The Best Chance Diet. LC 82-80894. 220p. 1982. pap. 9.95 (ISBN 0-89334-032-4). Humanics Ltd.

Goldstrom, J. M. The Social Content of Education, Eighteen Hundred Eight to Eighteen Seventy: A Study of the Working-Class School Reader in England & Ireland. 242p. 1978. Repr. of 1972 ed. text ed. 25.00x (ISBN 0-7165-1004-9, BBA 04710, Pub. by Irish Academic Pr Ireland). Biblio dist.

Goldstrom, J. M. & Clarkson, L. A., eds. Irish Population, Economy, & Society: Essays in Honour of the Late K. H. Connell. 1981. 49.95x (ISBN 0-19-822499-0). Oxford U Pr.

Goldstrom, Robert, jt. auth. see Hollyn, Lynn.

Goldstucker, Jac L., jt. auth. see Bellenger, Danny N.

Goldstucker, Jac L., ed. Marketing Information: A Professional Reference Guide. 1982. 60.00 (ISBN 0-88406-132-9). Ga St U Busn Pub.

Goldstucker, Jac L. & De la Torre, Jose R., eds. International Marketing. LC 72-172762. (American Marketing Association Bibliography Ser.: No. 19). pap. 31.50 (ISBN 0-317-10806-9, 2007722). Bks Demand UMI.

Goldstucker, Jac L., et al. New Developments in Retail Trading Area Analysis & Site Selection. LC 78-8033. (Research Monograph: No. 78). 1978. pap. 15.00 (ISBN 0-88406-115-9). Ga St U Busn Pub.

Goldsworthy, David. Tom MBoya: The Man Who Kenya Wanted to Forget. LC 81-22870. 308p. 1982. text ed. 35.00x (ISBN 0-8419-0787-0, Africana). Holmes & Meier.

Goldsworthy, Graeme. Gospel & Kingdom: A Christian Interpretation of the Old Testament. pap. cancelled (ISBN 0-85364-218-4, Pub. by Paternoster U K). Attic Pr.

--Gospel & Kingdom: A Christian's Guide to the Old Testament. 128p. 1983. pap. 6.95 (ISBN 0-86683-686-1). Winston Pr.

--The Lamb & the Lion: Gospel in Revolution. 180p. 1985. pap. 6.95 (ISBN 0-8407-5978-9). Nelson.

Goldsworthy, Graham J. Endocrinology. LC 80-18704. (Tertiarty Level Biology Ser.). 184p. 1980. 42.95x (ISBN 0-470-27034-9). Halsted Pr.

Goldsworthy, Lansdown. Ben Jonson & the First Folio. LC 72-1337. (Studies in Drama, No. 39: English Literature, No. 33). 1972. Repr. of 1931 ed. lib. bdg. 49.95x (ISBN 0-8383-1439-2). Haskell.

Goldsworthy, Maureen. Clothes for Children. LC 79-56465. (Illus.). 120p. 1980. 12.95 (ISBN 0-7134-2041-3, Pub. by Batsford England). David & Charles.

--Clothes for Disabled People. (Illus.). 120p. 1981. 14.95 (ISBN 0-7134-3929-7, Pub. by Batsford England). David & Charles.

--Mend It! LC 79-3709. (Illus.). 128p. 1980. 10.95 (ISBN 0-8128-2695-7); pap. 5.95 (ISBN 0-8128-6046-2). Stein & Day.

Goldsworthy, Peter R. & Fisher, N. M., eds. The Physiology of Tropical Field Crops. 664p. 1984. 74.95 (ISBN 0-471-10267-9). Wiley.

Goldsworthy, W. Lansdown. Ben Jonson & the First Folio. LC 72-191959. 1939. lib. bdg. 10.00 (ISBN 0-8414-4493-5). Folcroft.

--Shakespeare's Heraldic Emblems: Their Origin & Meaning. 1978. Repr. of 1928 ed. lib. bdg. 32.50 (ISBN 0-8414-4618-0). Folcroft.

Goldthorpe, J. E. An Introduction to Sociology. 3rd ed. LC 81-18048. 256p. 1985. 34.50 (ISBN 0-521-24545-1); pap. 12.95 (ISBN 0-521-28779-0). Cambridge U Pr.

--An Introduction to Sociology. 2nd ed. LC 73-83107. (Illus.). 200p. 1974. text ed. 37.50 (ISBN 0-521-20338-4); pap. text ed. 12.95 (ISBN 0-521-09826-2). Cambridge U Pr.

--The Sociology of the Third World: Disparity & Development. 2nd ed. LC 83-13506. 320p. 1984. 49.50 (ISBN 0-521-25303-9); pap. 14.95 (ISBN 0-521-27293-9). Cambridge U Pr.

Goldthorpe, John H., jt. auth. see Hirsch, Fred.

Goldthorpe, John H., ed. Order & Conflict in Contemporary Capitalism: Studies in the Political Economy of West European Nations. 1984. 34.95 (ISBN 0-19-878008-7); pap. 15.95 (ISBN 0-19-878007-9). Oxford U Pr.

Goldthorpe, John H., et al. Affluent Worker, in the Class Structure. (Studies in Sociology: No. 3). 1969. o. p. 37.50 (ISBN 0-521-07231-X); pap. 12.95x (ISBN 0-521-09533-6). Cambridge U Pr.

--Affluent Worker: Industrial Attitudes. LC 68-21192. (Cambridge Studies in Sociology: No. 1). 1968. 37.50 (ISBN 0-521-07109-7); pap. 11.95x (ISBN 0-521-09466-6). Cambridge U Pr.

--Affluent Worker: Political Attitudes. LC 68-21192. (Cambridge Studies in Sociology: No. 2). 1968. pap. 9.95 (ISBN 0-521-09526-3). Cambridge U Pr.

--Social Mobility & Class Structure in Modern Britain. (Illus.). 1980. text ed. 39.95x (ISBN 0-19-827239-1); pap. text ed. 17.95x (ISBN 0-19-827247-2). Oxford U Pr.

Goldthorpe, Rhiannon. Sartre: Literature & Theory. (Studies in French). 272p. 1984. 42.50 (ISBN 0-521-23791-2). Cambridge U pr.

Goldthwait, John T. Value, Language & Life. 250p. 1985. 24.95 (ISBN 0-87975-284-X). Prometheus Bks.

Goldthwait, John T., ed. see Kant, Immanuel.

Goldthwait, Richard P., ed. Till: A Symposium. LC 70-153422. (Illus.). 414p. 1972. 20.00x (ISBN 0-8142-0148-2). Ohio St U Pr.

Goldthwaite, John. Office Automation Conference Digest. 373p. 1985. 28.00 (ISBN 0-88283-045-7). AFIPS Pr.

Goldthwaite, Richard A. The Building of Renaissance Florence: A Social & Economic History. LC 80-7995. (Illus.). 480p. 1981. text ed. 37.50x (ISBN 0-8018-2342-0); pap. text ed. 10.95 (ISBN 0-8018-2977-1). Johns Hopkins.

Goldup, A., ed. see International Symposium on Gas Chromatography (5th: 1964: Brighton) Staff.

Goldwag, E. M., et al, eds. The Joy of Life. (Octopus Book). (Illus.). 1978. 19.95 (ISBN 0-7064-0755-5, Mayflower Bks); pap. 8.95 (ISBN 0-7064-0897-7). Smith Pubs.

Goldwasser, Anita. Planning for Profits: The Retailers Guide to Success. 1981. 20.95 (ISBN 0-86730-531-2). Lebhar Friedman.

Goldwasser, Dan L. & Makens, Hugh H. State Regulation of Capital Formation & Securities Transactions. LC 83-61006. (Corporate Law & Practice Course Handbook Ser.: No. 415). (Illus.). 848p. 1983. 30.00 (ISBN 0-317-12900-7). PLI.

Goldwasser, Dan L. & Practising Law Institute Staff. Accountants' Liability: 1981. LC 81-80633. (Litigation & Administrative Practice Ser.). 404p. 1981. write for info. PLI.

Goldwasser, E., ed. Regulation of Hemoglobin Biosynthesis. (Proceedings of the Third Annual Comprehensive Sickle Cell Center Symposium, Chicago: Vol. 3). 428p. 1983. 83.00 (ISBN 0-444-00768-7, Biomedical Pr). Elsevier.

Goldwasser, Janet & Dowty, Stuart. Huan-Ying: Workers' China. LC 74-7790. 416p. 1976. pap. 5.95 (ISBN 0-85345-389-6). Monthly Rev.

Goldwasser, M., tr. see Weinreich, Uriel.

Goldwater, Barry M. Delightful Journey: Down the Green & Colorado Rivers. LC 77-94876. 1970. 15.00 (ISBN 0-910152-01-2). AZ Hist Foun.

--Why Not Victory? A Fresh Look at American Foreign Policy. LC 79-28300. 201p. 1980. Repr. of 1962 ed. lib. bdg. 18.75x (ISBN 0-313-22316-5, GOWN). Greenwood.

Goldwater, Marge, et al. Jennifer Bartlett. LC 84-51359. (Illus.). 174p. 1985. 35.00 (ISBN 0-89659-519-6). Abbeville Pr.

Goldwater, Michael, jt. auth. see Twose, Nigel.

Goldwater, Robert. Gauguin. (Library of Great Painters Ser). (Illus.). 1957. 40.00 (ISBN 0-8109-0137-4). Abrams.

--Gauguin. 1984. 19.95 (ISBN 0-8109-0983-9). Abrams.

--Symbolism. LC 77-82780. (Icon Editions Ser.). (Illus.). 1979. (HarpT); pap. 10.95i (ISBN 0-06-430095-1, IN-95, HarpT). Har-Row.

--What Is Modern Sculpture. LC 76-86420. (Illus.). 1971. 12.50 (ISBN 0-87070-636-5, Pub. by Museum Mod Art). NYGS.

Goldwater, Robert, jt. auth. see Jordan, Jim M.

Goldwater, Robert & Treves, Marco, eds. Artists on Art: From the 14th to the 20th Century. LC 45-11131. 1974. pap. 8.95 (ISBN 0-394-70900-4). Pantheon.

Goldwater, Robert, tr. see Friedlaender, Walter.

Goldwater, Sam. Five Hundred Competencies for Firefighter Certification. LC 83-62587. 140p. 1983. pap. text ed. 10.00 (ISBN 0-87939-050-6). Intl Fire Serv.

Goldwater, Walter. Radical Periodicals in America, 1890-1950: A Bibliography with Brief Notes. 1977. 17.50 (ISBN 0-685-77028-1). Univ Place.

--Shashki: How to Read Russian Books on Spanish Pool Checkers. pap. 1.00 (ISBN 0-685-02664-7). Univ Place.

Goldway, David, jt. ed. see Selsam, Howard.

Goldwert, Marvin. Democracy, Militarism, & Nationalism in Argentina, 1930-1966: An Interpretation. (Latin American Monographs: No. 25). 267p. 1972. 14.95x (ISBN 0-292-71500-5). U of Tex Pr.

--History As Neurosis: Paternalism and Machismo in Spanish America. LC 80-5640. 85p. 1980. lib. bdg. 17.00 (ISBN 0-8191-1226-7); pap. text ed. 8.00 (ISBN 0-8191-1227-5). U Pr of Amer.

--Machismo & Conquest: The Case of Mexico. 96p. 1984. lib. bdg. 19.25 (ISBN 0-8191-3514-3); pap. text ed. 8.25 (ISBN 0-8191-3515-1). U Pr of Amer.

--Psyche & History. 85p. (Orig.). 1985. pap. 6.95 (ISBN 0-932269-41-9). Wyndham Hall.

--Psychic Conflict in Spanish America: Six Essays on the Psychohistory of the Region. LC 82-45059. 86p. (Orig.). 1982. lib. bdg. 20.50 (ISBN 0-8191-2413-3); pap. text ed. 8.00 (ISBN 0-8191-2414-1). U Pr of Amer.

--The Suicide & Rebirth of Western Civilization: A Collage of Psychohistorical Analogies. LC 81-40704. 76p. 1982. lib. bdg. 21.00 (ISBN 0-8191-1886-9); pap. text ed. 6.75 (ISBN 0-8191-1887-7). U Pr of Amer.

Goldwhite, Harold. Introduction to Phosphorus Chemistry. LC 79-27141. (Cambridge Texts in Chemistry & Biochemistry). 175p. 1981. 34.50 (ISBN 0-521-22978-2); pap. text ed. 14.95 (ISBN 0-521-29757-5). Cambridge U Pr.

Goldwin, Robert A., ed. America Armed: Essays on U. S. Military Policy. facsimile ed. LC 74-157338. (Select Bibliographies Reprint Ser.). Repr. of 1963 ed. 17.00 (ISBN 0-8369-5798-9). Ayer Co Pubs.

--Beyond the Cold War. LC 72-10851. (Essay Index Reprint Ser.). 1973. Repr. of 1965 ed. 21.00 (ISBN 0-8369-7218-X). Ayer Co Pubs.

--Bureaucrats, Policy Analysts, Statesmen: Who Leads? 1980. 10.25 (ISBN 0-8447-3383-0); pap. 5.25 (ISBN 0-8447-3375-X). Am Enterprise.

--Political Parties in the Eighties. 1980. 10.25 (ISBN 0-8447-3382-2); pap. 5.25 (ISBN 0-8447-3377-6). Am Enterprise.

--Why Foreign Aid. facs. ed. LC 71-134083. (Essay Index Reprint Ser). 1963. 14.00 (ISBN 0-8369-2036-8). Ayer Co Pubs.

Goldwin, Robert A. & Schambra, William A., eds. How Capitalistic Is the Constitution? 1981. 14.25 (ISBN 0-8447-3477-2); pap. 6.25 (ISBN 0-8447-3478-0). Am Enterprise.

--How Democratic Is the Constitution? 1980. 12.25 (ISBN 0-8447-3400-4); pap. 5.25 (ISBN 0-8447-3399-7). Am Enterprise.

Goldwin, Robert A. & Zetterbaum, Marvin, eds. Readings in Russian Foreign Policy. 1959. pap. 6.95x (ISBN 0-19-500893-6). Oxford U Pr.

Goldwin, Robert A., ed. see Meyer, Frank S., et al.

Goldworm, Hersh. Mishnah-Moed, Vol. 2. (Artscroll Mishnah Ser.). 416p. 1981. 16.95 (ISBN 0-89906-254-7); pap. 13.95 (ISBN 0-89906-255-5). Mesorah Pubns.

Goldworth, Amnon, ed. see Bentham, Jeremy.

Goldwurm, Hersh. Daniel. (The Art Scroll Tanach Ser.). 352p. 1979. 16.95 (ISBN 0-89906-079-X); pap. 13.95 (ISBN 0-89906-080-3). Mesorah Pubns.

Goldwurm, Hersh, et al. Mishnah-Moed, Vol. 3. (Art Scroll Mishnah Ser.). 1980. 16.95 (ISBN 0-89906-256-3); pap. 13.95 (ISBN 0-89906-257-1). Mesorah Pubns.

Goldwyn, Martin. You'd Better Believe It! (Illus.). 256p. 1982. pap. 5.95 (ISBN 0-8065-0792-6). Citadel Pr.

Goldwyn, Martin M. You'd Better Believe It. 1979. 10.00 (ISBN 0-8065-0672-5). Citadel Pr.

Goldwyn, Robert M. Long Term Results in Plastic & Reconstruction Surgery. 1980. text ed. 110.00 (ISBN 0-316-31972-4, Little Med Div) (ISBN 0-316-31973-2). Little.

--The Patient & the Plastic Surgeon. 1981. text ed. 25.00 (ISBN 0-316-31974-0). Little.

--Plastic & Reconstructive Surgery of the Breast. LC 75-25159. 1976. text ed. 75.00 (ISBN 0-316-31971-6). Little.

--The Unfavorable Result in Plastic Surgery. 2nd ed. 1134p. 1984. text ed. 150.00 2 vols. in slipcase (ISBN 0-316-31975-9). Little.

Goldyne, Joseph, jt. auth. see Johnson, Robert F.

Goldzband, Melvin G. Consulting in Child Custody: An Introduction to the Ugliest Litigation for Mental-Health Professionals. LC 81-48024. 208p. 1982. 28.50x (ISBN 0-669-05246-9). Lexington Bks.

--Custody Cases & Expert Witnesses: A Manual for Attorneys. 216p. 1980. 35.00 (ISBN 0-15-100016-6, H39840). HarBraceJ.

--Quality Time: Easing the Children Through Divorce. 224p. 1985. 17.95 (ISBN 0-07-023693-3). McGraw.

Goldziher, Ignac. Muslim Studies. Stern, S. M., ed. & tr. Incl. Vol. 1. Muhammedanische Studien. LC 67-20745. 1967. 39.50x (ISBN 0-87395-234-0); Vol. 2. Hadith: The 'Traditions', Ascribed to Muhammed. LC 72-11731. 1972. State U NY Pr.

Goldziher, Ignaz. Introduction to Islamic Theology & Law. Lewis, Bernard, ed. Hamori, Andras & Hamori, Ruth, trs. from Ger. LC 80-7523. (Modern Classics in Near Eastern Studies). 325p. 1981. 32.00 (ISBN 0-691-07257-4); pap. 12.50 LPE (ISBN 0-691-10099-3). Princeton U Pr.

--Mythology Among the Hebrews & Its Historical Development. Martineau, Russell, tr. LC 66-2396. Repr. of 1877 ed. 30.00 (ISBN 0-8154-0082-9). Cooper Sq.

Gole, James L. & Stwalley, William C., eds. Metal Bonding & Interactions in High Temperature Systems with Emphasis on Alkali Metals. LC 81-20555. (ACS Symposium Ser.: No. 179). 1982. 59.95 (ISBN 0-8412-0689-9). Am Chemical.

Gole, Linda, ed. Neo-Tech - Psychuous Testimonials. 240p. 1985. 27.50 (ISBN 0-911752-44-7). I & O Pub.

Gole, Susan. India Within the Ganges. 1983. 34.00x (ISBN 0-8364-1008-4, Pub. by Jayaprint India). South Asia Bks.

Golec, Anthony M. Techniques of Legal Investigation. 2nd ed. (Illus.). 522p. 1985. 39.75x (ISBN 0-398-05031-7). C C Thomas.

Goleeke, Thomas. Literature for Voice: An Index of Songs in Collections & Source Book for Teachers of Singing. LC 84-5461. 234p. 1984. 22.50 (ISBN 0-8108-1702-0). SCARECROW.

Goleman, Dan. Vital Lies, Simple Truths: The Psychology of Self-Deception & Shared Illusions. 1985. 17.95 (ISBN 0-671-45058-1). S&S.

Goleman, Daniel & Freedman, Johnathan. What Psychology Knows That Everyone Should. LC 81-8463. (Illus.). 288p. 1981. 12.95 (ISBN 0-86616-010-8). Greene.

Goleman, Daniel & Speeth, Kathleen. The Essential Psychotherapies. 1982. pap. 4.95 (ISBN 0-451-62356-8, Ment). NAL.

Goleman, Daniel & Davidson, Richard J., eds. Consciousness: The Brain, States of Awareness, & Alternate Realities. LC 79-2702. (Illus.). 220p. 1979. text ed. 29.50x (ISBN 0-89197-648-5); pap. 16.95 (ISBN 0-8290-0964-7). Irvington.

Golemba, Henry L. Frank R. Stockton. (United States Authors Ser.). 1981. lib. bdg. 13.50 (ISBN 0-8057-7288-X, Twayne). G K Hall.

Golembe, Carter H. State Banks & the Economic Development of the West, 1830-1844. LC 77-14780. (Dissertations in American Economic History Ser.). 1978. 43.00 (ISBN 0-405-11035-9). Ayer Co Pubs.

Golembe, Carter H. & Holland, David S. Federal Regulation of Banking - 1983-84. rev. ed. 244p. 1983. 12.45x (ISBN 0-9608840-1-7). Golembe Assocs.

--The Federal Regulation of Banking, 1981. rev. ed. 200p. 1981. 19.50x (ISBN 0-9608840-0-9). Golembe Assocs.

Golembiewski & Rabin. Public Budgeting & Finance. (Public Adminstration & Public Policy Ser.). 400p. 1983. 24.75 (ISBN 0-8247-1668-X). Dekker.

Golembiewski, Robert T. Humanizing Public Organizations: Perspectives on Doing Better-Than-Average When Average Ain't at All Bad. LC 83-81972. 400p. 1984. 26.50 (ISBN 0-912338-43-1); write for info. microfiche (ISBN 0-912338-44-X). Lomond.

--Public Administration As a Developing Discipline: Perspectives on Past & Present, Pt. 1. (Public Administration & Public Policy Ser.: Vol. 1). 1977. 29.75 (ISBN 0-8247-6565-6). Dekker.

Golembiewski, Robert T. & Gibson, Frank. Readings in Public Administration: Institutions, Processes, Behavior, Policy. 4th ed. LC 82-81584. 544p. 1982. 18.50 (ISBN 0-395-32765-2). HM.

Golembiewski, Robert T. & Hilles, Richard J. Toward the Responsive Organization: The Theory & Practice of Survey Feed. 354p. 1979. pap. text ed. 16.95 (ISBN 0-89832-001-1). Pub Horizons.

Golembiewski, Robert T. & White, Michael. Cases in Public Management. 4th ed. LC 82-81583. 336p. 1983. pap. text ed. 15.50 (ISBN 0-395-32767-9). HM.

Golembiewski, Robert T. & Wildavsky, Aaron. The Costs of Federalism: Essays in Honor of James W. Fesler. 320p. 1984. 29.95 (ISBN 0-88738-000-X). Transaction Bks.

Golembiewski, Robert T., ed. Approaches to Organizing. LC 81-70133. (PAR Classics: Vol. III). 1981. 11.95 (ISBN 0-936678-03-8). Am Soc Pub Admin.

--Perspectives on Public Management: Cases & Learning Designs. 2nd ed. LC 75-17317. 279p. 1976. text ed. 14.95 (ISBN 0-87581-186-8). Peacock Pubs.

Golembiewski, Robert T. & Eddy, William B., eds. Organization Development in Public Administration: Public Sector Applications of Organization Development Technology, Pt. 2. LC 77-27574. (Public Administration & Public Policy Ser.: Vol. 5). pap. 84.00 (ISBN 0-317-29567-5, 2021507). Bks Demand UMI.

Golembiewski, Robert T. & Rabin, Jack, eds. Public Budgeting & Finance: Readings in Theory & Practice. 2nd ed. LC 73-85768. (Illus.). 513p. 1975. text ed. 27.50 (ISBN 0-87581-162-0). Peacock Pubs.

Golembiewski, Thomas E. The Study of Obituaries as a Source for Polish Genealogical Research. (Illus.). 63p. 1985. pap. 10.95 (ISBN 0-318-17020-5). Polish Genealog.

Golembiuwski. Approaches to Planned Change: Pt. 2; Macro-Level Interventions & Change-Agent Strategies. (Public Administration & Public Policy Ser.; a Comprehensive Publication Program: Vol. 7). 1980. 29.75 (ISBN 0-8247-6804-3). Dekker.

Golen, S. P., jt. auth. see Caron, P. F.

Golen, Steven, et al, eds. Readings & Cases in Business Communication. LC 83-17066. (Buisness Communication Ser.: 1-573). 260p. 1984. pap. text ed. 13.95 (ISBN 0-471-86953-8). Wiley.

Golen, Steven P., et al. Report Writing for Business & Industry. (Business Communications Ser.). 448p. 1985. 23.95 (ISBN 0-471-80822-9). Wiley.

Golenberg, Edward, jt. auth. see Ginzberg, Lev R.

Golenbock, Peter. Bums: An Oral History of the Brooklyn Dodgers. LC 84-2167. (Illus.). 1984. 17.95 (ISBN 0-399-12846-8, Putnam); Ltd. ed. 60.00 (ISBN 0-399-13060-8). Putnam Pub Group.

--Dynasty: The New York Yankees 1949-1964. LC 75-4705. 1975. (Reward); pap. 5.95 (ISBN 0-13-222208-6). P-H.

--Dynasty: The New York Yankees 1949-1964. 640p. 1985. pap. 4.50 (ISBN 0-425-07652-0). Berkley Pub.

Golenbock, Peter, jt. auth. see Guidry, Ron.

Golenbock, Peter, jt. auth. see Nettles, Graig.

Golenbock, Peter, jt. auth. see Rose, Pete.

Golender, V. E. & Rozenblit, A. B. Logical & Combinatorial Algorithms for Drug Design. 289p. 1983. 68.95x (ISBN 0-471-90266-7, Pub by Res Stud Pr). Wiley.

Golf Digest, ed. The Golf Digest 1984 Almanac. (Annual Ser.). 771p. 1984. 14.95 (ISBN 0-914178-66-0). Golf Digest.

Golf Digest Editors. Golf Digest Almanac, 1985. LC 84-645998. 893p. 1985. pap. 12.95 (ISBN 0-914178-74-1). Golf Digest.

Golf Digest Editors & Aultman, Dick. Square-to-Square Golf Swing. 1975. pap. 9.95 (ISBN 0-671-21947-2, Fireside). S&S.

Golf Digest Editors, ed. The One Hundred Greatest Golf Courses- & Then Some. rev. ed. Davis, William H. LC 83-83246. (Illus.). 279p. 1984. 29.95 (ISBN 0-914178-62-8). Golf Digest.

Golf Digest Magazine Editors, ed. One Hundred Golf Courses & Then Some. rev. ed. Davis, William H. 279p. 1984. 14.95 (ISBN 0-671-49556-9). S&S.

Golf Magazine Editors, ed. Golf Magazine's Encyclopedia of Golf. rev. ed. LC 77-11818. (Illus.). 1979. 19.95i (ISBN 0-06-011552-1, HarpT). Har-Row.

Golf Magazine Editors, jt. ed. see Fishman, Lew.

Golfarb, Warren D., ed. see Herbrand, Jacques.

Golffing, Francis, tr. see Nietzsche, Friedrich.

Golf-Racht, T. Van see Van Golf-Racht, T.

Golia, Jack de see De Golia, Jack.

Golian, Milan. L Aspect Verbal en Francais. (Hamburger Phonetische Beitrage Ser.: No. 29). 279p. (Orig., Fr.). 1979. pap. text ed. 19.00x (ISBN 3-87118-390-3, Pub. by Helmut Buske Verlag Hamburg). Benjamins North Am.

Goliard, Roy. Scholar's Glossary of Sex. (Illus., Orig.). 1968. pap. 1.95 (ISBN 0-685-11982-3, 20). Heineman.

Goliaz-Benson, Ursula, jt. auth. see Fearn, Leif.

Goliber, Paul F. Refrigeration Servicing. LC 75-6064. 91p. 1976. pap. 8.40 (ISBN 0-8273-1005-6). Delmar.

Golick, M. A Parents Guide to Learning Problems. 1970. pap. 1.95x (ISBN 0-88432-009-X). J Norton Pubs.

--She Thought I Was Dumb but I Told Her I Had a Learning Disability. 1969. pap. 1.95x (ISBN 0-88432-010-3). J Norton Pubs.

Golick, Margie. Deal Me in! The Use of Playing Cards in Teaching & Learning. rev. ed. LC 73-14124. (Illus.). 189p. 1981. pap. 7.95 (ISBN 0-88432-077-4). J Norton Pubs.

--Deal Me In! The Use of Playing Cards in Teaching & Learning. 1985. pap. 8.95 (Pub. by Monarch Pr). S&S.

Golieb, D. E., jt. auth. see Ettinger, Richard P.

Goligher, John, et al. Surgery of the Anus, Rectum & Colon. 5th ed. (Illus.). 1185p. 1983. 125.00 (ISBN 0-7216-0954-6, Pub. by Bailliere-Tindall). Saunders.

Golightly, Cecelia K. Help with Career Planning: A Workbook for Nurses. (Help Series of Management Guides). 95p. 1979. pap. 11.95 (ISBN 0-933036-17-5). Ganong W L Co.

Golightly, Cecilia K. Creative Problem Solving for Health Care Professionals. LC 81-3631. 240p. 1981. text ed. 33.00 (ISBN 0-89443-371-7). Aspen Systems.

Golightly, Henry O. Consultants: Selecting, Using & Evaluating Business Consultants. 256p. 1985. 16.95 (ISBN 0-531-09591-6). Watts.

Golightly, Jean. Circuit Hikes in Virginia, West Virginia, Maryland & Pennsylvania. 3rd ed. LC 78-54231. 1981. pap. text ed. 2.50 (ISBN 0-915746-09-3). Potomac Appalach.

Golikhere, Vasanti R., ed. see Pandit, M. P.

Golin, Anne K. & Ducanis, Alex J. The Interdisciplinary Team: A Handbook for the Education of Exceptional Children. LC 81-738. 206p. 1981. text ed. 28.95 (ISBN 0-89443-346-6). Aspen Systems.

Golin, Anne K., jt. auth. see Ducanis, Alex J.

Golin, Carol B., et al. Medical Practice Building. (Illus.). 300p. Date not set. price not set (ISBN 0-7216-4167-9). Saunders.

Golin, E., ed. see Acton, Lord.

Golinkin, Noah. Ayn Keloheynu. LC 81-51960. (Illus.). 128p. 1981. pap. 6.95x (ISBN 0-88400-076-1). Shengold.

--Shalom Aleichem. 77p. 1978. pap. 4.50x (ISBN 0-317-26840-6). Hebrew Pub.

Golinkoff, Roberta M., ed. The Transition from Prelinguistic to Linguistic Communication: Issues & Implications. 344p. 1983. text ed. 36.00x (ISBN 0-89859-257-7). L Erlbaum Assocs.

Golino, Carlo L., jt. auth. see Speroni, Charles.

Golino, Carlo L., ed. Galileo Reappraised. LC 66-15485. (UCLA Center for Medieval & Renaissance Studies). 1966. 26.00x (ISBN 0-520-00490-6). U of Cal Pr.

Golino, Carlo L. & Quasimodo, Salvatore, eds. Contemporary Italian Poetry: An Anthology. LC 76-21754. 1977. Repr. of 1962 ed. lib. bdg. 24.75x (ISBN 0-8371-8998-5, GOCI). Greenwood.

Golinskii, B. L., et al. Thirteen Papers on Algebra & Analysis. LC 51-5559. (Translations Ser.: No. 2, Vol. 76). 1968. 35.00 (ISBN 0-8218-1776-0, TRANS 2-76). Am Math.

Golisz-Benson, Ursula, jt. auth. see Fearn, Leif.

Goliszek, Andrew. The Cholesterol & Sodium Book: A Guide to Dietary Cholesterol & Sodium for Health, Prevention & Diet Information. LC 84-70247. 66p. 1984. pap. 3.95 (ISBN 0-916833-01-1). Bio-Pub.

--A Guide to Medical School Preparation: Developing a System for Successful Admission. LC 84-70246. 104p. 1984. 4.95 (ISBN 0-916833-00-3). Bio Pub.

Golitsyn, Anatoliy. New Lies for Old: The Communist Strategy of Deception & Disinformation. 592p. 1984. 19.95 (ISBN 0-396-08194-0). Dodd.

Golka, F. W., ed. see Westerman, Claus.

Goll, August. Criminal Types in Shakespeare. LC 68-765. (Studies in Shakespeare, No. 24). 1969. Repr. of 1909 ed. lib. bdg. 49.95x (ISBN 0-8383-0558-X). Haskell.

Goll, Reinhold W. The Moon Twins & the Treasure. LC 78-61141. (Illus.). (gr. 5-8). 1978. 6.95 (ISBN 0-686-23765-X). R W Goll.

--Pedro Sails with Columbus. (gr. 6-10). 1981. 4.00 (ISBN 0-686-30643-0). R W Goll.

--Three Weird Animals & a Flying Monster. (gr. 6-9). 1981. 4.00 (ISBN 0-686-30642-2). R W Goll.

Goll, Yvan. Lackawanna Elegy. Kinnell, Galaway, tr. 1970. o. p. 7.50 (ISBN 0-912090-07-3); pap. 2.45 (ISBN 0-912090-06-5). Sumac Mich.

--Selected Poems. Schulte, Rainer & Bullock, Michael, trs. from Eng. & Ger. 110p. (Eng. & Ger.). 1981. pap. 8.00 (ISBN 0-939378-02-7). Mundus Artium.

Golladay, E. Stevers. Injuries to the Heart & Chest in Children. LC 83-80054. (Illus.). 256p. 1983. monograph 37.50 (ISBN 0-87993-196-5). Futura Pub.

Golladay, Frederick. Health. (Sector Policy Paper). 90p. 1980. 5.00 (ISBN 0-686-36197-0, PP-8001). World Bank.

--Health Issues & Policies in the Developing Countries. (Working Paper: No. 412). ii, 53p. 1980. 5.00 (ISBN 0-686-36198-9, WP-0412). World Bank.

Golladay, Frederick L. Economics: Problems, Principles, Priorities. LC 76-19511. 1978. 32.95 (ISBN 0-8053-3302-9); instr's. manual 6.95 (ISBN 0-8053-3304-5); study guide 11.95 (ISBN 0-8053-3303-7). Benjamin-Cummings.

Gollak, B., ed. see Strogonov, B. P., et al.

Gollan, Anne. The Tradition of Australian Cooking. 1978. text ed. 11.50 (ISBN 0-7081-0229-8, Pub by ANUP Australia). Australia N U P.

--The Tradition of Australian Cooking. (Illus.). 211p. 1984. pap. text ed. 9.95 (ISBN 0-7081-1318-4). Australia N U P.

Gollan, Robin. The Coalminers of New South Wales. 1963. 15.50x (ISBN 0-522-83614-3, Pub. by Melbourne U Pr). Intl Spec Bk.

--Revolutionaries & Reformists: Communism & the Australian Labour Movement, 1920-1955. 2nd ed. 340p. 1985. pap. text ed. 11.50x (ISBN 0-86861-471-8). Allen Unwin.

Gollance, I., ed. A Petite Pallace of Pettie His Pleasure Containing Many Pretie Histories by Him Set Forth in Comely Colours & Most Delightfully Discoursed, 2 vols. 396p. 1982. Repr. Set. lib. bdg. 65.00 (ISBN 0-89760-022-3). Telegraph Bks.

Gollancz, I., ed. Wynnere & Wastoure: Middle English Poem. LC 73-178508. Repr. of 1930 ed. 18.50 (ISBN 0-404-56690-1). AMS Pr.

Gollancz, I., ed. see De Bury, Richard.

Gollancz, I., jt. ed. see Furnivall, F. J.

Gollancz, Israel. Allegory & Mysticism in Shakespeare: A Medievalist on the Merchant of Venice. LC 72-8710. (Studies in Shakespeare, No. 24). 1973. Repr. of 1931 ed. lib. bdg. 31.95x (ISBN 0-8383-1669-7). Haskell.

--Allegory & Mysticism in Shakespeare. LC 73-266. 1931. lib. bdg. 12.50 (ISBN 0-8414-1440-8). Folcroft.

--Pearl: An English Poem of the Fourteenth Century, Re-Set in Modern English. 1918. Repr. 25.00 (ISBN 0-8274-3113-9). R West.

--Pearl & Boccaccio's Olympia. 1921. Repr. 25.00 (ISBN 0-8274-3115-5). R West.

--Studies in the First Folio. LC 73-14893. 1924. lib. bdg. 30.00 (ISBN 0-8414-4466-8). Folcroft.

Gollancz, Israel, ed. & tr. Ambales Saga: Hamlet in Iceland. LC 70-178569. Repr. of 1898 ed. 34.50 (ISBN 0-404-56502-6). AMS Pr.

Gollancz, Israel, ed. A Book of Homage to Shakespeare: To Commemorate the Three Hundred Anniversary of Shakespeare's Death. 556p. 1980. Repr. of 1916 ed. lib. bdg. 100.00 set (ISBN 0-8414-4632-6). Folcroft.

Gollancz, Israel, tr. Pearl. LC 66-27657. (Medieval Library). (Illus.). Repr. of 1926 ed. 17.50 (ISBN 0-8154-0084-5). Cooper Sq.

Gollancz, Victor. A Year of Grace. 1950. 15.95 (ISBN 0-575-00982-9, Pub. by Gollancz England). David & Charles.

Gollancz, Victor, jt. auth. see Greene, Barbara.

Gollancz, Victor, jt. ed. see Greene, Barbara.

Golland, A. Goldie: The Development History of the Gold Star BSA. 79p. pap. 7.95 (ISBN 0-85429-233-0, F233). Haynes Pubns.

Gollasch, Frederick, ed. Language & Literacy: The Selected Writings of Kenneth S. Goodman: Reading, Language & the Classroom Teacher, Vol. II. 200p. 1982. 31.95x (ISBN 0-7100-9005-6). Routledge & Kegan.

Gollattscheck, James F., jt. ed. see Deegan, William L.

Gollattscheck, James F., jt. ed. see Harlacher, Ervin L.

Gollattscheck, James F., et al. College Leadership for Community Renewal: Beyond Community-Based Education. LC 76-19497. (Higher Education Ser.). 1976. 19.95x (ISBN 0-87589-299-X). Jossey-Bass.

Gollay, Elinor & Bennett, Alwina. The College Guide for Students with Disabilities: A Detailed Directory of Higher Education Services, Programs, & Facilities Accessible to Handicapped Students in the United States. 554p. 1985. pap. text ed. 47.50 (ISBN 0-8191-4498-3). U Pr of Amer.

Gollay, Elinor, et al. Coming Back: The Community Experiences of Deinstitutionalized Mentally Retarded People. LC 78-68165. 1978. text ed. 19.50 (ISBN 0-89011-512-5). Abt Bks.

Golledge, Reginald G., jt. auth. see Amedeo, Douglas.

Golledge, Reginald G., jt. auth. see King, Leslie J.

Golledge, Reginald G. & Rayner, John N., eds. Proximity & Preference: Problems in the Multidimensional Analysis of Large Data Sets. LC 81-14634. (Illus.). xxxix, 304p. 1982. 35.00x (ISBN 0-8166-1042-8). U of Minn Pr.

Golledge, Reginald G. & Rushton, Gerard, eds. Spatial Choice & Spatial Behavior: Geographic Essays on the Analysis of Preferences & Perceptions. LC 76-889. (Illus.). 335p. 1976. 16.50x (ISBN 0-8142-0241-1). Ohio St U Pr.

Golledge, Reginald G., jt. ed. see Cox, Kevin R.

Gollehon, John. All about Blackjack. LC 85-70862. 64p. 1985. pap. 1.95 (ISBN 0-914839-02-0). Gollehon Pub Co.

--All about Craps. LC 85-70863. 64p. 1985. pap. 1.95 (ISBN 0-914839-03-9). Gollehon Pub Co.

--All about Slots & Video Poker. 64p. 1985. pap. 1.95 (ISBN 0-914839-04-7). Gollehon Pub Co.

Gollehon, John T. Pay the Line. LC 83-90421. 160p. 1983. pap. 5.95 (ISBN 0-914839-00-4). Gollehon Pub Co.

--Pay the Line. LC 83-90421. 160p. 1984. pap. 3.95 (ISBN 0-914839-01-2). Gollehon Pub Co.

Goller, Claudine. Algonkians of the Eastern Woodlands. (Native Peoples Ser.). 48p. (gr. 2-4). 1984. PLB 9.40 (ISBN 0-531-04683-4). Watts.

Goller, Jeffrey M. Emergency Medical Technician's Review. 120p. 1983. pap. 14.95 (ISBN 0-668-05738-6). ACC.

Goller, Karl H., ed. The Alliterative Morte Arthure: A Reassessment of the Poem. (Arthurian Studies: II). 186p. 1981. 29.50 (ISBN 0-85991-075-X, BAB-03786, Pub. by Boydell & Brewer). Longwood Pub Group.

Gollerbach, M. & Krasavina, L. K. Cumulative Index to the National Bibliography on Algae for 1737 to 1960. 1977. Repr. of 1971 ed. lib. bdg. 75.60x (ISBN 3-87429-118-9). Lubrecht & Cramer.

Gollery, F. B. & Werger, M. J., eds. Tropical Rain Forest Ecosystems, Part A: Structure & Function. (Ecosystems of the World Ser.: Vol. 14A). 382p. 1983. 113.00 (ISBN 0-444-41986-1, I-488-82). Elsevier.

Golley, F. B. & Medina, E., eds. Tropical Ecological Systems: Trends in Terrestrial & Aquatic Research. LC 74-8828. (Illus.). xvi, 398p. 1975. 43.00 (ISBN 0-387-06706-X). Springer-Verlag.

Golley, F. B., jt. ed. see Farnworth, E. G.

Golley, F. B., et al, eds. Small Mammals. LC 74-25658. (International Biological Programme Ser.: No. 5). (Illus.). 448p. 1975. 82.00 (ISBN 0-521-20601-4). Cambridge U Pr.

Golley, Frank B., ed. Ecological Succession. LC 76-52930. (Benchmark Papers in Ecology Ser.: Vol. 5). 1977. 46.50 (ISBN 0-87933-256-5). Van Nos Reinhold.

Golley, John. The Big Drop. (Illus.). 212p. 1982. 19.95 (ISBN 0-86720-635-7). Jane's Pub Inc.
Gollin, Alfred. No Longer an Island: Britain & the Wright Brothers, 1902-1909. LC 84-51314. 488p. 1984. 35.00 (ISBN 0-8047-1265-4). Stanford U Pr.
Gollin, Eugene S., ed. The Comparative Development of Adaptive Skills: Evolutionary Implications. 352p. 1985. text ed. 36.00 (ISBN 0-89859-519-3). L Erlbaum Assocs.
--Developmental Plasticity: Behavioral & Biological Aspects of Variations in Development. LC 80-2331. (Developmental Psychology Ser.). 1981. 37.50 (ISBN 0-12-289620-3). Acad Pr.
--Malformations of Development: Biological & Psychological Sources & Consequences. LC 83-10020. (Developmental Psychology Ser.). 1983. 49.00 (ISBN 0-12-289630-0). Acad Pr.
Gollin, Gillian L. Moravians in Two Worlds: A Study of Changing Communities. LC 67-19653. 302p. 1967. 29.00x (ISBN 0-231-03033-9). Columbia U Pr.
Gollin, James. Eliza's Galiardo. 160p. 1983. 10.95 (ISBN 0-312-24244-1). St Martin.
--Verona Passamezzo. LC 85-7079. (Crime Club Ser.). 192p. 1985. 12.95 (ISBN 0-385-19483-8). Doubleday.
Gollin, Rita, jt. auth. see Hilen, Andrew.
Gollin, Rita K. Portraits of Nathaniel Hawthorne: An Iconography. LC 83-12155. 122p. 1984. 30.00 (ISBN 0-87580-087-4). N Ill U Pr.
Gollmar, Robert. Edward Gein: America's Most Bizarre Murderer. LC 80-83932. (Illus.). 254p. 1981. 9.95 (ISBN 0-87319-020-3). C Hallberg.
Gollmar, Robert H. Edward Gein. 256p. 1984. pap. 3.50 (ISBN 0-523-42210-5). Pinnacle Bks.
--Tales of a Country Judge. LC 79-65286. (Illus.). 192p. 1981. 9.95x (ISBN 0-87319-018-1). C Hallberg.
Gollner, Andrew B. Social Change & Corporate Strategy: The Expanding Role of Public Affairs. Chase, W. Howard, ed. LC 83-81612. (Illus.). 205p. 1984. 29.95 (ISBN 0-913869-00-7). Issue Action Pubns.
Gollner, Marie-Louise, tr. see Georgiades, Thrysbulos.
Gollnick. Dynamic Structure of Household Expenditures in the Federal Republic of Germany. LC 74-84207. 1975. 30.00 (ISBN 0-444-10796-7, North-Holland). Elsevier.
Gollnick, Daniel A. Basic Radiation Protection Technology. (Illus.). 454p. 1983. text ed. 42.00 (ISBN 0-916339-01-7); pap. text ed. 33.00 (ISBN 0-916339-00-9). Pacific Rad.
--Experimental Radiological Health Physics. LC 77-7638. (Illus.). 260p. 1978. 30.00 (ISBN 0-08-023201-9); pap. 12.50 (ISBN 0-08-020524-0). Pergamon.
--Radiation Protection Technology: Student Manual, a Self-Study Course. 195p. 1984. wkbk. 175.00 (ISBN 0-916339-02-5). Pacific Rad.
Gollnick, James. Flesh As Transformation Symbol in the Theology of Anselm of Canterbury. LC 85-10502. (Texts & Studies in Religion: Vol. 22). 336p. 1985. 59.95x (ISBN 0-88946-810-9). E Mellen.
Golloch, Alfred, et al. Anorganisch-Chemische Praparate: Darstellung und Charakterisierung Ausgewahlter Verbindungen. (Illus.). xvi, 324p. (Ger.). 1985. 19.20x (ISBN 3-11-004821-3). De Gruyter.
Gollock, Georgina A. Daughters of Africa. LC 71-89000. (Illus.). Repr. of 1932 ed. 19.75x (ISBN 0-8371-1765-8, GOD&, Pub. by Negro U Pr). Greenwood.
--Lives of Eminent Africans. LC 70-91256. Repr. of 1928 ed. cancelled (ISBN 0-8371-2062-4, GOE&, Pub. by Negro U Pr). Greenwood.
--Sons of Africa. LC 75-89001. Repr. of 1928 ed. 19.75x (ISBN 0-8371-1746-1, GSA&). Greenwood.
Golloday, Frederick L. & Haveman, Robert H. The Economic Impacts of Tax-Transfer Policy: Regional & Distributional Effects. 1977. 19.50 (ISBN 0-12-288850-2). Acad Pr.
Gollomb, Joseph. Albert Schweitzer: Genius in the Jungle. (Illus.). 149p. (gr. 7-9). 1949. 10.95 (ISBN 0-8149-0308-8). Vanguard.
--Master Man Hunters. 1926. 25.00 (ISBN 0-932062-65-2). Sharon Hill.
--Spies. 399p. Repr. of 1928 ed. lib. bdg. 19.40x (ISBN 0-88411-571-2, Pub. by Aeonian Pr). Amereon Ltd.
Gollon, John E. Chess Variations: Ancient, Regional & Modern. LC 68-11975. (Illus.). 1973. pap. 6.25 (ISBN 0-8048-1122-9). C E Tuttle.
Gollub, J. P., jt. ed. see Swinney, H. L.
Gollub, Wendy L., jt. auth. see Shulkin, Sunny.
Gollwitzer, Gerhard. Drawing Step-by-Step. LC 83-4960. (Illus.). 160p. (Orig.). 1984. pap. 4.95 (ISBN 0-8069-7748-5). Sterling.
--Express Yourself in Drawing. 1976. pap. 1.95 (ISBN 0-346-12238-4). Cornerstone.
--Freehand Drawing. LC 83-27191. (Illus.). 128p. (Orig.). 1984. pap. 4.95 (ISBN 0-8069-7814-7). Sterling.
--Sex, Eros & Marital Love. pap. 0.75 (ISBN 0-87785-104-2). Swedenborg.
Gollwitzer, Heinz. Europe in the Age of Imperialism, Eighteen Eighty to Nineteen Fourteen. (Library of World Civilization). (Illus.). 1979. pap. 7.95x (ISBN 0-393-95104-9). Norton.
Gollwitzer, Helmut. An Introduction to Protestant Theology. Cairns, David, tr. LC 82-4798. 236p. 1982. pap. 12.95 (ISBN 0-664-24415-7). Westminster.
--Unwilling Journey: A Diary from Russia. LC 74-7610. 316p. 1974. Repr. of 1965 ed. lib. bdg. 35.00x (ISBN 0-8371-7585-2, GOUJ). Greenwood.
Gollwitzer, P. M., jt. auth. see Wicklund, R. A.
Golob, Eugene O. Isms: A History & Evaluation. facs. ed. LC 68-20302. (Essay Index Reprint Ser). 1954. 25.00 (ISBN 0-8369-0480-X). Ayer Co Pubs.
--Meline Tariff: French Agriculture & Nationalist Economic Policy. LC 68-58582. (Columbia University. Studies in the Social Sciences: No. 506). Repr. of 1944 ed. 21.50 (ISBN 0-404-51506-1). AMS Pr.
Gologie, Ralph V. A Study in Symbolism: An Empirical Foundation of Graphology. LC 73-86368. 256p. 1973. pap. 5.95x (ISBN 0-915286-00-9). Landrum & Assocs.
Golomb, Claire. Young Children's Sculpture & Drawing: A Study in Representational Development. LC 73-89707. 192p. 1974. 14.00x (ISBN 0-674-96600-7). Harvard U Pr.
Golomb, Harvey, jt. ed. see Coltman, Charles A., Jr.
Golomb, Louis. An Anthropology of Curing in Multiethnic Thailand. LC 84-8649. (Illinois Studies In Anthropolgy: No. 15). (Illus.). 328p. 1985. 23.95x (ISBN 0-252-01170-8). U of Ill Pr.
--Brokers of Morality: Thai Ethnic Adaptation in a Rural Malaysian Setting. LC 78-4141. (Asian Studies at Hawaii: No. 23). 1979. pap. text ed. 12.00x (ISBN 0-8248-0629-8). UH Pr.
Golomb, Morris. Know Jewish Living & Enjoy It. LC 78-54569. (Illus.). (gr. 3-7). 1981. 11.95 (ISBN 0-88400-054-0). Shengold.
--Know Your Festivals & Enjoy Them. 3rd ed. LC 72-90771. (Illus.). 189p. (gr. 3-6). 1973. 10.00 (ISBN 0-88400-035-4). Shengold.
Golomb, Patricia C., ed. see Cabot, Val.
Golomb, Patricia C., ed. see Fox, Claire R.
Golomb, S., et al. Digital Communications with Space Applications. (Illus.). 228p. 1981. 18.95 (ISBN 0-932146-05-8). Peninsula CA.
Golomb, Soloman. Shift Register Sequences. rev. ed. 1981. pap. 32.80 (ISBN 0-89412-048-4). Aegean Park Pr.
Golombeck, Harry. Beginning Chess. 220p. 1981. pap. 3.95 (ISBN 0-14-046412-3). Penguin.
Golombek, H. The Chess Artists. 1986. price not set (ISBN 0-08-024108-5); price not set (ISBN 0-08-024107-7). Pergamon.
--The Game of Chess. (Handbooks Ser.). 304p. 1955. pap. 3.95 (ISBN 0-14-046024-1). Penguin.
Golombek, H., jt. auth. see Reti, Richard.
Golombek, Harvey & Garfinkel, Barry D. Adolescent & Mood Disturbance. LC 82-13044. xvi, 285p. 1983. text ed. 27.50 (ISBN 0-8236-0085-8). Intl Univs Pr.
Golomber, H., jt. auth. see Griffith, R. C.
Golombok, Susan, jt. auth. see Curran, Valerie.
Golomshtok, Eugenii A. The Old Stone Age in European Russia. LC 76-44723. (Illus.). 368p. 1983. Repr. of 1938 ed. 76.50 (ISBN 0-404-15927-3). AMS Pr.
Golomshtok, Igor, jt. auth. see Rueschemeyer, Marilyn.
Golonka, Nancy. How to Protect What's Yours. LC 83-3825. 304p. 1983. 11.95 (ISBN 0-87491-557-0); pap. 6.95 (ISBN 0-87491-560-0). Acropolis.
Golopentia-Eretescu, Sanda, jt. auth. see Vasiliu, Emanuel.
Golos, Natalie & Golbitz, Frances G. If This Is Tuesday, It Must Be Chicken. 2nd ed. LC 83-47676. 150p. 1983. pap. 7.95 (ISBN 0-87983-339-4). Keats.
--If This Is Tuesday It Must Be Chicken or How to Rotate Your Food for Better Health. Martin, Joan, ed. LC 81-13509. 109p. (Orig.). 1981. pap. 6.95 (ISBN 0-941962-00-8). Keats Pub.
Golos, Natalie, et al. Coping with Your Allergies. 1979. 18.95 (ISBN 0-671-24078-1). S&S.
Golovanov, L. Todo Es Armonia en la Naturaleza. 200p. (Span.). 1982. pap. 3.95 (ISBN 0-8285-2498-X, Pub. by Mir Pubs USSR). Imported Pubns.
Golovin, I. N. Kurchatov, I. V., Biography of the Soviet Nuclear Scientist. Dougherty, William H., tr. LC 68-58753. 1968. pap. 4.00x (ISBN 0-911706-11-9). Selbstverlag.
Golovin, Nikolai N. & Bubnov, A. D. Problem of the Pacific in the Twentieth Century. LC 79-111758. (American Imperialism: Viewpoints of United States Foreign Policy, 1898-1941). 1970. Repr. of 1922 ed. 17.00 (ISBN 0-405-02023-6). Ayer Co Pubs.
Golovin, Pavel N. Civil & Savage Encounters: The Worldly Travel Letters of an Imperial Russian Navy Officer, 1860-61. Dmytryshyn, Basil, tr. from Russian. Crownhart-Vaughn, E. A., ed. (North Pacific Studies: No. 5). (Illus.). 224p. (Eng.). 1983. 21.95x (ISBN 0-295-95953-3, Pub by Oreg Hist Soc). U of Wash Pr.
--Civil & Savage Encounters: The Worldly Travel Letters of an Imperial Russian Navy Officer, 1860-61. Dmytryshyn, Basil & Crownhart-Vaughan, E. A., trs. from Rus. (North Pacific Studies: No. 5). (Illus.). 208p. (Orig.). 1983. 21.95 (ISBN 0-87595-067-1, Western Imprints); pap. 12.95 (ISBN 0-87595-095-7, Western Imprints). Oreg Hist Soc.
--The End of Russian America: Captain P. N. Golovin's Last Report, 1862. Dymtryshyn, Basil & Crownhart-Vaughan, E. A. P., trs. from Rus. LC 79-84285. (North Pacific Studies: No. 4). (Illus.). 249p. 1979. 21.95 (ISBN 0-295-95955-X); pap. 12.95. U of Wash Pr.
Golovin, S. A., jt. auth. see Puskar, A.
Golovina, L. & Yaglom, I. Induction in Geometry. 133p. 1979. pap. 2.95 (ISBN 0-8285-1534-4, Pub. by Mir Pubs USSR). Imported Pubns.
Golovina, L. I. & Yaglom, I. M. Induccion en la Geometria. 126p. (Span.). 1976. pap. 2.95 (ISBN 0-8285-1687-1, Pub. by Mir Pubs USSR). Imported Pubns.
Golovine, Nicholas N. The Russian Army in the World War. (Economic & Social History of the World War, Russian Ser.). 1931. 75.00x (ISBN 0-317-27553-4). Elliots Bks.
Golovkin, K. K. Parametric-Normed Spaces & Normed Massives. (Proceedings of the Steklov Institute of Mathematics: No. 106). 1971. 39.00 (ISBN 0-8218-3006-6, STEKLO-106). Am Math.
Golovkin, K. K., et al. Four Papers on Functions of Real Variables. LC 51-5559. (Translations Ser.: No. 2, Vol. 81). 1969. 36.00 (ISBN 0-8218-1781-7, TRANS 2-81). Am Math.
Golovnin, V. N. Around the World on the "Kamchatka," 1817-1819. Wiswell, Ella L., tr. from Rus. LC 79-15230. (Illus.). 1979. text ed. 20.00x (ISBN 0-8248-0640-9). UH Pr.
Golovsky, Valery. The Motion Picture Industry in the USSR, 1972-1982. Rimberg, John, ed. Hill, Steven, tr. 175p. 1985. 25.00 (ISBN 0-88233-970-2). Ardis Pubs.
Golphenee, Lucille B. Isaac's Chosen Wife. (Arch Book Ser.: No. 21). 1984. pap. 0.99 (59-1282). Concordia.
Golsan, Gordon G., jt. auth. see Nicholson, James A.
Golschmidt, Ernst F., jt. auth. see Boas, Ernest P.
Golson, G. Barry, ed. The Playboy Interview II. 736p. 1983. (Wideview); pap. 10.95 (ISBN 0-399-50769-8). Putnam Pub Group.
Golson, G. Barry, ed. see Sheff, David.
Golson, J., jt. auth. see Polach, H. A.
Gol'Stein, E. G. Theory of Convex Programming. LC 72-3180. (Translations of Mathematical Monographs: Vol. 36). 57p. 1972. 24.00 (ISBN 0-8218-1586-5, MMONO-36). Am Math.
Golstein, Larry Joel & Weist, Edward. TI 99-4A: User's Guide. cancelled 10.95 (ISBN 0-89303-890-3). Brady Comm.
Golstein, Pierre, jt. ed. see Clark, William R.
Golt, Rick & Lagundimao, Clemente, Jr. Hawai'i Hawai'i. LC 81-50935. (Illus.). 128p. 1981. 12.95 (ISBN 0-8248-0772-3). UH Pr.
Golt, Sidney. The GATT Negotiations: A Guide to the Issues, 1973-75. 82p. 1974. 2.50 (ISBN 0-902594-24-9, BN14). Inst C D Howe.
--The GATT Negotiations, 1973-79: The Closing Stage. LC 78-54114. (British-North American Committee Ser.). 70p. 1978. 3.00 (ISBN 0-902594-32-X). Natl Planning.
--Trade Issues in the Mid-Nineteen Eighties. (British-North American Committee: No. 32). 94p. 1982. 7.00 (ISBN 0-902594-42-7). Inst C D Howe.
--World Trade Issues in the Mid-1980s. (British-North American Committee Ser.). 112p. 1982. pap. 7.00 (ISBN 0-902594-42-7, BN32-NPA198). Natl Planning.
Golterman, H. Methods for Chemical Analysis of Fresh Waters. 2nd ed. (Blackwell Scientific Pubns.: IBP Handbk. No. 8). (Illus.). 1978. pap. 17.50 (ISBN 0-632-00459-2, B 1888-6). Mosby.
Golterman, H., jt. ed. see Povoledo, D.
Golterman, H. L., ed. Interactions Between Sediments & Fresh Water. 1977. pap. 34.00 (ISBN 90-6193-563-6, Pub. by Junk Pubs. Netherlands). Kluwer Academic.
--Interactions Between Sediments & Fresh Water. (Illus.). 1977. pap. 52.00 (ISBN 90-220-0632-8, PDC47, PUDOC). Unipub.
Golther, Wolfgang. Nordische Literaturgeschichte. (Ger.). 1973. Repr. of 1905 ed. 30.00 (ISBN 0-8274-0200-7). R West.
--Parzival und der Gral in der Dichtung des Mittelalters und der Neuzeit. LC 74-178535. Repr. of 1925 ed. 32.50 (ISBN 0-404-56611-1). AMS Pr.
Golton, Margaret A. Professional Potpourri: Seeds Are Sown. (Illus., Orig.). 1984. pap. 9.95 (ISBN 0-942952-01-4). Frank Pubns.
--Unlock Your Potential: Know Your Brain & How to Use It. LC 82-2490. 80p. (Orig.). 1982. pap. 5.95 (ISBN 0-942952-00-6). Frank Pubns.
--Your Brain at Work: A New View of Personality & Behavior. 114p. (Orig.). 1983. pap. 7.95 (ISBN 0-942952-01-4). Frank Pubns.
Goltry, T. S., jt. auth. see Akin, Johnnye.
Goltz, Ronald. Can High Blood Pressure Be Predicted? (Illus.). 1978. wkbk. 20.00 (ISBN 0-916750-13-2). Dayton Labs.
--Checking Cranial Nerves. 1978. wkbk. 20.00 (ISBN 0-916750-14-0, CX-17). Dayton Labs.
Goltz, Ronald E. G-Force & Man. (Illus.). 1978. 20.00 (ISBN 0-916750-22-1). Dayton Labs.
--Glucose: Up or Down. (Illus.). 1978. 20.00 (ISBN 0-916750-23-X). Dayton Labs.
Golub, Edward S. The Cellular Basis of the Immune Response. rev. & 2nd ed. LC 80-28080. (Illus.). 325p. 1981. pap. text ed. 18.95x (ISBN 0-87893-212-7). Sinauer Assoc.
Golub, Gene H. & Van Loan, Charles F. Matrix Computations. LC 83-7897. (Mathematical Sciences Ser.: No. 3). 496p. 1983. text ed. 49.50x (ISBN 0-8018-3010-9); pap. text ed. 24.95x (ISBN 0-8018-3011-7). Johns Hopkins.
Golub, Gene H., ed. Studies in Numerical Analysis. 422p. 1985. 42.00 (ISBN 0-88385-126-1, MAS-24); members 31.00 (ISBN 0-317-37231-9). Math Assn.
Golub, Gene H. & Oliger, Joseph, eds. Numerical Analysis: Symposia in Applied Mathematics, Vol. 22. LC 78-11096. (Proceedings of Symposia in Applied Mathematics). 135p. 1980. pap. 13.00 (ISBN 0-8218-0122-8, PSAPM-22). Am Math.
Golub, Gene H., jt. ed. see De Boor, Carl.
Golub, P. The Bolsheviks & the Armed Forces in Three Revolutions. 304p. 1979. 6.95 (ISBN 0-8285-0394-X, Pub. by Progress Pubs USSR). Imported Pubns.
Golub, Sharon, ed. Health & the Female Adolescent. LC 84-19772. 160p. 1985. pap. text ed. 8.95 (ISBN 0-918393-05-1). Harrington Pk.
--Health Care of the Female Adolescent. LC 84-4560. (Women & Health Ser.: Vol. 9, Nos. 2-3). 141p. 1984. text ed. 22.95 (ISBN 0-86656-298-2, B298); pap. text ed. 16.95 (ISBN 0-86656-434-9). Haworth Pr.
--Lifting the Curse of Menstruation. LC 84-19804. 176p. 1985. pap. text ed. 7.95 (ISBN 0-918393-06-X). Harrington Pk.
--Lifting the Curse of Menstruation: A Feminist Appraisal of the Influence of Menstruation on Women's Lives. LC 83-12723. (Women & Health Ser.: Vol 8, Nos. 2/3). 156p. 1983. text ed. 22.95 (ISBN 0-86656-242-7, B242); pap. text ed. 16.95 (ISBN 0-86656-422-5). Haworth Pr.
--Menarche: The Physiological, Psychological & Social Effects of the Onset of Menstruation. LC 82-48105. 352p. 1983. 30.00x (ISBN 0-669-05982-X). Lexington Bks.
Golub, Sharon & Freedman, Rita J., eds. Health Needs of Women as They Age. LC 85-7642. (Women & Health Ser.: Vol. 10, Nos. 2 & 3). 144p. 1985. text ed. 24.95 (ISBN 0-86656-413-6); pap. text ed. 19.95 (ISBN 0-86656-414-4). Haworth Pr.
--Health Needs of Women as They Age. LC 85-7642. 160p. 1985. pap. 7.95 (ISBN 0-918393-23-X). Harrington Pk.
Golub, Spencer. Evreinov: The Theatre of Paradox & Transformation. Beckerman, Bernard, ed. LC 84-80. (Theater & Dramatic Studies: No. 19). 328p. 1984. 44.95 (ISBN 0-8357-1540-X). UMI Res Pr.
Golubev, G. N. & Biswas, A. K., eds. Interregional Water Transfers: Projects & Problems: Proceedings of the Task Force Meeting, International Institute for Applied Systems Analysis, Laxenburg, Austria, Oct. 1977. 1979. text ed. 32.00 (ISBN 0-08-022430-X). Pergamon.
Golubev, V. Lyudmila Turisheva. 40p. 1979. pap. 2.95 (ISBN 0-8285-1546-8, Pub. by Progress Pubs USSR). Imported Pubns.
--Nikolai Andrianov. 48p. 1979. pap. 2.95 (ISBN 0-8285-1550-6, Pub. by Progress Pubs USSR). Imported Pubns.
--Soviet Gymnastics Stars. 220p. 1979. 22.00 (ISBN 0-8285-1650-2, Pub. by Progress Pubs USSR). Imported Pubns.
Golubev, V. S. & Garibyants, A. A. Heterogeneous Processes of Geochemical Migration. LC 73-140829. 145p. 1971. 27.50x (ISBN 0-306-10860-7, Consultants). Plenum Pub.
Golubitsky, M. & Guillemin, V. W. Stable Mappings & Their Singularities: Second Corrected Printing. (Graduate Texts in Mathematics: Vol. 14). (Illus.). 209p. 1974. 29.50 (ISBN 0-387-90072-1). Springer-Verlag.
Golubitsky, M. & Schaeffer, D. Bifurcations & Groups in Bifurcation Theory I. (Applied Mathematical Sciences Ser.: Vol. 51). (Illus.). 320p. 1985. 38.00 (ISBN 0-387-90999-0). Springer-Verlag.
Golubova, E. Art of the Autonomous Republics of the Russian Federation. 1973. 40.00x (ISBN 0-317-14221-6, Pub. by Collet's). State Mutual Bk.
Golubovskis, Georgs M. Crazy Dreaming: The Anderson Campaign 1980. LC 81-51946. 130p. 1981. pap. 4.95 (ISBN 0-9606322-0-4). Talking Seal.
Golumbic, Martin C. Algorithmic Graph Theory & Perfect Graphs. LC 79-22956. (Computer Science & Applied Mathematics Ser.). 1980. 47.50 (ISBN 0-12-289260-7). Acad Pr.
Goluzin, G. M. Geometric Theory of Functions of a Complex Variable. LC 70-82894. (Translations of Mathematical Monographs: Vol. 26). 676p. 1983. pap. 71.00 (ISBN 0-8218-1576-8, MONO-26). Am Math.
Golyakhovsky, Vladimir. Russian Doctor: A Surgeon's Life in Contemporary Russia & Why He Chose to Leave. (Illus.). 384p. 1983. 17.95 (ISBN 0-312-69609-4, Pub. by Marek). St Martin.
Golyshkin, V. Little Magicians of the Large House. 40p. 1982. pap. 2.99 (ISBN 0-8285-2362-2, Pub. by Raduga Pubs USSR). Imported Pubns.
Golz, Jon L. Europe Import Guide. LC 83-16697. 68p. 1983. pap. 4.95 (ISBN 0-914123-00-9). J L Golz Co.
Golz, Judy, jt. auth. see Briscoe, Jill.
Golze, Alfred R., ed. Handbook of Dam Engineering. 1977. 68.50 (ISBN 0-442-22752-3). Van Nos Reinhold.

Golzen, G. How Architects Get Work. 96p. 1984. pap. text ed. 19.50x (ISBN 0-317-18927-1, Pub. by Architectural Pr England). Humanities.
Golzen, Godfrey. Working for Yourself. 1981p. 1985. 18.75 (ISBN 0-85038-887-2). Nichols Pub.
Golzio, Vincent. Raphael: His Life, His Art, His Fortunes, 2 vols. (The Great Masters of the World Ser.). (Illus.). 765p. 1982. Repr. of 1968 ed. 237.45 (ISBN 0-89901-089-X). Found Class Reprints.
Goma, Eulalia. Diccionario Magico Infantil. 7th ed. 50p. (Span.). 1978. 10.75 (ISBN 84-324-0190-0, S-26065). French & Eur.
--Diccionario Magico Infantil En Seis Lenguas. 2nd ed. 96p. (Span., Catalan, Vasco, Gallic, Fr. & Eng.). 1978. 20.25 (ISBN 84-324-0249-4, S-50028). French & Eur.
Goma, F. S. De see Marole, L. T. & De Goma, F. S.
Gomara, Francisco Lopez De. The Conquest of the West India. Repr. of 1578 ed. 60.00x (ISBN 0-8201-1193-7). Schol Facsimiles.
--Cortes: The Life of the Conqueror of Mexico by His Secretary Francisco Lopez de Gomara. Simpson, Lesley B., ed. & tr. LC 64-13474. 1964. pap. 5.95 (ISBN 0-520-00493-0). U of Cal Pr.
Gomathi Krishnamachari & Kakar, I. B. Discovering Science, 2 bks. 205p. (Orig.). 1983. Bk. 1. pap. text ed. 3.95x (ISBN 0-86131-410-7); Bk. 2. pap. text ed. 3.95x (ISBN 0-86131-411-5). Apt Bks.
Gombas, P. & Kisdi, D. Wave Mechanics & Its Applications. LC 73-5789. 250p. 1974. text ed. 28.00 (ISBN 0-08-016979-1). Pergamon.
Gomberg, Adeline W. Reading Activities Manual to Aid the Disadvantaged. LC 66-19258. (Illus.). 1966. pap. text ed. 2.50x (ISBN 0-8134-6878-7, 6878). Interstate.
Gomberg, David R., jt. auth. see O'Hara, Robert P.
Gomberg, E. L., et al, eds. Alcohol, Science, & Society Revisited. (Illus.). 432p. 1982. text ed. 20.00x (ISBN 0-472-10024-6); pap. text ed. 14.95x (ISBN 0-472-08028-8). U of Mich Pr.
Gombin, Richard. The Radical Tradition: A Study in Modern Revolutionary Thought. LC 78-31150. 1979. 20.00 (ISBN 0-312-66186-X). St Martin.
Gombos, George M., ed. Handbook of Ophthalmologic Emergencies. 2nd ed. LC 76-62573. (Illus.). 1977. pap. 18.95 (ISBN 0-87488-633-3). Med Exam.
Gombos, Gyula, ed. Szabo Dezso Es a Magyar Miniszterelnokok. (Hungarian.). 1975. 6.00 (ISBN 0-911050-43-4). Occidental.
Gombosi, Marilyn. A Day of Solemn Thanksgiving: Moravian Music for the Fourth of July, 1783, in Salem, North Carolina. LC 75-6533. x, 218p. 1977. 25.00x (ISBN 0-8078-1275-7). U of NC Pr.
Gombosi, Marilyn, ed. Catalog of the Johannes Herbst Collection. (Illus.). 255p. 17.50 (ISBN 0-8078-1124-6). Moravian Music.
Gombosi, Otto, ed. see Capirola, Vincenzo.
Gombrich, E. H. The Heritage of Apelles: Studies in the Art of the Renaissance. LC 76-3080. 240p. 1976. 34.50x (ISBN 0-8014-1012-6). Cornell U Pr.
--Homage to Kokoschka. (Illus.). 64p. (Orig.). 1984. pap. 2.95 (ISBN 0-901486-94-9, Pub. by Victoria & Albert Mus UK). Faber & Faber.
--Ideals & Idols: Essays on Values in History & in Art. 232p. 1979. 50.00x (ISBN 0-7148-2009-1, Pub. by Phaidon Pr). State Mutual Bk.
--The Image & the Eye: Further Studies in the Psychology of Pictorial Representation. LC 81-68788. 320p. 1982. 42.50x (ISBN 0-8014-1484-9). Cornell U Pr.
--Meditations on a Hobby Horse: And Other Essays on the Theory of Art. LC 84-28112. (Illus.). 256p. 1985. pap. 14.95 (ISBN 0-226-30215-6). U of Chicago Pr.
--Norm & Form: Studies in the Art of the Renaissance, No. I. LC 84-28113. (Illus.). 316p. 1985. pap. 14.95 (ISBN 0-226-30216-4). U of Chicago Pr.
--The Sense of Order: A Study in the Psychology of Decorative Art. LC 77-83898. (Illus.). 422p. 1984. pap. text ed. 24.95x (ISBN 0-8014-9249-1). Cornell U Pr.
--The Story of Art. 14th ed. (Illus.). 528p. 1985. pap. text ed. 20.95 (ISBN 0-13-850066-5). P-H.
--Symbolic Images: Studies in the Art of the Renaissance, No. II. LC 84-28111. (Illus.). 356p. 1985. pap. 14.95 (ISBN 0-226-30217-2). U of Chicago Pr.
--Tributes: Interpreters of Our Cultural Tradition. LC 83-43149. (Illus.). 272p. 1984. 34.95x (ISBN 0-8014-1703-1). Cornell U Pr.
Gombrich, E. H., jt. auth. see Gregory, R. L.
Gombrich, E. H., et al. Art, Perception & Reality. LC 76-186514. (Alvin & Fanny Blaustein Thalheimer Lectures). (Illus.). 142p. 1972. pap. 4.95x (ISBN 0-8018-1552-5). Johns Hopkins.
Gombrich, Ernst. Nature & Art as Needs of the Mind: Fourth Leverhulme Memorial Lecture. 25p. 1981. 25.00x (ISBN 0-85323-354-3, Pub. by Liverpool Univ England). State Mutual Bk.
Gombrich, Ernst H. Art & Illusion: A Study in the Psychology of Pictorial Presentation. 2nd ed. (Bollingen Ser.: Vol. 35). (A. W. Mellon Lecture No. 5). 1961. 60.00x (ISBN 0-691-09785-2); pap. 14.50 (ISBN 0-691-01750-6, 156). Princeton U Pr.
--The Sense of Order: A Study in the Psychology of Decorative Art. LC 77-83898. (Illus.). 1979. 48.50x (ISBN 0-8014-1143-2). Cornell U Pr.
Gombrich, Richard, jt. ed. see Bechert, Heinz.
Gombrich, Richard, jt. ed. see Cone, Margaret.
Gombrowicz, Witold. A Kind of Testament. Hamilton, Alisdair, tr. from Polish. 160p. 1982. pap. 8.95 (ISBN 0-7145-0916-7, Dist by Scribner). M Boyars.
--Possessed: Or the Secret of Myslotch. Underwood, J. A., tr. from Polish. 221p. 1981. 7.95 (ISBN 0-7145-2738-6, Dist by Scribner). M Boyars.
--Three Novels: Ferdydurke, Pornografia, & Cosmos. Mosbacher, Eric & Hamilton, Alastair, trs. from Polish. 1978. pap. 9.95 (ISBN 0-394-17067-9, E720, Ever). Grove.
Gombrowitz, Witold. A Kind of Testament. Hamilton, Alastair, tr. LC 72-89199. 158p. 1973. 14.95 (ISBN 0-87722-051-4). Temple U Pr.
Gomel, Charles. Causes Financieres De la Revolution Francaise, 2 vols. 1892-93. Set. 55.00 (ISBN 0-8337-1374-4); 30.00 ea. B Franklin.
--Histoire Financiere De la Legislative & De la Convention, 2 vols. LC 76-6475. 1902-05. Repr. 55.00. B Franklin.
--Histoire Financiere De l'Assemblee Constituante, 2 vols. LC 70-6433. 1896-97. Repr. 55.00 (ISBN 0-8337-1374-4). B Franklin.
Gomel, Victor. Microsurgery in Female Infertility. 1983. 75.00 (ISBN 0-316-31988-0). Little.
Gomella, C & Mounier, J. P., eds. Eutrophication & Water Supply: Proceedings of the Specialised Conference of the IWSA held in Vienna, Austria, Oct. 7-9, 1981. (Illus.). 284p. 1983. pap. 66.00 (ISBN 0-08-030419-2). Pergamon.
Gomella, L. G. & Olding, M. J., eds. Clinician's Pocket Reference: A Scutmonkey's Handbook. 4th ed. 1983. pap. 17.50x (ISBN 0-8385-1163-5). ACC.
Gomer. Prisma Modern Engelsk-Svensk, Svensk-Engelsk Pocket Dictionary. pap. 11.00 (ISBN 0-317-19083-0, SW208). Vanous.
Gomer, Charles J., jt. auth. see Doiron, Daniel R.
Gomer, E. Swedish Modern Pocket Dictionary: Svensk-Engelsk, Engelsk-Svensk Grammatik Parlor. (Swedish & Eng.). 1981. text ed. 11.00x (ISBN 91-518-1148-0, SW-208). Vanous.
Gomer, R., ed. Interactions on Metal Surfaces, Vol. 4. LC 75-1281. (Topics in Applied Physics Ser). (Illus.). 340p. 1975. 46.00 (ISBN 0-387-07094-X). Springer-Verlag.
Gomer, Robert. Field Emission & Field Ionization. LC 60-15237. (Harvard Monographs in Applied Science: No. 9). (Illus.). pap. 51.80 (ISBN 0-317-09155-7, 2002823). Bks Demand UMI.
Gomersall, A. & Farmer, P. Robotics. (Illus.). 200p. 1984. 45.00 (ISBN 0-387-15010-2). Springer-Verlag.
Gomersall, Alan. Machine Intelligence: An International Bibliography with Abstracts of Sensors in Automated Manufacturing. 240p. 1984. 50.50 (ISBN 0-387-13191-4). Springer Verlag.
Gomersall, Alan & Farmer, Penny, eds. Robotics Bibliography: 1970-1981. 230p. 1982. text ed. 68.00x (ISBN 0-903608-19-7, Pub by IFSPUBS). Scholium Intl.
Gomersall, Robert. The Tragedie of Lodovisk Sforza, Duke of Millan: From Quarto of 1628. Pearn, B. R., ed. (Material for the Study of the Old English Drama Ser.: No. 2, Vol. 8). pap. 16.00 (ISBN 0-317-15233-5). Kraus Repr.
Gomery, Douglas. The Hollywood Studio System. 240p. 1985. 25.00 (ISBN 0-312-38845-4). St Martin.
Gomery, Douglas, jt. auth. see Allen, Robert C.
Gomery, Douglas, jt. ed. see Balio, Tino.
Gomes, jt. auth. see Lincoln.
Gomes, Albert M. All Papa's Children. 113p. (Orig.). (gr. 10-12). 1978. pap. 5.00x (ISBN 0-906403-00-6). Three Continents.
Gomes, Alberto G. Ecological Adaptation & Population Change: Semang Foragers & Temuan Horticulturists in West Malaysia. LC 82-18286. (East-West Environment & Policy Institute Research Report: No. 12). vii, 51p. (Orig.). 1982. pap. text ed. 3.00 (ISBN 0-86638-034-5). E W Center HI.
Gomes, Bernadette. Maile & the Marvelous One. LC 84-4715. (Treasury of Children's Hawaiian Stories Ser.). (Illus.). (gr. 3-6). 1984. 5.95 (ISBN 0-916630-40-4). Pr Pacifica.
Gomes, Celso P. & Keil, Klaus. Brazilian Stone Meteorites. LC 80-5333. (Illus.). 192p. 1980. 25.00x (ISBN 0-8263-0543-1). U of NM Pr.
Gomes, Edwin H. Seventeen Years Among the Sea Dyaks of Borneo: A Record of Intimate Association with the Natives of the Bornean Jungles. LC 77-86993. (Illus.). 408p. Repr. of 1911 ed. 46.50 (ISBN 0-404-16718-7). AMS Pr.
Gomes, Francisco L. Essai sur la Theorie De l'Economie Politique et De Ses Rapports Auec la Morale et le Droit. LC 77-140976. (Philosophy Ser). 1971. Repr. of 1867 ed. lib. bdg. 21.00 (ISBN 0-8337-1375-2). B Franklin.
Gomes, Leonard. International Economic Problems. 1979. 25.00x (ISBN 0-312-42158-3). St Martin.
Gomes, P. I., ed. Rural Development in the Caribbean. 272p. (Orig.). 1985. 32.50 (ISBN 0-312-69599-3); pap. 14.95 (ISBN 0-312-69598-5). St Martin.
Gomes, Paulo E. & Gomes, Salles. P's Three Women. 144p. 1984. pap. 3.50 (ISBN 0-380-86256-5, 86256-5, Bard). Avon.
Gomes, Peter. Lent. LC 84-18756. (Proclamation 3 C Ser.). 64p. 1985. pap. 3.50 (ISBN 0-8006-4127-2). Fortress.
Gomes, Peter, ed. The Pilgrim Society. 1971. 0.75 (ISBN 0-940628-30-9). Pilgrim Hall.
Gomes, Peter J., jt. auth. see Geller, Lawrence D.
Gomes, Peter J., jt. auth. see Kee, Howard C.
Gomes, Salles, jt. auth. see Gomes, Paulo E.
Gomes, Teresa M. Friendly Correspondence: Mazes to the Mind. Kamei, Marlene, ed. 35p. (Orig.). 1978. pap. 2.00 (ISBN 0-935684-01-8). Plumbers Ink Bks.
Gomes Teixeira, Francisco. Traite des Courbes Speciales Remarquables Planes et Gauches, 3 vols. 2nd ed. LC 73-113153. 1337p. (Fr.). 1972. text ed. 65.00 set (ISBN 0-8284-0255-8). Chelsea Pub.
Gomez. Engineering with Rigid PVC. (Plastics Engineering Ser.). 544p. 1984. 69.75 (ISBN 0-8247-7080-3). Dekker.
--Metodo Experimental. 1983. pap. text ed. write for info. (ISBN 0-06-313355-5, Pub. by HarLA Mexico). Har-Row.
Gomez, A. A. & Gomez, K. A. Multiple Cropping in the Humid Tropics of Asia. 248p. 1983. pap. text ed. 15.00 (ISBN 0-88936-304-8, IDRC176, IDRC). Unipub.
Gomez, Alberto Perez see Perez Gomez, Alberto.
Gomez, Alfredo. The Basics of BASIC. 1983. pap. text ed. 19.95 (ISBN 0-03-063069-X). HR&W.
Gomez, Angel I. Outline of Mexican American Education. 1980. pap. 4.00 (ISBN 0-686-32640-7). Impresora Sahuaro.
Gomez, Antonio E. Fernan Mendez Pinto: Comedia Famosa En Dos Partes. Cohen, Louise G., et al, eds. LC 74-15566. (Harvard Text from the Romance Languages: No. 5). 253p. 1974. pap. text ed. 12.50x (ISBN 0-674-29875-6). Harvard U Pr.
Gomez, Arturo A., jt. auth. see Gomez, Kwanchai A.
Gomez, Dolores, jt. auth. see Christensen, Terri.
Gomez, Efrain A. For the Dead, for the Living. LC 81-81612. 1983. 8.95 (ISBN 0-87212-154-2). Libra.
Gomez, Ermilo A. Canek: History & Legend of a Maya Hero. 80p. 1983. pap. 2.50 (ISBN 0-380-61937-7, 61937-7, Bard). Avon.
Gomez, Gloria. An Introductory Guide to Bilingual-Bicultural-Multicultural Education: Beyond Tacos, Eggrolls & Grits. 40p. 1982. saddle stitched 3.95 (ISBN 0-8403-2708-0). Kendall-Hunt.
Gomez, Harry. Angeles y Rameras. (Pimienta Collection Ser). (Sp.). 1977. pap. 1.00 (ISBN 0-88473-256-8). Fiesta Pub.
Gomez, Joan. Diccionario de Sintomas. 625p. (Span.). 1976. 20.95 (ISBN 84-7002-207-5, S-31421). French & Eur.
--A Dictionary of Symptoms. rev. ed. LC 82-42525. (Illus.). 324p. 1983. 16.95 (ISBN 0-8128-2887-9); pap. 8.95 (ISBN 0-8128-6230-9). Stein & Day.
Gomez, Joan, jt. auth. see Dally, Peter.
Gomez, Joseph A. Peter Watkins. (Filmmakers Ser.). 1979. lib. bdg. 13.50 (ISBN 0-8057-9267-8, Twayne). G K Hall.
Gomez, Judith. Turning Point: A Workbook on Self Transformation. 144p. (Orig.). 1980. pap. text ed. 11.95 (ISBN 0-8403-2178-3). Kendall-Hunt.
Gomez, K. A., jt. auth. see Gomez, A. A.
Gomez, Kwanchai A. & Gomez, Arturo A. Statistical Procedures for Agricultural Research. 2nd ed. LC 83-14556. 680p. 1984. 39.95x (ISBN 0-471-87092-7, Wiley-Interscience). Wiley.
Gomez, Luis-Duque. Gold Museum, Colombia. (Illus.). 238p. 1982. 52.00 (ISBN 0-86710-052-4). Edns Vilo.
Gomez, Luis O. see Woodward, Hiram W.
Gomez, Luis O. & Torretti, Roberto, eds. Problemas de la Filosofia: Textos Filosoficos y Contemporaneos. Castilla, Ramon, et al, trs. 1979. pap. 11.25 (ISBN 0-8477-2812-9). U of PR Pr.
Gomez, Luis O., jt. ed. see Lancaster, Lewis.
Gomez, Madeleine Angelique Poisson De see Poisson De Gomez, Madeleine Angelique.
Gomez, Manuel, ed. Radiation Hazards in Mining: Control, Measurement, & Medical Aspects. LC 81-70691. (Illus.). 1105p. 1982. 58.00x (ISBN 0-89520-290-5). Soc Mining Eng.
Gomez, Manuel, et al. At Work in Copper: Occupational Health & Safety in Copper Smelting, 3 vols. LC 79-63375. (Illus.). 1979. Set. pap. 70.00x (ISBN 0-918780-11-X); Vol. I. 40.00x; Vols. II & III. 20.00x ea. INFORM.
Gomez, Manuel R., ed. Tuberous Sclerosis. LC 78-94312. 264p. 1979. text ed. 37.50 (ISBN 0-89004-313-2). Raven.
Gomez, Maximo P. Lonquen. 303p. (Span.). 1980. 8.00 (ISBN 0-317-15033-2, 3013). Ediciones Norte.
Gomez, Mesa L. Cinema. 1976. lib. bdg. 59.95 (ISBN 0-8490-1632-0). Gordon Pr.
Gomez, Monica V., jt. tr. see Argadonna, Fernando.
Gomez, Monica Villa, tr. see Life in Christ.
Gomez, Q. J. & Egay, L. M., eds. Anaesthesia Safety for All: Proceedings of the 8th World Congress of Anaesthesiologists, Manila, Philippines, 22-28 January 1984. (International Congress Ser.: No. 637). 676p. 1984. 126.00 (ISBN 0-444-80614-8, Excerpta Medica). Elsevier.
Gomez, Rafael A., et al. Solitary Nodular Lesions of the Lung: Contribution to Its Diagnosis & Management. (Illus.). 250p. Date not set. 22.50 (ISBN 0-87527-245-2). Green.
Gomez, Rudolph & Cottingham, Clement. The Social Reality of Ethnic America. 1974. pap. text ed. 11.95x (ISBN 0-669-84111-0). Heath.
Gomez, Rudolph, jt. auth. see Martin, Curtis.
Gomez, Thelma J. & Simpson, Elizabeth, eds. Independent Activities for Learning Centers. 1971. pap. 4.75x (ISBN 0-8422-0145-9). Irvington.
Gomez, Victoria. Scream Cheese & Jelly! Jokes, Riddles, & Puns. LC 79-14575. (Illus.). (gr. 2-6). 1979. 10.25 (ISBN 0-688-41916-X); PLB 10.88 (ISBN 0-688-51916-4). Lothrop.
--Wags to Witches: More Jokes, Riddles, & Puns. LC 80-17405. (Illus.). 64p. (gr. 2-6). 1981. 10.00 (ISBN 0-688-41954-2); PLB 10.88 (ISBN 0-688-51954-7). Lothrop.
Gomez-Arcos, Augustin. The Carnivorous Lamb: A Novel. Rodarmor, William, tr. LC 84-47651. 320p. 1984. 14.95 (ISBN 0-87923-536-5). Godine.
Gomez Bedate, Pilar. Introduccion a la Poesia Lirica. Crespo, Angel, tr. LC 76-22636. (Coleccion Mente y Palabra). (Span.). 1977. 6.25 (ISBN 0-8477-0538-2); pap. 5.00 (ISBN 0-8477-0539-0). U of PR Pr.
Gomez-Campo, C., ed. Plant Conservation in the Mediterranean Area. (Geobotany Ser.). 1985. lib. bdg. 67.50 (ISBN 90-6193-523-7, Pub. by Junk Pubs Netherlands). Kluwer Academic.
Gomez-Campo, Cesar. Plant Conservation in the Mediterranean Area. Date not set. write for info. (ISBN 0-12-289640-8). Acad Pr.
Gomez-Canedo, Fray L. Guide to the Historical Archives of Puerto Rico. (Puerto Rico Ser.). 1979. lib. bdg. 59.95 (ISBN 0-8490-2930-9). Gordon Pr.
Gomez de Acevedo, Labor. Sanz, Promotor de la Conciencia Separatista en Puerto Rico. (UPREX, Humanidades: No. 35). pap. 1.85 (ISBN 0-8477-0035-6). U of PR Pr.
Gomez de Cadiz, Javier. Diccionario de Sigles de Organismos Nacionales e Internacionales. 64p. (Span.). 1976. pap. 1.75 (ISBN 84-203-0051-9, S-50584). French & Eur.
Gomez de la Serna, Ramon. Greguerias: The Wit & Wisdom of Ramon Gomez de la Serna. Ward, Philip, tr. from Span. (Oleander Language & Literature Ser.: Vol. 12). (Illus.). iv, 220p. 1982. 29.95 (ISBN 0-900891-45-9); pap. 16.50 (ISBN 0-900891-49-1). Oleander Pr.
Gomez de Segura Beaumont, Angel J. Diccionario Infantil Fher. 24p. (Span.). 1978. pap. 5.25 (ISBN 84-243-1456-5, S-50076). French & Eur.
Gomez De Toledo, Gaspar. Tercera Parte de la Tragicomedia de Celestina. Barrick, Mac E., ed. LC 70-137886. (Haney Foundation Ser.). (Illus.). 570p. 1973. 20.00x (ISBN 0-8122-7602-7). U of Pa Pr.
Gomez-Estrada, Norhma, jt. auth. see Holton, James S.
Gomez-Ibanez, Jose A., jt. auth. see Meyer, John R.
Gomez-Mejia, Luis R. & McCann, Joseph E. Meeting the Challenges of Foreign Expansion: An International Business Simulation. LC 84-22532. 47p. 1985. pap. text ed. 9.95 (ISBN 0-88244-276-7). Pub Horizons.
Gomez-Mejia, Luis R. & Powers, Kathleen J. The Practice of Collective Bargaining: An Experimential Approach. 1985. 13.95x (ISBN 0-256-03158-4). Business Pubns.
Gomez-Moreno, Manuel. Renaissance Sculpture in Spain. Bevan, Bernard, tr. from Span. LC 76-116354. (Illus.). 1971. Repr. of 1931 ed. buckram 45.00 (ISBN 0-87817-042-1). Hacker.
Gomezplata, A., jt. ed. see Marchello, J. M.
Gomez-Quinones, Juan. Development of the Mexican Working Class North of the Rio Bravo. (Popular Ser.: No. 2). 116p. 1982. pap. text ed. 7.50 (ISBN 0-89551-055-3). UCLA Chicano Stud.
--Sembradores: Ricard Flores Magon y el Partido Liberal Mexicano, a Eulogy & Critique. (Monograph: No. 5). 1979. pap. text ed. 7.50 (ISBN 0-89551-010-3). UCLA Chicano Stud.
Gomez-Quinones, Juan & Camarillo, Albert. Selected Bibliography for Chicano Studies. (Bibliographic & Reference Ser: No. 4). 1975. pap. 2.00 (ISBN 0-89551-009-X). UCLA Chicano Stud.
Gomez-Quintero, Ela R. Quevedo, Hombre y Escritor en Conflicto con su Epoca. LC 77-88534. 1978. pap. 10.00 (ISBN 0-89729-181-6). Ediciones.
Gomez-Quintero, Ella & Perez, Maria. Al Dia de los Negocios: Habla. 288p. (Span.). 1984. pap. text ed. 14.00 (ISBN 0-394-33654-2, RanC). Random.
Gomez-Sicre, Jose. Jose Luis Cuevas: Self-Portrait with a Model. LC 83-42605. (Illus.). 164p. 1983. 29.95 (ISBN 0-8478-0489-5). Rizzoli Intl.
Gomez Sicre, Jose see Sicre, Jose G.
Gomez-Vidal, Oscar. Sabes la Noticia...? Dios Llega Manana. LC 77-92328. (Senda Narrativa). (Orig., Span.). 1978. pap. 4.95 (ISBN 0-918454-04-2). Senda Nueva.
Gomez-Vidal, Oscar & Koch, Harry W. Communicating with the Spanish-Speaking: For People in Government, Business & the Professions. (gr. 10-12). 1976. pap. 5.00 (ISBN 0-913164-67-4). Ken-Bks.
Gomi, Taro. Coco Can't Wait. LC 83-17295. 32p. (ps-1). 1984. 11.75 (ISBN 0-688-02789-X); PLB 11.88 (ISBN 0-688-02790-3). Morrow.
--Coco Can't Wait. 1985. 3.95 (ISBN 0-14-050522-9). Penguin.

--Hi Butterfly. LC 84-1100. (Illus.). 40p. (ps-1). 1985. 10.25 (ISBN 0-688-04137-X, Morrow Junior Books); PLB 10.88 (ISBN 0-688-04138-8, Morrow Junior Books). Morrow.

--Shadows. (Fun Time Ser.). (Illus.). 22p. (ps-1). 1981. 2.95 (ISBN 0-89346-197-0). Heian Intl.

--Sharing. (Fun Time Ser.). (Illus.). 22p. (ps-1). 1981. 2.95 (ISBN 0-89346-198-9). Heian Intl.

--Where's the Fish? (Illus.). 32p. (ps-2). 1986. 10.25 (ISBN 0-688-06241-5); PLB 10.88 (ISBN 0-688-06242-3). Morrow.

Gomi, Yugi. Guide to Japanese Taxes: 1983-1984. 1983. pap. text ed. 20.50 (ISBN 90-654-4160-3, Pub. by Kluwer Law Netherlands). Kluwer Academic.

--Guide to Japanese Taxes: 1984-85. 1984. pap. text ed. 30.00 (ISBN 90-6544-206-5, Pub. by Kluwer Law Netherlands). Kluwer Academic.

Gomi, Yuji. Guide to Japanese Taxes, 1980-1981. LC 66-50788. (Illus.). 282p. (Orig.). 1980. pap. 27.50x (ISBN 0-8002-2764-6). Intl Pubns Serv.

--Guide to Japanese Taxes 1981-82. 280p. pap. 22.00 (ISBN 0-686-41015-7). Kluwer Academic.

Gomme, A. H., ed. Jacobean Tragedies. (Oxford Paperbacks Ser). 1969. pap. 7.95x (ISBN 0-19-281059-6). Oxford U Pr.

Gomme, A. H., ed. see Middleton, Thomas.

Gomme, A. W. A Historical Commentary on Thucydides. Incl. Vol. 1. Introduction & Commentary of Book 1. 1945. 47.50x (ISBN 0-19-814126-2); Vol. 2. The Ten Years' War, Bks. 2-3. 1956. 47.50x (ISBN 0-19-814003-7); Vol. 3. The Ten Years' War, Bks. 4-5. 1956. 47.50x (ISBN 0-19-814001-0). Oxford U Pr.

Gomme, A. W. & Sandbach, F. H. Menander: A Commentary. 1973. 69.00x (ISBN 0-19-814197-1). Oxford U Pr.

Gomme, A. W., et al. Historical Commentary on Thucydides Vol. IV: Books V-VII, XXV. 1970. 49.95x (ISBN 0-19-814178-5). Oxford U Pr.

Gomme, A. W., et al, eds. A Historical Commentary on Thucydides, Volume V: Book VIII. (Illus.). 1981. 79.00x (ISBN 0-19-814198-X). Oxford U Pr.

Gomme, Alice B. The Traditional Games of England, Scotland & Ireland. LC 83-50102. (Illus.). 1016p. 1984. pap. 18.95 (ISBN 0-500-27316-2). Thames Hudson.

Gomme, Alice B. & Sharp, Cecil J., eds. Children's Singing Games in Five Sets. LC 75-35071. (Studies in Play & Games). 1976. Repr. 14.00x (ISBN 0-405-07921-4). Ayer Co Pubs.

Gomme, Alice B. see Gomme, George L., et al.

Gomme, Andor & Jenner, Michael. Bristol: An Architectual History. 452p. 1980. 90.00x (ISBN 0-85331-409-8, Pub. by Lund Humphries England). State Mutual Bk.

Gomme, Andor H. Attitudes to Criticism. LC 66-10057. (Crosscurrents-Modern Critiques Ser.). 192p. 1966. 7.95 (ISBN 0-8093-0194-6). S Ill U Pr.

Gomme, Arnold W. Essays in Greek History & Literature. facs. ed. LC 67-23222. (Essay Index Reprint Ser). 1937. 19.00 (ISBN 0-8369-0481-8). Ayer Co Pubs.

Gomme, G. L. Folklore As Historical Science. 59.95 (ISBN 0-8490-0177-3). Gordon Pr.

Gomme, George L. Ethnology in Folklore. LC 79-75802. 1969. Repr. of 1892 ed. 30.00x (ISBN 0-8103-3832-7). Gale.

--Ethnology in Folklore. 59.95 (ISBN 0-8490-0134-X). Gordon Pr.

--Folklore As an Historical Science. LC 67-23898. (Illus.). 1968. Repr. of 1908 ed. 37.00x (ISBN 0-8103-3432-1). Gale.

--Folklore Relics of Early Village Life. Dorson, Richard, ed. (International Folklore Ser.). 1977. Repr. of 1883 ed. lib. bdg. 20.00x (ISBN 0-405-10096-5). Ayer Co Pubs.

--Index of Archaeological Papers, 1665-1890, 2 Vols. 1907. 55.50 (ISBN 0-8337-1378-7). B Franklin.

--Primitive Folk-Moots: Or, Open-Air Assemblies in Britain. LC 67-23899. 1968. Repr. of 1880 ed. 40.00x (ISBN 0-8103-3433-X). Gale.

Gomme, George L., ed. Handbook of Folk-Lore. (Folk-Lore Society London Monographs Ser.: Vol. 20). pap. 20.00 (ISBN 0-317-15243-2). Kraus Repr.

Gomme, George L., et al, eds. The Gentleman's Magazine Library: Being a Classified Collection of the Chief Contents of the Gentleman's Magazine from 1731-1868, 13 vols. Incl. Vol. 1. Manners & Customs. Repr. of 1886 ed (ISBN 0-8103-3434-8); Vol. 2. Dialect, Proverbs, & Word Lore. Repr. of 1886 ed (ISBN 0-8103-3435-6); Vol. 3. Popular Superstitions. Repr. of 1884 ed (ISBN 0-8103-3436-4); Vol. 4. English Traditional Lore. Repr. of 1885 ed (ISBN 0-8103-3437-2); Vols. 5 & 6. Archaeology. Repr. of 1886 ed (ISBN 0-8103-3438-0); Vols. 7 & 8. Romano-British Remains. Repr. of 1886 ed (ISBN 0-8103-3439-9); Vol. 9. Literary Curiosities & Notes. Gomme, Alice B., ed. Repr. of 1889 ed (ISBN 0-8103-3440-2); Vol. 10. Bibliographical Notes. Bickley, A. C., ed. Repr. of 1890 ed (ISBN 0-8103-3441-0); Vols. 11 & 12. Architectural Antiquities. Repr. of 1890 ed (ISBN 0-8103-3442-9); Vol. 13. Ecclesiology. Milne, F. A., ed. Repr. of 1886 ed (ISBN 0-8103-3443-7). LC 67-23900. Vols. 1-4, 9, 10, 13. 40.00x ea.; Vols. 5 & 6, 7 & 8, 11 & 12 (two Vol. Sets) 53.00x ea. Gale.

Gommes, R. A. Pocket Computers in Agrometeorology. (Plant Production & Protection Papers: No. 45). 149p. 1983. pap. 10.75 (ISBN 92-5-101336-5, F2449, FAO). Unipub.

Gomon, Audrey, jt. auth. see Smith, Donald E.

Gomont, M. Monographie Des Oscillariees: 1892-93, 2 parts in 1 vol. (Illus.). 1962. 28.00 (ISBN 3-7682-0038-8). Lubrecht & Cramer.

Gomori, G., ed. Az Ismeretlen Fa. LC 78-71064. (Hungarian.). 1978. 8.00 (ISBN 0-911050-46-9). Occidental.

Gomori, George, tr. see Radnoti, Miklos.

Gomori, Gyorgy. Nyugtalan Koranyar: Restless Early Summer Poems. 82p. (Hung.). 1984. 6.00 (ISBN 0-911050-56-6); Cloth 8.00 (ISBN 0-911050-57-4). Occidental.

Gomori, Gyorgy & Juhasz, Vilmos, eds. Uj Egtajak. LC 71-94112. (Hung). 1969. pap. 6.00 (ISBN 0-911050-35-3). Occidental.

Gomos, Peter J. Churches of the Not-So-Standing Order: 1809-1869. (Pilgrim Society Notes Ser.: No. 18). 1966. 1.00 (ISBN 0-940628-10-4). Pilgrim Hall.

Gomoyunova, M. V., jt. auth. see Dobretsov, L. N.

Gompel, Claude. Atlas of Diagnostic Cytology. LC 77-27068. 237p. 1978. 80.00x (ISBN 0-471-02278-0, Pub. by Wiley Medical). Wiley.

Gompel, Claude & Silverberg, Steven. Pathology in Gynecology & Obstetrics. 3rd ed. (Illus.). 640p. 1985. text ed. 87.50 (ISBN 0-397-50610-4, Lippincott Medical). Lippincott.

Gompers, Samuel. American Labor & the War. LC 74-75239. (The United States in World War I Ser.). 377p. 1974. Repr. of 1919 ed. lib. bdg. 18.95x (ISBN 0-89198-103-9). Ozer.

--Labor & the Common Welfare. LC 79-89735. (American Labor, from Conspiracy to Collective Bargaining, Ser. 1). 306p. 1969. Repr. of 1919 ed. 17.00 (ISBN 0-405-02124-0). Ayer Co Pubs.

--Labor & the Common Welfare. Robbins, Hayes, ed. LC 70-102240. (Select Bibliographies Reprint Ser). 1919. 26.50 (ISBN 0-8369-5125-5). Ayer Co Pubs.

--Labor & the Employer. LC 79-156413. (American Labor Ser., No. 2). 1971. Repr. of 1929 ed. 26.00 (ISBN 0-405-02921-7). Ayer Co Pubs.

--Seventy Years of Life & Labour, 2 Vols. LC 66-21674. Repr. of 1925 ed. Set. 75.00x (ISBN 0-678-00213-4). Kelley.

Gompers, Samuel, jt. auth. see Allen, Henry J.

Gomperts, B. D. The Plasma Membrane: Models for Its Structure & Function. 1977. 39.50 (ISBN 0-12-289450-2). Acad Pr.

Gompertz, G. M. Chinese Celadon Wares. 2nd ed. (Illus.). 224p. 1980. 48.00 (ISBN 0-571-18003-5). Faber & Faber.

Gompertz, Helen. First Prayers. (Illus.). 32p. (ps-3). 1983. 4.95 (ISBN 0-8170-1013-0). Judson.

Gompertz, M. Corn from Egypt: The Beginning of Agriculture. 1979. Repr. of 1928 ed. lib. bdg. 15.00 (ISBN 0-8495-2036-3). Arden Lib.

--Helps to the Study of Goldsmith's the Traveller. LC 77-21465. 1977. Repr. of 1900 ed. lib. bdg. 12.50 (ISBN 0-8414-4607-5). Folcroft.

--Helps to the Study of Goldsmith's The Traveller. 1973. Repr. of 1900 ed. 12.50 (ISBN 0-8274-0402-6). R West.

Gompertz, Martin L. Adventures in Sakaeland, Comprising Harilek: Wrexham's Romance, Being a Continuation of "Harilek", 2 vols. in 1. Reginald, R. & Melville, Douglas, eds. LC 77-84226. (Lost Race & Adult Fantasy Ser.). 1978. Repr. of 1935 ed. lib. bdg. 53.00x (ISBN 0-405-10978-4). Ayer Co Pubs.

Gompertz, Philip. A Child's View of Inflation. (Illus.). 40p. 1974. pap. 1.15 (ISBN 0-918248-01-9). Word Doctor.

Gompertz, Rolf. A Celebration of Life: With Menachem. LC 83-50872. 160p. 1983. velo binding 10.00 (ISBN 0-918248-06-X). Word Doctor.

--The Messiah of Midtown Park. LC 83-50871. 136p. 1983. velo binding 10.00 (ISBN 0-918248-05-1). Word Doctor.

--My Jewish Brother Jesus. LC 76-55591. 200p. 1977. 15.00 (ISBN 0-918248-03-5); pap. 10.00 (ISBN 0-918248-02-7). Word Doctor.

--Sparks of Spirit: A Handbook for Personal Happiness. LC 83-50870. 168p. 1983. velo binding 10.00 (ISBN 0-918248-04-3). Word Doctor.

Gomperz, Heinrich. Philosophical Studies by Heinrich Gomperz. Robinson, Daniel S., ed. 1953. 9.50 (ISBN 0-8158-0100-9). Chris Mass.

Gomperz, Theodor. Greek Thinkers: A History of Ancient Philosophy, 4 vols. Incl. Vol. 1. pap. text ed. (ISBN 0-7195-0498-8); Vol. 2. pap. text ed. o. p. (ISBN 0-7195-0499-6); Vol. 3. pap. text ed.; Vol. 4. 1964. text ed. 18.00x ea.; pap. text ed. 14.25x ea. Humanities.

--Griechische Denker: Eine Geschichte der antiken Philosophie, 3 Vol. 1789p. 1973. Repr. of 1931 ed. Set. 178.00x (ISBN 3-11-002499-3). De Gruyter.

Gomringer, Eugen. Book of Hours & Constellations. Rothenberg, Jerome, tr. LC 68-31588. 1968. 8.00 (ISBN 0-89366-054-X); pap. 3.50 (ISBN 0-89366-055-8). Ultramarine Pub.

Gona, Debbie. Lieutenant Governor: The Office & Its Powers. rev. ed. 12p. 1983. pap. 12.00. Coun State Govts.

--The Office & Duties of the Secretary of State. (Illus.). 80p. (Orig.). 1983. pap. text ed. 10.00 (ISBN 0-87292-048-8). Coun State Govts.

Gonatilleke, Godfrey. Participatory Development & Dependence: The Case of Sri Lanka. 140p. 1979. 5.00 (ISBN 0-318-16156-7). Overseas Dev Council.

Gonchar, O. Cyclone. 322p. 1972. pap. 3.95 (ISBN 0-8285-0974-3, Pub. by Progress Pubs USSR). Imported Pubns.

Goncharov, I. Same Old Story. 390p. 1975. 7.95 (ISBN 0-8285-0975-1, Pub. by Progress Pubs USSR). Imported Pubns.

Goncharov, Ivan. Oblomov. Hogarth, C. J., tr. from Rus. LC 79-19061. 1980. Repr. of 1915 ed. lib. bdg. 14.00x (ISBN 0-8376-0451-6). Bentley.

--Oblomov. (Classics Ser). 1978. pap. 4.95 (ISBN 0-14-044040-2). Penguin.

--Oblomov. 1981. pap. 3.95 (ISBN 0-451-51572-2, Sig Classics). NAL.

Goncharov, Ivan A. A Common Story. Garnett, Constance, tr. from Rus. LC 76-23878. (Classics of Russian Literature). 1977. 15.00 (ISBN 0-88355-485-2); pap. 10.00 (ISBN 0-88355-486-0). Hyperion Conn.

--The Precipice. Bryant, M., tr. from Russian. LC 76-23879. (Classics of Russian Literature). 1977. pap. 10.00 (ISBN 0-88355-487-9). Hyperion Conn.

Goncharov, V., jt. auth. see Brekhovskikh, L.

Goncourt, Edmond De see De Goncourt, Edmond & De Goncourt, Jules.

Goncourt, Edmond L. The Woman of the Eighteenth Century: Her Life, from Birth to Death, Her Love & Her Philosophy in the Worlds of Salon, Shop & Street. Le Clercq, Jacques & Roeder, Ralph, trs. from Fr. LC 79-2937. (Illus.). 347p. 1981. Repr. of 1927 ed. 27.25 (ISBN 0-8305-0103-7). Hyperion Conn.

Goncourt, Edmond L. & Goncourt, Jules A. De. Goncourt Journals, Eighteen Fifty-One to Eighteen Seventy. Galantiere, Lewis, tr. LC 69-10099. 1969. Repr. of 1958 ed. lib. bdg. 22.50x (ISBN 0-8371-0448-3, GOJ). Greenwood.

Goncourt, Edmond L. & Goncourt, Jules A. The Woman of the Eighteenth Century: Her Life, From Birth to Death, Her Love, & Her Philosophy in the Worlds of Salon, Shop, & Street. 20.75 (ISBN 0-8369-6937-5, 7817). Ayer Co Pubs.

Goncourt, Edmund de see De Goncourt, Edmond & De Goncourt, Jules.

Goncourt, Jules A., jt. auth. see Goncourt, Edmond L.

Goncourt, Jules A. De, jt. auth. see Goncourt, Edmond L.

Goncourt, Jules De see De Goncourt, Edmond & De Goncourt, Jules.

Goncourt, Jules de see De Goncourt, Edmond & De Goncourt, Jules.

Goncz, Arpad, tr. see McCullough, Colleen.

Gonda, J. The Aspectual Function of the Rgvedic Present & Aorist. (Disputationes Rheno-Trajectinae: No. 7). pap. 32.00x (ISBN 90-2790-033-7). Mouton.

--Concise Grammar of the Sanskrit Language. LC 66-24139. (Alabama Linguistic & Philological Ser: Vol. 11). 152p. 1967. o. p. 12.65 (ISBN 0-8173-0351-0); pap. 9.00 (ISBN 0-8173-0072-4). U of Ala Pr.

--Vision of the Vedic Poets. (Disputationes Rheno-Trajectinae Ser.: No. 8). (Orig.). 1963. pap. text ed. 28.80x (ISBN 90-2790-034-5). Mouton.

--Visnuism & Sivaism: A Comparison. LC 71-545904. 1976. 12.50x (ISBN 0-89684-465-X). Orient Bk Dist.

--Visnuism & Sivaism: A Comparison. (Jordan Lectures in Comparative Religion: No. IX). 228p. 1970. 38.50 (ISBN 0-485-17409-X, Pub. by Athlone Pr Ltd). Longwood Pub Group.

Gonda, Jan. Epithets in the Rgveda. (D. R. T. Ser: No. 3). 1959. pap. text ed. 29.60x (ISBN 90-2790-030-2). Mouton.

--Some Observations on the Relations Between Gods & Powers in the Veda, a Propos of the Phrase, Sunah Sahasah. (Disputationes Rheno-Trajectinae Ser.: No. 1). (Orig.). 1957. pap. text ed. 12.80x (ISBN 90-2790-027-2). Mouton.

Gonda, Jan, ed. see Tondl, Ales.

Gonda, Thomas A. & Ruark, John. Dying Dignified. 1983. pap. 13.95 (ISBN 0-201-10603-5, 002665, Med-Nurse). Addison-Wesley.

Gonder, Budd. The Coast Guard License from Six-Pac To Ocean Operator. 7th ed. LC 84-71365. (Illus.). 238p. 1984. lib. bdg. 24.95x (ISBN 0-9613913-0-8); pap. 21.95x (ISBN 0-9613913-1-6). Charters W.

Gondie, Andrew & Gardner, Rita. Discovering Landscape in England & Wales. (Illus.). 192p. 1985. 19.95 (ISBN 0-04-551076-8). Allen Unwin.

Gondin, William R. Handbook Dictionary of Parliamentary Prodecure. (Quality Paperback: No. 234). (Orig.). 1969. pap. 2.95 (ISBN 0-8226-0234-2). Littlefield.

Gondin, William R. & Mammen, Edward W. The Art of Speaking. rev. ed. LC 80-2671. (Made Simple Ser.). (Illus.). 192p. 1981. pap. 4.95 (ISBN 0-385-17485-3). Doubleday.

Gondin, William R. & Sohmer, Bernard. Advanced Algebra & Calculus Made Simple. (Made Simple Ser.). pap. 4.95 (ISBN 0-385-00438-9). Doubleday.

--Intermediate Algebra & Analytic Geometry Made Simple. (Made Simple Ser.). pap. 4.95 (ISBN 0-385-00437-0). Doubleday.

Gondolf, Edward W. Men Who Batter: An Integrated Approach for Stopping Wife Abuse. LC 83-83313. 224p. 1985. pap. text ed. 19.95 (ISBN 0-918452-56-2). Learning Pubns.

Gondos, Victor, Jr. J. Franklin Jameson & the Birth of the National Archives: 1906-1926. LC 80-54050. 1981. 27.50x (ISBN 0-8122-7799-6). U of Pa Pr.

Gondosch, Linda. The Strawberryland Choo-Choo. (Strawberry Shortcake Ser.). (Illus.). 40p. (ps-3). 1984. cancelled 5.95 (ISBN 0-910313-24-5). Parker Bro.

--Who Needs A Bratty Brother? Brosnan, Rosemary, ed. (Illus.). 112p. (gr. 9-11). 1985. 10.95 (ISBN 0-525-67170-6). Lodestar Bks.

Gondran, Michel & Minoux, Michel. Graphs & Algorithms. LC 82-1975. (Wiley Series in Discreet Mathematics: 1-484). 650p. 1984. text ed. 64.95x (ISBN 0-471-10374-8, Wiley-Interscience). Wiley.

Gonedes, Nicholas J. Accounting for Common Stockholders: An Eclectic Decision-Making & Motivational Foundation. LC 70-633563. (Studies in Accounting: No. 4). 1971. pap. text ed. 5.00 (ISBN 0-87755-131-6). Bureau Busn UT.

Gonella, Ronald R., jt. ed. see Altman, Liza.

Gonen, Amiram. Community Support System for Mentally Handicapped Adults: An Alternative to Spatially Distributed Human Service Facilities. (Discussion Paper: No. 96). 1977. pap. 3.25 (ISBN 0-686-32262-2). Regional Sci Res Inst.

Gonen, Rivka. Pottery in Ancient Times. LC 72-10796. (The Lerner Archaeology Ser.: Digging up the Past). (Illus.). 96p. (gr. 5 up). 1974. PLB 7.95 (ISBN 0-8225-0829-X). Lerner Pubns.

--Weapons & Warfare in Ancient Times. LC 72-10802. (Lerner Archaeology Ser: Digging up the Past). (Illus.). (gr. 5 up). 1976. PLB 7.95 (ISBN 0-8225-0832-X). Lerner Pubns.

Gonen, T. Electric Power Distribution System Engineering. (Electrical Engineering Ser.). 752p. 1986. 51.95 (ISBN 0-07-023707-7). McGraw.

Gong, Gerrit W. The Standard of "Civilization" in International Society. LC 83-17248. 1984. 32.50x (ISBN 0-19-821948-2). Oxford U Pr.

Gong, Gerrit W., et al. Areas of Challenge for Soviet Foreign Policy in the 1980s. LC 84-47701. (CSIS Publication Series on the Soviet Union in the 1980s). 176p. (Orig.). 1984. 20.00x (ISBN 0-253-30861-5); pap. 7.95x (ISBN 0-253-20333-3, MB 333). Ind U Pr.

Gong, Henry, Jr. & Drage, Charles W., eds. The Respiratory System: A Core Curriculum. (Illus.). 400p. 1982. 28.95x (ISBN 0-8385-8280-X). ACC.

Gong, Jeh-Tween. Super Unified Theory: The Foundations of Science. LC 84-90325. 104p. 1984. text ed. 35.00 (ISBN 0-916713-01-6); pap. 27.00 (ISBN 0-916713-02-4). Gong Ent.

Gong, Victor, ed. Understanding AIDS: A Comprehensive Guide. 224p. 1985. 20.00 (ISBN 0-317-18048-7); pap. 9.95 (ISBN 0-8135-1101-1). Rutgers U Pr.

Gongora. Gongora: Vingt Poemes. (Illus.). 176p. 50.00 (ISBN 0-8076-1133-6). Braziller.

Gongora, Luis de. Polyphemus & Galatea: A Study in the Interpretation of a Baroque Poem by Alexander A. Parker & Verse Translation by Gilbert F. Cunningham. LC 77-81914. 182p. 1977. 12.50x (ISBN 0-292-72421-7). U of Tex Pr.

--Sonetos: Luis De Gongora. Ciplijauskaite, Birute, ed. 691p. 1981. 35.00x (ISBN 0-942260-17-1). Hispanic Seminary.

Gongora, Mario. Studies in the Colonial History of Spanish America. LC 74-19524. (Cambridge Latin America Studies: vol. 20). pap. 76.30 (ISBN 0-317-28400-2, 2022450). Bks Demand UMI.

Gongoray Argote, Luis de see De Gongoray Argote, Luis.

Gonick, Larry. The Cartoon Guide to Computer Science. 1983. pap. 5.05 (ISBN 0-06-460417-9). Har-Row.

--The Cartoon History of the Universe, Book One: From the Big Bang to Babylon. (Illus.). 96p. (Orig.). 1980. pap. 3.45 (ISBN 0-89620-081-7). Rip Off.

Gonick, Larry & Hosler, Jay. Cartoon Guide to Computer Science. (Illus.). 224p. (Orig.). (gr. 11 up). 1983. pap. 4.76i (ISBN 0-06-460417-9, COS CO 417). B&N NY.

Gonick, Larry & Wheelis, Mark. Cartoon Guide to Genetics. (Illus.). 224p. (Orig.). 1983. pap. 4.76i (ISBN 0-06-460416-0, COS CO 416). B&N NY.

Gonina, J., tr. see Charnay, Desire.

Gonnella, Gary, jt. auth. see Teja, Ed.

Gonner, E. C. Common Land & Inclosure. rev. ed. 461p. 1966. 35.00x (ISBN 0-7146-1311-8, F Cass Co). Biblio Dist.

--Economic Essays of David Ricardo. 315p. 1966. Repr. of 1923 ed. 27.50x (ISBN 0-7146-1222-7, BHA-01222, F Cass Co). Biblio Dist.

Gonnewein, F., jt. ed. see Von, Egidy T.

Gonsalves, Carol. Sermon on the Mountain. (Arch Bk. Supplement Ser.). 1981. pap. 0.99 (ISBN 0-570-06149-0, 59-1304). Concordia.

Gonsalves, Milton. Fagothey's Right & Reason: Ethics in Theory & Practice. 7th ed. LC 80-39863. 574p. 1981. text ed. 25.95 (ISBN 0-8016-1541-0). Mosby.

Gonsalvo Mainar, Gonzalo. Diccionario de Metologia Estadistica. 184p. (Span.). 1978. pap. 19.95 (ISBN 84-7112-096-8, S-50010). French & Eur.
Gonser, B. W. see Hausner, Henry.
Gonser, U., ed. Moessbauer Spectroscopy II: The Exotic Side of the Methods. (Topics in Currents Physics Ser.: Vol. 25). (Illus.). 210p. 1981. 33.00 (ISBN 0-387-10519-0). Springer-Verlag.
--Mossbauer Spectroscopy. (Topics in Applied Physics Ser.: Vol. 5). (Illus.). 240p. 1975. 44.00 (ISBN 0-387-07120-2). Springer-Verlag.
Gonseth, Ferdinand. Time & Method: An Essay on the Methodology of Research. Guggenheimer, Eva H., tr. (Illus.). 468p. 1972. 39.75x (ISBN 0-398-02297-6). C C Thomas.
Gonsett, Robert. Scuba Regulators: Air Pressure Reduction Valves for Diving. (Illus.). 65p. 1975. text ed. 4.50 (ISBN 0-916974-08-1). NAUI.
--Scuba Tanks: High Pressure Cylinders for Diving. (Illus.). 1973. 4.50 (ISBN 0-916974-07-3). NAUI.
Gonsette, R. E. & Delmotte, P. H., eds. Immunological & Clinical Aspects of Multiple Sclerosis. 500p. 1983. text ed. 65.00 (ISBN 0-85200-762-0, Pub. by MTP Pr England). Kluwer Academic.
Gonshack, Sol. Little Stories for Big People. (Illus.). (gr. 7 up). 1976. pap. 4.25 (ISBN 0-88345-263-4, 18475). Regents Pub.
Gonshack, Sol & McKenzie, Joanna. Send Me a Letter: A Basic Guide to Letter Writing. (Illus.). 224p. 1982. pap. text ed. 12.95 (ISBN 0-13-806604-3). P-H.
Gonshorowski, Addie. No-Sugar Cookbook. 100p. 1983. pap. 5.99 (ISBN 0-318-00754-1). Ad Dee Pubs Inc.
Gonsiorek, John C., ed. A Guide to Psychotherapy with Gay & Lesbian Clients. LC 84-19275. 224p. 1985. pap. text ed. 8.95 (ISBN 0-918393-03-5). Harrington Pk.
--Homosexuality & Psychotherapy: A Practitioner's Handbook of Affirmative Models. LC 82-3072. (Research on Homosexuality Ser.: No. 4). 212p. 1982. text ed. 29.95 (ISBN 0-917724-63-1, B63). Haworth Pr.
Gontarek, Leonard. St. Genevieve Watching over Paris. Owen, Maureen, ed. 1984. pap. 2.00 (ISBN 0-916382-32-X). Telephone Bks.
Gontarski, S. Beckett's Happy Days: An Analysis of the Manuscript. LC 76-620056. 1977. 13.50x (ISBN 0-88215-041-3). Ohio St U Lib.
Gontarski, S. E. The Intent of Undoing in Samuel Beckett's Dramatic Texts. LC 84-47884. (Illus.). 272p. 1985. 24.50 (ISBN 0-253-33029-7). Ind U Pr.
Gontarski, S. E., jt. ed. see Beja, Morris.
Gontarski, Stanley, ed. Journal of Beckett Studies, No. 9. 96p. 1984. pap. 10.00 (ISBN 0-7145-3970-8). Riverrun NY.
--Journal of Beckett Studies, No. 10. 1985. pap. 10.00 (ISBN 0-7145-4054-4). Riverrun NY.
Gonte, Marilyn. It Can't Happen to Me. LC 83-61483. 240p. 1984. 12.95 (ISBN 0-9611760-0-8). Marnik.
Gontier, Fernande, tr. see De Beauvoir, Simone.
Gonul, M. Turkish Embroideries, Sixteenth to Nineteenth Centuries. (Illus.). 1975. pap. 7.50 (ISBN 0-686-77972-X). Heinman.
Gonzague-Frick, Louis de, jt. auth. see Artaud, Antonin.
Gonzales, Ambrose E. The Captain. facsimile ed. LC 78-37593. (Black Heritage Library Collection). Repr. of 1924 ed. 20.50 (ISBN 0-8369-8969-4). Ayer Co Pubs.
--Laguerre. facsimile ed. LC 71-37594. (Black Heritage Library Collection). Repr. of 1924 ed. 20.50 (ISBN 0-8369-8970-8). Ayer Co Pubs.
--With Aesop Along the Black Border. LC 73-97424. Repr. of 1924 ed. 19.75x (ISBN 0-8371-2732-7, GOW&). Greenwood.
Gonzales, Arlene. The Intrigues. 1985. 7.50 (ISBN 0-8062-2478-9). Carlton.
Gonzales, Catherin T. Cynthia of the Comanches. (Illus.). 48p. 1985. 7.95 (ISBN 0-89015-479-1). Eakin Pubns.
Gonzales, F. Jose. He Reigns from the Cross. Lemon, tr. 1962. 3.00 (ISBN 0-8198-0054-6). Dghtrs St Paul.
Gonzales, German, jt. auth. see Mairowitz, David Z.
Gonzales, Gertrude D. & Lewis, Arthur J., eds. Modern Drug Encyclopedia & Therapeutic Index. 16th ed. LC 34-12823. 1066p. 1981. text ed. 59.00 (ISBN 0-914316-21-4). Yorke Med.
Gonzales, Josemilio. Soledad Absoluta: Diario Poetico. (UPREX, Poesia: No. 3). pap. 1.85 (ISBN 0-8477-0003-8). U of PR Pr.
Gonzales, Juan L., Jr. Mexican-American Farm Workers: The California Agricultural Industry. LC 84-26401. 240p. 1985. write for info. (ISBN 0-03-002763-2). Praeger.
Gonzales, Laurence. Artificial Horizon. LC 85-71165. (Orig.). 1985. pap. 6.95 (ISBN 0-933532-52-0). BkMk.
--Computers for Doctors. 1984. pap. 6.95 (ISBN 0-345-31478-6). Ballantine.
--Computers for Lawyers. LC 99-943923. 1984. pap. 6.95 (ISBN 0-345-31479-4). Ballantine.
--Computers for Realtors: User Friendly Guides. 144p. 1984. 6.95 (ISBN 0-345-31477-8). Ballantine.
--Computers for Writers: User Friendly Guides. 144p. 1984. 6.95 (ISBN 0-345-31476-X). Ballantine.
--User Friendly Guides: Computers for Realtors. 144p. (Orig.). 1984. pap. 6.95 (ISBN 0-345-31477-8). Ballantine.
--User Friendly Guides: Computers for Writers. 144p. (Orig.). 1984. pap. 6.95 (ISBN 0-345-31476-X). Ballantine.
Gonzales, Laurence, et al. Four-Four-Four: Short Fiction by Laurence Gonzales, Grant Lyons, & Roger Rath. LC 76-56873. (Breakthrough Bks.). 200p. 1977. 12.95 (ISBN 0-8262-0207-1). U of Mo Pr.
Gonzales, Luis J. & Sanchez Salazar, Gustavo A. The Great Rebel: Che Guevara in Bolivia. 1969. pap. 1.45 (ISBN 0-394-17156-X, B227, BC). Grove.
Gonzales, Manuel. London in Seventeen Thirty-One. Repr. of 1888 ed. 15.00 (ISBN 0-8482-4211-4). Norwood Edns.
Gonzales, Manuel A. Sociedad y Tipos en las Novelas de Ramon Meza y Suarez Inclan. LC 82-84334. (Coleccion Polymita Ser.). 184p. (Orig., Span.). 1985. pap. 12.95 (ISBN 0-89729-326-6). Ediciones.
Gonzales, Manuel G. Andrea Costa & the Rise of Socialism in the Romagna. LC 79-6771. 419p. 1980. text ed. 27.50 (ISBN 0-8191-0952-5); pap. text ed. 16.75 (ISBN 0-8191-0953-3). U Pr of Amer.
Gonzales, Merce C. Roncho Finds a Home. LC 85-40407. (Stories from Around the World Ser.). (Illus.). 28p. (ps-3). 1985. pap. 3.95 (ISBN 0-382-09135-3). Silver.
Gonzales, Michael J. Plantation Agriculture & Social Control in Northern Peru, 1875-1933. (Institute of Latin American Studies Monograph Ser.: No. 62). (Illus.). 251p. 1985. text ed. 25.00x (ISBN 0-292-76491-X). U of Tex Pr.
Gonzales, Michael L. CP-M Software Review. 1984. pap. text ed. 19.95 (ISBN 0-8359-1101-2). Reston.
Gonzales, Mike, tr. see Vazquez, Adolfo S.
Gonzales, Mike, et al, eds. Economy & Society in the Transformation of the World. LC 84-40080. 208p. 1984. 19.95 (ISBN 0-312-23682-4). St Martin.
Gonzales, Pancho. Tennis. 128p. 1965. pap. 2.95 (ISBN 0-346-12328-3). Cornerstone.
Gonzales, Rafael, jt. ed. see Quarm, Joan.
Gonzales, Ron. Automotive Fuel & Emission Systems. 1985. text ed. 24.95 (ISBN 0-8359-0117-3); pap. text ed. 19.95 (ISBN 0-8359-0116-5). Reston.
Gonzales, Ronald, jt. auth. see Edmonds, I. G.
Gonzales, Ronald F. Automotive Electrical & Electronic Systems Lab Manual. 1985. pap. text ed. 16.95 (ISBN 0-8359-0019-3). Reston.
--Automotive Electricity & Electronics. LC 84-3450. 1984. text ed. 29.95 (ISBN 0-8359-0343-5); pap. text ed. 21.95 (ISBN 0-8359-0342-7). Reston.
Gonzales, Sylvia A. Hispanic American Voluntary Organizations. LC 84-19317. (Ethnic American Voluntary Organizations Ser.: No. 2). 320p. 1985. lib. bdg. 45.00 (ISBN 0-313-20949-9, GHL/). Greenwood.
Gonzales, Tobias M., jt. auth. see Vasquez, James A.
Gonzales de Mendoza, Juan. The Historie of the Great & Mightie Kingdome of China. Parke, R., tr. LC 72-5997. (English Experience Ser.: No. 522). 420p. 1973. Repr. of 1588 ed. 67.00 (ISBN 90-221-0522-9). Walter J Johnson.
Gonzales-Robles, Luis. Spanish Art Tomorrow. (Illus.). 72p. 1983. pap. 12.00x (ISBN 0-318-00546-8). Pub Ctr Cult Res.
Gonzales Torres, Rafael. Un Hombre Se Ha Puesto De Pie. LC 81-16190. 178p. 1981. pap. 3.00 (ISBN 0-8477-0725-3). U of PR Pr.
Gonzalez. The Fallacy of Social Science Research: A Critical Examination & New Qualitative Model. (PPS on Social Policy Ser.). 75p. 1981. 16.50 (ISBN 0-08-027549-4). Pergamon.
Gonzalez, Ananias, ed. see Sisemore, J. T.
Gonzalez, Andrew B. Language & Nationalism: The Philippine Experience Thus Far. 179p. 1980. 19.50 (ISBN 0-686-28647-2); pap. 10.75 (ISBN 0-686-28648-0). Cellar.
Gonzalez, Angel. Harsh World & Other Poems. Walsh, Donald D., tr. (Lockert Library of Poetry in Translation). 1977. 18.50 (ISBN 0-691-06326-5); pap. 5.95 (ISBN 0-691-01333-0). Princeton U Pr.
Gonzalez, Antonio. Analisis e Interpretacion de Don Juan De Castro de Lope de Vega. LC 79-54185. (Coleccion Polymita Ser.). 241p. (Orig., Span.). 1981. pap. 10.00 (ISBN 0-89729-235-9). Ediciones.
Gonzalez, Antonio J. & Zavala, Domingo F. Tratado Moderno de Economia General. (Span.). 1976. text ed. 15.00 (ISBN 0-538-22060-0, V06). SW Pub.
Gonzalez, Armando E., jt. ed. see Aguilar, Juan F.
Gonzalez, Caleb. Strabismus & Ocular Motility. (Illus.). 240p. 1983. lib. bdg. 57.00 (ISBN 0-683-03629-7). Williams & Wilkins.
Gonzalez, Calos. An Overview of the Mestizo Heritage: Implications for Teachers of Mexican-American Children. LC 75-38306. 1976. perfect bdg. softcover 10.95 (ISBN 0-88247-379-4). R & E Pubs.
Gonzalez, Carlos F., et al. Computed Brain & Orbital Tomography: Technique & Interpretation. LC 76-28530. (Diagnostic & Therapeutic Radiology Ser.). 276p. 1976. 70.00x (ISBN 0-471-01692-6, Pub. by Wiley-Med). Wiley.
Gonzalez, Casanova P. Democracy in Mexico. 1970. pap. 7.95 (ISBN 0-19-501533-9, GB). Oxford U Pr.
Gonzalez, Catherine, jt. auth. see Gonzalez, Justo.
Gonzalez, Catherine G., jt. auth. see Gonzalez, Justo L.
Gonzalez, Catherine T. Cynthia Ann Parker: Indian Captive. (Stories for Young Americans Ser.). 1980. 5.95 (ISBN 0-89015-244-6). Eakin Pubns.
--Jane Long, Mother of Texas. 1982. 5.95 (ISBN 0-89015-299-3). Eakin Pubns.
--Lafitte: The Terror of the Gulf. (Stories for Young Americans Ser.). (Illus.). 64p. 1981. 5.95 (ISBN 0-89015-284-5). Eakin Pubns.
--Rhome & Its Pioneers. 1979. 18.50 (ISBN 0-89015-226-8). Eakin Pubns.
--Sam Houston: Hero of San Jacinto. (Illus.). 88p. 5.95 (ISBN 0-89015-382-5). Eakin Pubns.
--Tour Guide to North Texas. 1982. 8.95 (ISBN 0-89015-356-6). Eakin Pubns.
Gonzalez, Celedonio. El Espesor Del Pellejo De un Gato Ya Cadaver. LC 77-88536. 1978. pap. 6.00 (ISBN 0-89729-170-0). Ediciones.
Gonzalez, Edward. Cuba Under Castro: The Limits of Charisma. 224p. 1974. pap. text ed. 17.50 (ISBN 0-395-14067-6). HM.
Gonzalez, Elaine. The Chocolate Artistry. (Illus.). 240p. 1983. pap. 12.95 (ISBN 0-8092-5274-0). Contemp Bks.
Gonzalez, Emilio, jt. auth. see Cioffari, Vincenzo.
Gonzalez, Emilio, et al. Spanish Cultural Reader. 1969. text ed. 12.95x (ISBN 0-669-49841-6). Heath.
Gonzalez, Fe Acosta De see Acosta de Gonzalez, Fe.
Gonzalez, Fernando L. Disco-File: The Discographical Catalog of American Race, Rhythm & Blues, Rock & Roll & Soul. 3rd ed. Date not set. 80.00x (ISBN 0-9601090-2-1). F L Gonzalez.
Gonzalez, Gilbert G. Progressive Education: A Marxist Interpretation. LC 81-5787. (Studies in Marxism: Vol. 8). 197p. 1982. 19.95x (ISBN 0-930656-15-6); pap. 9.95 (ISBN 0-930656-16-4). MEP Pubns.
Gonzalez, Gloria. Curtains. 1976. pap. 1.85x (ISBN 0-685-67169-0). Dramatists Play.
--Gaucho. 144p. (gr. 5 up). pap. 1.25 (ISBN 0-440-92803-6, LFL). Dell.
Gonzalez, Gloria M., et al. La Empresa y Su Medio. (Span.). 1983. text ed. 17.00 (ISBN 0-538-22730-3, V73). SW Pub.
Gonzalez, Guillermo. Microwave Transistor Amplifiers: Analysis & Design. (Illus.). 368p. 1984. text ed. 35.95 (ISBN 0-13-581646-7). P-H.
Gonzalez, Gustavo. The Acquisition of Spanish Grammar by Native Spanish Speaking Children. LC 79-103428. 79p. (Orig.). 1978. pap. 6.75 (ISBN 0-89763-002-5). Natl Clearinghse Bilingual Ed.
Gonzalez, Harvey J. & Fein, Lois. Datatran: A Comprehensive & Practical System for Developing & Maintaining Data Processing Systems. (Illus.). 432p. 1983. text ed. 41.95 (ISBN 0-13-196493-3). P-H.
Gonzalez, Helga, ed. see Larson, Barbara.
Gonzalez, Irma, jt. ed. see Wertheim, Bill.
Gonzalez, J. A. & Gonzalez, Magda. Native American Tarot Deck. 108p. 1982. pap. 9.00 incl. card deck (ISBN 0-88079-009-1). US Games Syst.
Gonzalez, Jean, jt. auth. see Bergerud, Marly.
Gonzalez, Jean, jt. auth. see Bergerud, Mary.
Gonzalez, Joe R. & Zufelt, David L., eds. Cognates: Vocabulary Enrichment for Bilinguals. (Span. - Eng.). 1973. pap. text ed. 8.95x (ISBN 0-8422-0311-7). Irvington.
Gonzalez, Jose E. Contemporary Poetry in Puerto Rico. (Puerto Rico Ser.). 1979. lib. bdg. 59.95 (ISBN 0-8490-2902-3). Gordon Pr.
Gonzalez, Jose L. Balada de otro tiempo. 156p. 1980. pap. 5.95 (ISBN 0-940238-55-1). Ediciones Huracan.
--En Nueva York y Otras Desgracias. LC 81-65310. 172p. 1981. pap. 4.25 (ISBN 0-940238-14-4). Ediciones Huracan.
--Llegada. 144p. 1980. pap. 6.95 (ISBN 0-940238-56-X). Ediciones Huracan.
--Pais de Cuatro Pisos. LC 80-67414. (Nave y el puerto). 122p. 1981. pap. 4.25 (ISBN 0-940238-32-2). Ediciones Huracan.
Gonzalez, Josue. Towards Quality in Bilingual Education-Bilingual Education in the Integrated School. 34p. 1979. pap. 5.25 (ISBN 0-89763-001-7). Natl Clearinghse Bilingual Ed.
Gonzalez, Julio Lopez see Lopez Gonzalez, Julio.
Gonzalez, Justo. Historia de un Amor. (Illus.). 168p. (Orig., Span.). 1979. pap. 3.95 (ISBN 0-89922-151-3). Edit Caribe.
--The Story of Christianity. LC 83-49187. (Reformation to the Present Day Ser.: Vol. II). (Illus.). 448p. (Orig.). 1984. pap. 12.45x kivar cover (ISBN 0-06-063316-6, RD 511, HarpR). Har-Row.
Gonzalez, Justo & Gonzalez, Catherine. In Accord-Let Us Worship. (Orig.). 1981. pap. 3.95 (ISBN 0-377-00110-4). Friend Pr.
Gonzalez, Justo L. La Era de las Tinieblas. (Y Hasta Lo Ultimo de la Tierra: una Historia Ilustrada del Christianismo Ser.: Tomo III). (Illus.). 199p. (Orig., Span.). 1978. pap. 5.95 (ISBN 0-89922-128-9). Edit Caribe.
--La Era de los Altos Ideales. (Y Hasta Lo Ultimo de la Tierra: una Historia Ilustrada Del Cristianismo Ser.: Tomo IV). (Illus.). 197p. (Orig., Span.). 1979. pap. 5.95 (ISBN 0-89922-135-1). Edit Caribe.
--La Era de los Conquistadores. (Y Hasta Lo Ultimo de la Tierra: una Historia Ilustrada del Cristianismo: Tomo VII). (Illus.). 218p. (Orig., Span.). 1981. pap. 5.95 (ISBN 0-89922-162-9). Edit Caribe.
--La Era de los Dogmas y las Dudas. (Y hasta lo ultimo de la tierra Ser.: Tomo No. 8). (Illus.). 224p. (Orig.). 1983. pap. 5.95 (ISBN 0-89922-171-8). Edit Caribe.
--La Era de los Gigantes. (Y Hasta Lo Ultimo de la Tierra: una Historia Ilustrada del Cristianismo Ser.: Tomo II). (Illus.). 184p. (Orig., Span.). 1978. pap. 5.95 (ISBN 0-89922-117-3). Edit Caribe.
--La Era de los Martires. (Y Hasta Lo Ultimo de la Tierra: una Historia Ilustrada del Christianismo Ser.: Tomo I). (Illus.). 189p. (Orig., Span.). 1978. pap. 5.95 (ISBN 0-89922-109-2). Edit Caribe.
--La Era de los Reformadores. (Y Hasta Lo Ultimo de la Tierra: una Historia Ilustrada del Cristianismo Ser.: Tomo VI). (Illus.). 219p. (Orig., Span.). 1980. pap. 5.95 (ISBN 0-89922-154-8). Edit Caribe.
--La Era de los Suenos Frustrados. (Y Hasta Lo Ultimo de la Tierra: una Historia Ilustrada del Cristianismo Ser.: Tomo V). (Illus.). 182p. (Orig., Span.). 1979. pap. 5.95 (ISBN 0-89922-139-4). Edit Caribe.
--History of Christian Thought, 3 vols. rev. ed. LC 74-109679. 1975. Set. 56.00 (ISBN 0-687-17181-4). Abingdon.
--The History of Christian Thought: From the Beginnings to the Council of Chalcedon in A. D. 451. rev. ed. LC 74-109679. Set. text ed. 52.95; Vol. II. text ed. 18.75; Vol. I & III. text ed. 20.00. Abingdon.
--Luces Bajo el Almud. LC 77-11753. 76p. (Orig., Span.). 1977. pap. 2.50 (ISBN 0-89922-102-5). Edit Caribe.
--The Story of Christianity, Volume 1: The Early Church to the Reformation. LC 83-48430. (Illus.). 448p. (Orig.). 1983. pap. 12.95x (ISBN 0-317-01107-3, RD 510, HarpR). Har-Row.
Gonzalez, Justo L. & Gonzalez, Catherine G. Liberation Preaching: The Pulpit & the Oppressed. LC 79-27858. (Abingdon Preacher's Library). 1980. pap. 5.95 (ISBN 0-687-21700-8). Abingdon.
Gonzalez, Justo, Sr. Historia de un Milagro. 166p. (Span.). 1984. pap. 3.75 (ISBN 0-89922-144-0). Edit Caribe.
Gonzalez, Luis. San Jose de Gracia: Mexican Village in Transition. Upton, John, tr. from Sp. LC 73-11495. (Texas Pan American Ser.). (Illus.). 406p. 1974. O.P. 19.95x (ISBN 0-292-77507-5); pap. 11.95x (ISBN 0-292-77571-7). U of Tex Pr.
Gonzalez, M., tr. see Abdel-Malek, Anouar.
Gonzalez, Magda, jt. auth. see Gonzalez, J. A.
Gonzalez, Margaret. Louis Souris, Vol. 1. 149p. 1984. pap. text ed. 5.50 (ISBN 0-88334-181-6). Ind Sch Pr.
--Louis Souris, Vol. 2. 207p. 1984. pap. text ed. 5.95 (ISBN 0-88334-182-4). Ind Sch Pr.
Gonzalez, Mike, tr. see Vazquez, Adolfo S.
Gonzalez, Mirza. La Novela y el Cuento Psicologicos Demiquel de Carrion (Estudio Psico-Social Cubano) LC 76-42900. (Coleccion Polymita). 1979. pap. 9.95 (ISBN 0-89729-102-6). Ediciones.
Gonzalez, N. V. Mindoro & Beyond: Twenty-One Stories. 1979. text ed. 15.00x (ISBN 0-8248-0661-1); pap. text ed. 8.50x (ISBN 0-8248-0662-X). UH Pr.
Gonzalez, Nancie L. Black Carib Household Structure: A Study of Migration & Modernization. LC 77-93024. (Illus.). 188p. 1980. pap. text ed. 8.95x (ISBN 0-295-95733-6). U of Wash Pr.
Gonzalez, Nelly de see Diaz, Jorge & De Gonzalez, Nelly.
Gonzalez, Nilda. Bibliografia De Teatro Puertorriqueno: Siglos XIX y XX. LC 77-16485. 1978. pap. 9.00 (ISBN 0-8477-2006-3). U of PR Pr.
Gonzalez, Rene, jt. auth. see Ban, Thomas A.
Gonzalez, Richard, et al, eds. Improving U. S. Energy Security. 336p. 1985. 29.95 (ISBN 0-88730-015-4). Ballinger Pub.
Gonzalez, Richard F. & Negandhi, Anant R. United States Overseas Executive: His Orientations & Career Patterns. LC 66-64923. 1967. pap. 2.00 (ISBN 0-87744-078-6). Mich St U Pr.
Gonzalez, Richard F., jt. auth. see Harris, Roy D.
Gonzalez, RoseAnn D. & Cruz, MaryCarmen E. Copy, Combine, & Compose: Controlling Composition. 336p. 1983. pap. text ed. write for info. (ISBN 0-534-01341-4). Wadsworth Pub.
Gonzalez, Servando. Observando. (Essay Ser.). 72p. (Orig., Span.). 1985. pap. 5.00 (ISBN 0-932367-03-8). Ediciones El.
Gonzalez-Arce, Jorge F. Market Segmentation by Consumer Perception. LC 74-620059. 134p. 1974. pap. 6.00 (ISBN 0-87744-124-3). Mich St U Pr.
Gonzalez-Balado, Jose. Mother Teresa: Always the Poor. Diaz, Olimpia, Sr., tr. from Span. LC 80-83484. 112p. (Orig.). 1980. pap. 2.50 (ISBN 0-89243-134-2). Liguori Pubns.

Gonzalez-Balado, Jose L. & Playfoot, Janet, eds. My Life for the Poor: The Story of Mother Teresa in Her Own Words. LC 85-42787. 128p. 1985. 10.95 (ISBN 0-06-068237-X, HarpR). Har-Row.

Gonzalez-Crussi, Frank. Notes of an Anatomist. 144p. 1985. 12.95 (ISBN 0-15-167285-7). HarBraceJ.

Gonzalez de Barcia Carballido y Zuniga, Andres see Barcia Carballido Y Zuniga, Andres Gonzalez de.

Gonzalez del Valle, Antolin, jt. auth. see Gonzalez del Valle, Luis.

Gonzalez-Del-Valle, Antolin, jt. auth. see Gonzalez-Del-Valle, Luis.

Gonzalez del Valle, Antolin, jt. auth. see Gonzalez del Valle, Luis.

Gonzalez Del Valle, L. & Cabrera, Vicente. La Nueva Ficcion Hispanoamericana A Traves de Miguel Angel Asturias Y Gabriel Garcia Marquez. 1972. 9.95 (ISBN 0-88303-008-X); pap. 6.95 (ISBN 0-685-73212-6). E Torres & Sons.

Gonzalez del Valle, Luis & Gonzalez del Valle, Antolin. Correspondencia Comercial: Fondo y Forma. (Span.). 1981. text ed. 7.00 wkbk. (ISBN 0-538-22300-6, V30). SW Pub.

--Dos Decadas del Hispanismo Norteamericano Ante la Literatura Espanola del Siglo XX. LC 79-63859. 1979. pap. 2.00 (ISBN 0-89295-009-9). Society Sp & Sp-Am.

Gonzalez-Del-Valle, Luis & Gonzalez-Del-Valle, Antolin. Ficcion De Luis Romero. LC 76-22177. (Literary Criticism Ser.: No. 101). 1976. pap. 5.00 (ISBN 0-89295-000-5). Society Sp & Sp-Am.

Gonzalez-Del-Valle, Luis, jt. auth. see Cabrera, Vicente.

Gonzalez-del-Valle, Luis T., ed. Antologia de Poesia Espanola. 130p. 1984. pap. text ed. 20.00 (ISBN 0-89295-036-6). Society SP & SP-Am.

Gonzalez-del-Valle, Luis T. & Nickel, Catherine, eds. Selected Proceedings: Mid-America Conference on Hispanic Literature. 200p. 1985. pap. 30.00 (ISBN 0-89295-039-0). Society Sp & Sp-Am.

Gonzalez-del-Valle, Luis T. & Villanueva, Dario, eds. Estudios en Honor a Ricardo Gullon. LC 83-51005. 280p. 1984. pap. 30.00 (ISBN 0-89295-028-5). Society Sp & Sp Am.

Gonzalez-del-Valle, Luis T., jt. ed. see Boudreau, H. L.

Gonzalez-del-Valle, Luis T., jt. ed. see Hernandez, Ramon.

Gonzalez De Mendoza, Juan. History of the Great & Mighty Kingdom of China & the Situation Thereof, 2 Vols. Staunton, George T., ed. LC 73-141353. (Hakluyt Society First Ser: Nos. 14 & 15). 1971. Repr. of 1854 ed. Set. 58.00 (ISBN 0-8337-2360-X). B Franklin.

Gonzalez Diaz, Emilio, ed. see Universidad De Puerto Rico Centro De Investigaciones Sociales.

Gonzalez-Echevarria, Robert. Alejo Carpentier: The Pilgrim at Home. LC 76-28013. 304p. 1977. 27.50x (ISBN 0-8014-1029-0). Cornell U Pr.

Gonzalez Echevarria, Roberto & Muller-Bergh, Klaus. Alejo Carpentier: Bibliographical Guide-Guia Bibliografica. LC 83-10879. xxvii, 271p. 1983. lib. bdg. 39.95 (ISBN 0-313-23923-1, EAC/). Greenwood.

Gonzalez-Gerth, Miguel & Schade, George D., Jr., eds. Ruben Dario: Centennial Studies. 120p. (Published by Institute of Latin American Studies and the Dept. of Spanish-Portuguese). 1970. 5.00x (ISBN 0-292-70054-7). U of Tex Pr.

Gonzalez Gutierrez, Orlando. Diccionario de Expresiones Idiomaticas y Modismo Ingleses. 2nd ed. 328p. (Span. & Eng.). 1976. 35.00 (ISBN 0-686-56683-1, S-33043). French & Eur.

Gonzalez Lopez, Emilio. La Poesia De Valle-Inclan: Del Simbolismo Al Expresionism. 6.25 (ISBN 0-8477-0506-4); pap. 5.00 (ISBN 0-8477-0507-2). U of PR Pr.

Gonzalez Mas, Ezequiel. Historia De la Literatura Espanola, 2 vols. Incl. Vol. 1. Epoca Medieval, Siglo V-XV. 6.25 (ISBN 0-8477-3125-1); pap. 5.00 (ISBN 0-8477-3129-4); Vol. 2. Renacimiento, Siglo XVI. 6.25 (ISBN 0-8477-3126-X); pap. 5.00 (ISBN 0-8477-3130-8). pap. U of PR Pr.

Gonzalez-Mena, Frank & Gonzalez-Mena, Janet. Experiencias En Espanol. Medrano, A., ed. Gonzalez-Mena, Frank & Gonzalez-Mena, Janet, trs. from Eng. (Illus.). 192p. (Orig., Span.). (gr. k-3). 1976. pap. text ed. 12.95 tchrs ed. (ISBN 0-88499-232-2); student wkbk. 3.95 (ISBN 0-88499-234-9); program package 48.95 (ISBN 0-88499-233-0). Inst Mod Lang.

Gonzalez-Mena, Frank, tr. see Gonzalez-Mena, Frank & Gonzalez-Mena, Janet.

Gonzalez-Mena, Janet. English Experiences. Incl. Teacher's Program for English Experiences. (Illus.). 142p. pap. 12.95 (ISBN 0-88499-225-X); My Book Workbook. (Illus.). 48p. pap. 3.95 (ISBN 0-88499-238-1). LC 75-5307. (ps). 1975. Program Package Set. 48.95 (ISBN 0-88499-244-6). Inst Mod Lang.

Gonzalez-Mena, Janet & Eyer, Dianne W. Infancy & Caregiving. LC 79-91838. (Illus.). 163p. 1980. pap. 9.95 (ISBN 0-87484-515-7). Mayfield Pub.

Gonzalez-Mena, Janet, jt. auth. see Garcia, Mary H.

Gonzalez-Mena, Janet, jt. auth. see Gonzalez-Mena, Frank.

Gonzalez-Mena, Janet, tr. see Gonzalez-Mena, Frank & Gonzalez-Mena, Janet.

Gonzalez-Polio, Edgardo, jt. auth. see Bamberger, Michael.

Gonzalez Porto-Bompiani. Diccionario Literario De Obras y Perssonajes De Todos los Tiempos y Paises, 2 vols. 1538p. (Espn.). 1979. Set. 100.00 (ISBN 0-686-57356-0, S-50244). French & Eur.

Gonzalez-Ruiz, Jose-Maria. The New Creation: Marxist & Christian? O'Connell, Mathew J., tr. from Spanish. LC 76-10226. Orig. Title: Marximo y Cristianismo Frente Al Hombre Nuevo. 160p. (Orig.). 1976. 6.95 (ISBN 0-88344-327-9). Orbis Bks.

Gonzalez Torres, Rafael A. La Obra Poetica de Felix Franco Oppenheimer: Estudio Tematico-Analitico-Estilistico. LC 79-17993. (Coleccion UPREX; Ser. Estudios Literarios: No. 59). 150p. (Orig., Sp.). 1981. pap. 1.85x (ISBN 0-8477-0059-3). U of PR Pr.

Gonzalez-Vales, Luis. Alejandro Ramirez y Su Tiempo: Ensayos De Historia Economica E Institutional. LC 78-1772. (Illus., Span.). 1979. pap. 10.00 (ISBN 0-8477-0853-5). U of PR Pr.

Gonzalez-Wippler, Migene. The Complete Book of Spells, Ceremonies, & Magic. (Illus.). 1977. 12.95 (ISBN 0-517-52885-1). Crown.

--A Kabbalah for the Modern World: Revealing the Oneness of All Things. 2nd, rev. & expanded ed. LC 83-80133. (New Age Ser.). 250p. 1985. pap. 9.95 (ISBN 0-87542-294-2, L-294). Llewellyn Pubns.

--Rituals & Spells of Santeria. pap. 6.95 (ISBN 0-942272-07-2). Original Pubns.

--The Santeria Experience. LC 81-13989. 228p. 1982. 10.95 (ISBN 0-13-791079-7); pap. 4.95 (ISBN 0-13-791087-8). P-H.

Gonzalez-Zambrano, Jose. Analisis Financiero Compuesto o Integral. (Span.). 1982. text ed. 8.20 (ISBN 0-538-22400-2, V40). SW Pub.

Gonzelez, Carlos F., et al, eds. Head & Spine Imaging. LC 84-15172. 1000p. 1985. text ed. 150.00 (ISBN 0-471-89747-7, Pub. by Wiley Med). Wiley.

Goo, Edna. Western Customs. 132p. 1980. 1.95 (ISBN 0-89955-151-3, Pub. by Mei Ya China). Intl Spec Bk.

Gooch, A. Diminutive, Augumentative & Pejorative Suffixes in Modern Spanish. 2nd ed. 1970. Pergamon.

Gooch, B., et al. Work: Pathway to Independence. (Illus.). 1979. 17.50 (ISBN 0-8269-4900-2). Am Technical.

Gooch, Bill & Carrier, Lois. Strategies for Success. 1983. pap. text ed. write for info. (ISBN 0-534-01410-0, Breton Pubs). Wadsworth Pub.

Gooch, Bill, jt. auth. see Stadt, Ronald.

Gooch, Bob. Bass Fishing: Stripers, White Bass, Yellow Bass & Perch. LC 75-17965. (Illus.). 159p. 1975. pap. 5.00 (ISBN 0-87033-206-6). Tidewater.

--Spinning for Trout. (Illus.). 192p. 1981. 14.95 (ISBN 0-684-16843-X, ScribT). Scribner.

--Spinning for Trout. (Illus.). 192p. 1984. pap. 7.95 (ISBN 0-684-18076-6, ScribT). Scribner.

--Squirrels & Squirrel Hunting. LC 72-81371. (Illus.). 160p. 1972. 6.00 (ISBN 0-87033-172-8). Tidewater.

--Virginia Hunting Guide. LC 84-21004. (Illus.). 236p. 1985. pap. 8.95 (ISBN 0-8139-1041-2). U Pr of VA.

Gooch, Brad. Billy Idol. 160p. (Orig.). 1986. pap. 2.95 (ISBN 0-345-32895-7). Ballantine.

--Daily News. (Orig.). 1977. pap. 5.00 (ISBN 0-915990-07-5). Z Pr.

--Hall & Oates. (Rock Bks.). 1984. pap. 2.95 (ISBN 0-345-32271-1). Ballantine.

--Jailbait & Other Stories. LC 51-375. 120p. (Orig.). 1984. pap. 6.95 (ISBN 0-933322-17-8). Sea Horse.

Gooch, Brison D., ed. Napoleon III - Man of Destiny: Enlightened Statesman or Proto-Fascist? LC 75-12666. (European Problem Studies). 128p. 1976. pap. 5.95 (ISBN 0-88275-323-1). Krieger.

Gooch, Brison D., ed. & intro. by see Napoleon, Louis, 3rd.

Gooch, Bryan N. & Thatcher, David. Musical Settings of British Romantic Literature. LC 81-48412. 1470p. 1982. lib. bdg. 182.00 (ISBN 0-8240-9381-X). Garland Pub.

Gooch, Bryan N. & Thatcher, David S. Musical Settings of Early & Mid-Victorian Literature: A Catalogue. LC 78-68274. (Reference Library of Humanities Ser.). 1979. lib. bdg. 109.00 (ISBN 0-8240-9793-9). Garland Pub.

--Musical Settings of Late Victorian & Modern British Literature: A Catalogue. LC 75-24085. 1112p. 1976. lib. bdg. 109.00 (ISBN 0-8240-9981-8). Garland Pub.

Gooch, F. Face to Face with the Mexicans. 1976. lib. bdg. 59.95 (ISBN 0-8490-1798-X). Gordon Pr.

Gooch, G. P. Germany & the French Revolution. 543p. 1965. Repr. of 1920 ed. 35.00x (ISBN 0-7146-1477-7, BHA-01477, F Cass Co). Biblio Dist.

--Goethe: Some Makers of the Modern Spirit. Macmurray, John, ed. 1933. 10.00 (ISBN 0-8274-2421-3). R West.

--History of Our Time: 1885-1911. 1977. Repr. lib. bdg. 12.50 (ISBN 0-8495-1905-5). Arden Lib.

--Hobbes. LC 77-5390. 1939. lib. bdg. 8.50 (ISBN 0-8414-4429-3). Folcroft.

--Maria Theresa & Other Studies. viii, 432p. 1965. Repr. of 1951 ed. 23.50 (ISBN 0-208-00019-4, Archon). Shoe String.

--Under Six Reigns. vii, 344p. 1971. Repr. of 1958 ed. 22.00 (ISBN 0-208-01263-X, Archon). Shoe String.

Gooch, G. P. & Masterman, J. H. Century of British Foreign Policy. LC 70-118471. 1971. Repr. of 1917 ed. 19.50x (ISBN 0-8046-1220-X, Pub. by Kennikat). Assoc Faculty Pr.

Gooch, G. P., ed. see Great Britain Foreign Office.

Gooch, G. P., ed. see Royal Society of Literature, United Kingdom.

Gooch, George P. Annals of Politics & Culture, Fourteen Nintey-Two to Eighteen Nintey Nine. LC 79-170959. (History, Economics & Social Science Ser: No. 291). 1971. Repr. of 1905 ed. lib. bdg. 22.50 (ISBN 0-8337-1380-9). B Franklin.

--Courts & Cabinets. LC 72-3304. (Essay Index Reprint Ser.). Repr. of 1946 ed. 25.00 (ISBN 0-8369-2901-2). Ayer Co Pubs.

--Louis the Fifteenth: The Monarchy in Decline. LC 75-36361. (Illus.). 1976. Repr. of 1956 ed. lib. bdg. 21.50x (ISBN 0-8371-8632-3, GOLO). Greenwood.

--Political Thought in England from Bacon to Halifax. LC 75-41115. Repr. of 1955 ed. 18.00 (ISBN 0-404-14754-2). AMS Pr.

--The Second Empire. LC 75-1151. (Illus.). 324p. 1975. Repr. of 1960 ed. lib. bdg. 19.75x (ISBN 0-8371-7985-8, GOSE). Greenwood.

--Studies in Modern History. facs. ed. LC 68-16934. (Essay Index Reprint Ser). 1931. 20.00x (ISBN 0-8369-0482-6). Ayer Co Pubs.

Gooch, George P., ed. In Pursuit of Peace. facs. ed. LC 72-128249. (Essay Index Reprint Ser). 1933. 15.00 (ISBN 0-8369-1832-0). Ayer Co Pubs.

Gooch, Jane L. The Lamentable Tragedy of Locrine. (Garland English Texts Ser.). 1981. lib. bdg. 30.00 (ISBN 0-8240-9407-7). Garland Pub.

Gooch, John. The Prospect of War: Studies in British Defence Policy 1847-1942. 174p. 1981. 28.00x (ISBN 0-7146-3128-0, F Cass Co). Biblio Dist.

Gooch, John & Perlmutter, Amos, eds. Military Deception & Strategic Surprise. (Illus.). 200p. 1982. text ed. 30.00x (ISBN 0-7146-3202-3, F Cass Co). Biblio Dist.

Gooch, John, jt. ed. see Beckett, Ian.

Gooch, John, jt. ed. see Perlmutter, Amos.

Gooch, Nancy & Sexton, J. David. How to Maximize Your Child's Potential: A Developmental Guide to the First Three Years. 128p. (Orig.). 1984. pap. 5.95 (ISBN 0-346-12638-X). Cornerstone.

Gooch, P. S., jt. auth. see Harris, J. R.

Gooch, Robert K. French Parliamentary Committee System. LC 69-19226. xvi, 259p. 1969. Repr. of 1935 ed. 21.00 (ISBN 0-208-00803-9, Archon). Shoe String.

Gooch, Sandy. If You Love Me Don't Feed Me Junk! (Illus.). 240p. 1983. pap. 9.95 (ISBN 0-8359-3029-7). Reston.

Gooch, Stan. The Secret Life of Humans. 224p. 1981. 30.00x (ISBN 0-686-79450-8, Pub. by Dent Australia). State Mutual Bk.

Gooch, Stan & Pringle, M. L. Four Years On: A Follow-up Study at School Leaving Age of Children Formerly Attending a Traditional & Progessive Junior School. (Studies in Child Development). (Orig.). 1966. pap. text ed. 4.00x (ISBN 0-582-32392-4). Humanities.

Gooch, Stapleton D; see O'Neal, William B.

Gooch, Steve. All Together Now. 96p. 1984. pap. 6.95 (ISBN 0-413-53480-4, NO. 4111). Methuen Inc.

--Female Transport. 1984. pap. 6.95 (ISBN 0-902818-62-7, NO. 4140). Methuen Inc.

--Will Wat? If Not, What Will? 88p. (Orig.). 1981. pap. 5.95 (ISBN 0-902818-63-5, NO. 4128). Pluto Pr.

Gooch, Steve & Thompson, Paul. The Motor Show. 88p. (Orig.). 1981. pap. 5.95 (ISBN 0-902818-64-3, NO. 4127). Pluto Pr.

Gooch, T. G., et al, eds. Behavior of Joints in High Temperature Materials. (Illus.). 272p. 1983. 52.00 (ISBN 0-85334-187-7, Pub. by Elsevier Applied Sci England). Elsevier.

Gooch, Tom. That's All for Today: Selected Writings of Tom Gooch. Turner, Decherd, ed. LC 55-12081. (Illus.). 1955. 9.95 (ISBN 0-87074-062-8). SMU Press.

Gooch, Wilbur I. Junior High School Costs. LC 75-176813. (Columbia University. Teachers College. Contributions to Education: No. 604). Repr. of 1934 ed. 22.50 (ISBN 0-404-55604-3). AMS Pr.

Goock, Roland. Enciclopedia Del "Hagalo Usted Mismo". 436p. (Espn.). 1975. 41.95 (ISBN 84-239-6599-6, S-50462). French & Eur.

--The World's One Hundred Best Recipes. Culinary Arts Institute, tr. from Ger. LC 73-9341. (Illus.). 208p. 1973. 14.95 (ISBN 0-8326-0542-5, 1650); pap. 8.95 (ISBN 0-686-67697-1, 2650). Delair.

Good, Alvin. Sociology & Education. 589p. 1981. Repr. of 1926 ed. lib. bdg. 40.00 (ISBN 0-89760-322-2). Telegraph Bks.

Good, Anthony, jt. auth. see Barnard, Alan.

Good, Byron, jt. ed. see Kleinman, Arthur.

Good, Charles M. Rural Markets & Trade in East Africa. LC 72-128466. (Research Papers Ser.: No. 128). 252p. 1970. pap. 10.00 (ISBN 0-89065-035-7). U Chicago Dept Geog.

Good, Dale, ed. Compton's Book of the Year, 1984. 1984. write for info. Ency Brit Inc.

Good, David A. Cost-Benefit & Cost-Effectiveness Analyses: Their Application in Evaluating Investment Decisions in Urban Public Services & Facilities. (Discussion Paper Ser.: No. 47). 1971. pap. 4.50 (ISBN 0-686-32215-0). Regional Sci Res Inst.

Good, David F. The Economic Rise of the Hapsburg Empire 1750-1914. LC 83-17959. 288p. 1984. text ed. 33.50x (ISBN 0-520-05094-0). U of Cal Pr.

Good, Edwin M. The Eddy Collection of Musical Instruments: A Checklist, No.3. LC 85-1657. (Fallen Leaf Reference Books in Music: No. 3). 70p. 1985. pap. 19.95 (ISBN 0-914913-02-6). Fallen Leaf.

--Giraffes, Black Dragons & Other Pianos: A Technological History from Cristofori to the Modern Concert Grand. LC 81-50787. (Illus.). 328p. 1982. 32.50x (ISBN 0-8047-1120-8). Stanford U Pr.

--Irony in the Old Testament. (Bible & Literature Ser.: No. 3). (Orig.). 1981. pap. text ed. 9.95x (ISBN 0-907459-05-6, Pub. by Almond Pr England). Eisenbrauns.

Good, Fred. The Success Factor. LC 85-50414. 84p. 1985. pap. 4.95 (ISBN 0-931117-02-X). Univ Pub.

Good Housekeeping Editors. Family Health & Medical Guide. LC 78-51129. (Illus.). 960p. 1979. 27.00 (ISBN 0-87851-023-0). Hearst Bks.

Good Housekeeping Magazine Editors. Good Housekeeping American Family Christmas. (Alan D Bragdon Bk.). 168p. Date not set. 19.95 (ISBN 0-916410-29-3). Bragdon A.

Good, I. J. Good Thinking: The Foundations of Probability & Its Applications. (Illus.). 351p. 1983. 35.00x (ISBN 0-8166-1141-6); pap. 14.95x (ISBN 0-8166-1142-4). U of Minn Pr.

Good, I. S. & Osteyee, D. B. Information Weight of Evidence, the Singularity Between Probability Measures & Signal Detection. LC 74-393. (Lecture Notes in Mathematics: Vol. 376). xi, 156p. 1974. pap. 12.00 (ISBN 0-387-06726-4). Springer-Verlag.

Good, James. Sub Wars, No. 1: Target Delta V. (Orig.). 1982. pap. 2.50 (ISBN 0-8217-1046-X). Zebra.

--Sub Wars, No. 2: Target Sosus. 1982. pap. 2.50 (ISBN 0-8217-1092-3). Zebra.

--Target Delta V. (Sub Wars Ser.: No. 1). (Orig.). 1981. pap. 2.50 (ISBN 0-89083-892-5). Zebra.

Good, James W. Irish Unionism. LC 70-102607. Repr. of 1920 ed. 21.50x (ISBN 0-8046-0784-2, Pub. by Kennikat). Assoc Faculty Pr.

Good, Joan M., et al, eds. Theatrical Seasonings-Encore! LC 83-50926. (Illus.). 336p. (Orig.). 1983. pap. 9.95 comb. binding (ISBN 0-9612330-0-1). Stage Guild.

Good, John F. The Aviator's Guide to Loran-C. LC 84-71683. (Illus.). 160p. 1984. pap. 12.00 (ISBN 0-930939-01-8). Aksunai Pr.

Good, John M., ed. Readings in Educational Management. LC 73-80183. pap. 47.50 (ISBN 0-317-07957-3, 2004503). Bks Demand UMI.

Good, John W. Studies in the Milton Tradition. LC 73-144619. Repr. of 1915 ed. 16.00 (ISBN 0-404-02862-4). AMS Pr.

--Studies in the Milton Tradition. Repr. of 1915 ed. 22.00 (ISBN 0-384-19150-9). Johnson Repr.

Good, Lawrence R., et al. Therapy by Design: Implications of Architecture for Human Behavior. (Illus.). 208p. 1965. photocopy ed. 19.75x (ISBN 0-398-00703-9). C C Thomas.

Good, Linda A. The Curriculum from A to Z. (Teacher Aid Ser.). 185p. 1984. wire-o bdg. 16.95 (ISBN 0-513-01775-5). Denison.

Good, Mrs. Marvin. The Good Samaritan. 1978. pap. 1.95 (ISBN 0-686-24049-9). Rod & Staff.

--How God Made the World. 1978. pap. 1.95 (ISBN 0-686-24050-2). Rod & Staff.

--My Book About Bartemaeus. 1978. pap. 1.95 (ISBN 0-686-24052-9). Rod & Staff.

--A Shepherd Boy. 1978. pap. 1.95 (ISBN 0-686-24054-5). Rod & Staff.

Good, Merle. Hazel's People. LC 73-158174. 168p. 1975. pap. 1.95 (ISBN 0-8361-1773-5). Herald Pr.

--Nicole Visits an Amish Farm. LC 81-71531. (Illus.). 48p. (gr. 3-5). 1982. 8.95 (ISBN 0-8027-6443-6); reinforced 10.95 (ISBN 0-8027-6444-4). Walker & Co.

--Who Are the Amish? LC 85-70283. (Illus.). 128p. (Orig.). 1985. 24.95 (ISBN 0-934672-28-8); pap. 15.95 (ISBN 0-934672-26-1). Good Bks PA.

Good, Merle & Good, Phyllis. Twenty Most Asked Questions About the Amish & Mennonites. LC 79-54804. (People's Place Booklet Ser.: No.1). 96p. 1979. pap. 3.50 (ISBN 0-934672-00-8). Good Bks PA.

Good, Patricia K. & Brantner, John. A Practical Guide to the MMPI: An Introduction for Psychologists, Physicians, Social Workers, & Other Professionals. 1974. 10.95x (ISBN 0-8166-0706-0). U of Minn Pr.

Good, Paul. The Trouble I've Seen: White Journalist - Black Movement. LC 74-10923. 272p. 1975. 11.95 (ISBN 0-88258-020-5). Howard U Pr.

Good, Phillip. Choosing a Word Processor. 1983. text ed. 21.95 (ISBN 0-8359-0761-9); pap. text ed. 15.95 (ISBN 0-8359-0760-0). Reston.

--The Critic's Guide to Word Processing for the IBM PC & PC Compatable Computers. 19.95 (ISBN 0-8019-7530-1). Chilton.

Good, Phillip I. Choosing a Word Processor. 1984. 10.95 (ISBN 0-910085-00-5); word porcessor, comparison tables 6.95, (ISBN 0-910085-01-3). Info Res MI.

--Computerize Your Business. LC 84-45159. 320p. (Orig.). 1984. pap. 17.95 (ISBN 0-8019-7519-0). Chilton.

--A Critical Guide to Software for the IBM PC & PC Compatible Computers: Computers for Professionals in Business, Agriculture, Law & Health. LC 83-17148. (Illus.). 284p. 1983. pap. 12.95 (ISBN 0-8019-7413-5). Chilton.

--A Critic's Guide to Apple II Computers. LC 83-72438. (Illus.). 254p. 1983. pap. 12.95 (ISBN 0-8019-7412-7). Chilton.

--A Critic's Guide to Software for CP-M Computers. (Illus.). 224p. 1983. pap. 12.95 (ISBN 0-8019-7404-6). Chilton.

--Critic's Guide to Software for the IBM PC & PC Compatible Computers. 2nd ed. LC 83-17148. 310p. (Orig.). 1984. pap. 14.95 (ISBN 0-8019-7538-7). Chilton.

--A Critic's Guide to Word Processing for the IBM-PC & PC Compatible Computers. LC 84-45160. 120p. (Orig.). 1984. pap. 10.95 (ISBN 0-8019-7530-1). Chilton.

--Increasing Your Business Effectiveness Through Computer Communications: PC Plus C Equals Productivity. LC 84-45691. 190p. (Orig.). 1985. pap. 17.95 (ISBN 0-8019-7559-X). Chilton.

--Managing Your Office with Macintosh. LC 84-45689. 176p. (Orig.). 1985. pap. 16.95 (ISBN 0-8019-7543-3). Chilton.

Good, Phillip I., jt. auth. see Franz, Martin.

Good, Phyllis & Kraybill, Donald B. Perils of Professionalism. LC 82-3052. 240p. 1982. pap. 9.95 (ISBN 0-8361-1997-5). Herald Hse.

Good, Phyllis, jt. auth. see Good, Merle.

Good, Phyllis P. Cooking & Memories. LC 82-84537. (People's Place Booklet Ser.: No. 5). (Illus.). 256p. (Orig.). 1983. pap. 3.50 (ISBN 0-934672-16-4). Good Bks PA.

Good, Phyllis P., jt. auth. see Kraybill, Donald B.

Good, Phyllis P. & Pellman, Rachel T., eds. Breads: From Amish & Mennonite Kitchens. (Pennsylvania Dutch Cookbooks Ser.). (Illus., Orig.). 1982. pap. 1.95 (ISBN 0-934672-06-7). Good Bks PA.

--Cakes: From Amish & Mennonite Kitchens. (Pennsylvania Dutch Cookbooks Ser.). (Illus., Orig.). 1983. pap. 1.95 (ISBN 0-934672-12-1). Good Bks PA.

--Candies, Beverages & Snacks: From Amish & Mennonite Kitchens. (Pennsylvania Dutch Cookbooks Ser.). (Illus., Orig.). 1983. pap. 1.95 (ISBN 0-934672-15-6). Good Bks PA.

--Casseroles: From Amish & Mennonite Kitchens. (Pennsylvania Dutch Cookbooks Ser.). (Illus., Orig.). 1983. pap. 1.95 (ISBN 0-934672-11-3). Good Bks PA.

--Cookies: From Amish & Mennonite Kitchens. (Pennsylvania Dutch Cookbooks Ser.). (Illus., Orig.). 1982. pap. 1.95 (ISBN 0-934672-05-9). Good Bks PA.

--Desserts: From Amish & Mennonite Kitchens. (Pennsylvania Dutch Cookbooks Ser.). (Illus., Orig.). 1983. pap. 1.95 (ISBN 0-934672-13-X). Good Bks PA.

--From Amish & Mennonite Kitchens. LC 84-80653. 420p. 1984. pap. 11.95 deluxe ed. (ISBN 0-934672-21-0). Good Bks PA.

--Jams, Jellies & Relishes: From Amish & Mennonite Kitchens. (Pennsylvania Dutch Cookbooks Ser.). (Illus., Orig.). 1983. pap. 1.95 (ISBN 0-934672-14-8). Good Bks PA.

--Meats & Meat Dishes: From Amish & Mennonite Kitchens. (Pennsylvania Dutch Cookbooks Ser.). (Illus., Orig.). 1982. pap. 1.95 (ISBN 0-934672-07-5). Good Bks PA.

--Pies: From Amish & Mennonite Kitchens. (Pennsylvania Dutch Cookbooks Ser.). (Illus., Orig.). 1982. pap. 1.95 (ISBN 0-934672-04-0). Good Bks PA.

--Salads: From Amish & Mennonite Kitchens. (Pennsylvania Dutch Cookbooks Ser.). (Illus., Orig.). 1983. pap. 1.95 (ISBN 0-934672-10-5). Good Bks PA.

--Soups: From Amish & Mennonite Kitchens. (Pennsylvania Dutch Cookbooks Ser.). (Illus., Orig.). 1982. pap. 1.95 (ISBN 0-934672-08-3). Good Bks PA.

--Vegetables: From Amish & Mennonite Kitchens. (Pennsylvania Dutch Cookbooks Ser.). (Illus., Orig.). 1982. pap. 1.95 (ISBN 0-934672-09-1). Good Bks PA.

Good, R., jt. auth. see Nicholls, A.

Good, R. A., jt. ed. see Day, N. K.

Good, R. A., jt. ed. see Day, S. R.

Good, R. A., jt. ed. see Twomey, J. J.

Good, R. J. & Stromberg, R., eds. Surface & Colloid Science, Vol. 11. LC 67-29459. (Illus.). 360p. 1979. 49.50x (ISBN 0-306-40108-8, Plenum Pr). Plenum Pub.

Good, Ralph E., et al, eds. Freshwater Wetlands: Ecological Processes & Management Potential. LC 78-2836. 1978. 45.00 (ISBN 0-12-290150-9). Acad Pr.

Good, Richard P., Jr., jt. auth. see Peva, James R.

Good, Robert, jt. auth. see Alexander, J. Wesley.

Good, Robert A., jt. auth. see Park, Byung H.

Good, Robert A., jt. auth. see Sigel, M. Michael.

Good, Robert A., jt. ed. see Bach, Fritz H.

Good, Robert A., jt. ed. see Dupont, Bo.

Good, Robert A., jt. ed. see Gupta, Sudhir.

Good, Robert A., jt. ed. see Lipkin, Martin.

Good, Robert A., jt. ed. see Litman, Gary W.

Good, Robert A., jt. ed. see Safai, Bijan.

Good, Robert A., et al, eds. Molecular Pathology. (Illus.). 888p. 1975. 85.50x (ISBN 0-398-02944-X). C C Thomas.

Good, Robert C. U. D. I. The International Politics of the Rhodesian Rebellion. 1973. 35.00x (ISBN 0-691-05647-1). Princeton U Pr.

Good, Robert C., jt. ed. see Hilsman, Roger.

Good, Robert J., jt. ed. see Matijevic, Egon.

Good, Robert M. The Sheep of His Pasture: A Study of the Hebrew Noun 'AM(M) & its Semitic Cognates. LC 83-90934. (Harvard Semitic Monographs). 214p. 1984. 15.00 (ISBN 0-89130-628-5, 04 00 29). Scholars Pr GA.

Good, Roger & Greensher, Arnold, eds. Guide to Ambulatory Surgery. (Monographs in Family Medicine Ser.). 240p. 1982. 32.50 (ISBN 0-8089-1418-9, 791655). Grune.

Good, Ronald. Features of Evolution in the Flowering Plants. LC 74-82210. (Illus.). 416p. 1974. pap. text ed. 6.95 (ISBN 0-486-61591-X). Dover.

--Features of Evolution in the Flowering Plants. (Illus.). 11.50 (ISBN 0-8446-5194-X). Peter Smith.

--The Geography of Flowering Plants. 4th ed. LC 73-85684. (Illus.). 584p. 1974. text ed. 33.00x (ISBN 0-582-46611-3). Longman.

--The Philosophy of Evolution. 192p. 1981. 27.00x (ISBN 0-9503518-6-5, Pub. by Dovecote England). State Mutual Bk.

Good, Ronald D. The Geography of the Flowering Plants. 4th ed. LC 73-85684. pap. 145.00 (ISBN 0-317-27714-6, 2025240). Bks Demand UMI.

Good, Ronald G. How Children Learn Science: Conceptual Development & Implications for Teaching. (Illus.). 1977. text ed. write for info. (ISBN 0-02-344640-4). Macmillan.

Good, Shirley R. & Rodgers, Susan S. Analysis for Action: Nursing Care of the Elderly. (Illus.). 1980. pap. text ed. 16.95 (ISBN 0-13-032623-2). P-H.

Good, Stephen. How to Get a Job with the Police Department. (Illus.). 160p. 1984. pap. 6.25i (ISBN 0-06-463587-2, EH 587). B&N NY.

Good, Stephen M. How to Get a Job with the Post Office. LC 79-2240. 1980. pap. 5.95 (ISBN 0-06-463500-7, EH 500, EH). B&N NY.

Good Thing Inc. Slim Goodbody & Your Body. (Illus.). 1981. pap. text ed. 141.00 (ISBN 0-89290-182-9, 433-SATC). Soc for Visual.

Good Thing Inc. & Burstein, John. Slim Goodbody: Your Body, Health & Feelings. (gr. 1-3). 1978. text ed. 190.00 (ISBN 0-89290-098-9, CM-43). Soc for Visual.

Good, Thomas, et al. Mathematics Instructions. LC 82-4646. (I. R. T. Ser.). (Illus.). 321p. 1983. 25.00 (ISBN 0-582-28342-6). Longman.

Good, Thomas L. & Biddle, Bruce J. Teachers Make a Difference. 288p. 1982. pap. text ed. 13.00 (ISBN 0-8191-2157-6). U Pr of Amer.

Good, Thomas L. & Brophy, Jere E. Educational Psychology. 2nd ed. 1980. text ed. 26.95 (ISBN 0-03-053191-8, HoltC); study guide 11.95 (ISBN 0-03-053201-9); instr's manual 25.00 (ISBN 0-03-053196-9). HR&W.

--Looking in Classrooms. 3rd ed. 416p. 1984. pap. text ed. 13.95scp (ISBN 0-06-042404-4, HarpC). Har-Row.

Good, Thomas L., jt. auth. see Brophy, Jere E.

Good, Thomas L., jt. auth. see Cooper, Harris M.

Good, Thomas L., jt. ed. see Doyle, Walter.

Good, Thomas L., jt. auth. see Greenwood, Gordon E.

Good, William & Nelson, Jefferson. Psychiatry Made Ridiculously Simple. (Illus.). 83p. (Orig.). 1984. pap. text ed. 9.50 (ISBN 0-940780-04-6). Medmaster.

Goodacre, Clive. Penrose International Review of the Graphic Arts 1982, Vol. 74. (Illus.). 288p. 1982. 59.95 (ISBN 0-7198-2669-1, Pub. by Northwood Pr England). Alphabet MA.

Goodacre, J. Kenneth. Marine Insurance Claims. 1050p. 1981. 125.00 (ISBN 0-900886-53-6, Pub. By Witherby & Co England). State Mutual Bk.

Goodacre, P. Worked Examples in Quantity Surveying Measurement. (Illus.). 175p. 1982. pap. 25.00 (ISBN 0-419-12340-7, NO. 6727, E & FN Spon). Methuen Inc.

Goodacre, P., et al. Cost Factors in Dimensional Co-ordination. 85p. 1982. pap. 9.95 (ISBN 0-902132-66-0, NO. 6723, Pub. by E & FN Spon England). Methuen Inc.

Goodale, Ernest. Wearing & the Warners Eighteen Seventy to Nineteen Seventy. 1981. 30.00x (ISBN 0-85317-004-5, Pub. by Lewis Pubs). State Mutual Bk.

--Weaving & the Warners, Eighteen Seventy to Nineteen Seventy. (Illus.). 1971. text ed. 25.50x (ISBN 0-85317-004-5, Pub. by A & C Black England). Humanities.

Goodale, James C. Communications Law 1983: A Course Handbook, 2 Vols. 1860p. 1983. pap. 35.00 (G6-3754). PLI.

Goodale, James C., ed. The New York Times Co. vs. U. S. Pentagon Papers Litigation, 2 vols. LC 72-173288. 82.50 (ISBN 0-405-00100-2). Ayer Co Pubs.

Goodale, James G. The Fine Art of Interviewing. LC 81-10716. (Illus.). 208p. 1982. text ed. 24.95 (ISBN 0-13-317008-X). P-H.

Goodale, James G., jt. auth. see Hall, Dougals T.

Goodale, Jane C. Tiwi Wives: A Study of the Women of Melville Island, North Australia. LC 72-11728. (Illus.). 392p. 1980. pap. text ed. 9.95x (ISBN 0-295-95354-3). U of Wash Pr.

Goodale, Jerry, jt. auth. see Petersen, Dan.

Goodale, Katherine. Behind the Scenes with Edwin Booth. LC 76-87121. (Illus.). 328p. 1931. 24.50 (ISBN 0-405-08564-8, Blom Pubns). Ayer Co Pubs.

Goodale, Katherine D. Pas de Trois, Fun with Ballet Words. (Illus.). 25p. (Orig.). (gr. k-7). 1982. pap. 5.95 (ISBN 0-9609662-0-X). Goodale Pub.

Goodale, Thomas & Witt, Peter A., eds. Recreation & Leisure: Issues in an Era of Change. LC 79-92646. 394p. (Orig.). 1980. pap. text ed. 14.95x (ISBN 0-910251-00-X). Venture Pub PA.

Goodale, Thomas L. & Witt, Peter A., eds. Recreation & Leisure: Issues in an Era of Change. Rev. ed. LC 85-50103. 406p. 1985. pap. text ed. 18.95x (ISBN 0-910251-10-X). Venture Pub PA.

Goodall, B. The Economics of Urban Areas. 376p. 1972. text ed. 22.00 (ISBN 0-08-016892-2). Pergamon.

Goodall, Blake. The Homilies of St. John Chrysostom on the Letters of St. Paul to Titus & Philemon. (Univ. of California Publications in Classical Studies: Vol. 20). 1979. 18.00x (ISBN 0-520-09596-0). U of Cal Pr.

Goodall, Charles S. How to Train Your Own Gun Dog. LC 77-92420. (Illus.). 160p. 1985. 11.95 (ISBN 0-87605-561-7). Howell Bk.

Goodall, Charles S. & Gasow, Julia. The New Complete English Springer Spaniel. 3rd ed. LC 84-9048. (Illus.). 288p. 1985. 16.95 (ISBN 0-87605-118-2). Howell Bk.

Goodall, D. W. & Perry, R. A., eds. Arid Land Ecosystems, Vol. 1. LC 77-84810. (International Biological Programme Ser.: No. 16). (Illus.). 1979. 140.00 (ISBN 0-521-21842-X). Cambridge U Pr.

--Arid-Land Ecosystems: Structure, Functioning & Management, Vol. 2. LC 77-84810. (International Biological Programme Ser.: No. 17). 550p. 1981. 130.00 (ISBN 0-521-22988-X). Cambridge U Pr.

Goodall, Daphne M. The Flight of the East Prussian Horses. (Illus.). 192p. 1985. 12.95 (ISBN 0-7153-6061-2). David & Charles.

Goodall, Daphne M., tr. see Klimke, Reiner.

Goodall, Daphne M., tr. see Mohr, Erna.

Goodall, David W., ed. Evolution of Desert Biota. (Illus.). 250p. 1976. 20.00x (ISBN 0-292-72015-7). U of Tex Pr.

Goodall, David W., jt. ed. see Frenkiel, Francois N.

Goodall, E. G., tr. see Von Cube, Hans L. & Staimle, Fritz.

Goodall, F. & Rishton, D. K. Electrical & Electronic Principles: Level II. (Illus.). 194p. 1983. pap. text ed. 17.50x (ISBN 0-7121-0592-1). Intl Ideas.

Goodall, H. Lloyd, Jr. Human Communication: Creating Reality. 360p. 1983. pap. write for info. (ISBN 0-697-04216-2); instr's. manual avail. (ISBN 0-697-04224-3). Wm C Brown.

--Small Group Communication in Organizations. 360p. 1984. pap. text ed. write for info. (ISBN 0-697-00233-0). Wm C Brown.

Goodall, H. Lloyd, Jr. & Phillips, Gerald M. Making It in Any Organization. 224p. 1984. 15.95 (ISBN 0-13-547241-5); pap. 7.95 (ISBN 0-13-547233-4). P-H.

Goodall, H. Lloyd, Jr., jt. auth. see Phillips, Gerald M.

Goodall, Harrison & Friedman, Renee. Log Structures, Preservation & Problem-Solving. LC 80-23896. (Illus.). 120p. 1980. pap. 10.95 (ISBN 0-910050-46-5). AASLH Pr.

Goodall, Helen S. & Cooper, Ella G. Daily Lessons Received at 'Akka, January 1908. rev. ed. LC 79-19806. 1979. pap. 4.95 (ISBN 0-87743-135-3, 332-041). Baha'i.

Goodall, Jane. In the Shadow of Man. 1983. pap. 9.95 (ISBN 0-395-33145-5). HM.

Goodall, John. Heaven & Earth: Album Leaves from a Ming Encyclopedia. LC 79-64329. (Illus.). 192p. 1979. 39.50 (ISBN 0-87773-168-3). Shambhala Pubns.

Goodall, John S. Above & Below Stairs. LC 83-48528. (Illus.). 64p. 1983. 9.95 (ISBN 0-689-50238-9, McElderry Bk). Atheneum.

--Adventures of Paddy Pork. LC 68-26425. (Illus.). (gr. k-3). 1968. 5.95 (ISBN 0-15-201589-2, HJ). HarBraceJ.

--Creepy Castle. LC 74-16836. (Illus.). 60p. (ps up). 1975. 6.95 (ISBN 0-689-50027-0, McElderry Bk). Atheneum.

--An Edwardian Christmas. LC 77-4580. (Illus.). 64p. (ps up). 1978. 8.95 (ISBN 0-689-50106-4, McElderry Bk). Atheneum.

--Edwardian Entertainments. LC 81-67668. (Illus.). 64p. 1981. PLB 9.95 (ISBN 0-689-50220-6, McElderry Bk). Atheneum.

--An Edwardian Holiday. LC 78-64773. (Illus.). 64p. (ps up). 1979. 8.95 (ISBN 0-689-50135-8, McElderry Bk). Atheneum.

--An Edwardian Summer. LC 76-336. (Illus.). 72p. (ps up). 1976. 6.95 (ISBN 0-689-50062-9, McElderry Bk). Atheneum.

--Jacko. LC 72-149750. (ps-3). 1972. 9.95 (ISBN 0-15-239493-1, HJ). HarBraceJ.

--Jacko. LC 72-149750. (Illus.). 60p. (ps-3). 1984. pap. 3.95 (ISBN 0-15-239494-X, VoyB). HarBraceJ.

--John S. Goodall's Theatre: The Sleeping Beauty. (Illus.). 1980. 3.95 (ISBN 0-689-50161-7, McElderry Bk). Atheneum.

--Lavinia's Cottage: A Pop-Up Story. LC 82-71160. (Illus.). 16p. 1983. 8.95 (ISBN 0-689-50257-5, McElderry Bk). Atheneum.

--The Midnight Adventures of Kelly, Dot, & Esmeralda. LC 75-190555. 64p. (ps up). 1973. 6.95 (ISBN 0-689-30305-X, McElderry Bk). Atheneum.

--Naughty Nancy. LC 74-18182. (Illus.). 64p. (ps up). 1975. 6.95 (ISBN 0-689-50002-5, McElderry Bk). Atheneum.

--Naughty Nancy Goes to School. LC 85-70230. (Illus.). 32p. 1985. 8.95 (ISBN 0-689-50329-6, McElderry Bk). Atheneum.

--Paddy Goes Traveling. LC 82-71159. (Illus.). 32p. 1982. 6.95 (ISBN 0-689-50239-7, McElderry Bk). Atheneum.

--Paddy Pork-Odd Jobs. LC 83-70453. (Illus.). 32p. 1983. 6.95 (ISBN 0-689-50293-1, McElderry Bk). Atheneum.

--Paddy Pork's Holiday. LC 75-28278. (Illus.). 60p. (ps up). 1976. 6.95 (ISBN 0-689-50043-2, McElderry Bk). Atheneum.

--Paddy under Water. LC 83-71901. (Illus.). 32p. 1984. 6.95 (ISBN 0-689-50297-4, McElderry Bk). Atheneum.

--Paddy's Evening Out. LC 72-98006. (Illus.). 64p. (ps up). 1973. 6.95 (ISBN 0-689-30412-9, McElderry Bk). Atheneum.

--Shrewbetinna's Birthday. LC 73-24238. (Illus.). 1971. 7.95 (ISBN 0-15-274080-5, HJ). HarBraceJ.

--Shrewbettina Goes to Work: A Pop-up Story. LC 81-43104. (Illus.). 12p. 1981. 6.95 (ISBN 0-689-50214-1, McElderry Bk). Atheneum.

--Shrewbettina's Birthday. LC 73-24238. (Illus.). 60p. (ps-3). 1983. pap. 3.95 (VoyB). HarBraceJ.

--The Story of an English Village. LC 78-56242. (Illus.). 60p. (ps-12). 1979. 8.95 (ISBN 0-689-50125-0, McElderry Bks). Atheneum.

--Victorians Abroad. LC 80-67431. (Illus.). 64p. (ps up). 1981. 8.95 (ISBN 0-689-50191-9, McElderry Bk). Atheneum.

Goodall, John S., illus. The Surprise Picnic. LC 76-28455. (Illus.). 64p. (ps up). 1977. 6.95 (ISBN 0-689-50074-2, McElderry Bk). Atheneum.

Goodall, Merrill, et al. California Water: A New Political Economy. LC 77-88255. 128p. 1978. text ed. 18.00x (ISBN 0-916672-86-7). Allanheld.

Goodall, Norman, ed. see World Council Of Churches - Fourth Assembly - 1968.

Goodard, Dwight, ed. see Asvaghosa.

Goodard, T. & Schoen, S. Equipment Planning Guide for Vocational & Technical Training & Education Programmes: Carpentry & Joinery, No. 8. 134p. 1982. 22.80 (ISBN 92-2-102930-1). Intl Labour Office.

Goodarzi, Prouchestia, jt. auth. see Banuazizi, Ali.

Goodavage, Joseph F. Our Threatened Planet. 1980. pap. 2.95 (ISBN 0-671-81640-3). PB.

--Write Your Own Horoscope. 3rd, rev. ed. 1979. pap. 3.50 (ISBN 0-451-13093-6, AE3093, Sig). NAL.

Gooday, G. W., et al, eds. The Eukaryotic Microbial Cell. LC 79-20741. (Society for General Microbiology Symposium: No. 30). (Illus.). 450p. 1980. 85.00 (ISBN 0-521-22974-X). Cambridge U Pr.

Goodban, Dale, jt. auth. see Meyers, Ray C.

Goodban, Dale F., jt. auth. see Mehaffy, Robert E.

Goodban, William T., et al. Architectural Drawing & Planning. 3rd ed. (Illus.). 1979. pap. text ed. 32.50 (ISBN 0-07-023771-9). McGraw.

Goodbar, Joseph E. Managing the People's Money. 1935. 75.00x (ISBN 0-685-89765-6). Elliots Bks.

Goodbody, A. M. Cartesian Tensors: With Applications to Mechanics, Fluid Mechanics & Elasticity. (Mathematics & Its Applications Ser.). 298p. 1982. 84.95 (ISBN 0-470-27254-6). Halsted Pr.

Goodbody, John. The Illustrated History of Gymnastics. (Illus.). 144p. 1983. 14.95 (ISBN 0-09-143350-9). Beaufort Bks NY.

Goodbody, John, jt. ed. see Kirkley, George.

Goodbody, Slim. The Force Inside You. (Illus.). (gr. 4-7). 1983. 9.95 (ISBN 0-698-20589-8, Coward); pap. 4.95 (ISBN 0-698-20593-6). Putnam Pub Group.

--The Healthy Habits Handbook. (Illus.). (gr. 4-7). 1983. 9.95 (ISBN 0-698-20590-1, Coward); pap. 4.95 (ISBN 0-698-20592-8). Putnam Pub Group.

Goodboy, Eadie, jt. auth. see Lawless, Agnes.

Goodboy, Eddie. God's Daughter. (Aglow Bible Study: Bk. 2). 64p. 1974. 2.95 (ISBN 0-930756-06-1, 4220-2). Aglow Pubns.

Goodburn, Roger. The Roman Inscriptions of Britain: Inscriptions on Stone-Epigraphic Indexes, Vol. 1. 96p. 1983. text ed. 24.75x (ISBN 0-86299-026-2, Pub. by Alan Sutton England). Humanities.

Goodby, J. W. & Gray, G. W. Smectic Liquid Crystals: Textures & Structures. 200p. 1984. write for info. (ISBN 0-9914000-0-3, Pub. by Blackie & Son UK). Heyden.

Goodchild, Jon. By Design. 1979. pap. 12.95 (ISBN 0-8256-3122-X, Quick Fox). Putnam Pub Group.

Goodchild, Peter. J. Robert Oppenheimer: Shatterer of Worlds. (Illus.). 1985. pap. 10.95 (ISBN 0-88064-021-9). Fromm Intl Pub.
--Survival Skills of the North American Indians. LC 84-23255. (Illus.). 224p. 1985. 16.95x (ISBN 0-914091-64-6); pap. 9.95x (ISBN 0-914091-69-7). Chicago Review.
Goodchild, Robin & Munton, Richard. Development & the Landowner: An Analysis of the British Experience. 192p. 1985. text ed. 30.00x (ISBN 0-04-333021-5). Allen Unwin.
Gooddard, Harold C. Atomic Peace. 1983. pap. 5.00x (ISBN 0-87574-057-X, 057). Pendle Hill.
Goodden, Robert. British Butterflies: A Field Guide. 13.50 (ISBN 0-7153-7594-6). David & Charles.
Goode. The Nuclear Energy Controversy. (gr. 7 up). 1980. PLB 9.90 (ISBN 0-531-04165-4, G05). Watts.
--Pride & Prejudice (Austen) (Book Notes Ser.). 1984. pap. 2.50 (ISBN 0-8120-3437-6). Barron.
Goode, jt. auth. see Rylant, Cynthia.
Goode, Clement. Byron As Critic. LC 65-15893. (Studies in Byron, No., 5). 1969. Repr. of 1923 ed. lib. bdg. 49.95x (ISBN 0-8383-0696-9). Haskell.
Goode, Clement G. & Shannon, E. F. An Atlas of English Literature. 75.00 (ISBN 0-87968-287-6). Gordon Pr.
Goode, Clement T. An Atlas of English Literature. LC 73-15573. 1925. lib. bdg. 20.00 (ISBN 0-8414-4458-7). Folcroft.
--Byron As Critic. LC 72-83616. 312p. 1972. Repr. of 1923 ed. 17.50 (ISBN 0-8337-1381-7). B Franklin.
Goode, Clement T. & Shannon, Edgar F. An Atlas of English Literature. 1979. Repr. of 1925 ed. lib. bdg. 20.00 (ISBN 0-8495-2022-3). Arden Lib.
Goode, Delmer M., ed. Improving College & University Teaching Yearbook 1975. 268p. 11.95x (ISBN 0-87071-475-9). Oreg St U Pr.
--Improving College & University Teaching Yearbook 1976. 292p. 11.95x (ISBN 0-87071-476-7). Oreg St U Pr.
--Improving College & University Teaching Yearbook 1977. 380p. 11.95x (ISBN 0-87071-477-5). Oreg St U Pr.
Goode, Diane, illus. My Little Library of Christmas Classics: The Night Before Christmas, Christmas Carols, the Fir Tree, the Nutcracker. (Illus.). 32p. (gr. 4-8). 1983. slipcased 5.95 (ISBN 0-394-85229-X). Random.
Goode, Elizabeth W., ed. Drug Abuse Bibliography for 1978-1979. 1863p. 1983. 100.00 set (ISBN 0-87875-222-6); Part I. 50.00 (ISBN 0-87875-269-2); Part II. 50.00 (ISBN 0-87875-270-6). Whitston Pub.
Goode, Elizabeth W., compiled by. Drug Abuse Bibliography for 1980, No. 10. LC 79-116588. xxxii, 689p. 1984. 48.50x (ISBN 0-87875-285-4). Whitston Pub.
Goode, Erich. Deviant Behavior. 2nd ed. 432p. 1984. text ed. 26.95 (ISBN 0-13-208280-2). P-H.
--Drugs in American Society. 2nd ed. 272p. 1984. pap. text ed. 10.00 (ISBN 0-394-33408-6, RanC). Random.
--Social Class & Church Participation. Zuckerman, Harriet & Merton, Robert K., eds. LC 79-9001. (Dissertations on Sociology Ser.). 1980. lib. bdg. 22.00x (ISBN 0-405-12970-X). Ayer Co Pubs.
--Sociology. (Illus.). 608p. 1984. text ed. 26.95 (ISBN 0-13-820720-8). P-H.
Goode, G. Brown. Game Fishes of the United States. (Illus.). 1972. Repr. of 1879 ed. 75.00x (ISBN 0-8329-0851-7, Pub. by Winchester Pr). New Century.
Goode, George B. The Smithsonian Institution Eighteen Hundred Forty-Six to Eighteen Hundred Ninety-Six: The History of Its First Half Century. Cohen, I. Bernard, ed. LC 79-3119. (Three Centuries of Science in America Ser.). (Illus.). 1980. Repr. of 1897 ed. lib. bdg. 76.00x (ISBN 0-405-12584-4). Ayer Co Pubs.
Goode, James B. Poets of Darkness. LC 80-29653. (The Center for the Study of Southern Culture Ser.). 1981. 7.95 (ISBN 0-87805-133-3). U Pr of Miss.
Goode, James M. Capital Losses: A Cultural History of Washington's Destroyed Buildings. LC 79-13219. (Illus.). 517p. 1981. pap. 19.95 (ISBN 0-87474-479-2). Smithsonian.
--The Outdoor Sculpture of Washington, D.C. A Comprehensive Historical Guide. LC 74-5111. (Illus.). 528p. 1974. pap. 12.50 (ISBN 0-87474-149-1). Smithsonian.
Goode, John. George Gissing: Ideology & Fiction. (Barnes & Noble Critical Study Ser). 181p. 1979. text ed. 26.50x (ISBN 0-06-492488-2). B&N Imports.
Goode, John see Egerton, George, pseud.
Goode, John, ed. George Gissing: The Nether World. LC 74-499. 432p. 1974. 24.50 (ISBN 0-8386-1543-0). Fairleigh Dickinson.
Goode, John, ed. see Gissing, George.
Goode, John W., Jr. & Barrows, Suzanne S., eds. Texas Guardianship Manual. LC 82-61569. 791p. 1983. law bk. binder 65.00 (ISBN 0-938160-31-1, 6335). State Bar TX.
Goode, Judith G., jt. auth. see Eames, Edwin.
Goode, Kenneth M. How to Turn People into Gold. 1929. 12.50 (ISBN 0-686-17732-0). Quest Edns.
Goode, Patrick. Karl Kautsky: Selected Political Writings. LC 83-11054. 172p. 1983. 22.50x (ISBN 0-312-45075-3). St Martin.
--Karl Korsch: A Study in Western Marxism. 1979. text ed. 30.50x (ISBN 0-333-23425-1). Humanities.
Goode, Patrick, jt. ed. see Bottomore, Tom.
Goode, Peter. The Atari 600XL Program Book. (Illus.). 160p. 1984. pap. 12.95 (ISBN 0-946576-11-4, Pub. by Phoenix Pub). David & Charles.
--Getting Started with the Atari 600XL. 140p. 1984. pap. 12.95 (ISBN 0-946576-14-9, Pub. by Phoenix Pub). David & Charles.
--The Memotech MTX Program Book. (Illus.). 128p. 1984. pap. 12.95 (ISBN 0-946576-18-1, Pub. by Phoenix Pub). David & Charles.
Goode, Peter, jt auth. see Jackson, Peter.
Goode, Polly T. Drug Abuse Bibliography for 1981, 2 vols. LC 79-116588. 1600p. 1985. Set. 100.00 (ISBN 0-87875-283-8); Part I. 50.00 (ISBN 0-87875-297-8); Part II. 50.00 (ISBN 0-87875-298-6). Whitston Pub.
Goode, Polly T., compiled by. Abortion Bibliography for 1981, Vol. 12. LC 72-78877. 405p. 1984. 38.50x (ISBN 0-87875-278-1). Whitston Pub.
Goode, Polly T., ed. Abortion Bibliography for 1982. LC 72-78877. 400p. 1985. 38.50 (ISBN 0-87875-290-0). Whitston Pub.
Goode, R. M., ed. Consumer Credit. 508p. 1978. 52.50x (ISBN 9-0286-0928-8). Sijthoff & Noordhoff.
Goode, R. M. & Simmonds, K. R., eds. Commercial Operations in Europe. 475p. 1978. 42.50x (ISBN 90-286-0547-9). Sijthoff & Noordhoff.
Goode, Richard. Government Finance in Developing Countries. LC 83-20989. (Studies of Government Finance). 334p. 1984. 31.95 (ISBN 0-8157-3196-5); pap. 11.95 (ISBN 0-8157-3195-7). Brookings.
--The Individual Income Tax. rev. ed. (Studies of Government Finance). 1976. 29.95 (ISBN 0-8157-3198-1); pap. 10.95 (ISBN 0-8157-3197-3). Brookings.
Goode, Ruth. A Book for Grandmothers. (Paperbacks Ser.). 1977. pap. 3.95 (ISBN 0-07-023740-9). McGraw.
--Hands up! LC 81-82018. (Illus.). 64p. (gr. 2-5). 1983. SBE 8.95 (ISBN 0-02-736550-6). Macmillan.
Goode, Ruth, jt. auth. see Hurok, Solomon.
Goode, Ruth, jt. auth. see McKenzie, Scotty.
Goode, Stephan. The End of Detente? U. S. Soviet-Relations. LC 81-11370. (Impact Ser.). 96p. 1981. lib. bdg. 9.90 (ISBN 0-531-04334-7). Watts.
Goode, Stephen. The CIA. 160p. (gr. 9 up). 1982. PLB 9.90 (ISBN 0-531-04404-1). Watts.
--The Controversial Court: Supreme Court Influences on American Life. LC 82-3498. (Illus.). 192p. (gr. 7 up). 1982. PLB 10.29 (ISBN 0-671-43656-2); pap. 4.95 (ISBN 0-671-49496-1). Messner.
--The Foreign Policy Debate: Human Rights & American Foreign Policy. (Impact Bks.). 96p. 1984. lib. bdg. 9.90 (ISBN 0-317-14358-1). Watts.
--The National Defense System. (Career Concise Guides Ser.). (Illus.). (gr. 7 up). 1977. PLB 6.90 s&l (ISBN 0-531-04758-X). Watts.
--The New Congress. LC 80-19111. 224p. (gr. 7 up). 1980. PLB 9.49 (ISBN 0-671-34031-X). Messner.
--The New Federalism. (Single Title Ser.). (Illus.). 160p. (gr. 7 up). 1983. PLB 9.90 (ISBN 0-531-04501-3). Watts.
--Reaganomics: Reagan's Economic Program. (Impact Bks). (Illus.). 96p. 1982. PLB 9.90 (ISBN 0-531-04422-X). Watts.
--The Right to Privacy. (Single Titles Ser.). 128p. (gr. 9 up). 1983. lib. bdg. 9.90 (ISBN 0-531-04585-4). Watts.
--Violence in America. LC 83-25033. 192p. (YA) (gr. 7-12). 1984. lib. bdg. 9.79 (ISBN 0-671-45810-8). Messner.
Goode, Stephen H. Index to American Little Magazines, 1900-1919, 3 vols. LC 77-97476. iv, 1487p. 1974. Set. 82.50x (ISBN 0-87875-026-6). Whitston Pub.
--Index to American Little Magazines, 1920-39. LC 77-97476. 1970. 12.50x (ISBN 0-87875-001-0). Whitston Pub.
--Index to Commonwealth Little Magazines, 1964-65. Repr. of 1966 ed. 15.00 (ISBN 0-384-19170-3). Johnson Repr.
--Index to Commonwealth Little Magazines, 1968-69. LC 66-28796. 1970. 10.50x (ISBN 0-87875-006-1). Whitston Pub.
--Index to Commonwealth Little Magazines, 1970-1973. LC 66-28796. 551p. 1975. 25.00 (ISBN 0-87875-027-4). Whitston Pub.
--Index to Commonwealth Little Magazines, 1974-1975. LC 66-28796. vii, 491p. 1976. 20.00x (ISBN 0-87875-085-1). Whitston Pub.
--Population & the Population Explosion: A Bibliography for 1970. LC 72-87106. xxv, 361p. 1973. 17.00x (ISBN 0-87875-032-0). Whitston Pub.
--Venereal Disease Bibliography for 1972. LC 71-189843. xxi, 210p. 1974. 11.00x (ISBN 0-87875-045-2). Whitston Pub.
--Venereal Disease Bibliography for 1973. LC 71-189843. xxiii, 276p. 1975. 15.00x (ISBN 0-87875-058-4). Whitston Pub.
--Venereal Disease Bibliography, 1966-1970. LC 71-189843. 400p. (First of a series with annual supplements). 1972. 22.50x (ISBN 0-87875-023-1). Whitston Pub.
Goode, Stephen H., ed. Index to Commonwealth Little Magazines, 1966-1967. Repr. of 1968 ed. 14.00 (ISBN 0-384-19180-0). Johnson Repr.
--Index to Little Magazines: 1940-42. Repr. of 1967 ed. 15.00 (ISBN 0-384-19190-8). Johnson Repr.
Goode, Teresa C. Gonzalo De Berceo. (Carl Ser.: No. 7). Repr. of 1933 ed. 21.00 (ISBN 0-404-50307-1). AMS Pr.
Goode, William. The Family. 2nd ed. 240p. 1982. 15.95 (ISBN 0-13-301762-1); pap. 11.95 (ISBN 0-13-301754-0, 013-301762). P-H.
Goode, William J. The Celebration of Heroes: Prestige As a Social Control System. LC 77-20322. 1979. 33.00x (ISBN 0-520-03602-6); pap. 9.95x (ISBN 0-520-03811-8). U of Cal Pr.
--Women in Divorce. LC 78-14243. 1978. Repr. of 1965 ed. lib. bdg. 25.75x (ISBN 0-313-21026-8, GOWD). Greenwood.
--World Revolution & Family Patterns. LC 63-13538. 1970. pap. text ed. 12.95 (ISBN 0-02-912460-3). Free Pr.
Goode, William J., jt. auth. see Tavuchis, Nicholas.
Goode, William J., et al. Social Systems & Family Patterns: A Propositional Inventory. LC 75-158851. 1971. 49.50x (ISBN 0-672-61151-1). Irvington.
Goode, William J., et al, eds. see Waller, Willard W.
Goodearl, K. R. Notes on Real & Complex C-Algebras. 180p. 1982. 60.00x (ISBN 0-906812-16-X, Pub. by Shiva Pub England); pap. 40.00x (ISBN 0-906812-15-1). State Mutual Bk.
--Singular Torsion & the Splitting Properties. LC 72-4344. (Memoirs: No. 124). 89p. 1972. pap. 10.00 (ISBN 0-8218-1824-4, MEMO-124). Am Math.
--Von Neumann Regular Rings. (Monographs & Studies: Vol. 4). 388p. 1979. text ed. 59.95 (ISBN 0-686-91967-X). Pitman Pub MA.
Goodearl, K. R. & Boyle, Ann K. Dimension Theory for Nonsingular Injective Modules. LC 76-26498. (Memoirs of the American Mathematical Society: 177). 112p. 1976. pap. 13.00 (ISBN 0-8218-2177-6, MEMO 177). Am Math.
Goodearl, K. R., ed. Notes on Real & Complex C-Algebra. (Shiva Mathematics Ser.: 5). 180p. 1982. text ed. 28.95x (ISBN 0-906812-16-X). Birkhauser.
Goodearl, K. R., et al. Affine Representations of Grothendieck Groups & Applications to Rickart C-Algebras & Aleph O-Continuous Regular Rings. LC 80-17018. (Memoirs: No. 234). 163p. 1980. pap. 9.00 (ISBN 0-8218-2234-9). Am Math.
Goodearl, Kenneth R. Ring Theory: Nonsingular Rings & Modules. (Lecture Notes in Pure & Applied Mathematics: Vol.33). 224p. 1976. 49.75 (ISBN 0-8247-6354-8). Dekker.
Goodefellowe, Robin, jt. auth. see Molin, Sven E.
Goodell, Greg. Independent Feature Film Production: A Complete Guide from Concept Through Distribution. 352p. 1983. pap. 7.95 (ISBN 0-312-41308-4). St Martin.
Goodell, Gregory. Independent Feature Film Production: A Complete Guide from Concept Through Distribution. LC 82-5746. 352p. 1982. 17.95 (ISBN 0-312-41307-6). St Martin.
Goodell, Helen, jt. auth. see Wolf, Stewart.
Goodell, John. The Triumph of Moralism in New England Piety: A Study of Lyman Beecher, Harriet Beecher Stowe & Henry Ward Beecher. 50.00 (ISBN 0-405-14113-0). Ayer Co Pubs.
Goodell, Larry. Dawn Ladder. pap. 2.00 (ISBN 0-317-13319-5). San Marcos.
Goodell, Larry, ed. see Crews, Judson.
Goodell, Margaret M. Three Satirists of Snobbery: Thackeray, Meredith, Proust. 59.95 (ISBN 0-8490-1212-0). Gordon Pr.
--Three Satirists of Snobbery: Thackery, Meredith, Proust. LC 76-25175. 1939. lib. bdg. 16.50 (ISBN 0-8414-4437-4). Folcroft.
Goodell, Thomas D. Athenian Tragedy. LC 75-86018. 1969. Repr. of 1920 ed. 22.50x (ISBN 0-8046-0612-9, Pub by Kennikat). Assoc Faculty Pr.
--Commemoration & Other Verses. 1921. 24.50x (ISBN 0-686-83507-7). Elliots Bks.
Goodell, William. American Slave Code in Theory & Practice. (Basic Afro-American Reprint Library). Repr. of 1853 ed. 24.00 (ISBN 0-384-19210-6). Johnson Repr.
--American Slave Code in Theory & Practice: Its Distinctive Features As Shown by Its Statutes, Judicial Decisions, & Illustrative Facts. LC 73-82194. (Anti-Slavery Crusade in America Ser). 1969. Repr. of 1853 ed. 18.00 (ISBN 0-405-00633-0). Ayer Co Pubs.
--American Slave Code in Theory & Practice: Its Distinctive Features Shown by Its Statutes, Judicial Decisions, & Illustrative Facts. LC 68-55888. 231p. Repr. of 1853 ed. 19.75x (ISBN 0-8371-0450-5, GOC&, Pub. by Negro U Pr). Greenwood.
--Slavery & Anti-Slavery. LC 71-118016. Repr. of 1853 ed. 45.00x (ISBN 0-678-00657-1). Kelley.
--Slavery & Anti-Slavery: A History of the Great Struggle in Both Hemispheres. LC 68-55889. Repr. of 1852 ed. 19.75x (ISBN 0-8371-0449-1, GOS&). Greenwood.
--Views of American Constitutional Law: Its Bearing Upon American Slavery. facs. ed. LC 78-138337. (Black Heritage Library Collection Ser.). 1845. 15.25 (ISBN 0-8369-8729-2). Ayer Co Pubs.
Gooden, Brett, jt. auth. see Elsner, Robert.
Gooden, Dwight & Woodley, Richard. Rookie: The Story of My First Year in the Major Leagues. LC 85-1590. 192p. 1985. 13.95 (ISBN 0-385-23093-1). Doubleday.
Gooden, George & Thomas, Frank. Sherlock Holmes, Bridge Detective. (Illus.). 288p. 1977. pap. 1.95 (ISBN 0-523-40038-1). Pinnacle Bks.
Gooden, Mona, ed. Poet's Cat. facsimile ed. LC 74-75711. (Granger Index Reprint Ser). 1946. 14.00 (ISBN 0-8369-6017-3). Ayer Co Pubs.
Gooden, Orville T. Missouri & North Arkansas Railroad Strike. LC 68-57567. (Columbia University. Studies in the Social Sciences: No. 275). Repr. of 1926 ed. 21.00 (ISBN 0-404-51275-5). AMS Pr.
Goodenough, Anna K., ed. The Chronicle of Muntaner, 2 vols. in 1. (Hakluyt Society Works Ser.: No. 2, Vols. 47 & 50). (Illus.). 1920-21. 101.00 (ISBN 0-8115-0342-X). Kraus Repr.
Goodenough, Caroline L. High Lights on Hymnists & Their Hymns. LC 72-1626. Repr. of 1931 ed. 32.50 (ISBN 0-404-08310-2). AMS Pr.
Goodenough, David J., jt. auth. see Reba, Richard.
Goodenough, Donald R., jt. auth. see Witkin, Herman A.
Goodenough, E. R. Jewish Symbols in the Greco-Roman Period, 13 vols. Incl. Vols. 1-3. Archeological Evidence from Palestine & the Diaspora. 1953; Vol. 4. The Problem of Method; Symbols from Jewish Cult. 1954; Vols. 5 & 6. Fish, Bread, & Wine, 2 vols. 1956; Vols. 7 & 8. Pagan Symbols in Judaism. 1958. o.p. (ISBN 0-691-09755-0); Vols. 9-11. Symbolism in the Dura Synagogue. 1964; Vol. 12. Summary & Conclusions. 1965. 27.50x (ISBN 0-691-09757-7); Vol. 13. General Index & Maps. 1969. (Bollingen Ser.). Princeton U Pr.
Goodenough, Erwin R. Church in the Roman Empire. LC 77-122754. 1970. Repr. of 1931 ed. lib. bdg. 23.50 (ISBN 0-8154-0337-2). Cooper Sq.
--Jewish Symbols in the Greco-Roman Period: The Problem of Method: Symbols from Jewish Cult, Vol.4. LC 52-10031. (Bollingen Ser.: No.37). pap. 69.80 (ISBN 0-317-11329-1, 2011980). Bks Demand UMI.
--Jurisprudence of the Jewish Courts in Egypt. 1929. 75.00x (ISBN 0-686-83604-9). Elliots Bks.
Goodenough, Erwin R. & Goodhart, H. L. Politics of Philo Judaeus. 1938. 75.00x (ISBN 0-685-69822-X). Elliots Bks.
Goodenough, Florence. Anger in Young Children. LC 77-141547. (University of Minnesota Institute of Child Welfare Monographs: No. 9). (Illus.). 278p. 1975. Repr. of 1931 ed. lib. bdg. 27.50x (ISBN 0-8371-5894-X, CWGA). Greenwood.
Goodenough, Florence & Maurer, Katharine. The Mental Growth of Children from Two to Fourteen Years: Study of the Predictive Value of the Minnesota Pre-School Scales. LC 70-141548. (Univ. of Minnesota Institute of Child Welfare Monographs: No. 20). (Illus.). 130p. 1975. Repr. of 1942 ed. lib. bdg. 22.50x (ISBN 0-8371-5895-8, CWGM). Greenwood.
Goodenough, Florence L. The Kuhlman-Binet Test for Children of Pre-School Age. LC 73-9226. 146p. 1973. Repr. of 1928 ed. lib. bdg. 18.75x (ISBN 0-8371-6990-9, CWGT). Greenwood.
--Measurement of Intelligence by Drawings. LC 74-21410. (Classics in Child Development Ser.). 196p. 1975. Repr. 22.00x (ISBN 0-405-06462-4). Ayer Co Pubs.
--Mental Testing: Its History, Principles & Applications. Repr. of 1949 ed. 30.00 (ISBN 0-384-19230-0). Johnson Repr.
Goodenough, Florence L. & Anderson, John E. Experimental Child Study. 546p. 1982. Repr. of 1931 ed. lib. bdg. 45.00 (ISBN 0-8495-2134-3). Arden Lib.
Goodenough, Florence L. & Tyler, Leona E. Developmental Psychology. 3rd ed. LC 59-6858. (Century Psychology Ser.). (Illus.). 1959. 22.50x (ISBN 0-89197-125-4); pap. text ed. 6.95x (ISBN 0-89197-727-9). Irvington.
Goodenough, George A. Principles of Thermodynamics. 3rd, rev. ed. (Illus.). Repr. of 1920 ed. 40.00 (ISBN 0-384-19240-8). Johnson Repr.
Goodenough, J. B. Dower Land. (CSU Poetry Ser.: No. XV). 84p. (Orig.). 1984. pap. 5.00 (ISBN 0-914946-44-7). Cleveland St Univ Poetry Ctr.
Goodenough, J. B., ed. Metal Complexes. (Structure & Bonding Ser.: Vol. 44). (Illus.). 202p. 1981. 59.00 (ISBN 0-387-10494-1). Springer-Verlag.
Goodenough, J. B., et al see Hellwege, K. H.
Goodenough, J. E. Animal Communication. Head, John J., ed. LC 83-70598. (Carolina Biology Readers). (Illus.). 16p. pap. 1.60 (ISBN 0-89278-343-5, 45-9743). Carolina Biological.
Goodenough, John B. Magnetism & the Chemical Bond. LC 76-8393. 410p. 1976. Repr. of 1963 ed. 23.50 (ISBN 0-88275-384-3). Krieger.
Goodenough, John B. & Whittingham, M. Stanley, eds. Solid State Chemistry of Energy Conversion & Storage: A Symposium Sponsored by the Division of Inorganic Chemistry at the 71st Meeting of the American Chemical Society. LC 77-20011. (Advances in Chemistry Ser.: No. 163). pap. 95.50 (ISBN 0-317-08982-X, 2015231). Bks Demand UMI.

Goodenough, Josephus, ed. Dr. Goodenough's Home Cures & Herbal Remedies. (Illus.). 800p. 1983. 7.98 (ISBN 0-517-36243-0, Avenel). Outlet Bk Co.
Goodenough, P. W. & Atkin, R. K. Quality of Stored & Processed Vegetables & Fruit. LC 81-66382. 1981. 62.00 (ISBN 0-12-289740-4). Acad Pr.
Goodenough, Simon. The Country Parson. (Illus.). 192p. 1983. 19.95 (ISBN 0-7153-8238-1). David & Charles.
--Tactical Genius in Battle. Deighton, Len, ed. 144p. 1979. 39.00x (ISBN 0-7148-1949-2, Pub. by Phaidon Pr). State Mutual Bk.
--War Maps. (Illus.). 192p. 1983. 18.95 (ISBN 0-312-85584-2). St Martin.
--World Maps: World War II from September 1939-August 1945. (Illus.). 1983. 18.95 (ISBN 0-686-42933-8). St Martin.
Goodenough, Simon, ed. see Doyle, Arthur Conan.
Goodenough, Ursula. Genetics. 3rd ed. LC 83-4438. 894p. 1984. text ed. 37.95x (ISBN 0-03-058212-1). SCP.
Goodenough, Ward. Language, Culture & Society. 2nd ed. 1981. pap. 12.95 (ISBN 0-8053-3341-X). Benjamin-Cummings.
--Native Astronomy in the Central Carolines. (University Museum Monographs: No. 10). (Illus.). vi, 46p. 1953. bound 3.75xsoft (ISBN 0-934718-02-4). Univ Mus of U PA.
Goodenough, Ward H. Cooperation in Change: An Anthropological Approach to Community Development. LC 63-20667. 544p. 1963. 11.95x (ISBN 0-87154-344-3). Russell Sage.
--Description & Comparison in Cultural Anthropology. LC 80-67925. (Lewis Henry Morgan Lectures). 192p. 1981. 34.50 (ISBN 0-521-23740-8); pap. 10.95 (ISBN 0-521-28196-2). Cambridge U Pr.
--Property, Kin & Community on Truk. rev. ed. 260p. 1978. 19.50 (ISBN 0-208-01696-1, Archon). Shoe String.
Goodenough, Ward H. & Sugita, Hiroshi. Trukese-English Dictionary. LC 79-54277. (Memoir Ser.: Vol. 141). (Turkish.). 1980. 10.00 (ISBN 0-87169-141-8). Am Philos.
Goodenow, Darlene. Night Woods. LC 83-50260. (Althea Bantree Mysteries Ser.). (Illus., Orig.). 1984. pap. 2.95 (ISBN 0-938232-30-4, Dist. by Baker & Taylor). Winston-Derek.
--Secrets Within. LC 83-50263. (Althea Bantree Mystery Ser.). (Illus.). 175p. (Orig.). 1984. pap. 2.95 (ISBN 0-938232-32-0, Dist. by Baker & Taylor). Winston-Derek.
Goodenow, J. M. Historical Sketches of the Principles & Maxims of American Jurisprudence. Mersky, Roy M. & Jacobstein, J. Myron, eds. (Classics in Legal History Reprint Ser.: Vol. 17). 426p. 1972. Repr. of 1819 ed. lib. bdg. 35.00 (ISBN 0-89941-016-2). W S Hein.
Goodenow, John M. Historical Sketches of the Principles & Maxims of American Jurisprudence, in Contrast with the Doctrines of the English Common Law on the Subject of Crimes & Punishments. LC 76-37973. (American Law Ser.: The Formative Years). 446p. 1972. Repr. of 1819 ed. 27.50 (ISBN 0-405-04013-X). Ayer Co Pubs.
Goodenow, Ronald, jt. ed. see Ravitch, Diane.
Goodenow, Ronald K. & Ravitch, Diane, eds. Schools in Cities: Consensus & Conflict in American Educational History. 326p. 1983. text ed. 39.50x (ISBN 0-8419-0850-8). Holmes & Meier.
Goodenow, Ronald K. & White, Arthur O., eds. Education & the Rise of the New South. 1981. lib. bdg. 21.00 (ISBN 0-8161-9019-4, Univ Bks). G K Hall.
Gooder, B. C., jt. auth. see Sweeney, A. J.
Gooder, R. D., ed. see James, Henry.
Gooders, jt. auth. see Keith.
Gooders, John. Bird Seeker's Guide. (Illus.). 208p. 1985. pap. 6.95 (ISBN 0-233-97380-X, Pub. by A Deutsch England). David & Charles.
--Birds That Came Back. 180p. 1983. 25.00 (ISBN 0-88072-050-6). Tanager Bks.
--Birds That Came Back. (Illus.). 180p. 1984. 24.95 (ISBN 0-233-97445-8). Andre Deutsch.
--Birds That Came Back. (Illus.). 180p. 1984. 24.95 (ISBN 0-233-97445-8, Pub. by A Deutsch England). David & Charles.
--Collins British Birds. (Illus.). 384p. 1983. 39.95 (ISBN 0-00-219121-0, Collins Pub England). Greene.
--Where to Watch Birds in Europe. LC 77-84451. (Illus.). 1978. 10.95 (ISBN 0-8008-8246-6). Taplinger.
Gooders, John, ed. The Second Bird-Watchers Book. LC 75-10531. (The Bird-Watchers Bk). (Illus.). 144p. 1975. 3.95 (ISBN 0-7153-7047-2). David & Charles.
Gooderson, Richard. Alibi. LC 78-305077. (Cambridge Studies in Criminology). 1977. text ed. 48.95x (ISBN 0-435-82357-4). Gower Pub Co.
Goodfellow, jt. auth. see Wiebe, A. J.
Goodfellow, Barbara. The Complete Make it Now Bake it Later. 224p. 1982. pap. 8.95 (ISBN 0-671-45082-4, Fireside). S&S.
Goodfellow, C. G. Understanding Dolls. (Illus.). 197p. 1985. 29.50 (ISBN 0-907462-19-7). Apollo.
Goodfellow, Caroline. Understanding Dolls. (Illus.). 240p. 1983. 29.50 (ISBN 0-907462-19-7). Antique Collect.
Goodfellow, David C. Apple II BASIC. (Illus.). 240p. (Orig.). 1983. o.p 19.95 (ISBN 0-8306-0113-9); pap. 13.50 (ISBN 0-8306-1513-X, 1513). TAB Bks.
Goodfellow, David M. Principles of Economic Sociology: The Economics of Primitive Life As Illustrated from the Bantu Peoples of South & East Africa. LC 78-106836. Repr. of 1939 ed. 22.50x (ISBN 0-8371-3458-7, GES&). Greenwood.
Goodfellow, Denis, jt. auth. see Boughton, Brian.
Goodfellow, E. J., jt. auth. see Rook, Lizzie.
Goodfellow, M. & Board, R. G. Microbiological Classification & Identification. (Society for Applied Bacteriology Symposium Ser.: No. 8). 1980. 57.50 (ISBN 0-12-289660-2). Acad Pr.
Goodfellow, M., jt. auth. see Jones, D.
Goodfellow, M., ed. The Biology of the Nocardiae. 1976. 82.50 (ISBN 0-12-289650-5). Acad Pr.
Goodfellow, M., et al, eds. Computer-Assisted Bacterial Systematics. (Society for General Microbiology Special Publications Ser.: No. 15). Date not set. 75.00 (ISBN 0-12-289665-3). Acad Pr.
Goodfellow, Michael & Minnikin, David E., eds. Chemical Methods in Bacterial Systematics. (Society for Applied Bacteriology Technical Ser.). 1985. 69.50 (ISBN 0-12-289675-0). Acad Pr.
Goodfellow, Michael, jt. ed. see Berkeley, Roger.
Goodfellow, Michael, et al. The Biology of the Actinomycetes. 1984. 95.00 (ISBN 0-12-289670-X). Acad Pr.
Goodfellow, P., ed. Genetic Analysis of the Cell Surface. (Receptors & Recognition Series B: Vol. 16). 300p. 1984. text ed. 59.95 (ISBN 0-412-25070-5, NO. 9010, Pub by Chapman & Hall England). Methuen Inc.
Goodfellow, Peter. Shakespeare's Birds. LC 83-42982. (Illus.). 96p. 13.95 (ISBN 0-87951-201-6). Overlook Pr.
Goodfellow, Thomas M. Your Future in Railroading. LC 76-104706. (Careers in Depth Ser). (Illus.). (gr. 9 up). 1975. PLB 8.97 (ISBN 0-8239-0222-6). Rosen Group.
Goodfield, G. J. Growth of Scientific Physiology. LC 74-26265. (History, Philosophy & Sociology of Science Ser). 1975. Repr. 16.00x (ISBN 0-405-06593-0). Ayer Co Pubs.
Goodfield, June. An Imagined World: A Story of Scientific Discovery. LC 79-1664. (Illus.). 288p. 1981. 14.37i (ISBN 0-06-011641-2, HarpT). Har-Row.
--An Imagined World: A Story of Scientific Discovery. 1982. pap. 5.95 (ISBN 0-14-006204-1). Penguin.
--Quest for the Killers. (Illus.). 300p. 1985. 24.95 (ISBN 0-8176-3313-8). Birkhauser.
--Reflections on Science & the Media. LC 81-66420. 113p. 1981. 9.00x (ISBN 0-87168-252-4). AAAS.
Goodfield, June, jt. auth. see Toulmin, Stephen.
Goodfriend, L., et al, eds. Mechanisms in Allergy: Reagin-Mediated Hypersensitivity. (Immunology Ser: Vol. 1). 608p. 1973. 85.00 (ISBN 0-8247-6074-3). Dekker.
Goodfriend, Lewis S., jt. auth. see Burris-Meyer, Harold.
Goodfriend, Ronnie S. Power in Perception for the Young Child: A Comprehensive Program for the Development of Pre-Reading Visual Perceptual Skills. LC 72-189232. 1972. pap. text ed. 7.95x (ISBN 0-8077-1430-5); pap. text ed. 6.95x suppl. (ISBN 0-8077-1429-1). Tchrs Coll.
Goodfriend, Theodore, ed. Hypertension Essentials: Concepts, Causes, Consequences & Control. 232p. 1983. 26.00 (ISBN 0-8089-1534-7, 791657); pap. 17.50 (ISBN 0-8089-1583-5, 791658). Grune.
Goodgame, Louis R. Delightful Discipline: Humorous Stories of Woodshed Wisdom & Biblical Principles. LC 77-22560. 1977. pap. 3.00 (ISBN 0-915134-43-8). Mott Media.
Goodge, Malcolm E. Semiconductor Device Technology. 481p. 1983. 34.95 (ISBN 0-672-22074-1, 22074). Sams.
Goodger, E. M. Alternative Fuels: Chemical Energy Resources. LC 80-11796. 238p. 1980. 53.95 (ISBN 0-470-26952-9). Halsted Pr.
Goodger, Eric & Vere, Ray. Aviation Fuels Technology. (Illus.). 350p. 1985. text ed. 65.00x (ISBN 0-333-35787-6, Pub. by Macmillan Londan). Sheridan.
Goodglass, Harold & Blumstein, Sheila. Psycholinguistics & Aphasia. LC 73-8667. pap. 88.00 (ISBN 0-317-19875-0, 2023100). Bks Demand UMI.
Goodglass, Harold & Kaplan, Edith. The Assessment of Aphasia & Related Disorders. 2nd ed. LC 83-9326. 102p. 1983. text ed. 27.50 (ISBN 0-8121-0901-5). Lea & Febiger.
Goodgold, Ed, jt. auth. see Carlinsky, Dan.
Goodgold, Ed, jt. auth. see Weiss, Ken.
Goodgold, Joseph. Anatomical Correlates of Clinical Electromyography. 2nd ed. (Illus.). 216p. 1984. 33.00 (ISBN 0-683-03687-4). Williams & Wilkins.
Goodgold, Joseph & Eberstein, Arthur. Electrodiagnosis of Neuromuscular Diseases. 3rd ed. (Illus.). 358p. 1983. lib. bdg. 38.00 (ISBN 0-683-03686-6). Williams & Wilkins.
Goodhart, Arthur L. Five Jewish Lawyers of the Common Law. facs. ed. LC 79-148212. (Biography Index Reprint Ser.). 1949. 14.00 (ISBN 0-8369-8059-X). Ayer Co Pubs.
--Poland & the Minority Races. LC 71-135809. (Eastern Europe Collection Ser). 1970. Repr. of 1920 ed. 14.00x (ISBN 0-405-02751-6). Ayer Co Pubs.
Goodhart, C. A. E. Monetary Theory & Practice: The U. K. Experience. 288p. 1984. 29.50x (ISBN 0-8448-1469-5). Crane-Russak Co.
Goodhart, Charles A. New York Money Market & the Finance of Trade, 1900-1913. LC 69-12723. (Economic Studies: No. 132). 1969. 14.00x (ISBN 0-674-61950-1). Harvard U Pr.
Goodhart, H. L., jt. auth. see Goodenough, Erwin R.
Goodhart, Rendel & Stuart, Harry. English Architecture since the Regency. 1981. Repr. lib. bdg. 59.00x. Scholarly.
Goodhart, Robert & Wohl, Michael G. Manual of Clinical Nutrition. LC 64-14481. pap. 69.80 (ISBN 0-317-28603-X, 2055428). Bks Demand UMI.
Goodhart, Robert S. & Shils, Maurice E., eds. Modern Nutrition in Health & Disease. 6th ed. LC 79-16842. (Illus.). 1370p. 1980. text ed. 47.50 (ISBN 0-8121-0645-8). Lea & Febiger.
Goodhart, Simon P., jt. auth. see Sidis, Boris.
Goodheart, Eugene. Culture & the Radical Conscience. LC 72-91910. 234p. 1973. 12.50x (ISBN 0-674-17966-8); pap. 3.95x (ISBN 0-674-17968-4). Harvard U Pr.
--The Failure of Criticism. LC 77-29055. 1978. 15.00x (ISBN 0-674-29115-8). Harvard U Pr.
--The Skeptic Disposition in Contemporary Criticism. LC 84-15076. (Essays in Literature Ser.). 200p. 1985. text ed. 22.50x (ISBN 0-691-06626-4). Princeton U Pr.
--Utopian Vision of D. H. Lawrence. LC 63-22817. 1963. 12.00x (ISBN 0-226-30288-1). U of Chicago Pr.
Goodheart, Pat. The Translator. 160p. 1983. pap. 4.95 (ISBN 0-941324-07-9). Van Vactor & Goodheart.
Goodheart, Pat, tr. see Cardinal, Marie.
Goodheartz, A. S. Commitment to Youth. 1967. 11.95x (ISBN 0-317-18407-5). New Coll U Pr.
Goodheir, Albert, tr. see Nimo, Ko.
Goodhew, P. J. Electron Microscopy & Analysis. (The Wykeham Science Ser.: No. 33). 200p. 1975. pap. cancelled. Taylor & Francis.
--Real Solids & Radiation. (The Wykeham Science Ser.: No. 35). 208p. 1975. pap. cancelled (ISBN 0-85109-011-7). Taylor & Francis.
--Speciman Preparation in Materials Science. (Practical Methods in Electron Microscopy: Vol. 1, No. 1). 1983. 17.00 (ISBN 0-444-10412-7, North-Holland). Elsevier.
Goodhew, P. J. & Cartwright, L. E. Electron Microscopy & Analysis. LC 74-32449. (Wykeham Science Ser.: No. 33). 200p. 1975. 9.95x (ISBN 0-8448-1160-2). Crane Russak Co.
Goodhew, Peter. Specimen Preparation for Transmission Electron Microscopy of Materials. (Royal Microscopical Society Handbooks Ser.). (Illus.). 1984. pap. 9.95 (ISBN 0-19-856403-1). Oxford U Pr.
Goodhew, Peter, jt. auth. see Chescoe, Dawn.
Goodhill, Ruth M., selected by see Heschel, Abraham J.
Goodhill, Victor. Ear Diseases, Deafness, & Dizziness. (Illus.). 1979. text ed. 83.50 (ISBN 0-06-140981-2, 14-09812, Harper Medical). Lippincott.
Goodhue, Horace R. Indian Bead-Weaving Patterns: Chain Weaving Designs & Bead Loom Weaving-An Illustrated "How-To" Guide. LC 84-71456. (Illus.). 64p. (gr. 3 up). 1984. pap. 4.95 (ISBN 0-9613503-0-X). Bead Craft.
Goodich, Michael. The Unmentionable Vice: Homosexuality in the Later Medieval Period. LC 78-13276. 179p. 1980. pap. 7.95 (ISBN 0-87436-300-4). Ross-Erikson.
Goodie, Dick. Running in Maine. (Illus.). 140p. 1984. pap. 8.95 (ISBN 0-930096-62-2). G Gannett.
Goodier, A. Public Life of Our Lord Jesus Christ, 2 vols. 1978. Set. 15.95 (ISBN 0-8198-0551-3); Set. pap. 13.95 (ISBN 0-8198-0552-1). Dghtrs St Paul.
Goodier, Alban. The Crown of Sorrow. 156p. 1982. 3.25 (ISBN 0-8198-1422-9, SP0093); pap. 2.25 (ISBN 0-8198-1423-7). Dghtrs St Paul.
--The Prince of Peace. 152p. 1982. 3.25 (ISBN 0-8198-5807-2, SP0585); pap. 2.25 (ISBN 0-8198-5808-0). Dghtrs St Paul.
--Saints for Sinners. LC 70-99637. (Essay Index Reprint Ser.). 1930. 18.00 (ISBN 0-8369-1504-6). Ayer Co Pubs.
Goodier, J. H. Dictionary of Painting & Decorating. 308p. 1974. 39.50x (ISBN 0-85264-224-5, Pub. by Griffin England). State Mutual Bk.
--Painting & Decorating: A Guide for Houseowner & Decorator. pap. 40.00 (ISBN 0-317-27866-5, 2025265). Bks Demand UMI.
Goodier, J. L., et al. Spill Prevention & Fail-Safe Engineering for Petroleum & Related Products. LC 83-2204. (Pollution Tech. Rev. 100). (Illus.). 329p. (Orig.). 1983. 36.00 (ISBN 0-8155-0944-8). Noyes.
Goodier, J. M., jt. auth. see Hurst, A. E.
Goodier, J. N., jt. auth. see Timoshenko, Stephen P.
Goodin, J. R., jt. auth. see Northington, David K.
Goodin, J. R. & Northington, David K., eds. Arid Land Plant Resources. 724p. 1979. 15.00 (ISBN 0-318-14552-9, 79-1). Intl Ctr Arid & Semi-Arid.
--Plant Resources of Arid & Semiarid Lands: A Global Perspective. Edited Treatise ed. Date not set. price not set (ISBN 0-12-289745-5). Acad Pr.
Goodin, J. R., jt. ed. see Traylor, Idris R.
Goodin, Robert E. Manipulatory Politics. LC 79-27682. 264p. 1980. 27.00x (ISBN 0-300-02463-0). Yale U Pr.
--Political Theory & Public Policy. LC 81-23120. 1982. lib. bdg. 27.50x (ISBN 0-226-30296-2). U of Chicago Pr.
--Political Theory & Public Policy. LC 81-23120. 286p. 1983. pap. 10.00x (ISBN 0-226-30297-0). U of Chicago Pr.
--The Politics of Rational Man. LC 75-35616. pap. 54.50 (ISBN 0-317-07750-3, 2022401). Bks Demand UMI.
--Protecting the Vulnerable: A Re-Analysis of Our Social Responsibilities. LC 85-1127. 248p. 1985. 25.00 (ISBN 0-226-30298-9). U of Chicago Pr.
Gooding, C. Thomas, jt. auth. see Pittenger, Owen E.
Gooding, Charles, jt. ed. see Margulis, Alexander.
Gooding, Charles A., jt. auth. see Margulis, Alexander R.
Gooding, D. W. The Account of the Tabernacle. (Texts & Studies, New Ser.: Vol. 6). Repr. of 1959 ed. 28.00 (ISBN 0-317-15418-4). Kraus Repr.
Gooding, D. W., ed. see Katz, Peter.
Gooding, David. Monarch Notes on Defoe's Moll Flanders. (Orig.). pap. 2.95 (ISBN 0-671-00705-X). Monarch Pr.
--Un Reino Inconmovible. Orig. Title: An Unshakeable Kingdom. 196p. 1983. pap. 3.75 (ISBN 0-8254-1275-7). Kregel.
Gooding, Earl. The West Indies at the Crossroads. 254p. 1982. pap. text ed. 9.95 (ISBN 0-87073-053-3). Schenkman Bks Inc.
Gooding, John D. Durango South Project: Archaeological Salvage of Two Basketmaker III Sites in the Durango District. LC 80-16361. (Anthropological Papers: No. 34). 200p. 1980. pap. 6.95x (ISBN 0-8165-0705-8). U of Ariz Pr.
Gooding, Judson. The Job Revolution. LC 74-188469. 256p. 1972. 7.95 (ISBN 0-8027-0383-6). Walker & Co.
Gooding, Kathleen. The Festival Summer. 176p. (gr. 7 up). 1984. 15.95 (ISBN 0-571-13352-5). Faber & Faber.
--The Rainbow Trail. LC 83-5672. 192p. (gr. 5-8). 1983. 12.95 (ISBN 0-571-11958-1). Faber & Faber.
Gooding, Marion F. & Hughes, Bernice. Nursing School Entrance Examinations. 320p. (Orig.). 1985. pap. 8.95 (ISBN 0-668-06142-1). Arco.
Goodings, Richard & Byram, Michael, eds. Changing Priorities in Teacher Education: An International Survey. 240p. 1982. 25.00 (ISBN 0-89397-141-3). Nichols Pub.
Goodings, Richard, jt. ed. see Coffield, Frank.
Goodis, Karen L. The Learning Center Book of Bible People. LC 81-67026. (Learning Center Book Ser.). (Illus.). 123p. (Orig.). 1981. pap. 14.50 (ISBN 0-86705-005-5). AIRE.
Goodisman, J. Contemporary Quantum Chemistry. LC 76-58510. (Illus.). 376p. 1977. 55.00x (ISBN 0-306-30947-5, Plenum Pr); pap. 15.00 (ISBN 0-306-20023-6). Plenum Pub.
Goodisman, Jerry. Diatomic Interaction Potential Theory, 2 vols. Incl. Vol. 1. Fundamentals. 1973. 73.50 (ISBN 0-12-290201-7); Vol. 2. Applications. 1973. 78.00 (ISBN 0-12-290202-5). (Physical Chemistry Ser.). Acad Pr.
Goodison, Lucy, jt. auth. see Ernst, Sheila.
Goodison, Nicholas. English Barometers 1680-1860. 2nd ed. (Illus.). 388p. 1977. Repr. of 1968 ed. 49.50 (ISBN 0-902028-52-9). Antique Collect.
Goodkin, Bob. A Therapist's Notebook. LC 81-90025. 127p. (Orig.). 1981. pap. 3.95 (ISBN 0-9605872-0-9). Lenox Bks.
Goodkin, Marie, jt. auth. see Billingham, Richard.
Goodkin, Richard E. The Symbolist Home & the Tragic Home: Mallarme & Oedipus. LC 84-9280. (Purdue University Monographs in Fomance Languages (PURML): Vol. 13). xv, 203p. (Orig.). 1984. pap. 24.00x (ISBN 0-915027-00-3). Benjamins North Am.
Goodkind, Herbert K. Violin Inconography of Antonio Stradivari. LC 73-169961. (Illus.). 780p. 1972. 300.00x (ISBN 0-9600498-1-9). H K Goodkind.
Goodkind, Herbert K., compiled by. Cumulative Index to the Musical Quarterly, 1915-1959. LC 16-24484. 1960. pap. 40.00x (ISBN 0-9600498-2-7); pap. 50.00x with 1960-64 supplement (ISBN 0-9600498-3-5). H K Goodkind.
Goodkind, Richard J., jt. auth. see Baker, James L.
Goodkind, Thomas, jt. auth. see Rowell, Elizabeth.
Goodlad. The Conventional & the Alternative in Education. LC 75-2780. 288p. 1975. 22.75x (ISBN 0-8211-0611-2); text ed. 20.50x 10 or more copies (ISBN 0-685-53835-4). McCutchan.
Goodlad, Douglas, jt. auth. see Balderson, Eileen.
Goodlad, J. I. A Place Called School. 416p. 1984. pap. 9.95 (ISBN 0-07-023627-5). McGraw.
Goodlad, J. S. Science for Non-Scientists. 1973. 14.50x (ISBN 0-19-858209-9). Oxford U Pr.
Goodlad, John I. School, Curriculum, & the Individual. LC 66-17796. (Blaisdell Book in Education). pap. 66.80 (ISBN 0-317-09498-X, 2055148). Bks Demand UMI.
--What Schools Are For. LC 79-54644. (Foundation Monograph Ser.). 136p. 1979. pap. 5.50 (ISBN 0-87367-422-7). Phi Delta Kappa.
Goodlad, John I., ed. Changing American School. LC 66-2225. (National Society for the Study of Education Yearbooks Ser: No. 65, Pt. 2). 1966. 7.50x (ISBN 0-226-60083-1). U of Chicago Pr.

...d, John I., ed. see Culver, Carmen M. & Hoban, Gary J.
Goodlad, John I., jt. ed. see Fenstermacher, Gary D.
Goodlad, John I., jt. ed. see Shane, Harold G.
Goodlad, Sinclair, ed. Economics of Scale in Higher Education. 100p. 1983. 24.00 (ISBN 0-946376-00-X). Taylor & Francis.
--Education for the Professions. 348p. 1984. pap. 26.00x (ISBN 1-85059-001-X, Pub. by NFER Nelson UK). Taylor & Francis.
--Study Service. 236p. 1982. 19.00x (ISBN 0-85633-242-9, Pub. by NFER Nelson UK). Taylor & Francis.
Goodland. Coronary Care. 3rd ed. 96p. 1978. pap. 10.50 (ISBN 0-7236-0466-5). PSG Pub Co.
--General Intensive Care. 112p. 1978. pap. 10.50 (ISBN 0-7236-0503-3). PSG Pub Co.
Goodland, E. A., tr. see De Andrade, Mario.
Goodland, R. J. & Irwin, H. S. Amazon Jungle: Green Hell to Red Desert. (Development in Landscape Management & Urban Planning Ser.: Vol. 1). 155p. 1975. 42.75 (ISBN 0-444-41318-9). Elsevier.
Goodland, Robert. Buildings & the Environment. LC 76-22811. (Illus.). 1976. pap. 10.00x (ISBN 0-89327-052-0). NY Botanical.
--Environmental Management in Tropical Agriculture. 200p. 1983. softcover 20.00x (ISBN 0-86531-715-1). Westview.
--Power Lines & the Environment. LC 73-89356. (Illus.). 1973. pap. 5.00x (ISBN 0-89327-050-4). NY Botanical.
--Tribal Peoples & Economic Development: Human Ecologic Considerations. 111p. 1982. 5.00 (ISBN 0-8213-0010-5). World Bank.
Goodland, Roger. A Bibliography of Sex Rites & Customs. LC 72-9839. Repr. of 1931 ed. 42.50 (ISBN 0-404-57445-9). AMS Pr.
--A Bibliography of Sex Rites & Customs. LC 77-11605. 1977. Repr. of 1931 ed. lib. bdg. 60.00 (ISBN 0-89341-193-0). Longwood Pub Group.
Goodloe, Abbie C. At the Foot of the Rockies. LC 72-4424. (Short Story Index Reprint Ser.). Repr. of 1935 ed. 28.00 (ISBN 0-8369-4177-2). Ayer Co Pubs.
Goodloe, Albert. Confederate Echoes. 1983. Repr. 21.95 (ISBN 0-89201-105-X). Zenger pub.
Goodloe, Alfred, et al. Managing Yourself: How to Control Emotion, Stress, & Time. 304p. 1984. 15.95 (ISBN 0-531-09578-9). Watts.
Goodloe, William H. Coconut Palm Frond Weaving. LC 72-79018. (Illus.). 1972. pap. 3.95 (ISBN 0-8048-1061-3). C E Tuttle.
Goodman. Collection of Accounts. (The Law in the District of Columbia Ser.). 24.95 (ISBN 0-686-90158-4). Harrison Co GA.
--Collection of Accounts. (The Law in Iowa Ser.). 24.95 (ISBN 0-686-90587-3). Harrison Co GA.
--Collection of Accounts. (The Law in Virginia Ser.). 24.95 (ISBN 0-686-91022-2). Harrison Co GA.
--Declaratory Judgment Remedy in Retirement Plan Cases. 24p. pap. 2.00 (ISBN 0-317-04306-4). Commerce.
--How to Troubleshoot & Repair Electronic Circuits. 378p. 1981. 18.95 (ISBN 0-8306-9656-3); pap. 13.50 (ISBN 0-8306-1218-1, 1218). TAB Bks.
--Industry - Geared Retirement Plans. 24p. 1983. pap. 2.00 (ISBN 0-317-04312-9, 4858). Commerce.
--Innovations in Employee Plan Designs. 24p. pap. 2.00 (ISBN 0-317-04313-7). Commerce.
--Investment of Exempt Employees' Trusts in the 1980's. 24p. pap. 2.00 (ISBN 0-317-04316-1). Commerce.
--The Mayor of Casterbridge (Hardy) (Book Note Ser.). 1985. pap. 2.50 (ISBN 0-8120-3525-9). Barron.
--Of Mice & Men (Steinbeck) (Book Notes Ser.). 1984. pap. 2.50 (ISBN 0-8120-3431-7). Barron.
Goodman & Grant. Psychological Astrology. 68p. 1974. 6.00 (ISBN 0-86690-107-8, 1148-01). Am Fed Astrologers.
Goodman & Mason. Experiencing Accounting: A Study Guide for Personal Computing. (Pt. 1). 1985. 12.86 (ISBN 0-205-08221-1, 058221). Allyn.
Goodman & Wang. Meteorological Instruments Laboratory Manual. 72p. 1984. pap. text ed. 9.95 (ISBN 0-8403-3313-7). Kendall-Hunt.
Goodman, jt. auth. see Winters.
Goodman, A. H. Music Education: Perspectives & Perceptions. 160p. 1982. pap. text ed. 8.95 (ISBN 0-8403-2689-0). Kendall-Hunt.
Goodman, A. Harold. Instrumental Music Guide. LC 77-7923. 1977. pap. 2.40 (ISBN 0-8425-1525-9). Brigham.
Goodman, A. W. Analytic Geometry & the Calculus. 4th ed. (Illus.). 1980. text ed. write for info.. (ISBN 0-02-344960-8). Macmillan.
--Analytic Geometry & the Calculus: Student Study Guide, 2 vols. 4th ed. (Illus.). 1980. pap. text ed. write for info. Vol. I (ISBN 0-02-344970-5). Vol. II (ISBN 0-02-344980-2). Macmillan.
--A Short Course in Algebra & Trigonometry. (Illus.). 139p. 1985. pap. text ed. 9.95 (ISBN 0-912675-11-X). Ardsley.
--Univalent Functions, 2 vols. LC 83-7930. 246p. Vol. I. 47.50 ea. (ISBN 0-936166-10-X). Vol. II (ISBN 0-936166-11-8). Set. 95.00 (ISBN 0-936166-12-6). Mariner Pub.
Goodman, A. W. & Ratti, J. S. Finite Mathematics with Applications. 1979. text ed. 23.95x (ISBN 0-02-344760-5); write for info. Macmillan.
--Mathematics for Management & Social Sciences. LC 78-11841. (Illus.). 1979. text ed. 28.95 (ISBN 0-03-022161-7, HoltC). HR&W.
Goodman, A. W. & Saff, Edward. Calculus: Concepts & Calculations. 1981. text ed. write for info. (ISBN 0-02-344740-0); Vol. 1. write for info. (ISBN 0-02-344750-8); Vol. 2. write for info. (ISBN 0-686-72521-2). Macmillan.
Goodman, A. W., et al. The Mainstream of Algebra & Trigonometry. 2nd ed. LC 79-90059. (Illus.). 1980. text ed. 29.50 (ISBN 0-395-26765-X); solutions manual 7.50 (ISBN 0-395-26761-7). HM.
Goodman, Allan E. Politics in War: The Bases of Political Community in South Vietnam. LC 72-96629. 328p. 1973. 18.50x (ISBN 0-674-68825-2). Harvard U Pr.
Goodman, Allan E., jt. ed. see Abramowski, Luise.
Goodman, Allen E., ed. Negotiating While Fighting: The Diary of Admiral C. Turner Joy at the Korean Armistice Conference. LC 77-77565. (Publication Ser: No. 175). (Illus.). 1978. 22.50x (ISBN 0-8179-6751-6). Hoover Inst Pr.
Goodman, Alvin S. Principles of Water Resources Planning. (Illus.). 576p. 1984. 38.95 (ISBN 0-13-710616-5). P-H.
Goodman, Andrew. Gilbert & Sullivan at Law. LC 82-12175. (Illus.). 264p. 1982. 25.00 (ISBN 0-8386-3179-7). Fairleigh Dickinson.
Goodman, Ann, jt. auth. see Elting, Mary.
Goodman, Anthony. The Loyal Conspiracy: The Lords Appellant Under Richard Second. LC 77-170141. 1971. 9.95x (ISBN 0-87024-215-6). U of Miami Pr.
--The Wars of the Roses: Military Activity & English Society, 1452-1497. (Illus.). 300p. 1981. 30.00x (ISBN 0-7100-0728-0). Routledge & Kegan.
Goodman, Anthony, jt. ed. see Newman, Michael.
Goodman, Arnold M. A Plain Pine Box: A Return to Simple Jewish Funerals & Eternal Traditions. 7.95x (ISBN 0-87068-895-2). Ktav.
Goodman, Becky, ed. see Mindell, Arnold.
Goodman, Bernice. The Lesbian: A Celebration of Difference. 1977. pap. 3.50 (ISBN 0-918314-04-6). Out & Out.
Goodman, Brian L. Manual for Activated Sludge Sewage Treatment. LC 79-173027. 203p. 1971. pap. 15.00 (ISBN 0-87762-070-9). Technomic.
Goodman, Budd & Leventhal, Howard. Charges to the Jury & Requests to Charge in a Criminal Case: 1968-1983, 2 vols. rev. ed. LC 83-15323. Set. 160.00. Callaghan.
Goodman, C. Helen Frankenthaller: Works of the Seventies. 1980. pap. 4.00 (ISBN 0-912303-20-4). Michigan Mus.
Goodman, C. H., ed. Crystal Growth: Theory & Techniques, 2 vols. Incl. Vol. 1. 309p. 1974. 45.00x (ISBN 0-306-35101-3); Vol. 2. 201p. 1978. 39.50x (ISBN 0-306-35102-1). LC 72-95388. (Illus., Plenum Pr). Plenum Pub.
Goodman, Calvin J. Art Marketing Handbook. 5th, Rev. ed. Goodman, Florence J., ed. 568p. 1985. 39.95x (ISBN 0-917232-18-6). Gee Tee Bee.
Goodman, Cary. Choosing Sides: Playground & Street Life on the Lower East Side. LC 79-12665. 1979. 12.95 (ISBN 0-8052-3718-6). Schocken.
Goodman, Celia, ed. see Koestler, Mamaine.
Goodman, Charles, jt. auth. see Cogan, Arlene.
Goodman, Charles, jt. auth. see Hodge, Charlie.
Goodman, Charles D., et al, eds. The PN Reaction & the Nucleon-Nucleon Force. LC 79-27785. 550p. 1980. 79.50 (ISBN 0-306-40351-X, Plenum Pr). Plenum Pub.
Goodman, Charles r. Bound by Blood. 1985. pap. 3.25 (ISBN 0-87067-829-9, BH829). Holloway.
Goodman, Christopher. How Superior Powers Ought to Be Obeyed of Their Subjects. LC 70-38197. (English Experience Ser.: No. 460). 240p. 1972. Repr. of 1548 ed. 22.00 (ISBN 90-221-0460-5). Walter J Johnson.
Goodman, Claire G. Copper Artifacts in Late Eastern Woodlands Prehistory. Cantwell, Anne-Marie, ed. 104p. 1984. 14.50 (ISBN 0-942118-16-2, E78.E2G66). Ctr Amer Arche.
Goodman, Clarke E. God's Plan for the Church As Revealed in the Bible. LC 81-50191. 71p. 1982. 7.95 (ISBN 0-533-04974-1). Vantage.
--Preaching the Gospel of Jesus Christ. LC 84-90077. 101p. 1985. 8.95 (ISBN 0-533-06156-3). Vantage.
Goodman, Cynthia, ed. see Hofmann, Hans.
Goodman, D., et al, eds. Differing Perspectives in Motor Learning, Memory, & Control: Advances in Psychology, Vol. 27. 340p. 1985. 46.50 (ISBN 0-444-87761-4, North Holland). Elsevier.
Goodman, D. C., ed. see Symposium Based on Papers Presented at the Cajal Club Meeting in Conjunction with the American Association of Anatomists, Dallas, Tex., April 1972.
Goodman, Danny. Going Places with the New Apple IIc: All You'll Ever Need to Know to Get There. 256p. 1984. pap. 3.95 (ISBN 0-671-53188-3). PB.
--Hands-On EXCEL. 1985. pap. 19.95 (ISBN 0-673-18369-6). Scott F.
--How to Buy An IBM PC Or Compatible Computer. PC World Editors, ed. 224p. 1984. pap. 14.95 (ISBN 0-671-49282-9, Pub. by Computer Bks). S&S.
--The Simon & Schuster Guide to the IBM PCjr. 160p. 1984. pap. 8.95 (ISBN 0-671-50904-7, Pub. by Computer Bks). S&S.
--The Simon & Schuster Guide to the TRS-80 Model 100. 128p. 1984. pap. 9.95 (ISBN 0-671-49254-3, Pub. by Computer Bks). S&S.
--The Simon & Schuster's Guide to Atari's "My First Computer". 128p. 1984. pap. 5.95 (ISBN 0-671-49255-1, Pub. by Computer Bks). S&S.
--Supermac. 250p. 1985. pap. 12.95 (ISBN 0-671-49256-X, Pub. by Computer Bks). S&S.
--Word Processing on the IBM Personal Computer. 1983. pap. 19.95 (ISBN 0-672-22081-4). Bobbs.
--Word Processing on the IBM Personal Computer. LC 83-50376. 464p. 1983. pap. 19.95 (ISBN 0-672-22081-4, 22081). Sams.
Goodman, Danny, jt. auth. see Consumer Guide Editors.
Goodman, David. Inner Power: Discovering Yourself & Manifesting Your Potentials. LC 81-23599. (Quality Paperback Ser.: No. 369). 172p. (Orig.). 1982. pap. text ed. 5.95 (ISBN 0-8226-0369-1). Littlefield.
Goodman, David & Peavy, John, III. Hyperprofits. LC 85-4504. (Illus.). 192p. 1985. 15.95 (ISBN 0-385-19599-0). Doubleday.
Goodman, David & Redclift, Michael. From Peasant to Proletarian: Capitalist Developments & Agrarian Transitions. 1981. 27.50x (ISBN 0-312-30779-9). St Martin.
Goodman, David, ed. see Barnes, Steve.
Goodman, David, tr. see Domes, Jurgen.
Goodman, David B., intro. by. Technology Impact: Potential Directions for Laboratory Medicine. (Annals of The New York Academy of Sciences Ser.: Vol. 428). 334p. 1984. lib. bdg. 64.00x (ISBN 0-89766-250-4); pap. 64.00x (ISBN 0-89766-251-2). NY Acad Sci.
Goodman, David B., jt. ed. see Scott, Walter N.
Goodman, David E., jt. auth. see Bassett, Ernest D.
Goodman, David M. Arizona Odyssey: Bibliographic Adventures in Nineteenth Century Magazines. LC 73-94875. 1969. 20.00 (ISBN 0-910152-02-0). AZ Hist Foun.
Goodman, David S. Beijing Street Voices: The Poetry & Politics of China's Democracy Movement. (Illus.). 208p. 1984. 20.00 (ISBN 0-7145-2717-3, Dist by Scribner); pap. 9.95 (ISBN 0-7145-2703-3). M Boyars.
--Emotional Well-Being Through Rational Behavior Training. (Illus.). 256p. 1978. pap. 25.75x spiral binding (ISBN 0-398-03750-7). C C Thomas.
Goodman, David S., ed. & intro. by. Groups & Politics in the People's Republic of China. LC 83-20310. 224p. 1984. 25.00 (ISBN 0-87332-231-2). M E Sharpe.
Goodman, Deborah L. The Throne of Zeus. (Choose Your Own Adventure Ser.: No. 40). 128p. 1985. pap. 1.95 (ISBN 0-553-24679-8). Bantam.
Goodman, Don. The Boy Who Made God Smile. LC 82-7532. (A Cory Story Ser.). (Illus.). 32p. (ps-4). 1982. pap. 2.95 (ISBN 0-8307-0859-6, 5608224). Regal.
--Cory Hears with His Heart. LC 82-12272. (A Cory Story Ser.). 32p. (ps-2). 1982. pap. 2.95 (ISBN 0-8307-0858-8, 5608318). Regal.
Goodman, Donald C. & Fisher, Harvey I. Functional Apparatus in Waterfowl: (Aus: Anatidae) LC 62-9267. (Illus.). 206p. 1962. 6.50x (ISBN 0-8093-0066-4). S Ill U Pr.
Goodman, Donald P., et al. Collective Bargaining Law in the Public Sector. 802p. 1980. 16.95 (ISBN 0-686-27396-6). Niagara U Pr.
Goodman, Edward. Study of Liberty & Revolution. 1975. 27.50x (ISBN 0-7156-0870-3); pap. 18.95x (ISBN 0-685-88347-7). Intl Ideas.
Goodman, Edward, jt. auth. see Charters, Alexander N.
Goodman, Edward J. The Exploration of South America: An Annotated Bibliography. LC 82-49177. 250p. 1983. lib. bdg. 43.00 (ISBN 0-8240-9180-9). Garland Pub.
Goodman, Ellen. At Large. 1981. 12.95 (ISBN 0-671-43306-7). Summit Bks.
--At Large. 352p. 1983. pap. 3.50 (ISBN 0-449-20145-7, Crest). Fawcett.
--Close to Home. 1981. pap. 2.50 (ISBN 0-449-24351-6, Crest). Fawcett.
--Turning Points. 320p. 1983. pap. 3.50 (ISBN 0-449-20103-1, Crest). Fawcett.
--Turning Points. 1982. pap. 5.95 (ISBN 0-449-90015-0, Columbine). Fawcett.
--Writing Television & Motion Picture Scripts That Sell. 256p. 1982. pap. 8.95 (ISBN 0-8092-5787-4). Contemp Bks.
Goodman, Elliot R. The Soviet Design for a World State. LC 60-7625. (Studies of the Russian Institute). 512p. 1960. 35.00x (ISBN 0-231-02339-1). Columbia U Pr.
Goodman, Emily J., jt. auth. see Chesler, Phyllis.
Goodman, Eric K. High on the Energy Bridge. LC 79-1930. 264p. 1980. pap. 6.95 (ISBN 0-03-056841-2). HR&W.
Goodman, Eugene B. All the Justice I Could Afford. Sandum, Howard E., ed. LC 82-22300. 274p. 1983. 16.95 (ISBN 0-15-104778-2). HarBraceJ.
Goodman, Evelyn. Writing Television & Motion Picture Scripts That Sell. (Orig.). Date not set. pap. text ed. 9.95 (ISBN 0-9613885-8-7). Westbourne Ent.
Goodman, F. D., et al. Trance, Healing, & Hallucination: Three Field Studies in Religious Experience. LC 80-20043. 414p. 1982. Repr. of 1974 ed. text ed. 24.50 (ISBN 0-89874-246-3). Krieger.
Goodman, F. L., jt. auth. see Payne, Joseph N.
Goodman, Felicitas D. Speaking in Tongues: A Cross-Cultural Study of Glossolalia. LC 70-182871. 224p. 1972. 16.00x (ISBN 0-226-30324-1). U of Chicago Pr.
Goodman, Felicitas D. & Henney, Jeannette H. Trance, Healing & Hallucination: Three Field Studies in Religious Experience. LC 74-4159. (Contemporary Religious Movements Ser.). pap. 78.10 (ISBN 0-317-08516-6, 2055086). Bks Demand UMI.
Goodman, Florence G. A Young Person's Philosophical Dictionary. (gr. 5-12). 1978. pap. 7.95 (ISBN 0-917232-06-2). Gee Tee Bee.
Goodman, Florence J. The A B C's of Feminine Happiness. 88p. 1980. 8.95x (ISBN 0-917232-10-0). Gee Tee Bee.
Goodman, Florence J. & Adler, Shelley. Voices of Two Women. 1974. 5.95 (ISBN 0-917232-01-1). Gee Tee Bee.
Goodman, Florence J., ed. see Goodman, Calvin J.
Goodman, Floyd G. & Schoedinger, George R. Questions & Answers in Orthopaedics: For Students, Interns, Residents & Board Aspirant. 3rd ed. LC 77-8188. 294p. 1977. pap. 24.50 (ISBN 0-8016-1900-9). Mosby.
Goodman, Frances B., jt. auth. see Colegrove, William.
Goodman, Frances B., jt. auth. see Diamond, Ann.
Goodman, Frances B., jt. auth. see Richard, John T.
Goodman, Frances B., ed. see Brennan, R. O.
Goodman, Frances B., ed. see Hudgins, Edgar H.
Goodman, Frances B., ed. see Prokop, Phyllis S.
Goodman, Frances B., ed. see Wesley, Monte C. & Sellars, Jan.
Goodman, Frank O & Wachman, Harold Y. Dynamics of Gas-Surface Scattering. 1976. 76.00 (ISBN 0-12-290450-8). Acad Pr.
Goodman, G. & Ross, M., eds. Laser Applications: Video Disc, Vol. 4. 1980. 55.00 (ISBN 0-12-431904-1). Acad Pr.
Goodman, G. T. & Bray, S. An Annotated Bibliography of Ecological Aspects of the Reclamation of Derelict & Disturbed Land. (Bibliography Ser.). 351p. 1980. 14.95x (ISBN 0-902246-52-6, Pub. by GEO Abstracts England). State Mutual Bk.
Goodman, G. T., jt. auth. see Chadwick, M. J.
Goodman, G. T. & Chadwick, M. H., eds. Environmental Management of Mineral Wastes. 382p. 1978. 42.50x (ISBN 9-0286-0054-X). Sijthoff & Noordhoff.
Goodman, G. T. & Rowe, W. D., eds. Energy Risk Management. LC 79-42931. 1980. 53.50 (ISBN 0-12-289680-7). Acad Pr.
Goodman, Gary. Reach Out & Sell Someone: Phone Your Way to Success Through the Goodman System of Telemarketing. 141p. 1983. 12.95 (ISBN 0-13-753632-1); pap. 5.95 (ISBN 0-13-753624-0). P-H.
--Winning by Telephone: Telephone Effectiveness for the Business Man & Consumer. 144p. 1982. 14.95 (ISBN 0-13-960971-7); pap. 5.95 (ISBN 0-13-960963-6). P-H.
Goodman, Gary S. Gary Goodman's Sixty Salesperson. 132p. 1985. 14.95 (ISBN 0-13-346883-6); pap. 6.95 (ISBN 0-13-346875-5). P H.
--Selling Skills for the Non-Salesperson: For People Who Hate to Sell But Love to Succeed. 144p. 1984. 13.95 (ISBN 0-13-805961-6); pap. 6.95 (ISBN 0-13-805953-5). P-H.
--You Can Sell Anything by Telephone. 144p. 1984. 14.95 (ISBN 0-13-976770-3); pap. 6.95 (ISBN 0-13-976762-2). P-H.
Goodman, Geoffrey. The Miners' Strike. 192p. (Orig.). 1985. pap. 5.95 (ISBN 0-7453-0073-1, Pub. by Pluto Pr). Longwood Pub Group.
Goodman, Gerald. Companionship Therapy. LC 72-6046. (Jossey-Bass Behavioral Science Ser.). pap. 79.00 (ISBN 0-317-08609-X, 2013788). Bks Demand UMI.
Goodman, Gerald & Dooley, David. Interpersonal Processes: Introductory Readings. 117p. 1972. pap. text ed. 9.50x (ISBN 0-8422-0197-1). Irvington.
Goodman, Gerre, et al. No Turning Back: Lesbian & Gay Liberation for the '80s. 154p. 1983. lib. bdg. 16.95 (ISBN 0-86571-019-8); pap. 7.95 (ISBN 0-86571-018-X). New Soc Pubs.
Goodman, Gordon, et al, eds. The European Transition from Oil: Societal Impacts & Constraints on Energy Policy. 1981. 55.00 (ISBN 0-12-290420-6). Acad Pr.
Goodman, Grant K. An Experiment in Wartime Intercultural Relations: Philippine Students in Japan, 1943-1945. 34p. 1962. pap. 2.00 (ISBN 0-87727-046-5, DP 46). Cornell SE Asia.
--Japan: The Dutch Experience. LC 84-21671. 240p. 1985. 25.00 (ISBN 0-485-11262-0, Pub. by Athlone Pr Ltd). Longwood Pub Group.
Goodman, Grant K. & Moos, Felix, eds. The United States & Japan in the Western Pacific. (Westview Replica Edition Ser.). (Illus.). 225p. 1981. lib. bdg. 27.50x (ISBN 0-89158-840-X). Westview.

Goodman, Hanna. Jewish Cooking Around the World: Gourmet & Holiday Recipes. LC 73-15174. (Illus.). 256p. 1974. 9.95 (ISBN 0-8276-0043-7, 349). Jewish Pubns.

Goodman, Hanna see Goodman, Philip.

Goodman, Hannah G. Story of Prophecy. LC 65-24925. (gr. 9 up). 1965. 5.95x (ISBN 0-87441-017-7). Behrman.

Goodman, Harriet W. & Morse, Barbar. Just What the Doctor Ordered. LC 81-6786. 678p. 1982. 25.00 (ISBN 0-03-051011-2). HR&W.

Goodman, Helen, jt. auth. see Fleischer, Eugene.

Goodman, Henry. The Selected Writings of Lafcadio Hearn. 566p. 1983. 35.00 (ISBN 0-89984-219-4). Century Bookbindery.

Goodman, Henry, ed. see Hearn, Lafcadio.

Goodman, Herman, jt. auth. see Fredericks, Carlton.

Goodman, Howard A. Planpak Number 83131: Model Rocket Launch Panel. (Illus.). 24p. (Orig.). 1984. pap. text ed. 3.95 (ISBN 0-914465-00-7, 83131). S S J Pubns.

Goodman, I., ed. Developments in Block Copolymers, Vol. 1. (Illus.). xiv, 358p. 1982. 81.50 (ISBN 0-85334-145-1, I-360-82, Pub. by Elsevier Applied Sci England). Elsevier.

Goodman, Irving & Schein, Martin, eds. Birds: Brain & Behavior. 1974. 49.50 (ISBN 0-12-290350-1). Acad Pr.

Goodman, Isidore. Assured Pensions. LC 83-200021. 24p. 1983. pap. 2.00 (ISBN 0-317-04072-3, 4925). Commerce.

--Compensating Employees with the Least Tax Consequences. 24p. 1983. pap. 2.00 (ISBN 0-317-04304-8, 4869). Commerce.

--Coping with the Rising Costs of Employee Benefits. 24p. 1984. pap. 2.00 (ISBN 0-317-19234-5, 4784). Commerce.

--Current Employee Plan Issues. 24p. 1984. pap. 2.00 (ISBN 0-317-19235-3, 4848). Commerce.

--Employee Benefit Plans under TRA of 1984. LC 85-114839. Date not set. pap. 2.00 (ISBN 0-317-27343-4). Commerce.

--Employee Turnover Under Tax-Qualified Plans. LC 84-249350. 23p. Date not set. price not set. Commerce.

Goodman, Ivy. Heart Failure. LC 83-9183. (Iowa Short Fiction Award Ser.: No. 14). 149p. (Orig.). 1983. 12.95 (ISBN 0-87745-119-2); pap. 8.95 (ISBN 0-87745-120-6). U of Iowa Pr.

Goodman, J. Employment Relations in Industrial Society. (Industrial Studies). 1984. text ed. 25.75x (ISBN 0-86003-533-6, Pub. by Alan England); pap. text ed. 13.00x (ISBN 0-86003-635-9, Pub. by Philip Alan England). Humanities.

Goodman, J. F., et al. Rulemaking & Industrial Peace: Industrial Relations in the Footwear Industry. 213p. 1977. 35.00x (ISBN 0-85664-430-7, Pub. by Croom Helm Ltd). Longwood Pub Group.

Goodman, J. F. B., et al. Ideology & Shopfloor Industrial Relations. 224p. 1981. 37.50 (ISBN 0-7099-0465-7, Pub. by Croom Helm Ltd). Longwood Pub Group.

Goodman, J. W., ed. Advanced Aluminum & Titanium Structures (AD-02) 52p. 1981. 14.00 (ISBN 0-686-34473-1, H00193). ASME.

Goodman, Jack, ed. While You Were Gone: A Report on Wartime Life in the United States. LC 73-19969. (FDR & the Era of the New Deal Ser). 625p. 1974. Repr. of 1946 ed. lib. bdg. 69.50 (ISBN 0-306-70605-9). Da Capo.

Goodman, James. Larksdale Successful Executive Day Book. 110p. 1984. wkbk 9.95 (ISBN 0-89896-201-3). Larksdale.

Goodman, James, jt. auth. see Coombe, Jack.

Goodman, James, ed. see Brumbaugh, J. Frank.

Goodman, James, ed. see Kilthau, Gustave F.

Goodman, James A., ed. Dynamics of Racism in Social Work Practice. LC 73-88446. 375p. 1973. pap. 12.00 (ISBN 0-87101-068-2). Natl Assn Soc Wkrs.

Goodman, James M. The Navajo Atlas: Environments, Resources, People, & History of the Dine Bikeyah. LC 81-40287. (The Civilization of the American Indian Ser.: Vol. 157). (Illus.). 120p. 1982. 22.50 (ISBN 0-8061-1621-8). U of Okla Pr.

Goodman, Jane G. Aging Parents: Whose Responsibility? LC 80-149450. (Workshop Models for Family Life Education Ser.). 168p. 1980. plastic comb 13.95 (ISBN 0-87304-175-5). Family Serv.

Goodman, Jay S. The Democrats & Labor in Rhode Island, 1952-1962: Changes in the Old Alliance. LC 67-26817. (Illus.). 166p. 1967. 15.00x (ISBN 0-87057-104-4). U Pr of New Eng.

Goodman, Jay S., jt. auth. see Cornwell, Elmer E., Jr.

Goodman, Jean & Moncreiffe, Iain. Debrett's Royal Scotland. (Illus.). 240p. 1983. 24.95 (ISBN 0-399-12831-X, Putnam). Putnam Pub Group.

Goodman, Jeffrey. The Genesis Mystery: Explaining the Sudden Appearance of Modern Man. LC 82-40362. 320p. 1983. 16.60 (ISBN 0-8129-1039-7). Times Bks.

--We Are the Earthquake Generation. 1983. pap. 3.50 (ISBN 0-425-06259-7). Berkley Pub.

Goodman, Jeremy & Hut, Piet, eds. Dynamics of Star Clusters. 1985. lib. bdg. 69.00 (ISBN 90-277-1963-2, Pub. by Reidel Holland); pap. text ed. 29.00 (ISBN 90-277-1965-9). Kluwer Academic.

Goodman, Jo. Passion's Bride. 528p. 1984. pap. 3.75 (ISBN 0-8217-1417-1). Zebra.

Goodman, Joan E. Teddy Bear, Teddy Bear. (Platt & Munk Peggy Cloth Bks.). (Illus.). 8p. (ps). 1979. 2.50 (ISBN 0-448-46837-9, G&D). Putnam Pub Group.

Goodman, Jocelyne B., ed. see Hopkinson, James.

Goodman, Joel & Huggins, Kenneth. Let the Buyer Be Aware: Valuable Skills for Consumers, Parents & Teachers in the Eighties. 246p. 1981. pap. 9.95 (ISBN 0-940156-00-8). Wright Group.

Goodman, Joel, jt. auth. see Knapp, Cliff.

Goodman, Joel, jt. auth. see Weinstein, Matt.

Goodman, Joel M., et al. Phylogenetic Development of Vertebrate Immunity, No. 2. new ed. (Illus.). 220p. 1972. text ed. 28.50x (ISBN 0-8422-7057-4). Irvington.

Goodman, John. The Regulation of Medical Care: Is the Price Too High? LC 80-25397. (Cato Public Policy Research Monograph: No. 3). (Orig.). 1980. pap. 5.00x (ISBN 0-932790-23-2). Cato Inst.

Goodman, John C. National Health Care in Great Britain: Lessons for the U. S. A. LC 79-55246. 200p. (Orig.). 1980. lib. bdg. 11.95 (ISBN 0-933028-05-9); pap. 6.95 (ISBN 0-933028-04-0). Fisher Inst.

--Social Security in the United Kingdom. 1981. pap. 4.25 (ISBN 0-8447-3460-8). Am Enterprise.

Goodman, John C. & Dolan, Edwin G. Economics of Public Policy. 3rd ed. (Illus.). 225p. 1985. pap. text ed. 13.95 (ISBN 0-314-85238-7). West Pub.

--Economics of Public Policy: The Micro View. 2nd ed. (Illus.). 225p. 1982. pap. text ed. 12.95 (ISBN 0-314-63240-9). West Pub.

Goodman, John C., ed. The Failure of Our Public Schools: The Causes & a Solution. 1983. 7.00 (ISBN 0-943802-06-7). Natl Ctr Pol.

--Privatization. 1985. pap. 6.95 (ISBN 0-943802-13-X). Natl Ctr Pol.

--Space, Our Next Frontier. 1985. spiral bd. 6.95 (ISBN 0-943802-14-8). Natl Ctr Pol.

Goodman, John, Jr. Regional Housing Assistance Allocations & Regional Housing Needs. 50p. 1979. pap. text ed. 6.00x (ISBN 0-87766-263-0). Urban Inst.

Goodman, John K. Ross Stefan: An Impressionistic Painter of the Contemporary Southwest. LC 77-79013. (Illus.). 1983. Repr. of 1977 ed. 30.00 (ISBN 0-87358-168-7). Northland.

Goodman, John L. Public Opinion During the Reagan Administration. (Changing Domestic Priorities Ser.). 1983. pap. text ed. 5.95x nfo. (ISBN 0-87766-330-0). Urban Inst.

Goodman, John L. & Tuccillo, John A. Housing Finance: A Changing System in the Reagan Era. 1983. pap. text ed. 8.95x (ISBN 0-87766-328-9). Urban Inst.

Goodman, John L., Jr., jt. auth. see Goedert, Jeanne E.

Goodman, Jonathan. The Crippen File. 128p. 1985. pap. 8.95 (ISBN 0-8052-8244-0, Pub. by Allison & Busby England). Schocken.

--The Master Eccentric: The Diaries of Raynar Heppenstall 1969-1981. 224p. 1984. 17.95 (ISBN 0-8052-8170-3, Pub. by Allison & Busby England). Schocken.

--The Stabbing of George Harry Storrs. LC 83-8267. (Illus.). 254p. 1983. 15.00 (ISBN 0-8142-0349-3). Ohio St U Pr.

Goodman, Jonathan, ed. The Master Eccentric: The Journals of Rayner Heppenstall. 224p. 1985. 17.95 (ISBN 0-8052-8170-3, Pub. by Allison & Busby England). Schocken.

--The Railway Murders. 176p. 1985. 13.95 (ISBN 0-8052-8223-8, Pub. by Allison & Busby England). Schocken.

Goodman, Jordan E. & Downes, John. Dictionary of Finance & Investment Terms. (Orig.). 1985. pap. 6.95 (ISBN 0-8120-2522-9). Barron.

Goodman, Joseph I. & Biggers, W. Watts. Diabetes Without Fear. LC 77-90663. 1980. pap. 5.95 (ISBN 0-87795-294-9). Arbor Hse.

--Diabetes Without Fear. LC 77-90663. 1978. 8.95 (ISBN 0-87795-181-0). Arbor Hse.

--Diabetes Without Fear. 1979. pap. 3.95 (ISBN 0-380-43562-4, 65631-0). Avon.

Goodman, Joseph T. Heroes, Badmen & Honest Miners: Joe Goodman's Tales of the Comstock Lode. LC 77-81520. (Illus.). 1977. pap. 2.95 (ISBN 0-930830-00-8). Great Basin.

Goodman, Joseph W. Introduction to Fourier Optics. (Physical & Quantum Electronics Ser). 1968. text ed. 48.00 (ISBN 0-07-023776-X). McGraw.

--Statistical Optics. LC 84-13160. (Pure & Applied Optics Ser.). 550p. 1985. 44.95 (ISBN 0-471-01502-4). Wiley.

Goodman, Judith, ed. Big Sur Women. (Illus.). 112p. (Orig.). 1985. pap. 7.95 (ISBN 0-9614678-0-0). Big Sur Women.

Goodman, Judy. The Maze Book. (Orig.). (gr. 3-10). 1974. pap. 5.50 (ISBN 0-918932-31-9). Activity Resources.

Goodman, Julie, jt. auth. see Smith, Marjorie.

Goodman, Julius. The Magic Path. (Choose Your Own Adventure Ser.: No. 26). 64p. (Orig.). (gr. 2). 1985. pap. 1.95 (ISBN 0-553-15318-8). Bantam.

--Space Patrol, No. 22. (Choose Your Own Adventure Ser.). (Illus.). 128p. 1983. pap. 1.95 (ISBN 0-553-23349-1). Bantam.

--Treasure Diver. (Choose Your Own Adventure Ser.: No. 32). 128p. (gr. 5-9). 1984. pap. 1.95 (ISBN 0-553-24050-1). Bantam.

Goodman, Kennard E., et al. Today's Business Law. 4th ed. LC 74-15662. (gr. 10-12). 1975. text ed. 15.40 (ISBN 0-02-831060-8); tchrs' manual 6.60 (ISBN 0-02-831090-X); wkbk. 5.20 (ISBN 0-02-831070-5); tests 2.40 (ISBN 0-02-831080-2). Glencoe.

Goodman, Kenneth, et al. Reading in the Bilingual Classroom: Literacy and Biliteracy. LC 79-84373. 50p. 1978. pap. 5.25 (ISBN 0-89763-011-4). Natl Clearinghse Bilingual Ed.

Goodman, Kenneth S. & Niles, Olive S. Reading: Process & Program. LC 77-139591. (Illus.). 74p. 1970. pap. 4.25 (ISBN 0-8141-3902-7). NCTE.

Goodman, Kenneth S., ed. Miscue Analysis: Applications to Reading Instruction. LC 73-84400. (Illus.). 120p. (Orig.). 1973. pap. 5.20 (ISBN 0-8141-3188-3). NCTE.

Goodman, Kenneth S., ed. & frwd. by. The Psycholinguistic Nature of the Reading Process. 2nd ed. LC 67-26383. 347p. 1973. 12.95x (ISBN 0-8143-1338-8). Wayne St U Pr.

Goodman, Kenneth S. & Goodman, Yetta M., eds. Linguistics, Psycholinguistics & the Teaching of Reading. 1980 ed. (Annotated Bibliographies Ser). 1980. pap. 3.50 (ISBN 0-87207-312-2, 312). Intl Reading.

Goodman, Kenneth S., et al. Choosing Materials to Teach Reading. 156p. 1967. pap. 5.95x (ISBN 0-8143-1517-8). Wayne St U Pr.

Goodman, L. & Ocko, J. Y. The Savvy Shopper. 1982. pap. 5.95 (ISBN 0-345-30173-0). Ballantine.

Goodman, L. A. & Kruskal, W. H. Measures of Association for Cross Classifications. (Springer Series in Statistics: Vol. 1). 1979. 18.00 (ISBN 0-387-90443-3). Springer-Verlag.

Goodman, L. M., ed. Early American Quilt Patterns. new ed. (Illus.). 1972. pap. 5.00 (ISBN 0-87282-075-0). CHB-ALF.

Goodman, L. M., jt. ed. see Leed, Gretel.

Goodman, Lawrence R. & Putman, Charles E. Intensive Care Radiology: Imaging of the Critically Ill. LC 78-64. 364p. 1978. text ed. 44.50 (ISBN 0-8016-1894-0). Mosby.

Goodman, Lawrence R. & Putnam, C. The Radiographic Evaluation of the Intensive Care Unit Patient. LC 78-50186. Date not set. write for info. (ISBN 0-87527-172-3). Green.

Goodman, Lawrence R. & Putman, Charles E. Intensive Care Radiology: Imaging of the Critically Ill. 2nd ed. (Saunders Monographs in Clinical Radiology: Vol. 20). (Illus.). 352p. 1983. 47.50 (ISBN 0-7216-4166-0). Saunders.

Goodman, Lenn E. The Case of the Animals versus Man Before the King of the Jinn. (International Studies & Translations Program Ser.). 1980. 20.95 (ISBN 0-8057-8161-7, Twayne). G K Hall.

--Hayy Ibn Yaqzan. 2nd ed. 247p. 1983. 29.95x (ISBN 0-917232-17-8); pap. 16.95x (ISBN 0-917232-16-X). Gee Tee Bee.

--Monotheism: A Philosophic Inquiry into the Foundations of Theology & Ethics. LC 79-24818. (Publications of the Oxford Centre for Postgraduate Hebrew Study). 228p. 1981. 22.50x (ISBN 0-86598-068-3). Allanheld.

--Rambam: Readings in the Philosophy of Moses Maimonides. Patterson, David & Edelman, Lily, eds. LC 75-14476. 423p. 1978. text ed. 10.00 (ISBN 0-917232-07-0). Gee Tee Bee.

Goodman, Lenn E., jt. auth. see Goodman, Madeleine J.

Goodman, Leo A. The Analysis of Cross-Classified Data Having Ordered Categories. 336p. 1984. text ed. 22.50x (ISBN 0-674-03145-8). Harvard U Pr.

--Analyzing Qualitative Categorical Data: Log-Linear Models & Latent-Strucutre Analysis. Magidson, Jay, ed. 1978. text ed. 28.00 (ISBN 0-89011-513-3). Abt Bks.

--Analyzing Qualitative-Categorical Date: Log-Linear Models & Latent Structure Analysis. Magidson, Jay & Davis, James A., eds. 484p. 1984. Repr. of 1978 ed. lib. bdg. 32.50 (ISBN 0-8191-4105-4). U Pr of Amer.

--Analyzing Qualitative-Categorical Data: Log-Linear Models & Latent Structure Analysis. Magidson, Jay, ed. 484p. 1985. pap. text ed. 22.75 (ISBN 0-8191-4686-2). U Pr of Amer.

Goodman, Leon. Aviculturalist's Handbook: Management & Treatment of Diseases, Disorders & Ailments. 200p. 1983. 13.50 (ISBN 0-86230-051-7). Triplegate.

Goodman, Leonard. Alternative Careers For Teachers, Librarians, & Counselors. 192p. (Orig.). 1982. pap. 7.95 (ISBN 0-671-44819-6). Monarch Pr.

Goodman, Leonard H. Current Career & Occupational Literature, 1984. LC 80-646591. 208p. 1984. 30.00x (ISBN 0-8242-0703-3). Wilson.

Goodman, Leonard H., compiled by. Current Career & Occupational Literature, 1982. LC 78-106850. 196p. 1982. 18.00 (ISBN 0-686-95208-1). Wilson.

Goodman, Leonard H., ed. Current Career & Occupational Literature, 1973-1977. LC 78-106850. 275p. 1978. 18.00 (ISBN 0-8242-0616-9). Wilson.

--Current Career & Occupational Literature, 1977-1979. LC 80-646591. 333p. 1980. 18.00 (ISBN 0-686-77550-3). Wilson.

Goodman, Linda. Linda Goodman's Love Signs: A New Approach to the Human Heart. (Illus.). 1981. pap. 7.95 (Columbine). Fawcett.

--Linda Goodman's Sun Signs. rev. ed. 512p. 1985. pap. 4.50 (ISBN 0-553-24926-6). Bantam.

--Linda Goodman's Sun Signs. 1979. pap. 10.95 (ISBN 0-553-34217-7). Bantam.

--Linda Goodman's Sun Signs. LC 68-31737. 1968. 16.95 (ISBN 0-8008-4900-0). Taplinger.

--Love Signs. 1984. pap. 9.95 (ISBN 0-449-90149-1). Fawcett.

--Music & Dance in Northwest Coast Indian Life. (Music & Dance Ser.). 37p. 1977. pap. 1.50 (ISBN 0-912586-28-1). Navajo Coll Pr.

Goodman, Lisl M. Death & the Creative Life. (Springer Series: Death & Suicide). 1981. text ed. 17.95 (ISBN 0-8261-3500-5). Springer Pub.

--Death & the Creative Life. 172p. 1983. pap. 5.95 (ISBN 0-14-006275-0). Penguin.

Goodman, Lori, jt. auth. see Baker, Andrew.

Goodman, Louis J. & Karol, R. H. Theory & Practice of Foundation Engineering. LC 68-12070. (Macmillan Series in Civil Engineering). (Illus.). pap. 111.80 (ISBN 0-317-10610-4, 2010517). Bks Demand UMI.

Goodman, Louis J. & Hawkins, John N., eds. Food & Agricultural Waste Development Projects: Planning & Management. (Pergamon Policy Studies on International Development). (Illus.). 192p. 1982. 22.00 (ISBN 0-08-026001-2, K110, L110). Pergamon.

Goodman, Louis J. & Love, Ralph N., eds. Biomass Energy Projects: Planning & Management. (Pergamon Policy Studies). 200p. 1981. 30.00 (ISBN 0-08-025564-7). Pergamon.

--Geothermal Energy Projects: Planning & Management. LC 79-27715. (Policy Studies). 1980. 39.00 (ISBN 0-08-025095-5). Pergamon.

--Management of Development Projects: An International Case Study Approach. LC 78-26673. (Pergamon Policy Studies: No. 11). 272p. 1979. 35.00 (ISBN 0-08-022493-8). Pergamon.

--Project Planning & Management: An Integrated Approach. LC 79-25990. (Pergamon Policy Studies). 312p. 1980. 39.00 (ISBN 0-08-024667-2); pap. 13.25 (ISBN 0-08-025962-6). Pergamon.

--Small Hydroelectric Projects for Rural Development: Planning & Management. (Pergamon Policy Studies). 250p. 1981. 22.00 (ISBN 0-08-025966-9). Pergamon.

Goodman, M. C. Junior History of the American Negro, 2 vols. Incl. Vol. 1. Discovery to Civil War. 1969 (ISBN 0-8303-0072-4); Vol. 2. Civil War to Civil Rights War. LC 73-76026. 1970 (ISBN 0-8303-0073-2). (Illus.). (gr. 6-12). 8.95 ea. teaching manual 1.00 ea. Fleet.

Goodman, Madeleine J. & Goodman, Lenn E. Sex Differences in the Human Life Cycle. rev., 3rd ed. 423p. 1983. 27.95x (ISBN 0-917232-15-1). Gee Tee Bee.

--The Sexes in the Human Population. (Illus.). 203p. (Orig.). pap. text ed. 16.95x (ISBN 0-917232-12-7). Gee Tee Bee.

Goodman, Mae W. Verge of Eden. 1962. 6.95 (ISBN 0-8159-7100-1). Devin.

Goodman, Mae W. & Scheele, William E. In Time of Swallows. (Illus.). 6.95 (ISBN 0-8159-5808-0). Devin.

Goodman, Marcia M., jt. auth. see Roller, Duane.

Goodman, Marguerite. Christmas Comes in Assorted Sizes. Ashton, Sylvia, ed. LC 77-80303. 1977. 14.95 (ISBN 0-87949-111-6). Ashley Bks.

Goodman, Mark. Hurrah for the Next Man Who Dies. LC 84-45048. 288p. 1985. 14.95 (ISBN 0-689-11482-6). Atheneum.

Goodman, Mark N. The Ninth Amendment: History, Interpretation & Meaning. 74p. 1981. 5.00 (ISBN 0-682-49630-8, University). Exposition Pr FL.

Goodman, Martin. State & Society in Roman Galilee, A. D. 132-212. (Publications in the Oxford Centre for Postgraduate Hebrew Studies: Vol. 4). 318p. 1983. text ed. 36.95x (ISBN 0-86598-089-6). Rowman & Allanheld.

Goodman, Martin, tr. see Reuchlin, Johann.

Goodman, Mary E. Culture of Childhood: Child's-Eye Views of Society & Culture. LC 75-106992. 1970. pap. 8.95x (ISBN 0-8077-1444-5). Tchrs Coll.

--The Mexican-American Population of Houston: A Survey in the Field 1965-1970. (Rice University Studies: Vol. 57, No. 3). 125p. 1971. pap. 10.00x (ISBN 0-89263-209-7). Rice Univ.

Goodman, Michael B. Contemporary Literary Censorship: The Case History of Burroughs' Naked Lunch. LC 80-28993. 340p. 1981. 20.00 (ISBN 0-8108-1398-X). Scarecrow.

--William S. Burroughs: An Annotated Bibliography of His Works & Criticism. LC 75-23007. (Reference Library of the Humanities: Vol. 24). 100p. 1975. lib. bdg. 25.00 (ISBN 0-8240-9989-3). Garland Pub.

--Write to the Point: Effective Communication in the Workplace. (Illus.). 464p. 1984. pap. text ed. 15.95 (ISBN 0-13-971762-5). P-H.

Goodman, Michael R. Study Notes in System Dynamics. LC 74-84407. (Illus.). 300p. 1974. pap. 18.50x (ISBN 0-262-57051-3). MIT Pr.

Goodman, Mike. How to Win. pap. 3.95 (ISBN 0-87067-617-2). Borden.

--How to Win. rev. ed. (Orig.). 1963. pap. 3.95 (ISBN 0-87067-617-2, BR617). Holloway.

--Mike Goodman's Your Best Bet. 1977. pap. 2.50 (ISBN 0-345-28863-7). Ballantine.
Goodman, Miriam. Signal Noise. LC 82-71819. 61p. 1982. 12.95 (ISBN 0-914086-40-5); pap. 6.95 (ISBN 0-914086-39-1). Alicejamesbooks.
Goodman, Miriam, jt. auth. see Aguero, Kathleen.
Goodman, Mitchell. The End of It. LC 79-66117. 288p. 1984. pap. 15.95 (ISBN 0-933256-10-8); pap. 7.95 (ISBN 0-933256-11-6); rack 5.95 (ISBN 0-933256-50-7). Second Chance.
--A Life in Common. 68p. (Orig.). 1984. pap. 5.95 (ISBN 0-937966-13-4). Dog Ear.
Goodman, Morris, ed. Macromolecular Sequences in Systematic & Evolutionary Biology. (Monographs in Evolutionary Biology). 432p. 1982. 45.00x (ISBN 0-306-41061-3, Plenum Pr). Plenum Pub.
Goodman, Morris & Tashian, Richard E., eds. Molecular Anthropology: Genes & Proteins in the Evolutionary Ascent of the Primates. LC 76-45445. (Advances in Primatology Ser.). (Illus.). 479p. 1977. 49.50x (ISBN 0-306-30948-3, Plenum Pr). Plenum Pub.
Goodman, Morris C. Astrology & Sexual Analysis. LC 78-109373. (Illus.). 1972. 9.95 (ISBN 0-8303-0094-5). Fleet.
--Astrology & Sexual Analysis. 1984. pap. 5.00 (ISBN 0-87980-405-X). Wilshire.
--Modern Numerology. pap. 5.00 (ISBN 0-87980-102-6). Wilshire.
Goodman, Morris E. & Garnett, Patricia. The Miracle Man: An Inspiring True Story of the Human Spirit. 234p. 1984. 15.95 (ISBN 0-13-585357-5, Busn). P-H.
Goodman, Murray & Morehouse, Frank. Organic Molecules in Action. LC 72-85025. (Illus.). 368p. 1973. 24.50x (ISBN 0-677-01810-X). Gordon.
Goodman, Murray, ed. Peptides, Polypeptides, & Proteins: Interactions & Their Biological Implications, Vol. 22. 588p. 1983. text ed. 47.50x (ISBN 0-471-88679-3, Pub. by Wiley-Interscience). Wiley.
Goodman, N., jt. auth. see Belkin, Gary S.
Goodman, Nathan G., ed. The Ingenious Dr. Franklin: Selected Scientific Letters of Benjamin Franklin. LC 74-81751. 256p. 1974. 22.00x (ISBN 0-8122-7680-9); pap. 7.95 (ISBN 0-8122-1067-0). U of Pa Pr.
--The Ingenious Dr. Franklin: Selected Scientific Letters of Benjamin Franklin. 244p. 1982. Repr. of 1931 ed. lib. bdg. 40.00 (ISBN 0-89987-312-X). Darby Bks.
Goodman, Nelson. Fact, Fiction & Forecast. 4th ed. 176p. 1983. text ed. 10.00x (ISBN 0-674-29070-4); pap. text ed. 4.95x (ISBN 0-674-29071-2). Harvard U Pr.
--Languages of Art. 2nd, new ed. LC 68-31825. (Illus.). 288p. 1976. 19.50 (ISBN 0-915144-35-2); pap. text ed. 8.50 (ISBN 0-915144-34-4). Hackett Pub.
--Of Mind & Other Matters. (Illus.). 224p. 1984. text ed. 17.50x (ISBN 0-674-63125-0). Harvard U Pr.
--Problems & Projects. LC 73-165221. 478p. 1973. 19.50 (ISBN 0-915144-37-9); pap. text ed. 8.50 (ISBN 0-915144-36-0). Hackett Pub.
--The Structure of Appearance: Boston Studies in the Philosophy of Science LIII. (Synthese Library: No. 107). 1977. lib. bdg. 42.00 (ISBN 90-277-0773-1; Pub. by Reidel Holland); pap. 11.00 (ISBN 90-277-0774-X). Kluwer Academic.
--Ways of Worldmaking. LC 78-56364. (Illus.). 160p. 1978. 15.00 (ISBN 0-915144-52-2); pap. 4.95 (ISBN 0-915144-51-4). Hackett Pub.
Goodman, Nelson, ed. see Lee, Sherman E.
Goodman, Norman & Marx, Gary. Society Today. 4th ed. 561p. 1982. text ed. 26.00 (ISBN 0-394-32550-8, RanC). Random.
Goodman, Paul. The Break-up of Our Camp, Stories 1932-1935: The Collected Stories, Vol. 1. Stoehr, Taylor, ed. 300p. 1978. 14.00 (ISBN 0-87685-330-0); pap. 8.50 (ISBN 0-87685-329-7). Black Sparrow.
--A Ceremonial, Stories 1936-1940: The Collected Stories of Paul Goodman, Vol. 2. Stoehr, Taylor, ed. 273p. 1978. 14.00 (ISBN 0-87685-354-8); deluxe ed. 25.00 (ISBN 0-87685-355-6); pap. 8.50 (ISBN 0-87685-353-X). Black Sparrow.
--The Commodore 64 Guide to Data Files & Advanced BASIC. (Illus.). 176p. 1984. pap. 12.95 (ISBN 0-89303-375-8); diskett 20.00 (ISBN 0-89303-370-7). Brady Comm.
--The Copernican Revolution. 1947. pap. 4.50 (ISBN 0-910664-37-4). Gotham.
--Don Juan: Or, the Continuum of the Libido. Stoehr, Taylor, ed. 225p. 1979. 14.00 (ISBN 0-87685-422-6); deluxe ed. 25.00 (ISBN 0-87685-423-4); pap. 6.00 (ISBN 0-87685-421-8). Black Sparrow.
--The Facts of Life Stories 1940-1949: The Collected Stories of Paul Goodman, Vol. 3. Stoehr, Taylor, ed. 329p. 1979. 14.00 (ISBN 0-87685-357-2); deluxe ed. 25.00 (ISBN 0-87685-358-0); pap. 8.50 (ISBN 0-87685-356-4). Black Sparrow.
--The Galley to Mytilene, Stories 1949-1960: The Collected Stories of Paul Goodman, Vol. 4. Stoehr, Taylor, ed. 350p. (Orig.). 1980. 14.00 (ISBN 0-87685-360-2); deluxe ed. 25.00 (ISBN 0-87685-361-0); pap. 8.50 (ISBN 0-87685-359-9). Black Sparrow.
--Growing Up Absurd. (YA) 1962. pap. 4.95 (ISBN 0-394-70032-5, V32, Vin). Random.
--A Message to the Military-Industrial Complex. 16p. 1969. lib. bdg. 12.95 (ISBN 0-88286-137-9); pap. 1.00 (ISBN 0-88286-112-3). C H Kerr.
--Parents' Day. (Illus.). 275p. 1985. 20.00 (ISBN 0-87685-635-0); deluxe ed. 30.00 (ISBN 0-87685-636-9); pap. 12.50 (ISBN 0-87685-634-2). Black Sparrow.
Goodman, Paul & Goodman, Percival. Communitas: Means of Livelihood & Ways of Life. rev. ed. 1960. pap. 3.95 (ISBN 0-394-70174-7, Vin). Random.
Goodman, Paul & Zeldin, Alan. The MacPascal Book. (Illus.). 320p. 1985. pap. 19.95 (ISBN 0-89303-644-7). Brady Comm.
Goodman, Paul, ed. Essays in American Colonial History. facs. ed. LC 72-117795. (Essay Index Reprint Ser). 1967. 31.00 (ISBN 0-8369-1878-9). Ayer Co Pubs.
--The Federalists vs. the Jeffersonian Republicans. LC 76-49811. (American Problem Studies). 128p. 1977. pap. text ed. 5.95 (ISBN 0-88275-472-6). Krieger.
Goodman, Paul S. Assessing Organizational Change: Rushton Quality of Work Experiment. LC 78-31857. (Organizational Behavior Assessment & Change Ser.). 391p. 1979. 38.95x (ISBN 0-471-04782-1, Pub. by Wiley-Interscience). Wiley.
Goodman, Paul S., et al. Change in Organizations: New Perspectives on Theory, Research, & Practice. LC 82-48069. (Social & Behavioral Science Ser.). 1982. text ed. 22.95x (ISBN 0-87589-547-6). Jossey Bass.
--Absenteeism: New Approaches to Understanding, Measuring, & Managing Employee Absence. LC 84-47985. (Management Ser.). 1984. 28.95x (ISBN 0-87589-617-0). Jossey-Bass.
--New Perspectives on Organizational Effectiveness. LC 77-82916. (Social & Behavioral Science Ser). 1977. text ed. 23.95x (ISBN 0-87589-349-X). Jossey-Bass.
Goodman, Percival, jt. auth. see Goodman, Paul.
Goodman, Peter, ed. Fifty Years of Electron Diffraction. xiv, 432p. 1981. 79.00 (ISBN 90-277-1246-8, Pub. by Reidel Holland). Kluwer Academic.
Goodman, Philip, ed. The Hanukkah Anthology. LC 75-44637. (Illus.). xxxiv, 466p. 1976. 10.95 (ISBN 0-8276-0080-1, 392). Jewish Pubns.
--Jewish Marriage Anthology. Goodman, Hanna. LC 65-17045. (Illus.). 1965. 13.95 (ISBN 0-8276-0145-X, 236). Jewish Pubns.
--Passover Anthology. LC 61-11706. (Illus.). 196p. 1961. 10.95 (ISBN 0-8276-0019-4, 250). Jewish Pubns.
--Purim Anthology. (Illus.). 525p. 1949. 7.50 (ISBN 0-8276-0022-4, 248). Jewish Pubns.
--Rosh Hashanah Anthology. LC 74-105069. (Illus.). 379p. 1970. 10.95 (ISBN 0-8276-0023-2, 246). Jewish Pubns.
--The Shavuot Anthology. LC 74-25802. (Illus.). 369p. 1975. 9.95 (ISBN 0-8276-0057-7, 366). Jewish Pubns.
--The Sukkot & Simhat Torah Anthology. LC 72-14058. (Illus.). 324p. 1973. 7.50 (ISBN 0-8276-0010-0, 324). Jewish Pubns.
--Yom Kippur Anthology. LC 72-151312. (Illus.). 399p. 1971. 9.95 (ISBN 0-8276-0026-7, 245). Jewish Pubns.
Goodman, R. E., ed. Annual Review in Automatic Programming, Vols. 1, 4. Incl. Vol. 1. 1960 (ISBN 0-08-009217-9); Vol. 2. 1961 (ISBN 0-08-009333-7); Vol. 3. 1963 (ISBN 0-08-009763-4); Vol. 4. rev. ed. 1964 (ISBN 0-08-010857-1). 56.00 ea. Pergamon.
Goodman, R. W. Nilpotent Lie Groups: Structure & Applications to Analysis. (Lecture Notes on Mathematics Ser.: Vol. 562). 1976. soft cover 17.00 (ISBN 0-387-08055-4). Springer-Verlag.
Goodman, Randolph. Drama on Stage. 2nd ed. LC 77-16442. 1978. pap. text ed. 21.95 (ISBN 0-03-020326-0, HoltC). HR&W.
Goodman, Randolph, ed. see Franklin, Benjamin.
Goodman, Raymond J. Management of Service for the Restaurant Manager. 320p. 1979. text ed. write for info. (ISBN 0-697-08409-4). Wm C Brown.
Goodman, Raymond J., Jr., jt. auth. see Durocher, Joseph F.
Goodman, Richard. Footnote to Lawrence. LC 77-7129. 1932. lib. bdg. 10.00 (ISBN 0-8414-4593-1). Folcroft.
--Methods of Geological Engineering in Discontinuous Rocks. LC 75-42152. (Illus.). 1975. text ed. 35.00 (ISBN 0-8299-0066-7). West Pub.
Goodman, Richard & Gen-Hua Shi. Block Theory & Its Application to Block Engineering. LC 84-3348. (Illus.). 336p. 1985. text ed. 55.95 (ISBN 0-13-078189-4). P-H.
Goodman, Richard A. Real Property Exchanges. LC 81-71805. 233p. 1982. 60.00 (ISBN 0-88124-061-3, RE-34530). Cal Cont Ed Bar.
Goodman, Richard A. & Morote, Julian P., eds. Planning for National Technology Policy. LC 83-13790. 460p. 1984. 35.95 (ISBN 0-03-061343-4). Praeger.
Goodman, Richard Alan. Temporary Systems: Professional Development, Manpower Utilization, Task Effectiveness, & Innovation. LC 81-15902. 204p. 1981. 35.95 (ISBN 0-03-055896-4). Praeger.
Goodman, Richard E. Rock Mechanics. LC 80-13155. 478p. 1980. text ed. 47.75x (ISBN 0-471-04129-7). Wiley.
Goodman, Richard E. & Hueze, Francios E., eds. Issues in Rock Mechanics: Twenty-Third Symposium. LC 82-71989. (Illus.). 1133p. 1982. 45.00x (ISBN 0-89520-297-2). Soc Mining Eng.
Goodman, Richard M. Genetic Disorders Among the Jewish People. LC 78-21847. 512p. 1979. text ed. 39.50x (ISBN 0-8018-2120-7). Johns Hopkins.
Goodman, Richard M. & Center for Auto Safety Staff. Automobile Design Liability, 2 Vols. 2nd ed. LC 83-81615. 129.00 (ISBN 0-318-00175-6); Suppl. 1984. 20.00. Lawyers Co-Op.
Goodman, Richard M. & Gorlin, Robert J. The Malformed Infant & Child: An Illustrated Guide. (Illus.). 1983. text ed. 39.50x (ISBN 0-19-503254-3); pap. text ed. 24.95x (ISBN 0-19-503255-1). Oxford U Pr.
Goodman, Richard M. & Motulsky, Arno G., eds. Genetic Diseases among Ashkenazi Jews. LC 77-90594. 454p. 1979. text ed. 57.00 (ISBN 0-89004-262-4). Raven.
Goodman, Robert. Color TV Case Histories Illustrated: Photo Guide to Troubles & Cures. LC 74-33619. (Illus.). 238p. 1975. pap. 7.95 (ISBN 0-8306-2302-7, 2302). TAB Bks.
--Indexed Guide to Modern Electronic Circuits. LC 83-18752. 216p. 1984. pap. text ed. 14.95 (ISBN 0-89874-683-3). Krieger.
--The Last Entrepreneurs: America's Regional Wars for Jobs & Dollars. 350p. pap. 8.00 (ISBN 0-89608-145-1). South End Pr.
--A Teacher's Guide to Jewish Holidays. LC 83-70197. 224p. 1983. pap. text ed. 15.00 (ISBN 0-86705-036-5). AIRE.
Goodman, Robert B. & Spicer, Robert A. Kaguya Hime: The Shimmering Princess. Johnson, Victor, ed. LC 75-18791. (Illus.). (gr. 1-7). 1974. 5.95 (ISBN 0-89610-005-7). Island Herit.
--The Magic Brush. Tabrah, Ruth, ed. LC 74-80513. (Illus.). (gr. 1-7). 1974. 5.95 (ISBN 0-89610-007-3). Island Herit.
--The Secret of Beaver Valley. LC 73-77781. (Illus.). (gr. 1-7). 1963. 5.95 (ISBN 0-89610-017-0). Island Herit.
--Urashima Taro. Tabrah, Ruth, ed. LC 73-79570. (Illus.). (gr. 1-7). 1973. 5.95 (ISBN 0-89610-013-8). Island Herit.
Goodman, Robert L. Color TV Case Histories Illustrated: Photo Guide to Trouble Cures, Vol. 2. 2nd ed. (Illus.). 1977. pap. 7.95 (ISBN 0-8306-6876-4, 876). TAB Bks.
--Maintaining & Repairing Videocassette Recorders. (Illus.). 416p. 1983. 22.95 (ISBN 0-8306-0103-1); pap. 15.95 (ISBN 0-8306-1503-2, 1503). TAB Bks.
--Practical Troubleshooting with Modern Electronic Test Instruments. (Illus.). 1979. pap. 9.95 (ISBN 0-8306-1177-0, 1177). TAB Bks.
--Practical Troubleshooting with the Modern Oscilloscope. (Illus.). 1979. pap. 8.95 (ISBN 0-8306-1162-2, 1162). TAB Bks.
--A Quick Guide to Food Additives. (Orig.). 1982. pap. 4.00 (ISBN 0-940988-00-3). Gnosis Pubns.
--Troubleshooting Microprocessors & Digital Logic. (Illus., Orig.). 1980. 16.95 (ISBN 0-8306-9950-3); pap. 10.95 (ISBN 0-8306-1183-5, 1183). TAB Bks.
Goodman, Roger B. & Ince, William. Basic Writing Skills. (Pre-GED Basic Skills Ser.). 1979. pap. 5.95 (ISBN 0-07-023741-7). McGraw.
--How to Prepare for the Test of English As a Foreign Language: TOEFL. (McGraw-Nhill Paperbacks). (Orig.). 1980. pap. 5.95 (ISBN 0-07-023761-1). McGraw.
--Power Skills in Writing I. 1979. pap. 4.95 (ISBN 0-07-023744-1). McGraw.
--Power Skills in Writing II. (Illus.). 1978. pap. text ed. 4.95 (ISBN 0-07-023731-X). McGraw.
Goodman, Roger B., ed. Seventy-Five Short Masterpieces: Stories from the World's Literature. (Orig.). (gr. 10-12). pap. 3.95 (ISBN 0-553-25141-4). Bantam.
Goodman, Ronald, jt. auth. see Ruch, Richard S.
Goodman, Ryah. New & Selected Poems. 79p. 1985. 10.95 (ISBN 0-87233-079-6). Bauhan.
Goodman, Ryah T. Suddenly It's Evening. LC 77-9026. 1977. 5.95 (ISBN 0-87233-042-7). Bauhan.
Goodman, S. E. & Hedetniemi, S. T. Introduction to the Design & Analysis of Algorithms. (Computer Science Ser.). (Illus.). 1977. text ed. 41.95 (ISBN 0-07-023753-0). McGraw.
Goodman, S. L. The Faith of Secular Jews. (Library of Judaic Learning). 25.00x (ISBN 0-87068-489-2). Ktav.
Goodman, Sam R. Increasing Corporate Profitability: Financial Techniques for Marketing, Manufacturing, Planning & Control. LC 82-3643. (Wiley Series on Systems & Controls for Financial Management). 300p. 1982. 37.95x (ISBN 0-471-09161-8, Pub. by Ronald Pr). Wiley.
Goodman, Sam R. & Reece, James S. Controller's Handbook. LC 77-91319. 1978. 50.00 (ISBN 0-87094-157-7). Dow Jones-Irwin.
Goodman, Sam R., ed. see Prentice-Hall Editorial Staff.
Goodman, Sid, jt. auth. see Schwartz, Seymour.
Goodman, Sidney, jt. auth. see Schwartz, Seymour.
Goodman, Stanley. Psychoanalytic Education & Research: The Current Situation & Future Possibilities. LC 76-44638. 424p. 1977. 22.50 (ISBN 0-8236-4410-3). Intl Univs Pr.
Goodman, Stanley, jt. auth. see Winters, Arthur.
Goodman, Stanley, jt. auth. see Winters, Arthur A.
Goodman, Stanley J. How to Manage a Turnaround: A Senior Manager's Blueprint for Turning an Ailing Business into a Winner. LC 82-70077. 256p. 1982. 18.95 (ISBN 0-02-912480-8). Free Pr.
Goodman, Stephen H., ed. Financing & Risk in Developing Countries. (Praeger Special Studies). 122p. 1978. 34.95 (ISBN 0-03-042281-7). Praeger.
Goodman, Stephen I. & Markey, Sanford P., eds. Diagnosis of Organic Acidemias by Gas Chromatography-Mass Spectrometry. LC 81-8228. (Laboratory & Research Methods in Biology & Medicine Ser.: Vol. 6). 170p. 1981. 28.00 (ISBN 0-8451-1655-X). A R Liss.
Goodman, Steven M., jt. auth. see Houlihan, Patrick F.
Goodman, Sue, jt. auth. see Porter, Tom.
Goodman, Susan. Gertrude Bell. (Women's Ser.). (Illus.). 144p. (Orig.). 1985. pap. 5.95 (ISBN 0-907582-68-0, Pub. by Berg Pubs). Longwood Pub Group.
--You & Your Child. LC 78-66294. (Joy of Living Library). (Illus.). 1979. pap. 8.95 (ISBN 0-528-88016-0). Rand.
Goodman, Susan, jt. auth. see Campbell, John.
Goodman, Terry A., et al. A Guidebook for Teaching Algebra. (Guidebook for Teaching Ser.). 332p. 1985. pap. 32.95x (ISBN 0-205-08117-7, 238117, Pub. by Longwood Div). Allyn.
Goodman, Thomas. The Skin Doctor's Skin Doctoring Book. LC 83-15815. (Illus.). 256p. 1984. pap. 7.95 (ISBN 0-8069-7784-1). Sterling.
Goodman, Thomas H. Elements of Esperanto: A Structural Approach. LC 77-6811. (Illus.). 1977. pap. text ed. 5.00 (ISBN 0-9601252-1-3). T H Goodman.
Goodman, W. Party System in America. 1980. pap. 17.95 (ISBN 0-13-652677-2). P-H.
Goodman, W. L. British Planemakers from Seventeen Hundred. 2nd ed. 50.00 (ISBN 0-904638-07-3). State Mutual Bk.
Goodman, W. L., tr. see Prishvin, Mikhail.
Goodman, Walter. The Committee: The Extraordinary Career of the House Committee on Un-American Activities. LC 68-13010. (Illus.). 564p. 1968. 15.00 (ISBN 0-374-12688-7). FS&G.
Goodman, Wolf, tr. see Michelson, Frida.
Goodman, Yetta M. & Burke, Carolyn L. Reading Strategies: Focus on Comprehension. LC 80-10257. 243p. 1980. pap. text ed. 19.95 (ISBN 0-03-044011-4, HoltC). HR&W.
Goodman, Yetta M., jt. ed. see Goodman, Kenneth S.
Goodman-Kraines, Linda & Kan, Esther J. Jump into Jazz: A Primer for the Beginning Jazz Dance Student. LC 82-73739. (Illus.). 115p. 1983. pap. 7.95 (ISBN 0-87484-571-8). Mayfield Pub.
Goodnight, Lynn. The Complete Resource Handbook of Issues on the Problem of National Defense: What Should the Level of United States Commitments Be for National Defense? LC 82-60490. (NTC Debate Bks.). Date not set. price not set. Natl Textbk.
Goodnough, David. Christopher Columbus. new ed. LC 78-18052. (Illus.). 48p. (gr. 4-7). 1979. PLB 7.89 (ISBN 0-89375-170-7); pap. 1.95 (ISBN 0-89375-162-6). Troll Assocs.
--Francis Drake. LC 78-18056. (Illus.). 48p. (gr. 4-7). 1979. PLB 7.89 (ISBN 0-89375-173-1); pap. 1.95 (ISBN 0-89375-165-0). Troll Assocs.
--John Cabot & Son. new ed. LC 78-18054. (Illus.). 48p. (gr. 4-7). 1979. PLB 7.89 (ISBN 0-89375-172-3); pap. 1.95 (ISBN 0-89375-164-2). Troll Assocs.
Goodnow, Frank J. City Government in the United States. LC 73-11903. (Metropolitan America Ser.). 330p. 1974. Repr. 20.00x (ISBN 0-405-05394-0). Ayer Co Pubs.
--Social Reform & the Constitution. 1911. 23.50 (ISBN 0-8337-1385-X). B Franklin.
Goodnow, Frank J., ed. Comparative Administrative Law: An Analysis of the Administrative Systems of the U. S., England, France & Germany. 1970. Repr. of 1893 ed. Set. text ed. 44.50 (ISBN 0-8337-1384-1). B Franklin.
Goodnow, Jacqueline. Children Drawing. Bruner, Jerome, et al, eds. (Developing Child Ser.). (Illus.). 1977. 10.00x (ISBN 0-674-11603-8); pap. 3.95 (ISBN 0-674-11604-6). Harvard U Pr.
Goodnow, Josephine A., jt. auth. see Creegan, Charles C.
Goodpaster, Andrew J. Toward a Consensus on Military Service: Report of the Atlantic Council's Working Group on Military Service. Elliott, Lloyd H., ed. (Illus.). 300p. 1982. 36.00 (ISBN 0-08-029399-9, K125); pap. 13.95 (ISBN 0-08-029398-0). Pergamon.
Goodpaster, K. E., jt. auth. see Matthews, J. B.
Goodpaster, K. E. & Sayre, K. M., eds. Ethics & Problems of the Twenty-First Century. LC 78-51522. 223p. 1980. pap. text ed. 7.95 (ISBN 0-268-00907-4). U of Notre Dame Pr.
Goodpaster, Kenneth, ed. Perspectives on Morality: Essays by William Frankena. LC 76-646. 208p. 1976. text ed. 19.95x (ISBN 0-268-01519-8); pap. 7.95x (ISBN 0-268-01520-1). U of Notre Dame Pr.

Goodpasture, B. C., ed. Biography & Sermons of Keeble. 2.50 (ISBN 0-89225-042-9). Gospel Advocate.

Goodpoaster, Andrew J. & Elliott, Lloyd H. Toward a Consensus on Military Service. 70p. 1983. pap. 6.00x. Transaction Bks.

Goodrich, Arthur & Palmer, Rose A. Caponsacchi: A Play in Three Acts, Prologue & Epilogue, Based Upon Robert Browning's Poem, 'the Ring & the Book' 1939. 25.00 (ISBN 0-8274-2001-3). R West.

Goodrich, Carter. Government Promotion of American Canals & Railroads, 1800-1890. LC 74-12954. (Illus.). 382p. 1974. Repr. of 1960 ed. lib. bdg. 24.25x (ISBN 0-8371-7773-1, GOAC). Greenwood.

--The Miner's Freedom: Study of the Working Life in a Changing Industry. Stein, Leon, ed. LC 77-70498. (Work Ser.). (Illus.). 1977. Repr. of 1925 ed. lib. bdg. 20.00x (ISBN 0-405-10169-4). Ayer Co Pubs.

Goodrich, Carter, et al. Migration & Economic Opportunity: Report of the Study of Population Redistribution. LC 36-18989. (History of American Economy). Repr. of 1936 ed. 43.00 (ISBN 0-384-19270-X). Johnson Repr.

--Canals & American Economic Development. LC 72-86271. 312p. 1972. Repr. of 1961 ed. 28.50x (ISBN 0-8046-1765-1, Pub. by Kennikat). Assoc Faculty Pr.

Goodrich, Caspar F. Rope Yarns from the Old Navy: New York Historical Society. LC 32-14293. (Illus.). 1931. 6.00x (ISBN 0-685-73925-2). U Pr of Va.

Goodrich, Charles H., et al. Welfare Medical Care: An Experiment. LC 77-85075. (Illus.). 1970. 20.00x (ISBN 0-674-94895-5). Harvard U Pr.

Goodrich, Chauncey A. Essays from Select British Eloquence. Baird, A. Craig, ed. LC 63-7978. (Landmarks in Rhetoric & Public Address Ser.). 407p. 1963. pap. 9.95x (ISBN 0-8093-0095-8). S Ill U Pr.

Goodrich, Dana C., Jr. Floral Marketing. LC 80-26287. 1980. 19.95 (ISBN 0-86730-311-5). Lebhar Friedman.

Goodrich, Donna. Central Coast Cuisine: Favorite Recipes from Favorite Restaurants. LC 83-63469. (Illus.). 112p. 1984. pap. 5.95 (ISBN 0-9613112-0-7). Rest Recipes.

--How to Set up & Run a Typing Service. LC 82-25090. (Wiley Small Business Ser.). 176p. 1983. pap. text ed. 8.95x (ISBN 0-471-86858-2, 1-382, Pub. by Wiley Pr). Wiley.

--Teacher Tune-Ups. LC 84-80655. 80p. (Orig.). 1985. pap. 2.25 (ISBN 0-88243-754-2, 02-0754). Gospel Pub.

Goodrich, Donna C. How to Set up & Run a Successful Tax Service. (Small Business Ser.: 1-382). 160p. 1985. pap. 9.95 (ISBN 0-471-81281-1, Pub. by Wiley Pr). Wiley.

Goodrich, Edwin S. Evolution: Essays on Aspects of Evolutionary Biology Presented to Professor E. S. Goodrich on His Seventieth Birthday. De Beer, G. R., ed. LC 77-86425. Repr. of 1938 ed. 28.00 (ISBN 0-404-16645-8). AMS Pr.

Goodrich, Frances & Hackett, Albert. Diary of Anne Frank, Drama. (YA) 1956. 9.95 (ISBN 0-394-40564-1). Random.

Goodrich, Frances C. Third Adam. LC 66-22003. 1967. 5.00 (ISBN 0-8022-0608-5). Philos Lib.

Goodrich, Frank B. History of the Sea: From the Ark to the Present Time. 1977. lib. bdg. 75.00 (ISBN 0-8490-2006-9). Gordon Pr.

Goodrich, Frank C. A Primer of Quantum Chemistry. LC 80-11938. 244p. 1982. Repr. of 1972 ed. lib. bdg. 17.50 (ISBN 0-89874-149-1). Krieger.

Goodrich, Gail & Levin, Rich. Winning Basketball. LC 76-11206. (Winning Ser.). (Illus.). 142p. 1976. 8.95 (ISBN 0-8092-8108-2); pap. 7.95 (ISBN 0-8092-8107-4). Contemp Bks.

Goodrich, Gwenyth B. Bunnechauk: Alaska - Then & Now. 128p. 1982. 7.00 (ISBN 0-682-49821-1). Exposition Pr FL.

Goodrich, Herbert F. Six Years of Conflict of Laws. LC 80-142529. (Significant Developments in the Law During the War Years Ser.). 72p. 1984. write for info. PLI.

Goodrich, Herbert F. & Carson, Ralph M. A Case on Appeal: A Judge's View & a Lawyer's View. 4th ed. 113p. 1967. pap. 2.31 (ISBN 0-317-30858-0, B109). Am Law Inst.

Goodrich, James W., ed. see Duden, Gottfried.

Goodrich, Jamie. How to Grow Money: An Introduction to the Time Value of Money. 160p. (Orig.). 1985. pap. 8.95 (ISBN 0-930369-31-9). Invest Info.

Goodrich, Jamie, jt. auth. see Perritt, Gerald W.

Goodrich, Jennie, et al. Kashaya Pomo Plants. 171p. 1980. softcover 15.00 (ISBN 0-935626-01-8). U Cal AISC.

Goodrich, John K., ed. see Sonsini-Goodrich, Melanie.

Goodrich, Kristina, ed. Industrial Design Excellence U. S. A. (Illus.). 96p. (Orig.). 1985. pap. 15.00 (ISBN 0-9614683-0-0). Indus Design.

Goodrich, L. Carrington & Fang, Chaoying, eds. Dictionary of Ming Biography, 1364-1644, 2 vols. (Illus.). 1976. 160.00x set (ISBN 0-231-03801-1). Vol. 1, 1054pgs (ISBN 0-231-03801-1). Vol. 2, 634pgs (ISBN 0-231-03833-X). Columbia U Pr.

Goodrich, Laurence B. Ralph Earl, Recorder for an Era. LC 66-64728. (Illus.). pap. 27.00 (ISBN 0-317-10010-6, 2010108). Bks Demand UMI.

Goodrich, Lawrence B. Ralph Earl: Recorder for an Era. LC 66-64728. (Illus.). 1967. 19.95x (ISBN 0-87395-020-8). State U NY Pr.

Goodrich, Leland M. Korea: A Study of U. S. Policy in the United Nations. LC 78-24120. 1979. Repr. of 1956 ed. lib. bdg. 24.75x (ISBN 0-313-20825-5, GOKO). Greenwood.

--Korea: A Study of U. S. Policy in the United Nations. LC 56-9751. Repr. of 1956 ed. 20.00 (ISBN 0-527-34450-8). Kraus Repr.

--The United Nations in a Changing World. LC 74-893. (Columbia University Studies in International Organization). 280p. 1976. 30.00x (ISBN 0-231-03824-0); pap. 13.00x (ISBN 0-231-08343-2). Columbia U Pr.

Goodrich, Leland M. & Simons, Anne P. The United Nations & the Maintenance of International Peace & Security. LC 74-6751. (The Brookings Ser. on the United Nations). 709p. 1974. Repr. of 1955 ed. lib. bdg. 40.25x (ISBN 0-8371-7556-9, GOUN). Greenwood.

Goodrich, Leland M. & Kay, David A., eds. International Organization: Politics & Process. 488p. 1973. 30.00x (ISBN 0-299-06250-3); pap. 13.50x (ISBN 0-299-06254-6). U of Wis Pr.

Goodrich, Lloyd. Americans: Individualists at Work. (Illus.). 16p. 1972. pap. 1.00 (ISBN 0-685-39822-6). Am Fed Arts.

--Edward Hopper. (Illus.). 159p. 1985. 14.98 (ISBN 0-317-30949-8). Abrams.

--Thomas Eakins, 2 vols. (The Ailsa Mellon Bruce Studies in American Art). (Illus.). 1983. 90.00 (ISBN 0-674-88490-6). Vol. I: 368p. Vol. II: 384p. Harvard U Pr.

Goodrich, Lois. Decentralized Camping. 183p. 1982. pap. 12.50 (ISBN 0-686-83992-7). Am Camping.

Goodrich, Marcus. Delilah. (Classics of Naval Literature Ser.). 500p. 1985. Repr. of 1941 ed. 16.95 (ISBN 0-87021-145-5). Naval Inst Pr.

--Delilah: A Novel. LC 77-26042. (Lost American Fiction Ser.). 520p. 1978. Repr. of 1941 ed. 11.85 (ISBN 0-8093-0739-1). S Ill U Pr.

Goodrich, Nancy M. A Profile of the Competent Nursing Administrator. Kalisch, Philip & Kalisch, Beatrice, eds. LC 82-8479. (Studies in Nursing Management: No. 3). 180p. 1982. 39.95 (ISBN 0-8357-1360-1). UMI Res Pr.

Goodrich, Norma L. Ancient Myths. (RL 9). pap. 3.95 (ISBN 0-451-62361-4, Ment). NAL.

--Giono: Master of Fictional Modes. LC 72-4041. 344p. 1973. 32.00 (ISBN 0-691-06239-0). Princeton U Pr.

--King Authur. 416p. 1985. 18.95 (ISBN 0-531-09701-3). Watts.

--Medieval Myths. rev. ed. (YA) (RL 9). 1977. pap. 3.95 (ISBN 0-451-62359-2, Ment). NAL.

Goodrich, Roy G. Physics Laboratory Textbook. (Illus.). 442p. 1985. pap. text ed. 17.95 (ISBN 0-89892-031-0). Contemp Pub Co of Raleigh.

Goodrich, Samuel G. Recollections of a Lifetime, or Men & Things I Have Seen. LC 67-23886. 1967. Repr. of 1857 ed. 43.00x (ISBN 0-8103-3041-5). Gale.

Goodrich, Wallace, tr. see Pirro, Andre.

Goodrich, Ward L. The Modern Clock: A Study of Time Keeping Mechanism, Its Construction, Regulation & Repair. LC 84-24277. (Illus.). 512p. 1985. pap. 19.95 (ISBN 0-930163-23-0). Arlington Bk.

Goodrich, William, jt. auth. see Sissors, Jack.

Goodrich, William D. The Sherlock Holmes Reference Guide. LC 80-67701. (Sherlock Holmes Reference Ser.). 1985. 39.95 (ISBN 0-934468-06-0). Gaslight.

Goodrich-Freer, A. Outer Isles. (Folklore Ser). 22.50 (ISBN 0-8482-4214-9). Norwood Edns.

Goodrich-Freer, Adela M. Arabs in Tent & Town: An Intimate Account. LC 77-87616. Repr. of 1924 ed. 26.00 (ISBN 0-404-16438-2). AMS Pr.

Goodrick, A. T., tr. see Grimmelshausen, H. J. Von.

Goodrick, Edward W. Do It Yourself Hebrew & Greek. 2nd ed. LC 79-25463. 1980. pap. text ed. 9.95 (ISBN 0-930014-35-9); with cassette 14.95 (ISBN 0-930014-42-1). Multnomah.

--Do It Yourself Hebrew & Greek: Everybody's Guide to the Language Tools. 256p. (Orig.). 1980. pap. 9.95 (ISBN 0-310-41741-4). Zondervan.

Goodrick, Edward W. & Kohlenberger, John P. The NIV Complete Concordance. 1056p. 1981. 19.95 (ISBN 0-310-43650-8). Zondervan.

Goodrick, Edward W. & Kohlenberger, John R., III. The NIV Handy Concordance. 384p. (Orig.). 1982. pap. 5.95 (ISBN 0-310-43662-1). Zondervan.

Goodridge, jt. auth. see Dietz.

Goodridge, J. F., tr. see Langland, William.

Goodridge, Janet. Creative Drama & Improvised Movement for Children. LC 70-131937. Orig. Title: Drama in the Primary School. 1970. 10.00 (ISBN 0-8238-0120-9). Plays.

Goodrum, Charles A. Treasures of the Library of Congress. (Illus.). 456p. 1980. 50.00 (ISBN 0-8109-1661-4, 1661-4). Abrams.

Goodrum, Charles A. & Dalrymple, Helen W. The Library of Congress. 2nd ed. LC 82-8457. (Library of Federal Department, Agencies, & Systems Ser.). 338p. 1982. lib. bdg. 32.00x (ISBN 0-86531-303-2); pap. 11.95x (ISBN 0-86531-497-7). Westview.

Goodryder, Ernest. How to Earn Money As a Consultant: Including Specimen Contracts. rev. & 5th ed. LC 78-58276. (Frontiers of Industry Ser.: Vol. 1). (Illus.). 1978. pap. 39.00x (ISBN 0-931918-01-4). Busn Psych.

Goodsell, Charles T. Administracion De una Revolucion: La Reforma Del Poder Ejecutivo En Puerto Rico Bajo el Gobernador Tugwell, 1941-1946. pap. 5.50 (ISBN 0-8477-2207-4). U of PR Pr.

--The Case for Bureaucracy: A Public Administration Polemic. 2nd ed. (Chatham House Series on Change in American Politics). 224p. 1985. pap. text ed. 11.95 (ISBN 0-934540-55-1). Chatham Hse Pubs.

Goodsell, Charles T., ed. The Public Encounter: Where State & Citizen Meet. LC 81-47007. (Illus.). 280p. 1981. 25.00x (ISBN 0-253-15363-8). Ind U Pr.

Goodsell, Jane. Daniel Inouye. LC 77-1405. (Biography Ser.). (Illus.). (gr. 1-4). 1977. PLB 11.89 (ISBN 0-690-01358-2). Crowell Jr Bks.

--Eleanor Roosevelt. LC 71-106573. (Biography Ser.). (Illus.). (gr. 2-5). 1970. PLB 11.89 (ISBN 0-690-25626-4). Crowell Jr Bks.

--The Mayo Brothers. LC 70-139104. (Biography Ser.). (Illus.). 48p. (gr. 2-5). 1975. pap. 1.45 (ISBN 0-690-00639-X). Crowell Jr Bks.

Goodsell, John W. On Polar Trails. 214p. 1984. 12.95 (ISBN 0-89015-431-7). Eakin Pubns.

Goodsell, Willystine. Conflict of Naturalism & Humanism. LC 74-176814. (Columbia University. Teachers College. Contributions to Education: No. 33). Repr. of 1910 ed. 22.50 (ISBN 0-404-55033-9). AMS Pr.

--A History of Marriage & the Family. rev. ed. LC 72-9641. Repr. of 1934 ed. 34.50 (ISBN 0-404-57446-7). AMS Pr.

Goodsell, Willystine, ed. Pioneers of Women's Education in the United States. (Illus.). Repr. of 1931 ed. 24.00 (ISBN 0-404-02864-0). AMS Pr.

Goodson, Barbara D., jt. auth. see Travers, Jeffrey.

Goodson, Bobby, jt. auth. see Lathrop, Ann.

Goodson, C. E. & Miertschin, S. L. Technical Algebra with Applications. 592p. 1985. 26.95 (ISBN 0-471-08241-4). Wiley.

--Technical Mathematics with Calculus. 1152p. 1985. 33.95 (ISBN 0-471-86639-3). Wiley.

--Technical Trigonometry with Applications. 448p. 1985. 25.95 (ISBN 0-471-08240-6). Wiley.

Goodson, Carcle E. & Miertschin, Susan L. Student Solutions to Accompany Technical Mathematics with Applications. 1983. pap. price not set (ISBN 0-471-89290-4). Wiley.

Goodson, Carole E. & Miertschin, Susan L. Technical Mathematics with Applications. 1002p. 1983. 31.95x (ISBN 0-471-08244-9); tchr's. manual avail. (ISBN 0-471-89075-8); study guide avail. (ISBN 0-471-87578-3); student manual 21.95 (ISBN 0-471-88515-0); student solutions manual avail. (ISBN 0-471-89290-4). Wiley.

Goodson, Dean. The Cleveland, Oklahoma Family Reader & Other Matters of National Importance. LC 82-60110. 64p. (Orig.). 1982. 5.50x (ISBN 0-935834-07-9). Rainbow Books.

Goodson, Felix. Sweet Salt. LC 75-40585. 1976. 8.95 (ISBN 0-8048-1173-3). C E Tuttle.

Goodson, Gar. Fishes of Hawaii. LC 84-40783. (Illus.). 96p. 1985. pap. 5.95 (ISBN 0-8047-1270-0, SP 91). Stanford U Pr.

--Fishes of the Atlantic Coast: Canada to Brazil, Including the Gulf of Mexico, Florida, Bermuda, the Bahamas, & the Caribbean. LC 84-51685. (Illus.). 216p. 1985. pap. 6.95 (ISBN 0-8047-1268-9, SP-173). Stanford U Pr.

Goodson, I. The Making of Curriculum: Essays in the Social History of Education. 1985. write for info. (Pub. by Falmer Pr). Taylor & Francis.

Goodson, Ivan, jt. ed. see Ball, Stephen.

Goodson, Ivor & McGivney, Veronica. European Dimensions & the Secondary School Curriculum. 208p. 1985. text ed. 27.00x (ISBN 1-85000-045-X, Falmer Pr); pap. text ed. 16.00x (ISBN 1-85000-046-8, Falmer Pr). Taylor & Francis.

Goodson, Ivor & Ball, Stephen, eds. Defining the Curriculum: Histories & Ethnographies of School Subjects. LC 84-4024. 305p. 1984. 38.00x (ISBN 0-905273-94-X, Pub. by Falmer Pr); pap. 21.00x (ISBN 0-905273-93-1, Pub. by Falmer Pr). Taylor & Francis.

Goodson, Ivor F. School Subjects & Curriculum Change: Case Studies in the Social History of Curriculum. (Curriculum Policy & research Ser.). 212p. 1983. 32.00 (ISBN 0-7099-1104-1, Pub. by Croom Helm Ltd); pap. 10.00 (ISBN 0-7099-1158-0). Longwood Pub Group.

--Social Histories of the Secondary Curriculum: Subjects for Study. 250p. 1984. 33.00x (ISBN 1-85000-016-6, Pub. by Falmer Pr); pap. 20.00x (ISBN 1-85000-015-8, Pub. by Falmer Pr). Taylor & Francis.

Goodson, J. M. & Johansen, E. L. Analysis of Human Mandibular Movement. (Monographs in Oral Science: Vol. 5). 1975. 25.25 (ISBN 3-8055-1416-6). S Karger.

Goodson, James A. Tumult in the Clouds: A Story of the Eagle Squadron. (Illus.). 256p. 1984. 13.95 (ISBN 0-312-82327-4). St Martin.

Goodson, Millie S. Sunday School Growth & Renewal: How to Reach, Teach, Care, Share. LC 84-71642. 76p. (Orig.). DR014B. pap. 3.75 (ISBN 0-88177-014-0). Discipleship Res.

Goodson, R. E., ed. see Joint Automatic Control Conference (1974: University of Texas at Austin).

Goodspeed. Goodspeed's General History of Tennessee. (Goodspeed's History of Tennessee Ser.). (Illus.). 1973. Repr. of 1887 ed. 35.00 (ISBN 0-918450-10-1). C Elder.

--Goodspeed's History of East Tennessee. (Goodspeed's History of Tennessee Ser.). (Illus.). 1972. Repr. of 1887 ed. 35.00 (ISBN 0-918450-08-X). C Elder.

--Goodspeed's History of Hamilton, Knox, & Shelby Counties of Tennessee. (Goodspeed's History of Tennessee Ser.). (Illus.). 1974. Repr. of 1887 ed. 16.00 (ISBN 0-918450-11-X). C Elder.

--This Is the Life. (gr. 7-12). 1981. text ed. 14.64 (ISBN 0-02-665910-7). Bennett IL.

Goodspeed & T, Harper. Plant Hunters in the Andes. 429p. 1984. Repr. of 1941 ed. lib. bdg. 50.00 (ISBN 0-8482-4252-1). Norwood Edns.

Goodspeed, Bennett W. The Tao Jones Averages: A Guide to Whole-Brained Investing. (Illus.). 156p. 1983. 9.95 (ISBN 0-525-24201-5, 0966-290). Dutton.

--The Tao Jones Averages: A Guide to Whole Brained Investing. 160p. 1984. pap. 4.95 (ISBN 0-14-007368-X). Penguin.

Goodspeed, Charles E. Nathaniel Hawthorne & the Museum of the East India Marine Society. 1946. pap. 1.00 (ISBN 0-87577-035-5). Peabody Mus Salem.

--Yankee Bookseller. LC 73-15401. (Illus.). 325p. 1974. Repr. of 1937 ed. lib. bdg. 24.75x (ISBN 0-8371-7173-3, GOYB). Greenwood.

Goodspeed, Edgar J. Buying Happiness. facs. ed. LC 68-29207. (Essay Index Reprint Ser.). 1968. Repr. of 1932 ed. 15.00 (ISBN 0-8369-0483-4). Ayer Co Pubs.

--Full History of the Wonderful Career of Moody & Sankey, in Great Britain & America. LC 70-168154. (Illus.). Repr. of 1876 ed. 39.00 (ISBN 0-404-07227-5). AMS Pr.

--History of Early Christian Literature. rev. & enl. ed. Grant, Robert M., ed. LC 66-13871. (Midway Reprint Ser.). 1966. pap. 9.00x (ISBN 0-226-30386-1). U of Chicago Pr.

--How Came the Bible ? (Festival Books). 1976. pap. 1.95 (ISBN 0-687-17524-0). Abingdon.

--Index Patristicus, sive clavis Patrum Apostolicorum operum. LC 60-52358. 1960. 12.50x (ISBN 0-8401-0863-X). A R Allenson.

--A Life of Jesus. LC 78-21540. 1979. Repr. of 1950 ed. lib. bdg. 24.75x (ISBN 0-313-20728-3, GOLJ). Greenwood.

--Story of the Bible. LC 36-21666. Repr. of 1967 ed. 44.00 (ISBN 0-8357-9657-4, 2013612). Bks Demand UMI.

--Strange New Gospels. 1979. Repr. of 1931 ed. lib. bdg. 22.50 (ISBN 0-8495-2000-2). Arden Lib.

--Strange New Gospels. facsimile ed. LC 70-156652. (Essay Index Reprint Ser). Repr. of 1931 ed. 12.00 (ISBN 0-8369-2364-2). Ayer Co Pubs.

--The Student's New Testament: The Greek Text & the American Translation. pap. 160.00 (ISBN 0-317-20700-8, 2024115). Bks Demand UMI.

--Things Seen & Heard. facs. ed. LC 68-29208. (Essay Index Reprint Ser). 1968. Repr. of 1925 ed. 17.00 (ISBN 0-8369-0484-2). Ayer Co Pubs.

Goodspeed, Edgar J., jt. auth. see Owen, William B.

Goodspeed, Edgar J., ed. Apocrypha. 1959. pap. 5.95 (ISBN 0-394-70163-1, V163, Vin). Random.

Goodspeed, George S. A History of the Babylonians & the Assyrians. LC 78-14269. 1978. Repr. lib. bdg. 47.50 (ISBN 0-8414-2008-4). Folcroft.

Goodspeed, Peter. A Rhinoceros Wakes Me up in the Morning. LC 81-21556. (Illus.). 32p. (ps-1). 1982. PLB 10.95 (ISBN 0-02-736590-5). Bradbury Pr.

--A Rhinoceros Wakes Me up in the Morning. (Picture Puffin Ser.). (Illus.). 32p. 1984. pap. 3.50 (ISBN 0-14-050455-9, Puffin). Penguin.

Goodspeed Pub. Co. Editors. General History of Arkansas. 128p. 1977. Repr. of 1884 ed. 20.00 (ISBN 0-89308-078-0). Southern Hist Pr.

Goodspeed Publishing Co. History of Tennessee Illustrated, History of Thirty East Tenn. Counties. 526p. 1979. Repr. of 1887 ed. 35.00 (ISBN 0-89308-188-4). Southern Hist Pr.

--Knox County, Tennessee. (History of Tennessee Illustrated Ser.). 299p. 1982. Repr. of 1887 ed. 25.00 (ISBN 0-89308-125-6). Southern Hist Pr.

--Memorial & Genealogical Record of (East) Texas. (Illus.). 1982. Repr. of 1895 ed. 40.00 (ISBN 0-89308-300-3). Southern Hist Pr.

--A Reminiscent History of the Ozark Region. 784p. 1978. Repr. of 1894 ed. 47.50 (ISBN 0-89308-106-X). Southern Hist Pr.

Goodspeed Publishing Company. History of Giles, Lincoln, Franklin & Moore Counties, Tennessee. 1979. Repr. of 1886 ed. 25.00 (ISBN 0-89308-116-7). Southern Hist Pr.

--History of Henderson, Chester, McNairy, Decatur & Hardin Counties, Tennessee. 1978. Repr. of 1886 ed. 17.50 (ISBN 0-89308-097-7). Southern Hist Pr.

--History of Lauderdale, Tipton, Haywood & Crockett Counties. 1978. Repr. of 1886 ed. 20.00 (ISBN 0-89308-099-3). Southern Hist Pr.

aurence, Wayne, Perry, Hickman & ties, Tennessee. 129p. 1979. Repr. of 1886 ed. .00 (ISBN 0-89308-113-2). Southern Hist Pr.

--History of Madison County, Tennessee. 120p. 1979. Repr. of 1887 ed. 20.00 (ISBN 0-89308-114-0). Southern Hist Pr.

--History of Montgomery, Robertson, Humphreys, Stewart, Dickson, Cheatham & Houston Counties, Tennessee. 1979. Repr. of 1886 ed. 37.50 (ISBN 0-89308-117-5). Southern Hist Pr.

--History of Northeast Arkansas. 1978. Repr. of 1884 ed. 42.50 (ISBN 0-89308-081-0). Southern Hist Pr.

--History of Northwestern Arkansas. 1978. Repr. of 1884 ed. 50.00 (ISBN 0-89308-082-9). Southern Hist Pr.

--History of South Arkansas. 1978. Repr. of 1884 ed. 47.50 (ISBN 0-89308-083-7, Goodspeed Pub Co). Southern Hist Pr.

--History of Sumner, Smith, Macon & Trousdale Counties. 194p. 1979. Repr. of 1887 ed. 25.00 (ISBN 0-89308-115-9). Southern Hist Pr.

--History of Western Arkansas. 1978. Repr. of 1884 ed. 37.50 (ISBN 0-89308-084-5). Southern Hist Pr.

--History of White, Warren, Dekalb, Coffee & Cannon Counties. 195p. 1979. Repr. of 1886 ed. 25.00 (ISBN 0-89308-118-3). Southern Hist Pr.

--Memorial & Genealogical Record of Southwest Texas. 661p. 1978. Repr. of 1894 ed. 40.00 (ISBN 0-89308-122-1). Southern Hist Pr.

Goodspeed, Robert C. From Greek to Graffiti: English Words That Survive & Thrive. (Illus.). 308p. (Orig.). 1981. 15.00 (ISBN 0-682-49696-0, University); pap. 10.00 (ISBN 0-682-49706-1, University). Exposition Pr FL.

Goodspeed, T. Harper. Plant Hunters in the Andes. 2nd rev. & enl. ed. LC 61-7533. 1961. 33.00x (ISBN 0-520-00495-7). U of Cal Pr.

Goodspeed, Thomas W. A History of the University of Chicago. 1973. pap. 3.95x (ISBN 0-226-30383-7, P542, Phoen). U of Chicago Pr.

Goodstadt, Leo. China's Watergate: Political & Economic Conflicts in China 1969-1977. LC 79-902871. 1979. text ed. 16.25x (ISBN 0-7069-0725-6). Humanities.

Goodstein, David & Newhouse, Rosalyn, eds. Glossary of Typesetting, Computer, & Communications Terms. 65p. 20.00 (ISBN 0-318-17397-2); members 10.00 (ISBN 0-318-17398-0). Print Indus Am.

Goodstein, David L. States of Matter. 512p. 1985. pap. 10.95 (ISBN 0-486-64927-X). Dover.

Goodstein, Jeffrey R. Attorney's Fees: Winning a Recovery in Federal Court. 114p. 1985. pap. 9.50 (ISBN 0-87215-898-5). Michie Co.

Goodstein, Leonard D. Consulting with Human Service Systems. LC 77-81194. (Illus.). 172p. 1978. pap. text ed. 11.95 (ISBN 0-394-34761-7, RanC). Random.

Goodstein, Leonard D. & Calhoun, James F. Understanding Abnormal Behavior: Description, Explanation, Management. LC 81-17669. (Illus.). 1982. text ed. 26.95 (ISBN 0-394-34768-4, RanC); study guide 6.95 (ISBN 0-394-34769-2). Random.

Goodstein, Leonard D. & Lanyon, Richard I. Adjustment, Behavior, & Personality. 2nd ed. LC 78-62553. (Illus.). 512p. 1979. text ed. 23.95 (ISBN 0-394-34764-1, RanC); wkbk. 7.95 (ISBN 0-394-34765-X). Random.

Goodstein, Leonard D., jt. auth. see Lanyon, Richard I.

Goodstein, Leonard D. & Lanyon, Richard I., eds. Readings in Personality Assessment. LC 77-149770. Repr. of 1971 ed. 120.00 (ISBN 0-8357-9972-7, 2012426). Bks Demand UMI.

Goodstein, Leonard D. & Pfeiffer, J. William, eds. Annual for Facilitators, Trainers, & Consultants, 1983. LC 73-92841. 294p. 1983. looseleaf ntbk. 59.50 (ISBN 0-88390-007-6); pap. 24.50 (ISBN 0-88390-008-4). Univ Assocs.

--The Annual, 1985: Developing Human Resources. (Series in Human Resource Development). 293p. (Orig.). 1985. looseleaf binder 59.50 (ISBN 0-88390-011-4); pap. 24.50 (ISBN 0-88390-012-2). Univ Assocs.

Goodstein, Leonard D., jt. ed. see Pfeiffer, J. William.

Goodstein, Marvin, jt. ed. see Weintraub, Sidney.

Goodstein, Phil H. The Theory of the General Strike from the French Revolution to Poland. 337p. 1984. 35.00x (ISBN 0-88033-050-3). East Eur Quarterly.

Goodstein, R. L. Fundamental Concepts of Mathematics. 2nd ed. 1979. text ed. 53.00 (ISBN 0-08-021665-X); pap. text ed. 19.25 (ISBN 0-08-021666-8). Pergamon.

--Fundamental Concepts of Mathematics. 2nd ed. 53.00 (ISBN 0-08-021665-X). Pergamon.

Goodstein, Richard L., ed. Eating & Weight Disorders: Advances in Treatment & Research. (Springer Series on Behavior Therapy & Behavioral Medicine: Vol. 8). 192p. 1983. 23.95x (ISBN 0-8261-3830-6). Springer Pub.

Goodstein, Sylvia, jt. ed. see Bundy, Mary L.

Goodstone, Tony, ed. The Pulps: Fifty Years of American Pop Culture. abr. ed. LC 80-68162. (Illus.). 300p. 1980. pap. 4.95 (ISBN 0-87754-222-8). Chelsea Hse.

--The Whole Fun Catalogue of Nineteen Twenty-Nine. LC 79-52938. Orig. Title: Nineteen Twenty-Nine Johnson Smith & Co. Catalogue. (Illus.). 512p. 1979. pap. 8.50 (ISBN 0-87754-079-9). Chelsea Hse.

Goodwater, Leanna. Women in Antiquity: An Annotated Bibliography. LC 75-23229. 1975. 15.00 (ISBN 0-8108-0837-4). Scarecrow.

Goodway, David. London Chartism, 1838-1848. LC 81-12259. (Illus.). 320p. 1982. 44.50 (ISBN 0-521-23867-6). Cambridge U Pr.

Goodwill, William P. Buying Your First Computer. LC 81-90311. 72p. (Orig.). 1982. pap. 5.95 (ISBN 0-942844-00-9). Castle Designs.

Goodwillie, Edward. The World's Memorials of Robert Burns. 1911. 35.00 (ISBN 0-8274-3769-2). R West.

Goodwin, A. W. & Darien-Smith, I., eds. Hand Function & the Neocortex. (Experimental Brain Research: Supplement 10). (Illus.). 345p. 1985. 34.50 (ISBN 0-387-13948-6). Springer-Verlag.

Goodwin, Albert. The French Revolution. 5th ed. 175p. 1983. pap. 8.95 (ISBN 0-09-105021-9, Pub. by Hutchinson Educ). Longwood Pub Group.

--The Friends of Liberty: The English Democratic Movement in the Age of the French Revolution. LC 78-15673. (Illus.). 1979. text ed. 32.50x (ISBN 0-674-32339-4). Harvard U Pr.

Goodwin, Arthur. Technique of Mosaic. (Illus.). 144p. 1985. 19.95 (ISBN 0-7134-4551-3, Pub. by Batsford England). David & Charles.

Goodwin, Astly J. & Lowe, C. V. The Stone Age Cultures of South Africa. LC 76-44725. Repr. of 1929 ed. 41.50 (ISBN 0-404-15928-1). AMS Pr.

Goodwin, B., ed. Analytical Physiology of Cells & Developing Organisms. 1977. 46.00 (ISBN 0-12-289360-3). Acad Pr.

Goodwin, B. C., ed. Development & Evolution. LC 82-14728. (British Society for Developmental Biology Symposium Ser.: No. 6). 350p. 1983. 89.50 (ISBN 0-521-24949-X). Cambridge U Pr.

Goodwin, B. L. Handbook of Intermediate Metabolism of Aromatic Compounds. 1976. 49.95x (ISBN 0-412-12920-5, NO. 6130, Pub. by Chapman & Hall). Methuen Inc.

Goodwin, B. M., ed. Properties of Pure Liquids. LC 80-25560. (AIChEMI Modular Instruction D. Ser.: Vol. 2). 70p. 1981. pap. 30.00 (ISBN 0-8169-0179-1, J-10); pap. 15.00 members (ISBN 0-317-03843-5). Am Inst Chem Eng.

--Selected Topics in Thermodynamics. LC 80-25560. (AIChEMI Modular Instruction D. Ser.: Vol. 4). 34p. 1983. pap. 30.00 (ISBN 0-8169-0238-0, J-22); pap. 15.00 members (ISBN 0-317-03847-8). Am Inst Chem Eng.

Goodwin, Bailey, et al. Subsidised Public Transport & the Demand for Travel. 234p. 1983. text ed. 33.95x (ISBN 0-566-00654-5). Gower Pub Co.

Goodwin, Barbara. Social Science & Utopia. (Harvester Studies in Philosophy: No. 4). (Illus.). 1978. text ed. 30.50x (ISBN 0-391-00855-2). Humanities.

--Using Political Ideas. LC 81-16009. 294p. 1982. 39.95 (ISBN 0-471-10115-X, Pub. by Wiley-Interscience); pap. 17.95x (ISBN 0-471-10116-8). Wiley.

Goodwin, Barbara & Taylor, Keith. The Politics of Utopia: A Study in Theory & Practice. LC 82-21556. 300p. 1984. 27.50x (ISBN 0-312-62933-8). St Martin.

Goodwin, Bennie E., II. The Effective Teacher. LC 84-28869. 48p. 1985. pap. 1.95 (ISBN 0-87784-333-3). Inter-Varsity.

Goodwin, Bonnie E. The Effective Leader. 64p. 1981. pap. 2.95 (ISBN 0-87784-620-0). Inter-Varsity.

Goodwin, Carole. The Oak Park Strategy: Community Control of Racial Change. LC 79-13651. (Studies of Urban Society). (Illus.). 1979. 15.95x (ISBN 0-226-30396-9). U of Chicago Pr.

Goodwin, Charles. Conversational Organization: Interaction Between Speakers & Hearers. LC 81-3573. (Language, Thought, & Culture Ser.). 1981. 35.00 (ISBN 0-12-289780-3). Acad Pr.

Goodwin, Charles, jt. auth. see Parkes, James C.

Goodwin, Clive E. A Bird-Finding Guide to Ontario. (Illus.). 256p. 1982. pap. 12.95 (ISBN 0-8020-6494-9). U of Toronto Pr.

Goodwin, Craufurd C. & Holley, I. B., Jr., eds. The Transfer of Ideas: Historical Essays. LC 68-26691. pap. 47.80 (ISBN 0-317-26757-4, 2023390). Bks Demand UMI.

Goodwin, Craufurd D. Canadian Economic Thought: The Political Economy of a Developing Nation, 1814-1914. LC 61-6223. (Duke University, Commonwealth-Studies Center Publication: No. 15). pap. 57.50 (ISBN 0-317-26751-5, 2023387). Bks Demand UMI.

--Economic Enquiry in Australia. LC 65-27768. (Duke University, Commonwealth Center Publication: No. 24). pap. 160.00 (ISBN 0-317-26753-1, 2023388). Bks Demand UMI.

--Exhortation & Controls: The Search for a Wage-Price Policy, 1945-1971. (Studies in Wage-Price Policy). 1975. 29.95 (ISBN 0-8157-3208-2). Brookings.

--The Image of Australia: British Perception of the Australian Economy from the Eighteenth to the Twentieth Century. LC 73-81711. (Duke University, Commonwealth-Studies Center Publication: No. 42). pap. 68.80 (ISBN 0-317-26755-8, 2023389). Bks Demand UMI.

Goodwin, Craufurd D., ed. Energy Policy in Perspective: Today's Problems, Yesterday's Solution. LC 80-22859. 600p. 1980. 32.95 (ISBN 0-8157-3202-3); pap. 15.95 (ISBN 0-8157-3201-5). Brookings.

Goodwin, D. W., ed. Advances in Quantum Electronics. Vol. 1, 1970. 55.00 (ISBN 0-12-035001-7); Vol. 2, 1974. 60.00 (ISBN 0-12-035002-5); Vol. 3, 1975. 85.00 (ISBN 0-12-035003-3). Acad Pr.

Goodwin, Daniel R. Southern Slavery in Its Present Aspects. LC 78-97452. Repr. of 1864 ed. 22.50x (ISBN 0-8371-2687-8, GSS&, Pub. by Negro U Pr). Greenwood.

Goodwin, David. Delivering Educational Services. LC 76-54166. 1977. pap. text ed. 9.50x (ISBN 0-8077-2507-2). Tchrs Coll.

Goodwin, Del & Chaffee, Dorcas, eds. Perspectives Seventy Six, a Compendium of Useful Knowledge About Old-Time Vermont & New Hampshire. (Illus.). (gr. 6-12). 1975. pap. text ed. 8.95 (ISBN 0-915892-02-2); 7.95 (ISBN 0-686-86694-0). Regional Ctr Educ.

Goodwin, Derek. Birds of Man's World. LC 77-74922. (Illus.). 190p. 1978. 17.50x (ISBN 0-8014-1167-X). Comstock.

--Crows of the World. LC 76-20194. (Illus.). 352p. 1976. 40.00x (ISBN 0-8014-1057-6). Comstock.

--Estrildid Finches of the World. LC 81-70702. (Illus.). 352p. 1982. 45.00x (ISBN 0-8014-1433-4). Cornell U Pr.

--Pigeons & Doves of the World. 3rd ed. LC 76-55484. (Illus.). 496p. 1983. 48.50x (ISBN 0-8014-1434-2). Comstock.

--Pigeons & Doves of the World. 3rd ed. LC 81-70700. (Illus.). 466p. 1983. 48.50x (ISBN 0-8014-1434-2). Cornell U Pr.

Goodwin, Derek H. Beef Management & Production: A Practical Guide for Farmers & Students. 200p. (Orig.). 1982. pap. text ed. 10.95x (ISBN 0-09-127061-8, Hutchinson & Co). Brookfield Pub Co.

--Pig Management & Production: A Practical Guide for Farmers & Students. 203p. (Orig.). 1982. pap. text ed. 12.25 (ISBN 0-09-110891-8, Hutchinson & Co). Brookfield Pub co.

--Sheep Management & Production. 2nd ed. 224p. (Orig.). 1982. pap. text ed. 12.25 (ISBN 0-317-03049-3, Hutchinson & Co). Brookfield Pub Co.

Goodwin, Diana, jt. auth. see Bolton, Elizabeth.

Goodwin, Donald. Is Alcoholism Hereditary? LC 75-32346. 1976. pap. 4.95 (ISBN 0-19-502432-X, GB 549, GB). Oxford U Pr.

--Is Alcoholism Hereditary? 171p. 1976. 10.95 (ISBN 0-318-15334-3). Natl Coun Alcoholism.

Goodwin, Donald, et al, eds. Longitudinal Research in Alcoholism. 1983. lib. bdg. 39.00 (ISBN 0-89838-133-9, KNP). Kluwer Nijhoff.

Goodwin, Donald W. Alcoholism: The Facts. (The Facts Ser.). (Illus.). 1981. text ed. 13.95x (ISBN 0-19-261297-2). Oxford U Pr.

--Anxiety. 288p. 1986. 16.95 (ISBN 0-19-503665-4). Oxford U Pr.

--Phobia. (The Facts Ser.). 1983. 13.95x (ISBN 0-19-261395-2). Oxford U Pr.

Goodwin, Donald W. & Guze, Samuel B. Psychiatric Diagnosis. 3rd ed. (Illus.). 292p. 1984. 19.95x (ISBN 0-19-503410-4); pap. 11.95x (ISBN 0-19-503411-2). Oxford U Pr.

Goodwin, Donald W. & Erickson, Carlton K., eds. Alcoholism & Affective Disorders: Clinical, Genetic, & Biochemical Studies with Emphasis on Alcohol-Lithium Interaction. (Illus.). 298p. 1979. 40.00 (ISBN 0-89335-073-7). SP Med & Sci Bks.

Goodwin, Dwight L. & Coates, Thomas J. Helping Students Help Themselves: How You Can Put Behavior Analysis into Action in Your Classroom. (Illus.). 256p. 1976. pap. text ed. 15.95 (ISBN 0-13-386482-0). P-H.

Goodwin, E. First Lessons in Manx. pap. 4.95 (ISBN 0-686-10842-6). British Am Bks.

Goodwin, E. H. & Duffy, Nellie. A Pictorial History of Glenwood. 56p. 1983. pap. 5.00 (ISBN 0-937080-10-1). Century One.

Goodwin, E. M. & Kemp, J. F. Marine Statistics: Theory & Practice. 336p. 1979. 35.00x (ISBN 0-540-07379-2). Sheridan.

Goodwin, Everett C. The Magistracy Rediscovered: Connecticut, 1636-1818. Berkhofer, Robert, ed. LC 80-28681. (Studies in American History & Culture: No. 24). 194p. 1981. 39.95 (ISBN 0-8357-1160-9). UMI Res Pr.

Goodwin, F. K., jt. ed. see Wehr, T. A.

Goodwin, Frank J. Harmony of the Life of St. Paul. 1951. pap. 7.95 (ISBN 0-8010-3797-2). Baker Bk.

Goodwin, G. C. & Payne, R. L., eds. Dynamic System Identification: Experimental Design & Data Analysis. 1977. 65.000007677p (ISBN 0-12-289750-1). Acad Pr.

Goodwin, G. L. New Dimensions of World Politics. 200p. 1975. 16.50 (ISBN 0-85664-241-X, Pub. by Croom Helm Ltd). Longwood Pub Group.

Goodwin, Gary C. Cherokees in Transition: A Study of Changing Culture & Environment Prior to 1775. LC 77-2709. (Research Papers: No. 181). (Illus.). 1977. pap. 10.00 (ISBN 0-89065-088-8). U Chicago Dept Geog.

Goodwin, Geoffrey. Ethics & Nuclear Deterence. LC 81-21449. 208p. 1982. 22.50x (ISBN 0-312-26555-7). St Martin.

Goodwin, Geoffrey & Mayall, James, eds. The New International Commodity Regime. 1980. 32.50 (ISBN 0-312-56812-6). St Martin.

Goodwin, George, Jr. The Little Legislatures: Committees of Congress. LC 75-103477. 304p. 1970. 17.50x (ISBN 0-87023-060-3); pap. 8.00x (ISBN 0-87023-073-5). U of Mass Pr.

Goodwin, George L. The Ontological Argument of Charles Hartshorne. LC 78-2821. 1978. pap. 9.95 (ISBN 0-89130-228-X, 01-01-20). Scholars Pr GA.

Goodwin, Gerain. Conversations with George Moore. LC 73-13738. 1940. lib. bdg. 17.50 (ISBN 0-8414-4440-4). Folcroft.

Goodwin, Gerald, jt. auth. see Current, Richard N.

Goodwin, Gordon, ed. see Hamilton, Anthony.

Goodwin, Graham C. & Sin, Kwai S. Adaptive Filtering, Prediction & Control. 688p. 1984. text ed. 47.95 (ISBN 0-13-004069-X). P-H.

Goodwin, Grenville. Western Apache Raiding & Warfare. Basso, Keith H., ed. LC 73-142255. 330p. 1971. pap. 11.95 (ISBN 0-8165-0297-8). U of Ariz Pr.

Goodwin, Grenville, ed. Myths & Tales of the White Mountain Apache. LC 39-33959. (AFS M). Repr. of 1939 ed. 29.00 (ISBN 0-527-01085-5). Kraus Repr.

Goodwin, H. Eugene. Groping for Ethics in Journalism. (Illus.). 336p. 1983. text ed. 38.00 (ISBN 0-8138-0816-2); pap. text ed. 16.95 (ISBN 0-8138-0817-0). Iowa St U Pr.

Goodwin, Harold. Cargo. LC 84-11027. (Illus.). 128p. (gr. 5-7). 1984. 10.95 (ISBN 0-02-736870-X). Bradbury Pr.

Goodwin, Harry & Knight. Through the Wordsworth Country. LC 78-1598. Repr. of 1887 ed. lib. bdg. 35.00x (ISBN 0-8414-4612-1). Folcroft.

Goodwin, Harry & Knight, William. Through the Wordsworth Country. 1887. Repr. 50.00 (ISBN 0-8274-3882-6). R West.

Goodwin, Hope. Acts of Love. 8.95 (ISBN 0-317-17554-8, Avalon). Bouregy.

--A Dream for Julie. (Caprice Ser.: No. 78). 144p. 1985. pap. 2.25 (ISBN 0-441-16681-4). Ace Bks.

--Home for the Heart. (Orig.). 1980. pap. 1.95 (ISBN 0-532-23135-X). Woodhill.

--The Love Match. (YA) (gr. 9-12). 1985. 8.95 (ISBN 0-8034-8513-1, Avalon). Bouregy.

Goodwin, Inge, tr. see Blaukopf, Kurt.

Goodwin, Irene & Silvers, Ruth. Polka Dotted Pencil Pushers: Comprehension. 142p. 1980. pap. 8.95 (ISBN 0-932970-12-5). Prinit Pr.

--Polka Dotted Pencil Pushers: Math. LC 79-63129. 156p. (Orig.). 1979. pap. 8.95 (ISBN 0-932970-08-7). Prinit Pr.

--Polka-Dotted Pencil Pushers: Story Starters. LC 79-63129. 1979. pap. 8.95 (ISBN 0-932970-06-0). Prinit Pr.

Goodwin, Irene, ed. see Jenkins, Sheila.

Goodwin, J. see Riecker, G., et al.

Goodwin, J. F., ed. Heart Muscle Disease. (Current Status of Clinical Cardiology). 1985. lib. bdg. 55.00 (ISBN 0-85200-722-1, Pub. by MTP Pr England). Kluwer-Academic.

Goodwin, J. R. & Rovelstad, J. M. Travel & Lodging Law: Principles, Statutes & Cases. 456p. 1980. 29.95 (ISBN 0-471-84162-5). Wiley.

Goodwin, Jacob. Brotherhood of Arms: General Dynamics & the Business of Defending America. LC 85-40268. (Illus.). 384p. 1985. 18.95 (ISBN 0-8129-1151-2). Times Bks.

Goodwin, James C. & Poe, Elmer C. S-100 & Other Micro Buses. 2nd ed. LC 81-50561. 208p. 1981. pap. 9.95 (ISBN 0-672-21810-0, 21810). Sams.

Goodwin, James S. Suppressor Cells in Human Disease. (Immunology Ser: Vol. 14). (Illus.). 376p. 1981. 49.75 (ISBN 0-8247-1290-0). Dekker.

Goodwin, Jean M. Sexual Abuse: Incest Victims & Their Families. LC 81-16300. (Illus.). 224p. 1982. text ed. 23.00 (ISBN 0-7236-7012-9). PSG Pub Co.

Goodwin, Jill. A Dyer's Manual. (Illus.). 128p. 1983. 17.95 (ISBN 0-7207-1327-7, Pub by Michael Joseph). Merrimack Pub Cir.

Goodwin, John. Gaming Control Law. LC 84-26442. (Illus.). 216p. 1985. 29.95x (ISBN 0-942280-08-3). Pub Horizons.

--High Points of Legal History: The Development of Business Law. LC 82-15127. 138p. (Orig.). 1982. pap. text ed. 9.95 (ISBN 0-942280-01-6). Pub Horizons.

--A Short Guide to Shakespeare's Plays. (Orig.). 1979. pap. text ed. 4.50x (ISBN 0-435-18371-0). Heinemann Ed.

Goodwin, John, ed. see Hall, Peter.

Goodwin, John C. Insanity & the Criminal. (Historical Foundations of Forensic Psychiatry & Psychology Ser.). 308p. 1980. Repr. of 1924 ed. lib. bdg. 32.50 (ISBN 0-306-76061-4). Da Capo.

--Insanity & the Criminal. 1924. 17.50 (ISBN 0-686-17699-5). Quality Lib.

Goodwin, John F., jt. ed. see Maseri, Attilio.

Goodwin, John F., jt. ed. see Yu, Paul N.

Goodwin, John R. Business Law, Bk. 102. 3rd ed. (Illus.). 776p. 1980. 26.95 (ISBN 0-256-02266-6). Irwin.

--Student Workbook to Accompany Business Law. 3rd ed. 1980. pap. 9.50x (ISBN 0-256-02267-4). Irwin.

--Twenty Feet from Glory. 1970. 10.00 (ISBN 0-87012-087-5). McClain.

Goodwin, John R. & Rovelstad, James M. Travel & Lodging Law. LC 79-12189. (Law Ser.). 456p. 1980. text ed. 30.95 (ISBN 0-88244-188-4, Pub. by Grid). Wiley.

Goodwin, John W. Agricultural Economics. 2nd ed. (Illus.). 400p. 1982. text ed. 25.95 (ISBN 0-8359-0182-3); instr's manual free (ISBN 0-8359-0183-1). Reston.

Goodwin, Joseph, ed. see Ayensu, Edward S., et al.

Goodwin, June. Cry Amandla! South African Women & the Question of Power. (Illus.). 252p. 1984. text ed. 27.50x (ISBN 0-8419-0899-0, Africana); pap. text ed. 14.50x (ISBN 0-8419-0911-3). Holmes & Meier.

Goodwin, Ken. Understanding African Poetry: A Study of Ten Poets. 256p. 1982. text ed. 25.00x (ISBN 0-435-91325-5); pap. text ed. 12.50x (ISBN 0-435-91326-3). Heinemann Ed.

Goodwin, L. M., jt. auth. see Buck, L. E.

Goodwin, Lee M., jt. auth. see Buck, Linda E.

Goodwin, Leonard. Can Social Science Help Resolve National Problems? Welfare, a Case in Point. LC 74-11752. (Illus.). 1975. 11.95 (ISBN 0-02-912500-6). Free Pr.

--Causes & Cures of Welfare: New Evidence on the Social Psychology of the Poor. LC 82-48634. 224p. 1983. 24.00x (ISBN 0-669-06370-3); pap. 11.00. Lexington Bks.

--Do the Poor Want to Work? A Social-Psychological Study of Work Orientations. LC 72-146. pap. 48.00 (ISBN 0-317-29362-1, 2055941). Bks Demand UMI.

Goodwin, Mark D. Level II ROMs. (Illus.). 532p. 1983. 24.95 (ISBN 0-8306-0275-5, 1575); pap. 17.50 (ISBN 0-8306-0175-9). TAB Bks.

Goodwin, Mary T. & Pollen, Gerry. Creative Food Experiences for Children. rev. ed. (Illus.). 256p. 1980. text ed. 12.95 (ISBN 0-89329-028-9). Ctr Sci Public.

--Creative Food Experiences for Children. 2nd rev. ed. (Illus.). 256p. (gr. k-6). 1980. pap. 5.95 (ISBN 0-89329-027-0). Ctr Sci Public.

Goodwin, Matthew O. Numerology: The Complete Guide. LC 82-4143. 1981. Repr. Set. lib. bdg. 49.90x (ISBN 0-89370-999-9); Vol. 1. lib. bdg. 24.95x ea. (ISBN 0-89370-653-1). Vol. 2 (ISBN 0-89370-654-X). Borgo Pr.

--Numerology: The Complete Guide. (Orig.). 1981. Set. pap. 25.90 (ISBN 0-87877-999-X); Vol. 1. pap. 12.95 (ISBN 0-87877-053-4); Vol. 2. pap. 12.95 (ISBN 0-87877-054-2). Newcastle Pub.

Goodwin, Maud, jt. auth. see Bellamy, Blanche W.

Goodwin, Maud W. The Colonial Cavalier: Or, Southern Life Before the Revolution. facsimile ed. LC 75-1849. (Leisure Class in America Ser.). (Illus.). 1975. Repr. of 1895 ed. 21.00x (ISBN 0-405-06916-2). Ayer Co Pubs.

--Dolly Madison. LC 67-30157. 1967. Repr. of 1896 ed. 16.50 (ISBN 0-87152-039-7). Reprint.

Goodwin, Maud W., jt. auth. see Bellamy, Blanche W.

Goodwin, Maud W see Johnson, Allen & Nevins, Allan.

Goodwin, Maud W., et al, eds. Historic New York, 4 Vols, Series One & Two. LC 74-83482. (Empire State Historical Publications Ser.). (Illus.). 1969. Repr. of 1898 ed. Set. 75.00x (ISBN 0-87198-064-9). Friedman.

Goodwin, Maude W. Dutch & English on the Hudson. 1919. 8.50x (ISBN 0-686-83529-8). Elliots Bks.

Goodwin, Michael, ed. see Twentieth Century.

Goodwin, Michael C. My Stars! 128p. 1980. pap. 5.95 (ISBN 0-914350-50-1). Vulcan Bks.

Goodwin, Murray, jt. auth. see Jurgensen, Barbara.

Goodwin, Nathaniel. Genealogical Notes, or Contributions to Family History of Some of the First Settlers of Connecticut & Massachusetts. LC 75-76817. 362p. 1982. Repr. of 1856 ed. 18.50 (ISBN 0-8063-0159-7). Genealog Pub.

Goodwin, Norma L., jt. auth. see Tilley, Nannie M.

Goodwin, Parke. The Last Rainbow. LC 84-91010. 368p. 1985. pap. 7.95 (ISBN 0-553-34142-1). Bantam.

Goodwin, Paul H. & Hinkley, Edith. Physical Foundations of Radiology. LC 70-106337. pap. 102.30 (ISBN 0-317-08404-6, 2006252). Bks Demand UMI.

Goodwin, Paul N. & Rao, Dandamudi V. An Introduction to the Physics of Nuclear Medicine. (Illus.). 164p. 1977. 23.75x (ISBN 0-398-03569-5). C C Thomas.

Goodwin, Peter. Nuclear War: The Facts on Your Survival. (Illus.). 128p. 1981. (Rutledge Pr); pap. 5.95 (ISBN 0-8317-6458-9). Smith Pubs.

Goodwin, Phillip H., jt. auth. see Douglass, Merrill E.

Goodwin, R. Essays in Economic Dynamics. 180p. 1983. Repr. text ed. 42.50x (ISBN 0-333-29094-1, Pub. by Macmillan England). Humanities.

--Essays in Linear Economic Structures. 190p. 1983. text ed. 37.50x (ISBN 0-333-29102-6, Pub. by Macmillan England). Humanities.

Goodwin, R. Christopher & Walker, Jefferey B. The Villa Taina de Boqueron: Excavation of an Early Taino Site in Puerto Rico. LC 74-30903. (Illus.). 144p. 1975. 15.00 (ISBN 0-913480-21-5); pap. 6.50 (ISBN 0-913480-33-9). Inter Am U Pr.

Goodwin, R. M. Elementary Economics from the Higher Standpoints. LC 72-116842. 1970. 37.50 (ISBN 0-521-07923-3). Cambridge U Pr.

Goodwin, R. M., et al, eds. Nonlinear Models of Fluctuating Growth: An International Symposium, Siena, Italy, March 24-27, 1983. (Lecture Notes in Economics & Mathematical Systems Ser.: Vol. 228). xvii, 277p. 1984. pap. 20.00 (ISBN 0-387-13349-6). Springer-Verlag.

Goodwin, Reason A. Troika: Introduction to Russian Letters & Sounds. LC 80-81788. (Orig.). (gr. 11-12). 1980. text ed. 14.50 (ISBN 0-936368-00-4); pap. text ed. 6.95 (ISBN 0-936368-01-2). Lexik Hse.

Goodwin, Richard W., jt. ed. see Neufeld, Ronald D.

Goodwin, Robert P. Selected Writings: Aquinas. 1965. pap. text ed. write for info. (ISBN 0-02-345050-9). Macmillan.

Goodwin, Robert P., tr. see Thomas Aquinas, St.

Goodwin, Ruby B. It's Good to Be Black. LC 53-11462. (Arcturus Books Paperbacks). 256p. 1976. pap. 4.95 (ISBN 0-8093-0757-X). S Ill U Pr.

Goodwin, Ruby L. Passport to Sanity. (Illus.). 62p. 1969. pap. 3.95x (ISBN 0-934482-00-4). Hathor House Bks.

Goodwin, Ruby P., ed. see Parker & Parker.

Goodwin, Rufus, ed. see Lievegoed, Bernhard J.

Goodwin, Rutherfoord. Williamsburg in Virginia. LC 41-5562. (Illus., Orig.). 1968. 10.00 (ISBN 0-910412-39-1); leatherbound ed. 25.00 (ISBN 0-910412-40-5). Williamsburg.

Goodwin, Sandra, jt. ed. see Crittenden, Alan.

Goodwin, Stanley J. Black Destiny. 89p. 1983. pap. 2.40 (ISBN 0-686-28004-0). Northland Pubns WA.

--The Book of Desire. 1982. pap. 2.40 (ISBN 0-686-10271-1). Northland Pubns WA.

--Can Ice Cream & Oranges Prevent the Common Cold & Influenza? (Illus.). 1979. pap. 2.40 (ISBN 0-686-24961-5). Northland Pubns WA.

--The Devastating Eighties. 80p. 1980. pap. 2.40 (ISBN 0-686-27500-4). Northland Pubns WA.

Goodwin, Susanne, jt. auth. see Bennett, Jill.

Goodwin, Suzanne. Sisters. 336p. 1985. 15.95 (ISBN 0-312-72748-8). St Martin.

Goodwin, T. W. Biochemical Functions of Terpenoids in Plants Royal Society. LC 79-670276. (Illus.). 1979. Repr. of 1978 ed. text ed. 38.00x (ISBN 0-85403-105-7). Scholium Intl.

--Biochemistry of the Carotenoids, Vol. I. 2nd ed. (Plants). 377p. 1980. 75.00x (ISBN 0-412-21690-6, NO. 6412, Pub. by Chapman & Hall England). Methuen Inc.

--Biochemistry of the Carotenoids: Animals, Vol. II. 2nd ed. (Illus.). 400p. 1984. 55.00x (ISBN 0-412-23770-9, NO. 6787, Pub. by Chapman & Hall). Methuen Inc.

Goodwin, T. W. & Mercer, E. I. Introduction to Plant Biochemistry. 2nd ed. (Illus.). 400p. 1982. pap. 33.00 (ISBN 0-08-024921-3). Pergamon.

--Introduction to Plant Biochemistry. 2nd ed. 1972. 99.00 (ISBN 0-08-024922-1). Pergamon.

Goodwin, T. W., ed. Chemistry & Biochemistry of Plant Pigments, Vol. 1. 2nd ed. 1976. 90.00 (ISBN 0-12-289901-6). Acad Pr.

--Chemistry & Biochemistry of Plant Pigments, Vol. 2. 2nd ed. 1976. 70.00 (ISBN 0-12-289902-4). Acad Pr.

Goodwin, T. W., ed. see International Symposium on Carotenoids, Madison, 5th, U. S. A., July 23-28 1978.

Goodwin, T. W., ed. see International Symposium on Carotenoids, 6th, Liverpool, U. K., July 26-31, 1981.

Goodwin, Thomas. Holy Spirit in Salvation. 1979. 14.95 (ISBN 0-85151-279-8). Banner of Truth.

--Return of Prayers. (Summit Books Ser). 1979. pap. 2.95 (ISBN 0-8010-3729-8). Baker Bk.

--Works of Thomas Goodwin, 12 Vols. LC 74-168155. Repr. of 1866 ed. Set. lib. bdg. 450.00 (ISBN 0-404-02870-5); 37.50 ea. AMS Pr.

Goodwin, Thomas H., tr. see Zander, Maximilian.

Goodwin, Tony. Northern Adirondack Ski Tours: Thirty Selected Tours for the Novice to Expert Skier. LC 81-22785. (Illus.). 1982. pap. 7.95 (ISBN 0-935272-19-4). ADK Mtn Club.

Goodwin, Tony, ed. see Adirondack Mountain Club, Inc.

Goodwin, W. W. & Gulick, Charles B. Greek Grammar. (College Classical Ser.). 460p. (gr. 11-12). lib. bdg. 25.00 (ISBN 0-89241-118-X); pap. text ed. 12.50x (ISBN 0-89241-332-8). Caratzas.

Goodwin, William J. & Augustine, James, eds. Primate Research. LC 76-14940. 127p. 1976. 29.50x (ISBN 0-306-34506-4, Plenum Pr). Plenum Pub.

Goodwin, William L. & Driscoll, Laura A. Handbook for Measurement & Evaluation in Early Childhood Education: Issues, Measures, & Methods. LC 79-88768. (Social & Behavioral Science Ser.). 1980. text ed. 32.95x (ISBN 0-87589-440-2). Jossey-Bass.

Goodwin, William L. & Klausmeier, Herbert J. Facilitating Student Learning: An Introduction to Educational Psychology. 612p. 1975. text ed. 24.50 scp (ISBN 0-06-042377-3, HarpC); instructor's manual avail. (ISBN 0-06-362400-1); scp student field guide 9.50 (ISBN 0-06-042378-1). Har-Row.

Goodwin, William W. Greek Grammar. 2nd ed. 1879. 19.95 (ISBN 0-312-34825-8). St Martin.

--Syntax of the Moods & Tenses of the Greek Verb. (Illus.). 264p. 1981. Repr. of 1878 ed. lib. bdg. 35.00 (ISBN 0-8495-1972-1). Arden Lib.

Goodwin-Gill, Guy S. International Law & the Movement of Persons Between States. 1978. 57.00x (ISBN 0-19-825333-8). Oxford U Pr.

--The Refugee in International Law. 1984. 47.50x (ISBN 0-19-825372-9); pap. 14.95x (ISBN 0-19-825518-7). Oxford U Pr.

Goodworth, C. T. Effective Interviewing for Employment Selection. 138p. 1983. pap. text ed. 13.95 (ISBN 0-09-150331-0, Pub. by Busn Bks England); text ed. 31.50 (ISBN 0-09-150330-2). Brookfield Pub Co.

Goodworth, Clive T. Effective Speaking & Presentation for the Company Executive. 204p. 1980. text ed. 31.50x (ISBN 0-220-67028-5, Pub. by Busn Bks England). Brookfield Pub Co.

--How to Be a Super-Effctive Manager: A Guide to People Management. 158p. (Orig.). 1984. pap. text ed. 11.95x (ISBN 0-09-151851-2, Pub. by Busn Bks England). Brookfield Pub Co.

--How You Can Do More in Less Time. 176p. 1984. text ed. 24.95x (ISBN 0-09-159050-7, Pub. by Business Bks). Brookline Book.

Goodwyn, Floyd L., Jr. Image Pattern & Moral Vision in John Webster. (Salzburg Studies in English Literature: Jacobean Drama Ser: 71). 1977. pap. text ed. 25.50x (ISBN 0-391-01389-0). Humanities.

Goodwyn, Lawrence. Democratic Promise: The Populist Moment in America. LC 75-25462. (Illus.). 1976. 29.95x (ISBN 0-19-501996-2). Oxford U Pr.

--The Populist Moment: A Short History of the Agrarian Revolt in America. 1978. 22.50x (ISBN 0-19-502416-8). Oxford U Pr.

--The Populist Moment: A Short History of the Agrarian Revolt in America. 1978. pap. 8.95 (ISBN 0-19-502417-6, GB 536, GB). Oxford U Pr.

Goody, Esther N. Contexts of Kinship: An Essay in the Family Sociology of the Gonja of Northern Ghana. LC 72-78892. (Cambridge Studies in Social Anthropology: No. 7). (Illus.). 300p. 1973. 37.50 (ISBN 0-521-08583-7). Cambridge U Pr.

--Parenthood & Social Reproduction: Fostering & Occupational Roles in West Africa. LC 80-42177. (Cambridge Studies in Social Anthropology: No. 35). 368p. 1982. 47.50 (ISBN 0-521-22721-6). Cambridge U Pr.

--Questions & Politeness: Strategies in Social Interaction. LC 77-86577. (Cambridge Papers in Social Anthropology: No. 8). pap. 83.00 (ISBN 0-317-20622-2). Bks Demand UMI.

Goody, Esther N., ed. From Craft to Industry: The Ethnography of Proto-Industrial Cloth Production. LC 82-4205. (Cambridge Papers in Social Anthropology: No. 10). 304p. 1983. 42.50 (ISBN 0-521-24614-8). Cambridge U Pr.

Goody, Jack. Comparative Studies in Kinship. LC 73-76227. 1969. 20.00x (ISBN 0-8047-0678-6). Stanford U Pr.

--Cooking, Cuisine & Class: A Study in Comparative Sociology. LC 81-17035. (Themes in the Social Sciences Ser.). (Illus.). 304p. 1982. 37.50 (ISBN 0-521-24455-2); pap. 11.95 (ISBN 0-521-28696-4). Cambridge U Pr.

--Death, Property, & the Ancestors: A Study of the Mortuary Customs of the LoDagaa of West Africa. (Illus.). 1962. 32.50x (ISBN 0-8047-0068-0). Stanford U Pr.

--The Development of the Family & Marriage in Europe. LC 82-23465. (Past & Present Publications Ser.). (Illus.). 328p. 1983. 42.50 (ISBN 0-521-24739-X); pap. 13.95 (ISBN 0-521-28925-4). Cambridge U Pr.

--Succession to High Office. LC 79-52487. (Cambridge Papers in Social Anthropology: No. 4). (Illus.). 1979. pap. 10.95x (ISBN 0-521-29732-X). Cambridge U Pr.

Goody, Jack & Tambiah, S. J. Bridewealth & Dowry. LC 72-95407. (Cambridge Papers in Social Anthropology Ser.: No. 7). (Illus.). 128p. 1973. 24.95 (ISBN 0-521-20169-1); pap. 10.95x (ISBN 0-521-09805-X). Cambridge U Pr.

Goody, Jack, ed. The Character of Kinship. LC 73-82448. (Illus.). 242p. 1973. 34.50 (ISBN 0-521-20290-6); pap. 13.95 (ISBN 0-521-29002-3). Cambridge U Pr.

--The Domestication of the Savage Mind. (Themes in the Social Sciences Ser.). (Illus.). 1977. 34.50 (ISBN 0-521-21726-1); pap. 11.95 (ISBN 0-521-29242-5). Cambridge U Pr.

--Literacy in Traditional Societies. LC 69-10427. pap. 89.50 (ISBN 0-317-20621-4, 2024575). Bks Demand UMI.

--Production & Reproduction. LC 76-4238. (Cambridge Studies in Social Anthropology: No.17). (Illus.). 1977. 34.50 (ISBN 0-521-21294-4); pap. 10.95 (ISBN 0-521-29088-0). Cambridge U Pr.

--Technology, Tradition & the State in Africa. (Illus.). 88p. 1980. pap. 8.95x (ISBN 0-521-29892-X). Cambridge U Pr.

Goody, Jack, et al, eds. Family & Inheritance. LC 76-10402. (Past & Present Publications Ser.). (Illus.). 1976. 57.50 (ISBN 0-521-21246-4); pap. 18.95x (ISBN 0-521-29354-5). Cambridge U Pr.

Goody, Peter. Horse Anatomy. (Illus.). 11.95 (ISBN 0-85131-230-6, BL2351, Dist. by Miller). J A Allen.

Goody, Peter C. Horse Anatomy. 1978. 25.00 (ISBN 0-87556-610-3). Saifer.

Goody, Phyllis B. Julio, the Shoeshine Boy. (gr. 2-5). 1977. 6.50 (ISBN 0-682-48790-2). Exposition Pr FL.

Goody, Richard & Walker, James C. Atmospheres. (Foundations of Earth Science Ser). (Illus.). 160p. 1972. ref. ed. o.p. 8.95 (ISBN 0-13-050096-8); pap. 15.95 ref. ed. (ISBN 0-13-050088-7). P-H.

Goody, Roy W. The Intelligent Microcomputer. 354p. 1982. text ed. 28.95 (ISBN 0-574-21560-3, 13-4560); instr. guide avail. (ISBN 0-574-21561-1, 13-4561). SRA.

--Microcomputer Fundamentals. 300p. 1980. pap. text ed. 16.95 (ISBN 0-574-21540-9, 13-4540); instr's. guide avail. (ISBN 0-574-21541-7, 13-4541). SRA.

--The Versatile Microcomputer: The Motorola Family. 360p. 1984. text ed. 28.95 (ISBN 0-574-21595-6, 13-4595); free tchr's. ed (ISBN 0-574-21596-4, 13-4596). SRA.

Goodyear, Carmen. The Sheep Book. (Illus.). 25p. (Orig.). (ps-1). 1972. pap. 3.25 (ISBN 0-914996-02-9). Lollipop Power.

Goodyear, Don L., jt. ed. see Bitter, James A.

Goodyear, F. H., intro. by. A Growing American Treasure: Acquisition since 1978. (Illus.). 64p. 1984. 6.95 (ISBN 0-317-19587-5). Penn Acad Art.

Goodyear, F. R., jt. ed. see Diggle, J.

Goodyear, Frank. Neil Welliver. 1985. 60.00 (ISBN 0-8478-0597-2). Rizzoli Intl.

Goodyear, Frank H., Jr. Contemporary American Realism Since 1960. (Illus.). 256p. 1981. 37.50 (ISBN 0-8212-1126-9, 153621); pap. 22.00 (ISBN 0-8212-1561-2, 153648). NYGS.

Goodyear, Frank, Jr. American Paintings in the Rhode Island Historical Society. LC 73-91890. (Illus.). 116p. 1974. 10.00 (ISBN 0-917012-33-X). RI Hist Soc.

Goodyear, Imogene, jt. auth. see Brunson, Madelon.

Goodyear, Imogene, ed. The Beauty of Wholeness: Program Resource for Women 1981. 1980. pap. 5.00 (ISBN 0-8309-0294-5). Herald Hse.

--Daily Bread. 1983. pap. 6.00 (ISBN 0-8309-0374-7). Herald Hse.

Goodyear, Peter. Commodore 64 LOGO: A Learning & Teaching Guide. 206p. 1984. pap. 14.95 (ISBN 0-471-81964-6). Wiley.

Goodyear, W. H. Renaissance & Modern Art. 1978. Repr. of 1908 ed. lib. bdg. 30.00 (ISBN 0-8495-1945-4). Arden Lib.

--Roman & Medieval Art. (Illus.). 307p. 1985. Repr. of 1893 ed. lib. bdg. 60.00 (ISBN 0-918377-78-1). Russell Pr.

Goodyear, William H. Greek Refinements. (Illus.). 1912. 125.00x (ISBN 0-685-69823-8). Elliots Bks.

Goodykoontz, Colin B. Home Missions on the American Frontier. LC 76-120619. 1970. Repr. lib. bdg. 31.50 (ISBN 0-374-93198-4). Octagon.

Goof, Chan. Ma-Ma Fu-Fu. 1984. 7.50 (ISBN 0-533-05975-5). Vantage.

Googe, B., tr. see Neogeorgus, Thomas.

Googe, Barnabe. Eglogs, Epytaphes, & Sonettes, (1563) LC 68-24209. (Illus.). 1969. Repr. of 1563 ed. lib. bdg. 25.00x (ISBN 0-8201-1060-4). Schol Facsimiles.

--Eglogs, Epytaphes & Sonnettes: 1563. Arber, Edward, ed. 128p. 1983. pap. 12.50 (ISBN 0-87556-103-9). Saifer.

--Selected Poems of Barnabe Googe. Stephens, Alan, ed. LC 80-29155. (Books of the Renaissance Ser.). 60p. 1981. Repr. of 1961 ed. lib. bdg. 22.50x (ISBN 0-313-22830-2, GOSEP). Greenwood.

Googe, Barnabe, tr. see Palingenius, Marcellus.

Googenough, J. B. & Jorgensen, C. K., eds. Cation Ordering & Electron Transfer. (Structure & Bonding Ser.: Vo. 61). (Illus.). 170p. 1985. 35.00 (ISBN 0-387-15446-9). Springer-Verlag.

Gookin, Daniel. Historical Account of the Doings & Sufferings of the Christian Indians in New England in the Years 1675, 1676, 1677. LC 76-141098. (Research Library of Colonial Americana). 1972. Repr. of 1836 ed. 21.00 (ISBN 0-405-03307-9). Ayer Co Pubs.

--Historical Collections of the Indians in New England, of Their Several Nations, Numbers, Customs, Manners, Religion & Government, Before the English Planted There. LC 70-141099. (Research Library of Colonial Americana). 1972. Repr. of 1792 ed. 23.50 (ISBN 0-405-03308-7). Ayer Co Pubs.

Gool, W. Van see Hagenmuller, Paul & Van Gool, W.

Goold, Douglas, jt. auth. see Dockrill, Michael.

Goold, G. P., ed. Catullus. (Duckworth Classical, Medieval & Renaissance Editions Ser.). 272p. 1983. pap. 13.50x (ISBN 0-7156-1710-9, BPA-04893, Pub. by Duckworth England). Biblio Dist.

--Harvard Studies in Classical Philology. Incl. Vol. 63. 528p. 1958. 22.50x (ISBN 0-674-37914-4); Vol. 71. 352p. 1967. 18.50x (ISBN 0-674-37917-9); Vol. 72. 405p. 1968. 20.00x (ISBN 0-674-37918-7); Vol. 73. 333p. 1969. 18.50x (ISBN 0-674-37919-5); Vol. 74. 226p. 1970. 18.50x (ISBN 0-674-37920-9); Vol. 75. 1971. 14.00x (ISBN 0-674-37921-7); Vol. 76. 1972. 17.50x (ISBN 0-674-37922-5); Vol. 77. 1973. 15.00x (ISBN 0-674-37923-3). LC 44-32100. (Illus.). Harvard U Pr.

s. Harvard Studies in Classical -81. Incl. Vol. 78. text ed. 6-64021-7); Vol. 79. text ed. 4-37926-8); Vol. 80. text ed. 4-37927-6); Vol. 81. text ed. 20.00x (ISBN 0-674-37928-4). LC 44-32100. 296p. 1974. Harvard U Pr.

Goold, Nathan. The Wadsworth-Longfellow House. (Illus.). 1969. pap. 3.00 (ISBN 0-915592-04-5). Maine Hist.

--The Wadsworth-Longfellow House: Longfellow's Old Home. Repr. of 1915 ed. lib. bdg. 17.50 (ISBN 0-8492-4907-4). R West.

Goold-Adams, Richard. John Foster Dulles: A Reappraisal. LC 74-9272. 309p. 1974. Repr. of 1962 ed. lib. bdg. 55.00x (ISBN 0-8371-7638-7, GOJD). Greenwood.

Goolden, Jill, jt. auth. see Luxon, Bettina.

Gooley, Frank B., jt. ed. see Cooley, June H.

Goolrich, Robert, jt. auth. see Bach, Laurence.

Goolrick, Robert M. Public Policy Toward Corporate Growth: The ITT Merger Cases. 224p. 1978. 22.00x (ISBN 0-8046-9198-3, 9198). Assoc Faculty Pr.

Goolrick, William & Tanner, Ogden. The Battle of the Bulge. Time-Life Books Editors, ed. (World War II Ser.). 1980. 14.95 (ISBN 0-8094-2530-0). Time-Life.

Goolrick, William K. Rebels Resurgent. LC 84-23984. (Civil War Ser.). 1985. lib. bdg. 19.94 (ISBN 0-8094-4749-5, Pub. by Time-Life). Silver.

Goolsby, Elwin. Our Timberland Home: A History of Grant County. (Illus.). 450p. 1984. 25.00 (ISBN 0-914546-52-X). Rose Pub.

Goolsby, Leroy. How Bitter Are the Sweets. 64p. 1983. 7.95 (ISBN 0-89962-321-2). Todd & Honeywell.

Goolsby, Sam. Great Southern Wild Game Cookbook. LC 79-27954. (Illus.). 191p. 1980. 14.95 (ISBN 0-88289-226-6). Pelican.

Goonatilake, Susantha. Aborted Discovery: Science & Creativity in the Third World. (Third World Studies). 201p. 1984. pap. 9.25 (ISBN 0-86232-089-5, Pub. by Zed Pr England). Biblio Dist.

--Aborted Discovery: Science & Creativity in the Third World. (Third World Studies). 201p. Date not set. 23.25 (ISBN 0-86232-088-7, Pub. by Zed Pr England). Biblio Dist.

--Crippled Minds: An Exploration into Colonial Culture. 280p. 1982. text ed. 35.00x (ISBN 0-7069-1772-3, Pub. by Vikas India). Advent NY.

Gooneratne, Edmund R., ed. The Dhatu Katha Pakarana & Its Commentary. LC 78-72426. Repr. of 1892 ed. 21.50 (ISBN 0-404-17287-3). AMS Pr.

Gooneratne, Wilbert, jt. auth. see Richards, Peter.

Gooneratne, Yasmine. Alexander Pope. LC 76-4758. (British Authors Ser.). 160p. 1976. 29.95 (ISBN 0-521-21127-1); pap. 9.95 (ISBN 0-521-29051-1). Cambridge U Pr.

--Jane Austen. LC 75-123669. (British Authors Ser: Introductory Critical Studies). 1970. 29.95 (ISBN 0-521-07843-1). Cambridge U Pr.

Gooneratne, Yasmine, ed. Poems from India, Sri Lanka, Malaysia & Singapore. (Writing in Asia Ser.). 1980. 4.50x (ISBN 0-686-66066-8, 00219). Heinemann Ed.

--Stories from Sri Lanka. (Writing in Asia Ser.). 1979. pap. text ed. 5.50x (ISBN 0-686-58249-7, 00218). Heinemann Ed.

Goonetileke, H. A. Sri Lanka. (World Bibliographical Ser.: No. 20). Date not set. write for info. (ISBN 0-903450-33-X). ABC Clio.

Goonetilleke, D. C. Developing Countries in British Fiction. 282p. 1977. 19.50x (ISBN 0-87471-908-9). Rowman.

Goor, Daniel A. & Lillehei, C. Walton. Congenital Malformations of the Heart. (Illus.). 450p. 1975. 95.00 (ISBN 0-8089-0810-3, 791670). Grune.

Goor, J. van see Van Goor, J.

Goor, Kornelius Van see Block, Walter D. & Van Goor, Kornelius.

Goor, Nancy, jt. auth. see Goor, Ron.

Goor, Ron & Goor, Nancy. All Kinds of Feet. LC 83-45239. (A Let's-Read-&-Find-Out Science Bk.). (Illus.). 48p. (ps-3). 1984. 10.53i (ISBN 0-690-04384-8); PLB 11.89g (ISBN 0-690-04385-6). Crowell Jr Bks.

--In the Driver's Seat. LC 81-43885. (Illus.). 96p. (gr. 1-4). 1982. 10.53i (ISBN 0-690-04176-4); PLB 11.89g (ISBN 0-690-04177-2). Crowell Jr Bks.

--Shadows: Here, There, & Everywhere. LC 81-43036. (Illus.). 48p. (gr. k-3). 1981. 9.57i (ISBN 0-690-04132-2); PLB 9.89 (ISBN 0-690-04133-0). Crowell Jr Bks.

--Signs. LC 83-47649. (Illus.). 40p. (ps-1). 1983. 10.53i (ISBN 0-690-04354-6); PLB 10.89g (ISBN 0-690-04355-4). Crowell Jr Bks.

Gooriah, B. D. & Williams, F. P. The Investigation of Air Pollution: National Survey of Smoke & Sulphur Dioxide--Annual Summary Statistics for the Period 1963-4 to 1977-8, 1979. 1981. 60.00x (ISBN 0-686-97088-8, Pub. by W Spring England). State Mutual Bk.

Goormaghtigh, John, frwd. by see Freymond, Jacques.

Goorney, Howard. The Theatre Workshop Story. Hay, M. & Roberts, P., eds. 226p. 1981. pap. 11.95 (ISBN 0-413-48760-1, NO. 3454). Methuen Inc.

Goos, G., jt. auth. see Waite, W. M.

Goos, G., ed. see Hartmann, A. C.

Goos, G., jt. ed. see Reichertz, P. L.

Goos, G., et al, eds. Diana: An Intermediate Language for Ada. 201p. 1983. pap. 14.00 (ISBN 0-387-12695-3). Springer Verlag.

Goos, M., jt. ed. see Christophers, E.

Goose, D. H. & Appleton, J. Human Dentofacial Growth. LC 81-17895. (Illus.). 175p. 1982. 44.00 (ISBN 0-08-026394-1, H233); pap. 17.95 (ISBN 0-08-026393-3). Pergamon.

Goose, Edmund & Wise, Thomas J., eds. Selections from A. C. Swinburne. 288p. Date not set. lib. bdg. 25.00 (ISBN 0-8495-2101-7). Arden Lib.

Goosen, Kenneth R. Introduction to Managerial Accounting: A Business Game. 1976. pap. text ed. 17.95x (ISBN 0-673-15300-2). Scott F.

Goosens, Leon & Roxburgh, Edwin. Oboe. LC 77-15886. (The Yehudi Menuhin Music Guides Ser.). (Illus.). 1978. 14.95 (ISBN 0-02-871450-4); pap. 7.95 (ISBN 0-02-871460-1). Schirmer Bks.

Goosens, Louis, jt. auth. see Driven, Rene.

Goosey, M. T. Plastics for Electronics. 368p. 1985. 67.50 (ISBN 0-85334-338-1, Pub. by Elsevier Applied Sci England). Elsevier.

Goossen, Irvy W. Navajo Made Easier. 7th ed. LC 68-1360. 7.95 (ISBN 0-87358-023-0). Northland.

Goossens, Eugene. Overture & Beginners: A Musical Autobiography. LC 71-138240. (Illus.). 327p. 1972. Repr. of 1951 ed. lib. bdg. 19.50x (ISBN 0-8371-5597-5, GOOB). Greenwood.

Goossens, Mathias, ed. With the Church. 6.95 (ISBN 0-8199-0148-2, L39000). Franciscan Herald.

Goot, Henry V. Vander see Vander Goot, Henry V.

Goot, Henry Vander, ed. Creation & Method: Critical Essays on Christocentric Theology. LC 80-6245. 162p. 1982. lib. bdg. 23.50 (ISBN 0-8191-1921-0); pap. text ed. 11.25 (ISBN 0-8191-1922-9). U Pr of Amer.

Goot, Mary Vander see Vander Goot, Mary.

Gootesman, Meir U. Sparks from the Torah. 141p. pap. 7.95 (ISBN 0-88795-024-8). W W Pro Inter.

Gootlieb, William, ed. see Prevention Magazine Editors.

Gotman, Norman & Gootman, Phyllis M., eds. Perinatal Cardiovascular Function. (Illus.). 408p. 1983. 65.00 (ISBN 0-8247-1671-X). Dekker.

Gootman, Phyllis M., jt. ed. see Gootman, Norman.

Gootnick, David. Getting a Better Job. (Illus.). 1978. pap. 6.95 (ISBN 0-07-023745-X). McGraw.

Gootnick, David & Gootnick, Margaret M., eds. The Standard Handbook of Business Communication. 432p. 1984. 29.95x (ISBN 0-02-912660-6). Free Pr.

Gootnick, Margaret M. Action Tools for Managing the Accounting Staff. 224p. 1984. 29.95 (ISBN 0-02-912350-X). Free pr.

Gootnick, Margaret M., jt. ed. see Gootnick, David.

Gootzeit, Jack M. The Multihandicapped: Serving the Severely Disabled. 300p. 1981. text ed. 29.50x (ISBN 0-8290-0556-0); pap. text ed. 14.95x (ISBN 0-8290-0269-3). Irvington.

Gootzeit, Michael J. David Ricardo. (Essays on the Great Economists Ser.). 90p. 1975. pap. 10.00x (ISBN 0-231-03916-6). Columbia U Pr.

Goovaerts, M. J., et al. Insurance Premiums: Theory & Applications. 406p. 1983. 57.75 (ISBN 0-444-86772-4, I-404-83, North Holland). Elsevier.

Gooze, Mitchell. The S6800 Family. 224p. pap. 18.95 (ISBN 0-201-03399-2). Addison-Wesley.

Goozner, Calman. Arithmetic Skills Workbook. (gr. 7-12). 1973. text ed. 11.67 (ISBN 0-87720-238-9); pap. text ed. 7.58 (ISBN 0-87720-237-0); workbook 9.00, (ISBN 0-87720-236-2). AMSCO Sch.

--Business Math the Easy Way. (The Easy Way Ser.). 256p. 1983. pap. 7.95 (ISBN 0-8120-2513-X). Barron.

--Clerical Practice Skills. (gr. 10 up). 1978. pap. text ed. 8.92 (ISBN 0-87720-403-9). AMSCO Sch.

--Computational Skills for College Students. 1976. pap. text ed. 7.60 (ISBN 0-87720-976-6). AMSCO Sch.

Gopal. How India Struggled for Freedom. 1967. 8.75x (ISBN 0-89684-412-9). Orient Bk Dist.

Gopal, jt. auth. see Sharma, Rama.

Gopal, Bhargava. Urban Problems & Policy Perspectives. 531p. (Orig.). 1981. 49.95 (ISBN 0-317-12338-6, Pub. by Abhinav Pub India). Asia Bk Corp.

Gopal, Brij & Bhardwaj, N. Elements of Ecology. (Illus.). 200p. 1979. text ed. 15.00x (ISBN 0-7069-0754-X, Pub. by Vikas India). Advent NY.

Gopal, Erode S. Specific Heats at Low Temperatures. LC 65-11339. (International Cyrogenics Monographs). 240p. 1966. 45.00x (ISBN 0-306-30222-5, Plenum Pr). Plenum Pub.

Gopal, Kokila K., jt. auth. see Gopal, Krishan.

Gopal, Krishan & Gopal, Kokila K. West Asia & North Africa: A Documentary Study of Major Crises, 1974-78. 434p. 1981. 37.50x (ISBN 0-86590-012-4). Apt Bks.

Gopal, Lallanji. Economic Life of Northern India. 1965. 4.50 (ISBN 0-89684-200-2). Orient Bk Dist.

Gopal, M. Modern Control System Theory. 644p. 1984. 27.95 (ISBN 0-470-27424-7). Halsted Pr.

Gopal, M., jt. auth. see Nagrath, I. J.

Gopal, Madan. Sir Chhotu Ram: A Political Biography. 1977. 9.00x (ISBN 0-88386-946-2). South Asia Bks.

Gopal, R., et al, eds. Energy Conservation in Building Heating & Air Conditioning Systems. 112p. 1978. 18.00 (ISBN 0-685-66798-7, H00116). ASME.

Gopal, R., et al, eds. see American Society of Mechanical Engineers.

Gopal, Ram. India, China, Tibet Triangle. 1966. pap. 2.00 (ISBN 0-88253-139-5). Ind-US Inc.

--Trials of Jawaharlal Nehru. 133p. 1964. 24.00x (ISBN 0-7146-1557-9, F Cass Co). Biblio Dist.

Gopal, S. The Mind of Jawaharlal Nehru. 50p. 1980. pap. text ed. 3.95x (ISBN 0-86131-205-8, Pub. by Orient Longman Ltd India). Apt Bks.

--Selected Works of Jawaharlal Nehru, Vol. 14. cancelled (ISBN 0-8364-0904-3, Orient Longman). South Asia Bks.

Gopal, S., jt. auth. see Nehru, J.

Gopal, S., ed. Selected Works of Jawaharlal Nehru. (Second Ser.). (Illus.). 1984. Vol. 1. 34.95x (ISBN 0-19-561636-7); Vol. 2. 29.95x. Oxford U Pr.

Gopal, S., ed. see Nehru, J.

Gopal, Sarvepalli. British Policy in India, Eighteen Fifty-Eight to Nineteen Five. LC 65-19149. (Cambridge South Asian Studies: No. 1). pap. 108.80 (ISBN 0-317-11306-2, 2051395). Bks Demand UMI.

--Jawaharlal Nehru: A Biography, Vol. 2, 1947-1956. LC 75-33411. (Illus.). 1979. 22.50x (ISBN 0-674-47311-6). Harvard U Pr.

--Jawaharlal Nehru: A Biography, Vol. 1, 1889-1947. 416p. 1976. 25.00x (ISBN 0-674-47310-8). Harvard U Pr.

--Jawaharlal Nehru: A Biography, 1956-1964, Vol. III. LC 75-33411. (Illus.). 352p. 1984. text ed. 22.50x (ISBN 0-674-47312-4). Harvard U Pr.

Gopal, Sarvepalli, ed. see Nehru, Jawaharlal.

Gopal, Surendra. Patna in Nineteenth Century. 1983. 9.00x (ISBN 0-8364-0933-7, Pub. by Naya Prokash India). South Asia Bks.

Gopalakrishnan, Chennat, ed. Emerging Marine Economy of the Pacific. (Illus.). 256p. 1984. text ed. 39.95 (ISBN 0-250-40637-3). Butterworth.

Gopalakrishnan, P., jt. auth. see Sandilya, M. S.

Gopalakrishnan, R. The Geography & Politics of Afghanistan. 275p. 1982. text ed. 22.00x (ISBN 0-391-02726-3, Pub. by Concept). Humanities.

Gopalakrishnan, S. & Cooper, P., eds. Performance Prediction of Centifugal Pumps & Compressors. 296p. 1980. 38.00 (ISBN 0-317-33593-6, 100127); members 19.00 (ISBN 0-317-33594-4). ASME.

Gopaleen, Myles na, pseud. The Best of Myles. 400p. 1983. pap. 6.95 (ISBN 0-14-006366-8). Penguin.

Gopalkrishnan, S. & Salant, R. F., eds. Fluid Mechanics of Mechanical Seals. 1982. 14.00 (H00232). ASME.

Gopen, George D. Writing from a Legal Perspective. LC 80-27849. 225p. 1981. text ed. 14.95 (ISBN 0-8299-2123-0). West Pub.

Gopi Krishna. The Inner World. 12p. 1978. pap. 1.95 (ISBN 0-88697-001-6). Life Science.

--To Those Concerned Citizens. (Illus.). 16p. 1978. pap. 1.95 (ISBN 0-88697-002-4). Life Science.

Gopinath, B. see Levin, Simon.

Gopinath, Santha. Customer Satisfaction in the Postal Services. 105p. 1980. text ed. 11.25x (ISBN 0-391-02125-7). Humanities.

Gopinathan, V. Plasticity Theory & Its Application in Metal Forming. 211p. 1982. 21.95 (ISBN 0-470-27529-4). Halsted Pr.

Gopiparanadhana dasa Adhikari, ed. see Hridayananda dasa Goswami Acaryadeva.

Gopiparanadhana dasa Adhikari, et al, eds. see Hridayananda dasa Goswami Acaryadeva.

Goplerud, C. Peter, III. Coal Development & Use: The Legal Constraints & Incentives. LC 80-8890. 320p. 1982. 31.50x (ISBN 0-669-04403-2). Lexington Bks.

Goplerud, C. Peter, III, jt. auth. see Beck, Robert E.

Goplerud, Dena, jt. auth. see Fleming, Jo Ellen.

Gopnik, I. & Gopnik, Myrna. From Models to Modules. Pylyshyn, Zenon, ed. (Theoretical Issues in Cognitive Science Ser.). 288p. 1986. text ed. 32.50 (ISBN 0-89391-355-3). Ablex Pub.

Gopnik, Myrna. Linguistic Structures in Scientific Texts. (Janua Linguarum, Ser. Minor: No. 129). 1972. text ed. 15.20x (ISBN 90-2792-295-0). Mouton.

Gopnik, Myrna, jt. auth. see Gopnik, I.

Goppelt, Leonard. Theology of the New Testament: Jesus & the Gospels, Vol I. Alsup, John E., tr. LC 80-28947. 316p. 1981. 15.95 (ISBN 0-8028-2384-X). Eerdmans.

--Typos: The Typological Interpretation of the Old Testament in the New. 1982. 15.95 (ISBN 0-8028-3562-7). Eerdmans.

Goppelt, Leonhard. Theology of the New Testament: The Variety & Unity of the Apostolic Witness to Christ, Vol. II. 248p. 1983. 17.95 (ISBN 0-8028-2385-8). Eerdmans.

Gora, J. M. Due Process of Law. Haiman, Franklyn S., ed. (To Protect These Rights Ser.). 278p. 1983. pap. 10.00 (ISBN 0-8442-6003-7, 6003-7, Passport Bks.). Natl Textbk.

Gora, Joanne. The New Female Criminal: Empirical Reality or Social Myth. LC 82-7685. 160p. 1982. 23.95 (ISBN 0-03-062007-4). Praeger.

Gora, Michael H. Blood Coast: A Novel of South Florida. 1980. 12.50 (ISBN 0-682-49606-5, Banner). Exposition Pr FL.

Gora, Thomas, tr. see Kristeva, Julia.

Goran, Horris. A Preface to Astronomy. LC 74-81581. (Illus.). 150p. 1975. pap. 4.95x (ISBN 0-87762-158-6). Technomic.

Goran, Lester. Mrs. Beautiful. 1985. 14.95 (ISBN 0-88282-010-9). New Horizon NY.

Goran, Marjorie & Goran, Morris. The Lure of Longevity: The Art & Science of Living Longer. LC 82-83979. 120p. (Orig.). 1984. pap. text ed. 12.95 (ISBN 0-88247-709-9). R & E Pubs.

Goran, Morris. Can Science Be Saved? LC 81-121. 94p. 1981. perfect bound 9.95 (ISBN 0-88247-593-2). R & E Pubs.

--Conquest of Pollution. LC 81-184272. 281p. 1982. 30.00x (ISBN 0-915250-37-3). Environ Design.

--Fact, Fraud, & Fantasy: The Occult & Pseudosciences. (Quality Paperback Ser.: No. 356). 189p. 1980. pap. 3.95 (ISBN 0-8226-0356-X). Littlefield.

--Story of Fritz Haber. (Illus.). 1967. 15.95x (ISBN 0-8061-0756-1). U of Okla Pr.

--Ten Lessons of the Energy Crisis. LC 80-130511. 1980. 19.80x (ISBN 0-915250-35-7). Environ Design.

Goran, Morris, jt. auth. see Goran, Marjorie.

Goran, Ruth, jt. auth. see Hale, Lloyd S.

Goran, Ulf. Play Guitar. Britten, Paul, tr. (Illus.). 1974. pap. 5.75 (ISBN 0-19-322210-8). Oxford U Pr.

--Play Together for Voices & Guitar. Britten, Paul, tr. 1974. pap. 3.25 (ISBN 0-19-322212-4). Oxford U Pr.

Goran, Ulf., et al. Play a Tune on Recorder & Guitar. Pehrsson, Clas, ed. (Illus., Incl. a 33.3 record). 1975. pap. 6.00 (ISBN 0-19-322206-X). Oxford U Pr.

Gorbach, Sherwood L. & Zimmerman, David R. The Doctor's Anti-Breast Cancer Diet: How the Right Foods Can Reduce Your Risk of Breast Cancer. 1984. 15.95 (ISBN 0-671-49552-6). S&S.

Gorbach, Sherwood L., et al. Manual of Surgical Infections. (The Spiral Manual Ser.). 384p. 1984. spiral bdg. 17.95 (ISBN 0-316-32070-6). Little.

Gorbachev, et al. The Soviets Want Peace. (Illus.). 128p. (Orig.). 1985. pap. 3.25 (ISBN 0-7178-0635-9). Intl Pubs Co.

Gorbachev, V. M. & Zamyatnin, A. A. Nuclear Reactions in Heavy Elements: A Data Handbook. LC 79-40928. 460p. 1980. 140.00 (ISBN 0-08-023595-6). Pergamon.

Gorbanevskaia, Natal'Ia. Dereviannyi Angel. 1981. 22.50 (ISBN 0-88233-662-2). Ardis Pubs.

Gorbanevskaya, Natalia, tr. see Milosz, Czeslaw.

Gorbanevskaya, Natalya. Chuzhie Kamni. (Russica Poetry Ser.: No. 3). 70p. (Orig., Rus.). 1983. 13.00 (ISBN 0-89830-077-0); pap. 5.95. Russica Pubs.

Gorbatskii, Vitalii G. Exploding Stars & Galaxies. Lerman, Z., ed. LC 72-184984. (U. S. National Aeronautics & Space Administration. NASA Technical Translation Ser.: TT F-559). (Illus.). 1970. pap. 31.80 (2003732). Bks Demand UMI.

Gorbaty, Martin L. & Harney, Brian M., eds. Refining of Synthetic Crudes. LC 79-21098. (Advance in Chemistry: No. 179). 1979. 39.95 (ISBN 0-8412-0456-X). Am Chemical.

Gorbaty, Martin L. & Ouchi, K., eds. Coal Structure. LC 80-24104. (ACS Advances in Chemistry Ser.: No. 192). 1981. 39.95 (ISBN 0-8412-0524-8). Am Chemical.

Gorbaty, Martin L., et al, eds. Coal Science, Vol. 3. LC 82-179203. (Serial Publication Ser.). 1984. 90.00 (ISBN 0-12-150703-3). Acad Pr.

Gorbea, J. Q. Tecnicas Mecanograficas Modernas. 3rd ed. 240p. 14.72 (ISBN 0-07-023791-3). McGraw.

Gorbea, Josefina Q. see De Gorbea, Josefina Q., et al.

Gorbet, Larry P. A Grammar of Diegueno Nominals. LC 75-25116. (American Indian Linguistics Ser.). 1976. lib. bdg. 51.00 (ISBN 0-8240-1967-9). Garland Pub.

Gorbman, Aubrey, et al. Comparative Endocrinology. LC 82-13455. 572p. 1983. 34.95 (ISBN 0-471-06266-9, Pub. by Wiley-Interscience). Wiley.

Gorce, Pierre F. La see La Gorce, Pierre F.

Gorchakov, Nikolai. Stanislavsky Directs. Goldina, Marina, tr. 416p. 1985. pap. 10.95 (ISBN 0-87910-051-6). Limelight Edns.

Gorchakov, Nikolai A. Theater in Soviet Russia. Lehrman, E., tr. LC 72-2996. (Select Bibliography Reprint Ser.). 1972. Repr. of 1957 ed. 43.00 (ISBN 0-8369-6869-7). Ayer Co Pubs.

Gorchakov, Nikolai M. Stanislavsky Directs. Goldina, Miriam, tr. LC 73-15243. 402p. 1974. Repr. of 1954 ed. lib. bdg. 45.00x (ISBN 0-8371-7164-4, GOSD). Greenwood.

Gorchakov, O., ed. see Furmanov, Dmitry A.

Gorczynski, Renata, tr. see Zagajewski, Adam.

Gorczynski, Wladyslaw. Comparison of Climate of the United States & Europe: Especially Poland & Her Baltic Coast. 288p. 1945. 8.00 (ISBN 0-940962-03-9). Polish Inst Art & Sci.

Gordan, Gilbert S. & Vaughan, Cynthia. Clinical Management of the Osteoporoses. LC 77-353507. pap. 54.30 (ISBN 0-317-26193-2, 2052073). Bks Demand UMI.

Gordan, Joan, ed. Margaret Mead: The Complete Bibliography 1925-1975. 1976. text ed. 20.80x (ISBN 90-2793-026-0). Mouton.

Gordan, John D. Arnold Bennett, the Centenary of His Birth: An Exhibition in the Berg Collection. LC 68-21054. (Illus.). 1968. pap. 5.00 (ISBN 0-87104-015-8). NY Pub Lib.

Gorday, Peter. Principles of Patristic Exegesis: Romans 9-11 in Origen, John Chrysostom & Augustine. LC 83-20588. (Studies in the Bible & Early Christianity: Vol. 4). 424p. 1984. 69.95x (ISBN 0-88946-602-5). E Mellen.
Gorden, Morton, jt. auth. see Lerner, Daniel.
Gorden, Raymond L. Interviewing: Strategy, Techniques & Tactics. 3rd ed. 1980. 27.00x (ISBN 0-256-02370-0). Dorsey.
--Living in Latin America. 1974. text ed. 9.00 (ISBN 0-8442-9341-5). Natl Textbk.
--Unidimensional Scaling of Social Variables: Concepts & Procedures. LC 76-26443. 1977. 18.00 (ISBN 0-02-912580-4). Free Pr.
Gorden, William I. & Miller, John R. Managing Your Communication: In & for the Organization. (Illus.). 280p. 1983. pap. 9.95x (ISBN 0-88133-007-8). Waveland Pr.
Gordenker, Leon, jt. auth. see Baehr, Peter R.
Gordenker, Leon, ed. The United Nations in International Politics. LC 71-132239. (Center of International Studies Ser.). 1971. 26.00x (ISBN 0-691-05615-3). Princeton U Pr.
Gordenker, Leon, jt. ed. see Davison, W. Phillips.
Gorder, Cheryl. Home Schools: An Alternative. 201p. (Orig.). 1985. pap. 7.95 (ISBN 0-933025-00-9). Blue Bird Pub.
Gorder, Cheryl, ed. Who's Who in Antiques. (Illus.). 1985. 14.95 (ISBN 0-933025-01-7); pap. 18.95 (ISBN 0-933025-02-5). Blue Bird Pub.
Gordett, Marea. Freeze Tag. 15.00x (ISBN 0-8195-2117-5); pap. 6.95 (ISBN 0-8195-1118-8). Wesleyan U Pr.
Gordeyev, S. Vladimir: A Guide. 143p. 1983. 7.95 (ISBN 0-8285-2683-4, Pub. by Raduga Pubs USSR). Imported Pubns.
Gordh & Gordon. The Privately Printed Papers of A. A. Girault: Memoir Twenty-Eight. 400p. 1979. 30.00 (ISBN 0-686-40426-2). Am Entom Inst.
Gordh, Gordon & Trjapitzin, V. Taxonomic Studies of the Encyrtidae with the Desriptions of New Species & a New Genus: Hymenoptera: Chalcidoidea. (Publications in Entomology: Vol. 93). 1982. pap. 10.00 (ISBN 0-520-09629-0). U of Cal Pr.
Gordian Associates for the U. S. Department of Energy. Heat Pump Technology: A Survey of Technical Developments, Market Prospects & Research Needs. 464p. 1980. Repr. of 1978 ed. 44.95x (ISBN 0-89934-017-2, H-010PP). Solar Energy Info.
Gordillo, Agustin. Participation in Latin America. 1983. 7.95 (ISBN 0-533-05291-2). Vantage.
Gordimer, Nadine. Burger's Daughter. 362p. 1980. pap. 5.95 (ISBN 0-14-005593-2). Penguin.
--Burger's Daughter. 1979. 10.95 (ISBN 0-670-19475-1). Viking.
--The Conservationist. 288p. 1975. 12.95 (ISBN 0-670-23883-X). Viking.
--The Conservationist. 1983. pap. 4.95 (ISBN 0-14-004716-6). Penguin.
--A Guest of Honour. 1983. pap. 5.95 (ISBN 0-14-003696-2). Penguin.
--July's People. 1982. pap. 5.95 (ISBN 0-14-006140-1). Penguin.
--July's People. LC 80-24877. 192p. 1981. 10.95 (ISBN 0-670-41048-9). Viking.
--Late Bourgeois World. 1983. pap. 3.95 (ISBN 0-14-005614-9). Penguin.
--Selected Stories. LC 75-29460. 381p. 1976. 11.95 (ISBN 0-670-63197-3). Viking.
--Selected Stories. 448p. 1983. pap. 5.95 (ISBN 0-14-006737-X). Penguin.
--Soldier's Embrace. 1982. pap. 4.95 (ISBN 0-14-005925-3). Penguin.
--A Soldier's Embrace. 144p. 1980. 8.95 (ISBN 0-670-65638-0). Viking.
--Something Out There. 1984. 15.95 (ISBN 0-670-65660-7). Viking.
--Something Out There. (Fiction Ser.). 208p. 1986. pap. 5.95 (ISBN 0-14-007711-1). Penguin.
--A World of Strangers. 272p. 1984. pap. 6.95 (ISBN 0-14-001704-6). Penguin.
Gordin, Abba. Communism Unmasked. 1976. lib. bdg. 59.95 (ISBN 0-8490-1649-5). Gordon Pr.
Gordin, Morris. Utopia in Chains: An American's Experience in Red Russia. 1976. lib. bdg. 59.95 (ISBN 0-8490-2792-6). Gordon Pr.
Gordis, Leon. Epidemiology of Chronic Lung Diseases in Children. LC 72-11516. pap. 39.50 (ISBN 0-317-19874-2, 2023101). Bks Demand UMI.
Gordis, Leon, jt. auth. see Markowitz, Milton.
Gordis, Leon, jt. auth. see Nathanson, Neal.
Gordis, Leon, jt. ed. see Nathanson, Neal.
Gordis, Philip L. Property & Casualty Insurance. 28th ed. 750p. 1983. lib. bdg. 30.00 (ISBN 0-942326-09-1, 26520). Rough Notes.
Gordis, R. The Book of Job: Commentary, New Translation & Special Studies. (Moreshet Ser: No. 2). 39.50x (ISBN 0-87334-003-5, Pub. by Jewish Theol Seminary). Ktav.
Gordis, Robert. The Biblical Text in the Making: A Study of the Kethibh-Qere. rev. ed. 1971. 24.95x (ISBN 0-87068-157-5). Ktav.
--The Book of God & Man. LC 65-25126. 1978. pap. 8.95x (ISBN 0-226-30410-8, P771, Phoen). U of Chicago Pr.
--The Book of Job: Commentary, New Translation & Special Studies. LC 78-2305. 1977. 49.50x (ISBN 0-87334-003-5). Ktav.
--Faith for Moderns. 2nd rev. ed. LC 76-136424. 1971. pap. 7.95 (ISBN 0-8197-0001-0, 10001). Bloch.
--Koheleth: The Man & His World: A Study of Ecclesiastes. rev. ed. LC 67-26988. 1968. pap. 10.95 (ISBN 0-8052-0166-1). Schocken.
--Love & Sex: A Modern Jewish Perspective. 290p. 1978. 8.95 (ISBN 0-374-19252-9). FS&G.
--Megillat Esther: The Mascretic Hebrew Text with Introduction, New Translation & Commentary. 1977. 3.95x (ISBN 0-87068-763-8). Ktav.
--Poets, Prophets, & Sages: Essays in Biblical Interpretation. LC 79-98984. pap. 111.50 (2055498). Bks Demand UMI.
--Root & the Branch: Judaism & the Free Society. LC 62-17133. 1962. 20.00x (ISBN 0-226-30411-6). U of Chicago Pr.
--The Song of Songs & Lamentations: A Commentary & Translation. 1974. 25.00x (ISBN 0-87068-256-3). Ktav.
--Understanding Conservative Judaism. 15.00x (ISBN 0-87068-680-1). Ktav.
Gordley, James R., jt. auth. see Von Mehren, Arthur.
Gordo-Guarinos, Francisco. Diccionario De Sinonimos y Antonimos. 300p. (Span.). 1979. pap. 4.50 (ISBN 84-346-0311-X, S-29130). French & Eur.
Gordo Guarinos, Francisco. Diccionario Escolar Roble. 5th ed. 712p. (Span.). 1975. pap. 4.50 (ISBN 84-346-0191-5, S-50046). French & Eur.
Gordo-Guarinos, Francisco. Diccionario Manual De la Lengua Espanol a-Z. 3rd ed. 688p. (Span.). 1979. pap. 5.25 (ISBN 84-346-0083-8, S-27485). French & Eur.
--Diccionario Manual De la Lengua Espanol A-Z. 3rd ed. 688p. (Span.). 1979. 6.95 (ISBN 84-346-0084-6, S-27486). French & Eur.
Gordon. Clinical Management of the Osteophoroses. 38.50 (ISBN 0-85602-059-1). Wiley.
--Ordeal. 1984. pap. 3.95 (ISBN 0-425-07987-2, Medallion). Berkley Pub.
--Wordforms: Contexts, Strategies & Practice Book, 2 vols. 2nd ed. 1985. Bk. 1, 272 pgs. write for info. (ISBN 0-534-03389-X); Bk. 2, 272 pgs. write for info. (ISBN 0-534-03957-X). Wadsworth Pub.
Gordon & Rosenfield. Immigration Law & Procedure. 1983. write for info. (#325). Bender.
Gordon, jt. auth. see Lally.
Gordon, ed. Charles Lamb: Prose & Poetry with Essays. 1978. Repr. of 1921 ed. lib. bdg. 17.50 (ISBN 0-8414-5750-6). Folcroft.
Gordon, et al. Cases in Introductory Accounting. 104p. 1983. pap. 6.95 (ISBN 0-8403-3136-3). Kendall-Hunt.
Gordon, jt. auth. see Gordh.
Gordon, A. Studies in Physical Oceanography, 2 vols. 456p. 1972. Set. 113.50 (ISBN 0-677-12910-6); Vol. 1. 57.75 (ISBN 0-677-15160-8); Vol. 2. 69.50 (ISBN 0-677-15170-5). Gordon.
Gordon, A., jt. auth. see Fulton, O.
Gordon, A. C. & Page, Thomas N. Befo' de War: Echoes in Negro Dialect. facsimile ed. LC 79-154076. (Black Heritage Library Collection). 1888. 15.25 (ISBN 0-8369-8787-X). Ayer Co Pubs.
Gordon, A. D. Businessmen & Politics: Rising Nationalism & a Modernising Economy in Bombay, 1918-1933. 1978. 15.00 (ISBN 0-8364-0194-8). South Asia Bks.
--Classification: Methods for the Exploratory Analysis of Multivariate Data. 240p. 1981. 27.50 (ISBN 0-412-22850-5, NO.6547, Pub. by Chapman & Hall). Methuen Inc.
--Selected Essays. LC 73-2201. (The Jewish People; History, Religion, Literature Ser.). Repr. of 1938 ed. 25.50 (ISBN 0-405-05266-9). Ayer Co Pubs.
--Selected Essays. Silberschlag, E., ed. Burnce, Frances, tr. 1938. Repr. 20.00 (ISBN 0-8274-3349-2). R West.
Gordon, A. D., jt. auth. see Birks, H. J.
Gordon A Friesen International, Inc. The Ready Foods Systems for Health Care Facilities. LC 72-95360. 736p. 1973. 16.95 (ISBN 0-8436-0562-6). Van Nos Reinhold.
Gordon, A. H. Electrophoresis of Proteins in Polyacrylamide & Starch Gels, Vol. 1, Pt. 1. Rev. ed. LC 68-54514. (Laboratory Techniques in Biochemistry & Molecular Biology Ser.). 213p. 1975. pap. 18.00 (ISBN 0-444-10864-5, North-Holland). Elsevier.
Gordon, A. J., jt. auth. see Smith, R. F.
Gordon, A. J., et al. Hemodynamics of Aortic & Mitral Valve Disease. 144p. 1961. 32.50 (ISBN 0-8089-0157-5, 791670). Grune.
Gordon, A. M. Practical Programming for Non-Computer Professionals. 100p. 1984. pap. text ed. 18.10x (ISBN 0-471-81048-7). Wiley.
Gordon, A. V., jt. auth. see Tolskaya, M. S.
Gordon, Adele. Somebody's Mother. 48p. 1983. 6.95 (ISBN 0-89962-325-5). Todd & Honeywell.
Gordon, Adoniram J. Holy Spirit in Missions. pap. 2.25 (ISBN 0-87509-094-X). Chr Pubns.
--Ministry of Healing. pap. 2.95 (ISBN 0-87509-107-5). Chr Pubns.
Gordon, Adrian H. & Taylor, Ronald C. Computations of Surface Layer Air Trajectories, & Weather, in the Oceanic Tropics. LC 72-92065. (International Indian Ocean Expedition Meterological Monographs: No. 7). (Illus.). 112p. 1975. text ed. 20.00x (ISBN 0-8248-0253-5, Eastwest Ctr). UH Pr.
Gordon, Alan. Economics & Social Policy: An Introduction. 224p. 1982. 34.95x (ISBN 0-85520-527-X). Basil Blackwell.
--How to Choose School Leaves for Jobs. (Institute of Manpower Studies: No. 1). 110p. 1984. text ed. 21.50x (ISBN 0-566-00699-5). Gower Pub Co.
--Redundancy in the Nineteen Eighties: The Take-Up of Voluntary Schemes. LC 84-21052. (Institute of Manpower Studies: No. 6). 112p. 1984. pap. text ed. 23.50 (ISBN 0-566-00826-2). Gower Pub Co.
Gordon, Alan, et al. Employer Sponsorship of Undergraduate Engineers. 166p. 1985. text ed. 27.00x (ISBN 0-566-00993-5). Gower Pub Co.
Gordon, Albert I. Intermarriage: Interfaith, Interracial, Interethnic. LC 80-19279. (Illus.). xiii, 420p. 1980. Repr. of 1966 ed. lib. bdg. 32.50x (ISBN 0-313-22711-X, GOIN). Greenwood.
--Jews in Suburbia. LC 73-11749. 264p. 1973. Repr. of 1959 ed. lib. bdg. 15.00x (ISBN 0-8371-7088-5, COJS). Greenwood.
Gordon, Albert S., ed. Regulation of Hematopoiesis, 2 vols. Incl. Vol. 1. Red Cell Production. 780p. 79.50 (ISBN 0-306-50021-3); Vol. 2. White Cell & Platelet Production. 890p. 89.50 (ISBN 0-306-50022-1). LC 72-8589. 1970 (Plenum Pr). Plenum Pub.
Gordon, Albert S., jt. ed. see LoBue, Joseph.
Gordon, Albert S., et al, eds. Contemporary Hematology-Oncology, Vol. 3. 288p. 1984. 39.50x (ISBN 0-306-41535-6, Plenum Pr). Plenum Pub.
Gordon, Alexander, ed. Milton on the Son of God & the Holy Spirit (From the Treatise on Christian Doctrine) LC 73-4827. 1973. lib. bdg. 15.00 (ISBN 0-8414-2028-9). Folcroft.
Gordon, Alison. Foul Ball: Five Years in American League. 204p. 1985. 14.95 (ISBN 0-396-08651-9). Dodd.
Gordon, Alvin. Brooms of Mexico. (Illus.). 48p. 1973. 7.50 (ISBN 0-8165-0407-5, PS-3557065-B7). U of Ariz Pr.
Gordon, Andrew. An American Dreamer: A Psychoanalytic Study of the Fiction of Norman Mailer. LC 77-79778. 240p. 1981. pap. 8.95 (ISBN 0-8386-3066-9). Fairleigh Dickinson.
--The Evolution of Labor Relations in Japan: Heavy Industy, 1853-1955. (Harvard East Asian Monographs: No. 117). 400p. 1985. text ed. 25.00x (ISBN 0-674-27130-0). Harvard U Pr.
Gordon, Andrew C. & Heinz, John P., eds. Public Access to Information. LC 78-63009. 400p. 1979. Repr. 19.95 (ISBN 0-87855-278-2). Transaction Bks.
Gordon, Andrew J., jt. ed. see Seiber, R. Timothy.
Gordon, Andrew M. An American Dreamer: A Psychoanalytic Study of the Fiction of Norman Mailer. LC 77-89778. 240p. 1980. 22.50 (ISBN 0-8386-2158-9). Fairleigh Dickinson.
Gordon, Ann. Women Carved of Sun. (Illus.). 1974. 2.00 (ISBN 0-88447-034-2). Diana Pr.
Gordon, Ann & Browne, Kathryn W. Beginning & Beyond: Foundations in Early Childhood Education. LC 84-23000. 512p. 1985. text ed. 23.80 (ISBN 0-8273-2282-8); instr's. guide 3.60t (ISBN 0-8273-2283-6). Delmar.
Gordon, Anne. Death Is for the Living. 196p. 1984. 39.00 (ISBN 0-86228-089-3, Pub. by P Harris Scotland). State Mutual Bk.
Gordon, Armistead C. Allegra. LC 72-2103. (Studies in Byron, No. 5). 1972. Repr. of 1926 ed. lib. bdg. 39.95x (ISBN 0-8383-1474-0). Haskell.
--Allegra. 1926. 24.45 (ISBN 0-8274-1843-4). R West.
Gordon, Arnold J. & Ford, Richard A. Chemist's Companion: A Handbook of Practical Data, Techniques, & References. LC 72-6660. 560p. 1973. 49.95x (ISBN 0-471-31590-7, Pub. by Wiley-Interscience). Wiley.
Gordon, Arthur. Through Many Windows. 192p. 1982. 10.95 (ISBN 0-8007-1319-2). Revell.
--Touch of Wonder. (Orig.). pap. 2.95 (ISBN 0-515-07416-0). Jove Pubns.
--Touch of Wonder. 256p. 1974. 11.95 (ISBN 0-8007-0695-1). Revell.
--A Touch of Wonder. 256p. 1976. pap. 2.95 (ISBN 0-8007-8239-9, Spire Bks). Revell.
--A Touch of Wonder. 256p. 1984. pap. 6.95 (ISBN 0-8007-5172-8, Power Bks). Revell.
Gordon, Arthur, jt. auth. see Blanton, Smiley.
Gordon, Arthur E. Illustrated Introduction to Latin Epigraphy. LC 79-63546. (Illus.). 336p. 1983. text ed. 42.50x (ISBN 0-520-03898-3); pap. text ed. 19.95x (ISBN 0-520-05079-7, CAMPUS 313). U of Cal Pr.
--The Inscribed Fibula Praenestina: Problems of Authenticity. LC 75-620010. (University of California Publications: Classical Studies Ser.: Vol. 16). pap. 24.00 (ISBN 0-317-29518-7, 2021269). Bks Demand UMI.
Gordon, Arthur E., jt. auth. see Gordon, Joyce.
Gordon, Asa H. Sketches of Negro Life & History in South Carolina. 2nd ed. LC 76-122358. xxiv, 338p. 1971. pap. 6.95 (ISBN 0-87249-202-8). U of SC Pr.
Gordon, Audrey & Klass, Dennis. They Need to Know: How to Teach Children About Death. (Illus.). 1979. 10.95 (ISBN 0-13-917104-5, Spec); pap. 5.95 (ISBN 0-13-917096-0, Spec). P-H.
Gordon, B. L., et al. Apache Indians, Vol. VI. Horr, David A., ed. (American Indian Ethnohistory Ser.). 1978. lib. bdg. 51.00 (ISBN 0-8240-0708-5). Garland Pub.
Gordon, B. Le Roy. Human Geography & Ecology in the Sinu Country of Columbia. LC 77-4433. (Ibero-Americana: No. 39). 1977. Repr. of 1957 ed. lib. bdg. 15.00x (ISBN 0-8371-9047-9, GOHU). Greenwood.
Gordon, Barbara. Defects of the Heart. LC 82-48144. 336p. 1983. 14.37i (ISBN 0-06-015032-7, HarpT). Har-Row.
--Defects of the Heart. 1984. pap. 3.95 (ISBN 0-440-11866-2). Dell.
--I'm Dancing As Fast As I Can. 1980. pap. 3.95 (ISBN 0-553-23226-6). Bantam.
--I'm Dancing As Fast As I Can. LC 78-20165. 1979. 13.41i (ISBN 0-06-011499-1, HarpT). Har-Row.
Gordon, Barbara & Gordon, Elliott. How to Survive in the Free Lance Jungle. LC 80-68580. (Illus.). 119p. 1980. pap. 9.95 (ISBN 0-917168-06-2). Executive Comm.
Gordon, Barbara, jt. auth. see Lickey, Marvin E.
Gordon, Barclay F., ed. Olympic Architecture: Building for the Summer Games. LC 83-1228. (Illus.). 200p. 1983. 32.50 (ISBN 0-471-06069-0, Pub. by Wiley-Interscience); pap. 19.95 (ISBN 0-471-88281-X). Wiley.
Gordon, Barry. Astrophotography. 2nd ed. (Illus.). 224p. 1985. pap. text ed. 18.95 (ISBN 0-943396-07-7). Willmann-Bell.
--Economic Doctrine & Tory Liberalism Eighteen Twenty-Four to Eighteen Thirty. 1979. text ed. 28.50x (ISBN 0-06-492498-X). B&N Imports.
Gordon, Barry J. Non-Ricardian Political Economy. (Kress Library Publications: No. 20). 1967. pap. 8.95x (ISBN 0-678-09914-6, Baker Lib). Kelley.
Gordon, Belita, jt. auth. see Elifson, Joan.
Gordon, Benjamin L. New Judea: Jewish Life in Modern Palestine & Egypt. Davis, Moshe, ed. LC 77-70697. (America & the Holy Land Ser.). (Illus.). 1977. Repr. of 1919 ed. lib. bdg. 30.00x (ISBN 0-405-10251-8). Ayer Co Pubs.
Gordon, Bernard L. A Guide to Historical Southern New England. (Illus.). 24p. 0.75 (ISBN 0-910258-06-6). Book & Tackle.
--The Marine Fishes of Rhode Island. (Illus.). 148p. 1974. pap. 5.00 (ISBN 0-910258-00-7). Book & Tackle.
--Secret Lives of Fishes. rev. ed. (Illus.). 306p. 1980. pap. text ed. 7.95 (ISBN 0-910258-12-0). Book & Tackle.
Gordon, Bernard L., jt. auth. see Charlier, Roger H.
Gordon, Bernard L., ed. Energy from the Sea: Marine Resource Readings. new ed. (Illus.). 1977. pap. 12.50 (ISBN 0-910258-07-4). Book & Tackle.
--Energy from the Sea: Marine Resource Readings. LC 79-8826. (Illus.). 1980. pap. text ed. 16.75 (ISBN 0-8191-0887-1). U Pr of Amer.
--Hurricane in Southern New England: An Analysis of the Great Storm of 1938. LC 75-38912. (Illus.). 64p. 1976. pap. 4.00 (ISBN 0-910258-05-8). Book & Tackle.
--Man & the Sea. rev. ed. (Illus.). 1980. pap. text ed. 7.50 (ISBN 0-910258-10-4). Book & Tackle.
--Marine Careers: Selected Papers. 42p. 1974. 2.00 (ISBN 0-910258-02-3). Book & Tackle.
Gordon, Bertram. Collaborationism in France During the Second World War. LC 79-25281. (Illus.). 424p. 1980. 29.95x (ISBN 0-8014-1263-3). Cornell U Pr.
Gordon, Beverly. Domestic American Textiles: A Bibliographic Sourcebook. 217p. pap. 14.95 (ISBN 0-318-13870-0); pap. 12.95 members (ISBN 0-318-13871-9). Ctr Hist Am Needle.
--Feltmaking: Traditions, Techniques & Contemporary Explorations. (Illus.). 1980. 17.50 (ISBN 0-8230-1647-1). Watson-Guptill.
--The Final Steps: Traditional Methods & Contemporary Applications for Finishing Cloth by Hand. LC 82-81232. (Illus.). 36p. 1982. pap. 5.00 (ISBN 0-934026-07-6). Interweave.
--Shaker Textile Arts. LC 78-69899. (Illus.). 343p. 1980. 27.50x (ISBN 0-87451-158-5); pap. 15.95 (ISBN 0-87451-242-5). U Pr of New Eng.
Gordon, Beverly S. The First Year Alone. (Orig.). 1985. pap. 7.95 (ISBN 0-87233-082-6). Bauhan.
Gordon, Bezalel. House Divided: Israel in Crisis. 1984. 13.95 (ISBN 0-88015-022-X). Empire Bks.
Gordon, Bezalel, et al, trs. see Kahan, Yitzhak & Barak, Aharon.
Gordon, Bob. Early Electrical Appliances. (Shire Album Ser.: No. 124). (Illus.). 32p. (Orig.). 1984. pap. 2.95 (ISBN 0-85263-694-6, Pub. by Shire Pubns England). Seven Hills Bks.
Gordon, Bonnie. The Anatomy of Proteus: According to Merriam-Webster's Third International Dictionary of the English Language. LC 82-70153. (Artists' Bk.). (Illus.). 20p. (Orig.). 1982. pap. 4.50 (ISBN 0-89822-026-2). Visual Studies.
--The Anatomy of the Image Maps According to Merriam-Webster's Third International Dictionary of the English Language: Unabridged. LC 82-50789. (Artists' Book Ser.). 48p. (Orig.). 1983. pap. 10.00 (ISBN 0-89822-028-9). Visual Studies.
Gordon, Bonnie, ed. Songs from Unsung Worlds: Science In Poetry. 250p. 1985. 14.95 (ISBN 0-8176-3236-0); pap. 11.95 (ISBN 0-8176-3296-4). Birkhauser.

Gordon, Bonnie B. A Childhood in Reno. 32p. (Orig.). 1983. pap. text ed. 3.00 (ISBN 0-935252-33-9). Street Pr.
Gordon, Burgess. Understanding & Promoting the Resources of Aging People: A Guide to Care, Proper Environment & Well Being. 92p. 1981. 5.50 (ISBN 0-682-49599-9). Exposition Pr FL.
Gordon, Burton. A Panama Forest & Shore. (Illus., Orig.). 1983. 15.00 (ISBN 0-910286-88-4). Boxwood.
Gordon, Burton L. Monterey Bay Area: Natural History & Cultural Imprints. 2nd ed. LC 74-13912. (Illus.). 192p. 1977. pap. text ed. 7.95 (ISBN 0-910286-37-X). Boxwood.
Gordon, C. G. Colonel Gordon in Central Africa, 1874-1879. Hill, G. B., ed. Repr. of 1881 ed. 34.00 (ISBN 0-527-34600-4). Kraus Repr.
Gordon, C. W. & Canuto, V. The Earth One: The Upper Atmosphere, Ionisphere & Magnetosphere. (Handbook of Astronomy, Astrophysics & Geophysics Ser.: Vol. I). 420p. 1978. 103.95 (ISBN 0-677-16100-X). Gordon.
--Handbook of Astronomy, Astrophysics & Geophysics Vol. 1. (The Earth 1: The Upper Atmosphere, Ionosphere & Magnetosphre). 420p. 1978. 103.95. Gordon.
Gordon, C. Wayne, ed. The Uses of Sociology in Education. LC 6-16938. (National Society for the Study of Education Yearbooks Ser: No. 73, Pt. 2). xviii, 518p. 1974. 10.00x (ISBN 0-226-60115-3). U of Chicago Pr.
Gordon, Carl E. & Hindman, Neil. Elementary Set Theory: Proof Techniques. LC 74-14794. 1975. text ed. 13.95x (ISBN 0-02-845350-6). Hafner.
Gordon, Caroline. Aleck Maury, Sportsman. LC 74-164531. 1972. Repr. of 1934 ed. 18.50 (ISBN 0-8154-0400-X). Cooper Sq.
--Aleck Maury, Sportsman: A Novel. LC 80-14493. (Lost American Fiction Ser.). 308p. 1980. 12.95 (ISBN 0-8093-0972-6); pap. 6.95 (ISBN 0-8093-0988-2). S Ill U Pr.
--The Collected Stories. 352p. 1981. 17.95 (ISBN 0-374-12630-5); pap. 9.95 (ISBN 0-374-51675-8). FS&G.
--The Forest of the South. LC 83-45772. Repr. of 1945 ed. 25.00 (ISBN 0-404-20111-3). AMS Pr.
--Garden of Adonis. LC 70-164530. 1972. Repr. of 1937 ed. 22.50 (ISBN 0-8154-0399-2). Cooper Sq.
--Green Centuries. LC 76-164529. 1972. Repr. of 1941 ed. 23.50 (ISBN 0-8154-0398-4). Cooper Sq.
--Old Red & Other Stories. LC 79-164527. 1972. Repr. of 1963 ed. 18.50 (ISBN 0-8154-0396-8). Cooper Sq.
--The Southern Mandarins: Letters of Caroline Gordon to Sally Wood, 1924-1937. Wood, Sally, ed. LC 83-16229. 224p. 1984. text ed. 25.00x (ISBN 0-8071-1137-6). La State U Pr.
--Strange Children. LC 71-164525. 1972. Repr. of 1951 ed. 19.50 (ISBN 0-8154-0394-1). Cooper Sq.
--Women on the Porch. LC 78-164524. 1972. Repr. of 1944 ed. 19.50 (ISBN 0-8154-0393-3). Cooper Sq.
Gordon Centennial Book Committee, ed. Gordon, Nebraska: The First Hundred Years. (Illus.). 472p. 1984. 55.00 (ISBN 0-88107-020-3). Natl ShareGraphics.
Gordon, Chad & Johnson, Gayle, eds. Readings in Human Sexuality: Contemporary Perspectives. 2nd ed. 1980. pap. text ed. 12.50 scp (ISBN 0-06-042399-4, HarpC). Har-Row.
Gordon, Charles. The Two Tycoons: Charles Clore & Jack Cotton. (Illus.). 288p. 1984. 19.95 (ISBN 0-241-11256-7, Pub. by Hamish Hamilton England). David & Charles.
Gordon, Charles & Gordon, Ellen. Immigration & Nationality Law. LC 84-233728. 1984. write for info. Bender.
Gordon, Charles G. Journals of Major-Gen. Gordon, C. B. at Kartoum. LC 78-97401. (Illus.). Repr. of 1885 ed. 27.00x (ISBN 0-8371-2655-X, GOJ&, Pub. by Negro U Pr). Greenwood.
Gordon, Charlotte. How to Find What You Want in the Library. LC 77-12534. 1978. pap. 5.95 (ISBN 0-8120-0696-8). Barron.
Gordon, Clark. In Defense of Theology. 1984. 12.95 (ISBN 0-88062-123-0). Mott Media.
Gordon, Claude. Thirty Velocity Studies for Trumpet. (Ger. Fr. & Span.). 1981. pap. 6.95 (ISBN 0-8258-0213-X, 05092). Fischer Inc NY.
Gordon, Clifford K., ed. Coke & Other Solid Fuel Derivatives from Coal. LC 74-26747. 1976. text ed. 29.50x (ISBN 0-685-55477-5). Irvington.
Gordon, Coco. Raw Hands & Bagging. (Illus.). 1978. pap. 6.00 (ISBN 0-931956-00-5). Water Mark.
Gordon, Coco, jt. auth. see Roux, Barbara.
Gordon, Colin. Beyond the Looking Glass: Reflections of Her & Family. (Illus.). 1983. 19.95 (ISBN 0-15-112022-6). HarBraceJ.
Gordon, Colin, ed The Atlantic Alliance: A Selective Bibliography. 1978. 25.00x (ISBN 0-89397-041-7). Nichols Pub.
Gordon, Cosmo. Life & Genius of Lord Byron. LC 74-16130. 1974. Repr. of 1824 ed. lib. bdg. 12.50 (ISBN 0-8414-4401-3). Folcroft.
Gordon, Cyrus H. Adventures in the Nearest East. 1957. 6.95 (ISBN 0-911566-10-4). Ventnor.
--Ancient Near East. 1965. pap. 7.95 (ISBN 0-393-00275-6, Norton Lib). Norton.
--Before the Bible. LC 72-10828. (Essay Index Reprint Ser.). 1973. Repr. of 1962 ed. 24.00 (ISBN 0-8369-7219-8). Ayer Co Pubs.
--Common Background of Greek & Hebrew Civilizations. (Illus.). 1965. pap. 7.95 (ISBN 0-393-00293-4, Norton Lib). Norton.
--Evidence for the Minoan Language. 1966. 12.00 (ISBN 0-911566-06-6). Ventnor.
--Forgotten Scripts: Their Ongoing Discovery & Decipherment. rev. ed. LC 81-68822. 1982. 14.95 (ISBN 0-465-02484-X). Basic.
--Homer & Bible: The Origin & Character of East Mediterranean Literature. 1967. pap. 2.95 (ISBN 0-911566-03-1). Ventnor.
Gordon, D., ed. see Saxl, Fritz.
Gordon, D. I. Regional History of the Railway of Great Britain, Vol. 5. 1976. 19.95 (ISBN 0-7153-7431-1). David & Charles.
Gordon, D. L., jt. auth. see Smyth, Gordon D.
Gordon, Dane R. The Old Testament: A Beginning Survey. (Illus.). 400p. 1985. pap. text ed. 18.95 (ISBN 0-13-634031-8). P-H.
--Rochester Institute of Technology: Industrial Development & Educational Innovation in a American City. LC 82-6389. (Illus.). 450p. 1982. fine binding 89.95 (ISBN 0-88946-150-3). E Mellen.
Gordon, David. The Myths of School Self-Renewal. 1984. text ed. 26.95x (ISBN 0-8077-2755-5). Tchrs Coll.
--Problems in the Law of Mass Communications: Programmed Instruction. 1982 ed. 183p. 1982. pap. text ed. write for info. problems bk. (ISBN 0-88277-104-3). Foundation Pr.
--Therapeutic Metaphors. LC 78-58574. 1978. 10.95x (ISBN 0-916990-04-4). Meta Pubns.
--Translations from Lu Yu. (Juniper Bks: No. 25). 1978. pap. 4.00 (ISBN 0-685-60002-5). Juniper Pr Wi.
Gordon, David & Meyers-Anderson, Maribeth. Phoenix: Therapeutic Patterns of Milton H. Erickson. LC 81-85263. 1981. 14.00x (ISBN 0-916990-10-9). Meta Pubns.
Gordon, David, tr. from Chinese. Equinox: A Gathering of T'ang Poets. LC 73-181682. xx, 88p. 1975. 9.95x (ISBN 0-8214-0162-9, 82-81628). Ohio U Pr.
Gordon, David, tr. see Lu Yu.
Gordon, David B., ed. Hypertension: The Renal Basis. LC 79-6598. (Benchmark Papers in Human Physiology Ser.: Vol. 13). 448p. 1980. 51.50 (ISBN 0-87933-356-1). Van Nos Reinhold.
Gordon, David C. The Republic of Lebanon: A Nation in Jeopardy. LC 82-20108. (Profiles-Nations of the Contemporary Middle East). 171p. 1983. 20.00x (ISBN 0-86531-450-0); pap. text ed. 11.95x (ISBN 0-8133-0031-2). Westview.
Gordon, David F. The State & Decolonization in Kenya. (Westview Special Studies on Africa). 210p. 1985. pap. 21.00 (ISBN 0-8133-7111-2). Westview.
Gordon, David L. Employment & Development of Small Enterprises. (Sector Policy Paper). 93p. 1978. 5.00 (ISBN 0-686-36181-4, PP-7803). World Bank.
Gordon, David M. Merchants & Capitalists: Industrialization & Provincial Politics in Mid-Nineteenth-Century France. LC 83-18266. (Illus.). xi, 249p. 1985. 29.75 (ISBN 0-8173-0210-7). U of Ala Pr.
--Problems in Political Economy: An Urban Perspective. 2nd ed. 1977. pap. text ed. 15.95 (ISBN 0-669-92841-0). Heath.
--Theories of Poverty & Underemployment. 1973. pap. text ed. 12.95 (ISBN 0-669-89268-8). Heath.
--The Working Poor: Towards a State Agenda. Barker, Michael, ed. LC 79-67382. (Studies in State Development Policy: Vol. 4). 91p. 1979. pap. 9.95 (ISBN 0-934842-03-5). Coun State Plan.
Gordon, David M., et al. Segmented Work, Divided Workers: The Historical Transformation of Labor in the United States. LC 81-17010. (Illus.). 272p. 1982. 39.50 (ISBN 0-521-23721-1); pap. 11.95 (ISBN 0-521-28921-1). Cambridge U Pr.
Gordon, David R. The Hidden Weapon: The Story of Economic Warfare. Dangerfield, Royden, ed. LC 76-5473. (World War II Ser.). 1976. Repr. of 1947 ed. 29.50 (ISBN 0-306-70769-1). Da Capo.
Gordon, Debbie, jt. auth. see Adler-Golden, Rachel.
Gordon, Dennis. Quartered in Hell: The Story of the American North Russia Expeditionary Force 1918-1919. LC 81-71127. (Illus.). 320p. (Orig.). 1982. pap. 12.95 (ISBN 0-942258-00-2). Gos Inc.
Gordon, Diana R. Toward Realistic Reform: A Commentary on Proposals for Change in New York City's Criminal Justice System. 1981. 3.00 (ISBN 0-318-02048-3). Natl Coun Crime.
Gordon, Dillian. The National Gallery, London: One Hundred Great Paintings: Duccio to Picasso. (Illus.). 224p. 1984. 12.95 (ISBN 0-00-217066-3, Pub. by Salem Hse Ltd). Merrimack Pub Cir.
Gordon, Don. Excavations. 64p. (Orig.). 1980. pap. 3.00 (ISBN 0-915596-30-X). West Coast.
--On the Ward. 1977. pap. 3.00 (ISBN 0-915596-15-6). West Coast.
Gordon, Don E. Electronic Warfare: Element of Strategy & Multiplier of Combat Power. (Pergamon Policy Studies on Security Affairs). (Illus.). 200p. 1982. 17.50 (ISBN 0-08-027189-8). Pergamon.
Gordon, Donald C. Australian Frontier in New Guinea, 1870-1885. LC 68-58583. (Columbia University. Studies in the Social Sciences: No. 562). Repr. of 1951 ed. 25.00 (ISBN 0-404-51562-2). AMS Pr.
Gordon, Donald I. see Thomas, David J.
Gordon, Donald J. W. B. Yeats: Images of a Poet. LC 79-9441. 1979. Repr. of 1961 ed. lib. bdg. 24.75x (ISBN 0-313-22069-7, GOWBY). Greenwood.
Gordon, Douglas. The Energy. (Science in Today's World Ser.). (Illus.). 72p. (gr. 7-12). 1984. 14.95 (ISBN 0-7134-4484-3, Pub. by Batsford England). David & Charles.
--Managing the Dental Practice in the 21st Century. 1985. text ed. 22.00 (ISBN 0-8359-4179-5). Reston.
Gordon, Douglas H. The Pre-Historic Background of Indian Culture. Barrett, D. & Madhuri, Desai, eds. LC 75-31825. (Illus.). 199p. 1976. lib. bdg. 22.50x (ISBN 0-8371-8440-1, GOIC). Greenwood.
Gordon, Douglas H. & Torrey, Norman L. Censoring of Diderot's Encyclopedia & the Re-Established Text. LC 78-168156. Repr. of 1947 ed. 15.00 (ISBN 0-404-02865-9). AMS Pr.
Gordon, Dudley. The Birch Bark Poems of Charles F. Lummis. (Illus.). 29p. 1969. 10.00 (ISBN 0-317-11688-6). Dawsons.
--Charles F. Lummis: Crusader in Corduroy. (Illus.). xxii, 344p. 1972. leatherette 12.50 (ISBN 0-317-11661-4). Dawsons.
Gordon, Duncan. Rheumatoid Arthritis: Discussions in Patient Management. 1981. text ed. 24.00 (ISBN 0-87488-951-0). Med Exam.
Gordon, E. Legal & Financial Aspects of the Iranian Hostage Settlement, 2 vols. 1982. 90.00 (ISBN 0-317-30271-X). Oceana.
Gordon, E., ed. A Basis & Practice of Neuroanaesthesia. 2nd ed. (Monographs in Anaesthesiology: Vol. 2). 354p. 1981. 82.75 (ISBN 0-444-80252-5, Biomedical Pr). Elsevier.
Gordon, E. B., jt. auth. see Sim, Myre.
Gordon, E. O. Prehistoric London. LC 84-72709. (Illus.). 176p. 1985. pap. 6.00 (ISBN 0-934666-16-4). Artisan Sales.
Gordon, E. V., ed. The Battle of Maldon. (Old English Ser.). 1966. pap. text ed. 3.95x (ISBN 0-89197-565-9). Irvington.
Gordon, E. V., jt. ed. see Tolkien, J. R.
Gordon, E. V., tr. see Shetelig, Haakon.
Gordon, Earnest B. Adoniram Judson Gordon. Dayton, Donald W., ed. (The Higher Christian Life Ser.). 386p. 1985. 50.00 (ISBN 0-8240-6421-6). Garland Pub.
Gordon, Edmond W. & Miller, LaMar P., eds. Equality of Educational Opportunity: A Handbook for Research. LC 73-9244. 1974. lib. bdg. 35.00 (ISBN 0-404-10535-1). AMS Pr.
Gordon, Edmund F., jt. auth. see Harrington, Daniel J.
Gordon, Edmund F., jt. auth. see Meier, John P.
Gordon, Edmund W., ed. Human Diversity & Pedagogy. 800p. Date not set. 36.50 (ISBN 0-912056-04-5). Mediax.
Gordon, Edmund W., jt. ed. see Zigler, Edward F.
Gordon, Edward J. Writing about Imaginative Literature. 196p. 1973. pap. text ed. 10.95 (ISBN 0-15-597850-0, HC). HarBraceJ.
Gordon, Edwin. Psychology of Music Teaching. (Contemporary Perspectives in Music Education Ser.). (Illus.). 1971. ref. ed. o.p. 14.95 (ISBN 0-13-736215-3). P-H.
--A Three-Year Longitudinal Predictive Validity Study of the Musical Aptitude Profile. (Studies in the Psychology of Music Ser: Vol. 5). 78p. 1967. pap. 3.95x (ISBN 0-87745-009-9). U of Iowa Pr.
--Tonal & Rhythm Patterns. LC 76-7947. 1976. 39.50x (ISBN 0-87395-354-1). State U NY Pr.
Gordon, Edwin, ed. & intro. by. Experimental Research in the Psychology of Music. LC 73-632181. (Studies in the Psychology of Music Ser.: Vol. 10). (Illus.). 192p. 1975. text ed. 15.00x (ISBN 0-87745-052-8). U of Iowa Pr.
Gordon, Edwin, ed. Experimental Research in the Psychology of Music, Vols. 6-9. Incl. Vol. 6. LC 73-632181. 123p. 1970. 4.75x (ISBN 0-87745-018-8); Vol. 7. LC 73-632181. 186p. 1971. 6.95x (ISBN 0-87745-024-2); Vol. 8. LC 73-632181. 142p. 1972. 7.95x (ISBN 0-87745-034-X); Vol. 9. LC 73-632181. 242p. 1974. text ed. 15.00x (ISBN 0-87745-048-X). (Studies in the Psychology of Music Ser). U of Iowa Pr.
Gordon, Edwin E. Learning Sequences in Music (Skill, Content, & Patterns) 289p. 1980. 16.95 (ISBN 0-686-28115-2). GIA Pubns.
Gordon, Eleanor H., et al. FSI Vietnamese Basic Course: Guide to Pronunciation & Lessons 1-10. 1969. pap. text ed. 11.95X (ISBN 0-686-10797-7); 22 cassettes 132.00x (ISBN 0-686-10798-5). Intl Learn Syst.
Gordon, Eleanora C., jt. auth. see Baird, Henry W.
Gordon, Elinor. Collecting Chinese Export Porcelain. rev. ed. LC 84-865. (Illus.). 176p. 1984. 20.00 (ISBN 0-915590-50-6); pap. 12.95 (ISBN 0-915590-44-1). Main Street.
Gordon, Elinor, ed. Treasures from the East: Chinese Export Porcelain for the Collector. rev. ed. LC 84-15515. (Illus.). 192p. 1984. pap. 11.95 (ISBN 0-915590-58-1). Main Street.
Gordon, Ellen, jt. auth. see Gordon, Charles.
Gordon, Elliott, jt. auth. see Gordon, Barbara.
Gordon, Emanuel. Uranium Nineteen Eighty. (Technical & Economic Reports: Nuclear Fuel Cycle). 61p. 1981. avail.; members 20.00 (ISBN 0-318-13600-7). Atomic Indus Forum.
Gordon, Enid & Shirley, Midge. The Belgian Cookbook. LC 99-943990. (Illus.). 224p. 1984. 18.95 (ISBN 0-356-09501-0, Pub. by Salem Hse Ltd). Merrimack Pub Cir.
Gordon, Eric V. Introduction to Old Norse. 2nd ed. Taylor, A. R., ed. 1957. pap. 17.95x (ISBN 0-19-811184-3). Oxford U Pr.
Gordon, Eric V., ed. Pearl. 1980. Repr. of 1953 ed. 10.95x (ISBN 0-19-812675-1). Oxford U Pr.
Gordon, Ernest. Miracle on the River Kwai. LC 83-51673. 228p. 1984. pap. 3.50 (ISBN 0-8423-4356-3). Tyndale.
--Through the Valley of the Kwai. LC 83-12967. (Illus.). 257p. 1983. Repr. of 1962 ed. lib. bdg. 35.00x (ISBN 0-313-24220-8, G0VK). Greenwood.
Gordon, Fee D., jt. ed. see Epp, Eldon J.
Gordon, Felice D. After Winning: The Legacy of the New Jersey Suffragists, 1920-1947. LC 85-11745. 1985. 28.00 (ISBN 0-8135-1137-2). Rutgers U Pr.
Gordon, Frank J. Growing in Grace. (Illus.). 111p. (Orig.). 1981. pap. 6.00 (ISBN 0-686-34382-4). G Lutheran Foun.
Gordon, Frank S. & Hemnes, Thomas. The Legal Word Book. 1978. 7.95 (ISBN 0-395-26662-9). HM.
Gordon, Frank S. & Hemnes, Thomas M. S. The Legal Word Book. 2nd ed. 1982. 7.95 (ISBN 0-395-32942-6). HM.
Gordon, G & Gordon, L. Sky Will Be Blue. 160p. 1984. 5.95 (ISBN 0-8285-2819-5, Pub. by Mir Pubs USSR). Imported Pubns.
Gordon, G., ed. Active Touch-The Mechanism of Recognition of Objects by Manipulation: A Multidisciplinary Approach. 1978. text ed. 69.00 (ISBN 0-08-022647-7); pap. text ed. 41.00 (ISBN 0-08-022667-1). Pergamon.
--Continental Film Review Anthology, 1953-55, 2 vols. 1976. lib. bdg. 200.00 (ISBN 0-8490-1670-3). Gordon Pr.
Gordon, G. & Dicks, B., eds. Scottish Urban History. (Illus.). 280p. 1983. 25.00 (ISBN 0-08-025762-3). Pergamon.
Gordon, G., ed. see Raleigh, Walter A.
Gordon, G. B. Hieroglyphic Stairway: Ruins of Copan. (HU PMM). Repr. of 1902 ed. 21.00 (ISBN 0-527-01154-1). Kraus Repr.
--Prehistoric Ruins of Copan, Honduras: A Preliminary Report of the Explorations by Museum, 1891-1895. (HU PMM). Repr. of 1896 ed. 31.00 (ISBN 0-527-01150-9). Kraus Repr.
--Researches in the Uloa Valley, 1898. (HU PMM). Repr. of 1898 ed. 21.00 (ISBN 0-527-01153-3). Kraus Repr.
Gordon, G. S. Robert Bridges: The Rede Lectures, 1931. 1946. lib. bdg. 8.50 (ISBN 0-8414-4657-1). Folcroft.
Gordon, Garry, jt. auth. see Walker, Morton.
Gordon, Gary J. Products Liability Litigation. 1980. pap. 27.50 (ISBN 0-917126-20-3). Butterworth MN.
Gordon, Gary R., et al. A Field Guide to Criminal Justice Internships. 150p. (Orig.). 1984. pap. text ed. 11.95 (ISBN 0-87084-325-7). Anderson Pub Co.
Gordon, Geoffrey. The Application of GPSS Five to Discrete System Simulation. (Illus.). 336p. 1975. 35.00 (ISBN 0-13-039057-7). P-H.
--System Simulation. 2nd ed. LC 77-24579. (Illus.). 1978. ref. ed. 37.95 (ISBN 0-13-881797-9). P-H.
Gordon, George. Charles Lamb, Prose & Poetry. LC 74-9967. 1937. 17.50 (ISBN 0-8414-4517-6). Folcroft.
--The Discipline of Letters (Lamb, Shelley, Lang, Walter Raleigh, Hopkins, Bridges) 1973. lib. bdg. 17.50 (ISBN 0-8414-4658-X). Folcroft.
--More Companionable Books. 127p. Repr. of 1947 ed. lib. bdg. 35.00 (ISBN 0-89760-254-4). Telegraph Bks.
--Persuasion: Theory & Practice of Manipulative Communication. (Studies in Public Communication). 1971. pap. text ed. 10.00x (ISBN 0-8038-5777-2). Hastings.
--Poetry & the Moderns. LC 77-8027. 1935. lib. bdg. 10.00 (ISBN 0-8414-4592-3). Folcroft.
--Shakespeare's English. LC 77-7091. 1928. lib. bdg. 10.00 (ISBN 0-8414-4594-X). Folcroft.
--Shelley & the Oppressors of Mankind. LC 76-15981. 1973. lib. bdg. 10.00 (ISBN 0-8414-4421-8). Folcroft.
--Three Oxford Ironies: Being Copelston's "Advice to a Young Reviewer", Mansels' "Phrontisterion or Oxford in the Nineteenth Century" and the "Oxford Are Poetica". (Victorian Age Ser). 1927. Repr. 20.00 (ISBN 0-8482-4224-6). Norwood Edns.
Gordon, George & Byron, Lord. Don Juan. 24.95 (ISBN 0-89190-660-6, Pub. by Am Repr). Amereon Ltd.
Gordon, George, ed. Perspectives of the Scottish City. 224p. 1985. text ed. 37.25x (ISBN 0-08-030371-4, Pub. by Aberdeen U Scotland). Humanities.
--Perspectives of the Scottish City, Eighteen Thirty-One to Nineteen Eighty-One. (Illus.). 224p. 1985. 28.00 (ISBN 0-08-030371-4). Pergamon.

Gordon, George B. In the Alaskan Wilderness. LC 74-5840. Repr. of 1917 ed. 25.75 (ISBN 0-404-11645-0). AMS Pr.

Gordon, George J. Public Administration in America. 2nd ed. LC 81-51847. 623p. 1982. text ed. 25.95 (ISBN 0-312-65388-3); instr's. manual avail. St Martin.

Gordon, George K. & Stryker, Ruth. Creative Long-Term Care Administration. (Illus.). 406p. 1983. 34.50x (ISBN 0-398-04822-3). C C Thomas.

Gordon, George N. Classroom Television: New Frontiers in ITV. (Studies in Media Management). 1970. pap. text ed. 5.80x (ISBN 0-8038-1149-7). Hastings.

--The Communications Revolution: A History of Mass Media in the United States. LC 77-3037. (Humanistic Studies in the Communication Arts). 1977. pap. 9.95x (ISBN 0-8038-1219-1). Hastings.

--Erotic Communications: Studies in Sex, Sin & Censorship. new ed. (Humanistic Studies in the Communication Arts). (Illus.). 352p. 1980. 20.50 (ISBN 0-8038-1959-5, Communication Arts); pap. 12.50 (ISBN 0-8038-1960-9). Hastings.

--Languages of Communication. (Communication Arts Bk). 1969. 12.95 (ISBN 0-8038-4262-7). Hastings.

Gordon, George N. & Falk, Irving. The War of Ideas: America's International Identity Crisis. (Communication Arts Bks.). 1973. 8.50 (ISBN 0-8038-8064-2). Hastings.

Gordon, George N. & Falk, Irving A. Videocassette Technology in American Education. LC 72-81494. 176p. 1972. 21.95 (ISBN 0-87778-035-8). Educ Tech Pubns.

Gordon, George N., ed. Communications & Media: Constructing a Cross-Discipline. (Humanistic Studies in Communication Arts). 224p. 1975. 13.95 (ISBN 0-8038-1198-5); pap. text ed. 6.95x (ISBN 0-8038-1199-3). Hastings.

Gordon, George S. Anglo-American Literary Relations: The Watson Chair Foundation Lectures of the Sulgrave Manor Board. LC 76-167346. (Essay Index Reprint Ser.). (Delivered in University College, London, March 1931). Repr. of 1942 ed. 13.00 (ISBN 0-8369-2649-8). Ayer Co Pubs.

--Companionable Books Series One. facs. ed. LC 68-16935. (Essay Index Reprint Ser). 1927. 17.00 (ISBN 0-8369-0485-0). Ayer Co Pubs.

--Lives of Authors. facs. ed. LC 76-117796. (Essay Index Reprint Ser). 1950. 18.00 (ISBN 0-8369-1750-2). Ayer Co Pubs.

--Shakespeare's English. LC 71-168157. Repr. of 1928 ed. 13.50 (ISBN 0-404-02866-7). AMS Pr.

--Virgil in English Poetry. LC 74-19279. 1974. Repr. of 1931 ed. lib. bdg. 10.00 (ISBN 0-8414-4433-1). Folcroft.

Gordon, Gerald. Role Theory & Illness. 9.95x (ISBN 0-8084-0270-6); pap. 6.95x (ISBN 0-8084-0271-4). New Coll U Pr.

Gordon, Gerald & Fisher, G. Lawrence, eds. The Diffusion of Medical Technology: Policy & Research Planning Perspectives. LC 75-17638. 176p. 1975. prof ref 22.50 (ISBN 0-88410-129-0). Ballinger Pub.

Gordon, Gerald, et al. Disease, the Individual & Society. 1968. pap. 19.95x (ISBN 0-8084-0107-6). New Coll U Pr.

Gordon, Gilbert. Stage Fights: A Simple Handbook of Techniques. LC 73-75918. (Illus.). 1974. 7.95 (ISBN 0-87830-131-3). Theatre Arts.

Gordon, Gilbert & Pressman, Israel. Quantitative Decision Making for Business. 2nd ed. (Illus.). 576p. 1983. text ed. 30.95 (ISBN 0-13-746685-4). P-H.

Gordon, Giles, jt. auth. see Urquhart, Fred.

Gordon, Giles, ed. Shakespeare Stories. LC 83-207182. (Illus.). 224p. 1983. 16.95 (ISBN 0-241-10879-9, Pub. by Hamish Hamilton England). David & Charles.

Gordon, Glen, jt. auth. see Connolly, William H.

Gordon, Guanetta. Petals from the Moon. LC 72-15540. 96p. 1971. 4.50 (ISBN 0-8233-0162-1). Golden Quill.

--Red Are the Embers. LC 83-66878. 159p. 1980. 8.50 (ISBN 0-8233-0317-9). Golden Quill.

--Shadow Within the Flame. LC 73-80455. 96p. 1973. 5.00 (ISBN 0-8233-0189-3). Golden Quill.

Gordon, H. A., jt. ed. see Csaky, T. Z.

Gordon, H. L. New Chemotherapy in Mental Illness. 1958. 15.00 (ISBN 0-8022-0610-7). Philos Lib.

Gordon, H. R. & Morel, A. Y. Remote Assessment of Ocean Color for Interpretation of Satellite Visible Imagery: A Review. (Lecture Notes on Coastal & Estuarine Studies: Vol. 4). (Illus.). 130p. 1983. pap. 22.00 (ISBN 0-387-90923-0). Springer-Verlag.

Gordon, Haim. Martin Buber: A Centenary Volume. 1983. 49.50x (ISBN 0-88125-026-0). Ktav.

Gordon, Hampden. Antiques, the Amateur's Questions. (Illus.). 1951. pap. 3.95 (ISBN 0-7195-0511-9). Transatlantic.

Gordon, Harold H. Chaplain on Wings. Zahavy, Zev, ed. LC 81-51749. (Illus.). 192p. 1981. 12.95 (ISBN 0-88400-075-3). Shengold.

Gordon, Harold J. & Gordon, Nancy M., eds. The Austrian Empire: Abortive Federation. (Problems in European Civilization Ser.). 1974. pap. text ed. 5.50 (ISBN 0-669-90456-2). Heath.

Gordon, Harold J., Jr. Hitler & the Beer Hall Putsch. LC 73-166383. 632p. 1972. 59.00 (ISBN 0-691-05189-5); pap. 16.50 (ISBN 0-691-00775-6). Princeton U Pr.

Gordon, Harry G. More on Interest-Free Loans. rev. ed. 123p. (Orig.). 1982. pap. 19.95 (ISBN 0-9612184-1-X). H G Gordon.

--Tax Savings Through Interest-Free Loans: Corporate Loans, Interest-Free Loans, Vol. II. 1984. 34.95; pap. 19.95 (ISBN 0-13-885310-X). P-H.

--Tax Savings Through Interest-Free Loans: Intra-Family Loans-How to Reduce Taxes by Shifting to Low-Tax-Bracket Family Members, Vol. I. 244p. 1984. 34.95 (ISBN 0-13-885302-9); pap. 12.95 (ISBN 0-13-885294-4). P-H.

--Tax Savings thru Interest-Free Loans. rev. ed. Orig. Title: Tax Avoidance thru Interest-Free Loans. 162p. (Orig.). 1981. pap. 19.95 (ISBN 0-9612184-0-1). H G Gordon.

Gordon, Harvey C. Baby Power. LC 83-63488. (A Book About the Indignities of Babyhood). (Illus.). 112p. (Orig.). 1984. pap. 4.95 (ISBN 0-9601402-4-7); prepack 59.40. Punster's Pr.

--Pundemonium: Puns Are Everywhere! LC 83-61419. (Illus.). 108p. (Orig.). 1983. pap. 3.95 (ISBN 0-9601402-2-0); prepack 47.40. Punster's Pr.

Gordon, Helen H. From Copying to Creating. 237p. 1981. pap. text ed. 14.95 (ISBN 0-03-053551-4, HoltC). HR&W.

Gordon, Herbert. The Canoe Book. (Illus.). 1978. pap. 6.95 (ISBN 0-07-023783-2). McGraw.

Gordon, Herbert, jt. auth. see Gordon, Lucy.

Gordon, I. Controlled Breeding in Farm Animals. 200p. 1983. 60.00 (ISBN 0-08-024410-6); pap. 30.00 (ISBN 0-08-024409-2). Pergamon.

Gordon, I. & Shapiro, H. A. Forensic Medicine: A Guide to Principles. 2nd ed. LC 82-4119. (Illus.). 451p. 1983. text ed. 50.00 (ISBN 0-443-02393-X). Churchill.

Gordon, I. L., ed. The Seafarer. (Old English Ser.). 1966. pap. text ed. 3.95x (ISBN 0-89197-570-5). Irvington.

Gordon, I. R. A Preface to Pope. LC 75-25572. (Preface Books). (Illus.). 136p. 1976. pap. text ed. 8.95x (ISBN 0-582-31506-9). Longman.

Gordon, Ian. Basic Business Letters. 1973. pap. text ed. 3.50x (ISBN 0-435-28358-8). Heinemann Ed.

--John Galt. 1978. 12.50x (ISBN 0-7073-0218-8, Pub. by Scottish Academic Pr Scotland). Columbia U Pr.

--John Skelton, Poet Laureate. LC 70-96157. 1970. Repr. of 1943 ed. lib. bdg. 20.00x (ISBN 0-374-93211-5). Octagon.

--Practical Letter Writing. 1967. pap. text ed. 3.50x (ISBN 0-435-28359-6). Heinemann Ed.

Gordon, Ian, ed. The Last of the Lairds. 1976. 10.00x (ISBN 0-7073-0170-X, Pub. by Scottish Academic Pr Scotland). Columbia U Pr.

Gordon, Ian A. The Movement of English Prose. (English Language Ser.). 192p. 1980. pap. text ed. 10.95x (ISBN 0-582-29106-2). Longman.

Gordon, Ian A; see Blackstone, Bernard.

Gordon, Ian A., ed. Shenstone's Miscellany 1759-1763. 164p. 1983. lib. bdg. 50.00 (ISBN 0-89984-222-4). Century Bookbindery.

Gordon, Ian A., ed. see Galt, John.

Gordon, Ian A., intro. by see Mansfield, Katherine.

Gordon, Ira J. Baby Learning Through Baby Play: A Parent's Guide for the First Two Years. (Griffin Ser.). (Illus.). 128p. 1970. pap. 5.95 (ISBN 0-312-06405-5). St Martin.

--Baby to Parent, Parent to Baby: A Guide to Loving & Learning in a Child's First Year. LC 76-62768. (Illus.). 1978. 8.95 (ISBN 0-312-06448-9); pap. 4.95 (ISBN 0-312-06449-7). St Martin.

Gordon, Ira J., ed. Early Childhood Education. LC 6-16938. (National Society for the Study of Education Yearbooks Ser: No. 71, Pt. 2). (Illus.). xvi, 400p. 1975. pap. 6.00x (ISBN 0-226-60110-2). U of Chicago Pr.

Gordon, Ira. J, et al. Child Learning Through Child Play: Learning Activities for Two & Three-Year-Olds. (Griffin Paperback Ser). (Illus.). 128p. 1972. 8.95 (ISBN 0-312-13230-1, C16800); pap. 6.95 (ISBN -0312-13195-X, C16700). St Martin.

Gordon, Irene, ed. see Mead, Sidney M., et al.

Gordon, Irving. World History Review Text. 2nd ed. (gr. 10-12). 1979. text ed. 15.83 (ISBN 0-87720-625-2); pap. text ed. 10.75 (ISBN 0-87720-624-4). AMSCO Sch.

Gordon, Irving L. American Studies: A Conceptual Approach. LC 76-359753. (gr. 11). 1975. text ed. 16.25 (ISBN 0-87720-600-7); pap. text ed. 11.25 (ISBN 0-87720-603-1). AMSCO Sch.

--Review Text in American History. (Illus., Orig.). (gr. 10-12). 1968. pap. text ed. 8.58 (ISBN 0-87720-606-6). AMSCO Sch.

--Review Text in World History. (Illus., Orig.). (gr. 10-12). 1968. pap. text ed. 8.58 (ISBN 0-87720-604-X). AMSCO Sch.

Gordon, J. California Real Estate Law: Text & Cases. (Illus.). 1980. pap. text ed. 19.95 (ISBN 0-13-112524-9). P-H.

Gordon, J., et al, eds. Protein Phosphorylation & Bio-Regulation. (Illus.). x, 234p. 1980. 35.00 (ISBN 3-8055-1168-X). S Karger.

Gordon, J. Arthur. The Irregardless Cooks. LC 83-40028. (Illus.). 144p. 1983. pap. 9.95 (ISBN 0-89815-103-1). Ten Speed Pr.

Gordon, J. E. The New Science of Strong Materials or Why You Don't Fall Through the Floor. LC 83-43103. (Illus.). 288p. 1984. pap. 9.95x (ISBN 0-691-02380-8). Princeton U Pr.

--Structures: Or Why Things Don't Fall Down. LC 81-9755. (Quality Paperbacks Ser.). (Illus.). 395p. 1981. pap. 9.95 (ISBN 0-306-80151-5). Da Capo.

Gordon, J. E., ed. Structures: Or Why Things Don't Fall Down. LC 78-19068. 395p. 1978. 19.95x (ISBN 0-306-40025-1, Plenum Pr). Plenum Pub.

Gordon, J. E., tr. see Du Camp, Maxime.

Gordon, J. K., ed. Canada's Role in Science & Technology for Development: Proceedings of a Symposium Held at the Ontario Science Centre, Toronto, Canada, 10-13 May 1979. 136p. 1979. pap. 5.00 (ISBN 0-88936-230-0, IDRC141, IDRC). Unipub.

Gordon, J. L., jt. auth. see Roach, F. E.

Gordon, J. L., ed. Platelets in Biology & Pathlogy. (Research Monographs in Cell & Tissue Physiology: Vol. 1). 1977. 56.25 (ISBN 0-7204-0601-3, North-Holland). Elsevier.

--Platelets in Biology & Pathology, Vol. 2. (Research Monographs in Cell & Tissue Physiology: Vol. 5). 512p. 1981. 92.00 (ISBN 0-444-80308-4, Biomedical Pr). Elsevier.

Gordon, J. L., jt. ed. see Dingle, J. T.

Gordon, Jaimy. The Bend, the Lip, the Kid: Real Life Stories. LC 78-15579. 1978. pap. 6.00 (ISBN 0-915342-25-1). SUN.

--Circumspections from an Equestrian Statue. (Burning Deck Fiction Ser.). (Illus.). 1979. 15.00 (ISBN 0-930900-77-4); pap. 4.00 (ISBN 0-930900-78-2). Burning Deck.

--Private T. Pigeon's Tale. (Treade Story Ser.: No. 5). (Illus.). 36p. 1979. signed 8.00 (ISBN 0-914232-19-3); pap. 2.50 (ISBN 0-914232-18-5). McPherson & Co.

--Shamp of the City-Solo. rev. ed. LC 79-24979. 131p. 1980. 12.50 (ISBN 0-914232-38-X); pap. 3.95 (ISBN 0-914232-37-1). McPherson & Co.

Gordon, Jaimy, et al. The Treacle Story Series, Vol. Two (5-10) LC 76-43558. (Illus.). 304p. 1980. 15.00 (ISBN 0-914232-34-7). McPherson & Co.

Gordon, James. The Stone Boy. 256p. 1984. pap. 3.50 (ISBN 0-441-78634-0). Ace Bks.

Gordon, James S., jt. auth. see Rosenthal, Raymond F.

Gordon, James S., et al, eds. Mind Body & Health: Toward an Integral Medicine. 368p. 1984. 39.95 (ISBN 0-89885-150-5); pap. 16.95 (ISBN 0-89885-188-2). Human Sci Pr.

Gordon, Jan. Modern French Painters. LC 73-99697. (Essay Index Reprint Ser). 1923. 19.50 (ISBN 0-8369-1573-9). Ayer Co Pubs.

Gordon, Janet & Reische, Diana. Volunteer Powerhouse. 252p. 15.95 (ISBN 0-87469-038-2). Sammis Pub.

Gordon, Janet, jt. ed. see Yen, D. E.

Gordon, Jeffie R. Jacquelyn. 368p. (Orig.). (gr. 7 up). 1985. pap. 2.95 (ISBN 0-590-33432-8, Sunfire). Scholastic Inc.

Gordon, Jesse E. Testing, Counseling & Supportive Services for Disadvantaged Youth. (Orig.). 1969. pap. 4.95x (ISBN 0-87736-309-9). U of Mich Inst Labor.

Gordon, Joan. Joe Haldeman. LC 80-25936. (Starmont Reader's Guide: No. 4). 80p. 1980. Repr. lib. bdg. 13.95x (ISBN 0-89370-035-5). Borgo Pr.

--Reader's Guide to Joe Haldeman. Schlobin, Roger C., ed. LC 80-21388. (Starmont Reader's Guide to Contemporary Science Fiction & Fantasy Author Ser.: Vol. 4). (Illus., Orig.). 1980. 13.95x (ISBN 0-916732-15-0). Starmont Hse.

Gordon, Joan & Bennett, Janet. Complete Yorkshire Terrier. LC 75-30417. (Complete Breed Book). (Illus.). 320p. 1984. 15.95 (ISBN 0-87605-360-6). Howell Bk.

Gordon, Joel R. Focus on Growth in the Church. rev. ed. (To Live in Christ Ser.). 1980. pap. write for info. (ISBN 0-697-01724-9); instrs.' manual avail. (ISBN 0-697-01722-2). Wm C Brown.

Gordon, John. The Edge of the World. LC 83-2783. 192p. (gr. 5up). 1983. 10.95 (ISBN 0-689-50279-6, Argo). Atheneum.

--Englands & Scotlands Happiness in Being Reduced to Unitie of Religion. LC 75-38190. (English Experience Ser.: No. 461). 50p. 1972. Repr. of 1604 ed. 7.00 (ISBN 90-221-0461-3). Walter J Johnson.

--The Ghost on the Hill. LC 76-28316. 176p. 1977. 8.95 (ISBN 0-670-33784-6). Viking.

--Irish Wolfhound. LC 73-91146. 1974. 7.50 (ISBN 0-668-03435-1). Arco.

--James Joyce's Metamorphoses. 218p. 1981. 27.50x (ISBN 0-389-20167-7, 06937). B&N Imports.

--MCQ Tutor for Students of Microbiology. 1979. pap. text ed. 19.50 (ISBN 0-8151-3805-9). Year Bk Med.

--One Hundred Programs for the BBC Microcomputer. (Illus.). 1984. pap. 11.95 (ISBN 0-13-634741-X); cassette 9.95 (ISBN 0-13-634733-9). P-H.

Gordon, John & McLean, Ian. One Hundred Programs for the Commodore 64. (Illus.). 368p. 1984. pap. 14.95 (ISBN 0-13-634650-2). P-H.

Gordon, John C. Verbal Deficit: A Critique. 181p. 1981. 25.00 (ISBN 0-85664-990-2, Pub. by Croom Helm Ltd). Longwood Pub Group.

Gordon, John C., ed. German History & Society Eighteen Seventy to Nineteen Twenty. LC 85-4233. (Illus.). 128p. (Orig.). 1985. pap. text ed. 6.95 (ISBN 0-907582-54-0, Pub. by Berg Pubs). Longwood Pub Group.

Gordon, John D. George Gissing, Eighteen Fifty-Seven to Nineteen Three: An Exhibition from the Berg Collection. 1978. Repr. of 1954 ed. lib. bdg. 10.00 (ISBN 0-8414-4615-6). Folcroft.

--Landmarks in English Literature in First or Early Editions 1490-1900. 1959. lib. bdg. 10.00 (ISBN 0-8414-4659-8). Folcroft.

--Nathaniel Hawthorne: The Years of Fulfillment 1804-1853. 1973. Repr. of 1954 ed. 10.00 (ISBN 0-8274-0381-X). R West.

--Ralph Waldo Emerson Eighteen Hundred Three to Eighteen Eighty-Two. LC 73-16267. 1973. lib. bdg. 10.00 (ISBN 0-8414-4481-1). Folcroft.

--William Wordsworth, Seventeen Seventy to Eighteen Fifty. LC 73-12439. 1950. lib. bdg. 10.00 (ISBN 0-8414-4406-4). Folcroft.

Gordon, John E. How to Succeed in Organic Chemistry. LC 78-21496. (Wiley Self-Teaching Guides Ser.). 594p. 1979. pap. text ed. 10.95 (ISBN 0-471-03010-4, Pub. by Wiley Pr). Wiley.

--The Organic Chemistry of Electrolyte Solutions. LC 75-16139. 576p. 1975. 38.50 (ISBN 0-471-31620-2). Krieger.

Gordon, John E., jt. auth. see Plunkett, Richard J.

Gordon, John E., jt. auth. see Wyon, John B.

Gordon, John F. All about the Boxer. 164p. 1970. 9.95 (ISBN 0-7207-0317-4, Pub. by Michael Joseph). Merrimack Pub Cir.

--All about the Cocker Spaniel. 147p. 1971. 8.95 (ISBN 0-7207-0424-3, Pub. by Michael Joseph). Merrimack Pub Cir.

--All about the Staffordshire Bull Terrier. (Illus.). 184p. 1984. 14.95 (ISBN 0-7207-1497-4, Pub. by Michael Joseph). Merrimack Pub Cir.

--The Spaniel Owner's Encyclopedia. 183p. 1967. 7.95 (ISBN 0-7207-0098-1, Pub. by Michael Joseph). Merrimack Pub Cir.

--The Staffordshire Bull Terrier Owner's Encyclopedia. 2nd ed. (Illus.). 240p. 1977. 12.95 (ISBN 0-7207-0944-X, Pub. by Michael Joseph). Merrimack Pub Cir.

Gordon, John L., ed. Tillopidine: Quo Vadis? (Agents & Actions Supplement Ser.: No. 15). 312p. 1984. text ed. 43.95x (ISBN 0-317-18425-3). Birkhauser.

Gordon, Joseph C. The Education of Deaf Children. 59.95 (ISBN 0-8490-0089-0). Gordon Pr.

Gordon, Joyce & Gordon, Arthur E. Contributions to the Palaeography of Latin Inscriptions. LC 57-9881. (University of California Publications in Classical Archaeology: Vol. 3, No. 3). pap. 47.50 (ISBN 0-317-29114-9, 2021333). Bks Demand UMI.

Gordon, Judith. A Diagnostic Approach to Organizational Behavior. 700p. 1983. scp 32.00 (ISBN 0-205-07811-7, 087811). Allyn.

Gordon, Judith, jt. auth. see Gordon, Sol.

Gordon, Judith R., jt. ed. see Marlatt, G. Alan.

Gordon, K. F., jt. ed. see Hahn, W. A.

Gordon, Karen E. The Transitive Vampire: A Handbook of Grammar for the Innocent, the Eager & the Doomed. LC 83-40086. (Illus.). 144p. 1984. 9.95 (ISBN 0-8129-1101-6). Times Bks.

--The Well-Tempered Sentence: A Punctuation Handbook for the Innocent, the Eager & the Doomed. LC 82-19704. (Illus.). 96p. (gr. 7 up). 1983. 7.95 (ISBN 0-89919-170-3). Ticknor & Fields.

Gordon, Katherine, jt. auth. see Gordon, Richard E.

Gordon, Kenneth R. & Plane, Donald R. The Economics of Property Tax Postponement. 1978. 2.50 (ISBN 0-686-64185-X). U CO Busn Res Div.

Gordon, Kent H. Phonology of Dhangar-Kurux. 153p. 1976. pap. 2.50x (ISBN 0-88312-853-5); microfiche (2) 2.86 (ISBN 0-88312-488-2). Summer Inst Ling.

Gordon, Kermit, ed. Agenda for the Nation: Papers on Domestic & Foreign Policy Issues. LC 68-58977. pap. 158.00 (ISBN 0-317-20846-2, 2025380). Bks Demand UMI.

Gordon, L. Growth Policies & the International Order. 1979. pap. 8.95 (ISBN 0-07-023813-8). McGraw.

--Music & Modern Media of Transmission. 1975. lib. bdg. 75.00 (ISBN 0-87968-328-7). Gordon Pr.

Gordon, L., jt. auth. see Gordon, G.

Gordon, L., tr. see Gide, Andre.

Gordon, L. A. Adult Crossword Puzzles. (Illus.). 96p. 1984. pap. 3.95 (ISBN 0-8092-5356-9). Contemp Bks.

Gordon, L. D., jt. auth. see Baddeley, St. Clair.

Gordon, L. L. British Battles & Medals. 1979. 45.00 (ISBN 0-685-51512-5, Pub by Spink & Son England). S J Durst.

Gordon, Laura B. Behavioral Intervention in Health Care. (Behavioral Sciences for Health Care Professionals Ser.). 128p. 1981. 17.00x (ISBN 0-86531-018-1). Westview.

Gordon, Laura K., jt. auth. see Davidson, Laurie.

Gordon, Lawrence & Pinches, George. Improving Capital Budgeting: A Decision Support System. LC 83-15864. 144p. (Orig.). 1984. pap. 9.95 (ISBN 0-201-04319-X). Addison-Wesley.

Gordon, Lawrence A., et al. The Pricing Decision. 52p. pap. 6.95 (ISBN 0-86641-001-5, 80123). Natl Assn Accts.

--Normative Models in Managerial Decision-Making. 121p. 15.95 (ISBN 0-86641-040-6, 7578). Natl Assn Accts.

Gordon, Leonard. Bengal: The Nationalist Movement, 1876-1940. LC 73-12974. 407p. 1973. 31.00x (ISBN 0-231-03753-8). Columbia U Pr.

--Sociology & American Social Issues. LC 77-78577. (Illus.). 1978. pap. text ed. 30.50 (ISBN 0-395-25369-1); study guide 11.50 (ISBN 0-395-25371-3); instr's. manual 1.00 (ISBN 0-395-25370-5). HM.

Gordon, Leonard, jt. auth. see Mayer, Albert J.

Gordon, Leonard A. & Miller, Barbara S. A Syllabus of Indian Civilization. LC 70-168868. (Companions to Asian Studies). 182p. 1971. pap. 12.00x (ISBN 0-231-03560-8). Columbia U Pr.

Gordon, Leonard H., ed. Taiwan: Studies in Chinese Local History. LC 78-108096. (East Asian Institute Ser). 124p. 1970. 16.00x (ISBN 0-231-03376-1). Columbia U Pr.

Gordon, Lesley. A Country Herbal. (Illus.). 208p. 1980. 19.95 (ISBN 0-8317-4446-4, Mayflower Bks). Smith Pubs.

--The Mystery & Magic of Trees & Flowers. (Illus.). 112p. 1985. 12.95 (ISBN 0-86350-050-1, Pub. by Salem Hse Ltd). Merrimack Pub Cir.

--Old Roses. (Picture-Perfect Miniatures Ser.). (Illus.). 48p. 1983. 4.95 (ISBN 0-8253-0175-0). Beaufort Bks NY.

--Trees. (Picture-Perfect Miniatures Ser.). (Illus.). 48p. 1983. 4.95 (ISBN 0-8253-0174-2). Beaufort Bks NY.

--A Year of Fruits. (Picture-Perfect Miniatures Ser.). (Illus.). 48p. 1983. 4.95 (ISBN 0-8253-0177-7). Beaufort Bks NY.

Gordon, Lina. Story of Assisi. 1977. lib. bdg. 59.95 (ISBN 0-8490-2675-X). Gordon Pr.

Gordon, Lina D., jt. auth. see Symonds, Margaret.

Gordon, Lincoln. Growth Policies & the International Order. (Council on Foreign Relations 1980's Project). (Illus.). 1979. text ed. 18.95 (ISBN 0-07-023812-X). McGraw.

Gordon, Linda. Woman's Body, Woman's Right: A Social History of Birth Control in America. 1976. 14.95 (ISBN 0-670-77817-6, Grossman). Viking.

--Woman's Body, Woman's Right: Birth Control in America. 1977. pap. 7.95 (ISBN 0-14-004683-6). Penguin.

Gordon, Linda, Jr. Cossack Rebellions: Social Turmoil in the Sixteenth-Century Ukraine. 272p. 1982. 39.50x (ISBN 0-87395-654-0); pap. 13.95x (ISBN 0-87395-653-2). State U NY Pr.

Gordon, Lois. Donald Barthelme. (United States Author Ser.). 1981. lib. bdg. 14.50 (ISBN 0-8057-7347-9, Twayne). G K Hall.

--Robert Coover: The Universal Fictionmaking Process. LC 82-10337. (Crosscurrents-Modern Critques-New Ser.). 192p. 1983. 15.95x (ISBN 0-8093-1092-9). S Ill U Pr.

Gordon, Louise. How to Draw the Human Figure. (Illus.). 1979. 12.95 (ISBN 0-670-38329-5, Studio). Viking.

--How to Draw the Human Figure: An Anatomical Approach. 1980. pap. 7.95 (ISBN 0-14-046477-8). Penguin.

--How to Draw the Human Head: Techniques & Anatomy. (Illus.). 1983. pap. 7.95 (ISBN 0-14-046560-X). Penguin.

Gordon, Louise, illus. ABC Zoo. (Shape Board Play Bks.). (Illus.). (ps-2). 1976. 3.95g (ISBN 0-89828-001-X, 05002). Tuffy Bks.

--The Shoelace Book of Rhymes. (Shape Board Play Bks.). (Illus.). (ps-2). 1978. 3.95g (ISBN 0-89828-006-0, 05007). Tuffy Bks.

Gordon, Lucie D. Letters from Egypt. 416p. 1983. pap. 9.95 (ISBN 0-86068-455-5, Pub. by Virago Pr). Merrimack Pub Cir.

Gordon, Lucy & Gordon, Herbert. Sheer Romance: The Story of Pierre Dulaine, Yvonne Marceau & the American Ballroom Theatre Company. (Ballroom Dancing Ser.). (Illus.). 1985. lib. bdg. 79.95 (ISBN 0-8490-3245-8); pap. text ed. 39.95 (ISBN 0-8490-3246-6). Gordon Pr.

Gordon, Lydia L. From Lady Washington to Mrs. Cleveland. LC 72-5675. (Essay Index Reprint Ser.). 1972. Repr. of 1888 ed. 22.00 (ISBN 0-8369-2990-X). Ayer Co Pubs.

Gordon, Lyndall. Eliot's Early Years. (Illus.). 1977. 16.95x (ISBN 0-19-812078-8). Oxford U Pr.

--Eliot's Early Years. LC 76-29809. 1977. pap. 4.95 (ISBN 0-19-520086-1, GB 561, GB). Oxford U Pr.

--Virginia Woolf: A Writer's Life. (Illus.). 1985. 17.95 (ISBN 0-393-01891-1). Norton.

Gordon, Lynn, ed. see Werner, David & Bower, Bill.

Gordon, M. Manual of Nursing Diagnosis, 1984-1985. 240p. 1984. 11.95 (ISBN 0-07-023827-8). McGraw.

--Nursing Diagnosis: Process & Application. 400p. 1982. text ed. 25.00x (ISBN 0-07-023815-4). McGraw.

Gordon, M. & Green, E. L. Modules with Cores & Amalgamations of Indecomposable Modules. LC 77-3560. (Memoirs Ser.: No. 187). 145p. 1977. pap. 14.00 (ISBN 0-8218-2187-3, MEMO-187). Am Math.

Gordon, M., ed. Liquid Crystal Polymers I. (Advances in Polymer Science, Fortschritte der Hochpolymerenforschung: Vol. 59). (Illus.). 180p. 1984. 41.00 (ISBN 0-387-12818-2). Springer Verlag.

Gordon, M. & Plate, N. A., eds. Liquid Crystal Polymers II-III. (Advances in Polymer Science Ser.: Vol. 60-61). (Illus.). 1984. 54.00 (ISBN 0-387-12994-4). Springer-Verlag.

Gordon, M., jt. ed. see Mooney, H.

Gordon, M., et al. Edinburgh LCF: A Mechanised Logic of Computation. (Lecture Notes in Computer Sciences: Vol. 78). 159p. 1979. pap. 15.00 (ISBN 0-387-09724-4). Springer-Verlag.

Gordon, M., jt. ed. see Meadows, A. J.

Gordon, M. S., ed. see Conference on Poverty in America.

Gordon, Malcolm, et al. Animal Physiology. 4th ed. 1982. write for info. (ISBN 0-02-345320-6). Macmillan.

Gordon, Manya. Workers Before & After Lenin. LC 74-22743. Repr. of 1941 ed. 31.50 (ISBN 0-404-58495-0). AMS Pr.

Gordon, Margaret. Supermarket Mice. (Illus.). 32p. (ps-1). 1984. 10.95 (ISBN 0-525-44145-X, 01063-320). Dutton.

--Wilberforce Goes on a Picnic. LC 82-3476. (Illus.). 32p. (gr. k-3). 1982. 11.75 (ISBN 0-688-01481-X). Morrow.

--Wilberforce Goes Shopping. LC 84-40846. (Illus.). 32p. (ps-1). 1985. 8.95 (ISBN 0-670-80701-X). Viking.

--Wilberforce Goes to a Party. LC 85-40383. (Illus.). 32p. (ps-1). 1985. 8.95 (ISBN 0-670-80148-8). Viking.

Gordon, Margaret S. Barriers to World Trade. LC 82-48303. (The World Economy Ser.). 530p. 1982. lib. bdg. 66.00 (ISBN 0-8240-5359-1). Garland Pub.

--Economics of Welfare Policies. LC 63-14113. 159p. 1964. 22.00x (ISBN 0-231-02639-0). Columbia U Pr.

--Employment Expansion & Population Growth: The California Experience. LC 76-5893. 192p. 1976. Repr. of 1954 ed. lib. bdg. 16.25x (ISBN 0-8371-8805-9, GOEE). Greenwood.

Gordon, Margaret S., ed. Poverty in America. (Essay Index Reprint Ser.). 485p. Repr. of 1965 ed. lib. bdg. 27.00 (ISBN 0-8290-0829-2). Irvington.

Gordon, Marilyn. The Flaming Spirit: A Treasury of Poetry & Thought. LC 82-90789. 48p. 1983. 4.50 (ISBN 0-9609542-0-1). M Gordon Pub.

Gordon, Marilyn, ed. The Northeast Bronx Poets & Writers Forum Anthology, Vol. 1. LC 82-83783. 48p. 4.50 (ISBN 0-9609542-1-X). M Gordon Pub.

Gordon, Marjory. Manual of Nursing Diagnosis. (Illus.). 240p. 1982. pap. text ed. 11.95x (ISBN 0-07-023816-2). McGraw.

Gordon, Mark & Nachbar, Jack. Currents of Warm Life: Popular Culture in American Higher Education. LC 80-80344. 1980. 15.95 (ISBN 0-87972-152-9); pap. 8.95 (ISBN 0-87972-153-7). Bowling Green.

Gordon, Marsha. Government in Business. 289p. 1981. 10.00 (ISBN 0-88806-075-0). Inst C D Howe.

Gordon, Marshall, jt. auth. see Simonsen, Clifford.

Gordon, Martin. Gordon's Print Price Annual, 1984. 900p. 1984. 260.00 (ISBN 0-931036-12-7). Martin Gordon.

--Gordon's Print Price Annual, 1985. 900p. 1985. 285.00 (ISBN 0-931036-13-5). Martin Gordon.

Gordon, Martin, ed. Gordon's Print Price Annual, 1978, 2 vols. 1978. 175.00 (ISBN 0-931036-02-X). Vol. 1 (ISBN 0-931036-00-3). Vol. 2 (ISBN 0-931036-01-1). Martin Gordon.

--Gordon's Print Price Annual, 1979. 1979. 175.00 (ISBN 0-931036-05-4). Martin Gordon.

Gordon, Martin K. Imprint on the Nation. (Illus.). 98p. 1983. pap. text ed. 7.50x (ISBN 0-89745-039-6). Sunflower U Pr.

Gordon, Mary. Chase of the Wild Goose: The Story of Lady Eleanor Butler & Miss Sarah Ponsonby. LC 75-12319. 1975. Repr. of 1936 ed. 17.00x (ISBN 0-405-07354-2). Ayer Co Pubs.

--The Company of Women. 304p. 1982. pap. 2.95 (ISBN 0-345-29861-6). Ballantine.

--The Company of Women. LC 80-5284. 293p. 1981. 12.95 (ISBN 0-394-50508-5). Random.

--Final Payments. 320p. 1981. pap. 2.75 (ISBN 0-345-29554-4). Ballantine.

--Final Payments. 1985. pap. 3.95 (ISBN 0-345-32951-1). Ballantine.

--Final Payments. LC 77-90259. 1978. 10.95 (ISBN 0-394-42793-9). Random.

--Men & Angels. LC 84-45761. 241p. 1985. 16.45 (ISBN 0-394-52403-9). Random.

Gordon, Mary & Swinburne, Algernon C. The Children of the Chapel: A Tale. Lougy, Robert E., intro. by. LC 82-6436. 1185p. 1982. lib. bdg. 18.95x (ISBN 0-8214-0631-0, 82-84044). Ohio U Pr.

Gordon, Mary M., ed. see Reid, Bernard J.

Gordon, Maurice B. Naval & Maritime Medicine During the American Revolution. LC 76-52769. 1978. 17.50 (ISBN 0-685-78818-0, 911566-12). Ventnor.

--Problem of Alcholism: Past, Present & Future. 1968. pap. 1.95 (ISBN 0-911566-01-5). Ventnor.

Gordon, Maurice B., et al. Book of the Descendants of Doctor Benjamin Lee & Dorothy Gordon. LC 73-169910. 1972. 8.50 (ISBN 0-911566-11-2). Ventnor.

Gordon, Maurice R. Aesculapius Comes to the Colonies. LC 70-101590. (Illus.). 1969. Repr. of 1949 ed. 17.50 (ISBN 0-87266-014-1). Argosy.

Gordon, Max. Live at the Village Vanguard. (Quality Paperbacks Ser.). 146p. 1982. pap. 6.95 (ISBN 0-306-80160-4). Da Capo.

Gordon, Maxwell, ed. Psychopharmacological Agents, 3 vols. Incl. Vol. 1. 1964. 90.00 (ISBN 0-12-290550-4); Vol. 2. 1967. 80.00 (ISBN 0-12-290556-3); Vol. 3. 1974. 80.00 (ISBN 0-12-290558-X). (Medicinal Chemistry Ser.). Acad Pr.

Gordon, Maxwell, jt. ed. see Vida, Julius A.

Gordon, Maxwell, et al. A Review of Approaches to Viral Chemotherapy. 96p. 1981. 20.00 (ISBN 0-915340-08-9). PJD Pubns.

Gordon, Maynard M. The Iacocca Style of Management: The Successful Managerial Techniques of Chrysler's Chairman. 192p. 1985. 14.95 (ISBN 0-396-08494-X). Dodd.

Gordon, Mel. Lazzi: Comic Routines of the Commedia dell'Arte. LC 83-62613. 104p. 1983. pap. 7.95 (ISBN 0-933826-69-9). Performing Arts.

--Performing Arts Resources, Vol. 7: Lazzi: The Comic Routines of Commedia Dell' Arte. Cocuzza, Ginnine & Cohen-Stratyner, Barbara N., eds. Vincentini, Claudio, tr. LC 75-646287. (Illus.). 82p. 1981. 25.00x (ISBN 0-932610-03-X); members 10.00. Theatre Lib.

Gordon, Melvin, jt. auth. see Bromberg, Murray.

Gordon, Michael. The American Family in Social-Historical Perspective. 3rd ed. LC 82-60478. 602p. 1983. pap. text ed. 13.95 (ISBN 0-312-02313-8). St Martin.

--The American Family: Past, Present, & Future. 1977. text ed. 20.00 (ISBN 0-394-31722-X, RanC). Random.

--The Evaluation of Research Papers by Primary Journals in the U. K. 76p. 1978. 25.00x (ISBN 0-906083-03-6, Pub. by Primary Com England). State Mutual Bk.

--Old Enough to Feel Better: A Medical Guide for Seniors. LC 80-70351. 384p. 1981. 14.95 (ISBN 0-8019-6991-3). Chilton.

Gordon, Michael, et al, eds. Dictionary of New Information Technology Acronyms. 217p. 1983. 56.00x (ISBN 0-8103-4309-6, Pub. by Kogan Page UK). Gale.

Gordon, Michael J. C. The Denotational Description of Programming Languages: An Introduction. LC 79-15723. 160p. 1979. pap. 16.95 (ISBN 0-387-90433-6). Springer-Verlag.

Gordon, Michael Lewis, et al. Helping the Trainable Mentally Retarded Child Develop Speech & Language: A Guidebook for Parents, Teachers & Paraprofessionals. 80p. 1979. 12.75x (ISBN 0-398-02453-7). C C Thomas.

Gordon, Michael R. Conflict & Consensus in Labour's Foreign Policy, 1914-1965. 1969. 27.50x (ISBN 0-8047-0686-7). Stanford U Pr.

Gordon, Michael S. Self Assessment in Clinical Cardiology, Vol. 2. 349p. 1976. pap. 23.25 (ISBN 0-8151-3801-6). Year Bk Med.

Gordon, Michael W. The Cuban Nationalization: The Demise of Foreign Private Property. LC 76-17458. 239p. 1976. lib. bdg. 35.00 (ISBN 0-930342-13-5). W S Hein.

--Multinational Corporations Law: Mexico & Central America. 1979. 200.00 (ISBN 0-379-20373-1). Oceana.

Gordon, Michael W., ed. Commercial, Business, & Trade Laws: Mexico. LC 84-121476. 1983. (BDR) looseleaf 125.00 (ISBN 0-379-22012-1). Oceana.

Gordon, Michael W., tr. from Span. The Mexican Civil Code. LC 80-24556. 619p. 1980. lib. bdg. 40.00 (ISBN 0-379-20690-0). Oceana.

Gordon, Milton M. Assimilation in American Life: The Role of Race, Religion & National Origins. 1964. pap. 8.95x (ISBN 0-19-500896-0). Oxford U Pr.

--Human Nature, Class, & Ethnicity. (Illus.). 1978. 18.95x (ISBN 0-19-502236-X); pap. 7.95x (ISBN 0-19-502237-8). Oxford U Pr.

Gordon, Milton M. & Lambert, Richard D., eds. America As a Multicultural Society. LC 80-70879. (Annals of the American Academy of Political & Social Science Ser.: No. 454). 250p. 1981. pap. text ed. 7.95 (ISBN 0-87761-261-7). Am Acad Pol Soc Sci.

Gordon, Morton. Daytime School for Adults. 1967. write for info. (ISBN 0-87060-015-X, OCP 15). Syracuse U Cont Ed.

Gordon, Mrs. Christopher North: A Memoir of John Wilson. 1973. Repr. of 1880 ed. 30.00 (ISBN 0-8274-1396-3). R West.

Gordon, Murray, ed. Conflict in the Persian Gulf. (Checkmark Book Ser.). 200p. 1981. lib. bdg. 19.95 (ISBN 0-87196-158-X). Facts on File.

Gordon, Myron. How to Plan & Conduct A Successful Meeting. LC 85-9851. (Illus.). 176p. 1985. pap. 6.95 (ISBN 0-8069-6256-9). Sterling.

--Making Meetings More Productive. LC 80-52335. (Illus.). 192p. 1980. 12.95 (ISBN 0-8069-0206-X); lib. bdg. 15.69 (ISBN 0-8069-0207-8). Sterling.

Gordon, Myron, jt. auth. see Whitern, Wilfred L.

Gordon, Myron, ed. Pigment Cell Growth: Proceedings. 1953. 65.50 (ISBN 0-12-290956-9). Acad Pr.

Gordon, Myron J. The Investment, Financing & Valuation of the Corporation. LC 82-2968. (The Irwin Series in Economics). (Illus.). xiv, 256p. 1982. Repr. of 1962 ed. lib. bdg. 33.00x (ISBN 0-313-23542-2, G0RI). Greenwood.

Gordon, N. & Schutt, W. Paediatric Neurology for the Clinician. (Clinics in Developmental Medicine Ser.: Vols. 59 & 60). 228p. 1976. text ed. 35.50 (ISBN 0-433-12410-5, Pub. by Spastics Intl England). Lippincott.

Gordon, Nancy M., jt. ed. see Gordon, Harold J.

Gordon, Nancy M., tr. see Strieder, P.

Gordon, Naomi. Classroom Experiences: The Writing Process in Action. LC 84-6560. 128p. (Orig.). 1984. pap. text ed. 6.50x (ISBN 0-435-08210-8). Heinemann Ed.

Gordon, Neal J., jt. ed. see Farley, Frank.

Gordon, Neil & McKinlay, Ian, eds. Helping Clumsy Children. (Illus.). 200p. 1980. pap. text ed. 16.25 (ISBN 0-443-01868-5). Churchill.

Gordon, Oakley, ed. see Pacific Northwest Conference On Higher Education, 1968.

Gordon, P., jt. auth. see Guiltinan, J.

Gordon, P. F. & Gregory, P. Organic Chemistry in Colour. (Illus.). 300p. 1983. 73.50 (ISBN 0-387-11748-2). Springer-Verlag.

Gordon, P. J. The Renaissance Imagination: Essays & Lectures. Orgel, Stephen, ed. LC 74-81432. 1976. 49.75x (ISBN 0-520-02817-1); pap. 8.95 (ISBN 0-520-04092-9). U of Cal Pr.

Gordon, Patrick. Passages from the Diary of General Patrick Gordon of Auchleuchries. (Russia Through European Eyes Ser). 1968. Repr. of 1859 ed. lib. bdg. 39.50 (ISBN 0-306-12210-3). Da Capo.

Gordon, Paul. Policing Immigration: Britain's Internal Controls. 160p. (Orig.). 1985. pap. 7.50 (ISBN 0-86104-623-4, Pub. by Pluto Pr). Longwood Pub Group.

--Principles of Phase Diagrams in Materials Systems. LC 82-14073. 248p. 1983. Repr. of 1968 ed. 19.50 (ISBN 0-89874-408-3). Krieger.

Gordon, Paul A. The Sanctuary, Eighteen Forty-Four & the Pioneers. Wheeler, Gerald, ed. LC 83-17611. 160p. (Orig.). 1984. pap. 9.95 (ISBN 0-8280-0217-7). Review & Herald.

Gordon, Paul L., ed. The Book of Film Care. (H-23 Ser.). (Illus.). 130p. (Orig.). 1983. pap. text ed. 12.95 (ISBN 0-87985-321-2). Eastman Kodak.

Gordon, Pauline N. Sydney. 1983. 6.50 (ISBN 0-8062-2120-8). Carlton.

Gordon, Pearl S. Simply Elegant: A Guide for Elegant but Simple Entertaining. 10th ed. LC 77-13166. (Illus.). 208p. (Includes recipes and menues.). 1984. lib. bdg. 16.95 (ISBN 0-9600492-4-X). Simply Elegant.

Gordon, Peter. Selection for Secondary Education. 269p. 1980. 25.00x (ISBN 0-7130-0157-7, Pub. by Woburn Pr England) (ISBN 3-7165-0122-0). Biblio Dist.

--Study of Curriculum. 192p. 1981. 31.50 (ISBN 0-7134-2109-6, Pub. by Batsford England); pap. 13.50 (ISBN 0-7134-2092-8, Pub. by Batsford England). David & Charles.

--The Victorian School Manager: A Study in the Management of Education, 1800-1902. 337p. 1974. 27.50x (ISBN 0-7130-0125-9, Pub. by Woburn Pr England). Biblio Dist.

Gordon, Peter & Lawton, Denis. Curriculum Change in the Nineteenth & Twentieth Centuries. LC 78-23803. 258p. 1979. pap. 18.00x (ISBN 0-8419-6216-2). Holmes & Meier.

Gordon, Peter & Lawton, Dennis. A Guide to English Educational Terms. LC 84-5305. 238p. 1985. 26.50x (ISBN 0-8052-3922-7). Schocken.

Gordon, Peter, jt. auth. see Davison, A.

Gordon, Peter, ed. The Study of Education: A Collection of Inaugural Lectures, Vol. I--Early & Modern, Vol. II--The Last Decade. (The Woburn Education Ser.). 662p. 1980. Vol. I. 32.50x (ISBN 0-7130-0171-2, Pub. by Woburn Pr England); Vol. I. pap. 15.00x (ISBN 0-7130-4005-X); Vol.II. 32.50x (ISBN 0-7130-0170-4); Vol. II. pap. 15.00 (ISBN 0-7130-4006-8). Biblio Dist.

Gordon, Philip. The Availability of Contemporary American Music for Performing Groups in High Schools & Colleges. LC 72-176815. (Columbia U. Teachers College Contributions to Education Ser.: No. 961). Repr. of 1950 ed. 22.50 (ISBN 0-404-55961-1). AMS Pr.

Gordon, Phillip, jt. auth. see Kurtzman, Joel.

Gordon Press Editorial Staff, ed. Directory of American Film Scholars: Who's Who in American Film Scholarship. 1977. 75.00 (ISBN 0-87968-226-4). Gordon Pr.

Gordon, R. Carl Laemmle & Universal Pictures: A Tribute. 1976. lib. bdg. 69.95 (ISBN 0-8490-1579-0). Gordon Pr.

--Deutschen Filmschaffenden of 1935. 1976. lib. bdg. 120.00 (ISBN 0-8490-1712-2). Gordon Pr.

--The Yiddish Film. 1977. lib. bdg. 59.95 (ISBN 0-8490-2851-5). Gordon Pr.

Gordon, R. & Spaulding, M. L. Numerical Models for Tidal Rivers, Estuaries & Coastal Waters: Bibliography. (Technical Report Ser.: No. 32). 55p. 1974. 2.00 (ISBN 0-938412-31-0, P376). URI MAS.

--Play Ball, Kate! LC 81-4855. (Illus.). 32p. (gr. k-2). 1981. pap. text ed. 9.89 (ISBN 0-89375-525-7); pap. text ed. 1.95 (ISBN 0-89375-526-5). Troll Assocs.

--Sam the Scarecrow. (Illus.). 32p. (gr. k-2). 1980. PLB 4.81 (ISBN 0-89375-387-4); pap. 1.75 (ISBN 0-89375-287-8). Troll Assocs.

--Samuel el Espantapajaros. (Illus.). 32p. (Sp.). (gr. k-2). 1981. PLB 4.81 (ISBN 0-89375-556-7). Troll Assocs.

--The Spelling Bee. LC 81-4648. (Illus.). 32p. (gr. k-2). 1981. PLB 9.89 (ISBN 0-89375-535-4); pap. 1.95 (ISBN 0-89375-536-2). Troll Assocs.

--Surprise Party. LC 81-4869. (Illus.). 32p. (gr. k-2). 1981. PLB 9.89 (ISBN 0-89375-521-4); pap. 1.95 (ISBN 0-89375-522-2). Troll Assocs.

--Three Little Witches. (Illus.). 32p. (gr. k-2). 1980. PLB 4.81 (ISBN 0-89375-390-4); pap. 1.50 (ISBN 0-89375-290-8). Troll Assocs.

--Tick Tock Clock. LC 81-11393. (Now I Know Ser.). (Illus.). 32p. (gr. k-2). 1982. PLB 9.89 (ISBN 0-89375-676-8); pap. 1.25 (ISBN 0-89375-677-6). Troll Assocs.

--Trees. LC 82-20291. (Now I Know Ser.). (Illus.). 32p. (gr. k-2). 1982. lib. bdg. 9.89 (ISBN 0-89375-901-5). Troll Assocs.

--What a Dog. (Illus.). 32p. (gr. k-2). 1980. PLB 4.81 (ISBN 0-89375-393-9); pap. 1.50 (ISBN 0-89375-293-2). Troll Assocs.

Gordon, Sherry, tr. see Toguchi, Seikichi.

Gordon, Shirley. The Boy Who Wanted a Family. 96p. (gr. 1-4). 1982. pap. 1.95 (ISBN 0-440-40786-9, YB). Dell.

--The Boy Who Wanted a Family. LC 79-2003. (Illus.). 96p. (gr. 1-4). 1980. PLB 9.89 (ISBN 0-06-022052-X). HarpJ.

--Caribbean Generations. LC 82-17976. (Illus.). 320p. 1984. pap. text ed. 5.95 (ISBN 0-582-76568-4). Longman.

--Crystal Is the New Girl. LC 75-24500. 32p. (ps-3). 1976. PLB 9.89 (ISBN 0-06-022025-2). HarpJ.

--Grandma Zoo. LC 78-52402. (Illus.). (ps-2). 1978. PLB 9.89 (ISBN 0-06-022050-3). HarpJ.

--Happy Birthday, Crystal. LC 80-8941. (Illus.). 32p. (gr. k-4). 1981. 7.95 (ISBN 0-06-022006-6). HarpJ.

--Me & the Bad Guys. LC 79-9611. (Illus.). 80p. (gr. 3-6). 1980. HarpJ.

--Me & the Bad Guys. 80p. (gr. 3-7). 1984. pap. 1.95 (ISBN 0-440-45520-0, YB). Dell.

Gordon, Shirley C., jt. ed. see Augier, F. R.

Gordon, Sol. Facts About STD-Sexually Transmitted Diseases. LC 72-12089. (Illus., Orig.). (gr. 7-12). 1983. pap. 5.95 (ISBN 0-934978-04-2). Ed-U Pr.

--The New You. 1981. pap. 4.95 (ISBN 0-686-91582-8). Ed-U Pr.

--Protect Yourself from Becoming an Unwanted Parent. (Illus.). 20p. (Orig.). (gr. 9-12). 1983. pap. 1.00 (ISBN 0-934978-08-5). Ed U Pr.

--Psychology for You. 500p. pap. 9.95 (ISBN 0-317-36553-3); pap. 7.96, ea. 6 copies or more (ISBN 0-317-36554-1). Ed-U Pr.

--The Teenage Survival Book. 150p. 1-5 copies 9.95 ea.; 6-25 copies 8.46 ea.; 26 copies or more 6.97 ea. Ed-U Pr.

--The Teenage Survival Book: The Complete Revised, Updated Edition of YOU. 150p. 1981. pap. 9.95 (ISBN 0-8129-0972-0). Times Bks.

Gordon, Sol & Cohen, Judith. Did the Sun Shine Before You Were Born: A Sex Education Primer. LC 74-82733. (ps-2). 1974. 6.95 (ISBN 0-89388-179-1). Okpaku Communications.

Gordon, Sol & Gordon, Judith. A Better Safe than Sorry Book. (Illus., Orig.). (ps-4). 1984. pap. 5.95x (ISBN 0-934978-13-1). Ed U Pr.

--Did the Sun Shine Before You Were Born? A Sex Education Primer. (ps-3). 1982. pap. 6.95 (ISBN 0-934978-03-4). Ed-U Pr.

--Raising a Child Conservatively in a Sexually Permissive World. 1983. 13.95 (ISBN 0-671-46748-4). S&S.

Gordon, Sol, jt. auth. see Snyder, Susan U.

Gordon, Sol, jt. ed. see Williams, Gertrude j.

Gordon, Solon A. & Cohen, Melvin J., eds. Gravity & the Organism. LC 70-156302. pap. 121.00 (ISBN 0-317-20702-4, 2024116). Bks Demand UMI.

Gordon, Stephen D., et al. Minnesota Public Sector Labor Law. 1983. Looseleaf 55.00 (ISBN 0-86678-115-3). Butterworth MN.

Gordon, Stephen L., ed. see American Academy of Orthopedic Surgeons.

Gordon, Steven I. Computer Models in Environmental Planning. (Illus.). 240p. 1985. 34.50 (ISBN 0-442-22974-7). Van Nos Reinhold.

Gordon, Stewart. Gunswift. 1979. pap. 1.50 (ISBN 0-505-51347-1, Pub. by Tower Bks). Dorchester Pub Co.

Gordon, Stuart. Fire in the Abyss. 336p. (Orig.). 1983. pap. 2.95 (ISBN 0-425-06081-0). Berkley Pub.

--Gordonstown, a New Design for America. (Illus.). 288p. 1980. pap. 5.95 (ISBN 0-9603942-0-6). Gordonstown.

Gordon, Susan. Match of the Season. 1982. 11.95 (ISBN 0-8027-0708-4). Walker & Co.

Gordon, Susan, jt. ed. see Fooden, Myra.

Gordon, Susan J. The Road I Travel. 1964. 3.50 (ISBN 0-911566-02-3). Ventnor.

Gordon, Suzanne. Off Balance: The Real World of Ballet. LC 82-18806. 256p. 1983. 15.45 (ISBN 0-394-51985-X). Pantheon.

--Off Balance: The Real World of Ballet. (Illus.). 256p. 1984. pap. 7.95 (ISBN 0-07-023770-0). McGraw.

--A Talent for Tomorrow: Life Stories of South African Servants. 275p. 1985. pap. text ed. 16.95x (ISBN 0-86975-243-X, Pub. by Ravan Pr). Ohio U Pr.

Gordon, Suzanne & McFadden, Dave, eds. Economic Conversion: Revitalizing America's Economy. 280p. 1984. 28.00x (ISBN 0-88730-012-X); pap. 12.95x (ISBN 0-88410-967-4). Ballinger Pub.

Gordon, Sydney, jt. auth. see Allan, Ted.

Gordon, Taylor. Born to Be. LC 75-26561. (Illus.). 290p. 1975. pap. 7.95x (ISBN 0-295-95428-0). U of Wash Pr.

Gordon, Theodore H. California Real Estate Law: Text & Cases. 2nd ed. (Illus.). 304p. 1985. pap. text ed. 23.95 (ISBN 0-13-112517-6); pap. text ed. 17.95 student ed. (ISBN 0-317-11404-2). P-H.

Gordon, Theodore J. Life-Extending Technologies: A Technology Assessment. 1980. 39.00 (ISBN 0-08-023132-2). Pergamon.

Gordon, Theron L. How to Build, Customize & Design Plastic Models. (Illus.). 192p. (Orig.). 1982. pap. 10.95 (ISBN 0-8306-1192-4, 1192). TAB Bks.

Gordon, Thomas. Gazetteer of Pennsylvania. (Illus.). 1975. 20.00 (ISBN 0-686-20868-4). Polyanthos.

--Leader Effectiveness Training. 1980. pap. 9.95 (ISBN 0-553-34138-3). Bantam.

--Parent Effectiveness Training: The Tested New Way to Raise Responsible Children. LC 74-130756. 1970. 12.95 (ISBN 0-88326-039-5, Wyden). McKay.

--P.E.T, Parent Effectiveness Training: The Tested New Way to Raise Responsible Children. 352p. 1975. pap. 6.95 (ISBN 0-452-25252-0, Z5252, Plume). NAL.

--Teacher Effectiveness Training. 1975. 12.95 (ISBN 0-88326-080-8, Wyden). McKay.

Gordon, Thomas & Sands, Judith S. P.E.T. in Action. 1978. pap. 4.95 (ISBN 0-553-24556-2). Bantam.

Gordon, Thomas, jt. auth. see Trenchard, John.

Gordon, Thomas F. Gazetteer of the State of New Jersey. 1975. 15.00 (ISBN 0-686-20869-2). Polyanthos.

--History of America Containing the History of the Spanish Discoveries Prior to 1520, 2 Vols. LC 73-128434. Repr. of 1831 ed. 49.50 (ISBN 0-404-02867-5). AMS Pr.

--The History of Pennsylvania, from Its Discovery by Europeans to the Declaration of Independence in 1776. LC 66-25100. 1967. Repr. of 1829 ed. 22.50 (ISBN 0-87152-036-2). Reprint.

--War on the Bank of the United States. (Research & Source Works Ser.: No. 1622). 1966. Repr. of 1834 ed. 18.50 (ISBN 0-8337-1389-2). B Franklin.

--War on the Bank of the United States. LC 68-18219. Repr. of 1834 ed. 25.00x (ISBN 0-678-00380-7). Kelley.

Gordon, Thomas F. & Verna, Mary E. Mass Communication Effects & Processes: A Comprehensive Bibliography, 1950-1975. LC 77-26094. pap. 57.50 (ISBN 0-317-10682-1, 2021907). Bks Demand UMI.

Gordon, Tulo. Milbi: Aboriginal Tales from Queensland's Endeavor River. LC 79-53376. (Illus.). 59p. (Orig.). (gr. 1-4). 1980. text ed. 5.95 (ISBN 0-7081-1299-4, 0548). Australia N U P.

Gordon, V. O. A Course in Descriptive Geometry. 1980. 10.00 (ISBN 0-8285-1870-X, Pub. by Mir Pubs USSR). Imported Pubns.

Gordon, V. O. & Ivanov, Y. A. Worked Problems in Descriptive Geometry. 332p. 1979. 9.45 (ISBN 0-8285-1536-0, Pub. by Mir Pubs USSR). Imported Pubns.

Gordon, Victoria. Always the Boss. (Harlequin Romances Ser.). 192p. 1982. pap. 1.50 (ISBN 0-373-02469-X). Harlequin Bks.

--Battle of Wills. (Harlequin Romances Ser.). 192p. 1983. pap. 1.75 (ISBN 0-373-02540-8). Harlequin Bks.

--Dinner at Wyatt's. (Harlequin Romances Ser.). 192p. 1983. pap. 1.50 (ISBN 0-373-02531-9). Harlequin Bks.

--Dream House. (Harlequin Romances Ser.). 192p. 1982. pap. 1.50 (ISBN 0-373-02458-4). Harlequin Bks.

--Wolf at the Door. (Harlequin Romances Ser.). 192p. 1981. pap. 1.50 (ISBN 0-373-02433-9). Harlequin Bks.

Gordon, Virginia N. The Undecided College Student: An Academic & Career Advising Challenge. (Illus.). 140p. 1984. 16.75x (ISBN 0-398-04989-0). C C Thomas.

Gordon, Vivian V. The Self-Concept of Black Americans. 118p. 1977. pap. text ed. 8.75 (ISBN 0-8191-0151-6). U Pr of Amer.

Gordon, Vivian V., ed. Lectures: Black Scholars on Black Issues. LC 79-63259. 1979. pap. text ed. 14.00 (ISBN 0-8191-0709-3). U Pr of Amer.

Gordon, W. J. The Horse World of London. (Illus.). 7.95 (ISBN 0-85131-144-X, NL51, Dist. by Miller). J A Allen.

Gordon, W. R. Albany Hudson Fast Line: Third Rails, Pantographs & Trolley Poles. (Illus.). 112p. 1985. 6.00 (ISBN 0-317-18221-8). W R Gordon.

--Elmira & Chemung Valley Trolleys. (Illus.). 176p. 1985. 6.00 (ISBN 0-317-18222-6). W R Gordon.

Gordon, W. Terrence. A History of Semantics. (Studies in the History of Linguistics Ser.: Vol. 30). 284p. 1982. 33.00x (ISBN 90-272-4512-6). Benjamins North Am.

--Semantics: A Bibliography Nineteen Sixty-Five to Nineteen Seventy-Eight. LC 79-24719. 321p. 1980. 22.50 (ISBN 0-8108-1300-9). Scarecrow.

Gordon, Walter K., ed. Literature in Critical Perspectives: An Anthology. LC 68-15855. 1968. text ed. 28.95 (ISBN 0-13-537613-0). P-H.

Gordon, Walter K., jt. ed. see Sanderson, James L.

Gordon, Walter L., III. Crime & Criminal Law: The California Experience, 1960-1975. LC 81-67855. (New Studies on Law & Society). 164p. (Orig.). 1981. 24.00x (ISBN 0-86733-002-3, 5998). Assoc Faculty Pr.

Gordon, Wendell. Institutional Economics: The Changing System. 366p. 1980. text ed. 25.00x (ISBN 0-292-77022-7); pap. 13.95x (ISBN 0-292-73823-4). U of Tex Pr.

Gordon, Wendell C. The Expropriation of Foreign Owned Property in Mexico. Bruchey, Stuart & Bruchey, Eleanor, eds. LC 76-5013. (American Business Abroad Ser.). 1976. Repr. of 1941 ed. 20.00x (ISBN 0-405-09281-4). Ayer Co Pubs.

--The Expropriation of Foreign-Owned Property in Mexico. LC 73-16647. 1975. Repr. of 1941 ed. lib. bdg. 15.00x (ISBN 0-8371-7212-8, GOPM). Greenwood.

--The Political Economy of Latin America. LC 65-19444. 401p. 1965. 30.00x (ISBN 0-231-02675-7); pap. 16.00x (ISBN 0-231-08572-9). Columbia U Pr.

Gordon, William. History of the Rise, Progress, & Establishment of the Independence of the United States of America, 4 Vols. facs. ed. LC 75-85455. (Select Bibliographies Reprint Ser). 1788. Set. 164.00 (ISBN 0-8369-5024-0). Ayer Co Pubs.

Gordon, William A. Mind & Art of Henry Miller. LC 67-12215. xxxii, 232p. 1967. o. p. 22.50x (ISBN 0-8071-0512-0); pap. 6.95x (ISBN 0-8071-0142-7). La State U Pr.

--The Reading Curriculum: A Reference Guide to Criterion-Based Skill Development in Grades K-8. LC 82-9103. 272p. 1982. 38.95 (ISBN 0-03-062128-3). Praeger.

Gordon, William C. Bible Word Search. (Quiz & Puzzle Bks.). 112p. 1983. 2.95 (ISBN 0-8010-3679-8). Baker Bk.

--Social Ideals of Alfred Tennyson As Related to His Times. LC 68-812. (Studies in Tennyson, No. 27). 1969. Repr. of 1906 ed. lib. bdg. 49.95x (ISBN 0-8383-0661-6). Haskell.

Gordon, William C., jt. auth. see Logan, Frank A.

Gordon, William R. Buffalo & Lake Erie Traction Co. (Illus.). 224p. 1985. 10.50 (ISBN 0-317-18220-X). W R Gordon.

--Ninety Four Years of Rochester Railroads, 2 vols. (Illus.). 280p. (LC 74-21709, Vol. 1; LC 75-18651, Vol. 2). 1975. Vol. 1. pap. 9.50 (ISBN 0-910662-12-6); Vol. 2. pap. 10.00 (ISBN 0-685-48907-8). W R Gordon.

Gordon, William R. & Platukis, Joseph G. Syracuse & South Bay Railway to Oneida Lake. Cox, Harold E., ed. (Illus.). 48p. (Orig.). 1985. pap. 7.00 (ISBN 0-911940-40-5). W R Gordon.

Gordon, William Reed & Wagner, Richard M. The Overlook Route: The Dayton, Covington & Piqua Traction Co. LC 72-82992. 1972. 4.15 (ISBN 0-914196-12-X). Trolley Talk.

Gordon, William S. Recollections of the Old Quarter. facsimile ed. LC 75-39084. (Black Heritage Library Collection). Repr. of 1902 ed. 17.50 (ISBN 0-8369-9022-6). Ayer Co Pubs.

Gordon, Yvonne. Escape to Ecstasy. DeRoin, Gene, ed. (Aston Hall Presents Ser.). (Orig.). 1979. pap. 1.50 (ISBN 0-89936-001-7). Aston Hall.

Gordon-Ashworth, Fiona. International Commodity Control 1929-1977. LC 81-48262. 368p. 1984. 32.50 (ISBN 0-312-41994-5). St Martin.

Gordon-Bowe, Nicola. Harry Clarke: His Graphic Art. (Illus.). 160p. 1983. 40.00 (ISBN 0-943842-01-8); limited ed. 150.00 (ISBN 0-943842-00-X). H Keith Burns.

Gordon-Cumming, M. Money in Industry. 59.95 (ISBN 0-8490-0660-0). Gordon Pr.

Gordon-Cumming, Roualeyn G. The Lion Hunter of South Africa: Five Years Adventures in the Far Interior of South Africa, with Notices of the Native Tribes & Savage Animals. 20.75 (ISBN 0-8369-9187-7, 9056). Ayer Co Pubs.

Gordon-Smith, Eileen L. In His Time. 1984. pap. 1.95 (ISBN 9971-972-04-2). OMF Bks.

Gordon-Smith, Maria, jt. auth. see Marek, George R.

Gordon-Watson, Mary. Handbook of Riding. LC 82-47795. 1982. 22.50 (ISBN 0-394-52110-2). Knopf.

Gordus, A. A. Schaum's Outline of Analytical Chemistry. 256p. 8.95 (ISBN 0-07-023795-6). McGraw.

Gordus, Jeanne P. Leaving Early: Perspectives & Problems in Current Retirement Practice & Policy. LC 80-39653. 88p. (Orig.). 1980. pap. text ed. 6.95 (ISBN 0-911558-78-0). W E Upjohn.

Gordus, Jeanne P., jt. ed. see Ferman, Louis A.

Gordus, Jeanne P., et al. Plant Closings & Economic Dislocation. LC 81-16188. 173p. 1981. text ed. 16.95 (ISBN 0-911558-89-6); pap. text ed. 11.95 (ISBN 0-911558-90-X). W E Upjohn.

Gordy, Berry, Sr. Movin' Up: Pop Gordy Tells His Story. LC 78-22493. (Illus.). 160p. (gr. 5 up). 1979. 11.49 (ISBN 0-06-022053-8); PLB 10.89 (ISBN 0-06-022054-6). HarpJ.

Gordy, Louise J., ed. see Gray, Roscoe N.

Gordy, W. & Cook, L., eds. Technique of Organic Chemistry: Vol. 9, Pt. 2, Microwave Molecular Spectra. LC 80-16243. 747p. 1970. 67.50 (ISBN 0-471-93161-6). Krieger.

Gore, A. J., ed. Mires: Swamp, Fog, Fen & Moor. (Ecosystems of the World Ser.: Vol. 4). 1983. Set. (ISBN 0-444-42005-3); Pt. A: Analytical Studies. 161.75 (ISBN 0-444-42003-7); Pt. B: Descriptive Studies. 161.75 (ISBN 0-444-42004-5, I-493-82). Elsevier.

Gore, Alan & Chambers, James. The English House. (Illus.). 1985. 24.95 (ISBN 0-393-02241-2). Norton.

Gore, Alan, jt. auth. see Fleming, Laurence.

Gore, C. G. Regions in Question: Space Development Theory & Regional Policy. (Development & Underdevelopment Ser.). 304p. 1984. text ed. 29.95 (ISBN 0-416-31410-4, 4031); pap. text ed. 12.95 (ISBN 0-416-31420-1, 4021). Methuen Inc.

Gore, Catherine F. The Book of Roses or, the Rose Fancier's Manual. LC 78-9788. (Old Roses Reprint Ser.). 1978. Repr. of 1838 ed. text ed. 25.00 (ISBN 0-930576-09-8). E M Coleman Ent.

Gore, Catherine G. Cecil, a Peer, 3 vols. in 2. LC 79-8274. Repr. of 1841 ed. Set. 84.50 (ISBN 0-404-61879-0). Vol. 1 (ISBN 0-404-61880-4). Vol. 2 (ISBN 0-404-61881-2). AMS Pr.

--Cecil; or the Adventures of a Coxcomb, 3 vols. in 2. LC 79-8273. Repr. of 1841 ed. Set. 84.50 (ISBN 0-404-61875-8). Vol. 1 (ISBN 0-404-61876-6). Vol. 2 (ISBN 0-404-61877-4). AMS Pr.

--The Money-Lender, 3 vols. in 1. LC 79-8275. Repr. of 1843 ed. 44.50 (ISBN 0-404-61883-9). AMS Pr.

--Soldier of Lyons: A Tale of the Tuileries. LC 71-162906. (Bentley's Standard Novels: No. 82). Repr. of 1841 ed. 18.50 (ISBN 0-404-54482-7). AMS Pr.

Gore, Charles. Philosophy of Good Life. 1976. 12.95x (ISBN 0-460-00924-9, Evman). Biblio Dist.

--The Philosophy of the Good Life. LC 77-27197. (Gifford Lectures: 1929-30). Repr. of 1930 ed. 24.00 (ISBN 0-404-60484-6). AMS Pr.

--The Social Doctrine of the Sermon on the Mount. 59.95 (ISBN 0-8490-1063-2). Gordon Pr.

Gore, Daniel. To Know a Library: Essays & Annual Reports, 1970-1976. LC 77-84769. (New Directions in Librarianship: No. 1). 1978. lib. bdg. 35.00 (ISBN 0-8371-9881-X, GTK/). Greenwood.

Gore, Daniel, ed. Farewell to Alexandria: Solutions to Space, Growth & Performance Problems of Libraries. LC 75-35345. 224p. 1976. lib. bdg. 27.50 (ISBN 0-8371-8587-4, GGP/). Greenwood.

Gore, Daniel, ed. see Florida Atlantic University Conference.

Gore, Daniel, ed. see International Seminar on Approval & Gathering Plans in Large & Medium Size Academic Libraries, 3rd.

Gore, Daniel, et al, eds. Requiem for the Card Catalog: Management Issues in Automated Cataloging. LC 78-7129. (New Directions in Librarianship Ser.: No. 2). 1979. lib. bdg. 29.95 (ISBN 0-313-20608-2, GMI/). Greenwood.

Gore, Elizabeth. Child Psychiatry Observed. Nursten, Jean, ed. LC 75-6926. 264p. 1976. pap. text ed. 15.50 (ISBN 0-08-017278-4). Pergamon.

Gore, Francis, jt. auth. see Giraudeau, A.

Gore, G. The Scientific Basis of National Progress, Including That of Morality. 218p. 1970. Repr. of 1882 ed. 26.00x (ISBN 0-7146-2407-1, BHA-02407, F Cass Co). Biblio Dist.

Gore, George W. In-Service Professional Improvement of Negro Public School Teachers in Tennessee. LC 76-176816. (Columbia University. Teachers College. Contributions to Education: No. 786). Repr. of 1940 ed. 22.50 (ISBN 0-404-55786-4). AMS Pr.

Gore, Gerry. Handguns for Self Defense: A South African Guide. (Illus.). 164p. 1982. pap. 12.95x (ISBN 0-86954-079-3, Pub. by Macmillan S Africa). Intl Spec Bk.

Gore, H. & Lindroth, D. What to Do When There's No One but You. (Illus.). 1974. 4.95 (ISBN 0-13-955070-4). P-H.

Gore, Irene. Add Years to Your Life & Life to Your Years. LC 73-92183. 1975. pap. 1.95 (ISBN 0-8128-1849-0). Stein & Day.

Gore, James A. Restoration of Rivers & Streams. 320p. 1985. text ed. 39.95 (ISBN 0-250-40505-9). Butterworth.

Gore, Joel M. & Alpert, Joseph S. Handbook of Hemodynamic Monitoring. 240p. 1984. pap. text ed. 13.95 (ISBN 0-316-32085-4). Little.

Gore, John. The Ghosts of Fleet Street. 1973. 17.50 (ISBN 0-8274-0734-3). R West.

--King George V: A Personal Memoir. 26.00 (ISBN 0-8369-6938-3, 7819). Ayer Co Pubs.

Gore, Kay, jt. auth. see Bitter, Gary G.

Gore, Marjorie. Marble Dust: A Biography of Elizabet Ney. 320p. 1984. 16.95 (ISBN 0-89015-430-9). Eakin Pubns.

Gore, Marvin & Stubbe, John. Elements of Systems Analysis. 3rd ed. 568p. 1983. text ed. write for info. (ISBN 0-697-08169-9). instrs.' resource manual avail. (ISBN 0-697-08178-8); alternate casebook avail. (ISBN 0-697-00092-3); avail. solutions manual to alternate casebook (ISBN 0-697-00267-5). Wm C Brown.

Gore, Marvin R. & Stubbe, John W. Computers & Information Systems. 2nd ed. (Illus.). 512p. 1984. text ed. 32.95 (ISBN 0-07-023807-3). McGraw.

Gore, Mirkalice. Lessons. 19p. pap. 3.00 (ISBN 0-942494-43-1). Coleman Pub.

Gore, Nancy. Wireline Operations. LC 83-62077. (Oil & Gas Production Ser.: Lesson 10). (Illus.). 80p. (Orig.). 1983. pap. text ed. 5.00 (ISBN 0-88698-043-7, 3.31010). PETEX.

Gore, Patrick D. & Masoncup, John E. Teaching Energy Awareness. rev. ed. (Illus.). 309p. (gr. 6-12). pap. 16.95 (ISBN 0-943804-00-0). U of Denver Teach.

Gore, Sheila M. & Altman, Douglas G. Statistics in Practice. 100p. 1982. 19.00x (ISBN 0-7279-0085-4, Pub. by British Med Assoc UK). Taylor & Francis.

Gore, T. S., et al, eds. Recent Progress in the Chemistry of Natural & Synthetic Colouring Matters & Related Fields. 1962. 81.00 (ISBN 0-12-291650-6). Acad Pr.

Gore, Thomas P. Gore's Forms for Tennessee Annotated, 4 vols. 3rd ed. 1970. 80.00 (ISBN 0-87215-088-7). Michie Co.

Gore, W., ed. Microcircuits & Their Applications. 262p. 1970. 83.25 (ISBN 0-677-61390-3). Gordon.

Gore, William, et al. Rails in the North Woods. rev. ed. 1978. Repr. of 1973 ed. 14.95 (ISBN 0-932052-16-9). North Country.

Gore, William J. & Dyson, James. Making of Decisions. LC 64-23084. 1964. 18.00 (ISBN 0-02-912590-1). Free Pr.

Goreau, Angeline. The Whole Duty of a Woman. LC 84-12042. 360p. 1985. pap. 12.95 (ISBN 0-385-27878-0, Dial). Doubleday.

Goreau, Eloise K. Integrity of Life: Allegorical Imagery in the Plays of John Webster. (Salzburg Studies in English Literature, Jacobean Drama Studies: No. 32). 194p. 1974. pap. text ed. 25.50x (ISBN 0-391-01390-4). Humanities.

Goreau, Laurraine. Just Mahalia, Baby: The Mahalia Jackson Story. 612p. 1984. pap. 13.95 (ISBN 0-88289-441-2). Pelican.

Gore-Booth, Lord, ed. Satow's Guide to Diplomatic Practice. 6th ed. LC 77-12580. 1979. text ed. 45.00x. Longman.

Gorecki, Danuta M. & Wajenberg, Arnold. Cannon Law: History, Sources, & a Proposed Classification Scheme. Date not set. price not set. Am Assn Law Libs.

Gorecki, Jan. Capital Punishment: Criminal Law & Social Evolution. LC 83-1875. 176p. 1983. 26.00x (ISBN 0-231-05658-3). Columbia U Pr.

--Divorce in Poland. (Studies in the Social Sciences: No. 5). (Orig.). 1970. pap. text ed. 18.40x (ISBN 90-2790-548-7). Mouton.

--A Theory of Criminal Justice. LC 78-31559. 192p. 1979. 24.00x (ISBN 0-231-04670-7). Columbia U Pr.

Gorecki, Jan, ed. Sociology & Jurisprudence of Leon Petrazycki. LC 75-38551. (Office of International Programs & Studies Ser). 150p. 1975. 12.50x (ISBN 0-252-00525-2). U of Ill Pr.

Gorecki, Paul K. & Stanbury, W. T. The Objective of Canadian Competition Policy 1888-1983. 236p. 1984. pap. text ed. 15.00x (ISBN 0-88645-002-0, Pub. by Inst Res Pub Canada). Brookfield Pub Co.

Goree, Langston J., ed. see Goree, Thomas J.

Goree, Langston J., et al, eds. Master Index to the Huguenot. 325p. 1985. lib. bdg. 35.00 (ISBN 0-943162-05-X); microfilm of source material 35.00 (ISBN 0-943162-07-6); microfilm master index 15.00 (ISBN 0-943162-06-8). Family History.

Goree, Thomas J. Thomas Jewett Goree Letters: The Civil War Correspondence, Vol. 1. Goree, Langston J., ed. LC 81-67136. (Illus.). 338p. 1982. lib. bdg. 65.00 (ISBN 0-943162-00-9). Family History.

Gorelick, L. & Williams-Forte, E., eds. Ancient Seals & the Bible. (Occasional Papers on the Near East: Vol. 2, Issue 1). (Illus.). 84p. 1984. pap. 13.00x (ISBN 0-89003-045-6). Undena Pubns.

Gorelick, Sherry. City College & the Jewish Poor: Education in New York, 1880-1924. (Illus.). 264p. 1981. 25.00 (ISBN 0-8135-0905-X). Rutgers U Pr.

--City College & the Jewish Poor: Education in New York 1880-1924. LC 80-22128. (Illus.). 288p. 1982. pap. 9.95 (ISBN 0-8052-0712-0). Schocken.

Gorelik, A. G., jt. ed. see Vinnichenko, N. K.

Gorelik, George, tr. see Bogdanov, A.

Gorelik, Mordecai. New Theatres for Old. LC 75-14002. 553p. 1975. Repr. of 1940 ed. lib. bdg. 37.50x (ISBN 0-374-93213-1). Octagon.

Gorelik, S. S. Recrystallization in Metals & Alloys. 479p. 1981. 13.00 (ISBN 0-8285-2065-8, Pub. by Mir Pubs USSR). Imported Pubns.

Gorell, Lord. John Keats: The Principle of Beauty. LC 73-13743. 1948. lib. bdg. 17.50 (ISBN 0-8414-4434-X). Folcroft.

Gorell, Ronald. Keats: The Principle of Beauty. LC 72-122978. (Studies in Keats, No. 19). 1970. Repr. of 1948 ed. lib. bdg. 27.95x (ISBN 0-8383-1110-5). Haskell.

Gorell, Ronald G. John Keats: The Principle of Beauty. 126p. 1980. Repr. of 1948 ed. lib. bdg. 15.00 (ISBN 0-8495-2044-4). Arden Lib.

Goren. Contract Bridge for Beginners. pap. 5.95 (ISBN 0-671-21052-1, Fireside). S&S.

Goren, Arthur A. The American Jews. (Dimensions of Ethnicity Ser.). 128p. 1982. pap. text ed. 4.95x (ISBN 0-674-02516-4). Harvard U Pr.

--New York Jews & the Quest for Community. LC 76-129961. 1979. 31.50x (ISBN 0-231-03422-9); pap. 16.00x (ISBN 0-231-08368-8). Columbia U Pr.

Goren, Arthur A., ed. Dissenter in Zion: From the Writings of Judah L. Magnes. (Illus.). 576p. 1982. text ed. 32.50X (ISBN 0-674-21283-5). Harvard U Pr.

Goren, Charles. Goren's New Complete Bridge. LC 85-10344. 744p. 1985. 19.95 (ISBN 0-385-23324-8). Doubleday.

--New Contract Bridge in a Nutshell. 1973. pap. 2.95 (ISBN 0-346-12347-X). Cornerstone.

--Point Count Bidding. rev. ed. 1958. pap. 1.95 (ISBN 0-671-59230-0, Fireside). S&S.

Goren, Charles & Von der Porten, Ronald P. Introduction to Competitive Bidding. LC 83-25396. 192p. 1984. pap. 7.95 (ISBN 0-385-18892-7). Doubleday.

Goren, Charles H. Bridge Is My Game. 1967. pap. 3.95 (ISBN 0-346-12306-2). Cornerstone.

--Charles H. Goren's New Contract Bridge in a Nutshell. rev. ed. LC 76-182838. 168p. 1972. 8.95 (ISBN 0-385-00740-X). Doubleday.

--Fundamentals of Contract Bridge. 1984. pap. 3.50 (ISBN 0-671-49351-5). PB.

--Modern Backgammon Complete. 208p. 1975. pap. 2.95 (ISBN 0-346-12296-1). Cornerstone.

--Play Winning Bridge with Any Partner. 1965. pap. 2.95 (ISBN 0-346-12333-X). Cornerstone.

--The Precision System of Contract Bridge Bidding. 225p. 1972. pap. 2.95 (ISBN 0-346-12061-6). Cornerstone.

--The Precision System of Contract Bridge Bidding. rev. ed. 224p. 1984. pap. 6.95 (ISBN 0-671-53232-4, Fireside). S&S.

Goren, Leyla. Elements of Brahmanism in the Transcendentalism of Emerson. LC 80-2534. Repr. of 1959 ed. 18.50 (ISBN 0-404-19260-2). AMS Pr.

Goren, Roberta. The Soviet Union & Terrorism. Becker, Jillian, ed. LC 84-12366. (Illus.). 280p. 1984. text ed. 27.50 (ISBN 0-04-327073-5); pap. text ed. 11.50 (ISBN 0-04-327074-3). Allen Unwin.

Goren, Simon. Mining & Drilling: Germany, Austria, Hungary. 1985. write for info. looseleaf. Oceana.

Goren, Simon L., tr. from German. German Civil Code & the Introductory Act to the German Civil Code & the Marriage Law of the Federal Republic of Germany: 1981 Supplement. v, 73p. 1982. pap. text ed. 12.50x (ISBN 0-8377-0615-7). Rothman.

Goren, Simon L. & Forrester, Ian S., trs. from Ger. The German Commercial Code: As Amended to January 1, 1978. LC 78-65551. xx, 210p. 1979. text ed. 37.50x (ISBN 0-8377-0606-8). Rothman.

Goren, Simon L. & Forrester, Jan S., trs. The German Commercial Code: An English Translation of the German Commercial Code (As Amended to January 1, 1978) 250p. 1979. lib. bdg. 48.00 (ISBN 90-271-1559-1, Pub. by Kluwer Law Netherlands). Kluwer Academic.

Goren, Simon L., tr. see Forrester, Ian S.

Gorenberg, Hyman & American Institute of Certified Public Accountants. Continuing Professional Education Division. Income Taxation of Estates & Trusts. LC 85-105286. (Illus.). 288p. Date not set. price not set. Am Inst CPA.

Gorenflo, Louise, et al. Farm & Rural Energy Planning Manual. (Illus.). 120p. (Orig.). 1981. pap. 5.00 (ISBN 0-937786-04-7). Inst Ecological.

Gorenflo, Rudolf & Hoffmann, Karl-Heinz. Applied Nonlinear Functional Analysis. (Methoden und Verfahren der Mathematischen Physik Ser.: Vol. 25). 337p. 1983. pap. 38.40 (ISBN 3-8204-7297-5). P Lang Pubs.

Gorenstein, Daniel. Finite Groups. 2nd ed. xvii, 517p. 1980. 24.50 (ISBN 0-8284-0301-5). Chelsea Pub.

--Finite Simple Groups: An Introduction to Their Classification. LC 81-23414. (The University Series in Mathematics). 344p. 1982. 32.50x (ISBN 0-306-40779-5, Plenum Pr). Plenum Pub.

Gorenstein, Daniel & Harada, Kaichiro. Finite Groups Whose 2-Subgroups Are Generated by at Most 4 Elements. LC 74-11282. (Memoirs: No. 147). 464p. 1974. pap. 15.00 (ISBN 0-8218-1847-3, MEMO-147). Am Math.

Gorenstein, Daniel & Lyons, Richard. The Local Structure of Finite Groups of Characteristic Two Type. LC 82-24354. (Memoirs of the American Mathematical Society: No. 276). 731p. 1983. pap. 51.00 (ISBN 0-8218-2276-4). Am Math.

Gorenstein, David G., ed. Phosphorous-31 NMR: Principles & Applications. LC 83-7154. 1984. 79.00 (ISBN 0-12-291750-2). Acad Pr.

Gorenstein, Friedrich. Iskuplenie. LC 84-27974. 158p. 1985. pap. 8.50 (ISBN 0-938920-51-0). Hermitage.

Gorenstein, Paul, jt. ed. see Cornell, James.

Gorer, Geoffrey. American People: A Study in National Character. rev. ed. 1964. pap. 3.25x (ISBN 0-393-00262-4, Norton Lib). Norton.

--Death, Grief, & Mourning. Kastenbaum, Robert, ed. LC 76-19573. (Death & Dying Ser.). (Illus.). 1977. Repr. of 1965 ed. lib. bdg. 24.50x (ISBN 0-405-09571-6). Ayer Co Pubs.

--Exploring English Character. LC 55-11159. 18.95 (ISBN 0-87599-040-1). S G Phillips.

--The Life & Ideas of the Marquis de Sade. LC 77-16240. 1978. Repr. of 1963 ed. lib. bdg. 22.50x (ISBN 0-313-20023-8, GOMDS). Greenwood.

--Sex & Marriage in England Today: A Study of the Views & Experience of the Under 45's. 318p. 1971. text ed. 10.50x (ISBN 0-391-00236-8). Humanities.

Gorer, Geoffrey & Rickman, John. People of Great Russia: A Psychological Study. 1962. pap. 3.25x (ISBN 0-393-00112-1, Norton Lib). Norton.

Gores, Joe. Dead Skip. 1981. pap. 2.25 (ISBN 0-345-29206-5). Ballantine.

--Gone, No Forwarding. 1981. pap. 2.25 (ISBN 0-345-29208-1). Ballantine.

--Interface. LC 73-91882. 216p. 1974. 5.95 (ISBN 0-87131-146-1). M Evans.

--A Time of Predators. LC 84-60551. 1984. pap. 3.95 (ISBN 0-89296-084-1). Mysterious Pr.

Gores, Stan. The Attempted Assassination of Teddy Roosevelt. (Wisconsin Stories Ser.). 12p. pap. 1.75 (ISBN 0-686-76153-7). State Hist Soc Wis.

--Presidential Campaign Memorabilia with Prices. (Illus.). 156p. pap. 12.95 (ISBN 0-87069-370-0). Wallace-Homestead.

Goresky, C. A. & Fisher, M. M., eds. Jaundice. LC 75-8782. (Hepatology Ser.: Vol. 2). 431p. 1975. 55.00x (ISBN 0-306-34802-0, Plenum Pr). Plenum Pub.

Goreux, L. M. & Manne, A. S., eds. Multi-Level Planning: Case Studies in Mexico. 1973. 47.00 (ISBN 0-444-10434-8, North-Holland). Elsevier.

Goreux, Louis M. Interdependence in Planning: Multilevel Programming Studies of the Ivory Coast. LC 77-4793. (A World Bank Research Publication Ser.). (Illus.). 1978. text ed. 30.00x (ISBN 0-8018-2001-4); pap. text ed. 15.00x (ISBN 0-8018-2006-5). Johns Hopkins.

Goreux, Louis-Marie. Agricultural Productivity & Economic Development in France: Eighteen Fifty-Two to Nineteen Fifty. Bruchey, Stuart, ed. LC 77-77171. (Dissertations in European Economic History Ser.). (Illus., Fr. & Eng.). 1977. lib. bdg. 24.50x (ISBN 0-405-10784-6). Ayer Co Pubs.

Gorev, A. Jawaharlal Nehru. 341p. 1982. 8.95 (ISBN 0-8285-2455-6, Pub. by Progress Pubs USSR). Imported Pubns.

Gorevich, Donald. Triggers. 32p. 1984. pap. 3.50 (ISBN 0-939180-25-1). Tombouctou.

Gorey, Edward. Amphigorey. (Illus.). 1980. 9.95 (ISBN 0-399-50433-8, Perigee). Putnam Pub Group.

--Amphigorey Also. (Illus.). 256p. 1983. 20.00 (ISBN 0-312-92023-7); ltd., signed, numbered, slipcased 50.00. Congdon & Weed.

--Amphigorey Also. (Illus.). 256p. 1985. 13.95 (ISBN 0-312-92028-8). Congdon & Weed.

--Amphigorey Too. (Illus.). 224p. 1980. 9.95 (ISBN 0-399-50420-6, Perigee). Putnam Pub Group.

--The Awdrey-Gore Legacy. LC 72-478. (Illus.). 64p. 1982. pap. 4.95 (ISBN 0-312-92032-6). Congdon & Weed.

--The Broken Spoke. LC 76-13327. (Illus.). 64p. 1982. pap. 6.95 (ISBN 0-312-92066-0). Congdon & Weed.

--The Curious Sofa. LC 61-12368. (Illus.). 64p. 1982. pap. 5.95 (ISBN 0-312-92112-8). Congdon & Weed.

--Curious Sofa, Ogdred Weary. (Illus.). 1961. pap. 4.75 (ISBN 0-8392-1020-5). Astor-Honor.

--Dancing Cats & Neglected Murderesses. LC 79-56533. (Illus.). 96p. 1980. pap. 2.50 (ISBN 0-89480-082-5, 400). Workman Pub.

--The Doubtful Guest. LC 57-10200. (Illus.). 64p. 1982. pap. 5.95 (ISBN 0-312-92145-4). Congdon & Weed.

--Les Echanges Malandreux. (Limited Edition Ser.: No. 10). (Illus.). 64p. (Orig.). 1985. pap. 25.00 (ISBN 0-911381-09-0). Metacom Pr.

--The Eclectic Abecedarium. LC 85-13499. (Illus.). 1985. 6.95 (ISBN 0-915361-31-0). Adama Pubs Inc.

--The Epiplectic Bicycle. LC 75-93550. (Illus.). 64p. 1982. pap. 6.95 (ISBN 0-312-92185-3). Congdon & Weed.

--Fatal Lozenge. (Illus.). 1960. pap. 4.75 (ISBN 0-8392-1031-0). Astor-Honor.

--The Gilded Bat. LC 66-22413. (Illus.). 1979. 5.95 (ISBN 0-396-07688-2). Dodd.

--The Glorious Nosebleed. LC 74-10119. (Illus.). 64p. 1982. pap. 5.95 (ISBN 0-312-92252-3). Congdon & Weed.

--Hapless Child. 1961. pap. 4.75 (ISBN 0-8392-1044-2). Astor-Honor.

--The Hapless Child. LC 61-6959. (Illus.). 64p. 1982. pap. 5.95 (ISBN 0-312-92282-5). Congdon & Weed.

--The Loathsome Couple. LC 76-13353. (Illus.). 64p. 1982. pap. 4.95 (ISBN 0-312-92453-4). Congdon & Weed.

--Sinking Spell. (Illus.). 1965. pap. 4.75 (ISBN 0-8392-1150-3). Astor-Honor.

--The Sopping Thursday. (Illus.). 72p. (Orig.). 1971. pap. 4.95 (ISBN 0-88496-176-1). Capra Pr.

--The Tunnel Calamity. (Magic Windows Ser.). (Illus.). 9p. (Orig.). 1984. pap. 4.95 (ISBN 0-399-21055-5, Putnam). Putnam Pub Group.

--The Waterflowers. LC 82-73193. (Illus.). 64p. 1982. 6.95 (ISBN 0-312-92928-5). Congdon & Weed.

--The Willowdale Handcar. LC 62-17515. (Illus.). 64p. 1982. pap. 5.95 (ISBN 0-312-92946-3). Congdon & Weed.

Gorey, Edward & Evans, Larry. Gorey Games. Ltd. ed. (Illus.). 64p. (Orig.). (gr. 1-12). 1979. pap. 4.50 (ISBN 0-8431-4000-3); 45.00 (ISBN 0-8431-4017-8). Troubador Pr.

Gorey, Edward & Neumeyer, Peter. Donald Has a Difficulty. (Illus.). 48p. 1982. pap. 4.95 (ISBN 0-88496-175-3). Capra Pr.

--Why We Have Day & Night. (Illus.). 42p. 1982. pap. 4.95 (ISBN 0-88496-174-5). Capra Pr.

Gorey, Edward & Neumeyer, Peter F. Donald & the... LC 83-15002. (Illus.). 42p. 1983. pap. 4.95 (ISBN 0-88496-203-2). Capra Pr.

Gorey, Edward, jt. auth. see Lamport, Felicia.

Gorey, Edward, jt. auth. see Moss, Howard.

Gorey, Edward, illus. Monster Festival: Classic Tales of the Macabre. 296p. 1985. 12.50 (ISBN 0-8149-0377-0). Vanguard.

Gorey, Mark E. La see Blau, Judith R. & La Gory, Mark E.

Gorgan, Joseph M., jt. auth. see Obayashi, Alan W.

Gorgas, J. Confederate Ordinance Manual. (Illus.). 1975. Repr. 25.00 (ISBN 0-89029-033-4). Pr of Morningside.

Gorgas, Michael J. Inversion for Health & Fitness. LC 83-90337. (Illus.). 80p. 1983. pap. 5.95 (ISBN 0-913001-09-0). Gravity Research.

Gorge, Peter, tr. see Schindler, Maria.

Gorgen, Hermann M. Brazil: Impressions & Insight. (Illus.). 159p. 1982. 29.95 (ISBN 0-8044-5435-3). Ungar.

Gorges, A., tr. see Bacon, Francis.

Gorges, Arthur see Bacon, Francis.

Gorges, Raymond. History of the Family of Gorges. 289p. 1944. 35.00 (ISBN 0-686-36478-3). Mass Hist Soc.

Gorgey, Laszlo C. Bonn's Eastern Policy, 1964-71: Evolution & Limitations. ix, 191p. 1972. 17.50 (ISBN 0-208-01272-9, Archon). Shoe String.

Gorgol, John Francis. The Military-Industrial Firm: A Practical Theory & Model. LC 75-170024. (Special Studies in U.S. Economic, Social, & Political Issues). 1972. 29.50x (ISBN 0-275-28229-5); pap. text ed. 12.50x (ISBN 0-89197-848-8). Irvington.

Gorgolini, Pietro. The Fascist Movement in Italian Life. Petre, M. D., ed. LC 78-63674. (Studies in Fascism: Ideology & Practice). Repr. of 1923 ed. 27.00 (ISBN 0-404-16936-8). AMS Pr.

Gorgoni, Gianfranco, photos by. Beyond the Canvas. LC 85-43057. (Illus.). 300p. 1985. 45.00 (ISBN 0-8478-0662-6). Rizzoli Intl.

Gorham, Charles. Life Story of Robert Ingersoll. 56p. pap. cancelled (ISBN 0-911826-54-8). Am Atheist.

Gorham, Deborah. The Victorian Girl & the Feminine Ideal. LC 82-47944. 240p. 1982. 20.00X (ISBN 0-253-36258-X). Ind U Pr.

Gorham, Georgia & Warth, Jeanne. Charted Designs for Holidays & Special Occasions: Over 224 Motifs for Counted Cross-Stitch & Other Needlecrafts. (Illus.). 48p. (Orig.). 1981. pap. 2.00 (ISBN 0-486-24192-0). Dover.

--A Treasury of Charted Designs for Needleworkers. (Dover Needlework Ser.). (Illus.). 1978. pap. 1.95 (ISBN 0-486-23558-0). Dover.

Gorham, Hazel H. Japanese & Oriental Ceramics. LC 70-130416. (Illus.). 1970. 22.50 (ISBN 0-8048-0927-5). C E Tuttle.

Gorham, John P. Bookkeeping Simplified & Self-Taught. LC 82-11316. (Simplified & Self-Taught Ser.). 128p. 1983. pap. 4.95 (ISBN 0-668-05456-5, 5456). Arco.

Gorham, M. Ireland from Old Photographs. 1979. pap. 10.50 (ISBN 0-7134-2195-9, Pub. by Batsford England). David & Charles.

Gorham, Melvin. The Ancient Story of Selentag. 46p. 1970. pap. 1.00 (ISBN 0-914752-01-4). Sovereign Pr.

--Curse of the Ring. 1975. pap. 1.50 (ISBN 0-914752-06-5). Sovereign Pr.

--The Pagan Bible. 296p. 1982. 8.95 (ISBN 0-914752-22-7). Sovereign Pr.

--Pagan Reality. 201p. 1970. pap. 5.00 (ISBN 0-914752-02-2). Sovereign Pr.

--The Ring Cycle. LC 79-64509. (Orig.). 1979. 8.95 (ISBN 0-914752-11-1); pap. 5.00 (ISBN 0-914752-10-3). Sovereign Pr.

--The Six Disciplines of Man's Being & Man's Relation to Government. rev. ed. 128p. 1983. pap. 5.00 (ISBN 0-914752-16-2). Sovereign Pr.

--The Valkyrie, a Play in Three Acts: An Interpretation of Wagner's Opera. 60p. (Orig.). 1976. pap. 5.00 (ISBN 0-914752-07-3). Sovereign Pr.

Gorham, William & Glazer, Nathan, eds. The Urban Predicament. 363p. 1976. 19.95x (ISBN 0-87766-161-8, 14700); pap. 9.95x (ISBN 0-87766-160-X, 14500). Urban Inst.

Gori, G. K. Changing Phase of Tribal Area of Manipur. (Illus.). 1984. text ed. 27.50x (ISBN 0-86590-320-4, Pub. by B R Pub Corp Delhi). Apt Bks.

Gori, Gio B. & Bock, Fred G., eds. Banbury Report 3: A Safe Cigarette? LC 79-47999. (Banbury Report Ser.: Vol. 3). (Illus.). 364p. 1980. 52.00x (ISBN 0-87969-202-2). Cold Spring Harbor.

Gorin. Clinical Glaucoma. (Ophthalmology Ser.: Vol. 1). 1977. 75.00 (ISBN 0-8247-6456-0). Dekker.

Gorin, Edward, jt. auth. see Baron, Howard C.

Gorin, George. Echoes & Shadows: Poems. LC 85-90616. 72p. 1985. 12.00 (ISBN 0-9613974-1-1). G Gorin.

--History of Ophthalmology. LC 82-61325. xvi, 630p. 1982. text ed. 40.00 (ISBN 0-914098-25-X). Publish or Perish.

--A History of Ophthalmology. 646p. 1982. text ed. 49.50 (ISBN 0-914098-25-X). Raven.

--Intermezzo: Poems. LC 84-91184. 72p. 1984. 12.00 (ISBN 0-9613974-0-3). G Gorin.

Gorin, Ralph E. Introduction to DECsystem 20: Assembly Language Programming. 545p. 1981. pap. 39.00 (ISBN 0-932376-12-6, EY-AX017-DP). Digital Pr.

Gorina, R. Russian Fare. pap. 3.95 (ISBN 0-87557-106-9, 106-9). Saphrograph.

Goring, Charles. The English Convict: A Statistical Study to Which Is Added the Schedule of Measurements & General Anthropological Data. LC 71-129314. (Criminology, Law Enforcement, & Social Problems Ser.: No. 137). (Illus.). 530p. (With intro. essay added, Quarto). 1972. Repr. of 1913 ed. lib. bdg. 50.00x (ISBN 0-87585-137-1). Patterson Smith.

Goring, Cleve A. & Hamaker, John W., eds. Organic Chemicals in the Soil Environment. LC 71-179384. (Books in Soils & the Environment Ser.: Vol. 1). pap. 114.00 (ISBN 0-317-28661-7, 2055084). Bks Demand UMI.

Goring, J. J. & Wake, Joan, eds. Northamptonshire Lieutenancy Papers & Other Documents, 1580-1614. 1975. 40.00x (ISBN 0-686-87015-8, Pub. by Northamptonshire). State Mutual Bk.

Goring, Kaui, ed. Maui Cooks. (Illus.). 146p. (Orig.). 1984. pap. 11.95 (ISBN 0-915013-00-2). Editions Ltd.

Goring, Loris. The Care & Repair of Marine Gasoline Engines. LC 80-84623. (Illus.). 146p. 1981. 17.50 (ISBN 0-87742-139-0). Intl Marine.

--The Care & Repair of Marine Petrol Engines. (Illus.). 134p. (Orig.). 1985. pap. 14.50 (ISBN 0-229-11744-9, Pub. by Adlard Coles). Sheridan.

Goringe, M. J., ed. Electron Microscopy & Analysis, 1981. 570p. 1982. 90.00x (ISBN 0-85498-152-7, Pub. by A Hilger). State Mutual Bk.

Goringe, Michael J., jt. auth. see Thomas, Gareth.

Gorini, Giovanni. La Monetazione Incusa Della Magna Graecia. 1975. 37.50 (ISBN 0-318-03946-X). Numismatic Fine Arts.

Gorini, S., jt. ed. see Mannucci, P. M.

Gorio, A., jt. ed. see Weiss, D. G.

Gorio, Alfredo & Haber, Bernard. Neurobiology of Gangliosides. 390p. 1985. 48.00 (ISBN 0-8451-0240-0). A R Liss.

Gorio, Alfredo, jt. ed. see Rapport, Maurice M.

Gorio, Alfredo, et al, eds. Post-Traumatic Peripheral Nerve Regeneration: Experimental Basis & Clinical Implications. 658p. 1981. text ed. 71.50 (ISBN 0-89004-754-5). Raven.

Goris. Dictionary of American Idioms for Japanese Speakers. 1984. pap. 24.95 (ISBN 0-8120-2867-8). Barron.

Goris, Jan A. Etude Sur Les Colonies Marchandes Meridionales a Anvers De 1488 a 1567, 2 vols. in 1. 1925. 46.50 (ISBN 0-8337-1390-6). B Franklin.

Goris, Michael L. & Briandet, Philippe A. A Clinical & Mathematical Introduction to Computer Processing of Scintigraphic Images. (Illus.). 308p. 1983. text ed. 77.00 (ISBN 0-89004-766-9). Raven.

Gorjanc, Adele A. Italian Conversation: A Practical Guide for Students & Travelers. 7.50 (ISBN 0-8283-1670-8). Branden Pub Co.

Gorjanovic-Kramberger, Dragutin. Der Diluviale Mensch Von Krapina in Kroatien. LC 78-72695. Repr. of 1906 ed. 76.50 (ISBN 0-404-18266-6). AMS Pr.

Gorki, Maxim. Bystander. Guerney, Bernard G., tr. 1930. lib. bdg. 25.00 (ISBN 0-8414-4660-1). Folcroft.

--Fragments from My Diary. 1924. lib. bdg. 25.00 (ISBN 0-8414-4662-8). Folcroft.

--Her Lover. Goldberg, Isaac, ed. Bain, R. Nisbet, tr. (International Pocket Library). pap. 3.00 (ISBN 0-8283-1450-0). Branden Pub Co.

--The Lower Depths: Scenes from Russian Life. Hopkins, Edwin, tr. pap. 3.00 (ISBN 0-8283-1445-4, IPL). Branden Pub Co.

Gorki, Maxim see Goldberg, Isaac.

Gorkii, Maksim, ed. Belomor: An Account of the Construction of the New Canal Between the White Sea & the Baltic Sea. LC 75-37339. (Russian Studies). 1977. Repr. of 1935 ed. lib. bdg. 30.25 (ISBN 0-88355-432-1). Hyperion Conn.

Gorkill, W. A. A Beginner's Guide to Railway Modeling. (Illus.). 64p. 1982. 9.95 (ISBN 0-7153-8127-X). David & Charles.

Gorkin, Julian, jt. auth. see Sanchez Salazar, Leandro A.

Gorkin, V. Z. Amine Oxidases in Clinical Research. LC 82-18132. (Illus.). 300p. 1982. 88.00 (ISBN 0-08-025523-X). Pergamon.

Gorkom, J. W. Van see Van Gorkom, J. W.

Gorkov, L. P., jt. auth. see Abrikosov, A. A.

Gorky, M. Selected Short Stories. 410p. 1974. 6.45 (ISBN 0-8285-0981-6, Pub. by Progress Pubs USSR). Imported Pubns.

Gorky, M., jt. auth. see Lenin, Vladimir I.

Gorky, M., et al. About Lenin. 1980. 9.45 (ISBN 0-8285-1835-1, Pub. by Progress Pubs USSR). Imported Pubns.

--Anton Makarenko: His Life and His Work in Education. 393p. 1976. 4.95 (ISBN 0-8285-0421-0, Pub. by Progress Pubs USSR). Imported Pubns.

Gorky, Maksim. The Lower Depths & Other Plays. Bakshy, Alexander & Nathan, Paul S., trs. LC 75-41116. Repr. of 1945 ed. 17.25 (ISBN 0-404-14773-9). AMS Pr.

Gorky, Maxim. Autobiography of Maxim Gorky. Schneider, Isidor, tr. 1969. pap. 5.95 (ISBN 0-8065-0199-5). Citadel Pr.

--The Autobiography of Maxim Gorky, 3 vols. in 1. Schneider, Isidore, tr. Incl. My Childhood; In the World; My Universities. 13.25 (ISBN 0-8446-2143-9). Peter Smith.

--Childhood. (Soviet Authors' Library). (Illus.). 232p. 1975. 11.95x (ISBN 0-8464-0242-4). Beekman Pubs.

--Childhood. 232p. 1973. 5.45 (ISBN 0-8285-0976-X, Pub. by Progress USSR). Imported Pubns.

--The City of the Yellow Devil. 138p. 1972. 4.45 (ISBN 0-8285-0977-8, Pub. by Progress Pubs USSR). Imported Pubns.

--Collected Works of Maxim Gorky, 10 vols. 1983. Set. 76.00 (ISBN 0-8285-2546-3, Pub. by Progress Pubs USSR). Imported Pubns.

--Collected Works of Maxim Gorky, Vol. 1. 517p. 1979. 6.45 (ISBN 0-8285-1557-3, Pub. by Progress Pubs USSR). Imported Pubns.

--Collected Works of Maxim Gorky, Vol. 2. 272p. 1979. 6.45 (ISBN 0-8285-0978-6, Pub. by Progress Pubs USSR). Imported Pubns.

--Collected Works of Maxim Gorky, Vol. 3. 384p. 1979. 6.95 (ISBN 0-8285-1558-1, Pub. by Progress Pubs USSR). Imported Pubns.

--Collected Works of Maxim Gorky, Vol. 4. 861p. 1979. 7.95 (ISBN 0-8285-1597-2, Pub. by Progress Pubs USSR). Imported Pubns.

--Collected Works of Maxim Gorky, Vol. 5. 595p. 1980. 7.95 (ISBN 0-8285-1708-8, Pub. by Progress Pubs USSR). Imported Pubns.

--Collected Works of Maxim Gorky, Vol. 6. 430p. 1980. 7.95 (ISBN 0-8285-1709-6, Pub. by Progress Pubs USSR). Imported Pubns.

--Collected Works of Maxim Gorky, Vol. 7. 549p. 1981. 10.00 (ISBN 0-8285-2044-5, Pub. by Progress Pubs USSR). Imported Pubns.

--Collected Works of Maxim Gorky, Vol. 8. 336p. 1981. 6.40 (ISBN 0-8285-2040-2, Pub. by Progress Pubs USSR). Imported Pubns.

--Collected Works of Maxim Gorky, Vol. 9. 390p. 1982. 9.45 (ISBN 0-8285-2520-X, Pub. by Progress Pubs USSR). Imported Pubns.

--Collected Works of Maxim Gorky, Vol. 10. 455p. 1982. 10.95 (ISBN 0-8285-2376-2, Pub. by Progress Pubs USSR). Imported Pubns.

--Culture & the People. facs. ed. LC 79-119930. (Select Bibliographies Reprint Ser.). 1939. 19.00 (ISBN 0-8369-5373-8). Ayer Co Pubs.

--Danko's Burning Heart. Wettlin, Margaret, tr. 24p. 1983. pap. 2.99 (ISBN 0-8285-2756-3, Pub. by Raduga Pubs USSR). Imported Pubns.

--Decadence. Dewey, Veronica, tr. LC 84-3637. xiv, 351p. 1984. pap. 8.95 (ISBN 0-8032-7012-7, BB 881, Bison). U of Nebr Pr.

--Enemies: A Play. Brooks, Jeremy & Hunter-Blair, Kitty, trs. from Rus. (Richard Seaver Books). 96p. 1972. 9.95 (ISBN 0-670-29492-6). Viking.

--Foma Gordeyev. 264p. 1981. Repr. of 1956 ed. lib. bdg. 25.00 (ISBN 0-89984-237-2). Century Bookbindery.

--Foma Gordeyev. LC 74-10361. 264p. 1974. Repr. of 1956 ed. lib. bdg. 29.75x (ISBN 0-8371-7670-0, GOFG). Greenwood.

--Ilya's Childhood & Children. Birkett, G. A., ed. LC 66-52019. (Rus.). 1966. pap. text ed. 1.75x (ISBN 0-89197-488-1). Irvington.

--Letters. 199p. 1973. 4.95 (ISBN 0-8285-1085-7, Pub. by Progress Pubs USSR). Imported Pubns.

--The Lower Depths & Other Plays. Bakshy, Alexander & Nathan, Paul S., trs. Bd. with The Theater of Maxim Gorky. Bakshy, Alexander. xx, 220p. 1959. pap. 5.95 (ISBN 0-300-00100-2, Y-4). Yale U Pr.

--Mother. Wettlin, Margaret, tr. (Soviet Authors' Library Ser.). (Illus.). 1976. Repr. of 1949 ed. 4.40 (ISBN 0-8285-8080-4, Pub. by Progress Pubs USSR). Imported Pubns.

--Mother. Schneider, Isadore, tr. from Rus. 416p. 1984. pap. 6.95 (ISBN 0-8065-0890-6). Citadel Pr.

--My Apprenticeship. Wilks, Ronald, tr. (Classics Ser.). (Orig.). 1974. pap. 4.95 (ISBN 0-14-044291-X). Penguin.

--My Apprenticeship: My Universities. (Illus.). 485p. 1975. 16.00x (ISBN 0-8464-0660-8). Beekman Pubs.

--My Apprenticeship, My Universities. 484p. 1973. 6.95 (ISBN 0-686-80438-4, Pub. by Progress Pubs USSR). Imported Pubns.

--My Childhood. Wilks, Ronald, tr. (Classics Ser.). (Orig.). 1966. pap. 3.95 (ISBN 0-14-044178-6). Penguin.

--My Universities. Wilks, Ronald, tr. from Rus. (Classics Ser.). 1979. pap. 3.95 (ISBN 0-14-044302-9). Penguin.

--On Literature. 397p. 1975. 12.00x (ISBN 0-8464-0684-5). Beekman Pubs.

--On Literature. 347p. 1979. 9.45 (ISBN 0-8285-1713-4, Pub. by Progress Pubs USSR). Imported Pubns.

--On Literature. LC 72-11682. 400p. 1975. pap. 7.95x (ISBN 0-295-95453-1). U of Wash Pr.

--Orloff & His Wife: Tales of the Barefoot Brigade. 15th ed. Hapgood, Isabel F., tr. from Russian. LC 72-11934. (Short Story Index Reprint Ser). 1973. Repr. of 1901 ed. 29.00 (ISBN 0-8369-4232-9). Ayer Co Pubs.

--Outcasts & Other Stories. LC 75-113664. (Short Story Index Reprint Ser.). 1905. 18.00 (ISBN 0-8369-3393-1). Ayer Co Pubs.

--Reminiscences of Leo Nikilaevich Tolstoy. Koteliansky, S. S. & Woolf, Leonard, trs. LC 77-23858. 1977. Repr. of 1920 ed. lib. bdg. 15.00 (ISBN 0-8414-4455-2). Folcroft.

--Reminiscences of Leo Nikolaevich Tolstoy. 86p. 1981. Repr. of 1920 ed. lib. bdg. 15.00 (ISBN 0-8495-2048-7). Arden Lib.

--Reminiscences of My Youth. 334p. 1980. Repr. of 1924 ed. lib. bdg. 25.00 (ISBN 0-8492-4961-9). R West.

--Selected Short Stories. 410p. 1975. 12.95x (ISBN 0-8464-0834-1). Beekman Pubs.

--Stories of the Steppe. LC 72-121552. (Short Story Index Reprint Ser). 1918. 10.00 (ISBN 0-8369-3508-X). Ayer Co Pubs.

--Tales of Two Countries. facsimile ed. LC 70-160933. (Short Story Index Reprint Ser.). Repr. of 1914 ed. 15.00 (ISBN 0-8369-3912-3). Ayer Co Pubs.

--Twenty-Six & One: And Other Stories. LC 72-11935. (Short Story Index Reprint Ser.). 1973. Repr. of 1902 ed. 15.00 (ISBN 0-8369-4233-7). Ayer Co Pubs.

--Twenty Six Men & a Girl & Other Stories. LC 74-103510. (Short Story Index Reprint Ser.). 1902. 21.00 (ISBN 0-8369-3252-8). Ayer Co Pubs.

Gorky, Maxim, ed. see Sergieev-Tsensky, Sergiei N.

Gorky, Maxim, et al. Classic Soviet Plays. 829p. 1979. 12.50 (ISBN 0-8285-1727-4, Pub. by Progress Pubs USSR). Imported Pubns.

Gorky, Maxim, et al, eds. The History of the Civil War in the U. S. S. R. The Prelude of the Great Proletarian Revolution. 560p. 1985. 25.00 (ISBN 0-916650-28-6); pap. 12.95 (ISBN 0-916650-27-8). Banner Pr NY.

Gorlach, Manfred, jt. ed. see Bailey, Richard W.

Gorlach, Manfred, ed. see Busch, Wilhelm.

Gorland, Emanuel. Urban Renewal Administration: A Guide for Administrative Practices, Procedures & Record Keeping. LC 79-111041. 145p. 1971. 9.95x (ISBN 0-8143-1425-2). Wayne St U Pr.

Gorlick, Allan, jt. auth. see Karp, Robert E.

Gorlick, Lillian. Beskrivelse af Danske og Norske Monter: History of Danish & Norwegian Coins 1448-1923. LC 83-72146. (Illus.). 456p. 1983. Repr. of 1926 ed. 65.00 (ISBN 0-913799-01-7). Bengor Pubns.

Gorlick, S. Now That You've Incorporated. 4th ed. 1983. 24.95 (ISBN 0-87489-272-4). Med Economics.

--The Whys & Wherefores of Corporate Practice. 4th ed. 1982. 24.95 (ISBN 0-87489-264-3). Med Economics.

Gorlin, Harriet, jt. auth. see Lusterman, Seymour.

Gorlin, Richard. Coronary Artery Disease. LC 76-14680. (Major Problems in Internal Medicine Ser.: Vol. XI). (Illus.). Repr. of 1976 ed. 62.90 (ISBN 0-8357-9538-1, 2016664). Bks Demand UMI.

Gorlin, Robert J., jt. auth. see Goodman, Richard M.

Gorlin, Robert J., ed. Morphogenesis & Malformation of the Ear. LC 80-18892. (Birth Defects: Original Article Ser.: Vol XVI, No. 4). 367p. 1980. 58.00 (ISBN 0-8451-1038-1). A R Liss.

--Morphogenesis & Malformation of the Ear. LC 80-18892. (Alan R. Liss: Vol. 16,No. 4). 1980. 53.00 (ISBN 0-8451-1038-1). March of Dimes.

Gorlitz, Axel. Diccionario de Ciencia Politica. (Span.). 1979. pap. pns (S-50085). French & Eur.

Gorlitz, Dietmar. Perspectives on Attribution Research & Theory: The Bielefeld Symposium. 1981. prof ref 27.50 (ISBN 0-88410-375-7). Ballinger Pub.

Gorlitz, Dietmar & Wohlwill, Joachim, eds. Curiosity Imagination & Play: On the Development of Spontaneous Cognitive & Motivational Processes. 480p. 1985. text ed. 49.95 (ISBN 0-89859-683-1). L Erlbaum Assocs.

Gorlitz, Walter. History of the German General Staff, 1657-1945. Battershaw, Brian, tr. from Ger. LC 75-3867. (Illus.). 508p. 1975. Repr. of 1953 ed. lib. bdg. 33.00x (ISBN 0-8371-8092-9, GOGG). Greenwood.

--Paulus & Stalingrad. Stevens, R. H., tr. LC 74-5782. (Illus.). 301p. 1974. Repr. of 1963 ed. lib. bdg. 35.00x (ISBN 0-8371-7497-X, GOPS). Greenwood.

Gorlitz, Walter, jt. auth. see Keitel, Wilhelm.

Gorlow, Leon, jt. auth. see Katkosky, Walter.

Gormally, J., jt. ed. see Wyn-Jones, E.

Gorman, B. S. & Wessman, A. E., eds. The Personal Experience of Time. LC 77-21964. (Emotions, Personality, & Psychotherapy Ser.). (Illus.). 310p. 1977. 32.50x (ISBN 0-306-31039-2, Plenum Pr). Plenum Pub.

Gorman, Beth. Gentle Lover. DeRoin, Gene, ed. (Aston Hall Presents Ser.). (Orig.). 1980. pap. 1.50 (ISBN 0-89936-019-X). Aston Hall.

Gorman, Brian, compiled by. Finding Lost Alumni: Tracing Methods Used by 19 Institutions. 30p. 1981. 10.50 (ISBN 0-89964-181-4). Coun Adv & Supp Ed.

Gorman, C. N. & Cockain, G. D. Westby-Nunn's. 1977. 40.00x (ISBN 0-686-44519-8, Pub. by Oyez Longman Pub England). State Mutual Bk.

Gorman, Colum A., et al, eds. The Eye & Orbit in Thyroid Disease. (Illus.). 352p. 1984. text ed. 69.50 (ISBN 0-88167-036-7). Raven.

Gorman, D. B. The Histology of the Striped Bass. (AFS Monographs: No. 3). 116p. 1982. 15.00 (ISBN 0-913235-14-8); members 12.00 (ISBN 0-317-32538-8). Am Fisheries Soc.

Gorman, D. J. Free Vibration Analysis of Rectangular Plates. 324p. 1981. 77.50 (ISBN 0-444-00601-X). Elsevier.

Gorman, Damian & McGuckian, Medbh. Trio Poetry Two. 72p. (Orig.). 1981. pap. 6.95 (ISBN 0-85640-216-8, Pub. by Blackstaff Pr). Longwood Pub Group.

Gorman, Edward. New, Improved Murder. 192p. 1985. 12.95 (ISBN 0-312-56768-5). St Martin.

--Roughcut. 176p. Date not set. 11.95 (ISBN 0-312-69360-5). St Martin.

Gorman, G. E. The South African Novel in English Since 1950: An Information & Resource Guide. 1978. 36.50 (ISBN 0-8161-8178-0, Hall Reference). G K Hall.

Gorman, G. E. & Gorman, Lyn. Theological & Religious Reference Materials: General Resources & Biblical Studies. LC 83-22759. (Bibliographies & Indexes in Religious Studies: No. 1). xvi, 526p. 1984. 49.95 (ISBN 0-313-20924-3, GRM/). Greenwood.

--Theological & Religious Reference Materials: Systematic Theology & Church History. LC 83-22759. (Bibliographies & Indexes in Religious Studies: No. 2). xiv, 401p. 1985. lib. bdg. 47.50 (ISBN 0-313-24779-X, GOS/). Greenwood.

Gorman, Gary E. & Mahoney, Maureen M. Guide to Current National Bibliographies in the Third World. 328p. 1983. lib. bdg. 37.00 (ISBN 3-598-10446-4). K G Saur.

Gorman, George. The Society of Friends. 1978. pap. 3.15 (ISBN 0-08-021412-6). Pergamon.

Gorman, Gregory X. Waiting for Something to Happen. 80p. 1984. pap. 4.00 (ISBN 0-942582-05-5). Erie St Pr.

Gorman, Herbert. The Incredible Marquis: Alexandre Dumas. 1929. 25.00 (ISBN 0-8274-2568-6). R West.

--James Joyce. LC 74-30368. (Studies in Joyce Ser., No. 96). 1974. lib. bdg. 49.95x (ISBN 0-8383-2015-5). Haskell.

Gorman, Herbert S. Hawthorne: A Study in Solitude. LC 66-13474. 1927. 10.00x (ISBN 0-8196-0170-5). Biblo.

--James Joyce: His First Forty Years. 1978. Repr. of 1926 ed. lib. bdg. 30.00 (ISBN 0-8495-1927-6). Arden Lib.

--James Joyce: His First Forty Years. LC 74-11431. 1924. lib. bdg. 30.00 (ISBN 0-8414-4527-3). Folcroft.

--Procession of Masks. LC 77-99698. (Essay Index Reprint Ser.). 1923. 19.00 (ISBN 0-8369-1352-3). Ayer Co Pubs.

--A Victorian American: Henry Wadsworth Longfellow. 1979. Repr. of 1926 ed. lib. bdg. 35.00 (ISBN 0-8492-4933-3). R West.

Gorman, Hugh. Beacon Small-Group Bible Studies: Hosea, "The Triumph of Love". 96p. (Orig.). 1984. pap. 2.50 (ISBN 0-8341-0914-X). Beacon Hill.

Gorman, J. L. The Expression of Historical Knowledge. 123p. 1982. 20.00x (ISBN 0-85224-427-4, Pub by Edinburgh U Pr Scotland). Columbia U Pr.

Gorman, Jack. Pere Murray & the Hounds. (Illus.). 196p. 1977. 9.95 (ISBN 0-88826-069-5). Superior Pub.

Gorman, James. First Aid for Hypochondriacs. LC 82-60060. (Illus.). 160p. 1982. 4.95 (ISBN 0-89480-173-2, 489). Workman Pub.

Gorman, James E. Simplified Guide to Construction Management for Architects & Engineers. LC 75-34480. 288p. 1976. 19.95 (ISBN 0-8436-0160-4). Van Nos Reinhold.

Gorman, John A. Western Horse. LC 66-12997. (Illus.). (gr. 9-12). 1967. 16.50 (ISBN 0-8134-0126-7); text ed. 12.50x. Interstate.

Gorman, Joseph B. Kefauver: A Political Biography. 1971. 25.00x (ISBN 0-19-501481-2). Oxford U Pr.

Gorman, Judy. The Culinary Craft. LC 84-50427. (Illus.). 416p. 1984. 17.95 (ISBN 0-89909-038-9). Yankee Bks.

Gorman, Kenneth A., jt. auth. see Crowningshield, Gerald.

Gorman, Kenneth A., jt. auth. see Daiute, Robert J.

Gorman, LeRoy. Cutout Moons. 24p. 1980. 7.00 (ISBN 0-913719-44-7); pap. 2.00 (ISBN 0-913719-41-2). High-Coo Pr.

--Wind in the Keys. 40p. 1981. 10.00 (ISBN 0-913719-18-8); pap. 3.50 (ISBN 0-913719-16-1). High-Coo Pr.

Gorman, Lyn, jt. auth. see Gorman, G. E.

Gorman, M. L. Island Ecology. 1979. pap. 6.95 (ISBN 0-412-15540-0, NO.6131, Pub. by Chapman & Hall). Methuen Inc.

Gorman, Margaret. General Semantics & Contemporary Thomism. LC 62-9136. pap. 53.00 (ISBN 0-317-10288-5, 2022431). Bks Demand UMI.

Gorman, Margaret, ed. Psychology & Religion: A Reader. pap. 11.95 (ISBN 0-8091-2684-2). Paulist Pr.

Gorman, Marion. Cooking with Fruit. Gerras, Charles, ed. (Illus.). 352p. 1983. 6.95 (ISBN 0-87857-414-X, 07-003-0). Rodale Pr Inc.

Gorman, Martha, jt. auth. see Campbell, Gil L.

Gorman, Martha G. Psycho-Physiology of Fatigue: Subject Analysis & Reference Guidebook with Bibliography. LC 84-45990. 150p. 1985. 29.95 (ISBN 0-88164-302-5); pap. 21.95 (ISBN 0-88164-303-3). ABBE Pubs Assn.

Gorman, Martha Garcy. Science & Medicine of Backache: Subject Analysis & Research Guide With Bibliography. LC 83-45533. 140p. 1984. 29.95 (ISBN 0-88164-114-6); pap. 21.95 (ISBN 0-88164-115-4). ABBE Pubs Assn.

Gorman, Marvin, jt. ed. see Morin, Robert B.

Gorman, Michael. The Concise AACR2. LC 81-3496. 174p. 1981. pap. 8.00x (ISBN 0-8389-0325-8). ALA.

Gorman, Michael, ed. Crossroads: Proceedings of the First National Conference of the Library & Information Technology Association September 1983. LC 84-10965. (Library & Information Technology: No. 1). 262p. 1984. pap. text ed. 40.00x (ISBN 0-8389-3307-6). ALA.

Gorman, Michael & Height, Frank, eds. Design for Tourism: An I.C.S.I.D. Interdesign Report. 64p. 1977. text ed. 18.00 (ISBN 0-08-021481-9). Pergamon.

Gorman, Michael & Winkler, Paul, eds. Anglo-American Cataloguing Rules. 2nd ed. LC 78-13789. 640p. 1978. text ed. 20.00x (ISBN 0-8389-3210-X); pap. text ed. 15.00x (ISBN 0-8389-3211-8); looseleaf Lib Bdg 12.50 (ISBN 0-8389-3230-4). ALA.

Gorman, Michael J. Abortion & the Early Church: Christian, Jewish, & Pagan Attitudes. 120p. (Orig.). 1982. pap. 4.95 (ISBN 0-87784-397-X). Inter-Varsity.

Gorman, Michael M. Managing Database: Four Critical Factors. LC 83-83114. 216p. pap. 32.50 (ISBN 0-89435-103-6). QED Info Sci.

Gorman, N. T., jt. ed. see Bourne, F. J.

Gorman, Nana & Gorman, Papa. Billy & Bonnie Meet Christopher Caterpillar. (Illus.). 32p. (ps-3). 1984. 5.95 (ISBN 0-89962-415-4). Todd & Honeywell.

Gorman, Papa, jt. auth. see Gorman, Nana.

Gorman, Peter. Pythagoras: A Life. 1978. 19.95 (ISBN 0-7100-0006-5). Routledge & Kegan.

Gorman, R. H. Hobby Tools & How to Use Them. pap. 5.00x (ISBN 0-392-09558-0, SpS). Sportshelf.

Gorman, Ralph. Last Hours of Jesus. 1960. 4.50 (ISBN 0-8362-0221-X, Pub. by Sheed). Guild Bks.

Gorman, Robert. Catholic Apologetical Literature in the United States (1784-1858) LC 73-3582. (Catholic University of America. Studies in American Church History: No. 28). Repr. of 1939 ed. 23.00 (ISBN 0-404-57778-4). AMS Pr.

Gorman, Robert A. Neo-Marxism: The Meanings of Modern Radicalism. LC 81-13404. (Contributions in Political Science Ser.: No. 77). 320p. 1982. lib. bdg. 35.00 (ISBN 0-313-23264-4, GON/). Greenwood.

Gorman, Robert A., jt. auth. see Latman, Alan.

Gorman, Robert F. Political Conflict on the Horn of Africa. LC 81-5183. 256p. 1981. 33.95 (ISBN 0-03-059471-5). Praeger.

Gorman, Robert F., ed. Private Voluntary Organizations as Agents of Development. 160p. 1984. pap. 22.50x (ISBN 0-86531-997-9). Westview.

Gorman, Stephen M., jt. auth. see Maghroori, Ray.

Gorman, Stephen M., ed. Post-Revolutionary Peru: The Politics of Transformation. (Special Studies on Latin America & the Caribbean). 240p. (Orig.). 1982. pap. 26.50x (ISBN 0-86531-265-6). Westview.

Gorman, Walter & Sendell, Richard. Selling: Personality, Persuasion, Strategy. 2nd ed. LC 82-18592. 576p. 1983. text ed. 27.00 (ISBN 0-394-33003-X, RanC). Random.

Gorman, Walter H. Dynamic Psychiatry & the Sense of Justice. LC 70-96982. (Illus.). 320p. 1974. 22.50 (ISBN 0-87527-106-5). Green.

Gorman, Warren. Body Image & the Image of the Brain. LC 68-8293. (Illus.). 298p. 1969. 12.50 (ISBN 0-87527-037-9). Green.

--Flavor, Taste & the Psychology of Smell. (Illus.). 116p. 1964. 11.75x (ISBN 0-398-00704-7). C C Thomas.

Gormezano, C. & Leotta, G. G., eds. Heating in Toroidal Plasmas III: Proceedings of the 3rd Joint Varenna-Grenoble International Symposium, Grenoble, France, 22-26 March 1982, 3 vols. 1224p. 1982. pap. 165.00 set (ISBN 0-08-029984-9). Pergamon.

Gormezano, Keith. A Genealogical History of the Gormezano Family from the 1300's to the Present Day. LC 80-67022. 51p. (Orig.). 1980. pap. 2.95 (ISBN 0-935954-00-7). Gormezano Ref.

--Name Identification: Its Effect on Voter Choice & Election Outcome. LC 80-67021. 50p. (Orig.). 1980. pap. 12.95 (ISBN 0-935954-01-5). Gormezano Ref.

--Thirty-Six Flavours. LC 80-67023. (Orig.). 1980. pap. 2.95 (ISBN 0-935954-02-3). Gormezano Ref.

Gormezano, Keith, ed. Anthology of University of Iowa Poets, Artists & Authors. (Beacon Presse Poetry Ser.: No. 3). 124p. (Orig.). 1980. pap. 15.95 (ISBN 0-935954-07-4). Gormezano Ref.

Gormezano, Keith, jt. ed. see Gormezano Reference Publications Staff.

Gormezano, Keith S. Man Who Turned into a Woman. LC 81-69808. (New Authors Ser.: No. 3). 120p. 1981. pap. 6.95 (ISBN 0-935954-11-2). Gormezano Ref.

Gormezano, Keith S., ed. Hispanic Business, Professional & Community Directory of Greater Seattle & Puget Sound. LC 84-18854. 82p. (Orig.). 1985. pap. 19.95 (ISBN 0-935954-97-X). Gormezano Ref.

--Who's Who in Washington State, 1981-82: Five Thousand Brief Biographies. 2nd ed. LC 81-70643. (Who's Who Reference Ser.: No. 2). 124p. 1981. lib. bdg. 959.95 (ISBN 0-935954-12-0). Gormezano Ref.

Gormezano, Keith S., jt. ed. see Beacon Presse Staff.

Gormezano, Keith S., tr. see Gormezano, Shabetai B.

Gormezano Reference Publications Staff, ed. Who's Who in Alabama, 1982: Two Thousand Seven Hundred Brief Biographies. LC 81-70618. (Who's Who Reference Ser.: No. 27). 188p. 1982. lib. bdg. 959.95 (ISBN 0-935954-37-6). Gormezano Ref.

--Who's Who in Alaska, 1982: Five Hundred Brief Biographies. LC 81-70616. (Who's Who Reference Ser.: No. 50). 112p. 1982. lib. bdg. 949.95 (ISBN 0-935954-62-7). Gormezano Ref.

--Who's Who in Arizona, 1982: Four Thousand Brief Biographies. LC 81-70636. (Who's Who Reference Ser.: No. 9). 200p. 1981. lib. bdg. 959.95 (ISBN 0-935954-19-8). Gormezano Ref.

--Who's Who in Arkansas, 1982: Three Thousand Brief Biographies. LC 81-70623. (Who's Who Reference Ser.: No. 22). 196p. 1982. lib. bdg. 959.95 (ISBN 0-935954-32-5). Gormezano Ref.

--Who's Who in Colorado, 1982: Four Thousand Brief Biographies. LC 81-70633. (Who's Who Reference Ser.: No. 12). 212p. 1981. lib. bdg. 959.95 (ISBN 0-935954-22-8). Gormezano Ref.

--Who's Who in Connecticut, 1982: Two Thousand Brief Biographies. LC 81-70608. (Who's Who Reference Ser.: No. 41). 196p. 1982. lib. bdg. 959.95 (ISBN 0-935954-51-1). Gormezano Ref.

--Who's Who in Delaware, 1982: Fifteen Hundred Brief Biographies. LC 81-70605. (Who's Who Reference Ser.: No. 39). 120p. 1982. lib. bdg. 949.95 (ISBN 0-935954-49-X). Gormezano Ref.

--Who's Who in Florida, 1982: Three Thousand One Hundred Brief Biographies. LC 81-70649. (Who's Who Reference Ser.: No. 29). 204p. 1982. lib. bdg. 959.95 (ISBN 0-935954-39-2). Gormezano Ref.

--Who's Who in Georgia, 1982: Two Thousand Eight Hundred Brief Biographies. LC 81-70644. (Who's Who Reference Ser.: No. 28). 192p. 1982. lib. bdg. 959.95 (ISBN 0-935954-38-4). Gormezano Ref.

--Who's Who in Hawaii, 1982: Two Thousand One Hundred Brief Biographies. LC 81-70615. (Who's Who Reference Ser.: No. 49). 176p. 1982. lib. bdg. 949.95 (ISBN 0-935954-61-9). Gormezano Ref.

--Who's Who in Idaho, 1982: Four Thousand One Hundred Brief Biographies. LC 81-70641. (Who's Who Reference Ser.: No. 4). 204p. lib. bdg. 959.95 (ISBN 0-935954-14-7). Gormezano Ref.

--Who's Who in Illinois, 1982: Five Thousand Brief Biographies. LC 81-70625. (Who's Who Reference Ser.). 212p. 1981. lib. bdg. 959.95 (ISBN 0-935954-30-9). Gormezano Ref.

--Who's Who in Indiana, 1982: Three Thousand Brief Biographies. LC 81-70606. (Who's Who Reference Ser.: No. 33). 204p. 1982. lib. bdg. 959.95 (ISBN 0-935954-43-0). Gormezano Ref.

--Who's Who in Kansas, 1982: Three Thousand Brief Biographies. LC 81-70629. (Who's Who Reference Ser.: No. 16). 196p. 1981. lib. bdg. 59.95 (ISBN 0-935954-26-0). Gormezano Ref.

--Who's Who in Kentucky, 1982: Three Thousand One Hundred Brief Biographies. LC 81-770619. (Who's Who Reference Ser.: No. 26). 204p. 1982. lib. bdg. 959.95 (ISBN 0-935954-36-8). Gormezano Ref.

--Who's Who in Louisiana, 1982: Two Thousand Nine Hundred Brief Biographies. LC 81-70622. (Who's Who Reference Ser.: No. 23). 196p. 1982. lib. bdg. 959.95 (ISBN 0-935954-33-3). Gormezano Ref.

--Who's Who in Maine, 1982: Two Thousand Six Hundred Brief Biographies. LC 81-70611. (Who's Who Reference Ser.: No. 44). 156p. 1982. lib. bdg. 959.95 (ISBN 0-935954-54-6). Gormezano Ref.

--Who's Who in Maryland, 1982: Three Thousand One Hundred Brief Biographies. LC 81-70603. (Who's Who Reference Ser.: No. 37). 208p. 1982. lib. bdg. 959.95 (ISBN 0-935954-47-3). Gormezano Ref.

--Who's Who in Massachusetts, 1983: Three Thousand Brief Biographies. LC 81-70609. (Who's Who Reference Ser.: No. 42). 204p. 1982. lib. bdg. 959.95 (ISBN 0-935954-52-X). Gormezano Ref.

--Who's Who in Michigan, 1982: Three Thousand Brief Biographies. LC 81-70614. (Who's Who Reference Ser.: No. 47). 188p. 1982. lib. bdg. 959.95 (ISBN 0-935954-57-0). Gormezano Ref.

--Who's Who in Minnesota, 1982: Four Thousand Brief Biographies. LC 81-70627. (Who's Who Reference Ser.: No. 18). 204p. 1981. lib. bdg. 959.95 (ISBN 0-935954-28-7). Gormezano Ref.

--Who's Who in Mississippi, 1982: Two Thousand Nine Hundred Brief Biographies. LC 81-70621. (Who's Who Reference Ser.: No. 24). 186p. 1982. lib. bdg. 959.95 (ISBN 0-935954-34-1). Gormezano Ref.

--Who's Who in Missouri, 1982: Three Thousand Brief Biographies. LC 81-70624. (Who's Who Reference Ser.: No. 21). 192p. 1981. lib. bdg. 959.95 (ISBN 0-935954-31-7). Gormezano Ref.

--Who's Who in Nebraska, 1982: Three Thousand Brief Biographies. LC 81-70630. (Who's Who Reference Ser.: No. 15). 188p. 1981. lib. bdg. 959.95 (ISBN 0-935954-25-2). Gormezano Ref.

--Who's Who in Nevada, 1982: Four Thousand Two Hundred Brief Biographies. LC 81-70637. (Who's Who Reference Ser.: No. 8). 196p. 1981. lib. bdg. 959.95 (ISBN 0-935954-18-X). Gormezano Ref.

--Who's Who in New Hampshire, 1982: Two Thousand Five Hundred Brief Biographies. LC 81-70610. (Who's Who Reference Ser.: No. 43). 156p. 1982. lib. bdg. 959.95 (ISBN 0-935954-53-8). Gormezano Ref.

--Who's Who in New Jersey, 1982: Two Thousand Eight Hundred Brief Biographies. LC 81-70613. (Who's Who Reference Ser.: No. 46). 172p. 1982. lib. bdg. 959.95 (ISBN 0-935954-56-2). Gormezano Ref.

--Who's Who in New Mexico, 1982: Three Thousand Nine Hundred Brief Biographies. LC 81-70635. (Who's Who Reference Ser.: No. 10). 204p. 1981. lib. bdg. 959.95 (ISBN 0-935954-20-1). Gormezano Ref.

--Who's Who in New York State, 1982: Five Thousand Brief Biographies. LC 81-70607. (Who's Who Reference Ser.: No. 40). 302p. 1982. lib. bdg. 979.95 (ISBN 0-935954-50-3). Gormezano Ref.

--Who's Who in North Carolina, 1982: Three Thousand Brief Biographies. LC 81-70645. (Who's Who Reference Ser.: No. 31). 196p. 1982. lib. bdg. 959.95 (ISBN 0-935954-41-4). Gormezano Ref.

--Who's Who in North Dakota, 1982: One Thousand Five Hundred Brief Biographies. LC 81-70632. (Who's Who Reference Ser.: No. 13). 188p. lib. bdg. 959.95 (ISBN 0-935954-23-6). Gormezano Ref.

--Who's Who in Ohio, 1982: Three Thousand Brief Biographies. LC 81-70600. (Who's Who Reference Ser.: No. 34). 220p. 1982. lib. bdg. 959.95 (ISBN 0-935954-44-9). Gormezano Ref.

--Who's Who in Oklahoma, 1982: Three Thousand Brief Biographies. LC 81-70928. (Who's Who Reference Ser.: No. 17). 196p. 1981. lib. bdg. 959.95 (ISBN 0-935954-27-9). Gormezano Ref.

Gormezano Reference Publications Staff & Gormezano, Keith, eds. Who's Who in Oregon, 1982: Four Thousand Brief Biographies. LC 81-70642. (Who's Who Reference Ser.: No. 3). 216p. 1981. lib. bdg. 959.95 (ISBN 0-935954-13-9). Gormezano Ref.

Gormezano Reference Publications Staff, ed. Who's Who in Pennsylvania, 1982: Four Thousand Three Hundred Brief Biographies. LC 81-70601. (Who's Who Reference Ser.: No. 35). 216p. 1982. lib. bdg. 969.95 (ISBN 0-935954-45-7). Gormezano Ref.

--Who's Who in Rhode Island, 1982: One Thousand Five Hundred Brief Biographies. LC 81-70604. (Who's Who Reference Ser.: No. 38). 124p. 1982. lib. bdg. 949.95 (ISBN 0-935954-48-1). Gormezano Ref.

--Who's Who in South Carolina, 1982: Three Thousand Brief Biographies. LC 81-70651. (Who's Who Reference Ser.: No. 30). 196p. 1982. lib. bdg. 959.95 (ISBN 0-935954-40-6). Gormezano Ref.

--Who's Who in South Dakota, 1982: Two Thousand Five Hundred Brief Biographies. LC 81-70631. (Who's Who Reference Ser.: No. 14). 196p. 1981. lib. bdg. 959.95 (ISBN 0-935954-24-4). Gormezano Ref.

--Who's Who in Tennessee, 1982: Three Thousand Brief Biographies. LC 81-70620. (Who's Who Reference Ser.: No. 25). 192p. 1982. lib. bdg. 959.95 (ISBN 0-935954-35-X). Gormezano Ref.

--Who's Who in Texas. 1982: Five Thousand Brief Biographies. LC 81-70634. (Who's Who Reference Ser.: No. 11). 360p. 1981. lib. bdg. 959.95 (ISBN 0-935954-21-X). Gormezano Ref.

--Who's Who in Utah, 1982: Four Thousand One Hundred Brief Biographies. LC 81-70640. (Who's Who Reference Ser.: No. 5). 216p. 1981. lib. bdg. 959.95 (ISBN 0-935954-15-5). Gormezano Ref.

--Who's Who in Vermont, 1982: Two Thousand Seven Hundred Brief Biographies. LC 81-70612. (Who's Who Reference Ser.: No. 45). 162p. 1982. lib. bdg. 959.95 (ISBN 0-935954-55-4). Gormezano Ref.

--Who's Who in Virginia, 1982: Five Thousand Brief Biographies. LC 81-70650. (Who's Who Reference Ser.: No. 32). 312p. 1982. lib. bdg. 959.95 (ISBN 0-935954-42-2). Gormezano Ref.

--Who's Who in Wisconsin, 1982: Three Thousand Eight Hundred Brief Biographies. LC 81-70626. (Who's Who Reference Ser.: No. 19). 208p. 1981. lib. bdg. 959.95 (ISBN 0-935954-29-5). Gormezano Ref.

--Who's Who in Wyoming. 1982: Four Thousand One Hundred Brief Biographies. LC 81-70638. (Who's Who Reference Ser.: No. 7). 200p. 1981. lib. bdg. 959.95 (ISBN 0-935954-17-1). Gormezano Ref.

Gormezano, Shabetai, ed. Who's Who among American Jews: 1984-1985. LC 84-18858. (Illus.). 996p. 1985. lib. bdg. 989.95 (ISBN 0-935954-95-3). Gormezano Ref.

Gormezano, Shabetai B. Cousins: An Israeli War - Love Story. Gormezano, Keith S., tr. from Hebrew. LC 81-69807. (Foreign Artists, Poets & Authors Ser.: No. 2). 50p. 1981. pap. 14.95 (ISBN 0-935954-10-4). Gormezano Ref.

Gormezano, Stephen, ed. Oh, Say Can You See... One Hundred Collected Posters Reproduced. LC 80-67884. 108p. (Orig.). 1980. pap. 6.95 (ISBN 0-935954-08-2). Gormezano Ref.

Gormican, Annette. Controlling Diabetes with Diet. (Illus.). 232p. 1976. pap. 10.75x spiral (ISBN 0-398-00705-5). C C Thomas.

Gormley, Beatrice. Best Friend Insurance. (Illus.). 160p. (gr. 3-7). 1985. pap. 2.50 (ISBN 0-380-69854-4). Avon.

--Best Friends Insurance. (Illus.). 160p. (gr. 3-6). 1983. 10.95 (ISBN 0-525-44066-6, 01063-320). Dutton.

--Fifth Grade Magic. 144p. (gr. 3-6). 1982. 9.95 (ISBN 0-525-44007-0, 0966-290). Dutton.

--Fifth Grade Magic. (Illus.). 136p. (gr. 3-7). 1984. pap. 2.50 (ISBN 0-380-67439-4, 60216-4, Camelot). Avon.

--Mail-Order Wings. (Illus.). 176p. (gr. 3-6). 1981. 10.95 (ISBN 0-525-34450-0, 01063-320). Dutton.

--Mail-Order Wings. (Illus.). 164p. (gr. 3-7). 1984. pap. 2.25 (ISBN 0-380-67421-1, 67421, Camelot). Avon.

Gormley, Chuck. Group Backpacking: A Leader's Manual. (Illus.). 160p. 1979. pap. 7.95 (ISBN 0-916068-08-0). Groupwork Today.

Gormley, Gerard. A Dolphin Summer. LC 84-26841. 206p. 1985. 14.95 (ISBN 0-8008-2264-1). Taplinger.

Gormley, Joe. Battered Cherub. (Illus.). 288p. 1982. 19.95 (ISBN 0-241-10754-7, Pub. by Hamish Hamilton England). David & Charles.

Gormley, L. W. Prohibiting Restrictions on Trade Within the EEC: The Theory & Application of Articles 30-36 of the EEC Treaty. 466p. 1985. 55.75 (ISBN 0-444-86848-8, North-Holland). Elsevier.

Gormley, Mary J. Calligraphy: The Italic Alphabet for Right & Left-Handed Writers. 2nd, rev. ed. LC 83-90347. (Illus.). 85p. 1983. pap. 8.95 (ISBN 0-9611590-0-6). Inkspot Pr.

Gormley, R. James. The Law of Accountants & Auditors. 64.00 (ISBN 0-88262-517-9). Warren.

Gormley, William T., Jr. Effects of Newspaper-Television Cross-Ownership on News Homogeneity. LC 76-21859. (IRSS Research Report Ser.). 276p. 1976. pap. text ed. 5.00 (ISBN 0-89143-065-2). U NC Inst Res Soc Sci.

--The Politics of Public Utility Regulation. LC 82-42756. 281p. 1983. 26.95x (ISBN 0-8229-3479-5); pap. 9.95x (ISBN 0-8229-5351-X). U of Pittsburgh Pr.

Gormulicki, B. R. & Fielding, A. Statistics, 2 Vols. 1982. 59.00x set (ISBN 0-686-44551-1, Pub. by Natl Ext England). State Mutual Bk.

Gorn, Janice L. The Writer's Handbook. 128p. 1984. pap. 5.95 (ISBN 0-671-50424-X). Monarch Pr.

Gornall, Allan G., ed. Applied Biochemistry of Clinical Disorders. LC 80-23795. (Illus.). 544p. 1981. pap. text ed. 34.75x (ISBN 0-06-141010-1, 14-10109, Harper Medical). Lippincott.

Gornall, Thomas. The Letters & Diaries of John Henry Newman: Liberalism in Oxford, January 1835 to December 1836, Vol. 5. 1981. 65.00x (ISBN 0-19-920117-X). Oxford U Pr.

Gornall, Thomas, ed. see Newman, John H.

Gorner, P. A., tr. see Tugendhat, Ernst.

Gorney, Howard, jt. auth. see Johnson, Glenn S.

Gorney, Len. Queueing Theory: A Solving Approach. (Illus.). 300p. 1981. 23.95 (ISBN 0-89433-128-0). Petrocelli.

Gorney, Leonard. Invitation to Database Processing. (Illus.). 276p. 1985. text ed. 27.95 (ISBN 0-89433-217-1). Petrocelli.

Gornick, F., jt. ed. see McIntyre, Donald.

Gornick, Vivian. Women in Science: Portraits from a World in Transition. 177p. 1983. 15.95 (ISBN 0-671-41738-X). S&S.

--Women in Science: Portraits from a World in Transition. 176p. 1985. pap. 10.95 (ISBN 0-671-41739-8, Touchstone Bks). S&S.

Gornick, Vivian & Moran, Barbara K. Woman in Sexist Society. 1972. pap. 4.95 (ISBN 0-451-62325-8, ME2325, Ment). NAL.

Gornik, E., et al, eds. Physics of Narrow Gap Semiconductors: Proceedings. (Lecture Notes in Physics Ser.: Vol. 152). 485p. 1982. 30.00 (ISBN 0-387-11191-3). Springer-Verlag.

Gornitz, Vivien, ed. Geology of the Planet Mars. LC 78-13589. (Benchmark Papers in Geology Ser.: Vol. 48). 414p. 1979. 57.95 (ISBN 0-87933-339-1). Van Nos Reinhold.

Gorny, Joseph. The British Labour Movement & Zionism 1917-1948. 270p. 1983. text ed. 30.00x (ISBN 0-7146-3162-0, F Cass Co). Biblio Dist.

Gorochow, P. K. Russich-Deutsches Worterbuch der Funkechnik. 390p. (Rus. & Ger.). 1961. leatherette 6.95 (ISBN 0-686-92169-0). French & Eur.

Gorodess, Robert. How to Sell Remodeling. 240p. (Orig.). 1985. pap. 17.50 (ISBN 0-910460-47-7). Craftsman.

Gorodetsky, Gabriel. Stafford Cripps' Mission to Moscow, 1940-42. (Illus.). 377p. 1985. 44.50 (ISBN 0-521-23866-8). Cambridge U Pr.

Gorodetzky, Nadejda. The Humiliated Christ in Modern Russian Thought. LC 79-168159. Repr. of 1938 ed. 18.75 (ISBN 0-404-02883-7). AMS Pr.

Gorodezky, Sarah, jt. auth. see Lauffer, Armand.

Gorog, Judith. Caught in the Turtle. (Illus.). (gr. 5-8). 1983. 10.95 (ISBN 0-399-20981-6, Philomel). Putnam Pub Group.

--A Taste for Quiet: And Other Disquieting Tales. (Illus.). 124p. 1982. 9.95 (ISBN 0-399-20922-0, Philomel). Putnam Pub Group.

Gorog, Ralph De see De Gorog, Ralph.

Gorog, S. Quantitative Analysis of Steroids. (Studies in Analytical Chemistry: No. 5). 440p. 1983. 86.75 (ISBN 0-444-99698-2). Elsevier.

Gorog, S. & Szasz, G. Y. Analysis of Steroid Hormone Drugs. 426p. 1978. 72.50 (ISBN 0-444-99805-5). Elsevier.

Gorog, S., ed. Advances in Steroid Analysis: Proceedings of a Symposium in Egar, Hungary, May 1981. (Analytical Chemistry Symposia Ser.: Vol. 10). 552p. 1982. 95.75 (ISBN 0-444-99711-3). Elsevier.

Goroll, Allan H., et al. Primary Care Medicine: Office Evaluation & Management of the Adult Patient. (Illus.). 855p. 1981. text ed. 42.50 (ISBN 0-397-58256-0, 65-05598, Lippincott Medical). Lippincott.

Goromosov, M. S. Physiological Basis of Health Standards for Dwellings. (Public Health Papers Ser: No. 33). 99p. 1968. pap. 2.80 (ISBN 92-4-130033-7, 761). World Health.

Goronwy, Edwards J., ed. A Calender of Ancient Correspondence Concerning Wales. (History & Law Ser.: No. 2). 301p. 1935. text ed. 27.75x (ISBN 0-7083-0105-3, Pub. by Univ of Wales Pr England). Humanities.

Goronwy, Rees. A Bundle of Sensations: Sketches in Autobiography. 1978. Repr. of 1961 ed. lib. bdg. 17.50 (ISBN 0-8495-4518-8). Arden Lib.

Gorospe, Vitaliano R. The Four Faces of Asia: A Summary Report on the Asian Bishops' Meeting, Manila 1971. 1971. wrps. 2.50x (ISBN 0-686-09496-4). Cellar.

Gorospe, Vitaliano R., ed. Freedom & Philippine Population Control. 1976. wrps. 9.00x (ISBN 0-686-09435-2). Cellar.

--Responsible Parenthood in the Philippines. 1970. wrps. 7.50 (ISBN 0-686-09499-9). Cellar.

Gorospe, Vitaliano R. & Shinn, Larry D., eds. Incarnation & Avatara World Religions. (God Ser.). 200p. (Orig.). Date not set. text ed. 17.95 (ISBN 0-913757-12-8, Pub. by New Era Bks.); pap. text ed. 12.95 (ISBN 0-913757-13-6). Paragon Hse.

Gorostiaga, Xabier. The Role of the International Financial Centres in Underdeveloped Countries. Honeywell, Annette, tr. from Span. LC 83-40177. 148p. 1984. 25.00 (ISBN 0-312-68945-4). St Martin.

Gorostiaga, Xavier, jt. ed. see Irvin, George.

Gorostiza, C. El Color de Nuestra Piel. Soto-Ruiz, Luis & Trifilo, S. Samuel, eds. (Orig.). 1966. pap. text ed. write for info. (ISBN 0-02-345370-2). Macmillan.

Gorostiza, Jose. Death Without End. Villasenor, Laura, tr. (Literary Ser.). Orig. Title: Muerte sin fin. 1969. 10.00 (ISBN 0-87959-057-2). U of Tex H Ransom Ctr.

Gorostiza, L. G., jt. ed. see Fleming, W. H.

Gorove, Stephen. Legal Aspects of International Investment. (L.Q.C. Lamar Society of International Law, University of Mississippi Law Center Monograph: No. 1). 1977. pap. text ed. 15.00x (ISBN 0-8377-0607-6). U MS Law Ctr.

Gorove, Stephen, ed. Legal Aspects of International Investment. (L. Q. C. Lamar Society of International Law, University of Mississippi Law Center, Monograph: No. 1). viii, 79p. (Orig.). 1977. pap. text ed. 10.00x (ISBN 0-8377-0607-6). Rothman.

--United States Space Law: National & International Regulation, 2 BDRS. LC 81-22465. 1982. looseleaf 85.00 ea. (ISBN 0-379-20695-1); Set. 170.00. Oceana.

Gorovitz, Sam & Maklin, Ruth. Moral Problems in Medicine. 2nd ed. (Illus.). 640p. 1983. text ed. 28.95 (ISBN 0-13-600742-2). P-H.

Gorovitz, Samuel. Doctors' Dilemmas. 240p. 1985. pap. 7.95 (ISBN 0-19-503695-6). Oxford U Pr.

Gorovitz, Samuel, ed. Freedom & Order in the University. LC 66-28145. 1967. pap. 3.95 (ISBN 0-8295-0058-8). UPB.

Gorovitz, Samuel, ed. see Mill, John S.

Gorovitz, Samuel, et al. Philosophical Analysis: An Introduction to Its Language & Techniques. 3rd ed. LC 78-5661. 1979. pap. text ed. 9.00 (ISBN 0-394-32284-3, RanC). Random.

Gorowara, Krishna, tr. see Pritam, Amrita.

Gorr, Alan. The School in the Social Setting. 392p. 1974. text ed. 37.50x (ISBN 0-8422-5162-6); pap. text ed. 14.95x (ISBN 0-8422-0177-7). Irvington.

Gorr, Alan, ed. Problems in Todays Education. 1974. 29.00x (ISBN 0-8422-5141-3); pap. text ed. 8.95x (ISBN 0-8422-0364-8). Irvington.

Gorr, Samuel, ed. see Berniker, Bernard.

Gorrell, Donna. Bridges: Readings for Writers. 1984. pap. text ed. 10.95 (ISBN 0-316-32136-2); tchrs' manual avail. (ISBN 0-316-32137-0). Little.

--Copy-Write: Basic Writing Through Controlled Composition. (Orig.). 1982. pap. 11.95 (ISBN 0-316-32133-8); tchrs'. manual avail. (ISBN 0-316-32131-1). Little.

Gorrell, Robert & Laird, Charlton. Modern English Handbook. 6th ed. 1976. text ed. 18.95 (ISBN 0-13-594283-7); tchr's man. free (ISBN 0-13-594275-6). P-H.

Gorres, Joseph. Mythengeschichte der Asiatischen Welt: Mit einen Anhang: Beitrage aus den Heidelberger Jahrbuchern. Bolle, Kees W., ed. (Mythology Ser.). (Ger.). 1978. Repr. of 1935 ed. lib. bdg. 54.00x (ISBN 0-405-10538-X). Ayer Co Pubs.

Gorrod, J. W., ed. Drug Toxicity. 340p. 1979. 27.50x (ISBN 0-85066-179-X). Taylor & Francis.

Gorrod, J. W. & Damani, L. A., eds. Biological Oxidation of Nitrogen in Organic Molecules. 300p. 1985. lib. bdg. 58.00 (ISBN 0-89573-422-2). VCH Pubs.

Gorrod, J. W., jt. ed. see Bridges, J. W.

Gorry. Basic Molecular Spectroscopy. (Illus.). 160p. 1985. pap. text ed. 15.95 (ISBN 0-408-01553-5). Butterworth.

Gorse, Jean E. Forestry Terms - Terminologie Forestiere: A World Bank Glossary - Glosaire de la Banque Mondiale. 48p. Date not set. 5.00 (ISBN 0-318-02970-7, 175). World Bank.

Gorse, Naomi S., ed. see Koeninger, Kay, et al.

Gorshkov, G. & Yakushova, A. Physical Geology. Gurevich, A., tr. (Russian Monographs Ser.). 596p. 1969. 125.95x (ISBN 0-677-20790-5). Gordon.

Gorshkov, G. S. Volcanism & the Upper Mantle: Investigations in the Kurile Island Arc. LC 69-12530. (Monographs in Geoscience Ser.). 385p. 1970. 39.50x (ISBN 0-306-30407-4, Plenum Pr). Plenum Pub.

Gorshkov, George & Yakushova, Alexandra. Physical Geology. (Illus.). 596p. 1975. text ed. 17.50x (ISBN 0-8464-0718-3). Beekman Pubs.

Gorshkov, S. G. Sea Power of the State. (Illus.). 1979. text ed. 46.00 (ISBN 0-08-021944-6). Pergamon.

--World Ocean Atlas, Vol. 2: Atlantic & Indian Oceans. 3504p. 1979. 430.00 (ISBN 0-08-021953-5). Pergamon.

Gorshkov, Sergei G., ed. World Ocean Atlas: Arctic Ocean, Vol. 3. LC 78-40616. 184p. 1983. 400.00 (ISBN 0-08-028735-2). Pergamon.

Gorshkov, V. S., ed. Pacific Ocean. 350p. 1976. text ed. 430.00 (ISBN 0-08-021144-5). Pergamon.

Gorsini, G. U., ed. Current Trends in Lithium & Rubidium. 1984. lib. bdg. 49.50 (ISBN 0-85200-782-5, Pub. by MTP Pr England). Kluwer Academic.

Gorski, Andrew, tr. see Manteuffel, Tadeusz.

Gorski, Berni. Beyond Limitations: The Creative Art of the Mentally Retarded. (Illus.). 152p. 1979. photocopied 16.75x (ISBN 0-398-03897-X). C C Thomas.

Gorski, N. N., et al. Deutsch-Russisches Worterbuch fur Ozeanographie. 240p. (Ger. & Rus.). 1957. leatherette 4.95 (ISBN 0-686-92378-2, M-9104). French & Eur.

Gorski, Robert V., jt. ed. see Dudick, Thomas S.

Gorski, Roger A. & Whalen, Richard E., eds. Brain & Behavior: Brain & Gonadal Function, Vol. 3. LC 65-27542. (UCLA Forum in Medical Sciences Ser.). 1966. 75.00x (ISBN 0-520-00506-6). U of Cal Pr.

Gorski, Susan M., jt. ed. see Keane, Donna M.

Gorski, Terence T. & Miller, Merlene. Counseling for Relapse Prevention. 1982. pap. 9.95 (ISBN 0-8309-0367-4, Co-Pub. by Independence Press). Herald Hse.

--The Management of Aggression & Violence. Date not set. pap. 4.95 (ISBN 0-317-19300-7, 0-83094255, Co-Pub. by Independence Pr). Herald Hse.

Gorski, Terence T., jt. auth. see Miller, Merlene.

Gorskii, F. K., ed. see Sirota, N. N.

Gorsky, Benjamin H. Pain: Origin & Treatment Contemporary Patient Management. LC 80-15857. 1981. 22.00 (ISBN 0-87488-448-9); pap. 15.00 (ISBN 0-87488-447-0). Med Exam.

Gorsky, D. P. Definition. 272p. 1981. 7.20 (ISBN 0-8285-2089-5, Pub. by Progress Pubs USSR). Imported Pubns.

Gorsky, Susan R. Virginia Woolf. (English Authors Ser.). 1978. 13.50 (ISBN 0-8057-6712-6, Twayne). G K Hall.

--Virginia Woolf. (English Authors Ser.). 174p. 1984. pap. 5.95 (ISBN 0-8057-6890-4, Twayne). G K Hall.

Gorsline, Douglas, jt. auth. see Gorsline, Marie.

Gorsline, Douglas, illus. Nursery Rhymes. LC 76-24168. (Picturebacks Ser). (Illus.). (ps-2). 1977. pap. 1.95 (ISBN 0-394-83550-6, BYR). Random.

Gorsline, George W. Computer Organization: Hardware-Software. (Illus.). 400p. 1986. text ed. 36.95 (ISBN 0-13-165325-3). P-H.

--Sixteen-Bit Modern Microcomputers: The Intel I8086 Family. (Illus.). 496p. 1985. text ed. 32.95 (ISBN 0-13-811415-3). P-H.

Gorsline, Marie & Gorsline, Douglas. Cowboys. LC 78-1131. (Picturebacks Ser.). (Illus.). 32p. (ps-2). 1980. PLB 4.99 (ISBN 0-394-93935-2, BYR); pap. 1.95 (ISBN 0-394-83935-8). Random.

--North American Indians. LC 77-79843. (Picturebacks Ser.). (ps-2). 1978. 4.99 (ISBN 0-394-93702-3, BYR); pap. 1.95 (ISBN 0-394-83702-9). Random.

--The Pioneers. LC 78-54960. (Picturebacks Ser.). (Illus.). 32p. (ps-3). 1982. PLB 4.99 (ISBN 0-394-93905-0); pap. 1.50 saddle stitched (ISBN 0-394-83905-6). Random.

Gorst, Harold E. The Earl of Beaconsfield. 232p. 1981. Repr. of 1900 ed. lib. bdg. 45.00 (ISBN 0-89984-244-5). Century Bookbindery.

Gorsuch, Edwin N. & Hinds, Dudley S., eds. The Future of Atlanta's Central City. LC 77-9257. (Research Monograph Ser.: No. 73). 1977. spiral bdg. 12.95 (ISBN 0-88406-110-8). Ga St U Busn Pub.

Gorsuch, Richard L. Factor Analysis. 2nd ed. 448p. 1983. text ed. 36.00x (ISBN 0-89859-202-X). L Erlbaum Assocs.

Gorsuch, Richard L. & Malony, H. Newton. The Nature of Man: A Social Psychological Perspective. (Illus.). 228p. 1976. 18.75x (ISBN 0-398-03327-7). C C Thomas.

Gort, Michael. Diversification & Integration in American Industry. LC 84-10730. xxi, 238p. 1984. Repr. of 1962 ed. lib. bdg. 45.00x (ISBN 0-313-24423-5, GDIV). Greenwood.

Gorter, Wytze. United States Shipping Policy. LC 77-6767. 1977. Repr. of 1956 ed. lib. bdg. 20.00x (ISBN 0-8371-9657-4, GOUS). Greenwood.

Gorth, William P., et al. Comprehensive Achievement Monitoring: A Criterion-Referenced Evaluation System. LC 75-11788. 288p. 1975. 27.95 (ISBN 0-87778-080-3). Educ Tech Pubns.

Gortler, Leon B. & Tripp, Robert C., eds. Techniques & Experiments in Organic Chemistry. 2nd ed. (Illus.). 1978. lab manual 9.95 (ISBN 0-89529-016-2). Avery Pub.

Gortmaker, Gwen, jt. auth. see Goeldner, C. R.

Gortner, Harold J. Administration in the Public Sector. 2nd ed. LC 80-19757. 413p. 1981. text ed. 27.50 (ISBN 0-471-06320-7). Wiley.

Gortner, Willis A. Ancient Rock Carvings of the Central Sierra: The North Folk Indian Petroglyphs. (Illus., Orig.). 1984. 14.50 (ISBN 0-317-07249-8). Portola Pr.

Gortner, Willis A. & Freydberg, Nicholas. The Food Additives Book. 1982. 17.95 (ISBN 0-553-05012-5). Bantam.

Gorton, Audrey A. Venison Book: How to Dress, Cut up & Cook Your Deer. LC 57-13401. 1957. pap. 4.95 (ISBN 0-8289-0001-9). Greene.

Gorton, Eddie. Swimming. (Competitive Sports Ser.). (Illus.). 64p. (YA) (gr. 7-12). 1982. 12.95 (ISBN 0-7134-4079-1, Pub. by Batsford England). David & Charles.

Gorton, Jacquelyne & Partridge, Rebecca, eds. Practice & Management of Psychiatric Emergency Care. LC 82-3514. (Illus.). 430p. 1982. pap. text ed. 17.95 (ISBN 0-8016-1936-X). Mosby.

Gorton, Keith & Carr, Isobel. Low Cost Market Research: A Guide for Small Businesses. LC 82-17390. 111p. 1983. 23.95x (ISBN 0-471-90077-X, Pub. by Wiley-Interscience). Wiley.

Gorton, L. & Ihre, R. Contracts of Affreightment. 1985. write for info. (ISBN 1-85044-060-3). Lloyds London Pr.

Gorton, Richard A. School Administration & Supervision: Important Issues, Concepts & Case Studies. 2nd ed. 385p. 1980. text ed. write for info. (ISBN 0-697-06234-1). Wm C Brown.

--School Administration & Supervision: Leadership Challenges & Opportunities. 2nd ed. 576p. 1982. text ed. write for info (ISBN 0-697-06246-5). Wm C Brown.

Gorton, Richard A. & McIntyre, Kenneth E. The Senior High School Principalship: The Effective Principal, Vol. II. Koerner, Thomas F., ed. 1978. pap. 7.00 (ISBN 0-88210-094-7). Natl Assn Principals.

Gorton, Ron. The Lawyers of Hell. LC 78-27011. 225p. 1979. 9.95 (ISBN 0-8119-0319-2). Fell.

Gorun, Joel R. All Kinds of Growing. (New Creation Ser.). 62p. (gr. 3). 1984. pap. 2.95 (ISBN 0-697-01987-X); tchrs.' manual 4.50 (ISBN 0-697-01988-8). Wm C Brown.

--New Creation Program Manual. (New Creation Ser.). 76p. 1984. pap. 5.00 (ISBN 0-697-01999-3). Wm C Brown.

--People to Grow With. (New Creation Ser.). 62p. (gr. 2). 1984. 2.95 (ISBN 0-697-01985-3); tchr's. manual 4.50 (ISBN 0-697-01986-1). Wm C Brown.

--Someone Special. (New Creation Ser.). 1984. tchers man 2.95 (ISBN 0-697-01983-7); pap. 4.50 (ISBN 0-697-01984-5). Wm C Brown.

Gorun, Joel R. & Gorun, Marilyn B. Changing & Becoming. (New Creation Ser.). 62p. (gr. 4). 1984. pap. 3.00 (ISBN 0-697-01989-6); tchr's. manual 4.50 (ISBN 0-697-01990-X). Wm C Brown.

Gorun, Marilyn B., jt. auth. see Gorun, Joel R.

Gorvine, B., et al. Health Care of Women Labor & Delivery. LC 81-16202. 150p. 1982. pap. text ed. 15.25 pub net (ISBN 0-8185-0510-9). Brooks-Cole.

Gorvine, Beverly, jt. auth. see Hawkins, Joellen W.

Gorvine, Beverly, jt. ed. see Watson, Joellen.

Gorwen, Leonard. How to Find & Land Your First Full-Time Job. LC 82-6742. 144p. 1983. lib. bdg. 9.95 (ISBN 0-668-05458-1); pap. 4.95 (ISBN 0-668-05463-8). Arco.

Gory, Mark E. La see Pipkin, John S. & La Gory, Mark E.

Goryunova, N. A., jt. ed. see Nasledov, Dmitrii N.

Gorz, Andre. Ecology As Politics. Vigderman, Patsy & Cloud, Jonathan, trs. LC 79-64086. 215p. 1980. 15.00 (ISBN 0-89608-089-7); pap. 6.50 (ISBN 0-89608-088-9). South End Pr.

--Farewell to the Working Class. 250p. 1982. 20.00 (ISBN 0-89608-168-0); pap. 7.50 (ISBN 0-89608-167-2). South End Pr.

Gorzalka, Ann L. The Saddlemakers of Sheridan County, Wyoming. LC 82-23043. write for info. (ISBN 0-87108-634-4). Pruett.

Gorzelany, James A. Nevada Supplement for Modern Real Estate Practice. (Orig.). 1979. pap. 8.95 (ISBN 0-88462-346-7, 1510-29, Real Estate Ed). Longman USA.

--North Dakota Supplement for Modern Real Estate Practice. 120p. (Orig.). 1980. pap. 8.95 (ISBN 0-88462-377-7, 1510-41, Real Estate Ed). Longman USA.

Gorzelany, James A. & Reus, Violet. Indiana Supplement for Modern Real Estate Practice. 128p. (Orig.). 1980. pap. 8.95 (ISBN 0-88462-379-3, Real Estate Ed). Longman USA.

Gorzelany, James A., jt. auth. see Ballou, John D.

Gorzny, Willi, ed. Gesamtverzeichnis des Deutschsprachiger Hoshschulschriften, 1966 to 1980, 28 vols. 1983. Set. lib. bdg. 5000.00 (ISBN 3-598-30600-8). K G Saur.

Gos, Francois & Baldausky, Karen. Alpine Flower Designs for Artists & Craftsmen. (Illus.). 64p. (Orig.). 1980. pap. 4.95 (ISBN 0-486-23982-9). Dover.

Gos, Michael W. Brackish Aquariums. (Illus.). 1979. 4.95 (ISBN 0-87666-519-9, KW-046). TFH Pubns.

--Doves. (Illus.). 96p. 1981. 4.95 (ISBN 0-87666-828-7, KW-123). TFH Pubns.

Gosch, Marvin, jt. auth. see Hammer, Richard.

Goschen, George J. Essays & Addresses on Economic Questions (1865-1893) With Introductory Notes (1905) LC 82-48184. (Gold, Money, Inflation & Deflation Ser.). 382p. 1983. lib. bdg. 50.00 (ISBN 0-8240-5237-4). Garland Pub.

--The Theory of the Foreign Exchanges. Wilkins, Mira, ed. LC 78-3918. (International Finance Ser.). 1978. Repr. of 1892 ed. lib. bdg. 17.00x (ISBN 0-405-11221-1). Ayer Co Pubs.

Goschie, Susan. Fashion Direction & Coordination. 2nd ed. 1980. pap. 14.47 scp (ISBN 0-672-97266-2); scp tchr's manual 3.67 (ISBN 0-672-97267-0). Bobbs.

Gosciak, Josh, ed. see Ginsberg, Allen, et al.

Gosciak, Josh, ed. see Purdy, James.

Gosciak, Josh, ed. see Sanders, Ed, et al.

Gosciewski, F. William. Effective Child Rearing: The Behaviorally Aware Parent. LC 76-3620. 158p. 1976. 19.95 (ISBN 0-87705-262-X). Human Sci Pr.

Goscilo, Helena, ed. Russian & Polish Women's Fiction. LC 84-20915. 360p. 1985. text ed. 29.95x (ISBN 0-87049-456-2); pap. text ed. 14.95x (ISBN 0-87049-472-4). U of Tenn Pr.

Goscilo, Helena, ed. & tr. see Lermontov, Mikhail.

Goscilo, Helena, tr. see Nagibin, Yuri.

Goscinny & Uderzo. Asterix & Cleopatra. (Asterix Ser.). pap. 4.95 (ISBN 2-205-06905-5, Pub. by Dargaud Canada). C Berke.

--Asterix & Cleopatra. Bell, Anthea & Hockridge, Derek, trs. from Fr. (Illus.). 1979. pap. 3.95 (ISBN 0-340-17220-7, Pub. by Dargaud Canada). C Berke.

--Asterix & the Banquet. (Asterix Ser.). pap. 3.95 (ISBN 2-205-06923-3, Pub. by Dargaud Canada). C Berke.

--Asterix & the Big Fight. (Asterix Ser.). pap. 4.95 (ISBN 2-205-06906-3, Pub. by Dargaud Canada). C Berke.

--Asterix & the Big Fight. Bell, Anthea & Hockridge, Derek, trs. from Fr. (Illus.). 1979. pap. 3.95 (ISBN 0-340-19167-8, Pub. by Dargaud Canada). C Berke.

--Asterix & the Cauldron. Bell, Anthea & Hockridge, Derek, trs. from Fr. (Illus.). 1979. pap 3.95 (ISBN 2-205-06912-8, Pub. by Dargaud Canada). C Berke.

--Asterix & the Chieftain's Shield. Bell, Anthea & Hockridge, Derek, trs. from Fr. (Illus.). 1979. pap. 3.95 (ISBN 2-205-06910-1, Pub. by Dargaud Canada). C Berke.

--Asterix & the Golden Sickle. Bell, Anthea & Hockridge, Derek, trs. from Fr. (Illus.). 1979. pap. 3.95 (ISBN 2-205-06901-2, Pub. by Dargaud Canada). C Berke.

--Asterix & the Goths. (Asterix Ser.). pap. 3.95 (ISBN 2-205-06902-0, Pub. by Dargaud Canada). C Berke.

--Asterix & the Great Crossing. (Asterix Ser.). 1979. pap. 3.95 (ISBN 2-205-06921-7, Pub. by Dargaud Canada). C Berke.

--Asterix & the Laurel Wreath. (Asterix Ser.). 1979. pap. 3.95 (ISBN 2-205-06917-9, Pub. by Dargaud Canada). C Berke.

--Asterix & the Mansions of the Gods. Bell, Anthea & Hockridge, Derek, trs. from Fr. (Illus.). 1979. pap. 3.95 (ISBN 2-205-06916-0, Pub. by Dargaud Canada). C Berke.

--Asterix & the Normans. (Asterix Ser.). 1979. pap. 3.95 (ISBN 2-205-06908-X, Pub. by Dargaud Canada). C Berke.

--Asterix & the Roman Agent. (Asterix Ser.). 1979. pap. 4.95 (ISBN 2-205-06914-4, Pub. by Dargaud Canada). C Berke.

--Asterix & the Soothsayer. (Asterix Ser.). 1979. pap. 3.95 (ISBN 2-205-06918-7, Pub. by Dargaud Canada). C Berke.

--Asterix at the Olympic Games. (Asterix Ser.). 1979. pap. 4.95 (ISBN 2-205-06911-X, Pub. by Dargaud Canada). C Berke.

--Asterix Gladiator. (Asterix Ser.). 5.95 (ISBN 84-7419-065-7, Pub. by Dargaud Canada). C Berke.

--Asterix in Britain. (Asterix Ser.). 1979. pap. 4.95 (ISBN 2-205-06907-1, Pub. by Dargaud Canada). C Berke.

--Asterix in Corsica. Bell, Anthea & Hockridge, Derek, trs. (Illus.). 1980. pap. 3.95 (ISBN 0-340-24074-1). C Berke.

--Asterix in Corsica. (Asterix Ser.). 1979. pap. 3.95 (ISBN 2-205-06919-5, Pub. by Dargaud Canada). C Berke.

--Asterix in Spain. (Asterix Ser.). pap. 4.95 (ISBN 2-205-06913-6, Pub. by Dargaud Canada). C Berke.

--Asterix in Switzerland. (Asterix Ser.). 1979. pap. 4.95 (ISBN 2-205-06915-2, Pub. by Dargaud Canada). C Berke.

--Asterix the Gaul. (Asterix Ser.). pap. 4.95 (ISBN 2-205-06900-4, Pub. by Dargaud Canada). C Berke.

--Asterix the Gladiator. (Asterix Ser.). 1979. pap. 4.95 (ISBN 2-205-06903-9, Pub. by Dargaud Canada). C Berke.

--Asterix the Goth. Bell, Anthea & Hockridge, Derek, trs. from Fr. (Illus.). 1979. pap. 3.95 (ISBN 2-205-06902-0, Pub. by Dargaud Canada). C Berke.

--Asterix the Legionary. (Asterix Ser.). 1979. pap. 4.95 (ISBN 2-205-06909-8, Pub. by Dargaud Canada). C Berke.

--Asterix y los Godos. (Asterix Ser.). 5.95 (ISBN 84-7419-041-X, Pub. by Dargaud Canada). C Berke.

--El Escudo Arverno. (Asterix Ser.). 5.95 (ISBN 84-7419-020-7, Pub. by Dargaud Canada). C Berke.

--The Mansion of the Gods. (Asterix Ser.). pap. 3.95 (ISBN 2-205-06916-0, Pub. by Dargaud Canada). C Berke.

--Obelix & Co. (Asterix Ser.). pap. 3.95 (ISBN 2-205-06922-5, Pub. by Dargaud Canada). C Berke.

--Obelix & Company. Hall, Anthea & Hockridge, Derek, trs. (Illus.). 1979. pap 3.95 (ISBN 2-205-06922-5). C Berke.

Goscinny, R. & Uderzo, M. El Adivino. (Illus., Span.). 7.95 (ISBN 0-686-56236-4). French & Eur.

--Der Arvernerschild. (Illus., Ger.). 7.95 (ISBN 0-686-56259-3). French & Eur.

--Asterix als Gladiator. (Illus., Ger.). 7.95 (ISBN 0-686-56251-8). French & Eur.

--Asterix als Legionar. (Illus., Ger.). 7.95 (ISBN 0-686-56258-5). French & Eur.

--Asterix & Caesar's Gift. (Illus.). 7.95 (ISBN 0-686-56217-8). French & Eur.

--Asterix & Cleopatra. (Illus.). 7.95 (ISBN 0-686-56200-3). French & Eur.

--Asterix & the Big Fight. (Illus.). 7.95 (ISBN 0-686-56204-6). French & Eur.

--Asterix & the Chieftain's Shield. (Illus.). 7.95 (ISBN 0-686-56216-X). French & Eur.

--Asterix & the Goths. (Illus.). 7.95 (ISBN 0-686-56209-7). French & Eur.

--Asterix & the Laurel Wreath. (Illus.). 7.95 (ISBN 0-686-56211-9). French & Eur.

--Asterix & the Normans. (Illus.). 7.95 (ISBN 0-686-56218-6). French & Eur.

--Asterix & the Roman Agent. (Illus.). 7.95 (ISBN 0-686-56207-0). French & Eur.

--Asterix apud Gothos. (Illus., Lat.). 7.95 (ISBN 0-686-56273-9). French & Eur.

--Asterix at the Olympic Games. (Illus.). 7.95 (ISBN 0-686-56206-2). French & Eur.

--Asterix auf Korsika. (Illus., Ger.). 7.95 (ISBN 0-686-56268-2). French & Eur.

--Asterix bei den Briten. (Illus., Ger.). 7.95 (ISBN 0-686-56256-9). French & Eur.

--Asterix bei den Olympischen Spielen. (Illus., Ger.). 7.95 (ISBN 0-686-56260-7). French & Eur.

--Asterix bei den Schweizern. (Illus., Ger.). 7.95 (ISBN 0-686-56264-X). French & Eur.

--Asterix chez les Belges. (Illus., Fr.). 7.95 (ISBN 0-686-56247-X). French & Eur.

--Asterix der Gallier. (Illus., Ger.). 7.95 (ISBN 0-686-56249-6). French & Eur.

--Asterix el Galo. (Illus., Span.). 7.95 (ISBN 0-686-56223-2). French & Eur.

--Asterix en Bretana. (Illus., Span.). 7.95 (ISBN 0-686-56222-4). French & Eur.

--Asterix en Corcega. (Illus., Span.). 7.95 (ISBN 0-686-56237-2). French & Eur.

--Asterix en Corse. (Illus., Fr.). 7.95 (ISBN 0-686-56244-5). French & Eur.

--Asterix en Helvecia. (Illus., Span.). 7.95 (ISBN 0-686-56233-X). French & Eur.

--Asterix en los Juegos Olimpicos. (Illus., Span.). 7.95 (ISBN 0-686-56230-5). French & Eur.

--Asterix Gallus. (Illus., Lat.). 7.95 (ISBN 0-686-56271-2). French & Eur.

--Asterix Gladiador. (Illus., Span.). 7.95 (ISBN 0-686-56227-5). French & Eur.

--Asterix Gladiator. (Illus., Lat.). 7.95 (ISBN 0-686-56274-7). French & Eur.

--Asterix in Britain. (Illus.). 7.95 (ISBN 0-686-56202-X). French & Eur.

--Asterix in Spain. (Illus.). 7.95 (ISBN 0-686-56205-4). French & Eur.

--Asterix in Spanien. (Illus., Ger.). 7.95 (ISBN 0-686-56262-3). French & Eur.

--Asterix in Switzerland. (Illus.). 7.95 (ISBN 0-686-56208-9). French & Eur.

--Asterix iter Gallicum. (Illus., Lat.). 7.95 (ISBN 0-686-56275-5). French & Eur.

--Asterix Legionario. (Illus., Span.). 7.95. French & Eur.

--Asterix the Gaul. (Illus.). 7.95 (ISBN 0-686-56199-6). French & Eur.

--Asterix the Gladiator. (Illus.). 7.95 (ISBN 0-686-56201-1). French & Eur.

--Asterix the Legionary. (Illus.). 7.95 (ISBN 0-686-56203-8). French & Eur.

--Asterix und die Goten. (Illus., Ger.). 7.95 (ISBN 0-686-56255-0). French & Eur.

--Asterix und Kleopatra. (Illus., Ger.). 7.95 (ISBN 0-686-56250-X). French & Eur.

--Asterix y Cleopatra. (Illus., Span.). 7.95 (ISBN 0-686-56228-3). French & Eur.

--Asterix y el Caldero. (Illus., Span.). 7.95 (ISBN 0-686-56231-3). French & Eur.

--Asterix y los Godos. (Illus., Span.). 7.95 (ISBN 0-686-56225-9). French & Eur.

--Asterix y los Normandos. (Illus., Span.). 7.95 (ISBN 0-686-56229-1). French & Eur.

--Le Cadeau de Cesar. (Illus., Fr.). 7.95 (ISBN 0-686-56245-3). French & Eur.

--The Caldron. (Illus.). 7.95 (ISBN 0-686-56215-1). French & Eur.

--La Cizana. (Illus., Span.). 7.95 (ISBN 0-686-56232-1). French & Eur.

--El Combate de los Jefes. (Illus., Span.). 7.95 (ISBN 0-686-56221-6). French & Eur.

--Les Douze Travaux d'Asterix. (Illus., Fr.). 7.95 (ISBN 0-686-56248-8). French & Eur.

--El Escudo Arverno. (Illus., Span.). 7.95. French & Eur.

--Falx Aurea. (Illus., Lat.). 7.95 (ISBN 0-686-56272-0). French & Eur.

--Das Geschenk Casars. (Illus., Ger.). 7.95 (ISBN 0-686-56269-0). French & Eur.

--Die Goldene Sichel. (Illus., Ger.). 7.95 (ISBN 0-686-56253-4). French & Eur.

--La Gran Travesia. (Illus., Span.). 7.95 (ISBN 0-686-56239-9). French & Eur.

--La Grande Traversee. (Illus., Fr.). 7.95 (ISBN 0-686-56246-1). French & Eur.

--The Great Crossing. (Illus.). 7.95 (ISBN 0-686-56214-3). French & Eur.

--Die Grosse Uberfahrt. (Illus., Ger.). 7.95 (ISBN 0-686-56270-4). French & Eur.

--La Hoz de Oro. (Illus., Span.). 7.95 (ISBN 0-686-56224-0). French & Eur.

--Der Kampf der Hauptlinge. (Illus., Ger.). 7.95 (ISBN 0-686-56252-6). French & Eur.

--Der Kupferkessel. (Illus., Ger.). 7.95 (ISBN 0-686-56261-5). French & Eur.

--Los Laureles del Cesar. (Illus., Span.). 7.95 (ISBN 0-686-56235-6). French & Eur.

--Les Lauriers de Cesar. (Illus., Fr.). 7.95 (ISBN 0-686-56243-7). French & Eur.

--Die Lorbeeren des Casar. (Illus., Ger.). 7.95 (ISBN 0-686-56266-6). French & Eur.

--The Mansions of the Gods. (Illus.). 7.95 (ISBN 0-686-56210-0). French & Eur.

--Die Normannen. (Illus., Ger.). 7.95 (ISBN 0-686-56257-7). French & Eur.

--El Regalo del Cesar. (Illus., Span.). 7.95 (ISBN 0-686-56238-0). French & Eur.

--La Residencia de los Dioses. (Illus., Span.). 7.95 (ISBN 0-686-56234-8). French & Eur.

--Der Seher. (Illus., Ger.). 7.95 (ISBN 0-686-56267-4). French & Eur.

--La Serpe d'Or. (Illus., Fr.). 7.95 (ISBN 0-686-56240-2). French & Eur.

--The Soothsayer. (Illus.). 7.95 (ISBN 0-686-56212-7). French & Eur.

--Streit Um Asterix. (Illus., Ger.). 7.95 (ISBN 0-686-56263-1). French & Eur.

--Tour de France. (Illus., Ger.). 7.95 (ISBN 0-686-56254-2). French & Eur.

--Le Tour de Gaulle. (Illus., Fr.). 7.95 (ISBN 0-686-56241-0). French & Eur.

--Die Trabantenstadt. (Illus., Ger.). 7.95 (ISBN 0-686-56265-8). French & Eur.

--La Vuelta a la Galia. (Illus., Span.). 7.95 (ISBN 0-686-56226-7). French & Eur.

--La Zizanie. (Illus., Fr.). 7.95 (ISBN 0-686-56242-9). French & Eur.

Goscinny, R., jt. auth. see Sempe, J. J.

Goscinny, Rene. Asterix et la Serpe d'or. (Illus., Fr.). (gr. 3-8). 5.95 (ISBN 0-685-28431-X). French & Eur.

--Le Tour de Gaulle. (Fr., Also avail. in Span.). (gr. 3-8). 5.95 (ISBN 0-685-23428-2). French & Eur.

Goscinny, Rene & Uderzo, Albert. El Adivino. (Asterix the Gaul Ser.). (Illus.). 48p. 7.95. Dargaud Pub.

--Asterix & the Great Crossing. (Asterix the Gaul Ser.). (Illus.). 48p. 1984. pap. 4.95 (ISBN 2-205-06921-7). Dargaud Pub.

--Asterix apud Gothos. (Asterix the Gaul Ser.). (Illus.). 48p. 7.95. Dargaud Pub.

--Asterix at the Olympic Games. 2nd ed. (Asterix the Gaul Ser.). (Illus.). 48p. (gr. 10). 1984. pap. 4.95 (ISBN 2-205-06911-X). Dargaud Pub.

--Asterix el Galo. (Asterix the Gaul Ser.). (Illus.). 48p. 7.95. Dargaud Pub.

--Asterix en Bretana. (Asterix the Gaul Ser.). (Illus.). 48p. 7.95. Dargaud Pub.

--Asterix en Corcega. (Asterix the Gaul Ser.). (Illus.). 48p. 7.95. Dargaud Pub.

--Asterix en Helvecia. (Asterix the Gaul Ser.). (Illus.). 48p. 7.95. Dargaud Pub.

--Asterix en los Juegos Olimpicos. (Asterix the Gaul Ser.). (Illus.). 48p. 7.95. Dargaud Pub.

--Asterix Gallus. (Asterix the Gaul Ser.). (Illus.). 48p. 7.95. Dargaud Pub.

--Asterix Gladiator. (Asterix the Gaul Ser.). (Illus.). 48p. 7.95. Dargaud Pub.

--Asterix Legionario. (Asterix the Gaul Ser.). (Illus.). 48p. (Span.). 7.95 (ISBN 0-686-56219-4). Dargaud Pub.

--Asterix y Cleopatra. (Asterix the Gaul Ser.). (Illus.). 48p. 7.95. Dargaud Pub.

--Asterix y el Caldero. (Asterix the Gaul Ser.). (Illus.). 48p. 7.95. Dargaud Pub.

--Asterix y los Godos. (Asterix the Gaul Ser.). (Illus.). 48p. 7.95. Dargaud Pub.

--Asterix y los Normandos. (Asterix the Gaul Ser.). (Illus.). 48p. 7.95. Dargaud Pub.

--Certamen Principum. (Asterix the Gaul Ser.). (Illus.). 48p. 7.95. Dargaud Pub.

--La Cizana. (Asterix the Gaul Ser.). (Illus.). 48p. 7.95. Dargaud Pub.

--El Combate de los Jefes. (Asterix the Gaul Ser.). (Illus.). 48p. 7.95. Dargaud Pub.

--El Escudo Arverno. (Asterix the Gaul Ser.). (Illus.). 48p. 7.95 (ISBN 0-686-56220-8). Dargaud Pub.

--La Gran Traversia. (Asterix the Gaul Ser.). (Illus.). 48p. 7.95. Dargaud Pub.

--La Hoz de Oro. (Asterix the Gaul Ser.). (Illus.). 48p. 7.95. Dargaud Pub.

--Iter Gallicum. (Asterix the Gaul Ser.). (Illus.). 48p. 7.95. Dargaud Pub.

--Los Laureles del Cesar. (Asterix the Gaul Ser.). (Illus.). 48p. 7.95. Dargaud Pub.

--El Regalo del Cesar. (Asterix the Gaul Ser.). (Illus.). 48p. 7.95. Dargaud Pub.

--La Residencia de los Dioses. (Asterix the Gaul Ser.). (Illus.). 48p. 7.95. Dargaud Pub.

--La Vuelta a la Galia. (Asterix the Gaul Ser.). (Illus.). 48p. 7.95. Dargaud Pub.

Goscinny, Rene & Uderzo, M. The Golden Sickle. (Illus.). 7.95 (ISBN 0-686-56213-5). French & Eur.

Goscinny, Rene, et al. Falx Aurea. (Asterix the Gaul Ser.). (Illus.). 48p. (gr. 10up). 7.95. Dargaud Pub.

Goscinny, Rene de. Asterix alle Olimpiadi. (Italian.). 1976. 4.95x (ISBN 0-686-16878-X). Intl Learn Syst.

--Asterix bei den Olympischen Spielen. (German.). 1976. 7.95x (ISBN 0-686-16871-2). Intl Learn Syst.

--Asterix der Gallier. (German.). 1976. 5.95x (ISBN 0-686-16874-7). Intl Learn Syst.

--Asterix e gli Elvezi. (Italian.). 4.95x (ISBN 0-686-16877-1). Intl Learn Syst.

--Asterix e la Zizzania. (Italian.). 1976. 4.95x (ISBN 0-686-16876-3). Intl Learn Syst.

--Asterix Legionario. (Italian.). 1976. 5.95x (ISBN 0-686-16879-8). Intl Learn Syst.

--Canyon Apache. (Lucky Luke Series). (French.). 1976. 7.95x (ISBN 2-205-00517-0). Intl Learn Syst.

--Le Cavalier Blanc. (Lucky Luke Series). (French.). 1976. 7.95x (ISBN 2-205-00867-6). Intl Learn Syst.

--Le Chasseur De Primes. (Lucky Luke Series). (French.). 1976. 7.95x (ISBN 2-205-00604-5). Intl Learn Syst.

--Dalton City. (Lucky Luke Ser.). (French.). 1976. 7.95x (ISBN 2-205-00340-2). Intl Learn Syst.

--La Diligence. (Lucky Luke Series). (French.). 1976. 7.95x (ISBN 2-205-00304-6). Intl Learn Syst.

--Falx Aurea. (Asterix Series). (Latin.). 1976. 7.95x (ISBN 0-686-16872-0). Intl Learn Syst.

--Le Grand-Duc. (Lucky Luke Series). (French.). 1976. 5.95x (ISBN 2-205-00693-2). Intl Learn Syst.

--La Guerison Des Dalton. (Lucky Luke Series). (French.). 1976. 5.95x (ISBN 2-205-00920-6). Intl Learn Syst.

--L' Heritage De Ran-Tan-Plan. (Lucky Luke Series). (French.). 1976. 7.95x (ISBN 2-205-00747-5). Intl Learn Syst.

--Jesse James. (Lucky Luke Ser.). (French.). 1976. 7.95x (ISBN 2-205-00393-3). Intl Learn Syst.

--Ma Dalton. (Lucky Luke Ser.). (French.). 1976. 7.95x (ISBN 2-205-00585-5). Intl Learn Syst.

--Le Pied Tendre. (Lucky Luke Series). (French.). 1976. 7.95x (ISBN 2-205-00305-4). Intl Learn Syst.

--Sept Aventures Completes. (Lucky Luke Series). (French.). 1976. 5.95x (ISBN 0-686-16870-4). Intl Learn Syst.

--Western Circus. (Lucky Luke Series). (French.). 1976. 7.95x (ISBN 2-205-00425-5). Intl Learn Syst.

Goscinny, Rene De see De Goscinny, Rene.

Goscinny, Rene de see De Goscinny, Rene.

Gosden, R. C. Biology of Menopause: The Causes & Consequences of Ovarian Ageing. (Monographs). 1985. 37.50 (ISBN 0-12-291850-9). Acad Pr.

Gose, Charles J., Jr., ed. Corrugator Roll Wear Measurement. 1983. TAPPI members 20.07 (ISBN 0-89852-415-6); nonmembers 29.95. TAPPI.

Gose, Elliott B., Jr. Imagination Indulged: The Irrational in the Nineteenth-Century Novel. 184p. 1972. 17.50x (ISBN 0-7735-0085-5). McGill-Queen's U Pr.

--The Transformation Process in Joyce's Ulysses. 1980. 30.00x (ISBN 0-8020-5492-7). U of Toronto Pr.

--The World of the Irish Wonder Tale. 256p. 1985. 30.00 (ISBN 0-8020-5646-6); pap. 12.95 (ISBN 0-8020-6585-6). U of Toronto Pr.

Gosebrink, Jean E., ed. see Sweetland, James H.

Gosen, Patrica E. New York City Metropolitan Area Map Studies Program: Activity Manual. Irvin, J. L., ed. (Illus.). 76p. (gr. 4). 1981. Duplication Master 49.00 (ISBN 0-943068-12-6); Teacher's Guide 5.00 (ISBN 0-943068-11-8). Graphic Learning.

Gosen, Patricia E. & Irvin, J. L. New York City Metropolitan Area Studies Program. (Work-A-Text Ser.). (Illus.). 1981. of 105 435.00 set (ISBN 0-943068-95-9). Graphic Learning.

Gosh, Bijan, ed. Organization of Prokaryotic Cell Membranes, Vol. III. 288p. 1985. 87.00 (ISBN 0-8493-5659-8). CRC Pr.

Goshal, Sarat C., ed. & intro. by see Devendra Gani.

Goshay, Robert C. Corporate Self Insurance & Risk Retention Plans. 1964. 10.25x (ISBN 0-256-00646-6). Irwin.

--Statement of Financial Accounting Standards No. 5: Impact on Corporate Risk & Insurance Management. LC 78-65314. (The Financial Accounting Standards Board Research Report). (Illus.). 68p. (Orig.). 1978. pap. 2.50 (ISBN 0-910065-05-5). Finan Acct.

Goshen, Charles E. Documentary History of Psychiatry. 25.00 (ISBN 0-685-24842-9). Philos Lib.

--Drinks, Drugs, & Do-Gooders. LC 72-93309. (Illus.). 1973. 12.95 (ISBN 0-02-912620-7). Free Pr.

--Society & the Youthful Offender. (Illus.). 192p. 1974. 19.75x (ISBN 0-398-02934-2). C C Thomas.

Goshen, Robert P. Tuna Chopper. LC 80-50122. 14.95 (ISBN 0-9602964-0-9). Zoom.

Goshen-Gottstein, Moshe H. Syriac Manuscripts in the Harvard College Library: A Catalogue. LC 77-13132. (Harvard Semitic Studies: No. 23). 1979. 15.00 (ISBN 0-89130-189-5, 040423). Scholars Pr GA.

Goshgarian, Gary. Atlantis Fire. 1981. pap. 2.75 (ISBN 0-380-56093-3, 56093). Avon.

--The Contemporary Reader from Little, Brown. 1984. pap. text ed. 11.95 (ISBN 0-316-32152-4); tchr's. manual avail. (ISBN 0-316-32153-2). Little.

--Exploring Language. 3rd ed. 1983. pap. 11.95 (ISBN 0-316-32150-8); write for info tcher's manual (ISBN 0-316-32151-6). Little.

Gosink, Barbara B. & Squire, Lucy F. Diagnostic Radiology. 2nd ed. (Series of Exercises in Diagnostic Radiology: Vol. 8). (Illus.). 220p. 1981. text ed. 17.95 (ISBN 0-7216-4175-X). Saunders.

Goslee, Catherine L. Handling "Problem" Employees. Reilly, Harry A., ed. 76p. 1981. pap. 125.00 (ISBN 0-89290-142-X, SMP-214); pap. text ed. 45.00 participants manual (ISBN 0-89290-143-8). Soc for Visual.

Goslee, Catherine L., ed. see Yunker, Mary J.

Goslee, Catherine L., ed. see Yunker, Mary Jo.

Goslee, Nancy M. Uriel's Eye: Miltonic Stationing & Statuary in Blake, Keats, & Shelley. LC 84-8815. 312p. 1985. 32.50 (ISBN 0-8173-0243-3). U of Ala Pr.

Goslich, Siegfried. Beitrage Zur Geschicte der Deutschen Romantischen Oper Zwischen Spohrs "Faust" und Wagner's "Lohengrin". LC 80-2281. Repr. of 1937 ed. 31.50 (ISBN 0-404-18846-X). AMS Pr.

Goslin, David A. The Search for Ability: Standardized Testing in Social Perspective. LC 63-12591. 204p. 1963. 7.95x (ISBN 0-87154-357-5). Russell Sage.

--Teachers & Testing. LC 67-25912. 202p. 1967. 8.95x (ISBN 0-87154-358-3). Russell Sage.

Goslin, Lewis N. & Rethans, Arno J. Basic Systems for Decision Making. 2nd ed. 208p. 1980. pap. text ed. 10.95 (ISBN 0-8403-2191-0). Kendall-Hunt.

Goslin, Thomas S., II. The Church Without Walls. LC 84-63037. 104p. (Orig.). 1985. pap. 3.95 (ISBN 0-932727-00-X). Hope Pub Hse.

Gosline, William A. Functional Morphology & Classification of Teleostean Fishes. LC 77-151454. (Illus.). 216p. 1971. pap. text ed. 10.00x (ISBN 0-87022-300-3). UH Pr.

Gosling, C. T. Applied Air Conditioning & Refrigeration. 2nd ed. (Illus.). 410p. 1980. 44.50 (ISBN 0-85334-877-4, Pub. by Elsevier Applied Sci England). Elsevier.

Gosling, Craig, jt. auth. see Ritter, Merrill A.

Gosling, D. & Maitland, B. Design & Planning of Retail Systems. (Illus.). 208p. 1976. text ed. 103.95x (ISBN 0-85139-142-7, Pub. by Architectural Pr England). Humanities.

Gosling, E. M., jt. ed. see Wilkins, N. P.

Gosling, J. A. & Dixon, J. S. Functional Anatomy of the Urinary Tract: An Integrated Text & Color Atlas. (Illus.). 164p. 1982. text ed. 85.00 (ISBN 0-8391-1772-8, 19518). Univ Park.

Gosling, J. A., jt. ed. see O'Reilly, P. H.

Gosling, J. C. Plato: Arguments of the Philosophers. 319p. 1984. pap. 9.95 (ISBN 0-7102-0018-8). Routledge & Kegan.

Gosling, J. C. & Taylor, C. C. The Greeks on Pleasure. 1982. 37.50x (ISBN 0-19-824666-8); pap. 15.95x (ISBN 0-19-824775-3). Oxford U Pr.

Gosling, J. C., tr. & notes by see Plato.

Gosling, Nalda. Sucessful Herbal Remedies. (Nature's Way Ser.). 128p. (Orig.). 1985. pap. 4.95 (ISBN 0-7225-0941-3). Thorsons Pubs.

Gosling, Paula. Fair Game. 256p. 1985. pap. 2.95 (ISBN 0-445-20108-8, Popular Lib). Warner Bks.

--The Monkey Puzzle. LC 84-24689. (Crime Club Ser.). 312p. 1985. 12.95 (ISBN 0-385-19963-5). Doubleday.

--Solo Blues. 256p. 1983. pap. 2.50 (ISBN 0-345-30643-0). Ballantine.

--The Woman in Red. LC 83-11606. (Crime Club Ser.). 192p. 1984. 11.95 (ISBN 0-385-19105-7). Doubleday.

--The Woman in Red. 240p. 1985. pap. 2.95 (ISBN 0-445-20019-7, Pub. by Popular Lib). Warner Bks.

Gosling, R., et al. The Use of Small Groups in Training. 144p. 1968. pap. 24.50 (ISBN 0-8089-0630-5, 791685). Grune.

Gosling, William, jt. auth. see Dunkling, Leslie.

Gosling, William G. Life of Sir Humphrey Gilbert, England's First Empire Builder. LC 76-109737. Repr. of 1911 ed. lib. bdg. 17.00x (ISBN 0-8371-4227-X, GOHG). Greenwood.

Goslinga, C. The Dutch in the Caribbean & in the Guianas: 1680-1791. (Anjer-Publications Ser.: Vol. 18). 720p. 1984. text ed. 38.50x (ISBN 90-232-2060-9, Pub. by Van Gorcum Holland). Humanities.

Goslinga, Cornelis C. Dutch in the Caribbean & on the Wild Coast, 1580-1680. LC 72-93193. (Illus.). 1971. 20.00. U Presses Fla.

--A Short History of the Netherlands Antilles & Surinam. 1978. pap. 20.00 (ISBN 90-247-2118-0, Pub. by Martinus Nijhoff Netherlands). Kluwer Academic.

Goslinga, H. Blood Viscosity & Shock: The Role of Hemodilution, Hemoconcentration & Defibrination. (Anaesthesiology & Intensive Care Medicine Ser.: Vol. 160). (Illus.). 215p. 1984. pap. 30.60 (ISBN 0-387-12620-1). Springer-Verlag.

Goslng, John A., et al. Atlas of Human Anatomy: With Intetgrated Text. (Illus.). 300p. 1985. text ed. 29.75 (ISBN 0-397-58284-6, Lippincott Medical). Lippincott.

Gosman, Martin, ed. La Lettre du Pretre Jean: Edition des Versions en Ancien Francais et en Ancien Occitan Textes et Commentaires. (Mediaevalia Groningana). xi, 637p. (Fr.). 1982. 38.00x (ISBN 90-6088-080-3, Pub. by Boumas Boekhuis Netherlands). Benjamins North AM.

Gosman, Martin L. Accounting Graffiti. LC 75-4144. (Illus.). 152p. 1975. pap. text ed. 10.95 (ISBN 0-8299-0058-6). West Pub.

Gosman, Martin L., jt. auth. see Backer, Morton.

Gosnell, Cullen B. Fundamentals of American Government: National, State & Local. LC 75-100160. (Illus.). 1971. Repr. of 1957 ed. lib. bdg. 23.75x (ISBN 0-8371-3932-5, GOAG). Greenwood.

Gosnell, Davina J. Help with the Nursing Process. 2nd ed. LC 80-66120. (Help Series of Management Guides). 1986. pap. 13.75 (ISBN 0-933036-27-2). Ganong W L Co.

Gosnell, Harold F. Boss Platt & His New York Machine - A Study of the Political Leadership of Thomas C. Platt, Theodore Roosevelt, & Others. LC 70-145047. (Illus.). 1971. Repr. of 1924 ed. 49.00 (ISBN 0-403-00991-X). Scholarly.

--Boss Platt & His New York Machine: A Study of the Political Leadership of Thomas C. Platt, Theodore Roosevelt, & Others. LC 75-95153. Repr. of 1924 ed. 27.00 (ISBN 0-404-02884-5). AMS Pr.

--Democracy, the Threshold of Freedom. LC 77-1256. 1977. Repr. of 1948 ed. lib. bdg. 22.50x (ISBN 0-8371-9509-8, GODE). Greenwood.

--Getting Out the Vote: An Experiment in the Stimulation of Voting. LC 75-41117. Repr. of 1927 ed. 12.50 (ISBN 0-404-14547-7). AMS Pr.

--Getting Out the Vote: An Experiment in the Stimulation of Voting. LC 77-734. 1977. Repr. of 1927 ed. lib. bdg. 15.00x (ISBN 0-8371-9496-2, GOGV). Greenwood.

--Machine Politics: Chicago Model. LC 70-100507. Repr. of 1937 ed. 11.50 (ISBN 0-404-00591-8). AMS Pr.

--Machine Politics: Chicago Model. LC 37-20974. (Illus.). 1969. Repr. of 1937 ed. lib. bdg. 15.50x (ISBN 0-8371-0451-3, GOMP). Greenwood.

--Machine Politics: Chicago Politics. 2nd ed. LC 68-16692. (Midway Reprint Ser.). (Illus.). 1977. pap. text ed. 10.00x (ISBN 0-226-30495-7). U of Chicago Pr.

--Negro Politicians: The Rise of Negro Politics in Chicago. LC 66-30216. pap. 104.00 (ISBN 0-317-09963-9, 2020067). Bks Demand UMI.

--Truman's Crises: A Political Biography of Harry S. Truman. LC 79-7360. (Contributions in Political Science: No. 33). 1980. lib. bdg. 35.00 (ISBN 0-313-21273-2, GTC/). Greenwood.

Gosnell, Harold F., jt. auth. see Merriam, Charles E.

Gosnell, Stephen. Modern Interiors: Lithographs & Confessions. LC 84-73436. 1985. pap. 12.95 (ISBN 0-933532-46-6). BkMk.

Gosner, K. L. Guide to Identification of Marine & Estuarine Invertebrates: Cape Hatteras to the Bay of Fundy. 693p. 1974. pap. 35.50x (ISBN 0-471-31901-5). Wiley.

Gosner, Kenneth. A Field Guide to the Atlantic Seashore. (Peterson Field Guide Ser.). (Illus.). 416p. 1982. 16.95 (ISBN 0-395-24379-3); pap. 11.95 (ISBN 0-395-31828-9). HM.

Gosner, Kenneth L. Working Decoys of the Jersey Coast & Delaware River Valley. LC 82-70005. (Illus.). 256p. 1982. 50.00 (ISBN 0-87982-500-6). Art Alliance.

--Working Decoys of the Jersey Coast & Delaware Valley. LC 83-14312. (Illus.). 184p. 1985. 45.00 (ISBN 0-8453-4711-X). Cornwall Bks.

--Working Decoys of the Jersey Coast & Delaware Valley. LC 83-14312. (Illus.). 184p. 1985. 45.00 (ISBN 0-317-19123-3). Art Alliance.

Gosner, Pamela. Caribbean Georgian: The Great Houses & Small of the West Indies. LC 78-72966. (Illus.). 324p. (Orig.). 1982. 40.00x (ISBN 0-89410-011-4); pap. 22.00x (ISBN 0-89410-012-2). Three Continents.

Gosney, E. S. & Popenoe, Paul. Sterilization for Human Betterment. Grob, Gerald N., ed. LC 78-22561. (Historical Issues in Mental Health Ser.). 1979. Repr. of 1929 ed. lib. bdg. 16.00x (ISBN 0-405-11915-1). Ayer Co Pubs.

Gosney, Michael. Excerpts from L-Seven: A New World Mythos. new ed. (Illus., Orig.). 1979. pap. 8.00 cancelled (ISBN 0-932238-02-5, Pub. by Avant Bks). Slawson Comm.

--We Are It. LC 82-71920. (Illus., Orig.). 1984. pap. 8.95 (ISBN 0-932238-19-X, Pub. by Avant Bks). Slawson Comm.

Gosney, W. B. Principles of Refrigeration. LC 80-42210. (Illus.). 700p. 1982. 105.00 (ISBN 0-521-23671-1). Cambridge U Pr.

Gospel Advocate. Commentaries on the New Testament. Incl. Matthew. Boles, H. Leo (ISBN 0-89225-001-1); Mark. Dorris, C. E (ISBN 0-89225-002-X); Luke. Boles, H. Leo (ISBN 0-89225-003-8); John. Dorris, C. E (ISBN 0-89225-004-6); Acts. Boles, H. Leo (ISBN 0-89225-005-4); Romans. Lipscomb, David & Shepherd, J. W. (ISBN 0-89225-006-2); Corinthians I. Lipscomb, David & Shepard, J. W. (ISBN 0-89225-007-0); Corinthians II - Galatians. Lipscomb, David & Shepherd, J. W. (ISBN 0-89225-008-9); Ephesians - Colossians. Shepherd, J. W (ISBN 0-89225-009-7); Thess. I, II; Tim. I, II; Titus; Philomen. Shepherd, J. W (ISBN 0-89225-010-0); Hebrews. Milligan, Robert (ISBN 0-89225-011-9); James. Woods, Guy N (ISBN 0-89225-012-7); Peter I, II; John I, II, III; Jude. Woods, Guy N (ISBN 0-89225-013-5); Revelation. Hinds, John T (ISBN 0-89225-014-3). Set. 135.00 (ISBN 0-89225-000-3); 10.95 ea. Gospel Advocate.

Goss, Agnes G., jt. auth. see Grenell, Zelotes.

Goss, Albert E. & Nodine, Calvin F. Paired-Associates Learning: The Role of Meaningfulness, Similarity & Familiarization. 1965. 61.50 (ISBN 0-12-292350-2). Acad Pr.

Goss, Ann, ed. Harris Illinois Industrial Directory Annual. 1106p. 1985. 93.00 (ISBN 0-916512-42-8). Harris Pub.

--Illinois Buyers Industrial Directory. 720p. 25.00 (ISBN 0-916512-40-1). Harris Pub.

Goss, B. & Yamey, B. S. Economics of Future Trading. LC 75-6266. 236p. 1976. 37.95x (ISBN 0-470-97115-0). Halsted Pr.

Goss, Blaine. Communication in Everyday Life. 320p. 1982. pap. text ed. write for info (ISBN 0-534-01215-9). Wadsworth Pub.

--Processing Communications: Information Processing in Intrapersonal Communication. 144p. 1981. pap. text ed. write for info. (ISBN 0-534-01010-5). Wadsworth Pub.

Goss, Clav see Harrison, Paul C.

Goss, Clay. Homecookin' Five Plays. LC 74-5367. 101p. 1974. 8.95 (ISBN 0-88258-021-3). Howard U Pr.

Goss, Clay see Harrison, Paul C.

Goss, Dinah, et al. L. A. Bride Guide, the Orange County Bride Guide, the San Diego Bride Guide. 2nd ed. (Illus.). 250p. (Orig.). 1981. Repr. 10.95 (ISBN 0-939884-00-3). Bride Guide.

Goss, Dinah B. & Schram, Marla S. The Bride Guide: The Perfect Wedding Planner. LC 82-19777. (Illus.). 192p. (Orig.). 1983. comb bdg. 13.95 (ISBN 0-934878-22-6). Dembner Bks.

Goss, Elbridge H. The Life of Colonel Paul Revere, 2 vols. facsimile ed. LC 78-157339. (Select Bibliographies Reprint Ser). Repr. of 1891 ed. Set. 49.50 (ISBN 0-8369-5799-7). Ayer Co Pubs.

--The Life of Colonel Paul Revere, 2 vols. LC 72-8757. (American Revolutionary Ser.). (Illus.). 768p. Repr. of 1891 ed. Set. lib. bdg. 45.50x (ISBN 0-8398-0670-1). Irvington.

Goss, Ethel E. The Winds of God. 2nd ed. (Illus.). 288p. 1958. pap. 4.95 (ISBN 0-912315-26-1). Word Aflame.

Goss, Fred, jt. ed. see Bogan, James.

Goss, Gordon J. National Square Dance Directory. rev. ed. 168p. 1981. pap. 8.50 (ISBN 0-9605494-2-0). Natl Sq Dance.

Goss, Gordon J., ed. National Square Dance Directory. 1984 ed. 304p. 1984. pap. 10.00 (ISBN 0-9605494-4-7). Natl Sq Dance.

--National Square Dance Directory: 1983 Edition. 4th ed. 256p. 1983. pap. 9.50 (ISBN 0-9605494-3-9). Natl Sq Dance.

--National Square Dance Directory, 1985. 6th ed. 288p. 1985. pap. 10.00 (ISBN 0-9605494-5-5). Natl Sq Dance.

Goss, Gordon J. & McCoard, Winston, eds. Mississippi Construction Directory. 1984-85 ed. 248p. 1984. 14.95 (ISBN 0-9605494-9-8). Natl Sq Dance.

Goss, J. R., jt. auth. see Kaupp, A.

Goss, Janet L. & Harste, Jerome C. It Didn't Frighten Me. Holland, Margaret, ed. LC 84-52558. (The Predictable Reading Bks.). (Illus.). 24p. (gr. k-3). 1985. 7.95 (ISBN 0-87406-001-X, Dist. by Sterling). Willowisp Pr.

Goss, Jim. Tall Tales of the Outdoors. 1981. 4.95 (ISBN 0-8062-1739-1). Carlton.

Goss, Jocelyn, et al. Rhetoric & Readings for Writing. 4th ed. 1979. pap. text ed. 12.95 (ISBN 0-8403-2490-1). Kendall-Hunt.

Goss, John D. History of Tariff Administration in the United States from Colonial Times to the McKinley Administrative Bill. 2nd ed. LC 68-56658. (Columbia University, Studies in the Social Sciences Ser.: No. 2). Repr. of 1897 ed. 12.50 (ISBN 0-404-51002-7). AMS Pr.

Goss, K. David & Zarowin, David, eds. Massachusetts Officers & Soldiers in the French & Indian Wars, 1755-1756. LC 84-27224. 376p. 1985. pap. 14.95 (ISBN 0-88082-010-1). New Eng Hist.

Goss, L. Barry, ed. Factors Affecting Power Plant Waste Heat Utilization: Proceedings of a Workshop Held in Atlanta, Georgia, 28 Nov. - 1 Dec., 1978. LC 79-29656. (Illus.). 230p. 1980. 24.00 (ISBN 0-08-025548-5). Pergamon.

Goss, Laurence R., et al. Orange County Bride Guide. abridg. ed. Hess, Loretta, ed. Hess, Loretta, ed. (Buying Guide Ser.). 250p. 1981. 12.95 (ISBN 0-939884-02-X). Bride Guide.

--L. A. Bride Guide. 2nd rev. ed. (Buying Guide Ser.). 250p. 1981. 12.95 (ISBN 0-939884-01-1). Bride Guide.

--San Diego Bride Guide. abridg. ed. Hess, Loretta, ed. (Buying Guide Ser.). 250p. 1981. 12.95 (ISBN 0-939884-03-8). Bride Guide.

Goss, Leonard G., ed. see Besson, Clyde C.

Goss, Leonard G., ed. see Payne, Franklyn E., Jr.

Goss, Leonard G., ed. see Redmond, Howard.

Goss, Leonard G., ed. see Stobbe, Les.

Goss, Louise & McArtot, Marion. Technic Time, Pt. A. (Frances Clark Library for Piano Students). 48p. (Orig.). (gr. k-6). 1955. pap. text ed. 7.95 (ISBN 0-87487-189-1). Birch Tree Gr.

Goss, Louise, jt. auth. see Clark, Frances.

Goss, Louise, ed. Themes from Masterworks, 3 bks. (Frances Clark Library for Piano Students). 16p. (Orig.). (gr. k-12). 1970. pap. text ed. 5.95 Bk. 1 (ISBN 0-87487-191-3); pap. text ed. 5.95 Bk. 2 (ISBN 0-87487-192-1); pap. text ed. 5.95 Bk. 3 (ISBN 0-87487-193-X). Birch Tree Gr.

Goss, Louise, jt. ed. see Clark, Frances.

Goss, Louise, ed. see Dittenhaver, Sarah L., et al.

Goss, Louise, ed. see George, Jon.

Goss, Louise, ed. see George, Jon & Kraehenbuehl, David.

Goss, Louise, ed. see Kraehenbuehl, David.

Goss, Louise, ed. see Kraehenbuehl, David, et al.

Goss, Luoise, jt. auth. see Clark, Frances.

Goss, Madeleine. Modern Music-Makers: Contemporary American Composers. LC 73-97345. Repr. of 1952 ed. lib. bdg. 22.50x (ISBN 0-8371-2957-5, GOMM). Greenwood.

Goss, Mary E. Physicians in Bureaucracy: A Case Study of Professional Pressures on Organizational Roles. Zuckerman, Harriet & Merton, Robert K., eds. LC 79-9002. (Dissertations on Sociology Ser.). 1980. lib. bdg. 17.00x (ISBN 0-405-12971-8). Ayer Co Pubs.

Goss, Michael. The Evidence of Phantom Hitch-Hikers. (Illus.). 160p. (Orig.). 1985. pap. 5.95 (ISBN 0-85030-376-1, Pub. by Aquarian Pr England). Sterling.

Goss, Michael, compiled by. Poltergeists: An Annotated Bibliography of Works in English, Circa 1880-1975. LC 78-11492. 389p. 1979. 20.00 (ISBN 0-8108-1181-2). Scarecrow.

Goss, R. J., jt. ed. see Nowinski, W. W.

Goss, R. O. Studies in Maritime Economics. LC 68-29328. (Illus.). 1968. 42.50 (ISBN 0-521-07329-4). Cambridge U Pr.

Goss, R. O., ed. Advances in Maritime Economics. LC 76-1135. pap. 75.50 (ISBN 0-317-26400-1, 2024457). Bks Demand UMI.

Goss, Ralph. Roofing Ready Reckoner. 160p. 1969. 8.00x (ISBN 0-246-11430-4, Pub. by Granada England). Sheridan.

--Roofing Ready Reckoner for Timber Roofs of Any Span or Pitch. 2nd ed. 75p. 1979. pap. text ed. 11.25x (ISBN 0-258-96690-4, Pub. by Granada England). Brookfield Pub Co.

Goss, Richard J. Adaptive Growth. 1965. 61.50 (ISBN 0-12-292750-8). Acad Pr.

--The Physiology of Growth. 1978. 55.00 (ISBN 0-12-293055-X). Acad Pr.

--Principles of Regeneration. 1969. 51.00 (ISBN 0-12-293050-9). Acad Pr.

Goss, Richard J., ed. Deer Antlers: Regeneration, Function, & Evolution. LC 82-22795. (Monograph). 1983. 45.00 (ISBN 0-12-293080-0). Acad Pr.

Goss, Robert C. The San Xavier Altarpiece. LC 73-87715. (Illus.). 94p. 1974. pap. 4.95 (ISBN 0-8165-0323-0). U. of Ariz Pr.

Goss, Warren L. Recollections of a Private. LC 84-2679. (Collector's Library of the Civil War Ser.). 1984. Kivar binding 26.60 (ISBN 0-8094-4466-6, Pub. by Time-Life). Silver.

Gossage. Self-Paced Business Mathematics. 1986. pap. text ed. price not set (ISBN 0-538-13010-5, M01). SW Pub.

Gossage, Howard, et al. The Great International Paper Airplane Book. 1967. pap. 8.95 (ISBN 0-671-21129-3, Fireside). S&S.

Gossage, John & Sines, Denise. The Pond. Date not set. price not set. Aperture.

Gossage, Loyce C. Basic Mathematical Skills: A Text Workbook. 2nd ed. (Illus.). 320p. 1975. pap. text ed. 25.95 wkbk (ISBN 0-07-023852-9). McGraw.

--Basic Mathematics Review. 1985. text ed. 4.90 (ISBN 0-538-14220-0, N22). SW Pub.

--Business Mathematics: A College Course. 1984. text ed. 15.95 (ISBN 0-538-13090-3, M09). SW Pub.

--Mathematics Skill Builder. 5th ed. (gr. 9-12). 1985. pap. text ed. 5.10 (ISBN 0-538-13940-4, M95). SW Pub.

Gossage, Loyce C., jt. auth. see Rodriguez, Cristina.

Gossard, E. E. Waves in the Atmosphere. LC 73-89155. (Developments in Atmospheric Science Ser.: Vol. 2). 456p. 1975. 121.50 (ISBN 0-444-41196-8). Elsevier.

Goss-Custard, J. D., jt. ed. see Evans, P. R.

Gosse, Carol A., jt. auth. see Rother, Kathleen.

Gosse, E. Aspects & Impressions. 1973. Repr. of 1922 ed. 9.50 (ISBN 0-8274-0383-6). R West.

--From Shakespeare to Pope. 59.95 (ISBN 0-8490-0205-2). Gordon Pr.

--Robert Browning Personalia. LC 73-17095. (Studies in Browning, No. 4). 1974. lib. bdg. 46.95x (ISBN 0-8383-1728-6). Haskell.

Gosse, Edmund. Aspects & Impressions. 1979. Repr. of 1928 ed. lib. bdg. 20.00 (ISBN 0-8495-2027-4). Arden Lib.

--Books on the Table. 1921. Repr. 19.50 (ISBN 0-8274-1965-1). R West.

--Books on the Table: Disraeli, Chekhon, Tolstoi, Poe, Thackeray, Carlyle, Goethe. 347p. 1984. Repr. of 1921 ed. lib. bdg. 40.00 (ISBN 0-89760-449-0). Telegraph Bks.

--Continuity of Literature. LC 76-28547. lib. bdg. 8.50 (ISBN 0-8414-4516-8). Folcroft.

--Critical Kit-Kats. 1977. Repr. of 1896 ed. lib. bdg. 20.00 (ISBN 0-8495-1908-X). Arden Lib.

--Critical Kit Kats. 1913. Repr. 20.00 (ISBN 0-8274-3841-9). R West.

--English Literature: An Illustrated Record from the Age of Johnson to the Age of Tennyson, 4 vols. 1904. Repr. Set. 100.00 (ISBN 0-8274-2260-1). R West.

--English Men of Letters: Jeremy Taylor. 234p. 1980. Repr. of 1903 ed. lib. bdg. 25.00 (ISBN 0-89984-228-3). Century Bookbindery.

--Father & Son. 1963. pap. 6.95 (ISBN 0-393-00195-4, Norton Lib). Norton.

--Father & Son. 1916. Repr. 25.00 (ISBN 0-8274-2340-3). R West.

--Father & Son. 1983. pap. 3.95 (ISBN 0-14-000700-8). Penguin.

--From Shakespeare to Pope: An Inquiry into the Causes & Phenomena of the Rise of Classical Poetry in England. 1885. Repr. 13.50 (ISBN 0-8274-3820-6). R West.

--Gossip in a Library. 1913. Repr. 17.50 (ISBN 0-8274-2433-7). R West.

--Gray. 1902. Repr. 12.00 (ISBN 0-8274-2436-1). R West.

--History of Eighteenth Century Literature. LC 74-39396. (Select Bibliographies Reprint Ser.). 1972. Repr. of 1889 ed. 18.50 (ISBN 0-8369-9909-6). Ayer Co Pubs.

--A History of Eighteenth Century Literature. 1891. lib. bdg. 30.00 (ISBN 0-8414-4663-6). Folcroft.

--A History of Eighteenth Century Literature (1660-1780) 415p. Repr. of 1889 ed. lib. bdg. 50.00 (ISBN 0-89984-215-1). Century Bookbindery.

--Jeremy Taylor. 1904. Repr. 9.50 (ISBN 0-8274-2609-7). R West.

--Life of William Congreve. LC 73-270. 1973. lib. bdg. 20.00 (ISBN 0-8414-1428-9). Folcroft.

--Malherbe & the Classical Reaction in the Seventeenth Century. LC 73-503. 1973. lib. bdg. 8.50 (ISBN 0-8414-1543-9). Folcroft.
--Malherbe & the Classical Rendition in the Seventeenth Century. 1978. Repr. of 1920 ed. lib. bdg. 6.50 (ISBN 0-8495-1923-3). Arden Lib.
--Modern English Literature. 408p. 1980. Repr. lib. bdg. 35.00 (ISBN 0-89987-300-6). Darby Bks.
--Modern English Literature. 1897. Repr. 35.00 (ISBN 0-8274-2750-6). R West.
--More Books on the Table. 1914. Repr. 21.50 (ISBN 0-8274-2763-8). R West.
--Northern Studies. LC 75-103225. 1970. Repr. of 1890 ed. 23.00x (ISBN 0-8046-0862-8, Pub. by Kennikat). Assoc Faculty Pr.
--Northern Studies. 1973. Repr. of 1890 ed. 11.50 (ISBN 0-8274-0384-4). R West.
--Portraits & Sketches. Repr. of 1912 ed. lib. bdg. 25.00 (ISBN 0-8482-4165-7). Norwood Edns.
--Questions at Issue. LC 72-3465. (Essay Index Reprint Ser.). Repr. of 1893 ed. 18.00 (ISBN 0-8369-2902-0). Ayer Co Pubs.
--Questions at Issue. 1973. lib. bdg. 20.00 (ISBN 0-8414-4664-4). Folcroft.
--Robert Browning, Personalia. LC 72-5358. 1973. lib. bdg. 12.50 (ISBN 0-8414-0050-4). Folcroft.
--Seventeenth Century Studies. 1897. Repr. 10.95 (ISBN 0-8274-3366-2). R West.
--A Short History of Modern English Literature. 1900. 35.00 (ISBN 0-8274-3401-4). R West.
--Silhouettes. 1973. Repr. of 1925 ed. 25.00 (ISBN 0-8274-0382-8). R West.
--Swinburne: An Essay Written in 1875 & Now First Printed. LC 73-7959. 1925. lib. bdg. 10.00 (ISBN 0-8414-2036-X). Folcroft.
Gosse, Edmund, jt. auth. see Gide, Andre.
Gosse, Edmund, ed. The Poetical Works of Thomas Lovell Beddoes, 2 vols. (Illus.). Date not set. Repr. of 1890 ed. Set. lib. bdg. 150.00 (ISBN 0-89760-259-5). Vol.1: 254p. Vol. 2: 284p. Telegraph Bks.
--Restoration Plays. 1974. 11.95x (ISBN 0-460-00604-5, Evman); pap. 6.95x (ISBN 0-460-01604-0, Evman). Biblio Dist.
Gosse, Edmund & Wise, Thomas J., eds. Selections from A. C. Swinburne. 1979. Repr. of 1919 ed. lib. bdg. 20.00 (ISBN 0-8495-2011-8). Arden Lib.
Gosse, Edmund, ed. see Beddoes, Thomas L.
Gosse, Edmund, ed. see Gray, Thomas.
Gosse, Edmund, ed. see Swinburne, Algernon C.
Gosse, Edmund, tr. see La Motte-Foque, Friedrich H.
Gosse, Edmund, et al, trs. see Ibsen, Henrik, et al.
Gosse, Edmund W. Aspects & Impressions. LC 77-105016. (Essay Index Reprint Ser). 1922. 17.00 (ISBN 0-8369-1469-4). Ayer Co Pubs.
--Aspects & Impressions. (English Literary Reference Ser). Repr. of 1922 ed. 17.00 (ISBN 0-384-19320-X). Johnson Repr.
--Aspects & Impressions. LC 73-145048. 1971. Repr. of 1922 ed. 15.00x (ISBN 0-403-00992-8). Scholarly.
--Books on the Table. facsimile ed. LC 74-156653. (Essay Index Reprint Ser). Repr. of 1921 ed. 22.00 (ISBN 0-8369-2365-0). Ayer Co Pubs.
--Coventry Patmore. LC 71-131720. 1971. 10.00 (ISBN 0-403-00607-4). Scholarly.
--Critical Kit-Kats. 1971. Repr. of 1914 ed. 19.00x (ISBN 0-403-00993-6). Scholarly.
--English Odes. 259p. 1980. Repr. of 1881 ed. lib. bdg. 25.00 (ISBN 0-8414-4625-3). Folcroft.
--French Profiles. LC 70-108638. (Essay Index Reprint Ser.). 1913. 21.50 (ISBN 0-8369-1574-7). Ayer Co Pubs.
--French Profiles. 1973. Repr. of 1913 ed. 19.00 (ISBN 0-8274-1379-3). R West.
--From Shakespeare to Pope: An Inquiry into the Causes & the Phenomena of the Rise of Classic Poetry. LC 68-57907. (Research & Source Works Ser: No. 292). 1969. Repr. of 1885 ed. 17.00 (ISBN 0-8337-1395-7). B Franklin.
--From Shakespeare to Pope: An Inquiry into the Causes & Phenomena of the Rise of Classical Poetry in England. LC 11-21320. 1968. Repr. of 1885 ed. 17.00 (ISBN 0-527-34750-7). Kraus Repr.
--Gossip in a Library. 29.00x (ISBN 0-403-00773-9). Scholarly.
--Gray. Morley, John, ed. LC 68-58380. (English Men of Letters). Repr. of 1889 ed. 12.50 (ISBN 0-404-51712-9). AMS Pr.
--Henrik Ibsen. LC 77-51434. 1977. Repr. of 1907 ed. lib. bdg. 25.00 (ISBN 0-8414-4417-X). Folcroft.
--Inter Arma: Being Essays Written in Time of War. facs. ed. LC 68-29209. (Essay Index Reprint Ser). 1968. Repr. of 1916 ed. 17.00 (ISBN 0-8369-0486-9). Ayer Co Pubs.
--Jacobean Poets. LC 75-131721. 1970. Repr. of 1894 ed. 13.00x (ISBN 0-403-00608-2). Scholarly.
--Jeremy Taylor. LC 4-1683. 1969. Repr. of 1904 ed. 11.00x (ISBN 0-403-00088-2). Scholarly.
--Leaves & Fruit. LC 70-105017. (Essay Index Reprint Ser.). 1927. 21.50 (ISBN 0-8369-1505-4). Ayer Co Pubs.
--More Books on the Table. LC 71-93340. (Essay Index Reprint Ser.). 1923. 24.50 (ISBN 0-8369-1410-4). Ayer Co Pubs.
--Portraits & Sketches. LC 70-99699. (Essay Index Reprint Ser.). 1912. 21.50 (ISBN 0-8369-1411-2). Ayer Co Pubs.
--Portraits & Sketches. 1971. Repr. of 1914 ed. 19.00x (ISBN 0-403-00994-4). Scholarly.
--Raleigh. LC 74-14939. 1974. Repr. of 1888 ed. lib. bdg. 17.50 (ISBN 0-8414-4532-X). Folcroft.
--Selected Essays. 1973. Repr. of 1928 ed. 14.50 (ISBN 0-8274-0619-3). R West.
--Selected Essays, First Series. facs. ed. LC 68-29210. (Essay Index Reprint Ser). 1928. 17.00 (ISBN 0-8369-0487-7). Ayer Co Pubs.
--Selected Essays, First Series. 1973. Repr. of 1928 ed. 14.50 (ISBN 0-8274-0618-5). R West.
--Selected Essays, 2nd Series. facs. ed. LC 68-8464. (Essay Index Reprint Ser). 1928. 17.00 (ISBN 0-8369-0488-5). Ayer Co Pubs.
--Seventeenth Century Studies. LC 70-136381. Repr. of 1914 ed. 18.50 (ISBN 0-404-02885-3). AMS Pr.
--Seventeenth Century Studies. 1971. Repr. of 1913 ed. 16.00x (ISBN 0-403-00995-2). Scholarly.
--Silhouettes. facsimile ed. LC 78-156654. (Essay Index Reprint Ser). Repr. of 1925 ed. 24.50 (ISBN 0-8369-2399-5). Ayer Co Pubs.
--Sir Thomas Browne. LC 75-98837. Repr. of 1905 ed. lib. bdg. 18.75x (ISBN 0-8371-2952-4, GOTB). Greenwood.
--Some Diversions of a Man of Letters. facsimile ed. LC 70-157964. (Essay Index Reprint Ser). Repr. of 1919 ed. 20.00 (ISBN 0-8369-2225-5). Ayer Co Pubs.
--Some Diversions of a Man of Letters. 1973. Repr. of 1919 ed. 17.50 (ISBN 0-8274-0620-7). R West.
--Three French Moralists & the Gallantry of France. facs. ed. LC 67-23223. (Essay Index Reprint Ser). 1918. 15.00 (ISBN 0-8369-0489-3). Ayer Co Pubs.
--The Unequal Yoke. LC 75-31652. 52p. 1975. lib. bdg. 30.00x (ISBN 0-8201-1163-5). Schol Facsimiles.
Gosse, Edmund W., jt. auth. see Garnett, Richard.
Gosse, Fayette. William Gosse Hay. pap. 5.00x (ISBN 0-392-09463-0, ABC). Sportshelf.
Gosse, J. P. Freshwater Aquarium Fish: A Color Guide. (Illus.). 184p. 1983. 12.95 (ISBN 0-88254-759-3). Hippocrene Bks.
Gosse, Philip. Bibliography of the Works of Captain Charles Johnson. LC 72-127189. 1970. Repr. of 1927 ed. lib. bdg. 18.50 (ISBN 0-8337-1391-4). B Franklin.
--History of Piracy. (Illus.). 1969. Repr. of 1932 ed. 23.50 (ISBN 0-8337-1392-2). B Franklin.
--The History of Piracy. LC 75-16396. (Illus.). xvi, 349p. 1976. Repr. of 1934 ed. 40.00x (ISBN 0-8103-4156-5). Gale.
--My Pirate Library. LC 73-143670. (Research & Source Works Ser.: No. 619). (Illus.). 1971. Repr. of 1926 ed. lib. bdg. 22.75 (ISBN 0-8337-1393-0). B Franklin.
--Pirates Who's Who. LC 68-56594. (Bibliography & Reference Ser.: No. 119). (Illus.). 1968. Repr. of 1924 ed. 26.50 (ISBN 0-8337-1394-9). B Franklin.
--The Pirates' Who's Who. 1977. lib. bdg. 59.95 (ISBN 0-8490-2446-3). Gordon Pr.
--Traveller's Rest. facs. ed. LC 70-84308. (Essay Index Reprint Ser.). 1937. 17.50 (ISBN 0-8369-1132-6). Ayer Co Pubs.
Gosse, Philip H. Letters from Alabama (U. S.) Chiefly Relating to Natural History. annotated facsimile ed. LC 82-61822. (Illus.). 324p. 1983. pap. 12.95 (ISBN 0-910773-00-9). Overbrook Hse.
Gosse, Richard. How to Sell to Vertical Markets. 224p. 1985. wkbk. 49.95 (ISBN 0-934377-00-6). Marin Pubns.
--Looking for Love in All the Right Places. LC 84-60394. 230p. (Orig.). 1985. pap. 9.95 (ISBN 0-88247-735-8). R & E Pubs.
Gossec, Francois-Joseph. Eight Symphonic Works. Brook, Barry S., ed. (The Symphony Ser.). 424p. 1983. lib. bdg. 90.00 (ISBN 0-8240-3839-8). Garland Pub.
Gossel, Thomas A. & Bricker, J. Douglas. Principles of Clinical Toxicology. (Illus.). 368p. 1984. text ed. 39.50 (ISBN 0-89004-951-3). Raven.
Gosselin, C. C., jt. auth. see Briston, J. H.
Gosselin, Edward A. Listing of the Printed Editions of Nicolaus of Lyra. 1970. pap. 4.00x (ISBN 0-8232-0040-X). Fordham.
--A Listing of the Printed Editions of Nicolaus of Lyra. 28p. 1970. pap. 4.00 (ISBN 0-8232-0040-X). Fordham.
Gosselin, Edward A. & Lerner, Lawrence S., eds. Giordano Bruno: The Ash Wednesday Supper (la Cena De le Ceneri) (Illus.). 238p. 1977. 25.00 (ISBN 0-208-01610-4, Archon). Shoe String.
Gosselin, Louis L. Flight of Marie Antoinette. LC 73-168160. (Illus.). Repr. of 1906 ed. 27.50 (ISBN 0-404-07128-7). AMS Pr.
Gosselin, Robert E. Clinical Toxicology of Commercial Products: Acute Poisoning. 5th ed. 2012p. 1984. 95.00 (ISBN 0-683-03632-7). Williams & Wilkins.
Gossen, Gary. Chamulas in the World of the Sun: Time & Space in a Maya Oral Tradition. (Illus.). 382p. 1984. pap. text ed. 10.95x (ISBN 0-88133-091-4). Waveland Pr.
Gossen, Hermann H. The Laws of Human Relations & the Rules of Human Actions Derived Therefrom. Blitz, Rudolph C., tr. from German. (Illus.). 336p. 1983. text ed. 47.50x (ISBN 0-262-07090-1). MIT Pr.
Gosset, ed. see Donizetti.
Gosset, Adelaide L. Shepherds of Britain: Scenes from Shepherd Life Past & Present. LC 78-174415. (Illus.). Repr. of 1911 ed. 24.50 (ISBN 0-405-08565-6, Pub. by Blom). Ayer Co Pubs.
Gosset, Melinda Lu. Doggerelimericks I. (Limericklets Ser.: No. 12). (Illus.). 16p. 1982. pap. 1.00 (ISBN 0-938338-23-4). Winds World Pr.
--Doggerelimericks II. (Limericklets Ser.: No. 13). (Illus.). 16p. 1982. pap. 1.00 (ISBN 0-938338-24-2). Winds World Pr.
--Doggerelimericks III. (Limericklets Ser.: No. 14). (Illus.). pap. 1.00cancelled (ISBN 0-938338-25-0). Winds World Pr.
Gosset, Philip & Rosen, Charles, eds. La Favorite. (Early Romantic Opera Ser.). 198.00 (ISBN 0-8240-2927-5). Garland Pub.
Gosset, Philip, ed. see Bellini, Vincenzo.
Gosset, Philip, ed. see Fioravanti, Vincenzo.
Gosset, Philip, ed. see Marliani, Marco A.
Gosset, Philip, ed. see Mehul, Etienne N.
Gosset, Philip, ed. see Mercadante, Saverio.
Gosset, Philip, ed. see Nicolai, Otto.
Gosset, Philip, ed. see Pugni, Cesare.
Gosset, Philip, ed. see Ricci, Luigi.
Gossett, ed. see Rossini.
Gossett, Don. How to Conquer Fear. Orig. Title: How You Can Rise Above Fear. 160p. 1981. pap. 3.50 (ISBN 0-88368-092-0). Whitaker Hse.
--If Nobody Reaches, Nobody Gets Touched. 128p. (Orig.). 1983. pap. 3.50 (ISBN 0-88368-127-7). Whitaker Hse.
--I'm Sold on Being Bold. 1979. pap. 2.25 (ISBN 0-88368-085-8). Whitaker Hse.
--Praise Avenue. 128p. 1976. pap. 3.50 (ISBN 0-88368-059-9). Whitaker Hse.
--There's Dynamite in Praise. rev. ed. 1974. pap. 3.50 (ISBN 0-88368-048-3). Whitaker Hse.
--What You Say Is What You Get. 192p. 1976. pap. 3.50 (ISBN 0-88368-066-1). Whitaker Hse.
Gossett, Gretta P. Beyond the Bend. (Illus.). 1980. 18.95 (ISBN 0-87770-213-6). Ye Galleon.
Gossett, John T. & Lewis, Jerry M. To Find a Way: The Outcome of Treatment of Disturbed Adolescents. LC 82-17900. 200p. 1983. 25.00 (ISBN 0-87630-326-2). Brunner-Mazel.
Gossett, Philip. Anna Bolena & the Artistic Maturity of Gaetano Donizetti. (Studies in Musical Genesis & Structure). (Illus.). 1985. 29.95x (ISBN 0-19-313205-2). Oxford U Pr.
Gossett, Philip, jt. auth. see Coccia, Carlo.
Gossett, Philip, jt. auth. see Generali, Pietro.
Gossett, Philip, jt. auth. see Giovanni, Facini.
Gossett, Philip, jt. auth. see Mercadante, Saverio.
Gossett, Philip, ed. Medea in Corinto. (Itlaian Opera Ser., 1810-1840). 85.00 (ISBN 0-8240-6561-1). Garland Pub.
Gossett, Philip & Rosen, Charles, eds. I. Capuleti e i Montecchi. (Early Romantic Opera Ser.). 99.00 (ISBN 0-8240-2902-X). Garland Pub.
Gossett, Philip, ed. see Alessandro, Nini.
Gossett, Philip, ed. see Bellini, Vincenzo.
Gossett, Philip, ed. see Cherubini, Maria L.
Gossett, Philip, ed. see Donizetti.
Gossett, Philip, ed. see Donizetti, Gaetano.
Gossett, Philip, ed. see Halevy, Jacques-Francois.
Gossett, Philip, ed. see Levi, Samuel.
Gossett, Philip, ed. see Mehul, Etienne.
Gossett, Philip, ed. see Mercadante, Saverio.
Gossett, Philip, ed. see Meyerbeer, Giacomo.
Gossett, Philip, ed. see Morlacchi, Francesco.
Gossett, Philip, ed. see Pacini, Giovanni.
Gossett, Philip, ed. see Ricci, Federico.
Gossett, Philip, ed. see Rossini, Gioachino.
Gossett, Philip, ed. see Scribe, Eugene & Delestre-Poirson, Charles-Gaspard.
Gossett, Philip, ed. see Vaccaj, Nicola.
Gossett, Philip, tr. see Rameau, Jean-Philipe.
Gossett, Philip, tr. see Verdi, Giuseppe.
Gossett, Phillip, ed. see Cherubini, Maria L.
Gossett, Phillip, ed. see Mehul, Etienne N.
Gossett, Phillip, ed. see Meyerbeer, Giacomo.
Gossett, Phillip, ed. see Rossini, Gioachino.
Gossett, Phillip, ed. see Spontini, Gasparo.
Gossett, Suzanne, ed. Hierarchomachia, or the Antibishop. LC 78-75201. 300p. 1981. 35.00 (ISBN 0-8387-2151-6). Bucknell U Pr.
Gossett, Thomas F. Race: The History of an Idea in America. rev. ed. LC 63-21187. (Sourcebooks in Negro History Ser.). (YA) (gr. 7 up). 1965. pap. 9.50 (ISBN 0-8052-0106-8). Schocken.
--Race: The History of an Idea in America. LC 63-21187. 1963. 17.95 (ISBN 0-87074-065-2). SMU Press.
--Uncle Tom's Cabin & American Culture. (Illus.). 500p. 1985. 29.95 (ISBN 0-87074-189-6). SMU Press.
Gossez, J. P., et al, eds. Nonlinear Operators & the Calculus & Variations: Summer School Held in Bruxelles, 8-19 Sept. 1975. (Lecture Notes in Mathematics: Vol. 543). 1976. soft cover 17.00 (ISBN 0-387-07867-3). Springer-Verlag.
Gossip, C. J. An Introduction to French Classical Tragedy. 204p. 1981. 28.50x (ISBN 0-389-20163-4). B&N Imports.
Gossling, Harry R., et al, eds. Complications of Fracture Management. (Illus.). 700p. 1983. text ed. 72.50 (ISBN 0-397-50584-1, 65-07461, Lippincott Medical). Lippincott.
Gossling, W. F. Productivity Trends in a Sectoral Macroeconomic Model: A Study of American Agriculture & Supporting Industries, 1919-1964. 1972. lib. bdg. 37.50x (ISBN 0-678-08072-0). Kelley.
Gossling, W. F., ed. Capital Coefficients & Dynamic Input-Output Models. 1975. lib. bdg. 30.00x (ISBN 0-678-08073-9). Kelley.
--Input-Output & Throughput: The Norwich Conference. 1975. lib. bdg. 25.00x (ISBN 0-678-08074-7). Kelley.
--Medium-Term Dynamic Forecasting: The 1975 London Conference. 1977. lib. bdg. 40.00x (ISBN 0-678-08075-5). Kelley.
Gossling, W. F., jt. ed. see Gielnik, S. J.
Gossman, Charles S., et al. Migration of College & University Students in the United States. LC 68-24090. (Illus.). 198p. 1968. 20.00x (ISBN 0-295-73738-7). U of Wash Pr.
Gossman, Lionel. The Empire Unpossess'd: An Essay on Gibbon's "Decline & Fall". LC 80-24008. (Illus.). 176p. 1981. 24.95 (ISBN 0-521-23453-0). Cambridge U Pr.
--Medievalism & the Ideologies of the Enlightenment: The World & Work of la Curne de Sainte-Palaye. LC 68-16274. 377p. 1968. 35.00x (ISBN 0-8018-0227-X). Johns Hopkins.
--Men & Masks: A Study of Moliere. 325p. 1969. pap. 7.95x (ISBN 0-8018-1043-4). Johns Hopkins.
--Orpheus Philogus Bachofen versus Mommsen on the Study of Antiquity. 90p. 1983. 8.00 (ISBN 0-87169-735-1). Am Philos.
Gossman, N. J., jt. auth. see Baylen, J. O.
Gossman, Norbert J., jt. ed. see Baylen, Joseph O.
Gossom, W. J. Control of Projects, Purchasing & Materials. 128p. 1983. 29.95 (ISBN 0-87814-219-3, P-4325). Pennwell Bks.
Gosson, Stephen. The Ephemerides of Phialo. LC 73-170404. (The English Stage Ser.: Vol. 3). lib. bdg. 61.00 (ISBN 0-8240-0586-4). Garland Pub.
--Playes Confuted in Five Actions. LC 74-170407. (The English Stage Ser.: Vol. 6). lib. bdg. 61.00 (ISBN 0-8240-0589-9). Garland Pub.
--Plays Confuted in Five Actions. 128p. Repr. of 1582 ed. 22.00 (ISBN 0-384-19335-8). Johnson Repr.
--Pleasant Quippes for Upstart Newfangled Gentlewomen. Howard, Edwin J., ed. 1942. wrappers, limited to 200 copies 10.00x (ISBN 0-686-17402-X). R S Barnes.
--School of Abuse. Collier, John P., ed. LC 77-126658. Repr. of 1841 ed. 12.00 (ISBN 0-404-02886-1). AMS Pr.
--The Schoole of Abuse, Conteining a Pleasaunt Invective Against Poets, Pipers, Plaiers, Iesters & Such Like Catepillers of the Commonwelth. LC 72-5998. (English Experience Ser.: No. 523). 104p. 1973. Repr. of 1579 ed. 8.00 (ISBN 90-221-0523-7). Walter J Johnson.
--Schoole of Abuse Fifteen Seventy-Nine & a Short Apologie of the Schoole of Abuse Eighteen Sixty-Eight. 80p. pap. 12.50 (ISBN 0-87556-104-7). Saifer.
Gossop, M. Theories of Neurosis. (Illus.). 161p. 1981. 37.00 (ISBN 0-387-10370-8). Springer-Verlag.
Gossrau, H. R. Die Lysosomen Des Darmepithels. (Advances in Anatomy, Embryology, & Cell Biology Ser.: Vol. 51, Pt. 5). (Illus.). 95p. 1975. pap. 42.50 (ISBN 0-387-07271-3). Springer-Verlag.
Gostelow, J. P. Cascade Aerodynamics. (Thermodynamics & Fluid Mechanics for Mechanical Engineers Ser.). 300p. 1983. 50.00 (ISBN 0-08-020428-7); pap. 22.50 (ISBN 0-08-020427-9). Pergamon.
Gostelow, Mary. Blackwork. (Illus.). 168p. 1976. Repr. 10.95 (ISBN 0-7134-3259-4, Pub. by Batsford England). David & Charles.
--Blackwork. (Illus.). 168p. 1985. pap. 10.95 (ISBN 0-7134-4621-8, Pub. by Batsford England). David & Charles.
--Dress Sense. (Illus.). 120p. 1985. 19.95 (ISBN 0-7134-4559-9, Pub. by Batsford England); pap. 11.95 (ISBN 0-7134-4560-2, Pub. by Batsford England). David & Charles.
--Embroidery: Traditional Designs, Techniques & Patterns from All over the World. (Illus.). 1983. 21.95 (ISBN 0-668-05905-2); pap. 14.95 (ISBN 0-668-05910-9). Arco.
Gostin, Larry & Rassaby, Elaine. Representing the Mentally Ill & Handicapped. 211p. 1980. 25.00x (ISBN 0-905898-10-9, Pub. by Quartermaine England). State Mutual Bk.
Gostling, F. H. Lure of the Riviera. 1976. lib. bdg. 59.95 (ISBN 0-8490-2187-1). Gordon Pr.
Gostling, Frances M., tr. see Le Braz, Anatole.
Gostling, John, compiled by. The Gostling Manuscript. LC 77-1563. 442p. 1977. text ed. 40.00x (ISBN 0-292-72713-5). U of Tex Pr.
Gostony, Colman G. Dictionnaire d'Etymologie Sumerienne et Grammaire Comparee. 204p. (Fr.). 1975. pap. 52.50 (ISBN 0-686-57306-4, M-6283). French & Eur.
Gostwick, Harrison, jt. auth. see Gostwick, J.
Gostwick, J. & Gostwick, Harrison. Outlines of German Literature. 1973. Repr. of 1873 ed. 25.00 (ISBN 0-8274-0737-8). R West.
Gostwick, Joseph. Hand-book of American Literature: Historical, Biographical & Critical. LC 78-121942. 1971. Repr. of 1856 ed. 32.00x (ISBN 0-8046-1304-4, Pub. by Kennikat). Assoc Faculty Pr.
Gosvami, O. The Story of Indian Music: Its Growth & Synthesis. LC 79-181165. 332p. 1961. Repr. 59.00x (ISBN 0-403-01567-7). Scholarly.
Goswami, Amit. The Concepts of Physics. 1979. text ed. 24.95 (ISBN 0-669-01897-X). Heath.

Goswami, Amit & Goswami, Maggie. The Cosmic Dancers: Exploring the Physics of Science Fiction. (Illus.). 288p. 1983. 17.79i (ISBN 0-06-015083-1, HarpT). Har-Row.

--The Cosmic Dancers: Exploring the Science of Science Fiction. 304p. 1985. 7.95 (ISBN 0-07-023867-7). McGraw.

Goswami, B. C., et al. Textile Yarns: Technology, Structure & Applications. LC 77-398. 482p. 1977. 56.50x (ISBN 0-471-31900-7, Pub. by Wiley-Interscience). Wiley.

Goswami, Chitta R. Sri Aurobindo's Concept of the Superman. 260p. 1976. 8.00 (ISBN 0-89071-211-5). Matagiri.

Goswami, Dixie, ed. see Emig, Janet.

Goswami, Hridayananda das see Das Goswami, Hridayananda.

Goswami, Maggie, jt. auth. see Goswami, Amit.

Goswami, P. K. Ups & Downs of Indo-U. S. Relations, 1948-1983. 1984. 12.00x (ISBN 0-8364-1122-6, Pub. by Mukhopadhay India). South Asia Bks.

Goswami, Satavarupa das see Das Goswami, Satsvarupa.

Goswami, Satsvarupa D. Opening a Temple in Los Angelos: A Visit to Boston. Dasa, Mandalesvara, et al, eds. (Prabhupada-lila Ser.). 72p. 1981. pap. 2.25 (ISBN 0-911233-01-6). Gita Nagari.

Goswami, Satsvarupa das. Prabhupada Nectar, Bk. 1. Dasi, Bimali, ed. 134p. pap. 4.99 (ISBN 0-911233-22-9). Gita-Nagari.

Goswami, Satsvarupa das see Das Goswami, Satsvarupa.

Goswami, Satsvarupa Das see Das Goswami, Satsvarupa.

Goswami, Satsvarupa das see Das Goswami, Satsvarupa.

Goswami, Satsvarupa dasa see Dasa Goswami, Satsvarupa.

Goswami, Satsvarupa Dasa see Dasa Goswami, Satsvarupa.

Goswami, Shrivatsa & Shinn, Larry, eds. In Search of the Divine. (God Ser.). (Orig.). Date not set. text ed. 12.95 (ISBN 0-913757-28-4, Pub. by New Era Bks.); pap. text ed. price not set (ISBN 0-913757-29-2). Paragon Hse.

Goswami, Shyam S. Layayoga: An Advanced Method of Concentration. (Illus.). 1980. 35.00 (ISBN 0-7100-0078-2). Routledge & Kegan.

Goswami, Srila Hridayananda dasa, ed. The Glories of Sri Caitanya Mahaprabhu. Kusakratha dasa, tr. LC 83-7078. 64p. (Orig.). 1984. pap. 6.00 (ISBN 0-89647-018-0). Bala Bks.

Goswamy, B. N. & Dallapiccola, A. L. A Place Apart: Painting in Kutch, 1720-1820. (Illus.). 1984. 74.00x (ISBN 0-19-561311-2). Oxford U Pr.

Goswamy, B. N., ed. Early Document of Indian Art: The Citralaksana of Nagnajit. LC 76-903518. 1976. 16.00x (ISBN 0-88386-845-8). South Asia Bks.

Goswitz, Francis A., et al, eds. Clinical Uses of Radionuclides: Critical Comparison with Other Techniques: Proceedings. LC 72-660271. (AEC Symposium Ser.). 718p. 1972. 26.00 (ISBN 0-87079-002-1, CONF-711101); microfiche 4.50 (ISBN 0-87079-164-8, CONF-711101). DOE.

Gosz, James R., jt. auth. see Potter, Loren D.

Gosztonyi, Eva, tr. see Bernat, Ivan.

Gotaas, H. B. Composting: Sanitary Disposal & Reclamation of Organic Wastes. (Monograph Ser: No. 31). (Illus.). 205p. (Eng. & Fr.). 1956. 14.00 (ISBN 92-4-140031-5). World Health.

Gotaas, Mary C. Bossuet & Vieira. LC 75-128929. (Catholic Univ. of American Studies in Romance Lang. & Lit. Ser.: No. 46). Repr. of 1953 ed. 21.00 (ISBN 0-404-50346-2). AMS Pr.

Gotama. The Nyaya Sutras of Gotama. Satisa Chandra Vidyabhusana, tr. LC 73-3795. (Sacred Books of the Hindus: No. 8). Repr. of 1913 ed. 29.00 (ISBN 0-404-57808-X). AMS Pr.

Gotch, A. F. Birds: Their Latin Names Explained. (Illus.). 288p. 1981. 22.50 (ISBN 0-7137-1175-2, Pub. by Blandford Pr England). Sterling.

--Mammals: Their Latin Names Explained. (Illus.). 1979. 18.95 (ISBN 0-7137-0939-1, Pub. by Blandford Pr England). Sterling.

Gotch, Christopher, jt. auth. see Scutt, R. W.

Gotch, Rosamund B., ed. see Thompson, Frances A.

Gotesky, Rubin. Personality: The Need for Liberty & Rights. 1967. 3.50 (ISBN 0-87212-012-0). Libra.

Gotesky, Rubin & Laszlo, Ervin, eds. Evolution-Revolution. LC 74-160019. (Current Topics of Contemporary Thought Ser.). (Illus.). 364p. 1971. lib. bdg. 49.95 (ISBN 0-677-15090-3). Gordon.

--Human Dignity: This Century & the Next. (Current Topics in Contemporary Thought Ser.). 390p. 1970. lib. bdg. 57.75 (ISBN 0-677-14240-4). Gordon.

Goth, Andres. Medical Pharmacology: Principles & Concepts. 10th ed. LC 81-2861. (Illus.). 815p. 1981. text ed. 31.95 (ISBN 0-8016-1949-1). Mosby.

Goth, Andres & Vesell, Elliot S. Medical Pharmacology: Principles & Concepts. 11th ed. (Illus.). 716p. 1984. adhesive notchbound 31.00 (ISBN 0-8016-1962-9). Mosby.

Gotham, Halwick A. Methods in Behavior Therapy: Guidebook for Medicine & Psychology. LC 84-45169. 150p. 1985. 29.95 (ISBN 0-88164-174-X); pap. 21.95 (ISBN 0-88164-175-8). ABBE Pubs Assn.

Gothard, Bill. The Eagle Story. LC 81-85536. (Illus.). 64p. (gr. 3-12). 1982. 8.00 (ISBN 0-916888-07-X). Inst Basic Youth.

--Institute in Basic Youth Conflicts: Research in Principles of Life. Rev. ed. LC 79-92142. (Illus.). 192p. 1981. 15.00 (ISBN 0-916888-05-3). Inst Basic Youth.

--Men's Manual, Vol. II. LC 79-88994. (Illus.). 270p. 1983. 20.00 (ISBN 0-916888-09-6). Inst Basic Youth.

--Men's Manual, Vol. 1. LC 79-88994. (Illus.). 160p. 1979. 25.00 (ISBN 0-916888-04-5). Inst Basic Youth.

--Rebuilder's Guide. LC 80-80352. (Illus.). 250p. 1982. 15.00 (ISBN 0-916888-06-1). Inst Basic Youth.

Gothard, J. W. & Branthwaite, M. A. Anaesthesia for Thoracic Surgery. (Illus.). 199p. 1982. pap. text ed. 26.50 (ISBN 0-632-00578-5, B1940-8). Mosby.

Gothard, W. P. Brightest & Best. 1980. 30.00x (ISBN 0-905484-25-8, Pub. by Nafferton England). State Mutual Bk.

--Vocational Guidance: Theory & Practice. LC 84-23780. 198p. 1985. 29.00 (ISBN 0-7099-1161-0, Pub. by Croom Helm Ltd). Longwood Pub Group.

Gothberg, Helen M. Television & Video in Libraries & Schools. 246p. 1983. 22.50 (ISBN 0-208-01859-X, Lib Prof Pubns). Shoe String.

Gothefors, Leif, jt. auth. see Davies, Pamela.

Gothein, Marie-Luise. A History of Garden Art, 2 vols. LC 67-4274. (Illus.). 1979. Set. lib. bdg. 120.00 (ISBN 0-87817-008-1). Hacker.

Gotherman, John E. & Babbit, Harold W. Ohio Municipal Law, 3 vols. 2nd rev. ed. (Baldwin's Ohio Practice Ser.). 4376p. 1975. Set, annual cum. supp. 210.00 (ISBN 0-8322-0015-8). Banks-Baldwin.

Gotherman, John E., ed. Gotherman's Ohio Municipal Service. 1985. 115.00 (ISBN 0-8322-0121-9); prior yrs. 65.00; Combined with Ohio Municipal Law 288.00 (ISBN 0-8322-0015-8). Banks-Baldwin.

Gothie, Daniel L. A Selected Bibliography of Applied Ethics in the Professions, 1950-1970: A Working Sourcebook. LC 73-80627. 176p. 1973. 14.95x (ISBN 0-8139-0412-9). U Pr of Va.

Gothmann, W. Electronics: A Contemporary Approach. 1980. 31.95 (ISBN 0-13-252254-3). P-H.

Gothmann, William H. Contemporary Mathematics for Electronics. (Illus.). 560p. 1982. 31.95 (ISBN 0-13-170274-2). P-H.

--Digital Electronics. 2nd ed. (Illus.). 400p. 1982. 31.95 (ISBN 0-13-212159-X). P-H.

Gothot-Mesch, ed. see Flaubert, Gustave.

Gotleib, Phyllis. O Master Caliban. LC 76-5540. 244p. 1976. 15.00 (ISBN 0-06-011621-8). Ultramarine Pub.

Gotlieb, C. C. Computers in the Home. 65p. 1978. pap. text ed. 3.00x (ISBN 0-920380-10-7, Pub. by Inst Res Pub Canada). Brookfield Pub Co.

--The Economics of Computers: Costs, Benefits, Policies & Strategies. (Illus.). 272p. 1985. text ed. 36.95 (ISBN 0-13-224452-7). P-H.

Gotlieb, C. C. & Gotlieb, Leo R. Data Types & Structures. (Illus.). 1978. ref. ed. 33.95 (ISBN 0-13-197095-X). P-H.

Gotlieb, Leo R., jt. auth. see Gotlieb, C. C.

Gotlieb, Phillis. Emperor, Swords, Pentacles. 304p. 1985. pap. 2.95 (ISBN 0-441-20547-X, Pub. by Ace Science Fiction). Ace Bks.

Gotlieb, Phyllis. A Judgement of Dragons. 272p. 1985. pap. 2.95 (ISBN 0-441-42032-X, Pub. by Ace Science Fiction). Ace Bks.

--The Kingdom of the Cats. 288p. 1985. pap. 2.95 (ISBN 0-441-44453-9). Ace Bks.

--Son of the Morning & Other Stories. 240p. 1983. pap. 2.95 (ISBN 0-441-77221-8, Pub. by Ace Science Fiction). Ace Bks.

--Sunburst. LC 78-21597. 160p. 1978. 15.00 (ISBN 0-8398-2500-5). Ultramarine Pub.

Gotlieb, Randie & Gotlieb, Steven. Once to Every Man & Nation: Stories about Becoming a Bahar. 1985. price not set (ISBN 0-85398-210-4); pap. price not set (ISBN 0-85398-211-2). G Ronald Pub.

Gotlieb, Sondra. A Woman of Consequence. 1983. 12.95 (ISBN 0-312-88643-8). St Martin.

Gotlieb, Steven, jt. auth. see Gotlieb, Randie.

Gotlieb, Yosef. Self-Determination in the Middle East. LC 82-13239. 190p. 1982. 28.50 (ISBN 0-03-062408-8). Praeger.

Gotlin, Ronald W., jt. auth. see Alsever, Robert N.

Gotlin, Stanley. Test Wise Tactics for Higher Scores in English. 128p. (gr. 9-12). pap. 0.75 (ISBN 0-8120-2578-4). Barron.

Gotlin, Stanley, jt. auth. see Dore, Anita W.

Goto, E., et al, eds. RIMS Symposia on Software Science & Engineering: Proceedings, Kyoto, Japan, 1982. (Lecture Notes in Computer Science Ser.: Vol. 147). 232p. 1983. pap. 13.50 (ISBN 0-387-11980-9). Springer-Verlag.

Goto, H. E. Animal Toxonomy. (Studies in Biology Ser.: No. 143). 64p. 1982. pap. text ed. 8.95 (ISBN 0-7131-2847-X). E Arnold.

Goto, Joseph & Jordy, William H. Joseph Goto: Sculpture. LC 71-177398. (Illus.). 1971. 2.50 (ISBN 0-686-05418-0). Mus of Art RI.

Goto, Y. & Horiuchi, A., eds. Diabetic Neuropathy: Proceeding International Symposium on Diabetic Neuropathy & its Treatment, Tokyo, September 18-19, 1981. (International Congress Ser.: Vol. 581). 390p. 1982. 83.00 (ISBN 0-444-90259-7, I-327-82, Excerpta Medica). Elsevier.

Gotobed, Jabez. Darts: Fifty Ways to Play the Game. (Oleander Games & Pastimes Ser.: Vol. 2). (Illus.). 1979. 9.95 (ISBN 0-900891-71-8); pap. 4.95 (ISBN 0-900891-72-6). Oleander Pr.

Gotoff, Harold C. Cicero's Elegant Style: An Analysis of the Pro Archia. LC 79-10245. 153p. 1979. 15.00x (ISBN 0-252-00730-1). U of Ill Pr.

--Transmission of the Text of Lucan in the Ninth Century. LC 72-133212. (Loeb Classical Monographs Ser). 1971. 14.00x (ISBN 0-674-90466-4). Harvard U Pr.

Gotow, K., jt. ed. see Blecher, M.

Gotrick, K. Apidan Theatre. 271p. 1984. text ed. 26.00x (ISBN 91-22-00694-X, Pub. by Almqvist & Wiksell Sweden). Humanities.

Gots & Kaufman. People's Hospital Book. 1981. pap. 3.95 (ISBN 0-380-53058-9, 53058-9). Avon.

Gots, Barbara A., jt. auth. see Gots, Ronald E.

Gots, Ronald E. Truth about Medical Malpractice: The Patient's Rights, the Doctor's Rights. LC 75-11801. 1975. 7.95 (ISBN 0-8128-1831-8). Stein & Day.

Gots, Ronald E. & Gots, Barbara A. Caring for Your Unborn Child. 1979. pap. 3.95 (ISBN 0-553-24412-4). Bantam.

Gotsch, Carl & Brown, Gilbert. Prices, Taxes & Subsidies in Pakistan Agriculture, 1960-1976. (Working Paper: No. 387). 108p. 1980. 5.00 (ISBN 0-686-36073-7, WP-0387). World Bank.

Gotsch, Linda, ed. Criminal Justice Educational Opportunities: 1982-1983. (Special Editions Ser.). 199p. pap. 7.00 (ISBN 0-935530-09-6). Natl Employment.

Gotshalk, D. W. Human Aims in Modern Perspective: Outlines of a General Theory of Value. LC 66-13391. Repr. of 1966 ed. 25.30 (ISBN 0-8357-9366-4, 2014596). Bks Demand UMI.

--Patterns of Good & Evil: A Value Analysis. LC 63-17047. 147p. 1963. 15.00x (ISBN 0-252-72601-4). U of Ill Pr.

Gotshalk, Dilman W. The Promise of Modern Life: An Interrelational View. LC 58-8735. pap. 24.40 (ISBN 0-317-08853-X, 2014597). Bks Demand UMI.

--Structure & Reality: A Study of First Principles. LC 68-19273. 1968. Repr. of 1937 ed. lib. bdg. 15.75x (ISBN 0-8371-0088-7, GOSR). Greenwood.

Gotshall, Daniel W. Marine Animals of Baja California. LC 82-50492. (Illus.). 112p. 1982. pap. 17.95 (ISBN 0-930030-24-9). Western Marine.

--Marine Animals of Baja California. LC 82-50492. (Illus.). 112p. 1982. ltd. ed. 29.95 (ISBN 0-930118-08-1, Dist. by Western Marine Enterprises); pap. 17.95 (ISBN 0-930030-24-9). Sea Chall.

--Pacific Coast Inshore Fishes. rev. ed. LC 80-53027. (Illus.). 96p. 1981. ltd. ed. 22.95 (ISBN 0-930118-07-3); pap. 12.95 (ISBN 0-930118-06-5, Pap. dist. by Western Marine). Sea Chall.

--Pacific Coast Inshore Fishes. LC 80-5327. 96p. 1981. pap. 12.95 (ISBN 0-930030-31-1). Western Marine Ent.

Gotshall, Daniel W. & Laurent, Laurence L. Pacific Coast Subtidal Marine Invertebrates, a Fishwatchers' Guide. LC 79-64128. 112p. 1979. (Western Marine Enterprises); pap. 12.95 (ISBN 0-930118-03-0). Sea Chall.

--Pacific Coast Subtidal Marine Invertebrates. LC 79-64128. (Illus.). 112p. pap. 12.95 (ISBN 0-930118-03-0). Western Marine Ent.

Gotshall, Daniel W. & Zimbleman. Fishes of the Pacific Coast: An Underwater Guide, Alaske to the Baja. (Illus.). 96p. 1974. text ed. 12.50 (ISBN 0-87098-060-2). Livingston.

Gotshlich, Emil C., ed. Harvey Lectures, Vol. 78. 1984. 45.00 (ISBN 0-12-312078-0). Acad Pr.

Gotsick, Pricilla S., et al. Information for Everyday Survival. LC 76-13554. 416p. 1976. pap. text ed. 10.00x (ISBN 0-8389-0211-1). ALA.

Gotsman, M. S., jt. ed. see Borman, J. B.

Gott, Frank S. & Terry, Kristi. Thinning While Grinning: Thirty Day Diet Handbook. (Illus.). 160p. 1985. pap. 8.95 (ISBN 0-932849-00-8). Welcome Pub.

Gott, George. Here & There. 64p. (Orig.). 1985. pap. 3.95x (ISBN 0-943512-08-5, 961EP). Linwood Pub.

Gott, John K. Abstracts of Fauquier County, Virginia Wills, Inventories & Accounts, 1759-1800. LC 80-67141. 348p. 1980. pap. 15.00 (ISBN 0-8063-0898-2). Genealog Pub.

Gott, V. This Amazing, Amazing, Amazing but Knowable Universe. 253p. 1977. 5.45 (ISBN 0-8285-0837-2, Pub. by Progress Pubs USSR). Imported Pubns.

Gottardi, G. & Galli, E. Natural Zeolites. (Minerals & Rocks Ser.: Vol. 18). (Illus.). 390p. 1985. 59.00 (ISBN 0-387-13939-7). Springer-Verlag.

Gottcent, John H. The Bible As Literature: A Selective Bibliography. 1979. lib. bdg. 26.00 (ISBN 0-8161-8121-7, Hall Reference). G K Hall.

Gottdiener, M. The Social Production of Urban Space. 328p. 1985. text ed. 27.50x (ISBN 0-292-77586-5). U of Tex pr.

Gotte, Johannes. Augustine's Concept of Providence. 1.00 (ISBN 0-686-23373-5). Classical Folia.

Gottehrer, Dean M. Natural Landscaping. 182p. 1978. 10.95 (ISBN 0-87690-280-8). Brown Bk.

Gottelmann, Gabriele. Staatliche Regulierung Sozialer Innovation in der Bundesrepublik und in Frankreich. (European University Studies: No. 31, Vol. 35). 313p. (Ger.). 1983. 36.30 (ISBN 3-8204-7760-8). P Lang Pubs.

Gottemoller, Bartholomew. How to Find Happiness. LC 79-88324. 1979. pap. 1.95 (ISBN 0-87973-529-5). Our Sunday Visitor.

Gottenberg, W. G., ed. see Symposium on Applications of Holography in Mechanics (1971: University ofSouthern California).

Gottesfeld, Harry. Alternatives to Psychiatric Hospitalization: With Annotated Readers Guide. 1977. 0.23.95 (ISBN 0-89876-057-7). Gardner Pr.

Gottesfeld, Harry, et al. Strategies in Innovative Human Services Programs, Vol. 1, No. 3. LC 73-6871. (Developments in Human Services Ser). 100p. 1973. pap. text ed. 7.95 (ISBN 0-87705-078-3). Human Sci Pr.

Gottesfeld, Mary & Pharis, Mary. Profiles in Social Work. LC 76-20697. 238p. 1977. text ed. 24.95 (ISBN 0-87705-296-4). Human Sci Pr.

Gottesfeld, Mary, ed. Case Studies in Clinical Social Work. (A Special Issue of Clinical Social Work Journal Ser.). 96p. 1979. pap. 9.95 (ISBN 0-87705-397-9). Human Sci Pr.

--Education for Clinical Social Work: A Special Issue of Clinical Social Work Journal. LC 77-81412. 123p. 1977. text ed. 14.95 (ISBN 0-87705-323-5). Human Sci Pr.

Gottesfeld, Mary L., ed. Modern Sexuality. LC 73-643802. (A Special Issue of Clinical Social Work Journal). 72p. 1974. text ed. 12.95 (ISBN 0-87705-153-4). Human Sci Pr.

Gottesman, Alice J. & Burlingame, Beverley, eds. The Michigan League Cookbook. LC 84-50923. (Illus.). 200p. (Orig.). 1984. pap. 10.50 (ISBN 0-9613460-0-0). U of Mich Alumnae.

Gottesman, Irving I. & Shields, James. Schizophrenia & Genetics. (Personality & Psychopathology Ser.: Vol. 13). 1972. 65.00 (ISBN 0-12-293450-4). Acad Pr.

--Schizophrenia: The Epigenetic Puzzle. LC 81-18181. (Illus.). 275p. 1982. 37.50 (ISBN 0-521-22573-6); pap. 12.95 (ISBN 0-521-29559-9). Cambridge U Pr.

Gottesman, M. Molecular Cell Genetics. 944p. 1985. 79.95 (ISBN 0-471-87925-8). Wiley.

Gottesman, Meir, jt. ed. see Wolins, Martin.

Gottesman, Meir U. Shpeter: Book One. (Judaica Youth Ser.). (Illus.). (gr. 1-3). 1981. 5.95 (ISBN 0-910818-35-5); pap. 4.95 (ISBN 0-910818-36-3). Judaica Pr.

--Shpeter: Book Two. (Judaica Youth Ser.). (Illus.). (gr. 1-3). 1981. 5.95 (ISBN 0-910818-39-8); pap. 4.95 (ISBN 0-910818-40-1). Judaica Pr.

Gottesman, Rita S. Arts & Crafts in New York, Seventeen Twenty-Six to Seventeen Seventy-Six. LC 70-127254. (Architecture & Decorative Art Ser.: Vol. 35). 1970. Repr. of 1938 ed. lib. bdg. 45.00 (ISBN 0-306-71129-X). Da Capo.

Gottesman, Roberta. The Child & the Law. LC 81-3402. 223p. 1981. pap. text ed. 8.95 (ISBN 0-314-58803-5). West Pub.

Gottesman, Ronald. Upton Sinclair: An Annotated Checklist. LC 72-634010. (Serif Ser.: No. 24). pap. 141.00 (ISBN 0-8357-9375-3, 2014598). Bks Demand UMI.

Gottesman, Ronald & Geduld, Harry M. Guidebook to Film: An Eleven in One Reference. LC 77-167811. 1972. pap. text ed. 4.95 (ISBN 0-03-085292-7). Irvington.

Gottesman, Ronald & Silet, Charles. The Literary Manuscripts of Upton Sinclair. LC 72-751. (Calendars of American Literary Manuscripts: No. 2). (Illus.). 492p. 1973. 12.50x (ISBN 0-8142-0169-5). Ohio St U Pr.

Gottesman, Ronald & Geduld, Harry, eds. The Girl in the Hairy Paw. 1976. pap. 6.45 (ISBN 0-380-00610-3, 28688-2). Avon.

Gottesman, Ronald, ed. see Seidman, Steve.

Gottesman, Ronald, ed. see Van Wert, William F.

Gottesman, Ronald, ed. see Wead, George & Lellis, George.

Gottesman, Ronald, et al, eds. The Norton Anthology of American Literature. 1979. Vol I. text ed. 19.95x (ISBN 0-393-95026-3); Vol II. text ed. 19.95x (ISBN 0-393-95033-6); Vol. I. pap. text ed. 16.95x (ISBN 0-393-95030-1); Vol II. pap. text ed. 16.95x (ISBN 0-393-95035-2). Norton.

--The Norton Anthology of American Literature: Shorter Edition. 1980. pap. text ed. 16.95x (ISBN 0-393-95112-X). Norton.

Gottfredson, Floyd, intro. by. Mickey Mouse. LC 78-15264. (Walt Disney Best Comics Ser.). (Illus.). 204p. 1978. 15.95 (ISBN 0-89659-005-4). Abbeville Pr.

Gottfredson, Gary D. & Holland, John L. Dictionary of Holland Occupational Codes. 520p. (Orig.). 1982. pap. 18.50 (ISBN 0-89106-020-0, 7889). Consulting Psychol.

Gottfredson, Michael, jt. ed. see Hirshi, Travis.

Gottfredson, Michael R., jt. auth. see Goldkamp, John S.

Gottfridsson. Swedish Mitten Book. 1984. pap. 8.95 (ISBN 0-937274-14-3). Dodd.

Gottfridsson, Inger & Gottfridsson, Ingrid. The Swedish Mitten Book: Traditional Patterns from Gotland. Net Works Inc., tr. from Swedish. Orig. Title: Gotlandska Stickmonster. (Illus.). 104p. (Orig.). 1985. pap. 8.95 (ISBN 0-937274-14-3). Lark Bks.

Gottfridsson, Ingrid, jt. auth. see Gottfridsson, Inger.

Gottfried. Infant Stress under Intensive Care. (Illus.). 328p. 1984. text ed. 29.50 (ISBN 0-8391-1869-4, 19569). Univ Park.

Gottfried, Allen, jt. ed. see Brown, Catherine C.

Gottfried, Allen W., ed. Home Environment & Early Cognitive Development: Longitudinal Research. LC 83-13057. (Developmental Psychology Ser.). 1984. 49.00 (ISBN 0-12-293460-1). Acad Pr.

Gottfried, B. S. Programming with Pascal. (Schaum's Outline Ser.). 320p. 1983. 8.95 (ISBN 0-07-023849-9). McGraw.

--Schaum's Outline of Programming with BASIC. 2nd ed. (Schaum's Outline Ser.). 1982. pap. 9.95 (ISBN 0-07-023855-3). McGraw.

Gottfried, Bert A., jt. ed. see Clark, Donald T.

Gottfried, Byron S. Elements of Stochastic Process Simulation. (Illus.). 304p. 1984. 21.95 (ISBN 0-13-272500-2). P-H.

--Introduction to Engineering Calculations. (Schaum's Outline Ser.). (Illus.). 1979. pap. 7.95 (ISBN 0-07-023837-5). McGraw.

--Programming with FORTRAN IV. 2nd ed. (Illus.). 384p. 1984. pap. text ed. 19.95 (ISBN 0-13-729699-1). P-H.

Gottfried, Byron S. & Weisman, Joel. Introduction to Optimization Theory. (Illus.). 592p. 1973. ref. ed. 34.95 (ISBN 0-13-491472-4). P-H.

Gottfried, Chet. The Steel Eye. LC 84-5444. 160p. (Orig.). 1984. pap. 5.95 (ISBN 0-917053-00-1). Space And.

--The Steel Eye. LC 84-14467. 160p. 1984. Repr. lib. bdg. 15.95x (ISBN 0-89370-855-0). Borgo Pr.

Gottfried, Herbert & Jennings, Jan. American Vernacular Design: Eighteen Seventy to Nineteen Forty. (Illus.). 272p. (Orig.). 1985. pap. 24.95 (ISBN 0-442-22739-6). Van Nos Reinhold.

Gottfried, Herbert, tr. see Haller, Jurgen.

Gottfried, Kurt & Weisskopf, Victor F. Concepts of Particle Physics, Vol. I. (Illus.). 1984. 22.50x (ISBN 0-19-503392-2). Oxford U Pr.

Gottfried, Martin. Broadway Musicals. (Illus.). 1979. 24.95 (ISBN 0-8109-8060-6). Abrams.

--In Person: The Great Entertainers. (Illus.). 256p. 1985. 49.50 (ISBN 0-8109-1613-4). Abrams.

--Jed Harris: The Curse of Genius. (Illus.). 304p. 1984. 19.45i (ISBN 0-316-32156-7). Little.

Gottfried, Nathan, jt. auth. see Seay, Bill M.

Gottfried, Paul. Conservative Millenarians: The Romantic Experience in Bavaria. LC 74-20028. viii, 176p. 1979. 25.00 (ISBN 0-8232-0982-2). Fordham.

Gottfried, Paul, ed. Continuity: A Journal of History. 144p. ann. subscr. 10.00, biannual (ISBN 0-318-14484-0); back issues 5.00 ea. Intercoll Studies.

Gottfried, Robert S. The Black Death: Natural & Human Disaster in Medieval Europe. LC 82-48745. 240p. 1983. 16.95 (ISBN 0-02-912630-4); pap. 8.95w. Free Pr.

--Bury St. Edmunds & the Urban Crisis, 1290-1539. LC 81-11984. (Illus.). 324p. 1981. 32.00x (ISBN 0-691-05340-5). Princeton U Pr.

--Epidemic Disease in Fifteenth Century England: The Medical Response & the Demographic Consequences. (Illus.). 1978. 25.00x (ISBN 0-8135-0861-4). Rutgers U Pr.

Gottfried, Rosalie. Getting into American Medical-Veterinary Schools: A Practical "How to" Guide. LC 77-93397. (gr. 10 up). 1978. pap. text ed. 5.50x (ISBN 0-931084-01-6). Argee Pub.

Gottfried, Roy K. The Art of Joyce's Syntax in "Ulysses". LC 79-10294. 200p. 1980. 16.50x (ISBN 0-8203-0478-6). U of Ga Pr.

Gottfried, Rudolf see Spenser, Edmund, et al.

Gottfried, Rudolf B., tr. see Bembo, Pietro.

Gottfried, Sandra S. & Kelly, James L. Fundamentals in Laboratory Microbiology. (Illus.). 72p. (gr. 9-10). 1984. pap. text ed. 6.95 (ISBN 0-8138-1146-5). Iowa St U Pr.

Gottfried, Strassburg. Tristan und Isolde in Auswahl. 4th ed. Maurer, Friedrich, ed. (Sammlung Goeschen, No.2204). 1977. 3.90x (ISBN 3-11-006841-9). De Gruyter.

Gottheil, E. L., et al, eds. see Coatesville-Jefferson Conference on Addiction, 1st, October 1977.

Gottheil, Edward, et al. Alcohol, Drug Abuse & Aggression. (Illus.). 378p. 1983. 34.50x (ISBN 0-398-04787-1). C C Thomas.

--Etiologic Aspects of Alcohol & Drug Abuse. (Illus.). 360p. 1983. 39.75x (ISBN 0-398-04732-4). C C Thomas.

Gottheil, Edward, et al, eds. The Combined Problems of Alcoholism, Drug Addiction & Aging. 386p. 1985. 39.75x (ISBN 0-398-05046-5). C C Thomas.

--Substance Abuse & Psychiatric Illness: Proceedings of the Second Annual Coatesville--Jefferson Conference on Addiction. LC 79-25407. 224p. 1980. 33.00 (ISBN 0-08-025547-7). Pergamon.

Gottheil, Edward A., et al. Matching Patient Needs & Treatment Methods in Alcoholism & Drug Abuse. (Illus.). 432p. 1981. 39.75x (ISBN 0-398-04513-5). C C Thomas.

Gottheil, Fred M. Marx's Economic Predictions. 1967. 15.95 (ISBN 0-8101-0105-X). Northwestern U Pr.

Gottheil, Richard, ed. see New York Public Library.

Gottheil, Richard J., ed. Fragments from the Cairo Genizah in the Freer Collection. Repr. of 1927 ed. 37.00 (ISBN 0-384-38813-2). Johnson Repr.

Gottheiner, Till, tr. see Suret-Canale, Jean.

Gottheinerova, Till, tr. see Vana, Zdenek.

Gotthelf, Jeremias. Black Spider. Waidson, H. M., tr. from Ger. 1980. 12.95 (ISBN 0-7145-0125-5); pap. 5.95 (ISBN 0-7145-0126-3). Riverrun NY.

Gotthilf, Daniel L. Treasurer's & Controller's Desk Book. 512p. 1977. 54.95 (ISBN 0-13-930727-3). P-H.

Gotthilf, Daniel L., jt. auth. see Blecke, Curtis J.

Gottier, Karin P. Teaching Culture Through Folk Dance. (Ethnic Studies Bulletins: No. 10). 16p. 1983. 1.00. Thut World Ed Ctr.

Gottilly, Doris R. Creative Dollmaking: From Papier Mache, Cloth, Clothespins & Appleheads to Yarn, Corn Cob, Bottle & Seashell Dolls. LC 76-23722. (Illus.). 1976. 10.95 (ISBN 0-686-77157-5). CHB-ALF.

Gottinger, H. W. & Leinfellner, W. Decision Theory & Social Ethics. (Theory & Decision Library: No. 17). 1978. 50.00 (ISBN 90-277-0887-8, Pub. by Reidel Holland); pap. 24.00 (ISBN 90-277-0937-8, Pub. by Reidel Holland). Kluwer Academic.

Gottinger, Hans W. Coping with Complexity. 1983. lib. bdg. 44.00 (ISBN 90-277-1510-6, Pub. by Reidel Holland). Kluwer Academic.

--Elements of Statistical Analysis. 224p. 1980. text ed. 28.60 (ISBN 3-11-007169-X). De Gruyter.

Gottleib. The Fragments. 1974. 7.95 (ISBN 0-87306-105-5). Feldheim.

Gottleib, Alan, ed. Celebrity Address Book. 160p. (Orig.). pap. cancelled (ISBN 0-915463-12-1). Jameson Bks.

Gottleib, Benjamin M., ed. Unconventional Methods in Exploration for Petroleum & Natural Gas II. (Illus.). 280p. 1981. 50.00 (ISBN 0-87074-179-9). SMU Press.

Gottleib, Elaine, et al, trs. see Singer, Isaac B.

Gottleib, J. Educating Mentally Retarded Persons: Social & Behavioral Aspects. LC 79-20014. (Illus.). 304p. 1980. 14.00 (ISBN 0-8391-1522-9). Pro Ed.

Gottleib, Richard M., jt. auth. see Thompson, Waite.

Gottlie, Irving M. Power Supplies, Switching Regulators, Inverters & Converters. (Illus.). 448p. (Orig.). 1984. 21.95 (ISBN 0-8306-0665-3, 1665); pap. 15.95 (ISBN 0-8306-1665-9). TAB Bks.

Gottlieb & Mlotek. Ghetto Songs. 4.45 (ISBN 0-87677-126-6). Hartmore.

Gottlieb, A. A., et al, eds. Fundamental Aspects of Neoplasia. (Illus.). 450p. 1975. 49.50 (ISBN 0-387-07230-6). Springer-Verlag.

Gottlieb, Alan. The Rights of Gun Owners. 216p. (Orig.). 1981. pap. 6.95 (ISBN 0-89803-056-0). Green Hill.

Gottlieb, Annie, jt. auth. see Sher, Barbara.

Gottlieb, Arlan J., et al. The Whole Internist Catalog: A Compendium of Clues to Diagnosis & Management. LC 79-66034. (Illus.). 509p. 1980. pap. text ed. 22.50 (ISBN 0-7216-4179-2). Saunders.

Gottlieb, Beatrice, tr. see Febvre, Lucien.

Gottlieb, Benjamin, ed. Social Networks & Social Support in Community Mental Health. (Sage Studies in Community Mental Health: Vol. 4). 300p. 1981. 25.00 (ISBN 0-8039-1669-8); pap. 12.50 (ISBN 0-8039-1670-1). Sage.

Gottlieb, Benjamin H. Social Support Strategies: Guidelines for Mental Health Practice. (Sage Studies in Community Mental Health: Vol. 7). 240p. 1983. 25.00 (ISBN 0-8039-2031-8); pap. 12.50 (ISBN 0-8039-2032-6). Sage.

Gottlieb, Benjamin M., jt. ed. see Davidson, Martin J.

Gottlieb, Bill, ed. see Prevention Magazine Editors.

Gottlieb, Carla. Beyond Modern Art. 416p. 1976. pap. 11.95 (ISBN 0-525-47370-X, 01160-350). Dutton.

--The Restoration of the "Nereid" Monument at Xanthos. LC 80-53356. (Illus.). xxii, 349p. 1980. lib. bdg. 75.00 (ISBN 0-9604420-0-6); pap. 60.00 (ISBN 0-9604420-3-0). Boian Bks.

--Self-Portraiture: From Ancient Egypt to World War II. (Illus.). 480p. Date not set. 45.00 (ISBN 0-525-93298-4, 04369-1310). Dutton.

--The Window As a Symbol in Western Painting: From Divinity to Doubt. LC 80-53355. (Illus.). 550p. 1985. 100.00 (ISBN 0-9604420-1-4); pap. 75.00 (ISBN 0-9604420-2-2). Boian Bks.

--The Window in Art. LC 77-86219. (Illus.). 512p. 1981. 60.00 (ISBN 0-913870-40-4). Abaris Bks.

--The Window in Painting: A Study of Its Morphology As Basis for Motif Classification. LC 81-69473. (Illus.). 350p. 1985. 75.00 (ISBN 0-9604420-4-9); pap. 60.00 (ISBN 0-9604420-5-7). Boian Bks.

Gottlieb, D. The Germination of Fungus Spores. 180p. 1977. 39.00x (ISBN 0-904095-22-3, Pub. by Meadowfield Pr England). State Mutual Bk.

Gottlieb, D. & Shaw, P. D., eds. Antibiotics, 2 vols. Incl. Vol. 1: Mechanism of Action. xii, 785p; Vol. 2: Biosynthesis. xii, 466p. 1967. 89.00 (ISBN 0-387-03725-X). (Illus.). 1967. Springer-Verlag.

Gottlieb, Dale. Ontological Economy: Substitutional Quantification & Mathematics. (Clarendon Library of Logic & Philosophy Ser.). 1980. 29.95x (ISBN 0-19-824420-7). Oxford U Pr.

Gottlieb, Darcy. No Witness But Ourselves. LC 73-85459. 64p. 1973. 6.95 (ISBN 0-8262-0154-7). U of Mo Pr.

Gottlieb, David & Orszag, Steven A. Numerical Analysis of Spectral Methods: Theory & Applications. (CBMS-NSF Regional Conference Ser.: No. 26). v, 170p. (Orig.). 1977. pap. text ed. 17.50 (ISBN 0-89871-023-5). Soc Indus-Appl Math.

Gottlieb, David, intro. by. Youth in Contemporary Society. LC 72-84050. pap. 96.00 (ISBN 0-317-09700-8, 2021908). Bks Demand UMI.

Gottlieb, David I. The Gay Tapes: A Candid Discussion About Male Homosexuality. LC 76-57987. 1977. pap. 2.50 (ISBN 0-8128-7021-2). Stein & Day.

Gottlieb Duttweiler Institut. Die Unregierbarkeit der Staedte. 250p. (Ger.). 1982. pap. 13.00 (ISBN 0-89192-368-3). Interbk Inc.

Gottlieb Duttweiler Institut. Die Allgemeinpraxis: Das Zentrum der Psychosozialen Grundversorgung? 97p. (Ger.). 1984. pap. 6.00 (ISBN 0-89192-363-2). Interbk Inc.

--Elektronisches Geld. 88p. (Ger. & Fr.). 1983. pap. 30.00 (ISBN 0-89192-367-5). Interbk Inc.

--The Future of Political Institutions as Seen by Different Regional Cultures. 181p. 1982. pap. 12.50 (ISBN 0-89192-364-0). Interbk Inc.

--Kohlendioxid: Eine Gefahr Fuer Unsere Umwelt? 171p. (Orig., Ger.). 1983. pap. 13.00 (ISBN 0-89192-366-7). Interbk Inc.

--Waldschaeden Durch Immissionen? 227p. (Ger.). 1983. pap. 13.00 (ISBN 0-89192-365-9). Interbk Inc.

--Die Zukunft der Mikroelektronik und Mikrotechnik in der Schweiz. 281p. (Orig., Ger.). 1983. pap. 45.00 (ISBN 0-89192-362-4). Interbk Inc.

Gottlieb Duttweiler Institute, ed. Electronic Marketing-Electronic Shopping. 260p. (Eng. & Ger.). 1984. pap. text ed. 30.00. Interbk Inc.

Gottlieb, E. Systematic Tabulation of Indo-European Animal Names. (LD). 1931. pap. 16.00 (ISBN 0-527-00754-4). Kraus Repr.

Gottlieb, Elaine, ed. see Hemley, Cecil.

Gottlieb, Eli J. The Inescapable Truth: A Sound Approach to Genuine Religion. 8.95 (ISBN 0-87306-062-8). Feldheim.

Gottlieb, Fichte J. Addresses to the German Nation. Jones, R. F. & Turnbull, G. H., eds. LC 78-12431. 1979. Repr. of 1922 ed. lib. bdg. 24.75x (ISBN 0-313-21207-4, FIAG). Greenwood.

Gottlieb, G. Early Children's Books & Their Illustration. (Illus.). 1975. 40.00 (ISBN 0-87598-051-1). Pierpont Morgan.

Gottlieb, Gay. The Hungarian Vizsla. 320p. 1985. 36.00 (ISBN 0-947647-09-0, Pub. by Fanciers Supplies). Longwood Pub Group.

Gottlieb, Gilbert & Krasnegor, Norman. Measurement of Audition & Vision in the First Year of Postnatal Life. 496p. 1985. text ed. 57.50 (ISBN 0-89391-130-5). Ablex Pub.

Gottlieb, Gilbert, ed. Studies on the Development of Behavior & the Nervous System, 4 vols. Incl. Vol. 1. Behavioral Embryology. 1973. 68.00 (ISBN 0-12-609301-6); Vol. 2. Aspects of Neurogenesis. 1974. 65.00 (ISBN 0-12-609302-4); Vol. 3. Development of Neural & Behavioral Specificity. 1976. 68.00 (ISBN 0-12-609303-2); Vol. 4. Early Influences. 1978. 49.50 (ISBN 0-12-609304-0). Acad Pr.

Gottlieb, Herbert H. Physics: Lab Experiments & Correlated Computer Aids. 1981. 10.50 (ISBN 0-318-01172-7). Microphys Prog.

Gottlieb, Irving. Solid State High Frequency Power. 1981. text ed. 29.95 (ISBN 0-8359-7048-5). Reston.

--Switching Regulators & Power Supplies with Practical Inverters & Converters. LC 75-41722. (Illus.). 252p. 1976. 13.95 (ISBN 0-8306-6828-4); pap. 6.95 (ISBN 0-8306-5828-9, 828). TAB Bks.

Gottlieb, Irving, jt. auth. see Gottlieb, Isser.

Gottlieb, Irving M. Electric Motors & Control Techniques. (Illus.). 252p. 1982. 16.95 (ISBN 0-8306-2565-8, 1465); pap. 10.25 (ISBN 0-8306-1465-6). TAB Bks.

--Power Control with Solid State Devices. 1985. text ed. 24.95 (ISBN 0-8359-5592-3). Reston.

--Regulated Power Supplies. 3rd ed. LC 81-52157. 424p. 1981. pap. 19.95 (ISBN 0-672-21808-9). Sams.

Gottlieb, Isser & Gottlieb, Irving. Gottlieb's Bakery Cookbook. Gaede, Sarah, ed. 132p. (Orig.). Date not set. pap. 8.95 (ISBN 0-939114-90-9). Gottlieb's Bakery.

Gottlieb, Jack, ed. see Bernstein, Leonard.

Gottlieb, Jacques S., jt. ed. see Tourney, Garfield.

Gottlieb, Jay & Strichart, Stephen S., eds. Developmental Theory & Research in Learning Disabilities. LC 80-25155. (Illus.). 352p. 1981. 16.00 (ISBN 0-8391-1624-1). Pro Ed.

Gottlieb, Karen. Aloe Vera Heals. 1980. 1.95x (ISBN 0-918738-05-9). Cancer Control Soc.

Gottlieb, Laura Moss, ed. see Ginsberg, Elaine.

Gottlieb, Leon. The Best of Gottlieb's Bottom Line: A Practical Profit Guide for Today's Food Service Operator. LC 80-16535. 1980. 19.95 (ISBN 0-86730-229-1). Lebhar Friedman.

--Foodservice-Hospitality Advertising & Promotion. 363p. 1982. text ed. 22.39 scp (ISBN 0-672-97868-7). Bobbs.

Gottlieb, Leon S. Gold-Mining Surgeon: Hugh Huger Toland, M. D., Founder of the University of California, San Francisco, School of Medicine. (Illus.). 108p. 1985. pap. text ed. 8.00x (ISBN 0-89745-063-9). Sunflower U Pr.

Gottlieb, Leonard. Factory Made: How Things Are Manufactured. (Illus.). 144p. (gr. 5 up). 1978. 7.95 (ISBN 0-395-26450-2). HM.

Gottlieb, Linda, jt. auth. see Silver, Joan.

Gottlieb, Linda L., jt. auth. see Colangelo, Cheryl.

Gottlieb, Lois C. Rachel Crothers. (United States Authors Ser.). 1979. lib. bdg. 14.50 (ISBN 0-8057-7222-7, Twayne). G K Hall.

Gottlieb, Louise, jt. auth. see Bailey, David H.

Gottlieb, Malke, jt. auth. see Mlotek, Eleanor G.

Gottlieb, Manuel. The German Peace Settlement & the Berlin Crisis. 275p. 1960. 14.95 (ISBN 0-87855-033-X). Transaction Bks.

--Health Care Financing in Mainland Tanzania. (Foreign & Comparative Studies, Eastern African Ser.: No. 20). 104p. (Orig.). 1975. pap. text ed. 5.50x (ISBN 0-915984-17-2). Syracuse U Foreign Comp.

--Long Swings in Urban Development. (Urban & Regional Studies: No. 4). (Illus.). 360p. 1976. 17.50 (ISBN 0-87014-226-7, Dist. by Columbia U Pr). Natl Bur Econ Res.

--A Theory of Economic Systems (Monographs) LC 83-9995. (Studies in Social Discontinuity). 1984. 49.50 (ISBN 0-12-293780-5). Acad Pr.

Gottlieb, Marvin. Oral Interpretation. (Illus.). 1980. text ed. 27.95x (ISBN 0-07-023838-3). McGraw.

Gottlieb, Marvin, jt. auth. see Cohn, Sidney A.

Gottlieb, Marvin I., et al, eds. The Learning-Disabled Child. (Current Issues in Developmental Pediatrics Ser.). 448p. 1979. 40.50 (ISBN 0-8089-1179-1, 791692). Grune.

Gottlieb, Michael S. & Groopman, Jerome E. Acquired Immune Deficiency Syndrome. LC 84-15409. (UCLA Symposia on Molecular & Cellular Biology, Ser.: Vol. 16). 460p. 1984. 60.00 (ISBN 0-8451-2615-6). A R Liss.

Gottlieb, Milton, et al. Electro-Optical & Acoustic-Optical Scanning & Deflection. (Optical Engineering Ser.: Vol. 3). (Illus.). 208p. 1983. 35.00 (ISBN 0-8247-1811-9). Dekker.

Gottlieb, Moshe R. American Anti-Nazi Resistance, Nineteen Thirty-Three to Nineteen Forty-One: An Historical Analysis. LC 81-8144. 426p. 1982. 49.50x (ISBN 0-87068-889-8). Ktav.

Gottlieb, N. The Production & Properties of Warp-Knitted Fabrics. 100p. 1975. 70.00x (ISBN 0-686-63786-0). State Mutual Bk.

Gottlieb, Naomi. The Welfare Bind. LC 73-17259. 206p. 1974. 26.00x (ISBN 0-231-03762-7). Columbia U Pr.

Gottlieb, Naomi, ed. Alternative Social Services for Women. LC 80-164. 1980. 31.50x (ISBN 0-231-04212-4); pap. 16.00x (ISBN 0-231-04213-2). Columbia U Pr.

Gottlieb, Nathan. A Jewish Child Is Born. LC 60-16833. 1976. pap. 5.95 (ISBN 0-8197-0017-7). Bloch.

Gottlieb, Otto R. Micromolecular Evolution, Systematics, & Ecology: An Essay into a Novel Botanical Discipline. (Illus.). 170p. 1982. 36.00 (ISBN 0-387-11655-9). Springer-Verlag.

Gottlieb, Richard. The Directory of Mail Order Catalogs. 2nd ed. 350p. 1983. 99.00x (ISBN 0-87196-142-3). Facts on File.

Gottlieb, Richard, ed. The Directory of Mail Order Catalogs. 360p. 100.00; pap. 85.00 (ISBN 0-939300-00-1). Grey Hse Pub.

Gottlieb, Richard & Oddo, Sandra, eds. The Solar Energy Directory. LC 83-5498. 376p. 1983. 50.00 (ISBN 0-8242-0680-0). Wilson.

Gottlieb, Richard & Otto, Sandra, eds. Directory of Solar Energy. 320p. 1983. 50.00x (ISBN 0-939300-06-0). Grey Hse Pub.

Gottlieb, Richard M., jt. auth. see Thompson, Waite.

Gottlieb, Robert & Wiley, Peter. America's Saints: The Rise of Mormon Power. LC 84-3304. 1984. 16.95 (ISBN 0-399-12924-3, Putnam). Putnam Pub Group.

Gottlieb, Robert, jt. auth. see Wiley, Peter.

Gottlieb, Robert, jt. ed. see Craft, Robert.

Gottlieb, Robert, ed. see Deighton, Len.

Gottlieb, Robert, ed. see Dickinson, Charles.

Gottlieb, Robert, ed. see Eberstadt, Fernanda.

Gottlieb, Robert, ed. see Grau, Shirley A.

Gottlieb, Robert, ed. see Handl, Irene.

Gottlieb, Robert, ed. see Hyde, Anthony.

Gottlieb, Robert, ed. see Johnson, Denis.

Gottlieb, Robert, ed. see Johnston, Jill.

Gottlieb, Robert, ed. see Krementz, Jill.

Gottlieb, Robert, ed. see Lessing, Doris.

Gottlieb, Robert, ed. see Lukas, J. Anthony.

Gottlieb, Robert, ed. see Morgan, Janet.

Gottlieb, Robert, ed. see Mueller, John.

Gottlieb, Robert, ed. see O'Brien, Tim.

Gottlieb, Robert, ed. see Osborne, Charles.

Gottlieb, Robert, ed. see Portis, Charles.

Gottlieb, Robert, ed. see Thomson, David.

Gottlieb, Robert, ed. see Vanderbilt, Gloria.

Gottlieb, Robert, ed. see Whelan, Richard.

Gottlieb, Robin. Publishing Children's Books in America: An Annotated Bibliography, 1919-1976. 208p. pap. 10.00 (ISBN 0-317-33907-9). Child Bk Coun.

Gottlieb, Sondra. The Wife of... Confessions of an Ambassador's Wife. 160p. 1985. 12.95 (ISBN 0-87491-797-2). Acropolis.
Gottlieb, Steven, photos by. Washington: Portrait of a City. LC 85-4035. (Illus.). 160p. 1985. 38.00 (ISBN 0-87491-771-9). Acropolis.
Gottlieb, Sybil, jt. ed. see Davis, Harold B.
Gottlieb, Vera. Chekhov & the Vaudeville: A Study of Chekhov's One-Act Plays. LC 81-18142. 280p. 1982. 49.50 (ISBN 0-521-24170-7). Cambridge U Pr.
--Chekhov in Performance in Russia & Soviet Russia. (Theatre in Focus Ser.). (Illus.). 90p. 1984. pap. 55.00 incl. 50 slides (ISBN 0-85964-119-8). Chadwyck Healey.
Gottlieb, William. The Golden Age of Jazz. (Quality Paperbacks Ser.). (Illus.). 158p. 1985. pap. 10.95 (ISBN 0-306-80237-6). Da Capo.
Gottlieb, William, ed. see Prevention Magazine Editors.
Gottlieb, William P. Science Facts You Won't Believe. LC 82-20080. (Single Titles Ser.). (Illus.). 128p. (gr. 6 up). 1983. PLB 9.90 (ISBN 0-531-02875-5). Watts.
Gottlieb, Wolf, tr. see Rosen, Moses.
Gottlieb, Yaffa. A Thousand Guests for Shabbos. Zakutinsky, Ruth, ed. (Orig.). (gr. 1-5). 1984. pap. write for info. (ISBN 0-911643-04-4). Aura Pub.
Gottlieb's Bakery. Gottlieb's Bakery: One Hundred Years of Recipes. 132p. 1983. 8.95 (ISBN 0-939114-90-9). Wimmer Bks.
Gottling. Electronics. 792p. 1982. 75.00 (ISBN 0-8247-1840-2). Dekker.
Gottman, John, jt. ed. see Asher, Steven.
Gottman, John, et al. A Couple's Guide to Communication. LC 76-23968. 252p. 1976. pap. text ed. 12.95 (ISBN 0-87822-127-1, 1271). Res Press.
Gottman, John M. Marital Interaction: Experimental Investigations. LC 78-22527. 1979. 39.50 (ISBN 0-12-293150-5). Acad Pr.
--Time Series Analysis: A Comprehensive Introduction for Social Scientists. LC 80-25644. (Illus.). 368p. 1982. 29.95 (ISBN 0-521-23597-9). Cambridge U Pr.
Gottman, John M., jt. auth. see Williams, Esther A.
Gottman, John M., ed. see Glass, Gene V.
Gottman, John W. Wasatch Quartzite. (Illus.). 1979. pap. 3.00 (ISBN 0-915272-23-7). Wasatch Pubs.
Gottmann, Jean. The Coming of the Transactional City. 128p. 1983. pap. 12.00 (ISBN 0-913749-00-1). U MD Geography.
--The Significance of Territory. LC 72-87807. (Page-Barbour Lecture Ser). (Illus.). 169p. 1973. 15.00x (ISBN 0-8139-0413-7). U Pr of Va.
--Virginia in Our Century. LC 68-8541. pap. 160.00 (ISBN 0-317-28909-8, 2020269). Bks Demand UMI.
Gottmann, Jean, ed. Centre & Periphery: Spatial Variation in Politics. LC 79-21564. (Sage Focus Editions: Vol. 19). 1980. 24.00 (ISBN 0-8039-1344-3); pap. 12.00 (ISBN 0-8039-1345-1). Sage.
Gotto & Grosshan. Semisimple Lie Algebras. (Lecture Notes: Vol. 38). 1978. 75.00 (ISBN 0-8247-6744-6). Dekker.
Gotto, A. M., Jr., et al, eds. Atherosclerosis Five: Proceedings of the Fifth International Symposium. (Illus.). 848p. 1980. 57.00 (ISBN 0-387-90473-5). Springer-Verlag.
Gotto, Anthony M., Jr., jt. auth. see DeBakey, Michael E.
Gotto, Antonio M., Jr. & Paoletti, Rodolfo, eds. Atherosclerosis Reviews, Vol. 9. 174p. 1982. text ed. 32.00 (ISBN 0-89004-751-0). Raven.
--Atherosclerosis Reviews, Vol. 11. 264p. 1983. text ed. 57.50 (ISBN 0-89004-910-6). Raven.
Gotto, Antonio M., Jr., jt. ed. see Paoletti, Rodolfo.
Gotts, Edward E. The Home Visitors Kit: Training & Practictioner Materials for Paraprofessionals in Family Settings. Incl. Pt. 1. Home Visitors Notebook. 16.95 (ISBN 0-87705-352-9); Pt. 2. Parents Notebook. 4.95 (ISBN 0-87705-362-6); Pt. 3. Home Visitors Resource Materials. 6.95 (ISBN 0-87705-363-4). 1977. 19.95 set (ISBN 0-87705-364-2). Human Sci Pr.
Gotts, Edward E. & Purnell, Richard F. Improving Home-School Communications. LC 85-61791. (Fastback Ser.: No. 230). 50p. (Orig.). 1985. pap. 0.75 (ISBN 0-87367-230-5). Phi Delta Kappa.
Gottschald, Max. Deutscche Namenkunde: Unsere Familiennamen nach ihrer Entstehung und Bedeutung. 1982. 47.20 (ISBN 3-11-008618-2). De Gruyter.
--Deutsche Namenkunde: Unsere Familiennamen nach ihrer Entstehung und Bedeutung. 4th ed. (Ger). 1971. 44.00x (ISBN 3-11-006467-7). De Gruyter.
Gottschalk. Antique Motortoys. LC 85-50671. (Illus.). 328p. Date not set. 50.00 (ISBN 0-904568-46-6, Pub. by New Cavendish England). Schiffer.
Gottschalk, Alfred. The Chemistry & Biology of Sialic Acids & Related Substances. LC 60-50363. pap. 33.30 (ISBN 0-317-08958-7, 2050783). Bks Demand UMI.
Gottschalk, Ash. Growing up in Blooming Glen, Bk. 1. 1983. 6.75 (ISBN 0-8062-2208-5). Carlton.
Gottschalk, C. M., jt. auth. see Del Bigio, G.
Gottschalk, Carl W., jt. auth. see Earley, Lawrence E.
Gottschalk, Fruma, tr. see Gogol, Nikolay.
Gottschalk, Fruma, tr. see Wiles, Timothy J.
Gottschalk, G. Bacterial Metabolism. LC 78-7880. (Springer Ser. in Microbiology). (Illus.). 1979. 27.50 (ISBN 0-387-90308-9). Springer-Verlag.
Gottschalk, H. B. Heraclides of Pontus. 1980. 39.95x (ISBN 0-19-814021-5). Oxford U Pr.
Gottschalk, Herbert. Lexikon der Mythologie der Eurpaeischen Voelker. (Ger.). 42.00 (ISBN 3-7934-1184-2, M-7246). French & Eur.
Gottschalk, L. A. & Cravey, R. H. Toxicological & Pathological Studies on Psychoactive Drug-Involved Deaths. LC 79-56928. 470p. 1980. text ed. 21.00 (ISBN 0-931890-05-5). Biomed Pubns.
Gottschalk, Lars, et al, eds. Stochastic Processes in Water Resources Engineering. LC 77-78942. 1977. 18.00 (ISBN 0-918334-21-7). WRP.
Gottschalk, Louis. Jean-Paul Marat. 59.95 (ISBN 0-8490-0438-1). Gordon Pr.
--The United States & Lafayette. LC 58-49303. (Augustana College Library Occasional Papers: No. 3). 19p. 1958. pap. 0.50 (ISBN 0-910182-24-8). Augustana Coll.
Gottschalk, Louis & Lach, Donald F. Toward the French Revolution: Europe & America in the Eighteenth-Century World. LC 72-1905. (Illus.). 1973. 37.50x (ISBN 0-684-13170-6). Irvington.
Gottschalk, Louis & Maddox, Margaret. Lafayette in the French Revolution: From the October Days Through the Federation. LC 69-12572. 1973. 25.00x (ISBN 0-226-30547-3). U of Chicago Pr.
Gottschalk, Louis, ed. Pharmacokinetics of Psychoactive Drugs: Further Studies. new ed. LC 79-9430. 140p. 1979. text ed. 35.00 (ISBN 0-89335-092-3). SP Med & Sci Bks.
Gottschalk, Louis & Bill, Shirley, eds. The Letters of Lafayette to Washington, 1777-1799. 2nd rev. ed. LC 76-8599. (Memoirs Ser.: Vol. 115). 1976. 10.00 (ISBN 0-87169-115-9). Am Philos.
Gottschalk, Louis, et al. Use of Personal Documents in History, Anthropology, & Sociology. LC 45-2844. 1945. pap. 5.00 (ISBN 0-527-03282-4). Kraus Repr.
Gottschalk, Louis, et al, eds. Lafayette: A Guide to the Letters, Documents, & Manuscripts in the United States. LC 75-18724. 296p. 1975. 55.00x (ISBN 0-8014-0953-5). Cornell U Pr.
Gottschalk, Louis A. How to Understand & Analyze Your Own Dreams. LC 84-45110. 96p. 1983. pap. 15.00x (ISBN 0-87668-714-1). Aronson.
--How to Understand & Analyze Your Own Dreams. 3rd ed. LC 84-62473. 101p. 1985. pap. 10.00x (ISBN 0-533-01652-5). Art Repro Pr.
--The Tree of Knowledge. LC 85-71701. (Illus.). 125p. (gr. 8 up). 1985. text ed. 12.50x (ISBN 0-318-12116-6). Art Repro Pr.
Gottschalk, Louis A. & Auerbach, Arthur H. Methods of Research in Psychotherapy. LC 65-24563. 672p. 1966. 59.50x (ISBN 0-306-50027-2, Plenum Pr). Plenum Pub.
Gottschalk, Louis A. & Gleser, Goldine C. The Measurement of Psychological States Through the Content Analysis of Verbal Behavior. 1979. Repr. of 1969 ed. 24.50x (ISBN 0-520-03813-4). U of Cal Pr.
Gottschalk, Louis A., ed. The Content Analysis of Verbal Behavior: Further Studies. LC 77-28623. 350p. 1979. 45.00x (ISBN 0-470-26367-9). Halsted Pr.
Gottschalk, Louis A., et al. Manual of Instructions for Using the Gottschalk-Gleser Content Analysis Scales: Anxiety, Hostility, Social Alienation - Personal Disorganization. 1979. Repr. of 1969 ed. 16.00x (ISBN 0-520-03814-2). U of Cal Pr.
Gottschalk, Louis M. A Compendium of Piano Music. List, Eugene, ed. (Illus.). 64p. 1971. pap. 5.95 (ISBN 0-8258-0226-1, 0-4818). Fischer Inc NY.
--The Little Book of Louis Moreau Gottschalk: Seven Previously Unpublished Piano Pieces. new ed. Jackson, Richard & Ratliff, Neil, eds. LC 75-38850. (Americana Collection Music Series: No. 2). (Illus.). 1976. 20.00 (ISBN 0-87104-266-5, Co-Pub by Continuo Music Press Inc.); pap. 12.50 (ISBN 0-87104-262-2, Co-Pub by Continuo Music Press Inc.). NY Pub Lib.
--Notes of a Pianist. (Music Reprint Ser.). 1979. Repr. of 1964 ed. 45.00 (ISBN 0-306-79508-6). Da Capo.
--Piano Music of Louis Moreau Gottschalk: 26 Complete Pieces from Original Editions. Jackson, Richard, ed. LC 73-75872. 320p. (Orig.). 1973. pap. 10.00 (ISBN 0-486-21683-7). Dover.
--Piano Music of Louis Moreau Gottschalk: 26 Complete Pieces from Original Editions. Jackson, Richard, ed. & intro. by. 13.25 (ISBN 0-8446-4746-2). Peter Smith.
--Understanding History: A Primer of Historical Method. 1969. pap. 10.95 (ISBN 0-394-30215-X, KnopfC). Knopf.
Gottschalk, Louis R. Jean Paul Marat: A Study in Radicalism. LC 66-29542. Repr. of 1927 ed. 15.00 (ISBN 0-405-08566-4, Blom Pubns). Ayer Co Pubs.
--Jean Paul Marat: A Study in Radicalism. LC 67-16987. pap. 59.80 (ISBN 0-317-20703-2, 2024117). Bks Demand UMI.
--Lafayette & the Close of the American Revoluation. pap. 118.00 (ISBN 0-317-28090-2, 2024095). Bks Demand UMI.
--Lafayette Comes to America. LC 35-15130. pap. 49.50 (ISBN 0-317-28095-3, 2024093). Bks Demand UMI.
--Lafayette Joins the American Army. LC 37-38848. pap. 95.00 (ISBN 0-317-28092-9, 2024094). Bks Demand UMI.
Gottschalk, Rita. People Season. 1983. 7.50 (ISBN 0-8062-2121-6). Carlton.
Gottschalk, Stephen. The Emergence of Christian Science in American Religious Life. LC 72-85530. 1974. 18.95 (ISBN 0-520-02308-0); pap. 4.95 (ISBN 0-520-03718-9, CAL 398). U of Cal Pr.
Gottschalk, W. & Wolff, G. Induced Mutations in Plant Breeding. (Monographs on Theoretical & Applied Genetics Ser.: Vol. 7). (Illus.). 250p. 1983. 44.50 (ISBN 0-387-12184-6). Springer-Verlag.
Gottschalk, W., jt. auth. see Taylor, Ronald J.
Gottschalk, W. H. & Hedlund, G. A. Topological Dynamics. LC 55-12710. (Colloquium Pbns. Ser.: Vol. 36). 167p. 1982. pap. 29.00 (ISBN 0-8218-1036-7, COLL-36). Am Math.
Gottschall, Edward M. Graphic Communication Eighties' (Illus.). 200p. 1981. 33.95 (ISBN 0-13-363382-9). P-H.
Gottschang, Jack L. A Guide to the Mammals of Ohio. LC 80-27661. (Illus.). 188p. 1981. 37.50 (ISBN 0-8142-0242-X). Ohio St U Pr.
Gottsche, K. M., et al. Synopsis Hepaticarum. 1967. Repr. of 1844 ed. 56.00 (ISBN 3-7682-0516-9). Lubrecht & Cramer.
Gottsched, Johann C. Ausgewaehlte Werke. Mitchell, P. M., ed. Incl. Vol. 1. Gedichte und Gedichtuebertragungen. vi, 533p. 1968. 62.50x (ISBN 3-11-000351-1); Vol. 2. Saemtliche Dramen. iv, 481p. 1970. 72.50x (ISBN 3-11-000363-5); Vol. 3. Saemtliche Dramenuebertragungen. vi, 393p. 1970. 62.50x (ISBN 3-11-000364-3); Vol. 4. 481p. 1968. 60.00x (ISBN 3-11-000353-8). (Ausgaben Deutscher Literatur Des Fuenfzehnten Bis Achtzehnten Jahrhunderts). (Ger.). De Gruyter.
--Ausgewahlte Werke, Vol. 2. 164p. (Ger.). 1983. Set. 44.80 (ISBN 3-11-007934-8). De Gruyter.
--Johann Christoph Gottsched Ausgewahlte Werke: Versuch Einer Critischen Dichtkunst, Kommentar, Vol. 6. Mitchell, P. M., ed. (Ausgaben Deutscher Literature Des XV. Bis XVIII. Jahrhunderts: Pt. 4). 1978. 91.20x (ISBN 3-11-007581-4). De Gruyter.
Gottschling, E. see Siegel, C. L.
Gottsegen, Abby J., jt. ed. see Gottsegen, Gloria B.
Gottsegen, Gloria B., ed. Group Behavior: A Guide to Information Sources. LC 79-63744. (Psychology Information Guide Ser.: Vol. 2). 1979. 60.00x (ISBN 0-8103-1439-8). Gale.
Gottsegen, Gloria B. & Gottsegen, Abby J., eds. Humanistic Psychology: A Guide to Information Sources. (Psychology Information Guide Ser.: Vol. 6). 175p. 1980. 60.00x (ISBN 0-8103-1462-2). Gale.
Gottsegen, Katherine. Cooking Is an Act of Love. (Illus.). 165p. (Orig.). 1983. 9.95 (ISBN 0-686-38740-6). Buckminster Pr.
Gottselig, Cheryl. Probate Guide for Alberta. 2nd ed. 99p. 1983. 9.95 (ISBN 0-88908-226-X); Forms 12.95 (ISBN 0-88908-224-3). Self Counsel Pr.
--Wills for Alberta. 4th ed. 106p. 1982. 5.50 (ISBN 0-88908-222-7). Self Counsel Pr.
Gottshall, Franklin H. How to Make Colonial Furniture. LC 79-20825. 1980. 17.95 (ISBN 0-02-544840-4). Macmillan.
--Masterpiece Furniture Making. LC 79-12. (Illus.). 224p. 1979. 24.95 (ISBN 0-8117-0974-4). Stackpole.
--Provincial Furniture, Design & Construction. (Illus.). 1983. 9.98 (ISBN 0-517-54930-1). Crown.
--Wood Carving & Whittling for Everyone. LC 77-23224. (Illus.). 1980. pap. 9.95 (ISBN 0-684-16742-5, SL 921, ScribT). Scribner.
Gottsleben, Robert & Tyack, Dorothy. Golden Gate Reading & Spelling Series. Incl. Teacher's Manual. pap. text ed. 3.50x (ISBN 0-89106-009-X, 1901); Reader 1. pap. text ed. 5.00x (ISBN 0-89106-001-4, 1911); Workbook 1. pap. text ed. 2.90x (ISBN 0-89106-002-2, 1921); Reader 2. pap. text ed. 6.00x (ISBN 0-89106-003-0, 1912); Workbook 2. pap. text ed. 3.95x (ISBN 0-89106-004-9, 1922); Reader 3. pap. text ed. 4.00x (ISBN 0-89106-005-7, 1913); Workbook 3. pap. text ed. 2.80x (ISBN 0-89106-006-5, 1923); Reader 4. pap. text ed. 4.50x (ISBN 0-89106-007-3, 1914); Workbook 4. pap. text ed. 3.95x (ISBN 0-89106-008-1, 1924). (Illus.). 1979. Set. pap. text ed. 32.75 (ISBN 0-89106-013-8, 1909). Consulting Psychol.
Gottwald, Norman K. The Hebrew Bible-A Socio-Literary Introduction. LC 84-48719. (Illus.). 736p. 1985. 34.95 (ISBN 0-8006-0853-4, 1-1853); pap. 19.95 (ISBN 0-8006-1853-X, 1-853). Fortress.
--The Tribes of Yahweh: A Sociology of the Religion of Liberated Israel, 1250-1050 B.C. LC 78-24333. 944p. (Orig.). 1979. pap. 19.95 (ISBN 0-88344-499-2). Orbis Bks.
Gottwald, Norman K., ed. The Bible & Liberation: Politics & Social Hermeneutics. LC 82-22242. 624p. (Orig.). 1983. 35.00 (ISBN 0-88344-043-1); pap. 18.95 (ISBN 0-88344-044-X). Orbis Bks.
Gottwald, Paul, tr. see Luthi, Max.
Gottwald, Sigrun R. Der Mutige Narr im Dramatischen Werk Friedrich Durrenmatts. Strelka, ed. LC 83-48647. (New Yorker Studien zur Neueren Deutschen Literaturgeschichte Ser.: Vol. 3). 344p. (Orig., Ger.). 1983. pap. text ed. 32.65 (ISBN 0-8204-0027-0). P Lang Pubs.
Gottzman, C. F. Cryogenic Processes & Equipment in Energy Systems. 200p. 1980. 40.00 (ISBN 0-686-69847-9, H00164). ASME.
Gotwald, Frederick G. Offertory Prayers. 31p. 1976. pap. 2.75 (ISBN 0-89536-171-X). CSS of Ohio.
Gotwald, Luther A., Jr. Ushers & Offerings. 1973. 12.75 (ISBN 0-89536-241-4). CSS of Ohio.
Gotwald, William & Golden, Gale. Human Sexuality: Biological & Behavioral Foundations. 1981. text ed. write for info. (ISBN 0-02-344170-4). Macmillan.
Gotwald, William K. Ecclesiastical Censure at the End of the Fifteenth Century. LC 78-64124. (Johns Hopkins University. Studies in the Social Sciences. Forty-Fifth Ser. 1927: 3). Repr. of 1927 ed. 13.50 (ISBN 0-404-61238-5). AMS Pr.
Gotwals, Vernon, ed. Haydn: Two Contemporary Portraits. Orig. Title: Joseph Haydn: Eighteenth-Century Gentleman & Genius. 1963. 21.50x (ISBN 0-299-02791-0); pap. 7.95x (ISBN 0-299-02794-5). U of Wis Pr.
Gotz, Adriani. Edgar Degas. LC 84-24402. (Illus.). 269p. 1985. 75.00 (ISBN 0-89659-530-7). Abbeville Pr.
Gotz, D., ed. The Major Histocompatibility System in Man & Animals. 1977. 46.00 (ISBN 0-387-08097-X). Springer-Verlag.
Gotz, Ignacio L. No Schools. 198p. 1971. pap. text ed. 10.95x (ISBN 0-8422-0163-7). Irvington.
Gotzche, Anne. The Fluoride Question: Panacea or Poison? 176p. 7.95 (ISBN 0-318-15657-1). Natl Health Fed.
Gotze, H. Black & White Negatives: Exposure & Development. (Photo Tips Ser.). (Illus.). 96p. (Orig.). 1980. pap. 4.95 (ISBN 0-85242-709-3, Fountain Press). Morgan.
--Prints: Processing & Enlarging in Black & White. (Photo Tips Ser.). (Illus.). 1980. pap. 4.95 (ISBN 0-85242-632-1). Morgan.
Gotzen, L., jt. ed. see Tscherne, H.
Gotzkowsky, Bodo, ed. see Adelphus, Johannes.
Gotzsche, Henning. Electrocardiographic Atlas. (Illus.). 200p. 1977. pap. 19.95 (ISBN 0-8151-3825-3). Year Bk Med.
Goubert, Pierre. The Ancien Regime: French Society 1600-1750. Cox, Steve, tr. from Fr. 1974. pap. 6.95xi (ISBN 0-06-131822-1, TB1822, Torch). Har-Row.
--Clio Parmi les Hommes: Recueil D'articles. (Civilisations et Societes: No. 52). (Fr.). 1976. pap. text ed. 17.60x (ISBN 90-2797-833-6). Mouton.
--Louis the Fourteenth & the Twenty Million Frenchmen. 352p. 1972. pap. 3.95 (ISBN 0-394-71751-1, V751, Vin). Random.
Goubet, jt. auth. see Aubert.
Gouchou, Henry J. Le Dictionnaire Astrologique. 670p. (Fr.). 1975. 67.50 (ISBN 0-686-57307-2, M-6284). French & Eur.
Goudaillier, Jean-Pierre. Phonologie Fonctionelle et Phonetique Experimentale. (Hamburger Phonetische Beitrage Ser.: No. 36). 476p. (Orig.). 1981. pap. text ed. 38.00x (ISBN 3-87118-467-5, Pub. by Helmut Buske Verlag Hamburg). Benjamins North Am.
Goudar, Ange, pseud. Le Brigandage de la Musique Italienne. LC 76-43941. (Music & Theatre in France in the 17th & 18th Centuries). Repr. of 1777 ed. 19.00 (ISBN 0-404-60196-0). AMS Pr.
Goudard, Sr. M. Lucien. Etude Sur les Epistres Morales D'Honore D'Urfe. LC 70-94204. (Catholic University of America Studies in Romance Languages & Literatures Ser: No. 8). (Fr). Repr. of 1933 ed. 21.00 (ISBN 0-404-50308-X). AMS Pr.
Goudas, C. L., jt. auth. see Kopal, Z.
Goudas, C. L. & Pande, G. C., eds. Computers: Applications in Industry & Management. 450p. 1980. 59.75 (ISBN 0-444-86053-3, North Holland). Elsevier.
Goudas, C. L., ed. see International Conference on Selenodesy & Lunar Topograph, 2nd, University of Manchester, England May 30-June 4, 1966.
Goude, Jean-Paul & Hayes, Harold. Jungle Fever. (Illus.). 144p. 1982. 32.50 (ISBN 0-937950-01-7). Xavier-Moreau.
Goudey, Alice E. Here Come the Bears. LC 54-5924. (Illus.). 96p. (gr. 1-5). 1954. 5.95 (ISBN 0-684-13365-2, ScribJ). Scribner.
Goudge, Eileen. Afraid to Love. (Seniors Ser.: No. 4). (Orig.). (gr. k-12). 1984. pap. 2.25 (ISBN 0-440-90092-1, LFL). Dell.
--Bad Girl. (Senior Ser.: No. 11). (Orig.). (gr. k-12). 1985. pap. 2.25 (ISBN 0-440-90467-6, LFL). Dell.
--Before It's Too Late. (Senior Ser.: No. 5). (Orig.). (gr. k-12). 1985. pap. 2.25 (ISBN 0-440-90542-7, LFL). Dell.
--Don't Say Goodbye. (Senior Ser.: No. 12). (Orig.). (gr. k-6). 1985. pap. 2.25 (ISBN 0-440-92108-2, LFL). Dell.
--Forbidden Kisses. (Senior Ser.: No. 8). (gr. k-12). 1985. pap. 2.25 (ISBN 0-440-92674-2, LFL). Dell.
--Hands Off, He's Mine. (Senior Ser.: No. 7). (Orig.). (gr. 5-12). 1985. pap. 2.25 (ISBN 0-440-93359-5, LFL). Dell.
--Looking for Love. (Senior Ser.: No. 14). (Orig.). 1986. pap. 2.25 (ISBN 0-440-94730-8, LFL). Dell.
--Presenting Superhunk. (Senior Ser.: No. 10). (Orig.). (gr. k-12). 1985. pap. 2.25 (ISBN 0-440-97172-1, LFL). Dell.

--Smart Enough to Know. (Seniors Ser.: No. 2). (Orig.). (gr. 7-12). 1984. pap. 2.25 (ISBN 0-440-98168-9, LFL). Dell.
--Too Hot to Handle. (Seniors Ser.: No. 6). 192p. (gr. 7 up). pap. 2.25 (ISBN 0-440-98812-8, YB). Dell.
--Too Much Too Soon. (Senior Ser.: No. 1). 160p. (gr. 7-12). 1984. pap. 2.25 (ISBN 0-440-98974-4). Dell.
--A Touch of Ginger. (Senior Ser.: No. 9). (Orig.). (gr. 7-12). 1985. pap. 2.25 (ISBN 0-440-98816-0, LFL). Dell.
--Winner All the Way. (Senior Ser.: No. 3). 160p. (Orig.). (gr. 7-12). 1984. pap. 2.25 (ISBN 0-440-99480-2, LFL). Dell.
Goudge, Elizabeth. The Bird in the Tree. 339p. 1976. lib. bdg. 17.95x (ISBN 0-89966-099-1). Buccaneer Bks.
--The Blue Hills. 288p. 1976. lib. bdg. 16.95x (ISBN 0-89966-100-9). Buccaneer Bks.
--The Castle on the Hill. 379p. 1983. Repr. lib. bdg. 15.95x (ISBN 0-89966-101-7). Buccaneer Bks.
--A City of the Bells. 380p. 1979. Repr. lib. bdg. 15.95x (ISBN 0-89966-102-5). Buccaneer Bks.
--The Golden Skylark. 337p. 1976. lib. bdg. 17.95x (ISBN 0-89966-103-3). Buccaneer Bks.
--Heart of the Family. 317p. 1979. Repr. lib. bdg. 17.95x (ISBN 0-89966-104-1). Buccaneer Bks.
--Island Magic. 352p. 1979. Repr. lib. bdg. 16.95x (ISBN 0-89966-105-X). Buccaneer Bks.
--Linnets & Valerians. (YA) (gr. 7 up). 1978. pap. 1.75 (ISBN 0-380-01934-5, 37838). Avon.
--Little White Horse. (YA) 1978. pap. 1.95 (ISBN 0-380-01875-6, 52050). Avon.
--The Middle Window. 302p. 1976. lib. bdg. 19.95x (ISBN 0-89966-106-8). Buccaneer Bks.
--Pedlar's Pack. facs. ed. LC 78-132116. (Short Story Index Reprint Ser). 1937. 16.00 (ISBN 0-8369-3673-6). Ayer Co Pubs.
--Pilgrim's Inn. Large Print ed. LC 83-18023. 612p. 1984. Repr. of 1948 ed. 16.95 (ISBN 0-89621-502-4). Thorndike Pr.
--The Rosemary Tree. 381p. 1979. Repr. lib. bdg. 16.95x (ISBN 0-89966-107-6). Buccaneer Bks.
--Smoky-House. 391p. 1983. Repr. lib. bdg. 17.95x (ISBN 0-89966-108-4). Buccaneer Bks.
--Towers in the Midst. 386p. 1979. Repr. lib. bdg. 16.95x (ISBN 0-89966-109-2). Buccaneer Bks.
Goudie, A. & Wilkinson, J. The Warm Desert Environment. LC 76-9731. (Topics in Geography Ser). (Illus.). 1977. 16.95 (ISBN 0-521-21330-4); pap. 8.95 o. p. (ISBN 0-521-29105-4); slides 27.95x (ISBN 0-521-21912-4). Cambridge U Pr.
Goudie, A. S. & Pye, K., eds. Chemical Sediments & Geomorphology. 1983. 58.00 (ISBN 0-12-293480-6). Acad Pr.
Goudie, Andrew. Environmental Change. 2nd ed. (Contemporary Problems in Geography Ser.). (Illus.). 1983. 34.95x (ISBN 0-19-874132-4); pap. 12.50x (ISBN 0-19-874135-9). Oxford U Pr.
--The Human Impact: Man's Role in Environmental Change. (Illus.). 328p. 1982. pap. text ed. 11.95x (ISBN 0-262-57058-0). MIT Pr.
--The Nature of the Environment: An Advanced Physical Geography. 352p. 1985. 39.95x (ISBN 0-631-13143-4); pap. 12.95x (ISBN 0-631-13144-2). Basil Blackwell.
Goudie, Andrew & Wilkinson, John. The Warm Desert Environment. LC 76-9731. (Cambridge Topics in Geography Ser.). pap. 24.00 (ISBN 0-317-26407-9, 2024463). Bks Demand UMI.
Goudie, Andrew, ed. Geomorphological Techniques. (Illus.). 395p. 1981. text ed. 60.00x (ISBN 0-04-551042-3); pap. text ed. 29.95x (ISBN 0-04-551043-1). Allen Unwin.
Goudimel. Claude Goudimel OEuvres Completes 1964-1983, Pts. 1-7. Pidoux, Pierre & Dittmer, Luther, eds. (Gesamtausgaben - Collected Works Ser.: No. 3). (Fr., Ger. & Eng.). Pt. 1, 250p. lib. bdg. 30.00 (ISBN 0-912024-45-3); Pt. 2, 250p. lib. bdg. 30.00 (ISBN 0-912024-46-1); Pt. 3, 250p. lib. bdg. 30.00 (ISBN 0-912024-47-X); Pt. 4, 250p. lib. bdg. 30.00 (ISBN 0-912024-48-8); Pt. 5, 250p. lib. bdg. 30.00 (ISBN 0-912024-49-6); Pt. 6, 250p. lib. bdg. 30.00 (ISBN 0-912024-50-X); Pt. 7, 250p. lib. bdg. 30.00 (ISBN 0-912024-51-8). Inst Mediaeval Mus.
--Claude Goudimel OEuvres Completes 1964-1983, Pts. 8-14. Pidoux, Pierre & Dittmer, Luther, eds. (Gesamtausgaben - Collected Works Ser.: No. 3). (Fr., Ger. & Eng.). Pt. 8, 250p. lib. bdg. 30.00 (ISBN 0-912024-52-6); Pt. 9, 250p. lib. bdg. 30.00 (ISBN 0-912024-53-4); Pt. 10, 350p. lib. bdg. 60.00 (ISBN 0-912024-54-2); Pt. 11, 250p. lib. bdg. 30.00 (ISBN 0-912024-55-0); Pt. 12, 350p. lib. bdg. 60.00 (ISBN 0-912024-56-9); Pt. 13, 350p. lib. bdg. 60.00 (ISBN 0-912024-57-7); Pt. 14, 350p. lib. bdg. 60.00 (ISBN 0-912024-58-5). Inst Mediaeval Mus.
Goudimel, Claude see Expert, Henry.
Goudinoff, Peter, jt. auth. see Tobias, Sheila.
Goudis, C. The Orion Complex. 1982. 59.50 (ISBN 90-277-1298-0, Pub. by Reidel Holland). Kluwer Academic.
Goudiss, Maria H. WordStar in Everyday English. 157p. 1983. pap. 9.95 (ISBN 0-8159-7221-0). Devin.
Goudket, Michael. Audiovisual Primer. rev. ed. LC 72-93755. (Illus.). 77p. 1974. pap. text ed. 3.50x (ISBN 0-8077-2437-8). Tchrs Coll.
Goudoever, H. D. von see Van Goudoever, H. D.
Goudoever, V. P. van see Van Goudoever, A. P.
Goudriaan, J. Crop Micrometeorology: A Simulation Study. (Simulation Monographs). 1977. pap. 16.50 (ISBN 90-220-0614-X, PDC24, PUDOC). Unipub.
Goudriaan, J., jt. auth. see De Wit, C. T.
Goudriaan, J., jt. auth. see Kozai, T.
Goudriaan, T., tr. Kasyapa's Book of Wisdom: A Ritual Handbook of the Vaikhanasas. (Disputationes Rheno-Trajectinae Ser.: No. 10). 1965. pap. text ed. 37.60 (ISBN 90-2790-036-1). Mouton.
Goudriaan, Teun. Maya Divine & Human. 1978. 19.95 (ISBN 0-89684-040-9, Pub. by Motilal Banarsidass India). Orient Bk Dist.
--Maya, Divine & Human. 1979. 26.00x (ISBN 0-685-95754-3). South Asia Bks.
Goudsblom, Johan. Nihilism & Culture. 213p. 1980. 27.50x (ISBN 0-8476-6766-9). Rowman.
--Sociology in the Balance: A Critical Essay. LC 77-4368. 232p. 1977. 26.50x (ISBN 0-231-04290-6). Columbia U Pr.
Goudsmit, Samuel A. Alsos. (History of Modern Physics 1800-1950 Ser.: Vol. 1). (Illus.). 1983. Repr. of 1947 ed. 28.00x (ISBN 0-938228-09-9). Tomash Pubs.
Goudsouzian, Nishan & Karamanian, Agop. Physiology for the Anesthesiologist. 2nd ed. (Illus.). 432p. 1984. 39.00 (ISBN 0-8385-7857-8). ACC.
Goudy, Frederic W. Alphabet & Elements of Lettering. rev. ed. 13.00 (ISBN 0-8446-2145-5). Peter Smith.
--Goudy's Type Designs: His Story & Specimens. 2nd ed. LC 77-14886. (Treasures of Typography Ser: Vol. II). (Illus.). 1978. 14.95 (ISBN 0-918142-05-9); pap. 9.95 (ISBN 0-918142-04-0). Myriade.
--Typologia: Studies in Type Design & Type Making with Comments on the Invention of Typography, the First Types, Legibility & Fine Printing. 1978. 28.50x (ISBN 0-520-03308-6); pap. 3.95 (ISBN 0-520-03278-0, CAL 334). U of Cal Pr.
Goudy, Frederick W. Alphabet & Elements of Lettering. (Illus.). 1922. pap. 4.95 (ISBN 0-486-20792-7). Dover.
Goudy, Henry, ed. see Muirhead, James.
Goudy, Linda M., ed. Hart's Petroleum Professionals, 1985. 2nd ed. 568p. 1985. pap. text ed. 40.00 (ISBN 0-912553-06-5). Hart Pubns.
Goudy, William J., et al. Community: References from Selected Sociology & Other Social Science Journals, Nos. 1280-1282. 1977. 12.50 (ISBN 0-686-19692-9). CPL Biblios.
Goudzwaard, B. Aid for the Overdeveloped West. 1975. pap. 3.50 (ISBN 0-88906-100-9). Wedge Pub.
Goudzwaard, Bob. Capitalism & Progress: A Diagnosis of Western Society. LC 79-20818. 1979. pap. 9.95 (ISBN 0-8028-1809-9). Eerdmans.
--Capitalism & Progress: A Diagnosis of Western Society. 1979. pap. 9.95 (ISBN 0-88906-106-8). Radix Bks.
--Idols of Our Time. Vennen, Mark V., tr. from Dutch. LC 84-652. 120p. (Orig.). 1984. pap. 4.95 (ISBN 0-87784-970-6). Inter-Varsity.
Goudzwaard, Maurice B., jt. ed. see Weston, J. Fred.
Gouedy, Terrence. Everything You Never Wanted to Know about Yourself, or the Cancer Syndrome. (Illus.). 64p. 1980. 12.50 (ISBN 0-682-49640-5). Exposition Pr FL.
Gouffe, Jules. The Royal Cookery Book. (Illus.). 1977. Repr. of 1869 ed. 21.00x (ISBN 0-85409-809-7). Charles River Bks.
Gouffe, Marie A. Treasures Beyond the Snows. LC 77-95392. Orig. Title: Jigme. (Illus.). (gr. 3-9). 1970. 3.75 (ISBN 0-8356-0026-2, Quest). Theos Pub Hse.
Gougaud, Dom L. Gaelic Pioneers of Christianity: The Work & Influence of Irish Monks & Saints in Continental Europe. Collins, Victor, tr. from Fr. 166p. 1983. lib. bdg. 85.00 (ISBN 0-89984-223-2). Century Bookbindery.
Gougaud, Henri & Gouvion, Colette. Egypt Observed. (Observed Ser.). (Illus.). 1979. 24.95 (ISBN 0-19-520132-9). Oxford U Pr.
Gouge, Eileen. Kiss & Make Up. (Senior Ser.: No. 13). (Orig.). (gr. k-12). 1986. pap. 2.25 (ISBN 0-440-94514-3, LFL). Dell.
Gouge, Gerald, jt. auth. see Boserup, Dan.
Gouge, William. Commentary on Hebrews, 3 vols. in 1. LC 79-2541. (Kregel Limited Edition Library). 1980. 34.50 (ISBN 0-8254-2725-8). Kregel.
--Of Domesticall Duties. LC 76-57385. (English Experience Ser.: No. 803). 1977. Repr. of 1622 ed. lib. bdg. 66.00 (ISBN 90-221-0803-1). Walter J Johnson.
Gouge, William M. Curse of Paper-Money & Banking. LC 68-28633. 1968. Repr. of 1833 ed. lib. bdg. 22.50x (ISBN 0-8371-0452-1, GOCP). Greenwood.
--Fiscal History of Texas. LC 68-18226. Repr. of 1852 ed. 35.00x (ISBN 0-678-00364-5). Kelley.
--Fiscal History of Texas: An Account of Its Revenues, Debts, & Currency from the Commencement of the Revolution in 1834 to 1851-52 with Remarks on American Debts. 1969. Repr. of 1852 ed. 20.00 (ISBN 0-8337-1397-3). B Franklin.
--Short History of Paper Money & Banking in the United States. LC 65-26366. Repr. of 1833 ed. 37.50x (ISBN 0-678-00307-6). Kelley.
Gougenheim, jt. auth. see Mauger.
Gougeon, Helen. Helen Gougeon's Original Canadian Cookbook. rev. ed. LC 75-30482. Orig. Title: Good Food. (Illus.). 1975. pap. 5.95 (ISBN 0-00-211598-0). Tundra Bks.
Gougeon, M. & Knog, T. Evolution of Modern Sailboat Design. 1974. pap. 6.95 (ISBN 0-02-001400-7, Collier). Macmillan.
Gough. Problems of Solar & Stellar Oscillations. 1983. lib. bdg. 84.50 (ISBN 90-277-1554-8, Pub. by Reidel Holland). Kluwer Academic.
Gough, Aidan. Standards Relating to Non-Criminal Misbehavior. LC 76-14394. (IJA-ABA Juvenile Justice Standards Project Ser.). 96p. 1982. prof ref 17.50 (ISBN 0-88410-232-7); pap. 10.00 (ISBN 0-88410-832-5). Ballinger Pub.
Gough, Aidan, jt. ed. see Teitelbaum, Lee E.
Gough, Barry. Gold Rush! Focus on Canadian History. (gr. 6-8). PLB 8.40 (ISBN 0-317-06516-5). Watts.
Gough, Barry M. Gunboat Frontier: British Maritime Authority & Northwest Coast Indians 1846-1890. (Pacific Maritime Studies Ser.: Vol. 4). (Illus.). 256p. 1984. 27.95 (ISBN 0-7748-0175-1, Pub. by U of BC). Intl Spec Bk.
Gough, Barry M., ed. Canada. (Modern Nations in Historical Perspective Ser.). (Illus.). 192p. 1975. (Spec); pap. 3.25 (ISBN 0-13-112771-3, Spec). P-H.
--In Search of the Visible Past: History Lectures at Wilfrid Laurier University 1973-1974. v, 89p. 1975. text ed. 7.50x (ISBN 0-88920-019-X, Pub. by Wilfrid Laurier U Pr Canada). Humanities.
--To the Pacific & Arctic with Beechey: The Journal of Lieutenant George Peard of HMS Blossom, 1825-1828. 272p. 1973. 55.00x (ISBN 0-686-79463-X, Pub. by Hakluyt Soc England). State Mutual Bk.
Gough, C. & Innes, A. The Sikhs & the Sikh Wars. 254p. 1984. text ed. 24.50x (ISBN 0-391-03263-1, Pub. by Natl Bk Shop India). Humanities.
Gough, Chet & Srikantaiah, Taverekere. Systems Analysis in Libraries: A Question & Answer Approach. (Illus.). 1978. 16.00 (ISBN 0-208-01753-4, Linnet). Shoe String.
Gough, D. The Control of Diarrhoea in Clinical Practice. (Royal Society of Medicine International Congress & Symposium Ser.). 48p. 1979. pap. 16.00 (ISBN 0-8089-1170-8, 791705). Grune.
Gough, D., ed. New Advances in the Treatment of Candida Vaginitis. (Royal Society of Medicine Internationl Congress & Symposium Ser.: No. 7). 48p. 1979. pap. 16.00 (ISBN 0-8089-1188-0, 791706). Grune.
Gough, Edward. The Philosophy of the Upanishads. 268p. 1979. Repr. of 1882 ed. 19.95 (ISBN 0-89684-158-8). Orient Bk Dist.
Gough, H. A Glossary of Terms Used in Heraldry. 59.95 (ISBN 0-8490-0239-7). Gordon Pr.
Gough, H., jt. auth. see Collins, M. E.
Gough, Henry, ed. General Index to the Publications of the Parker Society. 1855. 61.00 (ISBN 0-384-19400-1). Johnson Repr.
Gough, Hubert. Soldiering On. 9.95 (ISBN 0-8315-0010-7). Speller.
Gough, Hugh. Europe, Seventeen Sixty-Three to Nineteen Seventy. (Illus.). 288p. (Orig.). (gr. 7-12). 1976. pap. text ed. 11.95x (ISBN 0-582-22053-X). Longman.
Gough, Ian. The Political Economy of the Welfare State. (Critical Texts in Social Work & the Welfare State Ser.). 1979. pap. text ed. 13.50x (ISBN 0-333-21599-0). Humanities.
Gough, Irene. Golden Lamb. LC 68-20643. (Foreign Lands Bks.). (gr. 3-6). 1968. PLB 3.95g (ISBN 0-8225-0360-3). Lerner Pubns.
--Here in the Grass. 10.00x (ISBN 0-392-03212-0, ABC). Sportshelf.
Gough, J. W., ed. see Locke, John.
Gough, Jamie & MacNair, Mike. Gay Liberation in the Eighties. 160p. (Orig.). 1985. pap. 7.50 (ISBN 0-86104-685-4, Pub. by Pluto Pr). Longwood Pub Group.
Gough, Jeff. Unseen Faces. LC 79-50224. (Illus.). 1979. pap. 3.50 (ISBN 0-89395-019-X). Cal Living Bks.
Gough, John. Into Print. 1979. 16.95 (ISBN 0-7134-0739-5, Pub. by Batsford England). David & Charles.
Gough, John W. Mines of Mendip. LC 67-105992. (Illus.). Repr. of 1930 ed. 27.50x (ISBN 0-678-05688-9). Kelley.
--The Social Contract: A Critical Study of Its Development. 2nd ed. LC 78-6099. 1978. Repr. of 1957 ed. lib. bdg. 24.00x (ISBN 0-313-20494-2, GOSO). Greenwood.
Gough, Kathleen. Rural Society in Southeast India. (Cambridge Studies in Social Anthropology: No. 38). (Illus.). 512p. 1982. 52.50 (ISBN 0-521-23889-7). Cambridge U Pr.
--Ten Times More Beautiful: The Rebuilding of Vietnam. LC 78-14890. 277p. 1978. 12.50 (ISBN 0-85345-464-7). Monthly Rev.
Gough, Kathleen & Sharma, Hari P., eds. Imperialism & Revolution in South Asia. LC 78-14890. (Illus.). 480p. 1973. pap. 6.95 (ISBN 0-85345-305-5). Monthly Rev.
Gough, Kathleen, jt. ed. see Schneider, David M.
Gough, Malcolm & Gear, Michael. Plain X-Ray in the Diagnosis of the Acute Abdomen. (Illus.). 194p. 1971. 9.50 (ISBN 0-8016-2019-8, B 2019-8, Blackwell). Mosby.
Gough, Pauline. Sexism: New Issue in American Education. LC 76-16876. (Fastback Ser.: No.81). (Orig.). 1976. pap. 0.75 (ISBN 0-87367-081-7). Phi Delta Kappa.
Gough, Richard. The History of Myddle. 1979. Repr. text ed. 25.50x (ISBN 0-686-58501-1). Humanities.
--The History of Myddle. 336p. 1981. pap. 5.95 (ISBN 0-14-005841-9). Penguin.
--The History of Myddle. Razzell, Peter, ed. 216p. 1979. 16.50 (ISBN 0-904573-14-1). Caliban Bks.
--History of Myddle, 17th Century England. 35.00 (ISBN 0-87556-105-5). Saifer.
--Human Nature Displayed in the History of Myddle. 1983. 90.00x (ISBN 0-900000-25-2, Pub. by Centaur Pr England). State Mutual Bk.
Gough, Richard, jt. auth. see Nichols, John.
Gough, T. J. & Taylor, T. W. The Building Society: Price Cartel. (Hobart Paper Ser.: No. 83). (Orig.). 1979. technical 4.75 (ISBN 0-255-36124-6). Transatlantic.
Gough, Terrence J, intro. by. The History of the Joint Chiefs of Staff: The Joint Chiefs of Staff & National Policy, 4 vols. Incl. Vol. 1. 1945-1947. Schnabel, James P; Vol. 2. 1947-1949. Condit, Kenneth W; Vol. 3. The Korean War, 2 pts. Schnabel, James F. & Watson, Robert J. Vol. 4, 1950-1952. 49.00 (ISBN 0-686-31793-9). Set. 245.00 (ISBN 0-89453-148-4); per vol. 49.00 (ISBN 0-686-86303-8). M Glazier.
Gough, Terry. Around the Branch Lines: Southern, Vol. 1. 96p. 30.00x (ISBN 0-86093-159-5, Pub. by ORPC Ltd UK). State Mutual Bk.
--Cross-Country Routes of the Southern Railway. 128p. 30.00x (ISBN 0-86093-267-2, Pub. by ORPC Ltd UK). State Mutual Bk.
--The Southern West of Salisbury. 96p. 35.00x (ISBN 0-86093-341-5, Pub. by ORPC Ltd UK). State Mutual Bk.
Gough, Terry A. The Southern in Kent & Sussex. 96p. 39.00x (ISBN 0-86093-273-7, Pub. by ORPC Ltd UK). State Mutual Bk.
Gough, Vera & Grier, B. R. Planned Speaking & Your Career. 1967. pap. 4.20 (ISBN 0-08-012588-3). Pergamon.
Gough, W. & Richards, J. P. Vibrations & Waves. 278p. 1983. 64.95 (ISBN 0-470-27446-8). Halsted Pr.
Gough, W. James, ed. see Seiden, Rudolph.
Gougher, Ronald L; see Dodge, James W.
Goug-Sigman, Margarete. Animals of the Night. LC 83-60109. (Strange but True Ser.). 64p. (gr. 6 up). 1983. 10.00 (ISBN 0-382-06687-1). Silver.
Gouhier. La Pensee Metaphysique de Descartes. 26.50 (ISBN 0-685-34225-5). French & Eur.
Gouillard, Jean. La Vie Religieuse A Byzance. 364p. 1981. 65.00x (ISBN 0-86078-077-5, Pub. by Variorum). State Mutual Bk.
Gouin, Michelle D. & Cross, Thomas B. Intelligent Buildings: Strategies for Technology & Architecture. 250p. 1985. 29.95 (ISBN 0-87094-667-6). Dow Jones-Irwin.
Gouin, Pierre. Earthquake History of Ethiopia & the Horn of Africa. 258p. 1979. pap. 25.00 casebound (ISBN 0-88936-194-0, IDRC118, IDRC). Unipub.
Gouinlock, James. John Dewey's Philosophy of Value. 1972. text ed. 15.50x (ISBN 0-391-00229-5). Humanities.
--Moral Writings of John Dewey. 1976. 13.75x (ISBN 0-317-30529-8). Free Pr.
--The Moral Writings of John Dewey: A Selection. LC 75-29826. 1976. 13.75x (ISBN 0-02-845420-0). Hafner.
Goulaeff, E. E., tr. see Saint John of Kronstadt.
Goulard, Robert J., ed. see Project Squid Workshop on Combustion Measurement in Jet Propulsion System.
Goulart, Frances. Bum Steers. LC 75-4499. 1975. 8.50 (ISBN 0-85699-117-1). Chatham Pr.
Goulart, Frances S. The Caffeine Book: A User's & Abuser's Guide. 1984. pap. 8.95 (ISBN 0-396-08371-4). Dodd.
--Eating to Win. LC 77-8756. 1978. pap. 2.95 (ISBN 0-8128-7055-7). Stein & Day.
--How to Write a Cookbook: And Sell It. LC 80-13092. 117p. 1981. 14.95 (ISBN 0-87949-180-9). Ashley Bks.
--Nutritional Self-Defense: Protecting Yourself from Yourself. (Illus.). 288p. 1984. 16.95 (ISBN 0-396-08362-5). Dodd.
--Nutritional Self-Defense: Protecting Yourself from Yourself. LC 85-40581. 302p. (Orig.). 1985. pap. 8.95 (ISBN 0-8128-6246-5). Stein & Day.
--The Official Eating to Win Cookbook. 287p. 1985. pap. 3.50 (ISBN 0-8128-8142-7). Stein & Day.
--The Official Eating to Win Cookbook: Super Foods for Super Athletic Performance. LC 81-40806. 224p. 1983. 16.95 (ISBN 0-8128-2832-1). Stein & Day.
--One Hundred One Allergy-Free Desserts. 1983. pap. 7.95 (ISBN 0-671-45785-3, Wallaby). S&S.
--The Vegetarian Weight Loss Cookbook. LC 81-18305. 176p. 1982. pap. 7.95 (ISBN 0-671-42826-8, Wallaby). S&S.
--The Whole Meal Salad Book. LC 84-73450. 224p. 1985. 9.95 (ISBN 0-917657-24-1). D I Fine.

Goulart, Francis S. Beyond Baby Fat: Weight-Loss Plans for Children & Teenagers. LC 84-28948. 208p. 1985. 15.95 (ISBN 0-07-023831-6). McGraw.
Goulart, Ron. After Things Fell Apart. 192p. 1985. pap. 2.75 (ISBN 0-425-07647-4). Berkley Pub.
--Brainz, Inc. 208p. 1985. pap. 2.75 (ISBN 0-88677-042-4). DAW Bks.
--A Graveyard of My Own. 1985. 13.95 (ISBN 0-8027-5605-0). Walker & Co.
--The Hellhound Project. LC 74-27582. (Science Fiction Ser.). 168p. 1975. 5.95 (ISBN 0-385-06275-3). Doubleday.
--The Prisoner of Blackwood Castle. 176p. 1984. pap. 2.50 (ISBN 0-380-88005-9, 88005-9). Avon.
--Suicide, Inc. 160p. 1985. pap. 2.75 (ISBN 0-425-07586-9). Berkley Pub.
Goulart, Ron, jt. auth. see Larson, Glen A.
Goulart, Ron, ed. The Great British Detective. 1982. pap. 3.50 (ISBN 0-451-62089-5, ME2089, Ment). NAL.
Goulay, Jack G. The Negro Salaried Worker. LC 65-17086. (AMA Research Study Ser.: No. 70). pap. 25.80 (ISBN 0-317-09070-4, 2000102). Bks Demand UMI.
Gould. Food Quality Assurance. rev. ed. 1983. 32.00 (ISBN 0-87055-430-1). AVI.
--Maine Lingo. 1975. 11.00 (ISBN 0-89272-010-7). Down East.
Gould & Whiteley. Cicero de Amicitia. 178p. 1983. 11.00x (ISBN 0-86516-042-2). Bolchazy-Carducci.
Gould, jt. auth. see Sheville.
Gould, Alan. Icelandic Solitaries. (Paperback Poets, Ser. 2: No. 16). 1978. 9.95x (ISBN 0-7022-1159-1); pap. 4.95x (ISBN 0-7022-1165-6). U of Queensland Pr.
Gould, Augustus, jt. auth. see Agassiz, Louis.
Gould, B., et al. Monetarism or Prosperity? 1981. text ed. 28.00x (ISBN 0-333-30782-8, Pub. by Macmillan England); pap. text ed. 15.50x (ISBN 0-333-31973-7). Humanities.
Gould, Barry K., et al. Galactorrhea. (Illus.). 128p. 1974. photocopy ed. 15.75x (ISBN 0-398-02978-4). C C Thomas.
Gould, Benjamin A. Investigations in the Military & Anthropological Statistics of American Soldiers. Kohn, Richard H., ed. LC 78-22380. (American Military Experience Ser.). 1979. Repr. of 1869 ed. lib. bdg. 51.50x (ISBN 0-405-11857-0). Ayer Co Pubs.
Gould, Bette, jt. auth. see Madsen, Sheila.
Gould, Bruce. Bruce Gould on Commodoties, Vol. 3. 213p. 1977. 30.00 (ISBN 0-686-84396-7). B Gould Pubns.
--Bruce Gould on Commodoties, Vol. 4. 213p. 1978. 30.00 (ISBN 0-686-84397-5). B Gould Pubns.
--Bruce Gould on Commodoties, Vol. 5. 213p. 1978. 30.00 (ISBN 0-686-84398-3). B Gould Pubns.
--Bruce Gould on Commodoties, Vol. 6. 213p. 1979. 30.00 (ISBN 0-686-84399-1). B Gould Pubns.
Gould, Bruce & Gould, Christine. We Love You Tiffany Anne: Book of Poems. 99p. 1985. pap. 9.95 (ISBN 0-918706-00-9). B Gould Pubns.
Gould, Bruce, jt. auth. see Fokker, Anthony H.
Gould, Bruce G. Bruce Gould on Commodities. 213p. 1983. Vol. 1, Pt. 1 & 2. pap. 30.00 ea. Vol. 1, Pt. 1 (ISBN 0-918706-05-X). Vol. 1, Pt. 2 (ISBN 0-918706-07-6). B Gould Pubns.
--Bruce Gould on Commodities. 1983. Vol. 3, Pt. 1, 231 pgs. pap. 30.00 (ISBN 0-918706-10-6); Vol. 3, Pt. 2, 244 pgs. pap. 12.95 (ISBN 0-918706-12-2). B Gould Pubns.
--Bruce Gould on Commodities. (Illus.). 218p. 1983. pap. 30.00 ea. Vol. 2, Pt. 1 (ISBN 0-918706-08-4). Vol. 2, Pt. 2 (ISBN 0-918706-06-8). B Gould Pubns.
--Bruce Gould On Commodoties, Vol. 2. 213p. 1977. 30.00 (ISBN 0-686-84395-9). B Gould Pubns.
--Commodity Trading Manual. 128p. 1983. pap. 65.00 (ISBN 0-918706-11-4). B Gould Pubns.
--The Dow Jones-Irwin Guide to Commodities Trading. rev. ed. LC 80-70272. 360p. 1981. 37.50 (ISBN 0-87094-193-3). Dow Jones-Irwin.
--The Greatest Money Book Ever Written. (Illus.). 420p. (Orig.). 1984. 100.00 (ISBN 0-918706-14-9); pap. 29.95 (ISBN 0-918706-24-6). B Gould Pubns.
--The Greatest Money Book Ever Written. (Illus.). 400p. 1985. pap. 7.95 (ISBN 0-918706-42-4). B Gould Pubns.
--How to Make Money in Commodities. 2nd ed. (Illus.). 186p. (Orig.). 1982. pap. 10.95 (ISBN 0-918706-09-2). B Gould Pubns.
--The Most Dangerous Money Book Ever Written. 444p. (Orig.). 1983. pap. 100.00 (ISBN 0-918706-13-0). B Gould Pubns.
Gould, Byrant P. Planning the New Corporate Headquarters. LC 82-23897. 196p. 1983. 39.95x (ISBN 0-471-09025-5, Pub. by Wiley-Interscience). Wiley.
Gould, Carol, ed. Beyond Domination: New Perspectives on Women & Philosophy. LC 83-10894. 321p. 1984. text ed. 24.95x (ISBN 0-8476-7202-6); pap. text ed. 11.95x (ISBN 0-8476-7236-0). Rowman & Allanheld.
Gould, Carol C. Marx's Social Ontology. 1978. pap. 6.95x (ISBN 0-262-57056-4). MIT Pr.
Gould, Cecil. Bernini in France: An Episode in Seventeenth-Century History. LC 81-47998. (Illus.). 192p. 1982. 29.00x (ISBN 0-691-03994-1). Princeton U Pr.
Gould, Charles. Mythical Monsters. 1976. lib. bdg. 134.95 (ISBN 0-8490-2324-6). Gordon Pr.
--Mythical Monsters. LC 81-50199. (Secret Doctrine Reference Ser.). (Illus.). 412p. 1981. Repr. of 1886 ed. 20.00 (ISBN 0-913510-38-6). Wizards.
--Red Cats Climbing in the Apple Trees. (Nebraska Review Chapbook Ser.: No. 1). 20p. (Orig.). 1980. pap. 1.00 (ISBN 0-937796-00-X). Nebraska Review.
Gould, Charles E., Jr. The Toad at Harrow: P. G. Wodehouse in Perspective. (Wodehouse Monograph: No. 3). 10p. (Orig.). 1982. pap. 7.50 (ISBN 0-87008-102-0). Heineman.
Gould, Charles N. Covered Wagon Geologist. (Illus.). Repr. of 1959 ed. 78.00 (ISBN 0-8357-9723-6, 2010150). Bks Demand UMI.
Gould, Chester. Dick Tracy: The Thirties, Tommy Guns & Hard Times. Galewitz, Herb, ed. LC 78-56876. (Illus.). 1978. 15.00 (ISBN 0-87754-071-3); slipcase signed & ltd. ed. 75.00 (ISBN 0-87754-090-X). Chelsea Hse.
Gould, Christine, jt. auth. see Gould, Bruce.
Gould, Christine A. Consider Your Options: Business Opportunities for Liberal Arts Graduates. (Liberal Learning & Careers Ser.). 1983. pap. 5.00 (ISBN 0-911696-13-X). Assn Am Coll.
Gould, Christopher & Morgan, Richard P. South Carolina Imprints, 1731-1800: A Descriptive Bibliography. 324p. 1985. lib. bdg. 75.00 (ISBN 0-87436-415-9). ABC-Clio.
Gould, Clarence P. The Land System in Maryland, 1720-1765. LC 78-63943. (Johns Hopkins University. Studies in the Social Sciences. Thirty-First Ser. 1913: 1). Repr. of 1913 ed. 24.50 (ISBN 0-404-61192-3). AMS Pr.
--Land System in Maryland, 1720-1765. Bruchey, Stuart, ed. LC 78-53540. (Development of Public Land in the U. S. Ser.). 1979. Repr. of 1913 ed. lib. bdg. 12.00x (ISBN 0-405-11376-5). Ayer Co Pubs.
--Money & Transportation in Maryland, 1720-1765. LC 78-63951. (Johns Hopkins University. Studies in the Social Sciences. Thirty-Third Ser. 1915: 1). Repr. of 1915 ed. 24.50 (ISBN 0-404-61199-0). AMS Pr.
Gould, D. On the Spot: The Sinking of the 'Belgrano' 80p. 1984. text ed. 12.25x (ISBN 0-900821-72-8, Pub. by C Woolf UK). Humanities.
Gould, Daniel, jt. ed. see Weiss, Maureen R.
Gould, David J. Law & the Administrative Process: Analytic Frameworks for Understanding Public Policy Making. LC 79-63850. 1979. pap. text ed. 13.75 (ISBN 0-8191-0746-8). U Pr of Amer.
Gould, David J. & Amaro-Reyes, Jose A. The Effects of Corruption on Administrative Performance: Illustrations from Developing Countries. LC 83-16905. 1983. write for info. (ISBN 0-8213-0259-0). World Bank.
Gould, Dennis, ed. From Protest to Resistance. 64p. lib. bdg. 12.95 (ISBN 0-88286-143-3); pap. 3.00 (ISBN 0-88286-118-2). C H Kerr.
Gould, Dick. Tennis, Anyone? 1976. pap. 2.50 (ISBN 0-451-12239-9, Sig). NAL.
--Tennis, Anyone? 4th ed. 1985. pap. 6.95 (ISBN 0-87484-720-6). Mayfield Pub.
Gould, Donald. The Black & White Medicine Show: How Doctors Serve & Fail Their Customers. 288p. 1985. 22.00 (ISBN 0-241-11540-X, Pub. by Hamish Hamilton England). David & Charles.
Gould, Douglas W. Explosion: Some Sources, Causes & Effects in Man's Affairs. 1985. 6.95 (ISBN 0-533-06615-8). Vantage.
Gould, Dudley C., jt. ed. see Sanders, Clyde.
Gould, E. American Woman Today: Free or Frustrated. 2nd ed. 1977. pap. text ed. 9.24 (ISBN 0-13-032359-4). P-H.
Gould, E. R; see Shaw, Albert.
Gould Editiorial Staff. Penal Law of New York: Spanish Edition. (Supplemented annually). looseleaf 10.00 (ISBN 0-87526-230-9). Gould.
Gould Editorial Dept. Criminal Laws of Florida. annual 1982. 12.00x; slide rule study guide 4.00. Gould.
--Dictionary of Criminal Justice Terms. 250p. 1983. text ed. 6.95 Soft cover (ISBN 0-87526-276-7). Gould.
--Michigan Motor Vehicle Laws: Slide Rule. 1982. 9.95; slide rule study guide 4.00 (ISBN 0-87526-286-4). Gould.
--Slide Rule for Ohio Criminal Code. annual slide rule study guide 4.00 (ISBN 0-87526-273-2). Gould.
--Slide Rule for Pennsylvania Vehicle Law. annual 1982. slide rule study guide 4.00 (ISBN 0-87526-290-2). Gould.
Gould Editorial Staff. Administrative Law 1981. 1981. pap. text ed. 6.50x (ISBN 0-87526-190-6). Gould.
--Agency Law of U. S., 1981. 1981. pap. text ed. 5.75x (ISBN 0-87526-191-4). Gould.
--Bailments Law of New York, 1962. 1962. pap. text ed. 1.50x (ISBN 0-87526-004-7). Gould.
--Banking Law of New York. (Updated annually). text ed. 40.00 (ISBN 0-87526-235-X). Gould.
--Building Code of New York City. text ed. 40.00 looseleaf (ISBN 0-87526-128-0). Gould.
--California Penal Code. 600p. 1982. text ed. 12.95 looseleaf (ISBN 0-87526-268-6); slide rule 4.00 (ISBN 0-87526-291-0). Gould.
--Chicago Municipal Code Handbook. 350p. (Annual update). 1984. loose-leaf bdg. 13.95 (ISBN 0-87526-264-3). Gould.
--Confessions & Admission, 1977. 1977. pap. text ed. 8.50x (ISBN 0-87526-152-3). Gould.
--Crime Code of Pennsylvania. 400p. (Supplemented annually). looseleaf 15.95 (ISBN 0-87526-216-3). Gould.
--Criminal Code of Ohio. (Annual). looseleaf 12.00x (ISBN 0-87526-202-3). Gould.
--Criminal Law Digest of Pennsylvania. looseleaf 14.50 (ISBN 0-87526-237-6). Gould.
--Criminal Laws of Florida. (Annual). text ed. 12.50x (ISBN 0-87526-188-4); Slide Rule 4.00. Gould.
--Criminal Laws of Massachusetts. 400p. (Supplemented annually). looseleaf 16.00 (ISBN 0-87526-135-3); slide rule study guide 4.00 (ISBN 0-87526-275-9). Gould.
--Criminal Laws of Michigan. 300p. loose leaf 12.50 (ISBN 0-87526-200-7). Gould.
--Criminal Procedure Law of New York: Question & Answer. (Supplemented annually). looseleaf 5.50x (ISBN 0-685-80905-6). Gould.
--Evidence Code-Federal. 300p. (Supplemented annually). looseleaf 10.00 (ISBN 0-87526-207-4). Gould.
--Evidence Law of New York Quizzer 1981. 1981. cancelled 7.50x (ISBN 0-87526-220-1). Gould.
--Florida Motor Vehicle Laws. 350p. (Updated annually). loose-leaf bdg. 11.00 (ISBN 0-87526-256-2); slide rule study guide 4.00 (ISBN 0-87526-280-5). Gould.
--Illinois Code of Civil Procedure. annual 470p. 1982. text ed. 10.95 looseleaf (ISBN 0-87526-279-1). Gould.
--Illinois Criminal Law & Procedure. (Annual). text ed. 13.95x (ISBN 0-87526-199-X); slide rule study guide 4.00 (ISBN 0-87526-270-8). Gould.
--Illinois Vehicle Code. 525p. (Updated annually). loose-leaf bdg. 13.95 (ISBN 0-87526-259-7); slide rule study guide 4.00. Gould.
--Insurance Laws of the United States. (Supplemented annually). looseleaf 7.50 (ISBN 0-87526-179-5). Gould.
--Massachusetts Motor Vehicle Laws. (Supplemented annually). looseleaf 15.00x (ISBN 0-87526-231-7); slide rule study guide 4.00 (ISBN 0-87526-281-3). Gould.
--Motor Vehicle Laws of Ohio. 300p. (Updated annually). loose-leaf bdg. 11.00 (ISBN 0-87526-257-0); slide rule 4.00 (ISBN 0-87526-283-X). Gould.
--Navigation Law of New York. annual looseleaf 5.00 (ISBN 0-87526-234-1). Gould.
--New Jersey Criminal Justice Code. annual 300p. looseleaf 14.50 (ISBN 0-87526-024-1); abridged ed. 8.95 (ISBN 0-87526-271-6); slide rule study guide 4.00 (ISBN 0-87526-272-4). Gould.
--New Jersey Motor Vehicle & Traffic Laws. (Supplemented annually). looseleaf 14.50x (ISBN 0-87526-232-5); slide rule study guide 4.00 (ISBN 0-87526-284-8). Gould.
--New York City Housing Maintenance Code. 300p. 1983. text ed. 15.00 looseleaf (ISBN 0-87526-278-3). Gould.
--New York Family Court Act. 450p. (Supplemented annually). looseleaf 11.00 (ISBN 0-87526-143-4); abridged ed. 6.95 (ISBN 0-87526-277-5). Gould.
--New York Law Digest. 330p. (Supplemented annually). looseleaf 7.50 (ISBN 0-87526-252-X). Gould.
--New York Multiple Dwelling Law. 300p. (Supplemented annually). 15.00x (ISBN 0-87526-285-6). Gould.
--New York Vehicle & Traffic Law. 400p. (Supplemented annually). looseleaf 7.95 (ISBN 0-87526-130-2). Gould.
--New York Vehicle & Traffic Law: Slide Rule. annual 1982. slide rule study guide 4.00 (ISBN 0-87526-288-0). Gould.
--Patents. 1981. 77.50 (ISBN 0-87526-078-0). Gould.
--Penal Law of New York Question & Answers. (Supplemented annually). looseleaf 6.50 (ISBN 0-87526-225-2). Gould.
--Slide Rule for Pennsylvania Crimes Code. annual 1982. slide rule study guide 4.00 (ISBN 0-87526-265-1). Gould.
--Surrogate's Court Procedure Act (N. Y.) (Supplemented annually). looseleaf 8.00 (ISBN 0-87526-129-9). Gould.
--Vehicle Laws of Pennsylvania. (Supplemented annually). looseleaf 14.95 (ISBN 0-87526-233-3). Gould.
Gould Editorial Staff, ed. Commercial Law Handbook. 1100p. 1985. looseleaf 15.95 (ISBN 0-87526-312-7). Gould.
--Federal Criminal Rules. 700p. 1985. looseleaf 15.00 (ISBN 0-87526-315-1). Gould.
--Michigan Motor Vehicle Laws: With Uniform Traffic Code. annual 1450p. text ed. 14.00 (ISBN 0-87526-253-8); slide rule study guide 4.00 (ISBN 0-87526-282-1). Gould.
--Michigan Penal Code. annual 2nd ed. 400p. text ed. 12.50 (ISBN 0-87526-200-7); slide rule study guide 4.00 (ISBN 0-87526-286-4). Gould.
--New Jersey Civil Practice Rules. 350p. 1983. text ed. 10.95 looseleaf (ISBN 0-87526-299-6). Gould.
--New York Criminal Law Handbook. 600p. 1985. pap. 15.00 looseleaf (ISBN 0-87526-309-7). Gould.
--New York Criminal Procedure: Law Questions & Answers. 200p. 1985. looseleaf 6.50 (ISBN 0-87526-314-3). Gould.
--New York Environmental Conservation Law, 2 vols. 1008p. (Supplemented annually). Set. looseleaf ed. 18.50 (ISBN 0-87526-255-4). Gould.
--New York Insurance Law. 600p. 1985. looseleaf 14.95 (ISBN 0-87526-316-X). Gould.
--New York Magistrate's Desk Book. 200p. 1985. looseleaf 25.00 (ISBN 0-87526-310-0). Gould.
--New York Penal Law: Questions & Answers. 1985. looseleaf 6.50 (ISBN 0-87526-313-5). Gould.
--New York Village Law. 300p. 1985. pap. 12.95 looseleaf (ISBN 0-87526-308-9). Gould.
--Pennsylvania Civil Procedure Law & Rules, 2 vol. 600p. 1983. text ed. 14.00 looseleaf (ISBN 0-87526-295-3). Gould.
--Pennsylvania Transportation Code. 900p. looseleaf 17.50 (ISBN 0-87526-317-8). Gould.
--Pertinent Commercial Statutes. 400p. 1983. looseleaf 8.50 (ISBN 0-87526-293-7). Gould.
--UCC-Pertinent Commercial Statutes, 2 vols. Set. text ed. 15.95 looseleaf (ISBN 0-686-47976-9). Gould.
--UCC State Service, 3 vols. 1983. Set. looseleaf 45.00 (ISBN 0-87526-296-1). Gould.
Gould Editorial Staff, ed. see Gallet, Jeffry.
Gould, Elaine & Gould, Loren. Arts & Crafts for Physically & Mentally Disabled: The How, What & Why of It. (Illus.). 368p. 1978. spiral 38.00x (ISBN 0-398-03783-3). C C Thomas.
--Crafts for the Elderly. (Illus.). 224p. 1976. 22.75x (ISBN 0-398-00710-1). C C Thomas.
Gould, Elgin R. The Social Condition of Labor. LC 78-63816. (Johns Hopkins University. Studies in the Social Sciences. Eleventh Ser. 1893: 1). Repr. of 1893 ed. 11.50 (ISBN 0-404-61079-X). AMS Pr.
--The Social Condition of Labor. 1973. pap. 9.00 (ISBN 0-384-19420-6). Johnson Repr.
Gould, Elizabeth P. Anne Gilchrist & Walt Whitman. LC 73-444. 1972. Repr. of 1900 ed. lib. bdg. 15.00 (ISBN 0-8414-1506-4). Folcroft.
--Anne Gilchrist & Walt Whitman. 1979. Repr. of 1900 ed. lib. bdg. 17.00 (ISBN 0-8482-0907-9). Norwood Edns.
Gould, Ellen. The Blue Number Counting Book. (Illus.). 13p. (ps-2). pap. 6.00 (ISBN 0-317-18942-5). Learning Tools.
--The Red Letter Alphabet Book. (Illus.). 29p. (gr. k up). 1983. pap. 7.00 (ISBN 0-317-19157-8). Learning Tools.
Gould, Eric. Mythical Intentions in Modern Literature. LC 81-47132. 304p. 1981. 29.00 (ISBN 0-691-06482-2). Princeton U Pr.
--Reading into Writing: A Rhetoric, Reader, & Handbook. 1982. pap. text ed. 18.95 (ISBN 0-395-32607-9); instr's manual 2.00 (ISBN 0-395-32608-7). HM.
Gould, Eric, ed. The Sin of the Book: Edmond Jabes. LC 84-5270. (Illus.). xxvi, 252p. 1985. 23.95x (ISBN 0-8032-2115-0). U of Nebr Pr.
Gould, Ezra P. see Hovey, Alvah.
Gould, F. J. The Children's Plutarch. 1910. Repr. 10.00 (ISBN 0-8274-2054-4). R West.
--Thomas Paine: Seventeen Thirty-Seven to Eighteen Hundred Nine. 192p. 1980. Repr. lib. bdg. 30.00 (ISBN 0-8492-4951-1). R West.
Gould, F. J. & Randolph, Vance. The Life Story of Auguste Comte: With a Digest Review of Ancient: Religious; & Modern Philosophy. 180p. (Orig.). 1984. pap. 4.95 (ISBN 0-911826-56-4). Am Atheist.
Gould, F. J., jt. auth. see Eppen, Gary D.
Gould, Frank W. Common Texas Grasses: An Illustrated Guide. LC 78-6368. (W. L. Moody, Jr. Natural History Ser.: No. 3). (Illus.). 280p. 1978. 15.95 (ISBN 0-89096-057-7); pap. 8.95 (ISBN 0-89096-058-5). Tex A&M Univ Pr.
--The Grasses of Texas. LC 75-18688. (Illus.). 672p. 1975. 27.50 (ISBN 0-89096-005-4). Tex A&M Univ Pr.
--Grasses of the Southwestern United States. (Illus.). 352p. 1973. pap. 8.95 (ISBN 0-8165-0406-7). U of Ariz Pr.
Gould, Frank W. & Shaw, Robert B. Grass Systematics. 2nd ed. LC 82-45894. (Illus.). 416p. 1983. text ed. 25.00 (ISBN 0-89096-145-X); pap. text ed. 15.00x (ISBN 0-89096-153-0). Tex A&M Univ Pr.
Gould, G., jt. auth. see Chilver, P.
Gould, G. W. & Corry, Janet E. Microbial Growth & Survival in Extremes of Environment. LC 79-41561. (Society for Applied Bacteriology Technical Ser.: No. 15). 1980. 42.50 (ISBN 0-12-293680-9). Acad Pr.
Gould, G. W., jt. auth. see Shapton, D. A.
Gould, G. W. & Hurst, A., eds. The Bacterial Spore, Vol. 2. 1984. 55.00 (ISBN 0-12-293652-3). Acad Pr.
Gould, G. W., jt. ed. see Barker, A. N.
Gould, George. Corrigenda & Explanations. 1884. 25.00 (ISBN 0-932062-66-0). Sharon Hill.
Gould, George M. Righthandedness & Lefthandedness: With Chapters Treating of the Writing Posture, the Rule of the Road, Etc. LC 78-72794. Repr. of 1908 ed. 26.50 (ISBN 0-404-60859-0). AMS Pr.
Gould, Gerald. Democritus or the Future of Laughter. 1929. 15.00 (ISBN 0-932062-67-9). Sharon Hill.

--English Novel of To-Day. facsimile ed. LC 73-150184. (Select Bibliographies Reprint Ser.). Repr. of 1924 ed. 18.00 (ISBN 0-8369-5697-4). Ayer Co Pubs.
--Journey, Odes & Sonnets. 1921. 24.50x (ISBN 0-686-83603-0). Elliots Bks.
Gould, Gerald L. Groundwork: Exercises in Perceiving & Understanding Grammar. 340p. 1977. pap. text ed. 11.95 (ISBN 0-15-529695-7, HC). HarBraceJ.
Gould, Glenn. Bach's Well-Tempered Clavier, Vol. 1. 1972. pap. 4.95 (ISBN 0-8256-2144-5). Music Sales.
--Bach's Well-Tempered Clavier, Vol. 2. 1972. pap. 4.95 (ISBN 0-8256-2145-3). Music Sales.
--The Glenn Gould Reader. Page, Tim, ed. LC 84-47819. 441p. 1984. 20.00 (ISBN 0-394-54067-0). Knopf.
Gould, H. & Matthews, H. R. Separation Methods for Nucleic Acids & Oligonucleotides. (Laboratory Techniques in Biochemistry & Molecular Biology: Vol. 4, Pt. 2). 1976. 23.50 (ISBN 0-444-10868-8, North-Holland). Elsevier.
Gould, H. E., ed. see Virgil.
Gould, Henry. Stone. (Illus.). 46p. (Orig.). 1979. pap. 4.50 (ISBN 0-914278-23-1). Copper Beech.
Gould, Heywood. Cocktail. LC 84-11726. 352p. 1984. 14.95 (ISBN 0-312-14633-7). St Martin.
Gould, Howard E. & Whiteley, Joseph L., eds. Selections from Five Roman Poets: Catullus, Virgil, Horace, Tibullus, Ovid. (Illus., Lat.). 1941. 12.95 (ISBN 0-312-71225-1). St Martin.
Gould, Howard E., ed. see Livy.
Gould, I. IFIP-Sach Worterbuch der Datenverarbeitung. 170p. (Ger.). 1977. 19.95 (ISBN 3-87144-335-2, M-7467, Pub. by Verlag Harri Deutsch). French & Eur.
Gould, J. K. Controllers & Control Elements. 1982. pap. text ed. 29.95x (ISBN 0-87664-622-4); instr's guide 10.00x (ISBN 0-87664-623-2). Instru Soc.
Gould, J. P. & Ferguson, C. E. Microeconomic Theory. 5th ed. 1980. 29.95x (ISBN 0-256-02157-0). Irwin.
Gould, J. Sutherland. Don't Throw it Out--Sell It: Convert the Clutter in Your Closets into Cash in Your Pocket. (Illus.). 138p. 1983. 14.95 (ISBN 0-13-218487-7); pap. 6.95 (ISBN 0-13-218479-6). P-H.
--How to Publicize Yourself, Your Family, & Your Organization. (Illus.). 216p. 1983. 15.95 (ISBN 0-13-430645-7); pap. 7.95 (ISBN 0-13-430637-6). P-H.
Gould, James. Classic Philosophical Questions. 5th ed. 728p. 1984. pap. 19.95 (ISBN 0-675-20264-7). Merrill.
--Marketing Anthology. (Illus.). 1979. pap. text ed. 15.95 (ISBN 0-8299-0255-4). West Pub.
--Men of Aldridge: A Local History of the Urban District of Aldridge. rev ed. 160p. 1983. pap. text ed. 13.00x (ISBN 0-86299-058-0, Pub. by Alan Sutton England). Humanities.
--A Treatise on the Principles of Pleading, in Civil Actions. LC 70-37974. (American Law Ser.: The Formative Years). 540p. 1972. Repr. of 1832 ed. 23.00 (ISBN 0-405-04014-8). Ayer Co Pubs.
Gould, James A. & Iorio, John J. Love, Sex & Identity. LC 78-176093. 184p. 1972. pap. 8.00x (ISBN 0-87835-033-0). Boyd & Fraser.
--Violence in Modern Literature. LC 71-182676. 208p. 1972. pap. 8.00x (ISBN 0-87835-037-3). Boyd & Fraser.
Gould, James A. & Truitt, Willis H. Political Ideologies. 576p. 1973. pap. text ed. write for info. (ISBN 0-02-345470-9, 34547). Macmillan.
Gould, James A., jt. auth. see Bierman, Arthur K.
Gould, James A., jt. auth. see Dewey, Robert E.
Gould, James L. Ethology: The Mechanisms & Evolution of Behavior. (Illus.). 1982. text ed. 23.95x (ISBN 0-393-01488-6). Norton.
Gould, James P. When I Eat I Hurt. 168p. (Orig.). 1980. pap. 5.95 (ISBN 0-89288-029-5). Maverick.
--When I Eat I Hurt: Freedom from Abdominal Pain. rev. ed. Moyer, Joyce, ed. (Illus.). 149p. 1983. pap. 7.95 (ISBN 0-9602506-0-3). Keller-Burns & McGuirk.
Gould, James W. United States & Malaysia. LC 76-78518. (American Foreign Policy Library). (Illus.). 1969. 16.50x (ISBN 0-674-92615-3). Harvard U Pr.
Gould, Jan. The Boathouse Question. 132p. 1978. pap. 6.95 (ISBN 0-686-74132-3). Superior Pub.
Gould, Jay. Delaware County, New York. 1977. Repr. 20.00 (ISBN 0-686-22207-5). Polyanthos.
--Saga of Belle Lea Acres: Any Fool Can Do It. (Orig.). pap. write for info. J Gould.
Gould, Jay & Losano, Wayne. Opportunities in Technical Communications. (VGM Career Bks.). (Illus.). 160p. 1983. 7.95 (ISBN 0-8442-6246-3, 6246-3, Passport Bks.); pap. 5.95 (ISBN 0-8442-6247-1, 6247-1). Natl Textbk.
Gould, Jay M. Input-Output Databases to Analyze Business. 25.00 (ISBN 0-8240-7058-5). Trinet.
Gould, Jay M. & Paykin, Bentley H. The Structure of U. S. Business. Trinet Inc., ed. LC 81-65730. 250p. 1981. pap. 100.00 (ISBN 0-86692-003-X). Trinet.
Gould, Jay R. & Losano, Wayne A. Opportunities in Technical Writing Today. LC 75-18013. (Illus.). 137p. (gr. 8-12). 1975. text ed. 6.60 (ISBN 0-8442-6429-6); pap. text ed. 4.95 (ISBN 0-8442-6428-8). Natl Textbk.
Gould, Jay R., jt. auth. see Ulman, Joseph N., Jr.
Gould, Jay R., ed. Directions in Technical Writing & Communication. LC 77-75832. (Technical Writing & Communications Ser.: Vol. 1). 1978. pap. 7.95x (ISBN 0-89503-006-3). Baywood Pub.
Gould, Jean. All about the Old English Sheepdog. 2nd ed. 136p. 1973. 8.95 (ISBN 0-7207-0619-X, Pub. by Michael Joseph). Merrimack Pub Cir.
--American Women Poets. (Illus.). 332p. 1980. 14.95 (ISBN 0-396-07828-1); pap. 8.95 (ISBN 0-396-08433-8). Dodd.
--Divorcing Your Grandmother. LC 85-347. 240p. 1985. 15.95 (ISBN 0-688-04970-2). Morrow.
--Modern American Women Poets. (Illus.). 426p. 1985. 17.95 (ISBN 0-396-08443-5). Dodd.
Gould, Jean & Gould, Maurice. Story of Israel in Coins. pap. 2.00 (ISBN 0-87980-150-6). Wilshire.
Gould, John. Next Time Around. (Illus.). 1983. 12.95 (ISBN 0-393-01777-X). Norton.
--No Other Place: A Novel. 192p. 1984. 12.95 (ISBN 0-393-01850-4). Norton.
--Stitch in Time. 1985. 12.95 (ISBN 0-393-01976-4). Norton.
Gould, John & Bittlingmayer, George. Economics of the Davis-Bacon Act: An Analysis of Prevailing Wage Laws. 89p. 1980. pap. 4.25 (ISBN 0-8447-3381-4). Am Enterprise.
Gould, John M. How to Camp Out. 144p. 1982. pap. 4.95 (ISBN 0-915850-06-0). Walking News Inc.
Gould, Joseph C. & Mott, Charles J. Earth Science: An Individualized Approach. 3rd ed. (Illus.). 250p. 1982. pap. text ed. 13.95x (ISBN 0-89459-185-1). Hunter Textbks.
Gould, Joseph C., et al. Earth Science: An Individualized Approach. 4th ed. 250p. 1985. pap. 14.95 (ISBN 0-88725-031-9). Hunter Textbks.
Gould, Joseph E. Chautauqua Movement. LC 61-8734. (Illus.). 1961. 39.50x (ISBN 0-87395-003-8); pap. 10.95x (ISBN 0-87395-004-6). State U NY Pr.
Gould, Josiah B. The Philosophy of Chrysippus. LC 78-112606. pap. 57.50 (ISBN 0-317-09064-X, 2010109). Bks Demand UMI.
Gould, Judith. Sins. 1982. pap. 3.95 (ISBN 0-451-11859-6, AE1859, Sig). NAL.
Gould, Julius & Kolb, W. J. UNESCO Dictionary of the Social Sciences. LC 64-20307. 1964. 40.00 (ISBN 0-02-917490-2). Free Pr.
Gould, Karen. The Psalter & Hours of Yolande of Soissons. LC 78-55888. 1978. 11.00x (ISBN 0-910956-78-2, SAM4); pap. 5.00x (ISBN 0-910956-64-2). Medieval Acad.
Gould, Karen, jt. ed. see Birn, Randi.
Gould, Karen L. Claude Simon's Mythic Muse. 152p. 1979. 14.95. Summa Pubns.
Gould, L A., jt. auth. see Taylor, S H.
Gould, L. Harry. Marxist Glossary. 99p. 1980. pap. text ed. 2.95 (ISBN 0-89380-018-X). Proletarian Pubs.
Gould, Lawrence, ed. Drug Treatment of Cardiac Arrhythmias. LC 82-83705. 448p. 1983. monograph 49.50 (ISBN 0-87993-190-6). Futura Pub.
Gould, Lawrence D., et al. Essentials for College Mathematics: A Programmed Text. (Illus.). 1970. pap. text ed. 7.95x (ISBN 0-89197-152-1); access pen 0.65x (ISBN 0-8290-1391-1). Irvington.
Gould, Leroy, et al. Connections: Notes from the Heroin World. LC 73-86896. 308p. 1974. 25.00x (ISBN 0-300-01731-6). Yale U Pr.
Gould, Lewis L. The Presidency of William McKinley. LC 80-16022. (The American Presidency Ser.). 298p. 1981. 19.95x (ISBN 0-7006-0206-2). U Pr of KS.
--Progressives & Prohibitionists: Texas Democrats in the Wilson Era. (Illus.). 355p. 1973. 21.50x (ISBN 0-292-76407-3); pap. 11.95x (ISBN 0-292-76428-6). U of Tex Pr.
--Reform & Regulation: American Politics from Roosevelt to Wilson. 200p. 1986. pap. text ed. 9.95 (ISBN 0-394-34154-6, KnopfC). Knopf.
--Reform & Regulation: American Politics 1900-1916. 197p. 1978. pap. text ed. 10.95 (ISBN 0-394-32182-1, RanC). Random.
--The Spanish-American War & President McKinley. LC 82-13672. (Illus.). x, 166p. 1982. pap. text ed. 5.95x (ISBN 0-7006-0227-5). U Pr of KS.
Gould, Lewis L. & Greffe, Richard. Photojournalist: The Career of Jimmy Hare. (Illus.). 179p. 1977. 19.95 (ISBN 0-292-74004-2). U of Tex Pr.
Gould, Lewis L., ed. The Progressive Era. LC 73-20783. (Illus.). 270p. 1974. text ed. 11.95x (ISBN 0-8156-2163-9); pap. text ed. 4.95x (ISBN 0-8156-2164-7). Syracuse U Pr.
Gould, Lewis L., jt. ed. see Curtis, James C.
Gould, Lois. Final Analysis. 1975. pap. 1.75 (ISBN 0-380-00234-5, 22343). Avon.
--La Presidenta. 1982. pap. 3.50 (ISBN 0-671-44310-0). PB.
--A Sea-Change. 1977. pap. 1.95 (ISBN 0-380-01695-8, 33704). Avon.
--Such Good Friends. 1978. pap. 2.95 (ISBN 0-440-18376-6). Dell.
Gould, Loren, jt. auth. see Gould, Elaine.
Gould, Lyman J. La Ley Foraker: Raices De la Politica Colonial De los Estados Unidos. 2nd ed. (UPREX, C. Sociales: No. 40). pap. 1.85 (ISBN 0-8477-0040-2). U of PR Pr.
Gould, Marjorie, jt. auth. see Larson, Carroll B.
Gould, Mary E. Antique Tin & Tole Ware: Its History & Romance. LC 57-8796. (Illus.). 1957. 27.50 (ISBN 0-8048-0026-X). C E Tuttle.
--Early American Wooden Ware. LC 69-13499. (Illus.). 1962. 15.00 (ISBN 0-8048-0153-3). C E Tuttle.
Gould, Maurice. Gould's Gold & Silver Guide to Coins. LC 70-76025. (Illus.). 1969. 10.95 (ISBN 0-8303-0077-5). Fleet.
Gould, Maurice, jt. auth. see Gould, Jean.
Gould, Meredith, et al. Invertebrate Oogenesis, Vol. 2. 300p. 1972. 32.50x (ISBN 0-8422-7030-2). Irvington.
Gould, Milton S. A Cast of Hawks. LC 84-19885. (Illus.). 374p. 1985. 24.50 (ISBN 0-913938-28-9). Copley Bks.
Gould, Morgan. Guide to California Foundations. 6th ed. 1985. 17.00 (ISBN 0-318-04665-2). Northern Cal.
Gould, Murray, jt. auth. see Hill, George R.
Gould, Murray J. Paths to Musical Thought: An Approach to Ear Training Through Sight Singing. LC 78-18383. 1979. pap. text ed. 17.95 (ISBN 0-03-020421-6, HoltC). HR&W.
Gould, Nathaniel D. Church Music in America. 1980. lib. bdg. 59.75 (ISBN 0-8490-3192-3). Gordon Pr.
--Church Music in America, Comprising Its History & Its Peculiarities at Different Periods. LC 78-144620. Repr. of 1853 ed. 19.25 (ISBN 0-404-02888-8). AMS Pr.
Gould, Nicholas. Looking at Place-Names. 80p. 1982. 30.00x (ISBN 0-85937-128-X, Pub. by Mason England). State Mutual Bk.
Gould, P. & Olsson, G., eds. A Search for Common Ground. 270p. 1982. 25.00x (ISBN 0-85086-093-8, NO. 8006, Pub by Pion England). Methuen Inc.
Gould, P., et al. The Structure of Television. (Illus.). 178p. 1984. 29.95 (ISBN 0-85086-110-1, 9195, Pub. by Pion England). Methuen Inc.
Gould, P. L. Introduction to Linear Elasticity. (Illus.). 195p. 1983. 24.00 (ISBN 0-387-90876-5). Springer Verlag.
Gould, P. L., et al, eds. Natural Draught Cooling Towers: Proceedings of the Second International Symposium, Ruhr University Bochum, Germany, September 5-7, 1984. (Illus.). xv, 548p. 1984. 34.40 (ISBN 0-387-13703-3). Springer-Verlag.
Gould, P. R. Spatial Diffusion. LC 79-94260. (CCG Resource Papers Ser.: No. 4). (Illus.). 1969. pap. text ed. 4.00 (ISBN 0-89291-051-8). Assn Am Geographers.
Gould, Peter. The Complete Taupo Fishing Guide. (Illus.). 248p. 1982. 19.95 (ISBN 0-00-216969-X, Pub. by W Collins New Zealand). Intl Spec Bk.
--The Geographer at Work. (Illus.). 320p. 1985. 39.95x (ISBN 0-7102-0459-0); pap. 16.95x (ISBN 0-7102-0494-9). Routledge & Kegan.
--Spatial Diffusion: The Spread of Ideas & Innovations in Geographic Space. (CISE Learning Package Ser.: No. 11). (Illus.). 55p. (Orig.). 1975. pap. text ed. 3.00x (ISBN 0-936876-26-3). Learn Res Intl Stud.
Gould, Philip. Les Cadiens d'Asteur-Today's Cajuns. 3rd. ed. Hebert, Sandy, ed. Ancelet, Barry, tr. LC 84-80584. (Illus.). 144p. (Eng. & Cajun Fr.). Repr. of 1980 ed. 23.95 (ISBN 0-917541-00-6). Galerie Pr.
Gould, Philip, photos by. Louisiana: A Land Apart. Spitzer, Nicholas. Ancelet, Barry, et al, eds. LC 84-72896. (Illus.). 144p. 1985. 35.00 (ISBN 0-917541-01-4). Galerie Pr.
Gould, Phillip. Finite Element Analysis of Shells of Revolution. (Surveys in Structural Engineering & Structural Mechanics Ser.). 1985. text ed. 34.95 (ISBN 0-273-08654-5). Pitman Pub MA.
Gould, R. A. Living Archaeology. LC 79-20788. (New Studies in Archaeology). (Illus.). 1980. pap. 12.95 (ISBN 0-521-29959-4). Cambridge U Pr.
Gould, R. G. & Lum, L. F., eds. Communication Satellite Systems: An Overview of the Technology. LC 75-39327. 1976. 24.90 (ISBN 0-87942-065-0, PC00703). Inst Electrical.
Gould, R. T. Captain Cook. 2nd ed. (Illus.). 135p. 1978. 20.00x (ISBN 0-7156-1061-9, BPA-02552, Pub. by Duckworth England). Biblio Dist.
Gould, R. W. & Morris, K. J. The Army of India Medal Roll: 1799-1826. 123p. 1981. text ed. 39.00x (ISBN 0-903754-08-8, Pub. by Picton England). State Mutual Bk.
Gould, Richard, ed. Shipwreck Anthropology. (School of American Research Advanced Seminar Ser.). (Illus.). 272p. 1983. 27.50x (ISBN 0-8263-0687-X). U of NM Pr.
Gould, Richard A. Archaeology of the Point St. George Site, & Tolowa Prehistory. LC 67-63726. (U. C. Publ. in Anthropology: Vol. 4). Repr. of 1966 ed. 37.30 (ISBN 0-8357-9626-4, 2014837). Bks Demand UMI.
Gould, Richard A. & Natural History Magazine, eds. Man's Many Ways: The Natural History Reader in Anthropology. 2nd ed. LC 77-4701. (Illus.). 1977. pap. text ed. 14.50 scp (ISBN 0-06-042436-2, HarpC). Har-Row.
Gould, Richard A. & Schiffer, Michael, eds. Modern Material Culture: The Archaeology of the U. S. LC 80-2332. (Studies in Archaeology). 1981. 37.50 (ISBN 0-12-293580-2). Acad Pr.
Gould, Robert N., jt. auth. see Hutton, Cynthia A.
Gould, Robert W. British Campaign Medals: Waterloo to the Falklands. (Illus.). 1984. 12.95 (ISBN 0-85368-672-6, Arms & Armour Pr). Sterling.
Gould, Roberta. Writing Air, Written Water. 96p. (Orig.). 1980. 5.95 (ISBN 0-936628-00-6). Waterside.
Gould, Roger L. Transformations. 1979. 7.95 (ISBN 0-671-25066-3, Touchstone Bks). S&S.
Gould, Rosalind. Mona. 224p. 1981. 9.95 (ISBN 0-89962-214-3). Todd & Honeywell.
Gould, Roy R. Going Sour: Science & Politics of Acid Rain. LC 84-21700. 200p. 1985. 11.95 (ISBN 0-8176-3251-4). Birkhauser.
Gould, Rupert. Marine Chronometer. (Illus.). 45.00x (ISBN 0-87556-106-3). Saifer.
Gould, Rupert T. The Case for the Sea Serpent. LC 72-75791. 1969. Repr. of 1930 ed. 35.00x (ISBN 0-8103-3833-5). Gale.
--Enigmas: Another Book of Unexplained Facts. (Illus.). 1965. 5.00 (ISBN 0-8216-0074-5). Univ Bks.
--The Loch Ness Monster. (Illus.). 1976. pap. 3.95 (ISBN 0-8065-0555-9). Citadel Pr.
Gould, S. Baring. Devon. 384p. 1983. pap. 7.50 (ISBN 0-907746-22-5, Pub. by A Mott Ltd). Longwood Pub Group.
Gould, S. E., ed. Pathology of the Heart & Blood Vessels. 3rd ed. (Illus.). 1218p. 1968. 59.75x (ISBN 0-398-00708-X). C C Thomas.
--Trichinosis in Man & Animals. (Illus.). 556p. 1970. 56.50x (ISBN 0-398-00709-8). C C Thomas.
Gould, S. H. Contemporary Chinese Research Mathematics, Vol. 2: A Report on Chinese-English Mathematical Dictionaries. 19p. 1964. 4.00 (ISBN 0-8218-0016-7, CED). Am Math.
--A Manual for Translaters of Mathematical Russian. 44p. 1980. Repr. of 1973 ed. 10.00 (ISBN 0-8218-0028-0, MTR). Am Math.
--Russian for the Mathematician. LC 72-76762. (Illus.). 224p. 1972. pap. 21.00 (ISBN 0-387-05811-7). Springer-Verlag.
Gould, S. H. & Liu, P. H. Kinship, Marriage & Mathematics. LC 80-2333. (Pure & Applied Mathematics Ser.). Date not set. write for info. (ISBN 0-12-293720-1). Acad Pr.
Gould, S. H. & Obreanu, P. E., eds. Romanian-English Dictionary & Grammar for the Mathematical Sciences. 51p. (Eng. & Romanian.). 1979. pap. 12.00 (ISBN 0-8218-0038-8, ROMA). Am Math.
Gould, S. H., tr. see Aleksandrov, A. D., et al.
Gould, Samuel B. & Cross, K. Patricia, eds. Explorations in Non-Traditional Study. LC 74-186578. (Higher Education Ser.). 1972. 18.95x (ISBN 0-87589-127-6). Jossey-Bass.
Gould, Sara. Struggling Through Tight Times: Introductory Handbook for Women's & Other Non-Profit Organizations on Fiscal Management. 125p. 1984. pap. 8.00 (ISBN 0-9605828-5-1). Women's Action.
Gould, Shirley. Challenge of Friendship: Helping Your Child Become a Friend. 124p. 1981. 16.95 (ISBN 0-8015-1172-0, Hawthorn). Dutton.
--How to Raise a Responsible Child. 192p. 1982. pap. 4.95 (ISBN 0-312-39580-9). St Martin.
--Swimming the Shane Gould Way. 160p. 1973. pap. 1.50 (ISBN 0-346-12093-4). Cornerstone.
Gould, Shirley G. Teenagers: The Continuing Challenge. 1977. (Hawthorn); pap. 6.95 (ISBN 0-8015-5801-8, 0674-210, Hawthorn). Dutton.
Gould, Sidney H. Sciences in Communist China: A Symposium Presented at the New York Meeting of the American Association for Advanced Science. LC 74-7534. 872p. 1975. Repr. of 1961 ed. lib. bdg. 47.50x (ISBN 0-8371-7583-6, GOSC). Greenwood.
Gould Staff Editors. New York Estates, Powers & Trusts Law. 150p. (Supplemented annually). looseleaf 7.50 (ISBN 0-87526-140-X). Gould.
Gould, Stephen J. Ever Since Darwin: Reflections in Natural History. (Illus.). 1979. pap. 4.95 (ISBN 0-393-00917-3). Norton.
--Ever Since Darwin: Reflections in Natural History. (Illus.). 1977. 14.95 (ISBN 0-393-06425-5). Norton.
--The Flamingo's Smile: Reflections in Natural History. 1985. 17.95 (ISBN 0-393-02228-5). Norton.
--Hen's Teeth & Horse's Toes: Further Reflections in Natural History. (Illus.). 1983. 15.50 (ISBN 0-393-01716-8). Norton.
--Hen's Teeth & Horse's Toes: Further Reflections in Natural History. (Illus.). 416p. 1984. pap. 5.95 (ISBN 0-393-30200-8). Norton.
--The Mismeasure of Man. (Illus.). 1981. 14.95 (ISBN 0-393-01489-4). Norton.
--The Mismeasure of Man. (Illus.). 352p. 1983. pap. 5.95 (ISBN 0-393-30056-0). Norton.
--Ontogeny & Phylogeny. 1977. 25.00x (ISBN 0-674-63940-5, Belknap Pr). Harvard U Pr.
--Ontogeny & Phylogeny. 520p. 1985. pap. 8.95 (ISBN 0-674-63941-3, Belknap Pr). Harvard U Pr.
--The Panda's Thumb: More Reflections in Natural History. (Illus.). 344p. 1982. pap. 4.95 (ISBN 0-393-30023-4). Norton.
--The Panda's Thumb: More Reflections in Natural History. (Illus.). 1980. 15.95 (ISBN 0-393-01380-4). Norton.

Gould, Stephen J., ed. The Complete Works of Vladimir Kovalevsky: Original Anthology. LC 79-8354. (The History of Paleontology Ser.). (Illus., Fr., Ger., Eng.). 1980. lib. bdg. 68.50x (ISBN 0-405-12750-2). Ayer Co Pubs.

--The Evolution of Gryphaea: Original Anthology. LC 79-8357. (The History of Paleontology Ser.). (Illus.). 1980. lib. bdg. 37.00x (ISBN 0-405-12751-0). Ayer Co Pubs.

--The History of Paleontology, 34 bks, Vols. 1-20. (Illus.). 1980. Repr. Set. lib. bdg. 2077.00x (ISBN 0-405-12700-6). Ayer Co Pubs.

--Louis Dollo's Papers on Paleontology & Evolution: Original Anthology. LC 79-8355. (The History of Paleontology Ser.). (Illus., Fr & Eng.). 1980. lib. bdg. 63.00x (ISBN 0-405-12752-9). Ayer Co Pubs.

Gould, Stephen J., ed. see Abel, Othenio.

Gould, Stephen J., ed. see Agassiz, Louis.

Gould, Stephen J., ed. see Beecher, Charles E.

Gould, Stephen J., ed. see Bernard, Felix.

Gould, Stephen J., ed. see Buckland, William.

Gould, Stephen J., ed. see Cuvier, Georges.

Gould, Stephen J., ed. see Dacque, Edgar.

Gould, Stephen J., ed. see Department of the Interior, U. S. Geologicaal Survey, Monograph & Osborn, Henry F.

Gould, Stephen J., ed. see Deperet, Charles.

Gould, Stephen J., ed. see D'Orbigny, Alcide D.

Gould, Stephen J., ed. see Gaudry, Albert.

Gould, Stephen J., ed. see Hatcher, John B.

Gould, Stephen J., ed. see Hyatt, Alpheus.

Gould, Stephen J., jt. ed. see Kummel, Bernhard.

Gould, Stephen J., ed. see Mantell, Gideon A.

Gould, Stephen J., ed. see Matthew, William D.

Gould, Stephen J., ed. see Mayr, Ernst.

Gould, Stephen J., ed. see Miller, Hugh.

Gould, Stephen J., ed. see Moore, C. Raymond & Laudon, Lowell R.

Gould, Stephen J., ed. see Newell, Norman D.

Gould, Stephen J., ed. see Nicholson, Henry A.

Gould, Stephen J., ed. see Osborn, Henry F.

Gould, Stephen J., ed. see Owen, Richard.

Gould, Stephen J., ed. see Phillips, John.

Gould, Stephen J., ed. see Pictet, Francois J.

Gould, Stephen J., ed. see Quenstedt, Friedrich A.

Gould, Stephen J., ed. see Romer, Alfred S. & Price, Llewellyn I.

Gould, Stephen J., ed. see Schindewolgf, Otto H.

Gould, Stephen J., jt. ed. see Schopf, Thomas J.

Gould, Stephen J., ed. see Scilla, Agostino.

Gould, Stephen J., ed. see Simpson, George G.

Gould, Stephen J., ed. see Stensio, Erik A.

Gould, Stephen Jay, ed. see Dobzhansky, Theodosius.

Gould, Sydney H. Variational Methods for Eigenvalue Problems: An Introduction to the Weinstein Method of Intermediate Problems. 2nd ed. LC 66-76289. (Mathematical Expositions Ser.). 1966. 27.50x (ISBN 0-8020-1404-6). U of Toronto Pr.

Gould, T. & Herington, J., eds. Greek Tragedy. LC 76-8156. (Yale Classical Studies: No. 25). 1977. 47.50 (ISBN 0-521-21112-3). Cambridge U Pr.

Gould, T. R. Tragedian: An Essay On-Junius Brutus Booth. LC 70-87122. 190p. 1868. 15.00 (ISBN 0-405-08567-2, Pub. by Blom). Ayer Co Pubs.

Gould, Thomas. Platonic Love. LC 81-6881. vii, 216p. 1981. Repr. of 1963 ed. lib. bdg. 19.75x (ISBN 0-313-22520-6, GOPT). Greenwood.

Gould, Toni. The Adventures of Mel & Tess. (Learn to Read Ser.). (Illus.). 1984. PLB 12.85 (ISBN 0-8027-9188-3); pap. text ed. 6.95 (ISBN 0-8027-9189-1). Walker & Co.

--Animal Tales, 6 bk. set. LC 83-5913. (Learn to Read Ser.). (Illus.). 1984. PLB 12.85 set (ISBN 0-8027-9186-7); pap. text ed. 6.95 set (ISBN 0-8027-9187-5). Walker & Co.

--Fun with the Fumble Families. LC 83-5928. (Learn to Read Ser.). (Illus.). 1984. PLB 12.85 (ISBN 0-8027-9190-5); pap. 6.95 (ISBN 0-8027-9191-3). Walker & Co.

--Fun with Water & Ice. LC 83-5938. (Learn to Read Ser.). (Illus.). 1984. PLB 12.85 (ISBN 0-8027-9192-1); pap. text ed. 6.95 (ISBN 0-8027-9194-8). Walker & Co.

--Home Guide to Early Reading. LC 75-40825. 1976. 9.95 (ISBN 0-8027-0531-6). Walker & Co.

--Science Fiction Fun. LC 83-5943. (Learn to Read Ser.). (Illus.). 1984. PLB 12.85 (ISBN 0-8027-9197-2); pap. 6.95 (ISBN 0-8027-9198-0). Walker & Co.

Gould, Toni S. Home Guide to Early Reading. (Illus.). 1978. pap. 4.95 (ISBN 0-14-004567-8). Penguin.

Gould, Toni S. & Stern, Margaret B. Gould-Stern Early Reading Activities, 2 bks. Incl. Bk. 1. Sound-Symbol Activities. 128p (ISBN 0-8027-9072-0); Bk. 2. Decoding Activities. 96p (ISBN 0-8027-9073-9). LC 79-83806. 1980. pap. text ed. 9.50x ea. Walker & Co.

Gould, Tony. Absolute Macinnes: The Best of Colin Macinnes. 256p. 1985. pap. 6.95 (ISBN 0-8052-8224-6, Pub. by Allison & Busby England). Schocken.

--In Limbo: The Story of Stanley's Rear Column. (Illus.). 269p. 1980. 25.00 (ISBN 0-241-10125-5, Pub. by Hamish Hamilton England). David & Charles.

--Inside Outsider: The Life & Times of Colin MacInnes. 288p. 1983. 16.95 (ISBN 0-7011-2678-7, Pub. by Chatto & Windus). Merrimack Pub Cir.

Gould, W, ed. Yeats Annual, Number Four. (Literary Annuals Ser.). 328p. 1985. text ed. 54.50x (ISBN 0-333-35332-3, Pub. by Macmillian England). Humanities.

Gould, W. J. & Lawrence, V. L. Surgical Care of Voice Disorders. (Disorders of Human Communication: Vol. 7). (Illus.). 130p. 1984. 24.50 (ISBN 0-387-81777-8). Springer-Verlag.

Gould, W. T. The Resources of Merseyside. 192p. 1982. 40.00x (ISBN 0-85323-384-5, Pub. by Liverpool Univ England). State Mutual Bk.

Gould, Walker. Talking Dog Stories. LC 83-5733. (Learn to Read Ser.). (Illus.). 1984. PLB 12.85 (ISBN 0-8027-9195-6); pap. 6.95 (ISBN 0-8027-9196-4). Walker & Co.

Gould, Wilbur A. Tomato Production, Processing & Quality Evaluation. 2nd ed. (Illus.). 1983. text ed. 57.50 (ISBN 0-87055-426-3). AVI.

Gould, William, ed. see Urdang, Laurence.

Gould, William B. Black Workers in White Unions: Job Discrimination in the United States. LC 76-50263. 512p. 1977. 39.95x (ISBN 0-8014-1062-2). Cornell U Pr.

--Japan's Reshaping of American Labor Law. (Illus.). 272p. 1984. text ed. 19.95x (ISBN 0-262-07091-X). MIT Pr.

--A Primer on American Labor Law. 272p. 1982. text ed. 30.00x (ISBN 0-262-07087-1); pap. text ed. 9.95x (ISBN 0-262-57060-2). MIT Pr.

--Strikes, Dispute Procedures, & Arbitration: Essays on Labor Law. LC 85-944. (Contributions in American Studies). write for info. Amer Bar Assn.

Gould, William B., IV. Strikes, Dispute Procedures, & Arbitration: Essays on Labor Law. LC 85-944. (Contributions in American Studies: No. 82). 320p. 1985. lib. bdg. 39.95 (ISBN 0-313-24468-5, GSD/). Greenwood.

Gould, William S. Baring see Doyle, Arthur Conan.

Gould-Caskey, Kay. Within the Bones of Memory. 168p. 1984. 10.95 (ISBN 0-932229-00-X). Falling Water.

Goulden, ed. see Judge, Clark S.

Goulden, Clyde E., ed. The Changing Scenes in the Natural Sciences 1776-1976. (Special Publication: No. 12). 362p. 1977. 27.00 (ISBN 0-910006-39-3). Acad Nat Sci Phila.

Goulden, Dorothy. The Illustrated Book of Flowers: A Collection of the Greatest Paintings of Flowers by the Greatest Artists. (Illus.). 1980. deluxe ed. 237.45 (ISBN 0-930582-54-3). Gloucester Art.

Goulden, I. P. & Jackson, D. M. Combinatorial Enumeration. 569p. 1983. 54.95x (ISBN 0-471-86654-7, Pub. by Wiley-Interscience). Wiley.

Goulden, J. C. Korea: The Untold Story of the War. 736p. 1983. pap. 12.95 (ISBN 0-07-023580-5). McGraw.

Goulden, Joseph, jt. auth. see Dickson, Paul.

Goulden, Joseph C. Korea: The Untold Story. LC 81-21262. (Illus.). 640p. 1982. 24.95 (ISBN 0-8129-0985-2). Times Bks.

--The Million Dollar Lawyer's. 336p. 1981. pap. 2.95 (ISBN 0-425-05149-8). Berkley Pub.

Goulden, Joseph C. & Raffio, Alexander W. The Death Merchant: The Rise & Fall of Edwin P. Wilson. LC 84-5547. 453p. 1984. 17.95 (ISBN 0-671-49341-8). S&S.

Goulden, Joseph C., jt. auth. see Dickson, Paul.

Goulden, Paula. Medical Science & the Law. rev. ed. 224p. 1983. 19.95 (ISBN 0-87196-818-5). Facts on File.

Goulden, Shirley. Royal Book of Ballet. LC 64-16319. (Illus.). (gr. 5 up). 1964. 7.95 (ISBN 0-695-90040-4, Dist. by Caroline Hse). Modern Curr.

Goulden, Steven L., jt. ed. see Turner, Roland.

Goulder, ed. Channel West & Solent Almanac: A Nautical Almanac for Yachtsmen. 1985 ed. (Illus.). 200p. (Orig.). 1984. spiral bdg. 18.50 (ISBN 0-229-11723-6, Pub. by Adlard Coles). Sheridan.

Goulder, Lois & Lutwak, Leo. The Strong Bones Diet. 272p. 1985. 14.95 (ISBN 0-937404-20-9). Triad Pub FL.

Goulder, Lois, jt. auth. see James, Janet.

Goulder, Michael, ed. Incarnation & Myth: The Debate Continued. LC 79-16509. pap. 67.30 (ISBN 0-317-19819-X, 2023212). Bks Demand UMI.

Goulder, Michael D. The Psalms of the Sons of Korah. (Journal for the Study of the Old Testament, Supplement Ser.: No. 20). xiv, 302p. 1983. 27.50x (ISBN 0-905774-40-X, Pub. by JSOT Pr England); pap. text ed. 14.95x (ISBN 0-905774-41-8). Eisenbrauns.

Goulding, Brian, jt. auth. see Garbett, Mike.

Goulding, Daniel J. Liberated Cinema: The Yugoslav Experience. LC 84-42835. (Illus.). 240p. 1985. 25.00x (ISBN 0-253-14790-5). Ind U Pr.

Goulding, Daniel J., jt. ed. see Wolfe, W. Dean.

Goulding, Dorothy J. The Gift of the Drum. 1955. in collection of 3 christmas plays 3.00x (ISBN 0-88020-097-9). Coach Hse.

--Mr. Bunch's Toys. 1981. pap. 3.00x in anthology Three Christmas Plays (ISBN 0-88020-096-0). Coach Hse.

--The Nativity: A Christmas Short Play for Children. 1955. pap. 3.00x in anthology Three Christmas Plays (ISBN 0-88020-074-X). Coach Hse.

--Three Christmas Plays. 20p. (gr. 3-6). Repr. of 1955 ed. 3.00 (ISBN 0-88020-103-7). Coach Hse.

Goulding, F. J., tr. see Musavi, Sayyed M.

Goulding, Francis R. The Young Marooners. 1973. Repr. of 1852 ed. lib. bdg. 59.95 (ISBN 0-8490-1344-5). Gordon Pr.

Goulding, J., jt. auth. see Gaines, M.

Goulding, James, jt. auth. see Sweetman, Bill.

Goulding, Jeanne H. Fanny Osborne's Flower Paintings. (Illus.). 84p. 1983. 24.50 (ISBN 0-86863-396-8, Pub. by Heinemann Pub. New Zealand). Intl Spec Bk.

Goulding, Mary & Goulding, Robert L. Changing Lives Through Redecision Therapy. LC 79-9979. 1979. 25.00 (ISBN 0-87630-191-X). Brunner-Mazel.

Goulding, Mary M. & Goulding, Robert. Changing Lives Through Redecision Therapy. LC 81-48537. 320p. 1982. pap. 9.95 (ISBN 0-394-17980-3, E-800, Ever). Grove.

Goulding, Michael. The Fishes & the Forest: Explorations in Amazonian Natural History. LC 80-41201. (Illus.). 250p. 1981. 24.50x (ISBN 0-520-04131-3). U of Cal Pr.

--Man & Fisheries of an Amazon Frontier. (Developments in Hydrobiology Ser.: Vol. 4). 140p. 1982. 47.50 (ISBN 90-6193-755-8, Pub. by Junk Pubs Netherlands). Kluwer Academic.

Goulding, Ray, jt. auth. see Elliot, Bob.

Goulding, Ray, jt. auth. see Elliott, Bob.

Goulding, Ray, jt. auth. see Elliott, Bob G.

Goulding, Robert, jt. auth. see Goulding, Mary M.

Goulding, Robert L., jt. auth. see Goulding, Mary.

Gouldman, W. Clyde & Hess, Amy M. Virginia Forms, Vol.I. 1978. 75.00 (ISBN 0-87215-205-7); 1983 supplement 10.00 (ISBN 0-87215-765-2). Michie Co.

Gouldner, Alvin W. Against Fragmentation: The Origins of Marxism & the Sociology of Intellectuals. Gouldner, Janet & Disco, Cornelis, eds. 1985. 27.95 (ISBN 0-19-503303-5). Oxford U Pr.

--Coming Crisis of Western Sociology. 1971. pap. text ed. 5.45 (ISBN 0-380-01109-3, 22186, Equinox). Avon.

--The Coming Crisis of Western Sociology. LC 77-75252. 528p. 1980. pap. 8.95x (ISBN 0-465-01279-5, TB-5066). Basic.

--The Dialectic of Ideology & Technology: The Origins, Grammar, & Future of Ideology. 1982. pap. 8.95 (ISBN 0-19-503064-8, GB). Oxford U Pr.

--The Future of Intellectuals & the Rise of the New Class. 1982. pap. 5.95 (ISBN 0-19-503065-6, GB). Oxford U Pr.

--Patterns of Industrial Bureaucracy: A Case Study of Modern Factory Administration. 1964. 14.95 (ISBN 0-02-912730-0); pap. text ed. 11.95 (ISBN 0-02-912740-8). Free Pr.

--The Two Marxisms: Contradictions & Anomalies in the Development of Theory. 1982. pap. 10.95 (ISBN 0-19-503066-4, GB). Oxford U Pr.

Gouldner, Alvin W. & Peterson, Richard A. Notes on Technology & the Moral Order. LC 62-20957. 1962. 19.95x (ISBN 0-672-51159-2). Irvington.

Gouldner, Alvin W., ed. see Durkheim, Emile.

Gouldner, Helen. Teacher's Pets, Troublemakers, & Nobodies: Black Children in Elementary School. LC 78-53660. (Contributions in Afro-American & African Studies: No. 41). (Illus.). 1978. lib. bdg. 27.50 (ISBN 0-313-20417-9, GOE/). Greenwood.

Gouldner, Janet, ed. see Gouldner, Alvin W.

Gouldsbury, Cullen & Sheane, Hubert. Great Plateau of Northern Rhodesia. LC 78-77201. (Illus.). Repr of 1911 ed. 24.00x (ISBN 0-8371-1289-3, GOG&, Pub. by Negro U Pr). Greenwood.

Goulet, A. S. L' Univers Theatral De Corneille: Paradoxe et Subtilite Heroiques. LC 78-1756. (Studies in Romance Languages: No. 33). 1978. 14.00x (ISBN 0-674-92928-4). Harvard U Pr.

Goulet, Alain. Caves du Vatican d'Andre Gide: Etude methodologigue. new ed. (La Collection themes et textes). 288p. (Orig., Fr.). 1972. pap. 6.75 (ISBN 2-03-035006-0, 2693). Larousse.

Goulet, Bertrand H., Jr. & Rochefort, David A. Barriers to the Establishment & Operation of Halfway Houses. (State Institutional Care Ser.). (Illus.). 55p. (Orig.). 1979. pap. 5.95 (ISBN 0-89995-056-6, M 405-6). Social Matrix.

Goulet, Denis. The Cruel Choice: A New Concept in the Theory of Development. LC 85-3313. 384p. 1985. pap. text ed. 14.75 (ISBN 0-8191-4612-9). U Pr of Amer.

--Looking at Guinea-Bissau: A New Nation's Development Strategy. (Occasional Papers: No. 9). 72p. 1978. 2.50 (ISBN 0-318-16154-0). Overseas Dev Council.

--Mexico: Development Strategies for the Future. LC 82-40379. 208p. 1983. text ed. 16.95 (ISBN 0-268-01355-1); pap. text ed. 8.95 (ISBN 0-268-01356-X). U of Notre Dame Pr.

--The Uncertain Promise: Valve Conflicts in Technology Transfer. 324p. 1977. pap. 5.95 (ISBN 0-318-16161-3). Overseas Dev Council.

Goulet, Denis & Kallab, Valeriana, eds. Development from Tradition: Views from Several Cultures. 322p. 1981. write for info. Overseas Dev Council.

Goulet, L. R. & Baltes, Paul B., eds. Lifespan Developmental Psychology: Research & Theory. 1970. 50.00 (ISBN 0-12-293850-X). Acad Pr.

Goulet, Rosalina M., jt. auth. see Ramos, Teresita.

Goulian, Dicran & Courtiss, Eugene H., eds. Symposium of Surgery of the Aging Face, Vol. 19. LC 78-12298. (Symposia of the Educational Foundation of the American Society of Plastic & Reconstructive Surgeons Inc. Ser.). 206p. 1978. text ed. 54.50 (ISBN 0-8016-1941-6). Mosby.

Goulooze, William. Comfort for the Sorrowing. pap. 0.45 (ISBN 0-686-23474-X). Rose Pub MI.

--The Shepherd's Care. pap. 0.45 (ISBN 0-686-23475-8). Rose Pub MI.

Goulson, Cary F. A Source Book of Royal Commissions & Other Major Governmental Inquiries in Canadian Education 1787-1978. 248p. 1981. 50.00x (ISBN 0-8020-2408-4). U of Toronto Pr.

Goulston, S. J. & McGovern, V. J. Fundamnetals of Colitis. (Illus.). 144p. 1981. 26.00 (ISBN 0-08-026862-5); pap. 11.50 (ISBN 0-08-026861-7). Pergamon.

Goult, R. J. Applied Linear Algebra. LC 78-40608. (Mathematics & Its Applications Ser.). 196p. 1979. pap. text ed. 25.95x (ISBN 0-470-26864-6). Halsted Pr.

Gounaris, John, et al. Dining in Hampton Road. Lotzgar, Elaine, ed. (Dining in Ser.). (Illus., Orig.). 1984. pap. 8.95 (ISBN 0-89716-136-X). Peanut Butter.

Gounaud, Karen J. A Very Mice Joke Book. (Illus.). 1981. PLB 6.95 (ISBN 0-395-30445-8); pap. 2.95 (ISBN 0-395-30442-3). HM.

Goundry, J. H., jt. auth. see Thiery, P.

Gounod, Charles. Autobiographical Reminiscences: With Family Letters & Notes on Music. LC 68-16235. (Music Ser.). 1970. Repr. of 1896 ed. lib. bdg. 29.50 (ISBN 0-306-71081-1). Da Capo.

Gounod, Charles F. Mozart's Don Giovanni: A Commentary. LC 78-125050. (Music Ser). 1970. Repr. of 1895 ed. lib. bdg. 21.50 (ISBN 0-306-70015-8). Da Capo.

Goupil, Armand. Jules Verne. new ed. Barberis, Pierre & Jean, Georges, eds. (Textes pour aujourd'hui). (Illus.). 191p. (Orig., Fr.). 1975. pap. 3.95 (ISBN 2-03-038006-7). Larousse.

Gour, Hari S. The Spirit of Buddhism. LC 78-72432. Repr. of 1929 ed. 57.50 (ISBN 0-404-17299-7). AMS Pr.

Gouran, Dennis S. Making Decisions in Groups. 1982. pap. text ed. 11.90x (ISBN 0-673-15386-X). Scott F.

Gouraud, Charles. Histoire De la Politique Commerciale De la France et De Son Influence Sur les Progres De la Richesse Publique Depuis le Moyen Age Jusqu'a Nos Jours, 2 vols. LC 79-171408. (Research & Source Works Ser.: No. 851). (Fr.). 1972. Repr. of 1854 ed. lib. bdg. 49.00 (ISBN 0-8337-1400-7). B Franklin.

Gourd, L. M. Introduction to Engineering Materials. 192p. 1982. pap. text ed. 18.50x (ISBN 0-7131-3444-5). Intl Ideas.

Gourdie, Tom. Calligraphic Styles. LC 78-52316. (Illus.). 106p. 1982. pap. 2.95 (ISBN 0-8008-1190-9, Pentalic). Taplinger.

--Calligraphic Styles. LC 78-52316. (Illus., Orig.). 1979. pap. 6.95 (ISBN 0-8008-1181-X, Pentalic). Taplinger.

--Calligraphy for the Beginner: Giant. LC 78-63439. (Illus.). 1979. pap. 4.50 (ISBN 0-8008-1185-2, Pentalic). Taplinger.

--Handwriting. (gr. 4 up). 2.50 (ISBN 0-7214-0216-X). Merry Thoughts.

--Handwriting for Today. 1978. pap. 3.95 (ISBN 0-8008-3812-2, Pentalic). Taplinger.

--Handwriting Made Easy: A Simple Modern Approach. LC 87-50225. (Illus.). 64p. 1981. pap. 3.95 (ISBN 0-8008-4597-8). Taplinger.

--Improve Your Handwriting. (Illus.). 80p. 1975. pap. 8.95x (ISBN 0-686-60815-1). Beekman Pubs.

--Puffin Book of Lettering. (Picture Bks.). 32p. (ps-3). 1962. pap. 2.95 (ISBN 0-14-049117-1, Puffin). Penguin.

Gourdin, M. Formalisme Langrangien et Lois de Symetrie. (Cour & Documents de Mathematiques & de Physique Ser.). 108p. (Fr) 1967. 37.25 (ISBN 0-677-50070-X). Gordon.

--Langrangian Formalism & Symmetry Laws. (Documents on Modern Physics Ser.). 108p. 1969. 27.95 (ISBN 0-677-30070-0). Gordon.

Gourdin, Peter G., 4th. The Gourdin Family. (Illus.). 713p. 1981. 35.00 (ISBN 0-89308-198-1). Southern Hist Pr.

Goure, Jim. Family. (Orig.). 1981. pap. 3.00 (ISBN 0-915235-06-4). United Res.

--The Great Light Way. 24p. (Orig.). 1980. pap. 3.50 (ISBN 0-915235-03-X). United Res.

--Seven Concentric Circles. 56p. (Orig.). 1983. pap. 5.00 (ISBN 0-915235-05-6). United Res.

--The Tree of Life. (Illus.). 62p. (Orig.). 1981. pap. 5.00 (ISBN 0-915235-04-8). United Res.

Goure, Leon. Shelters in Soviet War Survival Strategy. LC 78-57652. (Monographs in International Affairs). (Illus.). 1978. pap. text ed. 6.95 (ISBN 0-933074-32-8). AISI.

--The Siege of Leningrad. LC 62-8662. 1962. 27.50x (ISBN 0-8047-0115-6). Stanford U Pr.

--War Survival in Soviet Strategy: USSR Civil Defense. LC 76-12185. (Monographs in International Affairs). 1976. 11.95 (ISBN 0-933074-00-X); pap. 8.95 (ISBN 0-933074-01-8). AISI.

Goure, Leon & Rothenberg, Morris. Soviet Penetration of Latin America. LC 75-7513. (Monographs in International Affairs). 203p. 1975. text ed. 9.95 (ISBN 0-933074-10-7); pap. text ed. 6.95 (ISBN 0-933074-11-5). AISI.

Goure, Leon, ed. see Kohler, Foy D., et al.

Goure, Leon, et al. The Emerging Strategic Environment: Implications for Ballistic Missile Defense. LC 79-53108. 75p. 1979. 6.50 (ISBN 0-89549-008-0). Inst Foreign Policy Anal.

--Convergence of Communism & Capitalism: The Soviet View. LC 72-96761. (Monographs in International Affairs). 168p. 1973. text ed. 7.95 (ISBN 0-933074-12-3); pap. text ed. 4.95 (ISBN 0-933074-13-1). AISI.

--The Role of Nuclear Forces in Current Soviet Strategy. LC 74-81601. (Monographs in International Affairs). 131p. 1974. text ed. 9.95 (ISBN 0-933074-02-6); pap. text ed. 6.95 (ISBN 0-933074-03-4). AISI.

Gourevitch, Doris-Jean & Stadler, Eve M. Premiers Textes Litteraires. 2nd ed. LC 74-83346. 244p. 1975. pap. text ed. 16.50x (ISBN 0-471-00811-7). Wiley.

Gourevitch, Doris-Jeanne & Fourestier, Marie-Francoise, eds. La Bonne Lecture. LC 83-14659. 234p. 1984. pap. text ed. 15.95 (ISBN 0-471-89050-2). Wiley.

Gourevitch, Peter A. Paris & the Provinces: The Politics of Local Government Reform in France. LC 79-64666. 256p. 1981. 28.00x (ISBN 0-520-03971-8). U of Cal Pr.

Gourfinkel, Nina. Gorky. Feshbach, Ann, tr. LC 75-11423. (Illus.). 192p. 1975. Repr. of 1960 ed. lib. bdg. 22.50x (ISBN 0-8371-8190-9, GOGO). Greenwood.

--Lenin. Thornton, Maurice, tr. LC 75-11424. (Illus.). 189p. 1975. Repr. of 1961 ed. lib. bdg. 22.50x (ISBN 0-8371-8191-7, GOLE). Greenwood.

Gourgues, Harold W., Jr. Financial Planning Handbook. 443p. 1983. 35.00 (ISBN 0-13-316398-9). NY Inst Finance.

Gourieres, D. le see Le Gourieres, D.

Gourlay, A. R. & Watson, G. A. Computational Methods for Matrix Eigenproblems. LC 73-2783. 130p. 1973. pap. text ed. 22.95x (ISBN 0-471-27586-7). Wiley.

Gourlay, Alastair. Games for Your VIC-20. (The Dell Computer Games Ser.). 128p. (gr. 6-8). 1983. pap. 5.95 comb-bound (ISBN 0-440-52789-9, Dell Trade Pbks). Dell.

Gourlay, Carol. Computers & Mathematics. LC 82-50387. (Visual Science Ser.). 48p. (gr. 6 up). PLB 13.72 (ISBN 0-382-06662-6). Silver.

Gourlay, Logan. The Beaverbrook I Knew. (Illus.). 256p. 1985. 19.95 (ISBN 0-7043-2331-1, Pub. by Quartet Bks). Merrimack Pub Cir.

Gourlay, Robert F. General Introduction to Statistical Account of Upper Canada. Repr. of 1822 ed. 29.00 (ISBN 0-384-19440-0). Johnson Repr.

--Statistical Account of Upper Canada, 2 Vols. 1967. Repr. of 1822 ed. 60.00 set (ISBN 0-384-19475-3). Johnson Repr.

Gourley, D. R. Pharmacy College Admission Test (PCAT) 208p. (Orig.). 1983. pap. 12.00 (ISBN 0-668-05682-7). Arco.

Gourley, G. Douglas. Patrol Administration. 2nd ed. (Illus.). 400p. 1974. photocopy ed. 24.75x (ISBN 0-398-03126-6). C C Thomas.

--Public Relations & the Police. (Illus.). 134p. 1953. photocopy ed. 16.50x (ISBN 0-398-04268-3). C C Thomas.

Gourley, Ira M. & Vasseur, Phillip B. General Small Animal Surgery. (Illus.). 1248p. 1985. text ed. 95.00 (ISBN 0-397-52110-3, Lippincott Medical). Lippincott.

Gourman, Jack. The Gourman Report: A Rating of Graduate & Professional Programs in American & International Universities. 2nd, rev. ed. LC 82-73149. 176p. 1983-84. pap. 14.95 (ISBN 0-918192-07-2). Natl Ed Stand.

--The Gourman Report: A Rating of Undergraduate Programs in American & International Universities. 4th, rev. ed. LC 82-73150. 178p. 1983-84. pap. 14.95 (ISBN 0-918192-06-4). Natl Ed Stand.

Gourmant, Remy De see De Gourmont, Remy.

Gourmet Magazine, ed. The Gourmet Cookbook, Vol. I. 2nd, rev. ed. (Illus.). 1965. 27.50 (ISBN 0-394-54032-8). Gourmet Bks.

--The Gourmet Cookbook, Vol II. 2nd rev. ed. (Illus.). 1965. Repr. 24.00 (ISBN 0-933166-01-X). Gourmet Bks.

--Gourmet's France. LC 78-58144. (Illus.). 1978. 30.00 (ISBN 0-394-54035-2). Gourmet Bks.

--Gourmet's Menu Cookbook. (Illus.). 1963. 24.00 (ISBN 0-933166-02-8). Gourmet Bks.

Gourmet Magazine, ed. see Diat, Louis.

Gourmet Magazine, ed. see Langseth-Christensen, Lillian.

Gourmet Magazine Editors, jt. auth. see Righter, Evie.

Gourmont, Remy De. Le Latin mystique: Les Poetes de l'antiphonaire et la symbolique au moyen age. LC 77-10268. 400p. Repr. of 1895 ed. 37.50 (ISBN 0-404-16320-3). AMS Pr.

--Le Probleme du style. LC 78-64031. (Des Imagistes: Literature of the Imagist Movement). Repr. of 1907 ed. 27.00 (ISBN 0-404-17109-5). AMS Pr.

--Remy De Gourmont, Selections from All His Works. Aldington, Richard, ed. Aldington, Richard, tr. from Fr. LC 77-10269. (Illus.). Repr. of 1928 ed. 49.50 (ISBN 0-404-16321-1). AMS Pr.

Gourmont, Remy De see De Gourmont, Remy.

Gourou, Pierre. Etudes de Geographic Tropicale Offertes a Pierre Gourou. (Le Monde D'outre-Mer Passe et Present: Etudes 38). (Illus.). 1972. 46.00x (ISBN 90-2797-052-1); pap. 40.00x (ISBN 0-686-21243-6). Mouton.

--Lecons De Geographie Tropicale: Lecons Donees Au College De France De 1947 a 1970. (Le Savoir Geographique: No. 1). 1971. pap. 14.00x (ISBN 90-2796-841-1). Mouton.

Gourse, Leslie. Every Day: The Story of Joe Williams. (Illus.). 294p. 1985. 15.95 (ISBN 0-7043-2466-0, Pub. by Quartet Bks). Merrimack Pub Cir.

--Louis' Children: American Jazz Singers. LC 83-13178. (Illus.). 366p. 1984. 19.95 (ISBN 0-688-02241-3); pap. 12.95 (ISBN 0-688-02243-X). Morrow.

--Student Guide to New York. (Illus.). 1984. pap. 8.95 (ISBN 0-88254-895-6). Hippocrene Bks.

Gourvish, T. R. Railways in the British Economy: 1830-1914. (Studies in Economic & Social History). 64p. 1980. pap. text ed. 6.00x (ISBN 0-333-28365-1, Pub. by Macmillan England). Humanities.

Gourvitch, Alexander. Survey of Economic Theory on Technological Change & Employment. LC 66-23421. Repr. of 1940 ed. 27.50x (ISBN 0-678-00113-8). Kelley.

Gousen, Doeko. Aerial Photo Interpretation in Soil Survey. (Soils Bulletins: No. 6). 116p. (Eng., Fr. & Span., 3rd. Printing 1976). 1967. pap. 8.50 (ISBN 92-5-100105-7, F1151, FAO). Unipub.

Goutel, Beatrice, jt. auth. see Carillon, Annie.

Goutel, Beatrice de, jt. auth. see Carillon, Annie.

Gouvernet, Gerard R. Le Type du Valet chez Moliere et Ses Successeurs: Regnard, Dufresny, Dancourt, et Lesage. Caracteres et Evolution. LC 84-47806. (American University Studies II (Romance Languages & Literature): Vol. 15). 358p. (Fr.). 1985. text ed. 29.00 (ISBN 0-8204-0141-2). P Lang Pubs.

Gouverneur, Jacques. Contemporary Capitalism & Marxist Economics. Le Janu, Richard, tr. LC 83-9992. 300p. 1983. 29.95x (ISBN 0-389-20416-1, 07301). B&N Imports.

Gouvion, Colette, jt. auth. see Gougaud, Henri.

Gouvion, Colette, jt. auth. see Philippe, Daniel.

Gouw, jt. auth. see Altgelt.

Gouw, T. H. Guide to Modern Methods of Instrumental Analysis. LC 79-171913. 510p. 1972. 38.00 (ISBN 0-471-31925-2). Krieger.

Gouwenius, Peder. Power to the People: South Africa in Struggle, a Pictorial History, Pt. 1. (Illus.). 96p. (Orig.). 1981. (Pub. by Zed Pr England); pap. 8.95x (ISBN 0-905762-66-5, Pub. by Zed Pr England). Biblio Dist.

Gouy, Louis P. De see De Gouy, Louis P.

Gouy, Manlo, jt. auth. see Gautier, Christian.

Gov. Rockefeller Symposium Winrock, Arkansas, Oct. 1970. Technology Utilization Ideas for the 70's & Beyond. Forbes, Fred W. & Dergarabedian, Paul, eds. (Science & Technology Ser.: Vol. 26). 1971. lib. bdg. 30.00x (ISBN 0-87703-057-X, Pub. by Am Astronaut). Univelt Inc.

Govan, Alastair D., et al. Pathology Illustrated. (Illus.). 880p. (Orig.). 1981. pap. text ed. 37.50 (ISBN 0-443-01647-X). Churchill.

Govan, F. A., et al, eds. Thermal Insulations Materials, & Systems for Energy Conservation in the '80s - STP 789. LC 82-70616. 890p. 1983. text ed. 68.00 (ISBN 0-8031-0230-5, 04-789000-10). ASTM.

Govan, Gilbert E. & Livingood, James W. A Different Valor, the Story of General Joseph E. Johnston, C.S.A. LC 73-9372. (Illus.). 470p. 1973. Repr. of 1956 ed. lib. bdg. 24.75x (ISBN 0-8371-7012-5, GOVD). Greenwood.

Govan, Gilbert E. & Livingwood, James W. The Chattanooga Country, 1540-1976: From Tomahawks to TVA. 3rd ed. LC 77-21751. (Illus.). 1977. 17.95 (ISBN 0-87049-234-9). U of Tenn Pr.

Govan, Thomas P. Banking & the Credit System in Georgia, 1810-1860. LC 77-14786. (Dissertations in American Economic History Ser.). 1978. 26.00 (ISBN 0-405-11036-7). Ayer Co Pubs.

--Nicholas Biddle, Nationalist & Public Banker, 1786-1844. LC 59-12286. (Midway Reprint Ser.). pap. write for info. (2024042). Bks Demand UMI.

Govan-Kleckley, Robyn. Community Efforts to Improve Local Schools: Pt. II, An Inventory of Programs & Resources in New York City, Pt. 2. 23p. (Orig.). 1983. pap. 2.00 (ISBN 0-88156-014-6). Comm Serv Soc NY.

Gove, Doris. Miracle at Egg Rock: The Story of Puffin Q7. (Illus.). 48p. (Orig.). (gr. 4-6). 1985. pap. 6.95t (ISBN 0-89272-205-3). Down East.

Gove, Philip B. The Imaginary Voyage in Prose Fiction. LC 74-15972. (Science Fiction Ser). 459p. 1975. Repr. of 1941 ed. 29.00x (ISBN 0-405-06328-8). Ayer Co Pubs.

--The Imaginary Voyage in Prose Fiction. 445p. 1975. Repr. of 1941 ed. lib. bdg. 27.50x (ISBN 0-374-93223-9). Octagon.

Gove, Samuel, ed. Higher Education Policy. (Orig.). 1981. pap. 8.00 (ISBN 0-918592-48-8). Policy Studies.

Gove, Samuel & Wirt, Frederick, eds. Critical Issues in Educational Policy. 1976. pap. 8.00 (ISBN 0-918592-15-1). Policy Studies.

Gove, Samuel K. & Kitsos, Thomas R. Revision Success: The Sixth Illinois Constitutional Convention. 185p. 1974. 1.00 (ISBN 0-318-15814-0). Citizens Forum Gov.

Gove, Samuel K. & Masotti, Louis H. After Daley: Chicago Politics in Transition. LC 81-10302. (Illus.). 280p. 1982. 19.95x (ISBN 0-252-00902-9); pap. 7.95x (ISBN 0-252-00936-3). U of Ill Pr.

Gove, Samuel K., et al. Illinois Legislature: Structure & Process. LC 76-21238. 208p. 1976. pap. 7.95x (ISBN 0-252-00621-6). U of Ill Pr.

Gove, Walter, jt. auth. see Geerken, Michael.

Gove, Walter, jt. ed. see Langland, Elizabeth.

Gove, Walter, et al. Overcrowding in the Household: An Analysis of Determinants & Effects (Monograph) LC 83-12318. (Quantitative Studies Social Relations). 1983. 42.50 (ISBN 0-12-294060-1). Acad Pr.

Gove, Walter R. & Carpenter, G. Russell. The Fundamental Connection Between Nature & Nurture: A Review of the Evidence. LC 80-8961. 320p. 1981. 31.50x (ISBN 0-669-04483-0). Lexington Bks.

Gove, Walter R., ed. The Labelling of Deviance: Evaluating a Perspective. 2nd ed. LC 80-50397. (Illus.). 428p. 1980. pap. 14.95 (ISBN 0-8039-1471-7). Sage.

Govea, Rodger M. & Wolohojian, George G. Good Federalism Game: Participant's Manual for a Simulation of Intergovernmental Relations. (Learning Packages in Policy Sciences Ser.: No. 9). (Illus.). 56p. (Orig.). 1975. pap. text ed. 3.00x (ISBN 0-936876-03-4). Pol Stud Assocs.

Goveia, Elsa V. Slave Society in the British Leeward Islands at the End of the Eighteenth Century. LC 80-13. (Caribbean Ser.: No. 8). (Illus.). ix, 370p. 1980. Repr. of 1965 ed. lib. bdg. 32.50x (ISBN 0-313-22156-1, GOSL). Greenwood.

--A Study on the Historiography of the British West Indies to the End of the Nineteenth Century. LC 75-20036. 192p. 1980. pap. 8.95 (ISBN 0-88258-048-5). Howard U Pr.

Goven, Phoebe, et al. The Use of Sensory Stimulation in Teaching Mentally Impaired Students. (Illus.). 266p. 1984. spiral 29.75x (ISBN 0-398-04907-6). C C Thomas.

Govenar, Alan B., jt. auth. see St. Clair, Leonard L.

Gover, Harvey R. Keys to Library Research on the Graduate Level: A Guide to Guides. LC 80-5841. 75p. 1981. pap. text ed. 7.00 (ISBN 0-8191-1370-0). U Pr of Amer.

Gover, Robert. J. C. Kitten Trilogy. 600p. 1982. 10.00 (ISBN 0-915520-52-4). Ross-Erikson.

--One Hundred Dollar Misunderstanding. LC 62-20506. 256p. 1981. pap. 2.95 (ISBN 0-394-17764-9, B448, BC). Grove.

--Tomorrow Now Occurs Again. LC 75-6142. 1975. pap. 4.95 (ISBN 0-915520-00-1). Ross-Erikson.

--Voodoo Contra. LC 84-52293. 160p. (Orig.). 1985. pap. 6.95 (ISBN 0-87728-619-1). Weiser.

Government Information Office, ed. Republic of China: A Reference Book, 1983. (Illus.). 470p. 1983. 37.50x (ISBN 0-8002-3130-9). Intl Pubns Serv.

Government Institutes Staff, ed. Cogeneration in California, 1984. 200p. 1984. 3-ring binder 69.00 (ISBN 0-86587-071-3). Gov Insts.

Government Land Office. A Collection of Original Instructions to Surveyors of the Public Lands 1815-1881. (Illus.). 517p. Repr. of 1881 ed. 30.00 (ISBN 0-910845-08-5, 520). Landmark Ent.

Government of Bangladesh, National Institute for Population Research & Training. Basic Methods of Evaluative & Action Research. 166p. 1984. text ed. 15.95x (ISBN 0-89914-006-8). Third Party Pub.

Government Printing Office. America's Medal of Honor Recipients. LC 85-152004. 1110p. 1980. 18.95 (ISBN 0-9615009-0-5). Highland Pub.

Government Printing Office, ed. Glossaries for Surveyors. 517p. (Orig.). pap. 18.00 (ISBN 0-910845-07-7, 521). Landmark Ent.

Governmental Research Association, ed. GRA Directory 1981-82. 1981. 25.00 (ISBN 0-686-20612-6). GRA.

Governor's Conference on Crime, the Criminal & Society, Sep 30-Oct 3, 1935, New York. Proceedings. facsimile ed. Fogeleson, Robert M., ed. LC 74-3848. (Criminal Justice in America). 1974. Repr. 92.50x (ISBN 0-405-06161-7). Ayer Co Pubs.

Governors in the White House, Conference, Washington D.C., May 13-15, 1908, jt. ed. see McGee, W. J.

Govett, G. J. Rock Geochemistry in Mineral Exploration. (Handbook of Mineral Exploration Geology Ser.: Vol. 3). 462p. 1983. 100.00 (ISBN 0-444-42021-5). Elsevier.

Govett, G. J. & Govett, M. H., eds. World Mineral Supplies. (Developments in Economic Geology: Vol. 3). 476p. 1976. 72.50 (ISBN 0-444-41366-9). Elsevier.

Govett, M. H. & Larsen, J. World Aluminium Statistics: Update of the World Aluminium Industry, Vols. 1 & 2 of 1983. 1983. pap. 307.00 (ISBN 0-85000-003-3, Pub. by Aluminium W Germany). Heyden.

Govett, M. H., jt. ed. see Govett, G. J.

Govett, R. English Derived from Hebrew with Glances at Greek & Latin. LC 77-7661. 1977. Repr. of 1869 ed. lib. bdg. 15.00 (ISBN 0-89341-151-5). Longwood Pub Group.

Govier. A Practical Study of Argument. 1984. write for info. (ISBN 0-534-03333-4). Wadsworth Pub.

Govier, George W. & Aziz, Khalid. The Flow of Complex Mixture in Pipes. LC 77-2591. 842p. 1977. Repr. of 1972 ed. 55.50 (ISBN 0-88275-547-1). Krieger.

Govier, Jacquie. Create Your Own Stage Props. (Illus.). 192p. 1984. 18.95 (ISBN 0-13-189044-1); pap. 9.95 (ISBN 0-13-189036-0). P-H.

Govier, Katherine. Going Through the Motions. 256p. 1982. St Martin.

Govil, G. & Hosur, R. Conformation of Biological Molecules. (NMR - Basic Principles & Progress Ser.: Vol. 20). (Illus.). 220p. 1982. 72.50 (ISBN 0-387-10769-X). Springer-Verlag.

Govinda A., intro. by see Winkler, Kenneth D.

Govinda, L. Anagarika. Foundations of Tibetan Mysticism. (Illus.). 331p. 1969. pap. 7.95 (ISBN 0-87728-064-9). Weiser.

Govinda, Lama A. Creative Meditation & Multi-Dimensional Consciousness. LC 75-31616. (Illus.). 288p. (Orig.). 1976. 11.00x (ISBN 0-8356-0475-6, Quest); pap. 8.50 (ISBN 0-8356-0472-1, Guest). Theos Pub Hse.

--Psycho-Cosmic Symbolism of the Buddhist Stupa. LC 76-797. (Illus.). 144p. 1976. pap. 6.50 (ISBN 0-913546-36-4). Dharma Pub.

--The Way of the White Clouds. (Illus.). 305p. 1970. pap. 10.95 (ISBN 0-87773-007-5). Shambhala Pubns.

Govinda, Lama Anagarika. The Inner Structure of the I Ching: The Book of Transformations. LC 81-11491. (Illus.). 224p. 1981. 29.95 (ISBN 0-8348-0165-5). Weatherhill.

Govinda, Li G. Tibetan Fantasies. (Illus.). (gr. 1-6). 1977. 5.95 (ISBN 0-913546-48-8). Dharma Pub.

Govindagraj. Poems of Govindagraj. 2nd ed. Namjoshi, Sarojini & Namjoshi, Suniti, trs. 1976. lib. bdg. 8.00 (ISBN 0-89253-099-5); flexible bdg. 4.80 (ISBN 0-89253-145-2). Ind-US Inc.

Govindarajulu, Zakkula. The Sequential Statistical Analysis of Hypothesis Testing, Point & Interval Estimation, & Decision Theory. LC 80-68287. (The American Sciences Press Ser. in Mathematical & Management Sciences: Vol. 5). 1981. text ed. 48.50 (ISBN 0-935950-02-8). Am Sciences Pr.

Govinda Rao, C. Generalised Circuit Theory of Electrical Machines. 248p. 1981. 30.00x (ISBN 0-86131-028-4, Pub. by Orient Longman India). State Mutual Bk.

Govinda Rao, N. S. Mechanics of Fluids. 490p. 1981. 35.00x (ISBN 0-86125-671-9, Pub. by Orient Longman India). State Mutual Bk.

Govindjee, ed. Bioenergetics of Photosynthesis. 1975. 85.00 (ISBN 0-12-294350-3). Acad Pr.

--Photosynthesis: Vol. 1: Energy Conversion by Plants & Bacteria. (Cell Biology: A Series of Monographs). 690p. 1982. 79.00 (ISBN 0-12-294301-5). Acad Pr.

--Photosynthesis: Vol. 2, Carbon Metabolism and Plant Productivity. (Cell Biology: Monographs). 1983. 65.00 (ISBN 0-12-294302-3). Acad Pr.

Govlin, Robert J., jt. auth. see Konigsmark, Bruce W.

Govoni, Laura E. & Hayes, Janice E. Drugs & Nursing Implications. 4th ed. (Illus.). 1155p. 1982. 24.50x (ISBN 0-8385-1786-2). ACC.

Govoni, Norman A. & Jeannet, Jean-Pierre. Cases in Marketing. 2nd ed. LC 82-6076. (Marketing Ser.). 274p. 1983. text ed. 13.95 (ISBN 0-88244-252-X, Pub. by Grid); pap. 15.95 (ISBN 0-471-84163-3). Wiley.

Govoni, Norman A., et al. Promotional Management. (Illus.). 608p. 1986. text ed. 29.95 (ISBN 0-13-731019-6). P-H.

Govorchin, Gerald G. Americans from Yugoslavia. 1961. 10.00 (ISBN 0-686-61036-9). Ragusan Pr.

--Americans from Yugoslavia. LC 61-11312. 1961. 9.00 (ISBN 0-8130-0087-4). U Presses Fla.

Gow, A. S. A. E. Housman. LC 72-699. (English Literature Ser.: No. 33). 1972. Repr. of 1936 ed. lib. bdg. 32.95x (ISBN 0-8383-1423-6). Haskell.

Gow, A. S., tr. The Greek Bucolic Poets. LC 72-179529. xxvii, 156p. 1972. Repr. of 1953 ed. 15.00 (ISBN 0-208-01250-8, Archon). Shoe String.

Gow, Andrew S. & Page, D. L. Greek Anthology: Hellenistic Epigrams, 2 Vols. 1965. Set. 165.00 set (ISBN 0-521-05124-X). Cambridge U Pr.

Gow, Andrew S., ed. Bucolici Graeci. (Oxford Classical Texts). 1952. 14.95x (ISBN 0-19-814517-9). Oxford U Pr.

Gow, Bonar A. Madagascar & the Protestant Impact. LC 78-11216. (Dalhousie African Studies). 256p. 1980. text ed. 49.50x (ISBN 0-8419-0463-4, Africana). Holmes & Meier.

--Madagascar & the Protestant Impact: The Work of the British Missions, 1818-95. (Dalhousie African Studies Ser.). pap. 71.00 (ISBN 0-317-27749-9, 2025229). Bks Demand UMI.

Gow, David D., jt. ed. see Morss, Elliot R.

Gow, Doris T. A Curriculum Analysis of Individualized Science. 107p. 1977. 2.00 (ISBN 0-318-14707-6). Learn Res Dev.

Gow, Douglas J. I Like to Read Because It's Fun & Easy! LC 77-86209. (Illus.). 1977. pap. 9.95 (ISBN 0-9601378-1-5). Royale Pubs.

Gow, I. T. & Wallmott, H. P. Okinawa Nineteen Forty-Five: Gateway to Japan. LC 85-4386. (Illus.). 224p. 1985. 16.95 (ISBN 0-385-19918-X). Doubleday.

Gow, J. G. Surgical Procedures: Boari Bladder Flap Procedure, Vol. 7. (Single Surgical Procedures Ser.). 1983. 25.95 (ISBN 0-87489-505-7). Med Economics.

Gow, James. Short History of Greek Mathematics. LC 68-21639. 1968. 14.95 (ISBN 0-8284-0218-3). Chelsea Pub.

Gow, Kathleen M. How Nurses' Emotions Affect Patient Care: Self Studies by Nurses. 1982. text ed. 24.95 (ISBN 0-8261-3430-0). Springer Pub.

--Yes, Virginia, There Is Right & Wrong. 255p. 1985. pap. 6.95 (ISBN 0-8423-8561-4). Tyndale.

Gow, Kay, jt. auth. see Ricks, Betty.

Gow, Lesley & McPherson, Andrew. Tell Them from Me. 137p. 1980. 19.00 (ISBN 0-08-025738-0); pap. 10.00 (ISBN 0-08-025739-9). Pergamon.

Gow, Rosalie. Modern Ways with Traditional Scottish Recipes. LC 81-15756. (Illus.). 112p. 1981. Repr. of 1980 ed. spiral bdg. 8.95 (ISBN 0-88289-304-1). Pelican.

Gowa, Joanne. Closing the Gold Window: Domestic Politics & the End of Bretton Woods. LC 83-7184. (Cornell Studies in Political Economy). 248p. 1983. 29.95x (ISBN 0-8014-1622-1); pap. 13.95x (ISBN 0-8014-9260-2). Cornell U Pr.

Gowan, Donald E. Bridge Between the Testaments: Reappraisal of Judaism from the Exile to the Birth of Christianity. 2nd ed. LC 76-49996. (Pittsburgh Theological Monographs: No. 14). 1984. text ed. 21.95 (ISBN 0-915138-47-6). Pickwick.

--Ezekiel. Hayes, John, ed. (Preaching Guides). pap. 7.95 (ISBN 0-8042-3223-7). John Knox.

--Reclaiming the Old Testament for the Christian Pulpit. LC 79-87743. 163p. 1980. 13.95 (ISBN 0-8042-0166-8). John Knox.

--When Man Becomes God: Humanism & Hybris in the Old Testament. LC 75-17582. (Pittsburgh Theological Monographs: No. 6). 1975. pap. 8.75 (ISBN 0-915138-06-9). Pickwick.

Gowan, J. C. The Development of the Psychedelic Indiviual. 300p. 1974. pap. 4.00 (ISBN 0-686-27924-7). Snyder Inst Res.

--Enveloped in Glory. 160p. (Orig.). 1982. pap. 5.00x (ISBN 0-9606822-1-X). Gowan.

--Operations of Increasing Order. 408p. (Orig.). 1980. pap. 5.00x (ISBN 0-9606822-4-4). Gowan.

--Trance, Art & Creativity. 450p. 1975. 5.00 (ISBN 0-686-27925-5). Snyder Inst Res.

Gowan, John, et al. Creativity: Its Educational Implications. 2nd ed. 344p. 1981. pap. text ed. 11.95 (ISBN 0-8403-2467-7). Kendall-Hunt.

Gowan, John C. & Demos, George D. The Education & Guidance of the Ablest. (Illus.). 528p. 1964. 45.50x (ISBN 0-398-00714-4). C C Thomas.

Gowan, John C., jt. auth. see Gallagher, James J.

Gowan, Susanne, et al. Moving Toward a New Society. LC 75-30449. 296p. 1976. pap. 5.00 (ISBN 0-86571-007-4). New Soc Pubs.

Gowans, Adam L. The Twelve Best Short Stories in the English Language. 1920. 30.00 (ISBN 0-932062-68-7). Sharon Hill.

Gowans, Alan. Images of American Living: Four Centuries of Architecture & Furniture As Cultural Expression. (Icon Editions). (Illus.). 498p. 1976. pap. 12.95i (ISBN 0-06-430072-2, IN-72, HarpT). Har-Row.

--Learning to See. LC 81-80213. 1981. 29.95 (ISBN 0-87972-182-0). Bowling Green.

--Two Classics of Modern American Art. LC 75-22524. (Illus.). 1982. 20.00 (ISBN 0-89257-005-9). Am Life Foun.

Gowans, Fred. Rocky Mountain Rendezvous. LC 84-27586. (Illus.). 1985. pap. 9.95 (ISBN 0-87905-193-0). Gibbs M Smith.

Gowans, Fred R. & Campbell, Eugene E. Fort Bridger: Island in the Wilderness. LC 75-5827. (Illus.). 150p. 1975. 4.95 (ISBN 0-8425-0419-2). Brigham.

--Fort Supply: Brigham Young's Green River Experiment. 1976. pap. 2.95 (ISBN 0-8425-0248-3). Brigham.

Gowar, Norman. An Invitation to Mathematics. (Illus.). 1979. text ed. 32.50x (ISBN 0-19-853002-1); pap. 12.95x (ISBN 0-19-853001-3). Oxford U Pr.

Gowar, R. G., ed. Developments in Fire Protection of Offshore Platforms, Vol. 1. (Illus.). 232p. 1978. text ed. 46.25 (ISBN 0-85334-792-1, Pub. by Elsevier Applied Sci England). Elsevier.

Gowaskie, Joseph M. The Polish Community in America: An Annotated & Classified Bibliographical Guide. LC 77-25290. (Burt Franklin Ethnic Bibliographic Guides). (Illus.). 1978. lib. bdg. 14.50 (ISBN 0-89102-058-6). B Franklin.

Gowda, H. H., jt. auth. see Wells, Henry.

Gowdey, Eve B., jt. auth. see Jenkins, Richard L.

Gowdy, Eve. Job Hunting with Employment Agencies. LC 78-414. 1978. text ed. 3.25 (ISBN 0-8120-0610-0). Barron.

Gowen, Herbert H. Five Foreigners in Japan. facs. ed. LC 67-28735. (Essay Index Reprint Ser). 1936. 20.00 (ISBN 0-8369-0491-5). Ayer Co Pubs.

--History of Indian Literature from Vedic Times to the Present Day. LC 68-23292. 1968. Repr. of 1931 ed. lib. bdg. 32.50x (ISBN 0-8371-0089-5, GOHI). Greenwood.

--The Napoleon of the Pacific, Kamehameha the Great. LC 75-35193. Repr. of 1919 ed. 26.00 (ISBN 0-404-14221-4). AMS Pr.

--A Precursor of Perry; or, the Story of Takano Nagahide. 1928. Repr. 20.00 (ISBN 0-8482-4215-7). Norwood Edns.

Gowen, James A. English Review Manual: A Program for Self-Instruction. 3rd rev. ed. Talkington, William A., ed. 1980. pap. text ed. 18.95 (ISBN 0-07-023895-2). McGraw.

--Progress in Writing: A Learning Program. 230p. 1973. pap. text ed. 18.95 (ISBN 0-07-023859-6). McGraw.

Gowen, Marcia. Computational Manual for Renewable Energy Assessment. 250p. Date not set. pap. price not set (ISBN 0-86638-065-5). E W Center HI.

Gowen, Vincent. Village by the Yangtze. LC 72-87751. 424p. 1975. 12.50 (ISBN 0-913264-08-3). Douglas-West.

Gower, A M. Water Quality in Catchment Ecosystems. LC 79-42907. (Institution of Environmental Sciences Ser.). 335p. 1980. 69.95x (ISBN 0-471-27692-8, Pub. by Wiley-Interscience). Wiley.

Gower, Calvin W. Kansas Towns & Trade from Pike's Peak Gold Seekers, 1858-1860. 75p. 1980. pap. text ed. 8.00x (ISBN 0-89126-097-8). MA-AH Pub.

Gower, Charlotte D. Northern & Southern Affiliations of Antillean Culture. LC 28-7691. (Amer. Anthro. Association Memoirs). 1927. pap. 15.00 (ISBN 0-527-00534-7). Kraus Repr.

Gower, D. B. Steroid Hormones. 120p. 1980. 35.00x (ISBN 0-85664-838-8, Pub. by Croom Helm England). State Mutual Bk.

--Steroid Hormones. 1980. pap. 12.95 (ISBN 0-8151-3832-6). Year Bk Med.

Gower, D. M., jt. auth. see Lewis, D. B.

Gower Economic Publications. Leisure Industries Review, 1974. 1973. 60.00x (ISBN 0-8464-0552-0). Beekman Pubs.

Gower Economic Publications, ed. Business Atlas of Western Europe in English, French, German & Spanish Languages. (Illus.). 144p. 1974. 35.00x (ISBN 0-8464-0224-6). Beekman Pubs.

--One Hundred Center Guide, 1976: Market Feasibility Studies of Major Business Areas in England. 1976. 40.00x (ISBN 0-8464-0686-1). Beekman Pubs.

Gower, G. L. A Glossary of Surrey Words: A Supplement to No. 12. (English Dialect Society Publications Ser.: No. 70). pap. 15.00 (ISBN 0-317-16097-4). Kraus Repr.

Gower, H. D., et al. The Camera As Historian. LC 72-9202. (The Literature of Photography Ser.). Repr. of 1916 ed. 24.50 (ISBN 0-405-04911-0). Ayer Co Pubs.

Gower, Herschel. Faces in a Nashville Arcade. 183p. 1983. pap. 6.95 (ISBN 0-9613156-0-1). Herschel Gower.

Gower, Herschel, ed. see Haun, Mildred.

Gower, Iris. Beloved Captive. 256p. 1984. pap. 3.50 (ISBN 0-441-05321-1). Ace Bks.

--Copper Kingdom. 320p. 1984. 13.95 (ISBN 0-312-16971-X). St Martin.

--Proud Mary. 1985. 14.95 (ISBN 0-312-65225-9). St Martin.

Gower, J. F., ed. Oceanography from Space. LC 81-12060. (Marine Science Ser.: Vol. 13). 998p. 1981. 125.00x (ISBN 0-306-40808-2, Plenum Pr). Plenum Pub.

Gower, John. Complete Works of John Gower, 4 vols. Macaulay, G. C., ed. LC 1-21828. 1968. Repr. of 1899 ed. Set. 250.00x (ISBN 0-403-00087-4). Scholarly.

--Confessio Amantis. Peck, Russell A., ed. (Medieval Academy Reprints for Teaching Ser.). 570p. 1981. pap. 7.95 (ISBN 0-8020-6438-8). U of Toronto Pr.

--English Works of John Gower, 2 Vols. Macualay, G. C., ed. Vol. 1, 1900. 24.95x (ISBN 0-19-722530-6); Vol. 2 1901. 19.95x (ISBN 0-19-722531-4). Oxford U Pr.

Gower, Joseph F. & Leliaert, Richard M., eds. The Brownson-Hecker Correspondence. LC 76-20160. 1979. text ed. 25.00x (ISBN 0-268-00656-3). U of Notre Dame Pr.

Gower, Laurence C. Independent Africa, the Challenge to the Legal Profession. LC 67-20877. (Oliver Wendell Holmes Lecture Ser: 1966). 1967. 11.00x (ISBN 0-674-44800-6). Harvard U Pr.

Gower, P. E. PC Nephrology. (Illus.). 261p. 1983. pap. text ed. 13.95 (ISBN 0-86286-025-3, B1958-0). Mosby.

Gower Publications, ed. Business Atlas of Great Britain 1974. 1974. 35.00x (ISBN 0-8464-0223-8). Beekman Pubs.

--East Anglia: A Guide to Business Locations & Expansion 1973. 1973. 25.00x (ISBN 0-8464-0347-1). Beekman Pubs.

--Managing Buildings & Building Services in Great Britain. 1973. 19.95x (ISBN 0-8464-0595-4). Beekman Pubs.

--Who's Who in Marketing in Great Britain. 500p. 1974. 36.00x (ISBN 0-8464-0972-0). Beekman Pubs.

Gower Publishing Co., Ltd. Staff, ed. A Planning Guide to Office Automation. 123p. 1984. text ed. 41.95x (ISBN 0-566-02503-5). Gower Pub Co.

Gower, Roger & Walters, Steve. Teaching Practice Handbook: A Reference Book for EFL Teachers in Training. 188p. (Orig.). 1983. pap. text ed. 12.50x (ISBN 0-435-28995-0). Heinemann Ed.

Gower, Ronald C. Last Days of Marie Antoinette: An Historical Sketch. LC 74-168163. Repr. of 1886 ed. 15.00 (ISBN 0-404-07129-5). AMS Pr.

Gower, Susan, jt. auth. see Ulmer, Jefferson G.

Gowers, Ernest, ed. see Fowler, Henry W.

Gowers, William R. A Manual of Diseases of the Nervous System, 2 vols. Taylor, James, ed. Incl. Vol. 1. Diseases of the Nerves & Spinal Cord. (Illus.); Vol. 2. Diseases of the Brain & Crainal Nerves: General & Functional Diseases of the Nerves System. (Illus.). 1970. Repr. of 1899 ed. Set. 76.00x (ISBN 0-02-845390-5). Hafner.

Gowin, D. Bob. Educating. LC 81-66646. 222p. 1981. 24.50x (ISBN 0-8014-1418-0). Cornell U Pr.

Gowin, D. Bob, jt. auth. see Novak, Joseph D.

Gowing, Clara. The Alcotts As I Knew Them. LC 78-27322. 1978. Repr. of 1909 ed. lib. bdg. 22.50 (ISBN 0-8414-4617-2). Folcroft.

--The Alcotts As I Knew Them. 134p. 1980. Repr. of 1909 ed. lib. bdg. 22.50 (ISBN 0-8482-4188-6). Norwood Edns.

Gowing, Laurence. Lucian Freud. LC 82-80250. (Illus.). 1984. pap. 15.95f (ISBN 0-500-27333-2). Thames Hudson.

Gowing, Lawrence. Matisse. (World of Art Ser.). (Illus.). 216p. 1985. pap. 9.95f (ISBN 0-500-20170-6). Thames Hudson.

Gowing, Lawrence, ed. The Encyclopedia of Visual Arts, 2 vols. 1983. 100.00 set (ISBN 0-13-276543-8); Vol. 1. 60.00 (ISBN 0-13-276527-6); Vol. 2. 40.00 (ISBN 0-13-276535-7). P-H.

Gowing, M. M., jt. auth. see Hancock, W. K.

Gowing, N. F. Color Atlas of Tumor Histopathology. (Illus.). 240p. 1980. 104.50 (ISBN 0-8151-3837-7). Year Bk Med.

Gowing, Peter G. Muslim Filipinos: Heritage & Horizon. (Illus.). 1979. pap. 10.00x (ISBN 0-686-25217-9, Pub. by New Day Pub). Cellar.

Gowing, Peter G., jt. auth. see Diamond, Michael J.

Gowing, Peter Gordon. Mandate in Moreland: The American Government of Muslim Filipinos, 1899-1920. (Illus.). ixx, 411p. 1983. pap. 15.00 (ISBN 971-10-0101-2, Pub. by New Day Phillippines). Cellar.

Gowing, Roland. Roger Cotes: Natural Philosopher. LC 82-1154. (Illus.). 200p. 1983. 42.50 (ISBN 0-521-23741-6). Cambridge U Pr.

Gowland, D. A. Methodist Secessions. 192p. 1979. 24.00 (ISBN 0-7190-1335-6, Pub. by Manchester Univ Pr). Longwood Pub Group.

Gowland, D. A., jt. auth. see Hayes, A. J.

Gowland, D. A., jt. ed. see Hayes, A. J.

Gowland, D. H. Modern Economic Analysis 2. 224p. (Orig.). 1982. 19.95 (ISBN 0-408-10771-5); pap. 14.95 (ISBN 0-408-10772-3). Butterworth.

Gowland, David. Controlling the Money Supply. rev. ed. 244p. 1984. pap. 11.95 (ISBN 0-7099-1170-X, Pub. by Croom Helm Ltd). Longwood Pub Group.

--International Economics. LC 83-21386. 202p. 1984. 28.50x (ISBN 0-389-20438-2, 08000). B&N Imports.

--Money, Inflation & Unemployment: The Role of Money in the Economy. LC 84-24373. 208p. 1985. 28.95x (ISBN 0-389-20553-2, 08115). B&N Imports.

Gowland, David & Paterson, Anne. Microeconomic Analysis: A Modern Introduction. 256p. 1984. 24.50 (ISBN 0-7108-0289-7, Pub. by Salem Hse Ltd). Merrimack Pub Cir.

Gowland, David, jt. auth. see Dosser, Douglas.

Gowland, David H., ed. Modern Economic Analysis. (Illus.). 1979. 19.95 (ISBN 0-408-10632-8). Butterworth.

Gowland, Peter. Gowland's Guide to Glamour Photography. (Illus.). 160p. 1972. 9.95 (ISBN 0-517-50189-9). Crown.

--The Secrets of Photographing Women. Michelman, Herbert, ed. (Illus.). 224p. 1981. 12.95 (ISBN 0-517-54180-7, Michelman Books). Crown.

Gowlett, John. Ascent to Civilization: The Archaeology of Early Man. LC 83-48713. (Illus.). 208p. 1984. pap. 14.95 (ISBN 0-394-72266-3); pap. text ed. 9.95 (ISBN 0-394-34294-1). Knopf.

Goy, E. D., tr. see Konstantinovic, Radomir.

Goy, Joseph. Les Fluctuations Du Produit De la Dime: Conjoncture Decimale et Domaniale De la Fin Dumoyen Age Au XV11le Siecle. (Cahiers Des Etudes Rurales: No. 3). 1972. pap. 34.40x (ISBN 90-2797-000-9). Mouton.

Goy, Joseph, jt. auth. see Ladurie, Emmanuel Le Roy.

Goy, Peter A. & Miller, Laurence H., eds. A Biographical Directory of Librarians in the Field of Slavic & East European Studies. LC 67-28101. pap. 24.30 (ISBN 0-317-10487-X, 2001783). Bks Demand UMI.

Goy, R. S. & Jenkins, J. A. Industrial Applications of Textile. 65p. 1970. 70.00x (ISBN 0-686-63770-4). State Mutual Bk.

Goy, Richard J. Chioggia & the Villages of the Venetian Lagoon: Studies in History. (Illus.). 350p. Date not set. price not set (ISBN 0-521-30275-7). Cambridge U Pr.

Goy, Robert W. & McEwen, Bruce S., eds. Sexual Differentiation of the Brain. (Illus.). 1980. text ed. 30.00x (ISBN 0-262-07077-4). MIT Pr.

Goya. Drawings of Goya. (Master Draughtsman Ser). treasure trove bdg. 9.95x (ISBN 0-87505-010-7); pap. 4.95 (ISBN 0-87505-163-4). Borden.

Goya, Francisco. Los Caprichos. 1970. pap. 4.95 (ISBN 0-486-22384-1). Dover.

--Disasters of War. (Illus., Bilingual). (gr. 7-12). 1968. pap. 4.50 (ISBN 0-486-21872-4). Dover.

--Disparates. LC 68-28063. 1969. pap. 6.00 (ISBN 0-486-22319-1). Dover.

--The Disparates: Or, the Proverbs. (Illus.). 10.75 (ISBN 0-8446-0655-3). Peter Smith.

--Tauromaquia & the Bulls of Bordeaux. LC 69-15666. (Illus.). 1969. pap. 7.95 (ISBN 0-486-22342-6). Dover.

Goya, Fred & Moriarty, Mike. What a Way to Go. (Illus.). 96p. 1984. pap. 4.95 (ISBN 0-8065-0888-4). Citadel Pr.

Goyal, jt. auth. see Gerba.

Goyal, et al. Applied & Ecological Aspects of Phagebiology. Date not set. price not set (ISBN 0-471-82419-4). Wiley.

Goyal, B. R. Educating Harijans. 1982. 11.50x (ISBN 0-8364-0863-2, Pub by Academic India). South Asia Bks.

Goyal, Bhagwat S. The Strategy of Survival. 244p. 1975. text ed. 13.50x (ISBN 0-391-02714-X, Pub. by UBS India). Humanities.

Goyal, Des Raj. Rashtriya Swayamsevak Sangh. 1979. 10.00x (ISBN 0-8364-0566-8, Pub. by Radha Krishna India). South Asia Bks.

Goyal, R. K., jt. ed. see Spechler, S. J.

Goyder, Catherine, jt. auth. see Cousins, William J.

Goyder, D. G., jt. auth. see Neale, Alan D.

Goyder, Jane, jt. auth. see Lowe, Philip.

Goyen, Judith & Philip, Hugh. Innovation in Reading in Britain. (Experiments & Innovations in Education Ser.: No. 3). 36p. (Orig., 2nd Printing). 1973. pap. 5.00 (ISBN 92-3-101112-X, U312, UNESCO). Unipub.

Goyen, William. Arcadio. 1983. 12.95 (ISBN 0-517-55053-9, C N Potter Bks). Crown.

--Arcadio. (Obelisk Ser.). 160p. 1984. pap. 7.95 (ISBN 0-525-48130-3, 0772-230). Dutton.

--Had I a Hundred Mouths: New & Selected Stories 1947-1983. 224p. 1985. 15.95 (ISBN 0-517-55764-9, C N Potter). Crown.

--Savata: My Fair Sister. 1970. 13.50 (ISBN 0-7206-7695-9). Dufour.

Goyer, Doreen S. The International Population Census Bibliography: 1945-1977. rev. ed. LC 79-25890. (Studies in Population). 1980. 44.00 (ISBN 0-12-294380-5). Acad Pr.

Goyer, Doreen S. & Domschke, Eliane. The Handbook of National Population Censuses: Latin America & the Caribbean, North America & Oceania. LC 82-9390. (Illus.). 736p. 1983. lib. bdg. 75.00 (ISBN 0-313-21352-6, GHP/). Greenwood.

Goyer, Doreen S., compiled by. National Population Censuses, 1945-1976: Some Holding Libraries. LC 79-4232. 44p. (Orig.). 1979. pap. 8.00 (ISBN 0-933438-00-1, SP 1). APLIC Intl.

Goyer, Robert S., jt. auth. see Sincoff, Michael Z.

Goyet. L' Humanisme de Bossuet. 48.25 (ISBN 0-685-34207-7). French & Eur.

Goyet de la Sarthe, Charles L., jt. auth. see Constant, Benjamin.

Goyne, Minetta A., ed. Lone Star & Double Eagle: Civil War Letters of a German-Texas Family. LC 82-5491. 1982. pap. 15.00 (ISBN 0-912646-68-3). Tex Christian.

Goytisolo, Juan. Duelo en el Paraiso. Bleznick, Donald W., ed. 226p. (Span.). pap. text ed. cancelled (ISBN 0-8290-0894-2). Irvington.

--Juan the Landless. Lane, Helen R., tr. LC 76-55024. (Richard Seaver Bk). 1977. 14.95 (ISBN 0-670-41004-7). Viking.

--Makbara. Lane, Helen R., tr. from Span. LC 81-5808. 256p. 1981. 13.95 (ISBN 0-394-51803-9). Seaver Bks.

--Paisajes despues de la Batalla. 199p. (Span.). 1982. pap. 8.00 (ISBN 84-85859-54-5, 2008). Ediciones Norte.

Goytortua, Jesus. Lluvia Roja. Walsh, Donald D., ed. (Orig., Span.). 1962. pap. text ed. 14.95 (ISBN 0-13-538876-7). P-H.

--Pensativa. Walsh, Donald D., ed. (Orig., Span.). (gr. 10-12). 1962. pap. text ed. 15.95. P-H.

Goyvaerts, D. Phonology of the Nineteen Eighties. (Story-Scientia Linguistics Ser.: No. 4). 1980. text ed. 92.25x (ISBN 90-6439-150-5). Humanities.

Goyvaerts, D. L. Present-Day Historical & Comparative Linguistics: An Introductory Guide to Theory & Method Part One General Background-Phonological Change. 231p. 1975. pap. text ed. 22.25x (ISBN 0-391-01588-5). Humanities.

Goyvaerts, Didier. Aspects of Post-SPE Phonology. (Illus.). 1979. pap. text ed. 34.00x (ISBN 0-391-01602-4). Humanities.

Goyvaerts, Didier & Pullum, Geoffrey, eds. Essays on the Sound Pattern of English. (Illus.). 1975. text ed. 94.50x (ISBN 0-391-01602-4). Humanities.

Goyvaerts, Didier, jt. ed. see Coppieters, Frank.

Goyvaerts, Didier L., ed. Phonology in the Nineteen-Eighties. (Studies in the Sciences of Language Ser.: No. 4). viii, 647p. (Orig.). 1981. pap. 65.00x (ISBN 90-6439-150-5, Pub. by J Benjamins Publ Holland). Benjamins North Am.

Goyvaerts, Didier L. & Pullum, Geoffrey K., eds. Essays on the Sound Pattern of English. (Studies in the Sciences of Language Ser.: No. 1). 580p. (Orig.). 1975. pap. 68.00x (ISBN 90-6439-116-5, Pub. by J Benjamins Publ Holland). Benjamins North Am.

Goza, William M., ed. see Brinton, Daniel G.

Gozansky, Sue. Championship Volleyball Techniques & Drills. LC 83-4250. 228p. 1983. 17.95 (ISBN 0-13-127639-5, Parker); pap. 7.95 (ISBN 0-13-127621-2). P-H.

Gozmany, L., et al, eds. Septemlingual Dictionary of the Names of European Animals, 2 vols. 2232p. (Eng., Rus., Span., Ger., Hungarian, Fr., & Lat.). 1979. Set. 230.00 (ISBN 963-05-1381-1, Pub. by Akademiai Kaido Hungary). Heyden.

Gozmany, Laslo. Septemligual Dictionary of the Names of European Animals, 2 vols. 2188p. 1980. 500.00x (ISBN 0-569-08577-2, Pub. by Collet's). State Mutual Bk.

Gozzi, Raymond. Tropes & Figures: A Psychological Study of Henry David Thoreau. LC 80-2506. 1981. 62.50 (ISBN 0-404-19054-5). AMS Pr.

Gozzi, Raymond D., ed. Thoreau's Psychology: Eight Essays. LC 83-6870. 206p. (Orig.). 1983. lib. bdg. 24.25 (ISBN 0-8191-3261-6); pap. text ed. 12.25 (ISBN 0-8191-3262-4). U Pr of Amer.

Gozzini, A., ed. Topics of Radiofrequency Spectroscopy. (Italian Physical Society: Course 17). 1962. 75.00 (ISBN 0-12-368817-5). Acad Pr.

GP-Info Symposium, 13-15 March, 1980, London. Computers & the General Practitioner: Proceedings. Malcolm, A. & Poyser, J., eds. (Illus.). 142p. 1981. 22.00 (ISBN 0-08-026865-X). Pergamon.

Graaf, A. M. De see Hooper, H. O. & De Graaf, A. M.

Graaf, Frank de see De Graaf, Frank.

Graaf, H. J. De see De Graaf, H. J.

Graaf, Janny de see Schmid, Alex & De Graaf, Janny.

Graaf, Kaspar de see De Graaf, Kaspar & Garrett, Malcolm.

Graaf, Kasper de see De Graaf, Kasper & Garrett, Malcolm.

Graaff, John H. Van De see Van De Graaff, John H., et al.

Graaff, Kent M. Van De see Van De Graaff, Kent M. & Fox, Stuart I.

Graah, Wilhelm A. Narrative of an Expedition to the East Coast of Greenland. LC 74-5842. Repr. of 1837 ed. 14.50 (ISBN 0-404-11647-7). AMS Pr.

Grab, Walter, ed. Jahrbuch des Instutus fur Deutsche Geschichte, Vol. 12. 586p. (Ger.). 1983. lib. bdg. 41.00 (ISBN 3-598-21154-6). K G Saur.

Grabar, Andre. Christian Iconography: A Study of Its Origins. LC 67-31114. (A. W. Mellon Lectures in the Fine Arts No. 10, Bollingen Ser: No. Xxxv). (Illus.). 432p. (Orig.). 1980. 62.50x (ISBN 0-691-09716-X); pap. 14.95 (ISBN 0-691-01830-8). Princeton U Pr.

--L'art Du Moyen Age en Occident: Influences Byzantines et Orientales. 352p. 1980. 125.00x (ISBN 0-86078-057-0, Pub. by Variorum). State Mutual Bk.

--L'Art Paleochretien et L'Art Byzantin. 388p. 1979. 115.00x (ISBN 0-86078-045-7, Pub. by Variorum). State Mutual Bk.

Grabar, Igor. Valentin Aleksandrovich Serov: His Life & Work 1865-1911. 548p. 1980. 110.00x (ISBN 0-317-14305-0, Pub. by Collet's). State Mutual Bk.

Grabar, O. Persian Art Before & After the Mongol Conquest. 1959. pap. 0.50 (ISBN 0-912303-00-X). Michigan Mus.

--Sasanian Silver. 1967. pap. 3.50 (ISBN 0-912303-02-6). Michigan Mus.

Grabar, Oleg. The Alhambra. 1978. 15.00x (ISBN 0-674-01556-8). Harvard U Pr.

--The Formation of Islamic Art. LC 72-75193. (Illus.). 352p. 1973. pap. 14.95x (ISBN 0-300-02187-9). Yale U Pr.

--The Illustrations of the Maqamat. LC 83-24274. (Studies in Medieval Manuscript Illumination, CVL: No. 45). (Illus.). x, 196p. 1984. 40.00 (ISBN 0-226-69057-1). U of Chicago Pr.

Grabar, Oleg & Blair, Sheila. Epic Images & Contemporary History: The Illustrations of the Great Mongol Shahnama. LC 80-305. 1980. lib. bdg. 27.50x (ISBN 0-226-30585-6). U of Chicago Pr.

Grabar, Oleg, ed. Muqarnas: An Annual on Islamic Art & Architecture: The Art of the Mamluks, Vol. II. LC 83-643765. (Illus.). 240p. 1984. 35.00x (ISBN 0-300-03137-8). Yale U Pr.

--Muqarnas: An Annual on Islamic Art & Architecture, Volume I. (Illus.). 246p. 1983. 31.00x (ISBN 0-300-02837-7). Yale U Pr.

Grabar, Oleg, et al. City in the Desert. (Harvard Middle East Monographs: Vols. 23 & 24). 1978. 40.00x (ISBN 0-674-13195-9). Harvard U Pr.

Grabau, Richard F., tr. see Jaspers, Karl.

Grabb, William C. & Myers, M. Bert, eds. Skin Flaps. LC 74-20219. 440p. 1975. 75.00 (ISBN 0-316-32267-9). Little.

Grabb, William C., jt. ed. see Feller, Irving.

Grabb, William X. & Smith, James W., eds. Plastic Surgery. 3rd ed. 1980. text ed. 49.50 (ISBN 0-316-32269-5). Little.

Grabbe, Alexander. The Private World of the Last Tsar. Grabbe, Paul & Grabbe, Beatrice, eds. LC 84-19473. 192p. 1985. 25.00 (ISBN 0-316-32271-7). Little.

Grabbe, Beatrice, ed. see Grabbe, Alexander.

Grabbe, George. Dogmat Tserkvi v Sovrjemjennom Mire. 1975. pap. 1.50 (ISBN 0-317-30381-3). Holy Trinity.

--Orthodox Christian Education of Children in Our Days. 30p. 1976. pap. 1.00x (ISBN 0-913026-17-4). St Nectarios.

--Otritsanije vmesto utverzhdenije. 48p. 1971. pap. 2.00 (ISBN 0-317-30377-5). Holy Trinity.

--Pravda o Russkoj Tserkvi na Rodinje i za Rubjezhom. 216p. 1961. pap. 8.00 (ISBN 0-317-30359-7). Holy Trinity.

Grabbe, Lester L. Comparative Philology & the Text of Job: A Study in Methodology. LC 77-23489. (Society of Biblical Literature. Dissertation Ser.). 1977. pap. 9.95 (ISBN 0-89130-139-9, 060134). Scholars Pr GA.

Grabbe, Paul, ed. see Grabbe, Alexander.

Grabe, Erna F., jt. auth. see Ferrell, Paul C.

Grabendorff, Wolf & Krumwiede, Heinrich. Change in Central America: Internal & External Dimensions. (Special Studies in Latin America & the Caribbean). 175p. 1984. lib. bdg. 24.00x (ISBN 0-86531-609-0). Westview.

Grabendorff, Wolf & Roett, Riorden, eds. Latin America, Western Europe & the U. S. Reevaluating the Atlantic Triangle. 320p. 1985. 37.95 (ISBN 0-03-000533-7). Praeger.

Graber, Alan L., et al. Diabetes & Pregnancy: A Guide for the Prospective Mother with Diabetes. Pearson, Patricia C., ed. LC 73-6653. (Illus.). 80p. 1973. pap. 3.95x (ISBN 0-8265-1192-9). Vanderbilt U Pr.

--Diabetes & Pregnancy: A Guide for the Prospective Mother with Diabetes. (Vanderbilt University Press Bks.). 80p. 1973. pap. 3.95 (ISBN 0-8265-1192-9). U of Ill Pr.

Graber, Ana Maria R., jt. auth. see Rosenbusch, Marcia H.

Graber, B., ed. Circumvaginal Musculature & Sexual Function. (Illus.). x, 126p. 1982. 21.00 (ISBN 3-8055-3017-X). S Karger.

Graber, Benjamin, jt. auth. see Kline-Graber, Georgia.

Graber, David, ed. Tsese-Ma'Heone-Nemeototse: Cheyenne Spiritual Songs. LC 82-83401. 227p. (Eng. & Cheyenne.). 1982. 29.95 (ISBN 0-87303-078-8). Faith & Life.

Graber, Doris. Crime News & the Public. LC 80-16032. 256p. 1981. 38.95x (ISBN 0-03-055756-9). Praeger.

--Mass Media & American Politics. 2nd ed. 385p. 1984. pap. 11.95 (ISBN 0-87187-320-6). Congr Quarterly.

--Media Power in Politics: Myths & Realities. LC 83-23921. 348p. 1983. pap. 13.95 (ISBN 0-87187-285-4). Congr Quarterly.

Graber, Doris A. Development of the Law of Belligerent Occupation, 1863-1914. LC 68-58584. (Columbia University. Studies in the Social Sciences: No. 543). Repr. of 1949 ed. 24.50 (ISBN 0-404-51543-6). AMS Pr.

--Processing the News: How People Tame the Information Tide. LC 83-19537. (Political Communication & Policy Ser.). (Illus.). 256p. 1984. text ed. 27.50x (ISBN 0-582-28394-9); 15.95x (ISBN 0-582-28510-0). Longman.

--Verbal Behavior & Politics. LC 75-25830. 390p. 1976. 19.95x (ISBN 0-252-00262-8). U of Ill Pr.

Graber, Doris A., ed. The President & the Public. LC 82-3032. 324p. 1982. text ed. 19.95 (ISBN 0-89727-038-X); pap. text ed. 9.95 (ISBN 0-89727-042-8). ISHI PA.

Graber, Edith E., jt. auth. see Colton, David L.

Graber, Edward A., jt. auth. see Barber, Hugh R.

Graber, Edward A., jt. ed. see Schaefer, George.

Graber, Glenn C., et al. Ethical Analysis of Clinical Medicine: A Guide to Self-Evaluation. 1985. pap. text ed. write for info. (ISBN 0-8067-0701-1). Urban & S.

Graber, Kay, compiled by. Nebraska Pioneer Cookbook. LC 74-77089. (Illus.). x, 164p. 1974. 13.50 (ISBN 0-8032-0945-2); pap. 4.50 (ISBN 0-8032-5801-1, BB 573, Bison). U of Nebr Pr.

Graber, Kay, ed. see Eastman, Elaine G.

Graber, Kay, ed. see Tibbles, Thomas H.

Graber, R. Pay Your Respects. 224p. (gr. 7 up). 1981. pap. 1.95 (ISBN 0-440-97317-1, LE). Dell.

Graber, Richard. Black Cow Summer. LC 80-7767. 224p. (YA) (gr. 7 up). 1980. 9.95 (ISBN 0-06-022118-6). HarpJ.

--Pay Your Respects. LC 78-22486. 240p. (gr. 7 up). 1979. 9.57i (ISBN 0-06-022063-5). HarpJ.

Graber, T. M. Orthodontics: Principles & Practice. 3rd ed. LC 73-186950. (Illus.). 953p. 1972. text ed. 39.50 (ISBN 0-7216-4182-2). Saunders.

Graber, T. M. & Neumann, Bedrich. Removable Orthodontic Appliances. LC 76-14681. (Illus.). 1977. text ed. 39.50 (ISBN 0-7216-4190-3). Saunders.

--Removable Orthodontic Appliances. 2nd ed. (Illus.). 700p. 1984. 49.50 (ISBN 0-7216-1238-5). Saunders.

Grabert, H. Projection Operator Techniques in Nonequilibrium Statistical Mechanics. (Springer Tratcs in Modern physics Ser.: Vol. 95). (Illus.). 220p. 1982. 34.00 (ISBN 0-387-11635-4). Springer-Verlag.

Grabes, H. Fictitious Biographies: Vladimir Nabokov's English Novels. 1977. 16.00x (ISBN 90-279-3345-6). Mouton.

Grabes, Herbert. The Mutable Glass: Mirror Imagery in Titles & Texts of the Middle Ages & the English Renaissance. Collier, Gordon, tr. LC 82-4263. (Illus.). 532p. 1983. 72.50 (ISBN 0-521-22203-6). Cambridge U Pr.

Grabhorn, Robert. A Commonplace Book of Cookery. 192p. 1985. 13.50 (ISBN 0-86547-181-9). N Point Pr.

Grabiel, Federico. Theory of Energy Transfers & Conversions. LC 67-23440. (Illus.). pap. 57.80 (ISBN 0-317-07883-6, 2006350). Bks Demand UMI.

Grabill, James. In the Coiled Light. 28p. (Orig.). 1984. pap. text ed. 3.50 (ISBN 0-318-04284-3). Skydog OR.

--To Other Beings. 70p. (Orig.). 1981. pap. 6.00 (ISBN 0-89924-028-3). Lynx Hse.

Grabiner, Judith V. The Origins of Cauchy's Rigorous Calculus. 264p. 1981. text ed. 40.00x (ISBN 0-262-07079-0). MIT Pr.

Grabiner, Sandy. Derivations & Automorphisms of Banach Algebras of Power Series. LC 74-7124. (Memoirs: No. 146). 124p. 1974. pap. 11.00 (ISBN 0-8218-1846-5, MEMO-146). Am Math.

Grabmaier, J., ed. Silicon. (Crystals-Growth, Properties, & Applications Ser.: Vol. 5). (Illus.). 215p. 1981. 57.00 (ISBN 0-387-10932-3). Springer-Verlag.

Grabmuller, H. Singular Perturbation Techniques Applied to Integro-Differential Equations. (Research Notes in Mathematics: No. 20). 148p. (Orig.). 1978. pap. text ed. 22.95 (ISBN 0-273-08409-7). Pitman Pub MA.

Grabner, John R. & House, Robert E. Comprehensive Profile of the Motor Carrier Salesman. 1975. pap. text ed. 50.00 (ISBN 0-88711-038-X). Am Trucking Assns.

Grabner, John R., Jr., jt. auth. see Farouka, Saleh.

Grabner Haider, Anton. Vocabulario Practico De la Biblia. 892p. (Espn.). 1975. 41.95 (ISBN 84-254-0964-0, S-50206). French & Eur.

Grabo, Carl. Shelley's Eccentricities. LC 73-7623. 1950. lib. bdg. 17.50 (ISBN 0-8414-2030-0). Folcroft.

Grabo, Carl A. Newton Among Poets: Shelley's Use of Science in Prometheus Unbound. LC 68-19138. 1968. Repr. of 1930 ed. 20.00 (ISBN 0-8154-0085-3). Cooper Sq.

Grabo, Carl H. Newton Among Poets: Shelly's Use of Science in Prometheus Unbound. LC 68-24046. 1968. Repr. of 1930 ed. 7.50x (ISBN 0-87752-044-5). Gordian.

--Prometheus Unbound: An Interpretation. LC 68-19149. 1968. Repr. of 1935 ed. 9.00x (ISBN 0-87752-045-3). Gordian.

--Shelley's Eccentricities. LC 50-63247. 84p. 1982. lib. bdg. 22.95x (ISBN 0-89370-732-5). Borgo Pr.

--Technique of the Novel. LC 64-8178. 1964. Repr. of 1928 ed. 9.00 (ISBN 0-87752-046-1). Gordian.

Grabo, Carl H., ed. Romantic Prose of the Early Nineteenth Century. 1978. Repr. of 1927 ed. lib. bdg. 25.00 (ISBN 0-8495-1915-2). Arden Lib.

Grabo, Norman S. The Coincidental Art of Charles Brockden Brown. LC 80-39797. xiii, 209p. 1981. 19.00x (ISBN 0-8078-1474-1). U of NC Pr.

--Edward Taylor. (Twayne's United States Authors Ser.). 1961. pap. 5.95x (ISBN 0-8084-0117-3, T8, Twayne). New Coll U Pr.

Graboff, Abner. In a Cat's Eye. (Illus.). 1976. pap. 2.50 (ISBN 0-912846-25-9). Bookstore Pr.

Graboff, Abner, illus. Old Macdonald Had a Farm. (Illus.). (gr. k-3). 1970. pap. 2.50 (ISBN 0-590-33790-4); pap. 3.95 bk. & record (ISBN 0-590-09098-4). Scholastic Inc.

Grabois, Ayreh. The Illustrated Encyclopedia of Medieval Civilization. (Illus.). 752p. 1980. 25.00 (ISBN 0-7064-0856-X, Mayflower Bks). Smith Pubs.

Grabois, Martin, jt. ed. see Halstead, Lauro S.

Grabow, Anna, tr. see Jacobsen, Jens P.

Grabow, Patricia. The Renaissance: From the World of Fear to the World of Love. 331p. (Orig.). 1984. pap. 9.95 (ISBN 0-942494-82-2). Coleman Pub.

Grabow, Stephen. Christopher Alexander: The Search for a New Paradigm in Architecture. (Illus.). 306p. 1984. 30.00 (ISBN 0-85362-199-3, Oriel). Routledge & Kegan.

Grabowicz, George G. The Poet as Mythmaker: A Study of Symbolic Meaning in Taras Sevcenko. LC 82-81227. (Harvard Ukrainian Research Institute Monograph). 186p. 1982. text ed. 12.50x (ISBN 0-674-67852-4). Harvard Ukrainian.

--Toward a History of Ukrainian Literature. (Harvard Ukrainian Research Institute Monograph). 112p. 1981. pap. text ed. 8.50x (ISBN 0-674-89676-9). Harvard U Pr.

Grabowicz, George G., tr. see Ingarden, Roman.

Grabowicz, Paul, jt. auth. see Kotkin, Joel.

Grabowski, Casimer. Human Reproduction & Development. 1983. pap. text ed. 16.95 (ISBN 0-03-061534-8, CBS C). SCP.

Grabowski, Henry G. Drug Regulation & Innovation. LC 76-25709. 1976. pap. 4.25 (ISBN 0-8447-3217-6). Am Enterprise.

Grabowski, John, jt. ed. see Thompson, Travis.

Grabowski, John, jt. ed. see Van Tassel, David D.

Grabowski, Kathryn & Dumville, David. Chronicles & Annals of Medieval Ireland & Wales. (Studies in Celtic History: Vol. IV). 242p. 1984. 41.50 (ISBN 0-85115-167-1, Pub. by Boydell & Brewer). Longwood Pub Group.

Grabowski, Stanley, ed. Paulo Freire: A Revolutionary Dilemma for the Adult Educator. LC 72-7971. (Occasional Papers Ser., No. 32). 75p. (Orig.). 1972. pap. 6.00 (ISBN 0-87060-054-0). Syracuse U Cont Ed.

Grabowski, Stanley M. Training Teachers of Adults: Models & Innovative Programs. LC 76-23432. (Occasional Paper: No. 46). 75p. 1976. pap. text ed. 3.50 (ISBN 0-87060-071-0, OCP 46). Syracuse U Cont Ed.

Grabowski Stanley M., & Associates. Preparing Educators of Adults. LC 80-8910. (Higher Education Ser.). 1981. text ed. 19.95x (ISBN 0-87589-509-3). Jossey-Bass.

Grabowsky, Casimer T. & Kavlock, Robert J. Abnormal Functional Development of the Heart, Lungs, & Kidneys: Approaches to Functional Teratology. LC 83-19940. (Progress in Clinical & Biological Research Ser.: Vol. 140). 396p. 1983. 58.00 (ISBN 0-8451-0140-4). A R Liss.

Graburn, Nelson H., ed. Ethnic & Tourist Arts: Cultural Expressions from the Fourth World. 1977. 35.00 (ISBN 0-520-02949-6); pap. 10.95 (ISBN 0-520-03842-8). U of Cal Pr.

Grace, Alicia. Clovecrest. 1978. pap. 1.25 (ISBN 0-532-12534-7). Woodhill.

--Hawksbill Manor. 1976. pap. 1.25 (ISBN 0-532-12431-6). Woodhill.

--Head of Medusa. 1978. pap. 1.25 (ISBN 0-532-12547-9). Woodhill.

--House at Swansea. 1976. pap. 1.25 (ISBN 0-532-12387-5). Woodhill.

--House of the Darkest Death. 1976. pap. 1.25 (ISBN 0-532-12428-6). Woodhill.

--Mass for a Dead Witch. 1976. pap. 1.25 (ISBN 0-532-12413-8). Woodhill.

--The Terrified Heart. 1976. pap. 1.25 (ISBN 0-685-72357-7, LB383ZK, Leisure Bks). Dorchester Pub Co.

--The Terrified Target. 1978. pap. 1.25 (ISBN 0-532-12537-1). Woodhill.

--Wharf Sinister. 224p. 1976. pap. 1.25 (ISBN 0-532-12404-9). Woodhill.

Grace, Alonzo G; see Bree, Germaine.

Grace, Curtis. Cooking with Curtis Grace. LC 85-62174. (Illus.). 200p. 1985. pap. price not set (ISBN 0-913383-05-8). McClanahan Pub.

Grace, Eileen, illus. Three Little Pigs. LC 80-27483. (Illus.). 32p. (gr. k-2). 1981. PLB 7.89 (ISBN 0-89375-462-5); pap. text ed. 1.95 (ISBN 0-89375-463-3). Troll Assocs.

Grace, Evelyn. Introduction to Fashion Merchandising. LC 78-1318. (Illus.). 1978. ref. ed. 24.95 (ISBN 0-13-483206-X). P-H.

Grace, Fran. Branigan's Dog. LC 81-6188. 224p. (gr. 7 up). 1981. 10.95 (ISBN 0-02-736660-X). Bradbury Pr.

--A Very Private Performance. LC 83-6378. 182p. (YA) 1983. 11.95 (ISBN 0-02-736650-2). Bradbury Pr.

Grace, George. An Essay on Language. 1981. 14.50 (ISBN 0-917496-18-3); pap. 9.95 (ISBN 0-917496-17-5). Hornbeam Pr.

Grace, George W. The Position of the Polynesian Language within the (Austronesian Malayo-Polynesian) Language Family. LC 59-7612. (Indiana University Publications in Anthropology & Linguistics Ser.: No. 16). pap. 21.30 (ISBN 0-317-27811-8, 2015201). Bks Demand UMI.

Grace, Gerald, ed. Education & the City: Theory, History & Contemporary Practice. 350p. (Orig.). 1984. pap. 16.95x (ISBN 0-7100-9918-5). Routledge & Kegan.

Grace, Harvey. French Organ Music, Past & Present. LC 77-94581. 1979. Repr. of 1919 ed. lib. bdg. 25.00 (ISBN 0-89341-409-3). Longwood Pub Group.

--Musician at Large. LC 78-107703. (Essay Index Reprint Ser.). 1928. 18.00 (ISBN 0-8369-1506-2). Ayer Co Pubs.

--The Organ Works of Bach. LC 77-94581. 1979. Repr. of 1922 ed. lib. bdg. 35.00 (ISBN 0-89341-408-5). Longwood Pub Group.

Grace, Harvey, jt. auth. see Davies, Henry W.

Grace, Helen K. & Camilleri, Dorothy. Mental Health Nursing: A Socio-Psychological Approach. 2nd ed. 624p. 1981. pap. text ed. write for info. (ISBN 0-697-05517-5); instrs.' manual avail. (ISBN 0-697-05518-3). Wm C Brown.

Grace, Helen K., jt. auth. see Knafl, Kathleen A.

Grace, Helen K., jt. ed. see McCloskey, Joanne C.

Grace, J. Plant-Atmosphere Relationships. LC 82-19177. (Outline Studies in Ecology). 80p. 1983. pap. 7.50 (ISBN 0-412-23180-8, NO. 6783, Pub. by Chapman & Hall). Methuen Inc.

--Plant Response to Wind. (Experimental Botany Ser.). 1978. 47.50 (ISBN 0-12-294450-X). Acad Pr.

Grace, J., et al. Plants & Their Atmospheric Environment. (British Ecological Society Symposia Ser.). 419p. 1981. 89.95x (ISBN 0-470-27125-6). Halsted Pr.

Grace, J. Peter. Burning Money: The Waste of Your Tax Dollars. 192p. 1984. 14.95 (ISBN 0-02-544930-3). Macmillan.

Grace, James H. God, Sex, & the Social Project: The Glassboro Papers on Religion & Human Sexuality. LC 78-65496. (Symposium Ser.: Vol. 2). x, 203p. 1978. 19.95x (ISBN 0-88946-900-8). E Mellen.

--Sex & Marriage in the Unification Movement: A Sociological Study. LC 85-2961. (Studies in Religion & Society: Vol. 13). 308p. 1985. 49.95x (ISBN 0-88946-861-3). E Mellen.

Grace, Joan, jt. auth. see Grace, William.

Grace, Joan C. Tragic Theory in the Critical Works of Thomas Rymer, John Dennis, & John Dryden. LC 73-2892. 143p. 1975. 15.00 (ISBN 0-8386-1312-8). Fairleigh Dickinson.

Grace, John A. & Young, Alfred. The Algebra of Invariants. LC 65-11860. 1965. 16.95 (ISBN 0-8284-0180-2). Chelsea Pub.

Grace, John R. & Matsen, John M., eds. Fluidization. LC 80-16314. 622p. 1980. 89.50x (ISBN 0-306-40458-3, Plenum Pr). Plenum Pub.

Grace, Joyce, jt. auth. see Grace, Mike.

Grace, Julie, ed. Bulbs & Perennials. (Know Your Garden Ser.). (Illus.). 282p. 1984. 24.95 (ISBN 0-917304-85-3). Timber.

--Ornamental Conifers. (Illus.). 224p. 1983. 34.95 (ISBN 0-917304-83-7). Timber.

--Trees & Shrubs. (Know Your Garden Ser.). (Illus.). 179p. 1983. Repr. of 1973 ed. 24.95 (ISBN 0-917304-84-5). Timber.

Grace, Louise P. Leaving Home. 208p. (Orig.). 1984. pap. 11.95 (ISBN 0-318-03523-5). L P Grace.

Grace, M. R. Cassava Processing. Rev. ed. (Plant Production & Protection Papers: No. 3). 155p. 1977. pap. 10.00 (ISBN 92-5-100171-5, F1453, FAO). Unipub.

Grace, Mary. Mohawk Glory. 1980. 2.00 (ISBN 0-8198-4700-3); pap. 1.25 (ISBN 0-8198-4701-1). Dghtrs St Paul.

Grace, Mary, tr. see Navantes, S.

Grace, Mike & Grace, Joyce. A Joyful Meeting: Sexuality in Marriage. rev. ed. (Illus.). 100p. 1981. pap. 3.00 (ISBN 0-936098-29-5). Intl Marriage.

Grace, Patricia. The Dream Sleepers & Other Stories. (Pacific Paperperbacks Ser.). 106p. (Orig.). (gr. 10-12). 1980. pap. 7.00x (ISBN 0-582-70620-3, Pub. by Longman Paul Pubs New Zealand). Three Continents.

--Mutuwhenua: The Moon Sleeps. 155p. (Orig.). 1978. pap. 7.00x (ISBN 0-582-71762-0, Pub. by Longman Paul New Zealand). Three Continents.

--Waiariki. 91p. (gr. 10 up). 1976. pap. 7.00x (ISBN 0-582-71743-4, Pub. by Longman Paul New Zealand). Three Continents.

Grace, Patrick W. The Gulf of Maine. 1977. pap. 2.95 (ISBN 0-911764-18-6). Durrell.

Grace, Peter J. War On Waste: President's Private Sector Survey On Cost Control. 608p. 9.95 (ISBN 0-02-074660-1). Macmillan.

Grace, V. Stamped Amphora Handles Found in the Athenian Agora 1931-1932. 1977. 15.00 (ISBN 0-685-00187-3). Ares.

Grace, Vilma Janke. Latin American & Cholesterol Conscious Cooking. LC 79-15727. (Illus.). 1979. spiral 5.95 (ISBN 0-87491-280-6). Acropolis.

Grace, Virginia R. Amphoras & the Ancient Wine Trade. (Excavations of the Athenian Agora Picture Bks.: No. 6). (Illus.). 1979. pap. 1.50x (ISBN 0-87661-619-8). Am Sch Athens.

Grace, William. Monarch Notes on Spenser's Faerie Queene & Other Works. (Orig.). pap. 3.50 (ISBN 0-671-00512-X). Monarch Pr.

Grace, William & Grace, Joan. Art of Communicating Ideas. 1952. 5.00 (ISBN 0-8159-5014-4). Devin.

Grace, William J. Ideas in Milton. LC 68-12290. 1969. Repr. of 1968 ed. 6.95x (ISBN 0-268-00126-X). U of Notre Dame Pr.

Grace, William J., Jr. The ABC'S of IRA'S: The Complete Guide to Individual Retirement Accounts. 1984. pap. 4.95 (ISBN 0-440-50398-1, Dell Trade Pbks). Dell.

--The Phoenix Approach. 272p. (Orig.). 1985. pap. 3.95 (ISBN 0-553-24513-9). Bantam.

Gracenin, Carolyn T. Thoughts, Troubles & Things About Reading from the Cradle Through Grade Three. LC 80-65611. 180p. 1981. perfect bdg. 14.95 (ISBN 0-86548-038-9). R & E Pubs.

Gracey, Colin B., jt. auth. see Ames, David A.

Gracey, D. R. Pulmonary Diseases in the Adult. (Illus.). 448p. 1981. 48.95 (ISBN 0-8151-3850-4). Year Bk Med.

Gracey, Douglas R. Tuberculosis. Addington, Whitney W., ed. LC 79-88043. (Contemporary Patient Management Ser.). 1979. pap. 15.00 (ISBN 0-87488-875-1). Med Exam.

Gracey, H. L., jt. auth. see Wrong, Dennis H.

Gracey, Harry L. Curriculum or Craftmanship: Elementary School Teacher in a Bureaucratic System. LC 71-188235. 1972. text ed. 17.00x (ISBN 0-226-30595-3). U of Chicago Pr.

Gracey, J. F. Thornton's Meat Hygiene. 7th ed. (Illus.). 444p. 1981. 61.00 (ISBN 0-7216-0788-8, Pub. by Bailliere-Tindall). Saunders.

Gracey, Michael & Falkner, Frank, eds. Nutritional Needs & Assessment of Normal Growth. (Nestle Nutrition Workshop Ser.: Vol. 7). 240p. 1985. text ed. 32.50 (ISBN 0-88167-044-8). Raven.

Gracey, William. Measurement of Aircraft Speed & Altitude. LC 80-23503. 262p. 1981. 54.50x (ISBN 0-471-08511-1). Wiley.

Grachev, A. In the Grip of Terror. 150p. 1984. pap. 2.95 (ISBN 0-8285-2399-1, Pub. by Progress Pubs USSR). Imported Pubns.

Grachev, A. & Yermoshkin, N. New Information Order of Psychological Warfare? 264p. 1985. pap. 2.95 (ISBN 0-8285-2813-6, Pub. by Progress Pubs USSR). Imported Pubns.

Gracia, Debbie. My Birthday on Christmas Day. (Illus.). 30p. (Orig.). (ps-7). 1980. pap. 3.75 (ISBN 0-915347-05-9). Pueblo Acoma Pr.

Gracia, Jorge J. Suarez on Individuation. Robb, James, ed. 304p. 1981. pap. 24.95 (ISBN 0-87462-223-9); price not set med phil texts. Marquette.

Gracia, Jorge J., ed. El Hombre y su Conducta: Ensayos filosoficos en honor de Risieri Frondizi. Bilingual ed. Bd. with Man & His Conduct: Philosophical Essays in Honor of Risieri Frondizi. LC 79-988. 346p. (Span. & Eng.). 1980. pap. 10.00 (ISBN 0-8477-2820-X). U of PR Pr.

Gracia, Jorge J. E. Introduction to the Problem of Individuation in Early Middle Ages: 500-1200 A.D. LC 83-1947. 301p. 1984. 54.95 (ISBN 0-8132-0588-3). Cath U Pr.

Gracia-Bouza, Jorge, jt. auth. see Harari, Denyse.

Gracie, David M., tr. see Harnack, Adolf.

Gracie, Gordon, jt. auth. see Mikhail, Edward M.

Gracq, Julien. Andre Breton, Quelques Aspects de l'Ecrivain. 212p. 17.50 (ISBN 0-686-54016-6). French & Eur.

--Au Chateau d'Argol. 180p. 1970. 15.00 (ISBN 0-686-54017-4). French & Eur.

--Un Balcon en Foret. 256p. 1958. 16.50 (ISBN 0-686-54018-2). French & Eur.

--Un Beau Tenebreux. 206p. 1970. 16.50 (ISBN 0-686-54019-0). French & Eur.

--Les Eaux Etroites. 80p. 1976. 8.50 (ISBN 0-686-54020-4). French & Eur.

--Lettrines, 2 vols. 1967. 16.50 ea. French & Eur.

--Lettrines, Vol. 2. 256p. 1974. 16.50 (ISBN 0-686-54021-2). French & Eur.

--Liberte Grande. 156p. 1958. 12.50 (ISBN 0-686-54022-0). French & Eur.

--Penthesilee, de Kleist. 128p. 15.00 (ISBN 0-686-54023-9). French & Eur.

--Preferences. 256p. 1961. 17.50 (ISBN 0-686-54024-7). French & Eur.

--La Presqu'ile: Avec: La Route, Le Roi Cophetua. 256p. 1970. 19.95 (ISBN 0-686-54025-5). French & Eur.

--Le Rivage des Syrtes. 1952. 22.50 (ISBN 0-686-54026-3). French & Eur.

--Le Roi Pecheur. 156p. 1955. 15.00 (ISBN 0-686-54027-1). French & Eur.

Gracy, Alice, jt. auth. see Sumner, Jane.

Gracy, David & Carefoot, Jean. Ships of the Texas Navy. (Illus.). 1979. 45.00 (ISBN 0-935978-04-6). Presidial.

Gracy, David B., II. Archives & Manuscripts: Arrangement & Description. rev. ed. LC 77-13527. (SAA Basic Manual Ser.). 49p. 1977. pap. 5.00 (ISBN 0-931828-07-4). Soc Am Archivists.

Gracy, David B., 2nd. Littlefield Lands: Colonization on the Texas Plains, 1912-1920. (M. K. Brown Range Life Ser.: No. 8). (Illus.). 175p. 1968. 11.95 (ISBN 0-292-78359-0). U of Tex Pr.

Gracy, David B., 2nd, ed. see Austin, Stephen F.

Gracza, Margaret, jt. auth. see Rezsoe Gracza.

Gracza, Margaret Y. Bird in Art. LC 65-29035. (Fine Art Books). (Illus.). (gr. 5-11). 1966. PLB 5.95g (ISBN 0-8225-0158-9). Lerner Pubns.

--Ship & Sea in Art. LC 64-8203. (Fine Art Books). (Illus.). (gr. 5-11). 1965. PLB 5.95 (ISBN 0-8225-0153-8). Lerner Pubns.

Grad, A. Dictionary French-Slovene. 1402p. (Fr. & Slovene.). 1975. 35.00 (ISBN 0-686-92263-8, M-9693). French & Eur.

--Dictionnaire Moderne: Slovene-French-Slovene. 745p. (Slovenian & Fr.). 1978. leatherette 14.95 (ISBN 0-686-92561-0, M-9705). French & Eur.

--Dizionario Moderno Slovene-Italian-Slovene. 445p. (Ital. & Slovene.). 1979. leatherette 14.95 (ISBN 0-686-97353-4, M9704). French & Eur.

Grad, A., jt. auth. see Kotnik, J.

Grad, A., ed. Diccionario Esloveno-Espanol. 747p. (Span.). 1979. 49.95 (ISBN 0-686-92391-X, S-37817). French & Eur.

Grad, A., et al. English-Slovene Dictionary. 1120p. (Eng. & Slovene.). 1979. 49.95 (ISBN 0-686-97378-X, M-9695). French & Eur.

Grad, Andrew J. Formosa Today: An Analysis of the Economic Development & Strategic Importance of Japan's Tropical Colony. LC 75-30057. (Institute of Pacific Relations). Repr. of 1942 ed. 21.50 (ISBN 0-404-59526-X). AMS Pr.

--Modern Korea. 1979. Repr. of 1944 ed. lib. bdg. 24.00x (ISBN 0-374-93226-3). Octagon.

Grad, Arthur see Schaeffer, A. C. & Spencer, D. C.

Grad, Bonnie L. Milton Avery. (Illus.). 132p. 1981. 140.00 (ISBN 0-931554-19-5). Strathcona.

Grad, Bonnie L. & Riggs, Timothy. Visions of City & Country: Prints & Photographs of Nineteenth Century France. (Illus.). 228p. (Orig.). 1982. pap. text ed. 11.60 (ISBN 0-917418-69-7). Am Fed Arts.

Grad, Bonnie L. & Riggs, Timothy A. Visions of City & Country: Prints & Photographs of Nineteenth-Century France. LC 82-50258. (Illus.). 288p. (Orig.). 1982. pap. 14.95 (ISBN 0-87023-409-9). U of Mass Pr.

Grad, Burton, et al. Management Systems. 2nd ed. 504p. 1979. text ed. 33.95x (ISBN 0-03-047541-4); instr's. manual 10.00 (ISBN 0-03-047546-5). Dryden Pr.

Grad, Eli & Roth, Bette. Congregation Shaarey Zedek: 5622-5742 1861-1981. LC 82-48650. (Illus.). 198p. 1982. 25.00 (ISBN 0-8143-1713-8). Wayne St U Pr.

Grad, Frank, ed. Public Health Law Manual. LC 74-120960. 234p. 1973. 6.50x (ISBN 0-87553-058-3, 060). Am Pub Health.

Grad, Frank & O'Connor, Martha, eds. Constitution of the U. S. National & State, 1974-1976, 6 vols. 2nd ed. 450.00 set (ISBN 0-379-00186-1); includes supps, releases & index 1285.00 set. Oceana.

Grad, Frank P. & Marti, Noelia. Physicians' Licensure & Discipline. LC 79-21925. 471p. 1980. lib. bdg. 45.00 (ISBN 0-379-20463-0). Oceana.

Grad, Frank P., et al. Alcoholism & the Law. LC 72-116057. 311p. 1971. 20.00 (ISBN 0-379-00457-7). Oceana.

--Environmental Control: Priorities, Policies & the Law. LC 79-155361. 311p. 1971. 33.00x (ISBN 0-231-03563-2). Columbia U Pr.

--The Automobile & the Regulation of Its Impact on the Environment. LC 74-31051. 500p. 1975. 32.50x (ISBN 0-8061-1270-0); pap. 14.50x (ISBN 0-8061-1273-5). U of Okla Pr.

Grad, H., ed. see Symposia in Applied Mathematics - New York - 1965.

Grad, Laurie B. Dining In-Los Angeles. Rev. ed. (Dining In Ser.). (Illus.). 190p. 1982. pap. 8.95 (ISBN 0-89716-121-1). Peanut Butter.

--Make It Easy Entertaining. LC 84-2751. (Illus.). 336p. 1984. 15.95 (ISBN 0-87477-289-3). J P Tarcher.

--Make It Easy in Your Kitchen. LC 81-85208. (Illus.). 352p. 1982. pap. 9.95 (ISBN 0-87477-349-0). J P Tarcher.

--Make It Easy in Your Kitchen. 1985. pap. 9.95. HM.

Grad, Rae, et al. The Father Book: Pregnancy and Beyond. LC 80-27800. (Illus.). 200p. 1981. 17.50 (ISBN 0-87491-618-6); pap. 8.95 (ISBN 0-87491-422-1). Acropolis.

Graddy, Duane B. The Bank Holding Company Performance Controversy. LC 78-65842. 1979. pap. text ed. 30.00 (ISBN 0-8191-0678-X). U Pr of Amer.

Grade, Arnold, ed. Family Letters of Robert & Elinor Frost. LC 71-152518. (Illus.). 1972. 49.50x (ISBN 0-87395-087-9). State U NY Pr.

Grade, Chaim. The Agunah. Leviant, Curt, tr. from Yiddish. 1978. pap. 3.95 (ISBN 0-932232-00-0). Menorah Pub.

--Rabbis & Wives. LC 82-14. 1982. 15.95 (ISBN 0-394-50979-X). Knopf.

--Rabbis & Wives. LC 83-5855. 320p. 1983. pap. 5.95 (ISBN 0-394-71647-7, Vin). Random.

--The Yeshiva, Vols. 1 & 2. Leviant, Curt, tr. from Yiddish. 1979. pap. 11.95 (ISBN 0-932232-05-1). Menorah Pub.

Gradel, Morris, tr. see Yahil, Leni.

Gradenwitz, Peter. Music & Musicians in Israel. LC 75-166232. 226p. 1959. Repr. 39.00 (ISBN 0-403-01568-5). Scholarly.

Gradidge, Roderick. Dream Houses: The Edwardian Ideal. LC 80-17866. 272p. 30.00 (ISBN 0-8076-0988-9). Braziller.

--Edwin Lutyens: Architect Laureate. (Illus.). 160p. 1982. 24.50 (ISBN 0-04-720023-5). Allen Unwin.

--Edwin Lutyens: Architect Laureate. 160p. 1981. 30.00x (ISBN 0-85967-618-8, Pub. by Scolar England). State Mutual Bk.

Gradin, Hartley, Jr. Primer on Finite Element Method. 519p. 1986. text ed. price not set (ISBN 0-02-345480-6). Macmillan.

Gradinger, Gilbert P., jt. auth. see Kaye, Bernard L.

Gradish, Stephen. The Manning of the British Navy during the Seven Years' War. 1982. 65.00 (ISBN 0-901050-58-X, Royal Hist Soc England). State Mutual Bk.

Gradish, Steven. Manning of the British Navy During the Seven Years' War. (Royal Historical Society Studies in History: Vol. 21). 235p. 1980. text ed. 38.75x (ISBN 0-901050-58-X, Pub. by Swiftbks England). Humanities.

Gradl, M. J., ed. Authentic Art Nouveau Stained Glass Designs in Full Color. (Crafts Ser.). (Illus.). 32p. 1982. pap. 4.50 (ISBN 0-486-24362-1). Dover.

Gradman, Barry. Metamorphosis in Keats. LC 79-3756. 160p. 1980. 26.00x (ISBN 0-8147-2977-0); pap. 13.50x (ISBN 0-8147-2978-9). NYU Pr.

Gradon, F. Maintenance Engineering: Organisation & Management. (Illus.). 209p. 1973. 39.00 (ISBN 0-85334-555-4, Pub. by Elsevier Applied Sci England). Elsevier.

Gradon, P. O. Cynewulf's Elene. 115p. 1982. pap. text ed. 5.50x (ISBN 0-85989-087-2, Pub. by U Exeter England). Humanities.

Gradon, P. O., ed. see Cynewulf.

Gradshteyn, I. S., et al. Tables of Integrals, Series & Products. 1980. 25.00 (ISBN 0-12-294760-6). Acad Pr.

Gradstein, Bonnie, jt. auth. see Friedman, Rochelle.

Gradstein, S. R., jt. auth. see Vitt, D. H.

Graduate Institute Of International Studies - Geneva. World Crisis by the Professors of the Institute. facs. ed. LC 73-86753. (Essay Index Reprint Ser). 1938. 19.00 (ISBN 0-8369-1133-4). Ayer Co Pubs.

Graduate School of Planning. Indicadores de la Calidad de la Vida: Municipios de Puerto Rico. Navas, Gerardo, intro. by. (Social Planning Ser.: No. S-6). (Illus., Sp.). 1979. pap. 3.00 (ISBN 0-8477-2452-2). U of PR Pr.

Graduck, I. I. Prestressed Concrete. 150p. 1970. 42.95 (ISBN 0-677-61730-5). Gordon.

Gradus, Yehuda. Spatial Distribution of Political Power & Regional Disparities: The Israeli Case. (Working Papers Ser.: No. 82-4). 34p. 1982. pap. 6.00 (ISBN 0-686-82541-1, CRD138, UNCRD). Unipub.

Gradwohl, David M. & Osborn, Nancy M. Exploring Buried Buxton. (Illus.). 178p. 1984. text ed. 19.95 (ISBN 0-8138-0244-X). Iowa St U Pr.

Grady & Lim. Biological Wastewater Treatment: Theory & Applications. LC 80-20171. (Pollution Engineering & Technology Ser.: Vol. 12). 984p. 1980. 95.00 (ISBN 0-8247-1000-2). Dekker.

Grady & Wooton. Precalculus. 2nd ed. 662p. write for info. (ISBN 0-534-02841-1). Wadsworth Pub.

Grady, A., jt. auth. see Gilfoyle, E.

Grady, Ann, jt. auth. see Gilfoyle, Elnora.

Grady, Denice. Basic Skills Creative Writing Workbook. (Basic Skills Workbooks). 32p. (gr. 5-9). 1983. 0.99 (ISBN 0-8209-0549-6, EW-3). ESP.

--Creative Writing. (Language Arts Ser.). 24p. (gr. 3-5). 1977. wkbk. 5.00 (ISBN 0-8209-0326-4, LA-12). ESP.

Grady, Henry F. British War Finance, Nineteen Fourteen to Nineteen Nineteen. LC 73-76688. (Columbia University. Studies in the Social Sciences: No. 279). Repr. of 1926 ed. 24.50 (ISBN 0-404-51279-8). AMS Pr.

Grady, Henry W. The Complete Orations & Speeches of Henry W. Grady. Shurter, Edwin, ed. 1976. lib. bdg. 59.95 (ISBN 0-8490-1657-6). Gordon Pr.

--The New South & Other Addresses. 69.95 (ISBN 0-87968-024-5). Gordon Pr.

--New South & Other Addresses. LC 68-24979. (American History & Americana Ser., No. 47). 1969. Repr. of 1904 ed. lib. bdg. 39.95x (ISBN 0-8383-0948-8). Haskell.

Grady, James. Hard Bargains. 288p. 1985. 15.95 (ISBN 0-02-544960-5). Macmillan.

--Razor Game. 256p. (Orig.). 1985. pap. 3.50 (ISBN 0-553-24826-X). Bantam.

--Runner in the Street. 288p. 1984. 14.95 (ISBN 0-02-544940-0). Macmillan.

Grady, James, jt. auth. see Frangiamore, Roy.

Grady, James, jt. auth. see Hester, James J.

Grady, James H; see O'Neal, William B.

Grady, John C., Jr., jt. auth. see Felm, Bradford K.

Grady, John L. Abortion: Yes or No? LC 79-53228. 32p. 1968. pap. 1.00 (ISBN 0-89555-117-9). TAN Bks Pubs.

Grady, Liz. Heart of Gold. (Second Chance at Love Ser.: No. 260). 192p. 1985. pap. 1.95 (ISBN 0-425-08018-8). Berkley Pub.

--Heart of the Hunter. (Second Chance at Love Ser.: No. 283). 192p. 1985. pap. 2.25 (ISBN 0-425-08464-7). Berkley Pub.

--Hearts at Risk. (Second Chance at Love Ser.: No. 232). 192p. 1984. pap. 1.95 (ISBN 0-515-08206-6). Jove Pubns.

--Too Close for Comfort. (Second Chance at Love Ser.: No. 198). 192p. 1984. pap. 1.95 (ISBN 0-515-07814-X). Jove Pubns.

--Touch of Moonlight. (Second Chance at Love Ser.: No. 210). 192p. 1984. pap. 1.95 (ISBN 0-515-07958-8). Jove Pubns.

Grady, Michael. A la New Orleans: Restaurant Recipes. (Orig.). 1980. pap. 9.95 (ISBN 0-937070-02-5). Crabtree.

--Syntax & Semantics of the English Verb Phrase. LC 75-118277. (Janua Linguarum, Ser. Practica: No. 112). (Illus., Orig.). 1970. pap. text ed. 9.60x (ISBN 90-2790-745-5). Mouton.

Grady, Michael & Luecke, Emily. Education & the Brain. LC 78-50378. (Fastback Ser.: No. 108). 1978. pap. 0.75 (ISBN 0-87367-108-2). Phi Delta Kappa.

Grady, Mike, jt. auth. see Beckenbach, Edwin.

Grady, Perry L. & Mock, Gary N. Glossaries of Terms & Bibliographic Citations for Computers in the Textile Industry. 40p. 1983. pap. text ed. 4.95x (ISBN 0-87664-782-4). Instru Soc.

--Microprocessors & Minicomputers in the Textile Industry. LC 80-82119. 488p. 1983. text ed. 59.95 (ISBN 0-87664-485-X, 1485-X). Instru Soc.

Grady, Tom, jt. auth. see Lansky, Vicki.

Grady, Tom, ed. see Lansky, Bruce.

Grady, Tom, ed. see Simkin, Penny, et al.

Grady Crabtree, Catherine see Crabtree, Catherine G.

Grae, Camarin. PAZ. LC 84-72157. (Orig.). 1984. pap. 8.95 (ISBN 0-913017-02-7). Blazon Bks.

--Soul Snatcher. (Illus., Orig.). 1985. pap. 8.95 (ISBN 0-913017-03-5). Blazon Bks.
--The Winged Dancer. LC 83-71353. (Orig.). 1983. pap. 6.95 (ISBN 0-913017-01-9). Blazon Bks.
Grae, Ida. Dressing the Loom. 1975. Repr. of 1953 ed. 6.00 (ISBN 0-686-11143-5). Robin & Russ.
--Nature's Colors: Dyes from Plants. LC 73-11836. (Illus.). 230p. 1979. pap. 10.95 (ISBN 0-02-012390-6, Collier). Macmillan.
Graebe, Chris & Graebe, Julie. The Hornby Gauge O System. (Hornby Companion Ser. V). (Illus.). 312p. 1985. 55.00 (ISBN 0-904568-35-0, Pub. by New Cavendish England). Schiffer.
Graebe, Julie, jt. auth. see Graebe, Chris.
Graeber, Andreas. Untersuchungen zum Spaetromischen Korporationswesen. (European University Studies: No. 3, Vol. 196). 194p. (Ger.). 1983. 23.15 (ISBN 3-8204-7704-7). P Lang Pubs.
Graeber, Charlotte. The Hard Luck Mutt. (Mr. T & Me Ser.). 24p. (gr. 1-4). 1985. pap. 1.95 (ISBN 0-8407-6661-0). Nelson.
--I'm So-So, So What? (Mr. T & Me Ser.). 24p. (gr. 1-4). 1985. pap. 1.95 (ISBN 0-8407-6659-9). Nelson.
--In, Out & about Catfish Pond. (Early Readers Ser.). (Illus.). (gr. 1-4). 1984. 4.95 (ISBN 0-89191-841-8); pap. 2.95 (ISBN 0-89191-798-5). Cook.
--The Muscle Tussle. (Mr. T & Me Ser.). (Illus.). 24p. (gr. 1-4). 1985. pap. 1.95 (ISBN 0-8407-6668-8). Nelson.
--Mustard. LC 81-20764. (Illus.). 48p. (gr. 2-5). 1982. 9.95 (ISBN 0-02-736690-1). Macmillan.
--Mustard. (Skylark Choose Your Own Adventure). (Illus.). 1983. pap. 2.25 (ISBN 0-553-15384-6). Bantam.
--My Mr. T Doll. (Mr. T & Me Ser.). (Illus.). 24p. (gr. 1-4). 1985. pap. 1.95 (ISBN 0-8407-6662-9). Nelson.
--The Not So Great Place. (Mr. T & Me Ser.). (Illus.). 24p. (gr. 1-4). 1985. pap. 1.95 (ISBN 0-8407-6658-0). Nelson.
--Tackle Block Stop. (Mr. T & Me Ser.). 24p. (gr. 1-4). 1985. pap. 1.95 (ISBN 0-8407-6660-2). Nelson.
--Up, Down, & Around the Raintree. (Early Readers Ser.). (gr. 1-4). 1984. 4.95 (ISBN 0-89191-840-X); pap. 2.95 (ISBN 0-89191-786-1). Cook.
Graeber, Charlotte T. The Thing in Katy's Attic. LC 84-8117. (Illus.). 80p. (gr. 1-4). 1984. 9.95 (ISBN 0-525-44146-8, 0966-290). Dutton.
Graeber, Geoffrey M., jt. auth. see Seyfer, Alan E.
Graeber, Isacque & Britt, Steuart H. Jews in a Gentile World: The Problem of Anti-Semitism. LC 78-26329. (Illus.). 1979. Repr. of 1942 ed. lib. bdg. 32.50x (ISBN 0-313-20878-6, GRJE). Greenwood.
Graeber, Laurel. Are you Dying for a Drink? Teenagers & Alcohol Abuse. (Illus.). 128p. (gr. 7 up). 1985. 9.79 (ISBN 0-671-50818-0). Messner.
Graeber, R. Curtis, jt. ed. see Brown, Frederick M.
Graebner, Alan. Uncertain Saints. LC 75-1573. (Contributions in American History: No. 42). 320p. 1975. lib. bdg. 29.95 (ISBN 0-8371-7963-7, GUS/). Greenwood.
Graebner, Norman. The Cold War. 2nd ed. (Problems in European Civilization). 1976. pap. text ed. 5.50 (ISBN 0-669-81984-0). Heath.
--Nationalism & Communism in Asia: The American Response. (Problems in American Civilization Ser.). 1976. pap. text ed. 5.95 (ISBN 0-669-00683-1). Heath.
Graebner, Norman A. America As a World Power: A Realist Appraisal from Wilson to Reagan. LC 84-10706. 336p. 1984. 30.00 (ISBN 0-8420-2230-9); pap. text ed. 11.95 (ISBN 0-8420-2232-5). Scholarly Res Inc.
--Empire on the Pacific: A Study in American Continental Expansion. LC 82-22680. 278p. 1983. lib. bdg. 25.00 (ISBN 0-87436-033-1). ABC Clio.
--Foundations of American Foreign Policy: A Realist Appraisal from Franklin to McKinley. 400p. (Orig.). 1985. write for info. (ISBN 0-8420-2244-9); pap. write for info. (ISBN 0-8420-2245-7). Scholarly Res Inc.
Graebner, Norman A., ed. Freedom in America: A Two Hundred Year Perspective. LC 76-43022. 1977. 22.50x (ISBN 0-271-01234-X). Pa St U Pr.
--An Uncertain Tradition: American Secretaries of State in the Twentieth Century. LC 79-26791. (McGraw-Hill Ser. in American History). 341p. 1980. Repr. of 1961 ed. lib. bdg. 27.50x (ISBN 0-313-22317-3, GRUT). Greenwood.
Graebner, Norman A. & Thompson, Kenneth W., eds. Traditions & Values: American Diplomacy, 1865-1945. (American Values Projected Abroad Ser.: Vol. VIII). 218p. (Orig.). 1985. lib. bdg. 22.00 (ISBN 0-8191-4650-1, Co-pub. by White Miller Center); pap. text ed. 10.75 (ISBN 0-8191-4651-X, Co-pub. by White Miller Center). U Pr of Amer.
--Traditions & Values: American Diplomacy, 1790-1865. LC 85-7334. (American Values Projected Abroad Ser.: Vol. VII). 192p. (Orig.). Date not set. lib. bdg. 23.50 (ISBN 0-8191-4388-X); pap. text ed. 12.00 (ISBN 0-8191-4389-8). U Pr of Amer.
Graebner, Norman A., compiled by. American Diplomatic History Before 1900. LC 77-85991. (Goldentree Bibliographies in American History). 1978. text ed. 24.95x (ISBN 0-88295-573-X); pap. text ed. 14.95x (ISBN 0-88295-543-8). Harlan Davidson.
Graebner, Norman A., et al. A History of the American People, 2 vols. 2nd ed. LC 74-26670. (Illus.). 1975. Vol. 1. pap. text ed. 28.95 (ISBN 0-07-023885-5); Vol. 2. pap. text ed. 28.95 (ISBN 0-07-023886-3). McGraw.
Graebner, Walter, jt. ed. see Michie, Allan A.
Graebner, William. Coal-Mining Safety in the Progressive Period: The Political Economy of Reform. LC 75-38215. 256p. 1976. 23.00x (ISBN 0-8131-1339-3). U Pr of Ky.
--A History of Retirement: The Meaning & Function of An American Institution, 1885-1978. LC 79-28849. 328p. 1984. pap. 9.95 (ISBN 0-300-03300-1, Y-513). Yale U PR.
Graebner, William & Richards, Leonard. The American Record. LC 81-13748. 1981. Vol. 1. pap. text ed. 11.00 (ISBN 0-394-32216-9, KnopfC); Vol. 2. pap. text ed. 11.00 (ISBN 0-394-32665-2). Knopf.
Graedel, T. E. Chemical Compounds in the Atmosphere. LC 78-12264. 1979. 49.50 (ISBN 0-12-294480-1). Acad Pr.
Graedon, Joe. The New People's Pharmacy: Drug Breakthroughs of the '80s. 19.95 (ISBN 0-553-05072-9); pap. 8.95 (ISBN 0-553-34134-0). Bantam.
--The People's Pharmacy. 1977. pap. 5.95 (ISBN 0-380-00902-1, 76299-4). Avon.
--The People's Pharmacy. rev. ed. (Illus.). 432p. 1985. 16.95 (ISBN 0-312-60026-7). St Martin.
Graef, H. C. The Way of the Mystics. 1977. lib. bdg. 59.95 (ISBN 0-8490-2811-6). Gordon Pr.
Graef, Hilda. Mary: A History of Doctrine & Devotion, 2 vols. 1985. Set. pap. 18.95 (ISBN 0-87061-113-5). Pt. I, 371 pgs. Pt. II, 160 pgs. Chr Classics.
Graef, John R. Stability of Dynamical Systems: Theory & Application. (Lecture Notes in Pure & Applied Mathematics: Vol. 28). 1977. 55.00 (ISBN 0-8247-6410-2). Dekker.
Graef, John W., ed. see Children's Hospital, Boston, Department of Medicine Staff.
Graef, John W., ed. see Children's Hospital Medical Center, Boston.
Graef, Judy & Strom, J. Concepts in Clothing. 1976. 21.40 (ISBN 0-07-023889-8). McGraw.
Graef, Martin, et al. Organization & Operation of a Computer Center. Goldman, Abram F., tr. from Ger. 406p. 1985. text ed. 34.95x (ISBN 0-02-949990-9). Macmillan.
Graefe, E., jt. auth. see Eaton-Krauss, M.
Graeff, Arthur D., et al. The Pennsylvania Germans in Ontario, Canada: Bd. with Coppersmithing in Pennsylvania; & Lexical Differences Between Four Pennsylvania German Regions. (Penn. German Folklore Ser.: Vol. 11). Repr. of 1946 ed. 25.00 (ISBN 0-911122-19-2). Penn German Soc.
Graeff, G., et al, eds. Present Status & Aims of Quantum Electrodynamics: Proceedings. (Lecture Notes in Physics Ser.: Vol. 143). 302p. 1981. pap. 22.00 (ISBN 0-387-10847-5). Springer-Verlag.
Graeff, H. & Kuhn, W. Coagulation Disorders in Obstetrics: Pathobiochemistry-Pathophysiology-Diagnosis-Treatment. Davis, A., tr. from Ger. LC 79-48020. (Major Problems in Obstetrics & Gynecology Ser.: No. 13). 1980. 10.00 (ISBN 0-7216-4192-X). Saunders.
Graeff, H., jt. ed. see Henschen, A.
Graeff, Roderich W. Solar Energy Calculations. 280p. (Orig.). 1979. pap. text ed. 28.00x (ISBN 0-9604570-0-3). Graeff.
--Solar Energy Calculations. 280p. 1982. pap. text ed. 28.00 (ISBN 0-317-12237-1). Graeff.
Graeffe, Arnold D. Creative Education in the Humanities. LC 70-167347. (Essay Index Reprint Ser.). Repr. of 1951 ed. 17.00 (ISBN 0-8369-2691-9). Ayer Co Pubs.
Graeme, Jerald G. Application of Operational Amplifiers: Third Generation Techniques. (Illus.). 1973. 43.00 (ISBN 0-07-023890-1). McGraw.
--Designing with Operational Amplifiers: Applications, Alternatives. (Illus.). 1977. 44.50 (ISBN 0-07-023891-X). McGraw.
Graendorf, Werner, jt. auth. see Mattson, Lloyd.
Graendorf, Werner, ed. Introduction to Biblical Christian Education. LC 81-1608. 1981. 15.95 (ISBN 0-8024-4128-9). Moody.
Graesbeck, R. & Alstrom, T., eds. Reference Values in Laboratory Medicine: The Current State of the Art. LC 80-42312. 413p. 1982. 54.95x (ISBN 0-471-28025-9, Pub. by Wiley-Interscience). Wiley.
Graesch, Heinz. Wooden Toys: Projects & Plans. LC 83-4747. (Home Craftsman Bk.). (Illus.). 128p. (Orig.). 1984. pap. 6.95 (ISBN 0-8069-7606-3). Sterling.
Graeser, Andreas. Zenon von Kition: Positionen und Probleme. 1975. 48.00x (ISBN 3-11-004673-3). De Gruyter.
Graeser, Andreas, ed. Die Logischen Fragmente des Theophrast. (Kleine Texte fuer Vorlesungen und Uebungen Vol. 191). 96p. (Ger.). 1973. 9.60x (ISBN 3-11-003999-0). De Gruyter.
Graeser, Andreas, ed. see Gigon, Olof.
Graeser, Kathi, ed. Who's Who in Electronics 1985 Annual. pap. 1029.00 (ISBN 0-916512-72-X). Harris Pub.
Graeser, Kathie & Loesner, Bonnie, eds. Electronic Representative Directory 1985. 192p. 1985. 20.00 (ISBN 0-916512-73-8). Harris Pub.
Graesse, J. G. Fuhrer Fur Sammler Von Porzellan und Fayence. (Illus.). 862p. (Ger.). 1985. 45.00 (ISBN 3-7814-0202-9, Pub. by Klinkhardt & Biermann WG). Seven Hills Bks.
Graesser, A. C. Prose Comprehension Beyond the Word. (Illus.). 310p. 1981. 33.00 (ISBN 0-387-90544-8). Springer-Verlag.
Graesser, Arthur C. & Clark, Leslie F. Structures & Procedures Implicit Knowledge. LC 85-7336. 336p. 1985. text ed. 37.50 (ISBN 0-89391-192-5); pap. 24.95 (ISBN 0-89391-362-6). Ablex Pub.
Graesser, Arthur C. & Black, John B., eds. The Psychology of Questions. 392p. 1985. text ed. 39.95 (ISBN 0-89859-444-8). L Erlbaum Assocs.
Graesser, Erich. Das Problem der Parusieverzoegerung in den Synoptischen Evangelien und in der Apostelgeschichte. 3rd ed. (Beihefte zur Zeitschrift fuer die Alttestamentliche Wissenschaft 22). 1977. 36.40x (ISBN 3-11-007512-1). De Gruyter.
Graesser, Erich, et al. Jesus in Nazareth. (Beiheft 40 zur Zeitschrift fuer die alttes tamentliche Wissenschaft). 153p. 1972. 31.60x (ISBN 3-11-004004-2). De Gruyter.
Graesser, Neil. Fly Fishing for Salmon. (Illus.). 126p. 1982. 16.50 (ISBN 0-85115-172-8, Pub. by Boydell & Brewer). Longwood Pub Group.
--Fly Fishing for Salmon. (Illus.). 128p. 1985. Repr. of 1982 ed. 14.95 (ISBN 0-913276-50-2). Stone Wall Pr.
Graesser, Neil, jt. auth. see Mills, Derek.
Graesser, R. F., jt. auth. see Peterson, Gordon M.
Graesslin, D., jt. ed. see Radola, R. J.
Graetz, Heinrich. The Structure of Jewish History & Other Essays. 25.00x (ISBN 0-87068-466-3); pap. 11.95x (ISBN 0-685-56206-9). Ktav.
Graetz, Michael J. Federal Income Taxation, Principles & Policies: Successor Edition. (University Casebook Ser.). 1100p. 1985. text ed. write for info. (ISBN 0-88277-244-9). Foundation Pr.
Graetz, Michael J., jt. auth. see Griswold, Erwin N.
Graetz, R. D. & Howes, K. M. Studies of the Australian Arid Zone: Chenopod Shrublands, Pt. 4. 202p. 1981. 40.00x (ISBN 0-643-00347-9, Pub. by CSIRo Australia). State Mutual Bk.
Graetz, Rick. Beautiful Montana. 2nd ed. LC 78-102354. (Illus.). 72p. 1984. 14.95 (ISBN 0-317-07727-9); pap. 7.95 (ISBN 0-317-07728-7). Beautiful Am.
Graetzer, G. Universal Algebra. 2nd ed. LC 68-55539. xvi, 368p. 1979. 39.50 (ISBN 0-387-90355-0). Springer-Verlag.
Graetzerk, Hans G. & Anderson, David L. The Discovery of Nuclear Fission. Cohen, I. Bernard, ed. LC 80-2123. (Development of Science Ser.). (Illus.). 1981. lib. bdg. 12.00x (ISBN 0-405-13846-6). Ayer Co Pubs.
Graevenitz, Alexander Von see Von Graevenitz, Alexander & Rubin, Sally Jo.
Graevenitz, Alexander Von see Von Graevenitz, Alexander & Seligson, David.
Graf, Alfred B. Exotic House Plants. 10th ed. LC 72-97182. (Illus.). 1976. 8.95 (ISBN 0-911266-10-0). Roehrs.
--Exotic Plant Manual. 5th ed. (Illus.). 1975. 37.50 (ISBN 0-911266-13-5, ScribT). Scribner.
--Exotic Plant Manual: Exotic Plants to Live with. 5th ed. LC 74-75310. (Illus.). 1978. 37.50 (ISBN 0-911266-13-5). Roehrs.
--Exotica IV: Pictorial Cyclopedia of Exotic Plants & Trees. (Illus.). 2580p. 1985. 187.00 (ISBN 0-684-17477-4). Scribner.
--Exotica Series IV International: Pictorial Cyclopedia of Exotic Plants, 2 vols. LC 81-52361. (Illus.). 1985. 187.00x (ISBN 0-911266-20-8). Roehrs.
--Tropica: Color Cyclopedia of Exotic Plants. 2nd ed. 1981. 115.00 (ISBN 0-684-16771-9, ScribT). Scribner.
--Tropica: Color Encyclopedia of Exotic Plants. 2nd ed. LC 77-82461. (Illus.). 1981. 115.00x (ISBN 0-911266-16-X). Roehrs.
Graf, Calvin R. Exploring Light, Radio & Sound Energy: With Projects. (Illus.). 240p. (Orig.). 1985. 17.95 (ISBN 0-8306-0758-7, 1758); pap. 10.95 (ISBN 0-8306-1758-2). TAB Bks.
Graf, Calvin R., jt. auth. see Graf, Rudolf F.
Graf, David F., jt. ed. see Freedman, David N.
Graf, David K., jt. auth. see Freeman, M. Herbert.
Graf, Diane R., jt. auth. see Schroeder, Betty L.
Graf, Dieter. Master Drawings of the Roman Baroque. (Illus.). 320p. (Orig.). 1984. pap. 10.95 (ISBN 0-901486-56-6, Pub. by Victoria & Albert Mus UK). Faber & Faber.
Graf, Edward R., jt. auth. see Irwin, J. David.
Graf, Ernst, ed. Phytic Acid: Chemistry & Applications. (Illus.). 350p. 1986. 46.50 (ISBN 0-9614915-0-7). Pilatus Pr.
Graf, Fritz. Eleusis und die orphische Dichtung Athens in vorhellenistischer Zeit. (Religionsgeschichtliche Versuche und Vorarbeiten, Vol. 33). xii, 224p. 1974. 33.60x (ISBN 3-11-004498-6). De Gruyter.
Graf, Herbert. The Opera & Its Future in America. LC 78-154712. (Illus.). 305p. 1973. Repr. of 1941 ed. 29.50x (ISBN 0-8046-1744-9, Pub. by Kennikat). Assoc Faculty Pr.
--Opera for the People. LC 68-23811. (Music Reprint Ser.). 1973. Repr. of 1951 ed. lib. bdg. 35.00 (ISBN 0-306-70984-8). Da Capo.
Graf, K., jt. auth. see Ploog, K.
Graf, Lee A., jt. auth. see Certo, Samuel C.
Graf, LeRoy P. & Haskins, Ralph W., eds. Papers of Andrew Johnson, 5 vols. Incl. Vol. 1. 1822-1851. (Illus.). 752p. 1967. 27.50x (ISBN 0-87049-079-6); Vol. 2. 1852-1857. (Illus.). 608p. 1970. 27.50x (ISBN 0-87049-098-2); Vol. 3. 1858-1860. (Illus.). 796p. 1972. 27.50x (ISBN 0-87049-141-5); Vol. 4. 1860-1861. 796p. 1976. 27.50x (ISBN 0-87049-183-0); Vol. 5. 1861-1862. 752p. 1979. text ed. 27.50x (ISBN 0-87049-273-X). LC 67-25733. U of Tenn Pr.
--The Papers of Andrew Johnson, Vol. 6: 1862-1864. LC 67-25733. (Illus.). 892p. 1983. text ed. 27.50 (ISBN 0-87049-346-9). U of Tenn Pr.
Graf, Max. Composer & Critic: Two Hundred Years of Musical Criticism. LC 81-6376. 331p. 1981. Repr. of 1969 ed. lib. bdg. 35.00x (ISBN 0-313-23110-9, GRCR). Greenwood.
--From Beethoven to Shostakovich: The Psychology of the Composing Process. LC 73-94607. Repr. of 1947 ed. lib. bdg. 19.00x (ISBN 0-8371-2452-2, GRBS). Greenwood.
--Modern Music: Composers & Music of Our Time. Maier, Beatrice R., tr. LC 77-27613. 1978. Repr. of 1946 ed. lib. bdg. 25.50x (ISBN 0-313-20185-4, GRMM). Greenwood.
Graf, Nanette. Beowulf Notes. (Orig.). 1966. pap. 3.95 (ISBN 0-8220-0228-0). Cliffs.
Graf, R. & Whalen, G. Home Wiring. 1982. 24.95 (ISBN 0-13-392977-9). P-H.
Graf, Rudolf E. Directory of Toll Free Numbers. (Orig.). 1983. pap. 4.95 (ISBN 0-671-46729-8). PB.
Graf, Rudolf F. Electronic Databook. 3rd ed. (Illus.). 416p. (Orig.). 1983. 24.95 (ISBN 0-8306-0138-4, 1538); pap. 17.50 (ISBN 0-8306-1538-5). TAB Bks.
--The Encyclopedia of Electronic Circuits. (Illus.). 768p. 1985. 50.00 (ISBN 0-8306-0938-5, 1938); pap. 29.95 (ISBN 0-8306-1938-0). TAB Bks.
--Modern Dictionary of Electronics. 6th ed. LC 83-51223. (Illus.). 1152p. 1984. 39.95 (ISBN 0-672-22041-5). Sams.
--Safe & Simple Electrical Experiments. Orig. Title: Safe & Simple Book of Electricity. 1973. pap. 4.50 (ISBN 0-486-22950-5). Dover.
--Safe & Simple Electrical Experiments. (Illus.). 14.00 (ISBN 0-8446-4747-0). Peter Smith.
Graf, Rudolf F. & Graf, Calvin R. Emergency Lighting & Power Projects. LC 84-8865. (Illus.). 304p. (Orig.). 1985. 18.95 (ISBN 0-8306-0788-9); pap. cancelled (1788). TAB Bks.
Graf, Rudolf F. & Whalen, George J. The Build-It Book of Electronic Projects. (Illus.). 272p. (Orig.). 1983. 18.95 (ISBN 0-8306-0498-7); pap. 10.25 (ISBN 0-8306-1498-2, 1498). TAB Bks.
--The TAB Handbook of Hand & Power Tools. (Illus.). 512p. (Orig.). 1984. 26.95 (ISBN 0-8306-0638-6, 1638); pap. 17.95 (ISBN 0-8306-1638-1). TAB Bks.
Graf, T. & Jaenisch, R., eds. Tumorviruses, Neoplastic Transformation & Differentiation. (Current Topics in Microbiology & Immunology: Vol. 101). (Illus.). 198p. 1982. 42.00 (ISBN 0-387-11665-6). Springer-Verlag.
Graf, W. H. Hydraulics of Sediment Transport. LC 79-128788. 513p. 1984. 45.00 (ISBN 0-918334-81-0). WRP.
Graf, W. H. & Mortimer, C. H., eds. Hydrodynamics of Lakes: Proceeding of the Symposium, Switzerland, Oct. 1978. LC 79-17492. (Developments in Water Science Ser.: Vol. 11). 360p. 1979. 72.50 (ISBN 0-444-41827-X). Elsevier.
Graf, Walter H. Water Resources & Environmental Engineering. LC 79-128788. 1984. 45.00 (ISBN 0-918334-56-X). WRP.
Graf, William D. The German Left since Nineteen Forty-Five. 256p. 1976. 35.00 (ISBN 0-902675-54-0); pap. 25.00 (ISBN 0-902675-68-0). Oleander Pr.
Graf, William D., tr. see Lukacs, Georg.
Grafarend, E. W. & Rapp, R. H., eds. Advances in Geodesy. 320p. 1984. 23.00 (ISBN 0-87590-235-9). Am Geophysical.
Grafbury, Norman J. A New Power Bloc in the Making: The Euro-Arab Economic & Political Coalition. (Illus.). 1979. deluxe ed. 89.85x (ISBN 0-930008-51-0). Inst Econ Pol.
Grafchik, Gail & Schultz, Margaret A., eds. Lawyer's Register by Specialties & Fields of Law. 7th ed. 1985. 89.50 (ISBN 0-934607-00-1). Jury Verdict.
Grafe, Blanche. Down in the Valley. 1982. 8.95 (ISBN 0-533-05143-6). Vantage.
Grafe, Louis. Get Rich in Spite of Yourself. 1962. pap. 2.95 (ISBN 0-910140-22-7). C & R Anthony.
--Get Rich in Spite of Yourself. pap. 1.95 (ISBN 0-912576-10-3). R Collier.
Grafenberg, Wirnt von see Wirnt Von Grafenberg.
Graff, Arden. Arden Graff's Interior Design Kit. (Illus., Orig.). 1979. wkbk. 9.95 (ISBN 0-934892-00-8). Interiors.
--The Best Building on the Block. (Orig.). 1981. pap. 4.95 (ISBN 0-934892-01-6). Interiors.
Graff, C. M. The Wreck of the Casperus. LC 81-83467. 236p. (Orig.). 1981. pap. 5.95 (ISBN 0-9607018-0-X). Penelope Pr.
Graff, Gerald. Literature Against Itself: Literary Ideas in Modern Society. LC 78-9879. 1979. 17.00x (ISBN 0-226-30600-3). U of Chicago Pr.

--Literature Against Itself: Literary Ideas in Modern Society. LC 78-9879. x, 250p. 1981. pap. 8.50x (ISBN 0-226-30598-8). U of Chicago Pr.
--Poetic Statement & Critical Dogma. LC 80-14318. 208p. 1980. lib. bdg. 7.00x (ISBN 0-226-30601-1). U of Chicago Pr.
Graff, Gerald & Gibbons, Reginald, eds. Criticism in the University. 250p. 1985. 25.95 (ISBN 0-8101-0670-1); pap. 9.95 (ISBN 0-8101-0671-X). Northwestern U Pr.
Graff, Gerald, ed. see Scott, W. B.
Graff, Gil. Separation of Church & State: Dina de-Malkhuta Dina in Jewish Law, 1750-1848. LC 84-24061. (Judaic Studies Ser.). 224p. 1985. 29.50 (ISBN 0-8173-0264-6). U of Ala Pr.
Graff, Harvey J. Literacy in History: An Interdisciplinary Research Bibliography. 1981. lib. bdg. 61.00 (ISBN 0-8240-9460-3). Garland Pub.
Graff, Harvey J., ed. Literacy & Social Development in the West: A Reader. LC 81-10208. (Cambridge Studies in Oral & Literate Culture: No. 3). (Illus.). 336p. 1982. 44.50 (ISBN 0-521-23954-0); pap. 13.95 (ISBN 0-521-28372-8). Cambridge U Pr.
Graff, Harvey J., et al. Dallas, Texas: A Bibliographical Guide to the Sources of Its Social History to 1930. 64p. 1979. text ed. 6.95x (ISBN 0-292-71522-6, Pub. by U of Tex. at Dallas). U of Tex Pr.
Graff, Harvey L. The Literacy Myth: Literacy & Social Structure in the Nineteenth Century City. LC 79-51702. (Studies in Social Discontinuity). 1979. 29.50 (ISBN 0-12-294520-4). Acad Pr.
Graff, Henry F. America: The Glorious Republic. 1985. text ed. 24.64 (ISBN 0-395-33992-8); tchr's. manual 12.00 (ISBN 0-395-33993-6); Voice of America Reasings 12.00 (ISBN 0-395-35986-4). HM.
--America: The Glorious Republic, from 1877, Vol. 2. Date not set. text ed. price not set (ISBN 0-395-38175-4); price not set tchr's. manual (ISBN 0-395-38176-2); price not set resource bk. (ISBN 0-395-38177-0); price not set student wkbk. (ISBN 0-395-38178-9); price not set tchr's. wkbk. (ISBN 0-395-38179-7). HM.
--America: The Glorious Republic, to 1877, Vol. 1. Date not set. text ed. price not set; price not set tchr's. manual (ISBN 0-395-38154-1); price not set resource bk. (ISBN 0-395-38155-X); price not set student wkbk. (ISBN 0-395-38156-8); price not set tchr's. wkbk. (ISBN 0-395-38157-6). HM.
--The Presidents: A Reference History. LC 83-20225. 700p. 1984. lib. bdg. 65.00 (ISBN 0-684-17607-6, ScribR). Scribner.
Graff, Henry F., jt. auth. see Barzun, Jacques.
Graff, Henry F., jt. auth. see Morris, Richard B.
Graff, John R. Variety Is. 55p. 1974. 5.00 (ISBN 0-87881-015-3). Mojave Bks.
Graff, Karl F. Wave Motion in Elastic Solids. LC 74-3040. (Illus.). 667p. 1975. 25.00 (ISBN 0-8142-0232-2). Ohio St U Pr.
Graff, Kent M. van de see Van De Graaff, Kent M.
Graff, Sr. Laurine. Handbook of Routine Urinalysis. (Illus.). 304p. 1983. pap. text ed. 24.95 (ISBN 0-397-52111-1, Lippincott Medical). Lippincott.
Graff, Lois & Cohen, Neil. Financial Analysis with Symphony. 384p. 1985. 19.95 (ISBN 0-89303-448-7); incl. disk 41.95 (ISBN 0-89303-450-9). Brady Comm.
Graff, Lois & Goldstein, Larry. Applesoft BASIC for the Apple II & IIe. LC 83-15527. 336p. 1983. 16.95 (ISBN 0-89303-320-0). Brady Comm.
Graff, Lois & Goldstein, Larry J. Apple IIc: An Introduction to Applesoft BASIC. (Illus.). 384p. 1984. pap. 16.95 (ISBN 0-89303-291-3). Brady Comm.
Graff, Lois, jt. auth. see Cohen, Neil.
Graff, Michelle & Reese, Loretta. Thirty-Four Craft Stick Projects. LC 82-61453. (Illus.). 48p. 1983. pap. 4.50 (ISBN 0-87239-622-3, 2104). Standard Pub.
Graff, Polly A., jt. auth. see Graff, Stewart.
Graff, Richard A. Elements of Non-Linear Functional Analysis. LC 78-14727. (Memoirs: No. 206). 196p. 1980. pap. 12.00 (ISBN 0-8218-2206-3). Am Math.
Graff, Robert. Communications for National Development: Lessons From Experience (Published for the Salzburg Seminar) LC 82-18763. 196p. 1983. text ed. 30.00 (ISBN 0-89946-161-1). Oelgeschlager.
Graff, Stewart. The Story of World War II. (Illus.). (gr. 3-6). 1978. 9.25 (ISBN 0-525-40355-8, 0898-270). Dutton.
Graff, Stewart & Graff, Polly A. Helen Keller. (Illus.). 80p. (gr. 2-7). 1966. pap. 1.95 (ISBN 0-440-43566-8, YB). Dell.
--Helen Keller: Toward the Light. LC 65-14550. (Discovery Bks.). (gr. 2-5). 1965. PLB 7.47 (ISBN 0-8116-6288-8). Garrard.
--Squanto: Indian Adventurer. LC 65-10158. (Indians Ser.). (Illus.). (gr. 2-5). 1965. PLB 7.47 (ISBN 0-8116-6601-8). Garrard.
Graff, Thomas, et al. Arkansas: A Geography. (Geographies of the United States Ser.). 350p. 1985. 35.00x (ISBN 0-86531-219-2). Westview.
Graff, Werner. Es Kommit der Neue Fotograf. Sobieszk, Robert A. & Bunnell, Peter C., eds. LC 76-24682. (Sources of Modern Photography Ser.). (Illus., Ger.). 1979. Repr. of 1929 ed. lib. bdg. 17.00x (ISBN 0-405-09656-9). Ayer Co Pubs.
Graff, Willem L. Rainer Maria Rilke: Creative Anguish of a Modern Poet. LC 56-8381. pap. 90.80 (ISBN 0-317-26667-5, 2055991). Bks Demand UMI.
Graff, William J. Introduction to Offshore Structures: Design, Fabrication, Installation. LC 81-6259. 372p. 1981. 29.95x (ISBN 0-87201-694-3). Gulf Pub.
Graffagnino, J. Kevin. The Shaping of Vermont: From the Wilderness to the Centennial 1749-1877. LC 82-84526. (Illus.). 180p. 1983. 49.50 (ISBN 0-911853-01-4). Vermont Herit Pr.
Graffagnino, J. Kevin, intro. by see Hard, Walter.
Graffenreid, Diane De & Wheaton, Philip, eds. Panama: Sovereignty for a Land Divided. LC 76-53993. (Illus.). 127p. 1976. pap. 2.50 (ISBN 0-918346-01-0). EPICA.
Graffi, D. Nonlinear Partial Differential Equations in Physical Problems. (Research Notes in Mathematics Ser.: No. 42). 105p. (Orig.). 1980. pap. text ed. 21.95 (ISBN 0-273-08474-7). Pitman Pub MA.
Graffigny, Francoise. Letters Written by a Peruvian Princess, 1748. Shugrue, Michael F., ed. LC 74-16070. (Novel in England, 1700-1775 Ser.). 1975. lib. bdg. 61.00 (ISBN 0-8240-1121-X). Garland Pub.
Graffis, Don W., et al. Approved Practices in Pasture Management. 4th ed. 1985. 19.95 (ISBN 0-8134-2449-6, 2249); text ed. 14.95x (ISBN 0-317-19931-5). Interstate.
Graffis, H. B., ed. see Esquire Magazine.
Graffman, Gary. I Really Should be Practicing: Reflections on the Pleasures & Perils of Playing the Piano in Public. 368p. 1982. pap. 4.95 (ISBN 0-380-59873-6, 59873-6, Discus). Avon.
Grafsky, Albert J., jt. auth. see Johnson, Milo P.
Grafstein, Joel M., jt. auth. see Caron, Denis R.
Grafstein, Paul & Schwarz, Otto M. Pictorial Handbook of Technical Devices. (Illus.). 1971. 14.00 (ISBN 0-8206-0234-5). Chem Pub.
Graft, J. C. De see De Graft, J. C.
Graft, Joe De see De Graft, Joe.
Grafteaux, Serge. Meme Santerre: A French Woman of the People. Tilly, Louise A. & Tilly, Kathryn L., trs. from Fr. 192p. 1985. 15.95 (ISBN 0-8052-3954-5). Schocken.
Grafton, A. H. Autobiography & Political Correspondence. LC 5-875. Repr. of 1898 ed. 34.00 (ISBN 0-527-35150-4). Kraus Repr.
Grafton, Anthony. Joseph Scaliger: A Study in the History of Classical Scholarship: Textual Criticism & Exegesis, Vol. I. (Oxford-Warburg Studies). 1983. 59.95x (ISBN 0-19-814850-X). Oxford U Pr.
Grafton, Anthony, et al, trs. see Wolf, F. A.
Grafton, C. W. Beyond a Reasonable Doubt. LC 75-44977. (Crime Fiction Ser). 1976. Repr. of 1940 ed. lib. bdg. 21.00 (ISBN 0-8240-2371-4). Garland Pub.
--Beyond a Reasonable Doubt. LC 80-7840. 338p. 1980. pap. 1.95i (ISBN 0-06-080519-6, P 519, PL). Har-Row.
--The Rat Began to Gnaw the Rope. LC 82-48243. 256p. 1983. pap. 2.84i (ISBN 0-06-080639-7, P 639, PL). Har-Row.
Grafton, Carl & Permaloff, Anne. Big Mule & Branchheads: James E. Folsom & Political Power in Alabama. LC 84-24006. (Illus.). 360p. 1985. text ed. 27.50 (ISBN 0-8203-0770-X). U of Ga Pr.
Grafton, Carol. Historic Alphabets & Initials. (Dover Pictorial Archive Ser.). (Illus.). 1977. pap. 6.00 (ISBN 0-486-23480-0). Dover.
Grafton, Carol, jt. auth. see Weiss, Rita.
Grafton, Carol B. Banners, Ribbons & Scrolls: An Archive For Artists & Designers, Five Hundred & Three Copyright Free Designs. (Illus.). 96p. (Orig.). 1983. pap. 4.50 (ISBN 0-486-24443-1). Dover.
--Baseball Stars: Sixty Full-Color Pressure Seneitive Stickers. (Sports, Out-of-Door Activities). 8p. (Orig.). (gr. 2up). 1984. pap. 2.95 (ISBN 0-486-24565-9). Dover.
--Bizarre & Ornamental Alphabets. (Illus.). 128p. (Orig.). 1981. pap. 4.50 (ISBN 0-486-24105-X). Dover.
--Children: A Pictorial Archive from Nineteenth-Century Sources. (Illus.). 12.00 (ISBN 0-8446-5765-4). Peter Smith.
--Decorative Alphabets for Needleworkers, Craftsmen & Artists. (Illus.). 128p. (Orig.). 1981. pap. 4.50 (ISBN 0-486-24175-0). Dover.
--Early American Patchwork Patterns. (Orig.). 1980. pap. 3.50 (ISBN 0-486-23882-2). Dover.
--Full-Color Bicentennial Needlepoint Designs. 1975. pap. 2.50 (ISBN 0-486-23233-6). Dover.
--Geometric Needlepoint Designs. LC 74-21225. (Illus.). 48p. 1975. pap. 2.95 (ISBN 0-486-23160-7). Dover.
--Geometric Patchwork Patterns: Full-Size Cut-Outs & Instructions for 12 Quilts. LC 74-31894. (Illus.). 64p. (Orig.). 1975. pap. 3.25 (ISBN 0-486-23183-6). Dover.
--Old English Tile Designs for Artists & Craftspeople. (Pictorial Archive Ser.). 128p. 1985. pap. 4.95 (ISBN 0-486-24777-5). Dover.
--Optical Designs in Motion with Moire Overlays. (Illus.). 32p. (Orig.). 1976. pap. 5.95 (ISBN 0-486-23284-0). Dover.
--Ready-to-Use Accents & Attention-Getters. 64p. 1984. pap. 2.95 (ISBN 0-486-24692-2). Dover.
--Ready-to-Use Borders on Layout Grids. (Clip Art Ser.). 48p. 1985. pap. 3.75 (ISBN 0-486-24812-7). Dover.
--Ready-to-Use Victorian Stickers: 96 Pressure-Sensitive Seals. (Stationery Ser.). 8p. (gr. 4up). 1983. pap. 2.95 (ISBN 0-486-24551-9). Dover.
--Shapes & Colors: Cutouts for Creative Geometric Designs. (Illus.). 32p. (Orig.). 1976. pap. 3.00 (ISBN 0-486-23290-5). Dover.
--Traditional Patchwork Patterns. (Illus.). 14.75 (ISBN 0-8446-5038-2). Peter Smith.
--Traditional Patchwork Patterns: Full-Size Cut-Outs & Instructions for 12 Quilts. (Illus.). 64p. (Orig.). 1974. pap. 3.50 (ISBN 0-486-23015-5). Dover.
--Treasury of Art Nouveau Design & Ornament. (Pictorial Archive Ser.). (Illus.). 144p. (Orig.). 1980. pap. 5.00 (ISBN 0-486-24001-0). Dover.
--Treasury of Victorian Printers' Frames, Ornaments, & Initials. 128p. 1984. pap. 5.00 (ISBN 0-486-24703-1). Dover.
--Victorian Color Vignettes & Illustrations for Artists & Craftsmen: 344 Antique Chromolithographs. (Illus.). 48p. (Orig.). 1983. pap. 3.95 (ISBN 0-486-24477-6). Dover.
--Victorian Cut & Use Stencils: 55 Full-Size Stencils Printed on Durable Stencil Paper. (Illus., Orig.). 1976. pap. 3.95 (ISBN 0-486-23385-5). Dover.
--Victorian Floral Illustrations: Three Hundred Forty-Four Wood Engravings of Exotic Flowers & Plants. (Pictorial Archive Ser.). 112p. 1985. pap. 4.95 (ISBN 0-486-24822-4). Dover.
--Victorian Pictorial Borders: One Hundred Twenty-Four Full-Page Designs. 128p. 1984. pap. 5.95 (ISBN 0-486-24693-0). Dover.
Grafton, Carol B., ed. Alphabet Cut & Use Stencils. (Cut & Use Stencils Ser.). 64p. 1984. pap. 4.50 (ISBN 0-486-24623-X). Dover.
--Art Nouveau Frames & Borders: 250 Copyright-Free Illustrations for Artists & Craftsmen. (Pictorial Archive Ser.). (Illus.). 128p. 1983. pap. 4.95 (ISBN 0-486-24513-6). Dover.
--Authentic Victorian Stencil Designs. (Illus.). 64p. (Orig.). 1982. pap. 3.50 (ISBN 0-486-24337-0). Dover.
--Borders & Frames of the Art Nouveau Period. (Pictorial Archive Ser.). 128p. 1984. pap. 4.95 (ISBN 0-486-24610-8). Dover.
--Children: A Pictorial Archive from Nineteenth Century Sources; 242 Copyright-Free Illustrations for Artists & Designers. (Pictorial Archive Ser.). (Illus.). 1978. pap. 4.50 (ISBN 0-486-23694-3). Dover.
--Fanciful Victorian Initials. (Pictorial Archive Ser.). 128p. 1984. pap. 4.95 (ISBN 0-486-24604-3). Dover.
--Historic Alphabets & Initials: Woodcut & Ornamental. 16.25 (ISBN 0-8446-5580-5). Peter Smith.
--Humorous Victorian Spot Illustrations. (Illus.). 128p. 1985. pap. 5.95 (ISBN 0-486-24896-8). Dover.
--More Silhouettes: Eight Hundred Sixty-Eight Copyright-Free Copy Illustrations for Artists & Craftsmen. (Illus.). 112p. 1982. pap. 4.50 (ISBN 0-486-24256-0). Dover.
--Pictorial Archive of Decorative & Illustrative Mortised Cuts: 551 Eye-Catching Designs for Advertisisng & Other Uses. (Pictorial Archive Ser.). 112p. (Orig.). 1984. pap. 4.95 (ISBN 0-486-24540-3). Dover.
--Pictorial Archive of Decorative Frames & Labels: 550 Copyright Free Designs. (Illus.). 128p. 1982. pap. 4.50 (ISBN 0-486-24277-3). Dover.
--Pictorial Archive of Printer's Ornaments from the Renaissance to the 20th Century. (Pictorial Archive Ser.). (Illus., Orig.). 1980. pap. 5.00 (ISBN 0-486-23944-6). Dover.
--Ready-to-Use Small Frames & Borders (Clip Art) (Pictorial Archive Ser.). (Illus.). 64p. (Orig.). 1982. pap. 2.95 (ISBN 0-486-24375-3). Dover.
--Silhouettes: A Pictorial Archive of Varied Illustrations. (Illus.). 1979. pap. 4.95 (ISBN 0-486-23781-8). Dover.
--Three Hundred Art Nouveau Designs & Motifs in Full Color. (Illus.). 48p. pap. 6.00 (ISBN 0-486-24354-0). Dover.
--Treasury of Japanese Designs & Motifs for Artists & Craftsmen. (Illus.). 96p. (Orig.). 1982. pap. 3.95 (ISBN 0-486-24435-0). Dover.
--Victorian Spot Illustrations, Alphabets & Ornaments from Porret's Type Catalog. (Illus.). 96p. (gr. 5 up). 1982. pap. 4.50 (ISBN 0-486-24271-4). Dover.
Grafton, Carol B., ed. see Gesner, Konrad.
Grafton, Carol Belanger. Treasury of Art Nouveau Design & Ornament. 1983. 17.75 (ISBN 0-8446-5949-5). Peter Smith.
Grafton, Carol Belanger, ed. More Silhouettes. 1983. 12.75 (ISBN 0-8446-5935-5). Peter Smith.
--Pictorial Archive of Decorative Frames & Labels. 1983. 13.25 (ISBN 0-8446-5936-3). Peter Smith.
Grafton, Fiona. Cooking Afloat. 224p. 1982. 15.00x (ISBN 0-333-31928-1, Pub. by Nautical England). State Mutual Bk.
Grafton, John. The American Revolution: A Picture Sourcebook. (Pictorial Archive Ser.). (Illus.). 160p. 1975. pap. 5.50 (ISBN 0-486-23226-3). Dover.
--New York in the Nineteenth Century: Engravings from Harper's Weekly & Other Contemporary Sources. LC 77-73339. (Illus.). 1977. pap. 8.95 (ISBN 0-486-23516-5). Dover.
--Sports Picture Quiz Book. LC 76-20845. (Illus.). 144p. 1977. pap. 4.95 (ISBN 0-486-23404-5). Dover.
--Sports Picture Quiz Book. LC 76-20845. (Illus.). 1977. lib. bdg. 11.50x (ISBN 0-88307-587-3). Gannon.
Grafton, John, jt. auth. see Sugar, Bert.
Grafton, John, ed. New York in the Nineteenth Century: 321 Engravings from Harper's Weekly & Other Contemporary Sources. 16.50 (ISBN 0-8446-5581-3). Peter Smith.
Grafton, Nora P. My Own True Psychic Adventures. LC 75-28590. 270p. 1977. cl.-vinyl 5.95 (ISBN 0-916498-01-8). Tolff.
Grafton, Sue. A Is for Alibi: A Kinsey Millhone Mystery. LC 81-7128. 256p. 1982. 12.95 (ISBN 0-03-059048-5). HR&W.
--A Is for Alibi: A Kinsey Millhone Mystery. 192p. 1984. pap. 2.75 (ISBN 0-451-12862-1, Sig). NAL.
--B Is for Burglar. LC 84-158. 1985. 14.95 (ISBN 0-03-001889-7). HR&W.
Graf Von Beust, Friedrich F. Memories of Friedrich Ferdinand Count Von Beust, 2 vols. 1981. Repr. Set. lib. bdg. 59.00x (ISBN 0-686-71932-8). Scholarly.
Gragert, Steven K., ed. Cumulative Index: The Writings of Will Rogers. 200p. 1983. 6.95 (ISBN 0-914956-27-2). Okla State Univ Pr.
--He Chews to Run: Will Rogers Life Magazine Articles, 1928. LC 82-80415. (The Writings of Will Rogers Ser.: Ser. V, Vol. 1). (Illus.). 133p. 1982. 9.95 (ISBN 0-914956-20-5). Okla State Univ Pr.
Gragert, Steven K., ed. see Rogers, Will.
Gragg, Alan. Charles Hartshorhe. new ed. Patterson, Bob E., ed. LC 70-188063. (Makers of Modern Theological Minds Ser.). 128p. 1973. 5.95 (ISBN 0-87680-270-6, 80270). Word Bks.
--George Burman Foster: Religious Humanist. LC 77-92499. (Special Studies Ser.: No. 3). 1978. pap. 3.50 (ISBN 0-932180-02-7). NABPR.
Gragg, Florence A., ed. The Latin Writings of the Italian Humanists. (College Classical Ser.). xxxvi, 434p. (gr. 11-12). 1981. pap. text ed. 17.50x (ISBN 0-89241-370-0); lib. bdg. 30.00x (ISBN 0-89241-356-5). Caratzas.
Gragg, Gerald R., ed. see Wesley, John.
Gragg, Larry D. Migration in Early America: The Virginia Quaker Experience. Berkhofer, Robert, ed. LC 80-15188. (Studies in American History & Culture: No. 13). 144p. 1980. 39.95 (ISBN 0-8357-1095-5). UMI Res Pr.
Gragg, Rod. Bobby Bagley POW. 1978. pap. 3.95 (ISBN 0-89728-022-9, 678434). Omega Pubns OR.
--The Civil War Quiz & Fact Book. LC 84-48162. (Illus.). 224p. 1985. pap. 8.61i (ISBN 0-06-091226-X, CN 1226, CN). Har-Row.
--The Civil War Quiz & Fact Book. LC 84-48162. (Illus.). 224p. 1985. 15.34 (ISBN 0-06-015395-4, HarpT). Har-Row.
--Pirates, Planters & Patriots: Historical Tales from the South Carolina Grand Strand. (Illus.). 160p. (Orig.). 1984. pap. 6.95 (ISBN 0-916253-00-7). Bk Serv Assocs.
Graggerud, Egil, ed. Symoblae Osloenses Fifty-Nine. 144p. (Orig.). 1984. pap. 25.00x (ISBN 82-00-06883-8). Universitet.
Graglia, Lino A. Disaster by Decree: The Supreme Court Decisions on Race & the Schools. LC 75-36997. 352p. 1976. 24.50x (ISBN 0-8014-0980-2). Cornell U Pr.
Gragoe, Elizabeth. The Untidy Gardener. 192p. 1982. 18.50 (ISBN 0-241-10759-8, Pub. by Hamish Hamilton England). David & Charles.
Graham. Colony & Mother City in Ancient Greece. 1985. pap. 12.50 (ISBN 0-89005-520-3). Ares.
--Jazz Chants for Children Kit. 1985. 75.00 (ISBN 0-19-434167-4). Oxford U Pr.
--Please Sir I've Broken My Arm. 11.50x (ISBN 0-392-06921-0, SpS). Sportshelf.
Graham & Gramm. The Discovery of the Sleepers & the Striking for the Speculative Leaders in Wall Street. (Illus.). 187p. 1984. 97.45x (ISBN 0-86654-128-4). Inst Econ Finan.
Graham, jt. auth. see Cleary.
Graham, et al. A Compendium of Alfalfa Disease. LC 79-88555. (Illus.). 65p. 1979. saddle stitched 17.00 (ISBN 0-89054-026-8). Am Phytopathol Soc.
Graham, et al, eds. Glasgow Story of a Missouri Rivertown. (Illus.). 237p. 1984. 8.00 (ISBN 0-930552-03-2). Tech Ed Serv.
Graham, A., jt. auth. see Fretter, V.
Graham, A., jt. auth. see Martelli, L.
Graham, A. C. Reason & Spontaneity. LC 84-12358. 320p. 1985. 26.50x (ISBN 0-389-20510-9, BNB 08068). B&N Imports.
Graham, A. C., tr. Chuang Tzu: The Inner Chapters. 1981. text ed. 28.50x (ISBN 0-04-299010-6). Allen Unwin.
--Poems of the Late T'ang. (Classics Ser.). 1977. pap. 4.95 (ISBN 0-14-044157-3). Penguin.
Graham, A. Kenneth. Electroplating Engineering Handbook. 3rd ed. 880p. 1971. 46.50 (ISBN 0-318-12534-X); members 39.50 (ISBN 0-318-12535-8). Am Electroplate.
Graham, A. L., et al. Catalogue of Meteorites. 4th ed. 1985. 50.00x (ISBN 0-8165-0912-3). U of Ariz Pr.
--Catalogue of Meteorites. 4th ed. 400p. 1985. text ed. 84.50x (ISBN 0-565-00941-9, Pub. by Brit Mus Nat Hist England). Sabbot-Natural Hist Bks.

Graham, A. Richard. An Introduction to Engineering Measurements. (Illus.). 224p. 1975. ref. ed 29.95 (ISBN 0-13-482406-7). P-H.

Graham, A. Stephens, jt. auth. see Rankin, Fred W.

Graham, Ada & Graham, Frank. Alligators. LC 79-50671. (Audubon Readers Ser.: No. 5). (Illus.). (gr. 4-6). 1979. 7.95 (ISBN 0-440-00390-3); PLB 9.95 (ISBN 0-385-28042-4). Delacorte.

--Bears in the Wild. LC 80-68732. (Audubon Reader: No. 6). (Illus.). 128p. (gr. 4-7). 1981. 8.95 (ISBN 0-440-00532-9); PLB 8.44 (ISBN 0-440-00538-8). Delacorte.

--Bears in the Wild. (Illus.). 176p. (gr. 4-8). 1983. pap. 2.25 (ISBN 0-440-40897-0, YB). Dell.

--The Big Stretch: The Complete Book of the Amazing Rubber Band. LC 83-25615. (Books for Young Readers Ser.). (Illus.). 96p. (gr. 3-7). 1985. 9.95 (ISBN 0-394-85758-5); PLB 10.99 (ISBN 0-394-95758-X). Knopf.

--Busy Bugs. LC 82-22085. (Illus.). 64p. (gr. 5 up). 1983. 9.95 (ISBN 0-396-08126-6). Dodd.

--The Changing Desert. (Illus.). 96p. (gr. 5 up). 1981. 11.95 (ISBN 0-684-17146-5, ScribJ). Scribner.

--Three Million Mice: A Story of Modern Medical Research. (Illus.). 96p. (gr. 4-7). 1981. 9.95 (ISBN 0-684-17150-3, ScribJ). Scribner.

--We Watch Squirrels. (Illus.). 48p. (gr. 2-5). 1985. PLB 9.95 (ISBN 0-396-08740-X). Dodd.

--Whale Watch. LC 77-20531. (Audubon Readers: No. 1). (Illus.). (gr. 5 up). 1978. 7.95 (ISBN 0-440-09505-0); PLB 7.89 (ISBN 0-440-09506-9). Delacorte.

--Whale Watch: An Audubon Reader. (Illus.). 128p. (gr. 4-8). 1983. pap. 2.25 (ISBN 0-440-49250-5, YB). Dell.

Graham, Alan, jt. auth. see Taylor, James.

Graham, Alan K., jt. auth. see Alfeld, Louis.

Graham, Alastair, jt. auth. see Fretter, Vera.

Graham, Alexander. Kronecker Products & Matrix Calculus with Applications. LC 81-7132. (Mathematics & Its Applications Ser.). 160p. 1981. 48.95x (ISBN 0-470-27300-3). Halsted Pr.

--Matrix Theory & Applications for Engineers & Mathematicians. LC 79-40988. (Mathematics & Its Applications Ser.). 295p. 1980. pap. 39.95x (ISBN 0-470-27072-1). Halsted Pr.

--Roman Africa. facs. ed. LC 70-157369. (Black Heritage Library Collection Ser). 1902. 26.75 (ISBN 0-8369-8807-8). Ayer Co Pubs.

Graham, Alice H. Desert Ballet. LC 70-129878. (Illus.). 1970. 4.00 (ISBN 0-912472-01-4). Miller Bks.

Graham, Alistair. The Gardeners of Eden. (Illus.). 246p. 1973. 14.50x (ISBN 0-87471-633-0). Rowman.

Graham, Allison. Lindsay Anderson. (Filmmakers Ser.). 1981. lib. bdg. 16.95 (ISBN 0-8057-9283-X, Twayne). G K Hall.

Graham, Alma, jt. auth. see Martelli, Len.

Graham & Trotman Conference, 1980. Corporate Investment & Acquistions by Foreign Companies in the USA: Proceedings. 194p. 1980. 110.00x (ISBN 0-86010-208-4, Pub. by Graham & Trotman England). State Mutual Bk.

Graham & Trotman Ltd. Assessment of Manganese Nodules Resources. 90p. 1982. 80.00x (ISBN 0-86010-347-1, Pub. by Graham & Trotman England). State Mutual Bk.

--Business Yearbook of Brazil, Mexico & Venezuela 1985. 300p. 1980. 95.00x (ISBN 0-86010-212-2, Pub. by Graham & Trotman England). State Mutual Bk.

Graham & Trotman Ltd., jt. auth. see Oxford University Press.

Graham & Trotman Ltd., ed. Boiler Operators Handbook. 155p. 1981. 13.00x (ISBN 0-86010-244-0, Pub. by Graham & Trotman England). State Mutual Bk.

--Coke Oven Techniques. 350p. 1982. 50.00x (ISBN 0-86010-366-8, Pub. by Graham & Trotman England). State Mutual Bk.

--Fluidised Combustion: Systems & Applications. 512p. 1981. 85.00x (ISBN 0-686-80925-4, Pub. by Graham & Trotman England). State Mutual Bk.

--The Gulf States: Business Opportunities in the 1980's. 1981. 350.00x (ISBN 0-686-78880-X, Pub. by Graham & Trotman England). State Mutual Bk.

--International Energy Options: An Agenda for the 1980's. 1980. 59.00x (ISBN 0-86010-303-X, Pub. by Graham & Trotman England). State Mutual Bk.

--Nigeria: Its Petroleum Geology, Resources & Potential, Vol. 1. 176p. 1982. 110.00x (ISBN 0-86010-264-5, Pub. by Graham & Trotman England). State Mutual Bk.

--North Africa: Business Opportunities in the 1980's. 1981. 350.00x (ISBN 0-686-78881-8, Pub. by Graham & Trotman England). State Mutual Bk.

--The Regulation of Banks in the Member States of EEC. 267p. 1981. 97.00x (ISBN 0-686-81497-5, Pub. by Graham & Trotman England). State Mutual Bk.

--Seabed Minerals Series: Analysis of Exploration, Vol. 2. 120p. 1982. 50.00x (Pub. by Graham & Trotman England). State Mutual Bk.

--Seabed Minerals Series: Vol. 3, Analysis of Processing Technology for Manganese Nodules. 90p. 1982. 50.00x (ISBN 0-86010-349-8, Pub. by Graham & Trotman England). State Mutual Bk.

Graham & Trotman Ltd. & Barrow, S. M., eds. Major Companies of the Far East, 1983, Vols. 1 & 2. 700p. 1983. Set. 149.00 (ISBN 0-317-09552-8). Nichols Pub.

--Major Companies of the Far East, 1983, Vol. 2. (Major Companies Ser.). 350p. 1983. 80.00 (ISBN 0-86010-326-9); 149.00 set. Nichols Pub.

Graham & Trotman Ltd., jt. ed. see Whiteside, R. M.

Graham & Trotman Ltd., et al. Arab Business Yearbook: 1985. 500p. 1982. 290.00x (ISBN 0-86010-204-1, Pub. by Graham & Trotman England). State Mutual Bk.

Graham, Angela, jt. auth. see Osmond, John.

Graham, Anila, ed. Eastern Cultures. LC 74-147794. (Illus.). 135p. 1971. 12.75 (ISBN 0-582-34101-9, UM19, UNESCO). Unipub.

Graham, Ann H. Subject Guide to Statistics in the Presidential Reports of the Brazilian Provinces, 1830-1889. (Institute of Latin American Studies Guides & Bibliographies Ser.: No. 9). 484p. 1977. pap. 8.95x (ISBN 0-292-77536-9). U of Tex Pr.

Graham, Ann H. & Woods, Richard D., eds. Latin America in English-Language Reference Books: A Selected Annotated Bibliography. LC 80-28880. 56p. 1981. pap. text ed. 7.75 (ISBN 0-87111-267-1). SLA.

Graham, Anne D. Bird in My Bed. LC 72-155090. (Illus.). 1971. 6.95 (ISBN 0-8008-0745-6). Taplinger.

Graham, B. D., jt. auth. see Reeves, P. D.

Graham, Benjamin. The Intelligent Investor: A Book of Practical Counsel. 4th rev. ed. LC 78-156524. (Illus.). 1973. 18.22 (ISBN 0-06-011591-2, HarpT). Har-Row.

Graham, Benjamin & McGolrick, Charles. The Interpretation of Financial Statements. 3rd rev. ed. LC 74-15829. 128p. 1975. 13.41i (ISBN 0-06-011566-1, HarpT). Har-Row.

Graham, Benjamin, et al. Security Analysis. 4th ed. LC 62-17368. 1962. text ed. 41.95 (ISBN 0-07-023957-6). McGraw.

Graham, Betsy P. Magazine Article Writing: Substance & Style. LC 79-23249. 224p. (Orig.). 1980. pap. text ed. 20.95 (ISBN 0-03-047156-7, HoltC). HR&W.

Graham, Beverly T. Suzuki Pianist's List of Supplementary Materials: An Annotated Bibliography. LC 81-65666. 1981. pap. 4.95 (ISBN 0-918194-11-3). Accura.

Graham, Billie J. & Thomas, William N. An Introduction to Physics for Radiologic Technologist. LC 74-12911. pap. 64.80 (ISBN 0-317-08967-6, 2015279). Bks Demand UMI.

Graham, Billy. Los Angeles: Agentes Secretos de Dios. Rojas, Juan, tr. from Eng. LC 76-20259. 168p. (Span.). 1976. pap. 4.95 (ISBN 0-89922-069-X). Edit Caribe.

--Angels. 1984. pap. 3.50 (ISBN 0-671-54147-1). PB.

--Approaching Hoofbeats. 256p. 1985. pap. 3.95 (ISBN 0-8499-4170-9, 4170-9). Word Bks.

--Approaching Hoofbeats: The Four Horsemen of the Apocalypse. 288p. 1985. pap. 3.95 (ISBN 0-380-69921-4). Avon.

--A Biblical Standard for Evangelists. 144p. 1984. pap. 5.95 (ISBN 0-89066-057-3). World Wide Pubs.

--Billy Graham Christian Worker's Handbook. 240p. 1982. price not set (ISBN 0-89066-042-5); pap. 7.95. World Wide Pub.

--El Espiritu Santo. Sipowicz, A. Edwin, tr. from Eng. Orig. Title: The Holy Spirit. 252p. (Span.). 1981. pap. 6.25 (ISBN 0-311-09096-6). Casa Bautista.

--Hasta el Armagedon. Sipowicz, Edwin, tr. from Eng. Orig. Title: Till Armageddon. 272p. 1983. pap. 7.95 (ISBN 0-311-09097-4). Casa Bautista.

--How to Be Born Again. LC 77-76057. 1977. 2.95 (ISBN 0-8499-4119-9). Word Bks.

--El Mundo en Llamas. Orig. Title: World Aflame. 272p. (Span.). 1982. pap. 5.25 (ISBN 0-311-46091-7). Casa Bautista.

--Nacer a Una Nueva Vida. Ward, Rhode, tr. from Eng. LC 78-52622. 191p. (Span.). 1978. pap. 4.50 (ISBN 0-89922-110-6). Edit Caribe.

--Paz Con Dios. Muntz, Carrie, tr. from Eng. Orig. Title: Peace with God. 272p. 1981. pap. 3.75 (ISBN 0-311-43037-6). Casa Bautista.

--Peace with God. LC 53-5967. 1953. 7.95 (ISBN 0-385-04349-X). Doubleday.

--Peace with God. rev. ed. 288p. 1985. 10.95 (ISBN 0-8499-0464-1, 0464-1); pap. text ed. 7.95 (ISBN 0-8499-2991-1, 2991-1). Word Bks.

--The Secret of Happiness. rev. & enl. ed. 160p. 1985. 9.95 (ISBN 0-8499-0508-7, 0508-7); pap. 7.95 (ISBN 0-8499-3034-0, 3034-0). Word Bks.

--El Secreto de la Felicidad. Orig. Title: The Secret of Happiness. 192p. (Span.). 1981. pap. 2.75 (ISBN 0-311-04352-6). Casa Bautista.

--Till Armageddon. 224p. 1984. pap. 6.95 (ISBN 0-8499-2998-9, 2998-9). Word Bks.

Graham, Billy & Ten Boom, Corrie. To God Be the Glory. 62p. 1985. pap. text ed. 4.95 large print ed. (ISBN 0-8027-2473-6). Walker & Co.

Graham, Mrs. Billy. Our Christmas Story. LC 73-84958. (Illus.). 96p. 1973. Repr. of 1959 ed. 5.95 (ISBN 0-89066-004-2); pap. 2.95 (ISBN 0-89066-005-0). World Wide Pubs.

Graham, Blanche, jt. auth. see Noble, Mary.

Graham, Bob. Libby, Oscar & Me. LC 84-45430. (Illus.). 32p. (ps-3). 1985. 10.95 (ISBN 0-911745-89-0, Bedrick Blackie). P Bedrick Bks.

--Pearl's Place. LC 85-47503. 32p. (gr. 1-5). 1985. 10.95 (ISBN 0-87226-019-4). P Bedrick Bks.

--Pete & Roland. (Illus.). 28p. (gr. 1). 1983. lib. bdg. 9.95 (ISBN 0-00-184344-3, Pub. by W Collins Australia). Intl Spec Bk.

--Pete & Roland. LC 83-23402. (Illus.). 32p. (ps-2). 1984. 5.95 (ISBN 0-670-54912-6, Viking Kestrel). Viking.

--Workdays: Finding Florida on the Job. Mahoney, Lawrence, ed. LC 78-4177. (Illus.). 1978. pap. 5.95 (ISBN 0-916224-34-1). Banyan Bks.

Graham, Bob, jt. auth. see Smith, Peter.

Graham Brash Editorial Staff, ed. Short Stories of the Far East. (Illus.). 184p. 1984. pap. 8.00 (ISBN 9971-947-62-5, Pub. by Graham Brash Singapore). Three Continents.

Graham, Brenda K. Juliana of Clover Hill. 192p. 1984. pap. 1.95 (ISBN 0-310-46422-6, Serenade-Saga). Zondervan.

--Stone Gables. LC 78-52615. (gr. 9-12). 1978. 6.95 (ISBN 0-8054-7222-3). Broadman.

Graham, Bruce. Music & the Synthesiser. 144p. 1985. pap. 8.50 (ISBN 0-85242-695-X, Pub. by Argus). Aztex.

Graham, C. C. & McGehee, O. C. Essays in Commutative Harmonic Analysis. LC 79-13096. (Grundlehren der Mathematischen Wissenschaften: Vol. 238). (Illus.). 1979. 58.00 (ISBN 0-387-90426-3). Springer-Verlag.

Graham, C. D., Jr., ed. see AIP Conference.

Graham, C. D., Jr., ed. see AIP Conference, Chicago, 1971.

Graham, C. D., Jr., ed. see AIP Conference, Denver, 1972.

Graham, C. D., Jr., et al, eds. see Conference on Magnetism & Magnetic Materials 20th, Dec 3-6, 1974 San Francisco.

Graham, C. F. & Wareing, P. F. Developmental Control in Animals & Plants. 2nd ed. (Illus.). 424p. 1984. pap. text ed. 32.50x (ISBN 0-632-00758-3, Pub. by Blackwell Sci UK). Blackwell Pubns.

--Developmental Control in Plants & Animals. 2nd ed. (Illus.). 400p. 1983. pap. text ed. 24.00 (ISBN 0-632-00758-3, B1935-1). Mosby.

Graham, Carol, ed. see Common Ground Community Restaurant, Inc.

Graham, Carolyn. The Carolyn Graham Turn-of-the-Century Songbook. (Illus.). 95p. (gr. 7-12). 1982. pap. text ed. 5.75 (ISBN 0-88345-488-2, 21129). Regents Pub.

--The Electric Elephant & Other Stories. (Illus., Orig.). 1982. pap. text ed. 5.50x (ISBN 0-19-503229-2). Oxford U Pr.

--Jazz Chants. 1978. pap. text ed. 7.25x (ISBN 0-19-502407-9); cassette 10.95x (ISBN 0-19-502410-9); text & cassette 13.95x (ISBN 0-19-502429-X). Oxford U Pr.

--Jazz Chants for Children. (Illus.). 1979. pap. text ed. 7.50x (ISBN 0-19-502496-6); tchrs ed. 10.95x (ISBN 0-19-502497-4); cassette 12.00x (ISBN 0-19-502575-X); tchrs' ed & cassette 16.00x (ISBN 0-19-502576-8). Oxford U Pr.

Graham, Carroll & Graham, Garrett. Queer People: A Novel. LC 76-3478. (Lost American Fiction Ser.). 285p. 1976. Repr. of 1930 ed. 7.95 (ISBN 0-8093-0784-7). S Ill U Pr.

Graham, Charles E. & Bowen, James A. Clinical Management of Infant Great Apes. LC 84-25019. 228p. 1985. 48.00 (ISBN 0-8451-3404-3). A R Liss.

Graham, Charles E., ed. Reproductive Biology of the Great Apes: Comparative & Biomedical Perspectives. LC 80-89417. 1981. 60.00 (ISBN 0-12-295020-8). Acad Pr.

Graham, Charles K. History of Education in Ghana from the Earliest Times to the Declaration of Independence. 232p. 1971. 27.50x (ISBN 0-7146-2457-8, F Cass Co). Biblio Dist.

Graham, Charles L., jt. ed. see Wilson, Charles L.

Graham, Clayton R. A Man of Taste. LC 84-9671. 249p. (Orig.). 1984. pap. 6.95 (ISBN 0-915175-01-0). Knights Pr.

--Walkin' Matilda. LC 84-19413. 249p. (Orig.). 1985. pap. 6.95 (ISBN 0-915175-08-8). Knights Pr.

Graham, Colin, jt. auth. see Collins, Peter.

Graham, Cooper C., et al. D. W. Griffith & the Biograph Company. LC 85-2170. (Filmmakers Ser.: No. 10). 343p. 1985. 27.50 (ISBN 0-8108-1806-X). Scarecrow.

Graham, Courtenay P. IME. 45p. 1969. 4.00 (ISBN 0-913219-07-X); pap. 2.00 (ISBN 0-913219-08-8). Pym-Rand Pr.

Graham, D. & Eddie, T. X-Ray Techniques in Art Galleries & Museums. 136p. 1985. 22.00 (ISBN 0-9903003-3-1, Pub. by A Hilger England). Heyden.

Graham, Daniel. High Frontier. 320p. (Orig.). 1984. pap. 3.50 (ISBN 0-8125-9420-7). Tor Bks.

Graham, Daniel & Thomson, John. Grenz Rays: An Illustrated Guide to the Theory & Practical Applications of Soft X-Rays. LC 79-42745. (Illus.). 164p. 1980. 26.00 (ISBN 0-08-025525-6). Pergamon.

Graham, Daniel A. Microeconomics: The Analysis of Choice. 1980. text ed. 22.95 (ISBN 0-669-02273-X). Heath.

Graham, Daniel O. High Frontier: A Strategy for National Survival. (Tor Bks.). 314p. (Orig.). 1983. pap. 7.95 (ISBN 0-523-48078-4). Pinnacle Bks.

--A New Strategy for the West: NATO After Detente. LC 77-89607. 1977. 3.00 (ISBN 0-89195-020-6). Heritage Found.

--The Non-Nuclear Defense of Cities: The High Frontier Space-Based Defense Against ICBM Attack. 1983. Repr. of 1982 ed. text ed. 25.00 (ISBN 0-89011-586-9). Abt Bks.

--The Non-Nuclear Defense of Cities: The High Frontier Space-Based Defense Against ICBM Attack. (Illus.). 160p. 1984. Repr. of 1983 ed. lib. bdg. 25.00 (ISBN 0-8191-4101-1). U Pr of Amer.

Graham, Daniel O. & Fossedal, Gregory A. A Defense that Defends: Blocking Nuclear Attack. (Illus.). 172p. 1984. 17.50 (ISBN 0-8159-5317-8). Devin.

Graham, Darol L. & Yestingsmeier, Jan L. Clinical Manual for Respiratory Therapy Education. 2nd ed. LC 82-74058. (Illus.). 366p. 1985. pap. text ed. 35.00 (ISBN 0-933195-02-8). Cal College Pr.

Graham, David. Common Sense & the Muses. 1925. lib. bdg. 20.00 (ISBN 0-8414-4665-2). Folcroft.

--Down to a Sunless Sea. 352p. 1982. pap. 3.50 (ISBN 0-449-24513-6, Crest). Fawcett.

Graham, David & Dennis, Larry. The Way to Winning Golf. LC 84-63139. (Illus.). 168p. 1985. 18.95 (ISBN 0-914178-72-5). Golf Digest.

Graham, David C. The Tribal Songs & Tales of the Ch'uan-Miao. (Asian Folklore & Social Life Monographs: Vol. 102). 1981. 22.00 (ISBN 0-89986-333-7). Oriental Bk Store.

Graham, David R. Role of Business in the Economic Redevelopment of the Rural Community. (Research Monograph: No. 36). 1973. pap. 4.00 (ISBN 0-87755-175-8). Bureau Busn UT.

Graham, Desmond. The Truth of War: Owen, Rosenburg & Blunder. (Illus.). 220p. 20.00 (ISBN 0-85635-496-1). Carcanet.

Graham, Desmond, intro. by see Douglas, Keith.

Graham, Dominick, jt. auth. see Bidwell, Shelford.

Graham, Don. Cowboys & Cadillacs: How Hollywood Looks at Texas. Rodriquez, Barbara, ed. (Illus.). 192p. 1983. pap. 10.95 (ISBN 0-932012-37-X). Texas Month Pr.

--Critical Essays on Frank Norris. 1980. lib. bdg. 26.00 (ISBN 0-8161-8307-4, Twayne). G K Hall.

--The Fiction of Frank Norris: The Aesthetic Context. LC 77-18298. (Illus.). 192p. 1978. text ed. 15.00x (ISBN 0-8262-0252-7). U of Mo Pr.

--Texas: A Literary Portrait. LC 85-71202. (Illus.). 228p. 1985. 45.00x (ISBN 0-931722-40-3); pap. 16.95 (ISBN 0-931722-41-1). Corona Pub.

Graham, Don, jt. ed. see Pilkington, William T.

Graham, Donald K., et al. Manual for Notaries Public of Virginia. LC 82-72541. (Illus.). viii, 83p. 1982. 5.95. Am Soc Notaries.

Graham, Dougal. Collected Writings of Dougal Graham, Skellat Bellman of Glasgow, 2 vols. LC 69-16478. 1968. Repr. of 1883 ed. Set. 40.00x (ISBN 0-8103-3535-2). Gale.

Graham, Douglas, jt. auth. see Herzlich, Claudine.

Graham, Douglas H., jt. auth. see Merrick, Thomas W.

Graham, Douglas H., jt. auth. see Schulz, Donald E.

Graham, Douglas J., tr. see Pogony, G. E.

Graham, Earl C. & Mullen, Marjorie. Rehabilitation Literature, 1950 to 1955: A Bibliographic Review of the Medical Care, Education, Employment, Welfare & Psychology of Handicapped Children & Adults. Phillips, William R. & Rosenberg, Janet, eds. LC 79-6901. (Physically Handicapped in Society Ser.). 1980. Repr. of 1956 ed. lib. bdg. 55.50x (ISBN 0-405-13112-7). Ayer Co Pubs.

Graham, Edgar. Maintenance Welding. LC 84-11439. (Illus.). 368p. 1985. text ed. 25.95 (ISBN 0-13-545468-9). P-H.

Graham, Edmund C. Surgical Procedures: Lumbar Discography, Vol. 14. (Single Surgical Procedures Ser.). 1984. 25.95 (ISBN 0-87489-513-8). Med Economics.

Graham, Edward D., Jr. & Gwyn, Charles W. Microwave Transistors. LC 74-82594. Repr. of 1975 ed. 146.50 (ISBN 0-8357-9037-1, 2015321). Bks Demand UMI.

Graham, Edward H. Natural Principles of Land Use. Repr. of 1944 ed. lib. bdg. 17.00x (ISBN 0-8371-2394-1, GRLU). Greenwood.

Graham, Eleanor, ed. Thread of Gold, an Anthology of Poetry. LC 75-99030. (Granger Index Reprint Ser). 1964. 13.00 (ISBN 0-8369-6104-8). Ayer Co Pubs.

Graham, Elizabeth. L' Aigle de la Vallee. (Harlequin Romantique Ser.). 192p. 1983. pap. 1.95 (ISBN 0-373-41210-X). Harlequin Bks.

--Le Coeur Naufrage. (Collection Harlequin Ser.). 192p. 1983. pap. 1.95 (ISBN 0-373-49363-0). Harlequin Bks.

--Highland Gathering. (Harlequin Presents Ser.). 192p. 1983. pap. 1.95 (ISBN 0-373-10617-3). Harlequin Bks.

--La Lune Dansait Sur la Mer. (Collection Harlequin Ser.). 192p. 1983. pap. 1.95 (ISBN 0-373-49347-9). Harlequin Bks.

--Passionate Impostor. (Harlequin Presents Ser.). 192p. 1982. pap. 1.75 (ISBN 0-373-10493-6). Harlequin Bks.

--Sans Attendre. (Harlequin Romantique Ser.). 192p. 1984. pap. 1.95 (ISBN 0-373-41233-9). Harlequin Bks.

--Stormy Vigil. (Harlequin Romances Ser.). 192p. 1982. pap. 1.75 (ISBN 0-373-10543-6). Harlequin Bks.

--Thief of Copper Canyon. (Harlequin Presents Ser.). 192p. (Orig.). 1981. pap. 1.50 (ISBN 0-373-10403-0). Harlequin Bks.

--Vision of Love. (Harlequin Presents Ser.). 192p. 1983. pap. 1.95 (ISBN 0-373-10583-5). Harlequin Bks.

Graham, Esther, jt. ed. see Graham, Neil.

Graham, F. Lanier, ed. The Rainbow Book. rev. ed. LC 77-3490. 1979. pap. 7.95 (ISBN 0-394-72365-1, Vin). Random.

Graham, Frances K., jt. auth. see Ouzinkie Botanical Society adj staff.

Graham, Frank & Buffinghon, Charles. Power Plant Engineers Guide. 3rd ed. LC 83-17779. (Illus.). 816p. 1983. 16.95 (ISBN 0-672-23329-0). Audel.

Graham, Frank, jt. auth. see Graham, Ada.

Graham, Frank D. Abolition of Unemployment. LC 72-137944. (Economic Thought, History & Challenge Ser). 1971. Repr. of 1932 ed. 22.50x (ISBN 0-8046-1447-4, Pub.by Kennikat). Assoc Faculty Pr.

--Exchange, Prices & Production in Hyper-Inflation: Germany, 1920-1923. LC 66-27086. 1967. Repr. of 1930 ed. 11.00x (ISBN 0-8462-1020-7). Russell.

Graham, Frank D. & Buffington. Power Plant Engineers Guide. 3rd ed. LC 82-17779. (Audel Ser.). (Illus.). 960p. 1983. 16.95 (ISBN 0-672-23329-0). G K Hall.

Graham, Frank D. & Whittlesey, Charles R. Golden Avalanche. Wilkins, Mira, ed. LC 78-3919. (International Finance Ser.). (Illus.). 1978. Repr. of 1939 ed. lib. bdg. 20.00x (ISBN 0-405-11222-X). Ayer Co Pubs.

Graham, Frank, Jr. The Adirondack Park: A Political History. LC 78-54900. (Illus.). 346p. 1984. pap. 13.95 (ISBN 0-8156-0192-1). Syracuse U Pr.

--Dragon Hunters: The Coming Victory over Man's Ancient Enemies-the Superpests. (Illus.). 416p. 1984. 22.95 (ISBN 0-525-24249-X, 02229-660, Truman Talley Bk). Dutton.

--Great No Hit Games of the Major Leagues. (Major League Baseball Library: No. 9). (Illus.). (gr. 1-6). 1968. (BYR); PLB 3.69 (ISBN 0-394-90189-4). Random.

Graham, Franklin. Histrionic Montreal. LC 68-20225. (Illus.). 360p. 1902. 26.50 (ISBN 0-405-08568-0, Blom Pubns). Ayer Co Pubs.

Graham, Franklinn & Lockerbie, Jeanette. Bob Pierce: This One Thing I Do. 1983. 9.95 (ISBN 0-8499-0097-2). Word Bks.

Graham, Fred, jt. auth. see Report of the Twentieth Century Fund Task Force on the Government & the Press.

Graham, G. Historical Explanation Reconsidered. (Scots Philosophical Monographs: No. 4). 96p. 1983. text ed. 19.00x (ISBN 0-08-028495-7, Pub. by Aberdeen U Scotland); pap. text ed. 12.50x (ISBN 0-08-028478-7). Humanities.

Graham, G., ed. Historical Explanation Reconsidered. (Scots Philosophical Monographs: No. 4). 96p. 1983. pap. 11.00 (ISBN 0-08-028478-7). Pergamon.

Graham, G. E. & Floering, Ingrid. The Modern Plantation in the Third World. Fieldhouse, David, ed. & frwd. by. LC 84-15924. 240p. 1984. 35.00 (ISBN 0-312-54128-7). St Martin.

Graham, G. M., ed. see International Conference on Low Temperature Physics.

Graham, G. R. & Rossi, E. Heart Diseases in Infants & Children. (Illus.). 495p. 1980. 99.95 (ISBN 0-8151-3854-7). Year Bk Med.

Graham, Garrett, jt. auth. see Graham, Carroll.

Graham, George, jt. ed. see Pieron, Maurice.

Graham, George, et al. Children Moving: A Reflective Approach to Teaching Physical Education. LC 79-91832. (Illus.). 497p. 1980. text ed. 24.95 (ISBN 0-87484-467-3); pap. 8.95 study guide (ISBN 0-87484-562-9). Mayfield Pub.

Graham, George J., Jr. & Graham, Scarlett G. Founding Principles of American Government: Two Hundred Years of Democracy on Trial. rev. ed. LC 83-21085. 400p. 1984. pap. text ed. 12.95x (ISBN 0-934540-25-X). Chatham Hse Pubs.

Graham, George P., jt. auth. see Easton, Richard J.

Graham, Gerald. Tides of Empire: Discussions on the Expansion of Britain Overseas. LC 72-82242. pap. 30.00 (ISBN 0-317-26049-9, 2023840). Bks Demand UMI.

Graham, Gerald H. Understanding Human Relations: The Individual, Organization & Management. 416p. 1982. text ed. 26.95 (ISBN 0-574-19520-3, 13-2520); instr. guide avail. (ISBN 0-574-19521-1, 13-2521). SRA.

Graham, Gerald H., jt. auth. see Wichita State University Staff.

Graham, Gerald S. British Policy & Canada, Seventeen Seventy-Four to Seventeen Ninety-One. LC 74-136532. (Imperial Studies: No. 4). 161p. 1974. Repr. of 1930 ed. lib. bdg. 15.00x (ISBN 0-8371-5453-7, GRPC). Greenwood.

--The China Station: War & Diplomacy 1830-1860. (Illus.). 1978. 59.00x (ISBN 0-19-822472-9). Oxford U Pr.

--Sea Power & British North America, 1783-1820: A Study in British Colonial Policy. LC 69-10101. 1969. Repr. of 1941 ed. lib. bdg. 19.00x (ISBN 0-8371-0453-X, GRBP). Greenwood.

Graham, Gerald S. & Alexander, John. Secular Abyss: An Interpretation of History & the Human Situation. 1968. pap. 1.95 (ISBN 0-8356-0019-X, Quest). Theos Pub Hse.

Graham, Gerald S., ed. Walker Expedition to Quebec, 1711. LC 69-14509. 1969. Repr. of 1953 ed. lib. bdg. 26.75x (ISBN 0-8371-5072-8, GRWE). Greenwood.

Graham, Gordon. Automated Inventory Management for the Distributor. LC 80-17655. 234p. 1980. 22.50 (ISBN 0-8436-0794-7). Van Nos Reinhold.

Graham, Gordon, et al. California Condominium & Planned Development Practice. LC 84-70332. (Illus.). xiv, 844p. 1984. 95.00. Cal Cont Ed Bar.

Graham, Grace. The Public School in the New Society: The Social Foundations of Education. pap. 104.00 (ISBN 0-8357-9149-1, 2013229). Bks Demand UMI.

Graham, Gregory S. Metalworking: An Introduction. 1980. text ed. write for info. (ISBN 0-534-00843-7, Breton Pubs). Wadsworth Pub.

Graham, Gwethalyn & Rolland, Solange C. Dear Enemies: A Dialogue on French & English Canada. 1965. 6.50 (ISBN 0-8159-5300-3). Devin.

Graham, H., et al, eds. Marek's Disease II: Pathogenicity & Immunology. (Herpesvirus-Related Diseases Ser.). 320p. 1974. text ed. 28.50x (ISBN 0-8422-7167-8). Irvington.

Graham, H. D. Food Colloids. (Illus.). 1977. lib. bdg. 57.50 (ISBN 0-87055-201-5). AVI.

Graham, H. D., jt. ed. see Chichester, C. O.

Graham, H. T. Human Resources Management. 269p. 1983. pap. 14.95x (ISBN 0-7121-0822-X). Trans-Atlantic.

Graham, Harold. The Contented Amish: An Inside View. LC 84-90033. 1984. 7.95 (ISBN 0-533-06120-2). Vantage.

Graham, Harriet C. Peanuts, Popped Corn, & Lemonade. 1982. 4.95 (ISBN 0-533-05286-6). Vantage.

Graham, Harry. Splendid Failures. 1913. Repr. 20.00 (ISBN 0-8274-3496-0). R West.

Graham, Harry E. The Paper Rebellion: Development & Upheaval in Pulp & Paper Unionism. LC 79-131059. 170p. 1970. 13.00x (ISBN 0-87745-019-6). U of Iowa Pr.

Graham, Harry L., jt. auth. see Gaona, Victor D.

Graham, Heather. An Angel's Share. (Candlelight Supreme Ser.: No. 94). (Orig.). 1985. pap. 2.75 (ISBN 0-440-10350-9). Dell.

--Arabian Nights. (Candlelight Ecstasy Supreme Ser.: No. 37). 288p. (Orig.). 1984. pap. 2.50 (ISBN 0-440-10214-6). Dell.

--Forbidden Fruit. (Candlelight Ecstasy Supreme Ser.: No. 10). (Orig.). 1983. pap. 2.50 (ISBN 0-440-12686-X). Dell.

--Golden Surrender. 336p. 1985. pap. 3.50 (ISBN 0-440-12973-7). Dell.

--Hold Close the Memory. (Candlelight Ecstasy Ser.: No. 335). 192p. (Orig.). 1985. pap. 2.25 (ISBN 0-440-13696-2). Dell.

--Hours to Cherish. (Candlelight Ecstasy Ser.: No. 241). (Orig.). 1984. pap. 1.95 (ISBN 0-440-13780-2). Dell.

--Night, Sea & Stars. (Supreme Ser.: No. 10). 288p. pap. 2.50 (ISBN 0-440-16384-6). Dell.

--The Queen of Hearts. (Candelight Supreme Ser.: No. 67). 1985. pap. 2.50 (ISBN 0-440-17165-2, Banbury). Dell.

--Quiet Walks the Tiger. (Candlelight Ecstasy Ser.: No. 177). 192p. (Orig.). 1983. pap. 1.95 (ISBN 0-440-17227-6). Dell.

--Red Midnight. (Candlelight Ecstasy Supreme Ser.: No. 17). 288p. (Orig.). 1984. pap. 2.50 (ISBN 0-440-17431-7). Dell.

--A Season for Love. (Candlelight Ecstasy Ser.: No. 154). (Orig.). 1983. pap. 1.95 (ISBN 0-440-18041-4). Dell.

--Sensuous Angel. (Candlelight Ecstasy Ser.: No. 359). 1985. pap. 2.25 (ISBN 0-440-17636-0). Dell.

--Serena' Magic. (Candlelight Ecstasy Ser.: No. 271). 192p. (Orig.). 1984. pap. 1.95 (ISBN 0-440-17860-6). Dell.

--Tempestuous Eden. (Candlelight Ecstasy Supreme Ser.: No. 1). 288p. (Orig.). 1983. pap. 2.50 (ISBN 0-440-18646-3). Dell.

--Tender Deception. (Candlelight Ecstasy Ser.: No. 214). 192p. (Orig.). 1984. pap. 1.95 (ISBN 0-440-18591-2). Dell.

--Tender Taming. (Candlelight Ecstasy Ser.: No. 125). (Orig.). 1983. pap. 1.95 (ISBN 0-440-18803-2). Dell.

--When Next We Love. (Candlelight Ecstasy Ser.: No. 117). (Orig.). 1983. pap. 1.95 (ISBN 0-440-19588-8). Dell.

Graham, Henry G. Literary & Historical Essays. 1973. Repr. of 1908 ed. 30.00 (ISBN 0-8274-0198-1). R West.

--Scottish Men of Letters in the Eighteenth Century. 1973. Repr. of 1908 ed. 35.00 (ISBN 0-8274-1568-0). R West.

--The Social Life of Scotland in the Eighteen-Century, 2 Vol. set. 265p. 1982. Repr. of 1899 ed. lib. bdg. 100.00 (ISBN 0-89984-903-2). Century Bookbindery.

--The Social Life of Scotland in the Eighteenth-Century. 2nd ed. LC 73-173169. Repr. of 1901 ed. 30.00 (ISBN 0-405-08569-9, Blom Pubns). Ayer Co Pubs.

--The Social Life of Scotland in the Eighteenth-Century. 545p. 1982. Repr. of 1909 ed. lib. bdg. 65.00 (ISBN 0-89760-251-X). Telegraph Bks.

--What Faith Really Means. LC 82-74243. 94p. 1982. Repr. of 1914 ed. pap. 2.00 (ISBN 0-89555-204-3). TAN Bks Pubs.

--Where We Got the Bible... Our Debt to the Catholic Church. 153p. 1977. pap. 3.00 (ISBN 0-89555-137-3). TAN Bks Pubs.

Graham, Hilary. Health & Welfare. (Issues in Sociology Ser.). 152p. (Orig.). 1985. pap. text ed. 12.95x (ISBN 0-333-37191-7, Pub. by Macmillan London). Sheridan.

--Women, Health & the Family. 208p. 1984. 21.00 (ISBN 0-7108-0732-5, Pub. by Salem Hse Ltd); pap. 8.95 (ISBN 0-7108-0727-9). Merrimack Pub Cir.

Graham, Horace D. Safety of Foods. 2nd ed. (Illus.). 1980. lib. bdg. 59.00 (ISBN 0-87055-337-2). AVI.

Graham, Horace D., jt. auth. see Telek, Lehel.

Graham, Hugh. An American Treasury. 1977. Repr. of 1949 ed. 12.50 (ISBN 0-89984-188-0). Century Bookbindery.

Graham, Hugh, jt. auth. see Carlson, Jack.

Graham, Hugh D. Crisis in Print: Desegregation & the Press in Tennessee. LC 67-21654. (Illus.). 1967. 15.95x (ISBN 0-8265-1105-8). Vanderbilt U Pr.

--The Uncertain Triumph: Federal Education Policy in the Kennedy & Johnson Years. LC 83-23424. 300p. 1984. 22.00 (ISBN 0-8078-1599-3). U of NC Pr.

Graham, Hugh D., jt. auth. see Bartley, Numan V.

Graham, Hugh D. & Gurr, Ted R., eds. Violence in America: Historical & Comparative Perspectives. rev., college ed. LC 78-21934. (Illus.). 528p. 1979. 29.95 (ISBN 0-8039-0963-2); pap. 14.95 (ISBN 0-8039-0964-0). Sage.

Graham, Hugh Davis, et al, eds. Violence: The Crisis of American Confidence. LC 79-171554. 180p. 1972. 18.00x (ISBN 0-8018-1299-2). Johns Hopkins.

Graham, Hugh F., ed. & tr. The Moscovia of Antonio Possevino, S. J. LC 77-12648. (Ser. in Russian & East European Studies: No. 1). (Illus.). 1977. 20.00x (ISBN 0-8229-4202-X). U of Pittsburgh Pr.

Graham, Hugh F., ed. see Skrynnikov, R. G.

Graham, I., jt. auth. see Myring, L.

Graham, Ian. The Art of Maya Hieroglyphic Writing. 1971. pap. 2.25x (ISBN 0-87365-998-8). Peabody Harvard.

--Computer & Video Games. (Usborne Electronics Ser.). (gr. 5-9). 1982. pap. 5.95 (ISBN 0-86020-681-5, Usborne-Hayes); PLB 12.95 (ISBN 0-88110-010-2). EDC.

--Computers. (Inside Stories Ser.). (Illus.). 40p. (gr. 4-6). 1983. PLB 9.90 (ISBN 0-531-03462-3). Watts.

--Computers & Video Games. write for info. EDC.

--Corpus of Maya Hieroglyphic Inscriptions, Vol. 1. LC 75-19760. 1976. pap. 12.00x (ISBN 0-87365-779-9). Peabody Harvard.

--Corpus of Maya Hieroglyphic Inscriptions: Naranjo, Chunhuitz, Xunantunich, Vol. 2, Pt. 2. LC 77-90960. 1978. pap. 12.00x (ISBN 0-87365-781-0). Peabody Harvard.

--Corpus of Maya Hieroglyphic Inscriptions: Ucanal, Ixtutz, Ixkun, Naranjo, Vol. 2, Pt. 3. LC 75-19760. pap. 12.00 (ISBN 0-87365-786-1). Peabody Harvard.

--Corpus of Maya Hieroglyphic Inscriptions: Yaxchilan, Vol. 3, Pt. 2. LC 75-19760. 1979. pap. 12.00 (ISBN 0-87365-789-6). Peabody Harvard.

--Corpus of Maya Hieroglyphic Inscriptions: Yaxchilan, Vol. 3, Pt. 3. LC 75-19760. (Illus.). 64p. (Orig.). 1982. pap. 12.00x (ISBN 0-87365-799-3). Peabody Harvard.

Graham, Ian & Varley, Helen. The Home Computer Handbook. 224p. 1984. 12.95 (ISBN 0-671-47221-6). S&S.

Graham, Ian & Von Euw, Eric. Corpus of Maya Hieroglyphic Inscriptions: Naranjo, Vol. 2, Pt. 1. LC 75-39917. 1976. pap. 12.00x (ISBN 0-87365-780-2). Peabody Harvard.

--Corpus of Maya Hieroglyphic Inscriptions: Yaxchilan, Vol 3, Pt. 1. LC 77-78741. (Illus.). 1977. pap. 12.00 (ISBN 0-87365-788-8). Peabody Harvard.

Graham, Ian, jt. auth. see Von Euw, Eric.

Graham, Ilse. Schiller: A Master of the Tragic Form: His Theory in His Practice. (Philological Ser.: No. 16). 185p. 1974. text ed. 13.00x (ISBN 0-391-00344-5). Duquesne.

Graham, Ilse. Goethe: Portrait of the Artist. LC 76-54974. 1977. 36.40x (ISBN 3-11-006928-8). De Gruyter.

--Heinrich Von Kleist, Word into Flesh: A Poet's Quest for the Symbol. 1977. 32.00x (ISBN 3-11-007165-7). De Gruyter.

Graham, Irvin. Encyclopedia of Advertising. 2nd ed. LC 68-14544. (Illus.). 1969. 20.00 (ISBN 0-87005-014-1). Fairchild.

Graham, J., jt. auth. see Currie, George.

Graham, J. A., ed. Use of Computers in Managing Material Property Data. (MPC: No. 14). 64p. 1980. 18.00 (ISBN 0-686-69865-7, G00192). ASME.

Graham, J. D. P., ed. Cannabis & Health. 1976. 74.00 (ISBN 0-12-294650-2). Acad Pr.

Graham, J. T. Scales & Balances. (Shire Album Ser.: No. 55). (Illus.). 32p. (Orig.). 1981. pap. 2.95 (ISBN 0-85263-547-8, Pub. by Shire Pubns England). Seven Hills Bks.

Graham, J. W., ed. see Woolf, Virginia.

Graham, James, pseud. The Khufra Run. 224p. 1985. pap. 2.95 (ISBN 0-425-07060-3). Berkley Pub.

Graham, James. So! You're Going to the Hospital! LC 68-20945. 178p. 1968. 5.00 (ISBN 0-87527-013-1); pap. 3.50 (ISBN 0-87527-038-7). Green.

Graham, James, jt. auth. see Higgins, Jack.

Graham, James Q., jt. auth. see Rowney, Don Karl.

Graham, James R. The Planting of the Presbyterian Church in Northern Virginia Prior to the Organization of Winchester Presbytery, December Fourth, Seventeen Ninenty Four. LC 26-22114. 168p. 1904. 15.00x (ISBN 0-685-65067-7). Va Bk.

Graham, James W. Let Us Affirm Our Faith. 1979. pap. 6.75 (ISBN 0-89536-369-0). CSS of Ohio.

Graham, Jamie M., ed. The Best of Hardy's Anglers Guides. 1983. 100.00x (ISBN 0-904265-94-3, Pub. by Macdonald Pub UK); pap. 50.00x (ISBN 0-904265-95-1). State Mutual Bk.

Graham, Jamie R. Urban Affairs Subject Heading Comparisons. 184p. 1979. pap. 7.00 (ISBN 0-318-00030-X, INS 19). Inst for Urban & Regional.

Graham, Jean Ann & Kligman, Albert M., eds. The Psychology of Cosmetic Treatments. LC 84-26657. 272p. 1985. 33.95 (ISBN 0-03-070717-X). Praeger.

Graham, Joan, jt. auth. see Shade, Carolyn.

Graham, John. Ancient Mesoamerica: Selected Readings. rev. ed. (Illus.). 334p. 1982. pap. text ed. 14.95 (ISBN 0-917962-70-2). Peek Pubns.

--The Coming New Wave of God's Spirit. LC 84-80226. 212p. 1984. pap. 7.95 (ISBN 0-916333-01-9). King's Hse Pub.

--Facts on File Dictionary of Telecommunications. (Illus.). 224p. 1983. 15.95 (ISBN 0-87196-120-2). Facts on File.

--The Facts on File Dictionary of Telecommunications. 224p. 1984. pap. 6.95 (ISBN 0-87196-876-2). Facts on File.

--Fast Reactor Safety. (Nuclear Science & Technology Ser.: Vol. 8). 1971. 76.00 (ISBN 0-12-294950-1). Acad Pr.

--I Love You, Mouse. LC 76-8022. (Illus.). (gr. k-2). 1976. 12.95 (ISBN 0-15-238005-1, HJ). HarBraceJ.

--I Love You, Mouse. LC 78-6214. (Illus.). (ps-3). 1978. pap. 6.95 (ISBN 0-15-644106-3, VoyB). HarBraceJ.

--Lavater's Essays on Physiognomy. (European University Studies: Series 18,Comparative, Literature Vol. 18). (Illus.). 130p. 1980. pap. 15.30 (ISBN 3-261-03153-0). P Lang Pubs.

--The Literature of Chess. LC 83-26759. (Illus.). 256p. 1984. lib. bdg. 18.95x (ISBN 0-89950-099-4). McFarland & Co.

--Mold Me & Shape Me. 176p. 1983. 9.95 (ISBN 0-310-60170-3, Pub by Chosen Bks). Zondervan.

--Novels in English: The Eighteenth & Nineteenth-Century Holdings at Schloss Corvex, Hoxter, Germany. (American University Studies IV: Vol. 2). 153p. (Orig.). 1983. pap. text ed. 18.95 (ISBN 0-8204-0030-0). P Lang Pubs.

Graham, John, jt. auth. see Brown, Skip.

Graham, John, ed. & intro. by see Sinclair, Upton.

Graham, John A. The Hieroglyphic Inscriptions & Monumental Art of Altar de Sacrificios. LC 70-186984. (Peabody Museum Papers: Vol. 64, No. 2). 1972. pap. 7.50 (ISBN 0-87365-184-7). Peabody Harvard.

Graham, John K. God's Gift: The Secrets of Financial Freedom, No. 1. LC 83-83273. (God's Gift Ser.). (Illus.). 112p. 1984. 12.95 (ISBN 0-916333-00-0). King's Hse Pub.

Graham, John L. & Sano, Yoshihiro. Business Negotiations, Smart Bargaining, John Wayne Style: And Other Problems for Americans Bargaining in Japan. 1984. 19.95i (ISBN 0-88410-729-9). Har-Row.

--Smart Bargaining: Doing Business with the Japanese. LC 84-404. 184p. 1984. 19.95 (ISBN 0-88410-729-9). Ballinger Pub.

Graham, John M., II & Wedgwood, Hensleigh C. Wedgwood. LC 71-128384. (Brooklyn Museum Publications in Reprint Ser.). (Illus.). 122p. Repr. of 1948 ed. 17.00 (ISBN 0-405-00878-3). Ayer Co Pubs.

Graham, John R. Constitutional History of the Military Draft. 5.95 (ISBN 0-87018-065-7); pap. 2.95 (ISBN 0-87018-070-3). Ross.

--The MMPI: A Practical Guide. 1977. text ed. 16.95x (ISBN 0-19-502304-8). Oxford U Pr.

Graham, John R. & Lilly, Roy S. Psychological Testing. (Illus.). 480p. 1984. text ed. 29.95 (ISBN 0-13-732652-1). P-H.

Graham, John T. Donoso Cortes: Utopian Romanticist & Political Realist. LC 73-85460. (Illus.). 352p. 1974. 24.00x (ISBN 0-8262-0155-5). U of Mo Pr.

Graham, John W. Conscription & Conscience: A History, 1916-1919. LC 76-147643. (Library of War & Peace; Conscrip. & Cons. Object.). lib. bdg. 46.00 (ISBN 0-8240-0413-2). Garland Pub.

--Conscription & Conscience: A History 1916-1919. LC 78-81509. Repr. of 1922 ed. 35.00x (ISBN 0-678-00507-9). Kelley.

--The Harvest of Ruskin. 1973. Repr. of 1920 ed. 20.00 (ISBN 0-8274-0647-9). R West.

--Sejanus: The Secret Ruler of Rome. (The Golden Age of Rome Ser.). 1978. pap. 2.50 (ISBN 0-89083-353-2). Zebra.

Graham, John W. & Jones, Susan K. Selling by Mail: An Entrepreneurial Guide to Direct Marketing. 1985. cancelled (ISBN 0-684-18215-7). Scribner.

Graham, Jorie. Erosion. LC 82-61365. (Princeton Series of Contemporary Poet). 83p. 1983. 13.50x (ISBN 0-691-06570-5); pap. 6.95 (ISBN 0-691-01405-1). Princeton U Pr.

--Hybrids of Plants & of Ghosts. LC 79-84010. (Princeton Series of Contemporary Poets). 1980. 13.00 (ISBN 0-691-06421-0); pap. 6.95 (ISBN 0-691-01335-7). Princeton U Pr.

Graham, Jory. In the Company of Others. LC 78-22252. 288p. 1981. 10.95 (ISBN 0-15-144642-3). HarBraceJ.

Graham, Jory, et al, eds. see Fishman, Joan & Anrod, Barbara.

Graham, Joseph F., ed. Difference in Translation. LC 84-15622. 256p. 1985. text ed. 32.50x (ISBN 0-8014-1704-X); pap. text ed. 9.95x (ISBN 0-8014-9287-4). Cornell U Pr.

Graham, Josephine. Suggin Cookbook. 164p. 1974. pap. 6.98 (ISBN 0-686-09048-9). J Graham.

--Suggin Painting. 1976. pap. 3.00 (ISBN 0-686-17966-8). J Graham.

Graham, Judith. Hawaiian Voices. LC 81-71631. (Illus.). 152p. (Orig.). 1982. pap. 6.95 (ISBN 0-935848-06-1). Bess Pr.

Graham, Judy. Evening Primrose Oil: Its Remarkable Properties & Its Use in the Treatment of a Wide Range of Conditions. 96p. (Orig.). 1984. pap. 4.95 (ISBN 0-7225-0743-7). Thorsons Pubs.

--Multiple Sclerosis: A Self-Help Guide to Its Management. 1981. 24.00x (ISBN 0-7225-0625-2, Pub. by Thorsons England). State Mutual Bk.

--Multiple Sclerosis: A Self-Help Guide to its Management. 160p. (Orig.). 1984. pap. 6.95 (ISBN 0-7225-0804-2). Thorsons Pubs.

Graham, Julia B. & Wiedeman, Varley E. Biology of Populations. 136p. 1982. pap. text ed. 8.95 (ISBN 0-8403-2784-6). Kendall-Hunt.

Graham, Juliet. Reflections. 32p. 1982. 5.95 (ISBN 0-89962-267-4). Todd & Honeywell.

Graham, K. J., jt. auth. see Kinney, G. F.

Graham, Katherine A., jt. auth. see Feldman, Lionel D.

Graham, Katherine A., et al. The Administration of Mineral Exploration in the Yukon & Northwest Territories. 60p. (Orig.). 1979. pap. text ed. 4.00x (ISBN 0-686-63144-7, Pub. by Ctr Resource Stud Canada). Brookfield Pub Co.

Graham, Kathy. Hope for God's People. (Bible Puzzle Time). 16p. (Orig.). (gr. 3-6). 1982. pap. 0.60 (ISBN 0-87239-521-9, 2176). Standard Pub.

Graham, Keith, ed. Contemporary Political Philosophy: Radical Studies. (Illus.). 140p. 1982. 27.95 (ISBN 0-521-24551-6); pap. 9.95 (ISBN 0-521-28783-9). Cambridge U Pr.

Graham, Kennard C. Industrial & Commercial Wiring. 2nd ed. (Illus.). 1963. 12.00 (ISBN 0-8269-1500-0). Am Technical.

--Understanding & Servicing Fractional Horsepower Motors. LC 61-11419. pap. 66.00 (ISBN 0-317-10141-2, 2004575). Bks Demand UMI.

Graham, Kenneth see Swan, D. K.

Graham, Kenneth G. & Robinson, H. Alan. The Study Skills Handbook: A Guide for All Teachers. (IRA Bk.: No. 858). 136p. 1984. 9.00 (ISBN 0-87207-858-2). Intl Reading.

Graham, L. J. & Field, T. Your IBM PC. 400p. 1983. 17.95 (ISBN 0-88134-120-7, 112-6, Osborne-McGraw). Mcgraw.

Graham, L. R. Soviet Academy of Sciences & the Communist Party, 1927-1932. (Studies of the Russian Institute). 1968. 35.00x (ISBN 0-691-08038-0). Princeton U Pr.

Graham, Lawrence. Conquering College Life: How to Be a Winner at College. 1983. pap. 3.95 (ISBN 0-671-46976-2). WSP.

--Jobs in the Real World: The Student Job-Search Handbook. LC 81-85476. 160p. 1982. pap. 6.95 (ISBN 0-448-12268-5, G&D). Putnam Pub Group.

--Ten-Point Plan for College Acceptance. (Illus.). 144p. 1981. pap. 6.95 (ISBN 0-399-50678-0, Perigee). Putnam Pub Group.

--Your Ticket to Business School. 144p. 1985. pap. 4.95 (ISBN 0-553-34146-4). Bantam.

--Your Ticket to Law School. 144p. 1985. pap. 4.95 (ISBN 0-553-34144-8). Bantam.

--Your Ticket to Medical or Dental School. 144p. 1985. pap. 4.95 (ISBN 0-553-34145-6). Bantam.

Graham, Lawrence & Hamdan, Lawrence. F. L. Y. E. R. S. Fun Loving Youth en Route to Success. 1985. pap. 4.95 (ISBN 0-671-60369-8, Fireside). S&S.

Graham, Lawrence S. Civil Service Reform in Brazil: Principles vs. Practice. (Latin American Monographs: No. 13). 247p. 1968. 12.50x (ISBN 0-292-78356-6). U of Tex Pr.

--Romania: A Developing Socialist State. (Nations of Contemporary Eastern Europe Ser.). 136p. 1982. lib. bdg. 20.00x (ISBN 0-89158-925-2). Westview.

Graham, Lawrence S., jt. auth. see Thurber, Clarence E.

Graham, Lawrence S. & Makler, Harry M., eds. Contemporary Portugal: The Revolution & Its Antecedents. LC 78-11213. 401p. 1979. text ed. 27.50x (ISBN 0-292-71047-X); pap. text ed. 12.95x (ISBN 0-292-71048-8). U of Tex Pr.

Graham, Lawrence S. & Wheeler, Douglas L., eds. In Search of Modern Portugal: The Revolution & its Consequences. LC 81-69819. 384p. 1983. text ed. 32.50x (ISBN 0-299-08990-8). U of Wis Pr.

Graham, Leroy. Baltimore: The Nineteenth Century Black Capital. 346p. (Orig.). 1982. lib. bdg. 27.25 (ISBN 0-8191-2624-1); pap. text ed. 14.25 (ISBN 0-8191-2625-X). U Pr of Amer.

Graham, Lillian S., jt. auth. see Wackerbarth, Marjorie.

Graham, Lisa J. A Porcelain Perspective. LC 84-90362. 64p. 1984. 6.50 (ISBN 0-8233-0383-7). Golden Quill.

Graham, Lloyd A. Ingenious Mathematical Problems & Methods. 1959. pap. 4.95 (ISBN 0-486-20545-2). Dover.

--Surprise Attack in Mathematical Problems. (Illus., Orig.). 1968. pap. 4.50 (ISBN 0-486-21846-5). Dover.

Graham, Loren & Lepenies, Wolf, eds. Functions & Uses of Disciplinary Histories. 1983. lib. bdg. 44.00 (ISBN 90-277-1520-3, Pub. by Reidel Holland); pap. text ed. 29.00 (ISBN 90-277-1521-1, Pub. by Reidel Holland). Kluwer Academic.

Graham, Loren R. Between Science & Values. 448p. 1981. 24.00 (ISBN 0-231-05192-1); pap. 12.50x (ISBN 0-231-05193-X). Columbia U Pr.

Graham, Loren R., ed. see Bogdanov, Alexander.

Graham, Lorenz. John Brown: A Cry for Freedom. LC 79-7903. (Illus.). 192p. (gr. 7 up). 1980. 11.49i (ISBN 0-690-04023-7); PLB 11.89 (ISBN 0-690-04024-5). Crowell Jr Bks.

--Song of the Boat. LC 74-5183. (Illus.). (gr. 2-5). 1975. 9.57i (ISBN 0-690-75231-8); PLB 9.89 (ISBN 0-690-75232-6). Crowell Jr Bks.

Graham, Lou. Fanny G. (Orig.). 1980. pap. text ed. 2.25 (ISBN 0-505-51569-5, Pub. by Tower Bks). Dorchester Pub Co.

--Fragments. 288p. (Orig.). 1981. pap. 2.50 (ISBN 0-505-51708-6, Pub. by Tower Bks). Dorchester Pub Co.

--Fragments. 288p. 1985. pap. 3.25 (ISBN 0-8439-2250-8, Leisure Bks). Dorchester Pub Co.

--The Seventh Sister. 480p. (Orig.). 1985. pap. 3.95 (ISBN 0-8439-2266-4, Leisure Bks). Dorchester Pub Co.

Graham, Lou & Bibb, John. Mastering Golf. LC 77-91155. 1978. o. p. 9.95 (ISBN 0-8092-7763-8); pap. 8.95 (ISBN 0-8092-7761-1). Contemp Bks.

Graham, Lyle & Field, Tim. Your IBM PC: A Guide to the IBM PC (D05 2.0) and XT. 600p. (Orig.). 1983. pap. 17.95 (ISBN 0-07-881120-1, 120-1). Osborne-McGraw.

Graham, Lyle J. Your IBM PC: A Guide to the IBM Personal Computer. 384p. (Orig.). 1983. pap. text ed. 17.95 (ISBN 0-07-931085-0, 85-0). Osborne-McGraw.

Graham, M., jt. ed. see Davy, B.

Graham, M. A., jt. auth. see Burghes, D. N.

Graham, M. G., ed. see AIP Conference, Corning, N.Y., 1971.

Graham, M. W., Jr. New Governments of Eastern Europe. LC 27-20024. (Illus.). 1969. Repr. of 1927 ed. 40.00 (ISBN 0-527-35250-0). Kraus Repr.

Graham, Malbone W. American Diplomacy in the International Community. facs. ed. LC 70-76900. (Essay Index Reprint Ser). 1948. 17.75 (ISBN 0-8369-1037-0). Ayer Co Pubs.

Graham, Malcolm. Henry Taunt in Oxford. 8.95 (ISBN 0-902280-14-7, P914). Haynes Pubns.

--Modern Elementary Mathematics. 4th ed. 576p. 1984. text ed. 26.95 (ISBN 0-15-561043-0, HC); instr's manual avail. (ISBN 0-15-561044-9). HarBraceJ.

Graham, Malcolm & House, William F., eds. Disorders of the Facial Nerve: Anatomy, Diagnosis & Management. (House Ear Institute Ser.). 576p. 1982. text ed. 90.50 (ISBN 0-89004-624-7). Raven.

Graham, Malcolm D. Cleft Palate: Middle Ear Disease & Hearing Loss. (Illus.). 168p. 1978. 18.25x (ISBN 0-398-03667-5). C C Thomas.

Graham, Marcus. Marxism & a Free Society. 1984. lib. bdg. 79.95 (ISBN 0-87700-646-6). Revisionist Pr.

Graham, Margaret. Stories of the Foot Hills. LC 76-94727. (Short Story Index Reprint Ser.). 1895. 17.00 (ISBN 0-8369-3106-8). Ayer Co Pubs.

Graham, Margaret A. Katie. 1981. pap. 3.50 (ISBN 0-8423-2028-8). Tyndale.

Graham, Margaret B. Be Nice to Spiders. LC 67-17101. (gr. k-3). 1967. 12.02i (ISBN 0-06-022072-4); PLB 11.89 (ISBN 0-06-022073-2). HarpJ.

--Benjy & the Barking Bird. LC 79-129856. (Illus.). (ps-3). 1971. PLB 11.89 (ISBN 0-06-022080-5). HarpJ.

--Benjy's Boat Trip. LC 77-6393. (Illus.). (ps-3). 1977. 10.53i (ISBN 0-06-022092-9); PLB 11.89 (ISBN 0-06-022093-7). HarpJ.

--Benjy's Dog House. LC 72-9854. (Illus.). 32p. (ps-3). 1973. 12.02i (ISBN 0-06-022083-X); PLB 11.89 (ISBN 0-06-022084-8). HarpJ.

Graham, Marteen D. Ariane. (Orig.). 1984. pap. 3.50 (ISBN 0-440-10279-0). Dell.

Graham, Martha. The Notebooks of Martha Graham. LC 72-75416. (Illus.). 1973. 27.50 (ISBN 0-15-167265-2). HarBraceJ.

Graham, Matthew. New World Architecture. LC 84-81137. 50p. (Orig.). 1985. 6.50 (ISBN 0-913123-07-2); pap. 4.50 (ISBN 0-913123-05-6). Galileo.

Graham, Maynard. One Small Coal Company's Struggle for Survival. 1983. 8.95 (ISBN 0-8062-2023-6). Carlton.

Graham, Michael. Cleary & Graham's Handbook of Illinois Evidence. 4th ed. LC 83-82693. 816p. 1984. 60.00 (ISBN 0-316-32299-7). Little.

--Map of the World. 1982. pap. 4.95 (ISBN 0-14-051114-8). Penguin.

--A Natural Ecology. (Illus.). 251p. 1973. 17.50x (ISBN 0-87471-024-3). Rowman.

Graham, Michael, jt. ed. see Davy, F. Brian.

Graham, Michael, jt. ed. see Sharp, Donald.

Graham, Michael H. Evidence: Text, Rules, Illustrations & Problems. 937p. 1985. 49.95 (ISBN 0-318-11873-4). Natl Inst Trial Ad.

--Federal Evidence Handbook Nineteen Eighty-Five Pocket Part. (West's Handbook Ser.). 301p. 1985. 11.00 (ISBN 0-314-88027-5). West Pub.

--Federal Rules of Evidence in a Nutshell. LC 81-1498. (Nutshell Ser.). 429p. 1981. pap. text ed. 8.95 (ISBN 0-314-58806-X). West Pub.

--Supplement to Illinois Evidence, 1985. 4th ed. LC 83-82693. 80p. 1985. pap. write for info. (ISBN 0-316-32301-2). Little.

--Tightening the Reins of Justice in America: A Comparative Analysis of the Criminal Jury Trail in England & the United States. LC 82-12029. (Contributions in Legal Studies Ser.: No. 26). (Illus.). xiii, 341p. 1983. lib. bdg. 35.00 (ISBN 0-313-23598-8, GJA/). Greenwood.

--Witness Intimidation: The Law's Response. LC 84-11780. xiii, 317p. 1985. lib. bdg. 39.95 (ISBN 0-89930-104-5, GRW/, Quorum). Greenwood.

Graham, Milton D., ed. Science & Blindness: Retrospective & Prospective. LC 72-82240. 212p. 1972. pap. 3.60 (ISBN 0-89128-052-9, PIP052). Am Foun Blind.

Graham, N., jt. ed. see Dewitt, B. S.

Graham, Nancy. Quality Assurance in Hospitals: Strategies for Assessment & Implementation. LC 81-12677. 326p. 1982. text ed. 33.95 (ISBN 0-89443-391-1). Aspen Systems.

Graham, Neil & Graham, Esther, eds. What Are Their Memorable Songs? 1984. 12.50 (ISBN 0-533-05992-5). Vantage.

Graham, Neill. Artificial Intelligence. LC 78-26512. (Illus.). 1979. pap. 10.25 (ISBN 0-8306-1076-6, 1076). TAB Bks.

--Computing & Computers: An Introduction Through BASIC. (Illus.). 525p. 1982. text ed. 21.95 (ISBN 0-8299-0382-8). West Pub.

--Introduction to Computer Science: A Structured Approach. 2nd ed. (Illus.). 568p. 1982. text ed. 29.95 (ISBN 0-314-63243-3). West Pub.

--The Mind Tool: Computers & Their Impact on Society. 3rd ed. (Illus.). 410p. 1983. pap. text ed. 21.95 (ISBN 0-314-69650-4); study manual avail. (ISBN 0-314-71093-0); instrs.' manual avail. (ISBN 0-314-71094-9). West Pub.

--Programming the IBM Personal Computer: Fundamentals of BASIC. 1984. 17.95 (ISBN 0-03-059561-4). HR&W.

--Programming the IBM Personal Computer: BASIC. LC 82-11706. 256p. 1983. 17.50 (ISBN 0-03-063667-1). HR&W.

--Programming the IBM Personal Computer: COBOL. 1984. 20.45 (ISBN 0-03-059563-0); 40.50. HR&W.

--Programming the IBM Personal Computer: Pascal. 1984. 19.45 (ISBN 0-03-061982-3). HR&W.

Graham, Norma S. Carrots Are a Girl's Best Friend. (Illus.). 110p. (Orig.). 1985. pap. 5.95 (ISBN 0-89288-109-7). Maverick.

Graham, Norman A. & Edwards, Keith L. Demographic, Economic, & Resource-Use Trends in Seventeen Caribbean Basin Countries. (Replica Edition Ser.). 145p. 1984. 18.50xsoftcover (ISBN 0-86531-830-1). Westview.

Graham, Norman A. & Jordan, Robert S., eds. The International Civil Service: Changing Role & Concepts. LC 79-19471. (Pergamon Policy Studies). 200p. 1980. 32.00 (ISBN 0-08-024643-5). Pergamon.

Graham, O. J. The Six-Pointed Star. LC 84-60276. 1984. pap. text ed. 2.50 (ISBN 0-932050-24-7). New Puritan.

Graham, Ora L. Season of the Carnival. LC 83-25032. 168p. 1984. pap. 4.95 (ISBN 0-8407-5888-X). Nelson.

Graham, Otis, jt. auth. see Borden, Morton.

Graham, Otis L. Toward a Planned Society: From Franklin D. Roosevelt to Richard Nixon. 1976. 22.50x (ISBN 0-19-501985-7). Oxford U Pr.

Graham, Otis L., jt. auth. see Borden, Morton.

Graham, Otis L., Jr. Encore for Reform: The Old Progressives & the New Deal. 1967. 19.95x (ISBN 0-19-500558-9). Oxford U Pr.

--Illegal Immigration & the New Reform Movement. 1980. pap. text ed. 2.50 (ISBN 0-935776-01-X). F A I R.

--Toward a Planned Society: From Roosevelt to Nixon. LC 75-10189. 1976. pap. 8.95 (ISBN 0-19-502181-9, 486, GB). Oxford U Pr.

Graham, Otis L., Jr. & Litwack, Leon. The Great Campaigns--Reform & War in America Nineteen Hundred to Nineteen Twenty-Eight. LC 79-24302. 400p. 1980. pap. 11.95 (ISBN 0-89874-022-3). Krieger.

Graham, Otis L., Jr., ed. From Roosevelt to Roosevelt, 1901-1941. LC 70-151116. (Literature of History Ser). (Orig.). 1971. 24.50x (ISBN 0-89197-181-5); pap. text ed. 9.95x (ISBN 0-89197-182-3). Irvington.

Graham, Otis L., Jr. & Wander, Meghan R., eds. Franklin D. Roosevelt, His Life & Times: An Encyclopedia View. LC 84-25149. (Presidential Encyclopedia Ser.). (Illus.). 472p. 1985. lib. bdg. 27.50 (ISBN 0-8161-8667-7). G K Hall.

Graham, P. Anderson. Nature in Books. 1891. Repr. 25.00 (ISBN 0-8274-3014-0). R West.

--The Victorian Era: With Seventy Five Illustrations and Two Maps. (Illus.). 1973. Repr. of 1897 ed. 25.00 (ISBN 0-8274-0738-6). R West.

Graham, P. Anderson, ed. see Blackburne, Joseph H.

Graham, Patricia. Rigby Graham. 1981. 79.00x (ISBN 0-686-75523-5, Pub. by Brewhouse Private England). State Mutual Bk.

Graham, Patricia A. Progressive Education: From Arcady to Academe: A History of the Progressive Education Association: 1919-1955. LC 67-26480. 1967. text ed. 10.95x (ISBN 0-8077-1452-6). Tchrs Coll.

Graham, Pearson & Bodenhorn, Diran. Managerial Economics. LC 78-67945. (Economics Ser.). (Illus.). 1980. text ed. 23.95 (ISBN 0-201-02470-5); instrs' manual 3.50 (ISBN 0-201-02482-9). Addison-Wesley.

Graham, Peter. International Herald Tribune Guide to Business Travel & Entertainment in Europe. LC 83-82526. 224p. 1984. pap. 9.95 (ISBN 0-03-070772-2). HR&W.

Graham, Peter, tr. see Stierlin, Henri.

Graham, Peter J. & Klar, Lawrence R. Planning & Delivering Leisure Services. 350p. 1979. text ed. write for info. (ISBN 0-697-07384-X). Wm C Brown.

Graham, Peter J. & Ueberhorst, Horst. The Modern Olympics. new ed. LC 76-27945. 1976. pap. text ed. 12.95 (ISBN 0-918438-05-5). Leisure Pr.

Graham, Peter W. Byron's Bulldog: The Letters of John Cam Hobhouse to Lord Byron. LC 84-5250. (Illus.). 378p. 1984. 25.00x (ISBN 0-8142-0367-1). Ohio St U Pr.

Graham, Philip. The Art of the Knock: Stories. LC 84-11584. 188p. 1985. 11.95 (ISBN 0-688-04117-5). Morrow.

--The Vanishings. LC 78-504343. (Illus.). 1978. pap. 3.00 (ISBN 0-913722-12-X, Pub. by Release). Small Pr Dist.

Graham, Philip & Jones, Joseph. A Concordance to the Poems of Sidney Lanier: Including the Poem Outlines & Certain Uncollected Items. (English Literary Reference Ser). 1969. Repr. of 1939 ed. 45.00 (ISBN 0-384-19610-1). Johnson Repr.

Graham, Philip see Anderson, Charles R.

Graham, Pierre, ed. see International Symposium on Immunopathology 3rd.

Graham, R. Officiating Soccer. 139p. 1979. pap. 3.95 (ISBN 0-8092-7477-9). Contemp Bks.

Graham, R. A., jt. auth. see Percival, G. S.

Graham, R. B. A Brazilian Mystic: Life & Miracles of Antonio Conselheiro. 1976. lib. bdg. 59.95 (ISBN 0-87968-786-X). Gordon Pr.

--Jose Antonio Paez. LC 72-112799. 1970. Repr. of 1929 ed. 24.50x (ISBN 0-8046-1069-X, Pub. by Kennikat). Assoc Faculty Pr.

--Pedro De Valdivia, Conqueror of Chile. LC 74-3619. (Illus.). 227p. 1974. Repr. of 1926 ed. lib. bdg. 15.75x (ISBN 0-8371-7454-6, GRPV). Greenwood.

--The South American Sketches of R. B. Cunninghame Graham. Walker, John, ed. LC 77-18604. 1978. 18.95 (ISBN 0-8061-1468-1). U of Okla Pr.

Graham, R. Cunninghame. Conquest of New Granada: Being the Life of Gonzalo Jimenez De Quesada. LC 66-30734. Repr. of 1922 ed. 23.50 (ISBN 0-8154-0086-1). Cooper Sq.

--The Conquest of New Grenada, Being the Life of Gonzalo Jimenez De Quesada. LC 77-88572. 1977. Repr. of 1922 ed. lib. bdg. 30.00 (ISBN 0-89341-279-1). Longwood Pub Group.

--The Conquest of the River Plate. LC 77-17167. 1977. Repr. of 1924 ed. lib. bdg. 25.00 (ISBN 0-89341-287-2). Longwood Pub Group.

--Jose Antonio Paez. LC 72-118638. (Illus.). 1970. Repr. of 1929 ed. lib. bdg. 23.50 (ISBN 0-8154-0329-1). Cooper Sq.

--Pedro De Valdivia, Conqueror of Chile. LC 77-88575. 1977. Repr. of 1926 ed. lib. bdg. 25.00 (ISBN 0-89341-281-3). Longwood Pub Group.

Graham, R. D. Rough Passage. 256p. (Orig.). 1984. pap. 11.50 (ISBN 0-246-12311-7, Pub. by Granada England). Sheridan.

--Rough Passage. 256p. 1985. pap. 7.95 (ISBN 0-246-12311-7, Pub. by Granada England). Academy Chi Pubs.

Graham, Richard. Britain & the Onset of Modernization in Brazil, 1850-1914. LC 68-21393. (Cambridge Latin American Studies: No. 4). pap. 100.30 (ISBN 0-317-28004-X, 2025583). Bks Demand UMI.

--Cuisine for Cats. 1980. 15.00 (ISBN 0-686-96956-1, Pub. by J Landesman England). State Mutual Bk.
--The Good Dog's Cook Book. LC 79-92259. (Illus., Orig.). 1980. pap. 4.95 (ISBN 0-932966-06-3). Permanent Pr.
--The Good Dog's Cookbook. 1982. 15.00 (ISBN 0-905150-21-X, Pub. by J Landesman England). State Mutual Bk.
--Latin America. (Studies in World Civilization). 192p. 1972. pap. text ed. 7.50 (ISBN 0-394-31641-X, KnopfC). Knopf.
--The Masters of Victorian Literature. 1973. Repr. of 1897 ed. 25.00 (ISBN 0-8274-0739-4). R West.
Graham, Richard & Goldston, Angela. Social Studies: History. (Latin American Curriculum Units for Junior & Community Colleges Ser.). v, 46p. 1981. pap. text ed. 3.95x (ISBN 0-86728-008-5). U TX Inst Lat Am Stud.
Graham, Richard, jt. auth. see Beer, Alice S.
Graham, Richard, tr. see Lecourt, Edith.
Graham, Rigby. Leicestershire. 1981. 200.00x (ISBN 0-905837-07-X, Pub. by Sycamore Pr England). State Mutual Bk.
--String & Walnuts: Hans Erni on Enthusiasm. 1981. 100.00x (ISBN 0-905837-04-5, Pub. by Sycamore Pr England). State Mutual Bk.
Graham, Robert. Iran: The Illusion of Power. LC 78-65258. (Illus.). 272p. 1980. pap. 6.95 (ISBN 0-312-43589-4). St Martin.
--Spain: A Nation Comes of Age. 327p. 1984. 14.95 (ISBN 0-312-74958-9). St Martin.
Graham, Robert A. Vatican Diplomacy: A Study of Church & State on the International Plane. LC 59-13870. pap. 113.00 (ISBN 0-317-08423-2, 2015012). Bks Demand UMI.
Graham, Robert B. Brought Forward. facsimile ed. LC 77-169552. (Short Story Index Reprint Ser.). Repr. of 1916 ed. 15.00 (ISBN 0-8369-4014-8). Ayer Co Pubs.
--The Ipane. facsimile ed. LC 70-169553. (Short Story Index Reprint Ser.). Repr. of 1899 ed. 15.00 (ISBN 0-8369-4015-6). Ayer Co Pubs.
--Success. LC 71-103512. (Short Story Index Reprint Ser.). 1902. 17.00 (ISBN 0-8369-3254-4). Ayer Co Pubs.
--Thirteen Stories. LC 78-103511. (Short Story Index Reprint Ser.). 1900. 17.00 (ISBN 0-8369-3253-6). Ayer Co Pubs.
--Thirty Tales & Sketches. facs. ed. LC 76-125213. (Short Story Reprint Ser.). Repr. of 1929 ed. 20.00 (ISBN 0-8369-3580-2). Ayer Co Pubs.
--Vanished Arcadia: Being Some Account of the Jesuits in Paraguay. LC 68-25238. (Studies in Spanish Literature, No. 36). 1969. Repr. of 1901 ed. lib. bdg. 50.95x (ISBN 0-8383-0949-6). Haskell.
Graham, Robert E., Jr., ed. see U. S. Office Of Business Economics.
Graham, Robert J. Project Management: Combining Technical & Behavioral Approaches for Effective Implementation. (Illus.). 256p. 1985. 34.50 (ISBN 0-442-23018-4). Van Nos Reinhold.
Graham, Robert K. The Future of Man. rev. ed. LC 74-112341. (Illus.). 101p. 1981. pap. 3.50 (ISBN 0-939794-00-4). Foun Adv Man.
Graham, Robert M. Principles of Systems Programming. LC 74-19390. 422p. 1975. text ed. 40.00 (ISBN 0-471-32100-1). Wiley.
Graham, Robert W., jt. auth. see Hsu, Yih-Yun.
Graham, Robert W., ed. Primary Electrochemical Cell Technology: Advances Since 1977. LC 81-38329. (Energy Tech. Rev. 66; Chem. Tech. Rev. 191). 388p. 1981. 48.00 (ISBN 0-8155-0853-0). Noyes.
--Rechargeable Batteries: Advances Since 1977. LC 80-13152. (Energy Technology Review Ser. No. 55; Chemical Technology Review Ser. No.160). 452p. 1980. 54.00 (ISBN 0-8155-0802-6). Noyes.
Graham, Robin & Gill, Derek. The Boy Who Sailed Round the World Alone. 192p. 1985. 8.95 (ISBN 0-8499-0477-3, 0477-3). Word Bks.
Graham, Robin & Roy, Ronald. Slipper Orchids: The Art of Digby Graham. (Illus.). 128p. 1982. 39.95 (ISBN 0-589-01387-4, Pub. by Reed Pub). David & Charles.
Graham, Robin L. & Gill, Derek. Dove. LC 73-181623. (Illus.). 192p. 1972. 14.95i (ISBN 0-06-011603-X, HarpT). Har-Row.
--Home Is the Sailor. LC 82-48835. (Illus.). 224p. 1983. 13.41 (ISBN 0-06-015154-4, HarpT). Har-Row.
Graham, Robin L. & Gill, L. T. Dove. (Illus.). (gr. 6 up). 1978. pap. 3.50 (ISBN 0-553-25485-5). Bantam.
Graham, Roger. Practical Pascal for Microcomputers. LC 83-10213. 230p. 1984. pap. 14.95 (ISBN 0-471-88234-8, Pub. by Wiley Pr). Wiley.
Graham, Ronald. The Aluminum Industry & the Third World. 288p. 1983. pap. 12.50x (ISBN 0-86232-057-7, Pub. by Zed Pr England). Biblio Dist.
Graham, Ronald, et al. Ramsey Theory. LC 80-14110. (Wiley-Interscience Series in Discrete Mathematics). 174p. 1980. 34.50x (ISBN 0-471-05997-8, Pub. by Wiley Interscience). Wiley.
Graham, Ronald L. Rudiments of Ramsey Theory. LC 80-29667. (CBMS Ser.: No. 45). 1983. pap. 8.00 (ISBN 0-8218-1696-9). Am Math.
Graham, Roy E. Ellen G. White: Co-Founder of the Seventh-Day Adventist Church. (American University Studies in Theology & Religion: No. VII, Vol. 12). 507p. 1986. text ed. 39.00 (ISBN 0-8204-0255-9). P Lang Pubs.
Graham, Russell W., et al. Taphonomy & Paleoecology of the Christensen Bog Mastodon Bone Bed, Hancock County, Indiana. (Reports of Investigations Ser.: No. 38). (Illus.). 29p. (Orig.). 1983. pap. 4.00 (ISBN 0-89792-097-X). Ill St Museum.
Graham, Ruth B. It's My Turn. (Illus.). 192p. 1982. 12.95 (ISBN 0-8007-1274-9). Revell.
--Navidad en Nuestra Familia. Gama, Roberto, tr. from Eng. Orig. Title: Our Christmas Story. 128p. (Orig., Span.). pap. 5.25 (ISBN 0-311-08225-4). Casa Bautista.
--Sitting by My Laughing Fire. LC 77-75457. 1977. 10.95 (ISBN 0-8499-2933-4). Word Bks.
Graham, Ruth M. The Cytologic Diagnosis of Cancer. 3rd ed. LC 70-176206. pap. 121.50 (ISBN 0-317-07914-X, 2011495). Bks Demand UMI.
Graham, S. Graham on Bread. 1983. pap. 3.95x (ISBN 0-686-76735-7). B of A.
Graham, S., ed. see Sologub, Fiodor K.
Graham, S. D. The Lyric Poetry of A. K. Tolstoi. (Studies in Slavic Literature & Poetics: Vol. VII). 221p. 1985. pap. text ed. 23.50x (ISBN 0-317-17974-8, Pub. by Rodopi Holland). Humanities.
Graham, Sally. Working Your Way Through WordStar. (gr. 9-12). 1985. tutorial text 4.95 (ISBN 0-538-23101-7, W10). SW Pub.
Graham, Sam D., Jr., ed. Urologic Oncology. 1985. text ed. price not set (ISBN 0-88167-144-4). Raven.
Graham, Samuel R., jt. auth. see Barron, Michael M.
Graham, Scarlett G., jt. auth. see Graham, George J., Jr.
Graham, Sharon K. One Thousand & One Tips for Successful Gardening: Easy Ways to Grow the Best Vegetables, Fruits, Herbs, Flowers & Houseplants. 160p. 1983. 7.95 (ISBN 0-525-93278-X, 0772-230). Dutton.
Graham, Sheila Y. Harbrace College Workbook, Form 9A. 337p. 1982. pap. text ed. 9.95 (ISBN 0-15-531841-1, HC); instructors key avail. (ISBN 0-15-531842-X). HarBraceJ.
--Harbrace College Workbook: Form 9B. 353p. 1984. pap. text ed. 9.95 (ISBN 0-15-531843-8, HC); instr's ed. avail. (ISBN 0-15-531844-6). HarBraceJ.
--HarBrace College Workbook: Form 9C, Writing for the World of Work. 339p. 1982. pap. text ed. 9.95 (ISBN 0-15-531845-4, HC); instr's edition avail. (ISBN 0-15-531846-2); tests avail. (ISBN 0-15-531839-X). HarBraceJ.
--Sentencecraft. (Illus.). 128p. 1976. pap. text ed. 11.95 (ISBN 0-13-806224-2). P-H.
--Writingcraft: The Paragraphs & the Essays. (Illus.). 192p. 1976. pap. text ed. 11.95x (ISBN 0-13-970152-4). P-H.
Graham, Shelia. Hollywood Revisited: A Fiftieth Anniversary Celebration. (Illus.). 256p. 1985. 15.95 (ISBN 0-312-38844-6). St Martin.
Graham, Shirley. Paul Robeson, Citizen of the World. LC 75-152393. Repr. of 1946 ed. 27.50x (ISBN 0-8371-6055-3, GRR&). Greenwood.
Graham, Sidney W. & Vaaler, Jeffrey D., eds. Topics in Analytic Number Theory. 352p. 1985. text ed. 35.00x (ISBN 0-292-75530-9). U of Tex Pr.
Graham, Stephen. Alexander of Yugoslavia: The Story of the King Who Was Murdered at Marseilles. LC 73-122414. (Illus.). 329p. 1972. Repr. of 1939 ed. 22.00 (ISBN 0-208-01082-3, Archon). Shoe String.
--Boris Godunof. (Illus.). ix, 290p. 1970. Repr. of 1933 ed. 19.50 (ISBN 0-208-00969-8, Archon). Shoe String.
--Children of the Slaves. (Basic Afro-American Reprint Library). 1970. Repr. of 1920 ed. 16.00 (ISBN 0-384-19620-9). Johnson Repr.
--The Death of Yesterday. 1973. Repr. of 1930 ed. 25.00 (ISBN 0-8274-0209-0). R West.
--Great American Short Stories. 1979. Repr. of 1931 ed. lib. bdg. 22.50 (ISBN 0-8495-2019-3). Arden Lib.
--Great Russian Short Stories. 1979. Repr. of 1959 ed. lib. bdg. 35.00 (ISBN 0-8495-2020-7). Arden Lib.
--Peter the Great: A Life of Peter I of Russia. LC 75-138241. (Illus.). 1971. Repr. of 1950 ed. lib. bdg. 39.75x (ISBN 0-8371-5598-3, GRPG). Greenwood.
--Soul of John Brown. LC 70-109915. Repr. of 1920 ed. 25.00 (ISBN 0-404-00162-9). AMS Pr.
--Stalin. LC 73-112803. 1970. Repr. of 1931 ed. 17.50x (ISBN 0-8046-1070-3, Pub. by Kennikat). Assoc Faculty Pr.
--Tramping with a Poet in the Rockies. 1973. Repr. of 1922 ed. 40.00 (ISBN 0-8274-1569-9). R West.
--Tsar of Freedom: The Life & Reign of Alexander Second. (Illus.). xii, 324p. 1968. Repr. of 1935 ed. 21.00 (ISBN 0-208-00067-4, Archon). Shoe String.
--With Poor Immigrants to America. LC 73-13133. (Foreign Travelers in America, 1810-1935 Ser.). 366p. 1974. Repr. 26.50x (ISBN 0-405-05455-6). Ayer Co Pubs.
Graham, Stephen, ed. see Romanov, Panteleimon S.
Graham, Stephen, ed. see Teternikov, Fedor K.
Graham, Susan. This Land I Love: New Zealand. (Illus.). 1962. 10.00 (ISBN 0-686-00958-4). Wellington.
Graham, Susan M. Idaho Divorce Book. 1979. pap. 17.95 (ISBN 0-932722-02-4). NC Bk Express.
Graham, Sylvester. The Greatest Health Discovery. (Illus.). 241p. pap. 2.95 (ISBN 0-318-12866-7, A-37). Am Nat Hygiene.
--A Lecture to Young Men. LC 73-20625. (Sex, Marriage & Society Ser.). 84p. 1974. Repr. 14.00 (ISBN 0-405-05801-2). Ayer Co Pubs.
Graham, T. The "Interests of Civilization"? Reaction in the United States Against the "Seizure" of the Panama Canal Zone, 1903-1904. (Lund Studies in International History: No. 19). 282p. 1983. text ed. 15.25x (ISBN 91-24-32548-1, Pub. by Almqvist & Wiksell Sweden). Humanities.
Graham, T. C., jt. ed. see Livingston, K. C.
Graham, Terry. Let Loose on Mother Goose. LC 81-80248. (Illus.). 96p. (gr. k-1). 1982. pap. text ed. 6.95 (ISBN 0-86530-030-5, IP 30-5). Incentive Pubns.
Graham, Terry, tr. see Nurbakhsh, Javad.
Graham, Terry, tr. see Nurbakhsh, Jawad.
Graham, Terry, et al, trs. see Javad, Nurbakhsh.
Graham, Terry L. Fingerplays & Rhymes for Always & Sometimes. (Illus.). 160p. 1984. pap. text ed. 12.95 (ISBN 0-89334-083-9). Humanics Ltd.
Graham, Terry L., jt. auth. see Knight, Michael E.
Graham, Tether. Fudge Dream Supreme. LC 73-16815. (ps-2). 1975. 6.99 (ISBN 0-87955-109-7); PLB 5.95 (ISBN 0-686-57941-0). O'Hara.
Graham, Thomas. The Awakening of St. Augustine, the Anderson Family & the Oldest City: 1821-1924. LC 84-154673. (Illus.). 289p. 1979. 25.00 (ISBN 0-917553-07-1); pap. 8.95 (ISBN 0-917553-08-X). St Augustine Hist.
--Impact of Tokyo Round Agreements on U. S. Export Competitiveness, No. 10. LC 80-67709. (Significant Issues Ser.: Vol. II). 80p. 1980. 5.95 (ISBN 0-89206-024-7). CSI Studies.
Graham, Thomas, intro. by see Sewall, Rufus K.
Graham, Thomas F. Parallel Profiles. 4.95 (ISBN 0-8199-0082-6, L38621). Franciscan Herald.
Graham, Thomas F., jt. auth. see Crow, Lester D.
Graham, Thomas R., jt. ed. see Rubin, Seymour J.
Graham, Tim. On the Royal Road: A Decade of Photographing the Royal Family. (Illus.). 160p. 1984. 19.45 (ISBN 0-316-32300-4). Little.
--Royal Review. 1985. pap. 8.95 (ISBN 0-03-000133-1, Owl Bks). HR&W.
--The Royal Year. 1983. pap. 7.95 (ISBN 0-03-064168-3). HR&W.
Graham, Timothy R., jt. auth. see Jander, Klaus H.
Graham, Tom M. Biology Laboratory Manual for the Nonscience Major I. 2nd ed. 1978. pap. text ed. 10.95 (ISBN 0-8403-1137-0). Kendall-Hunt.
--Biology: The Essential Principles. LC 81-53071. 736p. 1982. text ed. 33.95x (ISBN 0-03-057838-8). SCP.
Graham, Virginia L. & Tulcea, C. Ionescu. Casino Gambling. 1984. pap. 2.95 (ISBN 0-671-50759-1). PB.
Graham, W. English Political Philosophy from Hobbes to Maine. 59.95 (ISBN 0-8490-0115-3). Gordon Pr.
Graham, W. A. see Carroll, John M.
Graham, W. S. Selected Poems. LC 80-11534. 128p. 1980. 12.95 (ISBN 0-912946-73-3). Ecco Pr.
--Selected Poems. Halpern, Daniel, ed. LC 80-11534. 112p. 1981. pap. 6.95 (ISBN 0-912946-74-1). Ecco Pr.
Graham, Walter. The Reader's Browning. 486p. 1980. Repr. lib. bdg. 30.00 (ISBN 0-8492-4984-8). R West.
--The Reader's Browning: Selected Poems. 1934. ltd. ed. 30.00 (ISBN 0-8482-4217-3). Norwood Edns.
--Tory Criticism in the Quarterly Review, 1809 - 1853. LC 77-110570. 1970. Repr. of 1921 ed. 11.50 (ISBN 0-404-02889-6). AMS Pr.
Graham, Walter B., jt. auth. see Abbott, David P.
Graham, Walter J. The Beginnings of English Literary Periodicals, 1665-1715. LC 74-159190. ix, 92p. 1971. Repr. of 1926 ed. lib. bdg. 13.00x (ISBN 0-374-93229-8). Octagon.
--English Literary Periodicals. 1967. lib. bdg. 27.50x (ISBN 0-374-93230-1). Octagon.
Graham, Walter W. & Rowan, William H. Plane Analytic Geometry. (Quality Paperback Ser.: No. 47). 169p. (Orig.). 1968. pap. 3.50 (ISBN 0-8226-0047-1). Littlefield.
Graham, William. English Political Philosophy from Hobbes to Maine. (Research & Source Works Ser: No. 741). 1971. Repr. of 1899 ed. lib. bdg. 23.50 (ISBN 0-8337-1404-X). B Franklin.
--Last Links with Byron, Shelley & Keats. LC 72-196918. 1898. lib. bdg. 15.00 (ISBN 0-8414-4666-0). Folcroft.
--Socialism: New & Old. (The International Scientific Ser.). 1979. Repr. of 1891 ed. lib. bdg. 40.00 (ISBN 0-8495-2030-4). Arden Lib.
Graham, William A. Divine Word & Prophetic Word in Early Islam: A Reconsideration of the Sources, with Special Reference to the Divine Saying or Hadith Qudsi. (Religion & Society Ser.). 1977. text ed. 28.40x (ISBN 90-279-7612-0). Mouton.
Graham, William C., jt. ed. see Sprengling, Martin.
Graham, William H. What Is a Woman. 2nd ed. (Illus.). 1967. 12.50 (ISBN 0-910550-16-6). Elysium.
Graham, William P., III, jt. ed. see Kilgore, Eugene S., Jr.
Graham, William T. The Lament for the South: Yu Hsin's Ai Chiang Nan Fu. LC 79-50503. (Cambridge Studies in Chinese History, Literature & Institutions). 1980. 39.50 (ISBN 0-521-22713-5). Cambridge U Pr.
Graham, Winifred. The Vegetarian Treasure Chest. Fraser, Lisa, ed. 224p. 1983. pap. 6.95 (ISBN 0-930356-33-0). Quicksilver Prod.
Graham, Winston. The Black Moon, 2 vols. (Reader's Request Ser.). 1979. Set. lib. bdg. 18.95 (ISBN 0-8161-6680-3, Large Print Bks). G K Hall.
--Demelza, 2 vols. (Reader's Request Ser.). 1979. Set. lib. bdg. 17.95 (ISBN 0-8161-6677-3, Large Print Bks). G K Hall.
--Jeremy Poldark. (Reader's Request Ser.). 1979. lib. bdg. 14.95 (ISBN 0-8161-6678-1, Large Print Bks). G K Hall.
--Loving Cup: The Tenth Poldark Novel. LC 85-4362. 456p. 1985. 17.95 (ISBN 0-385-19834-5). Doubleday.
--Merciless Ladies. (General Ser.). 1980. lib. bdg. 14.95 (ISBN 0-8161-3119-8, Large Print Bks). G K Hall.
--Poldark's Cornwall. (Illus.). 224p. 1983. 21.95 (ISBN 0-370-30518-3, Pub. by the Bodley Head). Merrimack Pub Cir.
--Poldark's Cornwall. (Illus.). 224p. 1985. pap. 10.95 (ISBN 0-370-30678-3, Pub. by the Boadley Head). Merrimack Pub Cir.
--Ross Poldark, 2 vols. (Reader's Request Ser.). 1979. lib. bdg. 16.95 (ISBN 0-8161-6676-5, Large Print Bks). G K Hall.
--Warleggan. (Poldark Ser.: No. 4). 1977. pap. 2.25 (ISBN 0-345-26003-1). Ballantine.
--Warleggan, 2 vols. (Reader's Request Ser.). 1979. Set. lib. bdg. 17.95 (ISBN 0-8161-6679-X, Large Print Bks). G K Hall.
Graham-Barber, Lynda. The Kit Furniture Book. (Illus.). 1982. pap. 9.95 (ISBN 0-394-70674-9). Pantheon.
--Round Fish, Flatfish & Other Animal Changes. 48p. (gr. 5-8). 1982. 1.98 (ISBN 0-517-54631-0). Crown.
Graham-Brown, Sarah. Palestinians & Their Society. (Illus.). 192p. 1981. 25.00 (ISBN 0-7043-2225-0, Pub. by Quartet England); pap. 14.95 (ISBN 0-7043-3343-0). Charles River Bks.
Graham-Bryce, I., jt. auth. see Hartley, G. S.
Graham-Bryce, I. J., jt. ed. see Fowden, L.
Graham-Bryce, I. J., ed. see Hartley, G. S.
Graham-Cameron, M. The Farmer. (Cambridge Dinosaur Information Ser.). (Illus.). 26p. (gr. 7-10). 1983. pap. 1.95 (ISBN 0-521-27162-2). Cambridge U Pr.
Grahame, A., jt. ed. see Shoham, S. G.
Grahame, Anthony see Shoham, S. Giora.
Grahame, George. The Life & Art of Claude Lorrain. (Illus.). 117p. 1984. 87.45x (ISBN 0-86650-107-X). Gloucester Art.
Grahame, James. The History of the U. S. of North America: From the Plantation of the British Colonies till Their Assumption of National Independence, 2 vols. 2nd facsimile ed. LC 74-152985. (Select Bibliographies Reprint Ser). Repr. of 1845 ed. Set. 66.00 (ISBN 0-8369-5737-7). Ayer Co Pubs.
Grahame, Kenneth. Adventures in the Wild Wood. LC 81-16417. (The Wind in the Willows Ser.). (Illus.). 32p. (gr. 2-5). 1982. PLB 9.79 (ISBN 0-89375-638-5); pap. text ed. 2.50 (ISBN 0-89375-639-3). Troll Assocs.
--The Adventures of Mole, Rat & Toad. LC 81-16422. (The Wind in the Willows Ser.). (Illus.). 32p. (gr. 2-5). 1982. PLB 9.79 (ISBN 0-89375-636-9); pap. text ed. 2.50 (ISBN 0-89375-637-7). Troll Assocs.
--The Battle at Toad Hall. LC 81-16407. (The Wind in the Willows Ser.). (Illus.). 32p. (gr. 2-5). 1982. PLB 9.79 (ISBN 0-89375-642-3); pap. text ed. 2.50 (ISBN 0-89375-643-1). Troll Assocs.
--Dream Days. (Illus.). 1975. pap. 4.95 (ISBN 0-380-00288-4, 23994, Equinox). Avon.
--Dream Days. (gr. 4 up). 1985. 14.95 (ISBN 0-8253-0281-1). Beaufort Bks NY.
--Dream Days. 275p. Repr. of 1899 ed. lib. bdg. 25.00 (ISBN 0-89760-258-7). Telegraph Bks.
--The Golden Age. (Illus.). 1975. pap. 4.95 (ISBN 0-380-00289-2, 23986). Avon.
--The Golden Age. 241p. Repr. of 1898 ed. lib. bdg. 25.00 (ISBN 0-89760-257-9). Telegraph Bks.
--The Golden Age. (Illus.). 288p. (gr. 4 up). 1985. Repr. of 1898 ed. 14.95 (ISBN 0-8253-0331-1). Beaufort Bks NY.
--Mole's Christmas: Or Home Sweet Home. LC 82-12333. (Illus.). 32p. (gr. k-3). 1983. 10.95 (ISBN 0-13-599738-0). P-H.
--More Adventures with Mr. Toad. LC 81-16412. (The Wind in the Willows Ser.). (Illus.). 32p. (gr. 2-5). 1982. PLB 9.79 (ISBN 0-89375-640-7); pap. text ed. 2.50 (ISBN 0-89375-641-5). Troll Assocs.
--The Open Road. LC 79-22614. (Illus.). 32p. (gr. 1 up). 1980. 9.95 (ISBN 0-684-16471-X, ScribJ). Scribner.
--Pagan Papers. LC 72-3427. (Essay Index Reprint Ser.). Repr. of 1898 ed. 15.00 (ISBN 0-8369-2903-9). Ayer Co Pubs.
--The Penguin Kenneth Grahame. 320p. (Orig.). 1984. pap. 6.95 (ISBN 0-14-006856-2). Penguin.
--Reluctant Dragon. (Illus.). 58p. (gr. 3-6). 1953. 6.95 (ISBN 0-8234-0093-X). Holiday.

--The Reluctant Dragon. LC 83-209. (Illus.). 48p. (gr. 1-4). 1983. 11.50 (ISBN 0-03-064031-8). HR&W.

--Wayfarers All: From the Wind in the Willows. (Encore Edition). (Illus.). 32p. (gr. 1 up). 1981. 2.98 (ISBN 0-684-16876-6, ScribJ). Scribner.

--Wind in the Willows. (Illus.). (gr. 2-6). 1967. pap. 1.50 (ISBN 0-448-17188-0, Pub. by Tempo). Ace Bks.

--Wind in the Willows. (Classics Ser). (gr. 4 up). pap. 1.25 (ISBN 0-8049-0105-8, CL-105). Airmont.

--The Wind in the Willows. 253p. Repr. of 1908 ed. lib. bdg. 15.95x (ISBN 0-88411-877-0, Pub. by Aeonian Pr). Amereon Ltd.

--Wind in the Willows. 234p. 1981. Repr. lib. bdg. 14.95x (ISBN 0-89966-305-2). Buccaneer Bks.

--Wind in the Willows. (Illus.). deluxe ed. 10.95 (ISBN 0-448-06028-0, G&D); Companion lib. ed. o.p. 2.95 (ISBN 0-448-05481-7). Putnam Pub Group.

--The Wind in the Willows. LC 80-197. (Illus.). 216p. (gr. 2-7). 1980. 17.95 (ISBN 0-03-056294-5). HR&W.

--Wind in the Willows. (Illus.). 240p. (Orig.). (RL 4). 1969. pap. 1.95 (ISBN 0-451-51733-4, CJ1733, Sig Classics). NAL.

--Wind in the Willows. 75th ed. (Anniversary Edition). (Illus.). (gr. 4 up). 1933. reinforced bdg. 17.95 (ISBN 0-684-17957-1, ScribJ); reg. ed. 12.95 (ISBN 0-684-12819-5); pap. 6.95 (ISBN 0-684-71788-3, SL66, ScribJ); pap. 3.95 rack size (ISBN 0-684-18025-1). Scribner.

--The Wind in the Willows. (Bantam Classics Ser.). (Illus.). 256p. (gr. 4-12). 1982. pap. 1.95 (ISBN 0-553-21129-3). Bantam.

--The Wind in the Willows. (Illus.). 240p. (gr. 1 up). 1983. 15.75 (ISBN 0-670-77120-1). Viking.

--The Wind in the Willows. Green, Peter, ed. (The World's Classics Ser.). (YA) 1983. pap. 2.50 (ISBN 0-19-281640-3). Oxford U Pr.

--The Wind in the Willows. LC 83-11573. (Illus.). 256p. (gr. 5 up). 1983. PLB 17.95 (ISBN 0-684-17957-1). Scribner.

--The Wind in the Willows. (Puffin Story Bks.). 240p. 1984. pap. 2.50 (ISBN 0-14-031544-6, Puffin). Penguin.

--The Wind in the Willows. LC 85-13538. (Illus.). 224p. (gr. 2 up). 1985. 12.95 (ISBN 0-915361-32-9). Adama Pubs Inc.

--The Wind in the Willows. (Illus.). 256p. pap. 2.95 (ISBN 0-440-49555-5, YB). Dell.

--The Wind in the Willows Coloring Book. 64p. 1976. pap. 2.50 (ISBN 0-486-23292-1). Dover.

--The Wind in the Willows Pop-up-Book. LC 83-80060. (Illus.). 12p. (gr. k-4). 1983. 11.95 (ISBN 0-03-063862-3). HR&W.

Grahame, R. Low Back Pain, Vol. 1. Horrobin, D. F., ed. (Annual Research Reviews Ser.). 1980. 18.00 (ISBN 0-88831-068-4). Eden Pr.

Grahame, R. & Anderson, J. A. Low Back Pain, Vol. 2. (Annual Research Reviews). 83p. 1981. 14.00 (ISBN 0-88831-095-1). Eden Pr.

Grahame, R. B. Cunningham see Cunningham Grahame, R. B. & Cunningham, B.

Grahame, Simon. Anatomie of Humors. (Bannatyne Club, Edinburgh. Publications: No. 36). Repr. of 1830 ed. 17.50 (ISBN 0-404-52742-6). AMS Pr.

Grahame-Smith. Clinical Psychopharmacology, Pt. 2. (Psychopharmacology Ser.: Vol. 2, Pt. 2). Date not set. write for info. Elsevier.

Grahame-Smith, D. G. & Aronson, J. K. Oxford Textbook of Clinical Pharmacology & Drug Therapy. (Illus.). 1984. 42.50x (ISBN 0-19-261492-4); pap. 26.95x (ISBN 0-19-261172-0). Oxford U Pr.

Grahame-Smith, D. G. & Cowen, P. J. Preclinical Psychopharmacology, Pt. 1. (Psychopharmacology Ser.: Vol. 2). Date not set. write for info. (ISBN 0-444-90350-X). Elsevier.

Grahame-Smith, D. G. & Hippius, H., eds. Psychopharmacology, Vol. 1. 935p. 1983. Part 1: Basic Preclinical Neuropharmacology. 93.75 (ISBN 0-444-90240-6, Excerpta Medica); Part 2: Clinical Psychopharmacology. 93.50 (ISBN 0-444-90282-1); 166.00 set (ISBN 0-444-90294-5). Elsevier.

Grahame-White, G. K., ed. see Horner, J. G.

Graham-Jones, Oliver. First Catch Your Tiger. LC 72-8320. 1973. 7.95 (ISBN 0-8008-2739-2). Taplinger.

Graham-Jones, Susanna, tr. see Goldoni, Carolo.

Graham-Lujan, James, tr. see Garcia Lorca, Federico.

Graham-Lujan, James, tr. see Lorca, Federico Garcia.

Graham-Moore, Brian & Ross, Timothy. Productivity Gainsharing: How Employee Incentive Programs Can Improve Business Performance. (Illus.). 173p. 1983. 18.95 (ISBN 0-13-725051-7); pap. 9.95 (ISBN 0-13-725044-4). P-H.

Graham-Mulhall, Sara. Opium the Demon Flower. Grob, Gerald N., ed. LC 80-1229. (Addiction in America Ser.). 1981. Repr. of 1926 ed. lib. bdg. 28.00x (ISBN 0-405-13587-4). Ayer Co Pubs.

Graham-Pole, John, ed. Non-Hodgkin's Lymphomas in Children. LC 80-81990. (Masson Monographs in Pediatric Hematology - Oncology: Vol. 2). (Illus.). 192p. 1980. 32.50x (ISBN 0-89352-068-3). Masson Pub.

Graham-Walker, Ross, jt. auth. see Anthony, Robert N.

Graham-White, Anthony. The Drama of Black Africa. 220p. 1925. 9.95 (ISBN 0-573-69024-3). French.

Graham-Yooll, Andrew. A Matter of Fear: Portrait of an Argentinian Exile. 136p. 1982. 12.95 (ISBN 0-88208-144-6); pap. 7.95 (ISBN 0-88208-145-4). Lawrence Hill.

Grahan, Frank. Hattie. (Illus.). 80p. cancelled (ISBN 0-89962-269-0). Todd & Honeywell.

Grahl, Bart, ed. see International Telos Conference, 1st, Waterloo, Ont., Oct. 8-11, 1970.

Grahl, Bart, tr. see Goldmann, Lucien.

Grahl, Wolfgang de. The Parrot Family. LC 83-17940. (Illus.). 176p. 1984. 12.95 (ISBN 0-668-06039-5). Arco.

Grahl, Wolfgang de see De Grahl, Wolfgang.

Grahl-Madsen, Atle. Territorial Asylum. LC 80-10498. (Studies in International Law: Vol. 1). 231p. 1980. lib. bdg. 28.00 (ISBN 0-379-20706-0). Oceana.

Grahl-Madsen, Atle & Toman, Jiri, eds. The Spirit of Uppsala. xviii, 601p. 1984. 79.20x (ISBN 3-11-008822-3). De Gruyter.

Grahm, Marteen D. Silver Sundown. (Orig.). 1982. pap. 3.50 (ISBN 0-440-17806-1). Dell.

Grahm, Milton L., jt. auth. see Szafarz, Henry F.

Grahman, Martin & Furbank, P. N., eds. Twentieth Century Poetry. 464p. 1975. pap. 15.00x (ISBN 0-335-05117-0, Pub. by Open Univ Pr). Taylor & Francis.

Grahn, Judy. Another Mother Tongue: Gay Words, Gay Worlds. LC 83-45953. 324p. 1984. 19.95 (ISBN 0-8070-6716-4, BP701); pap. 9.95 (ISBN 0-8070-6717-2). Beacon Pr.

--The Common Woman Poems. (Illus.). 1974. 1.00 (ISBN 0-88447-017-2). Diana Pr.

--Edward the Dyke. (Illus.). 1971. 2.50 (ISBN 0-88447-018-0). Diana Pr.

--The Highest Apple: Sappho & the Lesbian Poetic Tradition. 180p. (Orig.). 1985. pap. 5.95 (ISBN 0-933216-12-2). Spinsters Ink.

--The Queen of Wands. LC 82-17115. 112p. 1982. 16.95 (ISBN 0-89594-095-7); pap. 6.95 (ISBN 0-89594-094-9). Crossing Pr.

--She Who. LC 77-22333. (Illus.). 1977. pap. 6.00 (ISBN 0-88447-015-6). Diana Pr.

--A Woman Is Talking to Death. (Illus.). 1974. 2.50 (ISBN 0-88447-019-9). Diana Pr.

--The Work of a Common Woman: Collected Poetry (1964-1977) (The Feminist Ser.). 158p. 1984. 16.95 (ISBN 0-89594-156-2); pap. 6.95 (ISBN 0-89594-155-4). Crossing Pr.

Grahn, Judy, ed. Lesbians Speak Out. (Illus.). 1974. pap. 5.00 (ISBN 0-88447-028-8). Diana Pr.

Grahn, Judy, intro. by. True to Life Adventure Stories, Vol. 1. LC 78-16251. 1978. pap. 6.00 (ISBN 0-88447-025-3). Diana Pr.

Grahn, Judy, ed. True to Life Adventure Stories, Vol. 1. (Feminist Ser.). 1983. 15.95 (ISBN 0-89594-110-4); pap. 7.95 (ISBN 0-89594-098-1). Crossing Pr.

--True to Life Adventure Stories, Vol. 2. 224p. 1981. 15.95 (ISBN 0-89594-067-1); pap. 7.95 (ISBN 0-89594-068-X). Crossing Pr.

Grahn, Judy, intro. by. True to Life Adventure Stories, Vol. 2. LC 78-16251. 1980. pap. 6.00 (ISBN 0-88447-026-1). Diana Pr.

--True to Life Adventure Stories, Vol. 3. LC 78-16251. pap. 6.00 (ISBN 0-88447-027-X). Diana Pr.

Grahs, Lillebill & Korlen, Gustav, eds. Theory & Practice of Translation. 356p. 1978. pap. 31.60 (ISBN 3-261-03072-0). P Lang Pubs.

Graindor, Paul. Athens sous Hadrien. LC 72-7892. (Greek History Ser.). (Illus., Fr.). Repr. of 1934 ed. 25.50 (ISBN 0-405-04788-6). Ayer Co Pubs.

--Un Milliardaire Antique: Herode Atticus et sa famille. Finley, Moses, ed. LC 79-4977. (Ancient Economic History Ser.). (Illus., Fr.). 1980. Repr. of 1930 ed. lib. bdg. 23.00x (ISBN 0-405-12364-7). Ayer Co Pubs.

Grainge, Michael, et al. Plant Species Reportedly Possessing Pest-Control Properties: A Database. (East-West Resource Systems Institute RM Ser.: NO. 84-1). vi, 240p. 1984. velobound 20.00 (ISBN 0-86638-057-4). E W Center HI.

Grainger, David A., jt. auth. see Bell, Bruce.

Grainger, Gervais. Four Years with the Boys in Gray. (Facsimile Ser., No. 10). 50p. 1972. 7.50 (ISBN 0-89029-008-3); pap. 5.00 (ISBN 0-89029-008-3). Pr of Morningside.

Grainger, J. H. Character & Style in English Politics. LC 69-10428. pap. 74.80 (ISBN 0-317-09563-3, 2013252). Bks Demand UMI.

Grainger, J. M. & Lynch, J. M., eds. Microbiological Methods for Environmental Biotechnology. (Society for Applied Bacteriology, Technical Ser.: No. 19). 1984. 65.00 (ISBN 0-12-295040-2). ACad Pr.

Grainger, John A. The Flow Turning of Metals. 144p. 1981. 50.00x (ISBN 0-86108-029-7, Pub. by Portcullio Pr). State Mutual Bk.

Grainger, L. Coal: Modern Technology & Economics. 300p. 1980. 33.00x (ISBN 0-86010-213-0, Pub. by Graham & Trotman England). State Mutual Bk.

Grainger, L. & Gibson, J. Coal Utilisation: Technology, Economics & Policy. LC 81-7249. 503p. 1982. 53.95 (ISBN 0-470-27272-4). Halsted Pr.

Grainger, Margaret, ed. The Natural History Prose Writings of John Clare. (Illus.). 1983. 67.00x (ISBN 0-19-818517-0). Oxford U Pr.

Grainger, Percy. A Complete Catalogue of the Works of Percy Grainger. Balough, Teresa, ed. (Music Monograph: Vol. 2). 258p. 1982. pap. 13.50 (ISBN 0-916352-04-8, Pub. by U of W Austral Pr). Intl Spec Bk.

Grainger, Percy & Dreyfus, Kay. The Farthest North of Humanness: Letters of Percy Grainger. (Illus.). 568p. 1985. 39.50 (ISBN 0-918812-44-5). MMB Music.

Grainger, Roger. The Language of the Rite. 192p. 1984. pap. 8.95 (ISBN 0-232-51246-9). Chr Classics.

Grainger, Ronald G., jt. auth. see Verel, David.

Grainger, Ronald G., jt. ed. see Veiga-Pires, J. A.

Grainger, Stuart E. Creative Ropecraft. (Illus.). 1977. 12.95 (ISBN 0-393-08746-8). Norton.

Grainger, Sylvia. How to Make Your Own Moccasins. LC 77-4262. (gr. 5 up). 1977. 9.13i (ISBN 0-397-31754-9); pap. 3.95 (ISBN 0-397-31755-7). Lipp Jr Bks.

Grainville, Jean B. De see De Grainville, Jean B.

Grais, Wafik. Aggregate Demand & Macroeconomic Imbalances in Thailand: Simulations with the SIAM 1 Model. (Working Paper: No. 448). 70p. 1981. 5.00 (ISBN 0-686-36163-6, WP-0448). World Bank.

Grais, Wafik, jt. auth. see Drud, Arne.

Graivier, Pauline, jt. auth. see Hoffman, Gloria.

Grala. Say It in Polish. 1982. 12.00 (ISBN 0-317-18989-1, P557). Vanous.

Grala, M. & Retman, R. Polish, Say It In. 110p. 1982. pap. 12.50x (ISBN 83-01-03922-1, P-557). Vanous.

Gralapp, Leland W. Balinese Painting. (Illus.). pap. 2.50 (ISBN 0-686-15927-6). Taylor Museum.

Graley, A. M. & Nicolls, K. D. Sampling in Surveys of Exchangeable Potassium in Soils. 1980. 20.00x (ISBN 0-643-02486-7, Pub. by CSJRO Australia). State Mutual Bk.

Gralla, Arthur R., ed. see U.S. Naval Academy, Class of 1934.

Gralla, E. J. Scientific Consideration in Monitoring & Evaluating Toxicological Research. 1981. 29.50 (ISBN 0-07-024047-7). McGraw.

Gralla, E. J., ed. Scientific Considerations in Monitoring & Evaluating Toxicological Research. LC 80-21367. (Chemical Industry Institute of Toxicology Ser.). (Illus.). 221p. 1980. text ed. 39.95 (ISBN 0-89116-209-7). Hemisphere Pub.

Gralnick, Alexander, ed. Treatment of the Seriously Ill Psychiatric Patient. 133p. 1985. 30.00x (ISBN 0-8147-2998-3); pap. 11.50x (ISBN 0-8147-2999-1). NYU Pr.

Gralnick, Alexander, jt. ed. see Greenhill, Maurice H.

Gram, Harvey N., jt. auth. see Walsh, Vivian C.

Gram, J., ed. see NATO Advanced Study Institute, Kjeller, Norway, Aug., 1973.

Gram, M. S. & Klemke, E. D., eds. The Ontological Turn: Studies in the Philosophy of Gustav Bergmann. LC 73-78442. 322p. 1974. text ed. 25.00x (ISBN 0-87745-043-9). U of Iowa Pr.

Gram, Moltke. Kant, Ontology & the A Priori. LC 68-29324. pap. 50.50 (ISBN 0-8357-9462-8, 2016708). Bks Demand UMI.

Gram, Moltke S. Direct Realism. 1983. lib. bdg. 34.00 (ISBN 90-247-2870-3, Pub. by Martinus Nijhoff Netherlands). Kluwer Academic.

--The Transcendental Turn: Foundations of Kant's Idealism. LC 84-22047. xii, 260p. 1985. 25.00 (ISBN 0-8130-0787-9). U Presses Fla.

Gram, Moltke S., ed. Interpreting Kant. LC 82-13627. 1982. text ed. 16.00x (ISBN 0-87745-118-4). U of Iowa Pr.

Gram, Per. Chartering Documents. 1981. 44.00 (ISBN 0-907432-03-4). Lloyds London Pr.

Gram, Robert L. An Enemy Disguised. 224p. 1985. 10.95 (ISBN 0-8407-5942-8). Nelson.

Gram, T. E., ed. Extrahepatic Metabolism of Drugs & Other Foreign Compounds. (Monographs in Pharmacology & Physiology: Vol. 5). (Illus.). 470p. 1980. 60.00 (ISBN 0-89335-095-8). SP Med & Sci Bks.

Gram, W. A. see Carroll, John M.

Gramacke, Althea J. From Womb to Tomb. 1985. 8.95 (ISBN 0-8062-2485-1). Carlton.

Gramain, Andre. Topology of Surfaces. Boron, Leo F. & Christenson, Charles O., trs. from Fr. LC 84-70461. (Illus.). 160p. 1984. pap. text ed. 17.95 (ISBN 0-914351-01-X). BCS Assocs.

Gramatky, Hardie. Hercules. (Illus.). (gr. k-3). 1960. PLB 5.99 (ISBN 0-399-60240-2). Putnam Pub Group.

--Little Toot. (Illus.). (gr. k-3). 1959. 8.95 (ISBN 0-399-20144-0, Putnam); PLB 8.99 (ISBN 0-399-60422-7). Putnam Pub Group.

--Little Toot. LC 78-4801. (Illus.). (gr. k-2). 1978. pap. 5.95 (ISBN 0-399-20649-3, Putnam). Putnam Pub Group.

--Little Toot on the Thames. (Illus.). (gr. k-3). 1964. PLB 5.99 (ISBN 0-399-60424-3). Putnam Pub Group.

Grambeau, Rod, jt. auth. see Reznik, John W.

Grambeau, Rodney J., ed. Official National Touch & Flag Football Rules for Men & Women. rev. ed. 1977. soft bdg. 2.00 (ISBN 0-87670-033-4). Athletic Inst.

Grambs, David. Words about Words: A Dictionary of 2000 Words - Old, New, & Surprising - for the Styles, Devices, Defects & Oddities of the Craft of Prose Writing. 432p. 1984. 17.95 (ISBN 0-07-024048-5). McGraw.

Grambs, Jean D. & Carr, John C. Modern Methods in Secondary Education. 4th ed. LC 78-26995. 1979. text ed. 30.95 (ISBN 0-03-022391-1, HoltC). HR&W.

Grambs, Jean D., ed. Teaching About Women in the Social Studies: Concepts, Methods & Materials. LC 75-43431. 1976. pap. 6.95 (ISBN 0-87986-005-7, 498-15254). Nat Coun Soc Studies.

Grambs, Marya & Miller, Pam, eds. Dollars & Sense: A Community Fundraising Manual. 135p. (Orig.). 1983. pap. 18.00 (ISBN 0-912309-00-8). W States Shelter.

--Dollars & Sense: A Community Fundraising Manual. rev. ed. 135p. 1985. pap. 18.00 (ISBN 0-317-19746-0). W States Shelter.

Grambs, Peter H. & Bullock, Charles E., eds. Solar Electricity: Making the Sun Work for You. LC 81-82421. (Illus.). 231p. 1981. pap. 12.95 (ISBN 0-940520-00-1, Pub. by Future Syst Inc). Monegon Ltd.

Grame, Carl A. & O'Donnell, Daniel J. Learning BASIC Programming Essentials. 320p. 1984. pap. text ed. 17.95 (ISBN 0-574-21370-8, 13-4370); TRS 80 6.95 (ISBN 0-574-21372-4, 13-4372); Apple II 6.95 (ISBN 0-574-21374-0, 13-4374); IBM-PC 6.95 (ISBN 0-574-21377-5, 13-4377); instr's guide avail. (ISBN 0-574-21376-7, 13-4376); avail. audio tapes 62.50 (ISBN 0-574-21375-9, 13-4375). SRA.

Gramelsbach, Helen. Seventy-One Creative Bible Story Projects: Patterns for Crafts, Visuals, & Learning Centers. (Illus.). 64p. 1983. pap. 4.50 (ISBN 0-87239-607-X, 2103). Standard Pub.

Gramiak, Raymond, jt. auth. see Nanda, Navin C.

Gramlich, Edward M. Benefit-Cost Analysis of Government Programs. (Illus.). 304p. 1981. text ed. 28.95 (ISBN 0-13-074757-2). P-H.

Gramlich, Edward M. & Koshel, Patricia P. Educational Performance Contracting. LC 75-6592. (Brookings Institution Studies in Social Experimentation). pap. 22.50 (ISBN 0-317-20847-0, 2025381). Bks Demand UMI.

Gramlich, Edward M., jt. auth. see Courant, Paul N.

Gramling, Oliver. A P: Story of News. LC 77-94561. 1969. Repr. of 1940 ed. 39.75x (ISBN 0-8046-0690-0, Pub. by Kennikat). Assoc Faculty Pr.

--The Story of News. 1977. Repr. of 1940 ed. lib. bdg. 25.00 (ISBN 0-686-19826-3). Havertown Bks.

Gramling, Roger M. A Ministry of Hope: Portrait of Arthur J. Moore. LC 79-67099. 112p. (Orig.). 1979. pap. 1.75x (ISBN 0-8358-0395-3). Upper Room.

Gramm, jt. auth. see Graham.

Gramm, Anthony A. Original Stock Market Games for the Stimulation of Major Profits in Wall Street. (Illus.). 117p. 1984. 77.25x (ISBN 0-86654-107-1). Inst Econ Finan.

Gramm, Phil. The Role of Government in a Free Society: A Collection of Speeches & Articles. LC 82-70597. 150p. 1982. text ed. 11.95 (ISBN 0-933028-19-9); pap. text ed. 7.95 (ISBN 0-933028-20-2). Fisher Inst.

Gramm, R. J. The Energy Boom. (Illus.). 1976. pap. 10.00 (ISBN 0-918826-02-0). Time-Wise.

Gramm, W. Phillip see Anders, Gerhard, et al.

Gramm, William J. How to Select the Leaders in a Bull & in a Bear Market. (Illus.). 109p. 1983. 137.75x (ISBN 0-86654-094-6). Inst Econ Finan.

Grammage, Grady. Mission & Mediterranean Revival Railroad Stations. (RSHS Monograph: No. 4). (Illus.). 1973. softcover 3.00 (ISBN 0-685-60077-7). J-B Pub.

Grammel, Richard, ed. see International Union of Theoretical & Applied Mechanics Colloquium, Madrid, 1955.

Grammer, Norma R. & Mullins, Marion D. Marriage Record of Washington County, Tennessee, 1787-1840. LC 73-8035. 68p. 1981. pap. 5.00 (ISBN 0-8063-0564-9). Genealog Pub.

Gramophone Shop Inc. - New York. Gramophone Shop Encyclopedia of Recorded Music. Reid, Robert H., ed. Repr. of 1948 ed. lib. bdg. 33.75x (ISBN 0-8371-3718-7, GRSE). Greenwood.

Grampp, William D. The Manchester School of Economics. 1960. write for info. iniv. microfilm (ISBN 0-8047-0020-6). Stanford U Pr.

Grams, Betty J. Families Can Be Happy. LC 81-82420. 128p. (Orig.). 1981. pap. 2.50 (ISBN 0-88243-759-3, 02-0759); tchr's ed 3.95 (ISBN 0-88243-334-2, 02-0334). Gospel Pub.

--Women of Grace. LC 77-93409. 128p. 1978. pap. 1.95 (ISBN 0-88243-751-8, 02-0751, Radiant Books); teacher's ed 2.50 (ISBN 0-88243-336-9, 02-0336). Gospel Pub.

Grams, Marilyn. Breastfeeding Success for Working Mothers. LC 85-71326. (Illus.). 160p. 1985. 18.95 (ISBN 0-932707-13-0); pap. 15.00 (ISBN 0-932707-14-9). Achievement Pr.

--How to Make Money Writing with Your Macintosh & Get Published Instantly with a Laser Printer. LC 85-71821. (Illus.). 192p. 1985. pap. 14.95 (ISBN 0-932707-15-7). Achievement Pr.

Grams, Ralph R. Medical Information Systems: The Laboratory Module. LC 78-71496. (Illus.). 430p. 1979. 59.50 (ISBN 0-89603-004-0). Humana.

Grams, Ralph Raymond. Problem Solving, Systems Analysis, & Medicine. (Illus.). 244p. 1972. Set. 31.00x (ISBN 0-398-02298-4); companion volume - Systems Analysis wkbk. incl. (ISBN 0-398-02566-5). C C Thomas.

Gramsci, Antonio. Antonio Gramsci: Selections from Political Writings 1921-1926. 1978. pap. 19.95x (ISBN 0-8464-0140-1). Beekman Pubs.

--Antonio Gramsci: Selections from Political Writings, 1910-1920. LC 76-54252. 415p. 1977. 13.50 (ISBN 0-7178-0485-2). Intl Pubs Co.

--Antonio Gramsci: Selections from Political Writings, 1921-26. 560p. 1978. pap. 6.95 (ISBN 0-7178-0555-7). Intl Pubs Co.

--The Modern Prince & Other Writings. LC 67-25646. 192p. 1959. pap. 2.95 (ISBN 0-7178-0133-0). Intl Pubs Co.

--Prison Notebooks: Selections. Hoare, Quintin & Smith, Geoffrey N., trs. from It. LC 73-77646. 572p. 1971. 13.50 (ISBN 0-7178-0270-1); pap. 6.50 (ISBN 0-7178-0397-X). Intl Pubs Co.

--Selections from Cultural Writings. Forgacs, David & Nowell-Smith, Geoffrey, eds. Boelhower, William, tr. from Ital. 464p. 1985. text ed. 20.00x (ISBN 0-674-79985-2). Harvard U Pr.

Gran, Claurene du see Ugrann, Claurene.

Gran, Eldon. Knots for a Bored of Education: Ways to Individualize Your Basic Program. LC 77-81460. (Mandala Ser. in Education). (Illus.). 150p. 1977. pap. 8.95 (ISBN 0-916250-22-9). Irvington.

Gran, Guy. Development by People: Citizen Construction of a Just World. LC 82-22442. 506p. 1983. 36.95 (ISBN 0-03-063294-3); pap. 13.95 (ISBN 0-03-063296-X). Praeger.

--Zaire: The Political Economy of Underdevelopment. LC 79-19512. (Praeger Special Studies). 352p. 1979. 39.95 (ISBN 0-03-048916-4). Praeger.

Gran, Joseph A. Fanny Burney: An Annotated Bibliography. LC 80-9022. (British Literature Catalogue Ser.). 190p. 1981. lib. bdg. 36.00 (ISBN 0-8240-9325-9). Garland Pub.

Gran, Peter. Islamic Roots of Capitalism: Egypt, 1760-1840. (Modern Middle East Ser: No. 4). 296p. 1979. text ed. 25.00x (ISBN 0-292-70333-3). U of Tex Pr.

Grana, ed. Update in Arthoscopic Techniques. (Illus.). 128p. 1984. text ed. 40.00 (ISBN 0-8391-2001-X, 21016). Univ Park.

Grana, Janice, ed. Images: Women in Transition. LC 75-46441. 1977. pap. 4.95 (ISBN 0-88489-092-9). St Mary's.

Grana, Janice T. Images: Women in Transition. LC 75-46441. 1976. pap. 5.50 (ISBN 0-8358-0343-0). Upper Room.

Granacher, Robert P., jt. auth. see Mason, Aaron S.

Granade, Charles, jt. ed. see Conley, Diane.

Granade, Charles, jt. ed. see Goldstein, Amy J.

Granata, Fred A. Real Estate Buying-Selling Guide for Oregon. 111p. 1980. 3.95 (ISBN 0-88908-809-8). Self Counsel Pr.

Granath, Olle, jt. auth. see Hulten, Pontus.

Granatstein, J. L. & Stevens, Paul, eds. A Reader's Guide to Canadian History, No. 2: Confederation to the Present. 288p. 1982. pap. 9.95 (ISBN 0-8020-6490-6). U of Toronto Pr.

Granbeck, Marilyn. The Fifth Jade of Heaven. 352p. 1982. pap. 2.95 (ISBN 0-515-04628-0). Jove Pubns.

--Finding Your Job Skillbook. LC 66-40358. (Illus.). (gr. 7 up). 1980. write for info. (ISBN 0-912486-39-2); wkbk 3.75. Finney Co.

--Looking Forward to a Career: Metals & Plastics. 2nd ed. LC 74-864. (Looking Forward to a Career Ser.). (Illus.). (gr. 6 up). 1974. PLB 6.95 (ISBN 0-87518-068-X). Dillon.

Granberg, Ron. California Legal Research. 2nd ed. LC 77-89423. (Illus.). 1977. pap. 7.95 (ISBN 0-686-21803-5). R S Granberg.

Granberg-Michaelson, Karin. In the Land of the Living: Health Care & the Church. 1984. pap. 4.95 (ISBN 0-310-27491-5). Zondervan.

Granberg-Michaelson, Wesley. A Wordly Spirituality: The Call to Take Care of the Earth. LC 83-48997. 224p. 1984. 12.45 (ISBN 0-06-063380-8, HarpR). Har-Row.

Granberry, Nola, ed. Crucigramas Biblicos Y Otras Actividades. 80p. (Orig.). 1983. pap. 3.95 (ISBN 0-311-26609-6). Casa Bautista.

Granberry, Nola, tr. see Shely, Patricia.

Granberry, Nola, tr. see Woggon, Guillermo.

Granch, Ladislav. Room of Errors. 1985. 15.95 (ISBN 0-533-06480-5). Vantage.

Grancsay, Stephen V. & Lindsay, Merrill. Illustrated British Firearms Patents 1718-1853. limited ed. LC 77-99750. (Illus.). 450p. 1969. 75.00 (ISBN 0-87691-008-8). Arma Pr.

Grand, Alexander J. De see De Grand, Alexander J.

Grand, Julian Le see Le Grand, Julian & Robinson, Ray.

Grand, Samuel, jt. auth. see Grand, Tamar.

Grand, Sarah. The Beth Book. (A Virago Modern Classics Ser.). 544p. 1981. pap. 7.95 (ISBN 0-385-27180-8, Virago). Doubleday.

--Our Manifold Nature. LC 75-103513. (Short Story Index Reprint Ser.). 1894. 17.00 (ISBN 0-8369-3255-2). Ayer Co Pubs.

Grand, Stanley, jt. ed. see Freedman, Norbert.

Grand, Tamar. Holiday-Craft Kit for the Jewish Child. (Illus.). (ps). 1976. pap. text ed. 5.00 (ISBN 0-8074-0138-2, 103901). UAHC.

Grand, Tamar & Grand, Samuel. Children of Israel. (gr. 3-4). 1972. text ed. 5.50 (ISBN 0-8074-0131-5, 121320); tchr's guide 2.25 (ISBN 0-8074-0132-3, 201320); fun & act bk. 4.50 (ISBN 0-8074-0133-1, 121322). UAHC.

Granda, A. M. & Hayes, W. N., eds. Neural Mechanisms in Animal Behavior. (Illus.). 1972. 19.25 (ISBN 3-8055-1558-8). S Karger.

Granda, A. M. & Maxwell, J. H., eds. Neural Mechanisms of Behavior in the Pigeon. LC 78-24064. (Illus.). 452p. 1979. 59.50x (ISBN 0-306-40096-0, Plenum Pr). Plenum Pub.

Grandal, Bjorn, ed. Artificial Particles Beams in Space Plasma Studies. LC 82-470. (NATO ASI Series B, Physics: Vol. 79). 722p. 1982. 95.00 (ISBN 0-306-40985-2, Plenum Pr). Plenum Pub.

Grandal, Bjorn & Holtet, Jan A., eds. Dynamical & Chemical Coupling of the Neutral & Ionized Atmosphere. (Nato Advanced Study Institute Ser. C: No. 35). 1977. lib. bdg. 47.50 (ISBN 90-277-0840-1, Pub. by Reidel Holland). Kluwer Academic.

Grandamy, Rene. La Physiocratie: Theorie Generale Du Development Economique. 1973. pap. 8.80x (ISBN 90-2797-202-8). Mouton.

Grandaur, Georg, ed. & tr. Leben Des Abtes Eigil Von Fulda und der Aebtissin Hathumoda Von Gandersheim Nebst der Uebertragung Des Hl. Liborius und Des Hl. Vitus. (Ger). pap. 10.00 (ISBN 0-384-19640-3). Johnson Repr.

Grandaur, Georg, tr. see Genealogia Welforum.

Grandbois, Mildred, ed. Cumulative Index to Nursing & Allied Health Literature, Vol. 22. LC 78-643434. 1977. 70.00 (ISBN 0-910478-13-9). Glendale Advent Med.

--Cumulative Index to Nursing Literature, Vol. 20. LC 62-147. 1975. 60.00 (ISBN 0-910478-11-2). Glendale Advent Med.

--Cumulative Index to Nursing Literature, Vol. 21. LC 62-147. 1976. 60.00 (ISBN 0-910478-12-0). Glendale Advent Med.

Grandbois, Mildred, et al, eds. Cumulative Index to Nursing Literature. Incl. Vols. 1-5, 5 vols. in 1. 1956-1960; Vols. 6-8, 3 vols. in 1. 1961-1963. 40.00 (ISBN 0-910478-01-5); Vols. 9-11, 3 vols. in 1. 1964-1966; Vols. 12-13, 2 vols. in 1. 1967-1968; Vol. 14. 1969. 50.00 (ISBN 0-910478-04-X); Vol. 15. 1970. 50.00 (ISBN 0-910478-06-6); Vol. 16. 1971. 50.00 (ISBN 0-910478-07-4); Vol. 17. 1972. 50.00 (ISBN 0-910478-08-2); Vol. 18. 1973. 60.00 (ISBN 0-910478-09-0); Vol. 19. 1974. 60.00 (ISBN 0-910478-10-4). LC 62-147. Glendale Advent Med.

Grandbouche, John. A Declaration of Financial Independence. LC 84-147602. 214p. (Orig.). 1983. pap. 7.95 (ISBN 0-911805-03-6). S Judd Pubs.

Grande, Charles, Jr., ed. American Film Institute Guide to College Courses in Film & Television. 7th ed. LC 80-81121. 334p. 1980. pap. 11.50 (ISBN 0-87866-158-1). Petersons Guides.

Grande, Hypolite La see La Grande, Hypolite.

Grande, Hyppolite La see La Grande, Hyppolite.

Grandell, J. Doubly Stochastic Poisson Processes. (Lecture Notes in Mathematics: Vol. 529). 1976. soft cover 17.00 (ISBN 0-387-07795-2). Springer-Verlag.

Grandfather Drewsen, jt. auth. see Hans Christian Andersen.

Grandfield, Raymond J., jt. auth. see Gold, Faye.

Grandgent, C. H., ed. see Dante Alighieri.

Grandgent, C. H., jt. ed. see Singleton, Charles S.

Grandgent, Charles H. Dante. LC 73-12876. 1921. lib. bdg. 30.00 (ISBN 0-8414-4420-X). Folcroft.

--Dante Alighieri. 1978. lib. bdg. 30.00 (ISBN 0-8482-0938-9). Norwood Edns.

--From Latin to Italian: An Historical Outline of the Phonology & Morphology of the Italian Language. LC 79-102497. 1971. Repr. of 1927 ed. 11.00x (ISBN 0-8462-1513-6). Russell.

--Getting a Laugh: And Other Essays. facsimile ed. LC 77-128250. (Essay Index Reprint Ser). Repr. of 1924 ed. 16.00 (ISBN 0-8369-2226-3). Ayer Co Pubs.

--New Word. facs. ed. LC 75-121471. (Essay Index Reprint Ser). 1929. 17.00 (ISBN 0-8369-1707-3). Ayer Co Pubs.

--Old & New. facs. ed. LC 79-121472. (Essay Index Reprint Ser). 1920. 17.00 (ISBN 0-8369-1809-6). Ayer Co Pubs.

--Outline of the Phonology & Morphology of Old Provencal. LC 72-1627. Repr. of 1905 ed. 16.25 (ISBN 0-404-08348-X). AMS Pr.

--Prunes & Prism: With Other Odds & Ends. facsimile ed. LC 70-128251. (Essay Index Reprint Ser). Repr. of 1928 ed. 15.00 (ISBN 0-8369-2227-1). Ayer Co Pubs.

Grandidier, Alfred & Grandidier, Guillaume. Ethnographie de Madagascar, 4 vols. LC 77-87499. Repr. of 1928 ed. Set. 250.00 (ISBN 0-404-16720-9). AMS Pr.

Grandidier, Guillaume, jt. auth. see Grandidier, Alfred.

Grandilli, Peter A. Technician's Handbook of Plastics. 272p. 1981. 22.95 (ISBN 0-442-23870-3). Van Nos Reinhold.

--Technician's Handbook of Plastics. 246p. 1981. 23.00 (ISBN 0-686-48117-8, B327). T-C Pubns CA.

Grandin, Thomas. Political Use of the Radio. LC 73-161178. (History of Broadcasting: Radio to Television Ser). 1971. Repr. of 1939 ed. 15.00 (ISBN 0-405-03584-5). Ayer Co Pubs.

Grandine, Jonathan. Problem of Shape in the Prelude: The Conflict of Private & Public Speech. LC 68-54018. (LeBaron Russell Briggs Prize Honors Essays in English Ser.: 1968). (Orig.). 1968. pap. 1.75x (ISBN 0-674-70800-8). Harvard U Pr.

Grandis, Sue L. Instrumentation for Coronary Care. (Techniques of Measurement in Medicine Ser.: No. 5). (Illus.). 150p. 1981. 42.50 (ISBN 0-521-23548-0); pap. 14.95 (ISBN 0-521-28024-9). Cambridge U Pr.

Grandjean, E. & Gilgen, A. Environmental Factors in Urban Planning. 206p. 1976. text ed. 42.50x (ISBN 0-8290-0943-4). Irvington.

Grandjean, E., et al. Environmental Factors in Urban Planning. 220p. 1976. cancelled (ISBN 0-85066-084-X). Taylor & Francis.

Grandjean, Etienne. Ergonomics of the Home. LC 73-13221. (Illus.). 344p. 1973. 32.00x (ISBN 0-85066-067-X). Taylor & Francis.

--Fitting the Task to the Man: An Ergonomic Approach. 3rd ed. LC 79-3855. (Illus.). 379p. (Orig.). 1980. 42.00x (ISBN 0-8002-2225-3); pap. 25.00x (ISBN 0-85066-192-7). Intl Pubns Serv.

--Fitting the Task to the Man: An Ergonomic Approach. 3rd ed. LC 79-3855. 379p. 1980. 42.00x (ISBN 0-8002-2225-3); pap. 25.00x (ISBN 0-85066-192-7). Taylor & Francis.

Grandjean, Etienne, ed. Ergonomics & Health in Modern Offices. LC 84-8470. 510p. 1984. pap. 77.00 (ISBN 0-85066-270-2). Taylor & Francis.

--Sitting Posture. LC 70-23595. (Illus.). 253p. 1970. 33.00x (ISBN 0-85066-029-7). Taylor & Francis.

Grandjean, Etienne & Vigliani, E., eds. Ergonomic Aspects of Visual Display Terminals: Proceedings of the International Workshop, Milan, March 1980. (Illus.). 300p. 1980. 55.00x (ISBN 0-85066-211-7). Taylor & Francis.

Grandjean, Philippe, ed. Biological Effects of Organolead Compounds. 288p. 1984. 84.00 (ISBN 0-8493-5309-2). CRC PR.

Grandjean, Serge, et al. Gold Boxes. (The Waddesdon Catalogues Ser.). (Illus.). 368p. 1985. text ed. 75.00 (ISBN 0-7078-0023-4, Pub. by P Wilson Pubs). Sotheby Pubns.

Grandma, Marian, pseud. Georgie the Jovial Giraffe. LC 85-71331. (Illus.). 32p. (gr. 3 up). 1985. text ed. write for info. (ISBN 0-9614989-0-0). Banmar Inc.

Grandmaison, C. De see De Grandmaison, C.

Grandmont, Jean-Michel. Money & Value: A Reconsideration of Classical & Neoclassical Monetary Economics. LC 82-14763. (Econometric Society Monograph in Pure Theory: No. 5). 240p. 1983. 29.95 (ISBN 0-521-25141-9). Cambridge U Pr.

--Money & Value: A Reconsideration of Classical & Neoclassical Monetary Theories. (Econometric Society Monographs). 240p. Date not set. pap. price not set (ISBN 0-521-31364-3). Cambridge U Pr.

Grandolfo, M. & Micaelson, S. M., Jr., eds. Biological Effects & Dosimetry of Static & Elf Electromagnetic Fields. (Ettore Majorana International Science Series Life Sciences: 19 vols.). 652p. 1985. 97.50x (ISBN 0-306-41923-8, Plenum Pr). Plenum Pub.

Grandolfo, M., et al, eds. Biological Effects & Dosimetry of Nonionizing Radiation: Radiofrequency & Microwave Energies. (NATO ASI Series A, Life Sciences: Vol. 49). 682p. 1982. 89.50x (ISBN 0-306-41017-6, Plenum Pr). Plenum Pub.

Grandon, Ronald E., jt. auth. see Bergin, Edward J.

Grand Orient, pseud. Complete Manual of Occult Divination, 2 vols. 1972. 20.00 set (ISBN 0-8216-0063-X). Univ Bks.

Grandpre, De see De Grandpre.

Grandpre, V. P. Vocabulaire des assurances sur la vie. 14p. 1973. pap. 2.95 (ISBN 0-686-92148-8, M-9230). French & Eur.

Grandsaigne, J. de see De Grandsaigne, J.

Grandsen, James, jt. auth. see Zaloga, Stephen J.

Grandsen, James, jt. auth. see Zaloga, Steven J.

Grandsen, K. W., ed. Tudor Verse Satire. (Renaissance Library). 182p. 1970. pap. 16.95 (ISBN 0-485-12601-X, Pub. by Athlone Pr Ltd). Longwood Pub Group.

Grandsent, C. H. The Ladies of Dante's Lyrics. 59.95 (ISBN 0-8490-0479-9). Gordon Pr.

Grandstaff, Peter J. Interregional Migration in the U.S.S.R. Economic Aspects, 1959 to 1970. LC 78-57233. 192p. 1980. 18.75 (ISBN 0-8223-0413-9). Duke.

Grandstaff, Terry B. Shifting Cultivation in Northern Thailand: Possibilities for Development. (Resource Systems Theory & Methodology Ser.: No. 3). 44p. 1981. pap. 10.00 (ISBN 92-808-0192-9, TUNU120, UNU). Unipub.

Grandville. Bizarreries & Fantasies of Grandville. (Illus.). 11.25 (ISBN 0-8446-5039-0). Peter Smith.

Grandville, J. J. Bizarreries & Fantasies of Grandville. Appelbaum, Stanley, ed. 1974. pap. 6.50 (ISBN 0-486-22991-2). Dover.

--The Court of Flora. LC 80-70276. Orig. Title: Les Fleurs Animees. (Illus.). 120p. 1981. 30.00 (ISBN 0-8076-1014-3); pap. 12.95 (ISBN 0-8076-1006-2). Braziller.

Grandy, D. W., jt. auth. see Petrakis, L.

Grandy, James. Guide to Eastern Rocks & Minerals. (Illus.). 40p. pap. 3.50 (ISBN 0-88839-105-6). Hancock House.

Grandy, Richard E. Advanced Logic for Applications. (Synthese Library: No. 110). 1977. lib. bdg. 31.50 (ISBN 90-277-0781-2, Pub. by Reidel Holland). Kluwer Academic.

--Advanced Logic for Applications. (Pallas Paperbacks: No. 13). 1979. pap. 13.00 (ISBN 90-277-1034-1, Pub. by Reidel Holland). Kluwer Academic.

Grandy, Richard E., ed. Theories & Observation in Science. vii, 184p. 1980. lib. bdg. 24.00x (ISBN 0-917930-39-8); pap. 8.50x (ISBN 0-917930-19-3). Ridgeview.

Grandy, W. T., Jr., jt. ed. see Smith, C. Ray.

Grandy, Walter T., Jr. Introduction to Electrodynamics & Radiation. LC 78-117077. (Pure & Applied Physics Ser). 1970. 35.50 (ISBN 0-12-295250-2). Acad Pr.

Graneau, Peter. Underground Power Transmission: The Science, Technology, & Economics of High Voltage Cables. LC 79-15746. 515p. 1979. 57.95x (ISBN 0-471-05757-6, Pub. by Wiley-Interscience). Wiley.

Granell, Eugenio F. Picasso's "Guernica". The End of a Spanish Era. Kuspit, Donald, ed. LC 81-10508. (Studies in the Fine Arts: Art Theory: No. 4). 242p. 1981. 39.95 (ISBN 0-8357-1206-0). UMI Res Pr.

Granelle, Jean-Jacques. La Valeur du Sol Urbain et la Propriete Fonciere: Le Marche Des Terrains a Paris. (La Recherche Urbain: No. 12). (Illus.). 240p. (Fr.). 1976. pap. text ed. 20.80x (ISBN 90-2797-892-1). Mouton.

Granelli, Roger. Urban Black Housing: A Review of Existing Conditions in the Cape Peninsula with Some Guidelines for Change. (Illus.). 79p. 1977. pap. 10.00x (ISBN 0-8476-2401-3). Rowman.

Granet, Irving. Fluid Mechanics for Engineering Technology. 2nd ed. (Illus.). 416p. 1981. text ed. 28.95 (ISBN 0-13-322610-7). P-H.

--Modern Materials Science. (Illus.). 1980. text ed. 25.95 (ISBN 0-8359-4569-3); solutions manual avail. (ISBN 0-8359-4570-7). Reston.

--Statics & Strength of Materials. 1983. text ed. 31.95 (ISBN 0-03-060309-9). HR&W.

--Strength of Materials for Engineering Technology. 2nd ed. (Illus.). 448p. 1979. 26.95 (ISBN 0-8359-7074-4); solutions manual avail. (ISBN 0-8359-7075-2). Reston.

--Technical Mechanics: Applied Statics & Dynamics. 1984p. text ed. 28.95 (ISBN 0-03-061708-1). HR&W.

--Thermodynamics & Heat Power. 3rd ed. 1985. text ed. 36.95 (ISBN 0-8359-7674-2); instrs'. manual avail. Reston.

Granet, M. Festivals & Songs of Ancient China. lib. bdg. 79.95 (ISBN 0-87968-233-7). Krishna Pr.

Granet, Marcel. Chinese Civilization. LC 74-38068. Repr. of 1930 ed. 31.00 (ISBN 0-404-56974-9). AMS Pr.

--La Pensee Chinoise: Chinese Thought. LC 74-25753. (European Sociology Ser.). 642p. 1975. Repr. 46.50x (ISBN 0-405-06507-8). Ayer Co Pubs.

--The Religion of the Chinese People. Freedman, Maurice, tr. from Fr. 1977. pap. 5.95xi (ISBN 0-06-131905-8, TB 1905, Torch). Har-Row.

Granfield, Patrick, jt. auth. see Dulles, Avery.

Grange Book Company Editorial Board, ed. Poetry Index Annual, 1982. 372p. 1982. 54.99x (ISBN 0-89609-223-2). Granger Bk.

Grange, J. L., ed. Satellite & Computer Communications. 380p. 1984. 51.00 (ISBN 0-444-86730-9, North Holland). Elsevier.

Grange, J. M. Mycobacterial Diseases. (Current Topics in Infection Ser.: Vol. 1). 1981. 37.50 (ISBN 0-444-00625-7, Biomedical Pr). Elsevier.

Grange, J. M., jt. ed. see Collins, D. H.

Grange, Jane Des see Des Grange, Jane.

Grange, Jean-Louis & Gein, M., eds. Flow Control in Computer Networks: Proceedings of International Symposium Held in France, Feb. 1979. 430p. 1979. 64.00 (ISBN 0-444-85297-2, North Holland). Elsevier.

Grange, John. The Golden Aphroditis. LC 37-5556. 1978. Repr. of 1577 ed. 30.00x (ISBN 0-8201-1177-5). Schol Facsimiles.

Grange, Judith K., jt. ed. see Battilega, John A.

Grange, McQuilkin de see De Grange, McQuilkin.

Grange, Roger T. Fort Robinson, Outpost on the Plains. (Nebraska History Magazine Reprints: Vol. 39, No. 3). 241p. 1958. 3.00 (ISBN 0-318-17581-9). Nebraska Hist.

Grange, Roger T., jt. auth. see Heldman, Donald P.

Grange, Roger T., Jr. Archeological Investigations at the Red Willow Reservoir. (Publications in Anthropology: No. 9). (Illus.). 238p. (Orig.). 1980. pap. 10.00 (ISBN 0-686-28124-1). Nebraska Hist.

--Pawnee & Lower Loup Pottery. (Publications in Anthropology: No. 3). 235p. 1968. pap. 6.00 (ISBN 0-686-20020-9). Nebraska Hist.

Grange, S. G. M. The Constitutionality of Federal Intervention in the Marketplace: The Competition, Vol. 7. (HRI Commentary Ser.). 49p. 1975. 2.00 (ISBN 0-88806-011-4). Inst C D Howe.

Grange, William J. Manual for Corporations Officers: The Law, Procedures, & Forms. LC 67-14483. pap. 160.00 (ISBN 0-317-07960-3, 2015846). Bks Demand UMI.

Grange, William J. & Woodbury, Thomas C. Manual of Real Estate Law & Procedures. LC 67-26183. pap. 118.00 (ISBN 0-317-07959-X, 2015841). Bks Demand UMI.

Granger, Alfred H. Charles Follen McKim: A Study of His Life & Work. LC 70-168178. Repr. of 1913 ed. 12.00 (ISBN 0-404-02890-X). AMS Pr.

--Charles Follen McKim: A Study of His Life & Work. LC 79-152623. (Illus.). Repr. of 1913 ed. 15.00 (ISBN 0-405-08570-2, Blom Pubns). Ayer Co Pubs.

Granger, Alix. Trusts & Trust Companies in Canada: What You Need to Know to Avoid Getting Taken. 1st ed. 92p. 1978. 3.95 (ISBN 0-88908-046-1). Self Counsel Pr.

Granger, B. Noice. Health Without Drugs: A Practical Nature Cure. 1975. lib. bdg. 69.95 (ISBN 0-685-51373-4). Revisionist Pr.

Granger, Bill. The British Cross. 1984. pap. 3.50 (ISBN 0-671-52361-9). PB.

--The British Cross: The New "November Man" Novel. 1983. 3.98 (ISBN 0-517-55035-0). Crown.

--The November Man. 1979. pap. 1.95 (ISBN 0-449-14245-0, GM). Fawcett.

--Public Murders. 288p. (Orig.). 1984. pap. 3.50 (ISBN 0-515-08155-8). Jove Pubns.

--Queen's Crossing. 288p. (Orig.). 1982. pap. 2.95 (ISBN 0-449-14483-6, GM). Fawcett.

--Schism. 1982. pap. 3.50 (ISBN 0-671-45274-6). PB.

--The Shattered Eye. 320p. 1984. pap. 3.95 (ISBN 0-671-47756-0). PB.

--Sweeps. 1980. pap. 2.50 (ISBN 0-449-14351-1, GM). Fawcett.

--The Zurich Numbers. 256p. 1984. 14.95 (ISBN 0-517-55446-1). Crown.

--The Zurich Numbers. 1985. pap. 3.95 (ISBN 0-671-55399-2). PB.

Granger Book Co. Editorial Board. Index to Poetry in Periodicals: American Poetic Renaissance, 1915 to 1919. LC 81-80120. 228p. 1981. lib. bdg. 39.99x (ISBN 0-89609-212-7). Granger Bk.

--Survey of American Poetry: Vol. I-Colonial Period, 1607-1765. LC 81-83526. (The Granger Anthology, Series II). 220p. 1982. 34.95x (ISBN 0-89609-213-5). Granger Bk.

Granger Book Co., Editorial Board, ed. American Poetry Index, 1981-1982, Vol. I. LC 83-81682. 220p. 1983. 40.00x (ISBN 0-89609-238-0). Granger Bk.

Granger Book Co. Editorial Board, ed. Poetry Index Annual, 1983. LC 83-641946. 337p. 1983. 54.99x (ISBN 0-89609-237-2). Granger Bk.

--Survey of American Poetry: Early Nineteenth Century (1800-1829, Vol. III. LC 81-83526. (The Granger Anthology Ser.: Series II). 286p. 1984. 34.95x (ISBN 0-89609-215-1). Granger Bk.

Granger Book Co., Editorial Board, ed. Survey of American Poetry: Revolutionary Era, 1766-1799, Vol. II. LC 81-83526. (The Granger Anthology, Series Two). 200p. 1983. 34.95x (ISBN 0-89609-214-3). Granger Bk.

Granger Book Company Editoral Board. The World's Best Poetry for Children, 2 Vols. (Illus.). 800p. (gr. k-8). 1985. lib. bdg. 89.50x (ISBN 0-89609-260-7). Granger Bk.

Granger Book Company Editorial Board, ed. American Poetry Index, Vol. II: 1983. LC 83-81682. 1985. 40.00x (ISBN 0-89609-241-0). Granger Bk.

Granger Book Company Editorial Board. Poetry Index Annual 1984. 1984. 54.99x (ISBN 0-89609-240-2). Granger Bk.

--Survey of American Poetry: First Great Period (1830-1860, Vol. IV. LC 81-83526. (Anthology Ser.: No. II). 1984. 34.95x (ISBN 0-89609-216-X). Granger Bk.

--The World's Best Poetry: Critical Companion, Suppl. III. 400p. 1985. 49.95x (ISBN 0-89609-242-9). Granger Bk.

--The World's Best Poetry: Supplement One: Twentieth Century English & American Verse, 1900-1929. LC 82-84763. (The Granger Anthology Ser.: No. I). 352p. 1983. 39.95x (ISBN 0-89609-236-4). Granger Bk.

Granger Book Company Editorial Board, ed. World's Best Poetry: Supplement Two: Twentieth Century English & American Verse, 1930-1950. LC 82-84763. (Anthology Series I). 1984. 49.95x (ISBN 0-89609-239-9). Granger Bk.

Granger Book Company, Inc, ed. Index to Poetry in Periodicals: 1920 to 1924. LC 81-80120. 198p. 1983. 39.99x (ISBN 0-89609-224-0). Granger Bk.

Granger Book Company, Inc., ed. Index to Poetry in Periodicals: 1925 to 1929. LC 81-80120. 290p. 1984. 39.99x (ISBN 0-89609-235-6). Granger Bk.

Granger, Bruce I. American Essay Serials from Franklin to Irving. LC 78-4120. 1978. 21.95x (ISBN 0-87049-221-7). U of Tenn Pr.

--Benjamin Franklin: An American Man of Letters. LC 76-8167. 1976. pap. 6.95 (ISBN 0-8061-1336-7). U of Okla Pr.

Granger, Byrd. Arizona Names. 821p. 1983. 29.95 (ISBN 0-918080-18-5). Treasure Chest.

Granger, Byrd, ed. Arizona Place Names. LC 59-63657. 519p. 1982. pap. 14.95 (ISBN 0-8165-0729-5). U of Ariz Pr.

Granger, Byrd H. Grand Canyon Place Names. 26p. 1960. pap. 1.95 (ISBN 0-8165-0538-1). U of Ariz Pr.

--Motif Index for Lost Mines & Treasures, Applied to Redaction of Arizona Legends, & to Lost Mines & Treasure Legends Exterior to Arizona. LC 77-27331. 277p. 1978. text ed. 17.50x (ISBN 0-8165-0646-9). U of Ariz Pr.

Granger, C. W. Forecasting in Business & Economics. LC 79-91742. (Economic Theory, Econometrics & Mathematical Econometrics Ser.). 1979. text ed. 20.00i (ISBN 0-12-295180-8). Acad Pr.

Granger, C. W. & Hatanaka, M. Spectral Analysis of Economic Time Series. (Princeton Studies in Mathematical Economics Ser.: Vol. 1). 1964. 35.00x (ISBN 0-691-04177-6). Princeton U Pr.

Granger, C. W., ed. Forecasting Economic Time Series. (Economic Theory & Math. Economics Ser.). 1977. 35.00 (ISBN 0-12-295150-6). Acad Pr.

--Trading in Commodities: An Investors Chronicle Guide. 4th ed. 158p. 1983. 18.00 (ISBN 0-85941-179-6, Pub. by Woodhead-Faulkner); pap. 11.50 (ISBN 0-85941-178-8). Longwood Pub Group.

Granger, Carl V. & Gresham, Glenn. Functional Assessment in Rehabilitation Medicine. 424p. 1984. lib. bdg. 42.00 (ISBN 0-683-03731-5). Williams & Wilkins.

Granger, Colin. Play Games with English, Bk. I. (Orig.). 1981. pap. text ed. 2.95x (ISBN 0-435-28060-0); instr's manual 6.00x (ISBN 0-435-28061-9). Heinemann Ed.

Granger, Colin & Hicks, Tony. Contact English, Bk. 1. 1977. 5.95x (ISBN 0-435-28371-5); tchr's manual 14.95x (ISBN 0-435-28370-7); 3 tapes 90.00 (ISBN 0-435-28372-3); 3 cassettes 70.00x (ISBN 0-435-28373-1); wallcharts o.p. 40.00x (ISBN 0-435-28374-X). Heinemann Ed.

--Contact English, Bk. 2. 1978. pap. text ed. 5.95x (ISBN 0-435-28068-6); tchr's ed. 14.95x (ISBN 0-435-28067-8); three tapes 90.00x (ISBN 0-435-28066-X); three cassettes 70.00x (ISBN 0-435-28065-1). Heinemann Ed.

Granger, Colin & Plumb, John. Play Games With English, Bk. 2. (Orig.). 1981. pap. text ed. 2.95x (ISBN 0-435-28062-7); 6.50x (ISBN 0-435-28063-5). Heinemann Ed.

Granger, D. N., jt. ed. see Shepherd, A. P.

Granger, Edith. An Index to Poetry & Recitations, 2 vols. Set. lib. bdg. 300.00 (ISBN 0-87968-417-8). Gordon Pr.

Granger, Edith, ed. Granger's Index to Poetry & Recitations. LC 73-21544. 1974. Repr. of 1904 ed. 95.00 (ISBN 0-8369-9400-0). Ayer Co Pubs.

--Granger's Index to Poetry & Recitations. 2nd ed. LC 73-21545. 1974. Repr. of 1918 ed. 95.00 (ISBN 0-8369-9401-9). Ayer Co Pubs.

Granger, Gilles G. Formal Thought & the Sciences of Man. 1983. lib. bdg. 48.00 (ISBN 90-277-1524-6, Pub. by Reidel Holland). Kluwer Academic.

Granger, Harris J., ed. see Bishop, Vernon S.

Granger, J. T. A Brief Biographical Sketch of the Life of Major-General Grenville M. Dodge. Bruchey, Stuart, ed. LC 80-1310. (Railroads Ser.). 1981. Repr. of 1893 ed. lib. bdg. 15.00x (ISBN 0-405-13778-8). Ayer Co Pubs.

Granger, Jean. Mushroom Matings: The Best in Mushroom Cookery. LC 78-5407. 1978. pap. 2.95 (ISBN 0-89666-000-1). Cragmont Pubns.

Granger, John V. Technology & International Relations. LC 78-15363. (Illus.). 202p. 1979. text ed. 23.95 (ISBN 0-7167-1004-8); pap. text ed. 12.95 (ISBN 0-7167-1003-X). W H Freeman.

Granger, Joseph E., Jr. Meadowood Phase Settlement Pattern in the Niagara Frontier Region of Western New York State. (Anthropological Papers: No. 65). (Illus., Orig.). 1978. pap. 8.00x (ISBN 0-932206-76-X). U Mich Mus Anthro.

Granger, Judith. Amazing World of Dinosaurs. LC 81-7476. (Illus.). 32p. (gr. 2-4). 1982. PLB 9.89 (ISBN 0-89375-562-1); pap. text ed. 1.95 (ISBN 0-89375-563-X). Troll Assocs.

Granger, K. R. Alameda. (Orig.). 1978. pap. 2.25 (ISBN 0-89083-429-6). Zebra.

Granger, Katherine. Man of Her Dreams. (Second Chance at Love Ser.: No. 301). 192p. 1985. pap. 2.25 (ISBN 0-425-08629-1). Berkley Pub.

--A Man's Persuasion. (Second Chance at Love Ser.: No. 89). 1982. pap. 1.75 (ISBN 0-515-06851-9). Jove Pubns.

--Moments to Share, No. 13. 192p. 1984. pap. 1.95 (ISBN 0-515-06940-X). Jove Pubns.

--Private Lessons. (To Have & To Hold Ser.: No. 42). 192p. 1984. pap. 1.95 (ISBN 0-515-07844-1). Jove Pubns.

--Wanton Ways. (Second Chance at Love Ser.: No. 206). 192p. 1984. pap. 1.95 (ISBN 0-515-07822-0). Jove Pubns.

Granger, M. Savannah River Plantations. LC 71-187384. (Illus.). 532p. 1972. Repr. of 1947 ed. 30.00 (ISBN 0-87152-079-6). Reprint.

Granger, M. E., jt. ed. see Friedman, A. P.

Granger, Mary, tr. see Landry, Monica & Olivier, Julien.

Granger, Mary E., et al, eds. Pathophysiologic, Diagnostic & Therapeutic Aspects of Headache. (Research & Clinical Studies in Headache: Vol. 4). 135p. 1976. 26.50 (ISBN 3-8055-2282-7). S Karger.

Granger, P., jt. auth. see Brevard, C.

Granger, P., jt. auth. see Richard, C.

Granger, S., ed. The Be Past Participle Construction in Spoken English: With Special Emphasis on the Passive. (Linguistics Ser.: Vol. 49). 390p. 1983. 47.00 (ISBN 0-444-86744-9, I-255-83, North Holland). Elsevier.

Granholm, S., ed. Mining with Backfill: Proceedings of the International Symposium on Mining with Backfill, Lulea, 7-9 June 1983. 472p. 1983. lib. bdg. 37.50 (ISBN 90-6191-509-0, Pub. by Balkema RSA). IPS.

Granholm, Steve, jt. auth. see Beedy, Ted.

Granick, David. Enterprise Guidance in Eastern Europe: A Comparison of Four Socialist Economies. LC 75-2992. 536p. 1975. 50.00 (ISBN 0-691-04209-8); pap. 20.00 LPE (ISBN 0-691-10033-0). Princeton U Pr.

--The European Executive. Coser, Lewis A. & Powell, Walter W., eds. LC 79-6994. (Perennial Works in Sociology Ser.). (Illus.). 1979. Repr. of 1962 ed. lib. bdg. 28.50x (ISBN 0-405-12093-1). Ayer Co Pubs.

--Management of the Industrial Firm in the USSR. LC 74-6752. 346p. 1974. Repr. of 1954 ed. lib. bdg. 45.00x (ISBN 0-8371-7555-0, GRIF). Greenwood.

--The Red Executive: A Study of the Organization Man in Russian Industry. Coser, Lewis A. & Powell, Walter W., eds. LC 79-6993. (Perennial Works in Sociology Ser.). (Illus.). 1979. Repr. of 1960 ed. lib. bdg. 26.50x (ISBN 0-405-12094-X). Ayer Co Pubs.

--Soviet Metal-Fabricating & Economic Development: Practice Versus Policy. 382p. 1967. 30.00x (ISBN 0-299-04290-1). U of Wis Pr.

Granick, Lois. Thesaurus of Psychological Index Terms. 4th ed. 263p. (Orig.). 1985. pap. 45.00 (ISBN 0-912704-68-3, 3070043). Am Psychol.

Granick, Mark, jt. auth. see Thaller, Seth.

Granier, Camille. Essai de Bibliographie Charitable. LC 68-6155. (Fr). 1967. Repr. of 1891 ed. lib. bdg. 29.50 (ISBN 0-8337-1405-8). B Franklin.

Granier, Jacqueline P., jt. ed. see Kavaas, Igor I.

Granier, James A. Latin American Belles-Lettres in English Translation. 1976. lib. bdg. 69.95 (ISBN 0-8490-2132-4). Gordon Pr.

Granirer, Edmond E. Exposed Points of Convex Sets & Weak Sequential Convergence. LC 72-2682. (Memoirs: No. 123). 80p. 1972. pap. 10.00 (ISBN 0-8218-1823-6, MEMO-123). Am Math.

Granit, Arthur. I Am from Brownsville. LC 84-1789. (Illus.). 271p. 1985. 16.95 (ISBN 0-8022-2456-3). Philos Lib.

Granit, R., ed. see IBRO Symposium, Italy, September 1978.

Granit, Ragnar. Basis of Motor Control. 1970. 58.50 (ISBN 0-12-295350-9). Acad Pr.

--The Purposive Brain. 1977. text ed. 22.50x (ISBN 0-262-07069-3); pap. 6.95x (ISBN 0-262-57054-8). MIT Pr.

--Receptors & Sensory Perception. LC 75-14597. (Mrs. Hepsa Ely Silliman Memorial Lectures). (Illus.). 369p. 1975. Repr. of 1955 ed. lib. bdg. 24.75x (ISBN 0-8371-8213-1, GRRS). Greenwood.

--Sensory Mechanisms of the Retina. (Illus.). 1963. Repr. of 1947 ed. 17.95x (ISBN 0-02-845410-3). Hafner.

Granit, Robert. Another Run In the Night. 1985. pap. 3.95 (ISBN 0-451-13402-8, Sig). NAL.

Granite, Robert H. The Fortunes of Astrology. 128p. (Orig.). 1980. pap. 7.95 (ISBN 0-917086-27-9). A C S Pubns Inc.

Graniti, A., jt. ed. see Wood, R. K.

Granito, Anthony R. Fire Officer's Guide to Company Leadership & Operations. LC 75-13631. (Fire Officer's Guide Ser). (Illus.). 282p. 1975. 10.50 (ISBN 0-87765-036-5, F*S*P-43). Natl Fire Prot.

--Fire Service Instructor's Guidebook. Neale, Robert A., ed. LC 76-22898. 1976. pap. 6.50 (ISBN 0-87765-079-9, FSP-49). Natl Fire Prot.

Granito, Michael R. Bond Portfolio Immunization. LC 83-49012. 256p. 1984. 25.00x (ISBN 0-669-07660-0). Lexington Bks.

Granits. Mechanisms Regulating the Discharge of Motoneurons. 92p. 1982. 50.00x (ISBN 0-85323-340-3, Pub. by Liverpool Univ England). State Mutual Bk.

Granjard, Heri, ed. Quelques Lettres d'Ivan Tourguenev a Pauline Viardot: Texte Integral d'Apres l'Apres les Originaux de la Collection Maupoil de 29 Lettres de l'Edition Halperine-Kaminski avec en Appendice 8 Lettres Inedites en France d'Ivan Tourguenev a Pauline Viardot. (Etudes Sur l'Historie l'Economie et la Sociologie des Pays Slaves: No. 16). 1974. 16.40x (ISBN 90-2797-309-1). Mouton.

Granlund, Marvin. Nuclear Lore from the Vitamin Swamp. Dietz, Chris, ed. 48p. (Orig.). 1983. pap. 2.50x (ISBN 0-938196-04-9). Bisbee Pr.

Grannemann, Thomas W. & Pauly, Mark V. Controlling Medicaid Costs. 1983. 13.95 (ISBN 0-8447-3527-2); pap. 4.95 (ISBN 0-8447-3515-9). Am Enterprise.

Grannes, Alf. Loan Compounds in Bulgarian Reflecting the Turkish Indefinite Izafet-Construction. 70p. 1980. pap. 16.00x (ISBN 82-00-01951-9). Universitet.

Grannis, Alberta M. Something Diffrent Cookbook. 200p. (Orig.). 1985. pap. 10.95 (ISBN 0-9613774-0-2). A M Grannis.

Grannis, Chandler B., ed. What Happens in Book Publishing. 2nd ed. LC 67-19875. 467p. 1967. 34.00x (ISBN 0-231-02948-9). Columbia U Pr.

Grannis, Chandler B., et al. Century of a Modern Church. LC 83-4800. (Illus.). 120p. (Orig.). 1983. pap. 9.95 (ISBN 0-9610366-0-5). UCC UCC.

Grannis, G. F., jt. ed. see Dietz, A. A.

Grannis, Gary E. Modern Power Mechanics. LC 78-12106. 1979. scp 26.56 (ISBN 0-672-97130-5); pap. 12.04 scp student's manual (ISBN 0-672-97132-1); scp instructor's guide 3.67 (ISBN 0-672-97131-3). Bobbs.

Grannis, Gary E., jt. auth. see Groneman, Chris H.

Grannis, J. Christopher, et al. The Risk of the Cross: Christian Discipleship in the Nuclear Age. 128p. (Orig.). 1981. pap. 5.95 (ISBN 0-8164-2305-9, Pub. by Seabury). Winston Pr.

Granniss, Ruth S. A Descriptive Catalogue of the First Editions in Book Form of the Writings of Percy Bysshe Shelley. LC 74-9783. 1973. lib. bdg. 30.00 (ISBN 0-8414-4513-3). Folcroft.

Grano, Joseph D. Problems in Criminal Procedure. 2nd ed. LC 81-7577. (American Casebook Ser.). 176p. 1981. pap. text ed. 8.95 (ISBN 0-314-59979-7); pap. text ed. tchr's. manual avail. (ISBN 0-314-79133-7). West Pub.

Granof, Michael H. Accounting for Managers & Investors. 768p. 1983. 34.95 (ISBN 0-13-002725-1). P-H.

--Financial Accounting: Principles & Issues. 3rd ed. (Illus.). 656p. 1985. 30.95 (ISBN 0-13-316704-6). P-H.

--How to Cost Your Labor Contract. LC 73-77273. 158p. 1973. 17.50 (ISBN 0-87179-191-9). BNA.

Granof, Michael H. & Evans, Thomas G. Financial Accounting: Principles & Issues. 2nd ed. (Illus.). 352p. 1980. text ed. 30.95 (ISBN 0-13-314153-5); student guide 11.95 (ISBN 0-13-314179-9). P-H.

Granoff, Phyllis. Philosophy & Argument in Late Vedanta. (Studies of Classical India: No. 1). 1978. lib. bdg. 53.00 (ISBN 90-277-0878-9, Pub. by Reidel Holland). Kluwer Academic.

Granoff, Steve, et al. Framework Made Easier. 200p. 1985. 14.95 (ISBN 0-13-330531-7). P-H.

Granov, V. New Realities & the Struggle of Ideas. 1980. pap. 4.95 (ISBN 0-8285-1774-6, Pub. by Progress Pubs USSR). Imported Pubns.

Granovetter, Mark S. Getting a Job: A Study of Contacts & Careers. LC 73-89505. 1974. text ed. 10.00x (ISBN 0-674-35416-8). Harvard U Pr.

Granovsky, Abraham. Land Policy in Palestine. LC 75-6436. (The Rise of Jewish Nationalism & the Middle East Ser). 208p. 1975. Repr. of 1940 ed. 19.80 (ISBN 0-88355-323-6). Hyperion Conn.

Granovsky, Anatoli. I Was an NKVD Agent. 282p. 1982. pap. 4.95 (ISBN 0-88264-177-8). Diane Bks.

Granowsky, Al, jt. auth. see Thompkins, Steve.

Granowsky, Alvin & Mumford, Janice H. Building Life Skills, Level D. (Skillbooster Ser.: Bk. 1). 64p. (gr. 4). 1981. write for info. wkbk. (ISBN 0-87895-418-X). Modern Curr.

--Building Life Skills, Level E. (Skillbooster Ser.: Bk. 2). 64p. (gr. 5). 1981. write for info. (ISBN 0-87895-523-2). Modern Curr.

--Building Life Skills, Level F. (Skillbooster Ser.: Bk. 3). 64p. (gr. 6). 1981. write for info. wkbk. (ISBN 0-87895-617-4). Modern Curr.

Granqvist, Hilma N. Birth & Childhood Among the Arabs. LC 72-9643. Repr. of 1947 ed. 23.00 (ISBN 0-404-57447-5). AMS Pr.

--Marriage Conditions in a Palestinian Village, 2 vols. LC 72-9644. Repr. of 1935 ed. Set. 52.50 (ISBN 0-404-57450-5). AMS Pr.

Granrose, John T., jt. auth. see Frankena, William K.

Granrud, John E. The Organization & Objectives of State Teachers' Associations. LC 70-176817. (Columbia University. Teachers College. Contributions to Education: No. 234). Repr. of 1926 ed. 22.50 (ISBN 0-404-55234-X). AMS Pr.

Gransden, Antonia. Historical Writing in England: C. 550 to C. 1307. LC 73-3732. 634p. 1974. 69.50x (ISBN 0-8014-0770-2). Cornell U Pr.

--Historical Writing in England II: c. 1307 to the Early 16th Century, Vol. 2. LC 74-23267. 576p. 1980. 75.00x (ISBN 0-8014-1264-1). Cornell U Pr.

Gransden, K. W. Tennyson: In Memoriam. (Studies in English Literature). 1971. pap. text ed. 3.95x (ISBN 0-7131-5095-5). Dynamic Learn Corp.

--Virgil's Iliad: An Essay on Epic Narrative. 232p. 1985. 39.50 (ISBN 0-521-24504-4); pap. 13.95 (ISBN 0-521-28756-1). Cambridge U Pr.

Gransden, K. W., ed. see Virgil.

Granseth, Sandra, ed. see Better Homes & Gardens Editors.

Granskou, D., jt. ed. see Richardson, P.

Gransow, Volker, et al, trs. see Gerber, Margy, et al.

Granstrand, Ove. Technology, Management & Marketing. LC 82-16804. 300p. 1982. 25.00x (ISBN 0-312-79007-4). St Martin.

Granstrom, B., jt. ed. see Carlson, R.

Granstrom, E., jt. ed. see Pace-Asciak, C.

Grant. Bringing Teaching to Life: An Introduction to Education. 1985. 32.86 (ISBN 0-205-07635-1, 237635). Allyn.
--Nightmare Season. 2.95 (ISBN 0-317-31817-9). Tor Bks.
--Seventeen Eighty Nine. 4.50 (ISBN 0-318-01842-X). Am Fed Astrologers.
--Seventeen Eighty One. 4.50 (ISBN 0-318-01840-3). Am Fed Astrologers.
--Seventeen Eighty Seven. 4.50 (ISBN 0-318-01841-1). Am Fed Astrologers.
--Seventeen Ninety Two. 4.50 (ISBN 0-318-01843-8). Am Fed Astrologers.
--Seventeen Seventy Seven. 4.50 (ISBN 0-318-01838-1). Am Fed Astrologers.
--Seventeen Seventy Six. 4.50 (ISBN 0-318-01839-X). Am Fed Astrologers.
Grant & Leavenworth. Statistical Quality Control. 5th ed. 682p. 32.50 (ISBN 0-318-13252-4, P80). Am Soc QC.
Grant, jt. auth. see Anderson.
Grant, jt. auth. see Brennan.
Grant, jt. auth. see Goodman.
Grant, jt. auth. see Mackworth-Praed.
Grant, jt. auth. see Macworth-Praed.
Grant, A. J., ed. English Historians. LC 73-118472. 1971. Repr. of 1906 ed. 25.00x (ISBN 0-8046-1221-8, Pub. by Kennikat). Assoc Faculty Pr.
Grant, A. J., tr. see Eginhard & Monk of St. Gall.
Grant, A. T., tr. see Ivanov, Vsevolod V.
Grant, Alan. American Political Process. 1980. text ed. 30.00x (ISBN 0-435-83357-X); pap. text ed. 14.50x (ISBN 0-435-83356-1). Gower Pub Co.
Grant, Alexander. Independence & Nationhood: Scotland, 1306-1469. (New History of Scotland Ser.). 192p. 1985. pap. text ed. 14.95 (ISBN 0-7131-6309-7). E Arnold.
Grant, Alexander T. Study of the Capital Market in Britain from 1919-1936. 2nd ed. 320p. 1967. 35.00x (ISBN 0-7146-1224-3, F Cass Co). Biblio Dist.
Grant, Alice, et al. Shindano-Swahili Essays & Other Stories. (Foreign & Comparative Studies Program, African Special Publications Ser.: No.6). 55p. 1971. pap. 3.50x (ISBN 0-686-70992-6). Syracuse U Foreign Comp.
Grant, Allen. Flashlights on Nature: A Popular Account of the Life Histories of Some Familiar Insects, Birds, Plants, Etc. 1978. Repr. of 1898 ed. lib. bdg. 25.00 (ISBN 0-8492-0088-1). R West.
Grant, Andrew & Todd, Elizabeth. Enteral & Parenteral Nutrition: A Clinical Handbook. 1982. 9.50 (ISBN 0-632-00732-X, B1957-2). Mosby.
Grant, Anne. Memoirs of an American Lady: With Sketches of Manners & Scenes in America As They Existed Previous to the Revolution; With Unpublished Letters & a Memoir of Mrs. Grant, by James Grant Wilson. LC 77-38354. (Select Bibliographies Reprint Ser.). Repr. of 1901 ed. 32.00 (ISBN 0-8369-6771-2). Ayer Co Pubs.
Grant, Anne M. Essays on the Superstitions of the Highlanders of Scotland. LC 76-25997. 1976. Repr. of 1811 ed. Set. lib. bdg. 75.00 (ISBN 0-8414-4530-3). Folcroft.
Grant, Anne R., ed. Medical Malpractice 1984. (Trial Annuals Ser.). (Illus.). 72p. (Orig.). 1985. pap. 15.00 (ISBN 0-941916-19-7). Assn Trial Ed.
--Products Liability Eighty-Four. (Trial Annuals Ser.). (Illus., Orig.). 1985. pap. 18.00 (ISBN 0-941916-20-0). Assn Trial Ed.
--Trial Techniques Eighty-Four. (Trial Annuals Ser.). (Illus.). 144p. (Orig.). 1985. pap. 22.00 (ISBN 0-941916-21-9). Assn Trial Ed.
Grant, Arthur. In the Old Paths: Memories of Literary Pilgrimages. 1977. Repr. of 1913 ed. lib. bdg. 25.00 (ISBN 0-8492-1014-3). R West.
Grant, Arthur J. The French Monarchy (1483-1789, 2 vols. LC 75-41118. Repr. of 1925 ed. Set. 30.00 (ISBN 0-404-14930-8). AMS Pr.
--Greece in the Age of Pericles. LC 72-91204. (Illus.). xvi, 331p. 1972. Repr. of 1893 ed. lib. bdg. 24.50 (ISBN 0-8154-0444-1). Cooper Sq.
--Huguenots. 255p. 1969. Repr. of 1934 ed. 19.50 (ISBN 0-208-00745-8, Archon). Shoe String.
--Scott. 1973. Repr. of 1909 ed. 20.00 (ISBN 0-8274-0644-4). R West.
Grant, Audrey, jt. auth. see Rodwell, Eric.
Grant, Barbara M., jt. auth. see Hennings, Dorothy G.
Grant, Barry K., ed. Film Genre: Theory & Criticism. LC 77-8908. 1977. 16.00 (ISBN 0-8108-1059-X). Scarecrow.
--Film Study in the Undergraduate Curriculum. (Options for Teaching Ser.: No.5). 158p. 1983. 19.50x (ISBN 0-87352-304-0); pap. 12.50x (ISBN 0-87352-305-9). Modern Lang.
--Planks of Reason: Essays on the Horror Film. LC 84-10592. 442p. 1984. 27.50 (ISBN 0-8108-1713-6). Scarecrow.
Grant, Blanche C. The Taos Indians. (Beautiful Rio Grande Classic Ser.). (Illus.). 198p. 1984. pap. 7.50 (ISBN 0-87380-141-5). Rio Grande.
--The Taos Indians. LC 76-40917. (Beautiful Rio Grande Classics Ser.). 1985. pap. 10.50 (ISBN 0-87380-112-1). Rio Grande.
--When Old Trails Were New: The Story of Taos, N.M. LC 63-21230. (Beautiful Rio Grande Classics Ser.). 344p. 1983. Repr. of 1934 ed. softcover 12.00 (ISBN 0-87380-140-7). Rio Grande.
Grant, Brian W. From Sin to Wholeness. LC 81-16122. 174p. 1982. pap. 8.95 (ISBN 0-664-24399-1). Westminster.
Grant, Bruce. Encyclopedia of Rawhide & Leather Braiding. LC 72-10407. (Illus.). 556p. 1972. 20.00 (ISBN 0-87033-161-2). Cornell Maritime.
--Leather Braiding. (Illus.). 191p. 1950. 6.00 (ISBN 0-87033-039-X). Cornell Maritime.
Grant, Bruce & Rice, Lee M. How to Make Cowboy Horse Gear. 2nd ed. LC 56-10884. (Illus.). 192p. 1956. pap. 6.50 (ISBN 0-87033-034-9). Cornell Maritime.
Grant, Bruce K. A Guide to Korean Characters: Reading & Writing Hangul & Hanja. 2nd ed. 367p. (Eng. & Korean.). 1982. 21.95x (ISBN 0-930878-13-2). Hollym Intl.
--Korean Proverb. LC 85-80454. 150p. 1985. 9.95x (ISBN 0-930878-44-2). Hollym Intl.
Grant, C. D. Energy Conservation in the Chemical & Process Industries. 112p. 1981. 2.00x (ISBN 0-85295-118-3, Pub. by Inst Chem Eng England). State Mutual Bk.
Grant, C. David. God the Center of Value: Value Theory in the Theology of H. Richard Niebuhr. LC 84-40232. 160p. 1984. 16.95x (ISBN 0-912646-92-6). Tex Christian.
Grant, C. H. The Making of Modern Belize. LC 75-36022. (Cambridge Commonwealth Ser.). (Illus.). 400p. 1976. 62.50 (ISBN 0-521-20731-2). Cambridge U Pr.
Grant, C. H., jt. auth. see Mackworth-Praed, C. W.
Grant, C. L. A Quiet Night of Fear. (Orig.). 1981. pap. 2.25 (ISBN 0-425-04844-6). Berkley Pub.
Grant, C. L., et al, eds. Advances in X-Ray Analysis, Vol. 17. LC 58-35928. 600p. 1974. 65.00x (ISBN 0-306-38117-6, Plenum Pr). Plenum Pub.
Grant, Campbell. Canyon De Chelly: Its People & Rock Art. LC 75-8455. 290p. 1978. 25.00x (ISBN 0-8165-0632-9); pap. 12.50 (ISBN 0-8165-0523-3). U of Ariz Pr.
--Rock Art of the American Indian. (Illus.). 192p. 1981. pap. 7.95 (ISBN 0-89646-060-6). Outbooks.
--The Rock Art of the North American Indians. LC 82-23655. (The Imprint of Man Ser.). (Illus.). 144p. 1983. 21.95 (ISBN 0-521-25443-4). Cambridge U Pr.
Grant, Campbell & Diguet, Leon. Rock Art of Baja California: With "Notes on the Pictographs of Baja California" by Leon Diguet (1895) 36.00 (ISBN 0-317-11598-7). Dawsons.
Grant, Carl A. Preparing for Reflective Teaching. 1984. pap. text ed. 18.93 for info (ISBN 0-205-08092-8, 238092). Allyn.
Grant, Carl A., ed. Multicultural Education: Commitments, Issues & Applications. 1977. 7.00 (ISBN 0-87120-084-8). Assn Supervision.
Grant, Carl A., et al. The Public School & the Challenge of Ethnic Pluralism. LC 80-21315. 1981. pap. 2.95 (ISBN 0-8298-0421-8). Pilgrim NY.
Grant, Carol L., jt. auth. see Grant, John A.
Grant, Carolyn, jt. auth. see Wakeman, Frederic.
Grant, Catherine, jt. auth. see Grant, John.
Grant, Charles. An Economics Primer. 232p. 1985. 34.95x (ISBN 0-631-14091-3); pap. 9.95x (ISBN 0-631-14092-1). Basil Blackwell.
--The Nestling. 416p. (Orig.). 1982. pap. 3.50 (ISBN 0-671-41989-7). PB.
Grant, Charles, ed. The Gazetteer of the Central Provinces of India. 1985. Repr. of 1870 ed. 75.00x (ISBN 0-8364-1333-4, Pub. by Usha). South Asia Bks.
Grant, Charles L. A Glow of Candles & Other Stories. (Orig.). 1981. pap. 2.25 (ISBN 0-425-05145-5). Berkley Pub.
--Midnight. 288p. 1985. pap. 2.95 (ISBN 0-8125-1850-0). Tor Bks.
--Night Songs. 384p. (Orig.). 1984. pap. 3.95 (ISBN 0-671-45249-5). PB.
--Nightmare Seasons. LC 80-2051. (DD Science Fiction Ser.). 1982. 10.95 (ISBN 0-385-15956-0). Doubleday.
--Nightmare Seasons. (Tor Bks.). 256p. 1983. pap. 2.95 (ISBN 0-523-48076-8). Pinnacle Bks.
--Nightmares. LC 79-83966. (Orig.). 1984. pap. 2.95 (ISBN 0-425-07693-8). Berkley Pub.
--Shadows. LC 80-81628. 224p. 1983. pap. 2.50 (ISBN 0-425-05955-3). Berkley Pub.
--Shadows Eight. (Science Fiction Ser.). 192p. 1985. 12.95 (ISBN 0-385-19823-X). Doubleday.
--Shadows Four. 224p. 1985. pap. 2.95 (ISBN 0-425-07650-4). Berkley Pub.
--Shadows Three. LC 80-651. (DD Science Fiction Ser.). 224p. 1980. 10.95 (ISBN 0-385-15777-0). Doubleday.
--The Soft Whisper of the Dead. (Illus.). 208p. 1983. 15.00 (ISBN 0-937986-55-0); Signed & Slipcased ed. 40.00x (ISBN 0-937986-56-9). D M Grant.
--Tales from the Nightside. (Illus.). 240p. 1981. 11.95 (ISBN 0-87054-091-2). Arkham.
--The Tea Party. 1985. pap. 3.50 (ISBN 0-317-18906-9). PB.
Grant, Charles L., ed. The Dodd Mead Gallery of Horror. 408p. 1983. 15.95 (ISBN 0-396-08160-6); pap. 9.95 (ISBN 0-396-08266-1). Dodd.
--Fears. 288p. (Orig.). 1984. pap. 2.95 (ISBN 0-425-07694-6). Berkley Pub.
--Fears. Date not set. pap. 2.95 (ISBN 0-425-07691-1). Berkley Pub.
--Greystone Bay. 288p. (Orig.). 1985. pap. 2.95 (ISBN 0-8125-1852-7, Dist. by Warner Pub Services & St. Martin). Tor Bks.
--Horrors. LC 81-47255. 224p. (Orig.). 1984. pap. 2.95 (ISBN 0-425-07692-X). Berkley Pub.
--Shadows, No. 6. LC 82-45527. (DD Science Fiction Ser.). 192p. 1983. 11.95 (ISBN 0-385-18259-7). Doubleday.
--Shadows Seven. LC 82-45527. (Science Fiction Ser.). 192p. 1984. 11.95 (ISBN 0-385-18943-5). Doubleday.
--Shadows Three. 224p. 1985. pap. 2.95 (ISBN 0-425-07453-6). Berkley Pub.
--Shadows Two. 224p. 1984. pap. 2.95 (ISBN 0-425-08159-1). Berkley Pub.
--Terrors. LC 81-85822. 224p. (Orig.). 1984. pap. 2.95 (ISBN 0-425-07691-1). Berkley Pub.
Grant, Charles L., ed. see Morrell, David, et al.
Grant, Charles L., et al. Night Visions I. Ryan, Alan, ed. (Illus.). 325p. 1984. 18.00 (ISBN 0-913165-05-0); signed limited ed. 45.00 (ISBN 0-913165-04-2). Dark Harvest.
Grant, Charles S. Democracy in the Connecticut Frontier Town of Kent. LC 77-120201. (Columbia University. Studies in the Social Sciences: No. 601). Repr. of 1961 ed. 12.50 (ISBN 0-404-51601-7). AMS Pr.
Grant, Charles W. & Butah, Jon. Introduction to the UCSD p-System. LC 81-50655. (Illus.). 300p. 1982. pap. 15.95 (ISBN 0-89588-061-X, P370). SYBEX.
Grant, Cherri. Swingers Three. (Orig.). 1974. pap. 2.25 (ISBN 0-87067-047-6, BH047). Holloway.
Grant, Chet. Before Rockne at Notre Dame. LC 78-12487. (Illus.). 1978. 11.95 (ISBN 0-89651-050-6). Icarus.
Grant, Christian P. The Syrian Desert. LC 78-63341. (The Crusades & Military Orders: Second Ser.). (Illus.). Repr. of 1937 ed. 41.00 (ISBN 0-404-17017-X). AMS Pr.
Grant, Clay. Demon Samurai. 1978. pap. 1.50 (ISBN 0-505-51244-0, Pub. by Tower Bks). Dorchester Pub Co.
Grant, Colin D. Energy Consevation in the Chemical & Process Industries. 1979. 32.50x (ISBN 0-7114-5525-2). Intl Ideas.
Grant, Mrs. Colquhoun. Louise Renee de Kerouaille (Dutchess of Portsmouth) 1977. Repr. of 1909 ed. 20.00 (ISBN 0-8274-4302-1). R West.
Grant, Cynthia D. Big Time. LC 81-8075. 168p. (gr. 5-9). 1982. PLB 9.95 (ISBN 0-689-30879-5). Atheneum.
--Hard Love. LC 83-2603. 228p. (gr. 7 up). 1983. 10.95 (ISBN 0-689-30985-6). Atheneum.
--Hard Love. (gr. 7 up). pap. 2.25 (ISBN 0-317-13274-1, Juniper). Fawcett.
--Joshua Fortune. LC 80-11983. 156p. (gr. 5-9). 1980. 9.95 (ISBN 0-689-30777-2). Atheneum.
Grant, D., illus. In an Eighteenth Century Kitchen. 1968. text ed. 14.25x (ISBN 0-900821-00-0, Pub. by C Woolf UK). Humanities.
Grant, Damian. Realism. (Critical Idiom Ser.). 1970. pap. 5.50x (ISBN 0-416-17820-0, NO. 2216). Methuen Inc.
Grant, Daniel A., et al. Orban's Periodontics: A Concept-Theory & Practice. 4th ed. LC 75-189276. (Illus.). 715p. 1972. 27.50 (ISBN 0-8016-1960-2). Mosby.
--Periodontics in the Tradition of Orban & Gottlieb. 5th ed. LC 79-10615. (Illus.). 974p. 1979. text ed. 48.95 (ISBN 0-8016-1961-0). Mosby.
Grant, Daniel R. & Nixon, H. C. State & Local Government in America. 4th ed. 608p. 1981. text ed. 30.54 (ISBN 0-205-07705-6, 767707); free tchr's. ed. (ISBN 0-205-07706-4, 7677073); study guide 10.00 (ISBN 0-205-07707-2). Allyn.
Grant, Dave. The Ultimate Power. 192p. 1983. 9.95 (ISBN 0-8007-1337-0). Revell.
Grant, David. Emerald Decision. 352p. 1982. pap. 2.75 (ISBN 0-345-29645-1). Ballantine.
Grant, Dean E. How to Negotiate Physician Contracts. LC 79-66018. 254p. (Orig.). 1979. text ed. 26.95 (ISBN 0-931028-17-5); pap. text ed. 22.95 (ISBN 0-931028-10-8). Teach'em.
--How to Negotiate Physician Contracts. 254p. 1979. 22.95 (ISBN 0-931028-10-8, 1107). Healthcare Fin Mgmt Assn.
Grant, Donald L. Anti-Lynching Movement, Eighteen Eighty-Three to Nineteen Thirty-Two. LC 75-18122. 1975. soft bdg. 12.00 (ISBN 0-88247-348-4). R & E Pubs.
Grant, Donald P. Author & Key Word Index to Twenty-Four Conferences & Symposia on Environmental Design Research, Design Methods & Computer-Aided Design, Nos. 1034-1036. 1976. 12.50 (ISBN 0-686-20395-X). CPL Biblios.
--Creative Idea Production in Architecture: The Morphological Approach. LC 83-70986. iv, 56p. (Orig.). 1984. pap. 6.00x (ISBN 0-910821-01-1). Design Meth.
--Design by Objectives: Multiple Objective Design Analysis & Evaluation in Architectural, Environmental & Product Design. LC 82-73290. 50p. (Orig.). 1982. pap. text ed. 6.00x (ISBN 0-910821-00-3). Design Meth.
--The Dual Graph Approach: How to Use Planar Graphs & Their Duals As Design Aids. (Illus.). iii, 26p. (Orig.). 1983. pap. 3.60x (ISBN 0-911215-02-6). Small Master.
--A Partially Annotated Bibliography on Space Planning Methods for Architects & Physical Planners. (Architecture Ser.: A 1). 1978. pap. 8.50 (ISBN 0-88066-000-7). Vance Biblios.
--PERT & CPM: Network Methods for Project Planning, Scheduling & Control. LC 83-60947. (Illus.). vi, 58p. (Orig.). 1983. pap. 6.00x (ISBN 0-911215-01-8). Small Master.
Grant, Donald P., illus. Architectural Economics for Small-Scale Design & Construction. (Illus.). x, 240p. (Orig.). 1985. pap. 32.50x (ISBN 0-911215-03-4). Small Master.
Grant, Doris. Recipe for Survival: Your Daily Food. LC 73-93654. 224p. 1974. 6.95 (ISBN 0-87983-069-7); pap. 3.95 (ISBN 0-87983-078-6). Keats.
Grant, Doris & Joice, Jean. Food Combining for Health: A New Look at the Hay System. 240p. (Orig.). 1985. pap. 8.95. Thorsons Pubs.
Grant, Douglas. Robert Frost & His Reputation. LC 77-7604. 1977. Repr. of 1965 ed. lib. bdg. 9.50 (ISBN 0-8414-4595-8). Folcroft.
Grant, Douglas, ed. see Churchill, Charles.
Grant, Douglas, ed. see James, Henry.
Grant, E. Physical Science in the Middle Ages. LC 77-8393. (History of Science Ser.). (Illus.). 1978. pap. 10.95 (ISBN 0-521-29294-8). Cambridge U Pr.
Grant, E., jt. auth. see Wood, Irving F.
Grant, E. H., et al. Dielectric Behaviour of Biological Molecules in Solution. (Monographs on Physical Biochemistry). (Illus.). 1978. 55.00x (ISBN 0-19-854621-1). Oxford U Pr.
Grant, Edgar. Exploring Careers in the Travel Industry. (Careers in Depth Ser.). 144p. 1984. lib. bdg. 8.97 (ISBN 0-8239-0619-1). Rosen Group.
Grant, Edward. In Defense Of The Earth's Centrality & Immobility: Scholastic Reaction To Copernicanism In The Seventeenth Century. 67p. 10.00 (ISBN 0-87169-744-0). Am Philos.
--Much Ado about Nothing: Theories of Space & Vacuum from the Middle Ages to the Scientific Revolution. LC 80-13876. (Illus.). 545p. 1981. 70.00 (ISBN 0-521-22983-9). Cambridge U Pr.
--A Source Book in Medieval Science. LC 70-183977. (Source Books in the History of Science Ser). 896p. 1974. text ed. 45.00x (ISBN 0-674-82360-5). Harvard U Pr.
--Studies in Medieval Science & Natural Philosophy. 378p. 1981. 70.00x (ISBN 0-86078-089-9, Pub. by Variorum). State Mutual Bk.
Grant, Edward, ed. Nicole Oresme & the Kinematics of Circular Motion: Tractatus De Commensurabilitate Vel Incommensurabilitate Motuum Celi. Grant, Edward, tr. LC 79-133238. (Medieval Science Ser). (Illus.). 438p. 1971. 50.00x (ISBN 0-299-05830-1). U of Wis Pr.
Grant, Edward, tr. see Oresme, Nicole.
Grant, Elihu. The People of Palestine. rev. 2nd ed. LC 75-6434. (The Rise of Jewish Nationalism & the Middle East Ser). 1975. Repr. of 1921 ed. 25.00 (ISBN 0-88355-321-X). Hyperion Conn.
Grant, Elliott M. Career of Victor Hugo. (Harvard Studies in Romance Languages). 1945. 32.00 (ISBN 0-527-01119-3). Kraus Repr.
--French Poetry & Modern Industry, 1830-1870. (Harvard Studies in Romance Languages). 1927. 19.00 (ISBN 0-527-01104-5). Kraus Repr.
Grant, Ellsworth S. The Colt Legacy. LC 81-85196. (Illus.). 234p. 1982. pap. 17.00 (ISBN 0-917218-17-5). Mowbray.
--Yankee Dreamers & Doers. (Illus.). 269p. 1974. 9.95x (ISBN 0-686-26751-6). Conn Hist Soc.
Grant, Eric G. Scotland. Collision, Robert L., ed. (World Bibliographical Ser.: No. 34). 408p. 1982. lib. bdg. 55.00 (ISBN 0-903450-64-X). ABC-Clio.
Grant, Ernest R. Tables of Ascendants & Midheavens. 136p. 1954. 6.00 (ISBN 0-86690-108-6, 1151-01). Am Fed Astrologers.
Grant, Eugene L. & Bell, L. F. Basic Accounting & Cost Accounting. 2nd ed. 1964. text ed. 34.95 (ISBN 0-07-024094-9). McGraw.
Grant, Eugene L. & Leavenworth, Richard. Statistical Quality Control. 5th ed. (Industrial Engineering & Management Science Ser.). (Illus.). 1979. text ed. 44.95 (ISBN 0-07-024114-7). McGraw.
Grant, Eugene L., et al. Principles of Engineering Economy. 7th ed. 700p. (Arabic.). 1982. pap. 17.00 (ISBN 0-471-87183-4). Wiley.
Grant, Eugene L., et al, eds. Principles of Engineering Economy. 7th ed. LC 81-10399. 687p. 1982. text ed. 36.50 (ISBN 0-471-06436-X); Avail Tchr's Manual (ISBN 0-471-08439-5). Wiley.
Grant, Eva. I Hate My Name. LC 80-14428. (Life & Living from a Child's Point of View). (Illus.). 32p. (gr. k-5). 1980. PLB 14.25 (ISBN 0-8172-1362-7). Raintree Pubs.
--Will I Ever Be Older? LC 80-24782. (Life & Living from a Child's Point of View). (Illus.). (gr. k-5). 1981. PLB 14.25 (ISBN 0-8172-1363-5). Raintree Pubs.
Grant, F. Life of Samuel Johnson. Repr. of 1887 ed. lib. bdg. 20.00 (ISBN 0-8495-1904-7). Arden Lib.
Grant, F. C. Hellenistic Religions: Grant. 1953. pap. text ed. write for info. (ISBN 0-02-345640-X). Macmillan.
Grant, F. C., ed. see Weiss, Johannes.
Grant, F. S. & West, G. F. Interpretation Theory in Applied Geophysics. (Illus.). 1965. text ed. 69.95 (ISBN 0-07-024100-7). McGraw.

--The Conquest of a Continent: Of the Expansion of Races in America. LC 76-40680. (Anti-Movements in America). 1977. Repr. of 1933 ed. lib. bdg. 32.00x (ISBN 0-405-09953-3). Ayer Co Pubs.
--Passing of the Great Race, or, the Racial Basis of European History. LC 74-129398. (American Immigration Collection, Ser. 2). (Illus.). 1970. Repr. of 1918 ed. 16.00 (ISBN 0-405-00577-6). Ayer Co Pubs.
Grant, Malcolm. Veteran & Vintage Cars of Australia. LC 73-77577. (Illus.). 1973. 7.75 (ISBN 0-8048-1104-0). C E Tuttle.
Grant, Malcolm A., et al. Geothermal Reservoir Engineering. LC 82-4105. (Energy Science & Technology Ser.). 1983. 49.50 (ISBN 0-12-295620-6). Acad Pr.
Grant, Marcia M., et al. Case Studies in Clinical Pharmacology. LC 77-519. 169p. 1977. pap. text ed. 8.95x (ISBN 0-8036-4280-6). Davis Co.
Grant, Marcus. Alcoholism in Perspective. 178p. 1979. text ed. 24.50 (ISBN 0-8391-1332-3). Univ Park.
Grant, Marcus & Ritson, Bruce, eds. Alcohol: The Prevention Debate. LC 83-43003. 220p. 1983. 26.00 (ISBN 0-312-01705-7). St Martin.
Grant, Marcus, jt. ed. see Edwards, Griffith.
Grant, Marcus, et al, eds. Economics & Alcohol. 302p. 1983. 28.50 (ISBN 0-89876-089-5). Gardner Pr.
Grant, Margaret. Your Child & the Piano: How to Enrich & Share in Your Child's Musical Experience. 104p. 1980. pap. 5.95 (ISBN 0-8253-0027-4). Beaufort Bks NY.
Grant, Marion H. In & About Hartford: Tours & Tales. (Illus.). 360p. 1977. 2.50x (ISBN 0-940748-26-6); pap. 1.00x (ISBN 0-686-26746-X). Conn Hist Soc.
Grant, Mary K. The Tragic Vision of Joyce Carol Oates. LC 77-75617. 1978. 10.75 (ISBN 0-8223-0404-X). Duke.
Grant, Mary K., jt. ed. see Buback, Kenneth A.
Grant, Mary L., ed. see Dickens, Charles.
Grant, Mary M. & Berleant-Schiller, Riva, eds. Directory of Business & Financial Services. 8th ed. LC 83-20300. 200p. 1984. 35.00 (ISBN 0-87111-287-6). SLA.
Grant, Sr. Mary. Yes, Lord. LC 78-58587. 1978. pap. 2.50 (ISBN 0-87973-706-9). Our Sunday Visitor.
Grant, Matthew G. Buffalo Bill. LC 73-10073. 1974. PLB 7.95 (ISBN 0-87191-255-4). Creative Ed.
--Champlain. LC 73-13714. 1974. PLB 7.95 (ISBN 0-87191-287-2). Creative Ed.
--Chief Joseph. LC 73-9816. 1974. PLB 7.95 (ISBN 0-87191-251-1). Creative Ed.
--Crazy Horse. LC 73-12403. 1974. PLB 7.95 (ISBN 0-87191-269-4). Creative Ed.
--John Paul Jones. LC 73-18212. 1974. PLB 7.95 (ISBN 0-87191-300-3). Creative Ed.
--Kit Carson. LC 73-10063. 1974. PLB 7.95 (ISBN 0-87191-253-8). Creative Ed.
--Lewis & Clark. LC 73-14582. 1974. PLB 7.95 (ISBN 0-87191-277-5). Creative Ed.
--Osceola. LC 73-12407. 1974. PLB 7.95 (ISBN 0-87191-266-X). Creative Ed.
--Paul Revere. LC 73-18076. 1974. PLB 7.95 (ISBN 0-87191-303-8). Creative Ed.
--Squanto. LC 73-12813. 1974. PLB 7.95 (ISBN 0-87191-270-8). Creative Ed.
Grant, Maurice. A Chronological History of the Old English Landscape Painters in Oil 1760-1830, Vol. 5. (Illus.). 1974. Repr. of 1959 ed. text ed. 30.50x (ISBN 0-85317-590-X, Pub. by A & C Black England). Humanities.
--A Chronological History of the Old English Landscape Painters in Oil 1780-1865, Vol. 7. (Illus.). 1974. Repr. of 1960 ed. text ed. 30.50x (ISBN 0-85317-640-X, Pub. by A & C Black England). Humanities.
Grant, Maurice H. A Dictionary of British Painters: From the 16th Century to the Early 20th Century. 240p. 1981. 40.00x (ISBN 0-85317-250-1, Pub. by Lewis Pubs). State Mutual Bk.
Grant, Maxwell. Norgil: More Tales of Prestidigitection. LC 78-53497. (Illus.). 1979. 10.00 (ISBN 0-89296-041-8); limited ed. o.p. 25.00 (ISBN 0-89296-042-6). Mysterious Pr.
Grant, May B. Wildly Speaking. LC 75-122574. (Popular Ser.: No. 10). 1972. pap. 2.95 (ISBN 0-87768-005-1). Denver Mus Natl Hist.
Grant, Michael. Ancient History Atlas. LC 73-654430. (Illus.). 1981. pap. 10.00 (ISBN 0-915262-73-8). S J Durst.
--Atlas of Ancient History - 1700 BC to 565 AD. (Illus.). 120p. 1984. 17.95 (ISBN 0-88029-009-9). Hippocrene Bks.
--Blandford Book of Rock & Pop Crosswords. (Illus.). 128p. (Orig.). 1985. pap. 3.95 (ISBN 0-7137-1470-0, Pub. by Blandford Pr England). Sterling.
--The Etruscans. (Illus.). 352p. 1981. 17.50 (ISBN 0-684-16724-7, ScribT). Scribner.
--From Alexander to Cleopatra. 319p. 1982. pap. text ed. price not set (ISBN 0-02-345590-X, Pub. by Scribner). Macmillan.
--From Alexander to Cleopatra: The Hellenistic World. (Illus.). 480p. 1982. 19.95 (ISBN 0-684-17780-3, ScribT); pap. 14.95 (ISBN 0-684-17819-2). Scribner.
--From Imperium to Auctoritas: A Historical Study of Coinage in the Roman Empire. (Library Editions Ser). (Illus.). 1969. Repr. of 1946 ed. 79.50 (ISBN 0-521-07457-6). Cambridge U Pr.
--The History of Ancient Israel. (Illus.). 360p. 1984. pap. 14.95 (ISBN 0-684-18084-7, ScribT); 19.95 (ISBN 0-684-18081-2). Scribner.
--The History of Ancient Israel. 360p. 1984. pap. text ed. price not set (ISBN 0-02-345620-5, Pub. by Scribner). Macmillan.
--History of Rome. LC 78-12966. 537p. 1978. pap. text ed. 17.95 (ISBN 0-02-345610-8, Pub. by Scribner). Macmillan.
--Jesus: An Historian's Review of the Gospels. LC 77-70218. 1978. (ScribT); pap. text ed. 9.95 (ISBN 0-684-17439-1). Scribner.
--Jesus: An Historian's View of the Gospels. 261p. 1978. pap. text ed. price not set (ISBN 0-02-345630-2, Pub. by Scribner). Macmillan.
--Myths of the Greeks & Romans. (Illus.). 1964. pap. 4.95 (ISBN 0-451-62267-7, ME2267, Ment). NAL.
--The Roman Emperors: A Biographical Guide to the Rulers of Imperial Rome: 31 B.C.-476 A.D. (Illus.). 416p. 1985. 25.00 (ISBN 0-684-18388-9, ScribT). Scribner.
--Saint Paul. (Crossroad Paperback Ser.). 256p. pap. 7.95 (ISBN 0-686-85826-3). Crossroad NY.
--Saint Paul. 272p. 1976. (ScribT); pap. 8.95 (ISBN 0-684-17746-3). Scribner.
--T. S. Eliot: The Critical Heritage, 2 vols. (Critical Heritager Ser.). 1982. 55.00x (ISBN 0-7100-9226-1); Vol.1, 388p. 33.00x (ISBN 0-7100-9224-5); Vol.2, 402p. 33.00x (ISBN 0-7100-9225-3). Routledge & Kegan.
--Twelve Caesars. 1983. 15.95 (ISBN 0-684-14402-6). Scribner.
Grant, Michael & Hazel, John. Gods & Mortals in Classic Mythology: Dictionary. (Illus.). 320p. 1985. 19.95 (ISBN 0-88029-036-6, Pub. by Dorset Pr). Hippocrene Bks.
Grant, Michael, ed. Greek Literature: An Anthology. (Classics Ser.). 496p. 1977. pap. 5.95 (ISBN 0-14-044323-1). Penguin.
--Latin Literature: An Anthology. (Penguin Classics Ser.). 1979. pap. 5.95 (ISBN 0-14-044389-4). Penguin.
Grant, Michael, tr. see Cicero.
Grant, Michael, tr. see Cicero, Marcus T.
Grant, Michael, tr. see Tacitus.
Grant, Mildred B., compiled by. Indexes to "The Competitor". LC 77-15303. 1978. lib. bdg. 29.95x (ISBN 0-313-20032-7, GIC/). Greenwood.
Grant, Moeller M., jt. auth. see McFarland, Mary B.
Grant, Murray. Handbook of Community Health. 3rd ed. LC 80-26182. (Illus.). 368p. 1981. pap. 12.00 (ISBN 0-8121-0760-8). Lea & Febiger.
--Scaffold Falsework Design to BS 5975. (Viewpoint Publication Ser.). (Illus.). 1982. pap. text ed. 17.95x (ISBN 0-86310-005-8). Scholium Intl.
Grant, Myrna. Ivan & the Daring Escape. (Ivan Ser.). (gr. 3-8). 1976. pap. 3.50 (ISBN 0-8423-1847-X). Tyndale.
--Ivan & the Hidden Bible. (Ivan Ser.). (gr. 3-8). 1975. pap. 2.95 (ISBN 0-8423-1848-8). Tyndale.
--Ivan & the Informer. (Ivan Ser.). 1977. pap. 3.50 (ISBN 0-8423-1846-1). Tyndale.
--Ivan & the Moscow Circus. (gr. 4-8). 1980. pap. 3.50 (ISBN 0-8423-1843-7). Tyndale.
--Ivan & the Secret in the Suitcase. (Ivan Ser.). (gr. 3-8). 1975. pap. 3.50 (ISBN 0-8423-1849-6). Tyndale.
--Ivan & the Star of David. (Ivan Ser.). 1977. pap. 3.50 (ISBN 0-8423-1845-3). Tyndale.
--Ivan y el Delator. 112p. 1980. 2.25 (ISBN 0-88113-154-7). Edit Betania.
--Ivan y el Secreto en la Valija. 160p. 1978. 2.50 (ISBN 0-88113-152-0). Edit Betania.
--Ivan y la Biblia Escondida. 128p. 1978. 2.25 (ISBN 0-88113-150-4). Edit Betania.
--Ivan y la Estrella de David. 144p. 1980. 2.50 (ISBN 0-88113-155-5). Edit Betania.
--Ivan y la Fuga Audaz. 176p. 1978. 2.75 (ISBN 0-88113-151-2). Edit Betania.
--La Jornada. 208p. 1980. 3.25 (ISBN 0-88113-200-4). Edit Betania.
--Mision Secreta de Alexis. 144p. 1980. 2.50 (ISBN 0-88113-202-0). Edit Betania.
--Tanya y el Guarda Fronterizo. 96p. 1980. 1.95 (ISBN 0-88113-321-3). Edit Betania.
--Vanya. LC 73-89729. 1974. pap. 5.95 (ISBN 0-88419-009-9). Creation Hse.
--Vanya. 208p. 1976. 2.95 (ISBN 0-88113-310-8). Edit Betania.
Grant, Neil. Everyday Life in the Eighteenth Century. LC 83-60890. (Everyday Life Ser.). 64p. (gr. 4 up). 1983. 13.72 (ISBN 0-382-06695-2). Silver.
--Explorers. LC 82-50399. (History Eye Witness Ser.). PLB 15.96 (ISBN 0-382-06665-0). Silver.
Grant, Neil & Jones, Jo. Discovering the World. (Full Color Fact Books). (Illus.). 32p. (gr. 4-12). 1981. PLB 7.95 (ISBN 0-8219-0011-0, 35548). EMC.
Grant, Neville see Allen, W. S.
Grant, Nicholas J. & Giessen, Bill C., eds. Rapidly Quenched Metals. 1976. text ed. 47.50x (ISBN 0-262-07066-9). MIT Pr.
Grant, Nigel. Soviet Education. 4th, rev ed. 1979. pap. 6.95 (ISBN 0-14-020660-4, Pelican). Penguin.
Grant, P. J. Gulls: A Guide to Identification. 280p. 1982. 60.00x (ISBN 0-85661-030-5, Pub. by T & AD Boyser England). State Mutual Bk.
--Nuclear Science. (Illus.). 1971. pap. text ed. 17.95x (ISBN 0-245-50419-2). Intl Ideas.
Grant, P. M., jt. auth. see Cowan, C. F.
Grant, P. T. & Mackie, A. M., eds. Chemoreception in Marine Organisms. 1974. 57.00 (ISBN 0-12-295650-8). Acad Pr.
Grant, Parks. Music for Elementary Teachers. 2nd ed. LC 60-6665. (Illus.). 1960. 34.50x (ISBN 0-89197-311-7). Irvington.
Grant, Patrick. Images & Ideas in Literature of the English Renaissance. LC 78-53176. 264p. 1979. 17.50x (ISBN 0-87023-163-4). U of Mass Pr.
--Literature & the Discovery of Method in the English Renaissance. LC 84-23920. 188p. 1985. 22.50x (ISBN 0-8203-0764-5). U of Ga Pr.
--The Literature of Mysticism in Western Tradition. LC 83-5789. 200p. 1983. 22.50x (ISBN 0-312-48808-4). St Martin.
--Six Modern Authors & Problems of Belief. LC 79-14511. 175p. 1979. text ed. 28.50x (ISBN 0-06-492515-3). B&N Imports.
--The Transformation of Sin: Studies in Donne, Herbert, Vaughan & Traherne. LC 73-93174. 308p. 1974. 17.50x (ISBN 0-87023-158-8). U of Mass Pr.
--The Transformation of Sin: Studies in Donne, Herbert, Vaughan & Traherne. LC 73-93174. pap. 63.50 (ISBN 0-317-26444-3, 2023850). Bks Demand UMI.
Grant, Patrick, ed. A Dazzling Darkness: An Anthology of Western Mysticism. (Orig.). 1985. pap. 14.95 (ISBN 0-8028-0088-2). Eerdmans.
Grant, Percy S. Essays. facs. ed. LC 68-22916. (Essay Index Reprint Ser). 1968. Repr. of 1922 ed. 12.00 (ISBN 0-8369-0492-3). Ayer Co Pubs.
Grant, Peter. The Power of Intercession. 108p. (Orig.). 1984. pap. 4.95 (ISBN 0-89283-132-4). Servant.
Grant, Peter H. Holistic Therapy: The Risk & Pay-Offs of Being Alive. 1978. 8.95 (ISBN 0-8065-0633-4). Citadel Pr.
--The Risks & Payoffs of Being Alive: An Introduction to Holistic Therapy. 1979. pap. 4.95 (ISBN 0-8065-0688-1). Citadel Pr.
Grant, Peter J. Gulls: A Guide to Identification. LC 81-71625. (Illus.). 408p. 32.50 (ISBN 0-931130-08-5). Buteo.
Grant, Philip C. Employee Motivation: Principles & Practices. LC 84-90036. 159p. 1984. 14.95 (ISBN 0-533-06122-9). Vantage.
Grant, R. A., ed. Applied Protein Chemistry. (Illus.). 332p. 1980. 52.00 (ISBN 0-85334-865-0, Pub. by Elsevier Applied Sci England). Elsevier.
Grant, R. E., ed. Sing Along-Senior Citizens. 108p. 1973. spiral 11.75x (ISBN 0-398-02722-6). C C Thomas.
Grant, R. M. & Shaw, G. K., eds. Current Issues in Economic Policy. 340p. 1980. text ed. 32.00x (ISBN 0-86003-029-6, Pub. by Allan Pubs England); pap. text ed. 16.25x (ISBN 0-86003-128-4). Humanities.
Grant, Ray, jt. auth. see Iverson, Dick.
Grant, Raymond W. Checklist of Arizona Minerals. (Special Publications Ser.: No. 1). (Illus.). 78p. (Orig.). 1982. pap. 4.00 (ISBN 0-910011-00-1). Mineral Soc ARI.
Grant, Richard. Saraband of Lost Time. 336p. 1985. pap. 2.95 (ISBN 0-380-89533-1). Avon.
Grant, Richard & Thomas, Nigel. BMX Action Bike Book. (Illus.). 48p. 1985. 5.95 (ISBN 0-668-06345-9). Arco.
Grant, Richard B. Zola's Son Excellence Eugene Rougon. LC 60-6649. pap. 38.50 (ISBN 0-317-26760-4, 2023392). Bks Demand UMI.
Grant, Robert. Bachelor's Christmas & Other Stories. LC 70-94728. (Short Story Index Reprint Ser.). 1895. 21.00 (ISBN 0-8369-3107-6). Ayer Co Pubs.
--Face to Face. LC 74-22786. (Labor Movement in Fiction & Non-Fiction). Repr. of 1901 ed. 26.50 (ISBN 0-404-58433-0). AMS Pr.
--History of Physical Astronomy. 1966. Repr. of 1852 ed. 35.00 (ISBN 0-384-19670-5). Johnson Repr.
--The Law Breakers & Other Stories. 1972. Repr. of 1906 ed. 18.00 (ISBN 0-8422-8060-X). Irvington.
--The Orchid. LC 68-57527. (Muckrakers Ser). (Illus.). Repr. of 1905 ed. lib. bdg. 16.00 (ISBN 0-8398-0664-7). Irvington.
--Unleavened Bread. LC 68-20014. (Americans in Fiction Ser.). Repr. of 1900 ed. lib. bdg. 16.00 (ISBN 0-8398-0665-5). Irvington.
Grant, Robert, et al. The King's Men: A Tale of Tomorrow. LC 74-15973. (Science Fiction Ser). 276p. 1975. Repr. of 1884 ed. 20.00x (ISBN 0-405-06292-3). Ayer Co Pubs.
Grant, Robert B. Black Man Comes to the City: A Documentary Account from the Great Migration to the Great Depression, 1915-1930. LC 72-83821. 287p. 1975. 23.95x (ISBN 0-911012-45-1). Nelson-Hall.
Grant, Robert M. Eusebius As Church Historian. 1980. 34.95x (ISBN 0-19-826441-0). Oxford U Pr.
--U-Boat Intelligence, 1914-1918. (Illus.). 192p. 1969. 18.50 (ISBN 0-208-00898-5, Archon). Shoe String.
Grant, Robert M. & Tracy, David. A Short History of the Interpretation of the Bible. 2nd, rev. & enlarged ed. LC 83-18485. 224p. 1984. pap. 10.95 (ISBN 0-8006-1762-2, 1-1762). Fortress.
Grant, Robert M., ed. Gnosticism: A Source Book of Heretical Writings from the Early Christian Period. LC 77-85274. Repr. of 1961 ed. 23.50 (ISBN 0-404-16108-1). AMS Pr.
Grant, Robert M., ed. see Goodspeed, Edgar J.
Grant, Robert M., ed. see Theophilus Of Antioch.
Grant, Ron. Where the Light Was Burning. 192p. 1981. 8.95 (ISBN 0-89962-044-2). Todd & Honeywell.
Grant, Ronald M., ed. Ethno-Nationalism, Multinational Corporations, & the Modern State. Wellhofer, E. Spencer. LC 78-74237. (Monograph Series in World Affairs: Vol. 15, 1977-78, Bk. 4). 90p. (Orig.). 1979. pap. 5.95 perfect bdg (ISBN 0-87940-057-9). Monograph Series.
Grant, Rose. Fast & Delicious Cookbook. LC 81-81484. (Illus.). 183p. (Orig.). 1981. pap. 5.95 (ISBN 0-911954-62-7). Nitty Gritty.
Grant, Roy E., jt. auth. see Jordan, Myra J.
Grant, Russell. Concepts in Physical Fitness: A Self-Paced Program to Improved Health Fitness. 176p. 1985. pap. text ed. 12.95 (ISBN 0-8403-3548-2). Kendall-Hunt.
Grant, Ruthie. Scattered Moments. Richard, L. E. & Lorenzo, Thomas, eds. LC 82-74055. (Illus.). 96p. 1983. pap. 5.95 (ISBN 0-911657-00-2). Creative Gen.
Grant, Sam. A Communication Manager's Guide to Telecommunications in Great Britain. new ed. 1979. 75.00 (ISBN 0-936648-00-7). Telecom Lib.
Grant, Sea. First Aid for Boaters & Divers. 128p. 1980. pap. 6.95 (ISBN 0-8329-1425-8). New Century.
Grant, Sharon L., jt. auth. see Palmer, Phyllis M.
Grant, Sister Marie, jt. auth. see Ashlock, Patrick.
Grant, Stan. The Call of Mother Africa. (Illus.). Repr. of 1973 ed. 10.00 (ISBN 0-686-24749-3). Courier Pr FL.
--Jimmy Carter's Odyssey to Black Africa: Part One. (Illus.). 9.50 (ISBN 0-686-70153-4). Courier Pr FL.
Grant, Stephenson, jt. auth. see Christensen, Alice.
Grant, Steven A. Scholars' Guide to Washington, D.C. for Russian-Soviet Studies. rev. ed. Mayerchak, Patrick M., ed. LC 83-600231. (Scholars' Guides to Washington, D.C.). 403p. 1983. 29.95x (ISBN 0-87474-490-3); pap. 15.00x (ISBN 0-87474-489-X). Smithsonian.
Grant, Steven A., jt. auth. see Brown, John H.
Grant, Steven C. A Management Guide to Automatic Call Distributors. 240p. 1981. 125.00 (ISBN 0-686-98043-3). Telecom Lib.
--A Management Guide to Efficient Automatic Call Distributors. Brooks, Yvonne C., ed. 264p. 1981. pap. 125.00 (ISBN 0-936648-08-2). Telecom Lib.
Grant, Susan T. Beauty & the Beast: The Coevolution of Plants & Animals. 224p. 1984. 14.95 (ISBN 0-684-18186-X, ScribT). Scribner.
Grant, Theodore J. The Universe As Man's Chief Adversary in the Struggle for Life's Dominion: From Aristotle to Nietzsche. (Illus.). 129p. 1985. 88.85 (ISBN 0-89920-078-8). Am Inst Psych.
Grant, Thomas M. The Comedies of George Chapman: A Study in Development. (Salzburg Studies in English Literature, Jacobean Drama Studies: No. 5). 1972. pap. text ed. 25.50x (ISBN 0-391-01391-2). Humanities.
Grant, Tommy, ed. see Rotary Club of Chester, S. Carolina.
Grant, U. S. Letters of Ulysses S. Grant to His Father & His Youngest Sister. LC 12-24177. Repr. of 1912 ed. 12.00 (ISBN 0-527-35350-7). Kraus Repr.
--Personal Memoirs of U. S. Grant. (Quality Paperbacks Ser.). 608p. 1982. pap. 10.95 (ISBN 0-306-80172-8). Da Capo.
Grant, U. S., jt. auth. see Hertlein, Leo G.
Grant, Ulysses S. General Grant's Letters to a Friend, 1861-1880. Wilson, James G., ed. LC 73-168179. Repr. of 1897 ed. 14.25 (ISBN 0-404-04598-7). AMS Pr.
--The Papers of Ulysses S. Grant, Vol. 11, June 1 - August 15, 1864. Simon, John Y., ed. LC 67-10725. (Illus.). 512p. 1984. 45.00x (ISBN 0-8093-1117-8). S Ill U Pr.
--The Papers of Ulysses S. Grant, Vol. 12, August 16 - November 15, 1864. Simon, John Y., ed. LC 67-10725. (Illus.). 525p. 1984. 45.00 (ISBN 0-8093-1118-6). S Ill U Pr.
--The Papers of Ulysses S. Grant: Vol. 1 - 1837-1861. Simon, John Y., ed. LC 67-10725. (Illus.). 498p. 1967. 22.50x (ISBN 0-8093-0248-9). S Ill U Pr.
--The Papers of Ulysses S. Grant, Vol. 10: January 1 - May 31, 1864. Simon, John Y., ed. LC 67-10725. (Illus.). 648p. 1982. 40.00x (ISBN 0-8093-0980-7). S Ill U Pr.
--The Papers of Ulysses S. Grant, Vol. 2: April to September, 1861. Simon, John Y., ed. LC 67-10725. (Illus.). 437p. 1969. 22.50x (ISBN 0-8093-0366-3). S Ill U Pr.
--The Papers of Ulysses S. Grant, Vol. 4: January 8 to March 31, 1862. Simon, John Y. & Bridges, Roger D., eds. LC 67-10725. (Illus.). 558p. 1972. 22.50x (ISBN 0-8093-0507-0). S Ill U Pr.
--The Papers of Ulysses S. Grant, Vol. 5: April 1 to August 31, 1862. Simon, John Y. & Alexander, Thomas G., eds. LC 67-10725. (Illus.). 488p. 1973. 30.00x (ISBN 0-8093-0636-0). S Ill U Pr.

--The Papers of Ulysses S. Grant, Vol. 6: September 1 to December 8, 1862. Simon, John Y., ed. LC 67-10725. (Illus.). 516p. 1977. 30.00x (ISBN 0-8093-0694-8). S Ill U Pr.

--The Papers of Ulysses S. Grant, Vol. 7: December 9, 1862 to March 31, 1863. Simon, John Y., ed. LC 67-10725. (Illus.). 612p. 1979. 35.00x (ISBN 0-8093-0880-0). S Ill U Pr.

--The Papers of Ulysses S. Grant, Vol. 8: April 1 to July 6, 1863. Simon, John Y., ed. LC 67-10725. (Illus.). 634p. 1979. 35.00x (ISBN 0-8093-0884-3). S Ill U Pr.

--The Papers of Ulysses S. Grant, Vol. 9: July 7-December 31, 1863. Simon, John Y., ed. LC 67-10725. (Illus.). 724p. 1982. 40.00x (ISBN 0-8093-0979-3). S Ill U Pr.

--The Papers of Ulysses S. Grant, Vol.3: October 1, 1861 to January 7, 1862. Simon, John Y., ed. LC 67-10725. (Illus.). 513p. 1970. 22.50x (ISBN 0-8093-0471-6). S Ill U Pr.

--Personal Memoirs, 2 Vols in 1. Repr. of 1894 ed. 41.50 (ISBN 0-404-04599-5). AMS Pr.

--Personal Memoirs. abr. ed. 14.50 (ISBN 0-8446-0657-X). Peter Smith.

Grant, Ulysses S., 4th & Hertlein, L. G. The West American Cenozoic Echinoidea. 1967. Repr. of 1938 ed. 23.00 (ISBN 0-384-09680-8). Johnson Repr.

Grant, Verne. The Evolutionary Process: A Critical Review of Evolutionary Theory. 544p. 1985. 20.00x (ISBN 0-231-05752-0). Columbia U Pr.

--Genetics of Flowering Plants. LC 74-13555. (Illus.). 1975. 52.50x (ISBN 0-231-03694-9); pap. 22.00x (ISBN 0-231-08363-7). Columbia U Pr.

--Organismic Evolution. LC 76-54175. (Illus.). 418p. 1977. text ed. 31.95 (ISBN 0-7167-0372-6). W H Freeman.

--The Origin of Adaptations. LC 63-11695. (Illus.). 606p. 1963. 54.00x (ISBN 0-231-02529-7); pap. 22.00x (ISBN 0-231-08648-2). Columbia U Pr.

--Plant Speciation. 2nd ed. LC 81-6159. (Illus.). 544p. 1981. 52.50x (ISBN 0-231-05112-3); pap. 18.50x (ISBN 0-231-04460-7). Columbia U Pr.

Grant, Verne, jt. auth. see Grant, Karen A.

Grant, Vernon. Falling in Love: The Psychology of the Romantic Emotion. LC 75-44446. 200p. 1976. text ed. 11.00 (ISBN 0-8261-1890-9). Springer Pub.

Grant, Vernon W. The Psychology of Sexual Emotion: The Basis of Selective Attraction. LC 75-36356. 1979. Repr. of 1957 ed. lib. bdg. 24.75x (ISBN 0-8371-8631-5, GRPS). Greenwood.

Grant, W. A., ed. Low Energy Ion Beams: Proceedings of the Third LEIB Conference, Loughborough, UK, 28-31 March 1983. 120p. 1983. pap. 27.50 (ISBN 0-08-030553-9). Pergamon.

--Vacuum, Eighty-Four: Technological Aspects of Surface Treatment & Analysis: Proceedings of the Conference Held at the University of York, 1-4 April 1984. 204p. 1985. pap. 45.00 (ISBN 0-08-032555-6). Pergamon.

Grant, W. A. & Balfour, D., eds. Vacuum Eighty-Two: Proceedings of the Biennial Conference of the Vacuum Group of the Institute of Physics, Chester, 29-31 March 1982. 112p. 1983. pap. 28.00 (ISBN 0-08-029999-7). Pergamon.

Grant, W. A., jt. ed. see Ashworth, V.

Grant, W. E., tr. see Zlotin, R. I. & Khodashova, K. S.

Grant, W. J. Medical Gases: Their Properties & Uses. (Illus.). 1978. pap. 24.95 (ISBN 0-8151-3875-X). Year Bk Med.

Grant, W. L., ed. Voyages of Samuel De Champlain, Sixteen Four to Sixteen Eighteen. (Original Narratives). 374p. 1967. Repr. of 1907 ed. 21.50x (ISBN 0-06-480330-9). B&N Imports.

Grant, W. Morton. Toxicology of the Eye: Drugs, Chemicals, Plants, Venoms, 2 vols. 2nd ed. (Illus.). 1216p. 1974. 74.50x (ISBN 0-398-02299-2). C C Thomas.

Grant, Walter, tr. see Fastenrath, Fritz.

Grant, Will. The Act of Theatre. LC 77-92930. 1978. pap. text ed. 6.95 (ISBN 0-8403-1841-3). Kendall-Hunt.

Grant, William. Cable Television. 1983. pap. text ed. 24.95 (ISBN 0-8359-0616-7). Reston.

Grant, William D. & Long, P. E. Environmental Microbiology. LC 81-11685. (Tertiary Level Biology Ser.). 200p. 1981. pap. 29.95x (ISBN 0-470-27233-3). Halsted Pr.

Grant, William F. Plant Biosystematics: Symposium. 1984. 49.50 (ISBN 0-12-295680-X). Acad Pr.

Grant, William N. The P-50 One Mustang. (Illus.). 64p. 1983. pap. 4.95 (ISBN 0-13-647875-1). P-H.

Grant, Wilson W. The Caring Father. LC 82-72990. (Orig.). 1983. pap. 5.95 (ISBN 0-8054-5654-6). Broadman.

--De Padres a Hijos Acerca Del Sexo. La Valle, Maria T., et al, trs. from Eng. (Sexo en la Vida Christiana Ser.). (Illus.). 192p. (Span.). 1980. pap. 3.95 (ISBN 0-311-46255-3). Casa Bautista.

Grant, Wyn. Political Economy & Industrial Policy. 1982. 39.95 (ISBN 0-408-10765-0). Butterworth.

Grant, Wyn & Marsh, David. The Confederation of British Industry. 226p. 1977. text ed. 16.50x (ISBN 0-8419-6205-7). Holmes & Meier.

Grant, Wyn, ed. The Political Economy of Corporatism. 272p. 1985. 29.95 (ISBN 0-312-62260-0). St Martin.

Grant, Zalin. Survivors. 345p. 1975. 8.95 (ISBN 0-393-08727-1). Norton.

Granta Magazine Staff. Granta, No. 15. 1985. 6.95 (ISBN 0-14-007582-8). Penguin.

Grant-Adamson, Lesley. Death on Widow's Walk. 224p. 1985. 13.95 (ISBN 0-684-18318-8, ScribT). Scribner.

Grant Duff, M. E. Sir Henry Maine: A Brief Memoir of His Life. Stokes, Whitley, ed. 451p. 1979. Repr. of 1892 ed. lib. bdg. 35.00x (ISBN 0-8377-0609-2). Rothman.

Grant Duff, Mountstuart. Ernest Renan in Memoriam. 1893. Repr. 25.00 (ISBN 0-8274-2285-7). R West.

Grant-Duff, Mountstuart E. Studies in European Politics. LC 72-110901. 1970. Repr. of 1866 ed. 34.50x (ISBN 0-8046-0884-9, Pub. by Kennikat). Assoc Faculty Pr.

Grant Duff, Mountstuart E., ed. Anthology of Victorian Poetry. facs. ed. LC 72-133070. (Granger Index Reprint Ser). 1902. 24.00 (ISBN 0-8369-6200-1). Ayer Co Pubs.

Grant-Goddard, Betty S., jt. auth. see Kilchenstein, E. Delores.

Grantham, A. E. Porcelain Pagodas & Palaces of Jade. LC 78-57427. (Illus.). 1979. write for info. (ISBN 0-89344-025-6). ARS Ceramica.

Grantham, Alexandra E. Manchu Monarch: An Interpretation of Chia Ch'ing. (Studies in Chinese History & Civilization). 1977. Repr. of 1934 ed. 19.00 (ISBN 0-89093-076-7). U Pubns Amer.

Grantham, Charles E. Social Networks & Marital Interaction. Reed, R., ed. LC 81-83621. (Illus.). 125p. 1982. pap. 9.00 (ISBN 0-88247-617-3). R & E Pubs.

Grantham, Dewey W. Contemporary American History: The United States Since 1945. LC 75-883. (AHA Pamphlets: No. 215). 1975. pap. text ed. 1.50 (ISBN 0-87229-019-0). Am Hist Assn.

--Democratic South. 1965. pap. 1.45x (ISBN 0-393-00299-3, Norton Lib). Norton.

--The Regional Imagination: The South & Recent American History. LC 78-26556. 1979. 15.95x (ISBN 0-8265-1207-0). Vanderbilt U Pr.

--The Regional Imagination: The South & Recent American History. (Vanderbilt University Press Bks.). 283p. 1979. 15.95 (ISBN 0-8265-1207-0). U of Ill Pr.

--Southern Progressivism: The Reconciliation of Progress & Tradition. LC 82-25918. (Twentieth-Century America Ser.). (Illus.). 490p. 1983. text ed. 34.95x (ISBN 0-87049-389-2); pap. text ed. 16.95x (ISBN 0-87049-390-6). U of Tenn Pr.

--United States Since Nineteen Forty-Five: The Ordeal of Power. (Modern America Ser.). 1975. 19.95 (ISBN 0-07-024116-3). McGraw.

Grantham, Dewey W., ed. see Bunche, Ralph J.

Grantham, Dewey W., Jr. Hoke Smith & the Politics of the New South. LC 58-9209. (Southern Biography Ser.). (Illus.). 396p. pap. text ed. 9.95x (ISBN 0-8071-0118-4). La State U Pr.

Grantham, Dixie L. An Anthology. 64p. 1984. 5.95 (ISBN 0-87397-263-5). Strode.

Grantham, Donald, jt. auth. see Kennan, Kent.

Grantham, Donald J. Antennas, Transmission Lines, & Microwaves. LC 77-25369. (The Grantham Electronics-with-Mathematics Ser.: Vol. 6). (Illus.). 1977. pap. text ed. 18.95x (ISBN 0-915668-06-8). G S E Pubns.

--Basic Electronic Devices & Circuits. LC 77-22488. (The Grantham Electronics-with-Mathematics Ser.: Vol. 4). (Illus.). 1977. pap. text ed. 18.95x (ISBN 0-915668-04-1). G S E Pubns.

--Basic Radio & Television Systems. LC 79-11773. (Grantham Electronics-with-Mathematics Ser.: Vol. 5). (Illus.). 1979. pap. 17.95x (ISBN 0-915668-05-X). G S E Pubns.

--Fundamental Properties of AC Circuits. LC 75-18398. (Grantham Electronics-with-Mathematics Ser.: Vol. 2). (Illus.). 1976. pap. text ed. 15.95x (ISBN 0-915668-02-5). G S E Pubns.

--Geometry for Science & Technology. LC 76-40924. 121p. 1976. pap. text ed. 8.95x (ISBN 0-915668-28-9). G S E Pubns.

--Introductory Electricity with Mathematics. LC 75-2797. (Grantham Electronics-with-Mathematics Ser.: Vol. 1). (Illus.). 288p. 1975. pap. text ed. 16.95x (ISBN 0-915668-01-7). G S E Pubns.

--Mathematics for Basic Circuit Analysis. LC 76-40449. (Grantham Electronics-with-Mathematics Ser: Vol. 3). 1976. pap. text ed. 18.95x (ISBN 0-915668-03-3). G S E Pubns.

Grantham, Emily. PERT-CPM for Population Program Management. LC 75-29488. (PopCase Series B). (Illus.). 119p. 1975. pap. 3.00 (ISBN 0-89055-302-5). U of NC Dept Health.

Grantham, G. J. The Utilization of Krill. (Southern Ocean Fisheries Survey Programmes: GLO-SO-77-3). 67p. (Eng. & Span.). 1977. pap. 7.50 (ISBN 92-5-100416-1, F1314, FAO). Unipub.

Grantham, G. J. & Tuna, Charley. Minced Fish Technology: A Review. (Fisheries Technical Papers: No. 216). 79p. 1981. pap. 7.50 (ISBN 92-5-101130-3, F2242, FAO). Unipub.

Grantham, Jared J., jt. auth. see Sullivan, Lawrence P.

Grantham, Jared J. & Gardner, Kenneth D., Jr., eds. Problems in Diagnosis & Management of Polycystic Kidney Disease: Proceedings of the First International Workshop on PKD. (Illus.). 216p. 1985. 14.95 (ISBN 0-9614567-0-1). PKR Foundation.

Grantham, Rudolph E. Lay Shepherding. 1980. pap. 4.95 (ISBN 0-8170-0863-2). Judson.

--Love: Your Path to Health. 64p. 1982. pap. 3.95 (ISBN 0-8170-0938-8). Judson.

Grantham, Walter J., jt. auth. see Vincent, Thomas L.

Grant-Watson, Elliot L. Innocent Desires. facsimile ed. LC 76-121553. (Short Story Index Reprint Ser.). Repr. of 1924 ed. 19.00 (ISBN 0-8369-3509-8). Ayer Co Pubs.

Grantz, Gerald. Home Book of Taxidermy & Tanning. (Illus.). 160p. (Orig.). 1985. pap. 8.95 (ISBN 0-8117-2259-7). Stackpole.

Grantz, Gerald J. Home Book of Taxidermy & Tanning. LC 77-85651. (Illus.). 160p. 1970. 10.95 (ISBN 0-8117-0805-5). Stackpole.

Granville, Joseph. The Warning: The Coming Great Crash in the Stock Market. 414p. 1985. 17.95 (ISBN 0-88191-034-1). Freundlich.

Granville, Joseph E. Granville's New Strategy of Daily Stock Market Timing for Maximum Profit. 375p. 1976. 19.95 (ISBN 0-13-363432-9, Parker). P-H.

Granville, Joseph E. & Hoffer, William. The Book of Granville: Reflections of a Stock Market Prophet. 256p. 1984. 14.95 (ISBN 0-312-08902-3). St Martin.

Granville, Michael S. The Theory of Elitism in Education. (Illus.). 123p. 1984. 76.85x (ISBN 0-89266-438-X). Am Classical Coll Pr.

Granville, Samuel. How to Get Your Hands on Some Money. LC 79-91842. 229p. 1980. 19.95 (ISBN 0-935686-00-2); pap. 14.95 (ISBN 0-935686-01-0). Prosperity Pr.

Granville, Wiley J. A Practical Handbook of Ceramic Art with Important Technological Notes. (Illus.). 149p. 1980. 65.65 (ISBN 0-930582-85-3). Gloucester Art.

Granville, Wilfred. Theater Dictionary: British & American Terms in the Drama, Opera, and Ballet. Repr. of 1952 ed. lib. bdg. 55.00x (ISBN 0-8371-4428-0, GRTD). Greenwood.

Granville, William A. Plane Trigonometry & Four-Place Tables. LC 52-3178. pap. 69.00 (ISBN 0-317-08698-7, 2000160). Bks Demand UMI.

Granville, William A. & Smith, Percey F. Elements of the Differential & Integral Calculus. rev. ed. pap. 142.00 (ISBN 0-317-08569-7, 2019890). Bks Demand UMI.

Granville-Baker, Harley. Preface to Shakespeare: Volume 1, Hamlet. 1977. pap. 11.95 (ISBN 0-7134-2050-2, Pub. by Batsford England). David & Charles.

Granville-Barker, H. Associating with Shakespeare. LC 73-13543. 1932. lib. bdg. 15.00 (ISBN 0-8414-4422-6). Folcroft.

--From Henry V to Hamlet. LC 76-14978. 1973. lib. bdg. 15.00 (ISBN 0-8414-4423-4). Folcroft.

--The Study of Drama. 1934. lib. bdg. 15.00 (ISBN 0-8414-4624-5). Folcroft.

Granville-Barker, Harley. Exemplary Theatre. LC 74-114878. (Select Bibliographies Reprint Ser). 1922. 20.00 (ISBN 0-8369-5282-0). Ayer Co Pubs.

--Prefaces to Shakespeare. Incl. Vol. 1. Hamlet, King Lear, the Merchant of Venice, Anthony & Cleopatra. 30.00 (ISBN 0-691-06276-5); pap. 11.95 (ISBN 0-691-01350-0); Vol. 2. Othello, Coriolanus, Julius Caesar, Romeo & Juliet, Love's Labor Lost. pap. 10.95 (ISBN 0-691-01351-9). Princeton U Pr.

--Prefaces to Shakespeare: Caesar, Anthony & Cleopatra. 160p. 1982. pap. 11.95 (ISBN 0-7134-4511-4, Pub. by Batsford England). David & Charles.

--Prefaces to Shakespeare: Coriolanus. 160p. 1982. pap. 11.95 (ISBN 0-7134-4328-6, Pub. by Batsford England). David & Charles.

--Prefaces to Shakespeare: Cymbeline - The Winter's Tale. (Prefaces to Shakespeare Ser.). 104p. 1985. pap. 11.95 (ISBN 0-7134-4836-9, Pub. by Batsford England). David & Charles.

--Prefaces to Shakespeare: King Lear & Macbeth. 160p. 1982. pap. 11.95 (ISBN 0-7134-4512-2, Pub. by Batsford England). David & Charles.

--Prefaces to Shakespeare: Love's Labour's Lost, The Merchant of Venice, Romeo & Juliet. 160p. 1982. pap. 11.95 (ISBN 0-7134-4330-8, Pub. by Batsford England). David & Charles.

--Prefaces to Shakespeare: Vol. 3, Julius Caesar, Cymbeline, the Merchant of Venice. 192p. 1971. pap. 11.95 (ISBN 0-7134-2065-0, Pub. by Batsford England). David & Charles.

--Prefaces to Shakespeare: Vol. 6, a Winter's Tale, Twelfth Night, Midsummer Night's Dream, Macbeth, from Henry V to Hamlet. 176p. 1974. pap. 11.95 (ISBN 0-7134-2791-4, Pub. by Batsford England). David & Charles.

--The Study of Drama. 92p. 1980. Repr. of 1934 ed. lib. bdg. 15.00 (ISBN 0-8482-4195-9). Norwood Edns.

--The Study of Drama. 92p. 1983. Repr. of 1934 ed. lib. bdg. 15.00 (ISBN 0-8492-5025-0). R West.

Granville-Barker, Harley & Harrison, George B. Companion to Shakespeare Studies. 1934. 69.50 (ISBN 0-521-05132-0). Cambridge U Pr.

Granville-Barker, Harley, ed. see Fellows of the Royal Society of Literature of the UK.

Granville-Barker, Harley G. Exemplary Theatre. LC 70-84514. 286p. Repr. of 1922 ed. 24.50 (ISBN 0-405-08571-0, Blom Pubns). Ayer Co Pubs.

Granzer, F., et al, eds. see International Conference on Solid State Nuclear Track Detectors, 9th, Neuherberg-Munich, 1976.

Granzer, Randolf. Cyclical Indicators for Manufacturing Industries. (Occasional Economic Studies Ser.). 1973. 2.50x (ISBN 92-64-11148-4). OECD.

Granzotto, Gianni. Christopher Columbus. Sartorelli, Stephen, tr. from Ital. LC 85-4387. (Illus.). 336p. 1985. 18.95 (ISBN 0-385-19677-6). Doubleday.

Graovac, A., et al. Topological Approach to the Chemistry of Conjugated Molecules. (Lecture Notes in Chemistry: Vol. 4). 1977. pap. 14.00 (ISBN 0-387-08431-2). Springer-Verlag.

Graper, Elmer D. American Police Administration: A Handbook on Police Organization & Methods of Administration in American Cities. LC 69-14929. (Criminology, Law Enforcement, & Social Problems Ser.: No. 37). (With intro. added). 1969. Repr. of 1921 ed. 17.00x (ISBN 0-87585-037-5). Patterson Smith.

Graphic Artists Guild, tr. Corporate & Communications Design Annual. (Illus.). 80p. 1984. 24.95 (ISBN 0-912417-02-1). Annuals Pub Co.

--The Graphic Artists Guild Directory Four. (Illus.). 208p. 1984. comb. binding 25.95 (ISBN 0-912417-01-3). Annuals Pub Co.

Graphical Ray Tracing. Graphical Ray Tracing: An Advanced Text. (Illus.). pap. 20.00 (ISBN 0-317-07887-9, 2010138). Bks Demand UMI.

Grapp, Valera. Law Office Desk Book. 450p. 1982. 37.50 (ISBN 0-13-526574-6). P-H.

--Portfolio of Business Forms, Agreements & Contracts. LC 84-11647. 497p. 1984. 59.95 (ISBN 0-13-686791-X). P-H.

Grappa, Carol di see Di Grappa, Carol.

Grappa, Carol di see Di Grappa, Carol, et al.

Grappel, Robert D. & Hemenway, Jack E. Tracer: A 6800 Debugging Program. LC 78-7326. 1978. pap. 9.95 (ISBN 0-07-024121-X, BYTE Bks). McGraw.

Grappelli, Stephane, jt. auth. see Glaser, Matt.

Grappin, P. Dictionnaire moderne Larousse, francais-allemand et allemand-francais. (Fr. & Ger.). 29.95 (ISBN 2-03-020603-2, 3778). Larousse.

Grard, R. J., ed. see ESLAB Symposium, 6th, Noordwijk, the Netherlands, Sept. 1972.

Gras, Ann, jt. auth. see Frankel, Phillip.

Gras, Joseph Le see Le Gras, Joseph.

Gras, N. S. & Larson, H. M. Casebook in American Business History. (Illus.). 1939. 44.50x (ISBN 0-89197-065-7); pap. text ed. 14.95x (ISBN 0-89197-066-5). Irvington.

Gras, Norman S. Business & Capitalism: An Introduction to Business History. LC 68-55720. (Illus.). Repr. of 1939 ed. 37.50x (ISBN 0-678-00747-0). Kelley.

--History of Agriculture in Europe & America. 2nd ed. (History of American Economy Ser.). 1968. Repr. of 1946 ed. 37.00 (ISBN 0-384-19710-8). Johnson Repr.

--Industrial Evolution. LC 68-55722. Repr. of 1930 ed. 27.50x (ISBN 0-678-00462-5). Kelley.

--Introduction to Economic History. LC 68-55723. (Illus.). Repr. of 1922 ed. 35.00x (ISBN 0-678-00466-8). Kelley.

--The Massachusetts First National Bank of Boston, 1784-1934. LC 75-41759. (Companies & Men: Business Enterprises in America). (Illus.). 1976. Repr. of 1937 ed. 60.50x (ISBN 0-405-08075-1). Ayer Co Pubs.

Gras, S., ed. see Strieder, Jacob.

Graselli, Jeanette, jt. auth. see Brame, Edward.

Graselli, Rose N. & Hegner, Priscilla A. Playful Parenting. LC 80-39665. (Illus.). 320p. 1983. 7.95 (ISBN 0-399-50725-6, G&D). Putnam Pub Group.

Grases, Pedro J. & Beker G., Simon. Color Atlas of Liver Biopsy: A Clinical Pathological Guide. LC 80-28801. Orig. Title: Guia Practica De Biopsia Hepatica En el Adulto. (Illus.). 134p. 1981. 60.00 (ISBN 0-8451-0209-5). A R Liss.

Grasha, Anthony F. Practical Applications of Psychology. 2nd ed. 1982. pap. text ed. 16.95 (ISBN 0-316-32408-6); tchr's. manual avail. (ISBN 0-316-32409-4); students' guide 8.95 (ISBN 0-316-32411-6). Little.

Grasha, Anthony F. & Kirchenbaum, Daniel S. Psychology of Adjustment & Competence: An Applied Approach. (Orig.). 1980. text ed. 19.95 (ISBN 0-316-32412-4); tchr's. manual (ISBN 0-316-32421-3); study guide 8.95 (ISBN 0-316-32413-2). Little.

Grasha, Anthony F., jt. auth. see Fuhrmann, Babara S.

Grashio, Samuel C. & Norling, Bernard. Return to Freedom: Bataan Death March. LC 82-60732. 1982. 14.95 (ISBN 0-912958-20-0). MCN Pr.

Grasmick, Mary K., jt. auth. see Thornton, Russell.

Grass, Al, jt. auth. see Eberts, Tony.

Grass, Dean E. The Learning Block. 152p. (Orig.). 1981. pap. 6.95 (ISBN 0-930298-10-1). Westwood Pub Co.

Grass, Gunter. Cat & Mouse. pap. 2.50 (ISBN 0-451-12699-8, AE2699, Sig). NAL.

--Cat & Mouse. 10.95 (ISBN 0-8488-0112-1, Pub. by Amereon hse). Amereon Ltd.

--Davor: Ein Stuck in 13 Szenen. Lange, Victor & Lange, Frances, eds. 182p. 1973. pap. text ed. 4.95 (ISBN 0-15-516963-7, HC). HarBraceJ.

--Dog Years. 1979. pap. 2.95 (ISBN 0-449-24256-0, Crest). Fawcett.
--Drawings & Words Nineteen Fifty-Four to Nineteen Seventy-Seven. Arndt, Walter & Hamburger, Michael, trs. (A Helen & Kurt Wolff Bk.). (Illus.). 1983. Repr. of 1982 ed. 150.00 (ISBN 0-15-126559-3). HarBraceJ.
--Etchings & Words Nineteen Seventy-Two to Nineteen Eighty-Two. Hamburger, Michael, et al, trs. from Ger. (A Helen & Kurt Wolff Bk.). (Illus.). 148p. 1985. 99.95 (ISBN 0-15-129150-0). HarBraceJ.
--The Flounder. 1979. pap. 2.95 (ISBN 0-449-24180-7, Crest). Fawcett.
--The Flounder. Manheim, Ralph, tr. LC 78-53891. (Helen & Kurt Wolff Bks). 1978. 12.00 (ISBN 0-15-131486-1). HarBraceJ.
--Headbirths; or, The Germans Are Dying Out. 160p. 1983. pap. 2.95 (ISBN 0-449-20057-4, Crest). Fawcett.
--In the Egg & Other Poems. Hamburger, Michael & Middleton, Christopher, trs. LC 76-40441. 1977. pap. 5.95 (ISBN 0-15-672239-9, Harv). HarBraceJ.
--Katz und Maus. Brookes, H. F. & Fraenkel, C. E., eds. 272p. (Orig., Ger.). 1971. pap. text ed. 9.00x (ISBN 0-435-38370-1). Heinemann Ed.
--Kinderlied. (Illus.). 60p. 1983. 50.00 (ISBN 0-935716-18-1). Lord John.
--Local Anaesthetic. 1979. pap. 2.95 (ISBN 0-449-24257-9, Crest). Fawcett.
--Love Tested. 600.00 (ISBN 0-15-102570-3). Johnson Repr.
--Max: A Play. Wilson, Leslie A., tr. Manheim, Ralph. 122p. Date not set. pap. 3.25 (ISBN 0-15-657782-8). HarBraceJ.
--The Meeting at Telgte. Manheim, Ralph, tr. from Ger. LC 80-8749. (Helen & Kurt Wolff Bk.). 1981. 9.95 (ISBN 0-15-158588-1). HarBraceJ.
--The Meeting at Telgte. 224p. 1982. pap. 3.50 (ISBN 0-449-24504-7, Crest). Fawcett.
--On Writing & Politics: 1967-1983. Manheim, Ralph, tr. from Ger. (A Helen & Kurt Wolff Bk.). 192p. 1985. 13.95 (ISBN 0-15-169969-0). HarBraceJ.
--Die Plebejer Proben Den Aufstand. Brookes, H. F. & Fraenkel, C. E., eds. (Ger.). 1971. pap. text ed. 6.00x (ISBN 0-435-38372-8). Heinemann Ed.
--Speak Out: Speeches, Open Letters, Commentaries. Manheim, Ralph, tr. LC 69-12035. (Helen & Kurt Wolff Bk). 1969. 9.95 (ISBN 0-15-184704-5). HarBraceJ.
--Tin Drum. Manheim, Ralph, tr. 1971. 10.95 (ISBN 0-394-44902-9, V-300, Vin); pap. 5.95 (ISBN 0-394-74560-4). Random.

Grass, Martin, ed. Control of Working Capital: A Programme of Management Priorities. 1972. 17.95x (ISBN 0-8464-0286-6). Beekman Pubs.

Grass, Roland & Risley, William R., eds. Waiting for Pegasus: Studies of the Presence of Symbolism & Decadence in Hispanic Letters. LC 79-64810. 1979. pap. 5.00 (ISBN 0-934312-02-8). Essays in Lit W Ill U.

Grasse, P. P., ed. La Vie des Animaux, 4 vols. (Illus., Fr.). 1969. Vols. 1-3. 57.25x ea.; Vol. 4. 49.95x (ISBN 0-685-92813-6). Larousse.

Grasse, Pierre P. Evolution of Living Organisms: Evidence for a New Theory of Transformation. 1978. 47.50 (ISBN 0-12-295550-1). Acad Pr.
--Plus Beau Bestiaire du monde. (Fr). 49.95x (ISBN 2-03-017167-0). Larousse.

Grasse, Pierre P. & Tetry, Andree. Zoologie: Generalites, Protozoaires, Metazoaires I, Vol. 1. (Methodique Ser.). 1268p. 41.50 (ISBN 0-686-56434-0). French & Eur.
--Zoologie: Metazoaires, Vol. 2. (Methodique Ser.). 1056p. 39.95 (ISBN 0-686-56435-9). French & Eur.

Grassell, E. Milton, ed. see Pacific Northwest Conference on Higher Education, 1970.

Grasselli, A., ed. Automatic Interpretation & Classification of Images. (NATO Advanced Study Institute Ser.). 1969. 68.50 (ISBN 0-12-295850-0). Acad Pr.

Grasselli, J. & Ritchey, W., eds. Atlas of Spectral Data & Physical Constants for Organic Compounds, 6 vols. 2nd ed. LC 72-2452. 4688p. 1975. Set. 725.00 (ISBN 0-87819-317-0). CRC Pr.

Grasselli, Jeanette G., ed. The Analytical Approach. LC 82-22618. (Illus.). 239p. 1983. 29.95 (ISBN 0-8412-0753-4); pap. 19.95 (ISBN 0-8412-0755-0). Am Chemical.

Grasselli, Jeanette G., et al. Chemical Applications of Raman Spectroscopy. LC 81-1326. 198p. 1981. 45.00 (ISBN 0-471-08541-3, Pub. by Wiley-Interscience). Wiley.

Grasselli, Jeanette, jt. ed. see Brame, E. G.

Grasselli, Jeannette, jt. ed. see Brame, Edward G.

Grasselli, Margaret M., tr. see Brayer, Yves & Faxon, Alicia.

Grasserbauer, M. & Zacherl, M. K., eds. Progress in Materials Analysis, Vol. 1. (Mikrochimica Acta Ser.: Supplement 10). (Illus.). 350p. 1983. pap. 49.70 (ISBN 0-387-81759-X). Springer-Verlag.

Grasshoff, Klaus, ed. Methods of Seawater Analysis. 2nd ed. (Illus.). 419p. 1983. 70.00x (ISBN 0-89573-070-7). VCH Pubs.

Grassi, C. Vocabolarietto della Lingua Italiana. (Ital.). write for info. French & Eur.

Grassi, Carlo, ed. see International Congress of Chemotherapy, 11th & Interscience Conference on Antimicrobial Agents & Chemotherapy, 19th.

Grassi, Carlo, ed. see Symposium Milan, Italy, November 1978.

Grassi, Ernesto. Heidegger & the Question of Renaissance Humanism: Four Studies. LC 83-984. (Medieval & Renaissance Texts & Studies: Vol. 24). 110p. 1983. 12.00 (ISBN 0-86698-062-8). Medieval & Renaissance NY.
--Rhetoric As Philosophy: The Humanist Tradition. LC 79-25276. 1980. text ed. 20.00x (ISBN 0-271-00256-5). Pa St U Pr.

Grassi, G. & Palz, W., eds. Energy from Biomass. 1982. 39.50 (ISBN 90-277-1482-7, Pub. by Reidel Holland). Kluwer Academic.

Grassi, G., jt. ed. see Bloss, W. H.

Grassi, G., jt. ed. see Palz, W.

Grassi, Giacomo Di see Jackson, James L.

Grassi, Giuliana G., ed. see International Congress of Chemotherapy, 12th, Florence, Italy.

Grassi, Joseph A. Broken Bread & Broken Bodies: The Eucharist & World Hunger. LC 84-18888. 128p. (Orig.). 1985. pap. 6.95 (ISBN 0-88344-193-4). Orbis Bks.
--The Secret of Paul the Apostle. LC 77-29045. (Orig.). 1978. pap. 6.95 (ISBN 0-88344-454-2). Orbis Bks.
--Teaching the Way: Jesus, the Early Church & Today. LC 82-7054. 176p. 1982. lib. bdg. 24.00 (ISBN 0-8191-2501-6); pap. text ed. 11.25 (ISBN 0-8191-2502-4). U Pr of Amer.

Grassi, Joseph R. Grassi Block Substitution Test for Measuring Organic Brain Pathology. 2nd ed. (Illus.). 96p. 1970. photocopy ed. spiral 12.75x (ISBN 0-398-00717-9). C C Thomas.

Grassi, Rosanna & DeBlois, Peter. Composition & Literature: A Rhetoric for Critical Writing. (Illus.). 336p. 1984. pap. text ed. 13.95 (ISBN 0-13-163428-3). P-H.

Grassian, Victor. Moral Reasoning: Ethical Theory & Some Contemporary Moral Problems. 400p. 1981. pap. text ed. 19.95 (ISBN 0-13-600759-7). P-H.
--Perennial Philosophical Issues. 640p. 1984. text ed. 26.95 (ISBN 0-13-656769-X). P-H.

Grassick, Patrick. Making the Grade: How to Score High on All Scholastic Tests. LC 83-9966. 160p. (Orig.). 1983. pap. 6.95 (ISBN 0-668-05818-8, 5818). Arco.

Grassie, A. D. The Superconducting State. 40.00x (ISBN 0-686-97024-1, Pub. by Scottish Academic Pr Scotland). State Mutual Bk.

Grassie, J., ed. Highland Experiment: The Story of the Highlands & Islands Development Board. (Illus.). 200p. 1983. 18.00 (ISBN 0-08-025765-8); pap. 11.00 (ISBN 0-08-028473-6). Pergamon.

Grassie, N., ed. Developments in Polymer Degradation, Vol. 3. (Illus.). 319p. 1981. 72.25 (ISBN 0-85334-942-8, Pub. by Elsevier Applied Sci England). Elsevier.
--Developments in Polymer Degradation, Vol. 4. (Illus.). x, 300p. 1982. 70.50 (ISBN 0-85334-132-X, Pub. by Elsevier Applied Sci England). Elsevier.
--Developments in Polymer Degradation, Vol. 5. 240p. 1984. 52.00 (ISBN 0-85334-238-5, Pub. by Elsevier Applied Sci England). Elsevier.
--Developments in Polymer Degradation, Vol. 6. 256p. 1985. 54.00 (ISBN 0-85334-337-3, Pub. by Elsevier Applied Sci England). Elsevier.

Grassie, Norman & Scott, Gerald. Polymer Degradation & Stabilization. (Illus.). 200p. 1985. 54.50 (ISBN 0-521-24961-9). Cambridge U Pr.

Grassl, W., jt. ed. see Haller, R.

Grassl, Wolfgang, ed. Lectures in the Philosophy of Mathematics. Waismann, Friedrich. (Studien Zur Oesterreichischen Philosophie). 125p. 1981. pap. text ed. 19.00x (ISBN 90-6203-613-9, Pub. by Rodopi Holland). Humanities.

Grassle, J. F., et al, eds. Ecological Diversity in Theory & Practice. (Statistical Ecology Ser.: Vol. 6). 1979. 45.00 (ISBN 0-89974-003-0). Intl Co-Op.

Grassman, Peter. Physical Principles of Chemical Engineering. 928p. 1971. text ed. 125.00 (ISBN 0-08-012817-3). Pergamon.

Grassman, Sven & Lundberg, Erik, eds. World Economic Order: Past & Prospects. LC 79-18803. 1980. 42.50x (ISBN 0-312-89046-X). St Martin.

Grassman, W. K. Stochastic Systems for Management. 358p. 1981. 33.25 (ISBN 0-444-00449-1, North Holland). Elsevier.

Grassmann, Hermann. Gesammelte Mathematische und Physikalische Werke, 3 vols in 6 pts. (Ger). Repr. of 1911 ed. Set. 195.00 (ISBN 0-384-09730-8). Johnson Repr.

Grassmann, Hermann G. Ausdehungslehre Von 1878. 4th ed. LC 68-53944. (Ger). 1969. 27.50 (ISBN 0-8284-0222-1). Chelsea Pub.

Grassmick, John D. Mark: The Gospel of Action. (Everyman's Bible Commentary Ser.). Date not set. pap. 5.95 (ISBN 0-8024-2070-2). Moody.

Grassmuck, George & Salibi, Kamal. Reformed Administration in Lebanon. LC 66-3550. 1964. pap. text ed. 1.00x (ISBN 0-932098-00-2). Ctr for NE & North African Stud.

Grassmuck, George, et al, eds. Afghanistan: Some New Approaches. LC 72-11212. 1969. pap. text ed. 4.00x (ISBN 0-932098-01-0). Ctr for NE & North African Stud.

Grassmuck, George L. Sectional Bias in Congress on Foreign Policy. LC 78-64214. (Johns Hopkins University. Studies in the Social Sciences. Sixty-Eighth Ser. 1950: 3). 18.50 (ISBN 0-404-61318-7). AMS Pr.

Grasso, J. C. The Best of Southern Italian Cooking. 1984. 16.95 (ISBN 0-8120-5483-0). Barron.

Grasso, Joseph E., jt. auth. see Miller, Ernest L.

Grasso, Mary E. & Maney, Margaret. You Can Write. 1975. pap. text ed. 12.95 (ISBN 0-316-32422-1). Little.

Grasso, Patricia H. & Stump, Jan S. The Headache Cookbook: A Tool for Migraine Self-Help. (Illus.). 416p. 1984. pap. 12.95 (ISBN 0-89303-512-2). Brady Comm.

Grasswell, Peter. Houses in the Country. 15.00x (ISBN 0-392-05882-0, LTB). Sportshelf.

Grasty, William K & Sheinkopf, Kenneth. Successful Fundraising. 1983. 17.95 (ISBN 0-684-17493-6). Scribner.

Grastyan, E. & Molnar, P., eds. Sensory Functions: Proceedings of the 28th International Congress of Physiological Sciences, Budapest, 1980. LC 80-41852. (Advances in Physiological Sciences). (Illus.). 350p. 1981. 44.00 (ISBN 0-08-027337-8). Pergamon.

Gratarolus, Gulielmus. The Castel of Memorie. LC 72-38109. (English Experience Ser.: No. 382). 128p. 1971. Repr. of 1562 ed. 13.00 (ISBN 90-221-0382-X). Walter J Johnson.
--A Direction for the Health of Magistrates & Students. Newton, Thomas, tr. LC 72-38192. (English Experience Ser.: No. 462). 172p. 1972. Repr. of 1574 ed. 15.00 (ISBN 90-221-0462-1). Walter J Johnson.

Gratcap, L. P. The Substance of Literature. 1973. Repr. of 1913 ed. 20.00 (ISBN 0-8274-0205-8). R West.

Gratch, Alan S. Board Members Are Child Advocates. (Orig.). 1980. pap. text ed. 4.95 (ISBN 0-87868-197-3, AM-31). Child Welfare.

Gratch, Alan S. & Ubik, Virginia H. Ballots for Change: New Suffrage & Amending Articles for Illinois. LC 73-16472. (Studies in Illinois Constitution Making Ser). 139p. 1973. pap. 10.00x (ISBN 0-252-00433-7). U of Ill Pr.

Gratch, Bonnie, et al, eds. Sports & Physical Education: A Guide to the Reference Resources. LC 82-24159. xxi, 198p. 1983. lib. bdg. 35.00 (ISBN 0-313-23433-7, GED/). Greenwood.

Gratch, Serge, ed. see Symposium on Thermophysical Properties, 3rd, 1965, Purdue University.

Grate, Harriette G. English Pronunciation Exercises for Japanese Students. 188p. (gr. 12 up). 1974. pap. text ed. 7.95 (ISBN 0-88345-209-X, 18136); cassettes 150.00 (ISBN 0-685-42245-3, 58138). Regents Pub.

Grater, Fred A., tr. see Schwenckfeld, Caspar.

Grater, Michael. Complete Book of Paper Mask Making. 144p. 1984. pap. 4.50 (ISBN 0-486-24712-0). Dover.
--Creative Paper Toys & Crafts. Orig. Title: Paper Play. (Illus.). 224p. 1981. pap. 5.00 (ISBN 0-486-24184-X). Dover.
--Cut & Color Paper Masks. (Dover Coloring Book Ser.). 32p. (Orig.). 1975. pap. 2.25 (ISBN 0-486-23171-2). Dover.
--Cut & Color Toys & Decorations. (Illus.). 40p. (Orig.). (gr. 1-6). 1974. pap. 2.00 (ISBN 0-486-23013-9). Dover.
--Cut & Fold Extraterrestrial Invaders That Fly: Twenty-Two Full-Color Spaceships. (Illus.). 36p. (Orig.). 1983. pap. 2.95 (ISBN 0-486-24478-4). Dover.
--Cut & Fold Paper Spaceships That Fly. (Illus.). 48p. (Orig.). (gr. 1-5). 1981. pap. 2.50 (ISBN 0-486-23978-0). Dover.
--Cut & Make Monster Masks in Full Color. LC 77-87448. (Illus.). 1978. pap. 2.95 (ISBN 0-486-23576-9). Dover.
--Make It in Paper: Creative Three-Dimensional Paper Projects. (Illus.). 96p. (gr. 5 up). 1983. pap. 3.95 (ISBN 0-486-24468-7). Dover.
--One Piece of Paper. LC 75-165523. (Illus.). (gr. 4-6). 7.50 (ISBN 0-8008-5825-5). Taplinger.

Grater, Russel K. Snakes, Lizards & Turtles of the Lake Mead Region. LC 81-50464. (Illus.). 48p. 1981. pap. 5.95 (ISBN 0-911408-58-4). SW Pks Mnmts.

Grater, Russell K. Discovering Sierra Mammals. (Discovering Sierra Ser.). (Illus.). 174p. (Orig.). 1978. pap. 4.50 (ISBN 0-939666-02-2). Yosemite Natl Hist.
--The Interpreter's Handbook. Jackson, Earl, ed. LC 76-14116. (Technical Ser: No. 8). (Illus., Orig.). 1976. pap. 3.50 (ISBN 0-911408-40-1). SW Pks Mnmts.

Grathwohl, Manfred. Energieversorgung. 2nd ed. 1983. 54.40 (ISBN 3-11-008592-5). De Gruyter.
--Energieversorgung. 2nd ed. 1983. 54.40 (ISBN 3-11-008592-5). De Gruyter.
--World Energy Supply. (Illus.). 450p. 1982. 49.50 (ISBN 3-11-008153-9). De Gruyter.

Grathwol, Robert P. Stresemann & the DNVP: Reconciliation or Revenge in German Foreign Policy, 1924-1928. (Illus.). 352p. 1980. 29.95x (ISBN 0-7006-0199-6). U Pr of KS.

Gratian Of Paris. I Know Christ. (Spirit & Life Ser). 1957. 2.00 (ISBN 0-686-11569-4). Franciscan Inst.

Gratovich, ed. Sixteen Contemporary Violin Etudes for Study & Performance. Blank, et al. 8.95 (ISBN 0-318-18104-5). Am String Tchrs.

Gratry, A. Logic. Singer, Helen & Singer, Milton, trs. from Fr. xii, 640p. 1944. 34.95x (ISBN 0-87548-035-7). Open Court.

Gratsch, Edward, et al. Principles of Catholic Theology: A Synthesis of Dogma & Morals. LC 80-26272. 401p. (Orig.). 1981. pap. 10.95 (ISBN 0-8189-0407-0). Alba.

Gratsch, Edward J. Where Peter Is: A Survey of Ecclesiology. LC 74-34578. 290p. 1975. pap. 5.95 (ISBN 0-8189-0302-3). Alba.

Grattan, C. H. Why We Fought. Nelson, Keith, ed. LC 70-84163. 1969. 34.50x (ISBN 0-8290-1392-X). Irvington.

Grattan, C. Hartley. Bitter Bierce: A Mystery of American Letters. LC 66-24261. Repr. of 1929 ed. 22.50 (ISBN 0-8154-0087-X). Cooper Sq.
--The Deadly Parallel. 34.95 (ISBN 0-8490-0001-7). Gordon Pr.
--In Quest of Knowledge: A Historical Perspective on Adult Education. LC 77-165738. (American Education Ser, No. 2). 1971. Repr. of 1955 ed. 26.50 (ISBN 0-405-03608-6). Ayer Co Pubs.
--Preface to Chaos: War in the Making. 59.95 (ISBN 0-8490-0887-5). Gordon Pr.

Grattan, Clinton H., ed. Critique of Humanism: A Symposium. facs. ed. LC 68-20303. (Essay Index Reprint Ser). 1930. 20.00 (ISBN 0-8369-0493-1). Ayer Co Pubs.

Grattan, Clinton Hartley. Australian Literature. LC 77-1352. 1977. Repr. of 1929 ed. lib. bdg. 8.50 (ISBN 0-8414-4576-1). Folcroft.

Grattan, J. H. & Singer, Charles. Anglo-Saxon Magic & Medicine. LC 72-190385. 1952. lib. bdg. 35.00 (ISBN 0-8414-1075-5). Folcroft.

Grattan, J. H., jt. auth. see Chambers, R. W.

Grattan, J. H. & Sykes, G. F., eds. The Owl & the Nightingale. (EETS, ES Ser.: No. 119). Repr. of 1916 ed. 14.00 (ISBN 0-527-00322-0). Kraus Repr.

Grattan, Kevin. Go Away, Billy Wind! (Irish Play Ser.). pap. 2.95x (ISBN 0-912262-66-4). Proscenium.

Grattan, Thomas C. Civilized America, 2 Vols. (American Studies). 1969. Repr. of 1859 ed. Set. 85.00 (ISBN 0-384-19740-X). Johnson Repr.

Grattan, Virginia L. Mary Colter: Builder Upon the Red Earth. LC 79-52507. (Illus.). 1980. pap. 9.95 (ISBN 0-87358-198-9). Northland.

Grattan-Guinness, I., ed. Dear Russell-Dear Jourdain: A Commentary on Russall's Logic Based on His Correspondence with Philip Jourdain. LC 77-9431. 234p. 1977. 19.00x (ISBN 0-231-04460-7). Columbia U Pr.
--From the Calculus to Set Theory 1630-1910: An Introductory History. 306p. 1980. pap. text ed. 12.00x (ISBN 0-7156-1625-0, Pub. by Duckworth England). Biblio Dist.
--History & Philosophy of Logic, Vol. 1. 1980. 41.00 (ISBN 0-9961001-2-1, 906100121, Pub. by Abacus England). Heyden.

Grattan-Guinness, Ivor, ed. Psychical Research: A Guide to Its History, Principles & Practices. 416p. 1982. 35.00x (ISBN 0-85030-316-8, Pub. by Aquarian Pr England). State Mutual Bk.

Gratte, Ingvar. Starting with COMAL. 224p. 1985. pap. 15.95 (ISBN 0-13-843003-9). P-H.

Gratton, Brian. Urban Elders: Family, Work & Welfare among Boston's Aged, 1890 to 1950. 1985. 32.95 (ISBN 0-87722-390-4). Temple U Pr.

Gratton, Carolyn. Guidelines for Spiritual Direction. 8.95 (ISBN 0-87193-130-3). Dimension Bks.
--Trusting: Theory & Practice. LC 82-9760. 240p. 1982. 17.50 (ISBN 0-8245-0496-8). Crossroad NY.
--Trusting: Theory & Practice. LC 82-9760. 256p. 1983. pap. 9.95 (ISBN 0-8245-0548-4). Crossroad NY.

Gratton, L. High Energy Astrophysics. (Italian Physical Society: Course 35). 1967. 75.00 (ISBN 0-12-368835-3). Acad Pr.

Gratton, L., ed. see I.A.U. Symposium, No. 37, Rome, Italy, May 8-18, 1969.

Gratton, Livio, ed. Star Evolution. (Italian Physical Society: Course 28). (Illus.). 1966. 77.50 (ISBN 0-12-368828-0). Acad Pr.

Gratus, Jack. The False Messiahs: Prophets of the Millennium. LC 75-29890. 284p. 1976. 10.95 (ISBN 0-8008-2588-8). Taplinger.
--The Great White Lie: Slavery, Emancipation & Changing Racial Attitudes. LC 72-84113. 320p. 1973. pap. 3.95 (ISBN 0-85345-288-1). Monthly Rev.

Gratwick, William E. The Truth, Tall Tales, & Blatant Lies. LC 81-65246. (Illus.). 192p. 1981. 20.00 (ISBN 0-89822-016-5); pap. 10.95 (ISBN 0-89822-017-3). Visual Studies.

Gratz, David B. Fire Department Management: Scope & Method. (Fire Science Ser.). 1972. text ed. write for info. (ISBN 0-02-474620-7, 47462). Macmillan.

Gratz, Gustav & Schuller, Richard. Die Aussere Wirtschaftspolitik Osterreich-Ungarns: Mitteleuropaische Plane. (Wirtschafts-Und Sozialgeschichte des Weltkrieges (Osterreichische Und Ungarische Ser.)). (Ger.). 1925. 75.00x (ISBN 0-317-27415-5). Elliots Bks.

Graves, Alfred P., ed. The Book of Irish Poetry. rev. & enl. ed. LC 77-39394. (Granger Index Reprint Ser.). Repr. 20.00 (ISBN 0-8369-6345-8). Ayer Co Pubs.

Graves, Algernon. Art Sales from Early in the Eighteenth Century to Early in the 20th Century, 3 Vols. LC 77-108428. (Bibliography & Reference Ser.: No. 340). 1970. Repr. of 1918 ed. Set. lib. bdg. 78.00 (ISBN 0-8337-1408-2). B Franklin.

--Century of Loan Exhibition, 1813-1912, 3 vols. Repr. Set. 150.00 (ISBN 0-87556-259-0). Saifer.

--Century of Loan Exhibitions, 1813-1912, 5 Vols. 1913-1915. 165.00 (ISBN 0-8337-1415-5). B Franklin.

--Dictionary of Artists: London Exhibitions 1760-1893. 3rd rev. ed. 25.00 (ISBN 0-912729-04-X). Newbury Bks.

--Dictionary of Artists Who Have Exhibited Works in the Principal London Exhibitions from 1760-1893. LC 72-132538. (Bibliography & Reference Ser.: No. 372). 1971. Repr. of 1901 ed. 24.50 (ISBN 0-8337-1416-3). B Franklin.

--The Royal Academy of Arts, 8 vols. Repr. of 1905 ed. Set. 400.00 (ISBN 0-8482-4220-3). Norwood Edns.

--The Royal Academy of Arts, a Complete Dictionary of Contributors & Their Work from Its Foundation in 1769 to 1904, Compiled with the Sanction of the President & Council of the Royal Academy, 8 vols. in 4. LC 76-118750. 1972. Repr. of 1905 ed. Set. lib. bdg. 181.00 (ISBN 0-8337-1425-2). B Franklin.

Graves, Anne A., jt. ed. see Davies, Carole B.

Graves, B., jt. auth. see Schmidt-Joos, S.

Graves, Barbara F. & McBain, Donald J. Lyric Voices: Approaches to the Poetry of Contemporary Song. LC 77-165947. pap. 55.50 (ISBN 0-317-28457-6, 2055129). Bks Demand UMI.

Graves, C. B., et al. Catalogue of the Flowering Plants & Ferns of Connecticut Growing Without Cultivation. (Illus.). 1974. 21.00 (ISBN 3-7682-0952-0). Lubrecht & Cramer.

Graves, C. L. & Lucas, E. V. The War of the Wenuses. LC 74-15979. (Science Fiction Ser). (Illus.). 140p. 1975. Repr. of 1898 ed. 16.00x (ISBN 0-405-06293-1). Ayer Co Pubs.

Graves, Carson. The Zone System for 35mm Photographers: A Basic Guide to Exposure Control. (Illus.). 112p. 1982. pap. 13.95 (ISBN 0-930764-39-0). Curtin & London.

Graves, Charles. The Alchemist. 156p. (Orig.). 1981. pap. 1.95 (ISBN 0-441-01426-7, Pub. by Charter Bks). Ace Bks.

Graves, Charles L. Post-Victorian Music. LC 71-102838. 1970. Repr. of 1911 ed. 27.50x (ISBN 0-8046-0754-0, Pub. by Kennikat). Assoc Faculty Pr.

Graves, Charles L., ed. see Grove, George.

Graves, Charles P. Fourth of July. LC 63-13625. (Holiday Bks.). (Illus.). (gr. 2-5). 1963. PLB 8.37 (ISBN 0-8116-6550-X). Garrard.

--John F. Kennedy. (Illus.). 80p. (gr. 1-7). 1966. pap. 1.95 (ISBN 0-440-44242-7, YB). Dell.

--Paul Revere: Rider for Liberty. LC 64-10938. (Discovery Books Ser.). (Illus.). (gr. 2-5). 1964. PLB 7.47 (ISBN 0-8116-6282-9). Garrard.

--Robert F. Kennedy: Man Who Dared to Dream. LC 76-101302. (Americans All Ser.). (Illus.). (gr. 3-6). 1970. PLB 7.98 (ISBN 0-8116-4557-6). Garrard.

Graves, Clay. Hurry up, Christmas! LC 75-11504. (Easy Venture Ser.). (Illus.). 32p. (gr. k-2). 1976. PLB 7.47 (ISBN 0-8116-6068-0). Garrard.

Graves, Clotilde I. Headquarter Recruit & Other Stories. facsimile ed. LC 77-150544. (Short Story Index Reprint Ser.). Repr. of 1913 ed. 20.00 (ISBN 0-8369-3841-0). Ayer Co Pubs.

--Sailor's Home, & Other Stories. LC 77-122711. (Short Story Index Reprint Ser). 1919. 18.00 (ISBN 0-8369-3544-6). Ayer Co Pubs.

--Under the Hermes, & Other Stories. LC 70-121554. (Short Story Index Reprint Ser). 1917. 20.00 (ISBN 0-8369-3510-1). Ayer Co Pubs.

Graves, Donald. Writing: Teachers & Children at Work. LC 82-21177. 312p. (Orig.). 1982. pap. text ed. 11.00x (ISBN 0-435-08203-5). Heinemann Ed.

Graves, Donald & Stuart, Virginia. Write from the Start: How to Tap Your Child's Innate Writing Abilities. 16.95 (01646-490); pap. 11.95 (ISBN 0-525-48170-2, 01160-350). Dutton.

Graves, Donald H. Balance the Basics: Let Them Write. LC 78-51898. 32p. 1978. pap. 4.00 (ISBN 0-916584-09-7). Ford Found.

--A Reseacher Learns to Write: Selected Article & Monographs. LC 84-6525. 208p. (Orig.). 1984. pap. text ed. 11.00x (ISBN 0-435-08213-2). Heinemann Ed.

Graves, Donald H., jt. auth. see DeVore, R. William.

Graves, Donald H., jt. ed. see De Vore, R. William.

Graves, Donald H., jt. ed. see DeVore, R. William.

Graves, Dorothy, jt. auth. see Graves, F. T.

Graves, Douglas. Painting a Likeness. LC 84-1466. (Illus.). 144p. 1984. 19.95 (ISBN 0-89134-072-6, North Light). Writers Digest.

Graves, Douglas R. Drawing a Likeness. (Illus.). 1979. 19.95 (ISBN 0-8230-1359-6). Watson-Guptill.

--Drawing a Likeness. (Illus.). 176p. 1984. pap. 12.95 (ISBN 0-8230-1358-8). Watson-Guptill.

--Drawing Portraits. (Illus.). 160p. 1974. 18.50 (ISBN 0-8230-1430-4). Watson-Guptill.

--Drawing Portraits. 160p. (Orig.). 1983. pap. 14.95 (ISBN 0-8230-1431-2). Watson-Guptill.

--Life Drawing in Charcoal. (Illus.). 160p. 1979. pap. 11.95 (ISBN 0-8230-2766-X). Watson-Guptill.

Graves, Edgar B., ed. Bibliography of English History to Fourteen Eighty-Five. 1975. 135.00x (ISBN 0-19-822391-9). Oxford U Pr.

Graves, Edmund. The National Inventory of Family Planning Services: 1978 Survey Results. Shipp, Audrey, ed. (Series 14: No. 26). 50p. 1981. pap. text ed. 1.75 (ISBN 0-8406-0234-0). Natl Ctr Health Stats.

Graves, Edmund J., jt. auth. see Haupt, Barbara J.

Graves, Edward S., jt. auth. see Boyd, T. Munford.

Graves, Elizabeth. Minangkabau Response to Dutch Colonial Rule in the Nineteenth Century. (Monograph Ser.). 157p. 1981. 7.50 (ISBN 0-87763-000-3). Cornell Mod Indo.

Graves, Elizabeth, tr. see Simatupang, T. B.

Graves, Ernest & Hildreth, Steven A., eds. United States Security Assistance: The Political Process. LC 84-47688. 208p. 1984. 24.00x (ISBN 0-669-08355-0). Lexington Bks.

Graves, F. D. Windows of Tarot. LC 73-85990. 96p. 1973. pap. 6.95 (ISBN 0-87100-027-X, 2027). Morgan.

Graves, F. T. & Graves, Dorothy. Seeing Operative Surgery, Vol. 1. (Illus.). 260p. 1980. 72.50 (ISBN 0-8151-3916-0). Year Bk Med.

Graves, Frank P. Great Educators of Three Centuries. 75.00 (ISBN 0-8490-0258-3). Gordon Pr.

--A History of Education Before the Middle Ages. 75.00 (ISBN 0-87968-163-2). Gordon Pr.

--A History of Education Before the Middle Ages. (Educational Ser.). 1925. Repr. 40.00 (ISBN 0-8482-4208-4). Norwood Edns.

--History of Education During the Middle Ages & the Transition to Modern Times. Repr. of 1910 ed. lib. bdg. 15.00x (ISBN 0-8371-3933-3, GRHE). Greenwood.

--A History of Education During the Middle Ages & the Transition of Modern Times. (Educational Ser.). 1925. Repr. 40.00 (ISBN 0-8482-4209-2). Norwood Edns.

--A History of Education During the Middle Ages. 1980. lib. bdg. 75.00 (ISBN 0-87968-164-0). Gordon Pr.

--A History of Education in Modern Times. 75.00 (ISBN 0-87968-165-9). Gordon Pr.

--A History of Education in Modern Times. (Educational Ser.). 1915. Repr. 40.00 (ISBN 0-8482-4210-6). Norwood Edns.

--A Student's History of Education. rev. ed. LC 75-106716. (Illus.). xix, 567p. Repr. of 1936 ed. lib. bdg. 22.75x (ISBN 0-8371-3541-9, GRSH). Greenwood.

--A Student's History of Education. (Educational Ser.). 1925. Repr. 35.00 (ISBN 0-8482-4222-X). Norwood Edns.

Graves, Frank P., ed. Great Educators of Three Centuries: Their Work & Its Influence on Modern Education. LC 70-121285. Repr. of 1912 ed. 23.00 (ISBN 0-404-02891-8). AMS Pr.

Graves, Frederick. Mariner's Guide to Single Sideband. (Illus.). 108p. (Orig.). 1982. pap. 9.95. Stephens Eng Assocs.

--Mariner's Guide to Single Sideband. (Illus.). 112p. 1985. pap. 11.95 (ISBN 0-911677-00-3). Stephens Eng Assocs.

--Piloting. LC 80-84742. (Illus.). 288p. 1981. 8.95 (ISBN 0-87742-116-1). Intl Marine.

Graves, Ginny. Ginny Graves' Discovery Stuff. (Illus.). (gr. k-6). 1977. pap. 4.95 (ISBN 0-930484-01-0). Discovery Stuff.

--Santa Fe, A Tour of Americas Oldest Capital City. (Illus.). 1977. pap. 2.50 (ISBN 0-930484-02-9). Discovery Stuff.

Graves, Harold F. & Hoffman, L. Report Writing. 4th ed. 1965. text ed. 19.95 (ISBN 0-13-773671-1). P-H.

Graves, Harvey W. Nuclear Fuel Management. LC 78-19119. 327p. 1979. text ed. 51.75x (ISBN 0-471-03136-4). Wiley.

Graves, Henry S. & Guise, C. H. Forest Education. 1932. 59.50x (ISBN 0-686-51388-6). Elliots Bks.

Graves, Herbert S., jt. auth. see Ficker, Victor B.

Graves, Ian D. Enneagrams: A Game of Nine Letter-Words. (Oleander Games & Pastimes Ser.: Vol. 4). (Illus.). 64p. 1981. 9.95 (ISBN 0-900891-78-5); pap. 4.95 (ISBN 0-900891-79-3). Oleander Pr.

Graves, Jack A. What Is a California Sea Otter? 1977. pap. 3.50 (ISBN 0-910286-61-2). Boxwood.

Graves, James, ed. Roll of the Proceedings of the King's Council in Ireland for a Portion of the 16th Year of the Reign of Richard II, 1392-1393. (Rolls Ser.: No. 69). Repr. of 1877 ed. 44.00 (ISBN 0-317-16792-8). Kraus Repr.

Graves, James S., ed. Regulation & Development of Membrane Transport Processes. LC 84-11987. (Society of General Physiologists Ser.: Vol. 39). 304p. 1985. text ed. 39.95 (ISBN 0-471-81038-X, Pub. by Wiley-Interscience). Wiley.

Graves, Jay C. Training Boys to Be Men. 1981. 6.95 (ISBN 0-8062-1824-X). Carlton.

Graves, Jim, jt. auth. see Adams, Charles.

Graves, John. Blue & Some Other Dogs. (Illus.). 29p. 1981. 15.00 (ISBN 0-88426-058-5). Encino Pr.

--From a Limestone Ledge. LC 80-7641. (Illus.). 256p. 1980. 13.95 (ISBN 0-394-51238-3). Knopf.

--From a Limestone Ledge. 288p. 1984. Repr. pap. 7.95 (ISBN 0-932012-77-9). Texas Month Pr.

--Goodbye to a River. (YA) 1960. 13.95 (ISBN 0-394-42690-8). Knopf.

--Goodbye to a River. 306p. 1984. pap. 7.95 (ISBN 0-932012-75-2). Texas Month Pr.

--Hard Scrabble. 1974. 13.50 (ISBN 0-394-48386-3). Knopf.

--Hard Scrabble. 267p. 1984. pap. 7.95 (ISBN 0-932012-76-0). Texas Month Pr.

--The Last Running. (Illus.). 48p. 1974. 15.00 (ISBN 0-88426-036-4). Encino Pr.

Graves, John, jt. auth. see Bones, Jim, Jr.

Graves, John, ed. see Starr, Gail W.

Graves, John, illus. Landscapes of Texas. LC 79-5274. (Louise Lindsey Merrick Texas Environment Ser.: No. 3). (Illus.). 162p. 1980. 24.95 (ISBN 0-89096-088-7). Tex A&M Univ Pr.

Graves, John T. The Fighting South. LC 84-16320. (The Library of Alabama Classics). (Illus.). 304p. 1985. 20.00x (ISBN 0-8173-0245-X); pap. 9.95x (ISBN 0-8173-0246-8). U of Ala Pr.

Graves, Joseph A. The History of the Bedford Light Artillery. 83p. 1983. Repr. of 1903 ed. 9.90X (ISBN 0-913419-24-9). Butternut Pr.

Graves, Joseph J. Managing Investor Relations: Strategies & Techniques. LC 82-71348. 430p. 1982. 18.95 (ISBN 0-87094-346-4). Dow Jones-Irwin.

Graves, Joseph J., Jr. Investor Relations Today: A Compendium on the Trends, Problems, Challenges & Opportunities on the Investor Relations Scene Today & a Look at the 1990's. LC 84-62576. 72p. (Orig.). 1985. pap. 65.00 (ISBN 0-9614409-0-2). Investor Relations.

Graves, Joy D. Early Interventions in Child Abuse: The Role of the Police Officer. LC 81-85982. 125p. 1983. pap. 14.95 (ISBN 0-88247-697-1). R & E Pubs.

Graves, Judy, ed. Directory of Pathology Training Programs, 1986-87. 18th ed. (Illus.). 500p. 1985. pap. 45.00 (ISBN 0-937888-02-8). Intersoc Comm Path Info.

--Directory of Pathology Training Programs, 1985-1986. (Illus.). 500p. (Orig.). 1984. pap. 45.00 (ISBN 0-317-04534-2). Intersoc Comm Path Info.

Graves, Judy, ed. see Anlyan, William G., et al.

Graves, Katharine B. The Influence of Specialized Training on Tests of General Intelligence. LC 73-176818. (Columbia University. Teachers College. Contributions to Education: No. 143). Repr. of 1924 ed. 22.50 (ISBN 0-404-55143-2). AMS Pr.

Graves, Lawrence L., ed. History of Lubbock. 692p. 1962. 15.00 (ISBN 0-911618-01-5). West Tex Mus.

Graves, Maitland E. Art of Color & Design. 2nd ed. (Illus.). 1951. text ed. 45.95 (ISBN 0-07-024119-8). McGraw.

Graves, Merle D. Bubblin's An' B'ilin's at the Center. LC 75-122688. (Short Story Index Reprint Ser). (Illus.). 1934. 14.50 (ISBN 0-8369-3552-7). Ayer Co Pubs.

Graves, Michael. Michael Graves, Buildings & Projects, 1980-1985. (Illus.). 320p. 1985. pap. 24.00 (ISBN 0-910413-13-4). Princeton Arch.

Graves, Michael, et al. Easy Reading: Book Series & Periodicals for Less Able Readers. (IRA Reading Aids Ser.). (Orig.). 1979. pap. text ed. 4.50 (ISBN 0-87207-224-X, 224). Intl Reading.

Graves, Michael A. The House of Lords in the Parliaments of Edward VI & Mary I: An Institutional Study. LC 80-42225. 312p. 1981. 47.50 (ISBN 0-521-23678-9). Cambridge U Pr.

Graves, Michael A. & Silcock, Robin H. Revolution, Reaction, & the Triumph of Conservatism: English History, 1558-1700. 524p. 1984. pap. text ed. 17.95 (ISBN 0-582-68394-7). Longman.

Graves, N. J. Geography of the British Isles. 4th ed. 1976. pap. text ed. 9.95x (ISBN 0-435-34275-4). Heinemann Ed.

Graves, Nora C. Two Culture Theory in C. P. Snow's Novels. LC 73-170672. 1971. pap. 1.00 (ISBN 0-87805-006-X). U Pr of Miss.

Graves, Norman. Curriculum Planning in Geography. 1979. pap. text ed. 10.50x (ISBN 0-435-35312-8). Heinemann Ed.

--New Movements in the Study & Teaching of Geography. 252p. 1982. 30.00x (ISBN 0-85117-018-8, Pub. by M Temple Smith). State Mutual Bk.

Graves, Norman J. Geography in Education. 1975. text ed. 21.95x (ISBN 0-435-35310-1); pap. text ed. 9.95x (ISBN 0-435-35311-X). Heinemann Ed.

Graves, Norman J., ed. New UNESCO Source Book for Geography Teaching. 394p. (Co-published with Longman Group Ltd., Harlow). 1982. text ed. 17.95 (ISBN 92-3-101935-X, U1275, UNESCO). Unipub.

Graves, Oliver F., ed. see Pape, Ambrosius.

Graves, Paul A. Inter-Regional Migration & Urbanization in Sri Lanka. 1985. write for info. U MD Geography.

Graves, Perceval. A. E. Housman: The Scholar-Poet. (Encore Edition). 5.95 (ISBN 0-684-17678-5). Scribner.

Graves, Philip E., jt. auth. see Mills, Edwin S.

Graves, Philip E., jt. ed. see Tolley, George S.

Graves, Philip P. Palestine: The Land of Three Faiths. LC 75-6460. (Rise of Jewish Nationalism & the Middle East Ser.). 286p. 1975. Repr. of 1923 ed. 23.50 (ISBN 0-88355-324-4). Hyperion Conn.

Graves, Phillip E. & Crumm, Ronald J. Health & Air Quality: Evaluating the Effects of Policy. 1981. 14.25 (ISBN 0-8447-3442-X); pap. 6.25 (ISBN 0-8447-3443-8). Am Enterprise.

Graves, R. English Ballad. LC 70-155147. (Studies in Poetry, No. 38). 1971. Repr. of 1927 ed. lib. bdg. 27.95x (ISBN 0-8383-1284-5). Haskell.

--Mrs. Fisher; Or, the Future of Humor. LC 73-21511. (English Literature Ser., No. 33). 1974. lib. bdg. 29.95x (ISBN 0-8383-1755-3). Haskell.

--On English Poetry: Being an Irregular Approach to the Psychology of This Art from Evidence Mainly Subjective. LC 78-185878. (English Literature Ser., No. 33). 159p. 1972. Repr. of 1922 ed. lib. bdg. 39.95x (ISBN 0-8383-1386-8). Haskell.

Graves, R., jt. auth. see Riding, Laura.

Graves, R. L., jt. auth. see Thorelli, Hans B.

Graves, R. W., ed. see Geoscience Information Society Staff.

Graves, R. W., Jr. Geology of Hood Spring Quadrangle, Brewster County, Texas. (Report of Investigations Ser.: RI 21). (Illus.). 51p. 1954. 2.25 (ISBN 0-686-29331-2). Bur Econ Geology.

Graves, Ralph. August People. LC 84-24661. 330p. 1985. 16.95 (ISBN 0-385-19476-5). Doubleday.

Graves, Richard. Bushcraft. (Illus.). 1978. pap. 4.95 (ISBN 0-446-32747-6). Warner Bks.

--Bushcraft: A Serious Guide to Survival & Camping. LC 74-185329. (Illus.). 354p. 1972. pap. 7.95 (ISBN 0-8052-0333-8). Schocken.

--The Spiritual Quixote; or, the Summer's Ramble of Mr. Geoffrey Wildgoose, 1773, 3 vols. Shugrue, Michael F., ed. (The Flowering of the Novel 1740-1775 Ser: Vol. 102). 1975. Set. lib. bdg. 182.00 (ISBN 0-8240-1201-1). Garland Pub.

Graves, Richard, ed. Rhetoric & Composition: A Sourcebook for Teachers & Writers. 384p. 1984. pap. text ed. 12.00x (ISBN 0-86709-029-4). Boynton Cook Pubs.

Graves, Richard, tr. see Harrer, Heinrich.

Graves, Richard, tr. see Mann, Erika.

Graves, Richard L. C. L. A. W. LC 76-13620. 1976. 3.50 (ISBN 0-8128-8042-0). Stein & Day.

--Quicksilver. LC 75-35864. 224p. 1976. pap. 2.50 (ISBN 0-8128-7075-1). Stein & Day.

--Rhetoric & Composition: A Sourcebook for Teachers. LC 76-13016. 1976. pap. text ed. 9.25x (ISBN 0-8104-5984-1). Boynton Cook Pubs.

Graves, Richard P. The Brothers Powys. (Illus.). 384p. 1983. 29.50 (ISBN 0-684-17880-X, ScribT). Scribner.

Graves, Robert. An Ancient Castle. LC 81-17204. (Illus.). 72p. (YA) 1981. 10.95 (ISBN 0-935576-06-1). Kesend Pub Ltd.

--Apuleius' the Golden Ass. 293p. 1951. pap. 6.25 (ISBN 0-374-50532-2). FS&G.

--The Big Green Book. LC 84-42972. (Illus.). 64p. (gr. 1-4). 1985. 12.95 (ISBN 0-02-736810-6). Macmillan.

--Claudius the God. 1977. pap. 4.95 (ISBN 0-394-72537-9, Vin). Random.

--Claudius the God. LC 83-42945. 592p. 8.95 (ISBN 0-394-60812-7). Modern Lib.

--Collected Short Stories. (Penguin Fiction Ser.). 304p. 1985. pap. 4.95 (ISBN 0-14-002881-1). Penguin.

--Common Asphodel. LC 78-117590. (English Literature Ser., No. 33). 1970. Repr. of 1949 ed. lib. bdg. 49.95x (ISBN 0-8383-1023-0). Haskell.

--Contemporary Techniques of Poetry. LC 77-1225. 1949. lib. bdg. 17.00 (ISBN 0-8414-4588-5). Folcroft.

--Count Belisarius. 564p. 1982. pap. 9.25 (ISBN 0-374-51739-8). FS&G.

--Count Belisarius. 527p. Date not set. Repr. of 1938 ed. lib. bdg. 40.00 (ISBN 0-8482-4253-X). Norwood Edns.

--Crowning Privilege. facs. ed. LC 70-117797. (Essay Index Reprint Ser). 1955. 17.00 (ISBN 0-8369-1751-0). Ayer Co Pubs.

--English Ballad. LC 73-13765. 1927. lib. bdg. 20.00 (ISBN 0-8414-4436-6). Folcroft.

--Fairies & Fusiliers. LC 77-1323. 1919. lib. bdg. 27.50 (ISBN 0-8414-4580-X). Folcroft.

--Five Pens in Hand. LC 78-111834. (Essay Index Reprint Ser). 1958. 22.00 (ISBN 0-8369-1611-5). Ayer Co Pubs.

--Good-Bye to All That. rev. ed. LC 57-12294. pap. 5.95 (ISBN 0-385-09330-6, Anch). Doubleday.

--Good-Bye to All That: An Autobiography. 448p. 1980. Repr. lib. bdg. 38.00 (ISBN 0-8492-4985-6). R West.

--Greek Gods & Heroes. 125p. pap. 2.50 (ISBN 0-440-93221-1, LFL). Dell.

--Greek Myths. (Illus.). 244p. 1982. 25.00 (ISBN 0-385-17790-9). Doubleday.

--Greek Myths, 2 Vols. (Orig.). (YA) (gr. 9 up). 1955. Vol. 1. pap. 3.95 (ISBN 0-14-020508-X, Pelican); Vol. 2. pap. 3.95 (ISBN 0-14-020509-8). Penguin.

--Hercules, My Shipmate. 464p. 1945. pap. 8.95 (ISBN 0-374-51677-4). FS&G.

--Hercules, My Shipmate. LC 79-9879. (Illus.). 1979. Repr. of 1945 ed. lib. bdg. 37.50x (ISBN 0-313-20991-X, GRHR). Greenwood.

--Homer's Daughter. 238p. 1982. 14.95 (ISBN 0-89733-058-7); pap. 6.95 (ISBN 0-89733-059-5). Academy Chi Pubs.
--I, Claudius. (YA) 1977. pap. 4.95 (ISBN 0-394-72536-0, Vin). Random.
--I, Claudius. LC 37-27271. 448p. 8.95 (ISBN 0-394-60811-9). Modern Lib.
--John Kemp's Wager. LC 73-313. 1973. lib. bdg. 22.50 (ISBN 0-8414-1446-7). Folcroft.
--John Skelton, Laureate. lib. bdg. 20.00 (ISBN 0-8414-4668-7). Folcroft.
--King Jesus. 424p. 1946. 20.00 (ISBN 0-374-18114-4); pap. 8.95 (ISBN 0-374-51664-2). FS&G.
--King Jesus. 356p. 1983. Repr. of 1946 ed. lib. bdg. 25.00 (ISBN 0-8495-2139-4). Arden Lib.
--The More Deserving Cases: Eighteen Old Poems for Reconsideration. LC 77-1291. 1977. Repr. of 1962 ed. lib. bdg. 20.00 (ISBN 0-8414-4582-6). Folcroft.
--Mrs. Fisher: Or, the Future of Humor. LC 74-28463. 1928. lib. bdg. 17.00 (ISBN 0-8414-4581-8). Folcroft.
--My Head, My Head. LC 73-20386. (English Literature Ser., No. 33). 1974. lib. bdg. 49.95x (ISBN 0-8383-1757-X). Haskell.
--Occupation Writer. 1977. Repr. of 1950 ed. lib. bdg. 26.00x (ISBN 0-374-93237-9). Octagon.
--On English Poetry. 149p. 1980. Repr. of 1922 ed. lib. bdg. 20.00 (ISBN 0-8495-1955-1). Arden Lib.
--On English Poetry. LC 75-28419. 1975. Repr. of 1922 ed. lib. bdg. 17.50 (ISBN 0-8414-4544-3). Folcroft.
--Over the Brazier. LC 77-1283. Repr. of 1916 ed. lib. bdg. 22.00 (ISBN 0-8414-4587-7). Folcroft.
--Oxford Addresses on Poetry. LC 69-10102. 1969. Repr. of 1962 ed. lib. bdg. 24.75x (ISBN 0-8371-0090-9, GRAP). Greenwood.
--Oxford Addresses on Poetry. 129p. Date not set. Repr. of 1961 ed. lib. bdg. 35.00 (ISBN 0-8482-4254-8). Norwood Edns.
--The Pier-Glass. LC 73-11339. Repr. of 1921 ed. lib. bdg. 22.00 (ISBN 0-8414-2047-5). Folcroft.
--Poems, Nineteen Thirty-Eight to Nineteen Forty-Five. 58p. 1946. 4.95 (ISBN 0-374-23472-8). FS&G.
--Poetic Unreason & Other Studies. LC 68-59244. 1968. Repr. of 1925 ed. 12.00x (ISBN 0-8196-0227-2). Biblo.
--The Shout. LC 77-1292. Repr. of 1929 ed. lib. bdg. 22.50 (ISBN 0-8414-4578-8). Folcroft.
--They Hanged My Saintly Billy. (Illus.). 267p. 1980. 14.95 (ISBN 0-89733-030-7); pap. 5.95 (ISBN 0-89733-029-3). Academy Chi Pubs.
--To Whom Else? LC 77-4107. Repr. of 1931 ed. lib. bdg. 22.00 (ISBN 0-8414-4555-9). Folcroft.
--Watch the North Wind Rise. 290p. 1949. pap. 7.95 (ISBN 0-374-51679-0). FS&G.
--Weldman's Hose. LC 76-30507. Repr. of 1925 ed. lib. bdg. 25.00 (ISBN 0-8414-4508-7). Folcroft.
--Whipperginny. LC 76-39795. Repr. of 1923 ed. lib. bdg. 25.00 (ISBN 0-8414-4512-5). Folcroft.
--The White Goddess: A Historical Grammar of Poetic Myth. rev. & enl. ed. 511p. 1966. pap. 8.25 (ISBN 0-374-50493-8). FS&G.
--The White Goddess (amended & enlarged edition) 1983. 15.50 (ISBN 0-8446-5983-5). Peter Smith.
--Wife to Mr. Milton. 1979. Repr. of 1944 ed. lib. bdg. 26.00x (ISBN 0-374-93240-9). Octagon.
--Wife to Mr. Milton. (Penguin Fiction Ser.). 416p. 1984. pap. 6.95 (ISBN 0-14-001024-6). Penguin.
Graves, Robert & Hodge, Alan. Long Weekend: A Social History of Great Britain, 1918 to 1939. 1963. pap. 9.95 (ISBN 0-393-00217-9, Norton Lib). Norton.
Graves, Robert & Patai, Raphael. Hebrew Myths. 1966. pap. 5.95 (ISBN 0-07-024125-2). McGraw.
Graves, Robert, jt. auth. see Jackson, Laura R.
Graves, Robert, jt. auth. see Riding, Laura.
Graves, Robert, ed. English & Scottish Ballads, Fourteenth to Sixteenth Century. (The Poetry Bookshelf). 1957. pap. text ed. 5.00x (ISBN 0-435-15013-8). Heinemann Ed.
Graves, Robert, ed. see Frost, Robert.
Graves, Robert, tr. see Suetonius.
Graves, Robert L., jt. auth. see Telser, Lester G.
Graves, Robert P. Life of Sir William Rowan Hamilton, 3 vols. LC 74-26266. (History, Philosophy & Sociology of Science Ser). 1975. Repr. 158.00x (ISBN 0-405-06594-9). Ayer Co Pubs.
Graves, Robert W. Storm Centres of the Near East. LC 76-180344. Repr. of 1933 ed. 30.00 (ISBN 0-404-56269-8). AMS Pr.
Graves, Rolande J. Flamenca: Variations sur les Themes de l'Amour Courtois. (American University Studies II: Vol. 5). 206p. (Fr.). 1983. pap. text ed. 20.55 (ISBN 0-8204-0058-0). P Lang Pubs.
Graves, Rosewell H. Forty Years in China: Or China in Transition. LC 72-79822. (China Library Ser.). 1972. Repr. of 1895 ed. lib. bdg. 32.00 (ISBN 0-8420-1372-5). Scholarly Res Inc.
Graves, S. H. On the White Pass Payroll, - by the President of the White Pass & Yukon Route. LC 73-108120. Repr. of 1908 ed. 21.00 (ISBN 0-404-00631-0). AMS Pr.
Graves, Sharol, jt. auth. see Ortiz, Simon J.
Graves, Thornton S. Act Time in Elizabethan Theatres. (Studies in Drama, No. 39). 1970. pap. 16.95x (ISBN 0-8383-0043-X). Haskell.
--Court & the London Theatres During the Reign of Elizabeth. LC 72-194353. 1913. lib. bdg. 5.95 (ISBN 0-8414-4669-5). Folcroft.
Graves, Tom. Needles of Stone. (Illus.). 265p. 1983. pap. 5.95 (ISBN 0-586-04965-7, Pub. by Granada England). Academy Chi Pubs.
Graves, Tricia. Heart on Trial. (Rapture Romance Ser.: No. 38). 192p. 1983. pap. 1.95 (ISBN 0-451-12558-4, Sig). NAL.
Graves, W. B., ed. Intergovernmental Relations in the United States. (American Federalism-the Urban Dimension). (Illus.). 1978. Repr. of 1940 ed. lib. bdg. 20.00x (ISBN 0-405-10490-1). Ayer Co Pubs.
Graves, W. Brooke, ed. see Highsaw, Robert B. & Fortenberry, Charles N.
Graves, W. Brooke, ed. see Pi Sigma Alpha Committee on Publications.
Graves, W. H., jt. auth. see Bowman, James T.
Graves, Will. Raising Poultry Successfully. (Illus.). 196p. (Orig.). 1985. pap. 8.95 (ISBN 0-913589-09-8). Williamson Pub Co.
--Raising Your Own Meat for Pennies a Day. Stetson, Fred, ed. LC 83-1595. (Illus.). 160p. (Orig.). 1983. pap. 6.95 (ISBN 0-88266-330-5). Garden Way Pub.
Graves, William. America's Siberian Adventure. 59.95 (ISBN 0-87968-615-4). Gordon Pr.
Graves, William B. Public Administration in a Democratic Society. LC 77-148635. (Illus.). 759p. 1972. Repr. of 1950 ed. lib. bdg. 28.50x (ISBN 0-8371-6003-0, GRPA). Greenwood.
Graves, William H. On the Theory of Vector Measures. LC 77-12182. (Memoirs Ser.: No. 195). 72p. 1977. pap. 13.00 (ISBN 0-8218-2195-4, MEMO 195). Am Math.
Graves, William H., ed. Conference on Integration, Topology & Geometry in Linear Spaces: Proceedings. LC 80-25417. (Contemporary Mathematics Ser.: Vol. 2). 269p. 1980. pap. 19.00 (ISBN 0-8218-5002-4, CONM-2). Am Math.
Graves, William S. American Siberian Adventure. 11.75 (ISBN 0-8446-1205-7). Peter Smith.
--America's Siberian Adventure, 1918-1920. LC 76-150951. (Russia Observed Ser.). (Illus.). 1971. Repr. of 1931 ed. 19.00 (ISBN 0-405-03083-5). Ayer Co Pubs.
Graves, William W. The Church Teaching & Training. Viertel, Weldon & Viertel, Joyce, eds. 152p. 1982. Repr. of 1975 ed. 11.50 (ISBN 0-311-72681-X, Carib Pubns). Casa Bautista.
Graves-Morris, P. R. Pade Approximants & Their Applications. 1973. 56.50 (ISBN 0-12-295950-7). Acad Pr.
Graves-Morris, P. R., ed. Pade Approximants. (Illus.). 1973. pap. 24.75 (ISBN 0-9960018-4-0, Pub. by A Hilger England). Heyden.
Graves-Morris, P. R., et al, eds. Rational Approximation & Interpolation, Vol. 1105. (Lecture Notes in Mathematics Ser.). xii, 528p. 1984. pap. 28.00 (ISBN 0-387-13899-4). Springer-Verlag.
Graveson, R. H. Comparative Conflict of Laws, Vol. 1: Selected Essays. (European Studies in Law). 380p. 1977. 44.75 (ISBN 0-7204-0486-X, North-Holland). Elsevier.
--One Law, Comparative Conflict on Law: On Jurisprudence & the Unification of Law - Selected Essays, Vol. 2. 238p. 1977. 42.50 (ISBN 0-7204-0487-8, North-Holland). Elsevier.
Graves-Smith, Tom R. Linear Analysis of Frameworks. (Series in Engineering Science). (Illus.). 451p. 1983. 64.95 (ISBN 0-470-27449-2). Halsted Pr.
Gravett, K. Timber & Brick Building in Kent. 1971. 50.00x (ISBN 0-85033-006-8, Pub. by Phillimore England). State Mutual Bk.
Gravetter, Frederick J. & Wallanu, Larry B. Statistics for the Behavioral Sciences: A First Course for Students of Psychology & Education. 550p. 1985. text ed. 20.95 (ISBN 0-314-85241-7). West Pub.
Gravie, Francisca, tr. see Von Albertini, Rudolf.
Gravier, Gabriel. Les Voyages De Giovanni Verrazano Sur les Cotes D' Amerique Avec Des Marins Normands, Pour le Compte Du Roi De France. LC 74-17266. 1975. pap. 3.50 (ISBN 0-916346-10-2). Harbor Hill Bks.
Gravil, Richard & Newlyn, Lucy, eds. Coleridge's Imagination: Essays in Memory of Pete Laver. (Illus.). 280p. Date not set. 34.50 (ISBN 0-521-30302-8). Cambridge U Pr.
Gravil, Robert. The Anglo-Argentine Connection, 1900-1939. (Dellplain Latin American Studies Ser.: Vol. 16). 300p. 1985. softcover 22.00x (ISBN 0-317-06876-8). Westview.
Gravitz, Herbert L. & Bowden, Julie D. A Guide to Recovery: A Book for Adult Children of Alcoholics. LC 84-48494. 128p. (Orig.). 1985. pap. 9.95 (ISBN 0-918452-82-1). Learning Pubns.
Gravitz, Melvin A., ed. Medical Applications of Clinical Hypnosis. (Modern Techniques of Clinical Hypnosis: Vol. 1). 400p. Date not set. text ed. price not set (ISBN 0-8290-1460-8). Irvington.
--Psychotherapeutic Applications of Clinical Hypnosis. (Modern Techniques of Clinical Hypnosis Ser.: Vol. 2). 400p. 1985. text ed. write for info. (ISBN 0-8290-1461-6). Irvington.
Gravrock, Mark. Stewardship Preaching. (Ser. B). 56p. (Orig.). 1984. pap. 3.95 (ISBN 0-8066-2076-5, 10-6002). Augsburg.
Grawe, Paul H. Comedy in Space, Time, & the Imagination. LC 82-10603. 368p. 1983. text ed. 27.95x (ISBN 0-88229-631-0). Nelson-Hall.
Grawe, Roger. Ability in Pre-Schoolers, Earnings, & Home Environment. (Working Paper: No. 322). 92p. 1979. 5.00 (ISBN 0-686-36052-4, WP-0322). World Bank.
Grawitz, M; see Boudeville, J. R.
Grawoig, Dennis E. & Hubbard, Charles L. Strategic Financial Planning with Simulation. (Illus.). 1982. 39.95 (ISBN 0-89433-115-9). Petrocelli.
Grawoig, Dennis E., jt. auth. see Hughes, Ann J.
Grawunder, Mary. Practical Nursing Review. 3rd ed. LC 79-15916. 272p. 1984. pap. 14.95 (ISBN 0-8385-7874-8). ACC.
Gray. The Ecology of Soil Bacteria. 698p. 1982. 70.00x (ISBN 0-85323-161-3, Pub. by Liverpool Univ England). State Mutual Bk.
--Gray's Anatomy: The Unabridged Running Press Color Edition of the American Classic 1901. LC 74-19510. (Illus.). 800p. 1973. lib. bdg. 19.80 (ISBN 0-914294-49-0); pap. 8.95 (ISBN 0-914294-08-3). Running Pr.
--Quality Control in Diagnostic Imaging. (Illus.). 264p. 1982. text ed. 38.00 (ISBN 0-8391-1681-0). Univ Park.
Gray & Hidalgo. How to Hypnotize. 3.00 (ISBN 0-87505-083-2). Borden.
Gray, jt. auth. see Affleck.
Gray, jt. auth. see Groves.
Gray, jt. ed. see Drnevich.
Gray, et al. Synopsis of Children's Diseases. 6th ed. 1985. 29.50 (ISBN 0-7236-0743-5). PSG Pub Co.
Gray, A. see Wilkes, Charles.
Gray, A. A., ed. see Clavigero, Francisco J.
Gray, A. H., jt. auth. see Markel, J. E.
Gray, A. P. Mammalian Hybrids: A Check-List with Bibliography. 256p. 1971. cloth 40.00X (ISBN 0-85198-170-4, Pub. by CAB Bks England). State Mutual Bk.
Gray, Al. Algebra; Beginning: Syllabus. 2nd ed. 1976. pap. text ed. 7.25 (ISBN 0-89420-033-X, 367015); cassette recordings 164.35 (ISBN 0-89420-125-5, 367007). Natl Book.
Gray, Al & Matousek, Clifford H. General Mathematics: Syllabus. 2nd ed. 1972. pap. text ed. 6.75 (ISBN 0-89420-019-4, 350899); cassette recordings 103.55 (ISBN 0-89420-148-4, 350900). Natl Book.
Gray, Alasdair. Janine. (Fiction Ser.). 352p. 1985. pap. 6.95 (ISBN 0-317-19381-3). Penguin.
--Janine, 1982. LC 83-40655. 352p. 1984. 16.95 (ISBN 0-670-51387-3, E Sifton Bks). Viking.
--Lanark: A Life in Four Books. LC 84-20323. 560p. 1985. Repr. of 1981 ed. 20.00 (ISBN 0-8076-1108-5). Braziller.
Gray, Albert, ed. see Pyrard, Francois.
Gray, Alexander. The Development of Economic Doctrine: An Introductory Survey. LC 75-41121. Repr. of 1931 ed. 26.00 (ISBN 0-404-14750-X). AMS Pr.
Gray, Alfred, jt. ed. see Brooks, Robert.
Gray, Alice & Kasahara, Kunihiko. Magic of Origami. LC 77-74654. (Illus.). 1977. 13.75 (ISBN 0-87040-390-7). Japan Pubns USA.
Gray, Alice, et al. The Magic of Origami. LC 77-74654. (Illus.). 132p. 1985. pap. 9.95 (ISBN 0-87040-624-8, Dist. by Harper & Row). Japan Pubns USA.
Gray, Alisdair. Unlikely Stories, Mostly. (Illus.). 280p. 1984. pap. 6.95 (ISBN 0-14-006925-9). Penguin.
Gray, Allan W., jt. auth. see Bryson, Carlton W.
Gray, Allan W., jt. auth. see Williams, Lloyd B.
Gray, Allan W., ed. see Brunelle, Wallace & O'Neill, Robert.
Gray, Amlin. Kingdom Come. 1984. pap. 3.35x (ISBN 0-317-17218-2). Dramatists Play.
Gray, Andrea. Ansel Adams: An American Place, 1936. (Illus.). 132p. 1982. pap. 19.95 (ISBN 0-938262-06-8). U Ariz Ctr Photog.
Gray, Andrew, jt. auth. see Jenkins, W. I.
Gray, Andrew, tr. see Wagner, Richard.
Gray, Anne. The Wonderful World of San Diego. 2nd ed. LC 74-76733. (Illus.). (gr. 4 up). 1975. pap. 3.95 (ISBN 0-88289-081-6). Pelican.
Gray, Annette E. Guide to Thrift Shops in Seattle & the Puget Sound Area. 108p. (Orig.). 1981. pap. 5.95 (ISBN 0-9607154-0-1). C & G Ent.
Gray, Arthur. Chapter in the Early Life of Shakespeare. 1973. Repr. of 1926 ed. 13.50 (ISBN 0-8274-0645-2). R West.
--Chapter in the Early Life of Shakespeare: Polesworth in Arden. LC 72-130620. Repr. of 1926 ed. 14.00 (ISBN 0-404-02892-6). AMS Pr.
--How Shakespeare Purged Jonson, a Problem Solved. LC 72-153325. Repr. of 1928 ed. 11.50 (ISBN 0-404-02893-4). AMS Pr.
Gray, Arthur A. Men Who Built the West. facsimile ed. LC 73-167348. (Essay Index Reprint Ser). Repr. of 1945 ed. 25.00 (ISBN 0-8369-2591-2). Ayer Co Pubs.
Gray, Asa. Elements of Botany. LC 73-125739. (American Environmental Studies). 1970. Repr. of 1887 ed. 23.50 (ISBN 0-405-02664-1). Ayer Co Pubs.
--Letters of Asa Gray, 2 vols. Gray, Jane L., ed. LC 73-170952. 1973. Repr. of 1893 ed. Set. lib. bdg. 47.00 (ISBN 0-8337-1430-9). B Franklin.
Gray, Austin K. Teresa: The Story of Byron's Last Mistress. 1948. 25.00 (ISBN 0-8274-3586-X). R West.
Gray, Ava A., jt. auth. see Chesser, Barbara J.
Gray, B. Grammatical Foundations of Rhetoric. (Janua Linguarum Ser. Major: No. 51). 1977. 38.00 (ISBN 90-279-7915-4). Mouton.
Gray, B. F. Measurements, Instrumentation & Data Transmission. LC 76-49922. (Illus.). 1977. text ed. 13.50x (ISBN 0-582-41065-7); pap. text ed. 9.50x (ISBN 0-582-41066-5). Longman.
Gray, B. Kirkman. History of English Philanthropy. LC 67-23620. Repr. of 1905 ed. 30.00x (ISBN 0-678-05053-8). Kelley.
Gray, Mrs. B., jt. ed. see Cushing, Mrs. C. H.
Gray, Barbara & Issacs, Bernard. Care of the Elderly Mentally Infirm. 1979. 27.00x (ISBN 0-422-77190-2, NO.6364, Pub. by Tavistock England). Methuen Inc.
Gray, Barbara Q., jt. auth. see Fortune, Sarah D.
Gray, Basil. Sung Porcelain & Stoneware. LC 83-20668. (Illus.). 205p. 1984. 65.00 (ISBN 0-571-13048-8). Faber & Faber.
Gray, Basil & Gray, Mary. A Taste of Europe. (Illus.). 1985p. 25.00 (ISBN 0-318-01381-9); pap. 12.00 (ISBN 0-318-01382-7). CLCB Pr.
Gray, Basil, jt. auth. see Barrett, Douglas.
Gray, Basil, jt. auth. see Barrett, Douglas B.
Gray, Basil, ed. The Arts of India. LC 81-66537. (Cornell-Phaidon Bks.). (Illus.). 208p. 1981. 55.00 (ISBN 0-8014-1425-3). Cornell U Pr.
Gray, Benjamin K. History of English Philanthropy: From the Dissolution of the Monasteries to the Taking of the First Census. new ed. 302p. 1967. 30.00x (ISBN 0-7146-1112-3, F Cass Co). Biblio Dist.
Gray, Benna. Seasoned to Taste. (Orig.). 1981. pap. 1.95 (ISBN 0-8439-8046-X, Tiara Bks). Dorchester Pub Co.
Gray, Bennison. The Phenomenon of Literature. LC 74-77353. (De Proprietatibus Litterarum, Ser. Maior: No. 36). 594p. 1975. pap. text ed. 48.00x (ISBN 0-686-22585-6). Mouton.
--Style: The Problem & Its Solution. (De Proprietatibus Litterarum Ser. Major: No. 3). 1969. text ed. 13.20x (ISBN 90-2790-441-3). Mouton.
Gray, Betty, jt. auth. see Gray, William B.
Gray, Bettyanne. Manya's Story. LC 77-92305. (Adult & Young Adult Books). (Illus.). (gr. 5-9). 1978. PLB 7.95 (ISBN 0-8225-0762-5). Lerner Pubns.
Gray, Bonnie, et al. Every Woman Works: A Complete Manual for Women Re-Entering the Job Market or Changing Jobs. (Career Development Ser.). (Illus.). 315p. 1982. 19.95 (ISBN 0-534-97981-5); pap. 11.95 (ISBN 0-534-97928-9); leader's guide free avail. (ISBN 0-534-97954-8). Lifetime Learn.
Gray, Bradford H. Human Subjects in Medical Experimentation: A Sociological Study of the Conduct & Regulation of Clinical Research. LC 80-11612. 316p. 1981. Repr. of 1975 ed. lib. bdg. 22.50 (ISBN 0-89874-134-3). Krieger.
Gray, Brayton. Homotopy Theory: An Introduction to Algebraic Topology. 1975. 59.50 (ISBN 0-12-296050-5). Acad Pr.
Gray, C. G. & Gubbins, K. E. Theory of Molecular Fluids: Fundamentals, Vol. 1. (International Series of Monographs on Chemistry). (Illus.). 1984. 79.00x (ISBN 0-19-855602-0). Oxford U Pr.
Gray, C. H. & James, V. H. T. Hormones in Blood, Vol. 3. 3rd ed. LC 78-73882. 1980. 90.00 (ISBN 0-12-296203-6). Acad Pr.
Gray, C. H. & James, V. H., eds. Hormones in Blood, Vol. 4. 3rd ed. 1983. 77.50 (ISBN 0-12-296204-4). Vol. 5th. 55.00 (ISBN 0-12-296205-2). Acad Pr.
Gray, C. H. & James, V. H. T., eds. Hormones in Blood, Vol. 1. 3rd ed. 1979. 90.00 (ISBN 0-12-296201-X). Acad Pr.
--Hormones in Blood, Vol. 2. 3rd ed. 1979. 80.00 (ISBN 0-12-296202-8). Acad Pr.
Gray, Carol J., jt. auth. see Reams, Bernard D.
Gray, Carol J., jt. auth. see Reams, Bernard D, Jr.
Gray, Carol J., compiled by. Checklist of Federal Revised Laws: A Bibliography of Current Editions. (Bibliography Ser.). iii, 54p. (Orig.). 1984. pap. text ed. 8.00 (ISBN 0-318-11694-4). Wash U Law Lib.
Gray, Catherine D. & Gray, James. Tammy & the Gigantic Fish. LC 82-47732. (Illus.). 32p. (ps-2). 1983. PLB 8.89g (ISBN 0-06-022139-9). HarpJ.
Gray, Cecil. Carlo Gesualdo, Prince of Venosa, Musician & Murderer. LC 76-104268. (Illus.). 1971. Repr. of 1926 ed. lib. bdg. 22.50x (ISBN 0-8371-3934-1, GRCG). Greenwood.
--Contingencies & Other Essays. facs. ed. LC 75-134084. (Essay Index Reprint Ser). 1947. 17.00 (ISBN 0-8369-2159-3). Ayer Co Pubs.
--Forty-Eight Preludes & Fugues of J. S. Bach. (Music Reprint Ser.). 1979. Repr. of 1938 ed. 21.50 (ISBN 0-306-79559-0). Da Capo.
--The Forty-Eight Preludes & Fugues of J. S. Bach. (Encore Music Editions Ser.). (Illus.). 1979. Repr. of 1938 ed. 16.00 (ISBN 0-88355-742-8). Hyperion Conn.
--The History of Music. LC 78-10335. 1979. Repr. of 1935 ed. lib. bdg. 22.50x (ISBN 0-313-20655-4, GRHM). Greenwood.
--Musical Chairs. 352p. 1985. pap. 8.95 (ISBN 0-7012-0642-X, Pub. by Hogarth Pr.). Merrimack Pub Cir.

--Predicaments, or Music & the Future: An Essay in Constructive Criticism. LC 79-103652. (Select Bibliographies Reprint Ser). 1936. 24.50 (ISBN 0-8369-5152-2). Ayer Co Pubs.
--Sibelius. LC 78-66986. (Encore Music Editions Ser.). (Illus.). 1979. Repr. of 1931 ed. 21.75 (ISBN 0-88355-743-6). Hyperion Conn.
--Sibelius: The Symphonies. LC 78-114879. (Select Bibliographies Reprint Ser). 1935. 11.00 (ISBN 0-8369-5283-9). Ayer Co Pubs.
--Survey of Contemporary Music. LC 75-93341. (Essay Index Reprint Ser). 1924. 19.00 (ISBN 0-8369-1294-2). Ayer Co Pubs.
--A Survey of Contemporary Music. 2nd ed. LC 78-163551. 266p. 1972. Repr. of 1927 ed. lib. bdg. 22.50x (ISBN 0-8371-6211-4, GRCM). Greenwood.
Gray, Charles E., jt. auth. see Pierce, Walter D.
Gray, Charles G. Off at Sunrise: The Overland Journal of Charles Glass Gray. Clark, Thomas D., intro. by. LC 76-9350. (Illus.). 185p. 1976. 12.00 (ISBN 0-87328-069-5). Huntington Lib.
Gray, Charles H. Theatrical Criticism in London to Seventeen Ninety-Five. LC 64-14708. 1931. 18.00 (ISBN 0-405-08574-5). Ayer Co Pubs.
Gray, Charles, Jr. & Alson, Jeff. Methanol: The Transportation Fuel of the Future (The Optimal Solution to the Acid Rain & Energy Problems) 300p. 1985. text ed. 25.00x (ISBN 0-472-10071-8); pap. text ed. 12.50x (ISBN 0-472-08063-6). U of Mich Pr.
Gray, Charles M. Copyhold, Equity, & the Common Law. LC 63-11420. (Historical Monographs: No. 53). 1963. 16.50x (ISBN 0-674-17150-0). Harvard U Pr.
Gray, Charles M. see Blum, John, et al.
Gray, Charles M., ed. The Costs of Crime. LC 79-18871. (Sage Criminal Jusice System Annuals: Vol. 12). (Illus.). 280p. 1979. 28.00 (ISBN 0-8039-1198-X); pap. 14.00 (ISBN 0-8039-1199-8). Sage.
Gray, Charles M., ed. see Hale, Matthew.
Gray, Charles W. Dawgs: An Anthology about Them. Repr. of 1925 ed. 25.00 (ISBN 0-686-18763-6). Scholars Ref Lib.
Gray, Christopher. Cubist Aesthetic Theories. LC 53-6493. pap. 51.50 (ISBN 0-317-10011-4, 2007365). Bks Demand UMI.
--Sculpture & Ceramics of Paul Gauguin. LC 79-91819. (Illus.). 330p. 1980. Repr. of 1963 ed. lib. bdg. 75.00 (ISBN 0-87817-263-7). Hacker.
Gray, Clarence T. Deficiencies in Reading Ability, Their Diagnosis & Remedies. (Educational Ser.). 1922. Repr. 15.00 (ISBN 0-8482-4204-1). Norwood Edns.
--Types of Reading Ability as Exhibited Through Tests & Laboratory Experiments. (Educational Ser.). 1917. Repr. 20.00 (ISBN 0-8482-4250-5). Norwood Edns.
Gray, Clifford F. Essentials of Project Management. (Illus.). 288p. 1980. text ed. 17.50 (ISBN 0-89433-101-9). Petrocelli.
Gray, Clifton D., ed. The Samas Religious Texts Classified in the British Museum Catalogue As Hymns, Prayers, & Incantations. LC 78-72728. (Ancient Mesopotamian Texts & Studies). Repr. of 1901 ed. 17.50 (ISBN 0-404-18176-7). AMS Pr.
Gray, Colin S. American Military Space Policy. 1983. text ed. 28.00 (ISBN 0-89011-591-5). Abt Bks.
--American Military Space Policy: Information Systems, Weapon Systems & Arms Control. 138p. 1984. lib. bdg. 28.00 (ISBN 0-8191-4076-7); pap. text ed. 9.25 (ISBN 0-8191-4077-5). U Pr of Amer.
--Arms Control & European Security: Some Basic Issues. 54p. 1980. 15.00 (ISBN 0-318-14335-6, HI31572P). Hudson Inst.
--The Geopolitics of the Nuclear Era: Heartland, Rimlands, & the Technological Revolution. LC 77-83666. 70p. 1977. pap. 7.50x (ISBN 0-8448-1258-7). Crane-Russak Co.
--Missiles for the Nineties: ICBMs & Strategic Policy. (Replica Edition Ser.). 190p. 1984. pap. 17.85x (ISBN 0-8133-7001-9). Westview.
--The MX ICBM & National Security. LC 81-2557. 190p. 1981. 38.95 (ISBN 0-03-059442-1). Praeger.
--The Nuclear Strategy & National Style. 1984. 28.00 (ISBN 0-89011-599-0). Abt Bks.
--Nuclear Strategy & Strategic Planning. LC 83-20800. (Philadelphia Policy Papers). 130p. (Orig.). 1984. pap. 5.95 (ISBN 0-910191-07-7). For Policy Res.
--The Soviet-American Arms Race. 208p. pap. text ed. 44.00x (ISBN 0-347-01125-X). Gower Pub Co.
--Strategic Studies: A Critical Assessment. LC 81-6820. (Contributions in Political Science Ser.: No. 70). x, 213p. 1982. lib. bdg. 29.95 (ISBN 0-313-22862-0, GSS/). Greenwood.
--Strategic Studies & Public Policy: The American Experience. Davis, Vincent, ed. LC 80-5175. (Essays for the Third Century Ser.: America & a Changing World). 240p. 1982. 20.00 (ISBN 0-8131-0403-3). U Pr of Ky.
Gray, Colin S., jt. auth. see Payne, Keith B.
Gray, Colin S., jt. ed. see Payne, Keith B.
Gray, Collen. Peru. LC 83-8740. (World Education Ser.). (Illus.). 122p. (Orig.). 1983. pap. text ed. 2.00 (ISBN 0-910054-77-0). Am Assn Coll Registrars.
Gray, Constance S., ed. U. S. Government Directories, 1970-1981: A Selected, Annotated Bibilography. 1984. lib. bdg. 35.00 (ISBN 0-87287-414-1). Libs Unl.
Gray, D., jt. ed. see Stanley, E. G.
Gray, D. Dodson, jt. auth. see Gray, E. Dodson.
Gray, D. F., ed. Stellar Turbulence: Proceedings of Colloquium 51 of the International Astronomical Union, Held at the University of Western Ontario, London, Ontario, Canada, August 27-30, 1979. (Lecture Notes in Physics: Vol. 114). 308p. 1980. pap. 26.00 (ISBN 3-540-09737-6). Springer-Verlag.
Gray, D. M., ed. Handbook on the Principles of Hydrology. LC 73-82157. (Illus.). 720p. 1973. pap. text ed. 28.00 (ISBN 0-912394-07-2). Water Info.
Gray, D. M. & Male, D. H., eds. Handbook of Snow: Principles, Processes, Management & Use. (Illus.). 800p. 1981. 66.00 (ISBN 0-08-025375-X); pap. 29.00 (ISBN 0-08-025374-1). Pergamon.
Gray, Daniel S. In the Words of Napoleon. LC 77-71468. 1977. pap. 8.50x (ISBN 0-916624-07-2). Troy State Univ.
--Troy State University Writings & Research, Vol. III. 32p. 1974. pap. 1.95 (ISBN 0-686-97227-9). Troy State Univ.
Gray, Daniel S. & Starr, J. Barton. Alabama: A Place, a People, a Point of View. LC 76-25623. (History Ser.). 1977. pap. text ed. 10.95 (ISBN 0-8403-1561-9). Kendall-Hunt.
Gray, Darrell. Essays & Dissolutions. 1977. pap. 3.00 (ISBN 0-932868-02-9). Abraxas.
--Halos of Debris. 80p. Date not set. price not set. (ISBN 0-918395-00-3); pap. price not set. (ISBN 0-918395-01-1). Poltroon Pr.
--Scattered Brains. LC 74-32028. 1974. pap. 5.00 (ISBN 0-915124-04-1, Pub. by Toothpaste). Coffee Hse.
Gray, Darrell, jt. ed. see Sklar, Morty.
Gray, David. Ensign Russell. LC 74-130058. (Short Story Index Reprint Ser.). 1912. 15.00 (ISBN 0-8369-3644-2). Ayer Co Pubs.
--Gallops, 2 vols. in one. facs. ed. LC 73-75778. (Short Story Index Reprint Ser.). 1903. 19.00 (ISBN 0-8369-3003-7). Ayer Co Pubs.
Gray, David, jt ed. see Pratt, Keith.
Gray, David B., et al. Ecological Beliefs & Behaviors: Assessment & Change. LC 84-12833. (Contributions in Psychology Ser.: No. 4). (Illus.). 256p. 1985. lib. bdg. 35.00 (ISBN 0-313-24319-0, GRB/). Greenwood.
Gray, David F. The Mystery of Israel's Flag. Hall, J. L., ed. (Illus.). 112p. pap. 4.95 (ISBN 0-912315-38-5). Word Aflame.
--The Observation & Analysis of Stellar Photospheres. LC 75-19229. 471p. 1976. 49.95x (ISBN 0-471-32380-2, Pub. by Wiley-Interscience). Wiley.
Gray, David R. Non-Private Foundations. 1978. 80.00 (ISBN 0-07-024230-5, Shepard). McGraw.
Gray, Denis J. & Gray, Jill P., eds. The Medical Annual 1985: The Yearbook of General Practice. (Illus.). 344p. 1985. 20.00 (ISBN 0-7236-0822-9). PSG Pub Co.
Gray, Don. Dark Side of the Moon. 1970. pap. 2.50 (ISBN 0-685-01071-6); pap. 10.00x ea. signed ed. Twowindows Pr.
--Five Hours. 1969. signed ed. 25.00x (ISBN 0-685-20656-4); pap. 2.25 (ISBN 0-685-20657-2). Twowindows Pr.
Gray, Donald. Finding God among Us. 2nd ed. LC 77-89322. 1977. pap. 3.95 (ISBN 0-88489-090-2). St Mary's.
Gray, Donald & Leiser, Andrew. Biotechnical Slope Protection: Economic Methods for Earth Support & Erosion Control. 432p. 1982. 28.95 (ISBN 0-442-21222-4). Van Nos Reinhold.
Gray, Donald, ed. see Austen, Jane.
Gray, Donald J., ed. see Carroll, Lewis.
Gray, Donald P. Jesus: The Way to Freedom. LC 79-66823. (Illus.). 1979. pap. text ed. 4.95 (ISBN 0-88489-112-7). St Mary's.
--A New Creation Story: The Creative Sprirituality of Teilhard de Chardin. (Teilhard Studies). 1979. pap. 2.00 (ISBN 0-89012-014-5). Anima Pubns.
Gray, Doris E. Experiments in Biological Chemistry: A Laboratory Manual for Medical Students. pap. 42.30 (ISBN 0-317-28806-7, 2020774). Bks Demand UMI.
Gray, Dorothy L. Reluctant Memory. 1977. 4.00 (ISBN 0-682-48897-6). Exposition Pr FL.
Gray, Douglas. Start & Run a Profitable Consulting Business: A Step-by-Step Business Plan. 120p. 1984. pap. 12.95 (ISBN 0-88908-598-6). Self Counsel Pr.
--Start & Run a Profitable Consulting Business. pap. 12.95. TAB Bks.
Gray, Douglas & Stanley, E. G., eds. Middle English Studies: Presented to Norman Davis in Honour of His Seventieth Birthday. (Illus.). 1983p. 1983. text ed. 67.00x (ISBN 0-19-811183-5). Oxford U Pr.
Gray, Douglas, jt. ed. see Stanley, E. G.
Gray, Duncan. The Life & Work of Lord Byron. LC 76-41017. Repr. of 1946 ed. lib. bdg. 10.00 (ISBN 0-8414-4447-1). Folcroft.
Gray, Dwight E. So You Have to Write a Technical Report: Elements of Technical Report Writing. LC 70-120541. ix, 117p. 1970. pap. 7.00 (ISBN 0-87815-002-1). Info Resources.
Gray, E. Dodson. Patriarchy As a Conceptual Trap. 136p. 1982. pap. 8.95 (ISBN 0-934512-04-3). Roundtable Pr.
Gray, E. Dodson & Gray, D. Dodson. Children of Joy: Raising Your Own Home-Grown Christians. LC 74-80259. xviii, 258p. (Orig.). 1975. pap. 7.95 (ISBN 0-934512-03-5). Roundtable Pr.
Gray, E. G. The Synapse. rev. ed. Head, J. J., ed. LC 76-53173. (Carolina Biology Readers Ser.). (Illus.). 16p. (gr. 10 up). 1977. pap. 1.60 (ISBN 0-89278-235-8, 45-9635). Carolina Biological.
Gray, Eden. Complete Guide to the Tarot. 1971. pap. 3.95 (ISBN 0-553-23470-6). Bantam.
--Mastering the Tarot: Basic Lessons in an Ancient Mystic Art. 208p. 1973. pap. 3.50 (ISBN 0-451-12320-4, AE2320, Sig). NAL.
--Tarot Revealed: A Modern Guide to Reading the Tarot Cards. 1971. pap. 3.95 (ISBN 0-451-13700-0, AE1965, Sig). NAL.
Gray, Edmund R., ed. Business Policy & Strategy: Selected Readings. LC 78-59402. (Illus.). 1979. text ed. 15.00 (ISBN 0-914872-12-5); pap. text ed. 10.00 (ISBN 0-686-67375-1). Austin Pr.
Gray, Edward. Daniel Webster in England: Journal of Harriette Story Page. 1977. Repr. of 1917 ed. 45.00 (ISBN 0-8274-4283-1). R West.
--Gray's Journal: The First Correction. LC 82-83769. (Illus.). 80p. 1982. 25.00 (ISBN 0-9609842-0-8). Grays Sporting.
--Gray's Journal: The Second Correction. LC 84-82448. (Illus.). 80p. 1984. 25.00 (ISBN 0-9609842-2-4). Grays Sporting.
Gray, Edwyn. Crash Dive Five Hundred. 220p. 1985. 13.95 (ISBN 0-8027-0840-4). Walker & Co.
--Devil Flotilla. 192p. 1981. pap. 2.25 (ISBN 0-523-41405-6). Pinnacle Bks.
--Diving Stations. 222p. 1985. 13.95 (ISBN 0-8027-0815-3). Walker & Co.
--Lost with All Hands: The History of Submarine Disasters. LC 85-40327. (Illus.). 1985. 18.95 (ISBN 0-8128-3053-9). Stein & Day.
Gray, Elizabeth. The Taken Girl. (gr. 7 up). 1972. PLB 9.95 (ISBN 0-670-69099-6). Viking.
Gray, Elizabeth D., et al. Growth & Its Implications for the Future. LC 75-13809. (Illus.). 184p. (Orig.). 1975. pap. 5.95 (ISBN 0-915758-06-7). Roundtable Pr.
Gray, Elizabeth Dodson. Green Paradise Lost. LC 79-89193. x, 166p. 1979. pap. 7.95 (ISBN 0-934512-02-7). Roundtable Pr.
--Why the Green Nigger? Re-Mything Genesis. LC 79-89193. x, 166p. 1979. 12.95 (ISBN 0-934512-01-9). Roundtable Pr.
Gray, Elizabeth J. Adam of the Road. (Illus.). 320p. (gr. 4-8). 1942. 12.95 (ISBN 0-670-10435-3). Viking.
--Anthology with Comments. 1983. pap. 5.00x (ISBN 0-87574-018-9, 018). Pendle Hill.
--Contributions of the Quakers. 1983. pap. 5.00x (ISBN 0-87574-034-0, 034). Pendle Hill.
Gray, Elma E. & Gray, Leslie R. Wilderness Christians: The Moravian Mission to the Delaware Indians. LC 72-84988. (Illus.). xiv, 354p. 1973. Repr. of 1956 ed. 22.00x (ISBN 0-8462-1701-5). Russell.
Gray, Elmer L. Furious & Free. LC 83-25190. (gr. 10 up). 1984. 7.95 (ISBN 0-8054-7320-3). Broadman.
Gray, Ernest. Successful Business Resumes. 285p. 1981. 12.50 (ISBN 0-8436-0771-8). Van Nos Reinhold.
Gray, Ernest, ed. Man Midwife. 1946. 20.00 (ISBN 0-8274-4206-8). R West.
Gray, Ernest A. Profitable Methods for Small Business Advertising. LC 83-19884. (Wiley Series on Small Business Management: 1-471). 285p. 1984. 22.95 (ISBN 0-471-86962-7, Ronald Pr). Wiley.
Gray, Ethan. The Well of Silence: First Poems by Ethan Gray. LC 83-70134. 50p. 1983. 7.95 (ISBN 0-9610736-0-8). Trad Pr.
Gray, Floyd, ed. Anthologie de la Poesie Francaise du Seizieme Siecle. LC 67-10343. (Fr.). 1977. 39.50x (ISBN 0-89197-026-6); pap. text ed. 22.95x (ISBN 0-89197-659-0). Irvington.
Gray, Floyd, ed. see Beaujour, Michel, et al.
Gray, Floyd, ed. see Rabelais, Francois.
Gray, Floyd F., tr. see Rabelais, Francois.
Gray, Frances. John Arden. LC 82-47993. (Illus.). 180p. (Orig.). 1982. pap. 9.95 (ISBN 0-394-62415-7, E820, Ever). Grove.
Gray, Francine, frwd. by see Badinter, Elisabeth.
Gray, Francine du Plessix see Du Plessix Gray, Francine.
Gray, Francis C. Prison Discipline in America. LC 77-172599. (Criminology, Law Enforcement, & Social Problems Ser.: No. 189). (With intro. & index added). 1973. Repr. of 1847 ed. 15.00x (ISBN 0-87585-189-4). Patterson Smith.
Gray, Frank D. Pulmonary Embolism. LC 66-19290. pap. 58.50 (ISBN 0-317-07818-6, 2055298). Bks Demand UMI.
--Pulmonary Embolism. LC 66-19290. pap. 58.50 (ISBN 0-317-28602-1, 2055429). Bks Demand UMI.
Gray, Fred, jt. auth. see Merrett, Stephen.
Gray, G. & Hoel, L. Public Transportation: Planning, Operations & Management. 1979. 47.95 (ISBN 0-13-739169-2). P-H.
Gray, G. W., jt. auth. see Goodby, J. W.
Gray, G. W. & Winsor, P. A., eds. Liquid Crystals & Plastic Crystals: Preparation, Constitution & Applications, Vol. 1. LC 73-11504. (Illus.). 383p. 1974. 74.95 (ISBN 0-470-32339-6). Halsted Pr.
--Liquid Crystals & Plastic Crystals: Physico-Chemical Properties & Methods of Investigation, Vol. 2. LC 73-11505. (Illus.). 314p. 1974. 79.95 (ISBN 0-470-32340-X). Halsted Pr.
Gray, G. W., jt. ed. see Luckhurst, G. R.
Gray, Genevieve. Alaska Woman. LC 77-7040. (Time of Danger, Time for Courage Ser.). (Illus.). (gr. 3-9). 1977. PLB 6.95 (ISBN 0-88436-386-4, 35482); pap. 3.95 (ISBN 0-88436-387-2, 35300). EMC.
--Break-In. LC 73-4505. (Girl Stuff Ser.). (Illus.). (gr. 4-8). 1973. PLB 6.95 (ISBN 0-912022-64-7, 35560); pap. 3.95 (ISBN 0-912022-65-5, 35347). EMC.
--The Dark Side of Nowhere. LC 77-7110. (Time of Danger, Time for Courage Ser.). (Illus.). (gr. 3-9). 1977. PLB 6.95 (ISBN 0-88436-390-2, 35480); pap. 3.95 (ISBN 0-88436-391-0, 35298). EMC.
--Has Anyone Seen Buddy Bascom? LC 77-7926. (Time of Danger, Time for Courage Ser.). (Illus.). 40p. (gr. 3-9). 1977. PLB 6.95 (ISBN 0-88436-384-8, 35481); pap. 3.95 (ISBN 0-88436-385-6, 35299). EMC.
--Hot Shot. LC 73-4585. (Girl Stuff Ser). (Illus.). 32p. (gr. 4-8). 1973. pap. 3.95 (ISBN 0-912022-63-9). EMC.
--How Far, Felipe? LC 77-11846. (I Can Read History Bk.). (Illus.). 64p. (gr. k-3). 1978. 8.64i (ISBN 0-06-022107-0); PLB 9.89 (ISBN 0-06-022108-9). HarpJ.
--The Magic Bears. LC 75-29316. (Blessingway: Tales of a Navajo Family). (Illus.). 40p. (gr. 4-9). 1975. PLB 6.95 (ISBN 0-88436-223-X, ELA 129079); pap. 3.95 (ISBN 0-88436-224-8, ELA 129055). EMC.
--The Secret of the Mask. LC 75-30708. (Blessingway: Tales of a Navajo Family). (Illus.). 40p. (gr. 4-9). 1975. PLB 6.95 (ISBN 0-88436-221-3); pap. 3.95 (ISBN 0-88436-222-1). EMC.
--The Spiderweb Stone. LC 75-30529. (Blessingway: Tales of a Navajo Family). (Illus.). 40p. (gr. 4-9). 1975. PLB 6.95 (ISBN 0-88436-219-1, 129077); pap. 3.95 (ISBN 0-88436-220-5, ELA 129053). EMC.
--Stand-Off. LC 73-4722. (Girl Stuff Ser.). (gr. 4-8). 1973. PLB 6.95 (ISBN 0-912022-68-X, 35559); pap. 3.95 (ISBN 0-912022-69-8, 35345). EMC.
--Stray. LC 73-4587. (Girl Stuff Ser). (Illus.). 40p. (Orig.). (gr. 4-8). 1973. PLB 6.95 (ISBN 0-912022-66-3, 35561); pap. 3.95 (ISBN 0-912022-67-1, 35348). EMC.
--The Tall Singer. LC 75-30531. (Blessingway: Tales of a Navajo Family). (Illus.). 40p. (gr. 4-9). 1975. PLB 6.95 (ISBN 0-88436-217-5, ELA 129076); pap. 3.95 (ISBN 0-88436-218-3, ELA 129052). EMC.
--Two Tickets to Memphis. LC 77-23394. (Time of Danger, Time for Courage Ser.). (Illus.). 40p. (gr. 3-9). 1977. PLB 6.95 (ISBN 0-88436-388-0, 35483); pap. 3.95 (ISBN 0-88436-389-9, 35301). EMC.
Gray, George & Darley, H. C. Composition & Properties of Oil Well Drilling Fluids. 4th ed. LC 79-28157. 630p. 1980. 59.95x (ISBN 0-87201-129-1). Gulf Pub.
Gray, George B. A Critical Introduction to the Old Testament. 1978. Repr. of 1936 ed. lib. bdg. 25.00 (ISBN 0-8495-1939-X). Arden Lib.
--Studies in Hebrew Proper Names. (The International Library of Names). 338p. 1984. Repr. of 1896 ed. text ed. cancelled (ISBN 0-8290-1232-X). Irvington.
Gray, George W. Education on an International Scale: A History of the International Education Board, 1923-1938. LC 78-800. (Illus.). 1978. Repr. of 1941 ed. lib. bdg. 17.00x (ISBN 0-313-20268-0, GREI). Greenwood.
--Science at War. LC 72-4531. (Essay Index Reprint Ser.). Repr. of 1943 ed. 20.00 (ISBN 0-8369-2944-6). Ayer Co Pubs.
Gray, Gordon, jt. auth. see Linn, Jo W.
Gray, Gustave Le see Croucher, J. H. & Le Gray, Gustave.
Gray, H. B., jt. auth. see Ballhausen, C. J.
Gray, H. B., jt. ed. see Lever, A. B.
Gray, H. Dean & Tindall, Judy A. Peer Counseling: In-Depth Look at Peer Helpers. 2nd ed. LC 77-75892. (Illus.). 320p. 1985. pap. text ed. 12.45x (ISBN 0-915202-52-2). Accel Devel.
Gray, H. Dean, jt. auth. see Tindall, Judy.
Gray, H. J. & Isaacs, A., eds. A New Dictionary of Physics. rev. ed. LC 75-307635. Orig. Title: Dictionary of Physics. (Illus.). 640p. 1975. 40.00x (ISBN 0-582-32242-1). Longman.
Gray, H. Peter. Free Trade or Protection? A Pragmatic Analysis. 144p. 1985. 25.00 (ISBN 0-312-30374-2). St Martin.
--International Trade, Investment & Payments. LC 78-69573. (Illus.). 1979. text ed. 31.95 (ISBN 0-395-26659-9). HM.
Gray, Hamish. Cost of Council Housing. (Institute of Economic Affairs, Research Monographs: No. 18). (Orig.). pap. 2.50 technical (ISBN 0-255-69639-6). Transatlantic.
Gray, Harold. Little Orphan Annie. (Illus.). 64p. (gr. 2 up). 1982. pap. 1.95 (ISBN 0-486-24420-2). Dover.

--Little Orphan Annie in Cosmic City. (Illus.). 64p. (gr. 2 up). 1982. pap. 1.95 (ISBN 0-486-24421-0). Dover.
--Little Orphan Annie in the Great Depression. (Illus.). 58p. (Orig.). 1979. pap. 2.50 (ISBN 0-486-23737-0). Dover.
Gray, Harold S. Character "Bad". The Story of a Conscientious Objector. Brown, Kenneth I., ed. LC 72-147634. (Library of War & Peace; Conscrip. & Cons. Object.). lib. bdg. 46.00 (ISBN 0-8240-0410-8). Garland Pub.
Gray, Harry, ed. Change & Management in Schools. 84p. 1979. 15.00x (ISBN 0-905484-10-X, Pub. by Nafferton England). State Mutual Bk.
--Management in Education. 180p. 1980. 20.00x (ISBN 0-905484-13-4, Pub. by Nafferton England). State Mutual Bk.
--The School As an Organization. 84p. 1981. 20.00x (ISBN 0-905484-11-8, Pub. by Nafferton England). State Mutual Bk.
Gray, Harry B. Chemical Bonds: An Introduction to Atomic & Molecular Structure. LC 72-5014. 1973. pap. text ed. 21.95 (ISBN 0-8053-3402-5). Benjamin-Cummings.
--Electrons & Chemical Bonding. (Orig.). 1964. pap. 21.95 (ISBN 0-8053-3401-7). Benjamin-Cummings.
Gray, Harry B., jt. auth. see DeKock, Roger L.
Gray, Harry L., ed. The Management of Educational Institutions: Theory, Research & Consultancy. 294p. 1982. text ed. 28.00x (ISBN 0-905273-25-7, Pub. by Falmer Pr); pap. 18.00x (ISBN 0-905273-24-9, Pub. by Falmer Pr). Taylor & Francis.
Gray, Harry N. The Farmer & the Miner: Enoch & Big Mike. 1983. 8.00 (ISBN 0-533-05550-4). Vantage.
Gray, Henry. Gray's Anatomy. LC 76-52804. 1977. 10.00x (ISBN 0-517-22365-1, Pub. by Bounty). Formur Intl.
Gray, Henry D. Love's Labour's Lost. LC 77-3972. 1918. lib. bdg. 15.00 (ISBN 0-8414-4480-3). Folcroft.
Gray, Henry D., ed. see Shakespeare, William.
Gray, Herbi. On-loom Cardweaving: A Modern Extension of an Ancient Craft. (Illus.). 60p. (Orig.). 1982. pap. 8.95 (ISBN 0-9608406-0-5). H Gray.
Gray, Howard A. Some Factors in the Undergraduate Careers of Young College Students with Particular Reference to Columbia & Barnard Colleges. LC 77-176819. (Columbia University. Teachers College. Contributions to Education: No. 437). Repr. of 1930 ed. 22.50 (ISBN 0-404-55437-7). AMS Pr.
Gray, Howard L. English Field Systems. LC 76-29420. Repr. of 1915 ed. 39.50 (ISBN 0-404-15335-6). AMS Pr.
--English Field Systems. 1980. Repr. of 1915 ed. lib. bdg. 37.50x (ISBN 0-678-08069-0). Kelley.
Gray, Hugh, tr. & compiled by see Bazin, Andre.
Gray, Hugh, tr. see Bazin, Andre.
Gray, I. General & Industrial Management. LC 84-10747. 1984. 19.95 (ISBN 0-87942-178-9, PC01727). Inst Electrical.
Gray, Irvine. Antiquaries of Gloucestershire & Bristol. 208p. 1981. text ed. 18.50x (ISBN 0-900197-14-5, Pub. by Alan Sutton England). Humanities.
Gray, Irvine, tr. see De La Sale, Antoine.
Gray, Irwin. The Engineer in Transition to Management. LC 78-61533. 1979. 25.95 (ISBN 0-87942-111-8, PC01164). Inst Electrical.
--The Engineer in Transition to Management. LC 78-61533. 127p. 1979. 24.95x (ISBN 0-471-05212-4). Wiley.
Gray, J. Caltrop's Desire. 25.00x (ISBN 0-86036-108-X, Pub. by R Collings UK). State Mutual Bk.
--Formal Category Theory: Adjointness for 2-Categories. LC 74-7910. (Lecture Notes in Mathematics: Vol. 391). xii, 282p. 1974. pap. 17.00 (ISBN 0-387-06830-9). Springer-Verlag.
--The Social System: A Treatise on the Principle of Exchange. LC 5-20470. Repr. of 1831 ed. 24.00 (ISBN 0-527-35540-2). Kraus Repr.
Gray, J. & Ricketts, D. E. Cost & Managerial Accounting. 800p. 1982. 36.95x (ISBN 0-07-024220-8). McGraw.
Gray, J., jt. auth. see Leeson, J.
Gray, J., jt. auth. see McPherson, A.
Gray, J. & White, G., eds. China's New Development Strategy. LC 81-68984. 1982. 38.00 (ISBN 0-12-296840-9). Acad Pr.
Gray, J., tr. see Schubert, H.
Gray, J. A. Amerika Samoa. LC 79-6109. (Navies & Men Ser.). (Illus.). 1980. Repr. of 1960 ed. lib. bdg. 28.50x (ISBN 0-405-13038-4). Ayer Co Pubs.
--Elements of a Two-Process Theory of Learning. 1975. 49.00 (ISBN 0-12-296850-6). Acad Pr.
--The Neuropsychology of Anxiety: An Inquiry into the Functions of the Septo-Hippocampal System. (Oxford Psychology Ser.). (Illus.). 1982. 55.00x (ISBN 0-19-852109-X). Oxford U Pr.
Gray, J. A. & Barrow, R. W. Small Gas Engines. 357p. 1976. pap. text ed. 19.95 (ISBN 0-13-813113-9). P-H.
Gray, J. A. & Lovet, Mrs. Heather M. Take Care of Your Elderly Relative. (Illus., Orig.). 1980. 23.95 (ISBN 0-04-618015-X). Allen Unwin.
Gray, J. A., jt. ed. see Nebylitsyn, V. D.
Gray, J. A., jt. auth. see Wilcock, G. K.
Gray, J. C. Mirror up to Shakespeare: Essays in Honor of G. R. Hibbard. 328p. 1984. text ed. 35.00x (ISBN 0-8020-5639-3). U of Toronto Pr.
Gray, J. Glenn. Re-Thinking American Education: A Philosophy of Teaching & Learning. 304p. 1984. pap. 9.95 (ISBN 0-8195-5114-7). Wesleyan U Pr.
--The Warriors: Reflections on Men in Battle. pap. 5.72i (ISBN 0-06-090580-8, CN580, CN). Harrow.
Gray, J. Glenn, tr. see Heidegger, Martin.
Gray, J. H. China: A History of the Laws, Manners & Customs of the People, 2 vols. Gregor, W. G., ed. (Illus.). 800p. 1972. Repr. of 1878 ed. Set. 75.00x (ISBN 0-7165-2030-3, BBA 02126, Pub. by Irish Academic Pr Ireland). Biblio Dist.
Gray, J. M. James & William Tassie: A Biographical & Critical Sketch. 45.00 (ISBN 0-685-53307-7). ARS Ceramica.
--Thro' the Vision of the Night: A Study of Source, Evolution & Structure in Tennyson's "Idylls of the King". 189p. 1980. 25.00x (ISBN 0-7735-0519-9). McGill-Queens U Pr.
Gray, J. M., ed. Processing & Properties of Low Carbon Steel. LC 73-172124. pap. 106.30 (ISBN 0-317-08694-4, 2012653). Bks Demand UMI.
Gray, J. M. & Lowe, J. J., eds. Studies in the Scottish Lateglacial Environment. 1977. text ed. 35.00 (ISBN 0-08-020498-8). Pergamon.
Gray, J. M., ed. see Tennyson, Alfred.
Gray, J. M., illus. Hello Kitty's Christmas Book. LC 82-80921. (Sanrio Bks.). (Illus.). 16p. (ps). 1982. pap. 1.25 (ISBN 0-394-85432-2). Random.
Gray, J. O., jt. ed. see Billings, S. A.
Gray, J. Patrick. Primate Sociobiology. LC 85-60629. (Comparative Ser.). 550p. (Orig.). 1985. pap. price not set (ISBN 0-87536-344-X). HRAFP.
Gray, J. S. The Ecology of Marine Sediments. (Cambridge Studies in Modern Biology: No. 2). (Illus.). 170p. 1981. 39.50 (ISBN 0-521-23553-7); pap. 18.95 (ISBN 0-521-28027-3). Cambridge U Pr.
Gray, J. S. & Christianson, M. E. European Marine Biology, 18th Symposium: Marine Biology of the Polar Regions & Effects of Stress on Marine Organisms. 1985. 49.95 (ISBN 0-471-90465-1). Wiley.
Gray, J. W. Shakespeare's Marriage. 59.95 (ISBN 0-8490-1044-6). Gordon Pr.
--Shakespeare's Marriage. 1973. 9.95 (ISBN 0-8274-0642-8). R West.
Gray, J. W., ed. see Midwest Category Seminar, 5th.
Gray, Jack, jt. ed. see Brown, Archie.
Gray, James. Edna St. Vincent Millay. (Pamphlets on American Writers Ser: No. 64). (Orig.). 1967. pap. 1.25x (ISBN 0-8166-0437-1, MPAW64). U of Minn Pr.
--John Steinbeck. LC 74-633323. (University of Minnesota Pamphlets on American Writers Ser.: No. 94). pap. 20.00 (ISBN 0-317-29456-3, 2055935). Bks Demand UMI.
--University of Minnesota, 1851-1951. (Illus.). 1951. 9.50x (ISBN 0-8166-0069-4). U of Minn Pr.
--The Winning Image. LC 81-69372. pap. 48.00 (ISBN 0-317-19832-7, 2023074). Bks Demand UMI.
Gray, James, jt. auth. see Catton, Chris.
Gray, James, jt. auth. see Gray, Catherine D.
Gray, James, jt. auth. see Ochs, Robert.
Gray, James, ed. Ancient Proverbs & Maxims from Burmese Sources: The Niti Literature of Burma. LC 77-87014. Repr. of 1886 ed. 17.50 (ISBN 0-404-16822-1). AMS Pr.
Gray, James, ed. see Johnson, Samuel.
Gray, James, jt. ed. see Myers, Miles.
Gray, James, jt. ed. see Ochs, Robert.
Gray, James A., ed. see Childers, James S.
Gray, James, Jr. The Winning Image. 192p. 1982. 13.95 (ISBN 0-8144-5667-7). AMACOM.
--The Winning Image. LC 81-69372. 192p. 1984. pap. 6.95 (ISBN 0-8144-7611-2). AMACOM.
Gray, James M. Home Bible Study Commentary. LC 85-9750. 448p. 1985. pap. 12.95 (ISBN 0-8254-2727-4). Kregel.
Gray, James R. Modern Process Thought: A Brief Ideological History. LC 81-43672. 272p. 1982. lib. bdg. 27.25 (ISBN 0-8191-2310-2); pap. text ed. 12.25 (ISBN 0-8191-2311-0). U Pr of Amer.
--Process Ethics. LC 83-6564. 110p. 1983. lib. bdg. 21.00 (ISBN 0-8191-3237-3); pap. text ed. 9.00 (ISBN 0-8191-3238-1). U Pr of Amer.
Gray, Jane. Medicine. LC 74-76181. (Professions Ser.). (Illus.). 168p. 1974. 5.95 (ISBN 0-7153-6623-8). David & Charles.
Gray, Jane & Berry, William. Communities of the Past. LC 81-4069. 623p. 1981. 49.00 (ISBN 0-87933-362-6). Van Nos Reinhold.
Gray, Jane, ed. see Biology Colloquium, 37th, Oregon State University, 1976.
Gray, Jane L., ed. see Gray, Asa.
Gray, Janet. Hearts Are Wild. (Second Chance at Love: No. 298). 192p. 1985. pap. 2.25 (ISBN 0-425-08626-7). Berkley Pub.
Gray, Janet G. The French Huguenots. LC 81-67172. 200p. (Orig.). 1981. pap. 8.95 (ISBN 0-8010-3758-1). Baker Bk.
Gray, Jean M. The Term Structure of Interest Rates in the United States, 1884-1914. LC 77-14785. (Dissertations in American Economic History Ser.). 1978. 23.50 (ISBN 0-405-11037-5). Ayer Co Pubs.
Gray, Jeffrey. Psychology of Fear & Stress. LC 70-104742. (Illus., Orig.). 1971. pap. 3.95 (ISBN 0-07-024225-9). McGraw.
Gray, Jeffrey A. Ivan Pavlov. (Modern Masters Ser.). 1981. pap. 4.95 (ISBN 0-14-005326-3). Penguin.
--Ivan Pavlov. (Modern Masters Ser.). (Illus.). 1980. 12.95 (ISBN 0-670-40457-8). Viking.
Gray, Jennifer. Canvas Work. (Illus.). 120p. 1985. pap. 10.95 (ISBN 0-7134-4769-9, Pub. by Batsford England). David & Charles.
Gray, Jenny. Teacher's Survival Guide. 2nd ed. LC 73-83493. 1974. pap. 7.50 (ISBN 0-8224-6795-X). Pitman Learning.
--Teaching Without Tears: Your First Year in the Secondary School. LC 67-29159. 1968. pap. 6.95 (ISBN 0-8224-6920-0). Pitman Learning.
Gray, Jenny, ed. see Stevenson, Robert Louis.
Gray, Jeremy. Ideas of Space: Euclidean, Non-Euclidean & Relativistic. (Illus.). 1979. 39.50x (ISBN 0-19-853352-7). Oxford U Pr.
Gray, Jeremy, jt. auth. see Smith, David J.
Gray, Jerry & Starke, Frederick. Readings in Organizational Behavior: Concepts and Applications. (Business Ser.). 1976. pap. text ed. 14.95 (ISBN 0-675-08522-5). Merrill.
Gray, Jerry E. Floor Covering: The Only Complete Installation Guide. LC 83-70255. (Illus.). 188p. 1983. pap. 12.95 (ISBN 0-9610814-0-6). Cameo Pub.
Gray, Jerry L. Supervision: An Applied Behavioral Science Approach to Managing People. LC 83-22224. 544p. 1984. text ed. write for info. (ISBN 0-534-03129-3). Kent Pub Co.
Gray, Jerry L. & Starke, Fred. Organizational Behavior: Concepts & Applications. 3rd ed. 1984. Additional supplements may be obtained from publisher. text ed. 28.95 (ISBN 0-675-20098-9). Merrill.
Gray, Jerry L., ed. The Glacier Project: Concepts & Critiques-Selected Readings on the Glacier Theories of Organization & Management. LC 75-27252. (Illus.). 452p. 1976. 27.50x (ISBN 0-8448-0716-8). Crane-Russak Co.
Gray, Jesse G. Hegel's Hellenic Ideal. LC 83-48507. (The Philosophy of Hegel Ser.). 149p. 1984. lib. bdg. 25.00 (ISBN 0-8240-5630-2). Garland Pub.
Gray, Jill P., jt. ed. see Gray, Denis J.
Gray, Jim, et al. Interpersonal Conflict Management: A Trainer's Manual. 106p. (Orig.). 1980. pap. 19.95 (ISBN 0-937636-00-2). Gray Assoc.
Gray, Joanna, et al. Discovering English. 154p. 1984. pap. text ed. 9.95 (ISBN 0-03-062988-8). HR&W.
--Starting English. 125p. 1984. pap. text ed. 9.95 (ISBN 0-03-062992-6). HR&W.
Gray, John. City in Revolt: James Larkin & the Belfast Dock Strike of 1907. (Illus.). 192p. 1985. pap. 9.95 (ISBN 0-85640-289-3, Pub. by Blackstaff Pr). Longwood Pub Group.
--Essential Principles of the Wealth of Nations Illustrated. LC 68-55725. Repr. of 1797 ed. 25.00x (ISBN 0-678-00504-4). Kelley.
--First & Second Kings, a Commentary. rev. ed. 2nd ed. LC 73-134271. (Old Testament Library). (Illus.). 826p. 1978. 27.50 (ISBN 0-664-20898-3). Westminster.
--Good School, Bad School. 176p. 1984. 13.00x (ISBN 0-7005-0618-7, Pub. by NFER Nelson). Taylor & Francis.
--Hayek on Liberty. 200p. 1984. 29.95x (ISBN 0-85520-710-8). Basil Blackwell.
--Joshua, Judges & Ruth. rev. ed. (New Century Bible Ser). 337p. 1977. 17.50 (ISBN 0-551-00784-2). Attic Pr.
--Last Letters of Aubrey Beardsley. LC 73-12999. 1904. Repr. lib. bdg. 20.00 (ISBN 0-8414-4426-9). Folcroft.
--A Lecture on Human Happiness. LC 66-21675. (Reprints of Economic Classics). 83p. Repr. of 1826 ed. lib. bdg. 17.50x (ISBN 0-678-00293-2). Kelley.
--Lectures on the Nature & Use of Money. LC 68-55724. 1972. Repr. of 1848 ed. lib. bdg. 37.50x (ISBN 0-678-00828-0). Kelley.
--Near Eastern Mythology. LC 84-45599. (The Library of the World's Myths & Legends). (Illus.). 144p. 1985. 17.95 (ISBN 0-87226-004-6). P Bedrick Bks.
--Park: A Fantastic Story. Healy, Philip, ed. 128p. (Orig.). 1985. pap. 6.50 (ISBN 0-85635-538-0). Carcanet.
--Pocket Guide: Programming for the Apple. (Pitman Programming Pocket Guides Ser.). 64p. (Orig.). 1984. pap. 6.95 (ISBN 0-273-01991-0). Pitman Pub MA.
--Racewalking for Fun & Fitness. 176p. 1985. 15.95 (ISBN 0-13-944711-3); pap. 7.95 (ISBN 0-13-944703-2). P-H.
--Social System: A Treatise on the Principle of Exchange. LC 73-73. Repr. of 1831 ed. 37.50x (ISBN 0-678-00962-7). Kelley.
Gray, John, ed. VLSI Eighty-One: Very Large Scale Integration. LC 81-68035. 1981. 39.50 (ISBN 0-12-296860-3). Acad Pr.
Gray, John, jt. ed. see Pelczynski, Zbigniew.
Gray, John C. The Nature & Sources of Law. Reams, Bernard D., Jr., ed. LC 27-15000. (Historical Reprints in Jurisprudence & Classical Legal Literature Ser.). xiii, 348p. 1983-84. Repr. of 1921 ed. lib. bdg. 35.00 (ISBN 0-89941-250-5). W S Hein.
--Nature & Sources of the Law. 2nd ed. 11.75 (ISBN 0-8446-2156-0). Peter Smith.
--Number by Development: A Method of Number Instruction. (Educational Ser.). 1910. Repr. 17.50 (ISBN 0-8482-4212-2). Norwood Edns.
--Tranquebar: A Guide to the Coins of Danish India Circa 1620 to 1845. new ed. LC 74-84564. (Illus.). 96p. 1975. 20.00x (ISBN 0-88000-054-6). Quarterman.
Gray, John E. & Harned, Joseph W. Nuclear Power & Nuclear Weapons Proliferation, Vol. 1. (Atlantic Council Policy Papers). (Illus.). 164p. 1978. 6.00 (ISBN 0-317-33695-9). Atlantic Council US.
Gray, John H. China: A History of the Laws, Manners, & Customs of the People, 2 vols. LC 72-38070. Repr. of 1878 ed. 65.00 set (ISBN 0-404-56930-7). AMS Pr.
Gray, John M. History of Gambia. 508p. 1966. 35.00x (ISBN 0-7146-1668-0, F Cass Co). Biblio Dist.
--History of Zanzibar, from the Middle Ages to 1856. LC 75-3732. (Illus.). 314p. 1975. Repr. of 1962 ed. lib. bdg. 18.25x (ISBN 0-8371-8057-0, GRHZ). Greenwood.
--Lord Selkirk of Red River. (Illus.). xvii, 388p. 1964. 6.50 (ISBN 0-87013-082-X). Mich St U Pr.
Gray, John N. Mill on Liberty: A Defence. LC 82-16151. (International Library of Philosophy). 143p. 1983. 19.95x (ISBN 0-7100-9270-9). Routledge & Kegan.
Gray, John S. Pulmonary Ventilation & Its Physiological Regulation. 110p. 1950. 11.50x (ISBN 0-398-04269-1). C C Thomas.
Gray, John T. & Rowe, J. Phillip. An Alaska Census of Transportation. (ISER Report Ser.: No. 54). (Illus.). 84p. 1982. pap. 7.50 (ISBN 0-88353-032-5). U Alaska Inst Res.
Gray, John W. Communication & Leadership. LC 73-78227. 1973. pap. 6.00 (ISBN 0-88210-044-0). Natl Assn Principals.
--Forest Revenue Systems in Developing Countries: Their Role in Income Generation & Forest Management Strategies. (Forestry Papers: No. 43). 261p. 1984. pap. text ed. 20.50 (ISBN 92-5-101340-3, F2492, FAO). Unipub.
Gray, John W. & Rea, Richard. Parliamentary Procedure: A Programmed Introduction. 2nd ed. 1974. pap. 8.65x (ISBN 0-673-07671-7). Scott F.
Gray, John W., ed. Mathematical Applications of Category Theory. LC 84-9371. (Contemporary Mathematics Ser.: Vol. 30). 308p. 1984. pap. 28.00 (ISBN 0-8218-5032-6). Am Math.
Gray, Joseph B., jt. ed. see Uhl, Vincent.
Gray, Joseph M. Prophets of the Soul. facsimile ed. LC 71-156655. (Essay Index Reprint Ser). Repr. of 1936 ed. 18.00 (ISBN 0-8369-2277-8). Ayer Co Pubs.
Gray, Joseph W. Shakespeare's Marriage. LC 75-168182. Repr. of 1905 ed. 24.00 (ISBN 0-404-02894-2). AMS Pr.
Gray, Juanita & De Felice, Louise. Emotional Crisis: How to Cope, How to Recover. new ed. Ashton, Sylvia, ed. LC 74-77469. 1975. 12.95 (ISBN 0-87949-024-1). Ashley Bks.
Gray, Kenneth E., ed. Basic & Applied Rock Mechanics: Proceedings of the Symposium on Rock Mechanics, 10th, University of Texas at Austin, 1968. LC 74-161923. pap. 160.00 (ISBN 0-317-08700-2, 2012663). Bks Demand UMI.
--Nonequilibrium Superconductivity, Phonons, & Kapitza Boundaries. LC 81-1858. (NATO ASI Series B, Physics: Vol. 65). 710p. 1981. 95.00x (ISBN 0-306-40720-5, Plenum Pr). Plenum Pub.
Gray, Kevin, jt. auth. see Pearl, David.
Gray, Kevin J. Reallocation of Property on Divorce. 110.00x (ISBN 0-903486-36-9, Pub. by Prof Bks England). State Mutual Bk.
Gray, L. C., et al. Farm Ownership & Tenancy. LC 75-26319. (World Food Supply Ser). (Illus.). 1976. Repr. of 1924 ed. 12.00x (ISBN 0-405-07795-5). Ayer Co Pubs.
Gray, Laman A. Vaginal Hysterectomy: Indications, Technique, & Complications. 3rd ed. (Illus.). 242p. 1983. 48.75x (ISBN 0-398-04853-3). C C Thomas.
Gray, Laman A., Sr. Endometrial Carcinoma & Its Treatment: The Role of Irradiation, Extent of Surgery & Approach to Chemotherapy. (Illus.). 240p. 1977. 29.75x (ISBN 0-398-03608-X). C C Thomas.
Gray, Lawrence, jt. ed. see Serfaty, Simon.
Gray, Lawrence V. Simian Horizons. LC 82-90627. 1984. 10.95 (ISBN 0-533-05546-6). Vantage.
Gray, Lee L. Better & Faster Reading. pap. text ed. 7.33 (ISBN 0-8428-0006-9); key 1.00 (ISBN 0-8428-0034-4). Cambridge Bk.
--How We Choose a President. 5th ed. 1980. 8.95 (ISBN 0-312-39411-X). St Martin.
Gray, Lee L., jt. auth. see Hauser, Travis.
Gray, Leonard. Celestial Navigation Planning. LC 84-45264. (Illus.). 133p. (Orig.). 1984. pap. 12.95 (ISBN 0-87033-327-5). Cornell Maritime.
Gray, Leslie R., jt. auth. see Gray, Elma E.
Gray, Lewis C. History of Agriculture in the Southern United States to 1860, 2 Vols. LC 72-13878. Repr. of 1933 ed. Set. 75.00x (ISBN 0-678-00957-0). Kelley.
--History of Agriculture in the Southern United States to 1860, 2 vols. Set. 36.00 (ISBN 0-8446-1206-5). Peter Smith.

Gray, Lillian. Teaching Children to Read. 3rd ed. LC 63-11837. pap. 114.50 (ISBN 0-317-07747-3, 2012543). Bks Demand UMI.

Gray, Linda, ed. see Yallop, David A.

Gray, Louis H. Index to Mythology of All Races, Vol. XIII. (Mythology of All Races Ser). Repr. of 1932 ed. 25.00 (ISBN 0-8154-0088-8). Cooper Sq.

--Indo-Iranian Phonology. LC 79-168183. (Columbia University. Indo-Iranian Ser.: No. 2). Repr. of 1902 ed. 23.00 (ISBN 0-404-50472-8). AMS Pr.

--The Narrative of Bhoja (Bhojaprabandha) by Ballala of Benares. (American Oriental Ser.: Vol. 34). 1950. pap. 5.00x (ISBN 0-940490-34-X). Am Orient Soc.

Gray, Louis H., tr. see Subandhu.

Gray, Lynton & Waitt, Ian, eds. Perspectives on Academic Gaming & Simulation: Simulation in Management & Business Education, No. 7. 160p. 1982. 35.00 (ISBN 0-89397-139-1). Nichols Pub.

Gray, M., jt. auth. see Costin, A. B.

Gray, M. M. Influence of Spencer's Irish Experiences on the Faerie Queene. LC 77-2993. 1930. lib. bdg. 4.50 (ISBN 0-8414-4407-2). Folcroft.

Gray, Madeline. Changing Years: The Menopause Without Fear. 1970. pap. 3.50 (ISBN 0-451-11777-8, AE1777, Sig). NAL.

Gray, Malcolm. The Highland Economy: Seventeen Fifty to Eighteen Fifty. LC 75-31474. 1976. Repr. of 1957 ed. lib. bdg. 20.50x (ISBN 0-8371-8536-X, GRHIE). Greenwood.

Gray, Malcolm J., ed. see American Society for Metals Staff.

Gray, Malcom. The Fishing Industries of Scotland 1790-1914: A Study in Regional Adaptation. LC 78-40244. 1978. 27.95x (ISBN 0-19-714105-6). Oxford U Pr.

Gray, Margaret. The Donkey's Tale. (Illus.). 32p. 1984. casebound 3.95 (ISBN 0-8307-0963-0, 5111209). Regal.

Gray, Marlowe & Gray, Urna. The Lovers Guide to Sensuous Astrology. 1974. pap. 2.95 (ISBN 0-451-12364-6, AE2364, Sig). NAL.

Gray, Mary, jt. auth. see Gray, Basil.

Gray, Mary A. The Truth about Fathers. LC 81-21571. 192p. (gr. 7 up). 1982. 9.95 (ISBN 0-02-736700-2). Bradbury Pr.

Gray, Mary A., jt. auth. see Simpson, Elizabeth.

Gray, Mary Jane, jt. auth. see Burleigh, Robert.

Gray, Mary Jane, jt. auth. see Lutgendorf, Philip.

Gray, Mary L., jt. auth. see Bach, Ira J.

Gray, Mary Z. Ah, Bewilderness: Muddling Through Life. LC 83-45512. 288p. 1984. 14.95 (ISBN 0-689-11432-X). Atheneum.

Gray, Max, jt. auth. see Brandon, Dick H.

Gray, Maxwell. The Silence of Dean Maitland: A Novel, 3 vols. in 2. LC 79-8209. Repr. of 1886 ed. Set. 84.50 (ISBN 0-404-62188-0). AMS Pr.

Gray, May. In His Hands. 1979. 5.00 (ISBN 0-8233-0290-3). Golden Quill.

--In Love with Life. 1978. 5.00 (ISBN 0-8233-0289-X). Golden Quill.

--Moment Before Summer. LC 72-115218. 1970. 4.00 (ISBN 0-8233-0148-6). Golden Quill.

Gray, Melvin. Neuroses: A Comprehensive & Critical View. 1978. pap. 18.95 (ISBN 0-442-22814-7). Van Nos Reinhold.

Gray, Melvin, jt. auth. see Norback, Craig T.

Gray, Michael. The Art of Bob Dylan. (Illus.). 224p. 1982. pap. 9.95 (ISBN 0-312-05420-3). St Martin.

--The Lost Wizard. LC 84-51003. (Fantasy Forest Adventures Ser.). 80p. (gr. 2-5). Date not set. pap. 1.95 (ISBN 0-394-72787-8, Pub. by BYR). Random.

--Mother! Is the Story of Frank Zappa. (Illus.). 128p. 1984. 18.95 (ISBN 0-86276-147-6); pap. 10.95 (ISBN 0-86276-146-8). Proteus Pub NY.

Gray, Michael & James, Francis. Marlborough in Old Photographs. 128p. 1982. pap. text ed. 8.75x (ISBN 0-86299-018-1, Pub. by Alan Sutton England). Humanities.

Gray, Michael H. Beecham: A Centenary Discography. LC 79-21842. 129p. 1980. text ed. 32.50x (ISBN 0-8419-0582-7). Holmes & Meier.

Gray, Michael H. & Gibson, Gerald D. Bibliography of Discographies: Vol. 3: Popular Music. 200p. 1983. 49.95 (ISBN 0-8352-1683-7). Bowker.

Gray, Michael H., jt. ed. see Gibson, Gerald O.

Gray, Mike. Angle of Attack. Date not set. 15.95 (ISBN 0-393-01892-X). Norton.

Gray, Mike & Rosen, Ira. The Warning: Accident at Three Mile Island. (Illus.). 1982. 14.95 (ISBN 0-393-01522-X). Norton.

Gray, Mitchel & Kennedy, Mary. The Lingerie Book. 96p. 1982. pap. 10.95 (ISBN 0-312-48703-7). St Martin.

Gray, Mitchell & Kennedy, Mary. The Lingerie Book. (Illus.). 96p. 1980. 19.95 (ISBN 0-312-48701-0). St Martin.

Gray, Muir & Fowler, Godfrey, eds. Preventive Medicine in General Practice. (Oxford General Practice Ser.). (Illus.). 1983. pap. 26.95x (ISBN 0-19-261299-9). Oxford U Pr.

Gray, N. Rossetti, Dante & Ourselves. LC 74-6406. (Studies in Italian Literature, No. 46). 1974. lib. bdg. 47.95x (ISBN 0-8383-1917-3). Haskell.

Gray, Nada. Holidays: Victorian Women Celebrate in Pennsylvania. LC 83-8259. (Oral Traditions Projects Ser.). (Illus.). 76p. 1983. 8.95 (ISBN 0-271-00357-X). Pa St U Pr.

Gray, Nicholas S. The Seventh Swan. (Magic Quest Ser.: No. 3). 208p. 1984. pap. 2.25 (ISBN 0-441-75955-6). Ace Bks.

--A Wind from Nowhere. LC 78-321970. 160p. (gr. 4-9). 1979. 9.50 (ISBN 0-571-11182-3). Faber & Faber.

Gray, Nicolete. Lettering As Drawing. LC 81-84750. (Illus.). 195p. 1982. pap. 9.95 (ISBN 0-8008-4729-6, Pentalic). Taplinger.

--Nineteenth-Century Ornamented Type Faces. LC 75-17294. 1977. 62.50 (ISBN 0-520-03074-5). U of Cal Pr.

Gray, Nicolette. Rossetti, Dante & Ourselves. LC 74-11358. 1974. Repr. of 1947 ed. lib. bdg. 12.00 (ISBN 0-8414-4531-1). Folcroft.

Gray, Nicolette, ed. Jacob's Ladder: Bible Picture Book from Anglo-Saxon & 12th Century English MSS. 1978. Repr. of 1949 ed. lib. bdg. 25.00 (ISBN 0-8495-1948-9). Arden Lib.

Gray, Nigel. The Deserter. LC 76-58693. (gr. 4-7). 1977. 8.61i (ISBN 0-06-022061-9). HarpJ.

--It'll All Come Out in the Wash. LC 78-22482. (Illus.). (ps-2). 1979. 10.53i (ISBN 0-06-022067-8); PLB 10.89 (ISBN 0-06-022074-0). HarpJ.

--The Worst of Times: An Oral History of the Great Depression in Britain. (Illus.). 256p. 1985. 19.95x (ISBN 0-389-20574-5). B&N Imports.

Gray, Noel. Looking at China. LC 74-7046. (gr. 4-6). 1974. 11.06i (ISBN 0-397-31584-8). Lipp Jr Bks.

Gray, O. P. & Cockburn, F., eds. Children: A Handbook for Children's Doctors. 384p. 1984. text ed. 65.00 (ISBN 0-272-79702-2, Pub. by Pitman Bks Ltd UK). Urban & S.

Gray, Oscar S. Cases & Materials on Environmental Law. 2nd ed. LC 73-83169. pap. 160.00 (ISBN 0-317-29772-4, 2017240). Bks Demand UMI.

--Cases & Materials on Environmental Law: 1977 Supplement. 2nd ed. LC 73-83169. pap. 154.80 (ISBN 0-317-29770-8, 2017241). Bks Demand UMI.

Gray, P., et al. Midland Red: A History of the Company & Its Vehicles from 1940-1970. 223p. 1981. 60.00x (ISBN 0-903839-27-X, Pub. by Transport). State Mutual Bk.

--Midland Red: A History of the Company & Its Vehicles up to 1940. 175p. 1981. 40.00x (ISBN 0-903839-19-9, Pub. by Transport). State Mutual Bk.

Gray, P. M. Logic, Algebra & Database. (Computers & Their Applications Ser.). 294p. 1984. 34.95 (ISBN 0-470-20103-7). Halsted Pr.

Gray, P. R., et al, eds. Analog MOS Integrated Circuits. LC 80-22216. 1980. 38.45 (ISBN 0-87942-141-X, PC01347). Inst Electrical.

Gray, Patrick G. Letters & Papers. Thomson, Thomas, ed. LC 72-168184. (Bannatyne Club, Edinburgh. Publications: No. 48). Repr. of 1835 ed. 27.50 (ISBN 0-404-52758-2). AMS Pr.

Gray, Patsey. Barefoot a Thousand Miles. LC 83-40391. 96p. 1984. 11.95 (ISBN 0-8027-6528-9). Walker & Co.

--Double Standards. 160p. 1983. pap. 1.95 (ISBN 0-448-15694-6). Ace Bks.

Gray, Patsy see Weikel, Bill.

Gray, Paul. A Student Guide to IFPS. 384p. 1983. 19.95 (ISBN 0-07-024322-0). McGraw.

Gray, Paul, jt. auth. see Chinese, U. S. Symposium on Systems Analysis.

Gray, Paul, et al. Analog MOS Integrated Circuits. Brodersen, Robert W., ed. LC 80-22116. 405p. 1980. pap. 36.95x (ISBN 0-471-08966-4). Wiley.

Gray, Paul E. & Searle, Campbell L. Electronic Principles: Physics, Models & Circuits. LC 78-107884. 1969. text ed. 51.00 (ISBN 0-471-32398-5). Wiley.

Gray, Paul R. & Meyer, Robert G. Analysis & Design of Analog Integrated Circuits. 2nd ed. LC 83-17098. 771p. 1984. text ed. 39.95 (ISBN 0-471-87493-0); write for info. solutions (ISBN 0-471-87094-3). Wiley.

Gray, Paul S. Unions & Leaders in Ghana: A Model of Labor & Development. LC 80-18482. 1981. 35.00 (ISBN 0-914970-57-9); pap. text ed. 17.50 (ISBN 0-914970-58-5). Conch Mag.

Gray, Paula G. Dramatics for the Elderly: A Guide for Directors of Dramatics Groups in Senior Centers & Residential Care Settings. LC 74-3185. 1974. pap. text ed. 3.95x (ISBN 0-8077-2400-9). Tchrs Coll.

Gray, Peter. The Dictionary of the Biological Sciences. LC 81-19369. 622p. 1982. Repr. of 1967 ed. lib. bdg. 42.50 (ISBN 0-89874-441-5). Krieger.

--Encyclopedia of the Biological Sciences. LC 80-28590. 1056p. 1981. Repr. of 1970 ed. lib. bdg. 55.00 (ISBN 0-89874-326-5). Krieger.

--The Microtomists Formulary & Guide. LC 74-23818. 808p. 1975. Repr. of 1954 ed. 44.50 (ISBN 0-88275-247-2). Krieger.

Gray, Peter, ed. A. I. B. S. Directory of Bio-Science Departments & Facilities in the United States & Canada. 2nd ed. LC 75-33761. 1975. 60.00 (ISBN 0-12-786589-6). Acad Pr.

--Encyclopedia of Microscopy & Microtechnique. LC 80-29516. 654p. 1982. Repr. of 1973 ed. 39.50 (ISBN 0-89874-335-4). Krieger.

Gray, Phillip M., intro. by. Extraction Metallurgy '81. 441p. (Orig.). 1981. pap. text ed. 115.00x (ISBN 0-900488-59-X). IMM North Am.

Gray, Piers. T. S. Eliot: Intellectual & Poetic Development. 273p. 1982. text ed. 30.50x (ISBN 0-391-02506-6, Harvester England). Humanities.

Gray, R., ed. see Davies, G. J.

Gray, R. B. The Agricultural Tractor - 1855-1950. 160p. 1975. pap. 12.95 (ISBN 0-916150-01-1). Am Soc Ag Eng.

Gray, Ralph D., ed. The Hoosier State: Readings in Indiana History. Incl. Vol. 1. Indian Prehistory to 1880. 406p. pap. 6.95x (ISBN 0-8028-1842-0); Vol. 2. The Modern Era. 504p. pap. 6.95x (ISBN 0-8028-1843-9). LC 80-12496. (Orig.). 1982. pap. Ind U Pr.

Gray, Rebecca & Reeve, Cintra. Gray's Wild Game Cookbook: A Menu Cookbook. LC 83-82973. (Illus.). 220p. 1984. 25.00 (ISBN 0-9609842-1-6). Grays Sporting.

--Gray's Wild Game Cookbook: A Menu Cookbook. (Illus.). 220p. casebound 25.00 (ISBN 0-9609842-1-6). Globe Pequot.

Gray, Richard. A History of the Southern Sudan Eighteen Thirty-Nine to Eighteen Eighty-Nine. LC 78-5649. (Illus.). viii, 219p. 1978. Repr. of 1961 ed. lib. bdg. 19.25x (ISBN 0-313-20402-0, GRHS). Greenwood.

--The Two Nations. LC 73-21175. (Illus.). 373p. 1974. Repr. of 1960 ed. lib. bdg. 20.00x (ISBN 0-8371-6069-3, GRTN). Greenwood.

Gray, Richard, ed. American Fiction: New Readings. LC 83-2810. (Critical Studies). 240p. 1983. text ed. 28.50x (ISBN 0-389-20370-X, 07242). B&N Imports.

--American Verse of the Nineteenth Century. (Rowman & Littlefield University Library). 234p. 1973. 12.50x (ISBN 0-87471-404-4); pap. 4.95x (ISBN 0-87471-397-8). Rowman.

--American Verse of the Nineteenth Century. 234p. 1973. 11.50 (ISBN 0-460-10250-8, DEL 05224, Evman). Biblio Dist.

--Robert Penn Warren: A Collection of Critical Essays. (Twentieth Century Views Ser.). 1980. 11.95 (ISBN 0-13-781914-5, Spec); pap. 3.95 (ISBN 0-13-781906-4). P-H.

Gray, Richard A., compiled by. A Guide to Book Review Citations: A Bibliography of Sources. LC 67-63222. 240p. 1969. 7.00 (ISBN 0-8142-0056-7). Ohio St U Pr.

Gray, Richard A., ed. Serial Bibliographies in the Humanities & Social Sciences. LC 68-58895. 1969. 29.50 (ISBN 0-87650-004-1). Pierian.

Gray, Richard J. The Literature of Memory: Modern Writers of the American South. LC 76-18941. (Illus.). 384p. 1977. 34.00x (ISBN 0-8018-1803-6). Johns Hopkins.

Gray, Richard L., jt. auth. see Parham, Russell A.

Gray, Robert. The Aristocracy of Labour in Nineteenth Century Britain: 1850-1914. (Studies in Economic & Social History). 79p. (Orig.). 1981. pap. text ed. 6.50x (ISBN 0-333-25330-2, Pub. by Macmillan England). Humanities.

--Creekwater Journal. (Paperback Poets Ser.). 1974. 9.95x (ISBN 0-7022-0945-7); pap. 4.95x (ISBN 0-7022-0935-X). U of Queensland Pr.

--A Good Speed to Virginia. LC 70-25511. (English Experience Ser.: No. 253). 32p. 1970. Repr. of 1609 ed. 7.00 (ISBN 90-221-0253-X). Walter J Johnson.

--A History of London. LC 78-22605. 1979. 9.95 (ISBN 0-8008-3884-X); pap. 5.95 (ISBN 0-8008-3885-8). Taplinger.

Gray, Robert C. Biology Concepts: Illustrated Lecture Outline. (Illus.). 154p. (Orig.). 1982. pap. text ed. 5.75x (ISBN 0-9606666-1-3). Greenfield Pubns.

--Biology Laboratory Experiences. (Illus.). 160p. (Orig.). 1983. 6.90x (ISBN 0-9606666-2-1). Greenfield Pubns.

Gray, Robert C., jt. auth. see Sloan, Stanley R.

Gray, Robert F. The Sonjo of Tanganyika. LC 73-13319. (Illus.). 181p. 1974. Repr. of 1963 ed. lib. bdg. 25.00 (ISBN 0-8371-7119-9, GRST). Greenwood.

Gray, Robert L. Physics Problems: Electricity, Magnetism, & Optics. LC 73-20445. (Wiley Self-Teaching Guides Ser.). pap. 43.50 (ISBN 0-317-09209-X, 2012619). Bks Demand UMI.

--The Wings of Courage. LC 84-61223. 154p. (Orig.). pap. 4.95 (ISBN 0-943324-11-4). Omenana.

Gray, Robert M. & Davisson, Lee D. Random Processes: A Mathematical Approach for Engineers. (Illus.). 272p. 1985. text ed. 32.95 (ISBN 0-13-752882-5). P-H.

Gray, Robert M. & Davisson, Lee D., eds. Ergodic & Information Theory. (Benchmark Papers in Electrical Engineering & Computer Science: Vol. 19). 1977. 64.50 (ISBN 0-12-786590-X). Acad Pr.

Gray, Robert M., jt. ed. see Davisson, Lee D.

Gray, Rockwell, tr. see Pino-Saavedra, Yolando.

Gray, Rod. Drogas, Lujuria y Muerte. new ed. Castellanos, Juan, tr. from Eng. (Pimienta Collection Ser). (Illus.). 160p. (Span.). 1975. pap. 1.25 (ISBN 0-88473-240-1). Fiesta Pub.

--Los Trucos De Eva: La Ninta De G.O.C.E. new ed. Ibero, Jairo, tr. (Pimienta Collection Ser.). (Illus.). 160p. (Span.). 1975. pap. 1.25 (ISBN 0-88473-232-0). Fiesta Pub.

Gray, Roland P., ed. Songs & Ballads of the Maine Lumberjacks. LC 73-75944. 1969. Repr. of 1924 ed. 35.00x (ISBN 0-8103-3835-1). Gale.

Gray, Ronald. Christopher Wren & St. Paul's Cathedral. LC 81-13696. (Cambridge Topic Bks.). (Illus.). 52p. (gr. 6 up). 1982. PLB 7.95 (ISBN 0-8225-1222-X). Lerner Pubns.

--Hitler & the Germans. LC 83-996. (Cambridge Topic Bks.). (Illus.). 36p. (gr. 5 up). 1983. PLB 7.95 (ISBN 0-8225-1231-9). Lerner Pubns.

Gray, Ronald D. Brecht the Dramatist. LC 75-19575. 240p. 1976. 42.50 (ISBN 0-521-20937-4). Cambridge U Pr.

--Christopher Wren & St. Paul's Cathedral. LC 77-94370. (Cambridge Introduction to the History of Mankind Ser.). (Illus.). (YA) 1980. pap. 4.95 (ISBN 0-521-21666-4). Cambridge U Pr.

--Francis Kafka. LC 72-83576. 192p. 1973. pap. 13.95 (ISBN 0-521-09747-9). Cambridge U Pr.

--German Poetry: A Guide to Free Appreciation. rev. ed. LC 75-20834. 120p. 1976. pap. 11.95 (ISBN 0-521-29000-7). Cambridge U Pr.

--German Tradition in Literature. LC 65-17206. 1966. o. p. 49.50 (ISBN 0-521-05133-9); pap. 19.95 (ISBN 0-521-29278-6). Cambridge U Pr.

--Goethe: A Critical Introduction. (Orig.). pap. text ed. 16.95 (ISBN 0-521-09404-6). Cambridge U Pr.

--Goethe, the Alchemist: A Study of Alchemical Symbolism in Goethe's Literary & Scientific Works. LC 79-8612. Repr. of 1952 ed. 34.00 (ISBN 0-404-18476-6). AMS Pr.

--Hitler & the Germans. LC 81-3913. (Cambridge Introduction to the History of Mankind). (Illus.). 32p. 1982. pap. 4.50 (ISBN 0-521-22702-X). Cambridge U Pr.

--Ibsen: A Dissenting View. LC 77-5653. 1980. pap. 11.95 (ISBN 0-521-29835-0). Cambridge U Pr.

--Ibsen: A Dissenting View. LC 77-5653. 1977. 34.50 (ISBN 0-521-21702-4). Cambridge U Pr.

Gray, Roscoe N. Attorneys' Textbook Medicine, 16 vols. 3rd ed. Gordy, Louise J., ed. (Courtroom Medicine Ser.). 1984. Updates avail. looseleaf 925.00 (300); looseleaf 1983 462.50; looseleaf 1984 510.00. Bender.

Gray, Ruth, jt. auth. see Rudy, Ellen.

Gray, S. J. & Coenenberg, A. G. EEC Accounting Harmonization: Implementation & Impact of the Fourth Directive. (Advanced Management Ser.: Vol. 5). 1984. 36.75 (ISBN 0-444-86825-9). Elsevier.

Gray, S. J., ed. International Accounting & Transnational Decisions. 384p. 1983. 59.95 (ISBN 0-408-10841-X). Butterworth.

Gray, S. J., et al. Information Disclosure & the Multinational Corporation. LC 84-3565. (Wiley-IRM Series in Multinationals). 236p. 1984. 29.95 (ISBN 0-471-90424-4). Wiley.

Gray, S. J., et al, eds. International Financial Reporting: A Comparative International Survey of Accounting Requirements & Practices in Thirty Countries. LC 84-40409. 592p. 45.00 (ISBN 0-312-42202-4). St Martin.

Gray, Sam, ed. see Roberts, Derrel, et al.

Gray, Simon. Close of Play & Pig in a Poke. 92p. 1984. pap. 5.95 (ISBN 0-413-46960-3, 9236). Methuen Inc.

--The Common Pursuit: A Methuen Modern Play. 64p. 1984. pap. 6.95 (ISBN 0-413-55990-4, 9089, Pub. by Eyre Metheun England). Methuen Inc.

--Otherwise Engaged & Other Plays. 135p. 1984. pap. 5.95 (ISBN 0-413-34430-4, NO. 9237). Methuen Inc.

--Quartermaine's Terms. (Modern Plays Ser.). 79p. 1983. pap. 6.95 (ISBN 0-413-52830-8, NO. 3887). Methuen Inc.

--The Rear Column & Other Plays. (Methuen Modern Plays Ser.). 192p. (Orig.). 1985. pap. 5.50 (ISBN 0-413-39170-1, 9387). Methuen Inc.

--The Rear Column, Dog Days, & Other Plays. 1979. pap. 5.95 (ISBN 0-14-048155-9). Penguin.

--Stage Struck. LC 80-25312. 64p. 1981. 9.95 (ISBN 0-394-51804-7); pap. 4.95 (ISBN 0-394-17882-3). Seaver Bks.

Gray, Spalding. In Search of the Monkey Girl. (Illus.). 96p. 1982. 25.00 (ISBN 0-89381-095-9); ltd. ed. 300.00 (ISBN 0-89381-097-5). Aperture.

--Swimming to Cambodia. 176p. 1985. pap. 7.95 (ISBN 0-930452-50-X). Theatre Comm.

Gray, Stanley J. Psychological Foundations of Education. 534p. 1981. Repr. of 1935 ed. lib. bdg. 40.00 (ISBN 0-89984-236-4). Century Bookbindery.

Gray, Stephen. Arts & Crafts Furniture: Shop of the Crafters at Cincinnati. (Mission Furniture Catalogues Ser.: No. 7). 72p. 1983. pap. 6.95 (ISBN 0-940326-07-8). Turn of Cent.

--Douglas Blackburn. (World Authors Ser.: No. 719). 200p. 1984. lib. bdg. 19.95 (ISBN 0-8057-6566-2, Twayne). G K Hall.

--Limbert Furniture. (Mission Furniture Catalogues Ser.: No. 4). 128p. 1981. pap. 9.95 (ISBN 0-940326-04-3). Turn of Cent.

--Southern African Literature: An Introduction. LC 79-53358. (Illus.). 209p. 1979. text ed. 28.50x (ISBN 0-06-492530-7). B&N Imports.

Gray, Stephen, ed. Lifetime Furniture. (Mission Furniture Catalogues Ser.: No. 2). 112p. 1981. pap. 8.95 (ISBN 0-940326-02-7). Turn of Cent.

--The Mission Furniture of L. & J.G. Stickley. (Mission Furniture Catalogues Ser.: No. 6). 192p. 1983. pap. 18.50 (ISBN 0-940326-06-X). Turn of Cent.

--Quaint Furniture. (Mission Furniture Catalogues Ser.: No. 1). 80p. 1981. pap. 5.95 (ISBN 0-940326-01-9). Turn of Cent.

--Roycroft Furniture. (Mission Furniture Catalogues: No. 3). 52p. 1981. pap. 4.95 (ISBN 0-940326-03-5). Turn of Cent.

Gray, Stephen & Edwards, Robert, eds. Collected Works of Gustav Stickley. (Mission Furniture Catalogues Ser.: No. 5). 168p. 1981. pap. 17.50 (ISBN 0-940326-05-1). Turn of Cent.

Gray, Stephen W. & Skandalakis, John E. Atlas of Surgical Anatomy for General Surgeons. (Illus.). 368p. 1984. 148.00 (ISBN 0-683-03733-1). Williams & Wilkins.

Gray, Stephen W., jt. auth. see Skandalakis, John E.

Gray, Steven & Steffy, Wilbert. Hospital Cost Containment through Productivity Management. 256p. 1983. 22.95 (ISBN 0-442-22921-6). Van Nos Reinhold.

Gray, Susan, jt. auth. see Morse, Dean.

Gray, Susan H. No-Frills Statistics: A Guide for the First-Year Student. LC 83-11015. (Helix Bks.: No. 380). (Illus.). 188p. 1984. pap. text ed. 8.95 (ISBN 0-8226-0380-2). Rowman & Allanheld.

--Pascal Simplified: A Guide for the First-Time User. LC 85-14197. 150p. 1985. text ed. 21.50x (ISBN 0-8476-7428-2, Helix Bks.); pap. 9.95 (ISBN 0-8226-0394-2). Rowman & Allanheld.

Gray, Susan W. Psychologist in the Schools. LC 63-13760. 1963. text ed. 24.95x (ISBN 0-03-012220-1). Irvington.

Gray, Susan W., et al. Before First Grade: Training Project for Culturally Disadvantaged Children. LC 66-24872. (Orig.). 1966. pap. text ed. 7.95x (ISBN 0-8077-1464-X). Tchrs Coll.

--From Three to Twenty: The Early Training Project. LC 81-10485. (Illus.). 360p. 1982. 19.00 (ISBN 0-8391-1685-3). Pro Ed.

Gray, Suzanne K., et al, eds. NOVA: Science Adventures on Television. 1974. 2.50 (ISBN 0-89073-000-8). Boston Public Lib.

--NOVA: Science Adventures on Television II. 1975. 4.00 (ISBN 0-89073-006-7). Boston Public Lib.

Gray, T. C., et al. General Anesthesia, 2 vols. 4th ed. Incl. Vol. 1. text ed. 150.00 (ISBN 0-407-00144-1); Vol. 2. text ed. 150.00 (ISBN 0-407-00145-X). LC 79-42889. (Illus.). 1979. Set. text ed. 275.00 (ISBN 0-407-00146-8). Butterworth.

Gray, T. G. & Spence, John. Rational Welding Design. 315p. 1982. 39.95 (ISBN 0-408-01200-5). Butterworth.

Gray, T. K. & Gashus, O. K., eds. Tidal Power. LC 70-179031. 630p. 1972. 85.00x (ISBN 0-306-30559-3, Plenum Pr). Plenum Pub.

Gray, Thomas. Correspondence, 3 vols. Repr. of 1935 ed. 75.00 (ISBN 0-403-04017-5). Somerset Pub.

--The Correspondence of Thomas Gray & William Mason. (Illus.). 1853. Repr. lib. bdg. 50.00 (ISBN 0-8414-4670-9). Folcroft.

--Essays & Criticisms. Northup, Clark S., ed. 1911. Repr. lib. bdg. 22.50 (ISBN 0-8414-4671-7). Folcroft.

--Gray & His Friends. Tovey, Duncan C., ed. 1890. Repr. lib. bdg. 20.00 (ISBN 0-8414-4672-5). Folcroft.

--Gray: Poetry & Prose. LC 76-29472. Repr. of 1926 ed. 18.50 (ISBN 0-404-15304-6). AMS Pr.

--Poems, 4 vols. 1778. Set. 200.00 (ISBN 0-686-17753-3). Ridgeway Bks.

--Poems, Letters & Essays. 1970. Repr. of 1912 ed. 12.95x (ISBN 0-460-00628-2, Evman). Biblio Dist.

--The Poems of Thomas Gray. 1814. Repr. lib. bdg. 30.00 (ISBN 0-8414-4673-3). Folcroft.

--Scalacronica: A Chronicle of England & Scotland from A.D. 1066 to A. D. 1362. Stevenson, Joseph, ed. LC 70-168186. (Maitland Club. Glasgow. Publications: No. 40). Repr. of 1836 ed. 47.50 (ISBN 0-404-53015-X). AMS Pr.

--Selections from the Poetry & Prose of Thomas Gray. Phelps, William L., ed. 1894. Repr. lib. bdg. 17.50 (ISBN 0-8414-4674-1). Folcroft.

--The Works of Thomas Gray, 4 vols. Gosse, Edmund, ed. 1884. Repr. lib. bdg. 120.00 (ISBN 0-8414-4675-X). Folcroft.

--Works of Thomas Gray in Verse & Prose, 4 Vols. Gosse, Edmund, ed. LC 76-168185. Repr. of 1884 ed. Set. 70.00 (ISBN 0-404-02900-0). Vol. 1 (ISBN 0-404-02901-9). Vol. 2 (ISBN 0-404-02902-7). Vol. 3 (ISBN 0-404-02903-5). Vol. 4 (ISBN 0-404-02904-3). AMS Pr.

Gray, Tracy C., et al, eds. Current Status of Bilingual Education Legislation: An Update. LC 80-29021. (Bilingual Education Ser.: No. 9). 105p. 1981. 16.95x (ISBN 0-15-599076-4). Ctr Appl Ling.

Gray, Urna, jt. auth. see Gray, Marlowe.

Gray, V. Visible People. Rex Collings Ltd., ed. 25.00 (ISBN 0-86036-046-6, Pub. by R Collings UK). State Mutual Bk.

Gray, V. Katherine. Caresharing: How to Relate to the Frail Elderly. 80p. (Orig.). 1984. pap. 8.00 (ISBN 0-938846-15-9). Ebenezer Ctr.

Gray, V. Ruth, jt. auth. see Rudy, Ellen B.

Gray, Valeria B. Invisible Man's Literary Heritage: Benito Cereno & Moby Dick. (Costerus New Ser.: No. XII). 1978. pap. text ed. 17.75x (ISBN 90-6203-652-X). Humanities.

Gray, Vanessa. The Duke's Messenger. 1982. pap. 2.50 (ISBN 0-451-13885-6, Sig). NAL.

--The Dutiful Daughter. (Orig.). 1980. pap. 1.75 (ISBN 0-451-09017-9, E9017, Sig). NAL.

--The Reckless Gambler. 1985. pap. 2.50 (ISBN 0-451-13764-7, Sig). NAL.

--The Unruly Bride. 1985. pap. 2.50 (ISBN 0-451-13406-0, Sig). NAL.

Gray, Vic. Common Chronicle: Archival Treasures from the County Record Offices of England & Wales. (Illus.). 112p. (Orig.). 1984. pap. 9.95 (ISBN 0-905209-42-7, Pub. by Victoria & Albert Mus UK). Faber & Faber.

Gray, Virginia & Dye, Thomas. Determinants of Public Policy: Cities, States, Nations. 1979. pap. 8.00 (ISBN 0-918592-32-1). Policy Studies.

Gray, Virginia & Jacob, Herbert. Politics in the American States: A Comparative Analysis. 4th ed. 1982. pap. text ed. 21.95 (ISBN 0-316-32577-5). Little.

Gray, Virginia & Macrae, Alan. Mud, Space & Spirit: Handmade Adobes. Young, Noel, ed. LC 76-7958. (Illus.). 96p. (Orig.). 1976. pap. 9.95 (ISBN 0-88496-059-5). Capra Pr.

Gray, Virginia & Williams, Bruce. The Organizational Politics of Criminal Justice: Policy in Context. LC 77-18590. 1980. 27.50x (ISBN 0-669-02108-3). Lexington Bks.

Gray, Virginia, jt. auth. see Conover, Pamela J.

Gray, W. & Rizzo, N. D., eds. Unity Through Diversity: Festschriff in Honor of Ludwig, 2 vols. (Current Topics of Contemporary Thought Ser.). 1168p. 1973. Set. 123.75 (ISBN 0-677-14860-7); 69.50x ea. Vol. 1, 596p (ISBN 0-677-14840-2). Vol. 2, 572p (ISBN 0-677-14850-X). Gordon.

Gray, W., et al, eds. General Systems Theory & Psychiatry. (Systems Inquiry Ser.). 450p. (Orig.). 1982. pap. text ed. 13.95 (ISBN 0-914105-07-8). Intersystems Pubns.

Gray, W. A. & Muller, R. Engineering Calculations in Radiative Heat Transfer. LC 73-17321. 176p. 1974. text ed. 34.00 (ISBN 0-08-017786-7); pap. text ed. 14.50 (ISBN 0-08-017787-5). Pergamon.

Gray, W. Forbes. An Edinburgh Miscellany. 1973. Repr. of 1925 ed. 20.00 (ISBN 0-8274-0740-8). R West.

--The Poets Laureate of England. 1914. Repr. 25.00 (ISBN 0-8274-3180-5). R West.

--Scott in Sunshine & Shadow. 1973. Repr. of 1931 ed. 30.00 (ISBN 0-8274-0643-6). R West.

Gray, W. G., jt. auth. see Pinder, G. F.

Gray, W. H., jt. ed. see Akin, J. E.

Gray, W. J., jt. auth. see Macknight, C. C.

Gray, Wallace. Homer to Joyce. 256p. 1985. 17.95 (ISBN 0-02-545170-7). Macmillan.

Gray, Walter, Jr. Manual for Discussion Moderators. 1964. pap. 3.00 (ISBN 0-910092-00-1). Am Inst Disc.

Gray, Wanda. I Live Here Too. LC 77-82740. 1978. pap. 8.95 (ISBN 0-89334-013-8). Humanics Ltd.

Gray, Willaim, et al, eds. General Systems Theory & the Psychological Sciences, Vols. 1 & 2. (Systems Inquiry Ser.). 550p. 1982. pap. 26.50x set (ISBN 0-914105-10-8). Intersystems Pubns.

Gray, William, ed. see Sidney, Philip.

Gray, William A. Challenging the Gifted & Talented through Mentor-Assisted Enrichment Projects. LC 82-63056. (Fastback Ser.: No. 189). 50p. 1983. pap. 0.75 (ISBN 0-87367-189-9). Phi Delta Kappa.

Gray, William A. & Gerrard, Brian A. Learning by Doing: Developing Teaching Skills. (Education Ser.). 1977. pap. text ed. 10.35 (ISBN 0-201-02547-7, Sch Div). Addison-Wesley.

Gray, William B. & Gray, Betty. Episcopal Church Welcomes You: An Introduction to Its History, Worship & Mission. rev. ed. LC 73-17898. 168p. 1974. (Pub. by Seabury); pap. 3.95 (ISBN 0-8164-2087-4). Winston Pr.

Gray, William D. The Use of Fungi As Food & in Food Processing, Pt. 1. (Monotopic Reprint Ser.). 1971. 11.95 (ISBN 0-87819-104-6). CRC Pr.

--The Use of Fungi As Food & in Food Processing, Pt. 2. LC 76-141883. (Monotopic Reprint Ser.). 1973. 19.95 (ISBN 0-8493-0118-1). CRC Pr.

Gray, William F. The Diary of Col. Wm. Fairfax Gray: From Virginia to Texas: 1835-1836. (Illus.). 248p. 1982. 14.95 (ISBN 0-89896-036-3). Larksdale.

Gray, William G. Concepts of Qabalah. LC 82-62848. (The Sangreal Sodality Ser.: Vol.3). 1984. pap. 9.95 (ISBN 0-87728-561-6). Weiser.

--Inner Traditions of Magic. (Orig.). 1978. pap. 7.95 (ISBN 0-87728-447-4). Weiser.

--Ladder of Lights. 1981. 7.95 (ISBN 0-87728-536-5). Weiser.

--Magical Ritual Methods. 1980. pap. 8.95 (ISBN 0-87728-498-9). Weiser.

--An Outlook on Our Inner Western Way. 1980. pap. 6.95 (ISBN 0-87728-493-8). Weiser.

--Sangreal Ceremonies & Rituals. (Sangreal Sodality Ser.: Vol. 4). 1985. pap. 10.95 (ISBN 0-87728-583-7). Weiser.

--The Sangreal Sacrament. LC 82-62847. (The Sangreal Sodality Ser.: Vol. 2). 224p. 1983. pap. 8.95 (ISBN 0-87728-562-4). Weiser.

--A Self Made by Magic. LC 76-15547. 198p. (Orig.). 1984. pap. 8.95 (ISBN 0-87728-556-X). Weiser.

--The Talking Tree. LC 74-28905. (Orig.). 1981. pap. 12.50 (ISBN 0-87728-537-3). Weiser.

--The Tree of Evil. rev. ed. LC 84-51741. 1984. pap. 7.95 (ISBN 0-87728-539-X). Weiser.

--Western Inner Workings. LC 82-62846. (The Sangreal Sodality Ser.: Vol. 1). 188p. 1983. pap. 8.95 (ISBN 0-87728-560-8). Weiser.

Gray, William H. A History of Oregon, Seventeen Ninety-Two to Eighteen Forty-Nine. LC 72-9446. (The Far Western Frontier Ser.). (Illus.). 630p. 1973. Repr. of 1870 ed. 37.50 (ISBN 0-405-04974-9). Ayer Co Pubs.

--Journal of William H. Gray. 88p. 1980. 10.95 (ISBN 0-87770-241-1). Ye Galleon.

--Venezuela, Uncle Sam & OPEC: A Story for All Americans. 189p. (Orig.). 1982. pap. 7.50 (ISBN 0-686-94960-9, Pub by O. E. G. Foundation). Exposition Pr FL.

Gray, William R. Pacific Crest Trail. LC 74-1565. (Special Publications Ser.). 1975. 6.95 (ISBN 0-87044-149-3). Natl Geog.

Gray, William S. On Their Own in Reading: How to Give Children Independence in Analyzing New Words. 2nd ed. 1960. text ed. 11.90x (ISBN 0-673-05510-8). Scott F.

--Preliminary Survey on Methods of Teaching & Writing, Pt. 1: Survey of Theories & Practices (UNESCO) (Education Studies & Documents: No. 5). pap. 13.00 (ISBN 0-317-17854-7). Kraus Repr.

--Teaching of Reading: An International View. LC 58-6579. (Burton Lectures Ser: 1956). 1957. 5.95x (ISBN 0-674-87001-8). Harvard U Pr.

Gray, William S. & Liquori, Salvatore C. Hotel & Motel Management & Operations. (Illus.). 1980. text ed. 27.95 (ISBN 0-13-394908-7). P-H.

Gray, William S., ed. Reading in the High School & College. LC 57-6273. (National Society for the Study of Education Yearbooks Ser: No. 47, Pt. 2). 1948. 6.00x (ISBN 0-226-60002-5); pap. 4.50x (ISBN 0-226-60003-3). U of Chicago Pr.

Gray, William S., ed. see National Council of Teachers of English.

Gray, Wilson, tr. see Marvan, Jiri.

Gray, Winifred. You & Your Wedding. (Orig.). 1970. pap. 3.50 (ISBN 0-553-24749-2). Bantam.

Gray, Wood, et al. Historian's Handbook: A Key to the Study & Writing of History. 2nd ed. (Orig.). 1964. pap. text ed. 8.95 (ISBN 0-395-04537-1). HM.

Gray, Zane. Betty Zane. 1978. pap. 1.75 (ISBN 0-89083-363-X). Zebra.

Graybar, Lloyd J. Albert Shaw of the Review of Reviews: An Intellectual Biography. LC 73-80464. (Illus.). 256p. 1974. 23.00x (ISBN 0-8131-1300-8). U Pr of Ky.

Graybard, Carla A., jt. ed. see Taronowieski, Dale.

Graybill, Christopher. Modern Superstitions: When Bad Luck Happens to Good People. (Illus.). 96p. (Orig.). 1985. pap. 4.95 (ISBN 0-523-42316-0). Pinnacle Bks.

Graybill, Donald. Computer Mathematics: Essential Math for Computer Proficiency. LC 83-21539. 192p. (Orig.). 1984. lib. bdg. 14.95 (ISBN 0-668-06017-4); pap. 8.95 (ISBN 0-668-05845-5). Arco.

Graybill, Donald, et al. Computer Aptitude Tests. LC 83-15628. 224p. (Orig.). 1984. 12.95 (ISBN 0-668-06012-3); pap. 7.95 (ISBN 0-668-05854-4). Arco.

Graybill, Franklin A. Matrices with Applications in Statistics. 2nd ed. LC 82-8485. (Wadsworth Statistics-Probability Ser.). 461p. 1983. write for info. (ISBN 0-534-98038-4). Wadsworth Pub.

--Theory & Applications of the Linear Model. LC 75-41970. 1976. text ed. write for info. (ISBN 0-87872-108-8, Duxbury Pr). PWS Pubs.

Graybill, Nina & Rapoport, Maxine. The Pasta Salad Book. (Illus.). 175p. (Orig.). 1984. pap. 8.95 (ISBN 0-918535-00-X). Farragut Pub.

Graybill, Robert V. & Kindrick, Robert L., eds. Teaching the Middle Ages. 160p. (Orig.). pap. 6.95 (ISBN 0-942912-00-4). Smart.

Gray-Cobb, Geof. The Miracle of New Avatar Power. 1974. 14.95 (ISBN 0-13-585364-8, Parker). P-H.

Graydon, Alexander. Memoirs of His Own Time with Reminiscences of the Men & Events of the Revolution. Littell, John S. & Decker, Peter, eds. LC 71-76560. (Eyewitness Accounts of the American Revolution Ser., NO. 2). 1969. Repr. of 1846 ed. 26.00 (ISBN 0-405-01159-8). Ayer Co Pubs.

Graydon, Nell S. Nell Graydon's Cookbook: From My House to Your House. rev. ed. LC 84-22198. (Illus.). 200p. 1985. pap. 11.95 (ISBN 0-87844-057-7). Sandlapper Pub Co.

--South Carolina Ghost Tales. 10.95 (ISBN 0-910206-06-6). Beaufort SC.

--Tales of Beaufort. 10.50 (ISBN 0-685-06835-8). Beaufort SC.

--Tales of Edisto. 7th ed. (Illus.). 166p. 1983. Repr. of 1955 ed. 12.95 (ISBN 0-87844-053-4). Sandlapper Pub Co.

Grayeff, F. Kant's Theoretical Philosophy. 240p. 1970. pap. 7.50 (ISBN 0-7190-0441-1, Pub. by Manchester Univ Pr). Longwood Pub Group.

Grayling, A. C. An Introduction to Philosophical Logic. LC 82-6854. 300p. 1982. text ed. 29.50x (ISBN 0-389-20299-1); pap. text ed. 9.95x (ISBN 0-389-20300-9). B&N Imports.

Grayling, Anthony C. Refutation of Scepticism. LC 85-5032. 160p. 1985. cloth 22.95 (ISBN 0-87548-314-3). Open Court.

Graymer, LeRoy & Thompson, Frederick. Reforming Social Regulation: Alternative Public Policy Strategies. (Sage Focus Editions). (Illus.). 320p. 1982. 28.00 (ISBN 0-8039-1845-3); pap. 14.00 (ISBN 0-8039-1846-1). Sage.

Graymont, Barbara. Iroquois in the American Revolution. LC 73-170096. (New York State Studies). (Illus.). 1972. 17.95x (ISBN 0-8156-0083-6); pap. 9.95 (ISBN 0-8156-0116-6). Syracuse U Pr.

Graymont, Barbara, ed. Fighting Tuscarora: The Autobiography of Chief Clinton Rickard. LC 73-8208. (Iroquois Bks.). (Illus.). 212p. 1984. pap. 12.95 (ISBN 0-8156-0190-5). Syracuse U Pr.

Grayser, Stephen A., jt. auth. see Bursk, Edward C.

Grayshon, Jane, jt. auth. see Bailey, Rosemary E.

Grayshon, M. Towards a Social Grammar of Language. 1977. 11.80x (ISBN 90-279-7633-3). Mouton.

Graysmith, Robert. Zodiac. (Illus.). 384p. 1985. 16.95 (Pub. by Marek). St Martin.

Grayson. Diseases of the Cornea. LC 79-16021. 552p. 1979. 87.50 (ISBN 0-8016-1964-5). Mosby.

Grayson, jt. auth. see Rockwell.

Grayson, A. Kirk, jt. auth. see Donbaz, Veysel.

Grayson, Albert K. Babylonian Historical-Literary Texts. LC 74-80888. (Toronto Semitic Texts & Studies: No. 3). pap. 31.80 (ISBN 0-317-27039-7, 2023626). Bks Demand UMI.

Grayson, Ashley. Simon & Schuster Guide to Briefcase Computers. 1985. pap. 12.95 (Pub. by Computer Bks). S&S.

Grayson, Ashley D. & Vornholt, John. Computers to Go. Hagmann, Marnie, ed. (Illus.). 395p. 1985. pap. 12.95 (ISBN 0-671-50749-4, Pub. by Computer Bks). S&S.

Grayson, Benson L. Russian-American Relations in World War One. LC 78-20938. 1979. 13.50 (ISBN 0-8044-1309-6). Ungar.

--Saudi-American Relations. LC 82-40075. 178p. (Orig.). 1982. lib. bdg. 24.00 (ISBN 0-8191-2528-8); pap. text ed. 11.00 (ISBN 0-8191-2529-6). U Pr of Amer.

--United States-Iranian Relations. LC 81-40305. 194p. (Orig.). 1981. lib. bdg. 23.50 (ISBN 0-8191-1796-X); pap. text ed. 11.25 (ISBN 0-8191-1797-8). U Pr of Amer.

Grayson, Benson L., ed. The American Image of China. LC 79-4827. 1979. 15.95 (ISBN 0-8044-1311-8). Ungar.

Grayson, Bette J. My Guiding Light. 1983. 5.95 (ISBN 0-533-05712-4). Vantage.

Grayson, C. Jackson, Jr. Decisions Under Uncertainty: Drilling Decisions by Oil & Gas Operators. Bruchey, Stuart, ed. LC 78-22686. (Energy in the American Economy Ser.). (Illus.). 1979. Repr. of 1960 ed. lib. bdg. 32.50x (ISBN 0-405-11989-5). Ayer Co Pubs.

Grayson, Cary T. Woodrow Wilson: An Intimate Memoir. new ed. LC 60-10998. (Illus.). 154p. 1977. Repr. of 1960 ed. 7.50 (ISBN 0-87107-038-3). Potomac.

Grayson, Cary T., Jr. & Lukowski, Susan, eds. The Impeachment Congress: Ninety-Third U. S. Congress 1974. LC 66-18579. (Washington Ser.). 66p. (Orig.). 1975. pap. 3.50 (ISBN 0-87107-031-6). Potomac.

Grayson, Cary T., Jr., jt. ed. see Lukowski, Susan.

Grayson, Cecil. The World of Dante: Essays on Dante & His Times. (Illus.). 1980. text ed. 42.00x (ISBN 0-686-70060-0). Oxford U Pr.

Grayson, Cecil, jt. auth. see Chastel, Andre.

Grayson, David. Better Understanding Your Child Through Handwriting. Slavin, Marlene & Bitoy, Earl, eds. LC 81-90133. 190p. 1981. 14.95 (ISBN 0-9606228-1-0); pap. 9.95 (ISBN 0-9606228-0-2). GBC Pub.

Grayson, David, pseud. The Countryman's Year. LC 85-245. (Illus.). 288p. 1985. pap. 12.95 incl. dust jacket (ISBN 0-939650-47-9, Renaissance Hse). Jende-Hagan Bk.

Grayson, Donald K. A Bibliography of the Literature on North American Climates of the Past Thirteen Thousand Years. LC 75-5131. (Reference Library of Natural Science: No. 2). 160p. 1975. lib. bdg. 22.00 (ISBN 0-8240-9992-3). Garland Pub.

--Quantitative Zooarchaeology: Topics in the Analysis of Archaeological Faunas. Dimbleby, G. W., ed. (Studies in Archaeological Science). 1984. 34.50 (ISBN 0-12-297280-5). Acad Pr.

Grayson, Donald K., ed. The Establishment of Human Antiquity (Monograph) LC 82-11571. 280p. 1983. 29.50 (ISBN 0-12-297250-3). Acad Pr.

Grayson, Donald K., jt. ed. see Dunnell, Robert C.

Grayson, Donald K., jt. ed. see Sheets, Payson D.

Grayson, Ellis S. The Elements of Short-Term Group Counseling. rev. ed. (Illus.). 112p. 1978. pap. 5.00 (ISBN 0-942974-10-7). Am Correctional.

Grayson, Fred N. Household Budgeting & Accounting on Your Home Computer. LC 83-26235. (Illus.). 96p. 1984. pap. 5.95 (ISBN 0-399-50986-0, G&D). Putnam Pub Group.

--Learn to Type on Your Home Computer. LC 83-23728. (Illus.). 1984. pap. 5.95 (ISBN 0-399-50991-7, G&D). Putnam Pub Group.

--The Office Handbook for Civil Service Employees. LC 82-18480. 304p. 1983. pap. 8.00 (ISBN 0-668-05605-3). Arco.

--The Secretarial Handbook for the Modern Office. 256p. 1985. pap. 9.95 (ISBN 0-399-51138-5). Putnam Pub Group.

Grayson, George. United States & Mexico: Patterns of Influence. LC 83-24514. (Studies of Influence in International Relations Ser.). 236p. 1984. 27.95 (ISBN 0-03-061584-4); pap. 13.95 (ISBN 0-03-061586-0). Praeger.

Grayson, George W. The Politics of Mexican Oil. LC 80-5253. (Pitt Latin American Ser.). (Illus.). 1981. pap. 8.95 (ISBN 0-8229-5323-4). U of Pittsburgh Pr.

Grayson, Harry. They Played the Game: The Story of Baseball Greats. LC 77-167349. (Essay Index Reprint Ser.). Repr. of 1944 ed. 25.00 (ISBN 0-8369-2692-7). Ayer Co Pubs.

Grayson, Henry, ed. Short-Term Approaches to Psychotheraphy, Vol. III. LC 78-27605. (New Directions in Psychotherapy Ser.). 285p. 1979. 29.95 (ISBN 0-87705-345-6). Human Sci Pr.

Grayson, Henry & Loew, Clemens, eds. Changing Approaches to the Psychotherapies. LC 77-24270. 335p. 1978. 25.00X (ISBN 0-470-99177-1). Halsted Pr.

Grayson, Jan L., tr. see Puig, Manuel.

Grayson, Jane. Nabokov Translated: A Comparison of Nabokov's Russian & English Prose. (Oxford Modern Languages & Literature Monographs). 1977. 39.95x (ISBN 0-19-815527-1). Oxford U Pr.

Grayson, Janet. Structure & Imagery in "Ancrene Wisse". LC 73-77480. 251p. 1974. 22.50x (ISBN 0-87451-081-3). U Pr of New Eng.

Grayson, Joan. The Repair & Restoration of Pottery & Porcelain. (Illus.). 152p. 1982. 14.95 (ISBN 0-8069-5466-3). Sterling.

Grayson, John & Zingg, Walter, eds. Microcirculation, 2 vols. Incl. Vol. 1: Blood Vessel Interactions - Systems in Special Tissues. 443p. 1976. 52.50x (ISBN 0-306-37097-2); Vol. 2: Transport Mechanisms - Disease States. 378p. 1976. 52.50x (ISBN 0-306-37098-0). LC 76-26051. (Illus., Plenum Pr). Plenum Pub.

Grayson, L. E. National Oil Companies. 269p. 1981. 53.95 (ISBN 0-471-27861-0, Wiley-Interscience). Wiley.

Grayson, L. P. & Biedenbach, J. M., eds. Individualized Instruction in Engineering Education. 174p. 1974. 5.00 (ISBN 0-317-33257-0). Am Soc Ag Eng.

Grayson, L. P, jt. ed. see Biedenbach, J. M.

Grayson, Leslie, ed. Social & Economic Impact of New Technology. (IFI Data Base Library). 130p. 1984. 85.00x (ISBN 0-306-65209-9, Plenum Pr). Plenum Pub.

Grayson, Leslie E. & Tompkins, Curtis J. Management of Public Sector & Non-Profit Organizations. 1984. text ed. 23.95 (ISBN 0-8359-4240-6); solutions manual avail. (ISBN 0-8359-4246-5). Reston.

Grayson, Leslie E., ed. Economics of Energy: Readings on Environment, Resources, & Markets. LC 73-20718. 460p. 1975. 16.95 (ISBN 0-87850-022-7); pap. text ed. 6.95x (ISBN 0-87850-023-5). Darwin Pr.

Grayson, M. Information Retrieval in Chemistry & Chemical Patent Law. LC 82-24727. 116p. 1983. 24.95x (ISBN 0-471-89057-X, Pub. by Wiley-Interscience). Wiley.

Grayson, Marion. Let's Do Fingerplays. LC 62-10217. (Illus.). (ps-3). 1962. 9.95 (ISBN 0-88331-003-1). Luce.

Grayson, Martin. An Academy of One. 88p. 1984. 12.95x (ISBN 0-915639-00-9). Cos Cob Pr.

--Encyclopedia of Semiconductor Technology. LC 83-21587. (Encyclopedia Reprint Ser.). 941p. 1984. 69.95x (ISBN 0-471-88102-3). Wiley.

Grayson, Martin, ed. Antibiotics, Chemotherapeutics, & Antibacterial Agents for Disease Control. 513p. 1983. 64.95 (ISBN 0-471-87359-4, Pub. by Wiley-Interscience). Wiley.

--Encyclopedia of Composite Materials & Components. LC 82-23823. 1161p. 1983. 125.00x (ISBN 0-471-87357-8, Pub. by Wiley-Interscience). Wiley.

--Encyclopedia of Glass, Ceramics, Clay & Cement. (Encyclopedia Reprint Ser.). 960p. 1985. 89.95x (ISBN 0-471-81931-X, Pub. by Wiley-Interscience). Wiley.

--Encyclopedia of Textiles, Fibers & Non-Woven Fabrics. LC 84-13213. (Encyclopedia Reprint Ser.). 581p. 1984. 59.95x (ISBN 0-471-81461-X, 1-631). Wiley.

--Recycling, Fuel & Resource Recovery: Economic & Environmental Factors. LC 84-7516. (Encyclopedia Reprint Ser.). 232p. 1984. text ed. 39.95x (ISBN 0-471-81175-0). Wiley.

Grayson, Martin & Griffith, Edward J., eds. Topics in Phosphorus Chemistry, Vol. 10. (Topics in Phosphorus Chemistry Ser.). 517p. 1980. 109.50 (ISBN 0-471-05890-4, Pub. by Wiley-Interscience). Wiley.

--Topics in Phosphorus Chemistry, Vol. 11. (Topics in Phosphorous Chemistry Ser.). 451p. 1983. 92.00 (ISBN 0-471-89628-4, Pub. by Wiley-Interscience). Wiley.

Grayson, Martin, jt. ed. see Griffith, Edward J.

Grayson, Martin, jt. ed. see Othmer, Kirk.

Grayson, Merrill. Diseases of the Cornea. 2nd ed. LC 82-14530. (Illus.). 668p. 1983. text ed. 89.95 (ISBN 0-8016-1973-4). Mosby.

Grayson, Richard. Crime Without Passion. 224p. 1983. 10.95 (ISBN 0-312-17205-2). St Martin.

--Eating at Arby's: The South Florida Stories. 32p. (Orig.). 1983. pap. 3.00 (ISBN 0-88100-017-5). Grinning.

--I Brake for Delmore Schwartz. LC 82-63067. 96p. 1983. pap. 4.95 (ISBN 0-939010-03-8). Zephyr Pr.

--Lincoln's Doctor's Dog & Other Stories. LC 81-69117. 187p. 1982. 11.95 (ISBN 0-917976-13-4). White Ewe.

--The Monterant Affair. 208p. 1983. pap. 2.95 (ISBN 0-441-53623-9). Ace Bks.

--The Montmartre Murders. 196p. 1982. 10.95 (ISBN 0-312-54502-9). St Martin.

--The Murders at Impasse Louvain. 224p. 1982. pap. 2.75 (ISBN 0-441-54526-2). Ace Bks.

Grayson, Richard A. With Hitler in New York. LC 78-20695. 1979. 7.95 (ISBN 0-8008-8406-X). Taplinger.

Grayson, Robert. Crime Victim's Aid: A Regional Directory of Crime Victim Services for New York, New Jersey & Pennsylvania. 128p. (Orig.). 1983. pap. 19.95 (ISBN 0-935000-01-1). Bloom Bks.

Grayson, S. New Anecdota Americana: Jokes. 2.95x (ISBN 0-685-22058-3). Wehman.

Grayson, Stan. Catboats. LC 83-49415. (Illus.). 176p. 1984. 25.00 (ISBN 0-87742-162-5, C233). Intl Marine.

--The Dinghy Book. LC 80-84743. (Illus.). 272p. 1981. 7.95 (ISBN 0-87742-135-8). Intl Marine.

--Old Marine Engines: The World of the One Longer. LC 82-80402. (Illus.). 224p. 1982. 25.00 (ISBN 0-87742-155-2). Intl Marine.

Grayson, Stan, ed. Ferrari: The Man, the Machines. (Marque History Bks.). (Illus.). 348p. 1982. 29.95 (ISBN 0-915038-05-6). Auto Quarterly.

Grayson, Theodore J. Investment Trusts: Their Origin, Development & Operation. facsimile ed. LC 75-2636. (Wall Street & the Security Market Ser.). 1975. Repr. of 1928 ed. 36.50x (ISBN 0-405-06961-8). Ayer Co Pubs.

--Leaders & Periods of American Finance. facs. ed. LC 68-29211. (Essay Index Reprint Ser). 1932. 35.50 (ISBN 0-8369-1240-3). Ayer Co Pubs.

Grayson, William J. Hireling & the Slave, Chicora, & Other Poems. facs. ed. LC 78-83913. (Black Heritage Library Collection Ser). 1856. 12.00 (ISBN 0-8369-8581-8). Ayer Co Pubs.

Grayston, Donald. Thomas Merton: The Development of a Spiritual Theologian. LC 84-27299. (Toronto Studies in Theology: Vol. 20). 225p. 1985. 49.95x (ISBN 0-88946-758-7). E Mellen.

Grayston, Kenneth. The Johannine Epistles. Clements, Ronald & Black, Matthew, eds. (New Century Bible Commentary Ser.). 180p. (Orig.). 1984. pap. 5.95 (ISBN 0-8028-1981-8). Eerdmans.

--Philippians & Thessalonians. (Cambridge Bible Commentary on the New English Bible, New Testament Ser.). 1967. 16.95 (ISBN 0-521-04224-0); pap. 8.95 (ISBN 0-521-09409-7, 409). Cambridge U Pr.

Gray-Turner, Elston & Sutherland, F. M. History of the British Medical Association, Vol. II: 1932-1981. 375p. 1982. 35.00x (ISBN 0-7279-0090-0, Pub. by British Med Assoc UK); pap. 30.00x (ISBN 0-7279-0091-9). Taylor & Francis.

Graywon, J., jt. auth. see Catling, D. M.

Grayzel, Solomon. History of the Contemporary Jews from 1900 to the Present. LC 60-15542. (Temple Books). 1969. pap. text ed. 4.95x (ISBN 0-689-70080-6, T3). Atheneum.

--History of the Jews. rev. ed. (Illus.). 908p. 1968. Repr. of 1947 ed. 12.95 (ISBN 0-8276-0142-5, 190). Jewish Pubns.

--A History of the Jews. 768p. 1968. pap. 4.95 (ISBN 0-452-00694-5, Mer). NAL.

Graz, Liesl. The Omanis: Sentinels of the Gulf. (Illus.). 216p. 1982. text ed. 25.00x (ISBN 0-582-78348-8). Longman.

Grazda, Edward E., et al. Handbook of Applied Mathematics. 4th ed. LC 77-10309. 1128p. 1977. Repr. of 1966 ed. 56.50 (ISBN 0-88275-615-X). Krieger.

Graze, Sue. Visions: James Surls, 1974-1984. 19.95 (ISBN 0-9609622-5-5, Pub. by Dallas Museum). Texas Month Pr.

Grazer, Frederick M. & Klingbeil, Jerome R. Body Image: A Surgical Perspective. LC 79-23858. 422p. 1979. text ed. 84.50 (ISBN 0-8016-1965-3). Mosby.

Grazia, Alfred De. Apportionment & Representative Government. LC 83-12719. viii, 180p. 1983. Repr. of 1963 ed. lib. bdg. 27.50x (ISBN 0-313-23375-6, DGRA). Greenwood.

--The Burning of Troy: Essays on Catastrophe & Chronology. (Quantavolution Ser.: No. 12). 300p. (Orig.). 1984. pap. 17.00X (ISBN 0-940268-07-8). Metron Pubns.

--Cosmic Heretics: A Personal History of Attempts to Establish & Resist Theories of Quantavolution & Catastrophe in the Natural & Human Sciences, 1962-1983. (Quantavolution Ser.). 396p. 1984. pap. 23.00X (ISBN 0-940268-08-6). Metron Pubns.

--God's Fire: Moses & the Management of Exodus. (Quantavolution Ser.). (Illus.). 340p. 1983. pap. 20.00 (ISBN 0-940268-03-5). Metron Pubns.

--Homo Schizo: Human & Cultural Hologenesis, No. I. (Quantavolution Ser.). 278p. 1983. pap. 16.00 (ISBN 0-940268-01-9). Metron Pubns.

--Homo Schizo II: Human Nature & Behavior. (Quantavolution Ser.). 240p. 1983. pap. 15.00x (ISBN 0-940268-02-7). Metron Pubns.

Grazia, Alfred de & Milton, Earl R. Solaria Binaria: Origins & History of the Solar System. (Quantavolution Ser.). (Illus.). 292p. 1984. pap. 21.00x (ISBN 0-940268-04-3). Metron Pubns.

Grazia, Alfred de see De Grazia, Alfred.

Grazia, Alfred De see Michels, Roberto.

Grazia, Alfred De see Schlesinger, Arthur M., Jr. & De Grazia, Alfred.

Grazia, Anne-Marie de see De Grazia, Anne-Marie.

Graziani, M. & Giongo, G. M., eds. Fundamental Research in Homogeneous Catalysis, Vol. 4. 208p. 1984. 42.50x (ISBN 0-306-41512-7, Plenum Pr). Plenum Pub.

Graziani, Rene, ed. The Naked Astronaut: Poems on Birth & Birthdays. LC 83-20697. 352p. (Orig.). 1984. 22.95 (ISBN 0-571-13119-0); pap. 10.95 (ISBN 0-571-13193-X). Faber & Faber.

Graziani, Tommaso G. Mastering the Five Unknown Dimensions of the Art Expression. (Illus.). 129p. 1984. 77.45x (ISBN 0-86650-097-9). Gloucester Art.

Graziani, Vicenzo G. De see De Graziani, Vincenzo G.

Graziano, Anthony M. & Mooney, Kevin C. Children & Behavior Therapy. LC 83-25724. 486p. 1984. 29.95x (ISBN 0-202-26087-9). Aldine Pub.

Graziano, Anthony M., jt. auth. see Bugelski, Richard.

Graziano, Anthony M., ed. Behavior Therapy with Children, Vol. 2. LC 74-29461. 1975. lib. bdg. 39.95x (ISBN 0-202-26082-8). Aldine Pub.

Graziano, Frank. Duncan, the Potato Eaters, & Thanksgiving in the Shadow of Goat-Tit Mountain. 1979. pap. 3.00 (ISBN 0-931498-09-0). DuBois Zone Pr.

--From Sheepshead, from Paumanok. (Porch Chapbook Ser.: No. 3). (Illus.). 1979. pap. 3.00 (ISBN 0-932968-14-7); signed & numbered ed. 5.00 (ISBN 0-686-60167-X). Porch Pubns.

Graziano, Frank, ed. Homage to Robert Penn Warren. 96p. (Orig.). 1982. text ed. 14.00 (ISBN 0-937406-12-0); pap. 5.00 (ISBN 0-937406-11-2); ltd. ed. o.p. 35.00 (ISBN 0-937406-13-9). Logbridge-Rhodes.

Graziano, Frank, ed. see Trakl, Georg.

Graziano, Frank, jt. ed. see Wild, Peter.

Graziano, Luci. Hours... Days... Infinity. LC 82-60197. (Illus.). 59p. (gr. 7-10). 1982. 5.95 (ISBN 0-938232-15-0). Winston-Derek.

Graziano, Rocky. Somebody Down Here Likes Me, Too. 288p. 1984. pap. 3.95 (ISBN 0-8128-8041-2). Stein & Day.

Graziano, Rocky & Corsel, Ralph. Somebody Down Here Likes Me, Too. LC 81-40332. (Illus.). 288p. 1981. 12.95 (ISBN 0-8128-2828-3). Stein & Day.

Graziano, Rocky & Liss, Howard. Rocky's Boxing Book. (Illus.). 96p. 1980. PLB 7.95 (ISBN 0-686-63048-3); pap. 5.95 (ISBN 0-87460-377-3). Lion Bks.

Grazier, Kyle L. & Holbrook, Troy L. The Frequency of Occurrence, Impact & Cost of Musculoskeletal Conditions in the U.S. 187p. 1984. 10.00 (ISBN 0-89203-003-8, 4000032). Amer Acad Ortho Surg.

Grdinic, Eva. Fifty-Four Dobri Dol: A Letter from Yugoslavia. (Illus.). 92p. 1980. pap. 3.95 (ISBN 0-9604176-0-5). Grdinic.

Grdnic, Joy, jt. auth. see Stevens, Ron.

Gre, Gerald De see DeGre, Gerard.

Greacen, E. L. Soil Water Assessment by the Neutron Method. (Illus.). 140p. 1982. pap. text ed. 17.50 (ISBN 0-643-00414-9, Pub. by CSIRO). Intl Spec Bk.

--Soil Water Assessment by the Neutron Method. 1982. 60.00x (ISBN 0-686-97898-6, Pub. by CSIRO Australia). State Mutual Bk.

--Soil Water Assessment by the Neutron Method. 148p. 1982. pap. 21.75 (ISBN 0-643-00414-9, C063, CSIRO). Unipub.

Greacen, E. L., jt. auth. see Russell, J. S.

Greacen, Robert. Art of Noel Coward. LC 72-195441. 1953. lib. bdg. 17.00 (ISBN 0-8414-4676-8). Folcroft.

Greacon, Robert. The Art of Noel Coward. 1978. Repr. of 1953 ed. lib. bdg. 10.00 (ISBN 0-8495-1929-2). Arden Lib.

Greaf, Donald E. de see De Greaf, Donald E.

Grealey, S., jt. ed. see Jones, G. B.

Grealish, Charles & Grealish, Mary J. The Sneely-Mouth Snerds & the Wonderoctopus. 1975. 1.75 (ISBN 0-937540-05-6, C-1). Human Policy Pr.

Grealish, Charles A., jt. auth. see Grealish, Mary J.

Grealish, Mary J. & Grealish, Charles A. Amy Maura. 1975. 1.75 (ISBN 0-937540-09-9, C-2). Human Policy Pr.

Grealish, Mary J., jt. auth. see Grealish, Charles.

Grealy, Joseph I. School Crime & Violence: Problems & Solutions. LC 79-55399. 1980. 29.95 (ISBN 0-918214-05-X). F E Peters.

Grean, Stanley. Shaftesbury's Philosophy of Religion & Ethics: A Study in Enthusiasm. LC 67-15457. pap. 80.00 (ISBN 0-317-09231-6, 2006441). Bks Demand UMI.

Greaney, Richard B. & Gerber, Frederic H. Scintigraphic Review of the Hip. 1985. 22.50 (ISBN 0-87527-269-X). Green.

Greaney, Vincent, ed. Children: Needs & Rights. 200p. 1985. text ed. 24.50x (ISBN 0-8290-1553-1). Irvington.

--The Rights of Children. 250p. 1985. text ed. 24.50x (ISBN 0-8290-1297-4). Irvington.

Greanias, Francis. More Pasting Penguins. (Preschool Ser.). 24p. (ps). 1980. 5.50 (ISBN 0-88160-060-1, LW 608). Learning Wks.

--Pasting Penguin. (Preschool Ser.). 24p. (ps). 1980. 5.50 (ISBN 0-88160-059-8, LW 607). Learning Wks.

Greanias, George C. The Foreign Corrupt Practices Act: Anatomy of a Statute. LC 81-48265. (Illus.). 208p. 1982. 26.50x (ISBN 0-669-05254-X). Lexington Bks.

Greanias, George C. & Windsor, Duane, eds. The Changing Boardroom: Making Policy & Profits in an Age of Corporate Citizenship. LC 81-83531. 176p. 1981. 12.95x (ISBN 0-87201-103-8). Gulf Pub.

Grear, A. C. & Oxborough, J. Company Property Management in Great Britain. 1970. 24.00x (ISBN 0-8464-0264-5). Beekman Pubs.

Grear, J. W. A Revision of the American Species of Eriosema (Leguminosae-Lotoideae, Vol. 20(3) (Memoirs of the New York Botanical Garden Ser.). 98p. 1970. 10.00 (ISBN 0-317-35527-9). NY Botanical.

Grear, John W. A Revision of the New World Species of Rhynchosia (Leguminosae-Faboideae) LC 78-17663. (Memoirs Ser.: Vol. 31, No. 1). 1978. pap. 15.00x (ISBN 0-89327-208-6). NY Botanical.

Greaser, Galen D., tr. see Bayon, Damian.

Greaser, Galen D., tr. see Ortega, Julio.

Greasley, Mike. Rallycourse Nineteen Eighty-Four to Nineteen Eighty-Five. (Rally Annual Ser.). (Illus.). 200p. 1985. text ed. 36.95 (ISBN 0-905138-34-1, Pub. by Hazelton England). Motorbooks Intl.

Greasybear, Charley J. Songs. Trusky, Tom & Crews, Judson, eds. LC 78-58484. (Modern & Contemporary Poets of the West). (Orig.). 1979. pap. 3.00 (ISBN 0-916272-10-9). Ahsahta Pr.

Great Basin Foundation & Blackburn, Thomas C., eds. Woman, Poet, Scientist: Essays in New World Anthropology Honoring Dr. Emma Louise Davis. LC 85-6075. (Anthropological Papers). (Illus.). 256p. (Orig.). 1985. pap. 21.50 (ISBN 0-87919-106-6). Ballena Pr.

Great Britain. Sheffield Outrages Inquiry: Report Presented to the Trades Unions Commissioners. LC 72-108850. Repr. of 1867 ed. lib. bdg. 45.00x (ISBN 0-678-07766-5). Kelley.

Great Britain - Admiralty. Handbook of German East Africa. LC 75-90114. (Illus.). Repr. of 1920 ed. cancelled (ISBN 0-8371-2034-9, HGE&, Pub. by Negro U Pr). Greenwood.

Great Britain - Admiralty (Naval I) Handbook of Portuguese Nyasaland. LC 79-90115. Repr. of 1920 ed. cancelled (ISBN 0-8371-2033-0, HPN&, Pub. by Negro U Pr). Greenwood.

Great Britain Board of Agriculture. Agriculture State of the Kingdom, 1816. LC 78-108849. Repr. of 1816 ed. lib. bdg. 37.50x (ISBN 0-678-07767-3). Kelley.

Great Britain Cabinet Office. Principle War Telegrams & Memo, 1940-1943, 7 Vols. 1976. lib. bdg. 450.00x (ISBN 0-527-35650-6). Kraus Intl.

Great Britain, Census Office. Abstract of the Answers & Returns: The Census Report for 1801, 2 vols. LC 79-366591. 1968. Repr. of 1802 ed. Set. lib. bdg. 125.00x00347507x (ISBN 0-678-05225-5). Vol. 1, Enumeration. Vol. 2, Parish Registers. Kelley.

Great Britain Challenger Office. Report on the Scientific Results of the Voyage of H. M. S. Challenger During the Years 1873-1876, 50 Vols. (Illus.). 1880-1895. Set. 5000.00 (ISBN 0-384-19750-7). Johnson Repr.

Great Britain Commission of Inquiry into Condition of Crofters & Cottars of Scotland. Report of Her Majesty's Commissioners of Inquiry: Into the Conditions of the Crofters & Cottars in the Highlands & Islands of Scotland, 5 vols. LC 77-87677. Repr. of 1884 ed. 165.00 set (ISBN 0-404-16470-6). AMS Pr.

Great Britain Court of the Star Chamber. Reports of Cases in Courts of Star Chamber & High Commission. Gardiner, Samuel R., ed. 1886. 27.00 (ISBN 0-384-19760-4). Johnson Repr.

Great Britain, Factories Inquiry Commission. First Report of the Central Board of His Majesty's Commissioners Appointed to Collect Information in the Manufacturing Districts: As to the Employment of Children in Factories. LC 71-367641. 1968. Repr. of 1833 ed. lib. bdg. 75.00x (ISBN 0-678-05226-3). Kelley.

Great Britain Foreign Office. British Documents of the Origin of the War 1898-1914, Vols. 1-11. Gooch, G. P. & Temperley, Harold, eds. 1926-38. Set. 700.00 (ISBN 0-384-19770-1); Set. pap. 630.00 (ISBN 0-384-19770-1). Johnson Repr.

Great Britain, Foreign Office. Index to Foreign Office Correspondence Years 1920-1951, 131 vols. 1982. lib. bdg. 7546.00 (ISBN 3-262-02571-2). Kraus Intl.

Great Britain Foreign Office Historical Section. British Possessions, 2: The Congo. LC 70-79814. (Illus.). Repr. of 1920 ed. 20.50x (ISBN 0-8371-1474-8, BRP&, Pub. by Negro U Pr). Greenwood.

--German African Possessions, Late. LC 70-79815. (Illus.). Repr. of 1920 ed. 25.00x (ISBN 0-8371-1475-6, GAP&, Pub. by Negro U Pr). Greenwood.

--Spanish & Italian Possessions: Independent States. LC 74-79816. (Illus.). Repr. of 1920 ed. cancelled (ISBN 0-8371-1473-X, SIP&, Pub. by Negro U Pr). Greenwood.

Great Britain Gold & Silver Commission. Monetary Problem: Gold & Silver. LC 72-1685. Repr. of 1936 ed. 26.50 (ISBN 0-404-05362-9). AMS Pr.

Great Britain Historical Manuscripts Commission. Manuscripts of the Earl of Dartmouth, 3 vols. Billias, George, ed. LC 72-8795. (American Revolutionary Ser.). 1592p. Repr. of 1896 ed. Set. lib. bdg. 132.00x (ISBN 0-8398-0802-X). Irvington.

--Report of the Manuscripts of Mrs. Stopford-Sackville of Drayton House, Northamptonshire, 2 vols. Billias, George, ed. LC 72-8813. (American Revolutionary Ser.). Repr. of 1910 ed. Set. lib. bdg. 80.00 (ISBN 0-8398-0803-8). Irvington.

--Report on American Manuscripts in the Royal Institution of Great Britain, 4 vols. Billias, George, ed. LC 72-8703. (American Revolutionary Ser.). 1979. Repr. of 1909 ed. Set. lib. bdg. 180.00 (ISBN 0-8398-0801-1). Irvington.

Great Britain House Of Commons. Debates in the House of Commons in 1625. Gardiner, Samuel R., ed. 1873. 27.00 (ISBN 0-384-19810-4). Johnson Repr.

--Parliamentary Debates in 1610. 1862. 24.00 (ISBN 0-384-19780-9). Johnson Repr.

Great Britain House Of Lords - 1621. Notes of the Debates in the House of Lords. 1870. 19.00 (ISBN 0-384-19790-6). Johnson Repr.

Great Britain House of Lords - 1624. Notes of the Debates in the House of Lords. Gardiner, Samuel R., ed. 1879. 27.00 (ISBN 0-384-19800-7). Johnson Repr.

Great Britain Parliament. British West Indies at Westminster, 1789-1823. LC 70-100306. 1954. cancelled (ISBN 0-8371-3235-5, WII&, Pub. by Negro U Pr). Greenwood.

Great Britain. Parliament. Proceedings & Debates of the British Parliaments Respecting North America, 5 vols. Stock, Leo F., ed. LC 24-7105. 1976. Set. 290.00 (ISBN 0-527-35720-0). Kraus Repr.

Great Britain. Parliament. House of Commons. Fifth Report from the Select Committee of the House of Commons on the Affairs of the East India Company, 3 Vols. Firminger, Walter K., ed. LC 67-30063. Repr. of 1918 ed. lib. bdg. 150.00x (ISBN 0-678-00520-6). Kelley.

Great Britain, Parliament, House of Commons, Secret Committee on Joint Stock Banks. Report from the Secret Committee on Joint Stock Banks, 20 August 1836. LC 70-363560. 1968. Repr. of 1836 ed. lib. bdg. 37.50x (ISBN 0-678-05228-X). Kelley.

Great Britain, Parliament, House of Commons, Select Committee on Public Libraries. Report from the Select Committee on Public Libraries, 23 July 1849. LC 74-366370. 1968. Repr. of 1849 ed. lib. bdg. 45.00x (ISBN 0-678-05231-X). Kelley.

Great Britain, Parliament, House of Commons, Select Committee on the Health of Towns. Report from the Select Committee on the Health of Towns. LC 68-111978. 1968. Repr. of 1840 ed. lib. bdg. 37.50x (ISBN 0-678-05230-1). Kelley.

Great Britain, Parliament, House of Commons. Report from the Select Committee to Whom the Several Petitions Complaining of the Distressed State of the Agriculture in the United Kingdom Were Referred, 18 June 1821. LC 68-112457. 1968. Repr. of 1821 ed. lib. bdg. 50.00x (ISBN 0-678-05227-1). Kelley.

Great Britain, Parliament, House of Commons, Select Committee on Artizans & Machinery. Six Reports from the Select Committee on Artizans & Machinery, 23 February - 21 May 1824. LC 68-110405. 1968. Repr. of 1824 ed. lib. bdg. 57.50 (ISBN 0-678-05229-8). Kelley.

Great Britain Parliament House Of Commons. Substance of the Debate in the House of Commons, on the 15th of May, 1823. LC 72-82053. Repr. of 1823 ed. 19.75x (ISBN 0-8371-1874-3, DES&, Pub. by Negro U Pr). Greenwood.

Great Britain Patent Office. Alphabetical Index of Patentees of Inventions 1617-1852. Woodcroft, Bennett, ed. LC 68-58945. Repr. of 1854 ed. lib. bdg. 50.00x (ISBN 0-678-07755-X). Kelley.

Great Britain, Patent Office. Patents for Inventions, 2 vols. Bunnell, Peter C. & Sobieszek, Robert A., eds. LC 76-23063. (Sources of Modern Photography Ser.). (Illus.). 1979. Repr. of 1903 ed. Set. lib. bdg. 103.00x (ISBN 0-405-09626-7); lib. bdg. 45.00x ea. Vol. 1 (ISBN 0-405-09627-5). Vol. 2 (ISBN 0-405-09628-3). Ayer Co Pubs.

Great Britain Poor Law Board. Official Circulars of Public Documents & Information, Vols. 1-10 In 2. LC 68-56565. (Repr. of 1840-51 ed.). Set. lib. bdg. 95.00x (ISBN 0-678-00581-8). Kelley.

Great Britain Poor Law Commissioners. Reports of Special Assistant Poor Law Commissioners on the Employment of Women & Children in Agriculture. LC 68-141609. 378p. 1968. Repr. of 1843 ed. PLB 37.50 (ISBN 0-678-05232-8). Kelley.

Great Britain, Public Record Office. Lists & Indexes, 81 vols. LC 65-3164. (Supplementary Ser.: Nos.I-XVI). 1964. lib. bdg. 4692.00x (ISBN 0-527-02914-9). Kraus Intl.

Great Britain Public Record Office. Syllabus in English of the Documents Relating to England & Other Kingdoms, 3 Vols. LC 78-168243. Repr. of 1885 ed. Set. 172.50 (ISBN 0-404-03130-7). AMS Pr.

Great Britain, Royal Commission on Capital Punishment, 1949-1953. Report: Presented to Parliament by Command of Her Majesty, Sept, 1953. LC 79-25707. 505p. 1980. Repr. of 1953 ed. lib. bdg. 42.50x (ISBN 0-313-22121-9, GBCP). Greenwood.

Great Britain, Royal Institute of International Affairs & Foreign Office. Review of the Foreign Press, 1939-1945, 10 Ser. in 27 vols. 1980. lib. bdg. 1980.00x (ISBN 0-527-75543-5). Kraus Intl.

Great Britain Sovereigns. British Royal Proclamations Relating to America, 1603-1783. 1964. Repr. of 1911 ed. 29.00 (ISBN 0-8337-0373-0). B Franklin.

Great Britain - War Office - Intelligence Division. Report on the Egyptian Provinces of the Sudan, Red Sea & Equator. LC 79-140809. Repr. of 1883 ed. 14.75x (ISBN 0-8371-5840-0). Greenwood.

Great Northern Railroad. Dedication & Opening of the New Cascade Tunnel. (Shorey Historical Ser.). (Illus.). 20p. Repr. of 1929 ed. pap. 1.95 (ISBN 0-8466-0235-0, S235). Shorey.

Great Plains Flora Assn. Atlas of the Flora of the Great Plains. 1977. text ed. 26.00x (ISBN 0-8138-0135-4). Iowa St U Pr.

Greated, Clive A., jt. auth. see Durrani, Tariq S.

Greater Lansing Spinsters' Guild. The Greengathering Feast. (Illus.). 56p. 1981. pap. 6.00 (ISBN 0-940302-00-4). Tea Rose Pr.

Greater London Council. Introduction to Housing Layout. (Illus.). 192p. 1978. pap. text ed. 23.00x (ISBN 0-85139-298-9, Pub. by Architectural Pr England). Humanities.

--Survey of London. Incl. Vol. 31-32. St. James, Westminister, Pt. 2; Vol. 33-34. St. Anne, Soho. text ed. 91.50x (ISBN 0-485-48233-9); Vol. 35. Theatre Royal, Drury Lane, & the Royal Opera House, Covent Garden; Vol. 36. St. Paul, Covent Garden; Vol. 37. Northern Kensington. text ed. 78.50x (ISBN 0-485-48237-1). Athlone Pr). Humanities.

--Survey of London, Vol. 38: The Museum Area of South Kensington & Westminster. (Illus.). 480p. 1975. text ed. 83.75x (ISBN 0-485-48238-X, Athlone Pr). Humanities.

--The Urban School. (Illus.). 222p. 1983. pap. text ed. 23.00x (ISBN 0-85139-695-X, Pub. by Architectural Pr England). Humanities.

Greater London Council Department of Architecture & Civic Design. Detailing for Building Construction: A Designer's Manual of Over 350 Standard Details. (Illus.). 500p. 1980. pap. 37.75x (ISBN 0-85139-234-2). Nichols Pub.

--GLC Preferred Dwelling Plans. 2nd ed. (Illus.). 83p. 1981. 18.50 (ISBN 0-85139-252-0). Nichols Pub.

--Good Practice Details. (Illus.). 148p. 1980. 24.95 (ISBN 0-85139-241-5); pap. 17.50 (ISBN 0-85139-242-3). Nichols Pub.

--Introduction to Housing Layout. 1978. 27.50 (ISBN 0-89397-037-9). Nichols Pub.

Greater New York Fund, Inc. Boards of Directors: A Study of Current Practices in Board Management & Board Operations in Voluntary Hospitals, Health & Welfare Organizations. LC 74-8586. 266p. 1974. lib. bdg. 17.50 (ISBN 0-379-00275-2). Oceana.

Greater Portland Landmarks Research Committee, ed. Researching the Old House. (Illus.). 72p. 1981. pap. 3.95 (ISBN 0-9600612-9-0). Greater Portland.

Greathead, D. J. A Review of Biological Control in the Ethiopian Region. 162p. 1971. cloth 42.00x (ISBN 0-85198-022-8, Pub. by CAB Bks England). State Mutual Bk.

--A Review of Biological Control in Western & Southern Europe. 182p. 1976. 45.00X (ISBN 0-85198-369-3, CAB Bks). State Mutual Bk.

Greathouse, M., ed. see Martin, T. E.

Greathouse, Willam M. Beacon Bible Expositions: Vol. 6, Romans. Taylor, Willard H., ed. (Beacon Bible Exposition Ser.). 1975. 6.95 (ISBN 0-8341-0317-6). Beacon Hill.

Greathouse, William & Dunning, H. Ray. An Introduction to Wesleyan Theology. 1982. 4.95 (ISBN 0-8341-0762-7). Beacon Hill.

Greathouse, William M. From the Apostles to Wesley. 124p. 1979. pap. 3.50 (ISBN 0-8341-0588-8). Beacon Hill.

Greathouse, William M., jt. auth. see Bassett, Paul M.

Greathouse, William M., jt. auth. see Sanner, A. Elwood.

Greathouse, William M., ed. see Airhart, Arnold E.

Greathouse, William M, ed. see Martin, Sydney.

Greathouse, William M., ed. see Purkiser, W. T.

Greathouse, William M., ed. see Reed, Oscar F.

Greathouse, William M., ed. see Welch, Reuben.

Greathouse, William M., ed. see Young, Samuel.

Greatorex, Wilfred. Button Zone. 320p. 1984. 16.95 (ISBN 0-02-545200-2). Macmillan.

Greatsinger, Calvin. Alternatives to the Ditto: Resources for the Reading-Language Arts Teacher. (Illus.). 1977. 3.95 (ISBN 0-914634-46-1, 7712). DOK Pubs.

--Free Learning (for Learning Without Study Through Introductory Offers) (Illus.). 56p. 1981. pap. text ed. 4.95 (ISBN 0-914634-87-9). DOK Pubs.

Greaver, J. P., jt. auth. see Johnston, B. F.

Greaves, A. Descriptions of Seed Sources & Collections for Provenances of Pinus Caribaea. 1978. 30.00x (ISBN 0-85074-035-5, Pub. by For Lib Comm England). State Mutual Bk.

--A Regional Volume Table for Gmelina Arborea. 1978. 30.00x (ISBN 0-85074-044-4, Pub. by For Lib Comm England). State Mutual BK.

--Review of Pinus Caribaea. 1980. 30.00x (ISBN 0-85074-052-5, Pub. by For Lib Comm England). State Mutual Bk.

--Site Index Curves for Gmelina Arborea. 1978. 30.00x (ISBN 0-85074-043-6, Pub. by For Lib Comm England). State Mutual Bk.

Greaves, Bettina B. Free Market Economics: A Syllabus. 242p. 1975. pap. text ed. 6.00 (ISBN 0-910614-53-9). Foun Econ Ed.

Greaves, Bettina B., ed. Free Market Economics: A Basic Reader. 286p. (gr. 11-12). 1975. pap. text ed. 6.00 (ISBN 0-910614-56-3). Foun Econ Ed.

Greaves, Bettina B., tr. see Von Mises, Ludwig.

Greaves, C. Desmond. The Easter Rising in Song & Ballad. 88p. 1980. 10.00 (ISBN 0-900707-51-8, Pub. by Stanmore Pr England); pap. 5.95 (ISBN 0-686-36894-0). Facsimile Bk.

--Liam Mellows & the Irish Revolution. 400p. 1970. 18.00x (ISBN 0-8464-0565-2). Beekman Pubs.

--Sean O'Casey: Politics & Art. 1980. text ed. 18.75x (ISBN 0-391-01023-9). Humanities.

--Sean O'Casey: Politics & Art. 1980. 30.00x (ISBN 0-85315-431-7, Pub. by Lawrence & Wishart England). State Mutual Bk.

Greaves, Doris E. Cosmobiology: A Modern Approach. 136p. 1980. 10.00 (ISBN 0-86690-110-8, 1152-01). Am Fed Astrologers.

Greaves, Edward R. & Anderson, Lee P. One Hundred One Activities for Exceptional Children. (Illus.). 115p. pap. 7.95 (ISBN 0-917962-75-3). Peek Pubns.

Greaves, Fred. Nurse Education & the Curriculum: A Curricular Model. 108p. (Orig.). 1984. pap. 12.00 (ISBN 0-7099-1179-3, Pub. by Croom Helm Ltd). Longwood Pub Group.

Greaves, Harold R. The League Committees & World Order. LC 76-29430. Repr. of 1931 ed. 23.00 (ISBN 0-404-15336-4). AMS Pr.

Greaves, I. C. Modern Production among Backward Peoples. (London School of Economic & Political Science Studies in Economics & Commerce: Vol. 5). pap. 26.00 (ISBN 0-317-15415-X). Kraus Repr.

Greaves, Ida C. Colonial Monetary Conditions. pap. 28.00 (ISBN 0-384-19840-6). Johnson Repr.

--Modern Production Among Backward Peoples. LC 68-9759. Repr. of 1935 ed. 22.50x (ISBN 0-678-00419-6). Kelley.

Greaves, J. H. Rodent Control in Agriculture: A Handbook on the Biology & Control of Commensal Rodents as Agricultural Pests. (Plant Production & Protection Papers: No. 40). 95p. 1982. pap. text ed. 7.50 (ISBN 92-5-101295-4, F2407, FAO). Unipub.

Greaves, M. A. A Classification Scheme for Adult Education. 1966. 20.00x (ISBN 0-900008-07-5, Pub. by U of London England). State Mutual Bk.

--Education in British India Sixteen Ninety-Eight to Nineteen Forty-Seven: A Bibliography & Guide to the Sources of Information in London. 1962. 20.00x (ISBN 0-900008-15-6, Pub. by U of London England). State Mutual Bk.

Greaves, M. F. Cellular Recognition. 1975. pap. 6.95 (ISBN 0-412-13110-2, NO.6129, Pub. by Chapman & Hall). Methuen Inc.

Greaves, M. F., jt. ed. see Cuatrecasas, P.

Greaves, Margaret. Cat's Magic. LC 80-8451. 192p. (gr. 5 up). 1981. 10.10i (ISBN 0-06-022122-4); PLB 10.98 (ISBN 0-06-022123-2). HarpJ.

--A Little Box of Witches, 4 vols. LC 85-4436. (Illus.). 28p. (ps-3). 1985. Boxed Set. 8.95 (ISBN 0-8037-0225-6). Dial Bks Young.

--A Net to Catch the Wind. LC 78-20265. (Illus.). (gr. 1-4). 1979. PLB 11.89 (ISBN 0-06-022105-4). HarpJ.

--Once There Were No Pandas: A Chinese Legend. Durell, Ann, ed. LC 85-7033. (Illus.). 32p. (ps-3). 1985. 11.95 (ISBN 0-525-44211-1). Dutton.

--Stone of Terror. LC 74-2614. (Story of Suspense Ser). 176p. (gr. 7-12). 1974. HarpJ.

Greaves, P. & Faccini, J. M. Rat Histopathology. 260p. 1984. 52.00 (ISBN 0-444-90364-X). Elsevier.

Greaves, Percy L., Jr. Mises Made Easier: A Glossary for Ludwig Von Mises' Human Action. 175p. 1974. 12.00 (ISBN 0-930902-00-9). Free Market.

--Understanding the Dollar Crisis. Enlarged Ed. ed. LC 84-148895. 332p. (gr. 11-12). 1984. 14.00 (ISBN 0-930902-02-5); pap. 7.00 (ISBN 0-930902-03-3). Free Market.

Greaves, Percy L., Jr. & Martin, James J. Pearl Harbor: Revisionism Renewed. 128p. 1984. pap. 5.00 (ISBN 0-939484-18-8). Inst Hist Rev.

Greaves, Percy L., Jr., ed. see Von Mises, Ludwig.

Greaves, R. & Zaller, R., eds. Biographical Dictionary of British Radicals in the Seventeenth Century, Vol. 1 A-F. 308p. 1982. text ed. 75.50x (ISBN 0-85527-133-7, Pub. by Harvester England). Humanities.

--Biographical Dictionary of British Radicals in the Seventeenth Century, Vol. 3, P-Z. 371p. 1984. text ed. 75.50x (ISBN 0-7108-0486-5, Pub. by Harvester England). Humanities.

Greaves, Richard. The Puritan Revolution & Education Thought: Background for Reform. 1970. 18.00x (ISBN 0-8135-0616-6). Rutgers U Pr.

Greaves, Richard & Zaller, Robert, eds. Biographical Dictionary of British Radicals in the Seventeenth Century, Vol. 2, G-O. 352p. 1982. text ed. 75.50x (ISBN 0-7108-0430-X, Pub. by Harvester England). Humanities.

Greaves, Richard L. Elizabeth First, Queen of England. (Problems in European Civilization Ser). 1974. pap. text ed. 5.50 (ISBN 0-669-86371-8). Heath.

--Saints & Rebels: Seven Nonconformists in Stuart England. LC 84-22799. xiv, 224p. 1985. 18.95x (ISBN 0-86554-136-1, MUP-H127). Mercer Univ Pr.

--Society & Religion in Elizabethan England. 832p. 1981. 39.50x (ISBN 0-8166-1030-4). U of Minn Pr.

Greaves, Richard L., jt. auth. see Forrest, James F.

Greaves, Richard L., compiled by. An Annotated Bibliography of John Bunyan Studies. LC 72-177693. (Bibliographia Tripotamopolitana: No. 5). 1972. 7.00x (ISBN 0-931222-04-4). C E Barbour.

--Annotated Bibliography of John Bunyan Studies. LC 72-177693. 1972. 7.00 (ISBN 0-318-03615-0). Pitts Theolog.

Greaves, Richard L., ed. Triumph over Silence: Women in Protestant History. LC 85-961. (Contributions to the Study of Religion Ser.: No. 15). 320p. 1985. lib. bdg. 35.00 (ISBN 0-313-24799-4, GTS/). Greenwood.

Greaves, Richard L., ed. see Bunyan, John.

Greaves, Roger, tr. see Eisner, Lotte.

Greaves, Roger, tr. see Kaltenmark, Max.

Greaves, Roland E. Food Equipment Repair & Maintenance: A Manual to Help You Maintain Your Equipment. LC 83-71223. (Illus.). 320p. (Orig.). 1984. pap. 32.50 (ISBN 0-686-45568-1). FERM.

Greaves, Thomas & Culver, William, eds. Miners & Mining in the Americas. 320p. 1985. 40.00 (ISBN 0-7190-1761-0, Pub. by Manchester Univ Pr). Longwood Pub Group.

Greaves, W., jt. auth. see Benson, J.

Greaves, William, jt. auth. see Benson, James.

Grebanier, Bernard. The Angel in the Rock. limited ed. LC 79-176132. (Living Poets' Library Ser). pap. 2.50 (ISBN 0-686-01281-X). Dragons Teeth.

--Barron's Simplified Approach to Moliere. LC 64-8320. 1965. pap. text ed. 1.95 (ISBN 0-8120-0181-8). Barron.

--Barron's Simplified Approach to Shakespeare's Henry Fourth, Pt. 1. LC 64-8319. (Orig.). 1965. pap. text ed. 1.95 (ISBN 0-8120-0185-0). Barron.

--Barron's Simplified Approach to Shakespeare's Richard Second. LC 67-24535. 1967. pap. text ed. 1.95 (ISBN 0-8120-0263-6). Barron.

--English Literature, 2 Vols. (Orig.). (gr. 9 up). text ed. 7.00 ea. Vol. 1 1959 (ISBN 0-8120-5037-1). Vol. 2 1948. Vol. 1. pap. 5.95 (ISBN 0-8120-0065-X); Vol. 2. pap. 6.95 (ISBN 0-8120-0066-8). Barron.

--The Great Shakespeare Forgery: A New Look at the Career of William Henry Ireland. 308p. 1983. Repr. of 1966 ed. lib. bdg. 40.00 (ISBN 0-89760-170-X). Telegraph Bks.

--Playwriting: How to Write for the Theater. (Everyday Handbooks Ser.). 384p. 1979. pap. 5.29i (ISBN 0-06-463498-1, EH 498). B&N NY.

--Thornton Wilder. (Pamphlets on American Writers Ser: No. 34). (Orig.). 1964. pap. 1.25x (ISBN 0-8166-0318-9, MPAW34). U of Minn Pr.

Grebanier, Bernard, tr. see Racine, Jean B.

Grebanier, Bernard D. Barron's Simplified Approach to Rousseau: Emile & Other Works. LC 64-8318. 1965. pap. text ed. 1.95 (ISBN 0-8120-0183-4). Barron.

Grebanier, Bernard D., tr. see Moliere, Jean B.

Grebanier, Frances. Oscar Wilde & the Yellow Nineties. LC 79-8062. Repr. of 1940 ed. 37.00 (ISBN 0-404-18373-5). AMS Pr.

Grebe, Anthony Van see Van Grebe, Anthony.

Grebe, Paul, et al, eds. Deutscher Wortschatz-deutsch erklart. (Illus.). 444p. 1971. 7.50x (ISBN 3-468-96100-6). Intl Film.

Grebel, E. & Pogrund, P. Caring for Your Car. (On Your Own Ser.). (Illus.). 64p. (gr. 9 up). 1982. pap. text ed. 3.95 (ISBN 0-915510-59-6). Janus Bks.

Grebel, Rosemary & Pogrund, Phyllis. Becoming a Driver. 2nd ed. Katz, Elaine, ed. (Survival Guides Ser.). (Illus.). 64p. (gr. 7-12). 1981. pap. text ed. 3.95 (ISBN 0-915510-57-X). Janus Bks.

Greben, Stanley E. Love's Labor: The Experience & Practice of Psychotherapy. 1985. pap. 7.95 (ISBN 0-452-25736-0, Plume). NAL.

--Love's Labor: Twenty-Five Years of Experience in the Practice of Psychotherapy. LC 83-40460. 224p. 1984. 18.95 (ISBN 0-8052-3896-4). Schocken.

Greben, Stanley E., et al, eds. A Method of Psychiatry. 2nd ed. LC 85-6937. (Illus.). 475p. 1985. text ed. write for info. (ISBN 0-8121-0976-7). Lea & Febiger.

Grebene, A. B., ed. Analog Integrated Circuits. LC 78-59636. 1978. 20.25 (ISBN 0-87942-114-2, PC01099). Inst Electrical.

Grebene, Alan B. Analog Integrated Circuit Design. LC 78-15389. 416p. 1978. Repr. of 1972 ed. lib. bdg. 24.50 (ISBN 0-88275-710-5). Krieger.

--Bipolar & MOS Analog Integrated Circuit Design. 894p. 1983. 53.50x (ISBN 0-471-08529-4, Pub. by Wiley-Interscience). Wiley.

Grebenshchikov, O. S. Geobotanic Dictionary. (Rus., Eng., Ger. & Fr.). 1979. lib. bdg. 31.50x (ISBN 3-87429-164-2). Lubrecht & Cramer.

Greber, David, jt. auth. see Zimmer, Henry B.

Greber, Judith. Easy Answers. 256p. 1983. pap. 2.50 (ISBN 0-449-20269-0). Fawcett.

--The Silent Partner. 304p. 1984. 13.95 (ISBN 0-517-55295-7). Crown.

--The Silent Partner. 320p. 1985. pap. 3.95 (ISBN 0-345-32270-3). Ballantine.

Greber, N'omi. Recent Excavation at the Edwin Harness Mound Liberty Works, Ross County, Ohio. (MCJA Special Papers: No.5). (Illus.). 72p. 1984. pap. 9.95x (ISBN 0-87338-303-6). Kent St U Pr.

Greber, N'omi, jt. ed. see Brose, David S.

Grebing, Helga. The History of the German Labour Movement: A Survey. Korner, Edith, tr. from Ger. LC 84-73483. 204p. 1985. 22.50 (ISBN 0-907582-29-X, Pub. by Berg Pubs); pap. 8.95 (ISBN 0-907582-31-1). Longwood Pub Group.

Grebinger, P. Discovering Past Behavior: Experiments in the Archaeology of the American Southwest. (Library of Anthropology). 296p. 1978. 39.50 (ISBN 0-677-16080-1). Gordon.

Grebler, Leo. The Future of Thrift Institutions: A Study of Diversification Versus Specialization. 155p. 1971. pap. text ed. 2.50x (ISBN 0-8134-1428-8, 1428). Interstate.

Grebler, Leo, et al. Mexican American People: The Nation's Second Largest Minority. LC 73-81931. 1970. 45.00 (ISBN 0-02-912800-5). Free Pr.

Grebner, Bernice. Decanates: A Full View. rev. ed. 176p. 1980. 7.50 (ISBN 0-86690-109-4, 1153-01). Am Fed Astrologers.

--Everything Has a Phase. 216p. 1982. 12.00 (ISBN 0-86690-035-7, 2585-01). Am Fed Astrologers.

--Lunar Nodes. 72p. 1980. 6.00 (ISBN 0-86690-186-8, 1154-01). Am Fed Astrologers.

Grebnikov, E. A. & Ryabov, Yu A. Constructive Methods in the Analysis of Nonlinear Systems. 328p. 1983. 9.95 (ISBN 0-8285-2406-8, Pub. by Mir Pubs USSR). Imported Pubns.

Grebstein, Sheldon N. Hemingway's Craft. LC 70-183304. (Crosscurrents-Modern Critiques Ser.). 264p. 1973. 14.95 (ISBN 0-8093-0611-5). S Ill U Pr.

--John O'Hara. (Twayne's United States Authors Ser). 1966. pap. 5.95x (ISBN 0-8084-0187-4, T103, Twayne). New Coll U Pr.

--Sinclair Lewis. (Twayne's United States Authors Ser). 1962. pap. 5.95x (ISBN 0-8084-0278-1, T14, Twayne). New Coll U Pr.

--Sinclair Lewis. (United States Authors Ser.). lib. bdg. 13.95 (ISBN 0-8057-0448-5, Twayne). G K Hall.

Grech, P., ed. see Dun Karm.

Grech, P. F. Casualty Radiology. 1981. 46.95 (ISBN 0-8151-3998-5). Year Bk Med.

Grechko, A. The Armed Forces of the Soviet Union. 342p. 1977. 6.45 (ISBN 0-8285-0443-1, Pub. by Progress Pubs USSR). Imported Pubns.

Grechko, A., ed. Liberation Mission of the Soviet Armed Forces in Second World War. 512p. 1975. 5.45 (ISBN 0-8285-0483-0, Pub. by Progress Pubs USSR). Imported Pubns.

Greco, Ben. How to Get the Job That's Right for You: A Career Guide for the 80's. rev. ed. LC 79-56085. 210p. (Orig.). 1981. pap. 7.95 (ISBN 0-87094-194-1). Dow Jones-Irwin.

Greco, Eileen M. Ramblings in the Clover-Absorbing Shock. (Illus.). 48p. 1982. 5.00 (ISBN 0-682-49885-8). Exposition Pr FL.

Greco, F. Anthony, ed. Biology & Management of Lung Cancer. 1983. lib. bdg. 54.50 (ISBN 0-89838-554-7, Pub. by Martinus Nijhoff Netherlands). Kluwer Academic.

--Small Cell Lung Cancer. (Clinical Oncology Monograph). (Illus.). 463p. 1981. 49.00 (ISBN 0-8089-1345-X, 791721). Grune.

Greco, F. Anthony, jt. ed. see Fer, Mehmet.

Greco, M., ed. Proton-Antiproton Collider Physics 1985: Proceedings of the 5th Topical Workshop on Proton-Antiproton Collider Physics, Saint-Vincent Aosta Valley, 25 Feb.-March, 1985. 700p. 1985. 79.00 (ISBN 0-317-27165-2, Pub by World Sci Singapore). Taylor & Francis.

Greco, Marshall C. Group Life: The Nature & Treatment of Its Specific Conflicts. 357p. 1980. Repr. of 1950 ed. lib. bdg. 35.00 (ISBN 0-89984-229-1). Century Bookbindery.

Greco, S. & Salmon, P. Topics on M-Adic Topologies. LC 76-139730. (Ergebnisse der Mathematik und Ihrer Grenzgebiete: Vol. 58). 1971. 23.00 (ISBN 0-387-05091-4). Springer-Verlag.

Greco, S. & Strano, R., eds. Complete Intersections. (Lecture Notes in Mathematics Ser.: Vol. 1092). vii, 299p. 1984. pap. 18.50 (ISBN 0-387-13884-6). Springer-Verlag.

Grede, John F., jt. auth. see Harris, Norman C.

Gree & Camps. La Pandilla en el Zoo. 1980. 6.95 (ISBN 0-88332-253-6). Larousse.

--La Pandilla en la Carretera. 1980. 6.95 (ISBN 0-686-69157-1). Larousse.

Gree, Alain. Anchoring & Mooring Techniques Illustrated. Brackenbury, Mark, tr. from Fr. (Illus.). 176p. 1984. 22.50 (ISBN 0-229-11702-3, Pub. by Adlard Coles). Sheridan.

--Les Farfeluches aiment les Animaux-Love the Animals. (Illus., Fr.). 1980. 5.95 (ISBN 2-203-12313-3). Larousse.

--Farfeluches Apprennent a Compter. (Illus.). 1981. 5.95 (ISBN 0-88332-262-5, 2720). Larousse.

--Les Farfeluches font des achats. (Illus., Fr.). (gr. k-3). 1979. 5.95 (ISBN 0-88332-114-9, 2235). Larousse.

--Pandilla Elige un Oficio. (Illus.). (gr. 3). 1981. 6.95 (ISBN 84-261-1664-7). Larousse.

--Pandilla En la Orilla Del Mar. (Illus.). (gr. 3). 1981. 6.95 (ISBN 0-686-73331-2, 23980). Larousse.

--Sailing: A Basic Guide. (Illus.). 1980. 14.95 (ISBN 0-670-61523-4, The Vendome Pr.). Viking.

Gree, Alain & Camps, Luis. Les Farfeluches a la campagne. (Illus.). 1973. 5.95 (ISBN 0-88332-234-X, 2914). Larousse.

--Les Farfeluches a la maison. (Illus.). 1973. 5.95 (ISBN 0-88332-235-8, 2915). Larousse.

--Les Farfeluches a l'ecole. (Illus.). 1973. 5.95 (ISBN 0-88332-236-6, 2907). Larousse.

--Les Farfeluches au bord de la mer. (Illus.). 1973. 5.95 (ISBN 0-88332-237-4, 2913). Larousse.

--Les Farfeluches au cirque. (Illus.). 1973. 5.95 (ISBN 0-88332-238-2, 2916). Larousse.

--Les Farfeluches au marche. (Illus.). 1973. 5.95 (ISBN 0-88332-239-0, 2909). Larousse.

--Farfeluches autour du Monde. (Illus.). 1982. 5.95 (ISBN 2-203-12316-8, 2787). Larousse.

--La Pandilla en el Circo. (Illus., Span.). (gr. 3). 1979. 6.95 (ISBN 0-88332-112-2). Larousse.

--La Pandilla Va a las Tiendas. (Illus., Span.). (gr. 2). 1979. 6.95 (ISBN 0-88332-111-4). Larousse.

Greeber, Charlotte & Boddy, Joe. The Best Bike Ever. (The Mr. T & Me Ser.). (Illus.). 24p. (ps-4). 1985. pap. 1.95 (ISBN 0-8407-6641-6). Nelson.

--The Hand-Me-Down Cap. (The Mr. T & Me Ser.). (Illus.). 24p. (ps-4). pap. 1.95 (ISBN 0-8407-6637-8). Nelson.

--Phoney Baloney: The Counterfeit Kid. (The Mr. T & Me Ser.). (Illus.). 24p. (ps-4). 1985. pap. 1.95 (ISBN 0-8407-6642-4). Nelson.

--The Sidewalk Mockers. (The Mr. T & Me Ser.). (Illus.). 24p. (ps-4). 1985. pap. 1.95 (ISBN 0-8407-6639-4). Nelson.

--The Silver Squawk Box. (The Mr. T & Me Ser.). (Illus.). 24p. (ps-4). 1985. pap. 1.95 (ISBN 0-8407-6638-6). Nelson.

--The Somebody Kid. (Mr. T & Me Ser.). 24p. 1985. pap. 1.95 (ISBN 0-8407-6640-8). Nelson.

Greef, Albert O. The Commercial Paper House in the United States. facsimile ed. LC 75-2637. (Wall Street & the Security Market Ser.). 1975. Repr. of 1938 ed. 42.00x (ISBN 0-405-06962-6). Ayer Co Pubs.

Greeff, K., ed. Pharmacokinetics & Clinical Pharmacology of Caridac Clyscosides: Pharmacokinetics & Clinical Pharmacology of Caridac Clycosides. (Handbook of Experimental Pharmacology Ser.: Vol. 56). (Illus.). 394p. 1982. 126.00 (ISBN 0-387-10918-8). Springer-Verlag.

Gregg, R., jt. auth. see Hearle, J. W.

Greeley, A. M. Ethnicity. (Concilium Ser.: Vol. 101). 1977. pap. 6.95 (ISBN 0-8245-0261-2). Crossroad NY.

Greeley, Andrew. American Catholics Since the Council: An Unauthorized Report. (Illus.). 240p. (Orig.). 1985. pap. 14.95 (ISBN 0-88347-191-4). Thomas More.

--The Bottom Line Catechism for Contemporary Catholics. 304p. 1982. pap. 9.95 (ISBN 0-88347-135-3). Thomas More.

--The Catholic Why? Book. 167p. 1983. 9.95 (ISBN 0-88347-154-X). Thomas More.

--Death in April. 256p. (Orig.). 1984. pap. 3.95 (ISBN 0-440-01702-5, Emerald). Dell.

--Lord of the Dance. (Hall Large Print Bk.). lib. bdg. 18.95 (ISBN 0-8161-3797-8, Large Print Bks); pap. text ed. 11.95 (ISBN 0-8161-3807-9). G K Hall.

--The Magic Cup. 304p. 1985. pap. 3.50 (ISBN 0-446-32438-8). Warner Bks.

--Making of the Popes, Nineteen Seventy-Eight: The Politics of Intrigue in the Vatican. LC 79-14714. (Illus.). 1979. 12.95 (ISBN 0-8362-3100-7). Andrews McMeel Parker.

--Sexual Intimacy. 200p. 1982. pap. 8.95 (ISBN 0-88347-143-4). Thomas More.

Greeley, Andrew & Durkin, Mary. Angry Catholic Women. 1984. pap. 15.95 (ISBN 0-88347-165-5). Thomas More.

--A Church to Come Home to. 160p. 1982. 10.95 (ISBN 0-88347-141-8). Thomas More.

Greeley, Andrew & Durkin, Mary G. How to Save the Catholic Church. 288p. 1984. 16.95 (ISBN 0-670-38475-5, Elizabeth Sifton Bks). Viking.

Greeley, Andrew & McCready, William C. Ethnic Drinking Subcultures. LC 79-13904. 144p. 1980. 29.95 (ISBN 0-03-052731-7). Praeger.

Greeley, Andrew, ed. Ethnic Drinking Subcultures. 124p. 1980. 24.95x (ISBN 0-686-92320-0). Bergin & Garvey.

Greeley, Andrew, jt. ed. see Baum, Gregory.

Greeley, Andrew M. The American Catholic: A Social Portrait. LC 76-7683. (Illus.). pap. 8.95x (ISBN 0-465-09733-2, TB-5058). Basic.

--Ascent into Hell. LC 82-61879. 368p. (Orig.). 1984. 16.50 (ISBN 0-446-51254-0); pap. 3.95 (ISBN 0-446-30319-4). Warner Bks.

--Ascent into Hell. 633p. 1983. lib. bdg. 18.50 (ISBN 0-8161-3588-6, Large Print Bks). G K Hall.

--The Cardinal Sins. (Orig.). 1984. pap. 4.50 (ISBN 0-446-32839-1); 12.95 (ISBN 0-446-51236-2). Warner Bks.

--Catholic High Schools & Minority Students. LC 81-23131. (Illus.). 125p. 1982. 14.95 (ISBN 0-87855-452-1). Transaction Bks.

--Changing Catholic College. LC 67-27393. (NORC Monographs in Social Research Ser.: No. 13). 1967. 8.95x (ISBN 0-202-09011-6). NORC.

--The Communal Catholic: A Personal Manifesto. 220p. 1976. 2.00 (ISBN 0-8164-0299-X, Pub. by Seabury). Winston Pr.

--Denominational Society. LC 70-173239. 1975. pap. text ed. 8.95 (ISBN 0-394-33308-X, RanC). Random.

--Ethnicity in the United States: A Preliminary Reconnaissance. LC 74-11483. (Wiley Urban Research Ser.). Repr. of 1974 ed. 67.70 (ISBN 0-8357-9887-9, 2055177). Bks Demand UMI.

--The Great Mysteries: An Essential Catechism. 192p. (Orig.). 1976. pap. 8.95x (ISBN 0-8164-0309-0, AY7823, Pub. by Seabury). Winston Pr.

--Happy Are the Meek. 288p. 1985. pap. 3.95 (ISBN 0-446-32706-9). Warner Bks.

--The Irish Americans: The Rise to Money & Power. LC 81-47353. 215p. 1981. 14.37i (ISBN 0-06-038001-2). Har-Row.

--The Irish Americans: The Rise to Money & Power. 352p. cancelled (ISBN 0-8129-0907-0). Times Bks.

--The Jesus Myth. LC 75-160882. 200p. 1973. pap. 3.50 (ISBN 0-385-07865-X, Im). Doubleday.

--Lord of the Dance. 416p. (Orig.). 1985. 17.50 (ISBN 0-446-51292-3); pap. 4.50 (ISBN 0-446-32648-8). Warner Bks.

--The Magic Cup. LC 79-16720. 1979. 10.95 (ISBN 0-07-024250-X). McGraw.

--The Mary Myth: On the Femininity of God. 240p. 1977. 9.95 (ISBN 0-8164-0333-3, Pub. by Seabury). Winston Pr.

--Piece of My Mind on Just About Everything. LC 82-45966. 240p. 1985. pap. 7.95 (ISBN 0-385-23237-3, Im). Doubleday.

--Religion: A Secular Theory. 144p. 1982. text ed. 19.95 (ISBN 0-02-912870-6); pap. text ed. 8.95x (ISBN 0-02-912880-3). Free Pr.

--Religious Imagination. 14.95 (ISBN 0-8215-9876-7). Sadlier.

--Sexual Intimacy. 199p. 1975. pap. 6.95 (ISBN 0-8164-2591-4, Pub. by Seabury). Winston Pr.

--Thy Brother's Wife. LC 81-16239. 368p. (Orig.). 1982. 14.95 (ISBN 0-446-51245-1); pap. 3.95 (ISBN 0-446-30055-1). Warner Bks.

--Thy Brother's Wife. (General Ser.). 1982. lib. bdg. 15.95 (ISBN 0-8161-3416-2, Large Print Bks). G K Hall.

--Unsecular Man. rev. ed. 1985. pap. 8.95 (ISBN 0-8052-0794-5). Schocken.

--Virgin & Martyr. LC 84-40455. 448p. 1985. 17.50 (ISBN 0-446-51287-7). Warner Bks.

--Virgin & Martyr. 448p. 1986. pap. 4.95 (ISBN 0-446-32873-1). Warner Bks.

--Why Can't They Be Like Us? Facts & Fallacies About Ethnic Differences & Group Conflicts in America. LC 73-81091. (Institute of Human Relations Press Paperback Ser.). x, 76p. (Orig.). 1980. pap. 1.50 (ISBN 0-87495-009-0). Am Jewish Comm.

--Young Catholics in U. S. & Canada. 14.95 (ISBN 0-8215-9875-9). Sadlier.

Greeley, Andrew M. & Rossi, Peter H. Education of Catholic Americans. LC 66-10867. (NORC Monographs in Social Research Ser.: No. 6). 1966. 8.95x (ISBN 0-202-09003-5). NORC.

Greeley, Andrew M., ed. The Family in Crisis or in Transition. (Concilium: Vol. 121). (Orig.). 1979. pap. 6.95x (ISBN 0-8245-0282-5). Crossroad NY.

Greeley, Horace. American Conflict: A History of the Great Rebellion in the United States of America, 1860-1865, 2 vols. LC 69-18978. 1864-1866. Repr. 64.00x (ISBN 0-8371-1438-1, GAC&, Pub. by Negro U Pr). Greenwood.

--Divorce. LC 78-72342. (Free Love in America Ser.). Repr. of 1860 ed. 12.50 (ISBN 0-404-60952-X). AMS Pr.

--Essays Designed to Elucidate the Science of Political Economy. LC 73-38258. (The Evolution of Capitalism Ser.). 388p. 1972. Repr. of 1870 ed. 27.50 (ISBN 0-405-04122-5). Ayer Co Pubs.

--Essays Designed to Elucidate the Science of Political Economy, While Serving to Explain & Defend the Policy of Protection to Home Industry, As a System of National Cooperation for the Elevation of Labor. (The Neglected American Economists Ser.). 1975. lib. bdg. 61.00 (ISBN 0-8240-1006-X). Garland Pub.

--History of the Struggle for Slavery Extension or Restriction in the U. S. From the Declaration of Independence to the Present Day. facs. ed. LC 70-133154. (Black Heritage Library Collection Ser). 1856. 15.25 (ISBN 0-8369-8709-8). Ayer Co Pubs.

--Recollections of a Busy Life. facs. ed. LC 74-83912. (Black Heritage Library Collection Ser). 1868. 23.50 (ISBN 0-8369-8582-6). Ayer Co Pubs.

--Recollections of a Busy Life. LC 74-125695. (American Journalists Ser). 1970. Repr. of 1868 ed. 23.50 (ISBN 0-405-01674-3). Ayer Co Pubs.

--Recollections of a Busy Life, 2 Vols. LC 71-137913. (American History & Culture in the Nineteenth Century Ser). 1971. Repr. of 1873 ed. Set. 66.50x (ISBN 0-8046-1481-4, Pub. by Kennikat). Assoc Faculty Pr.

--What I Know of Farming. facsimile ed. LC 74-30631. (American Farmers & the Rise of Agribusiness Ser.). 1975. Repr. of 1871 ed. 30.00x (ISBN 0-405-06800-X). Ayer Co Pubs.

--What I Know of Farming: A Series of Brief & Plain Expositions of Practical Agriculture As an Art Based upon Science. LC 72-89058. (Rural America Ser.). 1973. Repr. of 1871 ed. 29.00 (ISBN 0-8420-1484-5). Scholarly Res Inc.

Greeley, Horace & Cleveland, John F. Political Text-Book for Eighteen Sixty. LC 69-18979. Repr. of 1860 ed. 25.00x (ISBN 0-8371-0986-8, GRP&). Greenwood.

Greeley, Horace, ed. The American Laborer, Devoted to the Cause of Protection to Home Industry, Embracing the Arguments, Reports & Speeches of the Ablest Civilians of the United States in Favor of the Policy of Protection to American Labor. (The Neglected American Economists Ser.). 1974. lib. bdg. 61.00 (ISBN 0-8240-1005-1). Garland Pub.

Greeley, Horace, ed. see Clay, Cassius M.

Greeley, Horace, ed. & pref. by see Clay, Cassius M.

Greeley, Horace, ed. see Sargent, Epes.

Greeley, Margaret. The Cancer Patient's Handbook. LC 78-70591. (Illus.). 1978. pap. 8.50 (ISBN 0-932904-01-7). Magoos Umbrella.

Greeley, Peg. Tennis Charting: The Graphic Way. Tucker, Jackie, ed. (Illus., Orig.). 1981. pap. 6.95 (ISBN 0-932904-02-5). Magoos Umbrella.

Greeley, R., jt. auth. see Guest, J. E.

Greeley, R. G., jt. auth. see Piermattei, D. L.

Greeley, Roger E., ed. The Best of Robert Ingersoll. rev. ed. LC 77-90495. 1982. pap. 11.95 (ISBN 0-87975-209-2). Prometheus Bks.

Greeley, Ronald. Planetary Landscapes. (Illus.). 256p. 1985. 39.95x (ISBN 0-04-551080-6). Allen Unwin.

Greeley, Valerie. A Book of Days. (Illus.). 128p. 1984. 7.95 (ISBN 0-911745-85-8, Bedrick Blackie). P Bedrick Bks.

--Farm Animals. LC 83-22508. (Illus.). 12p. 1984. bds. 3.50 (ISBN 0-911745-22-X, Bedrick Blackie). P Bedrick Bks.

Greeley, Valerie, illus. Field Animals. LC 83-22507. (Illus.). 12p. 1984. bds. 3.50 (ISBN 0-911745-23-8, Bedrick Blackie). P Bedrick Bks.

--Pets. LC 83-22509. (Illus.). 12p. 1984. bds. 3.50 (ISBN 0-911745-21-1, Bedrick Blackie). P Bedrick Bks.

--Zoo Animals. LC 83-22513. (Illus.). 12p. 1984. 3.50 (ISBN 0-911745-24-6, Bedrick Blackie). P Bedrick Bks.

Greeley, William B. Forests & Men. LC 72-2840. (Use & Abuse of America's Natural Resources Ser). 260p. 1972. Repr. of 1951 ed. 18.00 (ISBN 0-405-04508-5). Ayer Co Pubs.

Greely, Adolphus W. Handbook of Alaska: Its Resources, Products & Attractions in 1924. LC 70-118420. 1970. Repr. of 1925 ed. 33.50x (ISBN 0-8046-1372-9, Pub. by Kennikat). Assoc Faculty Pr.

Greely, John N., tr. see Ardant Du Picq, Charles J.

Greely, Margaret. Arabian Exodus. (Illus.). write for info. (ISBN 0-85131-223-3, NL51, Dist. by Miller). J A Allen.

Greeman, Phillip, tr. see Dvorak, Jiri, et al.

Greeman, Richard, tr. see Serge, Victor.

Green. Consumers in the Economy. (gr. 9-12). 1983. text ed. 10.70 (ISBN 0-538-08460-X, H46). SW Pub.

--Directions & Directing. 2.00 (ISBN 0-86690-111-6). Am Fed Astrologers.

--The Georgia Law of Evidence. 2nd ed. latest pocket part supplement 79.95_incl. (ISBN 0-686-90331-5); separate pocket part supplement, 1984 17.95. Harrison Co GA.

--A Hobbit's Journal. LC 79-20203. pap. 4.95 (ISBN 0-89471-090-7); 12.90 (ISBN 0-89471-089-3). Running Pr.

--A Hobbit's Travels. LC 78-15318. pap. 4.95 (ISBN 0-89471-040-0); 12.90 (ISBN 0-89471-041-9). Running Pr.

--Nutrition in Contemporary Nursing Practice. 2nd ed. Date not set. price not set (ISBN 0-471-82468-2). Wiley.

--The Rattlesnake. Schroeder, Howard, ed. LC 83-20865. (Wildlife Ser.: Habits & Habitat). (Illus.). 48p. (gr. 4-5). 1984. PLB 9.95 (ISBN 0-89686-247-X). Crestwood Hse.

--Speech Reading Theory & Application. cancelled (ISBN 0-8391-1838-4, 20044). Univ Park.

--The Thyroid. Date not set. price not set (ISBN 0-444-00858-6). Elsevier.

--The Unicorn Notebook. LC 81-10670. pap. 4.95 (ISBN 0-89471-146-6); 12.90 (ISBN 0-89471-147-4). Running Pr.

--Welcome to the Planet Earth. 8.95 (ISBN 0-89471-154-7); 19.80 (ISBN 0-89471-125-3). Running Pr.

Green & Bourne. Reliability Technology. 636p. 99.95 (ISBN 0-318-13243-5). Am Soc QC.

Green & Nessen. Problems, Cases & Materials on Evidence. 1983. text ed. 31.00 (ISBN 0-316-32646-1). Little.

Green, jt. auth. see Weiner.

Green, ed. see Shakespeare, William.

Green, jt. auth. see Brickel Assoc., Inc.

Green, A. Aynsley see Aynsley-Green, A.

Green, A. C. Texas Sketches. (Illus.). 160p. 1985. 14.95 (ISBN 0-87833-519-6). Taylor Pub.

Green, A. E. High Risk Safety Technology. LC 81-19781. 654p. 1982. 69.95x (ISBN 0-471-10153-2). Wiley.

--Safety Systems Reliability. LC 82-24863. 293p. 1984. 41.95x (ISBN 0-471-90144-X, Pub. by Wiley-Interscience). Wiley.

--Witches & Witch Hunters. (Folklore Ser). lib. bdg. 25.00 (ISBN 0-8482-4251-3). Norwood Edns.

Green, A. E. & Bourne, A. J. Reliability Technology. LC 73-161691. 636p. 1972. 114.00 (ISBN 0-471-32480-9). Wiley.

Green, A. E., ed. An Alternative to Oil: Burning Coal with Gas; the Benefits of Burning Coal & Natural Gas Mixtures in Boilers Originally Designed for Oil. LC 82-1894. (Illus.). xi, 140p. (Orig.). 1982. pap. 8.95 (ISBN 0-8130-0724-0). U Presses Fla.

--Coal Burning Issues. LC 79-25376. (Illus.). x, 390p. (Orig.). 1980. pap. 12.00 (ISBN 0-8130-0667-8). U Presses Fla.

Green, A. E., ed. see International Conference on The Nuclear Optical Model.

Green, A. E., et al. Nuclear Independent Particle Model. 1968. 77.00 (ISBN 0-12-297450-6). Acad Pr.

Green, A. H. & Hall, P. E. Production Control Implementation. 46p. 1977. pap. 19.00x (ISBN 0-85012-165-5). Intl Pubns Serv.

Green, A. Richard & Costain, David W. Pharmacology & Biochemistry of Psychiatric Disorders. 217p. 1981. 39.95x (ISBN 0-471-09998-8); pap. 19.95 (ISBN 0-471-10000-5). Wiley.

Green, A. Romney. A Craftman's Anthology. 1979. Repr. of 1948 ed. lib. bdg. 25.00 (ISBN 0-8495-2021-5). Arden Lib.

Green, A. S. Women's Place in the World of Letters. 1977. Repr. of 1913 ed. 10.00 (ISBN 0-8274-4321-8). R West.

Green, A. Wigfall. Inns of Court & Early English Drama. 1931. 49.50x (ISBN 0-686-83590-5). Elliots Bks.

--The Man Bilbo. LC 76-28416. 1976. Repr. of 1963 ed. lib. bdg. 15.00x (ISBN 0-8371-9103-3, GRTM). Greenwood.

Green, A. Wigfall, jt. ed. see Webb, James W.

Green, Abel & Laurie, Joe, Jr. Show Biz, from Vaude to Video. LC 82-49223. (Cinema Classics Ser.). 613p. 1985. lib. bdg. 60.00 (ISBN 0-8240-5761-9). Garland Pub.

Green Acres School. Going Places with Children in Washington. 11th, rev. ed. Shannon, Salley & Phang, Ruth A., eds. LC 84-81568. (Illus.). 256p. (Orig.). 1985. pap. 5.95 (ISBN 0-9608998-1-2). Green Acres Schl.

Green, Adam B. Advanced dBASE II User's Guide. (Illus.). 160p. 1984. pap. 29.00 (ISBN 0-13-011271-2). P-H.

--The dBASE II User's Guide. 151p. 1983. 29.00 (ISBN 0-13-196519-0). P-H.

Green, Adele, jt. auth. see Nitsche, Richard A.

Green, Alan, jt. auth. see Kahaner, Larry.

Green, Alan & Hogan, Bill, eds. City, State & Regional Media Directory. 160p. looseleaf 46.00 (ISBN 0-9614280-0-7). City Desk.

Green, Albert. That Girl from Texas. 72p. 1976. pap. 2.50 (ISBN 0-88680-190-7); royalty 35.00 (ISBN 0-317-03594-0). I E Clark.

Green, Alex, pseud. Money Magic: Incredible Low-Risk Way to Build your Fortune. LC 82-82535. (Illus.). 117p. (Orig.). 1983. pap. 5.95 (ISBN 0-910067-00-7). G K Pr.

Green, Alex E., ed. The Middle Ultraviolet: Its Science & Technology. LC 66-22839. (Wiley Series in Pure & Applied Optics). pap. 101.50 (ISBN 0-317-09204-9, 2007393). Bks Demand UMI.

Green, Alexander. Dative of Agency: A Chapter of Indo-European Case-Syntax. LC 14-1364. (Columbia University. Germanic Studies, Old Ser.: No. 17). Repr. of 1913 ed. 14.00 (ISBN 0-404-50417-5). AMS Pr.

Green, Alice S. Irish Nationality. 1977. Repr. lib. bdg. 12.50 (ISBN 0-8492-0911-0). R West.

--The Making of Ireland & Its Undoing 1200-1600. facsimile ed. LC 75-37883. (Select Bibliographies Reprint Ser). Repr. of 1908 ed. 27.50 (ISBN 0-8369-6720-8). Ayer Co Pubs.

--Town Life in the Fifteenth Century, 2 Vols. LC 70-171443. 920p. Repr. of 1894 ed. Set. 40.00 (ISBN 0-405-08575-3, Blom Pubns); 20.00 ea. Vol. 1 (ISBN 0-405-08576-1). Vol. 2 (ISBN 0-405-08577-X). Ayer Co Pubs.

Green, Andre. The Tragic Effect. Sheridan, Alan, tr. LC 76-12629. 1979. 34.50 (ISBN 0-521-21377-0). Cambridge U Pr.

Green, Andrew. Haunted Houses. (Shire Album Ser.: No. 7). 1985. pap. 3.50 (ISBN 0-85263-460-9, Pub. by Shire Pubns England). Seven Hills Bks.

Green, Andrew, ed. Emerging High Performance Structural Plastic Technology. LC 82-70767. 85p. 1982. pap. 16.00x (ISBN 0-87262-305-X). Am Soc Civil Eng.

Green, Ann, tr. see Peguy, Charles P.

Green, Anna K. The Circular Study. LC 75-44978. (Crime Fiction Ser). 1976. Repr. of 1900 ed. lib. bdg. 21.00 (ISBN 0-8240-2372-2). Garland Pub.

--Circular Study. 1976. lib. bdg. 12.95x (ISBN 0-89968-170-0). Lightyear.

--A Difficult Problem: The Staircase at the Heart's Delight. 1972. Repr. of 1900 ed. text ed. 26.00x (ISBN 0-8422-8061-8). Irvington.

--The Filigree Ball: Account of the Solution of the Mystery Concerning the Jeffrey-Moore Affair. LC 75-32778. (Literature of Mystery & Detection). (Illus.). 1976. Repr. of 1903 ed. 32.00x (ISBN 0-405-07873-0). Ayer Co Pubs.

--The Leavenworth Case. 352p. 1982. pap. 5.00 (ISBN 0-486-23865-2). Dover.

--The Leavenworth Case. 1976. lib. bdg. 12.95x (ISBN 0-89968-171-9). Lightyear.

--The Leavenworth Case: A Lawyer's Story. LC 79-104467. 481p. Repr. of 1878 ed. lib. bdg. 11.25 (ISBN 0-8398-0666-3). Irvington.

--Old Stone House, & Other Stories. facs. ed. LC 71-132117. (Short Story Index Reprint Ser). 1891. 13.00 (ISBN 0-8369-3674-4). Ayer Co Pubs.

Green, Anne. Flaubert & the Historical Novel: Salammbo Reassessed. LC 81-6085. 220p. 1982. 44.50 (ISBN 0-521-23765-3). Cambridge U Pr.

Green, Anthony. A Green Part of the World. 520p. 1984. pap. 9.95 (ISBN 0-14-007554-2). Penguin.

Green, Archie. Only a Miner: Studies in Recorded Coal-Mining Songs. LC 78-155499. (Music in American Life Ser). (Illus.). 518p. 1972. 20.00x (ISBN 0-252-00181-8). U of Ill Pr.

Green, Arnold H. The Tunisian Ulama 1873-1915: Social Structure & Response to Ideological Currents. (Social, Economic & Political Studies of the Middle East: No. 22). (Illus.). 1978. text ed. 55.25x (ISBN 90-04-05687-4). Humanities.

Green, Arthur. Child Maltreatment: A Handbook for Mental Health Professionals & Child Care Workers. LC 80-66923. 300p. 1980. 25.00 (ISBN 0-87668-420-7). Aronson.

--Tormented Master: A Life of Rabbi Nahman of Bratslav. LC 80-14668. 408p. 1981. pap. 11.95 (ISBN 0-8052-0663-9). Schocken.

--Tormented Master: A Life of Rabbi Nahman of Bratslav. LC 78-16674. (Judaic Studies: No. 9). (Illus.). 400p. 1979. 30.00 (ISBN 0-8173-6907-4). U of Ala Pr.

Green, Ashbel, ed. see Houston, James D.

Green, Ashbel, ed. see Junior League of Washington.

Green, Ashbel, ed. see Kahin, George McT.

Green, Ashbel, ed. see Morgentau, Hans J. & Thompson, Kenneth W.

Green, Ashbel, ed. see Norrell, Robert J.

Green, Ashbel, ed. see Wilford, John N.

Green, B. S. & Ashani, Y. Chemical Approaches to Understanding Enzyme Catalysis: Biomimetic Chemistry & Transition State Analogs. (Studies in Organic Chemistry: Vol. 10). 356p. 1982. 91.50 (ISBN 0-444-42063-0). Elsevier.

Green, B. S. & Johns, E. A. An Introduction to Sociology. 1967. pap. 7.00 (ISBN 0-08-012154-3). Pergamon.

Green, Barth, et al, eds. Intensive Care for Neurological Trauma & Disease. LC 82-8903. 390p. 1982. 37.00 (ISBN 0-12-788284-7). Acad Pr.

Green, Ben. Finest Kind: A Celebration of a Florida Fishing Village. LC 85-5664. (Illus.). 271p. 1985. 19.95 (ISBN 0-86554-159-0, MUP H149). Mercer Univ Pr.

Green, Ben K. The Color of Horses. LC 74-79459. (Illus.). 120p. 1974. O.P. 25.00 (ISBN 0-87358-131-8); softcover 12.95 (ISBN 0-87358-327-2). Northland.

--Horse Conformation: As to Soundness & Performance. LC 74-82362. (Illus.). 1974. Repr. 9.95 (ISBN 0-87358-135-0). Northland.

--Horse Tradin' (Illus.). (YA) 1967. 14.95 (ISBN 0-394-42929-X). Knopf.

--Some More Horse Tradin' (Illus.). (YA) 1972. 15.00 (ISBN 0-394-46123-1). Knopf.

--A Thousand Miles of Mustangin' LC 72-76378. (Illus.). 148p. 1972. 8.95 (ISBN 0-87358-098-2). Northland.

--Village Horse Doctor, West of the Pecos. LC 79-118716. (YA) 1971. 14.95 (ISBN 0-394-42922-2). Knopf.

--Wild Cow Tales. (Illus.). (YA) 1969. 13.95 (ISBN 0-394-45188-0). Knopf.

Green, Benjamin. The Basic Guide to Pictorial Perspective. (A Promotion of the Arts Library). (Illus.). 97p. 1981. 69.45 (ISBN 0-86650-001-4). Gloucester Art.

Green, Benny. Drums in My Ears: Jazz in Our Time. LC 72-96368. 1973. 5.95 (ISBN 0-8180-1209-9). Horizon.

--P. G. Wodehouse: A Literary Biography. (Illus.). 272p. 1981. 12.95 (ISBN 0-8317-6863-0, Rutledge Pr). Smith Pubs.

--The Reluctant Art: The Growth of Jazz. (New Reprints in Essay & General Literature Index Ser.). 1975. Repr. of 1963 ed. 20.25 (ISBN 0-518-10199-1, 10199). Ayer Co Pubs.

--The Streets of London: Moments in Time from the Albums of Charles White & London Transport. (Illus.). 192p. 1983. 19.95 (ISBN 0-907516-20-3, Pub. by Michael Joseph). Merrimack Pub Cir.

--The Streets of London: Moments in Time from the Albums of Charles White & London Transport. (Illus.). 192p. 1985. pap. 11.95 (ISBN 0-907516-59-9, Pub. by Michael Joseph). Merrimack Pub Cir.

Green, Benny, compiled by. London. (Small Oxford Bks.). 1984. 9.95 (ISBN 0-19-214143-0). Oxford U Pr.

Green, Bernard. Getting over Getting High: How to Overcome Dependency on Cocaine, Caffeine, Hallucinogens, Marijuana, Speed & Other Stimulants the Natural & Permanent Way. LC 84-10814. 256p. 1984. 15.95 (ISBN 0-688-03948-0); pap. 6.95 (ISBN 0-688-03949-9). Morrow.

--Your Child Is Bright. 192p. 1982. 11.95 (ISBN 0-312-89771-5). St Martin.

Green, Bernard & Schwarz, Ted. Goodbye, Blues: A Guide to Breaking the Tranquilizer Habit the Natural Way. LC 80-21551. 224p. 1981. 10.95 (ISBN 0-07-024337-9); pap. 5.95 (ISBN 0-07-024338-7). McGraw.

Green, Bert F., Jr., jt. ed. see Hulse, Stewart H.

Green, Bette. Summer of My German Soldier. 208p. 1981. pap. 2.50 (ISBN 0-553-24565-1). Bantam.

Green, Betty & Irish, Donald, eds. Death Education: Preparation for Living. LC 70-145965. 142p. 1971. pap. 8.95 (ISBN 0-87073-961-1). Schenkman Bks Inc.

Green, Bill. Alcoholism. Rahmas, Sigurd C., ed. (Topics of Our Times Ser.: No. 19). 32p. (Orig.). 1982. 3.50x (ISBN 0-87157-820-4); pap. text ed. 1.95 (ISBN 0-87157-320-2). SamHar Pr.

--The Dancing Was Lively: Fort Concho, Texas: A Social History, 1867 to 1882. LC 74-81921. (Illus.). 152p. 1974. 12.50 (ISBN 0-686-08963-4). Fort Concho.

--J. R. R. Tolkien, Master of Fantasy. Rahmas, Sigurd C., ed. (Outstanding Personalities Ser.: No. 91). 32p. (gr. 9-12). 1982. 3.50 (ISBN 0-87157-591-4); pap. text ed. 1.95 (ISBN 0-87157-091-2). SamHar Pr.

--Jack Dempsey: Champion Heavyweight Boxer. LC 74-14588. (Outstanding Personalities Ser.). 32p. 1974. lib. bdg. 3.50 incl. catalog cards (ISBN 0-87157-576-0); pap. 1.95 vinyl laminated covers (ISBN 0-87157-076-9). SamHar Pr.

Green, Billie. The Count from Wisconsin. (Loveswept Ser.: No. 75). 320p. 1985. pap. 2.25 (ISBN 0-553-21682-1). Bantam.

--Dreams of Joe. (Loveswept Ser.: No. 87). 208p. (Orig.). 1985. pap. 2.25 (ISBN 0-553-21661-9). Bantam.

--The Last Hero. (Loveswept Ser.: No. 65). 208p. (Orig.). 1984. pap. 2.25 (ISBN 0-553-21673-2). Bantam.

Green, Bob, jt. auth. see Bryant, Anita.

Green, Brain, jt. auth. see Jeeves, Malcolm A.

Green, Brian M. Confederate States Lithographs Issues. (Illus.). 66p. 1978. Set of Five. 5.60 (ISBN 0-911989-06-4). Philatelic Found.

--The Confederate States of America Two Cent Red Jack Intaglio Stamp. (Illus.). 62p. 1983. pap. 6.00 (ISBN 0-911989-12-9). Philatelic Found.

--Confederate States Typographs Issues. 40p. 1981. 4.00 (ISBN 0-911989-05-6). Philatelic Found.

Green, Bryan. Being & Believing. 96p. 1982. pap. 1.15 (ISBN 0-88028-016-6). Forward Movement.

--Saints Alive. 112p. 1977. pap. 1.10 (ISBN 0-88028-029-8). Forward Movement.

Green, Bryan S. Knowing the Poor: A Case Study in Textual Reality Construction. (International Library of Phenomology & Moral Sciences). 224p. 1983. 25.95x (ISBN 0-7100-9282-2). Routledge & Kegan.

Green, Bryn. Countryside Conservation. (The Resource Management Ser.: No. 3). (Illus.). 272p. 1981. text ed. 35.00x (ISBN 0-04-719001-9). Allen Unwin.

--Countryside Conservation. 2nd ed. (The Resource Management Ser.: No. 3). 256p. (Orig.). 1985. text ed. 35.00x (ISBN 0-04-719005-1); pap. text ed. 17.95x (ISBN 0-04-719006-X). Allen Unwin.

Green, Burchenal, jt. ed. see Ahl, David H.

Green, Burchenal, jt. ed. see Taylor, Robert.

Green, C. Tale of Theodore Bear. LC 68-56812. (Illus.). (gr. 1-2). 1968. PLB 9.26 (ISBN 0-87783-038-X). Oddo.

Green, C. & Bourgue, R. Theory & Servicing of AM, FM & FM Stereo Receivers. 1980. 31.95 (ISBN 0-13-913590-1). P-H.

Green, C. J. Animal Anaesthesia. 300p. 1981. 90.00x (ISBN 0-901334-08-1, Pub. by Lab Animals England). State Mutual Bk.

Green, C. J., et al, eds. Airframe & Systems Fitting. 2nd ed. (Engineering Craftsmen: No. H9). (Illus.). 1973. spiral bdg. 39.95x (ISBN 0-85083-218-7). Trans-Atlantic.

Green, Cadida L., jt. auth. see Evans, Tony.

Green, Calvin C. Counseling: With the Pastor & CPE Student in Mind. 1984. 12.95 (ISBN 0-533-05923-2). Vantage.

Green, Candida L., jt. auth. see Evans, Tony.

Green, Carl, jt. auth. see Sanford, William.

Green, Carl R., jt. auth. see Sanford, William R.

Green, Carol. Dressage Explained. (Practical Horse Guides Ser.). 96p. 1985. 7.95 (ISBN 0-668-06439-0); pap. 4.95 (ISBN 0-668-06443-9). Arco.

--Eventing Explained. (Horseman's Handbooks). 1978. 6.95 (ISBN 0-668-04383-0). Arco.

--Jumping Explained. (Practical Horse Guides Ser.). 1985. 7.95 (ISBN 0-668-06436-6); pap. 4.95 (ISBN 0-668-06440-4). Arco.

--Training Explained. (Illus.). 1977. 6.95 (ISBN 0-668-04110-2). Arco.

--Training Explained. (Practical Horse Guides Ser.). 1985. 7.95 (ISBN 0-668-06438-2); pap. 4.95 (ISBN 0-668-06442-0). Arco.

Green, Carol H., jt. ed. see Mason, Mary G.

Green, Carol Hurd, jt. ed. see Sicherman, Barbara.

Green, Carolyn & Jaeger, Christi. Teacher, Kids, & LOGO. 160p. 1984. pap. 18.95 (ISBN 0-9612226-0-3). Educomp Pubns.

Green, Carolyna. Vagabond Healer. LC 82-90766. 227p. 1983. pap. text ed. 6.95 (ISBN 0-936958-02-2). Emerald Hse.

Green, Catherine. George Bellows: Works from the Permanent Collection of the Albright-Knox Art Gallery. LC 81-68250. (Illus.). 24p. 1982. pap. 2.00 (ISBN 0-914782-41-X). Buffalo Acad.

Green, Cecile. The Tale of Theodore Bear. (Illus.). (gr. 1-2). 1978. pap. 1.25 (ISBN 0-89508-060-5). Rainbow Bks.

Green, Celia. Advice to Clever Children. 20.00x (ISBN 0-900076-07-0, Pub. by Inst Psyc Res UK). State Mutual Bk.

--The Decline & Fall of Science. 1977. 18.95x (ISBN 0-900076-06-2). State Mutual Bk.

--The Human Evasion. 18.95x (ISBN 0-900076-02-X, Pub. by Inst Psyc Res UK). State Mutual Bk.

--Lucid Dreams. 20.00x (ISBN 0-900076-00-3, Pub. by Inst Psyc Res UK). State Mutual Bk.

--Out-of-the-Body Experiences. 20.95x (ISBN 0-900076-01-1, Pub. by Inst Psyc Res UK). State Mutual Bk.

Green, Celia & McCreery, Charles. Apparitions. 1977. 18.95x (ISBN 0-900076-05-4, Pub. by Inst Psyc Res UK). State Mutual Bk.

Green, Charles. All about Crystal Sets: How to Build Crystal Set Radios. (Illus.). 58p. (Orig.). 1984. pap. 7.95 (ISBN 0-930003-00-4). Allabout Bks.

--Edward Albee: An Anotated Bibliography, 1968-1977. LC 79-8633. (AMS Studies in Modern Literature: No. 6). 1980. 22.50 (ISBN 0-404-18014-0). AMS Pr.

--Elitism Versus Democracy. 85p. (Orig.). 1985. pap. 6.95 (ISBN 0-932269-29-X). Wyndham Hall.

Green, Charles & Walker, Mortcompiled by. The National Cartoonists Society Album. (Illus.). 174p. 1980. pap. 8.50 (ISBN 0-318-15258-4). Natl Cartoonists.

Green, Christopher. Leger & the Avant-Garde. LC 75-11499. 1976. 62.00x (ISBN 0-300-01800-2). Yale U Pr.

--Making Maps. (Young Geologist Ser.). (Illus.). 24p. (gr. 1-4). 1982. 5.95 (ISBN 0-370-30465-9, Pub. by the Bodley Head). Merrimack Pub Cir.

--Polar Lands. (The Young Geographer Ser.). (Illus.). 24p. (gr. 1-5). 1984. 6.95 (ISBN 0-370-30812-3, Pub. by the Bodley Head). Merrimack Pub Cir.

--Toddler Taming. 256p. 1985. pap. 5.95 (ISBN 0-449-90155-6, Columbine). Fawcett.

Green, Clarence C. Neo-Classic Theory of Tragedy in England During the 18th Century. LC 65-27913. 1934. 15.00 (ISBN 0-405-08578-8, Pub. by Blom). Ayer Co Pubs.

Green, Clarence R. Technical Physics. (Illus.). 832p. 1984. 29.95 (ISBN 0-13-898387-9). P-H.

Green, Clifford, tr. see Bonhoeffer, Dietrich.

Green, Constance & Lomask, Milton. Vanguard: A History. LC 70-606624. (Illus.). 309p. 1971. text ed. 19.95x (ISBN 0-87474-112-2). Smithsonian.

Green, Constance M. Eli Whitney & the Birth of American Technology. (The Library of American Biography). 1965. pap. 6.95 (ISBN 0-316-32621-6). Little.

--Secret City: A History of Race Relations in the Nation's Capital. 1967. 38.00x (ISBN 0-691-04563-1); pap. 9.95 (ISBN 0-691-00568-0). Princeton U Pr.

--Washington: A History of the Capital. 1976. pap. 13.50 (ISBN 0-691-00585-0). Princeton U Pr.

--Washington: Capital City, 1879-1950, Vol. II. 1976. 38.00x (ISBN 0-691-04573-9). Princeton U Pr.

--Washington: Village & Capital, 1800-1878, Vol. I. 1976. 38.00x (ISBN 0-691-04572-0). Princeton U Pr.

Green, Cynthia B., jt. auth. see Caro, Francis G.

Green, D., jt. auth. see Perry, R. H.

Green, D., ed. Cobbett's Tour in Scotland. 224p. 1984. 20.00 (ISBN 0-08-030376-5); pap. 11.00 (ISBN 0-08-030384-6). Pergamon.

--Cobbett's Tour in Scotland. 201p. 1984. text ed. 24.25x (Pub. by Aberdeen U Scotland). Humanities.

Green, D. G. The Welfare State: For Rich or For Poor? (Institute of Economic Affairs, Occasional Papers Ser.: No. 63). pap. 4.75 technical (ISBN 0-255-36154-8). Transatlantic.

Green, D. H. The Art of Recognition in Wolfram's "Parzifal". LC 82-1283. 400p. 1982. 69.50 (ISBN 0-521-24500-1). Cambridge U Pr.

Green, D. M. An Introduction to Hearing. 353p. 1976. 24.95x (ISBN 0-89859-121-X). L Erlbaum Assocs.

Green, D. R. & Lewis, J. Science with Pocket Calculators. (The Wykeham Science Ser.: No. 48). 300p. 1978. write for info (ISBN 0-85109-660-3); pap. cancelled (ISBN 0-85109-560-7). Taylor & Francis.

Green, Dallas W. Chief Joseph's Alps. 1972. 5.95x (ISBN 0-87315-003-1). Golden Bell.

Green, Dan S., ed. see Du Bois, W. E. B.

Green, Dana S., ed. Chasms in the Americas. (Illus., Orig.). 1970. pap. 1.95 (ISBN 0-377-10251-2). Friend Pr.

Green, Daniel. Great Cobbett: The Noblest Agitator. (Illus.). 496p. 1984. 24.95 (ISBN 0-340-22378-2, Pub. by Hodder & Stoughton UK). David & Charles.

Green, David. Carving in Wood: A Personal Approach to an Old Craft. (Illus.). 144p. 1982. 19.95 (ISBN 0-575-02964-1, Pub. by Gollancz England). David & Charles.

--Marble Mountain Wilderness. Winnett, Thomas, ed. LC 79-57598. (Illus.). 168p. (Orig.). 1980. pap. 11.95 (ISBN 0-911824-93-6). Wilderness Pr.

--A Pacific Crest Odyssey. Winnett, Thomas, ed. LC 79-66298. (Illus.). 158p. (Orig.). 1979. pap. 7.95 (ISBN 0-911824-91-X). Wilderness Pr.

--Pottery Glazes. new rev. ed. (Illus.). 144p. (YA) 1973. 14.50 (ISBN 0-8230-4217-0). Watson-Guptill.

Green, David, ed. see Jewett, Sarah O.

Green, David B. & Wilson, Edwin G., eds. Keats, Shelley, Byron, Hunt & Their Circles: A Bibliography, July 1, 1950-June 30, 1962. LC 64-15181. Repr. of 1964 ed. 83.30 (ISBN 0-8357-9708-2, 2016337). Bks Demand UMI.

Green, David C. Julius Caesar & It's Sources. (Salzburg Institute for English Literature Jacobean Drama Studies: No. 86). (Orig.). 1980. pap. text ed. 25.50x (ISBN 0-391-01715-2). Humanities.

Green, David E., tr. see Becker, Joachim.

Green, David E., tr. see Botterweck, G. Johannes & Ringgren, Helmer.

Green, David E., tr. see Hahn, Ferdinand.

Green, David E., tr. see Ringgren, Helmer.

Green, David E., tr. see Schweizer, Eduard.

Green, David E., tr. see Westermann, Claus.

Green, David G. Plutarch Revisited. A Study of Shakespeare's Last Roman Tragedies & Their Source. (SSEL Jacobean Drama Studies: No. 78). (Orig.). pap. text ed. 25.50x (ISBN 0-391-01608-3). Humanities.

--Power & Party in an English City. (New Local Government Ser.: No. 20). 256p. 1981. text ed. 37.50x (ISBN 0-04-352094-4). Allen Unwin.

--Working-Class Patients & the Medical Establishment. 224p. 1985. 27.50 (ISBN 0-312-88980-1). St Martin.

Green, David, Jr. Accounting for Corporate Retained Earnings. Brief, Richard P., ed. LC 80-1496. (Dimensions of Accounting Theory & Practice Ser.). 1981. lib. bdg. 14.00x (ISBN 0-405-13490-8). Ayer Co Pubs.

Green, David M. & Swets, John A. Signal Detection Theory & Psychophysics. rev. ed. LC 66-21059. 494p. 1974. Repr. of 1966 ed. 27.50 (ISBN 0-88275-139-5). Krieger.

Green, David P. Operative Hand Surgery, 2 Vols. (Illus.). 1936p. 1982. 170.00 (ISBN 0-443-08090-9). Churchill.

Green, David P., jt. auth. see Rockwood, Charles A., Jr.

Green, David R. & Lewis, John. Science with Pocket Calculators. LC 78-57665. (Wykeham Science Ser.: No. 48). 220p. 1979. 27.50x (ISBN 0-8448-1361-3). Crane-Russak Co.

Green, Dennis H. Irony in the Medieval Romance. LC 78-14930. 1979. 72.50 (ISBN 0-521-22458-6). Cambridge U Pr.

--Millstatter Exodus: A Crusading Epic. 1966. 85.00 (ISBN 0-521-05139-8). Cambridge U Pr.

Green, Dennis H. & Johnson, Leslie P. Approaches to Wolfram von Eschenbach: Five Essays. (Methoden und Verfahren der Mathematischen Physik Ser.: Vol. 27). 346p. 1978. pap. 28.40 (ISBN 3-261-02908-0). P Lang Pubs.

Green, Donald C., jt. auth. see McDavid, Raven Ioor.

Green, Donald E. Fifty Years of Service to West Texas Agriculture: A History of Texas Tech University's College of Agricultural Sciences, 1925-1975. (Illus.). 182p. 1977. 11.95 (ISBN 0-89672-056-X). Tex Tech Pr.

--Land of the Underground Rain: Irrigation on the Texas High Plains, 1910-1970. LC 72-7589. (Illus.). 328p. 1973. pap. 8.95 (ISBN 0-292-74629-6). U of Tex Pr.

--Panhandle Pioneer: Henry C. Hitch, His Ranch, & His Family. LC 78-21390. (Oklahoma Heritage Association Trackmaker Ser.: Vol. 7). (Illus.). 1979. 15.95 (ISBN 0-8061-1529-7). U of Okla Pr.

Green, Donald R., ed. see Conference on Issues in Educational Measurement, 2nd, Carmel, Cal., 1974.

Green, Donald R., jt. ed. see Wargo, Michael J.

Green, Douglas A. An Index to Collected Essays on Educational Media & Technology. LC 81-18249. 197p. 1982. 15.00 (ISBN 0-8108-1490-0). Scarecrow.

Green, Douglas B. & Oermann, Robert K. Listener's Guide to Country Music. (Illus.). 144p. 1983. 11.95 (ISBN 0-87196-750-2). Facts on File.

Green, Douglas G. & Hearn, Michael H. W. W. Denslow. (Juvenile Ser.: No. 2). (Illus.). 225p. 1976. 9.00 (ISBN 0-916699-09-9). Clarke His.

Green, Douglass. Harmony Through Counterpoint: A Programmed Introduction to the Theory of Tonal Music-Harmonic Counterpoint in Two & Three Parts. 1970. pap. text ed. 19.50x (ISBN 0-89197-209-9). Irvington.

Green, Douglass M. Form in Tonal Music: An Introduction to Analysis. 2nd ed. LC 78-27072. 1979. text ed. 23.95 (ISBN 0-03-020286-8, HoltC). HR&W.

Green, E. Judicial Attitude in Sentencing. (Cambridge Studies in Criminology: Vol. 15). pap. 25.00 (ISBN 0-317-15411-7). Kraus Repr.

Green, E. L., jt. auth. see Gordon, M.

Green, Earl L. Genetics & Probability. (Illus.). 1981. text ed. 45.00x (ISBN 0-19-520159-0). Oxford U Pr.

Green, Edith. Fears & Fallacies: Equal Opportunities in the 1970's. (William K. McInally Memorial Lecture Ser.: No. 9). 28p. 1975. pap. 1.00 (ISBN 0-87712-167-2). U Mich Busn Div Res.

Green, Edith, jt. auth. see Bayer, Leona M.

Green, Edward. Judicial Attitudes in Sentencing. LC 74-17589. (Cambridge Studies in Criminology Ser.: Vol. 15). 149p. 1975. Repr. of 1961 ed. lib. bdg. 40.00 (ISBN 0-8371-7834-7, GRJA). Greenwood.

Green, Edward J. Psychology for Law Enforcement. LC 75-15634. Repr. of 1976 ed. 44.50 (ISBN 0-8357-9969-7, 2055143). Bks Demand UMI.

Green, Edward J., jt. auth. see Komoski, P. Kenneth.

Green, Edward T., jt. auth. see O'Reilly, Robert C.

Green, Edwin & Moss, Michael. Business of National Importance. 1982. 32.00x (ISBN 0-416-32220-4, NO. 6729). Methuen Inc.

Green, Edwin, jt. auth. see Cockerell, H. A.

Green, Edwin L. A History of Richland County, (South Carolina) 1732-1805, Vol. 1. LC 73-16485. (Illus.). 385p. 1974. Repr. of 1932 ed. 18.50 (ISBN 0-8063-0594-0). Regional.

Green, Eise F. Now We Can Face the Day. 1975. 2.25 (ISBN 0-87509-112-1). Chr Pubns.

Green, Elaine. Woman Between Men. 1979. pap. 1.75 (ISBN 0-532-17209-4). Woodhill.

Green, Elizabeth. The Negro in Contemporary American Literature. 1973. Repr. of 1928 ed. 15.00 (ISBN 0-8274-0742-4). R West.

Green, Elizabeth, jt. auth. see Galamian, Ivan.

Green, Elizabeth A. Mary Lyon & Mount Holyoke: Opening the Gates. LC 78-68857. (Illus.). 424p. 1979. pap. 16.00x (ISBN 0-87451-261-1). U Pr of New Eng.

--The Modern Conductor. 3rd ed. (Illus.). 288p. 1981. text ed. 27.95 (ISBN 0-13-590216-9); wkbk. 18.95 (ISBN 0-13-590224-X). P-H.

--Orchestral Bowings & Routines. 1963. pap. 6.25 (ISBN 0-87506-007-2). Campus.

--Orchestral Bowings & Routines. 108p. 1963. 6.25 (ISBN 0-317-20164-6). Campus.

Green, Elizabeth A. & Malko, Nicolai. The Conductor's Score. (Illus.). 208p. 1985. text ed. 22.95 (ISBN 0-13-167370-X). P-H.

Green, Elizabeth B., jt. auth. see Bittinger, Morton N.

Green, Ellen, jt. ed. see Buckley, Thomas C.

Green, Elton. Tuscarora Language. 1969. 5.00 (ISBN 0-930230-27-2). Johnson NC.

Green, Eric & Nesson, Charles. Federal Rules of Evidence with Selected Statutes & Cases, 1984. LC 81-86688. 250p. 1984. pap. text ed. 12.00 (ISBN 0-316-32649-6). Little.

--Problems Cases & Material on Evidence. 960p. 1983. 31.00 (ISBN 0-316-32646-1). Little.

Green, Eric D. & Boston Bar Association. Getting out of Court: Alternative Dispute Resolution in Complex Civil Cases: Mini Trials, Summary Jury Trials, Rent-a-Judge, Neutral Expert Reports. LC 81-82085. Date not set. price not set. Mass CLE.

Green, Eric D. & Marks, Jonathan B., eds. Disputing in America: The Lawyer's Changing Role. 1985. 50.00 (ISBN 0-317-29455-5, #H43996). HarBraceJ.

Green, Eric F., et al. Profitable Food & Beverage Management: Planning. 1978. text ed. 19.75x (ISBN 0-8104-9480-9). Hayden.

--Profitable Food & Beverage Management: Operations. 1978. text ed. 21.95 (ISBN 0-8104-9466-3). Hayden.

Green, Ernest J. Personal Relationships: An Approach to Marriage & Family. (Illus.). 1978. text ed. 32.95 (ISBN 0-07-024270-4). McGraw.

Green, Ernest S., ed. & tr. Mexican & South American Poems. 400p. 1974. lib. bdg. 75.00 (ISBN 0-8490-0612-0). Gordon Pr.

Green, Ernestene L., ed. Ethics & Values in Archaeology. LC 83-48644. 336p. 1984. 34.95x (ISBN 0-02-912750-5). Free Pr.

Green, Eugene & Sachse, William L. Names of the Land: Cape Cod, Nantucket, Martha's Vineyard & the Elizabeth Islands. LC 82-82167. (Illus.). 192p. (Orig.). 1983. pap. 8.95 (ISBN 0-87106-974-1). Globe Pequot.

Green, Evan. Alfa Romeo. (Illus.). 1977. 13.50 (ISBN 0-9596637-0-3, Pub. by Evan Green Pty. Ltd. England). Motorbooks Intl.

Green, Evelyn M. Your Basenji. LC 76-20959. (Your Dog Bk.). (Illus.). 1976. 12.95 (ISBN 0-87714-041-3). Denlingers.

Green, Ezra. Diary of Ezra Green, M.D., Surgeon on Board the Continental Ship of War Ranger Under John Paul Jones from November 1, 1777, to September 27, 1778. Preble, George H. & Green, Walter C., eds. LC 75-140867. (Eyewitness Accounts of the American Revolution Ser., No. 3). 1970. Repr. of 1875 ed. 11.50 (ISBN 0-405-01190-3). Ayer Co Pubs.

Green, F. C. Rousseau & the Idea of Progress. LC 77-3282. 1950. lib. bdg. 9.50 (ISBN 0-8414-4408-0). Folcroft.

Green, F. C., compiled by. French Short Stories of the Nineteenth & Twentieth Centuries. 1971. 12.95x (ISBN 0-460-00896-X, Evman); pap. 3.95x (ISBN 0-460-01896-5). Biblio Dist.

Green, F. C., ed. see De Maupassant, Guy.

Green, F. C., ed. see Diderot, Denis.

Green, F. L. Odd Man Out. LC 81-84722. (Rowan Tree Mystery Ser.: No. 2). 214p. 1982. pap. 5.95 (ISBN 0-937672-06-8). Rowan Tree.

Green, Fitzhugh. A Change in the Weather. (Illus.). 1977. 9.95 (ISBN 0-393-06429-8). Norton.

--Our Naval Heritage. 1977. lib. bdg. 69.95 (ISBN 0-8490-2390-4). Gordon Pr.

--The U. S. Information Agency. (WV Library of Federal Department Agencies & Systems Ser.). 285p. 1983. lib. bdg. 25.00 cancelled (ISBN 0-86531-228-1). Westview.

--Z R Wins. Reginald, R. & Melville, Douglas, eds. LC 77-84232. (Lost Race & Adult Fantasy Ser.). 1978. Repr. of 1924 ed. lib. bdg. 24.50x (ISBN 0-405-10980-6). Ayer Co Pubs.

Green, Fitzhugh & Frost, Holloway. Some Famous Sea Fights. facs. ed. LC 68-58792. (Essay Index Reprint Ser). 1927. 23.50 (ISBN 0-8369-0075-8). Ayer Co Pubs.

Green, Fletcher. Constitutional Development in the South Atlantic States, 1776-1860. LC 71-158485. (Civil Liberties in American History Ser.). 1971. Repr. of 1930 ed. lib. bdg. 42.50 (ISBN 0-306-70189-8). Da Capo.

Green, Fletcher M. Democracy in the Old South & Other Essays. Copeland, J. Isaac, ed. LC 68-9268. 1969. 15.00x (ISBN 0-8265-1128-7). Vanderbilt U Pr.

--Heroes of the American Revolution. 1931. lib. bdg. 10.00 (ISBN 0-8482-9977-9). Norwood Edns.

--Romance of the Western Frontier. LC 77-16305. 1977. Repr. of 1932 ed. lib. bdg. 10.00 (ISBN 0-8414-4609-1). Folcroft.

Green, Fletcher M., ed. Essays in Southern History: Presented to Joseph Gregoire De Roulhac Hamilton by His Former Students at the University of North Carolina. (James Sprunt Studies in History & Political Science: Vol. 31). 1977. Repr. of 1949 ed. lib. bdg. 15.00x (ISBN 0-8371-9326-5, NCES). Greenwood.

Green, Fletcher M. & Copeland, J. Isaac, eds. The Old South. LC 79-55730. (Goldentree Bibliographies in American History Ser.). 1980. pap. text ed. 14.95 (ISBN 0-88295-580-2). Harlan Davidson.

Green, Fletcher M., ed. see Smedes, Susan D.

Green, Francis & Nore, Petter, eds. Issues in Political Economy: A Critical Approach. 294p. 1980. text ed. 31.75x (ISBN 0-333-25376-0). Humanities.

Green, Frank. As Dickens Saw Them. 1973. Repr. of 1933 ed. 20.00 (ISBN 0-8274-0386-0). R West.

--London Homes of Dickens. 1928. lib. bdg. 25.00 (ISBN 0-8414-4678-4). Folcroft.

Green, Frank L. Captains, Curates & Cockneys: The English in the Pacific Northwest. LC 81-620029. (Illus.). 105p. 1982. pap. 6.00 (ISBN 0-917048-52-0). Wash St Hist Soc.

--A Guide to the Howard A. Hanson Collection. (Illus.). 17p. 1970. pap. 1.00 (ISBN 0-917048-15-6). Wash St Hist Soc.

--A Guide to the Thomas M. Chambers Collection. LC 72-619506. (Illus.). 29p. 1972. pap. 1.00 (ISBN 0-917048-16-4). Wash St Hist Soc.

Green, Fred, et al. Strategies for Improving Reading in Social Studies. 1979. pap. text ed. 9.95 (ISBN 0-8403-2098-1). Kendall-Hunt.

Green, Fred P., et al, eds. Partners in Praise. 176p. 1982. pap. 6.95 (ISBN 0-687-30130-0). Abingdon.

Green, Frederick C. Minuet: A Critical Survey of French & English Literary Ideas in the 18th Century. LC 75-158504. 1971. Repr. of 1935 ed. 49.00x (ISBN 0-403-01296-1). Scholarly.

Green, G. D., tr. see Fichte, J. G.

Green, G. H., et al. Cervical & Nasopharyngeal Carcinoma. LC 74-670. 213p. 1974. text ed. 23.50x (ISBN 0-8422-7206-2). Irvington.

Green, G. K. & Obe, R. P. Law of Pilotage. 2nd ed. 1984. 35.00 (ISBN 0-907432-66-2). Lloyds London Pr.

Green, Gareth M. & Daniel, Thomas M, eds. Koch Centennial Memorial. 136p. 1982. text ed. 12.50 (ISBN 0-915116-17-0). Am Lung Assn.

Green, Geoffrey. Literary Criticism & the Structures of History: Erich Auerbach & Leo Spitzer. LC 82-2654. x, 186p. 1982. 17.95x (ISBN 0-8032-2108-8). U of Nebr Pr.

Green, Geoffrey, jt. ed. see Cope, Jackson I.

Green, George. Green Grammar: A Simple System for Writing Superior Sentences. 192p. 1981. pap. text ed. 12.95 (ISBN 0-8403-2402-2). Kendall-Hunt.

--Mathematical Papers. LC 70-92316. 19.95 (ISBN 0-8284-0229-9). Chelsea Pub.

Green, George, jt. auth. see Mooney, Sean.

Green, George A. Editor Looks Back: South African & Other Memories, 1883-1946. LC 72-106874. (Illus.). Repr. of 1947 ed. 19.75x (ISBN 0-8371-3291-6, GRE&, Pub. by Negro U Pr). Greenwood.

Green, George D. Finance & Economic Development in the Old South: Louisiana Banking, 1804-1861. LC 73-153817. 1972. 22.50x (ISBN 0-8047-0792-8). Stanford U Pr.

Green, George F. Elementary School Mathematics: Activities & Materials. 1974. text ed. 18.95x (ISBN 0-669-84582-5). Heath.

Green, George N. The Establishment in Texas Politics: The Primitive Years, 1938 to 1957. LC 78-55340. (Illus.). 320p. 1984. pap. 9.95 (ISBN 0-8061-1891-1). U of Okla Pr.

--Liberal View of Texas Politics Since the 1930s. (Texas History Ser.). (Illus.). 52p. 1982. pap. text ed. 1.95x (ISBN 0-89641-088-9). American Pr.

--Liberal View of Texas Politics, 1890s-1930s. (Texas History Ser.). (Illus.). 45p. 1982. pap. text ed. 1.95x (ISBN 0-89641-087-0). American Pr.

Green, Georgia M. Semantics & Syntactic Regularity. LC 74-9947. 256p. 1974. 22.50x (ISBN 0-253-35160-X). Ind U Pr.

Green, Gerald. The Heartless Light. 1976. Repr. of 1961 ed. lib. bdg. 21.95 (ISBN 0-89190-123-X, Pub. by River City Pr). Amereon Ltd.

--The Hostage Heart. 1977. pap. 1.95 (ISBN 0-380-00944-7, 32037). Avon.

--Karpov's Brain. LC 83-946. 384p. 1983. 15.95 (ISBN 0-688-01889-0). Morrow.

--The Last Angry Man. 1976. Repr. of 1956 ed. lib. bdg. 23.95 (ISBN 0-89190-121-3, Pub. by River City Pr). Amereon Ltd.

--The Lotus Eaters. 1976. Repr. of 1959 ed. lib. bdg. 26.95 (ISBN 0-89190-122-1, Pub. by River City Pr). Amereon Ltd.

--Not in Vain. LC 84-81326. 279p. 1984. 15.95 (ISBN 0-917657-12-8). D I Fine.

--The Portofino PTA. 1976. Repr. of 1962 ed. lib. bdg. 13.95x (ISBN 0-89190-124-8, Pub. by River City Pr). Amereon Ltd.

Green, Gerald & Klingman, L. His Majesty O'keefe. 1976. Repr. of 1950 ed. lib. bdg. 18.95 (ISBN 0-89190-125-6, Pub. by River City Pr). Amereon Ltd.

Green, Gil. Cold War Fugitive. Smith, Betty, ed. 288p. 1984. 16.00 (ISBN 0-7178-0615-4); pap. 6.95 (ISBN 0-7178-0616-2). Intl Pubs Co.

--Cuba... the Continuing Revolution. 2nd ed. Smith, Betty, ed. 120p. 1985. pap. 3.75 (ISBN 0-7178-0628-6). Intl Pubs Co.

--Terrorism: Is It Revolutionary? 1970. pap. 0.50 (ISBN 0-87898-054-7). New Outlook.

--What's Happening to Labor. LC 76-14861. 312p. 1976. 12.00 (ISBN 0-7178-0465-8); pap. 4.50 (ISBN 0-7178-0464-X). Intl Pubs Co.

Green, Gion. Introduction to Security. 3rd ed. 1981. text ed. 22.95 (ISBN 0-409-95036-X); instr's manual avail. Butterworth.

Green, Gordon G. & Eiker, Earl E., eds. Accomplishments & Impacts of Reservoirs. 238p. 1983. pap. 24.00x (ISBN 0-87262-382-3). Am Soc Civil Eng.

Green, Gordon W., Jr. Getting Straight A's. 192p. 1985. pap. 6.95 (ISBN 0-8184-0380-2). Lyle Stuart.

Green, Griz. Life, Love & Laughter. LC 82-90300. 62p. 1983. 5.95 (ISBN 0-533-05397-8). Vantage.

Green, H. Benedict. The Gospel According to Matthew in the Revised Standard Version. (New Clarendon Bible Ser). 1975. pap. 9.95x (ISBN 0-19-836911-5). Oxford U Pr.

Green, H. D. Carving Realistic Birds: A Step-by-Step Manual with Full-Size Patterns. LC 76-55216. (Illus., Orig.). 1978. pap. 3.00 (ISBN 0-486-23484-3). Dover.

--Carving Realistic Birds: A Step-by-Step Manual with Full-Size Patterns. 12.75 (ISBN 0-8446-5582-1). Peter Smith.

--Patterns & Instructions for Carving Authentic Birds. (Illus.). 80p. (Orig.). 1982. pap. 2.75 (ISBN 0-486-24222-6). Dover.

Green, H. I. & Levy, M. H. Drug Misuse-Human Abuse. 1976. 55.00 (ISBN 0-8247-6273-8). Dekker.

Green, H. J. Godmanchester. (Cambridge Town, Town & County Ser.: Vol. 18). (Illus.). 1977. pap. 4.25 (ISBN 0-900891-16-5). Oleander Pr.

Green, H. S. & Raphael. Mundane Astrology. LC 77-86746. 1977. 3.95 (ISBN 0-912504-39-0). Sym & Sign.

Green, Hannah. I Never Promised You a Rose Garden. LC 64-11018. 1964. 14.95 (ISBN 0-03-043725-3). HR&W.

--In the City of Paris. LC 81-43649. (Illus.). 32p. (ps-3). 1985. 11.95 (ISBN 0-385-15692-8); lib. bdg. 11.95 (ISBN 0-385-15693-6). Doubleday.

Green, Harold P., ed. Energy Law Service, Vols. 1, 2, & 3. LC 78-12593. pap. 160.00 ea. (2017601). Bks Demand UMI.

Green, Harriet & Martin, Sue. Sprouts. (gr. 3-8). 1981. 9.95 (ISBN 0-86653-028-2, GA256). Good Apple.

Green, Harriet H. & Martin, Sue G. Treasure Hunts. 144p. (gr. 4-7). 1983. wkbk. 9.95 (ISBN 0-86653-115-7, GA 469). Good Apple.

Green, Harry J. A Study of the Legislature of the State of Maryland, with Special Reference to the Sessions of 1927 & 1929. LC 78-64137. (Johns Hopkins University. Studies in the Social Sciences. Forty-Eighth Ser. 1930: 3). Repr. of 1930 ed. 15.00 (ISBN 0-404-61249-0). AMS Pr.

Green, Harry L. Echoes of Thunder. LC 80-66322. 167p. 1980. 10.95 (ISBN 0-936958-00-6); pap. 5.95 (ISBN 0-936958-01-4). Emerald Hse.

Green, Harvey & Perry, Mary E. The Light of the Home: An Intimate View of the Lives of Women in Victorian America. LC 82-18867. (Illus.). 256p. 1983. 18.45 (ISBN 0-394-52746-1); pap. 8.95 (ISBN 0-394-71329-X). Pantheon.

Green, Helen H. & Morton, Margaret A. Transcription & Skill Building, Bk. 11. (Hedman Stenotype System Ser.). 354p. 1978. text ed. 18.00x (ISBN 0-939056-01-1). Hedman Steno.

Green, Helen H., et al. The Secretary Today: An Integrated Secretarial Block Program; Integrated Skill Builders. (Illus.). (gr. 12). 1978. pap. text ed. 14.32 (ISBN 0-07-024296-8). McGraw.

--The Secretary Today: An Integrated Secretarial Block Program; Training Handbooks, Pts. 1-4. (Illus.). (gr. 12). 1977. pap. text ed. 21.76 (ISBN 0-07-024295-X). McGraw.

Green, Henrietta. The Marinade Cookbook. LC 77-11534. (Illus.). 1979. 10.95i (ISBN 0-06-011553-X, HarpT). Har-Row.

Green, Henry. Andrea Alciati & His Books of Emblems. (Illus.). 1965. Repr. of 1872 ed. 24.50 (ISBN 0-8337-1435-X). B Franklin.

--Back. LC 81-721. 256p. 1981. pap. 5.95 (ISBN 0-8112-0798-6, NDP517). New Directions.

--Blindness. 1978. 11.95 (ISBN 0-670-17428-9). Viking.

--Caught. LC 70-83158. Repr. of 1950 ed. lib. bdg. 17.50x (ISBN 0-678-03157-6). Kelley.

--Concluding. LC 73-122055. Repr. of 1950 ed. 19.50 (ISBN 0-678-03158-4). Kelley.

--Concluding. LC 85-8526. 262p. 1961. pap. 7.95 (ISBN 0-226-30611-9). U of Chicago Pr.

--Doting. LC 70-122054. Repr. of 1952 ed. 19.50x (ISBN 0-678-03159-2). Kelley.

--Living. 1971. Repr. of 1929 ed. 39.00x (ISBN 0-403-01001-2). Scholarly.

--Loving, Living, & Party Going, 3 vols. in 1. 1978. pap. 6.95 (ISBN 0-14-004916-9). Penguin.

--Nothing. LC 72-122052. Repr. of 1950 ed. 19.50x (ISBN 0-678-03160-6). Kelley.

--Nothing Doting Blindness. 1980. pap. 6.95 (ISBN 0-14-005664-5). Penguin.

--Party Going. LC 76-122053. Repr. of 1951 ed. 19.50x (ISBN 0-678-03161-4). Kelley.

--Shakespeare & the Emblem Writers. (Illus.). 1967. Repr. of 1870 ed. 29.00 (ISBN 0-8337-1440-6). B Franklin.

Green, Henry, ed. see Whitney, Geoffrey.

Green, Henry M. Australian Literature, 1900-1950. 1963. pap. 3.50x (ISBN 0-522-83620-8, Pub. by Melbourne U Pr). Intl Spec Bk.

Green, Henry M., ed. Modern Australian Poetry. LC 78-73487. (Granger Poetry Library). 1979. Repr. of 1952 ed. 22.75x (ISBN 0-89609-113-9). Granger Bk.

Green, Hill, ed. see Hume, David.

Green, Hollis. Why Churches Die. 224p. (Orig.). 1972. pap. 5.95 (ISBN 0-87123-642-7, 210642). Bethany Hse.

Green, Hollis L. Dynamics of Christian Discipleship. 112p. 1962. 5.25 (ISBN 0-87148-251-7); pap. 4.25 (ISBN 0-87148-252-5). Pathway Pr.

Green, Holly W. Turning Fear to Hope. 228p. (Orig.). 1984. pap. 5.95 (ISBN 0-8407-5937-1). Nelson.

Green, Horace, ed. see Borah, William E.

Green, I. Conservation from A to Z. LC 66-11443. (Illus.). (gr. 4 up). 1968. PLB 9.26 (ISBN 0-87783-009-6); pap. 3.94 deluxe ed. (ISBN 0-87783-088-6). Oddo.

--Where Is Duckling Three? LC 68-16402. (Illus.). (gr. 1-2). 1967. PLB 9.26 (ISBN 0-87783-048-7). Oddo.

Green, I. M. The Re-Establishment of the Church of England, 1660-1663. (Oxford Historical Monographs). 1978. 35.00x (ISBN 0-19-821867-2). Oxford U Pr.

Green, Ira & Cohen, Stanley, eds. Mechanisms of Tumor Immunity. LC 76-48047. (Basic & Clinical Immunology Ser.). pap. 63.10 (ISBN 0-317-08534-4, 2015193). Bks Demand UMI.

Green, Ivah. Splash & Trickle. LC 68-56818. (Illus.). (gr. 2-3). 1968. PLB 9.26 (ISBN 0-87783-037-1); pap. 3.94 deluxe ed. (ISBN 0-87783-109-2); cassette 7.94x (ISBN 0-87783-226-9). Oddo.

--Splash & Trickle. (Illus.). (gr. 2-3). 1978. pap. 1.25 (ISBN 0-89508-062-1). Rainbow Bks.

Green, Ivah J. Loon. LC 65-22310. (Illus.). (gr. 4 up). 1968. PLB 9.26 (ISBN 0-87783-025-8). Oddo.

Green, J. Biology of Estuarine Animals. LC 68-21828. (Biology Ser.). (Illus.). 404p. 1968. 20.00x (ISBN 0-295-95122-2). U of Wash Pr.

--The Book of Political Quotes. 256p. 1983. pap. 8.95 (ISBN 0-07-024354-9). McGraw.

--Oeuvres Completes: Epaves, Le Visionnaire, Minuit, Varouna, Si j'estais vous, etc, Vol. 2. 1608p. 41.50 (ISBN 0-686-56519-3). French & Eur.

--Oeuvres Completes: Journal (1926-1955, Vol. 4. 1848p. 45.00 (ISBN 0-686-56521-5). French & Eur.

--Oeuvres Completes: Journal (1956-1972), Autobiographie, etc, Vol. 5. 1808p. 47.95 (ISBN 0-686-56522-3). French & Eur.

--Oeuvres Completes: Moira, Le Malfaiteur, Chaque Homme dans sa Nuit, L'Autre, Theatre Complet, Vol. 3. 1824p. 45.00 (ISBN 0-686-56520-7). French & Eur.

--Oeuvres Completes: Mont-Cinere, Leviathan, Adrienne Mesurat, L'Autre Sommeil, etc, Vol. 1. 1328p. 45.00 (ISBN 0-686-56518-5). French & Eur.

Green, J. & Laffont, J. J. Incentives in Public Decision Making. (Studies in Public Economics: Vol. 1). 294p. 1979. 55.50 (ISBN 0-444-85144-5, North Holland). Elsevier.

Green, J. see Barnes, R. S.

Green, J., jt. ed. see Dumont, H. J.

Green, J., jt. ed. see Thompson, R.

Green, J. A. Polynomial Representations of GLN. (Lecture Notes in Mathematics: Vol. 830). 118p. 1980. pap. 13.00 (ISBN 0-387-10258-2). Springer-Verlag.

Green, J. A., ed. Pestalozzi's Educational Writings. 59.95 (ISBN 0-8490-0822-0). Gordon Pr.

Green, J. Charles. First Words. 1975. 2.00 (ISBN 0-912678-21-6). Greenfld Rev Pr.

Green, J. Keith & Perkins, Philip H. Concrete Liquid Retaining Structures. (Illus.). 355p. 1979. 52.00 (ISBN 0-85334-856-1, Pub. by Elsevier Applied Sci England). Elsevier.

Green, J. R. Corpus Vasorum Antiquorum, New Zealand. (Corpus Vasorum Antiquorum Ser.: Fascicule 1). (Illus.). 1979. 98.00x (ISBN 0-19-725990-1). Oxford U Pr.

--Monuments Illustrating Old & Middle Comedy. (Bulletin Supplemtn Ser.: No. 39). 286p. 1981. 40.00x (ISBN 0-900587-38-5, Pub. by Inst Class Stud England). State Mutual Bk.

Green, J. R. & Margerison, D. Statistical Treatment of Experimental Data. rev. ed. (Physical Sciences Data Ser.: Vol. 2). 1978. 52.00 (ISBN 0-444-41725-7). Elsevier.

Green, J. R., ed. Some Aspects of the Foundations of General Equilibrium Theory: The Posthumous Papers of Peter J. Kalman. LC 78-14520. (Lecture Notes in Economics & Mathematical Systems: Vol. 159). 1978. pap. 14.00 (ISBN 0-387-08918-7). Springer-Verlag.

Green, J. R., jt. ed. see Thompson, Richard A.

Green, Jack. The Trust Account. 1982. 10.95 (ISBN 0-533-05345-5). Vantage.

Green, Jack, ed. Geological Problems in Lunar & Planetary Research. (Science & Technology Ser.: Vol. 25). (Illus.). 1971. lib. bdg. 45.00x (ISBN 0-87703-056-1, Pub. by Am Astronaut). Univelt Inc.

--Interpretation of Lunar Probe Data. (Science & Technology Ser.: Vol. 14). 1967. 25.00x (ISBN 0-87703-042-1, Pub. by Am Astronaut). Univelt Inc.

Green, Jack L. Leasing: Principles & Methods. 49.95 (ISBN 0-686-23598-3). Sound Pub.

--Tax Law Supplement to Leasing Principles & Methods: Covering ERTA '81 & TEFRA '82. LC 83-172395. (Illus.). 12p. 1983. write for info. Sound Pub.

Green, Jack P., jt. ed. see Weinstein, Harel.

Green, James & Lee, John. Positronium Chemistry. 1964. 35.00 (ISBN 0-12-298650-4). Acad Pr.

Green, James F. United Nations & Human Rights. (Brookings Institution Reprint Ser). 1958. Repr. of 1956 ed. lib. bdg. 28.50x (ISBN 0-697-00155-5). Irvington.

Green, James H. Automating Your Office: How to Do It, How to Justify It. 256p. 1984. 24.95 (ISBN 0-07-024318-2). McGraw.

--Local Area Networks: A User's Guide for Business Professionals. 1985. pap. 17.95 (ISBN 0-673-18065-4). Scott F.

Green, James J. Wendell Phillips. LC 44-5915. pap. 20.00 (ISBN 0-317-28069-4, 2025545). Bks Demand UMI.

Green, James R. Grass-Roots Socialism: Radical Movements in the Southwest, 1895-1943. LC 77-28205. 432p. 1978. 32.50x (ISBN 0-8071-0367-5); pap. 8.95x (ISBN 0-8071-0773-5). La State U Pr.

--The World of the Worker: Labor in Twentieth-Century America. Foner, Eric, ed. 1978. pap. 7.95 (ISBN 0-8090-0132-2). Hill & Wang.

Green, James R. & Donahue, Hugh C. Boston's Workers: A Labor History. (Illus.). 1978. 10.00 (ISBN 0-89073-056-3). Boston Public Lib.

Green, James R., ed. Workers' Struggles, Past & Present: A "Radical America" Reader. 437p. 1983. 32.95 (ISBN 0-87722-293-2); pap. 9.95 (ISBN 0-87722-315-7). Temple U Pr.

Green, James R., ed. see Ameringer, Oscar.

Green, James W. Cultural Awareness in the Human Services. (Illus.). 272p. 1982. 22.95 (ISBN 0-13-195362-1). P-H.

Green, Jane. You & Your Private I. LC 75-2320. (Illus.). 225p. 1975. pap. 4.95 (ISBN 0-87542-295-0). Llewellyn Pubns.

Green, Jane N. You & Your Private "I". Analytic Graphology. 2nd, enl. ed. LC 83-80848. 230p. pap. 8.95 (ISBN 0-87542-295-0, L-295). Llewellyn Pubns.

Green, Janet. US: Inside a Teenage Gang. (Illus.). 128p. (gr. 5 up). 1982. 9.95 (ISBN 0-8038-6753-0). Hastings.

Green, Janet & Janssen, Robert B. Minnesota Birds: Where, When, & How Many. LC 74-16980. (Illus.). xvi, 248p. 1975. 10.95x (ISBN 0-8166-0738-9). U of Minn Pr.

Green, Janet C. & Janssen, Robert B. Minnesota Birds: Where, When, & How Many. LC 74-16980. (Illus.). 1980. pap. 6.95 (ISBN 0-8166-0958-6). U of Minn Pr.

Green, Jay P. Interlinear Hebrew-English Old Testament, 3 vols. 1983. pap. 67.95 (ISBN 0-8010-3742-5). Baker Bk.

Green, Jay P., ed. The Pocket Interlinear New Testament. 1981. pap. 5.95 (ISBN 0-8010-3777-8). Baker Bk.

Green, Jeff. Pluto: The Evolutionary Cause of Incarnation, Vol. I. Buske, Terry, ed. (Modern Astrology Ser.). 360p. (Orig.). 1985. pap. 12.95 (ISBN 0-87542-296-9, L-296). Llewellyn Pubns.

Green, Jeffrey P. Edmund Thorton Jenkins: The Life & Times of an American Black Composer, 1894-1926. LC 81-23721. (Contributions to the Study of Music & Dance Ser.: No. 2). (Illus.). xii, 213p. 1982. lib. bdg. 27.50 (ISBN 0-313-23253-9, GRJ/). Greenwood.

Green, Jennifer. The Self-Sufficient Weaver. (Illus.). 120p. 1983. 18.95 (ISBN 0-7134-0763-8, Pub. by Batsford England). David & Charles.

Green, Jerald R. Direccion: Moncloa: An Intermediate Cultural Reader. 1977. pap. 16.50 (ISBN 0-395-30980-8). HM.

Green, Jerold. Revolution in Iran: The Politics of Countermobilization. LC 82-11295. 218p. 1982. 29.95 (ISBN 0-03-062409-6). Praeger.

Green, Jerry & Scheinkman, Jose A., eds. General Equilibrium, Growth & Trade: Essays in Honor of Lionel McKenzie. LC 79-50216. (Economic Theory, Econometrics & Mathematical Economics Ser.). 1979. 70.00 (ISBN 0-12-298750-0). Acad Pr.

Green, Jesse, ed. see Cushing, Frank H.

Green, Jo E. The Bargain Hunter's Guide to Houston. 176p. (Orig.). 1984. pap. 7.95 (ISBN 0-9613381-0-5). Little Tx Pr.

Green, Joann. The Small Theatre Handbook: A Guide to Management & Production. (Illus.). 192p. (Orig.). 1981. 11.95 (ISBN 0-916782-19-0); pap. 8.95 (ISBN 0-916782-20-4). Harvard Common Pr.

Green, Joe. More Money-Less Work. (Illus.). 184p. (Orig.). 1982. 12.00 (ISBN 0-9607678-0-0). Technico Bks.

Green, Joel B. How to Read Prophecy. LC 84-12838. 150p. (Orig.). 1984. pap. 5.95 (ISBN 0-87784-936-6). Inter-Varsity.

Green, Joey, ed. Cornell Widow Hundredth Anniversary Anthology: 1894-1994. LC 81-65708. (Illus.). 224p. (Orig.). 1981. pap. 9.95 (ISBN 0-9605870-0-4). Cornell Widow.

Green, Joey & Handy, Bruce, eds. Hellbent on Insanity. 1982. pap. 9.95 (ISBN 0-03-059981-4, Owl Bks). HR&W.

Green, John. Dakota Days: The True Story of John Lennon's Final Years. 320p. 1984. pap. 5.95 (ISBN 0-312-18177-9). St Martin.

Green, John, jt. ed. see Posner, Rebecca.

Green, John, tr. see Ahmad, Jalal Al-e.

Green, John, illus. Favorite Dogs Coloring Book. (Coloring Bks). (Illus.). 48p. (Orig.). (gr. 3up). 1984. pap. 2.50 (ISBN 0-486-24552-7). Dover.

Green, John, et al, trs. see Al-e Ahmad, Jalal.

Green, John A. Educational Ideas of Pestalozzi. Repr. of 1907 ed. lib. bdg. 15.00x (ISBN 0-8371-2398-4, GREP). Greenwood.

--Teacher-Made Tests. 2nd ed. 224p. 1975. pap. text ed. 10.95 scp (ISBN 0-06-042489-3, HarpC). Har-Row.

Green, John A., tr. see Pestalozzi, Johann H.

Green, John A., III. A Diagonsis for Man: Technology, the New Diseases, & Our Present Dilemma. 16p. 1985. 3.00 (ISBN 0-89756-016-7). Two Rivers.

Green, John C., Jr. Ritchie's First Steps in Latin. 3rd ed. 1978. text ed. 8.95x (ISBN 0-582-28085-0). Longman.

--Ritchie's Second Steps in Latin. 3rd ed. 1924. text ed. 8.85x (ISBN 0-582-28086-9). Longman.

Green, John H. Basic Clinical Physiology. 3rd ed. (Illus.). 1978. pap. text ed. 16.95x (ISBN 0-19-263331-7). Oxford U Pr.

--An Introduction to Human Physiology. 4th ed. (Illus.). 1976. pap. text ed. 25.00x (ISBN 0-19-263328-7). Oxford U Pr.

--Speak to Me. LC 62-14943. (Orig.). 1962. pap. 5.99 (ISBN 0-672-63116-4). Odyssey Pr.

Green, John H. & Kramer, Amihud. Food Processing Waste Management. (Illus.). 1979. text ed. 49.50 (ISBN 0-87055-331-3). AVI.

Green, John H. & Silver, P. H. An Introduction to Human Anatomy. (Illus.). 1981. pap. text ed. 29.95x (ISBN 0-19-261196-8). Oxford U Pr.

Green, John L. Pioneer Evangelists of the Church of God in the Pacific Northwest. 164p. pap. 2.00 (ISBN 0-686-29135-2). Faith Pub Hse.

Green, John L. & Barber, Allan W. A System of Cost Accounting for Physical Plant Operation in Institutions of Higher Education. LC 68-59245. 116p. 1968. pap. 4.50x (ISBN 0-8203-0227-9). U of Ga Pr.

Green, John N. see Posner, Rebecca.

Green, John R. Medical History for Students. (Illus.). 202p. 1968. 20.75x (ISBN 0-398-00722-5). C C Thomas.

--A Short History of the English People, 2 Vols. 1980. Repr. of 1960 ed. Vol. 1. 14.95x (ISBN 0-460-00727-0, Evman); Vol. 2. 14.95x (ISBN 0-460-00728-9). Biblio Dist.

--Stray Studies: Second Series. facs. ed. LC 72-3362. (Essay Index Reprint Ser.). Repr. of 1903 ed. 18.00 (ISBN 0-8369-2904-7). Ayer Co Pubs.

Green, John R., jt. auth. see Brooke, Stopford.

Green, John R., jt. ed. see Thompson, Richard A.

Green, Johnnie. Bentley Fifty Years of the Marque. 296p. 1981. 75.00x (ISBN 0-686-97071-3, Pub. by D Watson England). State Mutual Bk.

Green, Jonathan. American Photography: A Critical History 1945 to the Present. LC 83-15532. (Illus.). 248p. 1984. 35.00 (ISBN 0-8109-1814-5). Abrams.

--The Greatest Criminals of All Time: The Anti-Social Register. LC 81-48441. (Illus.). 288p. 1984. pap. 11.95 (ISBN 0-8128-6216-3). Stein & Day.

--Journal of a Tour on the Northwest Coast in 1829. Date not set. 7.50 (ISBN 0-87770-013-3). Ye Galleon.

--Morrow's International Dictionary of Contemporary Quotations. LC 82-12633. 1982. 17.95 (ISBN 0-688-01537-9). Morrow.

--Newspeak: A Dictionary of Jargon. 263p. 1984. 19.95 (ISBN 0-7100-9685-2). Routledge & Kegan.

--Sweet Nothings: Love Quotes for Lovers & Other Fools. LC 84-60209. 256p. 1984. pap. 5.95 (ISBN 0-688-03661-9). Morrow.

Green, Jonathan, ed. Snapshot. LC 74-18754. (Illus.). 128p. 1974. 20.00 (ISBN 0-912334-67-3); pap. 12.50 (ISBN 0-912334-68-1). Aperture.

Green, Jonathan H. Gambling Exposed, a Full Exposition of the Various Arts, Mysteries, Miseries of Gambling. LC 78-172603. (Criminology, Law Enforcement, & Social Problems Ser.: No. 193). (Illus., With intro. & index added). 1973. Repr. of 1857 ed. 15.00x (ISBN 0-87585-193-2). Patterson Smith.

--Secret Band of Brothers. (Illus.). 1980. 9.50 (ISBN 0-682-49368-6, University). Exposition Pr FL.

Green, Jonathon. The Cynic's Lexicon: A Dictionary of Amoral Advice. 240p. 1985. 13.95 (ISBN 0-312-18055-1). St Martin.

--The Dictionary of Contemporary Slang. LC 85-40247. 334p. 1985. 17.95 (ISBN 0-8128-3051-2). Stein & Day.

--Greatest Criminals of All Time. LC 81-48441. (Illus.). 288p. 1982. 20.00 (ISBN 0-8128-2847-X). Stein & Day.

--Newspeak: A Dictionary of Jargon. 263p. 1985. pap. 9.95 (ISBN 0-7102-0673-9). Routledge & Kegan.

--Sweet Nothings: Love Quotes for Lovers & Other Fools. LC 84-60210. 256p. 1984. pap. 5.95 (ISBN 0-688-03662-7, QUill NY). Morrow.

Green, Jonathon, compiled by. The Book of Rock Quotes. (Illus.). 128p. (Orig.). 1982. pap. 6.95 (ISBN 0-399-41000-7). Delilah Bks.

Green, Joseph R., ed. English Men of Science, 7 vols. Repr. of 1908 ed. Set. 125.45 (ISBN 0-404-07890-7). AMS Pr.

Green, Joseph S., et al. Continuing Education for the Health Professions. LC 83-49261. (Higher Education Ser.). 1984. text ed. 25.95x (ISBN 0-87589-604-9). Jossey-Bass.

Green, Judith. Review of Maternal Child Nursing. 1978. pap. text ed. 16.95 (ISBN 0-07-024302-6). McGraw.

Green, Judith & Wallat, Cynthia, eds. Ethnography & Language in Educational Settings. (Advances in Discourse Processes Ser.: Vol. 5). 368p. 1981. text ed. 39.50 (ISBN 0-89391-035-X); pap. 24.50 (ISBN 0-89391-078-3). Ablex Pub.

Green, Judith, ed. see Cochran-Smith, Marilyn.

Green, Judith, ed. see Corsaro, William.

Green, Judith, ed. see Genishi, Celia & Dyson, Anne.

Green, Judith, ed. see Mishler, Elliot G.

Green, Judith, ed. see Tannen, Deborah.

Green, Judith A. A City for Ransom. (Adult Basic Learner Ser.). (Illus.). 225p. (Orig., Reading level gr. 2, Interest level gr. 9-12, ABE). 1980. pap. text ed. 4.80x (ISBN 0-89061-216-1, 205). Jamestown Pubs.

--Dr. Valdez. (Adult Learner Ser.). (Illus.). 215p. (Orig., Reading level gr. 2, Interest level gr. 9-12, ABE). 1980. pap. text ed. 4.80x (ISBN 0-89061-211-0, 203). Jamestown Pubs.

--Killer in a Trance. (Illus.). 220p. 1985. pap. text ed. 4.80x (ISBN 0-89061-426-1). Jamestown Pubs.

--The Man Who Stopped Time. (Adult Learner Ser.). (Illus.). 189p. (Orig., Reading level gr. 2, Interest level gr. 9-12, ABE). 1979. pap. text ed. 4.80x (ISBN 0-89061-173-4, 201). Jamestown Pubs.

--The Man with the Scar. (Adult Learner Ser.). (Illus.). 203p. (Orig., Reading level gr. 2, Interest level gr. 9-12, ABE). 1979. pap. text ed. 4.80x (ISBN 0-89061-153-X, 202). Jamestown Pubs.

--Murder by Radio. (Adult Learner Ser.). (Illus.). 191p. (Orig., Reading level gr. 2, Interest level gr. 9-12, ABE). 1979. pap. text ed. 4.80x (ISBN 0-89061-152-1, 200). Jamestown Pubs.

--Nightmare Snow. (Illus.). 220p. 1985. pap. text ed. 4.80 (ISBN 0-89061-283-8). Jamestown Pubs.

--Peril on the Road. (Illus.). 220p. 1985. pap. text ed. 4.80 (ISBN 0-89061-427-X). Jamestown Pubs.

--The Secret of Room 401. (Adult Learner Ser.). (Illus.). 223p. (Orig., Reading level gr. 2, Interest level gr. 9-12, ABE). 1980. pap. text ed. 4.80x (ISBN 0-89061-210-2, 204). Jamestown Pubs.

Green, Judy. Natural Dyes from Northwest Plants. pap. 5.95 (ISBN 0-686-19929-4). Robin & Russ.

Green, Judy, et al. Lights Out at DOE: How Reagan Has Put America in the Dark about Energy. 49p. 1984. pap. 5.00 (ISBN 0-937188-26-3). Pub Citizen Inc.

Green, Julian. Diary: Nineteen Twenty-Eight to Nineteen Fifty-Seven. 313p. 1985. pap. 9.95 (ISBN 0-88184-119-6). Carroll & Graf.

Green, Julian, tr. see Peguy, Charles P.
Green, Julien. The Dark Journey. Holland, Vyvyan, tr. from Fr. LC 76-152597. 376p. Repr. of 1929 ed. lib. bdg. 22.50x (ISBN 0-8371-6031-6, GRDJ). Greenwood.
--God's Fool: The Life of Francis of Assisi. LC 84-48771. 256p. 1985. 16.30 (ISBN 0-06-063462-6, HarpR). Har-Row.
--Memories of Evil Days. Piriou, Jean-Pierre J., ed. LC 75-44037. 200p. 1976. 14.95x (ISBN 0-8139-0553-2). U Pr of Va.
--Memories of Happy Days. Repr. of 1942 ed. lib. bdg. 18.75x (ISBN 0-8371-2310-0, GRMD). Greenwood.
Green, Justin J., jt. ed. see Chipp, Sylvia A.
Green, K. Family Life Education: Focus on Student Involvement. LC 75-4098. 1975. pap. 3.00 (ISBN 0-686-14989-0, 261-08420). Home Econ Educ.
Green, K. & Coombs, Rod. The Effects of Microelectronic Technologies on Employment Prospects. 240p. 1980. text ed. 36.75x (ISBN 0-566-00418-6). Gower Pub Co.
Green, K. B. Test Item Construction in the Cognitive Domain. 1979. 2.00 (ISBN 0-686-34528-2, A261-08443). Home Econ Educ.
Green, Karen. Classic Cold Cuisine. LC 84-2752. (Illus.). 256p. 1984. 16.95 (ISBN 0-87477-322-9); pap. 9.95. J P Tarcher.
--The Great International Noodle Experience. LC 77-76546. (Illus.). 1977. 10.95 (ISBN 0-689-10807-9); pap. 4.95 (ISBN 0-689-70584-0, 247). Atheneum.
--Japanese Cooking for the American Table. LC 82-10397. (Illus.). 176p. 1982. 14.95 (ISBN 0-87477-215-X). J P Tarcher.
Green, Karen & Black, Betty. How to Cook His Goose: And Other Wild Games. LC 83-61149. 1977. pap. 8.95 (ISBN 0-8329-2293-5, Pub. by Winchester Pr). New Century.
Green, Kate. If the World is Running Out. LC 83-80592. (Illus.). 80p. (Orig.). 1983. pap. 5.00 (ISBN 0-930100-15-8). Holy Cow.
--Shattered Moon. (Orig.). 1986. pap. 3.95 (ISBN 0-440-17593-3). Dell.
Green, Kate, et al. Believing Everything: An Anthology of New Writing. Logue, Mary & Sutin, Laurence, eds. LC 79-91217. (Illus.). 160p. (Orig.). 1980. pap. 4.95 (ISBN 0-930100-06-9). Holy Cow.
Green, Kenneth & Van Dam, Rika. Appleworks & III E-Z Pieces: The Tutorial. 256p. 1985. pap. 14.95 (ISBN 0-88056-331-1). Dilithium Pr.
Green, Kenneth A. Positive Parenting. 1979. 3 ring notebook 24.00x (ISBN 0-88035-053-9); pap. text ed. 6.00x parent's wkbk. (ISBN 0-88035-054-7). Human Kinetics.
Green, Kenneth A., et al. Better Grades in College with Less Effort. LC 70-134238. 176p. (Orig.). 1971. pap. 4.95 (ISBN 0-8120-0415-9). Barron.
Green, Kenneth C. & Van Dam, Rika. The Joy of Macintosh: Recipes for Using Your Mac Productively. 1986. pap. 18.95 (ISBN 0-673-18329-7). Scott F.
--The Macintosh Apple: A Comprehensive Reference Guide. (Illus.). 256p. pap. 14.95 (ISBN 0-88056-332-X). Dilithium Pr.
Green, Kerry & Leocha, Charles. Escape Manual: Italy. Demers, W. A., ed. (Escape Manual Ser.). (Illus.). 160p. (Orig.). 1986. pap. 6.95 (ISBN 0-915009-04-8). World Leis Corp.
--Whole Europe Escape Manual: France, Holland, Belgium, with Luxembourg. Demers, W. A., ed. (Escape Manual Ser.). Orig. Title: Escape Manual: France, Holland, Belgium, with Luxembourg. (Illus.). 160p. (Orig.). 1985. pap. 6.95 (ISBN 0-915009-02-1). World Leis Corp.
Green, Kerry & Leocha, Charles A. The Whole Europe Escape Manual: UK, Ireland. Demers, W A., ed. (Escape Manual Ser.). Orig. Title: Escape Manual: UK, Ireland. (Illus.). 160p. 1984. pap. 6.95 (ISBN 0-915009-00-5). World Leis Corp.
Green, Kevin W., ed. The City As a Stage: Strategies for the Arts in Urban Economics. LC 82-82824. (Illus.). 164p. (Orig.). 1983. pap. 12.50 (ISBN 0-941182-04-5). Partners Livable.
Green, L. C. Essays on the Modern Law of War. 350p. 1985. lib. bdg. 37.50 (ISBN 0-941320-26-X). Transnatl Pubs.
Green, L. F., ed. Developments in Soft Drinks Technology, Vols. 1 & 2. Houghton, H. W. (Illus.). 1984. Vol. 1, 1978. 52.00 (ISBN 0-85334-767-0, Pub. by Elsevier Applied Sci England); Vol. 2, 1984. 44.50; Vol. 3, 1984. 48.25. Elsevier.
Green, L. F., jt. ed. see Birch, G. G.
Green, Landis K. The Astrologer's Manual. LC 74-16082. 256p. 1975. pap. 6.95 (ISBN 0-668-04200-1). Arco.
Green, Laura. Folktales from Hawaii. lib. bdg. 79.95 (ISBN 0-87968-521-2). Krishna Pr.
--Help: Getting to Know About Needing & Giving. LC 80-81082. (Juvenile Ser.). 32p. 1981. 10.95 (ISBN 0-87705-402-9). Human Sci Pr.
Green, Laurel & Beck, Trudy. My Birthday Memories. (Illus.). (ps-12). 1985. 5.00 (ISBN 0-9613079-1-9). Greenbeck.
Green, Laurence. America Goes to Press: The News of Yesterday. LC 79-145060. 1971. Repr. of 1936 ed. 29.00x (ISBN 0-403-01003-9). Scholarly.
Green, Laurence Craig see Craig-Green, Laurence.
Green, Lawrence & Kansler, Connie, eds. Professional & Scientific Literature on Patient Education: A Guide to Information Sources. (Health Affairs Information Guide Ser.: Vol. 5). 330p. 1980. 58.00x (ISBN 0-8103-1422-3). Gale.
Green, Lawrence S. & Johnston, Francis S., eds. Social & Biological Predictors of Nutritional Status, Physical Growth & Neurological Development. 1980. 37.50 (ISBN 0-12-299750-6). Acad Pr.
Green, Lawrence W. & Anderson, C. L. Community Health. 4th ed. LC 81-18785. (Illus.). 620p. 1982. text ed. 22.95 (ISBN 0-8016-0187-8). Mosby.
Green, Lawrence W., et al. Health Education Planning: A Diagnostic Approach. LC 79-89920. 306p. 1980. text ed. 20.95 (ISBN 0-87484-471-1). Mayfield Pub.
Green, Lee. Sportswit. LC 83-48840. 270p. 1984. 15.95 (ISBN 0-06-015272-9, HarpT). Har-Row.
--Sportswit. 256p. 1984. pap. 9.57i (ISBN 0-06-091133-6, CN 1133, CN). Har-Row.
--Teaching Tools You Can Make. 1978. pap. 6.95 (ISBN 0-88207-465-2). Victor Bks.
--Use Your Overhead. LC 78-64398. 71p. 1979. pap. 6.95 (ISBN 0-88207-467-9). Victor Bks.
Green, Lee & Dengerink, Don. Five Hundred One Ways to Use the Overhead Projector. 200p. pap. text ed. 18.50 (ISBN 0-87287-339-0). Libs Unl.
Green, Lee, jt. auth. see Christensen, Ann.
Green, Leon. The Litigation Process in Tort Law. 2nd ed. 656p. 1977. pap. text ed. 14.50 (ISBN 0-672-82836-7, Bobbs-Merrill Law). Michie Co.
Green, Leon, et al. Advanced Torts: Injuries to Business, Family & Political Interests. 2nd ed. 544p. 1977. write for info. West Pub.
--Cases & Materials on Torts. 2nd ed. 1360p. 1977. write for info. West Pub.
Green, Leslie. Law & Society: Essays in the Sociology of Law. 502p. 1975. text ed. 35.00 (ISBN 0-379-00307-4). Oceana.
Green, Leslie C. International Law Through the Cases. 4th ed. LC 78-1420. (Illus.). 865p. 1978. lib. bdg. 50.00 (ISBN 0-379-20404-5); pap. text ed. 29.50 (ISBN 0-379-20405-3). Oceana.
Green, Lewis. Bed & Breakfast Washington. Burton, Brenda, ed. LC 83-63518. (Illus.). 96p. (Orig.). 1984. pap. 7.95 (ISBN 0-915325-00-4, 19607). New Hor Pubs.
--Fairs & Festivals of the Pacific Northwest. LC 84-62199. (Illus.). 96p. (Orig.). 1985. pap. 9.95 (ISBN 0-915325-01-2). New Hor Pubs.
--The Silence of Snakes. 350p. 1984. 15.95 (ISBN 0-89587-040-1). Blair.
Green, Lewis W. And Scatter the Proud. LC 78-88672. 1969. 12.95 (ISBN 0-910244-54-5). Blair.
--The High-Pitched Laugh of a Painted Lady. LC 80-16382. 1980. 10.00 (ISBN 0-89587-017-7); pap. 5.95 (ISBN 0-89587-020-7). Blair.
Green, Lila. Tales from Africa. LC 78-54623. (The World Folktale Library). (Illus.). 1979. PLB 12.68 (ISBN 0-382-03350-7). Silver.
--Tales from Hispanic Lands. LC 78-54624. (The World Folktale Library). (Illus.). 1979. PLB 12.68 (ISBN 0-382-03349-3). Silver.
Green, Lowell C. How Melanchthon Helped Luther Discover the Gospel: The Doctrine of Justification in the Reformation. 274p. 9.95 (ISBN 0-89890-010-7). Attic Pr.
Green, Lucinda. Regal Realm: A World Champion's Story. (Illus.). 188p. 1984. 16.95 (ISBN 0-7207-1471-0). Merrimack Pub Cir.
Green, M. Igbo Village Affairs. 262p. 1964. Repr. of 1947 ed. 29.50x (ISBN 0-7146-1669-9, F Cass Co). Biblio Dist.
--Second Epistle Peter & Epistle of Jude. (Tyndale Bible Commentaries: Vol. 18). 1968. pap. 3.95 (ISBN 0-8028-1417-4). Eerdmans.
Green, M., jt. ed. see Domb, C.
Green, M., ed. see Olesha, Iurii.
Green, M., tr. see Olesha, Iurii.
Green, M A., jt. auth. see Studer, H.
Green, M. C. & Targett, B. R. Space Age Puppets & Masks. LC 77-89957. (Illus.). (gr. 4 up). 1969. 10.00 (ISBN 0-8238-0070-9). Plays.
Green, M. L., ed. see Royal Society Discussion Meeting, May 20-21, 1982.
Green, M. S., ed. Critical Phenomena. (Italian Physical Society: Course 51). 1973. 88.00 (ISBN 0-12-368851-5). Acad Pr.
Green, Malcolm. Through the Year in West Africa. (Through the Year Ser.). (Illus.). 72p. (gr. 7-10). 1982. 14.95 (ISBN 0-7134-3964-5, Pub. by Batsford England). David & Charles.
Green, Marc, jt. auth. see Farber, Stephen.
Green, Margaret. Lake Mary's Florida. 1985. price not set (ISBN 0-913122-50-5). Mickler Hse.
Green, Marge. A Life with Wings. 1966. 8.75 (ISBN 0-89137-403-5); pap. 4.95 (ISBN 0-89137-402-7). Quality Pubns.
--Martha, Martha! 1964. 8.75 (ISBN 0-89137-401-9); pap. 4.95 (ISBN 0-89137-400-0). Quality Pubns.
Green, Margerie. Chipped Stone Raw Material & the Study of Interaction. (Occasional Paper: No. 6). Date not set. price not set. (ISBN 0-88104-051-7). Center Archaeo.
Green, Marguerite. The National Civic Federation & the American Labor Movement. LC 73-9337. 537p. 1973. Repr. of 1956 ed. lib. bdg. 23.00x (ISBN 0-8371-7007-9, GRCF). Greenwood.
Green, Marian. Experiments in Aquarian Magic. 160p. 1985. pap. 7.95 (ISBN 0-8408-0407-5). Newcastle Pub.
--Magic for the Aquarian Age: A Contemporary Textbook of Practical Magical Techniques. 160p. 1983. pap. 7.95 (ISBN 0-85030-318-4). Newcastle Pub.
--Magic for the Aquarian Age: A Contemporary Textbook of Practical Magical Techniques. (Illus.). 144p. (Orig.). 1983. pap. 7.95 (ISBN 0-85030-318-4, Pub. by Aquarian Pr England). Sterling.
Green, Marilyn L. & Harry, Joann. Nutrition in Contemporary Nursing Practice. LC 80-22426. 864p. 1981. 29.50 (ISBN 0-471-03892-X, Pub. by Wiley Med). Wiley.
Green, Marion, jt. auth. see Gardner, Rosalyn.
Green, Marjorie, ed. see Polyani, Michael.
Green, Marjorie, tr. see Jahn, Janheinz.
Green, Mark. The Other Government. 318p. 1975. 12.50 (ISBN 0-686-36548-8). Ctr Responsive Law.
Green, Mark & Berry, John F. The Challenge of Hidden Profits: Reducing Corporate Bureaucracy & Waste. 382p. 1985. 19.95 (ISBN 0-688-03986-3). Morrow.
Green, Mark & Waldman, Michael. Who Runs Congress? 4th ed. (Orig.). 1984. pap. 3.95 (ISBN 0-440-19676-0). Dell.
Green, Mark, ed. The Big Business Reader: On Corporate America. rev. ed. 480p. (Orig.). 1983. pap. 12.95 (ISBN 0-8298-0439-0). Pilgrim NY.
--The Closed Enterprise System. 288p. 1972. pap. 1.95 (ISBN 0-686-36547-X). Ctr Responsive Law.
Green, Mark & MacColl, Gail, eds. There He Goes Again: Ronald Reagan's Reign of Error. 128p. 1983. pap. 4.95 (ISBN 0-394-72171-3). Pantheon.
Green, Mark J. The Other Government: The Unseen Power of Washington Lawyers. new ed. 1978. pap. 3.45 (ISBN 0-393-00865-7, N865, Norton Lib). Norton.
Green, Mark J. & Wasserstein, Bruce, eds. With Justice for Some: An Indictment of the Law by Young Advocates. LC 70-136235. 416p. 1972. pap. 5.95x (ISBN 0-8070-0541-X, BP429). Beacon Pr.
Green, Martin. The Great American Adventure: Action Stories from Cooper to Mailer & What They Reveal about American Manhood. LC 83-72386. 224p. 1984. 19.95 (ISBN 0-8070-6356-8). Beacon Pr.
--Home Pet Vet Guide: Cats. 1983. pap. 8.95 (ISBN 0-345-28945-5). Ballantine.
--The Home Pet Vet Guide: Dogs. 1980. 7.95 (ISBN 0-345-28944-7). Ballantine.
--Re-Appraisals: Some Commonsense Readings in American Literature. 1967. pap. 1.65x (ISBN 0-393-00400-7, Norton Lib). Norton.
--Tolstoy & Gandhi, Men of Peace (A Biography) LC 82-72397. 500p. 1983. 23.50 (ISBN 0-465-08631-4). Basic.
Green, Martin, ed. The Old English Elegies: New Essays in Criticism & Research. LC 82-48525. 240p. 1983. 32.50 (ISBN 0-8386-3141-X). Fairleigh Dickinson.
Green, Martin, jt. ed. see Ritterbush, Philip C.
Green, Martin A. Solar Cells: Operation Principles Technology & Systems Applications. (Illus.). 256p. 1982. 38.95 (ISBN 0-13-822270-3). P-H.
Green, Martin B. Science & the Shabby Curate of Poetry: Essays about the Two Cultures. LC 77-27419. 1978. Repr. of 1964 ed. lib. bdg. 17.00x (ISBN 0-313-20191-9, GRSS). Greenwood.
Green, Martin I. Lifesavers. (Orig.). 1982. pap. 8.95 (ISBN 0-345-29032-1). Ballantine.
--A Sigh of Relief: First-Aid Handbook for Childhood Emergencies. rev. ed. (Illus.). 1984. pap. 12.95 (ISBN 0-553-34090-5). Bantam.
Green, Marvin, jt. auth. see Behrendt, Hans.
Green, Mary & Gillmar, Stanley. How to Be an Importer & Pay for Your World Travels. LC 78-64971. 1979. pap. 6.95 (ISBN 0-89087-241-4). Celestial Arts.
Green, Mary A. Festive Crafts. (Illus.). 124p. 1984. 15.95 (ISBN 0-584-11035-9, Pub. by Salem Hse Ltd). Merrimack Pub Cir.
--The Teen I Want to Be. 224p. 1985. 12.95 (ISBN 0-8407-9040-6); pap. 8.95 (ISBN 0-8407-9544-0). Nelson.
Green, Mary A., ed. see Rous, John.
Green, Mary J. Louis Guilloux: An Artisan of Language. 184p. 1980. 15.95 (ISBN 0-917786-15-7). Summa Pubns.
Green, Mary L. The Little Almond Cookbook. Noonan, Patricia, ed. (Little Cookbooks). (Illus., Orig.). 1984. pap. 1.50 (ISBN 0-934030-10-3). Metagraphics.
--The Little Apple Cookbook. Noonan, Patricia, ed. (Little Cookbooks). 8p. (Orig.). 1984. pap. 1.50 (ISBN 0-934030-01-4). Metagraphics.
--The Little Artichoke Cookbook. Noonan, Patricia, ed. (Little Cookbooks). (Illus., Orig.). 1984. pap. 1.50 (ISBN 0-934030-06-5). Metagraphics.
--The Little Avocado Cookbook. Noonan, Patricia, ed. (Little Cookbooks). (Illus., Orig.). 1984. pap. 1.50 (ISBN 0-934030-16-2). Metagraphics.
--The Little Beer Cookbooks. Noonan, Patricia, ed. (Little Cookbooks). (Illus., Orig.). 1984. pap. 1.50 (ISBN 0-934030-08-1). Metagraphics.
--The Little Cake Cookbooks. Noonan, Patricia, ed. (Little Cookbooks). (Illus., Orig.). 1984. pap. 1.50 (ISBN 0-934030-26-X). Metagraphics.
--The Little Cashew Cookbook. Noonan, Patricia, ed. (Little Cookbooks). (Illus., Orig.). 1984. pap. 1.50 (ISBN 0-934030-18-9). Metagraphics.
--The Little Cheese Cookbook. Noonan, Patricia, ed. (Little Cookbooks). (Illus., Orig.). 1984. pap. 1.50 (ISBN 0-934030-11-1). Metagraphics.
--The Little Cheesecake Cookbook. Noonan, Patricia, ed. (Little Cookbooks). (Illus., Orig.). 1984. pap. 1.50 (ISBN 0-934030-20-0). Metagraphics.
--The Little Cherry Cookbook. Noonan, Patricia, ed. (Little Cookbooks). (Illus., Orig.). 1984. pap. 1.50 (ISBN 0-934030-04-9). Metagraphics.
--The Little Chocolate Cookbook. Noonan, Patricia, ed. (Little Cookbooks). (Illus., Orig.). 1984. pap. 1.50 (ISBN 0-934030-21-9). Metagraphics.
--The Little Cinnamon Cookbook. Noonan, Patricia, ed. (Little Cookbooks). (Illus., Orig.). 1984. pap. 1.50 (ISBN 0-934030-29-4). Metagraphics.
--The Little Coffee Cookbook. Noonan, Patricia, ed. (Little Cookbooks). (Illus., Orig.). 1984. pap. 1.50 (ISBN 0-934030-14-6). Metagraphics.
--The Little Croissant Cookbook. Noonan, Patricia, ed. (Little Cookbooks). (Illus., Orig.). 1984. pap. 1.50 (ISBN 0-934030-05-7). Metagraphics.
--The Little Egg Cookbook. Noonan, Patricia, ed. (Little Cookbooks). (Illus., Orig.). 1984. pap. 1.50 (ISBN 0-934030-27-8). Metagraphics.
--The Little Hamburger Cookbook. Noonan, Patricia, ed. (Little Cookbooks). (Illus., Orig.). 1984. pap. 1.50 (ISBN 0-934030-32-4). Metagraphics.
--The Little Honey Cookbook. Noonan, Patricia, ed. (Little Cookbooks). (Illus., Orig.). 1984. pap. 1.50 (ISBN 0-934030-15-4). Metagraphics.
--The Little Ice Cream Cookbook. Noonan, Patricia, ed. (Little Cookbooks). (Illus., Orig.). 1984. pap. 1.50 (ISBN 0-934030-25-1). Metagraphics.
--The Little Lemon Cookbook. Noonan, Patricia, ed. (Little Cookbooks). (Illus., Orig.). 1984. pap. 1.50 (ISBN 0-934030-03-0). Metagraphics.
--The Little Lobster Cookbook. Noonan, Patricia, ed. (Little Cookbooks). (Illus., Orig.). 1984. pap. 1.50 (ISBN 0-934030-17-0). Metagraphics.
--The Little Orange Cookbook. Noonan, Patricia, ed. (Little Cookbooks). (Illus., Orig.). 1984. pap. 1.50 (ISBN 0-934030-23-5). Metagraphics.
--The Little Pastry Cookbook. Noonan, Patricia, ed. (Little Cookbooks). (Illus., Orig.). 1984. pap. 1.50 (ISBN 0-934030-30-8). Metagraphics.
--The Little Pepper Cookbook. Noonan, Patricia, ed. (Little Cookbooks). (Illus., Orig.). 1984. pap. 1.50 (ISBN 0-934030-02-2). Metagraphics.
--The Little Pie Cookbooks. Noonan, Patricia, ed. (Little Cookbooks). (Illus., Orig.). 1984. pap. 1.50 (ISBN 0-934030-09-X). Metagraphics.
--The Little Pineapple Cookbook. Noonan, Patricia, ed. (Little Cookbooks). (Illus., Orig.). 1984. pap. 1.50 (ISBN 0-934030-19-7). Metagraphics.
--The Little Potato Cookbook. Noonan, Patricia, ed. (Little Cookbooks). (Illus., Orig.). 1984. pap. 1.50 (ISBN 0-934030-31-6). Metagraphics.
--The Little Shrimp Cookbook. Noonan, Patricia, ed. (Little Cookbooks). (Illus., Orig.). 1984. pap. 1.50 (ISBN 0-934030-28-6). Metagraphics.
--The Little Strawberry Cookbook. Noonan, Patricia, ed. (Little Cookbooks). (Illus., Orig.). 1984. pap. 1.50 (ISBN 0-934030-07-3). Metagraphics.
--The Little Tomato Cookbook. Noonan, Patricia, ed. (Little Cookbooks). (Illus., Orig.). 1984. pap. 1.50 (ISBN 0-934030-24-3). Metagraphics.
--The Little Wine Cookbook. Noonan, Patricia, ed. (Little Cookbooks). (Illus., Orig.). 1984. pap. 1.50 (ISBN 0-934030-22-7). Metagraphics.
Green, Maryan. International Law: The Law of Peace. 2nd ed. 336p. 1982. 26.50x (ISBN 0-7121-0956-0). Sheridan.
Green, Mason A. Nineteen Two in Vermont: The Flight for Local Option. 189p. 1912. 1.00x (ISBN 0-934720-01-0). VT Hist Soc.
Green, Mason S. The Maps of Fiji: A Selective & Annotated Cartobibliography. LC 78-24066. (Western Association of Map Libraries: Occasional Paper; No. 5). (Illus.). 90p. (Orig.). 1978. pap. 4.00x (ISBN 0-939112-06-X). Western Assn Map.
Green, Maurice B. & West, T. F. Chemicals for Crop Protection & Pest Control. 2nd ed. LC 77-4881. 1977. pap. text ed. 16.25 (ISBN 0-08-019013-8). Pergamon.
Green, Maurice R., ed. Violence & the Family. (AAAS Selected Symposium Ser.: No. 47). 200p. 1980. pap. text ed. 10.00x (ISBN 0-86531-141-2). Westview.
Green, Maurus, tr. see Goberna, M. Regina.
Green, Melinda. Rachel's Recital. LC 79-1510. (Illus.). (gr. 1-5). 1979. 6.95g (ISBN 0-316-32634-8, Pub. by Atlantic-Little Brown). Little.
Green, Melvin D. Agoraphobia; the Silent Epidemic: A Self Help, Step-by-Step Manual for Recovery. (The Skill Builder Ser.). 164p. (Orig.). cancelled (ISBN 0-943920-56-6); pap. cancelled (ISBN 0-943920-57-4). Metamorphous Pr.
Green, Merrill. A Practical Guide to Screen Printing. LC 84-71004. (Illus.). 96p. 1984. write for info. (ISBN 0-9613500-0-8). Adv Group.
Green, Michael. The Art of Coarse Acting. LC 80-20310. (Illus.). 128p. 1981. 9.95 (ISBN 0-89676-041-3). Drama Bk.
--The Art of Coarse Sex. 192p. 1981. 29.00x (ISBN 0-686-87314-9, Pub. by Hutchinson). State Mutual Bk.

--Creo en el Espiritu Santo. Vilela, Ernesto S., tr. from Eng. LC 77-164. (Serie Creo). 267p. (Span.). 1977. pap. 5.95 (ISBN 0-89922-090-8). Edit Caribe.
--The Day Death Died. LC 82-6522. 128p. (Orig.). 1982. pap. 3.25 (ISBN 0-87784-391-0). Inter-Varsity.
--The Empty Cross of Jesus. LC 84-19312. (The Jesus Library). 224p. 1984. pap. 6.95 (ISBN 0-87784-930-7). Inter-Varsity.
--Evangelism in the Early Church. 1970. pap. 7.95 (ISBN 0-8028-1612-6). Eerdmans.
--Evangelism: Now & Then. 150p. 1982. pap. 3.50 (ISBN 0-87784-394-5). Inter-Varsity.
--I Believe in Satan's Downfall. (I Believe Ser.). 256p. (Orig.). 1981. pap. 6.95 (ISBN 0-8028-1892-7). Eerdmans.
--I Believe in the Holy Spirit. (I Believe Ser). 224p. 1975. pap. 5.95 (ISBN 0-8028-1609-6). Eerdmans.
--New Life, New Lifestyle: A Fresh Look at the World. LC 84-25390. 159p. 1985. pap. 5.95 (ISBN 0-88070-073-4). Multnomah.
--Running from Reality. LC 83-18669. 128p. 1983. pap. 3.50 (ISBN 0-87784-349-X). Inter-Varsity.
--Second Peter & Jude. (Tyndale New Testament Commentaries Ser.). 1986. pap. 5.95 (ISBN 0-8028-0078-5). Eerdmans.
--Tonight Josephine: And Other Undiscovered Letters. 1982. 5.95 (ISBN 0-395-32510-2). HM.
--A Walk Through the Shire: Wherein We Discover Some Rare Drawings of Hobbit Life. LC 80-52955. (Illus., Orig.). 1980. lib. bdg. 12.90 (ISBN 0-89471-114-8); pap. 4.95 (ISBN 0-89471-115-6). Running Pr.
--What Is Christianity? 64p. 1982. 10.95 (ISBN 0-687-44650-3). Abingdon.
Green, Michael & Wilding, Michael. Cultural Policy in Great Britain. (Studies & Documents on Cultural Policies). (Orig.). 1971. pap. 5.00 (ISBN 92-3-100852-8, U122, UNESCO). Unipub.
Green, Michael, jt. auth. see Katsell, Jerome.
Green, Michael, jt. auth. see Zaloga, Steven.
Green, Michael, jt. auth. see Zaloga, Steven J.
Green, Michael, ed. Truck Facts Buyer's Guide, 1981. rev. ed. 96p. (Orig.). write for info. DMR Pubns.
Green, Michael, annotations by. & illus. Unicornis: On the History & Truth of the Unicorn. LC 83-3168. (Illus.). 64p. (Orig.). 1983. 14.95 (ISBN 0-89471-216-0); lib. bdg. 19.80 (ISBN 0-89471-207-1); pap. 7.95 (ISBN 0-89471-206-3). Running Pr.
Green, Michael, ed. see Buchanan, Duncan.
Green, Michael, ed. see Katsell, Jerome & Green, Michael.
Green, Michael, ed. see Kuzmin, Mikhail.
Green, Michael, tr. from Rus. The Russian Symbolist Theatre: An Anthology of Plays & Critical Texts. 350p. 1984. 37.50 (ISBN 0-686-82225-0); pap. 10.00 cancelled (ISBN 0-88233-798-X). Ardis Pubs.
Green, Michael, illus. The Unicorn Notebook: An Illustrated Book with Space for Notes. (Illus.). 96p. (gr. 5 up). 1985. pap. 5.98 (ISBN 0-89471-395-7). Running Pr.
Green, Michael D. The Creeks: A Critical Bibliography. LC 79-2166. (Newberry Library Center for the History of the American Indian Bibliographical Ser.). 132p. 1980. pap. 4.95x (ISBN 0-253-31776-2). Ind U Pr.
--The Politics of Indian Removal: Creek Government & Society in Crisis. LC 81-14670. xvi, 238p. 1982. 21.50x (ISBN 0-8032-2109-6). U of Nebr Pr.
--The Politics of Indian Removal: Creek Government & Society in Crisis. LC 81-14670. (Illus.). xvi, 238p. 1985. pap. 5.95x (ISBN 0-8032-7015-1, Bison). U of Nebr Pr.
Green, Michael E. & Turk, Amos. Safety in Working with Chemistry. (Illus.). 1978. pap. text ed. write for info. (ISBN 0-02-346420-8). Macmillan.
Green, Michael L. Truck Facts, 1980. (Truck Facts, 1980). 1979. pap. 2.25 (ISBN 0-89552-062-1). DMR Pubns.
Green, Michael L., ed. Audio Equipment. 1978. pap. 1.95 (ISBN 0-89552-018-4). DMR Pubns.
--Auto Ratings, 1978. 1978. pap. 1.95 (ISBN 0-89552-019-2). DMR Pubns.
--Autos, 1979: Ratings, Specifications & Best Buys. (Buyer's Guide Reports Ser.). 1978. pap. 1.95 (ISBN 0-89552-051-6). DMR Pubns.
--Car Facts, 1979. (Buyer's Guide Reports Ser.). 1978. pap. 1.95 (ISBN 0-89552-050-8). DMR Pubns.
--Car Facts, 1981. rev. ed. (Buyer's Guide Ser.). 96p. (Orig.). pap. 2.50 (ISBN 0-89552-069-9). DMR Pubns.
--CB, Carsound & Communication Equipment. 1978. pap. 1.95 (ISBN 0-89552-016-8). DMR Pubns.
--Economy Cars, 1981. rev. ed. (Buyer's Guide Ser.). 96p. (Orig.). pap. 2.50 (ISBN 0-89552-073-7). DMR Pubns.
--Foreign Car Prices. (Buyer's Guide Reports Ser.). 1978. pap. 1.95 (ISBN 0-89552-023-0). DMR Pubns.
--Franchise Handbook. rev. ed. 1981. 13.20 (ISBN 0-89552-027-3); pap. text ed. 8.95 (ISBN 0-89552-026-5). DMR Pubns.
--Franchise Handbook. 1978. pap. 6.95 (ISBN 0-89552-020-6). DMR Pubns.
--New & Used Foreign Car Prices. rev. ed. (Buyer's Guide Ser.). 1979. pap. 2.25 (ISBN 0-89552-057-5). DMR Pubns.
--New & Used Foreign Car Prices. rev. ed. (Buyer's Guide Ser.). 96p. (Orig.). pap. 2.50 (ISBN 0-89552-067-2). DMR Pubns.
--New Car Prices Buyer's Guide, 1979. (Buyer's Guide Reports Ser.). 1978. pap. 1.95 (ISBN 0-685-26098-4). DMR Pubns.
--New Car Prices Buyer's Guide, 1981. rev. ed. (Buyer's Guide Ser.). 128p. (Orig.). pap. 2.50 (ISBN 0-89552-068-0). DMR Pubns.
--New Truck & Van Prices, 1981. rev. ed. (Buyer's Guide Ser.). 96p. (Orig.). pap. 2.50 (ISBN 0-89552-070-2). DMR Pubns.
--Nineteen Eighty Autos: Rating, Specifications & Best Buys. (Buyer's Guide Ser.). 1979. pap. 2.25 (ISBN 0-89552-060-5). DMR Pubns.
--Nineteen Eighty Car Facts. (Buyer's Guide Ser.). 1979. pap. 2.25 (ISBN 0-89552-059-1). DMR Pubns.
--Nineteen Eighty Economy Cars. (Buyer's Guide Ser.). 1979. pap. 2.25 (ISBN 0-89552-063-X). DMR Pubns.
--Nineteen Eighty New Car Prices. (Buyer's Guide Ser.). 1979. pap. 2.25 (ISBN 0-685-95267-3). DMR Pubns.
--Nineteen Eighty New Truck & Van Prices. (Buyer's Guide Ser.). 1979. pap. 2.25 (ISBN 0-89552-061-3). DMR Pubns.
--Photo Equipment. 1978. pap. 1.95 (ISBN 0-89552-017-6). DMR Pubns.
--Truck & Van Prices Buyer's Guide, 1979. (Buyer's Guide Reports Ser.). 1978. pap. 1.95 (ISBN 0-89552-052-4). DMR Pubns.
--Truck Facts, 1979. (Buyer's Guide Reports Ser.). 1978. pap. 1.95 (ISBN 0-89552-053-2). DMR Pubns.
--U. S. Income Tax Guide, 1979. (Buyer's Guide Reports Ser.). 1978. pap. 1.95 (ISBN 0-89552-054-0). DMR Pubns.
--U. S. Income Tax Guide, 1980. (Buyer's Guide Ser.). 1979. pap. 2.25 (ISBN 0-89552-064-8). DMR Pubns.
--U. S. Income Tax Guide, 1981. rev. ed. (Buyer's Guide Ser.). 80p. (Orig.). pap. 2.50 (ISBN 0-89552-074-5). DMR Pubns.
--Used Car Prices. rev. ed. (Buyer's Guide Ser.). 1979. pap. 2.25 (ISBN 0-89552-055-9). DMR Pubns.
--Used Car Prices. 1978. pap. 1.95 (ISBN 0-89552-014-1). DMR Pubns.
--Used Truck & Van Prices. rev. ed. (Buyer's Guide Ser.). 1979. pap. 2.25 (ISBN 0-89552-056-7). DMR Pubns.
--Used Truck & Van Prices. 1978. pap. 1.95 (ISBN 0-89552-015-X). DMR Pubns.
Green, Mildred D. Black Women Composers: A Genesis. (Music Ser.). 1983. lib. bdg. 19.95 (ISBN 0-8057-9450-6, Twayne). G K Hall.
Green, Milton D. It's Legal to Laugh. 80p. 1985. 8.95 (ISBN 0-533-06070-2). Vantage.
Green, Mimi & Naab, Maxine. Lamaze Is for Chickens: A Manual for Prepared Childbirth. 2nd ed. (Avery's Childbirth Education Ser.). (Illus.). 192p. 1985. pap. 8.95 (ISBN 0-89529-181-9). Avery Pub.
Green, Miranda. Roman Technology & Crafts. Hodge, Peter, ed. (Aspects of Roman Life Ser.). 48p. (Orig.). (gr. 7-12). 1979. pap. text ed. 3.95 (ISBN 0-582-20162-4). Longman.
Green, Miranda J. The Gods of Roman Britain. (Shire Archeology Ser.: No. 34). (Illus.). 64p. (Orig.). 1983. pap. 5.95 (ISBN 0-85263-634-2, Pub. by Shire Pubns England). Seven Hills Bks.
Green, Morris. Pediatric Diagnosis: Interpretation of Symptoms & Signs in Different Age Periods. 3rd ed. LC 79-65454. (Illus.). 658p. 1980. text ed. 36.95 (ISBN 0-7216-4242-X). Saunders.
--The Psychosocial Aspects of the Family: The New Pediatrics. LC 84-48800. (Johnson & Johnson Round Table Ser.). (Illus.). 304p. 1985. 32.50x (ISBN 0-669-09768-3). Lexington Bks.
Green, Morris & Haggerty, Robert J. Ambulatory Pediatrics Three. (Illus.). 576p. 1984. 45.00 (ISBN 0-7216-4237-3). Saunders.
Green, N. W. Mormonism: Its Rise, Progress & Present Condition. LC 79-134401. Repr. of 1870 ed. 32.50 (ISBN 0-404-08445-1). AMS Pr.
Green, Nan, tr. see Carrillo, Santiago.
Green, Nancy L. Pletzl of Paris: Jewish Immigrant Workers in the Belle Epoque. 288p. 1985. 37.50 (ISBN 0-8419-0995-4). Holmes & Meier.
Green, Noel, jt. ed. see Magne, Lawrence.
Green, Norma. The Hole in the Dike. LC 74-23562. (Illus.). 32p. (gr. k-3). 1975. 11.49 (ISBN 0-690-00734-5); PLB 12.89 (ISBN 0-690-00676-4). Crowell Jr Bks.
Green, Norman E. Earthquake Resistant Building Design & Construction. 2nd ed. 216p. 1981. 21.95 (ISBN 0-442-28799-2). Van Nos Reinhold.
Green Oak Township Historical Society. Yesteryears of Green Oak, Eighteen Thirty to Nineteen Thirty. LC 81-2270. (Illus.). xii, 338p. 1981. 22.50 (ISBN 0-936792-00-0). Green Oak Township.
Green, Oliver P., tr. see Hirschfeld, Magnus.
Green, Otis H. Spain & the Western Tradition: The Castilian Mind in Literature from "El Cid" to Calderon, Vols. 1-4. 1963. pap. 7.95 ea.; Vol. 1. (ISBN 0-299-02954-9); Vol. 2. (ISBN 0-299-03294-9); Vol. 3. (ISBN 0-299-03794-0); Vol. 4. (ISBN 0-299-04084-4). U of Wis Pr.
--Spain & the Western Tradition: The Castilian Mind in Literature from El Cid to Calderon, Vols. 2-4. 1968. 17.50x ea.; Vol. 2. (ISBN 0-299-03290-6); Vol. 3. (ISBN 0-299-03790-8); Vol. 4. (ISBN 0-299-04080-1). U of Wis Pr.
Green, P. E. & Lucky, R. W., eds. Computer Communications. LC 74-82501. 1975. 36.35 (ISBN 0-87942-041-3, PC00380). Inst Electrical.
Green, P. V. The Need for Long Term Lagoons: A Literature Survey, 1980. 1981. 69.00x (ISBN 0-686-97125-6, Pub. by W Spring England). State Mutual Bk.
Green, Pat, ed. see Peaslee, Ann.
Green, Patrick, jt. auth. see Bruce, Vicki.
Green, Paul. The Common Glory. LC 72-11622. (Illus.). 273p. 1973. Repr. of 1948 ed. lib. bdg. 24.75x (ISBN 0-8371-7080-X, GRCH). Greenwood.
--The Field God, & in Abrahams's Bosom. LC 83-45773. Repr. of 1927 ed. 29.50 (ISBN 0-404-20112-1). AMS Pr.
--Hawthorn Tree: Some Papers & Letters on Life & the Theatre. facsimile ed. LC 79-134085. (Essay Index Reprint Ser). Repr. of 1943 ed. 15.00 (ISBN 0-8369-2228-X). Ayer Co Pubs.
--Land of Nod & Other Stories. LC 75-33880. v, 153p. 1976. 9.95 (ISBN 0-8078-1269-2). U of NC Pr.
--The Outdoor Leadership Handbook. 42p. 1982. pap. 3.50 (ISBN 0-913724-32-7). Survival Ed Assoc.
--This View from Above. 1970. signed 7.50 (ISBN 0-686-11434-5, Pub. by Ferry Pr); pap. 1.00 (ISBN 0-686-11435-3). Small Pr Dist.
--Wide Fields. LC 79-101911. Repr. of 1928 ed. 14.50 (ISBN 0-404-00625-6). AMS Pr.
Green, Paul & Abbott, Abbe. I Am Eskimo: Aknik My Name. LC 59-15891. (Illus., Orig.). 1959. pap. 3.95 (ISBN 0-88240-001-0). Alaska Northwest.
Green, Paul B., jt. auth. see Subtelny, Stephen.
Green, Paul E. Analyzing Multivariate Data. 1978. text ed. 36.95 (ISBN 0-03-020786-X). Dryden Pr.
Green, Paul E. & Carroll, Douglas. Mathematical Tools for Applied Multivariate Analysis: Student Edition. 1978. 27.50 (ISBN 0-12-297552-9). Acad Pr.
Green, Paul E. & Tull, Donald S. Research for Marketing Decisions. 4th ed. (Illus.). 1978. ref. 32.95 (ISBN 0-13-774158-8). P-H.
Green, Paul E., ed. Mathematical Tools for Applied Multivariate Analysis. 1976. 59.50 (ISBN 0-12-297550-2). Acad Pr.
Green, Paul E., Jr., ed. Computer Network Architectures & Protocols. LC 82-5227. (Applications of Communications Theory Ser.). 735p. 1982. 65.00x (ISBN 0-306-40788-4, Plenum Pr). Plenum Pub.
Green, Paul M., jt. auth. see Hill, Carmen P.
Green, Paul M., jt. ed. see Holli, Melvin G.
Green, Percy B. History of Nursery Rhymes. LC 72-191809. 195p. 1899. lib. bdg. 25.00 (ISBN 0-8414-4506-0). Folcroft.
--History of Nursery Rhymes. LC 68-31082. 1968. Repr. of 1899 ed. 34.00x (ISBN 0-8103-3481-X). Gale.
--A History of Nursery Rhymes. 59.95 (ISBN 0-8490-0340-7). Gordon Pr.
Green, Peter. Ancient Greece: An Illustrated History. (Illus.). 1979. pap. 8.95 (ISBN 0-500-27161-5). Thames Hudson.
--Beyond the Wild Wood: The World of Kenneth Grahame. LC 83-5553. (Illus.). 224p. 17.95 (ISBN 0-87196-740-5). Facts on File.
--Design Education: Problem Solving & Visual Experience. 1974. pap. 14.95 (ISBN 0-7134-2325-0, Pub. by Batsford England). David & Charles.
--Essays in Antiquity. 1960. 15.95 (ISBN 0-7195-0558-5). Dufour.
--The Shadow of the Parthenon: Studies in Ancient History & Literature. LC 72-87205. 1973. 32.00x (ISBN 0-520-02322-6). U of Cal Pr.
Green, Peter, jt. auth. see Green, Susan.
Green, Peter, ed. see Grahame, Kenneth.
Green, Peter, tr. see Beti, Mongo.
Green, Peter, tr. see Juvenal.
Green, Peter, tr. see Ovid.
Green, Philip. New Angles on Salmon Fishing. (Illus.). 300p. 1984. pap. 15.95x (ISBN 0-04-799020-1). Allen Unwin.
--The Pursuit of Inequality. 1981. 14.95 (ISBN 0-394-50676-6). Pantheon.
--The Pursuit of Inequality. 1982. pap. 6.95 (ISBN 0-394-70654-4). Pantheon.
--Retrieving Democracy: In Search of Civic Equality. LC 84-23798. 288p. 1985. 21.95x (ISBN 0-8476-7405-3); pap. text ed. 10.95x (ISBN 0-8476-7406-1). Rowman & Allanheld.
Green, Philip, compiled by. Planning Legislation in North Carolina. 274p. 1984. 13.00 (ISBN 0-686-39446-1). U of NC Inst Gov.
Green, Philip P. An Introduction to Municipal Zoning. Rev. ed. 54p. 1983. 4.50 (ISBN 0-686-39441-0). U of NC Inst Gov.
Green, Philip P., jt. auth. see Davenport, Stephen E.
Green, Philip S., ed. Acoustical Holography, Vol. 5. LC 69-12533. 752p. 1974. 95.00x (ISBN 0-306-37725-X, Plenum Pr). Plenum Pub.
Green, Phillip P. Legal Aspects of Building Code Enforcement in North Carolina. 225p. 1981. 11.00 (ISBN 0-686-39442-9). U of NC Inst Gov.
--Legal Responsibilities of the Local Housing Inspector in North Carolina. 3rd ed. 93p. 1977. 4.00 (ISBN 0-686-39443-7). U of NC Inst Gov.
--Legal Responsibilities of the Local Zoning Administrator in North Carolina. 102p. 1982. 5.00 (ISBN 0-686-39444-5). U of NC Inst Gov.
Green, Phyllis. Bagdad Ate It. (gr. k-3). 1980. PLB 8.60 (ISBN 0-531-02855-0). Watts.
--Eating Ice Cream with a Werewolf. LC 82-47727. (Illus.). 128p. (gr. 3-7). 1983. 10.53i (ISBN 0-06-022140-2); PLB 10.89g (ISBN 0-06-022141-0). HarpJ.
--Eating Ice Cream with a Werewolf. (gr. k-6). 1985. pap. 2.50 (ISBN 0-440-42182-9, YB). Dell.
--Gloomy Louie. Fay, Ann, ed. LC 79-28533. (Illus.). (gr. 3-6). 1980. PLB 7.50 (ISBN 0-8075-2962-1). A Whitman.
--It's Me, Christy. 96p. (gr. 4-6). 1983. pap. 1.95 (ISBN 0-590-32736-4, Apple Paperbacks). Scholastic Inc.
--Mildred Murphy How Does Your Garden Grow? (gr. k-6). 1980. pap. 1.75 (ISBN 0-440-45590-1, YB). Dell.
--A New Mother for Martha. LC 78-16731. 32p. 1978. 10.95 (ISBN 0-87705-330-8). Human Sci Pr.
--Wild Violets. 112p. (gr. k-6). 1980. pap. 1.50 (ISBN 0-440-49671-3, YB). Dell.
Green, R. Ford Madox Ford: Prose & Politics. LC 80-41566. 200p. 1981. 44.50 (ISBN 0-521-23610-X). Cambridge U Pr.
Green, R., jt. ed. see Pavoni, N.
Green, R., jt. ed. see Vyskcosil, P.
Green, R. A., jt. auth. see Coplans, M. P.
Green, R. C. & Kelly, M., eds. Studies in Oceanic Culture History, Vol. 3. (Pacific Anthropological Records: No. 11). 1972. pap. 4.00 (ISBN 0-910240-62-0). Bishop Mus.
Green, R. D. Hydrogen Bonding by C-H Groups. LC 74-11310. 207p. 1974. 58.95 (ISBN 0-470-32478-3). Halsted Pr.
Green, R. Elliot, jt. ed. see Parslow, R. D.
Green, R. K. & Schaefer, Arlene B. Forensic Psychology: A Primer for Legal & Mental Health Professionals. 288p. 1984. 29.75x (ISBN 0-398-04838-X). C C Thomas.
Green, R. L. The Tale of Thebes. LC 76-22979. (Illus.). 1977. o. p. 14.95 (ISBN 0-521-21410-6); pap. 6.95 (ISBN 0-521-21411-4). Cambridge U Pr.
Green, R. N., jt. auth. see Ramsden, E.
Green, Raleigh T. Genealogical & Historical Notes on Culpeper County, Virginia. LC 64-19758. xxvi, 280p. 1983. Repr. of 1900 ed. 17.50 (ISBN 0-8063-7957-X). Regional.
Green, Ralph. Works of Ralph Green. LC 81-51378. 112p. 1981. Repr. of 1955 ed. 24.95 (ISBN 0-932606-01-6). Ye Olde Print.
Green, Ralph C. Medical Overkill: Diseases of Medical Progress. (Illus.). 320p. 1983. 14.50 (ISBN 0-89313-065-6). G F Stickley.
Green, Rayna. Native American Women: A Contextual Bibliography. LC 82-48571. 128p. 1983. 19.50x (ISBN 0-253-33976-6). Ind U Pr.
Green, Rayna, ed. That's What She Said: Contemporary Poetry & Fiction by Native American Women. LC 83-49002. (Illus.). 328p. (Orig.). 1984. 29.95x (ISBN 0-253-35855-8); pap. text ed. 12.50x (ISBN 0-253-20338-4, 338). Ind U Pr.
Green, Reginald H., jt. auth. see Espiritu, Augusto C.
Green, Reginald H., et al, eds. Namibia, the Last Colony. LC 80-40465. pap. 80.00 (ISBN 0-317-27829-0, 2025249). Bks Demand UMI.
Green, Richard. Africa Review, 1985. (World of Information Ser.). (Illus.). 352p. (Orig.). 1985. pap. 24.95 (ISBN 0-345-32183-9). World Almanac.
--Anti-Methodist Publications Issued During the 18th Century. LC 71-83701. 175p. 1974. Repr. of 1902 ed. lib. bdg. 22.50 (ISBN 0-8337-1436-8). B Franklin.
--Asia & Pacific Review 1985. (World of Information Ser.). (Illus.). 336p. (Orig.). 1985. pap. 24.95 (ISBN 0-345-32186-3). World Almanac.
--Latin America & Caribbean Review. (World of Information Ser.). (Illus.). 240p. 1985. pap. 24.95, 1985 ed. (ISBN 0-911818-78-2); 1986 ed. 24.95, (ISBN 0-345-32837-X). World Almanac.
--The Works of John & Charles Wesley. 2nd rev. ed. LC 74-26049. Repr. of 1906 ed. 23.00 (ISBN 0-404-12924-2). AMS Pr.
Green, Richard, jt. auth. see Wagner, Gorm.
Green, Richard, ed. Middle East Review, Nineteen Eighty-Five. (World of Information Ser.). (Illus.). 320p. (Orig.). 1985. pap. 24.95 (ISBN 0-911818-77-4). World Almanac.
--Middle East Review: Nineteen Eighty-Five. 1985. 24.95 (ISBN 0-345-32184-7). Ballantine.
--Pacific Business Guide. 208p. 1984. pap. 9.95 (ISBN 0-904439-43-7, Pub. by World Info England). Hippocrene Bks.
Green, Richard, et al, eds. Transsexualism & Sex Reassignment. LC 69-15761. (Illus.). pap. 134.00 (ISBN 0-317-07865-8, 2013133). Bks Demand UMI.
Green, Richard A., ed. Neuropharmacology of Serotonin. (Illus.). 300p. 1985. cloth 35.00 (ISBN 0-19-261471-1). Oxford U Pr.
Green, Richard F. Poets & Princepleasers: Literature & the English Court in the Late Middle Ages. 1980. 30.00x (ISBN 0-8020-5409-9). U of Toronto Pr.

Green, Richard H. The Consolation of Philosophy: Boethius. 1962. pap. text ed. write for info. (ISBN 0-02-346450-X). Macmillan.

Green, Richard H., tr. see Boethius.

Green, Richard J. Dissolving Depression & Finding Peace. pap. 2.50 (ISBN 0-87516-278-9). De Vorss.

--Meditation, The Highway to Happiness. 3rd ed. 40p. 1980. pap. 3.00 (ISBN 0-87516-407-2). De Vorss.

Green, Richard L. & Gibson, John M. A Bibliography of A. Conan Doyle. (Soho Bibliographies Ser.). (Illus.). 1983. 49.95x (ISBN 0-19-818190-6). Oxford U Pr.

Green, Richard L., ed. see Doyle, Arthur Conan.

Green, Robert. R. C. Hutchinson: The Man & His Books. LC 85-2024. (Author Bibliographies Ser.: No. 70). 160p. 1985. 15.00 (ISBN 0-8108-1801-9). Scarecrow.

--Seditious Mandibles: Surrealist Drawings & Poems. (Illus.). 24p. 1981. pap. 3.00 (ISBN 0-941194-13-2). Black Swan Pr.

Green, Robert, jt. auth. see Kolevzon, Michael S.

Green, Robert, ed. see Hutchinson, R. C.

Green, Robert A. Jewelers Tradecards, 1800-1900. (Illus.). 256p. 20.00x (ISBN 0-9600266-8-1). R A Green.

--Marks of American Silversmiths, 1650-1850. LC 76-57343. (Illus.). 1977. lib. bdg. 30.00x (ISBN 0-9600266-5-7). R A Green.

--Marks of American Silversmiths, 1650-1900. rev. ed. LC 83-81781. (Illus.). 280p. 1984. pap. 20.00x (ISBN 0-9600266-7-3, Dist. by Seven Hills Bks). R A Green.

--Silver Collectors Address Book: Where to Find Over 350 Dealers, Manufacturers, Auction Houses & Booksellers Specializing in Old Silver. 64p. 1985. pap. 6.00x (ISBN 0-9600266-9-X). R A Green.

Green, Robert C., Jr., et al. The Care & Management of the Sick & Incompetent Physician. (Illus.). 116p. 1978. 12.75x (ISBN 0-398-03727-2). C C Thomas.

Green, Robert E., Jr. see Herman, Herbert.

Green, Robert E., Jr., jt. ed. see Ruud, Clay O.

Green, Robert H., jt. auth. see Hsiung, Gueh-Djen.

Green, Robert J. & Framo, James L., eds. Family Therapy: The Major Contributions. LC 81-14325. 620p. 1982. text ed. 35.00 (ISBN 0-8236-1885-4). Intl Univs Pr.

Green, Robert L., et al, eds. Discrimination & the Welfare of Urban Minorities. 260p. 1981. 26.75x (ISBN 0-398-04576-3). C C Thomas.

Green, Robert M. A Translation of Galen's Hygiene (De Sanitate Tuenda) 304p. 1952. 27.50x (ISBN 0-398-00723-3). C C Thomas.

Green, Robert T. Political Instability As a Determinant of U. S. Foreign Investment. (Studies in Marketing: No. 17). (Illus.). 1972. pap. 4.00 (ISBN 0-87755-172-3). Bureau Busn UT.

Green, Robert T. & Laxon, Veronica J. Entering the World of Number. (Illus.). 1978. pap. write for info. Thames Hudson.

Green, Robert W., jt. auth. see Bernstein, Paul.

Green, Robert W., ed. Protestantism & Capitalism & Social Science: The Webster Thesis Controversy. 2nd ed. (Problems in American Civilization Ser). 1973. pap. text ed. 5.50 (ISBN 0-669-81737-6). Heath.

Green, Roberta. Joshua: Promises to Keep. (Young Fisherman Bible Studyguide Ser.). (Illus.). 70p. (gr. 7-12). 1982. tchr's ed. 4.95 (ISBN 0-87788-434-X); student ed. 2.95 (ISBN 0-87788-433-1). Shaw Pubs.

Green, Robin. Spherical Astronomy. 480p. Date not set. price not set. (ISBN 0-521-23988-5); pap. price not set. (ISBN 0-521-31779-7). Cambridge U Pr.

Green, Robin M. Divorce: When It's the Only Answer. (Divorce & Local Law Ser.: No. 1). 224p. (Orig.). 1985. pap. 7.95 (ISBN 0-87833-468-8). Taylor Pub.

--Divorce Without Defeat. 194p. (Orig.). 1982. pap. 7.95 (ISBN 0-686-45654-8). Cimarron Pr.

Green, Rodney. Forecasting with Computer Models: Econometric, Population, & Energy Forecasting. LC 84-15934. 320p. 1985. 29.95 (ISBN 0-03-063788-0); pap. 12.95 (ISBN 0-03-063787-2). Praeger.

Green, Roger. Max Papart. LC 84-42754. (Illus.). 222p. 50.00 (ISBN 0-8478-0560-3). Rizzoli Intl.

Green, Roger, compiled by. The Train. (Small Oxford Books). (Illus.). 1982. 9.95 (ISBN 0-19-214127-9). Oxford U Pr.

Green, Roger C. Makaha Before Eighteen Eighty A. D. Makaha Valley Historical Project-Summary, Vol. 5. LC 80-67771. (Pacific Anthropological Records: No. 31). 90p. 1980. pap. 7.00 (ISBN 0-910240-72-8). Bishop Mus.

Green, Roger C., ed. Makaha Valley Historical Project: Interim Report No. 2. (Pacific Anthropological Records: No. 10). 46p. 1970. pap. 6.50 (ISBN 0-910240-61-2). Bishop Mus.

Green, Roger H. Sampling Design & Statistical Methods for Environmental Biologists. LC 78-24422. 257p. 1979. 32.50x (ISBN 0-471-03901-2). Wiley.

Green, Roger H., Jr. South Slav Settlement in Western Washington: Perception & Choice. LC 74-83372. 1974. 9.00 (ISBN 0-88247-286-0). Ragusan Pr.

Green, Roger J. The Fear of Samuel Walton. (Illus.). 234p. (gr. 6 up). 1984. 14.95 (ISBN 0-19-271474-0, Pub. by Oxford U Pr Childrens). Merrimack Pub Cir.

Green, Roger L. Adventures of Robin Hood. (Orig.). (gr. 2-5). 1984. pap. 2.25 (ISBN 0-14-035034-9, Puffin). Penguin.

--Andrew Lang. 1946. Repr. lib. bdg. 20.00 (ISBN 0-8414-4679-2). Folcroft.

--A Century of Humorous Verse 1850-1950. 1977. lib. bdg. 10.00 (ISBN 0-8495-1900-4). Arden Lib.

--Into Other Worlds: Space-Flight in Fiction, from Lucian to Lewis. LC 74-15976. (Science Fiction Ser.). 190p. 1975. Repr. of 1958 ed. 14.00x (ISBN 0-405-06329-6). Ayer Co Pubs.

--King Arthur & His Knights of the Round Table. (Orig.). (gr. 5-7). 1974. pap. 2.95 (ISBN 0-14-030073-2, Puffin). Penguin.

--King Arthur & the Knights of the Round Table. 1974. pap. 2.95 (ISBN 0-14-030073-2). Penguin.

--Myths of the Norsemen. 1970. pap. 2.95 (ISBN 0-14-030464-9, Puffin). Penguin.

--Old Greek Fairy Tales. (Illus.). 1979. cancelled (ISBN 0-7135-1849-9). Transatlantic.

--Tale of Troy. (Illus., Orig.). (gr. 5-7). 1974. pap. 3.50 (ISBN 0-14-030120-8, Puffin). Penguin.

--Tales of Ancient Egypt. (gr. k-3). 1972. pap. 2.95 (ISBN 0-14-030438-X, Puffin). Penguin.

--Tales of Greek Heroes. (Orig.). (gr. 5-7). 1974. pap. 2.95 (ISBN 0-14-030119-4, Puffin). Penguin.

Green, Roger L. & Hooper, Walter. C. S. Lewis: A Biography. LC 75-29425. 320p. 1976. pap. 7.95 (ISBN 0-15-623205-7, Harv). HarBraceJ.

Green, Roger L., pref. by. Alice in Wonderland. 1983. pap. 2.50 (ISBN 0-460-11836-6, DEL 04006, Evman). Biblio Dist.

Green, Roger L., ed. A Century of Humorous Verse: 1850-1950. 1973. Repr. of 1959 ed. 12.95 (ISBN 0-460-00813-7, Evman). Biblio Dist.

--Kipling: The Critical Heritage. 1971. 33.75x (ISBN 0-7100-6978-2). Routledge & Kegan.

Green, Roger L., ed. see Aesop.

Green, Roger L., ed. see Carroll, Lewis.

Green, Roger L., ed. & suppl. by see Dodgson, Charles L.

Green, Roland. Peace Company. (Peacekeeper Ser.: No. 1). 224p. 1985. pap. 2.75 (ISBN 0-441-65740-0) (ISBN 0-317-31872-1). Ace Bks.

--Wandor's Flight. 368p. 1981. pap. 2.75 (ISBN 0-380-77834-3, 77834-3). Avon.

--Wandor's Journey. pap. 1.95 (ISBN 0-380-00328-7, 45641-9). Avon.

--Wandor's Ride. 1973. pap. 1.95 (ISBN 0-380-00575-1, 45658-3). Avon.

--Wandor's Voyage. 1975. pap. 1.95 (ISBN 0-380-44271-X, 44271-X). Avon.

Green, Roland & Carr, John F. Great Kings' War. 288p. 1985. pap. 2.95 (ISBN 0-441-30200-9, Pub. by Ace Science Fiction). Ace Bks.

Green, Roland & Murray, Frieda. The Book of Kantela. (The Throne of Sherran Trilogy Ser.: Vol. 1). 1985. pap. 8.95 (ISBN 0-312-94035-1, Dist. by St. Martin). Bluejay Bks.

Green, Roland, jt. auth. see Dickson, Gordon R.

Green, Roland, jt. auth. see Pournelle, Jerry.

Green, Ronald. The Architect's Guide to Running a Job. 3rd ed. 140p. 1986. 14.50 (ISBN 0-85139-011-0). Nichols Pub.

Green, Ronald K. & Webster, Stephen A., eds. Social Work in Rural Areas: Preparation & Practice. 391p. 11.00 (ISBN 0-686-40925-6). U of Tenn Sch.

Green, Ronald K., jt. ed. see Morton, Thomas D.

Green, Ronald M. Religious Reason: The Rational & Moral Basis of Religious Belief. 1978. text ed. 16.95x (ISBN 0-19-502388-9); pap. text ed. 6.95x (ISBN 0-19-502389-7). Oxford U Pr.

Green, Rosalie, et al. Hortus Deiciarum' of Herrad of Hohenbourg (Landsberg) 1979. 750.00x (ISBN 0-686-79321-8, Pub. by U of London England). State Mutual Bk.

Green, Rosalie B., jt. ed. see Ragusa, Isa.

Green, Rose B. The Pennsylvania People. LC 83-20010. 120p. 1983. 12.95 (ISBN 0-8453-4781-0). Cornwall Bks.

--Primo Vino. 4.95 (ISBN 0-8453-1660-5). Cornwall Bks.

--Songs of Ourselves. LC 81-67779. 64p. 1982. 9.95 (ISBN 0-8453-4737-3). Cornwall Bks.

--To Reason Why. 4.95 (ISBN 0-8453-1042-9). Cornwall Bks.

--Woman, the Second Coming. 5.95 (ISBN 0-8453-2173-0). Cornwall Bks.

Green, Roy. Using Minicomputers in Distributed Systems. (Illus.). 1978. 28.50x (ISBN 0-85012-202-3). Intl Pubns Serv.

Green, Ruth H. The Book of Ruth. 1982. 7.00. Freedom Rel Found.

--The Born Again Skeptic's Guide to the Bible. 1979. 9.00. Freedom Rel Found.

Green, Ruth S., jt. ed. see Easterby, James H.

Green, Ruth S. see Easterby, James H. & Green, Ruth S.

Green, S. International Disaster Relief: Toward a Responsive System. 1977. pap. 3.95 (ISBN 0-07-024288-7). McGraw.

Green, S. J. The Classification of Pictures. rev. ed. (Illus.). 1984. cancelled (ISBN 0-9604656-1-8); pap. 15.00x (ISBN 0-9604656-2-6). Little Bks Co.

Green, Samuel & Long, John V. Marriage & Family Law Agreements. LC 83-24263. (Family Law Ser.). 494p. 1984. write for info. (ISBN 0-07-024275-5, Shepards-McGraw). McGraw.

Green, Samuel, ed. see Trager, Philip, et al.

Green, Samuel W. A Complete History of the New York & Brooklyn Bridge from Its Conception in 1866 to Its Completion in 1883. 1979. lib. bdg. 59.95 (ISBN 0-8490-1655-X). Gordon Pr.

Green, Scott E. Baby Sale at the Seven-Eleven. 32p. (Orig.). 1984. pap. 4.00 (ISBN 0-935000-02-X). Bloom Bks.

Green, Sharon. Chosen of Mida. (Jalav, Amazon Warrior Ser.: III). 368p. 1984. pap. 2.95 (ISBN 0-87997-927-5). DAW Bks.

--The Crystals of Mida. 352p. 1982. pap. 2.95 (ISBN 0-87997-735-3, UE1735). DAW Bks.

--Gateway to Xanadu. 1985. pap. 3.50 (ISBN 0-88677-089-0). DAW Bks.

--Mind Guest. 1984. pap. 3.50 (ISBN 0-87997-973-9). DAW Bks.

--An Oath to Mida. (Jalav Amazon Warrior Ser.: No. 2). 400p. 1983. pap. 2.95 (ISBN 0-87997-829-5). Daw Bks.

--The Warrior Enchained. 352p. 1983. pap. 2.95 (ISBN 0-87997-789-2). DAW Bks.

--The Warrior Rearmed. (Terrilian Ser.: No. 3). 256p. 1984. pap. 2.95 (ISBN 0-87997-895-3). DAW Bks.

--The Warrior Within. 1982. pap. 2.50 (ISBN 0-87997-707-8, UE1707). DAW Bks.

--The Will of the Gods. (Jalar-Amazon Warrior Ser.: Vol. 4). 384p. 1985. pap. 3.50 (ISBN 0-317-18680-9). DAW Bks.

Green, Sharon & Siemon, Michael. Barron's How to Prepare for the California High School Proficiency Examination (CHSPE) 2nd ed. LC 77-10521. 1983. pap. 7.95 (ISBN 0-8120-2327-7). Barron.

Green, Stanley. Broadway Musicals of the 30s. (Quality Paperbacks Ser.). (Illus.). 383p. 1982. pap. 14.95 (ISBN 0-306-80165-5). Da Capo.

--Broadway Musicals: Show by Show. (Illus.). 320p. 1985. pap. 9.95 (ISBN 0-88188-375-1, 00183117, Pub. by H Leonard Bks). H Leonard Pub Corp.

--Encyclopedia of the Musical Film. 1981. 35.00x (ISBN 0-19-502958-5). Oxford U Pr.

--Encyclopedia of the Musical Theatre. (Illus.). 1980. pap. 10.95 (ISBN 0-306-80113-2). Da Capo.

--The Great Clowns of Broadway. (Illus.). 1984. 19.95 (ISBN 0-19-503471-6). Oxford U Pr.

--The Rodgers & Hammerstein Story. (Illus.). 187p. 1980. pap. 6.95 (ISBN 0-306-80124-8). Da Capo.

--The World of Musical Comedy. 4th, rev. ed. LC 80-16915. 448p. 1980. 30.00 (ISBN 0-498-02344-3). A S Barnes.

--The World of Musical Comedy. 4th ed. (Quality Paperbacks Ser.). (Illus.). 494p. 1984. pap. 16.95 (ISBN 0-306-80207-4). Da Capo.

Green, Stanley, ed. Rodgers & Hammerstein Fact Book. (Illus.). 804p. (Orig.). 1980. pap. 17.95 (ISBN 0-9604002-0-6). Drama Bk.

Green, Stanton W. & Perlman, Stephen M., eds. The Archaeology of Frontiers & Boundaries. (Studies in Archaeology). 1985. 49.50 (ISBN 0-12-298780-2). Acad Pr.

Green, Stephen. Acts of Nature, Acts of Man: The Global Response to Natural Disasters. LC 77-81993. (Illus.). 1977. pap. 3.00 (ISBN 0-934654-16-6). UNA USA.

--Cricketing Bygones. (Shire Album Ser.: No. 90). (Illus.). 32p. 1982. pap. 2.95 (ISBN 0-85263-605-9, Pub. by Shire Pubns England). Seven Hills Bks.

--Taking Sides: America's Secret Relations with a Militant Israel. LC 83-61736. 320p. 1984. 14.95 (ISBN 0-688-02643-5). Morrow.

Green, Stephen A. Mind & Body: The Psychology of Illness. 280p. 1985. text ed. 22.50 (ISBN 0-88048-043-2, 48-043-2). Am Psychiatric.

Green, Stewart M. Pikes Peak Country: The Complete Guide to Natural Wonders, Historic Sites, Attractions & Outdoor Recreation. LC 85-60701. (Illus.). 104p. (Orig.). 1985. pap. 6.95 (ISBN 0-933393-07-5). Ponderosa Pr.

Green, Stuart A. Complications of External Skeletal Fixation: Causes, Prevention & Treatment. (Illus.). 208p. 1981. 32.75x (ISBN 0-398-04482-1). C C Thomas.

Green, Susan & Green, Peter. Salon Management. (Illus.). 160p. 1984. text ed. 21.95 (ISBN 0-13-788217-3). P-H.

Green, Susan E. Food Service Worktext, No. 213W. 220p. 1984. pap. 10.60 (ISBN 0-87356-213-5). Prentice-Media.

Green, T., jt. auth. see Smith, H. T.

Green, T. H., ed. see Hume, David.

Green, Thaddeus B. & Lee, Sang M. The Decision Science Process. (Illus.). 1979. text ed. 23.00 (ISBN 0-89433-060-8). Petrocelli.

Green, Theo, ed. see Gysin, Brion.

Green, Thomas. Weeds among the Wheat: Discernment: Where Prayer & Action Meet. LC 84-70663. 208p. (Orig.). 1984. pap. 4.95 (ISBN 0-87793-318-9). Ave Maria.

Green, Thomas, et al. Predicting the Behavior of the Educational System. (Illus.). 224p. 1980. 15.95x (ISBN 0-8156-2223-6); pap. 8.95x (ISBN 0-8156-2224-4). Syracuse U Pr.

Green, Thomas, et al, eds. The Psychology of Computer Use. (Computers & People Ser.). 1983. 23.00 (ISBN 0-12-297420-4). Acad Pr.

Green, Thomas A. Verdicts According to Conscience: The English Criminal Trial Jury, 1200-1800. LC 84-16227. 400p. 1985. lib. bdg. 35.00x (ISBN 0-226-30610-0). U of Chicago Pr.

Green, Thomas A., jt. auth. see Pepicello, W. J.

Green, Thomas E., et al. Glossary of Insurance Terms. 240p. 1980. pap. text ed. 11.95 (ISBN 0-930868-06-4). Merritt Co.

Green, Thomas H. Darkness in the Marketplace. LC 81-67559. 128p. (Orig.). 1981. pap. 3.95 (ISBN 0-87793-230-1). Ave Maria.

--Freedom & Politics in Ethical Behaviour, 2 vols. 301p. 1985. Repr. of 1883 ed. 227.50 (ISBN 0-89901-237-X). Found Class Reprints.

--Hume & Locke. 9.00 (ISBN 0-8446-2161-7). Peter Smith.

--Opening to God: A Guide to Prayer. LC 77-83197. 144p. 1977. pap. 3.95 (ISBN 0-87793-136-4). Ave Maria.

--Prolegomena to Ethics. 5th ed. Bradley, A. C., ed. LC 32-3225. 1968. Repr. of 1929 ed. 32.00 (ISBN 0-527-35800-2). Kraus Repr.

--When the Well Runs Dry: Prayer Beyond the Beginnings. LC 79-52404. 176p. (Orig.). 1979. pap. 4.95 (ISBN 0-87793-182-8). Ave Maria.

--Works of Thomas Hill Green, 3 Vols. 3rd ed. Nettleship, R. L., ed. Repr. of 1894 ed. Set. 135.00 (ISBN 0-404-02910-8). AMS Pr.

--Works of Thomas Hill Green, 3 Vols. 2nd ed. Nettleship, R. L., ed. LC 1-18259. 1968. Repr. of 1889 ed. Set. 116.00 (ISBN 0-527-35820-7). Kraus Repr.

Green, Thomas H., Jr. Gynecology: Essentials of Clinical Practice. 3rd ed. 1977. pap. 22.50 (ISBN 0-316-32632-1). Little.

Green, Thomas J. The Flowered Box: A Novel of Suspense. LC 80-22442. 192p. 1980. 9.95 (ISBN 0-8253-0010-X). Beaufort Bks NY.

--Journal of the Texian Expedition Against Mier. LC 72-9447. (The Far Western Frontier). (Illus.). 516p. 1973. Repr. of 1845 ed. 31.00 (ISBN 0-405-04975-7). Ayer Co Pubs.

Green, Thomas M. Historic Families of Kentucky: With Special Reference to Stocks Immediately Derived from the Valley of Virginia. LC 64-8604. 304p. 1982. Repr. of 1889 ed. 17.50 (ISBN 0-8063-7958-8). Genealog Pub.

--The Spanish Conspiracy: A Review of Early Spanish Movements in the South-West. Repr. of 1891 ed. 11.25 (ISBN 0-8446-1207-3). Peter Smith.

Green Tiger Press. Kites. (Envelope Bks.). (Illus.). 12p. 1985. pap. 2.50 (ISBN 0-88138-015-6). Green Tiger Pr.

Green Tiger Press, ed. Books & Readers. (Illus.). 12p. 1982. pap. 2.50 (ISBN 0-914676-99-7, Pub. by Envelope Bks). Green Tiger Pr.

--Bubbles & Bubble Blowers. (Illus.). 12p. 1982. pap. 2.50 (ISBN 0-88138-000-8, Pub. by Envelope Bks). Green Tiger Pr.

--Flying Horses. 12p. (Orig.). 1982. pap. 2.50 (ISBN 0-88138-005-9, Pub. by Envelope Bks). Green Tiger Pr.

--Mermaids. (Illus.). 12p. (Orig.). 1982. pap. 2.50 (ISBN 0-88138-001-6, Pub. by Envelope Bks). Green Tiger Pr.

--Women with Long Hair. (Illus.). 12p. (Orig.). 1982. pap. 2.50 (ISBN 0-88138-006-7, Pub. by Envelope Bks). Green Tiger Pr.

Green, Timothy. The New World of Gold. 1982. 15.95 (ISBN 0-8027-0692-4). Walker & Co.

Green, Timothy S. The New World of Gold. rev. ed. 260p. 1984. pap. 12.95 (ISBN 0-8027-7261-7). Walker & Co.

Green, Tom & Wooton, William. Intermediate Algebra. 608p. 1980. pap. text ed. write for info. (ISBN 0-534-00788-0). Wadsworth Pub.

Green, Trudell, jt. ed. see Wallace, Margaret.

Green, V. H. Renaissance & Reformation: A Survey of European History Between 1450 & 1660. 2nd ed. 462p. 1964. pap. text ed. 13.95 (ISBN 0-7131-5617-1). E Arnold.

Green, Vera M., jt. ed. see Nelson, Jack L.

Green, Victor, jt. auth. see Smith, Harvey.

Green, Vivian H. From St. Augustine to William Temple. facsimile ed. LC 72-148213. (Biography Index Reprint Ser.). 1948. 18.00 (ISBN 0-8369-8060-3). Ayer Co Pubs.

--Renaissance & Reformation. 2nd ed. (Illus.). 1974. pap. text ed. 16.95 (ISBN 0-312-67305-1). St Martin.

Green, W. C., ed. & tr. Translations from the Icelandic. 1976. lib. bdg. 59.95 (ISBN 0-8490-2757-8). Gordon Pr.

Green, W. Richard. Pathology of the Retina. LC 80-720249. (Lancaster Course in Ophthalmic Histopathology Ser.). (Illus.). 61p. text ed. 142.00 incl. 104 slides (ISBN 0-8036-3835-3). Davis CO.

--Pathology of the Vitreous. LC 80-720248. (Lancaster Course in Ophthalmic Histopathology Ser.). (Illus.). 29p. text ed. 43.00 incl. 29 slides (ISBN 0-8036-3834-5). Davis Co.

Green, Walford D. William Pitt. LC 73-14445. (Heroes of the Nation Ser.). Repr. of 1901 ed. 30.00 (ISBN 0-404-58263-X). AMS Pr.

Green, Walter C., ed. see Green, Ezra.

Green, Walter L., jt. auth. see Speckhart, Frank H.

Green, Wayne. Encyclopedia for the TRS-80, Vol. 2. McCarthy, Nan, et al, eds. (Encyclopedia for the TRS-80 Ser.). (Illus.). 283p. 1981. text ed. 19.95 (ISBN 0-88006-029-8, EN8102); pap. text ed. 10.95 (ISBN 0-88006-030-1, EN8082). Green Pub Inc.

Green, William. Shakespeare's Merry Wives of Windsor. 1962. 26.00 (ISBN 0-691-06120-3). Princeton U Pr.

Green, William & Cross, Roy. The Jet Aircraft of the World. Gilbert, James, ed. LC 79-7263. (Flight: Its First Seventy-Five Years Ser.). (Illus.). 1979. Repr. of 1956 ed. lib. bdg. 30.50x (ISBN 0-405-12173-3). Ayer Co Pubs.

Green, William & Pollinger, Gerald. The Aircraft of the World. Gilbert, James, ed. LC 79-7262. (Flight: Its First Seventy-Five Years Ser.). (Illus.). 1979. Repr. of 1956 ed. lib. bdg. 30.00x (ISBN 0-405-12172-5). Ayer Co Pubs.

Green, William & Swanborough, Gordon. An Illustrated Guide to the World's Airliners. (Illus.). 280p. 1982. 10.95 (ISBN 0-668-05612-6, 5612). Arco.

--Japanese Army Airforce Fighters. (World War II Aircraft Fact Files Ser.). (Illus.). 1977. pap. 4.95 (ISBN 0-668-04119-6). Arco.

--The Observer's Directory of Military Aircraft. LC 82-71835. (Illus.). 256p. 1983. 16.95 (ISBN 0-668-05649-5, 5649). Arco.

Green, William, ed. see Luukkanen, Eino.

Green, William A. British Slave Emancipation: The Sugar Colonies & the Great Experiment, 1830-1865. (Illus.). 1976. 52.00x (ISBN 0-19-822436-2). Oxford U Pr.

Green, William A., jt. auth. see DeLo, James S.

Green, William B. Digital Image Processing: A Systems Approach. (Van Nostrand Reinhold Electrical-Computer Science & Engineering Ser.). (Illus.). 204p. 1982. 34.50 (ISBN 0-442-28801-8). Van Nos Reinhold.

Green, William C. The Abbot of Montserrat: Or, the Pool of Blood. LC 77-2038. (Gothic Novels III). 1977. Repr. of 1826 ed. lib. bdg. 46.50x (ISBN 0-405-10137-6). Ayer Co Pubs.

--Soviet Nuclear Weapons Policy: A Research Guide. 250p. pap. 22.50x (ISBN 0-86531-817-4). Westview.

Green, William C., ed. Translations from the Icelandic. LC 66-30733. (Medieval Library). Repr. of 1926 ed. 17.50 (ISBN 0-8154-0089-6). Cooper Sq.

Green, William H. General Introduction to the Old Testament: The Canon. (Twin Brooks Ser.). 1980. pap. 6.95 (ISBN 0-8010-3755-7). Baker Bk.

--The Higher Criticism of the Pentateuch. (Twin Brooks Ser.). 1978. pap. 4.95 (ISBN 0-8010-3723-9). Baker Bk.

--Unity of Genesis. (Twin Books). 1979. pap. 9.95 (ISBN 0-8010-3738-7). Baker Bk.

Green, William M. The Romanov Connection: A Novel. 320p. 1984. 16.95 (ISBN 0-8253-0221-8). Beaufort Bks NY.

Green, William R. Computer-Aided Data Analysis: A Practical Guide. 256p. 1985. 29.95x (ISBN 0-471-80928-4). Wiley.

Green, William S. Approaches to Ancient Judaism, Vol. IV. (Brown Judaic Studies). 208p. 1983. pap. 17.00 (ISBN 0-89130-673-0, 14 00 27). Scholars Pr GA.

--Approaches to Ancient Judaism II. LC 76-57656. (Brown Judaic Studies). 1980. 15.00 (ISBN 0-89130-447-9, 14-00-09); pap. 10.50 (ISBN 0-89130-448-7). Scholars Pr GA.

--Approaches to Ancient Judaism: Theory & Practice. LC 76-57656. 1978. pap. 16.50 (ISBN 0-89130-130-5, 14-00-01). Scholars Pr GA.

Green, William S., ed. Approaches to Ancient Judaism, Vol. V. (Brown Judaic Studies: No. 32). 1985. 19.95 (ISBN 0-89130-797-4, 14 00 32); pap. 16.95 (ISBN 0-89130-798-2). Scholars Pr GA.

--Approaches to Ancient Judaism III. LC 76-57656. (Brown Judaic Studies). 220p. 1981. pap. 15.00 (14 00 11). Scholars Pr GA.

--Persons & Institutions in Early Rabbinic Judaism. LC 79-20712. (Brown University, Brown Judaic Studies: No. 3). 1977. pap. 13.50 (ISBN 0-89130-131-3, 14 00 03). Scholars Pr GA.

Greenacre, Francis & Epstace, Katherine. Robin Tanner. 56p. 1981. 30.00x (ISBN 0-317-20345-2, Pub. by Ashmolean Mus UK). State Mutual Bk.

Greenacre, Michael. Theory & Applications of Correspondence Analysis. 1984. 56.00 (ISBN 0-12-299050-1). Acad Pr.

Greenacre, Phyllis. Emotional Growth: Psychoanalytic Studies of the Gifted & a Great Variety of Other Individuals, 2 Vols. LC 75-129768. 1971. Set. text ed. 60.00 (ISBN 0-8236-1654-1). Intl Univs Pr.

--Quest for the Father: A Study of the Darwin-Butler Controversy. LC 63-13193. (The New York Psychoanalytic Institute Freud Anniversary Lecture Ser.). 1963. text ed. 17.50 (ISBN 0-8236-5760-4). Intl Univs Pr.

--Swift & Carroll: A Psychoanalytic Study of Two Lives. LC 55-8236. (Illus.). 306p. 1955. text ed. 30.00 (ISBN 0-8236-6280-2). Intl Univs Pr.

--Trauma, Growth, & Personality. LC 71-75188. 1969. Repr. of 1952 ed. text ed. 30.00 (ISBN 0-8236-6645-X). Intl Univs Pr.

Greenacre, Phyllis, ed. Affective Disorders: Psychoanalytic Contributions to Their Study. LC 53-11058. 211p. 1961. text ed. 22.50 (ISBN 0-8236-0100-5). Intl Univs Pr.

Greenall, R. L. A History of Northamptonshire. (The Darwen County History Ser.). (Illus.). 128p. 1979. 20.75x (ISBN 0-8476-3167-2). Rowman.

Greenauer, Felix. The Major Forces Which Dominate the World & the Destinies of Mankind. (Illus.). 1978. deluxe ed. 69.85x (ISBN 0-930008-02-2). Inst Econ Pol.

Greenawald, G. Dale, jt. auth. see Dillon-Peterson, Elizabeth.

Greenawalt, R. Kent. Discrimination & Reverse Discrimination. LC 82-18747. (Borzoi Books in Law & American Society Ser.). 260p. 1983. (RanC); pap. text ed. 7.00 (ISBN 0-394-33193-1). Random.

Greenawalt, R. Kent, jt. auth. see Gellhorn, Walter.

Greenawalt, R. Kent & Low, Peter W., eds. Model Penal Code & Commentaries, 3 vols, Pt. II. 1427p. 105.00 set (ISBN 0-686-69005-2) (ISBN 0-686-69006-0). Am Law Inst.

Greenaway, D. & Milner, C. Protectionism Again? (Institute of Economic Affairs, Hobart Papers Ser.: No. 84). pap. 5.95 technical (ISBN 0-255-36127-0). Transatlantic.

Greenaway, D. S. & Warman, E. A., eds. Eurographics 82: Proceedings of the International Conference & Exhibition, U.M.I.S.T., Manchester, U.K., 1982. xiv, 396p. 1983. 51.00 (ISBN 0-444-86480-6, North Holland). Elsevier.

Greenaway, David. Trade Policy & the New Protectionism. LC 82-10621. 232p. 1983. 25.00x (ISBN 0-312-81213-2). St Martin.

Greenaway, David & Shaw, G. K. Macroeconomics: Theory & Policy in the UK. 512p. 1984. 45.00x (ISBN 0-85520-533-4). Basil Blackwell.

Greenaway, David, jt. auth. see Milner, Chris.

Greenaway, David, ed. Current Issues in International Trade: Theory & Policy. 244p. 1985. 29.95 (ISBN 0-312-17927-8). St Martin.

Greenaway, Diana & Holdsworth, Christopher, eds. Tradition & Change: Essays in Honour of Marjorie Chibnall. 412p. Date not set. price not set. (ISBN 0-521-25793-X). Cambridge U Pr.

Greenaway, Everett A. English Art at the End of the Nineteenth Century. (A Promotion of the Arts Library). (Illus.). 111p. 1981. 97.45 (ISBN 0-86650-007-3). Gloucester Art.

Greenaway, Frank, ed. Time & the Sciences. (At the Crossroads of Culture Ser.). 182p. 1979. pap. 12.25 (ISBN 92-3-101657-1, U986, UNESCO). Unipub.

Greenaway, George W. Arnold of Brescia. LC 77-84710. Repr. of 1931 ed. 23.50 (ISBN 0-404-16116-2). AMS Pr.

Greenaway, Kate. A-Apple Pie. rev. ed. (Illus.). (ps-2). 1886. 8.95 (ISBN 0-7232-1801-3). Warne.

--Kate Greenaway's Birthday Coloring Book. (Illus.). 96p. (ps-2). 1974. pap. 2.95 (ISBN 0-486-23050-3). Dover.

--The Language of Flowers. LC 77-74518. (Illus.). (gr. 1 up). 1977. 5.95 (ISBN 0-7232-2006-9). Warne.

--Language of Flowers, with Value Guide. LC 66-29515. 1966. 4.50 (ISBN 0-87282-072-6). CHB-ALF.

--Marigold Garden. (Illus.). 58p. (gr. k-3). 1885. 8.95 (ISBN 0-7232-1800-5). Warne.

--Mother Goose Coloring Book. (Illus.). pap. 2.50 (ISBN 0-486-22883-5). Dover.

--Mother Goose: Or, the Old Nursery Rhymes. (Illus.). (gr. k-3). 1882. bds. 5.95 (ISBN 0-7232-0591-4). Warne.

Greenaway, Kate, illus. Mother Goose. (Illus.). 12p. (ps-5). 1973. pap. 2.50 (ISBN 0-914510-04-5). Evergreen.

Greenaway, Peter Van see Van Greenaway, Peter.

Greenaway, Peter van see Van Greenaway, Peter.

Greenbaum, Avraham, tr. see Nachman of Breslov.

Greenbaum, Avraham, tr. see Nachman of Breslov & Nathan of Breslov.

Greenbaum, Avraham, tr. see Nathan of Breslov.

Greenbaum, Dennis. Acute Cardiovascular Failure. (Clinics in Critical Care Medicine Ser.). (Illus.). text ed. write for info. (ISBN 0-443-08111-5). Churchill.

Greenbaum, Dorothy & Laiken, Deidre S. Lovestrong: A Woman Doctor's True Story of Marriage & Medicine. LC 83-45923. 288p. 1984. 15.50 (ISBN 0-8129-1110-5). Times Bks.

Greenbaum, Edward I. Radiographic Atlas of Colon Disease. (Illus.). 1980. 104.95 (ISBN 0-8151-3923-3). Year Bk Med.

Greenbaum, Edward I., ed. Radiology of the Emergency Patient: An Atlas Approach. LC 81-16282. 831p. 1982. 85.00 (ISBN 0-471-08562-6, Pub. by Wiley Med). Wiley.

Greenbaum, Everett. The Goldenberg Who Couldn't Dance. LC 79-3353. 160p. 1980. 8.95 (ISBN 0-15-136174-6). HarBraceJ.

Greenbaum, Howard H. Organizational Communication, Vol. 9. 383p. 1984. 36.00 (ISBN 0-8039-2298-1). Sage.

Greenbaum, Howard H. & Falcione, Raymond L. Organizational Communication: Abstracts, Analysis & Overview, Vol. 6. (Illus.). 357p. 1981. 36.00 (ISBN 0-8039-1606-X); pap. 17.95 (ISBN 0-8039-1607-8). Sage.

--Organizational Communication: Abstracts, Analysis & Overview, Vol. 7. (Illus.). 352p. 1982. 36.00 (ISBN 0-8039-1793-7); pap. 17.95 (ISBN 0-8039-1794-5). Sage.

--Organizational Communication Abstracts, 1974. 1975. pap. 3.60 (ISBN 0-931874-01-7). Assn Busn Comm.

--Organizational Communication Nineteen Seventy-Seven: Abstracts, Analysis, & Overview. new ed. 1979. pap. 9.00 (ISBN 0-931874-08-4). Assn Busn Comm.

Greenbaum, Howard H., jt. auth. see Falcione, Raymond L.

Greenbaum, Howard H., et al. Organizational Communication: Abstracts, Analysis & Overview, Vol. 8. 384p. 1985. 36.00 (ISBN 0-8039-2099-7). Sage.

Greenbaum, Joan M. In the Name of Efficiency: Management Theory & Shopfloor Practice in Data Processing Work. 210p. 1979. 27.95 (ISBN 0-87722-151-0). Temple U Pr.

Greenbaum, Lenora, jt. auth. see Bourguignon, Erika.

Greenbaum, S., et al, eds. Studies in English Linguistics: For Randolph Quirk. LC 79-41023. (Illus.). 304p. 1980. text ed. 46.00x (ISBN 0-582-55079-3); 16.95 (ISBN 0-582-29134-8). Longman.

Greenbaum, Sidney. Acceptability in Language. (Contributions to the Sociology of Langauge Ser.: No. 17). 1977. 12.80x (ISBN 90-279-7623-6). Mouton.

--Studies in English Adverbial Usage. LC 70-90047. (Miami Linguistics Ser: No. 5). 1969. 13.95x (ISBN 0-87024-137-0). U of Miami Pr.

--Verb-Intensifier Collocations in English. (Janua Linguarum, Ser. Minor: No. 86). (Orig.). 1970. pap. text ed. 10.00x (ISBN 90-2790-711-0). Mouton.

Greenbaum, Sidney & Quirk, Randolph. Elicitation Experiments in English: Linguistic Studies in Use & Attitude. LC 75-121857. (Miami Linguistics Ser: No. 10). (Illus.). 1970. 9.95x (ISBN 0-87024-155-9). U of Miami Pr.

Greenbaum, Sidney, jt. auth. see Quirk, Randolph.

Greenbaum, Walter W. The Gemstone Identifier. LC 82-4074. (Illus.). 196p. 1982. 13.95 (ISBN 0-668-05387-9); pap. 7.95 (ISBN 0-668-05391-7). Arco.

Greenbeg, Alan & George, Michael, eds. Monograph of the Work of McKim, Mead & White 1879-1915. (Illus.). 160p. 1981. pap. 10.95 student ed. (ISBN 0-8038-6775-1). Architectural.

Greenber, Fridaz. Great Barrier Reef Fishwatcher's Field Guide. (Illus.). 1984. plastic card 3.95x (ISBN 0-913008-15-X). Seahawk Pr.

Greenberg. Valvular Heart Disease. 1986. price not set (ISBN 0-88416-472-1). PSG Pub Co.

Greenberg, jt. auth. see Asimov.

Greenberg, jt. auth. see Carr.

Greenberg, et al. Prostaglandins. (Modern Pharmacology-Toxicology Ser.: Vol. 21). 440p. 1982. 65.00 (ISBN 0-8247-1682-5). Dekker.

Greenberg, et al, eds. Educating Learners of All Ages. (New Directions for Higher Education Ser.). 107p. 1980. 6.95 (ISBN 0-318-13434-9). Assn Exper Ed.

Greenberg, A., jt. ed. see Puschett, J. B.

Greenberg, Alan. Love in Vain. LC 80-2959. (Illus.). 240p. 1983. pap. 8.95 (ISBN 0-385-15679-0, Dolp). Doubleday.

Greenberg, Alan, tr. see Herzog, Werner.

Greenberg, Alan M. & McIver, Carole R. LC & AACR2: An Album of Cataloging Examples Arranged by Rule Number. LC 83-27144. 192p. 1984. 19.50 (ISBN 0-8108-1683-0). Scarecrow.

Greenberg, Allan C. Artists & Revolution: Dada & the Bauhaus, 1917-1925. Foster, Stephen, ed. LC 79-24156. (Studies in the Fine Arts: The Avant-Garde, No. 4). 300p. 1980. 39.95 (ISBN 0-8357-1080-7). UMI Res Pr.

Greenberg, Allen M. Standards Relating to Architecture of Facilities. (IJA-ABA Juvenile Justice Standards Project Ser.). 96p. 1980. prof ref 17.50 (ISBN 0-88410-249-1); pap. 10.00 prof ref (ISBN 0-88410-773-6). Ballinger Pub.

Greenberg, Alvin. And Yet. (Juniper Bk.: No. 35). 1981. 4.00 (ISBN 0-686-79780-9). Juniper Pr WI.

--Dark Lands. LC 73-159728. 68p. 1973. 2.95 (ISBN 0-87886-024-X). Ithaca Hse.

--Delta Q: Stories. LC 82-20075. (AWP Ser.: No.5). 208p. (Orig.). 1983. pap. 8.95 (ISBN 0-8262-0397-3). U of Mo Pr.

--The Discovery of America & Other Tales of Terror & Self-Exploration Short Stories. LC 79-13068. 160p. 1979. text ed. 14.95x (ISBN 0-8071-0591-0). La State U Pr.

--The House of the Would-Be Gardener. (Illus.). 1972. 5.00 (ISBN 0-685-27757-7); signed ltd ed 10.00 (ISBN 0-685-27758-5). New Rivers Pr.

--In-Direction. LC 77-94114. (Third Godine Poetry Chapbook Ser.). 1978. 5.00 (ISBN 0-87923-178-5). Godine.

--The Invention of the West. (Illus.). 1976. pap. 2.95 (ISBN 0-380-00596-4, 30296). Avon.

--The Man in the Cardboard Mask. LC 84-15533. 120p. (Orig.). 1985. pap. 8.95 (ISBN 0-918273-02-1). Coffee Hse.

--Metaform. LC 75-8448. 72p. 1975. 7.50x (ISBN 0-87023-188-X); pap. 3.50 (ISBN 0-87023-189-8). U of Mass Pr.

Greenberg, Alvin, et al. X-One: Experimental Fiction Project. Smith, Harry, ed. LC 76-20256. (Illus.). 1976. pap. 5.00 (ISBN 0-912292-41-5). The Smith.

Greenberg, Arnold. South America on Twenty-Five Dollars a Day. 432p. 1985. pap. 9.95 (ISBN 0-671-53156-5). Frommer-Pasmantier.

Greenberg, Arnold & Greenberg, Harriet. Rio Alive. 4th ed. (Alive Travel Ser.). (Illus.). 1980. pap. 4.95 (ISBN 0-935572-00-7). Alive Pubns.

Greenberg, Arnold, jt. auth. see Greenberg, Harriet.

Greenberg, Arnold, et al, eds. Standard Methods for the Examination of Water & Wastewater. 16th ed. 1268p. 1985. 90.00x (ISBN 0-87553-131-8). Am Pub Health.

Greenberg, Arnold E. & Hunt, Daniel A., eds. Laboratory Procedures for the Examination of Seawater & Shellfish. 5th ed. LC 84-24321. 80p. 1984. 15.00 (ISBN 0-87553-119-9). Am Pub Health.

Greenberg, Arnold L., jt. auth. see Greenberg, Harriet.

Greenberg, Arthur & Liebman, Joel. Strained Organic Molecules. (Organic Chemistry Ser.). 1978. 47.00 (ISBN 0-12-299550-3). Acad Pr.

Greenberg, Barbara. The Bravest Babysitter. LC 77-71516. (Illus.). (gr. k-3). 1977. PLB 6.46 (ISBN 0-8037-0364-3). Dial Bks Young.

Greenberg, Barbara L. Fire Drills: Stories. LC 81-69837. (Breakthrough Ser.: No. 38). 80p. 1982. pap. 6.95 (ISBN 0-8262-0363-9). U of Mo Pr.

--The Spoils of August. LC 73-15012. (Wesleyan Poetry Program: No. 71). 72p. 1974. 15.00x (ISBN 0-8195-2071-3); pap. 6.95 (ISBN 0-8195-1071-8). Wesleyan U Pr.

Greenberg, Barnett & Bellenger, Danny. The Classification of Consumer Goods: An Empirical Study. LC 74-621745. (Research Monograph: No. 56). 82p. 1974. spiral bdg. 10.00 (ISBN 0-88406-022-5). Ga St U Busn Pub.

Greenberg, Bernard. Flies & Disease, 2 vols. Incl. Vol. 1. Ecology Classification & Biotic Associations. LC 68-56210. 1970. 63.80 (ISBN 0-691-08071-2); Vol. 2. Biology & Disease Transmission. LC 68-56310. 1973. 55.00 (ISBN 0-691-08093-3). Set. 110.00 (ISBN 0-685-53050-7). Princeton U Pr.

Greenberg, Bette, jt. auth. see Rothenberg, Albert.

Greenberg, Bette, ed. How to Find Out in Psychiatry: A Guide to Sources of Mental Health Information. LC 78-16005. 1979. text ed. 17.25 (ISBN 0-08-021860-1). Pergamon.

Greenberg, Blu. How to Run a Traditional Jewish Household. 1983. 19.95 (ISBN 0-671-41700-2). S&S.

--On Women & Judaism: A View from Tradition. LC 81-11779. 192p. 1983. pap. 5.95 (ISBN 0-8276-0195-6, 482). Jewish Pubns.

Greenberg, Bonita R., jt. auth. see Haynes, William O.

Greenberg, Bradley S. Life on Television: Content Analysis of U.S. TV Drama. LC 80-14478. (Communication & Information Science Ser.). 224p. 1980. text ed. 29.50 (ISBN 0-89391-039-2); pap. text ed. 17.95 (ISBN 0-89391-062-7). Ablex Pub.

Greenberg, Bradley S. & Parker, Edwin B., eds. Kennedy Assassination & the American Public: Social Communication in Crisis. 1965. 30.00x (ISBN 0-8047-0257-8). Stanford U Pr.

Greenberg, Bradley S., et al. Mexican Americans & the Mass Media. LC 82-11658. (Communication & Information Science Ser.). 304p. 1983. text ed. 35.00 (ISBN 0-89391-126-7). Ablex Pub.

Greenberg, Brian. Worker & Community: Response to Industrialization in a 19th-Century American City, Albany, New York, 1850-1884. (Series in American Social History). 250p. 1985. lib. bdg. 34.50x (ISBN 0-88706-046-3); pap. text ed. 12.95x (ISBN 0-88706-048-X). State U NY Pr.

Greenberg, Bruce. Greenberg's Price Guide to Lionel Trains: 1901-1942. (Illus.). 1978. 12.95 (ISBN 0-517-53796-6). Crown.

Greenberg, Bruce & LaVoie, Roland. Greenberg's Price Guide To Lionel Fundimensions Trains 1970-1985. (Illus.). 192p. (Orig.). 1985. pap. 25.00 (ISBN 0-89778-022-1, 6535). Greenberg Pub Co.

Greenberg, Bruce C. Greenberg's Guide to American Flyer: Prewar 0 & Standard. (Orig.). 1986. pap. 35.00 (ISBN 0-89778-014-0, 6411). Greenberg Pub Co.

--Greenberg's Price Guide to Lionel Trains: Numerical Listing 1901-1942 & 1945-1984. 60p. (Orig.). 1984. pap. 5.95 (ISBN 0-317-14047-7, 6565). Greenberg Pub Co.

--Greenberg's Price Guide to Lionel Trains: Prewar-1901-1942. 160p. (Orig.). 1984. 35.00 (ISBN 0-89778-502-9). Greenberg Pub.

--Greenberg's Repair & Operating Manual for Lionel Trains. 4th ed. (Illus.). 736p. 1983. pap. 12.95 (ISBN 0-89778-074-4, NO. 6500). Greenberg Pub Co.

Greenberg, Bruce C. & LaVoie, Roland. Greenberg's Price Guide to Lionel Trains 1945-1969. (Illus., Orig.). 1985. pap. 26.95 (ISBN 0-89778-021-3, 6530). Greenberg Pub Co.

Greenberg, Bruce C., ed. Greenberg's Lionel Catalogues, Vol. 1: Nineteen Twenty-Three to Nineteen Thirty-Two. (Illus.). 490p. 1982. text ed. 95.00 (ISBN 0-89778-011-6). Greenberg Pub Co.

--Greenberg's Lionel Catalogues, Vol. 2: Nineteen Thirty-Three to Forty-Two, (Illus.). 516p. 1982. text ed. 95.00 (ISBN 0-89778-012-4). Greenberg Pub Co.

--Greenberg's Repair & Operating Manual for Lionel Trains. (Illus.). 736p. 1985. pap. 13.50 (ISBN 0-89778-040-X, 6610). Greenberg Pub Co.

Greenberg, Bruce C., ed. see McDuffie, Al.

Greenberg, Bruce C., ed. see Rosa, Vincent & Horan, George.

Greenberg, Calvin L. Profit Opportunities in Real Estate Investments. cancelled 12.95 (ISBN 0-13-726042-3, Parker). P-H.

Greenberg, Clement. Art & Culture: Critical Essays. pap. 9.95 (ISBN 0-8070-6681-8, BP212). Beacon Pr.

--Joan Miro. LC 77-91377. (Contemporary Art Ser). Repr. of 1948 ed. 17.00 (ISBN 0-405-00728-0). Ayer Co Pubs.

Greenberg, Clement, et al. Jack Bush. LC 84-81368. (Illus.). 224p. 1985. 65.00 (ISBN 0-933920-12-1, Dist. by Viking Penguin). Hudson Hills.

Greenberg, D. & Marcus, A. The Computer Image: Applications of Computer Graphics. 1982. text ed. 27.95 (ISBN 0-201-06192-9). Addison-Wesley.

Greenberg, D. M., ed. Metabolic Pathways. 3rd ed. Incl. Vol. 1. 1967. 82.00 (ISBN 0-12-299251-2); Vol. 2. 1968. 71.50 (ISBN 0-12-299252-0); Vol. 3. 1969. 95.00 (ISBN 0-12-299253-9); Vol. 4. 1970. 82.00 (ISBN 0-12-299254-7); Vol. 5. Vogel, Henry J., ed. 1971. 88.00; Vol. 6. Hokin, L. E., ed. 1972. 95.00 (ISBN 0-12-299256-3). Acad Pr.

Greenberg, Dan & Jacobs, Marcia. How to Make Yourself Miserable. 1976. pap. 4.95 (ISBN 0-394-73168-9). Random.

Greenberg, Dan & O'Malley, Suzanne. How to Avoid Love & Marriage. (Illus.). 150p. 1985. lib. bdg. 12.90 (ISBN 0-89471-373-6); pap. 4.95 (ISBN 0-89471-372-8). Running Pr.

Greenberg, David. Slugs. (Illus.). 32p. (gr. k-5). 1983. PLB 12.45i (ISBN 0-316-32658-5, Pub. by Atlantic Monthly Pr); pap. 4.70i (ISBN 0-316-32659-3, Pub. by Atlantic Monthly Pr). Little.

Greenberg, David & Bernards, Solomon S. The Living Heritage of Hanukkah. 47p. 1.50 (ISBN 0-686-74963-4). ADL.

Greenberg, David, jt. auth. see Kessler, Ronald.

Greenberg, David F. Mathematical Criminology. (Illus.). 1979. text ed. 32.50x (ISBN 0-8135-0873-8). Rutgers U Pr.

Greenberg, David F., ed. Crime & Capitalism: Essays in Marxist Criminology. LC 80-84018. 506p. (Orig.). 1981. 18.95 (ISBN 0-87484-505-X). Mayfield Pub.

Greenberg, Diane, jt. auth. see Block, Joel D.

Greenberg, Dolores. Financiers & Railroads, Eighteen Sixty-Nine to Eighteen Eighty-Nine: A Study of Morton, Bliss & Company. LC 78-66830. 288p. 1980. 27.50 (ISBN 0-87413-148-0). U Delaware Pr.

Greenberg, Douglas. Crime & Law Enforcement in the Colony of New York, 1691-1776. LC 76-13658. (Illus.). 256p. 1976. 27.50x (ISBN 0-8014-1020-7). Cornell U Pr.

Greenberg, Edward & Webster, Charles E. Advanced Econometrics: A Bridge to the Current Literature. LC 82-23770. (Wiley Series in Probability & Mathematical Statistics-Probability & Mathematical Statistics Section). 344p. 1983. text ed. 44.95 (ISBN 0-471-09077-8). Wiley.

Greenberg, Edward, ed. Capitalism & the American Political Ideal. LC 84-27722. 288p. 1985. 30.00 (ISBN 0-87332-292-4); pap. 12.95 (ISBN 0-87332-293-2). M E Sharpe.

Greenberg, Edward, et al. Estimating Economic Development Impacts: An Alternative Approach. 55p. 1977. pap. 4.00 (ISBN 0-686-15724-9, INS 17). Inst for Urban & Regional.

Greenberg, Edward S. The American Political System: A Radical Approach. 3rd ed. 1983. pap. text ed. 16.95 (ISBN 0-316-32657-7); tchr's. manual avail. (ISBN 0-316-32656-9). Little.

--Serving the Few: Corporate Capitalism & the Bias of Government Policy. LC 79-10104. 275p. 1974. pap. 17.95x (ISBN 0-471-32487-6). Wiley.

--Understanding Modern Government: The Rise & Decline of the American Political Economy. LC 78-10104. 197p. 1979. pap. text ed. 15.95 (ISBN 0-471-02913-0). Wiley.

Greenberg, Edward S., ed. Political Socialization. LC 75-105605. (Controversy Ser.). 199p. 1970. text ed. 11.95x (ISBN 0-88311-026-1); pap. text ed. 5.95x (ISBN 0-88311-027-X). Lieber-Atherton.

Greenberg, Eliezer, jt. ed. see Howe, Irving.

Greenberg, Eliezer, ed. see Peretz, I. L.

Greenberg, Ellen, jt. auth. see Greenberg, Hal.

Greenberg, Eric R. The Celebrant. LC 82-9236. 272p. 1983. 14.95 (ISBN 0-89696-171-0, An Everest House Book). Dodd.

Greenberg, Florence & Heffley, Anne P. Tradition & Dissent: A Rhetoric Reader. 2nd ed. LC 76-145858. 602p. 1971. pap. write for info. (ISBN 0-02-346620-0). Macmillan.

Greenberg, Frank, jt. auth. see Shangold, Jules.

Greenberg, Gary. C-BIMS: Cassette-Based Information Management System for the PET. (Illus.). 224p. (Orig.). 1983. 16.95 (ISBN 0-8306-0489-8); pap. 10.95 (ISBN 0-8306-1489-3, 1489). TAB Bks.

Greenberg, Gary & Tobach, Ethel, eds. Behavioral Evolution & Integrative Levels: Proceedings of the First T.C. Scneirla Conference on the Evolution & Development of Behavior. 320p. 1984. text ed. 29.95 (ISBN 0-89859-363-8). L Erlbaum Assocs.

Greenberg, Georgia, jt. auth. see Greenberg, Henry.

Greenberg, H. J. & Murphy, F. H. Advanced Techniques in the Practice of Operations Research. (Publications in Operations Research Ser.: Vol. 4). 470p. 1982. 56.50 (ISBN 0-444-00750-4, North Holland). Elsevier.

Greenberg, H. J., ed. Design & Implementation of Optimization of Software, No. 28. (Nato Advanced Study Institute, Applied Science Ser.). 566p. 1978. 45.00x (ISBN 90-286-0728-5). Sijthoff & Noordhoff.

Greenberg, H. M., et al, eds. Clinical Aspects of Life-Threatening Arrhythmias. (Annals of The New York Academy of Sciences Ser.: Vol. 427). 326p. 1984. lib. bdg. 75.00x (ISBN 0-89766-248-2); pap. 75.00x (ISBN 0-89766-249-0). NY Acad Sci.

Greenberg, Hal & Greenberg, Ellen. Inside Chocolate: The Chocolate Lover's Guide to Boxed Chocolates. (Illus.). 80p. (Orig.). 1984. pap. 14.95 (ISBN 0-8109-1111-6). Abrams.

Greenberg, Harold. Integer Programming. (Mathematics in Science & Engineering Ser.: Vol. 76). 1971. 47.50 (ISBN 0-12-299450-7). Acad Pr.

Greenberg, Harold, jt. auth. see Radin, Stephen.

Greenberg, Harold M., jt. auth. see Radin, Stephen.

Greenberg, Harriet. U. S. Virgin Islands Alive. 1983. pap. 5.95 (ISBN 0-935572-11-2). Alive Pubns.

Greenberg, Harriet & Greenberg, Arnold L. Caracas Alive. 3rd, rev. ed. 1979. pap. 4.95 (ISBN 0-935572-01-5). Alive Pubns.

--Caracas Alive. 2nd rev. ed. 1975. 2.95 (ISBN 0-686-02450-8). Alive Pubns.

Greenberg, Harriet & Greenberg, Arnold. Caracas Alive. rev. ed. 1971. pap. 2.50 (ISBN 0-686-23069-8). Alive Pubns.

--Guatemala Alive. 1976. pap. 2.50 (ISBN 0-686-23068-X). Alive Pubns.

Greenberg, Harriet & Greenberg, Arnold L. Lebendiges Rio. 1979. pap. 3.50 (ISBN 0-935572-07-4). Alive Pubns.

Greenberg, Harriet & Greenberg, Arnold. Rio Alive. rev. ed. 1977. pap. 2.95 (ISBN 0-686-23067-1). Alive Pubns.

Greenberg, Harriet & Greenberg, Arnold L. Venezuela Alive. 1974. pap. 2.00 (ISBN 0-935572-04-X). Alive Pubns.

Greenberg, Harriet, jt. auth. see Greenberg, Arnold.

Greenberg, Harvey & Maybee, John, eds. Computer-Assisted Analysis & Model Simplification. LC 80-28509. 1981. 44.50 (ISBN 0-12-299680-1). Acad Pr.

Greenberg, Harvey R. Hanging In: What You Should Know about Psychotherapy. 288p. (gr. 7 up). 1985. pap. 2.95 (ISBN 0-590-33244-9, Point). Scholastic Inc.

Greenberg, Hayim. Hayim Greenberg Anthology. Syrkin, Marie, ed. (Schaver Publication Fund for Jewish Studies Ser). 342p. 1968. 8.95x (ISBN 0-8143-1344-2). Wayne St U Pr.

Greenberg, Hazel, ed. see Equal Rights Amendment Project.

Greenberg, Henry & Greenberg, Georgia. Carl Gorman's World. LC 83-26072. (Illus.). 195p. 1984. 35.00 (ISBN 0-8263-0738-8). U of NM Pr.

Greenberg, Henry F., et al. Child Care Manual. 6th ed. St. Geme, Joseph W., Jr., ed. LC 75-21904. (Illus., Orig.). 1982. pap. text ed. 9.50 (ISBN 0-89119-000-7). Sutherland Learn Assocs.

Greenberg, Henry M., ed. Sudden Coronary Death, Vol. 382. 484p. 1982. 102.00x (ISBN 0-89766-153-2); pap. 102.00x (ISBN 0-89766-154-0). NY Acad Sci.

Greenberg, Herbert. Quest for the Necessary: W. H. Auden & the Dilemma of Divided Consciousness. LC 68-54019. Repr. of 1968 ed. 42.00 (ISBN 0-8357-9175-0, 2017009). Bks Demand UMI.

Greenberg, Herbert M. Coping with Job Stress. (Illus.). 288p. 1980. 12.95 (ISBN 0-13-172411-8, Spec); pap. 5.95 (ISBN 0-13-172403-7). P-H.

--Teaching with Feeling: Compassion & Self-Awareness in the Classroom Today. LC 69-13393. 1969. pap. 7.87scp (ISBN 0-672-63601-8). Pegasus.

--Teaching with Feeling: Compassion & Self-Awareness in the Classroom Today. 219p. 1969. pap. text ed. write for info. (ISBN 0-02-346610-3). Macmillan.

Greenberg, Herman D., ed. Applications of Fracture Toughness Parameters to Structural Metals. LC 65-27851. (Metallurgical Society Conference Ser.: Vol. 31). pap. 104.50 (ISBN 0-317-11263-5, 2001519). Bks Demand UMI.

Greenberg, Hinda F., ed. Bilingualism As a Learning Disability. (Journal of Reading, Writing & Learning Disabilities International Ser.). 112p. (Orig.). 1985. pap. text ed. write for info. Am Lib Pub Co.

Greenberg, Idaz. Field Guide to Marine Invertebrates. (Illus.). 1980. plastic card 3.95x (ISBN 0-913008-11-7). Seahawk Pr.

--Fishwatcher's Field Guide. (Illus.). 1979. plastic card 3.95x (ISBN 0-913008-10-9). Seahawk Pr.

--Guide to Corals & Fishes. (Illus.). 1977. saddlestitched 4.95x (ISBN 0-913008-08-7). Seahawk Pr.

--Hawaiian Fishwatcher's Field Guide. (Illus.). 1983. plastic card 3.95x (ISBN 0-913008-13-3). Seahawk Pr.

--Red Sea Fishwatcher's Field Guide. (Illus.). 1982. plastic card 3.95x (ISBN 0-913008-12-5). Seahawk Pr.

--Waterproof Guide to Corals & Fishes. (Illus.). 1977. soft plastic pages, rust-proof bdg. 9.95x (ISBN 0-913008-07-9). Seahawk Pr.

Greenberg, Idaz & Greenberg, Jerry. Sharks & Other Dangerous Sea Creatures. (Illus.). 64p. 1981. pap. 4.95 (ISBN 0-913008-09-5, G-095). Banyan Bks.

--Sharks & Other Dangerous Sea Creatures. (Illus.). 1981. saddlestiched 4.95x (ISBN 0-913008-09-5). Seahawk Pr.

Greenberg, Idaz, jt. auth. see Greenberg, Jerry.

Greenberg, Ira A. Psychodrama & Audience Attitude Change. LC 68-54532. 1968. 10.00 (ISBN 0-911958-00-2); pap. 5.95 (ISBN 0-685-06839-0). Behavioral Studies.

Greenberg, Ira A., ed. Group Hypnotherapy & Hypnodrama. LC 76-17012. 408p. 1977. 25.95x (ISBN 0-88229-256-0). Nelson-Hall.

Greenberg, Irving, jt. ed. see Rosenfeld, Alvin H.

Greenberg, J., et al see Maquet, J.

Greenberg, J. M., ed. see Symposium Organized by the International Astronomical Union, 52nd, the State Univ. of N.Y. at Albany, May-June, 1972.

Greenberg, Jack. Judicial Process & Social Change. 666p. 1977. write for info. West Pub.

--Race Relations & American Law. LC 59-11179. 481p. 1959. 31.50x (ISBN 0-231-02313-8). Columbia U Pr.

--Race Relations & American Law. LC 59-11179. pap. 123.30 (ISBN 0-317-26579-2, 2023967). Bks Demand UMI.

Greenberg, Jack & Lambert, Richard D., eds. Blacks & the Law. new ed. LC 72-93252. (Annals of the American Academy of Political & Social Science: No. 407). 250p. 1973. 15.00 (ISBN 0-87761-163-7); pap. 7.95 (ISBN 0-87761-162-9). Am Acad Pol Soc Sci.

Greenberg, Jack, et al, eds. The Long Road up from Barbarism: The Issues of Capital Punishment. LC 82-49327. 1983. write for info. (ISBN 0-669-06615-X); pap. 8.95x (ISBN 0-669-06616-8). Lexington Bks.

Greenberg, James A., jt. auth. see Kropf, Roger.

Greenberg, James B. Santiago's Sword: Chatino Peasant Religion & Economics. LC 80-6051. 250p. 1981. 21.00x (ISBN 0-520-04135-6). U of Cal Pr.

Greenberg, Jan. Bye, Bye, Miss American Pie. LC 85-47590. 150p. (gr. 7 up). 1985. 10.95 (ISBN 0-374-31012-2). FS&G.

--The Iceberg & Its Shadow. 128p. (gr. 5 up). 1982. pap. 1.75 (ISBN 0-440-93978-X, LFL). Dell.

--The Iceberg & Its Shadow. LC 80-20060. 132p. (gr. 7 up). 1980. 10.95 (ISBN 0-374-33624-5). FS&G.

--No Dragons to Slay. LC 83-17200. 119p. (gr. 7 up). 1984. 10.95 (ISBN 0-374-35528-2); pap. 3.45 (ISBN 0-374-45509-0). FS&G.

--The Pig-Out Blues. LC 82-2552. 150p. (gr. 7 up). 1982. 9.95 (ISBN 0-374-35937-7). FS&G.

--A Season In-Between. 144p. (gr. 7 up). 1981. pap. 1.75 (ISBN 0-440-97710-X, LFL). Dell.

--A Season In-Between. LC 79-17997. 120p. (gr. 5 up). 1980. 9.95 (ISBN 0-374-36524-5). FS&G.

--The Teenager's Guide to the Best Summer Opportunities. 208p. 1985. 16.95 (ISBN 0-916782-59-X); pap. 9.95 (ISBN 0-916782-58-1). Harvard Common Pr.

Greenberg, Jan W. Theater Careers. (Illus.). 216p. (gr. 7 up). 1983. 13.95 (ISBN 0-03-061568-2). HR&W.

--Theatre Business: From Auditions Through Opening Night. LC 80-20295. 1981. 10.95 (ISBN 0-03-051451-7). HR&W.

Greenberg, Janelle R., jt. auth. see Weston, Corinne.

Greenberg, Jay, et al. NHL: The World of Professional Ice Hockey. (Illus.). 256p. 1981. 24.95 (ISBN 0-8317-6370-1, Rutledge Pr). Smith Pubs.

Greenberg, Jay, jt. auth. see Eustis, Nancy.

Greenberg, Jay N., jt. ed. see Choi, Thomas.

Greenberg, Jay R. & Mitchell, Stephen A. Object Relations in Psychoanalytic Theory. 448p. 1983. 25.00x (ISBN 0-674-62975-2). Harvard U Pr.

Greenberg, Jerald, jt. auth. see Baron, Robert A.

Greenberg, Jerald & Cohen, Ronald, eds. Equity & Justice in Social Behavior. LC 82-1602. 1982. 42.50 (ISBN 0-12-299580-5). Acad Pr.

Greenberg, Jerrold, jt. auth. see Dintiman, George.

Greenberg, Jerrold S. Comprehensive Stress Management. 368p. 1983. pap. text ed. write for info. (ISBN 0-697-07199-5). Wm C Brown.

--Managing Stress: A Personal Guide. 256p. 1984. pap. 7.95 (ISBN 0-697-00282-9). Wm C Brown.

--Student-Centered Health Instruction: A Humanistic Approach. (Illus.). 270p. 1978. pap. text ed. 14.95 (ISBN 0-394-34874-5, RanC). Random.

Greenberg, Jerrold S. & Pargman, David. Physical Fitness: A Wellness Approach. (Illus.). 352p. 1985. pap. text ed. 16.95 (ISBN 0-13-668856-X). P-H.

Greenberg, Jerrold S., jt. auth. see Dintiman, George B.

Greenberg, Jerrold S., et al. Sexuality: Insights & Issues. 640p. 1986. text ed. price not set (ISBN 0-697-00466-X); pap. text ed. price not set (ISBN 0-697-00482-1); price not set instr's. manual (ISBN 0-697-00859-2); price not set transparencies (ISBN 0-697-00858-4). Wm C Brown.

Greenberg, Jerry. The Coral Reef. (Orig.). saddlestiched 4.95x (ISBN 0-913008-06-0). Seahawk Pr.

--Field Guide to Marine Invertebrates. plastic card 3.95 (ISBN 0-916224-79-1). Banyan Bks.

--Fishwatcher's Field Guide. plastic card 3.95 (ISBN 0-916224-78-3). Banyan Bks.

--Manfish with a Camera. (Illus.). 48p. pap. 2.50 (ISBN 0-686-75253-8). Banyan Bks.

Greenberg, Jerry & Greenberg, Idaz. Guide to Corals & Fishes of Florida, the Bahamas, the Caribbean. (Illus.). 64p. pap. 5.95 (ISBN 0-913008-08-7). Banyan Bks.

--The Living Reef. LC 70-187354. (Illus.). 126p. perfect bound 9.95x (ISBN 0-913008-01-X). Seahawk Pr.

--Waterproof Guide to Corals & Fishes of Florida, the Bahamas, & the Caribbean. (Illus.). 64p. pap. 8.95 special (ISBN 0-913008-07-9). Banyan Bks.

Greenberg, Jerry & Greenberg, Michael. The Radiant Reef. (Illus.). 1985. saddle stitched 3.50 (ISBN 0-913008-14-1). Seahawk Pr.

Greenberg, Jerry & Idaz. The Coral Reef. (Illus.). 64p. pap. 4.95 (ISBN 0-686-75254-6). Banyan Bks.

Greenberg, Jerry, jt. auth. see Greenberg, Idaz.

Greenberg, Jim. The Pig-Out Blues. 128p. (YA) (gr. 7 up). 1985. pap. 2.25 (ISBN 0-440-96977-8, LFL). Dell.

Greenberg, Joann & Vernon, McCay. The Language Arts Handbook: A Total Communication Approach. 1981. pap. 19.95 (ISBN 0-317-05966-1). Univ Park.

Greenberg, Joanne. The Far Side of Victory. 233p. 1983. 14.95 (ISBN 0-03-063252-8). HR&W.

--Founder's Praise. 1977. pap. 1.95 (ISBN 0-380-01757-1, 34702). Avon.

--High Crimes & Misdemeanors. 208p. 1981. pap. 2.95 (ISBN 0-380-55657-X, 55657, Bard). Avon.

--I Never Promised You a Rose Garden. movie ed. (Illus.). 1977. pap. 2.95 (ISBN 0-451-13136-3, AE3136, Sig). NAL.

--In This Sign. 288p. 1972. pap. 2.50 (ISBN 0-380-00941-2, 52712-X). Avon.

--In This Sign. 288p. 1984. pap. 5.95 (ISBN 0-03-000438-1, Owl Bks). HR&W.

--The King's Persons. LC 85-8466. 288p. 1985. pap. 6.95 (ISBN 0-03-005623-3). HR&W.

--Rites of Passage. 1985. pap. 6.95 (ISBN 0-03-003677-1, Owl Bks). HR&W.

--A Season of Delight. LC 80-20421. 240p. 1981. 12.95 (ISBN 0-03-057627-X). HR&W.

--A Season of Delight. 256p. 1982. pap. 2.95 (ISBN 0-380-60285-7, 60285-7). Avon.

Greenberg, Joanne C., et al. The Language Arts Handbook: A Total Communication Approach. 1982. 19.95 (ISBN 0-673-15808-X). Scott F.

Greenberg, Joel, jt. auth. see Higham, Charles.

Greenberg, Joseph. Language Typology: A Historical & Analytical Overview. LC 73-87532. (Janua Linguarum, Ser. Minor: No. 184). 82p. (Orig.). 1974. pap. text ed. 7.60x (ISBN 0-686-22575-9). Mouton.

Greenberg, Joseph H. Essays in Linguistics. LC 57-6273. 1963. pap. 1.95x (ISBN 0-226-30615-1, P119, Phoen). U of Chicago Pr.

--Language, Culture, & Communication: Essays by Joseph H. Greenberg. Dil, Anwar S., ed. LC 72-150323. (Language Science & National Development Ser). 384p. 1971. 27.50x (ISBN 0-8047-0781-2). Stanford U Pr.

--Language Universals: With Special References to Feature Hierarchies. (Janua Linguarum Ser. Minor: No. 59). (Orig.). 1966. pap. text ed. 10.00x (ISBN 0-686-22444-2). Mouton.

--A New Invitation to Linguistics. LC 76-42422. (Illus.). 1977. pap. 3.50 (ISBN 0-385-07550-2, Anch). Doubleday.

Greenberg, Joseph H., et al, eds. Universals of Human Language, 4 vols. Incl. Vol. I. Method & Theory. 22.50x (ISBN 0-8047-0965-3); Vol. II. Phonology. 40.00x (ISBN 0-8047-0966-1); Vol. III. Word Structure. 35.00x (ISBN 0-8047-0968-8); Vol. IV. Syntax. 45.00x (ISBN 0-8047-0969-6). LC 77-89179. 1978. Set. 142.50x (ISBN 0-8047-1012-0). Stanford U Pr.

Greenberg, Judith, jt. auth. see Carey, Helen.

Greenberg, Judith, tr. see D'Allonnes, Olivier R.

Greenberg, Judith E. What Is the Sign for Friend? (Illus.). 32p. (gr. 1-3). 1985. PLB 8.90 (ISBN 0-531-04939-6). Watts.

Greenberg, Judith E. & Carey, Helen. How to Participate in a Group. (Social Studies Skills Ser.). 96p. (YA) (gr. 7 up). lib. bdg. 9.40 (ISBN 0-531-04671-0). Watts.

Greenberg, Judith E. & Carey, Helen H. Jewish Holidays. (First Bks.). (Illus.). 32p. (gr. 4-6). 1985. lib. bdg. 9.40 (ISBN 0-531-04913-2). Watts.

Greenberg, Judith E., jt. auth. see Carey, Helen.

Greenberg, Kathy, jt. auth. see Kyte, Barbara.

Greenberg, Keith. Menudo. (Illus.). 64p. (Orig., Eng. & Sp.). (gr. 3 up). 1983. pap. 3.95 (ISBN 0-671-49896-7). PB.

Greenberg, Keith E. Cyndi Lauper. LC 85-10262. (Enterainment World Ser.). (Illus.). 32p. (gr. 4-10). 1985. PLB 8.95 (ISBN 0-8225-1605-5). Lerner Pubns.

Greenberg, Kenneth R. A Tiger by the Tail: Parenting in a Troubled Society. LC 73-93103. 272p. 1974. 20.95x (ISBN 0-911012-77-X). Nelson-Hall.

Greenberg, Kenneth S. Masters & Statesmen: The Political Culture of American Slavery. LC 85-9786. (New Studies in American Intellectual & Cultural History Ser.). 256p. 1985. text ed. 26.50x (ISBN 0-8018-2762-0). Johns Hopkins.

Greenberg, L. M., ed. Evolution, Extinction, & Catastrophism. 1982. pap. 5.00x (ISBN 0-917994-12-4). Kronos Pr.

Greenberg, L. M., et al, eds. see Velikovsky, et al.

Greenberg, Leo & Chaffin, Don B. Workers & Their Tools: A Guide to the Ergonomic Design of Hand Tools & Small Presses. (Illus.). 130p. 1978. 19.25 (ISBN 0-87812-161-7). Pendell Pub.

Greenberg, Leon, ed. Discontinuous Groups & Reimann Surfaces. LC 73-16783. (Annals of Mathematics Studies: No. 79). 450p. 1974. text ed. 38.00 (ISBN 0-691-08138-7). Princeton U Pr.

Greenberg, Leon A., jt. auth. see Haggard, Howard W.

Greenberg, Leonard H. Discoveries in Physics for Scientists & Engineers. 2nd ed. 1975. pap. text ed. 20.95 (ISBN 0-7216-4246-2, CBS C). SCP.

--Discovery in Physics for Scientists & Engineers. 2nd ed. LC 74-4565. (Illus.). 316p. 1975. pap. text ed. 20.95 (ISBN 0-7216-4246-2). HR&W.

Greenberg, Leslie S., jt. ed. see Rice, Laura N.

Greenberg, Lewis M., et al, eds. see Velikovsky, et al.

Greenberg, Linda, ed. see Barker, Thomas B.

Greenberg, Linda, ed. see Bradshaw, John.

Greenberg, Linda, ed. see Patteson, Jim.

Greenberg, Linda, ed. see Shantar, Stan.

Greenberg, Linda, ed. see Smith, Philip K. & Shantar, Stan.

Greenberg, Louis. Jews in Russia: The Struggle for Emancipation, 2 Vols. in 1. LC 79-161769. Repr. of 1965 ed. 27.50 (ISBN 0-404-09023-0). AMS Pr.

--The Jews in Russia: The Struggle for Emancipation, 1772-1917, 2 vols. in 1. Wishnitzer, Mark, ed. LC 75-36489. 234p. 1976. pap. 11.95 (ISBN 0-8052-0525-X). Schocken.

Greenberg, Louis M. Sisters of Liberty: Marseille, Lyon, Paris, & the Reaction to a Centralized State, 1868-1871. LC 70-134952. (Historical Monographs Ser: No. 62). 1971. 25.00x (ISBN 0-674-81000-7). Harvard U Pr.

Greenberg, M., jt. auth. see Olander, J.

Greenberg, M. J. & Harper, J. R. Algebraic Topology: A First Course. 1981. 47.95 (ISBN 0-8053-3558-7); pap. 29.95 (ISBN 0-8053-3557-9). Benjamin-Cummings.

Greenberg, M. J., tr. see Serre, J. P.

Greenberg, Margaret & Olds, Nancy J. The Sanibel Shell Guide. LC 82-71090. (Illus.). 117p. (Orig.). 1982. pap. 5.95 (ISBN 0-89305-041-5). Anna Pub.

Greenberg, Mark, et al, eds. Essentials of Body Computed Tomography. (Illus.). 576p. 1983. 55.00 (ISBN 0-7216-4243-8). Saunders.

Greenberg, Mark S. & Bocchino, Anthony J. Pennsylvania Evidence: Objections & Responses. 146p. 1983. 20.00 (ISBN 0-87215-629-X). Michie Co.

Greenberg, Marshall G., jt. auth. see Frank, Ronald E.

Greenberg, Marti H. Women Sleuths. (Mystery Short Novels Ser.: No. II). (Orig.). 1985. pap. 4.95 (ISBN 0-89733-157-5). Academy Chi Pubs.

Greenberg, Martin. Kafka: The Terror of Art. LC 68-54148. 256p. 1983. pap. 8.95 (ISBN 0-8180-1138-6). Horizon.

--A Short History of Communism. (Illus.). 80p. 0.95 (ISBN 0-686-74925-1). ADL.

Greenberg, Martin & Olander, Joseph. Science Fiction of the Fifties. 1979. pap. 4.95 (ISBN 0-380-46409-8, 46409-8). Avon.

Greenberg, Martin & Pronzini, Bill, eds. The Lawmen. 256p. 1984. pap. 2.50 (ISBN 0-449-12689-7, Gold Medal). Fawcett.

Greenberg, Martin & Waugh, Charles, eds. Tantalizing Locked Room Mysteries. LC 80-54817. 224p. 1982. 12.95 (ISBN 0-8027-0680-0). Walker & Co.

Greenberg, Martin, jt. ed. see Asimov, Isaac.

Greenberg, Martin, jt. ed. see Waugh, Charles.

Greenberg, Martin, tr. see Kafka, Franz.

Greenberg, Martin, tr. from Ger. see Kleist, Heinrich.

Greenberg, Martin, tr. see Rohmer, Eric & Kleist, Heinrich von.

Greenberg, Martin, jt. ed. see Asimov, Isaac.

Greenberg, Martin A. Auxiliary Police: The Citizen's Approach to Public Safety. LC 83-22683. (Contributions in Criminology & Penology Ser.: No. 3). (Illus.). xiv, 231p. 1984. lib. bdg. 29.95 (ISBN 0-313-23955-X, GAU/). Greenwood.

Greenberg, Martin H. The Jewish Lists: Physicists & General, Actors & Writers, & Hundreds of Other Lists of Accomplished Jews. LC 79-14349. 1979. 12.95 (ISBN 0-8052-3711-9). Schocken.

Greenberg, Martin H. & Nevins, Francis M., Jr. Hitchcock in Prime Time. 352p. 1985. pap. 9.95 (ISBN 0-380-89673-7). Avon.

Greenberg, Martin H. & Norton, Augustus R. Touring Nam: The Vietnamese War Reader. LC 84-62022. 384p. 1985. 16.95 (ISBN 0-688-03463-2). Morrow.

Greenberg, Martin H. & Pronzini, Bill. The Cowboys. 192p. (Orig.). 1985. pap. 2.50 (ISBN 0-449-12720-6, GM). Fawcett.

--The Warriors. 256p. (Orig.). 1985. pap. 2.95 (ISBN 0-449-12721-4, GM). Fawcett.

Greenberg, Martin H., jt. auth. see Norton, Augustus R.

Greenberg, Martin H. see Pronzini, Bill.

Greenberg, Martin H., jt. auth. see Pronzini, Bill.

Greenberg, Martin H., ed. The Arbor House Celebrity Book of Horror Stories. 600p. 1982. 20.95 (ISBN 0-87795-373-2, Pub. by Priam); pap. 9.95 (ISBN 0-87795-400-3). Arbor Hse.

--Astounding Science Fiction, July, 1939. (Alternatives Ser.). 180p. 1981. Repr. of 1939 ed. 12.95 (ISBN 0-8093-0991-2). S Ill U Pr.

--The Best of Marion Zimmer Bradley. 225p. 1985. 14.95 (ISBN 0-89733-165-6); pap. 4.95 (ISBN 0-89733-166-4). Academy Chi Pubs.

--Fantastic Lives: Autobiographical Essays by Notable Science Fiction Writers. LC 80-17592. (Alternatives Ser.). 226p. 1981. 15.95 (ISBN 0-8093-0987-4). S Ill U Pr.

--Police Procedurals. (Mystery Short Novels Ser.: No. I). (Orig.). 1985. pap. 4.95 (ISBN 0-89733-158-3). Academy Chi Pubs.

Greenberg, Martin H. & Asimov, Isaac, eds. Amazing Stories: Sixty Years of the Best Science Fiction. LC 85-51055. (Illus.). 256p. (YA) 1985. pap. 7.95 (ISBN 0-394-74167-6). Random.

Greenberg, Martin H. & Olander, Joseph D., eds. Tomorrow, Inc. SF Stories About Big Business. LC 76-11057. (YA) (gr. 10 up). 1976. 9.95 (ISBN 0-8008-7746-2). Taplinger.

Greenberg, Martin H. & Prozini, Bill, eds. Academy Mystery Novellas, 2 Vols. Incl. Women Sleuths (ISBN 0-89733-157-5); Police Procedurals (ISBN 0-89733-158-3). 250p. pap. 4.95 ea. Academy Chi Pubs.

Greenberg, Martin H. & Silverberg, Robert, eds. The Arbor House Treasury of Modern Science Fiction. LC 79-54005. 1980. 19.95 (ISBN 0-87795-246-9); pap. 8.95 (ISBN 0-87795-266-3). Arbor Hse.

Greenberg, Martin H. & Waugh, Charles, eds. Hollywood Unreel: Fantasies About Hollywood & the Movies. LC 81-16742. 304p. 1982. 14.95 (ISBN 0-8008-3197-7). Taplinger.

Greenberg, Martin H. & Waugh, Charles G., eds. The Arbor House Celebrity Book of the Greatest Stories Ever Told. 512p. 1983. 15.95 (ISBN 0-87795-448-8); pap. 8.95 (ISBN 0-87795-449-6). Arbor Hse.

--The Arbor House Treasury of Nobel Prize Winners. 294p. 1984. 15.95 (ISBN 0-87795-511-5); pap. 7.95 (ISBN 0-87795-613-8). Arbor Hse.

--Cults! An Anthology of Secret Societies, Sects, & the Supernatural. 368p. 1983. 17.95 (ISBN 0-8253-0159-9). Beaufort Bks NY.

Greenberg, Martin H., jt. ed. see Asimov, Isaac.

Greenberg, Martin H., ed. see Asimov, Isaac.

Greenberg, Martin H., jt. ed. see Asimov, Isaac.

Greenberg, Martin H., ed. see Brown, Fredric, Jr.

Greenberg, Martin H., jt. ed. see Clear, Val.

Greenberg, Martin H., ed. see Gardner, Erle Stanley.

Greenberg, Martin H., jt. ed. see Malzberg, Barry N.

Greenberg, Martin H., jt. ed. see Miller, Walter M., Jr.

Greenberg, Martin H., ed. see Neville, Kris.

Greenberg, Martin H., jt. ed. see Nevins, Francis M., Jr.

Greenberg, Martin H., jt. ed. see Olander, Joseph D.

Greenberg, Martin H., ed. see Overholser, Wayne D.

Greenberg, Martin H., jt. ed. see Pronzini, Bill.

Greenberg, Martin H., jt. ed. see Saberhagen, Fred.

Greenberg, Martin H., ed. see St. Clair, Margaret.

Greenberg, Martin H., jt. ed. see Silverberg, Robert.

Greenberg, Martin H., jt. ed. see Warrick, Patricia S.

Greenberg, Martin H., jt. ed. see Waugh, Carol-Lynn R.

Greenberg, Martin H., jt. ed. see Waugh, Charles G.

Greenberg, Martin H., jt. auth. see Asimov, Isaac.

Greenberg, Martin H., et al, eds. The Future, Vol. I. 384p. (Orig.). 1981. pap. 2.50 (ISBN 0-449-24366-4, Crest). Fawcett.

--Sociology Through Science Fiction. 350p. (Orig.). 1974. pap. text ed. 11.95 (ISBN 0-312-74165-0). St Martin.

--The Science Fictional Dinosaur. 224p. (Orig.). 1982. pap. 2.25 (ISBN 0-380-77974-9, 77974-9, Flare). Avon.

Greenberg, Martin H., jt. ed. see Asimov, Isaac.

Greenberg, Martin J. Wisconsin Real Estate, 2 Vols. LC 79-92516. (The Practice Systems Library). (Illus.). 1982. 159.00; Suppl. 1984. 45.00; Suppl. 1983. 32.00. Lawyers Co-OP.

Greenberg, Martin J., jt. auth. see Cooper-Hill, James.

Greenberg, Marvin. Your Children Need Music: A Guide for Parents & Teachers of Young Children. (Illus.). 1979. text ed. 16.95 (ISBN 0-13-977116-6, Spec); pap. 8.95 (ISBN 0-13-977108-5). P-H.

Greenberg, Marvin J. Euclidean & Non-Euclidean Geometries: Development & History. 2nd ed. LC 79-19348. (Illus.). 400p. 1980. text ed. 26.95 (ISBN 0-7167-1103-6); instrs. manual & answer book avail. W H Freeman.

--Lectures on Algebraic Topology. (Math Lecture Notes Ser.: No. 9). 1973. 27.95 (ISBN 0-8053-3557-9). Benjamin-Cummings.

Greenberg, Mel L., jt. auth. see Massachusetts Continuing Education-New England Law Institute Incorporated.

Greenberg, Michael. British Trade & the Opening of China, Eighteen Hundred to Eighteen Forty-Two. LC 78-20465. 1980. Repr. of 1951 ed. 21.45 (ISBN 0-88355-844-0). Hyperion Conn.

--British Trade & the Opening of China, 1800-1842. LC 79-12206. 238p. 1979. pap. 6.50 (ISBN 0-85345-497-3). Monthly Rev.

Greenberg, Michael, jt. auth. see Greenberg, Jerry.

Greenberg, Michael, jt. auth. see Michaelson, Connie.

Greenberg, Michael, et al. Environmental Impact Statements. Natoli, Salvatore J., ed. LC 78-59102. (Resource Papers for College Geography). (Illus.). 1978. pap. text ed. 4.00 (ISBN 0-89291-131-X). Assn Am Geographers.

--Local Population & Employment Projection Techniques. LC 78-1294. 1978. text ed. 17.95 (ISBN 0-88285-049-0). Ctr Urban Pol Res.

Greenberg, Michael D. Foundations of Applied Mathematics. LC 77-11125. (Illus.). 1978. ref. ed. 42.95 (ISBN 0-13-329623-7). P-H.

Greenberg, Michael I. Advanced Techniques in Resuscitation. 160p. 1985. pap. text ed. 21.95 (ISBN 0-683-03552-5). Williams & Wilkins.

Greenberg, Michael I. & Roberts, James R. Emergency Medicine: A Clinical Approach to Challenging Problems. LC 81-3182. (Illus.). 395p. 1981. 40.00x (ISBN 0-8036-4331-4). Davis Co.

Greenberg, Michael R. Urbanization & Cancer Mortality: The United States Experience, 1950-1975. (Monographs in Epidemiology & Biostatistics). (Illus.). 1983. 45.00x (ISBN 0-19-503173-3). Oxford U Pr.

Greenberg, Michael R. & Anderson, Richard F. Hazardous Waste Sites: The Credibility Gap. 293p. 1984. 15.00x (ISBN 0-88285-102-0). Ctr Urban Pol Res.

Greenberg, Michael R. & Anderson, Richard. Hazardous Waste Siting. 276p. 1984. 19.95 (ISBN 0-88285-097-0). Transaction Bks.

Greenberg, Michael R. & Neuman, Nancy. New Jersey Toward the Year Two Thousand: Projections of Population. LC 77-87163. (Illus.). 1977. pap. 10.00 (ISBN 0-88285-044-X). Ctr Urban Pol Res.

Greenberg, Milton, jt. auth. see Plano, Jack C.

Greenberg, Mitchell. Detours of Desire: Readings in the French Baroque. LC 83-19380. 175p. 1984. 17.50x (ISBN 0-8142-0359-0). Ohio St U Pr.

Greenberg, Moshe. Biblical Prose Prayer: As a Window to the Popular Religion of Ancient Israel. LC 83-47662. (Taubman Lectures in Jewish Studies: No. 6). 78p. 1983. 14.95x (ISBN 0-520-05011-8); pap. 3.95 (ISBN 0-520-05012-6). U of Cal Pr.

--Ezekiel, 1-20: A New Translation with Introduction & Commentary. LC 77-12855. (Anchor Bible Ser.: Vol. 22). (Illus.). 408p. 1983. 16.00 (ISBN 0-385-00954-2, Anchor Pr). Doubleday.

--The Hab-Piru. (American Oriental Ser.: Vol. 39). 1955. pap. 5.00x (ISBN 0-940490-39-0). Am Orient Soc.

--Introduction to Hebrew. 1964. text ed. 22.95 (ISBN 0-13-484469-6). P-H.

--Understanding Exodus. 214p. 1969. pap. 9.95x (ISBN 0-87441-265-X). Behrman.

Greenberg, Moshe, ed. see Speiser, Ephraim A.

Greenberg, Moshe, tr. see Kaufmann, Yehezkel.

Greenberg, Naomi S. A Genealogical History of an Extended Family. (Illus.). 160p. 1981. 19.95 (ISBN 0-9607262-0-9). Everlast Pr.

--Occupational Therapy Assistant's Handbook. (Allied Health Professions Monograph). (Illus.). 186p. Date not set. 11.50 (ISBN 0-87527-270-3). Green.

Greenberg, Noah, ed. An Anthology of Early Renaissance Music. 336p. 1978-1979. 40.00x (ISBN 0-686-79448-6, Pub. by Dent Australia). State Mutual Bk.

--Anthology of English Medieval & Renaissance Vocal Music: Part Songs for One to Six Voices. Orig. Title: English Song Book. (Illus.). 1968. pap. 6.95 (ISBN 0-393-00461-9, Norton Lib). Norton.

Greenberg, Noah & Auden, W. H., eds. Play of Daniel, a Thirteenth-Century Musical Drama. (Illus.). 1959. pap. 5.95x (ISBN 0-19-385195-4). Oxford U Pr.

Greenberg, Noah & Maynard, Paul, eds. Anthology of Early Renaissance Music. (Illus.). 304p. 1975. 20.00x (ISBN 0-393-02182-3). Norton.

Greenberg, Noah & Smoldon, W. L., eds. Play of Herod: A Twelfth-Century Musical Drama. (Illus.). 1965. pap. 4.25x (ISBN 0-19-385196-2). Oxford U Pr.

Greenberg, Noah, ed. see Auden, W. H. & Kallman, Chester.

Greenberg, Noah, et al, eds. Anthology of Elizabethan Lute Songs, Madriagals & Rounds. (Illus.). 1970. pap. 6.95 (ISBN 0-393-00520-8, Norton Lib.). Norton.

Greenberg, Norman. The Man with a Steel Guitar: A Portrait of Ambition, Desperation & Crime. LC 79-63084. 181p. 1980. 16.50x (ISBN 0-87451-175-5). U Pr of New Eng.

Greenberg, P., ed. see Sedunov, Yu. S.

Greenberg, Paul D. & Glaser, Edward M. Some Issues in Joint Union-Management Quality of Worklife Improvement Efforts. LC 80-14044. 80p. 1980. pap. 4.95 (ISBN 0-911558-70-5). W E Upjohn.

Greenberg, Pearl, tr. see Buhler, Charlotte.

Greenberg, Polly. I Know I'm Myself Because... LC 80-25358. 32p. 1981. 10.95x (ISBN 0-89885-045-2). Human Sci Pr.

--Oh Lord, I Wish I Was a Buzzard. LC 68-24103. (Illus.). 32p. (gr. k-2). 1968. 10.95 (ISBN 0-02-736730-4). Macmillan.

Greenberg, Reesa. The Drawings of Alfred Pellan. (National Gallery of Canada Ser.). (Illus.). 192p. 1981. pap. 15.95 (ISBN 0-88884-458-1, 56319-7, Pub. by Natl Mus Canada). U of Chicago Pr.

Greenberg, Richard & Brahic, Andre, eds. Planetary Rings. LC 84-125. 785p. 1983. 35.00x (ISBN 0-8165-0828-3). U of Ariz Pr.

Greenberg, Robert, ed. see Swift, Jonathan.

Greenberg, Robert A., jt. auth. see Hoole, Axalla J.

Greenberg, Robert A., jt. auth. see Miller, Ruth.

Greenberg, Robert A., ed. see Swift, Jonathan.

Greenberg, Roger P., jt. auth. see Fisher, Seymour.

Greenberg, Russell. The Winter Exploitation Systems of Bay-Breasted & Chestnut-Sided Warblers in Panama. LC 83-17412. (Zoology Ser.: Vol. 116). 1984. lib. bdg. 7.50x (ISBN 0-520-09670-3). U of Cal Pr.

Greenberg, S. The Ethical in the Jewish & American Heritage. (Moreshet Ser: No. 4). 25.00x (ISBN 0-87334-002-7, Pub. by Jewish Theol Seminary). Ktav.

Greenberg, S. D., ed. Computer-Assisted Image Analysis Cytology. (Monographs in Clinical Cytology: Vol. 9). (Illus.). x, 202p. 1984. 41.75 (ISBN 3-8055-3902-9). S Karger.

Greenberg, Samuel. Poems. Holden, Harold & McManis, Jack, eds. LC 73-136067. 1971. Repr. of 1947 ed. lib. bdg. 18.75x (ISBN 0-8371-5217-8, GRPO). Greenwood.

Greenberg, Selma. Right from the Start: A Guide to Nonsexist Child Rearing. 1979. pap. 4.95 (ISBN 0-395-27817-1). HM.

Greenberg, Sheldon & Ortiz, Elisabeth L. The Spice of Life. LC 84-70582. (Illus.). 192p. 1984. 17.95 (ISBN 0-943276-04-7). Amaryllis Pr.

Greenberg, Sheldon F. Stress & the Teaching Profession. LC 84-6379. 188p. (Orig.). 1984. pap. text ed. 15.95 (ISBN 0-933716-39-7, 397). P H Brookes.

Greenberg, Sheldon F. & Valletutti, Peter J. Stress & the Helping Professions. LC 80-20328. 156p. (Orig.). 1980. pap. text ed. 9.95 (ISBN 0-933716-09-5, 095). P H Brookes.

Greenberg, Sid. Ayn Rand & Alienation. 1977. pap. 9.95 (ISBN 0-915358-25-5). Bridgeberg.

--Philosophy Can Be Verse: The Re-Sounds & Re-Motions of Man's Loco-Notions. (Illus.). 1979. pap. 6.95 (ISBN 0-915358-26-3). Bridgeberg.

Greenberg, Sidney. Likrat Shabbat. LC 72-97593. 8.95x (ISBN 0-87677-076-6). Hartmore.

--Sabbath & Festival Services for Children. (gr. 1-6). 1.95 (ISBN 0-87677-003-0). Prayer Bk.

--Say Yes to Life: A Book of Thoughts for Better Living. 160p. 1982. text ed. 3.98 (ISBN 0-517-54653-1). Crown.

--Treasury of the Art of Living. pap. 5.00 (ISBN 0-87980-168-9). Wilshire.

Greenberg, Sidney & Levine, Jonathan. Likrat Shabbat. LC 78-669313. 8.95 (ISBN 0-87677-076-6); large type ed. 14.95; simulated leather 9.95. Prayer Bk.

Greenberg, Sidney & Silverman, Morris. Siddurenu. (gr. 3-7). 7.95 (ISBN 0-87677-099-5). Prayer Bk.

Greenberg, Sidney & Sugarman, Allan S. Junior Contemporary Prayer Book for the High Holidays. (gr. 3-8). pap. 4.95 (ISBN 0-87677-054-5). Prayer Bk.

Greenberg, Sidney, ed. Contemporary Prayers & Readings. 1972. pap. 3.95 (ISBN 0-87677-050-2). Prayer BK.

--New Model Seder. pap. 1.75 (ISBN 0-87677-058-8). Prayer Bk.

--Treasury of Comfort. 1967. 10.95 (ISBN 0-87677-022-7). Hartmore.

--Treasury of the Art of Living. 1964. 10.95 (ISBN 0-87677-019-7). Hartmore.

Greenberg, Sidney S., ed. Treasury of Comfort. pap. 5.00 (ISBN 0-87980-167-0). Wilshire.

Greenberg, Simon. A Jewish Philosophy & Pattern of Life. LC 81-2153. (Moreshet Series, Studies in Jewish History, Literature & Thought: Vol. 9). 550p. 1982. 25.00x (ISBN 0-87334-012-4, Pub. by Jewish Theol Seminary). Ktav.

Greenberg, Stan. The Guinness Book of Olympics Facts & Feats. (Illus.). 256p. 1984. 14.95 (ISBN 0-85112-273-6, Pub by Guinness Superlatives England); pap. 9.95 (ISBN 0-85112-288-4, Pub. by Guinness Superlatives England). Sterling.

Greenberg, Stanley B. Politics & Poverty: Modernization & Response in Five Poor Neighborhoods. LC 73-10273. (Wiley Series in Urban Research). pap. 75.30 (ISBN 0-317-09220-0, 2051329). Bks Demand UMI.

--Race & State in Capitalist Development: Studies on South Africa, Alabama, Northern Ireland, & Israel. LC 79-22324. (Illus.). 416p. 1980. text ed. 67.00x (ISBN 0-300-02444-4); pap. 15.95x (ISBN 0-300-02527-0). Yale U Pr.

Greenberg, Warren, ed. Competition in the Health Care Sector: Past, Present & Future. LC 78-24573. 420p. 1979. text ed. 48.50 (ISBN 0-89443-081-5). Aspen Systems.

Greenberg, Warren & Southby, Richard McK., eds. Health Care Institutions in Flux: Changing Reimbursement Patterns in the 1980's. LC 84-80513. (Illus.). xxii, 185p. 1984. text ed. 24.95 (ISBN 0-87815-049-8). Info Resources.

Greenberg, Wendy N. The Power of Rhetoric: Hugo's Metaphor & Poetics. (American University Studies in Romance Languages & Literature: No. II, Vol. 35). 290p. 1985. text ed. price not set (ISBN 0-8204-0254-0). P Lang Pubs.

Greenberg, William J. Aspects of a Theory of Singular Reference. (Outstanding Dissertations in Linguistics Ser.). 145p. Date not set. 25.00 (ISBN 0-8240-5429-6). Garland Pub.

Greenberg, William S., jt. auth. see New Jersey Institute for Continuing Legal Education Staff.

Greenberger. Medical Book of Lists. 1983. 11.95 (ISBN 0-8151-3939-X). Year Bk Med.

--Year Book of Digestive Diseases, 1984. 1984. 42.95 (ISBN 0-8151-3938-1). Year Bk Med.

Greenberger, Evelyn B. Arthur Hugh Clough: Growth of a Poet's Mind. LC 78-116735. 1970. 17.50x (ISBN 0-674-04849-0). Harvard U Pr.

Greenberger, Howard. Bogey's Baby. 1980. pap. 3.95 (ISBN 0-346-12433-6). Cornerstone.

Greenberger, Joel S., jt. auth. see Wright, Daniel G.

Greenberger, Martin. Caught Unawares: The Energy Decade in Retrospect. 456p. 1983. prof ref. 29.95 (ISBN 0-88410-916-X). Ballinger Pub.

Greenberger, Martin, ed. Computers, Communications, & the Public Interest. LC 74-140671. pap. 83.80 (ISBN 0-317-09278-2, 2020531). Bks Demand UMI.

--Electronic Publishing Plus: Media for a Technological Future. LC 85-12613. 330p. 1985. 45.00 (ISBN 0-86729-146-X, 432-BW). Knowledge Indus.

Greenberger, Martin, et al. On-Line Computation & Simulation: The OPS-3 System. 1965. pap. 20.00x (ISBN 0-262-07019-7). MIT Pr.

Greenberger, Martin, et al, eds. Networks for Research & Education: Sharing of Computer & Information Resources Nationwide. 1974. 25.00x (ISBN 0-262-07057-X). MIT Pr.

Greenberger, Monroe E. & Siegel, Mary-Ellen. What Every Man Should Know about His Prostate. (Illus.). 1983. 13.95 (ISBN 0-8027-0725-4). Walker & Co.

Greenberger, Norton J. Gastrointestinal Disorders. 1980. 29.95 (ISBN 0-8151-3926-8). Year Bk Med.

Greenberger, Norton J., et al. Drug Treatment of Gastrointestinal Disorders. Azarnoff, Daniel L., ed. (Monographs in Clinical Pharmacology: Vol. 3). (Illus.). 1979. text ed. 25.00 (ISBN 0-443-08007-0). Churchill.

Greenbery, Leonard. Changes in Podiatry: Trends in the Podiatric Profession. Stevenson, Taloria, ed. (Ser. 14: No.21). 1978. pap. text ed. 1.75 (ISBN 0-8406-0139-5). Natl Ctr Health Stats.

Greenbie, B. B. Design for Diversity. (Developments in Landscape Management & Urban Planning: Vol. 2). 210p. 1976. 55.50 (ISBN 0-444-41329-4). Elsevier.

Greenbie, B. B., jt. ed. see Esser, A. H.

Greenbie, Barrie B. Spaces: Dimensions of the Human Landscape. LC 81-50435. (Illus.). 448p. 1981. text ed. 50.00x (ISBN 0-300-02549-1); pap. 16.95x (ISBN 0-300-02560-2). Yale U Pr.

Greenbie, Majorie B. Personality & the Divers Methods by Which Some Men & Here & There a Woman Have Achieved It. 328p. 1984. Repr. of 1933 ed. lib. bdg. 50.00 (ISBN 0-89987-347-2). Darby Bks.

Greenbie, Marjorie B. My Dear Lady: The Story of Anna Ella Carroll, the "Great Unrecognized Member of Lincoln's Cabinet". LC 74-3953. (Women in America Ser). (Illus.). 330p. 1974. Repr. of 1940 ed. 26.50 (ISBN 0-405-06101-3). Ayer Co Pubs.

Greenbie, Marjorie B., jt. auth. see Greenbie, Sydney.

Greenbie, Marjorie L. In Quest of Contentment. LC 72-121473. (Essay Index Reprint Ser). 1936. 19.00 (ISBN 0-8369-1752-9). Ayer Co Pubs.

--Wordsworth's Theory of Poetic Diction. LC 75-28998. Repr. of 1917 ed. 18.75 (ISBN 0-404-14009-2). AMS Pr.

Greenbie, Sydney & Greenbie, Marjorie B. Gold of Ophir. LC 72-79823. (China Library). 1972. Repr. of 1937 ed. lib. bdg. 30.00 (ISBN 0-8420-1373-3). Scholarly Res Inc.

Greenblat, Cathy S., jt. auth. see Duke, Richard D.

Greenblat, Cathy S., jt. auth. see Gagnon, John H.

Greenblat, Sidney L. Social Interaction in Chinese Society. Wilson, Richard & Wilson, Amy A., eds. LC 82-15019. 272p. 1982. 39.95 (ISBN 0-03-058021-8). Praeger.

Greenblatt, Bernard. Responsibility for Child Care: The Changing Role of Family & State in Child Development. LC 76-50699. (Social & Behavioral Science Ser.). (Illus.). 1977. text ed. 27.95x (ISBN 0-87589-315-5). Jossey-Bass.

Greenblatt, Bernard S. A Doctor's Marital Guide. (Illus.). 1976. pap. 2.99 (ISBN 0-686-65547-8). Budlong.

Greenblatt, Cathy & Duke, Richard D. Principles & Practices of Gaming Simulation: Rationale Designs & Applications. rev. ed. 250p. 1981. 29.95 (ISBN 0-8039-1675-2); pap. 14.95 (ISBN 0-8039-1713-9). Sage.

Greenblatt, Charles L., jt. ed. see Spira, Dan T.

Greenblatt, D. J., jt. ed. see Miller, R. R.

Greenblatt, David. The IBM System 36: What's In It for You? (Illus.). 99p. (Orig.). 1984. pap. text ed. 59.00 (ISBN 0-930941-01-2). D G C Assocs Inc.

--Insights into the IBM System 38. (Illus.). 137p. (Orig.). 1984. pap. text ed. 95.00 (ISBN 0-930941-00-4). D G C Assocs Inc.

Greenblatt, David, jt. ed. see Davis, John M.

Greenblatt, David J. & Shader, Richard I. Pharmacokinetic Basis of Therapeutics. (Illus.). 150p. Date not set. pap. price not set (ISBN 0-7216-1148-6). Saunders.

Greenblatt, David J., jt. ed. see Miller, Russell R.

Greenblatt, Fred S. Drama with the Elderly: Acting at Eighty. (Illus.). 90p. 1985. 19.75x (ISBN 0-398-05061-9). C C Thomas.

Greenblatt, Gordon M. Cat Musculature: A Photographic Atlas. 2nd ed. LC 80-25610. (Illus.). 32p. 1981. pap. 6.00x (ISBN 0-226-30656-9). U of Chicago Pr.

Greenblatt, M. H. Multiple Sclerosis & Me. (Illus.). 86p. 1972. 13.75x (ISBN 0-398-02300-X). C C Thomas.

Greenblatt, Milton. Psychopolitics. 352p. 1978. 38.50 (ISBN 0-8089-1062-0, 791729). Grune.

Greenblatt, Milton, jt. auth. see Becerra, Rosina M.

Greenblatt, Milton, ed. Drugs in Combination with Other Therapies. LC 75-25846. (Seminars in Psychiatry Ser). 224p. 1975. 44.50 (ISBN 0-8089-0908-8, 791727). Grune.

Greenblatt, Milton & Shuckit, Marc A., eds. Alcoholism Problems in Women & Children. LC 76-42232. (Seminars in Psychiatry Ser.). (Illus.). 304p. 1976. 55.00 (ISBN 0-8089-0972-X, 791725). Grune.

Greenblatt, Milton, et al. From Custodial to Therapeutic Patient Care in Mental Hospitals. Grob, Gerald N., ed. LC 78-22562. (Historical Issues in Mental Health Ser.). 1979. Repr. of 1955 ed. lib. bdg. 37.00x (ISBN 0-405-11916-X). Ayer Co Pubs.

Greenblatt, Robert B. Geriatric Endocrinology. LC 75-43196. (Aging Ser.: Vol. 5). 256p. 1978. 35.50 (ISBN 0-89004-112-1). Raven.

--Search the Scriptures Illustrated: Modern Medicine & Biblical Personages. (Illus.). 238p. 1985. special illus. ed. 16.00x (ISBN 0-389-20545-1, BNB-08106). B&N Imports.

Greenblatt, Robert B., ed. Induction of Ovulation. LC 79-10757. (Illus.). 167p. 1979. text ed. 14.75 (ISBN 0-8121-0652-0). Lea & Febiger.

Greenblatt, Robert B., jt. auth. see Semm, Kurt.

Greenblatt, Sidney L., ed. The People of Taihang: An Anthology of Family Histories. LC 74-15389. (China Book Project). (Illus.). pap. 89.50 (ISBN 0-317-11084-5, 2021856). Bks Demand UMI.

Greenblatt, Sidney L., et al, eds. Organizational Behavior in Chinese Society. LC 80-26728. 288p. 1981. 39.95 (ISBN 0-03-053206-X). Praeger.

Greenblatt, Stanley. Understand Computers Through Common Sense. 1979. pap. 2.95 (ISBN 0-346-12374-7). Cornerstone.

--Understand Computers Through Common Sense. rev. ed. (Illus.). 160p. 1983. 6.95 (ISBN 0-346-12529-4). Cornerstone.

Greenblatt, Stephen. Renaissance Self-Fashioning: From More to Shakespeare. LC 80-13837. (Illus.). x, 322p. 1983. pap. 11.00x (ISBN 0-226-30654-2). U of Chicago Pr.

--Renaissance Self-Fashioning: More to Shakespeare. LC 80-13837. 272p. 1980. 20.00x (ISBN 0-226-30653-4). U of Chicago Pr.

Greenblatt, Stephen J., ed. Allegory & Representation: Selected Papers from the English Institute, 1979-80. LC 81-47595. (New Ser.: No. 5). (Illus.). 208p. 1981. text ed. 8.50x (ISBN 0-8018-2642-X). Johns Hopkins.

Greenblum, Joseph, jt. auth. see Sklare, Marshall.

Greenburg, Cara. Mid-Century Modern: Furniture of the 1950's. (Illus.). 1984. 30.00 (ISBN 0-517-55411-9, Harmony). Crown.

Greenburg, Dan. How to Be a Jewish Mother. (Illus.). 1965. pap. 2.95 (ISBN 0-8431-0030-3). Price Stern.

--Love Kills. 1979. pap. 3.50 (ISBN 0-671-50811-3). PB.

--What Do Women Want? 465p. 1982. 14.95 (ISBN 0-671-43793-3, Wyndham Bks). S&S.

--What Do Women Want? 1983. pap. 3.95 (ISBN 0-671-46735-2). PB.

Greenburg, Dan & O'Malley, Suzanne. How to Avoid Love & Marriage. (Illus.). 1983. 9.95 (ISBN 0-88191-009-0). Freundlich.

Greenburg, Emanuel & Greenburg, Madeline. Pocket Guide to Spirits & Liqueurs: A Connoisseur's International Guide. LC 82-20532. (Illus.). 144p. 1983. pap. 5.95 (ISBN 0-399-50730-2, Perigee). Putnam Pub Group.

Greenburg, Herbert J. & Murphy, Charlotte W. Intermediate Algebra. 512p. 1982. text ed. write for info. (ISBN 0-87150-324-7, 33L 2581, Prindle). PWS Pubs.

Greenburg, Joanne. Jack in the Beanstalk. (Illus.). 48p. (gr. 3 up). 1980. write for info. (ISBN 0-8299-1033-6). West Pub.

Greenburg, Madeline, jt. auth. see Greenburg, Emanuel.

Greenburg, S. Thomas, jt. ed. see O'Rourke, John J.

Greenburg, Samuel A. & Gilkey, Helen L. Guests in My House, Bk. 1. 212p. 1984. 10.95 (ISBN 0-533-05727-2). Vantage.

Greenburg, Sidney. Infinite in Giordano Bruno. 1971. lib. bdg. 17.00x (ISBN 0-374-93246-8). Octagon.

Greenburm, Dorothy & Laiken, Deidre S. Love Strong. 1985. pap. 3.95 (ISBN 0-451-13650-0, Sig). NAL.

Greendorfer, Susan, ed. see North American Society for the Study of Sport.

Greendyke, Robert M. Introduction to Blood Banking. 3rd ed. LC 79-91979. 1980. pap. 20.00 (ISBN 0-87488-975-8). Med Exam.

Greene & Dicker. Sign Language. 1981. 8.90 (ISBN 0-531-04195-6). Watts.

Greene, A. C. Cedar Springs. 64p. 1984. 5.95 (ISBN 0-911225-05-6). Clearstream Pr.

--Dallas: The Deciding Years - a Historical Portrait. (Illus.). 192p. 1974. 22.50 (ISBN 0-88426-034-8). Encino Pr.

--Dallas, U.S.A. Lubeck, Scott, ed. (Illus.). 256p. (Orig.). 1984. 15.95 (ISBN 0-932012-83-3). Texas Month Pr.

--The Fifty Best Books on Texas. 96p. 1982. 14.95 (ISBN 0-939722-16-X); pap. 9.95 (ISBN 0-939722-14-3). Pressworks.

--The Fifty Best Books on Texas. 96p. 1981. Ltd. Ed. 120.00 (ISBN 0-939722-10-0). Pressworks.

--The Highland Park Woman. 200p. 1983. 13.95 (ISBN 0-940672-12-X). Shearer Pub.

--The Last Captive. (Illus.). 185p. (gr. 6-9). 1972. 15.00 (ISBN 0-88426-004-6). Encino Pr.

--A Personal Country. LC 79-7410. (Illus.). 354p. 1979. 14.95 (ISBN 0-89096-077-1). Tex A&M Univ Pr.

Greene, A. C., intro. by. The Texas Hill Country: Interpretations by Thirteen Artists. LC 81-40400. (The Joe & Betty Moore Texas Art Ser.: No. 5). (Illus.). 122p. 1981. 35.00 (ISBN 0-89096-116-6). Tex A&M Univ Pr.

Greene, Albert G. Recollections of the Jersey Prison Ship. 1961. pap. 1.25 (ISBN 0-87091-007-8, AE). Corinth Bks.

Greene, Alfred A., jt. auth. see Law & Business Inc. Staff.

Greene, Amy & Pomerance, Molly. The Successful Face. (Illus.). 1985. 14.95. Summit Bks.

Greene, Ann. Lambs in March & Other Essays. facs. ed. LC 68-8466. (Essay Index Reprint Ser). 1928. 18.00 (ISBN 0-8369-0497-4). Ayer Co Pubs.

Greene, Anne Marie, ed. Designs & Utility Models Throughout the World. LC 82-20738. 1983. looseleaf 85.00 (ISBN 0-87632-378-6). Boardman.

Greene, Annie. Bright River Trilogy. 256p. 1985. 14.95 (ISBN 0-671-49815-0). S&S.

Greene, Asa. A Yankee Among the Nullifiers. LC 72-104468. Repr. of 1833 ed. lib. bdg. 14.50 (ISBN 0-8398-0667-1). Irvington.

Greene, Audrey. Audrey's Add No Salt Cookery. (Illus.). 1982. write for info. (ISBN 0-9608892-0-5). Greene Pubns.

Greene, Barbara. Too Late to Turn Back: Barbara & Graham Greene in Liberia. 1981. 35.00x (ISBN 0-907070-06-X, Pub. by Settle & Bendall UK). State Mutual BK.

Greene, Barbara & Gollancz, Victor. God of a Hundred Names. 1962. 12.95 (ISBN 0-575-00987-X, Pub. by Gollancz England). David & Charles.

Greene, Barbara, jt. auth. see Greene, Eva.

Greene, Barbara & Gollancz, Victor, eds. God of a Hundred Names. 304p. 1985. pap. 6.95 (ISBN 0-575-03645-1, Pub. by Gollancz England). David & Charles.

--God of a Hundred Names: Prayers & Meditations from Many Faiths & Cultures. 304p. 1985. pap. 6.95 (ISBN 0-575-03645-1, Pub. by Gollancz England). David & Charles.

Greene, Barbara, ed. see Bingham, Mindy, et al.

Greene, Barbara, ed. see Edmondson, Judy, et al.

Greene, Bernard L. A Clinical Approach to Marital Problems: Diagnosis, Prevention & Treatment. 2nd ed. (Illus.). 556p. 1981. 53.75x (ISBN 0-398-04138-5). C C Thomas.

Greene, Bert. Bert Greene's Kitchen Bouquets. LC 79-50976. (Illus.). 448p. 1979. 17.95 (ISBN 0-8092-7710-7). Contemp Bks.

--Greene on Greens. LC 83-40538. 416p. (Orig.). 1984. 19.95 (ISBN 0-89480-758-7, 758); pap. 12.95 (ISBN 0-89480-659-9, 659). Workman Pub.

--Honest American Fare. 304p. 1984. pap. 8.95 (ISBN 0-8092-5964-8). Contemp Bks.

Greene, Bert & Schulz, Phillip S. Cooking for Giving. (Great American Cooking Schools Ser.). (Illus.). 84p. (Orig.). 1984. pap. 5.95 (ISBN 0-941034-22-4). I Chalmers.

Greene, Bert & Vaughan, Denis. The Store Cookbook. LC 76-6894. 288p. 1976. pap. 8.95 (ISBN 0-8092-7970-3). Contemp Bks.

Greene, Bette. Get on Out of Here, Philip Hall. LC 79-50151. 160p. (gr. 3-6). 1981. 12.95 (ISBN 0-8037-2871-9); PLB 12.89 (ISBN 0-8037-2872-7). Dial Bks Young.

--Get on Out of Here, Philip Hall. 144p. (gr. 4-7). 1984. pap. 2.25 (ISBN 0-440-43038-0, YB). Dell.

--Morning Is a Long Time Coming. (gr. 7-9). 1979. pap. 1.95 (ISBN 0-671-42456-4). Archway.

--Morning Is a Long Time Coming. LC 76-42933. (gr. 9 up). 1978. 10.95 (ISBN 0-8037-5496-5). Dial Bks Young.

--Philip Hall Likes Me, I Reckon, Maybe. 144p. 1975. pap. 2.50 (ISBN 0-440-45755-6, YB). Dell.

--Philip Hall Likes Me. I Reckon Maybe. LC 74-2887. (Illus.). 160p. (gr. 3-6). 1974. 12.95 (ISBN 0-8037-6098-1); PLB 12.89 (ISBN 0-8037-6096-5). Dial Bks Young.

--Summer of My German Soldier. 224p. (gr. 7 up). 1973. 13.95 (ISBN 0-8037-8321-3, 01354-410). Dial Bks Young.

--Them That Glitter & Them That Don't. LC 92-13020. 224p. 1983. 10.95 (ISBN 0-394-84692-3); lib. bdg. 10.99 (ISBN 0-394-94692-8). Knopf.

--Them That Glitter & Them That Don't. 1984. pap. 2.25 (ISBN 0-449-70077-1). Fawcett.

Greene, Bill. Think Like a Tycoon. 1982. pap. 5.95 (ISBN 0-449-90068-1, Columbine). Fawcett.

Greene, Bob. American Beat. LC 83-45071. 288p. 1983. 15.95 (ISBN 0-689-11397-8). Atheneum.

--American Beat. 352p. 1984. pap. 5.95 (ISBN 0-14-007320-5). Penguin.

--Cheeseburgers: The Best of Bob Greene. LC 85-47602. 320p. 1985. 15.95 (ISBN 0-689-11611-X). Atheneum.

--Easy-to-Build Electronics Projects. 96p. 1985. pap. 7.95 (ISBN 0-86668-050-0). ARCsoft.

--Good Morning, Merry Sunshine. 1985. lib. bdg. 17.95 (ISBN 0-8161-3803-6, Large Print Bks). G K Hall.

--Good Morning, Merry Sunshine: A Father's Journal of His Child's First Year. LC 83-45510. 320p. 1984. 14.95 (ISBN 0-689-11434-6). Atheneum.

--Good Morning, Merry Sunshine: A Father's Personal Journey of His Child's First Year. 320p. 1985. pap. 5.95 (ISBN 0-14-007948-3). Penguin.

--Johnny Deadline Reporter: The Best of Bob Greene. LC 76-6932. 304p. 1976. 21.95x (ISBN 0-88229-361-3). Nelson-Hall.

--Quick-n-Easy Electronics Projects. 96p. 1985. pap. 7.95 (ISBN 0-86668-049-7). ARCsoft.

--Twenty-Five Easy-to-Build One-Night & Weekend Electronics Projects. (Illus.). 96p. (Orig.). 1982. text ed. 8.95 (ISBN 0-86668-710-6); pap. 4.95 (ISBN 0-86668-010-1). ARCsoft.

--Twenty Five Quick-N-Easy Electronics Projects. 96p. (Orig.). 1982. pap. 4.95 (ISBN 0-86668-023-3). ARCsoft.

Greene, Bruce M. & Robertson, David, eds. Problems in Internal Medicine. 368p. (Orig.). 1980. pap. text ed. 19.00 (ISBN 0-8391-1594-6). Univ Park.

Greene, Carla. Animal Doctors: What Do They Do? LC 67-14065. (I Can Read Bks.). (gr. k-3). 1967. PLB 9.89 (ISBN 0-06-022078-3). HarpJ.

--Cowboys: What Do They Do? LC 72-183160. (I Can Read Bks.). (Illus.). 64p. (gr. k-3). 1972. (HarpJ). HarpJ.

--Doctors & Nurses: What Do They Do? LC 62-13313. (I Can Read Books). (Illus.). (gr. k-3). 1963. PLB 9.89 (ISBN 0-06-022076-7). HarpJ.

--Soldiers & Sailors: What Do They Do? LC 63-15325. (I Can Read Bks.). (Illus.). (gr. k-3). 1963. PLB 9.89 (ISBN 0-06-022096-1). HarpJ.

Greene, Carol. Astronauts. LC 83-23142. (New True Bks.). (Illus.). 48p. (gr k-4). 1984. lib. bdg. 10.60 (ISBN 0-516-01722-5); pap. 3.95 (ISBN 0-516-41722-3). Childrens.

--Christmas on the Street. (Illus.). 1984. 7.95 (ISBN 0-570-04107-4, 56-1499). Concordia.

--A Computer Went A-Courting: A Love Song for Valentine's Day. LC 83-7346. (Sing-Along Holiday Stories Ser.). (Illus.). 32p. (ps-2). 1983. PLB 10.20 (ISBN 0-516-08232-9). Childrens.

--Congress. (Illus.). 48p. (gr. k-4). 1985. 3.95 (ISBN 0-516-41939-0). Childrens.

--England: Enchantment of the World Ser. LC 82-4471. (Illus.). (gr. 5-9). 1982. PLB 19.95g (ISBN 0-516-02763-8). Childrens.

--Hi, Clouds. LC 82-19854. (Rookie Readers Ser.). (Illus.). 32p. (ps-2). 1983. PLB 8.65 (ISBN 0-516-02036-6); pap. 2.50 (ISBN 0-516-42036-4). Childrens.

--Hinny Winny Bunco. LC 81-47720. (Illus.). 64p. (ps-3). 1982. 10.10i (ISBN 0-06-022128-3); PLB 9.89g (ISBN 0-06-022129-1). HarpJ.

--Holidays Around the World. LC 82-9734. (New True Books). (Illus.). (gr. k-4). 1982. PLB 10.60 (ISBN 0-516-01624-5); pap. 3.95 (ISBN 0-516-41624-3). Childrens.

--I am One: Prayers for Singles. 112p. (Orig.). 1985. pap. 5.95 (ISBN 0-8066-2186-9, 10-3190). Augsburg.

--I Can Be a Baseball Player. (Illus.). 32p. (ps-3). 1985. 2.95 (ISBN 0-516-41845-9). Childrens.

--I Can Be a Football Player. LC 84-9609. (I Can Be Bks.). (Illus.). 32p. (gr. k-3). 1984. lib. bdg. 10.60 (ISBN 0-516-01839-6); pap. 2.95 (ISBN 0-516-41839-4). Childrens.

--Ice Is...Whee! LC 82-19855. (Rookie Readers Ser.). (Illus.). 32p. (ps-2). 1983. PLB 8.65 (ISBN 0-516-02037-4); pap. 2.50 (ISBN 0-516-42037-2). Childrens.

--The Insignificant Elephant. LC 84-1531. (Illus.). 32p. (ps-3). 1985. 13.95 (ISBN 0-15-238730-7, HJ). HarBraceJ.

--Japan. LC 83-7603. (Enchantment of the World Ser.). (Illus.). 128p. (gr. 5-9). 1983. PLB 19.95 (ISBN 0-516-02769-7). Childrens.

--Kiri & the First Easter. (Arch Bks: Set 9). (Illus.). 32p. (ps-4). 1972. pap. 0.99 (ISBN 0-570-06064-8, 59-1182). Concordia.

--Language. LC 83-7421. (New True Bks.). (Illus.). 48p. (gr. k-4). 1983. PLB 10.60 (ISBN 0-516-01694-6). Childrens.

--Louisa May Alcott: Author, Nurse, Suffragette. LC 84-5902. (People of Distinction Ser.). (Illus.). 112p. (gr. 4 up). 1984. lib. bdg. 11.65 (ISBN 0-516-03208-9). Childrens.

--Marie Curie: Pioneer Physicist. LC 83-26273. (People of Distinction Ser.). (Illus.). 112p. (gr. 4 up). 1984. lib. bdg. 11.95 (ISBN 0-516-03203-8). Childrens.
--Mother Teresa: Friend of the Friendless. LC 83-7386. (Picture-Story Biographies Ser.). (Illus.). 32p. (gr. 2-5). 1983. PLB 10.60 (ISBN 0-516-03559-2). Childrens.
--Music. LC 83-7255. (New True Bks.). (Illus.). 48p. (gr. k-4). 1983. PLB 10.60 (ISBN 0-516-01701-2). Childrens.
--No More Than a Mustard Seed. 1980. pap. 0.99 (ISBN 0-570-06134-2, 59-1252, Arch Bk). Concordia.
--Please, Wind? LC 82-4548. (Rookie Readers Ser.). (Illus.). (ps-2). 1982. PLB 8.65g (ISBN 0-516-02033-1); pap. 2.50 (ISBN 0-516-42033-X). Childrens.
--Poland. LC 82-19737. (Enchantment of the World Ser.). (Illus.). 128p. (gr. 5-9). 1983. PLB 19.95 (ISBN 0-516-02783-2). Childrens.
--Presidents. LC 84-7719. (New True Bks.). (Illus.). 48p. (gr. k-4). 1984. lib. bdg. 10.60 (ISBN 0-516-01928-7); pap. 3.95 (ISBN 0-516-41928-5). Childrens.
--Proverbs-Important Things to Know. 1980. pap. 0.99 (ISBN 0-570-06140-7, 59-1303, Arch Bk). Concordia.
--Rain! Rain! LC 82-9509. (Rookie Readers Ser.). (Illus.). (ps-2). 1982. PLB 8.65g (ISBN 0-516-02034-X); pap. 2.50 (ISBN 0-516-42034-8). Childrens.
--Robots. LC 82-17872. (New True Bks.). (Illus.). 48p. (gr. k-4). 1983. PLB 10.60 (ISBN 0-516-01684-9); pap. 3.95 (ISBN 0-516-41684-7). Childrens.
--Sandra Day O'Connor: First Woman on the Supreme Court. LC 81-18038. (Picture Story Ser.). (Illus.). 32p. (gr. 1-4). 1982. PLB 10.60 (ISBN 0-516-03618-1). Childrens.
--Shine, Sun! LC 82-19853. (Rookie Readers Ser.). (Illus.). 32p. (ps-2). 1983. PLB 8.65 (ISBN 0-516-02038-2); pap. 2.50 (ISBN 0-516-42038-0). Childrens.
--Snow Joe. LC 82-9403. (Rookie Readers Ser.). (Illus.). (ps-2). 1982. PLB 8.65g (ISBN 0-516-02035-8); pap. 2.50 (ISBN 0-516-42035-6). Childrens.
--The Thirteen Days of Halloween. LC 83-7347. (Sing-Along Holiday Stories Ser.). (Illus.). 32p. (ps-2). 1983. PLB 10.20 (ISBN 0-516-08231-0); pap. 2.95 (ISBN 0-516-48231-9). Childrens.
--The United Nations. LC 83-10068. (New True Bks.). (Illus.). 48p. (gr. k-4). 1983. PLB 10.60 (ISBN 0-516-01710-1); pap. 3.95 (ISBN 0-516-41710-X). Childrens.
--Welcome the Stranger. (Illus.). 1984. 7.95 (ISBN 0-570-04105-8, 561497). Concordia.
--Yugoslavia. LC 83-21049. (Enchantment of the World Ser.). (Illus.). 128p. (gr. 5-9). 1984. lib. bdg. 19.95 (ISBN 0-516-02791-3). Childrens.
Greene, Carol, jt. ed. see Burow, Daniel R.
Greene, Caroline, jt. auth. see Greene, Gerald.
Greene, Charles N., et al. Management: For Effective Performance. (Illus.). 688p. 1985. text ed. 30.95 (ISBN 0-13-548504-5); wkbk. 11.95 (ISBN 0-13-549247-5). P-H.
Greene, Constance. Ask Anybody. 160p. (gr. k-6). 1984. pap. 2.50 (ISBN 0-440-40330-8, YB). Dell.
Greene, Constance C. Al(Exandra) the Great. LC 81-16058. 144p. (gr. 5-9). 1982. 10.95 (ISBN 0-670-11197-X). Viking.
--Al(exandra) the Great. 144p. (gr. 5-9). 1983. pap. 2.25 (ISBN 0-440-40350-2, YB). Dell.
--Ask Anybody. LC 82-17624. 156p. (gr. 4-6). 1983. 10.95 (ISBN 0-670-13813-4). Viking.
--Beat the Turtle Drum. 128p. (gr. 5-8). 1979. pap. 2.50 (ISBN 0-440-40875-X, YB). Dell.
--Beat the Turtle Drum. LC 76-14772. (Illus.). 128p. (gr. 4-6). 1976. 12.95 (ISBN 0-670-15241-2). Viking.
--Dotty's Suitcase. 144p. (gr. 3-7). 1982. pap. 2.25 (ISBN 0-440-42108-X, YB). Dell.
--Dotty's Suitcase. LC 80-10949. 168p. (gr. 4-6). 1980. 11.95 (ISBN 0-670-28050-X). Viking.
--Double-Dare O'Toole. LC 81-5102. 168p. (gr. 5-9). 1981. 11.50 (ISBN 0-670-28053-4). Viking.
--Double-Dare O'Toole. 176p. (gr. 4-7). 1983. pap. 2.50 (ISBN 0-440-41982-4, YB). Dell.
--The Ears of Louis. (Illus.). 96p. (gr. 3-7). 1974. PLB 9.95 (ISBN 0-670-28718-0). Viking.
--Getting Nowhere. 1977. 11.50 (ISBN 0-670-33762-5). Viking.
--A Girl Called Al. 128p. 1977. pap. 2.25 (ISBN 0-440-42810-6, YB). Dell.
--A Girl Called Al. (Illus.). (gr. 6-8). 1969. 10.95 (ISBN 0-670-34153-3). Viking.
--I & Sproggy. (Illus.). 144p. (gr. 5 up). pap. 2.50 (ISBN 0-440-43986-8, YB). Dell.
--I & Sproggy. LC 78-6096. (Illus.). (gr. 3-7). 1978. 11.50 (ISBN 0-670-38980-3). Viking.
--I Know You, Al. 1977. pap. 2.25 (ISBN 0-440-44123-4, YB). Dell.
--I Know You, Al. (Illus.). 128p. (gr. 4-8). 1975. 9.95 (ISBN 0-670-39048-8). Viking.
--Isabelle Shows Her Stuff. 144p. (YA) (gr. 8-12). 1984. 11.95 (ISBN 0-670-41103-5, Viking Kestrel). Viking.
--Isabelle the Itch. 128p. (gr. 2-4). 1974. pap. 2.25 (ISBN 0-440-44345-8, YB). Dell.
--Isabelle the Itch. (Illus.). 128p. (gr. 4-6). 1973. PLB 9.95 (ISBN 0-670-40177-3). Viking.
--Other Plans. 448p. 1985. 15.95 (ISBN 0-312-58958-1). St Martin.
--Starshine. LC 85-40458. 144p. (gr. 5-9). 1985. 11.95 (ISBN 0-670-80772-9). Viking.
--The Unmaking of Rabbit. 128p. (gr. 4-6). 1972. PLB 9.95 (ISBN 0-670-74136-1). Viking.
--Your Old Pal, Al. 160p. (gr. k-6). 1981. pap. 2.50 (ISBN 0-440-49862-7, YB). Dell.
--Your Old Pal, Al. LC 79-12350. (gr. 5-9). 1979. 10.95 (ISBN 0-670-79575-5). Viking.
Greene County Homemakers Extension Association. Between Greene Leaves. 256p. (Orig.). 1984. pap. 7.95 (ISBN 0-9613043-0-8). Greene Coun Home Ext Assn.
Greene, Craig E. Clinical Microbiology & Infectious Diseases of the Dog & Cat. (Illus.). 610p. 1984. 52.00 (ISBN 0-7216-4251-9). Saunders.
Greene, Curtis, ed. Combinatorics & Algebra. LC 84-18608. (Contemporary Mathematics Ser.: Vol. 34). 30.00 (ISBN 0-8218-5029-6). Am Math.
Greene, D. & Knuth, D. Mathematics for the Analysis of Algorithms. 144p. 1981. text ed. 10.00x (ISBN 3-7643-3046-5). Birkhauser.
Greene, D. & Knuth, D., eds. Mathematics for the Analysis of Algorithms. 2nd ed. (Progress in Computer Science: Vol. 1). 144p. text ed. 12.95x (ISBN 0-8176-3102-X). Birkhauser.
Greene, D., jt. ed. see Lepper, M. R.
Greene, D. B. Temporal Processes in Beethoven's Music. (Monographs on Musicology: Vol. 2). 202p. 1982. 28.00 (ISBN 0-677-05600-1). Gordon.
Greene, Dana, ed. Lucretia Mott: Her Complete Speeches & Sermons. LC 80-81885. (Studies in Women & Religion: Vol. 4). x, 412p. 1980. 69.95x (ISBN 0-88946-968-7). E Mellen.
Greene, Dana, ed. see Brown, Olympia.
Greene, Daniel E. Pastel: A Comprehensive Guide to Pastel Painting. Singer, Joe, ed. LC 74-13740. (Illus.). 160p. 1974. 19.95 (ISBN 0-8230-3899-8). Watson-Guptill.
Greene, Danny. Cruising Sailboat Kinetics: The Art, Science & Magic of Cruising Boat Design. LC 84-13989. (Illus.). 260p. 1985. 29.95 (ISBN 0-915160-69-2). Seven Seas.
Greene, David, ed. see Sophocles.
Greene, David B. Mahler, Consciousness & Temporality. 324p. 1984. 35.00 (ISBN 0-677-06160-9). Gordon.
Greene, David G. Steel & Economic Development: Capital Output Ratios in Three Latin American Steel Plants. LC 67-64602. 1967. 4.50 (ISBN 0-87744-077-8). Mich St U Pr.
Greene, David H., ed. An Anthology of Irish Literature, 2 vols. LC 70-164022. 1971. o.p. 15.00x set (ISBN 0-8147-2953-3); pap. 20.00x set (ISBN 0-8147-2954-1). NYU Pr.
--An Anthology of Irish Literature. 1985. 45.00 set (ISBN 0-8147-2953-3); Vol. I. 25.00 (ISBN 0-8147-3003-5); Vol. II. text ed. 5.00 (ISBN 0-8147-3004-3); pap. 22.50 set; Vol. I. pap. text ed. 12.50 (ISBN 0-8147-3005-1); Vol. II. pap. 12.50 (ISBN 0-8147-3006-X). NYU Pr.
Greene, David L. Dentition of Meroitic X-Group, & Christian Populations from Wadi Halfa, Sudan. (Nubian Ser.: No. 1). Repr. of 1967 ed. 22.50 (ISBN 0-404-60685-7). AMS Pr.
Greene, David M. The Frail Duration. 1966. pap. 1.95x (ISBN 0-916304-02-7). SDSU Press.
--Greene's Biographical Encyclopedia of Composers. LC 79-6863. (Illus.). 1392p. 1985. 30.00 (ISBN 0-385-14278-1). Doubleday.
Greene, Diana S. Whole Grain Baking. (Cookbook Ser.). (Illus.). 200p. (Orig.). 1984. 18.95 (ISBN 0-89594-148-1); pap. 8.95 (ISBN 0-89594-147-3). Crossing Pr.
Greene, Dolph, jt. auth. see Culligan, Matthew J.
Greene, Don D. Divorce: The Manual. Meyer, William, ed. (Illus.). 158p. (Orig.). pap. 12.95 (ISBN 0-9613371-1-7). Greene Pub.
Greene, Donald. The Age of Exuberance: Backgrounds to Eighteenth Century Literature, 1660-1785. (Language & Literature Studies). (Orig.). 1967. pap. text ed. 5.00 (ISBN 0-394-30638-4, RanC). Random.
Greene, Donald, ed. Samuel Johnson. (The Oxford Author Ser.). (Illus.). 1984. 29.95x (ISBN 0-19-254179-X); pap. 9.95 (ISBN 0-19-281340-4). Oxford U Pr.
Greene, Donald J., jt. auth. see Clifford, James L.
Greene, Donald J., ed. see Johnson, Samuel.
Greene, Douglas, ed. Diaries of the Popish Plot. LC 77-938. 1977. 50.00x (ISBN 0-8201-1288-7). Schol Facsimiles.
Greene, Edward F. & Toennies, J. Peter. Chemical Reactions in Shock Waves. 1964. 56.00 (ISBN 0-12-299850-2). Acad Pr.
Greene, Edward H. The Law & Your Horse. pap. 7.00 (ISBN 0-87980-202-2). Wilshire.
Greene, Edward J. T. S. Eliot, et la France. 248p. 1982. Repr. lib. bdg. 75.00 (ISBN 0-89760-252-8). Telegraph Bks.
Greene, Edward L. Landmarks of Botanical History, 2 vols. Egerton, Frank N., ed. LC 79-66057. (Illus.). 1983. Vol. 1: 520p., Vol. 2: 640p. 100.00x set (ISBN 0-8047-1075-9). Stanford U Pr.
Greene, Ella L., jt. auth. see Williams, Herman.
Greene, Ellin & Shannon, George. Storytelling: A Selected Annotated Bibliography. LC 84-48877. 125p. 1985. lib. bdg. 17.00 (ISBN 0-8240-8749-6). Garland Pub.
Greene, Ellin, jt. auth. see Baker, Augusta.
Greene, Ethel J., jt. auth. see Robinson, Kitty K.
Greene, Eunice G. Anatomy of the Rat. (Illus.). 1971. Repr. of 1935 ed. 75.00x (ISBN 0-02-845440-5). Hafner.
Greene, Eva & Greene, Barbara. Chance of a Lifetime: An Anthology for the Ageless. LC 67-16829. (Illus.). 1968. 8.95 (ISBN 0-87027-095-8). Cumberland Pr.
Greene, Evarts B. The Foundations of American Nationality. 614p. 1985. Repr. of 1935 ed. lib. bdg. 75.00 (ISBN 0-918377-65-X). Russell Pr.
--Provincial America, Sixteen Hundred Ninety to Seventeen Hundred Forty. LC 79-25852. (Field Museum of Natural History: Vol. 6). (Illus.). xxi, 356p. 1980. Repr. of 1905 ed. lib. bdg. 27.50x (ISBN 0-313-22242-8, GRPR). Greenwood.
--The Provincial Governor in the English Colonies of North America. 12.75 (ISBN 0-8446-1209-X). Peter Smith.
--Religion & the State: The Making & Testing of an American Tradition. LC 75-41122. Repr. of 1941 ed. 17.25 (ISBN 0-404-14548-5). AMS Pr.
Greene, Felix. Awakened China: The Country Americans Don't Know. LC 73-431. 425p. 1973. Repr. of 1961 ed. lib. bdg. 22.00x (ISBN 0-8371-6773-6, GRAC). Greenwood.
--The Enemy: What Every American Should Know About Imperialism. 1971. pap. 4.95 (ISBN 0-394-71457-1, Vin). Random.
--Let There Be a World: A Call for an End to the Arms Race. (Illus.). 65p. 1982. pap. 4.95 (ISBN 0-575-03136-0, Pub. by Gollancz England). David & Charles.
--Peking. (Illus.). 1978. 12.50 (ISBN 0-8317-6790-1, Mayflower Bks). Smith Pubs.
Greene, Francis B. History of Boothbay, Southport & Boothbay Harbor, Maine. LC 84-61010. (Illus.). 693p. 1984. Repr. of 1906 ed. 45.00 (ISBN 0-89725-046-X). NE History.
Greene, Francis T., et al, eds. Quality Assurance of Polymeric Materials & Products: STP 846. LC 83-73514. (Illus.). 145p. 1985. pap. text ed. 24.00 (ISBN 0-8031-0408-1, 04-846000-19). ASTM.
Greene, Francis V. General Greene. LC 72-120878. (American Bicentennial Ser.). 1970. Repr. of 1893 ed. 25.50x (ISBN 0-8046-1271-4, Pub. by Kennikat). Assoc Faculty Pr.
Greene, Frank, ed. Composers on Record: An Index to Biographical Information on 14,000 Composers Whose Music Has Been Recorded. LC 85-8238. 636p. 1985. 42.50 (ISBN 0-8108-1816-7). Scarecrow.
Greene, Fred. Stresses in U. S. -Japanese Security Relations. (Studies in Defense Policy). 120p. 1975. pap. 6.95 (ISBN 0-8157-3271-6). Brookings.
--U. S. Policy & the Security of Asia. LC 68-11606. (The United States & China in World Affairs Ser.). pap. 111.80 (ISBN 0-317-09320-7, 2002943). Bks Demand UMI.
Greene, Freda, jt. auth. see Camden, Thomas M.
Greene, Gael. Doctor Love. 1983. pap. 3.95 (ISBN 0-451-12242-9, Sig). NAL.
Greene, Gardiner C. How to Start & Manage Your Own Small Business. 243p. 1975. 24.95 (ISBN 0-07-024350-6). McGraw.
Greene, Gardiner G. How to Start & Manage Your Own Business. (Executive Library Ser.). 256p. 1975. pap. 4.50 (ISBN 0-451-62401-7, ME2146, Ment). NAL.
Greene, Gayle & Kahn, Coppelia, eds. Making a Difference. 288p. (Orig.). 1985. 22.00 (ISBN 0-416-37470-0, 4147); pap. 9.95 (ISBN 0-416-37480-8, 4069). Methuen Inc.
Greene, George W. Historical View of the American Revolution. LC 70-91044. 1970. Repr. of 1872 ed. 35.00 (ISBN 0-8046-0654-4, Pub. by Kennikat). Assoc Faculty Pr.
--The Life of Nathanael Greene: Major-General in the Army of the Revolution. LC 72-5507. (Select Bibliographies Reprint Ser.). 1972. Repr. of 1867 ed. 84.00 (ISBN 0-8369-6910-3). Ayer Co Pubs.
Greene, Gerald & Greene, Caroline. S-M: The Last Taboo. LC 74-7680. 1974. pap. 2.95 (ISBN 0-394-17832-7, B376, BC). Grove.
Greene, Geraldine. Love's Velvet Song. (Orig.). 1983. pap. 1.95 (ISBN 0-317-02745-X, BH093). Holloway.
Greene, Gloria K. The Jewish Holiday Cookbook: An International Collection of Recipes & Customs. LC 85-40437. (Illus.). 1985. 17.95 (ISBN 0-8129-1224-1). Times Bks.
Greene, Graham. Another Mexico. 288p. 1982. 16.95 (ISBN 0-670-12892-9). Viking.
--The Bear Fell Free. LC 77-3318. Repr. of 1935 ed. lib. bdg. 17.50 (ISBN 0-8414-4403-X). Folcroft.
--Brighton Rock. 1977. pap. 3.95 (ISBN 0-14-000442-4). Penguin.
--Brighton Rock. LC 38-15724. 316p. 1938. 14.95 (ISBN 0-670-19153-1). Viking.
--British Dramatists. LC 79-739. 1942. 12.50 (ISBN 0-8414-4619-9). Folcroft.
--A Burnt-Out Case. 1977. pap. 3.95 (ISBN 0-14-001894-8). Penguin.
--A Burnt-Out Case. 252p. 1961. 16.95 (ISBN 0-670-19715-7). Viking.
--Collected Essays. 354p. 1981. pap. 4.95 (ISBN 0-14-003159-6). Penguin.
--The Collected Essays. 1969. 20.95 (ISBN 0-670-22740-4). Viking.
--Collected Stories. 1973. 16.95 (ISBN 0-670-22911-3). Viking.
--The Comedians. 1976. pap. 3.95 (ISBN 0-14-002766-1). Penguin.
--The Comedians. 1966. 14.95 (ISBN 0-670-23208-4). Viking.
--The Confidential Agent. 208p. 1981. pap. 3.95 (ISBN 0-14-001895-6). Penguin.
--The Confidential Agent. 256p. 1982. 17.95 (ISBN 0-670-23725-6). Viking.
--Dr. Fischer of Geneva or the Bomb Party. 144p. 1981. pap. 2.50 (ISBN 0-380-55202-7, 55202-7). Avon.
--Dr. Fischer of Geneva or the Bomb Party. (Uniform Editions Ser.). 160p. Date not set. 20.00 (ISBN 0-670-27522-0). Viking.
--The End of the Affair. 1977. pap. 4.95 (ISBN 0-14-004696-8). Penguin.
--The End of the Affair. 1951. 16.95 (ISBN 0-670-29457-8). Viking.
--England Made Me. 208p. 1981. pap. 3.95 (ISBN 0-14-003146-4). Penguin.
--Getting to Know the General: The Story of an Involvement. LC 84-14013. 192p. 1984. 14.95 (ISBN 0-671-54160-9). S&S.
--A Gun for Sale. 1982. pap. 3.95 (ISBN 0-14-001896-4). Penguin.
--The Heart of the Matter. 1978. pap. 3.95 (ISBN 0-14-001789-5). Penguin.
--The Heart of the Matter. 1948. 14.95 (ISBN 0-670-36459-2). Viking.
--The Heart of the Matter. 16.95 (ISBN 0-88411-654-9, Pub. by Aeonian Pr). Amereon Ltd.
--The Honorary Consul. 1983. 20.95 (ISBN 0-670-37872-0). Viking.
--The Honorary Consul. 17.95 (ISBN 0-88411-655-7, Pub. by Aeonian Pr). Amereon Ltd.
--The Honorary Counsel. 1983. pap. 3.95 (ISBN 0-671-47271-2). PB.
--The Human Factor. 1978. pap. 3.95 (ISBN 0-380-41491-0, 69799-8). Avon.
--The Human Factor. 1983. 20.95 (ISBN 0-670-38625-1). Viking.
--In Search of a Character. 112p. 1981. pap. 3.95 (ISBN 0-14-002822-6). Penguin.
--It's a Battlefield. 1977. pap. 3.95 (ISBN 0-14-000257-X). Penguin.
--It's a Battlefield. 224p. 1982. 17.95 (ISBN 0-670-40431-4). Viking.
--J'Accuse: Nice, the Dark Side. 48p. (Eng. & Fr.). 1982. pap. 3.95 (ISBN 0-370-30930-8, Pub. by the Bodley Head). Merrimack Pub Cir.
--Journey Without Maps. 1978. pap. 3.95 (ISBN 0-14-003280-0). Penguin.
--Journey Without Maps. (Uniform Edition). 336p. 1983. 20.95 (ISBN 0-670-40974-X). Viking.
--The Lawless Roads. 1982. pap. 3.95 (ISBN 0-14-000559-5). Penguin.
--Lord Rochester's Monkey. (Illus.). 1974. 19.95 (ISBN 0-670-44055-8, Studio). Viking.
--Loser Takes All. 1977. pap. 3.95 (ISBN 0-14-003277-0). Penguin.
--The Man Within. 1981. 14.95 (ISBN 0-670-45383-8). Viking.
--The Man Within. 1982. pap. 3.95 (ISBN 0-14-003283-5). Penguin.
--May We Borrow Your Husband? And Other Comedies of the Sexual Life. 1978. pap. 3.95 (ISBN 0-14-003030-1). Penguin.
--The Ministry of Fear. 1978. pap. 3.95 (ISBN 0-14-001897-2). Penguin.
--The Ministry of Fear. 272p. 1982. 17.95 (ISBN 0-670-47682-X). Viking.
--Monsignor Quixote. (General Ser.). 1983. lib. bdg. 14.95 (ISBN 0-8161-3535-5, Large Print Bks). G K Hall.
--Monsignor Quixote. 1983. pap. 3.95 (ISBN 0-317-47470-7). PB.
--Orient Express: Uniform Edition. 272p. 1982. 16.95 (ISBN 0-670-52841-2). Viking.
--Our Man in Havana. 1979. pap. 3.95 (ISBN 0-14-001790-9). Penguin.
--Our Man in Havana. LC 58-11735. 248p. 1981. 14.95 (ISBN 0-670-53141-3). Viking.
--The Pleasure Dome: The Collected Film Criticism 1935-40. Taylor, John R., ed. (Illus.). 1980. pap. 8.95 (ISBN 0-19-281286-6, GB604, GB). Oxford U Pr.
--The Pleasure-Dome: The Collected Film Criticism 1935-40. Taylor, John R., ed. 288p. 1972. 25.00x (ISBN 0-436-18798-1, Pub. by Secker & Warburg England). State Mutual Bk.
--The Portable Graham Greene. Stratford, Philip, ed. LC 76-55791. 1977. pap. 7.95 (ISBN 0-14-015075-7). Penguin.
--The Power & the Glory. LC 76-104160. (Viking Critical Library: No. 6). (Illus.). 1977. pap. 3.95 (ISBN 0-14-001791-7). Penguin.
--The Power & the Glory. 276p. 1981. 16.95 (ISBN 0-670-56979-8). Viking.
--The Power & the Glory. 17.95 (ISBN 0-88411-656-5, Pub. by Aeonian Pr). Amereon Ltd.
--The Quiet American. 1977. pap. 3.95 (ISBN 0-14-001792-5). Penguin.
--The Quiet American. 228p. 1982. 16.95 (ISBN 0-670-58552-1). Viking.

--The Quiet American. 15.95 (ISBN 0-88411-657-3, Pub. by Aeonian Pr). Amereon Ltd.

--The Return of A. J. Raffles: An Edwardian Comedy in Three Acts Based Somewhat Loosely on E. W. Hornung's Characters in 'The Amateur Cracksman' 92p. 1975. 7.50 (ISBN 0-317-03942-3). Ultramarine Pub.

--The Shipwrecked: The Uniform Edition. 1982. 16.95 (ISBN 0-670-64038-7). Viking.

--A Sort of Life, Vol. 1. 1982. pap. 2.95 (ISBN 0-671-45198-7). WSP.

--Stamboul Train. 224p. 1983. pap. 3.95 (ISBN 0-14-001898-0). Penguin.

--The Tenth Man. 192p. 1985. 14.95 (ISBN 0-671-50794-X). S&S.

--The Third Man & the Fallen Idol. 1981. pap. 3.95 (ISBN 0-14-003278-9). Penguin.

--The Third Man, Loser Takes All. 208p. 1983. 20.95 (ISBN 0-670-70084-3). Viking.

--This Gun for Hire. 240p. 1982. 16.95 (ISBN 0-670-70172-6). Viking.

--Travels with My Aunt. 1977. pap. 3.95 (ISBN 0-14-003221-5). Penguin.

--Travels with My Aunt. LC 72-94848. 324p. 1981. 14.95 (ISBN 0-670-72524-2). Viking.

--Twenty-One Stories. 200p. 1981. pap. 3.95 (ISBN 0-14-003093-X). Penguin.

--Ways of Escape. 288p. 1982. pap. 3.95 (ISBN 0-671-43820-4). WSP.

--Ways of Escape & a Sort of Life. (Uniform Editions Ser.). 320p. 1985. 20.00 (ISBN 0-670-75262-2). Viking.

Greene, Graham & Greene, Hugh. The Spy's Bedside Book. 256p. 1985. pap. 7.95 (ISBN 0-88184-188-9). Carroll & Graf.

--Victorian Villainies: The Great Tontine, The Rome Express, In the Fog, The Beetle. 720p. 1986. pap. 7.95 (ISBN 0-14-006850-3). Penguin.

Greene, Graham, jt. auth. see Mesnet, B.

Greene, Graham, ed. see Saki.

Greene, Graham H. Victorian Villainies. 1985. 7.95 (ISBN 0-670-80046-5). Viking.

Greene, Greg. Database Manager in Microsoft BASIC. (Illus.). 176p. 1983. 18.95 (ISBN 0-8306-0167-8, 1567); pap. 12.50 (ISBN 0-8306-0567-3). TAB Bks.

Greene, H. L., jt. ed. see Winters, R. W.

Greene, Hank. Square & Folk Dancing. (Illus.). 416p. 1984. 18.22i (ISBN 0-06-015325-3); pap. 9.57i (ISBN 0-06-464088-4, BN4088). B&N NY.

Greene, Harlan. Why We Never Danced the Charleston. 176p. 1984. 12.95 (ISBN 0-312-87881-8, Pub. by Marek). St Martin.

--Why We Never Danced the Charleston. (Contemporary American Fiction Ser.). 160p. 1985. pap. 4.95 (ISBN 0-14-008218-2). Penguin.

Greene, Harlan & O'Neill, Frank Q., eds. South Carolina Historical Magazine Index 71-81, 1970-1980, with Additions & Corrections 1-53, 1900-1952. rev ed. LC 5-32201. 384p. 1981. pap. 25.00 (ISBN 0-87152-356-6). Reprint.

Greene, Harry A. & Jorgensen, Albert N. The Use & Interpretation of High School Tests. 614p. 1981. Repr. of 1939 ed. lib. bdg. 35.00 (ISBN 0-89760-324-9). Telegraph Bks.

Greene, Harry A., et al. Measurement & Evaluation in the Secondary Schools. 670p. 1981. Repr. of 1943 ed. lib. bdg. 35.00 (ISBN 0-89984-242-9). Century Bookbindery.

Greene, Harry P. Interpretation in Song. LC 79-4135. (Music Reprint Ser.). 307p. 1979. Repr. of 1912 ed. 35.00 (ISBN 0-306-79509-4). Da Capo.

Greene, Harry W. Holders of Doctorates Among American Negroes. 275p. 1974. Repr. 15.00x (ISBN 0-89020-010-6). Crofton Pub.

Greene, Henry C., tr. see Bernard, Claude.

Greene, Herb. Mind & Image: An Essay on Art & Architecture. LC 74-18932. (Illus.). 224p. 1976. 24.00x (ISBN 0-8131-1323-7). U Pr of Ky.

Greene, Herb & Greene, Nanine H. Building to Last. (Illus.). 168p. 1981. 26.95 (ISBN 0-8038-0028-2). Hastings.

Greene, Homer. Physical Therapy Manual. LC 76-715. 1976. pap. 7.00 (ISBN 0-87125-032-2). Cath Health.

Greene, Hugh, jt. auth. see Greene, Graham.

Greene, J. H. Production & Inventory Control Handbook. 1970. 73.50 (ISBN 0-07-024332-8). McGraw.

Greene, J. Lee. Time's Unfading Garden: Anne Spencer's Life and Poetry. LC 77-5960. xi, 204p. 1977. 22.50x (ISBN 0-8071-0294-6). La State U Pr.

Greene, J. R. An Atlas of the Quabbin Valley: Past & Present. 2nd, rev. ed. (Illus.). 28p. 1983. pap. 4.50 (ISBN 0-9609404-2-1). J R Greene.

--An Atlas of the Ware River Diversion. (Illus.). 20p. (Orig.). 1983. pap. 3.95 (ISBN 0-9609404-3-X). J R Greene.

--The Creation of Quabbin Reservoir: Death of the Swift River Valley. 2nd. Ed ed. (Illus.). 123p. 1982. pap. 9.95 (ISBN 0-9609404-0-5). J R Greene.

--The Day Four Quabbin Towns Died. (Illus.). 100p. (Orig.). 1985. pap. 4.95 (ISBN 0-9609404-4-8). J R Greene.

--Death of Disco & Other Poems. 40p. (Orig.). 1982. pap. 3.25 (ISBN 0-9609404-1-3). J R Greene.

Greene, J. Reay, jt. auth. see Carlyle, Thomas.

Greene, J. Reay, ed. see Carlyle, Thomas.

Greene, Jack. The Mudgrump. LC 80-68130. (Illus.). 56p. (Orig.). 1980. pap. text ed. 3.95 perfect binding (ISBN 0-9601258-3-3). Golden Owl Pub.

Greene, Jack P. Landon Carter: An Inquiry into the Personal Values & Social Imperatives of the Eighteenth-Century Virginia Gentry. LC 64-19201. 1976. pap. 4.95x (ISBN 0-8139-0111-1). U Pr of Va.

--Quest for Power: The Lower Houses of Assembly in the Southern Royal Colonies, 1689-1776. 1972. pap. 3.95x (ISBN 0-393-00591-7, Norton Lib). Norton.

--The Quest for Power: The Lower Houses of Assembly in the Southern Royal Colonies 1689-1776. (Institute of Early American History & Culture Ser.). xv, 528p. 1963. 27.50x (ISBN 0-8078-0900-4). U of NC Pr.

Greene, Jack P. & McLoughlin, William G. Preachers & Politicians: Two Essays on the Origins of the American Revolution. LC 77-88162. 1977. pap. 7.00x (ISBN 0-912296-14-3, Dist. by U Pr of Va). Am Antiquarian.

--Preachers & Politicians: Two Essays on the Origins of the American Revolution. 1983. pap. 7.00 (ISBN 0-317-01411-0). U Pr of Va.

Greene, Jack P., compiled by. American Colonies in the Eighteenth Century, 1689-1763. LC 73-79166. (Goldentree Bibliographies in American History Ser.). (Orig.). 1969. pap. 14.95x (ISBN 0-88295-514-4). Harlan Davidson.

Greene, Jack P., ed. Colonies to Nation, 1763-1789: A Documentary History of the American Revolution. 608p. 1975. pap. 11.95x (ISBN 0-393-09229-1). Norton.

--Encyclopedia of American Political History, 3 vols. LC 84-1355. 1984. Set. lib. bdg. 200.00 (ISBN 0-684-17003-5). Scribner.

--Great Britain & the American Colonies, 1606-1763. LC 78-95257. (Documentary History of the United States Ser). xlvii, 312p. 1970. 19.95x (ISBN 0-87249-167-6). U of SC Pr.

--Nature of Colony Constitutions: Two Pamphlets on the Wilkes Fund Controversy in South Carolina by Sir Egerton Leigh & Arthur Lee. LC 74-120577. (Tricentennial Edition Ser.: No. 1). vi, 232p. 1970. 17.95x (ISBN 0-87249-185-4). U of SC Pr.

Greene, Jack P., compiled by. The Reinterpretation of the American Revolution, 1763 to 1789. LC 78-27785. 1979. Repr. of 1968 ed. lib. bdg. 42.50x (ISBN 0-313-20930-8, GRRE). Greenwood.

Greene, Jack P., ed. Settlements to Society, 1607-1763: A Documentary History of Colonial America. 400p. 1975. pap. 7.95x (ISBN 0-393-09232-1). Norton.

Greene, Jack P. & Pole, J. R., eds. Colonial British America: Essays in the New History of the Early Modern Era. LC 83-48060. 520p. 1984. pap. 14.95x (ISBN 0-8018-3055-9). Johns Hopkins.

Greene, Jack P., jt. ed. see Cohen, David W.

Greene, Jack P., jt. ed. see Forster, Robert.

Greene, Jack P., et al. Society, Freedom & Conscience: The Coming of the Revolution in Virginia, Massachusetts, & New York. Jellison, Richard M., ed. 1977. pap. text ed. 3.95x (ISBN 0-393-09160-0). Norton.

--Magna Charta for America: James Abercromby's An Examination of the Acts of Parliament Relative to the Trade & the Government of Our American Colonies. LC 84-45900. (Memoirs Ser.: Vol. 165). 1985. 35.00 (ISBN 0-87169-165-5). Am Philos.

Greene, Jack R., ed. Managing Police Work: Issues & Analysis. (Perspectives in Criminal Justice: Vol. 4). (Illus.). 176p. 1982. 20.00 (ISBN 0-8039-1787-2); pap. 8.95 (ISBN 0-8039-1788-0). Sage.

Greene, Jacqueline D. Butchers & Bakers Rabbis & Kings. LC 83-22222. (Illus.). 40p. (gr. 1-6). 1984. 9.95 (ISBN 0-930494-27-X); pap. 4.95 (ISBN 0-930494-28-8). Kar Ben.

--A Classroom Hanukah. (Illus.). 32p. (Orig.). (gr. k-4). 1980. pap. 3.00 (ISBN 0-938836-01-3). Pascal Pubs.

--The Hanukah Tooth. LC 81-90033. (Illus.). 28p. (ps-2). 1981. pap. 3.00 (ISBN 0-938836-02-1). Pascal Pubs.

--The Leveller. LC 83-40383. 128p. 1984. 12.95 (ISBN 0-8027-6521-1). Walker & Co.

Greene, James. Organizing for Exporting. (Studies in Business Policy: No. 126). 64p. 1968. pap. 17.50 (ISBN 0-8237-0044-5); pap. 3.50 member. Conference Bd.

--Regulatory Problems & Regulatory Reform: The Perceptions of Business. (Report Ser.: No. 769). vi, 50p. (Orig.). 1980. pap. 15.00 (ISBN 0-8237-0205-7); pap. 5.00 member. Conference Bd.

Greene, James & Lewis, David. Know Your Own Mind. 114p. 1984. 14.95 (ISBN 0-89256-265-X); pap. 6.95 (ISBN 0-89256-268-4). Rawson Assocs.

Greene, James, jt. auth. see Lewis, David.

Greene, James, ed. see More, Thomas.

Greene, James H. Operations Management: Productivity & Profit. 1984. text ed. 39.95 (ISBN 0-8359-5250-9); instrs' manual avail. (ISBN 0-8359-5251-7). Reston.

--Production & Inventory Control: Systems & Decisions. rev. ed. 1974. text ed. 27.95x (ISBN 0-256-01431-0). Irwin.

Greene, James R., ed. see Atlantic Council's Working Group on Western Interest & U. S. Policy Options in the Caribbean Basin.

Greene, James W., jt. auth. see Favell, Judith E.

Greene, Jane B., tr. see Rilke, Rainer M.

Greene, Janice P., jt. auth. see Brewer, Gail S.

Greene, Jerome. Consumer Behavior Models for Non-Statisticians: The River of Time. LC 82-9076. 192p. 1982. 25.95x (ISBN 0-03-058932-0). Praeger.

Greene, Jerome A. Evidence & the Custer Enigma. rev. ed. (Illus.). 1979. pap. 3.95 (ISBN 0-89646-058-4). Outbooks.

--Indian Wars Veteran Organizations. (Guidon Monograph). (Illus.). 1985. write for info. (Pub. by J M C & Co). Amereon Ltd.

--Slim Buttes, Eighteen Seventy-Six: An Episode of the Great Sioux War. LC 81-40291. (Illus.). 208p. 1982. 16.95 (ISBN 0-8061-1712-5). U of Okla Pr.

Greene, John. Ciceronis Amor: Tullies Love (1589) & Quip for an Upstart (1592) LC 54-11901. 30.00x (ISBN 0-8201-1224-0). Schol Facsimiles.

Greene, John, jt. auth. see Curtis, John.

Greene, John see Heywood, Thomas.

Greene, John C. American Science in the Age of Jefferson. (Illus.). 1984. pap. text ed. 24.95 (ISBN 0-8138-0102-8). Iowa St U Pr.

--Darwin & the Modern World View. LC 61-15489. (Rockwell Lectures Ser.). 152p. 1973. pap. text ed. 4.95x (ISBN 0-8071-0062-5). La State U Pr.

--Death of Adam: Evolution & Its Impact on Western Thought. (Illus.). 1959. pap. 9.95x (ISBN 0-8138-0390-X). Iowa St U Pr.

--Science, Ideology, & World View: Essays in the History of Evolutionary Ideas. LC 80-20756. 1981. 19.50x (ISBN 0-520-04217-4); pap. 5.95 (ISBN 0-520-04218-2, CAL 511). U of Cal Pr.

Greene, John G. The Social & Psychological Origins of the Climacteric Syndrome. LC 84-13637. 247p. 1984. text ed. 35.50x (ISBN 0-566-00795-9). Gower Pub Co.

Greene, Jonathan. Idylls. (Orig.). 1983. pap. 12.50 (ISBN 0-317-12173-1). Iron Mtn Pr.

--Peripatetics. 48p. 1978. 15.00 (ISBN 0-916562-18-2); pap. 4.00 (ISBN 0-916562-14-X). Truck Pr.

--Scaling the Walls: Poems Nineteen Sixty-Seven to Nineteen Seventy-Four. LC 74-18770. 1975. limited ed. 25.00x (ISBN 0-917788-06-0); pap. 5.00 (ISBN 0-917788-05-2). Gnomon Pr.

--Small Change for the Long Haul. 64p. (Orig.). 1984. pap. 4.95 (ISBN 0-88268-009-9). Station Hill Pr.

--Trickster Tales. (Morning Coffee Chapbks.). (Illus.). 16p. 1985. pap. 7.50 (ISBN 0-915124-80-7). Coffee Hse.

Greene, Jonathan, ed. Kentucky Renaissance: An Anthology of Contemporary Writings. LC 75-39168. 1976. pap. 9.50 (ISBN 0-917788-09-5). Gnomon Pr.

Greene, Joseph. Pupa Digging. 1984. 25.00x (ISBN 0-317-07171-8, Pub. by FW Classey UK). State Mutual Bk.

Greene, Joshua, retold by. Krishna, Master of All Mystics. (Illus.). 16p. (gr. 1-4). 1981. pap. 4.00 (ISBN 0-89647-010-5). Bala Bks.

Greene, Joshua, ed. Sakshi Gopal: A Witness for the Wedding. Bhaktivedanta, A. C., tr. from Sanskrit. (Illus.). 17p. (gr. 2 up). 1981. pap. 1.50 (ISBN 0-89647-011-3). Bala Bks.

Greene, Josiah E. Not in Our Stars. LC 74-28361. Repr. of 1945 ed. 35.00 (ISBN 0-404-58520-5). AMS Pr.

Greene, Judith. Thinking & Language. (Essential Psychology Ser.). 1975. pap. 4.95x (ISBN 0-416-81880-3, NO. 2736). Methuen Inc.

Greene, Judith & D'Oliveira, Manuela. Learning to Use Statistical Tests in Psychology. 144p. 1982. pap. 15.00x (ISBN 0-335-10177-1, Pub. by Open Univ Pr). Taylor & Francis.

Greene, Judith, jt. auth. see Hicks, Carolyn.

Greene, Julia. Untamed Heart. 1978. pap. 2.25 (ISBN 0-505-51321-8, Pub. by Tower Bks). Dorchester Pub Co.

Greene, June. Chinese Brush Strokes, An Introduction: The Scholarly Bamboo. LC 81-69758. (Illus., Orig.). 1981. pap. 9.50 (ISBN 0-941284-11-5). Deco Design Studio.

--The Scholarly Bamboo. 1981. 9.50. Deco Design Studio.

Greene, Kenneth V. & Neenan, William B. Fiscal Interactions in a Metropolitan Area. 256p. 1974. 12.50 (ISBN 0-317-36117-1, 73000). Urban Inst.

Greene, Kevin. Archaeology an Introduction: The History, Principles & Methods of Modern Archaeology. (Illus.). 190p. 1983. text ed. 27.50x (ISBN 0-389-20362-9). B&N Imports.

Greene, L. F., ed. see Leland, John.

Greene, Larry A., jt. ed. see Duff, J. B.

Greene, Laura. Careers in the Computer Industry. (First Bks). (Illus.). 96p. (gr. 5 up). PLB 8.90 (ISBN 0-531-04636-2). Watts.

--Change: Getting to Know About Ebb & Flow. LC 80-81081. (Juvenile Ser.). 32p. 1981. 10.95 (ISBN 0-87705-401-0). Human Sci Pr.

--Computer Pioneers. (Computer Awareness First Book Ser.). (Illus.). 96p. (gr. 4 up). 1985. lib. bdg. 9.40 (ISBN 0-531-04906-X). Watts.

--Computers in Business & Industry. (A Computer Applications Bk.). 128p. (YA) (gr. 7 up). 1984. 9.90 (ISBN 0-531-04842-X). Watts.

--I Am Somebody. LC 79-22288. (Social Value Ser.). (Illus.). 32p. (gr. k-3). 1980. PLB 10.35 (ISBN 0-516-01476-5); pap. 3.95 (ISBN 0-516-41476-3). Childrens.

Greene, Laurence. America Goes to Press: The News of Yesterday. LC 74-128252. (Essay Index Reprint Ser). 1936. 21.50 (ISBN 0-8369-1929-7). Ayer Co Pubs.

Greene, Lawrence & Jones-Bamman, Leigh. Getting Smarter: A Study Skills Improvement Program. 1985. pap. 4.80 (ISBN 0-8224-3386-9). Pitman Learning.

Greene, Lawrence J. Kids Who Hate School. rev. ed. 264p. (Orig.). 1984. pap. 12.95 (ISBN 0-89334-035-9). Humanics Ltd.

Greene, Lawrence P., ed. Space-Enhancing Technological Leadership. LC 57-43769. (Advances in the Astronautical Sciences Ser.: Vol. 44). (Illus.). 630p. 1981. lib. bdg. 65.00x (ISBN 0-87703-147-9, Pub. by Am Astronaut); pap. text ed. 50.00x (ISBN 0-87703-148-7); Microfiche Supplement 5.00x (ISBN 0-87703-164-9). Univelt Inc.

Greene, Lawrence S., ed. Malnutrition, Behavior & Social Organization. 1977. 47.00 (ISBN 0-12-298050-6). Acad Pr.

Greene, Lee, jt. ed. see Williamson, Rene.

Greene, Lee S. Lead Me On: Frank Goad Clement & Tennessee Politics. LC 81-11459. (Illus.). 574p. 1982. 19.95 (ISBN 0-87049-335-3). U of Tenn Pr.

Greene, Lee S., jt. ed. see American Academy of Political & Social Science.

Greene, Lee S., et al. Government in Tennessee. 4th ed. LC 81-16428. (Illus.). 424p. 1982. 24.50x (ISBN 0-87049-338-8); pap. text ed. 12.50x (ISBN 0-87049-339-6). U of Tenn Pr.

Greene, Leonard M. Free Enterprise Without Poverty. 1981. 12.95 (ISBN 0-393-01470-3). Norton.

--Free Enterprise Without Poverty. 192p. 1983. pap. 4.50 (ISBN 0-393-30083-8). Norton.

Greene, Letha C. Long Live the Delta Queen. (Illus.). 1973. 7.50 (ISBN 0-8038-4286-4). Hastings.

Greene, Liz. The Astrology of Fate. LC 84-51742. (Illus.). 370p. (Orig.). 1984. pap. 10.95 (ISBN 0-87728-636-1). Weiser.

--The Dreamer of the Vine: A Novel About Nostradamus. 1981. 12.95 (ISBN 0-393-01434-7). Norton.

--Looking at Astrology. LC 77-83149. (Illus.). 30p. (gr. 2-7). 1981. pap. 5.95 (ISBN 0-916360-13-X). CRCS Pubns NV.

--The Outer Planets & Their Cycles: The Astrology of the Collective. LC 82-45633. (Lectures on Modern Astrology Ser.). 192p. 1983. pap. 7.95 (ISBN 0-916360-17-2). CRCS Pubns NV.

--Relating: An Astrological Guide to Living with Others on a Small Planet. LC 83-145084. (Orig.). 1978. pap. 7.95 (ISBN 0-87728-418-0). Weiser.

--Saturn: A New Look at an Old Devil. 1976. pap. 5.95 (ISBN 0-87728-306-0). Weiser.

--Star Signs for Lovers. LC 80-5890. (Illus.). 480p. 1980. 14.95 (ISBN 0-8128-2765-1); pap. 3.75 (ISBN 0-8128-7076-X). Stein & Day.

--Star Signs for Lovers. LC 80-5890. 400p. 1980. 7.95 (ISBN 0-916360-08-3). CRCS Pubns NV.

--Star Signs for Lovers. 480p. 1984. pap. 3.75 (ISBN 0-8128-7076-X). Stein & Day.

Greene, Liz, jt. auth. see Arroyo, Stephen.

Greene, Lorenzo J. Negro in Colonial New England. LC 68-16413. (Studies in American Negro Life). 1968. pap. text ed. 4.75x (ISBN 0-689-70081-4, NL1). Atheneum.

Greene, Lorenzo J. & Woodson, Carter G. Negro Wage Earner. LC 76-126671. Repr. of 1930 ed. 10.25 (ISBN 0-404-00163-7). AMS Pr.

Greene, Lorne & Allen, Robert. Propaganda Game. 12.00 (ISBN 0-911624-39-2). Wffn Proof.

Greene, M., ed. see Nekrasov, V.

Greene, M. Louise. Development of Religious Liberty in Connecticut. facs. ed. LC 79-126235. (Select Bibliographies Reprint Ser). 1905. 26.50 (ISBN 0-8369-5461-0). Ayer Co Pubs.

--Development of Religious Liberty in Connecticut. LC 74-99858. (Civil Liberties in American History Ser). 1970. Repr. of 1905 ed. lib. bdg. 59.50 (ISBN 0-306-71861-8). Da Capo.

Greene, Margaret. I, Prince Tudor, Wrote Shakespeare. 1973. 15.00 (ISBN 0-8283-1351-2). Branden Pub Co.

Greene, Marilyn. Marilyn Sew Simple Quilts. (Spiraling Log Cabin Design Ser.). (Illus.). 32p. (Orig.). 1985. pap. 8.95 (ISBN 0-9614798-0-9). Dav-a-Lynn Ent.

Greene, Marjorie, jt. auth. see Perry, Ronald W.

Greene, Mark I. & Nisonoff, Alfred, eds. The Biology of Idiotypes. 524p. 1984. 59.50x (ISBN 0-306-41646-8, Plenum Pr). Plenum Pub.

Greene, Mark R. Life & Health Insurance Companies As Financial Institutions. (FLMI Insurance Education Program Ser.). 60p. 1984. pap. text ed. 6.00 (ISBN 0-915322-51-X). LOMA.

--Risk Aversion, Insurance, & the Future. LC 70-633854. (Sequeinnial Insurance Ser.: No. 2). 1971. 7.50 (ISBN 0-685-00048-6). Ind U Busn Res.

Greene, Mark R. & Dince, Robert R. Personal Financial Management. 1983. text ed. 21.95 (ISBN 0-538-06500-1, F50). SW Pub.

Greene, Mark R. & Trieschmann, James S. Risk & Insurance. 1984. text ed. 21.35 (ISBN 0-538-06540-0, F54). SW Pub.

Greene, Mary L. & Noonan, Patricia. The Little Mushroom Cookbook. (Little Cookbooks). (Orig.). 1984. pap. 1.50 (ISBN 0-934030-12-X). Metagraphics.

--The Little Onion Cookbook. (Little Cookbooks). (Illus., Orig.). 1984. pap. 1.50 (ISBN 0-934030-13-8). Metagraphics.

Greene, Maxine. Landscapes of Learning. LC 78-6571. 1978. pap. text ed. 13.95x (ISBN 0-8077-2534-X). Tchrs Coll.

Greene, Melvyn. Marketing Hotels into the 90's: A Systematic Approach to Increasing Sales. (Illus.). 1984. text ed. 22.50 (ISBN 0-87055-475-1). AVI.

Greene, Michael H. Program Your Own Life. 230p. 1982. 10.00 (ISBN 0-9610136-0-5). Behavorial Sys Inc.

Greene, Mildred S. Madame de Lafayette. Greene, Mildred S., tr. from Fr. LC 79-14591. (Romance Monographs: No. 35). 199p. 1979. 18.00x (ISBN 84-499-2977-6); pap. 8.95 (ISBN 84-499-2977-6). Romance.

Greene, Mott T. Geology in the Nineteenth Century: Changing Views of a Changing World. LC 82-7456. (Illus.). 320p. 1982. 34.50x (ISBN 0-8014-1467-9). Cornell U Pr.

--Geology in the Nineteenth Century: Changing Views of a Changing World. LC 82-7456. (Illus.). 328p. (Orig.). 1985. 34.50x (ISBN 0-8014-1467-9); pap. text ed. 12.95x (ISBN 0-8014-9295-5). Cornell U Pr.

Greene, Myles. Adventures in Philosophical Poetry & Literature. 48p. 1983. 1.95 (ISBN 0-9606994-2-2). Greenview Pubns.

--CIRCA Nineteen Sixty-Eight. 24p. 1982. pap. text ed. 2.95 (ISBN 0-9606994-0-6). Greenview Pubns.

--A Diary of Thought. 52p. 1983. pap. text ed. 1.95 (ISBN 0-9606994-3-0). Greenview Pubns.

--Poems of Social Revolt. LC 85-70604. 52p. 1985. pap. text ed. 2.50 (ISBN 0-9606994-4-9). Greenview Pubns.

--Sketches in Fantasy. LC 83-82670. 52p. 1983. pap. text ed. 1.95 (ISBN 0-9606994-5-7). Greenview Pubns.

Greene, Nancy L. Hearing Tests for Health Sciences. (Illus.). 1978. 20.00 (ISBN 0-916750-26-4, CX-11). Dayton Labs.

Greene, Nanine H., jt. auth. see Greene, Herb.

Greene, Naomi. Rene Clair: A Guide to References & Resources. (Performing Arts: Film-Directors Ser.). 1985. lib. bdg. 48.00 (ISBN 0-8161-8503-4). G K Hall.

Greene, Nathan, jt. auth. see Frankfurter, Felix.

Greene, Nathanael. From Versailles to Vichy: The Third French Republic 1919-1940. LC 75-101945. (Europe Since 1500 Ser.). 1970. pap. 7.95x (ISBN 0-88295-737-6). Harlan Davidson.

Greene, Nathanael, ed. Fascism: An Anthology. LC 67-30582. (Orig.). 1968. pap. 11.95x (ISBN 0-88295-736-8). Harlan Davidson.

Greene, Nicholas M. Key Words in Anesthesiology. 2nd ed. LC 79-23939. 80p. (Orig.). 1980. pap. 8.95 (ISBN 0-683-03768-4). Krieger.

--Physiology of Spinal Anesthesia. 2nd ed. LC 75-43601. 256p. 1976. Repr. of 1969 ed. 17.50 (ISBN 0-88275-370-3). Krieger.

Greene, Norbert D., jt. auth. see Fontana, Mars G.

Greene, Norman N. Jean-Paul Sartre: The Existentialist Ethic. LC 80-12203. vii, 213p. 1980. Repr. of 1960 ed. lib. bdg. 22.50x (ISBN 0-313-22422-6, GRJP). Greenwood.

Greene, Orville & Durr, Frank. The Practical Inventor's Handbook. LC 78-26666. (Illus.). 1979. 39.95 (ISBN 0-07-024320-4). McGraw.

Greene, Owen, et al. Nuclear Winter: The Evidence & the Risks. 252p. 1985. pap. 9.95 (ISBN 0-7456-0177-4); 34.95 (ISBN 0-7456-0176-6). Basil Blackwell.

Greene, Owne & Rubin, Barry. London after the Bomb: What a Nuclear Attack Really Means. (Illus.). 1982. pap. 4.95 (ISBN 0-19-285123-3). Oxford U Pr.

Greene, Peggy R. Things to Make. LC 77-91652. (Picturebacks Ser.). (Illus.). 32p. (ps-3). 1981. PLB 4.99 (ISBN 0-394-93834-8). Random.

Greene, Peter D. Never Pay Rent Again. Spears, Kenneth, ed. LC 84-90345. (Illus.). 128p. (Orig.). 1984. pap. 9.95 (ISBN 0-917233-00-X); legal forms 3.00 (ISBN 0-917233-01-8). Greenes Pub.

Greene, R. E. & Krantz, S. G. Function Theory of One Complex Variable. 1985. 64.95 (ISBN 0-471-80468-1). Wiley.

Greene, R. E. & Wu, H. H. Function Theory on Manifolds Which Possess a Pole. (Lecture Notes in Mathematics Ser.: Vol. 699). 1979. pap. 17.00 (ISBN 0-387-09108-4). Springer-Verlag.

Greene, R. Edwin. Saint Simons Island. 2nd ed. (Illus.). 90p. (Orig.). 1983. pap. 10.95 (ISBN 0-914124-10-2). Arner Pubns.

Greene, R. W. The Chemical Engineering Guide to Valves. 250p. 1984. 37.50 (ISBN 0-07-024313-1). McGraw.

--The Chemical Engineering to Compressors. 250p. 1984. 37.50 (ISBN 0-07-024312-3). McGraw.

Greene, Ralph L. Dynamic & Inspirational Sermons for Today. 128p. 1980. 7.95 (ISBN 0-89962-021-3). Todd & Honeywell.

Greene, Ray J. How to Double the Payoff from Your Real Estate Advertising. 1974. 79.50 (ISBN 0-13-405548-9). P-H.

Greene, Raymond, ed. Current Concepts in Migraine Research. LC 77-83690. 181p. 1978. 33.00 (ISBN 0-89004-199-7). Raven.

Greene, Reynolds W., Jr. Crucial Questions with Christian Answers. 3.95 (ISBN 0-911866-76-0). Advocate.

Greene, Richard. Assuring Quality in Medical Care: The State of the Art. LC 75-37567. 320p. 1976. prof ref 27.50 (ISBN 0-88410-116-9). Ballinger Pub.

Greene, Richard, jt. ed. see Beutler, Larry E.

Greene, Richard C. The King of Instruments. LC 82-4282. (Illus.). 32p. (gr. 1-5). 1982. lib. bdg. 8.95g (ISBN 0-87614-186-6). Carolrhoda Bks.

Greene, Richard L. The Early English Carols. LC 76-161945. 461p. 1935. Repr. 79.00x (ISBN 0-403-01342-9). Scholarly.

Greene, Richard L. & Wheeling, Kenneth E. A Pictorial History of the Shelburne Museum. (Illus., Orig.). 1972. pap. 6.00 (ISBN 0-939384-04-3). Shelburne.

Greene, Richard L., ed. The Early English Carols. 2nd ed. 1977. 94.00x (ISBN 0-19-812715-4). Oxford U Pr.

--A Selection of English Carols. LC 77-13760. 1978. Repr. of 1962 ed. lib. bdg. 24.75x (ISBN 0-313-20002-5, GREC). Greenwood.

Greene, Richard M. The Hit Parade, Nineteen Twenty to Nineteen Seventy. LC 85-90721. 57p. (Orig.). 1985. pap. 6.50 (ISBN 0-934487-00-6). Greene & Assocs.

Greene, Richard S. & Yawkey, Thomas D., eds. Early & Middle Childhood: Growth, Abuse & Delinquency. 467p. 1982. 35.00 (ISBN 0-87762-313-9). Technomic.

Greene, Robert. Alphonsus King of Aragon. LC 82-45788. (Malone Society Reprint Ser.: No. 58). Repr. of 1926 ed. 40.00 (ISBN 0-404-63058-8). AMS Pr.

--Ciceronis Amor: Tullie's Love, a Critical Edition. Larson, Charles H., ed. (Salzburg Studies in English Literature, Elizabethan & Renaissance Studies: No. 36). 216p. 1974. pap. text ed. 25.50x (ISBN 0-391-01392-0). Humanities.

--Friar Bacon & Friar Bongay. LC 71-133670. (Tudor Facsimile Texts. Old English Plays: No. 70). Repr. of 1914 ed. 49.50 (ISBN 0-404-53370-1). AMS Pr.

--Friar Bacon & Friar Bungay. Lavin, J. A., ed. (New Mermaid Ser.). 1976. pap. 2.95x (ISBN 0-393-90013-4). Norton.

--Friar Bacon & Friar Bungay. Seltzer, Daniel, ed. LC 63-14697. (Regents Renaissance Drama Ser.). xxii, 106p. 1963. 10.95x (ISBN 0-8032-0263-6). U of Nebr Pr.

--Friar Bacon & Friar Bungay. LC 82-45789. (Malone Society Reprint Ser.: No. 59). Repr. of 1926 ed. 40.00 (ISBN 0-404-63059-6). AMS Pr.

--Green Pastures. Grosart, Alexander, ed. 1894. Repr. 25.00 (ISBN 0-8274-2449-3). R West.

--Groats-Worth of Witte Bought with a Million of Repentance. Repr. of 1923 ed. lib. bdg. 18.75 (ISBN 0-8371-3021-2, GRGW). Greenwood.

--Groatsworth of Witte Bought with a Million of Repentance. 1967. Repr. of 1592 ed. 11.00 (ISBN 0-8337-1443-0). B Franklin.

--The History of Orlando Furioso. LC 82-45738. Repr. of 1594 ed. 40.00 (ISBN 0-404-63002-2). AMS Pr.

--The Honourable History of Friar Bacon & Friar Bungay. Harrison, G. B., ed. 1927. Repr. 17.50 (ISBN 0-8274-2528-7). R West.

--James the Fourth. Lavin, J. A., ed. (New Mermaid Ser.). 1976. pap. 2.95x (ISBN 0-393-90012-6). Norton.

--James the Fourth. Sanders, Norman, ed. (The Revels Plays Ser.). 154p. 1970. 23.50 (ISBN 0-7190-1521-9, Pub. by Manchester Univ Pr); pap. 6.50 (ISBN 0-7190-1606-1). Longwood Pub Group.

--John of Bordeaux: Or, the Second Part of Friar Bacon. LC 82-45682. (Malone Society Reprint Ser.: No. 79). Repr. of 1935 ed. 40.00 (ISBN 0-404-63079-0). AMS Pr.

--Menaphon: Camila's Alarm to Slumbering Eupheus in the Melancholy Cell at Silexdra, Etc. Arber, Edward, ed. 1880. Repr. 20.00 (ISBN 0-8274-2726-3). R West.

--Plays & Poems, 2 vols. Collins, John C., ed. LC 79-130985. Repr. of 1905 ed. Set. 37.00 (ISBN 0-404-01634-0). Vol. 1 (ISBN 0-404-01635-9). Vol. 2 (ISBN 0-404-01636-7). AMS Pr.

--Plays & Poems of Robert Greene, 2 Vols. facs. ed. Collins, J. Churton, ed. LC 79-119957. (Select Bibliographies Reprint Ser). 1905. Set. 36.00 (ISBN 0-8369-5400-9). Ayer Co Pubs.

--The Scottish History of James the Fourth. LC 82-45781. (Malone Society Reprint Ser.: No. 50). Repr. of 1921 ed. 40.00 (ISBN 0-404-63050-2). AMS Pr.

--The Thirde & Last Part of Conny-Catching. 1923. 12.50 (ISBN 0-8495-6284-8). Arden Lib.

--The Tragical Reign of Selimus. Grosart, Alexander, ed. 1898. Repr. 20.00 (ISBN 0-8274-3643-2). R West.

Greene, Robert, jt. auth. see Lodge, Thomas.

Greene, Robert E. Black Defenders of America, 1775-1973. LC 73-15607. (Illus.). 432p. 1974. 17.95 (ISBN 0-87485-053-3). Johnson Chi.

--Delta Memories: A Historical Summary. LC 81-83202. (Illus.). 54p. 1981. pap. 5.00 (ISBN 0-9603320-3-0). R E Greene.

--Isometric Embeddings of Riemannian & Pseudo Riemannian Manifolds. LC 52-42839. (Memoirs: No. 97). 63p. 1970. pap. 9.00 (ISBN 0-8218-1297-1, MEMO-97). Am Math.

--The Leary-Evans Ohio's Free People of Color. LC 79-66917. (Illus., Orig.). 1979. pap. 5.00 (ISBN 0-9603320-0-6). R E Greene.

--They Rest Among the Known Black Defenders of America Who Have Responded to the Call of Taps. LC 80-67671. (Illus.). 62p. 1982. write for info. (ISBN 0-9603320-1-4). R E Greene.

Greene, Robert E., jt. auth. see Gamelin, Theodore W.

Greene, Robert F. Tennis Drills: On & off Court Drills & Exercises to Improve Your Game. (Illus.). 1977. pap. 12.95 (ISBN 0-8015-7527-3, 01258-370, Hawthorn). Dutton.

Greene, Robert Lee. Welfare Economics & Peak Load Pricing: A Theoretical Application to Municipal Water Utility Practices. LC 75-631068. (University of Florida Social Sciences Monographs: No. 42). (Illus.). 1970. pap. 3.50 (ISBN 0-8130-0309-1). U Presses Fla.

Greene, Robert W. The Poetic Theory of Pierre Reverdy. LC 68-63065. 108p. 1983. Repr. of 1967 ed. lib. bdg. 19.95x (ISBN 0-89370-758-9). Borgo Pr.

--Six French Poets of Our Time: A Critical & Historical Study. LC 78-70927. (Princeton Essays in Literature Ser.). 1979. 22.00x (ISBN 0-691-06390-7). Princeton U Pr.

--The Sting Man. 1982. pap. 2.95 (ISBN 0-345-30324-5). Ballantine.

Greene, Roberta M. & Heavenrich, Elaine. A Question in Search of an Answer: Understanding Learning Disability in Jewish Education. LC 8-18059. (Illus.). 262p. 1981. pap. 5.00 (ISBN 0-8074-0029-7). UAHC.

Greene, Robertson M., ed. Third Palenque Round Table, 1978, Pt. 2. (Palenque Round Table Ser.: Vol. V). (Illus.). 244p. 1980. text ed. 35.00x (ISBN 0-292-78037-0). U of Tex Pr.

Greene, Robertson M. & Jeffers, Donnan C., eds. Third Palenque Round Table, 1978, Pt. 1. LC 79-64960. (Palenque Round Table Ser.: Vol. IV). (Illus.). 232p. (Orig.). 1979. pap. text ed. 25.00x (ISBN 0-292-78036-2, Pub. by Pre-Columbian Mexico). U of Tex Pr.

Greene, Roger L. The MMPI: An Interpretive Manual. (Illus.). 306p. 1980. 28.00 (ISBN 0-8089-1279-8, 791720). Grune.

Greene, Ruth A. Hsiang-Ya Journal. LC 76-28526. Repr. of 1977 ed. 36.70 (2011504). Bks Demand UMI.

Greene, S. W., ed. see International Association of Briologists, Taxonomic Workshop, 1979.

Greene, Samuel S. An Analysis of the English Language. LC 82-10272. (American Linguistics Ser.). 1983. Repr. of 1874 ed. 50.00x (ISBN 0-8201-1384-0). Schol Facsimiles.

--First Lessons in Grammar. LC 81-16559. (Amer. Linguistics Ser.). 1982. Repr. of 1848 ed. 40.00x (ISBN 0-8201-1349-2). Schol Facsimiles.

--The Public Library Movement in the United States. 59.95 (ISBN 0-8490-0914-6). Gordon Pr.

Greene, Sarah P. Some Other Folks. LC 74-98570. (Short Story Index Reprint Ser.). 1884. 18.00 (ISBN 0-8369-3144-0). Ayer Co Pubs.

Greene, Serbein & Serbein. Risk Management: Text with Cases. 2nd ed. LC 82-23115. 1983. text ed. 29.95 (ISBN 0-8359-6736-0); instr's. manual free (ISBN 0-8359-6737-9). Reston.

Greene, Sharon, jt. auth. see Telzer, Ellen.

Greene, Shep. The Boy Who Drank Too Much. 144p. (YA) (gr. 7 up). 1980. pap. 2.25 (ISBN 0-440-90493-5, LFL). Dell.

--The Boy Who Drank Too Much. LC 78-26370. 160p. (gr. 7 up). 1979. 11.50 (ISBN 0-670-18381-4). Viking.

Greene, Sherwin & Calvan, Rita A. Cityshape: Research & References in Community Design. (CPL Bibliographies Ser.: No. 119). 73p. 1983. 12.00 (ISBN 0-86602-119-1). Coun Plan Librarians.

Greene, Suzanne E. Books for Pleasure: Popular Fiction 1914-1945. LC 74-17776. 208p. 1974. 10.95 (ISBN 0-87972-073-5). Bowling Green Univ.

Greene, Sylvia W. Longings. 352p. (Orig.). 1981. pap. 2.50 (ISBN 0-89083-706-6). Zebra.

Greene, Theodora W. Protective Groups in Organic Synthesis. LC 80-25348. 349p. 1981. 43.50 (ISBN 0-471-05764-9). Wiley.

Greene, Theodore M. The Arts & the Art of Criticism. LC 73-16391. 690p. 1973. Repr. of 1947 ed. 27.50x (ISBN 0-87752-162-X). Gordian.

Greene, Theodore M., ed. Meaning of the Humanities. LC 73-86020. (Essay & General Literature Index Reprint Ser.). 1969. Repr. of 1938 ed. 21.00x (ISBN 0-8046-0562-9, Pub. by Kennikat). Assoc Faculty Pr.

Greene, Thomas H. Comparative Revolutionary Movements: Search for Theory & Justice. 2nd ed. LC 83-9776. 224p. 1984. 14.95 (ISBN 0-13-154203-6). P-H.

--The Descent from Heaven: A Study in Epic Continuity. LC 63-7934. pap. 111.00 (ISBN 0-317-29582-9, 2021999). Bks Demand UMI.

Greene, Thomas M. The Light in Troy: Imitation & Discovery in Renaissance Poetry. LC 81-21816. (Elizabethan Club Ser.: No. 7). 368p. 1982. 28.50x (ISBN 0-300-02765-6). Yale U Pr.

Greene, Tom, ed. see Barham, Martha.

Greene, Vaughn. Diving for Gold. rev. ed. (Illus.). 120p. 1985. pap. 5.95 (ISBN 0-89288-040-6). Maverick.

--The Six Thousand Year Old Space Suit. (Illus.). 116p. 1985. 5.95 (ISBN 0-8048-1311-6). V Greene.

Greene, Vaughn M. Astronauts of Ancient Japan. rev. ed. (Illus.). 400p. 1985. pap. 12.95 (ISBN 0-89288-041-4). Maverick.

--The Six Thousand Year-Old Spacesuit. LC 81-86564. (Illus.). 104p. (Orig.). 1982. pap. 5.95 (ISBN 0-8048-1311-6). Merlin Engine Wks.

Greene, Vaughn M., illus. Astronauts of Ancient Japan. LC 78-78289. (Illus.). 164p. (Orig.). 1978. 7.95 (ISBN 0-318-03043-8). Merlin Engine Wks.

Greene, Victor. For God & Country: The Rise of Polish & Lithuanian Ethnic Consciousness in America, 1860-1910. LC 75-19017. (Illus.). 202p. 1975. 17.50 (ISBN 0-87020-155-7). State Hist Soc Wis.

Greene, Victor, et al, eds. American Immigration Collection: Series 2, 33 Vols. 1970. Repr. 568.50 (ISBN 0-405-00543-1). Ayer Co Pubs.

Greene, Victor R. Slavic Community on Strike: Immigrant Labor in Pennsylvania Anthracite. 1968. 15.95x (ISBN 0-268-00256-8). U of Notre Dame Pr.

Greene, W. T. Parrots in Captivity. (Illus.). 1979. 29.95 (ISBN 0-87666-979-8, H-1018). TFH Pubns.

Greene, Walter H. & Simons-Morton, Bruce G. Introduction to Health Education. (Illus.). 432p. 1984. text ed. write for info. (ISBN 0-02-346600-6). Macmillan.

Greene, Walter H., jt. auth. see Read, Donald A.

Greene, Walter H., et al. Health in the Elementary School: Teaching for Relevance. (Illus.). 1978. write for info. (ISBN 0-02-346590-5). Macmillan.

Greene, Warwick. Letters of Warwick Greene, 1915-28. facsimile ed. Hale, Richard W., ed. LC 77-179522. (Select Bibliographies Reprint Ser). Repr. of 1931 ed. 23.50 (ISBN 0-8369-6651-1). Ayer Co Pubs.

Greene, Wilhelmina F. Exotic Flowers to Color & Identify. (Floralibrary). (Illus.). 48p. (Orig.). 1984. pap. 3.95 (ISBN 0-88045-052-5). Stemmer Hse.

Greene, Wilhelmina F. & Blomquist, Hugo L. Flowers of the South: Native & Exotic. xiv, 208p. 1953. 9.95 (ISBN 0-8078-0635-8). U of NC Pr.

Greene, William B. The Blazing Star, with an Appendix Treating of the Jewish Kabbala. 1977. lib. bdg. 59.95 (ISBN 0-8490-1516-2). Gordon Pr.

--Mutual Banking. 59.95 (ISBN 0-87968-048-2). Gordon Pr.

--Poems of William B. Greene. 1977. lib. bdg. 59.95 (ISBN 0-8490-2447-1). Gordon Pr.

--Socialistic, Communistic, Mutualistic, & Financial Fragments. LC 75-319. (The Radical Tradition in America Ser.). 271p. 1975. Repr. of 1875 ed. 21.00 (ISBN 0-88355-223-X). Hyperion Conn.

--Transcendentalism; bd. with Equality. LC 81-8972. (Repr. of 1849 eds.). 1981. 35.00x (ISBN 0-8201-1366-2). Schol Facsimiles.

Greene, William C. The Achievement of Greece: (A Chapter in Human Experience) 1978. Repr. of 1923 ed. lib. bdg. 45.00 (ISBN 0-8492-4909-0). R West.

--Moira, Fate, Good & Evil in Greek Thought. 12.75 (ISBN 0-8446-0661-8). Peter Smith.

Greene, William C., ed. Scholia Platonica. LC 81-16610. (American Philological Association Monograph Ser.). 1981. pap. 37.50 (ISBN 0-89130-541-6, 40 00 08). Scholars Pr GA.

Greene, William N. Strategies of the Major Oil Companies. Farmer, Richard, ed. LC 84-24076. (Research for Business Decisions Ser.: No. 70). 362p. 1985. 49.95 (ISBN 0-8357-1606-6). UMI Res Pr.

Greene, Yvonne. Little Sister. (Sweet Dreams Ser.). (gr. 11 up). 1981. pap. 2.25 (ISBN 0-553-24319-5). Bantam.

Greene, Zula B. Skimming the Cream: Fifty Years with "Peggy of the Flint Hills". 214p. 1983. 14.95 (ISBN 0-941974-04-9). Baranski Pub Corp.

Greene-Mercier, Marie Z. Salzburg One-Hundred One Zeichnungen. 112p. 1969. pap. 3.50x (ISBN 0-910790-16-7). Intl Bk Co IL.

--Trieste One Hundred One Designi. (Orig., It.). 1969. pap. 3.50x (ISBN 0-910790-17-5). Intl Bk Co IL.

--Venezia One-Hundred-One Disegni. 111p. (Orig.). 1969. pap. 3.50x (ISBN 0-910790-18-3). Intl Bk Co IL.

Greene-Pepper, Dorothy. Hate Poems for X-Lovers, or How to Break up Laughing. 2nd ed. (Illus.). 1980. pap. 8.95 (ISBN 0-8065-0697-0). Woodstock Edns.

Greene Robertson, Merle, ed. First Palenque Round Table, 1973, Part 2. LC 74-83484. (Palenque Round Table Ser.: Vol. II). (Illus.). 143p. (Orig.). 1974. pap. text ed. 15.00x (ISBN 0-292-76465-0, Stevenson Sch). U of Tex Pr.

Greenewalt, C. H., Jr. Ritual Dinners in Early Historic Sardis. (Publications in Classical Studies: Vol. 17). 1978. pap. 18.50x (ISBN 0-520-09563-4). U of Cal Pr.

Greenewalt, Crawford H. The Flight of Birds. LC 75-7170. (Transaction Ser.: Vol. 65, Pt. 4). (Illus.). 1975. pap. 7.00 (ISBN 0-87169-654-1). Am Philos.

Greeney, William J., ed. Utilizing Scientific Information in Environmental Quality Planning: Proceedings of the Symposium Held in Las Vegas, Nevada, Sept. 26-27, 1979. LC 81-68086. (American Water Resources Association, Technical Publications Ser.: No. TPS81-2). (Illus.). pap. 54.00 (ISBN 0-317-09806-3, 2022208). Bks Demand UMI.

Greenfader, Hal. Living Together: And Loving Every (Other) Minute of It. pap. 8.95 (ISBN 0-915677-21-0). Roundtable Pub.

--Living Together... & Loving Every (Other) Minute of It: A Guide to Successful Cohabitation. LC 84-60764. (Illus.). 220p. 1985. 15.95 (ISBN 0-915677-11-3); pap. 8.95. Roundtable Pub.

Greenfeld. Advances in Neprology, Vol. 13. 1984. 59.95 (ISBN 0-8151-4136-X, YBMP). Year Bk Med.

Greenfeld, D., jt. auth. see Pretest Service, Inc. Staff.

Greenfeld, David. The Psychotic Patient: Medication & Psychotherapy. 192p. 1984. 20.00x (ISBN 0-02-912830-7). Free Pr.

Greenfeld, Howard. Bar Mitzvah. LC 81-5104. (Illus.). 32p. 1981. 7.95 (ISBN 0-03-053861-0). HR&W.

--Books: From Writer to Reader. LC 76-15991. (Illus.). (gr. 7 up). 1978. pap. 4.95 (ISBN 0-517-53493-2). Crown.

--Caruso. LC 82-13301. 304p. 1983. 17.95 (ISBN 0-399-12736-4, Putnam). Putnam Pub Group.

--Caruso. (Quality Paperbacks Ser.). (Illus.). 275p. 1984. pap. 9.95 (ISBN 0-306-80215-5). Da Capo.

--Chanukah. LC 76-6527. 1976. 6.95 (ISBN 0-03-015566-5). HR&W.

--Chanukah, Passover, Rosh Hashanah, Yom Kippur. 1982. boxed set 20.00 (ISBN 0-03-057626-1). HR&W.

--Gypsies. LC 77-23746. (Illus.). 160p. (gr. 6 up). 1977. 7.95 (ISBN 0-517-52842-8). Crown.

--Marc Chagall: An Introduction. LC 80-14277. (Illus.). 176p. 1980. Repr. of 1967 ed. 15.95 (ISBN 0-87951-115-X). Overlook Pr.

--Passover. LC 77-13910. (Illus.). 32p. (gr. 3-5). 1978. 6.95 (ISBN 0-03-039921-1). HR&W.

--Purim. LC 82-3058. (Illus.). 32p. (gr. 3-7). 1983. 9.95 (ISBN 0-03-061478-3). HR&W.

--Rosh Hashanah & Yom Kippur. LC 79-4818. (Illus.). (gr. k-4). 1979. 6.95 (ISBN 0-03-044756-9). HR&W.

Greenfeld, Howard, tr. see Memmi, Albert.

Greenfeld, Josh. A Place for Noah. 1978. 10.00 (ISBN 0-03-089896-X). HR&W.

--The Return of Mr. Hollywood. LC 83-45202. 312p. 1984. 15.95 (ISBN 0-385-18407-7). Doubleday.

Greenfeld, et al. An Introduction to the Humanities. 128p. 1984. pap. text ed. 8.95 (ISBN 0-8403-3223-8). Kendall-Hunt.

Greenfield, C., jt. auth. see Stull, E.

Greenfield, Concetta C. Humanist & Scholastic Poetics Twelve Fifty to Fifteen Hundred. LC 76-49779. 498p. 1979. 32.50 (ISBN 0-8387-1991-0). Bucknell U Pr.

Greenfield, Darby. Indonesia: A Traveler's Guide. Incl. Vol. 1 o.p. Java & Sumatra (ISBN 0-902675-46-X); Vol. 2 o.p. Bali & East Indonesia. 1976. 12.50 (ISBN 0-902675-48-6). Oleander Pr.

Greenfield, David, ed. Systemic Ichthyology: A Collection of Readings. 1972. 39.50x (ISBN 0-8422-5024-7); pap. text ed. 17.50x (ISBN 0-8290-0674-5). Irvington.

Greenfield, Edward & Layton, Robert, eds. The Complete Penguin Stereo Record & Cassette Guide. 3rd ed. 1344p. 1985. 12.95 (ISBN 0-14-046682-7). Penguin.

Greenfield, Eloise. Africa Dream. LC 77-5080. (Illus.). (gr. k-4). 1977. 11.49i (ISBN 0-381-90061-4, JD-J). Har-Row.

--Darlene. (Illus.). 32p. (ps). 1980. 8.95 (ISBN 0-416-30701-9, NO.0201). Methuen Inc.

--Daydreamers. (Illus.). 1981. 11.95 (ISBN 0-8037-2137-4, 01160-350); PLB 11.89 (ISBN 0-8037-2134-X). Dial Bks Young.

--Daydreamers. LC 80-27262. (Illus.). 1985. pap. 3.95 (ISBN 0-8037-0167-5). Dial Bks Young.

--Grandmama's Joy. LC 79-11403. (Illus.). 32p. (gr. 2-5). 1980. 9.95 (ISBN 0-399-21064-4, Philomel). Putnam Pub Group.

--Honey, I Love: And Other Love Poems. LC 77-2845. (Illus.). (gr. 1-3). 1978. 8.61i (ISBN 0-690-01334-5); PLB 9.89 (ISBN 0-690-03845-3). Crowell Jr Bks.

--Mary McLeod Bethune. LC 76-11522. (Biography Ser.). (Illus.). (gr. 2-5). 1977. PLB 11.89 (ISBN 0-690-01129-6). Crowell Jr Bks.

--Me & Neesie. LC 74-23078. (Illus.). 40p. (gr. 1-4). 1975. PLB 11.89 (ISBN 0-690-00715-9). Crowell Jr Bks.

--Me & Neesie. LC 74-23078. (Trophy Picture Bk.). (Illus.). 40p. (ps-3). 1984. pap. 3.80i (ISBN 0-06-443057-X, Trophy). HarpJ.

--Paul Robeson. LC 74-13663. (Biography Ser.). (Illus.). (gr. 1-5). 1975. PLB 11.89 (ISBN 0-690-00660-8). Crowell Jr Bks.

--Rosa Parks. LC 72-83782. (Biography Ser.). (Illus.). (gr. 1-5). 1973. PLB 11.89 (ISBN 0-690-71211-1). Crowell Jr Bks.

--She Come Bringing Me That Little Baby Girl. LC 74-8104. (gr. k-3). 1974. PLB 11.49 (ISBN 0-397-31586-4). Lipp Jr Bks.

--Sister. LC 73-22182. (gr. 5-12). 1974. 9.57i (ISBN 0-690-00497-4). Crowell Jr Bks.

Greenfield, Eloise & Little, Lessie J. Childtimes: A Three-Generation Memoir. LC 77-26581. (Illus.). (gr. 5 up). 1979. PLB 10.89 (ISBN 0-690-03875-5). Crowell Jr Bks.

Greenfield, Eloise & Revis, Alesia. Alesia. (Illus.). 80p. (gr. 5 up). 1981. 9.95 (ISBN 0-399-20831-3, Philomel). Putnam Pub Group.

Greenfield, Eloise, jt. auth. see Little, Lessie J.

Greenfield, Eric V. German Grammar. 3rd ed. (Orig., Ger.). 1968. pap. 4.95 (ISBN 0-06-460034-3, CO 34, COS). B&N NY.

--Spanish Grammar. 4th ed. (Orig.). 1972. pap. 4.95 (ISBN 0-06-460042-4, CO 42, COS). B&N NY.

Greenfield, Eric V., jt. auth. see D'Eca, Raul.

Greenfield, Freddie. The Amusement Business. 1976. pap. 3.00 (ISBN 0-915480-07-7). Good Gay.

Greenfield, George B. Radiology of Bone Diseases. 3rd ed. (Illus.). 736p. 1980. text ed. 74.50 (ISBN 0-397-50432-2, 65-05796, Lippincott Medical). Lippincott.

Greenfield, George B. & Hubbard, Lincoln B. Computers in Radiology. (Illus.). 200p. 1984. text ed. 30.00 (ISBN 0-443-08349-5). Churchill.

Greenfield, Guy. We Need Each Other. 1984. 8.95 (ISBN 0-8010-3799-9); pap. 5.95 (ISBN 0-8010-3800-6). Baker Bk.

--The Wounded Parent. LC 82-70463. 128p. 1982. 7.95 (ISBN 0-8010-3778-6); pap. 4.95 (ISBN 0-8010-3779-4). Baker Bk.

Greenfield, Harry, ed. Theory for Economic Efficiency: Essays in Honor of Abba P. Lerner. 1979. text ed. 40.00x (ISBN 0-262-07074-X). MIT Pr.

Greenfield, Harry I. Allied Health Manpower: Trends & Prospectives. LC 75-76249. (Illus.). 195p. 1969. 29.00x (ISBN 0-231-03226-9). Columbia U Pr.

--Manpower & the Growth of Producer Services. LC 66-28265. 144p. 1967. 26.00x (ISBN 0-231-03028-2). Columbia U Pr.

Greenfield, Harry I., jt. auth. see Fabozzi, Frank J.

Greenfield, Howard, jt. auth. see Jones, Jo Lynne.

Greenfield, Irving. Agent Out of Place. (Illus.). 304p. pap. 3.25 (ISBN 0-441-01027-X, Pub. by Charter Bks). Ace Bks.

--Barracuda. 256p. 1982. pap. 2.75 (ISBN 0-441-04900-1, Pub. by Charter Bks). Ace Bks.

--Barracuda. LC 77-90660. 1978. 8.95 (ISBN 0-87795-188-8). Arbor Hse.

--Doesn't Everyone. 1977. pap. 1.95 (ISBN 0-532-19147-1). Woodhill.

--The Face of Him. 1976. pap. 1.50 (ISBN 0-532-15202-6). Woodhill.

--Fort Bliss. 1977. pap. 1.95 (ISBN 0-685-89534-3). Woodhill.

--Star Trail. 1977. pap. 1.50 (ISBN 0-532-15276-X). Woodhill.

--Who Knows. 1977. pap. 1.95 (ISBN 0-532-19151-X). Woodhill.

Greenfield, Irving A. Depth Force. pap. 2.95 (ISBN 0-8217-1355-8). Zebra.

--Depth Force, No. 3: Bloody Seas. 1985. pap. 2.50 (ISBN 0-8217-1541-0). Zebra.

--Depth Force, No. 4: Battle Stations. 1985. pap. 2.50 (ISBN 0-8217-1627-1). Zebra.

--Julius Caesar Is Alive & Well. 1977. pap. 1.95 (ISBN 0-532-19160-9). Woodhill.

--Love Scent. 1978. pap. 1.75 (ISBN 0-532-17174-8). Woodhill.

--No Better World. LC 82-82117. 304p. 1982. pap. 2.95 (ISBN 0-86721-219-5). Jove Pubns.

--Tagget. LC 78-72920. 1979. 9.95 (ISBN 0-87795-209-4). Arbor Hse.

--Tagget. 224p. 1981. pap. 2.25 (ISBN 0-345-28802-5). Ballantine.

Greenfield, J. D. Microprocessor Handbook. (Electrical & Electronics Technology Handbook Ser.). 608p. 39.95 (ISBN 0-471-08791-2). Wiley.

Greenfield, Jane. Books, Their Care & Repair. (Illus.). 204p. 1983. 22.00 (ISBN 0-8242-0695-9). Wilson.

Greenfield, Jeff. Television: The First Fifty Years. (Illus.). 1977. 50.00 (ISBN 0-8109-1651-7). Abrams.

--Tiny Giant: Nate Archibald. LC 75-42035. (Sports Profiles). (Illus.). 48p. (gr. 4-11). 1976. PLB 13.31 (ISBN 0-8172-0124-6). Raintree Pubs.

Greenfield, Joel I., jt. auth. see Blonien, Rodney.

Greenfield, Joseph D. Practical Digital Design Using ICs. 2nd ed. LC 82-10931. (Electronic Technology Ser.). 717p. 1983. 31.95 (ISBN 0-471-05791-6). Wiley.

Greenfield, Joseph D. & Wray, William C. Using Microprocessors & Microcomputers: The 6800 Family. LC 80-18090. (Electronic Technology Ser.: No. 1-325). 460p. 1981. 32.95 (ISBN 0-471-02727-8); avail. solution manual (ISBN 0-471-09394-7). Wiley.

Greenfield, Josh. A Place for Noah. 302p. 1979. pap. 2.50 (ISBN 0-671-41909-9). WSP.

Greenfield, Kent R. American Strategy in World War II: A Reconsideration. LC 78-12870. 1979. Repr. of 1963 ed. lib. bdg. 25.00x (ISBN 0-313-21175-2, GRAW). Greenwood.

--American Strategy in World War II: A Reconsideration. LC 82-14881. 158p. 1982. pap. 7.50 (ISBN 0-89874-557-8). Krieger.

--American Strategy in World War II: A Reconsideration. LC 63-19554. Repr. of 1963 ed. 39.30 (ISBN 0-8357-9263-3, 2001185). Bks Demand UMI.

--Economics & Liberalism in the Risorgimento: A Study of Nationalism in Lombardy, 1814-1848. LC 78-17674. 1978. Repr. of 1965 ed. lib. bdg. 22.25x (ISBN 0-313-20510-8, GREL). Greenwood.

--Historian & the Army. LC 71-115869. 1971. Repr. of 1954 ed. 16.50x (ISBN 0-8046-1123-8, Pub. by Kennikat). Assoc Faculty Pr.

--The Museum, Its First Half Century: Annual I. (Illus.). 1968. pap. 7.50 (ISBN 0-912298-25-1). Baltimore Mus.

--Sumptuary Law in Nuernberg: A Study in Paternal Government. LC 78-63964. (Johns Hopkins University. Studies in the Social Sciences. Thirty-Sixth Ser. 1918: 2). Repr. of 1918 ed. 16.50 (ISBN 0-404-61211-3). AMS Pr.

Greenfield, Larry D. & Uszler, J. Michael, eds. Nuclear Medicine in Clinical Practice: Selective Correlation with Ultrasound & Computerized Tomography. LC 81-23155. (Illus.). 413p. 1982. 47.50x (ISBN 0-89573-110-X). VCH Pubs.

Greenfield, Lazar J. Complications in Surgery & Trauma. (Illus.). 960p. 1983. text ed. 75.00 (ISBN 0-397-50521-3, 65-06679, Lippincott Medical). Lippincott.

--Surgery in the Aged. LC 75-8177. (Major Problems in Clinical Surgery Ser.: Vol. 17). pap. 40.80 (ISBN 0-317-26435-4, 2024990). Bks Demand UMI.

Greenfield, Lazar J., ed. Surgery in the Aged. LC 75-8177. (Major Problems in Clinical Surgery: Vol. 17). (Illus.). 151p. 1975. text ed. 15.00 (ISBN 0-7216-4250-0). Saunders.

Greenfield, Lee T. How to Capture the Profit Potential of Option Trading & the Magical Device of Stock Market Leverage. (Illus.). 138p. 1981. 56.75x (ISBN 0-86654-010-5). Inst Econ Finan.

Greenfield, Louise. Poems for Drinkers & Other Thinkers. (Contemporary Poets of Dorrance Ser.). 64p. 1983. 6.95 (ISBN 0-8059-2879-0). Dorrance.

Greenfield, Louise S. Sobering Thoughts. 68p. 1984. 6.95 (ISBN 0-8059-2957-6). Dorrance.

Greenfield, Margaret. Medicare & Medicaid: The Nineteen Sixty-Five & Nineteen Sixty-Seven Social Security Amendments. LC 82-25157. x, 143p. 1983. Repr. of 1968 ed. lib. bdg. 25.00x (ISBN 0-313-23841-3, GRME). Greenwood.

--Meeting the Costs of Health Care: The Bay Area Experience & the National Issues. LC 72-5657. 182p. 1972. pap. 6.50x (ISBN 0-87772-086-X). Inst Gov Stud Berk.

Greenfield, Marie. Elvis, Legend of Love. 1981. 10.00 (ISBN 0-936848-01-4). Palos Verdes.

Greenfield, Michael, ed. see Thackery, William M.

Greenfield, Michael M. Consumer Transactions. LC 83-1523. (University Casebook Ser.). 733p. 1983. text ed. 26.00 (ISBN 0-88277-110-8); Statutory Suppl. 12.50 (ISBN 0-88277-114-0); write for info. tchr's guide (ISBN 0-88277-167-1). Foundation Pr.

Greenfield, Natalee. First Do No Harm. 176p. 1981. pap. 1.95 (ISBN 0-448-17227-5, Pub. by Tempo). Ace Bks.

Greenfield, Norman S. & Lewis, William C., eds. Psychoanalysis & Current Biological Thought. LC 64-7725. 1965. pap. 97.50 (ISBN 0-317-08160-8, 2021133). Bks Demand UMI.

Greenfield, Norman S., jt. ed. see Abroms, Gene M.

Greenfield, Norman S., jt. ed. see Roessler, Robert.

Greenfield, Patricia. Mind & Media: The Effects of Television, Video Games, & Computers. (The Developing Child Ser.). (Illus.). 232p. 1984. text ed. 12.50x (ISBN 0-674-57620-9); pap. 4.95 (ISBN 0-674-57621-7). Harvard U Pr.

Greenfield, Patricia & Tronick, Edward. Infant Curriculum. 1980. pap. text ed. 11.35x (ISBN 0-673-16378-4). Scott F.

Greenfield, Richard. One Shot. 1977. pap. 1.75 (ISBN 0-532-17156-X). Woodhill.

--The Wretched of the Horn: Forgotten Refugees in Black Africa. LC 80-13204. (Illus.). 144p. (Orig.). 1985. pap. 11.95x (ISBN 0-936508-01-9). Barber Pr.

Greenfield, Robert. Temple. 480p. 1983. 15.95 (ISBN 0-671-44735-1). Summit Bks.

--Temple. 432p. 1984. pap. 4.95 (ISBN 0-440-38488-5, LFL). Dell.

Greenfield, Roy, jt. auth. see Cohen, Jerrold.

Greenfield, S. E. The Architecture of Microcomputers. 366p. 1980. text ed. 27.95 (ISBN 0-316-32669-0). Little.

--The Architecture of Microcomputers, Vol. II. 1983. pap. text ed. 12.95 (ISBN 0-316-32675-5). Little.

--The Architecture of Microcomputers: Fundamentals, Vol. I. 1983. 15.95 (ISBN 0-316-32674-7). Little.

Greenfield, Sidney M. English Rustics in Black Skin: A Study of Modern Family Forms in a Pre-Industrialized Society. 1966. 9.95x (ISBN 0-8084-0121-1); pap. 6.95x (ISBN 0-8084-0122-X). New Coll U Pr.

Greenfield, Sidney M., jt. ed. see Strickon, Arnold.

Greenfield, Sidney M., et al, eds. Entrepreneurs in Cultural Context. LC 78-21433. (School of American Research Advanced Seminar Ser.). 1979. 25.00x (ISBN 0-8263-0504-0). U of NM Pr.

Greenfield, Stanley B. A Critical History of Old English Literature. LC 65-19516. (Gotham Library). (Orig.). 1965. 25.00x (ISBN 0-8147-0170-1); pap. 12.50x (ISBN 0-8147-2950-9). NYU Pr.

Greenfield, Stanley B. & Calder, Daniel G. A New Critical History of Old English Literature. rev. ed. (Illus.). 352p. 1986. text ed. 30.00x (ISBN 0-8147-3002-7). NYU Pr.

Greenfield, Stanley B. & Robinson, Fred C. Bibliography of Publications on Old English Literature to the End of Nineteen Seventy-Two. LC 78-4989. 1980. pap. 30.00 (ISBN 0-8020-6505-8). U of Toronto Pr.

Greenfield, Stanley B. & Weatherhead, A. Kingsley, eds. Poem: An Anthology. 2nd ed. LC 68-15582. (Orig.). 1972. pap. text ed. 18.95 (ISBN 0-13-684431-6). P-H.

Greenfield, Stanley B., tr. A Readable "Beowulf". The Old English Epic Newly Translated. LC 81-16933. (Illus.). 173p. 1982. pap. 10.95x (ISBN 0-8093-1060-0). S Ill U Pr.

Greenfield, Stuart B. Invitation to Modula, No. 2. (Illus.). 280p. 1985. 29.95 (ISBN 0-317-31163-8). Van Nos Reinhold.

--Invitation to MODULA-2. (Illus.). 280p. 1985. text ed. 29.95 (ISBN 0-89433-273-2). Petrocelli.

Greenfield, Sumner M., ed. La Generacion de 1898 ante Espana: Antologia de literatura de temas nacionales y universales. LC 80-80146. 300p. 1981. pap. 25.00 (ISBN 0-89295-013-7). Society Sp & Sp-Am.

Greenfield, Thelma N. The Eye of Judgment: Reading the New Arcadia. LC 81-65056. 232p. 1982. 24.50 (ISBN 0-8387-5025-7). Bucknell U Pr.

--The Induction in Elizabethan Drama. LC 74-11155. 1970. 6.00 (ISBN 0-87114-053-5). U of Oreg Bks.

Greenfield, Thelma N., jt. ed. see McNeir, Waldo F.

Greenfield, Thomas A. Work & the Work Ethic in American Drama, 1920-1970. LC 82-4909. 272p. 1982. 22.00 (ISBN 0-8262-0374-4). U of Mo Pr.

Greenfield Tool Company. Eighteen Fifty-Four Price List of Joiners' Bench Planes & Moulding Tools. Roberts, Kenneth D., ed. 32p. 1981. pap. 2.50 (ISBN 0-913602-43-4). K Roberts.

Greenfield, William. The Greek-English Lexicon to the New Testament. 216p. 1981. pap. 5.95 (ISBN 0-310-20351-1). Zondervan.

Greenfield, William, jt. auth. see Blumberg, Arthur.

Greengard, Olga, ed. Biochemical Bases of the Development of Physiological Functions. (Enzyme: Vol. 15, Nos. 1-6). (Illus.). 386p. 1974. pap. 41.00 (ISBN 3-8055-1713-0). S Karger.

Greengard, P. & Costa, E., eds. Role of Cyclic AMP in Cell Function. LC 73-84113. (Advances in Biochemical Psychopharmacology Ser.: Vol. 3). 386p. 1970. 35.50 (ISBN 0-911216-15-4). Raven.

Greengard, P. & Robison, G. A., eds. Advances in Cyclic Nucleotide Research, Vol. 6. LC 71-181305. 368p. 1975. 50.50 (ISBN 0-89004-042-7). Raven.

Greengard, Paul. Cyclic Nucleotides, Phosphorylated Proteins, & Neuronal Function. LC 78-66349. (Distinguished Lecture Series of the Society of General Physiologists: Vol. 1). 134p. 1978. 22.00 (ISBN 0-89004-281-0). Raven.

Greengard, Paul, jt. auth. see Nestler, Erie J.

Greengard, Paul & Robison, Alan, eds. Advances in Cyclic Nucleotide Research, Vol. 13. 352p. 1980. text ed. 54.50 (ISBN 0-89004-471-6). Raven.

Greengard, Paul & Robison, G. Alan, eds. Advances in Cyclic Nucleotide Research, Vol. 3. 416p. 1973. text ed. 50.50 (ISBN 0-911216-38-3). Raven.

--Advances in Cyclic Nucleotide Research, Vol. 4. LC 71-181305. 498p. 1974. 57.00 (ISBN 0-911216-76-6). Raven.

--Advances in Cyclic Nucleotide Research, Vol. 11. LC 71-181305. 397p. 1979. text ed. 57.00 (ISBN 0-89004-363-9). Raven.

Greengard, Paul, et al, eds. Advances in Cyclic Nucleotide & Protein Phosphorylation Research, Vol. 18. 298p. 1984. text ed. 54.50 (ISBN 0-88167-020-0). Raven.

--Cyclic Nucleotides & Protein Phosphorylation: Fifth International Conference, Milan, Italy. (Advances in Cyclic Nucleotide & Protein Phosphorylation Research). (Illus.). 722p. 1984. Vol. 17. text ed. 104.50 (ISBN 0-89004-349-3); Vol. 17A-Abstracts, 192. pap. 21.50 (ISBN 0-89004-409-0). Raven.

--New Assay Methods for Cyclic Nucleotides. (Advances in Cyclic Nucleotide Research Ser.: Vol. 2). 145p. 1972. text ed. 27.50 (ISBN 0-911216-21-9). Raven.

Greengard, Paul G. & Robison, Alan, eds. Advances in Cyclic Nucleotide Research, Vol. 15. 532p. 1983. text ed. 78.00 (ISBN 0-89004-881-9). Raven.

Greengarten, I. M. Thomas Hill Green & the Development of Liberal-Democratic Thought. 194p. 1981. 22.50x (ISBN 0-8020-5503-6). U of Toronto Pr.

Greengenes, ed. see Cervantes, Jorge.

Greenglass, E. R. A World of Difference: Gender Roles in Perspective. 350p. 1982. pap. 15.95 (ISBN 0-471-79949-1). Wiley.

Greengold, Jane. What I Know about Sam. Piche, Thomas, Jr., ed. LC 85-70892. (Illus.). 36p. 1985. pap. text ed. write for info. (ISBN 0-914407-03-1). Everson Mus.

Greengrass, M., jt. ed. see Potter, G. R.

Greengrass, Mark. France in the Age of Henri IV: The Struggle for Stability. (Studies in Modern History). (Illus.). 288p. 1984. pap. text ed. 14.95 (ISBN 0-582-49251-3). Longman.

Greenhalgh, Peter. West African Diamonds: An Economic History 1919-83. LC 85-268. 384p. 1985. 32.50 (ISBN 0-7190-1763-7, Pub. by Manchester Univ Pr). Longwood Pub Group.

Greenhalgh, Anne M. A Cordance to Elizabeth Bishop's Poetry. LC 84-48021. (Reference Library of Humanities). 890p. 1984. lib. bdg. 115.00 (ISBN 0-8240-8909-X). Garland Pub.

Greenhalgh, C. A., ed. The Causes of Unemployment. 1983. pap. 16.95x (ISBN 0-19-828484-5). Oxford U Pr.

Greenhalgh, G. The Necessity of Nuclear Power. 220p. 1980. 33.00x (ISBN 0-686-64708-4, Pub. by Graham & Trotman England). State Mutual Bk.

Greenhalgh, Geoffrey. The Necessity for Nuclear Power. 260p. 1981. pap. 19.00x (ISBN 0-8448-1409-1). Crane-Russak Co.

Greenhalgh, John. School Site Budgeting: Decentralized School Management. (Illus.). 206p. 1984. lib. bdg. 22.00 (ISBN 0-8191-3774-X); pap. text ed. 11.50 (ISBN 0-8191-3775-8). U Pr of Amer.

Greenhalgh, Kenneth. The Management of Microprocessors. 1979. 99.00x (ISBN 0-86176-030-1, Pub. by MCB Pubns). State Mutual Bk.

Greenhalgh, Marilyn E., jt. auth. see Gibbs, Dudley.

Greenhalgh, Michael. The Classical Tradition in Art. (Illus.). 272p. 1979. 34.00x (ISBN 0-7156-1277-8, BPA-02643, Pub. by Duckworth England); pap. 9.95x (ISBN 0-7156-1300-6, BPA-02553, Pub. by Duckworth England). Biblio Dist.

--The Classical Tradition in Art. LC 81-48063. (Icon Editions Ser.). (Illus.). 271p. 1982. 10.95 (ISBN 0-06-430118-4, IN-118). Har-Row.

--Donatello & His Sources. (Illus.). 200p. 1982. text ed. 54.50x (ISBN 0-8419-0827-3). Holmes & Meier.

Greenhalgh, Michael & Megaw, Vincent, eds. Art in Society: Studies in Style, Culture & Aesthetics. LC 78-69954. 1978. 40.00 (ISBN 0-312-05267-7). St Martin.

Greenhalgh, P. A. Early Greek Warfare. LC 72-87437. 228p. 1973. 42.50 (ISBN 0-521-20056-3). Cambridge U Pr.

Greenhalgh, Peter. Pompey: The Republican Prince. LC 81-708. (Illus.). 336p. 1982. text ed. 23.00x (ISBN 0-8262-0356-6). U of Mo Pr.

--Pompey, Vol. I: The Roman Alexander. LC 80-54460. 288p. 1981. text ed. 23.00 (ISBN 0-8262-0335-3). U of Mo Pr.

Greenhalgh, Peter & Eliopoulos, Edward. Deep into Mani: Journey to the Southern Tip of Greece. LC 84-25916. (Illus.). 200p. 1985. 19.95 (ISBN 0-571-13523-4); pap. 7.95 (ISBN 0-571-13524-2). Faber & Faber.

Greenhalgh, R. M. Hormones & Vascular Disease. 346p. text ed. cancelled (ISBN 0-272-79622-0, Pub. by Pitman Bks Ltd UK). Pitman Pub MA.

--Smoking & Arterial Disease. 320p. text ed. cancelled (ISBN 0-272-79604-2, Pub. by Pitman Bks Ltd UK). Pitman Pub MA.

Greenhalgh, R. M., ed. Smoking & Arterial Disease. 315p. 1981. text ed. 57.95x (ISBN 0-8464-1215-2). Beekman Pubs.

Greenhalgh, Roger M. & Rose, F. Clifford. Progress in Stroke Research, Vol. 1. (Illus.). 1980. 48.95 (ISBN 0-8151-3937-3). Year Bk Med.

--Progress in Stroke Research, No. 2. 526p. 1983. text ed. 67.50 (ISBN 0-272-79764-2, Pub. by Pitman Bks Ltd UK). Urban & S.

Greenhalgh, Roger M., ed. Hormones & Vascular Disease. 345p. 1981. text ed. 57.95x (ISBN 0-8464-1222-5). Beekman Pubs.

Greenhalgh, Sylvia H. Snow on the Roses. 1985. 6.50 (ISBN 0-8062-2514-9). Carlton.

Greenhall, Agnes, jt. ed. see Levey, Judith S.

Greenhall, Ken. Childgrave. 304p. (Orig.). 1982. pap. 3.50 (ISBN 0-671-42161-1). PB.

Greenhall, Vladimir. The Art Book of Pencil Sketching. (Illus.). 101p. 1984. 49.85x (ISBN 0-86650-098-7). Gloucester Art.

Greenham, Richard. The Works, Examined, Corrected & Published: By H. Holland. LC 72-5999. (English Experience Ser.: No. 524). 496p. 1973. Repr. of 1599 ed. 70.00 (ISBN 90-221-0524-5). Walter J Johnson.

Greenhaw, Lois. Backward Glances. (Orig.). 1980. pap. text ed. 2.25 (ISBN 0-505-51590-3, Pub. by Tower Bks). Dorchester Pub Co.

Greenhaw, Wayne. Elephants in the Cottonfields: Ronald Reagan & the New Republican South. 320p. 1982. 15.75 (ISBN 0-02-545500-1). Macmillan.

--Flying High: Inside Big-Time Drug Smuggling. 256p. 1984. 15.95 (ISBN 0-396-08360-9). Dodd.

Greenhill, Basil. Archaeology of the Boat: A New Introductory Study. LC 76-22928. (Illus.). 1976. 27.00x (ISBN 0-8195-5002-7). Wesleyan U Pr.

--James Cook: The Opening of the Pacific. (Pendragon Americana). (Illus.). 1978. pap. 2.95 (ISBN 0-685-23968-3). Pendragon Ltd.

--The Life & Death of the Merchant Sailing Ships. (The Ship Series, National Maritime Museum). (Illus.). 1980. 10.95 (ISBN 0-11-290317-7). Sheridan.

--A Quayside Camera, 1845-1917. LC 74-20469. (Illus.). 112p. 1975. 17.50x (ISBN 0-8195-4088-9). Wesleyan U Pr.

--Schooners: From Old Photographs. LC 79-91086. (Illus.). 168p. 1980. 27.95 (ISBN 0-87021-960-X). Naval Inst Pr.

--Schooners from Old Photographs. (Illus.). 168p. 1980. 27.95 (ISBN 0-87021-960-X); bulk rates avail. Naval Inst Pr.

Greenhill, Basil & Stonham, Denis. Seafaring Under Sail. (Illus.). 192p. 1982. 18.95 (ISBN 0-87021-876-X); bulk rates avail. Naval Inst Pr.

Greenhill, Basil & Stonham, Dennis. Seafaring under Sail. LC 81-83483. 192p. 1981. 18.95 (ISBN 0-87021-876-X). Naval Inst Pr.

Greenhill, Basil, ed. The National Maritime Museum. (Illus.). 144p. 1982. (Pub. by Sotheby Pubns England); pap. 12.50 (Pub. by Sotheby Pubns England). Biblio Dist.

--The National Maritime Museum. 144p. 1982. 50.00x (ISBN 0-85667-130-4, Pub. by Scala Wilson Chambers England). State Mutual Bk.

--The National Maritime Museum. (Illus.). 144p. 1985. pap. 13.95 (ISBN 0-85667-133-9). Scala Books.

Greenhill, George. Gyroscopic Theory. LC 66-30616. 22.50 (ISBN 0-8284-0205-1). Chelsea Pub.

Greenhill, Lawrence & Shopsin, Baron, eds. Psychobiology of Childhood. 288p. 1984. text ed. 40.00 (ISBN 0-89335-192-X). SP Med & Sci Bks.

Greenhill, Maurice H. & Gralnick, Alexander, eds. Psychopharmacology & Psychotherapy. 1982. text ed. 29.95 (ISBN 0-02-912780-7). Free Pr.

Greenhill, Ralph. Engineer's Witness: A Photographic Panorama of Nineteenth Century Engineering Triumphs. LC 84-48299. 208p. 1985. 35.00 (ISBN 0-87923-550-0). Godine.

--Spanning Niagara: The International Bridges, 1848-1962. (Illus.). 48p. (Orig.). 1985. pap. 10.00 (ISBN 0-295-96235-6). U of Wash Pr.

Greenhill, Richard. Employee Remuneration & Profit Sharing. 210p. (Orig.). 1980. 27.00 (ISBN 0-85941-123-0). Woodhead-Faulkner.

Greenhill, Richard, jt. auth. see Fyson, Nance L.

Greenhood, David. Mapping. rev. ed. LC 63-20905. 1964. 20.00x (ISBN 0-226-30696-8); pap. 9.95 (ISBN 0-226-30697-6, P521, Phoen). U of Chicago Pr.

Greenhouse, Bernard L. Political Postcards: A Price Guide 1900-1980. 109p. 1985. pap. 12.95 (ISBN 0-317-29288-9, 99104). Wallace-Homestead.

Greenhouse, Herbert B. The Astral Journey. 1976. pap. 1.95 (ISBN 0-380-00611-1, 28928). Avon.

Greenhowe, Jean. Costumes for Nursery Tale Characters. LC 75-23444. (Illus.). 87p. 1976. 10.95 (ISBN 0-8238-0199-3). Plays.

--Cuddly Toys & Dolls. LC 83-5052. (Illus.). 140p. 1983. 17.95 (ISBN 0-8069-5496-5); pap. 8.95 (ISBN 0-8069-7762-0). Sterling.

--Making a Victorian Dolls' House. LC 78-53796. 1978. 9.95 (ISBN 0-8008-5055-6). Taplinger.

--Making a Victorian Doll's House. (Illus.). 192p. 1985. pap. 8.95 (ISBN 0-7134-0871-5, Pub. by Batsford England). David & Charles.

--Making Mascot Dolls. (Illus.). 120p. 1981. 19.95 (ISBN 0-7134-2177-0, Pub. by Batsford England). David & Charles.

--Making Miniature Toys & Dolls. (Illus.). 120p. 1985. pap. 9.95 (ISBN 0-7134-0799-9, Pub. by Batsford England). David & Charles.

--Making Musical Miniatures. (Illus.). 120p. 1980. 19.95 (ISBN 0-7134-1631-9, Pub. by Batsford England). David & Charles.

--Small Cuddly Toys. (Illus.). 120p. 1985. 16.95 (ISBN 0-8069-5710-7); pap. 7.95 (ISBN 0-8069-7988-7). Sterling.

--Stage Costumes for Girls. LC 75-23205. (Illus.). 1976. 10.95 (ISBN 0-8238-0196-9). Plays.

Greenhut, Frederic A., II. The Tibetan Frontiers Question: From Curzon to the Colombo Conference. (Illus.). 178p. 1982. 24.95x (ISBN 0-940500-71-X, Pub by S Chand India). Asia Bk Corp.

Greenhut, M. L. & Stewart, Charles T., Jr. From Basic Economics to Supply Side Economics. (Illus.). 280p. (Orig.). 1984. lib. bdg. 22.50 (ISBN 0-8191-3426-0, Co-pub. by Pol Eco Res); pap. text ed. 10.25 (ISBN 0-8191-3427-9). U Pr of Amer.

Greenhut, Melvin L. Plant Location in Theory & in Practice: The Economics of Space. LC 81-20230. xiii, 338p. 1982. Repr. of 1956 ed. lib. bdg. 35.00x (ISBN 0-313-23338-1, GRPL). Greenwood.

--A Theory of the Firm in Economic Space. LC 71-112946. (Illus.). 389p. 1974. Repr. of 1970 ed. text ed. 20.00x (ISBN 0-914872-00-1). Austin Pr.

Greenhut, Melvin L. & Ohta, Hiroshi. Theory of Spatial Pricing & Market Areas. LC 74-83786. x, 265p. 1975. 22.75 (ISBN 0-8223-0333-7). Duke.

Greenia, Mark. Professional Word Processing in Business & Legal Environments. 1985. pap. text ed. 19.95 (ISBN 0-8359-5773-X). Reston.

Greenidge, A. H. Roman Public Life. LC 72-77323. 483p. 1970. Repr. of 1910 ed. lib. bdg. 25.00 (ISBN 0-8154-0320-8). Cooper Sq.

Greenidge, A. H. & Clay, A. M., eds. Sources for Roman History: 133-70 B.C. 2nd ed. 1960. 21.95x (ISBN 0-19-814242-0). Oxford U Pr.

Greenidge, Abel. A Handbook of Greek Constitutional History. 59.95 (ISBN 0-8490-0277-X). Gordon Pr.

Greening, J R. Fundamentals of Radiation Dosimetry. 2nd ed. (Medical Physics Handbooks: No. 15). 160p. 1985. pap. 25.00 (ISBN 0-85274-789-6, Pub. by A Hilger England). Heyden.

Greening, J. R., ed. Medical Physics: Proceedings of the International School of Physics Course, LXXCI, Varenna, Italy, June 25 - July 7, 1979. (Enrico Fermi International Summer School of Physics Ser.: Vol. 76). 526p. 1982. 102.25 (ISBN 0-444-85457-6, North Holland). Elsevier.

Greening, John R. Fundamentals of Radiation Dosimetry. (Medical Physics Handbook: No. 6). 190p. 1981. 40.00 (ISBN 0-9960020-5-7, Pub. by A Hilger England). Heyden.

Greening, Roy R. & Heslep, J. Haynes. The Chest. (Illus.). 1973. 58.50 (ISBN 0-8151-3962-4). Year Bk Med.

Greenkorn. Flow Phenomena. (Energy, Power & Environment Ser.). 520p. 1983. 75.00 (ISBN 0-8247-1861-5). Dekker.

Greenkorn, R. A., jt. auth. see Chao, K. C.

Greenland, Colin. The Entropy Exhibition: Michael Moorcock & the British "New Wave" in Science Fiction. 244p. 1983. 26.95x (ISBN 0-7100-9310-1). Routledge & Kegan.

Greenland, Cyril. Mental Illness & Civil Liberties. 126p. 1970. pap. text ed. 5.00 (ISBN 0-7135-1826-X, Pub. by Bedford England). Brookfield Pub Co.

Greenland, D. J., ed. Characterization of Soils in Relation to Their Classification & Management for Crop Productions. (Illus.). 1981. 84.00x (ISBN 0-19-854538-X). Oxford U Pr.

Greenland, D. J. & Hayes, M. H., eds. The Chemistry of Soil Constituents. LC 77-18552. 508p. 1978. 126.95 (ISBN 0-471-99619-X, Pub. by Wiley-Interscience). Wiley.

--The Chemistry of Soil Processes. LC 79-42908. 714p. 1981. 126.95 (ISBN 0-471-27693-6, Pub. by Wiley-Interscience). Wiley.

Greenland, D. J. & Lal, R., eds. Soil Conservation & Management in the Humid Tropics. LC 76-8908. 283p. 1977. 84.95 (ISBN 0-471-99473-1, Pub. by Wiley-Interscience). Wiley.

Greenland, D. J., jt. ed. see Lal, R.

Greenland, David. Guidelines for Modern Resource Management. 224p. 1983. pap. text ed. 13.50 (ISBN 0-675-20004-0). Merrill.

Greenlaw, Barry A. New England Furniture at Williamsburg. LC 73-90536. (Decorative Arts Ser). (Illus.). 195p. (Orig.). 1974. pap. 7.95 (ISBN 0-87935-019-9). Williamsburg.

--New England Furniture at Williamsburg. abr. ed. LC 74-18017. (Decorative Arts Ser). (Illus.). 20p. 1974. pap. 1.25 (ISBN 0-87935-022-9). Williamsburg.

--New England Furniture at Williamsburg. LC 73-90536. (The Williamsburg Decorative Arts Ser.). pap. 51.00 (ISBN 0-317-29065-7, 2017829). Bks Demand UMI.

Greenlaw, Edwin. An Outline of the Literature of the English Renaissance. LC 72-187102. 1916. lib. bdg. 10.00 (ISBN 0-8414-0529-8). Folcroft.

--Studies in Spenser's Historical Allegory. 1978. Repr. of 1932 ed. lib. bdg. 30.00 (ISBN 0-8414-4463-3). Folcroft.

Greenlaw, Edwin, ed. see Spenser, Edmund, et al.

Greenlaw, Edwin see Spenser, Edmund, et al.

Greenlaw, Edwin A. A Syllabus of English Literature. 1977. Repr. of 1914 ed. lib. bdg. 25.00 (ISBN 0-8492-0916-1). R West.

Greenlaw, M. Jean, jt. auth. see Wendelin, Karla H.

Greenlaw, Martha, ed. see Coenen, George L.

Greenlaw, Martha, jt. ed. see Leecraft, Jodie.

Greenlaw, P. S. & Hottenstein, M. P. Prosim: A Production Management Simulation. 1969. pap. text ed. 14.50 scp (ISBN 0-7002-2224-3, HarpC); instructor's manual avail. (ISBN 0-06-362455-9); scp 360 computer deck 45.95 (ISBN 0-352-07309-8); scp 700-7000 computer deck 23.50 (ISBN 0-352-07310-1). Har-Row.

Greenlaw, Patricia. Colorado Woman. (Orig.). 1980. pap. text ed. 2.50 (ISBN 0-505-51589-X, Pub. by Tower Bks). Dorchester Pub Co.

Greenlaw, Paul S. & Kniffin, Fred W. Marksim: A Marketing Decision Simulation. 1964. pap. text ed. 12.95 scp (ISBN 0-7002-2040-2, HarpC); 25.50, scp 1620 computer deck (ISBN 0-352-05307-0); 19.95, scp 700-7000 computer deck (ISBN 0-352-05305-4); 23.50, scp 360 computer deck (ISBN 0-352-05306-2). Har-Row.

Greenlaw, Paul S., et al. Finansim: A Financial Management Simulation. 2nd ed. 1979. pap. text ed. 16.95 (ISBN 0-8299-0248-1); instrs.' maual avail. (ISBN 0-8299-0613-4). West Pub.

Greenlaw, Ralph, et al. The World of Europe Since Seventeen Fifteen, Vol. II. rev. ed. LC 78-67276. 1979. pap. text ed. 13.95x (ISBN 0-88273-329-X). Forum Pr IL.

Greenlaw, Ralph W. The Social Origins of the French Revolution. pap. 5.95 (ISBN 0-669-91116-X). Heath.

Greenlea, Denice. Birchwood Hall. 208p. (Orig.). 1984. pap. 2.25 (ISBN 0-449-20122-8, Crest). FAwcett.

--Distant Relations. (Coventry Romance Ser.: No. 197). 192p. 1982. pap. 1.50 (ISBN 0-449-50300-3, Coventry). Fawcett.

--A Friend of the Family, No. 154. 224p. 1981. pap. 1.50 (ISBN 0-449-50227-9, Coventry). Fawcett.

--The Masquer. 224p. (Orig.). 1980. pap. 1.75 (ISBN 0-449-50054-3, Coventry). Fawcett.

Greenleaf, Ann. No Room for Sarah. (Illus.). (ps-3). 1983. 10.95 (ISBN 0-396-08213-0). Dodd.

Greenleaf, E. Pricky, a Pet Porcupine. LC 65-22311. (Illus.). (gr. 2-5). 1968. PLB 9.26 (ISBN 0-87783-031-2); pap. 3.94 deluxe ed. (ISBN 0-87783-158-0). Oddo.

--Who Wants to Nap? LC 68-56820. (Illus.). 31p. (gr. 2-3). PLB 9.26 (ISBN 0-87783-050-9). Oddo.

Greenleaf, E. E. Basic Music Work & Play. 1964. pap. 1.95 (ISBN 0-87511-593-4). Claitors.

Greenleaf, F. & Gulick, D., eds. Banach Algebras & Several Complex Variables Conference: Proceedings. LC 84-18443. (Contemporary Mathematics Ser.: Vol. 32). 28.00 (ISBN 0-8218-5034-2). Am Math.

Greenleaf, Frederick P., jt. auth. see Freilich, Gerald.

Greenleaf, J. Cameron. Excavations at Punta De Agua in the Santa Cruz River Basin, Southeastern Arizona. LC 74-83334. (Anthropological Papers: No. 26). 122p. 1975. pap. 4.95x (ISBN 0-8165-0497-0). U of Ariz Pr.

Greenleaf, Jean. Above All, Love. 192p. 1984. 12.95 (ISBN 0-8027-0779-3). Walker & Co.

Greenleaf, Moses. Survey of the State of Maine in Reference to Its Geographical Features, Statistics & Political Economy. LC 71-128108. 1970. 14.00 (ISBN 0-913764-00-0). Maine St Mus.

Greenleaf, N., jt. auth. see Alling, N. L.

Greenleaf, Nancy P., ed. The Politics of Self-Esteem. LC 78-55202. 84p. 1978. pap. text ed. 17.95 (ISBN 0-913654-48-5). Aspen Systems.

Greenleaf, Peter. Experiments in Space Science. rev. ed. LC 79-13299. (Illus.). 176p. 1980. lib. bdg. 8.95 (ISBN 0-668-05104-3). Arco.

Greenleaf, Richard E. The Roman Catholic Church in Colonial Latin America. LC 77-76836. 284p. 1977. pap. 6.50x (ISBN 0-87918-034-X). ASU Lat Am St.

--Zumarraga & the Mexican Inquisition: 1536-1543. (Monograph Ser.). (Illus.). 1962. 20.00 (ISBN 0-88382-053-6). AAFH.

Greenleaf, Richard E., ed. Zumarraga & His Family: Letters to Vizcaya 1536-1548. Kaveny, Neal, tr. (Documentary Ser.). 1979. pap. 25.00 (ISBN 0-88382-013-7). AAFH.

Greenleaf, Richard E. & Meyer, Michael C., eds. Research in Mexican History: Topics, Methodology, Sources, & a Practical Guide to Field Research. LC 72-86020. (Illus.). xiv, 226p. 1973. pap. 4.95x (ISBN 0-8032-5773-2, BB 516, Bison). U of Nebr Pr.

Greenleaf, Robert K. Servant Leadership: A Journey into the Nature of Legitimate Power & Greatness. LC 76-45678. 348p. 1977. 8.95 (ISBN 0-8091-2527-7). Paulist Pr.

Greenleaf, Simon. The Testimony of the Evangelists. 640p. 1984. Repr. of 1874 ed. 19.95 (ISBN 0-8010-3803-0). Baker Bk.

--A Treatise on the Law of Evidence, 3 vols. LC 73-37975. (American Law Ser.: The Formative Years). 2070p. 1972. Repr. of 1850 ed. Set. 120.00 (ISBN 0-405-04015-6); 40.00 ea. Vol. 1 (ISBN 0-405-04016-4). Vol. 2 (ISBN 0-405-04017-2). Vol. 3 (ISBN 0-405-04018-0). Ayer Co Pubs.

Greenleaf, Stephen. Death Bed. 1982. pap. 2.50 (ISBN 0-345-30189-7). Ballantine.

--The Ditto List. Wallach, Susan, ed. LC 84-40481. 368p. 16.95 (ISBN 0-394-54114-6, Pub. by Villard Bks). Random.

--Fatal Obsession. LC 82-22226. 264p. 1983. 14.95 (ISBN 0-385-27886-1, Dial). Doubleday.

--Grave Error. 240p. 1982. pap. 2.50 (ISBN 0-345-30188-9). Ballantine.

--State's Evidence. 288p. 1983. pap. 2.95 (ISBN 0-345-30869-7). Ballantine.

Greenleaf, W. H. The British Political Tradition, 4 Vols. Incl. Vol. 1. The Rise of Collectivism. 352p. 1983. 48.00 (ISBN 0-416-15570-7, NO. 3771); Vol. 2. The Ideological Heritage. 576p. 1983. 55.00 (ISBN 0-416-34660-X, NO. 3785). Methuen Inc.

--Order, Empiricism & Politics: Two Traditions of English Political Thought, 1500-1700. LC 80-10499. (University of Hull Publications). vi, 299p. 1980. Repr. of 1964 ed. lib. bdg. 27.50x (ISBN 0-313-22324-6, GROE). Greenwood.

Greenleaf, William. The Pandora Stone. 224p. 1984. pap. 2.75 (ISBN 0-441-65089-9). Ace Bks.

--The Tartarus Incident. 208p. 1984. pap. 2.50 (ISBN 0-441-79846-2, Pub. by Ace Science Fiction). Ace Bks.

--Timejumper. 1981. pap. 1.95 (ISBN 0-8439-0867-X). Dorchester Pub Co.

Greenleaf, William, ed. American Economic Development Since 1860. LC 68-63013. (Documentary History of the United States Ser.). (Illus.). viii, 392p. 1968. 19.95x (ISBN 0-87249-116-1). U of SC Pr.

Greenlee, Carolyn W. & Greenlee, Dennis L. Applied Electro-Acupoint Therapy Workshop Manual. rev. ed. (Illus.). 152p. 1982. 45.00 (ISBN 0-9607836-0-1). See Do Pr.

Greenlee, Dennis L., jt. auth. see Greenlee, Carolyn W.

Greenlee, Douglas. Peirce's Concept of Sign. LC 72-94469. (Approaches to Semiotics Ser.: No. 5). 148p. 1974. pap. text ed. 12.00 (ISBN 90-2792-494-5). Mouton.

Greenlee, Herbert B. Surgery of the Small & Large Intestine. (Illus.). 1973. 34.95 (ISBN 0-8151-3972-1). Year Bk Med.

Greenlee, J. Harold. Concise Exegetical Grammar of New Testament Greek. (Orig.). 1963. pap. 3.95 (ISBN 0-8028-1092-6). Eerdmans.

--Introduction to New Testament Textual Criticism. 1964. pap. 5.95 (ISBN 0-8028-1724-6). Eerdmans.

--Scribes, Scrolls, & Scripture: A Layperson's Guide to Textual Criticism. 112p. (Orig.). 1985. pap. 6.95 (ISBN 0-8028-0082-3). Eerdmans.

Greenlee, James W. Malraux's Heroes & History. LC 74-12819. 222p. 1975. 15.00 (ISBN 0-87580-051-3). N Ill U Pr.

Greenlee, Jerri, jt. auth. see Moore, Elaine.

Greenlee, Mark, tr. see Myrtek, Mihcael.

Greenlee, Sam. The Spook Who Sat by the Door. 182p. 1985. pap. 5.95 (ISBN 0-8052-8225-4, Pub. by Allison & Busby England). Schocken.

Greenlee, William B., compiled by. The Voyage of Pedro Alvares Cabral to Brazil & India. (Hakluyt Society Works Ser.: No. 2, Vol. 81). (Illus.). Repr. of 1937 ed. 38.00 (ISBN 0-317-17853-9). Kraus Repr.

Greenler, Robert. Rainbows, Halos & Glories. LC 80-143722. (Illus.). 304p. 1980. 32.50 (ISBN 0-521-23605-3). Cambridge U Pr.

Greenley, Beverly J., jt. auth. see McCarter, Charles C.

Greenley, James. Research in Community & Mental Health, Vol. 4. 1984. 47.50 (ISBN 0-89232-360-4). Jai Pr.

Greenley, Michael. The Communist Millionaire. 1983. 8.95 (ISBN 0-533-05626-8). Vantage.

Greenlow, Jean. The Droopy Dragon. (Texas Instruments Magic Wand Speaking Library). (Illus.). 48p. (ps-3). 1982. text ed. 7.30 (ISBN 0-89512-063-1). Tex Instr Inc.

Greenly, H. & Evans, Martin. Walschaerts' Valve Gear. (Illus.). 64p. 1985. pap. 3.95 (ISBN 0-317-14791-9, Pub. by Argus). Aztex.

Greenly, Henry, jt. auth. see Stuart-Turner, S. M.

Greenly, Robert B. How to Win Government Contracts. 256p. 1983. 24.95 (ISBN 0-442-23265-9). Van Nos Reinhold.

Greenmam, P. E., ed. Concepts & Mechanisms of Neuromuscular Functions. (Illus.). 190p. 1984. pap. 19.00 (ISBN 0-387-13470-0). Springer Verlag.

Greenman, Andrew B. Checklist of Shelter Marketing Requirements. rev. ed. 17p. 1977. pap. 3.50 (ISBN 0-86718-015-3); pap. 2.50 members. Natl Assn Home.

Greenman, D., jt. ed. see Streater, R. A.

Greenman, David, ed. Jane's Merchant Ships 1985-86. 2nd ed. (Jane's Yearbooks). (Illus.). 750p. 1985. 125.00 (ISBN 0-7106-0807-1). Jane's Pub Inc.

Greenman, Emerson F. The Younge Site: An Archaeological Record from Michigan. (Occasional Contributions Ser.: No. 6). (Illus.). 1937. pap. 3.00x (ISBN 0-932206-01-8). U Mich Mus Anthro.

Greenman, Frederick P. Wire-Tapping: Its Relation to Civil Liberties. 1938. ltd. ed. 49.50x (ISBN 0-686-51326-6). Elliots Bks.

Greenman, James T. & Fuqua, Robert W., eds. Making Day Care Better: Training, Evaluation & the Process of Change. LC 83-18261. (Early Childhood Education Ser.). (Orig.). 1984. pap. text ed. 18.95x (ISBN 0-8077-2750-4). Tchrs Coll.

Greenman, Joseph & Joachim, Ann, eds. Educational Film Guide for Middle Eastern Studies. xxxvii, 126p. 1980. pap. text ed. 6.00x (ISBN 0-932098-16-9). Ctr for NE & North African Stud.

Greenman, Philip E., jt. ed. see Buerger, A. A.

Greenman, Robert. Captive Vocabulary. (Illus.). 187p. 1980. pap. text ed. 4.50 (ISBN 0-912853-01-8). NY Times.

--Words in Action. LC 82-50042. 1983. 17.65 (ISBN 0-8129-1025-7). Times Bks.

Greenman, Russell L. & Schmertz, Eric J. Personnel Administration & the Law. 2nd ed. 486p. 1979. 24.00 (ISBN 0-87179-234-6). BNA.

Greeno, J. Ladd, et al. Environmental Auditing: Fundamental & Techniques. 296p. 1985. 60.00 (ISBN 0-471-81984-0). Wiley.

Greeno, James G. Constructions in Geometry Problem Solving. (Illus.). 104p. 1979. 2.00 (ISBN 0-318-14704-1). Learn Res Dev.

Greeno, James G., jt. auth. see Riley, Mary S.

Greeno, James G., et al. Individual Differences & Selective Processes in Cognitive Procedures. 54p. 1979. 1.50 (ISBN 0-318-14714-9). Learn Res Dev.

--Theory of Constructions & Set in Problem Solving. 54p. 1979. 1.50 (ISBN 0-318-14745-9). Learn Res Dev.

Greenoak, Francesca. Forgotten Fruit. (Illus.). 126p. 1984. 16.95 (ISBN 0-233-97396-6). Andre Deutsch.

--Forgotten Fruit. (Illus.). 126p. 1984. 16.95 (ISBN 0-233-97396-6, Pub. by A Deutsch England). David & Charles.

--God's Acre: The Flowers & Animals of the Parish Churchyard. (Illus.). 192p. 1985. 19.95 (ISBN 0-525-24315-1, 01937-580). Dutton.

Greenough, Chester N. Collected Studies. LC 78-128253. (Essay Index Reprint Ser). 1940. 19.00 (ISBN 0-8369-1879-7). Ayer Co Pubs.

Greenough, Chester N., jt. auth. see Wendell, Barrett.

Greenough, Frances, ed. Letters of Horatio Greenough. LC 70-96437. (Library of American Art Ser.). 1970. Repr. of 1887 ed. lib. bdg. 32.50 (ISBN 0-306-71828-6). Da Capo.

Greenough, Frances B., ed. see Greenough, Horatio.

Greenough, George B. A Critical Examination of the First Principles of Geology. Albritton, Claude C., Jr., ed. LC 77-6520. (History of Geology Ser.). 1978. Repr. of 1819 ed. lib. bdg. 27.50x (ISBN 0-405-10442-1). Ayer Co Pubs.

Greenough, Horatio. Form & Function: Remarks on Art, Design & Architecture. Small, Harold A., ed. 1947. pap. 5.95x (ISBN 0-520-00514-7, CAMPUS26). U of Cal Pr.

--Letters of Horatio Greenough to His Brother Henry Greenough. Greenough, Frances B., ed. LC 78-168199. Repr. of 1887 ed. 19.00 (ISBN 0-404-02897-7). AMS Pr.

--The Miscellaneous Writings of Horatio Greenough. LC 75-1118. 1975. lib. bdg. 25.00x (ISBN 0-8201-1152-X). Schol Facsimiles.

Greenough, J. B., jt. auth. see Allen, J. H.

Greenough, J. B., ed. see Livy.

Greenough, J. B., ed. see Virgil.

Greenough, James B. & Kittredge, George L. Words & Their Ways in English Speech. 1980. Repr. of 1901 ed. lib. bdg. 50.00 (ISBN 0-89341-482-4). Longwood Pub Group.

--Words & Their Ways in English Speech. 431p. 1985. Repr. of 1909 ed. lib. bdg. 45.00 (ISBN 0-8414-4344-0). Folcroft.

Greenough, Joseph W., jt. auth. see Joseph, James.

Greenough, Paul R. Prosperity & Misery in Modern Bengal: The Famine of 1943-1944. (Illus.). 1982. 39.95x (ISBN 0-19-503082-6). Oxford U Pr.

Greenough, Sarah & Hamilton, Juan. Alfred Stieglitz: Photographs & Writings. LC 82-7925. (Illus.). pap. 24.95 (ISBN 0-89468-026-9). Natl Gallery Art.

Greenough, Sarah & Hamilton, Juan, eds. Alfred Stieglitz: Photographs & Writings. LC 82-7925. (Illus.). 248p. 75.00 (ISBN 0-935112-09-X). Callaway Edns.

Greenough, William C. & King, Francis P. Pension Plans & Public Policy. LC 76-13608. 311p. 1976. 34.00x (ISBN 0-231-04070-9). Columbia U Pr.

Greenough, William T. & Juraska, Janice M., eds. Developmental Neuropsychobiology. (Behavioral Biology Ser.). Date not set. price not set (ISBN 0-12-300270-2). Acad Pr.

Greenough, William T., jt. ed. see Walsh, Roger N.

Greenow, Linda. Credit & Socioeconomic Change in Colonial Mexico: Loans & Mortgages in Guadalajara, 1720-1820. LC 82-62502. (Dellplain Latin American Studies: No. 12). 250p. 1982. softcover 20.00x (ISBN 0-86531-467-5). Westview.

Greensher, Arnold & Roemer, Howard. Ambulatory Protocols for Emergency Care. LC 83-15471. (Illus.). 224p. 1984. pap. text ed. 24.95 (ISBN 0-89303-304-9). Brady Comm.

Greensher, Arnold, jt. ed. see Good, Roger.

Greenshields, Bruce L. & Bellamy, Margot A., eds. Rural Development: Growth & Inequity. LC 83-16345. 320p. 1983. text ed. 28.90x (ISBN 0-566-00637-5). Gower Pub Co.

Greenshields, Bruce L., jt. ed. see Bellamy, Margot A.

Greenshields, Mark. Mastering the Commodore 64. 220p. 1984. pap. 11.95 (ISBN 0-13-559535-5). P-H.

Greenskin, E. The Phonology of Akkadian Syllable Structure. (Afroasiatic Linguistics Ser.). 72p. 1984. pap. 11.00x (ISBN 0-89003-156-8). Undena Pubns.

Greenslade, D. J., jt. ed. see Bullen, G. J.

Greenslade, M. W., ed. A History of the County of Stafford, Vol. 20. (The Victoria History of the Counties of England Ser.). (Illus.). 244p. 1985. 98.00x (ISBN 0-19-722765-1). Oxford U Pr.

--Staffordshire, Vol. VI. (The Victoria History of the Counties of England Ser.). (Illus.). 1979. 129.00x (ISBN 0-19-722733-3). Oxford U Pr.

Greenslade, Roy. Goodbye to the Working Class. LC 76-373483. 192p. 1979. 11.95 (ISBN 0-7145-2511-1, Dist by Scribner); pap. 6.95 (ISBN 0-7145-2523-5). M Boyars.

Greenslade, S. L. Early Latin Theology. LC 56-5229. (The Library of Christian Classics). 412p. 1978. pap. 8.95 (ISBN 0-664-24154-9). Westminster.

Greenslade, Stanley L. Church & State from Constantine to Theodosius. LC 79-8712. 93p. 1981. Repr. of 1954 ed. lib. bdg. 19.50x (ISBN 0-313-20793-3, GRCS). Greenwood.

Greenslade-Moore, Dianne, ed. see Kosbab, William H.

Greenslet, F. Walter Pater. LC 73-21634. (English Literature Ser., No. 33). 1974. lib. bdg. 33.95x (ISBN 0-8383-1798-7). Haskell.

Greenslet, Ferris. James Russell Lowell. 1973. Repr. of 1905 ed. 9.50 (ISBN 0-8274-1338-6). R West.

--Life of Thomas Bailey Aldrich. LC 65-21767. 1965. Repr. of 1908 ed. 25.00x (ISBN 0-8046-0181-X, Pub. by Kennikat). Assoc Faculty Pr.

--The Life of Thomas Bailey Aldrich. 1908. 12.00 (ISBN 0-8274-2941-X). R West.

Greenslet, Ferris, jt. auth. see Curtis, Charles P., Jr.

Greensmith, J. T. Petrology of the Sedimentary Rocks. 6th ed. (Textbook of Petrology Ser.). (Illus.). 1978. text ed. 30.00x (ISBN 0-04-552011-9); pap. text ed. 14.95x (ISBN 0-04-552012-7). Allen Unwin.

Greenson, Ralph R. Explorations in Psychoanalysis. LC 77-90230. 578p. 1978. text ed. 35.00 (ISBN 0-8236-1810-2). Intl Univs Pr.

--Greenson's "Unpopular" Lectures. 1982. write for info. Intl Univs Pr.

--Technique & Practice of Psychoanalysis. LC 67-15417. 452p. 1967. text ed. 35.00 (ISBN 0-8236-6420-1). Intl Univs Pr.

Greenspahn, Frederick E. Hapax Legomena in Biblical Hebrew. LC 83-20021. (SBL Dissertation Ser.). 274p. 1984. 16.50 (ISBN 0-89130-660-9, 06 01 74); pap. 10.95. Scholars Pr GA.

--The Human Condition in the Jewish & Christian Conditions. 1985. text ed. 25.00x (ISBN 0-88125-084-8). Ktav.

Greenspahn, Frederick E., ed. Scripture in the Jewish & Christian Traditions: Authority, Interpretation, Relevance. 240p. 1982. pap. 11.95 (ISBN 0-687-37065-5). Abingdon.

Greenspahn, Frederick E., et al, eds. Nourished with Peace: Studies in Hellenistic Judaism in Memory of Samuel Sandmel. (Scholars Press Homage Ser.: No. 9). 23.95 (ISBN 0-89130-740-0, 00 16 09). Scholars Pr GA.

Greenspan, Alice. Granny's Special Moments Book. (Florida Grandparents Guide Ser.). (Illus., Orig.). (ps-4). 1980. pap. 1.95 (ISBN 0-936076-01-1). Aaron Pubs.

--What God Gave Me. LC 84-50286. (Little Happy Day Bks.). (Illus.). 24p. (Orig.). (ps-1). 1984. pap. 0.45 (ISBN 0-87239-804-8, 2164). Standard Pub.

Greenspan, Donald. Arithmetic Applied Mathematics. LC 80-40295. (Illus.). 172p. 1980. 34.00 (ISBN 0-08-025047-5); pap. 12.00 (ISBN 0-08-025046-7). Pergamon.

--Computer-Oriented Mathematical Physics. (I.S. in Nonlinear Mathematics Ser.: Vol. 3). (Illus.). 179p. 1981. 25.00x (ISBN 0-08-026471-9); pap. 10.75 (ISBN 0-08-026470-0). Pergamon.

--Discrete Numerical Methods in Physics & Engineering. (Mathematics in Science & Engineering Ser.). 1974. 55.00 (ISBN 0-12-300350-4). Acad Pr.

Greenspan, Donald, ed. Numerical Solutions of Nonlinear Differential Equations. LC 66-29278. pap. 88.80 (ISBN 0-317-08570-0, 2006351). Bks Demand UMI.

Greenspan, Emily. Little Winners: Inside the World of the Child Sports Star. (Illus.). 320p. 1983. 16.45i (ISBN 0-316-32667-4). Little.

Greenspan, Ezra. The Schlemiel Comes to America. LC 83-14399. 258p. 1983. 18.50 (ISBN 0-8108-1646-6). Scarecrow.

Greenspan, Ezra M., ed. Clinical Interpretation & Practice of Cancer Chemotherapy. 679p. 1982. text ed. 83.50 (ISBN 0-89004-566-6). Raven.

Greenspan, Francis S. & Forsham, Peter H., eds. Basic & Clinical Endocrinology. LC 83-81569. 646p. 1983. 25.00 (ISBN 0-87041-280-9). Lange.

Greenspan, H., et al, eds. Computing Methods in Reactor Physics. 602p. (Orig.). 1968. 114.50 (ISBN 0-677-11890-2). Gordon.

Greenspan, H. P. Theory of Rotating Fluids. LC 68-12058. (Cambridge Monographs on Mechanics & Applied Mathematics). (Illus.). 1968. text ed. 57.50 (ISBN 0-521-05147-9). Cambridge U Pr.

--The Theory of Rotating Fluids. (Cambridge Monographs on Mechanics & Applied Mathematics). (Illus.). 328p. 1980. pap. 22.95 (ISBN 0-521-29956-X). Cambridge U Pr.

Greenspan, Jay Seth. Hebrew Calligraphy: A Step-by-Step Guide. LC 79-12718. (Illus.). 1980. pap. 8.95 (ISBN 0-8052-0664-7). Schocken.

Greenspan, Judy. To Lesbians Everywhere: Poems. LC 75-35019. (Illus.). 1976. pap. 3.50 (ISBN 0-912968-04-4). Violet Pr.

Greenspan, Kalman & Thies, William H. Medical Examination Review: Physiology. 7th ed. 1984. pap. text ed. write for info. (ISBN 0-87488-383-0). Med Exam.

Greenspan, Kalman & Fischer, John, eds. Cardiovascular Diseases. (Medical Examination Review Ser.: No. 28). 1973. spiral bdg. 23.00 (ISBN 0-87488-138-2). Med Exam.

Greenspan, Kalman & Giddings, John A., eds. Physiology Review. 6th ed. 1981. 12.75 (ISBN 0-87488-206-0). Med Exam.

Greenspan, M. A New Approach to Women & Therapy. 384p. 1983. 16.95 (ISBN 0-07-024349-2). McGraw.

Greenspan, Miriam. A New Approach to Women & Therapy. 1985. 6.95 (ISBN 0-07-024392-1). McGraw.

Greenspan, Nancy T., jt. auth. see Greenspan, Stanley.

Greenspan, Ralph J., jt. auth. see Hall, Jeffrey C.

Greenspan, Rick. Fixing Cars. LC 75-302457. 1974. pap. 5.00 (ISBN 0-9603356-0-9). Rose Pub Co CA.

Greenspan, Rick & Kahn, Hal. Backpacking: A Hedonist's Guide. (Illus.). 200p. (Orig.). 1985. pap. 7.95 (ISBN 0-918373-00-X). Moon Pubns CA.

Greenspan, Stanley & Greenspan, Nancy T. First Feelings: Milestones in the Emotional Development of Your Baby & Child from Birth to Age 4. LC 84-40471. (Viking Nonfiction Ser.). 240p. 1985. 17.95 (ISBN 0-670-80386-3). Viking.

Greenspan, Stanley I. The Clinical Interview of the Child: Theory & Practice. 224p. 1981. 26.95 (ISBN 0-07-024340-9). McGraw.

--A Consideration of Some Learning Variables in the Context of Psychoanalytic Theory. LC 74-19890. (Psychological Issues Monograph: No. 33, Vol. 9, No. 1). 1975. text ed. 17.50 (ISBN 0-8236-1050-0). Intl Univs Pr.

--Intelligence & Adaptation. LC 78-13893. (Psychological Issues Monograph: No. 47-48). (Illus.). 412p. 1980. text ed. 32.50 (ISBN 0-8236-2717-9, 002718); pap. text ed. 25.00 (ISBN 0-8236-2718-7). Intl Univs Pr.

Greenspan, Stanley I., ed. Infants in Multi-Risk: Case Studies in Preventive Intervention. (Clinical Infant Reports: No. 3). 1984. text ed. write for info. (ISBN 0-8236-2645-8). Intl Univs Pr.

Greenspoon, Leonard. Textual Studies in the Book of Joshua. LC 83-3434. (Harvard Semitic Monographs). 412p. 1983. 21.75 (ISBN 0-89130-622-6, 04 00 28). Scholars Pr GA.

Greenspun, Regina. Herman Perlman: His Life & Art. LC 81-85005. (Illus.). 128p. 1982. 21.50 (ISBN 0-910155-00-3). Bartleby Pr.

Greenstadt, Eugene W. & Dryer, Murray, eds. Exploration of the Outer Solar System. LC 76-54804. (Illus.). 237p. 1976. 29.00 (ISBN 0-915928-14-0, PAAS50); members 19.00 (ISBN 0-317-32143-9). AIAA.

Greensted, C. S. & Jardine, A. K. Essentials of Statistics in Marketing. 1978. pap. 14.95 (ISBN 0-434-90887-8, Pub. by W Heinemann Ltd). David & Charles.

Greensted, C. S., et al. Statistical Methods in Quality Control. 240p. 1975. pap. 8.50 (ISBN 0-434-91196-8, Pub. by W Heinemann Ltd). David & Charles.

Greenstein, Blanche, jt. auth. see Woodard, Thomas K.

Greenstein, Fred I. Children & Politics. rev. ed. LC 74-104613. (Studies in Political Science: No. 13). 1965. 8.95x (ISBN 0-300-01319-1); pap. 8.95x 1967 (ISBN 0-300-01320-5, Y191). Yale U Pr.

--The Hidden-Hand Presidency: Eisenhower as Leader. LC 82-70849. 1982. 16.95 (ISBN 0-465-02948-5). Basic.

--The Hidden-Hand Presidency: Eisenhower As Leader. LC 82-70847. 286p. 1984. pap. 8.95 (ISBN 0-465-02949-3, CN 5118). Basic.

Greenstein, Fred I. & Feigert, Frank B. The American Party System & the American People. 3rd ed. (Illus.). 190p. 1985. text ed. 16.95; pap. text ed. 14.95 (ISBN 0-13-028473-4). P-H.

Greenstein, Fred I., ed. The Reagan Presidency: An Early Assessment. LC 83-48056. 208p. 1983. pap. 7.95x (ISBN 0-8018-3057-5). Johns Hopkins.

Greenstein, Fred I., et al. Evolution of the Modern Presidency: A Bibliographical Survey. 1977. pap. 8.25 (ISBN 0-8447-3251-6). Am Enterprise.

Greenstein, George. Frozen Star. 227p. 1984. 16.95 (ISBN 0-88191-011-2). Freundlich.

--Frozen Star. 1985. 8.95 (ISBN 0-452-25693-3, Plume). NAL.

Greenstein, Howard. Turning Point: Zionism & Reform Judaism. LC 81-8996. (Brown BJS Ser.). 1981. pap. 12.00 (ISBN 0-89130-512-2, 140012). Scholars Pr GA.

Greenstein, Howard R. Judaism: An Eternal Covenant. LC 82-17601. 208p. 1983. pap. 10.95 (ISBN 0-8006-1690-1, 1-1690). Fortress.

Greenstein, Jack. What the Children Taught Me: The Experience of an Educator in the Public Schools. LC 83-3503. 256p. 1985. 15.00x (ISBN 0-226-30705-0); pap. 8.95 (ISBN 0-226-30706-9). U of Chicago Pr.

Greenstein, Jesse L., ed. Stellar Atmospheres. LC 61-9045. (Stars & Stellar Systems Ser: Vol. 6). (Illus.). 1961. 50.00x (ISBN 0-226-45958-6). U of Chicago Pr.

Greenstein, Jesse P. Biochemistry of Cancer. 2nd ed. 1954. 77.00 (ISBN 0-12-300550-7). Acad Pr.

Greenstein, Jesse P. & Haddow, Alexander. Advances in Cancer Research, Vol. 41. (Serial Publication). 1984. 49.00 (ISBN 0-12-006641-6). Acad Pr.

Greenstein, Jesse P. & Haddow, Alexander, eds. Advances in Cancer Research. Incl. Vol. 1. 1953. 80.00 (ISBN 0-12-006601-7); Vol. 2. 1954. 80.00 (ISBN 0-12-006602-5); Vol. 3. 1955. 80.00 (ISBN 0-12-006603-3); Vol. 4. 1956. 80.00 (ISBN 0-12-006604-1); Vol. 5. 1958. 80.00 (ISBN 0-12-006605-X); Vol. 6. Haddow, Alexander & Weinhouse, Sidney, eds. 1962. 80.00 (ISBN 0-12-006606-8); Vol. 7. 1963. 80.00 (ISBN 0-12-006607-6); Vol. 8. 1964. 80.00 (ISBN 0-12-006608-4); Vol. 9. 1965. 80.00 (ISBN 0-12-006609-2); Vol. 10. 1967. 70.00 (ISBN 0-12-006610-6); Vol. 11. 1969. 80.00 (ISBN 0-12-006611-4); Vol. 12. Klein, George & Weinhouse, Sidney, eds. 1969. 80.00 (ISBN 0-12-006612-2); Vol. 13. 1970. 80.00 (ISBN 0-12-006613-0); Vol. 14. 1971. 80.00 (ISBN 0-12-006614-9); Vol. 15. 1972. 75.00 (ISBN 0-12-006615-7); Vol. 16. 1972. 75.00 (ISBN 0-12-006616-5); Vol. 17. 1973. 77.00 (ISBN 0-12-006617-3); Vol. 18. 1973. 75.00 (ISBN 0-12-006618-1). Acad Pr.

--Advances in Cancer Research, Vol. 38. (Serial Publication). 1983. 60.00 (ISBN 0-12-006638-6). Acad Pr.

Greenstein, Jessie P. & Winitz, Milton. Chemistry of the Amino Acids, 3 vols. LC 83-13616. 1984. Repr. of 1961 ed. 248.50 (ISBN 0-89874-484-9). Krieger.

Greenwood, J. D. Hard Chromium Plating: A Handbook of Modern Practice. 216p. 1981. 60.00x (ISBN 0-86108-088-2, Pub. by Portcullio Pr). State Mutual Bk.
--Heavy Deposition. 216p. 1981. 60.00x (ISBN 0-85218-030-6, Pub. by Portcullio Pr). State Mutual Bk.
--Heavy Deposition. 216p. 1969. 31.00 (ISBN 0-318-12542-0); members 23.00 (ISBN 0-318-12543-9). Am Electroplate.
Greenwood, J. Michael & Tollar, Jerry R. Users' Guidebook to Computer-Aided Transcription. 1977. pap. 2.50 (ISBN 0-89656-016-3, R0031). Natl Ctr St Courts.
Greenwood, J. R. & Wilson, D. J. Public Administration in Britain. (Illus.). 248p. 1984. text ed. 28.50x (ISBN 0-04-352109-6); pap. text ed. 10.95x (ISBN 0-04-352110-X). Allen Unwin.
Greenwood, James. The Seven Curses of London. LC 82-195528. xxvi, 293p. 1982. Repr. of 1869 ed. 27.50x (ISBN 0-686-84020-8, Pub. by B Blackwell England). Porcupine Pr.
--The Seven Curses of London. LC 83-48479. (The World of Labour - English Workers 1850-1890 Ser.). 336p. 1984. lib. bdg. 40.00 (ISBN 0-8240-5707-4). Garland Pub.
--The Wilds of London. LC 84-48268. (The Rise of Urban Britain Ser.). 364p. 1985. 50.00 (ISBN 0-8240-6270-1). Garland Pub.
Greenwood, James W., III & Greenwood, James W., Jr. Managing Executive Stress: A Systems Approach. 270p. 1984. pap. 17.50 (ISBN 0-935310-04-5). Burrill-Ellsworth.
Greenwood, Jennifer, tr. see Tesch, F. W.
Greenwood, Jim. Parachuting for Sport. 2nd ed. (Modern Aircraft Ser.). 1978. 7.95 (ISBN 0-8306-9975-9); pap. 3.95 (ISBN 0-8306-2224-1, 2224). TAB Bks.
--Total Rugby. 304p. 1978. 27.50x (ISBN 0-86019-034-X, Pub. by Kimpton). State Mutual Bk.
Greenwood, Jim & Greenwood, Maxine. Stunt Flying in the Movies. (Illus.). 256p. 1982. 21.95 (ISBN 0-8306-0304-2, 2304). TAB Bks.
Greenwood, John. The Missing Mr. Mosley. (Mosley Mystery Ser.). 192p. 1985. 13.95 (ISBN 0-8027-5618-2). Walker & Co.
--Mosley by Moonlight. 1985. 12.95 (ISBN 0-8027-5606-9). Walker & Co.
--Murder, Mr. Mosley. LC 83-42881. (Mysteries Ser.). 192p. 1983. 12.95 (ISBN 0-8027-5574-7). Walker & Co.
--Worker Sit-Ins & Job Protection. 136p. 1977. text ed. 35.50x (ISBN 0-566-02015-7). Gower Pub Co.
Greenwood, John G., tr. see Suzuki, Yoshio.
Greenwood, John O. Greenwood's Guide to Great Lakes Shipping 1984. 25th ed. Dills, Michael J., ed. 500p. 1984. 39.00 (ISBN 0-912514-22-1). Freshwater.
--Greenwood's Guide to Great Lakes Shipping, 1985. 26th ed. Dills, Michael, ed. 520p. 1985. 39.75x (ISBN 0-912514-29-9). Freshwater.
--Henry Hodgkin: The Road to Pendle Hill. LC 79-91958. 1980. pap. 2.30x (ISBN 0-87574-229-7). Pendle Hill.
--Namesakes Nineteen Fifty-Six to Ninety Eighty. 1981. casebound 24.75 (ISBN 0-912514-15-9). Freshwater.
--Namesakes of the Eighties, Vol. II. Dills, Michael, ed. LC 84-72935. (Illus.). 328p. 1985. 23.75 (ISBN 0-912514-28-0). Freshwater.
--Namesakes: 1920-1929. LC 84-80858. (Illus.). 376p. 1984. 22.75 (ISBN 0-912514-27-2). Freshwater.
--Namesakes 1930-1955. 1978. 20.25 (ISBN 0-912514-19-1). Freshwater.
--Quaker Encounters: Friends & Relief, Vol. 1. 1975. 59.00x (ISBN 0-686-87288-6, Pub. by W Sessions). State Mutual Bk.
--Quaker Encounters: Vines on the Mountain, Vol. 2. 1977. 59.00x (ISBN 0-686-87289-4, Pub. by W Session). State Mutual Bk.
--Quaker Encounters: Whispers of Truth, Vol. 3. 1978. 59.00x (ISBN 0-686-87290-8, Pub. by W Session). State Mutual Bk.
Greenwood, John O. & Dills, Michael. Greenwood's & Dills' Lake Boats, 1983. 19th, rev. ed. 180p. 1983. 4.75 (ISBN 0-912514-04-3). Freshwater.
--Greenwood's & Dill's Lake Boats 1985. 21st ed. 300p. 1985. pap. 5.00 (ISBN 0-912514-30-2). Freshwater.
Greenwood, John O. & Dills, Michael J. Greenwoods' Guide to Great Lakes Shipping 1983. 19th, rev. ed. 530p. 1983. 39.00 (ISBN 0-912514-06-X). Freshwater.
Greenwood, Joseph A. & Hartley, H. O. Guide to Tables in Mathematical Statistics. LC 62-7040. pap. 160.00 (ISBN 0-317-13006-4, 2021559). Bks Demand UMI.
Greenwood, Judith G. Role of the Physician Assistants in Primary Care. 181p. 1981. 14.95 (ISBN 0-87762-302-3). Technomic.
Greenwood, Judy. Coping With Sexual Relationships. 1983. 30.00x (ISBN 0-86334-043-1, Pub. by Macdonald Pub UK); pap. 20.00x (ISBN 0-86334-042-3). State Mutual Bk.
Greenwood, K. Weaving: Control of Fabric Structure. 72p. 1975. 39.00 (ISBN 0-900541-65-2, Pub. by Meadowfield Pr England). State Mutual Bk.
Greenwood, Kathryn M. & Murphy, Mary F. Fashion Innovation & Marketing. (Illus.). 1978. write for info. (ISBN 0-02-346950-1). Macmillan.
Greenwood, Katy B., ed. Contemporary Challenges for Vocational Education. (AVA Yearbook: 1982). 308p. 1981. text ed. 18.00 (ISBN 0-89514-037-3, 01982). Am Voc Assn.
Greenwood, L. H., tr. see Aristotle.
Greenwood, L. Larry & Rohrer, Richard L. KWIC Index to the Commonwealth Bureau of Soils Annotated Bibliographies on Soils & Fertilizers. LC 73-621756. (Libraries Bibliography: No. 13). 1974. Repr. 10.00 (ISBN 0-686-20814-5). KSU.
Greenwood, Larry. How to Search for Information: A Beginner's Guide to the Literature of Psychology. LC 80-53708. (Basic Tools Ser.: No. 1). 50p. (Orig.). 1980. pap. text ed. 4.50 (ISBN 0-938376-00-4). Willowood Pr.
Greenwood, Larry, jt. auth. see Timberlake, Charles.
Greenwood, Leonard H. Aspects of Euripidean Tragedy. LC 74-180610. viii, 144p. 1972. Repr. of 1953 ed. 13.50x (ISBN 0-8462-1643-4). Russell.
Greenwood, M. R. C. Obesity. LC 82-20714. (Contemporary Issues in Clinical Nutrition Ser.: Vol. 4). (Illus.). 214p. 1983. text ed. 27.00 (ISBN 0-443-08186-7). Churchill.
Greenwood, Major. Epidemics & Crowd Diseases: Introduction to the Study of Epidemiology. Rosenkrantz, Barbara G., ed. LC 76-40628. (Public Health in America Ser.). (Illus.). 1977. Repr. of 1935 ed. lib. bdg. 33.00x (ISBN 0-405-09821-9). Ayer Co Pubs.
--Some British Pioneers of Social Medicine. LC 71-126320. (Biography Index Reprint Ser.: London University Heath Clark Lectures, 1946). Repr. of 1948 ed. 14.00 (ISBN 0-8369-8026-3). Ayer Co Pubs.
Greenwood, Major, jt. auth. see Collis, Edgar L.
Greenwood, Major, jt. auth. see Royal College of Physicians of London in February 1943, Fitzpatrick Lectures for the Years 1941 & 1943.
Greenwood, Marjorie. Roads & Canals in the Eighteenth Century. Reeves, Marjorie, ed. (Then & There Ser.). (Illus.). 92p. (Orig.). (gr. 7-12). 1977. pap. text ed. 3.75 (ISBN 0-582-20383-X). Longman.
Greenwood, Mary, jt. auth. see Greenwood, Frank.
Greenwood, Maxine, jt. auth. see Greenwood, Jim.
Greenwood, Michael. Migration & Economic Growth in the United States: National, Regional & Metropolitan Perspectives. LC 80-1773. (Studies in Urban Economics). 1981. 29.50 (ISBN 0-12-300650-3). Acad Pr.
Greenwood, Michael & Dodge, Douglas C. Management of Court Reporting Services. 1976. Manuscript R-025 3.72 (ISBN 0-89656-006-6). Natl Ctr St Courts.
Greenwood, Michael & Tollar, Jerry R., eds. Evaluation Guidebook to Computer-Aided Transcription. 124p. 1975. 3.84 (ISBN 0-89656-001-5, R0019). Natl Ctr St Courts.
Greenwood, Michael J., jt. auth. see National Center for State Courts.
Greenwood, Mimi, jt. auth. see Winans, Chip.
Greenwood, N. N. & Earnshaw, A. Chemistry of the Elements. LC 83-13346. (Illus.). 1542p. 1984. 120.00 (ISBN 0-08-022056-8); flexi-cover 34.95 (ISBN 0-08-022057-6). Pergamon.
Greenwood, Ned J. & Edwards, J. M. Human Environments & Natural Systems. 2nd ed. LC 78-13082. (Illus.). 1979. write for info. (ISBN 0-87872-168-1). Wadsworth Pub.
Greenwood, P. H. The Cichlid Fishes of Lake Victoria, East Africa: Biology & Evolution of a Species Flock. (Bulletin of the British Museum Natural History Zool. Ser.: No. 6). (Illus.). 1974. text ed. 22.50x (ISBN 0-565-00761-0, Pub. by Brit Mus Nat Hist); pap. text ed. 15.00x (ISBN 0-8277-4357-2). Sabbot-Natural Hist Bks.
--The Haplochromine Fishes of the East African Lakes. (Illus.). 764p. 1981. 85.00x (ISBN 0-8014-1346-X). Cornell U Pr.
--The Haplochromine Fishes of the East African Lakes. 839p. 1981. lib. bdg. 70.00 (ISBN 3-601-00483-6). Kraus Intl.
Greenwood, P. J., et al, eds. Evolution: Essays in Honour of John Maynard Smith. 300p. 1985. 49.50 (ISBN 0-521-25734-4). Cambridge U Pr.
Greenwood, Paul J., jt. ed. see Swingland, Ian R.
Greenwood, Peter H. & Norman, J. R. A History of Fishes. 3rd ed. 467p. 1976. pap. 26.95x (ISBN 0-470-99012-0). Halsted Pr.
Greenwood, Peter W. & California Legislature Assembly. Youth Crime & Juvenile Justice in California: A Report to the Legislature. LC 83-9530. 165p. 1983. 15.00 (ISBN 0-8330-0504-9). Rand Corp.
Greenwood, Peter W., et al. The Criminal Investigation Process. 1977. pap. 8.95x (ISBN 0-669-01067-7). Heath.
Greenwood Press for the Urban Documents Program. Contemporary Subject Headings for Urban Affairs. LC 82-25504. viii, 106p. 1983. lib. bdg. 25.00 (ISBN 0-313-23869-3, CSU/). Greenwood.
Greenwood, R. R. A Preface to Literature. 1978. Repr. of 1930 ed. lib. bdg. 10.00 (ISBN 0-8495-1914-4). Arden Lib.
--A Preface to Literature. 1930. Repr. 10.00 (ISBN 0-8274-3199-6). R West.
Greenwood, Richard & Brodzinski, Ignatius. Enjoying BASIC: A Comprehensive Guide to Programming. 368p. 1984. 19.50 (ISBN 0-06-042504-0, HarpC); write for info. instr's manual (ISBN 0-06-362461-3). Har-Row.
Greenwood, Robert. The California Outlaw: Tiburcio Vasquez. LC 73-14203. (The Mexican American Ser.). (Illus.). 296p. 1974. Repr. 20.00x (ISBN 0-405-05677-X). Ayer Co Pubs.
Greenwood, Robert K. Arcadia & Other Stories. 1985. 17.50 (ISBN 0-934614-08-3); pap. 9.95 (ISBN 0-934614-09-1). Talisman Research.
Greenwood, Ron, jt. auth. see Butler, Bryon.
Greenwood, Ronald G., jt. ed. see Zimet, Melvin.
Greenwood, Royston, et al. Patterns of Management in Local Government. (Government & Administration Ser.). (Illus.). 192p. 1980. 34.95x (ISBN 0-85520-244-0); pap. 11.95x (ISBN 0-85520-245-9). Basil Blackwell.
Greenwood, Sadja. Menopause, Naturally: Preparing for the Second Half of Life. LC 84-7333. (Illus.). 210p. (Orig.). 1984. pap. 10.00 (ISBN 0-912078-74-X). Volcano Pr.
Greenwood, Shiryayev. Contiguity & the Statistical Invariance Principle. (Stochasti Monographs). 244p. 1985. text ed. 39.00 (ISBN 2-88124-013-5). Gordon.
Greenwood, Sydney. Stoker Greenwood's Navy. (Illus.). 192p. 1983. 16.95 (ISBN 0-88254-744-5). Hippocrene Bks.
Greenwood, Ted. Knowledge & Discretion in Government Regulation. LC 84-15925. 300p. 1984. 34.95 (ISBN 0-03-000047-5). Praeger.
Greenwood, Theresa. Gospel Graffiti. LC 78-662. (Illus.). 96p. 1978. pap. 2.95 (ISBN 0-87131-253-0). M Evans.
Greenwood, Val D. The Researcher's Guide to American Genealogy. LC 73-6902. (Illus.). 535p. 1983. 15.00 (ISBN 0-8063-0560-6). Genealog Pub.
Greenwood, Walter. Love on the Dole. (Penguin Fiction Ser.). 256p. 1985. pap. 4.95 (ISBN 0-14-002827-7). Penguin.
Greenya, John, jt. auth. see Burford, Anne M.
Greenya, John, jt. auth. see Rose, Thomas.
Greep, J. M., et al, eds. Pain in Shoulder & Arm: An Integrated View. (Developments in Surgery Ser.: No. 1). 306p. 1980. lib. bdg. 47.35 (ISBN 90-247-2146-6). Kluwer Academic.
Greep, Roy. Recent Progress in Hormone Research: Proceedings of the 1982 Laurentian Hormone Conference. (Serial Publication Ser.: Vol. 39). 1983. 72.00 (ISBN 0-12-571139-5). Acad Pr.
Greep, Roy, ed. Recent Progress in Hormone Research, Vol. 37. (Serial Publication). 1981. 82.00 (ISBN 0-12-571137-9). Acad Pr.
Greep, Roy O., ed. Recent Progress in Hormone Research, Vol. 35. 1979. 70.00 (ISBN 0-12-571135-2). Acad Pr.
--Recent Progress in Hormone Research, Vol. 36. (Serial Pub.). 1980. 75.00 (ISBN 0-12-571136-0). Acad Pr.
--Reproductive Physiology IV. (International Review of Physiology Ser.: Vol. 27). (Illus.). 352p. 1983. text ed. 49.50 (ISBN 0-8391-1555-5, 14206). Univ Park.
Greep, Roy O. & Koblinsky, Majorie A., eds. Frontiers in Reproduction & Fertility Control. 1977. 55.00x (ISBN 0-262-07068-5). MIT Pr.
Greep, Roy O. see Laurentian Hormone Conferences.
Greep, Roy O., et al. Reproduction & Human Welfare: A Challenge to Research-A Review of the Reproductive Sciences & Contraceptive Development. 1976. text ed. 32.50x (ISBN 0-262-07067-7). MIT Pr.
Greer, Ann L. The Mayor's Mandate: Municipal Statecraft & Political Trust. 200p. 1974. pap. 9.95 (ISBN 0-87073-165-3). Schenkman Bks Inc.
Greer, Ann L. & Greer, Scott A. Cities & Sickness. LC 83-15422. (Urban Affairs Annual Reviews Ser.: Vol. 25). 303p. 1983. 28.00 (ISBN 0-8039-2127-6); pap. 14.00 (ISBN 0-8039-2128-4). Sage.
Greer, Anne L. Creative Mexican Cooking: Recipes from Great Texas Chefs. (Illus.). 224p. 1985. 19.95 (ISBN 0-932012-63-9). Texas Month Pr.
--Cuisine of the American Southwest. LC 83-650. (Cookbook Ser.). (Illus.). 304p. 1983. 21.63i (ISBN 0-06-181320-6, HarpT). Har-Row.
--Cuisine of the American Southwest. Barnard, Melanie, ed. (Illus.). 288p. 1983. 22.50 (ISBN 0-06-181320-6). Cuisinart Cooking.
--The Culinary Renaissance: Creative Food Processor Recipes. 5th rev. ed. 400p. 1979. pap. 9.00 (ISBN 0-936662-01-8, FP-782). Cuisinart Cooking.
Greer, Archie, jt. ed. see Clift, Charles, III.
Greer, Arthur E. No Grown-Ups in Heaven. 1977. pap. 3.95 (ISBN 0-8015-5403-9, Hawthorn). Dutton.
Greer, Ben. Slammer. 1977. pap. 1.75 (ISBN 0-380-01845-4, 36418). Avon.
Greer, Blanche. The Black Swan & the Green See Saw. LC 75-261399. (Illus.). (gr. 5 up). 1977. 3.95 (ISBN 0-930422-07-4). Dennis-Landman.
Greer, Charles. Water Management in the Yellow River Basin of China. 192p. 1979. text ed. 12.50x (ISBN 0-292-79011-2). U of Tex Pr.
Greer, Clark. Multi-Media Methods for Christian Ministries. LC 82-16132. 1982. pap. 2.95 (ISBN 0-87227-085-8). Reg Baptist.
Greer, Colin. The Great School Legend: A Revisionist Interpretation of American Public Education. 224p. 1976. pap. 3.95 (ISBN 0-14-004447-7). Penguin.
Greer, David, ed. Hamilton Harty: His Life & Music. (Music Reprint Ser.). (Illus.). 1980. Repr. lib. bdg. 22.50 (ISBN 0-306-76015-0). Da Capo.
Greer, Don, jt. auth. see McDowell, Ernie.
Greer, Donald. The Incidence of Emigration During the French Revolution. 1951. 12.00 (ISBN 0-8446-1210-3). Peter Smith.
--The Incidence of the Terror During the French Revolution: A Statistical Interpretation. 1935. 12.00 (ISBN 0-8446-1211-1). Peter Smith.
Greer, Donald M. Plastic Surgery Continuing Education Review. 1975. spiral bdg. 20.50 (ISBN 0-87488-354-7). Med Exam.
Greer, Douglas. Design for Music Learning. LC 79-21117. 1980. pap. text ed. 13.95x (ISBN 0-8077-2573-0). Tchrs Coll.
Greer, Douglas F. Business, Government, & Society. 640p. 1983. text ed. write for info. (ISBN 0-02-347050-X). Macmillan.
--Cases in Marketing: Orientation, Analysis, & Problems. 3rd ed. 1983. pap. text ed. write for info. (ISBN 0-02-347100-X); instrs'. manual avail. Macmillan.
--Industrial Organization & Public Policy. 2nd ed. 704p. 1984. text ed. write for info. (ISBN 0-02-347070-4). Macmillan.
Greer, E. Eugene & Greer, Elaine W. Daily Guide Toward Fitness. LC 81-65387. 1981. pap. 9.95 (ISBN 0-8054-7521-4). Broadman.
Greer, Edward. Big Steel: Black Politics & Corporate Power in Gary, Indiana. LC 79-13178. 287p. 1981. 16.50 (ISBN 0-85345-490-6); pap. 6.50 (ISBN 0-85345-562-7). Monthly Rev.
Greer, Elaine W., jt. auth. see Greer, E. Eugene.
Greer, Frances & Greer, Frances. Stenospeed Shorthand Twenty-five Thousand Word Dictionary. (Illus.). 384p. 1971. 8.50 (ISBN 0-911744-26-6). Intl Educ Systems.
Greer, Frances A. Instant Notetaking. (Illus.). 1974. 7.95 (ISBN 0-911744-28-2). Intl Educ Systems.
--Stenospeed Shorthand. 300p. 1974. 8.75 (ISBN 0-911744-31-2). Intl Educ Systems.
--Stenospeed Workbook. 150p. 1974. pap. 3.45 (ISBN 0-911744-32-0). Intl Educ Systems.
Greer, Frances A. & Mitchell, W. M. Advanced Dictation & Transcription. 384p. 1974. 9.45 (ISBN 0-911744-27-4). Intl Educ Systems.
Greer, Francesca. Bright Dawn. 400p. 1983. pap. 3.50 (ISBN 0-446-90942-4). Warner Bks.
Greer, Gaylon E. The Real Estate Investor & the Federal Income Tax. 2nd ed. LC 81-147933. (Real Estate for Professional Practitioners: A Wiley Ser.). 267p. 1982. text ed. 34.95x (ISBN 0-471-09738-1, Pub. by Ronald Pr). Wiley.
--The Real Estate Investor & the Federal Income Tax. 2nd ed. LC 81-14793. pap. 70.80 (ISBN 0-317-26098-7, 2025175). Bks Demand UMI.
Greer, Gaylon E. & Farrell, Michael D. Contemporary Real Estate: Theory & Practice. 480p. 1983. text ed. 35.95x (ISBN 0-03-056682-7); instr's manual 20.00 (ISBN 0-03-056683-5). Dryden Pr.
--Investment Analysis for Real Estate Decisions. 604p. 1984. text ed. 34.95x (ISBN 0-03-061247-0); instr's. manual incl. supplementary material 19.95 (ISBN 0-03-061248-9); newsletter avail. Dryden Pr.
Greer, Gaylon E., jt. auth. see Farrell, Michael.
Greer, George C. Early Virginia Immigrants, Sixteen Twenty-Three to Sixteen Sixty-Six. LC 62-453. 376p. 1982. Repr. of 1912 ed. 17.50 (ISBN 0-8063-0161-9). Genealog Pub.
Greer, Georgeanna H. American Stonewares: The Art & Craft of Utilitarian Potters. LC 81-51449. (Illus.). 286p. 1981. 40.00 (ISBN 0-916838-52-8). Schiffer.
Greer, Germaine. The Obstacle Race: The Fortunes of Women Painters & Their Work. (Illus.). 373p. 1979. 25.00 (ISBN 0-374-22412-9); pap. 12.95 (ISBN 0-374-51582-4). FS&G.
--Sex & Destiny: The Politics of Human Fertility. LC 83-48349. 560p. 1984. 19.18i (ISBN 0-06-015140-4, HarpT). Har-Row.
--Sex & Destiny: The Politics of Human Fertility. LC 83-48349. 544p. 1985. pap. 9.57i (ISBN 0-06-091250-2, CN 1250, CN). Har-Row.
Greer, Gery & Ruddick, Bob. Max & Me & the Time Machine. LC 82-48762. 140p. (gr. 4-6). 1983. PLB 11.95 (ISBN 0-15-253134-3, HJ). HarBraceJ.
Greer, Guy. Ruhr-Lorraine Industrial Problem. (Brookings Institution Reprint Ser). Repr. of 1925 ed. lib. bdg. 27.00x (ISBN 0-697-00156-3). Irvington.
Greer, Harold E. Greer's Guidebook to Available Rhododendrons, Species & Hybrids. LC 82-90128. (Illus.). 152p. 1982. pap. 12.95 (ISBN 0-910013-00-4). Offshoot Pub.
Greer, Harold E., Jr., jt. auth. see Ward, Harry M.
Greer, Hazel M. As the Stars Forever. LC 65-250000024. (Dest Ser.). 1984. pap. 4.95 (ISBN 0-317-28302-2). Pacific Pr Pub Assn.
Greer, James K., ed. Buck Barry, Texas Ranger & Frontiersman. LC 84-11863. (Illus.). xviii, 262p. 1984. 19.95x (ISBN 0-8032-2119-3); pap. 6.95 (ISBN 0-8032-7013-5, BB 892, Bison). U of Nebr Pr.

Greer, Joanne G., jt. auth. see Stuart, Irving R.

Greer, Joanne G. & Stuart, Irving R., eds. The Sexual Aggressor: Current Perspectives on Treatment. 384p. 1983. 29.95 (ISBN 0-442-22855-4). Van Nos Reinhold.

Greer, John G. & Anderson, Robert M. Strategies for Helping Severely & Multiply Handicapped Citizens. LC 81-11499. (Illus.). 448p. 1982. 19.00 (ISBN 0-8391-1692-6). Pro Ed.

Greer, John G., et al. Motivating Learners with Instructional Games. LC 77-75525. 1977. pap. text ed. 7.50 (ISBN 0-8403-1738-7). Kendall-Hunt.

Greer, L. F. Your Personal Plumber. LC 79-54891. 1979. 24.95 (ISBN 0-686-26464-9). Plumbing Pubns.

Greer, Laura B., jt. auth. see Ackley, Robert J.

Greer, Louise. Browning & America. LC 72-7819. (Illus.). 355p. 1973. Repr. of 1952 ed. lib. bdg. 24.75x (ISBN 0-8371-6525-3, GRBA). Greenwood.

Greer, Louise & Harold, Anthony. Flying Clothing: The Story of Its Development. 176p. 1982. 65.00x (ISBN 0-9504543-7-0, Pub. by Airlife England). State Mutual Bk.

Greer, M. A., jt. auth. see Langer, P.

Greer, Mary & Rubenstein, Bonnie. Will the Real Teacher Please Stand Up? 2nd ed. 1977. pap. 12.95 (ISBN 0-673-16153-6). Scott F.

Greer, Mary A., ed. see Autry, George.

Greer, Mary K. Tarot for Yourself. LC 84-21620. (Illus.). 128p. 1984. Repr. of 1984 ed. lib. bdg. 24.95x (ISBN 0-89370-677-9). Borgo Pr.

--Tarot for Yourself. (Illus.). 256p. (Orig.). 1984. pap. 12.95 (ISBN 0-87877-077-1). Newcastle Pub.

Greer, Michael. Your Future in Interior Design. 2nd rev. ed. LC 79-95600. (Illus.). (gr. 7 up). 1980. PLB 8.97 (ISBN 0-8239-0524-1). Rosen Group.

Greer, Peter S., jt. auth. see Kidwell, Ann M.

Greer, R. Dictionary of One Thousand Dreams. 1.00 (ISBN 0-685-02610-8, 00545193). Stein Pub.

--Trees & Hills: Methodology for Maximising Functions of Systems of Linear Relations. (Mathematical Studies, No. 96; Annals of Discrete Mathematics). 1984. 44.50 (ISBN 0-444-87578-6). Elsevier.

Greer, Rebecca. How to Live Rich When You're Not. 1977. pap. 1.75 (ISBN 0-345-25204-7). Ballantine.

Greer, Rita. Wheat-Free, Milk-Free, Egg-Free Cooking. 128p. (Orig.). 1984. pap. 3.95 (ISBN 0-7225-0832-8). Thorsons Pubs.

Greer, Robert O., et al. Tumors of the Head & Neck in Children. LC 82-19114. 430p. 1983. 49.95 (ISBN 0-03-060093-6). Praeger.

Greer, Rowan A., ed. Origen: Selected Writings. LC 79-84886. (Classics of Western Spirituality Ser.). 334p. 1979. 11.95 (ISBN 0-8091-0283-8); pap. 9.95 (ISBN 0-8091-2198-0). Paulist Pr.

Greer, Scott. The Urbane View: Life & Politics in Metropolitan America. LC 71-182424. 1972. pap. 4.95 (ISBN 0-19-501728-5, 397, GB). Oxford U Pr.

Greer, Scott, ed. Ethnics, Machines, & the American Urban Future. 192p. 1981. pap. text ed. 15.25x (ISBN 0-87073-227-7); pap. text ed. 9.95x (ISBN 0-87073-228-5). Schenkman Bks Inc.

Greer, Scott, et al, eds. Accountability in Urban Society: Public Agencies Under Fire. LC 78-17295. (Urban Affairs Annual Reviews: Vol. 15). 304p. 1978. 28.00 (ISBN 0-8039-1081-9); pap. 14.00 (ISBN 0-8039-1082-7). Sage.

Greer, Scott A. Governing the Metropolis. LC 81-4211. xi, 153p. 1981. Repr. of 1966 ed. lib. bdg. 20.50x (ISBN 0-313-23038-2, GRGM). Greenwood.

Greer, Scott A., jt. auth. see Greer, Ann L.

Greer, Stanley & Morrison, Brian. The Power of Bullied Pacifics. 128p. 35.00x (ISBN 0-86093-082-3, Pub. by ORPC Ltd UK). State Mutual Bk.

Greer, Thomas. Marketing Doctoral Dissertation Abstracts 1980, Bibliography Ser. 191p. pap. 16.00 (ISBN 0-686-81349-9). Am Mktg.

Greer, Thomas H. American Social Reform Movements: Their Pattern Since 1865. LC 80-11282. ix, 313p. 1980. Repr. of 1949 ed. lib. bdg. 32.50x (ISBN 0-313-22382-3, GRAR). Greenwood.

--A Brief History of the Western World. 4th ed. LC 76-29165. (Illus.). 597p. 1982. pap. text ed. 19.95 (ISBN 0-15-505571-2, HC); instructor's manual avail. (ISBN 0-15-505572-0). HarBraceJ.

--Classics of Western Thought, 4 Vols. 3rd ed. 1980. Vol. I-The Ancient World, 421p. pap. text ed. 11.95 (ISBN 0-15-507678-7, HC); Vol. II-Middle Ages, Renaissance, & Reformation, 575p. pap. text ed. 12.95 (ISBN 0-15-507679-5); Vol. III-The Modern World, 666p. pap. text ed. 12.95 (ISBN 0-15-507680-9); Vol. IV-The Twentieth Century, 660p. pap. text ed. 13.95 (ISBN 0-15-507681-7). HarbraceJ.

--The Development of Air Doctrine in the Army Air Arm, 1917-1941. (USAF Historical Studies: No. 89). 162p. 1955. pap. text ed. 16.50x (ISBN 0-89126-021-8). MA-AH Pub.

--What Roosevelt Thought: The Social & Political Ideas of Franklin D. Roosevelt. xv, 244p. 1958. 5.00 (ISBN 0-87013-034-X). Mich St U Pr.

Greer, Thomas J., Jr. Writing & Understanding U. S. Patent Claims. 125p. 1979. pap. 17.50 (ISBN 0-87215-238-3). Michie Co.

Greer, Tom. A Modern Daedalus. LC 74-15977. (Science Fiction Ser). 278p. 1975. Repr. 23.50x (ISBN 0-405-06294-X). Ayer Co Pubs.

Greer, William J., jt. auth. see Baker, James K.

Greerhalgh, L., jt. auth. see Wasmuth, W.

Greeson, Phillip E., ed. River-Quality Assessments: Proceedings of a Symposium Held in Tucson, Arizona, November 2-3, 1977. LC 79-87721. pap. 49.80 (ISBN 0-317-11245-7, 2017814). Bks Demand UMI.

Greet, Anne H. Jacques Prevert's Word Games. LC 68-65231. 87p. 1983. Repr. of 1968 ed. lib. bdg. 19.95x (ISBN 0-89370-768-6). Borgo Pr.

Greet, Anne H., tr. see Apollinaire, Guillaume.

Greet, Anne Hyde, tr. & annotations by see Apollinaire, Guillaume.

Greetham, D. C. & Speed Hill, W, eds. Text 1: Transactions of the Society for Textual Scholarship. LC 83-45281. (Illus.). 350p. 1984. 37.50 (ISBN 0-404-62550-9). AMS Pr.

Greetings Etc. by Alfreda. All Occasion, Any Occasion, Promise, Favor Card Plaque Gift Instruction Workbook. 1984. pap. text ed. 5.75 (ISBN 0-318-04360-2, Pub. by Greetings). Prosperity & Profits.

--Coffee Substitution Gift: Recipe Card Directory. 1984. pap. text ed. 10.95 (ISBN 0-318-04361-0, Pub. by Greetings). Prosperity & Profits.

--Congratulations in Prose for Any-All Occasions. 1984. pap. text ed. 1.00 (ISBN 0-318-04362-9, Pub. by Greetings). Prosperity & Profits.

--Food Gifts Series Poetry: Calligraphy Editions. 1984. pap. text ed. 3.95 (ISBN 0-318-04363-7, Pub. by Greetings). Prosperity & Profits.

--Honey Gift Card with Suggestions for Use. 1984. pap. text ed. 1.00 (ISBN 0-318-04364-5, Pub. by Greetings). Prosperity & Profits.

--Jams, Jellies, Marmalade, Gift Recipe Card Directory, No. 1. 1984. pap. text ed. 10.95 (ISBN 0-318-04365-3, Pub. by Greetings). Prosperity & Profits.

--Meeting Challenges: Scripture References. 1984. pap. text ed. 2.95 (ISBN 0-318-04372-6, Pub. by Greetings). Prosperity & Profits.

--Mother's Day, Holiday, Pet Birthday, Secretaries Day Etc. Promise, Favor Letters with Suggestions in Poetry. 1984. pap. text ed. 12.95 (ISBN 0-318-04373-4, Pub. by Greetings). Prosperity & Profits.

--Pattern Poetry Greeting Directory, No. 1. 1984. pap. text ed. 9.95 (ISBN 0-318-04376-9, Pub. by Greetings). Prosperity & Profits.

--Seed Gift Greeting Directory, No. 1. 1984. pap. text ed. 9.95 (ISBN 0-318-04378-5, Pub. by Greetings). Prosperity & Profits.

--Small Buisness Services Poetry, Bk. 1. 1984. pap. text ed. 1.50 (ISBN 0-318-04380-7, Pub. by Greetings). Prosperity & Profits.

--Small Business Services Poetry, Bk. 2. 1984. pap. text ed. 1.50 (ISBN 0-318-04381-5, Pub. by Greetings). Prosperity & Profits.

Greever, Garland. A Wiltshire Parson & His Friends: The Correspondence of William Lisle Bowles Together with Four Hitherto Unidentified Reviews by Coleridge. 1926. 25.00 (ISBN 0-8274-3720-X). R West.

Greever, Garland see Anderson, Charles R.

Greever, Jack. Marcos: Estudios Para un Joven En Busca De Identidad. Orig. Title: Mark: an Inductive Bible Study. 64p. (Span.). 1982. pap. 2.50 (ISBN 0-311-12325-2, Edit Mundo). Casa Bautista.

Greever, William S. Arid Domain. Bruchey, Stuart, ed. LC 78-56663. (Management of Public Lands in the U. S. Ser.). (Illus.). 1979. Repr. of 1954 ed. lib. bdg. 16.00x (ISBN 0-405-11334-X). Ayer Co Pubs.

Greeves, Ivan S. London Docks 1800-1980: A Civil Engineering History. 167p. 1980. 33.00x (ISBN 0-7277-0114-2). Am Soc Civil Eng.

Greevy, Doug, jt. ed. see Weinberger, Marvin I.

Grefe, Edward A. Fighting to Win: Business Political Power. 280p. 1981. 35.00 (ISBN 0-15-100023-9, H39956). HarBraceJ.

Grefe, John & Silman, Jeremy. Center Counter. (Illus.). 96p. (Orig.). 1983. pap. 5.50 (ISBN 0-931462-22-3). Chess Ent Inc.

Grefe, Mary, jt. auth. see Fulcher, Claire.

Greffe, Richard, jt. auth. see Gould, Lewis L.

Greg, Andrew. Charles Napier Hemy 1841-1917. (Illus.). 64p. 1985. pap. 15.00x (ISBN 0-8390-0348-X). Abner Schram Ltd.

Greg, Percy. Across the Zodiac, 2 vols. in 1. LC 73-13271. (Classics of Science Fiction Ser.). 602p. 1974. 16.50 (ISBN 0-88355-125-X); pap. 10.00 (ISBN 0-88355-154-3). Hyperion Conn.

Greg, Philo see Beharrel, Peter.

Greg, R. P. A Selection of Old Nursery Rhymes. LC 74-17263. 1975. Repr. of 1903 ed. lib. bdg. 15.00 (ISBN 0-88305-232-6). Norwood Edns.

Greg, W. Variants in the First Quarto of King Lear. LC 68-1839. (Studies in Shakespeare, No. 24). 1969. Repr. of 1940 ed. lib. bdg. 49.95x (ISBN 0-8383-0559-8). Haskell.

Greg, W. W. The Collected Papers of Sir Walter W. Greg. Maxwell, J. C., ed. 1978. Repr. of 1966 ed. lib. bdg. 85.00 (ISBN 0-8482-4173-8). Norwood Edns.

--Jonson's Masque of Gipsies: In the Burley Belvoir & Windsor Versions. 246p. 1979. 10.00x (ISBN 0-686-26937-3). State Mutual Bk.

--Lodge's "Rosalynde". Being the Original of Shakespeare's "As You Like It". 1973. Repr. of 1907 ed. lib. bdg. 15.00 (ISBN 0-8414-4443-9). Folcroft.

Greg, W. W., ed. Clyomon & Clamydes: The Historie of the Two Valiant Knights. LC 82-45768. (Malone Society Reprint Ser.: No. 36). Repr. of 1599 ed. 40.00 (ISBN 0-404-63036-7). AMS Pr.

--The Contention Between Liberality & Prodigality. LC 82-45771. (Malone Society Reprint Ser.: No. 39). Repr. of 1913 ed. 40.00 (ISBN 0-404-63039-1). AMS Pr.

--Everyman: From the Edition by John Skot at Britwell Court. (Material for the Study of the Old English Drama Ser.: No. 1, Vol. 4). pap. 11.00 (ISBN 0-317-15230-0). Kraus Repr.

--Fair Em. LC 82-45792. (Malone Society Reprint Ser.: No. 62). Repr. of 1927 ed. 40.00 (ISBN 0-404-63062-6). AMS Pr.

--Gesta Grayorum: Including the Masque of Proteus. LC 82-45776. (Malone Society Reprint Ser.: No.45). Repr. of 1914 ed. 40.00 (ISBN 0-404-63045-6). AMS Pr.

--The History of King Leir. LC 82-45741. (Malone Society Reprint Ser.: No. 5). Repr. of 1907 ed. 40.00 (ISBN 0-404-63005-7). AMS Pr.

--The Interlude of Johan the Evangelist. LC 82-45739. (Malone Society Reprint Ser.: No. 3). Repr. of 1907 ed. 40.00 (ISBN 0-404-63003-0). AMS Pr.

--The Interlude of Wealth & Health. LC 82-45740. (Malone Society Reprint Ser.: No. 4). Repr. of 1907 ed. 40.00 (ISBN 0-404-63004-9). AMS Pr.

--A Larum for London, or the Seige of Antwerp. LC 82-45770. (Malone Society Reprint Ser.: No. 38). Repr. of 1913 ed. 40.00 (ISBN 0-404-63038-3). AMS Pr.

--Look About You. LC 82-45769. (Malone Society Reprint Ser.: No. 37). Repr. of 1913 ed. 40.00 (ISBN 0-404-63037-5). AMS Pr.

--A Newe Enterlude of Godly Queene Hester, 1561. (Material for the Study of the Old English Drama Ser.: No. 1, Vol. 5). pap. 14.00 (ISBN 0-317-15231-9). Kraus Repr.

--The Pedlar's Prophecy. LC 82-45775. (Malone Society Reprint Ser.: No. 44). 1914. 40.00 (ISBN 0-404-63044-8). AMS Pr.

--The Rare Triumphs of Love & Fortune. LC 82-45799. (Malone Society Reprint Ser.: No. 69). 1930. 40.00 (ISBN 0-404-63069-3). AMS Pr.

--The Second Maiden's Tragedy. LC 82-45751. (Malone Society Reprint Ser.: No. 17). 1909. 40.00 (ISBN 0-404-63017-0). AMS Pr.

--The Tragedy of Claudius Tiberius Nero. LC 82-45778. (Malone Society Reprint Ser.: No. 47). 1914. 40.00 (ISBN 0-404-63047-2). AMS Pr.

--The True Tragedy of Richard the Third. LC 82-45797. (Malone Society Reprints Ser.: No. 67). 1929. 40.00 (ISBN 0-404-63067-7). AMS Pr.

--Two Elizabethan Stage Abridgements: The Battle of Alcazar & Orlando Furioso, 2 vols. LC 82-45784. (Malone Society Reprints Ser.: No. 53). Date not set. Repr. of 1922 ed. Set. 80.00 (ISBN 0-404-63053-7). AMS Pr.

--The Weakest Goeth to the Wall. LC 82-45764. (Malone Society Reprints Ser.: No. 32). 1912. 40.00 (ISBN 0-404-63032-4). AMS Pr.

--Wily Beguiled. LC 82-45765. (Malone Society Reprints Ser.: No. 33). 1912. 40.00 (ISBN 0-404-63033-2). AMS Pr.

--The Wit of a Woman. LC 82-45772. (Malone Society Reprint Ser.: No. 40). 1913. 40.00 (ISBN 0-404-63040-5). AMS PR.

Greg, W. W., jt. ed. see Evans, B. Ifor.

Greg, W. W., ed. see Jonson, Ben.

Greg, W. W. see Jonson, Ben.

Greg, W. W., ed. see Jonson, Ben.

Greg, W. W., ed. see Lodge, Thomas.

Greg, W. W., et al, eds. Collections of the Malone Society Reprint Series, 17 vols. Repr. of 1907 ed. Set. 560.00 (ISBN 0-404-63142-8). AMS Pr.

--The Malone Society Reprints, 143 Vols. Repr. of 1907 ed. Set. 5840.00 (ISBN 0-404-63000-6); 40.00 ea.; double vols. 80.00 (ISBN 0-317-11725-4). AMS Pr.

Greg, Walter. List of English Plays Written Before 1643 & Printed Before 1700. LC 68-25311. (Studies in Drama, No. 39). 1969. Repr. of 1900 ed. lib. bdg. 39.95x (ISBN 0-8383-0950-X). Haskell.

--List of Masques, Pageants, Etc. Supplementary to a List of English Plays. LC 68-25312. (Studies in Drama, No. 39). 1969. Repr. of 1902 ed. lib. bdg. 39.95x (ISBN 0-8383-0942-9). Haskell.

Greg, Walter W. Calculus of Variants. 1927. lib. bdg. 10.00 (ISBN 0-8414-4681-4). Folcroft.

--Capell's Shakesperiana. 1903. lib. bdg. 12.50 (ISBN 0-8414-4682-2). Folcroft.

--Henslowe Papers. 1978. Repr. lib. bdg. 30.00 (ISBN 0-8495-1968-3). Arden Lib.

--Henslowe's Diary, Vol. 1. LC 76-27877. 1904. lib. bdg. 42.00 (ISBN 0-8414-4584-2). Folcroft.

--Henslowe's Papers. LC 72-191805. 1907. lib. bdg. 30.00 (ISBN 0-8414-4683-0). Folcroft.

--A List of English Plays Written Before Sixteen Forty-Three; Printed Before Seventeen Hundred. LC 76-131724. xi, 158p. 1972. Repr. of 1900 ed. 25.00x (ISBN 0-403-00611-2). Scholarly.

--Principles of Emendation in Shakespeare. LC 72-195248. Repr. of 1928 ed. 11.00 (ISBN 0-8414-4523-0). Folcroft.

--Principles of Emendation in Shakespeare. 1971. Repr. of 1928 ed. 10.00x (ISBN 0-403-00613-9). Scholarly.

Greg, Sir Walter W., ed. see Cambridge. University. Trinity College. Library.

Greg, William R. Enigmas of Life. LC 72-323. (Essay Index Reprint Ser.). Repr. of 1879 ed. 21.00 (ISBN 0-8369-2794-X). Ayer Co Pubs.

Greger, Debora. And. LC 85-42670. (Princeton Series of Contemporary Poets). 88p. 1985. 14.95 (ISBN 0-691-06646-9); pap. 7.95 (ISBN 0-691-01423-X). Princeton U Pr.

--Cartography. 1980. signed 50.00x (ISBN 0-686-28114-4). Penumbra Press.

--Movable Islands. LC 79-83985. (Princeton Series of Contemporary Poets). 1980. 14.00 (ISBN 0-691-06422-9); pap. 5.95 (ISBN 0-691-01369-1). Princeton U Pr.

Greger, Janet L., jt. auth. see Christian, Janet L.

Greger, Margaret. Kites for Everyone. LC 84-90383. (Illus.). 136p. (Orig.). 1984. pap. 10.00 (ISBN 0-9613680-0-4). M Greger.

Greger, R., et al, eds. Renal Transport of Organic Substances. (Proceedings of Life Sciences Ser.). (Illus.). 330p. 1981. 39.00 (ISBN 0-387-10904-8). Springer-Verlag.

Greger, Reinhard. Zivilrechtliche Haftung im Strassenverkehr: Grosskommentar zu 7-20 Strassenverkehrsgeseth und zum Haftpflichtgesetz unter Beruecksichtigung des Delikts, Vertrags und Versicherungsrechts Sowie des Schadensregresses. (Grosskommentare der Praxis Ser.). xvi, 560p. (Ger.). 1984. half leather 111.20x (ISBN 3-11-008651-4). De Gruyter.

Gregerman, Ira B. Productivity Improvement: A Guide for Small Business. (Illus.). 240p. 1984. 24.95 (ISBN 0-442-22968-2). Van Nos Reinhold.

Gregersen, E., ed. Language in Africa: An Introductory Survey. (Library of Anthropology). 256p. 1977. 37.25 (ISBN 0-677-04380-5). Gordon.

Gregersen, Edgar. Sexual Practices. (Illus.). 320p. 1982. 18.95 (ISBN 0-531-09899-0). Watts.

Gregersen, H. Ibsen & Spain: A Study in Comparative Drama. 1936. 21.00 (ISBN 0-527-01108-8). Kraus Repr.

Gregersen, Hans M. & Contreras, Arnoldo. United States Investment in the Forest-Based Sector in Latin America: Problems & Potentials. LC 74-21754. pap. 32.00 (ISBN 0-317-26461-3, 2023797). Bks Demand UMI.

Gregersen, Hans & Contreras, Arnoldo H. Economic Analysis of Forestry Projects: Case Studies. (Forestry Papers: No. 17). 208p. (Eng., Fr. & Span., 2nd Printing 1981). 1979. pap. 15.00 (ISBN 92-5-100827-2, F1907, FAO). Unipub.

Gregerson, Kenneth. Predicate & Argument of Rengao Grammar. (Sil Publications in Linguistics Ser.: No. 61). 141p. (Orig.). 1979. pap. 6.50x (ISBN 0-88312-075-5); microfiche (2) 2.86x (ISBN 0-88312-485-8). Summer Inst Ling.

Gregerson, Kenneth & Thomas, David, eds. Mon-Khmer Studies V. 267p. 1976. pap. 7.00 (ISBN 0-88312-788-1); microfiche (3) 3.80 (ISBN 0-88312-358-4). Summer Inst Ling.

Gregerson, Kenneth, jt. ed. see Huttar, George.

Gregerson, Linda. Fire in the Conservatory. LC 82-71648. 65p. 1982. 13.00 (ISBN 0-937872-06-7); pap. 6.00 (ISBN 0-937872-07-5). Dragon Gate.

Gregerson, Marilyn & Thomas, Dorothy, eds. Notes from Indochina On Ethnic Minority Culture. LC 78-65445. (Museum of Anthropology: No. 6). 254p. (Orig.). 1980. pap. 9.45x (ISBN 0-88312-155-7); microfiche (3) 3.80x (ISBN 0-88312-244-8); 3.00 (ISBN 0-88312-335-5). Summer Inst Ling.

Gregg. Clave de Cuaderno Taquigrafia Gregg S90. 1982. 3.80 (ISBN 0-07-024485-5). McGraw.

--Communication & Culture. 2nd ed. write for info (ISBN 0-534-04626-6). Wadsworth Pub.

--Manual del Maestro Dictado y Transcripcion S90. 1982. 5.35 (ISBN 0-07-024486-3). McGraw.

Gregg & Russell. Science & Society: A Reading Writing Text in English. 384p. 1985. lib. bdg. write for info. (ISBN 0-534-04860-9). Wadsworth Pub.

Gregg, Alan. Furtherance of Medical Research. 1941. 29.50x (ISBN 0-685-89754-0). Elliots Bks.

Gregg, Alexander. History of the Old Cheraws. enl ed. LC 75-14029. 1975. Repr. of 1925 ed. 27.50 (ISBN 0-87152-211-X). Reprint.

Gregg, Barbara, jt. auth. see Gregg, John.

Gregg, Benjamin, tr. see Dubiel, Hulmet.

Gregg, Charles T. Plague: An Ancient Disease in the Twentieth Century. rev. ed. 352p. pap. 22.50 (ISBN 0-8263-0807-4); pap. 12.95 (ISBN 0-8263-0803-1). U of NM Pr.

--Tarawa. LC 83-42972. (Illus.). 272p. 1983. 18.95 (ISBN 0-8128-2906-9). Stein & Day.

--Tarawa. 384p. 1985. pap. 3.95 (ISBN 0-8128-8119-2). Stein & Day.

--A Virus of Love & Other Tales of Medical Detection. LC 84-17204. 320p. (Orig.). 1985. pap. 12.95 (ISBN 0-8263-0793-0). U of NM Pr.

Gregg, Chris, ed. see Fila, Larry V., Jr.

Gregg, David L. The Diaries of David Lawrence Gregg, 1853-1858: An American Diplomat in Hawaii. King, Pauline, ed. LC 82-80764. (Illus.). 605p. 1982. 25.00x (ISBN 0-8248-0861-4). UH Pr.

Gregg, Davis W. & Lucas, Vane B., eds. Life & Health Insurance Handbook. 3rd ed. 1973. 26.50x (ISBN 0-256-00169-3). Irwin.

Gregg, Edith, ed. see Tucker, Ellen L.

Gregg, Edith E., ed. The Letters of Ellen Tucker Emerson, 2 Vols. LC 82-10069. (Illus.). 1982. Set. 75.00x (ISBN 0-87338-274-9); Vol. 1, 700p. (ISBN 0-87338-275-7); Vol. 2, 700p. (ISBN 0-87338-276-5). Kent St U Pr.

Gregg, Edward. Queen Anne. (Illus.). 1984. 29.95x (ISBN 0-7100-0400-1); pap. 9.95 (ISBN 0-7448-0018-8, Ark Paperbks). Routledge & Kegan.

Gregg, Elizabeth & Boston Children's Medical Center Staff. What to Do When There's Nothing to Do. 1984. pap. 3.50 (ISBN 0-440-19471-7). Dell.

Gregg, Frank. Federal Land Transfers: The Case for a Westwide Program Based on the Federal Land Policy & Management Act. LC 82-8126. 34p. (Orig.). 1982. pap. 5.00 (ISBN 0-89164-071-1). Conservation Foun.

Gregg, Irwin. The Divine Science Way. 1975. 5.95 (ISBN 0-686-24352-8); pap. 3.95 (ISBN 0-686-24353-6). Divine Sci Fed.

Gregg, J. R. & Leslie, L. A. Gregg Shorthand Dictionary. (Gregg Shorthand Ser.: No. 90). 416p. 1983. 15.95 (ISBN 0-07-024599-1). Mcgraw.

Gregg, J. R. & Harris, F. T., eds. Form & Strategy in Science: Studies Dedicated to Joseph Henry Woodger on His 70th Birthday. 476p. 1964. lib. bdg. 39.50 (ISBN 90-277-0018-4, Pub. by Reidel Holland). Kluwer Academic.

Gregg, J. R., et al. Gregg Shorthand: Series 90. 320p. 1985. 19.95 (ISBN 0-07-024490-1). McGraw.

Gregg, James R. The Story of Optometry. LC 65-12749. (Illus.). pap. 78.80 (ISBN 0-317-07936-0, 2012411). Bks Demand UMI.

--Your Future in New Optometric Careers. (Careers in Depth Ser). (gr. 7 up). 1978. PLB 8.97 (ISBN 0-8239-0449-0). Rosen Group.

Gregg, Joan Y. & Russel, Joan. Past, Present, & Future: A Reading-Writing Text. 384p. 1982. pap. text ed. write for info. (ISBN 0-534-01218-3). Wadsworth Pub.

Gregg, John. How to Launder Money. 1982. pap. 8.00 (ISBN 0-317-03306-9). Loompanics.

Gregg, John & Gregg, Barbara. Best Loved Poems of the American West. LC 78-1241. (Illus.). 480p. 1980. 11.95 (ISBN 0-385-13309-X). Doubleday.

Gregg, John R. Frases y Palabras de Uso Mas Frecuente en Taguigrafi: A Gregg Edicio. (Span). 1971. 9.40 (ISBN 0-07-024598-3). McGraw.

--Gregg Shorthand Dictionary. anniversary ed. 1930. 17.24 (ISBN 0-07-024464-2). McGraw.

--Gregg Shorthand Manual. anniversary ed. 1929. 17.00 (ISBN 0-07-024501-0). McGraw.

--Taquigrafia Gregg, Primer Curso. 1974. 16.00 (ISBN 0-07-024620-3). McGraw.

--Taquigrafia Gregg, Segundo Curso: Edicion Diamante. (Span.). 1970. text ed. 17.25 (ISBN 0-07-024621-1). McGraw.

Gregg, John R. & Leslie, Louis A. Gregg Shorthand, Most-Used Words & Phrases. (Series 90). 128p. 1984. 7.95 (ISBN 0-07-024487-1). McGraw.

Gregg, John R., et al. Gregg Shorthand. (Diamond Jubilee Ser.). 1963. text ed. 17.00 (ISBN 0-07-024591-6). McGraw.

--Gregg Shorthand Dictionary. 2nd ed. (Diamond Jubilee Ser.). 1974. 17.00 (ISBN 0-07-024632-7). McGraw.

--Gregg Shorthand Dictionary Simplified. 1949. 19.95 (ISBN 0-07-024545-2). McGraw.

--Gregg Shorthand Manual, Simplified. 2nd ed. 1955. 14.95 (ISBN 0-07-024548-7); text ed. 17.00 (ISBN 0-07-024549-5). McGraw.

--Gregg Speed Building. 2nd ed. (Diamond Jubilee Ser.). 1972. text ed. 17.16 (ISBN 0-07-024635-1). McGraw.

--Gregg Shorthand. 2nd ed. (Diamond Jubilee Ser.). 1972. 17.00 (ISBN 0-07-024625-4). McGraw.

--Most Used Words & Phases. 1963. 7.48 (ISBN 0-07-024592-4). McGraw.

--Gregg Shorthand Dictionary. (Diamond Jubilee Ser.). 416p. 1972. 19.95 (ISBN 0-07-024631-9). McGraw.

--Gregg Shorthand Dictionary. 2nd ed. LC 73-12581. (Diamond Jubilee Ser.). 416p. (gr. 7 up). 1974. minature ed. 14.84 (ISBN 0-07-024633-5). McGraw.

Gregg, Josiah. The Commerce of the Prairies. Quaife, Milo M., ed. LC 27-1450. (Illus.). xxxiv, 343p. 1967. pap. 7.50x (ISBN 0-8032-5076-2, BB 324, Bison). U of Nebr Pr.

Gregg, Karl C., ed. An Index to the Spanish Theatre Collection in the London Library. LC 84-70405. 399p. 1984. 40.00 (ISBN 0-916613-00-3). Biblio Siglo.

Gregg, Kate L. Thomas Dekker: A Study in Economic & Social Backgrounds. LC 77-3181. 1924. Repr. lib. bdg. 8.50 (ISBN 0-8414-4425-0). Folcroft.

Gregg, L. W., ed. Knowledge & Cognition. 320p. 1974. 29.95x (ISBN 0-89859-468-5). L Erlbaum Assocs.

Gregg, Lee W., ed. Cognition in Learning & Memory: Symposium on Cognition 5th: 1969: Pittsburgh. LC 72-6107. (Illus.). pap. 51.50 (ISBN 0-317-08284-1, 2012427). Bks Demand UMI.

--Knowledge & Cognition. LC 74-16105. (Carnegie Mellon University Cognition Ser.). 320p. 1974. 16.50x (ISBN 0-470-32657-3). Halsted Pr.

Gregg, Lee W. & Steinberg, Erwin, eds. Cognitive Processes in Writing. LC 80-18624. (Illus.). 192p. 1980. text ed. 19.95x (ISBN 0-89859-032-9). L Erlbaum Assocs.

Gregg, Linda. Eight Poems: A Limited Edition. 24p. (Orig.). 1983. pap. 10.00x (ISBN 0-915308-39-8). Graywolf.

--Too Bright to See. LC 80-67983. 72p. 1982. pap. 5.00 (ISBN 0-915308-28-2). Graywolf.

--Too Bright to See. LC 80-67983. 72p. 1981. 9.00 (ISBN 0-915308-27-4). Graywolf.

Gregg, Martin. Dhow Patrol. 208p. 1985. 13.95 (ISBN 0-8027-0818-8). Walker & Co.

Gregg, O. W, jt. ed. see Freeman, T. M.

Gregg, Pauline. Free-Born John: A Biography of John Lilburne. LC 73-22752. (Illus.). 424p. 1974. Repr. of 1961 ed. lib. bdg. 20.00x (ISBN 0-8371-7346-9, GRFJ). Greenwood.

--King Charles I. (Illus.). 508p. 1981. text ed. 24.95x (ISBN 0-460-04437-0, BKA 03726, Pub. by J. M. Dent England). Biblio Dist.

--King Charles I. LC 83-17926. (Illus.). 528p. 1984. 26.95 (ISBN 0-520-05146-7). U of Cal Pr.

Gregg, Phillip, ed. Current Problems in Policy Theory. 1975. pap. 8.00 (ISBN 0-918592-10-0). Policy Studies.

Gregg, Richard. Discipline for Nonviolence. 39p. 1983. pap. 1.00 (ISBN 0-934676-48-8). Greenlf Bks.

Gregg, Richard B. A Discipline for Non-Violence. 1983. pap. 5.00x (ISBN 0-87574-011-1, 011). Pendle Hill.

--Pacifist Program. 1983. pap. 5.00x (ISBN 0-686-43957-0, 005). Pendle Hill.

--Power of Non-Violence. rev. ed. 192p. 1960. pap. 4.95 (ISBN 0-227-67567-3). Attic Pr.

--The Power of Nonviolence. 3rd ed. 192p. (Orig.). 1984. pap. 7.50 (ISBN 0-934676-70-4). Greenlf Bks.

--Symbolic Inducement & Knowing: A Study in the Foundations of Rhetoric. LC 83-26113. 200p. 1984. 17.95x (ISBN 0-87249-434-9). U of SC Pr.

--The Value of Voluntary Simplicity. 1983. pap. 5.00x (ISBN 0-87574-003-0, 003). Pendle Hill.

Gregg, Richard B., jt. auth. see Philbrick, Helen.

Gregg, Robert C. Consolation Philosophy. LC 75-21778. (Patristic Monograph Ser.: No. 3). 1975. pap. 7.50 (ISBN 0-915646-02-1). Phila Patristic.

Gregg, Robert C. & Groh, Dennis E. Early Arianism: A View of Salvation. LC 79-7379. 224p. 1981. 25.95 (ISBN 0-8006-0576-4, 1-576). Fortress.

Gregg, Robert C., ed. Athanasius: The Life of Antony & the Letter to Marcellinus. LC 79-56622. (Classics of Western Spirituality Ser.). 192p. 1980. 11.95 (ISBN 0-8091-0309-5); pap. 8.95 (ISBN 0-8091-2295-2). Paulist Pr.

Gregg, Robert D. The Influence of Border Troubles on Relations Between the United States & Mexico, 1876-1910. LC 78-64167. (Johns Hopkins University. Studies in the Social Sciences. Fifty-Fifth Ser. 1937: 3). Repr. of 1937 ed. 18.50 (ISBN 0-404-61277-6). AMS Pr.

Gregg, Robert E. The Ants of Colorado: Their Ecology, Taxonomy & Geographic Distribution. LC 62-63446. (Illus.). 1963. 23.50x (ISBN 0-87081-027-8). Colo Assoc.

Gregg, Robert S. Influence of Border Troubles on Relations Between the United States & Mexico, 1876-1910. LC 72-98181. (American Scene Ser). 1970. Repr. of 1937 ed. lib. bdg. 32.50 (ISBN 0-306-71833-2). Da Capo.

Gregg, Rodman W., ed. Who's Who in Television. LC 81-64574. (Illus.). 180p. (Orig.). 1984. pap. 17.95 (ISBN 0-941710-11-4). Packard.

--Who's Who in the Motion Picture Industry. 4th, rev. ed. LC 81-64574. 200p. (Orig.). 1985. pap. text ed. 17.95 (ISBN 0-941710-03-3). Packard.

--Who's Who Television: Writers, Directors, Producers & the Networks. 185p. 1985. pap. 16.95x (ISBN 0-941710-11-4). Packard.

Gregg, Rosalie, ed. see Wise County Historical Survey Committee.

Gregg, S. J. & Sing, K. S. Absorption, Surface Area & Porosity. 2nd ed. 1982. 55.00 (ISBN 0-12-300956-1). Acad Pr.

Gregg, S. J., ed. see Conference on Vacuum Microbalance Techniques (10th: 1972: Uxbridge, England.

Gregg, Stuart. The Complete Idiot's Guide to Dx. Bash, Richard M., ed. (Illus.). 144p. 1981. pap. 12.95 (ISBN 0-938408-03-8). Bash Educ Serv.

Gregg, Sylvia J., jt. auth. see Tamminen, Mildred.

Gregg, Thomas G., jt. auth. see Mettler, Lawrence E.

Gregg, Tosh, jt. auth. see Muir, John.

Gregg Typing. Gregg Typing: IBM Intermediate Course. 2nd ed. 1985. write for info. McGraw.

--Gregg Typing, IPM Basic Course, Units 1-5. 2nd ed. 250.00 ea. (ISBN 0-07-086200-1). Unit 1 (ISBN 0-07-086201-X). Unit 2 (ISBN 0-07-086202-8). Unit 3 (ISBN 0-07-086203-6). Unit 4 (ISBN 0-07-086204-4). Unit 5 (ISBN 0-07-086206-0). McGraw.

Gregg, Vernon. Human Memory. (Essential Psychology Ser.). 1975. pap. 4.50x (ISBN 0-416-81980-X, NO. 2737). Methuen Inc.

Gregg, W. W. The Printing of Mayne's Plays. Incl. Worcester College Library. Wilkinson, C. H. Repr. of 1927 ed. (Oxford Bibliographical Society Ser.: Vol. 1, Pt. 4). pap. 13.00 (ISBN 0-317-17861-X). Kraus Repr.

Greggains, Joanie. Joanie Greggains' Total Shape-Up. LC 83-25448. (Illus.). 224p. 1984. 16.95 (ISBN 0-453-00455-5). NAL.

Greggains, Joanie & Foreman, John. Joanie Greggains Total Shape-Up. pap. 8.95 (ISBN 0-452-25672-0, Plume). NAL.

Gregier, Don M. Chiefs Without Indians: Asquith, Lloyd George, & the Liberal Remnant, 1916-1935. LC 82-17546. (Illus.). 330p. (Orig.). 1983. lib. bdg. 26.75 (ISBN 0-8191-2806-6); pap. text ed. 14.00 (ISBN 0-8191-2807-4). U Pr of Amer.

Grego, Joseph. A History of Parliamentary Elections & Electioneering: From the Stuarts to Queen Victoria. LC 73-141755. (Illus.). 403p. 1974. Repr. of 1892 ed. 70.00x (ISBN 0-8103-4030-5). Gale.

Grego, M., jt. auth. see Lennie, Delia.

Gregoir, Edouard G. Gretry (Andre-Ernest-Modeste) celebre compositeur belge. LC 76-43919. (Music & Theatre in France in the 17th & 18th Centuries). Repr. of 1883 ed. 48.50 (ISBN 0-404-60163-4). AMS Pr.

Gregoire, Abbe Henri de see De Gregoire, Abbe Henri.

Gregoire, H. Recueil des Inscriptiones Grecques Chretiennes d'Asie Mineure. 1985. Repr. of 1922 ed. 15.00 (ISBN 0-89005-291-3). Ares.

Gregoire, Henri. Autbur de L'Epopee Byzantine. 366p. 1975. 60.00x (ISBN 0-902089-83-8, Pub. by Variorum). State Mutual Bk.

Gregoire, R. & Perlman, F. Worker-Student Action Committees: France, May 1968. 1969. 1.50x (ISBN 0-934868-08-5). Black & Red.

Gregoire, Reginald, et al. The Monastic Realm. LC 85-43046. (Illus.). 288p. 1985. 65.00 (ISBN 0-8478-0664-2). Rizzoli Intl.

Gregonis, Linda M. & Reinhard, Karl J. Hohokam Indians of the Tucson Bascu. 48p. 1979. pap. 4.95 (ISBN 0-8165-0700-7). U of Ariz Pr.

Gregor, jt. auth. see Wilson.

Gregor, A. J. & Chang, Maria H. The Republic of China & U. S. Policy: A Study in Human Rights. LC 83-14130. 160p. 1983. pap. 7.00 (ISBN 0-89633-073-7). Ethics & Public Policy.

Gregor, A. James. Crisis in the Philippines: A Threat to U. S. Interests. LC 84-21124. 128p. (Orig.). 1984. pap. 6.00 (ISBN 0-89633-087-7). Ethics & Public Policy.

--The Fascist Persuasion in Radical Politics. LC 73-2463. 424p. 1974. 40.00 (ISBN 0-691-07556-5). Princeton U Pr.

--Ideology & Development: Sun Yat-Sen & the Economic History of Taiwan. (China Research Monographs: No. 23). 1982. 8.00x (ISBN 0-686-86115-9). IEAS.

--Young Mussolini & the Intellectual Origins of Fascism. LC 78-64470. 1979. 31.00x (ISBN 0-520-03799-5). U of Cal Pr.

Gregor, A. James & Chang, Maria H. Essays on Sun Yat-Sen & the Economic Development of Taiwan. (Occasional Papers--Reprints Series in Contemporary Asian Studies: No. 1-1983 (54)). 54p. (Orig.). 1983. pap. 3.00 (ISBN 0-942182-53-7). U MD Law.

--The Iron Triangle: A U. S. Security Policy for Northeast Asia. (Publication 292). x, 160p. 1984. lib. bdg. 23.95x (ISBN 0-8179-7921-2); pap. 9.95x (ISBN 0-8179-7922-0). Hoover Inst Pr.

Gregor, Arthur. Animal Babies. (Illus.). (ps-3). 1976. pap. 1.95 (ISBN 0-06-443013-8, Trophy). HarpJ.

--Embodiment & Other Poems. LC 82-3268. 110p. 1982. 14.95 (ISBN 0-935296-28-X); pap. 7.95 (ISBN 0-935296-29-8). Sheep Meadow.

--The Little Elephant. new ed. (Illus.). (ps-3). 1976. pap. 1.95 (ISBN 0-06-443014-6, Trophy). HarpJ.

--A Longing in the Land: Memoir of a Quest. LC 82-17043. (Illus.). 288p. 1983. 18.95 (ISBN 0-8052-3834-4). Schocken.

Gregor, Arthur S. Life Styles: An Introduction to Cultural Anthropology. LC 78-3416. (Illus.). 1978. 9.95 (ISBN 0-684-15599-0, ScribT). Scribner.

Gregor, Carol. Working Out Together: A Complete Fitness Program for Partners. (Illus.). 224p. (Orig.). 1983. pap. 9.95 (ISBN 0-425-05878-6). Berkley Pub.

Gregor, Carol & Samon, Katherine A. Carol Gregor's Body Type Workout Book. (Illus.). 160p. 1984. pap. 10.95 (ISBN 0-396-08423-0). Dodd.

Gregor, D. B. Celtic: A Comparative Study. 400p. 1980. 90.00x (ISBN 0-900891-41-6, Pub. by Oleander Pr); pap. 16.00x (ISBN 0-900891-56-4, Pub. by Oleander Pr). State Mutual Bk.

--Friulan: Language & Literature. (Oleander Language & Literature Ser.: Vol. 5). (Illus.). 1975. 35.00 (ISBN 0-902675-39-7). Oleander Pr.

--Romagnol: Language & Literature. (Oleander Language & Literature Ser.). (Illus.). 1972. 35.00 (ISBN 0-902675-12-5). Oleander Pr.

Gregor, D. B., ed. Mad Nap-Pulon Matt: Anonymous Sixteenth Century Romagnol Poem in English Verse Translation. (Oleander Language & Literature Ser.: Vol. 7). 1976. 35.00 (ISBN 0-902675-37-0). Oleander Pr.

Gregor, Douglas B. Celtic: A Comparative Study. (Oleander Language & Literature Ser.). 1980. 35.00 (ISBN 0-900891-41-6); pap. 25.00 (ISBN 0-900891-56-4). Oleander Pr.

--Romontsch: Language & Literature: Sursilvan Rhaeto Romance of Switzerland. (Oleander Language & Literature Ser.: Vol. 11). viii, 388p. 1982. pap. 35.00 (ISBN 0-900891-39-4). Oleander Pr.

Gregor, Elinor. The Tooth Fairy. Munch, Helen, ed. (Illus.). 32p. 1983. pap. 4.50 (ISBN 0-88084-119-2). Alemany Pr.

Gregor, Harry P., ed. Biomedical Applications of Polymers. LC 75-6846. (Polymer Science & Technology Ser.: Vol. 7). 239p. 1975. 42.50x (ISBN 0-306-36407-7, Plenum Pr). Plenum Pub.

Gregor, Howard F. Industrialization of U. S. Agriculture: An Interpretive Atlas. (Special Study in Agriculture-Aquaculture Science & Policy). 275p. 1982. 29.50x (ISBN 0-86531-236-2). Westview.

Gregor, Ian. The Great Web: The Form of Hardy's Major Fiction. 240p. 1982. pap. 7.95 (ISBN 0-571-11852-6). Faber & Faber.

--Reading the Victorian Novel: Detail into Form. (Critical Studies). (Illus.). 314p. 1980. text ed. 28.50x (ISBN 0-06-492542-0). B&N Imports.

Gregor, Ian, jt. auth. see Kinkead-Weeks, Mark.

Gregor, Ian, ed. Brontes: A Collection of Critical Essays. LC 78-126819. (Twentieth Century Views Ser). 1970. 12.95 (ISBN 0-13-083899-3, STC92, Spec). P-H.

Gregor, J. Italian Fascism & Developmental Dictatorship. LC 79-83992. 1979. 40.00 (ISBN 0-691-05286-7). Princeton U Pr.

Gregor, Josef. Masks of the World. LC 68-18150. (Illus.). 1968. Repr. of 1930 ed. 33.00 (ISBN 0-405-08579-6, Blom Pubns). Ayer Co Pubs.

Gregor, Joseph. Kulturgeschichte der Oper. 2nd, rev. & enl. ed. LC 80-2282. Repr. of 1950 ed. 57.50 (ISBN 0-404-18847-8). AMS Pr.

Gregor, Joseph, jt. auth. see Fulop-Miller, Rene.

Gregor, Mary J., tr. see Vant.

Gregor, Richard see McNeal, Robert H.

Gregor, T. Manufacturing Processes: Ceramics. 1976. pap. text ed. 8.84 (ISBN 0-13-555664-3). P-H.

Gregor, Thomas. Anxious Pleasures: The Sexual Lives of an Amazonian People. (Illus.). 240p. 1985. 19.95 (ISBN 0-226-30742-5). U of Chicago Pr.

--Mehinaku: The Drama of Daily Life in a Brazilian Indian Village. LC 76-54659. xvi, 382p. 1980. lib. bdg. 12.00x (ISBN 0-226-30746-8, P898, Phoen). U of Chicago Pr.

--Mehinaku: The Drama of Daily Life in a Brazilian Indian Village. LC 76-54659. 1977. lib. bdg. 24.00x (ISBN 0-226-30744-1). U of Chicago Pr.

Gregor, U. & Patalas, E. Geschichte Des Films, 2 vols. 560p. (Ger.). 1976. pap. 13.95 (ISBN 3-499-16193-1, M-7421). French & Eur.

Gregor, W. G., ed. see Gray, J. H.

Gregor, Walter. Counting out Rhymes of Children. LC 77-26942. 1891. 15.00 (ISBN 0-8414-4461-7). Folcroft.

--An Echo of the Olden Time from the North of Scotland. LC 76-44449. 1976. Repr. of 1874 ed. lib. bdg. 30.00 (ISBN 0-8414-4510-9). Folcroft.

--Notes on the Folk-Lore of the North-East of Scotland. (Folk-Lore Society, London, Monographs: Vol. 7). pap. 24.00 (ISBN 0-317-17856-3). Kraus Repr.

Gregor, Walter, ed. see Rolland, John.

Gregoratos, Gabriel, jt. ed. see Karliner, Joel.

Gregor-Dellin, Martin. Richard Wagner: His Life, His Work, His Century, 2 Vols. Brownjohn, J. Maxwell, tr. from Ger. (Helen & Kurt Wolff Bk.). (Illus.). 592p. 1983. 25.00 (ISBN 0-15-177151-0). HarBraceJ.

Gregores, Emma & Suarez, Jorge A. Description of Colloquial Guarani: Containing a Phonology & Grammar of Spoken Guarani & a Guarani-English Vocabulary of 1130 Entries. (Janua Linguarum, Ser. Practica: No. 27). 1967. pap. text ed. 33.60x (ISBN 90-2790-644-0). Mouton.

Gregori, Mina & Christiansen, Keith. The Age of Caravaggio. (Illus.). 352p. 1985. 45.00 (ISBN 0-8478-0596-4). Rizzoli Intl.

Gregori, Mina, et al. The Age of Caravaggio. (Illus.). 200p. 1985. 35.00 (ISBN 0-87099-380-1); pap. 25.00 (ISBN 0-87099-382-8). Metro Mus Art.

Gregoriadis, G. & Allison, A. C. Liposomes in Biological Systems. LC 79-40507. 412p. 1980. 94.95 (ISBN 0-471-27608-1). Wiley.

Gregoriadis, G., et al, eds. Receptor-Mediated Targeting of Drugs. (NATO ASI Series A, Life Sciences). 492p. 1985. 79.50x (ISBN 0-306-41831-2, Plenum Press). Plenum Pub.

Gregoriadis, Gregory. Liposome Technology. 1984. Vol. I, 304. 83.00 (ISBN 0-8493-5316-5); Vol., 240. 64.00 (ISBN 0-317-05131-8); Vol. III, 320. 83.00 (ISBN 0-317-05132-6). CRC Pr.

Gregoriadis, Gregory, ed. Drug Carriers in Biology & Medicine. 1979. 67.50 (ISBN 0-12-301050-0). Acad Pr.

Gregoriadis, Gregory, et al, eds. Targeting of Drugs. (NATO ASI Series A, Life Sciences: Vol. 47). 440p. 1982. 55.00x (ISBN 0-306-41001-X, Plenum Pr). Plenum Pub.

Gregorian, Joyce. The Broken Citadel. LC 75-8869. (Illus.). 384p. (gr. 4-8). 1975. 8.95 (ISBN 0-689-30476-5). Atheneum.

Gregorian, Joyce B. The Broken Citadel. 1983. pap. 3.95 (ISBN 0-441-08099-5, Pub. by Ace Science Fiction). Ace Bks.

--Castledown: A Haunting Tale of Magic & Nature. 1983. pap. 2.95 (ISBN 0-441-09240-3, Pub. by Ace Science Fiction). Ace Bks.

Gregorian, Juanita L. Glorious Thunder. 144p. 1986. 10.95 (ISBN 0-89962-498-7). Todd & Honeywell.

Gregorian, Vartan. The Emergence of Modern Afghanistan: Politics of Reform & Modernization, 1880-1946. LC 69-13178. (Illus.). 1969. 37.50x (ISBN 0-8047-0706-5). Stanford U Pr.

Gregorian, Vartan, ed. Censorship: Five Hundred Years of Conflict. (Illus.). 144p. 1984. 29.95 (ISBN 0-19-503529-1). Oxford U Pr.

Gregorich, Barbara. Adjectives & Adverbs. (Horizons II Ser.). (Illus.). 24p. (gr. 3-4). 1980. wkbk. 2.50 (ISBN 0-89403-596-7). EDC.

--All about Animals. Hoffman, Joan, ed. (A Get Ready! Bk.). (Illus.). 32p. (ps). 1983. pap. text ed. 1.95 (ISBN 0-938256-68-8). Sch Zone Pub Co.

--Alphabet: Lowercase. Hoffman, Joan, ed. (A Get Ready! Bk.). (Illus.). 32p. (ps). 1983. pap. text ed. 1.95 (ISBN 0-938256-66-1). Sch Zone Pub Co.

--Alphabet: Uppercase. Hoffman, Joan, ed. (A Get Ready! Bk.). (Illus.). 32p. (ps). 1983. pap. text ed. 1.95 (ISBN 0-938256-65-3). Sch Zone Pub Co.

--Apostrophe, Colon, Hyphen. (Horizons II Ser.). (Illus.). 24p. (gr. 3-4). 1980. wkbk. 2.50 (ISBN 0-89403-593-2). EDC.

--Beep, Beep: Grades K-2. Hoffman, Joan, ed. (Start to Read! Ser.). (Illus.). 16p. (Orig.). 1984. pap. 1.95 (ISBN 0-88743-007-4, 06007). Sch Zone Pub Co.

--Beginning Sounds. Hoffman, Joan, ed. (A Get Ready! Bk.). (Illus.). 32p. (ps). 1983. pap. text ed. 1.95 (ISBN 0-938256-54-8). Sch Zone Pub Co.

--Blends. Hoffman, Joan, ed. (An I Know It! Bk.). (Illus.). 32p. (gr. 1-3). 1981. pap. text ed. 1.95 (ISBN 0-938256-39-4). Sch Zone Pub Co.

--Capital Letters. (Horizons II Ser.). (Illus.). 24p. (gr. 3-4). 1980. wkbk. 2.50 (ISBN 0-89403-604-1). EDC.

--Colors. Hoffman, Joan, ed. (A Get Ready! Bk.). (Illus.). 32p. (ps). 1983. pap. text ed. 1.95 (ISBN 0-938256-64-5). Sch Zone Pub Co.

--Comma. (Horizons II Ser.). (Illus.). 24p. (gr. 3-4). 1980. wkbk. 2.50 (ISBN 0-89403-595-9). EDC.

--The Comprehension Adventure. (Reading Ser.). 48p. (gr. 7-12). 1984. 4.95 (ISBN 0-88160-109-8, LW 1004). Learning Wks.

--Connect the Dots. Hoffman, Joan, ed. (Get Ready! Bk.). (Illus.). 32p. (ps). 1983. pap. text ed. 1.95 (ISBN 0-938256-58-0). Sch Zone Pub Co.

--Consonants. Hoffman, Joan, ed. (An I Know It! Bk.). (Illus.). 32p. (gr. 1-3). 1981. pap. text ed. 1.95 (ISBN 0-938256-37-8). Sch Zone Pub Co.

--Context Clues. (Horizons II Ser.). (Illus.). 24p. (gr. 3-4). 1980. wkbk. 2.50 (ISBN 0-89403-602-5). EDC.

--Counting One to Ten. Hoffman, Joan, ed. (A Get Ready! Bk.). (Illus.). 32p. (ps). 1983. pap. text ed. 1.95 (ISBN 0-938256-56-4). Sch Zone Pub Co.

--Dictionary Skills. (Horizons II Ser.). (Illus.). 24p. (gr. 3-4). 1980. wkbk. 2.50 (ISBN 0-89403-605-X). EDC.

--D'Nealian Home-School Activities. 1985. pap. 4.95 (ISBN 0-673-18176-6). Scott F.

--Does it Belong? Hoffman, Joan, ed. (A Get Ready! Bk.). (Illus.). 32p. (ps). 1983. pap. text ed. 1.95 (ISBN 0-938256-59-9). Sch Zone Pub Co.

--Elephant & Envelope. Hoffman, Joan, ed. (Start to Read! Ser.). (Illus.). 16p. (gr. k-2). 1985. pap. 1.95 (ISBN 0-88743-017-1, 06016). Sch Zone Pub Co.

--Expanding Your Vocabulary. LC 78-730053. (Illus.). 1978. pap. text ed. 135.00 (ISBN 0-89290-126-8, 327-SATC). Soc for Visual.

--Figures of Speech. (Horizons II Ser.). (Illus.). 24p. (gr. 3-4). 1980. wkbk. 2.50 (ISBN 0-89403-601-7). EDC.

--Following Directions. Hoffman, Joan, ed. (A Get Ready! Bk.). (Illus.). 32p. (ps). 1983. pap. text ed. 1.95 (ISBN 0-938256-62-9). Sch Zone Pub Co.

--The Fox on the Box. Hoffman, Joan, ed. (Start to Read! Ser.). (Illus.). 16p. (Orig.). (gr. k-2). 1984. pap. 1.95 (ISBN 0-88743-005-8, 06005). Sch Zone Pub Co.

--The Gum on the Drum. Hoffman, Joan, ed. (Start to Read! Ser.). (Illus.). 16p. (Orig.). (gr. k-2). 1984. pap. 1.95 (ISBN 0-88743-004-X, 06004). Sch Zone Pub Co.

--Hidden Pictures. Hoffman, Joan, ed. (A Get Ready! Bk.). (Illus.). 32p. (Orig.). (ps). 1983. pap. text ed. 1.95 (ISBN 0-938256-50-5). Sch Zone Pub Co.

--I Want a Pet. Hoffman, Joan, ed. (Start to Read! Ser.). (Illus.). 16p. (Orig.). (gr. k-2). 1984. pap. 1.95 (ISBN 0-88743-003-1, 06003). Sch Zone Pub Co.

--Jace, Mace, & the Big Race. Hoffman, Joan, ed. (Start to Read! Ser.). (Illus.). 16p. (Orig.). (gr. k-2). 1985. pap. 1.95 (ISBN 0-88743-018-X, 06018). Sch Zone Pub Co.

--Jog, Frog, Jog. Hoffman, Joan, ed. (Start to Read! Ser.). (Illus.). 16p. (Orig.). (gr. k-2). 1984. pap. 1.95 (ISBN 0-88743-006-6, 06006). Sch Zone Pub Co.

--Long Vowels. Hoffman, Joan, ed. (An I Know It! Bk.). (Illus.). 32p. (gr. 1-3). 1981. pap. text ed. 1.95 (ISBN 0-938256-41-6). Sch Zone Pub Co.

--Mazes. Hoffman, Joan, ed. (A Get Ready! Bk.). (Illus.). 32p. (ps). 1983. pap. text ed. 1.95 (ISBN 0-938256-57-2). Sch Zone Pub Co.

--My Friend Goes Left. Hoffman, Joan, ed. (A Start to Read! Ser.). (Illus.). 16p. (Orig.). (gr. k-2). 1984. pap. 1.95 (ISBN 0-88743-008-2, 06008). Sch Zone Pub Co.

--Nine Men Chase a Hen. Hoffman, Joan, ed. (Start to Read! Ser.). (Illus.). 16p. (Orig.). (gr. k-2). 1984. pap. 1.95 (ISBN 0-88743-009-0, 06009). Sch Zone Pub Co.

--Opposites. Hoffman, Joan, ed. (A Get Ready! BK.). (Illus.). 32p. (ps). 1983. pap. text ed. 1.95 (ISBN 0-938256-60-2). Sch Zone Pub Co.

--Period, Question Mark, Exclamation Mark. (Horizons II Ser.). (Illus.). 24p. (gr. 3-4). 1980. wkbk. 2.50 (ISBN 0-89403-592-4). EDC.

--Prefixes, Bases, & Suffixes. (Horizons II Ser.). (Illus.). 24p. (gr. 3-4). 1980. wkbk. 2.50 (ISBN 0-89403-600-9). EDC.

--Prepositions & Conjunctions. (Horizons II Ser.). (Illus.). 24p. (gr. 3-4). 1980. wkbk. 2.50 (ISBN 0-89403-597-5). EDC.

--Rhyming Families. Hoffman, Joan, ed. (An I Know It! Bk.). (Illus.). 32p. (gr. 1-3). 1981. pap. text ed. 1.95 (ISBN 0-938256-38-6). Sch Zone Pub Co.

--Rhyming Pictures. Hoffman, Joan, ed. (A Get Ready! Bk.). (Illus.). 32p. (ps). 1983. pap. text ed. 1.95 (ISBN 0-938256-53-X). Sch Zone Pub Co.

--Same or Different. Hoffman, Joan, ed. (A Get Ready! Bk.). (Illus.). 32p. (ps). 1983. pap. text ed. 1.95 (ISBN 0-938256-52-1). Sch Zone Pub Co.

--Say Good Night. Hoffman, Joan, ed. (Start to Read! Ser.). (Illus.). 16p. (Orig.). (gr. k-2). 1984. pap. 1.95 (ISBN 0-88743-010-4, 06010). Sch Zone Pub Co.

--School Time Fun. Hoffman, Joan, ed. (A Get Ready! Bk.). (Illus.). 32p. (ps). 1983. pap. text ed. 1.95 (ISBN 0-938256-67-X). Sch Zone Pub Co.

--Shapes. Hoffman, Joan, ed. (A Get Ready! Bk.). (Illus.). 32p. (ps). 1983. pap. text ed. 1.95 (ISBN 0-938256-63-7). Sch Zone Pub Co.

--Short Vowels. Hoffman, Joan, ed. (An I Know It! Bk.). (Illus.). 32p. (gr. 1-3). 1981. pap. text ed. 1.95 (ISBN 0-938256-40-8). Sch Zone Pub Co.

--Sue Likes Blue. Hoffman, Joan, ed. (Start To Read! Ser.). (Illus.). 16p. (Orig.). (gr. k-2). 1984. pap. 1.95 (ISBN 0-88743-011-2, 06011). Sch Zone Pub Co.

--That's Work! Hoffman, Joan, ed. (A Get Ready! Bk.). 32p. (ps). 1983. pap. text ed. 1.95 (ISBN 0-938256-69-6). Sch Zone Pub Co.

--Up Went the Goat. Hoffman, Joan, ed. (Start to Read! Ser.). (Illus.). 16p. (Orig.). (gr. k-2). 1984. pap. 1.95 (ISBN 0-88743-002-3, 06002). Sch Zone Pub Co.

--What Order? Hoffman, Joan, ed. (A Get Ready! Bk.). 32p. (ps). 1983. pap. text ed. 1.95 (ISBN 0-938256-61-0). Sch Zone Pub Co.

--What's Missing? Hoffman, Joan, ed. (A Get Ready! Bk.). 32p. (ps). 1983. pap. text ed. 1.95 (ISBN 0-938256-55-6). Sch Zone Pub Co.

--Where Is It? Hoffman, Joan, ed. (A Get Ready Bk.). 32p. (ps). 1983. pap. text ed. 1.95 (ISBN 0-938256-51-3). Sch Zone Pub Co.

--Word Problems: Grades 1-2 Math. Hoffman, Joan, ed. (An I Know It! Bk.). 32p. (gr. 1-2). 1982. pap. text ed. 1.95 (ISBN 0-938256-45-9). Sch Zone Pub Co.

--Word Problems: Grades 3-4 Math. Hoffman, Joan, ed. (An I Know It! Bk.). (Illus.). 32p. (gr. 3-4). 1982. pap. text ed. 1.95 (ISBN 0-938256-46-7). Sch Zone Pub Co.

Gregorich, Barbara & Odom, Clark. Fractions. LC 79-730045. (Illus.). 1978. 135.00 (ISBN 0-89290-094-6, A510-SATC). Soc for Visual.

Gregorich, Barbara & Waldowski, Therese F. Punctuation Through Proofreading. LC 78-730056. (Illus.). 1977. pap. text ed. 135.00 (ISBN 0-89290-124-1, A325). Soc for Visual.

--The Research Paper. LC 78-730060. (Illus.). 1977. pap. text ed. 135.00 (ISBN 0-89290-124-1, A323). Soc for Visual.

Gregorich, Barbara & Zack, Carol. The Newspaper: Reading Skills. LC 78-730963. (Illus.). 1978. pap. text ed. 135.00 (ISBN 0-89290-114-4, A160). Soc for Visual.

Gregorich, Barbara, ed. That's Not All! LC 6019. (Start to Read! Ser.). (Illus.). 16p. (Orig.). (gr. k-2). 1985. pap. 1.95 (ISBN 0-88743-019-8, 06019). Sch Zone Pub Co.

Gregorich, Barbara, ed. see Antle, Nancy.

Gregorich, Barbara, ed. see Johnson, Sharon S.

Gregorich, Barbara, ed. see Simon, Shirley.

Gregorio, M. Pauline, ed. Medical Record Library Science Examination Review Book. 3rd ed. 1976. spiral bdg. 14.00 (ISBN 0-87488-496-9). Med Exam.

Gregorio, Mario A. Di see Di Gregorio, Mario A.

Gregorius, Saint Histoire Ecclesiastique Des Francs, 4 vols. 1967. 154.00 (ISBN 0-384-19875-9); pap. 130.00 (ISBN 0-384-19874-0). Johnson Repr.

--Les Livres des Miracles & Autres Opuscules, 4 Vols. 1863. Set. 149.00 (ISBN 0-384-19888-0); 38.00 ea.; pap. 32.00 ea.; Set. pap. 125.00 (ISBN 0-384-19889-9). Johnson Repr.

--Zehn Bucher Frankischer Geschichte, 3 vols. 4th ed. Hellmann, S., ed. Von Geisebrecht, Wilhel M, tr. 1911-1913. 34.00 ea. (ISBN 0-384-19908-9). Johnson Repr.

Gregorius I. Life & Miracles of Saint Benedict: Book Two of Dialogues. Zimmermann, Odo J. & Avery, Benedict R., trs. from Latin. LC 80-19624. xv, 87p. 1980. Repr. of 1949 ed. lib. bdg. 18.75x (ISBN 0-313-22766-7, GRLI). Greenwood.

Gregorovius, Ferdinand. Lucretia Borgia. LC 68-20226. (Illus.). 401p. 1968. Repr. of 1903 ed. 24.50 (ISBN 0-405-08580-X, Blom Pubns). Ayer Co Pubs.

--Rome & Medieval Culture. Morrison, K. F., ed. Hamilton, Mrs. Gustavus, tr. from Ger. LC 72-142683. (Classic European Historians Ser). xxviii, 466p. 1973. pap. 4.75x (ISBN 0-226-30750-6, P427, Phoen). U of Chicago Pr.

Gregorovius, Ferdinand A. History of the City of Rome in the Middle Ages, 8 Vols. in 13 Pts. Hamilton, Annie, tr. LC 1-10138. Repr. of 1912 ed. Set. 520.00 (ISBN 0-404-02920-5); 40.00 ea. AMS Pr.

Gregorvich, Barbara & Manoni, Mary H. Learning to Spell Correctly. LC 78-730054. (Illus.). 1978. pap. text ed. 135.00 (ISBN 0-89290-127-6, 331-SATC). Soc for Visual.

Gregorvich, Barbara, jt. auth. see Mahoney, Susan.

Gregory. A Book of Saints & Wonders. 116p. 1971. Repr. of 1906 ed. text ed. 12.00x (ISBN 0-900675-36-5, Pub. by Colin Symthe England). Humanities.

--Irish Folk-History Plays: Second Series-The Tragic-Comedies. 198p. 1982. Repr. of 1912 ed. lib. bdg. 35.00 (ISBN 0-8495-2129-7). Arden Lib.

--The Kiltartan Poetry History & Wonder Books. 213p. 1971. Repr. of 1909 ed. text ed. 17.50x (ISBN 0-900675-33-0, Pub. by Colin Symthe England). Humanities.

--Seven Short Plays. 204p. 1982. Repr. of 1915 ed. lib. bdg. 30.00 (ISBN 0-8495-2130-0). Arden Lib.

--Teaching of Saint Gregory: An Early Armenian Catechism. Thomson, Robert W., et al, trs. from Arm. LC 78-115482. (Armenian Texts & Studies: No. 3). 1971. 14.00x (ISBN 0-674-87038-7). Harvard U Pr.

--Visions & Beliefs in the West of Ireland Collected & Arranged by Lady Gregory: With Two Essays & Notes by W.B. Yeats. 2nd ed. 1976. text ed. 17.50x (ISBN 0-7705-1412-X, Pub. by Colin Smythe); pap. text ed. 8.00x (ISBN 0-7705-1412-X). Humanities.

Gregory, A. Woodworking. (Illus.). 82p. 1970. 11.95 (ISBN 0-85219-601-6, Pub. by Batsford England). David & Charles.

Gregory, A. Charles & Gregory, Francis T. Journals of Australian Explorations. LC 68-55189. 1968. Repr. of 1884 ed. lib. bdg. 15.00x (ISBN 0-8371-0455-6, GRJO). Greenwood.

Gregory, Alexis K., ed. see Massie, Robert & Sweezey, Marilyn P.

Gregory, Allene. French Revolution & the English Novel. LC 68-764. (Studies in Comparative Literature, No. 35). 1969. Repr. of 1915 ed. lib. bdg. 51.95x (ISBN 0-8383-0560-1). Haskell.

--French Revolution & the English Novel. LC 65-27134. 1965. Repr. of 1915 ed. 24.50x (ISBN 0-8046-0183-6, Pub. by Kennikat). Assoc Faculty Pr.

Gregory, Andre, jt. auth. see Shawn, Wallace.

Gregory, Anita. The Strange Case of Rudi Schneider. LC 84-10591. 464p. 1985. 29.50 (ISBN 0-8108-1711-X). Scarecrow.

Gregory, Augusta. Irish Legends for Children. (Illus.). 90p. (gr. 6 up). 1983. pap. 3.95 (ISBN 0-85342-691-0, Pub. by Mercier Pr Ireland). Irish Bk Ctr.

Gregory, Augusta, tr. see Moliere, Jean B.

Gregory, Augusta I. Poets & Dreamers: Studies & Translations from the Irish by Lady Gregory, Including Nine Plays by Douglas Hyde. 5th ed. (The Coole Edition of the Collected Works of Lady Gregory Ser.). 1974. text ed. 25.00x (ISBN 0-19-519790-9). Oxford U Pr.

Gregory, B. A. An Introduction to Electrical Instrumentation & Measurement Systems. 2nd ed. LC 80-22869. 446p. 1981. pap. 34.95x (ISBN 0-470-27092-6). Halsted Pr.

Gregory - Bishop of Tours. History of the Franks. Brehaut, Ernest, tr. (Columbia University Records of Civilization Ser). 1969. pap. 7.95x (ISBN 0-393-09845-1, NortonC). Norton.

Gregory, C. A. Gifts & Commodities. (Studies in Political Economy: Vol. 2). 1983. 39.00 (ISBN 0-12-301460-3); pap. 18.00 (ISBN 0-12-301462-X). Acad Pr.

Gregory, C. E. Explosives for Australasian Engineers. 3rd ed. (Illus.). 1977. 25.00x (ISBN 0-7022-1391-8). U of Queensland Pr.

--Explosives for North American Engineers. 3rd ed. (Rock & Soil Mechanics Ser.). (Illus.). 1983p. 1979. 29.50x (ISBN 0-87849-025-6); 38.00x (ISBN 0-87849-051-5). Trans Tech.

--Explosives for North American Engineers. 3rd. ed. LC 83-80650. 316p. 1984. 37.95x (ISBN 0-87201-259-X). Gulf Pub.

--Rudiments of Mining Practice. LC 83-80651. 128p. 1983. 24.00x (ISBN 0-87201-783-4). Gulf Pub.

--Rudiments of Mining Practice. 1983. 24.00x (ISBN 0-87849-042-6). Trans Tech.

Gregory, Cedric E. Bucolic Bull: Fun on a Farm in Australia. 160p. 1982. 8.00 (ISBN 0-682-49892-0). Exposition Pr FL.

--A Concise History of Mining. LC 80-13925. 1981. 33.00 (ISBN 0-08-023882-3). Pergamon.

Gregory, Charles, et al. Cases & Materials on Torts: 1981 Supplement. 1982. pap. 6.95 (ISBN 0-316-32782-4). Little.

Gregory, Charles O. & Katz, Harold A. Labor & the Law. 3rd ed. 1979. pap. text ed. 10.95x (ISBN 0-393-09995-4). Norton.

Gregory, Charles O., jt. auth. see Epstein, Richard.

Gregory, Conal. A Caterer's Guide to Drinks. 240p. 1981. 25.00x (ISBN 0-7198-2674-8, Pub. by Northwood Bks). State Mutual Bk.

Gregory, D., jt. auth. see Fetter, F. W.

Gregory, D. P. A Hydrogen-Energy System, August 1972. 466p. 20.00 (ISBN 0-910091-24-2). Inst Gas Tech.

Gregory, D. P. & Djordevich, L. Thermodynamic Properties of a Lean Natural Gas at Cryogenic Conditions. (Technical Reports Ser.: No.11). xi, 83p. 1973. 5.00 (ISBN 0-317-34316-5). Inst Gas Tech.

Gregory, David. The Elements of Physical & Geometrical Astronomy, 2 vols. 1972. Repr. of 1726 ed. Set. 70.00 (ISBN 0-384-19920-8). Johnson Repr.

Gregory, David D. & Diot, A. The Easement as a Conservation Technique. (Environmental Policy & Law Papers: No. 1). 47p. 1972. pap. 10.00 (ISBN 2-88032-071-2, IUCN18, IUCN). Unipub.

Gregory, Denis, ed. Work Organization: Swedish Experience & British Context. 270p. 1978. 25.00x (ISBN 0-900296-72-0, Pub. by Social Sci Res). State Mutual Bk.

Gregory, Derek. Ideology, Science & Human Geography. 1979. 20.00x (ISBN 0-312-40477-8). St Martin.

--Regional Transformation & Industrial Revolutions: A Geography of the Yorkshire Woollen Industry. (Illus.). 1983. 39.50x (ISBN 0-8166-1139-4); pap. 15.95x (ISBN 0-8166-1140-8). U of Minn Pr.

Gregory, Derek & Urry, John, eds. Social Relations & Spatial Structures. 450p. 1985. 39.95 (ISBN 0-312-73586-3); pap. 14.95 (ISBN 0-312-73484-0). St Martin.

Gregory, Derek, jt. ed. see Baker, Alan R.

Gregory, Diana. Don't Forget Me. (Secret Dreams Ser.: No. 74). 160p. (Orig.). 1984. pap. 2.25 (ISBN 0-553-24381-0). Bantam.

--Forget Me Not. (Turning Points Ser.: No. 5). 1984. pap. 1.95 (ISBN 0-451-13170-3, Sig Vista). NAL.

Gregory, Dick. Dick Gregory's Bible Tales. 1978. pap. 1.95i (ISBN 0-06-080445-9, P 445, PL). Har-Row.

--Dick Gregory's Bible Tales. McGraw, James, ed. LC 83-42970. 192p. 1983. pap. 7.95 (ISBN 0-8128-6194-9). Stein & Day.

--Dick Gregory's Bible Tales, with Commentary. McGraw, James R., ed. LC 73-91859. 192p. 1974. pap. 7.95x (ISBN 0-8128-6194-9). Stein & Day.

--Dick Gregory's Natural Diet for Folks Who Eat: Cookin' with Mother Nature. McGraw, James R., ed. LC 72-9096. 185p. 1973. 9.95i (ISBN 0-06-011604-8, HarpT). Har-Row.

--Dick Gregory's Natural Diet for Folks Who Eat: Cookin' with Mother Nature. McGraw, James R. & Fulton, Alvenia M., eds. 192p. 1974. pap. 3.80i (ISBN 0-06-080315-0, P315, PL). Har-Row.

Gregory, Donald R., et al, eds. The Questions Behind the Answers: A Sampler in the Philosophy. LC 80-1373. 164p. 1983. lib. bdg. 23.50 (ISBN 0-8191-2703-5); pap. text ed. 9.25 (ISBN 0-8191-2704-3). U Pr Of Amer.

Gregory, E. R., ed. see Sayers, Dorothy L.

Gregory, Eileen. Summoning the Familiar: Powers & Rites of Common Life. 90p. 6.00 (ISBN 0-317-04709-4). Pegasus Found.

Gregory, Elizabeth. Alfred's Alphabet Antics. (Illus.). 1981. 6.95 (ISBN 0-933184-07-7); pap. 4.95 (ISBN 0-933184-08-5). Flame Intl.

--Beach Colors & Beach Creatures. (Illus.). 1981. 6.95 (ISBN 0-933184-17-4); pap. 5.50 (ISBN 0-933184-18-2). Flame Intl.

--Blinky & the Blends. (Illus.). 1981. 6.95 (ISBN 0-933184-11-5); pap. 4.95 (ISBN 0-933184-12-3). Flame Intl.

--The Short & Long. (Illus.). 1981. 6.95 (ISBN 0-933184-09-3); pap. 4.95 (ISBN 0-933184-10-7). Flame Intl.

Gregory, F. E. & Stack, F. M. Dilemmas of Government: Britain & the European Community. 200p. 1984. 34.95x (ISBN 0-85520-588-1). Basil Blackwell.

Gregory, Frances W. Nathan Appleton: Merchant & Entrepreneur, 1779-1861. LC 74-31433. (Illus.). 1976. 17.95x (ISBN 0-8139-0561-3). U Pr of Va.

Gregory, Francis T., jt. auth. see Gregory, A. Charles.

Gregory, G. Decision Analysis. 320p. (Orig.). 1985. pap. text ed. 22.50x (ISBN 0-7121-0671-5). Trans-Atlantic.

--The Life of Thomas Chatterton. 1789. 65.00 (ISBN 0-8274-2899-5). R West.

Gregory, G. Robinson. Forest Resource Economics. 548p. 1972. 37.50 (ISBN 0-471-06833-0, 40503). Wiley.

Gregory, Geoffrey. Mathematical Methods in Management. LC 82-238836. (Handbook of Applicable Mathematics Ser.). 184p. 1984. 31.95x (ISBN 0-471-90131-8, Pub. by Wiley-Interscience); pap. 31.95 (ISBN 0-471-90132-6). Wiley.

Gregory, George A. & Thibeault, Donald W. Neonatal Pulmonary Care. LC 78-7773. 1979. 44.50 (ISBN 0-201-02481-0, 02481, Med-Nurse). Addison-Wesley.

Gregory, Goerge A. Respiratory Failure in the Child. (Clinics In Critical Care Medicine Ser.: Vol. 3). (Illus.). 200p. 1981. text ed. 35.00 (ISBN 0-443-08112-3). Churchill.

Gregory, Grace C. Sagebrush, Gunnysacks & Bailing Wire. Guthridge, Sharyn G., ed. 1982. pap. 8.00 (ISBN 0-936204-36-2). Jelm Mtn.

Gregory, H. Controversies about Stuttering Therapy. LC 78-9923. (Illus.). 336p. 1978. 16.00 (ISBN 0-8391-1257-2). Pro Ed.

Gregory, H. F. & Thomas, David H., eds. A Caddo Sourcebook. (The North American Indian Ser.). 550p. 1985. 65.00 (ISBN 0-8240-5886-0). Garland Pub.

Gregory, Herbert E. Military Geology & Topography. 1918. 49.50x (ISBN 0-686-83626-X). Elliots Bks.

Gregory, Homer E. & Barnes, Kathleen. North Pacific Fisheries, with Special Reference to Alaska Salmon. 1976. Repr. of 1939 ed. 23.00 (ISBN 0-527-35850-9). Kraus Repr.

Gregory, Horace. Amy Lowell. facs. ed. LC 69-16855. (Select Bibliographies Reprint Ser). 1958. 25.00 (ISBN 0-8369-5008-9). Ayer Co Pubs.

--D. H. Lawrence: Pilgrim of the Apocalypse. facs. ed. LC 70-140355. (Select Bibliographies Reprint Ser). 1933. 15.00 (ISBN 0-8369-5598-6). Ayer Co Pubs.

--World of James McNeill Whistler. facs. ed. LC 70-80621. (Select Bibliographies Reprint Ser). 1959. 23.00 (ISBN 0-8369-5033-X). Ayer Co Pubs.

Gregory, Horace, intro. by. A Selection of Poems. 194p. 1985. pap. 3.95 (ISBN 0-15-680675-4). HarBraceJ.

Gregory, Horace, ed. see Longfellow, Henry W.

Gregory, Horace, tr. see Ovid.

Gregory, Howard. Southern California's Seacoast: Then & Now. 1982. 19.95 (ISBN 0-9607086-1-8); pap. 10.95 (ISBN 0-9607086-0-X). H Gregory.

Gregory, Hugh M. The Sea Serpent Journal: Hugh McCulloch Gregory's Voyage Around the World in a Clipper Ship, 1854-55. Burgess, Robert H., ed. LC 74-12382. (Illus.). 1975. 12.95x (ISBN 0-8139-0589-3). U Pr of Va.

Gregory, Hugo H., ed. Learning Theory & Stuttering Therapy. LC 68-15332. 1968. 14.95x (ISBN 0-8101-0107-6). Northwestern U Pr.

Gregory, Ian & Smeltzer, Donald J. Psychiatry: Essentials of Clinical Practice. 2nd ed. 1983. 21.95 (ISBN 0-316-32783-2). Little.

Gregory, Isabella A. Collected Plays, 4 vols. Saddlemyer, Ann, ed. Incl. Vol. 1. The Comedies; Vol. 2. The Tragedies & Tragic-Comedies; Vol. 3. Wonder & Supernatural. 32.50x (ISBN 0-19-519475-6); Vol. 4. Translations, Adaptions & Collaborations. 1970. Oxford U Pr.

--Gods & Fighting Men. LC 76-115243. 1971. Repr. of 1904 ed. 23.00x (ISBN 0-403-00400-4). Scholarly.

--Gods & Fighting Men: The Story of the Tuatha De Danaan & of the Fianna of Ireland. 2nd ed. 1976. pap. text ed. 8.75x (ISBN 0-7705-1413-8). Humanities.

--Gods & Fighting Men: The Story of the Tuatha de Danaan & of the Fianna of Ireland. 2nd ed. (The Coole Edition of the Collected Works of Lady Gregory Ser.). (Illus.). 1970. text ed. 25.00x (ISBN 0-19-519478-0). Oxford U Pr.

--Hugh Lane. (The Coole Edition of the Collected Works of Lady Gregory Ser.). (Illus.). 1973. text ed. 22.50x (ISBN 0-19-519725-9). Oxford U Pr.

--Ideals in Ireland. LC 75-28815. Repr. of 1901 ed. 11.00 (ISBN 0-404-13808-X). AMS Pr.

--Irish Folk History Plays, 2 Vols. LC 70-145063. 1971. Repr. of 1912 ed. 39.50 (ISBN 0-403-01006-3). Scholarly.

--The Journals of Lady Gregory, Vol. 1: Book 1-29, 1916-1925. (Coole Edition of the Works of Lady Gregory). 1978. 45.00x (ISBN 0-19-519886-7). Oxford U Pr.

--Lady Gregory's Journals, Vol. I: Books 1-29 (10 October 1916 to 24 February 1925) Murphy, Daniel J., ed. (Illus.). xvi, 707p. 1978. 39.95 (ISBN 0-87104-305-X, Pub. by Oxford University Press). NY Pub Lib.

--Mr. Gregory's Letter-Box, 1813-1830. 2nd ed. (The Coole Edition of the Collected Works of Lady Gregory Ser.). 1981. 39.95x (ISBN 0-19-520281-3). Oxford U Pr.

--Seven Short Plays. LC 77-131727. 1970. Repr. of 1909 ed. 29.00x (ISBN 0-403-00614-7). Scholarly.

--Three Last Plays. 1971. Repr. of 1928 ed. 39.00x (ISBN 0-403-00615-5). Scholarly.

Gregory, Isabella A., ed. Sir Williams Gregory K. C. M. G. An Autobiography. 3rd ed. (The Coole Edition of the Works of Lady Gregory). 1981. 59.00x (ISBN 0-19-520282-1). Oxford U Pr.

Gregory, Isabelle A. Seven Short Plays. LC 76-40386. (One-Act Plays in Reprint Ser.). 1976. Repr. of 1903 ed. 18.50x (ISBN 0-8486-2002-X). Core Collection.

Gregory, J. Solid-Liquid Separation. 363p. 1984. 87.95 (ISBN 0-470-20021-9). Halsted Pr.

Gregory, J., jt. auth. see Coulibaly, S.

Gregory, J. S. Jiang Jie-Shi: 1887-1975. LC 82-199758. (Leaders of Asia Ser.). (Illus.). 40p. 1982. write for info. (ISBN 0-7022-1800-6). U of Queensland Pr.

Gregory, J. S., jt. ed. see Clarke, Prescott.

Gregory, Jack & Strickland, Rennard. Sam Houston with the Cherokees, 1829-1833. (Illus.). 226p. 1967. pap. 6.95 (ISBN 0-292-77526-1). U of Tex Pr.

Gregory, Jackson. Captain Cavalier. 1976. Repr. of 1927 ed. lib. bdg. 17.95 (ISBN 0-88411-281-0, Pub. by Aeonian Pr). Amereon Ltd.

--Daughter of the Sun: A Tale of Adventure. Reginald, R. & Melville, Douglas, eds. LC 77-842333. (Lost Race & Adult Fantasy Ser.). 1978. Repr. of 1921 ed. lib. bdg. 24.50x (ISBN 0-405-10981-4). Ayer Co Pubs.

--The Everlasting Whisper. 1976. Repr. of 1922 ed. lib. bdg. 19.95 (ISBN 0-88411-282-9, Pub. by Aeonian Pr). Amereon Ltd.

--The Maid of the Mountain. 1976. Repr. of 1925 ed. lib. bdg. 18.95 (ISBN 0-88411-283-7, Pub. by Aeonian Pr). Amereon Ltd.

--Man to Man. 1976. Repr. of 1929 ed. lib. bdg. 19.95 (ISBN 0-88411-284-5, Pub. by Aeonian Pr). Amereon Ltd.

--The Silver Star. 1976. Repr. of 1931 ed. lib. bdg. 17.95x (ISBN 0-88411-285-3, Pub. by Aeonian Pr). Amereon Ltd.

Gregory, James, compiled by. Narratives of The Revolution in New York. LC 75-2526. (Illus.). 1975. 12.95x (ISBN 0-685-73917-1, New York Historical Society). U Pr of Va.

Gregory, James & Dunnings, Thomas, eds. Horatio Gates Papers, 1726-1828: A Guide to the Microfilm Edition. 212p. 1979. 9.75 (ISBN 0-667-00539-0). Microfilming Corp.

Gregory, James M. Frederick Douglass the Orator. LC 76-99380. 1969. Repr. of 1893 ed. lib. bdg. 15.50 (ISBN 0-8411-0051-9). Metro Bks.

Gregory, Janice, jt. auth. see Gregory, Neal.

Gregory, Jill. My True & Tender Love. 352p. 1985. pap. 6.95 (ISBN 0-425-07666-0). Berkley Pub.

--Promise Me the Dawn. 352p. (Orig.). 1985. pap. 5.95 (ISBN 0-425-06814-5). Berkley Pub.

--To Distant Shores. 416p. 1985. pap. 3.50 (ISBN 0-515-07728-3). Jove Pubns.

--The Wayward Heart. 480p. (Orig.). 1982. pap. 4.95 (ISBN 0-441-87630-7). Ace Bks.

--The Wayward Heart. 1982. pap. 4.95 (ISBN 0-686-80904-1). Dell.

--The Wayward Heart. 1985. pap. 3.50 (ISBN 0-515-07100-5). Jove Pubns.

Gregory, Jim & Vinson, Harvey. Bass Guitar. (Illus., Orig.). 1973. pap. 6.95 (ISBN 0-8256-4061-X, Consolidated). Music Sales.

Gregory, John. Legacy of the Stars. 1979. pap. 1.50 (ISBN 0-8439-0634-0, Leisure Bks). Dorchester Pub Co.

Gregory, John & Ukladnikov, Alexander. Leningrad's Ballet: Maryinsky to Kirov. (Illus.). 176p. 1982. 15.00x (ISBN 0-87663-391-2). Universe.

Gregory, John, ed. Quadratic Form Theory & Differential Equations. LC 80-520. (Mathematics in Science & Engineering Ser.). 1981. 39.50 (ISBN 0-12-301450-6). Acad Pr.

Gregory, John, ed. see International Symposium on Glycoconjugates, Fourth.

Gregory, John D., ed. see International Symposium on Glycoconjugates, Fourth.

Gregory, John M. Seven Laws of Teaching. 1954. 6.95 (ISBN 0-8010-3652-6). Baker Bk.

--The Seven Laws of Teaching. (Orig.). 1886. 1.95x (ISBN 0-9606952-1-4). PBBC Pr.

Gregory, John W. Foundation of British East Africa. LC 78-88412. Repr. of 1901 ed. cancelled (ISBN 0-8371-1727-5, GRB&, Pub. by Negro U Pr). Greenwood.

--Great Rift Valley. (Illus.). 422p. 1968. Repr. of 1896 ed. 38.50x (ISBN 0-7146-1812-8, F Cass Co). Biblio Dist.

--The Rift Valleys & Geology of East Africa. LC 76-44726. Repr. of 1921 ed. 47.50 (ISBN 0-404-15863-3). AMS Pr.

Gregory, Joseph T. Bibliography of Fossil Vertebrates. Incl. 1978. 384p. (Orig.). 1981. write for info. (ISBN 0-913312-52-5); 1979. LC 80-70567. 464p. (Orig.). 1981. write for info. (ISBN 0-913312-69-X); 1980. Bryant, Laurie J., ed. LC 80-70567. 1983. write for info.. Am Geol.

Gregory, Joseph T., et al, eds. Bibliography of Fossil Vertebrates 1981. LC 80-70567. 576p. (Orig.). 1984. pap. text ed. 115.00 (ISBN 0-918799-00-7). Soc Vertebrate.

Gregory, Judith & Marshall, Daniel, eds. Office Automation: Jekyll or Hyde. LC 83-60764. 240p. (Orig.). 1983. pap. 12.95 (ISBN 0-912663-00-6). Work Women Educ.

Gregory, Julia, jt. auth. see Bartlett, Hazel.

Gregory, Justina, tr. see Levine, David.

Gregory, K. J., ed. Background to Palaeohydrology: A Perspective. 408p. 1983. 59.95x (ISBN 0-471-90179-2, Pub. by Wiley-Interscience). Wiley.

Gregory, K. J. & Walling, D. E., eds. Fluvial Processes in Instrumented Watersheds: Studies of Small Watershed in the British Isles. (The Special Publication of the Institute of British Geographers: No. 6). 1980. 25.00 (ISBN 0-12-301150-7). Acad Pr.

--Man & Environmental Processes. (Studies in Physical Geography Ser.). 224p. 1980. (Pub. by Dawson England); pap. text ed. 14.00x (ISBN 0-89158-865-5). Westview.

Gregory, Kenneth. The Second Cuckoo: A Further Selection of Witty, Amusing & Memorable Letters to the Times. (Illus.). 320p. 1983. 14.50 (ISBN 0-04-808036-5). Allen Unwin.

Gregory, Kenneth, ed. The First Cuckoo: Letters to the Times 1900-1980. Rev. ed. (Illus.). 359p. 1983. 14.50 (ISBN 0-04-808031-4); pap. 7.95 (ISBN 0-04-808040-3). Allen Unwin.

Gregory, Lady A Book of Saints & Wonders. 116p. 1971. Repr. of 1906 ed. 12.50x (ISBN 0-7165-1334-X, BBA 02057, Pub. by Cuala Press Ireland). Biblio Dist.

--Coole. 64p. 1971. Repr. of 1913 ed. 12.50x (ISBN 0-7165-1372-2, BBA 02058, Pub. by Cuala Press Ireland). Biblio Dist.

--Cuchulain of Muirtheme. 272p. 1970. Repr. of 1902 ed. text ed. 15.75x (ISBN 0-900675-26-8, Pub. by Colin Symthe England). Humanities.

--Cuchulain of Muirthemhe: The Story of the Men of the Red Branch of Ulster. 5th ed. (Coole Edition of the Collected Works of Lady Gregory Ser.: Vol. 2). 1970. pap. 7.95x (ISBN 0-19-519739-9). Oxford U Pr.

--The Kiltartan Poetry Book. 76p. 1971. Repr. of 1918 ed. 12.50x (ISBN 0-7165-1353-6, BBA 02059, Pub. by Cuala Press Ireland). Biblio Dist.

--Our Irish Theater. 279p. 1972. Repr. of 1913 ed. text ed. 20.50 (ISBN 0-900675-28-4, Pub. by Colin Smythe England). Humanities.

--The Voyages of St. Brendan: The Navigator & Stories of the Saints of Ireland. pap. 4.95 (ISBN 0-686-22378-0). British Am Bks.

Gregory, Laura A. A Study of Data Base Processor Technology. LC 79-66678. (Data Base Monograph: No. 8). (Illus.). 77p. (Orig.). pap. 15.00 (ISBN 0-89435-035-8). QED Info Sci.

Gregory, Lee. Colorado Scenic Guide: Northern Region. LC 83-81011. (Illus.). 240p. (Orig.). 1983. pap. 8.95 (ISBN 0-933472-73-0). Johnson Bks.

--Colorado Scenic Guide: Southern Region. LC 84-80536. (Illus.). 208p. (Orig.). 1984. pap. 8.95 (ISBN 0-933472-83-8). Johnson Bks.

--Colorado Scenic Guide: Southern Region. LC 84-80536. (Illus.). 208p. (Orig.). 1984. pap. 8.95 (ISBN 0-933472-85-4). Johnson Bks.

Gregory, Lisa. Crystal Heart. 320p. 1982. pap. 3.25 (ISBN 0-515-06428-9). Jove Pubns.

--Light & Shadow. 304p. 1985. pap. 3.95 (ISBN 0-515-08182-5). Jove Pubns.

--The Rainbow Season. 256p. 1984. pap. 3.50 (ISBN 0-515-07923-5). Jove Pubns.

Gregory, Lydia. Unwilling Enchantress. (Candlelight Ecstasy Ser.: No. 103). (Orig.). 1982. pap. 1.95 (ISBN 0-440-19185-8). Dell.

Gregory, M. S. Introduction to Extremum Principles. (Illus.). 1970. 9.00 (ISBN 0-8088-3125-9). Davey.

Gregory, Marshall, jt. auth. see Booth, Wayne C.

Gregory, Martha F. Sexual Adjustment: A Guide for the Spinal Cord Injured. Cheever, Raymond C., ed. 70p. 1974. pap. 4.95 (ISBN 0-915708-00-0). Cheever Pub.

Gregory, Marty. Dark Star of Love. (Harlequin American Romance Ser.). 256p. 1983. pap. 2.25 (ISBN 0-373-16014-3). Harlequin Bks.

Gregory, Marvin, jt. auth. see Smith, P. David.

Gregory, Mary, jt. auth. see Ary, Sheila.

Gregory, Michael. Hunger Weather Nineteen Fifty-Nine to Nineteen Seventy-Five, Vol. 1. (Orig.). 1979. pap. 4.95x (ISBN 0-934600-02-3). Mother Duck Pr.

--Hunger Weather Nineteen Fifty-Nine to Nineteen Seventy-Five, Vol. 2. 216p. (Orig.). 1982. pap. 8.95x (ISBN 0-934600-03-1). Mother Duck Pr.

--The Valley Floor. (Orig.). 1978. 10.00x (ISBN 0-934600-07-4). Mother Duck Pr.

Gregory, Michael & Carroll, Susanne. Language & Situation: Language Varieties & Their Social Contexts. (Language & Sociaty Ser). 1978. pap. 8.95x (ISBN 0-7100-8773-X). Routledge & Kegan.

Gregory, Michael & Parrish, Margaret. Essential Law for Landowners & Farmers. 288p. 1980. 20.00x (ISBN 0-246-11213-1, Pub. by Granada England). Sheridan.

Gregory, Michael, ed. see Bisbee Press Collective.

Gregory, Michael S., et al, eds. Sociobiology & Human Nature: An Interdisciplinary Critique & Defense. LC 78-62559. (Social & Behavioral Science Ser.). (Illus.). 1978. text ed. 22.95x (ISBN 0-87589-384-8). Jossey-Bass.

Gregory, Miriam. Fingertip Phonics. Piequet Press Staff, ed. (Illus.). 290p. (Orig.). (gr. 1-12). 1985. write for info. (ISBN 0-914275-05-4). Piequet Pr.

--My Furry Bear. Piequet Press Staff, ed. (Illus.). 43p. (Orig.). (gr. 3-5). 1985. 15.00 (ISBN 0-914275-02-X). Piequet Pr.

Gregory, Mollie. Making Films Your Business. LC 79-14428. 1979. 14.50x (ISBN 0-8052-3728-3); pap. text ed. 7.95 (ISBN 0-8052-0639-6). Schocken.

Gregory, Neal & Gregory, Janice. When Elvis Died. LC 80-19862. (Illus.). 300p. (Orig.). 1980. casebound 13.95 (ISBN 0-89461-032-5). Comm Pr Inc.

Gregory, Norma, jt. auth. see Watling, Roy.

Gregory, P., jt. auth. see Gordon, P. F.

Gregory, P. H. & Maddison, A. C. Epidemiology of Phytophthora on Cocoa in Nigeria. 188p. 1981. 79.00x (ISBN 0-85198-478-9, Pub. by CAB Bks England). State Mutual Bk.

Gregory, Padric. Modern Anglo-Irish Verse. 1977. Repr. of 1914 ed. 20.00 (ISBN 0-89984-189-9). Century Bookbindery.

--Modern Anglo-Irish Verse. Repr. of 1914 ed. 20.00 (ISBN 0-686-18770-9). Scholars Ref Lib.

Gregory, Padric, ed. Modern Anglo-Irish Verse: An Anthology Selected from the Work of Living Irish Poets. LC 75-28816. Repr. of 1914 ed. 32.50 (ISBN 0-404-13809-8). AMS Pr.

Gregory, Patricia. Bean Banquets... from Boston to Bombay: Two Hundred International, High-Fiber Vegetarian Recipes. LC 84-3668. (Illus.). 240p. 1984. pap. 9.95 (ISBN 0-88007-139-7). Woodbridge Pr.

Gregory, Patrick, tr. see Crete, Liliane.

Gregory, Patrick, tr. see Girard, Rene.

Gregory, Patrick, tr. see Levine, David.

Gregory, Paul. Labor Force Participation: The Soviet Experience with Rapid Change. 80p. 5.60 (ISBN 0-318-16289-X, G-8). Public Int Econ.

Gregory, Paul & Ruffin, Roy J. Essentials of Economics. 1985. pap. text ed. 18.95x (ISBN 0-673-18095-6). Scott F.

Gregory, Paul & Stuart, Robert. Comparative Economic Systems. LC 79-87859. 1980. text ed. 27.95 (ISBN 0-395-28183-0); instr's. manual 1.00 (ISBN 0-395-28184-9). HM.

Gregory, Paul, jt. auth. see Ruffin, Roy.

Gregory, Paul, jt. auth. see Ruffin, Roy J.

Gregory, Paul R. Russian National Income, Eighteen Eighty-Five to Nineteen Thirteen. (Illus.). 350p. 1983. Repr. 32.50 (ISBN 0-521-24382-3). Cambridge U Pr.

Gregory, Paul R. & Stuart, Robert C. Comparative Economic Systems. 2nd ed. LC 84-80474. 450p. 1985. text ed. write for info. (ISBN 0-395-34241-4). HM.

--Soviet Economic Structure & Performance. 2nd ed. 419p. 1981. pap. text ed. 24.00 scp (ISBN 0-06-042508-3, HarpC). Har-Row.

Gregory, Peter. Industrial Wages in Chile. LC 67-63229. (International Report Ser.: No. 8). 128p. 1967. 5.50 (ISBN 0-87546-012-7); pap. 3.00 (ISBN 0-87546-042-9). ILR Pr.

--Polluted Homes. 64p. 1965. pap. text ed. 3.75x (ISBN 0-686-70853-9, Pub. by Bedford England). Brookfield Pub Co.

--Telephones for the Elderly. 128p. 1973. pap. text ed. 7.50x (ISBN 0-7135-1888-X, Pub. by Bedford England). Brookfield Pub Co.

Gregory, Peter N., jt. ed. see Gimello, Robert M.

Gregory, Philip H., ed. Phytophthora Disease of Cocoa. LC 73-85686. pap. 93.00 (ISBN 0-317-30075-X, 2020979). Bks Demand UMI.

Gregory, R. A., ed. Regulatory Peptides of Gut & Brain. (British Medical Bulletin Ser.: Vol. 38, No. 3). 99p. 1983. pap. text ed. 19.50 (ISBN 0-443-02660-2). Churchill.

Gregory, R. A. & Petersen, O. H., eds. The Control of Secretion: Proceedings. (Royal Society of London Ser.). (Illus.). 193p. 1982. text ed. 74.00x (ISBN 0-85403-179-0, Pub. by Royal Soc London). Scholium Intl.

Gregory, R. L. & Gombrich, E. H. Illusion in Nature & Art. (Illus.). 1974. pap. 22.50 (ISBN 0-684-14185-X, ScribT). Scribner.

Gregory, R. P. Biochemistry of Photosynthesis. 2nd ed. 221p. 1977. 44.95 (ISBN 0-471-32676-3). Wiley.

Gregory, R. T. & Krishnamurthy, E. V. Methods & Applications of Error-Free Computation. (Texts & Monographs in Computer Science). (Illus.). 200p. 1984. 29.80 (ISBN 0-387-90967-2). Springer-Verlag.

Gregory, Ralph. Sign Painting Techniques: Beginner to Professional. (Illus.). 1973. 15.00 (ISBN 0-911380-29-9). Signs of Times.

Gregory, Richard L. Mind in Science: A History of Explanations in Psychology & Physics. LC 81-7732. (Illus.). 648p. 1981. 34.50 (ISBN 0-521-24307-6). Cambridge U Pr.

Gregory, Robert. The Third Choice. LC 78-54131. 1979. 16.95 (ISBN 0-87949-117-5). Ashley Bks.

Gregory, Robert A. Sugar Maple Research: Sap Production Processing, & Marketing of Maple Syrup. 112p. 1982. pap. 4.50 (ISBN 0-318-11834-3). Gov Printing Office.

Gregory, Robert G. & Lewis, Richard E., eds. A Guide to Daily Correspondence of the Coast, Central, Rift Valley, & Northern Frontier Provinces: Kenya National Archives Microfilm. (Eastern Africa Occasional Bibliography Ser.: No. 28). 1984. pap. text ed. 10.00x (ISBN 0-915984-64-4). Syracuse U Foreign Comp.

--A Guide to the Secretariat Circulars: Kenya National Archives Microfilm. (Eastern African Occasional Bibliography Ser.: No. 29). 1984. pap. text ed. 10.00x (ISBN 0-915984-65-2). Syracuse U Foreign Comp.

Gregory, Robert L. Rays of Hope. LC 69-20332. 1969. 7.00 (ISBN 0-8022-2291-9). Philos Lib.

Gregory, Robert T. Error-Free Computation: Why It Is Needed & Methods for Doing It. LC 80-23923. 152p. (Orig.). 1980. pap. 9.50 (ISBN 0-89874-240-4). Krieger.

Gregory, Ross. Origins of American Intervention in First World War. LC 70-141588. (Essays in American History Ser). 1972. pap. 4.95x (ISBN 0-393-09980-6). Norton.

--Walter Hines Page: Ambassador to the Court of St. James's. LC 78-94067. (Illus.). 252p. 1970. 24.00x (ISBN 0-8131-1198-6). U Pr of Ky.

Gregory, Ruth W. Anniversaries & Holidays. 4th ed. LC 83-3784. 262p. 1983. lib. bdg. 20.00x (ISBN 0-8389-0389-4). ALA.

--Special Days: The Book of Anniversaries & Holidays. 1978. pap. 5.95 (ISBN 0-8065-0659-8). Citadel Pr.

Gregory, S. Statistical Methods & the Geographer. 4th ed. LC 77-7025. (Geographies for Advanced Study Ser). (Illus.). 1978. pap. text ed. 13.95x (ISBN 0-582-48186-4). Longman.

Gregory, Sadie. A New Dimension in Old Testament Study. 103p. (Orig.). 1980. pap. 5.00 (ISBN 0-917479-05-X). Guild Psy.

Gregory, Sadie, jt. auth. see McKenzie, George A.

Gregory, St. Life of St. Macrina. 1974. pap. 2.95 (ISBN 0-686-10202-9). Eastern Orthodox.

Gregory, Stephen. Bobsledding: Down the Chute! new ed. LC 75-23407. (Illus.). 32p. (gr. 5-10). 1976. PLB 9.79 (ISBN 0-89375-002-6); pap. 2.50 (ISBN 0-89375-018-2). Troll Assocs.

--Racing to Win: The Salt Flats. new ed. LC 75-21845. (Illus.). (gr. 5-10). 1976. PLB 9.79 (ISBN 0-89375-010-7); pap. 2.50 (ISBN 0-89375-026-3). Troll Assocs.

Gregory, Susan. Hey, White Girl. LC 79-90978. 1970. 8.95 (ISBN 0-393-07450-1). Norton.

Gregory, T. E. & Podlecki, Anthony, eds. Panathenaia: Studies in Athenian Life & Thought in the Classical Age. 8.50x (ISBN 0-87291-126-8). Coronado Pr.

Gregory, T. E., ed. see Helfferich, Karl T.

Gregory, Tappan. Deer at Night in the North Woods. (Illus.). 212p. 1930. photocopy ed. 19.75x (ISBN 0-398-04270-5). C C Thomas.

Gregory, Theodor E. The Gold Standard & Its Future. Wilkins, Mira, ed. LC 78-3920. (International Finance Ser.). (Illus.). 1978. Repr. of 1932 ed. lib. bdg. 16.00x (ISBN 0-405-11223-8). Ayer Co Pubs.

Gregory, Theodore. Ernest Oppenheimer & the Economic Development of Southern Africa. Wilkins, Mira, ed. LC 76-29778. (European Business Ser.). (Illus.). 1977. Repr. of 1962 ed. lib. bdg. 56.50x (ISBN 0-405-09790-5). Ayer Co Pubs.

Gregory, Theodore, ed. Select Statutes, Documents & Reports Relating to British Banking: 1832-1928, 2 vols. (Illus.). 1964. Repr. of 1929 ed. 85.00x set (ISBN 0-7146-1225-1, BHA-01225, F Cass Co). Biblio Dist.

Gregory, Theodore E. Tariffs: A Study in Method. LC 68-20038. Repr. of 1921 ed. 37.50x (ISBN 0-678-00420-X). Kelley.

Gregory, Theodore E., ed. Select Statutes, Documents & Reports Relating to British Banking, 1832-1928, 2 Vols. LC 67-93658. Repr. of 1929 ed. 75.00x (ISBN 0-678-05169-0). Kelley.

Gregory, Thomas B., jt. auth. see Harmin, Merrill.

Gregory, Thomas W., ed. Adolescence in Literature. LC 77-17719. (English & Humanities Ser.). 1978. pap. text ed. 14.95x (ISBN 0-582-28045-1). Longman.

Gregory, Timothy E. Vox Populi: Popular Opinion & Violence in the Religious Controversies of the Fifth Century A.D. LC 79-16885. 257p. 1979. 20.00x (ISBN 0-8142-0291-8). Ohio St U Pr.

Gregory, Tony. The Pocket Encyclopedia of Modern Roses. (Illus.). 192p. 1984. 9.95 (ISBN 0-7137-1261-9, Pub. by Blandford Pr England). Sterling.

Gregory, Vikki & Kaplan, Christine. Bridging the Skills Gap: Women & Job in a High Tech World. 1983. 10.00 (ISBN 0-934966-05-2). Wow Inc.

Gregory, Vikki, jt. auth. see Kaplan, Chris.

Gregory, W., ed. American Newspapers, Eighteen Twenty-One to Eighteen Thirty-Six: A Union List of Files Available in the United States & Canada. LC 37-12783. 1937. 130.00 (ISBN 0-527-02250-0). Kraus Repr.

Gregory, W. D., et al, eds. Science & Technology of Superconductivity, Vol. 1 & 2. LC 72-77226. 1973. Vol. 1, 476p. 65.00x (ISBN 0-306-37631-8, Plenum Pr); Vol. 2, 391p. 65.00x (ISBN 0-306-37632-6, Plenum Pr). Plenum Pub.

Gregory, William. Animal Magnetism: or Mesmerism & Its Phenomena. 5th ed. LC 75-7384. (Perspectives in Psychical Research Ser.). 1975. Repr. of 1909 ed. 20.00x (ISBN 0-405-07032-2). Ayer Co Pubs.

Gregory, William A., jt. auth. see Reuschlein, Harold Gill.

Gregory, William K. Evolution Emerging: A Survey of Changing Patterns from Primeval Life to Man, 2 vols. LC 73-17822. (Natural Sciences in America Ser.). (Illus.). 1808p. 1974. Repr. Set. 122.00x (ISBN 0-405-05738-5); 61.00 ea. Vol.1 (ISBN 0-405-05739-3). Vol.2 (ISBN 0-405-05740-7). Ayer Co Pubs.

--The Orders of Mammals. LC 78-72718. Repr. of 1910 ed. 67.50 (ISBN 0-404-18293-3). AMS Pr.

--The Origin & Evolution of the Human Dentition. LC 78-72696. Repr. of 1922 ed. 51.50 (ISBN 0-404-18267-4). AMS Pr.

--The Structure & Relationships of Notharctus, an American Eocene Primate. LC 78-72719. Repr. of 1920 ed. 47.50 (ISBN 0-404-18294-1). AMS Pr.

--Studies on the Evolution of the Primates. Bd. with The Dentition of Dryopithecus & the Origin of Man. Gegory, William K. LC 78-72720. 67.50 (ISBN 0-404-18295-X). AMS Pr.

Gregory, William K., et al. Original Descriptions of Siwalik Primates Collected Mostly by American Expeditions, Reprinted from Various Sources. LC 78-72724. 1980. 26.50 (ISBN 0-404-18299-2). AMS Pr.

--Studies of Early Fossil Primates in North America. LC 78-72713. 1980. Repr. 34.50 (ISBN 0-404-18283-6). AMS Pr.

Gregory Bishop of Tours. History of the Franks. Brehaut, Ernest, ed. 1965. lib. bdg. 27.50x (ISBN 0-374-90950-4). Octagon.

Gregory Nazianzen, St. & Ambrose, St. Funeral Orations. LC 67-28586. (Fathers of the Church Ser: Vol. 22). 344p. 1953. 18.95x (ISBN 0-8132-0022-9). Cath U Pr.

Gregory Of Nyssa, St. Ascetical Works. LC 64-13360. (Fathers of the Church Ser: Vol. 58). 288p. 1967. 16.95x (ISBN 0-8132-0058-X). Cath U Pr.

Gregory of Tours. The History of the Franks: Gregory of Tours. Thorpe, Lewis, tr. 720p. 1976. pap. 6.95 (ISBN 0-14-044295-2). Penguin.

Gregory Of Tours see Peters, Edward.

Gregory Seventh, Pope The Correspondence of Pope Gregory VII. Emerton, E., tr. (Columbia University Records of Civilization Ser.). 1969. pap. 5.95x (ISBN 0-393-09859-1). Norton.

--Correspondence of Pope Gregory VII. Emerton, Ephraim, ed. 1966. lib. bdg. 24.00x (ISBN 0-374-92565-8). Octagon.

Gregory The Great. The Life of Saint Benedict: Book II of the Dialogues of Gregory the Great. Uhlfelder, Myra L., tr. LC 66-30611. (Orig.). 1967. pap. 3.56 scp (ISBN 0-672-60468-X, LLA216). Bobbs.

--Remediarium Conversorum: A Synthesis in Latin of "Moralia in Job". Peter of Waltham & Gildea, Joseph, eds. LC 84-3693. 504p. 1984. 25.00 (ISBN 0-8453-4507-9). Villanova Univ.

Gregory The Great, St. Dialogues. (Fathers of the Church Ser.: Vol. 39). 287p. 1959. 29.95x (ISBN 0-8132-0039-3). Cath U Pr.

Gregory the Great, Saint Parables of the Gospel. 169p. 1960. 5.95 (ISBN 0-933932-12-X). Scepter Pubs.

Gregory VII, Pope. The Epistolae Vagantes of Pope Gregory Seven. Cowdrey, H. E., ed. (Oxford Medieval Texts). (Eng. & Lat.). 1972. 35.00x (ISBN 0-19-822220-3). Oxford U Pr.

Gregotti, Vittorio. New Directions in Italian Architecture. LC 68-57723. (New Directions in Architecture Ser). (Orig.). 7.95 (ISBN 0-8076-0480-1); pap. 3.95 (ISBN 0-8076-0484-4). Braziller.

Gregoy, Robert G., et al. The Guide to the Kenya National Archives. (Foreign & Comparative Studies Program, Eastern African Bibliographic Ser.: No. 2). 452p. 1969. 16.00x (ISBN 0-686-70996-9). Syracuse U Foreign Comp.

Gregson, Bob. Incredible Indoor Games Book: One Hundred & Sixty Group Projects, Games, & Activities. LC 82-81983. 1982. pap. 10.95 (ISBN 0-8224-0765-5). Pitman Learning.

Gregson, J. M. Public & Private Man in Shakespeare. LC 83-3750. 256p. 1983. text ed. 28.50x (ISBN 0-389-20394-7). B&N Imports.

Gregson, J. Randolph. Skid Row: A Wide-Ranging Bibliography. 1977. 2.50 (ISBN 0-686-19107-2, 1249). CPL Biblios.

Gregson, M. J., ed. Recent Theoretical Developments in Control. (Institute of Mathematics & Applications Conference Ser.). 1978. 70.00 (ISBN 0-12-301650-9). Acad Pr.

Gregson, Robert. Psychometrics of Similarity. 1975. 55.00 (ISBN 0-12-301550-2). Acad Pr.

Gregson, Robert A. Time Series in Psychology. 456p. 1983. text ed. 49.95x (ISBN 0-89859-250-X). L Erlbaum Assocs.

Gregson, Shaun & Livesey, Frank. Management & the Organization. 300p. 1984. pap. 18.95 (ISBN 0-434-90863-0, Pub. by W Heinemann Ltd). David & Charles.

Gregson, Stephen, ed. Arthur Oakman's Radio Sermons, Vol. 2. 193p. 1984. pap. 11.00 (ISBN 0-8309-0400-X). Herald Hse.

Gregson, Vernon. Lonergan, Spirituality, & the Meeting of Religions. LC 85-3312. (College Theology Society-Studies in Religion: No. 2). 170p. (Orig.). 1985. lib. bdg. 22.00 (ISBN 0-8191-4619-6, Co-Pub by College Theo Soc); pap. text ed. 10.75 (ISBN 0-8191-4620-X). U Pr of Amer.

Greguras, Fred M. Summary of Coopers & Lybrand Study of Computer-Assisted Legal Research for the Department of Justice. (Computer Law Monograph Ser). 19p. (Orig.). 1980. 5.00 (ISBN 0-935200-02-9). Ctr Comp Law.

Greguras, Fred M. & Kawashima, Kiyoshi. Legal Protection of Computer Software in Japan. 32p. 1982. pap. 15.00 (ISBN 0-910215-02-2). Law & Tech Pr.

Greguras, Fred M. & Wright, Ann. The Consumer-Financial Instituiton Relationship in Electronic Funds Transfer Legislation. LC 79-55491. (Computer Law Monograph Ser). 160p. (Orig.). 1979. 20.00 (ISBN 0-935200-00-2). Ctr Comp Law.

Greguras, Fred M., jt. auth. see Ellis, Martin B.

Greguss, P., jt. auth. see Bally, G. V.

Grehan, Ida. Pocket Guide to Irish Family Names. (Pocket Bk.). (Illus.). 96p. (Orig.). (YA) 1985. pap. 3.95 (ISBN 0-86281-133-3, Pub. by Appletree Pr). Irish Bks Media.

--Waterford: An Irish Art. (Illus.). 256p. 1982. 50.00 (ISBN 0-942620-05-4). Portfolio Pr.

Greibach, S. A. Theory of Program Structures: Schemes, Semantics, Verification. (Lecture Notes in Computer Science: Vol. 36). xvi, 364p. 1976. pap. 15.20 (ISBN 0-387-07415-5). Springer-Verlag.

Greico, William. O-My-God an Interview. 1978. perfect bdg. 3.50. Paladin Hse.

Greicus, Mike, ed. Three Short Novels from Papua New Guinea. Incl. The Fires of Dawn. Umba, Benjamin; The Flight of a Villager. Kituai, August; Tali. Baital, Jim. 140p. 1976. 12.00x (ISBN 0-582-71437-0, Pub. by Longman Paul Zealand). Three Continents.

Greidanus, Morris, et al. Welcome. LC 82-12907. 71p. 1982. pap. 3.35 (ISBN 0-933140-48-7); pap. 3.35 leader's guide (ISBN 0-933140-49-5). Bd of Pubns CRC.

Greidanus, T. B. Van Wimersma see Rodriguez, E. M. & Van Wimersma Greidanus, T. B.

Greidanus, T. B. Van Wimersma see Van Wimersma Greidanus, T. B. & Lamberts, W. J.

Greidanus, T. B. Van Wimersma see Van Wimersma Greidanus, T. B. & Rees, L. H.

Greider, Janice E. & Beadles, William T. Law & the Life Insurance Contract. 5th ed. (Irwin Series in Insurance & Economic Security). 1984. 23.95 (ISBN 0-256-02823-0). Irwin.

--Principles of Life Insurance, Vol. 1. rev. ed. 1973. pap. 12.00 (ISBN 0-256-01396-9). Irwin.

Greider, William. The Education of David Stockman & Other Americans. (Obelisk Ser.). 128p. 1982. pap. 5.95 (ISBN 0-525-48010-2, 0578-210). Dutton.

Greif, Ann C., jt. auth. see Montomery, Jill D.

Greif, Edwin C. Store Talk: An Introduction to Retail Merchandising. LC 78-60034. (gr. 9 up). 1979. pap. 11.00 (ISBN 0-02-831200-7); pap. 2.80 tchrs'. manual, 1981 (ISBN 0-02-831210-4). Glencoe.

Greif, Elaine & Matarazzo, Ruth. Behavioral Approaches to Rehabilitation: Coping with Change. (Series on Rehabilitation: Vol. 3). 1982. text ed. 16.95 (ISBN 0-8261-3530-7); student adoptions 13.95 (ISBN 0-686-86758-0). Springer Pub.

Greif, Geoffrey. Single Fathers. 208p. 1985. 21.00x (ISBN 0-669-09594-X); pap. text ed. 8.95 (ISBN 0-669-09595-8). Lexington Bks.

Greif, Martin. The Airport Book: From Landing Field to Modern Terminal. (Illus.). 1979. 12.95 (ISBN 0-8317-0150-1, Mayflower Bks). Smith Pubs.

--Depression Modern: The Thirties Style in America. LC 75-11140. (Illus.). 192p. 1975. pap. 9.95 (ISBN 0-87663-925-2). Universe.

--The Gay Book of Days. 224p. 1982. 17.95 (ISBN 0-8184-0332-2). Lyle Stuart.

--The Gay Book of Days. 234p. 1985. pap. 12.95 (ISBN 0-317-19322-8). Lyle Stuart.

--The Lighting Book: A Buyer's Guide to Locating Almost Every Kind of Lighting Device. (Illus.). 160p. (Orig.). 1985. pap. 12.95 (ISBN 0-915590-82-4). Main Street.

--The St. Nicholas Book. LC 76-5089. (Illus.). 60p. 1976. 5.95 (ISBN 0-87663-554-0). Universe.

--The St. Nicholas Book: A Celebration of Christmas Past. rev. ed. LC 84-15460. (Illus.). 80p. (YA) (gr. 8). 1984. pap. 6.95 (ISBN 0-915590-51-4). Main Street.

Greif, Martin, jt. auth. see Schorsch, Anita.

Greife, H. Jewish-Run Concentration Camps in the Soviet Union. 1982. lib. bdg. 59.95 (ISBN 0-87700-371-8). Revisionist Pr.

Greiff, Barrie S. & Munter, Preston K. Tradeoffs: Executive, Family, & Organizational Life. 1981. pap. 3.50 (ISBN 0-451-61960-9, ME1960, Ment). NAL.

--Tradeoffs: The Executive, Family & Organization. 1980. cancelled 9.95 (ISBN 0-671-22904-4). S&S.

Greiff, Constance M. John Notman, Architect. (Illus.). 1979. pap. 20.00 (ISBN 0-916530-10-8). Athenaeum Phila.

--John Notman, Architect. LC 75-18978. (Illus.). 253p. text ed. 20.00x (ISBN 0-87474-483-0). Smithsonian.

Greiff, Constance M., et al. Princeton Architecture: A Pictorial History of Town & Campus. LC 65-17138. (Illus.). 1967. 35.00 (ISBN 0-691-04556-9); pap. 11.50 (ISBN 0-691-00583-4). Princeton U Pr.

Greiffenberg, Catharina Regina von. Samtliche Werke, 10 vols. Bircher, Martin & Kemp, Friedhelm, eds. (Ger.). 1983. 500.00 (ISBN 0-527-35868-1). Kraus Repr.

Greifinger, David, et al. Glove Compartment Book. Jenny, Brian P., ed. 181p. (Orig.). 1984. pap. 5.95 (ISBN 0-915765-04-7). Natl Pr Inc.

Greig, C., tr. see Pliny.

Greig, D. M. Optimisation. LC 79-42892. (Longman Mathematical Texts). (Illus.). 179p. 1980. pap. text ed. 14.50x (ISBN 0-582-44186-2). Longman.

Greig, Gertrud B. Seasonal Fluctuations in Employment in the Women's Clothing Industry in New York. LC 74-76656. (Columbia University. Studies in the Social Sciences: No. 554). 1969. Repr. of 1949 ed. 16.50 (ISBN 0-404-51554-1). AMS Pr.

Greig, J., tr. see Hubner, Hans.

Greig, J. Y. Breaking Priscian's Head; or, English As She Will Be Spoke & Wrote. Repr. of 1928 ed. 10.00 (ISBN 0-8274-1975-9). R West.

--David Hume. LC 82-48332. (The Philosophy of David Hume Ser.). 436p. 1983. lib. bdg. 50.00 (ISBN 0-8240-5405-9). Garland Pub.

Greig, J. Y., ed. see Hume, David.

Greig, John Y. Psychology of Laughter & Comedy. LC 72-79198. 1969. Repr. of 1923 ed. 20.00 (ISBN 0-8154-0295-3). Cooper Sq.

Greig, Noel. Poppies. 45p. (Orig.). 1983. pap. 3.50 (ISBN 0-907040-27-6, Pub. by GMP England). Alyson Pubns.

Greig, Noel & Griffiths, Drew. Two Gay Sweatshop Plays. (Gay Modern Classics Ser.). 142p. (Orig.). 1981. pap. 5.50 (ISBN 0-907040-06-3, Pub. by GMP England). Alyson Pubns.

--Two Gay Sweatshop Plays: As Time Goes By & The Dear Love of Comrades. 144p. 1982. pap. 5.50 (ISBN 0-907040-06-3). Gay Mens Pr.

Greig, W. Smith. Economics & Management of Food Processing. (Illus.). 1984. text ed. 57.50 (ISBN 0-87055-449-2). AVI.

Greig-Smith, P. Quantitative Plant Ecology. 3rd ed. LC 83-1302. (Studies in Ecology: Vol. 9). 355p. 1983. text ed. 42.00x (ISBN 0-520-04989-6); pap. text ed. 22.00x (ISBN 0-520-05080-0). U of Cal Pr.

Greil, Arthur L. Georges Sorel & the Sociology of Virtue. LC 80-69046. 262p. (Orig.). 1982. lib. bdg. 25.25 (ISBN 0-8191-1988-1); pap. text ed. 12.50 (ISBN 0-8191-1989-X). U Pr of Amer.

Greiling, R., jt. ed. see Kroener, A.

Greim, Helmut, et al, eds. Biochemical Basis of Chemical Carcinogenesis. (Workshop-Conference HOECHST Ser.: Vol. 13). 326p. 1984. text ed. 67.00 (ISBN 0-89004-961-0). Raven.

Greimann, Milly see Orost, Jean H., et al.

Greimas, A. Essais de semiotique poetique: Avec des etudes sur Apollinaire, Bataille, Hugo, Jarry, Mallarme, Michaux, Nerval, Rimbaud, Roubaud. (Collection L). 240p. (Orig., Fr.). 1972. pap. 13.95 (ISBN 2-03-036002-3, 2666). Larousse.

Greimas, A. J. L' Ancien Francais. 271p. (Orig.). 1974. bds. 27.50 (ISBN 2-03-070335-4, 3609). Larousse.

--Semantique structurale. (Fr). pap. 12.95 (ISBN 0-685-14077-6, 3639). Larousse.

--Structural Semantics: An Attempt at a Method. McDowell, Daniele, et al, trs. from Fr. LC 83-5864. lvi, 325p. 1983. 28.95x (ISBN 0-8032-2112-6). U of Nebr Pr.

Greimas, A. J. & Courtes, J. Semiotics & Language: An Analytical Dictionary. Crist, Larry, et al, trs. LC 81-47828. (Advances in Semiotics Ser.). (Illus.). 432p. 1983. 45.00x (ISBN 0-253-35169-3). Ind U Pr.

Grein, Christian W. Sprachschatze der Angelsachsischen Dichter. 100.00 (ISBN 0-8490-1118-3). Gordon Pr.

Grein, Jacob T. Premieres of the Year. LC 77-93162. Repr. of 1900 ed. 15.00 (ISBN 0-405-08581-8, Blom Pubns). Ayer Co Pubs.

Greinacher, Norbert. The Poor & the Church. Muller, Alois, ed. (Concilium Ser.: Vol. 104). 1978. pap. 6.95x (ISBN 0-8245-0264-7). Crossroad NY.

Greinacher, Norbert, ed. Evangelization in the World Today. (Concilium Ser.: Vol. 114). 1979. pap. 6.95 (ISBN 0-8245-0274-4). Crossroad NY.

Greinacher, Norbert & Muller, Alois, eds. The Church & Human Rights. (Concilium Ser.: Vol. 124). 1979. pap. 4.95x (ISBN 0-8245-0285-X). Crossroad NY.

Greinacher, Norbert, jt. ed. see Elizondo, Virgil.

Greiner, Corrine, ed. see Nelson, Tom & Brown, Bruce.

Greiner, Donald J. Adultery in the American Novel: Updike, James, & Hawthorne. 200p. 1985. text ed. 17.95x (ISBN 0-87249-458-6). U of SC Pr.

--John Updike's Novels. LC 84-7213. xvi, 223p. 1984. text ed. 23.95X (ISBN 0-8214-0780-5). Ohio U Pr.

--John Updike's Novels. 2nd ed. xvi, 223p. 1985. pap. 9.95 (ISBN 0-8214-0792-9). Ohio U Pr.

--The Other John Updike: Poems, Short Stories, Prose, Play. LC 80-22377. xxii, 297p. 1981. text ed. 20.95x (ISBN 0-8214-0585-3, 82-83723); pap. 10.00x (ISBN 0-8214-0612-4, 82-83731). Ohio U Pr.

--Understanding John Hawkes. (Understanding Contemporary American Literature Ser.). 200p. 1985. 19.95 (ISBN 0-87249-460-8); pap. 9.95 (ISBN 0-87249-262-1). U of SC Pr.

Greiner, Donald J., ed. American Poets since World War II, 2 vols. (Dictionary of Literary Biography Ser.: Vol. 5). (Illus.). 1980. 170.00x set (ISBN 0-8103-0924-6, Bruccoli Clark). Gale.

Greiner, James. Wager with the Wind: The Don Sheldon Story. (Illus.). 256p. 1982. pap. 8.95 (ISBN 0-312-85337-8). St Martin.

Greiner, John & Hatry, Harry. Productivity & Motivation: A Review of State & Local Government Initiatives. LC 80-53981. 1981. 22.50x (ISBN 0-87766-283-5, 29600); pap. 10.95x (ISBN 0-87766-295-9, 31900). Urban Inst.

Greiner, John M., jt. auth. see Hatry, Harry P.

Greiner, John M., et al. Monetary Incentives & Work Standards in Five Cities: Impacts & Implications for Management & Labor. 94p. 1977. pap. 6.95x (ISBN 0-87766-187-1, 17300). Urban Inst.

Greiner, Keith. Halley's Comet: The Viewer's Essential Guide & Notebook. (Illus.). 33p. 1984. pap. 6.95 (ISBN 0-9614258-0-6); European Edition. pap. 6.95 (ISBN 0-9614258-1-4). Better Life.

Greiner, Larry E. & Metzger, Robert O. Consulting to Management. (Illus.). 336p. 1983. text ed. 25.95 (ISBN 0-13-548131-7). P-H.

Greiner, Lynn, jt. auth. see Dzielak, Ted.

Greiner, Norbert. Studien zu Much Ado About Nothing, Vol. 8. (Trierer Studien zur Literatur). 188p. (Ger.). 1983. 22.10 (ISBN 3-8204-7794-2). P Lang Pubs.

Greiner, P. C. & Stein, E. M. Estimates of the Neumann Problem. (Mathematical Notes Ser.: No. 19). 1977. 20.00 (ISBN 0-691-08013-5). Princeton U Pr.

Greiner, R. H. Polynesian Decorative Designs. (BMB). Repr. of 1923 ed. 28.00 (ISBN 0-527-02110-5). Kraus Repr.

Greiner, T., jt. auth. see Almroth, S.

Greiner, W., jt. auth. see Eisenberg, J. M.

Greiner, W., ed. Quantum Electrodynamics of Strong Fields. (NATO ASI Series B, Physics: Vol. 80). 912p. 1982. 125.00 (ISBN 0-306-41010-9, Plenum Pr). Plenum Pub.

Greiner, W., et al. Quantum Electrodynamics of Strong Fields. (Texts & Monographs in Physics). (Illus.). 610p. 1985. 43.00 (ISBN 0-387-13404-2). Springer-Verlag.

Greinke, Pamylle & King, Lise. Jacqueline & the Beanstalk. LC 83-63250. (Illus.). 64p. 1984. pap. 5.95 (ISBN 0-932966-52-7). Permanent Pr.

Greisen, Deanna H., ed. Citizen Evaluation of the Community Development Block Grant Program in Norman, Oklahoma. 92p. 1983. 6.00 (ISBN 0-318-01374-6). Univ OK Gov Res.

Greisen, Kenneth. The Physics of Cosmic X-Ray, Gamma-Ray & Particle Sources. 2nd ed. Cameron, A. G. W. & Field, G. B., eds. LC 78-135063. (Topics in Astrophysics & Space Physics Ser.). (Illus.). 124p. 1971. 28.95 (ISBN 0-677-03380-X). Gordon.

Greisman, Bernard, ed. J. K. Lasser's How You Can Profit from the New Tax Law. LC 81-21196. 160p. 1982. pap. 4.95 (ISBN 0-671-45976-7, Fireside). S&S.

Greisman, Joan, jt. auth. see Wittels, Harriet.

Greisman, Joan, jt. auth. see Wittles, Harriet.

Greison, Betty, et al. Black Hawk & Jim Thorp: Super Heroes; Sauk Indian Stories for Children. (gr. 5-12). 1983. pap. 4.95 (ISBN 0-89992-085-3). Coun India Ed.

Greist, Georgia L., jt. auth. see Greist, John H.

Greist, John H. & Greist, Georgia L. Fearless Flying: A Passenger Guide to Modern Airline Travel. LC 81-11031. 160p. 1981. 17.95 (ISBN 0-88229-710-4). Nelson-Hall.

Greist, John H. & Jefferson, James W. Depression & Its Treatment. 128p. 1985. pap. 3.95 (ISBN 0-446-32718-2). Warner Bks.

--Depression & Its Treatment: Help for the Nation's No. 1 Mental Problem. LC 83-25666. 128p. 1984. pap. 7.95x (ISBN 0-88048-025-4). Am Psychiatric.

Greist, John H. & Jefferson, James W., eds. Treatment of Mental Disorders. 1982. pap. text ed. 23.95x (ISBN 0-19-503107-5). Oxford U Pr.

Greist, John H., et al. Anxiety & Its Treatment: Help Is Available. 168p. 1985. pap. text ed. 14.95x (ISBN 0-88048-212-5, 48-212-5). Am Psychiatric.

Greitz, Torgny, et al, eds. The Metabolism of the Human Brain Studied with Positron Emission Tomography. (Illus.). 536p. 1985. text ed. 98.00 (ISBN 0-88167-056-1). Raven.

Greitzer, S. L., jt. auth. see Coxeter, H. S.

Greitzer, Samuel L., ed. International Mathematical Olympiads 1959-1977. LC 78-54027. (New Mathematical Library: No. 27). 210p. 1979. pap. 10.00 (ISBN 0-88385-627-1). Math Assn.

Greitzer, Samuel L., compiled by. International Mathematical Olympiads Nineteen Fifty-Nine to Nineteen Seventy-Seven. LC 78-54027. (Illus.). 204p. 1979. pap. 8.75 (ISBN 0-88385-600-X). NCTM.

Greive, Hermann. Studien zum juedischen Neuplatonismus: Die Religionsphilosophie des Abraham Ibn Ezra. (Studia Judaica Vol. 7). 225p. 1973. 35.60x (ISBN 3-11-004116-2). De Gruyter.

Grejda, Edward S. The Common Continent of Men: Racial Equality in the Novels of Herman Melville. LC 74-80067. 1974. 15.50x (ISBN 0-8046-9073-1, Pub. by Kennikat). Assoc Faculty Pr.

Grekov, A. A., jt. ed. see Fridkin, V. M.

Grekov, Boris. The Culture of Kiev Russia. Rose, Pauline, tr. 1977. lib. bdg. 59.95 (ISBN 0-8490-1694-0). Gordon Pr.

Grekova, I. Russian Women: Two Stories. Visson, Lynn, tr. from Russ. LC 83-8553. 266p. 1984. 17.95 (ISBN 0-15-179056-6). HarBraceJ.

Grele, Ronald. Envelopes of Sound: The Art of Oral History. 2nd ed. xvi, 283p. 1985. 20.95 (ISBN 0-317-18513-6); pap. cancelled (ISBN 0-913750-29-8). Precedent Pub.

Grele, Ronald J., ed. Envelopes of Sound: The Art of Oral History. 2nd ed. LC 83-72306. 283p. 1984. 20.95 (ISBN 0-913750-23-9); cassettes of panel discussion 17.95. Precedent Pub.

--Envelopes of Sound: The Art of Oral History. 2nd ed. 283p. 1985. 20.95 (ISBN 0-913750-23-9). Transaction Bks.

Grelewicz, Richard M. Take It with You: The Complete Guide to Portable Business Computing. LC 84-5208. 246p. 1984. pap. 14.95 (ISBN 0-471-88198-8). Wiley.

Grell, E., ed. Membrane Spectroscopy. (Molecular Biology, Biochemistry, & Biophysics Ser.: Vol. 31). (Illus.). 512p. 1981. 89.50 (ISBN 0-387-10332-5). Springer-Verlag.

Grell, E. H., jt. auth. see Lindsley, Dan L.

Grell, Rhoda F., ed. Mechanisms in Recombination. LC 74-20987. 471p. 1974. 47.50x (ISBN 0-306-30823-1, Plenum Pr). Plenum Pub.

Grella, P., jt. auth. see Onnis, A.

Grellier, J. J. History of the National Debt from the Revolution in 1688 to 1800. LC 73-121224. (Research & Source Works Ser: No. 764). 1971. Repr. of 1810 ed. lib. bdg. 26.00 (ISBN 0-8337-1452-X). B Franklin.

Gremetz, M., et al. Meeting of European Communist Workers' Parties for Peace & Disarmament. 205p. 1980. 4.45 (ISBN 0-8285-1887-4, Pub. by Progress Pubs USSR). Imported Pubns.

Gremillion, Joseph. Church & Culture since Vatican II: The Experience of North & Latin America. LC 84-40364. 224p. 1985. pap. text ed. 9.95 (ISBN 0-268-00753-5, 85-07535). U of Notre Dame Pr.

Gremillion, Joseph, ed. Food-Energy & the Major Faiths. LC 77-17975. 302p. (Orig.). 1978. pap. 9.95 (ISBN 0-88344-138-1). Orbis Bks.

--The Gospel of Peace & Justice: Catholic Social Teaching Since Pope John. LC 75-39892. 637p. (Orig.). 1976. pap. 12.95 (ISBN 0-88344-166-7). Orbis Bks.

Gremillion, Lee L. Managing MIS Implementation. Dickson, Gary, ed. LC 82-4787. (Management Information Systems Ser.: No. 1). 198p. 1982. 39.95 (ISBN 0-8357-1321-0). UMI Res Pr.

Gremmen, N. J. The Vegetation of the Subantartic Islands & Prince Edward. 1982. lib. bdg. 49.00 (ISBN 90-6193-683-7, Pub. by Junk Pubs Netherlands). Kluwer Academic.

Gremy, F., et al, eds. Medical Informatics Europe 1981: Proceedings. (Lecture Notes in Medical Informatics Ser.: Vol. 11). 975p. 1981. pap. 56.20 (ISBN 0-387-10568-9). Springer-Verlag.

Gren, Erik. Kleinasien und der Ostbalkan in der Wirtschaftlichen Entwicklung der Romischen Kaiserzeit. Finley, Moses, ed. LC 79-4978. (Ancient Economic History Ser.). (Ger.). 1980. Repr. of 1941 ed. lib. bdg. 19.00x (ISBN 0-405-12365-5). Ayer Co Pubs.

Gren, Jack. Executive's Guide to Successful Speechmaking. Rev. ed. LC 68-55430. 48p. 1984. pap. 3.50 (ISBN 0-87576-022-8). Pilot Bks.

Grenander, U. Pattern Analysis: Lectures in Pattern Theory II. (Applied Mathematical Sciences Ser.: Vol. 24). (Illus.). 1978. pap. 28.50 (ISBN 0-387-90310-0). Springer-Verlag.

--Pattern Synthesis: Lectures in Pattern Recognition, Vol. 1. LC 76-209. (Applied Mathematical Sciences: Vol. 18). 1976. pap. 24.00 (ISBN 0-387-90174-4). Springer-Verlag.

Grenander, Ulf. Abstract Inference. LC 80-22016. (Wiley Series in Probability & Mathematical Statistics-Probability & Mathematical Statistics Section). 526p. 1981. 44.95x (ISBN 0-471-08267-8, Pub. by Wiley Interscience). Wiley.

--Mathematical Experiments on the Computer. (Pure & Applied Mathematics Ser.). 1982. 44.50 (ISBN 0-12-301750-5). Acad Pr.

Grenander, Ulf & Rosenblatt, Murray. Statistical Analysis of Stationary Time Series. 2nd ed. LC 83-62687. 308p. 1984. text ed. 17.95 (ISBN 0-8284-0320-1). Chelsea Pub.

Grenander, Ulf & Szego, Gabor. Toeplitz Forms & Their Applications. LC 83-62686. ix, 245p. text ed. 16.95 (ISBN 0-8284-0321-X). Chelsea Pub.

Grenard, jt. auth. see Krause.

Grenard, F. Tibet: The Country & Its Inhabitants. De Mattos, A. Teiseira, tr. from Fr. 373p. 1974. Repr. of 1904 ed. 35.00 (ISBN 0-89684-143-X). Orient Bk Dist.

Grenard, Fernand. Babar, First of the Moguls. facsimile ed. White, Homer & Glaenzer, Richard, trs. LC 70-124236. (Select Bibliographies Reprint Ser.). Repr. of 1930 ed. 16.00 (ISBN 0-8369-5424-6). Ayer Co Pubs.

Grenard, Ross B. Requiem for the Narrow Gauge. 125p. 1984. 24.95 (ISBN 0-912113-13-8); pap. 12.95 (ISBN 0-912113-12-X). Railhead Pubns.

Grenard, S. Guide to the Hazards of Respiratory Therapy. 1978. 14.50 (ISBN 0-8151-3979-9). Year Bk Med.

--Introduction to Respiratory Therapy. 1981. 19.95 (ISBN 0-8151-3973-X). Year Bk Med.

Grenby, Mike. Mike Grenby's Money Book: How to Survive Canada's Inflation. 2nd ed. 169p. 1979. 4.50 (ISBN 0-88908-051-8). Self Counsel Pr.

--Mike Grenby's Tax Tips: How to Pay Less Tax This Year. 7th ed. 172p. 1986. price not set (ISBN 0-88908-623-0). Self Counsel Pr.

Grenby, T. H., et al, eds. Developments in Sweeteners, Vol. 2. (Illus.). 264p. 1983. 52.00 (ISBN 0-85334-202-4, I-206-83, Pub. by Elsevier Applied Sci England). Elsevier.

Grendler, Paul. Culture & Censorship in Late Renaissance Italy & France. 318p. 1981. 70.00x (ISBN 0-86078-084-8, Pub. by Variorum). State Mutual Bk.

Grendler, Paul F. Critics of the Italian World, Fifteen Thirty to Fifteen Sixty: Anton Francesco Doni, Nicolo Franco & Ortensio Lando. LC 69-16112. (Illus.). 296p. 1969. 30.00x (ISBN 0-299-05220-6). U of Wis Pr.

--The Roman Inquisition & the Venetian Press, 1540-1605. LC 76-45900. 1978. text ed. 40.00 (ISBN 0-691-05245-X). Princeton U Pr.

Grendon, Felix. Anglo-Saxon Charms. LC 74-3177. Repr. lib. bdg. 30.00 (ISBN 0-8414-4497-8). Folcroft.

Grene, David. Greek Political Theory: The Image of Man in Thucydides & Plato. 90p. 1965. pap. 1.95x (ISBN 0-226-30787-5, P201, Phoen). U of Chicago Pr.

Grene, David see Sophocles.

Grene, David & Lattimore, Richmond, eds. Greek Tragedies. Incl. Vol. 1. Agamemnon, Prometheus Bound, Oedipus the King, Antigone. 1960. pap. 5.95 (ISBN 0-226-30774-3, P41); Vol. 2. The Libation Bearers, Electra (Sophocles), Iphigenia in Tauris, Electra (Euripides), the Trojan Women. 1960. pap. text ed. 5.95 (ISBN 0-226-30775-1, P42); Vol. 3. The Eumenides, Philoctetes, Oedipus at Colonus, the Bacchae, Alcestis. 1960. pap. text ed. 5.95 (ISBN 0-226-30777-8, P43). LC 60-950. 1960. pap. (Phoen). U of Chicago Pr.

Grene, David, ed. see Aeschylus.

Grene, David, ed. see Euripides.

Grene, David, tr. see Aeschylus.

Grene, David see Euripides.

Grene, David see Sophocles.

Grene, M. Boston Studies in the Philosophy of Science, Vol. 23: The Understanding of Nature. Essays in the Philosophy of Biology. LC 74-76477. (Synthese Library: No. 66). 366p. 1974. 44.00 (ISBN 90-277-0462-7, Pub. by Reidel Holland); pap. 24.00 (ISBN 90-277-0463-5). Kluwer Academic.

Grene, M. & Mendelsohn, E., eds. Boston Studies in the Philosophy of Science, Vol. 27: Topics in the Philosophy of Biology. LC 75-12875. (Synthese Library: No. 84). 425p. 1975. 58.00 (ISBN 90-277-0595-X, Pub. by Reidel Holland); pap. 29.00 (ISBN 90-277-0596-8). Kluwer Academic.

Grene, Marjorie. Introduction to Existentialism. LC 84-2725. (Midway Ser.). x, 150p. 1984. pap. text ed. 6.00x (ISBN 0-226-30823-5). U of Chicago Pr.

--The Knower & the Known. 284p. 1984. pap. text ed. 12.25 (ISBN 0-8191-3758-8, Ctr Adv Res Phenom). U Pr of Amer.

--Philosophy in & Out of Europe & Other Essays. LC 75-27924. 1976. 21.00x (ISBN 0-520-03121-0). U of Cal Pr.

--A Portrait of Aristotle. LC 63-5566. 1979. pap. text ed. 8.00x (ISBN 0-226-30822-7, Midway Reprint). U of Chicago Pr.

--Sartre. (Current Continental Research Ser.). 312p. 1983. pap. text ed. 14.25 (ISBN 0-8191-3372-8). U Pr of Amer.

Grene, Marjorie, ed. The Anatomy of Knowledge: Papers Presented to the Study Group on Foundations of Cultural Unity, Bowdoin College, 1965 & 1966. LC 68-19672. 384p. 1969. 17.50x (ISBN 0-87023-043-3). U of Mass Pr.

--Dimensions of Darwinism: Themes & Counter Themes in Twentieth-Century Evolutionary Theory. LC 83-1795. (Illus.). 336p. 1983. 32.50 (ISBN 0-521-25408-6). Cambridge U Pr.

--Spinoza: A Collection of Critical Essays. LC 78-62973. (Modern Studies in Philosophy). 1979. text ed. 18.95x (ISBN 0-268-01692-5); pap. text ed. 9.95x (ISBN 0-268-01693-3). U of Notre Dame Pr.

--Toward a Unity of Knowledge. LC 69-17280. (Psychological Issues Monograph: No. 22, Vol. 6, No. 2). 302p. 1969. text ed. 22.50 (ISBN 0-8236-6610-7). Intl Univs Pr.

Grene, Marjorie, ed. see Polanyi, Michael.

Grene, Marjorie, jt. ed. see Smith, Thomas V.

Grene, Marjorie, tr. see Plessner, Helmuth.

Grene, Nicholas. Bernard Shaw: A Critical View. LC 83-24547. 188p. 1984. 22.50 (ISBN 0-312-07661-4). St Martin.

--Shakespeare, Jonson, Moliere: The Comic Contract. 246p. 1980. 29.50x (ISBN 0-389-20093-X, 06866). B&N Imports.

--Synge: A Critical Study of the Plays. 202p. 1975. 18.50x (ISBN 0-87471-775-2). Rowman.

Grene, Nicholas, ed. see Synge, J. M.

Grenell, Robert. From Nerve to Mind. 244p. 1972. 67.25 (ISBN 0-677-12310-8). Gordon.

Grenell, Robert & Gabay, Sabit, eds. Biological Foundations of Psychiatry, 2 vols. LC 74-15664. 1976. 63.00 ea.; Vol. 1, 613pgs. (ISBN 0-911216-96-0); Vol. 2, 477 Pgs. (ISBN 0-89004-126-1). Raven.

Grenell, Zelotes & Goss, Agnes G. The Work of the Clerk. 1967. pap. 2.95 (ISBN 0-8170-0383-5). Judson.

Grenelle, Lisa. No Scheduled Flight. 64p. 1973. 4.00 (ISBN 0-685-25030-X). Golden Quill.

--Self Is the Stranger. 1963. 2.75 (ISBN 0-8233-0034-X). Golden Quill.

--Women Walking. LC 77-99152. 77p. 1978. 5.00 (ISBN 0-8233-0271-7). Golden Quill.

Grenert, Gerald T. Ground Lease Practice. LC 78-634364. (California Practice Bks.: No. 54). (Illus.). xii, 225p. 1971. 45.00 (ISBN 0-88124-019-2). Cal Cont Ed Bar.

Grenet, Emilio. Popular Cuban Music. (Ballroom Dance Ser.). 1985. lib. bdg. 79.95 (ISBN 0-87700-679-2). Revisionist Pr.

Grenfell, Cynthia. Stone Run: Tidings. LC 83-398. 96p. (Orig.). 1983. pap. 11.95 (ISBN 0-86534-023-4). Sunstone Pr.

Grenfell, Julian. Margot. 586p. 1984. 16.95 (ISBN 0-88191-002-3). Freundlich.

Grenfell, Russell. Bismarck Episode. (Illus.). 11.25 (ISBN 0-8446-4024-7). Peter Smith.

--Horatio Nelson: A Short Biography. LC 78-6150. (Illus.). 1978. Repr. of 1968 ed. lib. bdg. 24.25x (ISBN 0-313-20481-0, GRHN). Greenwood.

--Unconditional Hatred: German War Guilt Post W.W.II. 1953. 9.95 (ISBN 0-8159-7002-1). Devin.

Grenfell, Wilfred T. Down North on the Labrador. LC 70-122712. (Short Story Index Reprint Ser). 1911. 17.00 (ISBN 0-8369-3545-4). Ayer Co Pubs.

--Labrador Days: Tales of the Sea Toilers. facsimile ed. LC 73-167451. (Short Story Index Reprint Ser.). Repr. of 1919 ed. 15.00 (ISBN 0-8369-3977-8). Ayer Co Pubs.

--Off the Rocks. facs. ed. LC 70-134963. (Short Story Index Reprint Ser). 1906. 17.00 (ISBN 0-8369-3693-0). Ayer Co Pubs.

Grenier, Albert. Roman Spirit in Religion, Thought & Art. Dobie, M. R., tr. LC 76-118639. (Illus.). 423p. 1970. Repr. of 1926 ed. lib. bdg. 32.50 (ISBN 0-8154-0330-5). Cooper Sq.

Grenier, Albert, jt. auth. see Amiel-Tison, Claudine.

Grenier, Fernand, ed. Quebec. (Studies in Canadian Geography). (Illus., Fr.). 1972. pap. 6.00x (ISBN 0-8020-6159-1). U of Toronto Pr.

Grenier, M. Special Day Prayers for the Very Young Child. LC 56-1719. (gr. 1-4). 1983. 7.95 (ISBN 0-570-04076-0). Concordia.

Grenier, Mildred B. The Beginner's Guide to Writing for Profit. LC 83-23816. 43p. 1984. pap. text ed. 3.50 (ISBN 0-87576-108-9). Pilot Bks.

Grenier, Richard. The Marrakesh One-Two. LC 82-15818. 350p. 1983. 14.95 (ISBN 0-395-33099-8). HM.

--The Marrakesh One-Two. (Penguin Fiction Ser.). 224p. 1984. pap. 6.95 (ISBN 0-14-007372-8). Penguin.

Grenier, Robert. Dusk Road Games. 72p. 1967. 4.00 (ISBN 0-913219-00-2); pap. 2.00 (ISBN 0-913219-01-0). Pym-Rand Pr.

Grenier, Robert, ed. see Eigner, Larry.

Grenier-Sweet, Gail, ed. Pro-Life Feminism: Different Voices. 256p. (Orig.). 1985. pap. 7.95 (ISBN 0-919225-22-5). Life Cycle Bks.

Greniman, Deborah, tr. see Schweid, Eliezer.

Grenlee, Geraldine, et al. Kinesiology. Kneer, Marian, ed. (Basic Stuff Ser.: No. I, 2 of 6). (Illus.). 90p. (Orig.). 1981. pap. text ed. 6.55 (ISBN 0-88314-025-X). AAHPERD.

Grennan, David M. Rheumatology. (Illus.). 255p. Date not set. pap. price not set (Pub. by Bailliere-Tindall). Saunders.

Grennan, Margaret R. William Morris: Medievalist & Revolutionary. LC 76-102500. 1970. Repr. of 1945 ed. 10.00x (ISBN 0-8462-1459-8). Russell.

Grennan, Wayne. Argument Evaluation. 420p. (Orig.). 1985. lib. bdg. 27.50 (ISBN 0-8191-4266-2); pap. text ed. 15.50 (ISBN 0-8191-4267-0). U Pr of Amer.

Grennell, Dean, ed. Pistol & Revolver Digest. 3rd ed. LC 76-23196. (Illus.). 288p. 1982. pap. 11.95 (ISBN 0-910676-49-6). DBI.

Grennell, Dean A. ABC's of Reloading. 3rd ed. LC 73-91588. (Illus.). 288p. 1985. pap. 11.95 (ISBN 0-910676-84-4). DBI.

--Autoloading Pistols: Gun Digest Book. LC 83-72348. 288p. 1983. pap. 11.95 (ISBN 0-910676-59-3). DBI.

--Home Workshop Digest. LC 80-67742. 256p. 1981. pap. 7.95 (ISBN 0-910676-14-3). DBI.

Grennen, Joseph. Monarch Notes on Chaucer's Canterbury Tales. (Orig.). pap. 3.50 (ISBN 0-671-00511-1). Monarch Pr.

--Monarch Notes on Donne & the Metaphysical Poets. (Orig.). pap. 2.95 (ISBN 0-671-00731-9). Monarch Pr.

--Monarch Notes on Fielding's Joseph Andrews. (Orig.). pap. 3.25 (ISBN 0-671-00711-4). Monarch Pr.

Grennes, Thomas J. International Economics. (Illus.). 656p. Date not set. text ed. 27.95 (ISBN 0-13-472713-4). P-H.

Grenoble, Penelope B., jt. auth. see Soll, Robert W.

Grenoble Public Reference Library Staff, ed. General Catalogue of Printed Books to 1900 Grenoble Public Reference Library, 12 Vols. 1981. lib. bdg. 2075.00 (ISBN 3-598-10160-0). K G Saur.

Grenon, M. The Nuclear Apple & the Solar Orange: Alternatives in World Energy. LC 80-40836. (Illus.). 200p. 1981. 40.00 (ISBN 0-08-026157-4); pap. 17.25 (ISBN 0-08-026156-6). Pergamon.

Grenon, M., ed. Methods & Models for Assessing Energy Resources: First IIASA Conference on Energy Resources, 20-21 May, 1975, Laxenburg, Austria. (IIASA Proceedings: Vol. 5). (Illus.). 1979. 105.00 (ISBN 0-08-024443-2). Pergamon.

Grenough, Mildred C. English: Sing It! (Illus.). (gr. 9-12). 1976. pap. text ed. 3.33 (ISBN 0-07-024667-X). McGraw.

Grensemann, Hermann. Knidische Medizin, Part 1: Die Testimonien zur aeltesten knidischen Lehre und Analysen knidischer Schriften im Corpus Hippocraticum. (Ars Medica, Sect. 2, Griechisch-Lateinische Medizin, Vol. 4). 1974. 64.00x (ISBN 3-11-004141-3). De Gruyter.

Grenspan, Stanley I. Psychopathology & Adaptation in Infancy & Early Childhood. LC 81-19282. (Clinical Infant Reprots Ser.: No. 1). 263p. 1983. 27.50 (ISBN 0-8236-5660-8). Intl Univs Pr.

Grente, George F. Dictionnaire des Lettres Francaises, 19e Siecle: L-Z. 568p. (Fr.). 1973. 79.95 (ISBN 0-686-57315-3, M-6297). French & Eur.

Grente, Georges F. Dictionnaire des Lettres Francaises, le 19e Siecle: A-K. 549p. (Fr.). 1971. 75.00 (ISBN 0-686-57314-5, M-6296). French & Eur.

Grente, Georges Francois. Dictionnaire Des Lettres Francaises (le Moyen Age) 768p. (Fr.). 1972. 79.95 (ISBN 0-686-56780-3, M-6577). French & Eur.

--Dictionnaire Des Lettres Francaises, 18e Siecle (A-K, 2 vols. 672p. (Fr.). 1960. 75.00 (ISBN 0-686-56782-X, M-6578). French & Eur.

--Dictionnaire des Lettres Francaises, 18e siecle (L-Z, 2 vols. 568p. (Fr.). 1973. 75.00 (ISBN 0-686-56784-6, M-6580). French & Eur.

Grentzer, Rose M. & Hood, Marguerite V. A Comprehensive Book of Music & Activities for the Kindergarden. (Birchard Music Ser.). pap. 40.00 (ISBN 0-317-10024-6, 2005328). Bks Demand UMI.

Grenvik, Ake, jt. auth. see Safar, Peter.

Grenville, George, jt. auth. see Temple, Richard G.

Grenville, I. A. Generation of Blood. 1978. pap. 1.50 (ISBN 0-532-15318-9). Woodhill.

Grenville, J. A. Europe Reshaped Eighteen Forty-Eight to Eighteen Seventy-Eight. LC 80-66910. (History of Europe Ser.; Cornell Paperbacks Ser.). 412p. 1980. pap. 7.95x (ISBN 0-8014-9207-6). Cornell U Pr.

--A World History of the Twentieth Century Vol. 1: Western Dominance 1900-45. (Illus.). 605p. 1980. 35.00x (ISBN 0-389-20171-5, 06947). B&N Imports.

--A World History of the Twentieth Century: Vol. 1, Western Dominance, 1900-1945. LC 84-40300. (Illus.). 605p. 1984. pap. text ed. 15.00x (ISBN 0-87451-315-4). U Pr of New Eng.

Grenville, Kate. Bearded Ladies. 168p. 1985. 15.00 (ISBN 0-7022-1715-8). U of Queensland Pr.

Grenville, Peter. Kurt Tucholsky: The Ironic Sentimentalist, Vol. I. (German Literature & Society). 124p. 1981. pap. text ed. 11.25x (ISBN 0-391-02290-3, Pub. by Cecil Wolfe England). Humanities.

--Kurt Tucholsky: The Ironic Sentimentalist. (German Literature & Society Ser.: Vol. 1). 1980. pap. text ed. 10.75 (ISBN 0-85496-074-0). Humanities.

Grenville-Grey, Wilfred. All in an African Lifetime. (Orig.). 1971. pap. 1.50 (ISBN 0-377-11221-6). Friend Pr.

Grenville-Mathers, R. The Respiratory System, 2E. (Penguin Library of Nursing Ser.). 147p. 1983. pap. text ed. 7.25 (ISBN 0-443-02610-6). Churchill.

Grenz, Stanley. Isaac Backus - Puritan & Baptist. (Dissertation Ser.: No. 4). 1983. pap. 21.95 (ISBN 0-86554-067-5). NABPR.

--Isaac Backus: Puritan & Baptist; His Place in History, His Thought, & the Implications for Modern Baptist Theology. LC 83-12140. 352p. pap. 21.95x (ISBN 0-86554-067-5, P12). Mercer Univ Pr.

Grenz, Stanley J. The Baptist Congregation. 128p. 1985. pap. 7.95 (ISBN 0-8170-1083-1). Judson.

Grenzeback, Joe & Bergh, Haakon. Sing Ho for a Prince (Sleeping Beauty) (Children's Theatre Playscript with Music Ser.). 1957. pap. 2.50x (ISBN 0-88020-054-5); 15.00x (ISBN 0-88020-055-3). Coach Hse.

Grenzer, Louis E. Textbook Study Guide of Cardiology. 2nd ed. (Medical Examination Review Book: Vol. 2C). 1979. 13.95 (ISBN 0-87488-153-6). Med Exam.

Grenzke, Janet M. Influence, Change, & the Legislative Process. LC 82-9383. (Contributions in Political Science Ser.: No. 89). (Illus.). xi, 193p. 1983. lib. bdg. 35.00 (ISBN 0-313-23385-3, GRI/). Greenwood.

Greppin, John A. Classical & Middle Armenian Bird Names. LC 77-25361. 1978. 35.00x (ISBN 0-88206-017-1). Caravan Bks.

Gres, J. & Jung, H. German Employment Law. (Orig.). 1983. pap. text ed. 36.00 (ISBN 90-654-4144-1, Pub. by Kluwer Law & Taxation). Kluwer Academic.

--German Employment Law: From Hiring Through Dismissing Employees. (Illus.). 256p. 1983. 26.00 (ISBN 90-312-0128-6, Pub. by Kluwer Law, Netherlands). Kluwer Academic.

Gres, Joachim, jt. auth. see Jung, Harald.

Gresch, P. Managing Spatial Conflict: The Planning System in Switzerland. (Illus.). 94p. 1985. pap. 20.00 (ISBN 0-08-032731-1, Pub. by PPL). Pergamon.

Gresh, A. The P.L.O. The Struggle Within: Towards an Independent Palestinian State. Berrett, A. M., tr. 288p. 1985. 29.50x (ISBN 0-86232-272-3, Pub. by Zed Pr England); pap. 10.75 (ISBN 0-86232-273-1, Pub. by Zed Pr England). Biblio Dist.

Gresham, Charles R. Preach the Word. LC 83-71917. 200p. (Orig.). 1983. pap. 3.95 (ISBN 0-89900-198-X). College Pr Pub.

--What the Bible Says about Resurrection. LC 82-7411. (What the Bible Says Ser.). 351p. 1983. 13.50 (ISBN 0-89900-090-8). College Pr Pub.

Gresham, G. A. Primate Atherosclerosis. Kritchevsky, D., et al, eds. (Monographs on Atherosclerosis: Vol. 7). 1976. 21.00 (ISBN 3-8055-2270-3). S Karger.

--Reversing Atherosclerosis. 120p. 1980. 11.75x (ISBN 0-398-03931-3). C C Thomas.

Gresham, G. A., jt. ed. see Peeters, H.

Gresham, G. Austin. Color Atlas of Forensic Pathology. (Year Book Color Atlas Ser.). (Illus.). 320p. 1975. 49.95 (ISBN 0-8151-3992-6). Year Bk Med.

--Color Atlas of General Pathology. (Year Book Color Atlas Ser.). (Illus.). 1971. 39.95 (ISBN 0-8151-3990-X). Year Bk Med.

Gresham, G. Austin & Turner, Arthur F. Post-Mortem Procedures: An Illustrated Textbook. (Illus.). 1979. 39.95 (ISBN 0-8151-3994-2). Year Bk Med.

Gresham, Glenn, jt. auth. see Granger, Carl V.

Gresham, Grits. Fishes & Fishing in Louisiana. 1965. 6.00 (ISBN 0-685-08167-2); pap. 4.95 (ISBN 0-685-08168-0). Claitors.

--Fishing & Boating in Louisiana. pap. 2.95 (ISBN 0-87511-680-9). Claitors.

Gresham, John M. Biographical Cyclopedia of the Commonwealth of Kentucky. 736p. 1980. Repr. of 1896 ed. 40.00 (ISBN 0-89308-192-2). Southern Hist Pr.

Gresham, Matilda. Life of Walter Quintin Gresham 1832-1895, 2 Vols. facs. ed. LC 70-137378. (Select Bibliographies Reprint Ser). 1919. Set. 53.00 (ISBN 0-8369-5579-X); Vol. 1. 26.50 (ISBN 0-8369-9657-7); Vol. 2. 26.50 (ISBN 0-8369-9658-5). Ayer Co Pubs.

Gresham, Perry D. With Wings As Eagles. LC 80-66183. 1980. 10.95 (ISBN 0-89305-025-3); pap. 5.95 (ISBN 0-89305-026-1). Anna Pub.

Gresham, Stephan. Moon Lake. 1982. pap. 2.95 (ISBN 0-8217-1004-4). Zebra.

Gresham, Stephen. Half Moon Down. 1985. pap. 3.50 (ISBN 0-8217-1625-5). Zebra.

--Rockabye Baby. 1984. pap. 3.50 (ISBN 0-8217-1470-8). Zebra.

Gresham, William L. Houdini. (Illus.). 1975. pap. 1.50 (ISBN 0-532-15166-6). Woodhill.

Gresk, Grace E. Come Holy Spirit I Need Thee. 48p. 1985. 5.95 (ISBN 0-533-06177-6). Vantage.

Gresleri, Giuliano. Josef Hoffmann. 200p. 1985. pap. 12.50 (ISBN 0-8478-0554-9). Rizzoli Intl.

Gress, David. Peace & Survival: West Germany's National & Strategic Dilemma. (Publication Ser.: 309). 300p. 1985. 15.95 (ISBN 0-8179-8091-1). Hoover Inst Pr.

Gress, James R. & Kerber, James E., eds. Explorations into Teaching & Learning: School Based Teacher Education. 1976. pap. text ed. 5.00x (ISBN 0-89039-182-3). Ann Arbor FL.

Gress, James R. & Purpel, David E., eds. Curriculum: An Introduction to the Field. LC 77-23651. (National Society for the Study of Education Series on Contemporary Educ. Issues). 1978. 23.25x (ISBN 0-8211-0613-9); text ed. 21.25x 10 or more copies. McCutchan.

Gressel, David. Financing Techniques for Local Rehabilitation Programs. 98p. 1976. 9.00 (ISBN 0-318-14940-0, N585); members 7.00 (ISBN 0-318-14941-9). NAHRO.

Gressel, Jonathan, jt. ed. see Lebaron, Homer M.

Gresser, I. Interferon Five. 1984. pap. 22.00 (ISBN 0-12-302254-1). Acad Pr.

Gresser, I., ed. Interferons, 1980, Vol. 2. LC 79-41412. (Interferon Ser.). 1981. 23.00 (ISBN 0-12-302251-7). Acad Pr.

Gresser, Ion. Interferon: 1979. LC 79-41412. (Essays in Biochemistry Ser.). 1980. 27.50 (ISBN 0-12-302250-9). Acad Pr.

Gresser, Ion, ed. Interferon Eighty-Two. (Serial Publication). 1983. 22.00 (ISBN 0-12-302253-3). Acad Pr.

--Interferon 3: 1981. LC 79-4142. 164p. 1982. 22.00 (ISBN 0-12-302252-5). Acad Pr.

Gresser, Julian. Partners in Prosperity: Strategic Industries in the United States & Japan. LC 83-24925. 432p. 1984. 15.95 (ISBN 0-07-024671-8). McGraw.

Gresser, Julian & Fujikura, Koichiro. Environmental Law in Japan. (Illus.). 520p. 1980. text ed. 80.00x (ISBN 0-262-07076-6). MIT Pr.

Gresser, Sy. Fragments & Others. LC 82-73260. (Illus.). 50p. (Orig.). 1982. pap. 5.00 (ISBN 0-934996-18-0). Am Stud Pr.

Gresset, Michel. A Faulkner Chronology. LC 84-50873. (Illus.). 1985. pap. 7.95 (ISBN 0-87805-229-1). U Pr of Miss.

Gresset, Michel & Polk, Noel, eds. Intertextuality in Faulkner. LC 84-21943. 1985. 17.95x (ISBN 0-87805-249-6). U Pr of Miss.

Gresset, Michel & Samway, Patrick S., eds. Faulkner & Idealism: Perspectives from Paris. LC 83-3638. 168p. 1983. 12.50x (ISBN 0-87805-184-8). U Pr of Miss.

Gressitt, J. L. Biogeography & Ecology of New Guinea, 2 vols. 1982. lib. bdg. 195.00 (ISBN 90-6193-094-4, Pub. by Junk Pubs Netherlands). Kluwer Academic.

--The Coconut Rhinoceros Beetle with Particular Reference to the Palau Islands. (BMB). Repr. of 1953 ed. 19.00 (ISBN 0-527-02320-5). Kraus Repr.

Gressitt, J. L., jt. auth. see Bohart, G. E.

Gressitt, J. L., ed. Entomology of Antarctica. LC 67-62159. (Antarctic Research Ser.: Vol. 10). (Illus.). 395p. 1967. 22.00 (ISBN 0-87590-110-7). Am Geophysical.

Gressley, Gene M. The Twentieth-Century American West: A Potpourri. LC 76-56903. 232p. 1977. 19.00x (ISBN 0-8262-0218-7). U of Mo Pr.

Gressley, Gene M., ed. Voltaire & the Cowboy: The Letters of Thurman Arnold. LC 76-15772. (Illus.). 1977. 19.50x (ISBN 0-87081-073-1). Colo Assoc.

Gressley, Gene M., ed. see Livermore, Robert.

Gressman, Eugene, jt. auth. see Stern, Robert L.

Gresson, Aaron D., III. The Dialectics of Betrayal. LC 82-1783. (Modern Sociology Ser.). 160p. 1982. text ed. 24.50 (ISBN 0-89391-101-1); pap. text ed. 16.95. Ablex Pub.

Gress-Wright, D., tr. see Strangerup, Henry K.

Greston, Wilma, jt. ed. see Kleiner, George J.

Gresty, Hilary & Lewison, Jeremy, eds. Constructivism in Poland. (Illus.). 88p. (Orig.). 1984. pap. 12.50 (ISBN 0-87663-585-0). Universe.

Greteman, J. & Haverkamp, L. Divorce & Beyond: Facilitators Manual. LC 82-72048. 80p. 1984. pap. 3.95 (ISBN 0-915388-17-0). Buckley Pubns.

--Divorce & Beyond: Participants Book. LC 82-72048. 132p. 1984. pap. 3.95 (ISBN 0-915388-15-4). Buckley Pubns.

Greteman, Jim. Coping with Divorce. LC 81-65334. (Illus.). 80p. 1981. spiralbound 4.95 (ISBN 0-87793-226-3). Ave Maria.

Greth, Roma. Doctor Nostradamus. 1966. pap. 1.00x (ISBN 0-88020-078-2). Coach Hse.

--Narcissus. LC 77-82729. (Orig.). 1978. pap. 3.00 (ISBN 0-912292-46-6). The Smith.

Grethe, Guenter, ed. Isoquinolines, Vol. 38, Pt. 1. LC 80-11510. (Chemistry of Heterocyclic Compounds, a Series of Monographs). 561p. 1981. 222.95 (ISBN 0-471-37481-4). Wiley.

Grether, David M., jt. auth. see Nerlove, Marc.

Grether, Ewald T. Price Control under Fair Trade Legislation. LC 75-39245. (Getting & Spending: the Consumer's Dilemma Ser.). (Illus.). 1976. Repr. of 1939 ed. 38.50x (ISBN 0-405-08019-0). Ayer Co Pubs.

Gretler, Armin. The Training of Adult Middle-Level Personnel. LC 72-89860. (Illus.). 164p. (Orig.). 1972. pap. 7.00 (ISBN 92-3-100935-4, U685, UNESCO). Unipub.

Gretor, William, tr. see Bode, Wilhelm.

Gretry, Andre. La Caravane du Caire. Gevaert, F. A., ed. (Chefs-d'oeuvre classiques de l'opera francais Ser.: Vol. 12). (Illus.). 274p. (Fr.). 1972. pap. 25.00x (ISBN 0-8450-1112-X). Broude.

--Cephale et Procris. Gevaert, F. A., ed. (Chefs-d'oeuvre classiques de l'opera francais Ser.: Vol. 13). (Illus.). 372p. (Fr.). 1972. pap. 30.00x (ISBN 0-8450-1113-8). Broude.

--Memoires: Ou, Essais sur la Musique, 3 Vols. LC 73-160852. (Music Ser.). (Fr., Fr). 1971. Repr. of 1789 ed. Set. lib. bdg. 125.00 (ISBN 0-306-70194-4). Da Capo.

Gretry, Andre E. Reflexions d'un solitaire, 4 vols. Solvay, Lucien & Closson, Ernest, eds. LC 76-43920. (Music & Theatre in France in the 17th & 18th Centuries). Repr. of 1922 ed. Set. 135.00 (ISBN 0-404-60190-1). AMS Pr.

Gretsky, Neil E. Representation Theorems on Banach Function Spaces. LC 52-42839. (Memoirs: No. 84). 56p. 1968. pap. 9.00 (ISBN 0-8218-1284-X, MEMO-84). Am Math.

Gretten, R., jt. auth. see Digby, M.

Gretton, Ann, tr. see Romanov, Panteleimon S.

Gretton, M. Writings & Life of George Meredith. LC 70-117580. (Studies in George Meredith, No. 21). 1970. Repr. of 1926 ed. lib. bdg. 39.95x (ISBN 0-8383-1013-3). Haskell.

Gretton, Peter. Crisis Convoy. 1981. pap. 2.50 (ISBN 0-89083-852-6). Zebra.

Gretton, R. H. History. 1979. Repr. lib. bdg. 10.00 (ISBN 0-8495-2037-1). Arden Lib.

Gretz, J., et al, eds. Thermo-Mechanical Solar Power Plants: EURELIOS, the MWel Experimental Solar Thermal Electric Power Plant in the European Community. 1984. lib. bdg. 24.50 (ISBN 90-277-1728-1, Pub. by Reidel Holland). Kluwer Academic.

--Thermo-Mechnical Solar Power Plants. 1985. lib. bdg. 59.00 (ISBN 90-277-2049-5, Pub. by Reedel Netherlands). Kluwer Academic.

Gretz, Susanna. The Bears Who Went to the Seaside. (Picture Puffins Ser.). 32p. (gr. k-3). 1984. pap. 2.95 (ISBN 0-14-050111-8, Puffin). Penguin.

--It's Your Turn, Roger! (Illus.). 1985. pap. 10.95 (ISBN 0-318-11870-X). Dial Bks Young.

--It's Your Turn, Roger! LC 84-23879. (Illus.). 32p. (ps-2). 1985. 10.95 (ISBN 0-8037-0198-5). Dial Bks Young.

--Teddy Bears Cure a Cold. LC 84-4015. (Illus.). 32p. (ps-3). 1985. 11.95 (ISBN 0-02-736960-9). Macmillan.

Gretz, Susanna & Sage, Alison. Teddy Bears Cure a Cold. (Illus.). 32p. (gr. k-3). 1986. pap. 2.50 (ISBN 0-590-33993-1). Scholastic Inc.

Greub, W. Linear Algebra, Vol. 23. rev., 4th ed. (Graduate Texts in Mathematics Ser.: Vol. 23). (Illus.). 451p. 1975. 42.00 (ISBN 0-387-90110-8). Springer Verlag.

--Multilinear Algebra. 1978. pap. 29.50 (ISBN 0-387-90284-8). Springer-Verlag.

Greub, Werner, et al. Connections, Curvature, & Cohomology, 3 vols. Incl. Vol. 1. De Rham Cohomology of Manifold & Vector Bundles. 1972. 69.50 (ISBN 0-12-302701-2); Vol. 2. Lie Groups, Principal Bundles & Characteristic Classes. 1973. 79.50 (ISBN 0-12-302702-0); Vol. 3. Cohomology of Principle Bundles & Homogeneous Spaces. 1976. 94.00 (ISBN 0-12-302703-9). (Pure & Applied Mathematics Ser.). Acad Pr.

Greulach, Victor A. & Chiapetta, Vincent J. Biology. 1977. text ed. 26.65x (ISBN 0-673-15301-0); study guide 9.25x (ISBN 0-673-15302-9). Scott F.

Greulich, W. W. Handbook of Methods for the Study of Adolescent Children. (SRCD Ser.: Vol. 3, No. 2). 1938. 44.00 (ISBN 0-527-01502-4). Kraus Repr.

Greulich, William W. Somatic & Endocrine Studies of Puberal & Adolescent Boys. (SRCD: Vol. 7, No. 3). 1942. pap. 16.00 (ISBN 0-527-01524-5). Kraus Repr.

Greulich, William W. & Pyle, S. Idell. Radiographic Atlas of Skeletal Development of the Hand & Wrist. 2nd ed. (Illus.). 1959. 45.00x (ISBN 0-8047-0398-1). Stanford U Pr.

Greunke, Lowell R. Football Rankings: College Teams in the Associated Press Poll, 1936-1984. LC 83-25595. 208p. 1984. lib. bdg. 15.95x (ISBN 0-89950-108-7). McFarland & Co.

Greusel, J. R. The Poor Devil: A Memory of Robert Reitzel. (Men & Movements in the History & Philosophy of Anarchism). 1979. lib. bdg. 59.95 (ISBN 0-87700-301-7). Revisionist Pr.

Greutyner, jt. auth. see Johnson.

Grevalsky, Robin, jt. auth. see Herman, John.

Greve, E. L., ed. International Visual Field Symposium, 3rd. (Documenta Ophthalmologica Proceedings Ser.: Vol. 19). 1979. lib. bdg. 87.00 (ISBN 90-6193-160-6, Pub. by Junk Pubs Netherlands). Kluwer Academic.

--Symposium on Medical Therapy in Gloucoma. (Documenta Ophthalmologica Proceedings: Vol. 12). 1976. lib. bdg. 26.00 (ISBN 90-6193-152-5, Pub. by Junk Pubs Netherlands). Kluwer Academic.

Greve, E. L. & Heijl, A., eds. Visual Field Symposium, Fifth International: Documenta Ophthalmoligica Proceedings. 1983. lib. bdg. 86.00 (ISBN 90-619-3731-0, Pub. by Junk Pubs Netherlands). Kluwer Academic.

Greve, E. L. & Raitta, C., eds. Second European Glacoma Symposium Helsinki, May 1984. (Documenta Ophthalmogica Prooceedings Ser.). 1985. lib. bdg. 69.50 (ISBN 90-6193-526-1, Pub. by Junk Pubs Netherlands). Kluwer Academic.

Greve, E. L. & Verriest, G., eds. Fourth International Visual Field Symposium, 1980. (Documenta Ophthalmologica Proceedings Ser.: Vol. 26). 416p. 1981. 89.00 (ISBN 90-6193-165-7, Pub. by Junk Pubs Netherlands). Kluwer Academic.

Greve, Erik L., ed. Glaucoma Symposium Amsterdam: Diagnosis & Therapy. (Documenta Opthalmologica Proceedings Ser.: No. 22). 419p. 1980. lib. bdg. 92.00 (ISBN 90-6193-164-9, Pub. by Junk Pubs Netherlands). Kluwer Academic.

--International Visual Field Symposium; Second. (Documenta Ophalmologica Proceedings Ser.: No. 14). (Illus.). 1977. lib. bdg. 79.00 (ISBN 90-6193-154-1). Kluwer Academic.

Greve, J., et al. Homelessness in London. 1971. 17.50x (ISBN 0-7073-0195-5, Pub. by Scottish Academic Pr Scotland). Columbia U Pr.

Greve, J. Terrence, jt. auth. see Wallner, Nicholas.

Greve, John. London's Homeless. 76p. 1964. pap. text ed. 3.75x (ISBN 0-686-70849-0, Pub. by Bedford England). Brookfield Pub Co.

--Private Landlords in England. 54p. 1965. pap. text ed. 3.75x (ISBN 0-686-70855-5, Pub. by Bedford England). Brookfield Pub Co.

Greve, Tim, et al, eds. The Impact of Space Science on Mankind. LC 76-26652. (Nobel Foundation Symposia Ser.). 125p. 1976. 35.00x (ISBN 0-306-33701-0, Plenum Pr). Plenum Pub.

Greven, Philip. The Protestant Temperament. 15.00 (ISBN 0-394-40423-8). Knopf.

--The Protestant Temperament: Patterns of Child Rearing, Religious Experience, & the Self in Early America. 1979. pap. 8.95 (ISBN 0-452-00563-9, F563, Mer). NAL.

Greven, Philip J., Jr. Four Generations: Population, Land, & Family in Colonial Andover, Massachusetts. 349p. 1972. pap. 8.95x (ISBN 0-8014-9134-7). Cornell U Pr.

Greves, Beryl, jt. auth. see Butler, Margaret.

Grevich, J. D. Testing Procedures for Automotive AC & DC Charging Systems. 1972. text ed. 26.90 (ISBN 0-07-024673-4). McGraw.

Greville, Fulke. Life of the Renowned Sir Philip Sidney. LC 83-4483. 1984. Repr. of 1652 ed. 40.00 (ISBN 0-8201-1390-5). Schol Facsimiles.

Greville, G. D., jt. ed. see Campbell, Paul N.

Greville, R. K. Descriptions of New & Rare Diatoms. (Trans. Microscop. Soc. Ser.). (Illus.). 1968. 28.00 (ISBN 3-7682-0570-3). Lubrecht & Cramer.

Greville, T. N. United States Life Tables by Dentulous or Edentulous Condition, 1971 & 1957-58. LC 74-7204. (Data Evaluation & Methods Research Ser. 2: No. 64). 60p. 1974. pap. text ed. 1.50 (ISBN 0-8406-0018-6). Natl Ctr Health Stats.

Grevisse. Le Bon Usage: Grammaire Francaise. 29.95 (ISBN 0-685-36692-8). French & Eur.

--Code de Dictees Francaises. 11.95 (ISBN 0-685-36703-7). French & Eur.

--Code de l'Orthographe. 11.50 (ISBN 0-685-36702-9). French & Eur.

Grevisse, M. Le Bon Usage. (Fr). 49.95 (ISBN 0-685-20226-7). Schoenhof.

--Nouveaux Exercices Francais. (gr. 10-12). text ed. 11.95 (ISBN 0-685-36072-5); tchrs. manual 13.95 (ISBN 0-685-36073-3). French & Eur.

--Precis de Grammaire Francaise. (gr. 10-12). text ed. 11.25 (ISBN 0-685-36074-1). French & Eur.

Grevisse, Maurice. Grevisse's Correct French: A Practical Guide. Kendris, Christopher, tr. from Fr. (gr. 11-12). 1982. pap. text ed. 9.95 (ISBN 0-8120-2169-X). Barron.

Grevlich, Richard C., jt. ed. see Slavkin, Harold C.

Grevstad, Eric P., jt. auth. see Held, James C.

Grew, David. Beyond Rope & Fence. 14.95 (ISBN 0-8488-0135-0, Pub. by Amereon Hse). Amereon Ltd.

Grew, Eva & Grew, Sidney. Bach. (The Master Musicians Ser.). (Illus.). 230p. 1977. Repr. of 1947 ed. 13.50 (ISBN 0-460-02113-3, Pub. by J. M. Dent England). Biblio Dist.

Grew, Eva M. & Grew, Sydney. Bach. (The Master Musicians Ser.: No. M113). (Illus.). 1979. pap. 7.95 (ISBN 0-8226-0703-4). Littlefield.

Grew, F. & Hobley, B., eds. Roman Urban Topography in Britain & the Western Empire. (CBA Research Reports: No. 59). (Illus.). 136p. 1985. pap. text ed. 31.50x (ISBN 0-906780-47-0, Pub. by Coun Brit Archaeology). Humanities.

Grew, Frederick. Wealth & Common Man. 1969. 4.95 (ISBN 0-8022-0629-8). Philos Lib.

Grew, James H. & Olivier, Daniel D. One Thousand & One Pitfalls in French. rev. ed. LC 73-7323. (gr. 9up). 1974. pap. text ed. 5.95 (ISBN 0-8120-0471-X). Barron.

Grew, James H; see Bottiglia, William F.

Grew, Joseph C. Ten Years in Japan: A Contemporary Record. LC 72-4275. (World Affairs Ser.: National & International Viewpoints). (Illus.). 578p. 1972. Repr. of 1944 ed. 36.50 (ISBN 0-405-04600-6). Ayer Co Pubs.

--Ten Years in Japan: A Contemporary Record Drawn from the Diaries & Private & Official Papers of Joseph C. Grew, United States Ambassador to Japan, 1932-1942. LC 72-12556. (Illus.). 554p. 1973. Repr. of 1944 ed. lib. bdg. 23.50x (ISBN 0-8371-6723-X, GRTY). Greenwood.

--Turbulent Era: A Diplomatic Record of Forty Years, 1904-1945, 2 Vols. Johnson, Walter, ed. LC 72-114880. (Select Bibliographies Reprint Ser). 1952. Set. 88.00 (ISBN 0-8369-5284-7). Ayer Co Pubs.

Grew, Marion E. William Bentinck & William Third. LC 77-118473. 1971. Repr. of 1924 ed. 25.50x (ISBN 0-8046-1222-6, Pub. by Kennikat). Assoc Faculty Pr.

Grew, N. Experiments in Consort of the Luctation Arising from the Affusion of Several Menstrums upon All Sorts of Bodies, etc. 118p. 1985. 12.50 (ISBN 0-87556-632-4); pap. write for info. (ISBN 0-87556-114-4). Saifer.

Grew, Nehemiah. The Anatomy of Plants, with an Idea of a Philosophical History of Plants & Several Other Lectures. 1965. Repr. of 1682 ed. Facsimile Ed. 60.00 (ISBN 0-384-19950-X). Johnson Repr.

Grew, Raymond. Sterner Plan for Italian Unity: The Italian National Society in the Risorgimento. 1963. 48.00x (ISBN 0-691-05155-0). Princeton U Pr.

Grew, Raymond, ed. Crisis of Political Development in Europe & the United States. LC 78-51166. (Studies in Political Development: No. 9). 1978. 46.00 (ISBN 0-691-07598-0); pap. 10.95 (ISBN 0-691-02183-X). Princeton U Pr.

Grew, Raymond & Steneck, Nicholas H., eds. Society & History: Essays by Sylvia L. Thrupp. LC 75-31056. 352p. 1977. text ed. 18.50x (ISBN 0-472-08880-7). U of Mich Pr.

Grew, Sidney, jt. auth. see Grew, Eva.

Grew, Sydney, jt. auth. see Grew, Eva M.

Grewal, B. S., et al, eds. The Economics of Federalism. LC 79-54070. 432p. 1981. text ed. 18.50 (ISBN 0-7081-1301-X, 0457, Pub. by ANUP Australia). Australia N U P.

Grewe, Eugene F. & Sullivan, John F. The College Research Paper. 4th ed. 162p. 1957. write for info. wire coil (ISBN 0-697-03760-6). Wm C Brown.

Grewe, Georgeann, jt. auth. see Glover, Susanne.

Grewe, Georgeann, jt. auth. see Glover, Suzanne.

Grewe, Guenther. Games for Criminal Status: Justice as Order Through Structural Social Inequality. (European University Studies, Series 2: Vol. 210). 129p. 1979. 18.30 (ISBN 3-8204-6480-8). P Lang Pubs.

Grewe, Horst-Eberhard & Kremer, Karl. Atlas of Surgical Operations. Incl. Vol. 1. Grewe, Horst-Eberhard & Kremer, karl. Hirsch, H. J., tr. 1981. 69.50 (ISBN 0-7216-4273-X); Vol. 2. Grewe, Horst-Eberhard & Kremer, Karl. Rotzscher, Volker M. & Zammit, Anthony, trs. (Illus.). 434p. 1980. text ed. 69.50 (ISBN 0-7216-4274-8). LC 77-84671. Set. 139.00 (ISBN 0-7216-4272-1). Saunders.

Grewe, Wilhelm G. Friede Durch Recht? (Schriftenreihe der Juristischen Gesellschraft zu Berlin Ser.: Heft 94). 32p. (Ger.). 1985. pap. 8.00x (ISBN 3-11-010581-0). De Gruyter.

Grewell, Joy see Stortz, Diane, et al.

Grewlich, Klaus W. Transnational Enterprises in a New International System. 240p. 1981. 42.50 (ISBN 90-286-0650-5). Sijthoff & Noordhoff.

Grey, A., tr. see Svetloff, V.

Grey, Alan L., ed. Man, Woman & Marriage: Studies of Small Group Process in the Family. LC 72-105607. (Controversy Ser.). 225p. 1970. text ed. 11.95x (ISBN 0-202-25057-1). Lieber-Atherton.

Grey, Anthony. The Chinese Assassin. 272p. 1982. pap. 2.95 (ISBN 0-441-10438-X, Pub. by Charter Bks). Ace Bks.

--Saigon. 825p. 1982. 19.95 (ISBN 0-316-32822-7). Little.

--Saigon. 752p. 1983. pap. 4.95 (ISBN 0-440-17580-1). Dell.

--Saigon. pap. 4.95 (ISBN 0-317-00274-0). Dell.

Grey, Charles E. Colonial Policy of Lord John Russell's Administration, 2 vols. in 1. LC 79-118121. Repr. of 1853 ed. lib. bdg. 57.50x (ISBN 0-678-00660-1). Kelley.

Grey, Charlotte. Golden Butterfly. (Coventry Romance Ser.: No. 193). 192p. 1982. pap. 1.50 (ISBN 0-449-50291-0, Coventry). Fawcett.

--The London Ladies. (Coventry Romance Ser: No. 192). 192p. 1982. pap. 1.50 (ISBN 0-449-50295-3, Coventry). Fawcett.

Grey, David L. Supreme Court & the News Media. LC 68-17732. Repr. of 1968 ed. 51.50 (ISBN 0-8357-9473-3, 2015423). Bks Demand UMI.

Grey, Edward, ed. see Della Valle, Pietro.

Grey, Elizabeth. Behind the Scenes in a Film Studio. (Behind the Scenes Ser). (Illus.). 102p. 1970. Repr. of 1967 ed. 6.50x (ISBN 0-460-06011-2, Pub. by J. M. Dent England). Biblio Dist.

Grey, Elizabeth & Grey, Michael. The Executive Baby: Creating a Truly Superior Child. (Illus.). 128p. (Orig.). 1984. pap. 8.95 (ISBN 0-920792-36-7). Eden Pr.

Grey, Evelyn. Camberleigh. 464p. 1985. pap. 3.95 (ISBN 0-425-07643-1). Berkley Pub.

Grey Friars Of London. Chronicle of the Grey Friars of London. 1852. 19.00 (ISBN 0-384-33445-8). Johnson Repr.

Grey, Gene W. & Deneke, Frederick J. Urban Forestry. LC 78-5275. 279p. 1978. text ed. 33.95 (ISBN 0-471-01515-6). Wiley.

Grey, George. Ko Nga Whakapepeha: Proverbial & Popular Sayings of the Ancestors of the New Zealand Race. LC 75-35252. Repr. of 1857 ed. 10.75 (ISBN 0-404-14424-1). AMS Pr.

--Polynesian Mythology & Ancient Traditional History of the New Zealanders As Furnished by Their Priests & Chiefs. LC 75-35253. Repr. of 1906 ed. 20.50 (ISBN 0-404-14425-X). AMS Pr.

Grey, Georgina. The Belle of Brighton, No. 157. 224p. 1981. pap. 1.50 (ISBN 0-449-50230-9, Crest). Fawcett.

--Both Sides of the Coin. (Regency Love Story Ser.). 224p. (Orig.). 1980. pap. 1.75 (ISBN 0-449-50043-8, Coventry). Fawcett.

--Franklin's Folly. (Orig.). 1980. pap. 1.75 (ISBN 0-449-50026-8, Coventry). Fawcett.

--Lingering Laughter. (Coventry Romance Ser.: No. 172). 224p. 1982. pap. 1.50 (ISBN 0-449-50273-2, Coventry). Fawcett.

--The Queen's Quadrille. 224p. 1981. pap. 1.50 (ISBN 0-449-50212-0, Crest). Fawcett.

--Turn of the Cards. (Regency Romance Ser.). 1979. pap. 1.75 (ISBN 0-449-23969-1, Crest). Fawcett.

Grey, H. A Key to the Waverley Novels. LC 73-6987. (English Literature Ser., No. 33). 1973. Repr. of 1898 ed. lib. bdg. 47.95x (ISBN 0-8383-1699-9). Haskell.

Grey, H. G. Colonial Policy of Lord John Russell's Administration, 2 vols. in 1. LC 9-34540. Repr. of 1853 ed. 36.00 (ISBN 0-527-35900-9). Kraus Repr.

Grey, Henry. The Classics for the Million: Being an Epitome in English of the Works of the Principal Greek & Latin Authors. 1898. 30.00 (ISBN 0-89984-221-6). Century Bookbindery.

--Key to the Waverly Novels. 1973. Repr. of 1884 ed. lib. bdg. 15.00 (ISBN 0-8414-4685-7). Folcroft.

--The Plots of Some of the Most Famous Old English Plays. LC 72-13684. 1973. lib. bdg. 15.00 (ISBN 0-8414-1265-0). Folcroft.

Grey, Herman. Tales from the Mohaves. LC 69-16731. (Civilization of the American Indian Ser.: Vol. 107). 96p. 1980. pap. 4.95 (ISBN 0-8061-1655-2). U of Okla Pr.

Grey House Publishers, ed. Directory of Mail Order Catalogs. 384p. 1981. 85.00x (ISBN 0-87196-523-2). Facts on File.

Grey, Ian. Catherine the Great: Autocrat & Empress of All Russia. LC 75-14598. (Illus.). 254p. 1975. Repr. of 1961 ed. lib. bdg. 39.50x (ISBN 0-8371-8219-0, GRCTG). Greenwood.

Grey, J. The Turtle Who Wanted to Run. LC 68-56813. (Illus.). (gr. 1-3). 1968. PLB 9.26 (ISBN 0-87783-045-2). Oddo.

Grey, J. David, et al, eds. The Scribner Jane Austen Companion. (Illus.). 480p. 1986. lib. bdg. 25.00 (ISBN 0-684-18285-8). Scribner.

Grey, Jane. Arizona Ames. 17.95 (ISBN 0-88411-659-X, Pub by Aeonian Pr). Amereon Ltd.

--Majesty's Rancho. 16.95 (ISBN 0-88411-661-1, Pub. by Aeonian Pr). Amereon Ltd.

--Strangers from the Tonto. 14.95 (ISBN 0-88411-662-X, Pub. by Aeonian Pr). Amereon LTD.

--The Turtle Who Wanted to Run. (Illus.). (gr. 1-3). 1978. pap. 1.25 (ISBN 0-89508-057-5). Rainbow Bks.

--Wanderer of the Wasteland. 21.95 (ISBN 0-88411-660-3, Pub. by Aeonian Pr). Amereon Ltd.

--Wildfire. 16.95 (ISBN 0-89190-769-6, Pub. by Am Repr). Amereon Ltd.

Grey, Jerry. Aeronautics in China. LC 81-19083. (Illus.). 199p. 1981. 24.00 (ISBN 0-915928-59-0, AAS4); members 20.00 (ISBN 0-317-32128-5). AIAA.

--Aerospace Technology & Commercial Nuclear Power. 19.50 (ISBN 0-915928-69-8). AIAA.

--Beachheads in Space: A Blueprint for the Future. (Illus.). 288p. 1983. 14.95 (ISBN 0-02-545590-7). Macmillan.

Grey, Jerry, ed. Space Tracking & Data Systems. LC 81-19080. (Illus.). 236p. 1981. 27.00 (ISBN 0-915928-55-8, AAS8); members 22.00 (ISBN 0-317-32195-1). AIAA.

Grey, Jerry & Hamdan, Lawrence A., eds. International Aerospace Review. LC 82-3883. (Illus.). 313p. 1982. 30.00 (ISBN 0-915928-63-9, AAS6); members 25.00 (ISBN 0-317-32155-2). AIAA.

Grey, Jerry & Hamdan, Lawrence A, eds. Space Manufacturing Facilities--Four: Proceedings of the Princeton American Institute of Aeronautics & Astronautics Conference on Space Manufacturing. (Illus.). 585p. 37.50 (ISBN 0-915928-61-2, SMF3); members 30.00 (ISBN 0-317-32193-5). AIAA.

Grey, Jerry, jt. ed. see Newman, Martin.

Grey, Jerry, jt. ed. see Butler, George V.

Grey, Jonathan. How to Get Out of Debt & Stay Out. 1st ed. LC 67-18355. 120p. (Orig.). 1967. pap. 4.95 (ISBN 0-910610-01-0). Fortuna.

Grey, Judith. Mud Pies. LC 81-4042. (Illus.). 32p. (gr. k-2). 1981. PLB 9.89 (ISBN 0-89375-541-9); pap. text ed. 1.95 (ISBN 0-89375-542-7). Troll Assocs.

--What Time Is It? LC 81-5113. (Illus.). 32p. (gr. k-2). 1981. PLB 9.89 (ISBN 0-89375-509-5); pap. text ed. 1.95 (ISBN 0-89375-510-9). Troll Assocs.

--Yummy, Yummy. LC 81-2360. (Illus.). 32p. (gr. k-2). 1981. PLB 9.89 (ISBN 0-89375-543-5); pap. text ed. 1.95 (ISBN 0-89375-544-3). Troll Assocs.

Grey, Laura & Katz, Rachel. Fun Folds. 163p. (Orig.). 1984. pap. text ed. 16.95 (ISBN 0-88450-888-9, 7200-B). Communication Skill.

Grey, Linda, ed. see Bosse, Malcolm.

Grey, Linda, ed. see Glasco, Gordon.

Grey, Linda, ed. see Savage, Christina.

Grey, Linda, ed. see Thomas, Craig.

Grey, Loren. Discipline Without Fear. 192p. 1982. pap. 6.00 (ISBN 0-939654-02-4). Social Interest.

--Discipline Without Tyranny. 192p. 1982. pap. 6.00 (ISBN 0-939654-03-2). Social Interest.

--Zane Grey: A Photographic Odyssey. 224p. 1985. 19.95 (ISBN 0-87833-462-9). Taylor Pub.

Grey, Loren, jt. auth. see Dreikurs, Rudolf.

Grey, Loren, ed. see Grey, Zane.

Grey, Loren Z. Lassiter. 1985. pap. 2.95 (ISBN 0-671-52885-8). PB.

Grey, Louis D. Course in APL with Applications. 2nd ed. LC 76-5079. 300p. 1976. pap. text ed. 23.95 (ISBN 0-201-02563-9). Addison-Wesley.

Grey, Margot. Return from Death: An Exploration of the Near-Death Experience. 224p. (Orig.). 1985. pap. 8.95 (ISBN 1-85063-019-4, Ark Paperbacks). Routledge & Kegan.

Grey, Marianne, ed. see Bakema, J. B.

Grey, Michael, jt. auth. see Grey, Elizabeth.

Grey, Millie. Suspicion. (Loveswept Ser.: No. 104). 208p. 1985. pap. 2.25 (ISBN 0-553-21674-0). Bantam.

Grey, Pamela G. Shepherd's Crowns: A Volume of Essays. facs. ed. LC 67-30216. (Essay Index Reprint Ser). 1923. 15.00 (ISBN 0-8369-0498-2). Ayer Co Pubs.

Grey, R., et al. Readings in Embryology. 1969. pap. text ed. 4.95x (ISBN 0-8290-1182-X). Irvington.

Grey, Robert D., et al. A Laboratory Text for Developmental Biology. 160p. 1982. pap. text ed. 12.95 (ISBN 0-8403-2801-X). Kendall-Hunt.

Grey, Robert W., jt. ed. see Stone, Nancy.

Grey, Robin. Studies in Music. LC 74-24092. Repr. of 1901 ed. 27.50 (ISBN 0-404-12937-4). AMS Pr.

Grey, Rodney. United States Trade Policy Legislation: A Canadian View. 130p. (Orig.). 1982. pap. text ed. 7.95x (ISBN 0-920380-86-7, Pub. by Inst Res Pub Canada). Brookfield Pub Co.

Grey, Rodney De C. The Development of the Canadian Anti-Dumping System. (Illus.). 113p. 1973. 3.00 (ISBN 0-88806-001-7). Inst C D Howe.

Grey, Romer Z. King of the Outlaw Horde. (Zane Grey's Arizona Ames Ser.). 288p. 1984. pap. 2.75 (ISBN 0-8439-2158-7, Leisure Bks). Dorchester Pub Co.

--Siege at Forlorn River. (Zane Grey's Yaqui Ser.). 288p. 1985. pap. 2.75 (ISBN 0-8439-2192-7, Leisure BKs). Dorchester Pub Co.

--Zane Grey's Arizona Ames: Gun Trouble in Tonto Basin. (Zane Grey Westerns Ser.). 288p. 1984. pap. 2.75 (ISBN 0-8439-2098-X). Dorchester Pub Co.

--Zane Grey's Arizona Ames: King of the Outlaw Horde. (Orig.). 1980. pap. 1.95 (ISBN 0-505-51509-1, Pub. by Tower Bks). Dorchester Pub Co.

--Zane Grey's Buck Duane: King of the Range. (Orig.). 1980. pap. 1.95 (ISBN 0-505-51499-0, Pub. by Tower Bks). Dorchester Pub Co.

--Zane Grey's Buck Duane: King of the Range. (Zane Grey Westerns Ser.). 288p. 1984. pap. 2.75 (ISBN 0-8439-2136-6, Leisure Bks). Dorchester Pub Co.

--Zane Grey's Buck Duane: Rider of Distant Trails. 352p. 1984. pap. 2.75 (ISBN 0-8439-2082-3). Dorchester Pub Co.

--Zane Grey's Laramie Nelson: Other Side of the Canyon. 288p. 1983. pap. 2.75 (ISBN 0-8439-2041-6, Leisure Bks). Dorchester Pub Co.

--Zane Grey's Laramie Nelson: The Lawless Land. (Zane Grey Westerns). 288p. 1984. pap. 2.75 (ISBN 0-8439-2116-1). Dorchester Pub Co.

--Zane Grey's Laramie Nelson: The Other Side of the Canyon. 1980. pap. 1.95 (ISBN 0-505-51489-3, Pub. by Tower Bks). Dorchester Pub Co.

--Zane Grey's Nevada Jim Lacy: Beyond the Mogollon Rim. (Orig.). 1980. pap. 1.95 (ISBN 0-505-51529-6, Pub. by Tower Bks). Dorchester Pub Co.

--Zane Grey's Nevada Jim Lacy: Beyond the Mogollon Rim. (Romer Zane Grey Ser.). 288p. 1985. pap. 2.75 (ISBN 0-8439-2213-3, Leisure Bks). Dorchester Pub Co.

Grey, Rowland, jt. auth. see Dark, Sidney.

Grey, Sally. Index to Commonwealth Little Magazines 1976-1979, 2 vols. LC 66-28796. 1641p. 1984. 125.00 set (ISBN 0-87875-268-4); Part I. 56.25 (ISBN 0-87875-295-1); Part II. 56.25 (ISBN 0-87875-296-X). Whitston Pub.

Grey, Seymour. Beyond the Veil: The Adventures of an American Doctor in Saudi Arabia. (Bessie Bks.). 320p. 1983. 19.18i (ISBN 0-06-039014-X, HarpT). Har-Row.

Grey, Thomas C. The Legal Enforcement of Morality. (Law & American Society Ser.). 259p. 1983. pap. text ed. 7.00 (ISBN 0-394-33192-3, RanC). Random.

Grey, Vivian. The Chemist Who Lost His Head: The Story of Antoine Lavoisier. (Illus.). 112p. 1982. 9.95 (ISBN 0-698-20559-6, Coward). Putnam Pub Group.

Grey, Zachary. Critical, Historical & Explanatory Notes on Shakespeare with Emendations of the Text & Metre, 2 Vols. LC 76-168205. Repr. of 1754 ed. 52.50 (ISBN 0-404-02905-1). AMS Pr.

--A Free & Familiar Letter to That Great Refiner of Pope & Shakespear, the Rev. Mr. William Warburton, Preacher of Lincoln's-Inn. LC 78-131490. Repr. of 1750 ed. 11.00 (ISBN 0-404-02908-6). AMS Pr.

--Word or Two of Advice to William Warburton. LC 71-131491. Repr. of 1746 ed. 11.00 (ISBN 0-404-02909-4). AMS Pr.

Grey, Zane. Amber's Mirage & Other Stories. 1983. pap. 2.50 (ISBN 0-671-45781-0). PB.

--Bernardo's Revenge & Other Western Yarns. Clauss, J. E., ed. 1976. lib. bdg. 15.95 (ISBN 0-89190-751-3, Pub. by River City Pr). Amereon Ltd.

--Betty Zane. 1976. Repr. of 1903 ed. lib. bdg. 18.95 (ISBN 0-89190-752-1, Pub. by River City Pr). Amereon Ltd.

--The Border Legion. 288p. 1984. pap. 3.50 (ISBN 0-671-50071-6). PB.

--Buffalo Hunter. 1979. pap. 1.75 (ISBN 0-505-51334-X, Pub. by Tower Bks). Dorchester Pub Co.

--The Call of the Canyon. large print ed. LC 82-10448. 355p. 1982. Repr. of 1921 ed. 12.95 (ISBN 0-89621-386-2). Thorndike Pr.

--Captives of the Desert. 1984. pap. 2.95 (ISBN 0-671-52847-5). PB.

--The Deer Stalker. 1985. pap. 2.95 (ISBN 0-671-50147-X). PB.

--Desert Gold. 1984. pap. 2.95 (ISBN 0-671-54384-9). PB.

--The Desert of Wheat. large print ed. LC 82-19117. 583p. 1982. Repr. of 1918 ed. 13.95 (ISBN 0-89621-406-0). Thorndike Pr.

--Drift Fence. 272p. 1984. pap. 2.95 (ISBN 0-671-50224-7). PB.

--The Dude Ranger. (General Ser.). 1982. lib. bdg. 13.95 (ISBN 0-8161-3220-8, Large Print Bks). G K Hall.

--The Dude Ranger. 1982. pap. 2.50 (ISBN 0-671-46835-9). PB.

--Fighting Caravans. 1982. pap. 2.50 (ISBN 0-671-46288-1). PB.

--Fresh Water Fishing. 298p. Repr. lib. bdg. 16.95x (ISBN 0-89190-762-9, Pub. by River City Pr). Amereon Ltd.

--Greatest Indian Stories. 1978. pap. 1.50 (ISBN 0-505-51303-X, Pub. by Tower Bks). Dorchester Pub Co.

--Heritage of the Desert. 298p. Repr. of 1910 ed. lib. bdg. 16.95x (ISBN 0-89190-757-2, Pub. by River City Pr). Amereon Ltd.

--Heritage of the Desert. 1976. lib. bdg. 12.95x (ISBN 0-89968-151-4). Lightyear.

--Heritage of the Dessert. 1985. pap. 2.95 (ISBN 0-671-60674-3). PB.

--Ken Ward in the Jungle. 312p. Repr. of 1912 ed. lib. bdg. 17.95x (ISBN 0-89190-763-7, Pub. by River City Pr). Amereon Ltd.

--King of the Royal Mounted & the Great Jewel Mystery. Repr. lib. bdg. 16.95x (ISBN 0-89190-758-0, Pub. by River City Pr). Amereon Ltd.

--The Last of the Plainsmen. LC 78-5380. 1976. Repr. of 1908 ed. lib. bdg. 17.95x (ISBN 0-89190-753-X, Pub. by River City Pr). Amereon Ltd.

--The Last Ranger. 272p. 1981. pap. 2.25 (ISBN 0-505-51748-5, Pub. by Tower Bks). Dorchester Pub Co.
--The Last Trail. 1976. Repr. of 1909 ed. lib. bdg. 15.95 (ISBN 0-89190-754-8, Pub. by River City Pr). Amereon Ltd.
--The Last Trail. 256p. 1981. pap. 2.25 (ISBN 0-505-51761-2, Pub. by Tower Bks). Dorchester Pub Co.
--The Light of Western Stars. (Zanes Grey's West Ser.). 288p. 1985. Repr. lib. bdg. 12.95 (ISBN 0-915643-05-7). Santa Barb Pr.
--The Lone Star Ranger. 376p. Repr. of 1915 ed. lib. bdg. 19.95x (ISBN 0-89190-764-5, Pub. by River City Pr). Amereon Ltd.
--Lone Star Ranger. 256p. 1984. pap. 2.95 (ISBN 0-671-50991-8). PB.
--The Lord of Lackawaxen Creek. (Miniature Bk.). (Illus.). 64p. 1981. 17.50 (ISBN 0-915998-18-1). Lime Rock Pr.
--Lost Pueblo. 1984. pap. 2.95 (ISBN 0-671-50141-0). PB.
--Majesty's Rancho. Large Print ed. LC 82-709. 501p. 1982. Repr. of 1937 ed. 12.95 (ISBN 0-89621-347-1). Thorndike Pr.
--Majesty's Rancho. (Zane Grey's West Ser.). 288p. 1985. Repr. lib. bdg. 12.95 (ISBN 0-915643-06-5). Santa Barb Pr.
--Man of the Forest. 1982. pap. 2.95 (ISBN 0-671-45937-6). PB.
--Maverick Queen. 1984. pap. 2.95 (ISBN 0-671-53153-0). PB.
--Raider of the Spanish Peaks. 1983. pap. 2.50 (ISBN 0-671-49234-9). PB.
--Rainbow Trail. (Zane Grey's West Ser.). 288p. 1985. Repr. lib. bdg. 12.95 (ISBN 0-915643-04-9). Santa Barb Pr.
--Red-Headed Outfield. 302p. Repr. of 1920 ed. lib. bdg. 16.95x (ISBN 0-89190-759-9, Pub. by River City Pr). Amereon Ltd.
--Riders of the Purple Sage. 1984. pap. 3.50 (ISBN 0-671-52766-5). PB.
--Riders of the Purple Sage. (Zane Grey's West Ser.). 288p. 1985. Repr. lib. bdg. 12.95 (ISBN 0-915643-03-0). Santa Barb Pr.
--Round-up. 192p. (Orig.). 1976. pap. text ed. 1.50 (ISBN 0-532-15189-5). Woodhill.
--The Rustlers of Pecos County. 256p. 1982. pap. 2.50 (ISBN 0-505-51831-7, Pub. by Tower Bks). Dorchester Pub Co.
--Rustlers of Silver River. 226p. Repr. of 1920 ed. lib. bdg. 14.95 (ISBN 0-89190-765-3, Pub. by River City Pr). Amereon Ltd.
--Savage Kingdom. 1978. pap. 1.50 (ISBN 0-505-51293-9, Pub. by Tower Bks). Dorchester Pub Co.
--Seafishing Yarns. 276p. Repr. lib. bdg. 16.95x (ISBN 0-89190-766-1, Pub. by River City Pr). Amereon Ltd.
--The Secret of Quaking ASP Cabin & Other Stories. 1983. pap. 2.50 (ISBN 0-671-45782-9). PB.
--Shark. Grey, Loren, ed. 1978. pap. 1.50 (ISBN 0-505-51265-3, Pub. by Tower Bks). Dorchester Pub Co.
--The Shepherd of Guadaloupe. 1984. pap. 2.95 (ISBN 0-671-83594-7). PB.
--Short Stop. 298p. Repr. of 1909 ed. lib. bdg. 16.95 (ISBN 0-89190-760-2, Pub. by River City Pr). Amereon Ltd.
--The Spirit of the Border. 1976. Repr. of 1904 ed. lib. bdg. 17.95 (ISBN 0-89190-755-6, Pub. by River City Pr). Amereon Ltd.
--Spirit of the Border. 256p. (Orig.). 1981. pap. 2.25 (ISBN 0-505-51739-6, Pub. by Tower Bks). Dorchester Pub Co.
--Stairs of Sand. 1983. pap. 2.50 (ISBN 0-671-47347-6). PB.
--Sunset Pass. 1982. pap. 2.50 (ISBN 0-671-45642-3). PB.
--Tales of Freshwater Fishing. Erikson, George, ed. (Illus.). 320p. 1986. pap. 14.50 (ISBN 0-915643-11-1). Santa Barb Pr.
--Tales of the Great Game Fish. 304p. Repr. of 1928 ed. lib. bdg. 16.95x (ISBN 0-89190-767-X, Pub. by River City Pr). Amereon Ltd.
--Tenderfoot. 208p. 1982. pap. 2.25 (ISBN 0-505-51813-9, Pub. by Tower Bks). Dorchester Pub Co.
--Tex Thorne Comes out of the West. 300p. Repr. of 1937 ed. lib. bdg. 16.95x (ISBN 0-89190-761-0, Pub. by River City Pr). Amereon Ltd.
--Thunder Mountain. 1985. pap. 2.50 (ISBN 0-671-55814-5). PB.
--The Thundering Herd. large print ed. LC 81-2827. 519p. 1981. Repr. of 1925 ed. 12.95 (ISBN 0-89621-276-9). Thorndike Pr.
--The Thundering Herd. 1984. pap. 3.50 (ISBN 0-671-52848-3). PB.
--To the Last Man. 1983. pap. 2.50 (ISBN 0-671-49236-5). PB.
--The Trail Driver. 1982. pap. 2.50 (ISBN 0-671-45646-6). PB.
--Twin Sombreros. 1981. pap. 2.25 (ISBN 0-671-43947-2). PB.
--The U. P. Trail. 1983. pap. 2.95 (ISBN 0-671-49844-4). PB.
--The U. P. Trail. Large Print ed. LC 82-711. 608p. 1982. Repr. of 1981 ed. 12.95 (ISBN 0-89621-348-X). Thorndike Pr.
--The Undiscovered Zane Grey Fishing Stories. Reiger, George, ed. LC 83-17082. (Illus.). 200p. 1983. deluxe slipcased ed. 29.95 (ISBN 0-8329-0342-6, Pub. by Winchester Pr). New Century.
--Undiscovered Zane Grey Fishing Stories. Reiger, George, ed. LC 83-17082. (Illus.). 200p. 1983. 16.95 (ISBN 0-8329-0316-7). New Century.
--The Vanishing American. (General Ser.). 1984. lib. bdg. 16.95 (ISBN 0-8161-3502-9, Large Print Bks). G K Hall.
--The Vanishing American: The Epic of the Indian. (Orig.). 1984. pap. 3.50 (ISBN 0-671-47724-2). PB.
--Western Union. (General Ser.). 1982. lib. bdg. 12.95 (ISBN 0-8161-3354-9, Large Print Bks). G K Hall.
--Wild Horse Mesa. (General Ser.). 1981. lib. bdg. 12.95 (ISBN 0-8161-3239-9, Large Print Bks). G K Hall.
--Wildfire. (General Ser.). 1984. lib. bdg. 13.95 (ISBN 0-8161-3466-9, Large Print). G K Hall.
--The Wolftracker & Other Animal Tales. LC 84-50123. (Zane Grey West Ser.). 176p. (Orig.). 1984. pap. 7.95 (ISBN 0-915643-01-4). Santa Barb Pr.

Greyarz, Kaspar von see Von Greyerz, Kaspar.

Greyber, Howard D., jt. ed. see Morgenthaler, George W.

Greydanus, Rose. Animals at the Zoo. (Illus.). 32p. (gr. k-2). 1980. PLB 4.81 (ISBN 0-89375-371-8); pap. 1.50 (ISBN 0-89375-271-1). Troll Assocs.
--Big Red Fire Engine. (Illus.). 32p. (gr. k-2). 1980. PLB 4.81 (ISBN 0-89375-372-6); pap. 1.50 (ISBN 0-89375-272-X). Troll Assocs.
--Un Carro De Bomberos Grande y Rojo. (Illus.). 32p. (Span.). (gr. k-2). 1981. PLB 4.81 (ISBN 0-89375-555-9). Troll Assocs.
--Changing Seasons. LC 82-19959. (Now I Know Ser.). (Illus.). 32p. (gr. k-2). 1983. PLB 9.89 (ISBN 0-89375-902-3). Troll Assocs.
--Double Trouble. LC 81-2358. (Illus.). 32p. (gr. k-2). 1981. PLB 9.89 (ISBN 0-89375-529-X); pap. text ed. 1.95 (ISBN 0-89375-530-3). Troll Assocs.
--Federiquito el Sapo. (Illus.). 32p. (Span.). (gr. k-2). 1981. PLB 4.81 (ISBN 0-89375-549-4). Troll Assocs.
--Freddie the Frog. (Illus.). 32p. (gr. k-2). 1980. PLB 4.81 (ISBN 0-89375-376-9); pap. 1.50 (ISBN 0-89375-276-2). Troll Assocs.
--Hocus Pocus, Magic Show! LC 81-2637. (Illus.). 32p. (gr. k-2). 1981. PLB 9.89 (ISBN 0-89375-539-7); pap. text ed. 1.95 (ISBN 0-89375-540-0). Troll Assocs.
--Horses. LC 82-20296. (Now I Know Ser.). (Illus.). 32p. (gr. k-2). 1983. lib. bdg. 9.89 (ISBN 0-89375-900-7). Troll Assocs.
--Let's Pretend. LC 81-2357. (Illus.). 32p. (gr. k-2). 1981. PLB 9.89 (ISBN 0-89375-545-1); pap. text ed. 2.50 (ISBN 0-89375-546-X). Troll Assocs.
--Mike's New Bike. (Illus.). 32p. (gr. k-2). 1980. PLB 4.81 (ISBN 0-89375-382-3); pap. 1.50 (ISBN 0-89375-282-7). Troll Assocs.
--My Secret Hiding Place. (Illus.). 32p. (gr. k-2). 1980. PLB 4.81 (ISBN 0-89375-383-1); pap. 1.50 (ISBN 0-89375-283-5). Troll Assocs.
--Susie Goes Shopping. (Illus.). 32p. (gr. k-2). 1980. PLB 4.81 (ISBN 0-89375-389-0); pap. 1.50 (ISBN 0-89375-289-4). Troll Assocs.
--Tree House Fun. (Illus.). 32p. (gr. k-2). 1980. PLB 4.81 (ISBN 0-89375-391-2); pap. 1.50 (ISBN 0-89375-291-6). Troll Assocs.
--Trouble in Space. LC 81-5114. (Illus.). 32p. (gr. k-2). 1981. PLB 9.89 (ISBN 0-89375-517-6); pap. text ed. 1.95 (ISBN 0-89375-518-4). Troll Assocs.
--Valentine's Day Grump. LC 81-4712. (Illus.). 32p. (gr. k-2). 1981. PLB 9.89 (ISBN 0-89375-515-X); pap. text ed. 1.95 (ISBN 0-89375-516-8). Troll Assocs.
--Willie the Slowpoke. (Illus.). 32p. (gr. k-2). 1980. PLB 4.81 (ISBN 0-89375-394-7); pap. 1.50 (ISBN 0-89375-294-0); cassette 8.95. Troll Assocs.

Grey De Wilton, Arthur G. Commentary of the Services & Charge of William Lord Grey of Wilton. De Malpas Grey Egerton, Philip, ed. LC 71-161716. (Camden Society, London. Publications. First Ser.: No. 40). Repr. of 1847 ed. 19.00 (ISBN 0-404-50140-0). AMS Pr.
--Commentary of the Services & Charges of William Lord Grey of Wilton, K. G. 1847. 19.00 (ISBN 0-384-19970-4). Johnson Repr.

Grey Egerton Philip De, Malpas see Grey De Wilton, Arthur G.

Greyerz, Kaspar Von see Von Greyerz, Kaspar.

Greynolds, Elbert B. Financial Analysis Using Calculators. (Calculating & Computing Bks.). 472p. 1980. pap. 20.95 (ISBN 0-317-27321-3, LCB4531). Tex Instr Inc.

Greynolds, Elbert B. & Aronofsky, Julius S. Practical Real Estate Financial Analysis: Using the HP-12C Calculator. LC 83-563. 233p. (Orig.). 1983. pap. text ed. 19.95 (ISBN 0-88462-497-8, 1512-15, Real Estate Ed). Longman USA.

Greynolds, Elbert B., Jr. Time Sharing: Computer Programs & Applications in Accounting. (Research Monograph: No. 57). 1974. spiral bdg. 30.00 (ISBN 0-88406-021-7). Ga St U Busn Pub.

Grey of Fallodon. Wordsworth's "Prelude". 1923. Repr. lib. bdg. 8.50 (ISBN 0-8414-4476-5). Folcroft.

Greyser, Stephen A. Cases in Advertising & Communications Management. 2nd ed. 300p. 1981. text ed. 31.95 (ISBN 0-13-118513-6). P-H.

Greyser, Stephen A., jt. auth. see Young, Robert F.

Greyson, Bruce & Flynn, Charles P. The Near-Death Experience: Problems, Prospects, Perspectives. 304p. 1984. text ed. 29.75x (ISBN 0-398-05008-2). C C Thomas.

Grey-Wilson & Blamey. The Alpine Flowers of Britain & Europe. 1979. pap. 19.95 (ISBN 0-00-219288-8, Collins Pub England). Greene.

Grey-Wilson, Christine, illus. The Kew Five-Year Gardener's Diary. (Illus.). 304p. 1984. 29.95 (ISBN 0-913643-01-7). Capability's.

Grey-Wilson, Christopher & Mathew, Brian. Bulbs: The Bulbous Plants of Europe & Their Allies. (Illus.). 1983. 32.95 (ISBN 0-00-219211-X, Collins Pub England). Greene.

Greywolf, Elizabeth S. The Single Mother's Handbook. LC 83-17350. (Orig.). 1984. 12.95 (ISBN 0-688-02260-X); pap. 6.70 (ISBN 0-688-02261-8). Morrow.

Grianna, Seamus O. Nuair a Bhi Me OG. O'Donaill, Niall, ed. 224p. (Orig.). 1979. pap. 4.95 (ISBN 0-85342-604-X, Pub. by Mercier Pr Ireland). Irish Bk Ctr.

Griaule, Marcel. Conversations with Ogotemmeli: An Introduction to Dogon Religious Ideas. (Illus.). 1975. pap. 6.95x (ISBN 0-19-519821-2). Oxford U Pr.
--Conversations with Ogotemmeli: An Introduction to Dogon Religious Ideas. LC 65-3614. pap. 57.50 (ISBN 0-317-28624-2, 2055384). Bks Demand UMI.

Grib, Philip J. Divorce Laws & Morality: A New Catholic Jurisprudence. LC 84-21968. 254p. (Orig.). 1985. lib. bdg. 24.50 (ISBN 0-8191-4385-5); pap. text ed. 12.75 (ISBN 0-8191-4386-3). U Pr of Amer.

Gribben, Alan. Mark Twain's Library: A Reconstruction, 2 vols. 958p. 1980. Set. lib. bdg. 78.00 (ISBN 0-8161-8156-X). G K Hall.

Gribben, John, jt. auth. see Orgill, Douglas.

Gribben, Trish. Pajamas Don't Matter (or: What Your Baby Really Needs) LC 79-90081. (Illus.). 1980. pap. 5.95 (ISBN 0-915190-21-4). Jalmar Pr.

Gribben, Trish & Geddis, David. Nits & Other Nasties: Battling the Bugs That Attack Children. (Illus.). 80p. 1984. 10.50 (ISBN 0-437-06205-8, Pub. by Worlds Work). David & Charles.

Gribbin, jt. auth. see Orgill.

Gribbin, David, jt. auth. see Gribbin, Jill.

Gribbin, J., ed. Climatic Change. LC 76-52185. 1978. 77.50 (ISBN 0-521-21594-3); pap. 24.95x (ISBN 0-521-29205-0). Cambridge U Pr.

Gribbin, Jill & Gribbin, David. Japanese Antique Dolls. (Illus.). 180p. 1984. 70.00 (ISBN 0-8348-0194-9, Pub. by John Weatherhill Inc Tokyo). C E Tuttle.

Gribbin, John. Future Weather & the Greenhouse Effect. 320p. 1982. 15.95 (ISBN 0-385-28274-5, E Friede). Delacorte.
--Future Weather & the Greenhouse Effect. 310p. 1983. pap. 9.95 (ISBN 0-385-29279-1, Delta). Dell.
--Future Worlds. LC 81-5135. 225p. 1981. (full discount avail.) 14.95 (ISBN 0-306-40780-9, Plenum Pr). Plenum Pub.
--Genesis: The Origins of Man & the Universe. (Illus., Orig.). 1982. pap. 8.95 (ISBN 0-385-28321-0, Delta). Dell.
--Genesis: The Origins of Man & the Universe. 352p. 1981. 35.00x (ISBN 0-460-04505-9, Pub. by Dent Australia). State Mutual Bk.
--In Search of Schrodinger's Cat: Quantum Physics & Reality. 320p. 1984. pap. 9.95 (ISBN 0-553-34253-3). Bantam.
--Spacewarps. 224p. 1984. pap. 9.95 (ISBN 0-385-29366-6, Delta). Dell.
--Timewarps. 1980. pap. 4.95 (ISBN 0-385-29078-0, Delta). Dell.

Gribbin, John & Cherfas, Jeremy. The Monkey Puzzle: Reshaping the Evolutionary Tree. 1982. pap. 7.95 (ISBN 0-07-024739-0). McGraw.

Gribbin, John & Gribbin, John. Amateur Astronomer. (Octopus Bk.). (Illus.). 1979. 9.95 (ISBN 0-7064-1034-3, Mayflower Bks). Smith Pubs.

Gribbin, John, jt. auth. see Cherfas, Jeremy.

Gribbin, John, jt. auth. see Orgill, Douglas.

Gribbin, John R. & Plagemann, Stephen H. The Jupiter Effect Reconsidered. LC 81-70315. (Illus., Orig.). 1982. pap. 3.95 (ISBN 0-394-70827-X, Vin). Random.
--The Jupiter Effect: The Planets As Triggers of Devastating Earthquakes. 1976. pap. 3.95 (ISBN 0-394-70827-X, 72221, Vin). Random.

Gribbin, Lenore S. Who's Whodunit. LC 71-627563. (North CArolina University Library Studies: No. 5). pap. 46.00 (ISBN 0-317-09228-6, 2004350). Bks Demand UMI.

Gribbin, William. The Churches Militant: The War of 1812 & American Religion. LC 72-91313. pap. 55.00 (ISBN 0-317-29581-0, 2022000). Bks Demand UMI.

Gribbin, William J., jt. ed. see Anderson, Carl A.

Gribble, C. D. & Hall, A. J. A Practical Introduction to Optical Mineralogy. (Illus.). 200p. 1985. text ed. 30.00x (ISBN 0-04-549007-4); pap. text ed. 14.95x (ISBN 0-04-549008-2). Allen Unwin.

Gribble, C. D., jt. ed. see Atherton, M. P.

Gribble, Charles E. Medieval Slavic Texts, Vol. 1: Old & Middle Russian Texts. 320p. 1973. 17.95 (ISBN 0-89357-011-7); soft cover 10.95 (ISBN 0-89357-010-9). Slavica.
--Russian Root List with a Sketch of Russian Word Formation. 2nd ed. 62p. (Rus.). 1982. soft cover 3.95 (ISBN 0-89357-052-4). Slavica.
--Short Dictionary of Eighteenth Century Russian. 103p. (Rus.). 1976. soft cover 8.95 (ISBN 0-89357-039-7). Slavica.

Gribble, Charles E., ed. Studies Presented to Professor Roman Jakobson by His Students. 333p. 1968. 19.95 (ISBN 0-89357-001-X); soft cover 12.95 (ISBN 0-89357-000-1). Slavica.

Gribble, Colin D., jt. auth. see McLean, Adam C.

Gribble, Francis. Balzac: The Man & the Lover. 1973. 25.00 (ISBN 0-8274-0711-4). R West.
--Dumas: Father & Son. 1973. Repr. of 1930 ed. 25.00 (ISBN 0-8274-0387-9). R West.
--Lake Geneva & Its Literary Landmarks. 1978. Repr. of 1901 ed. lib. bdg. 25.00 (ISBN 0-8495-1918-7). Arden Lib.
--Lake Geneva & Its Literary Landmarks. 1901. Repr. 30.00 (ISBN 0-8274-2793-X). R West.
--The Love Affairs of Lord Byron. 1910. Repr. 30.00 (ISBN 0-8274-2998-3). R West.
--Madame De Stael & Her Lovers. 1979. Repr. of 1907 ed. lib. bdg. 35.00 (ISBN 0-8495-2023-1). Arden Lib.
--Madame De Stael & Her Lovers. 1907. Repr. 25.00 (ISBN 0-8274-2658-5). R West.
--Rachel: Her Stage Life & Her Real Life. LC 70-93163. (Illus.). 1972. Repr. of 1911 ed. lib. bdg. 22.00 (ISBN 0-405-08582-6, Blom Pubns). Ayer Co Pubs.
--The Romantic Life of Shelley & the Sequel. LC 72-3624. (Studies in Shelley, No. 25). 1972. Repr. of 1911 ed. lib. bdg. 58.95x (ISBN 0-8383-1566-6). Haskell.
--The Romantic Life of Shelley & the Sequel. 1977. Repr. lib. bdg. 35.00 (ISBN 0-8492-1018-6). R West.
--Rousseau & the Women He Loved. 443p. 1983. Repr. of 1908 ed. lib. bdg. 40.00 (ISBN 0-89760-368-0). Telegraph Bks.
--Royal House of Portugal. LC 73-110904. 1970. Repr. of 1915 ed. 26.50x (ISBN 0-8046-0887-3, Pub. by Kennikat). Assoc Faculty Pr.

Gribble, Francis H. George Sand & Her Lovers. LC 76-44500. 1976. lib. bdg. 42.50 (ISBN 0-8414-4504-4). Folcroft.

Gribble, George, ed. see Casanova, Jacques.

Gribble, George D. Scarecrows. (Illus.). 32p. 1985. 25.00x (ISBN 0-930126-16-5). Typographeum.

Gribble, J., ed. Matthew Arnold. 1967. pap. text ed. 1.95x (ISBN 0-02-973840-7). Macmillan.

Gribble, James. Literary Education: A Re-Evaluation. LC 82-23527. 165p. 1983. 32.50 (ISBN 0-521-25315-2); pap. 9.95 (ISBN 0-521-27308-0). Cambridge U Pr.

Gribble, Jennifer. The Lady of Shalott in the Victorian Novel. 222p. 1984. 24.00 (ISBN 0-333-35019-7, Pub. by Salem Hse Ltd). Merrimack Pub Cir.

Gribble, Leonard. Profiles from Notable Modern Biographies. 1978. Repr. lib. bdg. 20.00 (ISBN 0-8492-4924-4). R West.

Gribble, McPhee. Body Tricks: To Teach Yourself. (Practical Puffins Ser.). 32p. (gr. 5 up). 1982. pap. 2.95 (ISBN 0-14-049138-4, Puffin). Penguin.
--Gardening: How to Grow Things. (Practical Puffins Ser.). (gr. 6 up). 1976. pap. 2.95 (ISBN 0-14-049143-0, Puffin). Penguin.
--Strange Things to Do & Make. (Practical Puffins Ser.). (gr. 5 up). 1976. pap. 2.95 (ISBN 0-14-049146-5, Puffin). Penguin.

Gribble, Mercedes & Friedmann, Hope. Two Hundred Rooms in the Inn: The Story of Providence Mission Homes. LC 83-15367. (Illus.). 112p. (Orig.). 1983. pap. 3.95 (ISBN 0-87808-195-X). William Carey Lib.

Gribbon, H. D. History of Water Power in Ulster. LC 69-12248. (Illus.). 1969. 24.95x (ISBN 0-678-05528-9). Kelley.

Gribbon, R. T. Students, Churches & Higher Education. 128p. 1981. pap. 6.95 (ISBN 0-8170-0931-0). Judson.

Gribbon, Sybil. Edwardian Belfast: A Social Profile. 64p. 1981. pap. 5.95 (ISBN 0-86281-104-X, Pub. by Appletree Pr). Irish Bks Media.

Gribbons, Warren D. & Lohnes, Paul R. Careers in Theory & Experience: A Twenty-Year Longitudinal Study. LC 82-762. 208p. 1982. 44.50x (ISBN 0-87395-611-7); pap. 19.95x (ISBN 0-87395-612-5). State U NY Pr.
--Emerging Careers. LC 68-20557. 1968. text ed. 11.00x (ISBN 0-8077-1474-7). Tchrs Coll.

Gribik & Kortanek. Extremal Methods of Operations Research. (Pure & Applied Mathematics Ser.). 456p. 1986. price not set (ISBN 0-8247-7474-4). Dekker.

Gribkovskii, V. P., jt. auth. see Stepanov, B. I.

Gribnau, A. A. & Geijsberts, L. G. Morphogenesis of the Brain in Staged Rhesus Monkey Embryos. (Advances in Anatomy, Embryology & Cell Biology Ser.: Vol. 91). (Illus.). 70p. 1985. pap. 19.50 (ISBN 0-387-13709-2). Springer-Verlag.

Gribnau, T. C., et al, eds. Affinity Chromatography & Related Techniques: Theoretical Aspects. (Analytical Chemistry Symposia Ser.: Vol. 9). 584p. 1981. 89.50 (ISBN 0-444-42031-2). Elsevier.

Gribomont, Jean, et al. St. Bede: A Tribute. LC 85-8214. (Word & Spirit Ser.: Vol. VII). 1985. 7.00. St Bedes Pubns.

Gribov, Lev A. Intensity Theory for Infrared Spectra of Polyatomic Molecules. LC 64-17204. 120p. 1964. 30.00x (ISBN 0-306-10689-2, Consultants). Plenum Pub.

Grice, Charles R., Jr. Fifteen Tips on Handling Job Interviews. McFadden, S. Michele, ed. 1981. pap. text ed. 37.50 30 copy pack 1.25 ea. (ISBN 0-89262-043-9). Career Pub.

Grice, Elizabeth. Rogues & Vagabonds. (Illus.). 1979. 29.00 (ISBN 0-900963-78-6, Pub. by Terence Dalton England). State Mutual Bk.

Grice, Ettalene M. Chronology of the Larsa Dynasty. Bd. with Pt. 1. Grice, Ettalene M; Patesis of the Ur Dynasty, Pt 2. Kelser, Clarence E; An Old Babylonian Version of the Gilgamesh Epic on the Basis of Recently Discovered Texts, Pt 3. Jastrow, Morris & Clay, Albert T.. LC 80-21416. (Yale Oriental Ser. Researches). 1979. 37.50 (ISBN 0-404-60274-6). AMS Pr.

--Records from Ur & Larsa Dated in the Larsa Dynasty. LC 78-63534. (Yale Oriental Series: Babylonian Texts: No. 5). (Illus.). Repr. of 1919 ed. 42.50 (ISBN 0-404-60255-X). AMS Pr.

Grice, Frederick. Francis Kilvert & His World. 268p. 1982. 16.50 (ISBN 0-904573-52-4); pap. 8.50 (ISBN 0-904573-78-8). Caliban Bks.

Grice, G. D. & Reeve, M. R., eds. Marine Mesocosms: Biological & Chemical Research in Experimental Ecosystems. (Illus.). 450p. 1981. 49.00 (ISBN 0-387-90579-0). Springer Verlag.

Grice, H. C., ed. Interpretation & Extrapolation of Chemical & Biological Carcinogenicity Data to Establish Human Safety Standards. (Current Issues in Toxicology Ser.). 150p. 1984. pap. 18.50 (ISBN 0-387-13696-7). Springer-Verlag.

--The Selection of Doses in Chronic Toxicity-Carcinogenicity Studies. (Current Issues in Toxicology Ser.). (Illus.). 130p. 1984. pap. 17.00 (ISBN 0-387-12845-X). Springer-Verlag.

Grice, Julia. Emerald Fire. 1978. pap. 3.50 (ISBN 0-380-38596-1, 82347-0). Avon.

--Enchanted Nights. (Scarlet Ribbons Ser.). 352p. 1984. pap. 2.95 (ISBN 0-451-12897-4, Sig). NAL.

--How to Find Romance after Forty. 256p. 1985. 14.95 (ISBN 0-87131-461-4). M Evans.

--How to Find Romance after 40. (X). price not set. M Evans.

--Lovefire. 1977. pap. 3.50 (ISBN 0-380-01741-5, 84863-5). Avon.

--Satin Embraces. 1984. pap. 3.50 (ISBN 0-451-13242-4, Sig). NAL.

--Wild Roses. 1980. pap. 2.95 (ISBN 0-380-75069-4, 78022-4). Avon.

Grice, William A. Badminton. 3rd ed. (Illus.). 91p. 1981. pap. text ed. 3.95x (ISBN 0-89641-068-4). American Pr.

Grice, William A., jt. auth. see Barton, Joel R., III.

Grice, William A., jt. auth. see Dowell, Linus J.

Grice-Hutchinson, Marjorie. Early Economic Thought in Spain 1177-1740. 1978. text ed. 27.50x (ISBN 0-04-946011-0). Allen Unwin.

Grichting, Wolfgang L. Security vs. Liberty: Analyzing Social Structure & Policy. LC 84-15321. (Illus.). 274p. (Orig.). 1985. lib. bdg. 22.75 (ISBN 0-8191-4223-9); pap. text ed. 13.25 (ISBN 0-8191-4224-7). U Pr of Amer.

Grider, J. Kenneth. Born Again & Growing. 118p. 1982. pap. 3.50 (ISBN 0-8341-0758-9). Beacon Hill.

Grider, John D., jt. auth. see Denhard, J. G.

Grider, Sylvia A. The Wendish Texas. (Illus.). 120p. 1982. 8.95 (ISBN 0-86701-000-2); pap. 5.95 (ISBN 0-86701-001-0). U of Tex Inst Tex Culture.

Gridgeman, N. T. Biological Sciences at the National Research Council of Canada: The Early Years to 1952. 153p. 1979. text ed. 15.50x (ISBN 0-88920-082-3, Pub. by Wilfrid Laurier U Pr Canada). Humanities.

Gridley, Josephine B., tr. see Warcollier, Rene.

Gridley, Marion E. Maria Tallchief. LC 73-8382. (Story of an American Indian Ser.). (Illus.). 74p. (gr. 5 up). 1973. PLB 7.95 (ISBN 0-87518-060-4). Dillon.

Gridley, Mark C. Jazz Styles. (Illus.). 352p. 1978. pap. text ed. 18.95 (ISBN 0-13-509877-7). P-H.

--Jazz Styles. 2nd ed. (Illus.). 448p. 1985. pap. text ed. 18.95 (ISBN 0-13-509134-9). P-H.

Gridley, Roy E. The Brownings & France: A Chronicle with Commentary. 331p. 1982. 38.00 (ISBN 0-485-11231-0, Pub. by Athlone Pr Ltd). Longwood Pub Group.

Grieb, Conrad. Uncovering the Forces for War. 115p. pap. 4.00 (ISBN 0-89562-096-0). Sons Lib.

Grieb, Kenneth J. Guatemalan Caudillo: The Regime of Jorge Ubica, Guatemala, 1931-1944. LC 78-14339. 384p. 1979. 26.95x (ISBN 0-8214-0379-6, 82-82774). Ohio U Pr.

--The Latin American Policy of Warren G. Harding. LC 74-26229. (A.M. Pate, Jr., Series on the American Presidency: No. 1). 223p. 1977. 12.50x (ISBN 0-912646-46-2). Tex Christian.

--Research Guide to Central America & the Caribbean. LC 84-40496. 464p. 1985. text ed. 35.00x (ISBN 0-299-10050-2). U of Wis Pr.

--The United States & Huerta. LC 69-10906. (Illus.). xvi, 232p. 1969. 19.95x (ISBN 0-8032-0060-9). U of Nebr Pr.

Grieb, Lyndal C. The Operas of Gian Carlo Menotti, 1937-1972: A Selective Bibliography. LC 74-16310. 193p. 1974. 16.50 (ISBN 0-8108-0743-2). Scarecrow.

Grieb, William E., Jr. The Small Business Computer Today & Tomorrow. 1984. pap. 6.95 (ISBN 0-671-55907-9, Pub. by Baen Bks). PB.

Grieco, Joseph. The One Hundred Seventy-Five Thousand-Mile-Car. Myers, Marye, ed. (Illus.). 40p. (Orig.). 1984. pap. 7.95 (ISBN 0-931843-00-6). Grieco.

Grieco, Joseph M. Between Dependency & Autonomy: India's Experience with the International Computer Industry. LC 83-4866. (Science, Technology, & the Changing World Order Ser.). 224p. 1984. text ed. 37.50x (ISBN 0-520-04819-9). U of Cal Pr.

Grieco, M. H. Immunodiagnosis for Clinicians: Interpretation of Immunassays. 1983. 32.95 (ISBN 0-8151-4003-7). Year Bk Med.

Grieco, Michael H., ed. Infections in the Abnormal Host. LC 79-65400. (Illus.). 1980. 85.00 (ISBN 0-914316-18-4). Yorke Med.

Grieder, Calvin, et al. Public School Administration. 3rd ed. LC 76-75638. (Illus.). pap. 160.00 (ISBN 0-8357-9971-9, 2012544). Bks Demand UMI.

Grieder, Jerome B. Hu Shih & the Chinese Renaissance: Liberalism in the Chinese Revolution, 1917-1937. LC 78-106958. (East Asian Ser: No. 46). 1970. 25.00x (ISBN 0-674-41250-8). Harvard U Pr.

--Intellectuals & the State in Modern China: A Narrative History. Sheridan, James E., ed. LC 81-66436. (The Transformation of Modern China Ser.). 352p. 1981. 22.50 (ISBN 0-02-912810-2). Free Pr.

--Intellectuals & the State in Modern China. LC 81-66436. 1983. 11.95x (ISBN 0-02-912670-3). Free Pr.

Grieder, Josephine, jt. auth. see Grieder, Theodore.

Grieder, Terence. The Art & Archaeology of Pashash. LC 77-10677. (Illus.). 278p. 1978. 27.50x (ISBN 0-292-70328-7). U of Tex Pr.

--Origins of Pre-Columbian Art. (Texas Pan American Ser.). (Illus.). 251p. 1982. text ed. 19.95x (ISBN 0-292-76021-3). U of Tex Pr.

Grieder, Terence, jt. ed. see Catlin, Stanton L.

Grieder, Theodore. Acquisitions: Where, What, & How - A Guide to Orientation & Procedures for Students in Librarianship, Librarians, & Academic Faculty. LC 77-84762. (Contributions in Librarianship & Information Science: No. 22). 1978. lib. bdg. 35.00 (ISBN 0-8371-9890-9, GAL/). Greenwood.

Grieder, Theodore & Grieder, Josephine. A Student's First Aid to Writing. LC 72-81176. (Quality Paperback Ser.: No. 254). (Orig.). 1979. pap. 4.95 (ISBN 0-8226-0254-7). Littlefield.

Grieder, Theodore, ed. see New York University Libraries.

Grieg, Edward. Peer Gynt Suite No. 1 for Piano. Gahn, Joseph, ed. (Carl Fischer Music Library: No. 315). 1910. pap. 3.50 (ISBN 0-8258-0105-2). Fischer Inc NY.

Grieg, Margot, ed. see Doherty, Joseph C.

Grieg, Nordahl. Around the Cape of Good Hope: Poems of the Sea by Nordahl Grieg. Egede-Nissen, Lars, tr. from Norwegian. (Illus., Eng.). 1979. 6.95 (ISBN 0-933748-02-7); pap. 3.25 (ISBN 0-933748-01-9). Nordic Bks.

Grieger, Ingrid Z., jt. ed. see Grieger, Russell.

Grieger, Russell & Boyd, John. Rational-Emotive Therapy: A Skills-Based Approach. 304p. 1980. 19.95 (ISBN 0-442-22874-0). Van Nos Reinhold.

Grieger, Russell, jt. auth. see Ellis, Albert.

Grieger, Russell & Grieger, Ingrid Z., eds. Cognition & Emotional Disturbance. LC 81-6461. 232p. 1982. 26.95x (ISBN 0-89885-022-3). Human Sci Pr.

Griego, Jose & Maestas. Cuentos: Tales from the Hispanic Southwest. Anaya, Rudolfo, tr. from Sp. (Illus.). 1981. pap. 6.95 (ISBN 0-89013-111-2). Museum NM Pr.

Griego, Margot C., et al. Tortillitas Para Mama: And Other Spanish Nursery Rhymes. LC 81-4823. (Illus.). 40p. (gr. k-3). 1981. 9.95 (ISBN 0-03-056704-1). HR&W.

Griehl. Snakes. (Pet Care Ser.). 1984. pap. 3.95 (ISBN 0-8120-2813-9). Barron.

Griem, Hans R. Spectral Line Broadening by Plasmas. (Pure & Applied Physics: A Series of Monographs & Textbooks, Vol. 39). 1974. 79.50 (ISBN 0-12-302850-7). Acad Pr.

Griem, Hans R. see Marton, L.

Griem, M. L., ed. Breast Cancer: A Challenging Problem. LC 73-78194. (Recent Results in Cancer Research Ser.: Vol. 42). (Illus.). 150p. 1973. 38.00 (ISBN 0-387-06273-4). Springer-Verlag.

Griep, John A., ed. Clinical Uses of Frozen-Thawed Red Blood Cells: Proceedings of a Symposium Held in Indianapolis, April 29-30, 1976. LC 76-467663. (Progress in Clinical & Biological Research: Vol. 11). 228p. 1976. 27.00 (ISBN 0-8451-0011-4). A R Liss.

Griep-Ruiz, L. J. Daily in All the Small. Alurista & Xelina, eds. (Serie milpa poetica). 64p. 1985. pap. 5.00x (ISBN 0-939558-06-8). Maize Pr.

Grier, B. R., jt. auth. see Gough, Vera.

Grier, Barbara see Damon, Gene, pseud.

Grier, Barbara & Reid, Coletta, eds. Lesbian Lives. (Illus.). 1976. pap. 6.95 (ISBN 0-88447-012-1). Diana Pr.

--The Lesbians Home Journal: Stories from the Ladder. (Illus.). 1976. pap. 6.95 (ISBN 0-88447-013-X). Diana Pr.

Grier, Barbara, et al. The Lesbian in Literature: A Bibliography. 3rd ed. 200p. (Orig.). 1981. pap. 7.95 (ISBN 0-930044-23-1). Naiad Pr.

Grier, Edward F., ed. see Whitman, Walt.

Grier, James W. Biology of Animal Behavior. 704p. 1983. pap. text ed. 27.95 (ISBN 0-8016-1971-8). Mosby.

Grier, Margaret R., jt. auth. see Werley, Harriet H.

Grier, Sam. Pascal for the Eighties. LC 84-28518. (Computer Science Ser.). 448p. 1985. pap. text ed. 18.50 pub net (ISBN 0-534-04674-6). Brooks-Cole.

Grier, W. J. The Momentous Event. 1976. pap. 2.95 (ISBN 0-85151-020-5). Banner of Truth.

Grier, William H. & Cobbs, Price M. Black Rage. LC 68-29925. 213p. 1980. pap. 7.95x (ISBN 0-465-00703-1, TB-5055). Basic.

Grierson, Alice K. An Army Wife's Cookbook. Williams, Mary L., ed. LC 72-91099. (Popular Ser.: No. 13). 1972. pap. 3.75 (ISBN 0-911408-27-4). SW Pks Mnmts.

Grierson, D., jt. ed. see Smith, H.

Grierson, Donald & Covey, Simon. Plant Molecular Biology. (Tertiary Level Biology Ser.). 184p. (Orig.). 1985. 39.95 (ISBN 0-317-17304-9, NO. 9028, Pub. by Chapman & Hall England); pap. 17.95 (ISBN 0-412-00661-8, NO. 9029, Pub. by Chapman & Hall England). Methuen Inc.

Grierson, E. Things Seen in Florence. 1924. 15.00 (ISBN 0-89984-016-7). Century Bookbindery.

Grierson, Edward. The Second Man. LC 80-8411. 320p. 1981. pap. 2.25i (ISBN 0-06-080528-5, P 528, PL). Har-Row.

--The Second Man. Barzun, J. & Taylor, W. H., eds. LC 81-47400. (Crime Fiction 1950-1975 Ser.). 308p. 1982. lib. bdg. 18.00 (ISBN 0-8240-4969-1). Garland Pub.

Grierson, Flora. Haunting Edinburgh. 1979. Repr. of 1929 ed. lib. bdg. 50.00 (ISBN 0-8495-2039-8). Arden Lib.

--Haunting Edinburgh. 1929. Repr. 20.00 (ISBN 0-8274-2473-6). R West.

--Haunting Edinburgh. 1929. 30.00 (ISBN 0-686-17237-X). Scholars Ref Lib.

Grierson, Flora, tr. see Piccolomini, Enea S.

Grierson, Francis. Celtic Temperament & Other Essays. LC 71-108701. (Essay & General Literature Index Reprint Ser). 1970. Repr. of 1901 ed. 20.50x (ISBN 0-8046-0922-5, Pub. by Kennikat). Assoc Faculty Pr.

--The Celtic Temperament & Other Essays. 1913. Repr. 20.00 (ISBN 0-8274-2017-X). R West.

--The Humour of the Underman & Other Essays. 1911. Repr. 15.00 (ISBN 0-8274-2550-3). R West.

--Invincible Alliance. facs. ed. LC 77-86754. (Essay Index Reprint Ser.). 1913. 16.75 (ISBN 0-8369-1134-2). Ayer Co Pubs.

--Modern Mysticism. 1977. lib. bdg. 59.95 (ISBN 0-8490-2271-1). Gordon Pr.

--Modern Mysticism. LC 77-102570. 1970. Repr. of 1899 ed. 19.50x (ISBN 0-8046-0730-3, Pub. by Kennikat). Assoc Faculty Pr.

--The Valley of Shadows. Simonson, Harold P., ed. (Masterworks of Literature Ser.). 1970. 8.95x (ISBN 0-8084-0309-5); pap. 5.95x (ISBN 0-8084-0310-9). New Coll U Pr.

Grierson, G. A., ed. Linguistic Survey of India, 11 vols., 19 pts. 1973. Repr. 600.00 setx (ISBN 0-89684-245-2). Orient Bk Dist.

Grierson, H. Sir Walter Scott. LC 72-95427. (English Biography Ser., No. 31). 1969. Repr. of 1938 ed. lib. bdg. 49.95x (ISBN 0-8383-0977-1). Haskell.

Grierson, H. & Smith, J. C. A Critical History of English Poetry. 536p. 1983. text ed. 25.50x (ISBN 0-391-02866-9, Athlone Pr); pap. text ed. 16.50x (ISBN 0-391-02867-7). Humanities.

Grierson, H. J; see Doughty, Oswald.

Grierson, H. J., ed. see Scott, Walter.

Grierson, H. J., tr. see Heredia, Jose M. De.

Grierson, Herbert. The Background of English Literature: Classical & Romantic & Other Collected Essays & Addresses. 290p. 1983. Repr. of 1962 ed. lib. bdg. 45.00 (ISBN 0-89987-321-9). Darby Bks.

--Carlyle & Hitler. LC 73-18348. 1930. lib. bdg. 8.50 (ISBN 0-8414-4460-9). Folcroft.

--Criticism & Creation. LC 73-733. 1949. lib. bdg. 17.50 (ISBN 0-8414-1603-6). Folcroft.

--Cross Currents in English Literature of the XVIIth Century or the World, the Flesh & the Spirit, Their Actions & Reactions: Being the Messenger Lectures on the Evolution of Civilization. 1979. Repr. of 1965 ed. lib. bdg. 30.00 (ISBN 0-8495-2008-8). Arden Lib.

--Don Quixote. LC 73-13607. 1921. lib. bdg. 8.50 (ISBN 0-8414-4430-7). Folcroft.

--Edinburgh Essays on Scots Literature. 1973. lib. bdg. 15.00 (ISBN 0-8414-4687-3). Folcroft.

--Essays & Addresses. LC 72-195906. 1940. lib. bdg. 20.00 (ISBN 0-8414-4686-5). Folcroft.

--First Half of the Seventeenth Century. LC 76-40232. 1906. lib. bdg. 30.00 (ISBN 0-8414-4419-6). Folcroft.

--Lang, Lockhart & Biography. LC 73-14791. 1834. Repr. lib. bdg. 8.50 (ISBN 0-8414-4444-7). Folcroft.

--Lord Byron: Arnold & Swinburne. LC 74-17202. 1920. lib. bdg. 8.50 (ISBN 0-8414-4538-9). Folcroft.

--Rhetoric & English Composition. 1945. Repr. 15.00 (ISBN 0-8274-3276-3). R West.

--Seventeenth Century Studies Presented to Sir Herbert Grierson. 1967. Repr. lib. bdg. 24.50x (ISBN 0-374-93268-9). Octagon.

--Sir Walter Scott, Bart. LC 72-193213. 1938. lib. bdg. 20.00 (ISBN 0-8414-4688-1). Folcroft.

--Sir Walter Scott: Broadcast Lectures to the Young. LC 72-194438. 1932. lib. bdg. 12.50 (ISBN 0-8414-4689-X). Folcroft.

--Sir Walter Scott to-Day. LC 73-14912. 1832. Repr. lib. bdg. 20.00 (ISBN 0-8414-4462-5). Folcroft.

--Thomas Carlyle. 1940. lib. bdg. 8.50 (ISBN 0-8414-4690-3). Folcroft.

--Verse Translation. LC 77-4114. 1948. lib. bdg. 9.50 (ISBN 0-8414-4478-1). Folcroft.

Grierson, Herbert & Clifford, John. Byron: Arnold & Swinburne. 1978. Repr. of 1921 ed. lib. bdg. 15.00 (ISBN 0-8495-1926-8). Arden Lib.

Grierson, Herbert, et al. Sir Walter Scott Lectures, 1940-1948. LC 74-25563. (Illus.). 170p. 1975. Repr. of 1950 ed. lib. bdg. 18.75x (ISBN 0-8371-7869-X, GRSL). Greenwood.

Grierson, Herbert J. Background of English Literature, Classical & Romantic, & Other Collected Essays & Addresses. LC 78-58258. (Essay Index in Reprint Ser.). 1978. 23.75x (ISBN 0-8486-3020-3). Core Collection.

--The Background of English Literature: Classical & Romantic, & Other Collected Essays & Addresses. LC 78-2920. 1978. Repr. of 1970 ed. lib. bdg. 24.75x (ISBN 0-313-20306-7, GRBE). Greenwood.

--Criticism & Creation. LC 78-58259. (Essay Index in Reprint Ser.). 1978. 17.50x (ISBN 0-8486-3021-1). Core Collection.

--Lyrical Poetry from Blake to Hardy. LC 74-158903. 1971. Repr. of 1928 ed. 29.00x (ISBN 0-403-01309-7). Scholarly.

--Lyrical Poetry of the Nineteenth Century. LC 70-124768. Repr. of 1929 ed. 15.00 (ISBN 0-404-02915-9). AMS Pr.

--Metaphysical Lyrics & Poems of the Seventeenth Century. LC 78-12842. 1979. Repr. of 1921 ed. lib. bdg. 24.75x (ISBN 0-313-21163-9, GRML). Greenwood.

--Rhetoric & English Composition. LC 73-3435. 1945. lib. bdg. 15.00 (ISBN 0-8414-2009-2). Folcroft.

--Sir Walter Scott, Baronet. LC 76-153326. Repr. of 1938 ed. 12.50 (ISBN 0-404-02914-0). AMS Pr.

Grierson, Herbert J., ed. Metaphysical Lyrics & Poems of the Seventeenth Century: Donne to Butler. (Oxford Paperbacks Ser.). 1959. pap. 6.95x (ISBN 0-19-881102-0). Oxford U Pr.

Grierson, Herbert J. & Bullough, Geoffrey, eds. Oxford Book of Seventeenth Century Verse. 1934. 45.00x (ISBN 0-19-812125-3). Oxford U Pr.

Grierson, Herbert J., ed. see Donne, John.

Grierson, Herbert J. C., ed. Metaphysical Lyrics & Poems of the Seventeenth Century. (Poetry Library). 302p. 1985. Repr. of 1921 ed. 26.50x (ISBN 0-89609-251-8). Granger Bk.

Grierson, John. Grierson on Documentary. Hardy, Forsyth, ed. 208p. 1979. pap. 6.95 (ISBN 0-571-11367-2). Faber & Faber.

--Grierson on the Movies. Hardy, H. Forsyth, ed. 200p. 1981. 16.95 (ISBN 0-571-11665-5). Faber & Faber.

Grierson, Mary. Donald Francis Tovey: A Biography Based on Letters. LC 70-104237. (Illus.). xi, 337p. Repr. of 1952 ed. lib. bdg. 17.00x (ISBN 0-8371-3935-X, GRDT). Greenwood.

Grierson, Mary, jt. auth. see Hunt, P. Francis.

Grierson, Philip. Byzantine Coinage. (Byzantine Collection Publications Ser.: No. 4). (Illus.). 32p. 1982. pap. 4.50x (ISBN 0-88402-112-2). Dumbarton Oaks.

--Byzantine Coins. LC 82-50853. (The Library of Numismatics: Vol. 2). (Illus.). 479p. 1983. 95.00 (ISBN 0-520-04897-0). U of Cal Pr.

--Dark Age Numismatics. 414p. 1979. 70.00x (ISBN 0-86078-041-4, Pub. by Variorum). State Mutual Bk.

--Later Medieval Numismatics (11th-16th Centuries) 1980. 60.00x (ISBN 0-86078-043-0, Pub. by Variorum England). State Mutual Bk.

--Numismatics. (Illus.). 1975. pap. 5.95 (ISBN 0-19-888098-7, GB440, GB). Oxford U Pr.

Grierson, Philip, tr. see Ganshof, Francois L.

Grierson, Ronald. Woven Rugs. (Illus.). 50p. 1979. pap. 3.00 (Pub. by Batsford England). David & Charles.

Gries, David. Compiler Construction for Digital Computers. 493p. 1971. 42.50 (ISBN 0-471-32776-X). Wiley.

--The Science of Programming. (Texts & Monographs in Computer Science). 366p. 1981. 22.00 (ISBN 0-387-90641-X). Springer-Verlag.

Gries, David, jt. auth. see Conway, Richard.

Gries, David, ed. Programming Methodology: A Collection of Articles by Members of IFIP WG 2.3. LC 78-16539. (Texts & Monographs in Computer Science). (Illus.). 1978. 36.00 (ISBN 0-387-90329-1). Springer-Verlag.

Gries, John M., ed. see President's Conference On Home Building & Home Ownership.

Griesbach, C. B. Historic Ornament: A Pictorial Archive. LC 75-12174. Orig. Title: Historischer Anordnung Muster-Ornamentel Aus Allen Stilen in. (Illus.). 288p. 1975. pap. 8.95 (ISBN 0-486-23215-8). Dover.

Griesbach, Ellen & Taylor, Jerry. The Prentice-Hall Encyclopedia of Mathematics. Taylor, Louis, ed. (Illus., Orig.). (YA) (gr. 6 up). 1982. 35.00 (ISBN 0-13-696013-8). P-H.

Griesbach, G. B. Historic Ornament: A Pictorial Archive; 900 Fine Examples from Ancient Egypt to 1800 Suitable for Reproduction. (Illus.). 15.25 (ISBN 0-8446-5195-8). Peter Smith.

Griesbach, Heinz. Aktuell & Interessant, 3 vols. 78p. (Ger.). 1975. Vol. 1,Die Deutschsprachigen Laender, 80 p. 3.95 (ISBN 3-468-49561-7); Vol 2: Die Laender der Bundesrepublik Deutschland, 80p. 3.95 (ISBN 3-468-49661-3); Vol 3, Einigestaedte der Bundesrepublik Deutschland,80p. 3.95 (ISBN 3-468-49761-X). Langenscheidt.

--Deutsch Mit Erfolg, Level 2 y Lehrbuch 2. 240p. 9.95 (ISBN 3-468-49780-6); Cassette 2A lektionstexte 13.25 (ISBN 0-317-30510-7). Langenscheidt.

--Deutsch mal Drei: Level One. (Ger.). 1974. lernbuch 5.95 (ISBN 3-468-49501-3); lehrerheft 2.50 (ISBN 3-468-49506-4); glossar Englisch 2.50 (ISBN 3-468-49511-0); glossar Franzoesisch 2.50 (ISBN 3-468-49512-9); write for info. additional supplementary materials avail. Langenscheidt.

--Deutsch mal Drei: Level Three. (Ger.). 1977. lernbuch 5.95 (ISBN 3-468-49701-6); Lehrerheft 2.50 (ISBN 3-468-49706-7); Glossar Deutsch-Deutsch 2.50 (ISBN 3-468-49711-3); Loesungsheft 3 2.50 (ISBN 3-468-49741-5); Uebungsbuch 4.50 (ISBN 3-468-49751-2); leseheft 3.95 (ISBN 3-468-49761-X); Cassette text 11.50 (ISBN 3-468-84761-0). Langenscheidt.

--Deutsch mal Drei: Level Two. (Ger.). 1975. Lernbuch 5.95 (ISBN 3-468-49601-X); Lehrerheft 2.50 (ISBN 3-468-49606-0); Glossar Englisch 2.95 (ISBN 3-468-49611-7); Glossar Franzoesisch 2.95 (ISBN 3-468-49612-5); Loesungsheft 2.95 (ISBN 3-468-49641-9); Uebungsbuch 5.50 (ISBN 3-468-49651-6); write for info. additional supplementary material avail. Langenscheidt.

--Deutsch mit Erfolg. 256p. (Ger.). 1983. lernbuch 1 for beginners 9.95 (ISBN 3-468-49770-9); write for info. Self-instruction Manual 1 for Eng. speaking students (ISBN 3-468-49771-7); Cassette 1A 13.25 (ISBN 3-468-84720-3); Cassette 1B 13.25 (ISBN 3-468-84721-1); Cassette 1C 13.25 (ISBN 3-468-84722-X). Langenscheidt.

--Deutsch X 3. Incl. Gespraechsbuch I mit Uebungen, "Unterwegs". (Illus.). 1975. pap. text ed. 4.30x (ISBN 3-468-49556-0); Glossary I, German-English. 1974. pap. text ed. 2.10x (ISBN 3-468-49511-0); Glossary II, German-English. 1976. pap. text ed. 2.65x (ISBN 3-468-49611-7); Lehrerheft I. (Illus.). 1974. pap. text ed. 2.10x (ISBN 3-468-49506-4); Lehrerheft II. 1976. pap. text ed. 2.10x (ISBN 3-468-49606-0); Lernbuch I. Horn, Herbert, illus. 1974. pap. text ed. 4.85x (ISBN 3-468-49501-3); Lernbuch II. Horn, Herbert, illus. 1975. pap. text ed. 4.85x (ISBN 3-468-49601-X); Lernbuch III. (Illus.). 1977. pap. text ed. 4.85x (ISBN 3-468-49701-6); Leseheft I mit Uebungen, "Aktuell und interessant". (Illus.). 1975. pap. text ed. 3.75x (ISBN 3-468-49561-7); Leseheft II mit Uebungen, "Aktuell und interessant". Die Laender der Bundesrepublik Deutschland. (Illus.). 1977. pap. text ed. 3.75x (ISBN 3-468-49661-3); Loesungsheft I. 1974. pap. text ed. 2.10x (ISBN 3-468-49541-2); Loesungsheft II. 1976. pap. text ed. 2.65x (ISBN 3-468-49641-9); Sprachlabor-Cassetten, Saemtliche Sprechuebungen, Doppelspur Mitnachsprechpausen, 10 Casetten. 1974. pap. text ed. 136.80x (ISBN 3-468-84722-X); Sprachlabor-Tonbaender saemtliche Sprechuebungen, Vollspur mit Nachsprechpausen, 10 Tonbaender. 1974. pap. text ed. 239.40x (ISBN 3-468-84726-2); Sprechuebungem I - Textheft. 1974. pap. text ed. 3.75x (ISBN 3-468-49546-3). pap. M S Rosenberg.

Griesbach, Heinz & Schulz, Dora. Tausend Redensarten Deutsch. 248p. 7.95 (ISBN 3-468-43112-0). Langenscheidt.

Griesbach, Heinz, jt. auth. see Schulz, Dora.

Griesbach, Marc F., jt. auth. see Jones, John D.

Griesbach, Marc F. & Carmichael, John P., eds. The ACPA in Today's Intellectual World: Proceedings, 1983, Vol. 57. LC 82-73233. 250p. 1984. pap. 12.00 (ISBN 0-918090-17-2). Am Cath Philo.

Griese, Arnold. At the Mouth of the Luckiest River. LC 72-7548. (Illus.). 80p. (gr. 2-5). 1973. PLB 10.89 (ISBN 0-690-10787-0). Crowell Jr Bks.

--The Way of Our People. LC 74-23086. (Illus.). 90p. (gr. 2-5). 1975. PLB 11.89 (ISBN 0-690-00707-8). Crowell Jr Bks.

Griese, Arnold A. Do You Read Me? Practical Approaches to Teaching Reading Comprehension. LC 76-9913. (Illus.). 1977. pap. 12.95 (ISBN 0-673-16354-7); 13.95 (ISBN 0-673-16353-9). Scott F.

--The Wind Is Not a River. LC 77-5082. (Illus.). (gr. 4-7). 1978. PLB 10.89 (ISBN 0-690-03842-9). Crowell Jr Bks.

--Your Philosophy of Education-What Is It? (Illus.). 350p. (Orig.). 1981. pap. 15.45x (ISBN 0-673-16541-8). Scott F.

Griese, Bob, jt. auth. see Sayers, Gayle.

Griesemer, Bernard, jt. auth. see Pfister, Fred.

Griesemer, James R. Accountants' & Administrators' Guide: Budgeting for Results in Government. 208p. 1983. 55.95x (ISBN 0-471-89392-7, Pub. by Ronald Pr). Wiley.

--Microcomputers in Local Government. LC 83-18367. (Practical Management Ser.). 150p. (Orig.). 1983. 19.95 (ISBN 0-87326-040-6). Intl City Mgt.

Grieser, R. H., jt. auth. see Wilkins, Freida L.

Grieser, R. Henry. How to Play Cucamonga Gin: The Newest Card Game with Step-by-Step Pictorial Instructions, the Official Rules & Comments on the Strategy of the Game. LC 83-72412. (Illus.). 60p. 1983. 5.95 (ISBN 0-939260-02-6). Contract Data.

Grieser, Robert H. Clews to the Analysis or Preparation of a Request for Contract Adjustment (Claim) LC 84-73115. (Illus.). 52p. (Orig.). 1984. pap. 22.00x (ISBN 0-939260-04-2). Contract Data.

--A Guide to Developing the Contract Pricing Proposal (DD 633) for Small Businesses. (Illus.). 130p. 1981. 95.00x (ISBN 0-939260-00-X). Contract Data.

--How to Compute & Add Cost-of-Money to Government Contracts. LC 81-71235. (Illus.). 85p. 1982. 85.00x (ISBN 0-939260-01-8). Contract Data.

Grieshaber, Erich & Grieshaber, Jean. Expose of Jehovah's Witnesses. 128p. 1983. pap. text ed. 2.95 (ISBN 0-936728-08-6). Word for Today.

Grieshaber, Jean, jt. auth. see Grieshaber, Erich.

Griesinger, Theodor. The Jesuits: A Complete History of Their Open & Secret Proceedings, 2 vols. 1977. Set. lib. bdg. 200.00 (ISBN 0-8490-2092-1). Gordon Pr.

Grieson, Ronald E. Antitrust & Regulation. 1985. write for info. (ISBN 0-669-09301-7). Lexington Bks.

Grieson, Ronald E., ed. The Urban Economy & Housing. LC 81-48269. 256p. 1982. 31.50X (ISBN 0-669-05331-7). Lexington Bks.

Griesser, G. Data Protection in Health Information Systems: Considerations & Guidelines. 218p. 1980. 42.75 (ISBN 0-444-86052-5, North Holland). Elsevier.

Griesser, G, ed. see IFIP-WG Working Conference, Germany, 1976.

Griesser, G., et al. Data Protection in Health Information Systems. 2nd ed. 1983. 42.75 (ISBN 0-444-86713-9, I-410-83). Elsevier.

Griessman, B. Eugene, jt. ed. see Lewis, W. David.

Griest, Ellwood. John & Mary. facsimile ed. LC 78-178473. (Black Heritage Library Collection). Repr. of 1873 ed. 17.50 (ISBN 0-8369-8922-8). Ayer Co Pubs.

Griethuysen, Ted Van see Kranz, Sheldon.

Grieve, B. J. How to Know Western Australian Wildflowers, Pt. IV, Supplement 1982. (Illus.). 110p. (Orig.). 1983. pap. 21.00x (ISBN 0-85564-200-9, Pub. by U of W Austral Pr). Intl Spec Bk.

Grieve, B. J. & Blackall, W. E. How to Know Western Australian Wildflowers, Pt. 4. 1977. 37.95x (ISBN 0-85564-078-2, Pub. by U of W Austral Pr). Intl Spec Bk.

Grieve, B. J., jt. auth. see Blackall, W. E.

Grieve, B. J. & Blackall, W. E., eds. How to Know Western Australian Wildflowers: A Key to the Flore of the Flora of the Extratropical Regions of Western Australia, Pt. IIIA. 350p. 1980. 39.00x (ISBN 0-85564-160-6, Pub. by U of West Australia Pr Australia). Intl Spec Bk.

Grieve, Gregory P. Mobilzation of the Spine. 4th ed. (Illus.). pap. text ed. 18.50 (ISBN 0-443-02795-1). Churchill.

Grieve, Gregory P., ed. Common Vertebral Joint Problems. (Illus.). 500p. 1981. text ed. 79.00 (ISBN 0-443-02106-6). Churchill.

Grieve, M. Culinary Herbs & Condiments. 1954. pap. 3.95 (ISBN 0-486-21513-X). Dover.

--Culinary Herbs & Condiments. 13.00 (ISBN 0-8446-0117-9). Peter Smith.

--A Modern Herbal. Leyel, Mrs. C. F., ed. LC 72-169784. (Illus.). 1971. pap. 7.95; Vol. 1. pap. 7.95 (ISBN 0-486-22798-7); Vol. 2. pap. 8.50 (ISBN 0-486-22799-5). Dover.

Grieve, M. J., jt. auth. see Donelan, M. D.

Grieve, Mrs. M. A Modern Herbal, 2 vols. LC 72-169782. (Illus.). Set. 32.00 (ISBN 0-8446-0302-3). Peter Smith.

Grieve, Michael, ed. see MacDiarmid, Hugh.

Grieve, R., jt. ed. see Fraser, W. I.

Grieves, Forest L. Conflict & Order: An Introduction to International Relations. LC 76-10901. (Illus.). 1977. pap. text ed. 25.95 (ISBN 0-395-24332-7); inst. manual 1.65 (ISBN 0-395-24335-1). HM.

--Supranationalism & International Adjudication. LC 69-17362. (Illus.). 281p. 1969. 19.95x (ISBN 0-252-00012-9). U of Ill Pr.

Grieves, Forest L., ed. Transnationalism in World Politics & Business. LC 79-1397. (Pergamon Policy Studies). 240p. 1979. 39.00 (ISBN 0-08-023892-0). Pergamon.

Grieve-Smith, John. Business Strategy: An Introduction. 180p. 1985. 24.95x (ISBN 0-631-13986-9); pap. 9.95 (ISBN 0-631-13987-7). Basil Blackwell.

Griff, Allan L. Plastics Extrusion Technology. 2nd ed. LC 75-45329. 364p. 1976. Repr. of 1968 ed. 23.50 (ISBN 0-88275-386-X). Krieger.

Griff, Catherine, jt. auth. see Scott, John.

Griff, Leonard C., jt. auth. see Konikiewicz, Leonard W.

Griffeath, D. Additive & Cancellative Interacting Particle Systems. (Lecture Notes in Mathematics: Vol. 724). 1979. pap. 13.00 (ISBN 3-540-09508-X). Springer-Verlag.

Griffee, Dale. Listen & Act: Scenes for Language Learning. Rost, Michael, ed. (Illus.). 96p. 1982. pap. text ed. 7.50 (ISBN 0-940264-18-8); 2 cassettes 27.00 (ISBN 0-940264-21-8); 20 cards o.p. 10.00 (ISBN 0-940264-20-X); pap. 5.35 workbook (ISBN 0-940264-19-6). Lingual Hse Pub.

Griffel, D. H. Applied Functional Analysis. LC 81-6598. (Mathematics & Its Applications Ser.). 386p. 1981. 84.95x (ISBN 0-470-27196-5); pap. 27.95x (ISBN 0-470-20136-3). Halsted Pr.

Griffel, William. Beam Formulas. LC 68-31449. 1970. 15.00 (ISBN 0-8044-4338-6). Ungar.

--Handbook of Formulas for Stress & Strain. LC 66-17539. 1966. 30.00 (ISBN 0-8044-4332-7). Ungar.

--Plate Formulas. LC 67-26127. 1968. 18.00 (ISBN 0-8044-4335-1). Ungar.

Griffen, Clyde & Griffen, Sally. Natives & Newcomers: The Ordering of Opportunity in Mid-Nineteenth-Century Poughkeepsie. (Studies in Urban History). 1977. 20.00x (ISBN 0-674-60325-7). Harvard U Pr.

Griffen, Dana T., jt. auth. see Phillips, W. Revell.

Griffen, Edmund & Dodge, Daniel. Washington Playland. 1976. pap. 1.95 (LB403, Leisure Bks). Dorchester Pub Co.

Griffen, Edward. World Without Cancer: The Story of Vitamin B-17. 526p. 3.95 (ISBN 0-318-15699-7). Natl Health Fed.

Griffen, Elizabeth. Dog's Book of Bugs. (Illus.). 64p. (gr. 1-4). 1967. pap. 2.95 (ISBN 0-689-70408-9, A-34, Aladdin). Atheneum.

Griffen, Garnet M. Teenager & Safe Driving. Rosen, Ruth C., ed. LC 68-10029. (Personal Guidance, Social Adjustment Ser). (gr. 7 up). 1967. PLB 8.97 (ISBN 0-8239-0110-6). Rosen Group.

Griffen, Jeff. How to Raise & Train Your Puppy. pap. 5.00 (ISBN 0-87980-330-4). Wilshire.

Griffen, M. R., ed. see Pliny.

Griffen, Martin B., jt. auth. see Bowden, Charles L.

Griffen, Robert A., ed. see Meriwether, David.

Griffen, Sally, jt. auth. see Griffen, Clyde.

Griffen, Ward O., Jr., jt. auth. see Maull, Kimball I.

Griffen, William B. Culture Change & Shifting Populations in Central Northern Mexico. LC 69-16327. (Anthropological Papers, No. 13). 192p. 1969. pap. 5.95x (ISBN 0-8165-0140-8). U of Ariz Pr.

--Indian Assimilation in the Franciscan Area of Nueva Vizcaya. LC 78-14546. (Anthropological Papers: No. 33). 122p. 1979. pap. 6.75x (ISBN 0-8165-0584-5). U of Ariz Pr.

Griffen, William L. & Marciano, J. D. Education for a Culture in Crisis. LC 72-86266. 177p. 1972. pap. text ed. 6.95x (ISBN 0-8422-0219-6). Irvington.

Griffen, William L. & Marciano, John. Teaching the Vietnam War: A Critical Examination of School Texts & Interpretive Comparative History Utilizing the Pentagon Papers & other Documents. LC 78-73553. 204p. 1980. text ed. 16.50x (ISBN 0-916672-23-9); pap. text ed. 6.50x (ISBN 0-916672-27-1). Allanheld.

Griffes, Ernest J., ed. Employee Benefits Programs: Management, Planning & Control. LC 82-73627. 250p. 1983. 19.95 (ISBN 0-87094-247-6). Dow Jones-Irwin.

Griffeth, Benjamin. Pocket Guide to Literature & Language Terms. 176p. 1985. pap. 2.95 (ISBN 0-8120-2512-1). Barron.

Griffeth, Bill, ed. see Burke, Dennis R.

Griffeth, Bill, ed. see Hayes, Stephen K.

Griffeth, Robert & Thomas, Carol G., eds. The City-State in Five Cultures. LC 81-7897. 237p. 1981. lib. bdg. 25.00 (ISBN 0-87436-316-0). ABC-Clio.

Griffey, Carl H. The History of Local School Control in the State of New York. LC 71-176820. (Columbia University. Teachers College. Contributions to Education Ser.: No. 683). Repr. of 1936 ed. 22.50 (ISBN 0-404-55683-3). AMS Pr.

Griffhorn, Thelma. Things for Kids to Do. 132p. 1985. pap. 6.95 (ISBN 0-89693-525-6). Victor Bks.

Griffin. Conservative vs. Surgical Management of Foot Disorders. 1979. 32.95 (ISBN 0-8151-4002-9, YBMP). Year Bk Med.

Griffin & Beale. World of Electronics, 4 Bks. (Electronic World Ser.). (gr. 4-8). 12.95 (ISBN 0-86020-643-2). EDC.

Griffin & Foster. California After the U. S. Conquest. An Original Anthology. Cortes, Carlos, ed. & intro. by. LC 76-5225. (Chicano Heritage Ser.). (Illus.). 1976. 31.00x (ISBN 0-405-09535-X). Ayer Co Pubs.

Griffin, jt. auth. see D'Arcy.

Griffin, et al. Welding Processes. 2nd ed. LC 76-28745. (gr. 9-12). 1978. 20.60 (ISBN 0-8273-1257-1); instr.'s guide 5.10 (ISBN 0-8273-1259-8). Delmar.

--Welding Processes. 3rd ed. 400p. 1984. text ed. 20.60 (ISBN 0-8273-2133-3); instrs' guide 4.80 (ISBN 0-8273-2136-8). Delmar.

Griffin, A. Clark, ed. see Annual Symposium on Fundamental Cancer Research, No. 31.

Griffin, A. F. A List of Books on Puerto Rico with References to Periodicals. 1976. lib. bdg. 59.95 (ISBN 0-8490-2169-3). Gordon Pr.

Griffin, A. J. How to Avoid People Problems & Increase Laboratory Production. 112p. 1980. pap. 12.00 (ISBN 0-931386-17-9). Quint Pub Co.

Griffin, A. P. Bibliography of American Historical Societies. 59.95 (ISBN 0-87968-736-3). Gordon Pr.

Griffin, A. R. The Collier. (Shire Album: No. 82). (Illus.). 32p. (Orig.). 1982. pap. 2.95 (ISBN 0-85263-590-7, Pub. by Shire Pubns England). Seven Hills Bks.

--Mining in the East Midlands: 1550-1947. 338p. 1971. 35.00x (ISBN 0-7146-2585-X, F Cass Co). Biblio Dist.

Griffin, Adelaide, jt. auth. see Adams, Sexton.

Griffin, Alan R. Miners of Nottinghamshire, 1914-1944. LC 67-1377. 1962. 27.50x (ISBN 0-678-06017-7). Kelley.

Griffin, Alice V. Pageantry on the Shakespearean Stage. (Orig.). 1951. pap. 7.95x (ISBN 0-8084-0239-0). New Coll U Pr.

Griffin, Andrew. A Brief Guide to Sources for the Study of Burma. (Illus.). 25p. (Orig.). 1979. pap. 3.00 (ISBN 0-903359-19-7, Pub. by British Lib). Longwood Pub Group.

Griffin, Anne. Quebec: The Challenge of Independence. LC 81-72054. 260p. 1983. 27.50 (ISBN 0-8386-3135-5). Fairleigh Dickinson.

Griffin, Anselm C. & Johnson, Julian F., eds. Liquid Crystals & Ordered Fields, Vol. 4. 1162p. 1984. 135.00x (ISBN 0-306-41394-9, Plenum Pr). Plenum Pub.

Griffin, Appleton P. Bibliography of American Historical Societies. 2nd ed. rev. ed. LC 67-480. 1966. Repr. of 1907 ed. 75.00x (ISBN 0-8103-3080-6). Gale.

--Index of the Literature of American Local History. LC 65-27165. 160p. Repr. of 1896 ed. 10.50 (ISBN 0-405-03672-8). Ayer Co Pubs.

Griffin, Appleton P., compiled by. A Catalogue of the Washington Collection in the Boston Athenaeum. (Illus.). xi, 555p. 1897. 10.00 (ISBN 0-934552-06-1). Boston Athenaeum.

Griffin, Arthur. New England: The Four Seasons. 1980. 35.00 (ISBN 0-395-29164-X). HM.

Griffin, Audrey. Sikyon. (Oxford Classical & Philosophical Monographs). (Illus.). 1982. 39.95x (ISBN 0-19-814718-X). Oxford U Pr.

Griffin, Augustus. Griffin's Journal. 19.95 (ISBN 0-89190-408-5, Pub. by Am Repr). Amereon Ltd.

Griffin, Betty F. Family to Family. 78p. 1980. pap. text ed. 6.75 (ISBN 0-88200-140-X, 16008). Alexander Graham.

Griffin, Bobby. The Search. pap. 1.75 (ISBN 0-686-12739-0). Grace Pub Co.

Griffin, Brenda S. & Griffin, Charles T. Juvenile Delinquency in Perspective. (Illus.). 1978. text ed. 23.50 scp (ISBN 0-06-042512-1, HarpC). Harper-Row.

Griffin, Brian & Wingrove, David. Apertures: A Study of the Writings of Brian W. Aldiss. LC 83-5514. (Contributions to the Study of Science Fiction & Fantasy Ser.: No. 8). xvi, 261p. 1984. lib. bdg. 29.95 (ISBN 0-313-23428-0, GRA/). Greenwood.

Griffin, Bryan F. Panic among the Philistines. LC 82-60663. 259p. 1983. 12.95 (ISBN 0-89526-633-4). Regnery-Gateway.

--Panic among the Phillistines. (Christian Activist Ser.). 259p. 1985. pap. 8.95 (ISBN 0-89526-817-5). Regnery-Gateway.

Griffin, C. J. & McGrath, Philomena. Embryogenesis: Development & Some Anomalies of the Upper Respiratory Tract Including the Septo-Maxillary Syndrome & Its Treatment. 1978. 26.00x (ISBN 0-424-00049-0, Pub. by Sydney U Pr). Intl Spec Bk.

Griffin, C. J., et al, eds. The Temporomandibular Joint Syndrome: Masticatory Apparatus of Man in Normal & Abnormal Function. (Monographs in Oral Science: Vol. 4). (Illus.). 200p. 1975. 39.75 (ISBN 3-8055-2106-5). S Karger.

Griffin, C. S. Ferment of Reform, Eighteen Thirty to Eighteen Sixty. LC 67-13380. (American History Ser.). (Orig.). 1968. pap. 5.95x (ISBN 0-88295-738-4). Harlan Davidson.

Griffin, C. W. AIA: Manual of Built-Up Roof Systems. 2nd ed. 1982. 44.50 (ISBN 0-07-024783-8). McGraw.

Griffin, Charles C. United States & the Disruption of the Spanish Empire, 1810-1822. 1968. lib. bdg. 21.50x (ISBN 0-374-93287-5). Octagon.

Griffin, Charles D., jt. ed. see Fraker, Anna C.

Griffin, Charles H., et al. Advanced Accounting. 4th ed. 1980. 33.95x (ISBN 0-256-02328-X). Irwin.

Griffin, Charles T., jt. auth. see Griffin, Brenda S.

Griffin, Christine. Typical Girls: Young Women from School to the Full-Time Job Market. 1985. 22.95x; pap. 12.95 (ISBN 0-317-17175-5). Routledge & Kegan.

Griffin, Clarence W. History of Old Tryon & Rutherford Counties, North Carolina, 1730-1936. LC 77-24691. (Illus.). 1977. Repr. of 1937 ed. 35.00 (ISBN 0-87152-252-7). Reprint.

Griffin, Clifford S. Their Brothers' Keepers: Moral Stewardship in the United States, 1800 to 1865. LC 83-8563. xv, 332p. 1983. Repr. of 1960 ed. lib. bdg. 45.00 (ISBN 0-686-46564-4, GRTB). Greenwood.

--The University of Kansas: A History. LC 73-12349. (Illus.). 808p. 1974. 25.00x (ISBN 0-7006-0106-6). U Pr of KS.

Griffin, Colin. Curriculum Theory in Adult & Lifelong Education. 216p. 1983. 28.50 (ISBN 0-89397-162-6). Nichols Pub.

Griffin, D. M. Ecology of Soil Fungi. LC 72-247. (Illus.). 208p. 1972. text ed. 19.95x (ISBN 0-8156-5035-3). Syracuse U Pr.

Griffin, D. R., ed. Animal Mind - Human Mind: Report on the Dahlem Workshop. (Dahlem Workshop Report Ser.: Vol. 21). (Illus.). 427p. 1982. 29.00 (ISBN 0-387-11330-4). Springer-Verlag.

Griffin, David E., jt. auth. see Cole, Jim E.

Griffin, David H. Fungal Physiology. LC 81-3344. 383p. 1981. 37.50x (ISBN 0-471-05748-7). Wiley.

Griffin, David R., jt. auth. see Cobb, John B., Jr.

Griffin, David R. & Altizer, Thomas J., eds. John Cobb's Theology in Process. LC 77-23135. 212p. 1977. 17.50 (ISBN 0-664-21292-1). Westminster.

Griffin, David R. & Cobb, John B., Jr., eds. Mind in Nature: Essays on the Interface of Science & Philosophy. 1977. pap. text ed. 10.25 (ISBN 0-8191-0157-5). U Pr of Amer.

Griffin, Des. Descent into Slavery? (Illus.). 354p. 1980. pap. 8.00 (ISBN 0-941380-01-7). Emissary Pubns.

--Fourth Reich of the Rich. (Illus.). 297p. (Orig.). 1981. pap. 7.00 (ISBN 0-941380-00-9). Emissary Pubns.

Griffin, Diane. Slow Learners: A Break in the Circle. (Woburn Educational Ser.). 1978. 18.00x (ISBN 0-7130-0137-2, Pub. by Woburn Pr England); pap. 8.95x (ISBN 0-7130-4003-3). Biblio Dist.

Griffin, Dick, jt. ed. see Warden, Rob.

Griffin, Donald. The Question of Animal Awareness. 2nd ed. LC 81-51221. (Illus.). 221p. pap. 9.95 (ISBN 0-86576-002-0). W Kaufmann.

Griffin, Donald R. Animal Thinking. 256p. 1984. text ed. 17.50x (ISBN 0-674-03712-X). Harvard U Pr.

--Animal Thinking. 256p. 1985. pap. 7.95 (ISBN 0-674-03713-8). Harvard U Pr.

--Bird Migration. LC 74-76321. (Illus.). 192p. 1974. pap. 4.95 (ISBN 0-486-20529-0). Dover.

--Question of Animal Awareness: Evolutionary Continuity of Mental Experience. rev. ed. LC 81-51221. 224p. 1981. 13.95x (ISBN 0-87470-035-3). Rockefeller.

--The Question of Animal Awareness: Evolutionary Continuity of Mental Experience. LC 76-18492. 144p. 1976. 7.00x (ISBN 0-87470-020-5). Rockefeller.

Griffin, Donald R. & Novick, A. Animal Structure & Function. 2nd ed. LC 70-77810. (Modern Biology Ser). 1970. pap. text ed. 16.95 (ISBN 0-03-077505-1, HoltC). HR&W.

Griffin, Donald R., intro. by. Animal Engineering: Readings from Scientific American. LC 74-12112. (Illus.). 120p. 1974. pap. text ed. 10.95 (ISBN 0-7167-0508-7). W H Freeman.

Griffin, Donald S., jt. ed. see Cruse, Thomas A.

Griffin, Dustin H. Alexander Pope: The Poet in the Poems. LC 78-51167. 1978. 31.00x (ISBN 0-691-06371-0). Princeton U Pr.

--Satires Against Man: The Poems of Rochester. LC 72-95304. 1974. 29.50x (ISBN 0-520-02394-3). U of Cal Pr.

Griffin, E., tr. see Brichant, Francis.

Griffin, E. Glenn, jt. auth. see Williams, Cecil B.

Griffin, Edward. World Without Cancer. 5.95. Cancer Control Soc.

Griffin, Edward M. Jonathan Edwards. (Pamphlets on American Writers Ser: No. 97). (Orig.). 1971. pap. 1.25x (ISBN 0-8166-0601-3, MPAW97). U of Minn Pr.

--Old Brick: Charles Chauncy of Boston, Seventeen Five to Seventeen Eighty-Seven. (Minnesota Monographs in the Humanities: No. 11). 1980. 20.00x (ISBN 0-8166-0907-1). U of Minn Pr.

Griffin, Eldon. Clippers & Consuls: American Consular & Commercial Relations with Eastern Asia, 1845-1860. LC 72-79824. (China Library Ser.). (Illus.). 1972. Repr. of 1938 ed. lib. bdg. 42.00 (ISBN 0-8420-1368-7). Scholarly Res Inc.

Griffin, Eleanor D. Step by Step Success, Bks 1-4. 1970. prepaid 1.00 ea. Bk. 1 (ISBN 0-913692-05-0). Bk.2 (ISBN 0-913692-06-9). Bk. 3 (ISBN 0-913692-07-7). Bk.4 (ISBN 0-913692-08-5). Learning Inc.

Griffin, Elinor F. Island of Childhood: Education in the Special World of Nursery Schools. LC 81-9256. (Early Childhood Education Ser.). 1982. pap. text ed. 18.95x (ISBN 0-8077-2690-7). Tchrs Coll.

Griffin, Em. Getting Together: A Guide for Good Groups. LC 82-7131. (Illus.). 240p. (Orig.). 1982. pap. 6.95 (ISBN 0-87784-390-2). Inter-Varsity.

--The Mind Changers. 1976. pap. 6.95 (ISBN 0-8423-4290-7). Tyndale.

Griffin, Emilie. Clinging: The Experience of Prayer. LC 83-48989. 96p. 1984. 10.53 (ISBN 0-06-063461-8). Har-Row.

--Turning: Reflections on the Experience of Conversion. LC 79-6652. 224p. 1982. pap. 4.50 (ISBN 0-385-17892-1, Im). Doubleday.

Griffin, Ernest G. John Middleton Murray. LC 68-24284. (English Authors Ser.). 1969. lib. bdg. 11.95 (ISBN 0-89197-812-7); pap. text ed. 6.95x (ISBN 0-89197-998-0). Irvington.

Griffin, Frances. Less Time for Meddling: A History of Salem Academy & College, 1772-1866. LC 79-20697. 1979. 14.95 (ISBN 0-89587-012-6). Blair.

Griffin, Frank. Industrial Gases. (Illus.). (gr. 7 up). 13.75x (ISBN 0-392-03372-0, SpS). Sportshelf.

Griffin, Frank M., Jr., jt. auth. see Cobbs, C. Glenn.

Griffin, Frank W., jt. auth. see Smith, Sanderson M.

Griffin, G. Edward. Fearful Master: A Second Look at the United Nations. LC 64-22761. (Illus.). 1964. pap. 4.95 (ISBN 0-88279-102-8). Western Islands.

--The Life & Words of Robert Welch, Founder of the John Birch Society. LC 74-3311. (Illus.). 428p. 1975. 12.50 (ISBN 0-912986-07-7). Am Media.

--World Without Cancer: The Story of Vitamin B 17. LC 74-83649. (Illus., Orig.). 1974. 14.95 (ISBN 0-912986-08-5); pap. 5.95 (ISBN 0-912986-09-3). Am Media.

Griffin, G. W. Studies in Literature. 1973. Repr. of 1870 ed. 20.00 (ISBN 0-8274-0204-X). R West.

--Studies in Literature (Shakespeare, Hawthorne, Shelley, Thackeray, Dante, Hugo) 1978. Repr. of 1870 ed. lib. bdg. 20.00 (ISBN 0-8414-2007-6). Folcroft.

Griffin, Gary A., ed. Staff Development, Pt. II. LC 82-62382. (The National Society for the Study of Education Ser.: Bk. 82). 275p. 1983. lib. bdg. 17.00x (ISBN 0-226-60136-6). U of Chicago Pr.

--Staff Development, Pt. II. LC 82-62382. (National Society for the Study of Education Ser.: Bk. 82). 275p. 1984. pap. text ed. 10.00x (ISBN 0-226-60093-9). U of Chicago Pr.

Griffin, Gayle. Food for Temple & Table. 1981. spiral bdg. 9.95 (ISBN 0-89323-018-9). Bible Memory.

Griffin, Georgia B. Griffin: Generations of John W. & Jane Griffin. 183p. 1983. 16.00 (ISBN 0-318-11856-4). Griffin Herit.

--Ochlocknee: Land of Crooked Waters. (Illus.). 276p. 1982. 16.00 (ISBN 0-318-11704-5). Ochlocknee.

Griffin, Gerald. Gabriele D'Annunzio. LC 77-113312. 1970. Repr. of 1935 ed. 21.00x (ISBN 0-8046-0995-0, Pub. by Kennikat). Assoc Faculty Pr.

--Life & Works of Gerald Griffin, 8 Vols. LC 78-148792. Repr. of 1843 ed. Set. 135.00 (ISBN 0-404-08860-0); 17.00 ea. AMS Pr.

--The Rivals & Tracy's Ambition. LC 79-8278. Repr. of 1830 ed. 44.50 (ISBN 0-404-61892-8). AMS Pr.

--Wild Geese, Pen Portraits of Famous Irish Exiles. LC 77-2922. 1938. lib. bdg. 20.00 (ISBN 0-8414-4405-6). Folcroft.

Griffin, Gerald, tr. see Gritzbach, Erich.

Griffin, Gerald, tr. see Schebesta, Paul.

Griffin, Gerald R. A Study of Relationships Between Level of College Education & Police Patrolmen's Performance. LC 79-65262. 120p. 1980. 11.95 (ISBN 0-86548-012-5). R & E Pubs.

Griffin, Gerry, ed. see Johnson, Patti L.

Griffin, Glen C. About You...& Other Important People. LC 79-17256. (Illus.). (gr. 5-8). 1979. 5.95 (ISBN 0-87747-752-3). Deseret Bk.

--Not about Birds. LC 79-16653. (gr. 6-8). 1979. 5.95 (ISBN 0-87747-753-1). Deseret Bk.

Griffin, Graeme M. & Tobin, Des. In the Midst of Life: The Australian Response to Death. (Illus.). 177p. (Orig.). 1983. pap. 9.95x (ISBN 0-522-84248-8, Pub. by Melbourne U Pr Australia). Intl Spec Bk.

Griffin, H. J., ed. Ancient Hebrew & Solomonic Building Construction, 1983. 20.00 (ISBN 0-7201-1677-5). Mansell.

--Comparative History of Metrology. 1983. Mansell.

Griffin, Harry L. Attakapas Country: A History of Lafayette Parish. (Illus.). 261p. 1975. 20.00 (ISBN 0-88289-036-0). Pelican.

Griffin, Henry W. Jesus for Children. 132p. 1985. 12.95 (ISBN 0-86683-867-8); pap. 4.95 (ISBN 0-86683-866-X). Winston Pr.

Griffin, Honor M., jt. auth. see Chaffee, Wilber A., Jr.

Griffin, Howard. Conversations with Auden. LC 80-24381. 134p. 1981. 12.95 (ISBN 0-912516-55-0); pap. 5.95 (ISBN 0-912516-56-9). Grey Fox.

Griffin, Howard R., ed. see McGlynn Gaffney, Edward, Jr. & Sorensen, Philip C.

Griffin, I., et al. Basic Oxyacetylene Welding. 4th ed. LC 83-782061. 96p. 1984. pap. text ed. 7.60 (ISBN 0-8273-2137-6); instr's. guide 4.00 (ISBN 0-8273-2138-4). Delmar.

Griffin, I. H., et al. Basic TIG & MIG Welding: GTAW & GMAW. 3rd ed. LC 83-18844. 128p. 1984. pap. text ed. 8.60 (ISBN 0-8273-2129-5); instrs' guide 3.00 (ISBN 0-8273-2130-9). Delmar.

--Pipe Welding Techniques. 2nd ed. LC 76-51121. 1978. pap. text ed. 8.80 (ISBN 0-8273-1256-3). Delmar.

--Pipe Welding Techniques. 128p. 1985. pap. text ed. 14.00t (ISBN 0-8273-2248-8); instr's. guide 4.00 (ISBN 0-8273-2249-6). Delmar.

Griffin, Ivan H., et al. Basic Arc Welding (SMAW) 4th ed. 96p. 1984. pap. text ed. 7.60 (ISBN 0-8273-2131-7); instr's guide 3.00 (ISBN 0-8273-2132-5). Delmar.

Griffin, J. D., et al. Mental Hygiene: A Manual for Teachers. 1978. Repr. of 1940 ed. lib. bdg. 25.00 (ISBN 0-8495-1920-9). Arden Lib.

Griffin, J. F. & Duax, eds. Molecular Structure & Biological Activity. 422p. 1982. 80.00 (ISBN 0-444-00751-2, Biomedical Pr). Elsevier.

Griffin, J. Morgador, jt. auth. see Jeavons, John.

Griffin, J. P., jt. auth. see D'Arcy, P. F.

Griffin, J. P. see D'Arcy, P. F. & Griffin, J. P.

Griffin, James. Manual of Clinical Endocrinology & Metabolism. (PreTest Manuals of Clinical Medicine Ser.). 317p. (Orig.). 1982. 17.95 (ISBN 0-07-024776-5). McGraw.

--Papua New Guinea: A Political History. 1980. pap. text ed. 16.00x (ISBN 0-85859-197-9). Heinemann Ed.

Griffin, James, ed. Papua New Guinea Portraits: The Expatriate Experience. LC 78-52790. (Illus.). 1979. text ed. 18.50 (ISBN 0-7081-0232-8, 0410, Pub. by ANUP Australia); pap. text ed. 13.95 (ISBN 0-7081-1149-1, Pub. by ANUP Australia). Australia N U P.

Griffin, James A. The Priestly Heart. LC 83-26611. 149p. (Orig.). 1984. pap. 6.95 (ISBN 0-8189-0460-7). Alba.

--Sackcloth & Ashes: Liturgical Reflections for Lenten Weekdays. LC 74-44463. 1976. pap. 4.00 (ISBN 0-8189-0336-8). Alba.

Griffin, James B. The Fort Ancient Aspect. (Anthropological Papers: No. 28). (Illus.). 1966. pap. 6.00x (ISBN 0-932206-28-X). U Mich Mus Anthro.

Griffin, James B., jt. auth. see Price, James E.

Griffin, James B., et al. Burial Complexes of the Knight & Norton Mounds in Illinois & Michigan. (Memoirs Ser.: No. 2). (Illus.). 1970. pap. 7.00x (ISBN 0-932206-64-6). U Mich Mus Anthro.

Griffin, James B., jt. auth. see Braun, David P.

Griffin, James E. & Karselis, Terence C. Physical Agents for Physical Therapists. 2nd ed. (Illus.). 480p. 1982. 29.50x (ISBN 0-398-04579-8). C C Thomas.

Griffin, James M. Energy Conservation in the OECD: 1980 to 2000. LC 78-24109. 320p. 1979. prof ref 32.50 (ISBN 0-88410-087-1). Ballinger Pub.

Griffin, James M. & Steele, Henry B. Energy Economics & Policy. 1980. text ed. 21.75 (ISBN 0-12-303950-9). Acad Pr.

Griffin, James M. & Teece, David J., eds. OPEC Behavior & World Oil Prices. 256p. 1982. text ed. 28.50x (ISBN 0-04-338102-2); pap. text ed. 9.95x (ISBN 0-04-338103-0). Allen Unwin.

Griffin, James S. How to Make Money in Commercial Land: A Guide for Investors & Residential Salespersons. Ainsworth, Fay, ed. (Illus., Orig.). 1984. pap. 7.95 (ISBN 0-916682-37-4). Outdoor Empire.

Griffin, Jasper. Homer. (Past Masters Ser.). 1980. pap. 3.95 (ISBN 0-19-287532-9). Oxford U Pr.

--Homer on Life & Death. 1980. pap. 11.95x (ISBN 0-19-814026-6). Oxford U Pr.

Griffin, Jasper, compiled by. Snobs. (Small Oxford Books). (Illus.). 1982. 9.95 (ISBN 0-19-214128-7). Oxford U Pr.

Griffin, Jeff W. Cold Weather Flying. (Modern Aviation Ser.). 1980. 9.95 (ISBN 0-8306-9711-X). TAB Bks.

--Foundations of Flying. (Illus.). 144p. 1982. pap. 9.95 (ISBN 0-8306-2345-0, 2345). TAB Bks.

--Hangar Tales & War Stories: The Humor & Adventure of Flying. (Illus.). 154p. (Orig.). 1984. pap. 9.95 (ISBN 0-8306-2355-8, 2355). TAB Bks.

--How to Become a Flight Engineer. (Illus.). 160p. 1982. pap. 6.95 (ISBN 0-8306-2318-3, 2318). TAB Bks.

--Passing Your Instrument Pilot's Written Exam. (Modern Aviation Ser.). (Illus.). 1979. 7.95 (ISBN 0-8306-9818-3); pap. 4.95 (ISBN 0-8306-2255-1). TAB Bks.

--Pilot's Guide to Weather Forecasting. (Illus.). 144p. 1984. pap. 9.25 (ISBN 0-8306-2331-0, 2331). TAB Bks.

Griffin, Jocelyn. Battle With Desire. (Superromances Ser.). 384p. 1983. pap. 2.95 (ISBN 0-373-70069-5, Pub. by Worldwide). Harlequin Bks.

Griffin, John, intro. by. Narrative of a Voyage to the Spanish Main, in the Ship "Two Friends". The Occupation of Amelia Island, by McGregor. & C.- Sketches of the Province of East Fla; & Anecdotes Illustrative of the Habits & Manners of the Seminole Indians (London 1819) LC 78-9785. (Floridana Facsimile & Reprint Ser.). 1978. 12.00 (ISBN 0-8130-0416-0). U Presses Fla.

Griffin, John, ed. see Bookbinder, Susan R.

Griffin, John A., jt. ed. see Swanson, Ernst W.

Griffin, John H. Black Like Me. 2nd ed. 1977. 14.95 (ISBN 0-395-25102-8). HM.

--Black Like Me. (YA) (RL 8). pap. 2.95 (ISBN 0-451-13735-3, AE2711, Sig). NAL.

--The Hermitage Journals. LC 82-45833. (Illus.). 240p. 1983. pap. 6.95 (ISBN 0-385-18470-0, Im). Doubleday.

--Twelve Photographic Portraits. LC 74-134755. (Keepsake Ser.: Vol. 4). (Illus.). 1973. 8.00 (ISBN 0-87775-036-X); pap. 3.00 (ISBN 0-87775-077-7). Unicorn Pr.

Griffin, John H. & Simon, Yves R. Jacques Maritain: Homage in Words & Pictures. LC 73-85056. (Illus.). 1974. 12.95x (ISBN 0-87343-046-8). Magi Bks.

Griffin, John H., jt. auth. see Merton, Thomas.

Griffin, John I. Statistics Essential for Police Efficiency. (Illus.). 248p. 1972. 12.75x (ISBN 0-398-00734-9). C C Thomas.

--Strikes: A Study in Quantitative Economics. LC 68-58585. (Columbia University. Studies in the Social Sciences: No. 451). Repr. of 1939 ed. 17.50 (ISBN 0-404-51451-0). AMS Pr.

Griffin, John Q. Motorcycles on the Move. LC 75-17435. (Superwheels & Thrill Sports Bks.). (Illus.). 52p. (gr. 5-10). 1976. PLB 8.95 (ISBN 0-8225-0414-6). Lerner Pubns.

Griffin, John R. Binocular Anomalies: Procedures for Vision Therapy. LC 75-18293. (Illus.). 1976. 50.00 (ISBN 0-87873-020-6). Prof Press.

--Binocular Anomalies: Procedures for Vision Therapy. 2nd ed. LC 82-61252. 1982. 50.00 (ISBN 0-686-43308-4). Prof Press.

--Newman: A Bibliography of Secondary Studies. LC 80-68760. 150p. (Orig.). 1980. pap. text ed. 12.00 (ISBN 0-931888-04-2, Chr Coll Pr). Christendom Pubns.

Griffin, John R. & Fatt, Helene. Genetics for the Primary Eye Care Practitioner. LC 83-61488. 1983. 28.00 (ISBN 0-87873-037-0). Prof Press.

Griffin, John R., jt. auth. see Mackie, Peter H.

Griffin, John W. & Bullen, Ripley P., eds. The Safety Harbor Site, Pinellas County, Florida. 1950. pap. 7.00 (ISBN 0-384-19990-9). Johnson Repr.

Griffin, Jonathan. In This Transparent Forest. LC 76-58108. 1977. 12.00 (ISBN 0-940580-03-9); pap. 6.00 (ISBN 0-940580-04-7). Green River.

Griffin, Jonathan, jt. tr. see Caws, Mary Ann.

Griffin, Jonathan, tr. see De Sena, Jorge.

Griffin, Jonathan, tr. see Giono, Jean.

Griffin, Joseph. The Small Canvas: An Introduction to Dreiser's Short Stories. LC 83-49347. 176p. 1985. 24.50 (ISBN 0-8386-3217-3). Fairleigh Dickinson.

Griffin, Joseph A. The Contribution of Belgium to the Catholic Church in America (1523-1857) LC 73-3568. (Catholic University of America. Studies in American Church History: No. 13). Repr. of 1932 ed. 28.00 (ISBN 0-404-57763-6). AMS Pr.

Griffin, Joseph P., ed. Current Issues in International Antitrust. 47p. 1981. pap. 5.00 (ISBN 0-935328-08-4). Intl Law Inst.

--The Export Trading Company Act of 1982. 55p. 1982. 10.00 (ISBN 0-318-03976-1). Intl Law Inst.

Griffin, Joyanne. Love, Vanity & the Mirage. 32p. 1984. pap. 5.50 (ISBN 0-682-40166-8). Exposition Pr FL.

Griffin, Kathryn. Teaching Teens the Truth. LC 78-58567. 1978. pap. 4.95 (ISBN 0-8054-3425-9, 4234-25). Broadman.

Griffin, Keith. International Inequality & National Poverty. LC 78-7002. 191p. 1978. text ed. 39.50x (ISBN 0-8419-0394-8). Holmes & Meier.

--Land Concentration & Rural Poverty. LC 75-34149. 300p. 1976. 29.50x (ISBN 0-8419-0246-1). Holmes & Meier.

--Land Concentration & Rural Poverty. 2nd ed. LC 80-13808. 300p. 1981. 32.50x (ISBN 0-8419-0745-5); pap. text ed. 15.50x (ISBN 0-8419-0526-6). Holmes & Meier.

Griffin, Keith & James, Jeffrey. The Transition to Egalitarian Development. 1981. 22.50 (ISBN 0-312-81465-8). St Martin.

Griffin, Keith & Saith, Ashwani. Growth & Equality in Rural China. International Labour Office, ed. (Asian Employment Programme (ARTEP) Ser.). 166p. (Orig.). 1981. 15.00 (ISBN 92-2-102427-X); pap. 10.00 (ISBN 92-2-102422-9). Intl Labour Office.

Griffin, Keith, ed. Institutional Reform & Economic Development in the Chinese Countryside. LC 84-5335. 350p. 1984. 37.50 (ISBN 0-87332-285-1); pap. 18.95 (ISBN 0-87332-286-X). M E Sharpe.

Griffin, Keith & Kahn, Azizur R., eds. Growth & Inequality in Pakistan. LC 70-190776. 278p. 1972. 26.00 (ISBN 0-312-35175-5). St Martin.

Griffin, Kelley, jt. auth. see Nader, Ralph.

Griffin, LaDean. Cancer & the Parasite. 2.95 (ISBN 0-89557-009-2). Bi World Indus.

--Escape the Drug Scene. pap. 3.95 (ISBN 0-89036-141-X). Hawkes Pub Inc.

--Eyes: Windows of the Body & Soul. 9.95 (ISBN 0-89557-007-6). Bi World Indus.

--Health in the Space Age. pap. 19.95 (ISBN 0-89557-068-8). Bi World Indus.

--Herbs to the Rescue. 2.95 (ISBN 0-89557-003-3). Bi World Indus.

--Herbs to the Rescue, Vol. II. pap. 2.95 (ISBN 0-89557-058-0). Bi World Indus.

--Hyper & Hypo-Glycemia. 2.95 (ISBN 0-89557-008-4). Bi World Indus.

--Iridology Chart. pap. write for info. (ISBN 0-89557-072-6). Bi World Indus.

--Is Any Sick Among You. 8.95 (ISBN 0-89557-001-7). Bi World Indus.

--Is Any Sick Among You? 8.95x (ISBN 0-89557-001-7). Cancer Control Soc.

--No Side Effects: Return to Herbal Medicine. 7.95x (ISBN 0-89036-073-1). Cancer Control Soc.

--Please Dr., I'd Rather Do It Myself with Herbs. 1979. pap. 3.95 (ISBN 0-89036-058-8). Hawkes Pub Inc.

--Please Dr., I'd Rather Do It Myself with Vitamins & Minerals. 1979. pap. 3.95 (ISBN 0-89036-120-7). Hawkes Pub Inc.

--The Return to Herbal Medicine. 1979. pap. 6.95 (ISBN 0-89036-073-1). Hawkes Pub Inc.

Griffin, Lepel H. The Great Republic. LC 73-13134. (Foreign Travelers in America, 1810-1935 Ser.). 202p. 1974. Repr. 14.00x (ISBN 0-405-05456-4). Ayer Co Pubs.

Griffin, Lib U. The Pains & Pleasures of Parenthood. 1985. pap. 5.95 (ISBN 0-8054-5915-4). Broadman.

Griffin, Martin I. Frank R. Stockton: A Critical Biography. LC 65-18606. 1965. Repr. of 1939 ed. 24.50x (ISBN 0-8046-0185-2, Pub. by Kennikat). Assoc Faculty Pr.

--Story of Commodore John Barry: Father of the American Navy. 1977. lib. bdg. 59.95 (ISBN 0-8490-2678-4). Gordon Pr.

Griffin, Marvin A., et al. Computer Science Using BASIC. 1978. 13.95 (ISBN 0-8403-1965-7, 40196502). Kendall-Hunt.

Griffin, Marvin I. General Stephen Moylan, Muster-Master General, Secretary & Aide-De-Camp to General Washington. 1972. Repr. of 1909 ed. 18.50x (ISBN 0-8422-8062-6). Irvington.

Griffin, Merv. Merv: An Autobiography. Barsocchini, Peter, ed. 1981. pap. 2.95 (ISBN 0-671-43141-2). PB.

Griffin, Merv & Barsocchini, Peter. From Where I Sit: Merv Griffin's Book of People. LC 82-72054. (Illus.). 1982. 14.95 (ISBN 0-87795-416-X). Arbor Hse.

--From Where I Sit: Merv Griffin's Book of People. (Illus.). 256p. 1983. pap. 3.50 (ISBN 0-523-42086-2). Pinnacle Bks.

Griffin, Michael D., tr. from Span. Lingering with my Lord: Post-Communion Experiences of St. Teresa of Avila. LC 84-18590. Orig. Title: Obras Completas de Teresa de Jesus Doctora de la Iglesia. 79p. 1985. pap. 3.95 (ISBN 0-317-19366-X). Alba.

Griffin, Michael M. Motorcycles: From the Inside Out (& How to Keep Them Right Side up) (Illus.). 1978. ref. ed. 18.95 (ISBN 0-13-604041-1); pap. text ed. 9.95 (ISBN 0-13-604033-0). P-H.

Griffin, Miriam. Nero: The End of a Dynasty. LC 85-51761. (Illus.). 328p. 1985. 25.00x (ISBN 0-300-03285-4). Yale U Pr.

Griffin, Miriam D. Seneca: A Philosopher in Politics. 1976. 75.00x (ISBN 0-19-814365-6). Oxford U Pr.

Griffin, N. B., ed. see Dummer, Geoffrey W.

Griffin, Nathanial E., ed. see Delle Colonne, G.

Griffin, Nathaniel E., tr. see Boccaccio, Giovanni.

Griffin, Neil. The Bluegrass Banjo Method. 1976. pap. 5.95 (ISBN 0-89328-005-4). Lorenz Pr.

Griffin, Neil, jt. auth. see Flint, Tommy.

Griffin, Nicholas. Relative Identity. (Clarendon Library of Logic & Philosophy Ser.). 1977. 32.50x (ISBN 0-19-824409-6). Oxford U Pr.

Griffin, O. M., ed. Ocean Thermal Energy Conversion: OED, Vol. 5. 1978. 18.00 (ISBN 0-685-66808-8, G00139). ASME.

Griffin, O. M. & Gianotti, J. G., eds. Ocean Engineering for OTEC. (OED: Vol. 9). 96p. 1980. 14.00 (ISBN 0-317-33589-8, 100129); members 7.00 (ISBN 0-317-33590-1). ASME.

Griffin, Orwin B. Evolution of the Connecticut State School System with Special Reference to the Emergence of the High School. LC 75-176821. (Columbia University. Teachers College. Contributions to Education: No. 293). Repr. of 1928 ed. 22.50 (ISBN 0-404-55293-5). AMS Pr.

Griffin, P., jt. auth. see Richardson, J.

Griffin, P., ed. see Barrie, J. M.

Griffin, P. Bion, jt. ed. see Tuggle, H. David.

Griffin, Patricia. The Chinese Communist Treatment of Counter-Revolutionaries, 1924-1949. LC 75-30193. (Studies in East Asian Law). 312p. 1976. text ed. 32.00 (ISBN 0-691-09232-X). Princeton U Pr.

Griffin, Patricia, jt. auth. see Richardson, John.

Griffin, Paul A. Usefulness to Investors & Creditors of Information Provided by Financial Reporting: A Review of Empirical Accounting Research. LC 82-71093. (The Financial Accounting Standards Board Research Report). (Illus.). 232p. (Orig.). 1982. pap. 20.00 (ISBN 0-910065-15-2). Finan Acct.

Griffin, Paul R. Black Theology As the Foundation of Three Methodist Colleges: The Educational Views & Labors of Daniel Payne, Joseph Price, Isaac Lane. LC 84-13070. 148p. (Orig.). 1984. lib. bdg. 18.75 (ISBN 0-8191-4160-7); pap. text ed. 9.25 (ISBN 0-8191-4161-5). U Pr of Amer.

Griffin, Peg, ed. see Dieterich, T., et al.

Griffin, Peter. Along with Youth: Hemingway, the Early Years. (Illus.). 275p. 1985. 17.95 (ISBN 0-19-503680-8). Oxford U Pr.

Griffin, Richard F., jt. auth. see Patterson, Walter C.

Griffin, Ricky W. Management. LC 83-80786. 704p. 1983. text ed. 29.95 (ISBN 0-395-34280-5); instr's manual 3.50 (ISBN 0-395-34281-3); study guide 10.95 (ISBN 0-395-34282-1); practicing management (a case bk) 13.95 (ISBN 0-395-34285-6); instr's manual 2.00 (ISBN 0-395-34286-4); manager (a simulation package) 11.95 (ISBN 0-395-34287-2); instr's manual computerized 2.00 (ISBN 0-395-34288-0); test bank 2.50 (ISBN 0-395-34806-4); write for ancellaries info. HM.

--Task Design: An Integrative Approach. (The Scott, Foresman Series in Management & Organizations). 1982. pap. text ed. 13.65x (ISBN 0-673-16544-2). Scott F.

Griffin, Robert. Clement Marot & the Inflections of Poetic Voice. LC 73-84394. 1976. 34.50x (ISBN 0-520-02586-5). U of Cal Pr.

--I Never Said I Didn't Love You. LC 76-24442. (Emmuas Book Ser.). 128p. 1977. pap. 1.95 (ISBN 0-8091-1989-7). Paulist Pr.

--John Webster: Politics & Tragedy. (Salzburg Studies in English Literature, Jacobean Drama Studies: No. 12). 179p. 1972. pap. text ed. 25.50x (ISBN 0-391-01394-7). Humanities.

Griffin, Robert, jt. auth. see Thaine, Marina.

Griffin, Robert F. The Continuing Conversation. 200p. (Orig.). 1985. pap. 7.50 (ISBN 0-87973-828-6, 828). Our Sunday Visitor.

Griffin, Roger C., jt. auth. see Sacharow, Stanley.

Griffin, Roger C., Jr., jt. auth. see Sacharow, Stanley.

Griffin, Roger C., Jr., et al. Principles of Package Development. 2nd ed. (Illus.). 1985. text ed. 47.50 (ISBN 0-87055-465-4). AVI.

Griffin, Russell M. The Timeservers. 240p. 1985. pap. 3.50 (ISBN 0-380-89525-0). Avon.

Griffin, Sam. West Virginia Central & Pittsburg Railway. 1981. Repr. of 1899 ed. 5.00 (ISBN 0-87012-418-8). McClain.

Griffin, Sid. Gram Parsons: A Music Biography. Delgatto, John, et al, eds. (Illus.). 200p. (Orig.). 1985. 23.95 (ISBN 0-916003-00-0); pap. 10.95 (ISBN 0-916003-01-9). Sierra Bks.

Griffin, Sidney. Anthology: One Man's Experience with God & Nature. 1985. 5.75 (ISBN 0-8062-2479-7). Carlton.

Griffin, Steve. Children's Guitar Hymnal. 32p. 1978. wkbk 1.95 (ISBN 0-89228-052-2). Impact Bks MO.

Griffin, Steven. Ice Fishing: Methods & Magic. (Illus.). 160p. (Orig.). 1985. pap. 9.95 (ISBN 0-934802-25-4). ICS Bks.

Griffin, Stuart. Japanese Food & Cooking. LC 55-10617. 1955. pap. 5.25 (ISBN 0-8048-0299-8). C E Tuttle.

Griffin, Sue, jt. auth. see Shoden, Rebecca.

Griffin, Susan. Made from This Earth: An Anthology of Writings. LC 82-48229. 288p. 1983. pap. 6.68i (ISBN 0-06-090995-1, CN 995, CN). Har-Row.

--Woman & Nature: The Roaring Inside Her. LC 77-11812. 1979. pap. 6.25i (ISBN 0-06-090744-4, CN 744, CN). Har-Row.

Griffin, Susan, jt. auth. see Miner, Valerie.

Griffin, Suzanne. Follow Me to San Francisco. (Illus.). 128p. (Orig.). (gr. 9-12). 1981. pap. text ed. 6.95 (ISBN 0-582-79794-2); tchr's manual 3.50x (ISBN 0-582-79795-0); video cassette-Betamax 380.00x (ISBN 0-582-79792-6); video cassette-Sony u-matic 395.00 (ISBN 0-582-79793-4); video cassette-VHS 380.00 (ISBN 0-582-79791-8). Longman.

Griffin, Suzanne M. & Dennis, John. Reflections: A Reader for Intermediate Level ESL Students. LC 78-26469. 1979. pap. text ed. 8.95 (ISBN 0-88377-129-2). Newbury Hse.

Griffin, Ted. Namu: Quest for the Killer Whale. 1982. 14.95 (ISBN 0-943482-00-3). Gryphon West Pubs.

Griffin, Ted, ed. see Stafford, Bill.

Griffin, Thomas. A Practical Guide for Beginning Painters. (Art & Design Ser.). (Illus.). 184p. 1981. 19.95 (ISBN 0-13-689513-1, Spec); pap. 11.95 (ISBN 0-13-689505-0). P-H.

Griffin, Thomas K. Pelican Guide to New Orleans. 6th ed. LC 74-182889. (Pelican Guide Ser.). (Illus.). 160p. 1980. pap. 4.95 (ISBN 0-88289-010-7). Pelican.

Griffin, Thomas M. Paying the Price. (Orig.). 1985. pap. 1.75 (ISBN 0-89486-290-1). Hazelden.

Griffin, Tom, jt. auth. see Svendsen, Roger.

Griffin, W. E. The Berets. (Brotherhood of War Ser.: Bk. V). 400p. 1985. pap. 3.50 (ISBN 0-515-07909-X). Jove Pubns.

--Brotherhood of War, Bk. I: The Lieutenants. 432p. 1982. pap. 3.50 (ISBN 0-515-05643-X). Jove Pubns.

--Brotherhood of War, Bk. II: The Captains. 432p. 1982. pap. 3.50 (ISBN 0-515-05644-8). Jove Pubns.

--Brotherhood of War, Bk. III: The Majors. 384p. 1983. pap. 3.50 (ISBN 0-515-05645-6). Jove Pubns.

--Brotherhood of War, Bk. IV: The Colonels. 496p. 1983. pap. 3.50 (ISBN 0-515-07351-2). Jove Pubns.

--The Captains. (Brotherhood of War Ser.: No. II). 416p. 1985. pap. 3.50 (ISBN 0-515-08150-7). Jove Pubns.

--The Colonels. 496p. 1984. pap. 3.50 (ISBN 0-515-07698-8, Jove). Berkley Pub.

--The Colonels. (Brotherhood of War Ser.: Bk. IV). 480p. 1984. pap. 3.95 (ISBN 0-515-08302-X). Jove Pubns.

--The Lieutenants. (Brotherhood of War Ser.: No. I). 416p. 1985. pap. 3.95 (ISBN 0-515-08424-7). Jove Pubns.

--The Majors. (Brotherhood of War Ser.: No. III). 384p. 1984. pap. 3.95 (ISBN 0-515-08303-8). Jove Pubns.

Griffin, W. R. Food Service: Health, Sanitation & Safety. (Illus.). lab. manual 26.00 (ISBN 0-9601054-4-1). Cleaning Consultant.

Griffin, Walter. Blood Lines. 1973. 1.00 (ISBN 0-685-67930-6). Windless Orchard.

--How to Publish Your Poems. 120p. (Orig.). 1984. pap. write for info (ISBN 0-87397-277-5). Strode.

--Port Authority. (Illus.). 1976. pap. 3.95 (ISBN 0-917838-00-9). Brevity.

Griffin, William, ed. Teaching Effective Writing in All Disciplines. LC 81-48585. (Teaching & Learning Ser.: No. 12). 1982. 8.95x (ISBN 0-87589-926-9). Jossey-Bass.

Griffin, William D. A Portrait of the Irish in America. (Illus.). 272p. 1982. pap. 14.95 (ISBN 0-684-17856-7, ScribT). Scribner.

Griffin, William D., ed. & compiled by. Ireland Six Thousand B.C. to Nineteen Seventy-Two: A Chronology & Fact Book. LC 73-12694. (World Chronology Ser.). 154p. 1973. lib. bdg. 8.50x (ISBN 0-379-16302-0). Oceana.

--The Irish in America 550-1972: Chronology & Factbook. LC 73-3405. (Ethnic Chronology Ser.: No. 10). 154p. 1973. 8.50 (ISBN 0-379-00501-8). Oceana.

Griffin, William R. Instructors Guide to Comprehensive Custodial Training Programs. 1977. tchr's. ed 65.00 (ISBN 0-9601054-2-5). Cleaning Consul.

--Supervisors' Guide to Successful Training. (Illus.). 1977. pap. text ed. 21.00 (ISBN 0-9601054-3-3). Cleaning Consul.

Griffin, Wm. R. How to Start & Operate a Successful Service Business. (Illus.). 1980. 24.95x (ISBN 0-9601054-5-X). Cleaning Consul.

Griffing, Arnold. On Sensations from Pressure & Impact. Bd. with Association. Calkins, Mary W. Repr. of 1896 ed; The Mental Development of a Child. Moore, Kathleen C. Repr. of 1896 ed; A Study of Kant's Psychology. Buchner, Edward F. Repr. of 1897 ed. (Psychology Monographs General & Applied: Vol. 1). Repr. of 1895 ed. 45.00 (ISBN 0-317-15444-3). Kraus Repr.

Griffin-King, J. Indoor Gardening. (Illus.). (gr. 3-5). 1969. 2.50 (ISBN 0-7214-0232-1). Merry Thoughts.

Griffinn, S. G. & Whitcomb, M. A. A History of the Town of Keene, NH, Seventeen Thirty-Two to Nineteen Hundred & Four. (Illus.). 792p. (Orig.). 1980. Repr. of 1904 ed. 55.00 (ISBN 0-917890-21-3). Heritage Bk.

Griffis, Nixon, ed. Mariner's Guide to Oceanography. LC 84-10869. (Illus.). 236p. 1984. 19.95 (ISBN 0-688-03976-6, Hearst Marine Bk). Morrow.

Griffis, W. E. China's Story in Myth, Legend, Art & Annals. 1980. lib. bdg. 64.95 (ISBN 0-8490-3145-1). Gordon Pr.

Griffis, William E. Corea, the Hermit Nation. rev. ed. 9th ed., enl ed. LC 74-158615. Repr. of 1911 ed. 37.50 (ISBN 0-404-02916-7). AMS Pr.

--Japanese Fairy World. LC 78-67714. (The Folktale). (Illus.). Repr. of 1887 ed. 28.00 (ISBN 0-404-16091-3). AMS Pr.

--Religions of Japan: From the Dawn of History to the Era of Meiji. facsimile ed. LC 70-37469. (Essay Index Reprint Ser). Repr. of 1895 ed. 21.00 (ISBN 0-8369-2550-5). Ayer Co Pubs.

--Townsend Harris: First American Envoy in Japan. facsimile ed. LC 74-175698. (Select Bibliographies Reprint Ser). Repr. of 1895 ed. 21.00 (ISBN 0-8369-6613-9). Ayer Co Pubs.

Griffism, William E. The Romance of American Colonization: How the Foundation Stones of Our History Were Laid. 1898. Repr. 15.00 (ISBN 0-8482-4218-1). Norwood Edns.

Griffiss, James, ed. see Edwards, O. C., et al.

Griffiss, James E. Church, Ministry & Unity: A Divine Commission. 118p. 1984. 24.95x (ISBN 0-631-13185-X); pap. 8.95x (ISBN 0-631-13227-9). Basil Blackwell.

--A Silent Path to God. LC 79-8903. 112p. 1980. pap. 4.95 (ISBN 0-8006-1384-8, 1-1384). Fortress.

Griffith. Forward into Battle: Fighting Tactics from Waterloo to Vietnam. 1982. 20.00 (ISBN 0-907319-01-7). Hippocrene Bks.

Griffith, Anna. Balance: A Modern Christian Challenge. pap. 4.95 (ISBN 0-89137-425-6). Quality Pubns.

Griffith, Anna M. From Paul to Philippi with Love. pap. 4.95 (ISBN 0-89137-434-5). Quality Pubns.

Griffith, B. Barret. Investing is Adventure. 1965. Repr. of 1949 ed. flexible cover 6.00 (ISBN 0-87034-012-3). Fraser Pub Co.

Griffith, B. C., et al, eds. Monologues & Novelties. LC 70-38599. (Granger Index Reprint Ser.). Repr. of 1896 ed. 19.00 (ISBN 0-8369-6331-8). Ayer Co Pubs.

Griffith, Beatrice. American Me. LC 72-14087. (Illus.). 341p. 1973. Repr. of 1948 ed. lib. bdg. 21.00x (ISBN 0-8371-6756-6, GRAN). Greenwood.

Griffith, Belver C., ed. Key Papers in Information Science. LC 79-24288. (American Society for Information Sciences Ser.). 439p. 1980. 25.00x (ISBN 0-914236-50-4, 341-BW). Knowledge Indus.

Griffith, Ben, et al. Banking on Sickness: The Politics of Private Health Care. 180p. 1984. 16.50x (ISBN 0-85315-597-6, Pub. by Salem Hse Ltd). Merrimack Pub Cir.

Griffith, Benjamin W., jt. auth. see Walker, Kenneth E.

Griffith, Benjamin W., Jr., ed. see Beaumont, Francis & Fletcher, John.

Griffith, Benjamin W., Jr., ed. see Gay, John.

Griffith, Bill. Are We Having Fun Yet? Zippy the Pinhead's 29-Day Guide to Random Activities & Arbitrary Donuts. (Illus.). 128p. 1985. pap. 6.95 (ISBN 0-525-48184-2). Dutton.

--Time For Frankie Coolin. 1982. 13.50 (ISBN 0-394-52123-4). Random.

--Zippy: Nation of Pinheads. LC 82-72747. (Illus.). 96p. (Orig.). 1982. pap. 4.95 (ISBN 0-915904-71-3). And-Or Pr.

Griffith, Bob & Griffith, Nancy. Blue Water: A Guide to Self-Reliant Sailboat Cruising. LC 79-10264. (Illus.). 267p. 1979. 17.95 (ISBN 0-914814-19-2). Sail Bks.

Griffith, Bonnie. The Tree House Gang: Puppet Plays for Children. 48p. (Orig.). (gr. k-6). 1983. pap. 3.50 (ISBN 0-87239-648-7, 3352). Standard Pub.

Griffith, Carol F., ed. Christianity & Politics: Catholic & Protestant Perspectives. LC 81-19412. 124p. 1981. pap. 6.00 (ISBN 0-89633-050-8). Ethics & Public Policy.

Griffith, Celeste, jt. auth. see Timmerman, Maurine.

Griffith, Charles A., jt. auth. see Edginton, Christopher.

Griffith, Clark. The Long Shadow: Emily Dickinson's Tragic Poetry. LC 63-16234. pap. 79.50 (ISBN 0-317-09665-6, 2000988). Bks Demand UMI.

Griffith, Clelye L. Legal Problem Solver. rev. ed. 100p. 1980. 14.50 (ISBN 0-318-15845-0, MG410). Natl Restaurant Assn.

Griffith, Clifford, ed. see Fibonacci, Leonardo & Elliott, Ralph N.

Griffith, Coleman R. Psychology Applied to Teaching & Learning. 650p. 1981. Repr. of 1939 ed. lib. bdg. 40.00 (ISBN 0-89984-247-X). Century Bookbindery.

Griffith, Connie G., ed. Inventory of the Louisiana Historical Association Collection on Deposit in the Howard-Tilton Memorial Library, Tulane University, New Orleans, Louisiana. 201p. 1983. pap. 10.00 (ISBN 0-318-01103-4). LA Hist Assn.

Griffith, Cyril E. The African Dream: Martin R. Delany & the Emergence of Pan-African Thought. LC 74-20559. 176p. 1975. 18.75x (ISBN 0-271-01181-5). Pa St U Pr.

Griffith, Daniel A. Dynamical Spatial Models. 451p. 1981. 49.50 (ISBN 90-286-2721-9). Sijthoff & Noordhoff.

--Evolving Geographical Structures. 1983. lib. bdg. 65.00 (ISBN 90-2472-858-4, Pub. by Martinus Nijhoff Netherlands). Kluwer Academic.

Griffith, Donald M. Charlie Romo's Flying Field. 243p. 1980. 10.00 (ISBN 0-931980-03-8); pap. 6.00 (ISBN 0-931980-04-6). Iroquois Hse.

Griffith, Dotty. Wild about Chili. (Wild about Ser.). (Illus.). 96p. 1985. pap. 5.95 (ISBN 0-8120-3498-8). Barron.

Griffith, Dove. Life's Roadmap. (Illus.). 184p. (Orig.). 1985. pap. 6.95 (ISBN 0-89769-092-3, Dist. by Caroline Hse). Pine Mntn.

Griffith, Dudley. Origin of the Griselda Story. LC 73-9823. 1931. lib. bdg. 15.00 (ISBN 0-8414-2042-4). Folcroft.

--The Origin of the Griselda Story. 1973. Repr. of 1931 ed. 12.50 (ISBN 0-8274-0195-7). R West.

Griffith, Earle G. The Pastor As God's Minister. LC 76-50694. 1978. 7.95 (ISBN 0-87227-054-8). Reg Baptist.

Griffith, Edward J. & Grayson, Martin, eds. Topics in Phosphorus Chemistry, Vol. 8. LC 64-17051. 664p. 1976. 45.00 (ISBN 0-471-32789-1). Krieger.

--Topics in Phosphorus Chemistry, Vol. 9. LC 64-17051. 516p. 1977. 49.00 (ISBN 0-471-32782-4). Krieger.

Griffith, Edward J., jt. ed. see Grayson, Martin.

Griffith, Edward J., et al, eds. Environmental Phosphorus Handbook. LC 72-11574. 718p. 1973. 42.50 (ISBN 0-471-32779-4, Pub. by Wiley). Krieger.

Griffith, Elisabeth. In Her Own Right: The Life of Elizabeth Cady Stanton. LC 83-25120. (Illus.). 1984. 19.95 (ISBN 0-19-503440-6). Oxford U Pr.

Griffith, Elizabeth. Morality of Shakespeare's Drama. LC 78-130241. (Illus.). Repr. of 1775 ed. 24.50 (ISBN 0-404-02917-5). AMS Pr.

--Morality of Shakespeare's Drama Illustrated. 528p. 1971. Repr. of 1775 ed. 35.00x (ISBN 0-7146-2533-7, F Cass Co). Biblio Dist.

--Morality of Shakespeare's Drama Illustrated. LC 70-96358. Repr. of 1775 ed. lib. bdg. 37.50x (ISBN 0-678-05125-9). Kelley.

Griffith, Elmer C. The Rise & Development of the Gerrymander. LC 73-19149. (Politics & People Ser.). 124p. 1974. Repr. 11.00x (ISBN 0-405-05872-1). Ayer Co Pubs.

Griffith, Ernest S. The American Presidency: The Dilemmas of Shared Power & Divided Government. LC 76-4599. 1976. 27.50x (ISBN 0-8147-2961-4). NYU Pr.

--The American System of Government. 3rd ed. 1976. 13.95x (ISBN 0-416-70400-X, NO.2738). Methuen Inc.

--The American System of Government. 6th ed. LC 83-8226. 224p. 1984. 23.00 (ISBN 0-416-35090-9, NO. 3963); pap. 9.95 (ISBN 0-416-35100-X, NO. 3962). Methuen Inc.

--History of American City Government. LC 72-3615. (Law, Politics & History Ser.). 1972. Repr. of 1938 ed. lib. bdg. 55.00 (ISBN 0-306-70526-5). Da Capo.

--A History of American City Government: The Conspicuous Failure, 1870-1900. LC 82-23872. 320p. 1983. lib. bdg. 30.00 (ISBN 0-8191-3001-X, Co-pub. by Natl Municipal League); pap. text ed. 16.50 (ISBN 0-8191-3002-8). U Pr of Amer.

--A History of American City Government: The Progressive Years & Their Aftermath, 1900-1920. 364p. 1983. lib. bdg. 31.00 (ISBN 0-8191-3003-6, Co-pub. by Natl Municipal League); pap. text ed. 17.75 (ISBN 0-8191-3004-4). U Pr of Amer.

Griffith, Ernest S. & Adrian, Charles R. A History of American City Government: The Formation of Traditions, 1775-1870. LC 82-23877. 240p. 1983. lib. bdg. 28.00 (ISBN 0-8191-2999-2, Co-pub. by Natl Municipal League); pap. text ed. 15.25 (ISBN 0-8191-3000-1). U Pr of Amer.
Griffith, Ernest S. & Valeo, Francis R. Congress: Its Contemporary Role. 5th ed. LC 74-21660. (James Stokes Lectureship on Politics). 1975. 27.50x (ISBN 0-8147-8779-7). NYU Pr.
Griffith, Ernest S., ed. Research in Political Science. LC 77-86021. (Essay & General Literature Index Reprint Ser). 1969. Repr. of 1948 ed. 19.50x (ISBN 0-8046-0563-7, Pub. by Kennikat). Assoc Faculty Pr.
Griffith, F. L. & Thompson, Herbert, eds. The Leyden Papyrus: An Egyptian Magical Book. LC 73-90639. 224p. 1974. pap. 4.50 (ISBN 0-486-22994-7). Dover.
Griffith, Fitzclarence. Sparky the Rascal. 1984. 4.95 (ISBN 0-533-06143-1). Vantage.
Griffith, Francis. Handbook for the Observation of Teaching & Learning. LC 72-96794. 350p. 1973. text ed. 14.85 (ISBN 0-87812-051-3). Pendell Pub.
--Pocket Guide to Correct Spelling. 256p. (gr. 6-12). 1982. pap. 2.95 (ISBN 0-8120-2620-9). Barron.
Griffith, Francis, jt. auth. see Mersand, Joseph.
Griffith, Frank, jt. auth. see Griffith, Rubye.
Griffith, G. Artistry in Singing: Lieder for the American Singer. (Illus.). 1966. pap. 12.50 (ISBN 0-685-11993-9). Heinman.
Griffith, G. T. The Mercenaries of the Hellenistic World. pap. 10.00 (ISBN 0-89005-085-6). Ares.
Griffith, G. T., jt. auth. see Hammond, N. G. L.
Griffith, George. Angel of the Revolution. LC 73-13254. (Classics of Science Fiction Ser.). (Illus.). 410p. 1973. 13.95 (ISBN 0-88355-109-8); pap. 10.00 (ISBN 0-88355-138-1). Hyperion Conn.
--A Honeymoon in Space. LC 74-15978. (Science Fiction). (Illus.). 302p. 1975. Repr. 23.50x (ISBN 0-405-06295-8). Ayer Co Pubs.
--The Mummy & Miss Nitocris: A Phantasy of the Fourth Dimension. Reginald, R. & Menville, Douglas, eds. LC 75-46273. (Supernatural & Occult Fiction Ser.). 1976. Repr. of 1906 ed. lib. bdg. 24.50x (ISBN 0-405-08131-6). Ayer Co Pubs.
--Olga Romanoff. LC 73-13255. (Classics of Science Fiction Ser). 390p. 1973. 13.50 (ISBN 0-88355-110-1); pap. 4.25 (ISBN 0-88355-139-X). Hyperion Conn.
--The Romance of Golden Star. Reginald, R. & Melville, Douglas, eds. LC 77-84234. (Lost Race & Adult Fantasy Ser.). (Illus.). 1978. Repr. of 1897 ed. lib. bdg. 24.50x (ISBN 0-405-10982-2). Ayer Co Pubs.
Griffith, Guy T. The Mercenaries of the Hellenistic World. LC 75-41123. Repr. of 1935 ed. 19.50 (ISBN 0-404-14667-8). AMS Pr.
Griffith, Gwilym O. Interpreters of Reality: Lao-Tse, Heraclitus & the Christian Faith. 1977. lib. bdg. 59.95 (ISBN 0-8490-2065-4). Gordon Pr.
--John Bunyan. 1973. Repr. of 1927 ed. lib. bdg. 20.00 (ISBN 0-8414-4623-7). Folcroft.
Griffith, H. Winter. Complete Guide to Prescription & Non-Prescription Drugs. LC 83-82397. 888p. 1983. H P Bks.
--Complete Guide to Symptoms, Illness & Surgery. 896p. 1985. pap. 12.95 (ISBN 0-89586-334-0). H P Bks.
--Instructions for Patients. 3rd ed. 395p. 1982. pap. 39.50 (ISBN 0-7216-4286-1). Saunders.
Griffith, H. Winter & Mofenson, Howard. Pediatrics for Parents: A Guide to Child Health. (Mosby Medical Library). 1983. pap. 9.95 (ISBN 0-452-25459-0, Plume). NAL.
Griffith, H. Winter, et al. Instructions for Obstetric & Gynecologic Patients. (Illus.). 235p. 1984. pap. 29.95 (ISBN 0-7216-1230-X). Saunders.
--Information & Instructions for Pediatric Patients. LC 80-51712. 320p. 1980. 35.00 (ISBN 0-938372-00-9). Winter Pub Co.
Griffith, Harry C. The Ways of God: Paths into the New Testament. 128p. (Orig.). pap. cancelled (ISBN 0-8164-2629-5, Pub. by Seabury). Winston Pr.
Griffith, Helen. Dauntless in Mississippi: The Life of Sarah A. Dickey. LC 75-35885. 1976. Repr. of 1966 ed. 12.95 (ISBN 0-89201-006-1). Zenger Pub.
Griffith, Helen V. Alex & the Cat. LC 81-11608. (Read-Alone Bks.). (Illus.). 64p. (gr. 1-3). 1982. 11.75 (ISBN 0-688-00420-2); PLB 11.88 (ISBN 0-688-00421-0). Greenwillow.
--Alex Remembers. LC 82-11913. (Illus.). 32p. (gr. k-3). 1983. 10.25 (ISBN 0-688-01800-9); PLB 10.88 (ISBN 0-688-01801-7). Greenwillow.
--Foxy. LC 83-16392. 144p. (gr. 5-9). 1984. reinforced 9.25 (ISBN 0-688-02567-6). Greenwillow.
--Mine Will, Said John. LC 79-27886. (Illus.). 32p. (ps). 1980. PLB 11.88 (ISBN 0-688-84267-4). Greenwillow.
--More Alex & the Cat. LC 83-1411. (Illus.). 56p. (gr. 1-3). 1983. 13.00 (ISBN 0-688-02292-8); PLB 12.88 (ISBN 0-688-02293-6). Greenwillow.
--Nata. LC 85-727. (Illus.). 24p. (gr. k-3). 1985. 11.75 (ISBN 0-688-04976-1); lib. bdg. 11.88 (ISBN 0-688-04977-X). Greenwillow.
Griffith, J. A. The Politics of the Judiciary. LC 77-88391. (Political Issues of Modern Britain Ser.). 1977. text ed. 20.00x (ISBN 0-391-00551-0). Humanities.
Griffith, J. A., jt. auth. see Hartley, T. C.
Griffith, J. Neal. Linton Park: American Primitive. 125p. (Orig.). 1982. pap. 5.00 (ISBN 0-935648-11-9). Halldin Pub.
Griffith, J. S. Mathematical Neurobiology: An Introduction to the Mathematics of the Nervous System. 162p. 1971. 33.00 (ISBN 0-12-303050-1). Acad Pr.
Griffith, Jack D. Electron Microscopy in Biology, Vol. 1. (Electron Microscopy in Biology Ser.). 296p. 1981. 69.95x (ISBN 0-471-05525-5, Pub. by Wiley-Interscience). Wiley.
Griffith, Jack D., ed. Electron Microscopy in Biology, Vol. 2. (Electron Microscopy in Biology Ser.). 349p. 1982. text ed. 97.50x (ISBN 0-471-05526-3). Wiley.
Griffith, Jack S. Laboratory Manual for Man & His Environment. 128p. 1983. pap. 9.95 (ISBN 0-8403-3146-0). Kendall-Hunt.
Griffith, Jane & Powers, Robert L. An Adlerian Lexicon: Fifty-Nine Terms Associated with the Individual Psychology of Alfred Alder. LC 84-11100. 73p. (Orig.). 1984. pap. text ed. 10.00 (ISBN 0-918287-00-6). AIAS.
Griffith, Jane, jt. auth. see Mullen, Edwin.
Griffith, Janet W. & Christensen, Paula J. Nursing Process: Application of Theories, Frameworks & Models. LC 81-14191. (Illus.). 301p. 1982. pap. text ed. 14.95 (ISBN 0-8016-1984-X). Mosby.
Griffith, Jerry. Persons with Hearing Loss. (Illus.). 240p. 1969. 24.50x (ISBN 0-398-00737-3). C C Thomas.
Griffith, Jerry & Miner, Lynn E. Phonetic Context Drill Book. 1979. pap. 16.95. P-H.
Griffith, Jerry & Strandberg, Twila. A Guide to Nursing Home Living. 108p. 13.95 (ISBN 0-318-17112-0, 00024); 6.95, member (ISBN 0-318-17113-9). Am Health Care Assn.
Griffith, Jerry & Strandberg, Twila E. A Guide to Nursing Home Living. LC 81-82592. 132p. (Orig.). 1982. pap. 6.95 (ISBN 0-9606392-0-9). Generations Pub.
Griffith, Jim N. Sure You Can. LC 77-91269. 1978. 5.95 (ISBN 0-8054-5263-X). Broadman.
Griffith, John, ed. Socialism in a Cold Climate. (Counterpoint Ser.). 256p. 1983. pap. 8.95 (ISBN 0-04-335050-X). Allen Unwin.
Griffith, John L. & Weston, Edward G. Programmed Newswriting. (Basic Skills in Journalism Ser.). (Illus.). 1978. pap. text ed. 14.95 (ISBN 0-13-730630-X). P-H.
Griffith, John Q., Jr., jt. ed. see Farris, Edmond J.
Griffith, John R. Legal Environment of Business. LC 83-19843. 459p. 1984. text ed. 31.45 (ISBN 0-471-86857-4). Wiley.
--Measuring Hospital Performance. LC 78-793. xiii, 87p. (Orig.). 1978. pap. text ed. 10.00 (ISBN 0-914818-03-1, Inquiry Bk). Blue Cross & Shield.
--Study Guide to Accompany the Legal Environment of Business. 76p. 1984. pap. 10.95 (ISBN 0-471-80357-X). Wiley.
Griffith, John R., et al. Cost Control in Hospitals. 447p. 1976. 17.50 (ISBN 0-686-68582-2, 14916). Healthcare Fin Man Assn.
Griffith, John R., et al, eds. Cost Control in Hospitals. LC 75-28579. 462p. 1976. text ed. 17.50x (ISBN 0-914904-12-4). Health Admin Pr.
Griffith, John W. & Frey, Charles H. Classics of Children's Literature. 1980. write for info. (ISBN 0-02-347190-5). Macmillan.
Griffith, Kate, tr. see Camus, Albert.
Griffith, Kathryn M. Evil Stalks the Night. 368p. 1984. pap. 3.50 (ISBN 0-8439-2063-7). Dorchester Pub Co.
--Evil Stalks the Night. 368p. 1985. pap. 3.50 (ISBN 0-8439-2329-6, Leisure Bks). Dorchester Pub Co.
--The Heart of the Rose. 480p. (Orig.). 1985. pap. 3.95 (ISBN 0-8439-2216-8, Leisure Bks). Dorchester Pub Co.
Griffith, Kathryn P. Enduring Political Ideas. 230p. (Orig.). 1984. lib. bdg. 22.75 (ISBN 0-8191-3535-6); pap. text ed. 11.25 (ISBN 0-8191-3536-4). U Pr of Amer.
--Judge Learned Hand & the Role of the Federal Judiciary. LC 72-9254. 363p. 1973. 16.50x (ISBN 0-8061-1071-6); pap. 7.95x (ISBN 0-8061-1369-3). U of Okla Pr.
Griffith, Kelly, Jr. Writing Essays about Literature: A Guide & Style Sheet. 195p. 1982. pap. text ed. 9.95 (ISBN 0-15-597860-8, HC). HarBraceJ.
Griffith, Leonard. Take Hold of the Treasure. 128p. 1983. pap. 5.95 (ISBN 0-8170-0997-3). Judson.
Griffith, Liddon R. Mugging: You Can Protect Yourself. LC 78-4265. (Illus.). 1978. 11.95 (ISBN 0-13-604876-5, Spec); pap. 4.95 (ISBN 0-13-604868-4). P-H.
Griffith, Louise. Seekers Long Ago & Now. (FGC). 148p. (gr. 7-8). 1965. 0.75 (ISBN 0-318-14153-1). Friends Genl Conf.
Griffith, Lucille. Alabama: A Documentary History to 1900. LC 73-169499. 688p. 1972. 22.50 (ISBN 0-8173-5221-X). U of Ala Pr.
Griffith, Luther G., jt. auth. see Galbraith, John K.
Griffith, Malcolm A., jt. auth. see Kartiganer, Donald M.
Griffith, Mark. The Authenticity of Prometheus Bound. LC 76-14031. (Cambridge Classical Studies). 1977. 49.50 (ISBN 0-521-21099-2). Cambridge U Pr.
Griffith, Mark, ed. see Aeschylus.
Griffith, Marlene, jt. auth. see Muscatine, Charles.
Griffith, Mary. Road in the Dark. LC 85-875. 1985. pap. 11.95 (ISBN 0-87949-257-0). Ashley Bks.
Griffith, Nancy, jt. auth. see Griffith, Bob.
Griffith, Nancy S. & Person, Laura. Albert Schweitzer: An International Bibliography. 1981. lib. bdg. 47.00 (ISBN 0-8161-8531-X, Hall Reference). G K Hall.
Griffith, O. Hayes, jt. auth. see Jost, Patricia C.
Griffith, P., jt. auth. see Dinter, E.
Griffith, Paddy. Napoleonic Wargaming for Fun. 1980. 14.95 (ISBN 0-7063-5813-9, Pub. by Ward Lock England). Hippocrene Bks.
Griffith, Paul. My Stillness. LC 72-83347. 212p. 1972. 8.95 (ISBN 0-8149-0724-5). Vanguard.
Griffith, Peter. The School Play: A Complete Handbook. (Illus.). 168p. 1981. 14.95 (ISBN 0-7134-3541-0, Pub. by Batsford England). David & Charles.
Griffith, Phillip A. Infinite Abelian Group Theory. LC 70-124398. (Chicago Lectures in Mathematics Ser). 1970. pap. text ed. 7.00x (ISBN 0-226-30870-7). U of Chicago Pr.
Griffith, R. A., ed. Boroughs of Medieval Wales. 338p. 1978. text ed. 32.00x (ISBN 0-7083-0681-0, Pub. by Univ of Wales Pr Emgland). Humanities.
Griffith, R. C. & Golomber, H. A Pocket Guide to Chess Openings. (Illus.). 128p. 1974. 9.50 (ISBN 0-7135-0515-X). Transatlantic.
Griffith, R. T. The Hymns of the Rigveda. rev. ed. 1976. 39.95 (ISBN 0-8426-0592-4). Orient Bk Dist.
Griffith, Ralph T., tr. from Sanskrit. Sam-Veda Sanhita. 338p. 1978. Repr. of 1907 ed. 22.00 (ISBN 0-89684-160-X). Orient Bk Dist.
Griffith, Reginald H. Alexander Pope: A Bibliography, 2 pts. in 1 vol. LC 77-161771. Repr. of 1927 ed. 45.00 (ISBN 0-404-09020-6). AMS Pr.
--Alexander Pope, A Bibliography, 2 vols. 1983. 60.00 (ISBN 0-686-89435-9). Saifer.
Griffith, Reynolds. Personal Finance. 1985. text ed. 27.95 (ISBN 0-8359-5502-8); instr's. manual avail. (ISBN 0-8359-5503-6). Reston.
Griffith, Richard. Frank Capra. (Film Ser.). 1979. lib. bdg. 59.95 (ISBN 0-8490-2922-8). Gordon Pr.
--The Talkies. LC 71-164734. (Dover Film Ser). (Orig.). 1971. pap. 8.95 (ISBN 0-486-22762-6). Dover.
--The World of Robert Flaherty. LC 72-166104. 1972. Repr. of 1953 ed. lib. bdg. 27.50 (ISBN 0-306-70296-7). Da Capo.
--World of Robert Flaherty. Repr. of 1953 ed. lib. bdg. 22.50x (ISBN 0-8371-3400-5, GRRF). Greenwood.
Griffith, Richard & Mayer, Arthur. The Movies. rev. ed. (Illus.). 576p. 1983. 14.50 (ISBN 0-671-45622-9, Fireside). S&S.
Griffith, Richard, et al. The Movies. rev. ed. (Illus.). 1981. 24.95 (ISBN 0-671-42765-2). S&S.
Griffith, Robert, ed. Ike's Letters to a Friend, Nineteen Forty-One to Nineteen Fifty-Eight. (Illus.). 224p. 1984. 19.95x (ISBN 0-7006-0257-7). U Pr of KS.
Griffith, Robert K., Jr. Men Wanted for the U. S. Army: America's Experience with an All-Volunteer Army Between the World Wars. LC 81-6686. (Contributions in Military History Ser.: No. 27). (Illus.). xvii, 259p. 1982. lib. bdg. 29.95 (ISBN 0-313-22546-X, GMU/). Greenwood.
Griffith, Roger & Braren, Ken. Homemade: One Hundred & One Easy-to-Make Things for Your Garden, House or Farm. LC 77-2887. (Illus.). 1977. 6.95 (ISBN 0-88266-103-5). Garden Way Pub.
Griffith, Roger & Tompkins, Enoch. Practical Beekeeping. LC 76-51401. (Illus.). 224p. 1977. o. p. 9.95 (ISBN 0-88266-092-6); pap. 8.95 (ISBN 0-88266-091-8). Garden Way Pub.
Griffith, Roger, jt. auth. see Rogers, Marc.
Griffith, Roger, ed. see Campbell, Stu.
Griffith, Roger, ed. see Chan, Peter.
Griffith, Roger, ed. see Gay, Larry.
Griffith, Roger, ed. see Kirkpatrick, Frank.
Griffith, Roger, ed. see Mahnken, Jan.
Griffith, Roger, ed. see Simmons, Paula.
Griffith, Roger, ed. see Twitchell, Mary.
Griffith, Roger, ed. see Woodier, Olwen.
Griffith, Rubye & Griffith, Frank. Fun of Raising a Colt. pap. 5.00 (ISBN 0-87980-190-5). Wilshire.
Griffith, S. K., et al. Wind Energy Systems: Export Market Potential. LC 83-51687. 308p. (Orig.). 1984. pap. 125.00 (ISBN 0-88016-011-X). Windbks.
Griffith, Samuel B. The Battle for Guadalcanal. 15.95 (ISBN 0-405-13281-6). Ayer Co Pubs.
Griffith, Samuel B., tr. & intro. by see Sun Tzu.
Griffith, Samuel B., II. The Battle for Guadalcanal. LC 79-90112. (Great War Stories Ser.). (Illus.). 282p. 1979. Repr. of 1963 ed. 18.95 (ISBN 0-933852-04-5). Nautical & Aviation.
Griffith, Susan. Traveller's Survival Kit to the East: Turkey, Iraq, Iran, Afghanistan, India, Nepal, Sri Lanka, Burma. 2nd ed. 176p. 1982. pap. 9.95 (ISBN 0-907638-03-1, Pub. by Vacation Wk). Bradt Ent.
--Work Your Way Around the World. LC 83-12437. (Illus.). 292p. (Orig.). 1983. pap. 10.95 (ISBN 0-89879-125-1). Writers Digest.
Griffith, Susan, ed. Summer Jobs in Britain 1986. 174p. (Orig.). 1985. pap. 8.95 (ISBN 0-907638-48-1, Pub. by Vacation-Work England). Writers Digest.
Griffith, T. G., ed. see Petrarch.
Griffith, Talbot. Population Problems of the Age of Malthus. 2nd ed. (Illus.). 280p. 1967. Repr. of 1926 ed. 35.00x (ISBN 0-7146-1155-7, BHA-01155, F Cass Co). Biblio Dist.
Griffith, Terry. Recipes of the Deep. 96p. 1982. 6.95 (ISBN 0-939114-56-9). Wimmer Bks.
--Recipes of the Wild. 96p. 1980. 6.95 (ISBN 0-918544-63-7). Wimmer Bks.
Griffith, Thomas. The Waist-High Culture. LC 72-10978. 275p. 1973. Repr. of 1959 ed. lib. bdg. 22.50x (ISBN 0-8371-6645-4, GRWC). Greenwood.
Griffith, W., ed. see Roosevelt, Theodore.
Griffith, Wayland, ed. see International Shock Tube Symposium, 9th, Stanford Univ., 1973.
Griffith, Wickham. Young Wives Encyclopedia. 13.50 (ISBN 0-392-08135-0, SpS). Sportshelf.
Griffith, William. Annual Law Register of the United States, Vols. 3 & 4. LC 77-37976. (American Law Ser.: The Formative Years). 1468p. 1972. Repr. of 1822 ed. 81.00 (ISBN 0-405-04019-9). Ayer Co Pubs.
--Icones Plantrum Asiaticarum, 8 vols. (Illus.). 1978. Repr. of 1849 ed. Set. 800.00x (ISBN 0-89955-284-6, Pub. by Intl Bk Dist). Intl Spec Bk.
Griffith, William E. The Ostpolitik of the Federal Republic of Germany. (MIT Studies in Communism, Revisionism, & Revolution Ser.). 1978. 35.00x (ISBN 0-262-07072-3). MIT Pr.
Griffith, William E., ed. The World & the Great-Power Triangles. LC 74-31219. 695p. 1975. text ed. 40.00x (ISBN 0-262-07064-2). MIT Pr.
Griffith, William E., ed. see Commission on Critical Choices.
Griffith, William E., ed. see Johnson, A. Ross.
Griffith, Winter H. Complete Guide to Prescription & Non-Prescription Drugs. 888p. 1985. 12.95 (ISBN 0-89586-404-5). H P BKS.
Griffith, Wyn, tr. see Roberts, Kate.
Griffith-Jones, Lionel. That's My Lot: An Anecdotal Autobiography of a British Ex-Singapore Colonial. 1984. 12.95 (ISBN 0-533-05930-5). Vantage.
Griffith-Jones, Stephany. International Finance & Latin America. LC 84-15908. 128p. 1984. 19.95 (ISBN 0-312-42196-6). St Martin.
--The Role of Finance in the Transition to Socialism. LC 81-12844. 208p. 1981. text ed. 29.95x (ISBN 0-86598-069-1). Allanheld.
Griffith-Jones, Stephany, et al, eds. World Prices & Development. 380p. 1985. text ed. write for info. (ISBN 0-566-00890-4). Gower Pub Co.
Griffiths. Washington, D. C. in Your Pocket. 160p. 1985. pap. 2.95 (ISBN 0-8120-2837-6). Barron.
Griffiths, A. L., ed. see Dervish, H. B. M.
Griffiths, A. P., ed. Of Liberty: (Royal Institute of Philosophy Lectures 15) LC 83-1895. 250p. 1983. pap. 13.95 (ISBN 0-521-27415-X). Cambridge U Pr.
Griffiths, A. Philips, ed. Knowledge & Belief. 1967. pap. 8.95x (ISBN 0-19-500328-4). Oxford U Pr.
Griffiths, A. R. Contemporary Australia. LC 76-62534. 1977. 25.00 (ISBN 0-312-16651-6). St Martin.
Griffiths, Adrian, et al. An Annotated Bibliography of Health Economics: Western European Sources. 1980. 14.95 (ISBN 0-312-03874-7). St Martin.
Griffiths, Alex, jt. auth. see Hamilton, Dorothy.
Griffiths, Anita. Teaching the Dyslexic Child. LC 78-12875. 1978. pap. 5.00x (ISBN 0-87879-205-8). Acad Therapy.
Griffiths, Anthony J. F., jt. auth. see Suzuki, David T.
Griffiths, Antong, jt. auth. see Carey, Frances.
Griffiths, Antony. Prints & Printmaking: An Introduction to the History & Techniques. 152p. 1981. text ed. 18.00 (ISBN 0-394-32673-3, KnopfC). Knopf.
Griffiths, Arthur. The Rome Express. LC 75-35443. (Literature of Mystery & Detection). 1976. Repr. of 1907 ed. 19.00x (ISBN 0-405-07874-9). Ayer Co Pubs.
--Secrets of the Prison House, or Goal Studies & Sketches: London, 1893, 2 vols. LC 83-49239. (Crime & Punishment in England, 1850-1922 Ser.). 996p. 1984. Set. lib. bdg. 120.00 (ISBN 0-8240-6219-1). Garland Pub.
Griffiths, Bede. Christ in India. pap. 8.95 (ISBN 0-87243-134-7). Templegate.
--The Cosmic Revelation: The Hindu Way to God. 128p. 1983. pap. 7.95 (ISBN 0-87243-119-3). Templegate.
--The Golden String. 192p. 1980. 8.95 (ISBN 0-87243-101-0). Templegate.
--The Marriage of East & West. 180p. 1982. pap. 8.95 (ISBN 0-87243-105-3). Templegate.
--Return to the Center. 1976. pap. 7.95 (ISBN 0-87243-112-6). Templegate.
--Vedanta & Christian Faith. LC 73-88179. 1973. pap. 3.95 (ISBN 0-913922-04-8). Dawn Horse Pr.
Griffiths, Brian. The Creation of Wealth. LC 85-5210. 160p. 1985. pap. 5.95 (ISBN 0-87784-566-2). Inter-Varsity.

--Inflation: The Price of Prosperity. LC 75-43789. 300p. 1976. text ed. 25.00x (ISBN 0-8419-0255-0). Holmes & Meier.

Griffiths, Brian & Wood, Geoffrey E. Monetarism in the United Kingdom. LC 83-23021. 305p. 1984. 27.95 (ISBN 0-312-54412-X). St Martin.

Griffiths, Brian, ed. Monetary Targets. Wood, Geoffrey E. 29.95 (ISBN 0-312-54421-9). St Martin.

Griffiths, C. Auditory Techniques. (Illus.). 232p. 1974. 22.75x (ISBN 0-398-03047-2). C C Thomas.

Griffiths, C. E., ed. see Tasso, T.

Griffiths, C. T., jt. ed. see Heintz, A. P.

Griffiths, C. Thomas & Fuller, Arlan F., Jr. Gynecologic Oncology. 1983. lib. bdg. 87.00 (ISBN 0-89838-555-5, Pub. by Martinus Nijhoff Netherlands). Kluwer Academic.

Griffiths, Curt T., jt. auth. see Ekstedt, John W.

Griffiths, D. Introduction to Electrodynamics. 1981. 36.95 (ISBN 0-13-481374-X). P-H.

Griffiths, D. A. & Bowman, C. E. Acarology Six, 2 Vols. 1984. Vol. 1, 645p. 119.95 (ISBN 0-470-27410-7); Vol. 2, 700p. 100.00 (ISBN 0-470-27411-5); Set. 219.95 (ISBN 0-470-27412-3). Halsted Pr.

Griffiths, D. F., jt. auth. see Mitchell, A. R.

Griffiths, D. F., ed. Numerical Analysis: Proceedings of the 10th Biennial Conference Held at Dundee, Scotland, June 28-July 1, 1983. (Lecture Notes in Mathematics Ser.: Vol. 1066). ix, 275p. 1984. pap. 16.50 (ISBN 0-387-13344-5). Springer-Verlag.

Griffiths, D. H. & King, R. F. Applied Geophysics for Engineers & Geologists. 2nd ed. 1965. 33.00 (ISBN 0-08-022071-1); pap. 14.50 (ISBN 0-08-022072-X). Pergamon.

--Applied Geophysics for Geologists & Engineers: The Elements of Geophysical Prospecting. 2nd ed. (Illus.). 224p. 1981. 33.00 (ISBN 0-08-022071-1); pap. 14.50 (ISBN 0-08-022072-X). Pergamon.

Griffiths, Daniel E., ed. Behavioral Science & Educational Administration: 63rd Yearbook. (National Society for the Study of Education Ser: No. 63, Pt. II). (Illus.). xii, 368p. 1974. pap. text ed. 4.50x (ISBN 0-226-60076-9). U of Chicago Pr.

Griffiths, Daniel E. & McCarty, Donald J., eds. The Dilemma of the Deanship. LC 78-61237. (Illus.). 304p. 1980. 11.95x (ISBN 0-8134-2041-5, 2041). Interstate.

Griffiths, David. Psychology & Medicine. (Psychology for Professional Groups Ser.). 320p. 1981. text ed. 23.75x (ISBN 0-333-31862-5, Pub. by Macmillan England); pap. text ed. 9.75x (ISBN 0-333-31877-3). Humanities.

Griffiths, David F., ed. The Mathematical Basis of Finite Element Methods: With Application to Partial Differential Equations. (The Institute of Mathematics & Its Applications Conference Ser.). (Illus.). 250p. 1985. 24.95 (ISBN 0-19-853605-4). Oxford U Pr.

Griffiths, Denis. Brunel's Great Western. (Illus.). 160p. 1985. 13.95 (ISBN 0-85059-743-9, Pub. by Salem Hse Ltd). Merrimack Pub Cir.

Griffiths, Derek J. Urodynamics: The Mechanics & Hydrodynamics of the Lower Urinary Tract. (Medical Physics Handbooks: No. 4). 139p. 1980. 29.50 (ISBN 0-9960019-5-6, Pub. by A Hilger England). Heyden.

Griffiths, Drew, jt. auth. see Greig, Noel.

Griffiths, E. C. & Bennett, G. W., eds. Thyrotropin-Releasing Hormone. 416p. 1983. text ed. 52.00 (ISBN 0-89004-801-0). Raven.

Griffiths, E. H. Weighing Machines: Application of Electricity & Electronics to Weighting Machines, Vol. 3. 248p. 1970. 49.75x (ISBN 0-85264-160-5, Pub. by Griffin England). State Mutual Bk.

Griffiths, Franklyn & Polanyi, John C., eds. The Dangers of Nuclear War. LC 79-18825. 1979. 25.00 (ISBN 0-8020-2356-8); pap. 10.00 (ISBN 0-8020-6389-6). U of Toronto Pr.

--The Dangers of Nuclear War. 193p. 1979. 4.95 (ISBN 0-317-33392-5). Arms Control.

Griffiths, G. C. Flies of the Nearctic Region: Cyclorhapha II (Schizophora, Calyptratae) Part 2 Anthomiidae, Vol. VIII, No. 1. (Illus.). 600p. 1984. pap. text ed. 51.85x (ISBN 3-51070-009-0). Lubrecht & Cramer.

--Flies of the Nearctic Region Vol. VIII: Cyclorrhapha II (Schizophora. Calyptratae, Pt. 2 Anthomyiidae, No. 1. (Illus.). 160p. (Orig.). 1982. pap. text ed. 53.76 (ISBN 3-510-70004-X). Lubrecht & Cramer.

Griffiths, Gareth. A Double Exile: African & West Indian Writing Between Two Cultures. 208p. 1980. 7.95 (ISBN 0-7145-2623-1, Dist by Scribner). M Boyars.

Griffiths, Graham C. Flies of the Nearctic Region: Vol. VIII-Cyclorrhapha II Schizophora: Calyptratae Pt. 2-Anthomylidae. (Illus.). 1984. pap. text ed. 38.14 (ISBN 3-510-70007-4). Lubrecht & Cramer.

Griffiths, Graham C., ed. see Hall, J. C. & Evenhuis, M. L.

Griffiths, Graham C., ed. see Hall, Jack C. & Evenhuis, N. L.

Griffiths, Graham C., ed. see Hall, Jack C. & Evenhuis, Neal L.

Griffiths, Graham C., ed. see Stone, Alan.

Griffiths, Grahm C., ed. see Hall, Jack C. & Evenhuis, N. L.

Griffiths, H. B. Surfaces. 2nd ed. 131p. 1981. 37.50 (ISBN 0-521-23570-7); pap. 14.95 (ISBN 0-521-29977-2). Cambridge U Pr.

Griffiths, H. B. & Hilton, P. J. A Comprehensive Textbook of Classical Mathematics: A Contemporary Interpretation. 1978. pap. 29.50 (ISBN 0-387-90342-9). Springer-Verlag.

Griffiths, Harry J. Radiology of Renal Failures. LC 74-17754. (Monographs in Clinical Radiology: Vol. 9). (Illus.). 1976. text ed. 25.00 (ISBN 0-7216-4283-7). Saunders.

Griffiths, Harry J. & Sarno, Robert C. Contemporary Radiology: An Introduction to Imaging. LC 78-64711. (Illus.). 356p. 1979. text ed. 19.50 (ISBN 0-7216-4282-9). Saunders.

Griffiths, Helen. Blackface Stallion. LC 80-15850. (Illus.). 160p. (gr. 5 up). 1980. 10.95 (ISBN 0-8234-0420-X). Holiday.

--The Dancing Horses. LC 81-6762. 160p. (gr. 7 up). 1982. 9.95 (ISBN 0-8234-0437-4). Holiday.

--The Dog at the Window. LC 84-3806. 128p. (gr. 4-7). 1984. 10.95 (ISBN 0-8234-0527-3). Holiday.

--Grip, a Dog Story. (Illus.). (gr. 5-7). 1981. pap. 1.75 (ISBN 0-671-56034-4). Archway.

--Grip, a Dog Story. LC 78-6819. (Illus.). 160p. (gr. 5-9). 1978. 9.95 (ISBN 0-8234-0335-1). Holiday.

--Just a Dog. (Illus.). (gr. 5-7). 1976. pap. 1.95 (ISBN 0-671-42166-2). Archway.

--The Last Summer. LC 79-10469. (Illus.). 160p. (gr. 5 up). 1979. 7.95 (ISBN 0-8234-0361-0). Holiday.

--Moshie Cat. LC 70-122905. (Illus.). 128p. (gr. 4-6). 1970. 3.95 (ISBN 0-8234-0178-2). Holiday.

--The Mysterious Appearance of Agnes. LC 74-21793. (Illus.). 160p. (gr. 7 up). 1975. 10.95 (ISBN 0-8234-0267-3). Holiday.

--Rafa's Dog. LC 83-4384. 112p. (gr. 3-6). 1983. 9.95 (ISBN 0-8234-0492-7). Holiday.

--Running Wild. LC 77-3814. (Illus.). 160p. (gr. 5 up). 1977. 6.95 (ISBN 0-8234-0309-2). Holiday.

--Russian Blue. LC 73-78454. (Illus.). 160p. (gr. 4-6). 1973. 4.50 (ISBN 0-8234-0233-9). Holiday.

Griffiths, Henry J. A Handbook of Veterinary Parasitology: Domestic Animals of North America. LC 78-50021. 1978. 20.00x (ISBN 0-8166-0834-2); pap. 12.95x (ISBN 0-8166-0828-8). U of Minn Pr.

Griffiths, Ian & Platt, Philip. Multiple Choice Questions in Rheumatology. 126p. (Orig.). 1984. pap. text ed. 8.50 (ISBN 0-272-79698-0, Pub. by Pitman Bks Ltd Uk). Urban & S.

Griffiths, Ian, tr. see Levy-Leboyer, Claude.

Griffiths, Ieuan. An Atlas of African Affairs. (Illus.). 200p. 1984. pap. 11.95 (ISBN 0-416-30940-2, NO. 3907). Methuen Inc.

Griffiths, J. Color & Constitution of Organic Molecules. 1976. 55.00 (ISBN 0-12-303550-3). Acad Pr.

Griffiths, J., ed. Developments in the Chemistry & Technology of Organic Dyes. (Illus.). 138p. (Orig.). 1984. text ed. 39.00x (ISBN 0-632-01304-4). Blackwell Pubns.

Griffiths, J. B. The Theory of Classical Dynamics. (Illus.). 320p. Date not set. price not set (ISBN 0-521-23760-2). Cambridge U Pr.

Griffiths, J. B., jt. ed. see Spier, R. E.

Griffiths, J. F. Climates of Africa. (World Survey of Climatology Ser.: Vol. 10). 604p. 1972. 157.50 (ISBN 0-444-40893-2). Elsevier.

Griffiths, J. Gwyn. The Conflict of Horus & Seth: A Study in Ancient Mythology from Egyptian & Classical Sources. 182p. 1960. 40.00x (ISBN 0-85323-071-4, Pub. by Liverpool Univ England). State Mutual Bk.

Griffiths, J. M. Local Telecommunications. (IEE Telecommunications Ser.). 208p. 1983. 49.00 (ISBN 0-906048-93-1, TE010). Inst Elect Eng.

Griffiths, J. N. The Golden Years of Bridge. (Master Bridge Ser.). (Illus.). 128p. (Orig.). 1981. pap. 9.95 (ISBN 0-575-02906-4, Pub. by Gollanz England). David & Charles.

Griffiths, Jeanne. The Photographer's Project Book: Shooting Like a Professional. (Illus.). 160p. 1985. 15.95 (ISBN 0-356-10166-5, Pub. by Salem Hse Ltd). Merrimack Pub Cir.

Griffiths, Jeremy, ed. see Boffey, Julia.

Griffiths, John. The Book of English International Rugby 1871-1982. 496p. 1982. 50.00x (ISBN 0-686-45524-X, Pub. by Col-Wil). State Mutual Bk.

--The Caribbean in the Twentieth Century. (Twentieth Century History Ser.). (Illus.). 72p. (gr. 7-12). 1984. 14.95 (ISBN 0-7134-3839-8, Pub. by Batsford England). David & Charles.

--Lasers & Holograms. LC 83-60895. (Exploration & Discovery Ser.). 36p. (gr. 5 up). 1983. 13.80 (ISBN 0-382-06698-7). Silver.

--Latin America in the Twentieth Century. (Twentieth Century World History Ser.). (Illus.). 72p. (gr. 7-12). 1985. 14.95 (ISBN 0-7134-3840-1, Pub. by Batsford England). David & Charles.

--A Loyal & Dedicated Servant. 320p. 1984. pap. 3.50 (ISBN 0-441-49825-6). Ace Bks.

--Memory Man. LC 82-81382. 320p. 1982. pap. 3.25 (ISBN 0-86721-207-1). Jove Pubns.

--The Paintings in the Buddhist Cave-Temples of Ajanta. (Illus.). 46p. 1983. Set. 500.50x (ISBN 0-391-03134-1, Pub. by Caxton Pubns); Vol. 1. write for info (ISBN 0-391-03135-X); Vol. 2. write for info. (ISBN 0-391-03136-8). Humanities.

--Three Tomorrows: American, British & Soviet Science Fiction. 217p. 1980. 28.50x (ISBN 0-389-20008-5); pap. 10.95x (ISBN 0-389-20009-3). B&N Imports.

--We Live in the Caribbean. (Living Here Ser.). (Illus.). 64p. 1984. PLB 10.90 (ISBN 0-531-03832-7). Watts.

Griffiths, John, ed. A Letter of Private Direction. LC 81-126. (The Spiritual Classics Ser.). 176p. 1981. 9.95 (ISBN 0-8245-0081-4). Crossroad NY.

--The Mirror of Simple Souls. LC 81-126. (The Spiritual Classics Ser.). 176p. 1981. 9.95 (ISBN 0-8245-0083-0). Crossroad NY.

Griffiths, John & Griffiths, Peter, eds. Cuba: The Second Decade. (Illus.). 272p. 1981. 15.00 (ISBN 0-906495-00-8); pap. 8.95 (ISBN 0-904613-75-5). Writers & Readers.

Griffiths, John, ed. see John Of Landsburg.

Griffiths, John, ed. see Kempe, Margery, et al.

Griffiths, John, ed. see Rahner, Karl.

Griffiths, John, tr. see Lepetit, Charles.

Griffiths, John, tr. see Markow-Totevy, Georges.

Griffiths, John C. Afghanistan: Key to a Continent. LC 80-71079. 232p. 1981. 25.00x (ISBN 0-86531-080-7). Westview.

--The Queen of Spades. 232p. 1984. 14.95 (ISBN 0-233-97497-0, Pub. by A Deutsch England). David & Charles.

Griffiths, John F. Climate & the Environment: The Atmospheric Impact on Man. LC 76-5801. (Environmental Studies Ser.: Vol. 2). 1976. pap. text ed. 12.00x (ISBN 0-236-40022-3). Westview.

Griffiths, John F. & Driscoll, Dennis M. Survey of Climatology. 368p. 1982. text ed. 27.95 (ISBN 0-675-09994-3). Merrill.

Griffiths, Jose-Marie, jt. auth. see King, Donald W.

Griffiths, Julia, ed. Autographs for Freedom, 2 Vols. facs. ed. LC 71-83965. (Black Heritage Library Collection Ser.). 1854. 27.50 (ISBN 0-8369-8583-4). Ayer Co Pubs.

Griffiths, L. & Spence, P. Woodworking: Tools, Materials, Processes. (Illus.). 634p. 1981. 20.95 (ISBN 0-8269-4833-2). Am Technical.

Griffiths, Lavinia. Personification in Piers Plowman. (Piers Plowman Studies: No. III). 125p. 1985. 25.00 (ISBN 0-85991-184-5, Pub. by Boydell & Brewer). Longwood Pub Group.

Griffiths, Leslie, jt. auth. see Gulas, Ivan.

Griffiths, M. & Tagg, E. D., eds. Role of Programming in Teaching Informatics: Proceedings of the IFIP TC3 Working Conference on Teaching Programming, Paris, France, 7-9 May, 1984. 212p. 1985. 37.00 (ISBN 0-444-87664-2, North-Holland). Elsevier.

Griffiths, M. M. see Halpern, M., et al.

Griffiths, Mary. Introduction to Human Physiology. 2nd ed. 1981. text ed. write for info. (ISBN 0-02-347230-8). Macmillan.

Griffiths, Mattie. Autobiography of a Female Slave. facs. ed. LC 79-89412. (Black Heritage Library Collection Ser.). 1856. 15.50 (ISBN 0-8369-8584-2). Ayer Co Pubs.

--Autobiography of a Female Slave. pap. 3.50 (ISBN 0-685-16778-X, N109P). Mnemosyne.

--Autobiography of a Female Slave. LC 71-92430. 1857. 14.00 (ISBN 0-403-00163-3). Scholarly.

Griffiths, Maurice. Dream Ships. 290p. 1980. 35.00x (ISBN 0-85177-076-2, Pub. by Cornell England). State Mutual Bk.

--The First of the Tide. 160p. 1980. 16.50x (ISBN 0-85177-164-5, Pub. by Conway Maritime England). State Mutual Bk.

--The Hidden Menace. 160p. 1980. 35.00x (ISBN 0-85177-186-6, Pub. by Conway Maritime England). State Mutual Bk.

--Little Ships & Shoal Waters. (Illus.). 192p. 1985. Repr. of 1937 ed. 23.95 (ISBN 0-85177-056-8, Pub. by Conway Maritime Press England). Sheridan.

--The Magic of the Swatchways. 236p. 1980. 25.00x (ISBN 0-85177-045-2, Pub. by Cornell England). State Mutual Bk.

--Round the Cabin Table: Yarns of an Old Cruising Man. (Illus.). 160p. (Orig.). 1985. pap. 13.95 (ISBN 0-85177-318-4, Pub. by Conway Maritime Press England). Sheridan.

Griffiths, Mel & Rubright, Lynnell. Colorado: A Geography. (Geographies of the United States Ser.). 350p. 1983. 36.00x (ISBN 0-89158-574-5); pap. 20.00x (ISBN 0-86531-478-0). Westview.

Griffiths, Mervyn. The Biology of the Monotremes. LC 78-4818. 1979. 59.00 (ISBN 0-12-303850-2). Acad Pr.

Griffiths, Michael. Encouraging New Christians. pap. 0.75 (ISBN 0-87784-106-3). Inter-Varsity.

--The Example of Jesus. LC 84-6739. (The Jesus Library). 180p. 1985. pap. 6.95 (ISBN 0-87784-929-3). Inter-Varsity.

--Get Your Church Involved in Missions. 1972. pap. 1.00 (ISBN 9971-83-784-6). OMF Bks.

--God's Forgetful Pilgrims: Recalling the Church to Its Reason for Being. 176p. 1975. pap. 4.95 (ISBN 0-8028-1619-3). Eerdmans.

--What on Earth Are You Doing? 1983. pap. 4.95 (ISBN 0-8010-3792-1). Baker Bk.

Griffiths, P. Exterior Differential Systems & the Calculus of Variations. (Progress in Mathematics Ser.: Vol. 25). 349p. 1982. text ed. 30.00 (ISBN 0-8176-3103-8). Birkhauser.

Griffiths, P. & Hill, I. D. Applied Statistics Algorithms. (Mathematics & Its Applications Ser.). 1985. 51.95 (ISBN 0-470-20184-3). Halsted Pr.

Griffiths, P., jt. auth. see Evans, E. G.

Griffiths, P. A. & Morgan, J. Rational Homotopy Theory & Differential Forms. 256p. 1981. text ed. 19.95x (ISBN 0-8176-3041-4). Birkhauser.

Griffiths, P. J. & Thomas, J. D. Calculations in Advanced Physical Chemistry. 280p. 1983. pap. text ed. 18.50 (ISBN 0-7131-3483-6). E Arnold.

Griffiths, P. R., ed. Transform Techniques in Chemistry. LC 77-29271. (Modern Analytical Chemistry Ser.). (Illus.). 403p. 1978. 55.00x (ISBN 0-306-31070-8, Plenum Pr). Plenum Pub.

Griffiths, Paul. Bartok. (Master Musicians Ser.). (Illus.). 238p. 1984. 21.95x (ISBN 0-460-03182-1, BKA-05225, Pub. by J M Dent England). Biblio Dist.

--Boulez. (Oxford Studies of Composers). (Illus.). 1979. pap. 11.50x (ISBN 0-19-315442-0). Oxford U Pr.

--Cage. (Oxford Studies of Composers). (Illus., Orig.). 1981. pap. 9.95x (ISBN 0-19-315450-1). Oxford U Pr.

--A Guide to Electronic Music. 128p. 1981. pap. 7.95 (ISBN 0-500-27203-4). Thames Hudson.

--Gyorgi Ligeti. (The Contemporary Composers Ser.). (Illus.). 128p. 1984. text ed. 15.00x (ISBN 0-87663-442-0). Universe.

--Modern Music. (World of Art Ser.). (Illus.). 216p. 1985. pap. 9.95f (ISBN 0-500-20164-1). Thames Hudson.

--Modern Music: The Avant Garde Since 1945. LC 81-10123. (Illus.). 331p. 1981. pap. 10.95 (ISBN 0-8076-1018-6). Braziller.

--Modern Music: The Avant Garde Since 1945. (Illus.). 332p. 1981. 35.00x (ISBN 0-460-04365-X, Pub. by J. M. Dent England). Biblio Dist.

--New Sounds, New Personalities: British Composers of the Ninteen Eighties. 200p. 1985. pap. 9.95 (ISBN 0-571-10061-9). Faber & Faber.

--Olivier Messiaen & the Music of Time. LC 84-45797. (Illus.). 280p. 1985. text ed. 24.95x (ISBN 0-8014-1813-5). Cornell U Pr.

--Peter Maxwell Davies. (The Contemporary Composer Ser.). 192p. 1982. text ed. 15.00x (ISBN 0-87663-386-6). Universe.

--String Quartet. 2nd ed. LC 83-70402. (Illus.). 1985. pap. 10.95f (ISBN 0-500-27383-9, Dist. by Norton). Thames Hudson.

--The String Quartet: A History. LC 83-70402. (Illus.). 240p. 1983. 19.95f (ISBN 0-500-01311-X). Thames Hudson.

Griffiths, Paul, ed. Igor Stravinsky: The Rake's Progress. LC 81-17071. (Cambridge Opera Handbooks Ser.). (Illus.). 120p. 1982. 22.95 (ISBN 0-521-23746-7); pap. 8.95 (ISBN 0-521-28199-7). Cambridge U Pr.

Griffiths, Paul, et al. The New Grove Second Viennese School. (New Grove Composer Biography Ser.). (Illus.). 1983. 16.50 (ISBN 0-393-01686-2); pap. 7.95 (ISBN 0-393-30090-0). Norton.

Griffiths, Percival. Modern India. 1962. pap. 2.00 (ISBN 0-88253-203-0). Ind-US Inc.

Griffiths, Peter. Exploring the Endgame. (Illus.). 224p. (Orig.). 1985. pap. 8.95 (ISBN 0-7136-2445-0, Pub. by A & C Black UK). Sterling.

Griffiths, Peter, jt. ed. see Griffiths, John.

Griffiths, Peter R. Chemical Infrared Fourier Transform Spectroscopy. LC 75-6505. (Chemical Analysis: A series of Monographs on Analytical Chemistry & Its Applications: Vol. 43). 340p. 1975. 58.00x (ISBN 0-471-32786-7, Pub by Wiley-Interscience). Wiley.

Griffiths, Peter R., ed. Transform Techniques in Chemistry. LC 77-29271. (Modern Analytical Chemistry). (Illus.). pap. 100.80 (ISBN 0-317-09433-5, 2019649). Bks Demand UMI.

Griffiths, Phillip. Topics in Algebraic & Analytic Geometry. LC 74-2968. (Mathematical Notes Ser.: No. 13). 227p. 1974. 22.00x (ISBN 0-691-08151-4). Princeton U Pr.

Griffiths, Phillip & Harris, Joseph. Principles of Algebraic Geometry. LC 78-6993. (Pure & Applied Mathematics: A Wiley Interscience Series of Texts, Monographs & Tracts). 813p. 1978. 64.95x (ISBN 0-471-32792-1, Pub. by Wiley-Interscience). Wiley.

Griffiths, Phillip A. Entire Holomorphic Mappings in One & Several Complex Variables. (Annals of Mathematics Studies: No. 85). 20.00 (ISBN 0-691-08171-9); pap. 10.95 (ISBN 0-691-08172-7). Princeton U Pr.

--An Introduction to the Theory of Special Divisors on Algebraic Curves. LC 80-16415. (Conference Board of Mathematical Sciences Ser.: Vol. 44). 1980. 9.00 (ISBN 0-8218-1694-2, CBMS 44). Am Math.

Griffiths, Phillip A., ed. Topics in Transcendental Algebraic Geometry. LC 82-42593. (Annals of Mathematics Studies: No. 106). 390p. 1984. 45.00x (ISBN 0-691-08335-5); pap. text ed. 12.50x (ISBN 0-691-08339-8). Princeton U Pr.

Griffiths, Phillips A., ed. Philosophy & Practice. (Royal Institute of Philosophy Lecture: No. 18). 250p. Date not set. pap. price not set (ISBN 0-521-31231-0). Cambridge U Pr.

Griffiths, R. Principality of Wales in the Later Middle Ages: The Structure & Personnel of Government, Volume 1; South Wales 1277-1536. (History & Law Ser.: No. 26). 634p. 1972. text ed. 32.00x (ISBN 0-7083-0450-8, Pub. by Univ of Wales Pr England). Humanities.

Griffiths, R. F., jt. auth. see Britter, R. E.

Griffiths, Ralph, ed. Patronage, the Crown & the Provinces in Later Medieval England. 224p. 1980. text ed. 21.25x (ISBN 0-391-02096-X). Humanities.

Griffiths, Ralph A. The Reign of Henry VI. LC 80-53771. (Illus.). 604p. 1981. 40.00 (ISBN 0-520-04356-1). U of Cal Pr.

Griffiths, Ralph A. & Thomas, Roger S. The Making of the Tudor Dynasty. 221p. 1985. 29.95 (ISBN 0-312-50745-3). St Martin.

Griffiths, Richard, ed. see Montherlant, Henry de.

Griffiths, Richard, ed. see Radiguet, Raymond.

Griffiths, Richard F. Dealing with Risk: The Planning, Management & Acceptability of Technological Risk. 144p. 1982. pap. 14.95X (ISBN 0-470-27341-0). Halsted Pr.

Griffiths, Richard T. Industrial Retardation in the Netherlands: 1830-1850. (Illus.). xviii, 235p. 1980. lib. bdg. 34.00 (ISBN 90-247-2199-7, Martinus Nijhoff Pub). Kluwer Academic.

Griffiths, Rose. The Puffin Calculator Book. (Puffin Story Bks.). 32p. (gr. k-5). 1984. pap. 2.95 (ISBN 0-14-031657-4, Puffin). Penguin.

--The Puffin Number & Shape Book. (Illus.). 32p. (gr. 4-6). 1985. pap. 2.95 (ISBN 0-14-031691-4, Puffin). Penguin.

--The Puffin Pre-Computer Book. (Illus.). 32p. (gr. k-5). 1985. pap. 2.95 (ISBN 0-14-031828-3, Puffin). Penguin.

--The Puffin Times Table Book. (Illus.). 32p. (gr. k-5). 1985. pap. 2.95 (ISBN 0-14-031827-5, Puffin). Penguin.

Griffiths, Ruth. Study of Imagination in Early Childhood & Its Function in Mental Development. Repr. of 1935 ed. lib. bdg. 19.75x (ISBN 0-8371-3427-7, GRIM). Greenwood.

Griffiths, Ruth & Harvey, Nathan A. A Study of Imagination in Early Childhood & Its Function in Mental Development: Imaginary Playmates & Other Mental Phenomena of Children. LC 74-21411. (Classics in Child Development Ser). 390p. 1975. Repr. 34.00x (ISBN 0-405-06463-2). Ayer Co Pubs.

Griffiths, Steve. Civilised Airs. LC 84-72522. 63p. 1985. pap. 8.95 (ISBN 0-907476-33-3, Pub. by Poetry Wales Pr UK). Dufour.

Griffiths, Stuart. How Plays Are Made: The Fundamental Elements of Play Construction. (Illus.). 168p. 1984. 13.95 (ISBN 0-13-428145-4); pap. 6.95 (ISBN 0-13-428137-3). P-H.

Griffiths, Thomas M. San Juan Country. LC 82-16544. (Illus.). 1984. 34.95 (ISBN 0-87108-505-4). Pruett.

Griffiths, Tom. Enjoy Your Retirement. (Illus.). 144p. 1973. 3.50 (ISBN 0-7153-5943-6). David & Charles.

--Sport Scuba Diving Depth: An Introduction to Basic Scuba Instruction & Beyond. LC 83-6310. (Illus.). 1984. pap. text ed. 14.50 (ISBN 0-916622-32-0). Princeton Bk Co.

Griffiths, Trevor. Apricots & Thermidor. 24p. (Orig.). 1981. pap. 2.50 (ISBN 0-86104-206-9, NO. 4130). Pluto Pr.

--Comedians. LC 76-16727. 1976. pap. 3.95 (ISBN 0-394-17913-7, E677, Ever). Grove.

--Mermaid Book of Old Roses. (Illus., Orig.). 1984. pap. 14.95 (ISBN 0-7181-2421-9). Merrimack Pub Cir.

--Occupations. new ed. 74p. 1981. pap. 7.50 (ISBN 0-571-11667-1). Faber & Faber.

--Oi for England. 48p. 1982. pap. 4.95 (ISBN 0-571-11977-8). Faber & Faber.

--The Party. 1974. pap. 4.95 (ISBN 0-571-10647-1). Faber & Faber.

Griffiths, Trevor R. Stagecraft: The Complete Guide to Theatrical Practice. (Illus.). 192p. 1982. 15.95x (ISBN 0-89009-530-2). Drama Bk.

Griffiths, V. Problems of Rural Education. (Fundamentals of Educational Planning: No. 7). 38p. (Orig., 3rd Printing 1980). 1968. pap. 6.00 (ISBN 92-803-1022-4, U484, UNESCO). Unipub.

Griffiths, Valerie, tr. see Miura, Ayako.

Griffiths, Walter G. The Kol Tribe of Central India. LC 76-44727. (Asiatic Society, Calcutta. Monograph Ser.: Vol. 2). (Illus.). Repr. of 1946 ed. 31.50 (ISBN 0-404-15864-1). AMS Pr.

Griffiths, William. Behavior Difficulties of Children As Perceived & Judged by Parents, Teachers, & Children Themselves. LC 75-142313. (Illus.). xxi, 116p. Repr. of 1952 ed. lib. bdg. 18.75x (ISBN 0-8371-8080-5, CWGB). Greenwood.

Griffitt, William & Hatfield, Elaine. Human Sexual Behavior. 1985. text ed. 24.95x (ISBN 0-673-15057-7). Scott F.

Griffitts, C. H. see Dillingham, Louise B.

Griffore, Robert J. Child Development: An Educational Perspective. 224p. 1981. pap. 16.75x (ISBN 0-398-04490-2). C C Thomas.

Grifone, J., jt. ed. see Crumeyrolle, A.

Grigarick, A. A. & Stange, L. A. The Pollen-Collecting Bees of the Anthidiini of California (Hymenoptera: Megachilidae) (Bulletin of the California Insect Survey Ser.: Vol. 9). 1968. pap. 13.50x (ISBN 0-520-09034-9). U of Cal Pr.

Grigarick, Albert A. & Schuster, Robert O. Discrimination of Genera of Euplectini of North & Central America. (Publications n Entomology Ser.: Vol. 87). 1980. pap. 23.00x (ISBN 0-520-09609-6). U of Cal Pr.

Grigg, Carolyn D., compiled by. Music Translation Dictionary: An English, Czech, Danish, Dutch, French, German, Hungarian, Italian, Polish, Portuguese, Russian, Spanish, Swedish Vocabulary of Music. LC 78-60526. (Eng., Czech., Danish, Dutch, Fr., Ger., Hungarian, Ital., Pol., Port., Rus., Span. & Swedish.). 1978. lib. bdg. 39.95 (ISBN 0-313-20559-0, GMT/). Greenwood.

Grigg, David. The Dynamics of Agricultural Change: The Historical Experience. LC 82-24034. (Illus.). 304p. 1983. 29.50x (ISBN 0-312-22316-1). St Martin.

--An Introduction to Agricultural Geography. LC 84-12824. 204p. 1984. 23.00 (ISBN 0-09-156710-6, Pub. by Hutchinson Educ); pap. 9.75 (ISBN 0-09-156711-4). Longwood Pub Group.

Grigg, David B. Agricultural Revolution in South Lincolnshire. (Cambridge Studies in Economic History). 1966. 42.50 (ISBN 0-521-05152-5). Cambridge U Pr.

--The Agricultural Systems of the World. LC 73-82451. (Cambridge Geographical Studies). (Illus.). 348p. 1974. pap. 22.95 (ISBN 0-521-09843-2). Cambridge U Pr.

--Population Growth & Agrarian Change. LC 79-4237. (Cambridge Geographical Studies: No. 13). 368p. 1981. 59.50 (ISBN 0-521-22760-7); pap. 21.95 (ISBN 0-521-29635-8). Cambridge U Pr.

Grigg, E. R. Trail of the Invisible Light: From X-Strahlen to Radiobiology. (Illus.). 1016p. 1965. 49.75x (ISBN 0-398-00739-X). C C Thomas.

Grigg, Jessie S. Of Roots & Petals. LC 79-57290. 1980. 10.95 (ISBN 0-89754-009-3); pap. 5.00 (ISBN 0-89754-008-5). Dan River Pr.

Grigg, John. Lloyd George: From Peace to War Nineteen Twelve to Nineteen Sixteen. LC 84-16150. (Illus.). 512p. 1985. 30.00x (ISBN 0-520-05417-2). U of Cal Pr.

--Lloyd George: The People's Champion, 1902-1911. LC 77-91762. 1979. 40.00x (ISBN 0-520-03634-4). U of Cal Pr.

--Nineteen Forty-Three: The Victory That Never Was. (Illus.). 254p. 1980. 12.50 (ISBN 0-8090-7377-3). Hill & Wang.

--Nineteen Forty-Three: The Victory That Never Was. 1982. pap. 2.95 (ISBN 0-89083-971-9). Zebra.

--The Young Lloyd George. 1978. Repr. of 1973 ed. 34.50x (ISBN 0-520-02677-2). U of Cal Pr.

Grigg, N. S. Water Resources Planning. 39.95 (ISBN 0-07-024771-4). McGraw.

Grigg, Neil S., ed. Water Knowledge Transfer. LC 78-63016. 1978. 25.00 (ISBN 0-918334-25-X). WRP.

Grigg, Richard. Symbol & Empowerment: Paul Tillich's Post-Theistic System. 165p. 1985. text ed. 14.50x (ISBN 0-86554-163-9, MUP H153). Mercer Univ Pr.

Grigg, Susan. The Dependent Poor of Newburyport: Studies in Social History, 1800-1830. Berkhofer, Robert, ed. LC 84-1286. (Studies in American History & Culture: No. 39). 160p. 1984. 49.95 (ISBN 0-8357-1416-0). UMI Res Pr.

Griggs, et al. The Mexican Experience in Arizona: An Original Anthology. Cortes, Carlos E., ed. & intro. by. LC 76-5566. (Chicano Heritage Ser.). (Illus.). 1976. 22.00x (ISBN 0-405-09539-2). Ayer Co Pubs.

Griggs, Clive, ed. The Trades Union Congress & the Struggle for Education, 1868-1925. 293p. 1983. text ed. 28.50x (ISBN 0-905273-38-9, Pub. by Falmer Pr). Taylor & Francis.

Griggs, Donald & Griggs, Patricia. Generations Learning Together. (Griggs Educational Resources Ser.). 1980. pap. 7.95 (ISBN 0-687-14050-1). Abingdon.

--Teaching & Celebrating Advent. rev. ed. (Griggs Educational Resources Ser.). 1980. pap. 6.50 (ISBN 0-687-41080-0). Abingdon.

Griggs, Donald, jt. auth. see Griggs, Patricia.

Griggs, Donald L. Basic Skills for Church Teachers. (Griggs Educational Resources Ser.). 112p. 1985. pap. 7.50 (ISBN 0-687-02488-9). Abingdon.

--Teaching Teachers to Teach: A Basic Manual for Church Teachers. (Griggs Educational Resources Ser.). 1983. pap. 7.95 (ISBN 0-687-41120-3). Abingdon.

--Translating the Good News Through Teaching Activities. (Griggs Educational Resources Ser.). 1980. pap. 6.95 (ISBN 0-687-42527-1). Abingdon.

--Twenty New Ways of Teaching the Bible. (Griggs Educational Resources Ser.). 1979. pap. 6.95 (ISBN 0-687-42740-1). Abingdon.

Griggs, Earl L. Coleridge Fille: A Biography of Sara Coleridge. LC 73-3457. 1972. Repr. of 1940 ed. lib. bdg. 27.00 (ISBN 0-8414-2015-7). Folcroft.

--Hartley Coleridge. LC 72-194098. 1929. lib. bdg. 20.00 (ISBN 0-8414-1062-3). Folcroft.

--Thomas Clarkson: The Friend of Slaves. LC 75-107476. Repr. of 1936 ed. 17.50x (ISBN 0-8371-3754-3, GRC&). Greenwood.

Griggs, Earl L., ed. see Christophe, Henri.

Griggs, Earl L., ed. see Coleridge, Hartley.

Griggs, Earl L., ed. see Coleridge, Samuel T.

Griggs, Edward H. American Statesmen: An Interpretation of Our History & Heritage. LC 76-121474. (Essay Index Reprint Ser). 1927. 21.50 (ISBN 0-8369-1810-X). Ayer Co Pubs.

--Goethe's "Faust". A Handbook of Ten Lectures. LC 76-42256. 1976. Repr. of 1906 ed. lib. bdg. 10.00 (ISBN 0-8414-4409-9). Folcroft.

--Great Leaders in Human Progress. facs. ed. LC 70-86755. (Essay Index Reprint Ser). 1939. 14.50 (ISBN 0-8369-1135-0). Ayer Co Pubs.

--The Poetry & Philosophy of Browning. 59.95 (ISBN 0-8490-0858-1). Gordon Pr.

Griggs, Gary B. & Gilchrist, John A. Geologic Hazards, Resources, Environmental Planning. 528p. 1983. text ed. write for info. (ISBN 0-534-01226-4). Wadsworth Pub.

Griggs, Gary B. & Savoy, Lauret E., eds. Living with the California Coast. (Living with the Shore Ser.). (Illus.). 424p. 1985. 27.95 (ISBN 0-8223-0632-8); pap. 14.95 (ISBN 0-8223-0633-6). Duke.

Griggs, Grace E., ed. see Coleridge, Hartley.

Griggs, Irwin & Llewellyn, Robert. Basic Writer & Reader. LC 70-171888. (Orig.). pap. 11.50 (ISBN 0-442-22276-9). Krieger.

Griggs, James K. & Porta, Carol B. O. W. Duncan Family. (Illus.). 1977. pap. text ed. 25.00 (ISBN 0-685-87275-0). Griggs Print.

Griggs, John. The Films of Gregory Peck. 256p. 19.95 (ISBN 0-8065-0897-3). Citadel Pr.

Griggs, John D. Ringing Ears: An Original Tinnitus Guide. Buddy, Cynthia M., et al, eds. (Illus.). 60p. (Orig.). 1982. pap. 10.00x (ISBN 0-9612648-1-0). Natl Tinn Fund.

Griggs, John E. Evaluating Marketing Change: An Application of Systems Theory. LC 75-628281. 1970. 8.00 (ISBN 0-87744-097-2). Mich St U Pr.

Griggs, Lewis, jt. auth. see Copeland, Lennie.

Griggs, M., jt. auth. see Spitze, H.

Griggs, M. J., ed. Selections from the Ars Amatoria. LC 74-139865. 1971. text ed. 8.95 (ISBN 0-312-04970-6). St Martin.

Griggs, Patricia. Creative Activities in Church Education. (Griggs Educational Resources Ser.). 1980. pap. 5.95 (ISBN 0-687-09812-2). Abingdon.

Griggs, Patricia & Griggs, Donald. Teaching & Celebrating Lent-Easter. (Griggs Educational Resources Ser.). 1980. pap. 6.95 (ISBN 0-687-41081-9). Abingdon.

Griggs, Patricia, jt. auth. see Griggs, Donald.

Griggs, Patricia, jt. auth. see Williams, Doris.

Griggs, Patricia R. Using Storytelling in Christian Education. LC 80-26468. 64p. (Orig.). 1981. pap. 6.95 (ISBN 0-687-43117-4). Abingdon.

Griggs, R. F. Botanical Survey of the Sugar Grove (Hocking Hills) Region. 1972. Repr. of 1914 ed. 3.50 (ISBN 0-86727-002-0). Ohio Bio Survey.

Griggs, Silas & Rulon, Curt M. English Verb Inflection: A Generative View. LC 74-75445. (Janua Linguarum, Ser. Minor: No. 211). 69p. 1974. pap. text ed. 7.60 (ISBN 90-2793-262-X). Mouton.

Griggs, Sutton E. Hindered Hand. LC 77-100533. Repr. of 1905 ed. 9.50 (ISBN 0-404-00164-5). AMS Pr.

--Hindered Hand: Or, Reign of the Repressionist. facs. ed. LC 72-79025. (Black Heritage Library Collection Ser.). 1905. 15.75 (ISBN 0-8369-8585-0). Ayer Co Pubs.

--Hindred Hand. pap. 3.25 (ISBN 0-685-16786-0, N273P). Mnemosyne.

--Imperium in Imperio. LC 70-168206. Repr. of 1899 ed. 8.00 (ISBN 0-404-00165-3). AMS Pr.

--Imperium in Imperio. facs. ed. LC 76-79026. (Black Heritage Library Collection Ser). 1899. 12.50 (ISBN 0-8369-8586-9). Ayer Co Pubs.

--Imperium in Imperio. LC 69-18591. (American Negro: His History & Literature Ser., No. 2). 1969. 12.50 (ISBN 0-405-01865-7); pap. 2.45 (ISBN 0-405-01957-2). Ayer Co Pubs.

--Imperium in Imperio. pap. 2.50 (ISBN 0-685-16787-9, N274P). Mnemosyne.

--Overshadowed. LC 71-144621. Repr. of 1901 ed. 12.50 (ISBN 0-404-00166-1). AMS Pr.

--Overshadowed. facsimile ed. LC 79-161261. (Black Heritage Library Collection). Repr. of 1901 ed. 17.00 (ISBN 0-8369-8820-5). Ayer Co Pubs.

--Pointing the Way. LC 75-144622. Repr. of 1908 ed. 12.50 (ISBN 0-404-00167-X). AMS Pr.

--Unfettered. LC 79-144623. Repr. of 1902 ed. 14.00 (ISBN 0-404-00168-8). AMS Pr.

--Wisdom's Call. facs. ed. LC 75-89411. (Black Heritage Library Collection Ser). 1911. 15.50 (ISBN 0-8369-8587-7). Ayer Co Pubs.

Griggs, William H. & Iwakiri, Ben T. Asian Pear Varieties in California. 1977. pap. 3.00 (ISBN 0-931876-00-1, 4068). Ag & Nat Res.

Grigoli, Valorie. Patriotic Holidays & Celebrations. (First Bk.). (Illus.). 72p. (gr. 7 up). Date not set. PLB 9.40 (ISBN 0-531-10044-8). Watts.

--Service Industries. (First Books-Economic Ser.). 72p. (gr. 4-8). 1984. lib. bdg. 9.40 (ISBN 0-531-04832-2). Watts.

Grigolia, Alexander. Custom & Justice in the Caucasus: The Georgian Highlanders. LC 77-87659. Repr. of 1939 ed. 24.00 (ISBN 0-404-16406-4). AMS Pr.

Grigor, Jean C. Grow to Love. 1977. pap. 5.75x (ISBN 0-7152-0437-8). Outlook.

Grigorenko, Petro. Memoirs. (Illus.). 1983. 19.95 (ISBN 0-393-01570-X). Norton.

--Spohady Memoirs. Smyk, Michael, ed. Kyslycia, Dmytro, tr. from Russian. Orig. Title: Ukranian. 751p. 1984. 30.00 (ISBN 0-912601-01-9). Ukrainian News.

Grigorescu, Dan, illus. Ciucurencu. (Illus., Rumanian, Rus. Fr. Ger.). 1965. text ed. 59.50x (ISBN 0-8290-0366-5). Irvington.

Grigor'ev, Apollon. Turgenev i Ego Deiatel'nost' 136p. 1985. Repr. of 1915 ed. cancelled 24.50 (ISBN 0-88233-960-5). Ardis Pubs.

Grigorian, S. V, jt. auth. see Beus, A. A.

Grigorieff, W. W., ed. Abundant Nuclear Energy: Proceedings. LC 71-600642. (AEC Symposium Ser.). 352p. 1969. pap. 16.75 (ISBN 0-87079-130-3, CONF-680810); microfiche 4.50 (ISBN 0-87079-131-1, CONF-680810). DOE.

Grigoriev, Apollon. Sochineniya. (Rus). 1876. 50.00 (ISBN 0-384-20000-1). Johnson Repr.

Grigoriev, V. J., jt. ed. see Whetstone, G. W.

Grigoriu, D., ed. Champignons "Opportunistes". (Dermatologica: Vol. 159, Supplement 1, 1979). (Illus.). 1979. pap. 33.00 (ISBN 3-8055-0084-X). S Karger.

Grigorovich, Y. & Vanslov, V. Bolshoi Ballet. Sviridov, Yuri, tr. from Rus. (Illus.). 317p. 1984. text ed. 39.95 (ISBN 0-86622-043-7, Z-95). Paganiniana Pubns.

Grigoryev, Igor P., tr. see Kolbin, Vyacheslav V.

Grigoryev, L. & Platek, Y. Khrennikov: His Life & Times. Sviridov, Yuri, tr. from Rus. (Life & Times Ser.). 173p. 1983. 12.95 (ISBN 0-87666-797-3, Z-79). Paganiniana Pubns.

Grigoryev, V. & Myakishev, G. Forces of Nature. (Illus.). 346p. 1975. 14.95x (ISBN 0-8464-1099-0). Beekman Pubs.

Grigsby, Charles, jt. auth. see Brey, Ron.

Grigsby, Daryl R. Reflections on Liberation. LC 84-72421. (Illus.). 176p. (Orig.). 1985. pap. 5.95 (ISBN 0-9614210-0-2). Asante Pubns.

Grigsby, Gordon. Tornado Watch. LC 77-8855. 71p. 1978. 9.00 (ISBN 0-8142-0281-0). Ohio St U Pr.

Grigsby, Hugh B. History of the Virginia Convention of 1788, 2 Vols. LC 70-75319. (American History, Politics & Law Ser). 1969. Repr. of 1890 ed. Set. lib. bdg. 85.00 (ISBN 0-306-71280-6). Da Capo.

--The History of the Virginia Federal Convention of 1788, with Some Account of the Eminent Virginians of That Era Who Were Members of the Body, 2 vols. Brock, R. A., ed. LC 73-590. (Virginia Historical Society. Publications: Nos. 9 & 10). Repr. of 1891 ed. Set. 49.00 (ISBN 0-404-57658-3); 24.50 ea. AMS Pr.

--Virginia Convention of 1776. LC 75-75320. (American History, Politics & Law Ser.). 1969. Repr. of 1855 ed. lib. bdg. 29.50 (ISBN 0-306-71281-4). Da Capo.

--Virginia Convention of 1829-1830. LC 79-75321. (American History, Politics & Law Ser). 1969. Repr. of 1854 ed. lib. bdg. 25.00 (ISBN 0-306-71282-2). Da Capo.

Grigsby, John L. The Middle French Liber Fortunae. LC 68-63446. 276p. 1983. Repr. of 1967 ed. lib. bdg. 19.95x (ISBN 0-89370-764-3). Borgo Pr.

Grigsby, Leonard L., jt. auth. see Blackwell, William A.

Grigsby, Red. Bass, & How to Catch Them. 1966. pap. 0.50 (ISBN 0-87511-590-X). Claitors.

Grigsby, Wayne, ed. A Toronto Lampoon. (Illus.). 160p. (Orig.). 1984. pap. 9.95 (ISBN 0-920792-38-3). Eden Pr.

Grigson, G. A Master of Our Time. LC 72-3175. (English Literature Ser., No. 33). 1972. Repr. of 1951 ed. lib. bdg. 29.95x (ISBN 0-8383-1534-8). Haskell.

Grigson, Geoffrey. Before the Romantics: An Anthology of the Enlightenment. 368p. 1985. pap. 9.95 (ISBN 0-907540-59-7, Pub. by Salem Hse Ltd). Merrimack Pub Cir.

--Blessings, Kicks & Curses. 256p. 1983. 17.00 (ISBN 0-8052-8120-7, Pub. by Allison & Busby England). Schocken.

--Collected Poems, 1963-1980. 256p. 1983. 17.00 (ISBN 0-8052-8121-5, Pub. by Allison & Busby England). Schocken.

--The Contrary View: Glimpses of Fudge & Gold. 243p. 1974. 17.50x (ISBN 0-87471-152-5). Rowman.

--The Cornish Dancer & Other Poems. 64p. 1984. 10.50 (ISBN 0-436-18805-8, Pub. by Secker & Warburg UK). David & Charles.

--Freedom of the Parish. 208p. 1982. pap. 7.50 (ISBN 0-907746-02-0, Pub. by A Mott Ltd). Longwood Pub Group.

--A Master of Our Time: A Study of Wyndham Lewis. LC 73-13534. 1951. lib. bdg. 25.00 (ISBN 0-8414-4428-5). Folcroft.

--A Master of Our Time: Wyndham Lewis. 59.95 (ISBN 0-87968-010-5). Gordon Pr.

--Montaigne's Tower. 72p. 1984. 12.95 (ISBN 0-436-18806-6, Pub. by Secker & Warburg UK). David & Charles.

--Poems & Poets. LC 68-55232. 1969. 13.00 (ISBN 0-8023-1195-4). Dufour.

--The Private Art: A Poetry Notebook. 256p. 1983. 17.00 (ISBN 0-8052-8125-8, Pub. by Allison & Busby England). Schocken.

--Rainbows, Fleas, & Flowers: A Nature Anthology. 280p. 1985. 12.95 (ISBN 0-8149-0754-7). Vanguard.
--Recollections: Mainly of Artists & Writers. 224p. 1985. 17.95 (ISBN 0-7011-2791-0, Pub. by Chatto & Windus). Merrimack Pub Cir.
--Shapes & People. LC 76-11954. 64p. (gr. 9 up). 12.95 (ISBN 0-8149-0662-1). Vanguard.
--Shapes & Stories: A Book About Pictures. LC 65-25262. (Illus.). 72p. (gr. 5 up). 12.95 (ISBN 0-8149-0311-8). Vanguard.
--Skull in Salop & Other Poems. LC 68-8309. 1969. 12.00 (ISBN 0-8023-1183-0). Dufour.
Grigson, Geoffrey & Grigson, Jane. More Shapes & Stories: A Book About Pictures. LC 67-20942. (Illus.). 72p. (gr. 8 up). 1967. 12.95 (ISBN 0-8149-0310-X). Vanguard.
--Shapes, Animals & Special Creatures. LC 72-77789. (Illus.). 64p. (gr. 5 up). 1985. 12.95 (ISBN 0-8149-0717-2). Vanguard.
Grigson, Geoffrey, ed. The Cherry Tree. (Illus.). 538p. 1985. 17.50 (ISBN 0-8149-0309-6). Vanguard.
--Country Poems. (Pocket Poet Ser.). 1959. pap. 2.00 (ISBN 0-8023-9046-3). Dufour.
--The Faber Book of Love Poems. 408p. (Orig.). 1983. pap. 6.95 (ISBN 0-571-13118-2). Faber & Faber.
--The Faber Book of Nonsense Verse. 352p. 1982. pap. 7.95 (ISBN 0-571-11787-2). Faber & Faber.
--The Faber Book of Nonsense Verse. 352p. 1979. 12.95 (ISBN 0-571-11356-7). Faber & Faber.
--Faber Book of Reflective Verse. 240p. 1984. 18.95 (ISBN 0-571-13299-5); pap. 8.95 (ISBN 0-571-13300-2). Faber & Faber.
--The Gambit Book of Popular Verse. 384p. 1985. pap. 19.95 (ISBN 0-87645-123-7, Pub. by Gambit). Harvard Common Pr.
--The Oxford Book of Satirical Verse. 1980. 29.95x (ISBN 0-19-214110-4); pap. 10.95 (ISBN 0-19-281425-7). Oxford U Pr.
--The Romantics. LC 78-57858. (Granger Poetry Library). 1978. Repr. of 1942 ed. 25.00x (ISBN 0-89609-096-5). Granger Bk.
--Selected Poems-John Dryden. 1977. Repr. of 1950 ed. lib. bdg. 12.50 (ISBN 0-8482-0540-5). Norwood Edns.
Grigson, Geoffrey, intro. by. The Faber Book of Poems & Places. 480p. 1980. pap. 7.95 (ISBN 0-571-13008-9). Faber & Faber.
Grigson, Jane. The Art of Making Sausages, Pates & Other Charcuterie. (Illus.). 1976. pap. 7.95 (ISBN 0-394-73252-9). Knopf.
--Good Things. LC 84-45031. 384p. 1984. pap. 13.95 (ISBN 0-689-70677-4, 317). Atheneum.
--Jane Grigson's Book of European Cookery. LC 83-45072. (Illus.). 256p. 1983. 24.95 (ISBN 0-689-11398-6). Atheneum.
--Jane Grigson's British Cookery. LC 84-48442. (Illus.). 256p. 1985. 24.95 (ISBN 0-689-11524-5). Atheneum.
--Jane Grigson's Fruit Book. LC 82-45168. (Illus.). 528p. 1982. 19.95 (ISBN 0-689-11305-6). Atheneum.
--Jane Grigson's Vegetable Book. (Handbook Ser.). 1981. pap. 6.95 (ISBN 0-14-046352-6). Penguin.
--The Mushroom Feast. 1975. 16.95 (ISBN 0-394-48124-0). Knopf.
--The Mushroom Feast. (Illus.). 305p. 1983. pap. 5.95 (ISBN 0-14-046273-2). Penguin.
Grigson, Jane, jt. auth. see Grigson, Geoffrey.
Grigson, JAne, jt. auth. see Grigson, Geoffrey.
Grigulevich, I. Historia de la Inquisicion. 414p. (Span.). 1980. 8.95 (ISBN 0-8285-1813-0, Pub. by Progress Pubs USSR). Imported Pubns.
--Papado Siglo XX. 354p. 1982. 5.95 (ISBN 0-8285-2323-1, Pub. by Progress Pubs USSR). Imported Pubns.
Grigulevich, I. R. Ethnocultural Processes & National Problems in the Modern World. 383p. 1981. 8.00 (ISBN 0-8285-1968-4, Pub. by Progress Pubs USSR). Imported Pubns.
Grigulevich, J. La Iglesia Catolica y el Movimiento de Liberacion en America Latina. 510p. 1984. 8.95 (ISBN 0-8285-2803-9, Pub. by Progress Pubs USSR). Imported Pubns.
Grigull, H., ed. Properties of Water & Steam in SI-Units. 3rd, rev. ed. (Illus.). 194p. 1982. 32.50 (ISBN 0-387-09601-9). Springer-Verlag.
Grigull, U. & Sandner, H. Heat Conduction. Kestin, Joseph, tr. from Ger. LC 83-16616. (International Series in Heat & Mass Transfer). Orig. Title: Warmeleitung. (Illus.). 187p. 1984. text ed. 34.00 (ISBN 0-89116-358-1); pap. text ed. 22.50 (ISBN 0-89116-366-2). Hemisphere Pub.
Grigull, U., ed. see International Heat Transfer Conference, 7th, Munich, 1982.
Grigull, U., et al, eds. Steam Tables in SI-Units Wasserdampftafeln: Concise Steam Tables in SI-Units (Student's Tables)-Properties of Ordinary Water Substance up to 1000 degrees & 100 Megapascal. 2nd, Rev. ed. (Illus.). 96p. 1984. pap. 8.50 (ISBN 0-387-13503-0). Springer-Verlag.
Grijalva, Josue, tr. see Sisemore, J. T.
Grikscheit, Gary M., et al. Handbook of Selling: Psychological, Managerial & Marketing Basis. LC 80-19371. (Ronald Series on Marketing Management). 671p. 1981. 51.50x (ISBN 0-471-04482-2, Pub. by Ronald Pr). Wiley.
Griliches, Z. & Intriligator, M. D., eds. Handbook of Econometrics, 3 Vols. 1200p. 1984. Set. 195.00 (ISBN 0-444-86188-2, I-340-82, North Holland); 65.00 ea. Vol. 1 (ISBN 0-444-86185-8). Vol. 2 (ISBN 0-444-86186-6). Vol. 3 (ISBN 0-444-86187-4). Elsevier.
Griliches, Zvi. R & D, Patents, & Productivity. LC 83-18121. (National Bureau of Economic Research Conference Ser.). 528p. 1984. lib. bdg. 50.00x (ISBN 0-226-30883-9). U of Chicago Pr.
Griliches, Zvi, ed. see Schmookler, Jacob.
Grilikhes, Alexandra. Isabel Rawsthorne Standing in a Street in Soho. 72p. 1972. 6.00x (ISBN 0-913152-08-0); pap. 3.25x (ISBN 0-913152-07-2). Folder Edns.
--On Women Artists: Poems Nineteen Seventy-Five to Nineteen Eighty. LC 81-65430. (Illus.). 96p. (Orig.). 1981. pap. 4.95 (ISBN 0-939416-00-X). Cleis Pr.
Grill. Report Typing. 1980. text ed. 5.45 (ISBN 0-538-20060-X, T06). SW Pub.
Grill & Brown. ASBO, the First Fifty Years: The Building of the School Business Management Profession. (Research Bulletin: No. 20). pap. 0.69 (ISBN 0-685-57188-2). Assn Sch Busn.
Grill, Andre. Carnival of Innocence. LC 82-6852. 1985. 14.95 (ISBN 0-87949-215-5). Ashley Bks.
Grill, Johnpeter H. The Nazi Movement in Baden, 1920-1945. LC 82-13383. xvii, 720p. 1983. 32.00x (ISBN 0-8078-1472-5). U of NC Pr.
Grill, Tom & Scanlon, Mark. The Art of Scenic Photography: Technical & Aesthetic Guidelines for the Creative Photographer. (Illus.). 144p. 1982. 19.95 (ISBN 0-8174-3538-7, Amphoto). Watson-Guptill.
--The Essential Darkroom Book: A Complete Guide to Black & White Processing. (Illus.). 176p. 1983. pap. 14.95 (ISBN 0-8174-3838-6, Amphoto). Watson-Guptill.
--Photographic Composition: Guidelines for Total Image Control Through Effective Design. 144p. 1983. 22.50 (ISBN 0-8174-5419-5, Amphoto). Watson-Guptill.
--Photography: Turning Pro. (Illus.). 176p. 1982. 17.95 (ISBN 0-8174-5517-5, Amphoto). Watson-Guptill.
--Twenty-Five Projects to Improve Your Photography. (Illus.). 168p. 1981. 19.95 (ISBN 0-8174-6298-8, Amphoto); pap. 12.95 (ISBN 0-8174-6299-6). Watson-Guptill.
Grillet, Sophie, jt. auth. see Paczuska, Anna.
Grilley, Kate, jt. auth. see Venderheiden, Gregg C.
Grilley, Kate, jt. ed. see Vanderheiden, Gregg C.
Grilli, Enzo R. Italian Commercial Policies in the 1970's. (Working Paper: No. 428). 47p. 1980. pap. 3.00 (ISBN 0-686-39767-3, WP-0428). World Bank.
Grilli, Enzo R., ed. The Outlook for Primary Commodities. (Working Paper: No. 9). vi, 156p. 1982. pap. 5.00 (ISBN 0-686-39660-X, CP-0009). World Bank.
Grilli, Enzo R., et al. The World Rubber Economy: Structure, Changes, & Prospects. LC 80-554. (World Bank Occasional Papers). (Illus.). 224p. 1981. pap. text ed. 10.00x (ISBN 0-8018-2421-4). Johns Hopkins.
Grilli, Peter. Furo: The Japanese Bath. LC 85-40063. 176p. 1985. 35.00 (ISBN 0-87011-601-0). Kodansha.
Grilli, Peter, ed. Japan in Film: A Comprehensive Annotated Catalogue of Documentary & Theatrical Films on Japan Available in the United States. (Orig.). 1984. pap. text ed. 10.00 (ISBN 0-913304-20-4). Japan Soc.
Grilli, Sam. Sam Grilli's Complete Guide to Lake Erie Walleye. (Illus.). 160p. (gr. 4-12). 1980. 5.95 (ISBN 0-9604304-0-7); pap. 5.95 (ISBN 0-686-64677-0). Sport Fishing.
Grilliot, Harold J. Introduction to Law & the Legal System. 3rd ed. LC 39-532732. 672p. 1983. text ed. 28.95 (ISBN 0-395-32701-6); study guide 9.50 (ISBN 0-395-32703-2); instr's manual 2.00 (ISBN 0-395-32702-4). HM.
Grillius. Grillius, ein Beitrag Zur Geschichte der Retorik, Von Dr. Josef Martin. 1927. pap. 15.00 (ISBN 0-384-20025-7). Johnson Repr.
Grillmeier, Aloys. Christ in Christian Tradition: From the Apostolic Age to Chalcedon, Vol. 1. rev. ed. Bowden, John S., tr. from Ger. LC 75-13456. 451p. 1975. 29.95 (ISBN 0-8042-0492-6). John Knox.
Grillner, S. & Lindblom, B., eds. Speech Motor Control: Proceedings of an International Symposium on the Functional Basis of Ocular Motility Disorders, Wenner-Gren Center, Stockholm, Sweden, Aug. 31 to Sept. 3, 1981. LC 82-2223. (Wenner-Gren Ser.: Vol. 36). (Illus.). 306p. 1982. 60.00 (ISBN 0-08-028892-8). Pergamon.
Grillo, Ernesto. Shakespeare & Italy. LC 73-10197. (Studies in Shakespeare, No. 24). 1973. Repr. lib. bdg. 49.95x (ISBN 0-8383-1719-7). Haskell.
--Studies in Modern Italian Literature. 1973. Repr. of 1930 ed. 25.00 (ISBN 0-8274-0203-1). R West.
Grillo, Francesco. Tommaso Campanella in America: A Critical Bibliography & a Profile. 109p. 1954. 6.75x (ISBN 0-913298-43-3). S F Vanni.
--Tommaso Campanella in America: A Supplement to the Critical Bibliography. 48p. 1957. 5.00x (ISBN 0-913298-49-2). S F Vanni.
Grillo, Hermes C., jt. ed. see Choi, Noah C.
Grillo, John P. Color Computer Applications. LC 83-7034. (Recreational Computing Ser.: No. 1-704). 134p. 1983. pap. text ed. 10.95 (ISBN 0-471-86922-8). Wiley.
Grillo, John P. & Robertson, J. D. Apple Sampler: A Guide to Good BASIC Subroutines for the IIe-IIc. 1985. pap. 14.95 (ISBN 0-471-81729-5). Wiley.
--Data & File Management for the IBM Personal Computer. (Microcomputer Power Ser.). 191p. 1983. pap. 16.95 (ISBN 0-697-00349-3); incl. disk 32.95 (ISBN 0-697-00335-3). Wm C Brown.
--Data & File Management for the TI 99-4A. (Microcomputer Power Ser.). 196p. 1984. pap. 15.95 (ISBN 0-697-00245-4). Wm C Brown.
--Microcomputer Systems: An Applications Approach. 275p. 1979. pap. text ed. write for info. (ISBN 0-697-08132-X); instrs.' man. avail. (ISBN 0-697-08161-3). Wm C Brown.
--More Color Computer Applications: High Resolutions Graphics, Vol. 35. LC 84-2321. (Recreational Computing Ser: 1-704). 160p. 1984. pap. 14.95 (ISBN 0-471-86923-6, Wiley Professional Software); incl. disk 39.90 (ISBN 0-471-80767-2). Wiley.
--More Subroutine Sandwich. LC 82-13506. 260p. 1983. pap. text ed. 12.95 (ISBN 0-471-86921-X). Wiley.
--Subroutine Sandwich. LC 82-13516. 251p. 1983. pap. text ed. 12.95 (ISBN 0-471-86920-1). Wiley.
--Subroutine Sandwiches Set. 224p. 1983. pap. 25.90 (ISBN 0-471-88923-7). Wiley.
Grillo, John P. & Robertson, J. Douglas. Graphics for the Macintosh: An Idea Book. 1985. 17.95 (ISBN 0-03-000477-2). CBS Ed.
Grillo, John P., et al. Introduction to Graphics for the TI 99-4A. (Microcomputer Power Ser.). 130p. 1984. 14.95 (ISBN 0-697-00237-3). Wm C Brown.
Grillo, Paul. Vibes of the Saints. LC 76-48211. (Illus.). 1977. signed 20.00x (ISBN 0-916156-11-7). Cherry Valley.
Grillo, Paul J. Form, Function & Design. LC 74-18717. (Illus.). 238p. 1975. pap. 8.50 (ISBN 0-486-20182-1). Dover.
--Form, Function & Design. (Illus.). 16.25 (ISBN 0-8446-5196-6). Peter Smith.
Grillo, Peter, ed. La Chretiente de Corbaran: Part One, The Jerusalem Continuations. LC 83-7001. (The Old French Crusade Cycle Ser.: Vol. VII). lxvii, 102p. (Fr.). 1984. 27.50 (ISBN 0-8173-0134-8). U of Ala Pr.
Grillo, R. D. African Railwaymen. LC 73-79302. (African Studies: No. 10). (Illus.). 228p. 1973. 34.50 (ISBN 0-521-20276-0). Cambridge U Pr.
Grillo, R. D., ed. Nation & State in Europe: Anthropological Perspectives. LC 80-49766. 1981. 31.50 (ISBN 0-12-303060-9). Acad Pr.
Grillo, Ralph. Ideologies & Institutions in Urban France: The Representation of Immigrants. (Illus.). 368p. 1985. 44.50 (ISBN 0-521-30179-3). Cambridge U Pr.
Grillo, Ralph & Rew, Alan, eds. Social Anthropology & Development Policy. (ASA Monographs). 240p. 1985. 35.00 (ISBN 0-422-79790-1, 9524, Pub. by Tavistock England); pap. 13.95 (ISBN 0-422-79620-4, 952, Pub. by Tavistock England). Methuen Inc.
Grillo, Salvatore. The Gospel According to Barabbas. Cavoto, Nino, tr. from Italian. Orig. Title: Vangelo Secondo Barabba. 294p. (Orig.). 1982. pap. 4.95 (ISBN 0-89944-041-X, P 041-X). Don Bosco Multimedia.
Grillo, Virgil. Charles Dickens' Sketches by Boz: End in the Beginning. LC 73-89257. (Illus.). 1974. 17.50x. Colo Assoc.
Grillone, Lisa & Gennaro, Joseph. Small Worlds Close up. LC 77-15860. (Illus.). 64p. (gr. 3-5). 1978. 8.95 (ISBN 0-517-53289-1). Crown.
Grillos, Steve J. Ferns & Fern Allies of California. (California Natural History Guides: No. 16). (Illus., Rita Whittmore). 1966. pap. 2.65 (ISBN 0-520-00519-8). U of Cal Pr.
Grillot, Gerald F. A Chemical Background for the Paramedical Sciences. 2nd ed. (Illus.). 1974. text ed. 27.50 scp (ISBN 0-06-042511-3, HarpC). Har-Row.
Grillot, Peggy J., jt. auth. see Abegg, Lynda R.
Grillot De Givry. Witchcraft, Magic & Alchemy. Locke, J. Courtney, tr. from Fr. (Illus.). 395p. 1971. pap. 8.95 (ISBN 0-486-22493-7). Dover.
Grillparzer, F. Hero & Leander. Burkhard, Arthur, tr. 5.00x (ISBN 0-685-57219-6). M S Rosenberg.
--The Jewess of Toledo. Burkhard, Arthur, tr. 5.00x (ISBN 0-685-57218-8). M S Rosenberg.
--King Ottokar, His Rise & Fall. Burkhard, Arthur, tr. 5.00x (ISBN 0-685-57217-X). M S Rosenberg.
--Traum Ein Leben. Yates, W. E., ed. 1968. text ed. 9.95x (ISBN 0-521-05154-1). Cambridge U Pr.
Grillparzer, Franz. Medea. Burkhard, Arthur, tr. from Ger. pap. text ed. 5.00x (ISBN 0-685-48947-7). M S Rosenberg.
--Sappho. Burkhard, Arthur, tr. from Ger. 100p. (Orig.). 1953. pap. 5.00x (ISBN 0-686-74815-8). Register Pr.
Grills, Norma J. & Bosscher, Marcia V. Manual of Nutrition & Diet Therapy. 10th ed. 1981. pap. text ed. write for info. (ISBN 0-02-347280-4). Macmillan.
Grim, Gary & Dey, Denny. Storytelling. (gr. k-8). 1979. 8.95 (ISBN 0-916456-46-3, GA99). Good Apple.
Grim, John. Reflections on Shamanism: The Tribal Healer & the Technological Trance. (Teilhard Studies: No. 6). 20p. (Orig.). 1981. pap. 2.00 (ISBN 0-89012-029-3). Anima Pubns.
Grim, John A. The Shaman: Patterns of Siberian & Ojibway Healing. LC 83-47834. (Civilization of the American Indian Ser.: Vol. 165). (Illus.). 264p. 1984. pap. 19.95 (ISBN 0-8061-1809-1). U of Okla Pr.
Grim, Patrick. Philosophy of Science & the Occult. LC 81-13552. 320p. 1982. 39.50x (ISBN 0-87395-572-2); pap. 9.95x (ISBN 0-87395-573-0). State U NY Pr.
Grim, Ralph E. Applied Clay Mineralogy. LC 61-12035. (International Earth Science Ser.). pap. 105.50 (ISBN 0-317-28224-7, 2055970). Bks Demand UMI.
--Clay Mineralogy. 2nd ed. LC 67-24951. (McGraw-Hill International Earth & Planetary Science Ser.). pap. 149.00 (ISBN 0-317-28217-4, 2055969). Bks Demand UMI.
Grim, Ronald E., ed. Historical Geography of the United States & Canada: A Guide to Information Sources. (Geography & Travel Information Guide Ser.: Vol. 5). 350p. 1982. 60.00x (ISBN 0-8103-1471-1). Gale.
Grimal, ed. see De Voltaire, Francois-Marie A.
Grimal, Pierre. Dictionnaire de la Mythologie Grecque et Romaine. 5th ed. 612p. (Fr.). 1969. 59.95 (ISBN 0-686-57316-1, M-6299). French & Eur.
--Roman Cities: 'Les villes romaines'. Woloch, Michael, ed. & tr. from Fr. LC 81-69831. (Illus.). 349p. 1984. text ed. 30.00x (ISBN 0-299-08930-4); pap. 12.50x (ISBN 0-299-08934-7). U of Wis Pr.
Grimaldi. Brantome et le Sens de l'Histoire. 12.50 (ISBN 0-685-34182-8). French & Eur.
Grimaldi, Alfonsina A. The Universal Humanity of Giambattista Vico. 1958. 12.50x (ISBN 0-913298-62-X). S F Vanni.
Grimaldi, John V. & Simonds, Rollin H. Safety Management. 4th ed. 1984. 29.95 (ISBN 0-256-01564-3). Irwin.
Grimaldi, Nuzzo, jt. auth. see Lorit, Sergius C.
Grimaldi, Paul L. Medicaid Reimbursement of Nursing-Home Care. 1982. 15.95 (ISBN 0-8447-3456-X); pap. 7.95 (ISBN 0-8447-3457-8). Am Enterprise.
--Setting Rates for Hospital & Nursing Home Care. LC 84-17838. 360p. 1985. text ed. 27.50 (ISBN 0-89335-207-1). SP Med & Sci Bks.
--Supplemental Security Income: New Federal Program for the Aged, Blind, & Disabled. 1980. pap. 5.25 (ISBN 0-8447-3356-3). Am Enterprise.
Grimaldi, Paul L. & Micheletti, Julie A. DRG Update: Medicare's Prospective Payment System. LC 83-62696. 113p. (Orig.). 1983. pap. 15.95 (ISBN 0-931028-44-2, GM-3). Pluribus Pr.
--DRGs: A Practitioner's Guide. 2nd ed. LC 82-80887. 324p. 1983. 34.95 (ISBN 0-931028-30-2); pap. 28.95 (ISBN 0-931028-29-9). Pluribus Pr.
--Prospective Payment: The Definitive Guide to Reimbursement. LC 84-62516. (Illus.). 400p. (Orig.). 1985. 37.95 (ISBN 0-931028-63-9); pap. 32.95 (ISBN 0-931028-61-2). Pluribus Pr.
Grimaldi, Ralph P. & Rose-Hulman. Discrete & Combinatorial Mathematics. LC 84-9359. 1985. text ed. 32.95 (ISBN 0-201-12590-0). Addison-Wesley.
Grimaldi, Sal. Orealis. 309p. (Orig.). 1981. pap. 5.95 (ISBN 0-9608856-0-9). Universal Bks.
Grimaldi, William M. Aristotle, Rhetoric I: A Commentary. LC 79-53372. viii, 362p. 1980. 50.00x (ISBN 0-8232-1048-0). Fordham.
Grimarest, Jean L. Traite du recitatif dans la lecture, dans l'action publique, dans la declamation, et dans le chant. LC 76-43921. (Music & Theatre in France in the 17th & 18th Centuries). 1977. Repr. of 1760 ed. 20.00 (ISBN 0-404-60164-2). AMS Pr.
Grimaud, Michel, jt. auth. see Hules, Virginia T.
Grimaudet, Francois & Von Humboldt, Alexander. Fluctuations of Gold Together with the Law of Payment. LC 75-157156. (Research & Source Works Ser.: No. 722). 1971. Repr. of 1900 ed. 18.50 (ISBN 0-8337-4622-7). B Franklin.
Grimaux, jt. auth. see Clifton, E.
Grimaux, Edouard. Lavoisier: Seventeen Forty-Three to Seventeen Ninety-Four. Cohen, I. Bernard, ed. LC 80-2124. (Development of Science Ser.). (Illus.). 1981. lib. bdg. 35.00x (ISBN 0-405-13963-2). Ayer Co Pubs.
Grimble, Ian. Scottish Clans & Tartans. (Illus.). 272p. 1982. pap. 7.95 (ISBN 0-517-54827-5, Harmony). Crown.
Grimbly, Shona, jt. ed. see Picknett, Lynn.
Grimbol, William. Perspectives on the Passion. 1984. 5.25 (ISBN 0-89536-665-7). CSS of Ohio.
Grimbol, William R. The Communion Clown Circle. 1985. 2.50 (ISBN 0-89536-734-3, 5818). CSS of Ohio.
Grimby, Gunner, jt. auth. see Carlsten, Arne.
Grime, G. K. Analytical Solution Calorimetry. (Chemical Analysis Ser.). 400p. 1985. 60.00 (ISBN 0-471-86942-2). Wiley.

Grime, G. W. & Watt, F. Beam Optics of Quadrupole Probe-Forming System. 280p. 1983. 49.00 (ISBN 0-9960027-8-2, Pub. by A Hilger England). Heyden.
Grime, J. P. Plant Strategies & Vegetation Processes. LC 78-18523. 222p. 1979. 54.95x (ISBN 0-471-99695-5); pap. 23.95x (ISBN 0-471-99692-0). Wiley.
Grime, Kitty. Jazz Voices. 184p. 1984. 24.95 (ISBN 0-7043-2390-7, Pub. by Quartet Bks). Merrimack Pub Cir.
Grime, Philip N., jt. ed. see Lipke, William C.
Grime, William E. Ethno-Botany of the Black Americans. Irvine, Keith, ed. LC 78-20356. 1979. Repr. of 1976 ed. 19.95 (ISBN 0-917256-10-7). Ref Pubns.
Grimes, Alan P. American Political Thought. rev. ed. LC 83-16877. 572p. 1984. pap. text ed. 17.75 (ISBN 0-8191-3596-8). U Pr of Amer.
--Democracy & the Amendments to the Constitution. LC 78-4342. (Illus.). 1978. 26.00x (ISBN 0-669-02344-2). Lexington Bks.
--The Puritan Ethic & Woman Suffrage. LC 80-21799. xiii, 159p. 1980. Repr. of 1967 ed. lib. bdg. 22.50x (ISBN 0-313-22689-X, GRPE). Greenwood.
Grimes, Barbara F., ed. Ethnologue: Languages of the World. 10th ed. LC 73-646678. 592p. (Orig.). 1984. pap. text ed. 18.00x (ISBN 0-88312-597-8); microfiche 6.66 (ISBN 0-88312-993-0). Summer Inst Ling.
--Index to the Tenth Edition of the Ethnologue. 225p. (Orig.). 1984. pap. 9.00x (ISBN 0-88312-931-0); (3) 3.80microfiche (ISBN 0-88312-987-6). Summer Inst Ling.
Grimes, Barry. Five Primary Lines. 1985. pap. 5.00 handsewn paper (ISBN 0-911287-06-X). Blue Begonia.
Grimes, Bobbie M. The Parable of Jesus & Santa. LC 84-90331. (Illus.). 40p. (ps-5). 1984. 14.95 (ISBN 0-9613328-0-8). B & D Pub.
Grimes, Brian. British Wild Birds. 1982. 45.00x (ISBN 0-340-27970-2, Pub. by Hodder & Stoughton England). State Mutual Bk.
Grimes, Charles I., jt. auth. see Feldman, Alan S.
Grimes, Charles W. & Battersby, Gregory J. The Law of Merchandising & Character Licensing. 1985. write for info. Boardman.
Grimes, Daphne. Journeyings. ix, 101p. 1984. pap. 5.95 (ISBN 0-932269-03-6). Wyndham Hall.
Grimes, Dennis & Kelly, Brian. The Personal Computer Buyer's Guide. 296p. (Orig.). 1983. pap. text ed. 16.95 (ISBN 0-88410-917-8). Ballinger Pub.
Grimes, Dennis J., jt. auth. see Kelley, Brian W.
Grimes, Dennis J., jt. auth. see Kelly, Brian W.
Grimes, Diane C., jt. auth. see Krasevec, Joseph A.
Grimes, Ellen & Russell, Caryl Ann. How to Prepare for the CPA Examination: Business Law Section. 1978. pap. text ed. 9.95 (ISBN 0-07-024827-3). McGraw.
Grimes, Emily S. & Richman, Suzanne H. Teasers & Appeasers: An Hors d'Oeuvre Cookbook. (Illus.). 174p. (Orig.). 1980. pap. 9.95 (ISBN 0-9606236-0-4). Mushrooms Etc.
Grimes, Frances H. Good Night! LC 79-87669. (Illus.). (ps-3). Date not set. price not set (ISBN 0-89799-181-8); pap. price not set (ISBN 0-89799-182-6). Dandelion Pr.
--Sunny Side Up. (First Love Ser.). 187p. 1984. pap. 1.95 (ISBN 0-671-53384-3). PB.
Grimes, Harriette H. & Knack, John W., Sr. Games Book. Reusable ed. (gr. 1-8). 1976. wkbk. 6.00 (ISBN 0-89039-163-7). Ann Arbor FL.
Grimes, J. Bryan. Abstracts of North Carolina Wills 1663-1760. LC 67-28615. 670p. 1980. Repr. of 1910 ed. 25.00 (ISBN 0-8063-0163-5). Genealog Pub.
Grimes, Janet & Daims, Diva. Novels in English by Women, Eighteen Ninety-One to Nineteen Twenty: A Preliminary Checklist. Robinson, Doris, ed. LC 79-7911. (Reference Library of Humanities Ser.: Vol. 202). 805p. 1981. lib. bdg. 121.00 (ISBN 0-8240-9522-7). Garland Pub.
Grimes, Janet, jt. auth. see Daims, Diva.
Grimes, Janice L., jt. auth. see Wilson, Theresa E.
Grimes, Jeff, jt. ed. see Thomas, Alex.
Grimes, John M. Institutional Care of Mental Patients in the United States. Grob, Gerald N., ed. LC 78-22563. (Historical Issues in Mental Health Ser.). 1979. Repr. of 1934 ed. lib. bdg. 14.00x (ISBN 0-405-11917-8). Ayer Co Pubs.
--When Minds Go Wrong. 1954. 6.95 (ISBN 0-8159-7206-7). Devin.
Grimes, John R. The Tribal Style: Selections from the African Collection at the Peabody Museum of Salem. (Illus.). 1984. pap. 12.50 (ISBN 0-87577-150-5). Peabody Mus Salem.
Grimes, John S. Clark on Surveying & Boundaries. 4th ed. LC 76-12906. 1156p. 1976. 27.50 (ISBN 0-672-82326-8, Bobbs-Merrill Law). Michie Co.
--Henry's Probate Law & Practice, 6 vols. 7th ed. 5500p. 1978. 150.00 (ISBN 0-672-83934-2); 1984 supplement 30.00 (ISBN 0-87215-836-5). Michie Co.
--Thompson on Real Property, 24 vols. Set. 400.00 (ISBN 0-672-84297-1, Bobbs-Merrill Law); 1981 cum. suppl. 100.00 (ISBN 0-87215-426-2). Michie Co.
Grimes, Johnie M., ed. Willis M. Tate: Views & Interviews. LC 77-25103. (Illus.). 1978. 12.50 (ISBN 0-87074-163-2). SMU Press.
Grimes, Jorge & Iannopollo, Elizabeth. Health Assessment in Nursing Practice. LC 81-13110. (Nursing Ser.). 835p. 1982. text ed. 23.25 pub net (ISBN 0-534-01100-4); pap. text ed. 15.50 pub net (ISBN 0-534-02730-X). Brooks-Cole.
Grimes, Joseph E. Affix Positions & Coocurrences: The Paradigm Program. LC 83-50293. (Publications in Linguistics Ser.: No. 69). 90p. (Orig.). 1983. pap. 9.95 (ISBN 0-88312-095-X); microfiche 1.93 (ISBN 0-88312-400-9). Summer Inst Ling.
--Network Grammars. (SIL Linguistic & Related Fields Ser: No. 45). 198p. 1975. 8.50x (ISBN 0-88312-055-0); microfiche (3) 3.80x (ISBN 0-88312-455-6). Summer Inst Ling.
--Papers on Discourse. (Publications in Linguistics & Related Fields Ser: No. 51). 389p. 1978. pap. 13.80x (ISBN 0-88312-061-5); microfiche (5) 5.72x (ISBN 0-88312-461-0). Summer Inst Ling.
--Phonological Analysis. 187p. 1969. microfiche (2) 2.86 (ISBN 0-88312-360-6). Summer Inst Ling.
Grimes, Joseph E., ed. Sentence Initial Devices. LC 83-51455. (Publications in Linguistics Ser.: No. 75). 350p. (Orig.). 1985. pap. price not set (ISBN 0-88312-096-8). Summer Inst Ling.
Grimes, Judith A. & Rushforth, S. R. Diatoms of Recent Bottom Sediments of Utah Lake, Utah, USA. (Bibliotheca Phycologica Ser.: No. 55). (Illus.). 180p. 1982. text ed. 21.00x (ISBN 3-7682-1310-2). Lubrecht & Cramer.
Grimes, Larry E. The Religious Design of Hemingway's Early Fiction. Litz, A. Walton, ed. (Studies in Modern Literature: No. 50). 166p. 1985. 34.95 (ISBN 0-8357-1635-X). UMI Res Pr.
Grimes, Larry M. El Tabu Linguistico en Mexico: El Lenguaje erotico de los mexicanos. LC 78-52419. 1978. lib. bdg. 15.00x (ISBN 0-916950-10-7); pap. 9.00x (ISBN 0-916950-09-3). Biling Rev-Pr.
Grimes, Martha. The Anodyne Necklace. 252p. 1983. 14.45 (ISBN 0-316-32882-0). Little.
--The Anodyne Necklace. (No. 75). 256p. 1985. pap. 3.50 (ISBN 0-440-10280-4). Dell.
--The Dirty Duck. 252p. 1984. 14.45i (ISBN 0-316-32883-9). Little.
--The Dirty Duck. 1985. pap. 3.50 (ISBN 0-440-12050-0). Dell.
--Help the Poor Struggler. 288p. 1985. 15.45i (ISBN 0-316-32884-7). Little.
--Jerusalem Inn. 288p. 1984. 15.45i (ISBN 0-316-28989-2). Little.
--Jerusalem Inn. 1985. pap. 3.50 (ISBN 0-440-14181-8). Dell.
--The Man with a Load of Mischief. (Murder Ink Ser.: No. 49). 1985. pap. 3.50 (ISBN 0-440-15327-1). Dell.
--The Man with a Load of Mischief. 255p. 1981. 12.95 (ISBN 0-316-32880-4). Little.
--The Man with a Load of Mischief. Large Print ed. LC 83-24148. (A Richard Jury Mystery Ser.). 455p. 1984. Repr. of 1981 ed. 13.95 (ISBN 0-89621-514-8). Thorndike Pr.
--The Old Fox Deceiv'd. 288p. 1982. 13.95 (ISBN 0-316-32881-2). Little.
--The Old Fox Deceiv'd. 304p. 1985. pap. 3.50 (ISBN 0-440-16747-7). Dell.
--The Old Fox Deceiv'd. large print ed. LC 84-8566. 468p. 1984. Repr. of 1982 ed. 13.95 (ISBN 0-89621-543-1). Thorndike Pr.
Grimes, Millard. The Last Linotype. 500p. 1985. 19.95 (ISBN 0-317-07166-1). Strode.
Grimes, Nikki. Something on My Mind. LC 77-86266. 1978. 8.95 (ISBN 0-8037-8229-2); PLB 8.44 (ISBN 0-8037-8225-X). Dial Bks Young.
Grimes, Orville, Jr. Housing for Low Income Urban Families: Economics & Policy in the Developing World. LC 76-4934. (A World Bank Research Publication Ser). 192p. 1976. 18.50x (ISBN 0-8018-1853-2); pap. 8.95x (ISBN 0-8018-1854-0). Johns Hopkins.
Grimes, Paul. The New York Times Practical Traveler. LC 84-40431. 412p. (Includes index). 1985. pap. 10.95 (ISBN 0-8129-1152-0). Times Bks.
Grimes, Richard. Law & the Elderly. 250p. 1985. 26.50 (ISBN 0-7099-1162-9, Pub. by Croom Helm Ltd). Longwood Pub Group.
--Rockefeller, Old Money, New Politics. (Illus.). 250p. 1984. 12.95 (ISBN 0-934750-31-9). Jalamap.
Grimes, Richard H. & Horgan, Patrick T. Introduction to Law in the Republic of Ireland. 370p. 1982. 50.00x (ISBN 0-905473-55-8, Pub. by Wolfhound Pr England). State Mutual Bk.
Grimes, Ronald L. Beginnings in Ritual Studies. LC 81-40521. 312p. (Orig.). 1982. lib. bdg. 28.75 (ISBN 0-8191-2210-6); pap. text ed. 14.00 (ISBN 0-8191-2211-4). U Pr of Amer.
--Research in Ritual Studies: A Programmatic Essay & Bibliography. LC 84-23474. (ATLA Bibliography Ser.: No. 14). 177p. 1985. 15.00 (ISBN 0-8108-1762-4). Scarecrow.
--Symbol & Conquest: Public Ritual & Drama in Santa Fe, New Mexico. LC 76-13657. (Symbol, Myth, & Ritual Ser.). (Illus.). 336p. 1976. 32.50x (ISBN 0-8014-1037-1). Cornell U Pr.
Grimes, Roy E. The Thread of Discourse. 3rd ed. LC 74-78506. (Janua Linguarum Series Minor: No. 207). 408p. (Orig.). 1984. pap. text ed. 19.95x (ISBN 90-2793-164-X). Mouton.
Grimes, Russell N. Carboranes. (Organometallic Chemistry Ser). 1970. 65.00 (ISBN 0-12-303250-4). Acad Pr.
Grimes, Russell N., ed. Metal Interactions with Boron Clusters. LC 82-9068. (Modern Inorganic Chemistry Ser.). (Illus.). 342p. 1982. 49.50x (ISBN 0-306-40933-X, Plenum Pr). Plenum Pub.
Grimes, Sara. West Lake Reflections: A Guide to Hangzhou. (Illus.). 149p. (Orig.). 1983. pap. 4.95 (ISBN 0-8351-1012-5). China Bks.
Grimes, Sara, ed. see Dehuai, Peng.
Grimes, Seamus, ed. Ireland in Eighteen Hundred & Four. 2nd ed. (Illus.). 64p. 1980. Repr. of 1806 ed. 10.00x (ISBN 0-906127-24-6, BBA 03843, Pub. by Irish Academic Pr Ireland). Biblio Dist.
Grimes, William A. Criminal Law Outline. (Ser. 1050). 1980. pap. 8.00 (ISBN 0-686-08768-2). Natl Judicial Coll.
Grimeston, E., tr. see Le Petit, Jean Francois.
Grimke, Angelina E. Appeal to the Christian Women of the South. LC 77-82195. (Anti-Slavery Crusade in America Ser). 1969. Repr. of 1836 ed. 9.50 (ISBN 0-405-00635-7). Ayer Co Pubs.
--Letters to Catherine E. Beecher. facs. ed. LC 71-138338. (Black Heritage Library Collection Ser). 1838. 13.00 (ISBN 0-8369-8730-6). Ayer Co Pubs.
--Letters to Catherine E. Beecher, in Reply to an Essay on Slavery & Abolitionism. LC 70-82196. (Anti-Slavery Crusade in America Ser). 1969. Repr. of 1838 ed. 13.00 (ISBN 0-405-00636-5). Ayer Co Pubs.
Grimke, Archibald H. William Lloyd Garrison, the Abolitionist. LC 73-168207. Repr. of 1891 ed. 12.50 (ISBN 0-404-00057-6). AMS Pr.
Grimke, Francis J. The Negro: His Rights & Wrongs. 59.95 (ISBN 0-8490-0717-8). Gordon Pr.
Grimke, Frederick. Nature & Tendency of Free Institutions. Ward, John W., ed. LC 68-15638. (The John Harvard Library). 1968. 40.00x (ISBN 0-674-60500-4, Belknap Pr). Harvard U Pr.
Grimke, Thomas S. Address on the Truth, Dignity, Power & Beauty of the Principles of Peace, & on the Unchristian Character & Influence of War & the Warrior. LC 72-137542. (Peace Movement in America Ser). 56p. 1972. Repr. of 1832 ed. lib. bdg. 9.95x (ISBN 0-89198-070-9). Ozer.
Grimley, Gordon, ed. Victorian Cookery Book. (Illus.). 132p. 1974. 9.50 (ISBN 0-200-72047-3). Transatlantic.
Grimley, Mildred H. Mattie Loves All. 22p. 1985. 5.95 (ISBN 0-87178-552-8). Brethren.
Grimley, Paul, ed. see Santayana, George, et al.
Grimm, Brothers see Holme, Bryan.
Grimm, Charlie & Prell, Ed. Jolly Cholly's Story: Grimm's Baseball Tales. rev ed. LC 83-7627. xiv, 242p. 1983. pap. 7.95 (ISBN 0-912083-01-8). Diamond Communications.
Grimm, Claus. The Book of Picture Frames. (Illus.). 208p. 45.00 (ISBN 0-913870-92-7). Abaris Bks.
Grimm, Ede, jt. auth. see Edney, Margon.
Grimm, Florence M. Astronomical Lore in Chaucer. LC 73-168207. (University of Nebraska Studies in Language, Literature & Criticism). 1970. Repr. of 1919 ed. 12.00 (ISBN 0-404-02919-1). AMS Pr.
Grimm, Gary & Mitchell, Don. Creative Writing. (gr. 3-8). 1976. 7.95 (ISBN 0-916456-04-8, GA61). Good Apple.
--Dandylions Never Roar Book. (gr. k-8). 1976. 5.95 (ISBN 0-916456-03-X, GA53). Good Apple.
--Good Apple Math Book. (gr. 3-8). 1975. 10.95 (ISBN 0-916456-00-5, GA59). Good Apple.
--The Good Apple Spelling Book. 107p. (gr. 3-8). 1976. 7.95 (ISBN 0-916456-05-6, GA60). Good Apple.
--Mostly Me. (gr. k-6). 1976. 10.50 (ISBN 0-916456-07-2, GA64). Good Apple.
--Spelling Book. (gr. 3-8). 1976. 7.95 (ISBN 0-916456-05-6, GA60). Good Apple.
Grimm, Georg, jt. ed. see Benton, Wilbourn E.
Grimm, George. Buddhist Wisdom: The Mystery of the Self. 2nd, rev. ed. Keller-Grimm, M., ed. Aikins, Carrol, tr. from Ger. 1982. 11.50 (ISBN 0-89684-041-7, Pub. by Motilal Banarsidass India). Orient Bk Dist.
--Perennial Question. Schoenwerth, Ponisch, tr. from Ger. 56p. 1979. text ed. 6.95 (ISBN 0-89684-096-4, Pub. by Motilal Banarsidass India). Orient Bk Dist.
Grimm, H. Life of Michaelangelo, 2 vols. 200.00 (ISBN 0-8490-0533-7). Gordon Pr.
Grimm, Hans. Answer of a German. 69.95 (ISBN 0-87968-642-1). Gordon Pr.
--Tradition & History of the Early Churches of Christ in Central Europe. pap. 1.00 (ISBN 0-88027-095-0). Firm Foun Pub.
Grimm, Harold J. Lazarus Spengler: A Lay Leader of the Reformation. LC 78-13508. (Illus.). 249p. 1979. 15.00x (ISBN 0-8142-0290-X). Ohio St U Pr.
--The Reformation. LC 72-76717. (AHA Pamphlets: No. 403). 1972. pap. text ed. 1.50 (ISBN 0-87229-003-4). Am Hist Assn.
--The Reformation Era: 1500-1650. 2nd ed. (Illus.). 700p. 1973. text ed. write for info. (ISBN 0-02-347270-7, 34727). Macmillan.
Grimm, Harold J. & Lehmann, Helmut T., eds. Luther's Works: Career of the Reformer I, Vol. 31. LC 55-9893. 1957. 16.95 (ISBN 0-8006-0331-1, 1-331). Fortress.
Grimm, Harold J., ed. see Luther, Martin.
Grimm, Herman. Essays on Literature. 1973. Repr. of 1888 ed. 25.00 (ISBN 0-8274-0216-3). R West.
--The Life & Times of Goethe. facsimile ed. LC 78-152986. (Select Bibliographies Reprint Ser). Repr. of 1880 ed. 29.00 (ISBN 0-8369-5738-5). Ayer Co Pubs.
--The Life & Times of Goethe. 1880. 25.50 (ISBN 0-8274-2874-X). R West.
--The Life & Times of Goethe. Adams, Sarah H., tr. 559p. 1983. Repr. of 1880 ed. lib. bdg. 75.00 (ISBN 0-8495-2136-X). Arden Lib.
--Literature. facsimile ed. LC 76-37520. (Essay Index Reprint Ser). Repr. of 1885 ed. 20.00 (ISBN 0-8369-2551-3). Ayer Co Pubs.
Grimm, Herman F. Life of Michael Angelo, 2 Vols. Bunnett, Fanny E., tr. Repr. of 1900 ed. Set. lib. bdg. 48.00x (ISBN 0-8371-2750-5, GRMA). Greenwood.
--Life of Michael Angelo, 2 Vols. 45.00x (ISBN 0-403-00399-7). Scholarly.
Grimm, Jacob. Teutonic Mythology, 4 Vols. 4th ed. Stallybrass, James S., tr. Set. 60.00 (ISBN 0-8446-2168-4). Peter Smith.
Grimm, Jacob & Grimm, Wihelm K. Grimm's Fairy Tales. (Illus.). 128p. (gr. k-6). 1984. pap. 9.95 (ISBN 0-7100-9997-5); 13.95 (ISBN 0-7100-0912-7). Routledge & Kegan.
Grimm, Jacob & Grimm, Wilhelm. The Bear & the Kingbird. Segal, Lore, tr. from Ger. LC 79-118605. (Illus.). 32p. (ps up). 1979. 10.95 (ISBN 0-374-30618-4). FS&G.
--Deutsche Sagen: German Legends, 2 vols. in 1. Dorson, Richard M., ed. LC 77-70597. (Inter National Folklore Ser.). (Illus.). Repr. of 1891 ed. lib. bdg. 37.50x (ISBN 0-405-10097-3). Ayer Co Pubs.
--Deutsches Woerterbuch, 33 vols. (Ger.). 1973. Repr. Set. 3150.00x (ISBN 0-685-30396-9). Adlers Foreign Bks.
--The Fisherman & His Wife. Jarrell, Randall, tr. from Ger. LC 79-3248. (Illus.). 32p. (ps-3). 1980. 11.95 (ISBN 0-374-32340-2). FS&G.
--Grimm: Selected Tales. Luke, David, tr. 1983. pap. 3.95 (ISBN 0-14-044401-7). Penguin.
--Grimm's Fairy Tales. (Bambi Classics Ser.). (Illus.). 256p. (Orig.). 1981. pap. 3.95 (ISBN 0-89531-050-3, 0221-48). Sharon Pubns.
--The Juniper Tree & Other Tales from Grimm, 2 vols. Segal, Lore & Jarrell, Randall, trs. from Ger. LC 73-82698. (Illus.). 332p. 1973. boxed set 20.00 (ISBN 0-374-18057-1); pap. 7.95 (ISBN 0-374-51358-9). FS&G.
--King Grisly-Beard. Taylor, Edgar, tr. from Ger. LC 73-77911. (Illus.). (ps-3). 1973. 8.95 (ISBN 0-374-34133-8); pap. 6.95 (ISBN 0-374-34134-6). FS&G.
--Snow-White & the Seven Dwarfs. Jarrell, Randall, tr. from Ger. LC 28-1489. (Illus.). 32p. (ps up). 1972. 12.95 (ISBN 0-374-37099-0). FS&G.
Grimm, Jacob & Grimm, Wilhelm K. German Fairy Tales. Brackert, Helmut & Sander, Volkmar, eds. (German Library: Vol. 29). 320p. 1984. 24.50x (ISBN 0-8264-0288-7); pap. 10.95 (ISBN 0-8264-0289-5). Continuum.
--German Folk Tales. Krappe, Alexander H. & Magoun, Francis P., Jr., trs. LC 59-5095. (Arcturus Books Paperbacks). 682p. (gr. 5 up). 1969. pap. 15.95x (ISBN 0-8093-0356-6). S Ill U Pr.
--The Golden Goose. Jennings, Linda, retold by. LC 85-40536. (Illus.). 26p. (ps-3). 1985. 7.45 (ISBN 0-382-09147-7). Silver.
--Hansel & Gretel. LC 84-52783. (Tell Me a Story Ser.). (Illus.). 18p. (ps-1). 1985. 3.75 (ISBN 0-382-09072-1). Silver.
--Hansel & Gretel. (Illus.). 32p. (gr. k-3). 1985. 11.95 (ISBN 0-13-383654-1). P-H.
--Hansel & Gretel. (ps-3). Date not set. price not set. Delacorte.
--The Musicians of Bremen. Jennings, Linda, retold by. LC 85-61398. (Illus.). 26p. (ps-3). 1985. 7.45 (ISBN 0-382-09155-8). Silver.
--Sleeping Beauty. LC 84-52780. (Tell Me a Story Ser.). (Illus.). 18p. (ps-1). 1985. 3.75 (ISBN 0-382-09068-3). Silver.
Grimm, Jacob, jt. auth. see Grimm, Wilhelm.
Grimm, Jacob, jt. auth. see Grimm, Wilhelm K.
Grimm, Jacob, et al. The Glass Mountain. LC 84-7848. (Illus.). 40p. (ps-3). 1985. PLB 11.99 (ISBN 0-394-96724-0); pap. 11.95 (ISBN 0-394-86724-6). Knopf.
--The Valiant Tailor. Boada, Francesc, retold by. Northam, Leland, tr. from Span. LC 85-40495. (Illus.). 24p. (ps-4). 1985. 3.95 (ISBN 0-382-09142-6). Silver.
Grimm, Jakob. Grimm's Household Tales. 59.95 (ISBN 0-87968-214-0). Gordon Pr.
Grimm, Jakob & Grimm, Wilhelm. Grimm's Household Stories. Crane, Lucy, tr. LC 79-12246. (Facsimile Classics Ser.). (Illus.). 1979. Repr. of 1882 ed. 8.95 (ISBN 0-8317-4582-7, Mayflower Bks). Smith Pubs.
--Hansel & Gretel. (Illus.). (gr. k-3). 1981. 9.95 (ISBN 0-19-520262-7). Oxford U Pr.

Grimm, Jakob & Grimm, Wilhelm K. Snow White & Rose Red. (Collection of Fairy Tales Ser.). (Illus.). 32p. 1984. 7.95 (ISBN 0-87191-938-9). Creative Ed.

Grimm, James K., jt. auth. see Gerardi, Michael H.

Grimm, Josef & Grimm, Wilhelm. The Complete Grimm's Fairy Tales. (YA) 1974. 17.00 (ISBN 0-394-49415-6). Pantheon.

Grimm, Michele, jt. auth. see Grimm, Tom.

Grimm, Michelle & Grimm, Tom. Away for the Weekend: Great Getaways Less Than 250 Miles from Los Angeles. LC 83-23796. pap. 9.95 (ISBN 0-517-54940-9, C N Potter Bks). Crown.

Grimm, Reinhold. Love, Lust & Rebellion: New Approaches to Georg Buchner. LC 84-40497. 192p. 1985. text ed. 25.00x (ISBN 0-299-09860-5). U of Wis Pr.

--Texturen: Essays und Anderes zu Hans Magnus Enzenberger. LC 83-48820. (New York University Ottendorfer Ser.: Vol. 19). 224p. 1985. text ed. 19.50 (ISBN 0-8204-0059-9). P Lang Pubs.

Grimm, Reinhold, ed. Philosophical Writings. LC 82-22075. (The German Library: Vol. 44). 320p. Date not set. 24.50x (ISBN 0-8264-0278-X); pap. 10.95 (ISBN 0-8264-0279-8). Continuum.

Grimm, Reinhold, ed. see Enzensberger, Hans M.

Grimm, Reinhold, et al, eds. From Kafka & Dada to Brecht & Beyond. LC 81-24056. 96p. 1982. text ed. 17.00x (ISBN 0-299-97014-0). U of Wis Pr.

Grimm, Robert H. & MacKay, Alfred F., eds. Society: Revolution & Reform. LC 79-99232. (Proceedings of the 1969 Oberlin Colloquium in Philosophy). 1971. 17.50 (ISBN 0-8295-0190-8). UPB.

Grimm, Robert H., jt. ed. see Care, Norman S.

Grimm, Ronald E., jt. ed. see Wolter, John A.

Grimm, Ruediger H. Nietzsche's Theory of Knowledge. (Monographien und Texte Zur Nietzsche-Forschung: Vol. 4). 1977. 36.50x (ISBN 3-11-006568-1). De Gruyter.

Grimm, Susan. How to Write Computer Manuals for Users. 211p. 1982. 21.00 (ISBN 0-534-97941-6). Van Nos Reinhold.

Grimm, Susan J. How to Write Computer Manuals for Users. (Computer Technology Ser.). (Illus.). 211p. 1982. 21.00 (ISBN 0-534-97941-6). Lifetime Learn.

Grimm, Tom & Grimm, Michele. All about Thirty-Five mm Photography. LC 78-24816. (Illus.). 236p. 1979. pap. 8.95 (ISBN 0-02-012380-9, Collier). Macmillan.

--The Basic Darkroom Book: A Complete Guide to Processing & Printing Color & Black-&-White Photographs. (Orig.). (RL 9). 1978. pap. 8.95 (ISBN 0-452-25544-9, Z5544, Plume). NAL.

--The Good Guide for Bad Photographers: How to Avoid Mistakes & Take Better Pictures. LC 82-2139. (Illus.). 256p. 1982. pap. 7.95 (ISBN 0-452-25474-4, Z5474, Plume). NAL.

Grimm, Tom, jt. auth. see Grimm, Michelle.

Grimm, Tona. Basic Book of Photography. rev. ed. LC 73-90907. 368p. (RL 9). 1979. pap. 7.95 (ISBN 0-452-25216-4, Z5216, Plume). NAL.

Grimm, Werner, tr. see Althoff, Karl F.

Grimm, Wihelm K., jt. auth. see Grimm, Jacob.

Grimm, Wilhelm & Grimm, Jacob. The Falling Stars. LC 85-7193. (Illus.). 32p. (gr. k-3). 1985. 10.95 (ISBN 0-03-005742-6). HR&W.

Grimm, Wilhelm, jt. auth. see Grimm, Jacob.

Grimm, Wilhelm, jt. auth. see Grimm, Jakob.

Grimm, Wilhelm, jt. auth. see Grimm, Josef.

Grimm, Wilhelm K. & Grimm, Jacob. Household Stories of the Brothers Grimm. Crane, Lucy, tr. (Illus.). x, 269p. (gr. 3-9). 1886. pap. 4.00 (ISBN 0-486-21080-4). Dover.

Grimm, Wilhelm K., jt. auth. see Grimm, Jacob.

Grimm, Wilhelm K., jt. auth. see Grimm, Jakob.

Grimm, William C. The Illustrated Book of Trees. (Illus.). 512p. 1983. pap. 14.95 (ISBN 0-8117-2220-1). Stackpole.

Grimm Brothers, see Brothers Grimm.

Grimme, Hubert. Altsinaitische Forschungen, Epigraphisches und Historisches. 1937. pap. 15.00 (ISBN 0-384-20050-8). Johnson Repr.

--Israelitische Pfingstfest und der Plejadenkult. 1907. pap. 12.00 (ISBN 0-384-20060-5). Johnson Repr.

--Texte und Untersuchungen Zur Safatenisch - Arabischen Religion. 1929. pap. 15.00 (ISBN 0-384-20070-2). Johnson Repr.

Grimmelshausen, H. J. Von. Adventurous Simplicissimus. Goodrick, A. T., tr. LC 62-8406. (Illus.). xxxiv, 398p. 1962. pap. 7.95x (ISBN 0-8032-5077-0, BB 134, Bison). U of Nebr Pr.

--The Runagate Courage. Hiller, Robert L. & Osborne, John C., trs. LC 64-19584. (Illus.). xiv, 200p. 1965. 16.95x (ISBN 0-8032-0061-7). U of Nebr Pr.

Grimmelshausen, Hans J. Adventures of a Simpleton. Wallich, Walter, tr. LC 63-21987. Orig. Title: Simplicius Simplicissimus. pap. 5.50 (ISBN 0-8044-6229-1). Ungar.

Grimmelshausen, Hans J. Von see Von Grimmelshausen, Hans J.

Grimmelshausen, Hans Von see Von Grimmelshausen, Hans.

Grimmer, Elsa H. Wave Crest Ware: An Illustrated Guide to the Victorian World of C. F. Monroe. 96p. 1979. pap. 5.95 (ISBN 0-87069-279-8); price guide 1.50 (ISBN 0-87069-289-5). Wallace-Homestead.

Grimmer, Gernot, ed. Environmental Carcinogens - Polycyclic Aromatic Hydrocarbons. 272p. 1983. 85.00 (ISBN 0-8493-6561-9). CRC Pr.

Grimmer, Glenna. Texas Birds from A to Z. (Stories for Young Americans Ser.). (Illus.). 40p. (gr. 4-6). 1985. 9.95 (ISBN 0-89015-533-X). Eakin Pubns.

Grimmett, Geoffrey & Stirzaker, David. Probability & Random Processes. (Illus.). 1982. pap. 24.95x (ISBN 0-19-853185-0). Oxford U Pr.

Grimmett, Jennifer, jt. auth. see Thomis, Malcolm.

Grimmett, John O. Barriers Against Recovery. 8p. pap. 0.60 (ISBN 0-89486-009-7). Hazelden.

Grimmett, Robert G. Cabal of Death. LC 77-15675. 292p. 1977. 7.95 (ISBN 0-89301-047-2). U Pr of Idaho.

Grimond, Jo. Memoirs. 316p. 1980. 27.50x (ISBN 0-8419-6106-9). Holmes & Meier.

--A Personal Manifesto. 200p. 1983. 34.95x (ISBN 0-85520-678-0). Basil Blackwell.

Grimond, John. Youth Unemployment & the Bridge from School to Work. 51p. 1980. 30.00x (ISBN 0-905492-23-4, Pub. by Anglo-German Found England). State Mutual Bk.

Grimond, Joseph. The Liberal Challenge. LC 75-2696. 317p. 1975. Repr. of 1963 ed. lib. bdg. 18.25x (ISBN 0-8371-8025-2, GRLC). Greenwood.

Grimsditch, Herbert. Character & Environment in the Novels of Thomas Hardy. LC 68-788. (Studies in Thomas Hardy, No. 14). 1969. Repr. of 1925 ed. lib. bdg. 39.95x (ISBN 0-8383-0662-4). Haskell.

Grimshaw, Allen D. Language As Social Resource: Essays by Allen D. Grimshaw. Dil, Anwar S., ed. LC 81-50704. (Language Science & National Development Ser.). 388p. 1981. 27.50x (ISBN 0-8047-1108-9). Stanford U Pr.

Grimshaw, Anne. Hippobibliography Eighteen Fifty-One to Nineteen Seventy-Six: A Bibliographic Social History of the Horse. 372p. 1981. 75.00x (ISBN 0-85365-533-2, Pub. by Lib Assn England). State Mutual Bk.

--The Horse: A Bibliography of British Books 1851-1976. (Illus.). 508p. 1982. 110.00x (ISBN 0-89774-067-X, Pub. by Lib Assn England). Oryx Pr.

Grimshaw, Beatrice. In the Strange South Seas. facs. ed. LC 72-152920. (Black Heritage Library Collection). 1908. 33.50 (ISBN 0-8369-8764-0). Ayer Co Pubs.

Grimshaw, James A., Jr. The Flannery O'Connor Companion. LC 80-26828. (Illus.). 160p. 1981. lib. bdg. 27.50 (ISBN 0-313-21086-1, GRO/). Greenwood.

--Robert Penn Warren: A Descriptive Bibliography, 1922-1979. LC 81-3003. (Illus.). 608p. 1982. 30.00x (ISBN 0-8139-0891-4). U Pr of Va.

Grimshaw, James A., Jr., ed. Robert Penn Warren's Brother to Dragons: A Discussion. LC 82-16207. (Southern Literary Studies). 309p. 1983. text ed. 27.50X (ISBN 0-8071-1065-5). La State U Pr.

Grimshaw, Jane. English WH-Constructions & the Theory of Grammar. (Outstanding Dissertations in Linguistics Ser.). 239p. 1985. 30.00 (ISBN 0-8240-5448-2). Garland Pub.

Grimshaw, Patricia, et al. Families in Colonial Australia. (Illus.). 227p. 1985. text ed. 27.50x (ISBN 0-86861-513-7); pap. text ed. 14.00x (ISBN 0-86861-521-8). Allen Unwin.

Grimshaw, Peter. Excavators. (Illus.). 160p. 1985. 14.95 (ISBN 0-7137-1335-6, Pub. by Blandford Pr England). Sterling.

Grimshaw, William. Black Politics in Chicago: The Quest for Leadership 1939-1979. LC 80-120296. (Urban Insights Ser.: No. 4). (Illus.). 48p. 1980. pap. 2.50 (ISBN 0-911531-03-3). Loyola U Ctr Urban.

Grimshaw, William H. Official History of Free Masonry Among the Colored People in North America. LC 74-91257. (Illus.). Repr. of 1903 ed. 20.50x (ISBN 0-8371-2051-9, GRF&, Pub. by Negro U Pr). Greenwood.

--Official History of Freemasonry Among the Colored People in North America. facs. ed. LC 74-157370. (Black Heritage Library Collection). 1903. 22.50 (ISBN 0-8369-8808-6). Ayer Co Pubs.

Grimsley, jt. auth. see Lowell.

Grimsley, Bob. Management Accounting Systems & Records. 1972. 14.95x (ISBN 0-8464-0588-1). Beekman Pubs.

--Management Accounting Systems & Records. 2nd ed. 132p. 1981. text ed. 42.00x (ISBN 0-566-02349-0). Gower Pub Co.

Grimsley, R. W. The Church That Jesus Built. 1969. pap. 2.75 (ISBN 0-88027-031-4). Firm Foun Pub.

Grimsley, Ronald. Jean-Jacques Rousseau. LC 82-24409. 202p. 1983. text ed. 28.50x (ISBN 0-389-20378-5). B&N Imports.

Grimsley, Ronald, ed. see Rousseau, Jean-Jacques.

Grimson, Eric L. From Images to Surfaces: A Computational Study of the Human Early Visual System. (Artificial Intelligence Ser.). (Illus.). 274p. 1981. 35.00x (ISBN 0-262-07083-9). MIT Pr.

Grimstad, Bill. The Six Million Reconsidered. 170p. 1977. pap. 8.00 (ISBN 0-911038-50-7). Inst Hist Rev.

Grimstad, Bill & Drake, Raymond L. The Last Gold Rush: A Pictorial History of the Cripple Creek & Victor Gold Mining District. LC 83-61768. (Illus.). 159p. 1983. 20.00 (ISBN 0-913933-01-5); pap. 10.00. Pollux Pr.

Grimstad, Kari. Masks of the Prophet: The Theatrical World of Karl Kraus. 280p. 1982. 37.50x (ISBN 0-8020-5522-2). U of Toronto Pr.

Grimstad, William. Antizion: The Jewish & Zionist Question Through the Ages. 1982. lib. bdg. 69.95 (ISBN 0-686-97529-4). Revisionist Pr.

Grimstad, William, jt. auth. see Committee for Truth in History.

Grimstad, William, compiled by. Antizion. 2nd rev. ed. 1980. pap. 6.00 (ISBN 0-911038-20-5). Noontide.

Grimstad, William N., ed. see Committee for Truth in History.

Grimsted, David. Melodrama Unveiled: American Theater & Culture, 1800-1850. LC 68-15575. pap. 75.80 (ISBN 0-317-26505-9, 2024043). Bks Demand UMI.

Grimsted, Patricia K. Archives & Manuscript Repositories in the USSR: Estonia, Latvia & Belorussia. LC 79-15427. (Studies of the Russian Institute, Columbia University & Harvard Ser. in Ukrainian Studies). (Illus.). 1981. 70.00x (ISBN 0-691-05279-4). Princeton U Pr.

--Archives & Manuscript Repositories in the U. S. S. R., Moscow & Leningrad: Supplement I; Biographical Addenda. 218p. 1980. 30.00x (ISBN 0-691-05290-5). Princeton U Pr.

--Archives & Manuscript Repositories in the U. S. S. R. Moscow & Leningrad. LC 73-166375. (Studies of the Russian Institute Ser.). 480p. 1972. 55.00x (ISBN 0-691-05149-6). Princeton U Pr.

--The Foreign Ministers of Alexander First: Political Attitudes & the Conduct of Russian Diplomacy, 1801-1825. LC 69-11615. (Illus.). 1969. 35.00x (ISBN 0-520-01387-5). U of Cal Pr.

Grimstone, A. V. Electron Microscope in Biology. 2nd ed. (Studies in Biology: No. 9). 72p. 1978. pap. text ed. 8.95 (ISBN 0-7131-2611-6). E Arnold.

Grimstone, A. V., ed. see Sekida, Katsuki.

Grimvall, G. The Electro-Phonon Interaction in Metals. (Selected Topics in Solid State Physics: Vol. 16). 304p. 1981. 64.00 (ISBN 0-444-86105-X, North Holland). Elsevier.

Grimwade, Arthur G. London Goldsmith's, Sixteen Ninety-Seven to Eighteen Thirty-Seven: Their Marks & Lives from the Original Registers at Goldsmiths' Hall & Other Sources. (Illus.). 728p. 1976. 97.50x (ISBN 0-87471-794-9). Rowman.

--London Goldsmiths, 1697-1837: Their Marks & Lives from the Original Registers at Goldsmiths's Hall. rev. ed. (Illus.). 740p. 1983. 99.00 (ISBN 0-571-18065-5). Faber & Faber.

Grimwade, M. F. Introduction to Precious Metals. (Illus.). 128p. 1985. pap. text ed. 15.95 (ISBN 0-408-01451-2). Butterworth.

Grimwood, Brian E. Coconut Palm Products: Their Processing in Developing Countries. (Plant Production & Protection Papers). (Illus.). 261p. (2nd Printing 1980). 1976. pap. 28.25 (ISBN 92-5-100853-1, F95, FAO). Unipub.

Grimwood, William. Replay. 1986. price not set (ISBN 0-87795-781-9). Arbor Hse.

Grin, A. Seeker of Adventure. 484p. 1978. 7.95 (ISBN 0-8285-1623-5, Pub. by Progress Pubs USSR). Imported Pubns.

Grin, Alexander. Selected Short Stories. Luker, Nicholas, ed. & tr. from Rus. 250p. 1984. 22.00 (ISBN 0-88233-684-3); pap. 6.00 (ISBN 0-686-85663-5). Ardis Pubs.

Grinaker, Robert L. & Pearson, Della A. Basin Oil Company: A Comprehensive Problem for Oil & Gas Financial Accounting. 56p. 1983. pap. 9.50 loose-leaf, shrink-wrapped (ISBN 0-940966-03-4). N Texas St U Pro Devel Inst.

Grindal, Bruce. Growing up in Two Worlds: Education & Transition Among the Sisala of Northern Ghana. Spindler, George & Spindler, Louise, eds. (Case Studies in Education & Culture). 128p. 1983. pap. text ed. 6.95x (ISBN 0-8290-0318-5). Irvington.

Grindal, Bruce T. & Warren, Dennis M. Essays in Humanistic Anthropology: Festschrift in Honor of Davis Bidney, LC 78-66121. (Orig.). 1979. pap. text ed. 17.25 (ISBN 0-8191-0682-8). U Pr of Amer.

Grindal, Edmund. Remains of Edmund Grindal, Successively Bishop of London, & Archbishop of York & Canterbury. Repr. of 1843 ed. 41.00 (ISBN 0-384-20090-7). Johnson Repr.

Grindal, Gracia. Sketches Against the Dark. (Poetry Ser.). 88p. (Orig.). 1981. pap. 6.95 (ISBN 0-933188-13-7). Blue Moon Pr.

Grindal, Harald. Telecare Ministry: Using the Telephone in a Care Ministry. 40p. 1984. pap. 3.25 (ISBN 0-8066-2099-4, 23-1899). Augsburg.

Grindal, Richard. Death Stalk. 192p. 1982. 10.95 (ISBN 0-312-18805-6). St Martin.

Grindall, Irene V. Teaching Gifts. LC 85-71784. 64p. (Orig.). Date not set. pap. 3.50 (ISBN 0-88177-020-5, DR020B). Discipleship Res.

Grinde, Nils. Contemporary Norwegian Music Nineteen Twenty to Nineteen Eighty. 125p. 1981. pap. 20.00 (ISBN 82-00-05693-7). Universitet.

Grinde, Olav, tr. Breath Exercise: Poems of Rolf Jacobsen. 1985. 5.50 (ISBN 0-934834-53-9). White Pine.

Grindea, Carola. We Make Our Own Music. 64p. 1982. pap. 4.95 (ISBN 0-8008-8115-X, Crescendo). Taplinger.

Grindel, Cecelia M., jt. auth. see Nowak, Janie B.

Grindel, John. The Books of Joshua & Judges. (Bible Commentary Ser.). 112p. 1985. pap. 2.50 (ISBN 0-8146-1414-0). Liturgical Pr.

Grindel, John A. First Book of Chronicles, Vol. 17. (Bible Ser.). (Orig.). 1974. pap. 1.00 (ISBN 0-8091-5170-7). Paulist Pr.

--Second Book of Chronicles. (Bible Ser.: Vol. 18). (Orig.). 1974. pap. 1.00 (ISBN 0-8091-5171-5). Paulist Pr.

Grindell, Robert, et al. American Readings. (Saxon Series in English AS a Second Language).). 1964. text ed. 6.00 (ISBN 0-07-024860-5). McGraw.

Grinder, Alison L. & McCoy, E. Sue. The Good Guide: A Sourcebook for Interpreters, Docents, & Tour Guides. new ed. 164p. (Orig.). 1985. pap. 10.95 (ISBN 0-932541-00-3). Ironwood Scottsdale.

Grinder, John & Bandler, Richard. The Structure of Magic, Vol. 2. LC 75-12452. 1976. 8.95 (ISBN 0-8314-0049-8). Sci & Behavior.

--Trance-Formations: Neuro-Linguistic Programming & the Structure of Hypnosis. Andreas, Connirae, ed. 252p. (Orig.). 1981. 10.00 (ISBN 0-911226-22-2); pap. 6.50 (ISBN 0-911226-23-0). Real People.

Grinder, John, jt. auth. see Bandler, Richard.

Grinder, John, jt. auth. see McMaster, Michael.

Grinder, Robert E. Adolescence. 2nd ed. LC 77-7239. (Illus.). pap. 157.00 (ISBN 0-317-09708-3, 2020341). Bks Demand UMI.

--A History of Genetic Psychology: The First Science of Human Development. LC 67-21330. (Illus.). pap. 65.30 (ISBN 0-317-10457-8, 2012527). Bks Demand UMI.

Grindle, Crosby R., jt. auth. see Giegold, William C.

Grindle, Juliet, jt. ed. see Clements, Patricia.

Grindle, Juliet, ed. see Hardy, Thomas.

Grindle, Merilee S. Bureaucrats, Politicians, & Peasants in Mexico: A Case Study in Public Policy. LC 76-7759. 1977. 29.50x (ISBN 0-520-03238-1). U of Cal Pr.

--State & Countryside: Development Policy & Agrarian Politics in Latin America. LC 85-8081. (Studies in Development). 256p. 1986. text ed. 25.00x (ISBN 0-8018-3278-0); pap. text ed. 11.95x (ISBN 0-8018-2935-6). Johns Hopkins.

Grindle, Merilee S., ed. Politics & Policy Implementation in the Third World. LC 79-3213. 1980. 32.00 (ISBN 0-691-07617-0); pap. 9.95 (ISBN 0-691-02195-3). Princeton U Pr.

Grindley, Kit. Systematics: A New Approach to Systems Analysis. (Illus.). 1977. text ed. 12.00 (ISBN 0-89433-020-9). Petrocelli.

Grindon, Leo H. Shakespere Flora. LC 77-168208. Repr. of 1883 ed. 23.00 (ISBN 0-404-02929-9). AMS Pr.

Grindrod, Muriel. The Rebuilding of Italy: Politics & Economics, 1945-1955. LC 77-9604. (Illus.). 1977. Repr. of 1955 ed. lib. bdg. 24.00x (ISBN 0-8371-9712-0, GRRI). Greenwood.

Grindstaff, Carl F. The Pharmacist & Family Planning. 192p. 1980. pap. 8.95 (ISBN 0-8158-0396-6). Chris Mass.

--Population & Society: A Sociological Perspective. 192p. 1981. pap. 8.95 (ISBN 0-8158-0397-4). Chris Mass.

Griner, Lynn A. Pathology of Zoo Animals: A Review of Necropsies Conducted over a Fourteen Year Period at the San Diego Zoo. LC 82-62698. (Illus.). 1983. 25.00 (ISBN 0-911461-11-6). Zoological Soc.

Grinfelds, Vesma, jt. auth. see Hultstand, Bonnie.

Gringhuis, Dirk. Lore of the Great Turtle: Indian Legends of Mackinac Retold. LC 73-636148. (Illus.). 96p. (Orig.). 1970. pap. 2.50 (ISBN 0-911872-11-6). Mackinac Island.

--Were-Wolves & Will-O-the-Wisps: French Tales of Mackinac Retold. (Illus.). 106p. (Orig.). 1974. pap. 2.50 (ISBN 0-911872-14-0). Mackinac Island.

--Young Voyageur: Trade & Treachery at Michilimackinac. rev. ed. (Illus.). 202p. (gr. 9 up). 1969. pap. 2.50 (ISBN 0-911872-34-5). Mackinac Island.

Gringhuis, Dirk, jt. auth. see Holman, J. Allan.

Gringhuis, Dirk, et al. Mackinac History, Vol. 2. (Illus.). 76p. (Orig.). 1982. pap. 5.00 (ISBN 0-911872-34-5). Mackinac Island.

Grings, William W. & Dawson, Michael E. Emotions & Bodily Responses: A Psychophysiological Approach. (Behavioral Biology & International Ser.). 1978. 29.50 (ISBN 0-12-303750-6). Acad Pr.

Grinial. Dictionnaire des Biographies, 2 Tomes. Set. 67.90 (ISBN 0-685-35950-6). French & Eur.

Grinich, Victor. Introduction to Integrated Circuits. (Illus.). 672p. 1975. text ed. 48.00 (ISBN 0-07-024875-3). McGraw.

Grinker, Roy R. Mid-Century Psychiatry. (Illus.). 192p. 1953. 17.50x (ISBN 0-398-04271-3). C C Thomas.

--Psychosomatic Concepts. LC 84-451254. 219p. 1983. 20.00x (ISBN 0-87668-698-6). Aronson.

Grinker, Roy R. & Spiegel, John P. War Neuroses. Kohn, Richard H., ed. LC 78-22381. (American Military Experience Ser.). 1979. Repr. of 1945 ed. lib. bdg. 12.00x (ISBN 0-405-11858-9). Ayer Co Pubs.

Grinker, Roy R., Sr. Fifty Years in Psychiatry: A Living History. 280p. 1979. 29.75x (ISBN 0-398-03876-7). C C Thomas.

--Psychiatry in Broad Perspective. LC 74-13012. 262p. 1975. deluxe ed. 28.95 (ISBN 0-87705-231-X). Human Sci Pr.

Grinker, Roy R., Sr. & Speigel, John. Men under Stress. 1979. Repr. of 1945 ed. 49.50x (ISBN 0-89197-645-0). Irvington.
--Men under Stress. 1985. pap. text ed. 24.50x (ISBN 0-8290-1166-8). Irvington.
Grinker, Roy R., Sr. & Werble, Beatrice. The Borderline Patient. LC 84-45089. 226p. 1983. 25.00x (ISBN 0-87668-676-5). Aronson.
Grinnell, Alan D. & Moody, William J., Jr. The Physiology of Excitable Cells. LC 83-12063. (Neurology & Neurobiology Ser.: Vol. 5). 620p. 1983. 72.00 (ISBN 0-8451-2704-7). A R Liss.
Grinnell, Alan D., et al, eds. The Regulation of Muscle Contraction: Excitation-Contraction Coupling. LC 81-4362. (UCLA Forum in Medical Sciences: Vol. 22). 1981. 35.00 (ISBN 0-12-303780-8). Acad Pr.
Grinnell, Elizabeth, ed. see Grinnell, Joseph.
Grinnell, George B. Beyond the Old Frontier. (Illus.). 374p. 1976. Repr. of 1913 ed. 16.95 (ISBN 0-87928-069-7). Corner Hse.
--Blackfoot Lodge Tales. 310p. 1972. Repr. of 1892 ed. 16.95 (ISBN 0-87928-030-1). Corner Hse.
--Blackfoot Lodge Tales: The Story of a Prairie People. LC 62-4146. xviii, 311p. 1962. pap. 5.95 (ISBN 0-8032-5079-7, BB 129, Bison). U of Nebr Pr.
--By Cheyenne Campfires. LC 79-158083. (Illus.). xxiv, 305p. 1971. pap. 6.50 (ISBN 0-8032-5746-5, BB 541, Bison). U of Nebr Pr.
--The Cheyenne Indians: Their History & Ways of Life, 2 vols. Incl. Vol. 1. x, 402p. pap. 10.95 (ISBN 0-8032-5771-6, BB 562, Bison); Vol. 2. viii, 478p. pap. 11.95 (ISBN 0-8032-5772-4, BB 563, Bison). LC 23-17688. (Illus.). 1972. pap. U of Nebr Pr.
--The Fighting Cheyennes. LC 56-10392. (The Civilization of the American Indian Ser.: Vol. 44). (Illus.). 450p. 1983. cloth 24.95 (ISBN 0-8061-0347-7); pap. 14.95 (ISBN 0-8061-1839-3). U of Okla Pr.
--Fighting Cheyennes. (Illus.). 431p. 1976. Repr. of 1915 ed. 20.00 (ISBN 0-87928-075-1). Corner Hse.
--The Indians of Today. LC 74-7970. (Illus.). Repr. of 1911 ed. 34.50 (ISBN 0-404-11857-7). AMS Pr.
--Last of the Buffalo. LC 78-125740. (American Environmental Studies). 1970. Repr. of 1893 ed. 11.00 (ISBN 0-405-02665-X). Ayer Co Pubs.
--Pawnee Hero Stories & Folk-Tales with Notes on the Origin, Customs & Character of the Pawnee People. LC 61-10153. (Illus.). xiv, 417p. 1961. 29.95x (ISBN 0-8032-0896-0); pap. 7.50 (ISBN 0-8032-5080-0, BB 116, Bison). U of Nebr Pr.
--The Punishment of the Stingy & Other Indian Stories. LC 81-21922. (Illus.). xx, 265p. 1982. 19.50x (ISBN 0-8032-2113-4); pap. 5.95 (ISBN 0-8032-7008-9, BB 783, Bison). U of Nebr Pr.
--The Story of the Indian. Repr. of 1909 ed. 35.00 (ISBN 0-8492-9965-9). R West.
--Two Great Scouts & Their Pawnee Battalion: The Experiences of Frank J. North & Luther H. North, Pioneers in the Great West, 1856-1882, & Their Defence of the Building of the Union Pacific Railroad. LC 29-2718. pap. 76.50 (ISBN 0-317-20462-9, 2023005). Bks Demand UMI.
--When Buffalo Ran. LC 66-13429. (Western Frontier Library: No. 31). (Illus.). 1966. pap. 4.95 (ISBN 0-8061-1271-9). U of Okla Pr.
Grinnell, George B. & Sheldon, Charles, eds. Hunting & Conservation. LC 71-125741. (American Environmental Studies). 1970. Repr. of 1925 ed. 33.00 (ISBN 0-405-02666-8). Ayer Co Pubs.
Grinnell, Ira. Study Paper on Parliamentary Procedure. 1971. write for info. U of SD Gov Res Bur.
Grinnell, Ira H. The Tribal Government of the Oglala Sioux of Pine Ridge, South Dakota. 1967. write for info. U of SD Gov Res Bur.
Grinnell, Isabel H. Greek Temples. LC 79-168420. (Metropolitan Museum of Art Publications in Reprint Ser.). (Illus.). 138p. 1972. Repr. of 1943 ed. 35.50 (ISBN 0-405-02258-1). Ayer Co Pubs.
Grinnell, J. Erle. Interpreting the Public Schools. 1937. 20.00 (ISBN 0-932062-69-5). Sharon Hill.
--Interpreting the Public Schools: A Manual of Principles & Practices of Public School Interpretation with Special Emphasis on Published Materials. 1978. Repr. of 1937 ed. lib. bdg. 17.50 (ISBN 0-8492-0950-1). R West.
Grinnell, Joseph. An Account of the Mammals & Birds of the Lower Colorado Valley, with Especial Reference to the Distributional Problems Presented. Sterling, Keir B., ed. LC 77-81116. (Biologists & Their World Ser.). (Illus.). 1978. Repr. of 1914 ed. lib. bdg. 22.00x (ISBN 0-405-10708-0). Ayer Co Pubs.
--Gold Hunting in Alaska. facsimile ed. (Shorey Historical Ser.). (Illus.). 96p. Repr. of 1901 ed. pap. 6.95 (ISBN 0-8466-0023-4, S23). Shorey.
--Gold Hunting in Alaska. Grinnell, Elizabeth, ed. (Illus.). 80p. 1983. pap. 7.95 (ISBN 0-88240-236-6). Alaska Northwest.
--Joseph Grinnell's Philosophy of Nature: Selected Writings of a Western Naturalist. facs. ed. LC 68-20304. (Essay Index Reprint Ser). 1943. 21.50 (ISBN 0-8369-0499-0). Ayer Co Pubs.
Grinnell, Lawrence, et al, trs. see DeMorant, George S.
Grinnell, Lawrence, et al, trs. see DeMorant, Soulie G.
Grinnell, Paula C. How Can I Prepare My Young Child for Reading? (Micromonograph Ser.). 1984. 0.50. Intl Reading.
Grinnell, Richard M., Jr. Social Work Research & Evaluation. 2nd ed. LC 83-63543. 550p. 1984. text ed. 25.95 (ISBN 0-87581-303-8). Peacock Pubs.
Grinnell-Milne, Duncan, et al. Wind in the Wires. Ulanoff, Stanley M. & Gilbert, James, eds. LC 79-7264. (Flight: Its First Seventy-Five Years Ser.). (Illus.). 1979. Repr. of 1968 ed. lib. bdg. 25.50x (ISBN 0-405-12174-1). Ayer Co Pubs.
Grinold, Richard C. & Marshall, Kneale T. Manpower Planning Models. LC 76-40243. (Publications in Operations Research Ser.: Vol. 1). (Illus.). 268p. 1977. 47.00 (ISBN 0-444-00190-5, North Holland). Elsevier.
Grinols, Anne B., ed. Critical Thinking: Reading Across the Curriculum. LC 83-73116. 292p. 1984. 10.95x (ISBN 0-8014-9281-5). Cornell U Pr.
Grinsberg, Leon, et al. Introduction to the Work of Bion. Hahn, Alberto, tr. from Sp. LC 77-7733. 1977. 12.50x (ISBN 0-87668-271-9). Aronson.
GRINSEC. Electronic Switching. (Studies in Telecommunication: Vol. 2). 680p. 1983. 89.00 (ISBN 0-444-86448-2, North Holland). Elsevier.
Grinsell, L. V. The Ancient Burial-Mounds of England. LC 73-13037. (Illus.). 278p. 1975. Repr. of 1953 ed. lib. bdg. 22.50x (ISBN 0-8371-7101-6, GRAB). Greenwood.
--The Bath Mint. 1973. 4.00 (ISBN 0-685-51513-3, Pub by Spink & Son England). S J Durst.
Grinsell, Leslie & Rantz, Phillip. The Preparation of Archaeological Reports. 2nd ed. LC 74-82135. 1974. 27.50 (ISBN 0-312-63945-7). St Martin.
Grinsell, Leslie V. Barrows in England & Wales. (Archaeology Ser.: No. 8). (Illus.). pap. 5.95 (ISBN 0-85263-669-5, Pub. by Shire England). Seven Hills Bks.
Grinspoon, Lester. Marihuana Reconsidered. rev. ed. LC 77-76767. 1977. 25.00x (ISBN 0-674-54833-7); pap. 9.95 (ISBN 0-674-54834-5). Harvard U Pr.
--Psychiatry 1982: The American Psychiatric Association Annual Review Psychiatry Update, Vol. I. Incl. Psychiatry Update: The American Psychiatric Association Annual Review, Vol. II. Grinspoon, Lester, ed. (Illus.). 616p. 1983. text ed. 45.00 (ISBN 0-88048-007-6, 48-007-6); Psychiatry Update: The American Psychiatric Association Annual Review, Vol. III. Grinspoon, Lester, ed. (Illus.). 648p. 1984. text ed. 45.00x (ISBN 0-88048-015-7, 48-015-7). (Illus.). 552p. 1982. 45.00x (ISBN 0-88048-000-9, 48-000-9). Am Psychiatric.
Grinspoon, Lester & Bakalar, James B. Psychedelic Drugs Reconsidered. 1981. pap. 9.50 (ISBN 0-465-06451-5, CN-5068). Basic.
--Psychedelic Drugs Reconsidered. LC 79-7336. 1979. 16.50x (ISBN 0-465-06450-7). Basic.
Grinspoon, Lester & Hedblom, Peter. The Speed Culture: Amphetamine Use & Abuse in America. LC 74-27257. 368p. 1975. 20.00e (ISBN 0-674-83192-6); pap. 8.95 (ISBN 0-674-83194-2). Harvard U Pr.
Grinspoon, Lester, jt. auth. see Bakalar, James B.
Grinspoon, Lester & Bakalar, James B., eds. Psychedelic Reflections. 256p. 1983. 26.95 (ISBN 0-89885-129-7). Human Sci Pr.
Grinstead, E. D., ed. Chinese Periodicals in British Libraries: Handlist, No. 3. 80p. (Orig.). 1969. pap. 7.50 (ISBN 0-7141-0639-9, Pub. by British Lib). Longwood Pub Group.
Grinstead, J. E. Maverick Guns. 1978. pap. 1.25 (ISBN 0-505-51269-6, Pub. by Tower Bks). Dorchester Pub Co.
Grinstein, Alexander. Freud's Rules of Dream Interpretation. LC 83-12952. 306p. 1983. text ed. 25.00 (ISBN 0-8236-2035-2). Intl Univs Pr.
--Sigmund Freud's Dreams. LC 79-2485. 486p. 1980. text ed. 35.00 (ISBN 0-8236-6074-5). Intl Univs Pr.
Grinstein, Alexander, ed. The Index of Psychoanalytic Writings, Vols. 1-5. 1956-60. Set. text ed. 200.00 (ISBN 0-8236-8400-8). Intl Univs Pr.
--The Index of Psychoanalytic Writings, Vols. 6-9. 1963-66. Set. text ed. 200.00 (ISBN 0-8236-8401-6). Intl Univs Pr.
--The Index of Psychoanalytic Writings, Vols. 10-14. LC 56-8932. 1971. Set. text ed. 200.00 (ISBN 0-8236-8402-4); Vol. 10. (ISBN 0-8236-2570-2); Vol. 11. (ISBN 0-8236-2571-0); Vol. 12. (ISBN 0-8236-2572-9); Vol. 13. (ISBN 0-8236-2573-7); Vol. 14. (ISBN 0-8236-2574-5). Intl Univs Pr.
--Sigmund Freuds Writings: A Comprehensive Bibliography. LC 76-46812. 181p. 1977. text ed. 22.50 (ISBN 0-8236-6076-1). Intl Univs Pr.
Grinstein, Hyman. A Short History of the Jews in the United States. 208p. 1980. 20.00 (ISBN 0-900689-50-1). Soncino Pr NY.
Grinstein, Louise & Michaels, Brenda, eds. Calculus: Readings from the Mathematics Teacher. (Illus.). 230p. 1977. pap. 6.75 (ISBN 0-87353-031-4). NCTM.
Grinter, Lawrence E., jt. ed. see Kihl, Young W.
Grioli, G., ed. Thermodynamics & Constitutive Equations. (Lecture Notes in Physics Ser.: Vol. 228). (Illus.). v, 257p. 1985. pap. 17.30 (ISBN 0-387-15228-8). Springer-Verlag.
Gripe, Maria. Elvis & His Secret. (Illus.). 208p. (gr. 3-7). pap. 1.75 (ISBN 0-440-42434-8, YB). Dell.
Gripkey, Sr. M. Vincentine. Blessed Virgin Mary As Mediatrix in the Latin & Old French Legend Prior to the Fourteenth Century. LC 72-94166. (Catholic University of America Studies in Romance Languages & Literatures Ser: No. 17). 1969. Repr. of 1938 ed. 26.00 (ISBN 0-404-50317-9). Ams Pr.
Gripp, R. Political System of Communism. 1973. pap. 12.95 (ISBN 0-442-30693-8). Van Nos Reinhold.
Grippando, Gloria M. Nursing: Perspectives & Issues. 2nd ed. LC 82-71087. 512p. 1983. pap. text ed. 14.40 (ISBN 0-8273-2078-7). Delmar.
Grippin, Pauline & Peters, Sean. Learning Theory & Learning Outcomes: The Connection. 268p. (Orig.). 1984. lib. bdg. 23.00 (ISBN 0-8191-3794-4); pap. text ed. 12.50 (ISBN 0-8191-3795-2). U Pr of Amer.
Gripton, James see Valentich, Mary.
Gripton, James & Valentich, Mary, eds. Social Work Practice in Sexual Problems. (Journal of Social Work & Human Sexuality Ser.: Vol. 4, Nos. 1-2). 224p. 1985. text ed. price not set (ISBN 0-86656-485-3). Haworth Pr.
Griqull, U., ed. Selected Publications of Wilhelm Nusselt & Ernst Schmidt. LC 82-9199. 272p. 1982. pap. text ed. 17.95 (ISBN 0-89116-329-8). Hemisphere Pub.
Grisanti, Benedict. The Fully Illustrated Analytical History of Italian, French, British & German Architecture, 2 vols. (Illus.). 318p. 1985. Set. 147.50 (ISBN 0-86650-146-0). Gloucester Art.
Grisanti, John. Wining & Dining with John Grisanti. Streich, Marianne & Coward, Jane, eds. (Illus.). 192p. 1984. deluxe edition 25.00 (ISBN 0-939114-89-5); pap. 11.95 (ISBN 0-939114-84-4). Wimmer Bks.
Grisar, Hartmann. History of Rome & the Popes in the Middle Ages, 3 vols. LC 70-154115. (Illus.). Repr. of 1912 ed. Set. 120.00 (ISBN 0-404-09370-1). AMS Pr.
--Martin Luther: His Life & Work. Preuss, Arthur, ed. LC 71-137235. Repr. of 1930 ed. 29.50 (ISBN 0-404-02935-3). AMS Pr.
Grisbrooke, Jardine W., ed. Spiritual Counsels of Father John of Kronstadt: Select Passages from "My Life in Christ". 256p. 1983. pap. 10.95 (ISBN 0-227-67856-7, Pub. by J Clarke UK). Attic Pr.
Grisbrooke, John. French for Catering Students. 160p. 1982. pap. text ed. 7.95 (ISBN 0-7131-0710-3). E Arnold.
Grisbrooke, W. Jardine. The Spiritual Counsels of Father John of Kronstadt. 230p. (Orig.). 1982. pap. 7.95 (ISBN 0-913836-92-3). St Vladimirs.
--Spiritual Counsels of Father John of Kronstadt: Select Passages from My Life in Christ. 256p. 1983. Repr. of 1967 ed. 8.95 (ISBN 0-227-67856-7). Attic Pr.
Grisby, Robert F. R. F. Grigsby's Sierra Madre Journal: 1864: An American Prospector's Adventures. Boudreau, Eugene H., ed. LC 76-43601. 1976. pap. 8.00 (ISBN 0-686-16316-8). Pleasant Hill.
Griscelli, C. & Vossen, J. Progress in Immunodeficiency Research & Therapy, Vol. 1. (International Congress Ser.: Vol. 645). 1984. 94.50 (ISBN 0-444-80602-4). Elsevier.
Grischen, N. Deutsch-Russische Wirtschaftssprache. 480p. (Ger. & Rus.). 1969. 27.50 (ISBN 3-19-006207-2, M-7332, Pub. by M. Hueber). French & Eur.
Griscom, Andy, et al. The Complete Book of Beer Drinking Games. LC 83-90179. (Illus.). 128p. (Orig.). 1984. pap. 4.95 (ISBN 0-914457-01-2). Mustang Pub.
Griscom, Hilda, jt. auth. see Rosenzweig, Norman.
Griscom, John H. The Sanitary Condition of the Laboring Population of New York, with Suggestions for Its Improvement. LC 75-125742. (American Environmental Studies). Repr. of 1845 ed. 12.00x (ISBN 0-405-02667-6). Ayer Co Pubs.
--Uses & Abuses of Air: Showing Its Influence in Sustaining Life & Producing Disease. LC 79-125743. (American Environmental Studies). 1970. Repr. of 1854 ed. 17.00 (ISBN 0-405-02668-4). Ayer Co Pubs.
Griscom, Morgan & Arthur, Griscom, eds. Heritage of Community. (Orig.). (YA) 1956. pap. 1.50x (ISBN 0-685-08537-6). Comm Serv.
Grise, Jeannette. Robert Benjamin & the Great Blue Dog Joke. LC 78-17006. (Illus.). 122p. (gr. 3-6). 1978. 8.95 (ISBN 0-664-32637-4). Westminster.
Grisebach, A. H. Flora of the British West Indian Islands. 1963. Repr. of 1864 ed. 70.00 (ISBN 3-7682-7054-8). Lubrecht & Cramer.
Griselda. Story of Griselda in Iceland. Hermannsson, Halldor, ed. (Islandica: Vol. 7). pap. 16.00 (ISBN 0-527-00337-9). Kraus Repr.
Grisell, R. Sufism. 120p. 1983. pap. 4.95 (ISBN 0-89496-038-5). Ross Bks.
Grisewood, John. Simon & Schuster's Illustrated Young Readers' Dictionary. rev. ed. Barish, Wendy, ed. (Illus.). 240p. (gr. 8 up). 1984. pap. 5.95 (ISBN 0-671-50821-0). Wanderer Bks.
Grisez, Germain. Beyond the New Theism: A Philosophy of Religion. LC 74-27885. 444p. 1975. text ed. 22.95x (ISBN 0-268-00567-2); pap. text ed. 8.95x (ISBN 0-268-00568-0). U of Notre Dame Pr.
--Christian Moral Principles. 1983. 35.00 (ISBN 0-8199-0861-4). Franciscan Herald.
Grisez, Germain & Boyle, Joseph M., Jr. Life & Death with Liberty & Justice: A Contribution to the Euthanasia Debate. LC 78-31249. 1979. text ed. 30.00 (ISBN 0-268-01262-8, 85-12626, Dist. by Harper & Row). U of Notre Dame Pr.
--Life & Death with Liberty & Justice: A Contribution to the Euthanasia Debate. LC 78-31249. 544p. 1980. pap. text ed. 9.95 (ISBN 0-268-01263-6). U of Notre Dame Pr.
Grisez, Germain & Shaw, Russell. Beyond the New Morality: The Responsibilities of Freedom. rev. ed. LC 80-18293. 240p. 1980. text ed. 14.95 (ISBN 0-268-00663-6); pap. 6.95 (ISBN 0-268-00665-2). U of Notre Dame Pr.
--A Grisez Reader for Beyond the New Morality. Casey, Joseph H., ed. LC 81-43481. 218p. (Orig.). 1982. lib. bdg. 26.00 (ISBN 0-8191-2243-2); pap. text ed. 11.50 (ISBN 0-8191-2244-0). U Pr of Amer.
Grisham, J. W., ed. Health Aspects of the Disposal of Waste Chemicals. 560p. 1985. 85.00 (ISBN 0-08-033159-9, Pub by PPI). Pergamon.
Grisham, Noel. Buffalo & Indians on the Great Plains. (Illus.). (gr. k-4). 1985. 8.95 (ISBN 0-89015-470-8). Eakin Pubns.
--Crossroads at San Felipe. 1980. 6.95 (ISBN 0-89015-262-4). Eakin Pubns.
--A Serpent for a Dove: The Suppression of the American Indian. (Illus.). 168p. 7.50 (ISBN 0-8363-0089-0). Jenkins.
--Tame the Restless Wind: The Life & Legends of Sam Bass. (Illus.). 6.95 (ISBN 0-685-13279-X). Jenkins.
Grisham, Noel, jt. auth. see Driskill, Frank.
Grisham, Noel, jt. auth. see Driskill, Frank A.
Grishanov, V. M., ed. Man & Sea Warfare. 226p. 1978. pap. 5.45 (ISBN 0-8285-0417-2, Pub. by Progress Pubs USSR). Imported Pubns.
Grishaver, Joel L. Being Torah. LC 85-50219. (Illus.). 224p. (Orig.). (gr. 2-4). 1985. pap. text ed. 6.95 (ISBN 0-933873-00-X). Torah Aura.
Grishchenko, A. Danger: NATO. 176p. 1985. pap. 3.95 (ISBN 0-8285-2976-0, Pub. by Progress Pubs USSR). Imported Pubns.
Grishin, M. Hydraulic Structures, 2 vols. 732p. 1982. 15.45 (ISBN 0-8285-2448-3, Pub. by Mir Pubs USSR). Imported Pubns.
Grishin, V. V. Selected Speeches & Writings. LC 84-3042. (World Leaders Ser.). 300p. 1984. 40.00 (ISBN 0-08-030856-2). Pergamon.
Grishman, Ralph. Assembly Language Programming for Control Data 6000 & Cyber Ser. (Illus.). 248p. 1981. 15.00x (ISBN 0-917448-04-9). Algorithmics.
--Assembly Language Programming for the Control Data 6000 Series & the Cyber Series. Date not set. pap. 15.00 (ISBN 0-686-46118-5). Algorithmics.
Grisholme, Nicholas E. Geriatrics & Medicine: Guidebook for Reference & Research. LC 83-46110. 150p. 1985. 29.95 (ISBN 0-88164-154-5); soft cover 21.95 (ISBN 0-88164-155-3). ABBE Pubs Assn.
Grislis, Egil & Hill, W. Speed. Richard Hooker: A Selected Bibliography. LC 79-32321. 1981. 5.50 (ISBN 0-931222-03-6). Pitts Theolog.
Grisman, Arnold. The Winning Streak. 308p. 1985. 15.95 (ISBN 0-312-88231-9, J Kahn). St Martin.
Grismer, Karl H. The Story of Fort Myers: The History of the Land of the Caloosahatchee & Southwest Florida. LC 82-80620. (Illus.). 360p. 1982. pap. 15.00 (ISBN 0-87208-226-1). Island Pr.
Grismer, R. L. Cervantes: A Bibliography, 2 Vols. Repr. of 1946 ed. 47.00 (ISBN 0-527-36201-8). Kraus Repr.
Grismer, Raymond L. Reference Index to Twelve Thousand Spanish American Authors. LC 79-123600. (Bibliography & Reference Ser.: No. 287). 1970. Repr. of 1939 ed. lib. bdg. 19.00 (ISBN 0-8337-1460-0). B Franklin.
Grismer, Raymond L., compiled by. Bibliography of Lope De Vega, 2 vols. in 1. LC 65-90686. Repr. of 1965 ed. 29.00 (ISBN 0-527-36195-X). Kraus Repr.
Grismer, Raymond Leonard. The Influence of Plautus in Spain Before Lope De Vega. 210p. 3.50 (ISBN 0-318-14276-7). Hispanic Inst.
Grisoli, Angelo. Guide to Foreign Legal Materials, Italian. LC 59-8608. (Parker School Studies in Foreign & Comparative Law & Parker School Guides to Foreign Law: Vol. 2). 272p. 1965. 17.50 (ISBN 0-379-11752-5). Oceana.
Grisolia, S., et al. Ramon y Cajal's Contribution to the Neurosciences. 1983. 81.00 (ISBN 0-444-80486-2). Elsevier.
Grisolia, Santiago, et al. The Urea Cycle. LC 76-7382. (A Wiley-Interscience Publication Ser.). pap. 150.30 (ISBN 0-317-26102-9, 2025174). Bks Demand UMI.
Grisolia, Santiago M. & Frederico Da Guena, Rafael. The Urea Cycle. 579p. 1976. 64.50x (ISBN 0-471-32791-3). Wiley.
Griss, P., et al, eds. Findings of Total Hip Replacement for Ten Years. Konstam, Peter, tr. from Ger. (Illus.). 99p. 1982. pap. 21.50 (ISBN 3-456-81046-6, Pub. by Hans Huber Switzerland). J K Burgess.

Grissen, Lillian V. & Spykman, Gordon J. Men & Women: Partners in Service. 100p. (Orig.). 1981. pap. text ed. 4.10 (ISBN 0-933140-36-3). Bd of Pubns CRC.

Grissim, John. Pure Stoke. LC 82-47551. (Illus.). 176p. (Orig.). 1983. pap. 9.57i (ISBN 0-06-090972-2, CN 972, CN). Har-Row.

Grisso, Thomas. Juveniles' Waiver of Rights: Legal & Psychological Competence. LC 80-20488. (Perspectives in Law & Psychology Ser.: Vol. 3). 308p. 1981. 32.50x (ISBN 0-306-40526-1, Plenum Pr). Plenum Pub.

Grisso, Thomas & Sales, Bruce Dennis, eds. Law & Professional Psychology. 164p. (Reprinted from Professional Psychology, August, 1978). 13.00 (ISBN 0-317-33158-2); members 10.00 (ISBN 0-317-33159-0). Am Psychol.

Grissom, Ken. Buckskins & Black Powder: A Mountain Man's Guide to Muzzle Loading. LC 83-2193. (Illus.). 224p. 1983. 15.95 (ISBN 0-8329-0285-3, Pub. by Winchester Pr). New Century.

Grissom, M. Catherine, ed. In-Situ Coal Gasification: A Bibliography. 520p. 1984. pap. 25.00 (ISBN 0-87079-536-8, DOE/TIC-3401); microfiche 4.50 (ISBN 0-87079-537-6, DOE/TIC-3401). DOE.

--Oil Shales & Tar Sands: A Bibliography, Supplement 2. 588p. 1984. pap. 38.25 (ISBN 0-87079-526-0, DOE/TIC-3367); microfiche 4.50 (ISBN 0-87079-527-9, DOE/TIC-3367). DOE.

Grissom, Mary A. Negro Sings a New Heaven. LC 70-168209. Repr. of 1930 ed. 11.50 (ISBN 0-404-08311-0). AMS Pr.

Grissom, Thomas. Other Truths. 1984. 8.00 (ISBN 0-8233-0376-4). Golden Quill.

Grissum, Marlene & Spengler, Carol. Womanpower & Health Care. LC 75-41571. 1976. pap. 12.95 (ISBN 0-316-32895-2). Little.

Grist, Donald H. Rice. 5th ed. LC 73-90193. (Tropical Agriculture Ser.). (Illus.). 1975. pap. 30.00x (ISBN 0-582-46033-6). Longman.

Grist, W., tr. see Puccini, Giacomo & Nicholas, John.

Grisvard, P. Elliptic Problems in Nonsmooth Domains. (Monographs & Studies in Mathematics: No. 24). 384p. 1985. text ed. 49.95 (ISBN 0-273-08647-2). Pitman Pub MA.

Grisvard, P., et al, eds. Singularities & Constructive Methods for Their Treatment. (Lecture Notes in Mathematics: Vol. 1121). ix, 346p. 1985. pap. 23.50 (ISBN 0-387-15219-9). Springer-Verlag.

Griswold, A. Whitney. Liberal Education & the Democratic Ideal & Other Essays. LC 76-43025. 1976. Repr. of 1962 ed. lib. bdg. 18.00x (ISBN 0-8371-8977-2, GRLE). Greenwood.

Griswold, Bert J., ed. Fort Wayne, Gateway of the West, 1802-1813: Garrison Orderly Books, Indian Agency Account Book. LC 75-180404. Repr. of 1927 ed. 41.50 (ISBN 0-404-07133-3). AMS Pr.

Griswold, David H. How to Study. 156p. (Orig.). 1983. pap. text ed. 4.95x (ISBN 0-88334-157-3). Ind Sch Pr.

Griswold, Deirde. Eyewitness Ethiopia: The Continuing Revolution. 49p. 1.50 (ISBN 0-89567-028-3). World View Pubns.

Griswold, Deirdre. Eyewitness Ethiopia: The Continuing Revolution. (Illus.). 49p. 1978. pap. 2.00 (ISBN 0-89567-028-3). WV Pubs.

--Indonesia: The Second Greatest Crime of the Century. 102p. 1970. pap. 2.00 (ISBN 0-89567-003-8). WV Pubs.

--Indonesia: The Second Greatest Crime of the Century. 102p. 2.00 (ISBN 0-89567-003-8). World View Pubns.

Griswold, Deirdre, jt. auth. see Marcy, Sam.

Griswold, Erwin N. Search & Seizure: A Dilemma of the Supreme Court. LC 74-15275. (Landmark Ed., Roscoe Pound Lecture Ser.). xiv, 79p. 1976. 8.95x (ISBN 0-8032-0850-2). U of Nebr Pr.

Griswold, Erwin N. & Graetz, Michael J. Federal Income Taxation, Principles & Policies: 1983 Supplement. (University Casebook Ser.). 363p. 1983. pap. text ed. 3.63 (ISBN 0-88277-156-6). Foundation Pr.

Griswold, Francis. Sea Island Lady. 19.85 (ISBN 0-685-06833-1). Beaufort SC.

Griswold, Glenn E. Griswold Family England: America, Vol. 2. 276p. 1982. Repr. of 1935 ed. 25.00 (ISBN 0-9607906-1-6). ACETO Bookmen.

Griswold, H. D. Religion of the Rigveda. 1971. 8.50 (ISBN 0-89684-305-X). Orient Bk Dist.

Griswold, H. E. Catalog of Law Books: Reference Catalogue of Law Books Published Prior to 1894. LC 76-52290. 1977. Repr. of 1894 ed. lib. bdg. 35.00 (ISBN 0-930342-31-3). W S Hein.

Griswold, H. T. Home Life of Great Authors. 1973. Repr. of 1887 ed. 25.00 (ISBN 0-8274-0640-1). R West.

Griswold, Madge T., jt. auth. see Griswold, Ralph E.

Griswold, P. R. Colorado's Loneliest Railroad: The San Luis Southern. LC 82-3714. (Illus.). 200p. 1980. 32.50 (ISBN 0-87108-554-2). Pruett.

Griswold, P. R., jt. auth. see Newell, John C.

Griswold, Ralph E. The Macro Implementation of SNOBOL4: A Case Study of Machine-Independent Software Development. LC 72-184097. 1972. text ed. 36.95 (ISBN 0-7167-0447-1). W H Freeman.

--Opportunities in Landscape Architecture. 2nd ed. LC 78-58665. (VGM Career Bks.). (Illus.). (gr. 8 up). 1978. 7.95 (6583-4); pap. 5.95 (6583-0). Natl Textbk.

Griswold, Ralph E. & Griswold, Madge T. The ICON Programming Language. (Illus.). 336p. 1983. pap. text ed. 21.95 (ISBN 0-13-449777-5). P-H.

--A Snobol Four Primer. (Illus.). 128p. 1973. pap. 16.95 (ISBN 0-13-815381-7). P-H.

Griswold, Ralph E. & Thompson, Dorothy B. Garden Lore of Ancient Athens. (Excavations of the Athenian Agora Picture Bks.: No. 8). (Illus.). 1963. pap. 2.00x (ISBN 0-87661-608-2). Am Sch Athens.

Griswold, Ralph E., jt. auth. see Nichols, Frederick D.

Griswold, Ralph E., et al. Snobol Four Programming Language. 2nd ed. (Automatic Computation Ser). 1971. pap. 21.95 (ISBN 0-13-815373-6). P-H.

Griswold, Robert L. Family & Divorce in California, 1850-1890: Victorian Illusions & Everyday Realities. (American Social History Ser.). 320p. 1982. 39.50x (ISBN 0-87395-633-8); pap. 13.95x (ISBN 0-87395-634-6). State U NY Pr.

Griswold, Rufus. The Prose Writers of America. 1977. Repr. of 1851 ed. 50.00 (ISBN 0-89984-190-2). Century Bookbindery.

Griswold, Rufus W. The Poets & Poetry of America. 1973. Repr. of 1855 ed. 22.00 (ISBN 0-8274-0639-8). R West.

--The Prose Writers of America. 1857. 30.00 (ISBN 0-8274-3217-8). R West.

--Republican Court. LC 79-176498. (American History & Americana Ser., No. 47). 1971. Repr. of 1867 ed. lib. bdg. 62.95x (ISBN 0-8383-1285-3). Haskell.

Griswold, Rufus W., ed. The Female Poets of America. 2nd ed. 1972. Repr. of 1873 ed. 18.00 (ISBN 0-8422-8063-4). Irvington.

--The Prose Writers of America. 1972. Repr. of 1857 ed. lib. bdg. 22.00 (ISBN 0-8422-8064-2). Irvington.

Griswold, W. M. A Descriptive List of Novels & Tales Dealing with American City Life. 1976. lib. bdg. 59.95 (ISBN 0-8490-1709-2). Gordon Pr.

Griswold, Whit. Berkshire Trails for Walking & Ski Touring. LC 79-4901. (Illus.). 192p. 1978. pap. 7.95 (ISBN 0-914788-13-2). East Woods.

Griswold, William H. Descriptive Lists of American, International, Romantic & British Novels, 2 Vols. (Bibliography & Reference Ser.: No. 134). 1968. Repr. of 1964 ed. 48.00 (ISBN 0-8337-1463-5). B Franklin.

Griswold del Castillo, Richard. The Los Angeles Barrio: 1850-1890-A Social History. LC 78-65460. (Illus.). 232p. 1982. 25.00x (ISBN 0-520-03816-9); pap. 6.95 (ISBN 0-520-04773-7). U of Cal Pr.

Gritchfield, C. L., jt. auth. see Gamow, George.

Gritsai, N. Anthony Van Dyck. 25p. 1982. pap. 8.95 (ISBN 0-8285-2341-X, Pub. by Aurora Pubs USSR). Imported Pubns.

Gritsch, E., tr. see Fries, Heinrich & Rahner, Karl.

Gritsch, Eric W. Born Againism: Perspectives on a Movement. LC 81-70595. 112p. 1982. pap. 6.95 (ISBN 0-8006-1625-1, 1-1625). Fortress.

--Martin - God's Court Jester: Luther in Retrospect. LC 83-48004. 304p. 1983. pap. 15.95 (ISBN 0-8006-1753-3, 1-1753). Fortress.

Gritsch, Eric W. & Jenson, Robert W. Lutheranism: The Theological Movement & Its Confessional Writings. LC 76-7869. 228p. 1976. pap. 8.95 (ISBN 0-8006-1246-9, 1-1246). Fortress.

Gritsch, Eric W., jt. auth. see Bainton, Roland H.

Gritsch, Eric W., & Lehmann, Helmut T., eds. Luther's Works: Church & Ministry I, Vol. 39. LC 55-9893. 1970. 18.95 (ISBN 0-8006-0339-7, 1-339). Fortress.

Gritsch, Eric W., ed. see Haendler, Gert.

Gritsch, Eric W., jt. ed. see Lehmann, Helmut T.

Gritsch, R., tr. see Fries, Heinrich & Rahner, Karl.

Gritsch, Ruth C., tr. see Haendler, Gert.

Gritschneder, Otto. Ullstein Lexikon des Rechts. (Ger.). 1971. 20.00 (ISBN 3-550-06018-1, M-7677, Pub. by Ullstein Verlag/VVA). French & Eur.

Gritta, Patricia E. & Maltz, Patricia M. The Complete Job Search Handbook. LC 81-80799. 1981. pap. 10.00 (ISBN 0-686-32560-5). Peregrine Assoc.

Gritter, George. Communion Mediations. 80p. 1984. pap. 5.95 (ISBN 0-8010-3805-7). Baker Bk.

--When God Was at Calvary: Messages on the Seven Words. (Pocket Pulpit Library). 144p. 1982. pap. 3.50 (ISBN 0-8010-3785-9). Baker Bk.

Gritter, Headley. Rock & Roll Asylum. (Illus.). 320p. 1984. pap. 9.95 (ISBN 0-933328-73-7). Delilah Bks.

Grittner, Frank M., ed. Second Language Learning. LC 79-91182. (The National Society for the Study of Education Ser.). 242p. 1980. lib. bdg. 12.00x (ISBN 0-226-60129-3). U of Chicago Pr.

Gritzbach, Erich. Hermann Goering: The Man & His Work. Griffin, Gerald, tr. LC 75-180404. Repr. of 1939 ed. 28.00 (ISBN 0-404-56128-4). AMS Pr.

Gritzen, Edward F. Introduction to Naval Engineering. LC 79-90773. 448p. 1980. text ed. 16.95x (ISBN 0-87021-319-9). Naval Inst Pr.

Gritzen, Edward F., ed. Introduction to Naval Engineering. (Illus.). 448p. 1980. 16.95 (ISBN 0-87021-319-9); bulk rates avail. Naval Inst Pr.

Gritzer, Glenn & Arluke, Arnold. The Making of Rehabilitation. LC 84-28008. 1985. 22.50x (ISBN 0-520-05302-8). U of Cal Pr.

Grivainis. The Latvian Gambit. 1985. pap. price not set (ISBN 0-938650-20-3). Thinkers Pr.

Grivart, De see Crawford, Williame & Kerstrat, Francoise.

Grivas, C. N. Greek-English, English-Greek Modern Dictionary. 715p. 1984. 30.00 (ISBN 0-318-04722-5, Pub. by P. Efstathiadis & Sons, Greece). Heinman.

Grivel, Charles. Production E l'interet Romanesque: Un Etat Du Texte (1870-1880), un Essai De Constitution De Sa Theorie. (Approaches to Semiotics: No. 34). 1973. 46.00x (ISBN 90-2792-413-9). Mouton.

Grivelet, Michel. Thomas Heywood et la Drama Domestique Elizabethan. 1957. Repr. 50.00 (ISBN 0-8274-3612-2). R West.

Grivet, P. Physics of Transmission Lines at High & Very High Frequencies, Vol. 1. (Fr). 1970. 72.00 (ISBN 0-12-303601-1). Acad Pr.

Grivet, P., ed. The Physics of Transmission Lines at High & Very High Frequencies: Microwave Circuits & Amplifiers, Vol. 2. 1976. 95.00 (ISBN 0-12-303602-X). Acad Pr.

Grivot, Denis & Zarnecki, George. Gislebertus, Sculptor of Autun. LC 84-80599. (Illus.). 162p. 1985. Repr. of 1961 ed. lib. bdg. 60.00 (ISBN 0-87817-296-3). Hacker.

Grize, Jean-B. Logique Moderne, 3 fascicules. Incl. Fascicule I. Logique des Propositions & des Predicats, Deduction Naturelle. (No. 10). 1969. pap. price not set (ISBN 90-2796-320-7); Fascicule II. Logique des Propositions & des Predicats, Tables de Verite & Axiomatisation. (No. 14). 1971. pap. 5.60x (ISBN 0-686-22174-5); Fascicule III. Implications-Modalites, Logiques Polyvalentes, Logique Combinatoire, Ontologie & Mereologie de Lesniewski. (No. 22). 1973. pap. 7.60x (ISBN 90-2797-286-9). (Mathematiques et Sciences De L'homme). pap. Mouton.

Grizzard, Lewis. Don't Sit under the Grits Tree with Anyone Else but Me. 1985. pap. 3.50 (ISBN 0-446-32763-8). Warner Bks.

--Elvis Is Dead & I Don't Feel So Good Myself. LC 84-60922. 269p. 1984. 11.95 (ISBN 0-931948-66-5). Peachtree Pubs.

--Elvis is Dead, & I Don't Feel so Good Myself. 288p. 1986. pap. 3.50 (ISBN 0-446-34099-5). Warner Bks.

--If Love Were Oil, I'd Be about a Quart Low: Grizzard on Women. LC 83-61915. 288p. 1983. 9.95 (ISBN 0-931948-45-2). Peachtree Pubs.

--Kathy Sue Loudermilk, I Love You. Elliott, Helen L., ed. LC 79-22309. 1979. 9.95 (ISBN 0-931948-05-3). Peachtree Pubs.

--Kathy Sue Loudermilk, I Love You. 352p. 1984. pap. 3.95 (ISBN 0-446-32435-3). Warner Bks.

--Shoot Low, Boys-They're Riding Shetland Ponies. 336p. 1985. 13.95 (ISBN 0-931948-79-7). Peachtree Pubs.

--They Tore out My Heart & Stomped That Sucker Flat. LC 82-18119. 140p. 1982. 9.95 (ISBN 0-931948-38-X). Peachtree Pubs.

--Won't You Come Home Billy Bob Bailey? 240p. 1980. 9.95 (ISBN 0-931948-10-X). Peachtree Pubs.

--Won't You Come Home, Billy Bob Bailey? 304p. 1985. pap. 3.50 (ISBN 0-446-32606-2). Warner Bks.

Grizzard, Lewis M. Don't Sit Under the Grits Tree with Anyone Else But Me. LC 81-15704. 195p. 1981. 9.95 (ISBN 0-931948-24-X). Peachtree Pubs.

Grizzard, Mary F. Mitchell see Mitchell-Grizzard, Mary F.

Grjotheim. Aluminum Electrolysis: Chemistry of Hall-Heroult Process. 2nd ed. 1982. 69.00 (ISBN 0-9960035-4-1). Heyden.

Grjotheim, K. & Krohn, C. Aluminium Electrolysis: Fundamentals of the Hall-Heroult Process. 2nd ed. 1982. 69.00 (ISBN 0-9960035-4-1, Pub. by Aluminium W Germany). Heyden.

Grjotheim, K. & Welch, B. J. Aluminium Smelter Technology-A Pure & Applied Approach. 1980. 34.00 (ISBN 0-9960033-9-8, Pub. by Aluminium W Germany). Heyden.

Grmela, M., ed. Global Analysis. (Lecture Notes in Mathematics: Vol. 755). 1979. pap. 25.00 (ISBN 0-387-09703-1). Springer-Verlag.

Groah, Linda. Operating Room Nursing. 1982. text ed. 26.95 (ISBN 0-8359-5248-7) (ISBN 0-8359-5249-5). Reston.

Groak, S., ed. Action Planning & Responsive Design: Issues of Housing, Building, Planning & Development in the Third World. 350p. 1983. pap. 67.50 (ISBN 0-08-031310-8). Pergamon.

Groarke, Leo & Tindale, Christopher. Informal Logic. 75p. (Orig.). 1985. pap. 6.95 (ISBN 0-932269-31-1). Wyndham Hall.

Groarke, Leo, jt. auth. see Fox, Michael.

Groat, C. G., jt. auth. see McGowen, J. H.

Groat, George G. Attitude of American Courts in Labor Cases. LC 78-77993. (Columbia University. Studies in the Social Sciences: No. 108). Repr. of 1911 ed. 27.50 (ISBN 0-404-51108-2). AMS Pr.

--Trade Unions & the Law in New York: A Study of Some Legal Phases of Labor Organizations. LC 68-56659. (Columbia University. Studies in the Social Sciences: No. 51). Repr. of 1905 ed. 16.50 (ISBN 0-404-51051-5). AMS Pr.

Groat, H. Theodore, et al. Labor Force Participation & Family Formation among Currently Married Women 15-44 Years of Age. Olmstead, Mary, ed. (United States Ser.: No. 9). 1981. pap. text ed. 1.75 (ISBN 0-8406-0233-2). Natl Ctr Health Stats.

Groat, Linda N. Contextual Compatability in Architecture: An Investigation of Non-designer's Conceptualizations. (Illus.). viii, 97p. 1985. 12.50 (ISBN 0-938744-31-3). U of Wis Ctr Arch-Urban.

Grob. Chromatographic Analysis of the Environment. 736p. 1983. 95.00 (ISBN 0-8247-1803-8). Dekker.

Grob, Alan. The Philosophic Mind: A Study of Wordsworth's Poetry & Thought, 1797-1805. LC 72-12783. 291p. 1973. 10.00 (ISBN 0-8142-0178-4). Ohio St U Pr.

Grob, B. Basic Electronics. 5th ed. 752p. 1984. 33.00 (ISBN 0-07-024928-8). McGraw.

--Direct & Alternating Current Circuits. 624p. 1985. price not set (ISBN 0-07-024959-8). McGraw.

--Mathematics for Basic Electronics. 2nd ed. 128p. 1985. text ed. price not set (ISBN 0-07-024919-9). McGraw.

Grob, Bernard. Basic Television. 4th ed. 1975. text ed. 33.00 (ISBN 0-07-024927-X). McGraw.

--Electronic Circuits & Applications. LC 81-14298. (Illus.). 576p. 1982. text ed. 34.00 (ISBN 0-07-024931-8). McGraw.

Grob, Bernard & Kiver, M. S. Applications of Electronics. 2nd ed. 1966. text ed. 32.45 (ISBN 0-07-024930-X). McGraw.

Grob, Billias. Interpretations of American History Vol. II: Since 1865. 4th ed. 501p. pap. text ed. 11.95 (ISBN 0-02-912700-9). Free Pr.

--Interpretations of American History Vol. I: To 1877. 4th ed. 456p. 1982. pap. text ed. 11.95 (ISBN 0-02-912690-8). Free Pr.

Grob, David, ed. Myasthenia Gravis, Vol. 274. (Annals of the New York Academy of Sciences). 682p. 1976. 80.50x (ISBN 0-89072-053-3). NY Acad Sci.

--Myasthenia Gravis: Pathophysiology & Management, Vol. 377. LC 82-2199. 899p. 1981. 182.00x (ISBN 0-89766-143-5); pap. 182.00x (ISBN 0-89766-144-3). NY Acad Sci.

Grob, Gerald, jt. auth. see Monk, Maria.

Grob, Gerald, ed. Anti-Catholicism in America, 1841-1851. Three Sermons: An Original Anthology. (Anti-Movements in America Ser.). 1977. Repr. of 1977 ed. lib. bdg. 17.00x (ISBN 0-405-09980-0). Ayer Co Pubs.

--A Course of Lectures on the Jews: By Ministers of the Established Church in Glasgow. LC 76-46095. (Anti-Movements in America). 1977. lib. bdg. 37.50x (ISBN 0-405-09968-1). Ayer Co Pubs.

--The Inner World of American Psychiatry, 1890 to 1940: Selected Correspondence. 296p. 1985. text ed. 25.00 (ISBN 0-8135-1081-3); pap. write for info. Rutgers U Pr.

--Pope, or President? Startling Disclosures of Romanism As Revealed by Its Own Writers: Facts for Americans. LC 76-46094. (Anti-Movements in America). 1977. lib. bdg. 27.50x (ISBN 0-405-09967-3). Ayer Co Pubs.

Grob, Gerald, ed. see American Legion. National Americanism Commission.

Grob, Gerald, ed. see Annual Meeting, 1st, North Carolina, July 1923.

Grob, Gerald, ed. see Asiatic Exclusion League, 1907-1913.

Grob, Gerald, ed. see Beecher, Lyman.

Grob, Gerald, ed. see Calhoun, William P.

Grob, Gerald, ed. see Dies, Martin.

Grob, Gerald, ed. see Evans, Hiram W.

Grob, Gerald, ed. see Fairchild, Henry P.

Grob, Gerald, ed. see Fund for the Republic, Inc.

Grob, Gerald, ed. see Hendrick, Burton J.

Grob, Gerald, ed. see Huntington, Ellsworth.

Grob, Gerald, ed. see James, Henry A.

Grob, Gerald, ed. see King, James M.

Grob, Gerald, ed. see McDougall, William.

Grob, Gerald, ed. see Murray, Nicholas.

Grob, Gerald, ed. see Nevins, William.

Grob, Gerald, ed. see Priest, Josiah.

Grob, Gerald, ed. see Roberts, Kenneth L.

Grob, Gerald, ed. see Ross, Edward A.

Grob, Gerald, ed. see Schaack, Michael J.

Grob, Gerald, ed. see Schultz, Alfred P.

Grob, Gerald, ed. see Stripling, Robert E.

Grob, Gerald, ed. see Tenney, Jack B.

Grob, Gerald, ed. see Timayenis, Telemachus T.

Grob, Gerald N. Edward Jarvis & the Medical World of Nineteenth Century America. LC 78-3771. pap. 78.00 (ISBN 0-317-26165-7, 2024380). Bks Demand UMI.

--The Medical Professions & Drug Addiction: Six Studies, 1882 to 1932, An Original Anthology. LC 80-1206. (Addiction in America Ser.). 1981. lib. bdg. 32.00x (ISBN 0-405-13560-2). Ayer Co Pubs.

--Mental Illness & American Society, 1875-1940. LC 83-3047. 432p. 1983. 25.00x (ISBN 0-691-08332-0). Princeton U Pr.

--Mental Institutions in America: Social Policy to 1875. LC 72-92868. 1973. 15.95 (ISBN 0-02-913040-9). Free Pr.

--The State & Public Welfare in Nineteenth-Century America: Five Investigations, 1833-1877. LC 75-17244. (Social Problems & Social Policy Ser.). (Illus.). 1976. 46.50x (ISBN 0-405-07515-4). Ayer Co Pubs.

Grob, Gerald N. & Billias, George A. Historical Interpretations, 3 vols. Incl. Vol. 1. From Puritanism to the First Party System. pap. text ed. 5.95 (ISBN 0-02-912900-1); Vol. 2. From Jacksonian Democracy to the Gilded Age; Vol. 3. From Progressivism to the Cold War. pap. text ed. 5.95 (ISBN 0-02-912920-6, 91292). LC 67-12834. 1972. Free Pr.

--Interpretations of American History, 2 vols. 4th ed. LC 77-14681. 1978. Vol. 1. pap. text ed. 11.95 (ISBN 0-02-912690-8); Vol. 2. pap. text ed. 11.95 (ISBN 0-02-912700-9). Free Pr.

Grob, Gerald N., ed. American Perceptions of Drug Addiction: Five Studies, 1872 to 1912. an original anthology ed. LC 80-1209. (Addiction in America Ser.). 1981. lib. bdg. 30.00x (ISBN 0-405-13558-0). Ayer Co Pubs.

Grob, Gerald N., compiled by. American Social History Before 1860. LC 72-102037. (Goldentree Bibliographies in American History Ser.). (Orig.). 1970. pap. 6.95x (ISBN 0-88295-515-2). Harlan Davidson.

Grob, Gerald N., ed. Anti-Movements in America Series, 41 vols. (Illus.). 1977. Repr. Set. lib. bdg. 1196.00 (ISBN 0-405-09937-1). Ayer Co Pubs.

--The Epidemiology of Drug Addiction: Three Studies, 1924 to 1926, An Original Anthology. LC 80-1205. (Addiction in America Ser.). (Illus.). 1981. lib. bdg. 19.00x (ISBN 0-405-13559-9). Ayer Co Pubs.

--Historical Issues in Mental Health Series, 45 bks. (Illus.). 1979. Repr. lib. bdg. 1139.00xset (ISBN 0-405-11900-3). Ayer Co Pubs.

--Immigrants & Insanity: An Original Anthology. LC 78-22566. (Historical Issues in Mental Health Ser.). (Illus.). 1979. lib. bdg. 21.00x (ISBN 0-405-11920-8). Ayer Co Pubs.

--Mental Hygiene in Twentieth-Century America, Four Studies, 1921-1924: An Original Anthology. LC 78-22586. (Historical Issues in Mental Health Ser.). (Illus.). 1979. lib. bdg. 37.00x (ISBN 0-405-11937-2). Ayer Co Pubs.

--The Mentally Ill in Urban America: An Original Anthology. LC 78-22575. (Historical Issues in Mental Health Ser.). (Illus.). 1979. lib. bdg. 44.00x (ISBN 0-405-11928-3). Ayer Co Pubs.

--Narcotic Addiction & American Foreign Policy: Seven Studies, 1924 to 1938, An Original Anthology. LC 80-1207. (Addiction in America Ser.). (Illus.). 1981. lib. bdg. 32.00x (ISBN 0-405-13561-0). Ayer Co Pubs.

--The National Association for the Protection of the Insane & the Prevention of Insanity, 2 vols. in 1. LC 78-22578. (Historical Issues in Mental Health Ser.). 1979. Repr. lib. bdg. 14.00x (ISBN 0-405-11930-5). Ayer Co Pubs.

--Nineteenth Century Medical Attitudes Toward Alcoholic Addiction: Six Studies, 1814 to 1867, An Original Anthology. LC 80-1204. (Addiction in America Ser.). 1981. lib. bdg. 35.00x (ISBN 0-405-13562-9). Ayer Co Pubs.

--Opium Eating. LC 80-1241. (Addiction in America Ser.). 1981. Repr. of 1876 ed. lib. bdg. 15.00x (ISBN 0-405-13611-0). Ayer Co Pubs.

--Origins of Medical Attitudes Toward Drug Addiction in America: Eight Studies, 1791 to 1858, An Original Anthology. LC 80-1203. (Addiction in America Ser.). 1981. lib. bdg. 32.00x (ISBN 0-405-13563-7). Ayer Co Pubs.

--Psychiatric Research in America: Two Studies, Nineteen Thirty-Six to Nineteen Forty-One, 2 vols. in one. LC 78-22583. (Historical Issues in Mental Health Ser.). 1979. Repr. lib. bdg. 28.50x (ISBN 0-405-11935-6). Ayer Co Pubs.

--Psychiatry & Medical Education: Two Studies, 2 vols. in one. LC 78-22582. (Historical Issues in Mental Health Ser.). (Illus.). 1979. Repr. lib. bdg. 48.00x (ISBN 0-405-11934-8). Ayer Co Pubs.

--Public Policy & Mental Illness: Four Investigations, 1915-1939, an Original Anthology. LC 78-22585. (Historical Issues in Mental Health Ser.). (Illus.). 1979. lib. bdg. 50.50x (ISBN 0-405-11936-4). Ayer Co Pubs.

--Public Policy & the Problem of Addiction: Four Studies, 1914 to 1924, an Original Anthology. LC 70-1208. (Addiction in America Ser.). 1981. lib. bdg. 15.00x (ISBN 0-405-13564-5). Ayer Co Pubs.

--Social Problems & Social Policy Ser, 51 vols. (Illus.). 1975. 1799.50x (ISBN 0-405-07474-3). Ayer Co Pubs.

Grob, Gerald N., ed. see American Association for the Cure of Inebriates.

Grob, Gerald N., ed. see American Association for the Study & Cure of Inebiety.

Grob, Gerald N., ed. see American Psychopathological Association.

Grob, Gerald N., ed. see Anslinger, H. J. & Tompkins, William F.

Grob, Gerald N., ed. see Anstie, Francis E.

Grob, Gerald N., ed. see Beard, George M.

Grob, Gerald N., ed. see Belknap, Ivan.

Grob, Gerald N., ed. see Berkley, Henry J.

Grob, Gerald N., ed. see Bond, Earl D. & Komora, Paul O.

Grob, Gerald N., ed. see Briggs, Lloyd V.

Grob, Gerald N., ed. see Burrow, Trigant.

Grob, Gerald N., ed. see Cahow, Clark R.

Grob, Gerald N., ed. see Calkins, Alonzo.

Grob, Gerald N., ed. see Carpenter, William B.

Grob, Gerald N., ed. see Clum, Franklin D.

Grob, Gerald N., ed. see Cobbe, William R.

Grob, Gerald N., ed. see Committee of the American Neurological Association for the Investigation of Eugenical Sterilization.

Grob, Gerald N., ed. see Cotton, Henry A.

Grob, Gerald N., ed. see Crothers, T. D.

Grob, Gerald N., ed. see Cutten, George B.

Grob, Gerald N., jt. ed. see Day, Horace.

Grob, Gerald N., ed. see Dayton, Neil A.

Grob, Gerald N., ed. see Dorchester, Daniel.

Grob, Gerald N., ed. see Eisenlohr, L. E.

Grob, Gerald N., jt. ed. see Emerson, Haven.

Grob, Gerald N., ed. see Fein, Rashi.

Grob, Gerald N., ed. see Gavit, John P.

Grob, Gerald N., ed. see Goldhamer, Herbert & Marshall, Andrew W.

Grob, Gerald N., ed. see Gosney, E. S. & Popenoe, Paul.

Grob, Gerald N., ed. see Graham-Mulhall, Sara.

Grob, Gerald N., ed. see Greenblatt, Milton, et al.

Grob, Gerald N., ed. see Grimes, John M.

Grob, Gerald N., ed. see Gurin, Gerald, et al.

Grob, Gerald N., ed. see Hawkins, John A.

Grob, Gerald N., ed. see Helbrant, Maurice.

Grob, Gerald N., ed. see Hinsie, Leland E.

Grob, Gerald N., ed. see Hubbard, Fred H.

Grob, Gerald N., ed. see Jaffe, Arnold.

Grob, Gerald N., ed. see Jahoda, Marie.

Grob, Gerald N., ed. see Jellinek, E. M.

Grob, Gerald N., ed. see Joint Commission on Mental Illness & Health.

Grob, Gerald N., ed. see Kane, H. H.

Grob, Gerald N., ed. see Keeley, Leslie E.

Grob, Gerald N., ed. see Kerr, Norman.

Grob, Gerald N., ed. see Koren, John.

Grob, Gerald N., jt. ed. see Kruse, H. D.

Grob, Gerald N., ed. see LaMotte, Ellen N.

Grob, Gerald N., ed. see Landis, Carney & Page, James D.

Grob, Gerald N., ed. see Levinstein, Edward.

Grob, Gerald N., ed. see Lewis, Nolan D.

Grob, Gerald N., ed. see Light, Arthur, et al.

Grob, Gerald N., ed. see Lowes, Peter D.

Grob, Gerald N., ed. see Macmartin, D. F.

Grob, Gerald N., ed. see Malzberg, Benjamin.

Grob, Gerald N., ed. see May, James V.

Grob, Gerald N., ed. see Merrill, Frederick T.

Grob, Gerald N., ed. see Myerson, Abraham.

Grob, Gerald N., ed. see National Committee for Mental Health.

Grob, Gerald N., ed. see National Research Council, the Committee on Psychiatric Investigations.

Grob, Gerald N., ed. see Palmer, Charles F.

Grob, Gerald N., ed. see Parrish, Joseph.

Grob, Gerald N., ed. see Partridge, G. E.

Grob, Gerald N., ed. see Pearl, Raymond.

Grob, Gerald N., ed. see Pettey, George E.

Grob, Gerald N., ed. see Plunkett, Richard J. & Gordon, John E.

Grob, Gerald N., ed. see Rapoport, Robert N. & Rapopart, Rhona.

Grob, Gerald N., ed. see Robison, Dale W.

Grob, Gerald N., ed. see Sicherman, Barbara.

Grob, Gerald N., ed. see Smith, Stephen.

Grob, Gerald N., ed. see Spillard, William J.

Grob, Gerald N., ed. see Stearns, Henry P.

Grob, Gerald N., ed. see Stelle, Charles C.

Grob, Gerald N., ed. see Towns, Charles B.

Grob, Gerald N., ed. see Trotter, Thomas.

Grob, Gerald N., ed. see Turner, J. E.

Grob, Gerald N., ed. see U. S. Surgeon General's Office.

Grob, Gerald N., ed. see Wertheimer, F. I. & Hesketh, Florence E.

Grob, Gerald N., ed. see White, William A.

Grob, Gerald N., ed. see Williams, Henry S.

Grob, Gerald N., ed. see Wright, T. L.

Grob, Gerald N., ed. see Youmans, Edward L.

Grob, Gerald N., et al, eds. Mental Illness & Social Policy: The American Experience, 41 bks. 1973. Set. 1390.50 (ISBN 0-405-05190-5). Ayer Co Pubs.

--Addiction in America Series, 55 bks. 1981. write for info. Ayer Co Pubs.

Grob, Mollie C. & Singer, Judith E. Adolescent Patients in Transition: Impact & Outcome of Psychiatric Hospitalization. LC 73-22379. 202p. 1974. text ed. 24.95 (ISBN 0-87705-137-2). Human Sci Pr.

Grob, Paul & Brown, Nina W., eds. Readings in Education & Psychology. 333p. 1969. pap. text ed. 12.95x (ISBN 0-686-84056-9). Irvington.

Grob, R. L. Modern Practice of Gas Chromatography. 2nd ed. 912p. 1985. 65.00 (ISBN 0-471-87157-5). Wiley.

Grob, R. L. & Kaiser, M. A. Environmental Problem Solving Using Gas & Liquid Chromatography. (Journal of Chromatography Lib.: Vol. 21). 240p. 1982. 54.00 (ISBN 0-444-42065-7). Elsevier.

Grob, Robert L., ed. Modern Practice of Gas Chromatography. 654p. 1977. text ed. 58.00 (ISBN 0-471-01564-4). Wiley.

Grobani, Anton, ed. Guide to Baseball Literature. LC 74-17223. 363p. 1975. 44.00x (ISBN 0-8103-0962-9). Gale.

--Guide to Football Literature. LC 75-1478. xvi, 319p. 1975. 36.00x (ISBN 0-8103-0964-5). Gale.

Grobe, Susan J. Computer Primer & Resource for Nurses. (Illus.). 180p. 1984. pap. text ed. 9.75 (ISBN 0-397-54485-5, Lippincott Nursing). Lippincott.

Grobel, Kendrick, tr. The Gospel of Truth. LC 78-63167. (Heresies of the Early Christian & Medieval Era: Second Ser.). Repr. of 1960 ed. 19.50 (ISBN 0-404-16083-2). AMS Pr.

Grobel, Lawrence. Conversations with Capote. LC 84-27324. (Illus.). 1985. 14.95 (ISBN 0-453-00494-6). NAL.

Groben, W. Ellis. Adobe Architecture: Its Design & Construction. facs. ed. (Shorey Lost Arts Ser.). 42p. pap. 4.95 (ISBN 0-8466-6042-3, U42). Shorey.

Groben, W. Ellis, jt. auth. see Fickes, Clyde P.

Groble, Patricia & Marks, Edward. Criminal Law in New York. 3rd ed. LC 84-12703. 1984. 160.00. Callaghan.

Grobman, Alex, ed. Simon Wiesenthal Center Annual, Vol. 1. (Illus.). 256p. 1984. text ed. 17.95 (ISBN 0-940646-30-7). Rossel Bks.

Grobman, Alex & Landes, Daniel, eds. Genocide-Critical Issues of the Holocaust: A Companion to the Film Genocide. LC 83-3052. (Illus.). 512p. 1983. 19.95 (ISBN 0-940646-04-8, Co-Pub by Simon Wiesenthal). Rossel Bks.

Grobman, Alexander & Salhuana, Ricardo S. Races of Maize in Peru: Their Origins, Evolution & Classification. LC 61-60080. (National Research Council, Publication: 915). pap. 96.00 (ISBN 0-317-28682-X, 2055288). Bks Demand UMI.

Grobman, Arnold B., ed. Social Implications of Biological Education. LC 77-131404. 134p. 1971. 3.95 (ISBN 0-87850-000-6). Darwin Pr.

Grobman, Jerald. Group Psychotherapy for Students & Teachers: A Selective Bibliography, 1946-1979. LC 81-43339. 125p. 1982. lib. bdg. 22.00 (ISBN 0-8240-9291-0). Garland Pub.

Grobman, W. D., jt. ed. see Folberth, D. G.

Grobsmith, Elizabeth S. Lakota of the Rosebud (CSCA) 1981. pap. text ed. 9.95 (ISBN 0-03-057438-2, HoltC). HR&W.

Grobstein, Clifford. A Double Image of the Double Helix: The Recombinant-DNA Debate. LC 78-26093. (Biology Ser.). (Illus.). 177p. 1979. text ed. 20.95 (ISBN 0-7167-1056-0); pap. text ed. 11.95 (ISBN 0-7167-1057-9). W H Freeman.

--The Strategy of Life. 2nd ed. LC 73-18061. (Biology Ser.). (Illus.). 174p. 1974. text ed. 20.95 (ISBN 0-7167-0591-5). W H Freeman.

Grobstein, Michael, et al. Auditing: A Risk Analysis Approach. 1985. 34.95x (ISBN 0-256-02791-9). Irwin.

Groce, Betty M. Seizure. (Better Living Ser.). 1977. pap. 0.99 (ISBN 0-8127-0142-9). Review & Herald.

Groce, Eva H. Rainbows Through Tears. (Illus.). 1979. pap. 2.00x (ISBN 0-9602440-2-6). Jesus-First.

Groce, George C. & Wallace, David H. New York Historical Society's Dictionary of Artists in America, 1564-1860. 1957. 57.00x (ISBN 0-300-00519-9). Yale U Pr.

Groce, George C., Jr. William Samuel Johnson: A Maker of the Constitution. LC 37-33132. Repr. of 1937 ed. 14.50 (ISBN 0-404-02936-1). AMS Pr.

Groce, Nora E. Everyone Here Spoke Sign Language: Hereditary Deafness on Martha's Vineyard. (Illus.). 192p. 1985. text ed. 17.50x (ISBN 0-674-27040-1). Harvard U Pr.

Grochla, E., jt. ed. see Szperski, N.

Grochla, Erwin & Szyperski, Norbert, eds. Information Systems & Organizational Structure. 1975. 59.20x (ISBN 3-11-004803-5). De Gruyter.

Grock. Life's a Lark. LC 73-84515. 286p. 1931. 22.00 (ISBN 0-405-08583-4, Blom Pubns). Ayer Co Pubs.

Grocock, C. W., ed. see Ruodleib.

Grocott, Allan M. Convicts, Clergymen & Churches. 356p. 1980. 38.00x (ISBN 0-424-00072-5, Pub. by Sydney U Pr Australia). Intl Spec Bk.

Groddeck, Georg. The Book of the It. LC 76-4610. 346p. 1976. 27.50 (ISBN 0-8236-0570-1). Intl Univs Pr.

--The Meaning of Illness: Selected Psychoanalytic Writings. LC 76-46813. 290p. 1977. 30.00 (ISBN 0-8236-3205-9). Intl Univs Pr.

Grode, Susan A., ed. see Beverly Hills Bar Association Barristers Committee for the Arts.

Grodecki, Louis. Bibliographie Henri Focillon. LC 62-16232. (Yale Publications in the History of Art Ser.: No. 15). pap. 33.50 (ISBN 0-317-10249-4, 2022001). Bks Demand UMI.

--Gothic Architecture. (History of World Architecture). (Illus.). 1977. 50.00 (ISBN 0-8109-1008-X). Abrams.

--Gothic Architecture. (History of World Architecture Ser.). (Illus.). 220p. 1985. pap. 18.50 (ISBN 0-8478-0473-9). Rizzoli Intl.

Grodecki, Louis & Brisac, Catherine. Gothic Stained Glass: Twelve Hundred to Thirteen Hundred. Boehm, Barbara D., tr. from Fr. LC 85-71277. (Illus.). 288p. 1985. text ed. 75.00x (ISBN 0-8014-1809-7). Cornell U Pr.

Groden, James, ed. see Joyce, James.

Groden, June, jt. auth. see Cautela, Joseph R.

Groden, Michael. James Joyce's Manuscripts: An Index. LC 78-64575. (Garland Reference Library of the Humanities). 190p. 1980. 31.00 (ISBN 0-8240-9540-5). Garland Pub.

--Ulysses in Progress. LC 77-1217. 1977. 24.00x (ISBN 0-691-06338-9). Princeton U Pr.

Groden, Michael, ed. Ulysses: "Ithaca" & "Penelope." A Facsimile of Manuscripts & Typescripts for Episodes 17 & 18. LC 77-10882. (James Joyce Archive Ser.: Vol. 16). 1978. lib. bdg. 125.00 (ISBN 0-8240-2826-0). Garland Pub.

--Ulysses: "Sirens," "Cyclops," "Nausicaa," & "Oxen of the Sun." A Facsimile of Placards for Episodes 11-14. LC 78-11931. (James Joyce Archive Ser.: Vol. 19). 1979. lib. bdg. 125.00 (ISBN 0-8240-2813-9). Garland Pub.

--Ulysses: "Wandering Rocks," "Sirens," "Cyclops," "Nausicaa": Facsimile of Drafts & Typescripts for Episodes 10-13. LC 77-10196. (James Joyce Archive Ser.). 1978. lib. bdg. 125.00 (ISBN 0-8240-2823-6). Garland Pub.

Groden, Michael, ed. see Joyce, James.

Groden, Suzy Q, tr. see Plato.

Grodeon, Thelma. Poetry. (Illus.). 42p. 1982. 5.95 (ISBN 0-533-04999-7). Vantage.

Groder, Martin G. & Von Hartz, John. Business Games. LC 80-19095. 250p. 1980. 50.00 (ISBN 0-932648-14-2). Boardroom.

Grodin, Joseph R. Union Government & the Law: British & American Experiences. (Monograph & Research Ser.: No. 8). 209p. 1961. 5.00 (ISBN 0-89215-010-6). U Cal LA Indus Rel.

Grodin, Joseph R. & Grodin, Sharon. High Sierra Hiking Guide to Silver Lake. LC 78-50994. (High Sierra Hiking Guide Ser: Vol. 17). (Illus.). 96p. (Orig.). 1983. pap. 3.95 (ISBN 0-911824-42-1). Wilderness Pr.

Grodin, Joseph R., jt. ed. see Stern, James L.

Grodin, Joseph R., et al. High Sierra Hiking Guide to Silver Lake. 2nd ed. Winnett, Thomas, ed. LC 82-62832. (High Sierra Hiking Guide Ser.: Vol. 17). (Illus.). 96p. (Orig.). 1983. pap. 5.95 (ISBN 0-89997-027-3). Wilderness Pr.

Grodin, Joseph R., et al see Labor Law Group.

Grodin, Sharon, jt. auth. see Grodin, Joseph R.

Grodins, Fred S. Control Theory & Biological Systems. LC 63-10521. 205p. 1963. 32.00x (ISBN 0-231-02517-3). Columbia U Pr.

Grodins, Fred S. & Yamashiro, Stanley M. Respiratory Function of the Lung & Its Control. (Illus.). 176p. 1978. text ed. write for info. (ISBN 0-02-348190-0); pap. text ed. write for info. (ISBN 0-686-71603-5). Macmillan.

Grodinsky, Julius. The Iowa Pool: A Study in Railroad Competition, 1870 to 1884. Bruchey, Stuart, ed. LC 80-1311. (Railroads Ser.). 1981. Repr. of 1950 ed. lib. bdg. 20.00x (ISBN 0-405-13779-6). Ayer Co Pubs.

--Jay Gould: His Business Career, 1867-1892. Bruchey, Stuart, ed. LC 80-1312. (Railroads Ser.). (Illus.). 1981. Repr. of 1957 ed. lib. bdg. 55.00x (ISBN 0-405-13785-0). Ayer Co Pubs.

Grodner, Murray. Comprehensive Catalog of Available Literature for the Double Bass. 3rd ed. LC 64-25242. 1974. pap. 7.50 (ISBN 0-686-21217-7). Lemur.

Grodner, Murray, ed. Concepts in String Playing: Reflections by Artist-Teachers at the Indiana University School of Music. LC 78-13811. (Illus.). pap. 47.50 (ISBN 0-317-09952-3, 2055499). Bks Demand UMI.

Grodzins, Morton. The American System: A New View of Government in the United States. Elazar, Daniel J., ed. LC 82-8449. (Political Theory Ser.). 404p. 1983. 19.95 (ISBN 0-87855-916-7). Transaction Bks.

--Americans Betrayed. (Midway Reprint Ser.). xviii, 445p. 1974. pap. text ed. 17.50x (ISBN 0-226-30940-1). U of Chicago Pr.

Grodzinski, W., et al, eds. Forest Ecosystems in Industrial Regions: Studies on the Cycling of Energy, Nutrients & Pollutants in the Niepotomice Forest, South Poland. (Ecological Studies: Analysis & Synthesis: Vol. 49). (Illus.). 270p. 1984. 49.50 (ISBN 0-387-13498-0). Springer-Verlag.

Grodzinsky, Stephen, jt. auth. see Kirwin, Gerald J.

Groebbels, F. Der Vogel Atmungs-und Nahrungswelt, Geschlecht und Fortoflanzung. 1969. 77.00 (ISBN 3-7682-0241-0). Lubrecht & Cramer.

Groebner, David & Shannon, Patrick. Business Statistics. 2nd ed. 800p. 1985. text ed. 28.95 (ISBN 0-675-20217-5). Additional supplements may be obtained from publisher. Merrill.

--Business Statistics: A Decision-Making Approach. (Illus.). 800p. 1981. text ed. 27.95 (ISBN 0-675-08083-5); student guide 9.95x (ISBN 0-675-08084-3). Additional supplements may be obtained from publisher. Merrill.

--College Math with Business Applications. 640p. 1985. text ed. 26.95 (ISBN 0-675-20260-4). Additional supplements may be obtained from publisher. Merrill.

Groebner, David E., jt. auth. see Merz, C. Mike.

Groeg, Otto J., ed. Who's Who in Austria, 1977-78. 9th ed. 600p. 1977. 90.00x (ISBN 3-921220-19-X). Intl Pubns Serv.

--Who's Who in Germany, 1980, 2 vols. 7th ed. LC 56-3621. 1500p. 1980. Set. 175.00x (ISBN 3-921220-28-9). Intl Pubns Serv.

--Who's Who in Technology: Austria, Germany, Switzerland, 2 vols. 1055p. 1979. Set. 195.00x (ISBN 3-921220-24-6). Intl Pubns Serv.

Groehoff, Edwin. Care & Concern of the Church. LC 81-69760. (Heritage Ser.: Vol. 8). 1984. 8.95 (ISBN 0-911802-59-2). Free Church Pubns.

Groen, David, jt. auth. see Groen, Jay.

Groen, Elaine & Rapp, Irene. Healthy Cooking on the Run. (Illus.). 216p. 1983. pap. 7.95 (ISBN 0-911954-75-9). Nitty Gritty.

Groen, Jay & Groen, David. Huey. 1984. pap. 2.95 (ISBN 0-317-03648-3). Ballantine.

Groen, Jim, jt. auth. see Hensley, Dennis E.

Groene, Bertram H. Tracing Your Civil War Ancestor. Rev. ed. LC 73-77903. (Illus.). 1981. 8.95 (ISBN 0-89587-026-6). Blair.

Groene, Janet. Cooking on the Go. 234p. 1980. 14.95 (ISBN 0-914814-26-5). Sail Bks.

--How to Live Aboard a Boat. 1982. 17.95 (ISBN 87851-217-9, Hearst Marine Bk). Morrow.

Groenegress, H. W. Flame Hardening. 1964. pap. 6.50 (ISBN 0-387-03137-5). Springer-Verlag.

Groeneveld, Judith, jt. auth. see Shain, Martin.

Groeneveld, K. O., et al, eds. Forward Electron Ejection in Ion Collisions. (Lecture Notes in Physics Ser.: Vol. 213). vii, 165p. 1984. pap. 12.00 (ISBN 0-387-13887-0). Springer-Verlag.

Groeneveld, Karl-Ontjes, jt. ed. see Berkowitz, Joseph.

Groenewaid, P. W. Learning to Speak Afrikaans: A Method Based on One Thousand Words. 6th ed. 115p. 1976. pap. 10.00 (ISBN 0-86985-278-7, Pub. by Shuter & Shooter South Africa). Heinman.

Groenewald, P. W. Learn to Speak Afrikaans: A Method Based on One Thousand Words. 6th, rev. ed. 115p. (Orig.). 1976. pap. 10.00 (ISBN 0-86985-278-7). Heinman.

Groenewald, T., jt. auth. see Rapson, W. S.

Groenewegen, P. D. The Economics of A. R. J. Turgot. 1977. 34.00 (ISBN 90-247-1953-4, Pub. by Martinus Nijhoff Netherlands). Kluwer Academic.

Groenewegen Frankfort, Mrs. H. & Ashmole, Bernard. Art of the Ancient World. (Janson Art History Ser). (Illus.). 512p. 1972. text ed. 32.95 (ISBN 0-13-047001-5). P-H.

Groenhoff, Ed. The Freshman. 1983. 4.95 (ISBN 0-89636-110-1). Accent Bks.

Groenhoff, Edwin L. Graduation Weekend. LC 84-72314. 196p. 1985. pap. 5.95 (ISBN 0-89636-149-7). Accent Bks.

--It's Your Choice. 1975. pap. 1.75 (ISBN 0-911802-38-X). Free Church Pubns.

--Psalms for Cloudy Days. 2nd ed. 1964. pap. 1.00 (ISBN 0-911802-09-6). Free Church Pubns.

--The Quiet Prince. new ed. LC 74-79531. 1974. text ed. 4.95 (ISBN 0-911802-36-3). Free Church Pubns.

Groenlendinga, Pattr. The Vinland Sagas: The Norse Discovery of America. LC 66-31936. pap. 31.00 (ISBN 0-317-08208-6, 2050271). Bks Demand UMI.

Groennings, Sven & Hawley, Jonathan P. To Be a Congressman: The Promise & the Power. LC 73-7946. 250p. 1973. pap. 6.95 (ISBN 0-87491-353-5). Acropolis.

Groenvald. Introduction to Probability & Statistics Using BASIC. (Statistics; Textbooks & Monographs: Vol. 26). 1979. 35.00 (ISBN 0-8247-6543-5). Dekker.

Groer, Leon de see De Groer, Leon.

Groer, Maureen E. & Shekleton, Maureen E. Basic Pathophysiology: A Conceptual Approach. LC 78-21170. (Illus.). 524p. 1979. pap. 21.95 (ISBN 0-8016-1983-1). Mosby.

Groer, Maureen W. Physiology & Pathophysiology of the Body Fluids. LC 80-28583. (Illus.). 299p. 1981. pap. text ed. 16.95 (ISBN 0-8016-1989-0). Mosby.

Groer, Maureen W. & Shekleton, Maureen E. Basic Pathophysiology: A Conceptual Approach. 2nd ed. LC 82-3579. (Illus.). 643p. 1983. pap. text ed. 19.95 (ISBN 0-8016-2023-6). Mosby.

Groeschel, Benedict J. The Courage to be Chaste. 144p. (Orig.). 1985. pap. 3.95 (ISBN 0-8091-2705-9). Paulist Pr.

--Listening at Prayer. 80p. (Orig.). 1984. 3.95 (ISBN 0-8091-0351-6). Paulist Pr.

--Spiritual Passages. LC 82-17139. 176p. 1983. 12.95 (ISBN 0-8245-0497-6). Crossroad NY.

Groetch, D. J., ed. see AMSE.

Groetsch, C. W. Generalized Inverses of Linear Operators: Representation & Approximation. (Pure & Applied Math Ser.: Vol. 37). 1977. 39.75 (ISBN 0-8247-6615-6). Dekker.

--The Theory of Tikhonov Regularization for Fredholm Equations of the First Kind. (Research Notes in Mathematics Ser.: No. 105). 128p. 1984. pap. text ed. 16.95 (ISBN 0-273-08642-1). Pitman Pub MA.

Groetsch, Charles W. Elements of Applicable Functional Analysis. (Pure & Applied Mathematics: Monographs & Textbooks: Vol. 55). (Illus.). 320p. 1980. 45.00 (ISBN 0-8247-6986-4). Dekker.

Grof, Baumann T., jt. auth. see Kamm, G.

Grof, Christina, jt. auth. see Grof, Stanislav.

Grof, P. & Saxena, B., eds. Recent Advances in Canadian Neuropsychopharmacology. x, 238p. 1981. pap. 41.75 (ISBN 3-8055-1459-X). S Karger.

Grof, Stanislav. Beyond the Brain: Birth, Death, & Transcendence in Psychotherapy. (Transpersonal & Humanistic Psychology Ser.). 256p. 1985. lib. bdg. 34.50x (ISBN 0-87395-953-1); pap. text ed. 10.50x (ISBN 0-87395-899-3). State U NY Pr.

--East & West: Ancient Wisdom & Modern Science. (Broadside Ser.). 30p. 1985. pap. 2.95 (ISBN 0-931191-00-9). Rob Briggs.

--LSD Psychotherapy. LC 79-65432. (Illus.). 352p. 1980. 29.95 (ISBN 0-89793-008-8). Hunter Hse.

--Realms of Human Unconscious: Observations from LSD Research. 1976. pap. 7.95 (ISBN 0-525-47438-2, 0772-230). Dutton.

Grof, Stanislav & Grof, Christina. Beyond Death: The Gates of Consiousness. (Illus.). 1980. pap. 10.95 (ISBN 0-500-81019-2). Thames Hudson.

Grof, Stanislav, ed. Ancient Wisdom & Modern Science. 360p. 1984. 34.50x (ISBN 0-87395-848-9); pap. 10.95x (ISBN 0-87395-849-7). State U NY Pr.

Groff, Betty & Wilson, Jose. Betty Groff's Country Goodness Cookbook. LC 80-1093. (Illus.). 336p. 1981. 19.95 (ISBN 0-385-12120-2). Doubleday.

--Good Earth & Country Cooking. 2nd ed. LC 73-23128. (Illus.). 256p. 1974. pap. 14.95 (ISBN 0-8117-2066-7). Stackpole.

Groff, Cora M. Crown of Jewels. 1985. pap. 6.00 (ISBN 0-682-40210-9). Exposition Pr FL.

Groff, Diller B., ed. Handbook of Pediatric Surgical Emergencies. 2nd. ed. 1981. 18.95 (ISBN 0-87488-642-2). Med Exam.

Groff, Gene K. & Muth, John F. Operations Management: Analysis for Decisions. LC 78-158048. (Irwin Series in Quantitative Analysis for Business). pap. 145.50 (ISBN 0-317-08906-4, 2021669). Bks Demand UMI.

Groff, James R., jt. auth. see Weinberg, Paul N.

Groff, John M. & Allen, Jane E. The Titanic & Her Era. (Illus.). 32p. 1982. pap. 2.00 (ISBN 0-913346-07-1). Phila Maritime Mus.

Groff, Russell E. Card Weaving or Tablet Weaving. (Illus.). 4.50 (ISBN 0-686-09825-0). Robin & Russ.

--Two Hundred Patterns for Multiple Harness Looms. (Illus.). 1980. 14.95 (ISBN 0-686-27272-2); pap. 9.95 (ISBN 0-686-28458-5). Robin & Russ.

Groff, Warren F. Prayer: God's Time & Ours! 144p. (Orig.). 1984. pap. 6.95 (ISBN 0-87178-714-8). Brethren.

--Story Time: God's Story & Ours. new ed. LC 74-23540. 144p. 1974. pap. 2.95 (ISBN 0-87178-815-2). Brethren.

Grofit, E. The Fishing Technology Unit: A Guide for the Planning, Establishment & Operations of National Fishing Technology Services in Developing Fisheries. (Fisheries Technical Papers: No. 199). 55p. 1980. pap. 7.50 (ISBN 92-5-100989-9, F2027, FAO). Unipub.

Grofman, Bernard & Lijphart, Arend. Electoral Laws & Their Political Consequences. LC 85-15609. Date not set. price not set (ISBN 0-87586-064-8). Agathon.

Grofman, Bernard & Lijphart, Arend, eds. Electoral Laws & Their Political Consequences. 400p. 1985. 38.00 (ISBN 0-87586-064-8). Agathon.

Grofman, Bernard, jt. ed. see Lijphart, Arent.

Grofman, Bernard, et al. Reapportionment Policy. (Orig.). 1981. pap. 8.00 (ISBN 0-918592-45-3). Policy Studies.

--Representation & Redistricting Issues. LC 81-47783. (A Policy Studies Organization Bk.). 304p. 1982. 31.00x (ISBN 0-669-04718-X). Lexington Bks.

Groft, Tammis K. Cast with Style: Nineteenth Century Cast-Iron Stoves from the Albany Area. rev. ed. (Illus.). 120p. pap. text ed. 11.95 (ISBN 0-939072-03-3). Albany Hist & Art.

--The Folk Spirit of Albany. (Illus.). 86p. 1978. pap. 6.95 (ISBN 0-939072-00-9). Albany Hist & Art.

Grogan, Denis. Practical Reference Work. (Outlines of Modern Librarianship Ser.). 144p. 1979. text ed. 12.00 (ISBN 0-85157-275-8, Pub. by Bingley England). Shoe String.

--Science & Technology: An Introduction to the Literature. 4th ed. 400p. 1982. 27.50 (ISBN 0-85157-315-0, Pub. by Bingley England); pap. 18.50 (Pub. by Bingley England). Shoe String.

Grogan, Emmett. Ringolevio. 1973. pap. 1.50 (ISBN 0-380-01530-7, 14449). Avon.

Grogan, Ewart S. & Sharpe, Arthur H. From the Cape to Cairo: The First Traverse of Africa from South to North. LC 72-5488. (Black Heritage Library Collection Ser.). 1972. Repr. of 1900 ed. 26.25 (ISBN 0-8369-9140-0). Ayer Co Pubs.

Grogan, Geoffrey W. What the Bible Teaches about Jesus. 1979. pap. 3.95 (ISBN 0-8423-7884-7). Tyndale.

Grogan, John C. & Conway, John T., eds. Masonry-STP 871: Research, Application & Problems. LC 85-3852. (Illus.). 253p. 1985. text ed. 36.00 (ISBN 0-8031-0402-2, 04-871000-07). ASTM.

Grogan, Kaye. The Teacher's Pet. 1982. 6.75 (ISBN 0-8062-1966-1). Carlton.

Grogan, Raymond G., et al, eds. Annual Review of Phytopathology, Vol. 16. LC 63-8847. (Illus.). 1978. text ed. 20.00 (ISBN 0-8243-1316-X). Annual Reviews.

--Annual Review of Phytopathology, Vol. 17. LC 63-8847. (Illus.). 1979. text ed. 20.00 (ISBN 0-8243-1317-8). Annual Reviews.

--Annual Review of Phytopathology, Vol. 18. LC 63-8847. (Illus.). 1980. text ed. 20.00 (ISBN 0-8243-1318-6). Annual Reviews.

--Annual Review of Phytopathology, Vol. 19. LC 63-8847. (Illus.). 1981. text ed. 20.00 (ISBN 0-8243-1319-4). Annual Reviews.

--Annual Review of Phytopathology, Vol. 20. LC 63-8847. (Illus.). 1982. text ed. 22.00 (ISBN 0-8243-1320-8). Annual Reviews.

--Annual Review of Phytopathology, Vol. 21. LC 63-8847. (Illus.). 1983. text ed. 27.00 (ISBN 0-8243-1321-6). Annual Reviews.

--Annual Review of Phytopathology, 1984, Vol. 22. (Illus.). viii, 487p. 1984. 27.00x (ISBN 0-8243-1322-4). Annual Reviews.

Groger, Molly. E. A. T. Eating Awareness Training. 224p. 1983. 12.95 (ISBN 0-671-46887-1). Summit Bks.

--E A T: Eating Awareness Training. 1985. 4.95 (ISBN 0-671-55486-7). Summit Bks.

Grogg, Evelyn. Bible Lessons for Little People: Revised with Learning Centers. rev. ed. Eberle, Sarah, rev. by. LC 80-53878. 144p. 1981. pap. 7.95 (ISBN 0-87239-430-1, 3368). Standard Pub.

--Kindergarten Pattern Book. Eberle, Sarah, rev. by. (Illus.). 48p. (Orig.). 1981. pap. 4.50 (ISBN 0-87239-431-X, 2159). Standard Pub.

Groggins, R. C. & Higson, N. Common Paediatric Emergincees. 128p. 1985. price not set (ISBN 0-7236-0847-4). PSG Pub Co.

Grogono, A. W. MCQ Tutor: Anaesthesia. 240p. 1983. pap. 14.00 (ISBN 0-433-15360-1, 991430115, Pub. by Heinemann Medical). Heyden.

Grogono, A. W. & Howells, T. Hilary. Self Assessment in Anesthesiology. (Illus.). 1976. pap. 17.95 (ISBN 0-8151-3995-0). Year Bk Med.

Grogono, P. & Nelson, S. H. Problem Solving & Computer Programming in. 1982. pap. text ed. 17.95 (ISBN 0-201-02460-8). Addison-Wesley.

Grogono, Peter. Mouse: A Language for Microcomputers. (Illus.). 200p. 1983. text ed. 17.50 (ISBN 0-89433-201-5). Petrocelli.

--Problem Solving Techniques Pascal. (Business & Computer Science Ser.). 320p. 1982. pap. text ed. 17.95 (ISBN 0-201-02460-8). Addison-Wesley.

--Programming in Pascal. rev. ed. LC 79-24640. 384p. 1980. pap. text ed. 19.95 (ISBN 0-201-02775-5). Addison-Wesley.

--Programming in Pascal: Computer Science. (Illus.). 512p. 1984. 23.95 (ISBN 0-201-12070-4). Addison-Wesley.

Groh, Dennis E., jt. auth. see Gregg, Robert C.

Groh, Dennis E. & Jewett, Robert, eds. The Living Text: Essays in Honor of Ernest W. Saunders. (Illus.). 272p. (Orig.). 1985. lib. bdg. 24.75 (ISBN 0-8191-4584-X); pap. text ed. 14.00 (ISBN 0-8191-4585-8). U Pr of Amer.

Groh, John E. Nineteenth Century German Protestantism: The Church As Social Model. LC 80-6286. 636p. (Orig.). 1982. lib. bdg. 37.50 (ISBN 0-8191-2077-4); pap. text ed. 24.25 (ISBN 0-8191-2078-2). U Pr of Amer.

Groh, John E. & Smith, Robert H., eds. The Lutheran Church in North American Life: 1776-1976, 1580-1980. LC 78-71233. 1979. 5.95 (ISBN 0-915644-17-7, Clayton). Luth Acad.

Groh, Lynn. P. T. Barnum. 80p. (gr. k-6). 1980. pap. 1.25 (ISBN 0-440-47177-X, YB). Dell.

Groh, Richard. The Dynamite Gang: The Three Hundred Sixtey-Seventh Fighter Group in World War II. (Illus.). 192p. 1983. pap. write for info. Aero.

--The Dynamite Gang: The 367th Fighter Group in World War II. 1982. pap. 12.95 (ISBN 0-8168-9770-0). Aero.

Groher, Michael E. Dysphagia: Diagnosis & Management. (Illus.). 256p. 1984. text ed. 29.95 (ISBN 0-409-95112-9). Butterworth.

Grohman, Joann S. Keeping a Family Cow. 256p. 1984. pap. 2.95 (ISBN 0-345-31626-6). Ballantine.

Grohmann, Gerbert. The Plant: A Guide to Understanding its Nature. Castelli, K., tr. Orig. Title: Die Pflanze, Vol. 1. (Illus.). 209p. 1974. 18.00 (ISBN 0-85440-282-9, Pub. by Steinerbooks). Anthroposophic.

Grohmann, R. Nystagmus as a Resultant in Accordance with the Theoretical Principals of the Physical Mechanisms of the Normal Human Labyrinths. Bd. with Acoustic Trauma & Cochlear Microcirculation. Kellerhals, B. (Advances in Oto-Rhino-Laryngology: Vol. 18). (Illus.). 1972. 31.50 (ISBN 3-8055-1357-7). S Karger.

Grohmann, Will. Klee. (Library of Great Painters Ser). 1967. 40.00 (ISBN 0-8109-0228-1). Abrams.

--Klee. (Master of Art Ser.). (Illus.). 128p. 1985. 19.95 (ISBN 0-8109-1208-2). Abrams.

Grohskopf, Bernice. End of Summer. 208p. (YA) 1982. pap. 2.25 (ISBN 0-380-79293-1, Flare). Avon.

--The Treasure of Sutton Hoo Ship: Burial for an Anglo-Saxon King. LC 74-86555. (Illus.). 1973. pap. text ed. 2.95x (ISBN 0-689-70362-7, 199). Atheneum.

Groht, Mildred A. Natural Language for Deaf Children. 1958. pap. text ed. 9.00 (ISBN 0-88200-086-1, C1887). Alexander Graham.

Groia, Philip. They All Sang on the Corner: A Second Look at New York City's Rhythm & Blues Vocal Groups. LC 83-61960. Orig. Title: They All Sang on the Corner: New York City's R&B Vocal Groups of the 1950's. (Illus.). 192p. 1983. pap. 15.00x (ISBN 0-9612058-0-6). Phillie Dee Ent.

Grolich, E., ed. Functional Analysis & Approximation. (ISNM Ser.: 60). 500p. 1981. text ed. 54.95x (ISBN 0-8176-1212-2). Birkhauser.

Grolier Club. Catalog of Original & Early Editions of Some of the Poetical & Prose Works from Langland to Prior, 4 Vols. in 1. 60.00x (ISBN 0-87556-116-0). Saifer.

Grolier Club - New York. Bibliographical Notes on One Hundred Books Famous in English Literature. Kent, Henry W., ed. 1903. 51.00 (ISBN 0-527-36290-5). Kraus Repr.

--One Hundred Books Famous in English Literature with 100 Facsimiles of the Title-Pages. 1902. 51.00 (ISBN 0-527-36300-6). Kraus Repr.

--One Hundred Influential American Books Printed Before 1900. 1947. 32.00 (ISBN 0-527-36310-3). Kraus Repr.

Grolier Editors, jt. auth. see Douglas, John H.

Grolier, Eric de see De Grolier, Eric.

Grolier Incorporated. Encyclopedia Science Supplement, 1984. Kondo, Herbert, ed. LC 64-7603. (Illus.). 1982. write for info. (ISBN 0-7172-1514-8). Grolier Ed Corp.

Groll, Sarah. Negative Verbal System of Late Egyptian. 260p. 1972. Repr. of 1970 ed. text ed. 27.50x (ISBN 0-19-711635-3, Pub. by Aris & Phillips England). Humanities.

Groll, Sarah I. Egyptological Studies. (Scripta Hierosolymitana Ser.: No. XXVIII). (Illus.). 537p. 1982. text ed. 35.00x (ISBN 0-85668-911-4, Pub. by Magnes Press). Humanities.

--The Negative Verbal System of Late Egyptian. 282p. 1972. 50.00x (ISBN 0-900416-41-6, Pub. by Griffith Inst). State Mutual Bk.

Grolle, Carl G. Electronic Workshop Manual & Guide. 240p. 1977. 16.95 (ISBN 0-13-252502-X, Parker). P-H.

--Electronic Workshop Manual & Guide. (Illus.). 1984. pap. 12.95 (ISBN 0-13-252635-2, Busn). P-H.

--Grolle's Complete Guide to Electronic Troubleshooting. 224p. 1979. 17.95 (ISBN 0-13-365080-4, Parker). P-H.

Grolle, Carl G. & Girosky, Michael B. Workbench Guide to Electronic Projects You Can Build in Your Spare Time. LC 81-2169. 256p. 1981. 17.95 (ISBN 0-13-965269-8, Parker). P-H.

Grollenberg, Luc H. The Penguin Shorter Atlas of the Bible. Hedlund, Mary F., tr. (Reference Ser). (Illus.). 1978. pap. 6.95 (ISBN 0-14-051056-7). Penguin.

Grollenberg, Lucas. Jesus. Bowden, John, tr. LC 78-13478. 138p. 1979. pap. 4.50 (ISBN 0-664-24232-4). Westminster.

--Paul. Bowden, John, tr. LC 78-14372. 186p. 1979. pap. 4.50 (ISBN 0-664-24234-0). Westminster.

Grollman, Earl A. Living: When a Loved One Has Died. LC 76-48508. (Illus.). 1977. pap. 6.95 (ISBN 0-8070-2741-3, BP560). Beacon Pr.

--Talking about Death: A Dialogue Between Parent & Child; With Parent's Guide & Recommended Resources. new ed. LC 75-36042. (Illus.). 112p. (YA) (gr. k-4). 1976. pap. 5.95 (ISBN 0-8070-2373-6, BP531). Beacon Pr.

--Talking about Divorce & Separation: A Dialogue Between Parent & Child. LC 75-5289. (Illus.). (YA) (gr. k-4). pap. 6.95 (ISBN 0-8070-2375-2, BP524). Beacon Pr.

--When Your Loved One Is Dying. LC 79-3780. 160p. 1980. 10.95 (ISBN 0-8070-3216-6). Beacon Pr.

Grollman, Earl A., ed. Concerning Death: A Practical Guide for the Living. LC 73-17117. 384p. 1974. pap. 9.95 (ISBN 0-8070-2765-0, BP484). Beacon Pr.

--Explaining Death to Children. LC 67-4891. 1969. pap. 8.95 (ISBN 0-8070-2385-X, BP317). Beacon Pr.

--Suicide: Prevention, Intervention, Postvention. LC 79-141873. (Illus.). 1971. pap. 7.95 (ISBN 0-8070-2775-8, BP392). Beacon Pr.

--What Helped Me: When My Loved One Died. LC 80-68166. 168p. 1982. pap. 6.95 (ISBN 0-8070-3229-8, BP 626). Beacon Pr.

Grollman, Sigmund. A Laboratory Manual of Mammalian Anatomy & Physiology. 4th ed. (Illus.). 266p. 1978. pap. text ed. 13.95x (ISBN 0-02-348090-4, 34809). Macmillan.

Grolund, Norman E. Measurement & Evaluation in Teaching. 5th ed. 64p. 1985. write for info. (ISBN 0-02-348250-8); text ed. write for info. (ISBN 0-02-348110-2). Macmillan.

Gromacki, Robert G. Are These the Last Days? LC 75-42165. 1975. pap. 3.50 (ISBN 0-87227-019-X). Reg Baptist.

--Called to Be Saints. 1977. pap. 3.95 (ISBN 0-87227-014-9). Reg Baptist.

--Called to Be Saints (I Corinthians) 1977. pap. 5.95 (ISBN 0-8010-3715-8). Baker Bk.

--Is Salvation Forever? 1981. pap. 5.95 (ISBN 0-8024-7507-8). Moody.

--Modern Tongues Movement. pap. 4.95 (ISBN 0-8010-3708-5). Baker Bk.

--Modern Tongues Movement. 1967. 4.95 (ISBN 0-87552-304-8). Presby & Reformed.
--New Testament Survey. 15.95 (ISBN 0-8010-3677-1). Baker Bk.
--New Testament Survey. LC 74-83793. 1974. 9.95 (ISBN 0-87227-018-1). Reg Baptist.
--Stand Firm in the Faith. LC 78-68055. (Illus.). 1978. pap. 4.95 (ISBN 0-87227-064-5). Reg Baptist.
--Stand Perfect in Wisdom: Colossians & Ephesians. 1981. pap. 5.95 (ISBN 0-8010-3767-0). Baker Bk.
--Stand True to the Charge: An Exposition of I Timothy. 200p. 1982. pap. 7.95 (ISBN 0-8010-3786-7). Baker Bk.
--The Virgin Birth of Christ. 200p. 1981. pap. 5.95 (ISBN 0-8010-3765-4). Baker Bk.
Gromada, Karen. Mothering Multiples. (Illus.). 52p. 1981. pap. 2.50 (ISBN 0-912500-16-6, 52). La Leche.
Groman, George L., ed. The City Today. 1978. pap. text ed. 10.95 scp (ISBN 0-06-160420-8, HarpC). Har-Row.
--Political Literature of the Progressive Era. xxii, 287p. 1967. 6.50 (ISBN 0-87013-107-9). Mich St U Pr.
Grombach, John V. The Great Liquidator. 1981. pap. 2.95 (ISBN 0-89083-749-X). Zebra.
Gromer, Terry J. Why People Do Not Get Well. (Illus.). 156p. (Orig.). 1983. pap. 4.95. Skylight Health.
Gromisch, Donald S., jt. auth. see Wasserman, Edward.
Gromme, Owen J. Birds of Wisconsin. (Illus.). 236p. 1963. 45.00 (ISBN 0-299-03001-6). U of Wis Pr.
Grommon, Alfred H., ed. Education of Teachers of English for American Schools & Colleges. LC 63-20362. 1963. 27.00x (ISBN 0-89197-132-7). Irvington.
Gromyko, A. Africa: Progress, Problems, Prospects. 254p. 1983. 6.95 (ISBN 0-8285-2563-3, Pub. by Progress Pubs USSR). Imported Pubns.
--Reports of the CPSU Central Committee Plenum & the Meeting of the Supreme Soviet of the USSR: Speakers; Y. Andropov, K. Chernenko, Nos. 1-4. Karsavina, Jean, et al, eds. Notosi Press. (Soviet Press Ser.). 1983. pap. 5.00 (ISBN 0-9606282-0-7). Compass Pubns NY.
Gromyko, A., ed. African Countries' Foreign Policy. 221p. 1983. 7.95 (ISBN 0-8285-2654-0, Pub. by Progress Pubs USSR). Imported Pubns.
Gromyko, A. A. Only for Peace. (Illus.). 1979. text ed. 49.00 (ISBN 0-08-023582-4); pap. text ed. 20.00 (ISBN 0-08-024513-7). Pergamon.
Gromyko, A. A. & Ponomarev, B. N., eds. Soviet Foreign Policy, Nineteen Forty-Five to Nineteen Eighty. 728p. 1981. 14.00 (ISBN 0-8285-2294-4, Pub. by Progress Pubs USSR). Imported Pubns.
--Soviet Foreign Policy, 1917-1945. 501p. 1981. 11.00 (ISBN 0-8285-2293-6, Pub. by Progress Pubs. USSR). Imported Pubns.
Gromyko, Anatolii A. Through Russian Eyes: President Kennedy's One Thousand Thirty-Six Days. Garon, Philip A., ed. LC 73-75637. 239p. 1973. 11.95 (ISBN 0-914250-00-0). Intl Lib.
Gron, P. & Ericsson, Y., eds. Monofluorophosphate Perspectives. (Journal: Caries Research: Vol. 17, Suppl. 1). (Illus.). iv, 140p. 1983. pap. 18.75 (ISBN 3-8055-3793-X). S Karger.
Grona, Nancy. Basic Electricity for the Petroleum Industry. 2nd ed. (Illus.). 146p. (Orig.). 1978. pap. text ed. 5.50 (ISBN 0-88698-079-8, 1.40020). PETEX.
Grona, Nancy & Skinner, Mary L. Operation of Electrified & Automatic Leases. 2nd ed. Gerding, Mildred, ed. (Illus.). 114p. (Orig.). 1978. pap. text ed. 5.50 (ISBN 0-88698-113-1, 3.20020). Petex.
Gronander, U. Regular Structures: Lectures in Pattern Theory III. (Applied Mathematical Sciences Ser: Vol. 33). 569p. 1981. pap. 28.50 (ISBN 0-387-90560-X). Springer-Verlag.
Gronau, Israel Christian, jt. auth. see Boltzius, John M.
Gronau, Israel Christian, jt. auth. see Boltzius, John Martin.
Gronbech, Bo. Hans Christian Andersen. (World Authors Ser.). 1980. lib. bdg. 13.50 (ISBN 0-8057-6454-2, Twayne). G K Hall.
Gronbech, Vilhelm. Religious Currents in the Nineteenth Century. Mitchell, P. M. & Paden, W. D., trs. from Danish. LC 72-11829. (Arcturus Bks. Paperbacks). 206p. 1973. lib. bdg. 7.00x (ISBN 0-8093-0629-8); pap. 2.45 (ISBN 0-8093-0630-1). S Ill U Pr.
Gronbeck, Bruce E. The Articulate Person: A Guide to Everyday Public Speaking. 2nd ed. 1983. pap. text ed. 16.25x (ISBN 0-673-15628-1). Scott F.
Gronbeck, Bruce E., jt. auth. see Ehninger, Douglas.
Gronberg, Margaret & Nutting, Linda. Rock Hunting in Texas: Where to Go & How to Get There. (Illus.). 128p. (Orig.). 1986. pap. 9.95x (ISBN 0-88415-786-5, Lone Star Bks). Gulf Pub.
Gronbjerg, Kirsten, et al. Poverty & Social Change. LC 78-876. viii, 248p. 1980. pap. 9.00x (ISBN 0-226-30963-0). U of Chicago Pr.
Gronbjerg, Kirsten A. Mass Society & the Extension of Welfare, 1960-1970. LC 76-8101. (Illus.). 1977. lib. bdg. 20.00x (ISBN 0-226-30964-9). U of Chicago Pr.
Gronbjerg, Kristen A., et al. Government Spending & the Nonprofit Sector in Cook County - Chicago. (The Nonprofit Sector Ser.). 79p. (Orig.). 1985. pap. text ed. 12.95x (ISBN 0-87766-348-3). Urban Inst.
Grondahl, Calvin. Freeway to Perfection: A Collection of Mormon Cartoons. (Illus.). 96p. (Orig.). 1980. pap. 4.50 (ISBN 0-9606760-1-5). Sunstone Found.
--Sunday's Foyer. (Illus.). 96p. 1983. pap. 4.75 (ISBN 0-9606760-3-1). Sunstone Found.
Grondahl, Illit. Landmarks of English Literature. 1973. Repr. of 1938 ed. 20.00 (ISBN 0-8274-0030-6). R West.
--Landmarks of English Literature: A Brief Survey. 1979. Repr. of 1938 ed. lib. bdg. 25.00 (ISBN 0-8495-2010-X). Arden Lib.
Grondahl, Illit & Raknes, Ola. Chapters in Norwegian Literature; Being the Substance of Public Lectures, Given at University College, London, During the Sessions 1918-1922. LC 74-102241. (Select Bibliographies Reprint Ser.). 1923. 26.50 (ISBN 0-8369-5126-3). Ayer Co Pubs.
Grondal, Florence A. The Romance of Astronomy: The Music of the Spheres. 1937. 22.50 (ISBN 0-686-17424-0). Ridgeway Bks.
Grone, Linda. Reach for a Different Sky. 1984. 5.95 (ISBN 0-8062-2411-8). Carlton.
Groneman, C. H. & Feirer, J. L. General Industrial Education & Technology. 7th ed. 640p. 1985. 25.96 (ISBN 0-07-025023-5); write for info. study guide (ISBN 0-07-025024-3). McGraw.
Groneman, C. H., jt. auth. see Feirer, J. L.
Groneman, Chris. Leathercraft. (gr. 9-12). 1963. pap. 15.92 (ISBN 0-02-664840-7). Bennett IL.
Groneman, Chris H. General Woodworking. 6th ed. Lindquist, Hal, ed. (Publications in Industrial Education Ser.). (Illus.). 344p. (gr. 9-10). 1981. text ed. 21.80 (ISBN 0-07-025003-0). McGraw.
--Leather Tooling & Carving. LC 74-75258. (Illus.). 128p. 1974. pap. 4.00 (ISBN 0-486-23061-9). Dover.
Groneman, Chris H. & Feirer, John L. General Industrial Education. 6th ed. (M Publications in Industrial Education Ser.). 1979. text ed. 22.64 (ISBN 0-07-024991-1). McGraw.
--Getting Started in Drawing & Planning. (M-H Publications in Industrial Ed.). (Illus.). 1979. pap. 7.64 (ISBN 0-07-024996-2). McGraw.
--Getting Started in Electricity & Electronics. LC 78-19120. (M-H Publications in Industrial Ed.). (Illus.). (YA) (gr. 7-9). 1979. pap. text ed. 7.64 (ISBN 0-07-024999-7). McGraw.
--Getting Started in Metalworking. (M-H Publications in Industrial Ed.). (Illus.). (YA) 1979. pap. 7.64 (ISBN 0-07-024998-9). McGraw.
Groneman, Chris H. & Glazener, E. R. Technical Woodworking. 2nd ed. 1975. 27.60 (ISBN 0-07-024964-4). McGraw.
Groneman, Chris H. & Grannis, Gary E. Exploring the Industries. LC 79-55313. 1981. pap. text ed. 19.60 (ISBN 0-8273-1757-3); instr's. guide 3.00 (ISBN 0-8273-1758-1). Delmar.
Groneman, Nancy J. Business Mathematics Using Electronic Calculators. (Illus.). 240p. 1982. 21.95 (ISBN 0-13-105205-5). P-H.
Gronemeyer, Horst, et al, eds. see Klopstock, F. G.
Groner & Fraisse, eds. Cognition & Eye Movements. 224p. 1983. 55.50 (ISBN 0-444-86354-0, I-110-82, North Holland). Elsevier.
Groner, Alex. Duplicate Bridge Direction: A Complete Handbook. rev ed. LC 67-29818. 1973. pap. 8.95 (ISBN 0-87643-012-4). Barclay Bridge.
Groner, Alex, jt. auth. see Boehm, George A.
Groner, Alfred M. The Monopoly Players. LC 81-22798. 1982. 16.50 (ISBN 0-87949-207-4). Ashley Bks.
Groner, Gabriel F. PL-One Programming in Technological Applications. LC 70-136713. Repr. of 1971 ed. 60.50 (ISBN 0-8357-9955-7, 2012585). Bks Demand UMI.
Groner, Judyth S. & Wikler, Madeline. My Very Own Jewish Community. LC 83-22215. (Illus.). 40p. 1984. pap. 4.95 (ISBN 0-930494-32-6). Kar Ben.
Groner, Pat N. Cost Containment Through Employee Incentives Program. LC 77-72514. 144p. 1977. 28.00 (ISBN 0-912862-42-4). Aspen Systems.
Groner, R., et al. Eye Movements & Psychological Functions. 376p. 1983. 49.95x (ISBN 0-89859-281-X). L Erlbaum Assocs.
Groner, Rudolph, et al, eds. Methods of Heuristics. 416p. 1983. text ed. 49.95x (ISBN 0-89859-251-8). L Erlbaum Assocs.
Groner, Samuel. Modern Business Law. 1982. text ed. 25.95 (ISBN 0-8359-4555-3); wkbk. 7.95 (ISBN 0-8359-4557-X); instrs'. manual avail. (ISBN 0-8359-4556-1). Reston.
Groner, Tsvi. The Legal Methodology of Hai Gaon. LC 84-5566. (Brown Judaic Studies: No. 66). 1985. 24.95 (ISBN 0-89130-748-6, 14 00 66); pap. 19.95 (ISBN 0-89130-841-5). Scholars Pr GA.
Grones, Freda. Fifteen Tips on Writing Resumes. McFadden, S. Michele, ed. 17p. (Orig.). 1981. pap. text ed. 1.25 (ISBN 0-89262-055-2); 30 copy pack 37.50 (ISBN 0-686-85766-6). Career Pub.
Gronewold, Sue. Beautiful Merchandise: Prostitution in China 1860-1936. LC 85-7672. 128p. 1985. pap. 6.95 (ISBN 0-918393-15-9). Harrington Pk.
Gronewold, Sue, ed. Beautiful Merchandise: Prostitution in China, 1860-1936. LC 82-6049. (Women & History Ser.: No. 1). 114p. 1982. text ed. 22.95 (ISBN 0-86656-134-X, B134). Haworth Pr.
Gronhaug, Reidar. Micro-Macro Relations: Social Organization in Antalya, Southern Turkey. (Bergen Studies in Social Anthropology: No. 7). (Illus.). 518p. (Orig.). 1985. pap. text ed. 9.95x (ISBN 0-936508-52-3, Pub. by Dept Soc Anthropology, University of Bergen, Norway). Barber Pr.
Gronhovd, G. H., et al. Low-Rank Coal Technology: Lignite & Subbituminous. LC 82-3433. (Energy Tech Rev.: No. 79). (Illus.). 609p. 1982. 52.00 (ISBN 0-8155-0896-4). Noyes.
Gronicka, Andre von see Von Gronicka, Andre.
Gronicka, Andre Von see Von Gronicka, Andre & Bates-Yakobson, Helen.
Groningen, B. A. Van see Van Groningen, B. A. & Finley, Moses.
Gronlie, Gisle. Geophysical Studies in the Norwegian-Greenland Sea. (Norsk Polarinstitutt Skrifter: Vol. 170). (Illus.). 117p. 1980. pap. 10.00 (ISBN 82-90307-05-5). Universitet.
Gronlund, Laurence. The New Economy. LC 75-320. (The Radical Tradition in America Ser.). 364p. 1975. Repr. of 1898 ed. 25.85 (ISBN 0-88355-224-8). Hyperion Conn.
--Our Destiny: The Influence of Socialism on Morals & Religion; an Essay on Ethics. LC 75-321. (The Radical Tradition in America Ser.). 170p. 1975. Repr. of 1890 ed. 17.50 (ISBN 0-88355-225-6). Hyperion Conn.
Gronlund, Norman E. Constructing Achievement Tests. 3rd ed. (Illus.). 176p. 1982. pap. 14.95 reference (ISBN 0-13-169151-1). P-H.
--Improving Marking & Reporting in Classroom Instruction. (Illus.). 64p. 1974. text ed. write for info. (ISBN 0-02-348140-4, 34814). Macmillan.
--Individualizing Classroom Instruction. 1974. pap. write for info. (ISBN 0-02-348280-X, 34828). Macmillan.
--Preparing Criterion-Referenced Tests for Classroom Instruction. 55p. 1973. pap. text ed. 3.95 (ISBN 0-02-348270-2). Macmillan.
--Stating Objectives for Classroom Instruction. 2nd ed. 1978. pap. text ed. write for info. (ISBN 0-02-348240-0, 34824). Macmillan.
--Stating Objectives for Classroom Instruction. 3rd ed. 80p. 1985. text ed. write for info. (ISBN 0-02-348000-9). Macmillan.
--Student Exercise Manual for Measurement & Evaluation in Teaching. 5th ed. 224p. 1985. text ed. write for info. (ISBN 0-02-348010-6). Macmillan.
Gronomov, A. Problems & Exercises in Organic Chemistry. 341p. 1974. 7.45 (ISBN 0-8285-0663-9, Pub. by Mir Pubs USSR). Imported Pubns.
Gronoovius, J. F. Flora Virginica Exhibens Plantas Quas V. C. Johannes Clayton in Virginia Observavit Atque Collegit. pap. 10.00 (ISBN 0-934454-35-3). Lubrecht & Cramer.
Gronoswska, R., jt. auth. see Gronowski, T.
Gronowicz, Anthony, ed. Oswald Garrison Villard: The Dilemmas of the Absolute Pacifist in Two World Wars. LC 72-147764. (Library of War & Peace; Documentary Anthologies). lib. bdg. 83.00 (ISBN 0-8240-0504-X). Garland Pub.
Gronowicz, Antoni. Polish Profiles: The Land, the People & Their History. LC 75-23929. (Illus.). 256p. 1976. 10.00 (ISBN 0-88208-060-1). Lawrence Hill.
Gronowitz, Salo. Thiophene & Its Derivatives, Vol. 44. 2nd ed. (Chemistry of Heterocyclic Compounds Monographs). 784p. 1985. 205.00 (ISBN 0-471-38120-9). Wiley.
Gronowski, T. & Gronoswska, R. Poland. (Illus.). 1977. 40.00 (ISBN 0-686-77973-8). Heinman.
Gronski, Claudette & Meeker, Judith. Power Pak for Preschool Programs. LC 83-83187. (Illus.). 240p. (ps-1). 1984. pap. text ed. 12.95 (ISBN 0-86530-025-9, IP 25-9). Incentive Pubns.
Gronsky, Paul P. & Astrov, N. J. The War & the Russian Government: The Central Government & the Municipal Government & the All-Russian Union of Towns. (Economic & Social History of the World War, Russian Ser.). 1929. 27.50x (ISBN 0-317-27652-2). Elliots Bks.
Grontved, Johannes see Thule Expedition.
Gronvik, Ottar. The Words of "Heir", "Inheritance", & "Funeral Feasts" in Early Germanic. 28p. (Orig.). 1982. pap. 11.00 (ISBN 82-00-05896-4). Universitet.
Gronwall, Anders. Dextran & Its Use in Colloidal Infusion Solutions. (Illus.). 1957. 39.00 (ISBN 0-12-304050-7). Acad Pr.
Groom, A. J. & Taylor, Paul, eds. Functionalism: Theory & Practice in International Relations. LC 73-93664. 354p. 1975. 34.50x (ISBN 0-8448-0305-7). Crane-Russak Co.
Groom, A. J., ed. see Centre for the Analysis of Conflict, London.
Groom, A. J. R. & Taylor, Paul, eds. The Commonwealth in the Nineteen Eighties: Challenges & Opportunities. 380p. 1984. 27.50x (ISBN 0-8448-1468-7). Crane-Russak Co.
Groom, A. J. R., jt. ed. see Light, Margot.
Groom, Bernard. On the Diction of Tennyson, Browning & Arnold. LC 77-4013. Repr. of 1939 ed. lib. bdg. 8.50 (ISBN 0-8414-4415-3). Folcroft.
--On the Diction of Tennyson, Browning & Arnold. 57p. 1970. Repr. of 1939 ed. 10.50 (ISBN 0-208-01027-0, Archon). Shoe String.
Groom, Bernard, ed. see Shakespeare, William.
Groom, Bob. The Blues Revival. (The Paul Oliver Blues Ser.). pap. 2.95 (ISBN 0-913714-28-3). Legacy Bks.
Groom, James N., jt. auth. see Harkness, Sarah.
Groom, Nigel. Arabic-English Dictionary of Arabic Topography & Placenames. 1983. 25.00x (ISBN 0-86685-331-6). Intl Bk Ctr.
Groom, Olive. Yasmin Meets a Yak. 1973. pap. 1.95 (ISBN 0-87508-806-6). Chr Lit.
Groom, Winston. Better Times Than These. 1984. pap. 3.95 (ISBN 0-425-07151-0); pap. 4.50. Berkley Pub.
--Only. LC 83-17745. 192p. 1984. 12.95 (ISBN 0-399-12905-7, Putnam). Putnam PUb Group.
Groom, Winston & Spencer, Duncan. Conversations with the Enemy. (Nonfiction Ser.). 416p. 1984. pap. 7.95 (ISBN 0-14-007369-8). Penguin.
--Conversations with the Enemy: The Story of PFC Robert Garwood. LC 82-23007. 416p. 1983. 16.95 (ISBN 0-399-12715-1, Putnam). Putnam Pub Group.
Groome, Francis H. Edward Fitzgerald: an Aftermath: With Miscellanies in Verse & Prose. LC 72-5596. (Select Bibliographies Reprint Ser.). 1972. Repr. of 1902 ed. 21.00 (ISBN 0-8369-6911-1). Ayer Co Pubs.
--Gypsy Folk-Tales. Dorson, Richard M., ed. LC 77-70599. (International Folklore Ser.). 1977. Repr. of 1899 ed. lib. bdg. 29.00x (ISBN 0-405-10098-1). Ayer Co Pubs.
--In Gypsy Tents. LC 73-13616. (Folklore Ser). 28.00 (ISBN 0-88305-233-4). Norwood Edns.
--Two Suffolk Friends. 133p. 1980. Repr. lib. bdg. 17.50 (ISBN 0-89984-227-5). Century Bookbindery.
Groome, Harry. Opportunities in Advertising Careers. (Illus.). (gr. 9 up). 1976. PLB 6.60 (ISBN 0-8442-6403-2); pap. text ed. 4.95 (ISBN 0-8442-6402-4). Natl Textbk.
Groome, Harry C., Jr. Opportunities in Advertising. (VGM Career Bks.). (Illus.). 160p. 1983. 7.95 (ISBN 0-8442-6271-4, 6271-4, Passport Bks.); pap. 5.95 (ISBN 0-8442-6272-2, 6272-2). Natl Textbk.
--This Is Advertising: 1975. 1975. 9.95x (ISBN 0-910190-04-6). IMS Pr.
Groome, Sarah C. Today's Flower Arranging Without Tears. LC 78-67256. (Illus.). 88p. 1978. 8.95 (ISBN 0-8059-2594-5). Dorrance.
Groome, Thomas H. Christian Religious Education: Sharing Our Story & Vision. LC 81-47847. 320p. 1982. pap. text ed. 12.45 (ISBN 0-06-063494-4, RD 371, HarpR). Har-Row.
Groomer, Vera. Dibe Yazhi. (ps). 1980. pap. 1.95 (ISBN 0-8127-0260-3). Review & Herald.
--Good Friends Again: Two - Three. (Come Unto Me Ser.: Year 2, Bk. 3). 32p. (ps). 1980. pap. 1.65 (ISBN 0-8127-0272-7). Review & Herald.
--Growing Stronger: Two - Two. (Come Unto Me Ser.: Year 2, Bk. 2). 32p. (ps). 1980. pap. 1.65 (ISBN 0-8127-0271-9). Review & Herald.
--Kind Kristy. (Come Unto Me Library). 1979. pap. 1.65 (ISBN 0-8127-0209-3). Review & Herald.
--Obedience Brings Happiness. (Come Unto Me Ser.). 16p. (ps). 1979. pap. 1.65 (ISBN 0-8127-0251-4). Review & Herald.
--Quiet Because. (Come Unto Me Ser.). (ps). 1979. pap. 1.65 (ISBN 0-8127-0253-0). Review & Herald.
--Talking to My Friend Jesus: Two - Four. (Come Unto Me Ser.: Year 2, Bk. 4). 32p. (ps). 1980. pap. 1.65 (ISBN 0-8127-0273-5). Review & Herald.
Grooms, Bernard. Formation & Use of Compound Epithets in English Poetry from 1579. 1937. lib. bdg. 8.50 (ISBN 0-8414-4692-X). Folcroft.
Grooms, Kathe, ed. see Lansky, Bruce.
Grooms, Kathe, ed. see Masters, M.
Grooms, Kathe, ed. see Whitman, John.
Grooms, Martha. Walk in My Footsteps. Hartman, Suzanne, ed. 160p. (Orig.). 1985. pap. 8.95 (ISBN 0-913678-15-5). New Day Pr.
Grooms, Steve. Modern Pheasant Hunting. (Illus.). 224p. 1984. pap. 8.95 (ISBN 0-8117-2208-2). Stackpole.
Grooms, Steve, ed. see Babe Winkelman.
Grooms, Steve, ed. see Winkelman, Babe.
Groopman, Jerome E., jt. auth. see Gottlieb, Michael S.
Groos, ed. see De Voltaire, Francois M.
Groos, G. W., tr. see Waldstein, Baron.
Groos, Karl. Play of Animals. LC 75-35072. (Studies in Play & Games). 1976. Repr. 29.00x (ISBN 0-405-07922-2). Ayer Co Pubs.
--Play of Man. Baldwin, Elizabeth L., tr. LC 75-35073. (Studies in Play & Games). 1976. Repr. 29.00x (ISBN 0-405-07923-0). Ayer Co Pubs.
Groot, Adriaan de see Frijda, Nico H.
Groot, Adrian D. de see De Groot, Adriaan D.
Groot, C. Hofstede De see De Groot, C. Hofstede.
Groot, C. Hofstede de see De Groot, C. Hofstede.
Groot, David de see Dalenburg, Cornelia & De Groot, David.
Groot, E. C. de see Mouwen, J. M. & De Groot, E. C.
Groot, Georg Van Der see Van Der Groot, Georg.
Groot, Gerard J. The Prehistory of Japan. facsimile ed. Kraus, Bertram S., ed. LC 79-37884. (Select Bibliographies Reprint Ser). Repr. of 1951 ed. 36.00 (ISBN 0-8369-6721-6). Ayer Co Pubs.

Gross, D. R. & Hwang, N. H. The Rheology of Blood, Blood Vessels & Associated Tissues. (NATO Advanced Study, Applied Science Ser.: No. 41). 382p. 1981. 42.50 (ISBN 90-286-0950-4). Sijthoff & Noordhoff.
Gross, D. R. & Hwang, N. H. C., eds. The Rheology of Blood Vessels & Associated Tissues. 1981. lib. bdg. 42.50 (ISBN 90-286-0950-4, Pub. Martinus Nijhoff Netherlands). Kluwer Academic.
Gross, D. R., jt. ed. see Hwang, N. H.
Gross, Darwin. The Atom. 130p. (Orig.). 1984. pap. 4.95 (ISBN 0-931689-01-5). D Gross.
--Awakened Imagination. 128p. (Orig.). 1985. pap. 9.95 (ISBN 0-931689-03-1). D Gross.
--Gems of Soul. LC 80-83548. 168p. (Orig.). 1980. pap. 4.95 (ISBN 0-914766-61-9, 0166). IWP Pub.
--You Can't Turn Back. 98p. (Orig.). 1985. pap. 4.95 (ISBN 0-931689-02-3). D Gross.
Gross, Darwin & Goddard, Neville. The Power of Awareness. rev. ed. 144p. 1984. pap. 9.95 (ISBN 0-931689-00-7). D Gross.
Gross, Darwin, jt. auth. see Twitchell, Paul.
Gross, David. Teach Yourself Rock Bass. 64p. pap. 6.95 (ISBN 0-8256-2202-6). Music Sales.
--The Writer & Society: Heinrich Mann & Literary Politics in Germany Eighteen Ninety to Nineteen Forty. LC 79-11707. 1980. text ed. 18.00x (ISBN 0-391-00972-9). Humanities.
Gross, David C. One Thousand & One Questions & Answers About Judaism. LC 76-42330. (Illus.). 1978. 8.95 (ISBN 0-385-11137-1). Doubleday.
--Pride of Our People: The Stories of One Hundred Outstanding Jewish Men & Women. LC 77-25592. (Illus.). 448p. 1979. 14.95 (ISBN 0-385-13573-4). Doubleday.
Gross, David C., ed. see Isaacson, Ben.
Gross, David R. Animal Models in Cardiovascular Research. 1985. lib. bdg. 99.50 (ISBN 0-89838-711-6, Pub. by Martinus Nijhoff Netherlands). Kluwer Academic.
Gross, Donald & Harris, Carl M. Fundamentals of Queueing Theory. (Wiley Series in Probability & Mathematical Statistics-Applied Probability & Statistics Section). 556p. 1974. 45.95x (ISBN 0-471-32812-X). Wiley.
Gross, E., tr. see Determann, H.
Gross, E. T., et al, eds. Coil Spring Making. 2nd ed. (Engineering Craftsmen: No. H6). (Illus.). 1974. spiral bdg. 45.00x (ISBN 0-85083-172-5). Trans-Atlantic.
Gross, Edmund J. Copy Stimulators. new ed. (Illus.). 128p. 1975. pap. 8.50 (ISBN 0-912256-07-9). Halls of Ivy.
--How to Do Your Own Pasteup for Printing. (Illus., Orig.). 1979. pap. 7.50 (ISBN 0-912256-13-3). Halls of Ivy.
--How to Get More Sales from Your Advertising. (Illus.). 48p. 1968. pap. 4.00 (ISBN 0-912256-03-6). Halls of Ivy.
--One Hundred-One Ways to Save Money on All Your Printing. (Illus.). 1971. pap. 12.00 (ISBN 0-912256-02-8). Halls of Ivy.
Gross, Edward & Etzoini, Amatai. Organizations in Society. (Illus.). 256p. 1985. text ed. 16.95 (ISBN 0-13-641861-9); pap. text ed. 14.95 (ISBN 0-13-641853-8). P-H.
Gross, Edward & Western, John S., eds. The End of a Golden Age: Higher Education in a Steady State. (Scholars' Library). (Illus.). 144p. 1982. pap. text ed. 31.00x (ISBN 0-7022-1625-9). U of Queensland Pr.
Gross, Edward, et al. The Child Health Manual. (Illus.). 224p. 1985. pap. text ed. 16.95x (ISBN 0-86542-021-1). Blackwell Sci.
Gross, Edwin J. Personal Leadership in Marketing. 189p. 1968. pap. 4.50x (ISBN 0-912598-04-2). Florham.
Gross, Elizabeth H. Public Library Service to Children. LC 67-24347. 152p. 1967. 9.00 (ISBN 0-379-00309-0). Oceana.
Gross, Ellen & Harithas, James. Drawings of John Singer Sargent in the Corcoran Gallery of Art. (Master Draughtsman Ser). (Illus., Orig.). treasure trove bdg. 10.50 (ISBN 0-87505-051-4); pap. 5.50 (ISBN 0-87505-204-5). Borden.
Gross, Erhard, ed. The Peptides: Analysis, Synthesis, Biology: Vol. 3 Protection of Functional Groups in Peptides Synthesis. 1981. 55.00 (ISBN 0-12-304203-8). Acad Pr.
Gross, Erhard & Meiehnhofer, Hohannes, eds. The Peptides: Analysis, Synthesis, Biology, Vol. 5. (Special Methods in Peptide Synthesis Ser.: Part B). 1983. 79.50 (ISBN 0-12-304205-4). Acad Pr.
Gross, Erhard & Meienhofer, Johannes, eds. The Peptides: Analysis, Synthesis, Biology: Vol. I, Pt. a, Major Methods of Peptide Bond Formation. LC 78-31958. 1979. 65.00 (ISBN 0-12-304201-1). Acad Pr.
--The Peptides: Analysis, Synthesis, Biology: Vol. 4, Modern Techniques of Peptide & Amino Acid Anaysis. 1981. 59.50 (ISBN 0-12-304204-6). Acad Pr.
Gross, Erhard & Meinhoper, Johannes, eds. The Peptides: Analysis, Synthesis, Biology, Vol. 2: Special Methods in Peptide Synthesis, Pt. A. LC 78-31958. 1980. 65.50 (ISBN 0-12-304202-X). Acad Pr.
Gross, Evelyn C., jt. auth. see Shangold, Mona M.
Gross, F. The Cardioprotective Action of Betablockers: Facts & Theories. 99p. 1977. 40.00 (ISBN 3-456-80491-1, Pub. by Holdan Bk Ltd UK). State Mutual Bk.
Gross, F., ed. International Experience with Nadolol, a Long-Acting B-Blocking Agent. (Royal Society of Medicine International Congress & Symposium Ser.). 248p. 1981. 40.50 (ISBN 0-8089-1368-9, 791743). Grune.
Gross, F., et al, eds. Antihypertensive Agents. (Handbook of Experimental Pharmacology: Band 39). 1977. 166.00 (ISBN 0-387-07594-1). Springer-Verlag.
Gross, F. H. Mild Hypertension. 1980. 41.95 (ISBN 0-8151-4005-3). Year Bk Med.
Gross, F. H. & Inman, W. H., eds. Drug Monitoring. 1978. 55.00 (ISBN 0-12-304550-9). Acad Pr.
Gross, Feliks. Ethnics in a Borderland: An Inquiry into the Nature of Ethnicity & Reduction of Ethnic Tensions in a One-Time Genocide Area. LC 77-94741. (Contributions in Sociology: No. 32). 1978. lib. bdg. 27.50 (ISBN 0-313-20310-5, GET/). Greenwood.
--Ideologies, Goals & Values. LC 84-3754. (Contributions in Sociology Ser.: No. 52). (Illus.). xxxv, 343p. 1985. lib. bdg. 65.00 (ISBN 0-8371-6377-3, GVS/). Greenwood.
--O Wartosciach Spolecznych: Studia I Szkice. 211p. 1961. pap. 3.00 (ISBN 0-940962-16-0). Polish Inst Art & Sci.
--Peace Planning for Central & Eastern Europe. 70p. 1944. 3.00 (ISBN 0-940962-21-7). Polish Inst Art & Sci.
--The Polish Worker: Study of a Social Stratum. LC 77-87525. Repr. of 1945 ed. 22.00 (ISBN 0-404-16602-4). AMS Pr.
--The Revolutionary Party: Essays in the Sociology of Politics. LC 72-806. (Contributions in Sociology Ser.: No. 12). 1974. lib. bdg. 35.00 (ISBN 0-8371-6376-5, GRV/). Greenwood.
--Seizure of Political Power in a Century of Revolutions. LC 68-54776. 1979. Repr. of 1958 ed. lib. bdg. 27.50x (ISBN 0-8371-4639-9, GRPP). Greenwood.
--Violence in Politics: Terror & Political Assassination in Eastern Europe & Russia. Van Nieuwenhuijze, C. A., ed. LC 77-189701. (Studies in the Social Sciences: No. 13). 82p. 1973. pap. text ed. 11.20x (ISBN 0-686-22549-X). Mouton.
Gross, Feliks, ed European Ideologies. facs. ed. LC 71-128254. (Essay Index Reprint Ser). 1948. 46.50 (ISBN 0-8369-2107-0). Ayer Co Pubs.
Gross, Felix. European Ideologies. 1955. 12.00 (ISBN 0-8022-0633-6). Philos Lib.
Gross, Fletcher, jt. ed. see Scott, William R.
Gross, Francis L., Jr. Passages in Teaching. LC 82-3865. 225p. 1982. 15.00 (ISBN 0-8022-2403-2). Philos Lib.
Gross, Franz, ed. Decision-Making in Drug Research. 256p. 1983. text ed. 41.50 (ISBN 0-89004-944-0). Raven.
Gross, Franz & Strasser, Toma, eds. Mild Hypertension: Recent Advances. 446p. 1983. text ed. 54.50 (ISBN 0-89004-808-8). Raven.
Gross, Franz, et al, eds. Enzymatic Release of Vasoactive Peptides: Eighth Workshop Conference HOECHST. (Illus.). 432p. 1980. text ed. 59.00 (ISBN 0-89004-458-9). Raven.
Gross, Franz B., ed. United States & the United Nations. 1965. 24.50 (ISBN 0-8061-0631-X). U of Okla Pr.
Gross, Gail & Finkelstein, Honora. Beautiful Skin. (Orig.). 1985. pap. 8.95 (ISBN 0-449-90108-4, Columbine). Fawcett.
Gross, Gerald. Editors on Editing. rev. ed. LC 84-48163. 352p. 1985. pap. 12.45i (ISBN 0-06-091120-4, CN). Har-Row.
Gross, Gerald, ed. Editors on Editing. 2nd, rev. ed. LC 84-48163. 352p. 1985. 22.07i (ISBN 0-06-015381-4, HarpT). Har-Row.
Gross, Gerald C., jt. auth. see Herring, James M.
Gross, Grant M. Ocean World. (Physical Science Ser.). (Orig.). 1976. pap. text ed. 9.95 (ISBN 0-675-08576-4) (ISBN 0-675-08575-6). Merrill.
Gross, Gwen. Knights of the Round Table. LC 85-2176. (Step-Up Adventures Ser.). (Illus.). 112p. (gr. 2-5). 1985. pap. 2.95 (ISBN 0-394-87579-6, BYR); PLB 4.99 (ISBN 0-394-97579-0). Random.
Gross, H. Privacy, Its Legal Protection. rev. ed. LC 76-43110. (Legal Almanac Ser.: No. 54). 108p. 1976. 5.95 (ISBN 0-379-11099-7). Oceana.
--Woerterbuch Chemie und Chemische Technik, Vol. 2. (Ger.). 68.00 (ISBN 0-686-56616-5, M-6965). French & Eur.
Gross, H. & Hildebrand, H. Kleines Worterbuch der Chemie und Chem. Technik, 2 vols, Vol. 1. 128p. (Ger. -Eng., Dictionary of Chemistry and Chemical Engineering). 1976. 9.95 (ISBN 3-87144-218-6, M-7511, Pub. by Verlag Harri Deutsch). French & Eur.
--Kleines Worterbuch der Chemie und Chem. Technik, Vol. 2. 128p. (Ger. & Eng., Dictionary of Chemistry and Chemical Engineering). 9.95 (ISBN 3-87144-219-4, M-7510, Pub. by Verlag Harri Deutsch). French & Eur.
Gross, H. & Waerden, B. Studien zur Theorie der Quadratischen Formen. (Mathemische Reihe Ser.: No. 34). (Illus.). 254p. (Ger.). 1968. 41.95x (ISBN 0-8176-0401-4). Birkhauser.
Gross, H., ed. Dictionary of Chemistry & Chemical Technology, English-German. 720p. 1985. 102.00 (ISBN 0-444-99617-6). Elsevier.
--Dictionary of Chemistry & Chemical Technology, English-German. 640p. 1984. 102.00 (ISBN 0-444-99618-4). Elsevier.
Gross, Hans. Criminal Psychology: A Manual for Judges, Practioniers & Student. Kallen, Horace M., tr. LC 68-55772. (Criminology, Law Enforcement, & Social Problems Ser.: No. 13). 1968. Repr. of 1911 ed. 24.00x (ISBN 0-87585-013-8). Patterson Smith.
Gross, Hans, ed. Electrical Feed-Drives for Machine Tools. 363p. 1983. 54.95x (ISBN 0-471-26273-0). Wiley.
Gross, Harriet, jt. auth. see Gerstel, Naomi.
Gross, Harriet & Sussman, Marvin B., eds. Alternatives to Traditional Family Living. LC 82-9250. (Marriage & Family Review: Vol. 5, No. 2). 128p. 1982. text ed. 20.00 (ISBN 0-917724-59-3, B59). Haworth Pr.
Gross, Harry. Current Techniques in Financing. 33p. 1975. pap. 2.00 (ISBN 0-87576-012-0). Pilot Bks.
--How to Do Business with the Government. Rev. ed. 34p. 1979. pap. 2.50 (ISBN 0-87576-020-1). Pilot Bks.
Gross, Harry & Levy, Robert S. Franchise Investigation & Contract Negotiation. rev. ed. LC 84-25418. 48p. 1985. pap. 3.95 (ISBN 0-87576-118-6). Pilot Bks.
Gross, Harry, jt. auth. see Rubin, Ira L.
Gross, Harvey. Sound & Form in Modern Poetry: A Study of Prosody from Thomas Hardy to Robert Lowell. 1968. pap. 9.95 (ISBN 0-472-06141-0, 141, AA). U of Mich Pr.
--The Structure of Verse. rev. ed. LC 78-6781. 320p. 1980. pap. 9.95 (ISBN 0-912946-59-8). Ecco Pr.
--The Structure of Verse. rev. ed. LC 78-6781. 1979. Repr. of 1966 ed. 17.50 (ISBN 0-912946-58-X). Ecco Pr.
Gross, Harvey, ed. see Erasmus, Desiderius.
Gross, Heinrich. Biblical Introduction to the Old Testament. 1968. pap. 1.45x (ISBN 0-268-00020-4). U of Notre Dame Pr.
Gross, Helmut. Chemie und Chemische Technik. 2nd ed. (Eng. -Ger., Chemistry and Chemical Engineering). 1978. 55.00 (ISBN 0-686-56598-3, M-7319, Pub. by VEB Verlag Technik). French & Eur.
Gross, Henry. Pure Magic. (Illus.). 1979. (ScribT); encore ed. 4.95 (ISBN 0-684-16544-9). Scribner.
Gross, Herbert. Quadratic Forms in Infinite Dimensional Vector Spaces. (Progress in Mathematics: Vol. 1). 431p. 1979. pap. 28.00x (ISBN 0-8176-1111-8). Birkhauser.
Gross, Herbert F. Algebra by Example: An Elementary Course. 1978. 19.95 (ISBN 0-669-00473-1); instr's manual 1.95 (ISBN 0-669-00474-X); solutions manual 9.95x (ISBN 0-669-01014-6); cassettes 150.00 (ISBN 0-669-01154-1); tapescript 1.95 (ISBN 0-669-01018-9); demo tape 1.95 (ISBN 0-669-01633-0). Heath.
Gross, Hyman. A Theory of Criminal Justice. 1979. 27.50x (ISBN 0-19-502349-8); pap. 9.95x (ISBN 0-19-502350-1). Oxford U Pr.
Gross, Hyman & Von Hirsch, Andrew, eds. Sentencing. 1981. pap. text ed. 11.95x (ISBN 0-19-502764-7). Oxford U Pr.
Gross, Ira & Downing, John. Sex Role Attitudes & Cultural Change. 1982. 35.95 (ISBN 90-277-1340-5, Pub. by Reidel Holland). Kluwer Academic.
Gross, Irene, jt. auth. see Friedland, Joyce.
Gross, Irman H., et al. Management for Modern Families. 4th ed. (Illus.). 1980. text ed. 27.95 (ISBN 0-13-549477-X). P-H.
Gross, J. Encyclopedia of Real Estate Forms. 1973. 32.95 (ISBN 0-13-276170-X); pap. 12.95 (ISBN 0-13-276188-2). P-H.
Gross, J. F., et al, eds. Modern Techniques in Physiological Sciences. 1974. 79.50 (ISBN 0-12-304450-2). Acad Pr.
Gross, James A. The Making of the National Labor Relations Board: 1933-1937. LC 74-5284. (Illus.). 1974. 49.50x (ISBN 0-87395-270-7). State U NY Pr.
--The Reshaping of the National Labor Relations Board: National Labor Policy in Transition, 1937-1947. LC 74-5284. 400p. 1981. 54.50x (ISBN 0-87395-516-1); pap. 32.50x (ISBN 0-87395-517-X). State U NY Pr.
Gross, Jan T. Polish Society under German Occupation: The Generalgouvernement 1939-1944. LC 78-70298. 1979. 38.50 (ISBN 0-691-09381-4). Princeton U Pr.
Gross, Jan. T., jt. ed. see Grudzenska-Gross, Irena.
Gross, Jan T., ed. see Staniszkis, Jadwiga.
Gross, Jeffrey T., jt. auth. see Brown, Thomas H.
Gross, Jerome S. New Encyclopedia of Real Estate Forms. LC 82-21582. 701p. 1983. 59.95 (ISBN 0-686-45921-0). P-H.
Gross, Jerry & Gross, Becky. Growing Through Conflict. pap. 5.25 (ISBN 0-89137-556-2). Quality Pubns.
Gross, Jim, ed. see Carey, Ken.
Gross, Jim, et al. April Fourth, Nineteen Eighty-One: Pivotal Day in a Critical Year. (Illus.). 1980. pap. 4.00 (ISBN 0-933646-12-7). Aries Pr.
Gross, Jody, jt. ed. see Johnson, Bonnie L.
Gross, Joel. The Books of Rachel. 1981. pap. 3.50 (ISBN 0-451-09561-8, E9561, Sig). NAL.
--Fourteen-O-Seven Broadway. 1980. pap. 2.50 (ISBN 0-440-12819-6). Dell.
--Home of the Brave. 1983. pap. 3.95 (ISBN 0-451-12223-2, Sig). NAL.
--The Lives of Rachel. LC 84-6866. 423p. 1984. 16.95 (ISBN 0-453-00467-9). NAL.
--The Lives of Rachel. 1985. pap. 4.50 (ISBN 0-451-13994-1, Sig). NAL.
--Maura's Dream. 1982. pap. 3.95 (ISBN 0-451-13137-1, AE3137, Sig). NAL.
--This Year in Jerusalem. 304p. 1983. 14.95 (ISBN 0-399-12812-3, Putnam). Putnam Pub Group.
--This Year in Jerusalem. 288p. 1984. pap. 3.95 (ISBN 0-451-12899-0, Sig). NAL.
Gross, John. John P. Marquand. (Twayne's United States Authors Ser). 1963. pap. 5.95x (ISBN 0-8084-0188-2, T33, Twayne). New Coll U Pr.
Gross, John, compiled by. The Oxford Book of Aphorisms. 1983. 15.95 (ISBN 0-19-214111-2). Oxford U Pr.
Gross, John, ed. see Seeley, John R.
Gross, John A. & Flicek, Barbara D. Electromyographic Technologists Handbook. (Allied Health Professions Monograph). 1985. write for info. (ISBN 0-87527-271-1). Green.
Gross, Jonathan L. & Rayner, Steve. Measuring Culture: A Paradigm for the Analysis of Social Organization. 144p. 1985. 32.50 (ISBN 0-231-06032-7). Columbia U Pr.
Gross, Joseph, tr. see Konnyu, Leslie.
Gross, Joseph B. Water over the Dam. 1982. 10.95 (ISBN 0-533-05118-5). Vantage.
Gross, Joseph F. & Popel, Aleksander, eds. Mathematics of Microcirculation Phenomena. 186p. 1980. text ed. 35.00 (ISBN 0-89004-449-X). Raven.
Gross, Joy & Freifeld, Karen. The Vegetarian Child. 224p. 1983. 12.00 (ISBN 0-8184-0342-X). Lyle Stuart.
Gross, Judith. Patterns from China: Sweater Ideas for Children. 100p. 1981. 17.95 (ISBN 0-442-20399-3). Van Nos Reinhold.
Gross, K. & Klooss, W., eds. Voices from Distant Lands. 172p. 1983. 15.50x (ISBN 3-88479-111-7, Pub. by Konigshausen & Neumann Germany). Humanities.
Gross, Ken. Illustrated BMW Buyer's Guide. (Buyer's Guide Ser.). (Illus.). 176p. 1985. pap. 13.95 (ISBN 0-87938-165-5). Motorbooks Intl.
Gross, Kenneth. Spenserian Poetics: Idolatry, Iconoclasm & Magic. LC 85-47701. 256p. 1985. text ed. 24.95x (ISBN 0-8014-1805-4). Cornell U Pr.
Gross, Kenneth I., ed. Mathematical Methods in Energy Research. LC 84-52185. (Illus.). ix, 242p. 1984. text ed. 28.50 (ISBN 0-89871-199-1). Soc Indus Appl Math.
Gross, Laila Z., jt. ed. see Wilhelm, James J.
Gross, Larry, ed. see Worth, Sol.
Gross, Larry P., jt. ed. see Gerbner, George.
Gross, Len & Stirling, John T. How to Build a Small Advertising Agency & Run It at a Profit. (Illus.). 270p. 1984. plastic ring bdg. 48.00 (ISBN 0-917855-00-0). Kentwood.
Gross, Leo. Essays on International Law & Organization, 2 vols. LC 83-9136. 1300p. 1983. Set. lib. bdg. 120.00 (ISBN 0-941320-15-4). Transnatl Pubs.
Gross, Leo, ed. The Future of the International Court of Justice, 2 vols. LC 76-2646. 1976. Set. text ed. 76.00 (ISBN 0-686-96818-2); Vol 1. text ed. 38.00 (ISBN 0-379-00298-1); Vol 2. text ed. 38.00 (ISBN 0-379-00299-X). Oceana.
Gross, Leonard. The Golden Years of the Hutterites. LC 80-10711. (Studies in Anabaptist & Mennonite History: Vol. 23). 1980. 14.95x (ISBN 0-8361-1227-X). Herald Pr.
--Harmonic Analysis on Hilbert Space. LC 52-42839. (Memoirs: No. 46). 62p. 1983. pap. 9.00 (ISBN 0-8218-1246-7, MEMO-46). Am Math.
--How Much Is Too Much? The Effects of Social Drinking. 192p. 1985. pap. 2.95 (ISBN 0-345-31602-9). Ballantine.
Gross, Leonard, jt. auth. see Morehouse, Laurence E.
Gross, Leonard, jt. auth. see Salinger, Pierre.
Gross, Leonard H., ed. The Parents' Guide to Teenagers. 385p. 1981. 14.95 (ISBN 0-02-545820-5). Macmillan.
Gross, LeRoy. Art of Selling Intangibles. rev. ed. LC 85-7224. (Illus.). 336p. 1985. 29.95 (ISBN 0-13-048786-4). NY Inst Finance.
Gross, Leslie. Guide to Antiques. 160p. 1976. pap. 1.95 (ISBN 0-346-12228-7). Cornerstone.
Gross, Linda & Bailey, Zeila. Enterostomal Therapy: Developing Institutional & Community Programs. LC 78-70682. 221p. 1979. pap. text ed. 27.50 (ISBN 0-913654-49-3). Aspen Systems.
Gross, Ludwik. Oncogenic Viruses, 2 vols. 3rd ed. LC 83-2314. 1200p. 1983. 200.00 (ISBN 0-08-026830-7). Pergamon.
Gross, Lynne S. The Internship Experience. 144p. 1981. pap. text ed. write for info. (ISBN 0-534-00945-X). Wadsworth Pub.
--The New Television Technologies. 208p. 1983. pap. text ed. write for info. (ISBN 0-697-04362-2). Wm C Brown.
--Telecommunications: An Introduction to Radio, Television & the Developing Media. 480p. 1983. pap. text ed. write for info. (ISBN 0-697-04359-2). Wm C Brown.

Grossberg, Stephen, ed. Mathematical Psychology & Psychophysiology. LC 81-3500. (SIAM: 13). 35.00 (ISBN 0-8218-1333-1). Am Math.

Grossblat, Martha & Sikes, Bette H., eds. Women Lawyers: Supplementary Data to the 1971 Lawyer Statistical Report. LC 52-1123. pap. 26.00 (ISBN 0-317-29201-3, 2022253). Bks Demand UMI.

--Women Lawyers: Supplementary Data to the 1971 Lawyer Statistical Report. 91p. 1973. pap. 5.00 (ISBN 0-910058-52-0). Am Bar Foun.

Grosse, David G. Beacon Small-Group Bible Studies, Job: Struggles & Triumphs. Wolf, Earl C., ed. 96p. (Orig.). 1986. pap. 2.50 (ISBN 0-8341-0960-3). Beacon Hill.

Grosse, E. Dictionnaire d'Antiphilosophisme ou Refutation des Erreurs du 18e Siecle. Migne, J. P., ed. (Troisieme et Derniere Encyclopedie Theologique Ser.: Vol. 18). 770p. (Fr.). Repr. of 1856 ed. lib. bdg. 97.50x (ISBN 0-89241-301-8). Caratzas.

Grosse, Ernst. The Beginnings of Art. 1978. Repr. of 1898 ed. lib. bdg. 30.00 (ISBN 0-8495-1913-6). Arden Lib.

Grosse, Lloyd T. & Lyster, Alan F. Fifteen Hundred Literary References Everyone Should Know. LC 82-18444. 304p. (Orig.). 1983. pap. 3.95 (ISBN 0-668-05596-0, 5596). Arco.

Grosse, P., ed. Advances in Solid State Physics, Vol. 22. 1982. 56.00 (ISBN 0-9940018-7-8, Pub. by Vieweg & Sohn Germany). Heyden.

Grosse, Peter. Advances in Solid State Physics, Vol. 23. write for info. (ISBN 0-9904000-1-8, Pub. by Vieweg & Sohn Germany). Heyden.

Grosse, Robert. Romische Militargeschichte Von Gallienus Bis Zum Beginn der Byzantinischen Themenverfassung. LC 75-7319. (Roman History Ser.). (Ger.). 1975. Repr. 26.50x (ISBN 0-405-07083-7). Ayer Co Pubs.

Grosse, Robert E. Foreign Investment Codes & the Location of Direct Investment. LC 80-15194. 174p. 1980. 36.95 (ISBN 0-03-057024-7). Praeger.

Grosse, Rudolf. The Christmas Foundation Meeting: Beginning of a New Cosmic Age. Collis, Johanna, tr. from Ger. 158p. (Orig.). 1984. pap. 14.00 (ISBN 0-919924-23-9, Steiner Bk Ctr). Anthroposophic.

Grossen, Neal E., jt. auth. see Meyers, Lawrence S.

Grosser, A. E., jt. auth. see Butler, I. S.

Grosser, Alfred. French Foreign Policy under De Gaulle. LC 77-21747. 1977. Repr. of 1967 ed. lib. bdg. 22.50x (ISBN 0-8371-9795-3, GRFR). Greenwood.

--The Western Alliance: European American Relations since 1945. 416p. 1980. 19.50 (ISBN 0-8264-0004-3). Continuum.

--The Western Alliance: European-American Relations since 1945. LC 81-69568. 1982. pap. 7.95 (ISBN 0-394-70815-6, Vin). Random.

Grosser, Arthur E. The Cookbook Decoder. 304p. 1983. pap. 3.50 (ISBN 0-446-30605-3). Warner Bks.

--The Cookbook Decoder: Or, Culinary Alchemy Explained. LC 81-2143. (Illus.). 192p. 1981. 13.95 (ISBN 0-8253-0033-9). Beaufort Bks NY.

Grosser, George H., et al, eds. Threat of Impending Disaster: Contributions to the Psychology of Stress. 1965. pap. 5.95x (ISBN 0-262-57027-0). MIT Pr.

Grosser, George S. & Zinn, William. Vitametrics I: The Human Formula for Self-Evaluation. 190p. 1984. 15.95 (ISBN 0-8290-1372-5). Irvington.

Grosser, Kurt. Plagued By Money Problems? You Can Be Financially Free. LC 83-61440. 112p. 1983. pap. 4.95 (ISBN 0-89221-107-5). New Leaf.

Grosser, Morton. Diesel: The Man & the Engine. LC 78-6196. (Illus.). 224p. (YA) 1978. 8.95 (ISBN 0-689-30652-0). Atheneum.

--The Discovery of Neptune. LC 78-68017. 1979. pap. 4.50 (ISBN 0-486-23726-5). Dover.

--The Discovery of Neptune. 12.50 (ISBN 0-8446-5766-2). Peter Smith.

--Gossamer Odyssey: The Triumph of Human-Powered Flight. (Illus.). 288p. 1981. 14.95 (ISBN 0-395-30531-4). HM.

Grosser, Paul E. & Halperin, Edwin G. Anti-Semitism: Causes & Effects. LC 83-11420. 1983. 20.00 (ISBN 0-8022-2418-0). Philos Lib.

--The Causes & Effects of Antisemitism: The Dimensions of a Prejudice. LC 77-75261. (Illus.). 1978. 20.00 (ISBN 0-8022-2207-2). Philos Lib.

Grosseteste, Robert. Carmina Anglo-Normannica: Chasteau d'Amour, to Which Is Added La Vie de Saint-Marie Egyptienne & an English Version of the Chasteau d'Amour. Cooke, M., ed. 1852. 24.00 (ISBN 0-8337-1467-8). B. Franklin.

--Hexameron on the Six Days of Creation. Dales, Richard & Gieben, Servus, eds. (British Academy Ser.). (Illus.). 1982. 120.00x (ISBN 0-19-726006-3). Oxford U Pr.

Grossett, Philip, ed. see Auber, Daniel F.

Grossett, Philip, ed. see Meyerbeer, Giacomo.

Grossett, Philip, ed. see Spontini, Gasparo.

Grossfeld, B. Bibliography of Targum Literature: Supplement, Vol. 2. (Bibliographica Judaica Ser: No. 8). 39,50x (ISBN 0-87820-905-0, HUC Pr). Ktav.

Grossfeld, B., jt. auth. see Aberbach, M.

Grossfeld, Bernard. Concordance of the First Targum to the Book of Esther. LC 83-11550. (SBL Aramaic Studies). 186p. 1984. pap. 11.25 (ISBN 0-89130-635-8, 06 13 05). Scholars Pr GA.

--A Critical Commentary on Targum Neofiti I to Genesis. Schiffman, L. H., ed. 75.00x (ISBN 0-87068-333-0). Ktav.

--The First Targum to Esther. (Illus.). xiv, 224p. (Aramaic & Eng.). 1983. pap. 19.50 (ISBN 0-87203-112-8). Hermon.

Grossfeld, Muriel. Body Moves. LC 83-20984. (Illus.). 176p. 1984. 15.95 (ISBN 0-399-12942-1, Putnam). Putnam Pub Group.

Grossfeld, Stan. Nantucket: The Other Season. LC 82-81182. (Illus.). 160p. 1982. pap. 12.95 (ISBN 0-87106-971-7). Globe Pequot.

Grossfeld, Stan, ed. The Eyes of the Globe: Twenty Years of Photography from the Boston Globe. (Illus.). 256p. (Orig.). 1985. pap. cancelled (ISBN 0-87106-859-1); casebound 24.95 (ISBN 0-87106-861-3). Globe Pequot.

Grossfield, B. A Bibliography of Targum Literature, Vol. 1. 1972. 39.50x. Ktav.

Grosshan, jt. auth. see Gotto.

Grosshans, A. Propagandist's Lament. 32p. 1980. pap. 5.00 (ISBN 0-941104-01-X). Real Comet.

Grosshans, Daniel. File Systems. (Illus.). 496p. 1986. text ed. 32.95 (ISBN 0-13-314568-9). P-H.

Grosshans, Henry. Hitler & the Artists. (Illus.). 146p. 1983. text ed. 29.50x (ISBN 0-8419-0746-3). Holmes & Meier.

Grossholtz, Jean. Forging Colonial Patriarchy: The Economic & Social Transformation of Feudal Sri Lanka & Its Impact on Women. LC 84-4209. (Policy Studies). 176p. 1984. 29.75 (ISBN 0-8223-0576-3). Duke.

Grossi, John A. Model State Policy, Legislation & State Plan Toward the Education of Gifted & Talented Students: A Handbook for State & Local Districts. 224p. (Orig.). 1980. pap. 14.95 (ISBN 0-86586-101-3). Coun Exc Child.

Grossi, John A., jt. ed. see Jordan, June B.

Grossi, Paolo. An Alternative to Private Property: Collective Property in the Juridical Consciousness of the 19th Century. Cochrane, Lydia G., tr. LC 81-1219. 1981. lib. bdg. 37.00x (ISBN 0-226-31002-7). U of Chicago Pr.

Grossin, William. Les Temps de la Vie Quotidienne. (Interaction, l'Homme et Son Environment Social Ser.: No. 3). 416p. (Fr.). 1975. pap. text ed. 29.60x (ISBN 90-2797-785-2). Mouton.

Grossinger, Jennie. Art of Jewish Cooking. 1958. 15.95 (ISBN 0-394-40106-9). Random.

Grossinger, Richard. The Book of Being Born Again into the World. 248p. 1974. pap. 5.00 (ISBN 0-913028-29-0). North Atlantic.

--Book of the Cranberry Islands. 320p. (Orig.). 1974. 10.00 (ISBN 0-87685-211-8). Black Sparrow.

--Book of the Cranberry Islands. 299p. 1981. pap. 5.95 (ISBN 0-913028-88-6). North Atlantic.

--The Continents. 200p. (Orig.). 1973. pap. 4.50 (ISBN 0-87685-161-8). Black Sparrow.

--Early Field Notes from the All-American Revival Church. 1973. pap. 3.50 (ISBN 0-913028-19-3). North Atlantic.

--The Long Body of the Dream. 256p. (Orig.). 1974. pap. 5.00 (ISBN 0-913028-28-2). North Atlantic.

--Mars: A Science Fiction Vision. (Illus.). 230p. (Orig.). 1971. pap. 3.50 (ISBN 0-913028-00-2). North Atlantic.

--Martian Homecoming at the All-American Revival Church. 124p. (Orig.). 1974. pap. 3.00 (ISBN 0-913028-21-5). North Atlantic.

--The Night Sky: The Science & Anthropology of the Stars & Planets. LC 81-5293. 544p. 1981. 16.95 (ISBN 0-87156-288-X). Sierra.

--The Provinces. 5.00 (ISBN 0-913028-31-2). North Atlantic.

--The Slag of Creation. 256p. (Orig.). 1975. pap. 5.00 (ISBN 0-913028-32-0). North Atlantic.

--Solar Journal: Oecological Sections. (Illus.). 130p. (Orig.). 1973. pap. 4.50 (ISBN 0-87685-011-5). Black Sparrow.

--Spaces Wild & Tame. (Illus.). 144p. (Orig.). signed, slip-cased 15.00 (ISBN 0-685-22800-2); 6.00 (ISBN 0-685-22801-0); pap. 3.50 (ISBN 0-685-22802-9). Mudra.

--The Unfinished Business of Doctor Hermes. 1976. pap. 4.00 (ISBN 0-913028-43-6). North Atlantic.

--The Windy Passage from Nostalgia. 256p. (Orig.). 1974. pap. 5.00 (ISBN 0-913028-30-4). North Atlantic.

Grossinger, Richard, ed. The Alchemical Tradition in the Late Twentieth Century. 2nd & rev ed. (Illus.). 320p. 1983. pap. 12.95 (ISBN 0-938190-11-3). North Atlantic.

--Baseball. (Illus.). 232p. (Orig.). 1971. pap. 5.00 (ISBN 0-913028-11-8). North Atlantic.

--Ecology & Consciousness. 2nd ed. 226p. (Orig.). 1980. pap. 6.95 (ISBN 0-913028-71-1). North Atlantic.

--The Temple of Baseball. (Io Ser.: No. 34). (Illus.). 268p. (Orig.). 1985. deluxe ed. 27.50 (ISBN 0-938190-44-X); pap. 12.95 (ISBN 0-938190-43-1). North Atlantic.

--Vermont. (Illus.). 350p. 1974. pap. 10.00 (ISBN 0-913028-26-6). North Atlantic.

Grossinger, Richard & Hough, Lindy, eds. Anima Mundi. (Earth Geography Booklet Ser: No. 4). (Illus.). 256p. (Orig.). 1973. pap. 4.00 (ISBN 0-913028-17-7). North Atlantic.

--Doctrines of Signatures. rev. ed. (Illus.). 160p. 1972. pap. 25.00 (ISBN 0-913028-07-X). North Atlantic.

--Dreams. rev. ed. (Illus.). 322p. (Orig.). 1971. pap. 12.00 (ISBN 0-913028-10-X). North Atlantic.

--Economics, Technology & Celestial Influence. (Earth Geography Booklet Ser: No. 1). (Illus.). 180p. (Orig.). 1972. pap. 12.00 (ISBN 0-913028-12-6). North Atlantic.

--Ethnoastronomy. (Illus.). 210p. 1971. pap. 6.00 (ISBN 0-913028-08-8). North Atlantic.

--Imago Mundi. (Earth Geography Booklet Ser.: No. 3). (Illus.). 1972. 6.50 (ISBN 0-913028-14-2). North Atlantic.

--Nuclear Strategy & the Code of the Warrior: Faces of Mars & Shiva in the Crisis of Human Survival. (Io Ser.: No. 33). 320p. (Orig.). 1984. 25.00 (ISBN 0-938190-50-4); pap. 12.95 (ISBN 0-938190-49-0). North Atlantic.

--Oecology. rev. ed. (Illus.). 1972. 6.00 (ISBN 0-913028-09-6). North Atlantic.

--Regions & Locales. (Earth Geography Booklet Ser: No. 2). (Illus.). 312p. (Orig.). 1973. pap. 4.00 (ISBN 0-913028-13-4). North Atlantic.

Grossinger, Richard, jt. ed. see Kerrane, Kevin.

Grossinger, Tania. Weekend. 1981. pap. 2.95 (ISBN 0-440-19375-3). Dell.

Grosskopf, Susan A. Sew Special. (Illus.). 56p. 1984. pap. 6.00 (ISBN 0-943574-25-0). That Patchwork.

--Signs of Our Times. (Illus.). 56p. 1984. pap. 6.00 (ISBN 0-943574-23-4). That Patchwork.

Grosskurth, Phyllis. Havelock Ellis. (Illus.). 512p. 1985. 14.95 (ISBN 0-8147-3000-0). NYU Pr.

--John Addington Symonds: A Biography. LC 75-12322. (Homosexuality). (Illus.). 1975. Repr. of 1964 ed. 22.00x (ISBN 0-405-07356-9). Ayer Co Pubs.

Grosskurth, Phyllis, ed. The Memoirs of John Addington Symonds. LC 84-42676. (Illus.). 320p. 1984. 19.45 (ISBN 0-394-54085-9). Random.

Grosslight, Jane. Light: Effective Use of Daylight & Electrical Lighting in Residential & Commercial Spaces. (Illus.). 208p. 1984. 24.95 (ISBN 0-13-536300-4); pap. 14.95 (ISBN 0-13-536292-X). P-H.

Grossman. Applied Calculus. 464p. 1985. write for info (ISBN 0-534-04245-7). Wadsworth Pub.

--Applied Math for the Management Life & Social Sciences. 896p. 1985. write for info (ISBN 0-534-04239-2). Wadsworth Pub.

--Applied Mathematical Analysis. 1985. text ed. write for info (ISBN 0-534-05766-7). Wadsworth Pub.

--Brief Introduction to Linear Algebra. 1984. lib. bdg. write for info (ISBN 0-534-03495-0). Wadsworth Pub.

--Peptic Ulcer. 1981. 29.95 (ISBN 0-8151-4009-6). Year Bk Med.

Grossman, A. Richard. Augmentation Mammoplasty. (Illus.). 108p. 1976. 18.75x (ISBN 0-398-03401-X). C C Thomas.

Grossman, Allen. Against Our Vanishing: Winter Conversations with Allen Grossman. Halliday, Mark, ed. LC 81-51048. (Poetics Ser.: No. 1). 128p. (Orig.). 1981. pap. 7.95 (ISBN 0-937672-04-1). Rowan Tree.

--Of the Great House: A Book of Poems. LC 81-22453. 96p. (Orig.). 1981. pap. 6.95 (ISBN 0-8112-0835-4, NDP535). New Directions.

--The Woman on the Bridge Over the Chicago River. LC 78-26802. 1979. 8.95 (ISBN 0-8112-0714-5); pap. 3.95 (ISBN 0-8112-0715-3, NDP473). New Directions.

Grossman, Alvin. Breeding Better Cocker Spaniels. LC 76-56011. (Other Dog Bks.). (Illus.). 1977. 24.95 (ISBN 0-87714-044-8). Denlingers.

--The Great American Dog Show Game. LC 83-24061. (Other Dog Bks.). (Illus.). 1985. 24.95 (ISBN 0-87714-109-6). Denlingers.

--The Standard Book of Dog Breeding. LC 74-29654. (Other Dog Bks.). (Illus.). 1983. 16.95 (ISBN 0-87714-054-5). Denlingers.

Grossman, Arnold, jt. auth. see Lamm, Richard.

Grossman, Arnold H., ed. see Dodson, Dan W.

Grossman, Arnold H., ed. see Kindy, Joan H., et al.

Grossman, Bernard A., ed. Letters Rogatory. 97p. 1956. 8.00 (ISBN 0-87945-015-0). Fed Legal Pubn.

Grossman, Bob. The New Chinese-Kosher Cookbook. rev. ed. LC 77-79248. (Illus.). 1978. 5.95 (ISBN 0-8397-6308-5); pap. 4.95 (ISBN 0-8397-6309-3). Eriksson.

Grossman, Bob, jt. auth. see Grossman, Ruth.

Grossman, Brigite S. Experiencing Jewish Boston. LC 80-85316. (Illus.). 54p. (Orig.). 1981. pap. 3.50 (ISBN 0-9605624-0-0). Jewish Comm Ctr.

Grossman, Bruce & Keyes, Carol. Early Childhood Administration. 300p. 1985. text ed. 19.00 (238308). Allyn.

--Helping Children Grow: The Adults Role. 1978. pap. 9.95 (ISBN 0-89529-034-0). Avery Pub.

Grossman, Bruce, jt. auth. see Keys, Carol.

Grossman, C. C., et al, eds. Diagnostic Ultrasound. LC 65-27810. 519p. 1966. 49.50x (ISBN 0-306-30226-8, Plenum Pr). Plenum Pub.

Grossman, Carol. Business English: Simplified & Self-Taught. 144p. pap. 5.95 (ISBN 0-668-05392-5). Arco.

Grossman, Chaika. The Underground Army: Fighters of the Blalystock Ghetto. 1985. 14.95 (ISBN 0-317-18106-8). Holocaust Pubns.

Grossman, Charles C., ed. Diagnostic Ultrasound: Proceedings of the First International Conference, University of Pittsburgh, 1965. LC 65-27810. pap. 133.00 (ISBN 0-317-27899-1, 2055788). Bks Demand UMI.

Grossman, Cheryl S. & Engman, Suzy. Jewish Literature for Children: A Teaching Guide. 200p. (Orig.). 1985. text ed. 19.00 (ISBN 0-86705-041-1); pap. text ed. 15.00. AIRE.

Grossman, David A. The Future of New York City's Capital Plant. (America's Urban Capital Stock Ser.: Vol. 1). 112p. (Orig.). 1979. pap. text ed. 6.00x (ISBN 0-87766-249-5, 25700). Urban Inst.

Grossman, David A. & Smolka, Geraldine. New York City's Poverty Budget: An Analysis of the Public & Voluntary Agency Expenitures Intended to Benefit the City's Low Income Population. LC 85-105302. 184p. (Orig.). 1984. pap. 12.50 (ISBN 0-88156-034-0). Comm Serv Soc Ny.

Grossman, Edith, tr. see Scorza, Manuel.

Grossman, Edith, tr. see Segre, Roberto & Kusnetzoff, Fernando K.

Grossman, Eli A. Life Reinsurance. 79p. (Orig.). 1980. pap. text ed. 4.50 (ISBN 0-915322-38-2). LOMA.

Grossman, Elizabeth, ed. see Abramowitz, Jack, et al.

Grossman, Ellie. Dilys. 220p. 1982. 13.50 (ISBN 0-02-545840-X). Macmillan.

Grossman, Elliot. Circumcision: A Pictorial Atlas of Its History, Instrument Development & Operative Technique. (Illus.). 128p. 1982. 19.95 (ISBN 0-89962-246-1). Todd & Honeywell.

Grossman, Elliot S. Capital Appropriations & Expenditures: A Quarterly Forecasting Model. LC 75-27056. (Report Ser: No. 668). 47p. (Orig.). 1975. pap. 45.00 (ISBN 0-8237-0099-2). Conference Bd.

--A Guide to the Determinants of Capital Investment. (Report Ser.: No. 721). 41p. 1977. pap. 15.00 (ISBN 0-8237-0155-7); pap. 5.00 member. Conference Bd.

Grossman, Elliott S., jt. auth. see Kendrick, John W.

Grossman, Florence. Getting from Here to There: Writing & Reading Poetry. LC 82-4319. 176p. (YA) (gr. 10-12). 1982. pap. 8.25x (ISBN 0-86709-033-2). Boynton Cook Pub.

Grossman, Frances K. Brothers & Sisters of Retarded Children: An Exploratory Study. LC 73-170664. (Special Education & Rehabilitation Monograph: No. 9). 1972. text ed. 9.50x (ISBN 0-8156-2154-X). Syracuse U Pr.

Grossman, Frances K., et al. Pregnancy, Birth, & Parenthood: Adaptations of Mothers, Fathers, & Infants. LC 80-16518. (Social & Behavioral Science Ser.). 1980. text ed. 23.95x (ISBN 0-87589-465-8). Jossey-Bass.

Grossman, Gary. Saturday Morning TV: The Shows You Waited All Week For. 432p. (Orig.). 1981. pap. 12.95 (ISBN 0-440-58361-6, Dell Trade Pbks). Dell.

Grossman, Gene, ed. see Bhagwati, Jagdish.

Grossman, Gene M. & Richardson, J. David. Strategic Trade Policy: A Survey of Issues & Early Analysis. LC 85-196. (Special Papers in International Economics: No. 15). 1985. pap. text ed. 4.50x (ISBN 0-88165-304-7). Princeton U Int Finan Econ.

Grossman, Gregory. Economic Systems. 2nd ed. (Foundations of Modern Economics Ser). (Illus.). 192p. 1974. ref. ed. o.p. 13.95 (ISBN 0-13-233486-0); pap. text ed. 15.95 (ISBN 0-13-233478-X). P-H.

--Soviet Statistics of Physical Output of Industrial Commodities: Their Compilation & Quality. LC 85-8016. (National Bureau of Economic Research: No. 69). xvi, 151p. 1985. Repr. of 1960 ed. lib. bdg. 35.00x (ISBN 0-313-24623-8, GSOS). Greenwood.

Grossman, Gregory, ed. Value & Plan. LC 76-6060. (Russian & East European Studies Ser.). 370p. 1976. Repr. of 1960 ed. lib. bdg. 27.75x (ISBN 0-8371-8804-0, GRVP). Greenwood.

Grossman, Gregory, et al. The Soviet Union's Hard-Currency Balance of Payments & Creditworthiness in 1985. LC 83-3146. xiii, 90p. 1983. write for info. (ISBN 0-8330-0485-9). Rand Corp.

Grossman, H. I., jt. auth. see Barro, R. J.

Grossman, Harold J. Grossman's Guide to Wines, Beers, & Liquors. Rev., 7th ed. (Illus.). 640p. 29.95 (ISBN 0-684-17772-2, ScribT). Scribner.

Grossman, Henryk. Das Akkumulations-und Zusammenbruchsgesetz des Kapitalistischen Systems. 1929. 23.50 (ISBN 0-8337-1468-6). B Franklin.

Grossman, Herbert. Educating Hispanic Students: Cultural Implications for Instruction, Classroom Management, Counseling & Assessment. 266p. 1984. 26.75x (ISBN 0-398-05057-0). C C Thomas.

Grossman, Herbert J., ed. Classification in Mental Retardation. LC 83-8779. 228p. 1983. text ed. 16.00x (ISBN 0-940898-12-8). Am Assn Mental.

Grossman, Herbert J., jt. ed. see Bernsohn, Joseph.

Grossman, Howard R. For Health's Sake: A Critical Analysis of Medical Care in the United States. LC 77-23828. 1977. 8.95 (ISBN 0-87015-222-X). Pacific Bks.

Grossman, I. & Magnus, W. Groups & Their Graphs. LC 64-8512. (New Mathematical Library: No. 14). 1975. pap. 10.00 (ISBN 0-88385-614-X). Math Assn.

Grossman, Ilene. Employment in the 1980s. 1983. 10.00 (ISBN 0-87292-046-1). Coun State Govts.

Grossman, Irwin & Wolanin, Ron. Twenty-Five Ski Tours in Eastern Massachusetts: Cross Country Trails from the Quabbin Reservoir to Cape Cod. LC 82-4019. (Twenty-Five Ski Tours Ser.). (Illus.). 144p. 1982. pap. 6.95 (ISBN 0-942440-03-X). Backcountry Pubns.

Grossman, J. B., et al. Social Science Approaches to the Judicial Process. LC 74-153371. (Symposia on Law & Society Ser). 1971. Repr. of 1966 ed. lib. bdg. 19.50 (ISBN 0-306-70135-9). Da Capo.

Grossman, Jack, jt. auth. see Friedman, Sherwood.

Grossman, James. James Fenimore Cooper. 1949. 25.00x (ISBN 0-8047-0320-5); pap. 7.95 (ISBN 0-8047-0321-3, SP45). Stanford U Pr.

Grossman, Jeffrey E., jt. auth. see Kravitt, Gregory I.

Grossman, Jeremy. Quick Typing: A Self-Teaching Guide. LC 79-26243. (Self-Teaching Guides Ser.). 157p. 1980. pap. text ed. 6.95 (ISBN 0-471-05287-6). Wiley.

--Quickhand. (Self-Teaching Guides Ser.). 128p. 1976. pap. text ed. 6.95 (ISBN 0-471-32887-1). Wiley.

Grossman, Joan A., jt. auth. see Isaacman, Clara.

Grossman, Joan D. Valery Bryusov & the Riddle of Russian Decadence. LC 83-14470. 1985. 32.50x (ISBN 0-520-05141-6). U of Cal Pr.

Grossman, Joan D., ed. The Diary of Valery Bryusov (1893-1905) With Reminiscences by V. F. Khodasevich & Marina Tsvetaeva. LC 78-66013. (Documentary Studies in Modern Russian Poetry). 200p. 1980. 21.50x (ISBN 0-520-03858-4). U of Cal Pr.

Grossman, Joan D., ed. see Dobroliubov, Aleksandr M.

Grossman, Joel B. & Tanenhaus, Joseph. Frontiers of Judicial Research. LC 68-55334. 492p. 1969. text ed. 23.00 (ISBN -686-86252-X, Pub. by Wiley). Krieger.

Grossman, Joel B. & Wells, Richard S. Constitutional Law & Judicial Policy Making. 2nd ed. LC 84-3313. 1984. cased 34.50 (ISBN 0-582-28543-7); pap. 10.95 (ISBN 0-582-28463-5). Longman.

Grossman, Joel M., jt. auth. see Bakaly, Charles G., Jr.

Grossman, John A. Minor Injuries & Disorders: Surgical & Medical Care. 384p. 1983. text ed. 39.50 (ISBN 0-397-50529-9, 65-06752). Lippincott.

Grossman, Jonathan P. William Sylvis, Pioneer of American Labor. 1972. lib. bdg. 22.00x (ISBN 0-374-93314-6). Octagon.

Grossman, Jorge, ed. Public Administration in Latin America: A Bibliography. 1976. lib. bdg. 59.95 (ISBN 0-8490-2488-9). Gordon Pr.

Grossman, Judith. Evidence of Fascism in Greece. Kaplan, Peter, ed. LC 75-24939. 1975. 3.00x (ISBN 0-915176-09-2). Pourboire.

Grossman, Karl. Cover Up: What You Are Not Supposed to Know About Nuclear Power. 312p. 8.95 (ISBN 0-932966-26-8). Permanent Pr.

--Cover-Up: What You Are Not Supposed to Know About Nuclear Power. LC 80-81394. 312p. 1980. 11.95 (ISBN 0-932966-10-1). Permanent Pr.

--Nicaragua: America's New Vietnam? LC 83-63242. (Illus.). 224p. 1984. 15.95 (ISBN 0-932966-40-3). Permanent Pr.

--Nicaragua: America's New Vietnam. 224p. 1985. pap. 19.95 (ISBN 0-932966-61-6). Permanent Pr.

--The Poison Conspiracy. 281p. 1983. 15.95 (ISBN 0-932966-26-8). Permanent Pr.

Grossman, Larry & Schwartz, Arthur, eds. World History, Pt. 2. LC 79-9409. (Arco College Outlines Ser.). 1979. pap. 3.95 (ISBN 0-668-04731-3). Arco.

Grossman, Lawrence. The Democratic Party & the Negro: Northern & National Politics, 1868-92. LC 75-30546. (Blacks in the New World). pap. 57.00 (ISBN 0-317-09504-8, 2020239). Bks Demand UMI.

Grossman, Lawrence see Colowick, Sidney P. & Kaplan, Nathan O.

Grossman, Lawrence C. Peasants, Subsistence Ecology & Development in the Highlands of Paupa New Guinea. LC 84-42581. (Illus.). 324p. 1984. 35.00 (ISBN 0-691-09406-3). Princeton U Pr.

Grossman, Lee. The Change Agent. LC 74-4744. 180p. 1974. 10.95 (ISBN 0-8144-5364-3). AMACOM.

--Executive Survival in a World of Change. rev. ed. LC 81-18664. 176p. 1982. 12.50 (ISBN 0-89874-458-X). Krieger.

--Fat Paper: Diets for Trimming Paperwork. 1978. pap. 3.95 (ISBN 0-07-024983-0). McGraw.

Grossman, Leonid, intro. by see Sukhovo-Kobylin, Aleksandr V.

Grossman, Leonid P. Confession of a Jew. Moab, Ranne, ed. LC 74-27990. (Modern Jewish Experience Ser.). (Eng.). 1975. 16.00x (ISBN 0-405-06717-8). Ayer Co Pubs.

Grossman, Louis, jt. ed. see Phillipson, David.

Grossman, Louis I. Diagnosis & Treatment of Endodontic Emergencies. (Continuing Dental Education Series). 100p. 1981. 18.00 (ISBN 0-931386-31-4). Quint Pub Co.

--Endodontic Practice. 10th ed. LC 81-3679. (Illus.). 458p. 1981. text ed. 26.50 (ISBN 0-8121-0798-5). Lea & Febiger.

Grossman, Louis I., ed. Mechanism & Control of Pain. LC 79-84476. (Masson Monographs in Dentistry: Vol. 1). 256p. 1979. 31.50x (ISBN 0-89352-048-9). Masson Pub.

Grossman, Loyd. The Millionaire's Diet. 96p. 1985. pap. 7.95 (ISBN 0-318-04498-6, Pub. by Salem Hse Ltd). Merrimack Pub Cir.

Grossman, Maria & Mazzoni, Bruno. Bibliographie de phonologie Romane. (Janua Linguarum, Ser. Practica: No. 232). 115p. (Orig., Fr.). 1974. pap. text ed. 13.20x (ISBN 90-2792-710-3). Mouton.

Grossman, Mark M. The Question of Arbitrability: Challenges to the Arbitrator's Jurisdiction & Authority. (Practitioner Guides Ser.). 128p. (Orig.). 1984. pap. 9.95 (ISBN 0-87546-106-9, 84-6568). ILR Pr.

Grossman, Martin. The Arable Mind. (Blue Mountain Press Chapbook). 1977. pap. 2.00 (ISBN 0-686-21109-X). Blue Mtn MI.

Grossman, Michael. The Demand for Health: A Theoretical & Empirical Investigation. (Occasional Paper Ser.: No. 119). 132p. 1972. pap. 8.00 (ISBN 0-87014-248-8, Dist. by Columbia U Pr). Natl Bur Econ Res.

Grossman, Michael B. & Kumar, Martha J. Portraying the President: The White House & the News Media. 368p. 1981. pap. 10.95x (ISBN 0-8018-2537-7). Johns Hopkins.

Grossman, Mordecai. Philosophy of Helvetius with Special Emphasis on the Educational Implications of Sensationalism. LC 79-176822. (Columbia University. Teachers College. Contributions to Education: No. 210). Repr. of 1926 ed. 22.50 (ISBN 0-404-55210-2). AMS Pr.

Grossman, Morris. Four Hundred Ideas for Design, Vol.4. 376p. 1980. 15.25 (ISBN 0-8104-0950-X). Hayden.

Grossman, Morris, ed. see Electronic Design.

Grossman, Morton, et al, eds. Gastrointestinal Hormones & Pathology of the Digestive System. LC 78-17547. (Advances in Experimental Medicine & Biology Ser.: Vol.106). 336p. 1978. 45.00x (ISBN 0-306-40023-5, Plenum Pr). Plenum Pub.

Grossman, Morton I., et al, eds. Cellular Basis of Chemical Messengers in the Digestive System. LC 81-2318. (UCLA Forum in Medical Sciences Ser.: No. 23). 1981. 30.00 (ISBN 0-12-304420-0). Acad Pr.

Grossman, Moses, jt. auth. see Pascoe, Delmer J.

Grossman, Patty. Recorder Fingering Book for Beginners. (Illus., Orig.). (gr. 4-12). 1957. pap. text ed. 3.50x (ISBN 0-910286-06-X). Boxwood.

Grossman, Paul, jt. auth. see Schlei, Barbara L.

Grossman, Philip see Maimonides, Moses.

Grossman, R., jt. ed. see Slaby, R. J.

Grossman, R. B., et al, eds. Soil Taxonomy - Achievements & Challenges. 76p. 1984. 12.00 (ISBN 0-89118-775-8). Soil Sci Soc Am.

Grossman, Reinhardt. The Categorial Structure of the World. LC 81-48615. 448p. 1983. 27.50x (ISBN 0-253-31324-4). Ind U Pr.

--Meinong. (Arguments of the Philosophers Ser.). 1974. 22.95x (ISBN 0-7100-7831-5). Routledge & Kegan.

--Phenomenology & Existentialism: An Introduction. 256p. 1984. 30.00x (ISBN 0-7102-0270-9); pap. 11.95 (ISBN 0-7102-0291-1). Routledge & Kegan.

Grossman, Reinhardt S. The Structure of Mind. LC 65-13505. pap. 64.00 (ISBN 0-317-08118-7, 2002041). Bks Demand UMI.

Grossman, Richard. The Animals. LC 81-50385. 516p. 1983. fine cloth with slipcase 30.00 (ISBN 0-939358-00-X). Zygote Pr.

--Tycoon Boy. LC 83-50108. 72p. 1983. pap. 5.00 (ISBN 0-939358-02-6). Zygote Pr.

Grossman, Richard & Daneker, Gail. Energy, Jobs & the Economy. (Illus.). 1979. pap. 3.45 (ISBN 0-932870-00-7, Alyson Pubns). Carrier Pigeon.

Grossman, Richard L. Other Medicines. LC 80-2857. (Illus.). 256p. 1985. 19.95 (ISBN 0-385-15834-3); pap. 10.95 (ISBN 0-385-15835-1). Doubleday.

--Salvation. (Literary Chapbook Ser.). 48p. 1977. pap. 3.00 (ISBN 0-916300-05-6). Gallimaufry.

Grossman, Richard L., jt. auth. see Kazis, Richard.

Grossman, Robert G., jt. auth. see Willis, William D., Jr.

Grossman, Robert G. & Gildenberg, Philip L., eds. Head Injury: Basic & Clinical Aspects. (Seminars in Neurological Surgery Ser.). 300p. 1982. text ed. 68.50 (ISBN 0-89004-615-8). Raven.

Grossman, Ronald. The Italians in America. rev. ed. LC 66-10149. (In America Bks.). (Illus.). (gr. 5-11). 1979. PLB 7.95 (ISBN 0-8225-0202-X). Lerner Pubns.

Grossman, Ruth & Grossman, Bob. The New Kosher-Cookbook Trilogy. rev. ed. (Illus.). 304p. 1985. pap. 9.95 (ISBN 0-8397-6310-7). Eriksson.

Grossman, Sebastian P. Essentials of Physiological Psychology. LC 72-1450. pap. 129.00 (ISBN 0-317-29981-6, 2051764). Bks Demand UMI.

Grossman, Sheldon, et al. Studies in the History of Art 1974, Vol. 6. LC 72-600309. (Illus.). 214p. pap. 9.95 (ISBN 0-89468-024-2, Dist. by U Pr of New Eng). Natl Gallery Art.

Grossman, Siegfried. Stewards of God's Grace. 192p. (Orig.). 1981. pap. text ed. 8.95 (ISBN 0-85364-287-7). Attic Pr.

Grossman, Stanley. Calculus: Multivariate Calculus, Linear Algebra, & Differential Equations, Pt. II. 1981. 27.25i (ISBN 0-12-304302-6). Acad Pr.

--Calculus: Pt. 1: The Calculus of One Variable. 816p. 1981. 22.50i (ISBN 0-12-304301-8). Acad Pr.

--Finite Mathematics. 528p. 1983. text ed. write for info. (ISBN 0-534-01246-9). Wadsworth PUb.

Grossman, Stanley, jt. auth. see Strain, James J.

Grossman, Stanley I. Calculus. 2nd ed. 1176p. 1981. 31.00i (ISBN 0-12-304360-3). Acad Pr.

--Calculus. 3rd ed. 1984. 31.00i (ISBN 0-12-304371-9); instr's. manual 9.25i (ISBN 0-12-304373-5); student manual 9.75i (ISBN 0-12-304372-7). Acad Pr.

--Calculus. 3rd ed. 1984. pap. text ed. 24.00 (ISBN 0-12-304376-X). Acad Pr.

--Elementary Linear Algebra. 2nd ed. 426p. write for info. (ISBN 0-534-02738-5). Wadsworth Pub.

Grossman, Stanley I., jt. auth. see Derrick, William R.

Grossman, Stanley I., ed. Calculus: International Edition. 2nd ed. Date not set. 14.75 (ISBN 0-12-304330-1). Acad Pr.

Grossman, Stefan. Contemporary Fingerpicking Guitar Workshop. 1981. 5.95 (ISBN 0-89898-055-0). Almo Pubns.

Grossman, Steven D. & Kratchman, Stanley H. College Accounting Principles-Working Papers. 319p. 1985. wkbk. 12.95 (ISBN 0-13-140765-1). P-H.

Grossman, Steven D., jt. auth. see Crumbley, D. Larry.

Grossman, Steven D., jt. auth. see Lindhe, Richard.

Grossman, Steven D., et al. College Accounting Principles. (Illus.). 608p. 1985. text ed. 26.95 (ISBN 0-13-140724-4). P-H.

Grossman, Troy A. Sexascopes of the Presidents. (Illus.). 128p. (Orig.). 1981. pap. 6.95x (ISBN 0-936560-01-0). DoubLeo Pubns.

Grossman, Vasily, jt. auth. see Ehrenburg, Iiya.

Grossman, Vigdor. Employing Handicapped Persons: Meeting EEO Obligations. 154p. 1980. pap. 19.50 (ISBN 0-87179-319-9). BNA.

Grossman, W. & Pflug, G., eds. Probability & Statistical Inference. 1982. lib. bdg. 49.50 (ISBN 90-277-1427-4, Pub. by Reidel Holland). Kluwer Academic.

Grossman, Walter. Johann Christian Edelmann: From Orthodoxy to Enlightenment. (Religion & Society Ser: No. 3). 209p. 1976. text ed. 19.20x (ISBN 90-2797-691-0). Mouton.

Grossman, William & Farrell, Jack. The Heart of Jazz. LC 76-75730. (Roots of Jazz Ser.). 1976. Repr. of 1956 ed. lib. bdg. 29.50 (ISBN 0-306-70811-6). Da Capo.

Grossman, William, ed. Cardiac Catheterization & Angiography. 2nd ed. LC 80-10331. (Illus.). 427p. 1980. text ed. 34.50 (ISBN 0-8121-0714-4). Lea & Febiger.

Grossman, William L., ed. Modern Brazilian Short Stories. LC 67-13379. 1974. 23.50x (ISBN 0-520-00523-6); pap. 2.25 (ISBN 0-520-02766-3). U of Cal Pr.

Grossman, William L., tr. see Machado de Assis, Joaquim M.

Grossman, Zachary D., et al. The Clinician's Guide to Diagnostic Imaging. 274p. 1983. pap. text ed. 17.50 (ISBN 0-89004-948-3). Raven.

Grossmann. Englisches Handelsvokabularium Nach Sachgebieten. 330p. (Ger. & Eng., English Commercial Vokabulary Subjects). 1950. pap. 15.95 (ISBN 3-87217-001-5, 7360, Pub. by Th. Grossmann). French & Eur.

Grossmann & Friedmann. Kaufmannisches Grundworte Buch Fur Schule und Praxis. 280p. (Ger. -Eng., Dictionary of Commerce for School and Practice). 14.50 (ISBN 3-87217-300-6, M-7494, Pub. by Fachverlag Th. Grossmann). French & Eur.

Grossmann, Edwina B. Edwin Booth, Recollections by His Daughter & Letters to Her & to His Friends. LC 76-114881. (Select Bibliographies Reprint Ser). 1894. 18.00 (ISBN 0-8369-5285-5). Ayer Co Pubs.

Grossmann, Mary Lou, jt. auth. see Dessem, Ralph E.

Grossmann, Reinhardt. Reflections on Frege's Philosophy. LC 77-78328. (Northwestern University Publications in Analytic Philosophy Ser). Repr. of 1969 ed. 52.70 (ISBN 0-8357-9468-7, 2010264). Bks Demand UMI.

Grossmann, Reinhart. Ontological Reduction. LC 72-85604. (Indiana University Humanities Ser.: No. 72). pap. 42.00 (ISBN 0-317-09304-5, 2055221). Bks Demand UMI.

Grossmann, Walter & Kahmen, Heribert. Vermessungskunde I: Fehlerlehre, Vermessungen und Berechnungen fur Grossmassstabige Karten und Plane, Nivellieren. (Sammlung Goeschen: No. 2160). 252p. (Ger.). 1985. pap. 9.90x (ISBN 3-11-010262-5). De Gruyter.

--Vermessungskunde II: Winkel- und Streckenmessgerate, Polygonierung, Triangulation und Trilateration. (Sammlung Goeschen: No. 2161). 294p. 1983. 10.70 (ISBN 3-11-009601-3). De Gruyter.

Grossmen, Gene M., ed. see Bhagwati, Jagdish M.

Grossmith, George & Grossmith, Weedon. Diary of a Nobody. 1977. 12.95x (ISBN 0-460-00963-X, DEL-04084, Evman); pap. 2.50x (ISBN 0-460-01963-5, DEL-04085, Evman). Biblio Dist.

--The Diary of a Nobody. 240p. 1975. pap. 2.95 (ISBN 0-14-000510-2). Penguin.

Grossmith, Weedon, jt. auth. see Grossmith, George.

Grossner, Nathan. Transformers for Electronic Circuits. 2nd ed. (Illus.). 400p. 1983. 46.95 (ISBN 0-07-024979-2). McGraw.

Grossnickle, Foster E. Capital Outlay in Relation to a State's Minimum Educational Program. LC 72-176823. (Columbia University. Teachers College. Contributions to Education: No. 464). Repr. of 1931 ed. 22.50 (ISBN 0-404-55464-4). AMS Pr.

--Discovering Meanings in Elementary School Mathematics. 7th ed. LC 82-21335. 401p. 1983. text ed. 30.95 (ISBN 0-03-059933-4). HR&W.

Grosso, Michael. The Final Choice: Playing the Survival Game. 350p. (Orig.). 1985. pap. 10.95 (ISBN 0-913299-18-9). Stillpoint.

Gross-Stein, Janice & Dewitt, David, eds. Middle East at the Crossroads: International Forces & External Powers. 184p. 1984. 19.95 (ISBN 0-88962-202-7, Pub by Mosaic Pr Canada); pap. 12.95 (ISBN 0-88962-201-9). Flatiron Book Dist.

Grossvogel, David I. Four Playwrights & a Postscript: Brecht, Ionesco, Beckett, Genet. Archival ed. LC 75-27654. 209p. 1976. Repr. of 1962 ed. lib. bdg. 45.00x (ISBN 0-8371-8438-X, GRFP). Greenwood.

--Limits of the Novel: Evolutions of a Form from Chaucer to Robbe-Grillet. 357p. 1971. pap. 6.95 (ISBN 0-8014-9115-0, CP-115). Cornell U Pr.

--Limits of the Novel: Evolutions of a Form from Chauser to Robbe-Grillet. LC 68-16381. 347p. 1968. 17.50x (ISBN 0-8014-0162-3). Lib Soc Sci.

--Mystery & Its Fictions: From Oedipus to Agatha Christie. LC 78-20516. 1979. 20.00x (ISBN 0-8018-2201-7) Johns Hopkins.

--Twentieth Century French Drama. LC 65-7487. 378p. 1958. pap. 11.50x (ISBN 0-231-08522-2). Columbia U Pr.

--Twentieth Century French Drama. LC 68-16434. 1966. Repr. of 1961 ed. 12.50x (ISBN 0-87752-048-8). Gordian.

Grossvogel, David I., ed. see Sagan, Francoise.

Grosswald, Blanche. Statistical Summary Report of the 1979 University of California Union Catalog Data Base. (Working Paper: No. 10). 1980. 5.00 (ISBN 0-686-87251-7). UCDLA.

Grosswald, E. Bessel Polynomials. (Lecture Notes in Mathematics: Vol. 698). 1978. pap. 14.00 (ISBN 0-387-09104-1). Springer-Verlag.

Grosswald, E., ed. Representations of Integers As Sums of Squares. (Illus.). 200p. 1985. 45.00 (ISBN 0-387-96126-7). Springer-Verlag.

Grosswald, Emil. Topics from the Theory of Numbers. 2nd ed. 352p. 1982. text ed. 29.95x (ISBN 0-8176-3044-9). Birkhauser.

Grosswald, Emil & Rademacher, Hans. Dedekind Sums. LC 72-88698. (Carus Monograph: No. 16). 102p. 1972. 19.00 (ISBN 0-88385-016-8, 7288698). Math Assn.

Grosswald, Emil, ed. see Rademacher, Hans.

Grosswirth, M. & Salny, A. The Mensa Genius Book. 1981. pap. 5.95 (ISBN 0-201-05959-2). Addison-Wesley.

Grosswirth, Marvin & Salny, Abbie. The Mensa Genius Quiz Book Two. LC 83-7244. 160p. 1983. pap. 5.95 (ISBN 0-201-05958-4). Addison-Wesley.

Grosswirth, Marvin, jt. auth. see Salny, Abbie.

Grosu, A. Approaches to Island Phenomena. (Linguistic Ser.: Vol. 45). 346p. 1981. 51.00 (ISBN 0-444-86278-1, North Holland). Elsevier.

Grosvenor, Charles, ed. see Potter, Reuben.

Grosvenor, Donna K. see National Geographic Society.

Grosvenor, Theodore P. Primary Care Optometry: A Clinical Manual. LC 81-84965. 1982. 84.00 (ISBN 0-87873-038-9). Prof Press.

Grosvold, Olav, jt. auth. see Flemmen, Asbjorn.

Grosz, George. Ecce Homo. LC 76-26191. (Illus.). 96p. 1976. pap. 4.50 (ISBN 0-486-23410-X). Dover.

--The Face of the Ruling Class. 96p. 1983. pap. 5.95 (ISBN 0-8052-8161-4, Pub. by Allison & Busby England). Schocken.

--George Grosz: An Autobiography. (Illus.). 336p. 1983. 19.95 (ISBN 0-02-545830-2). Macmillan.

--George Grosz: An Autobiography. rev. ed. Hodges, Nora, tr. from Ger. Orig. Title: Ein Kleines Ja Und ein Grosses Nein. (Illus.). 328p. pap. 9.95postponed (ISBN 0-915829-57-6). Imago Imprint Inc.

--Love above All. 80p. 1985. pap. 5.95 (ISBN 0-8052-8235-1, Pub. by Allison & Busby England). Schocken.

--Love Above All & Other Drawings. Appelbaum, Stanley, tr. (Illus., Orig., Ger.). 1971. pap. 6.50 (ISBN 0-486-22675-1). Dover.

--Der Spiesser-Spiegel. LC 68-9232. (Contemporary Art Ser.). (Illus.). 1969-1972. Repr. of 1932 ed. 16.00 (ISBN 0-405-00720-5). Ayer Co Pubs.

Grosz, Geroge. The Day of Reckoning. 96p. 1983. pap. 5.95 (ISBN 0-8052-8163-0, Pub. by Allison & Busby England). Schocken.

Grotch, Howard, jt. auth. see McKelvey, John P.

Grote. Script Analysis: Reading & Understanding the Playscript for Production. 1984. write for info. (ISBN 0-534-03711-9). Wadsworth Pub.

Grote, A. R. An Illustrated Essay of the Noctuidae of North America: With a "Colony of Butterflies". 85p. 1971. Repr. of 1882 ed. 45.00x (ISBN 0-317-07097-5, Pub. by EW Classey UK). State Mutual Bk.

Grote, Caroline. Housing & Living Conditions of Women Students in the Western Illinois State Teachers College at Macomb - School Years 1926-1927, 1927-1928, & 1928-1929. LC 76-176824. (Columbia University. Teachers College. Contributions to Education: No. 507). Repr. of 1931 ed. 22.50 (ISBN 0-404-55507-1). AMS Pr.

Grote, David. The Medicine Man. 44p. 1980. pap. 2.75 (ISBN 0-88680-129-X); royalty 35.00 (ISBN 0-317-03570-3). I E Clark.

--Staging the Musical: Planning, Rehearsing, & Marketing the Amateur Production. 250p. 1985. 16.95 (ISBN 0-13-840190-X); pap. 8.95 (ISBN 0-13-840182-9). P-H.

--Undercover Lover. (Illus.). 39p. (Director's Production Script). 1978. pap. 7.50 (ISBN 0-88680-200-8). I E Clark.

Grote, David G. The End of Comedy: Sit-Com & the Comedic Tradition. 206p. 1983. 19.50 (ISBN 0-208-01991-X, Archon Bks). Shoe String.

Grote, E. H. CNS Control Mechanisms on Glucose Metabolism. (Acta Neurochirurgia Supplementum Ser.: No. 31). (Illus.). 160p. 1981. pap. 26.90 (ISBN 0-387-81619-4). Springer-Verlag.

Grote, George. Aristotle. 2nd ed. Bain, Alexander & Robertson, G. Croom, eds. LC 72-9292. (Philosophy of Plato & Aristotle Ser.). Repr. of 1880 ed. 37.00 (ISBN 0-405-04843-2). Ayer Co Pubs.

--Fragments on Ethical Subjects. LC 78-179391. (Philosophy Monograph: No. 87). 242p. 1972. Repr. of 1876 ed. lib. bdg. 21.00 (ISBN 0-8337-1469-4). B Franklin.

--History of Greece, 10 Vols. new ed. LC 75-137236. Repr. of 1888 ed. Set. 400.00 (ISBN 0-404-02950-7); 40.00 ea. AMS Pr.

--The Minor Works of George Grote with Critical Remarks on His Intellectual Character Writings, & Speeches. Bain, Alexander, ed. 1873. 22.50 (ISBN 0-8337-1470-8). B Franklin.

Grote, Harriet. Philosophical Radicals of Eighteen Thirty-Two. 1967. Repr. of 1866 ed. 14.00 (ISBN 0-8337-1471-6). B Franklin.

Grote, J. D., ed. see NATO Advanced Study Institute, University of Warwick, Coventry England, August 27-September 6, 1974.

Grote, J. J., ed. Biomaterials in Otology. 324p. 1984. text ed. 52.00 (ISBN 0-89838-610-1, Pub. by Martinus Nijhoff Netherlands). Kluwer Academic.

Grote, Jim, jt. ed. see Mitcham, Carl.

Grote, Jurgon, et al, eds. Oxygen Transport to Tissue II. LC 75-25951. (Advances in Experimental Medicine & Biology Ser.: Vol. 75). 804p. 1976. 85.00x (ISBN 0-306-39075-2, Plenum Pr). Plenum Pub.

Grote, R. Positive Discipline. 1979. leader's guide o.p. 125.00 (ISBN 0-07-025007-3); 3-ring binder 50.00 (ISBN 0-07-025006-5). McGraw.

Groteluesehen, Arden D., et al. Evaluation in Adult Basic Education: How & Why. LC 76-8341. 274p. 1976. pap. text ed. 12.50x (ISBN 0-8134-6793-4, 6793). Interstate.

Groten, Dallas. Will the Real Winner Please Stand Up. 160p. 1985. pap. 4.95 (ISBN 0-87123-819-5). Bethany Hse.

--Winning Isn't Always First Place. LC 83-14930. 160p. (Orig.). 1983. pap. 4.95 (ISBN 0-87123-613-3). Bethany Hse.

Grotenhuis, Elizabeth T., tr. see Okazaki, Joji.

Grotenhuis, Elizabeth Ten see Okudaira, Hideo.

Grotenhuis, Elizabeth Ten see Rosenfield, John M. & Ten Grotenhuis, Elizabeth.

Grotenhuis, Elizabeth ten see Ten Grotenhuis, Elizabeth.

Grotevant, Harold D. & Cooper, Catherine R., eds. Adolescent Development in the Family. LC 83-82344. (Child Development Ser.: No. 22). 1983. pap. text ed. 8.95x (ISBN 0-87589-934-X). Jossey-Bass.

Grotewold, Andreas. The Regional Theory of World Trade. LC 79-83769. (Illus.). 1979. 10.50x (ISBN 0-933550-00-6). Ptolemy Pr.

Groth, A. N. Men Who Rape: The Psychology of the Offender. LC 79-18624. 245p. 1979. 19.95x (ISBN 0-306-40268-8, Plenum Pr). Plenum Pub.

Groth, Alexander J. Major Ideologies: An Interpretative of Democracy, Socialism & Nationalism. LC 82-18755. 256p. 1983. text ed. 11.50 (ISBN 0-89874-579-9). Krieger.

--Major Ideologies: An Interpretative Survey of Democracy, Socialism & Nationalism. LC 74-168636. 244p. 1971. pap. 11.50 (ISBN 0-471-32895-2). Krieger.

--Progress & Chaos. LC 83-17549. 242p. (Eng.). 1984. pap. text ed. 9.50 (ISBN 0-89874-677-9). Krieger.

Groth, Alexander J. & Wade, Larry L. Comparative Resource Allocation. LC 84-13427. 247p. 1984. 28.00 (ISBN 0-8039-2370-8); pap. 14.00 (ISBN 0-8039-2371-6). Sage.

Groth, Alexander J., et al. Contemporary Politics: Europe. 1976. text ed. 18.95 (ISBN 0-316-52498-0). Little.

Groth, Ivan. Jesus Has Returned to Planet Earth. (Orig.). 1984. pap. 4.95 (ISBN 0-89221-097-4, Pub. by Sonlife Intl). New Leaf.

Groth, J. L. Prayer: Learning How to Talk to God. LC 56-1395. (Concept Books Series Four). 1983. pap. 3.95 (ISBN 0-570-07799-0). Concordia.

Groth, Jeanette. Thank You for My Spouse. LC 12-2826. 1983. pap. 2.50 (ISBN 0-570-03885-5). Concordia.

--Thank You for This Child. (Illus.). 1980. pap. 1.95 (ISBN 0-570-03797-2, 12-2906). Concordia.

Groth, Jeanette L. Little Journeys with Jesus. pap. 5.95 (ISBN 0-570-03924-X, 12-2858). Concordia.

Groth, Lynn. God Cares for Me. (A Cradle Roll Program Ser.). 8p. (Orig.). (ps). pap. 1.25 (ISBN 0-938272-75-6). Wels Board.

--Jesus Loves Children. (A Cradle Roll Program Ser.). 16p. (Orig.). (ps). 1985. pap. 1.25 (ISBN 0-938272-78-0). Wels Board.

--A Very Special Baby-Jesus. (A Cradle Roll Program Ser.). 8p. (Orig.). (ps). 1985. pap. 1.25 (ISBN 0-938272-76-4). Wels Board.

--With You, Dear Child, in Mind. (A Cradle Roll Program Ser.). 16p. (Orig.). (ps). 1985. pap. 1.25 (ISBN 0-938272-77-2). Wels Board.

Groth, Patricia C. Before the Beginning. LC 84-71323. (Illus.). 84p. 1984. pap. 6.00x (ISBN 0-9610346-4-5). Belle Mead Pr.

Groth, Patricia C. & Druck, Kitty, eds. Stones & Poets: An Anthology of Poetry. 2nd ed. LC 80-66853. (Illus.). 90p. (Orig.). 1981. pap. 7.00 (ISBN 0-937158-01-1). Del Valley.

Grothe, Carolyn, jt. auth. see Warner-Reitz, Anne.

Grothe, Mardy, jt. auth. see Wylie, Peter.

Grothendieck, A. Local Cohomology: A Seminar Given by A. Grothendieck at Harvard University, 1961. Hartshorne, ed. (Lecture Notes in Mathematics: Vol. 41). 1967. pap. 10.70 (ISBN 0-387-03912-0). Springer-Verlag.

--Topological Vector Spaces. (Notes on Mathematics & Its Applications Ser.). 256p. 1973. 49.95 (ISBN 0-677-30020-4). Gordon.

Grothendieck, A. & Murre, J. P. Tame Fundamental Group of a Formal Neighbourhood of a Divisor with Normal Crossing on a Scheme. (Lecture Notes in Mathematics: Vol. 208). 1971. pap. 11.00 (ISBN 0-387-05499-5). Springer-Verlag.

Grothendieck, Alexander. Produits Tensoriels Topologiques et Espaces Nucleaires. LC 52-42839. (Memoirs: No. 16). 336p. 1979. pap. 18.00 (ISBN 0-8218-1216-5, MEMO-16). Am Math.

Groth-Marnat, Gary. Handbook of Psychological Assessment. LC 83-21812. 1984. 38.50 (ISBN 0-442-22927-5). Van Nos Reinhold.

Grotius, Hugo. The Freedom of the Seas. LC 71-38252. (The Evolution of Capitalism Ser.). 184p. 1972. Repr. of 1916 ed. 25.00 (ISBN 0-405-04123-3). Ayer Co Pubs.

--The Rights of War & Peace, Including the Law of Nature & of Nations. LC 78-20466. 1980. Repr. of 1901 ed. text ed. 33.00 (ISBN 0-88355-845-9). Hyperion Conn.

--True Religion Explained & Defended. Coventry, F., tr. LC 72-201. (English Experience Ser.: No. 318). 350p. 1971. Repr. of 1632 ed. 28.00 (ISBN 90-221-0318-8). Walter J Johnson.

Grotjahn, Martin. The Art & Technique of Analytic Group Therapy. LC 76-22916. 276p. 1977. 15.00x (ISBN 0-87668-252-2). Aronson.

--Voice of the Symbol. LC 76-148963. (Illus.). 1971. 8.00 (ISBN 0-87787-002-0). Mara.

Grotjahn, Martin & Kline, Frank M. A Handbook of Group Therapy. 320p. 1982. 27.95 (ISBN 0-442-21939-3). Van Nos Reinhold.

Grotke, Guy. Intermediate Commodore 64. 220p. (Orig.). 1984. pap. 14.95 (ISBN 0-88190-253-5, BO253). Datamost.

Grotpeter, John J. Historical Dictionary of Swaziland. LC 75-4734. (African Historical Dictionaries Ser.: No. 3). 265p. 1975. 20.00 (ISBN 0-8108-0805-6). Scarecrow.

--Historical Dictionary of Zambia. LC 79-342. (African Historical Dictionaries Ser.: No. 19). 429p. 1979. 30.00 (ISBN 0-8108-1207-X). Scarecrow.

Grotpeter, John J., jt. auth. see Weinstein, Warren.

Grotstein, James S. Splitting & Projective Identification. LC 84-45724. 236p. 1985. 25.00x (ISBN 0-87668-756-7). Aronson.

Grott, J. J. De see De Groot, J. J.

Grotta, Daniel. The Biography of J. R. R. Tolkien, Architect of Middle-Earth. rev. ed. LC 77-29209. 1978. lib. bdg. 12.90 (ISBN 0-89471-034-6); pap. 4.95 (ISBN 0-89471-035-4). Running Pr.

Grottian, Peter & Nelles, Wilfried. Grosstadtpolitik und Neue Soziale Bewegung. (Stadtforschung Ser.: Vol. 1). 314p. 1983. pap. text ed. 14.95 (ISBN 0-8176-1483-4). Birkhauser.

Grottke, Robert & Norris, James. Improving Productivity Profits in Wholesale Distribution: The Magnifying Glass Technique. 137p. 40.00 (ISBN 0-318-16897-9); NAW Commodity Line Association Members 36.00 (ISBN 0-318-16898-7); NAW members 32.00 (ISBN 0-318-16899-5). Natl Assn Wholesale Dists.

Grotz, George. The Current Antique Furniture Style & Price Guide. LC 77-27673. (Illus.). 1979. 13.95 (ISBN 0-385-13165-8, Dolp). Doubleday.

--From Gunk to Glow: The Gentle Art of Refinishing Antiques & Other Furniture. 1983. pap. 4.95 (ISBN 0-385-29204-X, Delta). Dell.

--The Fun of Refinishing Furniture. LC 78-22809. 1979. pap. 9.95 (ISBN 0-385-14916-6, Dolp). Doubleday.

--The Furniture Doctor. 265p. 1981. 20.00x (ISBN 0-257-65027-X, Pub. by Barrie & Jenkins England). State Mutual Bk.

--Furniture Doctor. rev. & exp. ed. LC 82-45936. (Illus.). 384p. 1983. 14.95 (ISBN 0-385-17971-5). Doubleday.

--How to Double Your Money in Antiques in Sixty Days. LC 85-10280. (Illus.). 240p. 1986. pap. 9.95 (ISBN 0-385-19515-X). Doubleday.

--Staining & Finishing Unfinished Furniture & Other Naked Woods. LC 68-25596. (Illus.). 1968. pap. 3.50 (ISBN 0-385-01906-8, Dolp). Doubleday.

Grotz, George, ed. Grotz's Second Antique Furniture Style & Price Guide. LC 81-43105. (Illus.). 352p. 1982. pap. 13.95 (ISBN 0-385-17426-8, Dolp). Doubleday.

Grou, Jean-Nicholas. How to Pray. Dalby, Joseph, tr. 154p. 1982. pap. 6.95 (ISBN 0-227-67485-5). Attic Pr.

Grou, Pierre. The Financial Structure of Multinational Capitalism. Tayar-Adams, Aline, tr. from Fr. Orig. Title: La Structure Financiere du Capitalisme Multinational. 240p. 1985. 24.95 (ISBN 0-907582-40-0, Pub. by Berg Pubs); pap. 9.95 (ISBN 0-907582-41-9). Longwood Pub Group.

Grouchko, Daniel, ed. Operations Research & Reliability. LC 72-172824. (Illus.). 642p. 1971. 132.95 (ISBN 0-677-14610-8). Gordon.

Grouchy, J. & Turleau, C. Atlas de las Enfermedades Cromosomicas. 356p. (Span.). 1978. 97.50 (ISBN 84-7102-959-6, S-31931). French & Eur.

Groueff, S. L' Homme et la mer. (Collection maitrise du monde). 64.50x (ISBN 0-685-36200-0, 2278). Larousse.

Groueff, S. & Cartier, J. P. L' Homme et le cosmos. Cartier, Raymond, ed. (Collection maitrise du monde). (Illus.). 396p. (Fr.). 1975. 64.50x (ISBN 2-03-013369-8). Larousse.

Grouls, V. & Helpap, B. The Development of the Red Pulp in the Spleen. (Advances in Anatomy, Embryology, & Cell Biology Ser.: Vol. 75). (Illus.). 70p. 1982. pap. 26.00 (ISBN 0-387-11408-4). Springer-Verlag.

Groulx, Lionel A. Roland-Michel Barrin de la Galissoni Ere, 1693-1756. LC 74-22181. (Canadian Biographical Studies: No. 2). pap. 26.00 (ISBN 0-317-27037-0, 2023627). Bks Demand UMI.

Ground Zero. Hope: Nuclear War & the 1984 Elections. 96p. (Orig.). 1983. pap. 3.95 (ISBN 0-671-50226-3, Long Shadow). PB.

--Nuclear War: What's in It for You? (Orig.). 1983. pap. 3.95 (ISBN 0-671-47509-6). PB.

--What about the Russians--And Nuclear War? 1983. pap. 3.95 (ISBN 0-671-47209-7). PB.

Grounds, Roger. Growing Vegetables & Herbs. (Orig.). 1980. pap. 6.95x (ISBN 0-8464-1016-8). Beekman Pubs.

--House Plants. LC 77-700394. (Illus.). (gr. 11-12). 1977. pap. 4.95 (ISBN 0-8120-0796-4). Barron.

--The Natural Garden. LC 76-12981. 1976. pap. 2.95 (ISBN 0-8128-2111-4). Stein & Day.

--Ornamental Grasses. 216p. 1981. 18.95 (ISBN 0-442-24707-9). Van Nos Reinhold.

Grounds, Roger, ed. Practical Pruning. LC 77-70395. (Illus.). 1978. pap. 3.95 (ISBN 0-8120-0797-2). Barron.

Grounds, Vernon. Radical Commitment: Getting Serious about Christian Growth. LC 84-3344. 1984. pap. 5.95 (ISBN 0-88070-051-3). Multnomah.

Group, David. Evidence for the Bermuda Triangle. (Illus.). 160p. (Orig.). 1985. pap. 5.95 (ISBN 0-85030-413-X, Pub. by Aquarian Pr England). Sterling.

Group for Environmental Education, Inc. Our Man-Made Environment, Book 7. 1973. pap. 7.95x (ISBN 0-262-07050-2); pap. 7.95 (ISBN 0-262-57037-8). MIT Pr.

Group for Environmental Education Inc. Philadelphia Architecture: A Guide. Gallery, John A., ed. (Illus.). 176p. (Orig.). 1984. pap. 12.95 (ISBN 0-262-56030-5). MIT Pr.

Group for Human Development in Higher Education Group. Faculty Development in a Time of Retrenchment. 90p. 1974. pap. 4.95 (ISBN 0-915390-01-9, Pub. by Change Mag). Transaction Pubs.

Group for the Advancement of Psychiatry. Application of Psychiatric Insights to Cross-Cultural Communications. (Group for the Advancement of Psychiatry, Symposium Ser.: No. 7). 1961. pap. 20.00 (ISBN 0-317-08151-9, 2021836). Bks Demand UMI.

--Considerations on Personality Development in College Students: Committee on the College Student. (Group for the Advancement of Psychiatry Report Ser.: No. 32). 1955. pap. 20.00 (ISBN 0-317-08148-9, 2021823). Bks Demand UMI.

--Death & Dying: Attitudes of Patient & Doctor, Vol. 5. LC 65-28440. (Symposium: No. 11). 1965. pap. 7.50 (ISBN 0-87630-366-1, Pub. by GAP). Brunner-Mazel.

Group for the Advancement of Psychiatry. Committee on the Family, ed. Divorce, Child Custody, & the Family. LC 80-25935. (Social & Behavioral Science Ser.). 1981. pap. text ed. 18.95x (ISBN 0-910958-10-6). Jossey-Bass.

Group for the Advancement of Psychiatry. Factors Used to Increase the Susceptibility of Individuals to Forceful Indoctrination; Observations & Experiments, Vol. 3. (Symposium: No. 3). 1956. pap. 2.00 (ISBN 0-87318-043-7, Pub. by GAP). Brunner-Mazel.

Group for the Advancement of Psychiatry Editiors. The Family, the Patient & the Psychiatric Hospital: Toward a New Model (GAP No. 117) 96p. Date not set. 17.50 (ISBN 0-87630-399-8); pap. 10.50 (ISBN 0-87630-398-X). Brunner-Mazel.

Group for the Advancement of Psychiatry Committee on Mental Health Service, ed. Interfaces: A Communications Case Book for Mental Health Decision Makers. LC 81-9551. (Social & Behavioral Science Ser.). 1981. text ed. 23.95x (ISBN 0-87589-510-7). Jossey-Bass.

Group for the Advancement of Psychiatry. Medical Uses of Hypnosis, Vol. 4. 72p. (Symposium No. 8). 1962. pap. 7.50 (ISBN 0-87630-357-2, Pub. by GAP). Brunner-Mazel.

--Misuse of Psychiatry in the Criminal Courts: Competency to Stand Trial. (Group for the Advancement of Psychiatry, Report Vol. 6: No. 89). pap. 20.00 (ISBN 0-317-29902-6, 2021833). Bks Demand UMI.

--Normal Adolescence: Its Dynamics & Impact. LC 68-12511. 1968. pap. 3.45 (ISBN 0-684-71781-6, SL 143, ScribT). Scribner.

Group for the Advancement of Psychiatry Conference. Pavlovian Conditioning & American Psychiatry, Vol. 5. (Symposium No. 9). 1964. pap. 3.00 (ISBN 0-87318-079-8, Pub. by GAP). Brunner-Mazel.

Group for the Advancement of Psychiatry Committee on Child Psychiatry. The Process of Child Therapy. LC 82-45469. (Publications Ser.: No. 111). 224p. 1982. 17.50 (ISBN 0-87630-310-6, Pub. by GAP). Brunner-Mazel.

Group for the Advancement of Psychiatry. Psychopathological Disorders in Childhood: Theoretical Considerations & a Proposed Classification. LC 73-17784. 175p. 1974. 17.50x (ISBN 0-87668-130-5). Aronson.

--Research & the Complex Causality of the Schizophrenias. LC 84-9535. (Report Ser.: No. 116). 104p. 1984. pap. text ed. 11.95 (ISBN 0-87630-373-4). Brunner-Mazel.

--The Right to Die: Decision & Decision Makers. LC 84-45126. 79p. 1983. 12.50x (ISBN 0-87668-721-4). Aronson.

--Treatment of Families in Conflict: The Clinical Study of Family Process. LC 84-45131. 329p. 1983. 30.00x (ISBN 0-87668-724-9). Aronson.

Group Health Cooperative of Puget Sound. Nurses' Guide to Telephone Triage & Health Care. 1984. pap. 34.95 (ISBN 0-935236-34-1). Nurseco.

--Nurses' Guide to Telephone Triage & Health Care. 436p. Date not set. pap. 34.95 (ISBN 0-683-09526-9). Williams & Wilkins.

Group of European Nutritionists, 10th Meeting, Saltsjoebaden, 1971. Complete Intravenous Nutrition. Wretlind, A., ed. (Nutrition & Metabolism: Vol. 14, Suppl.). (Illus.). 300p. 1972. pap. 16.75 (ISBN 3-8055-1450-6). S Karger.

Group of European Nutritionists, 12th Symposium, Cambridge, July 1973. Gut & Nutrition: Proceedings. Somogyi, J. C. & MacDonald, eds. (Bibliotheca Nutritio et Dieta: No. 22). 200p. 1975. pap. 30.75 (ISBN 3-8055-1738-6). S Karger.

Groupar. Le Singe a la Porte: Vers une Theorie de la Parodie. LC 84-47830. 177p. (French.). 1984. pap. text ed. 18.50 (ISBN 0-8204-0144-7). P Lang Pubs.

Groupe, Vincent, ed. Alcoholism Rehabilitation: Methods & Experiences of Private Rehabilitation Centers. LC 78-620026. (NIAAA-RUCAS Alcoholism Treatment Ser.: No. 3). 1978. pap. 6.00 (ISBN 0-911290-49-4). Rutgers Ctr Alcohol.

Grouse, Phil, jt. auth. see Brookes, Cyril.

Grousset, P. The Conquest of the Moon: A Story of the Bayouda. LC 74-16504. (Science Fiction Ser). (Illus.). 340p. 1975. Repr. 25.50x (ISBN 0-405-06302-4). Ayer Co Pubs.

Grousset, R. & Leonard, E. G. Histoire Universelle: De l'Islam a la Reforme, Vol. 2. (Historique Ser.). 2112p. write for info. French & Eur.

--Histoire Universelle: Des Origines a l'Islam, Vol. 1. (Historique Ser.). 2000p. pap. 46.95 (ISBN 0-686-56446-4). French & Eur.

Grousset, Rene. The Civilizations of the East, 4 vols. Phillips, Catherine Alison, tr. from Fr. Incl. Vol. 1. The Near & Middle East. (Illus.). 404p. 27.50 (ISBN 0-8154-0093-4); Vol. 2. Civilization of India. (Illus.). 404p. 27.50 (ISBN 0-8154-0094-2); Vol. 3. The Civilization of China. (Illus.). 363p. 27.50 (ISBN 0-8154-0095-0); Vol. 4. The Civilization of Japan. (Illus.). 341p. 27.50 (ISBN 0-8154-0096-9). LC 66-30807. (Eng.). 1967. Repr. of 1930 ed. Cooper Sq.

--In the Footsteps of the Buddha. facs. ed. Leon, Mariette, tr. from Fr. LC 77-124235. (Select Bibliographies Reprint Ser). 1932. 19.50 (ISBN 0-8369-5423-8). Ayer Co Pubs.

--The Rise & Splendour of the Chinese Empire. (Illus.). (YA) (gr. 9-12). 1953. pap. 8.95 (ISBN 0-520-00525-2, CAL19). U of Cal Pr.

Groussett, Rene. The Sum of History. Patterson, A. & Patterson, H. Temple, trs. LC 78-59024. 1979. Repr. of 1951 ed. 21.00 (ISBN 0-88355-697-9). Hyperion Conn.

Grout, jt. auth. see Jorgensen.

Grout, A. J. Mosses with Hand Lens & Microscope. 1972. 15.00 (ISBN 0-910914-03-6). J Johnson.

Grout, Bill. Talking Behind Masks: Socio-Drama for ESL Students. Munch, Helen, ed. (Orig.). 1982. pap. text ed. 5.95 (ISBN 0-88084-051-X); tchr's ed. 4.95 (ISBN 0-88084-050-1); class set 52.95 (ISBN 0-88084-052-8). Alemany Pr.

Grout, Bill, jt. auth. see Hewes, Jeremy.

Grout, Bill, jt. auth. see Kidd, Billy.

Grout, D., ed. see Scarlatti, Alessandro.

Grout, Donald, ed. see Scarlatti, Allessandro.

Grout, Donald J. Alessandro Scarlatti: An Introduction to His Operas. LC 78-54796. 1979. 24.50x (ISBN 0-520-03682-4). U of Cal Pr.

--A History of Western Music. 3rd ed. (Illus.). 1980. text ed. 24.95x (ISBN 0-393-95136-7). Norton.

--A Short History of Opera. 2nd ed. LC 64-11043. 852p. (gr. 9 up). 1965. 29.50x (ISBN 0-231-02422-3). Columbia U Pr.

Grout, Donald J. & Palisca, Claude. A History of Western Music. 3rd, shorter ed. (Illus.). 1981. 23.95x (ISBN 0-393-95142-1). Norton.

Grout, Donald J., ed. The Faithful Princess. (Operas of Alessandro Scarlatti Ser.: Vol. 4). 1977. pap. 25.00x (ISBN 0-674-64030-6). Harvard U Pr.

--The Operas of Alessandro Scarlatti: Eraclea, Vol. I. LC 70-188973. (Publications in Music Ser: No. 6). 192p. 1974. pap. text ed. 25.00x (ISBN 0-674-64026-8). Harvard U Pr.

--The Operas of Alessandro Scarlatti, Vol. 3: Griselda. (Publications in Music Ser.). 256p. 1976. pap. 25.00x (ISBN 0-674-64029-2). Harvard U Pr.

Grout, Donald J. & Accone, Frank D., eds. The Operas of Alessandro Scarlatti: Vol. VII, Gli Eqivoci nel Sembiante. LC 81-7171. (Harvard Publications in Music: No. 12). 224p. 1982. pap. text ed. 30.00x. Harvard U Pr.

Grout, Donald J. & Holmes, Willicam C., eds. The Operas of Alessandro Scarlatti, Volume IX: La Statira. (Publications in Music Ser.: No. 15). 224p. 1985. pap. text ed. 40.00x (ISBN 0-674-64035-7). Harvard U Pr.

Grout, Frank F. & Wolff, J. Fred. Geology of the Cuyuna District, Minnesota: A Progress Report. LC 55-9000. (Bulletin: No. 36). (Illus.). 1955. 3.00x (ISBN 0-8166-0106-2). Minn Geol Survey.

Grout, Jack. Jack Grout's Golf Clinic. (Illus.). 160p. (Orig.). 1985. pap. 12.95 (ISBN 0-87670-099-7, Dist. by Sterling). Athletic Inst.

--On the Lesson Tee. 1982. pap. text ed. 6.95 (ISBN 0-87670-064-4). Athletic Inst.

--On the Lesson Tee: Basic Golf Fundamentals. LC 81-86517. (Athletic Institute Bk.). (Illus.). 131p. (Orig.). 1982. pap. 6.95 (ISBN 0-8069-7622-5). Sterling.

Grout, Jack & Aultman, Dick. Let Me Teach You Golf As I Taught Jack Nicklaus. LC 75-13515. (Illus.). 1977. pap. 14.95 (ISBN 0-689-70557-3). Atheneum.

Grout, Jarrell C. Fundamental Computer Programming Using FORTRAN 77. (Software Ser.). (Illus.). 432p. 1983. pap. text ed. 21.95 (ISBN 0-13-335141-6). P-H.

--Programming with BASIC: A Structured Approach. 376p. 1985. pap. text ed. write for info. (ISBN 0-697-00077-X); instr's. manual avail. (ISBN 0-697-00505-4). Wm C Brown.

Grout, P. B., et al, eds. The Legend of Arthur in the Middle Ages. (Arthurian Studies: VII). 254p. 1983. 37.50 (ISBN 0-85991-132-2, BAB-04928, Pub. by Boydell & Brewer). Longwood Pub Group.

Grout, Paul, jt. auth. see Birchenhall, Chris.

Grout, Victor. Grout's Value Added Tax Cases. 1982. 70.00x (ISBN 0-85459-046-3, Pub. by Tolley Pub England). State Mutual Bk.

--Tolley's Tax Cases, 1984. 1984. 140.00x (ISBN 0-85459-061-7, Pub. by Tolley Pub England). State Mutual Bk.

Grove & Creswell. City Landscape. 1983. text ed. 79.95 (ISBN 0-408-01165-3). Butterworth.

Grove, jt. auth. see McAllan.

Grove, A. S. Physics & Technology of Semiconductor Devices. 366p. 1967. 43.50 (ISBN 0-471-32998-3). Wiley.

Grove, A. T. Africa. 3rd ed. (Illus.). 1978. pap. text ed. 21.95x (ISBN 0-19-913244-5). Oxford U Pr.

Grove, A. T. & Klein, F. Rural Africa. LC 77-82496. (Topics in Geography Ser.). (Illus.). 1979. pap. 9.95 (ISBN 0-521-29282-4). Cambridge U Pr.

Grove, Alvin R., Jr. The Lure & Lore of Trout Fishing. (Illus.). 336p. 1971. boxed 9.95 (ISBN 0-88395-010-3). Freshet Pr.

Grove, Andrew. High Output Management. 1985. pap. 3.95 (ISBN 0-394-72827-0, Vin). Random.

Grove, Andrew S. High-Output Management. 7th ed. LC 83-3412. 288p. 1983. 16.95 (ISBN 0-394-53234-1). Random.

Grove, Bob. Behind the Dial. Force, Rich, ed. 57p. (Orig.). 1977. pap. 4.95 (ISBN 0-88006-001-8, BK 7307). Green Pub Inc.

Grove, C. S., Jr., jt. auth. see Rosato, D. V.

Grove, Charles. The Religion of the Church. 1916. 10.00 (ISBN 0-8414-4694-6). Folcroft.

Grove, Cynthia, jt. auth. see Bargmann, Eve.

Grove, David C. Chalcatzingo: Excavations on the Olmec Frontier. LC 83-51427. (Illus.). 184p. 1984. 29.95 (ISBN 0-500-39019-3). Thames Hudson.

--The Olmec Paintings of Oxtotitlan Cave, Guerrero, Mexico. Bd. with A Study of Olmec Iconography. Joralemon, Peter D; An Olmec Figure at Dumbarton Oaks. Benson, Elizabeth P. (Studies in Pre-Columbian Art & Archaeology: Nos. 6-8). (Illus.). 1970-71. 15.00x (ISBN 0-88402-036-3). Dumbarton Oaks.

Grove, E. J., jt. auth. see Davies, E. L.

Grove, E. L., ed. Analytical Emission Spectroscopy. LC 79-134783. (Analytical Spectroscopy Ser.: Vol.1, Pt.1). pap. 104.30 (ISBN 0-317-08368-6, 2055079). Bks Demand UMI.

--Applied Atomic Spectroscopy. Incl. Vol. 1. 331p. 47.50x (ISBN 0-306-33905-6); Vol. 2. 364p. 55.00 (ISBN 0-306-33906-4). LC 77-17444. (Modern Analytical Chemistry Ser.). (Illus.). 1978. 2 vols. 80.00 (Plenum Pr). Plenum Pub.

Grove, E. L., ed. see Mid-America Spectroscopy Symposium (19th; 1968, Chicago, IL).

Grove, E. L., ed. see Mid-America Spectroscopy Symposium (20th; 1969; Chicago, IL).

Grove, Frank W. The Coins of Mexico. LC 80-54430. 480p. 1981. lib. bdg. 60.00x (ISBN 0-88000-123-2). Quarterman.

Grove, Fred. A Far Trumpet. LC 83-40131. (Double D Westerns Ser.). 192p. 1985. 11.95 (ISBN 0-385-19087-5). Doubleday.

--The Great Horse Race. LC 76-50907. (Double D Western Ser.). 1977. 5.95 (ISBN 0-385-12101-6). Doubleday.

--The Great Horse Race. 1982. pap. 2.25 (ISBN 0-441-30267-X). Ace Bks.

--Match Race. large print ed. LC 83-24378. 386p. 1984. Repr. of 1982 ed. 12.95 (ISBN 0-89621-520-2). Thorndike Pr.

--Phantom Warrior. LC 80-2747. (Double D Western Ser.). 192p. 1981. 10.95 (ISBN 0-385-17044-0). Doubleday.

--Phantom Warrior. large print ed. LC 82-713. 324p. 1982. Repr. of 1981 ed. 11.95 (ISBN 0-89621-349-8). Thorndike Pr.

Grove, George. Beethoven & His Nine Symphonies. 3rd ed. 1898. pap. 5.95 (ISBN 0-486-20334-4). Dover.

--Beethoven & His Nine Symphonies. 3rd ed. 14.75 (ISBN 0-8446-2171-4). Peter Smith.

--Life & Letters of Sir George Grove. Graves, Charles L., ed. LC 77-75177. 1977. Repr. of 1903 ed. lib. bdg. 50.00 (ISBN 0-89341-059-4). Longwood Pub Group.

Grove, Glen A. English Elements & Principles. 1931. 10.00 (ISBN 0-8274-2256-3). R West.

Grove, Hugh D., jt. auth. see Mock, Theodore J.

Grove, J. W., jt. auth. see MacKenzie, William J.

Grove, Joan. Diamond in the Rough. (Candlelight Ecstasy Ser.: No. 337). 192p. 1985. pap. 2.25 (ISBN 0-440-11892-1). Dell.

--One in a Million. (Candlelight Ecstasy Ser.: No. 277). 192p. (Orig.). 1984. pap. 1.95 (ISBN 0-440-16664-0). Dell.

--Token of Love. (Candlelight Ecstasy Ser.: No. 375). (Orig.). 1985. pap. 2.25 (ISBN 0-440-18715-X). Dell.

Grove, John. The Omnibus of Romance. Repr. of 1931 ed. lib. bdg. 25.00 (ISBN 0-8414-4695-4). Folcroft.

Grove, L. C. & Benson, C. T. Finite Reflection Groups. 2nd ed. (Graduate Texts in Mathematics Ser.: Vol. 99). (Illus.). 135p. 1985. 24.00 (ISBN 0-387-96082-1). Springer-Verlag.

Grove, Larry & Hinton, Ted. Ambush: The Real Story of Bonnie & Clyde. (Illus.). 1979. 12.50 (ISBN 0-88319-041-9). Shoal Creek Pub.

Grove, Larry C. Algebra. (Pure & Applied Mathematics Ser.). 1983. 35.00 (ISBN 0-12-304620-3). Acad Pr.

Grove, Lee. Last Dance. LC 83-25355. 324p. 1984. 15.95 (ISBN 0-571-12526-3). Faber & Faber.

Grove, Lilly. Dancing: A Handbook of the Terpsichorean Arts in Diverse Places & Times, Savage & Civilized. LC 76-76138. (Illus.). xviii, 454p. 1969. Repr. of 1895 ed. 40.00x (ISBN 0-8103-3469-0). Gale.

Grove, Linda & Daniels, Christian. State & Society in China: Japanese Perspectives on Ming-Qing Social & Economic Theory. 507p. 1984. 55.00x (ISBN 0-86008-356-X, Pub. by U of Tokyo Japan). Columbia U Pr.

Grove, Maria, jt. auth. see Stauffer, Marge.

Grove, Marjorie J. You'll Die Laughing. (Mystery Puzzler Ser.: No. 5). (Illus., Orig.). 1978. pap. 1.95 (ISBN 0-89083-408-3). Zebra.

--You'll Die Today. (Mystery Puzzlers Ser.: No. 22). (Illus., Orig.). 1979. pap. 1.95 (ISBN 0-685-94562-6). Zebra.

--You'll Die Tomorrow. (Mystery Puzzler Ser.: No. 9). (Illus., Orig.). 1978. pap. 1.95 (ISBN 0-89083-421-0). Zebra.

--You'll Die When You Hear This. (Mystery Puzzlers Ser.: No. 1). (Illus., Orig.). 1978. pap. 1.95 (ISBN 0-89083-395-8). Zebra.

--You'll Die Yesterday. (Mystery Puzzlers Ser.: No. 18). (Illus., Orig.). 1979. pap. 1.95 (ISBN 0-89083-453-9). Zebra.

Grove, Martin A. Beatle Madness. 1978. pap. 1.95 (ISBN 0-532-19179-X). Woodhill.

--Elvis: The Legend Lives. 1978. pap. 1.95 (ISBN 0-532-19197-8). Woodhill.

--The King Is Dead: Elvis Presley. 1977. pap. 1.95 (ISBN 0-532-19162-5). Woodhill.

--Paul McCartney: Beatle with Wings. 1978. pap. 1.75 (ISBN 0-532-17191-8). Woodhill.

--Teen Idols. (Orig.). 1979. pap. 1.95 (ISBN 0-532-19258-3). Woodhill.

--Visions. 496p. (Orig.). 1980. pap. 2.75 (ISBN 0-89083-695-7). Zebra.

Grove, Migs, ed. see Cummings, Paul.

Grove, Migs, ed. see Kraft, James.

Grove, Nancy. Isamu Noguchi: A Study of the Sculpture. Freedberg, S. J., ed. (Outstanding Dissertations in Fine Arts Ser.). (Illus.). 310p. 1985. Repr. of 1983 ed. 55.00 (ISBN 0-8240-6866-1). Garland Pub.

Grove, Nancy & Botnick, Diane. The Sculpture of Isamu Noguchi, Nineteen Twenty-Four to Nineteen Seventy-Nine: A Catalogue. LC 70-28698. (Garland Reference Library of the Humanities: Vol. 207). 625p. 1980. lib. bdg. 73.00 (ISBN 0-8240-9550-2). Garland Pub.

Grove, Pat. Sweet & Sour: Humorous Cartoons. 7.50 (ISBN 0-392-08426-0, SpS). Sportshelf.

Grove, Pearce S., ed. Nonprint Media in Academic Libraries. LC 74-23972. (ACRL Publications in Librarianship: No. 34). 239p. 1975. pap. 11.00x (ISBN 0-8389-0153-0). ALA.

Grove Press Victorian Library. Love Victorian Style: III. 1983. Boxed Set. pap. 15.80 (ISBN 0-394-62010-0, B497, BC). Grove.

Grove, Richard. The Cambridgeshire Coprolite Mining Rush. (Cambridge Town, Gown & County Ser.: Vol. 1). (Illus.). 1976. pap. 4.25 (ISBN 0-902675-61-3). Oleander Pr.

Grove, Robert B. Communication Monitoring & Communications Projects. 128p. 1979. pap. 6.50 (ISBN 0-8104-0894-5). Hayden.

Grove, Roger. Light Blue. 16p. (gr. 3-12). 1973. pap. text ed. 5.95 (ISBN 0-87487-648-6). Birch Tree Gr.

--Riches of Rag. (Frances Clark Library for Piano Students). 16p. (Orig.). (gr. k-12). 1976. pap. text ed. 5.95 (ISBN 0-87487-188-3). Birch Tree Gr.

Grove, Simon, tr. see Togawa, Masako.

Grove, Tami. A Collective History of the Early Years of Settlement in Surprise Valley. (ANCRR Research Paper: No. 4). 1977. 7.50 (ISBN 0-686-38933-6). Assn NC Records.

Grove, W. B. British Stem-&-Leaf-Fungi: Coelomysycetes, 2 vols. (Illus.). 1967. Set. pap. 35.00 (ISBN 3-7682-0500-2). Lubrecht & Cramer.

Grover, A. K. & Daniel, E. E., eds. Calcium & Contractility: Smooth Muscle. LC 84-28841. (Contemporary Biomedicine Ser.). (Illus.). 512p. 1985. 69.50 (ISBN 0-89603-066-0). Humana.

Grover, Carrie B. A Heritage of Songs. LC 77-25507. 1977. lib. bdg. 20.00 (ISBN 0-8414-4459-5). Folcroft.

Grover, David H. Debaters & Dynamiters: The Story of the Haywood Trial. LC 64-63331. (Studies in History Ser: No. 4). (Illus.). 328p. 1964. pap. 8.95 (ISBN 0-87071-318-3). Oreg St U Pr.

Grover, Dorys C. A Solitary Voice: A Collection of Essays on Vardis Fisher. 1973. 69.95 (ISBN 0-87700-198-7). Revisionist Pr.

--Vardis Fisher: The Novelist As Poet. (Vardis Fisher Ser.). 1973. 69.95 (ISBN 0-87700-197-9). Revisionist Pr.

Grover, Eulalie O. Robert Louis Stevenson: A Teller of Tales. LC 71-164308. x, 265p. (YA) 1975. Repr. of 1940 ed. 40.00x (ISBN 0-8103-4080-1). Gale.

Grover, Eulalie O., ed. My Caravan. LC 31-29146. (Granger Poetry Library). (Illus.). 1976. Repr. of 1931 ed. 19.50x (ISBN 0-89609-020-5). Granger Bk.

Grover, F & Wallace, P. Laboratory Organization & Management. (Illus.). 1979. text ed. 29.95 (ISBN 0-408-70793-3). Butterworth.

Grover, Frank R. A Brief History of Les Cheneaux Islands. (Illus.). 1982. pap. 7.75 (ISBN 0-912382-10-4). Black Letter.

Grover, Frederick W. Inductance Calculations: Working Formulas & Tables. LC 82-126260. 304p. 1982. Repr. of 1946 ed. text ed. 29.95x (ISBN 0-87664-557-0). Instru Soc.

Grover, J. R. Management of Plutonium Contaminated Waste. (Radioactive Waste Management Ser.: Vol. III). 196p. 1982. 30.00 (ISBN 3-7186-0110-9). Harwood Academic.

Grover, Jania Z., jt. auth. see Noggle, Anne.

Grover, John. Review of Waste Management Organizations. (Radioactive Waste Management & the Nuclear Fuel Cycle Ser. (Special Journal Issue)). 116p. 1984. pap. text ed. 28.00 (ISBN 3-7186-0202-4). Harwood Academic.

Grover, John H., ed. Allocation of Fisheries Resources. 623p. 1982. pap. 25.00 (ISBN 0-913235-23-7). AM Fisheries Soc.

Grover, Lee, jt. auth. see Grover, Ray.

Grover, Marshall. Feud at Mendoza. 1977. pap. 1.25 (ISBN 0-505-51187-8, Pub. by Tower Bks). Dorchester Pub Co.

Grover, Philip, jt. auth. see Pound, Omar.

Grover, Philip, ed. Ezra Pound: the London Years, Nineteen Eight to Nineteen Twenty: The London Years, 1908-1920. LC 77-78316. (Illus.). 1978. 29.50 (ISBN 0-404-16006-9). AMS Pr.

Grover, Philip L. Chemical Carcinogens & DNA, 2 vols. 1979. Vol. 1, 256p. 79.50 (ISBN 0-8493-5303-3); Vol. 2, 224p. 74.50 (ISBN 0-8493-5304-1). CRC Pr.

Grover, Ralph S. Ernest Chausson: The Man & His Music. LC 77-74404. 248p. 1979. 20.00 (ISBN 0-685-19067-6). Bucknell U Pr.

Grover, Ray. New Zealand. (World Bibliographical Ser.: No. 18). 254p. 1980. 36.25 (ISBN 0-903450-31-3). ABC-Clio.

Grover, Ray & Grover, Lee. Art Glass Nouveau. LC 67-10197. 1967. 49.50 (ISBN 0-8048-0032-4). C E Tuttle.

--Carved & Decorated European Art Glass. LC 71-94025. (Illus.). 1970. 55.00 (ISBN 0-8048-0707-8). C E Tuttle.

--English Cameo Glass. (Illus.). 482p. cancelled (ISBN 0-517-53815-6). Wallace-Homestead.

Grover, Robert, ed. Great Plains Libraries, Vol. 20. 1982. pap. 5.00 (ISBN 0-686-35859-7). Sch Lib Sci.

Grover, Satish. The Architecture of India-Buddhist & Hindu. (Illus.). 1980. text ed. 42.50x (ISBN 0-7069-0685-3, Pub. by Vikas India). Advent NY.

--The Architecture of India: Islamic. (Illus.). 280p. 1981. text ed. 45.00x (ISBN 0-7069-1130-X, Pub. by Vikas India). Advent NY.

--The Architecture of India: Islamic. 280p. 1982. 70.00x (ISBN 0-7069-1130-X, Pub. by Garlandfold England). State Mutual Bk.

Grover, Sonja. Analysis of Human Behavior: A Psychological Laboratory Manual. 130p. 1985. text ed. 8.95x (ISBN 0-8290-0725-3). Irvington.

Grover, Sonja C. The Cognitive Basis of the Intellect: A Response to Jensen's "Bias in Mental Testing". LC 81-40303. 148p. (Orig.). 1981. lib. bdg. 21.75 (ISBN 0-8191-1741-2); pap. text ed. 10.00 (ISBN 0-8191-1742-0). U Pr of Amer.

--Toward a Psychology of the Scientist: Implications of Psychological Research for Contemporary Philosophy of Science. LC 80-6092. 102p. (Orig.). lib. bdg. 18.25 (ISBN 0-8191-1574-6); pap. text ed. 8.50 (ISBN 0-8191-1575-4). U Pr of Amer.

Grover-Rogoff, Annis, ed. see Anderson, Ross & Perry, Barbara.

Groves & Gray. A Synopsis of Otolaryngology. 4th ed. 1985. write for info. (ISBN 0-7236-0772-9). PSG Pub Co.

Groves, jt. auth. see Ballantyne.

Groves, jt. auth. see Horwitz.

Groves, Byron W., jt. auth. see Lynch, Michael.

Groves, C. Ancestors for the Pigs: Taxonomy & Phylogeny of the Genus SUS. (Department of Prehistory, Research School of Pacific Studies Technical Bulletin: No. 3). 96p. 1982. pap. text ed. 8.80 (ISBN 0-909596-75-1, Pub. by ANUP Australia). Australia N U P.

Groves, D. L. & Groves, S. L. Developing a Time Budget. 35p. 1978. pap. text ed. 4.00 (ISBN 0-940414-00-7). Appalach Assoc.

--Planning & Organizing Leisure Resources. 15p. 1978. pap. text ed. 3.00 (ISBN 0-940414-02-3). Appalach Assoc.

Groves, D. L., jt. auth. see Groves, S. L.

Groves, David N. & Poirot, James L. Computers & Data Processing. (Illus.). 1978. text ed. 12.95 (ISBN 0-88408-101-X). Sterling Swift.

Groves, Donald G. & Hunt, Lee M. The Ocean World Encyclopedia. LC 79-21093. (Illus.). 1980. 49.95 (ISBN 0-07-025010-3). McGraw.

Groves, Donald G., jt. auth. see Hunt, Lee M.

Groves, Dulcie, jt. ed. see Finch, Janet.

Groves, E. W. Vascular Plant Collections from the Tristan de Cunha Group of Islands. 72p. 50.00x (ISBN 0-686-78669-6, Pub. by Brit Mus Pubns England). State Mutual Bk.

Groves, Ernest R. The American Woman: The Feminine Side of a Masculine Civilization. LC 72-2605. (American Women Ser.: Images & Realities). 478p. 1972. Repr. of 1944 ed. 26.50 (ISBN 0-405-04460-7). Ayer Co Pubs.

Groves, Ernest R. & Ogburn, William F. American Marriage & Family Relationships. LC 75-38129. (Demography Ser.). (Illus.). 1976. Repr. of 1928 ed. 40.00x (ISBN 0-405-07983-4). Ayer Co Pubs.

Groves, F. P. Nottingham City Transport. 96p. 1981. 35.00x (ISBN 0-903839-25-3, Pub. by Transport). State Mutual Bk.

Groves, H. E., jt. auth. see Sheridan, Lionel A.

Groves, Harold M. Federal Tax Treatment of the Family. LC 76-55946. (Brookings Institution, Studies of Government Finance Ser). xii, 116p. 1977. Repr. of 1963 ed. lib. bdg. 15.00x (ISBN 0-8371-9425-3, GRFT). Greenwood.

--Tax Philosophers: Two Hundred Years of Thought in Great Britain & the United States. Curran, Donald J., ed. LC 74-5901. 168p. 1974. 29.50x (ISBN 0-299-06660-6). U of Wis Pr.

Groves, Ivor D., Jr., ed. Acoustic Transducers. LC 81-4113. (Benchmark Papers in Acoustics Ser.: Vol. 14). 391p. 1981. 53.95 (ISBN 0-87933-387-1). Van Nos Reinhold.

Groves, James & Bullock-Webster, George R. The British Charophyta, 2 Vols. Repr. of 1920 ed. Set. 46.00 (ISBN 0-384-20130-X). Johnson Repr.
Groves, John, jt. ed. see Ballantyne, John.
Groves, L., ed. Physical Education for Special Needs. LC 78-68389. 1979. pap. 11.95 (ISBN 0-521-29471-1). Cambridge U Pr.
Groves, Leslie M. Now It Can Be Told: The Story of the Manhattan Project. (Quality Paperbacks Ser.). (Illus.). 464p. 1983. pap. 9.95 (ISBN 0-306-80189-2). Da Capo.
Groves, Leslie R. Now It Can Be Told: The Story of the Manhattan Project. LC 75-1001. (FDR & the Era of the New Deal Ser). 465p. 1975. Repr. of 1962 ed. lib. bdg. 39.50 (ISBN 0-306-70738-1). Da Capo.
Groves, Martha, jt. ed. see Warden, Rob.
Groves, Michael. Parental Technology Manual. 132p. 1985. pap. text ed. 29.95 (ISBN 0-935184-04-X). Interpharm.
Groves, Norris A. Christian Devotedness. pap. 1.95 (ISBN 0-937396-63-X). Walterick Pubs.
Groves, P. A., jt. auth. see Wiedel, J. W.
Groves, Philip M. & Schlesinger, Kurt. Introduction to Biological Psychology. 2nd ed. 752p. 1982. text ed. write for info. (ISBN 0-697-06644-4); instrs. manual avail. (ISBN 0-697-06646-0); study guide avail. (ISBN 0-697-06645-2); transparencies avail. (ISBN 0-697-06653-3). Wm C Brown.
Groves, R. H., jt. auth. see Costin, A. B.
Groves, R. H., ed. Australian Vegetation. LC 80-40421. (Illus.). 350p. 1981. 75.00 (ISBN 0-521-23436-0). Cambridge U Pr.
Groves, R. H. & Burdon, J. J., eds. The Ecology of Biological Invasions. (Illus.). 225p. Date not set. price not set (ISBN 0-521-30355-9). Cambridge U Pr.
Groves, R. H. & Ride, W. D., eds. Species at Risk: Research in Australia. 250p. 1982. 40.00 (ISBN 0-387-11416-5). Springer-Verlag.
Groves, Reginald. Conrad Noel & the Thaxted Movement. LC 68-3219. 1968. lib. bdg. 27.50x (ISBN 0-678-08010-0). Kelley.
--Sharpen the Sickle. LC 74-22744. (Labor Movement in Fiction & Non-Fiction). 1976. Repr. of 1949 ed. 20.00 (ISBN 0-404-58496-9). AMS Pr.
Groves, Richard & Camaione, David N. Concepts in Kinesiology. 2nd ed. pap. text ed. 18.95 (ISBN 0-03-062372-3, CBS C). SCP.
Groves, Robert M. & Kahn, Robert L. Surveys by Telephone: A National Comparison with Personal Interviews. LC 79-51703. (Quantitative Studies in Social Relations Ser.). 1979. 37.50 (ISBN 0-12-304650-5). Acad Pr.
Groves, S. L. & Groves, D. L. Self-Evaluation. 20p. 1978. pap. text ed. 4.00 (ISBN 0-940414-01-5). Appalach Assoc.
Groves, S. L., jt. auth. see Groves, D. L.
Groves, Seli & Associated Press Editors. Soaps: A Pictorial History of America's Daytime Dramas. (Illus.). 224p. (Orig.). 1983. pap. 9.95 (ISBN 0-8092-5577-4). Contemp Bks.
Groves, Sheila & Stowell, Gordon. All Change. (Tortoise Tales Ser.). (Orig.). 1981. pap. 0.79 (ISBN 0-8010-3773-5). Baker Bk.
--Dolly's Revenge. (Tortoise Tales Ser.). (Orig.). 1981. pap. 0.79 (ISBN 0-8010-3772-7). Baker Bk.
--Hedgehog Law. (Tortoise Tales Ser.). (Orig.). 1981. pap. 0.79 (ISBN 0-8010-3775-1). Baker Bk.
--Leapalong. (Tortoise Tales Ser.). (Orig.). 1981. pap. 0.79 (ISBN 0-8010-3770-0). Baker Bk.
--Whisperings. (Tortoise Tales Ser.). 1981. pap. 0.79 (ISBN 0-8010-3774-3). Baker Bk.
Groves, Theodore, ed. see Symposium, University of Wisconsin, Madison, October, 1974.
Groves, William. Native Education & Culture-Contact in New Guinea, a Scientific Approach. LC 75-32819. Repr. of 1936 ed. 17.50 (ISBN 0-404-14123-4). AMS Pr.
Grow, Douglas, jt. auth. see Barnidge, Thomas.
Grow, Gerald. Florida Parks: A Guide to Camping in Nature. (Illus., Orig.). 1983. pap. 9.95 (ISBN 0-939638-51-7); 14.95 (ISBN 0-939638-52-5). Longleaf Pubns.
Grow, Laurence. The Old House Book of Outdoor Living Spaces. (Illus.). 96p. (Orig.). 1981. 15.00 (ISBN 0-446-51219-2); pap. 8.95 (ISBN 0-446-97556-7). Warner Bks.
Grow, Lawrence. The Catalogue of Contemporary Design: A Style & Sourcebook Resource Book of Interior Design from 30's Modern to Post Modern. LC 83-15150. (Illus.). 256p. 1983. 10.95 (ISBN 0-02-085230-4). Macmillan.
--Classic Old House Plans. LC 84-881. (Illus.). 128p. (Orig.). 1984. pap. 8.95 (ISBN 0-915590-41-7). Main Street.
--Country Architecture: Old-Fashioned Designs for Gazebos, Summerhouses, Springhouses, Smokehouses, Stables, Greenhouses, Carriage Houses, Outhouses, Icehouses, Barns, Doghouses, Sheds, & Other Outbuildings. (Illus.). 128p. (Orig.). 1985. pap. 9.95 (ISBN 0-915590-80-8). Main Street.
--The Fourth Old House Catalog. LC 84-15488. (Illus.). 224p. (Orig.). 1984. pap. 11.95 (ISBN 0-915590-52-2). Main Street.
--Modern Style: A Catalogue of Contemporary Design. (Illus.). 224p. (Orig.). 1985. pap. 15.95 (ISBN 0-915590-83-2). Main Street.
--The Old House Book of Bedrooms. (Illus.). 96p. (Orig.). 1980. 15.00 (ISBN 0-446-51216-8); pap. 7.95 (ISBN 0-446-97553-2). Warner Bks.
--The Old House Book of Living Rooms & Parlors. (Illus.). 96p. (Orig.). 1980. 15.00 (ISBN 0-446-51215-X); pap. 7.95 (ISBN 0-446-97552-4). Warner Bks.
--The Warner Collector's Guide to Pressed Glass. (Illus.). 256p. (Orig.). 1982. pap. 9.95 (ISBN 0-446-97709-8). Warner Bks.
Grow, Lawrence & Von Zweck, Dina. American Victorian: A Style & Source Book. LC 83-48789. (Illus.). 244p. 1985. pap. 15.95i (ISBN 0-06-091283-9, PL 1283, PL). Har-Row.
Grow, Lawrence & Zweck, Dina von. American Victorian: A Style & Source Book. LC 84-48789. (Illus.). 223p. 1984. 33.65 (ISBN 0-06-015209-5, HarpT). Har-Row.
Grow, Lawrence, ed. The Old House Book of Kitchens & Dining Rooms. (Illus.). 96p. (Orig.). 1981. 16.95 (ISBN 0-446-51233-8); pap. 9.95 (ISBN 0-446-97544-3). Warner Bks.
Grow, Lawrence, jt. ed. see Lancaster, Clay.
Grow, Lucille. Early Childrearing by Young Mothers: A Research Study. LC 79-53504. 1979. pap. text ed. 9.95 (ISBN 0-87868-138-8, YF-1). Child Welfare.
Grow, Lucille J. & Shapiro, Deborah. Black Children-White Parents: A Study of Transracial Adoption. LC 74-29169. (Orig.). 1974. pap. 7.95 (ISBN 0-87868-152-3, A-37). Child Welfare.
--Transracial Adoption Today: Views of Adoptive Parents & Social Workers. LC 75-7553. 1975. pap. 5.95 (ISBN 0-87868-153-1, A-38). Child Welfare.
Grow, Lynn M. The Prose Style of Samuel Taylor Coleridge. (Salzburg Studies in English Literature, Romantic Reassessment: No. 54). 161p. 1976. pap. text ed. 25.50x (ISBN 0-391-01395-5). Humanities.
Grow, Michael. The Good Neighbor Policy & Authoritarianism in Paraguay: United States Economic Expansion & Great - Power Rivalry in Latin America During World War II. LC 81-11. (Illus.). 164p. 1981. 19.95x (ISBN 0-7006-0213-5). U Pr of KS.
--Scholars' Guide to Washington, D. C., for Latin American & Caribbean Studies. LC 78-21316. (Scholar's Guide to Washington, D. C. Ser.: No. 2). 346p. 1979. text ed. 25.00x (ISBN 0-87474-486-5); pap. text ed. 9.95x (ISBN 0-87474-487-3). Smithsonian.
Grow, Thomas A. Construction: A Guide for the Profession. (Illus.). 224p. 1975. ref. ed. 23.95 (ISBN 0-13-169326-3). P-H.
Growe, Bernd, jt. auth. see Franz, Erich.
Growing Child-Growing Parent Editors. Growing Parent: A Sourcebook for Families. 128p. (Orig.). 1983. pap. 6.95 (ISBN 0-8092-5486-7). Contemp Bks.
Growney, J. S. Mathematics in Daily Life: Making Decisions & Solving Problems. 496p. 1985. price not set (ISBN 0-07-025015-4). McGraw.
Growoll, Adolf. American Book Clubs: Their Beginnings & History & a Bibliography of Their Publications. 1965. 29.50 (ISBN 0-8337-1477-5). B Franklin.
--American Book Clubs: Their Beginnings & History & a Bibliography of Their Publications. 59.95 (ISBN 0-87968-595-6). Gordon Pr.
--Book-Trade Bibliography in the U. S. in the Nineteenth Century. 59.95 (ISBN 0-87968-774-6). Gordon Pr.
--Book Trade Bibliography in the United States in the 19th Century. 1898. 18.50 (ISBN 0-8337-1478-3). B Franklin.
Growse, F. S., tr. see Prasad, R. C.
Growse, F. S., tr. see Tulasidas.
Groymko, A. A., et al, eds. Soviet Peace Efforts on Eve of World War Two. 68p. 1976. 8.95 (ISBN 0-8285-0500-4, Pub. by Progress Pubs USSR). Imported Pubns.
Groza, Vivian & Shelley, Susanne. Precalculus Mathematics. LC 76-158479. 1972. text ed. 14.95x (ISBN 0-03-077670-8). Irvington.
Groza, Vivian S. Arithmetic. 1982. 27.95 (ISBN 0-03-060109-6, CBS C); instr's manual 10.95 (ISBN 0-03-060111-8). SCP.
--College Algebra. 1980. text ed. 27.95 (ISBN 0-03-040376-6, CBS C). SCP.
--Elementary Algebra. 3rd ed. LC 80-53936. (Illus.). 660p. 1981. pap. text ed. 28.95x (ISBN 0-03-057719-5). HR&W.
--Elementary Algebra. 4th ed. 1986. pap. text ed. 26.95 (ISBN 0-03-006079-6, CBS C); instr's manual 9.95 (ISBN 0-03-006069-9). SCP.
--Trigonometry. 1980. text ed. 27.95 (ISBN 0-7216-4325-6, CBS C). SCP.
Groza, Vivian S. & Sellers, Gene. Algebra & Trigonometry. 1982. pap. 29.95 (ISBN 0-03-060107-X, CBS C). SCP.
--Intermediate Algebra. 2nd ed. 1981. pap. text ed. 27.95 (ISBN 0-03-057722-5, CBS C); pap. 9.95 instr's manual (ISBN 0-03-058256-3). SCP.
--Plane Trigonometry. (Illus.). 1979. pap. text ed. 27.95 (ISBN 0-7216-4325-6). HR&W.
Grozdanic, S., jt. ed. see Pasic, N.
Grozdic, Oton. Serbo-Croatian Grammar & Reader. 1969. 12.95x (ISBN 0-02-845540-1). Hafner.
Grozier, Edwin A. One Hundred World's Best Novels Condensed. 535p. 1984. Repr. of 1919 ed. lib. bdg. 40.00 (ISBN 0-89984-748-X). Century Bookbindery.
--One Hundred World's Best Novels Condensed. 535p. Repr. of 1940 ed. lib. bdg. 40.00 (ISBN 0-8414-4325-4). Folcroft.
Grozny, Yvonne. The Fables of Phonecius. LC 78-68416. 1978. 10.00 (ISBN 0-932364-00-4). Ann Arbor Bk.
Grriswold, David H., jt. auth. see Merris, William E.
Grua, Gaston. Jurisprudence Universelle et Theodicee Selon Leibniz. Sleigh, R. C., Jr., ed. LC 84-48417. (The Philosophy of Leibniz Ser.). 415p. 1985. lib. bdg. 65.00 (ISBN 0-8240-6530-1). Garland Pub.
--La Justice Humaine Selon Leibniz. Sleigh, R. C., Jr., ed. LC 84-48418. (The Philosophy of Leibniz Ser.). 548p. 1985. lib. bdg. 80.00 (ISBN 0-8240-6531-X). Garland Pub.
Gruau, Rene. Rene Gruau. 136p. 1984. 45.00 (ISBN 0-8478-0566-2). Rizzoli Intl.
Grub, Phillip D., et al. Multinational Enterprise in Transition: Selected Readings & Essays. 2nd ed. LC 83-25187. xx, 588p. 1984. 24.95 (ISBN 0-87850-043-X); pap. 17.95x (ISBN 0-87850-044-8). Darwin Pr.
Grubaum, Adolf. Validation of Clinical Psychoanalysis. Date not set. price not set (BN#06722). Intl Univs Pr.
Grubb & Ellis, jt. auth. see Real Estate Education Company.
Grubb, C. A. & Phares, M. I. Industrialization: A New Concept for Housing. LC 75-143972. (Special Studies in U.S. Economic, Social & Political Issues). 1972. 38.50x (ISBN 0-89197-794-5). Irvington.
--Industrialization: A New Concept for Housing. (Special Studies in U.S. Economic, Social & Political Issues). 1984. pap. text ed. 9.95 (ISBN 0-8290-1561-2). Irvington.
Grubb, Chandra. Colour Atlas of Breast Cytopathology. LC 80-54912. (Illus.). 64p. 1981. 52.00 (ISBN 0-89640-049-2). Igaku-Shoin.
Grubb, David. Beneath the Visiting Moon. 186p. 1983. 13.95 (ISBN 0-907746-14-4, Pub. by A Mott Ltd). Longwood Pub Group.
Grubb, Davis. Ancient Lights. LC 81-51881. 544p. 1982. 25.00 (ISBN 0-670-12262-9); pap. text ed. 10.95 (ISBN 0-670-12263-7). Viking.
--The Siege of Three Eighteen: Thirteen Mystical Stories. LC 78-61067. 180p. 1978. 9.00 (ISBN 0-686-37046-5). Back Fork Bks.
Grubb, Frederick, ed. see Roberts, Michael.
Grubb, Jake. The Sailboard Book. (Illus.). 208p. 1985. pap. 15.95 (ISBN 0-393-30224-5). Norton.
Grubb, John D., ed. see King, C. D.
Grubb, Mary L, ed. see King, C. D.
Grubb, Norman. Liberating Secret. 1978. pap. 3.95 (ISBN 0-87508-225-4). Chr Lit.
--Who Am I? 1975. pap. 2.95 (ISBN 0-87508-227-0). Chr Lit.
--Yes I Am. 1982. pap. text ed. 4.95 (ISBN 0-87508-206-8). Chr Lit.
Grubb, Norman P. C. T. Studd. 1972. pap. 5.95 (ISBN 0-87508-202-5). Chr Lit.
--Continuous Revival. 1961. pap. 1.50 (ISBN 0-87508-210-6). Chr Lit.
--Deep Things of God. 1970. pap. 4.95 (ISBN 0-87508-209-2). Chr Lit.
--God Unlimited. 1972. pap. 4.95 (ISBN 0-87508-226-2). Chr Lit.
--Law of Faith. 1969. pap. 3.95 (ISBN 0-87508-223-8). Chr Lit.
--Leap of Faith. 1964. pap. 5.95 (ISBN 0-87508-215-7). Chr Lit.
--Once Caught, No Escape. 1969. pap. 4.95 (ISBN 0-87508-218-1). Chr Lit.
--Rees Howells: Intercessor. 1964-1967. pap. 4.95 (ISBN 0-87508-219-X). Chr Lit.
--Spontaneous You. 1970. pap. 3.50 (ISBN 0-87508-224-6). Chr Lit.
--Touching the Invisible. 1960. pap. 1.95 (ISBN 0-87508-222-X). Chr Lit.
Grubb, Norton & Glover, Robert. The Persistent Dilemmas of Preparing for Work: Occupational Training Programs in Texas. l ed. LC 83-81383. (PRP Ser.: No.55). 77p. 1983. 8.00 (ISBN 0-89940-657-2). LBJ Sch Pub Aff.
Grubb, Philip W. Patents for Chemists. (Illus.). 1982. 45.00x (ISBN 0-19-855153-3). Oxford U Pr.
Grubb, R. Genetic Markers of Human Immunoglobulins. LC 72-121989. (Molecular Biology, Biochemistry & Biophysics Ser.: Vol. 9). (Illus.). 1970. 31.00 (ISBN 0-387-05211-9). Springer-Verlag.
Grubb, R. E. A Design Language for Computer-Assisted Instruction. (Illus.). 155p. 1974. pap. text ed. 20.00 (ISBN 0-87567-103-9). Entelek.
Grubb, Reba D. Hospital Manuals: A Guide to Development & Maintenance. LC 81-8023. 183p. 1981. text ed. 49.00 (ISBN 0-89443-366-0). Aspen Systems.
Grubb, Reba D. & Mueller, Carolyn J. Designing Hospital Training Programs. (Illus.). 216p. 1975. 27.75x (ISBN 0-398-03316-1). C C Thomas.
Grubb, Reba D. & Ondov, Geraldine. Operating Room Guidelines: An Illustrated Manual. LC 78-31422. (Illus.). 320p. 1979. pap. text ed. 18.95 (ISBN 0-8016-1985-8). Mosby.
Grubb, Reba D., jt. auth. see Vukovich, Virginia C.
Grubb, Thomas. Singing in French: A Manual of French Diction & French Vocal Repertoire. LC 77-18473. 1979. pap. text ed. 13.95 (ISBN 0-02-870790-7). Schirmer Bks.
Grubb, W. Norton, jt. ed. see Lazerson, Marvin.
Grubb, W. Norton, et al. Far, Far to Go: Public Spending for Children & Youth in Texas. 78p. 1982. pap. 5.50 (ISBN 0-89940-805-2). LBJ Sch Pub Aff.
Grubbs, Daisy. Modeling a Likeness in Clay. (Illus.). 160p. 1982. 19.95 (ISBN 0-8230-3094-6). Watson-Guptill.
Grubbs, David. Claim What Is Yours. 1984. 8.95 (ISBN 0-87162-400-1, D3060). Warner Pr.
Grubbs, Donald H. Cry from the Cotton: The Southern Tenant Farmers' Union & the New Deal. LC 72-109464. (Illus.). xix, 218p. 1971. 20.00 (ISBN 0-8078-1156-4). U of NC Pr.
Grubbs, Donald S. Funding. (Rules for Operation of Qualified Plans Ser.). 27p. 1978. pap. 6.00 (ISBN 0-317-31173-5, B360). Am Law Inst.
--Integration of Plans with Social Security: No. B353. 2nd ed. (Requirements for Qualification of Plans Ser.). 27p. 1979. pap. 6.00 (ISBN 0-317-31157-3). Am Law Inst.
--Target Benefit Plans: No. B331. (Kinds of Qualified Plans Ser.). 29p. 1980. pap. 6.00 (ISBN 0-317-31069-0). Am Law Inst.
Grubbs, H. A. Damien Mitton. (Elliott Monographs: Vol. 29). 1932. pap. 15.00 (ISBN 0-527-02632-8). Kraus Repr.
Grubbs, Henry A. Paul Valery. LC 67-25204. (World Author Ser.). 1968. lib. bdg. 15.95 (ISBN 0-8057-2920-8). Irvington.
Grubbs, Henry A., jt. auth. see Wiley, W. Leon.
Grubbs, Jim. The Commodore Ham's Companion. Grubbs, Jon, ed. LC 85-61585. 100p. (Orig.). 1985. pap. 19.95 (ISBN 0-931387-24-8). Qsky Pub.
Grubbs, Jon, ed. see Grubbs, Jim.
Grubbs, R. & Weaver, D. H. Typing Improvement Practice for Manual Typists. 1984. write for info. (ISBN 0-07-025065-0). McGraw.
Grubbs, Robert & Popham, Estelle. Gregg Shorthand for Colleges, Speed Building. (Diamond Jubilee Ser). (Illus.). 448p. 1976. text ed. 30.40 (ISBN 0-07-025080-4). McGraw.
Grubbs, Robert L. & Ober, B. Scot. Gregg Shorthand for Colleges, Speed Building. Lemaster, A. James, ed. LC 79-11915. (Series 90). (Illus.). 448p. 1981. text ed. 30.40 (ISBN 0-07-025055-3). McGraw.
Grubbs, Robert L. & White, James L. Sustained Timed Writings. 4th ed. 96p. 1982. pap. 7.72 (ISBN 0-07-025063-4). McGraw.
Grubbs, Robert L., et al. Exploratory Business. 6th ed. (Illus.). (gr. 9-10). 1978. text ed. 9.32 (ISBN 0-07-025050-2). McGraw.
Grubbs, Sylvia. Friends, a Guest Book. 1982. gift, padded cover 7.95 (ISBN 0-87162-261-0, J1018). Warner Pr.
Grubbstrom, R. W. & Hunterhuber, H. H., eds. Production Economics Trends & Issues: Proceedings of the Third International Working Seminar on Production Economics, Igls, Austria Feb. 20-24 1985. (Studies in Production & Engineering Economics: No. 4). 328p. 1985. Repr. 83.50 (ISBN 0-444-42500-4). Elsevier.
Grube, Bruce F. Death, Politics, & the Hubris of Consciousness. LC 81-40600. 120p. (Orig.). 1982. lib. bdg. 20.50 (ISBN 0-8191-2037-5); pap. text ed. 9.25 (ISBN 0-8191-2038-3). U Pr of Amer.
Grube, Frank, ed. The Big Book of Sailing: The Sailors, the Ships, & the Sea. LC 79-11549. (Illus.). 309p. 1979. 49.95 (ISBN 0-8120-5324-9). Barron.
Grube, Frank W. Flashbacks to the Old Times. LC 84-90048. 101p. 1984. 7.95 (ISBN 0-533-06129-6). Vantage.
Grube, G. M. On Poetry & Style Aristotle. 1958. pap. text ed. write for info. (ISBN 0-02-348500-0). Macmillan.
--Plato's Thought. Zeyl, Donald J., ed. LC 80-14588. 368p. 1980. 25.00 (ISBN 0-915144-79-4); pap. text ed. 8.50 (ISBN 0-915144-80-8). Hackett Pub.
Grube, G. M., tr. see Aristotle.
Grube, G. M., tr. see Plato.
Grube, G. M., tr. & intro. by see Plato.
Grube, G. M., tr. see Plato.
Grube, G. M. A., ed. & tr. see Aurelius, Marcus.
Grube, George M. The Greek & Roman Critics. LC 68-90371. (Canadian University Paperbooks Ser.: No. 72). pap. 96.00 (ISBN 0-317-27036-2, 2023628). Bks Demand UMI.
Grube, Joel W., jt. auth. see Ball-Rokeach, Sandra.
Grube, Max. Story of Meininger. Cole, Wendell, ed. Koller, Anne M., tr. LC 63-23352. (Bks of the Theatre: No. 4). (Illus.). 1963. 8.95x (ISBN 0-87024-027-7). U of Miami Pr.
Grube, Oswald W., jt. auth. see Bush-Brown, Albert.
Grubel, Herbert F. International Economics. rev. ed. 1981. 27.95 (ISBN 0-256-02493-6). Irwin.
Grubel, Herbert G. Domestic Origins of the Monetary Approach to the Balance of Payments. LC 76-21698. (Princeton University, International Finance Section, Essays in International Finance Ser.: No. 117). pap. 20.00 (ISBN 0-317-29051-7, 2019247). Bks Demand UMI.
--Forward Exchange, Speculation, & the International Flow of Capital. LC 65-21490. 1966. 17.50x (ISBN 0-8047-0269-1). Stanford U Pr.

--The International Monetary System. (Education Ser.). 208p. 1984. pap. 6.95 (ISBN 0-14-080818-3). Penguin.

Grubel, Herbert G. & Scott, Anthony. The Brain Drain: Determinants, Measurement & Welfare Effects. 165p. 1977. text ed. 13.50x (ISBN 0-88920-037-8, Pub. by Laurier U Pr Canada); pap. text ed. 9.75x (ISBN 0-88920-036-X). Humanities.

Grubel, Herbert G., ed. World Monetary Reform: Plans & Issues. 1963. 30.00x (ISBN 0-8047-0169-5). Stanford U Pr.

Grubel, Ralph O., ed. Metallurgy of Elemental & Compound Semiconductors: Proceedings. LC 61-9443. (Metallurgical Society Conference Ser.: Vol. 12). pap. 126.80 (ISBN 0-317-08023-7, 2000675). Bks Demand UMI.

Gruber, jt. ed. see Elton.

Gruber, A., ed. Mignot De la Voye: Treatise on Music. (Musical Theorists in Translation Ser.: Vol. 11). 96p. 1972. lib. bdg. 20.00 (ISBN 0-912024-31-3). Inst Mediaeval Mus.

Gruber, Alain. Silverware. LC 82-50422. (Illus.). 306p. 1982. 75.00 (ISBN 0-8478-0440-2). Rizzoli Intl.

Gruber, Alan R. Children in Foster Care: Destitute, Neglected...Betrayed. LC 77-521. 226p. 1978. 24.95 (ISBN 0-87705-265-4). Human Sci Pr.

Gruber, Albion, ed. see Brossard.

Gruber, Arnold, jt. auth. see Spiegel, Herbert J.

Gruber, Barbara. Barbara Jean's Household Money Tips. 256p. 1983. pap. 9.95 (ISBN 0-525-93294-1, 0966-290). Dutton.

--Classroom Management. (Instant Idea Bks.). (Illus.). 64p. 1985. 5.95 (ISBN 0-86734-056-8, FS-8306). Schaffer Pubns.

--Managing Your Classroom. (Instant Idea Books). (Illus.). 64p. 1983. 5.95 (ISBN 0-86734-048-7, FS-8302). Schaffer Pubns.

--Reading Ideas Ready to Use! (Instant Idea Bks.). (Illus.). 64p. 1983. 5.95 (ISBN 0-86734-049-5, FS-8303). Schaffer Pubns.

--Time Saving Tips for Teachers. (Instant Idea Bks.). (Illus.). 64p. 1983. 5.95 (ISBN 0-86734-047-9, FS-8301). Schaffer pubns.

--Writing Ideas Ready to Use! (Instant Idea Bks.). (Illus.). 64p. 1983. 5.95 (ISBN 0-86734-050-9, FS-8304). Schaffer Pubns.

Gruber, Boris. Theory of Crystal Defects. 1966. 73.50 (ISBN 0-12-304750-1). Acad Pr.

Gruber, Bruno & Millman, Richard S., eds. Symmetries in Science. LC 80-18665. 505p. 1980. 65.00x (ISBN 0-306-40541-5, Plenum Pr). Plenum Pub.

Gruber, C., et al. Group Analysis of Classical Lattice Systems. LC 77-2821. (Lecture Notes in Physics: Vol. 60). 1977. pap. 21.00 (ISBN 0-387-08137-2). Springer-Verlag.

Gruber, Carol S. Mars & Minerva - World War One & the Uses of the Higher Learning in America. LC 74-82004. x, 293p. 1975. 27.50x (ISBN 0-8071-0096-X). La State U Pr.

Gruber, Clemens. Dictionary of Advertising & Marketing. (Eng. & Ger.). 1977. pap. 15.75x (ISBN 3-1900-6312-5). Adlers Foreign Bks.

--Woerterbuch der Werbung und des Marketing. (Eng. & Ger.). 1977. pap. 15.00 (ISBN 3-19-006312-5, M-6942). French & Eur.

Gruber, Dwight, jt. auth. see Stasiuk, Garry.

Gruber, Edward & Gruber, Gary R. Graduate Record Examination. rev. ed. 1977. pap. 8.95 (ISBN 0-671-18993-X). Monarch Pr.

Gruber, Edward C. Graduate Management Admissions Test. (Exam Preparation Ser.). 1975. pap. 8.95 (ISBN 0-671-18995-6). S&S.

--High School Equivalency Test. (Exam Preperation Ser.). 1983. pap. 8.95 (ISBN 0-671-18998-0). Monarch Pr.

--Miller Analogies Test. 1976. pap. 7.95 (ISBN 0-671-18981-6). Monarch Pr.

--Test of English As a Foreign Language (TOEFL) rev. ed. (Exam Preparation Ser.). 528p. (gr. 12). 1981. pap. text ed. 7.95 (ISBN 0-671-18987-5). Monarch Pr.

Gruber, Edward C. & Bramson, Morris. Scholastic Aptitude Test (SAT) (Exam Prep. Ser.). 1975. pap. 7.95 (ISBN 0-671-18969-7). Monarch Pr.

Gruber, Edward C. & Gruber, Gary R. Graduate Management Admission Test (GMAT) 1977. pap. 8.95 (ISBN 0-671-18995-6). Monarch Pr.

--Preparation for the Law School Admission Test: LSAT. (Exam Prep. Ser.). 1982. pap. 8.95 (ISBN 0-671-45883-3). Monarch Pr.

Gruber, Edward C., jt. auth. see Strand, Stanley.

Gruber, F. A., jt. auth. see Segalowitz, S. J.

Gruber, Frank. Bitter Sage. Bd. with The Bushwhackers. (Signet Pound Double Western Ser.). 1984. pap. 3.50 (ISBN 0-451-12920-2, Sig). NAL.

--Quantrell's Raiders. Bd. with Town Tamer. 352p. 1984. pap. 3.50 (ISBN 0-451-12777-3, Sig). NAL.

--Zane Grey. 1978. pap. 1.95 (ISBN 0-505-51281-5, Pub. by Tower Bks). Dorchester Pub Co.

--Zane Grey: A Biography. 298p. Repr. of 1969 ed. lib. bdg. 16.95x (ISBN 0-89190-756-4, Pub. by River City Pr). Amereon Ltd.

Gruber, Frederick C., ed. Education & the State. LC 77-665. (Series: The Martin G. Brumbaugh Lectures in Education; 4th Ser.). 1977. lib. bdg. 15.00x (ISBN 0-8371-9491-1, GRED). Greenwood.

--The Emergence of the Modern Mind. LC 78-14331. (The Martin G. Brumbaugh Lectures in Education Ser.: No. 2). 1978. Repr. of 1958 ed. lib. bdg. 15.00x (ISBN 0-313-21023-3, GREM). Greenwood.

Gruber, Gary. American College Test. (Exam Preparation Ser.). 528p. (Orig.). (gr. 11-12). 1978. pap. 8.95 (ISBN 0-671-18996-4). S&S.

--American College Testing Program (ACT) (Exam Preparation Ser.). 1983. pap. 8.95 (ISBN 0-671-18996-4). Monarch Pr.

--Professional & Administrative Career Examination. (Exam Prep Ser.). 1975. pap. 6.95 (ISBN 0-671-18090-8). Monarch Pr.

Gruber, Gary R. College Level Examination Program (CLEP) (Exam Prep. Ser.). 1983. pap. 8.95 (ISBN 0-671-47248-8). Monarch Pr.

--The Gruber S. A. T. Self Instruction Course. LC 83-25777. 1984. pap. 8.95 (ISBN 0-201-10865-8). Addison-Wesley.

--Inside Strategies for the SAT. 144p. (Orig.). 1982. pap. 5.95 (ISBN 0-87694-185-4). Ed Design Inc.

--Math Review for the GMAT. 288p. (Orig.). 1982. pap. 8.95 Softcover (ISBN 0-671-43985-5). Monarch Pr.

--Monarch's Preparation for the ACT: American College Testing Program. (Illus.). 522p. 1983. 8.95 (ISBN 0-671-18996-4). Monarch Pr.

--Preparation for the Standard Written English Test. (Exam Prep Ser.). 176p. (Orig.). 1982. pap. 6.75 (ISBN 0-671-45884-1). Monarch Pr.

--Professional & Administrative Career Examination (PACE) (Exam Preparation). 300p. 1976. pap. 6.95 (ISBN 0-671-18090-8). S&S.

Gruber, Gary R., jt. auth. see Gruber, Edward.

Gruber, Gary R., jt. auth. see Gruber, Edward C.

Gruber, Howard E. Darwin on Man: A Psychological Study of Scientific Creativity. 2nd ed. LC 80-28453. 336p. 1981. lib. bdg. 25.00x (ISBN 0-226-31008-6); pap. 7.95x (ISBN 0-226-31007-8). U of Chicago Pr.

Gruber, Howard E. & Voneche, J. Jacques, eds. The Essential Piaget. 1982. pap. 18.50 (ISBN 0-465-02059-3, CN-5076). Basic.

Gruber, Ira D. The Howe Brothers & the American Revolution. (Illus.). 416p. 1975. pap. 4.45x (ISBN 0-393-00756-1, Norton Lib). Norton.

--The Howe Brothers & the American Revolution. (Institute of Early American History & Culture Ser.). xv, 396p. 1972. 32.50 (ISBN 0-8078-1229-3). U of NC Pr.

Gruber, J., ed. Econometric Decision Models: Proceedings, Hagen, FRG, 1981. (Lecture Notes in Economics & Mathematical Systems Ser.: Vol. 208). (Illus.). 364p. 1983. pap. 26.00 (ISBN 0-387-11554-4). Springer-Verlag.

Gruber, Jacob W. A Conscience in Conflict: The Life of St. George Jackson Mivart. LC 79-17545. (Illus.). 1980. Repr. of 1960 ed. lib. bdg. 32.50x (ISBN 0-313-22041-7, GRCC). Greenwood.

Gruber, James & Pryor, Judith. Materials & Methods for Sociology Research. LC 79-14814. (Bibliographic Instruction Ser.). 1980. lib. bdg. 25.00 wkbk. (ISBN 0-918212-13-8); 5 or more workbks. 8.50 ea. (ISBN 0-918212-12-X). Neal-Schuman.

Gruber, James, jt. auth. see Benson, Tedd.

Gruber, James E. Self in Transition: Change & Continuity in Self-Esteem After High School. LC 79-65211. 145p. 1979. perfect bdg. 11.00 (ISBN 0-88247-582-7). R & E Pubs.

Gruber, Joachim. Kommmentar Zu Boethius De Consolatione Philosophiae. (Texte und Kommentare: Vol. 9). 1978. 62.00x (ISBN 3-11-007223-8). De Gruyter.

Gruber, Josef, ed. Czechoslovakia: A Survey of Economic & Social Conditions. LC 76-135810. (Eastern Europe Collection Ser). 1970. Repr. of 1924 ed. 18.00 (ISBN 0-405-02752-4). Ayer Co Pubs.

Gruber, Katherine. International Associations 1986. 20th ed. (The Encyclopedia of Associations Ser.: Vol. 4). 500p. 1985. 175.00x (ISBN 0-8103-1840-7). Gale.

Gruber, Katherine, ed. Encyclopedia of Associations 1985: International Organizations, Vol. 4. 19th ed. LC 76-46129. 508p. 1984. 170.00x (ISBN 0-8103-0128-8). Gale.

--Encyclopedia of Associations 1985: Updating Service, 2 vols. 300p. 1985. Set. pap. 125.00x (ISBN 0-8103-1693-5). Gale.

--International Organizations, 1984, 3 pts. (Encyclopedia of Associations: Vol. 4). 150p. 1984. Set. pap. 145.00x (ISBN 0-8103-0143-1). Gale.

Gruber, Katherine & Koek, Karin, eds. Encyclopedia of Associations, 1985: International Organizations Supplement. 300p. 1985. Set. pap. text ed. 125.00x (ISBN 0-8103-1694-3). Gale.

Gruber, Katnern F. & Moor, Pauline M., eds. No Place to Go. 89p. 1963. pap. 5.00 (ISBN 0-89128-022-7, PCP001). Am Foun Blind.

Gruber, L. Fritz, jt. auth. see Gruber, Renate.

Gruber, Loren C. & Loganbill, Dean, eds. In Geardagum II: Essays on Old & Middle English Language & Literature. (Orig.). 1977. pap. 2.50 (ISBN 0-936072-03-2). Soc New Lang Study.

--In Geardagum III: Essays on Old English Language & Literature. 1979. pap. 4.00 (ISBN 0-936072-05-9). Soc New Lang Study.

Gruber, Loren C., jt. ed. see Johnson, William C., Jr.

Gruber, M. J., jt. ed. see Elton, E. J.

Gruber, Mark, jt. auth. see Institute for Continuing Education (N.J.).

Gruber, Martin J., jt. auth. see Elton, Edwin J.

Gruber, May. Pandora's Pride. 280p. (Orig.). 1985. pap. 9.95 (ISBN 0-8184-0374-8). Citadel Pr.

Gruber, Michael, ed. see Leo, Miriam & Forlini, Gary.

Gruber, Murray L., ed. Management Systems in the Human Services. 378p. 1981. 29.95 (ISBN 0-87722-207-X); pap. 12.95 (ISBN 0-87722-214-2). Temple U Pr.

Gruber, Peter & Wills, Jorg. Convexity & Its Applications. 420p. 1983. text ed. 59.95 (ISBN 0-8176-1384-6). Birkhauser.

Gruber, R. & Rappaz, J. Finite Element Methods in Linear Ideal Magnetohydrodymanics. (Computational Physics Ser.). (Illus.). 200p. 1985. 34.00 (ISBN 0-387-13398-4). Springer Verlag.

Gruber, Renate & Gruber, L. Fritz. The Imaginary Photo Museum. 1982. 12.98 (ISBN 0-517-54844-5, Harmony); pap. 7.98 (ISBN 0-517-54797-X). Crown.

Gruber, Ruth. Haven: The Unknown Story of 1000 World War II Refugees. 272p. 1984. pap. 3.50 (ISBN 0-451-12865-6, Sig). NAL.

--Raquela: A Woman of Israel. 1985. pap. 3.95 (ISBN 0-451-13769-8, Sig). NAL.

Gruber, S., tr. see Goden, D.

Gruber, S., tr. see Walter, H. & Breckle, S. W.

Gruber, Suzanne. Chatty Chipmunk's Nutty Day. LC 84-8665. (Giant First Start Reader Ser.). (Illus.). 32p. (gr. k-2). 1985. PLB 9.89 (ISBN 0-8167-0360-4); pap. text ed. 2.50 (ISBN 0-8167-0440-6). Troll Assocs.

--Monster under My Bed. LC 84-45687. (Illus.). 32p. (gr. k-2). 1985. PLB 9.89 (ISBN 0-8167-0456-2); pap. text ed. 2.50 (ISBN 0-8167-0457-0). Troll Assocs.

Gruber, Terry. Fat Cats. LC 81-47086. (Illus.). 192p. (Orig.). 1981. pap. 8.61i (ISBN 0-06-090897-1, CN 897, CN). Har-Row.

--Working Cats. 1979. 10.95i (ISBN 0-397-01376-0); pap. 9.95i (ISBN 0-690-01951-3). Har-Row.

Gruber, Terry D. Cat High: The Yearbook. (Illus.). 128p. 1984. pap. 9.95 (ISBN 0-312-92085-7). Congdon & Weed.

Gruber, U. F. Blood Replacement. Oxtoby, L. & Armstrong, R. F., trs. LC 69-16845. (Illus.). 1969. 25.00 (ISBN 0-387-04496-5). Springer-Verlag.

Gruber, U. F., et al, eds. Progress in Surgery, Vol. 15. 1977. 29.50 (ISBN 3-8055-2365-3). S Karger.

Gruber, William H., jt. auth. see Synott, William R.

Gruberg, Martin. Women in American Politics: An Assessment & Sourcebook. 1968. 9.50 (ISBN 0-911880-02-X). Academia.

Grubiak, J., jt. auth. see Grubiak, O.

Grubiak, O. & Grubiak, J. The Guernsey Experiment. 59.95 (ISBN 0-8490-0267-2). Gordon Pr.

Grubin, H. L., et al, eds. The Physics of Submicron Structures. 370p. 1984. 57.50x (ISBN 0-306-41715-4, Plenum Pr). Plenum Pub.

Grubmueller, Klaus, jt. ed. see Fromm, Hans.

Gruchcow, Jack. The VisiCalc Applications Book. 1982. text ed. 22.95 (ISBN 0-8359-8390-0); pap. 17.95 (ISBN 0-8359-8389-7). Reston.

Gruchman, Bohdan. Training & Research for Regional Planning & Development in Asia: An International Survey Report. (Working Papers Ser.: No. 78-20). 13p. 1978. pap. 6.00 (ISBN 0-686-78504-5, CRD106, UNCRD). Unipub.

Gruchy, Allan G. Comparative Economic Systems: Competing Ways to Stability, Growth & Welfare. 2nd ed. LC 76-10899. (Illus.). 1977. 31.50 (ISBN 0-395-18606-4). HM.

--Contemporary Economic Thought. LC 79-184664. 1972. 27.50x (ISBN 0-678-00898-1). Kelley.

--Modern Economic Thought: The American Contribution. LC 66-22624. Repr. of 1947 ed. 45.00x (ISBN 0-678-00204-5). Kelley.

Gruchy, John W. De see De Gruchy, John W. & Villa-Vicencio, Charles.

Gruchy, John W. de see De Gruchy, John W. & Villa-Vicencio, Charles.

Grudem, Wayne A. The Gift of Prophecy in One Corinthians. LC 81-40583. 358p. (Orig.). 1982. lib. bdg. 28.75 (ISBN 0-8191-2083-9); pap. text ed. 15.50 (ISBN 0-8191-2084-7). U Pr of Amer.

Grudin, L. Mister Eliot Among the Nightingales. LC 78-174691. (Studies in T. S. Eliot, No. 11). 1972. Repr. of 1932 ed. lib. bdg. 29.95x (ISBN 0-8383-1346-9). Haskell.

Grudin, Louis. Mr. Eliot Among the Nightingales. LC 72-194759. 1932. lib. bdg. 20.00 (ISBN 0-8414-4696-2). Folcroft.

--Tales & Poems. LC 74-21885. 219p. 1976. 10.00 (ISBN 0-8180-1532-2). Horizon.

Grudin, Robert. Mighty Opposites: Shakespeare & Renaissance Contrariety. LC 78-51753. 1979. 25.00x (ISBN 0-520-03666-2). U of Cal Pr.

--Time & the Art of Living. LC 82-47744. (Illus.). 224p. 1982. 14.37i (ISBN 0-06-250355-3, HarpR). Har-Row.

Grudzenska-Gross, Irena & Gross, Jan. T., eds. War Through Children's Eyes: The Soviet Occupation of Poland & the Deportations, 1939-1941. LC 80-83832. (Archival Documentaries). 1985. pap. 7.95 (ISBN 0-317-29945-X). Hoover Inst Pr.

Grudzinskas, J. B. & Seppala, M., eds. Pregnancy Proteins: Biology, Chemistry & Clinical Application (Australia) 474p. 1982. 55.00 (ISBN 0-12-304850-8). Acad Pr.

Grudzinski, Ted. Winequest: The Wine Dictionary. 464p. 1985. 28.00 (ISBN 0-9615063-0-X). Winequest.

Gruebel-Lee, David, ed. Disorders of the Hip. (Illus.). 300p. 1983. text ed. 52.00 (ISBN 0-397-50465-9, 65-06067, Lippincott Medical). Lippincott.

Grueber, H., jt. auth. see Keary, C.

Gruelle, Johnny. Beloved Belindy. (Raggedy Ann Ser). (Illus.). (ps-3). 4.95 (ISBN 0-672-50219-4). Bobbs.

--Johnny Mouse & the Wishing Stick. (Raggedy Ann Ser). (ps-3). 4.95 (ISBN 0-672-51812-0). Bobbs.

--Marcella. (Raggedy Ann Ser). (Illus.). (ps-3). 1968. 4.95 (ISBN 0-672-50378-6). Bobbs.

--More Raggedy Ann & Andy Stories. LC 76-47112. (Illus.). 1977. 4.95 (ISBN 0-672-52248-9). Bobbs.

--Raggedy Andy Stories. (Raggedy Ann Ser). (ps-3). 4.95 (ISBN 0-672-50442-1). Bobbs.

--Raggedy Ann & Andy & the Camel with the Wrinkled Knees. (Raggedy Ann Ser). (ps-3). 4.95 (ISBN 0-672-50444-8). Bobbs.

--Raggedy Ann & Andy & the Camel with the Wrinkled Knees. (gr. 1-4). 1977. pap. 1.95 (ISBN 0-440-47390-X). Dell.

--Raggedy Ann & Andy & the Kindly Rag Man. Williams, Martin, ed. LC 74-23187. (Raggedy Ann Ser). 96p. (ps-3). 1975. 4.95 (ISBN 0-672-52007-9). Bobbs.

--Raggedy Ann & Andy & the Nice Fat Policeman. (Raggedy Ann Ser). (ps-3). 4.95 (ISBN 0-672-50454-5). Bobbs.

--Raggedy Ann & Andy & Witchie Kissabye. Williams, Martin, ed. LC 74-23188. (Raggedy Ann Ser). 96p. (ps-3). 1975. 4.95 (ISBN 0-672-52101-6). Bobbs.

--Raggedy Ann & Andy Giant Treasury: Four Adventures Plus 12 Short Stories. Golden, N., retold by. 1985. 3.98 (ISBN 0-517-45594-3). Outlet Bk Co.

--Raggedy Ann & Andy's Animal Friends. (Raggedy Ann Ser). (ps-3). 1925. 4.95 (ISBN 0-672-51933-X). Bobbs.

--Raggedy Ann & Andy's Merry Adventures. (Raggedy Ann Ser). (ps-3). 1925. 4.95 (ISBN 0-672-51920-8). Bobbs.

--Raggedy Ann & Andy's Sunny Stories. (Raggedy Ann Ser). (ps-3). 1925. 4.95 (ISBN 0-672-51919-4). Bobbs.

--Raggedy Ann & Betsy Bonnet String. (Raggedy Ann Ser). (ps-3). 4.95 (ISBN 0-672-50443-X). Bobbs.

--Raggedy Ann & Raggedy Andy's Alphabet & Numbers. (Raggedy Ann Ser). (ps-3). 4.95 (ISBN 0-672-51793-0). Bobbs.

--Raggedy Ann & the Golden Butterfly. (Raggedy Ann Ser). (ps-3). 4.95 (ISBN 0-672-50447-2). Bobbs.

--Raggedy Ann & the Golden Ring. (Raggedy Ann Ser). (ps-3). 4.95 (ISBN 0-672-50448-0). Bobbs.

--Raggedy Ann & the Golden Ring. 96p. 1978. pap. 1.95 (ISBN 0-440-47331-4, YB). Dell.

--Raggedy Ann & the Happy Meadow. (Raggedy Ann Ser). (ps-3). 4.95 (ISBN 0-672-50449-9). Bobbs.

--Raggedy Ann & the Happy Meadow. 96p. 1978. pap. 0.95 (ISBN 0-440-47326-8, YB). Dell.

--Raggedy Ann & the Hobby Horse. (Raggedy Ann Ser). (ps-3). 4.95 (ISBN 0-672-50450-2). Bobbs.

--Raggedy Ann & the Hobby Horse. 96p. (gr. 1-4). pap. 1.95 (ISBN 0-440-47327-6, YB). Dell.

--Raggedy Ann & the Paper Dragon. (Raggedy Ann Ser). (ps-3). 4.95 (ISBN 0-672-51813-9). Bobbs.

--Raggedy Ann & the Wonderful Witch. (Raggedy Ann Ser). (ps-3). 4.95 (ISBN 0-672-50458-8). Bobbs.

--Raggedy Ann in Cookie Land. (Raggedy Ann Ser). (ps-3). 4.95 (ISBN 0-672-50445-6). Bobbs.

--Raggedy Ann in Cookie Land. 112p. 1978. pap. 1.95 (ISBN 0-440-47325-X, YB). Dell.

--Raggedy Ann in the Deep, Deep Woods. (Raggedy Ann Ser). (ps-3). 4.95 (ISBN 0-672-50446-4). Bobbs.

--Raggedy Ann in the Magic Book. (Raggedy Ann Ser). (ps-3). 4.95 (ISBN 0-672-50453-7). Bobbs.

--Raggedy Ann in the Snow White Castle. (Raggedy Ann Ser). (ps-3). 4.95 (ISBN 0-672-50455-3). Bobbs.

--Raggedy Ann Stories. (Raggedy Ann Ser). (ps-3). 4.95 (ISBN 0-672-50456-1). Bobbs.

--Raggedy Ann's Friendly Fairies. (Raggedy Ann Ser). (ps-3). 4.95 (ISBN 0-672-50285-2). Bobbs.

--Raggedy Ann's Lucky Pennies. (Raggedy Ann Ser). (Illus.). (ps-3). 1968. 4.95 (ISBN 0-672-50451-0). Bobbs.

--Raggedy Ann's Magical Wishes. (Raggedy Ann Ser). (Illus.). (ps-3). 1968. 4.95 (ISBN 0-672-50452-9). Bobbs.

--Raggedy Ann's Very Own Fairy Stories. (Raggedy Ann Ser). (gr. 1-3). 4.95 (ISBN 0-685-36675-8). Bobbs.

--Raggedy Ann's Wishing Pebble. (Raggedy Ann Ser). (ps-3). 4.95 (ISBN 0-672-50457-X). Bobbs.

--Wooden Willie. (Raggedy Ann Ser). (Illus.). (ps-3). 1968. 4.95 (ISBN 0-672-50593-2). Bobbs.

Gruelle, Johnny, illus. Little Treasury of Raggedy Ann & Andy. (Illus.). 1984. 4.98 (ISBN 0-517-44730-4). Outlet Bk Co.

Gruen, Al. Contact Sheet: The Secret of Creative Photography. (Illus.). 192p. (Orig.). 1982. 19.95 (ISBN 0-8174-3705-3, Amphoto). Watson-Guptill.

Gruen, Bob. Listen to These Pictures: Photographs of John Lennon. LC 84-22763. (Illus.). 1985. pap. 14.95x (ISBN 0-688-04707-6). Morrow.

Gruen, Claude, jt. auth. see Gruen, Nina.

Gruen, D. M., ed. Chemistry of Fusion Technology. LC 72-89488. 394p. 1972. 55.00x (ISBN 0-306-30714-6, Plenum Pr). Plenum Pub.

Gruen, Erich S. The Hellenistic World & the Coming of Rome, 2 vols. LC 82-8581. 800p. 1984. 60.00 (ISBN 0-520-04569-6). U of Cal Pr.

--The Last Generation of the Roman Republic. LC 72-89244. 1974. 53.50x (ISBN 0-520-02238-6). U of Cal Pr.

--The Roman Republic. LC 72-94085. (AHA Pamphlets: No. 312). 1972. pap. text ed. 1.50 (ISBN 0-87229-009-3). Am Hist Assn.

Gruen, Ernest. Freedom to Grow. 128p. (Orig.). 1983. pap. 3.50 (ISBN 0-88368-123-4). Whitaker Hse.

Gruen, Ernest J. Freedom to Choose. 224p. 1976. pap. 3.50 (ISBN 0-88368-072-6). Whitaker Hse.

Gruen, F. H., ed. Surveys of Australian Economics, Vol. III. 272p. 1983. text ed. 35.00x (ISBN 0-86861-396-7). Allen Unwin.

--Surveys of Australian Economics, Vol. 1. LC 78-55055. 1978. text ed. 30.00x (ISBN 0-86861-208-1). Allen Unwin.

--Surveys of Australian Economics, Vol. 2. LC 78-55055. 1979. text ed. 30.00x (ISBN 0-86861-137-9). Allen Unwin.

Gruen, George E., ed. The Palestinians in Perspective: Implications for Mideast Peace & U. S. Policy. LC 82-71810. 112p. 1982. pap. 3.50 (ISBN 0-87495-042-2). Am Jewish Comm.

Gruen, Gerald E., jt. auth. see Wachs, Theodore D.

Gruen, Gerd. The Development of the Vertebrate Retina: A Comparative Survey. (Advances in Anatomy, Embryology, & Cell Biology Ser.: Vol. 78). (Illus.). 130p. 1982. pap. 26.00 (ISBN 0-387-11770-9). Springer-Verlag.

Gruen, John. Erik Bruhn: Danseur Noble. (Illus.). 1979. 18.95 (ISBN 0-670-29771-2). Viking.

--Menotti: A Biography. LC 77-9304. (Illus.). 1978. 19.95 (ISBN 0-02-546320-9). Macmillan.

--The Private World of Ballet. 1975. 19.95 (ISBN 0-670-57851-7). Viking.

Gruen, John, photos by. Objects. LC 80-7663. 1981. 75.00 (ISBN 0-394-51363-0). Knopf.

Gruen, Nina & Gruen, Claude. Demographic Changes & Their Effects on Real Estate Markets in the '80s. LC 82-60314. (Development Component Ser.). (Illus.). 27p. 1982. pap. 10.50 (ISBN 0-87420-609-X, D22). Urban Land.

Gruenbaum, Hannah. All Aboard the Aleph-Beth. (Illus.). (ps-1). 1.39 (ISBN 0-685-86205-4). Feldheim.

--Come, Count with Me. (Illus.). (ps-1). 1.39 (ISBN 0-685-86207-0). Feldheim.

--A King & His Nose. (Illus.). (ps-1). 1.39 (ISBN 0-685-86209-7). Feldheim.

--The Magic Carpet. (Illus.). (ps-1). 1.39 (ISBN 0-685-86206-2). Feldheim.

--The Mice, the Fox, & the Cheese. (ps-2). 1.39 (ISBN 0-685-86210-0). Feldheim.

--The Unhappy King. (Illus.). (ps-3). 1.39 (ISBN 0-685-86208-9). Feldheim.

Gruenbaum, Thelma. Before Seventeen Seventy-Six: The Massachusetts Bay Colony from Founding to Revolution. (Illus.). 38p. (gr. 4-10). 1974. pap. 3.75 (ISBN 0-936190-01-9); study guide 1.75 (ISBN 0-936190-02-7). ExPressAll.

Gruenbaum, Thelma, jt. auth. see Rivera, A. Ramon.

Gruenberg, Gladys W. Labor Peacemaker: The Life & Works of Father Leo. C. Brown, S. J. Ganss, George E., ed. LC 80-83552. (Original Studies Composed in English Ser.: No. 4). (Illus.). 176p. 1981. 8.50 (ISBN 0-912422-54-8); pap. 7.00 smythsewn paperbound (ISBN 0-912422-53-X); pap. 6.00 (ISBN 0-912422-52-1). Inst Jesuit.

Gruenberg, K. W. Linear Geometry. 2nd ed. LC 76-27693. (Graduate Texts in Mathematics Ser.). (Illus.). 1977. 25.00 (ISBN 0-387-90227-9). Springer-Verlag.

Gruenberg, Karl W. Cohomological Topics in Group Theory. LC 70-127042. (Lecture Notes in Mathematics: Vol. 143). 1970. pap. 14.70 (ISBN 0-387-04932-0). Springer-Verlag.

--Relation Modules of Finite Groups. LC 76-3645. (CBMS Regional Conference Ser. in Mathematics: Vol. 25). 82p. 1976. pap. 15.00 (ISBN 0-8218-1675-6, CBMS-25). Am Math.

Gruenberg, Karl W. & Roseblade, James E., eds. Group Theory: Essays for Phillip Hall. 1985. 65.00 (ISBN 0-12-304880-X). Acad Pr.

Gruenberg, Sidonie M. Wonderful Story of How You Were Born. rev. ed. LC 71-92055. (Illus.). 85p. (gr. 3-5). 1970. 11.95 (ISBN 0-385-03674-4). Doubleday.

Gruenberg, Sidonie M. & Kreche, Hilda S. The Many Lives of Modern Women. 1977. Repr. of 1952 ed. 25.00 (ISBN 0-8274-4304-8). R West.

Gruenberger, Fred. Computing with the Apple. 208p. 1984. pap. text ed. 14.95 (ISBN 0-8359-0866-6). Reston.

Gruenberger, Fred & Babcock, David. Computing with Mini Computers. LC 73-4793. Repr. of 1973 ed. 57.80 (ISBN 0-8357-9864-X, 2017409). Bks Demand UMI.

Gruendemann, Barbara J. & Meeker, Margaret H. Alexander's Care of the Patient in Surgery. 7th ed. LC 82-8212. (Illus.). 848p. 1983. text ed. 38.95 (ISBN 0-8016-4147-0). Mosby.

Gruendemann, Barbara J., jt. auth. see Rhodes, Marie J.

Gruener, Jennette R., jt. auth. see Costin, Lela B.

Gruenert, Horst. Sprache und Politik: Untersuchungen zum Sprachgebrauch der "Paulskirche". LC 74-80634. (Studia Linguistica Germanica Vol. 10). 1974. 35.60x (ISBN 3-11-003609-6). De Gruyter.

Gruenewald. Language Interaction in Teaching & Learning: The Hidden Curriculum. (Illus.). 192p. 1983. 15.00 (ISBN 0-8391-1888-0). Pro-Ed.

Gruenfeld, Elaine F. Performance Appraisal: Promise & Peril. LC 81-3920. (Key Issues Ser.: No. 25). 72p. 1981. pap. 5.00 (ISBN 0-87546-088-7). ILR Pr.

Gruenfeld, Joseph. Science & Values. 210p. (Orig.). 1973. pap. 22.00x (ISBN 90-6032-016-6, Pub. by B R Gruener). Benjamins North AM.

Gruenfelder, John K. Influence in Early Stuart Elections, 1604-1640. LC 80-28226. 294p. 1981. 22.50x (ISBN 0-8142-0316-7). Ohio St U Pr.

Gruenhagen, Robert W. Mustang: Story of the P-Fifty-One Fighter. LC 75-30278. (Illus.). 1980. pap. 9.95 (ISBN 0-668-04884-0). Arco.

Gruening, Ernest. Battle for Alaska Statehood. (Illus.). 122p. 1967. 9.95 (ISBN 0-912006-12-9). U of Alaska Pr.

Gruening, Ernest H. Mexico & Its Heritage. LC 68-9542. (Illus.). 1968. Repr. of 1940 ed. lib. bdg. 43.75x (ISBN 0-8371-0457-2, GRMH). Greenwood.

Gruening, Ernest H., ed. These United States, First Series. facs. ed. LC 70-134088. (Essay Index Reprint Ser). 1923. 22.00 (ISBN 0-8369-2109-7). Ayer Co Pubs.

--These United States, Second Series. facs. ed. LC 70-134088. (Essay Index Reprint Ser). 1924. 24.50 (ISBN 0-8369-2140-2). Ayer Co Pubs.

Gruenler, Royce G. The Inexhaustible God: Biblical Faith & the Challenge of Process Theism. 176p. 1983. pap. 11.95 (ISBN 0-8010-3794-8). Baker Bk.

--New Approaches to Jesus & the Gospels: A Phenomenological & Exegetical Study of Jesus & the Gospels. 208p. (Orig.). 1982. pap. 13.95 (ISBN 0-8010-3782-4). Baker Bk.

Gruenthal, E., et al, eds. Current Research in Neurosciences: Topical Problem in Psychiatry & Neurology. (Bibliotheca Psychiatrica: No. 143). 1970. pap. 30.25 (ISBN 3-8055-0331-8). S Karger.

Gruenthal, Lola, et al, trs. see Mrozek, Slawomir.

Gruenwald, George. New Product Development. LC 83-71075. 325p. 1985. 34.95 (ISBN 0-87251-085-9). Crain Bks.

Gruenwald, Myron E. One Cubit of Stature. (Illus.). 84p. 1985. pap. 5.00 (ISBN 0-9601536-2-4). M E Gruenwald.

--Two Worlds for Our Children. 2nd ed. (Illus.). 36p. 1985. pap. 3.50 (ISBN 0-9601536-3-2). M E Gruenwald.

Gruenwald, Oskar. The Yugoslav Search for Man: Marxist Humanism in Contemporary Yugoslavia. LC 82-4290. 448p. 1983. 35.00 (ISBN 0-89789-005-1). Bergin & Garvey.

Gruenwald, Oskar & Rosenblum-Cale, Karen. Human Rights in Yugoslavia. 1985. text ed. 24.50x (ISBN 0-8290-1054-8). Irvington.

Gruenwedel & Whitaker. Food Analysis, Vol. 1. 328p. 1984. 59.75 (ISBN 0-8247-7181-8). Dekker.

--Food Analysis, Vol. 2. 568p. 1984. 89.75 (ISBN 0-8247-7182-6). Dekker.

Gruenzner, Norman. Postal History of American Prisoners of War: World War II, Korea, Vietnam. LC 79-50817. (APS Handbook Ser.). 1979. 12.50 (ISBN 0-933580-00-2). Am Philatelic Society.

Gruff, Susan C., jt. auth. see Korf, Richard P.

Gruffudd, Haini. Welsh Personal Names. pap. 7.95 (ISBN 0-317-06852-0). British AM Bks.

Gruffudd, Heini. Look up the Welsh: A Phrasebook Guide to the Welsh Language. pap. 4.95 (ISBN 0-317-06849-0). British AM Bks.

Gruffydd, W. J. Folklore & Myth in the Mabinogion. LC 75-34083. 1958. lib. bdg. 9.50 (ISBN 0-8414-4522-2). Folcroft.

Grugel, Lee E. George Jacob Holyoake: A Study in the Evolution of a Victorian Radical. LC 76-8241. 225p. 1975. lib. bdg. 19.50x (ISBN 0-87991-619-2). Porcupine Pr.

--Society & Religion During the Age of Industrialization: Christianity in Victorian England. LC 78-65844. (Illus.). 1979. pap. text ed. 9.25 (ISBN 0-8191-0671-2). U Pr of Amer.

Gruhl, Jim, ed. see Kirsner, Gary.

Gruhl, Max. The Citadel of Ethiopia. LC 74-15043. (Eng.). Repr. of 1932 ed. 27.50 (ISBN 0-404-12073-3). AMS Pr.

Gruhn, Albert. Die Byzantinische Politik Zur der Zeit Kreuzzuege. 1904. 12.50 (ISBN 0-8337-1479-1). B Franklin.

Gruhn, William & Douglass, Harl R. The Modern Junior High School. 3rd ed. LC 78-110549. pap. 107.50 (ISBN 0-317-28308-1, 2016478). Bks Demand UMI.

Gruhn, William T., jt. auth. see Anderson, Vernon E.

Gruijter, J. J. De see De Gruijter, J. J.

Gruilow, Rebecca, jt. ed. see Gruliow, Leo.

Grujic, B. Dictionnaire Serbocrate-Francais, Francais-Serbocroate, suivi d'une courte grammaire de Langue Francaise. 631p. (Serbocroatian & Fr.). 19.95 (ISBN 0-686-92591-2). French & Eur.

--English-Croatian, Croatian-English Pocket Dictionary. 1982. pap. 18.00 (ISBN 0-317-19026-1, Y647). Vanous.

--Pocket English-Croatian-English Dictionary: Short Grammar. 33rd ed. 624p. (Serbocroatian & Eng.). 1982. text ed. 18.00x (ISBN 0-89918-647-5, Y-647). Vanous.

--Serbocroatian-English, English-Serbocroatian Dictionary. Rev. & enl. ed. (Serbocroatian & Eng.). 25.00 (ISBN 0-685-65374-9). Heinman.

Grujic, J. English-Serbo-Croat & Serbo-Croat-English Dictionary. 620p. (Eng. & Serbocroatian.). 1980. 40.00x (ISBN 0-569-03165-6, Pub. by Collet's). State Mutual Bk.

Grujic, V. C. English-Serbocroat & Serbocroat-English Dictionary. 620p. (Eng. & Serbocroatian.). 1971. 65.00x (ISBN 0-686-44712-3, Pub. by Collets). State Mutual Bk.

Gruliow, L., tr. see Okudzhava, Bulat.

Gruliow, Leo. Current Soviet Policies I: The Documentary Record of the 19th Communist Party Congress & the Reorganization after Stalin's Death. Current Digest of the Soviet Press Staff, tr. from Rus. 268p. 1953. 30.00 (ISBN 0-913601-21-7); pap. 25.00 (ISBN 0-913601-01-2). Current Digest.

Gruliow, Leo, ed. Current Soviet Policies: The Documentary Record of the Twentieth Communist Party Congress & Its Aftermath, Vol. II. Current Digest of the Soviet Press Staff, tr. from Rus. 247p. (Orig.). 1957. pap. 30.00 (ISBN 0-913601-22-5); pap. 25.00 (ISBN 0-913601-02-0). Current Digest.

Gruliow, Leo & Gruilow, Rebecca, eds. Current Soviet Policies: The Documentary Record of the Twenty-Fifth Congress of the Communist Party of the Soviet Union, Vol. VII. Current Digest of the Soviet Press Staff, tr. from Rus. 142p. (Orig.). 1976. pap. 12.00 (ISBN 0-913601-07-1). Current Digest.

Gruliow, Leo & Neuweld, Mark, eds. Current Soviet Policies: The Documentary Record of the Extraordinary Twenty-First Communist Party Congress, Vol. III. Current Digest of the Soviet Press Staff, tr. from Rus. 230p. (Orig.). 1960. 30.00 (ISBN 0-913601-23-3); pap. 25.00 (ISBN 0-913601-03-9). Current Digest.

Grulndman, Donna. A Distant Eden. (Orig.). 1982. pap. 3.50 (ISBN 0-440-12136-1). Dell.

Grum, Fran & Bartleson, C. James. Optical Radiation Measurements, Vol. 5. 1984. 110.00 (ISBN 0-12-304905-9). Acad Pr.

Grum, Fran & Bartleson, James, eds. Optical Radiation Measurements, Vol. 4. 1983. 55.00 (ISBN 0-12-304904-0). Acad Pr.

Grum, Franc & Becherer, Richard, eds. Optical Radiation Measurements, Vol. 3. 314p. 1982. 55.00 (ISBN 0-12-304903-2). Acad Pr.

Grum, Franc C. & Becherer, Richard. Optical Radiant Energy Vol. 1: Radiometry, Concepts, Components & Methods. LC 78-20043. 1979. 49.50 (ISBN 0-12-304901-6). Acad Pr.

Grum, Franc C. & Bartleson, C. James, eds. Optical Radiation Measurements: Color Measurements, Vol. 2. LC 78-31412. 1980. 47.50 (ISBN 0-12-304902-4). Acad Pr.

Grumach, Ernst & Grumach, Renate, eds. Goethe: Begenugen und Gesprache Band V: 1800-1805. iv, 754p. (Ger.). 1985. 129.60x (ISBN 3-11-010164-5). De Gruyter.

Grumach, Renate, ed. Goethe, Begegnungen und Gesprache: 1786-1792, Vol.3. 1977. 71.20x (ISBN 3-11-006836-2). De Gruyter.

Grumach, Renate, jt. ed. see Grumach, Ernst.

Gruman, Gerald J. A History of Ideas About the Prolongation of Life: The Evolution of Prolongevity Hypotheses to 1800. Kastenbaum, Robert, ed. LC 76-19574. (Death & Dying Ser.). (Illus.). 1977. Repr. of 1966 ed. lib. bdg. 17.00x (ISBN 0-405-09572-4). Ayer Co Pubs.

Gruman, Gerald J. & Kastenbaum, Robert, eds. The "Fixed Period" Controversy: Prelude to Modern Ageism, an Original Anthology. LC 78-22186. (Aging & Old Age Ser.). 1979. lib. bdg. 17.00x (ISBN 0-405-11804-X). Ayer Co Pubs.

--Roots of Modern Gerontology & Geriatrics: An Original Anthology. LC 78-22184. (Aging & Old Age Ser.). 1979. lib. bdg. 28.50x (ISBN 0-405-11801-5). Ayer Co Pubs.

Grumann, V. Biographisch-bibliographisches Handbuch der Lichenologie. Nach dem Tode des Verfassers ed. by O. Klement. 1979. lib. bdg. 87.50x (ISBN 3-7682-0907-5). Lubrecht & Cramer.

Grumbach, A., ed. see Olitzki, A.

Grumbach, Doris. Chamber Music. 1980. pap. 2.50 (ISBN 0-449-24271-4, Crest). Fawcett.

--Chamber Music. (Obelisk Ser.). 264p. 1985. pap. 7.95 (ISBN 0-525-48177-X, 0772-230). Dutton.

--The Ladies. 224p. 1984. 14.95 (ISBN 0-525-24263-5, 01451-440). Dutton.

--The Ladies. 224p. 1985. pap. 3.50 (ISBN 0-449-20818-4, Crest). Fawcett.

Grumbach, Jane & Emerson, Robert, eds. Actor's Guide to Monologues, Vol. II. rev ed. LC 73-21893. 48p. 1981. pap. 2.95x (ISBN 0-89676-043-X). Drama Bk.

--Actors Guide to Monologues, Vol. I. rev. ed. LC 74-23335. 88p. 1974. pap. 2.95 (ISBN 0-89676-021-9). Drama Bk.

--Actors Guide to Scenes. LC 73-75346. 28p. 1973. pap. text ed. 2.95x (ISBN 0-910482-42-X). Drama Bk.

--Monologues: Men, Vol. 2. 56p. (Orig.). 1983. pap. 3.95x (ISBN 0-89676-065-0). Drama Bk.

--Monologues: Women, Vol. 2. LC 76-1975. 56p. (Orig.). 1981. pap. 3.95x (ISBN 0-89676-066-9). Drama Bk.

Grumbach, Jane, jt. ed. see Emerson, Robert.

Grumelli, Antonio, jt. ed. see Caporale, Rocco.

Grumet, Joanne, ed. Papers from the Fourth & Fifth Annual Meetings. (Gypsy Lore Society, North American Chapter Publications: No. 2). 318p. 1985. 12.50 (ISBN 0-318-17807-9); members 10.00 (ISBN 0-318-17808-7). Gypsy Lore Soc.

Grumet, Michael. Statue of Liberty. 1986. pap. price not set (ISBN 0-87795-782-7). Arbor Hse.

--The Statue of Liberty. 1986. price not set (ISBN 0-87795-763-0). Arbor Hse.

Grumet, Priscilla H. How to Dress Well: A Complete Guide for Women. (Illus., Orig.). 1980. pap. 6.95 (ISBN 0-346-12510-3). Cornerstone.

Grumet, Robert. How to Do Your Own Divorce in Nevada. 3rd, rev. ed. LC 83-106037. (Illus.). 91p. 1982. pap. 9.95 (ISBN 0-911947-00-0). Utopia Pr.

Grumet, Robert S. Native Americans of the Northwest Coast: A Critical Bibliography. LC 79-2165. (Newberry Library Center for the History of the American Indian Bibliographical Ser.). 128p. 1980. pap. 5.95x (ISBN 0-253-30385-0). Ind U Pr.

Grumm, H. Peter. Geometrical Methods in Congruence Modular Algebras. LC 83-11810. (Memoirs: No. 286). 80p. 1983. pap. 8.00 (ISBN 0-8218-2286-1, MEMO 286). Am Math.

Grumm, John & Wasby, Stephen, eds. The Analysis of Policy Impact. 1980. pap. 8.00 (ISBN 0-918592-39-9). Policy Studies.

Grumm, John G. & Wasby, Stephen L., eds. The Analysis of Policy Impact. (A Policy Studies Orgnization Bk.). 224p. 1981. 28.50x (ISBN 0-669-03951-9). Lexington Bks.

Grumman, Joan, jt. auth. see Webber, Jeanette.

Grumme, Marguerite. Basic Principles of Parliamentary Law & Protocol. 64p. 1963. pap. 3.95 (ISBN 0-8007-0015-5). Revell.

Grummel, William C. English Word Building from Latin & Greek. (Orig.). 1961. pap. text ed. 6.95x (ISBN 0-87015-104-5). Pacific Bks.

Grummelshausen, Hans J. Von see Von Grimmelshausen, Hans J. C.

Grummer, Arnold E. Paper by Kids. LC 79-22904. (Doing & Learning Bks.). (Illus.). (gr. 5 up). 1980. PLB 9.95 (ISBN 0-87518-191-0). Dillon.

Grummon, Stuart E., tr. see Sarmiento, Domingo F., et al.

Grummond, Lena De see De Grummond, Lena & Delaune, Lynn.

Grummond, Nancy T. de, ed. A Guide To Etruscan Mirrors. new ed. (Illus.). 200p. 1982. 25.00 (ISBN 0-943254-00-0). Arch News Inc.

Grun, Bernard. The Timetables of History. rev. ed. 1982. pap. 16.95 (ISBN 0-671-24988-6). S&S.

Grun, M., jt. ed. see Liehr, H.

Grun, Max von der see Von der Grun, Max.

Grun, Paul. Cytoplasmic Genetics & Evolution. LC 75-43987. (Illus.). 435p. 1976. 50.00x (ISBN 0-231-03975-1). Columbia U Pr.

Grunauer-Von Hoerschelmann, Susanne. Die Muenzpraegung der Lakedaimonier. (Antike Muenzen und Geschnittene Steine: Vol. 7). (Illus.). 1978. 72.00x (ISBN 3-11-007222-X). De Gruyter.

Grunbaum, A. Boston Studies in the Philosophy of Science, Vol. 12: Philosophical Problems of Space & Time. 2nd ed. LC 73-75763. (Synthese Library: No. 55). 884p. 1973. 66.00 (ISBN 90-277-0357-4, Pub. by Reidel Holland); pap. 25.00 (ISBN 90-277-0358-2). Kluwer Academic.

Grunbaum, Adolf. The Foundations of Psychoanalysis: A Philosophical Critique. LC 83-9264. (Pittsburgh Series on Philosophy & History). 256p. 1984. 16.95x (ISBN 0-520-05016-9). U of Cal Pr.

--Geometry & Chronometry in Philosophical Perspective. LC 68-22363. 1968. 12.50x (ISBN 0-8166-0489-4); pap. 3.45x (ISBN 0-8166-0490-8, MP16). U of Minn Pr.

Grunbaum, B. Arrangements & Spreads. LC 71-38926. (CBMS Regional Conference Series in Mathematics: No. 10). 114p. 1980. pap. 11.00 (ISBN 0-8218-1659-4, CBMS-10). Am Math.

Grunbaum, B. & Shephard, G. C. Tillings & Patterns. 1985. write for info (ISBN 0-7167-1193-1); pap. write for info (ISBN 0-7167-1194-X). W H Freeman.

Grunbaum, Branko. Convex Polytopes. LC 67-20423. (Pure & Applied Mathematics (Wiley) Ser.: Vol. 16). pap. 117.50 (ISBN 0-317-08683-9, 2022541). Bks Demand UMI.

Grunbaum, Dorien, jt. auth. see Markstein, Linda.

Grunbaum, E., ed. Vacuum Technology: Selected Proceedings of the 6th Israeli Vacuum Congress, Haifa, Israel, 4-5 April, 1982. 64p. 1983. pap. 14.00 (ISBN 0-08-030567-9). Pergamon.

Grunberg, Emanuel, jt. auth. see Schnitzer, Robert J.

Grunberg, Leon. Failed Multinational Ventures. LC 80-8364. (Illus.). 192p. 1981. 28.50x (ISBN 0-669-04032-0). Lexington Bks.

Grunberger, Bela. Narcissism: Psychoanalytic Essays. Diamanti, Joyce, tr. from Fr. LC 77-92104. 322p. 1979. text ed. 30.00 (ISBN 0-8236-3491-4). Intl Univs Pr.

Grunberger, Dezider, jt. auth. see Singer, Bea.

Grunberger, Richard. The Twelve Year Reich. LC 69-16189. (Illus.). 1979. pap. 7.95 (ISBN 0-03-048226-7). HR&W.

Grunberg-Manago & Safer. Interaction of Translation & Transcriptual Controls in the Regulation of Gene Expression. (Developments in Biochemistry Ser.: Vol. 24). 524p. 1982. 93.00 (ISBN 0-444-00760-1, Biomedical Pr). Elsevier.

Grunchec, Philippe. Gericault's Horses: Drawings & Watercolors. Wheeler, Dan, tr. from Fr. LC 84-7308. (Illus.). 184p. Date not set. 60.00 (ISBN 0-86565-047-0). Vendome.

--Master Drawings by Gericault. Shuey, Barbara, ed. Despointes, Ann H., tr. LC 85-80174. (Illus.). 188p. (Orig.). 1985. pap. 11.40 (ISBN 0-88397-084-8); pap. text ed. 19.00 (ISBN 0-317-20239-1). Intl Exhibit Foun.

Grund. Benezit Dictionary of Artists, 10 Vols. 1976. 500.00 (ISBN 0-686-43137-5). Apollo.

Grund, D. W. & Harrison, K. A. Nova Scotian Boletes. (Bibliotheca Mycologica Ser.: No. 47). 1976. text ed. 21.00 (ISBN 3-7682-1062-6). Lubrecht & Cramer.

Grund, Fracis J. Aristocracy in America: From the Sketch-Book of a German Nobleman. 11.75 (ISBN 0-8446-0666-9). Peter Smith.

Grund, Francis J. Americans in Their Social & Political Relations, 2 Vols in 1. LC 70-124453. Repr. of 1837 ed. lib. bdg. 47.50x (ISBN 0-678-00741-1). Kelley.

Grundberg, Andy, jt. auth. see Olander, William.

Grundberg, Sibyl, jt. ed. see Dowrick, Stephanie.

Grunden, jt. auth. see Hunter.

Grundfast, Kenneth & Carney, Cynthia J. Childhood Ear Infections. (Illus.). 180p. 1985. pap. 6.95 (ISBN 0-936320-22-2, Pub. by Compact Bks). Interbook.

Grundfest, Jerry. George Clymer, Philadelphia Revolutionary, 1739-1813. 60.00 (ISBN 0-405-14082-7). Ayer Co Pubs.

Grundin, Elizabeth H. Literacy. 1979. text ed. 14.25 (ISBN 0-06-318128-2, IntlDept); pap. text ed. 9.25 (ISBN 0-06-318140-1). Har-Row.

Grundlehner, Philip. The Lyrical Bridge: Essays from Holderlin to Benn. LC 76-46765. (Illus.). 177p. 1978. 18.50 (ISBN 0-8386-1792-1). Fairleigh Dickinson.

--Sprich Deutsch! 2nd ed. (German.). 1983. pap. text ed. 15.95 (ISBN 0-03-060616-0). HR&W.

Grundlehner, Philip, jt. auth. see Campagna, Andrew.

Grundlehner, Philip, jt. auth. see Leetch, Beverly.

Grundler, Horst. The Study of Tooth Shapes: A Systematic Procedure. (Illus.). 104p. 1976. 28.00 (ISBN 3-87652-561-6). Quint Pub Co.

Grundler, Otto, jt. ed. see Chrisman, Miriam.

Grundman, Claire, jt. ed. see Pulliam, Tom.

Grundman, Clare, jt. auth. see Pulliam, Tom.

Grundman, Claudia B., compiled by. Calendar of Continental Congress Papers. viii, 133p. (Orig.). 1973. pap. text ed. 5.00 (ISBN 0-88490-028-2). VA State Lib.

Grundman, Donna. Days to Remember. (Orig.). 1984. pap. 3.50 (ISBN 0-440-11680-5). Dell.

Grundman, E. & Grunze, H., eds. Early Gastric Cancer. Orig. Title: Current Status of Early Diagnosis in Stomach Cancer. 1974. pap. 36.00 (ISBN 0-387-06802-3). Springer-Verlag.

Grundmann, Carol, jt. auth. see Williams, Barbara.

Grundmann, E. & Gross, R. Cytostatic Theory-A Double Edged Sword. LC 75-6742. (Recent Results in Cancer Research Ser.: No. 52). (Illus.). 200p. 1975. 35.00 (ISBN 0-387-07240-3). Springer-Verlag.

Grundmann, E., ed. Carcinogenesis. LC 79-10558. (Current Topics in Pathology Ser.: Vol. 67). 1979. 67.00 (ISBN 0-387-09344-3). Springer-Verlag.

--Drug Induced Pathology. (Current Topics in Phathology Ser.: Vol. 69). (Illus.). 384p. 1980. 72.00 (ISBN 0-387-10415-1). Springer-Verlag.

--Glomerulonephritis. LC 59-49162. (Current Topics in Pathology: Vol. 61). 320p. 1976. 59.00 (ISBN 0-387-07442-2). Springer-Verlag.

--Special Topics in Carcinogenesis. LC 73-11951. (Recent Results in Cancer Research: Vol. 44). (Illus.). 220p. 1974. 37.00 (ISBN 0-387-06460-5). Springer-Verlag.

Grundmann, E. & Kirsten, W. H., eds. Current Topics in Pathology, Vol. 59. 270p. 1974. 87.40 (ISBN 0-387-06737-X). Springer-Verlag.

--Current Topics in Pathology, Vol. 65. 1977. 60.00 (ISBN 0-387-08330-8). Springer-Verlag.

--Current Topics in Pathology: Continuation of Ergebnisse der Pathologie, Vol. 64. 1977. 60.00 (ISBN 0-387-08107-0). Springer-Verlag.

--Perinatal Pathology. LC 79-450. (Current Topics in Pathology: Vol. 66). (Illus.). 1979. 62.00 (ISBN 0-387-09207-2). Springer-Verlag.

Grundmann, E. & Oettgen, H. F., eds. Experimental & Clinical Effects of L-Asparaginase. LC 70-119455. (Recent Results in Cancer Research: Vol. 33). (Illus.). 1970. 44.00 (ISBN 0-387-04998-3). Springer-Verlag.

Grundmann, E. & Pedersen, E., eds. Cancer Registry. LC 74-23303. (Recent Results in Cancer Research: Vol. 50). (Illus.). vii, 191p. 1974. 33.00 (ISBN 0-387-07008-7). Springer-Verlag.

Grundmann, E., ed. see International Symposium of the "Gesellschaft Zur Bekampfung De Krebskran Kheiten Nordhrein-West-Falen E. V.", 7th, Dusseldorf, Oct. 1975.

Grundmann, E., ed. see International Symposium of the Gesellschaft Zur Bekaempfung der Krebskrankheiten Nordrhein-Westfalen E. V., Duesselford, Germany, October 17-18, 1974.

Grundmann, E., ed. see Symposium on the Epidemiology of Cancer, Lymphomas, Duesseldorf, Nov. 4-6, 1971.

Grundon, M. F., ed. The Alkaloids, Vols. 1-8. Incl. Vol. 1. 1969-70 Literature. 1971. 43.00 (ISBN 0-85186-257-8, Royal Soc Chem London); Vol. 2. 1970-71 Literature. 1972. 36.00 (ISBN 0-85186-267-5); Vol. 3. 1971-72 Literature. 1973. 37.00 (ISBN 0-85186-277-2); Vol. 4. 1972-73 Literature. 1974. 43.00 (ISBN 0-85186-287-X); Vol. 5. 1973-74 Literature. 1975. 47.00 (ISBN 0-85186-297-7); Vol. 6. 1974-75 Literature. 1976. 50.00 (ISBN 0-85186-307-8); Vol. 7. 1975-76 Literature. 1977. 65.00 (ISBN 0-85186-317-5); Vol. 8. 1976-77 Literature. 1978. 61.00 (ISBN 0-85186-327-2). LC 70-616637. Am Chemical.

Grundon, Michael F., jt. ed. see Waterman, Peter G.

Grundrey, Elizabeth. England by Bus. 1981. 5.95 (ISBN 0-600-20253-4, Pub. by B T A). Merrimack Pub Cir.

Grundstein, Nathan D. The Futures of Prudence: Pure Strategy & Aristotelian & Hobbesian Strategists. (Foundation for an Artificial Intelligence of Strategy Ser.: Vol. 2). 228p. 1984. 17.50 (ISBN 0-930305-00-0). Enter Achieve.

Grundstrom, Allan W. L'Analyse du Francais. LC 83-16768. (Illus.). 228p. (Orig., Fr.). 1984. lib. bdg. 24.00 (ISBN 0-8191-3568-2); pap. text ed. 12.50 (ISBN 0-8191-3569-0). U Pr of Amer.

Grundt, Eugene. A Cocktail of Poems. 64p. 1980. 5.00 (ISBN 0-682-49656-1). Exposition Pr FL.

Grundt, Leonard. Efficient Patterns for Adequate Library Service in a Large City: A Survey of Boston. (Monograph: No. 6). 121p. 1968. pap. 4.00x (ISBN 0-87845-028-9). U of Ill Lib Info Sci.

Grundtvig, N. F. What Constitutes Authentic Christianity? Nielsen, Ernest D., ed. & tr. from Ger. LC 84-48728. 128p. 1985. pap. 6.95 (ISBN 0-8006-1844-0, 1-1844). Fortress.

Grundtvig, Sven. Danish Fairy Tales. Cramer, J. Grant, tr. from Danish. (Illus.). vii, 115p. (gr. k-5). 1972. pap. 4.50 (ISBN 0-486-22891-6). Dover.

Grundtvig, Svendt. Danish Fairy Tales. Cramer, J. Grant, tr. 7.75 (ISBN 0-8446-4626-1). Peter Smith.

Grundy, Betty L. & Gravenstein, J. S. The Quality of Care in Anesthesia. (Illus.). 278p. 1982. 31.50 (ISBN 0-398-04641-7). C C Thomas.

Grundy, D. Gastroinestal Motility. 1985. lib. bdg. 38.75 (ISBN 0-85200-894-5, Pub. by MTP Pr England). Kluwer Academic.

Grundy, Denis. Secular, Compulsory & Free: The Education Act of 1872. (The Second Century in Australian Education Ser.: Vol. 5). (Illus.). 104p. 1972. pap. 8.50x (ISBN 0-522-84026-4, Pub. by Melbourne U Pr). Intl Spec Bk.

Grundy, Eddie E., jt. auth. see Sansone, Diane M.

Grundy, F. & Reinke, W. A. Health Practice Research & Formalized Managerial Methods. (Public Health Paper: No. 51). (Also avail. in French & Spanish). 1973. pap. 7.20 (ISBN 92-4-130051-5). World Health.

Grundy, George B. Great Persian War. LC 71-84875. (Illus.). Repr. of 1901 ed. 37.50 (ISBN 0-404-02945-0). AMS Pr.

Grundy, Isobel, ed. Samuel Johnson: New Critical Essays. LC 84-18401. (Critical Studies). 208p. 1984. 27.50x (ISBN 0-389-20534-6, BNB-08096). B&N Imports.

Grundy, Isobel, jt. ed. see Clements, Patricia.

Grundy, Isobel, ed. see Montagu, Mary W.

Grundy, J. R. Color Atlas of Conservative Dentistry. 1980. 49.95 (ISBN 0-8151-4018-5). Year Bk Med.

Grundy, J. T. Construction Technology, Vol. 1. (Illus.). 1977. pap. 19.95x (ISBN 0-7131-3387-2). Intl Ideas.

--Construction Technology, Vol. 2. (Illus.). 200p. 1979. pap. 19.95x (ISBN 0-7131-3403-8). Intl Ideas.

--Construction Technology, Vol. 3. (Illus.). 208p. 1981. pap. 19.95x (ISBN 0-7131-3419-4). Intl Ideas.

Grundy, Joan. Hardy & the Sister Arts. LC 78-20834. 204p. 1979. text ed. 28.50x (ISBN 0-06-492576-5). B&N Imports.

--The Poems of Henry Constable. 256p. 1960. 35.00x (ISBN 0-85323-262-8, Pub. by Liverpool Univ England). State Mutual Bk.

Grundy, Julia M. Ten Days in the Light of 'Akka. rev. ed. LC 79-12177. 1979. pap. 4.95 (ISBN 0-87743-131-0, 332-040). Baha'i.

Grundy, Kenneth W. Confrontation & Accomodation in Southern Africa. LC 72-78950. (Perspectives on Southern Africa Ser., No. 10). 1973. 36.50x (ISBN 0-520-02271-8). U of Cal Pr.

--Defense Legislation & Communal Politics. LC 77-620051. (Papers in International Studies: Africa Ser.: No. 33). 1977. pap. 5.00x (ISBN 0-89680-065-2, 82-91841, Ohio U Ctr Intl). Ohio U Pr.

--Soldiers Without Politics: Blacks in the South African Armed Forces. LC 82-2584. (Perspectives on Southern Africa Ser.: Vol. 33). 416p. 1983. text ed. 26.50x (ISBN 0-520-04710-9). U of Cal Pr.

Grundy, Kevin. Tackling Farm Waste. (Illus.). 250p. 18.95 (ISBN 0-85236-103-3, Pub. by Farming Pr UK). Diamond Farm Bk.

Grundy, Milton. The World of International Tax Planning. LC 83-15078. 1984. 39.50 (ISBN 0-521-25955-X). Cambridge U Pr.

Grundy, P. J. & Jones, G. A. Electron Microscopy in the Study of Materials. (Structure & Properties of Solids Ser.). 186p. 1976. pap. text ed. 17.50 (ISBN 0-7131-2522-5). E Arnold.

Grundy, Philip, tr. see Tsaloumas, Dimitris.

Grundy, R. F. Magnetohydrodynamic Energy for Electric Power Generation. LC 77-15220. (Energy Technology Review Ser.: No. 20). (Illus.). 1978. 36.00 (ISBN 0-8155-0689-9). Noyes.

Grundy, Richard D., jt. ed. see Epstein, Samuel S.

Grundy, Stuart, jt. auth. see Tobler, John.

Gruneau, Richard. Class, Sports, & Social Development. LC 82-21896. 224p. 1983. lib. bdg. 20.00x (ISBN 0-87023-387-4); pap. 10.50x (ISBN 0-87023-388-2). U of Mass Pr.

Gruneau, Richard, jt. ed. see Cantelon, Hart.

Grunebaum, G. E. von see Von Grunebaum, G. E.

Grunebaum, G. E. Von see Von Grunebaum, G. E.

Grunebaum, Gabriele, illus. How to Marbleize Paper. (Crafts (General) Ser.). 32p. 1984. pap. 2.50 (ISBN 0-486-24651-5). Dover.

Grunebaum, Gustave E., ed. Mediaeval Islam: A Study in Cultural Orientation. 2nd ed. 1961. pap. 5.95 (ISBN 0-226-31025-6, p69, Phoen). U of Chicago Pr.

Grunebaum, Gustave E. von see Abel, Armand, et al.

Grunebaum, Gustave E. Von see Von Grunebaum, Gustave E.

Grunebaum, Gustave E. von see Von Grunebaum, Gustave E.

Grunebaum, Gustave E. Von see Von Grunebaum, Gustave E. & Caillois, Roger.

Grunebaum, Gustave Von see Von Grunebaum, Gustave E.

Grunebaum, Henry & Weiss, Justin L. Mentally Ill Mothers & Their Children. 2nd ed. LC 82-10911. xvii, 378p. 1982. lib. bdg. 30.00x (ISBN 0-226-31029-9); pap. 9.95x (ISBN 0-226-31022-1). U of Chicago Pr.

Grunebaum, Henry U., jt. auth. see Cohler, Bertram J.

Gruneberg, M. M., jt. ed. see Oborne, D. J.

Gruneberg, Michael & Morris, Peter, eds. Applied Problems in Memory. 1979. 44.00 (ISBN 0-12-305150-9). Acad Pr.

Gruneberg, Michael & Oborne, David, eds. Psychology & Industrial Productivity. 340p. 1981. text ed. 40.50x (ISBN 0-333-27074-6, Pub. by Macmillan England). Humanities.

Gruneberg, Michael & Wall, Toby, eds. Social Psychology & Organizational Behaviour. LC 83-19871. 265p. 1984. text ed. 29.95x (ISBN 0-471-10326-8). Wiley.

Gruneberg, Michael M. Understanding Job Satisfaction. LC 78-20782. 170p. 1979. 44.95x (ISBN 0-470-26610-4). Halsted Pr.

Gruneberg, Michael M. & Oborne, David J. Industrial Productivity: A Psychological Perspective. LC 81-7521. 1982. 34.95x (ISBN 0-470-27194-9). Halsted Pr.

Gruneberg, Michael M. & Morris, Peter, eds. Aspects of Memory. 1978. pap. 12.50x (ISBN 0-416-71350-5, NO.2741). Methuen Inc.

Gruneberg, R. N. Microbiology for Clinicians. (Illus.). 200p. 1981. text ed. 21.50 (ISBN 0-8391-1682-9). Univ Park.

Grunelius, Elizabeth M. Early Childhood Education & the Waldorf School Plan. 1984. pap. 4.95 (ISBN 0-916786-06-4, Pub by Waldorf School Monographs). St George Bk Serv.

Gruner, Charles R. Plain Public Speaking. 192p. 1983. pap. text ed. write for info. (ISBN 0-02-348340-7). Macmillan.

--Understanding Laughter: The Workings of Wit & Humor. LC 78-16759. 272p. 1978. 22.95x (ISBN 0-88229-186-6). Nelson-Hall.

Gruner, Charles R., et al. Speech Communication in Society. 2nd ed. 1977. text ed. 22.86 (ISBN 0-205-05732-2, 4857321); instr's manual free (ISBN 0-205-05733-0). Allyn.

Gruner, Mark & Brown, Christopher K. Mark Gruner's Numbers of Life: An Introduction to Numerology. LC 78-57560. 1979. 9.95 (ISBN 0-8008-5639-2); pap. 3.95 (ISBN 0-08-805640-6). Taplinger.

Gruner, Rolf. Philosophies of History. 190p. 1985. text ed. write for info. Gower Pub Co.

--Theory & Power: On the Character of Modern Science. 1977. pap. text ed. 17.75x (ISBN 90-6032-087-5). Humanities.

Gruner, Shirley M. Economic Materialism & Social Moralism: A Study in the History of Ideas in France from the Latter Part of the 18th Century to the Middle of the 19th Century. LC 72-88191. (Studies in the Social Sciences: No. 11). 1973. pap. text ed. 17.60x (ISBN 90-2792-416-3). Mouton.

Grunes, Barbara. All Holiday Menus. (Illus.). 64p. (Orig.). 1984. pap. 3.50 (ISBN 0-8249-3041-X). Ideals.

--Chef's Kitchen Companion. (Illus.). 1040p. 1984. 39.95 (ISBN 0-8249-3045-2). Ideals.

--Dining In-Chicago, Vol. III. (Dining In Ser.). 192p. 1983. pap. 8.95 (ISBN 0-89716-125-4). Peanut Butter.

--Dining In-Chicago, Vol. 2. (Dining In Ser.). 200p. (Orig.). 1982. pap. 8.95 (ISBN 0-89716-108-4). Peanut Butter.

--Fish & Shellfish. (Illus.). 64p. (Orig.). 1985. pap. 3.50 (ISBN 0-8249-3044-4). Ideals.

--Lunch & Brunch. (Illus.). 64p. (Orig.). 1985. pap. 3.50 (ISBN 0-8249-3065-7). Ideals.

--Mexican Cookbook. 64p. (Orig.). 1981. pap. 3.50 (ISBN 0-8249-3000-2). Ideals.

--Oriental Express: Chinese Menus for the Food Processor. Horowitz, Maxine, ed. Orig. Title: Cuisine Die Chine. 1979. pap. 5.00 (ISBN 0-932398-01-4). Good Food Bks.

Grunes, Barbara, jt. auth. see Horowitz, Maxine.

Grunes, D. L. & Rendig, V. V., eds. Grass Tetany. (Illus.). 1979. pap. 5.00 (ISBN 0-89118-056-7). Am Soc Agron.

Grunewald, Alan E., jt. auth. see Nemmers, Erwin E.

Grunewald, Donald. What You Should Know about Small Business Management. LC 66-25580. (Business Almanac Ser.: No. 6). 96p. 1966. 5.95 (ISBN 0-379-11206-X). Oceana.

Grunewald, Donald, jt. ed. see Mercy College.

Grunewald, H., ed. Chemistry for the Future: Proceedings of the 29th IUPAC Congress, Cologne, Federal Republic of Germany, 5-10 June 1983. LC 83-23825. (IUPAC Symposium Ser.). 268p. 1984. 95.00 (ISBN 0-08-029249-6). Pergamon.

Grunewald, Mathais. The Drawings of Mathis Gothart Nithert, Called Grunewald. Schoenberger, Guido, ed. LC 83-45775. Repr. of 1948 ed. 49.50 (ISBN 0-404-20113-X). AMS Pr.

Grunfeld. Advances in Nephrology, Vol. 14. 1985. 65.00 (ISBN 0-8151-4137-8). Year Bk Med.

--The Jewish Dietary Laws, 2 vols. 1973. Set. 32.95x (ISBN 0-900689-09-9). Bloch.

Grunfeld, Dayan I. The Jewish Dietary Laws, 2 vols. 246p. 1972. Vol. 1, 246 pgs. pap. 29.95 (ISBN 0-900689-10-2); Vol. 2, 285 pgs. pap. 32.95 slipcased (ISBN 0-900689-11-0). Soncino Pr NY.

Grunfeld, Emil N. The Blessed Yoke. 304p. (Orig.). 1982. pap. 5.95 (ISBN 0-686-42885-4). Makor Pub.

Grunfeld, Frederic V. The Art & Times of the Guitar. (Music Reprint Ser.). 340p. 1985. Repr. of 1969 ed. 39.50 (ISBN 0-306-76257-9). Da Capo.

Grunfeld, I. The Sabbath. 4th rev. ed. (Sabbath & Festivals Ser.). 96p. (Orig.). 1982. 6.95; pap. 4.95 (ISBN 0-87306-266-3). Feldheim.

--The Sabbath: A Guide to Its Understanding & Observance. pap. 3.95 (ISBN 0-87306-099-7). Feldheim.

Grunfeld, Joseph. Method & Language. 208p. (Orig.). 1982. pap. 26.00x (ISBN 90-6032-110-3). Benjamins North Am.

--Method & Language. 208p. 1982. pap. text ed. 28.25x (ISBN 90-6032-110-3, Pub. by Gruner Amsterdam). Humanities.

--Science & Values. 210p. 1980. text ed. 23.50x (ISBN 90-6032-018-2). Humanities.

Grunfeld, Joseph, ed. Growth in a Finite World. LC 78-27457. (Illus.). 1979. pap. 7.95 (ISBN 0-89168-022-5). L Erlbaum Assocs.

Grunfeld, Judith. Shefford. 1980. pap. 7.50 (ISBN 0-900689-55-2). Soncino Pr NY.

Grunfeld, Nina. The Royal Shopping Guide. LC 83-13221. (Illus.). 256p. 1984. 15.95 (ISBN 0-688-04080-2). Morrow.

Grung, B L., jt. auth. see Warner, R M.

Grunhut, Max. Juvenile Offenders Before the Courts. LC 77-27073. (Illus.). vii, 143p. 1978. Repr. of 1956 ed. lib. bdg. 15.50x (ISBN 0-313-20194-3, GRJU). Greenwood.

--Penal Reform: A Comparative Study. LC 71-172568. (Criminology, Law Enforcement, & Social Problems Ser.: No. 149). 502p. 1972. Repr. of 1948 ed. 22.00x (ISBN 0-87585-149-5). Patterson Smith.

Grunig, James, ed. Decline of the Global Village: How Specialization Is Changing the Mass Media. LC 76-9295. (Illus.). 297p. 1976. lib. bdg. 28.95x (ISBN 0-930390-30-X); pap. text ed. 14.95x (ISBN 0-930390-29-6). Gen Hall.

Grunig, James E. & Hunt, Todd T. Managing Public Relations. 640p. 1984. text ed. 29.95x (ISBN 0-03-058337-3); instr's. manual 19.95 (ISBN 0-03-058338-1). Dryden Pr.

Grunin, Robert, jt. ed. see Gitter, A. George.

Gruning, Martha S., tr. see Seruzier, Charles.

Grunkemeier, Garry. A Performance Guide to Artificial Heart Valves. 1985. pap. text ed. 60.00 (ISBN 0-8391-2043-5, 21539). Univ Park.

Grunlan, Stephen & Reimer, Milton K., eds. Christian Perspectives on Sociology. 448p. (Orig.). 1982. pap. 10.95 (ISBN 0-310-36331-4). Zondervan.

Grunlan, Stephen A. Marriage & the Family: A Christian Perspective. 384p. 1984. pap. 10.95 (ISBN 0-310-36341-1). Zondervan.

--Serving with Joy: A Study in Philippians. LC 85-71352. 115p. 1985. pap. 4.95 (ISBN 0-87509-371-X); leader's guide 2.95 (ISBN 0-87509-372-8). Chr Pubns.

Grunlan, Stephen A. & Mayers, Marvin K. Cultural Anthropology: A Christian Perspective. 1979. 9.95 (ISBN 0-310-36321-7). Zondervan.

Grunmann-Gaudet, Minnette & Jones, Robin F., eds. The Nature of Medieval Narrative. LC 80-66330. (French Forum Monographs: No. 22). 216p. (Orig.). 1980. pap. 12.50x (ISBN 0-917058-21-6). French Forum.

Grunow, A., jt. auth. see Cleve, P. T.

Grunow, Dieter & Hegner, Friedhart, eds. Welfare or Bureaucracy: Problems of Matching Social Services to Clients' Needs. LC 80-20631. (Research on Service Delivery Ser.: Vol. 2). 256p. 1980. text ed. 35.00 (ISBN 0-89946-060-7). Oelgeschlager.

Grunow, Oskar, tr. see Jaspers, Karl.

Grunsell & Hill. Veterinary Annual Twenty Fifth Issue. 1985. 23.50 (ISBN 0-85608-039-X). PSG Pub Co.

Grunsell, et al. Veterinary Annual. 26th ed. 1986. price not set. PSG Pub Co.

Grunsell, Bob. Absent from School: The Story of a Truancy Centre. (Chameleon Education Ser.). Orig. Title: Born to Be Invisible. 128p. (Orig.). 1981. pap. 4.95 (ISBN 0-906495-42-3). Writers & Readers.

Grunsell, Rob. Beyond Control? Schools & Suspension. (Chameleon Education Ser.). 148p. (Orig.). 1981. pap. 4.95 (ISBN 0-906495-23-7). Writers & Readers.

Grunsky, H. General Stokes Theorem. (Surveys & Reference Works in Mathematics Ser.: No. 9). 112p. 1983. text ed. 35.95 (ISBN 0-273-08510-7). Pitman Pub Ma.

Grunt, Manfred, jt. auth. see Bessant, John.

Grunwald, Bernice B. & McAbee, Harold v. Guiding the Family. LC 84-70098. 250p. 1985. pap. 16.95 (ISBN 0-915202-43-3). Accel Devel.

Grunwald, Joseph & Flamm, Kenneth. The Global Factory: Foreign Assembly in International Trade. 300p. 1985. 29.95 (ISBN 0-8157-3304-6); pap. 10.95 (ISBN 0-8157-3303-8). Brookings.

Grunwald, Joseph & Musgrove, Philip. Natural Resources in Latin American Development. LC 77-108381. pap. 128.00 (ISBN 0-317-26462-1, 2023798). Bks Demand UMI.

Grunwald, Joseph, ed. Latin America & World Economy: A Changing International Order. LC 77-17031. (Latin American International Affairs Ser.: Vol. 2). 323p. Date not set. 22.50x (ISBN 0-8039-0864-4); Pub., 02/1978. pap. 12.50 (ISBN 0-8039-0966-7). Sage.

Grunwald, Kurt. Turkenhirsch: A Study of Baron Maurice de Hirsch. 158p. 1966. casebound 9.95x (ISBN 0-87855-182-4). Transaction Bks.

Grunwald, Kurt & Ronall, Joachim O. Industrialization in the Middle East. Shwadran, Benjamin, ed. LC 75-16486. (Illus.). 394p. 1975. Repr. of 1960 ed. lib. bdg. 22.50x (ISBN 0-8371-8192-5, GRIME). Greenwood.

Grunwald, Lisa. Summer. LC 85-40115. 224p. 1985. 14.95 (ISBN 0-394-54535-4). Knopf.

Grunwald, Stefan. The Renderings of Stefanos: Book I, Science & Technology. LC 79-10680. 1980. pap. 4.95 (ISBN 0-915442-91-4, Unilaw). Donning Co.

Grunwald, Stefan, jt. auth. see Burlage, L. Charles.

Grunwald, Stefan, ed. see Nau, Erika S.

Grunwald, Stefan, ed. see Noyle, Ken.

Grunwald, Stefan F. A Biography of Johann Michael Moscherosch (1601-1669) (European University Studies: Series 1, German Language & Literature: Vol. 18). 96p. 1969. pap. 6.55 (ISBN 3-261-00017-1). P Lang Pubs.

Grunwald-Beyer, A. Technisches Taschenwoerterbuch. 533p. (Ger. & Fr.). 25.00 (ISBN 3-87749-013-1, M-7646, Pub. by Georg Siemens Verlagsbuchhandlung). French & Eur.

Grunwaldt, H., jt. ed. see Schmidt, W. K.

Grunwedel, Albert. Buddhist Art in India. rev. ed. Burgess, James, ed. Gibson, Agnes C., tr. LC 65-3064. (Illus.). Repr. of 1901 ed. 25.00x (ISBN 0-678-07260-4). Kelley.

Grunwell, P. The Nature of Phonological Disability in Children. LC 80-42269. (Studies in Applied Linguistics). 256p. 1981. 46.00 (ISBN 0-12-305250-5). Acad Pr.

Grunwell, Pamela. Clinical Phonology. 224p. 28.50 (ISBN 0-89443-392-X). Aspen Systems.

Grunze, H., jt. ed. see Grundman, E.

Grunze, Richard. Bible History: Teachers' Manual. 228p. 1985. suedene vinyl 3-ring binder 12.95 (ISBN 0-938272-15-2). WELS Board.

--Paul: An Example for Christian Teachers. 1979. pap. text ed. 3.50 (ISBN 0-8100-0108-X, 07N0740). Northwest Pub.

--The Young Christian's Life. (gr. 7-8). 1979. 9.95 (ISBN 0-8100-0104-7, 06N0557). Northwest Pub.

Grunze, Richard, ed. Bible History. (WELS Lutheran Elementary Schools' Religion Curriculum Ser.). (Illus.). 556p. (gr. 5-6). 1984. 11.95 (ISBN 0-938272-14-4). WELS Board.

Grunze, Richard, ed. see Fehlauer, Adolph.

Grunzweig, Walter. Charles Sealsfield. LC 85-70131. (Western Writers Ser.: No. 71). (Illus.). 50p. (Orig.). 1985. pap. 2.00x (ISBN 0-88430-045-5). Boise St Univ.

Grupe, O., ed. see Scientific Congress Munich, Aug 21-25, 1972.

Grupenhoff, John T. National Health Directory, 1984. 752p. 1984. 59.00 (ISBN 0-89443-824-7). Aspen Systems.

Grupenhoff, John T., ed. National News Media Directory: Medicine Health, 1980-1981. 220p. text ed. 35.00 (ISBN 0-89443-350-4). Aspen Systems.

Grupo de Investigadores Puertorriquenos. Breakthrough from Colonialism: An Interdisciplinary Study of Statehood, 2 Vols. LC 83-1326. xxiv, 1532p. pap. 40.00 (ISBN 0-8477-2491-3). U of PR Pr.

Grupp, Fred W., Jr. & Maurer, Marvin, eds. Political Behavior in the United States: Readings in American Government. LC 71-182885. (Illus.). 1972. pap. text ed. 4.95x (ISBN 0-89197-348-6). Irvington.

Grupp, Gunter, ed. Interactions of Biomedical Communicators Within the Health Care System. (Biosciences Communications: Vol. 2, No. 4). (Illus.). 1976. 13.00 (ISBN 3-8055-2427-7). S Karger.

Grupp, Stanley. Marijuana. LC 72-157698. 1971. pap. text ed. 9.95 (ISBN 0-675-09834-3). Merrill.

Grupp, Stanley E., ed. Theories of Punishment. LC 73-165047. (Illus.). Repr. of 1971 ed. 101.80 (ISBN 0-8357-9247-1, 2012998). Bks Demand UMI.

Gruppe, Emil A. Brushwork for the Oil Painter. (Illus.). 1977. 18.95 (ISBN 0-8230-0525-9). Watson-Guptill.

Gruppe, Emile. Brushwork for the Oil Painter: Develop a Lively Painting Style Through Expressive Brushwork. Movalli, Charles, ed. (Illus.). 144p. 1983. 23.50 (ISBN 0-8230-0526-7). Watson-Guptill.

Gruppe, Henry. The Frigates. Time-Life Books Editors, ed. (Seafarers Ser.). (Illus.). 1980. 13.95 (ISBN 0-8094-2715-X). Time-Life.

Gruppe, M. The Frigates. LC 79-10643. (The Seafarers Ser.). (Illus.). 1979. lib. bdg. 21.27 (ISBN 0-8094-2716-8, Pub. by Time-Life); 17.28 (ISBN 0-8094-2717-6). Silver.

Gruppe, Otto. Griechische Mythologie und Religionsgeschichte, 2 vols. facsimile ed. LC 75-10638. (Ancient Religion & Mythology Ser.). (Ger.). 1976. Repr. of 1906 ed. 144.00x set (ISBN 0-405-07015-2). Ayer Co Pubs.

Grupper, David & Klein, David G. The Paper Shtetl: A Complete Model of an East European Jewish Town. LC 83-42714. (Illus., Orig.). (gr. 6-12). 1984. pap. 11.95 (ISBN 0-8052-0749-X). Schocken.

Gruppo Editoriale Fabbri. Arnold Newman. (Great Photographer's Ser.). Date not set. price not set. P-H.

--Jay Maisel. (Great Photographer's Ser.). Date not set. price not set. P-H.

--Jeanloup Sieff. (Great Photographer's Ser.). Date not set. price not set. P-H.

--Man Ray. (Great Photographer's Ser.). Date not set. price not set. P-H.

--Pete Turner. (Great Photographer's Ser.). Date not set. price not set. P-H.

Gruppo Professionale. Advanced Computations & Trials for Car Radiators. 62p. 1968. 9.30 (ISBN 0-317-34496-X, 124). Intl Copper.

Grusa, Jiri. Franz Kafka of Prague. Mossbacher, Eric, tr. from Ger. (Illus.). 128p. (Orig.). 1983. pap. 12.95 (ISBN 0-8052-0748-1). Schocken.

--The Questionnaire. LC 83-48031. (The Library of Contemporary World Literature). 304p. 1983. pap. 7.95 (ISBN 0-394-72212-4, Vin). Random.

--The Questionnaire: Or, Prayer for a Town & a Friend. Kussi, Peter, tr. from Czech. 288p. 1982. 15.95 (ISBN 0-374-24010-8). FS&G.

Gruschcow, Jack. SuperCalc One & Two: Applications Book. (Illus.). 1984. pap. 17.95 (ISBN 0-8359-7307-7). Reston.

Gruschka, H. & Wecken, F. Gasdynamic Theory of Detonation: Combustion Science & Technology. 210p. 1971. 57.75 (ISBN 0-677-03370-2). Gordon.

Grusec, Joan E., jt. auth. see Walters, Gary C.

Grush, Byron. The Shoestring Animator: Making Animated Films with Super Eight. (Illus.). 160p. 1981. pap. 6.95 (ISBN 0-8092-5884-6). Contemp Bks.

Grushcow, Jack. Business Worksheets for Lotus 1-2-3. (Illus.). 1984. pap. 16.95 (ISBN 0-8359-0547-0); Diskette. 49.00. Reston.

--The VisiCalc Applications Book for the Apple IIe. 16.95 (ISBN 0-8359-8388-9). Reston.

--VisiCalc Extensions for the Apple II & IIe. (Illus.). 1984. pap. 16.95 (ISBN 0-8359-8403-6); text ed. 21.95 (ISBN 0-8359-8404-4). Reston.

--VisiCalc Extensions for the IBM PC & PC XT. (Illus.). 1984. pap. 16.95 (ISBN 0-8359-8405-2). Reston.

Grushcow, Jack & Smith, Courtney. Profits Through Seasonal Trading. LC 80-11929. 200p. 1980. 58.95 (ISBN 0-471-06158-1). Wiley.

Grushka, E. New Developments in Separation Methods. 1976. 49.75 (ISBN 0-8247-6411-0). Dekker.

Grushkin, Paul, et al. Grateful Dead: The Official Book of the Deadheads. LC 82-62276. (Illus.). 224p. 1983. pap. 12.95 (ISBN 0-688-01520-4, Quill NY); deluxe ed. 24.95 (ISBN 0-688-01917-X). Morrow.

Grushkin, Paul D. The Rock Poster. (Illus.). 432p. 1985. 75.00 (ISBN 0-89659-584-6). Abbeville Pr.

Grushow, Ira. The Imaginary Reminiscences of Sir Max Beerbohm. LC 83-19504. xviii, 287p. 1984. text ed. 28.95x (ISBN 0-8214-0723-6). Ohio U Pr.

--The Imaginary Reminiscences of Sir Max Beerbohm. xviii, 287p. 1985. pap. 13.95 (ISBN 0-8214-0766-X). Ohio U Pr.

Gruska, J., ed. Mathematical Foundations of Computer Science 1977: Proceedings, 6th Symposium, Tatranska Lmnica, Sept. 5-9, 1977. LC 77-10135. (Lecture Notes in Computer Science: Vol. 53). 1977. pap. 28.00 (ISBN 0-387-08353-7). Springer-Verlag.

Gruska, J., ed. see Chytil, M.

Gruskin, Alan, jt. auth. see Fine, Richard N.

Gruskin, Alan B., ed. see Pediatric Nephrology, International, 5th, Symposium, 1980.

Gruskin, Edward. The Invincible Doc Savage. (Illus.). pap. 3.95x (ISBN 0-933752-25-3). Odyssey MA.

Grusko, I. I., et al. Eleven Papers from the Fourth Prague Conference on Information Theory, Statistical Decision Functions, & Random Processes. LC 61-9803. (Selected Translations in Mathematical Statistics & Probability, Ser.: Vol. 8). 1970. 30.00 (ISBN 0-8218-1458-3, STAPRO-8). Am Math.

Grusky, Oscar & Pollner, Melvin. The Sociology of Mental Illness. 1981. pap. text ed. 25.95 (ISBN 0-03-053211-6, HoltC). HR&W.

Grusky, Oscar & Miller, George A., eds. The Sociology of Organizations: Basic Studies. LC 80-1060. (Illus.). 1981. 24.95 (ISBN 0-02-913060-3); pap. text ed. 12.95 (ISBN 0-02-912930-3). Free Pr.

Grusky, Oscar, jt. auth. see Johnson, Allen W.

Gruss, Edmond C. Apostles of Denial. 1970. pap. 7.95 (ISBN 0-87552-305-6). Presby & Reformed.

--Cults & the Occult. rev. ed. 1980. pap. 2.95 (ISBN 0-87552-308-0). Presby & Reformed.

--Jehovah's Witnesses & Prophetic Speculation. pap. 3.75 (ISBN 0-8010-3710-7). Baker Bk.

--Jehovah's Witnesses & Prophetic Speculation. 1972. pap. 3.75 (ISBN 0-87552-306-4). Presby & Reformed.

--We Left Jehovah's Witnesses. pap. 3.95 (ISBN 0-8010-3696-8). Baker Bk.

--We Left Jehovah's Witnesses: A Non-Prophet Organization. 1974. pap. 3.95 (ISBN 0-87552-307-2). Presby & Reformed.

--What Every Mormon Should Know. (Orig.). 1975. micro book 1.45 (ISBN 0-916406-34-2). Accent Bks.

Gruss, Edmund C. Cults & the Occult in the Age of Aquarius. (Direction Bks). pap. 2.95 (ISBN 0-8010-3682-8). Baker Bk.

Gruss, Jane F. Counseling Stutterers. (Publications on Stuttering: No. 18). 80p. 1982. pap. 1.50 (ISBN 0-933388-18-7). Speech Found Am.

Gruss, Jane Fraser, ed. Stuttering Therapy, Transfer & Maintenance. LC 83-240657. 112p. 1985. pap. 1.50 (ISBN 0-933388-19-5). Speech Found Am.

Gruss, Robert. Dictionnaire de Marine, Francais et Anglais. 368p. (Fr. & Eng.). 1978. 49.95 (ISBN 0-686-57319-6, M-6302). French & Eur.

Grusz, Eva, tr. see Wellner, Istvan.

Grutchfield, Martha, ed. Music for Orchestra, Band & Large Ensemble, Vol. 3. (American Music Center Library Catalog). 204p. (Orig.). 1982. pap. 10.00 (ISBN 0-916052-05-2). Am Music Ctr.

Gruter, Arnoldus & Rood, Jean. Country Harvest. (Illus., Orig.). 1984. pap. 6.50 (ISBN 0-941284-23-9). Deco Design Studio.

Gruter, Margaret & Bohannon, Paul, eds. Law, Biology & Culture: The Evolution of Law. 226p. 1983. pap. 10.95 (ISBN 0-915520-63-X). Ross-Erikson.

Grutzmacher, Hal & Grutzmacher, Stephen. Generations. 80p. (Orig.). 1983. pap. 4.95 (ISBN 0-933180-47-0). Spoon Riv Poetry.

Grutzmacher, Stephen, jt. auth. see Grutzmacher, Hal.

Gruver, Bert. The Stage Manager's Handbook. rev. ed. LC 72-190641. (Illus.). 1972. pap. text ed. 7.95x (ISBN 0-89676-007-3). Drama Bk.

Gruver, Cynthia. Country Inns of the Southwest. LC 85-13675. (Country Inns Ser.). (Illus.). 240p. (Orig.). 1985. pap. 7.95 (ISBN 0-89286-254-8). One Hund One Prods.

Gruver, Rebecca B. An American History. 4th ed. 1985. text ed. 25.00 (ISBN 0-394-35041-3, RanC); Vol. 2. pap. text ed. 17.95 (ISBN 0-394-35043-X); Set. 8.95 (ISBN 0-394-35045-6). Random.

Gruver, Suzanne C. The Cape Cod Cookbook. (Cookbook Ser.). 1977. pap. 3.95 (ISBN 0-486-23564-5). Dover.

--The Cape Cod Cookbook. 11.25 (ISBN 0-8446-5685-2). Peter Smith.

Gruver, W. A. Simulation & Identification in Biological Science. 160p. 1985. Repr. lib. bdg. 19.95x (ISBN 0-89370-892-5). Borgo Pr.

Gruver, W. A. & Sachs, E. Algorithmic Methods in Optimal Control. (Research Notes in Mathematics Ser.: No. 47). 256p. 1981. pap. text ed. 27.50 (ISBN 0-273-08473-9). Pitman Pub MA.

Gruverman, I. J. & Seidel, C. W., eds. Mossbauer Effect Methodology, Vol. 10. LC 65-21188. 342p. 1976. 49.50x (ISBN 0-306-38810-3, Plenum Pr). Plenum Pub.

Gruverman, Irwin J., et al, eds. Mossbauer Effect Methodology, Vol 9. 344p. 1974. 35.00x (ISBN 0-306-38809-X, Plenum Pr). Plenum Pub.

Gruzalski, Bart, jt. ed. see Nelson, Carl.

Gruzanski, C. V. Spike & Chain. 7.50x (ISBN 0-685-38452-7). Wehman.

Gruzanski, Charles V. Spike & Chain: Japanese Fighting Arts. LC 68-15019. (Illus.). 1968. 7.50 (ISBN 0-8048-0540-7). C E Tuttle.

Gruzdyev, G., et al. Chemical Protection of Plants. 471p. 1983. 13.95 (ISBN 0-8285-2741-5, Pub. by Mir Pubs USSR). Imported Pubns.

Gruzelier, J., jt. ed. see Flor-Henry, P.

Gruzelier, J. H. & Flor-Henry, P. Hemisphere Asymetries of Function in Psychopathology. (Developments in Psychiatry Ser.: Vol. 3). 678p. 1980. 75.75 (ISBN 0-444-80189-8, Biomedical Pr). Elsevier.

Gruzenberg, O. O. Yesterday: Memoirs of a Russian-Jewish Lawyer. Rawson, Don C., ed. & tr. from Rus. LC 80-39850. 288p. 1981. 30.00x (ISBN 0-520-04264-6). U of Cal Pr.

Gryboski, Joyce. Gastrointestinal Problems in the Infant. LC 74-21012. (Major Problems in Clinical Pediatrics Ser.: Vol. 13). pap. 120.00 (ISBN 0-317-08715-0, 2016665). Bks Demand UMI.

Gryboski, Joyce D. & Walker, W. Allan. Gastrointestinal Problems in the Infant. (Illus.). 484p. 1983. 75.00 (ISBN 0-7216-4329-9). Saunders.

Grygar, Mojmir, jt. ed. see Van Der Eng, Jan.

Grygier, Tadeusz. Oppression. LC 73-14194. (International Library of Sociology & Social Reconstruction: A Study in Social & Criminal Psychology). 362p. 1974. Repr. of 1954 ed. lib. bdg. 27.50x (ISBN 0-8371-7145-8, GROP). Greenwood.

--Social Protection Code: A New Model of Criminal Justice. (American Series of Foreign Penal Codes: Vol. 22). xxiv, 96p. 1977. text ed. 15.00x (ISBN 0-8377-0605-X). Rothman.

Gryglewski, Richard J., et al, eds. Prostacyclin: Clinical Trials. 160p. 1985. text ed. 38.00 (ISBN 0-88167-051-0). Raven.

Grylls, Glynn R. Mary Shelley: A Biography. LC 74-12163. 1973. lib. bdg. 25.00 (ISBN 0-8414-4535-4). Folcroft.

Grylls, R. Trelawny. 1950. 20.00 (ISBN 0-8274-3648-3). R West.

Grylls, R. Glynn. Mary Shelley: A Biography. LC 76-95428. (English Biography Ser., No. 31). 1969. Repr. of 1938 ed. lib. bdg. 49.95x (ISBN 0-8383-0978-X). Haskell.

Grylls, Rosalie G. Portrait of Rosetti. LC 65-9497. (Illus.). 272p. 1970. pap. 2.45 (ISBN 0-8093-0420-1). S Ill U Pr.

--William Godwin & His Work. LC 74-13753. 1974. Repr. of 1953 ed. lib. bdg. 20.00 (ISBN 0-8414-4525-7). Folcroft.

--William Godwin & His World. 1978. Repr. of 1953 ed. lib. bdg. 30.00 (ISBN 0-8495-1930-6). Arden Lib.

Grymeston, Elizabeth. Miscelanea, Meditations, Memoratives. LC 79-84114. (English Experience Ser.: No. 933). 68p. 1979. Repr. of 1604 ed. lib. bdg. 8.00 (ISBN 90-221-0933-X). Walter J Johnson.

Grymkowski, Peter, et al. The Gold's Gym Training Encyclopedia. (Illus.). 256p. (Orig.). 1984. pap. 12.95 (ISBN 0-8092-5446-8). Contemp Bks.

Gryn, Tom. Growing Closer to God. 100p. (Orig.). 1982. pap. 2.50 (ISBN 0-89283-160-X). Servant.

Gryna, Frank M., Jr., jt. auth. see Juran, Joseph M.

Grynberg, G. & Stora, R., eds. New Trends in Atomic Physics: Proceedings of the Les Houches Summer School, Session XXXVIII, 28 June-29 July, 1982, 2 pts. (Les Houches Summer School Proceedings Ser.: Vol. 38). 1250p. 1985. Set. 259.25 (ISBN 0-444-86823-2, North Holland); Pt. I. 138.50 (ISBN 0-444-86908-5, North Holland); Pt. II. 163.50 (ISBN 0-444-86909-3, North Holland). Elsevier.

Gryndall, William. Hawking, Hunting, Fouling & Fishing; Newly Corrected by W. Gryndall Faulkener. LC 70-38194. (English Experience Ser.: No. 463). 88p. 1972. Repr. of 1596 ed. 13.00 (ISBN 90-221-0463-X). Walter J Johnson.

Gryniewicz, Deborah L., et al. Nuclear Medicine Technology Examination Review. LC 79-17328. (Orig.). 1980. pap. 14.95 (ISBN 0-668-04724-0). ACC.

Grynszpan, R. I., jt. ed. see Chappert, J.

Gryski, Camilla. Cat's Cradle, Owl's Eyes: A Book of String Games. (Illus.). 80p. (gr. 3 up). 1984. PLB 9.55 (ISBN 0-688-03940-5, Morrow Junior Books); pap. 6.95 (ISBN 0-688-03941-3). Morrow.

--Many Stars & More String Games. LC 85-4875. (Illus.). 80p. (gr. 3 up). 1985. lib. bdg. 10.88 (ISBN 0-688-05793-4); pap. 6.95 (ISBN 0-688-05792-6). Morrow.

Gryski, Gerard S. Bureaucratic Policy Making in a Technological Society. 320p. 1981. 18.95x (ISBN 0-87073-831-3); pap. text ed. 9.95x (ISBN 0-87073-829-1). Schenkman Bks Inc.

Gryskievicz, Stanley S., ed. Selected Readings in Creativity, 2 vols. (Creativity Week Ser.). 1983. Set. 35.00 (ISBN 0-912879-81-5). Ctr Creat Leader.

Gryskiewicz, Stanley S., ed. Creativity Week I: Nineteen Seventy Eight Proceedings. (Creativity Week Ser.). 144p. 1979. pap. 20.00 (ISBN 0-912879-75-0). Ctr Creat Leader.

--Creativity Week II: Nineteen Seventy Nine Proceedings. (Creativity Week Ser.). 151p. 1980. pap. 20.00 (ISBN 0-912879-76-9). Ctr Creat Leader.

--Creativity Week III: Nineteen Eighty Proceedings. (Creativity Week Ser.). 185p. 1981. pap. 20.00 (ISBN 0-912879-77-7). Ctr Creat Leader.

Gryskiewicz, Stanley S. & Shields, James, eds. Blueprint for Innovation: Proceedings. (Creativity Week Ser.: No. 6). 1984. 20.00 (ISBN 0-912879-80-7). Ctr Creat Leader.

Gryskiewicz, Stanley S. & Shields, James T., eds. Creativity Week IV: Nineteen Eighty One Proceedings. (Creativity Week Ser.). 171p. 1982. pap. 20.00 (ISBN 0-912879-78-5). Ctr Creat Leader.

--Creativity Week V: Nineteen Eighty Two Proceedings. (Creativity Week Ser.). 145p. 1983. pap. 20.00 (ISBN 0-686-89247-X). Ctr Creat Leader.

Gryson, R. Le Receuil Arien de Verone. 1983. 46.00 (ISBN 90-247-2705-7, Pub. by Martinus Nijhoff Netherlands). Kluwer Academic.

Gryst, Gary. Eden Hotel. 1978. 1.50 (ISBN 0-917554-08-6). Maelstrom.

Grzebieniowski. Langenscheidt Polish Pocket Dictionary. pap. 8.95 (ISBN 0-88729-109-0). Langenscheidt.

Grzegorczyk, A. An Outline of Mathematical Logic: Fundamental Results & Notions Explained with All Details. LC 72-97956. (Synthese Library: No. 70). 1974. lib. bdg. 66.00 (ISBN 90-277-0359-0, Pub. by Reidel Holland); pap. text ed. 34.25 (ISBN 90-277-0447-3, Pub. by Reidel Holland). Kluwer Academic.

Grzelak, Janusz, jt. ed. see Derlega, Valerian.

Grzesiek, David J. Financial Independence Through Buying & Investing in Single Family Homes. LC 84-1135. 281p. 1985. 14.95 (ISBN 0-88289-440-4). Pelican.

Grzesinski, Albert C. Inside Germany. Lipschitz, Alexander S., tr. LC 79-180405. Repr. of 1939 ed. 27.00 (ISBN 0-404-56129-2). AMS Pr.

Grzimek, Martin. Heartstop. Mitchell, Breon, tr. from Ger. LC 84-11546. Orig. Title: Stillstand des Herzens. 192p. 1984. 17.95 (ISBN 0-8112-0921-0); pap. 8.95 (ISBN 0-8112-0922-9, NDP583). New Directions.

Grzybowski, Joseph A. & Schnell, Gary D. Oklahoma Orinthology: An Annotated Bibliography. 192p. 19.95 (ISBN 0-317-12257-6). U of Okla Pr.

--Oklahoma Ornithology: An Annotated Bibliography. (Stovall Museum Publications Ser.: Vol. 5). 176p. 19.95 (ISBN 0-8061-1887-3). U of Okla Pr.

Grzybowski, Kazimierz. Soviet Legal Institutions: Doctrines & Social Functions. LC 62-12163. (Michigan Legal Publications). xiv, 285p. 1982. Repr. of 1962 ed. lib. bdg. 32.50 (ISBN 0-89941-172-X). W S Hein.

Grzybowski, Kazimierz, ed. East-West Trade. LC 73-22437. (Library of Law & Contemporary Problems Ser.). 307p. 1973. lib. bdg. 20.00 (ISBN 0-379-11519-0). Oceana.

Grzybowski, Stefan. Tuberculosis & Its Prevention. (Illus.). 126p. 1983. 19.75 (ISBN 0-87527-198-7). Green.

Grzynkowicz, Wineva. Basic Education for Children with Learning Disabilities. (Illus.). 296p. 1979. 19.75x (ISBN 0-398-03875-9). C C Thomas.

--Meeting the Needs of Learning Disabled Children in the Regular Class. 208p. 1975. spiral 17.50x (ISBN 0-398-03159-2). C C Thomas.

Grzynkowicz, Wineva M. Teaching Inefficient Learners. 148p. 1971. 15.75x (ISBN 0-398-00743-8). C C Thomas.

Gschneider, K. A. & Eyring, L., eds. Handbook of Physics & Chemistry of Rare Earths, 4 Vols. 1979. Vol. 1: Metals. 176.50 (ISBN 0-444-85020-1); Vol. 2: Alloys & Intermetallics. 130.00 (ISBN 0-444-85021-X); Vol. 3: Non-Metallic Compounds I. 134.00 (ISBN 0-444-85215-8); Vol. 4: Non Metallic Compounds II. 123.50 (ISBN 0-444-85216-6). Elsevier.

Gschneidner, K. A. & Eyring, L., eds. Handbook on the Physics & Chemistry of Rare Earths, Vol. 5. 700p. 1983. 153.25 (ISBN 0-444-86375-3, I-002-83, North Holland). Elsevier.

Gschneidner, K. A., Jr. & Eyring, L., eds. Handbook on the Physics & Chemistry of Rare Earths, Vol. 7. 584p. 1984. 129.00 (ISBN 0-444-86851-8, North-Holland). Elsevier.

--Handbook on the Physics & the Chemistry of Rare Earths, Vol. 6. 604p. 1984. 124.00 (ISBN 0-444-86592-6, North Holland). Elsevier.

Gschneidner, Karl, Jr., ed. Industrial Applications of Rare Earth Elements. LC 81-10875. (ACS Symposium Ser.: No. 164). 1981. 36.95 (ISBN 0-8412-0641-4). Am Chemical.

Gschossmann-Hendershot, E. Schaum's Outline of German Grammar. 2nd ed. (Schaum's Outline Ser.). 272p. 1982. pap. text ed. 6.95 (ISBN 0-07-025097-9). McGraw.

Gschwandtner, Gerhard. Superachievers: Portraits of Success from Personal Selling Power. 227p. 1984. 15.95 (ISBN 0-13-876384-4, Busn). P-H.

Gschwend, N. Surgical Treatment of Rheumatoid Arthritis. LC 79-3795. (Illus.). 248p. 1981. text ed. 35.00 (ISBN 0-7216-4332-9). Saunders.

Gschwender, Edward, jt. auth. see Charters, Alexander N.

Gschwind, Brigitte B., jt. auth. see Freiberger, Waltraud.

Gsovski, Vladimir, ed. see Mid-European Law Project.

Gsovski, Vladimir. Highlights of the Mid-European Law Project: Vols. 1- 8, 1953- 1960 (in 7 books) 1980. Repr. Set. lib. bdg. 245.00 (ISBN 0-89941-279-3). W S Hein.

Guacho, Juan N. & Burns, Donald H. Bosquejo Gramatical del Quichua de Chimborazo. 203p. (Orig., Span.). 1975. microfiche (3) 3.80 (ISBN 0-88312-373-8). Summer Inst Ling.

Guadalupe, Alma. Sea of Sadness. 64p. 1984. 5.95 (ISBN 0-89962-041-8). Todd & Honeywell.

Guadarrama, Argelia A. Steps to English Kindergarten Teacher's Manual. 128p. 1983. kit 372.00 (ISBN 0-07-033100-6). McGraw.

Guademet, Jean. La Societe Ecclesiastique Dans L'Occident Medieval. 338p. 1980. 60.00x (ISBN 0-86078-061-9, Pub. by Variorum). State Mutual Bk.

Guahar, Altaf. Third World Affairs 1985. 436p. 1985. pap. 25.00 (ISBN 0-8133-0289-7). Westview.

Gual, Charles, et al. Current Studies on Thyrotropin, II. 233p. 1974. text ed. 32.50x (ISBN 0-8422-7162-7). Irvington.

Guala, F., jt. auth. see Marinone, N.

Gual Camarena, Miguel. Vocabulario del Comercio Medieval. 2nd ed. 532p. (Span.). 1976. leather 59.95 (ISBN 84-7370-017-1, S-50115). French & Eur.

Gualterus, Abbot of Montier-En-der. Walteri Abbatis Dervensis Epistolae. Messiter, C., ed. 1850. 24.00 (ISBN 0-8337-3679-5). B Franklin.

Gualtieri, Antonio R. The Vulture & the Bull: Religious Responses to Death. 194p. (Orig.). 1984. lib. bdg. 23.50 (ISBN 0-8191-3963-7); pap. text ed. 11.50 (ISBN 0-8191-3964-5). U Pr of Amer.

Gualtierotti, T., ed. The Vestibular System: Function & Morphology. (Illus.). 560p. 1981. 99.00 (ISBN 0-387-90559-6). Springer-Verlag.

Guandolo, John. Federal Procedure Forms. 2nd ed. LC 61-6580. xxxiv, 2027p. 1961. lib. bdg. 75.00 (ISBN 0-89941-363-3). W S Hein.

--Transportation Law. 4th ed. 1072p. 1983. text ed. write for info. (ISBN 0-697-08516-3). Wm C Brown.

Guandolo, John, jt. auth. see Fair, Marvin L.

Guangtian, Li. A Pitiful Plaything & Other Essays. Yang, Gladys, tr. (Panda Ser.). 154p. (Orig.). 1982. pap. 2.95 (ISBN 0-8351-1024-9). China Bks.

Guangyuan, Yu. China's Socialist Modernization. 775p. 1984. pap. 12.95 (ISBN 0-8351-1011-7). China Bks.

Guanhua, Lin. Beijing: The Cornucopia of Classical Chinese Architecture. (Illus.). 205p. 1982. 75.00 (ISBN 9-97194-714-5, Pub. by Graham Brash Singapore). Three Continents.

Guannu, Joseph S., compiled by. The Inaugural Addresses of the Presidents of Liberia: From Joseph Jenkins Robert to William Richard Tolbert Jr., 1848 to 1976. 1980. 20.00 (ISBN 0-682-49444-5). Exposition Pr FL.

Guanzhong, Luo, jt. auth. see Shi, Nai'an.

Guappone, Carmen. Antique Chains. 1978. pap. 7.95x (ISBN 0-686-22994-0). Guappones Pubs.

--Antique Clocks. 1978. pap. 7.95 (ISBN 0-686-22995-9). Guappones Pubs.

--Antique Pocket Watches. 1978. pap. 7.95 (ISBN 0-686-22993-2). Guappones Pubs.

Guappone, Carmen A. New Geneva & Greensboro Pottery. (Illus., Orig., A660861). 1980. pap. 9.95 (ISBN 0-686-17799-1). Guappones Pubs.

Guaraldo, Richard & Zaker, Susan M. Marvel Super Heroes Computer Fun Book I. (Illus.). 96p. (gr. 4-9). 1984. pap. 7.95 (ISBN 0-917657-05-5, Parachute Pr Bks). D I Fine.

--Marvel Super Heroes Computer Fun Book II. (Illus.). 96p. (gr. 4-9). 1984. pap. 7.95 (ISBN 0-917657-06-3, Parachute Pr Bks). D I Fine.

Guarasci, Richard. The Theory & Practice of American Marxism, Nineteen Fifty-Seven to Nineteen Seventy. LC 80-1376. 170p. 1980. lib. bdg. 23.50 (ISBN 0-8191-1148-1); pap. text ed. 12.50 (ISBN 0-8191-1149-X). U Pr of Amer.

Guarascio, Massimo, et al, eds. Advanced Geostatistics in the Mining Industry. LC 76-13915. (Nato Mathematical& Physical Sciences Ser: No. C24). 1976. lib. bdg. 55.00 (ISBN 90-277-0669-7, Pub. by Reidel Holland). Kluwer Academic.

Guard, David. Deirdre: A Celtic Legend. LC 80-69774. (Illus.). 118p. (gr. 6). 1981. Repr. of 1977 ed. 9.95 (ISBN 0-89742-047-0). Celestial Arts.

--Hale-Mano: A Legend of Hawaii. LC 80-69773. (Illus.). 118p. (gr. 6). 1981. 9.95 (ISBN 0-89742-048-9). Celestial Arts.

Guardarrama, Alvaro, tr. see Steven, Hugh.

Guardia, Francisco Ferrer Y see Ferrer Y Guardia, Francisco.

Guardia, Ricardo F. History of the Discovery & Conquest of Costa Rica. Van Dyke, Harry W., tr. 1978. 75.00 (ISBN 0-8490-1381-X). Gordon Pr.

Guardia, Ricardo Fernandez see Fernandez Guardia, Ricardo.

Guardians Of The Poor. Compilation of the Poor Laws of the State of Pennsylvania from the Year 1700 to 1788, Inclusive. LC 76-137168. (Poverty U.S.A. Historical Record Ser). 1971. Repr. of 1788 ed. 13.00 (ISBN 0-405-03106-8). Ayer Co Pubs.

Guardini, Romano. Lord. 1978. pap. 9.95 (ISBN 0-89526-909-0). Regnery-Gateway.

Guardiola, Felix. Recordar Es. 148p. 1985. 10.00 (ISBN 0-917049-01-2). Saeta.

Guardiola, R. & Polls, A., eds. Quarks, Mesons & Isobars in Nuclei: Proceedings of the Fifth Topical School Motril, Granada, Spain, Sept. 6-11, 1982. vi, 328p. 1983. 41.00x (ISBN 9971-950-49-9, Pub. by World Sci Singapore). Taylor & Francis.

Guardiola, R. & Ros, J., eds. The Many-Body Problem Jastrow Correlations: Proceedings. (Lecture Notes in Physics Ser.: Vol. 138). 374p. 1981. pap. 25.00 (ISBN 0-387-10577-8). Springer-Verlag.

Guare, John. Rich & Famous. 1977. pap. 3.35x (ISBN 0-685-81648-6). Dramatists Play.

--Three Exposures. LC 82-47922. 256p. 1982. 16.95 (ISBN 0-15-190178-3). HarBraceJ.

Guarendi, Raymond N. You're a Better Parent Than You Think! 252p. 1985. 15.95 (ISBN 0-13-981861-8); pap. 7.95 (ISBN 0-13-981853-7). P-H.

Guaresch, Giovanni. Duncan & Clotilda. Conrad, L. K., tr. 1968. 4.95 (ISBN 0-686-63532-9). FS&G.

Guareschi. Don Camillo. (Easy Reader, B). 1972. pap. 4.25 (ISBN 0-88436-121-7, 55255). EMC.

Guareschi, Giovanni. The Little World of Don Camillo. 1951. 10.95 (ISBN 0-575-00991-8, Pub. by Gollancz England). David & Charles.

--The Little World of Don Camillo. 10.95 (ISBN 0-89190-215-5, Pub. by Am Repr). Amereon Ltd.

--The World of Don Camillo. 576p. 1982. 16.95 (ISBN 0-575-02933-1, Pub. by Gollancz England). David & Charles.

Guariglia, Sherry, jt. ed. see Ziemba, Joe.

Guarini, Battista. Il Pastor Fido (The Faithfull Shepherd) Whitfield, J. H., ed. Fanshawe, Richard, tr. from It. LC 76-11575. (Edinburgh Bilingual Library: No. 11). 423p. 1976. text ed. 20.00x (ISBN 0-292-76431-6). U of Tex Pr.

Guarino, Frank J. Relationship of Stock Market Fluctuations to Lunar Cycles. 80p. 1978. 5.00 (ISBN 0-86690-112-4, 1163-01). Am Fed Astrologers.

Guarino, Guido, tr. see Alberti, Leon B.

Guarino, Vincent J. Everyman's Guide to Better Home Security. (Illus.). 136p. 1981. pap. 7.95 (ISBN 0-87364-217-1). Paladin Pr.

Guarnaschelli, Maria, ed. see Davidson, Frank P. & Cox, John S.

Guarnaschelli, Maria, ed. see Faderman, Lillian.

Guarnaschelli, Maria, ed. see Polanski, Roman.

Guarnaschelli, Maria, ed. see Tobias, Sheila, et al.

Guarnieri, M. & Guarnieri, O. Dizionario Tecnico Tedesco-Italiano, Italiano-Tedesco Garzanti. 2032p. (Ger. & Ital.). 1979. 75.00 (ISBN 0-686-97355-0, M9184). French & eur.

Guarnieri, O., jt. auth. see Guarnieri, M.

Guasp, Ignacio. Diccionario de la Lengua Mechada. (Span.). 12.50 (ISBN 0-686-56701-3, S-5248). French & Eur.

Guaspari, John. I Know It When I See It: A Modern Fable about Quality. LC 84-45814. 96p. 1985. 9.95 (ISBN 0-8144-5787-8). Amacom.

Guastella, Sal. An American Nuclear Family in Watted Wise Living. (Illus.). 52p. (Orig.). 1981. pap. write for info (ISBN 0-9607230-0-5). Guastella Pubns.

Guattari, Felix. Molecular Revolution: Psychiatry & Politics. Sheed, Rosemary, tr. 320p. 1984. pap. 8.95 (ISBN 0-14-055160-3, Peregrine). Penguin.

Guattari, Felix, jt. auth. see Deleuze, Gilles.

Guay, E. Joseph & Bryant College Staff. Programming in Vax-BASIC. LC 84-14602. 288p. 1985. pap. text ed. 23.95 (ISBN 0-201-11566-2, 160A16); write for info. instrs' manual (ISBN 0-201-11567-0); write for info. tape of sample programs (ISBN 0-201-11568-9). Addison Wesley.

Guay, Terrie. The Personal Fertility Guide. (Illus., Orig.). 1983. 9.95. Emergence.

--Personal Fertility Guide, Pt. 2. LC 84-69345. (Orig.). 1984. pap. 4.50 (ISBN 0-317-06632-3). Emergence.

--The Personal Fertility Guide: How to Avoid or Achieve Pregnancy Naturally. 192p. (Orig.). 1980. pap. 9.95 (ISBN 0-936602-04-X). Kampmann.

--The Personal Fertility Guide: How to Avoid or Achieve Pregnancy Naturally. (Illus.). 240p. 1985. 17.95 (ISBN 0-8253-0332-X). Beaufort Bks NY.

Guazzo, Francesco M. Compendium Maleficarum. Summers, Montague, ed. Ashwin, E. A., tr. LC 79-8102. Repr. of 1929 ed. 25.50 (ISBN 0-404-18413-8). AMS Pr.

Guazzo, Stefano. Civile Conversation of M. Steeven Guazzo, 2 Vols. LC 25-14538. (Tudor Translations, Second Ser.: Nos. 7 & 8). Repr. of 1925 ed. Set. 90.00 (ISBN 0-404-51980-6); 45.00 ea. Vol. 1 (ISBN 0-404-51981-4). Vol. 2 (ISBN 0-404-51982-2). AMS Pr.

Guba, Egon G. & Lincoln, Yvonna S. Effective Evaluation: Improving the Usefulness of Evaluation Results Through Responsive & Naturalistic Approaches. LC 80-8909. (Social & Behavioral Science Ser.). 1981. text ed. 19.95x (ISBN 0-87589-493-3). Jossey-Bass.

Guba, Egon G., jt. auth. see Lincoln, Yvonna S.

Guback, Denise. Francais Commercial: Theorie et Correspondance. (Fr.). 1984. pap. text ed. 19.95 (ISBN 0-03-062919-5). HR&W.

Guback, Thomas & Varis, Tapio. Transnational Communication & Cultural Industries. (Reports & Papers on Mass Communication: No. 92). (Illus.). 55p. 1982. pap. 6.00 (ISBN 92-3-101882-5, U1261, UNESCO). Unipub.

Gubal, F., et al, eds. Mechanism of Muscle Adaptation to Functional Requirements: Proceedings of a Satellite Symposium of the 28th International Congress of Physiological Sciences, Szeged, Hungary, 1980. LC 80-42250. (Advances in Physiological Sciences Ser.: Vol. 24). (Illus.). 500p. 1981. 66.00 (ISBN 0-08-027345-9). Pergamon.

Gubanov, Alexsandr I. Quantum Electron Theory of Amorphous Conductors. LC 65-10526. 277p. 1965. 35.00x (ISBN 0-306-10703-1, Consultants). Plenum Pub.

Gubanova, I. I., jt. auth. see Panovko, Ya. G.

Gubar, Susan, jt. auth. see Gilbert, Sandra M.

Gubar, Susan, jt. ed. see Gilbert, Sandra.

Gubar, Susan, jt. ed. see Gilbert, Sandra M.

Gubarev, A. Russian Museum: A Guide. 175p. 1981. 5.95 (ISBN 0-8285-2298-7, Pub. by Progress Pubs USSR). Imported Pubns.

Gubbay, Jon, jt. auth. see Crompton, Rosemary.

Gubbins, John H. The Making of Modern Japan. facsimile ed. LC 73-169760. (Select Bibliographies Reprint Ser). Repr. of 1922 ed. 23.50 (ISBN 0-8369-5980-9). Ayer Co Pubs.

--The Making of Modern Japan. LC 72-82095. (Japan Library Ser.). (Illus.). 1973. Repr. of 1922 ed. lib. bdg. 30.00 (ISBN 0-8420-1390-3). Scholarly Res Inc.

--Progress of Japan, 1853-1871. LC 79-137237. Repr. of 1911 ed. 24.50 (ISBN 0-404-02939-6). AMS Pr.

Gubbins, K. E., jt. auth. see Gray, C. G.

Gubellini, C. E., jt. auth. see Keith, L. A.

Gubelman, M. H., et al. Transition Metal Complexes: Structure & Spectra. (Structure & Bonding Ser.: Vol. 55). (Illus.). 210p. 1984. 40.00 (ISBN 0-387-12833-6). Springer Verlag.

Gubelmann, Albert. Studies in the Lyric Poems of Friedrich Hebbel. 1973. Repr. of 1912 ed. 25.00 (ISBN 0-8274-1570-2). R West.

Gubelmann, Albert E. Studies in the Lyric Poems of Friedrich Hebbel. 1912. 23.50x (ISBN 0-685-89788-5). Elliots Bks.

Guber, Lynda, jt. auth. see Finger, Alan.

Guber, Rivka. Village of the Brothers. LC 78-54568. (Illus.). 1979. 10.00 (ISBN 0-88400-059-1). Shengold.

Guberlet, Muriel L. Explorers of the Sea: Famous Oceanographic Expeditions. LC 64-13332. (Illus.). pap. 58.50 (ISBN 0-317-09879-9, 2012588). Bks Demand UMI.

--Windows to His World: The Story of Trevor Kincaid. LC 73-91594. (Illus.). 1975. 9.95 (ISBN 0-87015-210-6). Pacific Bks.

Guberman, Igor. Bumerang. (Illus.). 128p. (Rus.). 1982. pap. 6.00 (ISBN 0-938920-15-4). Hermitage.

Guberman, Reuben. Handbook of Retail Promotion Ideas. LC 80-12276. 192p. 1981. text ed. 27.50 (ISBN 0-201-02720-8). Addison-Wesley.

Gubernatis, A. Zoological Mythology. 69.95 (ISBN 0-8490-1351-8). Gordon Pr.

Gubernatis, Angelo De. Zoological Mythology, 2 Vols. LC 68-58904. 1968. Repr. of 1872 ed. Set. 56.00x (ISBN 0-8103-3527-1). Gale.

Gubernatis, Angelo De see De Gubernatis, Angelo.

Gubernick, David J. & Klopfer, Peter H., eds. Parental Care in Mammals. LC 80-36692. 478p. 1981. 39.50x (ISBN 0-306-40533-4, Plenum Pr). Plenum Pub.

Gubert, Betty K. Early Black Bibliographies. LC 81-43340. 350p. 1982. lib. bdg. 51.00 (ISBN 0-8240-9290-2). Garland Pub.

Gubitosi, Camillo, ed. see Wright, Frank L.

Gubitz, Albert C., Jr. Instant Personal Problem Solving. (Illus.). 1984. pap. text ed. 2.50x (ISBN 0-8134-2348-1). Interstate.

Gubitz, Myron, tr. see Guggenbuhl-Craig, Adolf.

Gubitz, Myron, tr. see Jacoby, Mario.

Gubler, Clark J., jt. ed. see Sable, Henry Z.

Gubler, Clark J., et al, eds. Thiamine. LC 75-29485. pap. 100.80 (ISBN 0-317-28657-9, 2055087). Bks Demand UMI.

Gubrium, Jaber F. Late Life: Communities & Environmental Policy. (Illus.). 304p. 1975. 19.75x (ISBN 0-398-03249-1); pap. 15.25x (ISBN 0-398-03248-3). C C Thomas.

--Living & Dying at Murray Manor. LC 74-23279. 256p. (Orig.). 1975. pap. text ed. 10.95 (ISBN 0-312-48965-X). St Martin.

--The Myth of the Golden Years: A Socio-Environmental Theory of Aging. (Illus.). 244p. 1973. 14.75x (ISBN 0-398-02703-X). C C Thomas.

Gubrium, Jaber F. & Buckholdt, David. Describing Care: Image & Practice in Rehabilitation. LC 81-18774. 210p. 1982. text ed. 30.00 (ISBN 0-89946-135-2). Oelgeschlager.

Gubrium, Jaber F. & Buckholdt, David R. Toward Maturity: The Social Processing of Human Development. LC 76-57306. (Social & Behavioral Science Ser.). 1977. text ed. 23.95x (ISBN 0-87589-311-2). Jossey-Bass.

Gubrium, Jaber F., jt. auth. see Buckholdt, David R.

Gubrium, Jaber F., ed. Time, Roles & Self in Old Age. LC 74-12131. 363p. 1976. text ed. 39.95 (ISBN 0-87705-230-1); pap. text ed. 19.95 (ISBN 0-87705-350-2). Human Sci Pr.

Gubser, D. U., et al, eds. Inhomogeneous Superconductors, 1979. LC 79-57620. (AIP Conference Proceedings: No. 58). (Illus.). 325p. lib. bdg. 20.50 (ISBN 0-88318-157-6). Am Inst Physics.
Gubser, Elsie. Bobbin Lace. (Illus.). 6.00 (ISBN 0-686-09828-5). Robin & Russ.
Gubser, Mary. America's Bread Book: The Best Breads from Home Bakers All Across the Country. LC 84-27283. 1985. 22.50 (ISBN 0-688-04176-0). Morrow.
--Mary's Bread Basket & Soup Kettle. LC 75-18826. (Illus.). 320p. 1975. 12.95 (ISBN 0-688-02975-2). Morrow.
Gubser, Peter. Jordan. LC 82-8361. (Nations of Contemporary Middle East Ser.). (Illus.). 139p. 1982. 22.50x (ISBN 0-89158-986-4); pap. text ed. 12.95. Westview.
--Politics & Change in Al-Karak, Jordan. (Westview Encore Edition Ser.). (Illus.). 200p. 1985. pap. 22.50 (ISBN 0-8133-0281-1). Westview.
Guckenheimer, J., et al. Dynamical Systems: C.I.M.E. Lectures. (Progress in Mathematics Ser.: No. 8). 300p. 1980. pap. text ed. 20.00x (ISBN 0-8176-3024-4). Birkhauser.
Guckenheimer, John & Holmes, Philip. Nonlinear Oscillations, Dynamical Systems, & Bifurcations of Vector Fields. (Applied Mathematical Sciences Ser.: Vol. 42). (Illus.). 400p. 1983. 34.00 (ISBN 0-387-90819-6). Springer-Verlag.
Gucker, Philip. Essential English Grammar. (Orig.). 1966. pap. 2.95 (ISBN 0-486-21649-7). Dover.
Guckin, John P., jt. auth. see Kaufman, Fredrick.
Guckler, G. Zweisprachiges Woerterbuch fuer Angenaeherte Operationelle Analyse Semantischer Entsprechungen Mittels EDV. 300p. (Ger. & It.). 1975. pap. 30.00 (ISBN 3-87808-053-0, M-7693, Pub. by G. Narr). French & Eur.
Guclu, Meral. Turkey. (World Bibliographical Ser.: No. 27). 331p. 1981. lib. bdg. 49.00 (ISBN 0-903450-39-9). ABC-Clio.
Gucwa, David & Ehmann, James. To Whom It May Concern: An Inquiry into the Art of Elephants. (Illus.). 1985. 14.95 (ISBN 0-393-02240-4). Norton.
Gudas, jt. ed. see Shih.
Gudas, Fabian, ed. Extrasensory Perception. LC 75-7385. (Perspectives in Psychical Research Ser.). 1975. Repr. of 1961 ed. 16.00x (ISBN 0-405-07033-0). Ayer Co Pubs.
Guddat, J., jt. ed. see Bank, B.
Gudde, Elisabeth K., ed. see Gudde, Erwin G.
Gudde, Erwin G. California Gold Camps: A Geographical & Historical Dictionary of Camps, Towns, & Localities Where Gold Was Found & Mines, & of Wayside Stations & Trading Centers. Gudde, Elisabeth K., ed. LC 73-85788. (Illus.). 1975. 38.50 (ISBN 0-520-02572-5). U of Cal Pr.
--California Place-Names. (The International Library of Names). 431p. 1985. Repr. of 1949 ed. text ed. 39.50x (ISBN 0-8290-1243-5). Irvington.
--California Place Names: The Origin & Etymology of Current Geographical Names. LC 68-26529. 1969. 32.50 (ISBN 0-520-01574-6). U of Cal Pr.
--One Thousand California Place Names: Their Origin & Meaning. 3rd rev. ed. LC 68-11311. 1969. pap. 3.95 (ISBN 0-520-01432-4). U of Cal Pr.
Gudder. Stochastic Methods in Quantum Mechanics. (Probability & Applied Mathematics Ser.: Vol. 1). 220p. 1979. 39.50 (ISBN 0-444-00299-5, North Holland). Elsevier.
Gudder, Stanley. A Mathematical Journey. 1976. text ed. 28.95 (ISBN 0-07-025105-3). McGraw.
Gude, A. J. Three Dimension Models of Basic Crystal Forms: 111 Crystal Models. Construction Kit. 1948. pap. 11.50 (ISBN 0-686-47211-X). Polycrystal Bk Serv.
--Three Dimension Models of Simple Crystal Forms: Construction Kit. 1957. pap. 4.50 (ISBN 0-686-47218-7). Polycrystal Bk Serv.
Gude, G. K. Mollusca: Trochomorphidae & Janellidae, Vol. 2. xii, 522p. 1978. Repr. of 1914 ed. 30.00 (ISBN 0-88065-091-5, Pub. by Messers Today & Tomorrows Printers & Publishers India). Scholarly Pubns.
Gude, Gilbert. Where the Potomac Begins: A History of the North Branch Valley. (Illus.). 208p. 1985. 18.95 (ISBN 0-932020-32-1). Seven Locks Pr.
Gude, Gilbert, jt. auth. see Barnes, Irston R.
Gude, Mary L. Le Page Disgracie: The Text As Confession. LC 78-21281. 1979. 16.00x (ISBN 84-499-2554-1). Romance.
Gude, W. D., et al. Histological Atlas of the Laboratory Mouse. LC 81-8708. (Illus.). 164p. 1982. 29.50x (ISBN 0-306-40686-1, Plenum Pr). Plenum Pub.
Gudehus, G. Finite Elements in Geomechanics. (Wiley Series in Numerical Methods in Engineering). 573p. 1977. 105.95 (ISBN 0-471-99446-4). Wiley.
Gudehus, Jonas H. & Neff, Larry M. Journey to America, Vol. XIV. 1980. 25.00 (ISBN 0-686-79899-6). Penn German Soc.
Gudehus, Tim, et al, eds. Fundamental Interactions at High Energy One. 416p. 1969. 106.50 (ISBN 0-677-13660-9). Gordon.
Gudel, Paul, jt. ed. see Philipson, Morris.
Gudel, Paul J., jt. ed. see Philipson, Morris.
Gudelunas, William A., Jr. & Shade, William G. Before the Molly Maguires: The Emergence of the Ethno-Religious Factor in the Politics of the Lower Anthracite Region, 1844-1872. LC 76-6344. (Irish Americans Ser). 1976. 15.00 (ISBN 0-405-09339-X). Ayer Co Pubs.
Gudeman, Howard E., jt. auth. see Craine, James F.
Gudeman, Stephen. The Demise of a Rural Economy: From Subsistence to Capitalism in a Latin American Village. (International Library of Anthropology). 1978. pap. 10.95x (ISBN 0-7100-8836-1). Routledge & Kegan.
Gudemann, Moritz. Judische Apologetik. Katz, Steven, ed. LC 79-7133. (Jewish Philosophy, Mysticism & History of Ideas Ser.). 1980. Repr. of 1906 ed. lib. bdg. 23.00x (ISBN 0-405-12258-6). Ayer Co Pubs.
Gudenberg, Karl. A Charter for Improved Rural Youth Transition. 74p. 1978. 5.00 (ISBN 0-318-15734-9). Natl Inst Work.
Guder, Darrel L., tr. see Weber, Otto.
Guder, Darrell L. Be My Witnesses: The Church's Mission, Message, & Messengers. 256p. (Orig.). 1985. pap. 10.95 (ISBN 0-8028-0051-3). Eerdmans.
Guder, Darrell L., tr. see Jungel, Eberhard.
Guder, Darrell L., tr. see Weber, Otto.
Guder, Robert. How to Set Up a Successful Job Posting & Bidding System. 1981. pap. 15.95 (ISBN 0-917386-64-7). Exec Ent Inc.
Guder, Robert, ed. see Reck, Ross R. & Long, Brian.
Guder, Robert F. Managing for Productivity: Motivating Employees. Reilly, Harry, ed. 100p. 1980. binder 125.00 (ISBN 0-89290-090-3, SWB 111); participant 45.00 (ISBN 0-89290-089-X). Soc for Visual.
Guder, W. & Schmidt, U. Biochemical Nephrology. 484p. 1978. 95.00 (ISBN 3-456-80627-2, Pub. by Holdan Bk Ltd UK). State Mutual Bk.
Guder, W. G., jt. ed. see Ross, D. B.
Guderian, C., ed. Hold on Book: A Short Course in Survival English for International Secretaries. (Materials for Language Practice Ser.). (Illus.). 28p. 1982. 2.80 (ISBN 0-08-028638-0). Pergamon.
Guderian, Heinz. Panzer Leader. LC 79-19897. Repr. of 1952 ed. 19.95 (ISBN 0-89201-076-2). Zenger Pub.
Guderian, R. Air Pollution: Phytotoxicity of Acidic Gases & Its Significance in Air Pollution Control. LC 76-50626. (Ecological Studies: Vol. 22). 1977. 36.00 (ISBN 0-387-08030-9). Springer-Verlag.
Guderian, R., ed. Air Pollution by Photochemical Oxidants. (Ecological Studies, Analysis & Synthesis: Vol. 52). (Illus.). 380p. 1985. 55.50 (ISBN 0-387-13966-4). Springer-Verlag.
Guderjahn, Ernie L. A Children's Trilogy: Ali's Flying Rug, the Shadow Workers, & the Magic Cricket. (Orig.). (gr. 3 up). 1985. pap. text ed. 5.00 (ISBN 0-88734-504-2). Players Pr.
Gudgin, G. Industrial Location Processes & Employment Growth. 360p. 1977. text ed. 46.95x (ISBN 0-566-00144-6). Gower Pub Co.
Gudgin, Graham & Taylor, Peter J. Seats, Votes & the Spatial Organization of Elections. 254p. 1979. 25.50x (ISBN 0-85086-073-3, NO. 6380, Pub. by Pion England). Methuen Inc.
Gudgin, Graham, jt. auth. see Fothergill, Stephen.
Gudgin, Peter. British Army Equipment. 80p. 1982. 8.95 (ISBN 0-85368-377-8). Stackpole.
--German Tanks: Nineteen Forty-Five to the Present, No. 7. (Tanks Illustrated Ser.). (Illus.). 72p. 1984. pap. 7.95 (ISBN 0-85368-621-1, Pub. by Arms & Armour Pr). Sterling.
Gudiol, Jose. Goya. (Library of Great Painters). 1965. 40.00 (ISBN 0-8109-0149-8). Abrams.
--Goya. (Masters of Art Ser.). (Illus.). 128p. 1985. 19.95 (ISBN 0-8109-0992-8). Abrams.
Guditus, Charles, jt. auth. see Wynn, Richard.
Gudjedjiani, Chato & Palmaitis, Letas. Svan-English Dictionary. LC 85-4089. 1985. write for info. (ISBN 0-88206-062-7). Caravan Bks.
Gudkov, D. A. & Utkin, G. A. Nine Papers on Hilbert's Sixteenth Problem. LC 78-10201. (American Mathematical Society Translations Ser. 2: Vol. 112). 1978. 43.00 (ISBN 0-8218-3062-7, TRANS2-112). Am Math.
Gudmundson, Abel, et al. You Can Control Your Class: A Practical Guide to Classroom Management. 1979. pap. text ed. 3.50 (ISBN 0-89039-236-6). Ann Arbor FL.
Gudmundsson, J. Jon Gudmundsson & His Natural History of Iceland. (Islandica: Vol. 15). pap. 16.00 (ISBN 0-527-00345-X). Kraus Repr.
Gudmundsson, Margaret, jt. auth. see Norinsky, Marvin.
Gudnason, C. H. & Corlett, E. N., eds. Development of Production Systems: Proceedings of the 2nd International Conference on Production Research, Copenhagen, 1973. 920p. 1974. write for info (ISBN 0-85066-078-5). Taylor & Francis.
Gudorf, Christine E. Catholic Social Teaching on Liberation Themes. LC 80-5382. 394p. 1980. lib. bdg. 24.75 (ISBN 0-8191-1080-9); pap. text ed. 15.25 (ISBN 0-8191-1081-7). U Pr of Amer.
Gudschinsky, Sarah C. Literacy: The Growing Influence of Linguistics. 2nd ed. (Trends in Linguistics: State-of-the-Art Report: No. 2). (Orig.). 1982. pap. text ed. 13.50x (ISBN 90-279-3064-3). Mouton.
--A Manual of Literacy for Preliterate Peoples. 180p. 1973. pap. 8.00x (ISBN 0-88312-840-3); microfiche (2) 2.86x (ISBN 0-88312-354-1). Summer Inst Ling.
Gudykunst, William B. & Kim, Young Yun. Communicating With Strangers: An Introduction to Intercultural Communication. (Illus.). 256p. 1984. pap. text ed. 14.95 (ISBN 0-394-35006-5, RanC). Random.
Gudykunst, William B., ed. Intercultural Communication Theory: Current Perspectives, Vol. 7. (International & Intercultural Communication Annual). 312p. 1983. 28.00 (ISBN 0-8039-1970-0); pap. 14.00 (ISBN 0-8039-1969-7). Sage.
Gudykunst, William B., et al. Communication, Culture & Organizational Processes. 1985. 29.95 (ISBN 0-8039-2427-5); pap. 14.95 (ISBN 0-8039-2428-3). Sage.
Gudzinowicz. Analysis of Drugs, Vol. 6: Cardiovascular, Antihypertensive, Hypoglycemic & Thyroid-Related Agents. 1979. 89.75 (ISBN 0-8247-6757-8). Dekker.
--Drug Dynamics for Analytical, Clinical & Biological Chemists. (Drugs & the Pharmaceutical Sciences Ser.). 176p. 1984. 39.75 (ISBN 0-8247-7239-3). Dekker.
Gudzinowicz, B. J. Analysis of Drugs & Metabolites by Gas Chromatography - Mass Spectometry: Antipsychotic, Antiemetic & Antidepressant Drugs, Vol. 3. 1977. 49.75 (ISBN 0-8247-6586-9). Dekker.
--Gas Chromatographic Analysis of Drugs & Pesticides. (Chromatographic Science Ser: Vol. 2). 1967. 125.00 (ISBN 0-8247-1255-2). Dekker.
Gudzinowicz, B. J. & Gudzinowicz, M. J. Analysis of Drugs & Meta-Bolites by Gas Chromatography-Mass Spectometry: Analgesics, Local Anesthetics, & Antibiotics, Vol. 5. 1978. 89.75 (ISBN 0-8247-6651-2). Dekker.
Gudzinowicz, B. J., et al. Fundamentals of Integrated Gc-Ms, Pt. III: The Integrated Gç-Ms Analytical System. (Chromatographic Science Ser.: Vol. 7). 1977. 125.00 (ISBN 0-8247-6431-5). Dekker.
--Fundamentals of Integrated Gc-Ms, Pt. I: Gas Chromatograpghy. (Chromatographic Science Ser.: Vol. 7). 1976. 95.00 (ISBN 0-8247-6365-3). Dekker.
Gudzinowicz, Benjamin & Gudzinowicz, Michael. Analysis of Drugs & Metabolites by Gas Chromotography-Mass Spectrometry: Central Nervous Stimulants, Vol. 4. 1978. 89.75 (ISBN 0-8247-6614-8). Dekker.
Gudzinowicz, Benjamin J., jt. auth. see Gudzinowicz, Michael J.
Gudzinowicz, M. J., jt. auth. see Gudzinowicz, B. J.
Gudzinowicz, Michael, jt. auth. see Gudzinowicz, Benjamin.
Gudzinowicz, Michael J. & Gudzinowicz, Benjamin J. The Analysis of Drugs & Related Compounds by Gas Chromatography-Mass Spectometry: Respiratory Gases, Volatile Anesthetics, Ethyl Alcohol, & Related Toxicological Materials, Vol. 1. 1977. 89.75 (ISBN 0-8247-6576-1). Dekker.
--Analysis of Drugs & Related Compounds by Gas Chromatography-Mass Spectometry: Hypnotics, Anticonvulsants & Sedatives, Vol. 2. 1977. 89.75 (ISBN 0-8247-6585-0). Dekker.
Gue. Increased Profits Through Control of Work in Process. (Illus.). 1980. text ed. 18.95 (ISBN 0-8359-3062-9). Reston.
Guecioueur, Adda, ed. The Problems of Arab Economic Development & Integration. (Special Studies on the Middle East). 275p. 1984. 24.00x (ISBN 0-86531-595-7). Westview.
Guedalla, Philip. Argentine Tango. 254p. 1982. Repr. of 1933 ed. lib. bdg. 30.00 (ISBN 0-89987-313-8). Darby Bks.
--Bonnet & Shawl: An Album. LC 70-121475. (Essay Index Reprint Ser). 1928. 18.00 (ISBN 0-8369-1753-7). Ayer Co Pubs.
--The Duke. LC 75-38381. 523p. 1976. Repr. of 1974 ed. lib. bdg. 28.25x (ISBN 0-8371-8670-6, GUTD). Greenwood.
--Gladstone & Palmerston: Being the Correspondence of Lord Palmerston with Mr. Gladstone, 1851-1865. 367p. 1982. Repr. of 1928 ed. lib. bdg. 40.00 (ISBN 0-89987-314-6). Darby Bks.
--The Hundredth Year. 312p. 1982. Repr. of 1939 ed. lib. bdg. 35.00 (ISBN 0-89987-315-4). Darby Bks.
--Men of Letters. 1927. Repr. 20.00 (ISBN 0-8274-2724-7). R West.
--Mr. Churchill: A Portrait. 1977. Repr. of 1941 ed. lib. bdg. 20.00 (ISBN 0-8414-4603-2). Folcroft.
--Palmerston (1784-1865) 1978. Repr. of 1927 ed. lib. bdg. 20.00 (ISBN 0-8414-4494-3). Folcroft.
--Super & Superman. 1924. Repr. 20.00 (ISBN 0-8274-3554-1). R West.
Guedalla, Philip, ed. see Palmerston, H. J.
Guedalla, Philip, ed. see Palmerston, Henry T.
Guedalla, R. Basil Bunting Bibliography. 62.50 (ISBN 0-911156-46-1). Porter.
Guedalla, Roger. Basil Bunting: A Bibliography of Works & Criticism. LC 76-41745. 1976. lib. bdg. 20.00 (ISBN 0-8414-4514-1). Folcroft.
Guedella, Philip. Wellington. 1979. Repr. of 1931 ed. lib. bdg. 30.00 (ISBN 0-8495-2007-X). Arden Lib.
Guedella, Philip, ed. see Victoria, Queen.
Guedella, Roger. A Comprehensive Bibliography of the Works by & About Basil Bunting. 1973. 17.50 (ISBN 0-88305-236-9). Norwood Edns.
Guedes, M. Morphology of Seed Plants. (Plant Science Ser.: No. 2). (Illus.). 1979. lib. bdg. 16.80x (ISBN 3-7682-1195-9). Lubrecht & Cramer.
--Teratological Modifications & the Meaning of Flower Parts. (International Bioscience Monographs: No. 7). 62p. 1979. 8.00 (ISBN 0-88065-093-1, Pub. by Messers Today & Tomorrows Printers & Publishers India). Scholarly Pubns.
Guedj, Aime, ed. see Zola, Emile.
Guedj, R. A., ed. Methodology of Interaction: SEILLAC II. 410p. 1980. 42.75 (ISBN 0-444-85479-7, North Holland). Elsevier.
Guedj, R. A. & Tucker, H., eds. Methodology in Computer Graphics: Proceedings of the IFIP Workshop, France, May 1976. 206p. 1979. 32.00 (ISBN 0-444-85301-4, North Holland). Elsevier.
Guedon, Mary S. Regionalist Art, Thomas Hart Benton, John Steuart Curry, Grant Wood: A Guide to the Literature. LC 82-3334. 199p. 1982. 15.00 (ISBN 0-8108-1543-5). Scarecrow.
Guehenno, Jean. Jean-Jacques Rousseau, 2 vols. Weightman, John & Weightman, Doreen, trs. from Fr. LC 66-12112. 404p. 1966. Set. 65.00x (ISBN 0-231-08961-9). Columbia U Pr.
Gueho, Robert. Mobilite, Rupture, Vitesse. (Romanistik in Geschichte uno Gegenwart Ser.: No. 6). 275p. (Orig.). 1979. pap. text ed. 19.00x (ISBN 3-87118-375-X, Pub. by Helmut Buske Verlag Hamburg). Benjamins North Am.
Guelff, Richard, jt. ed. see Roberts, Adam.
Guelich, Robert. The Sermon on the Mount. 448p. 1982. 19.95 (ISBN 0-8499-0110-3). Word Bks.
Guelinboin, Marie T., illus. Childhood Pastimes & Friends. 16p. (gr. 2). 1978. pap. 2.50 (ISBN 0-89647-004-0). Bala Bks.
--Krishna & the Demons. 16p. (ps-2). 1978. pap. 2.50 (ISBN 0-89647-005-9). Bala Bks.
Guelke, Leonard T. Historical Understanding in Geography: An Idealistic Approach. LC 82-4356. (Cambridge Studies in Historical Geography: No. 3). 112p. 1982. 29.95 (ISBN 0-521-24678-4). Cambridge U Pr.
Guell, Francisco. Malas Hierbas, Diccionario Clasificatorio Ilustrado. 224p. (Span. & Lat.). 1970. pap. 18.75 (ISBN 84-281-0132-9, S-50018). French & Eur.
Guelle, Johnny. Raggedy Ann & Andy & the Nice Fat Policeman. (Illus.). 96p. (gr. 1-4). pap. 1.95 (ISBN 0-440-47451-5, YB). Dell.
Guelloz, Ezzedine. Pilgrimage to Mecca. (Illus.). 208p. 1982. 60.00 (ISBN 0-85692-059-2, Pub. By Salem House). Merrimack Pub Cir.
Guelph. Biophysics Handbook II. 208p. 1982. pap. text ed. 7.95 (ISBN 0-8403-2816-8). Kendall-Hunt.
Guemes, Eudaldo R. Matematicas Para su Aplicacion. (Span.). 1981. text ed. 11.70 (ISBN 0-538-22090-2, V09). SW Pub.
Guemple, D. L., ed. Alliance in Eskimo Society. LC 72-3423. 1972. 16.50x (ISBN 0-295-95236-9). U of Wash Pr.
Guendogar, Feruzan. Trivialliteratur und Orient: Karl Mays Vorderasiatische Reiseromane. (European University Studies: No. 1, Vol. 684). 233p. (Ger.). 1983. 31.05 (ISBN 3-8204-7376-9). P Lang Pubs.
Guenau, Louis. Lyon et le Commerce de la Soie. LC 70-140977. 272p. (Fr.). 1973. Repr. of 1923 ed. lib. bdg. 26.50 (ISBN 0-8337-1483-X). B Franklin.
Guenebault, L. J. Dictionnaire Iconographique des Figures Legendes et Actes des Saints. Migne, J. P., ed. (Encyclopedie Theologique Ser.: Vol. 45). 716p. (Fr.). Repr. of 1850 ed. lib. bdg. 91.00x (ISBN 0-89241-249-6). Caratzas.
Guenon, Rene. The Multiple States of Being. Godwin, Joscelyn, tr. from Fr. LC 84-80121. Orig. Title: Les Etats Multiples de l'Etre. 142p. 1984. smyth-sewn binding 13.95 (ISBN 0-943914-07-8); pap. 9.95 smyth-sewn binding (ISBN 0-943914-08-6). Larson Pubns Inc.
Guenter, C. H. Days of Vengeance. (Orig.). 1979. pap. 1.75 (ISBN 0-532-17218-3). Woodhill.
--Dead in Aqaba. (Mr. Dynamite Ser.). 1978. pap. 1.50 (ISBN 0-532-15319-7). Woodhill.
--Drop Dead in Havana. (Mr. Dynamite Ser.). 1978. pap. 1.25 (ISBN 0-532-12529-0). Woodhill.
--A Swindler Named Zefano. (Orig.). 1979. pap. 1.75 (ISBN 0-532-17225-6). Woodhill.
--To Know Is to Die. (Mr. Dynamite Ser.). 1977. pap. 1.25 (ISBN 0-532-12528-2). Woodhill.
--Web of Silence. 1977. pap. 1.25 (ISBN 0-532-12525-8). Woodhill.
Guenter, Clarence A. & Welch, Martin H., eds. Pulmonary Medicine. 2nd ed. (Illus.). 896p. 1982. text ed. 83.50 (ISBN 0-397-50444-6, 65-05895, Lippincott Medical). Lippincott.
Guenter, H. Jugendlexikon Wirtschaft. 192p. (Ger.). 1976. 5.95 (ISBN 3-499-16189-3, M-7492, Pub. by Rowohlt). French & Eur.
Guentert, Georges. Das Fremde Ich: Fernando Pessoa. 223p. 1971. 18.80x (ISBN 3-11-003835-8). De Gruyter.
Guentert, Margaret. Running Free. LC 75-22930. 64p. 1975. 5.00 (ISBN 0-8233-0229-6). Golden Quill.
Guenther & Liebenbery, eds. Optical Interferograms - Reduction & Interpretation- STP 666. 168p. 1979. pap. 22.50 (ISBN 0-8031-0709-9, 04-666000-46). ASTM.
Guenther, A. Andrew Garrett's Fische der Suedsee, 3 vols. in 1. (Illus.). 1966. 126.00 (ISBN 3-7682-0351-4). Lubrecht & Cramer.

Guenther, Albert. Catalogue of the Fishes in the British Museum (Natural History, 8 vols. 4368p. 1981. lib. bdg. 295.00 (ISBN 3-7682-7109-9). Lubrecht & Cramer.

Guenther, Albert C., jt. auth. see Playfair, R. Lambert.

Guenther, Arthur H., ed. see American Society for Testing & Materials.

Guenther, Bruce. Fifty Northwest Artists. LC 83-10159. (Illus.). 120p. 1983. 35.00 (ISBN 0-87701-311-X); pap. 16.95 (ISBN 0-87701-289-X). Chronicle Bks.

--State of War: New European & American Paintings. LC 84-52649. (Illus.). 64p. 1984. pap. 14.95 (ISBN 0-295-96294-1). U of Wash Pr.

--States of War: New European & American Paintings. LC 84-52649. (Illus.). 63p. (Orig.). 1985. pap. 14.95 (ISBN 0-932216-17-X). Seattle Mus WA.

Guenther, C., jt. ed. see Mueller, U.

Guenther, Charles, tr. from Fr. Jules LaForgue Selected Poems. 36p. 1984. 4.00 (ISBN 0-918476-10-0). Cornerstone Pr.

Guenther, Ernest, et al. The Essential Oils: Individual Essential Oils of the Plant Families, 6 vols. Vol. 1, 444p. 34.50 (ISBN 0-88275-073-9); Vol. 2, 866p. 66.50 (ISBN 0-88275-338-X); Vol. 3, 794p. 61.00 (ISBN 0-88275-163-8); Vol. 4, 766p. 59.00 (ISBN 0-88275-074-7); Vol. 5, 526p. 40.50 (ISBN 0-88275-354-1); Vol. 6, 498p. 40.50 (ISBN 0-88275-092-5); 257.00 set (ISBN 0-88275-953-1). Krieger.

Guenther, Franz & Gabbay, Dov, eds. Handbook of Philisophical Logic, Vol. 1. 1983. lib. bdg. 98.00 (ISBN 90-277-1542-4, Pub. by Reidel Holland). Kluwer Academic.

Guenther, Gloria. Contact. (Contemporary Problems Reading Ser.). (Illus.). (gr. 7-12). 1973. pap. 3.50 with tchrs'. guide (ISBN 0-914296-10-8). Ed Activities.

Guenther, Gloria M. Crisis. (Contemporary Problems Reading Ser). (Illus.). (gr. 7-12). 1972. pap. 3.50 with tchrs'. guide (ISBN 0-914296-05-1). Ed Activities.

--Drunk. (Contemporary Problems Reading Ser.). (Illus.). (gr. 7-12). 1972. pap. 3.50 with tchrs'. guide (ISBN 0-914296-07-8). Ed Activities.

--H As in Heroin. (Contemporary Problems Reading Ser). (Illus.). (gr. 7-12). 1973. pap. 3.50 with tchrs'. guide (ISBN 0-914296-09-4). Ed Activities.

--Help. (Contemporary Problems Reading Ser.). (Illus.). (gr. 7-12). 1972. pap. 3.50 with tchrs'. guide (ISBN 0-914296-06-X). Ed Activities.

--Secret. Harris, Norma, ed. (Contemporary Problems Reading Ser). (Illus.). 86p. (gr. 7-12). 1974. pap. 3.50 (ISBN 0-914296-20-5); tchr's guide avail. Ed Activities.

--Uptight. (Contemporary Problems Reading Ser.). (Illus.). (gr. 7-12). 1976. pap. cancelled (ISBN 0-914296-53-1). Ed Activities.

Guenther, H. V. Philosophy & Psychology in the Abhidharma. 2nd rev. ed. 1974. 13.95 (ISBN 0-87773-048-2). Orient Bk Dist.

Guenther, Harold. NMR Spectroscopy: An Introduction. LC 78-31736. 436p. 1980. 94.95x (ISBN 0-471-27580-8); pap. 32.95x (ISBN 0-471-27579-4). Wiley.

Guenther, Heinz O. The Footprints of Jesus' Twelve in Early Christian Traditions: A Study in the Meaning of Religious Symbolism. LC 84-48032. (American University Studies VII (Theology & Religion): Vol. 7). 156p. 1984. text ed. 20.90 (ISBN 0-8204-0164-1). P Lang Pubs.

Guenther, Herbert, et al. Questions & Answers on Guru & Disciple. (Illus.). 1978. pap. text ed. 3.00 (ISBN 0-931454-02-6). Timeless Bks.

Guenther, Herbert V. Matrix of Mystery: Scientific & Humanistic Aspects of rDzogs-chen Thought. LC 83-2306. (Illus.). 317p. 1984. 22.50 (ISBN 0-394-54073-5). Shambhala Pubns.

--Tibetan Buddhism in Western Perspective. LC 76-47758. (Illus.). 1977. pap. 6.95 (ISBN 0-913546-50-X). Dharma Pub.

Guenther, Herbert V. & Trungpa, Chogyam. The Dawn of Tantra. LC 74-10250. (Illus.). 92p. pap. write for info. (ISBN 0-87773-059-8). Shambhala Pubns.

Guenther, Herbert V., tr. see Klong-Chen Rab-'Byams-Pa.

Guenther, Herbert V., tr. see Klong-chen rab-byams pa.

Guenther, Herbert V., tr. see Ye-Shes Rgyal-Mtshan.

Guenther, Irma G. Memoirs of a Texas Pioneer Grandmother. 1982. 14.95 (ISBN 0-89015-341-8). Eakin Pubns.

Guenther, John. Fun with the Funnies: Fifty Motivating Activities for Language Arts, Writing, & Social Studies, Grades 4-6. 1983. pap. 7.95 (ISBN 0-673-15637-0). Scott F.

--Pearl Harbor: A Narrative Poem. LC 80-83810. (Illus.). 64p. (Orig.). 1980. pap. 4.95 (ISBN 0-938266-00-4). Purchase Pr.

--Quai Malaquais: A Story of Paris. 200p. 1984. pap. 5.00 (ISBN 0-938266-02-0). Purchase Pr.

Guenther, Maximilian. Defense of Shakespeare's Romeo & Juliet Against Modern Criticism. LC 72-144624. Repr. of 1876 ed. 11.50 (ISBN 0-404-02946-9). AMS Pr.

Guenther, Nancy A. Children & the Threat of Nuclear War: An Annotated Bibliography. (CompuBibs Ser.: No. 7). 42p. 1985. pap. 11.50x (ISBN 0-914791-06-0). Vantage Info.

--United States Supreme Court Decisions: An Index to Excerpts, Reprints & Discussions. 2nd ed. LC 82-10518. (Illus.). 864p. 1983. 52.50 (ISBN 0-8108-1578-8). Scarecrow.

Guenther, Roy, tr. see Orlova, Alexandra.

Guenther, Ruth. Nutritional Guide for the Problem Drinker. (Good Health Guide Ser.). 32p. (Orig.). 1983. pap. 1.45 (ISBN 0-87983-295-9). Keats.

Guenther, William B. Chemical Equilibrium: A Practical Introduction for the Physical & Life Sciences. LC 75-28028. (Illus.). 248p. 1975. 29.50 (ISBN 0-306-30850-9, Plenum Pr). Plenum Pub.

Guenther, William C. Scientific Sampling for Statistical Quality Control. LC 77-72042. (Griffin Statistical Monographs: No. 37). 1977. 16.25 (ISBN 0-02-845560-6). Macmillan.

Guentherodt, G., jt. ed. see Cardona, M.

Guenthner, F. & Guenthner-Reutter, M., eds. Meaning & Translation: Phlosophical & Linquistic Approaches. LC 78-57003. 1978. cusa 42.50x (ISBN 0-8147-2974-6). NYU Pr.

Guenthner, F. & Rohrer, C., eds. Studies in Formal Semantics: Intensionality, Temporality, Negation. (North Holland Linguistics Ser.: Vol. 35). 266p. 1978. 47.00 (ISBN 0-7204-0508-4, LIS, 35, North-Holland). Elsevier.

Guenthner, F. & Schmidt, S. J., eds. Formal Semantics & Pragmatics for Natural Languages. (Syntheses Language Library: No. 4). 1978. lib. bdg. 55.00 (ISBN 90-277-0778-2, Pub. by Reidel Holland); pap. 24.00 (ISBN 90-277-0930-0). Kluwer Academic.

Guenthner, Franz, jt. ed. see Gabbay, Dov.

Guenthner-Reutter, M., jt. ed. see Guenthner, F.

Guenzel, Pamela J., et al. General Interviewing Techniques: A Self-Instructional Workbook for Telephone & Personal Interviewer Training. 428p. 1983. tchrs' ed incl. training tape 60.00x (ISBN 0-87944-287-5); wkbk. 20.00x (ISBN 0-87944-288-3); audio training tape 12.00x (ISBN 0-317-01177-4). Inst Soc Res.

Guenzi, W. D., ed. Pesticides in Soil & Water. (Illus.). 1974. 14.00 (ISBN 0-89118-756-1). Soil Sci Soc Am.

Guerard, A. L. Five Masters of French Romance. 326p. 1980. Repr. lib. bdg. 25.00 (ISBN 0-89760-311-7). Telegraph Bks.

--Literature & Society. LC 35-27293. Repr. of 1935 ed. 27.00 (ISBN 0-527-36650-1). Kraus Repr.

Guerard, Albert. Christine-Annette. LC 84-25874. 272p. 1985. 17.95 (ISBN 0-525-24332-1, 01743-520, W Abrahams Bk). Dutton.

--France: A Modern History. rev. & enl. ed. LC 69-19782. (Illus.). 632p. 1969. 15.00 (ISBN 0-472-08390-2). U of Mich Pr.

--French Civilization. 59.95 (ISBN 0-8490-0197-8). Gordon Pr.

Guerard, Albert, tr. see Michelet, Jules.

Guerard, Albert J. Andre Gide. rev. ed. LC 74-88805. 1969. 20.00x (ISBN 0-674-03525-9). Harvard U Pr.

--Christie Annette: A Novel. Date not set. price not set (Pub. by W Abrahams Bk). Dutton.

--Conrad the Novelist. LC 58-8995. 1958. 20.00x (ISBN 0-674-16350-8). Harvard U Pr.

--The Triumph of the Novel: Dickens, Dostoevsky & Faulkner. LC 75-46357. 1976. 25.00x (ISBN 0-19-502066-9). Oxford U Pr.

Guerard, Albert L. Beyond Hatred: The Democratic Ideal in France & America. LC 71-89035. Repr. of 1925 ed. cancelled (ISBN 0-8371-1918-9, GUB&, Pub. by Negro U Pr). Greenwood.

--Five Masters of French Romance. 1916. Repr. 25.00 (ISBN 0-8274-2349-7). R West.

--Five Masters of French Romance: Anatole France, Pierre Loti, Paul Bourget, Maurice Barres, & Romain Rolland. 326p. 1981. Repr. of 1916 ed. lib. bdg. 35.00 (ISBN 0-89987-309-X). Darby Bks.

--French Civilization from Its Origins to the Close of the Middle Ages. LC 76-76562. 328p. Repr. of 1921 ed. 25.00 (ISBN 0-8154-0298-8). Cooper Sq.

--Literature & Society. LC 74-135271. 451p. 1971. Repr. of 1935 ed. lib. bdg. 25.00 (ISBN 0-8154-0364-X). Cooper Sq.

--Napoleon Third: A Great Life in Brief. LC 78-13974. 1979. Repr. of 1966 ed. lib. bdg. 22.50x (ISBN 0-313-21062-4, GUNA). Greenwood.

--A Short History of the International Language Movement. LC 78-14124. 1979. Repr. of 1922 ed. 23.50 (ISBN 0-88355-796-7). Hyperion Conn.

Guerard, Albert T. The Triumph of the Novel: Dickens, Dostoevsky, Faulkner. LC 81-16087. 1982. pap. 9.50x (ISBN 0-226-31034-5). U of Chicago Pr.

Guerard, Micahel. Michael Guerard's Cuisine Minceur. Chamberlain, Narcisse & Brennan, Fanny, trs. LC 76-49719. (Illus.). 1977. 12.95 (ISBN 0-688-03142-0). Morrow.

Guerard, Michel. Michel Guerard's Cuisine for Home Cooks. Hill, Judith & Ujlaki, Tina, trs. from Fr. LC 83-17247. 224p. 1984. 15.95 (ISBN 0-688-02658-3). Morrow.

--Michel Guerard's Cuisine Gourmande. Hyman, Philip & Hyman, Mary, trs. from Fr. LC 79-17165. (Illus.). 1979. 14.95 (ISBN 0-688-03508-6). Morrow.

Guerber, H. A. The Book of the Epic: The World's Great Epics Told in Story. 493p. 1983. Repr. of 1913 ed. lib. bdg. 75.00 (ISBN 0-8495-2100-9). Arden Lib.

--Legends of the Middle Ages: Narrated with Special Reference to Literature & Art. 59.95 (ISBN 0-8490-0506-X). Gordon Pr.

--Myths of Greece & Rome: Narrated with Special Reference to Literature & Art. 428p. 1985. Repr. of 1893 ed. 40.00 (ISBN 0-8495-2102-5). Arden Lib.

--Myths of Norsemen. 69.95 (ISBN 0-87968-280-9). Gordon Pr.

--Stories of the Wagner Operas. 1977. lib. bdg. 59.95 (ISBN 0-8490-2674-1). Gordon Pr.

--Stories of the Wagner Operas. LC 77-90804. 1978. Repr. of 1895 ed. lib. bdg. 20.00 (ISBN 0-89341-421-2). Longwood Pub Group.

Guerber, Helen A. Legends of the Middle Ages. (Illus.). 340p. 1977. Repr. of 1896 ed. 17.95 (ISBN 0-87928-080-8). Corner Hse.

Guerber, Helene. Myths & Legends of the Rhine. 1976. lib. bdg. 59.95 (ISBN 0-8490-2329-7). Gordon Pr.

Guerber, Helene A. The Book of the Epic: The World's Greatest Epics Told in Story. 1973. Repr. of 1913 ed. 50.00 (ISBN 0-8274-1385-8). R West.

Guerber, Robert. Dictonnaire de L'Automobile. 174p. (Fr.). 1967. pap. 12.50 (ISBN 0-686-57320-X, M-6303). French & Eur.

Guerber, Roger. Diccionario del Automovil. 4th ed. 237p. (Span., Eng., Fr. & Ger.). 1972. pap. 16.75 (ISBN 84-252-0065-2, S-14249). French & Eur.

Guercio, E., et al. General Mathematical Ability; Preparation & Review for the Mathematics Part of the High School Equivalency Diploma Test. LC 74-19738. (GED Preparation Ser.). 160p. (Orig.). 1975. pap. 6.00 (ISBN 0-668-03689-3). Arco.

--Reading Interpretation in Social Sciences, Natural Sciences & Literature: Preparation & Review for the Reading Parts of the High School Equivalency Diploma Test. LC 74-19739. (GED Preparation Ser.). 224p. (Orig.). 1975. pap. 5.00 (ISBN 0-668-03690-7). Arco.

Guercio, Francis M., ed. Anthology of Contemporary Italian Prose. LC 79-103226. 1970. Repr. of 1931 ed. 21.00x (ISBN 0-8046-0863-6, Pub by Kennikat). Assoc Faculty Pr.

Guercio, L. Multilingual Manual for Medical History Taking. 177p. (Fr. & Span. & Ger. & Ital. & Pol. & Rus. & Eng.). 1972. pap. 9.95 (ISBN 0-686-92420-7, M-9232). French & Eur.

Guercio, Louis R. Del see Del Guercio, Louis R.

Guerif, Francois. Brigitte Bardot: And God Created Woman. (Illus.). 128p. (Orig.). 1983. pap. 13.95 (ISBN 0-933328-78-8). Delilah Bks.

Gueriguian, J. L., et al, eds. Insulins, Growth Hormone, & Recombinant DNA Technology. 248p. 1981. 42.50 (ISBN 0-89004-544-5). Raven.

Guerin, Daniel. Anarchism: From Theory to Practice. Klopper, Mary, tr. from Fr. LC 71-105316. 1970. pap. 6.00 (ISBN 0-85345-175-3). Monthly Rev.

--Ci-Gft le Colonialisme: Algerie, Inde, Indo-Chine, Madagascar, Maroc, Palestine, Polynesie, Tunisie, Temoignage Militant. 1973. pap. 18.40x (ISBN 90-2797-262-1). Mouton.

--Fascism & Big Business. rev. 2nd ed. Merrill, Francis, et al, trs. from Fr. LC 73-80854. 352p. 1973. 24.00 (ISBN 0-913460-24-9, Dist. by Path Pr NY); pap. 7.95 (ISBN 0-913460-25-7). Monad Pr.

--One Hundred Years of Labor in the U. S. A. Adler, Alan, tr. (Ink Link Ser.). 1980. 13.95 (ISBN 0-906133-10-6); pap. 6.95 (ISBN 0-906133-11-4). Pluto Pr.

--One Hundred Years of Labor in the U. S. A. Adler, Alan, tr. from French. Orig. Title: Le Mouvement Ouvrier aux Etats-Unis de 1866 a Nos Jours. 252p. 1979. 13.95 (ISBN 0-906133-10-6, Pub. by Ink Link Ltd); pap. 6.95 (ISBN 0-906133-11-4). Longwood Pub Group.

Guerin, Daniel, ed. see Gauguin, Paul.

Guerin, Dominique. La Politique de l'Imaginaire. (Archontes Ser.: No. 1). 140p. (Fr.). 1975. pap. text ed. 15.20x (ISBN 90-2797-795-X). Mouton.

Guerin, E. J. Mountain Charley: Or the Adventures of Mrs. E. J. Guerin, Who Was Thirteen Years in Male Attire. LC 68-15671. 128p. (Orig.). 1985. pap. text ed. 4.95 (ISBN 0-8061-1964-0). U of Okla Pr.

Guerin, Florence. Le Prince Singh. (Collection Colombine Ser.). 192p. 1983. pap. 1.95 (ISBN 0-373-48072-5). Harlequin Bks.

--Tender Gazelle. (Collection Colombine Ser.). 192p. 1983. pap. 1.95 (ISBN 0-373-48080-6). Harlequin Bks.

Guerin, Gilbert & Maier, Arlee. Informal Assessment in Education. LC 81-84695. 418p. 1982. 14.95 (ISBN 0-87484-533-5). Mayfield Pub.

Guerin, L. F. Dictionnaire de l'Histoire Universelle de l'Eglise, 6 vols. Migne, J. P., ed. (Troisieme et Derniere Encyclopedie Theologique Ser.: Vols. 51-56). 4187p. (Fr.). Repr. of 1873 ed. lib. bdg. 532.50x (ISBN 0-89241-322-0). Caratzas.

Guerin, Marcel. Forain Aquafortiste. rev. ed. (Illus.). 336p. (Fr.). 1980. 100.00 (ISBN 0-915346-38-9). A Wofsy Fine Arts.

--Forain Lithographe. rev. ed. (Illus.). 208p. (Fr.). 1980. 75.00 (ISBN 0-915346-39-7). A Wofsy Fine Arts.

--Guaguin's Graphic Work. 272p. 1980. Repr. of 1927 ed. 100.00 (ISBN 0-915346-37-0). A Wofsy Fine Arts.

Guerin, Marcel, ed. see Gauguin, Paul.

Guerin, P., ed. Planetes et satellites: Mondes de l'espace. rev. ed. (Illus., Fr.). 1970. 40.50x (ISBN 0-685-14042-3). Larousse.

Guerin, Philip J., ed. Family Therapy: Theory & Practice. 1976. text ed. 29.50 (ISBN 0-89876-020-8). Gardner Pr.

Guerin, Polly. Fashion Writing. 1972. pap. text ed. 21.17 scp (ISBN 0-672-96033-8); scp tchr's manual 7.33 (ISBN 0-672-96034-6). Bobbs.

Guerin, Sanford M. Taxation of Real Estate Dispositions, 2 vols. 1100p. 1982. 140.00 (ISBN 0-07-025101-0, Shepards-McGraw). McGraw.

Guerin, Wilfred L., et al. A Handbook of Critical Approaches to Literature. 2nd ed. LC 78-12477. 1979. pap. text ed. 13.50 scp (ISBN 0-06-042554-7, HarpC). Har-Row.

Guerini, Vincenzo. History of Dentistry. LC 77-6990. 1977. Repr. of 1909 ed. lib. bdg. 40.00 (ISBN 0-89341-141-8). Longwood Pub Group.

Guerinot, Joseph V. & Jilg, Rodney. Contexts One: The Beggar's Opera. (Contexts Ser.). xii, 187p. (Orig.). 1976. 17.50 (ISBN 0-208-01488-8, Archon). Shoe String.

Guerke, W. R. A Monograph of the Genus Jubula Dumortier. (Bryophytorum Bibliotheca Ser.: No. 17). (Illus.). 1979. pap. 14.00 (ISBN 3-7682-1213-0). Lubrecht & Cramer.

Guerlac, Henry. Newton on the Continent. LC 81-3187. (Illus.). 160p. 1981. 18.95x (ISBN 0-8014-1409-1). Cornell U Pr.

Guerlac, Henry, ed. see Lavoisier, A. L. & Laplace, P. S.

Guerlac, Rita, ed. see Hutton, James.

Guerman, M. Art of the October Revolution. 1979. 90.00x (ISBN 0-569-08425-3, Pub. by Collet's). State Mutual Bk.

--Moiseyenko. 42p. 1975. 30.00x (ISBN 0-317-14313-1, Pub. by Collet's). State Mutual Bk.

Guermont, Claude & Frumkin, Paul. The Norman Table: The Traditional Cooking of Normandy. (Illus.). 288p. 1985. 19.95 (ISBN 0-684-18319-6, ScribT). Scribner.

Guern, J. & Peaud-Lenoel, C., eds. Metabolism & Molecular Activities of Cytokinins: Proceedings. (Proceedings in Life Sciences Ser.). (Illus.). 370p. 1981. 61.00 (ISBN 0-387-10711-8). Springer-Verlag.

Guern, M. Le see Le Guern, M. & Le Guern, M. R.

Guern, M. R. Le see Le Guern, M. & Le Guern, M. R.

Guernelli, Adelaida L. Eugenio Maria De Hostos: Essayist & Literary Critic. (Puerto Rico Ser.). 1979. lib. bdg. 59.95 (ISBN 0-8490-2909-0). Gordon Pr.

Guernelli, Giovanni. Gaspara Stampa, Louise Labe y Sor Juana Ines de la Cruz: Triptico Renacentista Barroco. 4.65 (ISBN 0-8477-3132-4). U of PR Pr.

Guernelli, J., ed. see Furioso.

Guerney, Bernard G., ed. Treasury of Russian Literature. LC 43-17369. (Illus.). 1050p. 19.50 (ISBN 0-8149-0113-1). Vanguard.

Guerney, Bernard G., tr. see Gorki, Maxim.

Guerney, Bernard G., tr. see Kuprin, Aleksandr I.

Guerney, Bernard G., tr. see Kuprin, Alexandre I.

Guerney, Bernard G., tr. see Turgenev, Ivan.

Guerney, Bernard G., Jr., et al. Relationship Enhancement: Skill-Training Programs for Therapy, Problem Prevention, & Enrichment. LC 76-11884. (Social & Behavioral Science Ser.). (Illus.). 1977. 21.95x (ISBN 0-87589-310-4). Jossey-Bass.

Guerney, Louise, jt. auth. see Keat, Donald B., II.

Guerney, Louise F. Parenting: A Skills Training Manual. (Illus.). 151p. (gr. 10-12). 1980. pap. 4.95 (ISBN 0-932990-00-2). Inst Dev Skills.

Guernica, Antonio & Kasperuk, Irene. Reaching the Hispanic Market Effectively: The Media, the Market, the Methods. LC 81-20687. (Illus.). 224p. 1982. 29.95 (ISBN 0-07-025107-X). McGraw.

Guernsey, Alfred H. Ralph Waldo Emerson. 1978. Repr. of 1901 ed. lib. bdg. 30.00 (ISBN 0-8492-0969-2). R West.

--Ralph Waldo Emerson: Philosopher & Poet. LC 72-12734. 1973. Repr. of 1901 ed. lib. bdg. 17.50 (ISBN 0-8414-0971-4). Folcroft.

Guernsey, Bruce. January Thaw. LC 81-70219. (Pitt Poetry Ser.). 64p. 1982. 12.95x (ISBN 0-8229-3459-0); pap. 5.95 (ISBN 0-8229-5339-0). U of Pittsburgh Pr.

Guernsey, Cindy. Cost of Recreation & Leisure Activities. 25p. 1984. pap. text ed. 15.00 (ISBN 0-89478-080-8). U CO Busn Res Div.

Guernsey, Dennis. Thoroughly Married. 100p. pap. 2.25 (ISBN 0-317-06918-7, 06416-5). Jove Pubns.

--Thoroughly Married. 145p. 1984. pap. text ed. 5.95 (ISBN 0-8499-3000-6, 3000-6). Word Bks.

Guernsey, Dennis B., jt. auth. see Anderson, Ray S.

Guernsey, H. H. The Application of the Principles & Practices of Homoeopathy to Obstetrics & the Disorders Peculiar to Women & Young Children. 1979. 40.00x (ISBN 0-686-78851-6, Pub. by Bks India England). State Mutual Bk.

Guernsey, JoAnn B. Five Summers. 192p. (gr. 6 up). 1983. 10.95 (ISBN 0-89919-147-9, Clarion). HM.

--Journey to Almost There. LC 85-2685. 156p. (gr. 5-9). 1985. 11.95 (ISBN 0-89919-338-2, Clarion). HM.

Guernsey, Kenneth L., et al. Advising California Nonprofit Corporations. Hone, Michael C., ed. LC 84-45135. 676p. 1984. text ed. 80.00 (ISBN 0-88124-128-8). Cal Cont Ed Bar.

Guernsey, Otis L. Best Plays 1981-1982. LC 20-21432. (The Burns Mantle Yearbook of the Theatre Ser.). 1983. 24.95 (ISBN 0-396-08124-X). Dodd.

Guernsey, Otis L., Jr., ed. The Best Plays of Nineteen Eighty-Four to Nineteen Eighty-Five: The Burns Mantle Yearbook of the Theater. (Illus.). 550p. 1985. 29.95 (ISBN 0-396-08612-8). Dodd.

--The Best Plays of 1978-1979. LC 20-21432. (The Burns Mantle Yearbook of the Theater Ser.). (Illus.). 1980. 20.00 (ISBN 0-396-07723-4). Dodd.

--The Best Plays of 1979-1980. LC 20-21432. (The Burns Mantle Yearbook of the Theatre Ser.). (Illus.). 550p. 1981. 24.95 (ISBN 0-396-07907-5). Dodd.

--The Best Plays of 1980-1981. (The Burns Mantle Yearbook of the Theater Ser.). (Illus.). 1982. 24.95 (ISBN 0-396-08012-X). Dodd.

--The Best Plays of 1982-83: The Burns Mantle Yearbook of the Theater. 27.95 (ISBN 0-396-08240-8). Dodd.

--Best Plays 1983-1984. (Burns Mantle Yearbook of the Theatre Ser.). (Illus.). 550p. 1985. 29.95 (ISBN 0-396-08347-1). Dodd.

--Broadway Song & Story: Theater. 480p. 1985. 22.95 (ISBN 0-396-08753-1). Dodd.

Guernsey, Rocellus S. Ecclesiastical Law in Hamlet: The Burial of Ophelia. LC 73-169263. (Shakespeare Society of New York. Publications: No. 1). Repr. of 1885 ed. 16.00 (ISBN 0-404-54201-8). AMS Pr.

Guernsey, Samuel J. Explorations in Northeastern Arizona. (HU PMP). 1931. 18.00 (ISBN 0-527-01224-6). Kraus Repr.

Guernsey, Samuel J. & Kidder, A. V. Basket-Maker Caves of Northeastern Arizona. (HU PMP). (Illus.). 1921. 12.00 (ISBN 0-527-01213-0). Kraus Repr.

Guerny, Gene & Skiera, Joseph A. Pilot's Handbook of Weather. 2nd ed. Reithmaier, Lawrence W., ed. LC 74-77535. (Illus.). 1974. pap. 10.95 (ISBN 0-8168-7355-0). Aero.

Guerny, Gene, jt. auth. see Elliot, James C.

Gueron, et al, eds. Grammatical Representation. (Studies in Generative Grammar: No. 22). viii, 360p. (Orig.). 1985. pap. 34.40 (ISBN 9-067-65116-8). Foris Pubns.

Gueroult, Martial. Descartes' Philosophy Interpreted According to the Order of Reasons: The Soul & God, Vol. 1. Ariew, Roger, tr. from Fr. LC 83-21771. 352p. 1984. 35.00x (ISBN 0-8166-1255-2); pap. 15.95 (ISBN 0-8166-1256-0). U of Minn Pr.

Guerra, Alfonso R. Systems of Higher Education: Mexico. (Systems of Higher Education). 98p. 1978. pap. 5.00 (ISBN 0-89192-203-2, Pub. by ICED). Interbk Inc.

Guerra, F. The Pre-Columbian Mind. LC 75-183465. 350p. 1972. 59.00 (ISBN 0-12-785286-7). Acad Pr.

Guerra, Francisco C., jt. ed. see Burton, Robert M.

Guerra, Frank & Aldrete, J. Antonio, eds. Emotional & Psychological Responses to Anesthesia & Surgery. 288p. 1980. 36.50 (ISBN 0-8089-1195-3, 791747). Grune.

Guerra, Sandra J., jt. auth. see Williams, Stephen J.

Guerrant, Dwight, jt. auth. see Twesten, Gary.

Guerrant, John, et al. Personality in Epilepsy. (Illus.). 128p. 1962. 14.75x (ISBN 0-398-00744-6). C C Thomas.

Guerreiro, Miriam, jt. auth. see Packard, Sidney.

Guerrera, Jeannette D. The Invisible Elf. LC 72-77555. (Illus.). (gr. 3-5). 1972. text ed. 5.00 (ISBN 0-912472-17-0). Miller Bks.

Guerrero, Leon M., tr. see Rizal, Jose.

Guerrero, Leon M., tr. see Rizal Y Alonso, Jose.

Guerrero, Linda D. John Adams' Vice Presidency, Seventeen Eighty-Nine to Seventeen Ninety-Seven: The Neglected Man in the Forgotten Office. 28.00 (ISBN 0-405-14083-5). Ayer Co Pubs.

Guerrero, M., jt. auth. see Gungwu, W.

Guerrero, Wilfrido M. My Favorite Eleven Plays. 1976. 8.00x (ISBN 0-686-09436-0). Cellar.

Guerrerosantos, J., jt. ed. see Fisher, J. C.

Guerrier, Yvonne, jt. auth. see Broussine, Michael.

Guerriere, Anne, ed. English-French Cross-World Puzzles: Bilingual Crossword Puzzles, No. 1. 96p. (Eng. & Fr.). 1985. pap. 3.95 (ISBN 0-940038-01-3). Andante Pub.

Guerrieri, Alfonso. The Inevitable Growth of Soviet Super-Nationalistic Drives Following the Demise of the Communist Order - & Its Meanings for the Political Equilibrium of the World. (Illus.). 137p. 1984. 112.50 (ISBN 0-86722-067-8). Inst Econ Pol.

Guerrieri, John A., jt. auth. see McClung, Christina J.

Guerrieri, John A., Jr. Business & Management Principles. 143p. 1971. pap. 5.00 (ISBN 0-318-13879-4, D6); pap. 2.50 members (ISBN 0-318-13880-8). Data Process Mgmt.

Guerriero, Diane. How to Use EasyWriter II. Zorn, K. Lee, ed. (Illus.). 42p. (gr. 7 up). 1983. wkbk. & tapes 57.00 (ISBN 0-318-01217-0). Flip Track.

--How to Use MultiMate. Menges, Patricia A., ed. (Illus.). 54p. (gr. 7 up). 1984. wkbk., tapes avail. 57.00 (ISBN 0-317-07254-4). Flip Track.

Guerriero, Graham & Devine, Charles. Urologic Injuries. (Illus.). 214p. 1984. 35.00 (ISBN 0-8385-9311-9). ACC.

Guerronnan, Anthony. Dictionnaire Synonymique. Bunnell, Peter C. & Sobieszek, Robert A., eds. LC 76-23055. (Sources of Modern Photography Ser.). (Fr.). 1979. Repr. of 1895 ed. lib. bdg. 17.00x (ISBN 0-405-09620-8). Ayer Co Pubs.

Guerry, Herbert, ed. A Bibliography of Philosophical Bibliographies. LC 77-71862. 1977. lib. bdg. 39.95x (ISBN 0-8371-9542-X, GUC/). Greenwood.

--Philosophy & Mysticism. pap. 2.95 (ISBN 0-685-61376-3). Dell.

Guerry, Moultrie. Weep Not for Me. 1984. 4.95 (ISBN 0-89536-974-5). CSS of Ohio.

Guerry, Vincent. Life with the Baoule. Hodges, Nora, tr. from Fr. LC 75-15876. Orig. Title: La Vie Quotidien Dans un Village Baoule. (Illus.). 172p. 1975. 12.00 (ISBN 0-89410-277-X); pap. 6.00 (ISBN 0-89410-278-8). Three Continents.

Guertin, Carolyn W., jt. auth. see Blank, Florence W.

Guertin, Robert P. & Suski, Wojciech, eds. Crystalline Electric Field Effects in f-Electron Magnetism. LC 82-5267. 604p. 1982. 85.00x (ISBN 0-306-41004-4, Plenum Pr). Plenum Pub.

Guertler, John T. & Newburger, Adele M. The Records of Baltimore's Private Organizations: A Guide to Archival Resources. LC 80-8976. 334p. 1981. lib. bdg. 48.00 (ISBN 0-8240-9360-7). Garland Pub.

Guertner, Beryl. Gregory's Guide to Better Outdoor Living. (Illus.). pap. 8.50x (ISBN 0-392-03159-0, ABC). Sportshelf.

Guesry, P., jt. ed. see Maupas, P.

Guess & Ellis. Guardian & Ward. (The Law in Georgia Ser.). incl. latest pocket part supplement 24.95 (ISBN 0-686-90396-X); separate pocket part supplement, 1982 9.45 (ISBN 0-686-90397-8). Harrison Co GA.

--Probate & Administration: With Forms. (The Law in Georgia Ser.). incl. latest pocket part supplement 24.95 (ISBN 0-686-90558-X); separate pocket part supplement, 1983 11.95. Harrison Co GA.

Guess, Doug, jt. auth. see Sailor, Wayne.

Guess, Doug, et al. Functional Speech & Language Training for the Severely Handicapped, Pt. 2. 1976. 10.00 (ISBN 0-89079-025-6); scoring form set 3.00 (ISBN 0-89079-026-4). Pro Ed.

--Functional Speech & Language Training for the Severely Handicapped, Pt. 3. 1977. 10.00 (ISBN 0-89079-027-2); scoring forms set 3.00 (ISBN 0-89079-028-0). Pro Ed.

--Functional Speech & Language Training for the Severely Handicapped, Part 1. 1976. 10.00 (ISBN 0-89079-023-X); scoring forms set 3.00 (ISBN 0-89079-024-8). Pro Ed.

Guess, Vincent C. Engineering: The Missing Link in MRP. LC 79-54859. (Illus.). 210p. 1979. 11.00x (ISBN 0-940964-00-7). PSE.

--How to Structure Product Data. LC 81-83133. (Illus.). 200p. (Orig.). 1981. pap. text ed. 12.95x (ISBN 0-940964-01-5). PSE.

--Manufacturing Control System User's Guide. (Illus.). 32p. (Orig.). 1982. pap. 10.00 (ISBN 0-940964-03-1). PSE.

Guessarian, Irene. Algebraic Semantics. (Lecture Notes in Computer Science Ser.: Vol. 99). 158p. 1981. pap. 14.00 (ISBN 0-387-10284-1). Springer-Verlag.

Guest. The Sword of Hachiman. 1981. 12.95 (ISBN 0-07-025108-8). McGraw.

Guest, Ann H. Dance Notation. 224p. 1984. 20.00 (ISBN 0-87127-141-9). Dance Horiz.

--Your Move: A New Approach to the Study of Movement & Dance. 343p. 1983. 39.50 (ISBN 0-677-06350-4); pap. 24.95 (ISBN 0-677-06365-2); tchrs' guide 15.00 (ISBN 0-677-06395-4). Gordon.

Guest, Ann H. see Ralov, Kirsten.

Guest, Anthony. Art & the Camera. LC 72-9203. (The Literature of Photography Ser.). Repr. of 1907 ed. 18.00 (ISBN 0-405-04912-9). Ayer Co Pubs.

Guest, Anthony G., jt. auth. see Anson, William R.

Guest, Barbara. Biography. (Burning Deck Poetry Ser.). 24p. (Orig.). 1980. pap. 3.00 (ISBN 0-930900-93-6); pap. 20.00 signed, special ed. (ISBN 0-930900-94-4). Burning Deck.

--The Countess from Minneapolis. (Burning Deck Poetry Ser.). 1976. pap. 4.00 (ISBN 0-930900-06-5). Burning Deck.

--Herself Defined: The Poet H. D. & Her World. LC 82-45482. (Illus.). 384p. 1984. 18.95 (ISBN 0-385-13129-1). Doubleday.

--Herself Defined: The Poet H. D. & Her World. LC 84-24886. (Illus.). 360p. 1985. pap. 12.95 (ISBN 0-688-04709-2, Quill). Morrow.

--Poems: The Location of Things. 1962. 9.95 (ISBN 0-911660-06-2). Yankee Peddler.

--Seeking Air. 260p. (Orig.). 1978. 14.00 (ISBN 0-87685-352-1); signed 17.50 (ISBN 0-87685-328-9); pap. 5.00 (ISBN 0-87685-327-0). Black Sparrow.

Guest, C. B. The Position of Women As Considered by Representative American Authors Since 1800. 59.95 (ISBN 0-8490-0885-9). Gordon Pr.

Guest, C. Z. C. Z. Guest's Datebook & Gardner Planner. 1985. 12.95 (ISBN 0-517-55306-6). Crown.

Guest, C. Z. & McDonald. C. Z. & Elvin's Weekly Garden Planner. LC 78-56254. 1978. pap. 6.95 (ISBN 0-87754-072-1). Chelsea Hse.

Guest, Carol L. Space Trip. 48p. 1981. 5.95 (ISBN 0-89962-047-7). Todd & Honeywell.

Guest, Charlotte. The Mabinogion. (Illus.). 504p. 1978. pap. 9.95 (ISBN 0-89733-000-5). Academy Chi Pubs.

Guest, David & Knight, Kenneth. Putting Participation into Practice. 346p. 1979. text ed. 46.95x (ISBN 0-566-02086-6). Gower Pub Co.

Guest, Dean. Discovering the Word of God. 64p. (Orig.). 1980. Repr. pap. 1.95 (ISBN 0-89841-011-8). Zoe Pubns.

--Tabernacle, God's Dwelling Place. 64p. (Orig.). 1979. pap. 1.95 (ISBN 0-89841-012-6). Zoe Pubns.

--Trees of Restoration. Date not set. 10.95 (ISBN 0-533-05752-3). Vantage.

Guest, Diana, jt. auth. see Harrison, Jim.

Guest, Diane. Twilight's Burning. 288p. 1982. pap. 3.25. Ace Bks.

Guest, Edgar. A Heap O'Living. 1976. lib. bdg. 13.95 (ISBN 0-89968-041-0). Lightyear.

--Just Folks. 192p. 1980. Repr. of 1917 ed. lib. bdg. 16.95 (ISBN 0-89968-190-5). Lightyear.

--Living Years. 192p. 1981. Repr. lib. bdg. 14.95 (ISBN 0-89968-221-9). Lightyear.

--Over Here. 192p. 1980. Repr. of 1918 ed. lib. bdg. 11.95x (ISBN 0-89968-192-1). Lightyear.

--Passing Through. 190p. 1980. Repr. of 1923 ed. lib. bdg. 11.95x (ISBN 0-89968-191-3). Lightyear.

--Rhymes of Childhood. 190p. 1981. Repr. lib. bdg. 14.95 (ISBN 0-89968-220-0). Lightyear.

--When Day Is Done. 191p. 1981. Repr. lib. bdg. 14.95 (ISBN 0-89968-219-7). Lightyear.

Guest, Edgar A. All in a Lifetime. facs. ed. LC 76-133071. (Granger Index Reprint Ser). 1938. 19.00 (ISBN 0-8369-6201-X). Ayer Co Pubs.

--Collected Verse. 60p. 17.95 (ISBN 0-8092-8828-1). Contemp Bks.

Guest, Edwin. History of English Rhythms. LC 68-29736. (Studies in Poetry, No. 38). 1969. Repr. of 1882 ed. lib. bdg. 59.95x (ISBN 0-8383-0287-4). Haskell.

--A History of English Rhythms. 1973. Repr. of 1882 ed. 75.00 (ISBN 0-8274-0032-2). R West.

--Origines Celticae: And Other Contributions to the History of Britain, 2 vols. LC 70-118474. 1979. Repr. of 1883 ed. Set. lib. bdg. 95.00x (ISBN 0-8046-1223-4). Irvington.

Guest, Elissa. Heart of Glass. Date not set. PLB price not set (ISBN 0-688-04148-5, Morrow Junior Books). Morrow.

Guest, Elissa H. The Handsome Man. 160p. (gr. 7 up). 1981. pap. 1.95 (ISBN 0-440-93437-0, LFL). Dell.

--Over the Moon. 176p. (gr. 7 up). 1986. 11.50 (ISBN 0-688-04148-5). Morrow.

Guest, Evan, ed. Flora of Iraq: Introduction to the Flora, Vol. 1. (Illus.). 213p. 1983. pap. 10.00 (ISBN 0-8139-1016-1). U Pr of Va.

Guest, Evan, jt. ed. see Townsend, C. C.

Guest, Francis F. Fermin Francisco De Lasuen: A Biography. (Monograph Ser.). (Illus.). 1973. 25.00 (ISBN 0-88382-059-5). AAFH.

Guest, G. Martin. Brief History of Engineering. (Illus.). 1974. pap. text ed. 17.50x (ISBN 0-245-52337-5). Intl Ideas.

Guest, Harry. Arrangements. 1968. 6.95 (ISBN 0-685-00947-5, Pub. by Anvil Pr); signed ed. 50 copies 12.50 ea.; pap. 3.95 (ISBN 0-685-00949-1). Small Pr Dist.

--Cutting-Room. 1970. 6.95 (ISBN 0-685-00950-5, Pub. by Anvil Pr); signed ed. 50 copies 15.00 ea.; pap. 3.95 (ISBN 0-685-00952-1). Small Pr Dist.

--Days. 1978. 6.95 (ISBN 0-685-99423-6, Pub. by Anvil Pr). Small Pr Dist.

--A House Against the Night. 1976. pap. 6.95 (ISBN 0-685-79181-5, Pub. by Anvil Pr). Small Pr Dist.

Guest, Ivor. Adventures of a Ballet Historian. LC 81-70096. (Illus.). 150p. 1982. 20.00 (ISBN 0-87127-131-1). Dance Horiz.

--The Alhambra Ballet. pap. 6.00 (ISBN 0-384-20260-8). Johnson Repr.

--The Ballet of the Second Empire. LC 73-15010. (Illus.). 299p. 1974. 22.00x (ISBN 0-8195-4067-6). Wesleyan U Pr.

--Fanny Cerrito: The Life of a Romantic Ballerina. 2nd, Rev ed. (Illus.). 176p. 1974. pap. 6.95 (ISBN 0-903102-09-9, Pub. by Dance Bks England). Princeton Bk Co.

--Fanny Elssler. LC 74-105507. (Illus.). 284p. 1970. 22.00x (ISBN 0-8195-4022-6). Wesleyan U Pr.

--Jules Perrot. 480p. 1984. 37.50 (ISBN 0-87127-140-0). Dance Horiz.

--The Romantic Ballet in England: Its Development, Fulfillment & Decline. 2nd ed. LC 77-172138. (Illus.). 176p. 1972. 22.00x (ISBN 0-8195-4050-1). Wesleyan U Pr.

--The Romantic Ballet in Paris. (Illus.). xix, 314p. 1980. 28.50 (ISBN 0-903102-45-5, Pub. by Dance Bks. England). Princeton Bk Co.

--Victorian Ballet Girl: The Tragic Story of Clara Webster. (Series in Dance). 1980. Repr. of 1958 ed. 22.50 (ISBN 0-306-76043-6). Da Capo.

Guest, Ivor, ed. Letters from a Ballet Master: The Correspondence of Arthur Saint-Leon. LC 81-65108. (Illus.). 200p. 1981. 20.00 (ISBN 0-87127-123-0). Dance Horiz.

Guest, J. E. & Greeley, R. Geology on the Moon. LC 77-371984. (Wykeham Science Ser.: No. 43). 235p. 1977. 17.95x (ISBN 0-8448-1170-X); pap. 12.50x (ISBN 0-8448-1346-X). Crane-Russak Co.

--Geology on the Moon. (Wykeham Science Ser.: No. 43). 220p. 1977. cancelled (ISBN 0-85109-580-1); pap. cancelled (ISBN 0-85109-540-2). Taylor & Francis.

Guest, Joan L. Self-Esteem. (Orig.). 1984. pap. 0.75 (ISBN 0-87784-066-0). Inter-Varsity.

Guest, John. In Search of Certainty. LC 83-19273. (In Search of...Ser.). 1984. 9.95 (ISBN 0-8307-0919-3, 5111001). Regal.

--Only a Prayer Away. 140p. (Orig.). 1985. pap. 5.95 (ISBN 0-89283-273-8, Pub. by Vine Books). Servant.

--Planetary Geology. LC 79-+011. 208p. 1979. 25.95x (ISBN 0-470-26887-5). Halsted Pr.

Guest, Judith. Ordinary People. 1982. pap. 2.95 (ISBN 0-345-30734-8). Ballantine.

--Ordinary People. (General Ser.). 1981. lib. bdg. 12.95 (ISBN 0-8161-3207-0, Large Print Bks). G K Hall.

--Ordinary People. LC 76-2368. 288p. (YA) 1976. 12.95 (ISBN 0-670-52831-5). Viking.

--Ordinary People. 1982. pap. 4.95 (ISBN 0-14-006517-2). Penguin.

--Second Heaven. LC 82-70124. 336p. 1982. 14.95 (ISBN 0-670-62830-1). Viking.

--Second Heaven. (General Ser.). 1983. PLB 17.95 (ISBN 0-8161-3515-0, Large Print Bks). G K Hall.

--Second Heaven. pap. 3.95 (ISBN 0-451-12499-5, Sig). NAL.

Guest, Lisa, jt. auth. see Smoke, Jim.

Guest, Lynn. The Sword of Hachiman. 416p. 1982. pap. 3.50 (ISBN 0-8217-1104-0). Zebra.

--Yedo. 1985. 14.95 (ISBN 0-312-89632-8). St Martin.

Guest, R. Compendious History of the Cotton Manufacture. (Illus.). 74p. 1968. Repr. of 1823 ed. 28.50x (ISBN 0-7146-1396-7, BHA-01396, F Cass Co). Biblio Dist.

Guest, R., et al. Organizational Change Through Effective Leadership. 1977. pap. text ed. 18.95 (ISBN 0-13-641308-0). P-H.

Guest, Robert H. Innovative Work Practices. (Work in America Institute Studies in Productivity: No. 21). 56p. 1982. pap. 35.00 (ISBN 0-08-029502-9, L120). Pergamon.

--Innovative Work Practices. (Studies in Productivity: Highlights of the Literature Ser.: Vol. 21). 52p. 1982. pap. 35.00 (ISBN 0-08-029502-9). Work in Amer.

--Robotics: The Human Dimension. (Work in America Institute Studies in Productivity: No. 36). 40p. 1984. pap. 35.00 (ISBN 0-08-031577-1). Pergamon.

Guest, Robert H., jt. auth. see Walker, Charles R.

Guest, S. Haden, ed. see Maynard, John.

Guetlich, P., et al. Moessbauer Spectroscopy & Transition Metal Chemistry. (Inorganic Chemistry Concepts: Vol. 3). (Illus.). 1978. 47.00 (ISBN 0-387-08671-4). Springer-Verlag.

Gue Trapier, Elizabeth Du see Du Gue Trapier, Elizabeth.

Guetti, James L. Word-Music: The Aesthetic Aspect of Narrative Fiction. 1980. 22.50x (ISBN 0-8135-0883-5). Rutgers U Pr.

Guetti, James L., Jr. The Rhetoric of Joseph Conrad. LC 76-18209. Repr. of 1860 ed. lib. bdg. 8.50 (ISBN 0-8414-4542-7). Folcroft.

Guettinger, W. & Eikemeier, H., eds. Structural Stability in Physics: Proceedings of Two International Symposia. (Springer Ser. in Synergetics). (Illus.). 1979. 43.00 (ISBN 0-387-09463-6). Springer-Verlag.

Guetzkow, Harold & Valadez, Joseph J., eds. Simulated International Processes: Theories & Research in Global Modeling. LC 80-29047. (Illus.). 400p. 1981. 29.95 (ISBN 0-8039-1574-8). Sage.

Guetzkow, Harold S. Groups, Leadership & Man: Research in Human Relations. LC 51-11130. (Illus.). pap. 76.50 (ISBN 0-317-10475-6, 2050540). Bks Demand UMI.

Gueulette, David, jt. auth. see Ohliger, John.

Gueulette, David G., ed. Microcomputers for Adult Learning: Potentials & Perils. 228p. pap. 29.27 (ISBN 0-8428-2205-4). Cambridge Bk.

Gueulette, Thomas S. Mogul Tales: or the Dreams of Man Awake, Pt. 2. LC 73-170593. (Novel in England, 1700-1775). 1972. lib. bdg. 61.00 (ISBN 0-8240-0576-7). Garland Pub.

Guevara, Antonio de. The Diall of Princes (with the Famous Booke of Marcus Aurelius) North, T., tr. LC 68-54646. (English Experience Ser.: No. 50). 536p. 1968. Repr. of 1557 ed. 69.00 (ISBN 90-221-0050-2). Walter J Johnson.

Guevara, Carlos I. & Sesman, Myrna. La Madre y el Aprendizaje del Nino: La Experiencia Urbana Puertorriquena. LC 77-9261. 1978. pap. 5.50 (ISBN 0-8477-2739-4). U of PR Pr.

Guevara, Che. Che Speaks: Selected Speeches & Writings. 1980. pap. 4.95 (ISBN 0-87348-602-1). Path Pr NY.

--Guerrilla Warfare. Loveman, Brian & Davies, Thomas M., Jr., eds. LC 84-13162. (Illus.). xiv, 440p. 1985. 22.95x (ISBN 0-8032-2116-9, BB 844); pap. 10.95 (ISBN 0-8032-7010-0, Bison). U Of Nebr Pr.

Guevara, E. Che. Guerrilla Warfare. 1968. (Vin). Random.

Guevara, Ernesto. Episodes of the Revolutionary War. LC 68-19920. pap. 38.00 (ISBN 0-317-28362-6, 2025542). Bks Demand UMI.

Guevara, Ernesto C. Socialism & Man. pap. 0.65 (ISBN 0-87348-079-1). Path Pr NY.

Guevara, Ernesto see also Che Guevara.

Guevera, Che. The Diary of Che Guevara. 13.95 (ISBN 0-89190-224-4, Pub. by Am Repr). Amereon Ltd.

Guevera, Jose M., jt. auth. see Tenah, Kwaku A.

Gueze, Raoul, jt. auth. see Carbone, Salvatore.

Guezou, J & Nilsen, O. Geological Survey of Norway. (No. 340, Bulletin 47). 1979. pap. 19.00x (ISBN 82-00-31373-5, Dist. by Columbia U Pr.). Universitet.

Guffey, George R. Concordance to the Poetry of Thomas Traherne. LC 73-76112. 1974. 58.50x (ISBN 0-520-02449-4). U of Cal Pr.

Guffey, George R., ed. A Concordance to the English Poems of Andrew Marvell. LC 73-21550. xiv, 623p. 1974. text ed. 35.00 (ISBN 0-8078-1230-7). U of NC Pr.

Guffey, Mary E. Business English. LC 82-21298. 352p. 1983. pap. text ed. write for info. (ISBN 0-534-01396-1); tchr's. ed. avail. Kent Pub Co.

Gufled, Eduard. Exploiting Small Advantages. (Illus.). 128p. 1985. pap. 8.95 (ISBN 0-7134-4822-9, Pub. by Batsford England). David & Charles.

Gugan, Keith. Unconfined Vapor Cloud Explosions. LC 78-74101. 168p. 1979. 37.50x (ISBN 0-87201-887-3). Gulf Pub.

--Unconfined Vapour Cloud Explosions. 168p. 1981. 100.00x (ISBN 0-686-75389-5, Pub. by Inst Chem Eng England). State Mutual Bk.

Gugelberger, Georg M. Nama Namibia: Diary & Letters of Nama Chief Hendrik Witbooi. (African Historical Documents: No. 5). x, 136p. (Orig.). 1984. pap. 9.00 (ISBN 0-915118-12-2). Boston U African.

Gugelberger, Georg M., ed. see Meister, Ernst.

Gugelberger, George M. Ezra Pound's Medievalism. (European University Studies: Series 18, Comparative, Literature Vol. 17). 214p. 1979. pap. 21.35 (ISBN 3-261-02510-7). P Lang Pubs.

Gugelberger, George M., tr. see Soik, Helmut M.

Gugelyk, Ted & Bloombaum, Milton. Ma'i Ho'oka'awale--The Separating Sickness: Interviews with Leprosy Patients Exiled at Kalaupapa, Hawaii. 1984. pap. text ed. 9.00x (ISBN 0-8248-0989-0). UH Pr.

Gugenheim, A. M., tr. see Gugenheim, V. K. & May, J. Peter.

Gugenheim, V. K. & May, J. Peter. On the Theory & Applications of Differential Torsion Products. Gugenheim, A. M., tr. LC 74-2164. (Memoirs: No. 142). 73p. 1974. pap. 10.00 (ISBN 0-8218-1842-2, MEMO-142). Am Math.

Gugenheim, V. K., jt. auth. see Bousfield, A. K.

Guggenberger, L. J., et al, eds. The Structural Aspects of Homogeneous, Heterogeneous & Biological Catalysis. (Transactions of the American Crystallographic Association: Vol. 14). 141p. 1978. pap. 15.00 (ISBN 0-686-60384-2). Polycrystal Bk Serv.

Guggenbuehl-Craig, A. Macht als Gefahr beim Helfer. 4th ed. (Psychologische Praxis: Vol. 45). vi, 106p. 1982. pap. 8.25 (ISBN 3-8055-3664-X). S Karger.

Guggenbuehl-Craig, A., jt. ed. see Probst, E.

Guggenbuhl-Craig, A. Marriage: Dead or Alive? Stein, Murray, tr. from German. 126p. 1977. pap. 10.00 (ISBN 0-88214-309-3). Spring Pubns.

Guggenbuhl-Craig, Adolf. Eros on Crutches: Reflections on Psychopathy & Amorality. Hartman, Gary V., tr. from Ger. 126p. (Orig.). 1980. pap. 10.00 (ISBN 0-88214-315-8). Spring Pubns.

--Power in the Helping Professions. Gubitz, Myron, tr. from Ger. 155p. 1971. pap. 10.00 (ISBN 0-88214-304-2). Spring Pubns.

Guggenheim. Thermodynamics. 6th ed. 390p. 1977. 42.75 (ISBN 0-7204-0021-X, North Holland). Elsevier.

Guggenheim & Nadelson, C., eds. Major Psychiatric Disorders. 388p. 1982. 21.25 (ISBN 0-444-00663-X, Biomedical Pr). Elsevier.

Guggenheim, Alan. Building Corporate Profiles: Sources & Strategies for Investigative Reporters. 124p. 1983. pap. 25.00x (ISBN 0-910377-05-7). Guggenheim.

Guggenheim, Alan, ed. see Guggenheim, Gus N.

Guggenheim, B., ed. Cardiology Today. (Illus.). xii, 396p. 1984. 70.00 (ISBN 3-8055-3761-1). S Karger.

--Health & Sugar Substitutes. 1979. pap. 41.00 (ISBN 3-8055-2961-9). S Karger.

Guggenheim, E. A. Thermodynamics: An Advanced Treatment for Chemists & Physicists. (Personal Library). 390p. 1985. pap. 22.50 (ISBN 0-444-86951-4, North-Holland). Elsevier.

Guggenheim, E. A., jt. auth. see Fowler, Ralph H.

Guggenheim, F. G., ed. Psychological Aspects of Surgery. (Advances in Psychosomatic Medicine: Vol. 15). (Illus.). viii, 272p. 1985. 77.50 (ISBN 3-8055-4090-6). S Karger.

Guggenheim, Frederick G. & Weiner, Myron F., eds. Manual of Psychiatric Consultation & Emergency Care. LC 84-477. 400p. 1984. 40.00 (ISBN 0-87668-666-8). Aronson.

Guggenheim, Gus N. Protocol for Productivity. Guggenheim, Alan, ed. (Textile Industry Management Ser.: No. 1). 132p. 1982. 17.95x (ISBN 0-910377-03-0); pap. 13.95x (ISBN 0-910377-00-6). Guggenheim.

Guggenheim, Hans. Dogon World: A Catalogue of Art & Myth for You to Complete. (Illus.). 50p. 1973. pap. 1.00 (ISBN 0-88397-021-X, Pub. by Intl Exhibitions). C E Tuttle.

--World of Wonderful Difference. (gr. 5-8). 5.00x (ISBN 0-87068-371-3, Pub. by Friendly Hse). Ktav.

Guggenheim, Hans G. Around the World in Eighty Ways. 128p. (Orig.). 1981. pap. 6.00 (ISBN 0-682-49683-9). Exposition Pr FL.

Guggenheim, Harry F. United States & Cuba. LC 79-111715. (American Imperialism: Viewpoints of United States Foreign Policy, 1898-1941). 1970. Repr. of 1934 ed. 18.00 (ISBN 0-405-02024-4). Ayer Co Pubs.

--United States & Cuba: A Study in International Relations. LC 78-102242. (Select Bibliographies Reprint Ser). 1934. 24.50 (ISBN 0-8369-5127-1). Ayer Co Pubs.

--United States & Cuba: A Study in International Relations. LC 79-131730. 1970. Repr. of 1934 ed. 22.00x (ISBN 0-403-00617-1). Scholarly.

Guggenheim, Martin & Sussman, Alan. The Rights of Young People. (American Civil Liberties Union Ser.). 352p. 1985. pap. 4.95 (ISBN 0-553-24818-9). Bantam.

Guggenheim, Michel, jt. auth. see Fanelli, Maresa.

Guggenheim, Paul. Survey on the Ways in Which States Interpret Their International Obligations. Bd. with Mission on the Teaching of the Social Sciences in Pakistan. Repr. of 1955 ed; Research Councils in the Social Sciences. Repr. of 1955 ed; The Social Sciences in Secondary Schools. Repr. of 1955 ed; Reserch Councils in the Social Sciences Addenda. Repr. of 1956 ed. (UNESCO SSSH RP Ser.: Nos. 1 & 6). pap. 49.00 (ISBN 0-317-15422-2). Kraus Repr.

Guggenheim, Peggy. Out of This Century: Confessions of an Art Addict. LC 78-68475. (Illus.). 456p. 1979. 17.50x (ISBN 0-87663-337-8). Universe.

Guggenheim, Peggy, ed. Art of This Century. LC 68-9242. (Contemporary Art Ser). (Illus.). 1968. Repr. of 1942 ed. 12.00 (ISBN 0-405-00721-3). Ayer Co Pubs.

Guggenheim, Scott E., jt. ed. see Weller, Robert P.

Guggenheim, Solomon R., Foundation & Barnett, Vivian E. Kandinsky in Paris: Nineteen Thirty-Four to Nineteen Forty-Four. (Illus.). 268p. (Orig.). 1985. pap. 19.50 (ISBN 0-89207-049-8). S R Guggenheim.

Guggenheimer, Elinor C. Planning for Parks & Recreation Needs in Urban Areas. LC 68-31141. (Illus.). 261p. 1969. text ed. 29.00x (ISBN 0-8290-0192-1). Irvington.

Guggenheimer, Eva H., tr. see Gonseth, Ferdinand.

Guggenheimer, Heinrich. Differential Geometry. pap. text ed. 6.95 (ISBN 0-486-63433-7). Dover.

Guggenheimer, Heinrich W. Mathematics for Engineering & Science. LC 76-28336. (Applied Math Ser.). 290p. 1976. pap. 18.50 (ISBN 0-88275-462-9). Krieger.

Guggenheimer, Henrich W. Applicable Geometry. LC 76-40007. 214p. 1977. pap. text ed. 15.00 (ISBN 0-88275-368-1). Krieger.

Guggenheimer, Richard. Sight & Insight. LC 68-15827. (Illus.). 1968. Repr. of 1945 ed. 22.50x (ISBN 0-8046-0186-0, Pub. by Kennikat). Assoc Faculty Pr.

Guggisberg, C. A. Wild Cats of the World. LC 74-21020. 1975. 15.95 (ISBN 0-8008-8324-1). Taplinger.

Guggisberg, C. A. W. S. O. S. Rhino. (Illus.). 1967. 9.50 (ISBN 0-8079-0116-4). October.

Guggisberg, Frederick G. Future of the Negro: Some Chapters in the Development of a Race. LC 71-97366. Repr. of 1929 ed. 15.00x (ISBN 0-8371-2427-1, GUF&, Pub. by Negro U Pr). Greenwood.

Gughemetti, Joseph M. & Wheeler, Eugene D. The Taking. Rev. ed. (Illus.). 197p. lib. bdg. cancelled (ISBN 0-9608474-1-3); pap. 9.95 (ISBN 0-9608474-0-5). Terra View.

Gugin, David A. An Inquiry into Rapid City's Rejection of Home Rule. 1965. write for info. U of SD Gov Res Bur.

Gugler, J. & Flanagan, W. Urbanization & Social Changes in West Africa. LC 76-9175. (Urbanisation in Developing Countries Ser.). (Illus.). 1978. 34.50 (ISBN 0-521-21348-7); pap. 11.95 (ISBN 0-521-29118-6). Cambridge U Pr.

Gugler, Josef, jt. auth. see Gilbert, Alan.

Gugli, William V., tr. see Chouraqui, Andre.

Guglielmi, Joseph. Translations, "B". Wellman, Don, ed. Duncan, Christopher, tr. (Translations: Experiments in Writing Ser.). 96p. (Orig.). 1983. pap. 4.50 (ISBN 0-942030-05-2). O ARS.

Guglielmo, L. Di see Di Guglielmo, L., et al.

Guglietti, Paul, jt. auth. see Germann, Sheridan.

Gugliotta, Bobette. Pigboat Thirty-Nine: An American Sub Goes to War. LC 84-15295. (Illus.). 288p. 1984. 19.50 (ISBN 0-8131-1524-8). U Pr of KY.

Guha, A. Evolutionary Theory of Economic Growth. 1981. 21.95x (ISBN 0-19-828431-4). Oxford U Pr.

Guha, Arun C. First Spark of Revolution: The Early Phase of India's Struggle for Independence, 1900-1920. 1971. 24.00x (ISBN 0-8046-8811-7, Pub. by Kennikat). Assoc Faculty Pr.

Guha, D. C. Navya Nyaya System of Logic. 3rd enlarged ed. 1979. 15.50 (ISBN 0-89684-059-X, Pub. by Motilal Banarsidass India). Orient Bk Dist.

Guha, J. P. India in the Seventeenth Century, 2 vols. 1976. 30.00 (ISBN 0-686-20251-1). Intl Bk Dist.

Guha, Naresh. W. B. Yeats: An Indian Approach. 1978. Repr. of 1968 ed. lib. bdg. 25.00 (ISBN 0-8495-1916-0). Arden Lib.

Guha, Nikhiles, tr. see Bhattacharya, Lokenath.

Guha, Ranajit. Elementary Aspects of Peasant Insurgency in Colonial India. (Illus.). 1983. 21.95x (ISBN 0-19-561517-4). Oxford U Pr.

--A Rule of Property for Bengal: An Essay on the Idea of Permanent Settlement. 2nd ed. 22p. 1982. text ed. 17.95x (ISBN 0-86131-289-9, Pub. by orient Longman Ltd India). Apt Bks.

Guha, Ranajit, ed. Subaltern Studies, Vol. III. 350p. 1985. 27.95x (ISBN 0-19-561653-7). Oxford U Pr.

--Subaltern Studies II: Writings on South Asian History & Society. (Illus.). 1984. 24.95x (ISBN 0-19-561502-6). Oxford U Pr.

--Subaltern Studies One: Writings on South Asian History & Society. (Illus.). 1982. 19.95x (ISBN 0-19-561355-4). Oxford U Pr.

Guha, Ushri. Introduction to Modern Mathematics. 364p. 1981. 30.00x (Pub. by Orient Longman India). State Mutual Bk.

Guha Majumdar, Rupendra see Majumdar, Rupendra G.

Guharaj, P. V. Forensic Medicine. (Illus.). viii, 452p. (Orig.). 1983. pap. text ed. 25.00x (ISBN 0-86131-292-9, Orient Longman Ltd India). Apt Bks.

Guha-Thakurta, P. Bengali Drama. LC 73-17927. 244p. 1974. Repr. of 1930 ed. lib. bdg. 18.75x (ISBN 0-8371-7271-3, GUBD). Greenwood.

Guha-Thakurta, S., jt. auth. see Bernitsas, Michael M.

Guhin, Michael A. John Foster Dulles: A Statesman & His Times. LC 72-5873. (Illus.). 404p. 1972. 34.00x (ISBN 0-231-03664-7). Columbia U Pr.

--Nuclear Paradox: Security Risks of the Peaceful Atom. 1976. pap. 4.25 (ISBN 0-8447-3204-4). Am Enterprise.

Guhler, Wolfgang & Merzbach, Joachim. Grundwissen Buchhandel-Verlag: Buchfuhrung, Vol. 3. 321p. 1984. lib. bdg. 17.50 (ISBN 0-317-13920-7). K G Saur.

Guiasu, S. & Malitza, M. Coalition & Connection in Games. 1980. text ed. 39.00 (ISBN 0-08-023033-4). Pergamon.

Guiasu, Silviu. Information Theory with New Applications. (Illus.). 1977. text ed. 65.00 (ISBN 0-07-025109-6). McGraw.

Guibe, Lucie. Hedges Ward, Korle Bu Hospital. (Illus.). 1982. 7.95 (ISBN 0-533-05193-2). Vantage.

Guibert, Joseph De see De Guibert, Joseph.

Guiberteau, Milton J., jt. auth. see Mettler, Fred A.

Guiberteau, Milton J., jt. auth. see Mettler, Fred A., Jr.

Guicciardini, Francesco. The History of Italy. Alexander, Sidney, tr. from Ital. LC 83-43221. (Illus.). 457p. 1984. 42.50x (ISBN 0-691-05417-7); pap. 12.50x (ISBN 0-691-00800-0). Princeton U Pr.

--Maxims & Reflections. LC 64-23752. 1972. pap. 8.95x (ISBN 0-8122-1037-9, Pa. Paperbks.). U of Pa Pr.

--The Political Philosophy of Francesco Guicciardini, 2 vols. (A Philosophy of History Library Bk.). (Illus.). 247p. 1985. Set. 189.75 (ISBN 0-89266-533-5). Am Classical Coll Pr.

Guicciardini, Franceso. Ricordi: Italian Text with English Translation. Thomson, Ninian H., tr. 1949. 8.95x (ISBN 0-913298-41-7). S F Vanni.

Guicciardini, Ludovico. The Description of the Low Countreys Gathered into an Epitome. LC 76-57386. (English Experience Ser.: No. 804). 1977. Repr. of 1593 ed. lib. bdg. 18.50 (ISBN 90-221-0804-X). Walter J Johnson.

Guiccioli, T. La Vie de Lord Byron en Italie, 9 vols. Hogg, James, ed. (Salzburg-Romantic Reassesment Ser.). Orig. Title: The Life of Lord Byron in Italy. 1800p. 1983. pap. text ed. 25.50x ea. (Pub. by Salzburg Austria). Vol. 1 (ISBN 0-391-02989-4). Vol. 2 (ISBN 0-391-02990-8). Vol. 3 (ISBN 0-391-02991-6). Vol. 4 (ISBN 0-391-02992-4). Vol. 5 (ISBN 0-391-02993-2). Vol. 6 (ISBN 0-391-02994-0). Vol. 7 (ISBN 0-391-02995-9). Vol. 8, ISBN 0-391-03996-7, Vol. 9, ISBN 0-391-02997-5; Vol. 9, ISBN 0-391-02997-5. Humanities.

Guicciradi, Francesco. Catholic Rome & Its Most Beautiful Paintings. (The Institute for the Promotion of the Arts Ser.). (Illus.). 1978. deluxe bdg. 75.65 (ISBN 0-930582-01-2). Gloucester Art.

Guiccoli, Countess. My Recollections of Lord Byron. 59.95 (ISBN 0-8490-0690-2). Gordon Pr.

Guice, Jackson, jt. auth. see Mantlo, Bill.

Guice, John D. The Rocky Mountain Bench: The Territorial Supreme Courts of Colorado, Montana, & Wyoming, 1861-1890. LC 72-75195. (Yale Western Americana Ser.: No. 23). pap. 58.50 (ISBN 0-317-29580-2, 2022002). Bks Demand UMI.

Guichard, ed. see Renard, Jules.

Guichard, Leon, ed. see Sand, George.

Guichardet, A. Lecons Sur Certaines Algebres Topologiques. (Cours & Documents de Mathematiques & de Physique Ser.). 194p. (Fr.). 1967. 57.75x (ISBN 0-677-50010-6). Gordon.

--Special Topics in Topological Algebras. (Notes on Mathematics & Its Applications Ser.). 202p. (Orig.). 1968. 65.95 (ISBN 0-677-30010-7). Gordon.

--Symmetric Hilbert Spaces & Related Topics. LC 72-76390. (Lecture Notes in Mathematics: Vol. 261). 102p. 1972. pap. 10.00 (ISBN 0-387-05803-6). Springer-Verlag.

Guichard-Meili, Jean. Matisse: Paper Cutouts. LC 83-72979. (Illus.). 195p. 1984. 75.00f (ISBN 0-500-23384-5). Thames Hudson.

Guicharnaud. Moliere. (Bibliotheque des Idees). 21.50 (ISBN 0-685-34244-1). French & Eur.

Guicharnaud, Jacques. Anthology of Twentieth Century French Theater. (Fr.). 1967. text ed. 19.95 (ISBN 0-686-46613-6). French & Eur.

--Raymond Queneau. LC 65-26340. (Columbia Essays on Modern Writers Ser.). (Orig.). 1965. pap. 2.50 (ISBN 0-231-02706-0, MW14). Columbia U Pr.

Guicharnaud, Jacques, ed. Seventeenth Century French Drama. Bishop, Morris & Muir, Kenneth, trs. Incl. Tartuffe. Moliere, Jean B; The Would Be Gentleman. Moliere, Jean B; Precious Damsels. Moliere, Jean B; Phaedra. Racine, Jean B; Athaliah. Racine, Jean B; Cid. Corneille, Pierre. LC 67-17879. (Modern Library College Editions Ser.). 1967. pap. text ed. 6.00 (ISBN 0-394-30977-4, 30977, RanC). Random.

Guicharnaud, June, tr. see Gide, Andre.

Guicharnaud, June, tr. see Halevy, Daniel.

Guicharnaud, June, tr. see Helias, Pierre-Jakez.

Guicharnaud, June, tr. see Toussaint, Auguste.

Guichelaar, P. J., ed. Gear Manufacture & Performance: American Society for Metals Metalworking Forum on Gear Manufacture & Performance, Troy, Mich., 1973. LC 74-86452. (Materials-Metalworking Technology Ser.). pap. 82.30 (ISBN 0-317-11077-2, 74-86452). Bks Demand UMI.

Guicheney, Peirre. Qu'est-ce Que le Medecin? Etude Psychologique de la Relation Medecin-Malade. (Interaction-l'Homme et Son Environnement Sociales Ser.: No. 1). 225p. (Fr.). 1974. pap. text ed. 12.80x (ISBN 90-2797-324-5). Mouton.

Guicherneau, June, ed. see Sullivan, Edward, et al.

Guida, G., jt. auth. see Bara, B. G.

Guidano, V. F. & Liotti, G. Cognitive Processes & Emotional Disorders. LC 83-13188. (Clinical Psychology & Psychotherapy Ser.). 347p. 1983. text ed. 24.50 (ISBN 0-89862-006-6, 2006). Guilford Pr.

Gui De Cambrai. Vengement Alixandre. Edwards, B., ed. (Elliott Monographs). 1928. 14.00 (ISBN 0-527-02626-3). Kraus Repr.

Guideline Publishing Co. Staff. The California Retail Liquor Store. 54p. (Orig.). 1972. pap. 9.95 (ISBN 0-917474-00-7). Guideline Pub.

Guideposts Associates. Guideposts Treasury of Faith. LC 78-22766. (Illus.). 1979. 12.95 (ISBN 0-385-14971-9). Doubleday.

Guidetti, Geri. A Seneca Garden. (Illus.). 26p. (Orig.). (gr. 2-8). 1981. pap. 1.95x (ISBN 0-938928-00-7). KMG Pubns OR.

Guidi, Angelo F., jt. auth. see Garlick, R. C., Jr.

Guidice, Paul J. del see Del Giudice, Paula J.

Guido, Daub, jt. auth. see Seese, William.

Guido, De Cauliaco. Guydos Questions Newly Corrected. LC 68-54627. (English Experience Ser.: No. 35). 390p. 1968. Repr. of 1579 ed. 50.00 (ISBN 90-221-0035-9). Walter J Johnson.

Guido, Margaret. Sicily: The Prehistoric & Roman Remains & the Greek Cities: An Archaeological Guide. (Illus.). 224p. 1977. pap. 7.95 (ISBN 0-571-10881-4). Faber & Faber.

--Southern Italy: An Archaeological Guide. Daniel, Glyn, ed. LC 72-85245. (Illus.). 1973. 16.00 (ISBN 0-8155-5011-1, NP). Noyes.

Guido, Raymond. Calculating with BASIC. (Da Capo Quality Paperbacks Ser.). (Illus.). 80p. 1981. pap. text ed. 8.95 (ISBN 0-306-80144-2). Da Capo.

Guido, Virginia W. Septal Defects: Atrial & Ventricular. (Continuing Education in Cardiovascular Nursing Ser.). (Illus.). 96p. 1982. 6.95x (ISBN 0-8385-8532-9). ACC.

Guidoni, Enrico. Primitive Architecture. (History of World Architecture Ser.). (Illus.). 1978. 50.00 (ISBN 0-8109-1026-8). Abrams.

Guidos, Barbara & Hamilton, Betty. MASA: Medical Acronyms, Symbols & Abbreviations. LC 83-4191. 186p. 1984. lib. bdg. 39.95 (ISBN 0-918212-72-3). Neal-Schuman.

Guidotti, C., jt. ed. see Rahman, N. K.

Guidry, Gail. Hold on Together. (Illus., Orig.). 1971. pap. 3.50 (ISBN 0-912284-20-X). New Rivers Pr.

Guidry, Ron & Golenbock, Peter. Guidry. 194p. 1981. pap. 2.50 (ISBN 0-380-55137-3, 55137-3). Avon.

Guie, H. Dean. Bugles in the Valley: Garnett's Fort Simcoe. rev. ed. LC 77-88149. (Illus.). 205p. 1977. Oreg Hist Soc.

Guie, Heister D., ed. & illus. see Mourning Dove.

Guiens, Lula P. Christianship Montgomery County, Virginia in the Heart of the Alleghenies. LC 80-68026. (Illus.). 256p. 1981. 12.00 (ISBN 0-9614765-1-6). Pat G Johnson.

--Highlights in Early History of Montgomery County, Virginia. LC 75-32949. (Illus.). 182p. 1976. 10.00 (ISBN 0-9614765-2-4). Pat G Johnson.

Guieu, Pierre. The Sixth Council Directive on Value Added Tax. pap. 15.00 (ISBN 90-200-0503-0, Pub. by Kluwer Law Netherlands). Kluwer Academic.

Guignard, M. Optimality & Stability in Mathematical Programming. (Mathematical Programming Studies: Vol. 19). 240p. 1982. 27.75 (ISBN 0-444-86441-5, I-346-82, North-Holland). Elsevier.

Guignet, Philippe. Mines, Manufactures & Ouvriers Du Valenciennois Au XVIII Siecle: Contribution a L'histoire Du Travail Dans L'ancuenne France, 2 vols. in 1. Bruchey, Stuart, ed. LC 77-77172. (Dissertations in European Economic History Ser.). (Illus., Fr.). 1977. lib. bdg. 68.50x (ISBN 0-405-10785-4). Ayer Co Pubs.

Guignon, Charles B. Heidegger & the Problem of Knowledge. LC 83-279. 272p. 1983. 27.50 (ISBN 0-915145-21-9); pap. text ed. 12.75 (ISBN 0-915145-62-6). Hackett Pub.

Guigo II. Guigo II: The Ladder of Monks & Twelve Meditations. Colledge, Edmund & Walsh, James, trs. (Cistercian Studies: No. 48). 1981. pap. write for info. (ISBN 0-87907-748-4). Cistercian Pubns.

Guigoile, E. Nobody Listens to Andrew. (gr. 4-6). pap. 1.95 (ISBN 0-695-36345-X, Dist. by Caroline Hse). Modern Curr.

Guigonnat, Henri. Daemon in Lithuania. Wright, Barbara, tr. from Fr. LC 84-22707. (Illus.). 160p. 1985. 14.00 (ISBN 0-8112-0930-X); pap. 7.95 (ISBN 0-8112-0939-3, NDP592). New Directions.

Guigou, Alberto. Dias Acratas: Sin Ley ni Dios. LC 80-53561. (Senda Narrativa). 276p. (Orig., Span.). 1981. pap. 8.95 (ISBN 0-918454-24-7). Senda Nueva.

Guiguet, Jean. Virginia Woolf & Her Works. Stewart, Jean, tr. 1976. 4.95 (ISBN 0-15-693630-5, Harv). HarBraceJ.

Guiho, Gerard, jt. auth. see Bierman, Alan W.

Guiho, Gerard, jt. auth. see Biermann, Alan W.

Guilbaud, P., jt. auth. see Prevert, Jacques.

Guilbault. Analytical Uses of Immobilized Enzymes. (Modern Monographs in Analytical Chemistry). 528p. 1984. 75.00 (ISBN 0-8247-7125-7). Dekker.

Guilbault, G. G. Modern Quantitative Analysis: Experiments for Non-Chemistry Majors. 256p. 1974. 22.75 (ISBN 0-8247-6106-5). Dekker.

--Practical Fluorescence: Theory, Methods, & Techniques. 680p. 1973. 99.75 (ISBN 0-8247-1263-3). Dekker.

Guilbault, G. G., ed. Fluorescence: Theory, Instrumentation, & Practice. 1967. 95.00 (ISBN 0-8247-1260-9). Dekker.

Guilbault, George. Handbook of Enzymatic Methods of Analysis. (Clinical & Biochemical Analysis Ser.: Vol. 4). 1976. 99.75 (ISBN 0-8247-6425-0). Dekker.

Guilbault, George G. & Hargis, Larry G. Instrumental Analysis Manual: Modern Experiments for the Laboratory. LC 78-126311. pap. 113.00 (ISBN 0-317-08385-6, 2055039). Bks Demand UMI.

Guilbaut, Adolfe, jt. auth. see Leautey, Eugene.

Guilbaut, Serge. How New York Stole the Idea of Modern Art: Abstract Expressionsm, Freedom, & the Cold War. LC 83-6506. (Illus.). x, 278p. 1983. 22.50x (ISBN 0-226-31038-8); pap. 9.95 (ISBN 0-226-31039-6). U of Chicago Pr.

Guilbeau, J. L. The St. Charles Streetcar or the New Orleans & Carrollton Railroad. (Illus.). 68p. 1977. pap. 3.00 (ISBN 0-686-32516-8). Transitour.

Guilbert. Le Vocabulaire de L'astronautique: Enquete Linguistique a travers la Presse d'information a L'occasion De Cinq Exploits de Cosmonautes. (Publ. de l'Univ. de Rouen Fac. des Lettres et Sc. Hum.). (Fr.). 15.95 (ISBN 0-685-36683-9). French & Eur.

Guilbert, Graeme, ed. Hill-Fort Studies. 216p. 1981. text ed. 35.50x (ISBN 0-7185-1200-6, Leicester). Humanities.

Guilbert, J. F., jt. auth. see Macchi, C.

Guilbert, John M., jt. auth. see Park, Charles F.

Guilbert, L. Le Vocabulaire De L'astronautique. 361p. (Fr.). pap. 45.00 (ISBN 0-686-57265-3, F-137130). French & Eur.

Guilbert, Louis. La Formation du Vocabulaire de L'Aviation. 712p. (Fr.). 1966. 37.50 (ISBN 0-686-57276-9, F-135660). French & Eur.

--Grand Larousse de la Langue Francaise, 7 vols. (Fr.). 1975. Set. 495.00 (ISBN 0-686-57308-0, M-6287). French & Eur.

Guilbert, Madeleine. Les Fonctions des Femmes Dans L'industrie. (Etudes Europeennes: No. 4). 1966. pap. 18.40x (ISBN 0-686-21232-C). Mouton.

Guild, Courtenay, jt. auth. see Bradbury, William.

Guild, I., jt. auth. see Potter, T.

Guild, June. Black Laws of Virginia. LC 78-98721. Repr. of 1936 ed. cancelled (ISBN 0-8371-2777-7, O, Pub. by Negro U Pr). Greenwood.

Guild, Laurence R., jt. auth. see Furniss, Edgar S.

Guild, Leah. Texas Passion. (Orig.). 1983. pap. 1.95 (ISBN 0-317-02747-6, BH064). Holloway.

Guild, Leo. Black Bait. rev. ed. 224p. (Orig.). 1985. pap. 2.50 (ISBN 0-87067-243-6, BH243). Holloway.

--Carlotta. (Orig.). 1980. pap. 2.25 (ISBN 0-87067-010-7, BH010). Holloway.

--Girl Who Loved Black. rev. ed. (Orig.). 1985. pap. 2.75 (ISBN 0-87067-715-2, BH715). Holloway.

--Street of Ho's. (Orig.). 1976. pap. 2.25 (ISBN 0-87067-025-5, BH025). Holloway.

--The Studio. (Orig.). 1969. pap. 1.75 (ISBN 0-87067-168-5, BH168). Holloway.

--World's Greatest Winning Systems. rev. ed. (Orig.). 1966. pap. 2.00 (ISBN 0-87067-614-8, BH614). Holloway.

--Zanuck: Hollywood's Last Tycoon. (Orig.). 1970. pap. 1.50 (ISBN 0-87067-409-9, BH409). Holloway.

Guild, Leo, ed. Confidential Sex Survey. (Orig.). pap. 1.25 (ISBN 0-87067-304-1, BH304). Holloway.

Guild, Leo, ed. see Pennington, Alberta L.

Guild, N. The Linz Tattoo. 320p. 1985. price not set (ISBN 0-07-025112-6). McGraw.

Guild, Nicholas. The Berlin Warning. 400p. 1985. pap. 3.95 (ISBN 0-441-05397-1, Pub. by Charter Bks). Ace Bks.

--Chain Reaction. 384p. 1983. 13.95 (ISBN 0-312-12785-5). St Martin.

--The Linz Tattoo. 1985. 16.95 (ISBN 0-07-025112-6). McGraw.

--The President's Man. 364p. 1982. 13.95 (ISBN 0-312-64128-1). St Martin.

Guild of Master Craftsman Publications, Ltd., ed. The First Book of Its Kind. 1981. 25.00x (ISBN 0-686-78734-X, Pub. by Guild Master England). State Mutual Bk.

Guild, Reuben A. Early History of Brown University, Including the Life, Times, & Correspondence of President Manning, 1756-1791. rev. ed. Gaustad, Edwin S., ed. LC 79-52594. (The Baptist Tradition Ser.). (Illus.). 1980. Repr. of 1897 ed. lib. bdg. 51.50x (ISBN 0-405-12461-9). Ayer Co Pubs.

--The Librarian's Manual: A Treatise on Bibliography, Comprising a Select & Descriptive List of Bibliographical Works; to Which Are Added, Sketches of Public Libraries. LC 70-174942. (Illus.). x, 304p. 1972. Repr. of 1858 ed. 46.00x (ISBN 0-8103-3811-4). Gale.

Guild, Stephen, et al. Teaching Non-Western Studies: A Handbook of Materials & Methods. 139p. (Orig.). 1972. pap. 4.00 (ISBN 0-932288-02-2). Ctr Intl Ed U of MA.

Guild, Thelma S. & Carter, Harvey L. Kit Carson: A Pattern for Heroes. LC 83-21628. (Illus.). xiv, 383p. 1984. 18.95 (ISBN 0-8032-2118-5). U of Nebr Pr.

Guild, Vera. Dollmakers' Workshop. 160p. 1981. 19.95 (ISBN 0-87851-049-4). Hearst Bks.

Guild, Vera P. Good Housekeeping Book of Quilt Making. LC 76-4189. (Illus.). 160p. 1976. 12.95 (ISBN 0-87851-017-6). Hearst Bks.

--Good Housekeeping New Complete Book of Needlecraft. LC 76-137519. (Illus.). 560p. 1971. 16.95 (ISBN 0-87851-002-8). Hearst Bks.

Guild, Warren R., et al. Physiology for Nurses: A Guide for Nurses, Allied Health Professionals & Physician Assistants. LC 73-5321. (Trainex Manual Ser.). (Illus.). 289p. 1973. 9.95 (ISBN 0-685-41086-2). Trainex Pr.

Guilday, Peter K. The English Catholic Refugees on the Continent, 1558-1795. LC 83-45582. Date not set. Repr. of 1914 ed. 55.00 (ISBN 0-404-19900-3). Ams Pr.

--History of the Councils of Baltimore, 1791-1884. LC 77-83421. (Religion in America, Ser. 1). 1969. Repr. of 1932 ed. 25.50 (ISBN 0-405-00246-7). Ayer Co Pubs.

--Life & Times of John England. LC 70-83422. (Religion in America, Ser. 1). 1969. Repr. of 1927 ed. 54.00 (ISBN 0-405-00247-5). Ayer Co Pubs.

Guilds, John C., ed. see Simms, William G.

Guile, A. E. & Paterson, W. Electrical Power Systems, Vol. 1. 2nd ed. LC 77-1789. 1977. text ed. 62.00 (ISBN 0-08-021728-1); pap. text ed. 18.75 (ISBN 0-08-021729-X). Pergamon.

--Electrical Power Systems, Vol. 2: In SI-Metric Units. 53.00 (ISBN 0-08-021730-3); pap. 18.75 (ISBN 0-08-021731-1). Pergamon.

Guilelmus. Godeffroy of Boloyne; or, the Siege & Conquest of Jerusalem. Colvin, Mary N., ed. (EETS, ES Ser.: No. 64). Repr. of 1893 ed. 29.00 (ISBN 0-527-00269-0). Kraus Repr.

Guiler, W. S., et al. Reading for Meaning, 6 bks. rev. ed. (gr. 4-9). Gr. 4-6. 1962. text ed. 1.88 ea.; Gr. 7-9. 1965. text ed. 1.88 ea. Har-Row.

Guiles, Cecil R. The In Crowd. 1976. pap. 3.95 (ISBN 0-87148-627-X). Pathway Pr.

--Ministering to Youth. 1973. 5.25 (ISBN 0-87148-551-6); pap. 4.25 (ISBN 0-87148-552-4); instrs. guide 4.95 (ISBN 0-87148-834-5). Pathway Pr.

Guiles, Fred L. Jane Fonda: The Actress in Her Time. 368p. 1983. pap. 3.95 (ISBN 0-523-41994-5). Pinnacle Bks.

--Legend: The Life & Death of Marilyn Monroe. LC 84-40243. (Illus.). 440p. 1984. 17.95 (ISBN 0-8128-2983-2). Stein & Day.

--Legend: The Life & Death of Marilyn Monroe. 1985. pap. 3.95. Stein & Day.

--Stan: The Life of Stan Laurel. LC 80-5806. (Illus.). 272p. 1980. 12.95 (ISBN 0-8128-2762-7). Stein & Day.

--Tyrone Power: The Last Idol. 1980. pap. 2.75 (ISBN 0-425-04619-2). Berkley Pub.

Guiles, R., jt. auth. see Hosmer, L. T.

Guiley, Rosemary. Lovelines. (Illus.). 316p. 1983. 15.95 (ISBN 0-87196-724-3); pap. 7.95 (ISBN 0-87196-826-6). Facts on File.

Guilfoile, Elizabeth. Nobody Listens to Andrew. (Beginning-to-Read Bks). (Illus.). (gr. 1-3). 1957. (Dist. by Caroline Hse); pap. 1.95 (ISBN 0-685-10944-5). Modern Curr.

--Valentine's Day. LC 65-10086. (Holiday Bks.). (Illus.). (gr. 2-5). 1965. PLB 8.37 (ISBN 0-8116-6556-9). Garrard.

Guilford, C., jt. auth. see Mackenzie, W. S.

Guilford, Carol. The Easiest Cookbook. 1979. 10.95i (ISBN 0-397-01366-3). Har-Row.

Guilford, Charles. Beginning College Writing. 1984. pap. text ed. 13.95 (ISBN 0-316-33127-9); tchr's. ed. avail. (ISBN 0-316-33128-7). Little.

Guilford, J. P. Cognitive Psychology with a Frame of Reference. LC 78-74137. 1979. 11.95 (ISBN 0-912736-22-4). EDITS Pubs.

--Intelligence, Creativity & Their Educational Implications. LC 68-26627. 1968. pap. text ed. 8.95 (ISBN 0-912736-09-7). EDITS Pubs.

--Way Beyond the I. Q. Guide to Improving Intelligence & Creativity. LC 77-80536. 1977. pap. 9.50 (ISBN 0-930222-01-6). Creat Educ Found.

Guilford, Joan S., et al. Guilford-Zimmerman Temperament Survey Handbook. LC 76-17988. 1976. 14.95 (ISBN 0-912736-19-4). EDITS Pubs.

Guilford, Joy P. & Fruchter, Benjamin. Fundamental Statistics in Psychology & Education. 6th ed. LC 77-5768. (McGraw-Hill Series in Psychology). (Illus.). 1977. text ed. 34.95 (ISBN 0-07-025150-9). McGraw.

Guilford, Nancy, jt. ed. see Brandt, Patricia.

Guilfoyle, Ann. Home Free: A Quick & Easy Guide to Housekeeping. 1985. price not set (ISBN 0-07-025145-2). McGraw.

--Home Free: The No-Nonsense Guide to House Care. LC 83-42666. (Illus.). 1984. 12.95 (ISBN 0-393-01778-8). Norton.

Guilfoyle, Ann & Rayfield, Susan. Wildlife Photography. (Illus.). 176p. 1982. 24.95 (ISBN 0-8174-6417-4, Amphoto). Watson-Guptill.

Guilfoyle, George, jt. auth. see Lerman, Alan.

Guilfoyle, George R. & Silverman-Dresner, Toby. Vocabulary Norms for Deaf Children. LC 72-83498. (Lexington School Ser.: Book 7). 1972. softcover 8.00 (ISBN 0-88200-060-8, C2344). Alexander Graham.

Guilfoyle, Merlin J. The Little "O". LC 72-86757. (Illus.). 1972. 10.00 (ISBN 0-912450-05-3). Willow Hse.

Guilhaudi, J. F., jt. auth. see Cot, J. P.

Guilhaumou, Jean. Lexique de L'Informatique. 3rd ed. 122p. (Fr.). 1976. pap. 18.95 (ISBN 0-686-57288-2, F-137140). French & Eur.

Guiliani, jt. auth. see Nasser.

Guiliani, Dorothy A. Complete Guide to Coaching Women's Basketball. 1982. 16.95 (ISBN 0-13-160465-1, Parker). P-H.

Guiliano, Edward. Lewis Carroll: An Annotated International Bibliography, 1960-1977. LC 80-13975. 253p. 1980. 15.00x (ISBN 0-8139-0862-0). U Pr of Va.

Guiliano, Edward & Kincaid, James R., eds. Soaring with the Dodo: Essays on Lewis Carroll's Life & Art. LC 82-83516. (Illus.). 140p. 1982. 15.00x (ISBN 0-930326-07-5, Pub. by Lewis Carroll Soc). U Pr of Va.

Guiliano, Edward, ed. see Carroll, Lewis.

Guiliano, William, jt. auth. see Resnick, Seymour.

Guilion, Fanny L. Raul Dufy: Catalogue Raisonne des Aquarelles, Gouaches, et Pastels, 2 Vols, Fr. 48p. 1981. 385.00x (ISBN 2-86574-002-1). Hacker.

Guillain, Robert. I Saw Tokyo Burning. LC 82-81999. 320p. 1982. pap. 2.95 (ISBN 0-86721-223-3). Jove Pubns.

Guillame, Gustave. Foundations for a Science of Language. Hirtle, Walter & Hewson, John, trs. (Current Issues in Linguistic Theory Ser.: No. 31). Orig. Title: French. 175p. 1984. 28.00x (ISBN 90-272-3523-6). Benjamins North Am.

Guillamin, Duch M. A Hurrian Musical Scare from Ugart: Sources & Monographs from the Ancient Near East, Vol. 2. (Sources & Monographs from the Ancient Near East). 32p. pap. 6.50x (ISBN 0-89003-158-4); tape 6.50x (ISBN 0-317-17531-9). Undena Pubns.

Guilland, Antoine. Modern Germany & Her Historians. Repr. of 1915 ed. lib. bdg. 17.00x (ISBN 0-8371-4506-6, GUMG). Greenwood.

Guillard, Joanny. Golonpoui: Analyse des Conditions de Modernisation d'un Village du Nord-Cameroun. (Le Monde d'outre Mer Passe et Present Documents: No. 7). 1965. pap. text ed. 36.00x (ISBN 90-2796-191-3). Mouton.

Guillard, Roddphe. Titres et Fonctions De L'Empire Byzantin. 528p. 1976. 60.00x (ISBN 0-902089-94-3, Pub. by Variorum). State Mutual Bk.

Guillaud, Jacqueline, jt. auth. see Guillaud, Maurice.

Guillaud, Maurice & Guillaud, Jacqueline. Altdorfer & Fantastic Realism in German Art. (Illus.). 496p. 1985. 45.00 (ISBN 0-8478-5410-8). Rizzoli Intl.

Guillaume, A., jt. auth. see Arnold, T. W.

Guillaume, A., intro. by see Ishaq, I.

Guillaume, Alfred. Islam. 1954. pap. 4.95 (ISBN 0-14-020311-7, Pelican). Penguin.

--The Traditions of Islam. LC 79-52552. (Islam Ser.). 1980. Repr. of 1924 ed. lib. bdg. 16.00x (ISBN 0-8369-9260-1). Ayer Co Pubs.

Guillaume De Berneville. La Vie De Saint Gilles. Paris, Gaston & Bos, Alphonse, eds. 34.00 (ISBN 0-384-20300-0); pap. 28.00 (ISBN 0-384-20285-3). Johnson Repr.

Guillaume de Dole. Le Roman de la Rose Ou de Guillaume de Dole. Servois, G., ed. 37.00 (ISBN 0-685-13581-0); pap. 31.00 (ISBN 0-384-20310-8). Johnson Repr.

Guillaume De Nangis. Chronique Latine De Guillaume De Nangis 1113 a 1300, 2 Vols. Geraud, H., ed. Set. 86.00 (ISBN 0-384-20360-4); Set. pap. 74.00 (ISBN 0-384-20361-2). Johnson Repr.

Guillaume, James. Internationale: Documents & Souvenirs Eighteen Sixty-Four to Seventy-Eight, 4 Vols. in 2. (Fr). 1969. 91.00 (ISBN 0-8337-1487-2). B Franklin.

Guillaume, Paul. Imitation in Children. Halperin, Elaine P., tr. from Fr. LC 77-135742. xviii, 214p. 1971. 13.00 (ISBN 0-226-31045-0). U of Chicago Pr.

--Imitation in Children. Halperin, Elaine P., tr. from Fr. LC 77-135742. xviii, 214p. 1973. pap. 2.95x (ISBN 0-226-31046-9, P423, Phoen). U of Chicago Pr.

Guillaume, Paul, jt. auth. see Apollinaire, Guillaume.

Guillaume De, Bertier De Sauvigny see De Bertier De Sauvigny, Guillaume.

Guillaume de Deguilleville. The Pilgrimage of the Lyf of the Manhode. Wright, W. A., ed. LC 78-178536. (Eng.). Repr. of 1869 ed. 28.50 (ISBN 0-404-56613-8). AMS Pr.

Guillaume De Machaut. Oeuvres de Guillaume de Machaut, 3 Vols. 120.00 (ISBN 0-384-20329-9); pap. 102.00 (ISBN 0-384-20330-2). Johnson Repr.

Guillaume de Normandie. Le Bestiare. LC 73-180441. Repr. of 1892 ed. 38.50 (ISBN 0-404-56615-4). AMS Pr.

Guillaume De Palerne. The Ancient English Romance of William & the Werewolf. Madden, Frederick, ed. LC 73-80173. (Literature & Criticism Ser.). 1971. Repr. of 1832 ed. 29.50 (ISBN 0-8337-2178-X). B Franklin.

Guillaumin, Emile. The Life of a Simple Man. Weber, Eugen, ed. Crosland, Margaret, tr. from Fr. LC 82-40339. 231p. 1982. 20.00x (ISBN 0-87451-247-6); pap. 8.95x (ISBN 0-87451-246-8). U Pr of New Eng.

Guillebaud, Claude W. Economic Recovery of Germany from 1933 to the Incorporation of Austria in March 1938. LC 72-180859. (Studies in Fascism, Ideology & Practice). Repr. of 1939 ed. 29.00 (ISBN 0-404-56135-7). AMS Pr.

Guillebaud, John. The Pill. (Illus.). 1980. pap. 9.95x (ISBN 0-19-286002-X). Oxford U Pr.

Guillemain, B. L' Eveil de l'Europe. (Histoire universelle Larousse de poche). (Fr). pap. 3.50 (ISBN 0-685-13913-1). Larousse.

Guillemard, Anne Marie. Old Age & the Welfare State. LC 82-42835. (Studies in International Sociology: No. 28). 265p. 1983. 28.00 (ISBN 0-8039-9784-1); 14.00 (ISBN 0-8039-9759-0). Sage.

Guillemard, Francis H. Life of Ferdinand Magellan & the First Circumnavigation of the Globe. LC 70-127901. Repr. of 1890 ed. 26.00 (ISBN 0-404-02947-7). AMS Pr.

Guillem de Saint-Didier. Poesies Du Troubadour Guillem de Saint-Didier. LC 80-2179. Repr. of 1956 ed. 31.00 (ISBN 0-404-19007-3). AMS Pr.

Guillemeau, Jacques. Child-Birth. LC 77-38196. (English Experience Ser.: No. 464). 396p. 1972. Repr. of 1612 ed. 55.00 (ISBN 90-221-0464-8). Walter J Johnson.

--Sixteenth Century Storehouse of Surgical Treasures. 288p. 1985. 25.00 (ISBN 0-89962-487-1). Todd & Honeywell.

Guillemin. Le Converti Paul Claudel. 25.95 (ISBN 0-685-37276-6). French & Eur.

Guillemin, Anne. The Kennedys Abroad: Ann & Peter in Brittany. 12.50 (ISBN 0-392-15943-0, SpS). Sportshelf.

Guillemin, Ernest A. Synthesis of Passive Networks: Theory & Methods Appropriate to the Realization & Approximation Problems. LC 76-50044. 760p. 1977. Repr. of 1957 ed. 42.50 (ISBN 0-88275-481-5). Krieger.

Guillemin, Jeanne. Urban Renegades: The Cultural Strategy of American Indians. new ed. LC 74-30434. 336p. 1975. 29.00x (ISBN 0-231-03884-4). Columbia U Pr.

Guillemin, Jeanne E., ed. Anthropological Realities: Readings in the Science of Culture. LC 79-66433. 528p. 1980. pap. 12.95 (ISBN 0-87855-783-0). Transaction Bks.

Guillemin, Roger, et al, eds. Neural Modulation of Immunity. 272p. 1985. text ed. 54.50 (ISBN 0-88167-049-9). Raven.

Guillemin, V. W. & Sternberg, Shlomo. Deformation Theory of Pseudogroup Structures. LC 52-42839. (Memoirs Ser.: No. 64). 80p. 1966. pap. 9.00 (ISBN 0-8218-1264-5, MEMO-64). Am Math.

Guillemin, V. W., jt. auth. see Golubitsky, M.

Guillemin, Victor & Pollack, Alan. Differential Topology. (Math. Ser). (Illus.). 324p. 1974. 36.95x (ISBN 0-13-212605-2). P-H.

Guillemin, Victor & Sternberg, Shlomo. Geometric Asymptotics. LC 77-8210. (Mathematical Surveys Ser.: No. 14). 474p. 1977. 58.00 (ISBN 0-8218-1514-8, SURV-14). Am Math.

--Symplectic Techniques in Physics. LC 83-7762. 464p. 1984. 49.50 (ISBN 0-521-24866-3). Cambridge U Pr.

Guillemin, Victor, jt. auth. see Boutet De Monvel, Louis B.

Guillemin, Victor, ed. Studies in Applied Mathematics: Volume Dedicated to Irving Segal. (Advances in Mathematics: Supplementary Studies: Vol. 8). 1983. 41.50 (ISBN 0-12-305480-X). Acad Pr.

Guillemin, Victor, et al. Seminar on Micro-Local Analysis. LC 78-70609. (Annals of Mathematics Studies: No. 93). 1979. 25.00x (ISBN 0-691-08228-6); pap. 10.95x (ISBN 0-691-08232-4). Princeton U Pr.

Guilleminault, C. Disorders of Sleep & Waking. 1981. text ed. 52.50 (ISBN 0-201-10500-4, Med-Nurse). Addison-Wesley.

Guilleminault, Christian & Dement, William C., eds. Sleep Apnea Syndromes: Proceedings. LC 78-416. (Kroc Foundation Ser.: Vol. 11). 390p. 1978. 52.00 (ISBN 0-8451-0301-6). A R Liss.

Guilleminault, Christian, jt. ed. see Czeisler, Charles A.

Guillen, Claudio, ed. Proceedings of the Tenth Congress of the International Comparative Literature Association: Comparative Poetics. LC 84-48469. 600p. 1985. lib. bdg. 70.00 (ISBN 0-8240-4012-0). Garland Pub.

Guillen, Claudio, jt. ed. see Balakian, Anna.

Guillen, Jorge. Affirmation: A Bilingual Anthology 1919-1966. Palley, Julian, tr. LC 68-15667. (Orig.). 1971. 14.95x (ISBN 0-8061-0764-2). U of Okla Pr.

--Guillen on Guillen: The Poetry & the Poet. Gibbons, Reginald & Geist, Anthony L., trs. LC 78-70299. 1979. pap. 7.95 (ISBN 0-691-01356-X). Princeton U Pr.

--Guirnalda Civil. LC 70-133836. (Orig., Span). 1970. 25.00 (ISBN 0-912604-01-8); pap. 3.00 (ISBN 0-912604-00-X). Halty Ferguson.

--Segun las Horas. 1.85 (ISBN 0-8477-3203-7); pap. 1.55 (ISBN 0-8477-3204-5). U of PR Pr.

Guillen, Michael. Bridges to Infinity. LC 83-15925. (Illus.). 216p. 1984. 12.95 (ISBN 0-87477-233-8). J P Tarcher.

--Bridges to Infinity. LC 83-15925. 216p. 1985. pap. 6.95 (ISBN 0-87477-345-8). J P Tarcher.

Guillen, Nicholas. Tengo. Carr, Richard, tr. 1974. 7.25 (ISBN 0-685-42550-9); pap. 4.25 (ISBN 0-910296-29-4). Broadside.

Guillen, Nicolas. The Great Zoo & Other Poems. Marquez, Robert, ed. & tr. from Span. LC 72-81758. 224p. (Eng. & Span.). 1973. pap. 8.00 (ISBN 0-85345-287-3). Monthly Rev.

--Man-Making Words: Selected Poems of Nicolas Guillen. Marquez, Robert & McMurray, David, eds. Marquez, Robert & McMurray, David, trs. LC 78-181363. 248p. (Span. & Eng.). 1972. 15.00x (ISBN 0-87023-101-4); pap. 7.95x (ISBN 0-87023-102-2). U of Mass Pr.

Guillerm-Kirk, Christine, jt. auth. see Kirk, Richard.

Guillermo, E. & Hernandez, J. A. La Novelistica Espanola De los Sesenta. 1971. 12.45 (ISBN 0-88303-002-0); pap. 9.00 (ISBN 0-685-73208-8). E Torres & Sons.

Guillermo, Luna A. Hacia una Administracion Eficaz. 128p. (Span.). 1985. 3.25 (ISBN 0-88113-114-8). Edit Betania.

Guillet, Alain & La Fauci, Nunzio, eds. Lexique-Grammaire dex Langues Romanes: Actes du Ier Colloque Europeen sur la Grammaire et le Lexique Compares des Langues Romanes, 23-26 Septembre 1981. (Linguisticae Investigationes Supplementa Ser.: No. 9). (Illus.). 319p. (Fr.). 1984. 40.00x (ISBN 90-272-3119-2). Benjamins North Am.

Guillet, David. Agrarian Reform & Peasant Economy in Southern Peru. LC 78-19644. 244p. 1979. text ed. 20.00x (ISBN 0-8262-0263-2). U of Mo Pr.

Guillet, David, ed. see Forman, Sylvia H., et al.

Guillet, Edwin C. The Great Migration: The Atlantic Crossing by Sailing-Ship Since 1770. LC 73-145482. (The American Immigration Library). xii, 316p. 1971. Repr. of 1937 ed. lib. bdg. 17.95x (ISBN 0-89198-013-X). Ozer.

--Pioneer Travel. LC 66-4464. (Illus.). 1966. pap. 7.50 (ISBN 0-8020-6052-8). U of Toronto Pr.

--Story of Canadian Roads. LC 66-31427. (Illus.). 1966. 30.00 (ISBN 0-8020-1414-3). U of Toronto Pr.

Guillet, Ernest B. Un Theatre francophone dans un milieu franco-americain. (Illus.). 52p. (Fr.). 1981. pap. text ed. 1.50 (ISBN 0-911409-37-8). Natl Mat Dev.

Guillet, J. Religious Experience of Jesus & His Disciples. Richards, M. Innocentia, tr. LC 75-210. (Religious Experience Ser: Vol. 9). 1975. pap. 2.95 (ISBN 0-87029-044-4, 20132-7). Abbey.

Guillet, J., ed. Polymers & Ecological Problems. LC 73-81406. (Polymer Science & Technology Ser.: Vol. 3). 230p. 1973. 42.50x (ISBN 0-306-36403-4, Plenum Pr). Plenum Pub.

Guillet, James. Polymer Photophysics & Photochemistry: An Introduction to the Study of Photoprocesses in Macromolecules. 391p. 1985. 79.50 (ISBN 0-521-23506-5). Cambridge U Pr.

Guillet de Montoux, Pierre. Action & Existence: Anarchism for Business Administration. 294p. 1983. text ed. 47.95 (ISBN 0-471-10217-2). Wiley.

Guillet-Rydell, Mirelle, tr. see Switzer, Richard.

Guillevic. Euclidians. Savory, Teo, tr. from Fr. (Illus.). 1977. pap. 5.00 (ISBN 0-87775-079-3). Unicorn Pr.

Guillevic, Eugene. Selected Poems. Levertov, Denise, tr. LC 74-88726. (Orig., Eng. & Fr.). 1969. 5.95 (ISBN 0-8112-0283-6). New Directions.

Guilliame, Patrice. Success & Higher Income: The Write Way. (Illus.). 57p. 1981. write for info. PW Pubns.

Guillien, Raymond & Vincent, Jean. Lexique des Termes Juridiques. 3rd ed. 354p. (Fr.). 1978. pap. 14.95 (ISBN 0-686-57321-8, M-6304). French & Eur.

Guillim, John. A Display of Heraldrie. LC 79-84115. (English Experience Ser.: No. 934). 308p. 1979. Repr. of 1611 ed. lib. bdg. 46.00 (ISBN 90-221-0934-8). Walter J Johnson.

Guillmin, Henri, ed. see Zola, Emile.

Guillois, Antoine. Salon de Madame Helvetius: Cabanis et les Ideologues. LC 74-159698. (Research & Source Works Ser: No. 892). 250p. (Selected essays in History, Economics, & Social Science, No. 323). 1972. Repr. of 1894 ed. lib. bdg. 23.50 (ISBN 0-8337-4145-4). B Franklin.

Guillory, John. Poetic Authority: Spenser, Milton, & Literary History. 224p. 1983. 25.00x (ISBN 0-231-05540-4); pap. 12.50x (ISBN 0-231-05541-2). Columbia U Pr.

Guillory, La Vera M. Expressive & Receptive Finger Spelling for Hearing Adults. 1966. pap. 2.25 (ISBN 0-87511-055-X). Claitors.

Guillory, William A. Realizations: Personal Empowerment Through Self-Awareness. LC 85-60283. (Illus., Orig.). 1985. pap. 7.95 (ISBN 0-933241-00-3). Innovations Inc.

Guillot, Bernard. La Terre Enkou: Recherches Sur les Structures Agraires Du Plateau Koukouya (Congo) (Atlas Des Structures Agraires Au Sud Du Sahara: No.8). 1973. pap. 22.40 (ISBN 0-686-21233-9). Mouton.

Guillot, Genevieve & Prudhommeau, Germaine. The Book of Ballet. (Reference Shelf Ser.). (Illus.). 384p. 1980. pap. 3.95 (ISBN 0-13-079764-2, Spec). P-H.

Guillot, Genevieve, jt. auth. see Prudhommeau, Germaine.

Guillot, J. Le Developpement Economique de L'Algerie. (Economies et Societes Series F: No. 15). 1960. pap. 26.00 (ISBN 0-317-16839-8). Kraus Repr.

Guillot, Rene. Grishka & the Bear. March, Gwenn, tr. LC 60-6265. (Illus.). (gr. 3-6). 1960. 9.57i (ISBN 0-200-00000-4, 329050, AbS-J). Har-Row.

--Prince of the Jungle. LC 59-60132. (Illus.). (gr. 7-9). 1959. 10.95 (ISBN 0-87599-045-2). S G Phillips.

--Sirga. LC 59-12198. (Illus.). (gr. 6-9). 1959. 10.95 (ISBN 0-87599-046-0). S G Phillips.

--Three Hundred Ninety-Seventh White Elephant. LC 57-6246. (Illus.). (gr. 4-6). 1957. 10.95 (ISBN 0-87599-043-6). S G Phillips.

--Wind of Chance. Dale, Norman, tr. (Illus.). (gr. 6-9). 1958. 10.95 (ISBN 0-87599-048-7). S G Phillips.

Guilloton, D. S., jt. auth. see Domandi, Agnes K.

Guillou, Andre. Culture et Societe en Italie Byzantine (VIe-XIes.) 336p. 1978. 60.00x (ISBN 0-86078-021-X, Pub. by Variorum). State Mutual Bk.

Guillou, Jean & Vitols, M. Le Francais Contemporain. LC 75-140658. 1972. pap. text ed. 20.95 (ISBN 0-03-081347-6, HoltC). HR&W.

Guillou, Louis A. Calculus with Analytic Geometry. 4th ed. (Illus.). 368p. 1984. 15.95 (ISBN 0-13-111824-2). P-H.

Guillou, P. J., ed. see European Dialysis & Transplant Association Staff.

Guillou, Pierre J., jt. ed. see Davison, Alex M.

Guilmant, Alexandre & Pirro, A., eds. Archives Des Maitres De L'orgue Des XVIe, XVIIe, et XVIIIe, 10 vols. 1898-1910. Set. 425.00 (ISBN 0-384-01893-9); 45.00 ea. Johnson Repr.

Guilmant, Alexandre, ed. see Campra, Andre.

Guilmant, Alexandre see Rameau, Jean Philippe.

Guilmartin, J. F., Jr. Gunpowder & Galleys. LC 73-83109. (Early Modern History Studies). (Illus.). 380p. 1975. 57.50 (ISBN 0-521-20272-8). Cambridge U Pr.

Guilpin, Everard. Skialethia Or a Shadowe of Truth, in Certaine Epigrams & Satyres. Carroll, D. Allen, ed. LC 73-14841. vii, 248p. 1974. 22.50x (ISBN 0-8078-1220-X). U of NC Pr.

Guiltinan, J. & Gordon, P. Readings in Marketing Strategy. (Marketing Ser.). 624p. 1982. 18.95 (ISBN 0-07-048922-X). McGraw.

Guiltinan, J. & Paul, G. Marketing Management: Strategies & Programs. 2nd ed. LC 84-19454. 448p. 1985. 29.95 (ISBN 0-07-048924-6). McGraw.

Guiltinan, J. P. & Paul, G. W. Marketing Management. (Marketing Ser.). 1982. 33.95 (ISBN 0-07-048920-3). McGraw.

Guimier, Claude. Prepositions: An Analytical Bibliography. (Library & Information Sources in Linguistics Ser.: No. 8). viii, 244p. 1981. 28.00x (ISBN 90-272-3734-4). Benjamins North Am.

Guimond, James. The Art of William Carlos Williams: A Discovery & Possession of America. LC 68-11028. 257p. 1969. pap. 7.50x (ISBN 0-252-00014-5). U of Ill Pr.

--Seeing & Healing: A Study of the Poetry of Galway Kinnell. LC 83-22335. (Modern & Contemporary Literature Ser.). 200p. 1985. 20.00 (ISBN 0-8046-9341-2, 9341, Natl U). Assoc Faculty Pr.

Guin, Ursala K. Le see Le Guin, Ursula K.

Guin, Ursula K. Le see Le Guin, Ursula K.

Guin, Ursula K. Le see LeGuin, Ursula K.

Guin, Ursula K. Le see Le Guin, Ursula K.

Guin, Ursula K. Le see Le Guinn, Ursula K.

Guin, Ursula Le see Le Guin, Ursula.

Guin, Ursula Le see Le Guin, Ursula K.

Guin, Ursula le see Le Guin, Ursula K.

Guin, Ursula Le see Le Guin, Ursula K.

Guinagh, Kevin. Inspired Amateurs. facs. ed. LC 67-26746. (Essay Index Reprint Ser). 1937. 18.00 (ISBN 0-8369-0500-8). Ayer Co Pubs.

Guinagh, Kevin & Dorjahn, Alfred P., eds. Latin Literature in Translation. 822p. 1983. Repr. of 1942 ed. lib. bdg. 35.00 (ISBN 0-89984-018-3). Century Bookbindery.

Guinagh, Kevin, jt. ed. see Lyle, Guy R.

Guinagh, Kevin, tr. Dictionary of Foreign Phrases & Abbreviations. 3rd ed. LC 82-8486. 288p. 1982. 30.00 (ISBN 0-8242-0675-4). Wilson.

Guinan, Betty F., jt. auth. see Springman, Mary J.

Guinan, John, jt. auth. see Fitzmaurice, George.

Guinan, Michael, tr. Gospel Poverty: Essays in Biblical Theology. 1977. 6.95 (ISBN 0-8199-0610-7). Franciscan Herald.

Guinan, Michael D. Covenant in the Old Testament. (Biblical Booklets Ser). 68p. 1975. pap. 1.25 (ISBN 0-8199-0520-8). Franciscan Herald.

--Gospel Poverty: Witness to the Risen Christ. LC 81-80051. 96p. (Orig.). 1981. pap. 3.95 (ISBN 0-8091-2377-0). Paulist Pr.

Guinane, George E. An Analysis of the SMP Policy: A Line-by-Line Explanation of the Special Multi-Peril Policy. 20.00 (ISBN 0-686-31022-5, 26625). Rough Notes.

Guinares, W. O., et al, eds. Lasers & Applications: Proceedings. (Springer Series in Optical Sciences: Vol. 26). (Illus.). 337p. 1981. 37.00 (ISBN 0-387-10647-2). Springer-Verlag.

Guinchat, Claire & Menou, Michel. General Introduction to the Techniques of Information & Documentation Work. 340p. 1983. pap. text ed. 33.75 (ISBN 92-3-101860-4, U1328, UNESCO). Unipub.

Guinchat, Claire, jt. auth. see Dumazedier, Joffre.

Guindey, Guillaume. The International Monetary Tangle: Myths & Realities. Hoffman, Michael L., tr. LC 77-77797. 128p. (Fr.). 1977. 25.00 (ISBN 0-87332-108-1). M E Sharpe.

Guindey, Guillaume & Coombs, Charles A. Reflections on the International Monetary System. (Per Jacobsson Lectures: 1980). pap. 20.00 (ISBN 0-317-29084-3, 2019265). Bks Demand UMI.

Guindi, Fadwa el see Callender, Charles & El Guindi, Fadwa.

Guindon, Kathleen M., ed. see Dawley, Gloria & Sorger, James.

Guindon, Richard. Cartoons by Guindon. (Illus.). 1982. pap. 6.95 (ISBN 0-399-50700-0, Perigee). Putnam Pub Group.

--The World According to Carp. (Illus., Orig.). 1983. pap. 5.95 (ISBN 0-8362-1214-2). Andrews McMeel Parker.

Guinee, P. A., jt. ed. see De Leeuw, P. W.

Guiness, Desmond. Georgian Dublin. 1979. 31.50 (ISBN 0-7134-1908-3, Pub. by Batsford England). David & Charles.

Guiness, Gerald, jt. auth. see Forastieri-Braschi, Eduardo.

Guiness, Os. The Gravedigger File. LC 83-10666. (Illus.). 204p. (Orig.). 1983. 12.95 (ISBN 0-87784-920-X); pap. 6.95 (ISBN 0-87784-817-3). Inter-Varsity.

Guiney, David. The Dunlop Book of the Olympics. 1979. 20.00 (ISBN 0-903214-12-1, Pub. by Terence Dalton England). State Mutual Bk.

--The Dunlop Book of the World Cup. 1979. 20.00 (ISBN 0-903214-10-5, Pub. by Terence Dalton England). State Mutual Bk.

Guiney, Grace C., jt. auth. see Guiney, Louise I.

Guiney, Louise. Three Heroines of New England Romance. 1894. Repr. 25.00 (ISBN 0-8274-3622-X). R West.

Guiney, Louise, tr. see Ansermet, Ernest.

Guiney, Louise, tr. see Bree, Germine.

Guiney, Louise, tr. see Follain, Jean.

Guiney, Louise I. Happy Ending: The Collected Lyrics of Louise I. Guiney. LC 78-11678. 1979. Repr. of 1927 ed. lib. bdg. 24.75x (ISBN 0-313-20702-X, GUHE). Greenwood.

--Patrins: To Which Is Added an Inquirendo into the Wit & Other Good Parts of His Late Majesty King Charles the Second. LC 72-4750. (Essay Index Reprint Ser.). Repr. of 1897 ed. 21.00 (ISBN 0-8369-2946-2). Ayer Co Pubs.

Guiney, Louise I. & Guiney, Grace C. Letters of Louise Imogen Guiney. 34.00 (ISBN 0-8369-6975-8, 7855). Ayer Co Pubs.

Guinier, A. The Structure of Matter: From the Blue Sky to Liquid Crystals. Duffin, W. J., tr. 240p. 1984. pap. text ed. 19.95 (ISBN 0-7131-3489-5). E Arnold.

Guinle, R. L. English-Spanish Technical Dictionary. (Eng & Span.). 37.50 (ISBN 0-87559-188-4). Shalom.

--A Modern Spanish-English & English-Spanish Technical & Engineering Dictionary. (Span. & Eng.). 1969. Repr. of 1938 ed. 27.95 (ISBN 0-7100-1478-3). Routledge & Kegan.

--Spanish-English Technical Dictionary. 37.50 (ISBN 0-87559-187-6). Shalom.

Guinness, Catherine, jt. auth. see Guinness, Jonathan.

Guinness, F. E., jt. auth. see Clutton-Brock, T. H.

Guinness, Jonathan & Guinness, Catherine. The House of Mitford. (Nonfiction Ser.). 604p. 1985. 19.95 (ISBN 0-670-48215-3). Viking.

Guinness, Michele. Child of the Covenant. 160p. 1985. pap. 2.95 (ISBN 0-345-32715-2). Ballantine.

Guinness, Paul & Bradshaw, Michael. North America: A Human Geography. LC 84-28434. (Illus.). 350p. 1985. pap. 23.50x (ISBN 0-389-20557-5). B&N Imports.

Guinness, Paul G. Hear O Israel. LC 81-50749. 235p. 1983. 12.95 (ISBN 0-533-04997-0). Vantage.

Guinot, B., jt. auth. see Debarbat, S.

Guinot, B., ed. see I.A.U. Symposium, 32nd, Stresa, Italy, 1967.

Guinot, Jean P., jt. auth. see Romeuf, Jean.

Guins, George C. Soviet Law & Soviet Society. LC 79-1604. 1980. Repr. of 1954 ed. 32.50 (ISBN 0-88355-907-2). Hyperion Conn.

Guins, S. G. & Tack, C. E., eds. Anthology of Rail Vehicle Dynamics: Freight Car Impact, Vol. I. Incl. Anthology of Rail Vehicle Dynamics: Effects of Train Action & Rail Car Vibration, Vol. II. Tack, C. E. & Guins, S. G., eds. 270p. 1972. pap. text ed. 25.00 (H00365); Anthology of Rail Vehicle Dynamics: Axles, Wheels & Rail - Wheel Interaction, Vol. III. Guins, S. G. & Tack, C. E., eds. 361p. 1973. pap. text ed. 30.00 (H00066). 115p. 1971. pap. text ed. 20.00 (ISBN 0-685-78338-3, H00064). ASME.

Guins, S. G. see Guins, S. G. & Tack, C. E.

Guinsburg, Thomas N. The Pursuit of Isolationism in the United States Senate from Versailles to Pearl Harbor. LC 80-8478. (Modern American History Ser.). 339p. 1982. lib. bdg. 44.00 (ISBN 0-8240-4854-7). Garland Pub.

Guinta, John L. Oral Pathology. 2nd ed. (Illus.). 142p. 1984. pap. text ed. 14.95 (ISBN 0-683-03547-9). Williams & Wilkins.

Guinther, John. Philadelphia: Dream for the Keeping. Silvey, Kitty & Mason, Sharon, eds. LC 81-86566. (American Portrait Ser.). (Illus.). 272p. 1982. 29.95 (ISBN 0-932986-23-4). Continent Herit.

Guinther, William & Taylor, Richard L. Positive Flying. 1983. 10.00 (ISBN 0-02-546570-8). Macmillan.

Guiora, Alexander Z. An Epistemology for the Language Sciences. 246p. 1984. 22.50 (ISBN 0-8143-1773-1). Wayne St U Pr.

Guiraud, Jean. The Medieval Inquisition. Messenger, E. C., tr. LC 78-63181. (Heresies of the Early Christian & Medieval Era: Second Ser.). Repr. of 1929 ed. 21.50 (ISBN 0-404-16222-3). AMS Pr.

Guiraud, Paul. Etudes Economiques Sur l'Antiquite. LC 77-126394. (Research & Source Ser.: No. 501). (Fr). 1970. Repr. of 1905 ed. 22.50 (ISBN 0-8337-1488-0). B Franklin.

--La Propriete Fonciere en Grece Jusqua la Conquete Romaine. Vlastos, Gregory, ed. LC 78-19357. (Morals & Law in Ancient Greece Ser.). 1979. Repr. of 1893 ed. lib. bdg. 46.00x (ISBN 0-405-11549-0). Ayer Co Pubs.

Guiraud, Pierre. Dictionnaire Erotique. 648p. (Fr.). 1978. pap. 39.95 (ISBN 0-686-57322-6, M-6306). French & Eur.

--Semiology. 1975. 18.00x (ISBN 0-7100-8005-0); pap. 7.95x (ISBN 0-7100-8011-5). Routledge & Kegan.

Guiraut D'Espanha. Die Lieder Des Trobadors Guiraut d'Espanha: Inaugural-Dissertation. Hoby, Otto, ed. LC 80-2178. Repr. of 1915 ed. 24.50 (ISBN 0-404-19008-1). AMS Pr.

Guirdham, Arthur. Cathars & Reincarnation. LC 77-17012. (Illus.). 1978. pap. 3.75 (ISBN 0-8356-0506-X, Quest). Theos Pub Hse.

--A Foot in Both Worlds. 224p. 15.00x (ISBN 0-85978-002-3, Pub. by Spearman England). State Mutual Bk.

--The Psyche in Medicine. 242p. 25.00x (ISBN 0-85978-031-7, Pub. by Spearman England). State Mutual Bk.

--The Psychic Basis of Psychiatry. 302p. 1981. 30.00x (ISBN 0-85500-130-5, Pub. by Thorsons England). State Mutual Bk.

Guirdham, M. Marketing: The Management of Distribution Channels. 222p. 1972. pap. text ed. 19.75 (ISBN 0-08-016965-1). Pergamon.

Guirguis, Wahuih, jt. auth. see Howells, John G.

Guirma, Frederic. Princess of the Full Moon. Garrett, John, tr. LC 76-89587. (Illus.). 32p. (gr. 2-4). 1970. 9.95 (ISBN 0-02-737710-5). Macmillan.

Guiry, M. D. A Consensus & Bibliography of Irish Seaweeds. (Bibliotheca Phycologica Ser.: No. 44). 1979. pap. text ed. 14.00x (ISBN 3-7682-1209-2). Lubrecht & Cramer.

Guise, C. H., jt. auth. see Graves, Henry S.

Guise, Giorgio De see De Guise, Giorgio.

Guiseppe, Verdi & Nicholas, John, eds. Falstaff. Porter, Andrew, tr. from Ital. (English National Opera Guide Ser.: No. 10). 128p. 1982. pap. 4.95 (ISBN 0-7145-3921-X). Riverrun NY.

--Flying Dutchman. Poutney, David, tr. from Ger. (English National Opera Guide Ser.: No. 12, Libretto, Articles). 128p. 1982. pap. 4.95 (ISBN 0-7145-3920-1). Riverrun NY.

--The Force of Destiny. Porter, Andrew, tr. from Ital. (English National Opera Guide: No. 23). 128p. (Orig.). 1984. pap. 5.95 (ISBN 0-7145-4007-2). Riverrun NY.

Guisewite, Cathy. Another Saturday Night of Wild & Reckless Abandon. LC 82-72415. 128p. 1982. pap. 5.95 (ISBN 0-8362-1201-0). Andrews McMeel Parker.

--Eat Your Way to a Better Relationship. LC 82-72420. 60p. (Orig.). 1983. pap. 2.95 (ISBN 0-8362-1987-2). Andrews McMeel Parker.

--How to Get Rich, Fall in Love, Lose Weight, & Solve All Your Problems by Saying "No". LC 82-72412. (Illus.). 60p. (Orig.). 1983. pap. 2.95 (ISBN 0-8362-1986-4). Andrews McMeel Parker.

--Men Should Come with Instruction Booklets. (Illus.). 128p. (Orig.). 1984. pap. 5.95 (ISBN 0-8362-2055-2). Andrews McMeel Parker.

--Sorry I'm Late. My Hair Won't Start. 1986. pap. price not set (ISBN 0-449-20925-3, Crest). Fawcett.

--Wake Me Up When I'm a Size Five. (Illus.). 128p. (Orig.). 1985. pap. 6.95 (ISBN 0-8362-2069-2). Andrews McMeel Parker.

Guisinger, Stephen, et al. Evaluation of MDTA Training in Correctional Institutions, Vol. 2. 1969. pap. 18.80x (ISBN 0-89011-453-6, CRJ-103). Abt Bks.

Guisinger, Stephen E., ed. Investment Incentives & Performance Requirements: Patterns of International Trade, Production, & Investment. LC 84-26374. 336p. 1985. 35.95 (ISBN 0-03-002443-9). Praeger.

--Trade & Investment Policies in the Americas. LC 73-84723. 1973. 7.95 (ISBN 0-87074-136-5). SMU Press.

Guisset Poch, Consuelo & Castellanos Alentorn, Prado. Diccionario Infantil Ilustrado Bruguera. 96p. (Span.). 1977. pap. 9.50 (ISBN 84-02-05211-8, S-50160). French & Eur.

Guisso, R. W. Wu Tse-t'ien & the Politics of Legitimation in T'ang China. LC 78-4840. (Occasional Papers: Vol. 11). (Illus.). 335p. 1978. 9.00 (ISBN 0-914584-11-1). West Wash Univ.

Guisti, E. Minimal Surfaces & Functions of Bounded Variation. (Monographs in Mathematics). 1984. text ed. 39.95 (ISBN 0-8176-3153-4). Birkhauser.

Guistini, F. G. & Keefer, F. J. Understanding Hysterectomy: A Woman's Guide. (Illus.). 1979. 12.95 (ISBN 0-8027-0633-9); pap. 7.95 (ISBN 0-8027-7150-5). Walker & Co.

Guitar, Barry, jt. auth. see Peters, Theodore.

Guitar Player Magazine Editors. The Guitar Player Book. LC 83-81371. (Illus.). 402p. 1983. pap. 11.95 (ISBN 0-394-62490-4, E869, Ever). Grove.

Guiterrez, Alfredo. Uruguay: Economic Memorandum. viii, 201p. 1979. pap. 15.00 (ISBN 0-686-36124-5, RC-7902). World Bank.

Guiterrez, Nancy A. A Bibliography of English Historical Poetry: 1476-1603. LC 82-49264. 350p. 1983. lib. bdg. 52.00 (ISBN 0-8240-9131-0). Garland Pub.

Guither, Harold D. The Food Lobbyists: Behind the Scenes of Food & Agri-Politics. LC 79-6734. 352p. 1980. 32.00x (ISBN 0-669-03539-4). Lexington Bks.

Guither, Harold D. & Thompson, W. N. Mission Overseas: A Handbook for U.S. Families in Developing Countries. LC 76-76828. 322p. 1969. pap. 12.50x (ISBN 0-252-00017-X). U of Ill Pr.

Guithes, Henry J., jt. auth. see Kim, Suk H.

Guithues, Henry J., jt. auth. see Kim, Suk H.

Guiton, Jacques, ed. see Le Corbusier.

Guiton, M. La Fontaine: Poet & Counterpoet. 1970. 5.00 (ISBN 0-8135-0360-4). Brown Bk.

Guiton, Margaret, jt. auth. see Bree, Germaine.

Guiton, Margaret, tr. see Le Corbusier.

Guiton, Shirley. A World by Itself: Tradition & Change in the Venetian Lagoon. (Illus.). 1978. 17.95 (ISBN 0-241-89434-4, Pub. by Hamish Hamilton England). David & Charles.

Guitor, Jean. From Equivalence of Degrees to Evaluation of Competence: Present Procedures & Practices, New Avenues. (Studies on the Evaluation of Qualifications at the Higher Education Level). (Illus.). 138p. 1977. pap. 11.00 (ISBN 92-3-101419-6, U788, UNESCO). Unipub.

Guiulnazarian, J. Sol de Arturito. 33p. (Span.). 1983. 4.95 (ISBN 0-8285-2596-X, Pub. by Raduga Pubs USSR). Imported Pubns.

Guizot, F. The History of Civilization from the Fall of the Roman Empire to the French Revolution, 4 vols. Repr. of 1861 ed. 75.00 (ISBN 0-686-19854-9). Ridgeway Bks.

Guizot, Francois, et al. Historical Essays & Lectures. Mellon, Stanley & Krieger, Leonard, eds. LC 72-76486. (Classic European Historians Ser.). xlvi, 442p. 1974. pap. 3.95x (ISBN 0-226-31050-7, P486, Phoen). U of Chicago Pr.

Guizot, Francois P. Corneille & His Times. LC 76-153271. 1971. Repr. of 1852 ed. 25.50x (ISBN 0-8046-1569-1, Pub. by Kennikat). Assoc Faculty Pr.

--Essais Sur L'histoire de France. x1865 ed. Mayer, J. P., ed. LC 78-67354. (European Political Thought Ser.). (Fr.). 1979. lib. bdg. 30.50x (ISBN 0-405-11700-0). Ayer Co Pubs.

--The History of Civilization in Europe. Hazlitt, William, tr. 322p. 1983. Repr. of 1893 ed. lib. bdg. 50.00 (ISBN 0-8495-2142-4). Arden Lib.

Guizot, Francois P., ed. Collections Des Memoires Relatifs a L'histoire De France, 31 Vols. LC 75-88788. (Fr). Repr. of 1835 ed. Set. 1240.00 (ISBN 0-404-02970-1); 40.00 ea. AMS Pr.

--History of France from the Earliest Times to the Year Eighteen Forty-Eight, 8 Vols. Black, Robert, tr. LC 73-91786. (Illus.). Repr. of 1881 ed. Set. 276.00 (ISBN 0-404-03010-6); 34.50 ea. AMS Pr.

--Memoirs to Illustrate the History of My Time, 8 Vols. Cole, John W., tr. LC 72-168212. Repr. of 1867 ed. Set. 260.00 (ISBN 0-404-08040-5); 32.50 ea. AMS Pr.

Gujarati, Damodar. Government & Business. 608p. 1984. text ed. 30.95 (ISBN 0-07-025186-X). McGraw.

--Pensions & New York City's Fiscal Crisis. 1978. pap. 4.25 (ISBN 0-8447-3314-8). Am Enterprise.

Gujral, M. L. Economic Failures of Nehru & Indira Gandhi. 1980. text ed. 22.50x (ISBN 0-7069-0835-X, Pub. by Vikas India). Advent NY.

Gujral, Sunil. Indian Hockey. 1979. 9.00x (ISBN 0-7069-0716-7, Pub. by Vikas India). Advent NY.

Gukiina, Peter. Uganda: A Case Study in African Political Development. LC 72-3511. 192p. 1972. text ed. 17.95x (ISBN 0-268-00473-0); pap. 3.25x (ISBN 0-268-00476-5). U of Notre Dame Pr.

Gula, Richard M. To Walk Together Again: The Sacrament of Reconciliation. LC 83-82021. (Orig.). 1984. pap. 7.95 (ISBN 0-8091-2603-6). Paulist Pr.

--What Are They Saying about Moral Norms? LC 81-83188. 128p. (Orig.). 1982. pap. 3.95 (ISBN 0-8091-2412-2). Paulist Pr.

Gula, Robert J. Exposition: Critical Writing & Thinking. 210p. 1984. pap. 5.95 (ISBN 0-88334-177-8). Ind Sch Pr.

--Nonsense: How to Overcome It. LC 79-65121. (Illus.). 200p. 1981. pap. 6.95 (ISBN 0-8128-6116-7); 11.95 (ISBN 0-8128-2677-9). Stein & Day.

--Precision: A Reference Handbook for Writers. LC 83-21810. 290p. 1984. pap. text ed. 10.25 (ISBN 0-8191-3688-3). U Pr of Amer.

Gula, Robert J., jt. auth. see Carpenter, Thomas H.

Gulaev, B. B., ed. Gases in Cast Metals. LC 65-15007. 257p. 1965. 45.00x (ISBN 0-306-10726-0, Consultants). Plenum Pub.

Gularte, Frank & Richardson, Jim. Prophecy. pap. 2.95 (ISBN 0-911739-23-8). Abbott Loop.

Gulas, Ivan & Griffiths, Leslie. Herpes, the Love Bug: Facts & Fears. LC 84-7293. (Illus.). 72p. (YA) (gr. 9-12). 1984. pap. 5.75 (ISBN 0-910707-06-5). Ohio Psych Pub.

Gulati, Basia, tr. see Bringuier, Jean-Claude.

Gulati, Basia, tr. see Dumont, Louis.

Gulati, Basia, tr. see France, Anatole.

Gulati, Basia M., tr. see Bucher, Bernadette.

Gulati, Basia M., tr. see Devereux, George.

Gulati, Basia M., tr. see Leenhardt, Maurice.

Gulati, Bodh R. College Algebra. 480p. 1982. text ed. 30.50 (ISBN 0-205-07683-1, 5676835); tchr's ed. free (ISBN 0-205-07684-X, 5676843); 8.93 (ISBN 0-205-07685-8, 5676851). Allyn.

--College Mathematics with Applications to the Business & Social Sciences. (Illus.). 1978. text ed. 27.50 scp (ISBN 0-06-042538-5, HarpC); ans. bklt. avail. (ISBN 0-06-362551-2). Har-Row.

--A Short Course in Calculus. LC 79-67409. 536p. 1981. text ed. 36.95x (ISBN 0-03-047466-3); solutions manual 20.00 (ISBN 0-03-057434-X). Dryden Pr.

--A Short Course in Calculus. 536p. 1981. text ed. 34.50x (ISBN 0-03-047466-3). SCP.

Gulati, Bodh R. & Bass, Helen. Algebra & Trigonometry: Precalculus Mathematics. 676p. 1982. text ed. 33.39 scp (ISBN 0-205-07686-6, 567688); tchr's ed. free (ISBN 0-205-07687-4, 567688); scp avail. study guide 10.14 (ISBN 0-205-07688-2). Allyn.

Gulati, I. S. International Monetary Development & the Third World: A Proposal to Readress the Balance. (R. C. Dutt Lectures on Political Economy Ser.: 1978). 48p. 1980. pap. text ed. 2.95x (ISBN 0-686-42711-4, Pub. by Orient Longman Ltd India). Apt Bks.

Gulati, Leela. Fisherwomen on the Kerala Coast: Demographic & Socio-Economic Impact of a Fisheries Development Project. (Women, Work & Development Ser.: No. 8). 1984. pap. 11.40 (ISBN 92-2-103626-X, ILO339, ILO). Unipub.

Gulati, Lella. Fisherwomen on the Kerala Coast: Demographic Socio-Economic Impact of a Fisheries Development Project. International Labour Office Staff, ed. (Women, Work & Development Ser.: No. 8). xi, 156p. (Orig.). 1984. pap. 11.40 (ISBN 92-2-103626-X). Intl Labour Office.

Gulati, R. D. & Parma, S. Studies on Lake Vechten & Tjeukemeer: The Netherlands. 1982. 87.00 (ISBN 90-6193-762-0, Pub. by Junk Pubs Netherlands). Kluwer Academic.

Gulcher, E., tr. see Blennerhassett, Charlotte J.

Gulczynski, Diane, jt. auth. see Allen, Norma C.

Guldberg, Jens, ed. Silicon. LC 81-7305. 515p. 1981. 75.00x (ISBN 0-306-40738-8, Plenum Pr). Plenum Pub.

Guldescu, Stanko. The Croatian-Slavonian Kingdom, 1526-1792. (Studies in European History: No. 21). 1970. 32.80x (ISBN 90-2790-536-3). Mouton.

Guldmann, Jean-Michel & Shefer, Daniel. Industrial Location & Air Quality Control: A Planning Approach. LC 80-15380. (Environmental Science & Technology: A Wiley-Interscience Series of Texts & Monographs). 237p. 1980. 75.00 (ISBN 0-471-05377-5, Pub. by Wiley-Interscience). Wiley.

Guldner, Francis J. BASIC Programming for Engineers & Technicians. LC 84-12061. 224p. 1985. pap. text ed. 18.00 (ISBN 0-8273-2363-8); instr's. guide 5.60 (ISBN 0-8273-2364-6). Delmar.

Guldner, W. G., jt. ed. see Murt, E. M.

Guleck, Charles J., jt. ed. see Paoletti, Rodolfo.

Gulezian, Ronald C. Elements of Business Statistics. 1979. 32.95x (ISBN 0-7216-4351-5); instr's. manual 10.00 (ISBN 0-03-057083-2). Dryden Pr.

--Statistics for Decision Making. LC 78-52729. (Illus.). 1979. text ed. 31.95x (ISBN 0-7216-4350-7). Dryden Pr.

Gulezian, Ronald C. & Weiland, Jerome. Elements of Business Statistics: Workbook. 1979. pap. text ed. 11.95 (ISBN 0-7216-4354-X). HR&W.

--Statistics for Decision Making: Workbook. 1979. pap. 11.95 (ISBN 0-7216-4353-1). HR&W.

Gulezian, Ronald T. & Tingey, Henry. Business Mathematics for College Students. LC 82-10986. 463p. 1983. pap. 26.95 (ISBN 0-471-08121-3); tchr's ed. (ISBN 0-471-87479-5); test bank avail. (ISBN 0-471-87232-6). Wiley.

Gulf Coast Offset, Inc. Staff, ed. see Young, Thomas R.

Gulf Publishing Co. Evaporite Deposits. LC 81-82357. 266p. 1981. 54.95x (ISBN 0-87201-277-8). Gulf Pub.

Gulhati, Ravi. Eastern & Southern Africa: Past Trends & Future Prospects. (Working Paper: No. 413). 24p. 1980. pap. 3.00 (ISBN 0-686-39673-1, WP-0413). World Bank.

Gulhati, Ravi & Sekhar, Uday. Industrial Strategy for Late Starters: The Experience of Kenya, Tanzania & Zambia. (Working Paper: No. 457). 63p. 1981. 3.00 (ISBN 0-686-36175-X, WP-0457). World Bank.

Gulhati, Ravi, et al. Exchange Rate Policies in Eastern & Southern Africa, 1965-1983. (Staff Working Paper: No. 720). 92p. 1985. 5.00 (ISBN 0-318-11955-2, WP 0720). World Bank.

Guli, Francesca. Be Gentle, April. LC 69-19408. 1969. 4.00 (ISBN 0-8233-0131-1). Golden Quill.

--Bitter Lime. LC 72-87817. 89p. 1973. 5.00 (ISBN 0-8233-0184-2). Golden Quill.

--Boy & the Stars. (Illus.). 1965. 5.50 (ISBN 0-8233-0036-6). Golden Quill.

--The Hollow Madonna: Poems. LC 76-1266. 95p. 1976. 6.00 (ISBN 0-8233-0246-6). Golden Quill.

--I Sing of Summer. 1964. 3.00 (ISBN 0-8233-0035-8). Golden Quill.

--Land of My Loving. LC 76-155241. 64p. 1971. 4.00 (ISBN 0-8233-0163-X). Golden Quill.

--Poems in Praise of the Man. 1980. 6.50 (ISBN 0-8233-0309-8). Golden Quill.

Gulian, Kevork H. Elementary Modern Armenian Grammar. LC 54-11490. 17.50 (ISBN 0-8044-0200-0). Ungar.

Gulick, Bill. Chief Joseph Country: Land of the Nez Perce. LC 79-51577. (Illus.). 316p. 1981. 29.95 (ISBN 0-87004-275-0). Caxton.

--Snake River Country. LC 71-140117. (Illus.). 1971. 35.00 (ISBN 0-87004-215-7). Caxton.

Gulick, C. A., et al, eds. see Lamar, Mirabeau B.

Gulick, Charles A. Austria from Habsburg to Hitler, 2 vols. Incl. Vol. I. Labor's Workshop of Democracy; Vol. II. Fascism's Subversion of Democracy. (California Library Reprint Ser.: No. 109). 1936p. 1981. Repr. of 1948 ed. Set. 87.50x (ISBN 0-520-04211-5). U of Cal Pr.

Gulick, Charles A., Jr. Labor Policy of the United States Steel Corporation. LC 68-57568. (Columbia University. Studies in the Social Sciences: No. 258). Repr. of 1924 ed. 17.50 (ISBN 0-404-51258-5). AMS Pr.

Gulick, Charles A., Jr., jt. auth. see Seager, Henry R.

Gulick, Charles A., Jr., ed. see Seager, Henry R.

Gulick, Charles B. The Life of the Ancient Greeks. LC 72-94074. (Illus.). 373p. 1973. Repr. of 1902 ed. lib. bdg. 25.00 (ISBN 0-8154-0456-5). Cooper Sq.

--Modern Traits in Old Greek Life. LC 63-10291. (Our Debt to Greece & Rome). 159p. Repr. of 1930 ed. 18.50x (ISBN 0-8154-0097-7). Cooper Sq.

Gulick, Charles B., jt. auth. see Goodwin, W. W.

Gulick, D., ed. see Conference on Harmonic Analysis, College Park, Md., 1971.

Gulick, D., jt. ed. see Greenleaf, F.

Gulick, Denny, jt. auth. see Ellis, Robert.

Gulick, Edward V. Europe's Classical Balance of Power. (Illus.). 1967. pap. 8.95x (ISBN 0-393-00413-9, Norton Lib). Norton.

--Europe's Classical Balance of Power: A Case History of the Theory & Practice of One of the Great Concepts of European Statecraft. LC 81-20253. xvii, 337p. 1982. Repr. lib. bdg. 35.00x (ISBN 0-313-23350-0, GUEC). Greenwood.

--Peter Parker & the Opening of China. LC 73-82628. (Harvard Studies in American-East Asian Relations: No. 3). 228p. 1974. text ed. 17.50x (ISBN 0-674-66326-8). Harvard U Pr.

Gulick, John. Cherokees at the Crossroads. rev. ed. 222p. 1973. pap. text ed. 7.00 (ISBN 0-89143-062-8). U NC Inst Res Soc Sci.

--The Middle East: An Anthropological Perspective. 264p. 1983. pap. text ed. 12.75 (ISBN 0-8191-3041-9). U Pr of Amer.

--Social Structure & Culture Changes in a Lebanese Village. 19.00 (ISBN 0-384-20440-6). Johnson Repr.

--Tripoli: A Modern Arab City. LC 67-14340. (Middle Eastern Studies: No. 12). (Illus.). 1967. 17.50x (ISBN 0-674-90915-1). Harvard U Pr.

Gulick, Luther H. Physical Education by Muscular Exercise. (Physical Education Reprint Ser). (Illus.). Repr. of 1904 ed. lib. bdg. 27.50x (ISBN 0-697-00102-4). Irvington.

Gulick, Luther H. & Urwick, Lydall, eds. Papers on the Science of Administration. LC 68-55727. (Illus.). Repr. of 1937 ed. 25.00x (ISBN 0-678-00512-5). Kelley.

Gulick, Robert Van see Van Gulick, Robert.

Gulick, Sidney L. American Democracy & Asiatic Citizenship. Daniels, Roger, ed. LC 78-54841. (Asian Experience in North America Ser.). (Illus.). 1979. Repr. of 1918 ed. lib. bdg. 19.00x (ISBN 0-405-11307-2). Ayer Co Pubs.

--A Chesterfield Bibliography to Eighteen Hundred. 2nd ed. 255p. 1979. 30.00 (ISBN 0-686-31066-7). Biblio Soc Am.

--Chesterfield Bibliography to Eighteen Hundred. LC 78-25886. 255p. 1979. 30.00x (ISBN 0-8139-0815-9). U Pr of Va.

--Mixing the Races in Hawaii: A Study of the Coming Neo-Hawaiian American Race. LC 75-35194. Repr. of 1937 ed. 24.50 (ISBN 0-404-14222-2). AMS Pr.

--Some Unpublished Letters of Lord Chesterfield. Repr. of 1937 ed. lib. bdg. 15.00 (ISBN 0-8414-4590-7). Folcroft.

Gulick, W. Lawrence. Hearing: Physiology & Psychophysics. (Illus.). 1971. 17.95x (ISBN 0-19-501299-2). Oxford U Pr.

Gulick, W. Lawrence & Lawson, Robert B. Human Stereopsis: A Psychophysical Approach. (Illus.). 1976. text ed. 17.95x (ISBN 0-19-501971-7). Oxford U Pr.

Gulik, R. H. Van see Uhlenbeck, Christianus C. & Van Gulik, R. H.

Gulik, R. H. Van see Van Gulik, R. H.

Gulik, Robert H. Van see Van Gulik, Robert H.

Gulik, Robert Van. The Haunted Monastery: A Judge Dee Mystery. 168p. 1983. pap. 2.95 rack-size (ISBN 0-684-17975-X, ScribT). Scribner.

Gulik, Robert Van see Van Gulik, Robert.

Gulik, Robert van see Van Gulik, Robert.

Gulik, Robert Van see Van Gulik, Robert.

Gulik, Robert van H. see Van Gulik, Robert H.

Gulik, W. R. Van see Van Gulik, W. R., et al.

Gulino, Bill. How to Ski the Bumps. (Illus.). 1984. pap. 6.00 (ISBN 0-915803-01-1). Sun Valley Pub.

--How Women Can Be Successful with Men: The Male Point of View. 60p. (Orig.). 1983. pap. 4.95 (ISBN 0-915803-00-3). Sun Valley Pub.

Gull, ed. see Ingleby, Leonard C.

Gull, Carol W., jt. auth. see Larsen, Judith L.

Gull, Cyril A. Oscar Wilde: Some Reminiscences. LC 72-13766. 1973. lib. bdg. 10.00 (ISBN 0-8414-1309-6). Folcroft.

Gull, Edward M. British Economic Interests in the Far East. LC 75-30058. (International Series of the Institute of Pacific Relations). 280p. 1983. Repr. of 1943 ed. 34.50 (ISBN 0-404-59528-6). AMS Pr.

Gull, K. & Oliver, S. G. The Fungal Nucleus. LC 81-6079. (British Mycological Society Symposium: No. 5). 358p. 1981. 75.00 (ISBN 0-521-23492-1). Cambridge U Pr.

Gulla, Kell, tr. see Malum, Amadu.

Gullace, Giovanni. Gabriele D'Annunzio in France: A Study in Cultural Relations. LC 66-20233. 1966. 12.95x (ISBN 0-8156-2097-7). Syracuse U Pr.

--Taine & Brunetiere on Criticism. 158p. 1982. 10.00x (ISBN 0-87291-160-8). Coronado Pr.

Gullace, Giovanni, tr. see Cotta, Sergio.

Gullace, Giovanni, tr. from Ital. see Croce, Benedetto.

Gullahorn, Jeanne E. Psychology & Women: In Transition. LC 78-16794. (Scripts Seriesin Personality & Social Psychology). 224p. 1979. 15.95x (ISBN 0-470-26459-4). Halsted Pr.

Gullan, Marjorie. Speech Choir. LC 71-116405. (Granger Index Reprint Ser). 1937. 19.00 (ISBN 0-8369-6146-3). Ayer Co Pubs.

Gulland, J. A. Fish Stock Assessment: A Manual of Basic Methods. (FAO Wiley Food & Agriculture Ser.). 223p. 1983. 37.95x (ISBN 0-471-90027-3, Pub. by Wiley-Interscience). Wiley.

--Manual of Methods for Fish Stock Assessment: Fish Population Analysis, Pt. 1. (Fisheries Ser.: No. 3). (Illus.). 154p. (Orig., 4th Printing 1976). 1969. pap. 13.25 (ISBN 92-5-100204-5, F262, FAO). Unipub.

--Manual of Methods for Fisheries Resource Survey & Appraisal: Objectives & Basic Methods, Pt. 4. (Fisheries Technical Papers: No. 145). (Illus.). 33p. (3rd Printing 1977). 1975. pap. 7.50 (ISBN 92-5-100118-9, F876, FAO). Unipub.

--Manual of Sampling & Statistical Methods for Fisheries Biology, Pt. 1. (Manuals in Fisheries Science: No. 3). (Orig.). 1972. pap. 5.25, 4 fascicules (ISBN 92-5-101605-4, F268, FAO). Unipub.

--Some Problems of the Management of Shared Stocks. (Fisheries Technical Papers: No. 206). 29p. (Eng. & Fr., 2nd Printing 1981). 1980. pap. 7.50 (ISBN 92-5-101022-6, F2149, FAO). Unipub.

Gulland, John A. Fish Population Dynamics. LC 75-45094. 372p. 1977. 74.95 (ISBN 0-471-01575-X). Wiley.

--The Management of Marine Fisheries. LC 74-2473. (Illus.). 206p. 1974. 25.00x (ISBN 0-295-95335-7). U of Wash Pr.

Gulland, John A. & Rothschild, Brian J., eds. Penaeid Shrimps - Their Biology & Management. (Illus.). 308p. 1985. pap. 72.00 (ISBN 0-85238-131-X, FN108, FNB). Unipub.

Gullander, Elizabeth. Oswald Hoot: The Owl Who Was Scared of the Dark. (Illus.). 64p. (ps-6). 1982. PLB 7.95 (ISBN 0-940828-06-5); pap. 4.95 (ISBN 0-940828-05-7). Still News.

Gullans, Charles. Bibliography of the Published Works of J. V. Cunningham. 44p. 1981. pap. 15.00 (ISBN 0-936576-06-5). Symposium Pr.

--The Bright Universe. 48p. 1984. 50.00 (ISBN 0-936576-10-3). Symposium Pr.

--Diatribe to Dr. Steele. 18p. 1982. s & l, wrappers 16.50 (ISBN 0-936576-09-X). Symposium Pr.

--Imperfect Correspondences. 1978. s & l, wrappers 10.00 (ISBN 0-936576-00-6). Symposium Pr.

--Local Winds. (Orig.). 1985. pap. 5.00 (ISBN 0-941150-36-4). Barth.

--Many Houses. 40p. 1981. s & l wrappers 30.00 (ISBN 0-936576-04-9). Symposium Pr.

Gullans, Charles, tr. see Schneider, Franz.

Gullan-Whur, Margaret. What Your Handwriting Reveals. 256p. 1984. pap. 9.95 (ISBN 0-85030-378-8). Newcastle Pub.

Gullar, Ferreira, tr. see De Moraes, Vinicius.

Gullason, Thomas A., ed. see Crane, Stephen.

Gullath, Brigitte. Untersuchungen Zur Geschichte Boiotiens In Der Zeit Alexanders Und Der Diadochen. (European University Studies: No. 3, Vol. 169). 249p. 1982. 30.55 (ISBN 3-8204-7026-3). P Lang Pubs.

Gullberg. Swedish-English Technical Dictionary. 200.00 (ISBN 0-317-19084-9, SW207). Vanous.

Gullberg, Elsa & Astrom, Paul. The Thread of Ariadne: A Study of Ancient Greek Dress. (Studies in Mediterranean Archaeology Ser.: No. XXI). (Illus.). 1970. pap. text ed. 15.50x (ISBN 91-85058-34-3). Humanities.

Gullberg, Hjalmar. Gentleman, Single, Refined & Selected Poems, 1937-1959: Poems. Moffett, Judith, tr. from Swedish. LC 79-4596. 96p. 1979. text ed. 13.95x (ISBN 0-8071-0371-3). La State U Pr.

Gullberg, Ingvar E. Swedish-English Dictionary of Technical Terms Used in Business, Industry, Administration, Education & Research. 2nd rev. & enl. ed. (Swedish & Eng.). 150.00 (ISBN 91-1-775052-0). Heinman.

--Swedish-English Fact Ordbok (Technical Terms) 2nd ed. (Swedish & Eng.). 1977. 200.00x (ISBN 91-177-5052-0, SW-207). Vanous.

Gulledge, A. Dale. Adult Psychiatry Case Studies. 1981. pap. text ed. 20.50 (ISBN 0-87488-039-4). Med Exam.

Gulledge, Dennis & McWhirter, David. An Index to the Evangelist & the Christian. LC 83-70079. 160p. (Orig.). 1983. pap. 3.95 (ISBN 0-89900-231-5). College Pr Pub.

Gulledge, Earl N. BASIC for Technicians. LC 84-7659. 352p. 1985. pap. text ed. 19.80 (ISBN 0-8273-2310-7); instr's. guide 4.00 (ISBN 0-8273-2311-5). Delmar.

Gulledge, W. P., jt. ed. see Conway, R. A.

Gullen, Harold V. & Rhodes, Geoffrey E. Management in the Hotel & Catering Industry. (Illus.). 144p. (Orig.). 1983. 12.95 (ISBN 0-7134-1932-6, Pub. by Batsford England). David & Charles.

Gulleserian, Papken. Armenian Church. Poladian, Vartapet T., tr. LC 70-131508. Repr. of 1939 ed. 11.50 (ISBN 0-404-02949-3). AMS Pr.

Gullestad, Marianne. Kitchen Table Society. 356p. 1984. pap. 24.00x (ISBN 82-00-06778-5). Universitet.

Gullett, C. Ray, jt. auth. see Hicks, Herbert G.

Gullett, H. S. see Bean, C. E.

Gullett, Jane Fellows, jt. auth. see Gullett, Walter.

Gullett, Walter & Gullett, Jane Fellows. Everyone's Guide to Food Self-Sufficiency. LC 81-481. 240p. 1981. 13.95 (ISBN 0-87961-096-4); pap. 7.95 (ISBN 0-87961-095-6). Naturegraph.

Gullette, Margaret M. The Lost Bellybutton. LC 76-26377. (Illus.). 32p. (Orig.). (ps-2). 1976. pap. 3.00 (ISBN 0-914996-11-8). Lollipop Power.

Gullette, Margaret M., ed. The Art & Craft of Teaching. (Harvard-Danforth Center for Teaching & Learning Ser.). 144p. 1984. pap. 6.95. Harvard U Pr.

Gulley, Elsie E. Joseph Chamberlain & English Social Politics. 1972. lib. bdg. 24.00x (ISBN 0-374-93322-7). Octagon.

Gulley, Hal & Gulley, Nadine. I Tell You Truly. LC 81-82218. 192p. 1983. pap. 4.95 (ISBN 0-89900-194-7). College Pr Pub.

Gulley, Judie. Rodeo Summer. LC 84-9129. 192p. (gr. 5-9). 1984. 11.95 (ISBN 0-395-36174-5). HM.

Gulley, Nadine, jt. auth. see Gulley, Hal.

Gulley, Norman R. Final Events on Planet Earth. LC 77-24206. (Horizon Ser.). 1977. pap. 4.95 (ISBN 0-8127-0144-5). Review & Herald.

Gullick, Eugenia L. & Peed, Steven F. The Health Practitioner in Family Relationships: Marital & Sexual Aspects. LC 77-83067. 1978. 9.95 (ISBN 0-87762-245-0). Technomic.

Gullick, John. Malaysia: Economic Expansion & National Unity. (Illus.). 272p. 1981. lib. bdg. 33.50x (ISBN 0-86531-089-0). Westview.

Gullickson, Gary R., ed. The Psychophysiology of Darrow. 1973. 35.00 (ISBN 0-12-305650-0). Acad Pr.

Gullickson, Stuart G. Structuring a General Practice Course. LC 76-7826. (Continuing Legal Education Library). (Illus.). 412p. 1976. text ed. 25.00 (B200). Am Law Inst.

Gulliford, Andrew. America's Country Schools. (Illus.). 292p. 1984. 18.95 (ISBN 0-89133-112-3). Preservation Pr.

Gulliford, Ron. Teaching Children with Learning Difficulties. 136p. 1984. 6.00x (ISBN 0-7005-0551-2, Pub. by NFER Nelson UK). Taylor & Francis.

Gulliksen. Oslo Info. (Illus.). 300p. 1981. pap. 8.00 (ISBN 0-317-19018-0, N543). Vanous.

Gullino, Pietro M., jt. ed. see Jain, Rakesh K.

Gullion, Gordon. Grouse of the North Shore. Smith, Steve, ed. (Illus.). 160p. 1984. 39.00 (ISBN 0-932558-19-4). Willow Creek.

Gulliver, Ashbel G. Introduction to the Law of Future Interests. 87p. 1959. pap. write for info. West Pub.

Gulliver, Hal. A Friendly Tongue. LC 84-6733. xvi, 312p. 1984. 24.95 (ISBN 0-86554-118-3, MUP-H111). Mercer Univ Pr.

Gulliver, Hal, ed. see Nunn, Sam.

Gulliver, Harold S. Thackeray's Literary Apprenticeship. 1979. Repr. of 1934 ed. lib. bdg. 30.00 (ISBN 0-8414-4631-8). Folcroft.

Gulliver, Lucile. Louisa May Alcott: A Bibliography. LC 76-102858. (Bibliography & Reference Ser.: No. 292). 71p. 1973. Repr. of 1932 ed. lib. bdg. 17.50 (ISBN 0-8337-1490-2). B Franklin.

Gulliver, Lucille. Louisa May Alcott: A Bibliography. 59.95 (ISBN 0-8490-0559-0). Gordon Pr.

Gulliver, P. H. Family Herds: A Study of Two Pastoral Tribes in East Africa, the Jie & Turkana. LC 79-129943. (Illus.). Repr. of 1955 ed. 19.75x (ISBN 0-8371-5032-9, GFH&, Pub. by Negro U Pr). Greenwood.

--Neighbours & Networks: The Idiom of Kinship Among the Ndendeuli of Tanzania. LC 71-115491. 1971. 37.50x (ISBN 0-520-01722-6). U of Cal Pr.

Gulliver, P. H., ed. Tradition & Transition in East Africa: Studies of the Tribal Factor in the Modern Era. LC 78-84787. 1969. 36.50x (ISBN 0-520-01402-2). U of Cal Pr.

Gulliver, Philip H. Disputes & Negotiations: A Cross-Cultural Perspective. LC 79-22735. (Studies on Law & Social Control). 1979. 26.50 (ISBN 0-12-305550-4). Acad Pr.

Gullo, Dominic F., jt. ed. see Mcloughlin, Caven S.

Gullo, John M., jt. auth. see Ellis, Albert.

Gullo, Stephen V., et al, eds. Death & Children: A Guide for Educators, Parents & Caregivers. 210p. 1985. 21.75 (ISBN 0-930194-15-2). Ctr Thanatology.

Gullon, Ricardo. De Goya Al Arte Abstracto. 2nd ed. pap. 4.35 (ISBN 0-8477-2104-3). U of PR Pr.

Gullon, Ricardo, ed. see Galdos, Benito Perez.

Gullon, Ricardo, tr. see Soby, James Thrall.

Gullotta, Thomas, jt. auth. see Adams, Gerald R.

Gullvag, Ingemund & Hoibraaten, Helge. Essays in Pragmatic Philosophy. (Norwegian University Press Pub. Ser.). 150p. 1985. 27.50 (ISBN 0-317-27973-4). Oxford U Pr.

Gullvag, Ingemund & Wetlesen, Jon, eds. In Skeptical Wonder: Inquiries into the Philosophy of Arne Naess on the Occasion of His 70th Birthday. 328p. 1982. 46.00 (ISBN 82-00-05867-0). Universitet.

Gullvag, Ingemund, jt. ed. see Hoibraaten, Helge.

Gulshaw, B., et al. Avalanche Diode Oscillators. LC 79-308906. 160p. 1978. pap. text ed. 27.00x (ISBN 0-85066-102-1). Taylor & Francis.

Gulstad, Daniel E. A Modern Theory of 'Langue' LC 73-82004. (Janua Linguarum, Ser. Minor: No. 180). 141p. 1973. pap. text ed. 15.20x (ISBN 90-2792-540-2). Mouton.

Gulvin, C. The Scottish Hosiery & Knitwear Industry, 1680-1980. 163p. 1984. text ed. 31.00x (ISBN 0-85976-120-7, Pub. by John Donald England). Humanities.

Gulvin, Harold E., jt. auth. see Stone, Archie.

Gulvin, J. The Garment Makers. 250p. text ed. cancelled (Pub. by Donald Scotland). Humanities.

Gulyaev, A. P. Physical Metallurgy, 2 vols. 650p. 1980. 11.00 set (ISBN 0-8285-2031-3, Pub. by Mir Pubs USSR). Imported Pubns.

Gulyas, G., tr. see Mesterhazi, Lajos.

Gulyas, Gyula, tr. see Nemeth, Laszlo.

Gulyga, Arsenij. Immanuel Kant. Despalatovic, Marijan, tr. 250p. 1985. 19.95 (ISBN 0-8176-3195-X). Birkhauser.

Guma, Alex La see La Guma, Alex.

Gumaer. History of Deer Park. 10.30x (ISBN 0-686-14958-0). T E Henderson.

Gumaer, J., jt. auth. see Duncan, J. A.

Gumaer, Jim. Counseling & Therapy for Children. 384p. 1984. 20.00x (ISBN 0-02-913350-5). Free Pr.

Gumb, Raymond. Evolving Theories. (Language, Logic & Linguistics Ser.). 96p. (Orig.). 1980. pap. text ed. 12.00 (ISBN 0-930586-14-X). Haven Pubns.

Gumbel, Emil J. Statistics of Extremes. LC 57-10160. 1958. 40.00x (ISBN 0-231-02190-9). Columbia U Pr.

Gumbert, David E., jt. ed. see Harvard Business Review Staff.

Gumbert, Edgar B. & Spring, Joel H. The Superschool & the Superstate: American Education in the Twentieth Century, 1918-1970. LC 73-22226. (Studies in the History of American Education Ser.). pap. 55.50 (ISBN 0-317-09296-0, 2013572). Bks Demand UMI.

Gumbert, J. P. & De Haan, M. J., eds. Texts & Manuscripts: Litterae Textuales. (Illus.). 110p. 1972. 46.50 (ISBN 0-8390-0105-3). Abner Schram Ltd.

--Varia Codicologica: Litterae Textuales. (Illus.). 110p. 1972. 46.50 (ISBN 0-8390-0106-1). Abner Schram Ltd.

Gumbert, Marc. Neither Justice nor Reason: A Legal & Anthropological Analysis of Aboriginal Rights. LC 84-3598. (Illus.). 215p. 1985. text ed. 18.50x (ISBN 0-7022-1746-8). U of Queensland Pr.

Gumbley, Walter. Parish Priests among the Saints. facs. ed. LC 76-148214. (Biography Index Reprint Ser.). 1947. 15.00 (ISBN 0-8369-8061-1). Ayer Co Pubs.

Gumbrell, Colin. Karl Marx. (Evergreen Lives Ser.). (Illus.). 128p. 1984. 6.95 (ISBN 0-312-45078-8). St Martin.

Gumenskii, B. M. & Komarov, N. S. Soil Drilling by Vibration. LC 61-12724. 80p. 1961. 29.50x (ISBN 0-306-10604-3, Consultants). Plenum Pub.

Gumerman, G. J., jt. ed. see Schiffer, M. B.

Gumerman, George J. A View from Black Mesa: The Changing Face of Archaeology. LC 84-8581. (Illus.). 184p. 1984. 18.95x (ISBN 0-8165-0848-8). U of Ariz Pr.

Gumerman, George J. & Euler, Robert C., eds. Papers on the Archaeology of Black Mesa, Arizona, Vol. I. LC 75-32340. (Illus.). 198p. 1976. 10.00x (ISBN 0-8093-0734-0); pap. 5.95x (ISBN 0-8093-0735-9). S Ill U Pr.

Gumerman, George J., jt. ed. see Spoerl, Patricia M.

Gumhalter, Hans. Power Systems in Communications Engineering: Principles, Pt. 1. LC 83-13666. 230p. 1984. 44.95x (ISBN 0-471-90290-X). Wiley.

Gumilev, Nikolai. K Sinei Zvezde. (Rus.). 1979. 10.00 (ISBN 0-88233-497-2); pap. 3.00 (ISBN 0-88233-498-0). Ardis Pubs.

--Koster. (Rus.). 1979. pap. 2.50 (ISBN 0-88233-499-9). Ardis Pubs.

--On Russian Poetry. Lapeza, David, tr. from Rus. 210p. 1977. 15.00 (ISBN 0-88233-100-0). Ardis Pubs.

Gumina, Deanna P. The Italians of San Francisco, Eighteen Fifty to Nineteen Thirty: (Gli Italiani Di San Francisco, 1850 to 1930) dual language ed. Are, Ennio T., tr. LC 77-89342. 1978. pap. text ed. 9.95x (ISBN 0-913256-28-5). Ctr Migration.

--The Italians of San Francisco: 1850-1930. rev. ed. (CMS Migration & Ethnicity Ser.). 250p. 1985. pap. 14.95 (ISBN 0-913256-93-5). Ctr Migration.

Guminsky, C., jt. auth. see Galus.

Gummer, E. N. Dickens' Works in Germany: 1837-1937. 59.95 (ISBN 0-8490-0030-0). Gordon Pr.

Gummer, Ellis N. Dickens' Works in Germany, 1837-1937. 1972. lib. bdg. 17.00x (ISBN 0-374-93323-5). Octagon.

Gummer, H. Managing Potentials of Food & Beverage Control. 1983. 12.95 (ISBN 0-7131-0732-4). E Arnold.

Gummere, Amelia M. Quaker: A Study in Costume. LC 68-56494. (Illus.). 1968. Repr. of 1901 ed. 20.00 (ISBN 0-405-08585-0, Blom Pubns). Ayer Co Pubs.

Gummere, Francis. The Beginnings of Poetry. 1973. Repr. of 1901 ed. 25.50 (ISBN 0-8274-1576-1). R West.

--A Handbook of Poetics. LC 73-15748. 1973. lib. bdg. 20.00 (ISBN 0-8414-4468-4). Folcroft.

Gummere, Francis, jt. auth. see Hinchman, Walter S.

Gummere, Francis B. Beginnings of Poetry. facs. ed. LC 71-114908. (Select Bibliographies Reprint Ser). 1901. 29.00 (ISBN 0-8369-5313-4). Ayer Co Pubs.

--Germanic Origins: A Study in Primitive Culture. 69.95 (ISBN 0-8490-0231-1). Gordon Pr.

--Handbook of Poetics. 59.95 (ISBN 0-87968-286-8). Gordon Pr.

--The Popular Ballad. 69.95 (ISBN 0-87968-285-X). Gordon Pr.

Gummere, John F. Neuter Plural in Vergil. (LD). 1934. pap. 16.00 (ISBN 0-527-00763-3). Kraus Repr.

Gummere, John F; see Bird, Thomas E.

Gummere, Richard M. Seneca, the Philosopher & His Modern Message. LC 63-10274. (Our Debt to Greece & Rome Ser.). 145p. 1963. Repr. of 1930 ed. 18.50 (ISBN 0-8154-0098-5). Cooper Sq.

--Seneca the Philosopher & His Modern Message. 1976. lib. bdg. 59.95 (ISBN 0-8490-2593-1). Gordon Pr.

--Seven Wise Men of Colonial America. LC 67-27084. 1967. 8.95x (ISBN 0-674-80250-0). Harvard U Pr.

Gummerman, G. S., jt. ed. see Evler, R. C.

Gummett, P. Scientists in Whitehall. 1980. text ed. 38.50x (ISBN 0-7190-0791-7). Humanities.

Gummett, P., jt. auth. see Johnston, R.

Gummett, Philip. Science & Technology Policy in the 1980's & Beyond. 275p. 1984. pap. text ed. 32.00 (ISBN 0-582-90200-2). Gale.

Gummett, Philip, jt. ed. see Gibbons, Michael.

Gummett, Philip, jt. ed. see Johnston, Ron.

Gumnit, Robert J. The Epilepsy Handbook: The Practical Management of Seizures. 120p. 1983. pap. text ed. 12.00 (ISBN 0-89004-882-7). Raven.

Gumowski, I. & Mira, C. Recurrence & Discrete Dynamic Systems. (Lecture Notes in Mathematics: Vol. 809). (Illus.). 272p. 1980. pap. 20.00 (ISBN 0-387-10017-2). Springer-Verlag.

Gumowski, Igor & Mira, C. Optimization in Control Theory & Practice. LC 68-12059. pap. 63.00 (ISBN 0-317-26399-4, 2024456). Bks Demand UMI.

Gump, Patricia L., ed. see Wallower, Lucille.

Gump, Paul V., jt. auth. see Barker, Roger G.

Gump, Paul V. see Hetherington, E. Mavis.

Gump, Richard. Jade: Stone of Heaven. LC 62-12100. (Illus.). 1962. 14.95 (ISBN 0-385-01705-7). Doubleday.

Gump, W. Robert, jt. auth. see Woodworth, James R.

Gumpel, Henry J. & Boettcher, Carl. Taxation in the Federal Republic of Germany. 2nd ed. LC 62-19737. 1969. pap. 17.50 (ISBN 0-685-08541-4, 4479). Commerce.

Gumpel, Liselotte. Concrete Poetry from East & West Germany: The Language of Exemplarism & Experimentalism. LC 74-43317. (Germanic Studies Ser.: No. 16). 1976. 27.00x (ISBN 0-300-01914-9). Yale U Pr.

--Metaphor Reexamined: A Non-Aristotelian Perspective. LC 84-47707. (Advances in Semiotics Ser.). 304p. 1984. 20.00x (ISBN 0-253-33781-X). Ind U Pr.

Gumpert, David & Timmons, Jeffrey. The Encyclopedia of Small Business Resources: Everything You Need to Know to Help Your Business Prosper. LC 83-48350. (Illus.). 448p. 1984. pap. 9.57i (ISBN 0-06-091111-5, CN 1111, CN). Har-Row.

Gumpert, David, jt. auth. see Rich, Stanley R.

Gumpert, David E., ed. see Harvard Business Review.

Gumpert, Gary & Cathcart, Robert, eds. Inter-Media: Interpersonal Communication in a Media World. 2nd ed. (Illus.). 1982. pap. text ed. 14.95x (ISBN 0-19-503078-8). Oxford U Pr.

Gumpert, Lynn. The End of the World: Contemporary Visions of the Apocalypse. LC 83-43253. (Illus.). 84p. (Orig.). 1983. pap. 13.50 (ISBN 0-915557-38-X). New Mus Contemp Art.

Gumpert, Martin. Trail-Blazers of Science: Life Stories of Some Half-Forgotten Pioneers of Modern Research. facs. ed. Shuman, Edwin L., tr. LC 68-29212. (Essay Index Reprint Ser). 1968. Repr. of 1936 ed. 18.00 (ISBN 0-8369-0501-6). Ayer Co Pubs.

Gumpert, Robert. Harlan County, a Photo-Document. (Illus.). 1976. 10.00 (ISBN 0-685-79287-0). Invisible-Red Hill.

Gumpert, T. Reminiscences of a Physician. (Illus.). 224p. 1983. 13.50 (ISBN 0-86230-048-7). Triplegate.

Gumpertz, Robert, jt. auth. see Thayer, Philip.

Gumpertz, W., ed. Single-Ply Roofing Technology-STP 790. 120p. 1982. pap. 14.25 (ISBN 0-8031-0778-1, 04-790000-10). ASTM.

Gumperz, John J. Discourse Strategies. LC 81-20627. (Studies in Interactional Sociolinguistics 1). 200p. 1982. 34.50 (ISBN 0-521-24691-1); pap. 11.95 (ISBN 0-521-28896-7). Cambridge U Pr.

--Language in Social Groups: Essays by John J. Gumperz. Dil, Anwar S., ed. LC 75-170982. (Language Science & National Development Ser). 366p. 1971. 37.50x (ISBN 0-8047-0798-7). Stanford U Pr.

Gumperz, John J., ed. Language & Social Identity. 2nd ed. LC 82-4331. (Studies in Interactional Sociologuistics 2). 250p. 1983. 37.50 (ISBN 0-521-24692-X); pap. 13.95 (ISBN 0-521-28897-5). Cambridge U Pr.

Gumplowicz, Ludwig. The Outlines of Sociology. Moore, Frederick W., tr. LC 74-25755. (European Sociology Ser.). 234p. 1975. Repr. 22.00x (ISBN 0-405-06509-4). Ayer Co Pubs.

--Outlines of Sociology. LC 78-62687. (Social Science Classics Ser.). 336p. 1980. 29.95 (ISBN 0-87855-309-6); pap. text ed. 6.95 (ISBN 0-87855-693-1). Transaction Bks.

Gumr, Charles J. Trade Financing. 190p. 1981. 88.00 (ISBN 0-8002-3402-2). Intl Pubns Serv.

Gumring, Steven G., jt. auth. see Weber, Eric.

Gumuchian & Cie. Les Livres de l'Enfance du Quinzieme au Dix-Neuvieme Siecle. (Illus.). Repr. 175.00x (ISBN 0-87556-117-9). Saifer.

Gumucio, Mariano B. Cultural Policy in Bolivia. (Studies & Documents on Cultural Policies). (Illus.). 81p. 1979. pap. 6.25 (ISBN 92-3-101519-2, U890, UNESCO). Unipub.

Gun, Guneli. The Adventures of Huru on the Road to Baghdad. 352p. 1985. 19.95 (ISBN 0-89793-033-9). Hunter Hse.

Gun, Nerin E. Day of the Americans. LC 66-16521. (Illus.). 1966. 10.95 (ISBN 0-8303-0038-4). Fleet.

Gunabhadra Acharya. Atmanushasana (Discourse to the Soul) Jaini, Rai B., ed. & tr. LC 73-3841. (Sacred Books of the Jainas: No. 7). Repr. of 1928 ed. 18.00 (ISBN 0-404-57707-5). AMS Pr.
Gunaratna, Henepola. The Path of Serenity & Insight. 1984. 22.50x (ISBN 0-8364-1149-8). South Asia Bks.
Gunaseker, Wickrema, jt. auth. see Fernando, Sunimal.
Gunasekera, Henry M., tr. Satvotpatti Vinischaya & Nirvana Vibhaga: An Enquiry into the Origin of Beings & Discussions about Nirvana. Dharmaratna, M., compiled by. LC 78-72424. Repr. of 1902 ed. 17.50 (ISBN 0-404-17285-7). AMS Pr.
Gunatilaka, Ananda, jt. auth. see Bowen, Robert.
Gunatilleke, Godfrey & Tiruchelvan, Nellan, eds. Ethical Dilemmas of Development in Asia. LC 81-47964. 288p. 1983. 23.00x (ISBN 0-669-05147-0). Lexington Bks.
Gunawardana, R. A. Robe & Plough: Monasticism & Economic Interest in Early Medieval Sri Lanka. LC 78-26090. (Association for Asian Studies Monographs: No. 35). 377p. 1979. 9.50x (ISBN 0-8165-0648-5); pap. 5.95x (ISBN 0-8165-0647-7). U of Ariz Pr.
Gunb, Raymond D. Rule-Governed Linguistic Behavior. (Janua Linguarum, Ser. Minor: No. 141). 139p. 1972. pap. text ed. 12.80x (ISBN 90-2792-316-7). Mouton.
Gunby, D. C., ed. see Webster, John.
Gunby, R. A. Sport Parachuting Manual. 5th ed. Jeppesen Sanderson, ed. (Illus.). 162p. 1974. pap. text ed. 4.95 (ISBN 0-88487-008-1, RE314751). Jeppesen Sanderson.
Guncheon, Mark C. The Incredible Dial-a-Message Directory: 3000 Informative, Exciting, & Entertaining Phone Numbers You Can Call. (Illus.). 128p. (Orig.). 1985. pap. 5.95 (ISBN 0-8092-5338-0). Contemp Bks.
Gunchuck, Roberta S. An Educator's Cry. 1985. 6.95 (ISBN 0-533-06475-9). Vantage.
Gunckel, J. E. Current Topics in Plant Science. 1969. 72.00 (ISBN 0-12-305750-7). Acad Pr.
Gunda, B., ed. The Fishing Culture of the World, 2 Vols. 1253p. 1984. Set. text ed. 85.50x (ISBN 963-05-2837-1, Pub. by Kultura Hungary). Vol. 1 (ISBN 963-05-3278-6). Vol. 2 (ISBN 963-05-3279-4). Humanities.
Gundel, K. Cookbook Hungarian. (Illus.). 137p. 1984. 9.50x (ISBN 0-317-18236-6, H261). Vanous.
--Hungarian Cook Book. 6th rev. ed. 7.50x (ISBN 0-89918-261-5, H261). Vanous.
Gundel, Karoly. Hungarian Cookery. (Illus.). 13.50x (ISBN 0-392-03341-0, LTB). Sportshelf.
Gundell, Glen, ed. Writing, from Idea to Printed Page: Case Histories of Stories & Articles Published in the Saturday Evening Post. LC 69-10104. Repr. of 1949 ed. lib. bdg. 42.50x (ISBN 0-8371-0458-0, GUW). Greenwood.
Gundell, Herb. Herb Gundell's Complete Guide to Rocky Mountain Gardening. 1985. 24.95 (ISBN 0-87833-385-1). Taylor Pub.
Gunden, Heidi Von see Von Gunden, Heidi.
Gunden, Kenneth Von see Von Gunden, Kenneth & Stock, Stuart H.
Gunder Frank, Andre. Critique & Anti-Critique: Essays on Dependence & Reformism. LC 83-13683. 320p. 1984. 34.95 (ISBN 0-03-063737-6); pap. 14.95 (ISBN 0-03-063738-4). Praeger.
Gundersen, Dennis F. & Hopper, Robert. Communication & Law Enforcement. LC 83-12986. 304p. 1983. 11.50 (ISBN 0-06-042556-3, HarpC). Har-Row.
Gundersen, James N. & Schwartz, George M. Geology of the Metamorphosed Biwabik Iron Formation, Eastern Mesabi District, Minnesota. LC 62-9302. (Bulletin: No. 43). 1962. 4.25x (ISBN 0-8166-0274-3). Minn Geol Survey.
Gundersen, Joan R., jt. auth. see Smelser, Marshall.
Gundersen, Roy M. Linearized Analysis of One-Dimensional Magnetohydrodynamic Flows. (Springer Tracts in Natural Philosophy: Vol. 1). (Illus.). 1964. 19.50 (ISBN 0-387-03216-9). Springer-Verlag.
Gundersheimer, Karen. ABC Say with Me. LC 84-47627. (Illus.). 32p. (ps-1). 1984. 3.80i (ISBN 0-06-022174-7); PLB 4.89g (ISBN 0-06-022175-5). HarpJ.
--Happy Winter. LC 81-48650. (Illus.). 40p. (gr. k-3). 1982. 9.57i (ISBN 0-06-022172-0); PLB 10.89g (ISBN 0-06-022173-9). HarpJ.
--One Two Three Play with Me. LC 84-47628. (Illus.). 32p. (ps-1). 1984. 3.80i (ISBN 0-06-022176-3); PLB 4.89g (ISBN 0-06-022177-1). HarpJ.
Gunderson, Carl. Quick Reference to Clinical Neurology. (Illus.). 448p. 1982. pap. text ed. 28.95 (ISBN 0-397-50498-5, Lippincott Medical). Lippincott.
Gunderson, David R. Writing Your Way up the Ladder. LC 81-67248. 175p. (Orig.). 1981. pap. 7.95 (ISBN 0-938442-02-3). Focus Pub.
Gunderson, E. K., ed. Human Adaptability to Antarctic Conditions. LC 74-18498. (Antarctic Research Ser.: Vol. 22). (Illus.). 131p. 1974. 17.00 (ISBN 0-87590-122-0). Am Geophysical.
Gunderson, E. K. & Rahe, Richard H., eds. Life Stress & Illness. (Illus.). 274p. 1979. 25.50x (ISBN 0-398-03003-0). C C Thomas.
Gunderson, Edna. Pletka. (Illus.). 125p. 1983. 50.00 (ISBN 0-87358-309-4). Northland.
Gunderson, Jeffrey. Fixin' Fish: A Guide to Handling, Buying, Preparing & Preserving Fish. 2nd ed. 64p. 1984. 12.95x (ISBN 0-8166-1330-3); pap. 6.95 (ISBN 0-8166-1333-8). U of Minn Pr.
Gunderson, John G. Borderline Personality Disorder. LC 84-18411. 224p. 1984. 23.50x (ISBN 0-88048-020-3, 48-020-3). Am Psychiatric.
--Get That Interview. 32p. (Orig.). 1980. pap. 3.00 (ISBN 0-938442-00-7). Focus Pub.
--Principles & Practices of Milieu Therapy. LC 80-70244. 224p. 1982. 25.00 (ISBN 0-87668-439-8). Aronson.
--Write a Winning Resume. 82p. (Orig.). 1983. pap. 3.95 (ISBN 0-938442-03-1). Focus Pub.
Gunderson, John G. & Mosher, Loren, eds. Psychotherapy of Schizophrenia. LC 75-6844. 448p. 1975. 30.00x (ISBN 0-87668-208-5). Aronson.
Gunderson, Keith. A Continual Interest in the Sun & Sea & Inland Missing the Sea. (Illus.). 154p. 1977. pap. 1.00 (ISBN 0-686-83870-X). Nodin Pr.
--Mentality & Machines. 2nd ed. Date not set. pap. 13.95 (ISBN 0-8166-1362-1). U of Minn Pr.
--To See a Thing. (Poetry Ser). (Illus.). 1975. pap. 1.00 (ISBN 0-685-79526-8). Nodin Pr.
Gunderson, Keith, ed. & intro. by. Language, Mind, & Knowledge. LC 74-22836. (Studies in the Philosophy of Science Ser: Vol. 7). 415p. 1975. 25.00x (ISBN 0-8166-0742-7). U of Minn Pr.
Gunderson, Loren. The Gold Book: The Businessman's Guide to the State of Montana's Procedures for the Procurement of Goods & Services. LC 83-80036. (Illus.). 150p. (Orig.). 1983. pap. 30.00 (ISBN 0-934318-12-3). Falcon Pr MT.
Gunderson, Morley, ed. Collective Bargaining in the Essential & Public Service Sectors: Proceedings of a Conference, April 3-4, 1975. LC 75-31677. pap. 43.30 (ISBN 0-317-27033-8, 2023630). Bks Demand UMI.
Gunderson, Richard U. The Power of Positive Shrinking: Appetite - Weight Control by Hypnosis & Behavior Modification. 54p. (Orig.). 1981. 12.95 (ISBN 0-686-36697-2). Gunderson.
Gunderson, Robert G. The Log-Cabin Campaign. LC 76-49604. (Illus.). 1977. Repr. of 1957 ed. lib. bdg. 20.50x (ISBN 0-8371-9395-8, GULC). Greenwood.
--Old Gentlemen's Convention: The Washington Peace Conference of 1861. LC 80-24747. (Illus.). xiii, 168p. 1981. Repr. of 1961 ed. lib. bdg. 19.25x (ISBN 0-313-22584-2, GUOG). Greenwood.
Gunderson, Vivian. Bible Learn & Do: Exodus. (Illus.). 1981. pap. 1.25 (ISBN 0-8323-0394-1); tchr's manual 2.50 (ISBN 0-8323-0435-2). Binford.
--Bible Learn & Do: Genesis, Pt. I. (Illus.). 1979. pap. 1.25 (ISBN 0-8323-0368-2); tchr's. manual 2.50 (ISBN 0-8323-0376-3). Binford.
--Bible Learn & Do: Genesis, Pt. II. (Illus.). 1980. pap. 1.25 (ISBN 0-8323-0369-0); tchr's. manual 2.50 (ISBN 0-8323-0377-1). Binford.
--Bible Learn & Do: Gospel of Mark. (Illus.). 1982. pap. 1.25 (ISBN 0-8323-0412-3); pap. 2.50 tchr's manual (ISBN 0-8323-0439-5). Binford.
--Bible Learn & Do: Numbers. (Illus.). 1981. pap. 1.25 (ISBN 0-8323-0393-3); tchr's. manual 2.50 (ISBN 0-8323-0436-0). Binford.
--What's the Bible Like: New Testament. (Illus.). 1983. pap. 1.25 (ISBN 0-8323-0418-2). Binford.
--What's the Bible Like: Old Testament. (Illus.). 1984. pap. 1.25 (ISBN 0-8323-0428-X). Binford.
Gunderson, Vivian D. The Enemy Guest. 1964. pap. 1.65 (ISBN 0-915374-11-0, 11-0). Rapids Christian.
--Island Prisoner. 1974. pap. 1.65 (ISBN 0-915374-12-9, 12-9). Rapids Christian.
--Over the Cliff. 1974. pap. 1.65 (ISBN 0-915374-13-7, 13-7). Rapids Christian.
--Saved on Monday. 1964. pap. 1.65 (ISBN 0-915374-14-5, 14-5). Rapids Christian.
--The Wrong Road. 1964. pap. 1.65 (ISBN 0-915374-15-3, 15-3). Rapids Christian.
Gundevia, Y. D. Outside the Archives. 392p. 1984. text ed. 40.00x. Apt Bks.
--War & Peace in Nagaland. LC 75-908123. 1975. 12.50x (ISBN 0-88386-580-7). South Asia Bks.
Gundevia, Y. D., ed. The Testament of Sheikh Abdulla. LC 74-900723. 1974. 8.00x (ISBN 0-88386-478-9). South Asia Bks.
Gundlach, jt. auth. see Kelsey.
Gundlach, H., jt. ed. see Rose, A. W.
Gundlach, Pat, jt. auth. see Kelsey, Keenan.
Gundolf, Friedrich. Caesar in der Deutschen Literatur. 18.00 (ISBN 0-384-20461-9); pap. 13.00 (ISBN 0-384-20460-0). Johnson Repr.
--Goethe. LC 79-170845. Repr. of 1930 ed. 44.50 (ISBN 0-404-02961-2). AMS Pr.
--Heinrich Von Kleist. LC 72-112914. Repr. of 1922 ed. 18.50 (ISBN 0-404-02962-0). AMS Pr.
Gundrey, Elizabeth. Painting & Decorating. (Orig.). 1980. pap. 8.95x (ISBN 0-8464-1036-2). Beekman Pubs.
--Staying off the Beaten Track. (Illus.). 248p. 1985. pap. 8.95 (Pub. by Auto Assn-British Tourist Authority England). Merrimack Pub Cir.
Gundry, D. W. Teacher & the World's Religions. 160p. 1968. 10.95 (ISBN 0-227-67456-1). Attic Pr.
Gundry, Patricia. The Complete Woman. 240p. 1984. pap. 2.95 (ISBN 0-515-07612-0). Jove Pubns.
--The Complete Woman. 240p. 1985. pap. 6.95 (ISBN 0-385-19749-7, Galilee). Doubleday.
--Heirs Together. 192p. 1982. pap. 5.95 (ISBN 0-310-25371-3). Zondervan.
--Woman Be Free. 1979. pap. 4.95 (ISBN 0-310-25361-6). Zondervan.
Gundry, Patricia, jt. ed. see Gundry, Stanley.
Gundry, R. Soma, in Biblical Theology, with Emphasis on Pauline Anthropology. LC 75-22927. (Society for New Testament Studies: No. 29). 300p. 1976. 54.50 (ISBN 0-521-20788-6). Cambridge U Pr.
Gundry, Robert. Matthew: A Commentary on His Literary & Theological Art. 600p. 1982. 24.95 (ISBN 0-8028-3549-X). Eerdmans.
Gundry, Robert H. The Church & the Tribulation. 224p. 1973. pap. 7.95 (ISBN 0-310-25401-9). Zondervan.
--Somain Biblical Theology: With Emphasis on Pauline Anthropology. LC 75-22975. (Society for New Testament Studies: No. 29). pap. 69.50 (ISBN 0-317-28002-3, 2025584). Bks Demand UMI.
--A Survey of the New Testament. (Illus.). 432p. 1982. 16.95 (ISBN 0-310-25410-8). Zondervan.
Gundry, Stanley & Gundry, Patricia, eds. The Wit & Wisdom of D. L. Moody. (Direction Bks.). 78p. 1982. pap. 2.95 (ISBN 0-8010-3780-8). Baker Bk.
Gundry, Stanley N. Love Them In: The Proclamation Theology of D. L. Moody. 252p. 1982. pap. 6.95 (ISBN 0-8010-3783-2). Baker Bk.
Gundry, Stanley N. & Johnson, Alan F., eds. Tensions in Contemporary Theology. 2nd ed. 478p. 1983. pap. 12.95 (ISBN 0-8010-3796-4). Baker Bk.
Gundtherodt, H. J., jt. ed. see Beck, H.
Gundy, Arthur B. Van see Van Gundy, Arthur B.
Gundy, Elizabeth. Bliss. 1977. 11.95 (ISBN 0-670-17431-9). Viking.
--The Disappearance of Gregory Pluckrose. 192p. 1985. 15.95 (ISBN 0-385-19517-6, Dial). Doubleday.
--Love, Infidelity, & Drinking to Forget. LC 83-2076. 408p. 1984. 15.95 (ISBN 0-385-27760-1, Dial). Doubleday.
Gundy, H. Pearson, ed. Letters of Bliss Carman. (Illus.). 416p. 1981. 25.00x (ISBN 0-7735-0364-1). McGill-Queens U Pr.
Gundy, John H. Assessment of the Child in Primary Health Care. (Illus.). 208p. 1981. pap. text ed. 14.95 (ISBN 0-07-025197-5). McGraw.
Gundy, Samuel C., jt. auth. see Quirk, Thomas C., Jr.
Gundy Jones, Dorothea Van see Lager, Mildred & Van Gundy Jones, Dorothea.
Gunfield, F. Wayfarers of the Thai Forest: The Akha. (Peoples of the Wild Ser.). (gr. 7 up). 1983. kivar bdg. 15.94 (ISBN 0-7054-0703-9, Pub. by Time-Life). Silver.
Gungwu, W. & Guerrero, M. Society & the Writer: Essays on Literature in Modern Asia. 322p. (Orig.). 1982. pap. text ed. 10.95 (ISBN 0-909596-69-7, Pub. by ANUP Australia). Australia N U P.
Gungwu, Wang. The Structure of Power in North China During the Five Dynasties. 1963. 20.00x (ISBN 0-8047-0786-3); pap. 6.95 (ISBN 0-8047-0603-4, SP61). Stanford U Pr.
Gunion, J. F. & Yager, P. M., eds. Multiparticle Dynamics, 1983: Proceedings of the XIV International Symposium on Multiparticle Dynamics Lake Tahoe, USA, June 22-27, 1983. 100p. 1984. 88.00x (ISBN 9971-966-41-7, Pub. by World Sci Singapore). Taylor & Francis.
Gunji, Masakatsu. Kabuki. LC 85-56. (Illus.). 240p. 1984. 50.00 (ISBN 0-317-19315-5). Kodansha.
Gunkel, Carroll R. Into the House of the Lord. 1973. pap. 2.25 (ISBN 0-89536-109-4). CSS of Ohio.
--They Met the Master: Sermons on Contemporary Saints. 1980. 4.50 (ISBN 0-89536-413-1). CSS of Ohio.
--The Unlikely Bride. 1976. pap. 4.00 (ISBN 0-89536-246-5). CSS of Ohio.
Gunkel, Hermann. The Influence of the Holy Spirit: The Popular View of the Apostolic Age & the Teaching of the Apostle Paul. Harrisville, Roy A. & Quanbeck, Philip A., II, trs. LC 78-20022. 144p. 1979. 12.95 (ISBN 0-8006-0544-6, 1-544). Fortress.
--The Legends of Genesis: The Biblical Saga & History. LC 64-22609. 1984. pap. 5.50 (ISBN 0-8052-0086-X). Schocken.
--Psalms: A Form-Critical Introduction. Reumann, John, ed. Horner, Thomas M., tr. from Ger. LC 67-22983. (Facet Bks.). 64p. (Orig.). 1967. pap. 2.50 (ISBN 0-8006-3043-2, 1-3043). Fortress.
Gunkel, Peter. Oeffentliche Investitionsentscheidungen im Fremdenverkehrssektor: Ueberpruefung und Konzeption von Bewertungsansatzen. (European University Studies: No. 5, Vol. 438). 323p. (Ger.). 1983. 36.85 (ISBN 3-8204-7727-6). P Lang Pubs.
Gunlicks, Arthur B., ed. Local Government Reform & Reorganization: An International Perspective. (National University Publications, Political Science Ser.). 1981. 19.50x (ISBN 0-8046-9272-6, Pub. by Kennikat). Assoc Faculty Pr.
--Local Government Reform & Reorganization: An International Perspective. 252p. 1981. 19.50x (ISBN 0-8046-9272-6, 9272). Assoc Faculty Pr.
Gunn. Manual of Document Microphotography. 1985. 99.95 (ISBN 0-240-51146-8). Focal Pr.
Gunn, A. D., jt. auth. see Lodewick, L.
Gunn, A. V. How to Design Better Products for Less Money. new ed. (Illus.). 1976. pap. 7.00 (ISBN 0-912256-09-5). Halls of Ivy.
Gunn, Aeneas. We of the Never-Never & the Little Black Princess. 256p. 1984. pap. 3.95 (ISBN 0-380-87791-0, Discus). Avon.
Gunn, Alan. Federal Income Taxation Cases & Materials. LC 81-1502. (American Casebook Ser.). 785p. 1981. text ed. 22.95 1981 teacher's manual (ISBN 0-314-58805-1); pap. text ed. incl. 1983 suppl. avail. (ISBN 0-314-87672-3); teacher's manual avail. (ISBN 0-314-63144-5). West Pub.
--Federal Income Taxation Cases & Other Materials. LC 81-1502. (American Casebook Ser.). 785p. 1981. text ed. 22.95 (ISBN 0-314-58805-1); write for info. 1981 tchr's. manual (ISBN 0-314-63144-5). West Pub.
--Federal Income Taxation, Cases & Other Materials, 1985 Supplement. (American Casebook Ser.). 77p. 1984. pap. text ed. 3.95 (ISBN 0-314-87672-3). West Pub.
--Federal Income Taxation: 1983 Supplement. (American Casebook Ser.). 67p. 1983. pap. text ed. 3.95 (ISBN 0-314-75417-2). West Pub.
Gunn, Alan M. The Mirror of Love: A Reinterpretation of the "Romance of the Rose". 592p. 1952. 24.00 (ISBN 0-89672-005-5). Tex Tech Pr.
Gunn, Albert E., ed. Cancer Rehabilitation. 238p. 1984. text ed. 46.50 (ISBN 0-89004-989-0). Raven.
Gunn, Alexander. Hermitage-Zoar Notebook & Journal of Travel, 2 Vols. 1902. 36.00 (ISBN 0-8337-1493-7). B Franklin.
Gunn, Alexander, ed. see Timbs, John.
Gunn, Ander, jt. auth. see Gunn, Thom.
Gunn, Angus M. Habitat: Human Settlements in an Urban Age. 1978. 15.00 (ISBN 0-08-021486-X). Pergamon.
Gunn, Anita. A Citizen's Handbook on Solar Energy. rev. ed. 90p. 1977. 3.50 (ISBN 0-318-16178-8); institutions & businesses 15.00 (ISBN 0-318-16179-6). PIRG.
Gunn, Anita & Courrier, Kathleen, eds. Shining Examples: Model Projects Using Renewable Resources. LC 80-67831. (Illus.). 210p. 1980. 6.95 (ISBN 0-937446-00-9, 211). Ctr Renew Resources.
Gunn, Betty R. Nurse Whitney's Paradise. (YA) 1981. 8.95 (ISBN 0-686-85731-3, Avalon). Bouregy.
Gunn, Bill. Black Picture Show. LC 75-27165. 1975. pap. 2.95 (ISBN 0-918408-03-2). Reed & Cannon.
--Rhinestone Sharecropping. LC 81-52032. 194p. (Orig.). 1981. pap. 5.95 (ISBN 0-918408-19-9). Reed & Cannon.
Gunn, Christopher E. Workers' Self-Management in the United States. LC 83-45937. 289p. 1984. 25.00x (ISBN 0-8014-1644-2). Cornell U Pr.
Gunn, Clare A. Tourism Planning. LC 79-15931. 378p. 1979. 22.50x (ISBN 0-8448-1301-X). Crane-Russak Co.
Gunn, D. L. & Rainey, R. C. Strategy & Tactics of Control of Migrant Pests. (Royal Society Discussion Ser.). (Illus.). 240p. 1980. text ed. 66.50x (ISBN 0-85403-117-0, Pub. by Royal Soc England). Scholium Intl.
Gunn, D. M. The Fate of King Saul. (Journal for the Study of the Old Testament, Supplement Ser.: No. 14). 1980. text ed. 18.95x (ISBN 0-905774-24-8, Pub. by JSOT Pr England). Eisenbrauns.
--The Story of King David: Genre & Interpretation. (Journal for the Study of the Old Testament Supplement Ser.: No. 6). 164p. 1978. (Pub. by JSOT Pr England); pap. text ed. 16.95x (ISBN 0-905774-05-1, Pub. by JSOT Pr England). Eisenbrauns.
Gunn, D. M., jt. auth. see Clines, D. J.
Gunn, Drewey W. American & British Writers in Mexico: 1556-1970. LC 74-8840. 313p. 1974. 20.00x (ISBN 0-292-70307-4). U of Tex Pr.
--Mexico in American & British Letters: A Bibliography of Fiction & Travel Books Citing Original Editions. LC 73-20354. 157p. 1974. 15.00 (ISBN 0-8108-0692-4). Scarecrow.
--Tennessee Williams: A Bibliography. LC 80-12714. (Scarecrow Author Bibliographies: No. 48). 270p. 1980. 20.00 (ISBN 0-8108-1310-6). Scarecrow.
Gunn, Edward M., ed. Twentieth Century Chinese Drama: An Anthology. LC 82-47923. (Midland Bks.: No. 310). (Illus.). 544p. (Orig.). 1983. 27.50x (ISBN 0-253-36109-5); pap. 15.00x (ISBN 0-253-20310-4). Ind U Pr.
Gunn, Edward M., Jr. Unwelcome Muse: Chinese Literature in Shanghai & Peking 1937-1945. LC 79-19754. 1980. 26.00x (ISBN 0-231-04730-4). Columbia U Pr.
Gunn, Elizabeth. A Daring Coiffeur: Reflections on "War & Peace" & "Anna Karenina". 146p. 1971. 7.50x (ISBN 0-87471-031-6). Rowman.
--Ella's Dream. 1979. 14.95 (ISBN 0-241-89847-1, Pub. by Hamish Hamilton England). David & Charles.
--Ethics & the Public Service: An Annotated Bibliography & Overview Essay. 47p. 1980. 3.50 (ISBN 0-686-32067-0). Univ OK Gov Res.
--Representative Bureaucracy in Oklahoma: A Comparison of Citizens' & Administrators' Characteristics & Attitudes. 58p. 1982. 4.00 (ISBN 0-318-01377-0). Univ OK Gov Res.
Gunn, Fenja. The Artificial Face: A History of Cosmetics. (Illus.). 220p. (gr. 9 up). 1983. pap. 9.95 (ISBN 0-88254-795-X). Hippocrene Bks.

Gunn, George S. Indispensable Christ: Sermons. 266p. 1962. 8.95 (ISBN 0-227-67661-0). Attic Pr.
--This Gospel of the Kingdom: Dilemmas in Evangelism. 167p. 1964. 6.95 (ISBN 0-227-67660-2). Attic Pr.
Gunn, Gertrude E. Political History of Newfoundland, 1832-1864. LC 67-397. 1966. pap. 10.95 (ISBN 0-8020-6323-3). U of Toronto Pr.
Gunn, Giles. The Bible & American Arts & Letters. LC 83-5634. (SBL Bible in American Culture Ser.). 256p. 1983. 15.95 (ISBN 0-89130-625-0, 06 12 03). Scholars Pr GA.
--F. O. Matthiessen: The Critical Achievement. LC 75-20363. 236p. 1975. 20.00x (ISBN 0-295-95430-2). U of Wash Pr.
--The Interpretation of Otherness: Literature Religion & the American Imagination. 1979. 24.95 (ISBN 0-19-502453-2). Oxford U Pr.
Gunn, Giles, ed. The Bible & American Arts & Letters. LC 83-5634. (The Bible in American Culture Ser.). 256p. 1983. 15.95 (ISBN 0-8006-0613-2, 1-613). Fortress.
--New World Metaphysics: Readings on the Religious Meaning of the American Experience. 1981. pap. text ed. 10.95x (ISBN 0-19-502874-0). Oxford U Pr.
Gunn, Giles, ed. see James, Henry.
Gunn, H. see Gunn, Hugh.
Gunn, Harry & Gunn, Violet C. The Test for Success Book. 100p. pap. 4.95 (ISBN 0-914091-22-0). Chicago Review.
Gunn, Hugh, ed. The British Empire, 12 vols. Incl. Vol. 1. Dominions & Dependencies of the British Empire. (Illus.). 20.00 (ISBN 0-404-54301-4); Vol. 2. The Story of the Empire. Lucas, C. 14.00 (ISBN 0-404-54302-2); Vol. 3. The Constitution, Administration & Laws of the Empire. Keith, A. B. 15.00 (ISBN 0-404-54303-0); Vol. 4. The Resources of the Empire & Their Development. Lewin, E. 15.00 (ISBN 0-404-54304-9); Vol. 5. Health Problems of the Empire, Past, Present & Future. Balfour, A. & Scott, H. H. 17.50 (ISBN 0-404-54305-7); Vol. 6. The Press & Communications of the Empire. Mills, J. S. 17.50 (ISBN 0-404-54306-5); Vol. 7. The Trade, Commerce...of the Empire. McLeod, C. C. 17.50 (ISBN 0-404-54307-3); Vol. 8. Makers of the Empire. Gunn, H. 17.50 (ISBN 0-404-54308-1); Vol. 9. The Native Races of the Empire. Lagden, G. 17.50 (ISBN 0-404-54309-X); Vol. 10. The Universities & Educational Systems of the British Empire. 17.50 (ISBN 0-404-54310-3); Vol. 11. The Literature of the Empire; the Art of the Empire. Salaman, E. & Longden, A. A. 17.50 (ISBN 0-404-54311-1); Vol. 12. Migration Within the Empire. Belcher, E. A. & Williamson, J. A. 17.50 (ISBN 0-404-54312-X). Repr. of 1924 ed. Set. 200.00 (ISBN 0-404-54300-6). AMS Pr.
Gunn, J. A. Beyond Liberty & Property: The Process of Self-Recognition in Eighteenth-Century Political Thought. (McGill-Queen's Studies in the History of Ideas). 336p. 1983. 35.00x (ISBN 0-7735-1006-0). McGill-Queens U Pr.
--Factions No More: Attitudes to Party in Government Opposition in Eighteenth Century England. 276p. 1972. 30.00x (ISBN 0-7146-2595-7, F Cass Co). Biblio Dist.
Gunn, J. A., et al, eds. Benjamin Disraeli: Letters, 1815-1834. 1982. 50.00x (ISBN 0-8020-5523-0). U of Toronto Pr.
--Benjamin Disraeli: Letters, 1835-1837. 1982. 50.00x (ISBN 0-8020-5587-7). U of Toronto Pr.
Gunn, J. E., jt. auth. see Williamson, J.
Gunn, Jack W. & Castle, Gladys C. A Pictorial History of Delta State University. LC 80-19085. 216p. 1980. 25.00x (ISBN 0-87805-112-0). U Pr of Miss.
Gunn, James. Christ: The Fullness of the Godhead, a Study in New Testament Christology. 256p. 1983. pap. 5.50 (ISBN 0-87213-283-8). Loizeaux.
--Isaac Asimov: The Foundations of Science Fiction. (Science-Fiction Writers Ser.). 1982. 19.95x (ISBN 0-19-503059-1); pap. 7.95 (ISBN 0-19-503060-5, GB). Oxford U Pr.
--The Joy Makers. (Classics of Modern Science Fiction Ser.). 1984. 7.95 (ISBN 0-517-55184-5). Crown.
--The Joymakers. Date not set. pap. 2.50 (ISBN 0-671-83302-2, Timescape). PB.
Gunn, James, ed. The Road to Science Fiction, No. 3. (Orig.). 1979. pap. 4.95 (ISBN 0-451-62427-0, ME1910, Ment). NAL.
Gunn, James E. The Listeners. 240p. 1985. pap. 2.95 (ISBN 0-345-30036-X, Del Rey). Ballantine.
Gunn, Janet V. Autobiography: Toward a Poetics of Experience. LC 81-43521. 160p. 1982. 18.95x (ISBN 0-8122-7834-8). U of Pa Pr.
Gunn, Joel, jt. ed. see Hill, James N.
Gunn, John. The Defeat of Distance: Qantas 1919-1939. LC 84-11978. (Illus.). 400p. 1985. 25.00 (ISBN 0-7022-1707-7). U of Queensland Pr.
--Violence in Human Society. 1973. 12.95x (ISBN 0-8464-0956-9). Beekman Pubs.
Gunn, John & Farrington, David P. Abnormal Offenders, Delinquency & the Criminal Justice System. LC 81-14657. (Current Research in Forensic Psychiatry & Psychology Ser.). 384p. 1982. 59.95x (ISBN 0-471-28047-X, Pub. by Wiley-Interscience). Wiley.
Gunn, John, ed. Epileptics in Prison. 1978. 29.50 (ISBN 0-12-306550-X). Acad Pr.
Gunn, John A. Bergson & His Philosophy. 1976. lib. bdg. 59.95 (ISBN 0-8490-1488-3). Gordon Pr.
Gunn, John M. Schat-Chen: History, Traditions & Narratives of the Queres Indians of Laguna & Acoma. LC 76-43720. Repr. of 1917 ed. 22.00 (ISBN 0-404-15553-7). AMS Pr.
Gunn, Mark R. History of the Clan Gunn. write for info. (ISBN 0-912951-07-9). ScotPr.
Gunn, Mary K. A Guide to Academic Protocol. LC 70-76250. 112p. 1969. 20.00x (ISBN 0-231-03036-3). Columbia U Pr.
Gunn, Peter. Byron: Selected Prose. Date not set. pap. 7.95 (ISBN 0-14-057007-1). Penguin.
--Vernon Lee: Violet Paget, 1856-1935. LC 75-12323. (Homosexuality). (Illus.). 1975. Repr. of 1964 ed. 14.00x (ISBN 0-405-07357-7). Ayer Co Pubs.
Gunn, Peter, ed. see Byron.
Gunn, Richard. The Search for Sensitivity & the Spirit. LC 80-26646. (Illus.). 216p. 1981. 7.95 (ISBN 0-87747-851-1). Deseret Bk.
Gunn, Richard L. Art & Politics in Wolfgang Koeppen's Postwar Trilogy. LC 83-48753. (American University Studies I (Germanic Languages & Literature): Vol. 26). 232p. (Orig.). 1983. pap. text ed. 25.25 (ISBN 0-8204-0048-3). P Lang Pubs.
Gunn, Robert D., jt. ed. see Krantz, William B.
Gunn, Robin. Billy 'n' Bear Series. Incl. Billy 'n' Bear Go to Sunday School (ISBN 0-570-08900-X, 56-1546); Billy 'n' Bear Go to Church (ISBN 0-570-08901-8, 56-1547); Billy 'n' Bear Go to the Grocery Store (ISBN 0-570-08902-6, 56-1548); Billy 'n' Bear Go to a Birthday Party (ISBN 0-570-08903-4, 56-1549); Billy 'n' Bear Go to the Doctor (ISBN 0-570-08904-2, 56-1550); Billy 'n' Bear Visit Grandma & Grandpa (ISBN 0-570-08905-0, 56-1551). (Illus.). 24p. (Orig.). (gr. 2-5). 1985. pap. 3.95 ea. (ISBN 0-317-20512-9). Concordia.
Gunn, Rodger S. Mormonism: Challenge & Defense. 1979. pap. 8.95 (ISBN 0-89036-126-6). Hawkes Pub Inc.
Gunn, Scout. Basic Terminology for Therapeutic Recreation & Other Action Therapies. 1975. pap. text ed. 3.60x (ISBN 0-87563-094-4). Stipes.
Gunn, Scout L., jt. auth. see Peterson, Carol A.
Gunn, Thom. Jack Straw's Castle. LC 75-18065. 1975. pap. 3.50 (ISBN 0-685-57066-5, Pub. by F Hallman). Small Pr Dist.
--Jack Straw's Castle & Other Poems. 78p. 1976. 8.95 (ISBN 0-374-17851-8); pap. 3.45 (ISBN 0-374-51417-8). FS&G.
--Moly & My Sad Captains. 104p. 1973. 7.50 (ISBN 0-374-21190-6); pap. 4.95 (ISBN 0-374-51072-5). FS&G.
--The Occasions of Poetry: Essays in Criticism & Autobiography. Wilmer, Clive, intro. by. 188p. 1982. 15.00 (ISBN 0-374-22418-8). FS&G.
--The Occasions of Poetry: Essays in Criticism & Autobiography. Wilmer, Clive, intro. by. 200p. 1985. pap. 8.50 (ISBN 0-86547-207-6). N Point Pr.
--The Passages of Joy. 96p. 1982. 10.00 (ISBN 0-374-22990-2); pap. 6.95 (ISBN 0-374-51796-7). FS&G.
--Positives: Verses by Thom Gunn. LC 66-29663. (Illus.). 1967. 10.00x (ISBN 0-226-31067-1). U of Chicago Pr.
--Selected Poems, Nineteen Fifty to Nineteen Seventy-Five. 140p. 1979. 12.95 (ISBN 0-374-25865-1); pap. 5.95 (ISBN 0-374-51595-6). FS&G.
--The Sense of Movement. 62p. 1968. pap. 3.95 (ISBN 0-571-08530-X). Faber & Faber.
--Talbot Road. (Illus.). 16p. (Orig.). 1981. pap. 7.00 (ISBN 0-914496-06-9); signed limited ed. 20.00 (ISBN 0-914496-05-0). Helikon NY.
--To the Air. Schreiber, Jan, ed. LC 73-89045. (Chapbook Series One). 1974. 5.00 (ISBN 0-87923-086-X). Godine.
Gunn, Thom & Gunn, Ander. Positives. 80p. 1966. pap. 4.95 (ISBN 0-571-10391-X). Faber & Faber.
Gunn, Thomas G., Jr. Computer Applications in Manufacturing. LC 81-6544. (Illus.). 224p. 1981. 28.95 (ISBN 0-8311-1087-2). Indus Pr.
Gunn, Violet C., jt. auth. see Gunn, Harry.
Gunn, W., tr. see Rimbaud, Arthur & Verlaine, Paul.
Gunnar, Peter M. & Burkhart, Judith A. The Management of Hotel & Motel Condominiums. (Illus.). 1978. text ed. 17.50 (ISBN 0-937056-01-4, A&F16). Cornell U Sch Hotel.
Gunnar, Rolf M., et al, eds. Shock in Myocardial Infarction. (Illus.). 310p. 1974. 35.50 (ISBN 0-8089-0830-8, 791760). Grune.
Gunnars, Kristjana. Wake-Pick Poems. (House of Anansi Poetry Ser.: No. 40). 85p. (Orig.). 1981. pap. 6.95 (ISBN 0-88784-089-2, Pub. by Hse Anansi Pr Canada). U of Toronto Pr.
Gunnarsson, Gunnar. Black Cliffs. Wood, Cecil, tr. from Danish. (Nordic Translation Ser). 260p. 1967. 17.50x (ISBN 0-299-04471-8). U of Wis Pr.
Gunnarsson, J. Production Systems & Hierarchies of Centres. (Studies in Applied Regional Science). 1977. pap. 16.00 (ISBN 90-207-0688-8, Pub. by Martinus Nijhoff Netherlands). Kluwer Academic.
Gunnel, John, ed. The Standard Catalog of American Cars, 1946-1975. LC 82-84065. (Illus.). 704p. 1982. pap. 19.95 (ISBN 0-87341-027-0). Krause Pubns.
Gunnell, John. Classic Motorbooks Chrysler 300, 1955-1961. (Photofacts). (Illus.). 80p. 1982. pap. 9.95 (ISBN 0-87938-137-X). Motorbooks Intl.
--Classic Motorbooks Pontiac Trans-Am, 1969-1973. (Photofacts Ser.). (Illus.). 80p. 1983. pap. 9.95 (ISBN 0-87938-161-2). Motorbooks Intl.
--Seventy Five Years of Pontiac-Oakland. Dammann, George H., ed. LC 81-71489. (Automotive Ser.). (Illus.). 528p. 1982. 34.95 (ISBN 0-912612-20-7). Crestline.
Gunnell, John G. Between Philosophy & Politics: The Alienation of Political Theory. LC 85-14106. 280p. 1986. lib. bdg. 25.00x (ISBN 0-87023-497-8); pap. text ed. 12.95x (ISBN 0-87023-498-6). U of Mass Pr.
--Convertibles: The Complete Story. (Illus.). 224p. 20.50 (ISBN 0-8306-2110-5, 2110). TAB Bks.
--Political Theory: Tradition & Interpretation. (Orig.). 1979. pap. text ed. 10.95 (ISBN 0-316-33150-3). Little.
Gunnell, Richard A. Adventures in Successful Thinking. 2nd ed. 1982. pap. text ed. 5.95 (ISBN 0-939530-01-5). Burtis Ent.
Gunnell, Robert. This Changing World. 14.50x (ISBN 0-392-04974-0, SpS). Sportshelf.
Gunnell, Sally, jt. auth. see Gardner, Hope C.
Gunnemann. The Moral Meaning of Revolution. LC 79-10219. 1979. 24.50x (ISBN 0-300-01997-1). Yale U Pr.
Gunnemann, Jon P., ed. The Nation-State & Transnational Corporations in Conflict. LC 75-3623. (Special Studies Ser.). 1975. pap. 3.50 (ISBN 0-685-99395-7). Coun Rel & Intl.
Gunnemann, Louis H. The Shaping of the United Church of Christ: An Essay in the History of American Christianity. LC 77-4900. 1977. 6.95 (ISBN 0-8298-0335-1). Pilgrim NY.
Gunner, Emily & McConky, Shirley. A Family in Australia. (Families Around the World Ser.). (Illus.). 32p. 1984. lib. bdg. 9.40 (ISBN 0-531-03824-6). Watts.
Gunner, Eugenia M. T. S. Eliot's Romantic Dilemma. Wilhelm, James, ed. LC 84-48372. (Comparative Literature Ser.). 225p. 1985. lib. bdg. 30.00 (ISBN 0-8240-6703-7). Garland Pub.
Gunner, Jean. Simple Repair & Preservation Techniques for Collection Curators, Librarians & Archivists. (Illus.). 14p. (Orig.). 1980. pap. 2.00x (ISBN 0-913196-32-0). Hunt Inst Botanical.
--Simple Repair & Preservation Techniques for Collection Curators, Librarians & Archivists. 3rd ed. (Illus.). 22p. 1984. pap. 3.00 (ISBN 0-913196-44-4). Hunt Inst Botanical.
Gunner, John. From Nineteen to Twenty-Three. 1984. 7.95 (ISBN 0-533-05964-X). Vantage.
Gunnerson, Charles G., ed. see ASCE National Convention, Environmental Analysis Research Council, Atlanta, 1979.
Gunnerson, Charles G., jt. auth. see Shuval, Hillel I.
Gunnerson, Dolores A. The Jicarilla Apaches: A Study in Survival. LC 72-2582. (Illus.). 327p. 1974. 17.50 (ISBN 0-87580-033-5). N Ill U Pr.
Gunnerson, James H. An Archeological Survey of the Fremont Area. (Utah Anthropological Papers: No. 28). Repr. of 1957 ed. 35.00 (ISBN 0-404-60628-8). AMS Pr.
--Excavations, Glen Canyon Area, 1957. (Glen Canyon Ser.: No. 10). Repr. of 1959 ed. 35.00 (ISBN 0-404-60643-1). AMS Pr.
--The Fremont Culture: A Study in Culture Dynamics on the Northern Anasazi Frontier. LC 79-76014. (Peabody Museum Papers: Vol. 59, No. 2). 1969. pap. 15.00x (ISBN 0-87365-172-3). Peabody Harvard.
Gunneweg, A. H. Understanding the Old Testament. Bowden, John, tr. LC 78-6696. (Old Testament Library). 272p. 1978. Westminster.
Gunneweg, Antonius H. & Schmithals, Walter. Achievement. Smith, David, tr. LC 80-26977. (Biblical Encounter Ser.). 208p. (Orig.). 1981. pap. 9.95 (ISBN 0-687-00690-2). Abingdon.
--Authority. Steely, John E., tr. LC 81-12889. (Biblical Encounter Ser.). 224p. (Orig.). 1982. pap. 10.95 (ISBN 0-687-02314-9). Abingdon.
Gunning, B. E. & Robards, A. W., eds. Intercellular Communication in Plants: Studies on Plasmodesmata. (Illus.). 300p. 1976. 46.00 (ISBN 0-387-07570-4). Springer-Verlag.
Gunning, Dennis. The Teaching of History. 197p. 1978. pap. 11.50 (ISBN 0-85664-762-4, Pub. by Croom Helm Ltd); 22.00 (ISBN 0-85664-326-2). Longwood Pub Group.
Gunning, Monica, tr. see Fry, Edward B.
Gunning, Monica, tr. see Mountain, Lee.
Gunning, Peter. Paschal or Lent Fast. LC 70-168214. (Library of Anglo-Catholic Theology: No. 7). Repr. of 1845 ed. 27.50 (ISBN 0-404-52088-X). AMS Pr.
Gunning, R. C. Problems in Analysis: A Symposium in Honor of Salomon Bochner. (Mathematical Series, No. 31). 1970. 39.00 (ISBN 0-691-08076-3). Princeton U Pr.
--Riemann Surfaces & Generalized Theta Functions. (Illus.). 1976. 31.00 (ISBN 0-387-07744-8). Springer-Verlag.
Gunning, Robert. Technique of Clear Writing. rev. ed. 1968. 16.95 (ISBN 0-07-025206-8). McGraw.
Gunning, Robert C. Lectures on Complex Analytic Varieties: Finite Analytic Mappings. LC 74-2969. (Mathematical Notes Ser.: No. 14). 170p. 1974. 19.95 (ISBN 0-691-08150-6). Princeton U Pr.
--Lectures on Modular Forms. (Annals of Mathematics Studies: No. 48). (Orig.). 1963. pap. 13.50 (ISBN 0-691-07995-1). Princeton U Pr.
--Lectures on Vector Bundles Over Riemann Surfaces. (Mathematical Notes Ser.: No. 6). (Orig.). 1967. pap. 25.00 (ISBN 0-691-07998-6). Princeton U Pr.
--On Uniformization of Complex Manifolds. LC 78-55534. (Mathematical Notes Ser: 22). 1978. pap. 16.50 (ISBN 0-691-08176-X). Princeton U Pr.
Gunning, Stella, et al. Topic Teaching in the Primary School: Teaching about Society Through Topic Work. 210p. 1981. pap. 9.00 (ISBN 0-7099-1118-1, Pub. by Croom Helm Ltd); 23.00 (ISBN 0-7099-0437-1). Longwood Pub Group.
Gunning, Thomas G. Amazing Escapes. LC 83-25401. (High Interest, Low Vocabulary Ser.). (Illus.). 111p. (gr. 5-9). 1984. PLB 8.95 (ISBN 0-396-08324-2). Dodd.
--Unexplained Mysteries. LC 82-19950. (High Interest, Low Vocabulary Ser.). (Illus.). 128p. (gr. 4 up). 1983. 8.95 (ISBN 0-396-08122-3). Dodd.
Gunnison, Binney. New Dialogues & Plays, 3 vols. in 1. LC 72-5829. (Granger Index Reprint Ser). 1972. Repr. of 1905 ed. 31.00 (ISBN 0-8369-6372-5). Ayer Co Pubs.
Gunnison, Binney, jt. ed. see Craig, A. H.
Gunnison, D., ed. Microbial Processes in Reservoirs. (Developments in Hydrobiology Ser.). 1985. lib. bdg. 52.50 (ISBN 90-6193-525-3, Pub. by Junk Pub Netherlands). Kluwer-Academic.
Gunnison, John W. The Mormons: Or, Latter-Day Saints, in the Valley of the Great Salt Lake; a History of Their Rise & Progress, Peculiar Doctrines, Present Condition & Prospects, Derived from Personal Observation During a Residence Among Them. LC 70-38355. (Select Bibliographies Reprint Ser.). Repr. of 1852 ed. 16.00 (ISBN 0-8369-6772-0). Ayer Co Pubs.
Gunnison, Nina. Alex Makes New Friends. LC 72-77596. (Illus.). 32p. (ps-2). 1972. 1.95 (ISBN 0-87397-019-5). Strode.
Gunns, Albert F. Civil Liberties in Crisis: The Pacific Northwest, 1917-1940. LC 82-49072. (Modern American History Ser.). 268p. 1985. 33.00 (ISBN 0-8240-5656-6). Garland Pub.
Gunsalus, I. C., ed. The Bacteria; a Treatise on Structure & Function, Vol. 8: Archaebacteria. Date not set. 85.00 (ISBN 0-12-307208-5). Acad Pr.
Gunsalus, I. C., et al, eds. Bacteria: A Treatise on Structure & Function, 7 vols. Incl. Vol. 1. Structure. 1960. 72.00 (ISBN 0-12-307201-8); Vol. 2. Metabolism. 1961. 72.00 (ISBN 0-12-307202-6); Vol. 3. Biosynthesis. 1962. 81.00 (ISBN 0-12-307203-4); Vol. 4. Physiology of Growth. 1963. 67.50 (ISBN 0-12-307204-2); Vol. 5. Heredity. 1964. 72.00 (ISBN 0-12-307205-0); Vol. 6. Bacterial Diversity. 1978. 68.50 (ISBN 0-12-307206-9); Vol. 7. Mechanism of Adaption. 1979. 60.50 (ISBN 0-12-307207-7). LC 59-13831. Acad Pr.
Gunsaulus, H. C. Japanese Sword-Mounts. (Field Museum of Natural History). (Illus.). 1923. 26.00 (ISBN 0-527-01876-7). Kraus Repr.
Gunsburg, Jeffrey A. Divided & Conquered: The French High Command & the Defeat of the West, Nineteen Forty. LC 78-22725. (Contributions in Military History Ser.: No. 18). (Illus.). 1979. lib. bdg. 29.95 (ISBN 0-313-21092-6, GDC/). Greenwood.
Gunsch, Emil. Family Homestead Reflections. 1985. 6.95 (ISBN 0-533-06707-3). Vantage.
Gunson, Niel. Messengers of Grace: Evangelical Missionaries in the South Seas 1797-1860. (Illus.). 1978. 47.50x (ISBN 0-19-550517-4). Oxford U Pr.
Gunson, Niel, ed. Australian Reminiscences & Papers of L. E. Threlkeld, Missionary to the Aborigines 1824-1859, 2 vols. (AIAS Ethnohistory Ser.: No. 2). (Illus.). 1974. pap. text ed. 24.00x (ISBN 0-85575-031-6). Humanities.
Gunst, Kathy. Condiments. (Illus.). 272p. 1984. 17.95 (ISBN 0-399-12919-7, Putnam). Putnam Pub Group.
Gunst, R. F. & Mason, R. L. Regression Analysis & Its Application: A Data Oriented Approach. (Statistics: Textbooks & Monographs Ser.: Vol. 34). 49.75 (ISBN 0-8247-6993-7). Dekker.
Gunsten, Paul. Tournament Scheduling the Easy Way. 84p. (Orig.). 1978. pap. text ed. 6.95x (ISBN 0-89459-203-3). Hunter Textbks.
Gunsteren, Herman R. van see Van Gunsteren, Herman R.
Gunston, Bill. Aircraft of the Soviet Union. (Illus.). 416p. 1983. 45.00 (ISBN 0-85045-445-X, Pub. by Osprey England). Motorbooks Intl.
--F-111. (Illus.). 11.95 (ISBN 0-668-05904-4). Arco.
--An Illustrated Guide to Allied Fighters of World War II. LC 80-70976. (Illustrated Military Guides Ser.). (Illus.). 160p. 1981. 9.95 (ISBN 0-668-05228-7, 5228). Arco.
--An Illustrated Guide to Future Fighters & Combat Aircraft. LC 84-71015. (Illustrated Military Guides Ser.). (Illus.). 160p. 1984. 9.95 (ISBN 0-668-06065-4). Arco.

--The Illustrated Guide to German, Italian & Japanese Fighters of World War II. LC 80-67627. (Illustrated Military Guides). (Illus.). 160p. 1981. 9.95 (ISBN 0-668-05093-4, 5093). Arco.
--An Illustrated Guide to Military Helicopters. LC 81-67084. (Illus.). 160p. 1981. 9.95 (ISBN 0-668-05345-3, 5345). Arco.
--An Illustrated Guide to Modern Airborne Missiles. LC 82-74478. (Illustrated Military Guides Ser.). (Illus.). 160p. 1983. 9.95 (ISBN 0-668-05822-6). Arco.
--The Illustrated Guide to Modern Fighters & Attack Aircraft. LC 80-65164. (Illustrated Military Guides Ser.). (Illus.). 160p. 1980. 9.95 (ISBN 0-668-04964-2, 4964-2). Arco.
--An Illustrated Guide to NATO Fighters & Attack Aircraft. LC 82-74479. (Illustrated Military Guides Ser.). (Illus.). 160p. 1983. 9.95 (ISBN 0-668-05823-4, 5823). Arco.
--An Illustrated Guide to Spyplanes & Electronic Warfare Aircraft. LC 83-2809. (Illustrated Military Guides Ser.). (Illus.). 160p. 1983. 9.95 (ISBN 0-668-05825-0). Arco.
--An Illustrated Guide to the Bombers of World War II. LC 80-67628. (Illustrated Guide Ser.). 1981. 9.95 (ISBN 0-668-05094-2). Arco.
--An Illustrated Guide to the Israeli Air Force. LC 81-71938. (Illustrated Military Guides Ser.). (Illus.). 160p. 1983. 9.95 (ISBN 0-668-05506-5, 5506). Arco.
--An Illustrated Guide to the Modern Soviet Air Force. LC 81-71863. (Illustrated Military Guides Ser.). (Illus.). 160p. 1982. 9.95 (ISBN 0-668-05496-4, 5496). Arco.
--An Illustrated Guide to the Modern U. S. Air Force. LC 81-71861. (Illustrated Military Guides Ser.). (Illus.). 160p. 1982. 9.95 (ISBN 0-668-05497-2, 5497). Arco.
--Jane's Aerospace Dictionary. 492p. 1980. 34.95 (ISBN 0-86720-573-3). Jane's Pub Inc.
--Water. LC 82-50389. (Visual Science Ser.). 48p. (gr. 6 up). 1982. PLB 13.72 (ISBN 0-382-06659-6). Silver.

Gunston, Bill & Taylor, David. Guinness Book of Speed Facts & Feats. (Illus.). 192p. 1985. 14.95 (ISBN 0-85112-267-1, Pub. by Guinness Superlatives England). Sterling.

Gunston, Bill, jt. auth. see Feldman, Anthony.

Gunston, Bill, ed. Aviation. (Octopus Bk.). (Illus.). 1979. 16.95 (ISBN 0-7064-0879-9, Mayflower Bks); pap. 7.95 (ISBN 0-7064-0899-3). Smith Pubs.

Gunston, C. A. Deutsch-Englishes Glossarium. 1292p. (Ger. & Eng., German-English Glossary of Financial and Economic Terms). 1977. 69.50 (ISBN 3-7819-2014-3, 7328, Pub. by Fritz Knapp Verlag). French & Eur.

Gunston, C. A. & Corner, C. M. Glossary of Financial & Economic Terms. 8th ed. 935p. (Orig., Eng. & Ger.). 1983. pap. text ed. 70.00x (ISBN 0-7121-5474-4). Trans-Atlantic.

Gunstone, Anthony, ed. Sylloge of Coins of the British Isles, Lincolnshire Collection: Coins in the Lincolnshire Collection. (Illus.). 1981. 79.00x (ISBN 0-19-725993-6). Oxford U Pr.

Gunstone, F. D. Guidebook to Stereochemistry. LC 75-12762. pap. 31.00 (ISBN 0-317-27819-3, 2025243). Bks Demand UMI.

Gunstone, F. D. & Norris, F. D. Lipids in Foods: Chemistry, Biochemistry & Application Technology. 175p. 1983. 29.00 (ISBN 0-08-025499-3); pap. 15.75 (ISBN 0-08-025498-5). Pergamon.

Gunstream, Stanley E. Human Biology: Laboratory Explorations. (Illus.). 288p. 1986. pap. price not set lab manual (ISBN 0-8087-4148-9). Burgess.

Gunstream, Stanley E. & Babel, John S. Explorations in Basic Biology. 3rd ed. 1982. pap. text ed. 14.95x (ISBN 0-8087-4122-5). Burgess.
--Explorations in Basic Biology. 4th, rev. ed. (Illus.). 368p. 1986. pap. price not set (ISBN 0-8087-4161-6). Burgess.

Gunter, A. Y. Big Thicket: A Challenge for Conservation. LC 73-184310. 1972. 14.95 (ISBN 0-8363-0120-X); pap. 8.50 (ISBN 0-685-02984-0). Jenkins.

Gunter, Archibald C. Bob Covington: A Novel. LC 72-3165. (Black Heritage Library Collection). Repr. of 1897 ed. 19.25 (ISBN 0-8369-9074-9). Ayer Co Pubs.

Gunter, B. G., et al, eds. Transitions to Leisure: Conceptual & Human Issues. 334p. (Orig.). 1985. lib. bdg. 26.50 (ISBN 0-8191-4769-9); pap. text ed. 14.25 (ISBN 0-8191-4770-2). U Pr of Amer.

Gunter, Barrie. Dimensions of Television Violence. LC 83-40145. 282p. 1985. 31.95 (ISBN 0-312-21077-9). St Martin.

Gunter, Christopher L. The Intelligent Understanding of Sculptures & Mosaics in the Early Church. (Illus.). 138p. 1982. 75.45 (ISBN 0-86650-037-5). Gloucester Art.

Gunter, Edmund. A Description & Use of His Majesties Dials in White-Hall Garden. LC 74-38198. (English Experience Ser.: No. 465). 64p. 1972. Repr. of 1624 ed. 9.50 (ISBN 90-221-0465-6). Walter J Johnson.
--The Description & Use of the Sector, the Crosse-Staffe & Other Instruments, 2 pts. LC 70-38418. (English Experience Ser.: No. 422). 500p. 1971. Repr. of 1624 ed. 53.00 (ISBN 90-221-0422-2). Walter J Johnson.

Gunter, Elizabeth E., jt. ed. see Lowry, Bullitt.

Gunter, F. A. & Gunter, J. Davies, eds. Residue Reviews, Vol. 57. (Illus.). 160p. 1975. 29.00 (ISBN 0-387-90118-3). Springer-Verlag.

Gunter, Hans. ILO Research on Multinational Enterprises & Social Policy: An Overview. International Labour Office, ed. (Working Paper Ser.: No. 15). ii, 33p. 1981. pap. 8.55 (ISBN 92-2-102918-2). Intl Labour Office.
--Transnational Industrial Relations. 1972. 36.00 (ISBN 0-312-81480-1). St Martin.
--The Tripartite Declaration of Principles Concerning Multinational Enterprises & Social Policy: History, Contents, Follow-up & Relationship with Relevant Instruments of Other Organisations. (Working Paper Ser.: No. 18). iii, 29p. (Orig.). 1981. pap. 8.55 (ISBN 92-2-102909-3). Intl Labour Office.

Gunter, Herman. Elevations in Florida. (Illus.). 1160p. 1948. 2.00 (ISBN 0-318-17294-1, B 32). FL Bureau Geology.

Gunter, J. Davies, jt. ed. see Gunter, F. A.

Gunter, J. E. Essentials of Forestry Investment Analysis. LC 83-63342. 1984. pap. 15.90x (ISBN 0-88246-077-3). Oreg St U Bkstrs.

Gunter, Jock. Ashton - Warner Literacy Method, No. 5. Clason, Carla, tr. from Span. (Technical Notes Ser.). 14p. (Orig.). 1972. pap. 1.00. Eng (ISBN 0-932288-12-X). Span (ISBN 0-932288-13-8). Ctr Intl Ed U of MA.
--Mercado, No. 4. Clason, Carla, tr. from Span. (Technical Notes Ser.). 13p. (Span.). 1972. pap. 1.00 ea. Eng (ISBN 0-932288-10-3). Span (ISBN 0-932288-11-1). Ctr Intl Ed U of MA.

Gunter, Jock & Clason, Carla. Letter Dice, No. 6. (Technical Notes Ser.). 17p. (Orig.). 1973. pap. 1.00 ea. Eng (ISBN 0-932288-14-6). Span (ISBN 0-932288-15-4). Ctr Intl Ed U of MA.
--Letter Fluency Games. (Technical Notes Ser.: No.9). 51p. (Orig.). 1975. pap. 1.00 ea. Eng (ISBN 0-932288-20-0). Span (ISBN 0-932288-21-9). Ctr Intl Ed U of MA.
--Math Fluency Games, No. 8. (Technical Notes Ser.). 25p. (Orig.). 1974. pap. 1.00 ea. Eng (ISBN 0-932288-18-9). Span (ISBN 0-932288-19-7). Ctr Intl Ed U of MA.
--Number Bingo, No. 7. (Technical Notes Ser.). 15p. (Orig.). 1973. pap. 1.00. Eng (ISBN 0-932288-16-2). Span (ISBN 0-932288-17-0). Ctr Intl Ed U of MA.

Gunter, Jonathan F. NFE-TV: Television for Nonformal Education. 286p. (Orig.). 1975. pap. 6.00 (ISBN 0-932288-33-2). Ctr Intl Ed U of MA.

Gunter, Laurie M. & Estes, Carmen A. Education for Gerontic Nursing. LC 78-10472. (Teaching of Nursing Ser.: Vol. 5). 1979. pap. text ed. 16.95 (ISBN 0-8261-2451-8). Springer Pub.

Gunter, Pete A. Bergson & the Evolution of Physics. LC 77-77844. pap. 90.00 (ISBN 0-317-08063-6, 2019683). Bks Demand UMI.
--River in Dry Grass. 232p. 1984. pap. 10.95 (ISBN 0-940672-26-X). Shearer Pub.

Gunter, Philip L., jt. ed. see Brady, Michael P.

Gunter, Richard. Reading Poems. 1975. pap. text ed. 1.95 (ISBN 0-917496-06-X). Hornbeam Pr.
--Sentences in Dialog. 1975. pap. 5.95 (ISBN 0-917496-03-5). Hornbeam Pr.

Gunter, Riley W., jt. auth. see Daniel, Larry J.

Gunter, Roy C., Jr., ed. Ethnic Stew: Colorful Menus from the Kitchens of Southbridge, Sturbridge & Charlton, Mass. LC 84-50704. (Illus.). 192p. (Orig.). 1984. pap. 6.95 (ISBN 0-917523-00-8). Worcester County.

Guntermann, C. Gail. Contemporary Latin American Culture: Unity & Diversity. LC 84-20061. 109p. 1984. pap. 9.95 (ISBN 0-87918-057-9). ASU Lat Am St.

Guntermann, Gail & Phillips, June K. Functional-Notional Concepts: Adapting the FL Textbook. (Language in Education Ser.: No. 44). 76p. (Orig.). 1982. pap. 6.00 (ISBN 0-15-599078-0). Ctr Appl Ling.

Guntern, G. Social Change, Stress, & Mental Health in the Alps: A Systematic Study of a Village Process. (Psychiatry Ser.: Vol. 22). (Illus.). 1979. 67.30 (ISBN 0-387-09631-0). Springer-Verlag.

Guntharp, Matthew G. Learning the Fiddler's Ways. LC 79-65825. (Keystone Bks.). (Illus.). 150p. 1980. 15.95 (ISBN 0-271-00237-9); pap. 8.95 (ISBN 0-271-00248-4). Pa St U Pr.

Gunthart, Lotte. Linger Golden Light. (Illus.). 245p. (Orig.). 1984. pap. 30.00 (ISBN 0-913196-46-0). Hunt Inst Botanical.
--The Paradise Island. (Illus.). 24p. 1984. pap. 15.00 (ISBN 0-913196-47-9). Hunt Inst Botanical.

Gunther, Albert. Catalogue of Colubrine Snakes in the Collection of the British Museum. xvi, 281p. 1971. Repr. of 1858 ed. 9.00x (ISBN 0-565-00709-2, Pub. by British Mus Nat Hist England). Sabbot-Natural Hist Bks.

Gunther, Albert E. A Century of Zoology at the British Museum: Through the Lives of Two Zoo Keepers 1815-1914. (Illus.). 533p. 1975. lib. bdg. 45.00 (ISBN 0-88202-040-4, Sci Hist). Watson Pub Intl.

Gunther, Bernard. Energy Ecstasy & Your Seven Vital Shakras. 200p. (Orig.). 1983. pap. 9.95 (ISBN 0-87877-066-6). Newcastle Pub.
--Energy Ecstasy & Your Seven Vital Shakras. LC 83-8822. 200p. 1983. lib. bdg. 21.95x (ISBN 0-89370-666-3). Borgo Pr.

Gunther, Dick, jt. auth. see Roberts, Jack.

Gunther, Erna. Art in the Life of the Northwest Coast Indians. (Illus.). 274p. (Orig.). 1966. pap. 12.95 (ISBN 0-89955-345-1, Pub. by Portland Art). Intl Spec Bk.
--Indian Life on the Northwest Coast of North America As Seen by the Early Explorers & Fur Traders During the Last Decade of the 18th Century. LC 72-188822. 320p. 1972. 15.00x (ISBN 0-226-31088-4). U of Chicago Pr.
--The Permanent Collection, Vol. 1. LC 75-32053. (Whatcom Museum). (Illus.). 64p. 1975. pap. 5.00 (ISBN 0-295-95579-1). U of Wash Pr.

Gunther, Erna, jt. auth. see Haeberlin, Hermann.

Gunther, Erna, tr. see Jacobsen, Johann A.

Gunther, Erna, tr. see Krause, Aurel.

Gunther, F. A., ed. Residue Reviews, Vols. 1-11. Incl. Vol. 1. (Illus.). iv, 162p. 1962; Vol. 2. (Illus.). iv, 156p. 1963; Vol. 3. (Illus.). iv, 170p. 1963; Vol. 4. (Illus.). iv, 175p. 1963; Vol. 5. Instrumentation for the Detection & Determination of Pesticides & Their Residues in Foods. (Illus.). viii, 176p. 1964; Vol. 6. (Illus.). iv, 165p. 1964; Vol. 7. vi, 161p. 1964; Vol. 8. (Illus.). viii, 183p. 1965. 25.00 (ISBN 0-387-03390-4); Vol. 9. (Illus.). viii, 175p. 1965; Vol. 10. With Comprehensive Cumulative Contents, Subjectmatter, & Author Indexes of Volume 1-10. (Illus.). viii, 159p. 1965; Vol. 11. (Illus.). viii, 164p. 1965. 25.00 (ISBN 0-387-03393-9). LC 62-18595. (Eng, Fr, Ger.). Springer-Verlag.
--Residue Reviews, Vols. 13-24. Incl. Vol. 13. (Illus.). viii, 136p. 1966; Vol. 14. (Illus.). viii, 131p. 1966. 25.00 (ISBN 0-387-03649-0); Vol. 15. (Illus.). vi, 121p. 1966. 25.00 (ISBN 0-387-03650-4); Vol. 16. (Illus.). viii, 158p. 1966. 29.00 (ISBN 0-387-03651-2); Vol. 17. (Illus.). viii, 184p. 1967. 29.00 (ISBN 0-387-03963-5); Vol. 18. (Illus.). viii, 227p. 1967; Vol. 19. (Illus.). viii, 155p. 1967; Vol. 20. With Cumulative Table of Subjects Covered, Detailed Subject-Matter Index, & Author Index of Volumes 11-20. x, 214p. 1968. 39.00 (ISBN 0-387-04310-1); Vol. 21. (Illus.). viii, 128p. 1968. 36.00 (ISBN 0-387-04311-X); Vol. 22. (Illus.). viii, 120p. 1968. 39.00 (ISBN 0-387-04312-8); Vol. 23. (Illus.). viii, 152p. 1968. 39.00 (ISBN 0-387-04313-6); Vol. 24. vii, 173p. 1968. 39.00 (ISBN 0-387-04314-4). LC 62-18595. (Eng, Fr, Ger.). Springer-Verlag.
--Residue Reviews, Vols. 25-35. Incl. Vol. 25. Special Volume: Seminar on Experimental Approaches to Pesticide Metabolism, Degradation & Mode of Action. United States-Japan Seminar, August 16-19, 1967, Nikko, Japan. (Illus.). x, 364p. 1969. 52.00 (ISBN 0-387-04687-9); Vol. 26. (Illus.). vii, 142p. 1969. 39.00 (ISBN 0-387-04688-7); Vol. 27. (Illus.). vii, 143p. 1969. 37.00 (ISBN 0-387-04689-5); Vol. 28. Insecticide Residues in California Citrus Fruits & Products. (Illus.). vii, 127p. 1969. 39.00 (ISBN 0-387-04690-9); Vol. 29. Special Volume: Symposium on Decontamination of Pesticide Residues in the Environment. Atlantic City Meetings of the ACS, Sept. 1968. (Illus.). viii, 213p. 1969. 43.00 (ISBN 0-387-04691-7); Vol. 30. With Cumulative Table of Subjects Covered, Detailed Subject-Matter Index & Author Index of Vols. 21-30. (Illus.). ix, 169p. 1969. 43.00 (ISBN 0-387-04692-5); Vol. 31. Leaf Structure As Related to Absorption of Pesticides & Other Compounds. Hull, H. M. vii, 155p. 1970. 42.50 (ISBN 0-387-05000-0); Vol. 32. Single-Pesticide Volume: Trianzine Herbicides. (Illus.). 420p. 1970. 42.00 (ISBN 0-387-05235-6); Vol. 33. (Illus.). 160p. 1970. 43.00 (ISBN 0-387-05236-4); Vol. 34. 160p. 1971. 43.00 (ISBN 0-387-05237-2); Vol. 35. (Illus.). viii, 156p. 1971. 39.00 (ISBN 0-387-05238-0). LC 62-18595. (Eng, Fr, Ger.). Springer-Verlag.
--Residue Reviews, Vols. 36-45. Incl. Vol. 36. Chemistry of Pesticides. Melnikov, N. N. (Illus.). xii, 492p. 1971; Vol. 37. (Illus.). 144p. 1971. 49.00 (ISBN 0-387-05374-3); Vol. 38. (Illus.). 144p. 1971; Vol. 39. The Carbinole Acaricides, Chlorobenzilate & Chloropropylate. 1971. 49.00 (ISBN 0-387-05409-X); Vol. 40. With Cumulative Table of Subjects, Vols. 31-40. (Illus.). 144p. 1971. 43.00 (ISBN 0-387-05410-3); Vol. 41. Rueckstandsberichte. (Illus.). 1972. 24.00 (ISBN 0-387-05568-1); Vol. 42. (Illus.). 1972. 24.00 (ISBN 0-387-05627-0); Vol. 43. (Illus.). 1972. 25.00 (ISBN 0-387-05779-X); Vol. 44. (Illus.). 1973. 39.50 (ISBN 0-387-90058-6); Vol. 45. 1972. 39.50 (ISBN 0-387-90059-4). LC 62-18595. (Eng, Fr, Ger,.). Springer-Verlag.
--Residue Reviews, Vol. 47. LC 62-18595. (Illus.). 199p. 1973. 39.50 (ISBN 0-387-90057-8). Springer-Verlag.
--Residue Reviews, Vol. 50. x, 192p. 1974. 39.50 (ISBN 0-387-90082-9). Springer-Verlag.
--Residue Reviews, Vol. 51. viii, 203p. 1974. 39.50 (ISBN 0-387-90079-9). Springer-Verlag.
--Residue Reviews, Vols. 52 & 61. Incl. Vol. 52. 1974. 33.00 (ISBN 0-387-90083-7); Vol. 61. 1976. 29.50 (ISBN 0-387-90149-3). Springer-Verlag.
--Residue Reviews, Vol. 75. (Illus.). 189p. 1980. 38.50 (ISBN 0-387-90534-0). Springer-Verlag.
--Residue Reviews, Vol. 76. (Illus.). 218p. 1981. 35.00 (ISBN 0-387-90535-9). Springer-Verlag.
--Residue Reviews, Vol. 77. (Illus.). 364p. 1981. 44.00 (ISBN 0-387-90538-3). Springer-Verlag.
--Residue Reviews, Vol. 79. (Illus.). 280p. 1981. 32.50 (ISBN 0-387-90539-1). Springer-Verlag.
--Residue Reviews, Vol. 82. (Illus.). 240p. 1982. 29.95 (ISBN 0-387-90678-9). Springer-Verlag.
--Residue Reviews, Vol. 85. (Illus.). 307p. 1983. 41.95 (ISBN 0-387-90751-3). Springer-Verlag.
--Residue Reviews, Vol. 86. (Illus.). 133p. 1983. 24.80 (ISBN 0-387-90778-5). Springer-Verlag.
--Residue Reviews, Vol. 87. (Illus.). 152p. 1983. 21.50 (ISBN 0-387-90781-5). Springer-Verlag.
--Residue Reviews: Residues of Pesticides & Other Contaminants in the Total Environment, 2 vols. LC 62-18595. (Residue Reviews Ser.). (Illus.). viii, 168p. 1973. Vol. 48. 29.00 (ISBN 0-387-90064-0); Vol. 49. 29.00 (ISBN 0-387-90068-3). Springer-Verlag.

Gunther, F. A. & Gunther, J. D., eds. Residue Reviews, Vol. 83. (Illus.). 174p. 1982. 26.50 (ISBN 0-387-90679-7). Springer-Verlag.

Gunther, F. A. & Gunther, J. Davies, eds. Residue Reviews. (Illus.). 166p. 1982. 28.50 (ISBN 0-387-90750-5). Springer-Verlag.
--Residue Reviews, Vol. 55. (Residues of Pesticides & Other Contaminants in the Total Environment Ser.). (Illus.). 180p. 1975. text ed. 25.00 (ISBN 0-387-90102-7). Springer-Verlag.
--Residue Reviews, Vol. 69. LC 62-18595. 1978. 27.50 (ISBN 0-387-90306-2). Springer-Verlag.
--Residue Reviews, Vol. 72. (Illus.). 1979. 25.00 (ISBN 0-387-90418-2). Springer-Verlag.
--Residue Reviews, Vol. 80. (Illus.). 198p. 1981. 32.50 (ISBN 0-387-90567-7). Springer-Verlag.
--Residue Reviews: Residues of Pesticides & Other Contaminants in the Total Environment, Vol. 64. LC 62-18595. (Illus.). 1976. 26.50 (ISBN 0-387-90214-7). Springer-Verlag.
--Residue Reviews: Residues of Pesticides & Other Contaminants in the Total Environment, Vol. 65. LC 62-18595. (Illus.). 1976. 23.50 (ISBN 0-387-90222-8). Springer-Verlag.
--Residue Reviews: Residues of Pesticides & Other Contaminants in the Total Environment, Vol. 66. LC 62-18595. 1977. 35.00 (ISBN 0-387-90251-1). Springer-Verlag.
--Residue Reviews: Residues of Pesticides & Other Contaminants in the Total Environment, Vol. 68. LC 62-18595. 1977. 29.50 (ISBN 0-387-90253-8). Springer-Verlag.
--Residue Reviews: Residues of Pesticides & Other Contaminants in the Total Environment, Vol. 73. (Illus.). 140p. 1980. 26.50 (ISBN 3-540-90470-0). Springer-Verlag.
--Residues of Pesticides & Other Contaminants in the Total Environment. (Residue Reviews Ser.: Vol. 67). 1977. 25.00 (ISBN 0-387-90252-X). Springer-Verlag.

Gunther, F. A., ed. see Futuko, T. R., et al.

Gunther, F. A., ed. see Kaemmerer, K. & Buntenkoetter, S.

Gunther, F. A., ed. see Mullla, M. S., et al.

Gunther, Francis A., ed. Residues of Pesticides & Other Contaminants in the Total Environment. (Residue Reviews: Vol. 91). (Illus.). 160p. 1984. 24.00 (ISBN 0-387-90998-2). Springer-Verlag.
--Residues of Pesticides & Other Contaminants in the Total Environment. (Residue Reviews Ser.: Vol. 92). (Illus.). 210p. 1984. 29.50 (ISBN 0-387-96018-X). Springer-Verlag.
--Residues of Pesticides & Other Contaminants in the Total Environment. (Residue Reviews Ser.: Vol. 93). (Illus.). 255p. 1984. 29.50 (ISBN 0-387-96019-8). Springer-Verlag.

Gunther, Gerald. Constitutional Law. 11th ed. (University Casebook Ser.). 1659p. 1985. text ed. write for info. (ISBN 0-88277-233-3). Foundation Pr.
--Constitutional Law, Cases & Materials on. 10th ed. LC 80-20484. (University Casebook Ser.). 1717p. 1980. text ed. 28.00 (ISBN 0-88277-010-1). Foundation Pr.
--Individual Rights in Constitutional Law, Cases & Materials on. 3rd, abr. ed. LC 80-70238. (University Casebook Ser.). 1337p. 1980. text ed. 23.00 (ISBN 0-88277-021-7). Foundation Pr.

Gunther, Gerald, jt. auth. see Schauer, Frederick F.

Gunther, Gerald, ed. John Marshall's Defense of "McCulloch Vs Maryland". 1969. 17.50x (ISBN 0-8047-0698-0); pap. 5.95 (ISBN 0-8047-0699-9, SP108). Stanford U Pr.

Gunther, Gerald, et al. Individual Rights in Constitutional Law, Cases & Materials, 1984 Supplement. 3rd ed. (University Casebook Ser.). 519p. 1984. pap. text ed. 9.95 (ISBN 0-88277-208-2). Foundation Pr.

Gunther, H. G. Private Hell. (Gunther Romance Ser.: No. 5). 208p. (Orig.). 1981. pap. 1.95 (ISBN 0-515-05677-4). Jove Pubns.
--The Ravishing Doctor. (Gunther Ser.). 1980. pap. 1.95 (ISBN 0-515-05676-6). Jove Pubns.
--Summer with Danica. (Gunther Ser.: No. 3). 224p. (Orig.). 1981. pap. 1.95 (ISBN 0-515-05674-X). Jove Pubns.

Gunther, Hans F. The Racial Elements of European History. 59.95 (ISBN 0-8490-0926-X). Gordon Pr.
--Racial Elements of Europeon History. Wheeler, G. C., tr. LC 77-110905. 1970. Repr. of 1927 ed. 21.50x (ISBN 0-8046-0888-1, Pub by Kennikat). Assoc Faculty Pr.

Gunther, Irene, jt. auth. see Cowen, Ida.

Gunther, J. D., jt. ed. see Gunther, F. A.

Gunther, J. Davies, jt. ed. see Gunther, F. A.

Gunther, Jack. The Gunther Papers. (Illus.). 1975. pap. 3.95 (ISBN 0-380-01238-3, 24000-9). Avon.

Gunther, John. Death Be Not Proud. new ed. LC 75-138730. (Memorial ed.). 1971. (HarpT); PLB 9.89i (ISBN 0-06-011633-1). Har-Row.

--Death Be Not Proud. LC 53-5344. 1953. 5.95 (ISBN 0-394-60469-5). Modern Lib.

--Death Be Not Proud: A Memoir. 1965. pap. 3.80i (ISBN 0-06-080111-5, P111, PL). Har-Row.

--Inside Africa. text ed. 45.25 (ISBN 0-8369-8197-9, 8335). Ayer Co Pubs.

--Inside Asia. LC 74-15554. (Illus.). 637p. 1974. Repr. of 1942 ed. lib. bdg. 26.00x (ISBN 0-8371-7825-8, GUIA). Greenwood.

--Inside Latin America. LC 74-27666. (Illus.). 498p. 1975. Repr. of 1941 ed. lib. bdg. 25.75x (ISBN 0-8371-7908-4, GULA). Greenwood.

--The Riddle of MacArthur: Japan, Korea, & the Far East. LC 74-11880. 240p. 1974. Repr. of 1951 ed. lib. bdg. 55.00x (ISBN 0-8371-7701-4, GURM). Greenwood.

Gunther, K. & Radtka, R. Electrical Properties & Weekly Nonideal Plasmas. (Experientia Supplementum Ser.: Vol. 49). 1984. text ed. 19.95x (ISBN 3-764316-35-7). Birkhauser.

Gunther, Konrad S. Hand Injuries: Medical Subject Analysis & Research Guidebook with Bibliography. LC 84-45874. 150p. 1985. 29.95 (ISBN 0-88164-272-X); pap. 29.95 (ISBN 0-88164-273-8). ABBE Pubs Assn.

Gunther, Louise. Anna's Snow Day. LC 78-22050. (For Real Ser.). (Illus.). (gr. k-6). 1979. PLB 6.69 (ISBN 0-8116-4310-7). Garrard.

--A Tooth for the Tooth Fairy. LC 77-16422. (For Real Ser.). (Illus.). (gr. k-6). 1978. PLB 7.47 (ISBN 0-8116-4308-5). Garrard.

--Where Is Maria? LC 79-11733. (For Real Ser.). (Illus.). (gr. 1-5). 1979. PLB 7.47 (ISBN 0-8116-4311-5). Garrard.

Gunther, Marc. Basepaths: From the Minor Leagues to the Majors & Beyond. (Illus.). 244p. (YA) (gr. 7up). 1984. 14.95 (ISBN 0-684-18175-4, ScribJ). Scribner.

Gunther, Max. D. B. Cooper: What Really Happened. (Illus.). 224p. 1985. 14.95 (ISBN 0-8092-5180-9). Contemp Bks.

--How to Get Lucky. LC 85-40245. 240p. 1985. 16.95 (ISBN 0-8128-3054-7). Stein & Day.

--The Very, Very Rich & How They Got That Way. LC 74-187402. 320p. 1973. pap. 2.95 (ISBN 0-86721-088-5). Jove Pubns.

--Writing the Modern Magazine Article. 4th ed. 225p. 1982. 12.95 (ISBN 0-87116-128-1). Writer.

--The Zurich Axioms: Investment Secrets of the Swiss Bankers. 1985. pap. 6.95 (ISBN 0-452-25659-3, Plume). NAL.

Gunther, N. Integrales De Stieltjes. LC 50-1366. (Fr). 19.95 (ISBN 0-8284-0063-6). Chelsea Pub.

Gunther, Peter F., ed. Sermon Classics by Great Preachers. LC 81-16899. 1982. pap. 4.95 (ISBN 0-8024-3328-6). Moody.

Gunther, R. Glass Melting Tank Furnaces. 232p. 1954. 69.00x (ISBN 0-686-79277-7, Pub. by Soc Glass Tech England). State Mutual Bk.

Gunther, R. T., ed. see Pratt, Roger.

Gunther, R. W., ed. Early British Botanists & Their Gardens. Repr. of 1922 ed. 29.00 (ISBN 0-527-36850-4). Kraus Repr.

Gunther, Richard. Public Policy in a No-Party State: Spanish Planning & Budgeting in the Twilight of the Franquist Era. LC 78-62839. 1980. 26.50x (ISBN 0-520-03752-9). U of Cal Pr.

Gunther, Richard, et al. Spain after Franco: The Making of a Competitive Party. LC 84-16172. 1985. 37.50x (ISBN 0-520-05183-1). U of Cal Pr.

Gunther, Richard C. A Management Methodology for Software Product Engineering. LC 78-711. 379p. 1978. 43.95x (ISBN 0-471-33600-9, Pub. by Wiley-Interscience). Wiley.

Gunther, Robert T. Astrolabes of the World, 2 vols. in one. (Illus.). 100.00 (ISBN 0-87556-604-9). Saifer.

Gunther, Samuel P. Current Issues in Financial Accounting for Lawyers. LC 83-61992. 1983. 35.00 (ISBN 0-317-04101-0). PLI.

Gunther, Samuel P., et al. Basic Accounting for Lawyers: A Video Handbook. LC 82-8163. 1982. 40.00 (ISBN 0-686-46286-6, V7-3910). PLI.

Gunther, Theresa C. Manipulative Participation in the Study of Elementary Industrial Arts. LC 70-176825. (Columbia University. Teachers College. Contributions to Education: No. 490). Repr. of 1931 ed. 22.50 (ISBN 0-404-55490-3). AMS Pr.

Gunther, W. A. Physics of Modern Electronics. (Illus.). 8.25 (ISBN 0-8446-2177-3). Peter Smith.

Guntherodt, G., jt. ed. see Cardona, M.

Guntherodt, H. J. & Beck, H., eds. Glassy Metals II. (Topics in Applied Physics: Vol. 53). (Illus.). 410p. 1983. 44.00 (ISBN 0-387-12787-9). Springer-Verlag.

Guntheroth, Warren G. Crib Death: The Sudden Infant Death Syndrome. LC 82-70102. (Illus.). 240p. 1982. 26.50 (ISBN 0-87993-175-2). Futura Pub.

Guntle, Gregory, jt. auth. see Hunter, James F.

Guntle, Gregory, jt. auth. see Hunter, James.

Gunton, Colin. Enlightenment & Alienation. 176p. (Orig.). 1985. pap. 10.95 (ISBN 0-8028-0052-1). Eerdmans.

--Yesterday & Today: Continuites in Christology. 240p. (Orig.). 1983. pap. 7.95 (ISBN 0-8028-1974-5). Eerdmans.

Gunton, Colin E. Becoming & Being: The Doctrine of God in Charles Hartshorne & Karl Barth. (Theological Monographs). 1978. text ed. 39.95x (ISBN 0-19-826713-4). Oxford U Pr.

Gunton, George. Wealth & Progress. facs. ed. LC 71-130549. (Select Bibliographies Reprint Ser). 1887. 21.00 (ISBN 0-8369-5522-6). Ayer Co Pubs.

Gunton, J. D. & Droz, M. Introduction to the Theory of Metastable & Unstable States. (Lecture Notes in Physics: Vol. 183). 140p. 1983. 9.00 (ISBN 0-387-12306-7). Springer-Verlag.

Gunton, Sharon R., ed. Contemporary Literary Criticism, Vol. 23. 600p. 1982. 85.00x (ISBN 0-8103-0113-X). Gale.

--Contemporary Literary Criticism, Vol. 24. LC 76-38938. 600p. 1983. 85.00x (ISBN 0-8103-0111-3). Gale.

--Contemporary Literary Criticism: Excerpts from the Criticism of the Works of Today's Novelists, Poets, Playwrights & Other Creative Writers, 22 vols. Incl. Vol. 1. 1973. (ISBN 0-8103-0100-8); Vol. 2. 1974. (ISBN 0-8103-0102-4); Vol. 3. 1975. (ISBN 0-8103-0104-0); Vol. 4. 1975. (ISBN 0-8103-0106-7); Vol. 5. 1976. (ISBN 0-8103-0108-3); Vol. 6. 1976. (ISBN 0-8103-0110-5); Vol. 7. 1977. (ISBN 0-8103-0112-1); Vol. 8. 1978. (ISBN 0-8103-0114-8); Vol. 9. 1978. (ISBN 0-685-92122-0); Vol. 10. 1979. (ISBN 0-8103-0118-0); Vol. 11. 1979; Vol. 12. 1979 (ISBN 0-8103-0122-9); Vol. 13. 1979 (ISBN 0-8103-0124-5); Vol. 14. 1980 (ISBN 0-8103-0101-6); Vol. 15. 1980 (ISBN 0-8103-0103-2); Vol. 16. 1981 (ISBN 0-8103-0105-9); Vol. 17. 1981 (ISBN 0-8103-0107-5); Vol. 18. 1981 (ISBN 0-8103-0123-7); Vol. 19. 1981 (ISBN 0-8103-0120-2); Vol. 20. 1982 (ISBN 0-8103-0119-9); Vol. 21. 1982 (ISBN 0-8103-0117-2); Vol. 22. 1982 (ISBN 0-8103-0115-6). LC 76-38938. (Contemporary Literary Criticism Ser.). 85.00x ea. Gale.

Guntrip, Harry. Personality Structure & Human Interaction: The Developing Synthesis of Psychodynamic Theory. LC 61-12135. 456p. 1964. text ed. 40.00 (ISBN 0-8236-4120-1). Intl Univs Pr.

--Psychoanalytic Theory, Therapy & the Self. LC 79-135563. 1973. pap. 8.95x (ISBN 0-465-09511-9, TB-5012). Basic.

--Schizoid Phenomena, Object Relations & the Self. LC 68-56426. 438p. 1969. text ed. 35.00 (ISBN 0-8236-5985-2). Intl Univs Pr.

Guntz. Nomenclature Anatomique Illustree. 512p. (Fr.). 1975. pap. 32.50 (ISBN 2-225-40623-5, M-6307). French & Eur.

Gunz, F. W. & Henderson, Edward S., eds. Leukemia. 4th ed. 1024p. 1982. 109.00 (ISBN 0-8089-1513-4, 791769). Grune.

Gunzberg, Doran. Bringing Work to Life. 1975. 90.00x (ISBN 0-7015-1680-1, Pub. by MCB Pubns). State Mutual Bk.

Gunzburg, D., et al, eds. Festschrift zu Ehren des Dr. A. Harkavy. LC 79-7160. (Jewish Philosophy, Mysticism & History of Ideas Ser.). 1980. Repr. of 1908 ed. lib. bdg. 60.00x (ISBN 0-405-12259-4). Ayer Co Pubs.

Gunzel, Dave, ed. see Lien, David A.

Guo, Zhou, ed. China & the World, No. 1. (Beijing Review Foreign Relations Ser.). 128p. (Orig.). 1982. pap. 1.95 (ISBN 0-8351-0932-1). China Bks.

--China & the World, No. 3. (Foreign Affairs Ser.). 100p. (Orig.). 1983. pap. 1.95 (ISBN 0-8351-1144-X). China Bks.

Guo-Gan, Gao, et al, eds. China Press & Publishing Directory, 1985. 400p. 1985. 55.00x (ISBN 0-317-19645-6). Gale.

Guohao, Li, et al, eds. Exploration in the History of Science & Technology in China. 835p. 1985. text ed. 79.95 (ISBN 0-88738-064-6). Transaction Bks.

Guojun, Liu & Rusi, Zheng. The Story of Chinese Books. Yicheng, Zhou, tr. from Chinese. (Illus.). 125p. (Orig.). 1985. pap. 2.95 (ISBN 0-8351-1304-3). China Bks.

Gup, B. E. The Basics of Investing. 3rd ed. 550p. 1985. write for info. (ISBN 0-471-82146-2). Wiley.

--Principles of Financial Management. 747p. 1983. 34.50 (ISBN 0-471-08194-9); study guide 14.45 (ISBN 0-471-09322-X); Gup Transp-Financial 150.00; Tables-Financial 5.00; TM-Financial 30.00. Wiley.

Gup, Benton. Management of Financial Institutions. LC 83-81686. 608p. 1984. text ed. 31.50 (ISBN 0-395-34243-0); instr's manual 2.95 (ISBN 0-395-34244-9). HM.

Gup, Benton & Kitchin, Thomas. How to Ask for a Business Loan. 1983. pap. 7.95 (ISBN 0-8359-2902-7). Reston.

Gup, Benton E. The Basics of Investing. 2nd ed. LC 78-17521. (Finance Ser.). 511p. 1983. text ed. 31.50 (ISBN 0-471-09638-5); tchrs.' manual 25.00 (ISBN 0-471-89536-9); tests 3.00 (ISBN 0-471-05663-4). Wiley.

--Financial Intermediaries: An Introduction. 2nd ed. LC 79-87858. 1980. text ed. 31.50 (ISBN 0-395-28138-5); instr's. manual 1.65 (ISBN 0-395-28157-1). HM.

--Guide to Strategic Planning. LC 79-21904. (McGraw-Hill Finance Guide Ser.). pap. 62.50 (ISBN 0-317-28229-8, 2055971). Bks Demand UMI.

Gup, Benton E. & Kitchin, Thomas W. How to Ask for a Business Loan. LC 81-67146. (Banking Ser.). 34p. (Orig.). pap. 3.00 (ISBN 0-936328-12-6). Dame Inc.

Gup, Benton E. & Meiburg, Chales. Cases in Bank Management. 495p. 1986. price not set (ISBN 0-02-348480-2). MacMillan.

Guppy, Henry, jt. auth. see Tyson, Moses.

Guppy, J. G., jt. auth. see Agrawal, A. K.

Guppy, James G., jt. ed. see Agrawal, Ashok K.

Guppy, Robert, ed. see Nietzsche, Friedrich.

Gupta, A. & Yagi, K. Petrology & Genesis of Leucite-Bearing Rocks. (Minerals & Rocks Ser.: Vol. 14). (Illus.). 250p. 1980. 44.00 (ISBN 0-387-09864-X). Springer-Verlag.

Gupta, A. & Toong, H. D., eds. Advanced Microprocessors. LC 83-6092. 1983. 41.50 (ISBN 0-87942-167-3, PC01602). Inst Electrical.

Gupta, A. & Toong, Hm, eds. Insights into Personal Computers. LC 84-29707. 1985. 29.50 (ISBN 0-87942-188-6, PCO1826). Inst Electrical.

Gupta, A. K. & Lilley, D. G. Flowfield Modeling & Diagnostics. (Energy & Engineering Sciences Ser.). 400p. 1984. 49.00 (ISBN 0-9901004-5-6, Pub. by Abacus England). Heyden.

--Swirl Flows. 1983. 62.00 (ISBN 0-9961004-2-3, Pub. by Abacus England). Heyden.

Gupta, A. N., jt. auth. see Maheshwari, R. P.

Gupta, A. P. Insect Hemocytes. LC 78-10477. 1979. 125.00 (ISBN 0-521-22364-4). Cambridge U Pr.

--Neurohemal Organs of Arthropods: Their Development, Evolution, Structures, & Functions. (Illus.). 646p. 1983. 74.50x (ISBN 0-398-04728-6). C C Thomas.

Gupta, A. R. Caste Hierarchy & Social Change: A Study of Myth & Reality. 1985. 17.00x (ISBN 0-317-19652-9, Pub. by Jyotsena Prakashan). South Asia Bks.

Gupta, Akshey K. Genetics & Wheat Improvement. 268p. 1981. 80.00x (ISBN 0-686-76640-7, Pub. by Oxford & IBH India). State Mutual Bk.

Gupta, Alka. UN Peacekeeping Activities in Korea: A Study of India's Role, 1947-1953. 1977. 11.00x (ISBN 0-88386-850-4). South Asia Bks.

Gupta, Amar & Toong, Hoo-min. Advanced Microprocessors. 359p. 1983. 41.50 (ISBN 0-471-88176-7, Pub. by Wiley-Interscience). Wiley.

Gupta, Amar, jt. auth. see Toong, Hoo-min D.

Gupta, Anandswarup. The Police in British India, Eighteen Sixty-One to Nineteen Forty-Seven. 1980. text ed. 23.50x (ISBN 0-391-01843-4). Humanities.

Gupta, Anil. The Logic of Common Nouns: An Investigation in Quantified Modal Logic. LC 79-19684. 196p. 1980. text ed. 23.50x (ISBN 0-300-02346-4). Yale U Pr.

Gupta, Anirudha. Government & Politics in Africa. 1975. 10.50 (ISBN 0-7069-0345-5). Intl Bk Dist.

Gupta, Arun K. Teacher Education: Current Prospects. 227p. 1984. text ed. 25.00 (ISBN 0-86590-268-2, Sterling Pubs India). Apt Bks.

Gupta, Ashin Das see Das Gupta, Ashin.

Gupta, Ayodhya P. Anthropod Phylogeny. 768p. 1979. 42.50 (ISBN 0-442-22973-9). Van Nos Reinhold.

Gupta, B. D. Mathematical Physics. 1977. 35.00x (ISBN 0-7069-0514-8, Pub. by Vikas India). Advent NY.

Gupta, B. K., jt. auth. see Agnihotri, O. P.

Gupta, Badlu R. The Aggarwals: A Socio-Economic Study. LC 75-908248. 1975. 7.75x (ISBN 0-88386-715-X). South Asia Bks.

Gupta, Bhabani. Communism in Indian Politics. LC 73-190190. (South Asian Institute Studies). 455p. 1972. 34.00x (ISBN 0-231-03568-3). Columbia U Pr.

Gupta, Bhabani S. Afghanistan: Politics, Economics & Society. Szajkowski, Bogdan, ed. LC 84-62667. (Marxist Regimes Ser.). (Illus.). 160p. 1985. lib. bdg. 22.50x (ISBN 0-931477-19-0); pap. text ed. 10.95 (ISBN 0-931477-20-4). Lynne Rienner.

Gupta, Bhabani Sen. Soviet Perspectives of Contemporary Asia. 187p. 1984. text ed. 16.50x (ISBN 0-391-03026-4). Humanities.

Gupta, Bhagwan Das. Life & Times of Maharaja Chhatrasal Bundela. 178p. 1980. text ed. 11.50x (ISBN 0-391-01771-3). Humanities.

Gupta, Brijan K. & Lopatin, Arthur D. Small Business Development in the Inner City Areas of Rochester. LC 78-58110. (Illus.). 231p. (Orig.). 1978. pap. 22.50x (ISBN 0-936876-15-8). Learn Res Intl Stud.

Gupta, Brijen & Kharbas, Datta, eds. India. (World Bibliographical Ser.: No. 26). 264p. 1984. lib. bdg. 42.00 (ISBN 0-903450-38-0). ABC-Clio.

Gupta, C., et al. Computer-Aided Design of Microwave Circuits. (Artech Microwave Library). (Illus.). 650p. 1981. 72.00x (ISBN 0-89006-106-8). Artech Hse.

Gupta, C. B. An Introduction to Statistical Methods. 9th ed. (Illus.). 776p. 1982. text ed. 35.00x (ISBN 0-7069-1258-6, Pub. by Vikas India). Advent NY.

Gupta, Chiananda D. Talking about Films. 218p. 1981. 70.00x (ISBN 0-86131-229-5, Pub. by Orient Longman India). State Mutual Bk..

Gupta, Chidananda Das see Das Gupta, Chidananda.

Gupta, D. C. Indian National Movement & Constitutional Development. 1976. 10.50 (ISBN 0-7069-0495-8). Intl Bk Dist.

--Indian National Movement & Constitutional Development. 4th ed. 475p. 1983. text ed. 40.00x (ISBN 0-7069-2093-7, Pub. by Vikas India). Advent NY.

--United States Attitude Toward China. 458p. 35.00x (ISBN 0-686-78838-9, Pub. by Bks India England). State Mutual Bk.

Gupta, D. C., ed. Semiconductor Processing - STP 850. 700p. 1984. 60.00 (ISBN 0-8031-0403-0, 04-850000-46). ASTM.

--Silicon Processing- STP 804. LC 82-83529. 559p. 1983. text ed. 60.00 (ISBN 0-8031-0243-7, 04-804000-46). ASTM.

Gupta, D. S., jt. ed. see Raychaudhuri, S. P.

Gupta, Derek. Radioimmunoassay of Steroid Hormones. 2nd ed. (Illus.). 265p. 1980. 48.80x (ISBN 3-5272-5863-9). VCH Pubs.

Gupta, Derek & Voelter, Wolfgang. Hypothalamic Hormones: Chemistry, Physiology & Clinical Applications. (Illus.). 766p. 1978. 75.30x (ISBN 3-527-25712-8). VCH Pubs.

--Hypothalamic Hormones: Structure, Synthesis, & Biological Activity. (Illus.). 328p. 1975. 34.20x (ISBN 3-527-25589-3). VCH Pubs.

Gupta, Derek, et al. Paediatric Neuroendocrinology. LC 84-26110. 256p. 1985. 48.00 (ISBN 0-8451-3012-9). A R Liss.

Gupta, Dharmendra K. Recent Studies in Sanskirt & Indology. 1982. 28.00x (ISBN 0-8364-0913-2, Pub. by Ajanta). South Asia Bks.

Gupta, Giri R., ed. Cohesion & Conflict in Modern India. LC 77-86741. (Main Currents in Indian Sociology Ser.: Vol. 3). 324p. 1978. 22.75 (ISBN 0-89089-103-6). Carolina Acad Pr.

--Contemporary India: Some Sociological Perspectives. LC 75-5479. (Main Currents in Indian Sociology Ser.: Vol. 1). 328p. 1976. 19.95 (ISBN 0-89089-052-8). Carolina Acad Pr.

--Family & Social Change in Modern India. LC 76-91216. (Main Currents in Indian Sociology Ser.: Vol. 2). 263p. 1977. 18.75 (ISBN 0-89089-060-9). Carolina Acad Pr.

--Urban India, Vol. 6. (Main Currents In Indian Sociology Ser.). 424p. 1984. text ed. 40.00x (ISBN 0-317-07654-X, Vikas India). Advent NY.

Gupta, Giri Raj, ed. Main Currents in Indian Sociology: Social & Cultural Context of Medicine in India, Vol. IV. 1982. text ed. 35.00x (ISBN 0-7069-0793-0, Pub. by Vikas India). Advent NY.

Gupta, H. Selected Topics in Number Theory. 1980. 55.00 (ISBN 0-9961004-6-6, Pub. by Abacus England). Heyden.

Gupta, H. & Rastogi, B. Dams & Earthquakes. (Developments in Geotechnical Engineering Ser.: Vol. 11). 230p. 1976. 70.25 (ISBN 0-444-41330-8). Elsevier.

Gupta, H. C. Economics for the Trade Unionists. 1976. 11.00x (ISBN 0-88386-501-7). South Asia Bks.

Gupta, H. K. Geothermal Resources: An Energy Alternative. (Developments in Economic Geology Ser.: Vol. 12). 288p. 1981. 66.00 (ISBN 0-444-41865-2). Elsevier.

Gupta, H. K. & Delany, F. M. Zagros, Hindu Kush, Himalaya: Geodynamic Evolution. (Geodynamics Series: Vol. 3). 323p. 1981. 36.00 (ISBN 0-87590-507-2). Am Geophysical.

Gupta, I. C. Use of Saline Water in Agriculture. 210p. 1981. 50.00x (ISBN 0-686-76671-7, Pub. by Oxford & IBH India). State Mutual Bk.

Gupta, J. P. Fundamentals of Heat Exchanger & Pressure Vessel Technology. LC 84-12865. (Illus.). 675p. 1985. 45.00 (ISBN 0-89116-344-1). Hemisphere Pub.

Gupta, J. S. Textbook of Algae. 348p. 1981. 60.00x (ISBN 0-686-84468-8, Pub. by Oxford & I B H India). State Mutual Bk.

--Textbook of Fungi. 305p. 1981. 60.00x (ISBN 0-686-84469-6, Pub. by Oxford & I B H India). State Mutual Bk.

Gupta, K. Multiple Choice Questions in Geriatrics. 192p. 1985. pap. 10.50 (ISBN 0-272-79779-0, Pub. by Pitman Med UK). Urban & S.

--One Hundred Short Cases for the MRCP. LC 82-23477. 144p. 1983. pap. 12.95 (ISBN 0-412-25230-9, NO. 6797, Pub. by Chapman & Hall). Methuen Inc.

Gupta, K., jt. auth. see Rao, J. S.

Gupta, K. C. Microwaves. LC 80-11904. 256p. 1980. 18.95x (ISBN 0-470-26966-9). Halsted Pr.

Gupta, K. C. & Garg, J. Microstrip Lines & Slotlines. LC 79-1375. 1979. 54.00 (ISBN 0-89006-074-6). Artech Hse.

Gupta, K. L. Finance & Economic Growth in Developing Countries. LC 84-14307. 242p. 1984. 31.00 (ISBN 0-7099-3803-9, Pub. by Croom Helm Ltd). Longwood Pub Group.

Gupta, K. M. Man & Forest: A New Dimension in the Himalaya. 349p. 1979. 15.00 (ISBN 0-88065-094-X, Pub. by Messers Today & Tomorrows Printers & Publishers India). Scholarly Pubns.

Gupta, K. N., jt. ed. see Rao, J. S.

Gupta, Kalyan Sen see Sen Gupta, Kalyan.

Gupta, Kanhaya L. & Islam, M Anisul. Foreign Capital, Savings & Growth. 1983. lib. bdg. 34.50 (ISBN 90-277-1449-5, Pub. by Reidel Holland). Kluwer Academic.

Gupta, L. C. Banking & Working Capital Finance, India. 1978. 12.50x (ISBN 0-8364-0209-X). South Asia Bks.

--Financial Ratios for Monitoring Corporate Sickness: Towards a More Systematic Approach. (Illus.). 1983. 16.95x (ISBN 0-19-561513-1). Oxford U Pr.

--Growth Theory & Strategy: New Directions. (Illus.). 1983. 13.95x (ISBN 0-19-561633-2). Oxford U Pr.

--Rates of Return on Equities: The Indian Experience. (Illus.). 1981. 17.95x (ISBN 0-19-561312-0). Oxford U Pr.

--Readings in Industrial Finance, India. 1976. 14.00x (ISBN 0-333-90136-3). South Asia Bks.

Gupta, M., jt. auth. see Kamthan, P. K.

Gupta, M., jt. ed. see Haenel, R.

Gupta, M. L., jt. auth. see Gupta, V. K.

Gupta, M. M. & Saridis, G. N. Fuzzy Automata & Decision Processes. 496p. 1977. 62.50 (ISBN 0-444-00231-6, North-Holland). Elsevier.

Gupta, M. M. & Sanchez, E., eds. Approximate Reasoning in Decision Analysis. 480p. 1983. 68.00 (ISBN 0-444-86492-X, North Holland). Elsevier.

--Fuzzy Information & Decision Processes. 480p. 1983. 68.00 (ISBN 0-444-86491-1, North Holland). Elsevier.

Gupta, M. M., ed. see Sanchez, E.

Gupta, M. M., et al, eds. Advances in Fuzzy Set Theory & Applications. 753p. 1979. 106.50 (ISBN 0-444-85372-3, North Holland). Elsevier.

Gupta, Madan, jt. auth. see Kaufmann, Arnold.

Gupta, Madhu S., ed. Electrical Noise: Fundamentals & Sources. LC 76-57816. 1977. 22.85 (ISBN 0-87942-086-3, PP00893). Inst Electrical.

Gupta, Mallika C., jt. auth. see Ray, Irene R.

Gupta, Mallika C., ed. see Gnaneswarananda, Swami.

Gupta, N. K., ed. Large Deformations: Proceedings of the Symposium in the Memory of Professor B. Karunes, Organized by the Department of Applied Mechanics, Indian Institute of Technology, New Delhi. LC 83-900047. 491p. 1982. 59.00 (ISBN 0-9605004-6-4, Pub. by South Asian Pubs India). Eng Pubns.

Gupta, N. S. Industrial Structure of India During Medieval Period. 262p. 1981. 30.00x (ISBN 0-686-78867-2, Pub. by Chand & Co India). State Mutual Bk.

Gupta, Nagendranath, tr. see Tagore, Rabindranath.

Gupta, Nagendranath S. The Ayurvedic System of Medicine, 2 vols. 1984. Set. text ed. 200.00x (ISBN 0-86590-346-8, Pub. by B R Pub Corp Delhi). Vol. 1, 590p. Vol. 2, 855p. Apt Bks.

Gupta, Narain. Oil in the Modern World. LC 75-6475. (The History & Politics of Oil Ser). 184p. 1975. Repr. of 1949 ed. 17.50 (ISBN 0-88355-293-0). Hyperion Conn.

Gupta, O. P. Aquatic Weeds: Their Menace & Control. (Illus.). 272p. 1979. 20.00 (ISBN 0-88065-096-6, Pub. by Messers Today & Tomorrows Printers & Publishers India). Scholarly Pubns.

--Commitment to Work. 260p. 1982. text ed. 13.50x (ISBN 0-391-02723-9, Pub. by Concept India). Humanities.

Gupta, O. P. & Lamba, P. S. Modern Weed Science. (Illus.). 325p. 1977. 25.00 (ISBN 0-88065-095-8, Pub. by Messers Today & Tomorrows Printers & Publishers India). Scholarly Pubns.

Gupta, P. K. Advanced Dynamics of Rolling Elements. (Illus.). 370p. 1984. 42.50 (ISBN 0-387-96031-7). Springer-Verlag.

Gupta, Partha S. Imperialism & the British Labour Movement 1914-1964. LC 74-28203. 438p. 1975. text ed. 45.00x (ISBN 0-8419-0191-0). Holmes & Meier.

Gupta, Pranab K. Life & Culture of Matrilineal Tribes of Meghalaya. (Tribal Studies of India Ser.: T 113). (Illus.). xiii, 210p. 1984. text ed. 40.00x (ISBN 0-86590-385-9, Pub. by Inter Pubns N Delhi). Apt Bks.

Gupta, Pranati Sen. The Art of Indian Cuisine: Everyday Menus, Feasts & Holiday Banquets. 1980. pap. 5.95 (ISBN 0-8015-0367-1, Hawthorn). Dutton.

Gupta, Pratul C., tr. see Gangarama.

Gupta, R. C. & Johari, J. C. Indian Freedom Movement & Thought, 1930-1947. 1983. text ed. 40.00x (ISBN 0-86590-159-7, Pub. by Sterling India). Apt Bks.

Gupta, R. D. Wage Flexibility & Full Employment. 1971. 4.50x (ISBN 0-686-20323-2). Intl Bk Dist.

Gupta, R. G. Planning & Development of Towns. 1984. 22.50x (ISBN 0-8364-1233-8, Pub. by Oxford IBH). South Asia Bks.

Gupta, R. P., ed. Multivariate Statistical Analysis: Proceedings of the Conference Held at Dalhousie University, Halifax, Nova Scotia, Canada, October 1979. 290p. 1980. 68.00 (ISBN 0-444-86019-3, North-Holland). Elsevier.

Gupta, R. S. A Handbook of Fire Technology. 292p. 1981. 30.00x (ISBN 0-86125-113-X, Pub. by Orient Longman India); cloth with jacket 30.00x (ISBN 0-86125-088-5). State Mutual Bk.

Gupta, Rajatananda D. Eastern Indian Manuscript Painting. (Illus.). xv, 112p. 1981. text ed. 45.00x (ISBN 0-86590-042-6, Pub. by Taraporevala India). Apt Bks.

Gupta, Rakesh. Bihar Peasantry & the Kisan Sabha: 1936 to 1947. 1983. 14.00x (ISBN 0-8364-0941-8, Pub. by Peoples Pub Hse). South Asia Bks.

Gupta, Ram C. Sri Krishna: A Socio-Political & Philosophical Study. xiv, 188p. 1984. text ed. 30.00x (ISBN 0-86590-376-X, Pub. by B R Pub Corp Delhi). Apt Bks.

Gupta, Ram N. & Sunshine, Irving, eds. Drugs, Vol. I & II. 1981. Vol. I, 384p. 66.00 (ISBN 0-8493-3031-9); Vol. II, 368p. 66.00 (ISBN 0-8493-3032-7). CRC Pr.

Gupta, Ramesh, jt. ed. see Cheremisinoff, Nicholas P.

Gupta, Rk. Bibliography of the Himalayas. 1981. 42.50x (ISBN 0-8364-0803-9, Pub. by Indian Doc Service). South Asia Bks.

Gupta, Rohini. Karna & Other Poems. 1976. 8.00 (ISBN 0-89253-825-2); flexible cloth 4.80 (ISBN 0-89253-826-0). Ind-US Inc.

Gupta, Rupa. Tales from Indian Classics. (Illus.). 136p. (gr. 1-9). 1981. 7.25 (ISBN 0-89744-233-4, Pub. by Hemkunt India). Auromere.

Gupta, S. C. Art of Bernard Shaw. LC 76-40161. lib. bdg. 22.50 (ISBN 0-8414-4439-0). Folcroft.

--Transform & State Variable Methods in Linear Systems. LC 66-17635. 444p. 1971. Repr. of 1966 ed. text ed. 26.50 (ISBN 0-88275-022-4). Krieger.

Gupta, S. K. Elephant in Indian Art & Mythology. LC 83-902433. 87p. 1983. text ed. 65.00x (ISBN 0-391-02833-2). Humanities.

--Madhusudan Saraswati on the Bhagavaddita. 1977. 28.00 (ISBN 0-89684-246-0, Pub. by Motilal Banarsidass India). Orient Bk Dist.

--Mercantile Law. 1984. text ed. 18.95x (ISBN 0-86590-187-2, Pub. by Sterling India). Apt Bks.

--Teaching Physical Sciences in Secondary Schools. rev., 2nd ed. 232p. 1985. text ed. 22.50x (ISBN 0-86590-422-7, Pub. by Sterling Pubs India). Apt Bks.

--Technology of Science Education. 103p. 1983. (Pub. by Vikas India); pap. text ed. 5.95x (ISBN 0-7069-2140-2, Pub. by Vikas India). Advent NY.

Gupta, S. K., jt. auth. see Iyengar, N. R.

Gupta, S. K., ed. Current Trends in Arid Zone Hydrology: Proceedings of Symposium Held at Physical Research Laboratory, Ahmedabad, April 5-8, 1978. 540p. 1979. 40.00 (ISBN 0-88065-097-4, Pub. by Messers Today & Tomorrows Printers & Publishers India). Scholarly Pubns.

Gupta, S. N. Quantum Electrodynamics. 238p. 1977. 56.75 (ISBN 0-677-04240-X). Gordon.

--Yoga Philosophy in Relation to Other Systems of Indian Thought. 1974. 18.00 (ISBN 0-89684-343-2). Orient Bk Dist.

Gupta, S. P. Archaeology of Central Asia & the Indian Border Lands, 2 vols. 1979. text ed. 53.00x ea. Vol. 1 (ISBN 0-391-01855-8). Vol. 2 (ISBN 0-391-02092-7). Humanities.

--Medical Emergencies in General Practice. 311p. 1978. 14.00x (ISBN 0-7069-0614-4, Pub. by Vikas India). Advent NY.

--Medical Emergencies in General Practice. 335p. 1983. text ed. 30.00x (ISBN 0-7069-1240-3, Pub. by Vikas India). Advent NY.

--Modern India & Progress in Science & Technology. 166p. 1979. 15.95x (ISBN 0-7069-0743-4, Pub by Vikas India). Advent NY.

--The Roots of Indian Art. (Illus.). 1980. text ed. 105.50x (ISBN 0-391-02172-9). Humanities.

--Science, Technology & Society in the Modern Age. 1977. 18.00x (ISBN 0-686-22672-0). Intl Bk Dist.

Gupta, S. P., jt. auth. see Majupuria, Trilok C.

Gupta, S. P., jt. auth. see Pandit, G. S.

Gupta, S. S. & Huang, D. Y. Multiple Statistical Decision Theory: Recent Developments. (Lecture Notes in Statistics Ser.: Vol. 6). 112p. 1981. pap. 12.00 (ISBN 0-387-90572-3). Springer-Verlag.

Gupta, S. V. & Kumar, N. S. A Business Challenge: A Simulation Game. 1981. 5.95 (ISBN 0-201-04583-4). Addison-Wesley.

Gupta, Samita. Architecture & the Raj. (Illus.). 171p. 1984. text ed. 80.00x (ISBN 0-86590-394-8, Pub. by B R Pub Corp Delhi). Apt Bks.

Gupta, Santosh & Gupta, Virendra. Ichneumonologia Orientalis, Part IX: The Tribe Gabuniini (Hym: Ichneumonidae) (Oriental Insects Monograph: No. 10). 300p. 1983. 45.00x (ISBN 0-318-01041-0). Oriental Insects.

Gupta, Satyadev. The World Zinc Industry. LC 81-47075. (Illus.). 224p. 1981. 29.00x (ISBN 0-669-04587-X). Lexington Bks.

Gupta, Shanti C. & Panchapakesan, S. Multiple Decision Procedures: Theory & Methodology of Selecting & Ranking Populations. LC 79-13119. (Probability & Mathematical Statistics: Applied Section). 573p. 1979. 58.95x (ISBN 0-471-05177-2, Pub. by Wiley-Interscience). Wiley.

Gupta, Shanti S. & Berger, James O., eds. Statistical Decision Theory & Related Topics III, Vol. II. 534p. 1982. 44.50 (ISBN 0-12-307502-5). Acad Pr.

--Statistical Decision Theory & Related Topics III, Vol. I. LC 82-11528. 526p. 1982. 44.50 (ISBN 0-12-307501-7). Acad Pr.

Gupta, Shanti S. & Moore, David S., eds. Statistical Decision Theory & Related Topics II. 1977. 55.00 (ISBN 0-12-307560-2). Acad Pr.

Gupta, Shanti S. & Yackel, James, eds. Statistical Decision Theory & Related Topics: Proceedings. 1971. 64.50 (ISBN 0-12-307550-5). Acad Pr.

Gupta, Shanti S., ed. see Berger, James O. & Wolpert, Robert L.

Gupta, Shanti S., ed. see Gaenssler, Peter.

Gupta, Shanti S., ed. see Knight, Frank B.

Gupta, Shanti S., ed. see Takemura, Akimichi.

Gupta, Shanti S., jt. ed. see Tong, Y. L.

Gupta, Shekhar. Assam: A Valley Divided. 224p. 1984. text ed. 30.00x (ISBN 0-317-14492-8, Pub. by Vikas India). Advent NY.

Gupta, Shiv K. & Cozzolino, John M. Fundamentals of Operations Research for Management. LC 73-94384. (Illus.). 1975. text ed. 32.00x (ISBN 0-8162-3476-0); solutions manual 6.50x (ISBN 0-8162-3486-8). Holden-Day.

Gupta, Shiv K. & Hamman, Ray T. Starting a Small Business: A Simulation Game. (Illus.). 64p. 1974. P-H.

Gupta, Sipra Das see Das Gupta, Sipra.

Gupta, Someshwar C. & Hasdorff, Lawrence. Fundamentals of Automatic Control. LC 82-20338. 602p. 1983. Repr. of 1970 ed. lib. bdg. 39.50 (ISBN 0-89874-578-0). Krieger.

Gupta, Sudhir, ed. Immunobiology of Clinical & Experimental Diabetes. 414p. 1984. 50.00x (ISBN 0-306-41402-3, Plenum Pr). Plenum Pub.

Gupta, Sudhir & Good, Robert A., eds. Cellular, Molecular & Clinical Aspects of Allergic Diseases. LC 79-867. (Comprehensive Immunology Ser.: Vol. 6). (Illus.). 648p. 1979. 65.00x (ISBN 0-306-40142-8, Plenum Med. Bk.). Plenum Pub.

Gupta, Suraj B. Monetary Planning for India. 1979. text ed. 19.95x (ISBN 0-19-561145-4). Oxford U Pr.

Gupta, Surendra K. Citizen in the Making. LC 75-903605. 1975. 12.75x (ISBN 0-88386-581-5). South Asia Bks.

Gupta, Suresh C., ed. Operations Research. (Core Business Program Ser.). (Illus.). 128p. Date not set. pap. 7.95 (ISBN 0-87196-804-5). Facts on File.

Gupta, Surinder N. British: The Magnificent Exploiters of India. 192p. 1981. 45.00x (ISBN 0-686-78868-0, Pub. by Chand & Co India). State Mutual Bk.

Gupta, Sushil K. Song of Life. new ed. (Illus.). 1979. 25.00 (ISBN 0-686-77178-8); pap. 15.00 (ISBN 0-685-91450-X). Sverge-Haus.

Gupta, T. C. & Pahwa, K. N. A Century of Soil Salinity Research in India. 400p. 1981. 72.00x (ISBN 0-686-76627-X, Pub. by Oxford & IBH India). State Mutual Bk.

Gupta, Tapas K. Das see Das Gupta, Tapas K.

Gupta, Tarun, tr. see Tagore, Rabindranath.

Gupta, U. S. Physiological Aspects of Dryland Farming. 392p. 1981. 80.00x (ISBN 0-686-76654-7, Pub. by Oxford & IBH India). State Mutual Bk.

Gupta, U. S., ed. Crop Physiology. 431p. 1981. 70.00x (ISBN 0-686-76632-6, Pub. by Oxford & IBH India). State Mutual Bk.

Gupta, V. K. & Gupta, M. L. Ichneumonologia Orientalis, Pt. V: Genus Dusona Cameron (Hym: Ichneumonidae) (Oriental Insects Monographs: No. 8). 1977. 45.00x (ISBN 0-318-01583-8). Oriental Insects.

Gupta, V. K. & Maheshwary, Sharda. Ichneumonolgia Orientalis, Pt. IV: The Tribe Porizontini (Hym: Ichneumonidae) (Oriental Insects Monographs: No. 5). 1977. 45.00x (ISBN 0-318-01582-X). Oriental Insects.

Gupta, V. K. & Tikar, D. T. Ichneumonologia Orientalis, Pt. I: The Tribe Pimplini (Hym: Ichneumonidae) (Oriental Insects Monograph: No. 1). 1976. 45.00x (ISBN 0-318-01579-X). Oriental Insects.

Gupta, V. K., jt. auth. see Bhat, Shama.

Gupta, V. K., jt. auth. see Chandra, Girish.

Gupta, V. K., jt. auth. see Jonathan, J. K.

Gupta, V. K., jt. auth. see Kamath, M. K.

Gupta, V. K., et al, eds. Marine Fish Marketing in India, 6 vols. 3064p. 1984. Set. text ed. 370.50x (ISBN 0-391-03276-3, Pub. by Indian Inst Mgt India). Vol. I (ISBN 0-391-03277-1). Vol. IIa (ISBN 0-391-03278-X). Vol. IIb (ISBN 0-391-03279-8). Vol. III (ISBN 0-391-03280-1). Vol. IV (ISBN 0-391-03281-X). Vol. V & VI (ISBN 0-391-03282-8). Humanities.

Gupta, Vijay. Obote: Second Liberation. v, 196p. 1983. text ed. 25.00x (ISBN 0-7069-2265-4, Pub. by Vikas India). Advent NY.

Gupta, Vinod. Natural Cooling of Buildings. 31p. 1981. pap. 4.75x (ISBN 0-910661-00-6). Innovative Inform.

Gupta, Vinod, ed. Energy & Habitat. 96p. 1984. text ed. 29.95x (ISBN 0-470-20069-3). Halsted Pr.

Gupta, Virendra, jt. auth. see Gupta, Santosh.

Gupta, Virendra K., jt. auth. see Townes, Henry.

Gupta, Yogi. Yoga & Long Life. 5th ed. LC 58-9502. (Illus.). 1983. 14.00 (ISBN 0-911664-01-7). Yogi Gupta.

--Yoga & Yogic Powers. LC 63-14948. (Illus.). 1963. 20.00 (ISBN 0-911664-02-5). Yogi Gupta.

Guptara, Prabhu. Beginnings. 8.00 (ISBN 0-89253-689-6); flexible cloth 4.80 (ISBN 0-89253-690-X). Ind-US Inc.

Gupte, Parag A., et al, eds. Documentation of the Basis for Selection of the Contents of Chapter 3 Vapor Pressure in Manual for Predicting Chemical Process Design Data. 130p. 1984. pap. 90.00 spiral (ISBN 0-8169-0313-1). Am Inst Chem Eng.

Gupte, Pranay. The Crowded Earth: People & the Politics of Population. LC 84-6145. 352p. 1984. 17.95 (ISBN 0-393-01927-6). Norton.

--Vengeance: India after the Assassination of Indira Gandhi. LC 85-7207. 1985. 16.95 (ISBN 0-393-02230-7). Norton.

Gupte, R. S. Iconography of the Hindus, Buddhists & Jains. 2nd ed. (Illus.). xviii, 201p. 1981. text ed. 45.00 (ISBN 0-86590-028-0, Pub. by Taraporevala India). Apt Bks.

Gupte, Sural. Know Your Child. 232p. 1984. text ed. 17.50x (ISBN 0-86590-220-8, Pub. by Sterling Pubs India). Apt Bks.

Guptill, Arthur L. Free Hand Drawing, Self Taught. 144p. 1980. pap. 10.95 (ISBN 0-8230-1920-9). Watson-Guptill.

--Rendering in Pen & Ink. Meyer, Susan E., ed. (Illus.). 1976. 19.95 (ISBN 0-8230-4530-7). Watson-Guptill.

--Rendering in Pencil. Meyer, Susan E., ed. (Illus.). 272p. 1977. 19.95 (ISBN 0-8230-4531-5). Watson-Guptill.

--Watercolor Painting Step-By-Step. rev. & enl. ed. (Illus.). 1967. 19.95 (ISBN 0-8230-5675-9). Watson-Guptill.

Guptill, David. Tuner Techniques. 72p. 1985. write for info. Guptill.

--Tunes & Variations for Bluegrass Banjo. 32p. (Orig.). 1984. pap. 10.95 incl. audio cassette (ISBN 0-916715-00-0). Guptill.

Gupton, James A., Jr. Getting Down to Business with Your Microcomputer. LC 78-68552. (Illus., Orig.). 1979. pap. 9.95 (ISBN 0-933422-00-8, A100). Sourcebooks CA.

Gupton, Oscar W. & Swope, Fred C. Trees & Shrubs of Virginia. LC 80-21585. (Illus.). 205p. 1981. 10.95 (ISBN 0-8139-0886-8). U Pr of Va.

--Wildflowers of the Shenandoah Valley & Blue Ridge Mountains. LC 78-21296. (Illus.). 1979. 10.95 (ISBN 0-8139-0814-0). U Pr of Va.

--Wildflowers of Tidewater Virginia. LC 81-16247. (Illus.). 207p. 1982. 10.95 (ISBN 0-8139-0922-8). U Pr of Va.

Gura, Philip. A Glimpse of Sion's Glory: Puritan Radicalism in New England, 1620-1660. (Illus.). xviii, 399p. 1986. pap. 12.95 (ISBN 0-8195-6154-1). Wesleyan U Pr.

Gura, Philip F. A Glimpse of Sion's Glory. Incl. 1984. 25.95 (ISBN 0-8195-5095-7); Puritan Radicalism in New England,1620-1660. (Illus.). 399p. 1986. pap. 12.95 (ISBN 0-8195-6154-1). 1984. 25.95 (ISBN 0-8195-5095-7). Wesleyan U Pr.

--The Wisdom of Words: Language, Theology & Literature in the New England Renaissance. LC 80-25041. 203p. 1981. 35.00x (ISBN 0-8195-5053-1). Wesleyan U Pr.

--The Wisdom of Words: Language, Theology & Literature in the New England Renaissance. x, 203p. 1985. pap. 10.95 (ISBN 0-8195-6120-7). Wesleyan U Pr.

Gura, Timothy, jt. auth. see Lee, Charlotte I.

Guraedy, Ila. Illustrated Gymnastics Dictionary for Young People. (Illus., Orig.). (gr. 4 up). pap. 2.50 (ISBN 0-13-450932-3). P-H.

Gurainik, David B., ed. Webster's New World Dictionary: Basic School Edition. 1976. 19.96 (ISBN 0-13-944652-4). P-H.

Guralnick. Early Intervention & the Integration of Handicapped & Nonhandicapped Children. LC 77-11946. (Illus.). 320p. 1977. 14.00 (ISBN 0-8391-1165-7). Pro Ed.

Guralnick, jt. auth. see Levitt.

Guralnick, Elissa S., jt. auth. see Levitt, Paul M.

Guralnick, Elissa S., jt. auth. see Levitt, Paula M.

Guralnick, Michael J. Pediatric Education & the Needs of Exceptional Children. LC 79-9167. (Illus.). 240p. 1979. 18.00 (ISBN 0-8391-1500-8). Pro Ed.

Guralnick, Peter. Feel Like Going Home: Portraits in Blues & Rock 'n' Roll. LC 80-6131. 256p. 1981. pap. 4.95 (ISBN 0-394-74706-2, V-706, Vin). Random.

--Listener's Guide to the Blues. 1982. 11.95 (ISBN 0-87196-567-4). Facts on File.

--Lost Highway: Journeys & Arrivals of American Musicans. LC 79-52636. (Illus.). 1979. 18.95 (ISBN 0-87923-293-5); pap. 8.95 (ISBN 0-87923-294-3). Godine.

--Lost Highway: Journeys & Arrivals of American Musicans. LC 81-52867. (Illus.). 384p. 1982. pap. 5.95 (ISBN 0-394-75215-5, Vin). Random.

Guralnick, Stanley M. Science & the Ante-Bellum American College. LC 75-12219. (Memoirs Ser: Vol. 109). 1975. pap. 5.00 (ISBN 0-87169-109-4). Am Philos.

Guralnik, David B., ed. Webster's New World Dictionary of the American Language. 704p. 1982. pap. 9.95 (ISBN 0-446-38240-X); pap. 3.50 (ISBN 0-446-31299-1). Warner Bks.

Guralsky, Jacob, tr. see Tolstoy, Leo.

Guralsky, T., tr. see Martynov, Ivan I.

Guratzsch, Herwig. Dutch & Flemish Painting. 305p. 1981. 39.95 (ISBN 0-86710-003-6). Edns Vilo.

--Dutch Paintings. (Alpine Fine Arts Collection). (Illus.). 304p. 1981. write for info (ISBN 0-933516-09-6, Pub by Alpine Fine Arts). Hippocrene Bks.

Guraya, S. S. Biology of Ovarian Follicles in Mammals. (Illus.). 340p. 1985. 69.50 (ISBN 0-387-15022-6). Springer-Verlag.

Gurbachan Singh Talib. Japuji: The Immortal Prayer-Chant. 1977. 7.00x (ISBN 0-88386-967-5). South Asia Bks.

Gurchot, Charles. Trophoblast Theory of Cancer. 1.50x (ISBN 0-686-29932-9). Cancer Control Soc.

Gurd, Frank R., ed. Chemical Specificity in Biological Interactions. 1954. 41.50 (ISBN 0-12-307950-0). Acad Pr.

Gurd, Patty. The Early Poetry of William Butler Yeats. Repr. of 1916 ed. lib. bdg. 20.00 (ISBN 0-8414-4611-3). Folcroft.

--The Early Poetry of William Butler Yeats. 1979. Repr. of 1916 ed. lib. bdg. 20.00 (ISBN 0-8482-4181-9). Norwood Edns.

Gurda, John. The Quiet Company: A Modern History of Northwestern Mutual Life. (Illus.). 334p. 1983. 14.95 (ISBN 0-9612010-0-2). NW Mutual Life.

Gurdji. Oriental Rug Weaving. facs. ed. 93p. pap. 8.95 (ISBN 0-8466-6002-4, U2). Shorey.

Gurdjian, E. S. Head Injury from Antiquity to the Present with Special Reference to Penetrating Head Wounds. (Illus.). 148p. 1973. 16.75x (ISBN 0-398-02689-0). C C Thomas.

--Impact Head Injury: Mechanistic, Clinical & Preventive Correlations. (Illus.). 388p. 1975. photocopy ed. 43.00x (ISBN 0-398-03301-3). C C Thomas.

Gurdjian, E. S. & Thomas, L. M. Neckache & Backache: Proceedings. (Illus.). 296p. 1970. photocopy ed. 34.50x (ISBN 0-398-00747-0). C C Thomas.

Gurdjian, E. S., et al, eds. Glossary of Neurotraumatology. LC 78-15626. (Acta Neurochirurgica: Supplementum 25). 63p. (Eng., Ger., Fr. & Span.). 1978. pap. 11.70 (ISBN 0-387-81481-7). Springer-Verlag.

Gurdjian, Elisha S., et al. Impact Injury & Crash Protection. (Illus.). 580p. 1970. photocopy ed. 54.75x (ISBN 0-398-00746-2). C C Thomas.

Gurdjieff Foundation of California & Driscoll, J. Walter. Gurdjieff: An Annotated Bibliography. LC 83-49296. (Reference Library of Social Science). 390p. 1984. 50.00 (ISBN 0-8240-8972-3). Garland Pub.

Gurdjieff, G. I. Beelzebub's Tales to His Grandson, 3 vols. in 1. 1973. 39.75 (ISBN 0-525-05222-4, 03883-117); pap. 29.95 (ISBN 0-525-47351-3, 02913-87). Dutton.

--Life Is Real Only Then, When "I Am". 177p. 1981. 17.50 (ISBN 0-525-14547-8, 01699-510). Dutton.

--Meetings with Remarkable Men. Orage, Alfred R., tr. 1969. pap. 6.95 (ISBN 0-525-47242-8, 0674-210). Dutton.

--Views from the Real World: Early Talks, 1918-1934. 1975. pap. 9.95 (ISBN 0-525-47408-0, 0966-290). Dutton.

Gurdon, Charles. Sudan at the Crossroads. 128p. (Orig.). 1984. pap. text ed. 12.50 (ISBN 0-906559-18-9). Lynne Rienner.

Gurdon, J. B. Gene Expression During Cell Differentiation. rev ed. Head, J. J., ed. LC 76-29376. (Carolina Biology Readers Ser.). (Illus.). 32p. (gr. 10 up). 1978. pap. 2.00 (ISBN 0-89278-225-0, 45-9625). Carolina Biological.

Gurdon, Philip R. The Khasis. LC 77-87036. Repr. of 1907 ed. 23.00 (ISBN 0-404-16823-X). AMS Pr.

Gurdus, Luba K. The Death Train. LC 78-54657. (Illus.). 1979. 10.00 (ISBN 0-8052-5005-0, Pub. by Holocaust Library). Schocken.

--The Death Train. LC 78-54657. (Illus.). 165p. (Orig.). 1978. 12.95 (ISBN 0-89604-005-4). Holocaust Pubns.

Gurel, Lois M. & Beeson, Marianne S. Dimensions of Dress & Adornment: A Book of Readings. 3rd ed. LC 74-20103. 1979. pap. text ed. 14.95 (ISBN 0-8403-2038-8). Kendall-Hunt.

Gurel, Lois M., jt. auth. see Horn, Marilyn J.

Gurel, O. Oscillations in Chemical Reactions. (Topics in Current Chemistry: Vol. 118). (Illus.). 130p. 1983. 28.00 (ISBN 0-387-12575-2). Springer-Verlag.

Gurel, Okan, ed. Bifurcation Theory & Applications in Scientific Disciplines, Vol. 316. Rossler, Otto E. (Annals of the New York Academy of Sciences). 708p. (Orig.). 1979. pap. 87.00x (ISBN 0-89766-000-5). NY Acad Sci.

Guren, Pamela, et al. Life & Times in Shoe City: The Shoe Workers of Lynn. Farnam, Anne, ed. (Illus.). 1979. pap. 4.00 (ISBN 0-88389-100-X). Essex Inst.

Guren, Peter. Ask Shagg. 72p. (Orig.). 1985. pap. 4.95 (ISBN 0-345-32632-6). World Almanac.

Gurevich, A. Nonlinear Phenomena in the Ionosphere. (Physics & Chemistry in Space Ser.: Vol. 10). (Illus.). 1978. 65.00 (ISBN 0-387-08605-6). Springer-Verlag.

Gurevich, A., tr. see Gorshkov, G. & Yakushova, A.

Gurevich, A. J. Categories of Medieval Culture. 224p. 1985. 39.95x (ISBN 0-7100-9578-3). Routledge & Kegan.

Gurevich, A. V. & Tsedilina, E. E. Long Distance Propagation of HF Radio Waves. (Physics & Chemistry in Space: Vol. 12). (Illus.). 350p. 1985. 79.00 (ISBN 0-387-15139-7). Springer-Verlag.

Gurevich, B. L., jt. auth. see Shilov, G. E.

Gurevich, David A., tr. see Schneersohn, Y. Y.

Gurevich, Ilya. The Fountains of Petrodvorets Near Leningrad. 124p. 1980. 60.00x (ISBN 0-686-97671-1, Pub. by Collet's). State Mutual Bk.

Gurevich, Inge, et al. The Theory & Practice of Infection Control. 444p. 1984. 39.95 (ISBN 0-03-063626-4). Praeger.

Gurevich, K. G., tr. see Klimentov, P.

Gurevich, Yu. Y., ed. Photoelectrochemistry. LC 78-21541. (Illus.). 255p. 1979. 49.50x (ISBN 0-306-10953-0, Consultants). Plenum Pub.

Gurevitch, Michael, jt. auth. see Katz, Elihu.

Gurevitch, Michael, et al, eds. Culture, Society & the Media. (Illus.). 1982. pap. 13.95x (ISBN 0-416-73510-X, NO. 3585). Methuen Inc.

Gurewitch, Morton. Comedy: The Irrational Vision. LC 74-15186. 245p. 1975. 22.50x (ISBN 0-8014-0843-1). Cornell U Pr.

Gurewitsch, Bonnie. Bibiliography. 2nd ed. LC 81-139241. 30p. 1985. pap. write for info. (ISBN 0-9609970-2-4). Ctr for Holo.

Gurewitsch, Brana, jt. auth. see Eliach, Yaffa.

Gureyev, P. P. & Sedugin, P. I. Legislation in the U. S. S. R. 269p. 1977. 3.95 (ISBN 0-8285-0338-9, Pub. by Progress Pubs USSR). Imported Pubns.

Gurfinkel, German. Wood Engineering. 560p. text ed. 18.95 (ISBN 0-8403-2476-6). Kendall-Hunt.

Gurganus, Allan. Breathing Lessons. 16p. (Orig.). 1981. pap. 1.50x (ISBN 0-933598-01-7); pap. 4.00 signed & numbered (ISBN 0-686-32882-5). N C Wesleyan Friends Lib.

Gurganus, Gene. The Great Omission: Fruit That Remains. (Illus.). 104p. 1983. pap. 3.50 (ISBN 0-89084-191-8). Bob Jones Univ Pr.

Gurganus, George P., ed. Guidelines for World Evangelism. 1977. 11.95 (ISBN 0-89112-040-8). Bibl Res Pr.

Gurian, Anita, jt. auth. see Formanek, Ruth.

Gurian, Jay. American Studies Singing. 18p. 1979. pap. 2.00 (ISBN 0-934996-04-0). Am Stud Pr.

--Western American Writing: Tradition & Promise. LC 74-82195. 1975. lib. bdg. 12.00 (ISBN 0-912112-04-2). Everett-Edwards.

Gurian, Jay P. & Gurian, Julia M. The Dependency Tendency: Returning to Each Other in Modern America. LC 82-17569. 176p. 1983. lib. bdg. 21.75 (ISBN 0-8191-2781-7); pap. text ed. 9.75 (ISBN 0-8191-2782-5). U Pr of Amer.

Gurian, Julia M., jt. auth. see Gurian, Jay P.

Gurian, Waldemar. Bolshevism: An Introduction to Soviet Communism. 1963. pap. 3.95x (ISBN 0-268-00367-X). U of Notre Dame Pr.

--Bolshevism: Theory & Practice. Watkin, E. I., tr. LC 70-104052. Repr. of 1932 ed. 28.50 (ISBN 0-404-02963-9). AMS Pr.

--Bolshevism: Theory & Practice. 402p. 1981. Repr. of 1934 ed. lib. bdg. 30.00 (ISBN 0-89760-316-8). Telegraph Bks.

--Hitler & the Christians. Peeler, E. F., tr. LC 78-63675. (Studies in Fascism: Ideology & Practice). 184p. Repr. of 1936 ed. 22.00 (ISBN 0-404-16937-6). AMS Pr.

Gurian, Waldemar, ed. Soviet Imperialism. LC 75-1099. (International Studies of the Comm. on International Relations, U. of Notre Dame). 166p. 1975. Repr. of 1953 ed. lib. bdg. 22.50x (ISBN 0-8371-7993-9, GUSI). Greenwood.

Gurin, Arnold, jt. auth. see Perlman, Robert.

Gurin, Gerald. National Attitude Study of Trainees in MDTA Institutional Programs. 258p. 1970. pap. 5.50x (ISBN 0-87944-086-4). Inst Soc Res.

Gurin, Gerald, et al. Americans View Their Mental Health. Grob, Gerald N., ed. LC 78-22564. (Historical Issues in Mental Health Ser.). (Illus.). 1979. Repr. of 1960 ed. lib. bdg. 34.50x (ISBN 0-405-11918-6). Ayer Co Pubs.

Gurin, Joel, jt. auth. see Bennett, William.

Gurin, Maurice. What Volunteers Should Know for Successful Fundraising. 151p. 1981. 10.50 (ISBN 0-318-17150-3, C64). Natl Ctr Cit Involv.

Gurin, Maurice G. Confessions of a Fund Raiser: Lessons of an Instructive Career. LC 84-26914. 175p. 1985. 23.95 (ISBN 0-914756-14-1). Taft Group.

--What Volunteers Should Know about Successful Fund Raising. 1981. pap. 14.95 (ISBN 0-686-31967-2). Public Serv Materials.

--What Volunteers Should Know for Successful Fund Raising. LC 81-48508. (Illus.). 144p. 1982. pap. 7.95 (ISBN 0-8128-6150-7). Stein & Day.

--What Volunteers Should Know for Successful Fund Raising. LC 80-51637. (Illus.). 144p. 1980. 10.00 (ISBN 0-8128-2739-2). Stein & Day.

Gurin, Patricia & Epps, Edgar. Black Consciousness, Identity, & Achievement: A Study of Students in Historical Black Colleges. LC 75-5847. pap. 139.80 (ISBN 0-317-09789-X, 2019891). Bks Demand UMI.

Gurin, Phillip. The James Bond Trivia Quiz Book: From Odd Job to Money Penny... Everything You Always Wanted to Know about Agent 007. 1984. pap. 4.95 (ISBN 0-87795-580-8); (10-copy prepack) 49.50 (ISBN 0-87795-615-4). Arbor Hse.

Gurkan, Ihsan. NATO, Turkey, & the Southern Flank: A Mideastern Perspective. 67p. 1980. pap. text ed. 3.95x (ISBN 0-87855-825-X). Transaction Bks.

Gurkaynak, M. R. & LeCompte, W. A., eds. Human Consequences of Crowding. LC 79-19152. (NATO Conference Ser. III, Human Factors: Vol. 10). 340p. 1979. 39.50x (ISBN 0-306-40298-X, Plenum Pr). Plenum Pub.

Gurkin, Kathryn B. Terra Amata. Bayes, Ronald H., ed. (Illus.). 1979. pap. 5.00 (ISBN 0-932662-31-5). St Andrews NC.

Gurko, Leo. Heroes, Highbrows & the Popular Mind. facs. ed. LC 73-134089. (Essay Index Reprint Ser.). 1953. 20.00 (ISBN 0-8369-2160-7). Ayer Co Pubs.

--Joseph Conrad: Giant in Exile. 1979. 14.95 (ISBN 0-02-546700-X). Macmillan.

--Thomas Wolfe: Beyond the Romantic Ego. LC 74-34204. (Twentieth Century American Writers Ser.). 153p. (gr. 6 up). 1975. 11.49i (ISBN 0-690-00751-5). Crowell Jr Bks.

Gurko, Miriam. The Ladies of Seneca Falls: The Birth of the Woman's Rights Movement. LC 76-9144. (Studies in the Life of Women). (Illus.). 1976. pap. 8.95 (ISBN 0-8052-0545-4). Schocken.

Gurland, Barry J., et al. Structured & Scaled Interview to Assess Maladjustment (SSIAM) 32p. 1973. 10 SSIAM for 24.00x (ISBN 0-8261-1420-2); special offer 3 samples 7.50x (ISBN 0-8261-1421-0). Springer Pub.

--The Mind & Mood of Aging: Mental Health Problems of the Community Elderly in New York & London. LC 83-294. 192p. 1983. text ed. 32.95 (ISBN 0-917724-28-3, B28). Haworth Pr.

Gurland, Barry J., jt. ed. see Bennett, Ruth.

Gurland, H. J. & Lysaght, M. J., eds. Plasma Separation & Plasma Fractionation. (Illus.). viii, 332p. 1982. 57.25 (ISBN 3-8055-3822-7). S Karger.

Gurland, John. Stochastic Models in Medicine & Biology: Proceedings of a Symposium Conducted by the Mathematics Research Center, 1963. LC 64-14509. (U. S. Army Mathematics Research Center Ser.: No. 10). pap. 102.50 (ISBN 0-317-12991-0, 2021134). Bks Demand UMI.

Gurley. Flexible Circuit Application & Design Guide. (Electrical Engineering & Electronics Ser.). 136p. 1984. 39.75 (ISBN 0-8247-7215-6). Dekker.

Gurley, George H., Jr. Fugues in the Plumbing. LC 80-71009. 1980. 4.50 (ISBN 0-933532-05-9). BKMK.

Gurley, John G. Challengers to Capitalism, Marx, Lenin, Stalin & Mao. rev. ed. (Illus.). 224p. 1980. 12.95 (ISBN 0-393-01224-7); pap. 5.95x (ISBN 0-393-95005-0). Norton.

--China's Economy & the Maoist Strategy. LC 76-26314. 325p. 1976. 15.00 (ISBN 0-85345-395-0). Monthly Rev.

--China's Economy & the Maoist Strategy. LC 76-26314. 1978. pap. 5.95 (ISBN 0-85345-431-0). Monthly Rev.

Gurley, John G. & Shaw, Edward S. Money in a Theory of Finance. 1960. 26.95 (ISBN 0-8157-3322-4). Brookings.

Gurley, LaVerne T. & Callaway, William J. Introduction to Radiologic Technology. LC 81-82005. (Illus.). 300p. (Orig.). 1982. pap. 16.95x (ISBN 0-940122-02-2). Multi Media CO.

Gurley, Ralph R. Life of Jehudi Ashmun. facs. ed. LC 73-149867. (Black Heritage Library Collection Ser). 1835. 22.50 (ISBN 0-8369-8749-7). Ayer Co Pubs.

--Life of Jehudi Ashmun, Late Colonial Agent in Liberia. LC 76-75532. Repr. of 1835 ed. 21.00x (ISBN 0-8371-1101-3, GUJ&, Pub. by Negro U Pr). Greenwood.

Gurlik, Philip, Jr. The Piano: A Piano Technicians Guide for the Piano Owner. 40p. (Orig.). 1985. pap. 2.95 (ISBN 0-918464-66-8). Bookman Hse.

Gurlitt, C. Easiest Velocity Studies for Beginners: Piano Op. 83. (Carl Fischer Music Library: No. 547). (Illus.). 1908. pap. 1.00 (ISBN 0-8258-0140-0). Fischer Inc NY.

Gurlitt, W. & Eggebrecht, H. Riemann Musiklexikon. 108p. (Ger.). 1967. 135.00 (ISBN 3-7957-0031-0, M-7602, Pub. by Schatt's Soehne). French & Eur.

Gurlitt, Wilibald. Johann Sebastian Bach: The Master & His Work. Rupprecht, O. C., tr. from Ger. (Music Reprint Ser.). 150p. 1985. Repr. of 1957 ed. 19.95 (ISBN 0-306-76262-5). Da Capo.

Gurlitt, Wilibald see Buxtehude, Dietrich.

Gurly, John G. Challenges to Communism. (Illus.). 184p. 1983. text ed. 23.95 (ISBN 0-7167-1506-6); pap. text ed. 12.95 (ISBN 0-7167-1507-4). W H Freeman.

Gurman, Alan S. & Kniskern, David P. Handbook of Family Therapy. LC 80-20357. 800p. 1981. 45.00 (ISBN 0-87630-242-8). Brunner Mazel.

Gurman, Alan S. & Razin, Andrew M. Effective Psychotherapy: A Handbook of Research. LC 76-23300. 1977. 42.00 (ISBN 0-08-019508-3). Pergamon.

Gurman, Alan S., ed. Casebook of Marital Therapy. 340p. 1985. text ed. write for info. (ISBN 0-89862-062-7). Guilford Pr.

--Questions & Answers in the Practice of Family Therapy, Vol. 1. LC 80-22460. 544p. 1981. 30.00 (ISBN 0-87630-246-0). Brunner-Mazel.

--Questions & Answers in the Practice of Family Therapy, Vol. 2. LC 80-22460. 320p. 1982. 30.00 (ISBN 0-87630-308-4). Brunner-Mazel.

Gurman, Richard, jt. auth. see Lucas, John T.

Gurnall, William. The Christian in Complete Armour. 1979. 25.95 (ISBN 0-85151-196-1). Banner of Truth.

Gurney, A. R. Children. 1977. pap. 3.35x (ISBN 0-685-81642-7). Dramatists Play.

--Four Plays. 208p. 1985. pap. 4.95 (ISBN 0-380-89498-X, Bard). Avon.

--The Snow Ball. LC 84-10971. 1984. 15.95 (ISBN 0-87795-621-9, Pub. by Belvedere Bks). Arbor Hse.

--The Wayside Motor Inn. 1978. pap. 3.35x (ISBN 0-685-08727-1). Dramatists Play.

Gurney, A. R., Jr. Entertaining Strangers. 1979. pap. 1.95 (ISBN 0-380-44313-9, 44313). Avon.

Gurney, Clare & Gurney, Gene. Unidentified Flying Objects. LC 75-105262. (Illus.). (gr. 5-10). 1970. 10.53i (ISBN 0-200-71677-8, B86600, AbS-J). Har-Row.

Gurney, Davis. The Demonists. rev. ed. 1977. pap. 1.95 (ISBN 0-532-19146-3). Woodhill.

Gurney, Edmund. Phantasms of the Living, 2 Vols. LC 71-119868. (Hist. of Psych. Ser.). 1970. Repr. of 1886 ed. Set. 130.00x set (ISBN 0-8201-1075-2). Schol Facsimiles.

Gurney, Eric. Eric Gurney's Pop-Up Book of Dogs. (Pop-Up Bks.: No. 26). (ps up). 1973. 5.95 (ISBN 0-394-82634-5). Random.

--Gurney's Gallery of Dogs... & Doggie Dictionary. LC 83-17081. (Illus.). 124p. 1983. pap. 4.95 (ISBN 0-88007-138-9). Woodbridge Pr.

--How to Live with a Calculating Cat. 1981. pap. 2.50 (ISBN 0-671-44140-X). PB.

--How to Live with a Headstrong Horse. (Illus.). 192p. 1982. 6.95 (ISBN 0-13-415406-1). P-H.

--Schnoodle & Sam. (Illus.). 104p. 1981. pap. 2.95 (ISBN 0-13-792036-9). P-H.

Gurney, Eric, jt. auth. see Armour, Richard.

Gurney, Eric, jt. auth. see Gurney, Nancy.

Gurney, G. Jeep Book. 1986. cancelled (ISBN 0-442-21912-1). Van Nos Reinhold.

Gurney, Gene. Five Down & Glory. (War Library). 288p. 1983. pap. 2.95 (ISBN 0-345-30799-2). Ballantine.

--Flying Aces of World War One. (gr. 5-9). 1965. (BYR); (BYR). Random.

--Kingdoms of Europe: An Illustrated Encyclopedia of Ruling Monarchs from Ancient Times to the Present. (Illus.). 640p. 1982. 20.00 (ISBN 0-517-54395-8). Crown.

--P-38 Lightning. LC 70-76218. (Famous Aircraft Ser). (Illus., Orig.). 1969. pap. 4.95 (ISBN 0-668-02015-6). Arco.

--A Pictorial History of the United States Army. rev. ed. (Illus.). 1978. 25.00 (ISBN 0-517-53316-2). Crown.

--Vietnam: The War in the Air: A Pictorial History of the U. S. Air Forces in the Vietnam War: Air Force, Army, Navy, & the Marines. LC 84-11327. (Illus.). 277p. 1985. text ed. 17.95 (ISBN 0-517-55350-3). Crown.

Gurney, Gene & Friedlander, Mark P. Higher, Faster & Farther. LC 73-9377. 1973. 7.95 (ISBN 0-688-00204-8). Aero.

Gurney, Gene & Friedlander, Mark P., Jr. Five Down & Glory: A History of the American Air Ace. LC 75-169419. (Literature & History of Aviation Ser.). 1972. Repr. of 1958 ed. 21.00 (ISBN 0-405-03764-3). Ayer Co Pubs.

Gurney, Gene, jt. auth. see Friedlander, Mark, Jr.

Gurney, Gene, jt. auth. see Gurney, Clare.

Gurney, Gene, jt. auth. see Willinger, Kurt.

Gurney, Gene & Gilbert, James, eds. Test Pilots. LC 79-7265. (Flight: Its First Seventy-Five Years Ser.). (Illus.). 1979. Repr. of 1962 ed. lib. bdg. 25.50x (ISBN 0-405-12175-X). Ayer Co Pubs.

Gurney, George. Sculpture & the Federal Triangle. (Illus.). 380p. 1985. text ed. 35.00 (ISBN 0-87474-492-X, GUSF). Smithsonian.

Gurney, Gerald. Tennis, Squash & Badminton Bygones. (Shire Album Ser.: No. 121). (Illus.). 32p. (Orig.). 1984. pap. 2.95 (ISBN 0-85263-676-8, Pub. by Shire Pubns England). Seven Hills Bks.

Gurney, Ivor. Collected Poems of Ivor Gurney. Kavanagh, P. J., ed. 1982. 24.95x (ISBN 0-19-200940-0). Oxford U Pr.

--The War Letters. Thornton, R. K., ed. 224p. 1982. text ed. 23.50x (ISBN 0-85635-408-2, 80753, Pub. by Carcanet Pr England). Humanities.

--War Letters. Thornton, R. K. R., ed. 272p. 1984. pap. 7.95 (ISBN 0-7012-0567-9, Pub. by Hogarth Pr). Merrimack Pub Cir.

Gurney, Jackie. National Trust Book of Picnics. LC 80-69355. (Illus.). 96p. 1982. 9.95 (ISBN 0-7153-8099-0). David & Charles.

Gurney, James & Kinkade, Thomas. The Artist's Guide to Sketching: A Handbook for Drawing on the Spot. (Illus.). 160p. 1982. 19.95 (ISBN 0-8230-0332-9). Watson-Guptill.

Gurney, Joseph J. Journey in North America. LC 71-159795. (The American Scene Ser.). 422p. 1973. Repr. of 1841 ed. lib. bdg. 49.50 (ISBN 0-306-70572-9). Da Capo.

--A Peculiar People: The Rediscovery of Primitive Christianity. LC 79-50100. 1979. pap. 11.95 (ISBN 0-913408-48-4). Friends United.

--Winter in the West Indies, Described in Familiar Letters to Henry Clay, of Kentucky. 2nd ed. LC 69-19356. (Illus.). Repr. of 1840 ed. 19.75x (ISBN 0-8371-1022-X, GUW&). Greenwood.

Gurney, Nancy & Gurney, Eric. King, the Mice & the Cheese. LC 65-21212. (Illus.). (gr. k-3). 1965. PLB 5.99 (ISBN 0-394-90039-1). Beginner.

Gurney, Oliver R. & Kramer, Samuel N., eds. Sumerian Literary Texts in the Ashmolean Museum. (Oxford Editions of Cuneiform Texts). (Illus.). 1976. pap. 45.00x (ISBN 0-19-815450-X). Oxford U Pr.

Gurney, R. Bibliography of the Larvae of Dacapod Crustaces & Larvae of Decapod Crustacea, 2 vols. in 1. 1960. 26.60 (ISBN 3-7682-0029-9). Lubrecht & Cramer.

Gurney, T. R. Fatigue of Welded Structures. 2nd ed. LC 78-21885. (British Welding Research Association Ser.). (Illus.). 1980. 79.50 (ISBN 0-521-22558-2). Cambridge U Pr.

Gurney, W. S., jt. auth. see Nisbet, R. M.

Gurney-Salter, Emma. Tudor England Through Venetian Eyes. 1977. lib. bdg. 59.95 (ISBN 0-8490-2778-0). Gordon Pr.

Gurock, Jeffrey. When Harlem Was Jewish, Eighteen Seventy to Nineteen Thirty. 216p. 1979. 26.00x (ISBN 0-231-04666-9). Columbia U Pr.

Gurock, Jeffrey S. American Jewish History: A Bibliograhical Guide. 1983. 6.95 (ISBN 0-88464-037-X). ADL.

Guroff. Molecular Neurobiology. LC 79-22812. 1980. 79.50 (ISBN 0-8247-6862-0). Dekker.

--Oncogenes & Growth Factors. 1986. price not set (ISBN 0-471-82595-6). Wiley.

Guroff, G. Growth & Maturation Factors, Vol. 1. (Growth & Maturation FActors Ser.). 1075p. 1983. 62.95 (ISBN 0-471-09709-8, Pub. by Wiley-Interscience). Wiley.

--Growth & Maturation Factors, Vol. 3. 344p. 1985. 74.50 (ISBN 0-471-09707-1). Wiley.

Guroff, Gordon, ed. Growth & Maturation Factors, Vol. 2. LC 82-17598. (Growth & Maturation Factors Ser.: 1-503). 340p. 1984. 69.50 (ISBN 0-471-09708-X, Pub. by Wiley-Interscience). Wiley.

Guroff, Gregory, ed. Entrepreneurship in Imperial Russia & the Soviet Union. Carstensen, Fred V. LC 82-15056. 384p. 1983. 42.50 (ISBN 0-691-05376-6); pap. 13.95 LPE (ISBN 0-691-10141-8). Princeton U Pr.

Guroff, Katherine S. Quality in Liberal Learning: Curricular Innovations in Higher Education. 272p. (Orig.). 1981. pap. 6.00 (ISBN 0-911696-09-1). Assn Am Coll.

Gurowski, Adam. Diary from March 4, 1861 Through April 15, 1865, 3 vols. in 2. (Research & Source Works Ser.). 1968. Repr. of 1862 ed. 49.00 (ISBN 0-8337-1496-1). B Franklin.

Gurowski, Adam De. America & Europe. LC 72-6042. (Select Bibliographies Reprint Ser.). 1972. Repr. of 1857 ed. 29.00 (ISBN 0-8369-6912-X). Ayer Co Pubs.

Gurpide, E. Tracer Methods in Hormone Research. (Monographs on Endocrinology: Vol. 8). (Illus.). xi, 188p. 1975. 45.00 (ISBN 0-387-07039-7). Springer-Verlag.

Gurpide, Erlio, ed. Biochemical Actions of Progesterone & Progestins, Vol. 286. (Annuals of the New York Academy of Sciences.). 449p. 1977. 43.00x (ISBN 0-89072-032-0). NY Acad Sci.

Gurr, Andrew. Hamlet & the Distracted Globe. (Text & Context). 1978. text ed. 9.75x (ISBN 0-85621-069-2). Humanities.

--The Shakespearean Stage, 1574-1642. 2nd ed. LC 80-40085. (Illus.). 220p. 1981. 54.50 (ISBN 0-521-23029-2); pap. 14.95 (ISBN 0-521-29772-9). Cambridge U Pr.

--Writers in Exile. (Harvester Studies in Contemporary Literature & Culture: No. 4). 160p. 1981. text ed. 25.50x (ISBN 0-391-02310-1, Pub. by Harvester England). Humanities.

Gurr, Andrew & Hanson, Clare. Katherine Mansfield. 160p. 1981. 18.95 (ISBN 0-312-45093-1). St Martin.

Gurr, Andrew, ed. King Richard II. (Illus.). 240p. 1984. 29.95 (ISBN 0-521-23010-1); pap. 6.95 (ISBN 0-521-29765-6). Cambridge U Pr.

Gurr, Andrew, ed. see Beaumont, Francis & Fletcher, John.

Gurr, Andrew J., ed. see Beaumont, Francis.

Gurr, Charles S., jt. ed. see Coleman, Kenneth.

Gurr, John E. Principle of Sufficient Reason in Some Scholastic Systems, 1750-1900. 1959. 12.95 (ISBN 0-87462-411-8). Marquette.

Gurr, M. I. & James, A. T. Lipid Biochemistry: An Introduction. 3rd ed. 1980. 18.95x (ISBN 0-412-22620-0, NO. 6335, Pub. by Chapman & Hall). Methuen Inc.

Gurr, M. I., ed. Role of Fats in Food & Nutrition. 176p. 1984. 36.00 (ISBN 0-85334-298-9, Pub. by Elsevier Applied Sci England). Elsevier.

Gurr, Robert H. Automobile Design, the Complete Styling Book. (Illus.). 1955. pap. 10.00 (ISBN 0-911160-55-8). Post-Era.

Gurr, Robin. Song Is a Mirror. 10.00 (ISBN 0-392-04683-0, ABC). Sportshelf.

Gurr, Ted R. Rogues, Rebels, & Reformers. LC 76-17370. pap. 25.50 (ISBN 0-317-09470-X, 2021909). Bks Demand UMI.

--Why Men Rebel. LC 74-84865. (Center of International Studies). 1970. 40.00x (ISBN 0-691-07528-X); pap. 11.95x (ISBN 0-691-02167-8). Princeton U Pr.

Gurr, Ted R., jt. auth. see Eckstein, Harry.

Gurr, Ted R., ed. Handbook of Political Conflict: Theory & Research. LC 79-6145. (Free Press Ser. on Political Behavior). (Illus.). 1980. 45.00 (ISBN 0-02-912760-2). Free Pr.

Gurr, Ted R., jt. ed. see Graham, Hugh D.

Gurr, Ted R., et al. Comparative Studies of Political Conflict & Change: Cross National Datasets. LC 78-59713. 1978. codebook write for info. (ISBN 0-89138-996-2); microfiche avail. (ISBN 0-89138-997-0). ICPSR.

--The Politics of Crime & Conflict: A Comparative History of Four Cities. LC 76-45429. 792p. 1977. 45.00 (ISBN 0-8039-0677-3). Sage.

--The Politics of Crime & Conflict: A Comparative History of Four Cities. LC 76-45429. pap. 160.00 (ISBN 0-317-29676-0, 2021910). Bks Demand UMI.

Gurren, Louise. Living Method Course in Better Speech. (YA) (gr. 9-12). 15.95, with 4 LP records & manual (ISBN 0-517-00137-3). Crown.

Gurrie, Michael & O'Connor, Patrick. Voice-Data Telecommunications Systems: An Introduction to Technology. (Illus.). 416p. 1986. text ed. 34.95 (ISBN 0-13-943283-3). P-H.

Gurry, Francis. Breach of Confidence. LC 83-23809. 1984. 59.00x (ISBN 0-19-825378-8). Oxford U Pr.

Gursan-Salzmann, Ayse & Salzmann, Laurence. Last Jews of Radauti. LC 82-22176. (Illus.). 192p. 1983. 29.95 (ISBN 0-385-27808-X, Dial). Doubleday.

Gursey, F., ed. see Istanbul Summer School Of Theoretical Physics - 1962.

Gurskaya, Galina Viktorovna. The Molecular Structure of Amino Acids: Determination by X-ray Diffraction Analysis. LC 68-18821. (Illus.). pap. 32.00 (ISBN 0-317-09387-8, 2020678). Bks Demand UMI.

Gursky, H. & Ruffini, R., eds. Neutron Stars, Black Holes & Binary X-Ray Sources. LC 75-15716. (Astrophysics & Space Science Library: No. 48). 441p. (Orig.). 1975. lib. bdg. 71.00 (ISBN 90-277-0541-0, Pub. by Reidel Holland); pap. 34.00 (ISBN 90-277-0542-9). Kluwer Academic.

Gursky, H., jt. ed. see Giacconi, R.

Gurteen, S. Humphreys. Arthurian Epic. LC 65-26457. (Arthurian Legend & Literature Ser., No. 1). 1969. Repr. of 1895 ed. lib. bdg. 49.95x (ISBN 0-8383-0562-8). Haskell.

--Epic of the Fall of Man. LC 65-15879. (Studies in Comparative Literature, No. 35). 1969. Repr. of 1896 ed. lib. bdg. 49.95x (ISBN 0-8383-0561-X). Haskell.

Gurthrie, Gary D. The Wisdom Tree. (Illus., Orig.). 1984. pap. 6.95 (ISBN 0-942494-87-3). Coleman Pub.

Gurti & Nash. Philanthropy in the Shaping of American Higher Education. LC 65-19399. 8.50 (ISBN 0-910294-27-5). Brown Bk.

Gurtin, M. E. On the Thermodynamics of Elastic Materials & of Reacting Fluid Mixtures. (CISM - International Centre for Mechanical Sciences, Courses & Lectures: Vol. 75). (Illus.). 47p. 1975. pap. 7.10 (ISBN 0-387-81178-8). Springer-Verlag.

--Topics in Finite Elasticity. LC 80-53711. (CBMS-NSF Regional Conference Ser.: No. 35). v, 58p. 1981. pap. text ed. 10.50 (ISBN 0-89871-168-1). Soc Indus-Appl Math.

Gurtin, Morton E. An Introduction to Continuum Mechanics. LC 80-2335. (Mathematics in Science & Engineering Ser.). 1981. 44.00 (ISBN 0-12-309750-9). Acad Pr.

Gurtin, Morton E., ed. Phase Transformations & Material Instabilities in Solids. (Mathematics Research Center Symposium Ser.). 1985. 17.00 (ISBN 0-12-309770-3). Acad Pr.

Gurtler, Mary. Let's Look at Thailand. 1983. pap. 1.50 (ISBN 9971-83-825-7). OMF Bks.

Gurtov, Melvin. China & Southeast Asia-The Politics of Survival: A Study of Foreign Policy Interaction. LC 74-24792. 256p. 1975. pap. 6.95x (ISBN 0-8018-1683-1). Johns Hopkins.

--The First Vietnam Crisis. LC 84-27928. xxiv, 228p. 1985. Repr. of 1967 ed. lib. bdg. 35.00x (ISBN 0-313-24736-6, GUFV). Greenwood.

--Making Changes: The Politics of Self Liberation. LC 79-88747. (Orig.). 1979. pap. 4.95 (ISBN 0-9602886-0-0). Harvest Moon.

--Southeast Asia Tomorrow: Problems & Prospects for U.S. Policy. LC 79-101457. 124p. 1970. 12.00x (ISBN 0-8018-1121-X); pap. 3.95x (ISBN 0-8018-1120-1). Johns Hopkins.

Gurtov, Melvin & Hwang, Byong-Moo. China under Threat: The Politics of Strategy & Diplomacy. LC 80-7990. 352p. 1981. text ed. 32.00x (ISBN 0-8018-2397-8). Johns Hopkins.

Gurtov, Melvin & Maghroori, Ray. Roots of Failure: United States Policy in the Third World. LC 84-10718. (Contributions in Political Science Ser.: No. 108). (Illus.). ix, 224p. 1984. lib. bdg. 27.95 (ISBN 0-313-24561-4, GUR/). Greenwood.

Guru, R. H. Teachings of Agni Yoga: Talk Does Not Cook the Rice. LC 81-70390. (Vol. 2). 224p. (Orig.). 1985. pap. 8.95 (ISBN 0-87728-535-7). Weiser.

Guru, R. H. H. The Teachings of Agni Yoga: Talk Does Not Cook the Rice. LC 81-70390. (Vol. 1). 416p. 1982. pap. 7.95 (ISBN 0-87728-530-6). Weiser.

Gurudas. Flower Essences. 314p. (Orig.). 1983. pap. cancelled (ISBN 0-914732-09-9). Bro Life Inc.

--Flower Essences & Vibrational Healing. 2nd ed. 314p. 1985. pap. 12.95 (ISBN 0-914732-09-9). Bro Life Inc.

Guruge, A. SNA: Theory & Practice. (Illus.). 200p. 1984. 53.95 (ISBN 0-08-028583-X). Pergamon.

Gurung, Deu B., et al. Gurung-Nepali-English Glossary. 223p. (Nepalese & Eng.). 1976. pap. 3.00xop (ISBN 0-88312-854-3); microfiche (3) 3.80 (ISBN 0-88312-391-6). Summer Inst Ling.

Gurung, K. K. Heart of the Jungle. (Illus.). 197p. 1984. 19.95 (ISBN 0-233-97595-0). Andre Deutsch.

--Heart of the Jungle. (Illus.). 197p. 1984. 19.95 (ISBN 0-233-97595-0, Pub. by A Deutsch England). David & Charles.

Gurung, Sant B. Economy, Ecology, & Migration in the Far Western Development Region, Nepal. (Working Papers Ser.: No. 78-12). 29p. 1978. pap. 6.00 (ISBN 0-686-78476-6, CRD100, UNCRD). Unipub.

Guruswami, M. N., jt. auth. see Iswaran, V.

Gurvich, Georgy D. & Moore, Wilbert E., eds. Twentieth Century Sociology. facs. ed. LC 78-134090. (Essay Index Reprint Ser). 1945. 38.50 (ISBN 0-8369-2110-0). Ayer Co Pubs.

Gurvich, L. V., ed. Thermodynamic Properties of Individual Substances, 2 vols, Pt. I. 3rd, rev. & enl. ed. (Illus.). 830p. 1986. Set. 150.00 (ISBN 0-08-027585-0). Pergamon.

Gurvitch, G. The Spectrum of Social Time. Korenbaum, Myrtle, ed. Bosserman, Phillip, tr. from Fr. (Synthese Library). 152p. 1964. lib. bdg. 21.00 (ISBN 90-277-0006-0, Pub. by Reidel Holland). Kluwer Academic.

Gurwitch, A. A., ed. see Panassie, Hugues & Gautier, Madeleine.

Gurwitsch, Aron. Das Bewusstseinsfeld. Froehlich, Werner D., tr. from Fr. LC 74-81087. (Phaenomenologisch-Psychologische Forschungen, Vol. 1). 1974. 55.60x (ISBN 3-11-002334-2). De Gruyter.

--Field of Consciousness. LC 63-13565. (Psychological Ser.: No. 2). 1976. pap. text ed. 15.00x (ISBN 0-8207-0043-6). Duquesne.

--Leibniz: Philosophie des Panlogismus. LC 73-88298. (Ger.). 1974. 55.60x (ISBN 3-11-004358-0). De Gruyter.

--Marginal Consciousness. Embree, Lester, ed. LC 84-11877. (Series in Continental Thought: Vol. 7). xlvi, 126p. 1985. text ed. 24.95x (ISBN 0-8214-0789-9). Ohio U Pr.

--Phenomenology & the Theory of Science. Embree, Lester, ed. LC 73-91997. (Studies in Phenomenology & Existential Philosophy). 1974. text ed. 21.95x (ISBN 0-8101-0559-4); pap. 8.95x (ISBN 0-8101-0544-6). Northwestern U Pr.

--Studies in Phenomenology & Psychology. (Studies in Phenomenology & Existential Philosophy Ser). 1966. 25.95 (ISBN 0-8101-0110-6); pap. 11.95 (ISBN 0-8101-0592-6). Northwestern U Pr.

Gurwitz, Aaron S., ed. The Economics of Public School Finance. (Rand Education Policy Ser.). 240p. 1982. prof ref 25.00 (ISBN 0-88410-859-7). Ballinger Pub.

Gurzadyan, G. A. Planetary Nebulae. 328p. 1969. 80.95 (ISBN 0-677-20220-2). Gordon.

--Planetary Nebulae. Hummer, D. G., ed. & tr. LC 69-11664. 314p. 1971. lib. bdg. 45.00 (ISBN 90-277-0117-2, Pub. by Reidel Holland). Kluwer Academic.

Guschlbauer, W. Nucleic Acid Structure: An Introduction. LC 75-11796. (Heidelberg Science Library: Vol. 21). (Illus.). 180p. 1976. pap. 16.00 (ISBN 0-387-90141-8). Springer-Verlag.

Gusdorf, Georges. Speaking. Brockelman, Paul T., tr. (Studies in Phenomenology & Existential Philosophy Ser). 1965. 17.95 (ISBN 0-8101-0111-4); pap. 5.95 (ISBN 0-8101-0531-4). Northwestern U Pr.

Guse, Ernst-Gerhard. Auguste Rodin: Drawing & Watercolors. LC 85-42873. (Illus.). 368p. 1985. 35.00 (ISBN 0-8478-0625-1). Rizzoli Intl.

Guseinov, Chinghiz. Name Unknown. Smith, Holly, tr. from Rus. 213p. 1983. 7.95 (ISBN 0-8285-2415-7, Pub. by Raduga Pubs USSR). Imported Pubns.

Gusev, B. V., et al. English-Russian Dictionary of Applied Geophysics. 488p. 1983. 50.00 (ISBN 0-08-028168-0). Pergamon.

Gusev, E. Cerebrovascular Diseases. 191p. 1982. 6.95 (ISBN 0-8285-2440-8, Pub. by Mir Pubs USSR). Imported Pubns.

Gusev, K. & Naumov, V. The U. S. S. R. A Short History. 353p. 1976. 4.95 (ISBN 0-8285-0508-X, Pub. by Progress Pubs USSR). Imported Pubns.

Gusev, N. G. & Dimitriev, P. P. Quantum Radiation of Radioactive Nuclides. new ed. 1979. text ed. 165.00 (ISBN 0-08-023058-X). Pergamon.

Gusfield, Joseph R. Community: A Critical Response. 1978. pap. 3.95i (ISBN 0-06-090642-1, CN 642, CN). Har-Row.

--The Culture of Public Problems: Drinking-Driving & the Symbolic Order. LC 80-17007. 1981. lib. bdg. 22.00x (ISBN 0-226-31093-0). U of Chicago Pr.

--The Culture of Public Problems: Drinking, Driving & the Symbolic Order. LC 80-17007. 278p. 1984. pap. 9.95 (ISBN 0-226-31094-9). U of Chicago Pr.

--Symbolic Crusade: Status Politics & the American Temperance Movement. LC 80-13342. viii, 198p. 1980. Repr. of 1963 ed. lib. bdg. 24.75x (ISBN 0-313-22423-4, GUSC). Greenwood.

--Symbolic Crusade: Status Politics & the American Temperance Movement. LC 63-10314. 206p. 1966. pap. 6.95x (ISBN 0-252-74518-3). U of Ill Pr.

Gush, George & Finch, Andrew. Guide to Wargaming. (Illus.). 257p. 1980. 19.95 (ISBN 0-88254-508-6, Pub. by Croom Helm England). Hippocrene Bks.

Gushee, Charles H., ed. see Financial Publishing Company Staff.

Gusikoff, Lynne. Guide to Musical America. (Illus.). 336p. 1984. 17.95 (ISBN 0-87196-701-4). Facts on File.

Gusinde, Martin. Die Yamana: Die Feuerland Indianer, Vienna 1937, Vol. 2. (Classics of Anthropology Ser.). 266.00 (ISBN 0-8240-9631-2). Garland Pub.

Guskey. Implementing Mastery Learning. 1984. write for info. (ISBN 0-534-04053-5). Wadsworth Pub.

Gusky, Jeff, et al. Medical Student Ward Survival Manual. LC 82-60882. (Illus.). 22p. (Orig.). 1982. pap. text ed. 13.95 (ISBN 0-910015-00-7). Med Student Pubs.

Gusler, Wallace. Furniture of Eastern Virginia. LC 78-3499. (Illus.). 1978. pap. 2.00 (ISBN 0-917046-04-8). VA Mus Arts.

Gusler, Wallace B. Furniture of Williamsburg & Eastern Virginia, 1710-1790. LC 78-27282. (Illus.). 195p. 1979. 24.00 (ISBN 0-917046-05-6). VA Mus Arts.

Gusler, Wallace B & Lavin, James D. Decorated Firearms, 1540-1870, from the Collection of Clay P. Bedford. LC 76-53750. 242p. 1977. 25.00 (ISBN 0-87935-041-5, Colonial Williamsburg Foundation). U Pr of Va.

Gusman, Sam, et al. Public Policy for Chemicals: National & International Issues. LC 80-68965. 152p. (Orig.). 1980. pap. 8.50 (ISBN 0-89164-062-2). Conservation Foun.

Gusmani, Roberto. Lydisches Woerterbuch. (Ger.). 1964. 49.95 (ISBN 3-533-00655-7, M-7546, Pub. by Carl Winter). French & Eur.

--Neue Epichorische Schriftzeugnisse Aus Sardis. LC 74-81203. (Archaeological Exploration of Sardis Monograph: No. 3). 176p. (Ger.). 1975. text ed. 10.00x. Harvard U Pr.

Gusmer, Charles W. And You Visited Me. (Studies in the Reformed Rites of the Catholic Church: Vol. VI). 160p. (Orig.). 1984. pap. 9.95 (ISBN 0-916134-61-X). Pueblo Pub Co.

Guss, David, ed. see De Civrieux, Marc.

Guss, David, jt. ed. see Koran, Dennis.

Guss, David, tr. see Bernstein, Charles, et al.

Guss, David M., ed. Language of the Birds: Tales, Texts & Poems of Interspecies Communication. 384p. 1985. 14.50 (ISBN 0-86547-106-1). N Point Pr.

Guss, David M., ed. see Huidobro, Vicente.

Guss, Margaret B., ed. OSU Theses & Dissertations 1966-1970. (Bibliographic Ser: No. 9). 1973. pap. 4.95x (ISBN 0-87071-129-6). Oreg St U Pr.

Guss, Sam. Management & Diseases of Dairy Goats. 16.50 (ISBN 0-686-26691-9). Dairy Goat.

Gussenhoven, Elma J. & Becker, Anton E. Congenital Heart Disease: Morphologic Echocardiographic Correlations. LC 82-4474. (Modern Pediatric Cardiology Ser.). (Illus.). 220p. 1983. text ed. 79.00 (ISBN 0-443-02262-3). Churchill.

Gussin, Gilda & Buxbaum, Ann. Developing Skills. (Self-Discovery Ser.). (Illus.). 171p. (Orig.). (gr. 7-11). 1984. pap. text ed. 11.95 (ISBN 0-913723-08-8); tchrs' guide 14.95 (ISBN 0-913723-09-6). Mgmt Sci Health.

Gussin, Gilda, jt. auth. see Buxbaum, Ann.

Gussin, Gilda, et al. Caring, Loving, & Sexuality: Using Skills to Make Tough Choices. (Self-Discovery Ser.). (Illus.). 80p. (Orig.). (gr. 7-11). 1984. pap. text ed. 6.95 (ISBN 0-913723-12-6); tchrs' guide 8.95 (ISBN 0-913723-13-4). Mgmt Sci Health.

Gussmann, Edmund. Studies in Abstract Phonology. (Linguistic Inquiry Monographs). 176p. (Orig.). 1981. 32.50x (ISBN 0-262-07081-2); pap. text ed. 15.95x (ISBN 0-262-57057-2). MIT Pr.

Gussow, Don. The New Merger Game: The Plan & the Players. 1978. 12.50 (ISBN 0-8144-5463-1). AMACOM.

--The New Merger Game: The Plan & the Players. LC 77-28480. pap. 69.00 (ISBN 0-317-20796-2, 2023918). Bks Demand UMI.

Gussow, Donald. The New Business Journalism: The People & Corporations Behind America's Business Publications. 193p. 1984. 14.95 (ISBN 0-15-165202-3). HarBraceJ.

Gussow, Joan. The Feeding Web: Issues in Nutritional Ecology. LC 78-8579. 1978. pap. 13.95 (ISBN 0-915950-15-4). Bull Pub.

Gussow, Joan D. & Thomas, Paul. Is Health Food Healthy? The Real Issues in Nutrition. 1985. 17.95 (ISBN 0-915950-66-9); pap. 9.95 (ISBN 0-915950-67-7). Bull Pub.

Gussow, Joan D., jt. auth. see Birch, Herbert G.

Gussow, Mel. Darryl F. Zanuck: "Don't Say Yes Until I Finish Talking". (Illus.). 323p. 1980. pap. 7.95 (ISBN 0-306-80132-9). Da Capo.

Gussow, W. Schaum's Outline of Basic Electricity. (Schaum Outline Ser.). 448p. 1983. pap. 9.95 (ISBN 0-07-025240-8). McGraw.

Gust, Katharine & Brown, Deborah. Between the Creeks: Recollections of Northeast Texas. (Illus.). 1976. 12.50 (ISBN 0-88426-048-8). Encino Pr.

Gust, Philip. Introduction to Machine & Assembly Language Programming. (Illus.). 528p. 1985. text ed. 32.95 (ISBN 0-13-486416-6). P-H.

Gustafson. Fundamentals of Electricity for Agriculture. cancelled (ISBN 0-317-14342-5). AVI.

Gustafson, Alrik. History of Swedish Literature. LC 61-7722. (Illus.). 1961. 25.00x (ISBN 0-8166-0236-0). U of Minn Pr.

--Six Scandinavian Novelists. LC 40-27695. 1940. 14.50x (ISBN 0-89067-051-X). Am Scandinavian.

--Six Scandinavian Novelists: Lie, Jacobsen, Heidenstam, Selma Lagerlof, Hamsun, Sigrid Undset. LC 69-19835. 1968. Repr. of 1940 ed. 12.00x (ISBN 0-8196-0230-2). Biblo.

Gustafson, Anita. Burrowing Birds. LC 80-29058. (Illus.). 64p. (gr. 4-6). 1981. 11.25 (ISBN 0-688-41977-1); PLB 11.88 (ISBN 0-688-51977-6). Lothrop.

--The Case of the Purloined Pork. (Illus.). 32p. (gr. 2-3). 1985. 7.95 (ISBN 0-88700-004-5). Natl Live Stock.

--Guilty or Innocent. LC 85-7608. (Illus.). 160p. (gr. 6-9). 1985. 12.95 (ISBN 0-03-002927-9). HR&W.

--Some Feet Have Noses. LC 81-15573. (Illus.). 96p. (gr. 4 up). 1983. 12.50 (ISBN 0-688-00925-5); PLB 12.88 (ISBN 0-688-00926-3). Lothrop.

Gustafson, Anita & Kriney, Marilyn. Monster Rolling Skull & Other Native American Tales. LC 79-7890. (Illus.). (gr. 4-6). 1980. PLB 8.89 (ISBN 0-690-04020-2). Crowell Jr Bks.

Gustafson, Arnold A. Life: Nineteen Hundred to Nineteen Eighty-One. LC 81-90487. (Illus.). 187p. 1982. 8.95 (ISBN 0-533-05207-6). Vantage.

Gustafson, Bruce. French Harpsichord Music of the Seventeenth Century: A Thematic Catalog of the Sources with Commentary, 3 vols. Buelow, George, ed. LC 79-23567. (Studies in Musicology: No. 11). 1328p. 1979. Set. 99.95 (ISBN 0-8357-1069-6). Vol. 1, 442p (ISBN 0-8357-1066-1). Vol. 2, 496p (ISBN 0-8357-1067-X). Vol. 3, 388p (ISBN 0-8357-1068-8). UMI Res Pr.

Gustafson, Charles. How to Buy the Best Sailboat: A Consumer's Guide to Selecting, Outfitting, & Negotiating the Purchase of a Sailboat. LC 85-19258. (Illus.). 192p. (Orig.). 1985. pap. 12.95 (ISBN 0-688-03981-2, Hearst Marine Bks). Morrow.

Gustafson, Charles H. & American Law Institute. Federal Income Tax Simplification. LC 79-51416. 573p. 1979. 40.00. Am Law Inst.

Gustafson, Dana, ed. Food from Afar. spiral 3.95 (ISBN 0-686-12747-1). Grace Pub Co.

Gustafson, David R. Plane Trigonometry. 2nd ed. LC 84-9446. 1984. text ed. 21.00 pub net (ISBN 0-534-03606-6). Brooks-Cole.

Gustafson, Donald F. & Tapscott, Bangs L., eds. Body, Mind, & Method. (Synthese Library: No. 138). 1979. lib. bdg. 28.95 (ISBN 90-277-1013-9, Pub. by Reidel Holland). Kluwer Academic.

Gustafson, Dorothy D., jt. auth. see Higgs, Zana R.

Gustafson, Eleanor K. Appalachian Spring. LC 83-11656. 272p. 1984. pap. 6.95 (ISBN 0-310-37381-6). Zondervan.

Gustafson, Gus. I Was...Called To Be A Layman. 176p. (Orig.). 1982. pap. 7.75 (ISBN 0-687-18604-8). Abingdon.

Gustafson, J. Louise & Poziemski, Christine L. Step-by-Step Through the Bible: Puzzles, Quizzes & Writing Experiences for Teaching Important Biblical Passages. (The Lerning Connections Ser.). 160p. (Orig.). 1984. pap. 9.95 (ISBN 0-86683-835-X, 8442). Winston Pr.

Gustafson, J. P., ed. Gene Manipulation in Plant Improvement. (Stadler Genetics Symposium Ser.). 680p. 1985. 75.00x (ISBN 0-306-41883-5, Plenum Pr). Plenum Pub.

Gustafson, James. Bright Eyes Talks Crazy to Rembrandt. LC 75-1483. 72p. 1976. pap. 4.00 (ISBN 0-914610-03-1). Hanging Loose.

Gustafson, James M. Can Ethics Be Christian? LC 74-11622. 1977. pap. 7.00x (ISBN 0-226-31102-3, P734, Phoen). U of Chicago Pr.

--Christ & the Moral Life. 1979. 8.00x (ISBN 0-226-31109-0, P830, Phoen). U of Chicago Pr.

--The Contributions of Theology to Medical Ethics. (Pere Marquette Theology Lectures). 1975. 7.95 (ISBN 0-87462-507-6). Marquette.

--Ethics from a Theocentric Perspective: Theology & Ethics, Vol. 1. LC 81-11603. 284p. 1981. 27.50x (ISBN 0-226-31110-4). U of Chicago Pr.

--Ethics from a Theocentric Perspective: Theology & Ethics, Vol. 1. LC 81-11603. xiv, 346p. 1983. pap. 12.00x (ISBN 0-226-31111-2). U of Chicago Pr.

--Ethics from a Theocentric Perspective, Vol. 2: Ethics & Theology. LC 81-11603. 370p. 1984. lib. bdg. 25.00x (ISBN 0-226-31112-0). U of Chicago Pr.

--Moral Education. 7.95x (ISBN 0-674-58660-3); pap. 3.95x (ISBN 0-674-58661-1). Harvard U Pr.

--Protestant & Roman Catholic Ethics: Prospects for Rapprochement. LC 77-21421. 1980. pap. 3.95x (ISBN 0-226-31108-2, P868). U of Chicago Pr.

--Protestant & Roman Catholic Ethics: Prospects for Rapprochement. LC 77-21421. 1978. 15.00x (ISBN 0-226-31107-4). U of Chicago Pr.

--Treasure in Earthen Vessels. (Midway Reprint Ser). 1976. pap. text ed. 8.95 (ISBN 0-226-31101-5). U of Chicago Pr.

Gustafson, James W. Philosophy: The Quest for Truth. LC 81-50212. (Illus.). 252p. (Orig.). 1981. pap. 15.95x (ISBN 0-686-39639-1). Slingerland.

Gustafson, John. Racquetball. (Illus.). 64p. 1983. pap. text ed. 6.95x (ISBN 0-88136-020-1). Jostens.

Gustafson, Karen, jt. auth. see Yee, Roger.

Gustafson, Karl E. Introduction to Partial Differential Equations & Hilbert Space Methods. LC 80-331. 270p. 1980. text ed. 38.50 (ISBN 0-471-04089-4). Wiley.

Gustafson, Karl E. & Reinhardt, William P., eds. Quantum Mechanics in Mathematics, Chemistry, & Physics. LC 81-5846. 512p. 1981. 75.00x (ISBN 0-306-40737-X, Plenum Pr). Plenum Pub.

Gustafson, Kristen, jt. auth. see Sohn, Louis B.

Gustafson, M. & Corcoran, S. Teachers' Desk Reference. 1978. pap. 12.95 (ISBN 0-87489-211-2). Med Economics.

Gustafson, Paula. Salish Weaving. LC 80-51075. (Illus.). 132p. 1980. 27.50 (ISBN 0-295-95755-7). U of Wash Pr.

Gustafson, R. D. & Frisk, Peter D. College Algebra. 2nd ed. LC 82-4389. (Mathematics Ser.). 475p. 1982. text ed. 21.50 pub net (ISBN 0-534-01202-7); single copy 29.25. Brooks-Cole.

--College Algebra & Trigonometry. LC 82-4388. (Mathematics Ser.). 600p. 1982. text ed. 22.75 pub net (ISBN 0-534-01203-5). Brooks-Cole.

Gustafson, R. David & Frisk, Peter D. Algebra for College Students. LC 84-23055. (Mathematics Ser.). 565p. 1985. text ed. 22.25 pub net (ISBN 0-534-05028-X). Brooks-Cole.

--Beginning Algebra. LC 84-23764. (Mathematics Ser.). 400p. 1985. text ed. 21.50 pub net (ISBN 0-534-04077-2). Brooks-Cole.

--Intermediate Algebra. LC 83-7585. (Mathematics Ser.). 512p. 1983. text ed. 20.75 pub net (ISBN 0-534-02906-X). Brooks-Cole.

Gustafson, Ralph. At the Ocean's Verge: Selected Poems. (Literary Ser.). 169p. 1984. 20.00 (ISBN 0-933806-16-7). Black Swan CT.

Gustafson, Ray L. Buying, Selling, Starting a Business. LC 82-90702. 152p. 1982. pap. 9.95 (ISBN 0-9609046-0-3, DEPT. OR-1). GHC.

Gustafson, Richard F. The Imagination of Spring: The Poetry of Afanasy Fet. LC 76-15198. 1976. Repr. lib. bdg. 29.75x (ISBN 0-8371-8146-1, GUIS). Greenwood.

Gustafson, Robert. The Degenerate Principal Series for Sp(2n) LC 81-13033. (Memoirs of the American Mathematical Society Ser.: No. 248). 88p. 1981. pap. 9.00 (ISBN 0-8218-2248-9). Am Math.

Gustafson, Robert, jt. auth. see Schmalleger, Frank.

Gustafson, Robert H., jt. auth. see Church, Albert M.

Gustafson, Robert J. Fundamentals of Electricity for Agriculture. (Illus.). 1980. pap. 21.00 (ISBN 0-87055-327-5). AVI.

Gustafson, Robert L., jt. auth. see Johnson, David G.

Gustafson, Robert R. Authors of Confusion. pap. 1.45 (ISBN 0-686-12743-9). Grace Pub Co.

Gustafson, Rosalie. Hollywood's Mother Goose. 1985. 6.95 (ISBN 0-533-06626-3). Vantage.

Gustafson, Roy D. & Frisk, Peter D. Elementary Plane Geometry. 2nd ed. LC 84-7259. 358p. 1985. 26.95 (ISBN 0-471-89047-2). Wiley.

Gustafson, S. A., jt. auth. see Glashoff, K.

Gustafson, Thane. Reform in Soviet Politics: The Lessons of Recent Policies on Land & Water. LC 80-24286. (Illus.). 224p. 1981. 34.50 (ISBN 0-521-23377-1). Cambridge U Pr.

--The Soviet Gas Campaign: Politics & Policy in Soviet Decisionmaking. LC 83-13942. 118p. 1983. 10.00 (ISBN 0-8330-0513-8). Rand Corp.

Gustafson, Thane, jt. ed. see Bialer, Seweryn.

Gustafson, Thomas J. Microcomputers & Educational Administration. (Illus.). 240p. 1985. pap. text ed. 18.95 (ISBN 0-13-580267-9). P-H.

Gustafson, W. Eric & Jones, Kenneth. Sources on Punjab History. LC 75-903111. 1975. 16.00 (ISBN 0-88386-584-X). South Asia Bks.

Gustafson, W. Eric, ed. see Mayer, Milton.

Gustafson, W. Eric, ed. see Mayer, Milton S.

Gustafson, William F., jt. auth. see Bosco, James S.

Gustafsson, Bo, ed. Post-Industrial Society. LC 78-18793. 1979. 26.00 (ISBN 0-312-63226-6). St Martin.

Gustafsson, J. A., jt. auth. see Eriksson, H.

Gustafsson, Lars. The Death of a Beekeeper. Swaffer, Janet K. & Weber, Guntram H., trs. from Swedish. LC 81-11182. 160p. 1981. 12.95 (ISBN 0-8112-0809-5); pap. 5.95 (ISBN 0-8112-0810-9, NDP523). New Directions.

--Selected Poems. Fulton, Robin, tr. from Swedish. LC 71-188436. (Illus.). 112p. 1972. signed ed 10.00 (ISBN 0-685-23801-6); 5.00 (ISBN 0-685-23802-4); pap. 2.50 (ISBN 0-685-23803-2). New Rivers Pr.

--Sigismund. Weinstock, John, tr. from Swedish. LC 84-1021. 224p. 1985. 16.50 (ISBN 0-8112-0923-7); pap. 7.95 (ISBN 0-8112-0924-5, NDP584). New Directions.

--The Tennis Players. Sandstroem, Yvonne L., tr. LC 82-22559. 96p. (Swedish.). 1983. 13.00 (ISBN 0-8112-0861-3); pap. 6.25 (ISBN 0-8112-0862-1, NDP551). New Directions.

--Warm Rooms & Cold. Sandstroem, Yvonne, tr. from Swedish. (Orig.). 1975. pap. 3.50 (ISBN 0-914278-05-3). Copper Beech.

--Warm Rooms & Cold. Sandstroem, Yvonne L., tr. from Swedish. 64p. 1975. pap. 3.50 (ISBN 0-914278-05-3, Pub. by Copper Beech). Small Pr Dist.

Gustafsson, Uwe. English-Kotia Oriya, Kotia Oriya-English Glossary. 150p. 1974. pap. 2.00x (ISBN 0-88312-748-2); microfiche (2) 2.86 (ISBN 0-88312-995-7). Summer Inst Ling.

--Kotia Oriya Adiwasi Oriya Phonemic Summary. 43p. 1974. pap. 1.93x (ISBN 0-88312-779-2); microfiche 1.50 (ISBN 0-88312-398-3). Summer Inst Ling.

Gustason, et al. Signing Exact English. 490p. 1980. 18.00 (ISBN 0-317-34989-9, SL025). Natl Assn Deaf.

Gustason, Gerilee. Beginning Curricula A, B & Affixes Used in Signing Exact English. 124p. (Orig.). 1983. pap. text ed. 8.50 student wkbk. (ISBN 0-916708-09-8). Modern Signs.

--Teaching & Learning Signing Exact English: An Idea Book. 535p. (Orig.). 1983. pap. 30.00 (ISBN 0-916708-08-X). Modern Signs.

Gustason, Gerilee, ed. Using Signing Exact English in Total Communication: A Collection of Articles. LC 80-84549. (Illus.). 68p. (Orig.). 1980. pap. 4.00x (ISBN 0-916708-04-7). Modern Signs.

Gustason, Gerilee, et al. Signing Exact English. 1980 ed. LC 80-80571. (Illus.). 460p. (gr. k-12). 1980. text ed. 24.00x (ISBN 0-916708-02-0); pap. text ed. 18.00x (ISBN 0-916708-03-9). Modern Signs.

Gustason, Gerilee, jt. auth. see Wojcio, Michael D.

Gustason, William & Ulrich, Dolph E. Elementary Symbolic Logic. LC 81-70028. 280p. 1982. Repr. of 1973 ed. text ed. 16.95x (ISBN 0-917974-78-6). Waveland Pr.

Gustav, Bergmann. Philosophy of Science. LC 77-5439. 181p. lib. bdg. 71.50x (ISBN 0-8371-9623-X, BEPH). Greenwood.

Gustaveson, David. Personal Life Notebook. 192p. 1980. pap. 8.95 spiral bdg. (ISBN 0-87123-467-X, 210467). Bethany Hse.

Gustaveson, Patricia, jt. auth. see Mandetta, Anne.

Gustavsen, Bjorn & Hunnius, Gerry. New Patterns of Work Reform: The Case of Norway. 207p. 1981. write for info. Universitet.

Gustavson, Bjorn & Hunius, Gerry. Improving the Quality of Life: The Case of Norway. 112p. 1981. pap. 11.00x (ISBN 82-00-05525-6). Universitet.

Gustavson, Carl. The Mansion of History. (McGraw-Hill Paperbacks). 384p. (Orig.). 1976. pap. 4.95 (ISBN 0-07-025276-9). McGraw.

Gustavson, Carl G. The Institutional Drive: A Study in Pluralistic Democracy. LC 66-14029. xviii, 199p. 1966. 15.00x (ISBN 0-8214-0019-3, 82-80216). Ohio U Pr.

--Preface to History. (YA) (gr. 9-12). 1955. pap. 5.95 (ISBN 0-07-025279-3). McGraw.

--The Small Giant: Sweden Enters the Industrial Era. 180p. 1985. text ed. 23.95x (ISBN 0-8214-0825-9). Ohio U Pr.

Gustavson, Frances & Sackson, Marian. Problem Solving & BASIC: A Modular Approach. LC 78-21904. 335p. 1979. pap. text ed. 17.95 (ISBN 0-574-21240-X, 13-4240); instr's guide avail. (ISBN 0-574-21241-8, 13-4241). SRA.

Gustavson, Frances G. The Automatic Revision of Storage Structures. Stone, Harold, ed. LC 82-6974. (Computer Science: Systems Programming Ser.: No. 11). 154p. 1982. 34.95 (ISBN 0-8357-1345-8). UMI Res Pr.

Gustavson, Reuben G. Humanity's Great Adventure. LC 60-2570. (Augustana College Library Occasional Papers: No. 6). 19p. 1960. pap. 0.50 (ISBN 0-910182-27-2). Augustana Coll.

Gustavson, Rolf. Training Therapy. Gilliar, Wolfgang, tr. from German. (Illus.). 178p. 1985. text ed. 19.00 (ISBN 0-86577-192-8). Thieme Stratton.

Gustavson, Sandra G., jt. auth. see Mehr, Robert I.

Gustavson, T. C., jt. auth. see Finley, R. J.

Gustavson, Thomas C., jt. auth. see Finley, Robert J.

Gustavsson, B. The Soul under Stress: A Study of the Poetics of John Berryman's Dream Songs. (Acta Universitatis Upsaliensis-Studia Anglistica Upsaliensia: No. 52). 135p. 1984. pap. text ed. 17.25x (ISBN 91-554-1503-2, Pub. by Acta Universitatis Upsaliensis Sweden). Humanities.

Gustavsson, Bengtove & Karlsson, Jan. Work in the Nineteen Eighties: Emancipation & Derogation. 220p. 1985. text ed. 34.50 (ISBN 0-566-00862-9). Gower Pub Co.

Guste, Bob. Mary at My Side. 64p. (Orig.). 1985. pap. 3.95 (ISBN 0-89622-247-0). Twenty-Third.

Guste, Roy F., Jr. Antoine's Restaurant Cookbook. (Illus.). 1980. pap. 9.95 (ISBN 0-393-00027-3). Norton.

--The Restaurants of New Orleans. (Illus.). 239p. 1983. 19.95 (ISBN 0-393-01746-X). Norton.

Gustilo, Ramon B. Management of Open Fractures & Their Complications. (Saunders Monographs in Clinical Orthopedics: Vol. 4). (Illus.). 224p. 1982. 41.00 (ISBN 0-7216-4357-4). Saunders.

Guston, Bill. The Harrier. LC 83-83421. (Modern Fighting Aircraft Ser.: No. 5). 64p. 1984. 11.95 (ISBN 0-668-06069-7, 6069). Arco.

Gustorf, Ernest A. Von see Von Gustorf, Ernest A.

Gustorf, Frederick & Gustorf, Gisela. Uncorrupted Heart: Journal & Letters of Frederick Julius Gustorf 1800-1845. LC 70-93049. 192p. 1969. 14.00x (ISBN 0-8262-0079-6). U of Mo Pr.

Gustorf, Gisela, jt. auth. see Gustorf, Frederick.

Guswa, J. H., et al. Groundwater Contamination & Emergency Response Guide. LC 84-14842. (Pollution Technology Review Ser.: No. 111). (Illus.). 490p. 1985. 48.00 (ISBN 0-8155-0999-5). Noyes.

Guszak, Frank J. Diagnostic Reading Instruction in the Elementary School. 2nd ed. 1978. pap. text ed. 19.50 scp (ISBN 0-06-042558-X, HarpC). Har-Row.

--Diagnostic Reading Instruction in the Elementary School. 3rd ed. 352p. 1985. pap. text ed. 23.50 scp (ISBN 0-06-042559-8, HarpC); instr's. manual avail. (ISBN 0-06-362553-9). Har-Row.

Gut, A. & Schmidt, K. D. Amarts & Set Function Processes. (Lecture Notes in Mathematics: Vol. 1042). 258p. 1983. pap. 15.00 (ISBN 0-387-12867-0). Springer Verlag.

Gut, I., et al, eds. Industrial & Environmental Xenobiotics. (Proceedings in Life Sciences Ser.). (Illus.). 409p. 1981. 46.50 (ISBN 0-387-10960-9). Springer Verlag.

Gutaj, R., jt. auth. see Schoen, S.

Gutas, Dimitri. Greek Wisdom Literature in Arabic Translation: A Study of the Graeco-Arabic Gnomologia. (American Oriental Ser.: Vol. 60). 1975. pap. 10.00x (ISBN 0-940490-60-9). Am Orient Soc.

Gutberlet, John E. On the Osteology of Some of the Loricati. (Illus.). pap. 8.00 (ISBN 0-384-20480-5). Johnson Repr.

Gutch, C. F. & Stoner, Martha H. Review of Hemodialysis for Nurses & Dialysis Personnel. 4th ed. LC 83-1004. (Illus.). 224p. 1983. pap. text ed. 18.95 (ISBN 0-8016-1991-2). Mosby.

--Review of Hemodialysis for Nurses & Dialysis Personnel. 3rd ed. LC 79-16882. (Illus.). 242p. 1979. pap. text ed. 18.95 (ISBN 0-8016-1994-7). Mosby.

Gutch, E., ed. County Folklore: Vol. II, Printed Extracts No. 4, Examples of Printed Folklore Concerning the North Riding of Yorkshire, York, & the Ainsty. (Folk-Lore Society, London, vol. 45). pap. 35.00 (ISBN 0-317-16267-5). Kraus Repr.

--County Folklore Vol. VI: Printed Extracts no. 8, Examples of Printed Folklore Concerning the East Riding of Yorkshire. (Folklore Society, London, vol. 69). pap. 35.00 (ISBN 0-317-16297-7). Kraus Repr.

Gutch, E. & Peacock, Mabel, eds. County Folklore Vol. IV: Printed Extracts No. 7, Examples of Printed Folklore Concerning Lincolnshire. (Folk-Lore Society, London: Vol. 63). pap. 35.00. Kraus Repr.

Gutch, John. Collectanea Curiosa, 2 vols. Straka, Gerald M., ed. LC 72-83163. (English Studies Ser.). 1972. Repr. of 1781 ed. Set. lib. bdg. 75.00 (ISBN 0-8420-1422-5). Scholarly Res Inc.

Gutcheon, Beth. The New Girls. 336p. 1981. pap. 2.50 (ISBN 0-380-50831-1, 50831-1). Avon.

--The Perfect Patchwork Primer. (Handbook Ser.). (Illus.). 1974. pap. 9.95 (ISBN 0-14-046212-0). Penguin.

--Still Missing. (General Ser.). 1981. lib. bdg. 14.95 (ISBN 0-8161-3327-1, Large Print Bks). G K Hall.

--Still Missing. 384p. pap. 3.50 (ISBN 0-440-17864-9, Dell Trade Pbks). Dell.

--Without a Trace. 384p. 1983. pap. 3.95 (ISBN 0-440-19496-2). Dell.

Gutcheon, Jeff. Teach Yourself Rock Piano. 72p. pap. 6.95 (ISBN 0-8256-2207-7). Music Sales.

Gutcheon, Jeffrey. Diamond Patchwork. (Illus.). 72p. 1984. pap. 9.95 (ISBN 0-525-48094-3, 0966-290). Dutton.

--Improvising Rock Piano. 1978. pap. 7.95 (ISBN 0-8256-4071-7). Music Sales.

Gutchess, Jocelyn F. Employment Security in Action: Strategies That Work. (Work in America Institute Ser.). 224p. 1985. 25.00 (ISBN 0-08-031594-1). Pergamon.

Gutcho, M. Textured Protein Products. LC 77-85662. (Food Technology Review Ser.: No. 44). (Illus.). 1978. 39.00 (ISBN 0-8155-0681-3). Noyes.

Gutcho, M. H. Tampons & Other Catamenial Receptors. LC 79-84431. (Chemical Technology Review Ser.: No. 129). (Illus.). 294p. 1979. 39.00 (ISBN 0-8155-0753-4). Noyes.

Gutcho, M. H., ed. Household & Industrial Fabric Conditioners. LC 79-27919. (Chemical Technology Review Ser.: No. 152). (Illus.). 431p. 1980. 54.00 (ISBN 0-8155-0793-3). Noyes.

--Inorganic Pigments: Manufacturing Processes. LC 80-16319. (Chemical Technology Review No. 166). 488p. 1980. 54.00 (ISBN 0-8155-0811-5). Noyes.

--Metal Surface Treatment: Chemical & Electrochemical Surface Conversions. LC 82-3404. (Chemical Tech. Rev.: No. 208). (Illus.). 404p. 1982. 48.00 (ISBN 0-8155-0900-6). Noyes.

Gutcho, Marcia, ed. Adhesives Technology: Developments Since 1979. LC 82-19096. (Chemical Technology Review: No. 215). (Illus.). 452p. 1983. 48.00 (ISBN 0-8155-0921-9). Noyes.

Gutek, Barbara, jt. auth. see Nieva, Veronica.

Gutek, Barbara A., ed. Sex Role Stereotyping & Affirmative Action Policy. (Monograph & Research Ser.: No. 32). 280p. 1982. 8.50 (ISBN 0-89215-116-1). U Cal LA Indus Rel.

Gutek, Gerald. Joseph Neef: The Americanization of Pestalozzianism 1800-1840. LC 77-1456. 176p. 1978. 12.00 (ISBN 0-8173-9110-X). U of Ala Pr.

Gutek, Gerald L. Basic Education: A Historical Perspective. LC 81-82470. (Fastback Ser.: No. 167). 50p. 1981. pap. 0.75 (ISBN 0-87367-167-8). Phi Delta Kappa.

--Education & Schooling in America. (Illus.). 416p. 1983. 26.95 (ISBN 0-13-240523-7, Busn). P-H.

--Education in the United States: An Historical Perspective. (Illus.). 400p. 1986. text ed. 27.95 (ISBN 0-13-235680-5). P-H.

--The Educational Theory of George S. Counts. LC 76-115428. (Studies in Educational Theory of the John Dewey Society: No. 8). 293p. 1971. 7.00 (ISBN 0-8142-0149-0). Ohio St U Pr.

--George S. Counts & American Civilization: The Educator as Social Theorist. LC 83-23762. 180p. 1984. 11.95x (ISBN 0-86554-091-8, MUP/H82). Mercer Univ Pr.

--Historical Introduction to American Education. 1970. pap. text ed. 12.20 scp (ISBN 0-690-39437-3, HarpC). Har-Row.

Gutelle, Pierre. The Design of Sailing Yachts. LC 83-82851. (Illus.). 210p. 1984. 35.00 (ISBN 0-87742-183-8, D340). Intl Marine.

Gutenberg, Janice P. Steens Mt. Scrapbook. LC 23-939860. 1982. write for info. (ISBN 0-939860-05-8). Tremaine Graph & Pub.

Gutenmacher, V., jt. auth. see Vasilyev, N.

Guter, Marvin & Serafini, Aldo. Chest Nuclear Medicine Case Studies. 1979. spiral bdg. 19.00 (ISBN 0-87488-083-1). Med Exam.

Guter, Marvin, jt. auth. see Serafani, Aldo N.

Guterbock, Carl. Bracton & His Relation to the Roman Law: A Contribution to the History of the Roman Law in the Middle Ages. Coxe, Brinton, tr. from Ger. 182p. 1979. Repr. of 1866 ed. lib. bdg. 18.50x (ISBN 0-8377-0608-4). Rothman.

Guterbock, Hans G., jt. ed. see Hoffner, Harry A., Jr.

Guterbock, K. E. Byzanz und Persien in ihren Diplomatisch Volkerrechtlichen Beziehungen im Zeitalter Justinians. 128p. (Ger.). Repr. of 1906 ed. lib. bdg. 22.50x (ISBN 0-89241-170-8). Caratzas.

Guterbock, Thomas M. Machine Politics in Transition: Party & Community in Chicago. LC 79-16131. (Studies in Urban Society). (Illus.). 1980. lib. bdg. 27.50x (ISBN 0-226-31114-7). U of Chicago Pr.

Guterman, Martin M. & Nitecki, Zbigniew H. Differential Equations. 1984. text ed. 35.95 (ISBN 0-03-062502-5, CBS C); study manual 11.95 (ISBN 0-03-062503-3). SCP.

Guterman, Norbert, jt. auth. see Lowenthal, Leo.

Guterman, Norbert, ed. see Sainte-Beuvel, Charles A.

Guterman, Norbert, jt. ed. see Steegmuller, Francis.

Guterman, Norbert, tr. see Afanas'Ev, Aleksandr.

Guterman, Norbert, tr. see Belaval, Yvon.

Guterman, Norbert, tr. see Hlasko, Marek.

Guterman, Norbert, tr. see Sainte-Beuvel, Charles A.

Guterman, Norbert see Zuckerkandl, Victor.

Guterman, Simeon L. Religious Toleration & Persecution in Ancient Rome. LC 70-104269. 160p. Repr. of 1951 ed. lib. bdg. 22.50x (ISBN 0-8371-3936-8, GURT). Greenwood.

Guterman, Stanley S. The Machiavellians: A Social Psychological Study of Moral Character & Organizational Milieu. LC 69-19104. xviii, 180p. 1970. 16.95x (ISBN 0-8032-0707-7). U of Nebr Pr.

Gutermuth, C. R. & Maunder, Elwood R. Pioneer Conservationist & the Natural Resources Council of America. (Illus.). 166p. 1974. 35.00 (ISBN 0-89030-016-X). Forest Hist Soc.

Gutfeld, Arnon. Montana's Agony: Years of War & Hysteria, 1917-1921. LC 78-31495. (University of Florida Social Sciences Monographs: No. 64). 174p. 1979. pap. 6.50 (ISBN 0-8130-0629-5). U Presses Fla.

Gutfreund, H. Biochemical Evolution. 320p. 1981. text ed. 80.00 (ISBN 0-521-23549-9); pap. text ed. 27.95 (ISBN 0-521-28025-7). Cambridge U Pr.

Gutfreund, H., jt. auth. see Edsall, J. T.

Gutfreund, H., et al. Felix Bloch & Twentieth Century Physics. Chodorow, M., et al, eds. (Rice University Studies: Vol. 66, No. 3). (Illus.). 247p. (Orig.). 1980. 25.00x (ISBN 0-89263-254-2); pap. 15.00 (ISBN 0-89263-246-1). Rice Univ.

Gutgesell, Steve. Guide to Ohio Newspapers, 1793-1973. 412p. 1976. 10.00 (ISBN 0-87758-004-9). Ohio Hist Soc.

Gutglass, Judith L., compiled by. Attorney's Fees & Law Office Management: A Selected Bibliography. LC 82-236288. (Washington University Law Library Bibliography Ser.: No. 3). vi, 24p. (Orig.). 1982. pap. text ed. 8.00 (ISBN 0-318-01099-2). Wash U Law Lib.

Guth. Handbook of Business Strategy. 1984. 68.00 (ISBN 0-88712-162-4). Warren.

Guth, Alan H., et al, eds. Asymptotic Realms of Physics: Essays in Honor of Francis E. Low. (Illus.). 336p. 1983. 40.00x (ISBN 0-262-07089-8). MIT Pr.

Guth, Chester & Shaw, Stanley. How to Put on Dynamic Meetings. (Illus.). 160p. 1980. 15.95 (ISBN 0-8359-2968-X). Reston.

Guth, Christine, tr. see Kageyama, Haruki.

Guth, David A. Suing in North Carolina Small Claims Court: A Practical Guide. 370p. 1983. 25.00 (ISBN 0-87215-623-0). Michie Co.

Guth, Deborah, jt. auth. see Schwartz, Anita K.

Guth, DeLloyd J. & McKenna, John W. Tudor Rule & Revolution. LC 82-4266. 400p. 1983. 52.50 (ISBN 0-521-24841-8). Cambridge U Pr.

Guth, DeLloyd J. & Wrone, David R.compiled By. The Assassination of John F. Kennedy: A Comprehensive Historical & Legal Bibliography, 1963-1979. LC 79-6184. (Illus.). lvi, 442p. 1980. lib. bdg. 49.95 (ISBN 0-313-21274-0, GJK/). Greenwood.

Guth, Dorothy L., compiled by see White, E. B.

Guth, Ekkehart P. Der Loyalitaetskonflikt des Deutschen Offizierkorps in der Revolution: 1918-1920. (European University Studies: No. 3, Vol. 198). 262p. (Ger.). 1983. 32.10 (ISBN 3-8204-7766-7). P Lang Pubs.

Guth, H. P. Advanced Composition. 2nd ed. (American English Today Ser.). 1980. text ed. 8.80 (ISBN 0-07-025013-8). McGraw.

--Basic Composition, 2 Bks. 2nd ed. (American English Today Ser.). 1980. text ed. 8.80 ea. Bk. 1 (ISBN 0-07-025011-1). Bk. 2 (ISBN 0-07-025012-X). McGraw.

Guth, Hans P. American English Today: A Text-Workbook for English Language & Composition, Level C. 3rd ed. Wilson, Paul H., ed. (Illus.). 160p. (gr. 9). 1979. pap. 6.24 (ISBN 0-07-025039-1). McGraw.

--American English Today: A Text-Workbook for English Language & Composition, Level D. 3rd ed. Wilson, Paul H., ed. (Illus.). 176p. (gr. 10). 1979. pap. text ed. 6.24 (ISBN 0-07-025040-5). McGraw.

--American English Today: Exploring English. 3rd Ed. ed. (gr. 7). 1980. text ed. 15.40 (ISBN 0-07-025027-8). McGraw.

--American English Today: Our Changing Language. 3rd ed. (Illus.). (gr. 12). 1980. text ed. 15.96 (ISBN 0-07-025022-7) (ISBN 0-07-025032-4). McGraw.

--American English Today: The Uses of Language. 3rd ed. (American English Today Ser.). (gr. 11). 1980. text ed. 15.96 (ISBN 0-07-025021-9). McGraw.

--American English Today: The World of English. 3rd ed. (American English Today Ser.). (Illus.). (gr. 10). 1980. text ed. 15.80 (ISBN 0-07-025020-0) (ISBN 0-07-025030-8). McGraw.

--New Concise Handbook. 384p. 1984. pap. text ed. write for info. (ISBN 0-534-05178-2). Wadsworth Pub.

--New English Handbook. 2nd ed. 592p. 1985. pap. text ed. write for info. (ISBN 0-534-04830-7). Wadsworth Pub.

--New English Manual. 176p. 1985. pap. text ed. write for info. (ISBN 0-534-04832-3). Wadsworth Pub.

--Wadsworth English Workbook. 160p. 1980. pap. text ed. write for info. (ISBN 0-534-00848-8). Wadsworth Pub.

--Words & Ideas. 5th ed. 528p. 1980. text ed. write for info. (ISBN 0-534-00815-1). Wadsworth Pub.

Guth, Hans P. & Hausmann, Renee V. Essay: Reading with the Writer's Eye. 534p. 1984. pap. text ed. write for info. (ISBN 0-534-03086-6). Wadsworth Pub.

Guth, Hans P. & Schuster, Edgar H. American English Today: A Text-Workbook for English Language & Composition, Level E. 3rd ed. (Illus.). 160p. (gr. 11). 1980. pap. text ed. 6.24 (ISBN 0-07-025041-3). McGraw.

--American English Today: A Text-Workbook for English Language & Composition, Level F. 3rd ed. Wilson, Paul H., ed. (Illus.). 160p. (gr. 12). 1980. pap. text ed. 6.24 (ISBN 0-07-025042-1). McGraw.

--American English Today: The Tools of English. 3rd ed. LC 79-4066. (American English Today Ser.). (gr. 9). 1980. text ed. 14.24 (ISBN 0-07-025019-7). McGraw.

--Our Common Language: American English Today. 3rd ed. (Illus.). 480p. (gr. 8). 1980. text ed. 17.40 (ISBN 0-07-025018-9). McGraw.

Guth, Hans P. & Wilson, Paul H. Today: A Text-Workbook for English Language & Composition, Level A. 3rd ed. (gr. 7). 1980. pap. text ed. 6.24 (ISBN 0-07-025037-5). McGraw.

--Today: A Text-Workbook for English Language & Composition, Level B. 3rd ed. (gr. 8). 1980. pap. text ed. 6.24 (ISBN 0-07-025038-3). McGraw.

Guth, Lloyd, tr. see Ramon y Cajal, Santiago.

Guth, Paul. Le Naif Aux Quarante Enfants. (Easy Readers, C). 1977. pap. 4.25 (ISBN 0-88436-294-9, 40274). EMC.

Guth, Phyllis & Goff, Georgeanna. Sewing with Scraps. (Illus.). (YA) (gr. 10 up). 1977. pap. 6.95 (ISBN 0-8306-6878-0, 878). TAB Bks.

Guth, W. Capital Exports to Less Developed Countries. rev. ed. Catty, F. B., tr. from Ger. 162p. 1963. 21.00 (ISBN 90-277-0095-8, Pub. by Reidel Holland). Kluwer Academic.

Guth DeLloyd, J. Late-Medieval England, 1377-1485. LC 75-23845. (Conference on British Studies Bibliographical Handbooks Ser.). 164p. 1976. 27.95 (ISBN 0-521-20877-7). Cambridge U Pr.

Guthe, C. E. A Possible Solution of the Number Series on Pages Fifty-One to Fifty-Eight of the Dresden Codex. (Harvard University Peabody Museum of Archaeology & Ethnology Papers). pap. 8.00 (ISBN 0-527-01207-6). Kraus Repr.

Guthe, Carl E. Management of Small History Museums. 2nd ed. 1964. pap. 5.50 (ISBN 0-910050-04-X). AASLH Pr.

--Pueblo Pottery Making: A Study of the Village of San Ildefonso. LC 76-43718. Repr. of 1925 ed. 30.00 (ISBN 0-404-15554-5). AMS Pr.

Guthe, T., jt. auth. see Idse, O.

Gutheil, Emil. Handbook of Dream Analysis. new ed. LC 78-114371. pap. 11.95 paper 1970 (ISBN 0-87140-219-X). Liveright.

--Music & Your Emotions. new ed. LC 75-131283. 1970. pap. 5.95 (ISBN 0-87140-232-7). Liveright.

Gutheil, Thomas & Applebaum, Paul. Clinical Handbook of Psychiatry & the Law. (McGraw-Hill Professional Publications). 253p. 1982. 32.95 (ISBN 0-07-025378-1, Pub. By Shepards-McGraw). McGraw.

Gutheim, Frederick. Alvar Aalto. LC 60-6080. (Masters of World Architecture Ser). 1960. pap. 3.95 (ISBN 0-8076-0226-4). Braziller.

--Worthy of the Nation: The History of Planning for the National Capital. LC 77-120. (Illus.). 416p. 1977. 29.95x (ISBN 0-87474-496-2). Smithsonian.

Gutheim, Frederick & Washburn, Wilcomb. The Federal City: Plans & Realities. LC 75-619412. (Illus.). 170p. 1976. pap. 8.95 (ISBN 0-87474-494-6). Smithsonian.

Gutheim, Frederick, ed. In the Cause of Architecture. (Illus.). 246p. 1975. 34.95 (ISBN 0-07-025350-1). McGraw.

Gutheridge, Anne. Barnes & Noble Thesaurus of Biology. (Illus.). 256p. 1984. pap. 6.68i (EH 581). B&N NY.

Gutherie, G. P. & Kotchen, T. A., eds. Hypertension & the Brain. 400p. 1984. 45.00 (ISBN 0-87993-211-2). Futura Pub.

Guthery, Scott B. Learning C with Tiny C. (Illus.). 176p. (Orig.). 1985. pap. 14.95 (ISBN 0-8306-1895-3). TAB Bks.

Guthiel, Emil A., ed. see Stekel, Wilhelm.

Guthikonda, R. N., ed. Indian Community Reference Guide & Directory of Indian Associations in North America. 1979. pap. 1.50 (ISBN 0-89684-075-1, Pub. by Federation of Indian Association-NY). Orient Bk Dist.

Guthke, Karl S. Erkundungen: Essays zur Literatur von Milton bis Traven. Mommsen, Katharina, ed. LC 83-48181. (Germanic Studies in America: Vol. 45). 432p. 1983. 62.10 (ISBN 0-8204-0019-X). P Lang Pubs.

Guthkelch, A. C., ed. see Swift, Jonathan.

Guthman, Judith. Metropolitan Libraries: The Challenge & the Promise. LC 71-78896. (Public Library Reporter: No. 15). pap. 20.00 (ISBN 0-317-26835-X, 2024212). Bks Demand UMI.

Guthman, William, ed. Guns & Other Arms. (Illus.). 160p. 1980. pap. 7.95 (ISBN 0-8317-4182-1, Mayflower Bks). Smith Pubs.

Guthman, William H., ed. The Correspondence of Captain Nathan & Lois Peters, April 25, 1775-Febuary 5, 1977. (Illus.). 1980. 6.50 (ISBN 0-940748-58-4). Conn Hist Soc.

Guthmann, Robert F., Jr. & Womack, Sharon K. Death, Dying & Grief: A Bibliography. LC 77-82084. 1978. pap. text ed. 5.50 (ISBN 0-918626-01-3, Pied Publications). Word Serv.

Guthmundsson, Barthi. The Origin of the Icelanders. Hollander, Lee M., tr. LC 66-19275. x, 173p. 1967. 15.95x (ISBN 0-8032-0063-3). U of Nebr Pr.

Guthorn, Peter. United States Coastal Charts, 1783-1860. LC 84-51187. (Illus.). 272p. 1984. 59.00 (ISBN 0-88740-019-1). Schiffer.

Guthorn, Peter J. American Maps & Map Makers of the Revolution. LC 66-30330. (Revolutionary War Bicentennial Ser.). (Illus.). 1966. lib. bdg. 9.95 (ISBN 0-912480-02-5). Freneau.

--British Maps of the American Revolution. LC 72-79889. (Revolutionary War Bicentennial Ser.). (Illus.). 1972. lib. bdg. 15.95 (ISBN 0-912480-07-6). Freneau.

--John Hills, Assistant Engineer: With a Collection of Plans of the Provinces of New Jersey. LC 76-1497. 1977. pap. text ed. 28.50 (ISBN 0-916762-01-7). Portolan.

--The Sea Bright Skiff & Other Shore Boats. rev. ed. LC 82-62951. (Illus.). 256p. 1983. pap. 13.95 (ISBN 0-916838-73-0). Schiffer.

Guthridge, Sharyn G., ed. see Gregory, Grace C.

Guthridge, Sue. Thomas A. Edison: Young Inventor. LC 82-17845. (Childhood of Famous Americans Ser.). (Illus.). 196p. (Orig.). (gr. 2 up). 1983. pap. 3.95 (ISBN 0-672-52751-0). Bobbs.

Guthrie, ed. see Cornford, F. M.

Guthrie, et al. Nuevo Comentario Biblico. Orig. Title: The New Bible Commentary Revised. 972p. 1983. pap. 43.75 (ISBN 0-311-03001-7). Casa Bautista.

Guthrie, A. B. Fair Land, Fair Land. 272p. (Orig.). 1984. pap. text ed. 3.50 (ISBN 0-553-23423-4). Bantam.

Guthrie, A. B., Jr. Arfive. large print ed. LC 84-16. 399p. 1984. Repr. of 1973 ed. 14.95 (ISBN 0-89621-521-0). Thorndike Pr.

--The Big It. 1985. pap. 2.50 (ISBN 0-345-32753-5). Ballantine.

--The Big Sky. 384p. (gr. 6 up). 1972. pap. 3.95 (ISBN 0-553-25015-9). Bantam.

--Fair Land, Fair Land. large print ed. LC 82-19484. 404p. 1983. Repr. of 1982 ed. 13.95 (ISBN 0-89621-417-6). Thorndike Pr.

--The Last Valley. Large Print ed. LC 83-18099. 472p. 1984. Repr. of 1972 ed. 15.95 (ISBN 0-89621-507-5). Thorndike Pr.

--Playing Catch-Up. (Cleveland Plain Dealer Ser.: No. 4). 192p. 1985. 13.95 (ISBN 0-395-35633-4). HM.

--The Way West. 352p. (gr. 8 up). 1972. pap. 3.95 (ISBN 0-553-24785-9). Bantam.

Guthrie, Al. Hospitality Route. LC 76-43383. 1977. pap. 1.95 (ISBN 0-9606526-0-4). A Guthrie.

Guthrie, Alfred B., Jr. Big Sky. 13.95 (ISBN 0-395-07762-1, 44, SenEd); pap. 9.95 (ISBN 0-395-08393-1). HM.

Guthrie, Andrew. Vacuum Technology. LC 63-20631. 532p. 1963. 50.50x (ISBN 0-471-33722-6, Pub. by Wiley-Interscience). Wiley.

Guthrie, Anna M. Wordsworth & Tolstoi & Other Papers. LC 74-7283. 1922. Repr. lib. bdg. 17.50 (ISBN 0-8414-4507-9). Folcroft.

Guthrie, Anne E. The Secret Word: A Guide to the Hidden Potential of Microsoft Word. 120p. (Orig.). 1985. pap. 17.95 (ISBN 0-9614335-0-7); pap. text ed. 14.50 (ISBN 0-317-20526-9). TechnoLiteracy Assocs.

Guthrie, Art, et al. Accounting: The Canadian Scene. 144p. 1980. pap. text ed. 8.95 (ISBN 0-8403-2234-8). Kendall-Hunt.

Guthrie, Bennett M. Three Winds of Death: The Saga of the 503rd Parachute Regimental Combat Team in the South Pacific. (Illus.). 272p. 1984. 13.50 (ISBN 0-682-40169-2). Exposition Pr FL.

Guthrie, Colin & Dann, Colin. Looking at Insects. 88p. 1982. 30.00x (ISBN 0-686-44647-X, Pub. by Mason England). State Mutual Bk.

Guthrie, D. M. Neuroethology: An Introduction. 221p. 1981. pap. 39.95x (ISBN 0-470-26993-6). Halsted Pr.

Guthrie, David. Burns from Various Aspects. LC 74-9967. Repr. of 1936 ed. lib. bdg. 8.50 (ISBN 0-8414-4515-X). Folcroft.

Guthrie, Diana W. & Guthrie, Richard A. Nursing Management of Diabetes Mellitus. 2nd ed. LC 81-14062. (Illus.). 389p. 1982. pap. text ed. 23.75 (ISBN 0-8016-1996-3). Mosby.

Guthrie, Donald. The Apostles. 432p. 1981. pap. 11.95 (ISBN 0-310-25421-3). Zondervan.

--The Epistle to the Hebrews: An Introduction & Commentary. (Tyndale New Testament Commentaries: Vol. 15). 288p. 1983. pap. 5.95 (ISBN 0-8028-1427-1). Eerdmans.

--Exploring God's World: A Guide to Ephesians, Philippians, & Colossians. 224p. (Orig.). 1985. pap. 6.95 (ISBN 0-8028-0084-X). Eerdmans.

--Galatians. rev. ed. Black, Matthew, ed. (New Century Bible Commentary Ser.). 176p. 1981. pap. 5.95 (ISBN 0-8028-1906-0). Eerdmans.

--Jesus the Messiah. 400p. 1981. pap. 12.95 (ISBN 0-310-25431-0). Zondervan.

--New Bible Commentary. rev. ed. 1970. 24.95 (ISBN 0-8028-2281-9). Eerdmans.

--New Testament Introduction. rev. ed. 1971. 24.95 (ISBN 0-87784-953-6). Inter-Varsity.

--New Testament Theology. 1056p. 1981. text ed. 24.95 (ISBN 0-87784-965-X). Inter-Varsity.

--Pastoral Epistles. (Tyndale Bible Commentary). 1957. pap. 4.95 (ISBN 0-8028-1413-1). Eerdmans.

--Shorter Life of Christ. LC 71-120039. (Contemporary Evangelical Perspectives Ser). 1970. kivar 5.95 (ISBN 0-310-25441-8). Zondervan.

--Teaching of the New Testament. 1983. pap. 4.50 (ISBN 0-87508-179-7). Chr Lit.

Guthrie, Donna. The Witch who Lives Down the Hall. LC 85-887. (Illus.). 32p. (gr. 5-8). 1985. pap. 11.95 (ISBN 0-15-298610-3). HarBraceJ.

Guthrie, E. R., tr. see Janet, Pierre.

Guthrie, Edwin. The Psychology of Learning. rev. ed. 1952. 12.00 (ISBN 0-8446-1213-8). Peter Smith.

Guthrie, Edwin R. The Psychology of Human Conflict: The Clash of Motives Within the Individual. LC 70-138115. 408p. 1938. Repr. lib. bdg. 24.75x (ISBN 0-8371-5691-2, GUPH). Greenwood.

Guthrie, Edwin R., jt. auth. see Smith, Stevenson.

Guthrie, Eileen & Miller, Warren S. Process Politics: A Guide for Group Leaders. LC 81-51484. Orig. Title: Making Change. (Illus.). 183p. 1981. pap. 12.95 (ISBN 0-88390-167-6). Univ Assocs.

Guthrie, Eileen, et al. A Trainer's Manual for Process Politics. LC 81-51484. Orig. Title: Making Change Trainer's Manual. 88p. 1981. pap. 9.95 (ISBN 0-88390-168-4). Univ Assocs.

Guthrie, Ellen E. Old Scottish Customs. LC 77-27438. 1885. 22.50 (ISBN 0-8414-4610-5). Folcroft.

Guthrie, F. E., jt. auth. see Hodgson, E.

Guthrie, F. E. & Perry, J. J., eds. Introduction to Environmental Toxicology. 484p. 1980. 39.50 (ISBN 0-444-00359-2, Biomedical Pr). Elsevier.

Guthrie, G., et al. M R N A: Current Research, 2 vols. (Illus.). 220p. 1972. Vol. 1. text ed. 27.50x (ISBN 0-8422-7049-3); Vol. 2. text ed. 27.50x (ISBN 0-8422-7050-7). Irvington.

Guthrie, Gary D. The Wisdom Tree. 56p. (Orig.). Date not set. pap. price not set (ISBN 0-9612980-0-6). Guthrie Gary.

Guthrie, Grace P. A School Dividend: An Ethnography of Bilingual Education in a Chinese Community. 264p. 1985. text ed. 27.50 (ISBN 0-89859-576-2). L Erlbaum Assocs.

Guthrie, H. M., tr. see Janet, Pierre.

Guthrie, Harvey H. Israel's Sacred Songs: A Study of Dominant Themes. 1978. pap. 6.95 (ISBN 0-8164-2178-1, Pub. by Seabury). Winston Pr.

Guthrie, Harvey H., Jr. Israel's Sacred Songs: A Study of Dominant Themes. 256p. 1984. pap. text ed. 11.25 (ISBN 0-8191-4027-9, Co-Pub. by Episcopal Div Sch). U Pr of Amer.
--Theology As Thanksgiving: From Israel's Psalms to the Church's Eucharist. 1981. 15.95 (ISBN 0-8164-0486-0, Pub. by Seabury). Winston Pr.

Guthrie, Helen. Introductory Nutrition. 5th ed. LC 82-8084. (Illus.). 675p. 1983. pap. text ed. 23.95 (ISBN 0-8016-1997-1). Mosby.

Guthrie, Helen A. & Braddock, Karen S. Programmed Nutrition. 2nd ed. LC 77-15942. (Illus.). 332p. 1978. pap. text ed. 15.95 (ISBN 0-8016-2003-1). Mosby.

Guthrie, Henry J., jt. auth. see Kim, Suk H.

Guthrie, J. T., jt. auth. see Hebeisch, A.

Guthrie, James M. Camp-Fires of the Afro-American: Or the Colored Man As a Patriot, Soldier, Sailor, & Hero, in the Cause of Free America. Repr. of 1899 ed. 48.00 (ISBN 0-384-20484-8). Johnson Repr.
--A Quarter Century in Lawrence County, Indiana 1917-1941. LC 84-8009. (Illus.). 432p. 1984. 40.00 (ISBN 0-318-03788-2). J M Guthrie.

Guthrie, James W. School Finance Policies & Practices: The Nineteen-Eighties: Decade of Conflict. (American Education Finance Association). 312p. 1981. pap. 14.95 (ISBN 0-88410-396-X). Ballinger Pub.

Guthrie, James W. & Reed, Rodney J. Educational Administration & Policy: Effective Leadership for American Education. (Illus.). 416p. 1986. 28.95 (ISBN 0-13-235672-4). P-H.

Guthrie, James W., et al, eds. Schools & Inequality. 1971. pap. 6.95x (ISBN 0-262-57047-5). MIT Pr.

Guthrie, John. Historical Dances for the Theatre: The Pavan & the Minuet. (Illus.). 79p. 1983. pap. text ed. 11.95 (ISBN 0-903102-68-4, Pub. by Dance Bks England). Princeton Bk Co.

Guthrie, John A. & Armstrong, George R. Western Forest Industry: An Economic Outlook. LC 61-9914. pap. 88.00 (ISBN 0-317-28864-4, 2020962). Bks Demand UMI.

Guthrie, John T. Cognition, Curriculum & Comprehension. 1977. pap. 8.50 (ISBN 0-87207-520-6). Intl Reading.

Guthrie, John T., ed. Aspects of Reading Acquisition. LC 75-36956. (Hyman Blumberg Symposiulm Ser.: Fifth Ser.). (Illus.). 240p. 1976. 22.50x (ISBN 0-8018-1800-1); pap. 6.95x (ISBN 0-8018-1801-X). Johns Hopkins.
--Comprehension & Teaching: Research Reviews. 338p. 1981. 13.50 (ISBN 0-87207-943-0). Intl Reading.
--Reading: A Research Retrospective, 1881-1941. 101p. 1984. 7.00. Intl Reading.

Guthrie, K. S., ed. see Plotinus.

Guthrie, Katherine B. Through Russia: From St. Petersburg to Astrakhan & the Crimea. LC 73-115541. (Russia Observed Ser 1). 1970. Repr. of 1874 ed. 32.00 (ISBN 0-405-03030-4). Ayer Co Pubs.

Guthrie, Kenneth S., tr. The Life of Zoroaster: In the Words of His Own Hymns the "Gathas". LC 73-131036. Repr. of 1914 ed. 14.50 (ISBN 0-404-02964-7). AMS Pr.

Guthrie, Lady, tr. see Vecchio, Giorgio del.

Guthrie, LaWanda. His Strange Ways. LC 81-10854. 1985. 13.95 (ISBN 0-87949-212-0). Ashley Bks.

Guthrie, Lou. The Valley Rose. 208p. (Orig.). 1984. pap. 7.95 (ISBN 0-939298-41-4, 414). J M Prods.

Guthrie, Mearl & Bunnell, Charlene. Practice Cases for Business: A Typing Simulation. 1984. pap. text ed. 13.95 (ISBN 0-8359-5609-1). Reston.

Guthrie, Mearl, et al. Business Mathematics for the Consumer. 3rd ed. (gr. 9-12). 1975. pap. 11.20 (ISBN 0-02-831250-3); man. 5.60tchrs'. (ISBN 0-02-831260-0). Glencoe.

Guthrie, Mearl R. Alphabetic Indexing. (gr. 9-12). 1981. text ed. 3.15 wkbk. (ISBN 0-538-11540-8, K54). SW Pub.

Guthrie, Peter & Page, Mary. Little Worlds. 274p. 1985. pap. text ed. 5.95 (ISBN 0-88334-184-0). Ind Sch Pr.

Guthrie, Ramon. Maximum Security Ward & Other Poems. Gall, Sally M., ed. (Lamplighter Ser.). 216p. 1984. 20.00 (ISBN 0-89255-079-1); pap. 9.95 (ISBN 0-89255-080-5). Persea Bks.

Guthrie, Ramon, tr. see Fay, Bernard.

Guthrie, Richard A., jt. auth. see Guthrie, Diana W.

Guthrie, Richard A., jt. auth. see Jackson, Robert L.

Guthrie, Robert V. Even the Rat Was White: A Historical View of Psychology. LC 75-26520. 256p. 1976. pap. text ed. 14.50 scp (ISBN 0-06-042561-X, HarpC). Har-Row.

Guthrie, Rufus K. Food Sanitation. 2nd ed. (Illus.). 1980. lib. bdg. 24.50 (ISBN 0-87055-361-5). AVI.

Guthrie, Shirley C., tr. see Cullmann, Oscar.

Guthrie, Shirley C., Jr. Christian Doctrine: Teachings of the Christian Church. (Orig.). 1969. pap. 7.95 (ISBN 0-8042-9051-2). John Knox.

Guthrie, Thomas. Anecdotes & Stories. Repr. of 1866 ed. 12.50 (ISBN 0-8274-4157-6). R West.
--Seed-Time & Harvest of Ragged Schools: Three Pleas for Ragged Schools. LC 75-172569. (Criminology, Law Enforcement, & Social Problems Ser.: No. 150). (With a new chapter & index added). 1973. Repr. of 1860 ed. lib. bdg. 10.00x (ISBN 0-87585-150-9). Patterson Smith.

Guthrie, Thomas A. Humour & Fantasy: Vice Versa, the Tinted Venus, a Fallen Idol, the Talking Horse, Salted Almonds, the Brass Bottle. Reginald, R. & Melville, Douglas, eds. LC 77-84195. (Lost Race & Adult Fantasy Ser.). 1978. Repr. of 1931 ed. lib. bdg. 90.50x (ISBN 0-405-10953-9). Ayer Co Pubs.
--Talking Horse. facsimile ed. LC 79-103514. (Short Story Index Reprint Ser.). 1891. 18.00 (ISBN 0-8369-3256-0). Ayer Co Pubs.

Guthrie, Thomas A. see Anstey, F., pseud.

Guthrie, Tyrone. In Various Directions: A View of the Theatre. LC 78-9989. 1979. Repr. of 1965 ed. lib. bdg. 27.50x (ISBN 0-313-21224-4, GUVD). Greenwood.
--A Life in the Theatre. LC 83-45776. Repr. of 1959 ed. 32.50 (ISBN 0-404-20114-8). AMS Pr.
--A Life in the Theatre. 368p. 1985. pap. 10.95 (ISBN 0-87910-048-6). Limelight Edns.

Guthrie, Vivian. A Cup of Cold Water. (Illus.). 96p. (Orig.). 1985. pap. 5.95 (ISBN 0-89114-150-2). Baptist Pub Hse.

Guthrie, W. D. Lectures on the Fourteenth Article of Amendment to the Constitution of the United States. LC 74-118030. (American Constitutional & Legal History Ser). 1970. Repr. of 1898 ed. lib. bdg. 35.00 (ISBN 0-306-71941-X). Da Capo.

Guthrie, W. K. Greek Philosophers: From Thales to Aristotle. pap. 4.95xi (ISBN 0-06-131008-5, TB 1008, Torch). Har-Row.
--A History of Greek Philosophy, 2 vols. LC 62-52735. 1979. Vol. 1. pap. 22.95 (ISBN 0-521-29420-7); Vol. 2. pap. 22.95 (ISBN 0-521-29421-5). Cambridge U Pr.
--A History of Greek Philosophy, 6 vols. LC 62-52735. 1975. 79.50; Vol. 1. 77.50 (ISBN 0-521-05159-2); Vol. 2. 79.50 (ISBN 0-521-05160-6); Vol. 3. 79.50 (ISBN 0-521-07566-1); Vol. 4. 79.50 (ISBN 0-521-20002-4); Vol. 5. 72.50; Vol. 6. 69.50 (ISBN 0-521-23573-1). Cambridge U Pr.

Guthrie, W. K., tr. see Plato.

Guthrie, William. The Christian's Great Interest. 208p. 1983. pap. 3.45 (ISBN 0-85151-354-9). Banner of Truth.

Guthrie, William & Holt, John. Essay upon English Tragedy & an Attempt to Rescue That Aunciente, English Poet, & Playwright, Maister Willaume Shakespere. LC 70-96347. Repr. of 1747 ed. lib. bdg. 30.00x (ISBN 0-678-05113-5). Kelley.
--Essay upon English Tragedy with Remarks upon the Abbe de Blane's Observations on the English Stage. 128p. 1971. Repr. 32.50x (ISBN 0-7146-2524-8, F Cass Co). Biblio Dist.

Guthrie, William D. Lectures on the Fourteenth Article of Amendment to the Constitution of the United States. Repr. of 1898 ed. 23.00 (ISBN 0-384-20485-6). Johnson Repr.
--Magna Carta & Other Addresses. facs. ed. LC 74-84309. (Essay Index Reprint Ser). 1916. 16.25 (ISBN 0-8369-1082-6). Ayer Co Pubs.
--Magna Carta & Other Addresses. LC 74-84309. (Essay Index Reprint Ser.). 282p. Repr. of 1916 ed. lib. bdg. 13.25x (ISBN 0-8290-0471-8). Irvington.

Guthrie, William K. Greeks & Their Gods. (Orig.). 1955. pap. 8.95 (ISBN 0-8070-5793-2, BP2). Beacon Pr.
--Socrates. 1971. pap. 13.95 (ISBN 0-521-09667-7). Cambridge U Pr.
--Sophists. 1971. pap. 16.95 (ISBN 0-521-09666-9). Cambridge U Pr.

Guthrie, William K., ed. see Cornford, Francis M.

Guthrie, William N. Modern Poet Prophets. 1979. Repr. of 1897 ed. lib. bdg. 30.00 (ISBN 0-8495-2032-0). Arden Lib.
--Modern Poet Prophets (Whitman) LC 72-6115. 1972. Repr. of 1897 ed. lib. bdg. 15.00 (ISBN 0-8414-0104-7). Folcroft.

Guthrie, Woody. Bound for Glory. LC 83-13424. 320p. 1984. pap. 6.95 (ISBN 0-452-25483-3, Plume). NAL.
--Bound for Glory. Date not set. 12.75 (ISBN 0-8446-6178-3). Peter Smith.

Gutierrez, Alfredo. Paraguay: Regional Development in Eastern Paraguay. vii, 50p. 1978. pap. 10.00 (ISBN 0-686-36114-8, RC-7802). World Bank.

Gutierrez, Armando, jt. auth. see Hirsch, Herbert.

Gutierrez, Carlos M. The Dominican Republic: Rebellion & Repression. Edwards, Richard E., tr. from Sp. LC 72-81763. 144p. 1973. pap. 2.95 (ISBN 0-85345-333-0). Monthly Rev.

Gutierrez, Donald. Lapsing Out: Embodiments of Death & Rebirth in the Last Writings of D. H. Lawrence. LC 78-75177. 184p. 1980. 18.50 (ISBN 0-8386-2293-3). Fairleigh Dickinson.
--The Maze in the Mind & the World: Labyrinths in Modern Literature. LC 85-70152. xi, 197p. 1985. 18.50 (ISBN 0-87875-293-5). Whitston Pub.

Gutierrez, Edna L., tr. see Mandeville, Sylvia.

Gutierrez, Edna L., tr. see Mandeville, Sylvia & Pierson, Lance.

Gutierrez, Edna L. de see Ton, Mary E.

Gutierrez, Edna L. de see Wood, Fred M.

Gutierrez, Elias R. Factor Proportions, Technology & Unemployment in Puerto Rico. LC 76-46435. (Planning Ser.: E-20). (Illus., Orig.). 1977. pap. 7.00 (ISBN 0-8477-2439-5). U of PR Pr.

Gutierrez, Felix, tr. see Gilly, Adolfo.

Gutierrez, Felix F. & Schement, Jorge R. Spanish-Language Radio in the Southwestern United States. (Mexican American Monographs: No. 5). (Illus.). 144p. 1979. pap. text ed. 9.95x (ISBN 0-292-77550-4, Pub. by Ctr Mex Am Stud). U of Tex Pr.

Gutierrez, G., jt. ed. see Geffre, C.

Gutierrez, Gustavo. Power of the Poor in History. Barr, Robert R., tr. from Span. LC 82-22252. Orig. Title: La Fuerza Historica de los Pobres. 256p. (Orig.). 1983. pap. 10.95 (ISBN 0-88344-388-0). Orbis Bks.
--A Theology of Liberation. Inda, Caridad, Sr. & Eagleson, John, trs. from Span. LC 72-85790. Orig. Title: Teologia de la Liberacion Prospectivos. 334p. (Orig.). 1973. 7.95 (ISBN 0-88344-477-1). Orbis Bks.
--We Drink from Our Own Wells: The Spiritual Journey of a People. O'Connell, Matthew J., tr. from Span. LC 83-22008. Orig. Title: Beber en Supropio Pozo: En el Itinerario Espiritual de un Pueblo. 208p. (Orig.). 1984. pap. 7.95 (ISBN 0-88344-707-X). Orbis Bks.

Gutierrez, Gustavo & Shaull, Richard. Liberation & Change. LC 76-44970. 1977. pap. 2.75 (ISBN 0-8042-0661-9). John Knox.

Gutierrez, Luis T. & Fey, Willard R. Ecosystem Succession: A General Hypothesis & a Test Model of a Grassland. (Illus.). 1980. text ed. 35.00x (ISBN 0-262-07075-8). MIT Pr.

Gutierrez, Marta & Velilla, Angie. Be Bilingual. (Span. & Eng.). 1984. text ed. write for info. (ISBN 0-538-22650-1, V65). SW Pub.

Gutierrez, Marta, jt. auth. see Bennett, Archie.

Gutierrez, O. & Schwartz, S. I. Atlas of Hepatic Tumors & Focal Lesions: Arteriographic & Tomographic. 200p. 1984. 50.00 (ISBN 0-07-055676-8). McGraw.

Gutierrez, Rolando. El Mensaje de los Salmos en Nuestro Contexto, Tomo II. 160p. 1980. pap. 5.50 (ISBN 0-311-04025-X). Casa Bautista.

Gutierrez, Rolando C. Mensaje de los Salmos, Tomo III. 160p. 1983. pap. 7.95 (ISBN 0-311-04028-4). Casa Bautista.
--El Mensaje de los Salmos en Nuestro Contexto Tomo I. 160p. 1984. Repr. of 1979 ed. 5.95 (ISBN 0-311-04023-3). Casa Bautista.

Gutierrez-Cortes, Rolando. Cuando la Familia Enfrenta Problemas. (Serie de la Familia). 96p. (Span.). 1985. pap. 3.40 (ISBN 0-311-46261-8). Casa Bautista.

Gutierrez De Lara, L. & Pinchon, Edgcumb. The Mexican People: Their Struggle for Freedom. 1976. lib. bdg. 59.95 (ISBN 0-8490-0619-8). Gordon Pr.

Gutierrez del Arroyo, Isabel. El Doctor Agustin Stahl, Hombre de Ciencia: Perspectiva humanistica. (Publicaciones de la Facultad de Humanidades). 56p. (Span.). 1976. pap. 1.85x (ISBN 0-8477-3400-5). U of PR Pr.

Gutierrez De La Solana, A. Maneras De Narrar: Contraste De Lino Novas Calvo y Alfonso Hernandez Cata. 1972. 10.95 (ISBN 0-88303-017-9); pap. 8.95 (ISBN 0-685-73219-3). E Torres & Sons.

Gutierrez De La Solana, Alberto. Investigacion y Critica Literaria y Linguistica Cubana, No. 1. LC 78-58525. (Senda Bibliografica Ser.). (Span.). 1978. pap. 9.95 (ISBN 0-918454-06-9); deluxe ed. 11.95 (ISBN 0-686-77021-8). Senda Nueva.

Gutierrez-Mouat, Ricardo. Jose Donoso, Impostura e Impostacion. LC 83-80599. 273p. (Orig., Span.). 1983. pap. 11.95 (ISBN 0-935318-11-9). Edins Hispamerica.

Gutierrez-Revueltas, Pablo, jt. ed. see Ezpinoza, Alurista H.

Gutilerrez-Vasquez, J. M. Microorganismos. 3rd ed. OAS General Secretariat, ed. (Biology Ser.: Monograph No. 6). (Illus.). 79p. (Span.). 1981. pap. 3.50. OAS.

Gutin, Bernard & Kessler, Gail. The High-Energy Factor. LC 82-13353. 175p. 1983. 14.95 (ISBN 0-394-52548-5). Random.

Gutirrez, Terry, ed. Washington Manufacturers Register, 1984-1985. 4th ed. LC 78-643574. 300p. 1984. 65.00 (ISBN 0-911510-89-3). Times-M Pr.

Gutjahr, H. Chapter Five - Direct Print Coloration. 75.00x (ISBN 0-686-98200-2, Pub. by Soc Dyers & Colour); pap. 50.00x (ISBN 0-686-98201-0). State Mutual Bk.

Gutjahr, Rainer. Sailboard Racing. 120p. 35.00x (ISBN 0-686-79111-8, Pub. by Nautical England). State Mutual Bk.
--Sailboard Racing. (Illus.). 119p. 1982. 14.95 (ISBN 0-914814-38-9). Sail Bks.

Gutkin, Terry B., jt. ed. see Reynolds, Cecil R.

Gutkind, C. W., jt. ed. see Cohen, Robin.

Gutkind, E. A. Community & Environment. LC 73-20381. (Studies in Philosophy, No. 40). 1974. lib. bdg. 33.95x (ISBN 0-8383-1797-9). Haskell.

Gutkind, Efraim. Patterns of Economic Behavior among the American Poor. 288p. 1985. 35.00 (ISBN 0-312-59818-1). St Martin.

Gutkind, Erwin A. International History of City Development, 8 vols. Incl. Vol. 1. Urban Development in Central Europe. 1964; Vol. 2. Urban Development in Alpine & Scandinavian Countries. 1965. 50.00 (ISBN 0-02-913260-6); Vol. 3. Urban Development in Southern Europe; Spain & Portugal. 1967. 50.00 (ISBN 0-02-913270-3); Vol. 4. Urban Development in Southern Europe; Italy & Greece. 1969. 50.00 (ISBN 0-02-913280-0); Vol. 5. Urban Development in Western Europe; France & Belgium. 1970. 50.00 (ISBN 0-02-913300-9); Vol. 6. Urban Development in Western Europe: The Netherlands & Great Britain. 1971. 50.00 (ISBN 0-02-913310-6); Vol. 7. Urban Development in East-Central Europe: Poland, Czechoslavia, & Hungary. 1972. 45.00 (ISBN 0-02-913320-3); Vol. 8. Urban Development in Eastern Europe: Bulgaria, Romania, & U.S.S.R. 1972. 50.00 (ISBN 0-02-913330-0). LC 64-13231. 300.00 (ISBN 0-02-913340-8). Free Pr.

Gutkind, Lee. Bike Fever. 1974. pap. 1.50 (ISBN 0-380-00046-6, 19497). Avon.
--God's Helicopter. LC 82-19533. (Slow Loris Press Fiction Ser.). (Illus.). 180p. 1983. pap. 9.50 (ISBN 0-918366-26-7). Slow Loris.
--Our Roots Grow Deeper Than We Know: Pennsylvania Writers-Pennsylvania Life. LC 85-40338. 336p. 1985. 19.95 (ISBN 0-8229-3523-6, Dist. by Harper & Row Publishers); pap. 8.95 (ISBN 0-8229-5374-9). U of Pittsburgh Pr.
--The People of Penn's Woods West. LC 84-2192. 152p. 1984. 14.95 (ISBN 0-8229-3494-9); pap. 5.95 (ISBN 0-8229-5360-9). U of Pittsburgh Pr.

Gutkind, Pete C. W. & Waterman, Peter, eds. African Social Studies: A Radical Reader. LC 75-43575. 481p. 1978. pap. 6.95 (ISBN 0-85345-460-4). Monthly Rev.

Gutkind, Peter & Wallerstein, Immanuel, eds. Political Economy of Contemporary Africa. 2nd ed. 1985. 29.95 (ISBN 0-8039-2096-2); pap. 14.95 (ISBN 0-8039-2097-0). Sage.

Gutkind, Peter C., jt. auth. see Jongmans, D. G.

Gutkind, Peter C. & Wallerstein, Immanuel, eds. The Political Economy of Contemporary Africa. LC 75-33470. (Sage Ser. on African Modernization & Development: Vol. 1). (Illus.). 318p. 1976. 29.95 (ISBN 0-8039-0506-8); pap. 14.95 (ISBN 0-8039-0592-0). Sage.

Gutkind, Peter C., et al, eds. African Labor History. LC 78-6635. (Sage Ser. on African Modernization & Development: Vol. 2). 280p. 1978. pap. 14.95 (ISBN 0-8039-1064-9). Sage.

Gutkind, Peter C., jt. ed. see Morrison, Minion K.

Gutkind, Peter C. W. & Waterman, Peter, eds. African Social Studies: A Radical Reader. LC 75-43575. 481p. 1977. 17.50 (ISBN 0-85345-381-0, CL3810). Monthly Rev.

Gutknecht, C. & Kerner, P., eds. Friedrich der Grosse: De la Litterature Allemande, Franzoesisch-Deutsch - Mit der Moeserschen. (Gegenschrift). 180p. (Orig.). 1969. pap. 9.00x (ISBN 3-87118-027-0, Pub. by Helmut Buske Verlag Hamburg). Benjamins North Am.

Gutknecht, Christoph, ed. Contemporary English. (Occasional Papers 1, Anglo-American Forum: Vol. 5). 174p. 1976. pap. 18.95 (ISBN 3-261-01768-6). P Lang Pubs.
--Contributions to Applied Linguistics (II) Forum Linguisticum, Vol. 7. 171p. 1975. pap. 25.85 (ISBN 3-261-01790-2). P Lang Pubs.
--Contributions to Applied Linguistics (III) Forum Linguisticum, Vol. 22. 138p. 1978. pap. 22.10 (ISBN 3-261-02616-2). P Lang Pubs.

Gutknecht, Douglas B., ed. Meeting Organization & Human Resource Challenges: Perspectives, Issues & Strategies. LC 84-7289. 476p. (Orig.). 1984. lib. bdg. 29.75 (ISBN 0-8191-3981-5); pap. text ed. 19.75 (ISBN 0-8191-3982-3). U Pr of Amer.

Gutknecht, Douglas B. & Butler, Edgar W., eds. Family, Self, & Society: Emerging Issues, Alternatives, & Interventions. LC 83-1199. (Illus.). 606p. (Orig.). 1983. lib. bdg. 39.25 (ISBN 0-8191-3077-X); pap. text ed. 24.25 (ISBN 0-8191-3078-8). U Pr of Amer.

Gutknecht, M., ed. see Rutishauser, H.

Gutknecht, Vereina, jt. ed. see Hirt, Walter.

Gutkoska, Joseph & Garner, Robert. Building Word Power: A Handbook for Parents & Teachers. 53p. (Orig.). (gr. 1-3). 1981. pap. 4.95 (ISBN 0-930723-01-5). Nutshell Enterprises.

Gutkoska, Joseph P. The Comprehensive Vocabulary Program, Vol. 1. 96p. (Orig.). (gr. 4-6). 1980. pap. 5.95 (ISBN 0-930723-02-3). Nutshell Enterprises.
--The Comprehensive Vocabulary Program, Vol. 2. 94p. (Orig.). (gr. 7-8). 1980. pap. 5.95 (ISBN 0-930723-03-1). Nutshell Enterprises.
--The Comprehensive Vocabulary Program, Vol. 3. 94p. (Orig.). (gr. 9-10). 1980. pap. 5.95 (ISBN 0-930723-04-X). Nutshell Enterprises.
--The Comprehensive Vocabulary Program, Vol. 4. 94p. (Orig.). (gr. 11-12). 1981. pap. 5.95 (ISBN 0-930723-05-8). Nutshell Enterprises.
--Developing Comprehension Skills Through the Use of Analogies. (Orig.). (gr. 5-12). 1985. pap. 6.95 (ISBN 0-930723-00-7). Nutshell Enterprises.

Gutkowski, Richard M. Structures: Fundamental Theory & Behavior. 592p. 1980. 36.50 (ISBN 0-442-22983-6). Van Nos Reinhold.

Gutman. How to Keep Product Costs in Line. (Costs Engineering Ser.). 328p. 1985. 35.00 (ISBN 0-8247-7265-2). Dekker.

Gutman, Bill. Baseball Stars of Tomorrow: An Inside Look at the Minor Leagues. 192p. 1982. pap. 2.50 (ISBN 0-448-16937-1, Pub. by Tempo). Ace Bks.

--Flame Throwers: Carlton & Gossage. (Baseball Ser.). (Illus.). 192p. 1982. pap. 2.50 (ISBN 0-448-16841-3, Pub. by Tempo). Ace Bks.

--Gamebreakers of the NFL. (NFL Punt, Pass & Kick Library: No. 18). (Illus.). (gr. 5 up). 1973. (BYR); PLB 3.69 (ISBN 0-394-92501-7). Random.

--Gridiron Superstars. 176p. 1983. pap. 2.25 (ISBN 0-441-30340-4). Ace Bks.

--The Harlem Globetrotters: Basketball's Funniest Team. LC 76-44411. (Sports Library). (Illus.). (gr. 4). 1977. lib. bdg. 7.98 (ISBN 0-8116-6680-8). Garrard.

--Modern Soccer Superstars. LC 79-52048. (High Interest-Low Vocabulary Ser.). (Illus.). (gr. 4-9). 1980. 8.95 (ISBN 0-396-07731-5). Dodd.

--Modern Women Superstars. LC 77-6503. (High Interest-Low Vocabulary Ser.). (Illus.). (gr. 4-9). 1977. 8.95 (ISBN 0-396-07489-8). Dodd.

--More Modern Women Superstars. LC 78-22433. (High Interest-Low Vocabulary Ser.). (Illus.). (gr. 4-9). 1979. 8.95 (ISBN 0-396-07680-7). Dodd.

--The Picture Life of Reggie Jackson. (gr. 1 up). 1978. pap. 1.95 (ISBN 0-380-40345-5, 58743-2, Camelot). Avon.

--Reggie Jackson, the Picture Life. LC 78-1335. (Picture Life Bks.). (gr. 2 up). 1978. PLB 9.90 (ISBN 0-531-01483-5). Watts.

--The Signal Callers: Sipe, Jaworski, Ferguson, Bartkowski. 1982. pap. 2.25 (ISBN 0-448-17268-2, Pub. by Tempo). Ace Bks.

--Women Who Work with Animals. (High Interest, Low Vocabulary). (Illus.). 160p. (gr. 5 up). 1982. PLB 8.95 (ISBN 0-396-08035-9). Dodd.

Gutman, Cheryl M. see Hejna, William F.

Gutman, Dan & Adams, Shay. The Greatest Games: The Ninety-Three Best Computer Games of All Time. Compute Editors, ed. (Orig.). 1985. pap. 9.95 (ISBN 0-942386-95-7). Compute Pubns.

Gutman, David. Prokofiev: His Life & Times. (Illus.). 150p. (gr. 7 up). Date not set. 25.00 (ISBN 0-88254-730-5, Pub. by Midas Bks England). Hippocrene Bks.

Gutman, Elana, ed. Art Directors Index U. S. A, Vol. 11. (Illus.). 488p. 1985. pap. 35.00 (ISBN 0-317-17672-2, Pub. by Rotovision). R Silver.

Gutman, Ernest M. A Travel Guide for the Disabled. 148p. 1967. 14.75x (ISBN 0-398-00748-9). C C Thomas.

--Wheelchair to Independence: Architectural Barriers Eliminated. (Illus.). 160p. 1968. photocopy ed. 17.50x (ISBN 0-398-00749-7). C C Thomas.

Gutman, Herbert G. Black Family in Slavery & Freedom, 1750-1925. (YA) 1977. pap. 6.95 (ISBN 0-394-72451-8, Vin). Random.

--Slavery & the Numbers Game: A Critique of Time on the Cross. LC 75-15899. (Blacks in the New World Ser.). (Illus.). 182p. 1975. pap. 5.95x (ISBN 0-252-00565-1). U of Ill Pr.

--Work Culture & Society in Industrializing America: Essays in America's Working Class & Social History. 1977. pap. 7.95 (ISBN 0-394-72251-5, Vin). Random.

Gutman, I. Industrial Uses of Mechanical Vibrations. (Illus.). 332p. 1968. 20.00x (ISBN 0-8464-1110-5). Beekman Pubs.

Gutman, Israel. Poles & Jews Between the Wars. 1985. 14.95 (ISBN 0-8052-5057-3); pap. 10.95 (ISBN 0-8052-5058-1). Schocken.

Gutman, Israel & Krakowski, Smuel. Poles & Jews Between The Wars. 1984. 14.95 (ISBN 0-89604-055-0); pap. 10.95 (ISBN 0-89604-056-9). Holocaust Pubns.

Gutman, Judith M. Through Indian Eyes. (Illus.). 1982. 16.50 (ISBN 0-19-503135-0). Oxford U Pr.

Gutman, Kellie O., jt. auth. see Gutman, Richard J.

Gutman, Myron P. War & Rural Life in the Early Modern Low Countries. LC 79-3237. (Illus.). 1980. 35.00x (ISBN 0-691-05291-3). Princeton U Pr.

Gutman, Richard, et al. American Diner. LC 79-1665. 192p. 1980. pap. 8.95i (ISBN 0-06-090811-4, CN 811, CN). Har-Row.

Gutman, Richard J. The Summer Camp Memory Book: A Pictorial Treasury of Everything-from Campfires to Color Wars You Loved about Camp. 4.98 (ISBN 0-517-54743-0). Crown.

Gutman, Richard J. & Gutman, Kellie O. John Wilkes Booth Himself. LC 78-71462. (Illus.). 1979. 20.00x (ISBN 0-9602256-0-9). Hired Hand.

Gutman, Stanley T. Mankind in Barbary: The Individual & Society in the Novels of Norman Mailer. LC 75-18290. 238p. 1975. text ed. 17.50x (ISBN 0-87451-118-6). U Pr of New Eng.

Gutman, Theodore E., tr. see Sapper, Karl.

Gutman, Walter. The Gutman Letter. LC 72-77962. (Illus.). 1969. 20.00 (ISBN 0-89366-056-6). Ultramarine Pub.

Gutman, Y. & Rothkirchen, L., eds. The Catastrophe of European Jewry: Antecedents, History, Reflections. 22.50x (ISBN 0-87068-336-5). Ktav.

Gutman, Y. & Zuroff, E., eds. Rescue Attempts During the Holocaust. 25.00x (ISBN 0-87068-345-4). Ktav.

Gutman, Yisrael. The Jews of Warsaw, 1939-1943: Ghetto, Underground, Revolt. Friedman, Ina, tr. LC 81-47570. (Illus.). 512p. 1982. 24.95x (ISBN 0-253-33174-9). Ind U Pr.

Gutman, Yisrael, ed. The Holocaust in Documents. 1982. 22.50 (ISBN 0-686-85569-8). ADL.

Gutmanis, June. Na Pule Kahiko: Ancient Hawaiian Prayers. LC 83-80256. (Illus.). 136p. 1983. 17.50 (ISBN 0-9607938-6-0); deluxe ed. 100.00 (ISBN 0-9607938-7-9). Editions Ltd.

Gutmann, Amy. Liberal Equality. LC 79-27258. 320p. 1980. 44.50 (ISBN 0-521-22828-X); pap. 16.95 (ISBN 0-521-29665-X). Cambridge U Pr.

Gutmann, Amy & Thompson, Dennis, eds. Ethics & Politics: Cases & Comments. LC 83-24996. 360p. 1984. text ed. 29.95x (ISBN 0-8304-1090-2); pap. text ed. 13.95x (ISBN 0-8304-1115-1). Nelson-Hall.

Gutmann, Emanuel & Caspi, Dan, eds. The Roots of Begin's Success: The 1981 Israeli Elections. LC 83-3120. 300p. 1983. 25.00x (ISBN 0-312-69309-5). St Martin.

Gutmann, Ernest, ed. Denervated Muscle. 486p. 1962. 50.00x (ISBN 0-306-10653-1, Consultants). Plenum Pub.

Gutmann, Felix & Lyons, Lawrence. Organic Semiconductors, Pt. A. rev. ed. LC 78-25782. 876p. 1981. Repr. of 1967 ed. lib. bdg. 54.50 (ISBN 0-88275-823-3). Krieger.

Gutmann, Felix & Bloom, Harry, eds. Electrochemistry: The Past Thirty & the Next Thirty Years. LC 76-49951. (Illus.). 450p. 1977. 69.50 (ISBN 0-306-30921-1, Plenum Pr). Plenum Pub.

Gutmann, Felix, jt. ed. see Keyzer, Hendrik.

Gutmann, Felix, et al. Organic Semiconductors, Pt. B. LC 78-25782. 742p. 1983. 46.50 (ISBN 0-89874-316-8). Krieger.

Gutmann, James, tr. see Schelling, Friedrich W.

Gutmann, Joseph. Beauty in Holiness: Studies in Jewish Ceremonial Art & Customs. 1970. 45.00x (ISBN 0-87068-012-9). Ktav.

--Hebrew Manuscript Painting. (Magnificent Paperback Art Ser.). 1978. 22.95 (ISBN 0-8076-0890-4); pap. 12.95 (ISBN 0-8076-0891-2). Braziller.

--The Jewish Sanctuary. (Inconography of Religions, Section Ser.: Vol. 23). (Illus.). 33p. 1983. 28.25x (ISBN 90-04-06893-7, Pub. by Brill Holland). Humanities.

--No Graven Images: Studies in Art & the Hebrew Bible. (Library of Biblical Studies). 1970. 45.00x (ISBN 0-87068-063-3). Ktav.

--The Synagogue: Studies in Origins, Archeology, & Architecture. 1974. 35.00x (ISBN 0-87068-265-2). Ktav.

Gutmann, Joseph, ed. Ancient Synagogues: The State of Research. LC 81-5252. (Brown Univ. BJS Ser.). 1981. pap. 14.00 (ISBN 0-89130-467-3, 140022). Scholars Pr GA.

--The Image & the Word: Confrontations in Judaism, Christianity & Islam. LC 77-23470. (American Academy of Religion & Society of Biblical Literature. Religion & the Arts Ser.: Vol. 4). 1977. pap. 9.00 (ISBN 0-89130-143-7, 09-01-04); pap. write for info. Scholars Pr GA.

--The Temple of Solomon: Archaeological Fact & Medieval Tradition in Christian, Islamic & Jewish Art. LC 75-19120. 1976. 9.00 (ISBN 0-89130-013-9, 090103). Scholars Pr GA.

Gutmann, Joseph & Chyet, Stanley F., eds. Moses Jacob Ezekiel: Memoirs from the Baths of Diocletian. LC 74-28009. (Schaver Pubns. Fund for Jewish Studies Ser). (Illus.). 509p. 1975. 25.00x (ISBN 0-8143-1525-9). Wayne St U Pr.

Gutmann, P. T., jt. auth. see Lomax, D. F.

Gutmann, V; see Dunitz, J. D., et al.

Gutmann, Viktor. Coordination Chemistry in Non-Aqueous Solutions. LC 68-13490. (Illus.). 1968. 29.50 (ISBN 0-387-80867-1). Springer-Verlag.

--The Donor-Acceptor Approach to Molecular Interactions. LC 77-25012. 295p. 1978. 45.00x (ISBN 0-306-31064-3, Plenum Pr). Plenum Pub.

Gutmann, Viktor, ed. International Review of Halogen Chemistry, 3 Vols. LC 66-30147. (Illus.). Vol. 1, 1967. 81.00 (ISBN 0-12-310901-9); Vol. 2, 1967. 76.00 (ISBN 0-12-310902-7); Vol. 3, 1968. 81.00 (ISBN 0-12-310903-5). Acad Pr.

Gutnam, Israel & Krakowski, Shmuel. Poles & Jews Between the Wars. 384p. 1985. 14.95 (ISBN 0-8052-5057-3, Dist. by Schocken Bks); pap. 10.95 (ISBN 0-8052-5058-1). Holocaust Pubns.

Gutnecht, Christoph, ed. Contributions to Applied Linguistics: Forum Linguisticum, Vol. 3. 234p. 1975. pap. 0.28.70 (ISBN 3-261-01780-5). P Lang Pubs.

Gutnik, Martin. Genetics. (Projects for Young Scientists). 128p. (gr. 7-12). 1985. PLB 10.40 (ISBN 0-531-04936-1). Watts.

Gutnik, Martin J. Ecology. (Projects for Young Scientists Ser.). 96p. (gr. 7 up). 1984. lib. bdg. 9.90 (ISBN 0-531-04765-2). Watts.

--How to Do a Science Project & Report. (gr. 7 up). 1980. PLB 8.90 (ISBN 0-531-04129-8). Watts.

--Science of Classification: Finding Order among Living & Nonliving Objects. (gr. 4 up). 1980. PLB 8.90 (ISBN 0-531-04160-3). Watts.

Gutnikov, G., tr. see Engelhardt, H.

Gutnov, Alexei, et al. The Ideal Communist City. 1978. text ed. 16.50x (ISBN 0-262-07073-1); pap. 6.95x (ISBN 0-262-57053-X). MIT Pr.

Gutowski, Armin, et al, eds. Financing Problems of Developing Countries: Proceedings of a Conference Held by the International Economic Association in Buenos Aires, Argentina. 400p. 1985. 39.95 (ISBN 0-312-28983-9). St Martin.

Gutowski, Michael & Field, Tracey. The Graying of Suburbia. (Illus.). 107p. (Orig.). 1979. pap. text ed. 6.00x (ISBN 0-87766-255-X). Urban Inst.

Gutowski, Michael, et al. The Pittsburgh Nonprofit Sector in a Time of Government Retrenchment. (Nonprofit Sector Ser.). 62p. (Orig.). 1984. pap. text ed. 12.95x (ISBN 0-87766-361-0). Urban Inst.

Gutridge, D. Foster, II. Your Secret Power: Creating Happiness, Vol. 2. (Your Secret Power Ser.). 96p. (Orig.). 1981. pap. 5.95 (ISBN 0-938014-02-1, 1001B). Freedom Unltd.

--Your Secret Power: Creating Harmony with Others, Vol. 4. 96p. (Orig.). 1981. pap. 5.95 (ISBN 0-938014-04-8, 301D). Freedom Unltd.

--Your Secret Power: Creating Love, Vol. 3. (Your Secret Power Ser.). 96p. (Orig.). 1981. pap. 5.95 (ISBN 0-938014-03-X, 2001C). Freedom Unltd.

--Your Secret Power: Creating Riches, Vol. 1. LC 80-69710. (Your Secret Power Ser.). 80p. (Orig.). 1981. pap. 5.95 (ISBN 0-938014-01-3, 901A). Freedom Unltd.

Gutsch, Kenneth U. & Daniels, Jack L. The Counselor's Desk Manual. (Illus.). 242p. 1985. 29.50x (ISBN 0-398-05114-3). C C Thomas.

Gutsch, Kenneth U. & Ritenour, Jacob V. Nexus Psychotherapy: Between Humanism & Behaviorism. (Illus.). 196p. 1978. 19.75x (ISBN 0-398-03734-5). C C Thomas.

Gutsch, Kenneth U. & Thornton, Larry L. Insights into Human Development: Commentaries. LC 77-17020. 1978. 9.95x (ISBN 0-87805-043-4); pap. 4.95x (ISBN 0-87805-044-2). U Pr of Miss.

Gutsch, Kenneth U., et al. Systems of Psychotherapy: An Empirical Analysis of Theoretical Models. (Illus.). 340p. 1984. 29.50x (ISBN 0-398-04922-X). C C Thomas.

Gutsche, C. David see Hart, Harold & Karabatsos, Gerasimos J.

Gutsche, George J. & Leighton, Lauren G., eds. New Perspectives on Nineteenth Century Russian Prose. 146p. (Orig.). 1982. pap. 9.95 (ISBN 0-89357-094-X). Slavica.

Gutstein, Solomon. Illinois Real Estate, 2 vols. LC 79-92517. (Practice Systems Library). (Illus.). 159.00; Suppl. 1984. 35.00. Lawyers Co-Op.

Gutteling, Johanna F. Hellenic Influence on the English Poetry of the Nineteenth Century. LC 74-28426. lib. bdg. 15.00 (ISBN 0-8414-4575-3). Folcroft.

Guttemtag, Marcia. The Evaluation of Training in Mental Health. LC 74-8506. 131p. 1975. 19.95 (ISBN 0-87705-161-5). Human Sci Pr.

Guttenberg, Barnett. Web of Being: The Novels of Robert Penn Warren. LC 74-26892. 192p. 1975. 11.95x (ISBN 0-8265-1198-8). Vanderbilt U Pr.

--Web of Being: The Novels of Robert Penn Warring. (Vanderbilt University Press Bks.). 192p. 1975. 11.95 (ISBN 0-317-06450-9). U of Ill Pr.

Guttenplan, Sammuel D. & Tamny, Martin. Logic: A Comprehensive Introduction. rev. 2nd ed. LC 77-20418. 1978. 13.95x (ISBN 0-465-04161-2). Basic.

Guttenplan, Samuel, ed. Mind & Language: Wolfson College Lectures 1974. 1975. pap. 6.95x (ISBN 0-19-875043-9). Oxford U Pr.

Guttentag, Jack & Herring, Richard. The Lender-of-Last Resort Function in an International Context. LC 83-8444. (Essays in International Finance Ser.: No. 151). 1983. pap. text ed. 2.50x (ISBN 0-88165-058-7). Princeton U Int Finan Econ.

Guttentag, Jack M. Branch Banking, Interstate Branching & Loan Production Offices: Analysis of the Issues. (Lec Occasional Paper Ser.). 1979. pap. 2.50 (ISBN 0-916770-10-9). Law & Econ U Miami.

Guttentag, Jack M. & Herring, Richard J. The Current Crisis in International Lending. (Studies in International Economics). 70p. 1985. pap. 6.95 (ISBN 0-8157-3325-9). Brookings.

Guttentag, Jack M., ed. Essays on Interest Rates, Vol. 2. (General Ser.: No. 93). 482p. 1971. 30.00 (ISBN 0-87014-224-0). Natl Bur Econ Res.

Guttentag, Marcia & Secord, Paul F. Too Many Women? The Sex Ratio Question. 336p. 1983. 28.00 (ISBN 0-8039-1918-2); pap. 14.00 (ISBN 0-8039-1919-0). Sage.

Guttentag, Marcia & Saar, Shalom, eds. Evaluation Studies Review Annual, Vol. 2. LC 77-81156. (Illus.). 736p. 1977. 40.00 (ISBN 0-8039-0724-9). Sage.

Guttentag, Marcia, jt. ed. see Struening, Elmer L.

Gutter. Atlas Linguistique et Ethnographique des Pyrenees-Orientales. 75.00 (ISBN 0-685-36660-X). French & Eur.

Gutter, Mae & Rooks, Nancy. The Maid, the Man, & the Fans: Elvis Is the Man. 1984. 6.95 (ISBN 0-533-06053-2). Vantage.

Gutterbock, Hans G. & Hoffner, Harry A., Jr., eds. The Hittite Dictionary, Vol. 3: Fascicle 2 (-ma to miyahuwant-) LC 79-53554. (The Hittite Dictionary of the Oriental Institute of the University of Chicago (CHD)). 127p. 1983. pap. 15.00x (ISBN 0-918986-38-9). Oriental Inst.

Gutteridge, Harold C. & Megrah, Maurice. The Law of Bankers' Commercial Credits. 6th ed. 318p. 1979. 22.50x (ISBN 0-905118-42-1). Intl Pubns Serv.

Gutteridge, John M., jt. auth. see Halliwell, Barry.

Gutteridge, Richard. Open Thy Mouth for the Dumb! The German Evangelical Church & the Jews, 1879-1950. LC 76-12068. 1976. text ed. 23.50x (ISBN 0-06-492620-6). B&N Imports.

Gutteridge, Thomas G., jt. auth. see Walker, James W.

Gutteridge, W. E. & Coombs, G. H. The Biochemistry of Parasitic Protozoa: An Introductory Text. (Illus.). 184p. 1977. pap. text ed. 21.00 (ISBN 0-8391-0886-9). Univ Park.

Gutteridge, W. F. South Africa's Military Capabilities. (Illus.). 200p. 1986. 20.00 (ISBN 0-08-031173-3, Pub. by BDP); pap. 11.00 (ISBN 0-08-031174-1). Pergamon.

Gutteridge, William, ed. European Security, Nuclear Weapons & Public Confidence. 1982. 29.95x (ISBN 0-312-27085-2). St Martin.

Gutteridge, William & Taylor, Trevor, eds. The Dangers of New Weapons Systems. LC 82-23066. 200p. 1983. 27.50 (ISBN 0-312-18217-1). St Martin.

Gutterman, Norman, tr. see Paracelsus.

Gutterman, Sy. Business Management for the Professional Photographer. (Illus.). 1980. text ed. 14.95 (ISBN 0-8174-3568-9, Amphoto). Watson-Guptill.

Guttery, T. E. Zeppelin. (Lifelines Ser.: No. 23). (Illus.). 64p. (Orig.). 1983. pap. 3.50 (ISBN 0-85263-210-X, Pub. by Shire Pubns England). Seven Hills Bks.

Guttgemans, Erhard T. Candid Questions Concerning Gospel Form Criticism: A Methodological Sketch of Fundamental Problematics of Form & Redaction Criticism. 2nd ed. Doty, William G., tr. LC 79-10167. (Pittsburgh Theological Monographs: No. 26). 1979. pap. 18.25 (ISBN 0-915138-24-7). Pickwick.

Gutting, Gary. Religious Belief & Religious Skepticism. LC 82-50287. 192p. 1982. text ed. 15.95 (ISBN 0-268-01613-5). U of Notre Dame Pr.

--Religious Belief & Religious Skepticism. LC 82-50287. xi, 192p. 1983. pap. text ed. 9.95x (ISBN 0-268-01618-6, 85-16189). U of Notre Dame Pr.

Gutting, Gary, ed. Paradigms & Revolutions: Appraisals & Applications of Thomas Kuhn's Philosophy of Science. LC 80-20745. 256p. 1980. text ed. 18.95 (ISBN 0-268-01542-2); pap. text ed. 9.95 (ISBN 0-268-01543-0). U of Notre Dame Pr.

Gutting, Robert. Chelation Therapy. 1.00x (ISBN 0-686-29933-7). Cancer Control Soc.

--Selenium. 1.39x (ISBN 0-686-29934-5). Cancer Control Soc.

Guttmacher, Alan. Pregnancy, Birth & Family Planning. (Reference Ser.). 352p. 1973. pap. 3.95 (ISBN 0-451-12741-2, AE2741, Sig). NAL.

--Pregnancy, Birth & Family Planning. 1984. pap. 9.95 (ISBN 0-452-25536-8, Plume). NAL.

Guttmacher, Manfred S. Mind of the Murderer. LC 72-10849. (Select Bibliographies Reprint Ser.). 1973. Repr. of 1960 ed. 19.00 (ISBN 0-8369-7111-6). Ayer Co Pubs.

Guttman, Alexander. Struggle Over Reform in Rabbinic Literature. LC 75-45046. 1977. 13.50 (ISBN 0-8074-0005-X, 382790). UAHC.

Guttman, Burton S. & Hopkins, Johns W., III. Understanding Biology. 978p. 1983. text ed. 31.95 (ISBN 0-15-592701-9, HC); pap. text ed. test file avail. (ISBN 0-15-592704-3); study guide 11.95 (ISBN 0-15-592702-7); pap. text ed. instr's manual avail. (ISBN 0-15-592703-5). HarBraceJ.

Guttman, Egon, jt. auth. see Israels, Carlos L.

Guttman, I. Linear Models: An Introduction. (Wiley Series in Probability & Mathematical Statistics-Probability & Mathematical Statistics Sectipon). 358p. 1982. 42.95x (ISBN 0-471-09915-5, Pub. by Wiley-Interscience). Wiley.

--Statistical Tolerance Regions: Classical & Bayesian. (Griffin's Statistical Monographs: No. 26). 150p. 1970. pap. text ed. 10.95X (ISBN 0-686-39549-2). Lubrecht & Cramer.

Guttman, Irwin, et al. Introductory Engineering Statistics. 3rd ed. 580p. 1982. text ed. 42.50 (ISBN 0-471-07859-X); solutions manual avail. (ISBN 0-471-08659-2). Wiley.

Guttman, Julius. Philosophies of Judaism: The History of Jewish Philosophy from Biblical Times to Franz Rosenzweig. LC 63-11875. 560p. 1973. pap. 11.95 (ISBN 0-8052-0402-4). Schocken.

Guttman, Julius W., ed. see Maimonodes, Moses.

Guttman, Linda, jt. auth. see Pocklington, Dorothy B.

Guttman, Lorrie. Guide to Dining Out in Tallahassee. (Illus.). 112p. 1981. pap. 3.95 (ISBN 0-942434-00-5). Old Fields Pubs.

Guttman, Michael. Experiments for Chemistry: 1046L. 1976. coil bdg. 4.95 (ISBN 0-88252-047-4). Paladin Hse.

Guttman, S. I., jt. ed. see Taylor, D. H.

Guttman, Samuel A., ed. see Waelder, Robert.

Guttman, Samuel A., et al. The Concordance to the Standard Edition of the Complete Works of Sigmund Freud, 6 vols. LC 83-22874. lxiii, 5512p. 1984. Set. text ed. 800.00x (ISBN 0-317-13817-0). Vol. 1 (ISBN 0-8236-1071-3). Vol. 2 (ISBN 0-8236-1072-1). Vol. 3 (ISBN 0-8236-1074-8). Vol. 4. Vol. 5. Vol. 6 (ISBN 0-8236-1076-4). Intl Univs Pr.
Guttman, V., ed. Phase Stability in High Temperature Alloys. (Illus.). vii, 155p. 1981. 42.75 (ISBN 0-85334-946-0, Pub. by Elsevier Applied Sci England). Elsevier.
Guttman, V. & Merz, M., eds. Corrosion & Mechanical Stress at High Temperatures. (Illus.). 477p. 1981. 52.00 (ISBN 0-85334-956-8, Pub. by Elsevier Applied Sci England). Elsevier.
Guttmann, Alexander. Rabbinic Judaism in the Making: The Halakhah from Ezra to I Judah. LC 69-10525. 344p. 1970. 17.95x (ISBN 0-8143-1382-5). Wayne St U Pr.
Guttmann, Allen. From Ritual to Record: The Nature of Modern Sports. (Illus.). 198p. 1979. 27.50x (ISBN 0-231-03993-X); pap. 10.50x (ISBN 0-231-08369-6). Columbia U Pr.
--The Games Must Go on: Avery Brundage & the Olympic Movement. LC 83-5360. (Illus.). 296p. 1983. 25.00x (ISBN 0-231-05444-0). Columbia U Pr.
Guttmann, Allen & Sappenfield, James, eds. Complete Works of Washington Irving: Life of George Washington, 5 vols. (Critical Editions Program Ser.). 1981. 83.50 (ISBN 0-8057-8511-6, Twayne). G K Hall.
Guttmann, Allen, jt. ed. see Filler, Louis.
Guttmann, Allen, ed. see Rigauer, Bero.
Guttmann, Jacob. Die Religionsphilosophischen Lehren des Isaak Abravanel. Katz, Steven, ed. LC 79-7134. (Jewish Philosophy, Mysticism & History of Ideas Ser.). 1980. Repr. of 1916 ed. lib. bdg. 14.00x (ISBN 0-405-12260-8). Ayer Co Pubs.
Guttmann, Mark J., jt. auth. see Simmons, Joseph W.
Guttmann, Yitzhak J. On the Philosophy of Religion. Herman, David V., tr. from Hebrew. 134p. 1976. text ed. 25.50x (Pub. by Magnes Israel). Humanities.
Guttorp. Statistics Inference for Branching Processes. (Probability & Mathematical Ser.). 1986. price not set (ISBN 0-471-82291-4). Wiley.
Guttridge, George H. Colonial Policy of William III in America & West Indies. new ed. 190p. 1966. 27.50x (ISBN 0-7146-1478-5, F Cass Co). Biblio Dist.
--English Whiggism & the American Revolution. LC 75-41125. Repr. of 1942 ed. 15.00 (ISBN 0-404-14668-6). AMS Pr.
Guttridge, George H. see Burke, Edmund.
Guttridge, Len, jt. auth. see Smith, Jay D.
Guttridge, Leonard F. & Smith, Jay D. The Commodores. (Classics of Naval Literature Ser.). 352p. 1984. 16.95 (ISBN 0-87021-133-1). Naval Inst Pr.
Guttschaik, George E., jt. ed. see Cangemi, Joseph P.
Guttschuss, Heather. Growing More Like Jesus. 128p. (ps). Date not set. pap. 5.95 (ISBN 0-8163-0486-6). Pacific Pr Pub Assn.
Guttsman, W. L. The German Social Democratic Party, 1875-1933. (Illus.). 1981. text ed. 37.50x (ISBN 0-04-943024-6). Allen Unwin.
Gutwein, Kenneth C. Third Palestine: A Regional Study in Byzantine Urbanization. LC 81-40340. 430p. 1982. lib. bdg. 31.00 (ISBN 0-8191-1907-5); pap. text ed. 18.25 (ISBN 0-8191-1908-3). U Pr of Amer.
Gutwinski, Waldemar, ed. see Linguistic Association of Canada & the U. S.
Gutwirth, Madelyn. Madame De Stael, Novelist: The Emergence of the Artist as Woman. LC 78-5836. 336p. 1978. 25.00 (ISBN 0-252-00676-3). U of Ill Pr.
Gutwirth, Samuel. You Can Learn to Relax. pap. 3.00 (ISBN 0-87980-177-8). Wilshire.
Gutzke, Manford. Plain Talk on Romans. 1976. pap. 6.95 (ISBN 0-310-25621-6). Zondervan.
Gutzke, Manford G. Plain Talk on Acts. 224p. 1972. pap. 6.95 (ISBN 0-310-25501-5). Zondervan.
--Plain Talk on Colossians. (Plain Talk Ser.). 112p. (Orig.). 1981. pap. 4.95 (ISBN 0-310-41961-1). Zondervan.
--Plain Talk on Corinthians. 1978. pap. 6.95 (ISBN 0-310-25641-0). Zondervan.
--Plain Talk on Deuteronomy. 1980. pap. 4.95 (ISBN 0-310-25691-7). Zondervan.
--Plain Talk on Ephesians. 224p. 1973. pap. 5.95 (ISBN 0-310-25511-2). Zondervan.
--Plain Talk on Exodus. new ed. 224p. (Orig.). 1974. pap. 6.95 (ISBN 0-310-25521-X). Zondervan.
--Plain Talk on Galatians. pap. 5.95 (ISBN 0-310-25651-8). Zondervan.
--Plain Talk on Genesis. 160p. 1975. pap. 4.95 (ISBN 0-310-25531-7). Zondervan.
--Plain Talk on Hebrews. 160p. 1976. pap. 4.95 (ISBN 0-310-25541-4). Zondervan.
--Plain Talk on Isaiah. 1977. pap. 6.95 (ISBN 0-310-25551-1). Zondervan.
--Plain Talk on James. 1969. pap. 5.95 (ISBN 0-310-25561-9). Zondervan.
--Plain Talk on John. LC 69-11646. (Prog. Bk.). 1969. pap. 5.95 (ISBN 0-310-25571-6). Zondervan.
--Plain Talk on Leviticus & Numbers. 144p. 1981. pap. 4.95 (ISBN 0-310-41951-4, 9872P). Zondervan.
--Plain Talk on Luke. 1966. pap. 5.95 (ISBN 0-310-25581-3). Zondervan.
--Plain Talk on Mark. 295p. 1975. pap. 6.95 (ISBN 0-310-25591-0). Zondervan.
--Plain Talk on Matthew. pap. 6.95 (ISBN 0-310-25601-1). Zondervan.
--Plain Talk on Peter & Jude. (Plain Talk Ser.). 1979. pap. 5.95 (ISBN 0-310-25671-2). Zondervan.
--Plain Talk on Philippians. 288p. 1973. pap. 6.95 (ISBN 0-310-25611-9). Zondervan.
--Plain Talk on Revelation. (Orig.). 1979. pap. 5.95 (ISBN 0-310-25681-X). Zondervan.
--Plain Talk on the Epistles of John. 1977. pap. 4.95 (ISBN 0-310-25631-3). Zondervan.
--Plain Talk on the Minor Prophets. (Plain Talk Series of Bible Study Bks.). 160p. (Orig.). 1980. pap. 4.95 (ISBN 0-310-41941-7, 9868P). Zondervan.
--Plain Talk on Thessalonians. (Plain Talk Bible Study Ser.). 128p. (Orig.). 1980. pap. 4.95 (ISBN 0-310-25701-8). Zondervan.
--Plain Talk on Timothy, Titus, & Philemon. (Plain Talk Ser.). 1978. pap. 6.95 (ISBN 0-310-25661-5). Zondervan.
Gutzkow, Karl, ed. Forum der Journal-Literatur: Eine antikritische Quartalsschrift, 2 vols. vol. 1, nos. 1-2 25.00 (ISBN 0-384-16443-9); vol. 2, nos. 1-14 14.00. Johnson Repr.
Gutzkow, Karl, jt. ed. see Duller, Edward.
Guy, et al, eds. Combinatorial Structures & Their Applications. 524p. 1970. 104.50 (ISBN 0-677-13890-3). Gordon.
Guy, A. G. Essentials of Materials Science. 1976. text ed. 42.00 (ISBN 0-07-025351-X). McGraw.
Guy, Alan J. Oeconomy & Discipline: Officership & Administration in the British Army, 1714-63. LC 84-1268. 188p. 1985. 37.50 (ISBN 0-7190-1099-3, Pub. by Manchester Univ Pr). Longwood Pub Group.
Guy, Albert G. & Hren, John J. Elements of Physical Metallurgy. 3rd ed. LC 72-9315. 1974. text ed. 31.95 (ISBN 0-201-02633-3). Addison-Wesley.
Guy, Basil, ed. see De Ligne.
Guy, Clifford M. Retail Location & Retail Planning in Britain. 208p. 1980. text ed. 36.50x (ISBN 0-566-00270-1). Gower Pub Co.
Guy, Dan M. An Introduction to Statistical Sampling in Auditing. LC 80-17279. (Wiley Series in Accounting & Information Systems). 229p. 1981. text ed. 27.45 (ISBN 0-471-04232-3); tchrs manual avail. (ISBN 0-471-09092-1). Wiley.
Guy, David. Football Dreams. 1982. pap. 2.50 (ISBN 0-451-12702-1, AE2702, Sig). NAL.
--The Man Who Loved Dirty Books. 1983. 14.95 (ISBN 0-453-00448-2). NAL.
--The Man Who Loved Dirty Books. 1985. pap. 3.50 (ISBN 0-451-13399-4, Sig). NAL.
--Second Brother. 264p. 1985. 14.95 (ISBN 0-453-00497-0). NAL.
Guy, Diana & Leigh, Guy I. The EEC & Intellectual Property. (European Practice Bks.). 375p. 1981. lib. bdg. 50.00 (ISBN 0-379-20712-5). Oceana.
Guy, Donna. Argentine Sugar Politics: Tucuman & the Generation of Eighty. LC 79-22922. 162p. 1980. text ed. 18.95x (ISBN 0-87918-043-9). ASU Lat Am St.
Guy, Edward T. & Merrigan, John J. Forms for Safety & Security Management. 448p. 1980. text ed. 39.95 (ISBN 0-409-95089-0). Butterworth.
Guy, Francis S. Edmund Bailey O'Callaghan: A Study in American Historiography (1797-1880) LC 73-3573. (Catholic University of America. Studies in American Church History: No. 18). Repr. of 1934 ed. 19.00 (ISBN 0-404-57768-7). AMS Pr.
Guy, Gary V. Easy to Make Candles. (Illus.). 1980. pap. 2.50 (ISBN 0-486-23881-4). Dover.
Guy, Henry. Essai sur la Vie & les Oeuvres Litteraires Du Trouvere Adam De la Hale. LC 79-101989. 605p. 1898. Repr. 32.50 (ISBN 0-8337-1498-8). B Franklin.
--Moneys Received & Paid for Secret Services of Charles II & James II. 19.00 (ISBN 0-384-20490-2). Johnson Repr.
--Moneys Received & Paid for Secret Services of Charles Second & James Second from 30th March, 1679 to 25th December, 1688. Akerman, John Y., ed. LC 77-158238. (Camden Socity, London. Publications. First Ser.: No. 52). Repr. of 1851 ed. 19.00 (ISBN 0-404-50152-4). AMS Pr.
Guy, J. A. The Cardinal's Court: The Impact of Thomas Wolsey in Star Chamber. 191p. 1977. 19.50x (ISBN 0-87471-815-5). Rowman.
--The Public Career of Sir Thomas More. LC 80-5391. 224p. 1980. 33.00x (ISBN 0-300-02546-7). Yale U Pr.
Guy, James. Metasphere: The Altered State of Word. LC 80-83463. (Illus.). 137p. (Orig.). 1980. pap. 7.00 (ISBN 0-9604918-7-2). Lampkin Pub.
Guy, Jeff. The Destruction of the Zulu Kingdom. (Illus.). 1979. text ed. 35.00x (ISBN 0-582-64686-3). Longman.
--The Heretic: A Study of the Life of John William Colenso, 1814-1883. 378p. 1983. pap. text ed. 25.95x (ISBN 0-86975-168-9, Pub. by Ravan Pr). Ohio U Pr.
Guy, John. Kent Castles. 264p. 39.00x (ISBN 0-905270-15-0, Pub. by Meresborough England). State Mutual Bk.
Guy, Julia. Human Anatomy: Introductory Laboratory Guide. 1982. wire coil bdg. 8.95 (ISBN 0-88252-091-1). Paladin Hse.
Guy, Ken, ed. Technological Trends & Employment: Volume 1: Basic Consumer Goods. LC 84-10125. (Illus.). 236p. 1984. text ed. 32.95 (ISBN 0-566-00706-1). Gower Pub Co.
Guy, Mary E. Professionals in Organizations: Debunking a Myth. LC 85-509. 208p. 1985. 33.95 (ISBN 0-317-18810-0). Praeger.
Guy, Maxine & Hickman, May. Care of the Wild Feathered & Furred: Treating & Feeding Injured Birds & Animals. 7th ed. LC 73-76670. (Illus.). 144p. 1983. pap. 9.95 (ISBN 0-935576-07-X). Kesend Pub Ltd.
Guy, May & Gilbert, Miriam. A Doctor Discusses the Care & Development of Your Baby. (Illus.). 1979. pap. 2.99 (ISBN 0-685-56949-7). Budlong.
Guy, N. G., ed. see International Conference on Fluid Sealing, 8th.
Guy, Patricia A. Women's Poetry Index. LC 84-42816. 192p. 1985. lib. bdg. 65.00 (ISBN 0-89774-173-0). Oryx Pr.
Guy, R. K., jt. auth. see Croft, H.
Guy, Randor. Indian Ribaldry. LC 77-113907. (Illus.). 1970. pap. 2.00 (ISBN 0-8048-0906-2). C E Tuttle.
Guy, Rebecca, jt. auth. see Allen, Donald.
Guy, Richard K., ed. Reviews in Number Theory II: Revnum II. 340p. pap. 500.00 set (ISBN 0-8218-0218-6); pap. 120.00 Vol. 1 (ISBN 0-8218-0219-4); Vol. 120.00 (ISBN 0-8218-0220-8); pap. 120.00 Vol.3 (ISBN 0-8218-0221-6); pap. 120.00 Vol.4 (ISBN 0-8218-0222-4); pap. 120.00 Vol.5 (ISBN 0-8218-0223-2); pap. 120.00 Vol.6 (ISBN 0-8218-0224-0). Am Math.
Guy, Rosa. Bird at My Window. 288p. 1985. pap. 5.95 (ISBN 0-8052-8234-3, Pub. by Allison & Busby England). Schocken.
--The Disappearance. LC 79-50672. 224p. 1979. 13.95 (ISBN 0-385-28129-3). Delacorte.
--The Disappearance. 256p. (gr. 7 up). pap. 2.50 (ISBN 0-440-92064-7, LFL). Dell.
--Edith Jackson. LC 77-28098. 180p. (gr. 7 up). 1978. 11.50 (ISBN 0-670-28906-X). Viking.
--The Friends. LC 72-11068. 176p. (gr. 7 up). 1973. reinforced bdg. 7.95 (ISBN 0-03-007876-8). HR&W.
--The Friends. (YA) 1983. pap. 2.25 (ISBN 0-553-20595-1). Bantam.
--A Measure of Time. LC 82-15461. 345p. 1983. 16.95 (ISBN 0-03-057653-9). HR&W.
--A Measure of Time. 1984. pap. 5.95 (ISBN 0-553-34112-X). Bantam.
--Mirror of Her Own. LC 80-69448. 192p. (gr. 7 up). 1980. 12.95 (ISBN 0-385-28636-8). Delacorte.
--Mother Crocodile: An Uncle Amadou Tale from Senegal. LC 80-393. (Illus.). 32p. (ps-3). 1981. 10.95 (ISBN 0-385-28454-3); PLB 10.95 (ISBN 0-385-28455-1). Delacorte.
--My Love, My Love, or, the Peasant Girl. 120p. 1985. 11.95 (ISBN 0-03-000507-8). HR&W.
--New Guys Around the Block. LC 82-72818. 192p. (gr. 7 up). 1983. 14.95 (ISBN 0-385-29247-3). Delacorte.
--Paris, Pee Wee & Big Dog. LC 85-1654. (Illus.). 112p. (gr. 4-8). 1985. 13.95 (ISBN 0-385-29407-7). Delacorte.
--Ruby. 1979. pap. 2.25 (ISBN 0-553-23367-X). Bantam.
Guy, W. & Messell, J. Norsk-Engelsk Ordbok Praktisk. 324p. (Norwegian & Eng.). 1979. 29.95 (ISBN 0-686-92442-8, M-9467). French & Eur.
Guy, W. & Ban, T. A., eds. The AGP System. 115p. 1985. pap. 9.50 (ISBN 0-387-15440-X). Springer-Verlag.
Guy, W & Ban, T. A., eds. The AMDP - System: Manual for the Assessment & Documentation of Psychopathology. (Illus.). 130p. 1982. pap. 12.00 (ISBN 0-387-11252-9). Springer-Verlag.
Guy, W. A; see Bucknill, John C.
Guy, Walter. Awakening the Slumbering Saints. 1985. 6.95 (ISBN 0-89536-997-4, 7551). CSS of Ohio.
Guy, William A. The Factors of the Unsound Mind. (Historical Foundations of Forensic Psychiatry & Psychology Ser.). xx, 232p. 1983. Repr. of 1881 ed. lib. bdg. 25.00 (ISBN 0-306-76186-6). Da Capo.
--Principles of Forensic Medicine. 3rd rev. enl. ed. LC 75-23715. (Illus.). Repr. of 1868 ed. 54.00 (ISBN 0-404-13268-5). AMS Pr.
Guyard, ed. see De Lamartine, Alphonse.
Guyard, ed. see Hugo, Victor.
Guyard, Marius Francois, jt. auth. see Chateaubriand, Rene de.
Guyard, S., tr. see Abu al-Fida.
Guyatt, E. J. The Training of Lay Primary Teachers in France from the Beginning of the Seventeenth Century to 1815. 1960. 29.00x (ISBN 0-900008-09-1, Pub. by U of London England). State Mutual Bk.
Guyatt, John. The American Revolution. Yapp, Malcolm, et al, eds. (World History Ser.). (Illus.). 32p. (gr. 10). 1980. lib. bdg. 6.95 (ISBN 0-89908-135-5); pap. text ed. 2.45 (ISBN 0-89908-110-X). Greenhaven.
--Ancient America. Killingray, Margaret, et al, eds. (World History Ser.). (Illus.). 32p. (gr. 10). 1980. lib. bdg. 6.95 (ISBN 0-89908-033-2); pap. text ed. 2.45 (ISBN 0-89908-008-1). Greenhaven.
--Bolivar. Yapp, Malcolm, et al, eds. (World History Ser.). (Illus.). 32p. (gr. 10). 1980. lib. bdg. 6.95 (ISBN 0-89908-045-6); pap. text ed. 2.45 (ISBN 0-89908-020-0). Greenhaven.
Guyau, Marie J. L' Art au Point de Vue Sociologique: Art from the Sociological Point of View. 11th ed. LC 74-25756. (European Sociology Ser.). 442p. 1975. Repr. 32.00x (ISBN 0-405-06510-8). Ayer Co Pubs.
Guyer, Foster E. Chretien De Troyes: Inventor of the Modern Novel. LC 73-168215. Repr. of 1957 ed. 19.50 (ISBN 0-404-02965-5). AMS Pr.
--The Main Stream of French Literature. 1973. Repr. of 1932 ed. 25.00 (ISBN 0-8274-0185-X). R West.
--Romance in the Making: Chretien de Troyes & the Earliest French. 1954. 7.00x (ISBN 0-913298-35-2). S F Vanni.
Guyer, Jane I. Family & Farm in Southern Cameroon. (African Research Studies: No. 15). (Orig.). 1984. pap. 11.00 (ISBN 0-915118-13-0). Boston U African.
Guyer, Mel, jt. auth. see Cross, John.
Guyer, Paul. Kant & the Claims of Taste. LC 78-19179. 1979. text ed. 25.00x (ISBN 0-674-50020-2). Harvard U Pr.
Guyer, Paul, jt. auth. see Cohen, Ted.
Guyer, Paul, jt. ed. see Cohen, Ted.
Guyette, Dale & Guyette, Gary. Decoys of Maritime Canada. LC 82-62953. (Illus.). 200p. 1983. text ed. 35.00 (ISBN 0-916838-76-5). Schiffer.
Guyette, Gary, jt. auth. see Guyette, Dale.
Guyette, Ralph L. Complete Guide to Successful Small Client Tax Practice. LC 81-5235. 392p. 1981. 37.50 (ISBN 0-13-160622-0, Busn). P-H.
--Tax Tactics Handbook: How to Exploit Tax-Savings Opportunities While Avoiding Audits. rev. ed. LC 83-9456. 376p. 1983. 39.95 (ISBN 0-13-886754-2, Busn). P-H.
Guyette, Susan. Community-Based Research: A Handbook for Native Americans. 358p. 1983. pap. 15.00 (ISBN 0-935626-10-7). U Cal AISC.
--Issues for the Future of American Indian Studies. Date not set. pap. price not set. U Cal AISC.
Guymon, E. Park, jt. auth. see Thomas, Joseph L.
Guymon, Ronald E., jt. auth. see Harrison, Grant V.
Guynn, Denise, ed. The Crow & the Pitcher. (Aesop's Fables Bks.). (Illus.). 16p. (ps). 1980. pap. 22.00 ten bks. & one cass. (ISBN 0-89290-077-6, BC14-5). Soc for Visual.
Guynn, Denise W., ed. The Boy Who Cried Wolf. (Aesop's Fable Bk.). (Illus.). 16p. (ps). 1980. pap. 22.00 ten bks & one cassette (ISBN 0-89290-076-8, BC14-4). Soc for Visual.
--The Country Mouse & the Town Mouse. (Aesop's Fables Bk). (Illus.). 16p. (ps). 1980. pap. 22.00 ten bks & one cass. (ISBN 0-89290-074-1, BC14-2). Soc for Visual.
--The Fox & the Crow. LC 74-736152. (Aesop's Fables Bk.). (Illus.). 16p. (ps). 1980. pap. 22.00 ten bks & one cass. (ISBN 0-89290-073-3, BC14-1). Soc for Visual.
--The Fox & the Grapes. (Aesop's Fables Bk.). (Illus.). 16p. (ps). 1980. pap. 22.00 ten bks & one cass. (ISBN 0-89290-075-X, BC14-3). Soc for Visual.
Guynn, Denise Y. Independent Living: Getting Started. Pozzi-Johnson, David, ed. LC 79-730911. (Illus.). 1979. pap. 135.00 (ISBN 0-89290-150-0, A581-SATC). Soc for Visual.
Guynn, J., jt. auth. see Bailey, William J.
Guynn, Stephen J., jt. auth. see Bailey, William J.
Guyon, Bernard, jt. auth. see Balzac, Honore De.
Guyon, Jean. Union with God. Edwards, Gene, rev. ed. 117p. 1981. pap. 4.95 (ISBN 0-940232-05-7). Christian Bks.
Guyon, Jeanne. The Book of Job. 1985. pap. 8.95 (ISBN 0-940232-23-5). Christian Bks.
--Christ Our Revelation. (Orig.). 1985. pap. 8.95 (ISBN 0-940232-21-9). Christian Bks.
--Genesis. 1983. pap. 5.95 (ISBN 0-940232-15-4). Christian Bks.
--Song of Songs. 1983. pap. 5.95 (ISBN 0-940232-16-2). Christian Bks.
--The Spiritual Adventure. 1985. pap. 7.95 (ISBN 0-940232-22-7). Christian Bks.
--The Way Out. (Orig.). 1985. pap. 7.95 (ISBN 0-940232-20-0). Christian Bks.
Guyon, Jeanne M. Experiencing the Depths of Jesus Christ. 3rd ed. Edwards, Gene, ed. 1975. pap. 4.95 (ISBN 0-940232-00-6). Christian Bks.
Guyon, Madame. Experiencing God Through Prayer. (Experiencing the Depths of Jesus Christ Ser.). 176p. 1984. pap. text ed. 3.50 (ISBN 0-88368-153-6). Whitaker Hse.
--Selections from the Autobiography of Madame Guyon. Hutchinson, Warner A., ed. Allen, Thomas T., tr. from Fr. LC 80-82328. (Shepherd Illustrated Classics Ser.). (Illus.). 1980. pap. 5.95 (ISBN 0-87983-234-7). Keats.
Guyon, Rene. The Ethics of Sexual Acts. 383p. 1974. Repr. of 1934 ed. lib. bdg. 29.00x (ISBN 0-374-93334-0). Octagon.
Guyon, Y. Limit-State Design of Prestressed Concrete, Vol. 2: The Design of the Member. Turner, F. H., tr. from Fr. LC 72-2655. 469p. 1974. 69.95x (ISBN 0-470-33791-5). Halsted Pr.

--Limit State Design of Prestressed Concrete Vol. 2: The Design of the Member, V. (Illus.). 469p. 1974. 57.50 (ISBN 0-85334-601-1, Pub. by Elsevier Applied Sci England). Elsevier.

Guyot, ed. see Leautaud, Paul.

Guyot, A., ed. International Symposium on Polyvinylchloride, 2nd: Proceedings. LC 77-73904. 1977. text ed. 48.00 (ISBN 0-08-021203-4). Pergamon.

Guyot, Arnold. Earth & Man: Lectures on Comparative Physical Geography in Its Relation to the History of Mankind. LC 72-125744. (American Environmental Studies). 1970. Repr. of 1849 ed. 20.00 (ISBN 0-405-02669-2). Ayer Co Pubs.

Guyot, Charles. The Legend of the City of Ys. Cavanagh, Deirdre, tr. from Fr. LC 78-10235. (Illus.). 128p. 1979. lib. bdg. 12.00x (ISBN 0-87023-264-9). U of Mass Pr.

Guyot, Edouard. John Galsworthy. 1978. Repr. of 1932 ed. lib. bdg. 45.00 (ISBN 0-8495-1934-9). Arden Lib.

--John Galsworthy. 1973. Repr. of 1933 ed. 30.00 (ISBN 0-8274-0388-7). R West.

Guyot, Genoveva C. Del Mar y Viento-of Sea & Wind. bilingual ed. Stickter, Jim, tr. LC 81-84453. 60p. (Orig., Eng. & Span.). 1981. pap. 7.50 (ISBN 0-930770-21-8). Hemisphere Hse.

Guyot, J. Atlas of Human Limb Joints. (Illus.). 252p. 1981. 159.00 (ISBN 0-387-10380-5). Springer-Verlag.

Guyot, Jacqueline & Raynal, Francois. Angela & Elton at Play. (Woofits Ser.). (Illus.). 24p. 1982. 3.95 (ISBN 0-8431-0980-7). Price Stern.

--Angela's House. (Woofits Ser.). (Illus.). 24p. 1982. 3.95 (ISBN 0-8431-0979-3). Price Stern.

--Flowers for Angela's Mother. (Woofits Ser.). (Illus.). 24p. 1982. 3.95 (ISBN 0-8431-0981-5). Price Stern.

Guyot, James F., jt. ed. see Wriggins, W. Howard.

Guyton, Anita. The Woman's Book of Natural Beauty. (Illus.). 160p. (Orig.). 1985. pap. 7.95 (ISBN 0-7225-1132-9). Thorsons Pubs.

Guyton, Arthur. Cardiovascular Physiology IV. (International Series of Sports Science: Vol. 26). 1982. text ed. 50.00 (ISBN 0-8391-1605-5). Univ Park.

Guyton, Arthur C. Arterial Pressure & Hypertension. LC 79-67792. (Circulatory Physiology Ser.: Vol. III). (Illus.). 564p. 1980. text ed. 36.95 (ISBN 0-7216-4362-0). Saunders.

--Basic Human Neurophysiology. 3rd ed. (Illus.). 345p. 1981. 22.00 (ISBN 0-7216-4367-1). Saunders.

--Human Physiology & Mechanisms of Disease. 3rd. ed. (Illus.). 720p. 1982. 26.50 (ISBN 0-7216-4384-1). Saunders.

--Physiology of the Human Body. 6th ed. 1984. text ed. 37.95 (ISBN 0-03-058339-X, CBS C). SCP.

--Textbook of Medical Physiology. 6th ed. (Illus.). 1237p. 1981. text ed. 45.95 (ISBN 0-7216-4394-9). Saunders.

Guyton, Arthur C., et al. Dynamics & Control of the Body Fluids. (Illus.). 397p. 1975. 28.95 (ISBN 0-7216-4361-2). Saunders.

Guyton, Emma J. W. The Wife's Trials; or, Lilian Grey, Repr. Of 1858 Ed. Wolff, Robert L., ed. Bd. with Married Life. Repr. of 1863 ed; Husbands & Wives. Repr. of 1873 ed. LC 75-492. (Victorian Fiction Ser.). 1975. lib. bdg. 73.00 (ISBN 0-8240-1568-1). Garland Pub.

Guyton, Robert, et al. Prerequisites for Winning Government R&D Contracts. rev. ed. LC 81-52984. (Project-Contract Acquisition & Management Ser.). 170p. 1983. pap. 28.00 (ISBN 0-912426-08-X). Univ Tech.

Guze, Samuel B. Criminality & Psychiatric Disorders. 1976. text ed. 21.95x (ISBN 0-19-501973-3). Oxford U Pr.

Guze, Samuel B., jt. auth. see Goodwin, Donald W.

Guze, Samuel B., et al, eds. Childhood Psychopathology & Development. (American Psychopathological Association Ser.). 320p. 1983. text ed. 59.00 (ISBN 0-89004-835-5). Raven.

Guzelimian, Vahe. Becoming a MacArtist. Compute!, ed. (Orig.). 1985. pap. 17.95 (ISBN 0-942386-80-9). Compute Pubns.

Guzie, Tad. The Book of Sacramental Basics. LC 81-83189. 160p. (Orig.). 1982. pap. 5.95 (ISBN 0-8091-2411-4). Paulist Pr.

Guzie, Tad W. Jesus & the Eucharist. LC 73-90069. 168p. 1974. pap. 4.95 (ISBN 0-8091-1858-0). Paulist Pr.

Guzman, jt. auth. see Enriquez.

Guzman, Domingo De see Domingo De Guzman, Saint.

Guzman, Emilio. Mind Control. write for info. (ISBN 0-913343-25-0). Inst Psych Inc.

Guzman, Fernan Perez de see Perez de Guzman, Fernan.

Guzman, Gaston. The Genus Psilocybe: Revision of the Known Species (Hallucinogenic Species) (Beiheft to Nova Hedwigia Ser.: No. 74). (Illus.). 650p. 1983. lib. bdg. 70.00 (ISBN 3-7682-1319-6). Lubrecht & Cramer.

Guzman, Jessie P. Crusade for Civic Democracy: The Story of the Tuskegee Civic Association, 1941-1970. 1984. 11.95 (ISBN 0-533-05700-0). Vantage.

Guzman, Jose L. & Fick, Carl. Undercover Cop. (Orig.). 1979. pap. 2.25 (ISBN 0-89083-488-1). Zebra.

Guzman, Juan P., tr. see Taylor, Jack R.

Guzman, Julia M. Realism & Naturalism in Puerto Rico. (Puerto Rico Ser.). 1979. lib. bdg. 59.95 (ISBN 0-8490-2993-7). Gordon Pr.

Guzman, M. De. Differentiation of Integrals in R to the nth Power. (Lecture Notes in Mathematics: Vol. 481). xii, 226p. 1975. pap. 16.00 (ISBN 0-387-07399-X). Springer-Verlag.

Guzman, Martin L. The Eagle & the Serpent. De Onis, Harriet, tr. 11.25 (ISBN 0-8446-0668-5). Peter Smith.

Guzman, Oscar, ed. Energy Use in Mexico: Perspectives on Efficiency & Conservation Policies. Yunez-Naude, Antonia. 330p. 1985. pap. 28.00 (ISBN 0-8133-0248-X). Westview.

Guzman, Rafael M. de & Melendez, Winifred A. Burnout: The New Academic Disease. Fife, Jonathan D., ed. LC 84-163478. (ASHE-ERIC Higher Education Research Report Ser.: No. 9, 1983). 90p. (Orig.). 1984. pap. 7.50 (ISBN 0-913317-08-X). Assn Study Higher Ed.

Guzman, Ralph C. The Political Socialization of the Mexican American People. Cortes, Carlos E., ed. LC 76-1264. (Chicano Heritage Ser.). (Illus.). 1976. 21.00x (ISBN 0-405-09504-X). Ayer Co Pubs.

Guzman Y Raz Guzman, Jesus. Bibliografia de la Reforma, la Intervencion y el Imperio, 2 vols. LC 79-153568. (Monographias Bibliographicas Mexicanas: Nos. 17 & 19). (Sp.). 1973. Repr. of 1931 ed. lib. bdg. 47.00 (ISBN 0-8337-1501-1). B Franklin.

Guzzetta, Charles, et al, eds. Education for Social Work Practice: Selected International Models. LC 84-12654. 130p. 1984. pap. text ed. 8.95 (ISBN 0-87293-005-X, 84-500-09). Coun Soc Wk Ed.

Guzzetti, Alfred. Two or Three Things I Know About Her: Analysis of a Film by Godard. LC 80-15832. (Film Studies). (Illus.). 376p. 1981. text ed. 27.50x (ISBN 0-674-91500-3). Harvard U Pr.

Guzzo, Richard A. Programs for Productivity & Quality of Working Life. (Work in America Institute Studies in Productivity: No. 32). 72p. 1983. pap. 35.00 (ISBN 0-08-030964-X). Pergamon.

Guzzo, Richard A. & Bondy, Jeffrey S. A Guide to Worker Productivity Experiments in the U. S., 1976-81. (Pergamon Press-Work in America Institute Ser.). 161p. 1983. 17.50 (ISBN 0-08-029548-7). Pergamon.

--A Guide to Worker Productivity Experiments in the U.S., 1976-1981. 125p. 17.50 (ISBN 0-686-84782-2). Work in Amer.

Guzzo, Richard A., ed. Improving Group Decision Making in Organization: Approaches from Theory & Research. LC 81-22827. (Organizational & Occupational Psychology Ser.). 1982. 21.50 (ISBN 0-12-310980-9). Acad Pr.

Guzzo, Sandra E. Fox & Heggie. Tucker, Kathleen, ed. LC 83-16672. (Just for Fun Bks.). (Illus.). 32p. (gr. k-3). 1983. PLB 10.25 (ISBN 0-8075-2546-4). A Whitman.

Guzzon, F., jt. auth. see Gennaro, L.

Guzzwell, John. Modern Wooden Yacht Construction: Cold-Molding Joinery, Fitting Out. LC 78-64787. (Illus.). 1979. 27.50 (ISBN 0-87742-106-4). Intl Marine.

--Trekka Round the World. (Illus.). 1980. 9.95 (ISBN 0-8286-0084-8). J De Graff.

--Trekka Round the World. (Illus.). 197p. 1980. Repr. 16.95 (ISBN 0-246-11322-7). Sheridan.

Gvillo, Doris. Musing, Meditations, & Meanderings. 1984. 5.95 (ISBN 0-89536-982-6, 7531). CSS of Ohio.

Gvishiani, A. D., jt. auth. see Kirillov, A. A.

Gvishiani, D. M., et al. Scientific Intelligentsia in the U. S. S. R. Structure & Dynamics of Personnel. Sayers, Jane, tr. from Russ. 1976. 12.95x (ISBN 0-8464-0820-1). Beekman Pubs.

Gvishiani, J. M., ed. Systems Research: Methodological Problems. 380p. 1983. 67.50 (ISBN 0-08-030000-6). Pergamon.

Gvozdetsky, N. A. Soviet Geographical Explorations & Discoveries: In the USSR, Antartica & World Oceans. (Illus.). 343p. 1975. 17.95x (ISBN 0-8464-0871-6). Beekman Pubs.

Gvozdetsky, N. Soviet Geography Today: Physical Geography. 280p. 1982. 6.95 (ISBN 0-8285-2352-5, Pub. by Progress Pubs USSR). Imported Pubns.

GW, ed. see Campbell, Ramsey.

GW, ed. see Wager, Walter.

Gwaltney, John L. Drylongso: A Self-Portrait of Black Americans. LC 79-5558. 1980. 12.95 (ISBN 0-394-51017-8). Random.

--Drylongso: A Self-Portrait of Black America. LC 80-6146. 324p. 1981. pap. 7.95 (ISBN 0-394-74713-5, V-713, Vin). Random.

--Thrice Shy: Cultural Accommodation to Blindness & Other Disasters in a Mexican Community. LC 71-118635. 219p. 1970. 26.00x (ISBN 0-231-03237-4). Columbia U Pr.

Gwara, Joseph J., Jr. The Sala Family Archives: A Handlist of Medieval & Early Modern Catalonian Charters. 156p. (Orig.). 1984. pap. 6.95 (ISBN 0-87840-090-7). Georgetown U Pr.

Gwartney, James D. & Stroup, Richard. Computer Test Bank for Economics: Private & Public Choice. 3rd ed. 1983. text ed. 125.00 (ISBN 0-12-311044-0). Acad Pr.

--Testbank for Economics: Private & Public Choice. 1983. text ed. 35.00i (ISBN 0-12-311048-3). Acad Pr.

Gwartney, James D. & Stroup, Richard, eds. Economics: Private & Public Choice. 3rd ed. LC 81-71896. 792p. 1983. text ed. 22.25i (ISBN 0-12-311045-9); instr's. manual 10.00i (ISBN 0-12-311047-5). Acad Pr.

--Macroeconomics: Private & Public Choice. 3rd ed. LC 81-71894. 1983. text ed. 15.25i (ISBN 0-12-311071-8). Acad Pr.

--Microeconomics: Private & Public Choice. 3rd ed. 447p. 1983. text ed. 15.25i (ISBN 0-12-311076-9). Acad Pr.

--Transparency Masters for Economics: Private & Public Choice. 3rd ed. 1984. text ed. 15.00i (ISBN 0-12-311049-1). Acad Pr.

Gwartney, James D., et al, eds. Coursebook for Economics: Private & Public Choice. 350p. 1983. text ed. 8.50i (ISBN 0-12-311046-7). Acad Pr.

Gwathkin, Nina W. Scenes for a Raja: Study of an Indian Kalamkari Found in Indonesia. (Monographs Ser.: No. 27). (Illus.). 32p. (Orig.). 1985. pap. text ed. 10.00 (ISBN 0-930741-06-4). UCLA Mus Hist.

Gwathmey, John H. Historical Register of Virginians in the Revolution: Soldiers, Sailors, Marines, 1775-1783. LC 73-4558. 872p. 1979. Repr. of 1938 ed. 32.50 (ISBN 0-8063-0557-6). Genealog Pub.

--Twelve Virginia Counties Where the Western Migration Began. LC 79-66025. (Illus.). 469p. 1981. Repr. of 1937 ed. 20.00 (ISBN 0-8063-0861-3). Genealog Pub.

Gwatkin, Davidson R. A Population Strategy for the Nineteen Eighties: Health, Mortality, & Development. 224p. 1981. write for info. Overseas Dev Council.

Gwatkin, Davidson R. & Wilcox, Janet R. Can Health & Nutrition Interventions Make a Difference? LC 80-80500. 76p. 1980. pap. 5.00 (ISBN 0-686-28117-9). Overseas Dev Council.

Gwatkin, H. M. Early Church History to A. D. 313, 2 vols. 1977. lib. bdg. 200.00 (ISBN 0-8490-1738-6). Gordon Pr.

Gwatkin, Henry M. The Arian Controversy. new ed. LC 77-84702. Repr. of 1903 ed. 19.00 (ISBN 0-404-16109-X). AMS Pr.

--Early Church History to A.D. 313, 2 Vols. LC 77-168216. Repr. of 1909 ed. 52.50 (ISBN 0-404-02966-3). AMS Pr.

--The Knowledge of God & Its Historical Development, 2 vols. LC 77-27219. (Gifford Lectures: 1904-05). 1978. Repr. of 1906 ed. Set. 49.50 (ISBN 0-404-60490-0). AMS Pr.

--Studies of Arianism: Chiefly Referring to the Character & Chronology of the Reaction Which Followed the Council of Nicaea. 2nd ed. LC 77-84703. Repr. of 1900 ed. 27.00 (ISBN 0-404-16110-3). AMS Pr.

Gwatkin, Ralph B. Fertilization Mechanisms in Man & Mammals. LC 77-1189. (Illus.). 171p. 1977. 29.50x (ISBN 0-306-31009-0, Plenum Pr). Plenum Pub.

Gwei-Djen, Lu, jt. auth. see Needham, Joseph.

Gwendolen, M. Carter, jt. ed. see Karis, Thomas.

Gwilt, Joseph. The Encyclopedia of Architecture: Historical, Theoretical & Practical. (Illus.). 1392p. 1982. pap. 10.95 (ISBN 0-517-54729-5). Crown.

Gwilym, Dafydd Ap. Selected Poems. Heseltine, Nigel, tr. 64p. 1971. Repr. of 1944 ed. 12.50x (ISBN 0-7165-1400-1, BBA 02060, Pub. by Cuala Press Ireland). Biblio Dist.

Gwin, Adrian. Never Grow Old with Our Man Gwin. LC 81-83055. (Illus.). 160p. (Orig.). 1982. pap. 5.95 (ISBN 0-934750-29-7). Jalamap.

--Rovin' The Years with Our Man Gwin. LC 82-83701. (Illus.). 188p. (Orig.). 1982. pap. 5.95 (ISBN 0-934750-33-5). Jalamap.

Gwin, Catherine, jt. auth. see Camps, Miriam.

Gwin, Mary M., jt. auth. see Gwin, William.

Gwin, Minrose, ed. Olden Times Revisited: W. L. Clayton's Pen Pictures. LC 81-21919. 160p. (Orig.). 1982. pap. 6.95 (ISBN 0-87805-153-8). U Pr of Miss.

Gwin, Minrose C. Black & White Women of the Old South: The Peculiar Sisterhood in American Literature. LC 85-3238. 248p. 1985. text ed. 19.95x (ISBN 0-87049-469-4). U of Tenn Pr.

Gwin, Paul, jt. auth. see Lionberger, Herbert F.

Gwin, Roy. The Great Adventure. Hodges, M. Constance, ed. 90p. 1980. pap. 5.95 (ISBN 0-934856-01-X). Delcon.

Gwin, Sherry. The Library: What's in It for You? 1973. text ed. 0.40x (ISBN 0-8134-1579-9, 1579). Interstate.

Gwin, William & Gwin, Mary M. Semiology, Symbolism & Architecture: A Selected & Partially Annotated Bibliography. (Architecture Ser.: Bibliography A 1346). 1985. pap. 3.00 (ISBN 0-89028-316-8). Vance Biblios.

Gwin, Yolande. Yolande's Atlanta: From the Historical to the Hysterical. LC 83-61918. 270p. 1983. 9.95 (ISBN 0-931948-43-6). Peachtree Pubs.

Gwinner, Robert F. & Smith, Edward M., eds. Sales Strategy: Cases & Readings. LC 75-77534. (Illus.). 1969. pap. text ed. 9.95x (ISBN 0-89197-388-5). Irvington.

Gwinner, Robert F., et al. Marketing: An Environmental Perspective. (Illus.). 1977. text ed. 27.95 (ISBN 0-8299-0119-1); instrs.' manual avail. (ISBN 0-8299-0484-0). West Pub.

Gwinup, Grant, jt. auth. see Elias, Alan N.

Gwinup, Thomas & Dickinson, Fidelia. Greek & Roman Authors: A Checklist of Criticism. 2nd ed. LC 82-690. 294p. 1982. 19.00 (ISBN 0-8108-1528-1). Scarecrow.

Gwirtsman, Harry, jt. auth. see Kaye, Walter H.

Gwon, Pu G. Dynamic Art of Breaking. 1977. 8.95x. Wehman.

--The Taegeuk Forms of Tae Kwon Do. Lee, Mike, ed. LC 83-63602. (Series 435). 224p. (Orig.). 1984. pap. 9.95 (ISBN 0-89750-097-0). Ohara Pubns.

Gwon, Pu Gill. Basic Training for Kicking. LC 81-85161. (Ser. 415). (Illus., Orig.). 1981. pap. 9.50 (ISBN 0-89750-078-4). Ohara Pubns.

Gwyer, M., tr. see Cocchia, Aldo.

Gwyn, Charles W., jt. auth. see Graham, Edward D., Jr.

Gwyn, John, jt. auth. see Atkyns, Richard.

Gwyn, Julian. The Enterprising Admiral: The Personal Fortune of Admiral Sir Peter Warren. (Illus.). 304p. 1974. 22.00x (ISBN 0-7735-0170-3). McGill-Queens U Pr.

Gwyn, Thomas. Ellis Wynne: Sixteen Seventy-One to Seventeen Thirty-Four. (Writers of Wales Ser.). 84p. 1984. pap. text ed. 6.75x (ISBN 0-7083-0865-1, Pub. by Univ of Wales Pr England). Humanities.

Gwyn, William B. Barriers to Establishing Urban Ombudsmen: The Case of Newark. new ed. LC 74-11446. 93p. 1974. pap. 4.50x (ISBN 0-87772-200-5). Inst Gov Stud Berk.

--Democracy & the Cost of Politics in Britain. LC 79-28340. (Illus.). vii, 256p. 1980. Repr. of 1962 ed. lib. bdg. 24.75x (ISBN 0-313-22257-6, GWDC). Greenwood.

--The Meaning of the Separation of Powers, Vol. 9. LC 66-4274. 1965. 10.00 (ISBN 0-930598-08-3). Tulane Stud Pol.

--Ombudsman Policy Innovation in the English-Speaking World. LC 80-15829. (IGS Research Report: No. 80-2). 51p. 1981. pap. 5.75 (ISBN 0-87772-274-9). Inst Gov Stud Berk.

Gwyn, William B. & Edwards, George C., III, eds. Perspectives on Public Policy Making, Vol. 15. LC 75-321771. xi, 241p. 1975. lib. bdg. 15.00 (ISBN 0-930598-15-6); pap. text ed. 10.00 (ISBN 0-930598-14-8). Tulane Stud Pol.

Gwyn, William B. & Rose, Richard, eds. Britain: Progress & Decline, Vol. 17. LC 81-165801. 154p. 1980. lib. bdg. 17.50 (ISBN 0-930598-18-0). Tulane Stud Pol.

Gwynedd, Viscount. Dame Margaret: The Life Story of His Mother by Viscount Gwynedd. 1978. Repr. of 1947 ed. lib. bdg. 20.00 (ISBN 0-8495-1921-7). Arden Lib.

Gwynn, Denis. The Life of John Redmond. facsimile ed. LC 77-169761. (Select Bibliographies Reprint Ser). Repr. of 1932 ed. 49.50 (ISBN 0-8369-5981-7). Ayer Co Pubs.

Gwynn, Edward, ed. Poems from the Dindshenchas. LC 78-72686. (Royal Irish Academy. Todd Lecture Ser.: Vol. 7). Repr. of 1900 ed. 16.50 (ISBN 0-404-60567-2). AMS Pr.

Gwynn, Frederick L. Sturge Moore & the Life of Art. 159p. 1980. Repr. of 1952 ed. lib. bdg. 30.00 (ISBN 0-89984-249-6). Century Bookbindery.

Gwynn, Frederick L. & Blotner, Joseph. The Fiction of J. D. Salinger. LC 58-14389. (Critical Essays in Modern Literature Ser.). 1958. pap. 4.95x (ISBN 0-8229-5019-7). U of Pittsburgh Pr.

Gwynn, Frederick L. & Blotner, Joseph L., eds. Faulkner in the University: Class Conferences at the University of Virginia, 1957-1958. LC 59-13713. (Illus.). 294p. 1977. Repr. of 1959 ed. 16.95x (ISBN 0-8139-0843-4). U Pr of Va.

Gwynn, Kate. Painting in Watercolour. 160p. 1982. 50.00x (ISBN 0-85223-221-7, Pub. by Ebury Pr England). State Mutual Bk.

Gwynn, Mary. Love, Mary: A Novel of New York City at Its Most Hilarious. LC 80-24996. 224p. 1981. 8.95 (ISBN 0-688-00429-6). Morrow.

Gwynn, Robin D. Huguenot Heritage: The History & Contribution of the Huguenots in England. (Illus.). 256p. 1985. 34.95x (ISBN 0-7102-0420-5). Routledge & Kegan.

Gwynn, S. Life of Horace Walpole. LC 76-160467. (English Biography Ser., No. 31). 1971. Repr. of 1932 ed. lib. bdg. 54.95x (ISBN 0-8383-1302-7). Haskell.

--Oliver Goldsmith. LC 74-30338. (English Literature Ser., No. 33). 1974. lib. bdg. 49.95x (ISBN 0-8383-1843-6). Haskell.

--Tennyson. LC 74-16313. (Studies in Tennyson, No. 27). 1974. lib. bdg. 43.95x (ISBN 0-8383-1796-0). Haskell.

Gwynn, Stephen. The Charm of Ireland: Her Places of Beauty, Entertainment, Sport, & Historic Association. Repr. of 1927 ed. 17.50 (ISBN 0-8482-4199-1). Norwood Edns.

--Fond Opinions. LC 70-122877. (Essay & General Literature Index Reprint Ser). 1971. Repr. of 1938 ed. 19.50x (ISBN 0-8046-1334-6, Pub. by Kennikat). Assoc Faculty Pr.

--For Second Reading. 1973. Repr. of 1918 ed. 20.00 (ISBN 0-8274-0184-1). R West.

--Henry Grattan & His Times. facsimile ed. LC 78-175699. (Select Bibliographies Reprint Ser.). Repr. of 1939 ed. 26.50 (ISBN 0-8369-6614-7). Ayer Co Pubs.

--Irish Literature & Drama in the English Language. LC 72-195442. 1936. lib. bdg. 28.50 (ISBN 0-8414-4699-7). Folcroft.

--The Life of Horace Walpole. facsimile ed. LC 73-160974. (Select Bibliographies Reprint Ser). Repr. of 1932 ed. 21.00 (ISBN 0-8369-5842-X). Ayer Co Pubs.

--Life of Horace Walpole. 1973. Repr. of 1932 ed. 13.00 (ISBN 0-8274-1273-8). R West.

--The Life of Sir Walter Scott. 1978. Repr. of 1936 ed. lib. bdg. 35.00 (ISBN 0-8492-0949-8). R West.

--Mrs. Humphrey Ward. 1917. Repr. 25.00 (ISBN 0-8274-2773-5). R West.

--Oliver Goldsmith. LC 74-9728. 1935. lib. bdg. 35.00 (ISBN 0-8414-4511-7). Folcroft.

--Robert Louis Stevenson. 1939. Repr. lib. bdg. 20.00 (ISBN 0-8414-4412-9). Folcroft.

--Tennyson. 59.95 (ISBN 0-8490-1186-8). Gordon Pr.

--Tennyson: A Critical Study. LC 72-8192. 1973. lib. bdg. 12.75 (ISBN 0-8414-0384-8). Folcroft.

--Thomas Moore. LC 73-13838. 1905. Repr. lib. bdg. 15.00 (ISBN 0-8414-4448-X). Folcroft.

--To-Day & To-Morrow in Ireland. 1973. Repr. of 1903 ed. 25.00 (ISBN 0-8274-0212-0). R West.

--Ulster. 59.95 (ISBN 0-8490-1241-4). Gordon Pr.

Gwynn, Stephen, ed. Scattering Branches: Tributes to the Memory of W. B. Yeats. 229p. 1981. Repr. of 1940 ed. lib. bdg. 35.00 (ISBN 0-89987-901-2). Darby Bks.

Gwynn, Stephen, ed. see Spring Rice, Cecil.

Gwynn, Stephen, ed. see Spring Rice, Cecil A.

Gwynn, Stephen L. Fond Opinions. facs. ed. LC 75-142636. (Essay Index Reprint Ser.). 1938. 14.00 (ISBN 0-8369-2050-3). Ayer Co Pubs.

--Garden Wisdom: Or, from One Generation to Another. facs. ed. LC 67-22061. (Essay Index Reprint Ser). 1922. 15.00 (ISBN 0-8369-0502-4). Ayer Co Pubs.

--Irish Books & Irish People. facs. ed. LC 74-86756. (Essay Index Reprint Ser.). 1920. 14.00 (ISBN 0-8369-1136-9). Ayer Co Pubs.

--Life of Horace Walpole. LC 79-153900. 1971. Repr. of 1932 ed. 23.50x (ISBN 0-8046-1599-3, Pub. by Kennikat). Assoc Faculty Pr.

--The Life of Sir Walter Scott. 17.00 (ISBN 0-8369-6939-1, 7820). Ayer Co Pubs.

--Masters of English Literature. facsimile ed. LC 71-177958. (Essay Index Reprint Ser.). Repr. of 1904 ed. 21.00 (ISBN 0-8369-2552-1). Ayer Co Pubs.

Gwynn, Zae H. Abstracts of the Records of Onslow County, North Carolina, 1734-1850, 2 vols. 1592p. 1961. 50.00. Genealog Pub.

--The Eighteen Fifty Census of Craven County, North Carolina. 185p. 1961. 12.50 (ISBN 0-685-34329-4). Genealog Pub.

Gwynne, jt. auth. see Miller.

Gwynne, Darryl T. & Morris, Glenn K. Orthopteran Mating Systems: Sexual Competition in a Diverse Group of Insects. (Westview Science Ser.). (Illus.). 375p. 1982. lib. bdg. 33.00x (ISBN 0-86531-391-1). Westview.

Gwynne, David & Murray, Robert. Weed Biology & Control in Agriculture & Horticulture. (Illus.). 256p. 1985. pap. 16.95 (ISBN 0-7134-3531-3, Pub. by Batsford England). David & Charles.

Gwynne, Fred. A Chocolate Moose for Dinner. LC 80-14150. (Illus.). 48p. (ps-3). 1981. Repr. of 1976 ed. PLB 8.79 (ISBN 0-671-43706-2). Messner.

--The King Who Rained. LC 80-12939. (Illus.). 40p. (ps-3). 1981. Repr. of 1970 ed. PLB 8.79 (ISBN 0-671-43705-4). Messner.

--The King Who Rained. (Illus.). 40p. (gr. 1 up). pap. 3.95 (ISBN 0-671-96070-9). Windmill Bks.

Gwynne, Fred & Basch, Peter. What's Nude? (Illus.). 1960. pap. 5.95 (ISBN 0-8392-1129-5). Astor-Honor.

Gwynne, H. The Cause of World Unrest: The Jews. 1982. lib. bdg. 69.95 (ISBN 0-87700-340-8). Revisionist Pr.

Gwynne, H. A., intro. by. The Cause of World Unrest. 1978. pap. 5.00x (ISBN 0-911038-40-X). Noontide.

Gwynne, M. D., jt. ed. see Pratt, D. J.

Gwynne, P. N. Pushkin Shove. 252p. 1984. 15.95 (ISBN 0-525-24224-4, 01549-460). Dutton.

Gwynne, Peter, jt. auth. see Hooper, Henry O.

Gwynne, Reid. The Illustrated Guidebook to Still-Life Painting. (Promotion of the Arts Library). (Illus.). 137p. 1982. 69.45 (ISBN 0-86650-025-1). Gloucester Art.

Gwynne, Walker. The Christian Year; Its Purpose & Its History. LC 74-89269. xiv, 143p. 1972. Repr. of 1917 ed. 43.00x (ISBN 0-8103-3814-9). Gale.

Gwynne-Thomas, E. H. A Concise History of Education to Nineteen Hundred A. D. LC 81-40315. 325p. (Orig.). 1981. lib. bdg. 25.25 (ISBN 0-8191-1659-9); pap. text ed. 13.00 (ISBN 0-8191-1660-2). U Pr of Amer.

--A Political History of the Roman Empire. LC 83-21611. (Illus.). 208p. (Orig.). 1984. lib. bdg. 22.75 (ISBN 0-8191-3642-5); pap. text ed. 11.50 (ISBN 0-8191-3643-3). U Pr of Amer.

Gwynns-Jones, A. How to Master the Art of Still Life, 2 vols. (A Promotion of the Arts Library Bk.). (Illus.). 201p. 1985. 157.45 (ISBN 0-86650-169-X). Gloucester Art.

Gwyther, D. N. Heat Transfer Fuels & Refractories Fluid Flow in Furnace Technology. 146p. 1985. pap. text ed. write for info. (ISBN 0-901462-25-X, Metals Soc). Brookfield Pub Co.

Gy, P. M. Sampling of Particulate Materials. 2nd ed. LC 79-16075. (Developments in Geomathematics Ser.: Vol. 4). 432p. 1982. 59.75 (ISBN 0-444-42079-7). Elsevier.

Gyalpo, Tangtong. A Technique for Developing Enlightened Consciousness: A Traditional Buddhist Meditation on Avalokiteshvara. Gyatso, Janet, tr. from Tibetan. (Basic Buddhism Ser.). 26p. (Orig.). 1980. pap. 1.50 (ISBN 0-915078-02-3, P-01). Buddhist Assn US.

Gyamfi, Enoch A. Success Control: Positive Thinking. 1985. 6.50 (ISBN 0-8062-2464-9). Carlton.

Gyan, Gopi. The Book of Numbers. Morningland Publications, Inc., ed. 620p. (Orig.). 1980. pap. 10.00 (ISBN 0-935146-13-X). Morningland.

--Lord Pluto. (Illus.). 171p. (Orig.). 1980. spiral bdg. 6.95 (ISBN 0-935146-22-9). Morningland.

--Morningland Color Book. 1979. pap. 7.95 (ISBN 0-935146-09-1). Morningland.

Gyan, Gopi, jt. auth. see Patricia.

Gyan, Gopi, jt. auth. see Patricia, Sri.

Gyarmathi, Samuel. Affinitas Linguae Hungaricae Cum Linguis Fennicae Originis, Grammatice Demonstrata, 1799. (Uralic & Altaic Ser: Vol. 95). (Lat). 1968. pap. text ed. 11.50x (ISBN 0-87750-040-1). Res Ctr Lang Semiotic.

--Grammatical Proof of the Affinity of the Hungarian Language with Languages of Fennic Origin: (Gottingen Dietrich, 1799) Hanzeli, Victor E., tr. from Ger. (Amsterdam Classics in Linguistics (ACIL): No. 15). 350p. 1983. 48.00x (ISBN 90-272-0976-6). Benjamins North Am.

Gyarmati, I. Non-Equilibrium Thermodynamics: Field Theory & Variational Principles. Heinz, W. F., tr. (Engineering Science Library). (Illus.). 1970. 28.00 (ISBN 0-387-04886-3). Springer-Verlag.

Gyatso, Geshe K. Buddhism in the Tibetan Tradition: A Guide. (Illus.). 144p. (Orig.). 1984. pap. 9.95 (ISBN 0-7102-0242-3). Routledge & Kegan.

--Clear Light of Bliss. Landaw, Jonathan, ed. Norbu, Tenzin, tr. from Tibetan. (Wisdom Advanced Book: Blue Ser.). (Illus.). 264p. (Orig.). 1982. pap. 10.95 (ISBN 0-86171-005-3, Pub. by Wisdom Pubns). Great Traditions.

Gyatso, Janet, tr. see Gyalpo, Tangtong.

Gyatso, Kalzang. Songs of Spiritual Change. Mullin, Glenn H., ed. LC 82-81034. 205p. 1982. lib. bdg. 16.00 (ISBN 0-937938-08-4); pap. 9.95 (ISBN 0-937938-07-6). Snow Lion.

Gyatso, Sonam & Gyatso, Tenzin. Essence of Refined Gold. Mullin, Glen, ed. LC 80-85453. 1982. lib. bdg. 16.00 (ISBN 0-937938-10-6); pap. 9.95 (ISBN 0-937938-09-2). Snow Lion.

Gyatso, Tenzin, jt. auth. see Gyatso, Sonam.

Gyatso, Tenzin, jt. auth. see Nagarjuna.

Gybels, J., et al, eds. Technical Advances. (Applied Neurophysiology: Vol. 45, No. 4-5). (Illus.). iv, 208p. 1981. pap. 32.25 (ISBN 3-8055-3499-X). S Karger.

--Advance in Stereotactic & Functional Neurosurgery: Proceedings of the Sixth Meeting of the European Society for Stereotatic & Functional Neurisurgery, Rome 1983. (Acta Neurochirurgica-Supplementum: No. 33). (Illus.). 600p. 1984. pap. 100.10 (ISBN 0-387-81773-5). Springer Verlag.

Gydikov, Alexander A., et al, eds. Motor Control. LC 73-19722. 270p. 1973. 37.50x (ISBN 0-306-30771-5, Plenum Pr). Plenum Pub.

Gyekye, Kwame, ed. & tr. Arabic Logic: Ibn Al-Tayyib on Porphyry's "Eisagoge". LC 76-4071. 1979. 49.50x (ISBN 0-87395-308-8). State U NY Pr.

Gyenes, I. Titration in Non-Aqueous Media. 474p. 1968. 24.00 (ISBN 0-442-32925-3, Pub. by Van Nos Reinhold). Krieger.

Gyepes, Michael, ed. Angiography in Infants & Childrens. LC 74-22253. (Illus.). 382p. 1974. 77.00 (ISBN 0-8089-0827-8, 791780). Grune.

Gyepes, Michael T. & Vincent, William R. Cardiac Catheterization & Angiocardiography in Severe Neonatal Heart Disease. (Illus.). 184p. 1974. 18.50x (ISBN 0-398-03088-X). C C Thomas.

Gyepi-Garbrah, Benjamin. Adolescent Fertility in Kenya. (Adolescent Fertility in Sub-Sahara Africa Ser.: Vol. 4). 62p. (Orig.). 1985. write for info. (ISBN 0-933853-03-3). Pathfinder Fund.

--Adolescent Fertility in Liberia. (Adolescent Fertility in Sub-Sahara Africa Ser.: Vol. 2). 55p. (Orig.). 1985. write for info. (ISBN 0-933853-01-7). Pathfinder Fund.

--Adolescent Fertility in Nigeria. (Adolescent Fertility in Sub-Sahara Africa Ser.: Vol. 3). 69p. (Orig.). 1985. write for info. (ISBN 0-933853-02-5). Pathfinder Fund.

--Adolescent Fertility in Sierra Leone. (Adolescent Fertility in Sub-Sahara Africa Ser.: Vol. 5). (Orig.). 1985. write for info. (ISBN 0-933853-04-1). Pathfinder Fund.

--Adolescent Fertility in Sub-Sahara Africa: An Overview. (Adolescent Fertility in Sub-Sahara Africa Ser.: Vol. 1). 51p. (Orig.). 1985. write for info. (ISBN 0-933853-00-9). Pathfinder Fund.

--Adolescent Fertility in Sub-Sahara Africa, 5 vols. 1985. Set. write for info. (ISBN 0-933853-05-X). Pathfinder Fund.

Gyeszly, S. W. Introduction to Packaging Materials. Date not set. price not set (ISBN 0-677-05090-9). Gordon.

Gyford, John. Local Politics in Britain. rev. ed. 192p. (Orig.). 1984. pap. 13.50 (ISBN 0-7099-1168-8, Pub. by Croom Helm Ltd). Longwood Pub Group.

--The Politics of Local Socialism. (Local Government Briefings Ser.). 170p. 1985. text ed. 25.00x (ISBN 0-04-352213-0); pap. text ed. 8.00x (ISBN 0-04-352214-9). Allen Unwin.

Gyford, John & James, Mari. National Parties & Local Politics. (New Local Government Ser.: No. 24). 240p. 1983. text ed. 35.00x (ISBN 0-04-352106-1). Allen Unwin.

Gyftopoulos, E. P., jt. auth. see Hatsopoulos, G. N.

Gyftopoulos, Elias P. & Cohen, Karen C., eds. Case Studies. (Industrial Energy-Conservation Manuals: No. 17). (Illus.). 112p. 1982. loose-leaf 30.00x (ISBN 0-262-09024-4). MIT Pr.

Gyftopoulos, Elias P., ed. see Anderson, M. & Lee, R.

Gyftopoulos, Elias P., ed. see Belding, John A.

Gyftopoulos, Elias P., ed. see Cho, Chun H.

Gyftopoulos, Elias P., ed. see Conta, Lewis D.

Gyftopoulos, Elias P., ed. see Dyer, D., et al.

Gyftopoulos, Elias P., ed. see Eckerlin, H. & Boyers, A.

Gyftopoulos, Elias P., ed. see Furbush, S. A.

Gyftopoulos, Elias P., ed. see Furgerson, W. F.

Gyftopoulos, Elias P., ed. see Harrison, Michael R.

Gyftopoulos, Elias P., ed. see Keller, George E., II.

Gyftopoulos, Elias P., ed. see Kenney, W. F.

Gyftopoulos, Elias P., ed. see Mix, T. W. & Dweck, J. S.

Gyftopoulos, Elias P., ed. see Monroe, Elmer S., Jr.

Gyftopoulos, Elias P., ed. see Seader, J. D.

Gyftopoulos, Elias P., ed. see Shinskey, F. G.

Gyftopoulos, Elias P., ed. see Stephanopoulos, G.

Gygi, Robert N. So Many Voices. (Illus.). 44p. (Orig.). 1981. pap. text ed. write for info. (ISBN 0-9607592-0-4). Gygi.

Gyi, Ko Ko. A Revision of Colubrid Snakes of the Subfamily Homalopsinae. (Museum Ser.: Vol. 20, No. 2). 177p. 1970. pap. 9.00 (ISBN 0-686-80361-2). U of KS Mus Nat Hist.

Gyi, M. The Crossed Swords. 44p. (Orig.). 1982. pap. write for info. Am Bando Assn.

Gyi, Maung. Burmese Political Values: The Socio-Political Roots of Authoritarianism. 288p. 1983. 29.95x (ISBN 0-03-063338-9). Praeger.

Gyires, B. Analytic Function Methods in Probability Theory. (Colloquia Mathematics Societatis Janos Bolyoi Ser.: Vol. 21). 379p. 1979. 85.00 (ISBN 0-444-85333-2, North Holland). Elsevier.

Gylden, Yves. Contribution of the Cryptographic Bureaus in the World War. Friedman, William F., ed. (Cryptographic Ser). 1978. 14.80 (ISBN 0-89412-027-1). Aegean Park Pr.

Gyldenals. Deluxe Ordboger: Danish-English. 120.00 (ISBN 0-317-19038-5, D726). Vanous.

Gyldendals. Norwegian Pocket Dictionary: English-Norwegian-English. 4th, rev. ed. (Norwegian & Eng.). 1983. 9.00x (ISBN 82-573-0212-0, N-407). Vanous.

--Rode Ordboger: Danish-English. 20.00 (ISBN 0-89918-282-8, D705). Vanous.

--Rode Ordboger: English-Danish. 20.00 (ISBN 0-317-19034-2, D704). Vanous.

Gyldenvand, Lily M. Joy in His Presence: Christian Reflections on Everyday Life. LC 81-67806. 112p. (Orig.). 1981. pap. 4.95 (ISBN 0-8066-1896-5, 10-3596). Augsburg.

Gyll, Gordon W. A Tractate on Language. 388p. 1981. Repr. of 1860 ed. lib. bdg. 85.00 (ISBN 0-89760-321-4). Telegraph Bks.

Gyllander, K. see Erdtman, G.

Gyllenskold, Karin. Breast Cancer. Crampton, Patricia, tr. 1982. 26.00x (ISBN 0-422-76820-0, NO.3623); pap. 12.95x (ISBN 0-422-76830-8, NO.3624). Methuen Inc.

--Breast Cancer: The Psychological Effects of the Disease & Its Treatment. Crampton, Patricia, tr. 1982. 26.00x (ISBN 0-422-76820-0, NO. 3623, Pub. by Tavistock); pap. 12.95x (ISBN 0-422-76830-8, NO. 3624). Methuen Inc.

Gyllensvard, Bo. Museum of Far Eastern Antiquities, Stockholm. LC 80-82645. (Oriental Ceramics Ser.: Vol. 8). (Illus.). 150p. 1982. 68.00 (ISBN 0-87011-447-6). Kodansha.

Gyllstoem, Walter, jt. ed. see Bryde, Konrad.

Gylys, Barbara A. & Wedding, Mary E. Medical Terminology: A Systems Approach. LC 82-12927. (Illus.). 421p. 1983. pap. text ed. 16.50x (ISBN 0-8036-4492-2); cassette 35.00x (ISBN 0-8036-4493-0). Davis Co.

Gymer, Roger G. Chemistry in the Natural World. 1976. text ed. 22.95 (ISBN 0-669-00343-3); instructor's manual free (ISBN 0-669-00352-2). Heath.

Gynn, Roger. The Guinness Book of the Marathon. (Illus.). 168p. 1984. 14.95 (ISBN 0-85112-410-0, Pub. by Guinness Superlatives England); pap. 9.95 (ISBN 0-85112-422-4, Pub. by Guinness Superlatives England). Sterling.

Gynn, Roger W., jt. auth. see Martin, David E.

Gynther, R. S. Accounting for Price Level Changes. 1966. pap. 10.75 (ISBN 0-08-011711-2). Pergamon.

Gyongyossy, Istvan. International Money Flows & Currency Crises. 1984. lib. bdg. 23.50 (ISBN 90-247-2647-6, Pub. by Martinus Nijhoff Netherlands). Kluwer Academic.

Gyorfi, Laszlo, jt. auth. see Devroye, Luc.

Gyorgy, Andrew. Geopolitics, the New German Science. 18.00 (ISBN 0-384-20585-2); pap. 12.00 (ISBN 0-384-20585-2). Johnson Repr.

--Governments of Danubian Europe. LC 77-26086. 1978. Repr. of 1949 ed. lib. bdg. 25.75x (ISBN 0-313-20081-5, GYGD). Greenwood.

Gyorgy, Anna, et al. No Nukes: Everyone's Guide to Nuclear Power. LC 78-71203. (Illus.). 478p. 1979. 20.00 (ISBN 0-89608-007-2); pap. 10.00 (ISBN 0-89608-006-4). South End Pr.

Gyorgy, P. & Kline, O. L., eds. Malnutrition Is a Problem of Ecology. (Bibliotheca Nutritio et Dieta: No. 14). 1970. pap. 14.50 (ISBN 3-8055-0164-1). S Karger.

Gyorgy, Paul see Sebrell, W. H., Jr. & Harris, Robert S.

Gyorgy, Szendy. Dictionary of Patent Law in Five Languages: German-English-French-Spanish-Russian. (3184005348). 950p. 1984. 46.00 (ISBN 0-317-13944-4, Pub. by VDI Verlag Gmbh Dusseldorf). Heyden.

Gyorgyey, Clara. Ferenc Molnar. (World Authors Ser.). 1980. lib. bdg. 16.95 (ISBN 0-8057-6416-X, Twayne). G K Hall.

Gyorke, Olivier. European Hydraulics Laboratories: A Survey. (Engineering Laboratories Ser.: No. 3). (Illus.). 128p. (Orig.). 1973. pap. 6.25 (ISBN 92-3-101064-6, U217, UNESCO). Unipub.

Gyory, Richard A. The Emergence of Being: Through Indian & Greek Thought. LC 78-70692. 1978. pap. text ed. 11.25 (ISBN 0-8191-0646-1). U Pr of Amer.

Gypsy Boots. Bare Feet & Good Things to Eat. 1965. 2.00x (ISBN 0-686-36336-1). Cancer Control Soc.

Gyr, K. E., et al. Pancreatitis: Concepts & Classification. (International Congress Ser.: Vol. 642). 1985. 90.75 (ISBN 0-444-80650-4). Elsevier.

Gyr, N E. Test of Cxocrine Pancreatic Function. 132p. 1975. 40.00 (ISBN 3-456-80215-3, Pub. by Holdan Bk Ltd UK). State Mutual Bk.

Gyrowit, Adalbert & Dussek, Jan L. Adalbert Gyrowitz & Jan Ladislav Dyssek. Brook, Barry S., et al, eds. LC 83-1634. (The Symphony Ser.). 304p. 1983. lib. bdg. 90.00 (ISBN 0-8240-3826-6). Garland Pub.

Gysbers, N. & Moore, E. Improving Guidance Programs. 1981. 18.95 (ISBN 0-13-452656-2). P-H.

Gysbers, Norman C., & Associates. Designing Careers: Counseling to Enhance Education, Work, & Leisure. LC 84-47986. (Higher Education Ser.). 1984. 35.95x (ISBN 0-87589-618-9). Jossey-Bass.

Gysi, Church, ed. Scanner Master Greater Philadelphia-South Jersey Guide. 2nd ed. (Scanner Master Frequency Guides Ser.: No. 5). (Illus.). 160p. 1985. 14.95 (ISBN 0-939430-04-5). Scanner Master.

Gysi, Lydia. Platonism & Cartesianism in the Philosophy of Ralph Cudworth. 163p. 1962. 14.35 (ISBN 3-261-00648-X). P Lang Pubs.

Gysin, Brion. Brion Gysin Let the Mice In. Herman, Jan, ed. LC 72-96737. (Illus.). 74p. 1973. 15.00 (ISBN 0-87110-105-X). Ultramarine Pub.

--Stories. Green, Theo, ed. 98p. (Orig.). 1984. pap. 6.95 (ISBN 0-934301-01-8). Inkblot Pubns.

Gysseling, Maurits. Corpus Van Middelnederlandse Teksten Tot en met het Jaar 1300, 9 vols. (Ambtelijke Bescheiden). 1979. Set. lib. bdg. 833.00 (ISBN 90-247-1808-2, Pub. by Martinus Nijhoff Netherlands). Kluwer Academic.

Gythiel, Anthony P., tr. see Spidlik, Tomas.

Gyugyi, L. & Pelly, B. R. Static Power Frequency Changers: Theory, Performance & Application. LC 76-6088. 442p. 1976. 66.95x (ISBN 0-471-67800-7, Pub. by Wiley-Interscience). Wiley.

Gyulay, Jo-Eileen. The Dying Child. 1977. pap. text ed. 19.95 (ISBN 0-07-025360-9). McGraw.

Gyulnazaryan, Hadjak. Little Arthur's Sun. Riordan, Jim & Solasko, Fainna, trs. 33p. 1983. 4.95 (ISBN 0-8285-2580-3, Pub. by Raduga Pubs USSR). Imported Pubns.

Gyure. The Colorado Report. 142p. 1981. pap. 6.95 (ISBN 0-938354-01-9). Stonehenge.

Gyure, Gerald A. The Colorado Report. LC 80-83983. (Illus.). 144p. (Orig.). 1981. pap. 3.95 (ISBN 0-938354-01-9). Hi Country Pubs.

Gywnn, Stephen L. Thomas More. 204p. 1980. Repr. of 1905 ed. lib. bdg. 22.50 (ISBN 0-8495-2045-2). Arden Lib.